HARRAP'S
STANDARD
FRENCH
AND ENGLISH
DICTIONARY

SUB-EDITORS

Hazel Curties, B.A. (née Catterall)
Flora Elphick, B.A.
H. R. Elphick
Muriel Holland Smith
Elizabeth A. H. Strick, M.A.
Helen Zarb, B.A.

PRINCIPAL COLLABORATORS AND TECHNICAL ADVISERS

Jean Bétesta, *Chevalier de la Légion d'Honneur*
Reginald Bowen, B.A., *Docteur de l'Université de Strasbourg*
Commander Ian Forbes, DSC, RN
F. G. S. Parker, M.A.

HARRAP'S
STANDARD FRENCH AND ENGLISH DICTIONARY

J.E. Mansion
Revised and edited by
D.M. Ledésert & R.P.L. Ledésert

1 A-I
French-English

HARRAP
London

Publisher in Great Britain

© Harrap Books Limited 1939, 1980

All rights reserved. No part of this publication
may be reproduced in any form or by any
means, without the prior permission of

Printed and bound in Singapore by
Intellicon Co.

*Published in Great Britain
by* Harrap Books Limited
Chelsea House, 26 Market Square,
Bromley, Kent BR1 1NA
Eighteenth impression: 1991

© *Harrap Books Limited* 1939, 1980

ISBN 0 245-50972-0

Printed and bound in Singapore by
Intellectual Publishing Co.

Preface

THIS work is a completely revised and greatly enlarged edition of *Harrap's Standard French and English Dictionary* and represents research work carried out over many years by a whole team of collaborators. As the card index of the original edition was destroyed during World War II, a new one was compiled after 1945 by the wearisome task of cutting up copies of the 1940 edition and pasting each headword on a separate card. These cards already formed an index of considerable dimensions, but it did not remain static, and in a very short space of time thousands of new cards had been added, representing words not appearing in the original dictionary and new acceptations of existing words. The new material was derived from a number of sources: the examination of the most modern unilingual dictionaries; the reading of periodicals and recently published books; suggestions sent in by users of the dictionary; and words or expressions gleaned quite fortuitously in the course of conversation. Our friends are no longer astonished to hear, "*What* did you say? I don't think we have that in our dictionary. Do you mind if I make a note of it in my little book?" In fact our research has gone much beyond the existing dictionaries in both languages.

By 1950 enough material had been gathered to publish a supplement, of which the second and third augmented editions appeared in 1955 and 1961. It was then evident that the additional material being collected was too extensive to make the publication of a fourth supplement a practical solution, so activities were directed towards the preparation of a completely new edition of the French–English part of the dictionary, which should not only incorporate the 1961 supplement and include further additional words and expressions, but should also comprise a complete revision of existing articles. Both the English and French languages have evolved rapidly over the last thirty to forty years, but not always in the same direction or at the same pace, so it stands to reason that what in 1934 was the best translation of a given expression is not necessarily the best translation today. In particular, many expressions which in the inter-war years were Americanisms have now become the standard English of the British Isles, and have superseded the expressions currently used in the twenties or thirties. Moreover, the French used in some of the examples relating to everyday conversation now appears stilted or old fashioned, so in these cases the more current expression has been substituted.

This must not be taken to mean that all words or expressions (including colloquialisms or even slang) no longer in current use have been deleted. This dictionary is intended not only for the user who requires an extensive vocabulary of modern French, but also for one who may be reading literature or scientific or technical works published in the past. Purely literary words or expressions are consequently marked *Lit.:*; obsolete or archaic ones *A.:*; and obsolescent ones, used currently largely by the older generations, *O.:*. It is also important to point out the distinction between *A.* preceding a category indication and *A:* following one; for example, the name of a ship no longer used (e.g. **galion**, *s.m.* galleon) would be labelled *A.Nau:*, while an expression indicating a nautical operation which has now been replaced by a more modern expression would be labelled *Nau: A:*.

No dictionary can contain a complete word list, and it has been difficult at times to know where to draw the line in order to produce within a reasonable space of time a work of manageable dimensions and of wide scope. The new material added pays particular attention to modern technical and scientific developments, including the fields of atomic physics, space travel and data processing, together with recent terms in connection with industries such as aircraft, automobiles, civil engineering, etc. The natural sciences, economics and finance have not been neglected; and a large number of colloquialisms (marked *F:*) and widely used slang expressions (marked *P:*) have been added. There is now a substantial list of French Canadianisms, and also words in use in French-speaking Switzerland and Belgium. It would, however, not have been practical to add all the compound words or combined forms deriving from prefixes such as **auto-**, **mono-**, **psycho-**, **sous-**, etc., so a broad representative selection has been included of the most widely used or those the translation of which presents difficulties.

Selection of words which may be described as *franglais* has been a difficult problem; we have included those which appear to be firmly established in the French language (e.g. **un parking, le pipeline**), though the user will note that we have used the symbol *F:* in many cases where purists might cast some doubt on their authenticity as wholly French words.

As far as the French word list is concerned widely used variants in spelling have been given, the variants appearing in their correct alphabetical place. For the English translations alternative spellings would not have been practicable, so the orthography used is that which appears to be the most current in the British Isles. Nevertheless, the American translation has been given alongside the British one (e.g. **essence**, *s.f.* petrol, *U.S:* gasoline; **voiture**, *s.f.* car, *U.S:* automobile), in cases where the usage differs considerably. And the attention of the North-American user or the Frenchman requiring, or more conversant with, the American form of spelling is drawn towards a few salient differences:

    (*a*) the English use of **-our** in words where American usage is **-or** (e.g. *Eng:* theatre, favour; *U.S:* color, favor);

    (*b*) the English use of the final **-re** where American usage is **-er** (e.g. *Eng:* theatre, kilometre, centre; *U.S:* theater, kilometer, center);

    (*c*) the doubling of the **l** in English usage before an ending beginning with a vowel, irrespective of accentuation (e.g. *Eng:* woollen, travelling; *U.S:* woolen, traveling);

    (*d*) the single **l** in English usage before a final syllable beginning with a consonant, where American usage is **ll** (e.g. *Eng:* skilful, enrolment; *U.S:* skillful, enrollment);

    (*e*) the use of **c** in certain words in which American usage is **s** (e.g. *Eng:* defence; *U.S:* defense);

    (*f*) the greater use in scientific words of **ae** where American usage prefers **e** (e.g. *Eng:* anaemia, *U.S:* anemia);

    (*g*) the English preference for **ph** in scientific words such as sulphur, sulphuric, in contrast to the American use of **f** (sulfur, sulfuric).

It should also be noted that for words with the alternative suffixes **-ise** or **-ize** and **-isation** or **-ization** the forms **-ize** and **-ization** have been adopted throughout, as English usage is about equally divided between the two, and American practice favours the **-ize**, **-ization**.

The general principles of layout as explained in the *Plan of the Dictionary* that accompanied the original edition (see p. xviii) have been maintained, though a few minor modifications have been made for the convenience of the user. Participial forms used as independent adjectives or nouns figure in their correct alphabetical position, and no longer follow the verb from which they are derived. The use of capital letters in the text has been abandoned except, naturally, in cases where they are essential, so that the user shall no longer be in doubt as to which word requires a capital. For reasons of space economy headwords appearing in examples in exactly the same form are not repeated, but are represented by the initial letter; in this way we estimate that we have saved probably some 150,000 words, which is the equivalent of a large book. Separate entries for feminine forms of adjectives and verb conjugations have also been largely suppressed, as it is considered that the users of *Harrap's New Standard French and English Dictionary* are sufficiently familiar with them to know without hesitation which headword to consult. In this way further space saving was achieved.

As far as the arrangement of the material under each headword is concerned, we have continued Mr Mansion's plan of using the subdivisions **1.**, **2.**, **3.**, etc. to denote important differences in the meaning or use of a word, and (*a*), (*b*), (*c*), etc. to show differences of lesser importance. In general the divisions (i), (ii), (iii), etc. are used to show different meanings of the same phrase, though in the longer articles they sometimes occur as subdivisions of (*a*), (*b*), etc. In addition to this the divisions I, II, etc. are sometimes used for very long articles when the word in question has several different grammatical functions, e.g. the word **sortir**, which is both an intransitive and a transitive verb and also a noun.

Two variants of the translation of a word or an expression are separated by a comma if the meaning is virtually identical; the semi-colon normally indicates a slight difference in meaning, but it is sometimes used to break up a complicated entry which might otherwise be confusing.

The use of the hyphen in the English translations has presented many problems as there is no hard and fast rule about it. As North-American usage seems to have to a large extent rejected the hyphen for compound nouns, and we in the United Kingdom are following this practice more and more, we have endeavoured to be forward-looking, and have printed most compound nouns either in two separate words or as one single word. Compound adjectives, however, are still presented with a hyphen, as this appears to be the general rule in both American and English practice. This will explain to the user the apparent contradiction of entries such as a **rolling mill** (two words) and **rolling-mill equipment** (hyphenated).

We have somewhat reduced the number of general cross references appearing in the dictionary. Cross references can at times be irritating to the user, particularly in a work of two or more volumes, so we have to an appreciable extent limited them to the longer references, where the inclusion of the examples under more than one headword would add too much to the bulk of the dictionary. Shorter examples usually appear under each of the main headwords concerned, though it must be pointed out that some idiomatic phrases appear only under the headword which to us seems to be the key word of the phrase.

We have maintained Mr Mansion's principle of giving the phonetics of every word listed, using the notation of the International Phonetic Association. The task has not been an easy one, particularly in view of the fact that we have had to supply the phonetics for a far longer list of words than any that has yet been published with phonetic transcription. Moreover, this work is not primarily a phonetic dictionary, and the phonetics are supplied to give the user a general guide to the most current way of pronouncing the words in question—of the way in which the average educated Frenchman pronounces them. We have therefore given relatively few alternative pronunciations, and have dispensed with nuances such as the introduction of the half-length sign [·], denoting a half lengthening within a phonetic group. We should also add that our task has been complicated by the fact that on certain points there is controversy among expert phoneticians as to what is the most usual pronunciation of certain words. We should like to take this opportunity of thanking M. B. Quémada for the help he has given us with the phonetic transcription.

The mechanics of the composition of a dictionary of this size is no small task. By the spring of 1967 it was felt that the research work had reached a sufficiently advanced stage to justify the preparation of the manuscript for the press, and work was started on letter A. As each letter (or part of a letter where the longer letters were concerned) was completed, the manuscript was sent to the printers, who duly supplied us with galley proofs. Their job was not easy as the copy, with many additions and amendments in handwriting, was by no means straightforward. This probably explains some of the amusing misprints we came across in the galleys, such as: *urine chargée*, clouded wine (for urine); *binoclard*, person who wears gloves (glasses); *arséniate diplomatique* (for diplombique); *écarts de régime*, overheating; *chien dressé à la propreté*, horse-trained dog; *voir grand*, to have pig ideas; *mouchoir de con* (cou), scarf; *l'industrie de la chaussure*, the boat and shoe industry; *pistolet*, bed wind (for urinal); *phantasme*, official illusion (for optical); *engager qn à l'heure*, to empty (for employ) s.o. by the hour; etc. We hasten to repeat that we blame our handwriting, not the printers, for these errors, for anything may be expected in a dictionary that lists extraordinary expressions such as the data-processing term 'eight-bit byte'; we can but express the hope that they helped our proof readers by bringing a little light relief to a most exacting task.

All the galley proofs were read by four or five readers, and when their corrections had been collated the work was set up in page proof, letter by letter. From that time onwards only minor amendments could be made, and additions were possible only if some existing item of lesser importance were deleted. In order to be able to publish the dictionary by 1972, the final version of letter A had to be passed for press early in 1970; it is therefore evident that any word beginning with A which appeared in the language for the first time in 1970 or 1971 could not be included. It is a matter of regret to us that the first volume (A–Cippe) of the 6-volume *Grand Larousse de la langue française* appeared too late in 1971 for us to be able to make use of it; we have, however, examined it, and are happy to be able to say that there are few words contained in it which we have not listed, and that the *New Standard* contains a number of words which do not appear in the *Grand Larousse*.

Our work necessitated the consultation of a vast number of dictionaries, books and periodicals. While it is impossible to list all the works to which reference has been made, we should like to acknowledge the considerable assistance offered to us by the following:

Dictionnaire alphabétique et analogique de la langue française (with supplement). P. Robert. (Société du nouveau Littré)

Le Petit Robert

Grand Larousse Encyclopédique (and supplement)

Petit Larousse

Dictionnaire du français contemporain (Larousse)

Dictionnaire Encyclopédique (Quillet)

Dictionnaire usuel Quillet-Flammarion

Encyclopédie internationale Focus (Bordas)

Le Bon Usage. M. Grevisse (J. Duculot, S.A.)

Dictionnaire des difficultés de la langue française. A. Thomas (Larousse)

Dictionnaire de la Prononciation française. L. Warnant (J. Duculot, S.A.)

Webster's New International Dictionary (second and third editions)

Webster's Seventh New Collegiate Dictionary

The Random House Dictionary of the English Language

The Penguin English Dictionary

Chambers's Twentieth Century Dictionary (with supplement)

The Penguin Dictionaries of Biology, Building, Civil Engineering, Electronics, Geography, Psychology and *Science*

Chambers's Technical Dictionary

Dictionnaire des termes techniques de médecine. Garnier et Delamare (Librairie Maloine, S.A.)

Stedman's Medical Dictionary (E. & S. Livingstone, Ltd)

Butterworth's Medical Dictionary

Dictionnaire technique des termes utilisés dans l'industrie du pétrole. Moureau et Rouge (Technip)

Vocabulaire franco-anglo-allemand de Géomorphologie. H. Baulig (Société d'édition: Les Belles Lettres)

Geological Nomenclature. J. Noorduijn en Zoon & N. V. Gorinchem (Ed. A. A. G. Schieferdecker)

A Dictionary of Geography. Monkhouse (Edward Arnold)

A Glossary of Geographical Terms. L. Dudley Stamp (Longmans)

Dictionary of Data Processing/Dictionnaire de l'Informatique. Camille & Dehaine (Harrap)

Dictionnaire d'Informatique. M. Ginguay (Masson, Paris)

Harrap's French–English Dictionary of Slang and Colloquialisms. J. Marks.

In this context we should like to express our thanks to the British Aircraft Corporation who made available to us their *Glossary of Aeronautical Terms*, French to English; and to Captain H. G. Sherwood (retired airline captain of B.O.A.C.), who was always ready to give us the benefit of his advice on aeronautical terms.

Our task would have been impossible without the assistance of the large army of helpers working in the Harrap offices and in all parts of the globe who have assisted us in our research work and in reading the proofs. We would like to pay a special tribute to M. Marcel Ferlin, whose association with the dictionary dates back to 1912 when, as a young *assistant* in Edinburgh, he began working with Mr Mansion in the early days of its conception. M. Ferlin continued his contributions to the dictionary throughout the years, sending in his *glanures* and correcting proofs until the time of his death in September 1970. It is a matter of great regret to us that he did not live to see the completion of the new dictionary, and in him we have lost not only a valuable helper but a great friend.

Another link with the original dictionary was provided by Mr H. R. Elphick, who was a member of Mr Mansion's office team. After the war he spent a number of years in New Zealand, and when he returned to England on his retirement he agreed to read the proofs of the new dictionary, and we are most grateful to him. In particular, his knowledge of the plan of the dictionary has enabled him to give us much valuable assistance in the matter of classification of the material in the longer articles.

Though in the later stages some of the preparation of the manuscript for the press was done in the office, much of it we did at home, with the indefatigable assistance of Miss Muriel Holland Smith. But we could not have accomplished it without the work of all the members of the office team who over the years have been responsible for research work and collation of material from outside sources, and we would like to express our sincere thanks to them. Some of them were with us for only a comparatively short space of time, others were able to give longer service, and among them we wish to mention particularly Mr P. H. Collin; Mrs Françoise Collin (*née* Laurendeau), who supplied us with French Canadianisms; Mrs E. A. H. Strick; Mrs A. Smetana-Thieberger; Mrs Valerie Deane; Mlle Christine Fontan; and Miss Vivien Flynn.

Apart from those mentioned in the prefaces to the Supplements (see p. xxii), outside contributors to whom we owe special thanks include MM. J. Bétesta, Michel Ginguay and Roland Ginguay, whose assistance, especially in the military and technical fields, has been of inestimable value; Mr H. T. Porter, who made a most valuable contribution on the names of European birds; Mrs Patricia Forbes, who was responsible for important additions to the vocabulary of natural history and the petroleum industry; and to Dr Feldblum, who supplied us with medical terms.

The assistance afforded to us by Professor L. C. Harmer did not cease with his contributions to the supplements, and we wish to thank him for continuing to help us with valuable additions and amendments and for reading some of the proofs. We also thank Dr Reginald Bowen, Mrs Patricia Forbes, Mr F. G. S. Parker, Mrs E. A. H. Strick and M. Michel Boutron for their help in reading the proofs.

Finally we should like to express our gratitude for their encouragement and for the help that they so frequently gave us, often unconsciously, in finding the word we were looking for, to all our friends living in and around Holyport, where we have our permanent home, and Les Pilles, the village in southern France where we have a house that was the scene of much of our labours.

RENÉ LEDÉSERT
MARGARET LEDÉSERT

December, 1971.

Préface

CET ouvrage est une édition complètement révisée et très agrandie du *Harrap's Standard French and English Dictionary* et représente le travail fait au cours de nombreuses années par toute une équipe de collaborateurs.

Le fichier rassemblé pour la préparation de la première édition a été détruit pendant la guerre mondiale. Il a donc fallu en créer un nouveau à partir de 1945, et ce travail fastidieux a été effectué en découpant des exemplaires de l'édition de 1940, et en collant chaque mot-clé sur une carte. Ces cartes formaient déjà un fichier très important, mais nous y avons travaillé sans relâche, et bientôt des milliers de nouvelles cartes y avaient été ajoutées pour les mots nouveaux et les sens nouveaux de mots qui figuraient déjà dans le dictionnaire. Nous avons réuni cette nouvelle documentation de toutes sortes de façons: la lecture des dictionnaires unilingues les plus récents, de revues et journaux, de livres récents; les usagers du dictionnaire nous ont envoyé de multiples suggestions; et des mots et expressions rassemblées par hasard au cours de conversations. Nos amis ne s'étonnent plus de nous entendre demander: "Qu'est-ce que vous dites? Je ne crois pas que ce soit dans le dictionnaire. Permettez-moi d'en prendre note dans mon calepin." En fait nos recherches ont de beaucoup dépassé les dictionnaires du français ou de l'anglais.

En 1950 nous avions déjà la documentation qui nous a permis d'éditer le premier supplément, suivi par une deuxième édition très augmentée de cet ouvrage en 1955, puis par une troisième en 1961. A cette date il était déjà évident que nous avions trop de nouveaux termes et expressions pour que la publication d'un quatrième supplément soit chose possible. Nous avons donc dirigé nos activités vers la préparation d'un nouveau texte du dictionnaire français-anglais qui comprendrait non seulement le supplément de 1961 mais la révision complète du texte original, ainsi que des milliers de mots et d'expressions supplémentaires. La langue française et la langue anglaise ont évolué rapidement au cours des trente ou quarante dernières années, mais cette évolution n'a pas toujours été parallèle. Il en résulte parfois que ce qui en 1934 était la meilleure traduction pour une expression donnée n'est plus la meilleure traduction aujourd'hui. Beaucoup d'expressions qui, entre les deux guerres, étaient des américanismes sont maintenant l'anglais standard des Iles Britanniques, et elles ont souvent remplacé des expressions courantes dans les années vingt ou trente. En outre, le français de beaucoup d'exemples de conversation courante était devenu guindé ou périmé, et chaque fois nous avons substitué l'expression courante.

Ceci ne signifie pas que tous les mots ou expressions (y compris expressions familières et argot) qui ne sont plus usités ont été supprimés. Ce dictionnaire est destiné non seulement à ceux qui veulent avoir accès à un vaste vocabulaire du français contemporain, mais aussi à ceux qui lisent des ouvrages scientifiques ou autres publiés dans le passé. Nous avons par conséquent indiqué les mots et expressions usités littérairement par l'abréviation *Lit:*; les mots anciens ou archaïques par *A:*; les mots qui vieillissent, mais qui sont toujours dans la bouche des générations nées vers 1910 par *O:*. Il faut noter d'autre part la distinction faite entre *A.* précédant l'indication d'une classification et *A:* suivant une classification. Par exemple, le nom d'un navire qui n'existe plus (**galion**, *s.m.* galleon) a l'étiquette *A.Nau:*, mais une expression indiquant une manœuvre navale qui a été remplacée par une expression moderne est mise dans la catégorie *Nau: A:*.

Il est impossible de faire un dictionnaire qui contienne tout le vocabulaire d'une langue. Il nous a été souvent difficile de décider où nous arrêter de façon à faire assez rapidement un ouvrage maniable et de portée universelle. La masse de nouveaux mots et expressions reflètent notre préoccupation d'expliquer l'évolution des techniques et des sciences, y compris les domaines des sciences atomiques, des voyages intersidéraux et de l'informatique, sans négliger les mots nouveaux d'industries plus anciennes, telles que l'aviation, l'automobile, ou le génie civil. Nous n'avons pas oublié les sciences naturelles, l'économie politique ou le monde de la finance. Et le lecteur verra que nous avons ajouté beaucoup d'expressions familières (*F:*) ou argotiques (*P:*). On trouvera aussi de nombreux canadianismes et des mots usités en Suisse et en Belgique. Il aurait été impossible d'inclure tous les mots composés formés à partir de préfixes comme **auto-, mono-, psycho-, sous-,** etc.; nous avons donc choisi les mots les plus courants, et ceux dont la traduction présente des difficultés.

Il nous a été difficile de faire le choix des mots que certains appellent *franglais*, mais nous avons noté ceux qui semblent fermement enracinés en France, comme par exemple **un parking**, ou **le pipeline**, et nous avons averti le lecteur quant à leur droit de cité dans le vocabulaire français en leur donnant l'étiquette *F:*.

Nous avons noté dans leur ordre strictement alphabétique les variantes orthographiques des mots français. En ce qui concerne les traductions anglaises, nous avons donné l'orthographe le plus couramment usité dans les Iles Britanniques. Cependant la traduction américaine accompagne la traduction anglaise quand l'usage est différent: par exemple **essence**, *s.f.* petrol, *U.S:* gasoline; **voiture**, *s.f.* car, *U.S:* automobile. D'autre part, nous attirons l'attention des Américains et Canadiens, ainsi que des Français qui veulent choisir l'orthographe américaine, sur une série de différences primordiales:

(*a*) l'usage en anglais de la terminaison **-our** alors que l'américain se sert de **-or** (par exemple, on écrit en anglais **colour, favour**, et en américain color, favor);

(*b*) la terminaison anglaise **-re** est remplacée par **-er** en américain (en anglais: theatre, kilometre, centre; en américain: theater, kilometer, center);

(*c*) dans l'usage anglais la lettre **l** est doublée quand la dernière syllabe comprend une voyelle, sans se préoccuper de l'accentuation (en anglais: woollen, travelling; en américain: woolen, traveling);

(*d*) l'usage anglais met un seul **l** devant une syllabe terminale commençant par une consonne alors que l'usage américain demande **ll** (en anglais: skilful, enrolment; en américain: skillful, enrollment);

(*e*) dans certains mots l'anglais met un **c** là où l'américain veut un **s** (en anglais: defence; en américain: defense);

(*f*) l'usage plus généralisé dans le vocabulaire scientifique de **ae** en anglais, alors qu'en Amérique on préfère **e** (en anglais: anaemia; en américain: anemia);

(*g*) dans le vocabulaire scientifique encore l'usage anglais est de mettre **ph** dans, par exemple, sulphur, sulphuric, alors que l'orthographe américaine est sulfur, sulfuric.

Enfin, il y a lieu de noter que dans le cas des suffixes **-ise** ou **-ize**, et **-isation, -ization**, nous avons retenu les formes **-ize** et **-ization**, car l'usage anglais hésite entre les deux orthographes, alors que l'usage américain préfère **-ize** et **-ization**.

Nous avons conservé la disposition typographique expliquée dans *Plan of the Dictionary* (p. xviii) de l'édition originale, mais nous avons fait quelques changements d'importance secondaire pour faciliter la lecture: les participes qui ont indépendamment fonction d'adjectifs ou de substantifs paraissent à leur ordre alphabétique et ne sont plus placés à la suite du verbe dont ils dérivent; nous avons supprimé l'usage des lettres majuscules dans le texte, sauf dans les cas où elles sont essentielles, afin que le lecteur sache immédiatement quels mots doivent commencer par une majuscule ou une minuscule; afin de réduire typographiquement la longeur du texte, les mots-clés qui sont utilisés dans les articles sont représentés seulement par leur lettre initiale lorsque leur orthographe ne comporte pas de variante, et nous avons ainsi économisé l'espace typographique d'environ 150.000 mots, ce qui est l'équivalent d'un livre de taille respectable; les entrées qui traitaient séparément des formes féminines

des adjectifs et des formes de la conjugaison des verbes ont été supprimées dans la plupart des cas, car nous avons considéré que les usagers du *Harrap's New Standard French and English Dictionary* ont suffisamment de connaissances grammaticales pour savoir immédiatement quel mot-clé ils doivent consulter. Nous avons ainsi réalisé une autre économie d'espace typographique.

Nous n'avons pas changé la classification établie par M. Mansion pour la présentation du texte: les différences importantes du sens ou de l'usage des mots sont indiquées par les numéros **1.**, **2.**, **3.**, etc., tandis que (*a*), (*b*), (*c*), etc. montrent des différences moindres. D'une manière générale (i), (ii), (iii), etc. marquent seulement les différents sens d'une locution, mais dans les longs articles nous nous en sommes servis parfois comme subdivisions de (*a*), (*b*), etc. Pour les très longs articles nous avons conservé les subdivisions I, II, etc., quand le mot expliqué a plusieurs fonctions grammaticales, comme par exemple **sortir**, qui est un verbe intransitif, un verbe transitif et un substantif.

Nous avons séparé par une virgule les traductions dont le sens est identique, mais le point et virgule indique généralement une petite différence de sens. Nous avons aussi utilisé le point et virgule pour décomposer les entrées trop compliquées qui auraient pu prêter à confusion.

Dans les traductions en anglais l'usage du trait d'union a présenté de nombreuses difficultés car il n'existe pas de règle absolue à cet égard. Comme l'usage américain semble avoir d'une manière générale abandonné le trait d'union pour les noms composés, et comme cette pratique est suivie de plus en plus dans le Royaume-Uni, nous avons écrit la plupart des noms composés soit en deux mots, soit en un seul. Les adjectifs composés ont cependant conservé le trait d'union car cela semble être la règle suivie à la fois en Amérique et dans l'usage anglais. Ceci explique la contradiction apparente d'entrées comme **rolling mill** (en deux mots) et **rolling-mill equipment** (avec trait d'union).

Nous avons diminué le nombre de renvois, qui peuvent être exaspérants pour l'usager, en particulier lorsqu'il s'agit d'un ouvrage en deux volumes. Ceux qui restent se réfèrent à des exemples assez longs afin d'éviter leur répétition sous plusieurs mots-clés. Les exemples plus courts paraissent généralement à chaque mot-clé, mais dans certains cas ils ne sont mentionnés que sous celui des mots-clés qui nous a semblé le plus important.

Nous avons suivi M. Mansion en donnant la notation phonétique de chaque mot selon les principes de *l'Association phonétique internationale*. Ce travail n'a pas été facile. En effet nous avons dû écrire la notation phonétique d'une multitude de mots pour lesquels cela n'avait jamais été fait. En outre cet ouvrage n'est pas un dictionnaire de phonétique, mais les transcriptions que nous avons données sont simplement un guide quant à la prononciation la plus courante des Français instruits. Nous avons par conséquent donné peu de variantes, et nous avons mis de côté des nuances telles que le signe [·] qui se réfère à une voyelle demi-longue. Notre tâche a été d'autre part compliquée parce que les phonéticiens ne sont pas d'accord sur la prononciation usuelle de certains mots. M. B. Quémada nous a guidés dans cette jungle et nous voudrions lui exprimer ici nos remerciements.

La composition typographique d'un dictionnaire de cette taille représente un travail considérable. Au printemps de 1967 nous avions suffisamment de matériaux pour nous permettre de commencer la rédaction du nouveau texte pour l'imprimerie, et nous avons commencé tout bêtement par la lettre A. Au fur et à mesure du travail, nous avons envoyé aux imprimeurs tout ou partie du texte de chaque lettre, et nous avons reçu en temps voulu les placards. Leur tâche a été difficile, car 30% de notre texte était écrit à la main. Ceci explique sans nul doute un certain nombre de coquilles amusantes que nous avons relevées dans les premières épreuves, par exemple: *urine chargée*, clouded wine (urine); *binoclard*, person who wears gloves (glasses); *arséniate diplomatique* (diplombique); *écarts de régime*, overheating; *chien dressé à la propreté*, horse-trained dog; *voir grand*, to have pig ideas; *mouchoir de con* (cou), scarf; *l'industrie de la chaussure*, the boat and shoe industry; *pistolet*, bed wind (urinal); *phantasme*, official (optical) illusion; *engager qn à l'heure*, to empty (employ) s.o. by the hour; etc. Nous insistons sur le fait que ces coquilles sont dûes à notre écriture, et non pas à la négligence de l'imprimeur qui interprétait ce qu'il croyait lire sur notre texte, car on peut s'attendre à tout dans un dictionnaire qui comprend des expressions bizarres comme, par exemple, le terme d'informatique 'eight-bit byte'; nous espérons que nos amis qui ont bien voulu lire les épreuves auront souri de ces écarts à la vérité linguistique au milieu de leur travail fatigant et fastidieux.

Quatre ou cinq lecteurs ont lu ces placards, et quand leur corrections ont été collationnées, l'ouvrage a été mis en pages lettre par lettre. A partir de ce moment-là seuls des changements d'importance typographique minime ont pu être effectués et lorsque nous avons fait quelques additions, cela n'a été possible que quand nous avons pu les mettre à la place d'entrées moins importantes. Pour nous permettre de publier le dictionnaire en 1972 nous avons dû donner le bon à tirer pour le texte final de la lettre A au début de 1970. Il en découle que les mots qui ont fait leur apparition dans la langue depuis cette date n'ont pas pu être ajoutés. Nous avons regretté que le premier volume (A–Cippe) du *Grand Larousse de la langue française* en six volumes ait paru trop tard en 1971 pour que nous puissions nous en servir. Mais nous l'avons étudié et nous sommes heureux de pouvoir dire que la plupart des mots et expressions qu'il contient figurent dans le *New Standard* alors que ce dernier comprend un vocabulaire important qui ne se trouve pas dans le *Grand Larousse*.

Notre travail nous a fait consulter une grande quantité de dictionnaires, de livres et de périodiques. Nous ne pouvons pas en donner une liste complète, mais nous voudrions mentionner l'aide précieuse que les ouvrages suivants nous ont apportée:

Dictionnaire alphabétique et analogique de la langue française (avec supplément). P. Robert (Société du nouveau Littré)

Le Petit Robert

Grand Larousse Encyclopédique (avec supplément)

Petit Larousse

Dictionnaire du français contemporain (Larousse)

Dictionnaire Encyclopédique (Quillet)

Dictionnaire usuel Quillet-Flammarion

Encyclopédie internationale Focus (Bordas)

Le Bon Usage. M. Grevisse (J. Duculot, S.A.)

Dictionnaire des difficultés de la langue française. A. Thomas (Larousse)

Dictionnaire de la Prononciation française. L. Warnant (J. Duculot, S.A.)

Webster's New International Dictionary (deuxième et troisième éditions)

Webster's Seventh New Collegiate Dictionary

The Random House Dictionary of the English Language

The Penguin English Dictionary

Chambers's Twentieth Century Dictionary (avec supplément)

The Penguin Dictionaries of Biology, Building, Civil Engineering, Electronics, Geography, Psychology and *Science*

Chambers's Technical Dictionary

Dictionnaire des termes techniques de médecine. Garnier et Delamare (Librairie Maloine, S.A.)

Stedman's Medical Dictionary (E. & S. Livingstone, Ltd)

Butterworth's Medical Dictionary

Dictionnaire technique des termes utilisés dans l'industrie du pétrole. Moureau et Rouge (Technip)

Vocabulaire franco-anglo-allemand de Géomorphologie. H. Baulig (Société d'édition: Les Belles Lettres)

Geological Nomenclature. J. Noorduijn en Zoon & N. V. Gorinchem (Ed. A. A. G. Schieferdecker)

A Dictionary of Geography. Monkhouse (Edward Arnold)

A Glossary of Geographical Terms. L. Dudley Stamp (Longmans)

Dictionary of Data Processing/Dictionnaire de l'Informatique. Camille et Dehaine (Harrap)

Dictionnaire d'Informatique. M. Ginguay (Masson, Paris)

Harrap's French–English Dictionary of Slang and Colloquialisms. J. Marks.

Nous voudrions aussi remercier la British Aircraft Corporation qui nous a permis de consulter son *Glossary of Aeronautical Terms* (French–English) et le Capitaine H. G. Sherwood (B.O.A.C.) qui nous a toujours donné son aide pour les termes d'aéronautique.

Notre tâche n'aurait pas pu être menée à bien sans l'assistance de tous nos collaborateurs, aussi bien ceux qui travaillent dans les bureaux de Harrap que ceux qui de tous les coins du globe nous ont aidés dans nos recherches et en lisant les épreuves. Nous voulons tout d'abord rendre hommage à M. Marcel Ferlin, qui lorsqu'il était Assistant à Edimbourg a commencé à travailler au dictionnaire avec M. Mansion en 1912, dès le début. Au cours des années, M. Ferlin a continué sa collaboration, avec ses 'glanures' et en corrigeant les épreuves jusqu'à sa mort en septembre 1970. Nous regrettons du fond du cœur qu'il soit mort avant que ce nouveau dictionnaire paraisse. En lui nous avons perdu non seulement un collaborateur de premier ordre mais aussi un très grand ami.

M. H. R. Elphick a lui aussi formé un lien direct avec le dictionnaire original car il travaillait immédiatement sous les ordres de M. Mansion jusqu'à sa publication. Lorsqu'il a pris sa retraite, après un long séjour en Nouvelle-Zélande, il a accepté de lire les épreuves, ce dont nous lui sommes très reconnaissants. Sa connaissance intime de la structure du dictionnaire nous a été d'une aide très considérable en ce qui concerne la classification du texte des longs articles.

Une partie du travail de préparation du manuscrit a été faite au bureau, mais nous en avons fait une très grosse tranche chez nous avec l'aide infatigable de Mlle Muriel Holland Smith. Nous n'aurions cependant pas encore terminé si nous n'avions pas eu l'aide au cours des années de tous les collaborateurs qui ont fait un gros travail de recherches et de vérification du matériel de provenance extérieure, et nous tenons a les en remercier. Certains ne sont restés que peu de temps avec nous en raison de circonstances personnelles, mais d'autres ont passé plusieurs années avec nous. Parmi eux nous voudrions mentionner tout particulièrement M. P. H. Collin; Mme Françoise Collin (*née* Laurendeau) qui nous a fourni les canadianismes; Mme E. A. H. Strick; Mme A. Smetana-Thieberger; Mme Valerie Deane; Mlle Christine Fontan; et Mlle Vivien Flynn.

Outre les collaborateurs extérieurs mentionnés dans les préfaces des Suppléments (voir p. xxii), nous voulons remercier tout particulièrement MM. J. Bétesta, Michel Ginguay et Roland Ginguay, dont l'aide dans les domaines militaires et techniques nous a permis d'inclure des quantités de termes qui ne se trouvent dans aucun autre dictionnaire; M. H. T. Porter, qui nous a procuré la liste des oiseaux européens; Mme Patricia Forbes, qui a ajouté des listes importantes dans les domaines de l'histoire naturelle et de l'industrie du pétrole; et le Dr I. Feldblum qui nous a aidés pour le vocabulaire médical.

L'aide du Professeur L. C. Harmer ne s'est pas tarie avec son travail sur les Suppléments, et nous tenons à le remercier de ses conseils, et d'avoir lu une partie des épreuves. Nous voulons aussi remercier le Dr Reginald Bowen, Mme Patricia Forbes, M. F. G. S. Parker, Mme E. A. H. Strick et M. Michel Boutron d'avoir bien voulu nous aider à la lecture des épreuves.

Nous voudrions enfin exprimer notre gratitude pour leur encouragement et pour l'aide qu'ils nous ont donnée —souvent inconsciemment—pour trouver des mots que nous cherchions à tous nos amis qui vivent à Holyport (Berkshire) où se trouve notre demeure permanente, et aux Pilles, le village du Midi de la France où notre maison a vu se dérouler beaucoup de nos travaux.

RENÉ LEDÉSERT
MARGARET LEDÉSERT

31 Décembre 1971.

Preface to the 1934 (Original) Edition

"THERE is not a satisfactory French Dictionary on the market." This constant reproach of the last thirty years renders less than justice to much excellent work done in the past by Elwall, Bellows, Boïelle, Tarver, and others; it is none the less true that no French and English dictionary hitherto available has proved adequate to the needs of the serious student.

The just grounds of complaint may be brought under the following heads. In the first place, existing dictionaries are, and always have been, a full generation behind their day in their content, and most of them are too small to be of any 'real use.' The range of human knowledge and invention has extended so greatly during the last two generations that it is materially impossible to cover it in any work of small bulk.

In the next place, bilingual dictionaries are not scientific in their treatment of words, and have not kept pace with the progress in philology that has been so notable in recent years.

Lastly, the mind of the lexicographer seems invariably to be anchored in the past; French phrases in current use are translated into early Victorian English, if not into that of Queen Anne, while a modern English or American colloquialism is rendered, *tant bien que mal*, in the language of Molière. This archaism of phrasing has become glaringly noticeable since the World War. In the vocabulary and phraseology of the peoples involved the reactions have been as violent as in the spheres of sociology and economics, and both French and English have been permanently affected to a degree that can no longer be ignored.

Messrs Harrap & Co. had already before the War laid their plans for the preparation of a new French and English dictionary that should mark a step in advance of what had been achieved up to that time. Material that had not been available to dictionary makers of the last century was at hand to facilitate the task. In France the publication of Hatzfeld and Darmesteter's *Dictionnaire Général* had been nothing short of epoch-making; in Britain the New English Dictionary was approaching completion; in Germany Plattner had finished the compilation of his *Ausführliche Grammatik* and of its Supplements.

In 1919 it was felt that the time was opportune for making a start, and a staff was brought together, whose first task it was to inventory the material ready to hand and to prepare some experimental pages of the French–English part. At the same time the general lines of the work were laid down, what it was proposed to include and what must be considered as lying outside our province.

In the first place this must be a dictionary of the present day, as far as it was possible for any work of reference ever to claim that it is up to date; and this must involve the clearing away of a large amount of archaic lumber still persisting in most dictionaries, echoes of short-lived fashions and of outworn technics that had their day and passed out of our civilization, without leaving any permanent mark on our phraseology. At the same time a modern work of reference must continue to provide a key to the great treasure-houses of French and English literature, within limits and dates which we had to fix.

With regard to France this is a matter of little difficulty. The great bulk of the educated classes live in full enjoyment of the patrimony handed down to them from their 'Grand Siècle'; their acquaintance with Montaigne and Ronsard may be scrappy and superficial, but they are nurtured on the 17th-century dramatists and moralists, on La Fontaine and Mme de Sévigné; in this school their style is formed; their literature of today is full of an allusiveness that takes for granted intimate acquaintance with the great works of this period, and not a few present-day writers, in a full-dress article or speech, will revert to a severely 'classical' French as their medium of expression. Thus no dictionary of the French language, however 'modern,' can leave out of account the vocabulary and syntax of the seventeenth century.

Where to draw the line in English is a question more controversial. Broadly speaking, and for all that the Bible, Shakespeare, and Milton are so 'full of quotations,' the language of the centuries preceding the nineteenth has aged much more than is the case with French; our school acquaintance with Fielding, Richardson, Burke, and Pope is negligible in comparison to the *lycéen*'s intimacy with his great classics, and does not condition our present-day idiom to nearly the same degree. At the same time the vocabulary of English is so extensive that considerations of space make the elimination of unessentials even more imperative than for French, and it was deemed wise to remain, broadly speaking, within the limits of the nineteenth and twentieth centuries.

In neither language, of course, is it possible to lay down hard and fast rules. A dictionary, as opposed to a word-list, must be a record of the diction, of the phrasing and idiom, peculiar to the languages under consideration, and much of this idiom enshrines words and phrases now forgotten, but which must of necessity be noted in order that a surviving use may be understood.

The next point to be decided was: what classes of readers and students we proposed to serve by the publication of this work. The aim was to supply the needs of 'everybody'; not only the general reader and the 'man in the street'—with his wife, but also the historian; the professional man, lawyer or physician, banker or stockbroker, architect or schoolmaster, soldier or sailor; the technician, builder or engineer, printer or binder.

The preparation of a few pages on this ambitious scale led to an early realization that a project conceived on these lines was impracticable; the work must assume the proportions of an encyclopaedia, and defeat its object through sheer wealth of material and the resultant laboriousness of consultation. In order therefore to keep within the limits of a volume easy to handle and reasonable

in cost, we decided that we should aim at helping 'everyman' to read, understand, and even translate, his foreign newspaper, from the leaders to the advertisements. This in itself is a very large undertaking. The better-class newspapers of today, whether French or English, reflect the whole of our daily life and activities, and cater for the most varied interests. Politics, literary and dramatic criticism, law and market reports, and advertisements of sales, constitute only a fraction of their daily contents; new inventions and scientific developments form the subject of articles by specialists who are no longer required to express themselves in strictly 'non-technical' language. For in an age of private motor cars, home-built wireless sets, and electricity 'on tap' for domestic purposes, we are all more or less engineers. Our interests are further taken up with flying displays, watched with critical appreciation of loops and zooms; with movies and talkies; with racing and gracing and the tote. We rely on our paper to keep us up to date regarding the quantum theory, relativity, and the ether-drift; we expect guidance from the same source on the psychics of bidding in the evening's game of bridge.

It has been our endeavour to build up a dictionary that shall deal, if not exhaustively, at any rate adequately, with all these things. Further on will be found a list of encyclopaedias and reference books that have been laid constantly under contribution; special mention should be made of the new and recast editions of Chambers's Encyclopaedia and the *Grand Dictionnaire Larousse;* most of the latter publication appeared in time to allow us to scan its pages. But from the start it was obvious that we could not hope to obtain immediate touch with the times we live in by means of textbooks and dictionaries alone, and that to supplement these we must collect and 'card' our own material. For ten years we have accumulated words and phrases from current works of fiction, from the daily press of both countries concerned, and from periodicals such as *La Science Moderne* and 'Nature.' We enrolled as unconscious collaborators many translators of French into English, of English into French—not all translations are bad, as is too frequently assumed. The number of cards thus collected approximates to 200,000. To establish translations of all these entries was not always an easy task. It entailed correspondence with specialists at home and abroad, and in a number of cases several years have elapsed before a card on the 'waiting list' was duly translated and filed. Most of this material was used in the first place in drafting the French–English section of the Dictionary, and then redistributed under an English head-word.

Thus, when we started on the preparation of the English–French section, a large amount of material lay ready to our hand; but every day produced its quota of English words and phrases that had not come under notice in the first part of the work, and for which renderings must be established. The latter were carded back under a French head-word, and utilized in due course for the revision and completion of the first draft of the French–English section. It is owing to this method of work that we flatter ourselves that in our renderings of much of the idiom of the two languages there will be found a breadth of vocabulary and a raciness that mark an advance on what has been achieved hitherto. In actual number of words we have not widely exceeded the range of the dictionaries already in common use. Under the French letter A, for instance, a count shows only three to four hundred new entries. As a matter of fact, new coinages in a language, of the type of *arpette, aspirine, paravane,* are of rare occurrence; more frequent as neologisms are compounds or derivatives of elements already in established use, such as *amérir, aéroflotte, accumètre, affût-trépied, autobus, autocar,* and the English 'aerobatics,' 'to entrain,' 'to detrain'; borrowings from dialect or from a foreign idiom, such as *braderie* and *batik;* the 'commonizing' of proper names: *un decauville,* or derivation from proper names: *bauxite.* Any new word, when well established, may generate a number of derivatives: the newly popular *braderie* has already given the back-formation '*Ici on bradera*'; *amérir* gives *amérissage;* from *batik* has been formed a verb *batiker,* and there is no reason why *batikage, débatiker, rebatiker,* should not come as readily to the tongue or from the pen.

The sum total of these additions to our store of words in the course of a generation is comparatively small; the real accretion to the vocabulary comes from the extension of the semantic range of the words already in common use. The manifold developments of the last fifty years, telephony, motoring, flying, cinematography, radiology, 'wireless,' psycho-analysis, and what not, have all been made to 'fit in' to the existing vocabulary. We steer a car with a wheel: French has extended the use of *volant* to meet this emergency; we emit and receive our broadcasts through a wire or wires stretched aloft: we have called into service the word 'aerial,' French has extended the range of the word *antenne;* we fire our motor engines with 'plugs,' the French use *bougies;* where at tennis we 'lob' a ball, the French play it *en chandelle.*

This enormous development in the uses of familiar words will be found more adequately mirrored in this dictionary than in any work hitherto available.

Another matter that required more care than is generally vouchsafed to it was the indication of the syntactical relations of the word, as a unit of speech, with its environment. Sentences are knit together by links—prepositions, phrases, conjunctions, concords, uses of tense and mood—according to a mechanism of which the grammar expounds the general principles; but it is the part of a dictionary to indicate the actual links required by, or commonly associated with, any given noun, pronoun, adjective, or verb. This we have done more fully, and more methodically, than has been heretofore attempted. For English syntactical uses we were able to found upon the *Concise Oxford Dictionary* and Mr H. W. Fowler's *Dictionary of Modern English Usage,* with reference, when this was needful, to the *New English Dictionary.* For French our chief source of reference has been Plattner's *Ausführliche Grammatik,* largely supplemented by material gleaned and carded from our own reading, and by that accumulated by Mr G. H. Clarke in his *Manuel-Lexique.*

In our range of words we have gone far beyond the *Dictionnaire de l'Académie;* and, besides technical terms, have admitted very freely what is commonly known as *argot* or 'slang,' at least such part of it as is well established in French and English, and indispensable to an understanding of the 'réalistes' and 'naturalistes' who have bulked so largely in modern literature. How far it is permissible to go in recording these lower strata of the vocabulary is, with regard to such a free-spoken language as French, a question of some delicacy; we established our own censorship, too strict, no doubt, from a French point of view, somewhat lax, perhaps, for Mrs Grundy.

We have extended a wide hospitality to Americanisms; many of these, indeed, have already taken out papers of naturalization; many more are old acquaintances, and by way of becoming intimate friends; they have qualities of terseness and breeziness that give them a value all their own. As regards the hundreds of English words that are current in French today, these are left unrecorded if they have been taken over unchanged in spelling and meaning (*e.g.* 'durbar'). But if they have been adapted (*doper, knockouter, turfiste, schampooing*), or mutilated (*un drop-goal, un shake-hand*), or contracted (*un dancing, un shaker, un skating*), or taken over with a change or extension of meaning (*carter, five-o'clock, flirt, footing, groom, mail-coach, snob*), we have thought them worthy of inclusion.

Two classes of words offer special difficulties to the dictionary maker: those pertaining to law and administration on the one hand, on the other those that cover the field of natural history.

The legal systems of France and England rest on different foundations, and for much of their technical phrasing there is no parallelism between the two languages. When possible we suggest approximate equivalents: and where none exist, we have provided adequate explanations.

As for the names of animals and plants, precision in translation will be unattainable so long as the Latin nomenclatures have not been standardized and internationalized. At present French works of reference are frequently at variance in their nomenclature not only with English works but among themselves, and the inquirer finds himself floundering in a morass of contradictions. The conclusions arrived at can only be offered 'sous toutes réserves.'

For assistance in the labour of compilation of material, and in the final arrangement of the matter under each vocable, we owe grateful thanks to a number of collaborators, some of whom were able to give us their assistance only for a time, and especially to Miss K. Wattie, M.A., and Mr H. R. Elphick, who have been associated with the undertaking since its inception. Mr Elphick has acted secretarially; his gift of organization and genius for ferreting out recondite information have been invaluable. We owe much also to the assistance given by M. A. Pruvot, L. ès L., L. en Dr., M. J. Guillemonat, L. ès L., L. en Dr., and M. E. Thévenot, L. ès L., who in turn joined in our labours; and special thanks are due to M. M. Ferlin, agrégé d'anglais, who for many years has sent us sheaves of '*glanures*,' and who has kindly read a large portion of the proofs. The whole work has been sub-edited from the beginning by Mr C. W. Bell, M.A., and in recent years also by Mr F. M. Atkinson. Their keen sense of language and fertility in constructive criticism have saved us from many sins of commission; for those that remain the Editor alone must assume responsibility.

Lastly we must pay our tribute to the unfailing helpfulness and resource of the printers, and in particular to the competency of the operator and the reader on whom fell the responsibility of transforming the MS. into almost impeccable proof.

J. E. MANSION

January, 1934.

Plan of the Dictionary

(for the original edition)

IN each part the entire contents have been arranged in one alphabetical order. The common practice of relegating biographical, geographical, and other proper names to special sections at the end of the volume entails double entries when, as is frequent, a proper name takes on new functions as a common noun, or *vice versa*, and is wasteful of both space and time. It was thought advisable, however, to group the current abbreviations of the language into a special alphabetical list, which will be found at the end of the volume.

Proper names of persons, gods, towns, rivers, etc., are entered only when they differ in spelling in the two languages, or offer some point of interest worth recording. They nevertheless form a very comprehensive list.

The pronunciation of every word has been given; in the French part the notation adopted is that of the *Association Phonétique Internationale*; its few special symbols can be memorized in a quarter of an hour, and there is no other satisfactory notation that can be mastered so readily. Where there is diversity of custom in the pronunciation of a word the alternatives have been shown.

'Etymologies' do not come within our province. In some French–English dictionaries they take up much valuable space, while merely duplicating information that is readily accessible elsewhere. But while we make no parade of philology, we have endeavoured to treat each word on a philological basis. In the first place care has been taken not to 'jumble up' words of totally different extraction. When under entries such as *appareiller*, *arbitre*, *arche*, *bachot*, *bander*, *barder*, *bille*, *binette*, two or sometimes three unrelated homonyms are treated as one word, their semantic values and development are hopelessly obscured. The present century has been productive of much valuable work in tracing words to their source and in discriminating between homonyms, but of this work no cognizance has been taken up to now in French–English dictionaries.

Again, in the unfolding of the various meanings of a word, its historical evolution has been taken as a basis, the earliest meaning or meanings being only omitted when they have passed out of the language, and are not today present to the mind of native speakers of French or English.

We have used numbers and letters to divide the word into semantic units, therein following Elwall and others; but we have departed from Elwall's practice in one important respect. Whereas he first tabulates the various meanings of the word under consideration, and then proceeds to deal with phrase and idiom, the course adopted here has been to bring together in one semantic group everything that belongs to that group. Language abounds in familiar phrases that pertain in the first place to the technics of sailing, of war, of industry or art; others are rooted in past religions, history, or literature; all such are illuminated, and best understood, when brought back within the semantic group from which they sprang, and first exemplified in their literal or technical use, if this has not become totally effaced. The matter has been arranged on this plan as nearly as is possible in our present state of knowledge of the history of French and English.

It is often difficult to decide under which catchword to enter a phrase that presents two or more 'centres of interest,' *e.g.* 'once bitten twice shy,' 'hunger is the best sauce,' 'to kill two birds with one stone.' In a bilingual dictionary choice will favour the key-word that is most apposite from the point of view of the translation suggested; but as this is a matter which the consulter of the dictionary cannot decide *a priori*, cross-references have been given in a great abundance. Intensive similes, of the type of 'as sharp as a needle,' 'as fit as a fiddle,' are regularly entered under the adjective.

The immediate business of a bilingual dictionary is to supply translations, to set the English word against the French word, and phrase against phrase. Therefore no definitions are given, and explanation is reduced to a minimum. *Râteau* is translated by 'rake' without mention of its being *un instrument de jardinage*. Sufficient that the catchword is followed by the abbreviation for 'Tools,' and that its 'rake's progress' is thereby limited to the garden path. The list of abbreviations of this type is very extensive, and these specifications of the uses of words will be found to leave little room for ambiguity.

There are no acknowledged 'quotations from standard authors'; on the contrary, the need for exercising the utmost economy of space has compelled resort to telegraphic style whenever possible. Points of vocabulary and syntax were gleaned in thousands from modern literature and standard works of reference, but the sentence in which they were embodied has in the majority of cases been shorn of its appendages, and commonly reduced to the infinitive form, in order to achieve compression. In many cases nevertheless the source of the entry remains immediately recognizable, whether, in this first part, it be Molière, the Code, or M. Francis Carco.

Pronominal verbs are dealt with in a separate article following the simple verb, provided that in the pronominal form the verb assumes new meanings or constructions. Thus the verb *battre* is followed by a special entry for the verb *se battre*, 'to fight'; *s'apercevoir de quelque chose* is treated apart from *apercevoir*, *se plaindre de quelqu'un* apart from *plaindre*. But if the pronominal form is merely a reflexive use of the simple verb, implying no change of meaning, it is not treated as a separate entity. Thus *se couper au doigt* is dealt with under *couper;* the reciprocal use *ils s'aiment*, 'they love one another,' will be found under *aimer;* the passive equivalent *cet article se vend bien* under *vendre*.

It is often a matter of some difficulty, and even of controversy, to decide when a past participle assumes a purely adjectival function. The two uses merge one into the other, and it has been deemed advisable to place the past participial adjective immediately after the verb, in order that the two articles may be read and consulted as one. The participle may further function as a noun, in which case the noun also will be found in this location. In many cases, *e.g. acquérir, acquis; mourir, mort*, this has involved a departure from alphabetical order. Whenever this is the case, the participial form will be found entered in its proper alphabetical place, with a reference to the relevant verb. All verbal forms that offer a departure from the stem of the infinitive have also been entered in their place, and referred to the verb under its infinitive form. For all 'irregular' verbs a skeleton of the conjugation is given immediately after the infinitive, but no full paradigms have been supplied. The student is assumed to possess a French grammar.

For convenience of abbreviation common nouns have been described as 'substantives' (masculine or feminine): *s.m., s.f.*, while proper names have been entered as *Pr.n.m., Pr.n.f.* (or in the case of most names of towns, merely as *Pr.n.*). It frequently happens that a proper name also functions as a common noun, and for the sake of compression both uses have been entered under one catchword. The description 'proper name' implies the use of a capital letter; the description 'substantive' implies a small initial. Thus also *parisien, italien,* and similar geographical derivatives are described as 'adjective and substantive' (*a. & s.*); they should be understood to take a capital in the latter function.

J. E. MANSION

Bibliography

OF SOME OF THE WORKS CONSULTED (FOR THE ORIGINAL EDITION)

Dictionnaire de la langue française. E. Littré. *Hachette.*
Dictionnaire général de la langue française. Hatzfeld et Darmesteter. *Delagrave.*
Larousse du XXᵉ Siècle.
Le Larousse pour tous.
Dictionnaire de la langue française. E. Littré et A. Beaujean. *Hachette.*
Petit Larive et Fleury. *Delagrave.*
Dictionnaire étymologique de la langue française. O. Bloch. *Les Presses universitaires de France.*
Dictionnaire des idées suggérées par les mots. P. Rouaix. *Colin.*
Les Synonymes. R. de Noter, H. Lécuyer, et P. Vuillermoz. *Rieder.*
Les Faux Amis. M. Kœssler et J. Derocquigny. *Vuibert.*
Mots anglais perfides. J. Derocquigny. *Vuibert.*
Les Traquenards de la Version anglaise. H. Veslot et J. Banchet. *Hachette.*
Petit Dictionnaire de Style. A. Reum et L. Chambille. *Weber.*
Dictionnaire de la Langue verte. H. France. *Librairie du Progrès.*
Le Langage populaire. H. Bauche. *Payot.*
Glossary of French Slang. O. Leroy. *Harrap.*
Le Slang. J. Manchon. *Payot.*

Comment on prononce le français. Ph. Martinon. *Larousse.*
Dictionnaire phonétique de la langue française. A. Barbeau et E. Rodhe. *Norstedt.*
Manual of French Pronunciation and Diction. J. W. Jack. *Harrap.*

Nouveau Dictionnaire des sciences et de leurs applications. Poiré, Perrier, et Joannis. *Delagrave.*
Dictionnaire des Sciences, des Lettres, et des Arts. M. N. Bouillet. *Hachette.*
Dictionnaire technique. Hoyer-Kreuter. New Edition. *Springer.*
Nouveau Dictionnaire de la Vie pratique. *Hachette.*
Dictionnaire des termes techniques de médecine. M. Garnier et V. Delamare. *Maloine.*
Dictionnaire illustré de médecine usuelle. Galtier-Boissière. *Larousse.*
Dictionnaire financier international. M. et A. Méliot. *Berger-Levrault.*
Dictionnaire juridique anglais-français. Fernand-Laurent et Georges Daumas. *Rousseau.*
Dictionnaire de droit et de termes juridiques anglais. L. E. F. Anspach et A. M. Coutanche. *Librairie générale de Droit.*
Le Langage maritime commercial. L. Bataille et D. H. Nash. *Société d'Éditions géographiques.*
Dictionnaire des termes de marine. J. Douady. *Challamel.*
Vocabulaire technique de l'Éditeur. (Published for the Congrès international des Éditeurs, 1913.)
Manuel d'Édition et de Librairie. G. Zelger. *Payot.*
Vocabulaire de télégraphie et téléphonie sans fil. H. Viard. *Gauthier-Villars.*
Dictionnaire anglais-français-allemand de physique et de chimie. R. Cornubert. *Dunod.*
La Technique photographique. L. P. Clerc. 2 vols. *Éditions P. Montel.*
Flore descriptive et illustrée de la France. Abbé Coste. 3 vols. *Klincksieck.*

Ausführliche Grammatik der französischen Sprache. Ph. Plattner. 7 vols. *Bielefeld.*
Grammaire historique de la langue française. Kr. Nyrop. 5 vols. *Picard.*
Syntaxe du Français contemporain. I. Les Pronoms. Kr. Sandfeld. *Champion.*
Grammaire française. C.-M. Robert. *Wolters.*
A Grammar of Present-Day French. J. E. Mansion. *Harrap.*

Phraséologie française. C.-M. ROBERT. *Wolters.*
L'Idiome français. M. A. VAN DE POEL. *Thieme.*
Traité de Stylistique française. CH. BALLY. 2 vols. *Winter.*
Manuel de langue et de style. FREY et GUÉNOT. *Masson.*
Stylistique française. E. LEGRAND. *De Gigord.*
Manuel-Lexique des difficultés linguistiques du français. G. H. CLARKE et A. CHARPENTIER. *Harrap.*
Le Français classique. G. CAYROU. *Didier.*

The New English Dictionary. *Clarendon Press.*
A Standard Dictionary of the English Language. *Funk and Wagnalls.*
The Practical Standard Dictionary. *Funk and Wagnalls.*
Webster's English Dictionary.
The Century Dictionary.
The Concise Oxford Dictionary of Current English. *Clarendon Press.*
The Little Oxford Dictionary of Current English. *Clarendon Press.*
A Dictionary of Modern English Usage. H. W. FOWLER. *Clarendon Press.*
SAITO's Idiomatic English–Japanese Dictionary. *S.E.G. Publishing Department, Tokio.*
English Idioms. J. M. DIXON. *Nelson.*
Slang, Phrase and Idiom in Colloquial English. T. R. G. LYELL. *Hokuseido Press.*
Chambers's Encyclopaedia.
Encyclopaedia Britannica. New Edition.
Nelson's Encyclopaedia.
Harmsworth's Universal Encyclopaedia.
GROVE's Dictionary of Music and Musicians. *Macmillan.*
A Dictionary of Military Terms. E. S. FARROW. *The Library Press.*
A French–English Military Technical Dictionary. C. DE WITT-WILLCOX.
British Standard Glossary of Aeronautical Terms. *Crosby Lockwood.*
A Glossary of Aeronautical Terms. L. F. PLUGGE. *H.M. Stationery Office.*
A Glossary of Botanical Terms. B. D. JACKSON. *Duckworth.*
Dictionary of Mechanical Engineering Terms. J. G. HORNER. *Crosby Lockwood.*
A French–English Dictionary for Chemists. A. M. PATTERSON. *Chapman and Hall.*
A Phraseological Dictionary of Commercial Correspondence. SCHOLL. *Scholl and McGhee.*

Preface to the 1950 Supplement

PART One (French–English) of *Harrap's Standard French and English Dictionary*, edited by J. E. Mansion, was first published in 1934; Part Two (English–French), in 1939. In the course of those five years Mr Mansion had collected much new material, which, together with the greater extent of the vocabulary of the English language, explains why Part Two of the Dictionary is so much larger than Part One. In 1940 a revised edition of the French–English Part was issued containing as many additions as possible without involving the most costly re-arrangement necessary if the two parts were to be brought into line. We have now incorporated in the French–English section of the Supplement the essential part of the remaining material, as well as many new articles compiled since Mr Mansion's death in 1942, and in consequence this section is substantially larger than the English–French section.

In compiling the Supplement, I had at my disposal:

(1) A large number of notes left by Mr Mansion.
(2) The lists of suggested additions supplied in the course of years by many correspondents, who have also solved knotty problems of translation.
(3) The whole field of modern French and English literature as expressed in books, periodicals, and newspapers.

In spite of our vigilance I am convinced that some recent words and idioms have evaded us and so have been omitted in both languages. Many are so familiar in our everyday language that they are often taken for granted by those whose task it is to keep up to date a work of such magnitude as this Dictionary.

Suggestions and criticism from users of the Dictionary will, therefore, be welcomed by the publishers, all the more so as they intend to publish in a few years' time a completely revised and enlarged edition of this Supplement, which will then become a clearing-house for the more modern words in both languages. This will be the first step towards the publication, in due course, of a completely revised edition of the main work, which will then incorporate those words and expressions which have come to stay.

The plan of the *Standard Dictionary* has been closely adhered to in the Supplement, and, therefore, it was not necessary to repeat the *Table of Phonetic Symbols* and the list of *Abbreviations used in the Dictionary*. The phonetic spelling, although not repeated in the case of words already appearing in the main work, has been given when an entirely new word is included. For the words for which supplementary meanings and explanations are necessary the numbers and classification given refer to the corresponding articles in the main work. Corrections to items appearing in the *Standard Dictionary* have not been included.

I should like to express my gratitude for the very valuable help given to me by Messrs M. Ferlin, F. Thomas, H. Montet, R. A. Sayce, E. M. Trehern, and G. C. Allen. Special thanks are due to M. M. Ferlin and Dr L. C. Harmer, who read the proofs of this Supplement, and who brought to my notice many omissions and errors that had escaped my attention.

R. P. L. LEDÉSERT

June, 1950

Preface to the Second Edition of the Supplement

Since the first Edition of this Supplement appeared in 1950, a large number of additions have been found to be necessary. Many correspondents have accepted my invitation to write to me, and I should like to thank them for their help. The contributions made by Messrs A. Élie, J. Gommy, N. Mayaud, F. G. S. Parker, J. Podgurski, H. T. Porter, E. Thévenot and Dr P. E. Thompson have been the most valuable, in addition to those of Messrs M. Ferlin, H. Montet, R. A. Sayce, E. M. Trehern, already mentioned in the preface to the First Edition. The proofs have been read this time again by M. M. Ferlin and Professor L. C. Harmer, who have as on the first occasion brought to my notice many omissions and errors that had escaped my attention.

R. P. L. LEDÉSERT

June, 1954

Preface to the Third Edition of the Supplement

In the course of the revision of *Harrap's Standard French and English Dictionary* it has become more and more obvious that many recent additions to the French and English languages should be made available (with their translations) as soon as is possible to users of the dictionary. It is for this reason that this very considerably enlarged supplement is now issued.

In addition to the contributors already mentioned in the two previous prefaces, we should like to thank for their help Mrs M. Davidson, Messrs D. Fortin, Ch. Arnaud le Foulon, Papineau-Couture, F. C. Townsend, and J. Watson.

We should also like to acknowledge the considerable assistance afforded us by the following works:

Dictionnaire alphabétique et analogique de la langue française. P. ROBERT. *Société du nouveau Littré.*
Grand Larousse Encyclopédique.
Petit Larousse.
Dictionnaire usuel Quillet-Flammarion.
Webster's New International Dictionary (Supplement).
and many Technical Dictionaries.

The proofs have been read by M. M. Ferlin, Professor L. C. Harmer and Messrs F. G. S. Parker and J. Watson, who have brought to our notice many omissions and imperfections that had escaped our attention.

R. P. L. LEDÉSERT
P. H. COLLIN

March, 1961

Pronunciation

Preface to the Supplement

THE symbols used are those of the International Phonetic Association, and the pronunciation given is the one used most frequently by educated Frenchmen. It is sometimes different from that given in previous editions of the dictionary, as allowance has been made for the evolution of the pronunciation from one generation to another. A few points, however, call for special explanation:

1. Although the accent on the letter *e* (é, è, ê) frequently indicates the pronunciation [e, ɛ, ɛː], this is not automatically so, as the proximity of certain sounds may modify the pronunciation. This modification has been represented, where it is most marked, by the nearest phonetic symbol available. Moreover, as unaccented vowels are always less closed or less open than those in a tonic position, [e] and [ɛ] are often reduced to an intermediate sound which is less closed than [e] and less open than [ɛ]. It has not, however, been considered desirable to show this intermediate sound.

2. The endings *-ation*, *-assion* have in general been represented as [asjɔ̃], though there is a modern tendency, particularly in some parts of France, for the pronunciation [ɑsjɔ̃] to be gaining ground in certain words.

3. Certain final syllables have been indicated as long [ː], notably before a final [j], [r], [v], [z] or [ʒ], and when a nasalized vowel is followed by a pronounced consonant. The user should note that in the table of phonetic symbols vowels followed by the lengthening sign have not been listed separately, though for each vowel, where applicable, examples of the lengthened syllable have been included. The half-length sign [ˑ], denoting a half lengthening within a phonetic group, has not been used at all, as it was felt that such discrimination, liable to give rise to a certain amount of controversy, would be out of place in a dictionary that is not primarily phonetic.

4. For the ending *-aille* the pronunciations [aːj] and [ɑːj] are both current; though in general the pronunciation [ɑːj] is associated with words that are pejorative in meaning, this is not always the case, and the user will note a certain number of words which are in no way pejorative for which we have considered that the pronunciation [ɑːj] is the more current.

5. The pronunciation of the unvoiced final *r* and *l* after a consonant has been given as [r̥] and [l̥], as in *mètre* [mɛtr̥] and *table* [tabl̥].

6. The pronunciation [œ̃] to represent *un* has been used throughout, despite the growing tendency, especially in some parts of France, for the pronunciation [ɛ̃] to be used in words such as *lundi* or *Verdun*.

7. The tonic accent is not indicated, but it may be assumed to fall, however slightly, on the last sounded syllable of a word, when that word is considered alone, apart from a word group. It should, however, be borne in mind that the tonic accent is much less pronounced in French than in English.

Prononciation

Les signes employés pour figurer la prononciation sont ceux de *l'Association phonétique internationale*.

La prononciation figurée est, dans chaque cas, la prononciation la plus courante chez les Français instruits. Elle est parfois différente de celle notée dans nos précédentes éditions; la prononciation française, comme la prononciation anglaise, évolue au cours des générations; nous avons autant que possible tenu compte de cette évolution.

Nous nous permettons d'attirer l'attention sur quelques particularités:

1. Il ne faut pas oublier que si dans un *e* accentué (é, è, ê) l'accent, dans beaucoup de cas, indique la prononciation [e, ɛ, ɛː], il n'en est pas toujours ainsi, car le voisinage de certains sons peut modifier cette prononciation. Nous avons noté cette modification, lorsqu'elle est patente, par le signe le plus approchant. D'autre part, les voyelles en position atone étant toujours moins fermées ou moins ouvertes qu'en position tonique, [e] ou [ɛ] sont souvent réduits à un son intermédiaire. Nous avons jugé superflu de noter spécialement cet *e* intermédiaire.

2. Pour les terminaisons *-ation*, *-assion* nous avons dans la plupart des cas choisi la prononciation [asjɔ̃]. Il faut cependant remarquer que la prononciation [ɑsjɔ̃] a une tendance à se répandre dans certaines régions, surtout pour certains mots.

3. Nous avons indiqué comme longues [ː] certaines syllabes finales, notamment celles qui se terminent en [j], [r], [v], [z], ou [ʒ] et celles dans lesquelles une voyelle nasale est suivie par une consonne prononcée. Dans la table des symboles phonétiques nous n'avons pas indiqué séparément les voyelles courtes et les voyelles longues ([i], [iː], [a], [aː], etc.) mais pour chaque voyelle où cela est nécessaire nous avons donné des exemples de syllabes courtes et longues. Nous n'avons pas considéré comme utile l'introduction du symbole [ˑ] qui se réfère à une voyelle demi-longue, car une distinction si minutieuse n'est pas à sa place dans un dictionnaire qui n'est pas primordialement un dictionnaire phonétique.

4. La terminaison *-aille* peut se prononcer ou [aːj] ou [ɑːj]; en général la prononciation [ɑːj] est associée aux mots qui ont un sens péjoratif, mais ceci n'est pas toujours le cas, et l'usager remarquera un certain nombre de mots avec la terminaison [ɑːj] dont le sens n'est aucunement péjoratif.

5. La prononciation de l'*r* ou de l'*l* final atone qui suit une consonne, comme dans des mots comme *mètre* ou *table*, est représentée par [ɾ] et [ḷ]: [mɛtɾ], [tabḷ].

6. Nous avons maintenu partout la figuration [œ̃] pour la graphie *un*; il faut cependant noter que la prononciation [ɛ̃] pour [œ̃] dans des mots comme *lundi*, *Verdun*, tend à se répandre, surtout dans certaines régions.

7. Nous n'avons pas noté l'accent tonique. L'accent *normal* (qu'il faut distinguer de l'accent *d'insistance*) porte, dans le mot isolé, sur la dernière syllabe (ou l'avant-dernière si la dernière comporte un *e* muet); mais il ne faut pas oublier que l'accent tonique est moins prononcé en français qu'en anglais.

Phonetic Symbols

VOWELS

[i] vite [vit]; signe [siɲ]; rire [riːr]; fille [fiːj]; Moïse [mɔiːz]; ami [ami]; sortie [sɔrti].

[e] été [ete]; donner, donné [dɔne]; légal [legal]; saisir [seziːr].

[ɛ] elle [ɛl]; très [trɛ]; parquet [parkɛ]; forêt [fɔrɛ]; mais [mɛ]; terre [tɛːr]; pèse [pɛːz]; rêve [rɛːv]; paire [pɛːr]; père [pɛːr].

[a] absent [absɑ̃]; chat [ʃa]; tache [taʃ]; toit [twa]; couramment [kuramɑ̃]; phare [faːr]; lave [laːv]; noir [nwaːr]; courage [kuraːʒ].

[ɑ] pas [pɑ]; âgé [ɑʒe]; âge [ɑːʒ]; tâche [tɑːʃ]; sable [sɑbl̩].

[ɔ] donner [dɔne]; Paul [pɔl]; album [albɔm]; fort [fɔːr]; éloge [elɔːʒ].

[o] dos [do]; impôt [ɛ̃po]; chaud [ʃo]; chapeau [ʃapo]; saumoneau [somɔno]; rose [roːz]; sauge [soːʒ].

[u] tout [tu]; goût [gu]; goutte [gut]; août [u]; cour [kuːr]; loup [lu]; louve [luːv].

[y] cru [kry]; crû [kry]; ciguë [sigy]; punir [pyniːr]; mur [myːr]; mûr [myːr]; gageure [gaʒyːr]; muse [myːz].

[ø] feu [fø]; nœud [nø]; heureux [œrø]; heureuse [œrøːz].

[œ] seul [sœl]; jeune [ʒœn]; œuf [œf]; cueillir [kœjiːr]; fleurir [flœriːr]; sœur [sœːr]; feuille [fœːj].

[ə]* le [lə]; ce [sə]; entremets [ɑ̃trəmɛ]; vendredi [vɑ̃drədi].

[ɛ̃] vin [vɛ̃]; plein [plɛ̃]; main [mɛ̃]; chien [ʃjɛ̃]; examen [egzamɛ̃]; syntaxe [sɛ̃taks]; impair [ɛ̃pɛːr]; faim [fɛ̃]; thym [tɛ̃]; prince [prɛ̃ːs]; plainte [plɛ̃ːt]; teindre [tɛ̃ːdr̩].

[ɑ̃] enfant [ɑ̃fɑ̃]; tambour [tɑ̃buːr]; temps [tɑ̃]; tant [tɑ̃]; tante [tɑ̃ːt]; paon [pɑ̃]; danse [dɑ̃ːs]; centre [sɑ̃ːtr̩]; exempt [egzɑ̃]; exempte [egzɑ̃ːt]; ample [ɑ̃ːpl̩]; branche [brɑ̃ːʃ].

[ɔ̃] mon [mɔ̃]; plomb [plɔ̃]; fronton [frɔ̃tɔ̃]; long [lɔ̃]; longe [lɔ̃ːʒ]; honte [ɔ̃ːt]; nombre [nɔ̃ːbr̩]; compte [kɔ̃ːt]; comte [kɔ̃ːt].

[œ̃] un [œ̃]; lundi [lœ̃di]; Verdun [vɛrdœ̃]; parfum [parfœ̃]; humble [œ̃ːbl̩]; lunch [lœ̃ːʃ].

CONSONANTS

[p] pain [pɛ̃]; frapper [frape]; tape [tap].

[b] beau [bo]; abbé [abe]; robe [rɔb].

[m] mon [mɔ̃]; aimer [ɛme]; madame [madam]; flamme [flam]; prisme [prism]; immatériel [im(m)aterjɛl].

[f] feu [fø]; effet [efɛ]; bref [brɛf]; phrase [fraːz]; Joseph [ʒɔzɛf].

[v] voir [vwaːr]; vie [vi]; wagon [vagɔ̃]; neuf heures [nœvœːr].

[t] table [tabl̩]; tête [tɛt]; nette [nɛt]; grand homme [grɑ̃tɔm]; théâtre [teɑːtr̩].

[d] donner [dɔne]; addition [adisjɔ̃]; sud [syd].

[n] né [ne]; animal [animal]; canne [kan]; amen [amɛn]; automne [otɔn]; penniforme [pɛn(n)ifɔrm].

[s] sou [su]; assassin [asasɛ̃]; tasse [tɑːs]; rébus [rebys]; prisme [prism]; cire [siːr]; leçon [ləsɔ̃]; scène [sɛn]; six [sis]; soixante [swasɑ̃ːt]; Bruxelles [brysɛl]; déhiscence [deis(s)ɑ̃ːs].

[z] cousin [kuzɛ̃]; les enfants [lɛzɑ̃fɑ̃]; vas-y [vazi]; zéro [zero]; deuxième [døzjɛm].

[l] lait [lɛ]; aile [ɛl]; facile [fasil]; aller [ale]; balle [bal]; illusion [il(l)yzjɔ̃].

[l̩] table [tabl̩]; sensible [sɑ̃sibl̩] hièble [jɛbl̩]; faible [fɛbl̩]; double [dubl̩]; noble [nɔbl̩].

[ʃ] chose [ʃoːz]; chercher [ʃɛrʃe]; schisme [ʃism].

[ʒ] Jean [ʒɑ̃]; gilet [ʒilɛ]; manger [mɑ̃ʒe]; âge [ɑːʒ]; changeable [ʃɑ̃ʒabl̩].

[k] camp [kɑ̃]; képi [kepi]; bifteck [biftɛk]; coq [kɔk]; quatre [katr̩]; queue [kø]; écho [eko]; chrétien [kretjɛ̃]; physique [fizik].

[g] garde [gard]; agrandir [agrɑ̃diːr]; aggraver [agrave]; guerre [gɛːr]; gui [gi]; second [səgɔ̃]; agnostique [agnɔstik]; gneiss [gnɛs]; grammaire [gram(m)ɛːr].

[ɲ] campagne [kɑ̃paɲ]; poignet [pwaɲɛ]; gnaf [ɲaf].

[ŋ] (in words of foreign origin) parking [parkiŋ]; smoking [smokiŋ].

[r] rare [raːr]; chariot [ʃarjo]; arbre [arbr̩]; marron [marɔ̃]; ménorrhée [menɔre]; rhume [rym]; sentir [sɑ̃tiːr]; irréparable [ir(r)eparabl̩].

[r̩] être [ɛːtr̩]; marbre [marbr̩]; neutre [nøtr̩]; notre [nɔtr̩]; moudre [mudr̩]; sabre [saːbr̩].

[ks] accident [aksidɑ̃]; exception [ɛksɛpsjɔ̃]; action [aksjɔ̃]; (la lettre) x [iks]; xénophobe [ksenɔfɔb]; xylophone [ksilɔfɔn].

[gz] exister [egziste]; examen [egzamɛ̃]; xanthéine [gzɑ̃tein].

SEMI-CONSONANTS

[j] yacht [jɔt]; yeux [jø]; yougoslave [jugɔslaːv]; yucca [juka]; piano [pjano]; mioche [mjɔʃ]; ration [rasjɔ̃]; voyager [vwajaʒe]; fauteuil [fotœːj]; travail [travaːj]; travailler [travaje]; ensoleillé [ɑ̃sɔlɛje]; œillade [œjad]; feuille [fœːj]; cahier [kaje]; levier [ləvje]; lévrier [levrije].

[w] ouate [wat]; ouest [west]; oui [wi]; jouer [ʒwe]; noir [nwaːr]; loin [lwɛ̃]; pingouin [pɛ̃gwɛ̃]; (also in words of foreign origin) water-closet [watɛrklɔzɛt]; wattage [wataːʒ]; whist [wist]; wellingtonia [wɛliŋtɔnja].

[ɥ] muet [mɥe]; huit [ɥit]; luire [lɥiːr]; aiguille [ɛgɥiːj]; distribuer [distribɥe].

---

* The symbol (ə) (in brackets) indicates that the 'mute' e is pronounced in careful speech but not in rapid speech.

Abbreviations Used in the Dictionary
Abréviations Utilisées dans le Dictionnaire

Abbr.	English	French
A:	archaism; ancient; in former use	désuet
a., adj.	adjective	adjectif
abbr.	abbreviation	abréviation
abs.	absolutely; absolute use	emploi absolu
Ac:	acoustics	acoustique
acc.	accusative	accusatif
Adm:	administration; civil service	administration
adv.	adverb	adverbe
adv.phr.	adverbial phrase	locution adverbiale
Aer:	aeronautics	aéronautique
Agr:	agriculture	agriculture
A.Hist:	ancient history	histoire ancienne
Alch:	alchemy	alchimie
Alg:	algebra	algèbre
Algae:	algae	algues
Amph:	Amphibia	amphibiens
Anat:	anatomy	anatomy
Ann:	Annelida, worms	annelés
Ant:	antiquity, antiquities	antiquité
Anthr:	anthropology	anthropologie
Ap:	apiculture	apiculture
approx:	approximately	sens approché
Ar:	arithmetic	arithmétique
Arach:	Arachnida	arachnides
Arb:	arboriculture	arboriculture; sylviculture
Arch:	architecture	architecture
Archeol:	archaeology	archéologie
Arm:	armour	armure
Arms:	arms; armaments	armes; armements
art.	article	article
Art:	art	beaux-arts
Artil:	artillery	artillerie
Astr:	astronomy	astronomie
Astrol:	astrology	astrologie
Astro-Ph:	astrophysics	astrophysique
Atom.Ph:	atomic physics	sciences atomiques
attrib.	attributive	attributif
Austr:	Australia; Australian	Australie; australien
Aut:	motoring; automobile industry	automobilisme; industrie automobile
aux.	auxiliary	auxiliaire
Av:	aviation; aircraft	aviation; avions
B:	Bible; biblical	Bible; biblique
Bac:	bacteriology	bactériologie
Bak:	baking	boulangerie
Ball:	ballistics	ballistique
Bank:	banking	opérations de banque
Belg:	Belgium; Belgian	Belgique; belge
B.Hist:	Bible history	histoire sainte
Bib:	bibliography	bibliographie
Bill:	billiards	jeu de billard
Bio-Ch:	biochemistry	biochimie
Biol:	biology	biologie
Bookb:	bookbinding	reliure
Book-k:	book-keeping	comptabilité
Bootm:	boot and shoe industry	cordonnerie; industrie de la chaussure
Bot:	botany	botanique
Box:	boxing	boxe
Breed:	breeding	élevage
Brew:	brewing	brasserie
Brickm:	brickmaking	briqueterie
card.a.	cardinal adjective	adjectif cardinal
Cards:	card games	jeu de cartes
Carp:	carpentry	charpenterie; menuiserie du bâtiment
Cav:	cavalry	cavalerie
Cer:	ceramics	céramique
cf.	refer to	conferatur
Ch:	chemistry	chimie
Chess:	chess	jeu d'échecs
Chr:	chronology	chronologie
Cin:	cinema	cinéma
Civ:	civilization	civilisation
Civ.E:	civil engineering	génie civil
Cl:	classical: Greek or Roman antiquity	classique; antiquité grecque ou romaine
Clockm:	clock and watch making	horlogerie
Coel:	Coelenterata	cœlentérés
cogn.acc.	cognate accusative	accusatif de l'objet interne
Cokem:	cokemaking	industrie du coke
coll.	collective	collectif
Com:	commerce; business term	(terme du) commerce
comb.fm.	combining form	forme de combinaison
Comest:	comestibles, food	comestibles
comp.	comparative	comparatif
Conch:	conchology	conchyliologie
condit.	conditional	conditionnel
conj.	conjunction	conjonction
conj. like	conjugated like	se conjugue comme
Const:	construction, building industry	industrie du bâtiment
Coop:	cooperage	tonnellerie
Corr:	correspondence, letters	correspondance, lettres
Cost:	costume; clothing	costume; habillement
cp.	compare	comparer
Cr:	cricket	cricket
Crust:	Crustacea	crustacés
Cryst:	crystallography	cristallographie
Cu:	culinary; cooking	culinaire; cuisine
Cust:	customs	douane
Cy:	cycles; cycling	bicyclettes; cyclisme
Danc:	dancing	danse
dat.	dative	datif
def.	(i) definitive; (ii) defective (verb)	(i) défini; (ii) (verbe) défectif
dem.	demonstrative	démonstratif
Dent:	dentistry	art dentaire
Dial:	dialectal	dialectal
dim.	diminutive	diminutif
Dipl:	diplomacy; diplomatic	diplomatie; diplomatique
Dist:	distilling	distillation
Dom.Ec:	domestic economy; household equipment	économie domestique; ménage
Draw:	drawing	dessin
Dressm:	dressmaking	couture (mode)
Dy:	dyeing	teinture

Abbr	English	French
Dyn:	*dynamics*	dynamique
E.	*east*	est
E:	*engineering*	industries mécaniques
Ecc:	*ecclesiastical*	église et clergé
Echin:	*Echinodermata*	échinodermes
e.g.	*for example*	par exemple
El:	*electricity; electrical*	électricité; électrique
El.Ch:	*electrochemistry*	électrochimie
Elcs:	*electronics*	électronique
El.E:	*electrical engineering*	électrotechnique
Eng:	*England; English*	Angleterre; anglais, britannique
Engr:	*engraving*	gravure
Ent:	*entomology*	entomologie
Equit:	*equitation*	équitation
esp.	*especially*	surtout
etc.	*et cetera*	et cætera
Eth:	*ethics*	morale
Ethn:	*ethnology*	ethnologie
Exp:	*explosives*	explosifs
f.	*feminine*	féminin
F:	*colloquial(ism)*	familier; style de la conversation
Farr:	*farriery*	maréchalerie
Fb:	*(Association) football*	football
Fenc:	*fencing*	escrime
Ferns:	*ferns*	fougères
Fin:	*finance*	finances
Fish:	*fishing*	pêche
For:	*forestry*	forêts
Fort:	*fortification*	fortification
Fr.	*France; French*	France; français
Fr.C:	*French Canadian*	canadien français
fu.	*future*	futur
Fuel:	*fuel*	combustibles
Fung:	*fungi*	champignons
Furn:	*furniture*	mobilier
Games:	*games*	jeux
Gaming:	*gaming; gambling*	le jeu; jeux d'argent
Gasm:	*gasmaking*	industrie du gaz
Geog:	*geography*	géographie
Geol:	*geology*	géologie
Geom:	*geometry*	géométrie
ger.	*gerund*	gérondif
Glassm:	*glassmaking*	verrerie
Gr.	*Greek*	grec
Gr.Alph:	*Greek alphabet*	alphabet grec
Gr.Ant:	*Greek antiquity*	antiquité grecque
Gr.Civ:	*Greek civilization*	civilisation grecque
Gr.Hist:	*Greek history*	histoire grecque
Gram:	*grammar*	grammaire
Gym:	*gymnastics*	gymnastique
Hairdr:	*hairdressing*	coiffure
Harn:	*harness; saddlery*	sellerie; harnais
Hatm:	*hatmaking*	chapellerie
Her:	*heraldry*	blason
Hist:	*history; historical*	histoire; historique
Hor:	*horology*	horométrie
Hort:	*horticulture*	horticulture
Hum:	*humorous*	humoristique
Husb:	*animal husbandry*	élevage
Hyd:	*hydraulics; hydrostatics*	hydraulique; hydrostatique
Hyg:	*hygiene; sanitation*	hygiène; installations sanitaires
i.	*intransitive*	intransitif
I.C.E:	*internal combustion engines*	moteurs à combustion interne
Ich:	*ichthyology; fish*	ichtyologie; poissons
Ill:	*illuminants; lighting*	illuminants; éclairage
imp.	*imperative*	impératif
impers.	*impersonal*	impersonnel
ind.	*indicative*	indicatif
Ind:	*industry; industrial*	industrie; industriel
indef.	*indefinite*	indéfini
ind.tr.	*indirectly transitive*	transitif avec régime indirect
inf.	*infinitive*	infinitif
Ins:	*insurance*	assurance
int.	*interjection*	interjection
Internat:	*international*	international
interr.	*interrogative*	interrogatif
inv.	*invariable*	invariable
Iron:	*ironic(ally)*	ironique(ment)
Jap:	*Japanese*	japonais
Jew:	*Jewish*	juif, juive
Jewel:	*jewellery*	bijouterie
Join:	*joinery*	menuiserie
Journ:	*journalism; journalistic*	journalisme; style journalistique
Jur:	*jurisprudence; legal term*	droit; terme de palais
Knitting:	*knitting*	tricot
Lacem:	*lacemaking*	dentellerie
Lap:	*lapidary arts*	arts lapidaires; taillerie
Laund:	*laundering*	blanchissage
Leath:	*leatherwork*	travail du cuir
Leg:	*legislation*	législation
Ling:	*linguistics; language*	linguistique; langue
Lit:	*literary use; literature; literary*	forme littéraire; littérature; littéraire
Lith:	*lithography*	lithographie
Locksm:	*locksmithery*	serrurerie
Log:	*logic*	logique
Lt.	*Latin*	latin
m.	*masculine*	masculin
Magn:	*magnetism*	magnétisme
Mapm:	*mapmaking*	cartographie
Matchm:	*match industry*	industrie des allumettes
Mch:	*machines; machinery*	machines; machines à vapeur
Mch.Tls:	*machine tools*	machines-outils
Meas:	*weights and measures*	poids et mesures
Mec:	*mechanics*	mécanique
Mec.E:	*mechanical engineering*	industries mécaniques
Med:	*medicine; illnesses*	médecine; maladies
Metall:	*metallurgy*	métallurgie
Metalw:	*metalworking*	travail des métaux
Metaph:	*metaphysics*	métaphysique
Meteor:	*meteorology*	météorologie
Mil:	*military; army*	militaire; armée de terre
Mill:	*milling*	meunerie
Min:	*mining and quarrying*	exploitation des mines et carrières
Miner:	*mineralogy*	minéralogie
M.Ins:	*marine insurance*	assurance maritime
Moll:	*molluscs*	mollusques
Moss:	*mosses and lichens*	muscinées
Mount:	*mountaineering*	alpinisme
Mth:	*mathematics*	mathématiques
Mus:	*music*	musique
Myr:	*Myriapoda*	myriapodes
Myth:	*mythology; myths and legends*	mythologie; mythes et légendes
n.		nous
N.	*north*	nord
N.Arch:	*naval architecture*	architecture navale
Nat.Hist:	*natural history*	histoire naturelle
Nau:	*nautical*	terme de marine
Nav:	*navigation*	navigation
Navy:	*Navy*	marine militaire
Needlew:	*needlework*	couture (travaux d'aiguille)
neg.	*negative*	négatif
neut.	*neuter*	neutre
nom.	*nominative*	nominatif
Num:	*numismatics*	numismatique
num.a.	*numeral adjective*	adjectif numéral
O:	*obsolescent*	vieilli
Obst:	*obstetrics*	obstétrique
Oc:	*oceanography*	océanographie
occ.	*occasionally*	parfois
onomat.	*onomatopoeia*	onomatopée
Opt:	*optics*	optique
Orn:	*ornithology; birds*	ornithologie; oiseaux
Ost:	*ostreiculture; oysters*	ostréiculture; huîtres
p.	*(i) past; (ii) participle*	(i) passé; (ii) participe
P:	*uneducated speech; slang*	expression populaire; argot
Paint:	*painting trade*	peinture en bâtiment
Pal:	*paleography*	paléographie
Paleont:	*paleontology*	paléontologie
Paperm:	*papermaking*	fabrication du papier

Parl:	parliament	parlement	*Soapm:*	soapmaking	savonnerie
Path:	pathology	pathologie	*Soc.H:*	social history	histoire sociale
p.d.	imperfect, *past descriptive* (tense)	imparfait (de l'indicatif), passé descriptif	*Sp:*	sport	sport
Pej:	pejorative	péjoratif	*Space:*	astronautics; space travel	astronautique; voyages interplanétaires
perf.	perfect (*tense*)	passé composé	*Spong:*	sponges	spongiaires
pers.	person(s); personal	personne(s); personnel	*St.Exch:*	Stock Exchange	terme de Bourse
p.h.	past historic, past definite (*tense*)	passé historique, passé simple	*sth.*	something	
Ph:	physics	physique	*Stonew:*	stoneworking	taille de la pierre
Pharm:	pharmacy	pharmacie	*sub.*	subjunctive	subjonctif
Ph.Geog:	physical geography	géographie physique	*suff.*	suffix	suffixe
Phil:	philosophy	philosophie	*Sug.-R:*	sugar refining	raffinerie du sucre
Phot:	photography	photographie	*sup.*	superlative	superlatif
Phot.Engr:	photo-engraving; *process work*	procédés photomécaniques; photogravure	*Surg:*	surgery	chirurgie
			Surv:	surveying	géodésie et levé de plans
phr.	phrase	locution	*Swim:*	swimming	natation
Phren:	phrenology	phrénologie	*Sw.Fr:*	Swiss French	mot utilisé en Suisse
Physiol:	physiology	physiologie	*Switz:*	Switzerland	la Suisse
Pisc:	pisciculture	pisciculture			
pl.	plural	pluriel	*Tail:*	tailoring	mode masculine
Plumb:	plumbing	plomberie	*Tan:*	tanning	tannage des cuirs
P.N:	public notice	affichage; avis au public	*Tchn:*	technical	terme technique, terme de métier
Poet:	poetical	poétique			
Pol:	politics; political	politique	*Telecom:*	telecommunications	télécommunications
Pol.Ec:	political economy, economics	économie politique	*Ten:*	tennis	tennis
poss.	possessive	possessif	*Ter:*	teratology	tératologie
Post:	postal services	postes et télécommunications	*Tex:*	textiles, textile industry	industries textiles
			Tg:	telegraphy	télégraphie
p.p.	past participle	participe passé	*Th:*	theatre; theatrical	théâtre
pr.	present (*tense*)	présent (de l'indicatif)	*Theol:*	theology	théologie
pref.	prefix	préfixe	*thg*	thing(s)	
Prehist:	prehistory	préhistoire	*Tls:*	tools	outils
prep.	preposition	préposition	*Toil:*	toilet; make up	toilette; maquillage
prep.phr.	prepositional phrase	locution prépositive	*Torp:*	torpedoes	torpilles
Pr.n.	proper name	nom propre	*Town P:*	town planning	urbanisme
pron.	pronoun	pronom	*Toys:*	toys	jouets
Pros:	prosody	prosodie; métrique	*Tp:*	telephony	téléphonie
Prot:	Protozoa	protozoaires	*tr.*	transitive	transitif
Prov:	proverb	proverbe	*Trans:*	transport	transports
pr.p.	present participle	participe présent	*Trig:*	trigonometry	trigonométrie
Psy:	psychology	psychologie	*Turb:*	turbines	turbines
Psychics:	psychics	métapsychisme	*Turf:*	turf, horse racing	turf
Publ:	publishing	édition	*T.V:*	television	télévision
Pyr:	pyrotechnics	pyrotechnie	*Typ:*	typography	typographie
			Typew:	typing; typewriters	dactylographie; machines à écrire
qch.		quelque chose			
qn		quelqu'un	*U.S:*	United States; American	États-Unis; américain
q.v.	which see	se reporter à ce mot	*usu.*	usually	d'ordinaire
Rac:	racing	courses	*v.*	verb	verbe
Rad.-A:	radioactivity	radioactivité	*v.*		vous
Rail:	railways, railroads	chemins de fer	*V:*	vulgar; not in polite use	trivial
R.C.Ch:	Roman Catholic Church	Église catholique	*Veh:*	vehicles	véhicules
Rec:	tape recorders; record players	magnétophones; tourne-disques	*Ven:*	venery; hunting	la chasse
			Vet:	veterinary science	art vétérinaire
rel.	relative	relatif	*v.i.*	intransitive verb	verbe intransitif
Rel:	religion(s)	religion(s)	*v.ind.tr.*	indirectly transitive verb	verbe transitif indirect
Rel.H:	religious history	histoire des religions	*Vit:*	viticulture	viticulture
Rept:	reptiles	reptiles	*voc.*	vocative	vocatif
Rh:	rhetoric	rhétorique	*v.pr.*	pronominal verb	verbe pronominal
Rom:	Roman	romain, romaine	*v.tr.*	transitive verb	verbe transitif
Ropem:	ropemaking	corderie			
Row:	rowing	aviron	*W.*	west	ouest
R.t.m	registered trade mark	marque déposée	*Wine-m:*	wine making	l'industrie du vin
Rubberm:	rubber manufacture	industrie du caoutchouc	*Woodw:*	woodworking	menuiserie
Rugby Fb:	Rugby (*football*)	le rugby	*Wr:*	wrestling	la lutte
Russ:	Russian	russe	*W.Tel:*	wireless telegraphy and telephony; radio	téléphonie et télégraphie sans fil; radio
S.	south	sud	*W.Tg:*	wireless telegraphy	télégraphie sans fil
s., sb.	substantive, noun	substantif, nom	*W.Tp:*	wireless telephony	téléphonie sans fil
s.a.	see also	voir			
Sch:	schools and universities; students' (*slang, etc.*)	université; écoles; (argot, etc.) scolaire	*Y:*	yachting	yachting
Scot:	Scotland; Scottish	Écosse; écossais	*Z:*	zoology; mammals	zoologie; mammifères
Scouting:	**Scout and Guide Movements**	scoutisme			
Sculp:	sculpture	sculpture	*=*	nearest equivalent (*of an institution, an office, etc., when systems vary in the different countries*)	équivalent le plus proche (d'un terme désignant une institution, une charge, etc., dans les cas où les systèmes varient dans les différents pays)
Ser:	sericulture	sériciculture			
sg.	singular	singulier			
Ski:	skiing	le ski			
Sm.a:	small arms	armes portatives			
s.o.	someone				

A

A, a [ɑ], *s.m.* (the letter) A, a; *F:* **il ne sait ni A ni B,** (i) he can't read, he doesn't know his ABC; (ii) he doesn't know A from B; *F:* he can't tell chalk from cheese; *Tp:* **A comme Anatole,** A for Andrew; **il vous prouvera par a plus b que . . .,** he will demonstrate that . . .; *Prov:* **A: qui a dit A doit dire B,** (i) one wrong step entails another; (ii) in for a penny in for a pound; **connaître un sujet depuis A jusqu'à Z,** to know a subject from A to Z, thoroughly, inside out; *A:* **marqué à l'A,** first-rate, eminent.

à [a], *prep.* (contracts with the article **le** into **au,** with the article **les** into **aux**). (*Note: in many uses* à *is found in competition with other prepositions or with constructions which do not include a preposition. The precise value of* à *is not always clear, and its uses sometimes tend to merge*). **I.** (à *with a non-infinitive complement*). **1.** (*denoting direction*) (*a*) (*towards some point or place, sometimes implying entry into a space*) **courir à qn,** to run to s.o.; **revenir à la surface,** to come (up) to the surface again; **aller à l'église, au cinéma,** to go to church, to the cinema; **monter à sa chambre,** to go up to one's room; **conduire les chevaux à l'écurie,** to lead the horses to the stable; **de Paris à Lyon,** from Paris to Lyons; **se rendre au Japon, aux Antilles, à la Guadeloupe, à Terre-Neuve,** to travel to Japan, to the West Indies, to Guadeloupe, to Newfoundland; (*elliptically*) **au feu! au voleur!** fire! stop thief! *W.Tel:* **à vous,** over (to you); (*b*) (*figuratively*) **courir à sa perte,** to head for disaster; **émouvoir qn aux larmes,** to move s.o. to tears; (*de*) **vingt à trente personnes,** between twenty and thirty people; (*c*) (*in the sense of* **vers,** *towards*) **lever les bras, les yeux, au ciel,** to raise one's arms, one's eyes, to heaven. **2.** (*denoting position*) (*a*) (*at a point, or more vaguely, denoting situation near or inside a space*) **au coin de la rue,** at the corner of the street, at the street corner; **à l'horizon,** on the horizon; **à la page deux,** on page two; **à l'ombre,** in the shade; **au grenier,** in the attic; **à la maison,** at home; **au théâtre,** at the theatre; **au Canada,** in Canada; **aux États-Unis,** in the United States; **à la Jamaïque,** in Jamaica; **à Cuba,** in Cuba; **à Paris,** in Paris; **à deux kilomètres d'ici,** two kilometres from here; *Sp:* **ils ne sont qu'à trois points,** they are only three points behind; **avoir un livre à la main,** to have a book in one's hand; (*b*) (*figuratively*) **être à la merci de qn,** to be at s.o.'s mercy; **au fond,** at bottom, fundamentally. **3.** (*denoting direction in time*) **du matin au soir,** from morning to night; **remettre une affaire à plus tard,** to put off a matter until later; **à jamais,** for ever; **à demain!** till tomorrow then! see you tomorrow!; **de lundi à vendredi,** from Monday to Friday, *U.S:* Monday through Friday; **au revoir,** good-bye (for the present). **4.** (*a*) (*denoting an attendant circumstance, sometimes with a causal implication*) **au premier mot,** at the first word; **à mon arrivée,** on my arrival; **se réveiller au tintement de la cloche,** to wake at the sound of the bell; (*b*) (*indicating a point or situation in time or in a wider sense*) **à deux heures,** at two o'clock; **au vingtième siècle,** in the twentieth century; **à l'avenir,** in (the) future. **5.** (*denoting opposition or succession*) **se battre homme à homme,** to fight man to man; (*elliptically*) *Ten:* **quinze à,** fifteen all; **monter l'escalier quatre à quatre,** to go upstairs four (steps) at a

time; **peu à peu,** little by little, gradually. **6.** (*introducing the indirect object of many verbs*) (*a*) (*expressing a great variety of ideas, including attribution, conformity, aim, purpose, etc.*) **attacher un cheval à un arbre,** to tie a horse to a tree; **attacher de l'importance à qch.,** to attach importance to sth.; **donner à qn,** to give sth. to s.o., to give s.o. sth.; **parler à qn,** to speak to s.o.; **penser à qn, à qch.,** to think of s.o., sth.; **s'habituer à qch.,** to become used to sth.; **viser à l'effet,** to aim at effect; **à quoi cela sert-il?** what is the use of that? (*b*) (*where the precise value of* à *is now less clear*) **survivre à qn, à qch.,** to survive, outlive s.o., sth.; **prendre qn à témoin,** to call s.o. to witness; (*c*) (*opposition*) **s'opposer à qch.,** to oppose sth.; **résister à qn, à qch.,** to resist s.o., sth.; (*d*) (*separation*) **cacher, voler, qch. à qn,** to hide, steal, sth. from s.o.; **échapper à la prison,** to escape imprisonment; **boire à (même) la bouteille,** to drink (straight) from the bottle. **7.** (*in the constructions*) **faire faire qch. à qn,** to get, cause, s.o. to do sth., to have sth. done by s.o.; **laisser,** *occ.* **entendre, voir, faire qch. à qn,** to let, hear, see, s.o. do sth.; **faire savoir qch. à qn,** to inform s.o. of sth.; **laisser croire à qn que . . .,** to allow s.o. to believe that . . .; **entendre dire qch. à qn,** to hear s.o. say sth.; **il avait vu faire le même geste à X,** he had seen X make the same gesture. **8.** (*denoting possession and cognate ideas*) **le livre est à Paul,** the book is Paul's; **la parole est à X,** X will now speak; **c'est à vous de décider,** it is for you to decide, it is up to you to decide; **c'est à vous,** it's your turn; **c'était à qui chanterait le plus fort,** each was trying to sing louder than the rest; **un ami à moi,** a friend of mine; **j'ai un bateau, de l'argent, à moi,** I have a boat, money, of my own; **son idée à elle serait à . . .,** her idea would be to . . .; **la société va ouvrir sa banque à elle,** the company is opening its own bank; *P:* **le livre à Paul,** Paul's book; (*in fixed phrases*) **un fils à papa,** a young man with an influential father; **bête à bon Dieu,** ladybird; **aucun mystère à . . .,** (there's) no mystery about . . . **9.** (*forming adjectival phrases*) (*a*) (*purpose*) **tasse à thé,** teacup; **brosse à dents,** toothbrush; (*b*) (*means, instrument*) **moulin à vent,** windmill; **travail à l'aiguille,** needlework; **travail fait à la main, à la machine,** work done by hand, by machine; (*c*) (*type*) **un repas à l'anglaise,** a meal in the English style, an English meal; **des scènes à la Dumas fils,** scenes after the manner of the younger Dumas; (*d*) (*special feature*) **ver à soie,** silkworm; **jeune fille aux cheveux noirs,** dark-haired girl; **des voitures à toit ouvrant,** cars with sunshine roofs; **les vieilles dames à pliant,** the old ladies with (their) camp-stools; **une enveloppe à mon nom,** an envelope with my name on it, addressed to me; **chambre à deux lits,** room with twin beds; **sauce à l'oignon,** onion sauce; (*e*) (*with a numeral*) **ménage à trois,** eternal triangle; *Fb:* **rugby à quinze,** Rugby union; (*f*) (*with a verbal noun*) **attachement à l'étude,** fondness for study; **une invitation à un bal,** an invitation to a ball, dance. **10.** (*forming adverbial phrases some of which may also be used adjectivally*) (*a*) (*purpose*) **à cet effet,** for this purpose; **à quoi bon se plaindre?** what is the use of complaining? (*b*) (*consequence*) **à mon étonnement,** to my surprise; **à notre grande joie,** to our great joy; (*c*) (*means, instrument*) **reconnaître qn à sa voix,** to recognize

s.o. by his voice; **passer de la viande au hachoir,** to put meat through the mincer; **aller à bicyclette,** to go by bicycle, to cycle; **lettre écrite au crayon,** letter written in pencil; **pêcher à la ligne,** to fish with rod and line; (*d*) (*rarely: agent*) **mangé aux mites,** moth-eaten; (*e*) (*manner*) **arriver à l'improviste,** to arrive unexpectedly; **filer à l'anglaise,** to take French leave; **à nouveau,** afresh, again; **faire qch. à qui mieux mieux,** to vie with one another in doing sth.; **recevoir qn à bras ouverts,** to welcome s.o. with open arms; **vendre des huitres à la douzaine,** to sell oysters by the dozen; **louer une maison à l'année,** to let a house by the year; **nous l'avons fait à deux, à trois,** there were two, three, of us doing it; (*f*) (*intensity*) **examiner qch. à fond,** to examine sth. thoroughly; **aux trois quarts ivre,** three parts drunk, *F:* three sheets in the wind; (*g*) (*price, rate*) **à quel prix vendez-vous cela?** at what price do you sell that? **deux timbres à un franc,** two one-franc stamps; *Nau:* **filer à vingt nœuds,** to proceed at twenty knots; (*h*) (*miscellaneous*) **à mon avis,** in my opinion; **à ce qu'il dit,** according to him, according to what he says; **au reste,** moreover, besides; **à sa manière,** in his (own) way; **à cette condition,** on this condition; *s.a.* CROIRE 1. **11.** (*introducing a complement to an adj. or adv., expressing various ideas, including a number related to verbs*); **indispensable à qn, à qch.,** indispensable to s.o., for sth.; **conforme à, conformément à,** in conformity with; **parallèle à, parallèlement à,** parallel to, in a parallel direction; **hostile à,** hostile to; **nuisible à,** harmful to; **c'est bien gentil à lui (de m'inviter),** it is very kind of him (to invite me). **12.** (*forming prepositional and conjunctional phrases*) **à défaut de,** in default of, for lack of; **à la différence de,** unlike, contrary to; **à la différence que,** with this difference that, except that; **à moins de, à moins que,** unless; *s.a.* MOINS 1(*a*). **II.** (à *introducing a verb in the infinitive*). **1.** (*denoting figurative direction in conjunction with* **de là**) **de là à signer la paix, il y avait loin,** from there to signing the peace treaty was still a long way. **2.** (*in conjunction with a verb*) (*a*) (*denoting figurative direction*) **en venir à faire qch.,** to come to the point of doing sth.; (*b*) (*denoting aim, purpose, and various attributive ideas, often analogous to construction in which* à *has a noun complement*) **aspirer à faire qch.,** to aspire to do sth.; **se préparer à faire qch.,** to prepare to do sth.; **encourager qn à faire qch.,** to encourage s.o. to do sth.; **penser à faire qch.,** to think of doing sth.; **s'habituer à faire qch.,** to become accustomed to doing sth.; (*c*) (*denoting figurative situation or circumstance, developing in some cases to a suggestion of cause or means*) *F: & occ:* **il est à travailler,** he is working; **se borner à faire qch.,** to content oneself with doing sth.; **s'épuiser à faire qch.,** to wear oneself out (with) doing sth.; **s'amuser à faire qch.,** to amuse oneself by doing sth.; **perdre son temps à faire qch.,** to waste one's time doing sth.; (*d*) (*expressing the ideas of obligation or possibility*) **j'ai à écrire une lettre,** I have to write a letter; **il n'y a qu'à continuer notre chemin,** there is nothing for it but to continue on our way; **il ne me reste qu'à vous remercier,** it only remains for me to thank you; **c'est-à-dire,** that is (to say); (*e*) (*with* **as** *a 'link-word'*) **commencer à, demander à, hésiter à, faire qch.,** to begin, ask, hesitate, to

do sth. 3. (*in adjectival relation to a noun or pronoun*) (*a*) (*purpose*) **machine à coudre,** sewing-machine; **bonne à tout faire,** maid-of-all-work; (*b*) (*nature*) **il est homme à se défendre,** he is the kind of man who will hit back; (*c*) (*obligation, possibility*) **j'ai une lettre à écrire,** I have a letter to write; **vous êtes à plaindre,** you are to be pitied; **maison à vendre,** house for sale; **enfants à naître,** unborn children; (*elliptically*) **donner à manger aux chevaux,** to feed the horses; (*d*) (*with abstract nouns*) **une tendance à exagérer,** a tendency to exaggerate; **son empressement à répondre,** his eagerness to reply; **son plaisir à nous revoir,** his pleasure at seeing us again. **4.** (*in adverbial phrases, with intensive force*) (*a*) (*modifying an adjective*) **elle est laide à faire peur,** she is frightfully ugly; (*b*) (*modifying a verb or clause*) **il gèle à pierre fendre,** it is freezing hard; **il imitait le maître à s'y méprendre,** he used to imitate the master to the life; **il a de l'argent à ne savoir qu'en faire,** he has so much money he doesn't know what to do with it. **5.** (*in adverbial phrases, with instrumental or restrictive force*) **à partager les mêmes périls on apprend à se connaître,** by sharing the same dangers we learn to know each other; **à vivre auprès d'elle il avait pris ses habitudes,** living with her he had acquired her ways; **à vous croire, tout serait perdu,** you would have us believe that all is lost; **à en juger par . . .,** judging by . . .; **à compter d'hier,** reckoning from yesterday. **6.** (*in adverbial relation to an adjective*) (*a*) **je suis prêt à vous écouter,** I am ready to listen to you; **lent à faire qch.,** slow to do sth.; **impuissant à faire qch.,** powerless to do sth.; (*b*) (*infin. with quasi-passive force*) **agréable à regarder,** pleasant to look at; **facile à comprendre,** easy to understand. **7.** (*in conjunction with numerals, etc.*) **être (le) seul à faire qch.,** to be the only one to do sth.; **vous êtes le premier, le troisième, le dernier, à le remarquer,** you are the first, the third, the last, to notice it; **nous étions cinq, plusieurs, à vous attendre,** there were five, several, of us waiting for you.

a(n)- [a(n)], *privative pref.* a(n)-; **aboulie,** aboulia, **amoralement,** amorally; **aphone,** aphonous; **astigmatique,** astigmatic.

aarite [aːrit], *s.f.* = ARITE.

Aaron [aːrɔ̃], *Pr.n.m. B.Hist:* Aaron.

ababouiné [ababwine], *a. A: Nau:* becalmed, in the doldrums.

abaca [abaka], *s.m.* **1.** *Bot:* abaca. **2.** manil(l)a hemp.

abacule [abakyl], *s.m.* abaculus.

Abaddon [abadɔ̃], *Pr.n.m. B:* (*a*) the Prince of Hell, Abaddon; (*b*) Hell, Abaddon.

abaissable [abɛsabl], *a.* lowerable (mast, etc.).

abaissant [abɛsɑ̃], *a.* lowering (to one's self-respect, etc.); humiliating.

abaisse [abɛs], *s.f. Cu:* pastry rolled out thin; undercrust.

abaissée [abese], *s.f. Orn:* (sweep of) downstroke.

abaisse-langue [abɛslɑ̃ːg], *s.m.inv. Med:* tongue-depressor.

abaissement [abɛsmɑ̃], *s.m.* **1.** lowering; state of being lowered; **a. du bras, de la voix, d'un store, des prix, des barrières douanières,** lowering of the arm, of the voice, of a blind, of prices, of tariff barriers, walls. **2.** (*a*) falling, abatement, subsidence, sinking; **a. des eaux,** falling of the waters; **a. de la température,** fall, drop, in temperature; **a. des prix,** fall, drop, in prices; **a. des valeurs,** deterioration in values; **a. de la valeur du franc, de la livre,** reduction in the value of the franc, of the pound; *Meteor:* **a. du baromètre,** fall of the barometer; *El:* **a. de courant,** decrease in current; (*b*) *Mth:* **a. d'une équation,** reduction of an equation; (*c*) *Artil:* **angle d'a.,** angle of negative jump. **3.** dip (of horizon, of the ground). **4.** (*a*) abasement, humbling, humiliation, degradation; **a. des grands, d'un état,** humbling of the great, of a state; (*b*) lowly state.

abaisser [abese], *v.tr.* **1.** to lower, pull down, draw down, let down; **a. un store, un pont-levis, un canon, son voile,** to pull down a blind, let down a drawbridge, depress a gun, pull down one's veil; **a. les yeux sur la foule,** to look down on the crowd; **abaissez la manette,** press the key down; **a. son jeu, ses cartes,** to lay one's cards on the table; *Nau:* **a. une voile, un mât,** to lower, strike, a sail, a mast. **2.** to lower (shelf, one's voice); to lower, reduce, lessen (prices, cost, pressure, etc.); **a. le taux de l'escompte,** to lower the bank rate; **a. le taux de natalité,** to lower, bring down, the birth rate. **3.** to humble, bring low, abase; **Dieu abaisse les superbes,** God humbles the proud; **il abaissa Babylone,** He brought Babylon low; **a. l'orgueil de qn,** to humble s.o.'s pride. **4.** (*a*) *Ar:* **a. un chiffre,** to bring down a figure; (*b*) *Mus:* to transpose (a semitone, a tone) down. **5.** *Geom:* **a. une perpendiculaire à une ligne,** to drop, let fall, a perpendicular to, on, a line. **6.** *Mth:* to reduce (an equation). **7.** *Cu:* to roll out (pastry, etc.).

s'abaisser. 1. to fall away, dip, slope downward, go down; **le terrain s'abaisse vers le sud,** the ground falls away to the south; **le terrain s'est abaissé,** the ground has subsided; **ses paupières s'abaissèrent,** her, his, eyelids drooped; **la température s'abaisse,** the temperature is falling; **les arts s'abaissent,** art is deteriorating, declining; **sa voix s'est abaissée,** his voice dropped. **2. s'a. devant Dieu,** to humble oneself before God. **3. s'a. à, jusqu'à, faire qch.,** (i) to demean, lower, oneself so far, to stoop so low, as to do sth., to stoop to doing sth.; (ii) to condescend to do sth; **il ne saurait s'a. jusqu'à mentir,** he is above telling a lie.

abaisseur [abɛsœːr]. **1.** *a. & s.m. Anat:* **(muscle) abaisseur,** depressor (muscle). **2.** *s.m. Ind:* depressant; **a. de point d'écoulement,** pour point depressant.

abajoue [abaʒu], *s.f.* **1.** *Z:* (monkey's) cheek-pouch; **se fourrer une noisette dans l'a.,** to pouch a nut. **2.** *pl. F:* flabby cheeks. **3.** *Cu:* (pig's, calf's) cheek, chap.

abalourdir [abalurdiːr], *v.tr. F:* to make (s.o.) dull, stupid.

s'abalourdir. *O: F:* to grow dull, slow-witted.

abandon [abɑ̃dɔ̃], *s.m.* abandonment. **1.** (*a*) surrender, relinquishment, cession, renunciation (of goods, rights, etc.); **a. du pouvoir,** relinquishing, leaving, of office; **faire (l')a. de qch. à qn,** to make over, give over, resign, surrender, sth. to s.o.; **a. des hostilités,** abandoning of hostilities; (*b*) *Sp:* (i) retirement, withdrawal (from race); (ii) *Wr:* submission; (*c*) *Jur:* **a. de poursuites,** nolle prosequi. **2.** neglect, forsaking (of home, children, duty, etc.); *Jur:* abandonment (of property, children), desertion (of home, wife, husband); *Mil:* **a. de poste (en présence de l'ennemi),** desertion, leaving, abandonment, of one's post (in face of the enemy); *Av:* **a. du bord en vol,** baling out (of an aircraft). **3.** forlornness, neglect; **mourir dans un a. général, universel,** to die in total neglect, forsaken by all; **à l'a.,** (i) neglected, in utter neglect; (ii) at random; (iii) *Nau:* (ship) derelict, adrift; **laisser aller à l'a.,** to neglect (business, etc.); **enfants à l'a.,** children running wild; **jardin à l'a.,** garden running wild. **4.** (*a*) lack, absence, of restraint, lack of reserve; abandon; **il me parla avec a.,** he spoke to me freely, without reserve; **il écrit avec un a. séduisant,** he writes with a charming lack of constraint; **a. de soi-même,** self-abandonment; (*b*) **a. au péché,** indulgence in sin.

abandonnable [abɑ̃dɔnabl], *a.* that can be abandoned.

abandonnateur, -trice [abɑ̃dɔnatœːr, -tris], *s. Jur:* releasor.

abandonnataire [abɑ̃dɔnatɛːr], *s.m. Jur:* releasee; *M.Ins:* abandonee.

abandonné, -ée, [abɑ̃dɔne]. *a. & s.* **1.** forsaken, deserted (person); **les abandonnés,** waifs and strays; **petit a.,** little waif; **navire a. en mer,** derelict (ship); *Jur:* **objet a.,** derelict. **2.** *O:* profligate, shameless, abandoned (person, conduct). **3.** untidy (appearance).

abandonnement [abɑ̃dɔnmɑ̃], *s.m. A:* **1.** = ABANDON 1, 2, 4. **2.** *O:* profligacy, shamelessness.

abandonnément [abɑ̃dɔnemɑ̃], *adv. A:* **1.** unreservedly, without restraint. **2.** shamelessly.

abandonner [abɑ̃dɔne], *v.tr.* **1.** (*a*) to forsake, desert, abandon; to throw over; to leave; to give up; **a. le pouvoir,** to leave, relinquish, office; *Nau:* **a. le bâtiment,** to abandon ship; **a. un homme sur une île déserte,** to maroon a man on a desert island; **ses amis l'abandonnent,** his friends are forsaking, deserting him; **mes forces m'abandonnent,** my strength is failing me; **abandonné de tous,** forsaken by all; **abandonné par les médecins,** given up by the doctors; **a. la garde de qch.,** to leave sth. unattended; **a. la partie,** to give up; *F:* to throw up the sponge, to throw in the towel; **a. l'étalon or,** to come off the gold standard; *Mil:* **a. son poste,** to desert one's post; *Av:* **a. le bord, un avion, en vol,** to bale out; (*b*) *abs. Sp:* (i) to give up (the race); to retire; (ii) *Wr:* to submit. **2.** to surrender, renounce, give up; to hand over, give over; **a. ses prétentions,** to renounce, throw up, surrender, one's claims; **a. ses biens à ses créanciers,** to surrender one's goods to one's creditors; **a. tout espoir de réussite,** to give up all hope of success; **a. un point à qn,** to concede a point to s.o.; **a. sa foi,** to renounce one's faith; **a. qn à son destin,** to leave s.o. to his fate; *s.a.* PRIME[2] 1. **3. a. les rênes,** to drop the reins; **ne pas a. les rênes,** to hold on to, cling to, the reins.

s'abandonner. 1. (*a*) to neglect oneself, to be careless of oneself; (*b*) to give way to despair, to grief; to lose courage. **2.** (*a*) to be unconstrained (in manners, in conversation); *F:* to let oneself go; **le soir je m'abandonnai à lui raconter mon enfance,** in the evening I relaxed and told him the story of my childhood; (*b*) (*of woman*) to give oneself (to a lover). **3. s'a. à qch.,** to give oneself up to sth.; to become addicted to (vice, etc.); to give way to (emotion); **s'a. au désespoir,** to give way to despair; **ne vous abandonnez pas à pleurer,** don't give way to tears. **4. s'a. à la Providence,** to commit oneself to, throw oneself on, Providence; **s'a. au sommeil,** to surrender oneself to sleep; **s'a. à son sort,** to resign oneself to one's fate.

abaquarrer [abakare], *v.tr.* to graph (on squared paper, etc.).

abaque [abak], *s.m.* **1.** *Archeol:* abacus. **2.** *Arch:* abacus. **3.** *Mth: etc:* (*a*) = BOULIER-COMPTEUR; (*b*) chart, graph, table, scale, diagram; nomograph, plotter; **a. cylindrique pour enregistrement de variable,** strip chart; **a. de restitution,** time graph; *Av:* **a. de centrage,** weight and balance chart.

abasie [abazi], *s.f. Med:* abasia.

abasourdir [abazurdiːr], *v.tr.* **1.** to deafen, stun, daze. **2.** to dumbfound, strike dumb, astound, bewilder, flummox, stun; **nous restâmes abasourdis de la nouvelle,** we were dumbfounded at, struck dumb by, flabbergasted by, the news.

abasourdissant [abazurdisɑ̃], *a.* **1.** deafening, stunning. **2. nouvelle abasourdissante,** astounding piece of news.

abasourdissement [abazurdismɑ̃], *s.m.* **1.** deafening (noise). **2.** bewilderment, stupefaction.

abat [aba], *s.m.* **1.** *A:* = ABATTAGE 3. **2. pluie d'a.,** *A:* **a. d'eau, de pluie,** sudden shower; downpour. **3.** *pl.* **abats,** (*a*) offal, *U.S:* variety meat; (*b*) giblets.

abatage [abataːʒ], *s.m.* = ABATTAGE.

abatant [abatɑ̃], *s.m.* = ABATTANT 2.

abâtardi [abɑtardi], *a.* degenerate; bastardized.

abâtardir [abɑtardiːr], *v.tr.* to cause to degenerate; to render degenerate, to debase; to bastardize.

s'abâtardir, to degenerate, to deteriorate.

abâtardissement [abɑtardismɑ̃], *s.m.* degeneracy, degeneration; retrogression.

abatée [abate], *s.f.* = ABATTÉE.

abat-faim [abafɛ̃], *s.m.inv. O: Cu: F:* substantial dish served early in the meal; entrée.

abat-foin [abafwɛ̃], *s.m.inv.* trap-door (of hay-loft).

abatis [abati], *s.m.* = ABATTIS.

abat-jour [abaʒuːr], *s.m.inv.* **1.** (*a*) lamp-shade; (*b*) eye-shade; **mettre la main en a.-j.,** to shade one's eyes with one's hand; (*c*) sun-blind, awning; (*d*) slanting shutter; (*e*) (*on prison window*) abat-jour. **2.** *Arch:* splayed window; **soupirail en a.-j.,** cellar light.

abat-son [abasɔ̃], *s.m.inv.* **1.** *Arch:* (*a*) louver (window); (*b*) *pl.* **abat-son(s),** louver-boards, louver-boarding. **2.** *Cin:* (sound-damping) flat, tormentor.

abattable [abatabl], *a.* that can be felled or demolished.

abattage [abataːʒ], *s.m.* **1.** (*a*) knocking down, throwing down; demolition (of wall, etc.); *F:* **recevoir un a.,** to get hauled over the coals; (*b*) felling, cutting down, clearing (of trees, etc.); (*c*) *Min:* cutting, working, stoping; **a. à la poudre,** blasting; **a. à ciel ouvert,** open mining; **face d'a.,** working face; **a. en gradins,** stoping; **a. en taille chassante,** drift-stoping; **a. à la lance,** hydraulic mining; **a. de la roche,** ground breaking; **a. par pinces,** barring down; (*d*) *Mil:* anchoring (of gun); *s.a.* CARÈNE 1. **2.** leverage, purchase; power (obtained by leverage). **3.** slaughtering, killing (of animal for food); **a. des bœufs,** slaughtering, pole-axing, knocking down, of oxen; **grand a. de gibier,** heavy slaughter, heavy bag, of game. **4.** *Cards:* (*a*) laying down of one's cards, putting down of one's hand; (*b*) exposed hand. **5.** (*a*) *P:* rushed work; (*b*) *Th:* dash; *F:* **elle a de l'a.,** she's full of go.

abattant [abatɑ̃]. **1.** *a.* (*a*) depressing; (*b*) **siège a.,** tip-up seat (of car, etc.). **2.** *s.m.* (*a*) (i) flap (of counter, table, etc.); (hinged) leaf (of table); drop front, fall front (of desk); flap (of envelope); flap-seat (of w.c. pan); (ii) drop-table; (iii) trap-door; (*b*) (pivoted) skylight; swinging ventilator.

abattée [abate], *s.f.* **1.** *Nau:* (*a*) falling off to leeward; casting (of ship); (*b*) alteration of course; (*c*) pitching (into waves). **2.** stall (of aircraft).

abattement [abatmɑ̃], *s.m.* **1.** (*a*) (physical) prostration; (*b*) despondency, dejection, low spirits; **un profond a.,** deep dejection; **tomber dans l'a.,** to become low-spirited. **2.** *Mth:* perpendicular depth. **3.** *Adm:* abatement (on declared income); **a. à la base,** basic abatement (Earned Income allowance or Personal allowance).

abatteur, -euse [abatœːr, -øːz], *s.* **1.** (*a*) person who knocks down, knocks over (things); *F:* **a. de besogne,** hard worker; *F:* slogger, *U.S:* plugger; *A:* **grand a. de quilles,** great braggart, boaster; **grand a. de bois,** lady-killer; (*b*) feller, hewer, cutter (of trees, coal); quarrier (of stone); (*c*) slaughterer (of animals). **2.** *s.f.* **abatteuse,** power-driven circular saw (for clearing brushwood).

abattis [abati], *s.m.* **1.** (*a*) felling, clearing (of trees); **sabre d'a.,** machete; (*b*) killing, slaughter (of game, enemy, etc.); **faire un grand a. de gibier,** to secure a big bag of game. **2.** *Const:* mass of rubble; **a. de maisons,** ruins of fallen houses. **3.** *pl.* (*a*) *Cu:* giblets; (*b*) *P:* limbs, hands and feet; **numéroter ses a.,** to make sure one is all in one piece (after an accident); **tu peux numéroter tes a.!** you had better take stock of yourself (i) before I thrash you, (ii) before you face the music; I'll break every bone in your body! **4.** *Mil:* abatis; **a. rapporté,** portable abatis; **a. sur place,** live abatis.

abattoir [abatwaːr], *s.m.* slaughter-house, abattoir.

abattre [abatr̥], *v.tr.* (*conj. like* BATTRE). **1.** (*a*) to knock down, throw down, batter down, pull down; to demolish, overthrow; **a. une maison,** to pull down a house; **a. un adversaire,** to overthrow, lay low, an opponent; *Box:* to down, floor, an opponent; **une fièvre l'a abattu,** he was laid low by fever; **a. les fruits d'un arbre,** to knock down the fruit from a tree; *F:* **a. de la besogne,** *P:* **en a.,** to get through a lot of work; *F:* **a. une lieue à pied,** to do, cover, three miles on foot; *s.a.* BOIS[1] 2; (*b*) to fell, cut down, hew down, cut away, clear (trees); to cut (corn); (*c*) to strike off, lop off, cut off, chop off (head, limb); (*d*) *Min:* to break down, stope, cut out (coal, ore); (*e*) *Mil:* to anchor (field-gun). **2.** to slaughter, kill, destroy; **a. un bœuf,** to slaughter, knock down, an ox; **a. un chien enragé,** to kill a mad dog; **a. un cheval blessé,** to destroy an injured horse. **3.** to bring down, shoot down; (*a*) **a. une perdrix,** to shoot, bring down, bag, a partridge; **a. un avion,** to bring down, shoot down, an aircraft; **j'abattis cinq faisans,** five pheasants fell to my gun; (*b*) **a. son sabre sur la tête de qn,** to bring down one's sword on s.o.'s head; **a. sur la table un grand coup de poing,** to bring one's fist down heavily on the table; **a. violemment le couvercle,** to bang down the lid. **4.** to lower; (*a*) **a. les tentes,** to strike tents; (*b*) **a. l'orgueil de qn,** to humble, break, s.o.'s pride. **5.** to lay (dust, wind); (*of rain*) to lay (crops) flat; to lodge (corn); *Prov:* **petite pluie abat grand vent,** small rain lays great dust. **6.** (*a*) (*of wind*) to blow down, beat down; **arbre abattu par le vent,** tree blown down by the wind; (*b*) **a. un navire,** to careen, heave down a ship; **a. un wagon,** to tip over a wagon, to lay a wagon on its side. **7.** to cast down, dishearten, depress; to take the heart out of (s.o.); **ne vous laissez pas abattre!** don't get disheartened! bear up! **ne pas se laisser a. par la mauvaise fortune,** to bear up against misfortune; **ils ne se laissèrent pas a.,** they refused to be disheartened, *F:* they wouldn't let (the situation, etc.) get them down. **8.** *Cards:* **a. ses cartes, son jeu,** to lay one's cards on the table, to lay down one's hand. **9.** *Tchn:* (*a*) to clinch (rivet); (*b*) to round, blunt (angle); to reduce (surface); **a. une arête,** to chamfer an edge; *Carp:* **a. l'arête d'une planche,** to beard a board; (*c*) to trim, cut back (sth. which sticks out). **10.** *v.i. Nau:* (*a*) **a. sur bâbord,** to cast to port; **a. sous le vent,** to fall off, cast off, pay off; **a. de bon bord,** to pay off on the right tack; **a. à contre-bord,** to pay off on the wrong tack; (*b*) **a. à la côte,** to drift on-shore; (*c*) to alter course.

s'abattre. 1. to fall, to crash down, to come down; to collapse; **le mât s'abattit,** the mast came crashing down; **l'avion s'est abattu sur la maison,** the plane crashed down on the house; **une bombe s'abattit au milieu de la foule,** a bomb dropped among the crowd; *F:* **il s'est abattu sur le nez,** he fell flat on his face. **2. s'a. sur qch.,** to pounce upon sth., to swoop down, sweep down, upon sth.; **le faucon s'abat sur sa proie,** the falcon pounces, swoops, *Ven:* stoops, on its prey; **l'orage s'abattit sur nous,** the storm swept down upon us. **3.** (*of fever, heat, etc.*) to abate, to subside; **le vent s'abat,** the wind is falling. **4.** to become disheartened, depressed, discouraged.

abattu [abaty], *a.* **1.** dejected, cast down, downcast, downhearted, low-spirited, heavy-hearted; **il a l'air a.,** he looks depressed, *F:* down in the mouth; **remonter les esprits abattus,** to revive drooping spirits; **a. par la chaleur,** limp with the heat; **visage a.,** drawn face. **2.** *s.a.* BRIDE 1. **3.** *s.m.* **mettre son fusil à l'a.,** to uncock one's rifle; **fusil à l'a.,** uncocked rifle.

abatture [abatyːr], *s.f.* (*a*) beating (of fruit trees); (*b*) *pl. Ven:* abature.

abat-vent [abavɑ̃], *s.m.inv.* **1.** louvre-boards (of steeple, etc.). **2.** (*a*) penthouse; (*b*) lean-to. **3.** chimney-cowl. **4.** *Hort:* wind-break.

abat-voix [abavwa], *s.m.inv.* sounding-board (of pulpit).

abbas(s)ide [abasid], *a. & s. Hist:* Abbas(s)id(e).

abbatial, -aux [abasjal, -o], *a.* **1.** abbatial; **dignité abbatiale,** abbacy; **droits abbatiaux, privilèges abbatiaux, juridiction abbatiale,** abbacy; **terres abbatiales,** abbey-lands; **église abbatiale,** minster, abbey church. **2.** *s.f.* **abbatiale,** abbey church.

abbatiat [abasja], *s.m.* abbacy, office of abbot.

abbaye [abei], *s.f.* **1.** abbey, monastery; *P:* **l'a. de monte-à-regret,** the gallows; the guillotine. *s.a.* MOINE 1, POUR I. 1. (i), THÉLÈME. **2.** benefice of an abbey; abbacy.

abbé [abe], *s.m.* **1.** abbot. **2.** beneficiary of an abbey. **3.** general designation of and mode of address for a (Roman Catholic) priest; **j'en parlerai à monsieur l'a.,** I shall mention it to the priest; **entrez donc, monsieur l'a.!** come in, Father! **l'A. Constantin,** Father Constantin, Abbé Constantin. **4.** *Hist:* (*as applied to one having no ecclesiastical duty*) abbé.

abbesse [abɛs], *s.f.* abbess.

abbevillien, -ienne [abviljɛ̃, -jɛn], *a. Prehist:* Abbevillian.

abbevillois, -oise [abvilwa, -waːz], *a. & s. Geog:* (inhabitant, native) of Abbeville.

abc [ɑbese], *s.m.inv.* **1.** alphabet, ABC. **2.** spelling-book, primer, ABC. **3.** rudiments, elements (of a science).

abcédation [apsedasjɔ̃], *s.f. Med:* (*a*) formation of an abscess; gathering; (*b*) suppuration.

abcéder [apsede], *v.i.* (il abcède, il abcédera). *Med:* (*a*) to form into an abscess, to gather; (*b*) to suppurate.

abcès [apsɛ], *s.m.* (*a*) *Med:* abscess, gathering; **a. au doigt,** abscess on the finger; **a. à la gencive,** gumboil; **a. de fixation,** fixation abscess; (*b*) *F:* explosive situation; **il faut vider, crever, l'a.,** we must take drastic measures to overcome the crisis; **vider un a.,** to drain an abscess.

Abdère [abdɛːr], *Pr.n.f. A.Geog:* Abdera.

abdéritain, -aine [abderitɛ̃, -ɛn], *a. & s.* Abderite.

Abdias [abdjɑːs], *Pr.n.m. B.Hist:* Obadiah.

abdicataire [abdikatɛːr]. **1.** *a.* (i) abdicating; (ii) abdicated (monarch). **2.** *s.* abdicator.

abdication [abdikasjɔ̃], *s.f.* abdication (of throne); resignation (of a post); renunciation, surrender (of authority, rights, etc.); **faire a. de ses biens, de ses droits,** to renounce, surrender, one's possessions, one's rights.

abdiquant [abdikɑ̃]. **1.** *a.* abdicating (monarch). **2.** *s.m.* abdicator.

abdiquer [abdike], *v.tr.* to abdicate (throne); to resign (post); to renounce, surrender (rights, possessions, etc.); *abs.* to abdicate.

abdomen [abdɔmɛn], *s.m.* (*a*) *Anat: Z: Ent: etc:* abdomen; (*b*) *F:* paunch, corporation.

abdominal, -aux [abdɔminal, -o]. **1.** *a. Anat: Z:* abdominal; **paroi abdominale,** abdominal wall; *Med:* **ceinture abdominale,** abdominal belt. **2.** *s.m.pl.* **faire des abdominaux,** to do stomach exercises.

abdomino- [abdɔminɔ]. *pref.* abdomino.

abdomino-génital, -aux [abdɔminɔʒenital, -o], *a. Anat:* abdominogenital.

abducteur [abdyktœːr], *a. & s.m.* **1.** *Anat:* **(muscle) abducteur,** abductor (muscle); abducent muscle; **nerf a. de l'œil,** abducent nerve; **a. du pouce,** abductor pollicis. **2.** *Tchn:* **tube a.,** delivery tube, pipe.

abduction [abdyksjɔ̃], *s.f. Physiol: Log:* abduction.

abeausir [abozi:r], *v.i. & pr. A: Nau:* (of weather) to clear (up); to turn finer.

abécédaire [ɑbesedɛːr]. **1.** *a. A:* **ordre a.,** alphabetical order. **2.** *s.m.* (*a*) ABC; spelling-book; (*b*) primer (of science, etc.).

abecquement [abɛkmɑ̃], *s.m.* feeding (of young birds by their parents).

abecquer [abeke], *v.tr.* (*of birds*) to feed (their young).

abée [abe], *s.f.* (*a*) mouth (of mill-leat); (*b*) leat, flume (of mill).

abeille [abɛj], *s.f.* (*a*) *Ent:* bee, honey bee; **a. domestique,** hive-bee, honey bee; **a. neutre, a. ouvrière,** worker (bee); **a. mâle,** drone; **a. mère,** queen bee; **a. âtre,** black bee, German bee; **a. des sables,** rufous bee; **a. géante,** giant bee, rock bee; **a. indienne,** Indian bee; **a. naine,** little bee; **nid d'abeilles,** bees' nest; *s.a.* COUPEUR, DÉCOUPEUR, FOUISSEUR, MAÇON, REINE, RUBICOLE, TERRASSIER. (*b*) *Tex:* **serviette nid d'abeilles,** honeycomb towel; *Aut:* **radiateur nid d'abeilles,** honeycomb radiator, cellular radiator; *W.Tel:* **bobine en nid d'abeilles,** honeycomb coil; *Needlew:* **nids d'abeilles,** smocking; *s.a.* HERBE 4.

abeiller, -ère [abeje, -ɛjɛːr]. *A:* **1.** (*a*) relating to bees; apiarian; **l'industrie abeillère,** bee-keeping. **2.** *s.m. Dial:* bee-hive.

abélien, -ienne [abeljɛ̃, -jɛn], *a. Mth:* abelian (integrals, equation, etc.).

aber [ɑbɛr], *s.m. Geog:* (*in Breton place-names*) river mouth; (*in Welsh place-names*) aber.

aberrance [abɛrɑ̃ːs], *s.f.* aberrance.

aberrant [abɛrɑ̃], *a.* (*a*) *Biol: etc:* aberrant; *s.a.* NORME; (*b*) deviating; (*c*) *Pol.Ec:* (*of price*) excessively high or low.

aberration [abɛrasjɔ̃], *s.f.* **1.** *Astr: Biol: Mth: Opt:* aberration; **a. moyenne,** constant of aberration; **a. de sphéricité,** spherical aberration; *s.a.* CHROMATIQUE 1. **2.** aberration (of mind, conduct, etc.); **dans un moment d'a.,** in a moment of aberration.

aberrer [abɛre], *v.i. A: Jur:* to wander from, to get off, away from, the point; to argue away from the point; to be mistaken, wrong.

abêtir [abetiːr]. **1.** *v.tr.* to stupefy, to render, make, (s.o.) stupid; to (make) dull. **2.** *v.i. & pr.* to stupefy, to become, grow, stupid; **il (s')abêtit de jour en jour,** he grows more stupid every day.

abêtissant [abetisɑ̃], *a.* stupefying.

abêtissement [abetismɑ̃], *s.m.* **1.** dullness, stupidity; **tomber dans l'a.,** to grow, become, stupid. **2.** making (s.o.) stupid.

abhorrer [abɔre], *v.tr.* to abhor, loathe, abominate, detest; **abhorré de, par, tous les honnêtes gens,** abhorred, shunned, by all decent people; **a. de faire qch.,** to loathe doing sth; **il abhorre qu'on lui fasse des éloges,** he loathes being praised.

Abia [abja], *Pr.n.m. B.Hist:* Abijah.

abies [abjɛs], *s.m. Bot:* abies; fir-tree.

abiétacées [abjetase], *s.f.pl. Bot:* Abietineae.

abiétate [abjetat], *s.m. Ch:* abietate.

abiétin [abjetɛ̃], *a. Bot: etc:* referring to fir-trees.

abiétique [abjetik], *a. Ch:* abietic (acid).

Abigaïl [abigail], *Pr.n.f. B.Hist:* Abigail.

abîme [abim], *s.m.* **1.** (*a*) abyss, chasm, unfathomable depth(s), abysmal space; **Dieu les précipita dans l'a.,** God hurled them into the abyss; **politique du bord de l'a.,** brinkmanship; **les profonds abîmes de l'océan,** ocean depths, deeps; the unfathomed deep; **un a. de science,** a mine of knowledge, a man of immense learning; *Lit:* **l'a. appelle l'a.,** deep calleth to deep; **un a. sépare les deux idéologies,** there is a gulf between the two ideologies; **la course à l'a.,** heading for disaster; (*b*) *Geol:* swallow (-hole). **2.** *Her:* fesse(e)-point; abyss, heart-point.

abîmé [abime], *a.* **1.** (*a*) *A:* **a. de dettes,** overwhelmed with debts; (*b*) **a. dans ses pensées,** deep, lost, in thought; (*c*) **a. de fatigue,** exhausted. **2. marchandises abîmées,** damaged, spoilt, goods; **caoutchouc a.,** perished rubber.

abîmer [abime], *v.tr.* **1.** (*a*) *A:* to engulf, sink, swallow up; (*b*) *A:* to overwhelm, destroy, lay low; **Dieu abîma les villes coupables,** God destroyed the guilty cities; *F:* **abîmer qn d'injures,** to overwhelm s.o. with abuse. **2.** (*a*) to spoil, damage, injure; **s'a. la santé,** to injure, undermine, one's health; **livre abîmé par la pluie,** book spoilt by the rain; *F:* **a. qn dans la presse,** to run down, slate s.o. in the papers; *P:* **se faire a.,** to get badly knocked about, to be beaten up; (*b*) *abs. P:* to exaggerate.

s'abîmer, *v.pr.* **1.** (*a*) **s'a. dans les flots,** to sink; to be engulfed, swallowed up, by the sea; (*b*) **s'a. dans la douleur, dans ses pensées,** to be sunk in grief, lost in thought. **2.** to get spoiled; to spoil.

ab intestat [abɛ̃tɛsta], *adv.phr. Jur:* intestate; **hériter ab i.,** to succeed to an intestate estate.

abiogenèse [abjɔʒənɛːz], *s.f.* abiogenesis.

abiose [abjoːz], *s.f. Biol:* abiosis.

abiotique [abjɔtik], *a.* abiotic.
abiotrophie [abjɔtrɔfi], *s.f. Biol:* abiotrophy.
abiotrophique [abjɔtrɔfik], *a. Biol:* abiotrophic.
abismal, -aux [abismal, -o], *a.* abysmal, fathomless.
abject [abʒɛkt], *a.* abject (poverty); mean, contemptible, despicable (person, conduct).
abjectement [abʒɛktəmɑ̃], *adv.* abjectly.
abjection [abʒɛksjɔ̃], *s.f.* **1.** abjection, abasement. **2.** abjectness, meanness (of thought, etc.).
abjuration [abʒyrasjɔ̃], *s.f.* abjuration; renunciation (on oath); recantation; **faire a. de . . .** = ABJURER.
abjuratoire [abʒyratwaːr], *a.* **acte, formule, a.,** act, formula, of abjuration, of recantation.
abjurer [abʒyre], *v.tr. & abs.* to abjure, forswear; to renounce (on oath); to recant, retract; **a. toute pudeur,** to cast off all sense of shame.
ablactation [ablaktasjɔ̃], *s.f.* ablactation, weaning.
ablater (s') [sablate], *v.pr.* to wear down, to wear away.
ablatif, -ive [ablatif, -iːv], *a. & s.m.* **1.** *Gram:* ablative (case); **à l'a.,** in the ablative; **a. absolu,** ablative absolute. **2.** *Ph:* ablative [əˈbleitiv].
ablation [ablasjɔ̃], *s.f.* **1.** *Surg:* excision, ablation, removal (of part, tumour, etc.). **2.** *Geol:* denudation; ablation. **3.** *Ph:* ablation (of cone of rocket, etc.).
able [abl̩], *s.m. Ich:* whitebait.
ablégat [ablega], *s.m. R.C.Ch:* ablegate.
ablépharie [ablefari], *s.f. Opt:* ablepharia.
ablepsie [ablɛpsi], *s.f. Med:* ablepsia.
ableret [ablərɛ], *s.m. Fish:* square dip(ping)-net.
ablette [ablɛt], *s.f. Ich:* bleak; *F:* **taquiner l'a.,** to do a bit of fishing.
abloc [ablɔk], *s.m. Constr:* foundation pier.
abluant [ablyɑ̃], *a. & s.m. A: Surg:* detergent.
abluer [ablye], *v.tr. Bookb: etc:* to wash, clean (soiled pages).
ablution [ablysjɔ̃], *s.f.* ablution, washing; *Ecc:* ablution, purification; *F:* **faire ses ablutions,** to perform one's ablutions; to wash.
ablutionner [ablysjɔne], *v.tr.* to wash; *Ecc:* **a. le calice,** to perform the ablution of the chalice.
abnégation [abnegasjɔ̃], *s.f.* abnegation, sacrifice; **a. de soi,** self-abnegation, self-denial, self-sacrifice; **faire a. de soi, de ses intérêts,** to sacrifice oneself, one's interests; **faire a. de sa volonté,** to abnegate one's will; **vie d'a.,** unselfish life.
Abner [abnɛːr], *Pr.n.m. B.Hist:* Abner.
aboi [abwa], *s.m.* **1.** *Ven:* bark, barking (of dog); bay, baying (of hound); yelp, yelping. **2. aux abois,** (i) (*of stag, enemy*) at bay, (ii) hard pressed, with his back against the wall; **réduire, mettre, qn aux abois,** to reduce s.o. to the last extremity, to press s.o. hard; **ils sont aux abois,** they are in desperate straits, they are hard pressed, sore pressed; **la police est aux abois,** the police are at their wits' end; **commerçant aux abois,** tradesman on his last legs.
aboiement [abwamɑ̃], *s.m.* bark, barking (of dog); bay, baying (of hound); (*of dog*) **pousser un a.,** to give a bark; *F:* **les aboiements des critiques,** the barking of critics.
abolir [abɔliːr], *v.tr.* to abolish, suppress; to cancel (a debt); **a. la haine,** to make an end of, do away with, hatred.
abolissable [abɔlisabl̩], *a.* abolishable.
abolissement [abɔlismɑ̃], *s.m.* = ABOLITION.
abolisseur [abɔlisœːr], *s.m.* abolisher (de, of).
abolitif, -ive [abɔlitif, -iːv], *a.* **décret a.,** decree of annulment.
abolition [abɔlisjɔ̃], *s.f.* **1.** abolition, abolishment; suppression. **2.** repeal, annulment, rescission (of decree, etc.).
abolitionnisme [abɔlisjɔnism], *s.m.* **1.** *U.S.Hist:* abolitionism. **2.** doctrine in favour of the abolition of customs duties, in favour of free trade.
abolitionniste [abɔlisjɔnist], *a. & s.* **1.** *U.S.Hist:* abolitionist. **2.** *a.* free-trade (propaganda, etc.); *s.* free-trader.
aboma [abɔma], *s.m. Rept:* aboma.
abomasum [abɔmazɔm], *s.m.,* **abomasus** [abɔmazys], *s.m.* abomasum, fourth stomach, rennet stomach (of ruminants).
abominable [abɔminabl̩], *a.* abominable, loathsome; heinous (crime); *F:* **temps a.,** foul, beastly, weather.
abominablement [abɔminabləmɑ̃], *adv.* abominably.
abomination [abɔminasjɔ̃], *s.f.* **1.** abomination, abhorrence, detestation; **être en a. à qn,** to be abominated, held in abomination, in abhorrence, by s.o.; to be an abomination to s.o.; **avoir qn, qch., en a.,** to abominate, loathe, s.o., sth. **2. assister à des abominations,** to witness abominations; **l'a. de la désolation,** the abomination of desolation; *F:* **ce café est une a.,** this coffee is filthy stuff, is abominable.
abominer [abɔmine], *v.tr.* to abominate, abhor, loathe; **abominé de, par, qn,** abominated by s.o.; *F:* **j'abomine le cacao,** I loathe cocoa.
à-bon-compte [abɔ̃kɔ̃ːt], *s.m.inv. A: Com:* advance, payment on account.
abondamment [abɔ̃damɑ̃], *adv.* abundantly, plentifully, profusely, copiously; **manger a.,** to make a hearty meal; **il a traité a. de cette question,** he dealt very fully with this question; **peu a.,** scantily, sparely.
abondance [abɔ̃dɑ̃ːs], *s.f.* **1.** abundance, plenty, large quantity; **une a. de fruits,** an abundance of fruit; *Prov:* **a. de bien(s) ne nuit pas,** store is no sore; *s.a.* CORNE[1] 4. **2.** (*a*) abundance, wealth, plenty; **société d'a.,** affluent society; **vivre dans l'a.,** to live in plenty; **année d'a.,** year of plenty; (*b*) abundance, wealth (of expression, details, thought); **parler avec a.,** to have a great flow of words; **parler d'a.,** to speak off-hand, extempore; *B:* **l'a. du cœur,** the abundance of the heart; (*c*) *Cards:* (*at solo whist*) abundance. **3.** *A: F:* wine diluted with water.
abondant [abɔ̃dɑ̃], *a.* (*a*) abundant, copious, plentiful; luxuriant (hair, foliage); rich (style); **moisson abondante,** plentiful harvest; **a. en qch.,** abounding in sth.; **peu a.,** scanty; (*b*) **faire un repas a.,** to have a hearty meal; **auteur a.,** prolific author; **hémorragie abondante,** profuse bleeding; (*c*) *Ar:* **nombre a.,** abundant number.
abondement [abɔ̃dmɑ̃], *s.m. Adm: Fin:* additional amount, increase (in a sum of money); agreed supplementary payment.
abonder [abɔ̃de], *v.i.* **1.** (*a*) to abound (**en,** in); **a. de biens,** to be blest with riches; **les rues abondaient de piétons,** the streets were teeming with pedestrians; **rivière qui abonde en poisson,** river well stocked with fish; (*b*) to be plentiful; **le poisson abonde dans cette rivière,** this river is well stocked with fish. **2. a. dans le sens de qn,** to be entirely of s.o.'s opinion, of the same opinion (as s.o.). **3.** *Jur:* to be superfluous; **ce qui abonde ne vicie pas,** superfluous words do not vitiate an act; *hence F:* you can't have too much of a good thing, store is no sore.
abonné, -ée [abɔne], *s.* **1.** subscriber (to paper, etc.). **2.** season-ticket holder; commuter. **3.** consumer; **abonnés du, au, gaz,** gas users, consumers.
abonnement [abɔnmɑ̃], *s.m.* **1.** (*a*) subscription (to paper, etc.); **prendre, souscrire, un a. au 'Times',** to subscribe to the 'Times'; (*b*) *Adm:* **l'a. aux eaux de la ville,** the water rate; **impôt forfaitaire fixé par voie d'a.,** composition tax; **a. pour le téléphone,** telephone rental; *Tp:* **ligne d'a.,** line always open; *Ins:* **police d'a.,** floating policy; (*c*) **payer par a.,** to pay on the instalment plan. **2. (carte d') a.,** season-ticket, *U.S:* commutation ticket (on railway, at theatre, etc.); contract (on railway); **prendre un a.,** to take out a season-ticket, *U.S:* to commute; *F:* **"les abonnements, s'il vous plaît!"** "(show) all seasons, please!" **3.** *Adm:* (*a*) *Excise:* composition (for dues); (*b*) fixed allowance (to prefects and subprefects) for administrative expenses.
abonner [abɔne], *v.tr.* to enrol (s.o.) in a list of subscribers; **a. qn à un journal,** to take out a subscription to a paper for s.o.; **être abonné à un journal,** to subscribe to, take, a paper.
s'abonner. 1. s'a. à un journal, to subscribe, take out a subscription, become a subscriber, to a paper. **2.** *Rail: etc:* to take a season-ticket, *U.S:* to commute. **3. s'a. au gaz, à l'électricité,** to have gas, electricity, installed, put in.
abonnir [abɔniːr], *A:* **1.** *v.tr.* to improve (wine etc.). **2.** *v.i. & pr.* (*of wine*) to improve.
abonnissement [abɔnismɑ̃], *s. A:* (*of wine*) improvement.
abord[1] [abɔːr], *s.m.* **1.** (*a*) access, approach (to land); (*b*) *Nau:* landing; **île d'un a. difficile,** island difficult of access; (*c*) *Mil:* **abords couverts,** covered approaches; **abords découverts,** open approaches; **bloquer les abords,** to block the approaches; **interdire à l'ennemi les abords de la Baltique,** to deny the Baltic approaches to the enemy. **2.** *pl.* approaches (**d'un endroit,** to a place); surroundings, outskirts (de, of). **3.** (*a*) manner in which a person approaches another; address; **son a. fut respectueux,** he approached, greeted, me respectfully; **avoir l'a. agréable,** to have a pleasing manner; **homme à l'a. agréable,** pleasant man; (*b*) manner in which a person receives those who approach him; **avoir l'a. facile, difficile, être d'un a. facile, difficile,** to be easy, difficult, to approach. **4.** (*a*) *adv.phr.* **d'a., tout d'a.,** (i) straight away, at once, right away; (ii) at first, to begin with; (iii) first, in the first place; **d'a. et avant tout,** first and foremost; **dès l'a.,** from the (very) first, from the outset; **à l'a., au premier a., de prime a.,** (i) at first sight, at (the) first glance, to begin with, (ii) (*of fighting*) at the onset; (*b*) *conj. phr. A:* **d'a. que** = AUSSITÔT QUE.
abord[2], *s.m. Nau: used in the phr.* **en a.,** close to the ship's side; (i) outboard, (ii) inboard; **en a. dans la cale,** in the wings.
abordable [abɔrdabl̩], *a.* **1.** easy to land on; easy of approach, easy of access; approachable, accessible; **côte a.,** coast easy of approach; *F:* **vos prix ne sont pas abordables,** your prices are beyond my purse, are not reasonable. **2.** easily approached, accessible, affable; kindly; **personne a. à tous,** person easily approached by all, accessible to all; **peu a.,** (i) stand-offish, (ii) grumpy (person); **il n'est pas a. aujourd'hui,** he's as cross as two sticks today, he's like a bear with a sore head today.
abordage [abɔrdaːʒ], *s.m. Nau:* **1.** boarding (as an act of war); grappling; **monter, sauter, à l'a. (d'un navire),** to board a ship; **refuser l'a.,** to refuse combat at close quarters. **2.** collision; running foul (of sth.); **il y a eu un a. causé par le brouillard,** two ships ran foul of each other, collided, in the fog. **3.** boarding; coming alongside (another boat, the quay); **a. à quai,** berthing.
abordé [abɔrde], *s.m.* (*a*) boarded ship; (*b*) rammed ship.
abordée [abɔrde], *s.f. A: used in the adv.phr.* **à l'a.,** on meeting. **d'a.,** forthwith.
aborder [abɔrde]. **1.** *v.i.* to land; to arrive (by water); to touch land, to make land; **a. à un port,** to reach a port; **a. dans un pays, en Afrique,** to reach a country, to land in Africa; **a. à quai,** to berth, come alongside. **2.** *v.tr.* (*a*) to land; **a. une côte,** to land on a coast; (*b*) to accost, approach (s.o.); **personne n'ose l'a.,** no one dare speak to him; **être abordé par un inconnu,** to be accosted by a stranger; (*c*) **a. une question, une difficulté,** to deal with, grapple with, tackle, attack, a question, a difficulty; to approach, broach, a question; **a. la lecture d'un livre,** to begin reading a book, to tackle a book; **a. de nouvelles études,** to take up new studies; **a. un problème,** to tackle a problem; (*d*) to board; to grapple (a ship in a fight); (*e*) to collide with, to foul, to run foul of, to run down, to run into (a ship); **a. (un navire) à l'éperon,** to ram (a ship); **navire qui a été abordé par un autre,** ship that has been in collision with another; (*f*) to board, accost (ship); to come alongside (ship); (*g*) **a. un navire au quai,** to fetch, moor, a vessel to the quay; to berth.
abordeur [abɔrdœːr], *a. & s.m.* colliding, ramming (ship).
aborigène [abɔriʒɛn]. **1.** *a.* aboriginal (**de,** in); indigenous, native (**de,** to); **plante a. d'une région,** plant native to a region. **2.** *s.m.* aboriginal, aborigine, *pl.* aborigines, *occ.* aboriginals; native.
abornement [abɔrnəmɑ̃], *s.m.* marking out (of field, etc.); delimitation, demarcation (of frontier).
aborner [abɔrne], *v.tr.* to mark out (field, etc.); to delimit, demarcate (frontier).
abortif, -ive [abɔrtif, -iːv], *a.* abortive. **1. fruit a.,** abortive fruit. **2. traitement a.,** abortive treatment (of disease). **3.** *a. & s.m.* abortifacient (drug); *Jur:* **manœuvres abortives,** procuring of abortion.
abot [abo], *s.m. A: Dial:* clog, hobble (of horse).
abouchement [abuʃmɑ̃], *s.m.* **1.** *A:* interview, conference; **ménager un a. entre deux personnes,** to bring two persons together, to bring about a meeting between two persons. **2.** *Tchn:* (*a*) **a. de deux tuyaux,** butt-joining, -junction, of two pipes; (*b*) *Med:* = ANASTOMOSE.
aboucher [abuʃe], *v.tr.* **1. a. deux personnes,** to bring two people together. **2. a. deux tuyaux,** to butt, to join up two pipes (end to end).
s'aboucher. 1. (*a*) to come, get, together (for a conference); to get into touch with one another; (*b*) to have an interview (**avec,** with); **s'a. avec l'ennemi,** to parley with the enemy. **2.** *Anat:* to join, communicate, inosculate.
Aboukir [abukiːr], *Pr.n.m. Geog:* Abukir, Aboukir; *Hist:* **la bataille d'A.,** the battle of the Nile.
abouler [abule], *v.tr. P:* to bring, to hand over; **aboule ça ici!** bring that to me! hand it over! **a. son fric, pognon,** to stump up; to fork out.

s'abouler. *P:* to arrive, come along; **s'a. en retard,** to turn up late.

aboulie [abuli], *s.f. Med:* aboulia, abulia.

aboulique [abulik], *a. Med:* aboulic, abulic.

about [abu], *s.m. Tchn:* butt(-end); abutment, end; junction-joint; **tenon en a.,** end-tenon; **joindre deux pièces en a.,** to join two pieces butt and butt, end to end; **joint d'a.,** butt-joint.

aboutage [abuta:ʒ], *s.m. Nau:* bending (of two cables).

aboutement [abutmɑ̃], *s.m. Tchn:* **1.** joining butt and butt, end to end. **2.** butt(ing), abutment, butt-joint, -scarf.

abouter [abute], *v.tr.* **1.** to join (timbers, etc.) end to end; to butt(-joint). **2.** *Nau:* to bend (two ropes) together. **3.** *Hort: Vit:* to prune back (vine).

aboutir [abuti:r], *v.i.* **1. a. à, dans, en, qch.,** to end at, in, sth., to lead to sth., to result in sth., to culminate in sth., to converge on sth; **ce sentier aboutit au grand chemin,** this path ends at, leads into, the high road; **les grands réseaux de chemins de fer aboutissent à Paris,** the main railway systems converge on Paris; **une pyramide aboutit en pointe,** a pyramid ends in a point; **observations qui aboutissent à une découverte,** observations that lead to, result in, a discovery; **à quoi cela aboutira-t-il?** how will it end? what will it lead to? what will be the outcome of it? **n'a. à rien,** to lead, come, to nothing; to prove abortive; *F:* to end in smoke, not to come off; **nous avons abouti à un accord général,** we have reached a general agreement; **pour a. aux fins que nous poursuivons,** to attain the end which we have in view; **mes efforts n'ont pas abouti à grand-chose,** my efforts were to little purpose; **a. à faire qch.,** to end by, in, effecting sth.; **sa conduite a abouti à le rendre suspect,** in the end his behaviour made him suspect; **j'ai abouti à ce qu'il soit décoré,** I succeeded in getting him decorated. **2.** *abs.* (*a*) (*of plan, etc.*) to succeed, materialize, *F:* to come off; **ne pas a.,** to fail, to fall through, to come to nothing; **les pourparlers n'ont pas abouti,** the negotiations were unsuccessful, came to nothing; **homme qui a abouti,** man who has achieved success; **faire a. qch.,** to bring sth. to a successful issue or conclusion, *F:* to bring, pull, sth. off; *Med:* (*of abscess, etc.*) to come to a head, to burst; **l'abcès a, est, abouti,** the abscess has come to a head. **3. ses terres aboutissent aux miennes,** his land abuts on mine.

aboutissant [abutisɑ̃]. **1.** *a.* bordering, abutting (**à,** on); **jardins aboutissants à la rivière,** gardens bordering, abutting, on the river. **2.** *s.m.* issue, outcome; **la nation est l'a. d'un long passé,** the nation is the product of a long history; *pl.* **aboutissants,** (i) abuttals, lands abutting on an estate; (ii) approaches (to station, etc.); (iii) circumstances; *s.a.* TENANT 3.

aboutissement [abutismɑ̃], *s.m.* **1.** issue, effect, outcome, result (of endeavours, etc.); materialization (of plans). **2.** *Med:* culmination; coming to a head, breaking (of abscess).

aboyant [abwajɑ̃], *a.* barking; baying.

aboyer [abwaje], *v.i.* (**j'aboie, n. aboyons; j'aboierai**) **1.** (*of dog*) to bark; to yelp; (*of hound*) to bay; **toute la meute aboie,** the whole pack is giving tongue, is in full cry; **a. à, après, contre, qn, qch.,** to bark at s.o., sth.; **a. à la lune,** (i) to bark at the moon; (ii) to complain uselessly. **2.** *F:* (*of pers.*) **a. après qn,** to pursue s.o. (with invective); **ses créanciers aboient après lui, après ses chausses,** his creditors are in full cry after him; *Prov:* **les chiens aboient, la caravane passe,** the dogs may bark, but the caravan moves on; **a. après qch.,** to clamour for sth.

aboyeur, -euse [abwajœ:r, -ø:z]. **1.** *a.* **chien a.,** dog given to barking; barking dog; *F:* **critique aboyeuse,** abusive, barking, carping, criticism. **2.** *s. F:* (*a*) carper, fault-finder; **certains critiques ne sont que des aboyeurs,** some critics only carp; (*b*) dun; (*c*) *A:* barker (in front of booth, etc.). **3.** *s.m. Orn:* sandpiper.

abracadabra [abrakadabra], *s.m.* abracadabra; magic keyword.

abracadabrant [abrakadabrɑ̃], *a. F:* stupendous, amazing, *F:* stunning; **histoire abracadabrante,** extraordinary yarn, cock-and-bull story.

Abraham [abraam], *Pr.n.m. B.Hist:* Abraham.

abraquer [abrake], *v.tr. A:* = EMBRAQUER.

abras [abra], *s.m.* iron mounting (of a tool).

abraser [abraze], *v.tr.* to abrade.

abrasif, -ive [abrazif, -i:v]. (*a*) *a.* abrasive; (*b*) *s.m.* abradant.

abrasijet [abraziʒɛ], *s.m. Min:* abrasijet.

abrasin [abrazɛ̃], *s.m. Bot:* tung tree; **huile d'a.,** tung oil.

abrasion [abrazjɔ̃], *s.f.* **1.** *Surg: Med:* abrasion, excoriation; *Phot:* **marques d'a.,** stress marks. **2.** *Geol: etc:* abrasion, attrition; **usé par a.,** abraded.

abraxas [abraksas], *s.m.* **1.** *Archeol: Lap:* abraxas. **2.** *Ent:* currant moth.

abréaction [abreaksjɔ̃], *s.f. Psy: Med:* abreaction.

abrégé [abreʒe], *s.m.* **1.** abridgment, précis, summary, epitome, abstract; **a. d'un discours,** abridgment, summary, of a speech; **faire un a. d'une correspondance,** to make a précis of a correspondence; **réduire un ouvrage en a.,** to summarize a work; **a. d'histoire de France,** short history of France; **voici les faits en a.,** here are the facts in a few words, stated briefly; **écrire qch. en a.,** to write sth. in an abridged, abbreviated, form. **2.** *pl.* **abrégés,** trackers (of organ).

abrégement [abrɛʒmɑ̃], *s.m.* **1.** (*a*) abridging, summarizing (of work, speech, etc.); (*b*) shortening (of syllable, etc.). **2.** abridgment, summary; **a. d'un ouvrage,** abridged edition of a work.

abréger [abreʒe], *v.tr.* (**abrégeant; j'abrège, n. abrégeons; j'abrégerai**). **1.** to shorten, to cut short (life, work, etc.); **il me faut a. mon discours,** I must cut my speech short; **a. une syllabe,** to shorten a syllable; **on l'appelle Toinon pour a.,** she is called Toinon for short; **pour a. . . .,** to be brief . . ., to cut it short. . . .; **son travail abrégeait les soirées d'hiver,** his work made the winter evenings seem shorter. **2.** to abridge, summarize, cut down (book, etc.). **3. a. un mot,** to abbreviate a word; *Ar:* **division abrégée,** abbreviated division.

s'abréger, (*of days, etc.*) to grow, become, get, shorter; to shorten.

abrêtier [abrɛ:tje], *s.m.* **abrêt-noir** [abrɛ'nwa:r], *s.m. Bot:* bilberry, whortleberry.

abreuvage [abrœva:ʒ], *s.m.*, **abreuvement** [abrœvmɑ̃], *s.m.* **1.** watering (of horses, etc.). **2.** watering, drenching (of meadows, etc.); seasoning (of casks); priming (of pump).

abreuver [abrœve], *v.tr.* **1.** to water (horses, cattle, etc.); to supply (animals) with drink. **2.** to soak, drench, flood, irrigate, saturate (**de,** with); to steep (**de, in**); **a. les prés,** to drench, irrigate, the meadows; **l'Égypte est abreuvée par le Nil,** Egypt is watered by the Nile; **a. un tonneau,** to season a cask; **a. une pompe,** to prime a pump; *Paint:* **a. un mur,** to prime (a wall). **3. a. qn de honte, d'injures,** to heap shame, insults, on s.o.

s'abreuver, (*of horse, etc.*) to drink; (*of pers.*) to drink deep; to quench one's thirst; **s'a. de larmes, de soleil,** to be steeped in tears; to bask in the sun, to sun-bathe; **s'a. de sang,** to slake, sate, one's thirst for blood.

abreuvoir [abrœvwa:r], *s.m.* (*a*) watering place (in river, etc.); horse-pond; **mener les chevaux à l'a.,** to water the horses, to take the horses to water; (*b*) watering-trough, drinking-trough (for cattle, poultry, etc.).

abréviateur, -trice [abrevjatœ:r, -tris], *s.* **1.** abridger (*of texts, etc.*). **2.** *s.m. Ecc: A:* drafter of Papal briefs; abbreviator.

abréviatif, -ive [abrevjatif, -i:v], *a.* abbreviatory.

abréviation [abrevjasjɔ̃], *s.f.* **1.** shortening (of term of imprisonment, etc.). **2.** contraction, abbreviation (of word); **nous l'appelons Toinon par a.,** we call her Toinon for short.

abréviativement [abrevjativmɑ̃], *adv.* in an abbreviated, shortened, form; for short.

abreyer [abreje], *v.tr. A:* **1.** *Hort:* to shelter, shield (plants). **2.** *Nau:* to becalm.

abri [abri], *s.m.* (*a*) shelter, cover; refuge; screen; *Hort:* (tent) cloche; **a. public,** public shelter; **chercher l'a. d'un arbre,** to seek shelter under a tree; **prendre a.,** to take cover; **famille sans a.,** homeless family; **a. contre le vent,** wind-screen; **a. à bateau,** boathouse; **a. du marin,** Sailor's Home; *For:* **peuplement d'a.,** nurse-crop; **arbre d'a.,** nurse-tree; *Meteor:* **a. (pour thermomètres)** thermometer screen; **température sous a.,** screened temperature; *Prehist:* **a. sous roche,** rock shelter; *Rail:* **a. du mécanicien, d'une locomotive,** driver's cab (of locomotive); *Min:* **a. de sondeur,** dog-house; **a. souterrain,** creep hole; *Mil:* shelter, dug-out, pit; **a. individuel,** fox hole, slit trench, rifle pit; **a. collectif,** unit shelter, crew shelter; **a. à l'épreuve des balles, des obus, des bombes, des éclats de projectiles, des gaz,** bullet-proof, shell-proof, bomb-proof, splinter-proof, gas-proof shelter; **a. bétonné,** bunker; **a. contre les attaques aériennes, de défense passive,** air raid shelter; **a. de champ de tir, de marqueur,** marker's shelter; **a. blindé,** armoured shelter; *Nau:* **a. de navigation,** wheelhouse; *Navy:* **a. de sous-marins,** submarine pen, U-boat pen; (*b*) *adv.phr.* **à l'a.,** sheltered, under shelter, under cover; **mettre qn à l'a.,** to shelter, screen s.o.; **se mettre à l'a.,** to take shelter, get under cover, retire to a place of safety; **se mettre à l'a. sous un arbre,** to shelter, take shelter, under a tree; **mettre la récolte à l'a.,** to house the crop; (*c*) *prep.phr.* **à l'a. de qch.,** sheltered, screened, secure from sth.; proof against sth.; **à l'a. du besoin,** secure, safe, from want; **se mettre à l'a. de la pluie,** to (take) shelter from the rain; **mettre une machine à l'a. de la chaleur,** to shield a machine from the heat; *Nau:* **à l'a. de la côte,** under the lee of the shore; *Mil:* **à l'a. des balles, des obus,** (i) bullet-proof, shell-proof; (ii) protected from infantry fire, artillery fire; **à l'a. des vues de l'ennemi,** protected, safe, from enemy observation.

abri-caverne [abrikavɛrn], *s.m. Mil:* cave shelter; *pl. abris-cavernes.*

abricot [abriko]. **1.** *s.m.* apricot. **2.** *a.inv.* apricot (-coloured).

abricoté [abrikɔte]. **1.** *a.* apricot-flavoured; **prune, pêche, abricotée,** apricot plum, apricot peach. **2.** *s.m.* slice of crystallized, *U.S:* candied, apricot.

abricotier [abrikɔtje], *s.m.* **1.** apricot(-tree). **2. a. de Saint-Domingue,** mammee.

abricotin [abrikɔtɛ̃], *s.m.* early apricot.

abricotine [abrikɔtin], *s.f.* **1.** apricot-plum. **2.** (*sort of*) Breccia marble.

abri-garage [abrigara:ʒ], *s.m.* carport.

abrier [abri(j)e], *v.tr. A:* = ABREYER.

abrité [abrite], *a.* sheltered; *W.Tel:* screened.

abriter [abrite], *v.tr.* **1.** to shelter; to give cover to (sth., s.o.); **a. une auto,** to put a car under cover. **2.** to shelter, screen, shield, shade, protect; **a. des plantes contre le vent,** to screen plants from the wind. **3.** *Nau:* to becalm; to blanket (another yacht, etc.). **4.** to house; **maison qui abrite plusieurs familles,** house accommodating, providing accommodation for, several families.

s'abriter, to shelter, take cover or shelter (**contre, de,** from).

abrivent [abrivɑ̃], *s.m.* **1.** (wind-)screen; windbreak; *Hort:* mat, matting. **2.** (*a*) penthouse; (*b*) *Mil:* (look-out man's) shelter.

abri-voûte [abrivut], *s.m. Mil:* bomb-proof vault; *pl. abris-voûtes.*

abrocome [abrɔkɔm], *s.m. Z:* abrocome.

abrogatif, -ive [abrɔgatif, -i:v], *a.* abrogative (statute, law).

abrogation [abrɔgasjɔ̃], *s.f.* abrogation, rescission, repeal (of statute, law).

abrogatoire [abrɔgatwa:r], *a.* annulling, rescinding (clause, etc.).

abrogeable [abrɔʒabl], *a.* repealable (statute, law).

abroger [abrɔʒe], *v.tr.* (**j'abrogeai(s), n. abrogeons**), to abrogate, annul, repeal, rescind (statute, law).

abroma [abrɔma], *s.m.*, **abrome** [abrɔ:m], *s.m. Bot:* abroma.

abrouti [abruti], *a. For:* (*of young shoots*) browsed on, nibbled, cropped, by animals.

abroutir [abruti:r], *v.tr. A:* (*of animals*) to nibble at, crop (young shoots of tree).

abroutissement [abrutismɑ̃], *s.m. For:* (*a*) browsing on, cropping (young shoots); (*b*) mutilation of tree (by repeated browsing of animals).

abrupt [abrypt], *a.* **1.** abrupt, sheer, steep, precipitous (descent). **2.** abrupt, blunt, short (speech); **style a.,** abrupt style; **répondre d'un ton a.,** to give an abrupt, short, curt, answer. **3.** *s.m.* precipice.

abruptement [abryptəmɑ̃], *adv.* abruptly. **1.** sheerly, steeply; **la falaise descend a. vers la mer,** the cliff falls abruptly, sheer, to the sea. **2. parler a.,** to speak bluntly, abruptly.

abruti, -ie [abryti], *s. F:* **1.** sot. **2.** idiot, fool; **quel a.!** what a clot!

abrutir [abryti:r], *v.tr.* to brutalize, stupefy, besot, deaden, bestialize; **l'alcool abrutit les hommes,** alcohol turns men into brutes; **abruti par la boisson,** sodden with drink; *F:* **je suis tout abruti de ce qui vient de se passer,** I am absolutely stupefied, dazed, by what has happened; **abruti de surprise,** stunned with surprise; *F:* **je suis complètement abruti,** I'm completely whacked.

s'abrutir, to become stupefied, besotted, sottish; **s'a. dans l'oisiveté, dans un trou de province,** to moulder in idleness, in a country hole.

abrutissant [abrytisɑ̃], *a.* besotting, stupefying; deadly dull, soul-destroying (task, etc.).

abrutissement [abrytismɑ̃], *s.m.* 1. degradation, debasement, sinking into sottishness; **le lent a. d'un esprit distingué,** the slow degradation of a rare intellect. 2. sottishness, brutishness; **vivre dans l'a.,** to live like a beast.
abrutisseur [abrytisœːr]. 1. *a.* stupefying. 2. *s.m.* stupefier.
Abruzzain, -aine [abryzɛ̃, -ɛn], **Abruzzais, -aise** [abryzɛ, -ɛːz]. 1. *a.* of the Abruzzi. 2. *s.* inhabitant of the Abruzzi. 3. *s.m. Ling:* dialect of the Abruzzi.
Abruzzes [abryːz], *Pr.n.m.pl. Geog:* **les A.,** the Abruzzi.
Absalon [apsalɔ̃], *Pr.n.m. B.Hist:* Absalom.
abscisse [apsis], *s.f. Mth:* abscissa; **axe des abscisses,** *x*-axis.
abscission [apsisjɔ̃], *s.f. Surg:* abscission, excision.
abscons [apskɔ̃(ːs)], *a.* obscure (style); abstruse (science).
absence [apsɑ̃ːs], *s.f.* 1. absence; **en, pendant, mon a.,** in, during my absence; **faire de fréquentes absences,** to be often away from home; **remarquer l'a. de qn,** to miss s.o.; **on ne s'est pas aperçu de leur a.,** they were never missed; **briller par son a.,** to be conspicuous by one's absence; **a. (de l'école),** non-attendance (at school); **faire des absences,** to play truant; *Mil:* **a. régulière,** absence with leave; **a. illégale,** absence without leave; **en position d'a. illégale,** absent without leave. 2. **a. de goût,** (i) lack of taste; (ii) tastelessness, lack of flavour; **a. d'imagination,** lack, want of imagination; **a. d'esprit,** absence of mind, abstraction; **il a des absences,** he is liable to be absent-minded; his mind wanders at times; he has fits of abstraction; *F:* **je lui ai écrit dans un moment d'a.,** I wrote to him in a moment of mental aberration. 3. *Med:* epileptic vertigo.
absent [apsɑ̃], *a.* 1. *(a)* absent, away (de, from); **a. par congé, régulièrement,** absent with leave; **a. sans permission,** absent without leave; *s.* (i) (the) absent (one); **les absents ont toujours tort,** the absent are always in the wrong; (ii) absentee; **liste des absents,** absentees' list; *(b)* missing, wanting, absent; **chez cet animal les dents sont absentes,** in this animal the teeth are absent. 2. **son esprit est a.,** his mind is, his thoughts are, far away; **d'un air a.,** idly, absently; **j'avais l'esprit a.,** I was wool-gathering.
absentéisme [apsɑ̃teism], *s.m.* absenteeism.
absentéiste [apsɑ̃teist], *s.m.* *(a)* *Hist:* absentee (landlord); *(b)* *Ind:* (habitual) absentee; slacker.
absenter(s') [sapsɑ̃te], *v.pr.* 1. **s'a. (de chez soi),** to absent oneself, to go away (from home); **s'a. pour affaires,** to go away on business. 2. **s'a. de l'école,** to stay, stop, away from school.
absid(i)al, -aux [apsid(j)al, -o], *a.* apsidal (chapel, etc.).
abside [apsid], *s.f. Ecc.Arch:* apse.
absidiole [apsidjɔl], *s.f.* 1. *Ecc.Arch:* apsidiole, apsidal chapel. 2. apsis, arched reliquary.
absinthe [apsɛ̃ːt], *s.f.* 1. *Bot:* wormwood; **la vie pour lui n'était que fiel et a.,** life to him was gall and wormwood; *s.a.* BOIS[1] 5. 2. absinth, absinthe (drink).
absinther [apsɛ̃te], *v.tr.* to mix (sth.) with absinthe, to add absinthe to (sth.).
s'absinther. *A: P:* to besot oneself with absinthe; to take to absinthe.
absinthine [apsɛ̃tin], *s.f. Ch:* absinthi(i)n.
absinthique [apsɛ̃tik], *a.* 1. *Ch:* absinthic. 2. *a. & s. Med:* (patient) addicted to absinthe, suffering from absinthism.
absinthisme [apsɛ̃tism], *s.m. Med:* absinthism.
absolu [apsɔly]. 1. *a.* absolute; *(a)* **ablatif a.,** ablative absolute; **construction absolue,** absolute construction; **poser une règle absolue,** to lay down a hard and fast rule; **démenti, refus, a.,** flat denial, refusal; **ignorance a.,** absolute ignorance; **cas de nécessité absolue,** case of absolute necessity; **un silence a.,** complete silence; **confiance absolue,** complete confidence, perfect trust; **majorité absolue,** absolute, clear, majority; **l'absolue désolation de toute cette région,** the stark desolation of the whole region; *Mth:* **valeur absolue,** absolute value; *Ph:* **température absolue,** absolute temperature; **zéro a.,** absolute zero; **alcool a.,** absolute alcohol; *Mil:* **l'arme absolue,** the ultimate weapon; **erreur absolue,** absolute error; *(b)* **pouvoir a.,** absolute, unrestricted power; **caractère a.,** autocratic character; **ne faites pas l'a.,** don't be so autocratic; *(c)* absolute, positive, peremptory (tone, voice, order). 2. *s.m. Phil:* **l'A.,** the Absolute; **la recherche de l'A.,** the quest for an Ultimate.
absolument [apsɔlymɑ̃], *adv.* 1. **régner a.,** to reign absolutely; **verbe employé a.,** verb used absolutely; **a. parlant . . .,** speaking generally . . ., on the whole. . . . 2. **c'est a. inutile,** it is entirely unnecessary; **a. impossible,** utterly impossible; **a. rien,** nothing whatever; **ça ne sert a. à rien,** it's not a bit of use; **j'ai a. oublié,** I clean forgot; **c'est a. vous!** it's you to a T! 3. **parler a.,** to speak peremptorily; **c'est a. défendu,** it is strictly forbidden; **je le veux a.,** I demand it, I insist upon it; **elle refuse a. de rentrer,** she simply won't come home; **nier a. qch.,** to deny sth. flatly.
absolution [apsɔlysjɔ̃], *s.f.* 1. *Jur:* acquittal, discharge. 2. *Theol:* absolution (de, from).
absolutisme [apsɔlytism], *s.m.* absolutism.
absolutiste [apsɔlytist], *a. & s.* absolutist.
absolutoire [apsɔlytwaːr], *a.* absolving, absolutory; *Jur:* **décision a.,** acquittal.
absorbable [apsɔrbabl̩], *a.* absorbable.
absorbant [apsɔrbɑ̃]. 1. *a. & s.m.* absorbent (substance). 2. *a.* *(a)* absorptive (function); *Bot:* **poils absorbants,** absorbing hairs; *(b)* absorbing, engrossing (task, book).
absorber [apsɔrbe], *v.tr.* 1. to absorb; *Ch:* to occlude (a gas); **les éponges absorbent l'eau,** sponges absorb, soak in, soak up, water; **l'Empire absorba tous les petits états,** the Empire absorbed all the lesser states; **le jeu a absorbé toute sa fortune,** gambling has run away with his entire fortune. 2. to consume; **elle n'a rien absorbé depuis deux jours,** she has had no food or drink for two days; to take (medicine); **a. de la bière,** to drink beer; **a. l'air du matin,** to drink in the morning air. 3. to absorb, engross; **son travail l'absorbe,** his work engrosses him, takes up all his time; **agréablement absorbé par la pensée de . . .,** pleasantly occupied by the thought of . . .; **entièrement absorbé par son travail,** wrapped up, buried, in his work.
s'absorber, to become absorbed, engrossed (**dans** in); to give oneself up entirely (to); **être absorbé dans ses pensées,** to be lost in thought; **esprit absorbé dans le recueillement,** mind absorbed in meditation; **s'a. dans la lecture d'un livre,** to become engrossed in a book, to pore over a book; **il est absorbé dans la télévision,** he is entirely taken up with television.
absorbeur, -euse [apsɔrbœːr, -øːz]. 1. *a.* absorbent. 2. *s.m. El: Ch: Ph:* absorber; *Telecom:* gate
absorptif, -ive [apsɔrptif, -iːv], *a. Ch: Ph:* absorptive, absorbent.
absorptiomètre [apsɔrpsjɔmɛtr̥], *s.m. Ch:* absorption-meter.
absorption [apsɔrpsjɔ̃], *s.f.* 1. absorption, absorbing; *Opt:* **raies d'a.,** absorption lines. 2. absorption, preoccupation. 3. *El: Ch: Ph:* absorption; **machine, réfrigérateur, à a.,** absorption refrigerator; **a. chimique,** chemisorption; **essence d'a.,** absorption petrol, *U.S:* gasoline; *Elcs:* **intervalle d'a.,** absorption range; **ondemètre d'a.,** absorption wavemeter. 4. *Med:* absorption, taking, intake; **a. de sang,** inhibition of blood. 5. *Fin:* take-over.
absorptivité [apsɔrptivite], *s.f. Ph: Ch:* absorptivity, absorptiveness.
absoudre [apsudr̥], *v.tr.* (*pr.p.* **absolvant;** *p.p.* **absous,** *f.* **absoute;** *pr.ind.* **j'absous, il absout, n. absolvons, v. absolvez, ils absolvent;** *pr.sub.* **j'absolve;** *p.d.* **j'absolvais;** *p.h. & p.sub.* are lacking; *fu.* **j'absoudrai**). 1. **a. qn de qch.,** (i) to forgive, pardon, s.o., sth.; (ii) to acquit s.o. of, exonerate s.o. from, sth.; (iii) to absolve s.o. from (blame, guilt, obligation). 2. **a. qn (de ses péchés),** to grant s.o. remission of his sins; to absolve s.o. (of his sins).
absoute [apsut], *s.f. Ecc:* 1. *A:* general absolution (on Holy Thursday). 2. *R.C.Ch:* absolution (at the end of a funeral mass).
abstème [apstɛm] *Ecc:* 1. *a.* abstaining (from wine). 2. *s.* abstainer (from wine).
abstenir (s') [sapstəniːr], *v.pr.* (*Conj. like* TENIR) **s'a. de qch.,** to abstain, refrain, from sth., to forgo sth.; **s'a. de faire qch.,** to abstain, refrain, forbear, from doing sth.; **s'a. (lorsqu'il s'agit de faire qch.),** to stand aside, aloof; *esp.* to abstain from voting; *Prov:* **dans le doute, abstiens-toi,** when in doubt, don't.
abstention [apstɑ̃sjɔ̃], *s.f.* abstention, abstaining (de, from); *Jur:* disclaiming of competence (by judge).
abstentio(n)nisme [apstɑ̃sjɔnism], *s.m. esp. Pol:* abstention, (the practice of) abstaining (from voting).
abstentio(n)niste [apstɑ̃sjɔnist], *a. & s. esp. Pol:* abstentionist.
abstergent [apstɛrʒɑ̃], *a. & s.m.* abstergent.
absterger [apstɛrʒe], *v.tr. Med: A:* to absterge, to cleanse.
abstersif, -ive [apstɛrsif, -iːv], *a.* abstersive.
abstersion [apstɛrsjɔ̃], *s.f. A:* abstersion.
abstinence [apstinɑ̃ːs], *s.f.* abstinence. 1. abstemiousness; **faire preuve d'a.,** to show oneself abstemious, temperate; *Ecc:* **jour d'a.,** day of abstinence; **faire a.,** to practise abstinence; **faire a. de,** to abstain from. 2. abstention (de, from); **l'a. des plaisirs,** abstinence from pleasure; *Med:* **symptômes d'a.,** withdrawal symptoms.
abstinent, -ente [apstinɑ̃, -ɑ̃ːt]. 1. *a.* abstemious, temperate; **être a. d'alcool,** to be a total abstainer from alcohol, *F:* to be teetotal. 2. *s.* *(a)* total abstainer, teetotaller; *(b)* *A:* = ABSTENTIO(N)NISTE.
abstracteur [apstraktœːr], *s.m.* 1. abstracter, abstractor. 2. person given to abstractions, abstractionist; **a. de quintessence,** hair-splitter.
abstractif, -ive [apstraktif, -iːv], *a.* abstractive.
abstraction [apstraksjɔ̃], *s.f.* abstraction; *(a)* **faire a. de qch.,** to leave sth. out of account, of consideration, to disregard sth.; **a. faite du style, le livre a du mérite,** style apart, the book is not without merit; *(b)* **se perdre dans des abstractions,** to lose oneself in abstractions; *(c)* **par a.,** absentmindedly; *(d)* *Art:* abstraction.
abstractionnisme [apstraksjɔnism], *s.m. Phil: etc:* abstractionism.
abstractionniste [apstraksjɔnist], *a. & s.m. & f. Phil: etc:* abstractionist.
abstractivement [apstraktivmɑ̃], *adv.* abstractively.
abstractivité [apstraktivite], *s.f. Log:* abstractiveness.
abstraire [apstrɛːr], *v.tr.* (*conj. like* TRAIRE); to abstract; to separate; to consider (sth.) apart (from sth.); **on ne peut a. un grand homme de son époque,** one cannot detach, isolate, a great man from his time, period.
s'abstraire. 1. **S'a. dans, en, qch.,** to become engrossed, to bury oneself, in sth. 2. **s'a. de qch.,** to withdraw oneself, hold aloof, from sth. 3. to cut oneself off from one's surroundings.
abstrait [apstrɛ]. 1. *a.* *A:* abstracted, absorbed; absent (-minded). 2. *(a)* abstract (idea, etc.); **nom a.,** abstract noun; **art a.,** abstract art; **avoir une connaissance abstraite de qch.,** to have a theoretical knowledge of sth.; **considérer qch. au point de vue a.,** to consider sth. in the abstract; *(b)* abstruse, deep, obscure (argument, author, etc.). 3. *s.m.* *(a)* **l'a.,** the abstract; *(b)* abstract artist.
abstraitement [apstrɛtmɑ̃], *adv.* 1. in the abstract. 2. *A:* abstractedly, in an absent-minded manner.
abstrus [apstry], *a.* abstruse, recondite (science, etc.).
absurde [apsyrd]. 1. *a.* absurd, preposterous, nonsensical, irrational; **revendication a.,** preposterous claim; **conclusion a.,** absurd, nonsensical, conclusion; **il est a. de le soupçonner,** it is absurd to suspect him; **il est a. que le gouvernement s'en prenne à lui,** it is absurd for the government to blame him. 2. *s.m.* **l'a.,** absurdity; **réduire une théorie à l'a.,** to reduce a theory *ad absurdum*; **raisonnement par l'a.,** *reductio ad absurdum* method of reasoning; **l'a. de cette hypothèse,** the absurd feature, the absurdity, in this hypothesis.
absurdement [apsyrdəmɑ̃], *adv.* absurdly, preposterously.
absurdité [apsyrdite], *s.f.* 1. absurdity, preposterousness, unreasonableness; **c'est le comble de l'a.,** it is the height of absurdity. 2. absurdity, nonsense; twaddle; **dire des absurdités,** to talk nonsense.
abus [aby], *s.m.* 1. *(a)* abuse, misuse (de, of); **employer un terme par a.,** to misuse a term; **l'a. n'enlève pas l'usage,** *abusus non tollit usum,* an abuse does not forfeit the legitimate use of a thing; *Jur:* **a. de pouvoir,** abuse of discretion; *(b)* over-indulgence (de, in); **faire a. de qch.,** to make too free a use of, to indulge too freely in, sth.; **il a été fait a. de cette permission,** this permission has been abused; *(c)* violation, infringement (of rights); *Jur:* **a. de confiance,** breach of trust, fraudulent misuse (of funds, etc.); **a. d'autorité,** use of undue (military or administrative) authority; misuse of authority; **commettre un a. de pouvoir, d'autorité,** to override one's commission; **a. de mineur,** undue influence upon a minor. 2. abuse, corrupt practice, evil custom or usage; **cette coutume dégénéra en a.,** this custom fell into abuse; **réformer un a.,** to redress, remedy, an abuse. 3. error, mistake; **c'est un a. (que) de croire que . . .,** it is a mistake to suppose that. . . . 4. *F:* **il y a de l'a.,** that's going too far, that's a bit thick.

abuser [abyze]. **1.** *v.i.* **a. de qch**; *(a)* to misuse, make ill use of, sth.; **vous abusez de vos forces,** you are over-exerting yourself; **a. du vin,** to indulge too freely in wine; **a. du tabac,** to smoke too much; **a. d'un privilège,** to abuse a privilege; **a. de son autorité,** to abuse one's authority; *(b)* to take (an unfair) advantage of sth.; **vous abusez de ma patience,** you make too great demands upon, overtax, my patience; **a. de l'amabilité de qn,** to impose upon s.o.'s kindness, to abuse s.o.'s good nature; **j'abuse de vos moments,** I am trespassing on your time; *(c)* **a. de qn,** to take advantage of s.o.; *(d)* **a. d'une femme,** to rape a woman; *(e) abs.* (i) **n'abusez point,** be moderate; (ii) **je ne voudrais pas a., j'ai peur d'a.,** I don't want to cause you any inconvenience; (iii) **vous abusez!** it's a bit much, thick! you exaggerate! **2.** *v.tr.* to deceive, delude; **a. qn par de fausses promesses,** to delude s.o. with false promises; **les sens abusent la raison,** our senses deceive our reason.

s'abuser, to delude oneself, to be mistaken; **s'a. sur le compte de qn,** to be mistaken regarding s.o.; **s'a. au point de croire que . . .,** to delude oneself, trick oneself, into the belief that . . ., into believing that . . .; **si je ne m'abuse,** if I am not mistaken.

abuseur [abyzœːr], *s.m. A:* deceiver, impostor.

abusif, -ive [abyzif, -iːv], *a.* **1.** improper, contrary to usage; **sens a. d'un mot,** misused sense, abusive meaning, of a word; **donner à un mot un sens a.,** to use a word in a wrong sense. **2.** excessive; **faire un emploi a. de la force,** to make an excessive use of force; **réquisition abusive,** unauthorized requisitioning (from inhabitants); **mère abusive,** possessive mother; **veuve abusive,** widow who exploits her late husband's fame.

abusivement [abyzivmɑ̃], *adv.* improperly, wrongly; abusively; **employer un mot a.,** to use a word in a wrong sense.

abutilon [abytilɔ̃], *s.m. Bot: Hort:* abutilon, flowering maple.

abut(t)er [abyte]. **1.** *v.i. Carp: etc:* to abut, to butt; **faire a. deux pièces,** to butt two timbers. **2.** *(a) v.tr.* **a. un camion à un quai,** to back a van against a platform; *(b) v.i. Games:* to throw a quoit, a bowl, etc., for the honour.

abyssal, -aux [abisal, -o], *a.* **1.** *Oc:* abyssal; **région, zone, abyssale,** the ocean deeps; **faune abyssale,** abyssal fauna; *Geol:* **roches abyssales,** plutonic rocks. **2.** unfathomable.

abysse [abis], *s.m. Oc:* the ocean deeps.

abyssin, -ine [abisɛ̃, -in], *a. & s.* = ABYSSINIEN.

Abyssinie (l') [labisini], *Pr.n.f. Geog:* Abyssinia; **en A.,** to, in, Abyssinia.

abyssinien, -ienne [abisinjɛ̃, -jɛn]. **1.** *a. & s.* Abyssinian. **2.** *s.f. Min:* **abyssinienne,** driven well, drive-well, Abyssinian well.

acabit [akabi], *s.m.* **1.** (good, bad) quality (of fruit, etc.). **2.** *F: often Pej:* nature, stamp (of person); **ils sont du même a.,** they are all of a piece, all of the same kidney, all tarred with the same brush; **des gens de votre a.,** people of your sort, people like you.

acacia [akasja], *s.m. Bot:* **1.** *(a)* **a. vrai,** acacia; *(b)* **(suc d') a.,** gum arabic. **2. a. vulgaire, faux a.,** locust (-tree), false acacia; *U.S:* **a. à trois épines,** honey-locust; *Austr:* **a. blanc,** silver wattle; **a. d'Arabie,** gum arabic tree; **a. de Farnèse,** sponge-tree.

académicien, -ienne [akademisjɛ̃, -jɛn], *s.m. & f.* academician, member of an academy, *esp. (m)* member of the *Académie française.*

académie [akademi], *s.f.* academy. **1.** *(a)* academy (of Plato, etc.); *(b)* educational district (of France); *s.a.* INSPECTEUR, OFFICIER[2] 3. **2.** academy, society (of letters, science, art); **l'A. française,** the French Academy (of letters); **le Dictionnaire de l'A.,** the Dictionary of the Academy. **3.** school; *(a)* riding-school, riding-academy; *(b)* **a. de dessin,** school of art, art school; **a. de danse, de musique,** academy, school, of dancing, of music; *A:* **tenir a.,** to conduct a school, hold classes (in dancing, riding, etc.). **4.** *(a)* study from the nude, academy figure; **dessiner, peindre, des académies,** to draw, paint, from the nude; *(b) F:* body.

académique [akademik], *a.* academic(al). **1. les palmes académiques,** insignia of decoration granted by the French Ministry of Education. **2.** *(a)* **séance a.,** sitting, meeting of an academy; *(b)* relating to the French Academy; **occuper un fauteuil a.,** to sit in the French Academy; *Lit:* **style a.,** academic, *Pej:* pedantic, style. **3.** *Art:* **figure a.,** nude, academy figure; **prendre une pose a.,** to assume a classic attitude. **4. débat a.,** academic discussion.

académiquement [akademikmɑ̃], *adv.* academically.

académisable [akademizabl], *a.* worthy of election to the French Academy.

académiser [akademize], *v.tr. Art:* to academize (pose, etc.).

académisme [akademism], *s.m. Art:* academism.

académiste [akademist], *s.m. A:* master, pupil, at a school of riding, fencing, etc.

Acadie (l') [lakadi], *Pr.n.f. Geog: A:* Acadia; **en A.,** in, to, Acadia.

acadien, -ienne [akadjɛ̃, -jɛn], *a. & s.* **1.** *Geog: A:* Acadian. **2.** *Geol:* acadian.

acaena [asena], *s.f. Bot:* acaena.

acagnarder [akaɲarde], *v.tr. Lit:* to make, render, slack, sluggish; to enervate.

acagnarder (s') [sakaɲarde], *v.pr. A. & Lit:* **1.** to drift into an idle, aimless way of living, to become a slacker, to drift. **2. s'a. dans un fauteuil,** to settle down comfortably in an armchair.

acajou [akaʒu], *s.m. Bot:* **1. a. mâle, à meubles,** mahogany (-tree, -wood). **2. a. femelle, à planches,** Honduras cedar. **3. a. à pommes,** cashew (nut tree); **noix d'a.,** cashew nut. **4.** *a.inv.* dark auburn (hair).

acalèphe [akalɛf], *s.m. Coel:* jellyfish; *Z: in pl.* Acalephae.

acanthacées [akɑ̃tase], *s.f.pl. Bot:* Acanthaceae.

acanthe [akɑ̃ːt], *s.f.* **1.** *Bot: (a)* acanthus, brankursine, *F:* bear's-breech; *(b)* **a. sauvage,** Scotch thistle; *(c)* **a. d'Allemagne,** hog-weed, cow-parsnip. **2.** *Arch:* acanthus.

acanthocarpe [akɑ̃tɔkarp], *a. Bot:* acanthocarpous.

acanthocéphales [akɑ̃tɔsefal], *s.m.pl. Ann:* Acanthocephala.

acanthoïde [akɑ̃tɔid], *a. Bot:* acanthoid, spiny.

acanthopanax [akɑ̃tɔpanaks], *s.m. Bot:* acanthopanax.

acanthophis [akɑ̃tɔfis], *s.m. Rept:* acantophis, death-adder.

acanthoptères [akɑ̃tɔptɛːr], *s.m.pl.,* **acanthoptérygiens** [akɑ̃tɔpteriʒjɛ̃], *s.m.pl. Ich:* Acanthopterygii.

acanthure [akɑ̃tyːr], *s.m. Ich:* acanthurus, surgeon fish.

acare [akaːr], *s.m. Arach:* acarus.

acariasis [akarjazis], *s.f.,* **acariose** [akarjoːz], *s.f. Med:* acariasis.

acariâtre [akarjɑːtr̥], *a.* crabbed, bad-tempered, cantankerous, (*especially of women, hence*) shrewish; **nature a.,** cantankerousness.

acariâtreté [akarjɑtrəte], *s.f.* bad temper, crabbedness, cantankerousness; (*of women*) shrewishness.

acarides [akarid], *s.m.pl.,* **acaridiens** [akaridjɛ̃], *s.m.pl.* **acariens** [akarjɛ̃], *s.m.pl. Arach:* Acarida; *F:* mites.

Acarnanie (l') [lakarnani], *Pr.n.f. Geog:* Acarnania.

Acarnane [akarnan], *s.m. & f. A.Geog:* Acarnanian.

acarnanien, -ienne [akarnanjɛ̃, -jɛn], *a. & s. A. Geog:* Acarnanian.

acarpe [akarp], *a. Bot:* acarpous, sterile.

acarus, -ri [akarys, -ri], *s.m. Arach:* acarus; **a. de la gale,** itch-mite.

acatalecte [akatalɛkt], **acatalectique** [akatalɛktik], *a. Pros:* acatalectic, complete in its syllables.

acatalepsie [akatalɛpsi], *s.f. Phil:* acatalepsy.

acataleptique [akatalɛptik], *a. Phil:* acataleptic.

acatène [akatɛn]. **1.** *a.* chainless. **2.** *s.f. O:* chainless bicycle.

acaudé [akode], *a. Anat: Z:* acaudate, tailless.

acaule [akoːl], *a. Bot:* acaulous, stemless.

accablant [akɑblɑ̃], *a.* **1.** overwhelming, crushing; **malheur a.,** overwhelming misfortune; **preuves accablantes,** overwhelming, damning, proofs (of guilt). **2.** oppressive, overpowering, sweltering (heat, etc.).

accablé [akɑble], *a.* **1.** overwhelmed; **a. de travail,** overwhelmed with work, *F:* up to the eyes in, snowed under with, work; **a. de douleur, par la douleur,** overcome, weighed down, with grief; **a. de fatigue,** worn out with fatigue, *F:* dog-tired; **a. par la peur,** overcome with fear; **a. sous le poids des années,** stricken in years; **a. par la chaleur, par la fièvre,** prostrated by the heat, by fever; *A:* **elle tomba accablée,** she collapsed; *s.a.* DETTE. **2. le malade est très a. aujourd'hui,** the patient is very low, quite prostrate, to-day.

accablement [akɑbləmɑ̃], *s.m.* **1.** (overwhelming) pressure; **l'a. des affaires,** the heavy pressure of business. **2.** *(a)* dejection, despondency; **tomber dans l'a.,** to become despondent; *(b) Med:* prostration; heaviness, torpor.

accabler [akɑble], *v.tr.* **1.** to overpower, overwhelm, crush; to bear down; **a. un adversaire,** to overcome, *F:* to floor, an opponent; **a. le peuple d'impôts,** to (over)burden the people with taxes; **a. qn d'injures,** to heap abuse upon s.o. **2.** to overwhelm (*in a favourable sense*); **a. qn de gentillesses,** to load, overwhelm, s.o. with kindnesses; **a. qn d'invitations,** to shower invitations on s.o.

accalmie [akalmi], *s.f.* **1.** lull (in the weather, in war, etc.); (period of) calm; smooth (in sea). **2.** period of quiet (in illness, etc.); slack time (in business). *Mil:* **a. dans la bataille,** lull in the battle.

accalminé [akalmine], *a. Nau:* becalmed.

accaparant [akaparɑ̃], *a.* engrossing; **un métier a.,** an all-absorbing occupation.

accaparement [akaparmɑ̃], *s.m.* monopolizing; cornering (of goods); buying up (of stocks); *A:* engrossing; *Jur: A:* coemption.

accaparer [akapare], *v.tr.* to corner, hoard (goods); to buy up (all available stocks, etc.); to seize upon (sth.); **a. la vente,** to capture the market; **a. la conversation, un hôte,** to monopolize the conversation, a guest; **a. les meilleures places,** to secure, *F:* bag, the best seats.

accapareur, -euse [akaparœːr, -øːz]. **1.** *a.* possessive (person). **2.** *s. (a)* buyer-up (of goods); monopolizer (of good things); monopolist; *(b) Pej:* grabber, shark.

accastillage [akastijaːʒ], *s.m. N. Arch:* **1.** superstructure (of ship); upper works; topsides. **2.** *A:* poop and forecastle.

accéder [aksede], *v.i.* **(j'accède, n. accédons; j'accéderai). 1.** *(a)* **a. quelque part, à qch.,** to have access to, to reach, sth.; **a. au trône,** to accede to the throne; **on accède à la porte par un escalier,** access to the door is by a flight of steps; **les sorties accèdent directement à la rue,** the exits open directly on to the street; **permettre d'a. à,** to provide access to; *(b)* **a. jusqu'à qn,** to obtain access to s.o. **2. a. à une requête,** to accede to, fall in with, comply with, a request; **a. à un pacte,** to accede to a pact; **a. à une condition,** to agree, assent, to a condition.

accelerando [akselerɑ̃do], *adv. Mus:* accelerando.

accélérateur, -trice [akseleratœːr, -tris]. **1.** *a.* accelerative, accelerating; *Physiol:* **nerfs accélérateurs,** accelerator nerves; **anode accélératrice (d'un tube oscillographique),** accelerator. **2.** *s.m.* accelerator; *Atom.Ph:* **a. de particules atomiques,** atomic accelerator; **a. de particules,** cyclotron; **a. d'électrons,** betatron; **a. d'inflammation,** ignition accelerator; *Aut:* **appuyer sur l'a.,** to accelerate, *F:* to step on the gas.

accélération [akselerasjɔ̃], *s.f.* acceleration. **1.** *(a) Mec:* **a. uniforme,** constant acceleration; **a. négative, retardatrice,** retardation, negative acceleration; **a. de la pesanteur,** gravitational acceleration; *(b) Aut:* **pédale d'a.,** accelerator pedal. **2.** speeding up (of work).

accéléré [akselere], *a.* **1.** accelerated, speeded up (motion). **2.** quick, fast; **pouls a.,** quick(ened) pulse; *Artil:* **Feu a.,** rapid fire; **machine à mouvement a.,** high-speed machine; *s.a.* PAS[1] 1. **3.** *s.m. Cin:* quick motion.

accélérer [akselere], *v.tr.* **(j'accélère, n. accélérons; j'accélérerai). 1.** to accelerate, quicken (rate of motion, etc.); to speed up (traffic, etc.); *abs.* to accelerate; *Mil:* **a. le pas,** to quicken the step. **2.** to hasten, speed up, expedite (undertaking, etc.).

s'accélérer, to become faster, to accelerate.

accéléro-compteur [akselerokɔ̃tœːr], *s.m.* statistical accelerometer.

accélérographe [akselerɔgraf], *s.m.* accelerograph, recording accelerometer.

accéléromètre [akselerɔmɛtr̥], *s.m. Mec:* accelerometer.

accent [aksɑ̃], *s.m.* **1.** accent; *(a)* stress; **a. oratoire,** sentence stress; **a. tonique,** tonic accent; **syllabe sans a.,** unaccented, unstressed, syllable; **mettre l'a. sur,** to stress, emphasize; *(b)* **a. grammatical,** grammatical accent; diacritic; **a. aigu,** acute accent. **2.** pronunciation, accent; **parler avec un a.,** to speak with an accent; **parler le français avec un a. anglais,** to speak French with an English accent; **a. irlandais,** Irish brogue. **3.** tone of voice; **d'un a. qui n'admet pas de réplique,** in a tone that admits of no reply; **son récit a l'a. de la vérité,** his account rings true. **4.** *pl. (a)* **les accents du désespoir,** the accents of despair; *(b)* **les accents de la Marseillaise,** the strains of the Marseillaise. **5.** *Art:* high light or deep shadow (in picture); accent.

accenteur [aksɑ̃tœːr], *s.m. Orn:* accentor; **a. alpin,** alpine accentor; **a. montanelle,** mountain accentor; **a. mouchet,** hedge accentor, hedge sparrow.

accentuable [aksɑ̃tɥabl̩], *a.* capable of bearing stress; which may be accentuated.

accentuation [aksɑ̃tɥasjɔ̃], *s.f.* **1.** stressing (of syllables, etc.); **syllabe à a. faible,** weak syllable, unstressed syllable. **2.** accentuation, placing of the grammatical accents.

accentuel, -elle [aksɑ̃tɥɛl], *a. Ling:* accented (syllable, etc.).

accentuer [aksɑ̃tɥe], *v.tr.* **1.** (*a*) to stress (word, syllable, note, etc.); **syllabe non accentuée,** unstressed, unaccented, syllable; (*b*) to accentuate; to mark (vowel) with a grammatical accent. **2.** (*a*) to emphasize (feature in landscape, etc.); **traits fortement accentués,** pronounced, strongly marked, features; (*b*) **sa réponse accentua mon opinion,** his answer strengthened my opinion; **cette mesure accentua le chômage,** this measure increased, added to, accentuated, the unemployment.

s'accentuer, to become accentuated; **le chômage s'accentue,** unemployment is on the increase; **le changement s'accentue,** the change is becoming more marked.

acceptabilité [aksɛptabilite], *s.f.* acceptableness, acceptability.

acceptable [aksɛptabl̩], *a.* **1.** acceptable (**à,** to); **offre a.,** acceptable, reasonable, decent, offer; **cadeau très a.** very acceptable, welcome, gift. **2.** in fair condition, that will pass muster.

acceptablement [aksɛptabləmɑ̃], *adv.* acceptably, in an acceptable manner.

acceptant, -ante [aksɛptɑ̃, -ɑ̃:t]. **1.** *s.* acceptant; *Com:* acceptor. **2.** *s.m.pl. Ecc. Hist:* acceptants.

acceptation [aksɛptasjɔ̃], *s.f.* (*a*) acceptance; *Com:* **refus d'a.,** non-acceptance (of goods, bill). *s.a.* HONNEUR 4, INTERVENTION; (*b*) submission, acceptance (of fate).

accepter [aksɛpte], *v.tr.* **1.** to accept; **j'accepte vos conditions,** I agree to, am agreeable to, your conditions; **a. un défi,** to take up, accept, a challenge; **a. la bataille,** to accept battle; **je n'accepte pas cette théorie,** I don't agree with this theory; **je vous accepte,** I'll take you (on), I'll engage you; **a. de faire qch.,** (i) to agree to do sth.; (ii) to accept an invitation to do sth., to consent to do sth.; **accepté!** agreed! **a. que qch. se fasse,** to agree to sth. being done; **a. à dîner,** to accept an invitation to dine, dinner; **faire a. qch.,** to get sth. accepted; **a. qn comme, pour, arbitre,** to accept s.o. as an arbitrator; *Com:* **a. un effet,** (i) to accept, sign, a bill, (ii) to honour a bill; **ne pas a. un effet,** to dishonour a bill; **si le "Times" accepte mon article,** if the 'Times' takes my article. **2.** to accept with resignation; **a. la mort,** to resign oneself to death.

accepteur [aksɛptœ:r], *s.m.* (*a*) *Com:* acceptor, drawee (of bill); (*b*) *Ch: Elcs:* acceptor.

acception [aksɛpsjɔ̃], *s.f.* **1.** (*a*) *A:* favouring, preference, partiality; (*b*) **sans a. de personne,** without respect of persons; **ne faire a. de personne,** to be no respector of persons. **2.** acceptation, meaning, sense (of word, etc.); **dans toute l'a. du mot,** in the full acceptation, meaning, of the word; in every sense of the word, in more than one sense; **a. figurée d'un mot,** figurative meaning of a word.

accès [aksɛ], *s.m.* **1.** (*a*) access, approach; **les a. de la gare,** the station approaches; *P.N:* **a. aux quais,** to the trains; *Nau:* **carte d'a. à bord,** embarkation card; **endroit difficile d'a.,** place difficult of access; **avoir a. à qch.,** to have access to sth.; **donner a. à qch.,** to give access, to lead, to sth.; **routes donnant a. en France,** roads of entry into France; **avoir a. auprès de qn,** to have access to s.o.; **trouver a. auprès de qn,** to gain admission to s.o.; (*b*) **a. gratuit,** admission free. **2.** fit, attack, outburst; **a. de fièvre,** attack, bout, of fever; **a. de faiblesse,** fainting fit; **a. de colère, de folie,** outburst of passion, fit of temper; fit of madness; **a. d'enthousiasme,** fit, burst, of enthusiasm; **dans un a. de fou rire,** in a fit of helpless, uncontrollable, laughter; **travailler par a.,** to work by fits and starts.

accessibilité [aksɛsibilite], *s.f.* accessibility, approachability, *F:* getatableness.

accessible [aksɛsibl̩], *a.* **1.** accessible; **livre peu a.** book difficult to get hold of; **emplois accessibles à tout le monde,** posts accessible, open, to all, within the reach of all; **connaissances accessibles à un enfant,** knowledge within the comprehension of a child; **être a. à un raisonnement,** to be willing to listen to an argument; **esprit a. à la conviction,** mind open to conviction; **endroit a.,** *F:* getatable place. **2.** (*of pers.*) (*a*) approachable; **il est peu, difficilement, a.,** he is (i) difficult to approach, to get at, (ii) stand-offish; **tribunal a. en tout temps,** court available at all times; (*b*) **a. à la pitié,** open to pity; **a. à l'intérêt,** liable to be swayed, influenced, by self-interest.

accession [aksɛsjɔ̃], *s.f.* **1.** (*a*) accession (to power, etc.); **a. au trône,** accession to the throne; (*b*) **a. à la propriété,** coming into ownership; **faciliter l'a. à la propriété,** to make home ownership easier. **2. l'a. de la Bretagne à la France,** the accession of Brittany to France. **3.** adherence, adhesion (to a contract, to a party).

accessit [aksesit], *s.m.* proxime accessit; honourable mention; certificate of merit.

accessoire [akseswa:r]. **1.** *a.* accessory, secondary; **jouer un rôle a.,** to play a subordinate, minor role, part; *s.a.* JEU 1. *Com:* **garantie a.,** collateral security; *s.m.* **laisser de côté l'a., les accessoires,** to ignore minor details. **2.** *s.m.* accessory, appurtenance, fitting, attachment (for machine, etc.); *Min:* **a. de pompe,** pump gear; **accessoires de soupapes,** valve trimmings; *pl. Th: Cin:* properties, *F:* props; **magasin des accessoires,** property-room; **jouer les accessoires,** to play small, minor parts; *Com:* **accessoires de, pour la, toilette,** toilet requisites.

accessoirement [akseswarmɑ̃], *adv.* accessorily, incidentally, as a secondary consideration, by the way.

accessoiriste [akseswarist], *s.m. or f. Th:* property-man, *F:* props; property mistress; *Com:* accessories supplier.

acciaccatura [atʃiakatura], *s.f. Mus:* acciaccatura.

accident [aksidɑ̃], *s.m.* **1.** accident; (*a*) **je l'ai retrouvé par a.,** I found it by accident, accidentally; (*b*) **être victime d'un a.,** to have, meet with, an accident; *F:* **elle a eu un a.,** she's had a miscarriage; **a. de chemin de fer,** railway accident, disaster, smash; **a. d'avion, d'aviation,** plane crash; **a. de la route, de la circulation,** road accident; **allez moins vite ou vous allez avoir un a.,** drive more slowly or you'll have an accident; **nous sommes arrivés sans a.,** we arrived safely; **en cas d'a.,** in case of accident; **accidents du travail,** industrial injuries; **la loi sur les accidents du travail** = the Factory Acts, the Workmen's Compensation Act; **a. de personne,** casualty; **a. mortel,** fatal accident, fatality; (*c*) (*sudden and unexpected*) sickness, disease. **2.** *Mus:* accidental. **3.** *Geog:* **a. de terrain,** undulation, unevenness, irregularity, of the ground; *Golf:* hazard. **4.** *Phil: Theol:* accident.

accidenté, -ée [aksidɑ̃te]. **1.** *a.* (*a*) eventful; **vie accidentée,** chequered career; (*b*) uneven, broken, rough, hilly (ground); **style a.,** (i) varied style, (ii) rugged, uneven, style; (*c*) **voiture accidentée,** damaged car; (*d*) restless; **vie peu accidentée,** calm, uneventful life. **2.** *s.* sufferer from, victim of, an accident; **les accidentés,** the injured, the casualties; **a. du travail,** victim of an occupational injury; *Philately:* wreck-cover.

accidentel, -elle [aksidɑ̃tɛl], *a.* **1.** accidental, undesigned, casual, adventitious. **2.** *Mus:* **signes accidentels,** (i) accidentals, (ii) key-signature.

accidentellement [aksidɑ̃tɛlmɑ̃], *adv.* **1.** accidentally, by accident, by chance; **faire qch. a.,** to happen to do sth. **2. mourir a.,** to die in, as the result of, an accident.

accidenter [aksidɑ̃te], *v.tr.* **1.** to give variety, a broken appearance, to (the landscape, etc.); to vary (one's style). **2.** *F:* to damage, injure, in an accident.

accipitres [aksipitr̩], *s.m.pl. Orn:* accipitres.

accipitrin [aksipitrɛ̃], *a. Orn:* accipitrine.

accise [aksi:z], *s.f.* excise (duty); **préposé à l'a.,** exciseman.

acclamateur [aklamatœ:r], *s.m.* acclaimer, applauder; shouter.

acclamatif, -ive [aklamatif, -i:v], *a.* acclamatory.

acclamation [aklamasjɔ̃], *s.f.* acclamation, cheering; **discours salué d'acclamations,** speech greeted with cheers; **la loi fut votée par a.,** the law was passed by a unanimous show of hands.

acclamer [aklame], *v.tr.* (*a*) to acclaim, applaud, cheer; to greet (s.o.) with cheers; (*b*) **a. qn empereur,** to acclaim s.o. emperor, to hail s.o. as emperor.

acclimatable [aklimatabl̩], *a.* acclimatizable.

acclimatation [aklimatasjɔ̃], *s.f.* acclimatization; *Pr.n.* **Le Jardin d'A.,** the Zoological Gardens (in Paris).

acclimatement [aklimatmɑ̃], *s.m.* acclimatation (**à,** to).

acclimater [aklimate], *v.tr.* to acclimatize (**à,** to); to import, introduce (new ideas, turns of phrase, customs).

s'acclimater, to become, get, acclimatized; (*of customs, etc.*) to become established, accepted.

acclimateur [aklimatœ:r], *s.m.* acclimatizer.

accoinçon [akwɛ̃sɔ̃], *s.m. Const:* hip-rafter.

accointance [akwɛ̃tɑ̃:s], *s.f. usu. pl., Pej:* intimacy; dealings; **avoir des accointances avec des escrocs,** to have dealings, relations, with sharpers.

accointé, -ée [akwɛ̃te]. **1.** *a.* in relations (with); **a. avec une bande,** mixed up with a gang. **2.** *s.* associate, partner (in fraud, etc.).

accointer (s') [sakwɛ̃te], *v.pr. Pej:* **s'a. avec qn,** to enter into relations with s.o.; *F:* to take up with s.o.; *F:* **s'a. avec une femme,** *abs.* **s'a.,** to go around with a woman, have an affair.

accolade [akɔlad], *s.f.* **1.** (*ceremonial*) embrace; **donner une a. à qn,** to embrace s.o. **2.** accolade; **donner l'a. à qn,** to confer the accolade, a knighthood, on s.o.; **recevoir l'a.,** to receive the accolade (conferring the *Légion d'honneur*); to be knighted. **3.** *Mus: Typ:* brace, bracket. **4.** *Arch:* **arc en a.,** four-centred arch, ogee arch, accolade.

accolader [akɔlade], *v.tr.* **1.** *A:* **a. qn,** (i) to embrace s.o., (ii) to confer the accolade on s.o., to knight s.o. **2.** *Mus: Typ:* to brace, bracket (staves, words, etc.).

accolage [akɔla:ʒ], *s.m. Hort: Vit:* tying up (of vine shoot, etc. to stakes or supports).

accolé [akɔle], coupled (joists, etc.); bracketed (words, sentences); *Bot:* united (flowers, leaves); conjugate (leaflets); *Her:* conjoined, *ac(c)ollé*; *Num:* accolled, accollated (heads); *Mil:* **unités accollées,** units disposed abreast.

accolement [akɔlmɑ̃], *s.m.* joining, uniting, bracketing; coupling together (with a brace); *Cryst:* **plan d'a.,** composition plane.

accoler [akɔle], *v.tr.* **1.** to join side by side, to couple; *Typ:* to brace, bracket; **église accolée aux murs de la ville,** church built on to the town walls. **2.** to tie up (vine, plants, to stakes or supports). **3.** *A:* (= ACCOLADER 1) to embrace. **4.** *Arch:* to interlace (decorative motifs).

s'accoler. 1. (*a*) (*of plants*) to intertwine; (*b*) **plante qui s'accole aux murs,** plant that clings to the walls. **2.** *F:* **s'a. avec une femme,** to associate, go around, with a woman.

accolure [akɔly:r], *s.f.* **1.** (*a*) piece of raffia, twine (for tying up plant); (*b*) withy, withe. **2.** *Bookb:* **accolures d'un livre,** bands of a book. **3.** raft (of floated timber).

accombant [akɔ̃bɑ̃], *a. Bot:* accumbent.

accommodable [akɔmɔdabl̩], *a.* **1.** adjustable, that can be settled. **2.** (*food*) that can be prepared, cooked, served (**avec,** with; **à la Provençale,** in the Provençal manner).

accommodage [akɔmɔda:ʒ], *s.m.* (*manner of*) preparing, serving (food).

accommodant [akɔmɔdɑ̃], *a.* good-natured, easy-going, easy to deal with, accommodating; **peu a.,** not easy to deal with, (*of pers.*) difficult.

accommodateur, -trice [akɔmɔdatœ:r, -tris], *a. Physiol:* which produces, aids, accommodation.

accommodation [akɔmɔdasjɔ̃], *s.f.* **1.** adapting, accommodation; **a. d'une salle aux usages d'un bureau,** adaptation, conversion, of a room for office use. **2.** *Physiol:* accommodation (of the eye).

accommodement [akɔmɔdmɑ̃], *s.m.* compromise, arrangement, coming to terms with; **entrer en a., en venir à un a.,** to arrange a settlement, to come to terms (**avec,** with); **politique d'a.,** policy of compromise, give-and-take policy; *Com:* **a. avec des créanciers,** composition with creditors.

accommoder [akɔmɔde], *v.tr.* **1.** (*a*) *A:* to make (s.o.) comfortable (in an armchair, etc.); (*b*) to suit (s.o.), to serve (s.o.), according to his wishes; **ceci vous accommodera-t-il?** will this suit you? will this answer your purpose? **difficile à a.,** difficult to please; (*c*) *A:* **a. deux personnes,** to reconcile, to adjust differences between, two people; **a. un différend,** to arrange amicably, to adjust, a dispute; (*d*) *A:* to make (things) fit together; to arrange, dispose (furniture, etc.); to dress, attire, accoutre (s.o.); **peu accommodé des biens de la fortune,** not greatly blessed with worldly goods; *F:* **a. qn de toutes pièces,** (i) to give s.o. a good dressing-down, (ii) to tear s.o. to pieces (behind his back). **2.** (*a*) to cook, season, prepare (food); **a. les restes,** to use up the scraps, leftovers; **veau accommodé à la sauce blanche,** veal prepared with white sauce; **a. une salade,** to dress a salad; *s.a.* SAUCE 1; (*b*) *A:* to dress, adjust (one's hair, etc.); to adjust (one's scarf); to arrange (house, furniture). **3. a. qch. à qch.,** to fit, adapt, sth. to sth.

s'accommoder. 1. (*a*) *A:* to make oneself comfortable, to settle down (in armchair, etc.); (*b*) **il s'accommode partout, à toutes les circonstances,** he makes himself at home everywhere, he is very adaptable; (*c*) *A:* to dress (up), to titivate. 2. **s'a. de qch., de qn,** to make the best of sth., of s.o.; to put up with sth., with s.o.; **je m'accommode de tout,** I put up, am pleased, with anything; anything suits me; **plante qui s'accommode de tous les sols,** plant that thrives in all soils, that adapts itself to any soil; **il s'accommoderait parfaitement qu'on le laissât à Paris,** he would be quite satisfied to be left in Paris. 3. **s'a. à qch.,** (i) to adapt, accommodate, oneself to sth.; (ii) (*of thg*) to suit sth. 4. **s'a. avec qn,** (i) to get on with s.o., (ii) to come to an agreement with s.o.; *Com:* to compromise with s.o., to compound (with creditor).

accompagnateur, -trice [akɔ̃paɲatœːr, -tris], *s.* 1. *Mus:* accompanist. 2. *s.m. St.Exch:* speculator. 3. courier (of conducted tour). 4. *s.m. Rail:* maintenance man (accompanying long-distance train).

accompagnement [akɔ̃paɲmɑ̃], *s.m.* 1. (*action of*) accompanying (s.o.). 2. (*a*) *A:* retinue, suite; (*b*) *pl. Cu:* garnish; (*c*) *Her:* **a. de l'écu,** accompaniments (about the shield); (*d*) concomitant (of sth); **le plaisir est parfois l'a. de la vertu,** pleasure sometimes goes hand in hand with, accompanies, virtue. 3. *Mus:* accompaniment; **chanter sans a.,** to sing unaccompanied. 4. *Mil: Av:* close support, escort; **engins d'a.,** close support weapons; **aviation d'a.,** close support aviation; **l'a. aérien,** close air support; **artillerie d'a.,** accompanying artillery; **chasseur d'a.,** escort fighter. 5. *Rail:* maintenance service.

accompagner [akɔ̃paɲe], *v.tr.* 1. to accompany; (*a*) to go, come, with (s.o.); **m'accompagnez-vous?** are you coming with me? **faites-vous a.,** take some one with you; **êtes-vous seul ou accompagné?** are you alone or is there anyone with you? **a. qn jusqu'à la porte, jusque chez lui,** to see s.o. to the door, home; **a. qn jusqu'au bateau, jusqu'à la gare, etc.,** to see s.o. off; **a. qn un bout de chemin,** to go part of the way with s.o., *s.a.* BAGAGE 2, VOYAGE; (*b*) to escort (s.o.); to attend (on) (s.o. as a retinue, etc.); to act as courier (to group of tourists); **accompagné de son secrétaire, par un général,** accompanied by his secretary, by a general; **rhume accompagné de fièvre,** feverish cold; **la vieillesse et les maux qui l'accompagnent,** old age and its attendant ills; **nos meilleurs vœux vous accompagnent,** our best wishes go with you; (*c*) *Mus:* **a. qn au piano,** to accompany s.o. on the piano; **elle s'accompagne elle-même,** she plays her own accompaniments; **a. son chant sur la guitare,** to sing to the guitar. 2. **a. des remontrances de menaces,** to join threats to remonstrances; **il accompagna ces mots d'un sourire,** he said this with a smile. 3. (*of article of dress, etc.*) to go with (sth.); to match (sth.).

accompli [akɔ̃pli], *a.* accomplished (musician, linguist, etc.); perfect, thorough; **elle est très accomplie,** she has many accomplishments; **a. en tout point,** perfect in everything; **scélérat a.,** thorough, out and out, rascal.

accomplir [akɔ̃pliːr], *v.tr.* 1. to accomplish, achieve (purpose, etc.); to carry out, perform, fulfil (order, promise, etc.); **que la volonté du Seigneur s'accomplisse,** the Lord's will be done; **le miracle s'est accompli tout seul,** the miracle came about of itself; *s.a.* MISSION 1. 2. to complete, finish (apprenticeship, service, etc.). **il a quarante ans accomplis,** he is turned forty; **fait accompli,** accomplished fact, *fait accompli.*

accomplissement [akɔ̃plismɑ̃], *s.m.* 1. accomplishment, performance, carrying out, achievement (of work, duty); fulfilment (of wish); **l'œuvre en a.,** the work in progress, in hand. 2. completion (of service, work, etc.).

accon [akɔ̃], *s.m.* = ACON.

acconage [akɔnaːʒ], *s.m.* = ACONAGE.

acconier [akɔnje], *s.m.* = ACONIER.

accorage [akɔraːʒ], *s.m. Nau: etc:* propping, shoring-up.

accord [akɔːr], *s.m.* 1. (*a*) agreement, understanding; bargain; settlement; **un a. est intervenu, d'après lequel . . .,** an agreement has been reached, by which . . .; (*b*) *pl. A. & Dial:* betrothal. 2. agreement (**sur, on**); harmony; **partout règne l'a.,** everywhere harmony reigns; **vivre en, de, bon a.,** to dwell in perfect harmony, to live in concord; **d'a.,** in agreement, in accordance (avec, with); **projets qui sont d'a. avec les nécessités,** plans that accord, harmonize, with requirements; **mettre d'a. deux points de vue,** to reconcile two points of view; **mettre une loi d'a. avec un principe,** to make a law conform to a principle; **se mettre d'a., tomber d'a., avec qn,** to come to an agreement with s.o.; **nous tombons d'a., nous sommes d'a., nous demeurons d'a. que . . .,** we agree, are at one in acknowledging that . . .; **être d'a. avec qn,** to agree, be at one, with s.o.; **nous sommes d'a. pour que . . .** we are of the same mind, of one mind, that . . .; **les témoins ne sont pas d'a.,** the witnesses disagree, differ, are at variance; **mettre tout le monde d'a.,** to square matters; **mes comptes sont d'a.,** my accounts balance; **tout est d'a.,** everything is settled, arranged; **je suis d'a. avec ce que vous dites,** I agree with what you say; **d'a.!** agreed! yes, I agree! quite so! *F:* O.K.! **d'un commun a.,** by common consent, with one accord, by mutual agreement; **en a. avec,** in harmony, keeping, with. 3. *Gram:* agreement concordance (avec, with); **les règles d'a.,** the concords. 4. *Mus:* chord; **a. parfait,** common chord; **faux a.,** discord; **a. arpégé, brisé, figuré,** broken chord; **a. à l'ouvert,** chord played on the open strings (of violin, etc.); **a. de sensible,** dominant seventh (chord); *Lit:* **de doux accords,** sweet strains. 5. (*a*) *Mus:* pitch, tune; **être d'a.,** to be in tune; **ne pas être d'a.,** to be out of tune; **mettre des instruments d'a.,** to tune instruments; (*of piano, etc.*) **tenir l'a.,** to keep in tune; (*b*) *W.Tel:* **a. précis,** fine-tuning; **effectuer l'a. d'un poste récepteur,** to tune a receiving-set, to tune in; **bobine, condensateur, d'a.,** tuning coil, condenser; **a. silencieux,** aural null; *Elcs:* **a. d'antenne,** alignment input; (*c*) *Mec.E:* tuning.

accordable [akɔrdabl̩], *a.* 1. reconcilable (facts, litigants). 2. *Mus:* tunable (piano, etc.). 3. such as can be granted; grantable.

accordage [akɔrdaːʒ], *s.m. Mus:* tuning; **marteau, clef, d'a.,** tuning-hammer, -key.

accordailles [akɔrdɑːj], *s.f.pl. A: Dial:* plighting of troths; party given for the signing of the marriage contract.

accordant [akɔrdɑ̃], *a. A:* 1. agreeing, accordant. 2. *Mus:* harmonious, in tune.

accordé, -ée [akɔrde], *s. A. & Dial:* betrothed; **le fiancé et son accordée,** the young man and his betrothed, his sweetheart; (*on wedding-day*) **les accordés,** the bride and bridegroom.

accordement [akɔrdəmɑ̃], *s.m. Mus:* tuning.

accordéon [akɔrdeɔ̃], *s.m.* 1. *Mus:* accordion; **a. hexagonal,** concertina; **en a.,** (i) pleated (garment); (ii) *F:* crumpled (up) (mudguard, trousers, etc.); *F:* **j'ai vu un a. sur l'autoroute,** I saw a row of cars which had concertinaed on the motorway; *s.a.* PLI 1. 2. *Aut: A:* folding hood.

accordéoniste [akɔrdeɔnist], *s.* accordionist, accordion-player; concertina-player.

accorder [akɔrde], *v.tr.* 1. (*a*) to reconcile (enemies, etc.); to reconcile (texts); (*b*) *abs. Gram:* to make the agreement. 2. *Mus: W.Tel:* to tune (piano, receiving-set, etc.); **a. les violons au ton du piano,** to tune the violins to the pitch of the piano. 3. (*a*) to grant, concede, admit (proposition); **il m'accorda qu'elle était bien élevée,** he admitted, agreed, that she was well-bred; (*b*) to grant (favour, etc.) (à, to); to bestow (gift, etc.) (à, on); **a. sa fille en mariage à qn,** to give one's daughter (in marriage) to s.o.; **a. des dommages-intérêts,** to award, adjudge, damages; **a. un escompte,** to allow a discount; **pouvez-vous m'a. quelques minutes?** can you spare me a few minutes? **a. à qn de faire qch.,** to grant s.o. leave to do sth.; **a. que qch. se fasse,** to consent to sth. being done; **les dieux ne lui accordèrent point de revoir sa patrie,** the gods did not permit him to see his country again; **on m'a accordé huit jours de congé,** I have been granted, given, a week's leave; **s'a. dix minutes de repos,** to allow oneself ten minutes' rest.

s'accorder. 1. (*of pers.*) (*a*) to agree, come to an agreement (concerning sth.); to come to terms (avec qn, with s.o.); **s'a. sur le prix,** to agree upon the price; **s'a. à, pour, faire qch.,** to agree to do sth.; **tous s'accordent à croire que . . .,** all concur in the belief that . . .; **l'on s'accorde à reconnaître que . . .,** it is universally acknowledged that . . .; (*b*) to get on (well, badly) (**avec qn,** with s.o.); **ils s'accordent mal ensemble,** they don't get on well; **ils s'accordent très bien,** they get on very well (together). 2. (*of fact or thg.*) to accord, tally, correspond, harmonize, *F:* to square, to fit in (avec, with); **son témoignage s'accorde avec les faits,** his evidence fits in (well) with the facts; **son récit s'accorde avec le vôtre,** his account tallies with yours; **les personnages s'acccordent avec le décor,** the characters fit into the setting; **cette action ne s'accorde pas avec son caractère,** this action is not in keeping, in line, with his character; **cela ne s'accorde pas avec mes idées,** it doesn't fit in with my ideas; *Com:* faire a. les livres, to agree the books. 3. **s'a. avec qch.** (*a*) to fit in with, to be consistent with (theory, plan); (*b*) *Gram:* to agree, to be in concord (with); **faire a. le verbe avec le sujet,** to make the verb agree with the subject; (*c*) (*of article of dress, etc.*) to go with, harmonize with, (sth.). 4. *Mus:* to tune (up); **s'a. sur le hautbois,** to tune to the oboe.

accordeur [akɔrdœːr], *s.m.* (*a*) tuner (of musical instruments); **marteau, clef, d'a.,** tuning-hammer, -key; (*b*) *Mec.E:* tuner.

accordoir [akɔrdwaːr], *s.m.* 1. (*piano*) tuning-hammer, -key. 2. tuning cone (for organ).

accore [akɔːr]. 1. *a.* (*of coast*) sheer, abrupt, perpendicular, bluff; steep-to. 2. *s.f.* edge (of reef). 3. *s.m. or f.* prop, shore (esp. in ship-building); stay, stanchion.

accorer [akɔre], *v.tr.* (*a*) to shore up (vessel); (*b*) to prop up, stay (wall, house); (*c*) to wedge, jam (an article in its place); to secure, chock (cask, etc.).

accorné [akɔrne], *a. Her:* horned.

accorner [akɔrne], *v.tr. Fort:* to cover with horn-work.

accort [akɔːr], *a.* (*rarely used in m.*) 1. pleasing, charming (girl). 2. *A:* affable, gracious.

accortement [akɔrtəmɑ̃], *adv. A:* pleasantly, affably, graciously.

accortise [akɔrtiːz], *s.f. A:* affability, courtesy, graciousness.

accostable [akɔstabl̩], *a.* approachable, easy of access; **plage peu a.,** beach difficult to land on.

accostage [akɔstaːʒ], *s.m.* 1. (*a*) *Nau:* drawing alongside (of ship, quay); (*b*) approaching, accosting (s.o.) (to speak to him). 2. *Welding:* **temps d'a.,** squeeze time.

accosté [akɔste], *a.* 1. *Nau:* alongside. 2. *Her:* accosted.

accoster [akɔste], *v.tr.* 1. to accost (s.o.), to go, come, up to (s.o.); **ils s'accostèrent,** they greeted each other, they stopped and spoke. 2. *Nau:* **a. un bateau le long du quai,** to moor, berth, lay, a boat alongside (the quay). 3. *Nau:* (*a*) to come, draw, alongside (ship, quay, etc.); *abs.* to come, draw, alongside; (*b*) to board, come on board (ship).

accot [ako], *s.m. Hort:* protective covering (of straw, etc., against frost).

accotar [akɔtaːr], *s.m. Nau:* shell chock.

accoté [akɔte], *a.* **a. contre,** leaning against; *Nau:* (ship) on her beam ends.

accotement [akɔtmɑ̃], *s.m.* (*a*) verge (of road); *Adm: P.N:* **a. non stabilisé,** soft verge; soft shoulder; **accotement interdit,** stopping prohibited on the shoulders; (*b*) *Rail:* shoulder.

accoter [akɔte], *v.tr.* 1. **a. qch. à qch.,** to lean sth. against sth. 2. to chock (barrel); to scotch (wheel). 3. *Const: Nau:* to shore (up), prop (up), stay (wall, vessel, etc.). 4. *v.i. Nau:* (*of ship*) to be laid on her beam ends.

s'accoter à, contre, un mur, to lean (sideways) against a wall.

accotoir [akɔtwaːr], *s.m.* 1. arm-rest, elbow-rest; **a. réversible,** drop side (of settee); **a. tête (de lit),** bed-head; **a. pied,** foot end (of bed). 2. *Nau:* = ACCORE 3.

accouardir [akwardiːr], *v.tr. A:* to turn (man) into a coward; to cow (s.o.).

s'accouardir. *A:* to turn coward, to lose one's daring.

accouchée [akuʃe], *s.f.* woman who has been confined; woman in childbed; mother (of newborn child); **salle des accouchées,** maternity ward.

accouchement [akuʃmɑ̃], *s.m.* childbirth; delivery; confinement; labour; accouchement; *Vet:* dropping (of young); **a. prématuré, avant terme,** premature delivery, premature confinement, premature birth; **a. sans douleur,** painless childbirth; **a. à domicile,** home confinement; **pratique des accouchements,** midwifery; **centre d'a.,** maternity centre, lying-in hospital; (*of doctor*) **faire un a.,** to attend a confinement.

accoucher [akuʃe]. 1. *v.i.* (*a*) to be confined; **elle accouchera dans un mois,** her baby is due in a month's time; **elle a accouché hier,** she had a baby yesterday; **elle a accouché, est accouchée, d'un garçon,** she has given birth to a boy; **a. avant terme,** to be confined prematurely; (*b*) *Hum:* **il a accouché d'un mauvais roman,** the result of his labours was a bad novel; *F:* **mais accouche(z) donc!** come on, out with it! *F:* spit it out! *U.S: P:* shoot! *s.a.* MONTAGNE 1. 2. *v.tr.* (*of doctor, etc.*) **a. une femme,** to deliver a woman.

accoucheur, -euse [akuʃœːr, -øːz], *s.m.* **1.** *Med:* accoucheur, obstetrician; *f. occ.* midwife. **2.** midwife toad.

accoudement [akudmɑ̃], *s.m.* **1.** leaning of, on, one's elbows (**sur, à,** on). **2.** *Mil:* (*a*) elbow-high parapet of trench; (*b*) feel of the elbows.

accouder (s') [sakude], *v.pr.* **1.** to lean on one's elbow(s); **s'a. à, sur la table,** to lean one's elbow(s) on the table. **2.** to fall into line elbow to elbow; to touch elbows.

accoudoir [akudwaːr], *s.m.* **1.** elbow-rest, arm (-rest) (of chair, railway carriage, etc.). **2.** *Arch:* balustrade; rail (of window, etc.).

accouer [akue], *v.tr.* to string (horses).

accouplage [akuplaːʒ], *s.m. Tchn:* coupling.

accouple [akupl], *s.f.* leash, couple; **chiens à l'a.,** leashed, coupled, hounds.

accouplé [akuple], *a. Arch: Mec.E: etc:* coupled (columns, wheels, etc.); dual; **haut-parleurs accouplés,** dual loudspeakers.

accouplement [akupləmɑ̃], *s.m.* **1.** coupling, join(ing), link(ing); (*a*) *Mec.E:* **a. à manchon,** box-coupling, **a. à cardan, a. articulé,** cardan; **a. à débrayage,** disengaging gear, clutch coupling; **barre d'a.,** (i) drag-link; (ii) *Aut:* cross-bar, tie-rod (of steering gear); *Aut:* **a. direct,** direct drive; *Av:* **a. bendix,** bendix drive; **a. à glissement,** slip clutch; *Av: Min:* **a. à griffe(s),** dog clutch, dog coupling; *Min:* **a. d'outils de sondage,** tool-joint; *Organ:* **pédale d'a.,** coupler (pedal), copula; (*b*) *El:* connecting, connection, coupling, grouping; **a. en quantité,** abreast connection. **2.** (*a*) pairing, mating; *s.a.* CONSANGUIN 2.; (*b*) copulation, coupling.

accoupler [akuple], *v.tr.* **1.** (*a*) to couple, to join in pairs; **a. des bœufs,** to yoke oxen; **ménage bien accouplé,** well-matched couple; (*b*) to couple (up) (parts); **a. deux claviers (d'un orgue),** to couple two manuals; (*c*) *El:* to connect, couple, group (batteries, etc.). **2.** *Husb:* to couple, mate, pair (male and female).

s'accoupler. **1.** to pair; to team up; **s'a. pour travailler,** to work in couples. **2.** (*a*) to mate, pair; (*b*) to copulate, to couple.

accourci [akursi], *s.m. A:* abridgment; abridged version (of narrative, etc.).

accourcie [akursi], *s.f. A: F:* short cut; **prendre (par) une a.,** to take a short cut.

accourcir [akursiːr], *v.tr. A:* to shorten (dress, syllable); to abridge (chapter, book); to curtail (speech).

s'accourcir. *A:* to become shorter; (*of days, etc.*) to draw in; (*of flannel, etc.*) to shrink.

accourcissement [akursismɑ̃], *s.m. A:* shortening; drawing-in (of days, etc.); shrinking (of materials).

accourir [akuriːr], *v.i.* (*conj. like* COURIR; *the aux. is avoir or* **être**; *the latter is more frequently used nowadays*); to run up, come running up, to hasten (up); to flock, rush, up; **accourez, mes enfants!** come here, children! **ils ont accouru, sont accourus, à mon secours,** they ran, came running, to my help.

accoutrement [akutrəmɑ̃], *s.m.* **1.** *A:* accoutrements, equipment; apparel. **2.** *usu. Pej:* dress, garb; *F:* rig-out, get-up.

accoutrer [akutre], *v.tr.* **1.** *A:* to accoutre, equip; *F:* **a. qn de toutes pièces,** (i) to give s.o. a dressing-down, a thrashing, a slating; (ii) to tear s.o. to pieces (behind his back). **2.** *usu. Pej:* to rig (s.o.) out, get (s.o.) up (**de, in**); **accoutré d'une vieille capote,** rigged out in an old military great-coat.

s'accoutrer, to dress, rig oneself out, to get oneself up (**de, in**).

accoutumance [akutymɑ̃ːs], *s.f.* **1.** (*a*) familiarization (**à,** with); **l'a. diminue le plaisir,** even pleasure palls on one; (*b*) inurement (to opium, etc.); (*c*) *Med:* **a. (à une drogue),** tolerance (to a drug; *F:* **cette drogue ne cause pas a.,** this drug is non-habit-forming. **2.** habit, usage, practice, use.

accoutumé, -ée [akutyme]. **1.** *a.* (*a*) accustomed, used (**à,** to); inured (to); **je n'étais pas a. à ce qu'on me parlât ainsi,** I was not accustomed to being spoken to in this way; (*b*) accustomed, customary, usual; **à l'heure accoutumée,** at the customary, usual, hour; *A. & Lit:* **avoir a. de faire qch.,** to be wont to do sth.; *A: adv.phr:* **à l'accoutumée,** usually; **comme à l'accoutumée,** as usual, as is customary, in the accustomed manner. **2.** *s.* **les visiteurs étaient des accoutumés,** the visitors were customary callers; **les dîneurs étaient des accoutumés,** the diners were regular customers.

accoutumer [akutyme], *v.tr.* (*a*) **a. qn à qch.,** to accustom s.o. to sth.; to inure s.o. (to hunger, cold, etc.); **a. qn à faire qch.,** to accustom s.o. to do sth.; to inure s.o. to do sth.; (*b*) *A:* **a. qn avec qn, qch.,** to familiarize s.o. with s.o., sth.

s'accoutumer, s'a. à qn, à qch., to become, get, accustomed to s.o., to sth.; **s'a. à la fatigue,** to become inured, used, to inure oneself, to fatigue; **s'a. à faire qch.,** to get accustomed to doing sth.; **je ne pouvais pas m'a. à ce qu'on me grondât,** I could not get accustomed, used, to being scolded.

accouvage [akuvaːʒ], *s.m. Husb:* artificial incubation.

accouvé [akuve], *Dial:* (*of hen*) sitting; *A: F:* **bonne femme accouvée au coin du feu,** old woman squatting by the fire, brooding over the fire.

accouver [akuve]. *Husb:* **1.** *v.tr.* (*a*) to set (hen, etc.); (*b*) to incubate eggs (artificially). **2.** *v.i.* (*of hen*) to sit, brood.

s'accouver, (*of hen*) to begin to sit; *F:* to squat down.

accouveur, -euse [akuvœːr, -øːz], *s. Husb:* hatchery operator.

accréditation [akreditasjɔ̃], *s.f.* accreditation, accrediting (of ambassador).

accréditement [akreditmɑ̃], *s.m.* accrediting; *Bank:* opening an account (for s.o.).

accrédité, -ée [akredite]. **1.** *a.* (*paper, etc.*) of good standing. **2.** *s. Com:* (*a*) holder of a letter of credit; (*b*) agent.

accréditer [akredite], *v.tr.* **1.** (*a*) *A:* **a. qn,** to give standing, give a good name to s.o.; (*b*) **a. (un ambassadeur, etc.) auprès de qn, auprès d'une cour,** to accredit s.o. to s.o., to, at, a court; **notre représentant dûment accrédité,** our duly authorized representative; (*c*) *Fin:* **a. un client,** to open a credit for a client; (*d*) **a. qch.,** to cause sth. to be credited, believed; **son témoignage accrédita ce bruit,** his testimony caused the rumour to be credited, gave colour to the rumour. **2. a. qch.** (*a*) to credit, accredit, sth.; (*b*) to sanction, countenance, give countenance to, sth.

s'accréditer. 1. s'a. auprès de qn, (i) to present one's letters of credit to s.o., (ii) *F:* to ingratiate oneself with s.o. **2.** (*of news, etc.*) to gain credence, to gain credit, to gain currency, to gain ground.

accréditeur [akreditœːr], *s.m. Fin:* surety, guarantor.

accréditif, -ive [akreditif, -iːv]. *Bank:* **1.** *a.* **lettre accréditive,** letter of credit. **2.** *s.m.* (*a*) letter of credit; (*b*) **loger un a.,** to open a credit (with a bank); **a. permanent,** permanent credit.

accrescent [akrɛsɑ̃], *a. Bot:* accrescent.

accrétion [akresjɔ̃], *s.f. Bot: Geol:* accretion.

accroc [akro], *s.m.* **1.** tear, rent (in clothes, etc.); **faire un a. à qch.,** to tear, to make a rent in, sth.; *F:* **elle a plus d'un a. à sa réputation,** her reputation is a little tainted. **2.** (*a*) *Fish:* snag; (*b*) hitch; difficulty; *F:* snag; **il y a eu un a.,** a hitch has occurred.

accrochage [akrɔʃaːʒ], *s.m.* **1.** (*a*) hooking, catching (by hooking), running foul, bumping, grazing (of vehicle, runner etc.); *Box:* clinch; (*b*) *Rail: etc:* hitching on, coupling; (*c*) hanging (up), hooking up (of picture, curtain, etc.); (*d*) *El.E:* putting (of alternators) into step; synchronization (of shock waves); **a. en phase,** synchronizing; *W.Tel:* **a. d'un poste,** picking up of a station; **limite d'a.,** oscillating point; (*e*) bond (welding); (*f*) *Sp:* recovery (from a losing position); (*g*) *Av:* **a. train rentré,** landing gear uplocking. **2.** *El.E: W.Tel:* falling into step. **3.** (*a*) *Min:* **a. (du fond, du jour),** (bottom, top) landing; (*b*) *Phot:* **a. à l'infini,** infinity catch. **4.** *Aut: Cy:* (*a*) clinch(er) of wheel-rim; rim edge; (*b*) bead (of pneumatic tyre). **5.** altercation, squabble; *Mil:* brush, skirmish; **zone d'a.,** fighting area.

accrochant [akrɔʃɑ̃], *a.* (*a*) striking; *F:* **un air a.,** a catching tune; (*b*) *Bot:* clinging.

accroche-assiette [akrɔʃasjɛt], *s.m. Furn:* plate-hanger; *pl. accroche-assiette(s).*

accroche-balai [akrɔʃbalɛ], *s.m. Dom.Ec:* brush-hanger; *pl. accroche-balais.*

accroche-casseroles [akrɔʃkasrɔl], *s.m. inv. Dom.Ec:* saucepan rack.

accroche-cœur [akrɔʃkœːr], *s.m.* love-lock, kiss-curl; *pl. accroche-cœur(s).*

accrochement [akrɔʃmɑ̃], *s.m.* **1.** = ACCROCHAGE 1 (*a*), (*b*). **2.** = ACCROC 2.

accroche-plat [akrɔʃpla], *s.m. Furn:* plate-hanger; *pl. accroche-plat(s).*

accrocher [akrɔʃe]. **1.** *v.tr.* (*a*) to hook; to catch (sth. by hooking) (*of tune*) to catch on; **a. un poisson, to hook a fish;** *F:* **essayer d'a. un mari,** to try to hook a husband, to angle for a husband; **réclame qui accroche l'œil,** advertisement that catches the eye; **nom qui accroche,** striking name; **ce titre accroche le lecteur,** this title attracts the reader's attention; **a. sa robe à un clou,** to catch one's dress on a nail; **a. une voiture,** to run, bump, into a car; **a. l'aile d'une voiture,** to catch the wing of a car; **en conduisant, surtout n'accrochez personne,** when driving, whatever you do, don't run into anyone; *F:* **a. qn dans la rue,** to buttonhole s.o. in the street; *Mil:* **se laisser a.,** to be compelled to make a stand; *abs. Phot:* **a. à l'infini,** to set the camera to infinity; (*b*) **a. une voiture au train,** to hitch, couple, a carriage on to the train; **a. la locomotive,** to couple up, on, the engine; (*c*) to grapple (ship); (*d*) to hang up, hook up (sth.); *Const:* to hang (door); *Min:* **a. une tige sur les élévateurs,** to latch on; **a. sa robe à un clou,** to hang (up) one's dress on a nail; **a. son chapeau à une patère,** to hang up one's hat; *P:* **a. sa montre,** to pawn, *P:* to pop, one's watch; *F:* **a. une affaire,** to clinch a deal; *P:* **être accroché,** (i) to be in debt; (ii) to be detained (after police raid); (iii) to have guts, to have what it takes; (*e*) *El.E:* to put (alternators, etc.) into step; **accroché en phase,** synchronized; *W.Tel:* **a. la longueur d'onde,** to get into tune; **a. un poste,** to pick up, tune in to, a station; (*f*) *Mec.E:* to throw (machinery) into gear; (*g*) *Mil:* **batterie accrochée,** battery in action. **2.** *v.i.* **les négociations ont accroché sérieusement,** there has been a serious hitch in the negotiations. **3.** *P:* **se l'a.,** to do without food, to fast; *F:* to tighten one's belt; **tu peux toujours te l'a.!** you can whistle for it! you've had it!

s'accrocher. 1. (*a*) **s'a. à qn, à qch.,** to fasten on to, to cling to, to grapple on to, s.o., sth.; **village accroché à la colline,** village clinging to the hillside; *Nau:* **s'a. à un navire,** to hang on to a ship, to follow a ship closely; *Rac: P:* **s'a. avec qn,** to catch up with s.o.; (*b*) **sous le toit s'accroche une petite cage,** a small cage hangs under the roof. **2.** to get caught (**à,** on). **3.** (*a*) *Box:* to clinch; (*b*) *F:* **s'a. avec qn,** to quarrel, have a row, with s.o.; (*c*) *W.Tel:* **les deux postes s'accrochent,** the two stations come into step; *F:* **nous ne nous accrochions pas,** we weren't on the same wavelength, we weren't making contact.

accroche-serviettes [akrɔʃsɛrvjɛt], *s.m.inv.* towel-hook.

accrocheur, -euse [akrɔʃœr, -øːz]. **1.** *s.m.* (*a*) *Ind: Min: etc:* hooker, hitcher; (*b*) *s. F:* wangler. **2.** (*a*) *s.m. Tls:* grab (for recovering broken boring tool); (*b*) *s. F:* (*pers.*) clinger, leech. **3.** *a. F:* stubborn, pig-headed; (*b*) striking; **un titre a.,** an eye-catching title.

accroi [akrwa], *s.f. Ch:* acrolein.

accroire [akrwaːr, -wɑːr], *v.tr. used only in the expressions* (**en**) **faire a. à qn, s'en faire a. 1. faire a. à qn que . . .,** to cause s.o. to believe, delude s.o. into believing, that. . . . **2. en faire a. à qn,** to impose (up)on s.o., to delude s.o., to humbug s.o. **3. s'en faire a.,** to overestimate one's own importance, to think too much of oneself, *F:* to fancy oneself, to have a swelled, swollen, head, to be swollen-headed.

accroissement [akrwasmɑ̃, -wɑ-], *s.m.* **1.** (*a*) growth, growing (of plant, etc.); (*b*) increase, increasing; **taux d'a.,** rate of increase; increment per cent; **un a. de revenus,** an increase in one's income; (*c*) *Jur:* accretion (of legacy, of rights of survivors through death of co-legatee or interested party). **2.** (Amount of) increase, growth; *Mth:* **a. d'une fonction,** increment of a function.

accroître [akrwatr, -wɑː-]. **1.** *v.tr.* (*pr.p.* **accroissant;** *p.p.* **accru;** *pr.ind.* **j'accrois, il accroît, n. accroissons, ils accroissent;** *p.d.* **j'accroissais;** *p.h.* **j'accrus;** *fu.* **j'accroîtrai**); to increase, enlarge, add to, augment; to enhance (reputation, etc.); **a. artificiellement la circulation fiduciaire,** to inflate the currency. **2.** *v.i.* **ses richesses ont accru par un heureux coup de bourse,** his wealth has increased through a fortunate speculation.

s'accroître, to increase, grow; **Rome s'accrut de la ruine d'Albe,** Rome expanded as a consequence of the fall of Alba.

accroupetonner (s') [sakruptɔne], *v.pr. F: A:* to squat down on one's heels; **vieille accroupetonnée au coin du feu,** old woman squatting by the fire.

accroupir (s') [sakrupiːr], *v.pr.* to sit (down) (on one's hams, on one's heels); to squat (down), to crouch (down); **accroupi au coin du feu,** squatting by the fire; **tigre accroupi avant de sauter,** tiger crouching, gathered, for a spring; *Her:* **accroupi,** (i) sejant; (ii) couchant.

accroupissement [akrupismɑ̃], *s.m.* squatting; crouching.

accru [akry], *s.m. Bot:* sucker.

accrue [akry], *s.f.* **1.** accretion (of land); accreted land. **2.** extension, encroachment, (of forest) by natural seeding.

accu [aky], *s.m. El: F:* = ACCUMULATEUR; **boîte d'accus,** storage battery.

accueil [akœj], *s.m.* reception, welcome, greeting; **centre d'a.,** rest centre; **service d'a.,** reception bureau; **cocktail d'a.,** reception with cocktails; **faire (bon) a. à qn,** to greet, welcome, s.o., to make s.o. welcome; **faire mauvais a. à qn,** to give s.o. an unfriendly reception; (*of plan, etc.*) **recevoir un a. favorable,** to be well received; **rencontrer un a. hostile,** to meet with a hostile reception; **on me fit un a. cordial,** I was given a hearty welcome, accorded a hearty reception, made very welcome; **faire bon a. à une demande,** to entertain a request, take a request into favourable consideration; *Com:* **faire (bon) a. à une traite,** to meet, honour, a bill; **réserver bon a. à une traite,** to be ready to meet a bill.

accueillant [akœjɑ̃], *a.* accessible; gracious, affable (person, manners); hospitable, welcoming; **le plus a. des hôtes,** the most gracious of hosts.

accueillir [akœjiːr], *v.tr.* (*conj. like* CUEILLIR); to receive, greet (s.o.); **bien a. qn, qch.,** to welcome s.o., sth., to make s.o. welcome, to give s.o., sth., a good, kind, courteous, hearty, reception; **a. qn à bras ouverts,** to receive s.o. with open arms; **a. qn avec joie, avec froideur,** to welcome s.o. with joy, coldly; **le livre a été accueilli favorablement,** the book has had a favourable reception; **mal a. qn,** to give s.o. a bad, unfriendly, reception; **a. favorablement une offre,** to entertain an offer; **a. une demande,** to accede to a request; **j'ai du mal à a. cette opinion,** I find it difficult to entertain this opinion; *Com:* **a. une traite,** to meet, honour, a bill.

accul [akyl], *s.m.* **1.** (*a*) *A:* blind alley, cul-de-sac; (*b*) *Min:* dead end; (*c*) *Nau:* creek. **2.** bottom of hole, burrow (of rabbit); *adv.phr.* **à l'a.,** (i) at bay, cornered; (ii) *F:* in a fix, in a hole; **mettre le renard à l'a.,** to drive the fox to earth. **3.** *Artil: A:* (*a*) breeching (of gun); (*b*) recoil buffer.

acculé [akyle], *a. Equit:* (*horse*) liable to throw itself on its haunches (when reined in); (*b*) *Her:* (*of horse*) cabré, rampant; (*c*) *Nau:* (*ship*) down at the stern; (*d*) *N.Arch:* **varangues acculées,** rising floor timbers.

acculée [akyle], *s.f. Nau:* (*a*) sternway; (*b*) **a. de l'hélice,** reversing of the propeller.

acculement [akylmɑ̃], *s.m.* **1.** cornering, bringing to bay. **2.** tilting backward (of cart). **3.** *Equit:* rearing; backing; jibbing. **4.** *Nau:* pitching by the stern. **5.** *N. Arch:* rising (of floor-timbers), deadrising.

acculer [akyle]. **1.** *v.tr.* to drive (s.o.) back (**contre,** against); to drive (s.o.) to the wall; to bring (animal) to bay, to a stand; to corner (s.o.); **le voilà acculé,** we have him cornered, in a corner; **il est acculé dans ses derniers retranchements,** he is fighting with his back to the wall; **être acculé à la faillite,** to be faced with, on the verge of, bankruptcy; **être acculé à faire qch.,** to be reduced to doing sth.; **a. qn à qch.,** to give s.o. no alternative to doing sth. **2.** *v.i. Nau:* (*a*) to pitch heavily astern; (*b*) to be down by the stern.

s'acculer, à, contre, qch., (*a*) to set one's back against sth.; (*b*) to stand at bay.

acculturation [akyltyrasjɔ̃], *s.f. Ethn: etc:* acculturation.

accumètre [akymɛtr], *s.m. El.E:* accumulator capacity indicator.

accumulateur, -trice [akymylatœːr, -tris], *s.* **1.** accumulator, hoarder (of money, etc.). **2.** *s.m.* (*a*) *El: Hyd.E: etc:* accumulator; *El:* storage cell; battery; **a. à oxydes rapportés, à pastilles,** pasted-plate accumulator; **a. au fer-nickel,** ferro-nickel accumulator; **a. à électrolyte liquide,** fluid accumulator; **a. à grillage,** grid-type accumulator; **a. de pression,** pressure accumulator; **bac, cuve, d'a.,** accumulator box; *Av:* **a. inversable,** non-spill battery; (*b*) *Computers:* accumulator; (*c*) **a. de départ (combustible),** fuel accumulator (flow increase for starting).

accumulation [akymylasjɔ̃], *s.f.* **1.** accumulating; hoarding (of money, etc.); **chauffage par a.,** storage heating; *Geol:* **formé par a.,** tectonic. **2.** accumulation, hoard, collection, pile; storage (of power, energy).

accumuler [akymyle], *v.tr.* to accumulate, amass; to gather (together); to hoard; to heap (up); *F:* to pile up.

s'accumuler, to accumulate, increase, gather; *F:* to pile up; (*of interest, etc.*) to accrue; (*of clouds*) to bank up.

accusable [akyzabl], *a.* accusable (**de,** of); chargeable (**de,** with); impeachable.

accusateur, -trice [akyzatœːr, -tris]. **1.** *a.* accusatory, incriminating, accusing. **2.** *s.* accuser, indicter, impeacher, arraigner; *Fr.Hist.* (*Revolution*): **l'accusateur public,** the Public Prosecutor.

accusatif, -ive [akyzatif, -iːv], *a. & s.m. Gram:* accusative, objective (case); **mot à l'a.,** word in the accusative; **a. de qualification,** cognate accusative.

accusation [akyzasjɔ̃], *s.f.* **1.** accusation, charge; **faire des accusations contre qn,** to make charges against s.o.; **lancer, porter, une a. contre qn,** to raise, bring, an accusation against s.o. **2.** *Jur:* (*a*) **acte d'a.,** indictment (for crime); arraignment, charge; **chef d'a.,** count (of indictment); particulars, specification (of charge); **mettre qn en a.,** to arraign s.o. to commit s.o. for trial; **mise en a.,** committal for trial; **chambre d'a.** = office of the Director of public prosecutions; *A:* **chambre des mises en a.** = Grand Jury; **prononcer la mise en a.,** to find a true bill; **refuser la mise en a.,** to ignore the bill; **dresser un acte d'a. contre tout un peuple,** to draw up an indictment against a whole people; (*b*) prosecution; (*c*) the case for the Crown. **3.** *Pol:* impeachment, arraignment.

accusatoire [akyzatwaːr], *a. Jur:* accusatory (procedure).

accusé, -ée [akyze]. **1.** *a.* prominent, pronounced, marked, bold (feature, etc.); **rides très accusées,** deep, strongly marked, wrinkles. **2.** *s.* accused (of crime); (*in court*) defendant, prisoner at the bar. **3.** *s.m.* **a. de réception d'une lettre,** acknowledgment (of receipt) of a letter; **envoyer un simple a. de réception,** to send a formal acknowledgment.

accuser [akyze], *v.tr.* **1. a. qn de qch.,** to accuse s.o. of sth.; to indict s.o. for sth.; to charge, tax, s.o. with sth.; **a. qn de faire qch.,** to accuse s.o. of, to charge, tax, s.o. with, doing sth.; **a. qn de haute trahison,** to impeach s.o. for high treason. **2. a. qch.,** to own to, profess, sth.; **a. ses péchés,** to confess one's sins. **3.** to define, show up, bring out, accentuate; **esquisse qui accuse tous les muscles,** sketch that brings out every muscle; **portrait qui accuse une ressemblance avec . . .,** portrait that reveals a resemblance to . . .; **paroles qui accusent une grande ignorance,** words that betray, show, great ignorance; **elle accuse trente ans,** she looks at least thirty; **la coupe de ses vêtements accuse le provincial,** the cut of his clothes shows he is from the provinces; **le thermomètre accuse une élévation de température,** the thermometer shows, indicates, a rise in temperature; **l'indicateur accusait une vitesse de 120 kilomètres à l'heure,** the speedometer marked 120 kilometres an hour. **4. a. réception de qch.,** to acknowledge (receipt of) sth.; *Fenc:* **a. un coup,** to acknowledge a hit. *F:* **a. le coup,** to react strongly.

s'accuser. 1. to accuse oneself. **2.** to be, become, accentuated; to stand out.

acène [asɛn], *s.f. Bot:* acaena.

acéphale [asefal]. **1.** *a.* acephalous, headless. **2.** *s.m. Ter:* acephalan.

acéphalie [asefali], *s.f. Ter:* acephalia.

acer [asɛːr], *s.m. Bot:* acer.

acéracées [aserase], **acérinées** [aserine], *s.f.pl. Bot:* aceraceae.

acérage [aseraːʒ], *s.m. A: Metall:* steeling; overlaying (with steel).

acérain [aserɛ̃], *a. A:* steely (iron, etc.).

acéras [aserɑːs], *s.m. Bot:* aceras, (green) man orchis.

acerbe [asɛrb], *a.* **1.** tart, sour (to the taste); (*of wine*) bitter. **2.** sharp, harsh; **réprimande a.,** sharp reproof; **discussion a.,** acrid discussion; **ton a.,** vinegary tone; **parler d'un ton a.,** to speak sharply.

acerbité [asɛrbite], *s.f.* acerbity. **1.** tartness, bitterness, sourness (to the taste). **2.** sharpness, harshness; **l'a. de cette critique,** the acerbity of this criticism; **répondre avec a.,** to give a sharp answer, to answer sharply.

acerdèse [asɛrdɛːz], *s.f. Miner:* manganite.

acère [asɛːr], *a. Ent:* acerous, hornless; without antennae.

acéré [asere], *a.* **1.** (*a*) sharp(-pointed) (dagger, needle, etc.); **les traits acérés de la calomnie,** the keen shafts of calumny; (*b*) sharp-edged, keen (blade, etc.); (*c*) stinging, cutting; **langue acérée,** sharp, stinging, tongue; cutting way of saying things. **2.** *A: Metall:* steeled.

acérer [asere], *v.tr.* (**j'acère, n. acérons; j'acérerai**). **1.** (i) to point, (ii) to give a keen edge to (sth.); **a. une épigramme,** to give a sting, to give point, to an epigram. **2.** *A: Metall:* to steel (tool, etc.).

acérure [aseryːr], *s.f. A: Metall:* steel edge (of tool, etc.).

acescence [asɛsɑ̃ːs], *s.f.* acescence; acescency; **tourner à l'a.,** to sour, to begin to turn sour.

acescent [asɛsɑ̃], *a.* acescent, tending to turn sour.

Aceste [asɛst], *Pr.n.m. Lt.Lit:* Acestes.

acetabularia [asetabylarja], *s.f. Algae:* Acetabularia, acetabulum.

acétabule [asetabyl], *s.f.,* **acetabulum** [asetabylɔm], *s.m.* **1.** *Rom.Ant:* acetabulum. **2.** *Anat: Z:* acetabulum.

acétal [asetal], *s.m. Ch:* acetal.

acétaldéhyde [asetaldeid], *s.f. Ch:* acetaldehyde.

acétamide [asetamid], *s.m. Ch:* acetamide.

acétate [asetat], *s.m. Ch:* acetate; **a. de cuivre,** copper acetate, verdigris; **a. de plomb,** lead acetate, sugar of lead; *Tex:* **a. de cellulose,** cellulose acetate.

acétaté [asetate], *a. Bookb:* **jaquette acétatée,** laminated jacket.

acéteux, -euse [asetø, -øːz], *a. Ch:* acetous.

acétification [asetifikasjɔ̃], *s.f. Ch:* acetification, acetifying.

acétifier [asetifje], *v.tr. Ch:* to acetify.

s'acétifier, to acetify; to turn sour.

acétimètre [asetimɛtr], *s.m.* acetimeter, acetometer.

acétimétrique [asetimetrik], *a.* **burette a.,** acetimeter, acetometer.

acétique [asetik], *a. Ch:* acetic; **acide a. concentré,** glacial acetic acid.

acétocellulose [asetoselyloːz], *s.f. Ch: Cin:* cellulose acetate, acetyl cellulose.

acétol [asetɔl], *s.m. Pharm:* acetol.

acétomètre [asetɔmɛtr], *s.m.* = ACÉTIMÈTRE.

acétone [asetɔn], *s.f. Ch:* acetone.

acétonémie [asetɔnemi], *s.f. Med:* acetonemia, acetonaemia.

acétonémique [asetɔnemik]. *a. Med:* acetonemic, acetonaemic.

acétonurie [asetɔnyri], *s.f. Med:* acetonuria.

acétophénone [asetɔfenɔn], *s.f. Ch:* acetophenone.

acétoselle [asetɔzɛl], *s.f. Bot:* wood-sorrel.

acétylation [asetilasjɔ̃], *s.f. Ch:* acetylation.

acétylcellulose [asetilselyloːz], *s.f. Tex:* = ACÉTOCELLULOSE.

acétylcholine [[asetilkɔlin], *s.f. Ch: Biol:* acetylcholine.

acétyle [asetil], *s.m. Ch:* acetyl.

acétylène [asetilɛn], *s.m. Ch: Ill:* acetylene; **lampe, lanterne, à a.,** acetylene lamp; **chalumeau à a.,** acetylene blow pipe, blow lamp.

acétylénique [asetilenik], *a. Ch:* acetylenic.

acétyler [asetile], *v.tr.* to acetylate.

acétylsalicyclique [asetilsalisiklik], *a. Ch:* acetylsalicyclic.

acétylure [asetilyːr], *s.m. Ch:* acetylide.

Achab [akab], *Pr.n.m. B.Hist:* Ahab.

Achaïe [akai], *Pr.n.f. A.Geog:* Achaia, Achaea.

achaïen, -ienne [akajɛ̃, -jɛn], *a. & s.,* **achaïque** [akaik], *a. A.Geog:* Achaian, Achaean.

achaine [akɛn], *s.m. Bot:* = AKÈNE.

achalandage [aʃalɑ̃daːʒ], *s.m. Com:* **1.** working up of a clientele. **2.** (*a*) custom, customers; **avoir un a. considérable,** to have considerable custom, a large clientele; (*b*) goodwill; **l'a. se vend avec l'établissement,** the goodwill is to be sold with the business; (*c*) *F:* stock (of shop).

achalandé [aʃalɑ̃de], *a.* **magasin bien a.,** (i) shop with a large custom, that does a thriving business; (ii) *F:* well-stocked shop.

achalander [aʃalɑ̃de], *v.tr.* (*a*) to provide (shop) with custom; **cette boutique s'achalande bien,** this shop is gathering custom; (*b*) *F:* to stock (shop).

achanti [aʃɑ̃ti]. **1.** *a. & s.m.* Ashanti. **2.** *Pr.n.m. Geog:* **l'A.,** Ashanti. **3.** *s.m. Ling:* **l'a.,** Ashanti.

achantin, -ine [aʃɑ̃tɛ̃, -in], *a. & s. Geog:* Ashanti.

achar [aʃar], *s.m. P:* **travailler d'a.,** to work like mad, to go at it tooth and nail.

acharné [aʃarne], *a.* **1.** eager in pursuit; **meute acharnée à la poursuite,** pack in hot, eager, pursuit; **hommes acharnés les uns contre les autres,** men fighting desperately against each other; **être a. contre qn,** to be a rabid enemy of s.o.; *F:* to be always going for s.o., always at s.o.; **a. à faire qch.,** bent on doing sth.; **a. à sa perte, à se perdre,** bent on his own ruin. **2. joueur a.,** inveterate, desperate, keen, gambler; **fumeur a.,** inveterate smoker; **haine acharnée,** fierce, bitter, hatred. **3. lutte acharnée,** bitter, desperate, struggle; **travail a.,** strenuous, desperately hard, work; **ils se font une concurrence acharnée,** they are engaged in cutthroat competition with each other.

acharnement [aʃarnəmɑ̃], *s.m.* (*a*) desperate eagerness; (*b*) relentlessness; obstinacy; **a. au travail, pour le travail,** passion for work; **a. à la vengeance,** tenaciousness, relentlessness, in revenge; **mettre de l'a. à faire qch.,** (i) to work desperately hard at sth.; (ii) to be relentless in doing sth.; **faire qch. avec a.,** to do sth. eagerly, furiously; **se battre avec a.,** to fight fiercely, to fight tooth and nail; **travailler avec a.,** to work (desperately) hard; *F:* to work like mad.

acharner [aʃarne], *v.tr.* **1.** *A:* **a. un piège,** to bait a trap. **2.** *Ven:* **a. un chien,** to flesh, blood, a dog. **3.** *Ven:* **a. la meute contre, sur, une bête,** to set the pack on (the track of) a quarry; *A:* **a. qn contre, sur, qn,** to set s.o. on, against s.o.

s'acharner. 1. s'a. contre, sur, après, qn, to be dead set against s.o., to go for s.o., to hound s.o., to be always on s.o.'s tracks, to have one's knife into, a down on, s.o.; **le sort s'acharne contre lui,** fate is against him; **le malheur s'acharne sur lui,** he is dogged by misfortune; **s'a. sur l'ennemi en fuite,** to pursue the retreating enemy hot-foot. **2. s'a. à qch.,** to work unceasingly at sth., to persist in sth.; **s'a. à un travail,** to slave, to work desperately hard, at a job; **elle s'acharne à ce mensonge,** she persists in this lie; **il s'acharne à vous nuire,** he is bent on harming you.

achat [aʃa], *s.m.* purchase. **1.** buying; **effectuer, faire un a.,** to effect, make a purchase; **faire l'a. de qch.,** to buy, purchase sth.; **aller faire ses achats,** to go shopping; *Book-k:* **livre, journal, des achats,** bought book; *Com:* **prix d'a.,** prime cost, actual cost, cost price, purchase price; **a. au comptant,** purchase for ready money, for cash; *Com:* **a. à terme, à crédit,** purchase on credit, credit purchase; *Fin:* **a. à terme,** purchase for the settlement, buying for the account; **facture d'a.,** invoice; *Com:* **ordre d'a.,** indent; **pouvoir, capacité, d'a.,** purchasing, spending power. **2.** thing bought; **voilà tous mes achats,** these are all my purchases.

Achate [akat], *Pr.n.m. Rom.Lit:* Achates; *Lit: A:* **son fidèle A.,** his *fidus Achates,* his faithful companion.

achatines [akatiːn], *s.f.pl. Moll:* Achatinas, Agate snails.

Achaz [akɑːz], *Pr.n.m. B:* Ahaz.

ache[1] [aʃ], *s.f. Bot:* wild celery, smallage, water-parsley; **a. des chiens,** fools' parsley; **a. de(s) montagne(s);** common lovage, Italian lovage; **a. d'eau,** water parsnip.

ache[2], *s.m. or f* (the letter) h, aitch.

achée [aʃe], *s.f. A: Fish:* gentles, bait, worm(s).

achéen, -enne [akeɛ̃, -ɛn], *a. & s. A.Hist:* Achaian, Achaean; **la Ligue achéenne,** the Achaean League.

Achéloos [akelɔɔs], *Pr.n.m.,* **Achéloüs** [akelɔys], *Pr.n.m. A.Geog:* Achelous.

acheminement [aʃminmɑ̃], *s.m.* **1. a. à, vers qch.,** step, preparatory measure, advance(ment), towards sth. **2.** (*a*) **a. d'un colis,** route to be followed by a consignment of goods; (*b*) flow, routing (of goods, mail, etc.); *Mil:* **l'a. des renforts,** the routing of reinforcements; **l'a. des circuits,** the routing of circuits; (*c*) forwarding, sending, dispatch (of goods, etc.); **durée d'a.,** forwarding time.

acheminer [aʃmine], *v.tr.* **1. a. qn (sur, vers, un endroit),** to direct, dispatch, s.o. (towards a place); **a. un élève sur l'université,** to prepare a pupil for university entrance; **a. qn vers un examen,** to bring s.o. on for an examination. **2. a. qch. sur, vers, un endroit,** to forward, dispatch, route, sth. to a place; **marchandises acheminées sur Nantes,** goods dispatched to Nantes; **a. le pétrole brut sur la raffinerie,** to carry, convey, the crude oil to the refinery.

s'acheminer sur, vers, (un endroit), to be on one's way to, towards (a place); **s'a. vers la maison,** to set out for, make one's way, home.

Achéron (l') [lakerɔ̃], *Pr.n.m. Myth:* Acheron.

achetable [aʃtabl̩], *a.* purchasable.

acheter [aʃte], *v.tr.* **(j'achète, n. achetons; j'achèterai). 1.** (*a*) **a. qch.,** to buy, purchase, sth.; **j'ai acheté ce livre cinq francs,** I bought this book for five francs; **a. qch. chez qn,** to buy sth. at s.o.'s; **a. qch. (à) bon marché, à vil prix,** to buy sth. cheap, dirt cheap; **a. chat en poche,** to buy a pig in a poke; **a. une conduite,** to turn over a new leaf; **j'achetais des bonbons sur l'argent de l'autobus,** I used to buy sweets out of my bus money; *Com:* **a. en gros, en détail,** to buy wholesale, retail; **a. en masse,** to buy up (stocks); **a. à crédit,** to buy on credit; **a. au comptant,** to buy for cash, for ready money; **a. à profit, à perte** to buy at a profit, at a loss; *s.a.* PRIME[2] 1; (*b*) **a. qch. à qn,** to buy sth. from s.o.; **je lui ai acheté pour dix milles francs de soieries,** I bought ten thousand francs' worth of silks from him; (*c*) *A:* **a. qch. de qn: j'ai acheté cela de votre représentant,** I bought that from your representative; (*d*) **a. qch. à, pour qn,** to buy sth. for s.o.; **je vais lui a. un livre,** I am going to buy him a book. **2. a. qn,** (i) to bribe s.o.; (ii) to buy s.o. off; (iii) *P:* to hoax s.o.; to take the mickey out of s.o.; **a. le silence de qn,** to bribe s.o. to silence, pay s.o. to keep his mouth shut; **on avait acheté les témoins,** *F:* the witnesses had been bribed; *P:* **on vous a acheté,** you've been had, sold.

acheteur, -euse [aʃtœːr, -øːz], *s.* **1.** (*a*) purchaser, buyer; *Jur:* vendee; **on ne put trouver d'acheteurs pour . . .,** they could find no purchasers, no market, for . . .; **je suis a.,** I'll take it; **je suis acheteur de . . .,** I am in the market for . . .; *St.Exch:* **a. de primes,** giver of option money; (*b*) **acheteurs à la recherche de soldes,** shoppers on the look-out for bargains. **2.** *Com:* buyer (for business house).

acheuléen, -enne [aʃœleɛ̃, -ɛn], *a. & s.* **1.** *Geog:* (native, inhabitant) of Saint-Acheul. **2.** *Paleont:* Acheulean, Acheulian.

achevage [aʃvaːʒ], *s.m. Cer:* finishing off.

achevaler [aʃvale], *v.tr. Mil:* **a. une rivière, une ligne de chemin de fer,** to occupy both sides of, to straddle, a river, a railway; to take up an *à-cheval* position.

achevé [aʃve]. **1.** *a.* (*a*) accomplished (horseman, etc.); perfect, finished (piece of work); **type a. du vieil aristocrate,** perfect type of the old aristocrat; (*b*) **sot a.,** downright, absolute, utter, fool; **menteur a.,** consummate, out and out, thoroughgoing, liar. **2.** *s.m.* finish, perfection of detail (of work of art, etc.).

achèvement [aʃɛvmɑ̃], *s.m.* completion, finishing, conclusion (of work); **travail en a.,** work in process of completion; **date d'a.,** target date; **navire en a.,** ship completing; **a. de la période budgétaire,** close of the financial period.

achever [aʃve], *v.tr.* **(j'achève, n. achevons; j'achèverai) 1.** to end, conclude, finish (off), complete (piece of work, etc.); to put, give, the finishing touch to (sth.); **a. la leçon,** to bring the lesson to an end; **avant d'a. ma lettre . . .,** before ending my letter . . .; **cette perte acheva sa ruine,** this loss completed his ruin; **j'eus bientôt achevé ce travail,** I soon got through this work; **avant que l'année soit achevée,** before the year is out; **mais achevez donc!** come on, out with it! **a. de faire qch.,** to finish doing something; **il n'a pas achevé de parler,** he has not finished speaking; **achève de boire ton café,** drink up your coffee; **le livre est achevé d'imprimer,** the book is printed off; **la maison achève de brûler,** the house is burning itself out. **2.** to dispatch (animal, etc.); to put (animal) out of pain; *F:* **il fut assommé puis achevé à coups de revolver,** he was knocked senseless and finished off with a revolver; *F:* **cette grosse perte l'acheva,** this heavy loss finished him off; *F:* **cette mauvaise nouvelle m'acheva,** this bad news was the last straw.

s'achever. 1. to draw to a close, to end; **le jour s'acheva tristement,** the day ended sadly. **2.** (*of work*) to reach completion.

achevoir [aʃəvwaːr], *s.m.* **1.** finishing tool. **2.** *Ind:* finishing shop.

achigan [aʃigɑ̃], *s.m. Fr.C: Ich:* (black) bass.

Achille [aʃil], *Pr.n.m. Gr.Lit:* Achilles; *s.a.* TALON 1, TENDON.

achillée [akile], *s.f. Bot:* achillea, milfoil, yarrow; **a. sternutatoire,** sneezewort.

achloropsie [aklɔrɔpsi], *s.f.* achloropsia, green-blindness.

acholie [akɔli], *s.f. Med:* acholuria.

achondroplasie [akɔ̃drɔplazi], *s.f. Med:* achondroplasia.

achoppement [aʃɔpmɑ̃], *s.m. A:* **1.** knock, stumble; **infirme qui craint les achoppements,** invalid (i) who fears to be jostled; (ii) who fears rough roads; (*still used in*) **pierre d'a.,** stumbling-block. **2.** obstacle, impediment; **voie semée d'achoppements,** path strewn with obstacles, rough road.

achopper [aʃɔpe], *v.i.* to stumble; **voilà où tous ont achoppé,** that has been everyone's stumbling-block, that is where all have stumbled; **a. contre, sur, une difficulté,** to stumble over, stick at, a difficulty.

s'achopper, to stumble (**à,** against).

achorion [akɔrjɔ̃], *s.m. Fung:* achorion.

achromatine [akrɔmatin], *s.f. Biol:* achromatin.

achromatique [akrɔmatik], *a. Mus: Opt:* achromatic; *Biol:* achromatic, achromatinic.

achromatisation [akrɔmatizasjɔ̃], *s.f. Opt:* achromatization.

achromatiser [akrɔmatize], *v.tr. Opt:* to achromatize.

achromatisme [akrɔmatism], *s.m. Opt:* achromatism.

achromatopsie [akrɔmatɔpsi], *s.f.* colour-blindness, achromatopsia, achromatopsy.

achrome [akroːm], *a.,* **achromique** [akrɔmik], *a.* colourless, achrom(at)ous (flame, etc.); *Med:* achromic.

achromie [akrɔmi], *s.f. Med:* achromia.

aciculaire [asikylɛːr], *a.* acicular, needle-shaped (leaf, crystal).

acicule [asikyl], *s.m. Ann:* aciculum.

aciculé [asikyle], *a. Nat.Hist:* aciculate(d).

aci(culi)forme [asi(kyli)fɔrm], *a.* aci(culi)form.

aciculite [asikylit], *s.f. Miner:* aikinite, needle ore.

acidage [asidaːʒ], *s.m. Tex:* acidification.

acide [asid]. **1.** *a.* (*a*) acid, sharp, tart, sour; **fruit a.,** acid, tart, fruit; **réponse a.,** sharp answer, tart reply; *Phot:* **fixateur a.,** acid fixer; (*b*) *Geol:* acidic (rock). **2.** *s.m. Ch:* acid; **indice d'a.,** acid value, acid number; **a. gras,** fatty acid; **acides verts,** green acids; **a. mort,** dead acid; **a. à boue,** mud acid; **inattaquable par les acides,** acid-proof; **a. aminé,** nucleic acid, amino-acid.

acidifère [asidifɛːr], *a.* acidiferous (rock, mineral, etc.).

acidifiable [asidifjabl̩], *a.* acidifiable.

acidifiant [asidifjɑ̃]. **1.** *a.* acidifying. **2.** *s.m.* acidifier.

acidification [asidifikasjɔ̃], *s.f.* acidification; acidization; *Min:* acidizing.

acidifier [asidifje], *v.tr.* (*pr.sub. & p.d.* **n. acidifiions, v. acidifiiez**) to acidify; to sour.

s'acidifier, (*a*) to become acid; to turn sour; (*b*) (*of wines, etc.*) to fox, to turn foxy.

acidimètre [asidimɛtr̥], *s.m.* **1.** acidimeter (for testing milk, butter, etc.). **2.** acidimeter, acidometer, acid tester (for accumulators); battery hydrometer.

acidisme [asidism], *s.m. Med:* acid dyspepsia.

acidité [asidite], *s.f.* acidity, sourness, sharpness, tartness; *F:* **avoir des acidités (d'estomac),** to suffer from acidity; *Ch:* **dosage de l'a.,** acid determination.

acidomètre [asidɔmɛtr̥], *s.m.* = ACIDIMÈTRE 2.

acidose [asidoːz], *s.f. Med:* acidosis.

acidulant [asidylɑ̃], *a. & s.m.* acidulent.

acidule [asidyl], *a.* subacid; acidulous.

acidulé [asidyle], *a.* acidulous; **bonbon acidulé,** acid drops.

aciduler [asidyle], *v.tr.* **1.** to acidulate (drink, etc.). **2.** to make, render, (stomach, etc.) acid.

s'aciduler, to become, turn, acid; to take on an acid taste.

acier [asje], *s.m.* **1.** (*a*) steel; **lame d'a., en a.,** steel blade; **a. inoxydable,** stainless steel; **a. doux,** mild, soft, steel; **a. trempé,** hardened steel; **a. fondu, coulé,** cast steel; **a. rapide,** high-speed steel; **a. demi-dur,** medium carbon steel, **a. allié,** alloy steel; **a. de cémentation,** carburizing steel; **a. cémenté,** case-hardened steel; **a. (r)affiné,** shear-steel; **a. tiré,** rolled steel; **a. poule,** blister steel; **a. au chrome, au nickel,** chrome steel, nickel steel; **a. méplat,** flat-ground steel; **a. en feuillards laminé à froid,** cold-rolled steel strip; **a. étiré à froid en profilés,** steel sections bright drawn; **a. de nitruration,** nitriding steel; **a. à ressort,** spring steel; **a. allié au plomb,** lead-alloy steel; **a. à coupe franche, de décolletage,** free-cutting steel; **a. en barres rectifiées avec précision,** precision-ground steel; *s.a.* CALMER 2, CORROYER 1; (*b*) **cœur d'a.,** heart of steel; **regard d'a.,** steely glance; **muscles d'a.,** muscles of steel. **2.** *A: Lit:* steel; sword, dagger.

aciérage [asjeraːʒ], *s.m.,* **aciération** [asjerasjɔ̃], *s.f.* **1.** *Metall:* (*a*) steeling; (*b*) case-hardening. **2.** *Electro-Ch:* steeling, steel-facing, acierage.

aciérer [asjere], *v.tr.* **(j'acière, n. aciérons; j'aciérerai) 1.** *Metall:* (*a*) to steel (tool, etc.); (*b*) to case-harden, face-harden. **2.** *Electro-Ch:* to steel(-face) (copper-plate, etc.). **3.** *Farr:* to rough (horse's shoes); to rough-shoe (horse).

aciéreux, -euse [asjerø, -øːz], *a. Metall:* steely (iron).

aciérie [asjeri], *s.f.* steel-works.

aciériste [asjerist], *s.m.* steel manufacturer.

acine [asin], *s.m.,* **acinus** [asinys], *s.m. Anat: Bot:* acinus.

acinèse [asinɛːz], *s.f. Med:* akinesia, akinesis.

acineta [asineta], *s.m. Bot:* acineta.

acinète [asinɛt], *s.m. Z:* acineta.

acinétidés [asinetide], *s.m.pl. Z:* Acinetae.

acineux, -euse [asinø, -øːz], *a. Anat: Bot:* acinose, acinous.

aciniforme [asinifɔrm], *a. Anat: Bot:* aciniform.

acipenséridés [asipɑ̃seride], *s.m.pl. Ich:* acipenseridae.

aclinique [aklinik], *a. Ph: Magn:* aclinic; **ligne a.,** aclinic line, magnetic equator.

acné [akne], *s.f. Med:* acne.

acnéique [akneik], *a.* covered with acne; suffering from acne.

acnodal, -aux [aknɔdal, -o], *a. Mth:* conjugate (point); **point a.,** acnode.

acœlomates [aselɔmat], *s.m.pl. Z:* Acœlomata.

acolytat [akɔlita], *s.m. Ecc: R.C.Ch:* acolythate.

acolyte [akɔlit], *s.m.* **1.** *Ecc:* acolyte. **2.** *(a)* assistant, attendant, acolyte; *(b) Pej:* confederate, accomplice.

acompte [akɔ̃ːt], *s.m.* instalment, partial payment, payment on account; **payer par acomptes,** to pay by instalments; **vente par acomptes,** hire purchase; **payer tant en a.,** to pay so much on account; **recevoir un a.,** to receive money on account; **un a. de cent francs,** a hundred francs on account (sur, of); (cp. **à compte,** under COMPTE.) *Fin:* **a. de, sur, dividende,** interim dividend.

acon [akɔ̃], *s.m. Nau:* **1.** (flat-bottomed) lighter; barge; (mud-)scow. **2.** punt.

aconage [akɔnaːʒ], *s.m. Nau:* lighterage.

aconier [akɔnje], *s.m.* **1.** lighterman. **2.** lighterage contractor.

aconit [akɔnit], *s.m. Bot:* aconite; **a. napel,** monkshood; **a. tue-loup,** wolf's-bane; **a. tue-chien,** dog's-bane.

aconitine [akɔnitin], *s.f. Ch:* aconitine.

aconitique [akɔnitik], *a. Ch:* aconitic.

acoquinant [akɔkinɑ̃], *a.* seductive, attractive, alluring (nook, armchair).

acoquiner [akɔkine], *v.tr. A:* *(a)* to debauch, degrade; *(b)* to allure, entice.

s'acoquiner. **1. s'a. auprès de qn,** to become degraded by s.o., by contact with s.o. **2. s'a. à un endroit,** (i) to sink to the level of one's surroundings, to renounce ambition; (ii) to make oneself comfortable in, to become attached, to a place; **s'a. dans un fauteuil,** to settle snugly in an armchair. **3. s'a. avec qn,** to take up with s.o.

acore [akɔːr], *s.m. Bot:* sweet rush, sweet flag.

Açores (les) [lezasɔːr], *Pr.n.f.pl. Geog:* the Azores.

acorie [akɔri], *s.f. Med:* acorea.

açorien, -ienne [asɔrjɛ̃, -jɛːn], *a. & s.* (native, inhabitant) of the Azores.

à-côté [akote], *s.m.* **1.** aside (remark). **2.** *usu. pl.* *(a)* **à-côtés d'une question,** side-issues of a question; **les à-côtés de l'histoire,** side-lights on history; *F:* **les petits à-côtés,** little extra profits, little extras, perks, a bit on the side; *(b)* **les à-côtés de l'exposition,** the side-shows of the exhibition.

acotylédone [akɔtiledɔn], **acotylédoné** [akɔtiledɔne]. *Bot:* **1.** *a.* acotyledonous. **2.** *s.f.* **acotylédone, acotylédonée,** acotyledon.

acoumètre [akumɛtʀ], *s.m. Med:* acoumeter, acousimeter.

à-coup [aku], *s.m.* jerk, jolt, jar, shock; sudden stoppage; *(a)* **machine qui fonctionne sans à-coups,** machine that works smoothly; **il travaille par à-coups,** he works by fits and starts; **la pièce fut jouée sans à-coups,** the play went off without incidents; *(b) Mil:* check, pull-up (in a column, line); *(c) El.E:* **à-c. de courant,** surge, rush, of current; **à-c. de surcharge,** sudden overload.

acousmie [akusmi], *s.f. Med:* acousma.

acousticien, -ienne [akustisjɛ̃, -jɛːn], *s.m. & f.* acoustician, acoustics expert.

acoustique [akustik]. **1.** *a.* acoustic (studies, properties, etc.); acoustic (nerve, etc.); **cornet a.,** ear-trumpet; **tuyau a.,** speaking-tube; **voûte a.,** whispering gallery; *s.a.* BRAS 2. **2.** *s.f.* *(a)* acoustics, (science of) sound; *(b)* **a. d'une salle,** acoustics of a room.

acoustiquement [akustikmɑ̃], *adv.* acoustically.

acquéreur, -euse [akerœːr, -øːz], *s.* acquirer; purchaser; buyer (on his own account); *Jur:* vendee.

acquérir [akeriːr], *v.tr.* (*pr.p.* **acquérant;** *p.p.* **acquis;** *pr.ind.* **j'acquiers, il acquiert, n. acquérons, ils acquièrent;** *pr.sub.* **j'acquière, n. acquérions, ils acquièrent;** *p.d.* **j'acquérais;** *p.h.* **j'acquis;** *fu.* **j'acquerrai**). **1.** to acquire, obtain, get, win, gain, secure; **il acquit une belle fortune,** he acquired a handsome fortune; **ce trait lui acquit l'estime publique,** this action won him the regard of the public, brought him into public esteem; **a. de mauvaises habitudes,** to get into bad habits; **ce droit vous est acquis,** you have that right; **sa protection m'est acquise,** I can count on his protection; *abs.* **le vin acquiert en vieillissant,** wine improves with age; *Prov:* **bien mal acquis ne profite jamais,** ill-gotten gains seldom prosper; **un bien en acquiert un autre,** money begets money. **2. a. une terre d'un voisin,** to purchase an estate from a neighbour.

acquêt [akɛ], *s.m.* **1.** *usu. pl. Jur:* acquest; **communauté réduite aux acquêts,** marriage settlement whereby only acquests accrue to the community. **2.** addition to one's worldly goods; acquisition; windfall.

acquiescement [akjɛsmɑ̃], *s.m.* acquiescence, assent, consent; **donner son a. à qch.,** to acquiesce in, give one's assent to, sth; *Jur:* **a. à un jugement,** acceptance of a judgment.

acquiescer [akjese], *v.ind.tr.* (**j'acquiesçai(s); n. acquiesçons**) **a. à qch.,** to acquiesce in sth.; to agree, assent, to sth.; **a. aux désirs de qn,** to fall in with s.o.'s desires, to comply with s.o.'s wishes.

acquis [aki]. **1.** *a.* *(a)* acquired (knowledge, etc.); **goût a.,** acquired taste; **biens mal a.,** ill-gotten goods; *(b)* **tenir pour a.,** to take for granted; **fait a.,** established fact; **fait a. à la science,** established scientific fact; **droits a.,** vested interests; **a. à l'aviation,** air-minded; **être tout a., entièrement a., à qn,** to be entirely devoted to s.o., to s.o.'s cause; **je vous suis tout a.,** I am entirely yours, I am your man; *s.a.* VITESSE. **2.** *s.m.* acquired knowledge, attainments, experience, background; **elle a de l'a.,** she has plenty of experience; (*of artist, writer, etc.*) **il a de l'a.,** he's gone through the mill; **ses a. intellectuels,** his intellectual attainments; **vivre sur son a.,** to mark time.

acquisitif, -ive [akizitif, -iːv], *a.* acquisitive; conferring a title, a right.

acquisition [akizisjɔ̃], *s.f.* acquisition. **1.** acquiring; **faire l'a. de qch.,** to acquire, purchase, sth. **2.** thing bought, obtained; purchase; **acquisitions de l'esprit,** intellectual attainments; (*in library*) **registre des acquisitions,** accessions list.

acquisivité [akizivite], *s.f.* acquisitiveness.

acquit [aki], *s.m.* **1.** *Com:* *(a)* receipt, acquittance; **donner a. de qch.,** to give a receipt for sth; **'pour a.',** 'received (with thanks),' 'paid'; **payer le solde à l'a. de qn,** to pay the balance on s.o.'s behalf; *s.a.* SOLDE[2] 1; *(b) Cust:* clearance (of ship). **2.** discharge, release (from engagement, etc.); **faire qch. par manière d'a.,** to do sth. as a matter of form, for form's sake; *s.a.* CONSCIENCE 2. **3.** *Bill:* **donner l'a.,** to break, to lead off; **donner un bon, mauvais, a.,** to leave the balls in a good, bad, position. **4.** *Jur:* **sentence, ordonnance, d'a.,** order of acquittal.

acquit-à-caution [akiakosjɔ̃], *s.m. Cus:* permit, transire, excise-bond, bond-note; *pl. acquits-à-caution.*

acquittable [akitabl̥], *a.* **1.** (*of prisoner, etc.*) worthy of acquittal. **2.** dischargeable, payable (debt, etc.).

acquittement [akitmɑ̃], *s.m.* **1.** discharge, payment (of debt, etc.). **2.** *Jur:* acquittal; **verdict d'a.,** verdict of not guilty.

acquitter [akite], *v.tr.* **1.** *(a)* **a. qn (d'une obligation, etc.),** to release s.o. (from an obligation, etc.); *(b)* **a. un accusé,** to acquit, discharge, an accused person. **2.** *(a)* **a. une obligation,** to fulfil an obligation; **a. une dette,** to discharge a debt; *Cust:* **a. les droits sur qch.,** to pay the duty on sth.; *(b)* **a. une facture,** to receipt a bill.

s'acquitter. **1. s'a. d'une obligation, d'un devoir,** to fulfil, carry out, discharge, an obligation, a duty; to implement a contract; **s'a. de son devoir,** to do one's duty; **comment pourrai-je m'a. envers vous?** how can I repay you? **s'a. d'une dette,** to discharge a debt. **2. se bien, mal, a.,** to acquit oneself well, badly; to put up a good, poor, fight; to give a good, poor, account of oneself.

acraeïdes [akreid], *s.m.pl. Ent:* Acraeidae.

acre [akʀ], *s.f. Fr.C:* acre; *in Fr. A:* (*approx.* =) acre.

âcre [ɑːkʀ], *a.* acrid, tart, bitter, pungent (taste, remark, etc.).

âcrement [ɑkrəmɑ̃], *adv.* acridly, pungently, bitingly.

âcreté [ɑkrəte], *s.f.* acridity, acridness, tartness, pungency (of smell, remark, etc.).

acrididés [akridide], *s.m.pl.* Acrididae, **acridien, -ienne** [akridjɛ̃, -jɛːn], *Ent:* **1.** *a.* acridian. **2.** *s.m.pl.* **acridiens,** Acrididae.

acridine [akridin], *s.f. Ch:* acridine.

acrimonie [akrimɔni], *s.f.* acrimony, acrimoniousness; bitterness (of speech, quarrel).

acrimonieusement [akrimɔnjøzmɑ̃], *adv.* acrimoniously, bitterly, acridly.

acrimonieux, -ieuse [akrimɔnjø, -jøːz], *a.* acrimonious, bitter (quarrel, etc.).

acro- [akrɔ-], *pref.* acro-; **acrocarpe,** acrocarpous; **acrogène,** acrogenous.

acrobate [akrɔbat], *s.m. & f.* **1.** acrobat; **tour d'a.,** acrobatic feat. **2.** *s.m. Z:* flying-phalanger, *Austr:* flying squirrel.

acrobatie [akrɔbasi], *s.f.* **1.** *(a)* acrobatics; *(b)* acrobatic feat. **2.** *Av:* **a. aérienne, acrobaties en vol,** trick flying; aerobatics; **faire des acrobaties,** to perform stunts, to stunt; *(c) F:* **a. politique,** brinkmanship.

acrobatique [akrɔbatik], *a.* **1.** acrobatic (feat, etc.). **2.** lifting (machinery).

acrobatisme [akrɔbatism], *s.m. A:* acrobatism, acrobatics.

acrocéphale [akrɔsefal], *a. & s. Anthr:* acrocephalic, acrocephalous (person).

acrocéphalie [akrɔsefali], *s.f.* acrocephalia, acrocephaly.

acrocéphalique [akrɔsefalik], *a.* acrocephalic.

acrocomia [akrɔkɔmja], *s.m. Bot:* acrocomia, macaw-tree.

acrodonte [akrɔdɔ̃t], *s.m. Rept:* acrodont.

acrodynie [akrɔdini], *s.f. Med:* acrodynia.

acroléine [akrɔlein], *s.f. Ch:* acrolein.

acromégalie [akrɔmegali], *s.f. Med:* acromegaly, acromegalia.

acromégalique [akrɔmegalik], *a. Med:* acromegalic.

acromial, -aux [akrɔmjal, -o], *a. Anat:* acromial.

acromion [akrɔmjɔ̃], *s.m. Anat:* acromion.

acron [akrɔ̃], *s.m. Z:* acron.

acronyque [akrɔnik], *a. Astr:* acronych(al), acronyctous (star).

acropodium [akrɔpɔdjɔm], *s.m. Art:* acropodium.

acropole [akrɔpɔl], *s.f.* acropolis.

acrosome [akrɔzoːm], *s.m. Biol:* acrosome.

acrospore [akrɔspɔːr], *s. Bot:* acrospore.

acrostiche [akrɔstiʃ], *a. & s.m.* acrostic.

acrostole [akrɔstɔl], *s.m. N.Arch:* acrostolium, acrostolion.

acrotère [akrɔtɛːr], *s.m.* acroter, acroterion, acroterium.

acryl-ester [akrilɛstɛːr], *s.m. Ch:* acrylate.

acrylique [akrilik], *a. Ch:* acrylic.

acte [akt], *s.m.* **1.** *(a)* action, act, deed; **a. de guerre,** act of war; **a. de courage,** brave action, deed; **faire a. de bonne volonté,** to give, show, proof of good will; **faire a. de volonté, d'autorité,** to exercise one's will, one's authority; **faire a. de souverain,** to exercise the royal prerogative; *Jur:* **faire a. de propriétaire,** to assume ownership. *s.a.* PRÉSENCE 2, GRATUIT; *(b)* **a. de foi, de contrition,** act of faith, of contrition. **2.** *Jur:* *(a)* instrument, deed, title, proof in writing; any instrument embodying a transaction in real estate; **a. de vente,** bill of sale; sale contract; **a. notarié, a. sur papier timbré,** deed executed and authenticated by a notary; **a. à l'écrit,** instrument in writing; **a. unilatéral,** deed poll; *s.a.* SINGE; **rédiger, dresser, un a.,** to draw up a document; *(b)* **a. judiciaire,** writ; **a. respectueux,** summons by son or daughter (to obtain parents' consent to marriage); **a. d'accusation,** bill of indictment; *(c)* record; **a. de naissance, de mariage, de décès,** birth, marriage, death certificate; **a. de dernière volonté,** last will and testament; **prendre a. de qch.,** to take (legal) cognizance of sth.; to note down, record, note sth.; **donner a. de . . ., que . . .,** to give official notice of . . ., that . . .; **dont a.,** (i) *Jur:* the following constitutes legal publication; (ii) *F:* noted; **donner a. de qch.,** to grant, to admit sth.; *(d) Nau:* **a. de nationalité,** (ship's) certificate of registry; *(e) pl.* records (of transactions, proceedings, etc.); transactions (of scientific body, etc.); **actes publics,** public registers; *B:* **les Actes des Apôtres,** the Acts of the Apostles. **3.** *Th:* act; **au second a.,** in the second act.

Actéon [akteɔ̃], **1.** *Pr.n.m. Myth:* Actaeon. **2.** *s.m. Moll:* actaeon.

actéonidés [akteɔnide], *s.m.pl. Moll:* Actaeonidae.

acter [akte], *v.tr. Jur:* **acter un document,** to publish a document officially.

acteur, -trice [aktœːr, -tris], *s.* actor, actress; player; **a. à transformations,** quick-change artist; **se faire a.,** to go on the stage.

actif, -ive [aktif, -iːv]. **1.** *a.* *(a)* active (supporter, drug, disease; *Gram:* verb, voice, etc.); potent (drug, etc.); **a. à défendre ses amis,** active in the defence of one's friends; **rallier la sympathie active de tous,** to receive the sympathy and

support of all; **citoyen a.,** voting and tax-paying citizen; **armée active,** regular army; **service dans l'armée active,** service with the colours; **service a.,** active service; **grenade active,** live grenade; *Pol.Ec:* **population active,** gainfully employed, working, population; (*b*) active, brisk, sprightly, agile, alert (person, etc.); **faire un commerce a.,** to be doing a good trade; (*c*) *Com:* **dettes actives,** debts due to us, to the firm. **2.** *s.m.* (*a*) *Com:* assets; credit (account); **mettre qch. à l'actif de qn,** to credit s.o. with sth.; **il a plusieurs bonnes actions à son a.,** he has several good deeds to his credit; **il avait cinq couples de perdrix à son actif,** he had accounted for five brace of partridges; (*b*) *Gram:* active voice; **verbe à l'actif,** verb in the active voice. **3.** *s.f.* regular army; **officier d'active,** officer in the regular army; **ancien officier d'active,** ex-regular officer.

actinal, -aux [aktinal, -o], *a. Z:* actinal (tentacles, etc.).

actiniaires [aktinjɛːr], *s.m.pl. Coel:* Actiniaria.

actinides [aktinid], *s.m.pl. Ch:* the actinium series.

actinie [aktini], *s.f. Coel:* actinia, sea-anemone.

actinifère [aktinifɛːr], *a. Ph:* actiniferous.

actinique [aktinik], *a. Ph:* actinic.

actinisme [aktinism], *s.m. Ph:* actinism.

actinium [aktinjɔm], *s.m. Ch:* actinium.

actinobacillose [aktinɔbasiloːz], *s.f. Vet:* actinobacillosis.

actinographe [aktinɔgraf], *s.m. Ph:* actinograph, recording actinometer.

actinographie [aktinɔgrafi], *s.f. Ph: Med:* x-ray photography.

actinologie [aktinɔlɔʒi], *s.f. Z:* actinology.

actinomètre [aktinɔmɛtr], *s.m. Ph: Phot:* actinometer.

actinométrie [aktinɔmetri], *s.f. Ph:* actinometry.

actinométrique [aktinɔmetrik], *a.* actinometric(al).

actinomorphe [aktinɔmɔrf], *a. Bot:* actinomorphic.

actinomycès [aktinɔmisɛs], *s.m. Bac:* actinomyces.

actinomycétales [aktinɔmisetal], *s.f.pl. Bac:* Actinomycetales.

actinomycète [aktinɔmisɛt], *s.f. Bac:* actinomycete.

actinomycine [aktinɔmisin], *s.f. Med:* actinomycin.

actinomycose [aktinɔmikoːz], *s.f. Vet: Med:* actinomycosis, lumpy jaw, wooden tongue.

actinon [aktinɔ̃], *s.m. Ch:* actinon.

actinote [aktinɔt], *s.f. Miner:* actinolite.

actinothérapie [aktinɔterapi], *s.f. Med:* actinotherapy.

actinotropisme [aktinɔtrɔpism], *s.m. Bot:* phototropism, inflexion towards a source of light.

action [aksjɔ̃], *s.f.* **1.** (*a*) action, act; **l'a. de marcher,** the action, act, of walking; **homme d'a.,** man of action; **obtenir qch. par l'a. de qn,** to obtain sth. through s.o.; **mettre en action un principe, une force,** to put a principle into practice, to carry a principle into action; to set a force at work; *s.a.* GRÂCE 5, OMISSION; (*b*) action, deed, exploit; **action d'éclat,** brilliant feat of arms. **2.** (*a*) (i) **a. sur qch., sur qn,** action, effect, on sth., on s.o.; (ii) **a. sur qn,** influence, power, over s.o.; **si l'on pouvait résister à l'a. de la vieillesse,** if one could check the progress of old age; **événements en dehors de notre a.,** events beyond our control; **sans a.,** ineffectual, ineffective; (*b*) **a. de l'eau, du feu, etc.,** agency, effect, of water, fire, etc.; (*c*) action, motion, working, functioning (of machine, etc.); (*of regulation, etc.*) **entrer en a.,** to come into force, operation; **suspendre l'a. d'une loi,** to suspend the operation of a law; **hors d'a.,** out of action, out of gear; (*d*) *Mec:* **principe de moindre a.,** principle of least action; *Mec.E:* **machine à simple, à double, a.,** single-, double-acting engine; **turbine d'a., à a.,** impulse turbine. **3.** (*a*) action, gesture (of orator, etc.); action (of horse); (*b*) *Th: Lit:* action; **scène qui retarde l'a.,** scene that delays the action; (*c*) plot (of play, novel). **4.** *Fin:* **a. (financière),** share, share certificate; **a. ordinaire,** ordinary share; **a. privilégiée,** preference share; **a. différée,** deferred share; **a. libérée,** fully paid-up share; **a. non entièrement libérée,** partly paid-up share; **a. libérée du tiers,** share on which one-third has been paid; **actions de dividende,** junior stocks; **actions de capital, de priorité,** senior shares; **actions gratuites,** bonus shares; **compagnie par actions,** joint-stock company; *F:* **ses actions montent, baissent, sont en hausse, en baisse,** his stock is going up, going down. **5.** *Jur:* action, lawsuit, trial; **intenter une a. à qn,** to bring an action against s.o., to sue s.o.; **a. civile,** civil action; **a. publique,** prosecution; **a. de la partie civile,** action instituted by private individual and joined to prosecution (in criminal case); **a. en paiement,** action for payment; **mandat d'a.,** receiving order (in bankruptcy); **a. en dommages et intérêts,** claim for damages; **a. en divorce,** divorce suit; **a. directe,** direct action; **a. indirecte, oblique,** indirect action. **6.** *Mil:* action, fight, engagement; **entrer en a.,** to go, come, into action; **a. d'ensemble,** concerted action; **a. interarmées, a. combinée (Terre, Air, Mer),** joint, combined action; **a. à distance,** long-range action. **7.** *Sw.Fr:* **vente a.,** bargain offer; **articles qui sont en a.,** goods which are selling at bargain prices.

actionnable [aksjɔnabl̩], *a. Jur:* actionable.

actionnaire [aksjɔnɛːr], *s.m. & f. Fin:* shareholder.

actionnariat [aksjɔnarja], *s.m.* shareholding; **a. ouvrier,** employee shareholding.

actionné [aksjɔne], *a.* busy, brisk; **marché très a.,** brisk market.

actionner [aksjɔne], *v.tr.* **1.** *Jur:* to sue (s.o.), to bring an action against (s.o.); **a. qn en dommages-intérêts,** to sue s.o. for damages. **2.** *Mec.E:* to set (sth.) in action, in motion; to operate, actuate, drive, work, run (sth.); **actionné par,** driven, powered by; **actionné à la main,** hand-operated; **actionné par la vapeur,** steam-driven; **a. les freins,** to apply, put on, the brakes.

s'actionner. *F:* to buck up, get a move on.

actionneur [aksjɔnœːr], *s.m.* actuator; *Av:* **a. de trim,** trim actuator.

activation [aktivasjɔ̃], *s.f. Ch:* activation.

activé [aktive], *a. Ch:* activated; *Bac: Hyg:* **boues activées,** activated (sewage) sludge.

activement [aktivmɑ̃], *adv.* actively, briskly, busily.

activer [aktive], *v.tr.* to quicken, to stir (up), to push on, to rouse; to activate (digestion, etc.); *Ch:* to activate; **a. le feu,** to stir up the fire, to make the fire burn up; **a. les gens,** to rouse, stir up, the people; **a. un cheval,** to whip up a horse; **a. un ouvrage,** to hasten, expedite, accelerate, a piece of work; *abs.* **activez!** hurry up! *F:* get a move on!

s'activer, (*a*) to keep oneself busy; (*b*) to hurry up, bestir oneself; to bustle (about); **s'a. à qch.,** (i) to busy oneself with (doing) sth., (ii) to press on with sth.

activeur [aktivœːr], *s.m. Ch:* activator.

activisme [aktivism], *s.m. Phil:* activism; *Pol:* militancy, activism.

activiste [aktivist], *s.m. & f. Pol:* **1.** *s.* activist. **2.** *a.* activist(ic), militant.

activité [aktivite], *s.f.* **1.** activity; potency (of a drug, etc.); **a. chimique d'un corps,** chemical activity of a body; **dans mon a. j'ai pu . . .,** in the course of my duties I was able to . . .; **dans ma sphère d'a. . . .,** in my sphere of action . . .; **il faut maintenir l'a. de l'industrie,** we must keep industry going. **2.** activity, quickness, briskness, dispatch; **travailler avec la plus grande a.,** to work with the greatest possible dispatch; **montrer de l'a. à faire qch.,** to show great activity in doing sth.; **déployer de l'a.,** to bustle (about); **nous sommes dans un moment de grande a.,** this is a very busy time for us; **c'est notre moment de plus grande a.,** we are now (*or* then) at our busiest; *Com:* **marché sans activité,** dull market; **le peu d'activité du marché,** the dullness, slackness, of the market; **rapport d'a.,** progress report; **il est débordant d'a.,** he is full of go. **3. en a.,** in activity, in action, in operation, in progress, at work; **l'usine est en a.,** the factory is in production; **volcan en a.,** volcano in eruption; **en pleine a.,** in full operation; (*furnace*) in full blast; **fête en pleine a.,** festivities in full swing; *Mil:* **être en a. (de service),** (i) to be on the active list; (ii) to be on active duty; (iii) (*rare*) to be on active service; *Sch: etc:* **activités dirigées,** organized spare-time activities; *Com:* **les activités d'une entreprise,** a firm's operations.

actrice. See ACTEUR.

actuaire [aktɥɛːr], *s.m. Ins: Fin:* actuary.

actualiser [aktɥalize], *v.tr.* **1.** to convert (sth.) into a fact, into a reality; to actualize. **2.** to bring (sth.) up-to-date.

s'actualiser, to become a reality.

actualisation [aktɥalizasjɔ̃], *s.f.* actualization.

actualité [aktɥalite], *s.f.* **1.** actuality, reality. **2.** question, event, of the (present) day, of the moment; **problème d'a.,** present-day problem; **cette question est toujours d'a.,** this question has always been with us; *pl.* (i) current events, passing events; (ii) *Cin:* news-reel; *s.a.* BULLETIN 1; **question dépourvue d'a.,** question not of current interest. **3.** up-to-dateness.

actuariat [aktɥarja], *s.m. Ins:* (*a*) functions of an actuary; (*b*) profession of actuary.

actuariel, -ielle [aktɥarjɛl], *a. Ins:* actuarial (calculation, etc.).

actuel, -elle [aktɥɛl], *a.* **1.** actual, real (service, etc.); *Theol:* **grâce actuelle,** actual grace. **2.** present-day, existing, current; **le gouvernement a.,** the present government; **l'état a. du pays,** the present state of the country; **dans les circonstances actuelles,** under existing circumstances; **à l'heure actuelle, à l'époque actuelle,** at the present time, *F:* in this day and age; **question actuelle,** topical question; *Com:* **valeur actuelle,** present value; **prix actuels,** ruling prices.

actuellement [aktɥɛlmɑ̃], *adv.* (just) now, at present, at the present time, currently, nowadays; *Scot:* presently; **les méthodes appliquées a.,** the methods now in force, present-day methods.

acuimètre [akɥimɛtr], *s.m. El: Meas:* Q meter.

acuité [akɥite], *s.f.* acuteness, sharpness, keenness (of point, pain, etc.); **a. d'un son,** shrillness, high pitch, of a sound; **a. de vision, a. visuelle,** keenness of sight; visual acuity.

aculé [akyle]. **1.** *a. Bot: Ent:* aculeate. **2.** *s.m.pl.* **aculés,** *Ent:* Aculeata.

aculéate [akyleat]. **1.** *a.* aculeate, sting-bearing (Hymenoptera, etc.). **2.** *s.m.pl. Ent:* Aculeata, the aculeate Hymenoptera.

aculéiforme [akyleifɔrm], *a. Bot:* aculeiform, spine-shaped.

acuminé [akymine], **acumineux, -euse** [akyminø, -øːz], *a. Bot: etc:* acuminate.

acuponcteur, acupuncteur [akypɔ̃ktœːr], *s.m. Med:* acupunctor.

acuponcture, acupuncture [akypɔ̃ktyːr], *s.f. Med:* acupuncture.

acutangle [akytɑ̃ːgl̩], *a.* **triangle a.,** acute-angled triangle.

acutangulaire [akytɑ̃gylɛːr], *a.* acute-angled, making an acute angle.

acutangulé [akytɑ̃gyle], *a. Bot:* acutangular.

acutesse [akytɛs], *s.f.* (*rare*) sharpness; keenness (of point, sight, etc.).

acuticaude [akytikod], *a. Z:* having a pointed tail.

acutifolié [akytifɔlje], *a. Bot:* acutifoliate.

acutilobé [akytilɔbe], *a. Bot:* acutilobate.

acutipenne [akytipɛn], *a. Orn:* acutipennate.

acyclique [asiklik], *a. Ch:* aliphatic, acyclic.

adactyle [adaktil], *a. Z:* adactylous.

adage [adaːʒ], *s.m.* adage, common saying; wise saw; proverb; **selon l'a.,** as the saying goes.

adagio [adaʒjo], *adv. & s.m. Mus:* adagio; *pl. adagios.*

Adam [adɑ̃], *Pr.n.m.* Adam; *F:* **dans le, en, costume d'Adam,** in the buff, in one's birthday suit; **nous sommes tous de la côte d'Adam,** we are all descended from Adam; **il se croit sorti de la côte d'Adam,** he thinks he is somebody; *s.a.* ÈVE, FOURCHETTE 1, POMME 1.

adamantin [adamɑ̃tɛ̃], *a. Miner:* adamantine; *Lit:* firm, hard, unyielding.

adamine [adamin], *s.f. Miner:* adamite, adamine.

adamique [adamik], *a.* Adamic (race, etc.).

adaptable [adaptabl̩], *a.* adaptable (à, to); adjustable.

adaptateur, -trice [adaptatœːr, -tris]. **1.** *s.m. El: Mec.E: Phot:* adapter. **2.** *s.m. W.Tel:* convertor. **3.** *s.* adapter (of book for film, etc.).

adaptation [adaptasjɔ̃], *s.f.* adaptation, adjustment, accommodation (à, to); *W.Tel:* matching; **faculté d'a.,** adaptability.

adapter [adapte], *v.tr.* (*a*) **a. qch. à qch.,** (i) to fit, adjust, sth. to sth., (ii) to adapt sth. to sth., to make sth. suitable for sth.; **a. un roman à la scène,** to adapt a novel for the stage; **pièce adaptée de Molière,** play adapted from Molière; **bien adapté à . . .,** well adapted for . . .; *s.a.* SURVIVANCE 1; *W.Tel:* to match.

s'adapter. 1. s'a. à qch, to fit, suit, sth.; to be suitable for sth. **2. s'a. aux conditions nouvelles,** to adapt, adjust oneself, to new conditions; **s'a. aux circonstances,** to adapt (oneself) to, make the best of, circumstances; **il sait s'a. aux circonstances,** he is very adaptable.

adapteur [adaptœr], *s.m. Phot:* (*plate*) adapter; *El: Mec.E:* adapter.

adaubages [adobaːʒ], *s.m.pl. A: Nau:* salted meat, pickled meat (for long voyages).

addax [adaks], *s.m. Z:* addax.

addenda [adɛ̃da], *s.m.inv.* addendum, addenda (à, to).

addeur [adœːr], *s.m. Computers:* adder.

Addis-Ababa, -Abéba [adisababa, -beba], *Pr.n. Geog:* Addis Ababa.

Addison [adisɔn], *Pr.n. Med:* **maladie d'A.,** Addison's disease.

additif, -ive [aditif, -iːv]. **1.** *a.* additive. **2.** *s.m.* (*a*) supplement, addition; (*b*) *Ch: etc:* additive; dope; **a. anti-boue,** sludge dispersal agent; **a. pour combustible,** fuel dope.

addition [adisjɔ̃], *s.f.* **1.** addition, (i) adding (**à**, to); (ii) adding up, totting up; **faire l'a. des chiffres,** to add up, tot up, the figures. **2.** (*a*) accession, accretion, addition; **faire une a. à un bâtiment,** to add to a building; **en a. au paragraphe 2 . . .,** in addition, further, to paragraph 2 . . .; (*b*) *Ar:* addition; (*c*) (*in restaurant, etc.*) bill; *U.S:* check; (*d*) *Typ:* marginal note.

additionnable [adisjɔnabl], *a.* addible, addable (sum).

additionnel, -elle [adisjɔnɛl], *a.* additional; *s.a.* CENTIME.

additionner [adisjɔne], *v.tr. & i.* **1.** (*a*) to add up, tot up; *abs.* **j'additionne,** I'm adding up, I'm totting up, I'm doing an, the, addition; (*b*) *F: A:* **a. la vanité à l'ignorance,** to add vanity to ignorance. **2. a. un liquide de qch.,** to increase the quantity of a liquid with sth.; **lait additionné d'eau,** watered milk, adulterated milk; **café additionné d'eau-de-vie,** coffee laced with spirits; **alcool additionné d'eau,** alcohol diluted with water.

additionneur [adisjɔnœːr], *s.m. Computers:* adder.

additionneuse [adisjɔnøːz], *s.f.* adding machine.

adducteur [ad(d)yktœːr]. **1.** *a.m.* (*a*) *Anat:* adducent (muscle); (*b*) *Tch:* feed(ing), supply. **2.** *s.m.* (*a*) *Anat:* adductor; (*b*) *Hyd.E:* supply main; *El.E:* **fil a.,** leading-in wire.

adduction [ad(d)yksjɔ̃], *s.f.* **1.** adduction, bringing forward. **2.** (*a*) *Mch: I.C.E:* admission (of steam, of gas); intake; (*b*) **a. d'eau,** canalization; **adductions d'eau,** water supply.

-ade[1] [ad], *s.suff.f.* -ad; (*a*) **monade,** monad; **triade,** triad; (*b*) **Iliade,** Iliad.

-ade[2], *s.suff.f.* -ade. **1.** (*derived product*) **orangeade,** orangeade; **arlequinade,** harlequinade; **cotonnade,** cotton fabric. **2.** *Coll:* **colonnade,** colonnade; **arcade,** arcade. **3. galopade,** gallop(ing); **débandade,** stampede.

Adélaïde [adelaid], *Pr.n.f.* Adelaide; *Geog:* Adelaide, S. Australia.

Adèle [adɛl]. **1.** *Pr.n.f.* Adela. **2.** *s.f. Ent:* Adela (butterfly).

adélides [adelid], *s.m.pl. Ent:* Adelidae.

Adelphes (les) [lezadɛlf], *m. Lt.Lit:* The Adelphi (of Terence).

Aden [adɛn], *Pr.n.m. Geog:* Aden.

adénectomie [adenɛktɔmi], *s.f. Surg:* adenoidectomy, removal of adenoids.

adénite [adenit], *s.f. Med:* adenitis, inflammation of the glands.

adéno-cancer [adenɔkɑ̃sɛːr], *s.m.*, **adéno-carcinome** [adenɔkarsinɔm], *s.m. Med:* adenocarcinoma.

adéno-fibrome [adenɔfibroːm], *s.m. Med:* adenofibroma.

adénoïde [adenɔid], *a. Med: Physiol:* adenoid, glandular; *Med:* **végétations adénoïdes,** adenoids.

adénoïdectomie [adenɔidɛktɔmi], *s.f. Surg:* = ADÉNECTOMIE.

adénoïdien, -ienne [adenɔidjɛ̃, -jɛn], *a.* adenoid(al).

adénome [adenoːm], *s.m. Med:* adenoma, glandular tumour; **adénomes nasopharyngiens,** adenoids.

adénopathie [adenɔpati], *s.f.* adenopathy.

adéno-sarcome [adenɔsarkoːm], *s.m. Med:* adenosarcoma.

adent [adɑ̃], *s.m.* **1.** dent, indentation, jag. **2.** *Carp:* indent, key, dovetail; **joint à, en, a.,** (i) notch-, cog-, joggle-, scarf-joint; (ii) dovetail (joint).

adenter [adɑ̃te], *v.tr. Carp: A:* to indent, dovetail, key.

adepte [adɛpt], *s.m. & f.* follower, adherent; adept; **art qui a peu d'adeptes,** art in which few are completely versed.

adéquat [adekwa], *a.* **1.** adequate; **production adéquate à la demande,** production adequate to, answering to, the demand. **2.** equivalent, synonymous (expressions, etc.).

adéquatement [adekwatmɑ̃], *adv.* adequately.

adéquation [adekwasjɔ̃], *s.f.* (*a*) adequation; (*b*) adequacy.

adéquatité [adekwatite], *s.f.* **1.** adequacy. **2.** equivalency.

adextré [adɛkstre], *a. Her:* dexterwise, dexterways; **a. d'une étoile,** with a star dexterwise, dexterways.

adhérence [aderɑ̃ːs], *s.f.* **1.** (*a*) adherence, adhesion; (*b*) **a. des roues (à la route),** grip of the wheels (on the road). **2.** *Med: Surg:* **adhérences,** adhesions.

adhérent, -ente [aderɑ̃, -ɑ̃ːt]. **1.** *a.* adherent (**à**, to); adhesive; *Rail:* **poids a.,** adhesion (weight); *Bot:* adnate (anther, etc.); **substance adhérente;** sticky substance. **2.** *s.* **a. d'un parti,** member, adherent, supporter, partisan, of a party.

adhérer [adere], *v.i.* (**j'adhère, n. adhérons; j'adhérerai**). **1.** to adhere, stick, cling (**aux doigts, etc.,** to the fingers, etc.); (*of wheels*) **a. à la route,** to grip the road. **2.** to adhere, cleave, hold (**à**, to opinion, etc.). **3.** to adhere (**à**, to); to approve (**à**, of); to confirm (act, decision, etc.). **4. a. à (un parti),** to join (a party).

adhésif, -ive [adezif, -iːv]. **1.** *a.* adhesive, sticky. **2.** *s.m.* adhesive; *Phot:* (i) dry-mounting tissue; (ii) **a. antihalo,** backing.

adhésion [adezjɔ̃], *s.f.* **1.** adhesion, sticking; **force d'a.,** adhesive force, adhesiveness. **2.** (*a*) joining, membership (of a party); adhesion, adherence (**à**, to); **délai d'a. le 30 juin,** last day for joining, for admission, June 30th; (*b*) agreement; approval; **donner son a. à un pacte, à un projet,** to accede to a covenant; to give, signify, one's adhesion to a plan.

adhésivité [adezivite], *s.f.* **1.** adhesiveness, stickiness; *Ch:* **agent d'a.,** adhesion promoter. **2.** *Phren:* adhesiveness.

ad hoc [adɔk], *Lt.adv.phr. & a.* ad hoc, for the purpose, special; **l'homme ad hoc,** the right man.

adiabatique [adjabatik], *a. & s. Ph: Meteor:* **1.** (*a*) adiabatic (curve, etc.); **courbe a.,** adiabat; **diagramme a.,** adiabatic chart. **2.** *s.f.* adiabat; **a. humide,** condensation adiabat; **a. sèche,** dry adiabat; **pseudo a., a. saturée,** pseudo adiabat.

adiabatiquement [adjabatikmɑ̃], *adv.* adiabatically.

adiabatisme [adjabatism], *s.m. Ph:* adiabatism, adiabatic state (of gas).

adiante [adjɑ̃ːt], *s.m. Bot:* adiantum; **a. capillaire,** maidenhair fern.

adiantum [adjɑ̃tɔm], *s.m. Bot:* maidenhair fern.

adieu, -ieux [adjø]. **1.** *int.* good-bye; (*Sw.Fr: in S. of Fr:*) hello! **dire a. à qn,** to bid s.o. farewell, goodbye; **dire a. à qch.,** to give up, renounce, sth.; **faire a. à qn,** to wave s.o. goodbye. **2.** *s.m.* farewell, parting, leave-taking; **faire ses adieux à qn,** to take one's leave of s.o., to say good-bye to s.o.; *Th:* **faire ses adieux à la scène,** to make one's farewell appearance; **j'ai reçu les adieux de M. X,** Mr X came, wrote, to say good-bye; **baiser d'a.,** parting kiss; **sans a.!** this is not good-bye!

à-Dieu-va(t)! [adjøva(t)], *int.* (*a*) *Nau: A:* about ship! 'bout ship! (*b*) we must chance it and trust to God.

adipeux, -euse [adipø, -øːz], *a. Physiol:* adipose, fatty (tissue, etc.); *F:* (*of pers.*) fat; **devenir a.,** to put on flesh, to grow stout.

adipique [adipik], *a. Ch:* adipic (acid).

adipocérite [adiposerit], *s.f. Geol:* adipocerite.

adipose [adipoːz], *s.f. Med:* adiposis.

adiposité [adipozite], *s.f.* adiposity.

adja [adʒa], *s.f. P: used in* **mettre l'a., les adjas,** to beat it, to do a bunk.

adjacence [adʒasɑ̃ːs], *s.f.* adjacency (of houses, angles, etc.).

adjacent [adʒasɑ̃], *a.* adjacent, contiguous (**à**, to); adjoining; bordering (**à**, on); *Geom:* **angles adjacents,** adjacent angles.

adjectif, -ive [adʒɛktif, -iːv]. **1.** *a.* (*a*) *Gram:* adjectival, adjective, (phrase, etc.); **proposition adjective,** adjectival, relative, clause; (*b*) *Tex:* **couleurs adjectives,** adjective colours. **2.** *s.m.* adjective; **a. attribut,** predicative adjective; **a. épithète,** attributive adjective.

adjectival, -aux [adʒɛktival, -o], *a. Gram:* adjectival.

adjectivement [adʒɛktivmɑ̃], *adv. Gram:* adjectivally.

adjectiver [adʒɛktive], *v.tr.* **1.** To use as an adjective. **2.** *P:* to call (s.o.) names; to blackguard (s.o.); **a. qn de la belle façon,** to call s.o. everything under the sun.

adjoindre [adʒwɛ̃ːdr], *v.tr.* (*conj. like* JOINDRE). **1. a. qch. à qch.,** to unite, associate, sth. with sth. **2. a. qn à qn,** to give s.o. to s.o. as an assistant, to appoint s.o. as an assistant to s.o.; **a. qn à un comité,** to add s.o. to a committee; **s'a. des collaborateurs,** to appoint assistants; **s'a. les capacités,** to call upon all the talent (of the nation).

s'adjoindre à d'autres, to join (in), to associate, with others.

adjoint, -ointe [adʒwɛ̃, -wɛ̃ːt]. **1.** *a.* assistant; deputy; *Mil:* **officier a.,** adjutant, *U.S:* executive officer; *Artil:* **lieutenant a.,** observation officer; *Sch: A:* **professeur a.** = *adjoint d'enseignement.* **2.** *s.* assistant; deputy; *Adm:* **a. (au maire),** deputy mayor; *Sch:* **a. d'enseignement** = assistant master with teaching and supervision duties.

adjonction [adʒɔ̃ksjɔ̃], *s.f.* **1.** adding, adjunction; **l'a. de deux nouveaux membres,** the addition of two new members; **a. des capacités,** enrolling of talent. **2.** anything added; **adjonctions faites à un texte,** additions made to a text; **hôpital et ses adjonctions,** hospital and its annexes.

adjudant [adʒydɑ̃], *s.m.* **1.** (*a*) *Mil:* warrant officer class II; *A:* sergeant-major, *U.S:* warrant officer (junior grade); *A:* **a. général,** adjutant general; **a. de garnison,** garrison adjutant; (*b*) *Lit:* assistant. **2.** *Orn:* adjutant-bird, -crane.

adjudant-chef [adʒydɑ̃ʃɛf], *s.m. Mil:* warrant officer class I, *A:* regimental sergeant-major, *U.S:* chief warrant officer.

adjudant-major [adʒydɑ̃maʒoːr], *s.m.* (**capitaine**) **a.-m.,** adjutant, *U.S.:* executive officer.

adjudicataire [adʒydikatɛːr]. **1.** *a.* **Partie a.,** (i) contracting party; (ii) purchasing party. **2.** *s.* (*a*) successful tenderer for a contract; contractor; **être déclaré a. de qch.,** to secure the contract for sth.; (*b*) highest bidder; purchaser (at auction); (*c*) lessee (of State fishery).

adjudicateur, -trice [adʒydikatœːr, -tris], *s.* adjudicator, awarder (of contract, etc.).

adjudicatif, -ive [adʒydikatif, -iːv], *a.* adjudicative, adjudging, awarding (decree, etc.).

adjudication [adʒydikasjɔ̃], *s.f. Adm: Com: Jur:* adjudication, allocation, award; (*a*) adjudicating, adjudging, awarding; (*b*) giving out, allocation (of contract); (*c*) knocking-down (of sth. to s.o.); **mettre qch. en a.,** (i) to invite tenders for sth., to put sth. out to tender; (ii) to put sth. up for sale by auction; **a. au rabais,** allocation to lowest tender(er); **a. à la surenchère,** allocation to the highest bidder; **par voie d'a.,** (i) by tender; (ii) by auction.

adjuger [adʒyʒe], *v.tr.* (**j'adjugeai(s) n. adjugeons**); **a. qch. à qn,** (i) to adjudge, award, allocate, sth. to s.o.; (ii) (*at auctions*) to knock down sth. to s.o.; **une fois! deux fois! adjugé!** going! going! gone! **a. les fournitures de bureau,** to give the contract for office furniture (after tender); *Jur:* **a. au demandeur ses conclusions,** to find for the plaintiff; **a. une récompense à qn,** to confer a reward on s.o.; **s'a. qch.,** to appropriate, take possession of, sth.; **s'a. un titre de noblesse,** to give oneself a title; **s'a. une course, un prix,** to win a race, a prize.

adjupète [adʒypɛt], *s.m. Mil: P:* = ADJUDANT.

adjuration [adʒyrasjɔ̃], *s.f.* adjuration. **1.** solemn entreaty. **2.** exorcism.

adjurer [adʒyre], *v.tr.* **a. qn de faire qch.,** to adjure, entreat, solemnly call upon, s.o. to do sth.

adjuteur [adʒytœːr], *s.m. A:* help(er), assistant; **a. du bourreau,** executioner's assistant.

adjuvant [adʒyvɑ̃]. **1.** *a.* auxiliary. **2.** *s.m.* (*a*) *Med:* adjuvant; (*b*) *Ind:* additive; (*c*) *Ch:* catalyst; (*d*) stimulus.

adlumie [adlymi], *s.f. Bot:* climbing fumitory.

Admète [admɛt], *Pr.n.m. Gr.Lit:* Admetus.

admetteur [admɛtœːr], *s.m. Mch:* high-pressure cylinder.

admettre [admɛtr], *v.tr.* (*conj. like* METTRE). **1.** to admit; to let (s.o., sth.) in; **a. qn chez soi,** to admit, allow, s.o. into one's house; **a. qn dans son intimité,** to admit s.o. to one's friendship; **a. qn à l'hôpital,** to admit s.o. to hospital; *Sch:* **être admis à un examen,** to pass, get through, an examination. **2. a. qn à faire qch.,** to allow, permit, authorize, s.o. to do sth; **être admis à passer un examen,** to be allowed to sit for an examination. **3.** (*a*) **a. qch.,** to admit, admit of, permit, allow, sth.; **a. une requête,** to allow a request; **l'usage admis,** the accepted custom; **a. qch. pour une vérité,** to admit, grant, sth. as a fact; **si l'on admet la vérité de . . .,** granting the truth of . . .; **cela n'admet aucun retard,** it admits of no delay; **le passage admet plusieurs interprétations,** the passage admits of several interpretations; **a. un compte,** to pass an account; (*b*) **a. que** + *ind.*, **il admet que c'est vrai,** he admits that it is true; **j'admets que j'ai tort,** I acknowledge, admit, agree, that I am in the wrong; *but* **je n'admets pas que j'aie tort,** I do not admit that I am in the wrong; **il n'admet pas qu'elle soit de santé délicate,** he will not have it that she is delicate; (*c*) **admettre que** + *sub.*, **admettons que j'aie tort,** let us assume, suppose, grant, that I am wrong; (*d*) **il n'admet pas d'être vaincu,** he will not admit to being defeated.

administrateur, -trice [administratœːr, -tris], *s.* 1. (*a*) administrator, *f.* administratrix (of colony, parish, charity, etc.); (*b*) a. foncier, land agent, estate agent; steward; cabinet d'a. foncier, estate agency; (*a*) a. civil, administrative officer. 2. director (of company, bank, etc.); business manager (of newspaper, etc.); a. délégué, gérant, managing director. 3. a. judiciaire, trustee, receiver (of estate, business, etc.). 4. Guardian (of the poor).

administratif, -ive [administratif, -iːv], *a.* administrative; détails d'ordre a., administrative details; bâtiment a., office building; office block; *Mil:* convoi a., supply column.

administration [administrasjɔ̃], *s.f.* 1. administering, dispensing (of justice, sacrament, etc.); *Jur:* producing (of proofs). 2. (*a*) administration, direction, management (of business, of public affairs, etc.); dépenses d'a., trade expenses; conseil d'a., board of directors; mauvaise a., mismanagement, maladministration; (*b*) governing (of country); administrations publiques, public offices; (*c*) *Jur:* trusteeship. 3. (*a*) governing body, board of directors, management; *Mil:* a. de l'armée, administrative services of the army; *Mil:* officier d'a., administration officer; *Nau:* a. de la marine, navy commissariat; (*b*) l'A., the civil service; entrer dans l'A., to become a civil servant, to enter government service.

administrativement [administrativmɑ̃], *adv.* administratively.

administré, -ée [administre], *s.m.* & *f.* person under s.o.'s administration, under s.o.'s jurisdiction; (*Mayor's speech*) mes chers administrés, Ladies and Gentlemen.

administrer [administre], *v.tr.* 1. to administer, manage, direct, conduct (business, undertaking, estate); to govern (country). 2. *Jur:* a. des preuves, etc., to produce proofs, etc. 3. a. qch. à qn, to administer, dispense, sth. to s.o.; a. la justice, to dispense justice; a. un purgatif à qn, to give s.o. a dose of laxative; *Hum:* s'a. un petit verre de rhum, to take a drop of rum for the good of one's health; *F:* a. une bonne raclée à qn, to give s.o. a good hiding; *Ecc:* a. (un sacrement), to administer (a sacrament); a. l'extrême onction à qn, *abs.* a. qn, to administer extreme unction to s.o.

admirable [admirabl̩], *a.* admirable, wonderful; conduite a. de fermeté, conduct admirable for its firmness; quel temps a.! what glorious weather! a. par la qualité, admirable in quality; *A:* médecin a. par ses remèdes, doctor admirable for his remedies.

admirablement [admirabləmɑ̃], *adv.* admirably, wonderfully, capitally.

admirateur, -trice [admiratœːr -tris]. 1. *a.* admiring. 2. *s.* admirer; fan.

admiratif, -ive [admiratif, -iːv], *a.* admiring (gesture, person, etc.).

admiration [admirasjɔ̃], *s.f.* admiration; regarder qch. avec a., to look at sth. with admiration, admiringly; avoir de l'a. pour qn, qch., être dans l'a., to admire, be full of admiration (for, s.o., sth.); être, devenir, faire, l'a. de qn, to be admired by s.o., to excite the admiration of s.o.; être, tomber, en a. devant qn, devant qch., to be lost in admiration of s.o., sth.; être saisi d'a., to be struck with admiration.

admirativement [admirativmɑ̃], *adv.* admiringly, with admiration.

admirer [admire], *v.tr.* 1. to admire; admiré de tous, admired by all, much admired; admiré même par ses ennemis, admired even by his enemies; je vous admire d'avoir eu ce courage, I admire you for having shown such courage. 2. *A:* (*still in occ. use*) to wonder at, be surprised at (sth.); to look on in wonder at (sth.); j'admire que vous ayez eu ce courage, I wonder that you could show such courage.

admis, -ise [admi, -iːz], *s.m.* & *f.* *Sch:* *etc:* successful candidate, competitor.

admissibilité [admisibilite], *s.f.* admissibility; eligibility; *Sch:* les candidats gardent leur a., candidates will be eligible for the oral without having to sit the written examination again.

admissible [admisibl̩], *a.* (*a*) admittable (à un endroit, to a place); (*b*) admissible, permissible, allowable (excuse, proof, conduct, etc.); (*c*) a. à un emploi, eligible for a job; *Sch:* candidats admissibles, *s.* les admissibles, candidates who have qualified for the oral examination.

admission [admisjɔ̃], *s.f.* 1. admission (à, dans, to); a. dans l'armée, à un club, admission to the army, to a club; cotisation d'a., entrance fee; *Art:* jury d'a., hanging committee. 2. *Cust:* entry (of goods); a. en franchise, duty-free entry; a. temporaire, duty-free entry (of products destined for re-export after processing). 3. *Mch:* *I.C.E:* admission; intake; induction; période d'a., induction stroke; a. anticipée, pre-admission; soupape d'a., inlet valve; *I.C.E:* pression d'a., boost pressure. 4. *St.Exch:* a. à la cote, admission to quotation.

admittance [admitɑ̃ːs], *s.f.* *El:* admittance.

admixtion [admikstjɔ̃], *s.f.* *Pharm:* admixture (à, with).

admonestation [admɔnɛstasjɔ̃], *s.f.* admonition, admonishment, reprimand.

admonester [admɔnɛste], *v.tr.* to admonish, censure, reprimand.

admoniteur, -trice [admɔnitœːr, -tris], *s.* (*rare*) admonisher.

admonitif, -ive [admɔnitif, -iːv], *a.* (*rare*) admonitory, admonishing (speech, tone, etc.).

admonition [admɔnisjɔ̃], *s.f.* admonition, admonishment, reprimand.

adné [adne], *a.* *Bot:* *Physiol:* adnate.

adobe [adɔb], *s.m.* *Const:* 1. adobe. 2. adobe house; mud-hut.

adolescence [adɔlɛsɑ̃ːs], *s.f.* adolescence.

adolescent, -ente [adɔlɛsɑ̃, -ɑ̃ːt]. 1. *s.* adolescent, youth; *f.* girl (in her teens); *F:* teenager. 2. *a.* adolescent, *F:* teenage; arbre a., young tree.

Adolphe [adɔlf], *Pr.n.m.* Adolphus.

adon [adɔ̃], *s.m.* *Fr.C:* *F:* coincidence.

adonc, adoncques, adonques [adɔ̃ːk], *adv.* *A:* then.

adonidine [adɔnidin], *s.f.* *Pharm:* adonidin.

adonien, -ienne [adɔnjɛ̃, -jɛn], **adonique** [adɔnik], *Gr.Lit:* 1. *a.* Adonic, Adonian. 2. *s.m.* Adonic, Adonian, verse.

Adonies [adɔni], *s.f.pl.* *Gr.Ant:* Adonia.

Adonis [adɔnis]. 1. *Pr.n.m.* *Myth:* Adonis. 2. *s.m.* (*a*) adonis; (*b*) *Ent:* adonis; (i) mazarine; (ii) clifton blue, clifden blue (butterfly). 3. *s.f.* *Bot:* pheasant's-eye, adonis.

adoniser (s') [sadɔnize], *v.pr.* *A:* (*of man*) to adonize, to adorn oneself, to dress elaborately.

adonner [adɔne], *v.i.* *Nau:* (*of wind*) to veer aft, abaft.

s'adonner, (*a*) s'a. à qch., to give oneself up to sth.; s'a. à l'étude, to devote oneself to study; s'a. à une profession, à une étude, to take up a profession, a study; ils se sont adonnés à la même profession, they follow, practise, the same profession; s'a. aux sports, à l'étude des langues, to go in for sport, for (the learning of) languages; il s'adonna au commerce, he took to trade, he went in for business; (*b*) s'a. à la boisson, (i) to take to drink; to become addicted to drink; (ii) to be given to drink; adonné à la boisson, à des habitudes coûteuses, given to drink, to expensive habits; s'a., être adonné, au tabac, au péché, to indulge in tobacco, in sin.

adoptable [adɔptabl̩], *a.* adoptable, acceptable (person, opinion).

adoptant, -ante [adɔptɑ̃, -ɑ̃ːt], *s.* adopter; adoptive parent.

adopté, -ée [adɔpte]. 1. *a.* adopted, adoptive. 2. *s.* adopted child, adoptive child; adoptee.

adopter [adɔpte], *v.tr.* 1. a. qn, to adopt s.o. 2. (*a*) a. une cause, to adopt, take up, embrace, a cause; a. un nom, to adopt, take, assume, a name; (*b*) a. un projet de loi, une résolution, to pass, carry, a bill, a resolution; a. un rapport, to accept a report; adopté à l'unanimité, carried unanimously.

adoptif, -ive [adɔptif, -iːv], *a.* adopted, adoptive (child, parent, country).

adoption [adɔpsjɔ̃], *s.f.* adoption; *Pol:* passage, carrying (of bill); mon pays d'a., my adopted country; *F:* je suis américain d'a., I am an American by adoption.

adorable [adɔrabl̩], *a.* 1. adorable, worthy of worship, adoration. 2. adorable, charming; vous êtes a. dans cette robe, you look charming in that dress.

adorablement [adɔrabləmɑ̃], *adv.* adorably, charmingly.

adorateur, -trice [adɔratœːr, -tris]. 1. *s.* (*a*) adorer, worshipper, votary (of a god); (*b*) ardent admirer. 2. *a.* adoring (people, etc.).

adoratif, -ive [adɔratif, -iːv], *a.* acte a., act of adoration, of worship.

adoration [adɔrasjɔ̃], *s.f.* adoration. 1. worship (of a god). 2. profound admiration (de, for); aimer qn à l'a., to adore s.o.; être en a. devant qn, to worship s.o.

adorer [adɔre], *v.tr.* 1. to adore, worship (a god). 2. to adore, idolize, to dote upon, to be passionately fond of (s.o., sth.); *F:* j'adore la salade, I love salad; j'adore monter à cheval, I adore riding; I'm crazy about riding; il adorait qu'on le regardât, he loved to be looked at.

adorner [adɔrne], *v.tr.* to adorn (heavily).

ados [ado], *s.m.* *Hort:* banked-up bed, border (facing the sun).

adossé [adose], *a.* 1. back to back; *Her:* addorsed. 2. a. à qch., (i) backed on to sth.; (ii) with one's back against sth.

adossement [adosmɑ̃], *s.m.* 1. leaning, backing (à, contre, against). 2. position back to back.

adosser [adose], *v.tr.* 1. to place (two things) back to back. 2. a. qn, qch., à, contre, qch., to place, lean, rest, s.o., sth. (with his, its, back) against sth.; to back sth. against sth.; *Const:* a. qch. à qch., to build sth. against sth.

s'adosser à, contre, qch., (*a*) to set, lean one's back against sth.; s'a. au mur, to lean (back) against the wall; (*b*) (*of village, etc.*) to stand against, to be backed by (hillside, etc.).

adouber [adube], *v.tr.* 1. *Hist:* (*a*) a. un chevalier, to equip a knight; (*b*) a. qn chevalier, to dub s.o. a knight. 2. *Chess:* *etc:* a. une pièce, to adjust a piece. 3. *Nav:* = radouber.

adoucir [adusiːr], *v.tr.* 1. to soften (voice, water); to tone down (contrast, colour); to subdue (light, one's tone); to sweeten (drink). 2. to alleviate, relieve, soothe, ease, assuage, mitigate, calm, allay (pain, sorrow, etc.). 3. to soften, pacify, mollify (person, animal). 4. to smooth down, polish (metal, wood); to smooth off (angle); to ease (curve). 5. (*a*) *Metall:* to let down (metal to quenching temperature); to temper; (*b*) *Metall:* to soften (cast iron); (*c*) *Glassm:* to polish (glass).

s'adoucir. 1. (*of voice*) to grow softer, to soften. 2. (*of weather*) to grow milder; (*of frost*) to yield, break. 3. (*of pain*) to be assuaged, mitigated; to grow less; to calm down. 4. (*of character*) to mellow.

adoucissage [adusisaːʒ], *s.m.* 1. smoothing, rough polishing; grinding. 2. *Metall:* (*a*) letting down (of metal to quenching temperature); tempering; (*b*) softening (of cast iron).

adoucissant [adusisɑ̃], *a.* & *s.m.* 1. *Med:* emollient, lenitive, demulcent (remedy); soothing (paste). 2. polishing (substance).

adoucissement [adusismɑ̃], *s.m.* 1. softening, mollifying, appeasement (of voice, temper, etc.); softening (of the truth). 2. alleviation, mitigation, assuagement, calming down (of pain, sorrow, etc.); l'a. de la température est dû à un anticyclone, the milder weather is due to an anticyclone. 3. smoothing off (of angles); easing (of curves); 4. (*a*) *Ind:* *Ch:* sweetening, softening; a. à l'air, air sweetening; a. au cuivre, copper sweetening; a. de l'eau, water softening; (*b*) *Metall:* *Tchn:* annealing; a. à la flamme, flame annealing.

adoucisseur, -euse [adusisœːr, -øːz], *s.* 1. *Sm.a:* *Artil:* fine-borer, finishing borer. 2. *Glassm:* *Metall:* (rough-)polisher. 3. *s.m.* a. d'eau, water-softener.

ad patres [adpatrɛs], *Lt. adv.phr.* *F:* envoyer a. p., to kill; *F:* to bump off.

adragante [adragɑ̃ːt], *a.f.* *Com:* *Pharm:* gomme a., gum tragacanth, gum dragon.

Adraste [adrast], *Pr.n.m.* *Myth:* Adrastus.

adrénaline [adrenalin], *s.f.* *Med:* adrenalin.

adresse [adrɛs], *s.f.* 1. (*a*) address, destination; écrire son a., to write down one's name and address; a. indéchiffrable, illegible address; lettre à l'a. de qn, letter addressed to s.o.; faire suivre une lettre à son a., to forward a letter to its destination; *F:* une observation à votre adresse, a dig at you; a remark aimed at you; c'est un compliment à votre a., it's a compliment to you; (*b*) section heading; headword (in dictionary). 2. (formal) address (to an assembly). 3. (*a*) skill, dexterity, adroitness; tour d'a., trick (of sleight-of-hand, etc.); feat (of skill, of dexterity); (*b*) shrewdness, adroitness, tact; dénué d'a., tactless, bungling (person); (*c*) craftiness, cunning, artfulness.

adresser [adrɛse, adrese], *v.tr.* 1. to address (packet, letter, etc.); lettre mal adressée, misdirected letter. 2. to recommend, direct; on m'a adressé à vous, I have been recommended to come to you; I have been referred to you; *A:* a. ses pas vers qn, qch., to turn, direct, one's steps towards s.o., sth. 3. to aim, address (remarks, reproaches, etc.); remarque adressée à qn, remark aimed at, intended for, meant for, s.o.; a. la parole à qn, to speak to, to address, s.o.; a. une prière à Dieu, to offer up a prayer to God; a. un sourire à qn, to smile at s.o.; a. une réprimande à qn, to administer a rebuke to s.o.

s'adresser. 1. to apply (à, to); **s'a. à qn pour avoir qch.**, to apply, make application, to s.o. for sth.; **"s'a. ici,"** "apply, enquire, here"; **adressez-vous à l'agent**, ask the policeman; *A: Dial:* **vous vous adressez mal**, you have come to the wrong person; *F:* to the wrong shop. 2. **s'a. à qn**, to address s.o., to speak to s.o.; **à qui pensez-vous vous a.?** to whom do you think you are speaking? 3. **s'a. à l'imagination, au bon sens, de qn**, to appeal to s.o.'s imagination, to s.o.'s common sense; **articles qui s'adressent à la femme**, articles that appeal to women; **c'est à vous que s'adresse cette observation**, that remark is meant for you.

adret [adrɛ], *s.m. Geog:* adret, (mountain) slope exposed to the sun.

Adriatique [adriatik]. 1. *a. Geog:* Adriatic. 2. *Pr.n.f.* **l'A.**, the Adriatic.

Adrien [adri(j)ɛ̃], *Pr.n.m.* 1. Adrian. 2. *Rom.Hist:* Hadrian.

Adrienne [adri(j)ɛn], *Pr.n.f.* Adrienne.

adroit [adrwa, -wɑ], *a.* 1. (*a*) dexterous, deft, skilful, handy; **il est a. dans la maison**, he is handy in the house; **être a. des mains, de ses mains**, to be skilful, good, clever, with one's hands, with one's fingers; to be handy; **joueur de football a. des pieds**, footballer clever at footwork; **a. à qch., à faire qch.**, dexterous, skilful, handy, at sth., at, in, doing sth.; **a. aux sports**, good at games; (*b*) **phrase adroite**, neat way of putting sth. 2. (*a*) shrewd, adroit (answer, diplomat); (*b*) artful, crafty (thief, liar).

adroitement [adrwatmɑ̃], *adv.* 1. skilfully, deftly, dexterously; **se servir a. de son crayon**, to be clever with one's pencil. 2. adroitly, shrewdly, artfully, cleverly.

adscrit [adskri], *a. Ling:* **iota a.**, iota adscript.

adsorber [adsɔrbe], *v.tr. Ph:* to adsorb.

adsorption [adsɔrpsjɔ̃], *s.f. Ph:* adsorption.

adulaire [adylɛ:r], *s.f. Lap:* moonstone, adularia.

adulateur, -trice [adylatœ:r, -tris]. 1. *a.* (*rare*) adulatory, flattering, fawning, sycophantic. 2. *s. Lit:* sycophant; toady; adulator, *f.* adulatress; flatterer.

adulatif, -ive [adylatif, -i:v], *a.* = ADULATEUR 1.

adulation [adylasjɔ̃], *s.f.* 1. *A:* adulation, (gross) flattery. 2. excessive admiration.

adulatoire [adylatwa:r], *a.* = ADULATEUR 1.

aduler [adyle], *v.tr.* 1. *O:* to adulate; to fawn upon (s.o.). 2. to heap admiration upon (s.o.).

adulte [adylt], *a. & s.* adult, grown-up, full-grown; **être arrivé à l'âge a.**, to be of adult age; **cours d'adultes**, courses of further education.

adultérant [adylterɑ̃]. 1. *a.* adulterating (ingredient). 2. *s.m.* adulterant.

adultérateur [adylteratœ:r], *s.m. A:* adulterator (of food); debaser (of coin).

adultération [adylterasjɔ̃], *s.f. A:* adulteration (of food, etc.); debasement, debasing (of coin); faking (of results); **a. d'un document**, falsification of, tampering with, a document.

adultère[1] [adyltɛ:r]. 1. *a.* adulterous. 2. *s.* adulterer, *f.* adulteress.

adultère[2], *s.m.* adultery; **commettre un a.**, to commit adultery (**avec**, with).

adultérer [adyltere], *v.tr.* (**j'adultère, n. adultérons; j'adultérerai**) *A:* to adulterate (food, etc.); to debase (coin); to fake (results); to falsify (document).

adultérin [adylterɛ̃], *a.* 1. adulterine (child). 2. *Hort:* hybrid.

adurol [adyrɔl], *s.m. Ch: Phot:* adurol.

aduste [adyst], *a.* (*rare*) sunburnt, scorched, burnt (complexion, etc.).

adustion [adystjɔ̃], *s.f. Med: A:* cauterization (of wound, etc.).

ad valorem [advalɔrɛm]. *Lt.adj.phr.* **payer des droits a. v.**, to pay an ad valorem duty.

advenir [advəni:r], *v.* (*conj. like* VENIR. *Used only in the third pers.*) to occur, happen; to come (about); to turn out. 1. *v.i.* **je ne sais ce qui en adviendra**, I don't know what will come of it, how it will turn out; **quand le cas adviendra**, when the case arises; **les événements advenus**, the events which have occurred; **advenant le décès de . . .**, in the event of the death of . . .; *Jur:* **le cas advenant que + sub.**, in the event of (something happening). 2. *v.impers.* **qu'est-il advenu de lui?** what has come of him? **il m'advient quelquefois d'oublier**, I sometimes happen to forget; **or, il advint que . . .**, now it chanced that . . .; **mais il est advenu que . . .**, but it turned out that . . .; **il advient qu'un compositeur écrive un bel opéra sur un livret médiocre**, it does happen that a composer will create a beautiful opera out of a poor libretto; **je ne sais ce qu'il en adviendra**, I don't know what will come of it; **il n'en advint que de la peine**, nothing but trouble came of it; **advienne que pourra, quoi qu'il advienne**, come what may; whatever happens.

adventice [advɑ̃tis], *a.* adventitious; casual (subject, weed, bud).

adventif, -ive [advɑ̃tif, -i:v], *a. Bot:* adventitious (root, etc.); *Geol:* parasitic (cone, etc.).

adventiste [advɑ̃tist], *a. & s. Rel:* adventist; **a. du septième jour**, Seventh-day Adventist.

adverbe [advɛrb], *s.m. Gram:* adverb.

adverbial, -aux [advɛrbjal, -o], *a. Gram:* adverbial; **locution adverbiale**, adverbial phrase.

adverbialement [advɛrbjalmɑ̃], *adv. Gram:* adverbially.

adversaire [advɛrsɛ:r], *s.m. & f.* (*a*) adversary, opponent, antagonist; (*b*) *Mil: Navy: Mil.Av:* enemy.

adversatif, -ive [advɛrsatif, -i:v], *a. Gram:* adversative (conjunction, etc.).

adverse [advɛrs], *a.* 1. (*a*) *Jur:* opposite, contrary, opposing, on the other side; **la partie adverse**, the opposing party, the other side; *Sp:* **l'équipe a.**, the opposing team; (*b*) adverse, unfortunate, unfavourable; **fortune adverse**, adverse fortune; adversity; bad luck; **critique adverse**, unfavourable criticism; (*c*) hostile. 2. *Bot:* adverse (leaves, anthers, etc.).

adversité [advɛrsite], *s.f.* 1. adversity, adverse circumstances; **être dans l'adversité**, to be in straitened circumstances. 2. misfortune, trial; **les adversités que Dieu nous envoie**, the misfortunes which God sends us.

advertance, advertence [advɛrtɑ̃:s], *s.f. Theol:* advertence, advertency; **pécher sans a.**, to sin inadvertently.

adynamie [adinami], *s.f. Med:* adynamia, adynamy; physical prostration.

adynamique [adinamik], *a. Med:* adynamic (state); prostrating (fever).

adyton, adytum [aditɔ̃, aditɔm], *s.m. Gr.Ant:* adyton, adytum.

aède [aɛd], *s.m. A.Lit:* (Greek) bard.

ægagropile [egagrɔpil], *s.m.* = ÉGAGROPILE.

ægériidés [eʒeriide], *s.m.pl. Ent:* Aegeriidæ.

ægle [egl̩], *s.m. Bot:* ægle.

ægocère [egɔsɛ:r], *s.m.* **ægocéros** [egɔserɔs], *s.m. Z:* egocerus.

ægopodium [egɔpɔdjɔm], *s.m. Bot:* ægopodium.

æpyornis [epjɔrnis], *s.m. Paleont:* æpyornis, *pl.* æpyornes.

aérable [aerabl̩], *a.* capable of ventilation, able to be ventilated, ventilable.

aérage [aera:ʒ], *s.m.* = AÉRATION.

aérateur, -trice [aeratœ:r, -tris]. 1. *a.* ventilating (system, etc.). 2. *s.m. Ind: etc:* ventilator, aerator, extractor fan.

aération [aerasjɔ̃], *s.f.* 1. ventilation, airing (of room, clothes, etc.); *Min:* **galerie d'a.**, ventilating course; **a. positive**, forced draught; **a. négative**, induced draught; **puits d'a.**, air-shaft; *s.a.* CLOISON 3; *Nau:* **sabord d'a.**, air-port, ventilation port. 2. aeration (of bread, water, etc.).

aéré [aere], *a.* (*a*) airy, well ventilated (room, etc.); (*b*) **couverture en maille aérée**, cellular blanket.

aérémie [aeremi], *s.f. Med:* aeremia.

aérenchyme [aerɑ̃ʃim], *s.m. Bot:* aerenchyma.

aérer [aere], *v.tr.* (**j'aère, n. aérons; j'aérerai**). 1. (*a*) to ventilate (mine); to air (room); **a. un malade**, to take an invalid for an airing; **il faut vous a. un peu**, you need (to go out for) a breath of air; (*b*) to air (linen); to expose (water) to the air. 2. to aerate (water, bread). 3. to space out; *Sch:* **vous auriez dû a. un peu votre discours**, you ought to have lightened your speech a bit.

aéricole [aerikɔl], *a. Bot:* aerial (orchid, etc.).

aéride [aerid], *s.f. Bot:* aeride.

aérien, -ienne [aerjɛ̃, -jɛn], *a.* 1. aerial, atmospheric (phenomenon, etc.); aerial (plant); **les couches aériennes**, the layers of the atmosphere; *Mil.Av:* **défense aérienne**, air defence; **les forces aériennes**, the air force; **attaque aérienne**, air raid; *Av:* **ligne aérienne**, airline; **poste aérienne**, airmail. 2. (light and) airy (footstep, texture). 3. (*a*) *Anat: O:* **voies aériennes**, air, wind, passages; (*b*) *Orn:* **sac a.**, air sac. 4. (*a*) *Mec.E: El.E: etc:* overhead (cable, conductor); **voie aérienne à câble**, aerial ropeway; (*b*) **voie ferrée aérienne, métro a.**, elevated railway. 5. *s.m. W.Tel: etc:* aerial, antenna.

aérifère [aerifɛ:r], *a.* air-conducting, aeriferous (pipe); air-bearing (vessel); *Anat:* **conduits aérifères**, air-, wind-passages.

ærifère [erifɛ:r], *a. Min: A:* copper-bearing (lode); copper (mine).

aérification [aerifikasjɔ̃], *s.f. Ch:* conversion into gas; aerification.

aérifier [aerifje], *v.tr. A:* (*p.d. & pr.sub.* **n. aérifiions, v. aérifiiez**), to aerify.

aériforme [aerifɔrm], *a.* aeriform, gaseous.

aériser [aerize], *v.tr. A:* to aerate (water, bread).

aérium [aerjɔm], *s.m.* (open-air) sanatorium.

aéro- [aerɔ-], *pref.* aero-; **aérophobie**, aerophobia.

aérobie [aerɔbi], *Biol:* 1. *a.* aerobic, aerobian (organism). 2. *s.m.* aerobe, aerobium, *pl.* aerobia. 3. *a. Aer:* aerobe.

aérobiose [aerɔbjo:z], *s.f. Biol:* aerobiosis.

aérobus [aerɔbys], *s.m. Av:* airbus, air-liner.

aérocâble [aerɔkɑbl̩], *s.m.* cableway.

aérocartographie [aerɔkartɔgrafi], *s.f.* aerocartography.

aérochimique [aerɔʃimik], *a.* **guerre a.**, aerochemical warfare, chemical warfare from the air; **attaque a.**, aerochemical attack, poison-gas attack from the air.

aérochir [aerɔʃi:r], *s.m. A: Mil:* (surgical) ambulance-plane.

aéro-club [aerɔklœb], *s.m.* flying-club, aero club; *pl. des aéro-clubs.*

aérocolie [aerɔkɔli], *s.f. Med:* aerocolia, aerocoly.

aérocondenseur [aerɔkɔ̃dɑ̃sœ:r], *s.m. Mec:* aerocondenser.

aérocyste [aerɔsist], *s.f. Algae:* air-bladder, aerocyst.

aérodrome [aerɔdro:m], *s.m. Av:* aerodrome, *U.S:* airdrome; airfield; **a. auxiliaire, de remplacement, de diversion**, alternative airfield; **a. de circonstance, de secours**, emergency airfield.

aérodynamicien [aerɔdinamisjɛ̃], *s.m.* aerodynamicist.

aérodynamique [aerɔdinamik], *Ph: Mec:* 1. *a.* aerodynamic (balance, etc.); **centre a.**, aerodynamic centre; **volets aérodynamiques**, aerodynamic surfaces; **carrosserie a.**, streamlined coachwork; *s.a.* TUNNEL. 2. *s.f.* aerodynamics.

aérodynamiste [aerɔdinamist], *s.m.* aerodynamicist.

aérodyne [aerɔdin], *s.m. Aer:* aerodyne.

aéro(-)élasticité [aerɔelastisite], *s.f.* aeroelasticity.

aéro(-)électronique [aerɔelɛktrɔnik], *s.f. Av:* avionics.

aéro(-)embolisme [aerɔɑ̃bɔlism], *s.m. Med:* aeroembolism.

aéroflotte [aerɔflɔt], *s.f.* air fleet.

aérofrein [aerɔfrɛ̃], *s.m. Av:* air-brake.

aérogare [aerɔgar], *s.f.* air(ways) terminal.

aérogastrie [aerɔgastri], *s.f. Med:* flatulence.

aérogène [aerɔʒɛn], *a. Med:* aerogenic.

aéroglisseur [aerɔglisœ:r], *s.m.* hovercraft.

aérogramme [aerɔgram], *s.m.* air letter (form).

aérographe [aerɔgraf]. 1. *s.m. & f. Meteor:* aerographer. 2. *s.m. Phot: Art:* air-brush; aerograph pencil.

aérographie [aerɔgrafi], *s.f.* aerography.

aérolit(h)e [aerɔlit], *s.m. Meteor:* aerolite, aerolith, meteorite.

aérologie [aerɔlɔʒi], *s.f.* meteorology, aerology.

aérologique [aerɔlɔʒik], *a.* meteorological, aerological.

aérologiste [aerɔlɔʒist], *s.m. & f.*, **aérologue** [aerɔlɔg], *s.m. & f.* aerologist.

aéromagnétique [aerɔmaɲetik], *a.* aeromagnetic.

aéromancie [aerɔmɑ̃si], *s.f.* aeromancy.

aéro-maritime [aerɔmaritim]. 1. *a.* air-sea (transport, etc.); **sauvetage a.-m.**, air-sea rescue. 2. *s.f.* marine aviation.

aéromètre [aerɔmɛtr̩], *s.m. Ph:* aerometer, air-poise.

aérométrie [aerɔmetri], *s.f.* aerometry.

aérométrique [aerɔmetrik], *a.* aerometric.

aéromodélisme [aerɔmɔdelism], *s.m.* (i) model aircraft construction; (ii) flying of model aircraft.

aéromoteur [aerɔmɔtœ:r], *s.m. Mch:* 1. windmill, wind-engine. 2. hot-air engine. 3. *A:* aero-engine.

aéronaute [aerɔno:t], *s.m.* aeronaut.

aéronautique [aerɔnotik]. 1. *a.* aeronautic(al); air (service, etc.). 2. *s.f.* aeronautics, aerial navigation; **ingénieur de l'a.**, aeronautical engineer; (*b*) **L'A. militaire** = the Air Force; **L'A. navale** = the Fleet Air Arm, *U.S:* the Naval Air Service.

aéronaval [aerɔnaval], *pl.* **-als.** 1. *a.* **la maîtrise aéronavale des Alliés**, the air and sea supremacy of the Allies. 2. *s.f.* **L'Aéronavale** = the Fleet Air Arm, Naval Aviation, *U.S:* the Naval Air Service; **l'aéronavale**, naval air forces.

aéronef [aerɔnɛf], *s.m.* 1. aircraft. 2. airship.

aéronomie [aerɔnɔmi], *s.f.* aeronomy.

aéro-otite [aerɔotit], *s.f. Med:* aero-otitis, aerotitis, aviator's ear.

aérophage [aerɔfa:ʒ], *s.m. & f. Med:* aerophagist.
aérophagie [aerɔfaʒi], *s.f. Med:* aerophagia.
aérophare [aerɔfa:r], *s.m. Av:* air beacon; aerial beacon.
aérophilatélie [aerɔfilateli], *s.f.* aerophilately.
aérophobie [aerɔfɔbi], *s.f.* aerophobia.
aérophotogrammétrie [aerɔfɔtɔgrametri], *s.f. Mapm:* air-photogrammetry.
aérophotogrammétrique [aerɔfɔtɔgrametrik), *a.* **levé, lever, a.,** aerial survey.
aérophotographie [aerɔfɔtɔgrafi], *s.f.* aerophotography, aerial photography.
aérophyte [aerɔfit], *a. & s.f. Bot:* aerophyte, epiphyte.
aéroplage [aerɔpla:ʒ], *s.f.* sand-yacht.
aéroplane [aerɔplan], *s.m. A:* (*now usu.* AVION) aeroplane, *U.S:* airplane.
aéroport [aerɔpɔ:r], *s.m.* airport.
aéroportable [aerɔpɔrtabl̩], *a.* transportable by air.
aéroporté [aerɔpɔrte], *a.* airborne; **troupes aéroportées,** airborne forces.
aéropostal, -aux [aerɔpɔstal, -o], *a.* airmail.
aéroroute [aerɔrut], *s.f. Av:* air-route, airway.
aéroscope [aerɔskɔp], *s.m. Bac: Meteor:* aeroscope.
aéroscopie [aerɔskɔpi], *s.f.* aeroscopy.
aérosite [aerɔzit], *s.f. Miner:* = PYRARGYRITE.
aérosol [aerɔsɔl, -zɔl], *s.m.* aerosol.
aérosolthérapie [aerɔsɔlterapi], *s.f. Med:* aerosol therapy.
aérosondage [aerɔsɔ̃da:ʒ], *s.m.* sounding of the atmosphere (by means of balloons).
aérospatial, -aux [aerɔspasjal, -o], *a.* aerospace (equipment, etc.).
aérosphère [aerɔsfɛ:r], *s.f.* aerosphere.
aérostat [aerɔsta], *s.m.* aerostat; lighter-than-air craft; balloon; airship.
aérostation [aerɔstasjɔ̃], *s.f: A:* (*a*) ballooning, aerostation, aeronautics; (*b*) *Mil.Av:* **L'A.,** the Balloon Service.
aérostatique [aerɔstatik]. **1.** *a.* aerostatic(al). **2.** *s.f.* aerostatics.
aérostier [aerɔstje], *s.m. Mil.Hist:* aeronaut; balloon (i) pilot, (ii) observer; **corps d'aérostiers militaires,** balloon corps.
aérotechnique [aerɔteknik], *a. & s.f.* **1.** *a.* aerotechnical. **2.** *s.f.* aerotechnics.
aérothérapie [aerɔterapi], *s.f.* aerotherapeutics.
aérotherme [aerɔterm], *s.m.* unit heater.
aérothermique [aerɔtermik], *a.* aerothermic.
aérothermodynamique [aerɔtermodinamik], *s.f.* aerothermodynamics *pl.*
aérotonomètre [aerɔtɔnɔmɛtr̥], *s.m. Med:* aerotonometer.
aérotonométrie [aerɔtɔnɔmetri], *s.f. Med:* aerotonometry.
aérotorpille [aerɔtɔrpij], *s.f.* aerial torpedo.
aérotrain [aerɔtrɛ̃], *s.m.* aerotrain, hover-train.
aérotransportable [aerɔtrɑ̃spɔrtabl̩], *a.* transportable by air.
aérotransporté [aerɔtrɑ̃spɔrte], *a.* air transported.
aérotransporter [aerɔtrɑ̃spɔrte], *v.tr.* to transport, carry, by air.
aérotriangulation [aerɔtriɑ̃gylasjɔ̃], *s.f.* stereotriangulation.
aérotropisme [aerɔtrɔpism], *s.m.* aerotropism.
æschynomène [eskinɔmɛn], *s.f. Bot:* sola; **casque colonial en moelle d'æ.,** sola topee.
æsthésiomètre [estezjɔmɛtr̥], *s.m. Physiol:* aesthesiometer.
æthuse [ety:z], *s.f. Bot:* aethusa, fools' parsley, lesser hemlock.
ætite [etit], **aétite** [aetit], *s.f. Miner:* aetites, eagle-stone.
Aétius [aesjys], *Pr.n.m. A.Hist:* Aetius.
affabilité [afabilite], *s.f.* graciousness, affability (**avec, envers,** to, towards).
affable [afabl̩], *a.* gracious, affable, kindly (**à, avec, envers,** to, towards, with).
affablement [afabləmɑ̃], *adv.* graciously, affably, with affability.
affabulation [afabylasjɔ̃], *s.f.* (*a*) plot (of a novel); (*b*) *A:* moral (of a fable).
affabuler [afabyle], *v.i.* to work out the plot (of a novel).
affadir [afadi:r], *v.tr.* **1.** (*a*) to render (food, etc.) insipid, tasteless; (*b*) **cela m'affadit le cœur,** it makes me feel rather sick. **2.** to make (sth.) dull, uninteresting, spiritless; **a. une anecdote,** to take the point out of an anecdote; **a. un chapitre,** to take all the interest, *F:* all the pep, out of a chapter.
s'affadir, to become insipid, to lose flavour.
affadissant [afadisɑ̃], *a.* which saps the vitality.
affadissement [afadismɑ̃], *s.m.* **1.** (*a*) loss of flavour (of food, etc.); (*b*) **a. de cœur,** nausea. **2.** making, growing, dull, insipid, flat; dulling (of taste, etc.).
affaiblir [afɛbli:r, -e-], *v.tr.* **1.** to weaken; (*a*) to enfeeble, debilitate; **s'a. la santé,** to impair one's health; **affaibli par la maladie,** weakened by illness; *Fin:* **a. la monnaie,** to debase the currency; (*b*) to lessen, reduce; **a. le courage de qn,** to damp s.o.'s courage; **a. la vérité,** to water down the truth; **a. une teinte,** to weaken, lighten, a tint; *Phot:* **a. un cliché,** to reduce (the contrasts of) a negative. **2.** *Carp:* to reduce the thickness of (plank, etc.).
s'affaiblir, to grow, become, weak(er), feeble(r), to lose one's strength; **le bruit s'affaiblit,** the sound is growing fainter; **ses forces s'affaiblissaient,** his strength was flagging; **la tempête s'affaiblit,** the storm is abating; *Nau:* **la marée, le vent, s'affaiblit,** the tide, the wind, is taking off.
affaiblissant [afɛblisɑ̃, -e-], *a.* weakening, enfeebling, debilitating.
affaiblissement [afɛblismɑ̃, -e-], *s.m.* **1.** (*a*) weakening, diminution (of strength, power, etc.); **a. d'odorat,** loss of sense of smell; (*b*) lessening, reducing; *El.E:* attenuation; **constante d'a.,** attenuation constant; *Phot:* **a. d'un cliché,** reducing of a negative; **agent d'a.,** reducing agent; (*c*) **a. d'une couleur,** fading of a colour. **2.** (state of) debility, enfeeblement, weakness.
affaiblisseur, -euse [afɛblisœ:r, -e-, -ø:z], *Phot:* **1.** *a.* reducing (bath, etc.). **2.** *s.m.* reducer, reducing agent.
affainéantir [afɛneɑ̃ti:r], *v.tr. O:* to render (s.o.) idle, lazy, slothful.
s'affainéantir. *A:* to become idle, lazy; to get into idle ways.
affaire [afɛ:r], *s.f.* **1.** (*a*) business, affair, concern; **savoir, connaître, son a.,** to know what one is doing, to know one's business; **ce n'est pas votre a.,** it's no business, concern of yours, it's none of your business; **c'est son a. (à lui),** that's his business, concern, *F:* his look-out, his pigeon; **ça, c'est l'a. du gérant,** (i) that is a matter, case, for the manager; (ii) that's the manager's business; **c'est l'a. d'un médecin,** it's a case for a doctor; **faire son a. de qch.,** (i) to specialize in sth.; (ii) to take charge of a matter; **j'en fais mon a.,** leave it to me, I will deal with it; **avoir pour unique a. de, n'avoir d'autre a. que de . . .,** to have nothing else to do except . . .; **ce métier n'est pas l'a. de tout le monde,** this trade is not everybody's job; **le théâtre est son a.,** he's in his element in the theatre; **être à son a.,** to be in one's element; **ne pas être à son a.,** to feel thoroughly ill at ease; **être tout à son a.,** to be wrapped up in what one is doing; (*b*) question, matter, affair; **a. d'intérêt, d'argent,** money matter; **a. de cœur, d'amour,** (love) affair; **l'a. du salut est la plus importante pour un chrétien,** the question of salvation is the most important one for a Christian; **affaire de conscience,** matter of conscience; **c'est (une) a. de goût,** it's a matter, question, of taste; **a. difficile,** difficult question; **a. épineuse,** thorny problem; **a. sans conséquence,** affair, matter, of no consequence, no importance; **c'est une a. de rien,** it's a trifling matter; **ce n'est que l'a. d'un instant,** it won't take a minute; **ce sera l'a. de cent francs,** it will be a matter of a hundred francs; **ça, c'est une autre a.,** that's another question altogether, that alters the case; **arranger une a.,** to solve a problem, to settle sth.; **le plus beau de l'a. c'est que . . .,** the best of the business, of the story, is that . . .; *A:* **point d'a.!** that's out of the question!; (*c*) thing, person, required; **faire l'a. de qn.,** to answer s.o.'s purpose; **ça fait, c'est, juste mon a.,** it's just what I need; it's the very thing (I was wanting); **cela ne fait pas l'a.,** it won't do, it's not suitable; **cela fera-t-il l'a.?** will that do? *F:* will that fill the bill?; **j'ai quelque chose qui ferait l'a.,** I have something that would do, suit, meet the case; **j'ai votre a.,** I have the very thing, person, you want; **il fera votre a.,** he is the very man for you; *F:* **il a fait ses affaires,** he has made his pile, his fortune; **faire son a. à qn,** (i) *F:* to give s.o. what (he is asking) for; (ii) *P:* to do s.o. in, to bump s.o. off; *Iron:* **son a. est faite,** he is done for, it's all up with him, *F:* he's had it; (*d*) (i) (serious, difficult) business, thing, matter; **vilaine, fâcheuse, sale, a.,** nasty, unpleasant, business; **c'est une malheureuse a.,** it's an unfortunate business; **ce n'est pas une a.,** it's not such a serious business, it's no great matter, think nothing of it; *F:* there's nothing to it; **ce n'est pas une petite a., c'est toute une a.,** it's quite an undertaking, quite a proposition, quite a (big) business; **je n'en fais pas une a.,** I don't make an issue of it; **en voilà une a.!** (i) here's a pretty kettle of fish!; (ii) what a lot of fuss about nothing!; *Iron:* **la belle a. (que cela)!,** is *that* all? *F:* what of it? *F:* so what? (ii) **tirer qn d'a.,** to get s.o. out of a difficulty, out of a tight corner; **être hors, tiré, d'a.,** to be out of one's difficulties, to be out of the wood; (*of sick person*) to be out of danger; **se tirer d'a.,** to get out of a difficulty, *F:* to save one's bacon; **se tirer d'a. le mieux possible,** to make the best of a bad bargain; **se tirer d'a. tant bien que mal,** to muddle through; **il sait se tirer d'a.,** he knows how to manage, how to make shift, how to get out of a difficulty; **s'attirer des affaires,** to get into trouble; **s'attirer une (mauvaise) a.,** to get into trouble, into a scrape, into hot water; **faire toute une a. de qch.,** to make a fuss over sth.; **se faire toute une a. de qch.,** *F:* to get all hot and bothered, all worked up, all het up, over sth.; **susciter des affaires à qn,** to get s.o. into trouble, into difficulties; **vous me faites des affaires pour dix francs!** all this fuss about ten francs! **2.** (*a*) affair, business, transaction, deal, (financial) venture; **faire, conclure, une a.,** to make, conclude, a deal; **traiter une a. avec qn,** to transact business with s.o.; **grosse, petite, a.,** big, small, deal; **(bonne) a.,** sound transaction; good speculation, good bargain, good buy; **une mauvaise a.,** a bad bargain; **a. d'or,** first-class speculation; splendid bargain; **c'est une a. d'or,** it will be a gold mine; **ils font des affaires d'or,** they are doing a roaring trade; they are making money hand over fist; they are simply coining money; **faire une bonne a.,** to get a bargain; to do a good stroke of business; *Iron:* **il a fait de belles affaires,** pretty things he's been up to! **faire a. avec qn,** to come to an agreement, to settle a deal, with s.o.; to do business with s.o.; **faire des affaires avec qn,** to do business with s.o.; **c'est une a. entendue!** agreed! it's agreed, it's fixed; **c'est une a. faite!** done! that's settled! **votre nomination est une a. faite,** your appointment is as good as settled; (*b*) **une grosse a.,** a large firm; **son usine est une grande a.,** his factory is a very big concern; **administrer, conduire, gérer, diriger, une a.,** to run a business; **s'intéresser dans, prendre part à, une a.,** to take an interest in a business; **se retirer d'une a.,** to back out, sell out, of a business; **être à la tête d'une a.,** to be at the head of a business; (*c*) **avoir a. avec qn,** to do business with s.o.; **avoir a. à qn,** to deal, have to deal, have to do, with s.o.; to have business with s.o.; **j'ai a. à vous,** I want a word with you; **vous aurez a. à moi,** (i) you will be hearing from me, you will hear from me again; (ii) *F:* I'll settle your hash! **je suis heureux de n'avoir plus a. à eux,** I'm glad to have no further dealings with them; **avoir a. à forte partie,** to be up against a strong opponent, to have met one's match; **qu'ai-je a. de toutes ces querelles, elles ne me regardent pas,** what have I to do with all these quarrels, they do not concern me. **3.** *pl.* (*a*) things, belongings; **ranger ses affaires,** to put away one's things; (*b*) business, trade; **chiffre d'affaires,** turnover; volume of business; **centre d'affaires,** business centre; **lettre d'affaires,** business letter; **homme d'affaires,** (i) business man; (ii) agent; (iii) steward, bailiff; (iv) lawyer; **bureau, agence, cabinet, d'affaires,** (i) (general) agency; (ii) estate agency; **parler affaires,** to talk business; *F:* to talk shop; **venir pour affaires,** to come on business; **déjeuner d'affaires,** business lunch; **avoir le génie des affaires,** to have a good head for business; **les affaires sont les affaires,** business is business; **quel est son genre d'affaires?** what's his line of business? **entrer dans les affaires,** to go into business; **il est dans les affaires,** he's in business; **mettre qn dans les affaires,** to set s.o. up in business; **faire des affaires,** to do business; **comment vont les affaires?** how's business? **les affaires vont mal,** business is bad; **faire de bonnes, de belles affaires,** to be successful (in business); **faire de mauvaises affaires,** to be doing badly, to be in difficulties; to work at a loss; **faire des affaires importantes,** to be in a large way of business; **être au-dessus de ses affaires,** to be doing well; (*c*) (public) affairs; **le courant des affaires,** the course of events; **les affaires de l'État,** affairs of State; **ce n'est pas une a. d'État,** it's a matter of no importance; **les Affaires étrangères,** foreign affairs; *Fr.C:* **les Affaires Extérieures,** External Affairs; **le ministère des Affaires étrangères** = the Foreign Office, *U.S:* the State Department; **affaires privées, domestiques,** private, domestic affairs; **arranger, régler ses affaires, mettre de l'ordre dans ses affaires,** to

put one's affairs in order; **s'occuper, se mêler, de ses (propres) affaires,** to mind one's own business; **raconter ses affaires,** to talk about one's own affairs; **les affaires temporelles et les affaires spirituelles,** affairs temporal and affairs spiritual; *F:* **faire ses affaires,** to go to the lavatory, to do one's duty; *F:* **elle a ses affaires,** she's got the curse. **4.** *Jur:* case, lawsuit; **plaider une a.,** to plead a case; **a. civile,** civil action; civil proceedings; **impliquer qn dans une a.,** to implicate s.o. in a case; **l'A. Dreyfus,** *F:* **l'Affaire,** the Dreyfus case; *F:* **son a. est claire,** I'll settle, I've settled, him. **5.** *(a)* **a. (d'honneur),** duel; *(b) F:* row, disturbance; *(c)* scandal; **quelle a.!** a *nice* business! **6.** *Mil:* engagement; **c'était la première fois que notre bataillon prenait part à une grosse a.,** it was the first time our battalion saw any heavy fighting; **l'a. d'Agadir,** the Agadir incident, affair.

affairé [afere], *a.* busy; **faire l'a.,** to pretend to be busy, to fuss around; **porteurs affairés,** bustling porters; **gens affairés de rien,** people busy, fussing, about trifles; **ils entraient et sortaient d'un air a.,** they were bustling in and out.

affairement [afɛrmɑ̃], *s.m.* **1.** hurry, bustle. **2. un grand a. à propos de rien,** a great ado, fuss, about nothing.

affairer (s') [safere], *v.pr.* to lead a busy life, to bustle about; **s'a. autour de qn,** to fuss round s.o.; **s'a. à tout remettre en place,** to busy oneself putting things away, tidying everything up.

affairisme [aferism], *s.m.* *(a)* intrusion of business into politics; *(b)* exclusive preoccupation with business deals.

affairiste [aferist], *s.m.* unscrupulous business man.

affaissé [afese], *a.* **1.** sunken (plain, etc.); sagging (beam, etc.). **2.** depressed (patient).

affaissement [afɛsmɑ̃], *s.m.* **1.** *(a)* subsidence, giving way; collapse (of floor, roof, tyre, etc.); sinking (in), settling (of foundation, wall, etc.); deflection (of materials); sagging (of floor, beam); depression (of rail); flabbiness (of muscles); *Pol.Ec:* **a. des prix,** drop in prices; *(b)* break up (of physical strength). **2.** depression, dejection, despondency; *Med:* prostration.

affaisser [afese], *v.tr.* **1.** to cause (sth.) to subside, sink, collapse; to cause (beam, etc.) to sag; to cause (earth) to settle. **2.** *(a)* to bend down, weigh down; **fleurs affaissées par le vent,** flowers blown down by the wind; *(b)* to depress, weigh down (by trouble, grief).

s'affaisser. 1. *(a)* *(of thg)* to subside, give way, cave in, collapse, sink in; *Pol.Ec:* **les cours s'affaissent,** prices are dropping; *(of material)* to give, yield; *(of beam, etc.)* to sag; *(of earth)* to settle; *(of ground)* to fall away; *(b)* *(of pers.)* to sink down, sink back (in chair); to crumple up, collapse; *(c)* **il s'affaisse de jour en jour,** he is gradually sinking. **2.** *(a)* to become bent, bowed down (by age); to sink (under weight); *(b)* to become depressed, dejected, downhearted.

affaitage, affaîtage [afɛtaːʒ], *s.m.,* **affaitement, affaîtement** [afɛtmɑ̃], *s.m.* manning, training (of hawk).

affaiter, affaîter [afete], *v.tr.* to man, to train (a hawk).

affaiteur, affaîteur [afetœːr], *s.m.* trainer (of hawks).

affalement [afalmɑ̃], *s.m. F:* **1.** discouragement, depression; exhaustion. **2. l'a. final,** the final crash, ruin.

affaler [afale], *v.tr. Nau:* **1.** *(a)* to haul down, overhaul (tackle, rope); *(b)* to pay down (rope). **2.** to lower (object); **affale!** lower away!

s'affaler. 1. *Nau:* *(a)* **s'a. par un cordage,** to slide down a rope; *(b)* *(of ship)* **s'a. à la côte,** to get embayed on a leeshore. **2.** *F:* *(a)* to sink to the ground; *(b)* **s'a. dans un fauteuil,** to drop, sink, *F:* flop, into an armchair; *Sch:* **ne vous affalez pas!** sit up! don't loll! *(c)* to confess, to come clean.

affamant [afamɑ̃], *a.* that causes hunger; **régime a.,** starvation diet; **l'air a. de la plage,** the sea air that gives one such an appetite.

affamé, -ée [afame], *a. & s.* hungry, starving, ravenous, famished (person); **regarder qch. d'un œil a.,** to look hungrily at sth; **être a. de qch.,** to hunger, hanker, after sth., to crave, yearn, long, for (pleasure, praise, etc.); **a. de savoir,** hungry for knowledge; *s.a.* VENTRE 1.

affamement [afammɑ̃], *s.m.* **1.** (act of) starving (s.o.). **2.** starvation.

affamer [afame], *v.tr.* to starve (s.o.); to deprive (s.o.) of food; *Med:* **s'a.,** to follow a starvation diet.

affameur [afamœːr], *s.m.* starver; **affameurs du peuple,** starvers of the people.

affangissements [afɑ̃ʒismɑ̃], *s.m.pl.* mud-bank(s) (in river-bed).

afféagement [afeaʒmɑ̃], *s.m. A.Jur:* subinfeudation.

afféager [afeaʒe], *v.tr.* **(afféageant, n. afféageons),** *A.Jur:* to grant (land) by subinfeudation; to subfeu.

affect [afɛkt], *s.m. Psy:* affect.

affectable [afɛktabl̩], *a.* **1.** impressionable; easily affected, excited or upset. **2.** *Jur:* (land) that may be mortgaged.

affectant [afɛktɑ̃], *a. O:* affecting, touching (story, scene, etc.).

affectation [afɛktasjɔ̃], *s.f.* **1.** affectation; *(a)* affectedness, conceit; **parler avec a.,** to talk affectedly; **sans a.,** unaffectedly; *(b)* simulation, pretence, show; **avec une a. de genérosité,** with an affectation, a show, of generosity; *(c) A:* predilection, partiality **(pour,** for). **2.** *(a)* **a. de qch. à qch.,** assignment, attribution, of sth. to a purpose; appropriation for a purpose; allotment (of money) to a purpose; *Fin:* **a. aux réserves,** allocation to reserve funds; **a. aux actions,** sum available for dividend; **a. de fonds,** appropriation of funds; **a. hypothécaire,** mortgage charge; *For:* **a. périodique,** periodic block; *(b) Mil: etc.* assignment, allotment, posting; **recevoir une a.,** to be posted; **nouvelle a.,** reassignment, reallotment, reposting; *Mil:* **a. d'unité à unité,** cross-posting; **avoir une, être en, a. spéciale** = to be in a reserved occupation.

affecté [afɛkte]. **1.** *a.* affected, conceited (person, manners, etc.); mincing (gait); **sourire a.,** simper. **2.** *s.m. Mil:* **a. spécial** = man in a reserved occupation; **être a. spécial,** to be in a reserved occupation.

affecter [afɛkte], *v.tr.* **1.** *(a)* **a. qch. à un certain usage,** to assign sth. to, to appropriate, set apart, earmark, allocate, sth. for, a certain use; **porte exclusivement affectée à la sortie,** exit only; *(b) Mil:* to detail, tell off, post, draft (soldier, detachment, for a particular service); **il sait se débrouiller; il s'est fait affecter à la météo . . .,** he knows the ropes; he got himself assigned to the met . . .; *Navy:* **être affecté à un navire,** to be posted to a ship. **2.** to affect, pretend, feign, simulate; **a. la mort,** to feign death; **a. de faire qch.,** to affect, pretend to do sth. **3.** to affect; to make great use of; to have a predilection for, a partiality for, to give preference to (sth.). **4.** to assume, take on (shape, colour, etc.). **5.** *(a)* to affect, move, touch (s.o.'s feelings); **vivement affecté par, de, la nouvelle,** much moved by the news; **il s'affecte aisément,** he is easily affected; *(b)* to affect, to have an effect upon, to concern (career, opinion, health, etc.); **loi qui affecte l'Alsace,** law that concerns Alsace; **ce gaz affecte les poumons,** this gas affects the lungs; **la grève affecte plusieurs usines,** the strike hits several factories; *Jur:* **domaine affecté d'hypothèques,** mortgaged, burdened, estate; *Mth:* **quantité affectée d'un exposant,** quantity bearing an index.

affectif, -ive [afɛktif, -iːv], *a.* affective; emotional; **pour des raisons affectives,** for emotional reasons.

affection [afɛksjɔ̃], *s.f.* affection. **1.** fondness, attachment, liking **(pour,** for); **faire qch. par a. pour qn,** to do sth. out of affection for s.o.; **porter de l'a. à qn, avoir qn en a.,** to be fond of s.o.; **nourrir une sincère a. pour qn,** to entertain a sincere affection for s.o.; **prendre qn en a., se prendre d'a. pour qn,** to become attached, to take a fancy, to s.o.; **placer son a. sur qn,** to set one's affections on s.o.; **avec a.,** affectionately. **2.** mental state; **les affections de l'âme,** the affections of the mind. **3.** *Med:* disease, complaint; **a. de la vue,** defect of eyesight; **a. courante,** common ailment.

affectionné [afɛksjɔne], *a.* affectionate, loving; *(at end of letter)* **votre affectionné(e) . . .,** your affectionate . . ., affectionately yours . . .

affectionnément [afɛksjɔnemɑ̃], *adv.* affectionately, lovingly.

affectionner [afɛksjɔne], *v.tr.* **1. a. qn, qch.,** to have an affection, a liking, a fondness, for s.o., sth.; to love, like, be fond of, s.o., sth.; to have a predilection for sth.; **le genre de robe qu'elle affectionne,** the style of dress she likes, persists in, wearing; **affectionné de tous,** loved by all. **2. s'a. qn,** to gain s.o.'s affection.

s'affectionner. *A:* **s'a. à qn, à qch.,** to become fond of, conceive a liking for, s.o., sth.

affectivité [afɛktivite], *s.f. Psy:* affectivity.

affectueusement [afɛktɥøzmɑ̃], *adv.* affectionately, lovingly, fondly.

affectueux, -euse [afɛktɥø, -øːz], *a.* affectionate, loving, fond.

affectuosité [afɛktɥozite], *s.f.* affectionateness.

affenage [afnaːʒ], *s.m. Husb:* foddering, feeding (of cattle).

affener [afne], *v.tr.* **(j'affène, n. affenons, j'affènerai)** *Husb:* to feed, fodder (cattle).

affenoir [afnwar], *s.m. Husb:* trap-door (of hayloft).

afférent[1] [aferɑ̃], *a.* **1.** assignable **(à,** to); **traitement a. à un emploi,** salary attaching to a post; **crédits afférents au budget,** credits falling into the budget; **les frais afférents à un achat,** the expenses incurred in making a purchase; **contributions afférentes à une terre,** rates assignable to an estate; *Jur:* **portion afférente à qn,** share falling (by right) to s.o., portion accruing to s.o. **2.** relating **(à,** to); **renseignements afférents à une affaire,** information relating to a matter.

afférent[2], *a. Anat:* afferent (vessel).

affermable [afɛrmabl̩], *a. Jur:* **1.** *(of farm, etc.)* *(a)* rentable; *(b)* leasable, demisable. **2.** *A:* **impôts affermables,** farmable taxes.

affermage [afɛrmaːʒ], *s.m.* **1.** *(a)* renting (of farm, land, etc.); *(b)* leasing; *(c)* contracting (for advertisements, etc.); *(d) A:* **a. des impôts,** farming (of) the taxes. **2.** rent (of land, farm).

affermataire [afɛrmatɛːr], *s.m. & f. A:* tenant farmer.

affermateur, -trice [afɛrmatœːr, -tris], *s. A:* lessor (of farm, etc.).

affermer [afɛrme], *v.tr.* **1.** *(a)* to lease (farm, etc.); *(b)* to let out (sth. on contract); *(c) A:* to farm out (taxes). **2.** *(a)* to rent; to take (land, etc.) on lease; *(b)* to contract for (sth.).

affermir [afɛrmiːr], *v.tr.* **1.** to strengthen, to harden, steady, make firm (pillar, table, foundations, etc.); to firm (the soil); **il affermit sa casquette,** he settled his cap (more) firmly on his head. **2.** to strengthen, establish, consolidate (power, credit, belief, health, etc.); **a. qn dans une croyance,** to strengthen s.o. in a belief.

s'affermir, to become stronger, firmer; to harden; **la gelée s'affermit,** the jelly is setting.

affermissement [afɛrmismɑ̃], *s.m.* **1.** Strengthening (of foundations, etc.); consolidation, strengthening (of power, credit, etc.). **2.** hardening (of road, muscle); setting (of jelly, etc.). **3.** support, strengthener; **la crainte est un a. de la vertu,** virtue is strengthened by a sense of fear.

affété [afete], *a. A:* affected, simpering, namby-pamby (air, tone); mincing (step); pretty-pretty (style).

afféterie [afetri], *s.f.* **1.** *Lit:* affectation, primness; affected manner. **2.** *pl. A:* simpering, mincing.

affichage [afiʃaːʒ], *s.m.* *(a)* bill-sticking, -posting; placarding, posting up (of bills); **tableau d'a.,** (i) notice-board; (ii) *Trans:* arrivals and departures (board); (iii) *Sp: Turf:* telegraph board, *U.S:* billboard, bulletin board; *(b)* show, display, flaunting (of opinions, etc.); *(c) Elcs:* display; *(d) Av:* visual indicator.

affichant [afiʃɑ̃], *a.* loud, showy, ostentatious (person, dress).

affiche [afiʃ], *s.f.* **1.** *(a)* **a. (murale),** placard, poster, bill; *Adm:* **a. blanche, sur papier blanc,** public notice (exempt from stamp duty); **a. à la main,** handbill; **a. illustrée,** picture poster; **poser une a.,** to stick a bill; **panneau à affiches,** hoarding; **annoncer une vente par voie d'affiches,** to bill, placard, a sale; **a. de théâtre,** play-bill; *Th:* **mettre une pièce à l'a.,** to bill a play; **la pièce a tenu l'a., est restée à l'a., pendant six mois,** the play ran for six months, had a six month's run, was on for six months; *Th:* **quitter l'a.,** to come off; **renouveler l'a.,** to change the bill; **faire, être en, tête d'a.,** to head, top, the bill; *(b)* stamp, mark, sign (of fault, quality). **2.** *Adm:* = AFFICHAGE.

affichement [afiʃmɑ̃], *s.m.* = AFFICHAGE.

afficher [afiʃe], *v.tr.* **1.** to post (up), stick (up), placard, display (bill, notice, etc.); **a. une vente,** to advertise, *U.S:* post a sale; *Th:* **a. une pièce,** to bill a play; **"défense d'a.," "stick,** *U.S:* **post, no bills", "billposting prohibited";** *F:* **c'est affiché,** it's a cert, it's in the bag. **2.** to parade, to show (off), to expose, air, flaunt (sth.); to make a display, a show, of (sth.); **a. son savoir,** to air, show off, one's knowledge; **a. son ignorance,** to expose, show, one's ignorance; **a. ses opinions,** to air, flaunt, one's opinions; **a. sa pauvreté,** to parade one's poverty; **a. des prétentions ridicules,** to set up ridiculous pretentions; **a. l'insouciance,** to show ostentatious carelessness.

s'afficher, to show off, to attract notice, to seek notoriety; **s'a. avec une femme,** to be seen everywhere with a woman.
affichette [afiʃɛt], *s.f.* small poster.
afficheur [afiʃœːr], *s.m.* bill-sticker, bill-poster.
affichiste [afiʃist], *s.m. & f.* poster artist, designer.
affidavit [afidavit], *s.m. Jur:* affidavit.
affidé, -ée [afide]. **1.** *a. A:* trusty, trustworthy, confidential (friend, servant). **2.** *s.* (*a*) *Pej:* confederate; **les affidés seuls connaissent ce fait,** only those who are in the know are acquainted with this fact; (*b*) secret agent, spy; **a. de la police,** police spy.
affilage [afilaːʒ], *s.m.* whetting (of scythe, etc.); sharpening (of sword, etc.); setting (of razor, saw, etc.).
affilé [afile], *a.* sharp (knife, etc.); **langue affilée,** (i) sharp tongue, (ii) glib tongue.
affilée [afile], *s.f.* (*used only in the adv. phr.* **d'a.,** *occ.* **à l'a.**); **cinq heures d'a.,** five hours at a stretch, at a time, on end; **pendant des heures d'a.,** for hours together; **lire vingt chapitres d'a.,** to read twenty chapters off the reel; **dormir neuf heures d'a.,** to sleep for nine hours solid.
affilement [afilmɑ̃], *s.m.* = AFFILAGE.
affiler [afile], *v.tr.* **1.** to sharpen, set, whet, to give an edge to, to put an edge on (blade, etc.). **2.** to (wire-)draw (gold, silver).
affilerie [afilri], *s.f. Ind:* grinding-shop, grindery.
affileur [afilœːr], *s.m.* sharpener, grinder (of tools).
affiliation [afiljasjɔ̃], *s.f.* affiliation.
affilié, -ée [afilje]. **1.** *a.* affiliated. **2.** *s.* (affiliated) member, associate; **a. à la Sécurité Sociale,** registered with the "*Sécurité Sociale*".
affilier [afilje], *v.tr.* (*p.d. & pr. sub.* **n. affiliions, v. affiliiez**) to affiliate (à, to, with); **la banque A s'est affilié la banque B,** the bank A has affiliated the bank B.
s'affilier à un parti, to affiliate oneself with, to join, a party; **s'a. à une bande de voleurs,** to join a band of thieves; to become an associate of thieves; **s'a. à un complot,** to join in a conspiracy.
affiloir [afilwaːr], *s.m. Tls:* (*a*) oilstone, hone, whetstone; (*b*) (razor) strop; (*c*) knife-sharpener; steel; (*d*) knife-sharpening machine.
affiloire [afilwaːr], *s.f. Tls:* oilstone.
affin [afɛ̃]. **1.** *a.* (*a*) related (by marriage); (*b*) akin, closely connected; **deux métiers affins,** two closely connected trades. **2.** *s.m. Jur:* relation (by marriage); connection, kinsman.
affinage [afinaːʒ], *s.m.* **1.** (*a*) *Metall:* fining, refining; **a. des minerais de fer,** smelting of iron ores; **a. de l'or, de l'argent,** refining of gold, of silver; **a. au vent,** converting; (*b*) ripening, maturing (of wine, cheese). **2.** pointing (of nails, needles, etc.). **3.** (*a*) thinning, fining down (of plank, etc.); (*b*) *Tex:* (fine-)shearing, cropping (of cloth). **4.** *Tex:* hackling (of hemp); dressing (of flax).
affinement [afinmɑ̃], *s.m.* refinement; **l'a. de l'intelligence,** sharpening of the intelligence; **l'a. du goût,** refinement of taste.
affiner [afine], *v.tr.* **1.** (*a*) to improve, refine, make better; **a. son goût en lisant,** to improve one's taste by reading; **devenir plus affiné,** to become more polished, more refined; (*b*) *Metall:* to (re)fine (iron, gold); **acier affiné,** refined steel, shear steel; (*c*) to ripen, mature (wine, cheese, etc.). **2.** (*a*) to sharpen (the intelligence, wits, etc.); (*b*) to point (nails, needles, etc.). **3.** (*a*) to thin, fine down (board, etc.); (*b*) *Tex:* to crop, shear (cloth). **4.** *Tex:* to hackle (hemp). **5.** *Agr:* to loosen, break up (soil).
s'affiner. **1.** (*of person, taste*) to become more refined. **2.** (*of wine, cheese, etc.*) to ripen, mature.
affinerie [afinri], *s.f.* **1.** *Metall:* (*a*) metal (re)finery; (re)fining works, hearth, or forge; bloomery; (*b*) wire-drawing mill. **2.** = AFFINAGE 1 (*a*). **3.** *Com:* sheet-iron in rolls.
affineur [afinœːr], *s.m.* **1.** *Metall: etc:* (re)finer. **2.** *Ind:* finisher (in various processes).
affineuse [afinøːz], *s.f.* **1.** *Ind:* finisher (in various processes). **2.** lace-worker.
affinité [afinite], *s.f.* affinity (**entre,** between); (*a*) *A:* relationship by marriage; (*b*) resemblance, similarity of character; **s'il trouve une âme qui ait des affinités avec la sienne,** if he finds a soul akin to his own, a kindred spirit; (*c*) liking, attraction; *Ch:* **a. pour un corps,** affinity for a body.
affinoir [afinwaːr], *s.m. Tex:* hackling machine.
affiquet [afikɛ], *s.m.* **1.** *A:* knitting-sheath (fastened at waist). **2.** *F: usu. pl.* brooch, clip, trinket (fastened to clothing). **3.** *Knitting:* stitch holder.
affirmatif, -ive [afirmatif, -iːv]. **1.** *a.* (*a*) affirmative, positive; **réponse affirmative,** answer in the affirmative; **signe a. (de la tête),** nod; **sur mon signe a. il ouvrit encore une bouteille,** at a nod from me he opened another bottle; (*b*) **personne affirmative,** assertive, positive, person; **prendre un ton a.,** to speak in a decisive way. **2.** *s.f.* **l'affirmative,** the affirmative; **dites-moi si vous pouvez venir demain; dans l'affirmative je vous attendrai à neuf heures,** tell me if you can come tomorrow; if so, if you can, I will expect you at nine o'clock; **répondre par l'affirmative,** to answer yes, to answer in the affirmative.
affirmation [afirmasjɔ̃], *s.f.* (*a*) affirmation, asseveration, assurance, averment; assertion, statement; **a. contraire,** assurance to the contrary; **a. trop générale,** sweeping assertion; *Jur:* **a. sous serment,** affidavit; **a. de créance,** proof of indebtedness; (*b*) **a. de soi-même,** self-assertion.
affirmativement [afirmativmɑ̃], *adv.* (*a*) affirmatively, in the affirmative; (*b*) positively, decisively.
affirmer [afirme], *v.tr.* **1.** (*a*) to affirm, assert, aver; to state positively; **j'affirme que j'ai payé, avoir payé, cette dette,** I solemnly declare (that) I have paid this debt; **je n'affirmerais pas que . . .,** I would not pledge my word that . . .; **je n'affirme rien, mais . . .,** I wouldn't swear to it, but . . .; **il affirme que j'ai tort,** he will have it that I am wrong; **je puis a. qu'il l'a fait,** I can testify to his having done it; **on affirme l'avoir vu à Paris,** he is stated to have been in Paris; **a. qch. sous, sur, par, serment,** to state sth. on oath, on affidavit; (*b*) **théorie affirmée par l'expérience,** theory supported by experience. **2. a. son existence, son autorité,** to make one's existence, one's authority, felt; to assert oneself.
s'affirmer. (*a*) to assert oneself, to assert one's authority; (*b*) **les qualités qui s'affirment dans son travail,** the qualities which stand out in his work; **sa maîtrise s'affirme dans . . .,** his mastery asserts itself in . . .; **beaucoup de ses observations se sont affirmées justes,** many of his observations have proved correct; (*c*) **l'épidémie s'affirme,** the epidemic is becoming a certainty, is asserting itself.
affistolement [afistɔlmɑ̃], *s.m. A:* = AFFUBLEMENT.
affistoler [afistɔle], *v.tr. A:* = AFFUBLER.
affixe [afiks]. *Ling:* **1.** *a.* affixed. **2.** *s.m.* affix. **3.** *s.f. Mth:* affix.
afflachi [aflaʃi], *a. A: F:* slack, flabby; **personne afflachie par l'oisiveté,** person grown slack through idleness; **câble a.,** slack cable.
affleurement [aflœrmɑ̃], *s.m.* **1.** *Arch: Carp: etc:* levelling, making flush. **2.** (*a*) *Geol:* outcrop; **filon sans a.,** blind lode; **a. oxydé,** blossom; (*b*) *Psy:* **a. de l'inconscient,** outcropping of the unconscious.
affleurer [aflœre]. **1.** *v.tr.* (*a*) to bring (timbers, etc.) to the same level; to level (two walls, etc.); to make flush; *N.Arch:* to fay (timbers); (*b*) **a. qch.,** to be level, even, flush, with sth. **2.** *v.i.* (*a*) to be even, level, flush; **a. à un trait,** to coincide with a gauge mark; **le fil de plomb affleure,** the wall, etc., is plumb; (*b*) *Geol:* (*of lode*) to outcrop.
afflictif, -ive [afliktif, -iːv], *a. Jur:* **peine afflictive,** punishment involving death, personal restraint, or penal servitude.
affliction [afliksjɔ̃], *s.f.* affliction, tribulation, sorrow.
affligé, -eé [afliʒe], *a. & s.* (*a*) afflicted; **être a. d'une infirmité,** to be afflicted with, to suffer from, an infirmity; **être a. de rhumatisme,** to be cursed with rheumatism; *s.* **les affligés,** (i) the afflicted (cripples, blind people, etc.); (ii) the bereaved; *B:* **heureux les affligés,** blessed are they that mourn; (*b*) **être a. d'une nouvelle,** to be grieved at a piece of news; **il en est profondément a.,** he's greatly distressed about it.
affligeant [afliʒɑ̃], *a.* distressing, painful, sad (news, etc.); **qu'y a-t-il d'a. à cela?** what is there distressing about that?
affliger [afliʒe], *v.tr.* (**j'affligeai(s); n. affligeons**) to afflict (de, with); to pain, distress, grieve.
s'affliger, to grieve, to be grieved, to be distressed, upset (de, at, about, over); **ne vous affligez pas ainsi,** don't take things so much to heart, *F:* don't be so cut up about it; **je m'afflige de les voir dans la misère,** it distresses, upsets, me to see them in (such) poverty; **s'a. de quitter qn,** to be very sorry to leave s.o., to be very unhappy at leaving s.o.
afflouage [afluaːʒ], *s.m.,* **afflouement** [aflumɑ̃], *s.m. Nau:* refloating, floating off (of stranded vessel).
afflouer [aflue], *v.tr. Nau:* to refloat, float off (stranded vessel).
affluence [aflyɑ̃ːs], *s.f.* **1.** *A:* flow, flowing, flood (of water, etc.); *Med:* afflux, rush (of blood). **2.** *A:* affluence, abundance, plenty; **vivre dans l'a.,** to live in affluence; **quelle a. de paroles!** what a flow of words! **3.** crowd, multitude (of people); **les heures d'a.,** the rush hours.
affluent [aflyɑ̃]. **1.** *a.* tributary (stream). **2.** *s.m.* tributary, affluent (of river).
affluer [aflye], *v.i.* **1.** (*of water, etc.*) to flow (**vers,** towards; **dans,** into); *Med:* (*of blood*) to rush, flow (à, to). **2.** to abound; to be plentiful; *F:* **les demandes de renseignements affluent,** inquiries are rolling in. **3. a. à, dans, un endroit,** to crowd, flock, to a place; to pour into (hall, country, etc.).
afflux [afly], *s.m.* (*a*) *Med: etc:* afflux, rush (of blood); (*b*) influx, crowd (of visitors); (*c*) *El:* surge (of current).
affolant [afɔlɑ̃], *a.* distracting; maddening; frightening; bewildering.
affolé [afɔle], *a.* **1.** crazy, distracted, demented, panic-stricken; **ils sont affolés,** they are scared out of their wits; **comme un a.,** as one demented; **épouvante affolée,** wild, crazed, terror. **2. aiguille affolée,** spinning, crazy, needle (of compass). **3.** *Mch:* **hélice affolée,** (i) racing; (ii) disconnected, propeller.
affolement [afɔlmɑ̃], *s.m.* **1.** distraction, panic, *F:* flap; **causer un a.,** to create a panic. **2.** *Meteor: Nau:* perturbation, unsteadiness, spinning (of magnetic needle). **3.** *Mch:* (*a*) racing (of engine, propeller, etc.); (*b*) disconnecting (of pulley, etc.).
affoler [afɔle], *v.tr.* **1.** to madden; to drive (s.o.) crazy; to throw (crowd) into a panic. **2.** to madden, infatuate (s.o.). **3.** *Meteor:* to disturb, perturb (needle of compass). **4.** *Mch:* (*a*) to let (machine) race; (*b*) to disconnect (part of machine).
s'affoler. **1.** (*a*) to fall into a panic; to stampede; (*b*) to go off the deep end. **2.** *O:* **s'a. de qn, de qch.,** to fall madly in love with s.o., to become infatuated with s.o., sth. **3.** (*a*) (*of compass-needle*) to begin to spin, to go crazy; (*b*) (*of machine*) to begin to race.
afforestage [afɔrɛstaːʒ], *s.m.* right to take firewood (from a forest).
afforestation [afɔrɛstasjɔ̃], *s.f. Adm:* (re-)afforestation.
afforester [afɔrɛste], *v.tr.* to grant (s.o.) the right to take firewood (from a forest).
affouage [afwaːʒ], *s.m.* **1.** right to cut firewood; **droit d'a.,** common of estovers. **2.** (laying-in of) (wood as) fuel (for works, forge, etc.).
affouagé, -ée [afwaʒe]. **1.** *a.* **bois a.,** wood that may be taken by privilege. **2.** *s.* holder of the privilege to cut firewood.
affouagement [afwaʒmɑ̃], *s.m. A.Adm:* allotment of estovers.
affouager[1], **-ère** [afwaʒe, -ɛːr]. **1.** *a.* **portion affouagère,** section of forest conceded as estovers. **2.** *s.* = AFFOUAGÉ 2.
affouager[2], *v.tr.* (**j'affouageai(s) n. affouageons**). **1. a. une commune,** to draw up the list of the inhabitants of a *commune* who have a right to take firewood from a communal forest. **2. a. un bois,** to mark off estovers in a wood.
affouagiste [afwaʒist], *s.m.* = AFFOUAGÉ 2.
affouillable [afujabl], *a.* liable to erosion, to undermining (through the action of running water).
affouillement [afujmɑ̃], *s.m.* **1.** *Geog:* undermining, underwashing, erosion (of river bank, etc.); **force d'a.,** scour. **2.** *Arms:* scoring (of gun).
affouiller [afuje], *v.tr.* (*a*) (*of water*) to undermine, erode, to scour, wash away, lay bare (bank, foundation, etc.); (*b*) **canon de fusil affouillé,** scored gun-barrel.
affouragement [afuraʒmɑ̃], *s.m.* **1.** foddering (of cattle). **2.** fodder, forage, provender.
affourager [afuraʒe], *v.tr.* (**j'affourageai(s) n. affourageons**) to fodder (cattle).
affourche [afurʃ], *s.f. Nau:* mooring tackle, moorings; **ancre d'a.,** small bower anchor.
affourcher [afurʃe], *v.tr.* **1. a. qn sur qch.,** to seat s.o. astride sth. **2.** *Join:* to join (two pieces) by tongue and groove or by open mortise. **3.** *Nau:* to moor (ship) (head to wind).
s'affourcher. **1.** *A:* **s'a. sur un âne,** to straddle a donkey. **2.** *Nau:* **s'a. sur ses ancres,** (i) to put out one's anchors; (ii) to retire from active life, to come to anchor.

affraîchie [afrɛʃi], *s.f. Nau:* freshening of the breeze.

affranchi, -ie [afrɑ̃ʃi]. **1.** *a.* (*a*) freed, manumitted, emancipated (slave); (*b*) free (**de**, of, from); **a. de tout préjugé,** free of any prepossessions; **a. de toute préoccupation,** free from all preoccupations; *a. & s. F:* (i) entirely unscrupulous (person); (ii) (person) who has nothing to learn about sex, vice, etc.

affranchir [afrɑ̃ʃiːr], *v.tr.* **1.** to free; to set free; to manumit, emancipate, affranchise, enfranchise, liberate (slave, etc.); **a. qn, qch., de qch.,** to free, release, deliver, s.o., sth., from sth. **2.** to pay the postage of, on (sth.); to frank, prepay; to stamp (letter); **colis affranchi,** prepaid parcel; **machine à a. (les lettres),** franking machine, franker, *U.S:* postal meter. **3.** *Cards:* to unblock (suit). **4.** *Metalw:* (*a*) to crop (the ends of a bar); **bout affranchi,** crop-end; (*b*) to give clearance to (cutting tool). **5.** *Nau:* **a. une pompe,** to suck a pump. **6.** *Husb:* to geld. **7.** *P:* to put (s.o.) in the picture; to tip (s.o.) off.

s'affranchir, to become free, independent, to throw off the yoke; **s'a. de qn, de qch.,** to free, rid, oneself of, to break free from, to shake off, s.o., sth.; **s'a. de règles rigoureuses,** to break away from rigorous rules; **s'a. du joug,** to cast off the yoke; **s'a. d'une habitude,** to break oneself of a habit.

affranchissable [afrɑ̃ʃisabl̥], *a.* **1.** that may be freed, set free, emancipated. **2.** *Post:* which should be franked, stamped.

affranchissement [afrɑ̃ʃismɑ̃], *s.m.* **1.** (*a*) emancipation, manumission, affranchisement, enfranchisement, liberation, setting free (of slave, etc.); **a. du joug de . . .,** liberation from the yoke of . . .; (*b*) release, deliverance, exemption (from taxes, charges, etc.). **2.** (*a*) prepayment, stamping, franking; **l'a. est insuffisant,** the letter is insufficiently stamped; (*b*) postage, carriage (of letter, parcel, etc.). **3.** (*a*) *Metalw:* cropping (of the ends of a bar); (*b*) *Mec.E:* rake, clearance (of cutting tool). **4.** *Husb:* gelding (of horse, etc.).

affranchisseur [afrɑ̃ʃisœːr], *s.m.* **1.** emancipator, liberator, deliverer, manumitter. **2.** *Husb:* gelder.

affres [aːfr̥], *s.f.pl.* (*a*) *A:* dread, horror; (*b*) anguish, spasm; **les a. de la mort,** (i) the pangs of death, the darkness of death; (ii) the death-throes, -struggle; **être en butte aux a. du mal de mer,** to be suffering from the pangs, from the horrors, of sea-sickness; to be in the throes of sea-sickness; **les a. de la faim,** the pangs of hunger.

affrètement [afrɛtmɑ̃], *s.m. Nau:* (*a*) freighting (= hiring out) (of ship); (*b*) chartering (of ship); **a. au voyage,** trip-charter; **a. à temps,** time-charter; **a. coque nue,** bare-boat charter; **acte, contrat, d'a.,** charter-party.

affréter [afrete], *v.tr.* (**j'affrète, n. affrétons; j'affréterai**) *Nau:* (*a*) to freight (= hire out) (ship); (*b*) to charter (ship); **a. un navire en travers,** to charter a ship by the bulk.

affréteur [afretœːr], *s.m. Nau:* (*a*) freighter; (*b*) charterer, shipper.

affreusement [afrøzmɑ̃], *adv.* terribly, frightfully, dreadfully, hideously, horribly, shockingly.

affreuseté [afrøzte], *s.f. F:* **1.** frightfulness, dreadfulness. **2.** (*a*) horrible deed; (*b*) dreadful thing.

affreux, -euse [afrø, -øːz], *a.* **1.** frightful, hideous, ghastly, atrocious (appearance, dress, etc.); *s.m. F:* (*pers.*) **un a.,** a nasty piece of work, a shocker. **2.** frightful, horrible, dreadful, shocking (news, poverty, crime, etc.); **il est a. qu'on ne puisse rien pour les sauver,** it is dreadful that nothing can be done to save them; **il a fait un temps a.,** it was a perfect beast of a day, the weather was awful; **mal de tête a.,** frightful, splitting, headache.

affriandant [afri(j)ɑ̃dɑ̃], *a. Lit:* attractive; enticing.

affriander [afri(j)ɑ̃de], *v.tr. Lit:* to attract; to entice.

affricher [afriʃe], *v.tr.* to leave fallow; to let (land) lie fallow.

affriolant [afri(j)ɔlɑ̃], tempting, appetizing, enticing; **des dessous affriolants,** sexy underwear.

affriolement [afri(j)ɔlmɑ̃], *s.m.* allurement, enticement.

affrioler [afri(j)ɔle], *v.tr.* **1. a. qn,** to entice, tempt, allure, s.o. **2. a. qch.,** to make sth. attractive, enticing.

s'affrioler de qch., to develop a liking, a taste, for sth.

affriquée [afrike], *s.f. Ling:* affricate (consonant).

affront [afrɔ̃], *s.m.* **1.** affront, indignity, insult, snub, slight, *F:* slap in the face; **faire, infliger, un a. à qn,** to slight s.o.; to snub s.o.; **avaler, dévorer, un a.,** to swallow, pocket, an affront; **doubler ses torts d'un a.,** to add insult to injury. **2.** *A:* disgrace, shame, reproach; **faire a. à qn,** to disgrace s.o., to cause s.o. to be ashamed; **faire a. de qch. à qn,** to reproach, upbraid, s.o. for sth.

affrontable [afrɔ̃tabl̥], *a.* (danger, etc.) that may be faced, tackled.

affronté [afrɔ̃te], *a.* **1.** (of panels, etc.) joined edgewise. **2.** *Her: Num:* affrontee (= front to front).

affrontement [afrɔ̃tmɑ̃], *s.m.* **1.** (*a*) facing (of enemy, of a problem, of an idea, etc.); (*b*) open defiance, opposition. **2.** joining edge to edge; *Surg:* bringing into apposition.

affronter [afrɔ̃te], *v.tr.* **1.** To face, confront, brave, tackle (s.o., sth.); to encounter (enemy); to affront (danger); **a. une épreuve avec courage,** to meet an ordeal bravely; **a. la mort avec calme,** to meet death calmly; **a. la colère de qn,** to brave the wrath of s.o., to beard the lion in his den; **a. les périls d'un voyage,** to face the perils of a journey; **a. les regards du public,** to venture before the public, to brave publicity. **2.** (*a*) to join face to face, edge to edge; to bring together (metal plates, etc.); (*b*) *Surg:* to bring into apposition. **3.** *A:* to insult (s.o.) openly, to affront (s.o.).

s'affronter, to come face to face, to clash.

affruiter [afrɥite]. **1.** *v.i. & pr.* to bear fruit, produce fruit. **2.** *v.tr.* to plant (ground) with fruit-trees.

affublement [afybləmɑ̃], *s.m. Pej:* get-up, rig-out; ridiculous dress.

affubler [afyble], *v.tr. Pej:* **a. qn de qch.,** to dress s.o. up in sth., to deck, rig, s.o. out in sth.

s'affubler, to dress, rig, oneself out (in sth.); **affublé d'un antique uniforme,** got up in an ancient uniform; **s'a. d'un faux nom,** to masquerade under an assumed name.

affusion [afyzjɔ̃], *s.f. Med:* affusion.

affût [afy], *s.m.* **1.** hiding-, lurking-place; post for lying in wait; hide (for ornithologist, etc.); **chasser un animal à l'a.,** to stalk an animal; **chasse au cerf à l'a.,** deer-stalking; **être, se mettre, à l'a. de qn, de qch.,** to lie in wait, be on the watch, for s.o., sth.; **attendre l'ennemi à l'a.,** to lie in wait for the enemy; **il est toujours à l'a. du scandale,** he keeps his ears open for scandal; **à l'a. de nouvelles,** on the look-out for news. **2.** (*a*) *Artil:* carriage, mount(ing); **a. de campagne,** field carriage; **a. automoteur,** self-propelled carriage; **a. à piédestal, à pivot,** pedestal carriage; **a. à éclipse,** disappearing carriage; (*b*) stand, frame, rest, mounting (of telescope, etc.); *Mil:* **a. de mitrailleuse,** machine-gun mount(ing).

affûtage [afytaːʒ], *s.m.* **1.** sharpening, grinding (of tool); setting (of saw). **2.** *Tls:* set of bench-tools.

affût-berceau [afybɛrso], *s. Machine-gun:* cradle-mounting.

affût-bipied [afybipje], *s.m. Mil:* bipod support (of automatic rifle); *pl. affûts-bipieds.*

affûté [afyte], *a.* **1.** (*a*) sharpened, whetted (tool); (*b*) fully-equipped (workman). **2.** (*of racehorse*) in form, at the top of its form.

affûter [afyte], *v.tr.* **1.** to grind, sharpen, whet (tool); to set (saw); *A: F:* **a. qn,** to sharpen s.o.'s wits; *Turf:* **a. un cheval,** to bring a horse to the top of its form; *F:* to wind up a horse; *P:* **s'a. le sifflet,** to wet one's whistle. **2.** to stock, equip, (shop) with tools. **3.** *A:* to mount (gun).

affûteur [afytœːr], *s.m.* **1.** *Ven:* (deer-)stalker. **2.** (tool-)grinder, sharpener; setter (of saws). **3.** *Tls:* saw file.

affûteuse [afytøːz], *s.f.* (*a*) sharpening machine (for taps); (*b*) grinding machine (for tools).

affûtiaux [afytjo], *s.m.pl.* **1.** *F:* trinkets, knick-knacks. **2.** *P:* tools.

affût-trépied [afytrepje], *s.m. Mil:* tripod mount(ing) (of machine-gun); *pl. affûts-trépieds.*

affût-truc [afytryk], *s.m. Artil:* railway-truck gun-carriage; *pl. affûts-trucs.*

afghan, -ane [afgɑ̃, -an], *a. & s. Geog:* Afghan.

Afghanistan (l') [lafganistɑ̃], *Pr.n.m. Geog:* Afghanistan.

afin [afɛ̃], *adv.* **1. a. de (faire qch.),** to, in order to, so as to (do sth.); **a. d'obtenir cette grâce,** in order to obtain this favour. **2. a. que** + *sub.,* that, so that, in order that; **a. que les autres puissent le voir,** in order that the others may see it.

afistoler [afistɔle], *v.tr.* = AFFUBLER.

africain, -aine [afrikɛ̃, -ɛn], *a. & s. Geog:* African.

africanisation [afrikanizasjɔ̃], *s.f. Pol:* Africanization.

africaniser [afrikanize], *v.tr.* to Africanize.

africanisme [afrikanism], *s.m.* Africanism.

africaniste [afrikanist], *s. & a.* (student) of African races and languages.

Afrikander [afrikɑ̃dɛːr], *s.m. Geog:* Afrikander.

afrika(a)ns [afrikɑ̃], *s.m. Ling:* Afrikaans.

Afrique [afrik], *Pr.n.f. Geog:* Africa; **l'A. du Nord,** North Africa; *s.a.* BATAILLON.

afrite [afrit], *s.m. Myth:* afreet, afrit(e).

afro-asiatique [afroazjatik], *a.* Afro-Asian.

aga [aga], *s.m. Turk. Civilization:* aga.

agaçant [agasɑ̃], *a.* **1.** annoying, irritating, provoking, *F:* aggravating. **2.** *O:* provocative, saucy (glance, smile, etc.).

agace, agasse [agas], *s.f. Orn: F: Dial:* magpie.

agacement [agasmɑ̃], *s.m.* irritation, annoyance; setting (of teeth, nerves) on edge.

agacer [agase], *v.tr.* (**j'agaçai(s), n. agaçons**). **1.** to set (teeth, nerves) on edge; to jar, grate, upon (nerves, ears). **2. a. qn,** (i) to provoke, annoy, irritate, s.o.; to get on s.o.'s nerves, *F:* to aggravate s.o.; (ii) to kindle, rouse, s.o.'s passions; to lead s.o. on; **a. un chien,** to tease a dog; **cela m'agace qu'il soit toujours là,** it gets on my nerves to see him always there.

s'agacer, to become irritated, to get annoyed.

agacerie [agasri], *s.f.* provocation, teasing; **faire des agaceries à qn,** to flirt with s.o., to lead s.o. on.

agaillardir [agajardiːr], *v.tr.* to cheer (s.o.) up, to hearten (s.o.).

s'agaillardir, to cheer up, become gay.

agalactie, agalaxie [agalaksi], *s.f. Vet: Med:* agalactia, agalaxy.

agalite [agalit], *s.f. Miner:* agalite.

agalmatolit(h)e [agalmatɔlit], *s.f. Miner:* agalmatolite, figure stone, pagodite.

agame[1] [agam], *Biol: Bot:* **1.** *a.* agamous, agamic. **2.** *s.f.pl.* agamae, cryptogams.

agame[2], *s.m. Rept:* agama.

agami [agami], *s.m. Orn:* agami, trumpeter.

agamidés [agamide], *s.m.pl. Rept:* Agamidae.

agan [agɑ̃], *s.m.* (sea-)wrack (left by the tide); *Jur:* wreck of the sea; *F:* jetsam.

aganter [agɑ̃te], *v.tr. Nau:* **1.** *A:* to overtake, overhaul (ship). **2.** to seize, catch (rope).

agape [agap], *s.f.* (*a*) *Ecc.Hist:* agape, love-feast, (*b*) *A:* reunion, get-together, of old friends, of old comrades; (*c*) *pl. Hum:* feast, spread.

agapètes [agapɛt], *s.f.pl. Ecc.Hist:* agapetae.

agapornis [agapɔrnis], *s.m. Orn:* agapornis, (African) love-bird.

Agar [agaːr], *Pr.n.f. B.Hist:* Hagar.

agar-agar [agaːragaːr], *s.m.* agar-agar, Bengal isinglass, Ceylon moss.

agaric [agarik], *s.m.* **1.** *Fung:* agaric. **2. a. minéral,** agaric-mineral, rock(-)milk.

agaricacées [agarikase], *s.f.pl. Fung:* Agaricaceae.

agarice [agaris], *s.m. Miner:* agaric-mineral, rock(-)milk.

agaristides [agaristid], *s.m.pl. Ent:* Agaristidae.

agasse [agas], *s.f.* = AGACE.

agassin [agasɛ̃], *s.m. Vit:* non-fruiting basal bud (of vine).

agate [agat], *s.f.* **1.** *Miner:* agate; **a. arborisée,** dendritic agate, tree-agate; **a. mousseuse,** moss-agate, mocha-stone; **a. œillée,** eye-agate; **a. noire, d'Islande,** obsidian; **a. onyx,** sardonyx. **2.** *Tls:* (agate) burnisher. **3.** glass marble.

agaté [agate], *a. Miner:* agaty (jasper).

agathais, -aise [agate, -ɛːz], *a. & s.* = AGATHOIS, -OISE.

Agathe [agat], *Pr.n.f.* Agatha.

agathée [agate], *s.f. Bot:* **a. amelloïde, céleste,** blue marguerite.

Agathocle [agatɔkl̥], *Pr.n.m. Gr.Hist:* Agathocles.

agathois, -oise [agatwa, -waːz], *a. & s. Geog:* (native, inhabitant) of Agde.

agatifère [agatifɛːr], *a.* agatiferous.

agatin [agatɛ̃], *a.* agatine.

agatiser [agatize], **agatifier** [agatifje], *v.tr.* to agatize.

agatoïde [agatɔid], *a.* agatoid.

agave, agavé [agaːv, agave], *s.m. Bot:* agave; **a. d'Amérique,** American aloe, sisal plant, *F:* century plant; **fibre d'a.,** aloe fibre, Mexican fibre, sisal-grass, -hemp.

-age [aːʒ], *s.suff.m.* **1.** -age; **hommage,** homage; **mariage,** marriage; **tonnage,** tonnage; **voyage,** voyage. **2.** (*a*) *expressing action,* -ing; **bavardage,** gossiping; **raccommodage,** mending; **outillage,** fitting out with tools; (*b*) *expressing*

result of action, **bavardages**, gossip; **raccommodage**, mend, repair; (*c*) *expressing place of action*, **pâturage**, pasturage, pasture (ground); **garage**, garage. 3. *Coll:* **feuillage**, foliage, leaves; **branchage**, branches; **outillage**, tools. 4. *expressing condition*, **apprentissage**, apprenticeship; **esclavage**, slavery; **servage**, serfdom; **veuvage**, widowhood.

âge [ɑːʒ], *s.m.* 1. age; (*a*) **quel â. avez-vous?** how old are you? **quand j'avais votre â. . . .**, when I was your age . . .; **à l'â. de six ans il jouait de l'orgue en public**, at six years old he was playing the organ in public; *P:* **je ne t'ai pas demandé ton â.**, mind your own business; **quel â. lui donnez-vous?** how old do you take him to be? **accuser son â.**, to look one's age; **elle ne porte pas, ne paraît pas, son â.**, she does not look her age; **dès son â. le plus tendre**, from his earliest years; **ils sont du même â.**, they are (of) the same age, of an age; **être d'â. à faire qch.**, to be of an age, old enough, to do sth.; **différence d'â.**, disparity in years; **il est président d'â.**, he is chairman by seniority; **être hors d'â.**, to be over age, superannuated; **mourir à un grand â., à un â. avancé, à un bel â.**, to die at a good old age; **être d'â. légal**, to be of age; **il n'est pas encore d'â.**, he is under age; **être en â. de se marier**, to be of an age to marry; **l'â. de la lune**, the age of the moon; **hors d'â.**, (*of horse*) aged; (*b*) **le bas â.**, infancy; **enfant en bas â.**, infant; **être à l'â. de raison, en â. de connaissance**, to have arrived at years, reached the age, of discretion; **l'â. d'homme**, manhood; **atteindre l'â. d'homme**, to reach man's estate; **l'â. mûr, moyen**, the middle of life, the years of maturity; **homme d'â. mûr, entre deux âges**, middle-aged man; **elle est d'un certain â.**, she's getting on; **sans â.**, of indeterminate age; **il est bien pour son â.**, he's marvellous for his age; **de tels amusements ne sont pas de son â.**, such amusements do not belong to his age; *s.a.* DEUX, CRITIQUE[1] 1, INGRAT 3, RETOUR 2; (*c*) old age; **un homme d'â.**, an old, aged, man; **avancer en â., tirer sur l'â., prendre de l'â.**, to be growing old, to be getting on in years; **à l'â. que j'ai, à mon â.**, at my age, at my time of day, at my time of life; **mourir avant l'â.**, to die before one's time; (*d*) *Psy:* **l'â. mental**, mental age; *s.a.* COEFFICIENT. 2. generation; **vivre, voir, trois âges d'homme**, to live through, see, three generations; **d'â. en â.**, from generation to generation; **il est d'un autre â.**, he belongs to a different generation. 3. age, period, epoch; **pendant des âges sans fin**, during aeons upon aeons; *Archeol:* **l'â. de (la) pierre**, the stone age; **l'â. de la pierre polie**, the neolithic age; **l'â. de, du, bronze**, the bronze age; **l'â. de, du, fer**, the iron age; *Hist:* **le moyen â.**, the middle ages; **costumes du moyen â.**, mediaeval costumes; *Myth:* **l'â. d'or**, the golden age; **l'â. d'airain**, the brazen age; **l'â. de fer**, the iron age.

age [aːʒ], *s.m. Husb:* beam (of plough).

âgé [ɑʒe], *a.* 1. old, aged; **â. de dix ans**, aged ten, ten years old, ten years of age; **jeune homme â. de vingt ans**, young man of twenty; **je suis plus â. que vous**, I am older than you; **je suis moins â. que vous**, I am younger than you. 2. aged, old, advanced in years; **femme un peu, assez, âgée**, elderly woman; **confier qch. à un homme â.**, to entrust sth. to a man of age.

âge-limite [ɑːʒlimit], *s.m.* maximum age; age limit.

agenais, -aise [aʒnɛ, -ɛːz], *a. & s. Geog:* (native, inhabitant) of Agen.

agence [aʒɑ̃ːs], *s.f.* 1. (*a*) agency (office); bureau; **a. d'affaires**, general business agency or office; **a. de renseignement(s)**, information bureau, enquiry agents; **a. de placement**, registry office, employment bureau; **a. de presse**, press agency; **a. télégraphique**, news agency; **a. de voyages**, tourist, travel, agency; **a. en douane**, customs agency; (*b*) branch office. 2. **obtenir l'a. d'une maison**, to obtain the agency of a firm.

agencement [aʒɑ̃smɑ̃], *s.m.* 1. arrangement, order(ing), disposition (of a house); fitting up, fitting together (of parts of machine, etc.); lay-out (of radio set, gear-box, etc.); furnishing (of aircraft); **a. des mots dans une phrase**, disposition, arrangement, of words in a sentence; **a. des figures dans un tableau**, grouping of figures in a picture. 2. *pl.* fixtures, fittings (of house, machine, etc.); appliances (of trade, etc.).

agencer [aʒɑ̃se], *v.tr.* (**j'agençai(s), n. agençons**), to arrange, dispose (house, etc.); to fit up, fit together, adjust (parts of machine, etc.); **local bien agencé**, well-designed, well-equipped, premises; **les figures, les couleurs, sont bien agencées**, the figures are well grouped, the colours harmonize, blend, well; the colour scheme is good; **phrases mal agencées**, ill-balanced, badly constructed, sentences; **régime bien agencé**, well-arranged, well-ordered, well-thought-out, diet.

s'agencer, (*of parts of whole*) to fit (together); to combine, to harmonize.

agenceur, -euse [aʒɑ̃sœːr, -øːz], *s.* arranger, contriver; **a. de magasins**, shop-fitter.

agenda [aʒɛ̃da], *s.m.* agenda, note-, memorandum-book; engagement book; diary; *pl. agendas.*

agénésie [aʒenezi], *s.f. Path:* 1. agenesia. 2. sterility.

agenois, -oise [aʒənwa, -waːz], *a. & s.* = AGENAIS.

agenouillé [aʒnuje], *a.* kneeling.

agenouillement [aʒnujmɑ̃], *s.m.* kneeling.

agenouiller [aʒnuje], *v.tr. A:* **a. qn**, to make s.o. kneel (down), to bring s.o. to his knees; **la peur l'agenouilla**, fear brought him to his knees.

s'agenouiller, to kneel (down); to fall on one's knees; **s'a. devant l'argent**, to worship Mammon.

agenouilloir [aʒnujwaːr], *s.m.* prie-Dieu; hassock (in church); bench (for kneeling in church).

agent, -ente [aʒɑ̃, -ɑ̃ːt]. 1. *s.m.* agent, agency, medium, acting power; **a. chimique**, chemical agent; *Geol:* **agents d'intempérisme**, weathering agents; **a. de circulation, a. monétaire**, circulating medium. 2. *s.* agent; (*a*) **a. d'affaires**, general agent, man of business; **a. de location, de publicité**, estate, advertising, agent; **seuls agents d'une maison**, sole agents, sole representatives, of a firm; **a. à demeure**, agent on the spot; **a. comptable**, accountant; **a. maritime**, shipping agent; **a. en douanes**, customs broker; **a. d'assurance(s)**, insurance agent; (*b*) *Adm:* agent, official; **a. diplomatique**, diplomatic agent; *Sch:* **a. (des lycées)**, school servant; **les agents des postes**, post-office officials; **a. (de police)**, policeman, police constable; **agents de la police**, police spies; **agents plongeurs**, riverside police; **a. de la circulation**, *A:* **a. pivot**, traffic policeman; *Nau:* **a. de la santé**, health officer (of port); *s.a.* PROVOCATEUR 1, VOYER[1]; (*c*) **a. de change**, (i) *Fin:* stock-broker, bill-broker, exchange-broker; (ii) *Com:* mercantile broker; *Com:* **a. de liaison**, contact man; **a. de recouvrements**, debt collector; *Ind:* **a. de maîtrise**, foreman. 3. *Mil:* **a. de liaison**, (i) liaison agent, liaison officer; (ii) connecting file; **a. de transmission**, runner, dispatch rider, *U.S:* messenger; **a. (du service des renseignements)**, agent; **a. secret**, secret agent; **a. double**, double agent.

agérate [aʒerat] *s.m.*, **ageratum** [aʒeratɔm], *s.m. Bot:* ageratum.

Agésilas [aʒezilɑːs], *Pr.n.m. Gr. Hist:* Agesilaus.

Aggée [agʒe]. *Pr.n.m. B.Hist:* Haggai.

agglomérant [aglɔmerɑ̃]. 1. *a.* binding (material). 2. *s.m.* binding material, binder.

agglomérat [aglɔmera], *s.m. Geol: Min:* agglomerate.

agglomératif, -ive [aglɔmeratif, -iːv]. 1. *a.* agglomerative; binding (material). 2. *s.m. Civ.E:* binder.

agglomération [aglɔmerasjɔ̃], *s.f.* agglomeration. 1. massing together; packing (of snow, etc.); caking, balling. 2. mass, cluster, aggregation; built-up area; **les grandes agglomérations urbaines**, the great urban centres, the great centres of population; **l'a. londonienne**, Greater London.

aggloméré [aglɔmere]. 1. *a.* conglomerate; **panneau de fibres agglomérées**, fibreboard. 2. *s.m.* (*a*) *Geol: Const:* conglomerate; (*b*) patent fuel, compressed fuel, (coal-dust) briquette; (*c*) fibreboard; **a. de liège**, agglomerated cork.

agglomérer aglɔmere], *v.tr.* (**j'agglomère, n. agglomérons j'agglomérerai**), to agglomerate; to bring together; to mass (people, etc.) together.

s'agglomérer, to agglomerate; to cohere, to bind; (*of fuel, etc.*) to cake, to ball; (*of particles, etc.*) to cluster together; (*of people*) to crowd together; *Geol:* to conglomerate.

agglutinant [aglytinɑ̃]. 1. *a.* (*a*) agglutinant, adhesive; (*b*) *Ling:* **langues agglutinantes**, agglutinative languages. 2. *s.m.* bond (of conglomerates).

agglutinateur, -trice [aglytinatœːr, -tris], *a.* agglutinative, adhesive; binding.

agglutinatif, -ive [aglytinatif, -iːv]. 1. *a.* agglutinative; binding. 2. *s.m.* agglutinant; binding material.

agglutination [aglytinasjɔ̃], *s.f.* 1. agglutination; binding; caking. 2. agglutinated mass, cake; *Bac:* clump (of microbes).

agglutiner [aglytine], *v.tr.* to agglutinate; to bind.

s'agglutiner, to agglutinate; to bind; (*of fuel, etc.*) to cake; (*of lips of wound*) to join, unite; (*of people*) to congregate.

agglutinine [aglytinin], *s.f. Physiol:* agglutinin.

agglutinogène [aglytinɔʒɛn], *s.m. Physiol:* agglutinogen.

aggravant [agravɑ̃], *a. Med: Jur: etc:* aggravating (symptom, circumstance).

aggravation [agravasjɔ̃], *s.f.* 1. aggravation (of disease, etc.); worsening (of weather, etc.). 2. augmentation (of penalty); increase (of taxation).

aggraver [agrave], *v.tr.* 1. to aggravate (disease, crime); to render (offence) more heinous; to worsen; **cambriolage aggravé de meurtre**, burglary aggravated by murder; **maladie aggravée par l'anxiété**, illness heightened by anxiety. 2. to increase, augment (penalty); to increase (difficulties, taxation).

s'aggraver, to worsen; to grow worse; **son état s'est subitement aggravé**, he has taken a turn for the worse.

agha [aga], *s.m.* = AGA.

agile [aʒil], *a.* agile, nimble; active, lithe; light-footed, light of foot; **avoir la langue a.**, to have a glib, ready, tongue; **esprit a.**, quick, agile, mind; **elle est a. de ses doigts**, she is clever with her fingers, nimble-fingered.

agilement [aʒilmɑ̃], *adv.* nimbly, lightly, with agility.

agilité [aʒilite], *s.f.* agility, nimbleness, litheness.

agio [aʒjo], *s.m. Fin:* 1. agio (of exchange); premium (on gold). 2. (*a*) money-changing; (*b*) jobbery, speculation.

agiotage [aʒjɔtaːʒ], *s.m. Pej: Fin:* stock-jobbing, agiotage; rigging the market; gambling (on Stock Exchange).

agioter [aʒjɔte], *v.i.* to speculate, gamble (on the Stock Exchange).

agioteur, -euse [aʒjɔtœːr, -øːz], *s.* speculator, gambler (on Stock Exchange).

agir [aʒiːr], *v.i.* to act. 1. **a. de soi-même**, to act on one's own initiative; **maintenant agissons**, now let's get going, get down to it; **a. selon le cas**, to act according to circumstances; **faire a. qn**, to get or cause s.o. to act; **le motif qui me fait a.**, the motive which actuates me; **faire a. qch.**, to set sth. going, working; to call sth. into action; to put sth. in motion; **faire a. certaines influences**, *F:* to pull the wires; to work the oracle; **c'est a. avec prudence que de . . .**, it is prudent to . . .; **bien, mal, a. envers qn**, to act behave, well, badly, towards s.o.; **je n'aime pas sa façon d'a.**, I don't like his ways, his behaviour; **est-ce ainsi que vous en agissez avec moi?** is that how you treat me? 2. to act, operate, take effect; **médecine qui agit vite**, medicine that acts, takes effect, quickly; **a. sur qch.**, to act (up)on sth.; **a. puissamment sur qch.**, to have a great effect on sth.; **a. sur un levier, sur un volant**, to bear on a lever, to turn a wheel; **a. sur qn**, to exercise an influence, bring an influence to bear, upon s.o.; **a. sur les sentiments de qn**, to work on s.o.'s feelings; **a. sur les superstitions du peuple**, to play on, upon, the superstitions of the people; *St. Exch:* **a. sur le marché**, to rig the market. 3. *Jur:* **a. contre qn**, to take action, proceedings, against s.o.; **a. au criminel, criminellement, contre qn**, to prosecute s.o.; **a. civilement contre qn**, to sue s.o.; **faire a. la loi contre qn**, to set the law in motion against s.o.

s'agir (de), *v.impers.* (*a*) to concern, to be in question, to be the matter; **de quoi s'agit-il?** what is the matter, the question, the business, in hand? what is it all about? what's up? **voici ce dont il s'agit, de quoi il s'agit**, this is the point; **l'affaire dont il s'agit**, the matter in hand, in question; **il ne s'agit pas d'argent**, it is not a question of money; **il s'agit de lui**, it is he who is concerned; **il s'agit de votre vie, de votre avenir**, your life, your future, is at stake; **il ne s'agit pas de cela**, that is not the question, not the point; that is neither here nor there; (*b*) **s'a. de faire qch.**, to be a matter, question, of doing sth.; **il ne s'agit que de les rendre heureux**, it is only a question of making them happy; **il s'agirait de savoir si . . .**, the (point in) question is whether . . .; **il s'agirait de faire vite, de se dépêcher**, we've got to look sharp, it's a case of now or never.

agissant [aʒisɑ̃], *a.* 1. active, busy, bustling; **collaboration agissante**, active collaboration. 2. efficacious (medicine, etc.).

agissements [aʒismɑ̃], *s.m.pl. usu. Pej:* doings, dealings, movements (of criminals, etc.); machinations (of a government, etc.).

agitable [aʒitabl], *a.* **1.** debatable (question). **2.** excitable (person).
agitant [aʒitɑ̃], *a.* **1.** agitating, disquieting (news, etc.). **2.** *Med:* **paralysie agitante,** paralysis agitans, Parkinson's disease.
agitateur, -trice [aʒitatœːr, -tris]. **1.** *s.* (political) agitator. **2.** *s.m.* (*a*) *Ch:* stirrer, stirring-rod, glass rod; (*b*) stirring machine, agitator, mixer; **a. pour charges,** batch mixer. **3.** *a.* stimulating, actuating, stirring.
agitation [aʒitasjɔ̃], *s.f.* **1.** (*a*) shaking, stirring; tossing (of sth.); waving (of handkerchief, flag); (*b*) roughness (of the sea); **a. sismique,** seismic disturbance. **2.** (*a*) agitation, tossing, restlessness; fidgetiness, *F:* the fidgets; (*b*) commotion, ferment, agitation; **l'a. ouvrière,** (labour) unrest; ferment; (*c*) (state of) perturbation; excitement; disturbance, flurry; **il le trouva dans un état de grande a.,** he found him greatly excited; (*d*) discussing, discussion (of question); (*e*) *Med:* jactitation.
agité [aʒite], *a.* **1.** choppy, rough (sea); wild (sky). **2.** (*a*) *Med:* feverish, restless (patient); (*b*) restless, sleepless (night); broken, fitful (sleep); **avoir le sommeil a.,** to be restless, to toss about, in one's sleep; (*c*) tumultuous (crowd). **3.** (*a*) restless, excited, fidgety (person); (*b*) perturbed, troubled (soul, mind); (*c*) unsettled, stirring (epoch); (*d*) **vie agitée,** hectic life; unsettled existence. **4.** *s.* **c'est un(e) agité(e),** he's, she's, a restless soul.
agiter [aʒite], *v.tr.* **1.** (*a*) to agitate; to wave (a handkerchief, a flag); **le chien agite sa queue, la queue,** the dog wags its tail; **le cheval agite la queue,** the horse whisks its tail about; **le vent agitait ses cheveux,** her hair was blowing in, ruffled by, the wind; (*b*) to shake (tree, bottle, etc.); to wave (arms); to flutter (fan, wings); to sway (tree, branches); to rouse (sea); *P:* **les a.,** to beetle off, to scram; **a. une épée au-dessus de sa tête,** to wave a sword above one's head; **il agita la menace d'une inspection,** he brandished the threat of an inspection; *Pharm:* **a. avant de s'en servir,** shake before use; (*c*) to stir (mixture, air); to fan (air). **2.** (*a*) to agitate; to excite (patient); **malade agité par la fièvre,** patient restless with fever; **le café m'agite,** coffee keeps me awake; (*b*) to perturb, to trouble; (*c*) to stir up; **a. le peuple, les masses,** to stir up, work up, the masses. **3.** to discuss, to debate (a question).
s'agiter. 1. (*a*) to be agitated, in movement; **s'a. dans l'eau,** to splash about, tumble (about), in the water; **quelque chose s'agitait sur l'eau,** something was bobbing on the water; **la mer s'agite,** the sea is rising; **l'enfant s'agite sur sa chaise,** the child fidgets, wriggles, on his chair; **s'a. dans son sommeil,** to toss in one's sleep; (*b*) to become, get, grow, agitated, excited, upset. **2. les passions qui s'agitent dans ce drame,** the passions that come into play in this drama.
Aglaé [aglae], *Pr.n.f. Gr.Myth:* Aglaia.
aglobulie [aglɔbyli], *s.f. Med:* aglobulia.
agnat, -ate [agna, -at], *s. A.Jur:* agnate.
agnathie [agnati], *s.f. Med:* agnathia.
agnation [agnasjɔ̃], *s.f. A.Jur:* agnation.
agnatique [agnatik], *a. A.Jur:* agnatic.
agneau, -eaux [aɲo], *s.m.* **1.** lamb; (**peau d')a.,** lambskin; **laine d'a.,** lamb's-wool; *Com: Furs:* **a. rasé,** shorn lamb; **doux comme un a.,** as gentle as a lamb. **2.** (*opposed to* AGNELLE) wether lamb. **3.** *Theol:* **l'A. sans tache,** the Lamb (of God). **4.** *Cu:* lamb.
agnelage [aɲ(ə)laːʒ], *s.m.,* **agnèlement** [aɲɛlmɑ̃], *s.m. Husb:* (*a*) lambing, yeaning; (*b*) lambing-season.
agnelée [aɲ(ə)le], *s.f. Husb:* fall (of lambs).
agneler [aɲ(ə)le], *v.i.* (**elle agnèle, elle agnèlera**), to lamb, to yean.
agnelet [aɲ(ə)lɛ], *s.m.* **1.** lambkin, yeanling. **2.** *A:* rustic who unites cunning with outward simplicity.
agnelin [aɲ(ə)lɛ̃], *s.m.* lambskin (as fur).
agneline [aɲ(ə)lin], *s.f. Tex:* lamb's-wool.
agnelle [aɲɛl], *s.f.* ewe-lamb.
Agnès [aɲɛs], *Pr.n.f.* Agnes.
agnosie [agnozi], *s.f. Med:* agnosia.
agnosticisme [agnɔstisism], *s.m.* agnosticism.
agnosticiste [agnɔstisist], *s.m.* agnostic.
agnostique [agnɔstik], *a. & s.* agnostic.
agnus-castus [agnyskastys], *s.m. Bot:* agnus castus, chaste-tree, Abraham's balm.
agnus-Dei [agnysdei], *s.m.inv. R.C.Ch:* agnus dei.
agone [agɔn], *a. & s.f. Magn:* agonic (line).
agonie [agɔni], *s.f.* **1.** *A: Lit:* anguish. **2.** death agony, death-struggle, pangs of death; **être à l'a.,** to be at one's last gasp; **lente a.,** lingering death, long-protracted death-bed; **il entre en a.,** his death-throes are beginning.
agonir [agɔniːr], *v.tr.* **a. qn d'injures,** heap abuse on s.o., to revile s.o.; **a. qn de malédictions,** to hurl curses at s.o.
agonisant, -ante [agɔnizɑ̃, -ɑ̃ːt]. **1.** *a.* dying, in the throes of death; **il était déjà a.,** he was already breathing his last; **de sa voix agonisante,** with his dying breath. **2.** *s.* dying person; **prières pour les agonisants,** prayers for the dying.
agoniser [agɔnize]. **1.** *v.i.* (*a*) to be dying, at the point of death; (*b*) (*of business, etc.*) to be on its last legs. **2.** *v.tr. F: in current use to-day in the sense of* AGONIR.
agonistique [agɔnistik], *a.* agonistic(al).
agonothète [agɔnɔtɛt], *s.m. Ant:* agonothete.
agora [agɔra], *s.f. Gr.Ant:* agora.
agoraphobe [agɔrafɔb]. *Med:* **1.** *a.* agoraphobic. **2.** *s.* sufferer from agoraphobia.
agoraphobie [agɔrafɔbi], *s.f. Med:* agoraphobia.
agouti [aguti], *s.m. Z:* agouti, agouty.
agrafage [agrafaːʒ], *s.m.* **1.** fastening, hooking up (of frock, etc.); clipping together (of papers); buckling (of strap). **2.** *Tchn:* (*a*) clamping; (*b*) dowelling; (*c*) *Plumb:* welting (of lead sheets).
agrafe [agraf], *s.f.* **1.** hook, fastener; clasp (of medal, of album); buckle (of strap); clip (for papers); staple (for stapler); *Surg: etc:* suture clip; **a. de diamants,** diamond clasp; **agrafes et portes (de couturière),** hooks and eyes; *Mil:* **a. d'un fourreau de sabre,** locket of a scabbard. **2.** *Const: etc:* (*a*) clamp; cleat; cramp, cramp-iron; (*b*) dowel; (*c*) joint; **a. à clavette,** cotter joint; **a. articulée,** knuckle joint; (*d*) casement fastener, hasp or catch (of window, etc.); (*e*) *Plumb:* welt(-joint) (of lead sheets); seam. **3.** *Arch:* (*ornamental*) keystone (of arch).
agrafer [agrafe], *v.tr.* **1.** to fasten by means of a hook, clasp, or clip; to buckle (belt); **a. une robe, un rideau, des papiers,** to do up a frock, hook up a curtain, clip papers together; **a. qn,** (i) to do up s.o.'s dress; *F:* to do s.o. up; (ii) *F:* to buttonhole s.o.; *F:* **agrafe-moi (ma robe),** do me up; zip me up; *F:* **a. un voleur,** to nab a thief. **2.** *Const: etc:* (*a*) to clamp, cramp; (*b*) to dowel; (*c*) to secure with a joint; (*d*) *Plumb:* to welt-joint (lead-sheets); (*e*) *Metalw:* to seam (metal).
s'agrafer à qn, à qch., to cling to, hang on, to, s.o., sth.
agrafeuse [agraføːz], *s.f.* stapler; staple gun.
agrainer [agrene], *v.tr.* to scatter grain for poultry and game-birds.
agraire [agrɛːr], *a.* agrarian; **mesures agraires,** land-measures; *Jur:* **loi agraire,** land-act; *Rom.Hist:* **les lois agraires,** agrarian laws.
agrandir [agrɑ̃diːr], *v.tr.* **1.** (*a*) to make (sth.) greater; to enlarge, to blow up (photograph, etc.); increase, extend, (sth.); **a. qch. en long, en large,** to lengthen, widen, sth.; **a. un trou,** to enlarge, open out, a hole; (*b*) to make (sth.) appear larger; to magnify; **a. sa taille,** to make oneself look taller; (*c*) to exaggerate, magnify (story, etc.); (*d*) to aggrandize (person, nation); (*e*) to raise (one's pretensions). **2.** to uplift, elevate, ennoble (the soul, etc.).
s'agrandir. 1. to grow larger; to become greater; to increase; to expand; **nous allons nous a.,** we are going to enlarge, extend, our premises. **2.** to become richer, more powerful, more important.
agrandissement [agrɑ̃dismɑ̃], *s.m.* **1.** (*a*) enlarging, extending; **a. en long, en large,** lengthening, widening; (*b*) enlargement, extension (of factory, etc.); increase (of holding, etc.); *Phot:* enlargement; **cône d'a.,** daylight, fixed-focus, enlarger; **lanterne d'a.,** condenser enlarger. **2.** advancement; increase in power, in importance; aggrandizement.
agrandisseur [agrɑ̃disœːr], *s.m. Phot:* enlarger.
agranulocytose [agranylɔsitoːz], *s.f. Med:* agranulocytosis.
agraphie [agrafi], *s.f.* agraphia.
agrarianisme [agrarjanism], *s.m. Pol:* agrarianism.
agrariat [agrarja], *s.m. Pol:* apportionment of land to those who cultivate it.
agrarien, -ienne [agrarjɛ̃, -jɛn], *a. & s. Pol:* agrarian.
agréable [agreabl], *a.* **1.** agreeable, pleasant, pleasing, nice; prepossessing, winsome (manner, countenance); gratifying (memory, etc.); **se rendre a. à qn,** to make oneself agreeable to s.o., to ingratiate oneself with s.o.; **a. au goût,** pleasant to the taste; **choses agréables à entendre,** things pleasant to hear; **réponse a.,** gratifying answer; **histoire a. à lire,** story that makes pleasant reading; **il est a. de (faire qch.),** it is pleasant, good, nice, to (do sth.); **tâche peu agréable,** disagreeable, invidious, task; **il n'y a rien de plus a. que de voyager à pied,** there is nothing like travelling on foot; **si cela peut vous être a.,** if you care to; if you like; **il lui est a. qu'on lui fasse des éloges,** he likes to be praised; **il nous est a. d'exprimer notre gratitude à,** it is a pleasure (for us) to express our gratitude to; **pour vous être a.,** to oblige, please, you; **nous venons de passer un moment très a.,** we have enjoyed ourselves very much; *s.* **faire l'a.,** to make oneself pleasant (**auprès de,** to); *s.m.* **joindre l'utile à l'a.,** to combine business with pleasure, the pleasant with the useful. **2. sacrifice a. à Dieu,** sacrifice acceptable to God.
agréablement [agreabləmɑ̃], *adv.* **1.** agreeably, pleasantly; comfortably; nicely. **2.** acceptably.
agréé [agree]. **1.** *a.* (*a*) approved (sample, etc.); (*b*) *Fr.C:* **comptable a.,** chartered accountant. **2.** *s.m. Jur:* solicitor, counsel, attorney (before a *tribunal de commerce*).
agréen, -enne [agreɛ̃, -ɛn], *a. & s.* (native, inhabitant) of Agra.
agréer [agree]. **1.** *v.tr.* to accept, recognize, approve (of), agree to (sth.); **a. un contrat,** to approve an agreement; **type agréé par le Gouvernement,** type approved by the Government; **a. les excuses de qn,** to accept s.o.'s apologies; **a. qn pour gendre,** to approve of s.o. as one's son-in-law; (*in letter*) **veuillez a., je vous prie d'a., l'assurance de mes salutations distinguées, empressées,** yours truly; yours faithfully; **veuillez a., je vous prie d'a., l'expression de mes sentiments distingués,** yours sincerely; **agréez, madame, que je vous fasse escorte,** allow me, madam, to escort you. **2.** *v.ind.tr.* to suit, please; **si cela lui agrée,** if that suits him, suits his convenience.
agréeur [agreœːr], *s.m.* **1.** wine-drawer. **2.** taster.
agreg [agrɛg], *s.f. Sch: F:* = AGRÉGATION 2 (*b*).
agrégat [agrega], *s.m.* aggregate.
agrégatif, -ive [agregatif, -iːv]. **1.** *a. Ch: Geol: etc:* aggregative. **2.** *s.* student working, reading for the *agrégation.*
agrégation [agregasjɔ̃], *s.f.* **1.** (*a*) aggregation, binding; **matière d'a.,** binding material (of road, etc.); (*b*) aggregate, agglomeration; *F:* conglomeration. **2.** (*a*) *A:* admission, admittance, reception (of s.o. to a society, etc.); (*b*) *Sch:* (**concours d') a.,** competitive examination conducted by the State for admission to posts on the teaching staff of *lycées* and universities.
agrégé, -ée [agreʒe]. **1.** *a.* aggregate (matter); *Geol:* **roches agrégées,** clastic rocks. **2.** *a. & s. Sch:* (one) who has passed the *agrégation* examination.
agréger [agreʒe], *v.tr.* (**j'agrège, n. agrégeons; j'agrégerai**) **1.** (*a*) to aggregate (particles together); (*b*) to admit, aggregate, incorporate. **2.** *Sch:* **a. qn,** to confer the title of *agrégé* on s.o.
s'agréger. 1. *A:* **s'a. à une secte,** to join a sect. **2.** (*of matter*) to unite, join together; to aggregate.
agrément [agremɑ̃], *s.m.* **1.** (*a*) pleasure, amusement; **trouver de l'a. à faire qch.,** to find pleasure, amusement, in doing sth.; **voyage d'a.,** pleasure-trip; **livres d'a.,** light reading; **ouvrages d'a.,** fancy work; *s.a.* ART 1; (*b*) agreeableness, attractiveness, pleasantness, charm. **2.** *usu. pl.* (*a*) amenities (of place); charms (of person); (*b*) ornament(ation), embellishment; *Cost:* trimmings (on dress, uniform); *Mus:* **notes d'a.,** *A:* **agréments,** grace-notes, ornaments; *A:* graces. **3. a. donné à qch.,** assent, consent, to sth.; approval, approbation, acceptance, of (proposal).
agrémenter [agremɑ̃te], *v.tr.* to embellish, ornament, deck; **robe agrémentée de dentelles,** dress trimmed with lace; **les murs s'agrémentaient d'assiettes peintes,** the walls were decorated with painted plates; **a. ses paroles de . . .,** to embellish one's speech with . . .
agréner [agrene], *v.tr. Nau:* (**j'agrène, n. agrénons; j'agrénerai**) to bale out, pump out (small boat).
agrès [agrɛ], *s.m.pl.* (*a*) tackle, gear (of ship, gun, etc.); *Jur:* **a. et apparaux,** tackle; (*b*) rigging (of ship); fittings (of gymnasium); **gymnastique aux a.,** apparatus work.
agresser [agrese], *v.tr.* to attack (without provocation).
agresseur [agresœːr], *s.m.* aggressor; assailant; attacker; *a.m.* **les peuples agresseurs de la France,** the nations that attacked France.
agressif, -ive [agresif, -iːv], *a.* aggressive, provocative (person, manner).

agression [agrɛsjɔ̃], s.f. aggression; unprovoked assault; être victime d'une a., to be assaulted; attacked; s.a. VOL.
agressivement [agrɛsivmɑ̃], adv. aggressively.
agressivité [agresivite], s.f. aggressiveness.
agreste [agrɛst], a. Lit: 1. rustic, uncultivated (country, plant, etc.); rural (site). 2. uncouth, countryfied (person, manners, etc.). 3. s.m. Ent: grayling (butterfly).
agrestement [agrɛstəmɑ̃], adv. Lit: 1. rustically. 2. uncouthly, in a countrified manner.
agreyeur, agréyeur [agrejœːr], s.m. wire-drawer.
agricher [agriʃe], v.tr. P: to grab; to arrest, run in (criminal).
agricole [agrikɔl], a. agricultural (country, produce, etc.); comice(s) agricole(s), agricultural show; grande exploitation a., farming on a large scale; large-scale farm; petite exploitation a., small-scale farming; small farm; smallholding.
agriculteur [agrikyltœːr]. 1. s.m. agriculturist, farmer. 2. a. agricultural (people).
agricultural, -aux [agrikyltyral, -o], a. agricultural.
agriculture [agrikyltyːr], s.f. agriculture, farming.
agriffer [agrife], v.tr. to claw; to seize hold of (sth.) with the claws; to clutch, grip; P: to arrest, run in (criminal).
s'agriffer. 1. to claw (à, at). 2. to clutch (à, at); to cling (à, to); le chat s'agriffe au rideau, the cat is clinging to the curtain (with his claws).
agriflamme [agriflɑːm], s.m. Hort: flame gun.
Agrigente [agriʒɑ̃ːt], Pr.n.f. (a) A.Geog: Agrigentum; (b) Geog: Agrigento.
agrigentin, -ine [agriʒɑ̃tɛ̃, -in], a. & s. A.Geog: (native, inhabitant) of Agrigentum; les Agrigentins, the Agrigenti.
agrile [agril], **agrilus** [agrilys], s.m. Ent: agrilus.
agrion [agri(j)ɔ̃], s.m. Ent: agrion, demoiselle.
agrionides [agriɔnid], **agrionidés** [agri(j)ɔnide], s.m.pl. Ent: Agrionidae.
agriote [agri(j)ɔt], s.m. Ent: agriotes.
agripaume [agripoːm], s.f. Bot: motherwort.
agripenne [agripɛn], s.m. Orn: bobolink.
agripper [agripe], v.tr. (a) to clutch, clutch at, grip (sth., s.o.); (b) to seize, snatch, grab; a. une place, to grab a job, to get one's hand on a job.
s'agripper, s'a. à qn, à qch., to cling to, clutch at, grab at, grip, s.o., sth.
agrippeur, -euse [agripœːr, -øːz], s. F: snatcher, grabber.
Agrippine [agripin], Pr.n.f. Rom.Hist: Agrippina.
agro- [agrɔ], pref. agro-.
agro [agrɔ], s.m. F: (a) = Institut national agronomique; (b) a student at this college.
agrobate [agrɔbat], s.m. Orn: a. roux, rubigineux, brown-backed, rufous, warbler.
agrologie [agrɔlɔʒi], s.f. Agr: agrology.
agromotive [agrɔmɔtiːv], s.f. Husb: portable engine (of threshing plant); tractor.
agronome [agrɔnɔm]. 1. a. = AGRONOMIQUE. 2. s.m. agronomist, agricultural economist; ingénieur a., agricultural expert.
agronométrie [agrɔnɔmetri], s.f. agronometry.
agronomie [agrɔnɔmi], s.f. agronomy; agronomics.
agronomique [agrɔnɔmik], a. agronomic(al); l'Institut national a., (university level) college for students of agronomics.
agropyre [agrɔpir], **agropyrum** [agrɔpirɔm], s.m. Bot: wheat-grass.
agrostemma [agrɔstema], s.f., **agrostemme** [agrɔstɛm], s.f. Bot: agrostemma; a. en couronne, rose-campion.
agrostide [agrɔstid], s.f., **agrostis** [agrɔstis], s.m. Bot: agrostis, bent(-grass).
agrostologie [agrɔstɔlɔʒi], s.f. Bot: agrostology.
agrostologue [agrɔstɔlɔg], s.m. Bot: pastoralist.
agrotide [agrɔtid], s.f., **agrotis** [agrɔtis], s.f. Ent: agrotis; a. des moissons, turnip-moth, common dart-moth.
agrouper [agrupe], v.tr. A: to group.
agroville [agrɔvil], s.f. Agr: agrogorod, agrotown.
agrume [agrym], s.f. Bot: plum (of species used for making Agen prunes).
agrumes [agrym], s.m.pl. citrus fruits.
agrumiculture [agrymikyltyːr], s.f. cultivation of citrus fruit.
aguerri [ageri], a. seasoned, trained (army, etc.); peu, mal, a., raw (soldier, etc.).
aguerrir [ageriːr], v.tr. to harden (s.o.) to war; to accustom, inure, to (the hardships of) war; to train (troops); a. qn à, contre, la fatigue, to accustom, inure, harden, s.o. to fatigue.
s'aguerrir, to grow hardened, seasoned (to war); s'a. à, contre, qch., to become accustomed, inured, hardened, used, to sth.
aguerrissement [agerismɑ̃], s.m. inurement; (i) inuring, (ii) becoming inured (à, contre, to); training.
aguets [agɛ], s.m.pl. used only in the adv. phr. aux a., watchful (de, for); être, se tenir, aux a., to be on the watch, on the look-out; avoir l'oreille aux a., to keep one's ears open; mettre qn aux a., to put s.o. on the watch; regard aux a. du détail, eyes on the watch for details.
agui [agi], s.m. Nau: (nœud d') a., 1. two bowlines. 2. (= nœud de chaise) bowline (knot).
aguichant [agiʃɑ̃], a. F: seductive, alluring, enticing, inviting.
aguicher [agiʃe], v.tr. F: 1. to excite, arouse (s.o.); to lead (s.o.) on; F: to give (s.o.) the glad eye. 2. to excite the curiosity of (s.o.).
aguicheur, -euse [agiʃœːr, -øːz]. 1. a. F: seductive; alluring. 2. s.f. F: une aguicheuse, an enticer.
ah [ɑ], int. ah! oh! ah, que c'est beau! isn't it beautiful! ah oui! well yes, of course; ah çà, dépêchez-vous donc! now then, do hurry up! pousser des ah! et des oh! to utter cries of admiration.
ahan [aɑ̃], s.m. A: deep (expiration of) breath; panting; suer d'a., to work like a slave, to toil and moil.
ahaner [aane], v.i. A: to breathe heavily with exertion; to pant; nos industries ahanent, our industries are hard put to it, are in difficulties.
Ahasvérus [aasverys], Pr.n.m. Ahasuerus, the Wandering Jew.
aheurtement [aœrt(ə)mɑ̃], s.m. A: 1. stumbling (à, against); sudden check. 2. obstinacy, stubbornness, perversity; c'est par pur a. que . . ., it's from sheer obstinacy that . . .
aheurter (s') [saœrte], v.pr. s'a. à qch., A: & Lit: 1. to come to a standstill before an obstacle, to come to grief over sth., to be brought up short by sth. 2. to persist in sth., to hold obstinately to sth.; s'a. à une opinion, to cling to an opinion, to be wedded to an opinion; s'a. à faire qch., to be bent on, to persist in, doing sth.
ahi [aj], int. = AÏE.
Ahriman [arimɑ̃], Pr.n.m. Rel.H: Ahriman.
ahuri, -ie [ayri]. 1. a. bewildered; (a) dumbfounded, flabbergasted; (b) confused, dazed, stupefied. 2. s. il reste planté là comme un a., he stands there gaping.
ahurir [ayriːr], v.tr. to bewilder. 1. to dumbfound, flabbergast. 2. to confuse, stupefy, daze.
ahurissant [ayrisɑ̃], a. bewildering; dumbfounding, flabbergasting; breath-taking.
ahurissement [ayrismɑ̃], s.m. bewilderment, confusion, dazed condition, stupefaction; il ne revient pas de son a., he can't get over it.
aï [ai], s.m. Z: ai, three-toed sloth.
aiche [ɛʃ], s.f. Fish: bait.
aicher [ɛʃe], v.tr. to bait (hook, line, etc.).
aidant [ɛdɑ̃]. 1. a. helpful (person). 2. Jur: s.m. aider, abettor.
aide[1] [ɛd], s.f. 1. (a) help, assistance, aid; venir en a. à qn, venir à l'aide de qn, donner a. à qn, to help s.o., to come to the assistance of s.o.; to befriend s.o.; A: Dieu vous soit en a.! God help you! recourir à l'a. d'un médecin, to call in a doctor; appeler à l'a., to call for help; à l'a.! help! prep.phr. à l'a. de qch., avec l'a. de qn, with the help, assistance, of sth., s.o.; faire qch. sans a., to do sth. without help, unassisted; (b) relief, succour; a. de l'État, A: aux pauvres = national assistance; recevoir une a. de l'État, to be on national assistance; Prov: un peu d'a. fait grand bien, every little helps; Pol.Ec: a. aux pays en voie de développement, aid for the developing countries. 2. pl. (a) Equit: aids; (b) Fr.Hist: custom dues, aids (paid by gentle and simple alike); A: cour des aides, Court of Aids = modern Board of Customs and Excise. 3. Ecc: A: chapel of ease.
aide[2], s.m. & f. 1. assistant, helper; Nau: mate; Surv: chain-man; a. de cuisine, under-cook; a. de camp, (i) Mil: aide-de-camp; (ii) Navy: flag-lieutenant; a. aux mères = home help; a. familiale = mother's help. 2. s.m. (thing) a. auditif, hearing aid.
aide-chauffeur [ɛdʃofœːr], s.m. Mch: assistant-stoker, assistant-fireman; pl. aides-chauffeurs.
aide-chirurgien [ɛdʃiryrʒjɛ̃], s.m. assistant-surgeon; pl. aides-chirurgiens.
aide-comptable [ɛdkɔ̃tabl], s.m. assistant-accountant; pl. aides-comptables.
aide-conducteur [ɛdkɔ̃dyktœːr], s.m. fireman; foot plateman; motorman; pl. aides-conducteurs.
aide-cuisinier [ɛdkɥizinje], s.m. assistant-cook, second cook; Nau: Navy: cook's mate.
aide-jardinier [ɛdʒardinje], s.m. under-gardener; pl. aides-jardiniers.
aide-maçon [ɛdmasɔ̃], s.m. mason's labourer, hodman; pl. aides-maçons.
aide-major [ɛdmaʒɔːr], s.m. Mil: assistant medical officer; pl. aides-majors.
aide-mécanicien [ɛdmekanisjɛ̃], garage-hand.
aide-mémoire [ɛdmemwaːr], s.m.inv., (a) pocket-book (of formulae, etc.); manual; (b) memorandum; (c) Dipl: aide-memoire.
aide-ouïe [ɛdwi], s.m.inv. hearing aid.
aider [ede]. 1. v.tr. aider qn, A: aider à qn, to help, assist, aid, s.o.; a. les pauvres, to succour, relieve, the poor; je me suis fait a., I got some help; je me suis fait a. par un ami, I got a friend to help me, to give a hand; a. qn de son avis, to help, assist, s.o. with one's advice, to give s.o. the benefit of one's advice; à qui se lève matin Dieu aide et prête la main, the early bird catches the worm; cette méthode aide la mémoire, this method assists the memory, is a help to the memory; a. qn à faire qch., to help s.o. to do sth.; to lend s.o. a hand; a. qn à monter, à descendre, à entrer, à sortir, to help s.o. up, down, in, out; a. qn à mettre, à ôter, son pardessus, to help s.o. on, off, with his overcoat; je vais vous a. à porter les bagages, I will help you with the luggage; Dieu aidant . . ., with God's help . . .; le temps aidant . . ., with, by, the help of time, in the course of time. . . . 2. v.ind.tr. a. à qch., to help towards sth., to contribute to(wards) sth.; a. au succès, to further the success, contribute to the success; une canne aide à sa marche, he helps himself along with a stick; Lit: a. à la lettre, to complete the sense, to read between the lines.
s'aider. 1. abs: aide-toi, do something to help yourself; Prov: aide-toi et le ciel t'aidera, God helps those who help themselves. 2. (a) s'a. de qch., to make use of, avail oneself of, sth.; s'a. de ses bras, de ses jambes, to make use of one's arms, of one's legs; (b) il faut s'aider les uns les autres, we must help one another; people must help each other.
aïe [aj], int. (indicating twinge of pain) ow! ouch!
aïeul [ajœl], s.m. 1. (pl. aïeuls) grandfather. 2. (pl. aïeux [ajø]) ancestor, forefather; pl. forbears.
aïeule [ajœl], s.f. 1. grandmother. 2. ancestress.
aïeux [ajø], s.m.pl. (see AÏEUL). (a) ancestors, forefathers; (b) int. F: (intensive) mes a.! good Lord! celui-là, mes a., il est impossible! as for him, damn it, he's impossible!
aigail [ɛgaj], s.m. = AIGUAIL.
aigle [ɛgl]. 1. (a) s.m. & f. Orn: eagle; a. impérial, imperial eagle; a. botté, booted eagle; a. criard, rough-footed spotted eagle; a. de Bonelli, à queue barrée, Bonelli's eagle; a. royal, fauve, doré, golden eagle; a. pomarin, lesser spotted eagle; a. des steppes, steppe eagle; a. ravisseur, tawny eagle; grand a. des mers, erne, sea-eagle; a. jean-le-blanc, harrier-eagle; a. des singes, monkey-eating forest eagle; a. bateleur, bateleur eagle; un regard, des yeux, d'a., keen, penetrating, glance; aux yeux d'a., eagle-eyed; nez en bec d'a., eagle nose; à vol d'a., eagle-winged; Miner: pierre d'a., eagle-stone; s.a. BOIS[1] 5; (b) s.m. Lit: genius, master-mind; ce n'est pas un a., he is no genius, is not brilliant. 2. s.m. (a) lectern, reading-desk; (b) Astr: l'A., (the constellation) Aquila. 3. s.m. Ich: a. de mer, eagle-ray. 4. (a) s.f. Her: eagle; a. de sable éployée, eagle displayed sable; double a., a. à deux têtes, double-headed eagle; (b) s.m. or f. Mil: eagle, standard; les aigles romaines, the Roman eagles; l'a. noir de Prusse, the black eagle of Prussia; a. impérial, imperial eagle; l'a impériale (des armées napoléoniennes), the imperial eagle; (c) s.m. Num: (United-States) eagle (of 10 dollars); (d) s.m. Paperm: elephant paper; grand a., double elephant; petit a., elephant; (e) s.m. Skating: grand a., spread-eagle.
aiglefin [ɛgləfɛ̃], s.m. Ich: haddock.
aiglette [ɛglɛt], s.f. Her: eaglet.
aiglon[1], **-onne** [ɛglɔ̃, -ɔn], s. Orn: eaglet, young eagle; Hist: L'A., Napoleon II.
aiglon[2], **-onne** [ɛglɔ̃, -ɔn], a. & s. Geog: (native, inhabitant) of Aigle (Switzerland).
aigre [ɛgr], a. (a) sour, sharp, acid, tart; s.m. tourner à l'a., (i) (of food, etc.) to turn sour; (ii) (of pers.) to become acrimonious, soured; (iii) (of quarrel) to turn nasty; sentir l'a., to smell sour; je n'aime pas l'a., I don't like sour things; (b) sour(-tempered), crabbed, tart (person, tone); (c) shrill, harsh, sharp; son a., harsh, shrill, sound; le son a. du banjo, the twang of the banjo; couleurs aigres, crude colours; vents aigres, bitter, raw, winds; s.m. il y a de l'a. dans l'air, there is a sharpness, a keenness, in the air; (d) Engr: harsh (line); (e) brittle, (cold-) short (iron); short (clay).

aigre-doux, -douce [ɛgrədu, -dus] *a.* bitter-sweet, (fruit, drink, sauce); sweet and sour (sauce); subacid (tone); **paroles aigres-douces,** cattish words.

aigrefin[1] [ɛgrəfɛ̃], *s.m. Ich:* = AIGLEFIN.

aigrefin[2], **-ine** [ɛgrəfɛ̃, -in], *s.* sharper, swindler, adventurer, adventuress; **aigrefins de la finance,** financial sharks.

aigrelet, -ette [ɛgrəlɛ, -ɛt], *a.* sourish, tart (fruit, sauce, etc.); **manière un peu aigrelette,** somewhat tart manner.

aigrelier [ɛgrəlje], *s.m. Bot:* wild service-tree.

aigrement [ɛgrəmɑ̃], *adv.* acrimoniously; bitterly; tartly.

aigremoine [ɛgrəmwan], *s.f. Bot:* agrimony; **a. eupatoire,** common agrimony.

aigret, -ette [ɛgrɛ, -ɛt], *a. Lit:* sourish.

aigrette [ɛgrɛt], *s.f.* **1.** (*a*) aigrette (of heron, of egret); crest (of peacock, etc.); horn, plumicorn (of owl); tuft; **héron à a.,** tufted heron; (*b*) *Cost:* aigrette, plume; tuft (of feathers, gems, etc.); osprey, spray (as head ornament); *Mil:* shaving-brush plume; *A: P:* **avoir son a.,** to be slightly elevated, sozzled; (*c*) *Bot:* egret, pappus; tassel (of maize); (*d*) *El:* aigrette, brush (discharge); (*e*) *Opt:* coma. **2.** *Orn:* egret; tufted heron; **a. blanche, grand a.,** great white heron, large, *U.S:* American, egret; **a. garzette, petite a.,** little egret.

aigretté [ɛgrɛte], *a. Bot:* bearing a pappus; tufted, crested.

aigreur [ɛgrœːr], *s.f.* (*a*) sourness, tartness, acidity; (*b*) sourness (of temper or manner); acerbity, acrimony, bitterness; **être plein d'a.,** to be full of rancour; *F:* **échanger des aigreurs,** to exchange bitter remarks, harsh words; (*c*) *Engr:* harshness (of line); *pl.* harsh lines; (*d*) *Metall:* brittleness, cold-shortness; (*e*) *pl.* **aigreurs,** acidity of the stomach; heartburn.

aigri [ɛgri], *a.* (*a*) turned sour; (*b*) embittered, soured (temper, etc.); *s.m.* **un a.,** an embittered man, a man with a grievance.

aigrin [ɛgrɛ̃], *s.m. Hort:* young wild pear-tree, young crabapple-tree.

aigrir [ɛgriːr]. **1.** *v.tr.* (*a*) to make or turn (sth.) sour; to sour (food, milk, etc.); (*b*) to sour, embitter (person). **2.** *v.i.* to turn or grow sour, to sour; (*of milk*) to turn; **son caractère a aigri,** his temper has soured; **faire a. qch.,** to turn sth. sour.

s'aigrir. 1. to turn sour, to sour. **2.** (*of pers.*) to become soured, embittered; **il s'aigrit de jour en jour,** he is getting more embittered, more bitter, every day. **3.** to get worse.

aigrissement [ɛgrismɑ̃], *s.m.* (*a*) souring (of food, etc.); (*b*) embittering, embitterment.

aigu, -uë [egy], *a.* **1.** sharp, pointed, sharp-pointed (instrument, etc.); sharp (corner); *Geom:* **angle a.,** acute angle; **triangle à angles aigus,** acute-angled triangle; *Const:* **angle (de mur) a.,** squint quoin. **2.** acute, sharp (pain); intense (curiosity); keen, bitter (conflict, jealousy); penetrating (look); keen (mind); **phase aiguë d'une maladie,** acute phase of an illness. **3.** shrill, sharp, piercing, high-pitched (sound); **dans les (tons) aigus,** in the high notes. **4.** *Gram:* **accent a.,** acute accent.

aiguade [ɛgad], *s.f. Nau:* **1.** watering place (for ships). **2. faire a., aller à l'a.,** to water.

aiguail [ɛgaːj], *s.m. Ven: & Dial:* dew (on the scent).

aiguayer [ɛgeje], *v.tr.* (**j'aiguaye, j'aiguaie, n. aiguayons; j'aiguayerai, j'aiguaierai**) *Dial:* **1.** to rinse (linen in a stream). **2.** to water (horse).

aigue-marine [ɛgmarin], *s.f. & a. inv.* aquamarine; *pl. aigues-marines.*

aiguière [ɛgjɛːr], *s.f.* aiguière; (mediaeval silver or crystal) ewer.

aiguiérée [ɛgjere], *s.f.* ewer-full.

aiguillage [eguijaːʒ], *s.m. Rail:* **1.** switching, shifting of points; shunting (of train); **erreur d'a.,** wrong setting of the points; **poste d'a.,** signal-box. **2.** *pl.* points, *U.S:* switches. **3.** *W.Tel:* directional filter. **4.** orientation; **faire une erreur d'a.,** to take the wrong turning, course.

aiguillat [eguija], *s.m. Ich:* pi(c)ked dog-fish, spiny dog-fish.

aiguille [eguij], *s.f.* **1.** needle; **a. à coudre,** sewing needle; **a. à repriser,** darning needle; **a. d'emballeur,** packing needle; **a. à passer, à lacet,** bodkin; **a. à filet,** netting needle; **a. à tricoter,** knitting needle; *Fish:* **a. à amorcer,** baiting needle; *Surg:* **a. à suture,** suture needle; **a. hypodermique,** hypodermic needle; **a. à charnière, à loquet, à palette, a. articulée,** latch needle; **a. composée, à deux éléments,** two-piece, compound, needle; **a. à bec, à barbe, a. faisant ressort,** bearded, spring, needle; **jeu d'aiguilles,** book of needles, needle-book; **en forme d'a.,** needle-shaped; *Bot: etc:* acicular; **travailler à l'a.,** to do needlework; **tirer à l'a.,** to sew; **je ne suis pas une femme d'a.,** I'm no needlewoman; **les travaux à l'a.,** needlework, needlecraft; **discuter sur la pointe d'une a.,** *A:* **sur des pointes d'a.,** to split hairs; **chercher une a. dans une botte de foin,** to look for a needle in a haystack, in a bundle of hay; *s.a.* FIL 1, TALON 1. **2.** (*thing shaped like a needle*) (*a*) **a. de glace,** icicle; **cristalliser en a.,** to needle; *Geol:* **a. (rocheuse),** needle; spine; **a. péléenne,** Pelean spine; **a. de pin,** pine-needle; *Bot:* **a. de berger** = AIGUILLETTE 2; *Ich:* **a. de mer,** sea-needle, pipe-fish, needle-fish, garfish; (*b*) **a. à tracer,** scriber; **a. de graveur,** etching needle; **a. de phonographe,** gramophone needle; **a. à graver,** record-cutter; **a. de fusil,** firing-pin, needle; *Mch:* **a. de réglage,** steam spindle (of injector); (*c*) *Rail:* tongue-rail, point-rail, blade; **a. de raccordement,** points, *U.S:* switches; **a. de prise en pointe,** catch points; **a. à contre-poids,** self-acting points; **changer l'a.,** to throw over the points; (*of train*) **franchir l'a.,** to take the points. **3.** (*a*) needle, point (of obelisk, peak, etc.); **a. d'un clocher d'église,** church spire. **4.** (*a*) (swinging) needle (of compass, galvanometer, etc.); **a. aimantée,** magnetic needle; (*b*) index, pointer (of barometer, balance, etc.); needle, pointer (of speedometer, pressure gauge, etc.); (*c*) hand (of watch, clock); **petite a.,** hour-hand; **grande a.,** minute-hand; **a. trotteuse,** second-hand; **grande a. trotteuse,** centre second-hand. *s.a.* SENS. **5.** (*a*) *Civ.E:* needle-beam (of bridge); (*b*) *Const:* king-post (of roof).

aiguillé [eguije], *a.* needle-shaped, acicular, aci(culi)form.

aiguillée [eguije], *s.f.* needleful (of thread, etc.).

aiguiller [eguije], *v.tr.* **1.** *Rail:* (*a*) to shunt, switch off, turn off (train); **a. un train sur un embranchement,** to shunt, *U.S:* switch a train, on to a branch line; **a. la conversation sur une autre voie,** to switch on to another subject, to divert the conversation; **a. la police sur une fausse piste,** to put, switch, the police on to the wrong track; (*b*) *abs.* to set, throw over, shift, the points. **2.** *P:* to have sexual intercourse with (s.o.); to sleep with (s.o.).

s'aiguiller, (*of line*) **s'a. sur une autre à tel endroit,** to join another at such and such a point.

aiguillerie [eguijri], *s.f.* **1.** needle-making. **2.** needle-factory. **3.** the needle trade.

aiguilletage [eguijtaːʒ], *s.m.* **1.** tagging (of laces, etc.); *Tex:* tufting (of felt). **2.** *Nau:* (*a*) lashing, seizing, frapping; (*b*) mousing (of hook). **3.** *Nau:* lashings.

aiguilleter [eguijte], *v.tr.* (**j'aiguillette, j'aiguillète, n. aiguilletons; j'aiguilletterai, j'aiguillèterai**) **1.** to tag (laces, etc.); *Tex:* to tuft (felt). **2.** *Nau:* (*a*) to lash, seize, frap; (*b*) to mouse (hook).

aiguillette [eguijet], *s.f.* **1.** (*a*) aiguillette, aglet, (tagged) lace; *A.Cost:* point; *Mil: Navy: etc:* shoulder-knot; (*b*) *Nau:* (i) lanyard, knittle; (ii) lashing. **2.** *Bot:* scandix, venus's-comb, lady's-comb, shepherd's-needle. **3.** *Cu:* aiguillette.

aiguilleur [eguijœːr], *s.m. Rail:* pointsman, *U.S:* switchman; *Tram:* point-boy, -man.

aiguillier [eguije], *s.m.* needlecase.

aiguillon [eguijɔ̃], *s.m.* **1.** (*a*) goad; **piquer un bœuf de, avec, l'a.,** to prick an ox with the goad, to goad (on) an ox; *Lit:* **l'a. du remords,** the pricks of remorse; (*b*) spur, incentive, whet, stimulus (of necessity, etc.); **la misère fut l'a. de son inertie,** poverty acted as a stimulus to his inertia; he was goaded into action by poverty. **2.** (*a*) *Bot:* prickle, thorn; (*b*) *Ent:* sting (of wasp, etc.). **3.** *Ich:* young pike. **4.** *Const:* pivot (of gate swivel-hinge, etc.).

aiguillonnant [eguijɔnɑ̃], *a.* goading (remorse); stimulating (applause); inciting (speech); compelling (curiosity).

aiguillonnement [eguijɔnmɑ̃], *s.m.* **1.** goading, incitement, spurring (of horse, etc.). **2.** pricking (of conscience, etc.).

aiguillonner [eguijɔne], *v.tr.* **1.** to goad, prod (oxen). **2.** to urge on, incite (to work, etc.); to spur on, inspire (by example); to rouse (s.o.), stir (s.o.) up; to goad on (by insults, etc.); to whet (appetite); **aiguillonné par la faim,** impelled by hunger.

aiguillot [eguijo], *s.m. Nau:* **1.** pintle (of rudder). **2. a. de gui,** goose-neck, swan-neck, of the boom. **3.** *Ich: Fr.C:* spring dogfish.

aiguisage [eg(ɥ)izaːʒ], *s.m.* whetting (of scythe); grinding, sharpening (of tool); setting (of saw).

aiguisé [eg(ɥ)ize], *a.* sharp (knife, appetite, teeth).

aiguisement [eg(ɥ)izmɑ̃], *s.m.* = AIGUISAGE.

aiguiser [eg(ɥ)ize], *v.tr.* **1.** (*a*) to whet (scythe); to sharpen, set, put, an edge on, grind (knife, etc.); to set (saw, razor); *s.a.* PIERRE[1]; (*b*) to point; to sharpen (tool) to a point; **a. un crayon,** to sharpen a pencil; **a. une épigramme,** to point an epigram. **2.** to make keen; to excite, stimulate, quicken (wits, appetite, etc.); to whet (appetite). **3.** *Pharm:* to acidulate (medicine); **aiguisé de vinaigre,** acidulated with vinegar.

s'aiguiser, (*of wits, etc.*) to become sharpened, keen; to grow sharper.

aiguiserie [eg(ɥ)izri], *s.f.* grindery, grinding-shop; grinding-mill.

aiguiseur, -euse [eg(ɥ)izœːr, -øːz], *s.* **1.** grinder, sharpener (of tools, etc.). **2.** *s.m. F:* (razor-) stropping machine.

aiguisoir [eg(ɥ)izwaːr], *s.m.* (*a*) (knife-)sharpener; (*b*) whetstone.

aiguité [eguite], *s.f.* (= ACUITÉ) sharpness (of angle); shrillness (of sound).

aigûment [egymɑ̃], *adv.* sharply, shrilly.

aikinite [ekinit], *s.f. Miner:* aikinite.

ail [aj], *s.m.* **1.** *Bot:* (*any species of*) allium; **a. doré,** wild garlic; moly; **a. des ours, des bois,** ramson. **2.** *Hort: Cu:* garlic; **gousse d'a.,** clove of garlic; *pl. ails, O: aulx* [o].

ailante [ɛlɑ̃ːt], *s.m. Bot:* ailantus, *esp.* tree of heaven.

aile [ɛl], *s.f.* **1.** (*a*) wing; **sur l'a.,** on the wing; **coup d'a.,** stroke, flap, of the wings, waft of the wing; **couper, rogner, les ailes à un oiseau, à qn,** to pinion, to clip the wings of a bird, to clip s.o.'s wings; **battre des ailes,** (*of bird*) to beat its wings; **battre de l'a.,** (i) (*of wounded bird*) to flutter; (ii) (*of pers.*) to be flustered, embarrassed; to be tired, exhausted; **entreprise qui bat de l'a.,** concern in a bad way; **ne (plus) battre que d'une a.,** (i) (*of bird*) to be wounded in one wing; (ii) (*of pers.*) to be on his last legs, to be in a bad way; **avoir du plomb dans l'a., en avoir dans l'a.,** (i) (*of bird*) to be winged; (ii) (*of pers.*) to be hard hit; *F:* **avoir un coup dans l'a.,** to be drunk; **j'entendis le bruit de ses ailes,** I heard the whir of its wings; **sous l'a. maternelle,** under the maternal wing; **la peur lui donnait des ailes,** fear lent him wings; **essayer ses ailes,** to try one's wings; **à tire-d'a.,** as swiftly as possible; **avoir des ailes,** to have wings on one's feet; **voler de ses propres ailes,** to depend on oneself, to stand on one's own (two) feet; **vouloir voler avant d'avoir ses ailes,** to want to run before one can walk; *s.a.* PLUME 1, TIRE-D'AILE (À); (*b*) *Av: F:* **coup d'a.,** hop; **l'avion couvre la distance Paris-Dakar d'un coup d'a.,** the aircraft makes a non-stop flight from Paris to Dakar; (*c*) flipper (of penguin); (*d*) *P:* arm, *P:* fin, flipper (of person). **2.** (*a*) wing (of building, of thumbscrew, of the stage); wing, flank (of army); vane (of wind pumping-engine); wing, sail, whip (of windmill); arm (of semaphore); blade (of propeller, of turbine, of ploughshare); aisle (of church); helix (of ear); wing (of papilionaceous flower); wing, ala (of nose); flange (of girder); came (of stained-glass window); brim (of hat); fluke (of anchor); wing (of motor car); **hélice à deux, trois, ailes,** two-, three-bladed propeller; *F: Aut:* **prendre un virage sur l'a.,** to take a corner on two wheels; **a. de mouche,** wing nail (of nailed shoes); *Av:* **a. de cornière,** angle section flange; *Civ.E:* **mur en a.,** wing-wall; **a. de soutènement, d'adossement,** retaining wing; *s.a.* DÉRIVE[1] 1, PIGEON 4. (*b*) *Av:* wing, airfoil; **a. battante,** flapping wing; **a. courbe,** cambered wing; **a. décalée,** staggered wing; **a. en delta,** delta wing; **a. en flèche, a. dièdre,** swept-back wing; **a. à fente,** slotted wing; **a. cantilever, a. en porte à faux,** cantilever wing; **a rentrante,** retractable wing; **a. surbaissée,** low wing; (*c*) *Fb:* wing; **les demi a.,** the wing halves; **jouer trois quarts a.,** to play wing three-quarters. **3.** *Mil:* flank, wing (of unit); **a. marchante,** wheeling flank; **a. pivotante,** pivoting flank; **faire avancer une a., porter une a. en avant,** to swing a flank forward.

ailé [ele], *a.* **1.** winged, feathered; *Nat. Hist:* alate; **gibier a.,** wing-game. **2. vis ailée,** butterfly screw; thumb screw.

aileron [ɛlrɔ̃], *s.m.* **1.** (*a*) pinion (of bird); *P:* arm, fin, flipper; (*b*) fin, paddle, flipper (of shark, etc.); (*c*) *pl. Ent:* balancers, poisers (of diptera). **2.** (*a*) console, scroll (of portal, etc.); (*b*) *Av:* aileron, wing-tip; **a. compensé,** balanced

aileron; **a. encastré,** built-in, pander type aileron; **a. en biais,** skew aileron; **profondeur d'a.,** aileron chord; (*c*) *Hyd.E:* ladle, float (-board), paddle-board (of water-wheel); (*d*) bilge-keel, fin-keel (of submarine); (*e*) *Aut: Av: etc:* **a. stabilisateur,** stabilizer fin; **stabilisateur à a.,** fin stabilizer; (*f*) *N.Arch:* **a. de passerelle,** bridge wing.

ailetage [ɛltaːʒ], *s.m.* blading, blades (of turbine).

ailette [ɛlɛt], *s.f.* **1.** small wing (of building, etc.). **2.** (*a*) radiating plate, (cooling) flange, rib, fin, gill (of radiator); **tube à ailettes,** fanned, gilled, tube; (*b*) lug, tenon (of machine part); stud (of shell); **vis à ailettes,** wing screw, thumb screw; (*c*) vane (of torpedo, fan, ventilator, etc.); wing, fin (of bomb, missile); fin (of aircraft); blade (of turbine); **à ailettes,** (i) (*of wheel, etc.*) bladed; (ii) (*of bomb, missile*) winged; (*d*) rib (of aircraft); (*e*) leaf (of hinge). **3.** *Tex:* flyer (of spindle).

ailier [elje], *s.m. Fb:* wing (player); winger.

aillade [ajad], *s.f.* garlic sauce; *A: F:* **servir une aillade à qn,** to give it hot to s.o.

-aille [aj, ɑːj], *s.suff.f.coll. The modern pronunciation tends to* [ɑːj], *esp. in Paris.* **1.** *appended to sbs and adjs;* (*a*) **rocaille,** rubble; **broussaille,** brushwood; *usu. Pej:* **ferraille,** old iron; **tripaille,** offal; (*b*) *A:* **menuaille,** quantity of trifling things. **2.** *appended to verbs;* (*a*) **épousailles,** (e)spousal(s); **fiançailles,** (marriage) engagement; (*b*) **mangeaille,** food, eatables; **trouvaille,** find, windfall.

ailler [aje], *v.tr. Cu:* to flavour with garlic.

-ailler [aje, ɑje], *v.suff. usu. Pej: the modern pronunciation tends to* [ɑje], *esp. in Paris.* **1.** *appended to verbs;* **écrivailler,** to scribble; **disputailler,** to wrangle, bicker; **rôdailler,** to prowl about, be on the prowl. **2.** *appended occ. to sbs;* **ferrailler,** to fence badly, to slash about with a sword; **fouailler,** to flog, lash.

-aillerie [ɑjri], *s.suff.f.coll: usu. Pej:* **criaillerie, boutiquaillerie,** *q.v.*

ailleurs [ajœːr], *adv.* **1.** elsewhere, somewhere else; **partout a.,** everywhere else, anywhere else; **nulle part a.,** nowhere else; **aimer a.,** to have another attachment; **il aimait a.,** his heart was elsewhere; **j'avais l'esprit a.,** my thoughts were elsewhere. **2.** *adv.phr.* (*a*) **d'a.,** (i) besides, furthermore, moreover, it must be added, again; (ii) from another place, from another source; **date fausse donnée par un historien d'a. digne de foi,** wrong date given by an historian otherwise worthy of credence; (iii) however; (iv) come to that; **tu n'y étais pas: moi non plus, d'a.,** you weren't there: neither was I, for that matter; (*b*) **par a.,** (i) by another way, route; (ii) in other respects, in another connection; (iii) **il est fiancé par a.,** he is engaged to someone else; (iv) **savoir une nouvelle par a.,** to have received news from another source, from another quarter; (v) (= **d'a.**) **par a., une locomotive électrique est toujours prête à prendre son service,** moreover an electric locomotive is always ready for duty; (vi) incidentally.

ailloli [ajɔli], *s.m.* (*in S. of Fr.*) mayonnaise containing pounded garlic.

ailloliser [ajɔlize], *v.tr. Cu:* to flavour with garlic.

-aillon [ajɔ̃, ɑjɔ̃], *s.suff.m. The modern pronunciation tends to* [ɑjɔ̃], *esp. in Paris; usu. Pej:* **écrivaillon,** scribbler; **poét(r)aillon,** poetaster, rhymester; **peintraillon,** dauber.

ailurinés [ɛlyrine], *s.m.pl. Z:* the Pandas, the Panda family.

aimable [ɛmabl], *a.* **1.** amiable, agreeable, pleasant; kind; nice; **faire l'a. avec qn,** to make oneself pleasant to s.o.; **être a. envers, pour, avec, qn,** to be nice to, with, s.o.; **vous êtes bien a., c'est très a. à vous,** that is very kind of you, very good of you; **vous êtes bien a. de m'avoir attendu,** it was very nice of you to wait for me; **voulez-vous être assez a. pour . . .,** will you be so kind as to . . .; *O:* **le sexe a.,** the fair sex; *O:* **a. lecteur,** gentle reader; **peu a.,** ungracious; *F:* **a. comme un crin, comme une porte de prison,** grumpy, disagreeable, like a bear with a sore head. **2.** lovable, attractive; **a. innocence,** refreshing innocence.

aimablement [ɛmabləmɑ̃], *adv.* amiably, pleasantly, kindly, nicely.

aimant[1] [ɛmɑ̃], *s.m.* magnet; **a. naturel, pierre d'a.,** magnetic iron ore, magnetite, loadstone, lodestone; **a. en fer à cheval,** horse-shoe magnet; *T.V:* **a. de cadrage,** scanning coil.

aimant[2], *a.* loving, affectionate.

aimantation [ɛmɑ̃tasjɔ̃], *s.f.* magnetization, magnetizing; **perméabilité à faible a.,** permeability under low magnetizing.

aimanter [ɛmɑ̃te], *v.tr.* to magnetize; **barreau aimanté,** bar magnet; **aiguille aimantée,** magnetic needle.

s'aimanter, to magnetize.

Aimée [ɛme], *Pr.n.f.* Amy.

aimer [eme], *v.tr.* **1.** (*a*) to like, care for, to be fond of (s.o., sth.); **je l'aime bien.,** I like him very much; **a. qn d'amitié,** to be good friends with s.o.; **ne guère a. qn, qch.,** not to care for, to have little liking for, s.o., sth.; **j'aime une pipe après dîner,** I like a pipe after dinner; **il n'aime pas les sucreries,** he doesn't care for sweet things; **une personne comme vous les aimez,** a person after your own heart; **je vous aime de l'avoir aimé,** I love you because you loved him; **elle l'aimait de ce qu'il avait cru en elle,** she liked him because he had believed in her; **elle dit que personne ne l'aime,** she says that nobody cares for her; **aimé de tous, par tout le monde,** loved by all; **on l'aime beaucoup,** he is held in great affection; **tout le monde l'aime,** he is a universal favourite; **se faire a. de qn,** to win s.o.'s affection; **j'aime beaucoup la musique,** I am very fond of music; **a. sa personne,** to fancy oneself; **elle aime son petit chien à la folie,** she dotes on her little dog; **plante qui aime un sol calcaire,** plant that likes, that does well in, a chalky soil; **a. faire qch., à faire qch.,** *A:* **de faire qch.,** to like to do sth., to like doing sth.; **il n'aime pas (à) sortir seul,** he doesn't like to go out alone, going out alone, he does not care to go out alone; **j'aime à voir comment vous l'instruisez,** I approve of the way you teach him; **le café aime à être bu chaud,** coffee ought to be drunk hot; **j'aurais aimé le voir,** I would like to have seen him; **il aime qu'on lui dise tout,** he likes to be told everything; *Prov:* **qui m'aime aime mon chien,** love me, love my dog; **qui m'aime me suive!** let those who love me follow me! *s.a.* CHÂTIER; (*b*) **a. autant: j'aime autant le cidre (que le vin),** I like cider just as much (as wine); **j'aime(rais) autant rester ici (que de . . .),** I would just as soon stay here (as . . .); **j'aime autant qu'il ne m'attende pas,** I would just as soon he didn't wait for me; (*c*) **a. mieux,** to prefer; **j'aime mieux le cidre (que le vin),** I prefer cider (to wine); **j'aime, j'aimerais, mieux rester ici,** I would rather, would sooner, stay here; **j'aime mieux qu'il vienne,** I would rather he came; *F:* **j'aime mieux pas,** I'd rather not. **2. a. qn (d'amour),** to love s.o., to be in love with s.o.; **ils s'aiment,** they are in love (with each other); **il l'aimait à la folie,** he was madly in love with her; **il n'a jamais aimé,** he was never in love; **se faire a. de qn,** to win s.o.'s love.

s'aimer. *F:* **il s'aime à la campagne,** he enjoys living in the country; **les oliviers s'aiment dans les lieux sablonneux,** olive trees like a sandy soil.

-ain, -aine [ɛ̃, ɛn]. **1.** *a. & s.suff.* (*a*) -an; **Américain,** American; **Napolitain,** Neapolitan; **Franciscain,** Franciscan; **Puritain,** Puritan; **urbain,** urban; (*b*) -ane; **humain,** humane; **mondain,** mundane; **ultramontain,** ultramontane. **2.** *s.suff.f.,* **neuvaine,** novena; **dizaine,** about ten, ten or so; **douzaine,** dozen; **vingtaine,** score, twenty or so, about twenty.

aine [ɛn], *s.f. Anat:* groin; **blessé à l'a.,** wounded in the groin.

aîné [ene], *a.* (*a*) elder (of two); eldest (of more than two); **mon frère a.,** (i) my elder brother; (ii) my eldest brother; **la branche ainée de la famille,** the elder, senior, branch of the family; *s.* **nos aînés,** our elders; **il est mon a.,** he is older than I (am); (*b*) senior; **M. Thomas a.,** Mr Thomas senior; **a. de trois ans,** senior by three years; *Sch:* **l'a. des deux Martin,** Martin major.

aînesse [ɛnɛs], *s.f.* **1.** primogeniture; **droit d'a.,** (i) law of primogeniture; (ii) birthright. **2.** *A:* seniority.

Aïno [aino], *s.m.,* **Aïnou** [ainu], *s.m.* **1.** *Ethn:* Ainu, Aino, Hairy Kurile. **2.** *Ling:* **aïnou,** Ainu, Aino.

ainsi [ɛ̃si]. **1.** *adv.* (*a*) thus; so; like this, like that; in this, in that, manner; *B:* **et Dieu parla a.,** and God spake on this wise; **a. parla le Seigneur,** thus spake the Lord; **c'est ainsi qu'il devint soldat,** and that was how he became a soldier; **s'il en est a.,** if that is the case, if (it is) so; **puisqu'il en est a. je n'ai plus rien à dire,** this being so, under the circumstances, I have nothing more to say; **les choses étant a.,** with things, things being, as they are; **ce travail doit être fait a.,** this work should be done as follows, like this; **il n'en est pas a. de vous,** it's different in your case; it's not the same for you; **je suis a. fait,** that's my nature, that's the way I'm made; **et a. du reste, et a. de suite,** and so on, and so forth; **nous sommes a. des milliers,** there are thousands of us like that; *adv.phr.* **pour a. dire,** so to speak, as it were; (*b*) **a. soit-il,** (i) so be it; (ii) *Ecc:* amen; (*c*) for example, for instance; **il m'arrive des aventures; a., l'autre jour . . .,** things happen to me; for instance, the other day . . . **2.** *conj.* so, thus; **a. vous ne venez pas?** so you are not coming? **de même que . . ., a. . . .,** (just) as; **faites en tout a. qu'il vous plaira,** do just as you please; **regarder qch. a. qu'un talisman,** to look on sth. as a talisman; (*b*) as also; **cette règle a. que la suivante me paraît, paraissent, inutile(s),** this rule, as also, as well as the next one, seems to me to be unnecessary.

aïoli [ajɔli], *s.m.* = AILLOLI.

air [ɛːr], *s.m.* **I. 1.** (*a*) air, atmosphere; **un cri fendit l'a., les airs,** a cry rent the air; **faire de l'a. à qn,** to fan s.o.; **privé d'a., sans a.,** airless; **cela manque d'a. ici,** it is a bit close, rather stuffy, here; **mettre des vêtements à l'a.,** to put clothes out to air; **donner de l'a à . . .,** (i) to ventilate (room); (ii) to give vent to (cask); **se donner de l'a.,** (i) to give oneself room to move, (ii) *F:* to show a clean pair of heels; *Typ:* **donner de l'a. à la composition,** to lead out, space out, the type; **prendre l'a.,** to enjoy the fresh air; **sortir prendre l'a.,** to go for a breath of (fresh) air, for a breather; **vivre de l'a. du temps,** to live on (next to) nothing, on air; **l'a. du temps,** the mood of the times; **prendre un a. de feu, de soleil,** to warm oneself at the fire, in the sun; **on va à Dieppe prendre un a. de mer,** we are going to Dieppe for a breath of sea air; **être à l'a.,** to have plenty of air; **"ne pas laisser à l'a.",** "not to be exposed to the air"; **au grand a., en plein a.,** in the fresh air, in the open air; **vie au grand a.,** open-air life; **jeux de plein a.,** outdoor games; **vie de plein a.,** outdoor life; **concert en plein a.,** open-air concert; *Tchn:* **amortisseur à a. comprimé,** pneumatic shock absorber; *Mch:* **moteur à a. chaud,** hot air engine; *Aut:* **poste d'a.,** air line; *s.a.* POCHE[1] 2, TROU 2; (*b*) **Ministère de l'A.,** Air Ministry; **avoir le mal de l'a.,** to be airsick; **tenir l'a.,** (*of aircraft*) (i) to keep in the air; (ii) to be airworthy; *F:* (*of aircraft*) **prendre l'a.,** to take off; *Mil: Av:* **Armée de l'A.** = (Royal) Air Force, *U.S:* (United States) Air Force; **École de l'A.** = R.A.F. College; (*c*) **en l'a.,** in the air; **nous écoutions, la fourchette en l'a.,** we listened with poised forks; **être en l'a.,** (i) to be in a state of confusion; (ii) (*of pers.*) to be in a flutter; (*of town*) to be all agog with excitement; (iii) *Mil:* (*of troops*) to be unsupported, exposed, to be in the air; (iv) (*of horse*) to be frisky; (v) (*of road*) to be up; **mettre tout en l'a.,** to throw everything into confusion; *V:* **elle s'est fait mettre en l'a.,** she's been laid; *P:* **mettre en l'a.,** (i) to bump (s.o.) off; (ii) to break in; (iii) to rob (s.o.); **regarder en l'a.,** to look up (into the sky), to look upwards; **curieux qui regardent en l'a.,** star-gazing sightseers; **aller le nez en l'a.,** to idle; **châteaux en l'a.,** castles in the air; **contes en l'a.,** idle tales, cock-and-bull stories; *F:* moonshine; **idées en l'a.,** idle notions; **paroles en l'a.,** unconsidered words, idle talk; **menaces en l'a.,** empty threats; **parler en l'a.,** to talk wildly, at random; *F:* **autant cracher en l'a.,** it's like talking to a brick wall; (*c*) **une voix dans les airs,** a voice from above; **l'idée était dans l'a.,** the idea was in the air; *P:* **flanquer, fiche(r) qch. en l'a.,** to chuck, throw, sth. out, away; **flanquer, fiche(r) qn en l'a.,** (i) to give s.o. the sack; (ii) to throw s.o. over; **il a envie de tout fiche en l'a.,** he wants to throw everything overboard; *F:* **il y a quelque chose dans l'a.,** there is something in the wind, something brewing; (*d*) *A:* gas. **2.** wind, draught; **il fait de l'a.,** it is windy, breezy; **il vient de l'a. par la serrure,** there's a draught coming through the keyhole; **courant d'a.,** draught; **il ne fait pas d'a.,** there's not a breath of air; **coup d'a.,** rush of air; **attraper un coup d'a.,** to catch a chill; **coup d'a. dans l'œil,** cold in the eye; *Metall:* **air chaud,** hot blast.

II. air, *s.m.* **1.** (*a*) appearance, look; **à l'a. triste,** sad-looking; **avoir grand a.,** to look impressive; **avoir bon a., grand a.,** (i) (*of pers.*) to look distinguished; (ii) (*of dress, etc.*) to look well, to be becoming; **il a bon a. en uniforme,** he looks well in uniform; **individu de mauvais a.,** unpleasant-looking customer; **a. de famille,** family likeness; **avoir un faux a. de qn,** to bear a slight, remote, resemblance to, to have a look of, s.o.; **il a de votre a.,** he is rather like you; **il avait un drôle d'a. avec cette casquette,** he looked a queer sight in that cap; **ça lui donnait**

l'a. d'un jockey, it made him look like a jockey; **la ville prend un a. de fête,** the town is beginning to look festive; (*b*) **avoir l'a.** (= SEMBLER, PARAÎTRE), to look, seem; **elle a l'a. fatigué(e),** she looks tired; **il a l'a. mauvais,** he looks vicious; **il a un peu l'a. étranger,** he has a slightly foreign appearance; **il avait si bien l'a. d'un Français que . . .,** he looked so like a Frenchman that . . .; **il hochait la tête, l'a. de dire "vous êtes fou,"** he nodded his head as if to say, "you're mad"; **ils ont l'a. d'avoir peur,** it looks as if they were afraid; **vous avez l'a. de vous amuser,** you seem to be enjoying yourself; **cela en a tout l'a.,** it looks like it; *F:* **il vous a dit non, ça en a tout l'a.,** he told you no by the look of things; **ceci m'a l'a. d'une entrée,** this looks to me like a way in; **le temps a l'a. d'être à la pluie,** *impers.* **il a l'a. de vouloir pleuvoir,** it looks like rain; *s.a.* TOUCHER I. 2. **2.** manner, way; (*a*) **il répondit d'un a. dégagé,** he answered in an easy manner; *O:* **prendre l'a. du monde,** to acquire society manners; **afficher de grands airs, prendre des airs, se donner des airs,** to give oneself airs, to put on a high-and-mighty manner; *F:* to put it on; **il prend des airs qui ne lui conviennent pas,** *F:* he's getting too big for his boots; *A:* **gens du bel a.,** fashionable people; (*b*) *Equit:* **les airs du manège,** the paces of a horse.

III. **air,** *s.m.* tune, air, melody; **l'a. ne fait pas la chanson;** all that glitters is not gold; **vieille chanson sur un a. nouveau,** old song to a new tune; **a. à boire,** drinking song; **a. varié,** theme with variations; **jouez-nous un a.,** play us a tune; **il joue encore le même a.,** he is still harping on the same (old) string; **je connais des paroles sur cet a.-là,** *F:* **a. connu!** I've heard that one before; *F:* **il en a l'a. et la chanson,** he not only looks it, he is.

airage [ɛraːʒ], *s.m.* **1.** angle of weather (of windmill-sails). **2.** *Min:* air-way.

airain [ɛrɛ̃], *s.m. A: or Lit:* bronze, brass; **vase d'a.,** brazen vessel; **bâtir sur l'a.,** to build upon a rock; **avoir un cœur, une âme, d'a.,** to have a heart of stone; *Pol.Ec:* **la loi d'a.,** (Lassalle's) iron law of wages; **homme d'a.,** man with an iron constitution; **voix d'a.,** brazen voice; **crier d'une voix d'a.,** to shout in brazen tones; **soleil d'a.,** fiery sun; **avoir un front d'a.,** to be brazen-faced, shameless; *Lit:* **l'a. tonne,** the cannon thunders; **l'a. retentit,** the trumpet sounds; **l'a. sonne,** the bells ring; *s.a.* ÂGE 3.

-aire [ɛːr], *a. & s.suff.* **1.** -ary; (*a*) *a.* **alvéolaire,** alveolary; **axillaire,** axillary; **élémentaire** elementary; **volontaire,** voluntary; **médullaire,** medullary; (*b*) *s.* **secrétaire** *m.f.,* secretary; **reliquaire,** *m.,* reliquary; **dictionnaire,** *m.,* dictionary; **statuaire** *f.,* statuary. **2.** *a.* -ar; **stellaire,** stellar; **angulaire,** angular; **linéaire,** linear. **3.** *a.* -arious; **grégaire,** gregarious; **téméraire,** temerarious; **précaire,** precarious. **4.** *a. & s.* -arian; (*a*) **humanitaire,** humanitarian; **sectaire,** sectarian; (*b*) (*person*) of an age; **octogénaire,** octogenarian; **nonagénaire,** nonagenarian. **5.** *s.m. & f.* -ee; **légataire,** legatee; **locataire,** lessee. **6.** *s.m.* -eer; **volontaire,** volunteer; **mousquetaire,** musketeer.

aire [ɛr], *s.f.* **1.** surface, flat space, floor; (*a*) sole (of furnace); **a. (d'une grange),** threshing floor; **a. d'un marteau,** face of a hammer; **a. d'une enclume,** flat, crown, of an anvil; (*b*) *Trans: etc:* (i) *Av: Civ.E:* **a. en dur,** hardstand, hard-surfaced, area; (ii) *Av:* **a. d'embarquement,** boarding area, the tarmac; **a. d'atterrissage,** (*on sea*) **d'amerrissage,** landing, alighting area; **a. de manœuvre,** apron; **a. de lavage,** wash-down, *U.S:* wash rack; **a. d'entretien,** servicing area; **a. de stationnement,** (parking) apron, tarmac; **a. de lancement,** launching site; **a. de compensation,** compass compensating base; (iii) **a. d'un pont,** roadway, floor, of a bridge; (*on motorway*) **a. de services principale,** service area; *Aut:* **a. de lavage,** washing bay; (*c*) (*in park*) **a. de jeu,** play area; (*d*) *Anat:* **a. germinative, embryonnaire,** germinal area; (*e*) *Z: Bot:* **a. de répartition,** range; (*f*) *Geol:* **a. continentale,** continental shield. **2.** area (of field, triangle, building, etc.); *Geog:* **a. de drainage,** drainage area, basin. **3.** eyrie (of eagle). **4.** *Nau:* rhumb; **les aires du vent,** the points of the compass; **prendre l'a. du vent,** to see which way the wind is blowing.

airée [ɛre], *s.f. Husb:* amount of grain that a threshing-floor will hold.

airelle [ɛrɛl], *s.f. Bot:* **a. myrtille, noire,** whortleberry, bilberry; *W. country dial:* whinberry, *Scot:* blaeberry; *U.S:* blueberry, huckleberry; **a. canche, rouge,** red bilberry, red whortleberry; **a. coussinette,** cranberry; **a. des marais,** mountain blaeberry, bog whortleberry, swamp-berry; **a. ponctuée,** cowberry.

airer [ɛre], *v.i.* (*of bird of prey*) to build an eyrie, a nest.

air lift [ɛrlift], *s.m. Min:* air lift.

airure [ɛryːr], *s.f. Min:* pinch-out, pinch.

ais [ɛ], *s.m.* (*a*) *A:* board, plank (of partition, etc.); (*b*) *Typ:* wetting board; *Bookb:* press-board; **a. de boucher,** butcher's block; **a. de marche (d'un escalier),** tread(-board); **a. de contre-marche,** riser; **a. d'un tonneau,** stave of a barrel; **a. à valve,** valve-board (of piano-player).

-ais, -aise [ɛ, ɛːz], *a. & s.suff. forming names of peoples:* -ese; **Japonais, -aise,** Japanese; **Milanais, -aise,** Milanese; **Portugais, -aise,** Portuguese; **Soudanais, -aise,** Sudanese.

aisance [ezɑ̃ːs], *s.f.* **1.** ease; (*a*) freedom (of movement, etc.); **faire qch. avec a.,** to do sth. easily, with ease; **avoir beaucoup d'a. dans un habit,** to have plenty of room in a coat; **donner de l'a. à qch.,** to ease sth.; **a. des coudes,** elbow-room; **a. de voirie,** easement; (*b*) **jouir de l'a., être dans l'a.,** to be well off, to be comfortably off; **un homme dans l'a.,** a well-to-do man; **assurer l'a. matérielle à qn,** to make provision for s.o.'s creature comforts; **acquérir une honnête a.,** to become reasonably well off; **ils ont une belle a.,** they are very well off. **2.** easing; **lieu, cabinet, d'aisances,** public convenience, lavatory; **fosse d'aisances,** cesspool.

aisceau, -eaux [ɛso], *s.m. Tls:* (*a*) (cooper's) adze; (*b*) tiling hammer.

aise [ɛːz]. **1.** *s.f.* (*a*) ease, comfort; **être à l'a., à son a.,** (i) to be comfortable, to have (elbow) room; (ii) to be well off, in easy circumstances; **vous êtes plus qu'à l'a.,** you have enough and to spare; **on tient à l'a. à six dans cette voiture,** this car holds six comfortably; **vous sentez-vous à l'a. dans ce pardessus?** is this overcoat comfortable? **ne pas être à son a., se sentir mal à l'a.,** (i) to feel awkward, to feel uncomfortable; (ii) to feel ill; **être (très) à l'a.,** to be relaxed, unworried; **mettre qn à son a.,** to put, set, s.o. at his ease; **mettez-vous à votre a.,** make yourself comfortable; **n'en prendre qu'à son a.,** to do only what one likes; **il en prend à son a.,** (i) he takes things, it, easy; (ii) he is a cool customer; **faire qch. à son a.,** to do sth. at one's own convenience; **en prendre à son a. avec qn,** to be off-hand with s.o.; **à votre a.!** just as you like! **vous en parlez à votre a.,** it's easy for you to talk; **aimer ses aises,** to be fond of comfort, to like one's comforts; (*b*) *A:* pleasure, joy; *still used in:* **tressaillir d'a.,** to thrill with pleasure; **ne pas se sentir d'a.,** to be overjoyed; *s.a.* PÂMER 1. **2.** *a.* **bien a., fort a.** [fɔrteːz], very glad; **je suis bien a. de vous voir,** I am very pleased, so pleased, so glad, to see you; **j'en suis bien a.,** I am very glad (*e.g.* to hear it); **je suis fort a. que vous soyez venu,** I am very glad you came.

aisé [eze], *a.* **1.** (*a*) easy, free (position, manner); comfortable (clothes); **morale aisée,** lax, facile, morals; **parler d'un ton a.,** to speak in a natural way; (*b*) in easy circumstances, well-to-do (person). **2.** easy, easily accomplished (task); **il est a. à fâcher,** he is easily annoyed; **c'est plus a. à dire qu'à faire,** it is more easily said than done; **il est a. de voir que . . .,** it is easy to see that . . .

aisément [ɛzemɑ̃], *adv.* **1.** (*a*) comfortably, freely; (*b*) **vivre a.,** to be comfortably off. **2.** easily, readily.

-aison [ɛzɔ̃], *s.suff.f.* (*a*) -ation; **combinaison,** combination; **exhalaison,** exhalation; **inclinaison,** inclination; (*b*) -ison; **comparaison,** comparison; **venaison,** venison.

aissante [ɛsɑ̃ːt], *s.f. Const:* shingle, wooden tile.

aissaugue [ɛsog], *s.m.* = ESSAUGUE.

aisseau, -eaux [ɛso], *s.m.* **1.** *Const:* shingle, wooden roofing tile. **2.** *Tls:* = AISCEAU.

aisselier [ɛsəlje], *s.m. Const:* brace, strut, angle-brace.

aisselle [ɛsɛl], *s.f.* **1.** armpit; **porter qch. sous l'a.,** to carry sth. under one's arm. **2.** *Arch:* haunch (of vault). **3.** *Bot:* axil(la).

aissette [ɛsɛt], *s.f. Tls:* (cooper's) adze.

aîtres [ɛːtr̥], *s.m.pl.* = ÊTRES.

Aix-la-Chapelle [ɛkslaʃapɛl], *Pr.n.f. Geog:* Aachen, Aix-la-Chapelle.

aixois, -oise [ɛkswa, -waːz], *a. & s. Geog:* (native, inhabitant) of Aix.

ajaccien, -ienne [aʒaksjɛ̃, -jɛn], *a. & s. Geog:* (native, inhabitant) of Ajaccio.

Ajax [aʒaks], *Pr.n.m. Gr.Lit:* Ajax.

ajisme [aʒism], *s.m.* (*a*) The Youth Hostel movement; (*b*) (youth) hostelling.

ajiste [aʒist], *s.m. & f.* (youth) hosteller.

ajointer [aʒwɛ̃te], *v.tr.* to join up; to fit (boards, pipes, etc.) end to end.

ajonc [aʒɔ̃], *s.m. Bot:* furze, gorse, whin; ulex.

ajour [aʒuːr], *s.m.* **1.** opening, hole, orifice (which lets the light through); **ménager un a. dans une cloison,** to allow an opening (for light) in a partition. **2.** (*a*) (ornamental) perforation, openwork (in wood-carving, metalwork, etc.); (*b*) *Needlew:* **faire les ajours d'un mouchoir,** to hemstitch a handkerchief.

ajourage [aʒuraːʒ], *s.m.* = AJOUR 2 (*a*).

ajouré [aʒure], *a.* (*of ornamental work*) perforated, pierced; *Needlew:* **travail a.,** drawn-(thread) work; **couture de raccord ajourée,** openwork seam; *Woodw:* **travail a.,** fretwork; **balustrade de bois a.,** wooden balustrade with openwork design; *Metalw:* **tôle ajourée,** perforated sheet of metal.

ajourer [aʒure], *v.tr.* (*a*) to pierce an opening (to let in light); **a. une mansarde,** to make a window in an attic; (*b*) (*of ornamental work*) to perforate, to pierce; (*c*) to hemstitch.

ajourné [aʒurne], *a. & s.m.* **1.** *Mil:* (conscript) deferred on medical grounds. **2.** *Sch:* referred (candidate).

ajournement [aʒurnəmɑ̃], *s.m.* **1.** (*a*) postponement, adjournment, putting off (of court proceedings, meeting, wedding, etc.); (*b*) *Sch:* referring (of examinee); *Mil:* deferment (of conscript on medical grounds, etc.). **2.** *Jur:* writ of summons (to appear); subpoena.

ajourner [aʒurne], *v.tr.* **1.** (*a*) to postpone, put off, adjourn, defer (meeting, decision, journey, etc.); to delay (plan); *Pol:* to table (bill), to allow (bill) to lie on the table; (*b*) *Sch:* to refer (candidate); *Mil:* to grant deferment to (conscript, on medical grounds). **2.** *Jur:* to summon (s.o.) to appear; to subpoena (s.o.).

s'ajourner, to adjourn; **la Chambre s'est ajournée à huitaine,** the House adjourned for a week; **le Parlement doit s'a. vers le 12 juillet,** Parliament is to rise about July 12th.

ajout [aʒu], *s.m.* addition (to MS, proof, contract).

ajoutable [aʒutabl̥], *a.* that may be added, joined (to sth.).

ajoute [aʒut], *s.m.* piece added on; eking-out piece; *Av:* **a. profilé,** fairing.

ajouté [aʒute], *s.m.* addition (to M.S., proof, contract).

ajouter [aʒute], *v.tr.* to add. **1. a. qch. à qch.,** to add sth. to sth.; **a. deux à sept,** to add two to seven; **a. des notes marginales,** to append marginal notes; **sans a. que . . .,** without adding that . . ., let alone the fact that . . .; **ajoutez au fait que . . .,** coupled with the fact that . . .; **a. l'action aux paroles,** (i) to suit the action to the word; (ii) to implement one's promise; *abs.* **son costume ajoute à sa beauté,** her dress adds to her beauty; **a. aux embarras de qn,** to add to s.o.'s difficulties. **2. "Venez aussi," ajouta-t-il,** "you come too," he added; **nous devons a. que . . .,** it should also be stated that . . .; **je n'ai rien à a.,** there is nothing else I need say, I have nothing to add; **il ajoute qu'il a fait son service militaire,** he also states that he has done his military service. **3. a. foi à qch.,** to believe sth.

ajoutoir [aʒutwaːr], *s.m.* = AJUTAGE.

ajust [aʒy(st)], *s.m. Nau:* **(nœud d')a.,** carrick bend.

ajustable [aʒystabl̥], *a.* adjustable.

ajustage [aʒystaːʒ], *s.m.* **1.** fitting, trying on (of dress, etc.). **2.** *Mec.E:* (*a*) assembly, fitting (of machine); **atelier d'a.,** fitting shop; (*b*) **a. d'une pièce,** finishing of a piece; **a. mécanique,** machining; (*c*) *Num:* gauging. **3.** fit; *Mec.E:* **a. serré,** tight fit; **a. lâche, à jeu,** loose fit.

ajustement [aʒystəmɑ̃], *s.m.* **1.** (*a*) adjusting, adjustment (of fittings, apparatus, prices, etc.); (*b*) arrangement, settlement (of quarrel, etc.). **2.** *A:* (*a*) garb, attire; (*b*) adornment. **3.** *pl.* fittings.

ajuster [aʒyste], *v.tr.* **1.** (*a*) to adjust, set (apparatus, tool); *Num:* to gauge; **tapis ajusté,** fitted carpet; **a. des poids,** to adjust, to try, weights; (*b*) to true (sth.) up, to finish; **a. une pièce à la lime,** to finish a piece with the file, to file a piece true; **a. une pièce à la machine,** to machine a piece; (*c*) to fit together, to set up (machine); (*d*) **a. son fusil,** to take aim with one's gun; **a. un coup,** to aim a shot; **a. qn, qch. (avec un fusil),** to aim (a gun) at s.o., sth.; *Abs:* **ajustez mieux une autre fois,** take better aim another time; **feu bien ajusté,** well-aimed fire; (*e*) **a. qch. à qch.,** to fit, adjust, adapt, suit, sth. to sth.; **cette clef s'ajuste à chacune des serrures,** this key fits each

of the locks; **a. un vêtement à qn**, to fit a garment on s.o.; **on a fait a. à sa taille le costume de son frère aîné**, they had his elder brother's suit cut down to fit him; **robe à corsage ajusté**, dress with a close-fitting bodice; **mi-ajusté**, semi-fitting; **a. sa voix à une salle**, to suit, adapt, one's voice to a hall; **a. un air ancien, à, sur des paroles nouvelles**, to set new words to an old tune; **s'a. sur qn**, to take one's cue from s.o.; to imitate s.o. **2.** to put (sth.) right, straight; to settle (sth.); *O:* **a. ses affaires**, to put one's affairs straight, in order; **ils s'efforcent d'a. des principes différents**, they are striving to reconcile different principles; **a. une querelle**, to arrange, settle; *F:* patch up, a quarrel; **a. son chapeau**, to set one's hat straight; **laissez-moi m'a.**, let me put myself straight, tidy myself up; *F:* **comme vous voilà ajusté!** what a sight you look! *A:* **on vous a bien ajusté!** they *did* run you down!

ajusteur [aʒystœ:r], *s.m.* **1.** *A:* adjuster, patcher-up (of quarrels, etc.). **2.** *Mec.E:* **a. sur métaux, a. mécanicien**, (metal) fitter, filer, bench-hand; **a. de tubes (de chaudières)**, tube setter; *Num:* gauger.

ajustoir [aʒystwa:r], *s.m.* = TRÉBUCHET 2.

ajut [aʒy], *s.m.* = AJUST.

ajutage [aʒyta:ʒ], *s.m.*, **ajoutoir** [aʒytwa:r], *s.m.* (*a*) *Ch: Hyd.E:* adjutage, ajutage; (*b*) *Mch: I.C.E: etc:* nozzle; delivery tube; jet; **a. à vapeur**, steam nozzle, steam cone (of injector).

akène [akɛn], *s.m. Bot:* achene, akene.

akinésie [akinezi], *s.f. Med:* akinesia.

akkadien [akadjɛ̃], *a. & s.m. A.Hist: Ling:* Akkadian, Accadian.

akromyodés [akrɔmjɔde], *s.m.pl. Orn:* Akromyodi (group of Passerine birds).

alabandine [alabɑ̃din], *s.f.*, **alabandite** [alabɑ̃dit], *s.f. Miner:* alabandite.

alabastrite [alabastrit], *s.f. Miner:* gypseous alabaster.

alacrité [alakrite], *s.f.* liveliness; alacrity.

Aladin [aladɛ̃], *Pr.n.m.* Aladdin.

Alain [alɛ̃], *Pr.n.m.* Allen, Allan, Alan.

Alains [alɛ̃], *s.m.pl. Hist:* Alans, Alani.

alaire [alɛ:r], *a. Av:* **charge a.**, wing load(ing); **surface a.**, wing area.

alaise [alɛ:z], *s.f. Med:* draw sheet.

Alamans [alamɑ̃], *s.m.pl. Hist:* Alamans, Alemanni.

alambic [alɑ̃bik], *s.m. Ch: Ind:* still; **passer qch. par., à, l'a.**, (i) to distil sth.; (ii) *O:* to scrutinize sth., to test sth. carefully.

alambiquage [alɑ̃bika:ʒ], *s.m.* excessive sublety, over-refinement.

alambiqué [alɑ̃bike], *a. Lit:* alembicated; fine-spun; over-subtle.

alambiquer [alɑ̃bike], *v.tr. Lit:* to refine (too much), to subtilize (style, thought, speech, etc.); **s'a. le cerveau (à approfondir qch.)**, to puzzle, rack, one's brains (over sth.).

alambiqueur, -euse [alɑ̃bikœ:r, -ø:z], *s. Lit:* **a. de phrases**, spinner of fine sentences.

alandier [alɑ̃dje], *s.m. Cer:* hearth of a hovel.

alandidés [alɑ̃dide], *s.m.pl. Orn:* Alandidae. the larks.

alangui [alɑ̃gi], *a.* languid, faint; **un regard a.**, a languishing look.

alanguir [alɑ̃gi:r], *v.tr.* (*usu. used in passive*) to make languid, to enfeeble.

s'alanguir, to grow languid; to languish, flag, droop.

alanguissement [alɑ̃gismɑ̃], *s.m.* languor, weakness; drooping, decline.

alanine [alanin], *s.f. Ch:* alanine.

Alaouites [alawit], *Pr.n.m. pl.* Alids.

alarguer [alarge], *v.i. Nau:* **1.** *A:* to shear off, bear off. **2.** to put to sea. **3.** to make more sail.

Alaric [alarik], *Pr.n.m. Hist:* Alaric.

alarmant [alarmɑ̃], *a.* alarming, startling (news); *St. Exch:* **bruits alarmants**, bear rumours.

alarme [alarm], *s.f.* alarm; **donner, jeter, sonner, l'a.**, to give, sound, the alarm; **fausse a.**, false alarm; **cloche d'a.**, tocsin; **canon d'a.**, alarm-gun; *Rail:* **tirer la sonnette d'a.**, to pull the communication cord; **tenir qn en a.**, to keep s.o. in a constant state of alarm; **porter l'a. dans un camp**, (i) to carry the alarm into a camp; (ii) to put fear into, raise a scare in, a political party, etc.; **prendre l'a.**, to take alarm; *Av:* warning signal; **a. lumineuse**, warning light.

alarmer [alarme], *v.tr.* **1.** to give the alarm to (s.o.). **2.** to frighten, startle, alarm (s.o.); **la nouvelle ne nous alarma pas**, the news did not alarm us; **alarmé de qch.**, alarmed at sth.

s'alarmer, to take alarm, to take fright (**de**, at); **ne vous alarmez pas**, don't be alarmed.

alarmiste [alarmist], *a. & s.* alarmist; **la presse a.**, the panic-press.

Alaska (l') [lalaska], *Pr.n.m. Geog:* Alaska; **en A.**, in Alaska.

alaterne [alatɛrn], *s.m. Bot:* alatern(us), buckthorn.

albacore [albakɔ:r], *s.m. Ich:* albacore; yellowfin tuna.

albain, -aine [albɛ̃, -ɛn], *a. & s. Rom.Hist:* (native, inhabitant) of Alba; **les Albains**, the Albani; **le mont A.**, the Mons Albanus.

albanais, -aise [albanɛ, -ɛ:z], *s.* **1.** *a. & s. Geog: Ling:* Albanian. **2.** *s.f. Bot:* white anemone.

Albanie (l') [lalbani], *Pr.n.f. Geog:* Albania; **en A.**, in Albania.

albâtre [albɑ:tr], *s.m.* alabaster; **a. calcaire**, travertine; **cou d'a.**, snow-white neck.

albatros [albatro:s], *s.m. Orn:* albatross; **a. fuligineux**, light-mantled sooty albatross; **a. hurleur**, wandering albatross; **a. à sourcils noirs**, black-browed albatross; **a. à tête grise**, grey-headed albatross; **a. à bec jaune**, yellow-nosed albatross.

Albe[1] [alb], *Pr.n.f. A.Geog:* **Albe(-la-Longue)**, Alba Longa.

Albe[2], *Pr.n. Hist:* **le duc d'A.**, the Duke of Alva, (*in modern times*) Alba.

albédo [albedo], *s.m. Ph: Astr:* albedo (of planet, snow, etc.).

albédomètre [albedɔmɛtr], *s.m. Astr:* albedometer.

albenassien, -ienne [albənasjɛ̃, -jɛn], *a. & s. Geog:* (native, inhabitant) of Aubenas.

alberge [albɛrʒ], *s.f. Hort:* clingstone apricot.

albergier [albɛrʒje], *s.m.* clingstone apricot(-tree).

Albert [albɛ:r], *Pr.n.m.* Albert; **A. le Grand**, Albertus Magnus.

albertin, -ine [albertɛ̃, -in], *a. & s. Geog:* (native, inhabitant) of Albert.

albertite [albɛrtit], *s.f. Miner:* albertite.

albertvillain, -aine [albɛrvilɛ̃, -ɛn], *a. & s. Geog:* (native, inhabitant) of Albertville.

albien, -ienne [albjɛ̃, -jɛn], *a. Geol:* **l'étage a.**, *s.m.* **l'albien**, gault.

albigeois, -oise [albiʒwa, -wa:z], *a. & s. Geog:* (inhabitant, native) of Albi; *Hist:* **les A.**, the Albigenses, Albigensians; **la Croisade des A.**, the Albigensian Crusade.

albin [albɛ̃], *a. Z:* white, unpigmented.

albinisme [albinism], *s.m. Path: Z: Bot:* albinism.

albinos [albino:s], *s. & a.inv.* albino.

Albion [albjɔ̃], *Pr.n.f. A.Geog:* Albion, Britain; *Lit:* **la perfide A.**, perfidious Albion.

albite [albit], *s.f. Miner:* albite, white feldspar.

albran [albrɑ̃], *s.m.* = HALBRAN.

albuginacées [albyʒinase], *s.f.pl. Fung:* Albuginaceae.

albuginé [albyʒine], *a.* albuginean, albugineous; white (tissue, membrane, sclerotic).

albugineux, -euse [albyʒinø, -ø:z], *a.* whitish.

albuginite [albyʒinit], *s.f. Med:* albuginitis.

albugo [albygo], *s.m. Med: Bot:* albugo.

albula [albyla], *s.m. Ich:* albula.

album [albɔm], *s.m.* **1.** album, sketch-book, scrap-book; **a. à feuilles mobiles**, loose-leaf album; **format a.**, cabinet size. **2.** picture-book. **3. a.(-tarif)**, trade catalogue.

albumen [albymɛn], *s.m. Biol: Bot:* albumen.

albuminage [albymina:ʒ], *s.m. A: Phot:* albumenizing.

albuminate [albyminat], *s.m. Ch:* albuminate.

albumine [albymin], *s.f. Ch: Biol:* albumin.

albuminé [albymine], *a.* **1.** albuminous. **2.** *A: Phot:* albumenized (paper).

albuminimètre [albyminimɛtr], *s.m.* albuminimeter, albuminometer.

albuminer [albymine], *v.tr. A: Phot:* to albumenize (paper).

albumineux, -euse [albyminø, -ø:z], *a. Biol: Bot:* albuminous, albuminose.

albumino-gélatineux, -euse [albyminoʒelatinø, -ø:z], *a. Anat: Biol:* albumino-gelatinous.

albuminoïde [albyminɔid], *a. Ch:* albuminoid.

albuminurie [albyminyri], *s.f. Med:* albuminuria.

albuminurique [albyminyrik], *a.* albuminuric.

albumose [albymo:z], *s.f. Med:* albumose.

albumosurie [albymozyri], *s.f. Med:* albumosuria.

alcade [alkad], *s.m.* (*in Spain*) (*a*) alcalde, mayor; (*b*) *A:* justice, sheriff.

alcaïque [alkaik], *a. & s.m. Pros:* Alcaic (strophe, etc.).

alcalescence [alkalesɑ̃:s], *s.f. Ch:* alkalescence, alkalescency.

alcalescent [alkalesɑ̃], *a. Ch:* alkalescent.

alcali [alkali], *s.m. Ch:* alkali; *A:* **a. volatil**, ammonia.

alcalifiant [alkalifjɑ̃], *a.* alcalizing.

alcaligènes [alkaliʒɛn], *s.m.pl. Bac:* alcaligenes *pl.*

alcalimètre [alkalimɛtr], *s.m. Ch:* alkalimeter.

alcalimétrie [alkalimetri], *s.f. Ch:* alkalimetry.

alcalin [alkalɛ̃], *a.* alkaline; **métal a.**, alkali metal, alkaline metal.

alcaliniser [alkalinize], *v.tr.* to alkalinize, alkalize.

alcalinité [alkalinite], *s.f.* alkalinity; **force d'a.**, alkali strength.

alcalino-terreux, -euse [alkalinotɛrø, -ø:z], *a. Ch:* alkaline-earth (metal, base, etc.).

alcalisation [alkalizasjɔ̃], *s.f.* alkalization.

alcaliser [alkalize], *v.tr.* to alkalize; to alkalify.

s'alcaliser, to become alkalized.

alcaloïde [alkalɔid], *a. & s.m. Ch:* alkaloid.

alcalose [alkalo:z], *s.f. Med:* alkalosis.

alcarazas [alkarazɑ:s], *s.m.* alcarraza, (porous) water-cooler, monkey(-pot).

alcédinidés [alsedinide], *s.m.pl. Orn:* Alcedinidae, the Kingfishers.

alcedo [alsedo], *s.m. Orn:* alcedo, kingfisher.

alcée[1] [alse], *s.f. Bot:* hollyhock, rose-mallow.

Alcée[2], *Pr.n.m. Myth: Gr.Lit:* Alcaeus.

alcélaphinés [alselafine], *s.m.pl. Z:* Alcelaphinæ.

alcène [alsɛn], *s.m. Ch:* olefin(e).

Alceste [alsɛst], *Pr.n.f. Gr.Lit:* Alcestis.

alchémille [alkemij], *s.f. Bot:* alchemilla; **a. vulgaire**, lady's-mantle; **a. des champs**, parsley-piert.

alchimie [alʃimi], *s.f.* alchemy.

alchimille [alkimij], *s.f.* = ALCHÉMILLE.

alchimique [alʃimik], *a.* alchemic(al), alchemistic(al).

alchimiste [alʃimist], *s.m.* alchemist.

Alcibiade [alsibjad], *Pr.n.m. Gr.Hist:* Alcibiades.

alcidés [alside], *s.m.pl.* Alcidæ, the Penguins.

alcool [alkɔl], *s.m.* alcohol, spirits, *U.S:* hard liquor; **a. absolu**, pure, absolute, alcohol; **a. éthylique, ordinaire**, ethyl, ordinary alcohol; **a. à brûler, dénaturé**, methylated spirits; **a. naturel**, raw spirits; *Med:* **a. à 90°** = surgical spirit, *U.S:* rubbing alcohol; *Cu:* **a. blanc**, clear spirits (*e.g. kirsch*); **lampe à a.**, spirit lamp, *U.S:* alcohol lamp; **a. carburant**, motor spirit; **impôt sur les alcools**, tax on spirits.

alcoolat [alkɔla], *s.m. Pharm:* spirit (of aromatic herbs).

alcoolate [alkɔlat], *s.m. Ch:* alcoholate.

alcoolature [alkɔlaty:r], *s.f. Pharm:* alcoholature, alcoholic tincture.

alcoolé [alkɔle], *s.m. Pharm:* alcoholic tincture.

alcoolémie [alkɔlemi], *s.f. Med:* alcoholemia.

alcoolique [alkɔlik]. **1.** *a.* (*a*) alcoholic, spirituous; **fermentation a.**, alcoholic fermentation; (*b*) *Med:* alcoholic (patient). **2.** *s.* (*a*) drunkard; (*b*) alcoholic.

alcoolisable [alkɔlizabl̩], *a.* alcoholizable.

alcoolisage [alkɔliza:ʒ], *s.m. Winem:* fortification.

alcoolisation [alkɔlizasjɔ̃], *s.f. Ch: Med:* alcoholization.

alcoolisé [alkɔlize], *a.* **boisson alcoolisée**, alcoholic drink.

alcooliser [alkɔlize], *v.tr.* to alcoholize; *Winem:* to fortify (wine); *F:* to make, get (s.o.) drunk.

s'alcooliser. *F:* (*of pers.*) to drink excessively; to get drunk; *F:* to soak.

alcoolisme [alkɔlism], *s.m. Med:* alcoholism.

alcoolomanie [alkɔlɔmani], *s.f. Path:* alcoholomania, dipsomania.

alcoolomètre [alkɔlɔmɛtr], *s.m.*, **alcoomètre** [alkɔmɛtr], *s.m.* alcohol(o)meter.

alcoolométrie [alkɔlɔmetri], **alcoométrie** [alkɔmetri], *s.f.* alcoholometry.

alcootest [alkɔtɛst], *s.m.* breathalyser test.

Alcoran (l') [lalkɔrɑ̃], *s.m.* = KORAN (LE).

alcôve [alko:v], *s.f.* alcove, (bed-)recess; **alcôves de dortoir**, cubicles; **les secrets d'a.**, the intimacies of married life.

alcoviste [alkɔvist], *s.m. A:* ladies' man, frequenter of literary salons (XVIIth century).

alcoylat [alkɔila], *s.m. Ch: Ind:* alkylate.

alcoylation [alkɔilasjɔ̃], *s.f. Ind: Ch:* alkylation.

alcoyle [alkɔil], *s.m. Ch:* alkyl.

alcoyler [alkɔile], *v.tr. Ch:* to alkylate.

alcyon [alsjɔ̃], *s.m.* **1.** *Myth:* halcyon. **2.** *Orn:* kingfisher; **a. pie**, pied kingfisher; **a. à collier**, belted kingfisher. **3.** *Coel:* alcyonium, dead man's fingers, cow-paps.

alcyon(n)aires [alsjɔnɛ:r], *s.m.pl. Coel:* Alcyonaria.

Alcyone [alsjɔn], *Pr.n.f. Myth: Astr:* Alcyone.

alcyonien, -ienne [alsjɔnjɛ̃, -jɛn]. **1.** *a.* **jours alcyoniens**, halcyon days. **2.** *s.m.pl.* **alcyoniens**; *Coel:* Alcyonaria(ns).

Alde [ald]. **1.** *Pr.n.m. Typ.Hist:* **A. Manuce**, Aldus Manutius. **2.** *s.m.* Aldine edition, an Aldine, an Aldus.

Aldébaran [aldebarɑ̃], *Pr.n.m. Astr:* Aldebaran, Aldeboran.

aldéhyde [aldeid], *s.m. Ch:* aldehyde; **a. formique,** formaldehyde.
aldin [aldɛ̃], *a. Typ:* Aldine (edition, type).
aldol [aldɔl], *s.m. Ch:* aldol.
aldolisation [aldɔlizasjɔ̃], *s.f. Ch:* aldolization.
aldose [aldoːz], *s.m. Ch:* aldose.
aldostérone [aldɔsterɔn], *s.f. Physiol:* electrocortin, aldosterone.
ale [ɛl], *s.f.* ale; **pale-ale** [pɛlɛl], *s.m. (rare)* pale ale.
aléa [alea], *s.m.* risk, hazard, chance; **l'affaire présente trop d'aléas,** the business is too hazardous.
aléatoire [aleatwaːr]. **1.** *a.* aleatory (contract, etc.); depending on contingencies, problematical, hazardous, risky, chancy, uncertain (result); random (sampling, fluctuation). **2.** *s.m.* **l'a. du marché,** the risks, the unsettled state, of the market; **l'a. d'une profession,** the uncertainties of a profession.
aléatoirement [aleatwarmɑ̃], *adv.* by chance; in an aleatory manner, riskily.
alem [alɛm], *s.m. Mohamm. Rel:* **1.** alim. **2.** *pl.* = OULÉMAS, ULÉMAS.
Aléman(n)ie [alemani], *Pr.n.f. A.Geog:* Alamannia, Alemannia (now Swabia).
aléman(n)ique [alemanik], *a. Hist:* Alemannian, Alemannic, Alamannian, Alamanic; *s.a.* SUISSE.
Alemans [almɑ̃], *s.m.pl. Hist:* Alemanni.
alençonnais, -aise [alɑ̃sɔnɛ, -ɛːz], *a. & s. Geog:* (native, inhabitant) of Alençon.
alêne [alɛn], *s.f.* **1.** *Tls:* awl; **a. plate,** bradawl; *Bot:* **en a.** = ALÉNÉ. **2.** *Ich:* sharp-nosed skate.
aléné [alene], *a.* awl-shaped, pointed. *Bot: (of leaf)* acuminate, subulate.
alénois [alenwa], *a.m. Bot:* **cresson a.,** garden cress.
alentir [alɑ̃tiːr], *v.tr. A:* = RALENTIR.
alentissement [alɑ̃tismɑ̃], *s.m. A:* = RALENTISSEMENT.
alentour [alɑ̃tuːr]. **1.** *adv.* around, round about; **le pays d'a.,** the surrounding, neighbouring, country; *prep.phr. A:* **alentour de la maison,** round about the house. **2.** *s.m.pl.* **alentours (d'une ville, etc.),** environs, neighbourhood, vicinity, surroundings (of a town, etc.); *A:* **les alentours d'une personne,** a person's companions, associates; *F:* **aux alentours de midi,** around mid-day, round about noon.
aléoute [aleut], *a. & s.*, **aléoutien, -ienne** [aleusjɛ̃, -jɛn], *a. & s. Geog:* Aleutian; **les (îles) Aléoutiennes,** the Aleutian Islands.
Alep [alɛp], *Pr.n.m. Geog:* Aleppo.
aleph [alef], *s.m. Hebrew Alph: Mth:* aleph.
alépin, -ine [alepɛ̃, -in], *a. & s.* **1.** *Geog:* Aleppine. **2.** *s.f. Tex: A:* **alépine,** alepine, alapeen, bombazine.
alérion [alerjɔ̃], *s.m. Her:* al(l)erion, eagle displayed, spread eaglet (without beak or talons).
alerte [alɛrt]. **1.** *int.* up! to arms! look out! **2.** *s.f.* alarm, (air-raid) warning; **donner l'a. au camp,** to give the alarm to, to rouse, the camp; **être en a.,** to be on the alert, on the qui-vive; **en état d'a.,** standing by, standing to; **tenir l'ennemi en a.,** to harass the enemy; **fausse a.,** false alarm; *Mil:* **fin d'a.,** 'all clear'; **dispositif d'a.,** warning system; *Av:* **a. en piste,** scramble; **point d'a.,** danger point (*e.g.* on river tide-gauge); **a. à la typhoïde,** typhoid warning; **une chaude a.,** a narrow escape, a close shave. **3.** *a.* (*a*) alert, brisk, quick, agile; **a. à faire qch.,** quick to do, at doing, sth.; (*b*) *A:* vigilant, watchful.
alertement [alɛrt(ə)mɑ̃], *adv.* briskly; **il descendit la rue a.,** he went briskly down the street.
alerter [alɛrte], *v.tr.* to alert, to give the alarm to, turn out (troops); to warn, send a warning to (police, headquarters, etc.).
alésage [alezaːʒ], *s.m.* **1.** *Metalw:* (*a*) boring (out); (*b*) broaching, reaming. **2.** bore (of rifle barrel); *I.C.E:* bore; internal diameter (of cylinder, etc.); **cylindre à deux alésages,** double-diameter cylinder; **a. cylindrique,** straight bore; **a. de gicleur,** jet bore.
alèse [alɛːz], *s.f. Med:* draw-sheet.
aléser [aleze], *v.tr.* **(j'alèse, n. alésons; j'aléserai)** *Metalw:* (*a*) to bore (out); **outil à a.,** boring tool; (*b*) to ream out, broach; to open out (hole).
aléseur, -euse [alezœːr, -øːz]. **1.** *s.m. Min:* (drill) reamer. **2.** *s.f.* **aléseuse,** *Metalw:* (*a*) boring, reaming machine; **a. équarrisseuse,** broaching machine; **a. fraiseuse,** boring mill; (*b*) drilling machine; **a. à revolver,** turret drill.
alésien, -ienne [alezjɛ̃, -jɛn], *a. & s.* (native, inhabitant) of Alès.
alésoir [alezwaːr], *s.m.* **1.** *Tls:* (*a*) borer; (*b*) broach; reamer(-bit); finishing bit; drift. **2.** boring machine, drilling mill.
alester [alɛste], **alestir** [alɛstiːr], *v.tr. Nau:* (*a*) to lighten (ship); (*b*) to trim up, tidy up (rigging).
alésures [alezyːr], *s.f.pl. Metalw:* borings, bore-chips, boring dust.
aleurode [alørɔd], *s.m. Ent:* aleurodes, *F:* mealy-wings.
aleurone [alørɔn], *s.f. Biol:* aleurone; protein grains.
alevin [alvɛ̃], *s.m. Pisc:* alevin, fry, young fish.
alevinage [alvinaːʒ], *s.m. Pisc:* stocking (of water) with young fish.
aleviner [alvine], *v.tr. Pisc:* **a. un étang,** to stock a pond (with fry).
alevinier [alvinje], *s.m.*, **alevinière** [alvinjɛːr], *s.f. Pisc:* breeding-pond, nursery; hatchery.
Alexandre [alɛksɑ̃ːdr], *Pr.n.m.* Alexander.
Alexandrette [alɛksɑ̃drɛt], *Pr.n.f. Geog:* Alexandretta, Iskenderon, Iskanderun.
Alexandrie [alɛksɑ̃dri], *Pr.n.f. Geog:* Alexandria.
alexandrin, -ine [alɛksɑ̃drɛ̃, -in], *a. & s.* alexandrine; Alexandrian (school); *Pros:* (vers) a., Alexandrine (line).
alexie [alɛksi], *s.f. Med:* alexia, word blindness.
alexine [alɛksin], *s.f. Med:* alexin.
alexipharmaque [alɛksifarmak], *a. & s.m. A: Med:* alexipharmic, antidote.
Alexis [alɛksi], *Pr.n.m.* Alexius, Alexis.
alezan, -ane [alzɑ̃, -an], *a. & s.* chestnut (horse); **a. châtain,** chestnut sorrel; **a. roux,** red bay.
alèze [alɛːz], *s.f.* **1.** *Med:* draw-sheet. **2.** wooden lining (of scabbard).
alfa [alfa], *s.m. Bot:* alfa(-grass), esparto(-grass).
alfange [alfɑ̃ːʒ], *s.f.* **1.** *A:* moorish scimitar. **2.** *Bot:* long-leaved lettuce.
alfénide [alfenid], *s.m. (type of)* German silver alloy.
alfortvillais, -aise [alfɔrvilɛ, -ɛːz], *a. & s. Geog:* (native, inhabitant) of Alfortville.
Alfred [alfrɛd], *Pr.n.m.* Alfred.
algarade [algarad], *s.f.* **1.** *A:* raid, foray. **2.** storm of abuse (directed at a person); **faire, faire essuyer, une a. à qn,** to storm at s.o.; to give s.o. a good dressing-down; to bite, snap, s.o.'s head off; to fling out at s.o.; to go for s.o.
algaroth [algarɔt], *s.m. Ch: A: Pharm:* powder of Algaroth.
algazelle [algazɛl], *s.f. Z:* algazel.
algèbre [alʒɛbr], *s.f.* algebra; **a. moderne,** modern algebra; **résoudre un problème par l'a.,** to solve a problem algebraically; *F:* **c'est de l'a. pour moi,** it's all Greek to me.
algébrique [alʒebrik], *a.* algebraic; **exactitude a.,** mathematical accuracy.
algébriquement [alʒebrikmɑ̃], *adv.* algebraically.
algébriste [alʒebrist], *s.m. & f.* algebraist, algebrist.
Alger [alʒe], *Pr.n.m. Geog:* **1.** Algiers. **2.** *s.m. Hist:* (the Department of) Alger.
Algérie (l') [lalʒeri], *Pr.n.f. Geog:* Algeria; **en A.,** in Algeria.
algérien, -ienne [alʒerjɛ̃, -jɛn], *a. & s.* Algerian; of Algeria; *Hist:* Algerine.
algérois, -oise, [alʒerwa,-waːz], *a.& s.* (inhabitant, native) of Algiers.
algésimètre [algezimɛtr], *s.m.* algesimeter.
Algésiras [alʒeziraːs], *Pr.n.m. Geog:* Algeciras.
algicide [alʒisid], *s.m.* algicide, algaecide.
algide [alʒid], *a. Med:* algid (cholera, fever, etc.).
algidité [alʒidite], *s.f. Med:* algidity.
-algie[1] [alʒi], *s.suff.f. Med:* -algia, -algy; **névralgie,** neuralgia; **coxalgie,** coxalgy.
algie[2], *s.f.* ache, pain.
alginate [alʒinat], *s.m. Ch:* alginate.
alginique [alʒinik], *a. Ch:* **acide a.,** alginic acid.
Algol [algɔl], *Pr.n.m. Astr:* Algol; the Demon star.
algologie [algɔlɔʒi], *s.f.* algology.
algologue [algɔlɔg], *s.m. & f.* algologist.
algonkien [algɔ̃kjɛ̃], *a. & s.m. Geol:* Algonkian.
Algonquin(s) [algɔ̃kɛ̃], *s.m.(pl.) Ethn:* **1.** Algonquin(s). **2.** Algonquian(s).
algorithme [algɔritm], *s.m. Mth:* algorism, algorithm.
algorithmique [algɔritmik], *a. Mth:* algorithmic.
alguazil [algwazil], *s.m.* alguazil, police-officer (in Spain).
algue [alg], *s.f. Bot:* alga, *pl.* algae, sea-weed.
Alhambra (l') [lalɑ̃bra], *s.m.* the Alhambra (at Granada); *A:* **un a.,** an Alhambresque building, 'a regular Alhambra.'
alias [aljaːs], *adv.* alias; otherwise (known as . . .).
alibi [alibi], *s.m.* **1.** *Jur:* alibi; **invoquer, plaider, un a.,** to fall back on, set up, plead, an alibi; **produire, fournir, un a.,** to produce an alibi; **établir, prouver, son a.,** to establish an alibi. **2.** excuse, pretext. **3.** diversion.
aliboron [alibɔrɔ̃], *s.m. Lit:* **un maître a.,** an ignoramus; (from La Fontaine's fable *Les Voleurs et l'âne*).
aliboufier [alibufje], *s.m. Bot: F:* styrax, storax.
alicante [alikɑ̃ːt], *s.m.* alicante (wine).
Alice [alis], *Pr.n.f.* Alice.
alichon [aliʃɔ̃], *s.m.* float (of water-wheel).
alidade [alidad], *s.f. Surv: Nau:* alidad(e); **a. à pinnules,** sight-rule, open-sight alidade; index (-bar) (of plane table); **a. à lunette,** telescopic alidade; **a. à éclimètre,** clinometer alidade; **a. de triangulation,** triangular alidade; **a. de réflexion,** pelorus.
aliénabilité [aljenabilite], *s.f. Jur:* alienability.
aliénable [aljenabl], *a. Jur:* alienable, transferable.
aliénant [aljenɑ̃], *a.* off-putting.
aliénataire [aljenatɛːr], *s.m. & f. Jur:* alienee.
aliénateur, -trice [aljenatœːr, -tris], *s. Jur:* alienator.
aliénation [aljenasjɔ̃], *s.f.* **1.** *Jur:* alienation, transfer (of rights, property, etc.). **2.** alienation, estrangement. **3. a. mentale,** alienation, derangement, of mind; insanity, lunacy; **j'ai vu en lui de l'a. mentale,** I saw that his mind was unhinged.
aliéné, -ée [aljene], *a. & s.* lunatic, mad(man), insane (person); *O:* **maison, asile, d'aliénés,** lunatic asylum; **hospice d'aliénés,** mental hospital; **a. interdit,** certified lunatic.
aliéner [aljene], *v.tr.* **(j'aliène, n. aliénons; j'aliénerai) 1.** (*a*) *Jur:* to alienate, part with, transfer, (property, rights, etc.); (*b*) **a. sa liberté,** to give up one's freedom. **2.** to alienate, estrange (affections, etc.); **a. l'affection, l'estime, de qn,** to estrange s.o.; **cet acte lui aliéna tous les cœurs,** this action alienated all hearts from him; **il s'est aliéné tous ses parents,** he has estranged all his relations. **3.** to derange, unhinge (the mind); **ce malheur lui aliéna l'esprit,** this misfortune unhinged his mind.
s'aliéner. 1. s'a. de qn, de qch., to become estranged from, a stranger to, s.o., sth. **2.** (*of the mind*) to become unhinged.
aliénisme [aljenism], *s.m.* alienism, study and treatment of mental diseases.
aliéniste [aljenist], *s.m. & f. Med:* alienist, mental specialist.
alifère [alifɛːr], *a. Ent:* aliferous, aligerous, wing-bearing.
aliforme [alifɔrm], *a.* aliform, wing-shaped.
aligère [aliʒɛːr], *a.* **les dieux aligères,** the winged gods.
alignée [aliɲe], *s.f.* line, row (of houses, trees, etc.).
alignement [aliɲmɑ̃], *s.m.* **1.** (*a*) alignment, alinement; laying out (of trees, etc.) in line; *Typ:* **a. des caractères,** (i) alignment of type, (ii) ranging of type; *Mil:* **a. d'un rang de soldats,** dressing of a line of soldiers; **perdre l'a.,** to get out of dress; **à droite a.!** right dress! (*b*) *Adm:* making up, balancing (of accounts, etc.); *Fin:* **a. des monnaies,** alignment of currencies; *Petrol. Ind:* **a. et pointage,** line and tack. **2.** (*a*) alignment, alinement, line (of wall, etc.); *Const:* **déborder, dépasser, l'a.,** to project beyond the building line; *Jur:* **servitude d'a.,** obligation upon landowners to observe the building line (of a street, etc.); **maison frappée d'a.,** house scheduled for realignment, threatened with a road-widening scheme; *Mil:* **rentrer dans l'a.,** to fall into line; **défaut d'a.,** misalignment; (*b*) *Nau:* leading mark(s). **3.** *Rail:* straight stretch (of line); *s.a.* PLASTIQUE 1, VOIRIE 1.
aligner [aliɲe], *v.tr.* **1.** to align, aline, lay out, draw up, line up; to put (thgs) in a line; **a. des maisons,** to lay out houses in a line; **a. un terrain,** to line out, mark out, a plot of ground; *Typ:* **a. des caractères,** (i) to align type; (ii) to range type; *Mil:* **a. des soldats,** to draw up, dress, a line of soldiers; **a. les tentes,** to dress the tents; **a. des phrases,** to string sentences together; **a. ses phrases,** to express oneself methodically, in well-ordered sentences; *Fin:* **la Belgique aligne sa monnaie sur la France,** Belgium aligns her currency on France. **2.** *Adm: etc:* **a. un compte,** to balance an account. **3.** (*of stag*) to cover, line (the doe).
s'aligner, to be in line with; to fall into line; *Mil:* to dress; **s'a. sur le terrain,** to take one's stand (for a duel); *P:* **tu peux toujours t'a.!** just you try it on! you're no match for him! *Pol:* **la Hongrie s'aligne sur l'URSS.,** Hungary takes her cue from the U.S.S.R.
aligoté [aligɔte], *s.m.* (*a*) white grape, (*b*) white wine (of Burgundy).
aliment [alimɑ̃], *s.m.* **1.** (*a*) aliment, food, nutriment, sustenance; *Physiol:* **a. complet,** complete food; **l'alcool n'est pas un a.,** alcohol has no food value; **a. de l'esprit,** food for the mind, mental pabulum; (*b*) *pl. Jur:* alimony. **2.** *Ins:* interest, risk, value.

alimentaire [alimɑ̃tɛːr], *a.* **1. régime a.,** diet; *Jur:* **pension, provision, a.,** alimony, allowances for necessaries; **auteur obligé de se consacrer à des besognes alimentaires,** author obliged to write pot-boilers; *Adm: Hist:* **carte a.,** ration card. **2.** alimentary, nutritious (food, plant, etc.); **produits alimentaires,** food (products); **conserves alimentaires,** tinned, canned, foods; *s.a.* PÂTE, 1. **3.** *Physiol:* **le canal, le tube, a.,** the alimentary canal; *Mch: etc:* **appareil a.,** feed(ing) apparatus; **pompe a.,** feed-pump, donkey-pump.

alimentateur, -trice [alimɑ̃tatœːr, -tris]. **1.** *a.* alimentary, nourishing, feeding (substance, etc.). **2.** *s.m. Mch: etc:* feed(er); **a. à bande articulée,** apron feeder.

alimentation [alimɑ̃tasjɔ̃], *s.f.* **1.** *(a)* alimentation, feeding (of plants, animals, etc.); supply (of town, market, etc.); **article d'a.,** foodstuff, food product; *Com:* **(magasin d') a.,** grocer's shop; **(rayon d')a.,** grocery department, food counter; *(b)* food, nourishment; nutrition; **a. défectueuse,** malnutrition. **2.** *Tchn: Mch: etc:* feed(ing) (of boiler, etc.); feed-mechanism (of gun); **pompe d'a.,** feed pump; **eau d'a.,** feed water; **foyer à a. sous grille,** grate with underfeed stoker; **a. par pesanteur, par gravité,** gravity feed; **a. par aspiration,** suction feed; **a. par pression,** pump feed; **a. en surface,** splash feed; **a. par gouttière,** chute feed; *El:* **bloc d'a.,** power supply; **groupe d'a.,** power equipment; **câble, fil, d'a.,** feeder; **appareil d'a.,** power pack; *W.Tel:* **puissance d'a.,** input.

alimenter [alimɑ̃te], *v.tr.* **1.** to feed, nourish (s.o.), to supply (market) with food; **ruisseaux qui alimentent une rivière,** streams that feed a river; **rivière qui alimente un moulin,** river that supplies a mill; **a. un journal,** to keep a paper supplied with news; **a. un foyer de charbon,** to feed a fire with coal; **a. une querelle,** to add fresh fuel to a quarrel; **a. la haine, la sédition,** to keep hatred, sedition, alive; *El.E:* **a. une usine en courant,** to deliver current to a factory, to furnish, supply, a factory with current; **centrale alimentée au mazout,** oil-fired power station; *Fb:* **a. les avants,** to feed the forward line; *s.a.* CONVERSATION 1. **2.** *Jur:* **a. son épouse,** to provide, (i) maintenance; (ii) alimony, for one's wife.

s'alimenter. *Med:* to eat.

alimenteur, -euse [alimɑ̃tœːr, -øːz], *s. Ind:* feeder (of machine, etc.).

alinéa [alinea], *s.m. Typ:* **1.** first line of paragraph, indented line; **en a.,** indented. **2.** paragraph, *F:* par; **multiplier les alinéas,** to break up copy.

alinger [alɛ̃ʒe], *v.tr. Tex:* to make supple, soft, by wear.

aliocentrique [aliɔsɑ̃trik], *a. Psy:* allocentric.

alios [aljos], *s.m. Geol:* iron pan.

aliphatique [alifatik], *a. Ch:* aliphatic, open chain (compound).

aliquante [alikɑ̃ːt], *a.f. Mth:* aliquant (part).

aliquote [alikɔt], *a. & s.f. Mth:* aliquot (part).

aliscaphe [aliskaf], *s.m. Trans:* hovercraft.

alise[1] [aliːz], *s.f. Nau:* (sheltered) creek.

alise[2], *s.f. Bot:* sorb-apple, fruit of the service-tree.

alisé [alize], *a.* = ALIZÉ.

alisier [alizje], *s.m. Bot:* service-tree; **a. des bois, a. aigrelier,** wild service-tree; **a. blanc, a. allouchier,** white-beam (tree).

alisma [alisma], *s.m. Bot:* alisma, water-plantain.

alismacées [alismase], *s.f.pl. Bot:* Alismaceae.

alisme [alism], *s.m. Bot:* = ALISMA.

alité [alite], *a.* confined to (one's) bed; *F:* laid up.

alitement [alitmɑ̃], *s.m.* confinement to bed; **trois jours d'a.,** three days in bed.

aliter [alite], *v.tr.* **1.** to confine (s.o.) to bed, to keep (s.o.) in bed. **2. a. des harengs,** to barrel herrings.

s'aliter, to take to one's bed.

alizari [alizari], *s.m.* madder root, alizari.

alizarine [alizarin], *s.f.* alizarin, madder dye.

alize [aliːz], *s.f. Bot:* = ALISE[2].

alizé [alize], *a. & s.m.* **les (vents) alizés,** the trade-winds.

alizéen, -enne [alizeɛ̃, -ɛn], *a.* of, relating to, the trade winds.

alizier [alizje], *s.m.* = ALISIER.

alkali [alkali], *s.m. Ch: A:* = ALCALI.

alkékenge [alkekɑ̃ːʒ], *s.f. Bot:* winter-cherry, strawberry-tomato, husk-tomato, physalis.

alkermès [alkermɛs], *s.m.* alkermes (liqueur, etc.).

Alkoran (l') [lalkɔrɑ̃], *s.m.* = KORAN (LE).

alkyd [alkid], *s.m. Ch:* alkyd (resin).

alkylat [alkila], *s.m. Ch: Ind:* alkylate.

alkylation [alkilasjɔ̃], *s.f. Ch:* alkylation.

alkylé [alkile], *a. Ch:* alkylated.

alkylique [alkilik], *a. Ch:* alkylic.

Allah [alla], *Pr.n.m.* Allah.

allaise [alɛːz], *s.f.* sand-bank (in river).

allaitant [alɛtɑ̃], *a. Husb:* suckling, nursing; **brebis allaitante,** milch-ewe.

allaite [alɛt], *s.f. Ven:* (wolf's) dug.

allaitement [alɛtmɑ̃], *s.m.* suckling, nursing, giving suck; **pendant l'a.,** during the nursing period; **a. artificiel, au biberon,** bottle-feeding, hand-feeding; **a. naturel,** breast-feeding.

allaiter [alete], *v.tr.* to suckle (child or young); to feed (child) at the breast; to nurse (child); **mère allaitante,** nursing mother.

allant [alɑ̃]. **1.** *a.* *(a)* active, busy, bustling, lively (person); *(b) (of old people)* active, able to move, walk about. **2.** *s.m.* initiative, drive; **avoir de l'a.,** to have plenty of energy, go; **manquer d'a.,** to lack energy, drive. **3.** *s.m.pl. O:* **allants et venants,** comers and goers, passers-by.

allantoïde [al(l)ɑ̃tɔid]. *Anat:* **1.** *a.* allantoid, allantoic. **2.** *s.f.* allantois.

allantoïne [al(l)ɑ̃tɔin], *s.f. Ch:* allantoin.

alléchant [al(l)ɛʃɑ̃], *a.* attractive, alluring, enticing, tempting (offer, advertisement, food); appetizing (smell, etc.).

allèchement [al(l)ɛʃmɑ̃], *s.m.* allurement, enticement, seduction, attraction.

allécher [al(l)eʃe], *v.tr.* **(j'allèche, n. alléchons; j'allécherai)** to allure, attract, entice, tempt.

allée [ale], *s.f.* **1.** *(action of)* going; **allées et venues,** coming and going, running about; *F:* **avoir l'a. pour la venue,** to go on a wild goose chase, to have one's journey for nothing. **2.** *(a)* walk (esp. lined with trees); lane, avenue (through wood, etc.); (carriage) drive; *s.a.* CAVALIER 1; *(b)* path (in garden); *(c)* passage, entrance, alley; *(d) Prehist:* **a. couverte,** passage grave, gallery tomb.

allégation [al(l)egasjɔ̃], *s.f.* allegation; averment.

allège [al(l)ɛːʒ], *s.f.* **1.** *Nau:* lighter, hopper, barge; *Com:* **frais d'a.,** lighterage; **franco a.,** free over side. **2.** *Arch: Const:* *(a)* breast-wall, dwarf-wall, basement (of window); *(b)* balustrade, rail (of window, etc.).

allégeable [al(l)eʒabl̩], *a.* that may be (i) lightened, (ii) alleviated.

allégeage [al(l)eʒaːʒ], *s.m.* lightening (of vessel).

allégeance[1] [al(l)eʒɑ̃ːs], *s.f.* **serment d'a.,** oath of allegiance.

allégeance[2], *s.f. Sp:* handicapping (of yachts).

allégeance[3], *s.f. O:* relief (of, from, anxiety).

allégement [al(l)eʒmɑ̃], *s.m.* **1.** lightening, unburdening (of vessel, floor); *N. Arch:* **trous d'a.,** lightening holes. **2.** alleviation, mitigation, relief (of pain, grief); **a. des impôts,** reduction, relief, in taxation, lightening of taxation.

alléger [al(l)eʒe], *v.tr.* **(j'allège, n. allégeons; j'allégeai(s); j'allégerai) 1.** *(a)* to lighten (ships, etc.); **a. les impôts,** to reduce, lighten, the taxes; *(b)* to unburden; to ease the strain on (timbers, etc.); *(c)* to alleviate, relieve, mitigate, soothe, allay (pain, grief). **2. a. qn de qch.,** to relieve s.o. of (the weight of) sth.; **allégé de tout souci,** relieved of all anxiety; *F:* **on m'a allégé de ma bourse,** I've had my purse lifted, pinched, I've been relieved of my purse. **3.** *Tchn:* to reduce the volume of (sth.); to plane down, file down, fine down (material).

s'alléger, to become, grow, lighter or easier.

Alleghany, Allegheny [al(l)egani], *Pr.n. Geog:* *(a)* **L'A.,** the Alleghany (river); *(b)* **les Monts A.,** the Alleghany Mountains, the Alleghanys.

allégir [al(l)eʒiːr], *v.tr.* = ALLÉGER 3.

allégorie [al(l)egɔri], *s.f.* allegory; **par a.,** allegorically.

allégorique [al(l)egɔrik], *a.* allegorical.

allégoriquement [al(l)egɔrikmɑ̃], *adv.* allegorically

allégorisation [al(l)egɔrizasjɔ̃], *s.f.* allegorization.

allégoriser [al(l)egɔrize], *v.tr. & i.* to allegorize.

allégoriste [al(l)egɔrist], *s.m. & f.* allegorist.

allègre [al(l)ɛːgr], *a.* lively, gay, jolly, merry, cheerful; **caractère a.,** cheerful disposition; **avoir le cœur a.,** to be light-hearted; **marcher d'un pas a.,** to walk with a lively step.

allégrement [al(l)ɛgrəmɑ̃], *adv.* briskly, nimbly; cheerfully, blithely, buoyantly.

allégresse [al(l)egrɛs], *s.f.* gladness, joy, cheerfulness, liveliness; **plein d'a.,** full of joy; *Ecc:* **les sept allégresses,** the Seven Joys of Mary.

allégretto [al(l)egrɛtto], *adv. & s.m. Mus:* allegretto; *pl. allégrettos.*

allégro [al(l)egro], *adv. & s.m. Mus:* allegro; *pl. allégros.*

alléguer [al(l)ege], *v.tr.* **(j'allègue, n. alléguons; j'alléguerai) 1.** to allege, urge, plead; **a. l'ignorance,** to plead ignorance; **a. l'impossibilité,** to put up a plea of impossibility; **a. un prétexte,** to advance a pretext. **2.** to cite, quote (author, authority); **a. une preuve,** to adduce a proof; to bring forward a proof.

allèle [al(l)ɛl], *s.m. Biol:* allele, allel, allelomorph.

allélomorphe [a(l)lelɔmɔrf], *a. Biol:* allelomorphic.

allélotrope [alelɔtrɔp], *Ch:* **1.** *a.* allelotropic. **2.** *s.m.* allelotropism, allelotropy.

alléluia [al(l)elyja). **1.** *s.m. & int. Ecc:* Hallelujah, alleluia(h). **2.** *s.m. Bot:* wood-sorrel.

Allemagne [almaɲ], *Pr.n.f. Geog:* Germany; **l'A. de l'ouest, de l'est,** West, East Germany; **l'empire d'A.,** the German Empire; **l'ambassadeur d'A.,** the German ambassador.

allemand, -ande [almɑ̃, -ɑ̃ːd]. **1.** *a. & s.* German; **querelle d'A.,** quarrel about nothing; **la langue allemande,** *s.m.,* **l'allemand,** the German language, German. **2.** *s.f.* **Allemande;** *(a) A. Danc: Mus:* Allemande; *(b) Cu:* Allemande sauce, white sauce.

allène [alɛn], *s.m. Ch:* allene, propadiene.

aller [ale] **I.** *v.i.* (*pr.p.* **allant;** *p.p.* **allé;** *pr.ind.* **je vais** (*A: & Dial:* **je vas**), **tu vas, il va, n. allons, v. allez, ils vont;** *pr. sub.* **j'aille, n. allions, ils aillent;** *imp.* **va** (**vas-y**), **allons, allez;** *p.d.* **j'allais;** *p.h.* **j'allai;** *fu.* **j'irai;** *the aux. is* **être.) 1.** to go; *(a)* **a. à Paris,** to go to Paris; **navire allant à Bordeaux,** ship bound for Bordeaux; **je vais à Versailles,** I am going to Versailles; **pour a. à X, s'il vous plait?** how do I get to X, please? **a. en autobus,** to go by bus; **a. à, en, bicyclette,** to go by bicycle, to cycle; **a. en bateau,** to go by boat; to go boating; **a. à la campagne, à l'église,** to go to the country, to church; **allez-vous encore à l'école?** are you still at school? do you still go to school? **a. chez qn,** to call on s.o.; **je vais chez des amis ce soir,** I am visiting, going to, friends tonight; **elle doit a. chez le boucher,** *P:* **au boucher,** she has to go to, to stop at, the butcher's; **il faut a. au ministre,** you must go to, apply to, the minister; **a. à l'eau,** (i) *A:* to go for water; (ii) to go into the water; **a. par bandes,** to go about in gangs; **a. à grands pas,** to stride along; **qui va là?** who goes there? *Nau:* **a. au fond,** to sink; **a. et venir,** to come and go, to go to and fro; *(of ferry)* to ply; **ne faire qu'a. et venir,** to be always on the go, on the move; **je ne ferai qu'a. et revenir,** I shall come straight back, I won't be a minute; **a. où va toute chose,** to go the way of all things, of all flesh; **où allons-nous?** (i) where are we going? (ii) *F:* what are things coming to? **où va le monde?** what is the world coming to? **a. contre la Providence,** to fly in the face of Providence; **nous allons vers l'emploi de l'énergie atomique dans la vie quotidienne,** we are on the way to using atomic energy in everyday life; **il va sur quarante ans,** he is getting on for forty, he is nearly forty (years old); **a. jusqu'à injurier qn,** to go so far as to call s.o. names; **il ira loin,** he will go far, will distinguish himself; **vous n'irez pas loin avec dix shillings,** you won't get very far with ten shillings, ten shillings won't get you very far; **soyez tranquille, cela n'ira pas plus loin,** don't worry, it won't go any further; **le pauvre vieux n'ira pas loin,** the poor old chap won't last long; **cet argent n'ira pas loin,** this money won't go far; **la recette ne va pas à une livre,** the takings don't come to a pound; **cette partie de l'héritage va à mon neveu,** this part of the inheritance goes, falls, to my nephew; **a. jusqu'au bout,** to see it through; **nous irons jusqu'au bout,** we shall carry on to the end; *s.a.* FEU[1] I 3, LAISSER 1; *Sp:* **allez!** go! *Box:* time! *F:* **faire a. qn,** to order s.o. about; *F:* **a. où le roi va seul, a. voir le roi de Prusse,** to have a look at the plumbing; *(b)* **a. en course, à la chasse, à la pêche, à pied, à cheval, en voiture, au galop, au trot:** *see these words;* *(c)* **a. à la selle,** *abs.* **aller,** to have a motion, a bowel movement; to have one's bowels opened; **allez-vous régulièrement?** do you clear your bowels regularly? are your bowels regular? *F:* **médecine qui fait a.,** laxative; *(d) with adv. acc.* **a. bon train,** to go at a good pace; **a. grand train,** to race along; *with cogn. acc.* **a. son chemin, son petit bonhomme de chemin,** to go one's way, to jog along; *(e)* **allez, je vous écoute,** go on, go ahead, I'm listening; *(f)* **sentier qui va à la gare,** path leading to the station; **tous les chemins vont à Rome,** all roads lead to Rome; **la frontière va du nord au sud,** the frontier runs from north to south; **la route va tout droit à travers le bois,** the road runs straight through the wood; *A:* **exemples qui vont à ébranler les**

mœurs, examples that tend to undermine morals; *A:* **exemples qui vont à prouver que . . .,** examples that go to prove that . . .; (*g*) **parc qui va jusqu'à la rivière,** park that extends, stretches, down to the river; (*h*) **plat qui va au feu, allant au feu, au four,** fire-proof, oven-proof dish. **2.** (*a*) to go, be going (well, badly); **les affaires vont, ne vont pas,** business is brisk, slack; **tout va bien,** everything is going well, things are all right; **ça ira!** we'll manage it! **ça n'irait pas du tout,** that would never do; **il y a quelque chose qui ne va pas,** there's something wrong; **voulez-vous de la bière?—va pour de la bière,** who's for beer?—right, beer it is; **je vous en offre cinq francs—va pour cinq francs!** I'll give you five francs for it—right, (we'll say) five francs! **cela va sans dire, cela va de soi,** that's understood, that is a matter of course, that goes without saying; **ainsi va le monde,** such is the way of the world; (*at roulette*) **rien ne va plus!** no more bets! (*b*) (*of machine, clock, etc.*) to go, act, work, run; **la pendule va bien, mal,** (i) the clock is right, wrong; (ii) the clock keeps good, bad, time; **vous êtes en retard si je vais bien,** you are late if my watch is right; **faire a. une montre,** to set a watch going; **faire a. un commerce,** to run a business; **tout va comme sur des roulettes,** everything is going like clockwork; **ça va tout seul,** it's all plain sailing; **cela ne va pas sans peine,** it involves, entails, some trouble; **la richesse ne va pas sans bien des soucis,** wealth brings, carries, many anxieties with it; (*c*) (*of clothes, etc.*) **ce veston ne va pas bien,** this jacket doesn't sit well; (*d*) **c'est trop grand pour a. dans le panier,** it's too big to go, get, into the basket; (*e*) **comment allez-vous?** *F:* **comment cela va-t-il? (comment) ça va?** how are you? **je vais bien,** *F:* **ça va,** I am well, I am all right; **cela va mieux,** I'm better; **cela ne va pas,** I am not feeling up to the mark. **3. aller à qn;** (*a*) (*of colours, clothes*) to suit s.o.; **le jaune vif me va bien,** bright yellow suits me; **ces grands airs ne vous vont pas,** putting on airs doesn't suit you; (*b*) (*of climate, food*) to agree with s.o.; (*c*) (*of clothes, etc.*) to fit s.o.; **cela vous va comme un gant,** *O:* **comme un bas de soie,** (i) it fits you like a glove; (ii) *F:* it suits you down to the ground, to a T; (*d*) (*of proposal, etc.*) to be to s.o.'s liking, to suit s.o.; **vos manières ne me vont pas,** I don't like your ways; **ça me va!** (i) agreed! done! (ii) that suits me; *F:* **ça va!** all right! O.K.! **ça ira comme ça,** we'll leave it at that; *F:* **ça va! ça va comme ça!** it's all right (as it is)! **n'allez pas croire cela!** don't you believe it! **s'il allait refuser,** should he refuse, if he should refuse, if he were to refuse; **et s'il allait refuser?** and what if he refuses? **4.** (*of colours, etc.*) **a. avec qch.,** to go well with sth., to match sth.; **a. (bien) ensemble,** to go well together, to match, to be a good match; *F:* **papier et enveloppes pour a. avec,** paper and envelopes to match; **bas qui ne vont pas ensemble,** stockings that are not a pair, odd stockings. **5.** (*a*) **aller** + *inf.*; **a. voir qn,** to go and, to, see s.o., to call on s.o.; **a. trouver qn,** to go and find s.o., to go to s.o.; **il était allé inspecter le terrain,** he had been to inspect the ground; **a. se promener,** to go for a walk, a stroll; *F:* **allez vous promener!** go (and) jump in the lake! **n'allez pas vous imaginer que . . .,** don't go and imagine that . . .; **allez donc savoir!** how is one to know? (*b*) (*aux. use of* **aller**, *pr. and p.d. only to form an immediate future*) to be going, to be about (to do sth.); **il va s'en occuper,** he is going to see about it; **il va venir,** he will come presently, he is going to come; **elle allait tout avouer,** she was about to confess everything; **nous allons maintenant écouter les leçons,** we shall now hear the lessons; **il y en a un qui va être surpris,** someone is in for a surprise; (*c*) **aller** + *pr.p. or ger.*; (i) (*forming a progressive tense*) **il va épiant, écoutant,** he goes on spying, listening. (ii) **sa santé va (en) empirant,** his health is steadily growing worse; **le fleuve va s'élargissant,** the river grows wider and wider. **6. y aller;** (NOTE: **y** *is omitted before forms of* **aller** *beginning with* **i**) (*a*) **j'y vais! on y va!** coming! **nous irons demain,** we will go there tomorrow; (*b*) **est-ce comme ça que vous y allez?** is that how you set about it, how you go to work? **allez-y doucement!** easy, gently (does it)! *s.a.* DOUCEMENT; **il faut y aller,** let's take the plunge; **comme vous y allez!** how fast you are working! *F:* you *do* go at it! **y a. de tout son cœur,** to put one's heart and soul into it; **il y va de toutes ses forces,** he goes at it for all he is worth; **y a. carrément, franchement,** to make no bones about it; **il n'y va pas par quatre chemins,** he doesn't mince matters, beat about the bush; **maintenant allons-y,** now (let's get down) to business; **allons-y!** well, here goes! **vas-y! allez-y!** go it! go ahead! get on with it! fire away! (*c*) *F:* **y a. de qch.,** to lay, stake, sth.; **y a. de son reste,** to stake one's all; **y a. de sa personne,** (i) to take a hand in it oneself; (ii) *F:* to do one's bit; **il y va de ses économies pour payer les dépenses de son fils,** he sacrifices his savings to pay (for) his son's expenses; **allez-y de vos compliments,** fire away with your compliments; **y a. de sa larme,** to squeeze out a tear; **il y est allé d'une bouteille,** he stood (us) a bottle; **il y est allé de ses vingt francs,** he put his name down for twenty francs. **7.** *v.impers.* **il va de soi que . . .,** it stands to reason, it is a matter of course, it goes without saying, that . . .; **il n'en va pas ainsi de son travail,** it's a different case, matter, with his work; **il en va de même pour lui, pour moi,** it's the same with him, with me; **il en va autrement de lui,** it's different with him; **il y va de vingt francs,** it's a matter of twenty francs; **il y allait de sa vie,** it was a matter of life and death (for him); his life was at stake. **8.** *int.* **allons, dépêchez-vous!** come on, hurry up! **allons, faisons une partie!** come on, let's have a game! **allons donc!** (i) come along! get a move on! (ii) nonsense! *F:* tell that to the marines! get on, along, with you! **allons bon!** there now! bother! **mais va donc!** get on with it! *P:* **va donc, sale vache!** get out, you dirty dog, skunk! **j'ai bien souffert, va! allez!** I have been through a lot, believe me!

II. **aller,** *s.m.* **1.** going, outward journey; **à l'a.,** on the way there; **nous avons eu bon vent à l'a.,** we had a fair wind on the outward passage; **cargaison d'a.,** outward cargo; **train d'a.,** down train; **a.-retour, voyage d'a. et retour,** journey there and back; *Nau:* voyage out and home; **billet a.-retour, d'a. et retour,** return ticket; **coupon d'a.,** outward half; *F:* **un a.,** a single ticket; **j'ai fait l'a.-retour en chemin de fer,** I went there and back by train; *M.Ins:* **police à l'a. et au retour,** round policy; *P:* **un a. et retour,** a box on the ears; *Sp:* **match a.,** away match. **2. gants pour tout a.,** gloves for all purposes. **3. pis a.,** last resort, makeshift, poor substitute; **accepter qch. comme pis a.,** to accept sth. as better than nothing; **ce serait un pis a.,** I hope it won't come to that; **au pis a.,** at the worst, if the worst comes to the worst. **4.** *Mec.E:* **a.-retour du piston,** up and down stroke; **a.-retour du train de tige du trépan,** round tripping.

s'en aller. (*pr.ind.* **je m'en vais;** *imp.* **va-t'en, allons-nous-en, allez-vous-en, ne t'en va pas, ne nous en allons pas;** *perf.* **je m'en suis allé(e), nous nous en sommes allé(e)s,** *F:* **je me suis en allé(e)**) **1.** to go away, to depart; to take one's departure; **faire s'en aller tout le monde,** to send everyone away; **les voisins s'en vont,** the neighbours are moving (house); **faire en a. des taches,** to remove stains; **les taches ne veulent pas s'en,** the stains won't come off, out; **allez-vous-en!** go away! **allons-nous-en!** let's go! **il faut que je m'en aille,** I must be going; **ses forces s'en allaient,** his strength was going; **le malade s'en va,** the patient is sinking; **votre lait s'en va,** your milk is boiling over; **s'en aller en fumée,** to end in smoke; **en allées, les vacances!** the holidays are over! **2.** (= ALLER I 5 (*b*)); **je m'en vais vous raconter ça,** I'll tell you all about it.

allergène [alɛrʒɛn], *s.m. Med:* allergen.

allergénique [alɛrʒenik], *a.* allergenic.

allergide [alɛrʒid], *s.f. Med:* allergic infection; illness caused by allergy.

allergie [alɛrʒi], *s.f. Med:* allergy; **a. aux œufs,** allergy to eggs.

allergique [alɛrʒik], *a. Med:* allergic (**à**, to); **je suis a. au poisson,** I'm allergic to fish.

allergologiste [alɛrgɔlɔʒist], *s.m.* & *f.* allergist.

alier-retour [aler(ə)tuːr], *s.m. F:* return (ticket).

alleu, -eux [alø], *s.m. Hist:* **(franc) a.,** allodium; freehold (land).

alliable [aljabl], *a.* (*a*) (*of metals, fluids, etc.*) miscible, that may be combined, mixed (**à**, with); (*b*) *A:* **idées alliables,** compatible ideas; **plaisir a. au devoir,** pleasure compatible with duty; **non, peu, alliable,** incompatible (**à**, with).

alliacé [aljase]. **1.** *a.* of, pertaining to, garlic; alliaceous. **2.** *s.f.pl. Bot:* **alliacées,** Alliaceae.

alliage [aljaːʒ], *s.m.* **1.** *Ch: Metall: etc:* (*a*) alloyage, combination, composition, (action of) alloying, blending; (*b*) alloy; (*c*) alloy, baser metal (mixed with finer); **sans a.,** pure, unalloyed. **2.** *Mth:* **règle d'a.,** Rule of Mixtures, alligation.

alliaire [aljɛːr], *s.f. Bot:* alliaria, *F:* jack-by-the-hedge, hedge garlic, sauce-alone.

alliance [aljɑ̃ːs], *s.f.* **1.** alliance; (*a*) match, marriage, union; **a. de deux maisons royales,** alliance, union, of two royal houses; **entrer par a. dans une famille,** to marry into a family; **parent par a.,** relation by marriage; (*b*) **a. de deux qualités,** union, blending, of two qualities; **a. de mots,** oxymoron; (*c*) **conclure un traité d'a., une a., avec un pays,** to conclude a treaty of alliance with a country; **renouer a. avec un pays,** to re-enter into an alliance with a country; *Hist:* **la Triple A.,** the Triple Alliance; *s.a.* ARCHE[1]. **2.** (*a*) wedding ring; (*b*) connecting piece (of harness).

alliciant [alisjɑ̃], *a. Lit:* attractive, enticing.

allié, -ée [alje]. **1.** *a.* (*a*) allied (nation, etc.); **être a. à une nation,** to be allied to, in alliance with, a nation; (*b*) **être bien a.,** to be well connected; **a. par le sang,** related by blood. **2.** *s.* (*a*) ally; *Hist:* **les Alliés,** the Allies; (*b*) relation by marriage; connection; **elle est l'alliée d'une famille très riche,** she is connected by marriage with a very rich family; **a. par le sang,** blood relation.

allier [alje], *v.tr.* (*p.d.* & *pr.sub.* **n. alliions, v. alliiez**) **1.** to ally, unite; **intérêts communs qui allient deux pays,** common interests that unite two countries; **a. une famille à, avec, une autre,** to unite one family with another by marriage. **2.** (*a*) to alloy, mix (metals); (*b*) to harmonize, blend, match (colours); (*c*) to combine, unite (qualities, words, etc.) (**à**, with).

s'allier. 1. (*a*) to form an alliance, to become allies, to ally; (*b*) to form a connection by marriage; **s'a. à une famille,** to marry into a family; **deux races qui s'allient souvent,** two races that often intermarry. **2.** (*a*) (*of fluids*) to mix; (*of metals*) to alloy; (*b*) (*of colours*) to harmonize, blend.

alligator [al(l)igatɔːr], *s.m. Rept:* alligator.

allitératif, -ive [al(l)iteratif, -iːv], *a.* alliterative.

allitération [al(l)iterasjɔ̃], *s.f.* alliteration.

allitérer [al(l)itere], to alliterate, to use alliteration.

allô, allo [alo], *int. Tp:* Hullo! hallo! *U.S:* Hello!

Allobroges [ɑl(l)ɔbrɔːʒ], *s.m.pl. Hist:* Allobroges.

allocataire [al(l)ɔkatɛːr], *s.m.* & *f. Adm:* recipient of an allowance; allocatee.

allocation [al(l)ɔkasjɔ̃], *s.f.* **1.** (*a*) allocation, apportionment, assignment, granting (of sum of money, of land, supplies, etc.); (*b*) *Fin:* allotment (of shares, etc.); (*c*) *Jur:* allocation, allowance (of items in an account, etc.). **2.** allowance, grant; **les allocations familiales,** family allowances, *U.S:* dependents' allowances; **a. de maternité,** maternity benefit; **a. (de) vieillesse,** old age, retirement, pension; **a. de chef de famille,** married allowance; **a. par tête,** capitation grant; **a. (faite) aux femmes de mobilisés,** separation allowance; **a. (de) chômage,** unemployment benefit; **demander une a.,** to apply for a grant.

allocentriste [al(l)ɔsɑ̃trist], *a. Psy:* allocentric.

allochtone [al(l)ɔktɔn]. **1.** *a.* & *s.* immigrant. **2.** *a. Geol:* allocht(h)onous; *s.m. Geol:* allochton(e).

allocution [al(l)ɔkysjɔ̃], *s.f.* (*a*) short speech, allocution; **prononcer, faire, une a.,** to deliver, give, an address (**à**, to); (*b*) *Ecc: Jur:* charge (by bishop; by judge to jury).

allodial, -iaux [al(l)ɔdjal, -jo], *a.* & *s.m. A.Jur:* allodial, freehold (estate).

allodialité [al(l)ɔdjalite], *s.f. A.Jur:* allodiality.

allogamie [al(l)ɔgami], *s.f. Bot:* allogamy, cross-fertilization.

allogène [al(l)ɔʒɛn]. **1.** *a. Geol:* allothogenous, allothogenic, allogenic. **2.** *a.* & *s. Ethn:* alien, foreign (element, race).

allométrie [al(l)ɔmetri], *s.f. Biol:* allometry.

allométrique [al(l)ɔmetrik], *a. Biol:* allometric.

allomorphe [al(l)ɔmɔrf], *a. Ch:* allomorphic.

allomorphie [al(l)ɔmɔrfi], *s.f. Ch:* allomorphism

allomorphite [al(l)ɔmɔrfit], *s.f. Miner:* allomorphite.

allonge [alɔ̃ːʒ], *s.f.* **1.** (*a*) **a.** lengthening-piece; extension(-piece); **mettre une a. à qch.,** to lengthen sth.; **a. d'une table,** leaf of a table; (*b*) *Phot:* extension bellows (for camera); **tube a.,** extension tube; **planchette d'a.,** extension board (of camera); (*c*) adaptor (of retort, pipe, etc.); lengthening-tube; (*d*) *Mch:* coupling-rod, sliding-rod; **a. de tige,** extension rod; *Min:* **a. de tige de pompage,** pony rod; (*e*) *N.Arch:* timber, futtock, stanchion; (*f*) **a. de boucher,** meat-hook. **2. a. d'une lettre de change,** allonge to a bill of exchange; **a. d'un document,** rider to a document. **3.** *Box:* reach; **être avantagé en a.,**

to have the longer reach. 4. *Equit:* lunging rein, longe, lunge.

allongé, -ée [alɔ̃ʒe]. 1. *a.* long; **cheval aux jambes allongées,** long-legged horse, horse long in the leg; *Equit:* **trot a.,** extended trot; **avoir une figure allongée,** (i) to have a long(-shaped) face; (ii) to have a face as long as a fiddle, to pull a long face; *Anat:* **la moelle allongée,** the medulla oblongata. 2. *a.* oblong; elongated (hexagon, etc.); prolate (ellipsoid); *s.a.* CYCLOÏDE 1. 3. *a. Sp:* **coup a.,** follow-through; *Artil:* **coup trop a.,** bye. 4. *s.m. & f.* (*a*) *Med:* recumbent patient; (*b*) *P:* **les allongés,** the dead and buried; **le boulevard des allongés,** the graveyard, *P:* the boneyard.

allongeable [alɔ̃ʒabl̩], *a.* that may be lengthened, extended; extensible.

allongeant [alɔ̃ʒɑ̃], *a. Cost:* giving an effect of height, of tallness.

allongement [alɔ̃ʒmɑ̃], *s.m.* 1. (*a*) lengthening, extension (of canal, etc.); lengthening (of dress); (*b*) elongation (of metals, etc.); strain; **a. spécifique,** unit elongation; **a. visqueux,** creep; *Mec.E:* **a. de rupture, à la rupture,** elongation at rupture, on break; **a. rémanent,** permanent set; (*c*) *Artil:* lifting (of fire); (*d*) *N.Arch:* jumboization. 2. protraction, extension (of time). 3. *F:* = LONGUEUR. 4. *Av:* aspect ratio (of wing).

allonger [alɔ̃ʒe], *v.tr.* **(j'allongeai(s); n. allongeons)** 1. (*a*) to lengthen, elongate; to let down (garment); **cette robe vous allonge,** this dress makes you look taller; **cette nouvelle lui allongea le nez, la mine, le visage,** this news made him pull a long face, his face fell at this news; (*b*) to add a piece to (sth.); (*c*) *s.a.* SAUCE 1; (*d*) *Artil:* to lift (fire); (*e*) *Sp:* **a. l'allure,** to increase the pace; (*f*) *N.Arch:* to jumboize. 2. (*a*) to stretch out (one's arm); to crane (one's neck); to extend, draw out (rope, etc.); **les piliers allongent de grandes ombres,** the pillars cast long shadows; *s.a.* PAS[1] 1; (*b*) *F:* **a. un coup à qn,** to aim a blow, strike out, at s.o.; **a. une gifle, une taloche, à qn,** to slap s.o. in the face; *F:* to fetch s.o. a clout; **a. l'argent,** to hand over, *F:* fork out, the money; *P:* **s'a. un bon dîner,** to stand oneself, treat oneself to, a good dinner; *cf.* APPUYER 2. 3. to protract, prolong (conversation, etc.); *Mus:* **a. un coup d'archet,** to prolong a stroke of the bow; **a. le temps,** to slacken the time.

s'allonger. 1. (*of days, hours, etc.*) to grow longer, lengthen; **son visage s'allongea,** he pulled a long face, his face fell; **un sourire s'allongea sur ses lèvres,** he grinned broadly. 2. to stretch oneself out, to lie down at full length; *F:* **s'a. par terre,** to come a cropper. 3. to extend; **de chaque côté de la nef s'allonge une file de stalles,** a row of stalls extends on either side of the nave; **chiens allongés sur la piste,** dogs strung out on the scent; **le peloton des coureurs allongé derrière,** the field strung out behind.

allonyme [al(l)ɔnim]. 1. *a.* allonymous; **livre a.,** allonymous book, allonym. 2. *s.* author who publishes under an allonym.

allopathe [al(l)ɔpat]. *Med:* 1. *a.* allopathic (remedy). 2. *s.* allopath.

allopathie [al(l)ɔpati], *s.f. Med:* allopathy.

allopathique [al(l)ɔpatik], *a. Med:* allopathic.

allophane [al(l)ɔfan], *s.f. Miner:* allophane.

allothigène [al(l)ɔtiʒɛn], *a. Geol:* allothogenous, allothogenic.

allotir [al(l)ɔtiːr], *v.tr.* 1. *Jur:* **a. des héritiers,** to share, apportion, an inheritance among heirs. 2. to group, to sort out (stores, etc.).

allotissement [al(l)ɔtismɑ̃], *s.m.* 1. apportionment, allotment. 2. grouping (of stores, etc.) into lots.

allotropie [al(l)ɔtrɔpi], *s.f. Ch:* allotropy.

allotropique [al(l)ɔtrɔpik], *a. Ch:* allotropic.

allotropisme [al(l)ɔtrɔpism], *s.m. Ch:* allotropism.

allouable [alwabl̩], *a.* grantable, allowable.

allouchier [al(l)uʃje], *s.m. Bot:* white-beam.

allouer [alwe], *v.tr. Adm:* (*a*) to grant (salary, etc.); **a. une dépense, un budget,** to allow, pass, an item of expenditure, a budget; (*b*) to allocate, apportion (shares, rations, etc.); *Jur:* **a. à qn une somme à titre de dommages-intérêts,** to award s.o. a sum as damages.

alluchon [alyʃɔ̃], *s.m. Mec.E:* (*a*) cog, tooth (of mortise wheel); (*b*) cam, wiper, lifter.

allumage [alymaːʒ], *s.m.* (*a*) lighting (of lamp, fire); kindling (of fire); switching on (of electric light); (*b*) firing (of mine); **a. défectueux,** misfiring; (*c*) *I.C.E:* ignition; *F:* **mettre, couper, l'a.,** to switch on, off; **a. à bobine,** coil ignition; **a. à dépression,** vacuum ignition; **a. par magnéto,** magneto ignition; **a. à rupture,** touch spark ignition; **a. à tube incandescent,** hot tube ignition; **a. avancé, retardé,** advanced, delayed, ignition; **foyer d'a.,** ignition point; **a. en retour,** arc-back; **point d'a.,** time of ignition; **pont d'a.,** spark gap; **ordre d'a.,** order of firing (of cylinders); **raté d'a.,** misfire; **a. prématuré,** pre-ignition; (i) pinking; (ii) backfire; **mettre de l'avance à l'a.,** to advance the spark.

allumé [alyme], *a.* 1. (*a*) alight; (*of fire*) kindled; **du charbon a.,** burning coals; **haut fourneau a.,** furnace in blast; (*b*) *F:* drunk, squiffy, lit up; **visage a.,** face flushed with wine. 2. *F:* (sexually) excited, *P:* randy.

allume-cigare [alymsigar], *s.m.* cigar lighter; *pl. allume-cigares.*

allume-feu [alymfø], *s.m.inv.* fire-lighter; kindling (-wood).

allume-gaz [alymgɑːz], *s.m.inv.* gas-lighter.

allumer [alyme], *v.tr.* 1. (*a*) to light (lamp, fire, pipe); to kindle, ignite, set fire to (sth.); *abs.* to light the lamps; to light up; to switch on the light; *F:* to light up (pipe, cigarette, etc.); *F:* **a. le salon,** to put the light(s) on in the drawing room; *F:* **a. le poste,** to switch, turn, put, on, the radio, the television; **a. un projecteur,** to switch on a searchlight; **a. sa cigarette à la bougie,** to light one's cigarette from the candle; (*b*) **a. une pompe,** to prime, fetch, a pump; *A:* **a. un fourneau de mine,** to fire a mine. 2. to inflame, excite (passions, persons); to stir up (war); *F:* **se faire a.,** to make oneself conspicuous; **a. l'imagination,** to fire the imagination; *F:* **a. un client,** to excite a customer's interest. 3. *P:* to plank down the money in advance (at cards, etc.). 4. *P:* **allume!** hurry up! look sharp! *Row:* pull hard! 5. *P:* to shoot (s.o.).

s'allumer. 1. to kindle, to take fire, to catch alight; **ses yeux s'allumèrent,** his eyes lit up; *I.C.E:* **s'a. prématurément,** to back fire. 2. (*of pers.*) (*a*) to warm up to one's subject; (*b*) to grow excited (*esp.* with drink).

allumette [alymɛt], *s.f.* 1. match; **a. de sûreté,** *A:* **a. suédoise,** safety match; **allumettes plates,** book matches; **pochette d'allumettes,** book of matches; **frotter une a.,** to strike a match; (*b*) *F:* long skinny leg. 2. *Cu:* **a. au fromage,** cheese straw; **a. glacée,** frosted stick; *s.a.* FLAMBER 1.

allumette-bougie [alymɛtbuʒi], *s.f.* wax-vesta; *pl. allumettes-bougies.*

allumette-tison [alymɛttizɔ̃], *s.f.* fusee; *pl. allumettes-tisons.*

allumettier, -ière [alymɛtje, -jɛːr], *s. Ind:* (*a*) match manufacturer; (*b*) worker in a match factory.

allumeur, -euse [alymœːr, -øːz], *s.* 1. lighter; igniter; **a. de réverbères,** lamp-lighter. 2. *s.f. P:* **allumeuse,** flirt, vamp. 3. *s.m.* (*a*) lighter, igniting device; **a. électrique,** electric igniter; **a. à gaz,** gas-lighter; (*b*) *I.C.E:* distributor; (*c*) *Av:* torch, igniter.

allumoir [alymwaːr], *s.m.* lighter; **a. à gaz,** gas-lighter.

allunir [alynir], *v.tr.* = ALUNIR.

allure [alyːr], *s.f.* 1. (*a*) walk, gait, tread, carriage, bearing; **a. dégagée,** free, easy carriage; **a. martiale,** soldierly bearing; **allures d'un cheval,** paces of a horse; **a. relevée,** high action (of horse); **avoir de l'a.,** (i) (*of horse*) to be a good stepper; (ii) (*of pers.*) to have style, a good presence; **reconnaître qn à son a.,** to know s.o. by his walk; **discours d'une a. guerrière,** speech with a warlike sound; (*b*) pace; **marcher à (une) vive a.,** to walk at a brisk pace; (*c*) speed; **à toute a.,** at full speed; *Rac:* at full stretch; **la voiture filait à toute a., à grande a.,** the car was going at top speed, *F:* all out; **pleine a.,** maximum speed; **a. économique de croisière,** cruising speed. (*d*) *Mch: etc:* working (of furnace, engine, etc.); **a. régulière,** smooth motion, running; **a. de marche,** rating; **le moteur fonctionne à l'a. normale,** the motor is running at its normal speed. 2. *Nau:* (*a*) point of sailing; (*b*) sailing trim. 3. (*a*) manner, ways; way(s) of dealing, of doing things; demeanour, behaviour, conduct (of pers.); **a. posée,** sedate behaviour; (*b*) aspect, look (of person, things, events); **il avait l'a. d'un professeur,** he looked like a schoolmaster; **l'a. des affaires,** the way things are going; the trend of affairs; **l'affaire prend une mauvaise a.,** the business is taking an ugly turn, looks bad; **prendre bonne allure,** to look promising, to look well; *Mth:* **a. d'une courbe,** trend of a curve; *s.a.* LIBRE 1.

allusif, -ive [al(l)yzif, -iːv], *a.* allusive.

allusion [al(l)yzjɔ̃], *s.f.* allusion (à, to); hint, innuendo; **une a. claire,** a broad hint; **une a. discrète,** a gentle hint; **faire a. à qn, qch.,** to refer to s.o., sth.; **faire une a. voilée à qch.,** to hint at sth; **faire une a. peu voilée à . . . ,** to make a pointed allusion to . . . ; **c'est à vous que s'adresse cette a.,** *F:* that's a dig, hit, at you, that's meant for you.

alluvial, -iaux [al(l)yvjal, -jo], **alluvien, -ienne** [al(l)yvjɛ̃, -jɛn], *a. Geol:* alluvial.

alluvion [al(l)yvjɔ̃], *s.f. Geol:* 1. *usu. pl.* alluvium, alluvial deposits. 2. *esp. Jur:* alluvion; **terrains d'a.,** alluvial tracts of land, alluvium.

alluvionnaire [al(l)yvjɔnɛːr], *a. Geol:* alluvial.

alluvionnement [al(l)yvjɔnmɑ̃], *s.m. Geog:* formation of alluvial deposits; aggradation.

allyle [al(l)il], *s.m. Ch:* allyl.

allylène [al(l)ilɛn], *s.m. Ch:* allylene.

allylique [al(l)ilik], *a. Ch:* allytic (alcohol, etc.).

almageste [almaʒɛst], *s.m. A.Astr:* almagest.

almanach [almana], *s.m.* 1. almanac; calendar; ephemeris. 2. directory guide; year-book; **a. de Gotha,** almanac listing members of the peerage and diplomatic corps; approx. = Debrett; *s.a.* NOBILIAIRE. 3. **faiseur d'almanachs,** fortune-teller.

almandin [almɑ̃dɛ̃], *s.m.*, **almandine** [almɑ̃din], *s.f. Miner:* almandite, almandine; *s.a.* GRENAT 1.

alme [alm], *s.f. Dial:* summer pasture (in the Alps).

almée [alme], *s.f.* alma(h), almeh, (Egyptian) dancing-woman.

almicantarat [almikɑ̃tara], *s.m. Astr:* almucantar.

aloès [alɔɛs], *s.m. Bot:* 1. aloe; *Pharm:* **amer d'a.,** bitter aloes. 2. *see* BOIS[1] 5.

aloétique [alɔetik], *a. Ch: Pharm:* aloetic.

aloi [alwa], *s.m.* 1. (*a*) *A:* (= TITRE) degree of fineness (of coin); **monnaie d'a.,** sterling money; (*b*) **pièce de mauvais a.,** base coin, light coin. 2. standard, quality, kind (of goods, persons); **de bon a.,** genuine; **argument de bon a.,** sound, valid, argument; **marchandises, homme, de bon a.,** goods of reliable quality, man of sterling worth; **noblesse de bon a.,** genuine old nobility; **plaisanterie de mauvais a.,** nasty joke; unkind joke; **de bas a.,** contemptible.

alopécie [alɔpesi], *s.f. Med:* alopecia.

alors [alɔːr], *adv.* 1. (*a*) then, at that time, at the time; **que faisiez-vous a.,** what were you doing then, at the time? **jusqu'a.,** until then; (*b*) *a.phr.* **d'a.,** of that time, of former days; **la vie d'a.,** life in those days; **le ministre d'a.,** the minister in power at the time; *F:* the then minister. 2. (*a*) then, well then, in that case, in such a case; **a. vous viendrez?** well then, you're coming? *F:* **a. comme a.,** we must wait and see; *F:* **et (puis) a.? a. quoi?** (i) and what then? (ii) so what? (*b*) therefore, so; **il n'était pas là, a. je suis revenu,** he wasn't there, so I came back again. 3. *conj. phr.* **a. (même) que,** (i) (at the very time) when, (ii) even when; (iii) even though, whereas; **vous économisez, a. qu'il faudrait dépenser,** you're saving, whereas you should be spending; **a. même que je le pourrais,** even though I could. 4. (= ENSUITE) then, next.

alose [aloːz], *s.f. Ich:* alosa; *esp.* alose; shad; **grande a.,** allice shad.

alosier [alozje], *s.m.*, **alosière** [alozjɛːr], *s.f. Fish:* shad-seine.

alouate [alwat], *s.m. Z:* alouatte, howler (monkey).

alouette [alwɛt], *s.f.* 1. *Orn:* (*a*) lark; **a. des champs,** skylark; **a. élégante,** bar-tailed desert lark; **a. leucoptère,** white-winged lark; **a. lulu, des bois,** wood-lark; **a. nègre,** black lark; **a. isabelline,** desert lark; **a. hausse-col, oreillarde,** shore lark; **a. calandre,** calandra lark; **a. pispolette,** lesser short-toed lark; *F:* **il attend que les alouettes lui tombent toutes rôties (dans le bec),** he's waiting for the plums to fall into his mouth; (*b*) **a. de mer,** summer-snipe, sea-lark, dunlin. 2. *Nau:* **tête d'a.,** (wall and) crown. 3. *Cu:* **a. sans tête,** veal olive.

alourdi [alurdi], *a.* heavy, dull; **a. de sommeil,** drowsy; **a. par le sommeil,** heavy with sleep; *Fin:* **le marché est alourdi,** the market is dull.

alourdir [alurdiːr], *v.tr.* 1. to make (sth.) heavy. 2. to make (s.o.) dull, stupid; to dull (the mind, etc.). 3. to weigh down (s.o., sth.); **a. qn de qch.,** to burden s.o. with sth.

s'alourdir, to grow, become, (i) heavy; (ii) dull, stupid.

alourdissant [alurdisɑ̃], *a.* oppressive (heat, weather, etc.).

alourdissement [alurdismɑ̃], *s.m.* 1. (process of) growing heavy; growing heaviness (of limbs, etc.). 2. dulling (of the mind).

aloyage [alwajaːʒ], *s.m.* alloyage (of metals).
aloyau, -aux [alwajo], *s.m. Cu:* sirloin (of beef).
aloyer [alwaje], *v.tr.* to alloy (metals).
alpaca [alpaka], *s.m.*, **alpaga** [alpaga], *s.m. Z: Tex:* alpaca.
alpage [alpaːʒ], *s.m. (in the Alps)* (*a*) alp, mountain pasture; (*b*) right of pasture (on mountain slopes); (*c*) season spent by sheep and cattle in mountain pastures.
alpax [alpaks], *s.m. Metall:* alpax.
alpe [alp], *s.f.* **1.** alp, mountain pasture (*esp.* in the Alps). **2.** (*a*) **Les Alpes**, the Alps; **les Alpes Cottiennes**, the Cottian Alps; **les Alpes Grées**, the Graian Alps; **cor des Alpes**, Alpine horn; **pavot des Alpes**, Alpine poppy; (*b*) **les Alpes australiennes**, the Australian Alps; **les Alpes néo-zélandaises, méridionales**, the Southern Alps.
alpenstock [alpɛnstɔk], *s.m.* alpenstock.
alpestre [alpɛstr̥], *a.* Alpine (scenery, climate, resort, plant, etc.); alpestrine (plant).
Alpette (l') [lalpɛt], *Pr.n.f. Geog: F:* the lower Alps (of France).
alpha [alfa], *s.m.* **1.** *Gr.Alph:* alpha; **l'a. et l'oméga**, Alpha and Omega, the beginning and the end. **2.** *Ph:* **particule a.**, alpha particle; **rayons a.**, alpha rays; **rayonnement a.**, alpha radiation, rays; **émetteur a.**, alpha radiator, emitter.
alphabet [alfabɛ], *s.m.* **1.** alphabet; **apprendre son a. à un enfant**, to teach a child his alphabet, his letters. **2.** *Sch:* spelling-book.
alphabétique [alfabetik], *a.* alphabetical; **par ordre a.**, in alphabetical order, alphabetically; **table a.**, index (of book).
alphabétiquement [alfabetikmɑ̃], *adv.* alphabetically.
alphabétisation [alfabetizasjɔ̃], *s.f.* elimination of illiteracy.
alphabétiser [alfabetize], *v.tr.* to teach s.o. to read and write.
alphabétisme [alfabetism], *s.m. Ling:* alphabetism.
alphagère [alfaʒɛːr], *s.m. Metall:* alpha phase stabilizer.
alphaméthylnaphtalène [alfametilnaftalɛn], *s.m. Ch:* alphamethylnaphthalene.
alphanumérique [alfanymerik], *a.* alphameric(al), alphanumeric(al).
Alphée [alfe]. **1.** *Pr.n.m. Gr.Myth:* Alpheus. **2.** *s.m. Crust:* alpheus.
alphénic [alfenik], *s.m. Pharm: A:* alphenic, white barley sugar.
Alphonse [alfɔ̃ːs]. **1.** *Pr.n.m.* Alphonso, Alfonso. **2.** *s.m. A: F:* procurer, pimp; (from A. Dumas's play *Monsieur Alphonse*).
alpicole [alpikɔl], *a. Bot:* alpine (plant).
alpin [alpɛ̃], *a.* alpine (club, plant, troops).
alpinisme [alpinism], *s.m.* mountaineering; **faire de l'a.**, to go in for mountaineering; to climb.
alpiniste [alpinist], *s.m. & f.* alpinist; mountaineer.
alpinum [alpinɔm], *s.m. Hort:* botanical garden of Alpine plants.
alpique [alpik], *a.* Alpine (range).
alpiste [alpist], *s.m. Bot:* alpist, alpia; canary-grass, -seed; **a. panaché**, gardener's garters.
alque [alk], *s.m. Orn:* auk.
alquifoux [alkifu], *s.m. Cer:* alquifou, potters' lead.
alréen, -enne [alreɛ̃, -ɛn], *a. & s.*, **alrien, -ienne** [alrijɛ̃, -jɛn], *a. & s. Geog:* (native, inhabitant) of Auray.
Alsace [alzas], *Pr.n.f. Geog:* Alsace.
alsacien, -ienne [alzasjɛ̃, -jɛn], *a. & s. Geog:* Alsatian.
alsatique [alzatik], *a.* (literature, etc.) of Alsace.
alsine [alsin], *s.f. Bot:* alsine, chickweed.
altaïque [altaik], *a. Ethn:* Altaic, Altaian (race).
altazimut [altazimyt], *s.m. Astr:* altazimuth.
altazimutal, -aux [altazimytal, -o], *a. Astr:* **théodolite a.**, altazimuth theodolite.
altérabilité [alterabilite], *s.f.* liability to deterioration.
altérable [alterabl̥], *a.* liable to deterioration.
altérant [alterɑ̃]. **1.** *a.* thirst-producing. **2.** *a. & s.m. Med:* alterative.
altérateur, -trice [alteratœːr, -tris]. **1.** *a.* adulterating. **2.** *s.* debaser (of coinage); adulterator (of food, wine, etc.).
altération [alterasjɔ̃], *s.f.* **1.** change (for the worse); impairing (of health, etc.); deterioration (of food, etc.); foxing (of paper); **a. de la voix**, (i) faltering of the voice, breaking of the voice (with emotion); (ii) break(ing) of the voice (after puberty); **a. d'une couleur**, fading of a colour; **a. des roches**, weathering of rocks; **a. du caoutchouc**, decomposition, perishing, of rubber. **2.** (*a*) debasing, debasement (of coinage); adulteration (of food); falsification (of document); garbling (of text); misrepresentation (of facts); deformation (of word); tampering (with key, etc.); (*b*) *Mus:* inflecting (of note). **3.** great thirst.
altercation [alterkasjɔ̃], *s.f.* altercation, dispute, wrangle, *F:* squabble; **avoir une a. avec qn**, to have words with s.o.
altéré [altere], *a.* **1.** faded (colour, etc.); drawn, haggard (face). **2.** thirsty; **a. de sang**, thirsty, athirst, for blood, *F:* out for blood.
alter ego [alterego], *s.m.* alter ego; **c'est mon a. e.**, he is my second self; *F:* **où est ton a. e.?** where's your other half?
altérer [altere], *v.tr.* **(j'altère, n. altérons; j'altérerai) 1.** to change (for the worse); to spoil, taint, corrupt (meat, wine, character); to impair (health); **le climat a altéré sa santé**, the climate has affected his health; **rien n'arriva pour a. notre bonheur**, nothing happened to spoil our happiness; **voix altérée par l'émotion**, voice faltering, husky, with emotion. **2.** (*a*) to tamper with (sth.); to adulterate (food); to debase (coinage); to falsify (document); to garble (text, history); to tamper with (key); **a. les faits**, to mis-state, give a garbled version of, the facts; **a. la vérité**, to twist the truth; (*b*) *Mus:* **a. une note**, to inflect a note. **3.** to make (s.o.) thirsty; *abs.* to cause thirst, to parch the mouth.
s'altérer. 1. to change, alter (for the worse); to deteriorate, spoil; (*of rocks*) to weather; (*of paper*) to fox; **sa voix s'altéra**, his voice faltered, broke. **2.** *A:* to grow thirsty.
altérité [alterite], *s.f. Phil:* otherness, alterity.
alternance [altɛrnɑ̃ːs], *s.f.* **1.** alternance (of seasons, leaves, strata, etc.); *Hort:* alternate bearing; **en a.**, alternately. **2.** *El.E:* alternation; **redresseur à deux alternances**, full-wave rectifier. **3.** *Ling:* **a. vocalique, de voyelles**, vowel gradation; ablaut.
alternant [altɛrnɑ̃], *a.* alternating (duties); rotating (crops); *Geol:* alternant (layers).
alternaria [altɛrnarja], *s.m. Fung:* Alternaria.
alternariose [altɛrnarjoz], *s.f. Fung:* alternariose.
alternat [altɛrna], *s.m.* **1.** *Agr:* = ASSOLEMENT. **2.** *Dipl:* alternat, rotation in precedence (in signing treaties, etc.).
alternateur [altɛrnatœːr], *s.m. El.E:* alternating-current generator; alternator; **a. monophasé**, single-phase alternator; **a. triphasé**, three-phase alternator.
alternatif, -ive [altɛrnatif, -iːv], *a.* **1.** (*a*) alternate (colours, etc.); (*b*) *El.E:* alternating (current); (*c*) *Mec.E:* reciprocating (engine, saw, motion). **2.** alternative (proposal, meaning, etc.). **3.** *s.f.* **alternative**; (*a*) alternation, succession; (*b*) alternative, option; **ce fait nous ôte toute alternative**, this fact leaves us no choice, no option.
alternation [altɛrnasjɔ̃], *s.f.* **1.** alternation; reciprocation (of motion). **2.** *Mth:* = PERMUTATION.
alternativement [altɛrnativmɑ̃], *adv.* alternately, by turns, in turn, turn and turn about, one after the other; **placer les rivets a.**, to stagger the rivets.
alterne [altɛrn], *a.* alternate (leaves, angles, etc.); *Geom:* **angles alternes-externes, alternes-internes**, alternate-exterior, alternate-interior angles.
alterné [altɛrne], *a.* **1.** alternate; *s.a.* UNILATÉRAL **1. 2.** staggered (poles of dynamo, etc.); *Mth:* **série alternée**, alternating series.
alterner [altɛrne]. **1.** *v.i.* (*a*) to alternate; **faire a. les larmes et les rires**, to make s.o. cry and laugh by turns; **l'éditeur alterne chez lui avec l'artiste**, he is publisher and artist by turns; (*b*) to take turns (**pour**, in + *ger.*); to take turn and turn about (**pour**, to + *inf.*, in + *ger.*), to take it in turns (**pour**, to + *inf.*); **il alterne avec les autres pour veiller**, he takes turns with the others in sitting up; **ils alternent pour veiller**, they take it in turns to sit up. **2.** *v.tr.* (*a*) to rotate (crops); to practise rotations on (field); (*b*) *Metalw:* **a. les joints**, to break joint.
alterniflore [altɛrniflɔːr], *a. Bot:* bearing alternate flowers.
alternifolié [altɛrnifɔlje], *a. Bot:* alternifoliate, alternate-leaved.
alternisépale [altɛrnisepal], *a. Bot:* alternisepalous.
alternomoteur [altɛrnɔmɔtœːr], *s.m. El.E:* alternating-current motor.
altesse [altɛs], *s.f.* highness; **son A. impériale**, his, her, Imperial Highness.
althæa [altea], *s.f. Bot:* althaea.
Althée [alte]. **1.** *Pr.n.f. Gr.Myth:* Althaea. **2.** *s.m. Bot:* althaea, marsh-mallow.
altier -ière [altje, -jɛːr], *a.* haughty, proud, arrogant (tone, bearing).
altièrement [altjɛrmɑ̃], *adv.* haughtily, proudly, arrogantly.
altigraphe [altigraf], *s.m. Av:* altigraph, barograph.
altimètre [altimɛtr̥], *s.m. Surv: Av:* altimeter; altitude indicator; **a. barométrique**, pressure altimeter; **a. électrostatique**, electrical-capacity altimeter; **a. indicateur d'altitude absolue**, absolute altimeter; *Av:* **a. à contact**, altitude switch.
altimétrie [altimetri], *s.f.* altimetry.
altimétrique [altimetrik], *a.* altimetric(al).
altiplanation [altiplanasjɔ̃], *s.f. Geol:* altiplanation.
altiport [altipɔr], *s.m.* high altitude airport.
altise [altiːz], *s.f. Ent:* Altica, flea-beetle; **a. potagère**, turnip-fly.
altissime [altisim], *a. sometimes Hum:* most high and mighty.
altiste [altist], *s.m. Mus:* viola player.
altitraceur [altitrasœːr], *s.m. Surv: Av:* altitude recorder.
altitude [altityd], *s.f.* altitude; **à cent mètres d'a.**, a hundred metres up; **en a.**, at a high altitude; **a. relative**, relative altitude; **a. absolue**, absolute altitude, height above sea level; *Av:* **prendre de l'a.**, to climb; **vol à haute a.**, altitude flight; **a. de croisière**, cruising altitude; **a. limite**, ceiling; **a. vraie, géométrique**, actual, true, altitude; **a. de ressource, de rétablissement**, pull-up, critical, altitude; **a. maximum en exploitation**, maximum operation height; *Med:* **cure d'a.**, high-altitude treatment; **mal d'a.**, (i) mountain sickness; (ii) altitude sickness; **ivresse d'a.**, altitude narcosis.
altitudinaire [altitydinɛːr], *a.* altitudinal (cold); of the upper regions.
alto [alto], *s.m. Mus:* **1.** alto, counter-tenor (voice). **2.** viola, tenor violin. **3.** tenor saxhorn, saxophone (in E flat); althorn.
altocumulus [altɔkymylys], *s.m.inv. Meteor:* altocumulus.
alto-fréquent [altofrekɑ̃], *a. Med:* high-frequency (current); *pl. alto-fréquents.*
altonais, -aise [altɔnɛ, -ɛːz], *a. & s. Geog:* (native) of Altona.
altostratus [altɔstratys], *s.m.inv. Meteor:* altostratus.
altrose [altroz], *s.m. Ch:* altrose.
altruisme [altryism], *s.m.* altruism.
altruiste [altryist]. **1.** *a.* altruistic. **2.** *s.* altruist.
alucite [alysit], *s.f. Ent:* **1.** alucita, plume-moth. **2. a. (des céréales)**, corn-moth.
alucité [alysite], *a.* (grain, etc.) containing dead corn-moths.
alude [alyd], *s.f. Leath: Book-b:* coloured sheepskin, coloured basil.
alule [alyl], *s.f. Orn:* alula, bastard wing.
alumelle [alymɛl], *s.f.* **1.** *A:* blade (of rapier). **2.** *Tls:* (*a*) scraper (for smoothing wood, ivory, etc.); (*b*) planisher. **3.** *Nau:* handspike hole (of capstan); bush (of rudder-head).
aluminage [alyminaːʒ], *s.m. Ch: Dy:* alumination, aluming.
aluminaire [alyminɛːr]. *Miner:* **1.** *a.* aluminiferous. **2.** *s.f.* aluminite.
aluminate [alyminat], *s.m. Miner: Ch:* aluminate.
alumine [alymin], *s.f.* alumina, aluminium oxide.
aluminer [alymine], *v.tr. Dy:* to aluminate; to alum.
aluminerie [alyminri], *s.f.* **1.** (*a*) aluminium works; (*b*) aluminium goods store. **2.** alum works.
alumineux, -euse [alyminø, -øːz], *a.* aluminous (water, etc.).
aluminiage [alyminjaːʒ], *s.m. Metalw: etc:* (process of) aluminizing.
aluminier [alyminje], *s.m.* aluminium worker, manufacturer.
aluminière [alyminjɛːr], *s.f.* = ALUNIÈRE.
aluminifère [alyminifɛːr], *a.* aluminiferous.
aluminilite [alyminilit], *s.f.* = ALUNITE.
aluminite [alyminit], *s.f. Miner:* aluminite.
aluminium [alyminjɔm], *s.m.* aluminium, *U.S:* aluminum; **sulfate d'a.**, aluminium sulphate; **diffusion d'a.**, aluminizing.
aluminosilicate [alyminosilikat], *s.m. Ch:* aluminosilicate.
aluminothermie [alyminotermi], *s.f. Metall:* aluminothermy, thermit welding.
alumnat [alymna], *s.m. Sch:* **1.** training college (for the priesthood); *R.C.Ch:* seminary. **2.** *U.S:* alumniate.
alun [alœ̃], *s.m.* alum; **a. ordinaire**, potash alum; **a. de chrome**, chrome alum; **a. de plume**, alum feather; *Toil:* **pierre d'a.**, shaving-block, styptic pencil.

alunage [alyna:ʒ], *s.m.* **1.** *Dy:* aluming. **2.** *Phot:* (alum-)hardening (of negatives, etc.).

alunation [alynasjɔ̃], *s.f.* **1.** formation of alum. **2.** *Dy:* aluming.

Alundum [alœ̃dɔm], *s.m. R.t.m: Ind:* Alundum.

aluner [alyne], *v.tr.* **1.** *Dy: etc:* to alum; *Phot:* **bain aluné,** hardening bath. **2.** *Phot:* to harden (emulsion, etc.).

alunerie [alynri], *s.f.* alum works.

aluneux, -euse [alynø, -ø:z], *a.* aluminous.

alunier [alynje], *s.m.* alum manufacturer.

alunière [alynjɛ:r], *s.f.* **1.** alum-pit. **2.** alum-works.

alunifère [alynifɛ:r], *a. Miner:* aluminiferous, alum-bearing; **schistes alunifères,** alum shales.

alunir [alyni:r], *v.i.* to land on the moon.

alunissage [alynisa:ʒ], *s.m.* moon landing.

alunite [alynit], *s.f. Miner:* alunite, alum-stone.

alunogène [alynɔʒɛn], *s.m. Miner:* alunogen.

alurgite [alyrʒit], *s.f. Miner:* alurgite.

alutacé [alytase], *a.* alutaceous.

alute [alyt], *s.f.* = ALUDE.

alvéolaire [alveɔlɛ:r], *a.* **1.** cell-like, alveolate; cellular; honeycomb (pattern, etc.). **2.** *Anat:* alveolar (nerve, vein); **bord a.,** alveolar process, ridge (of maxillary bone); **point a.,** alveolar point. **3.** *a. & s.f.* alveolar (consonant).

alvéole [alveɔl], *s.m. or f.* **1.** (*a*) alveole, alveolus; cell (of honeycomb, etc.); **alvéoles pulmonaires,** alveoli, air-cells, of the lungs; (*b*) pigeon-hole (of desk, etc.); (*c*) chamber (of revolver). **2.** socket (of tooth); socket, seat(ing) (of diamond); *Mec.E:* **a. d'une bille,** ball-bearing cup. **3.** cavity, pit (in stone, etc.); *El:* **alvéoles d'un grillage,** interstices, pockets, of an accumulator grid. **4.** (*a*) *Artil:* gun pit; (*b*) *Av:* **a. de départ,** revetted pen.

alvéolé [alveɔle], *a.* **1.** honeycombed, alveolate. **2.** pitted. **3.** *Av:* **abri a.,** revetted pen.

alvéolectomie [alveɔlɛktɔmi], *s.f. Dent:* alveolectomy.

alvéolisation [alveɔlizasjɔ̃], *s.f. Geol:* alveolation.

alvéolite[1] [alveɔlit], *s.f. Med:* alveolitis.

alvéolite[2], *s.m. Paleont:* alveolite.

alvéolodentaire [alveɔlodɑ̃tɛ:r], *a. Anat:* alveolodental.

alvin [alvɛ̃], *a.* alvine; **flux a.,** diarrhoea.

alvite [alvit], *s.f. Miner:* alvite.

alysse [alis], *s.f.,* **alysson** [alisɔ̃], *s.m. Bot:* alyssum, madwort; **a. saxatile,** gold-dust, rock alyssum.

alysséide [aliseid], *s.f. Geom:* catenoid.

alyte [alit], *s.m.,* **alytes** [alitɛs], *s.m. Amph:* alytes; obstetrical toad, midwife toad, nurse-frog.

amabilité [amabilite], *s.f.* **1.** amiableness, amiability; kindness; **auriez-vous l'a. de me dire . . .?** would you be so kind as to tell me . . .? **2.** *pl.* civilities, polite attention; **faites toutes sortes d'amabilités de ma part à . . .,** give my very kindest regards to . . .

Amadis [amadis]. **1.** *Pr.n.m.* Amadis. **2.** *s.m.* (*a*) *A:* gallant, lady-killer, dashing fellow; (*b*) *Moll:* admiral shell; (*c*) *A.Cost:* close-fitting sleeve buttoned at the wrist.

amadou [amadu], *s.m.* amadou, (German) tinder, touchwood, *U.S:* punk; *F:* **il prend feu comme de l'a.,** he is very touchy.

amadouement [amadumɑ̃], *s.m.* (*a*) wheedling, coaxing; (*b*) softening.

amadouer [amadwe], *v.tr.* (*a*) to coax, wheedle, persuade; (*b*) to soften.

amadoueur, -euse [amadwœ:r, -ø:z], *s. A:* **1.** coaxer, wheedler, flatterer. **2.** tinder-maker.

amadouvier [amaduvje], *s.m. Fung:* tinder fungus, tinder agaric.

amagnétique [amaɲetik], *a.* non-magnetic.

amaigrir [amɛgri:r, -e-], *v.tr.* **1.** (*a*) to make thin; to emaciate; (*b*) to thin down, reduce (column, beam, etc.). **2.** *Agr:* to impoverish (soil).

s'amaigrir, to grow thin, to lose flesh; **il s'est amaigri de dix livres,** he has lost ten pounds.

amaigrissant [amɛgrisɑ̃, -e-], *a.* slimming, reducing, banting (diet); **suivre un régime a.,** to follow a slimming diet.

amaigrissement [amɛgrismɑ̃, -e-], *s.m.* **1.** (*a*) wasting away, growing thin, loss of flesh, emaciation; (*b*) reducing, slimming; **cure d'a.,** slimming cure. **2.** reducing (in thickness), thinning down (of beam, etc.).

Amalécite [amalesit], *s.m. B.Hist:* Amalekite.

amalfitain, -aine [amalfitɛ̃, -ɛn], *a. & s. Geog:* Amalfitan, Amalphitan.

amalgamateur [amalgamatœ:r], *s.m. Ind:* amalgamator; **a. à cuve,** pan amalgamator.

amalgamation [amalgamasjɔ̃], *s.f.* **1.** amalgamation (of mercury with metal, of two races, etc.). **2.** *Fin:* merger.

amalgame [amalgam], *s.m.* **1.** *Ch: Dent:* amalgam. **2.** medley, mixture; **un a. de toutes les nations,** a mixture of every nation under the sun.

amalgamer [amalgame], *v.tr.* **1.** to amalgamate (*Metall:* gold, silver; *El.E:* zinc plates). **2.** to amalgamate (banks, companies, etc.); to blend (nations, parties, etc.).

s'amalgamer, to amalgamate; to blend.

Amalthée [amalte], *Pr.n.f. Myth:* Amalth(a)ea.

Aman[1] [amɑ̃], *Pr.n.m. B.Hist:* Haman.

aman[2], *s.m. & int.* (*in the Near East*) mercy (!); **demander l'a.,** to surrender, to submit.

amandaie [amɑ̃dɛ], *s.f.* almond grove.

amande [amɑ̃:d], *s.f.* **1.** almond; **amandes amères, douces,** bitter, sweet, almonds; **amandes pilées,** ground almonds; **amandes pralinées, lissées,** burnt almonds, sugar almonds; **huile d'amandes douces,** sweet-almond oil; **yeux en a.,** almond, almond-shaped, eyes. **2.** *Bot:* **a. d'une drupe,** kernel of a drupe. **3.** *Art:* **a. mystique,** vesica piscis.

amandé [amɑ̃de]. **1.** *a.* containing, flavoured with, almonds. **2.** *s.m. Pharm: A:* almond milk, milk of almonds, amygdalate.

amandier [amɑ̃dje], *s.m.* almond-tree.

amandon [amɑ̃dɔ̃], *s.m.* (*a*) green almond; (*b*) kernel of olive-stone.

amanite [amanit], *s.f. Fung:* amanita; **a. phalloïde,** death-cup; **a. tue-mouches,** fly agaric; **a. printanière,** destroying angel; **a. vireuse,** fool's mushroom; **a. panthère,** false blusher.

amant, -ante [amɑ̃, -ɑ̃:t], *s.* **1.** (*a*) *A:* lover, sweetheart; (*b*) **un amant de la nature,** a lover of nature. **2.** *s.m.* lover, paramour, gallant; **prendre un a.,** to take a lover; **a. de cœur,** fancy man.

amarante [amarɑ̃:t], *s.f.* **1.** *Bot:* amarant(h); **a. commune, à fleurs en queue,** love-lies-bleeding; **a. crête de coq,** cockscomb; **a. élégante,** prince's feather. **2.** *Com:* **bois d'a.,** kingwood, violet-wood. **3.** *s.m. & a.inv.* amaranth, (amaranth-) purple; purplish.

amarantacées [amarɑ̃tase], *s.f.pl. Bot:* Amarant(h)aceae.

amarantite [amarɑ̃tit], *s.f. Miner:* amarantite.

amareilleur [amarɛjœ:r], *s.m.* = AMAREYEUR.

amarescent [amarɛsɑ̃], *a.* bitterish, slightly bitter.

amareyeur [amarɛjœ:r], *s.m.* oyster-bed worker.

amaril [amaril], *a. Med:* amaril; **fièvre amarile,** yellow fever.

amarinage [amarina:ʒ], *s.m. Nau:* **1.** getting used to the sea, finding one's sea-legs, getting over sea-sickness; seasoning (of sailor). **2.** manning (of prize).

amarine [amarin], *s.f. Ch:* amarine.

amariner [amarine], *v.tr. Nau:* **1.** to inure to the sea, to season (sailor). **2.** to man (prize).

s'amariner, to get used to the sea, to overcome sea-sickness, to find one's sea-legs.

amarque [amark], *s.f. Nau:* leading buoy.

amarrage [amara:ʒ], *s.m. Nau:* **1.** (*a*) mooring, fastening; *Av:* mooring (aircraft); stowing (equipment); **droits d'a.,** berthage; *A: Aer:* **mât d'a.,** mooring mast; (*b*) berth, moorings. **2.** lashing, seizing; **faire un a. sur une corde,** to lash, seize, a rope; **a. plat avec bridure,** round seizing; **a. en étrive,** throat seizing; **a. en portugaise,** racking seizing; **fil d'a.,** binding wire. **3.** lanyard (of knife).

amarre [ama:r], *s.f.* (*a*) (mooring) rope or line; painter, warp; *pl.* moorings; **a. de l'arrière,** after-rope, stern-fast; **a. de travers,** breast-rope; **a. de l'avant,** bow-rope, head-rope; **a. du quai, de terre,** shore-fast; **a. de fond,** ground-tackle; **navire sur ses amarres,** ship at her moorings; **larguer les amarres,** to cast off the hawser, the moorings; (*of ship*) **rompre ses amarres,** to break adrift; (*b*) cable, hawser; **a. en fil d'acier,** steel hawser; **a. de retenue,** guy; (*c*) *Mil:* breast-line (of pontoon-bridge).

amarrer [amare], *v.tr. Nau: etc:* **1.** (*a*) to make fast, to moor (ship, etc.); **navire amarré à quai,** boat berthed, lying, at the quay; (*b*) to belay; to make (rope) fast; (*c*) to secure (gun); (*d*) *Const:* to brace (wall, etc.). **2.** (*a*) to seize, lash (hawsers, etc.); **a. une chaîne au cabestan,** to bring a chain to the capstan; (*b*) *P:* to get hold of, collar, nab.

s'amarrer, to make fast, to moor.

amarreur [amarœ:r], *s.m. A: Aut:* **a. pour malle,** trunk-brace.

amaryllid(ac)ées [amarilid(as)e], *s.f.pl. Bot:* Amaryllidaceae.

Amaryllis [amaril(l)is]. **1.** *Pr.n.f. Cl.Lit:* Amaryllis. **2.** *s.f. Bot:* amaryllis; **a. belle-dame,** belladonna lily, amaryllis belladonna.

amas [amɑ], *s.m.* **1.** (*a*) heap, pile, accumulation; **a. de sable,** heap of sand; *Nau:* **des a. de glace,** packs of ice; (*b*) store, hoard (of money, provisions); (*c*) concourse, gathering, mass (of people); (*d*) *Astr:* cluster; constellation; **a. ouvert,** open cluster; **a. globulaire,** globular cluster; **a. d'Hercule,** constellation Hercules; (*e*) *Cryst:* colony. **2.** *Min:* lode.

amassage [amɑsa:ʒ], *s.m.* **1.** (*a*) heaping-up; (*b*) storing up, hoarding up. **2.** heap, pile.

amasser [amɑse], *v.tr.* **1.** to heap up, pile up. **2.** to hoard up, store up; **a. une fortune,** to amass a fortune; **a. pour sa vieillesse,** to save up for one's old age; **il a amassé du bien,** he has made his pile, feathered his nest. **3.** to collect; to gather (troops, etc.) together.

s'amasser, to pile up, accumulate, collect, gather; **un orage s'amasse,** a storm is brewing.

amassette [amasɛt], *s.f.* palette-knife.

amasseur, -euse [amɑsœ:r, -ø:z], *s.* **1.** hoarder; **a. d'écus,** miser. **2.** gatherer; collector (of curios, etc.).

amateur [amatœ:r], *s.m.* **1.** (*a*) lover (of sth.); **a. d'art;** *O:* **a. des beaux-arts,** art-lover, lover of art, art enthusiast; **a. d'oiseaux, de chiens,** bird fancier, dog fancier; **édition d'a.,** collector's, booklover's, edition; **être a. de qch.,** to be fond of, have a taste for, sth.; (*b*) offerer, bidder (at sale); **est-ce qu'il y a des amateurs?** any takers? **2.** amateur; **elle joue bien pour un a.,** she plays well for an amateur; *Sp:* **championnat d'a.,** amateur championship; *s.a.* MARRON[2] 2; *adv. phr.* **en a.,** as an amateur, for a hobby, for the love of the thing; **travailler en a.,** to work in a dilettante fashion; **étudier la médecine en a.,** to dabble in medicine; **travail d'a.,** (i) amateur work; (ii) amateurish work.

amateurisme [amatœrism], *s.m. Art: Sp:* amateurism.

amatir [amati:r], *v.tr.* to mat, dull (surface, etc.); to deaden (gold).

amativité [amativite], *s.f.* amativeness.

amatol [amatɔl], *s.m. Exp:* amatol.

amaurose [amoro:z], *s.f. Med:* amaurosis.

amaurotique [amorɔtik], *a. & s. Med:* amaurotic (patient).

amazone [amazo:n], *s.f.* **1.** (*a*) *Myth.* Amazon; *Geog:* **l'A.,** *A:* **le fleuve des Amazones,** the (river) Amazon; (*b*) horsewoman, woman dressed in a riding-habit; **monter en a.,** to ride side-saddle. **2.** *Cost:* (lady's) riding habit. **3.** *Ent:* **fourmi) a.,** warrior, Amazon ant. **4.** *Orn:* Amazon parrot.

Amazonie [amazɔni], *Pr.n.f. Geog:* Amazonia.

ambasien, -ienne [ɑ̃bazjɛ̃, -jɛn], *a. & s.* = AMBOISIEN, -IENNE.

ambages [ɑ̃ba:ʒ], *s.f.pl. used only in* **parler sans a.,** to speak to the point, straight out; **parlez sans a.,** don't beat about the bush.

ambassade [ɑ̃basad], *s.f.* **1.** (*a*) *Dipl:* embassy, mission; **envoyer une a. extraordinaire,** to send a special mission; **obtenir une a.,** to obtain an ambassadorship; to be appointed ambassador; (*b*) mission, errand. **2.** (*a*) ambassador's staff, embassy; (*b*) (*building*) embassy.

ambassadeur [ɑ̃basadœ:r], *s.m.* **1.** ambassador; envoy; **a. extraordinaire,** ambassador extraordinary; **l'a. d'Angleterre,** the British ambassador; **a. auprès du roi d'Angleterre,** Ambassador to, at, the Court of St James's. **2.** deputy, messenger.

ambassadorial, -iaux [ɑ̃basadɔrjal, -jo], *a.* ambassadorial.

ambassadrice [ɑ̃basadris], *s.f.* **1.** ambassadress; (*a*) woman ambassador; (*b*) ambassador's wife. **2.** messenger (woman).

ambe [ɑ̃b], *s.m.* (*in lottery, game of chance*) combination of two numbers.

ambesas [ɑ̃b(ə)zɑ:s], *s.m. Backgammon:* Ambs-ace, (throw of a) double ace.

ambiance [ɑ̃bjɑ̃:s], *s.f.* surroundings, environment, atmosphere, ambience; *Dom.Ec:* **régulateur d'a.,** thermostat; *Fin: etc:* **l'a. générale,** the prevailing tone; *F:* **il y a de l'a. ici,** there's a cheerful atmosphere here.

ambiant [ɑ̃bjɑ̃], *a.* surrounding, encompassing. ambient (atmosphere, etc.); **milieu a.,** environment; **température ambiante,** room temperature; **les conditions ambiantes,** the ambient.

ambidextérité [ɑ̃bidɛksterite], *s.f.* = AMBIDEXTRIE.

ambidextre [ɑ̃bidɛkstr]. **1.** *a.* ambidextrous. **2.** *s.* ambidexter.

ambidextrie [ɑ̃bidɛkstri], *s.f.* ambidexterity, ambidextrousness.

ambigu, -uë [ɑ̃bigy]. **1.** *a.* ambiguous; (*a*) equivocal (phrase, etc.); cryptic; shady (character); (*b*) *Nat.Hist:* of doubtful classification. **2.** *s.m.* *A:* mixture, medley; *Cu: A:* cold collation.

ambiguïté [ɑ̃bigɥite], *s.f.* ambiguity, ambiguousness; **réponse sans a.,** unambiguous answer; **répondre sans a.,** to answer unambiguously.

ambigument [ɑ̃bigymɑ̃], *adv.* ambiguously.

ambitieusement [ɑ̃bisjøzmɑ̃], *adv.* **1.** ambitiously. **2.** pretentiously.

ambitieux, -ieuse [ɑ̃bisjø, -jøːz]. **1.** *a.* (*a*) ambitious; eager for; **être a. de qch., de faire qch.,** to be ambitious of sth., ambitious to do sth.; (*b*) **style a.,** pretentious, high-flown, studied, style. **2.** *s.* ambitious person; careerist; *U.S:* go-getter.

ambition [ɑ̃bisjɔ̃], *s.f.* ambition (**de,** of, for); **a. de la popularité,** hankering after popularity; **mettre son a. à faire qch.,** to make it one's ambition to do sth, to set one's heart on doing sth.; **dévoré d'a.,** eaten up with ambition; **l'a. de briller,** the ambition to shine; **sans a.,** unambitious(ly).

ambitionner [ɑ̃bisjɔne], *v.tr.* to be ambitious of, eager for (sth.); to covet (sth.); **a. de faire qch.,** to aspire, be eager, to do sth.

ambivalence [ɑ̃bivalɑ̃ːs], *s.f.* ambivalence.

ambivalent [ɑ̃bivalɑ̃], *a.* ambivalent.

amble [ɑ̃ːbl̩], *s.m.* amble, pace; *U.S:* single-foot; **a. rompu,** rack; *Equit:* **aller l'a.,** to amble; **chevaucher à l'a.,** to amble along, to ride at a leisurely pace.

ambler [ɑ̃ble], *v.i.* (*of horse, etc.*) to amble (along), to pace.

ambleur, -euse [ɑ̃blœːr, -øːz]. *Equit:* **1.** *a.* pacing, ambling (horse, mare). **2.** *s.* pacer, ambler.

amblycéphalidés [ɑ̃blisefalide], *s.m.pl. Rept:* Amblycephalidæ.

amblyope [ɑ̃bliɔp]. *Med:* **1.** *a.* amblyopic. **2.** *s.* amblyope.

amblyopie [ɑ̃bliɔpi], *s.f. Med:* amblyopia.

amblyopsidés, -ides [ɑ̃bliɔpside, -sid], *s.m.pl. Ich:* Amblyopsidæ.

amblyornis [ɑ̃bliɔrnis], *s.m. Orn:* (crestless) gardener (bower-)bird.

amblypode [ɑ̃blipɔd], *s.m. Paleont:* (*a*) amblypod; (*b*) *pl.* **amblypodes,** Amblypoda.

amblyrhynque [ɑ̃blirɛ̃ːk], *s.m. Z:* amblyrhynchus.

amblystome [ɑ̃blistɔm], *s.m. Amph:* amblystoma.

amblystomidés [ɑ̃blistɔmide], *s.m.pl. Amph:* Amblystomidae.

ambocepteur [ɑ̃bosɛptœːr], *s.m. Med:* amboceptor.

Amboine [ɑ̃bwan], *Pr.n.m. Geog:* Amboina; **bois d'A.,** *s.m.* **amboine,** Amboyna (wood).

amboisien, -ienne [ɑ̃bwazjɛ̃, -jɛn], *a. & s.* (native, inhabitant) of Amboise.

ambon [ɑ̃bɔ̃], *s.m.* **1.** *Ecc.Arch:* ambo. **2.** *Anat:* ambon.

ambre [ɑ̃ːbr̩], *s.m.* **1. a. gris,** ambergris; **parfumé d'a.,** amber scented; **pomme d'a.,** pomander. **2. a. jaune,** yellow amber, ordinary amber; **a. canadien,** chemawinite; *s.a.* FIN² 2.

ambré [ɑ̃bre], *a.* **1.** perfumed with amber(gris). **2.** amber-coloured; warm (complexion, tint). **3.** *O:* **cigarette à bout a.,** amber-tipped cigarette.

ambréine [ɑ̃brein], *s.f. Ch:* ambrain, ambrein.

ambrer [ɑ̃bre], *v.tr.* to amber; to scent (sth.) with amber(gris).

ambrette [ɑ̃brɛt], *s.f. Bot:* **1.** abel-musk, musk-mallow (of India); *Toil:* musk-seed; ambrette. **2.** sweet sultan; **a. musquée,** purple or white sweet sultan. **3.** *Hort:* **poire d'a.,** ambrette.

ambrin [ɑ̃brɛ̃], *a.* amber-like, amber-coloured; warm (tint).

ambrite [ɑ̃brit], *s.f. Miner:* ambrite.

ambroïne [ɑ̃brɔin], *s.f. Ind:* ambroid, ambroine.

Ambroise [ɑ̃brwaːz], *Pr.n.m.* Ambrose.

ambroisie [ɑ̃brwazi], *s.f.* **1.** *Gr.Myth:* ambrosia; **un parfum d'a.,** an ambrosial fragrance. **2.** *Bot:* ambrosia; wormseed.

ambroisien, -ienne [ɑ̃brwazjɛ̃, -jɛn], *a.* ambrosial.

ambrosiaque [ɑ̃brozjak], *a.* ambrosial.

ambrosien, -ienne [ɑ̃brozjɛ̃, -jɛn], *a. Ecc.Mus:* ambrosian (chant, etc.).

ambrosie [ɑ̃brɔzi], *s.f. Bot:* ambrosia; **a. maritime,** oak of Cappadocia.

ambulacre [ɑ̃bylakr̩], *s.m. Echin:* ambulacrum.

ambulance [ɑ̃bylɑ̃ːs], *s.f.* **1.** (*a*) ambulance; (*b*) *Mil: A:* **a. divisionnaire,** field ambulance; **a. chirurgicale,** mobile surgical unit; **a. chirurgicale automobile,** travelling operating theatre. **2.** *Adm: A:* itinerant collectorship (of excise, taxes, etc.).

ambulancier, -ière [ɑ̃bylɑ̃sje, -jɛːr], *s.* **1.** *A: Mil:* hospital orderly; *f.* nurse; stretcher-bearer. **2.** ambulance man; ambulance driver.

ambulancier-brancardier [ɑ̃bylɑ̃sjebrɑ̃kardje], *s.m.* stretcher-bearer, ambulance man; *pl. ambulanciers-brancardiers.*

ambulant [ɑ̃bylɑ̃]. **1.** *a.* strolling, itinerant, peripatetic, travelling, mobile; **épicier a.,** travelling grocer; **comédiens ambulants,** strolling players; **marchand ambulant,** itinerant dealer; pedlar, hawker; **cirque a.,** travelling circus; **brigade ambulante,** itinerant gang (of road workmen); *Rail:* **bureau a.,** *s.m.* **ambulant,** travelling post office; *Med:* **malade a.,** walking case; ambulatory, ambulant, patient; *Med:* **érysipèle a.,** migrant erysipelas. **2.** *s.m.* (*a*) pedlar, hawker; (*b*) *Adm:* itinerant collector (of excise, taxes, etc.); (*c*) *Rail: Post:* travelling sorter, clerk.

ambulation [ɑ̃bylasjɔ̃], *s.f.* ambulation, walking about.

ambulatoire [ɑ̃bylatwaːr], *a.* **1.** ambulatory; *Med:* **(fièvre) typhoïde a.,** ambulant typhoid (fever); **contrôle a.,** follow up. **2.** *Ent: Crust:* **patte a.,** ambulatory.

âme [ɑːm], *s.f.* **1.** soul; (*a*) **une bonne â.,** a well-meaning person, a good soul; **une grande â.,** a noble soul; *Ecc:* **avoir charge d'âmes,** to have a cure of souls; **se donner corps et â. à qn.,** to give oneself body and soul to s.o.; **rendre l'â.,** to give up the ghost, to die, to breathe one's last; **Dieu ait son â.,** God rest his soul; (*b*) (departed) soul, spirit; **invoquer l'â. de qn,** to call up the spirit of s.o.; **prier pour l'â. de qn,** to pray for someone's soul; **les âmes en peine,** the souls in Purgatory; **aller comme une â. en peine,** to wander around like a lost soul; *s.a.* DAMNÉ, PEINE 1; (*c*) heart, feeling, soul, spirit; **â. sœur,** kindred soul, spirit; **l'â. d'un peuple,** the heart of a nation; **en mon â. et conscience,** to the best of my knowledge and belief; **vous n'avez pas donc d'â.!** have you no feelings! **mettre de l'â. à faire qch.,** to do sth. with feeling; **désirer qch. de toute son â.,** to desire sth. ardently, with all one's heart; **joueur dans l'â.,** inveterate gambler; **être musicien dans l'â.,** to have a soul for music; **état d'â.,** mood, state of mind; **être tout â.,** to be all feeling; *A:* **sur mon â.,** upon my soul; (*d*) essence, inspiration, soul, life; **la discipline est l'â. de l'armée,** discipline is the soul of the army; **être l'â. d'une entreprise,** to be the moving spirit, the life and soul, of an enterprise; **ma chère â., mon â.,** my love; (*e*) **population de dix mille âmes,** population of ten thousand (souls); **ne pas rencontrer â. qui vive,** not to meet a (living) soul; (*f*) *Archeol:* **maison d'â.,** soul house. **2.** (*a*) bore (of gun, pump); **â. lisse,** smooth bore; **â. rayée,** rifled bore; *Artil:* **vérificateur d'â.,** bore gauge; (*b*) core (of statue, electric cable); heart, central strand (of rope, cable); (*c*) web (of girder, beam); centre-rib (of rail); **fer en U à â. verticale,** channel-iron with vertical web; *Av:* web (of wing); **â. de longeron,** spar web; **â. pleine,** fully stiffened web; (*d*) *Mus:* sound-post (of violin); *Paperm:* **â. (du carton),** filler; (*e*) *Her:* motto (of device).

Amédée [amede], *Pr.n.m.* Amadeus.

amélanche [amelɑ̃ːʃ], *s.f. Bot:* shadberry, serviceberry.

amélanchier [amelɑ̃ʃje], *s.m. Bot:* amelanchier, shadberry, shadbush; **a. à grappes,** June berry.

Amélie [ameli], *Pr.n.f.* Amelia.

améliorable [ameljɔrabl̩], *a.* improvable; perfectible.

améliorant [ameljɔrɑ̃], *a.* ameliorating, improving; *Agr:* **plante améliorante,** cover crop.

améliorateur, -trice [ameljɔratœːr, -tris], **amélioratif, -ive** [ameljɔratif, -iːv], *a.* ameliorative.

amélioration [ameljɔrasjɔ̃], *s.f.* **1.** amelioration, improvement, betterment; change for the better; **a. de santé,** improvement of, in, health; **il y a a. dans les affaires,** business is improving; **a. de traitement,** improvement in pay; **apporter des améliorations à qch.,** to effect improvements in sth.; **travaux d'a.,** improvements. **2.** appreciation (of property, etc.).

améliorer [ameljɔre], *v.tr.* to ameliorate, to better; to improve, to upgrade; **a. sa position, sa situation,** to better one's position, one's circumstances; *F:* to better oneself.

s'améliorer, to get better, to improve; to change, for the better; **sa santé s'améliore,** his health is improving; **le temps s'améliore,** the weather is improving.

amen [amen], *int. & s.m.inv. in pl.* amen; **dire a. à tout,** to agree to everything.

amenage [amnaːʒ], *s.m.* **1.** transport, conveyance, carriage (hither); **frais d'a.,** carriage (expenses). **2.** *Mec.E:* feed(ing), inching, (of tools to the work, of work to the tool).

aménageable [amenaʒabl̩], *a.* suitable for arranging, developing; improving; (*of stream*) suitable for harnessing (for power); (*of building*) suitable for conversion.

aménagement [amenaʒmɑ̃], *s.m.* **1.** parcelling out (of forest); planning (of mining operations, etc.); *Rail:* grading (of track). **2.** (*a*) fitting up, equipping, arranging, preparation (of house, etc.); fitting out (of new ship); (*b*) harnessing (of power). **3.** (*a*) arrangement, disposition (of house, etc.); (*b*) *pl.* appointments (of house), fittings (of office); amenities (of hotel); *pl.* fixtures (of kitchen, etc.); *Tchn:* installations; (*c*) *pl. Nau: Av:* accommodation, berthing; *Nav:* **les aménagements de l'équipage,** the mess decks; (*d*) *Town P:* development; *Pol.Ec:* **a. du territoire,** national development.

aménager [amenaʒe], *v.tr.* **(j'aménageai(s); n. aménageons) 1.** to divide, parcel out, distribute (supplies, trees for felling, water for irrigation, etc.); to plan (town); to organize (one's leisure); *Rail:* to grade (the track). **2.** (*a*) to fit up, to dispose, arrange, prepare (house, shop, etc.); to fit out (new ship); **étable aménagée,** converted cowshed; **plage aménagée,** beach with full amenities; *Adm:* **route non aménagée,** non made-up road; (*b*) to harness (water-power.)

amendable [amɑ̃dabl̩], *a. Agr:* (land) that can be improved; improvable.

amendage [amɑ̃daːʒ], *s.m. Agr:* improving, enriching (of soil).

amende [amɑ̃ːd], *s.f.* **1.** fine; **frapper qn d'une a., infliger une a. à qn, mettre qn a l'a.,** to impose a fine on s.o., to fine s.o.; **être condamné à l'a., à une a.,** to be fined; **défense d'entrer sous peine d'a.,** trespassers will be prosecuted; *Com:* **a. pour retard de livraison (etc.),** penalty; **être mis à l'a.,** (i) to be punished; (ii) *Games:* to have to pay a forfeit; *Golf:* **coup d'a.,** penalty stroke; *Prov:* **les battus payent l'a.,** the loser pays; the weakest goes to the wall. **2.** (*a*) *A:* judicial penance imposed on offender called on to make public confession of guilt; (*b*) **faire a. honorable,** (i) to make the *amende honorable,* to make amends; (ii) to make due apology.

amendement [amɑ̃dmɑ̃], *s.m.* **1.** improvement in conduct, of the soil, etc.); **employer le sable pour l'a. des terres argileuses,** to use sand for the improvement of clayey soils. **2.** (= ENGRAIS) ameliorator (of soil). **3.** *Pol:* amendment (to a bill, etc.).

amender [amɑ̃de], *v.tr.* (*a*) to make better, to improve (soil, etc.); **a. ses opinions,** to amend one's opinions; **a. l'enfance coupable,** to reclaim young delinquents; **a. sa conduite,** to mend one's ways; **terrain amendé,** improved, reclaimed, land; (*b*) *Pol: etc:* to amend (bill, etc.).

s'amender, to improve; (*a*) to grow better, to mend one's ways; to turn over a new leaf; (*b*) *Agr:* (*of soil*) to become more fertile.

amène [amɛn], *a. Lit:* pleasing, agreeable (place, manner, etc.).

amenée [amne], *s.f.* **1.** bringing, leading; **tuyau, conduite, d'a.,** (i) *Civ.E:* branch (drainage) pipe; (ii) *Hyd.E:* supply pipe, admission pipe, delivery pipe; *El.E:* lead; *s.a.* CANAL 1. **2.** inlet, intake (for air).

amener [amne], *v.tr.* **(j'amène, n. amenons; j'amènerai) 1.** (*a*) to bring; to lead (hither); to bring up (reserves, etc.); to bring forward (person to be introduced, etc.); to conduct (person, animal); **amenez votre ami avec vous,** bring your friend (along) with you; **quel bon vent vous amène?** what good wind brings you here? **faire a. son cheval,** to have one's horse led up, brought round; **a. qn à son opinion,** to bring s.o. round to one's opinion; **a. un sujet,** to lead up to a subject; **a. la conversation sur un sujet,** to bring the conversation round to a subject, to introduce a subject into the conversation; **remarque bien amenée,** apposite remark; **l'aqueduc amène les eaux à Paris,** the aqueduct brings, conveys, the water to Paris; **a. l'eau, le gaz (dans une maison),** to lay on the water, the gas; **a. qn à faire qch.,** to bring s.o. to do sth.; **amenez-le dîner avec nous,** bring him round to dine with us; **a. qn à faire qch.,** to get, lead, induce, s.o. to do sth.; **les faits nous amènent à cette conclusion,** the facts lead, bring, us to this conclusion; *Nau:* **a. un navire le long du quai,** to lay, berth, a boat alongside (the quay); *s.a.* MANDAT 2; *Th:* **a. un décor,** to run on a scene; (*b*) to bring (sth.) to pass; **a. une rupture,** to bring about, lead to, a rupture; **a. une mode,** to bring in a fashion; (*c*) *P:* = APPORTER 1. **2.** *Games:* to throw (number). **3.** *Nau:* to haul down (signal); to strike (colours); to lower (boat, sail); *abs.* **le navire amena,** the ship struck her colours.

s'amener, *F:* to turn up, to blow in; **allons, amène-toi!** now then, come here! come along! **il va s'a. dans dix minutes,** he will be along in ten minutes.

aménité [amenite], *s.f.* **1.** amenity, charm, graciousness (of manners, greeting, etc.); charm, grace (of style); *A:* amenity, mildness (of climate); **l'a. de leur accueil nous charma,** we were delighted with the charming way in which they welcomed us. **2.** *pl.* compliments; *esp. Iron:* **il y eut alors un échange d'aménités,** then compliments began to fly; *F:* then the fur began to fly.

aménorrhée [amenɔre], *s.f. Med:* amenorrhœa.

amentacées [amɑ̃tase], *s.f.pl. Bot:* amentaceae.

amentales [amɑ̃tal], *s.f.pl. Bot:* amentiferae.

amentifère [amɑ̃tifɛr], *Bot:* **1.** *a.* amentiferous. **2.** *s.f.pl.* **amentifères,** amentiferae.

amenuisement [amənɥizmɑ̃], *s.m.* **1.** thinning down (of board); whittling down (of stick). **2.** dwindling (of a party).

amenuiser [amənɥize], *v.tr.* to reduce, to thin (down) (board); to whittle down, pare down (stick).

s'amenuiser, to become thinner; (*of political party, etc.*) to dwindle.

amer[1], **-ère** [amɛːr]. **1.** *a.* (*a*) bitter (taste); **a. comme chicotin,** as bitter as wormwood; **j'ai la bouche amère,** I have a bitter taste in my mouth; *Poet:* **l'onde amère,** the briny deep; *s.a.* HERBE 4; (*b*) (*of pers.*) bitter; **douleur amère,** bitter grief; **ironie amère,** bitter irony; **expérience amère,** bitter, galling, experience. **2.** *s.m.* (*a*) *A:* **a. de bœuf,** ox gall; (*b*) bitters; **prendre un a.,** to have a bitters; *s.a.* ALOÈS 1.

amer[2], *s.m. Nau:* sea-mark, land-mark, leading-mark, day-mark.

Amerada [amerada], *Pr.n. R.t.m:* **manomètre A.,** Amerada (depth pressure recording) apparatus.

amèrement [amɛrmɑ̃], *adv.* bitterly.

américain, -aine [amerikɛ̃, -ɛn], *a.* & *s.* **1.** American; **idiotisme a.,** Americanism; *A: F:* **il a l'œil a.,** he keeps his eyes skinned; *adv.phr.* **à l'américaine,** (in the) American fashion; *Cu:* **homard à l'américaine,** lobster américaine; *s.a.* VOL[2] 1. **2.** *s.m. Ling:* American (English). **3.** *s.f.* **américaine** (*a*) *A.Veh:* American phaeton; (*b*) *Sp: Cy:* track relay (race).

américanisation [amerikanizasjɔ̃], *s.f.* Americanization.

américaniser [amerikanize], *v.tr.* to Americanize.

s'américaniser, to become Americanized, to begin to affect American manners.

américanisme [amerikanism], *s.m.* **1.** study of America. **2.** excessive admiration for America. **3.** *Ling:* American expression, Americanism.

américaniste [amerikanist], *s.m.* & *f.* Americanist, specialist in American studies.

américium [amerisjɔm], *s.m. Ch:* americium.

Améric Vespuce [amerikvɛspys], *Pr.n.m. Hist:* Amerigo Vespucci.

amérindien, -ienne [amerɛ̃djɛ̃, -jɛn], *a.* & *s. Ethn:* Amerind, Amerindian, American Indian.

Amérique [amerik], *Pr.n.f. Geog:* America; **l'A. du Nord, du Sud,** North, South, America; **l'A. latine,** Latin America.

amérir [ameriːr], *v.i.,* **amérissage** [amerisaːʒ], *s.m.* = AMERRIR, AMERRISSAGE.

Amerlo(t), Amerloque [amɛrlo, amɛrlɔk], *Pr.n.m. P:* American, Yank.

amerrir [ameriːr], *v.i.* (*a*) *Av:* to alight, 'land' (on the sea); (*b*) (*of space capsule*) to splash down.

amerrissage [amerisaːʒ], *s.m.* (*a*) *Av:* alighting (on the sea); **a. trop piqué, trop dur,** alighting too steeply; **a. forcé,** ditching; **faire un a. forcé,** to ditch; (*b*) splashdown (of space capsule).

amertume [amɛrtym], *s.f.* bitterness (of quinine, etc., of sorrow, etc.); **remplir qn d'a.,** to embitter s.o.; **ressentir beaucoup d'a. de qch.,** to feel, resent, sth. bitterly.

amétabole [ametabɔl], *a. Ent:* ametabolic, ametabolous.

améthyste [ametist]. **1.** *s.f.* amethyst. **2.** *a.inv.* **rubans améthyste,** amethyst ribbons. **3.** *s.f. Orn:* ruby-throated humming-bird.

améthystin [ametistɛ̃], *a.* amethystine, amethyst-coloured, violet-purple.

amétrope [ametrɔp], *a. Med:* ametropic.

amétropie [ametrɔpi], *s.f. Med:* ametropia.

ameublement [amœbləmɑ̃], *s.m.* **1.** furnishing (of house, office, etc.). **2.** (*a*) set, suite of furniture; (*b*) furniture; **tissu d'a.,** furnishing fabric.

ameublir [amœbliːr], *v.tr.* **1.** *Agr:* to loosen, break up, mellow (soil). **2.** *Jur:* (*a*) to convert (realty) into personalty; (*b*) to bring (one's realty) into the communal estate.

ameublissement [amœblismɑ̃], *s.m.* **1.** *Agr:* loosening, breaking-up (of soil). **2.** *Jur:* (*a*) conversion (of realty) into personalty; (*b*) inclusion (of realty) in the communal estate.

ameulonner [amølɔne], *v.tr.* to stack (hay, etc.).

ameutable [amøtabl̩], *a.* easily formed into a mob.

ameutement [amøtmɑ̃], *s.m.* **1.** *Ven:* (*a*) gathering (of hounds) into a pack; (*b*) pack (of hounds). **2.** (*a*) gathering (of persons) into a mob; rising; (*b*) mob.

ameuter [amøte], *v.tr.* **1.** *Ven:* to form (hounds) into a pack; to pack (hounds). **2.** (*a*) to assemble collect (riotous crowd); (*b*) to stir up (the mob).

s'ameuter, to gather into a mob; to assemble, to band together.

ami, -e [ami]. **1.** *s.* (*a*) friend; **c'est un de mes meilleurs amis,** he's one of my best friends, he's a particular friend of mine; **a. intime,** bosom friend, close friend; **a. d'enfance,** childhood friend; old playmate; **un a. de la maison,** a friend of the family; **un de mes vieux amis, un vieil a. à moi,** an old friend of mine; **un de mes amis qui est célibataire, un célibataire de mes amis,** a bachelor friend of mine; **un a. de toujours,** a lifelong friend; **a. de cour,** pretended, so-called, friend; **c'est un service d'a. que je vous demande,** will you do me a friendly turn; **se faire un a.,** to make a friend; **être a. avec qn,** to be friendly, friends, with s.o.; **être a. de qch.,** to like, have a taste for, sth.; **mon a.,** (i) (*between friends*) my dear fellow; (ii) (*from wife to husband*) my dear; (iii) *A:* (*to inferior*) my good man; **mon amie,** *A:* **m'amie,** my dear, my love; *A:* **bel a.,** fair friend; *A:* **il n'y a pas à dire mon bel a.,** there's no getting away from it (with fair words); **être sans amis,** to be friendless, without friends; *adv.phr.* **en ami(e),** in a friendly manner, as a friend; *s.a.* BESOIN 2, MALHEUR 2; (*b*) *F:* man- or boy-friend; *F.* woman- or girl-friend; lover, sweetheart; (*c*) *F:* **sa bonne amie,** **sa petite amie,** his sweetheart; (*d*) **un a. des arts,** a patron of art; **les amis des livres, de la nature,** book-lovers, nature-lovers; (*of words*) **faux amis,** deceptive cognates; (*e*) *Geog:* **les Iles des Amis,** the Friendly Islands, Tonga; (*f*) **société des amis,** Society of Friends, *F:* Quakers. **2.** *a.* (*a*) friendly, (de, to); **peuple a.,** ally, friendly state; (*b*) kind, kindly, favourable (wind, hand, etc.); (*c*) **couleurs amies,** colours that match.

amiable [amjabl̩], *a. Jur:* **1.** friendly, conciliatory, amicable; **a. compositeur,** arbitrator; *Mth:* **nombres amiables,** amicable numbers. **2. à l'a.;** (*a*) *adv.phr.* amicably; **différons à l'a.,** let us agree to differ; *Jur:* **arranger une affaire à l'a.;** to settle a difference out of court; (*b*) *adj.phr.* amicable, private, by mutual agreement; **arrangement à l'a.,** amicable arrangement; **vente à l'a.,** private sale, sale by private contract, agreement.

amiablement [amjabləmɑ̃], *adv. Jur:* amicably, in a friendly manner; privately.

amiante [amjɑ̃ːt], *s.m. Miner:* asbestos; amiant(h)us; **a. floconneux,** flaked asbestos; **a. projeté,** sprayed (limpet) asbestos; *Const:* **carton d'a.,** asbestos-board, -sheet.

amianté [amjɑ̃te], *a.* covered, treated, with asbestos; *Const:* **toile métallique amiantée,** asbestos wire gauze.

amiante-ciment [amjɑ̃ːtsimɑ̃], *s.m.* asbestos cement; *pl. amiantes-ciments.*

amiantifère [amjɑ̃ːtifɛːr], *a.* asbestos-bearing (rock, etc.).

amiantin [amjɑ̃tɛ̃], *a.* amiant(h)ine; asbestine.

amiantose [amjɑ̃toːz], *s.f. Med:* asbestosis.

amibe [amib], *s.f. Prot:* amoeba.

amibiase [amibjɑːz], *s.f. Med:* amoebiasis.

amibien, -ienne [amibjɛ̃, -jɛn]. **1.** *a. Med:* amœbic (dysentery). **2.** *s.m.pl. Prot:* **amibiens,** Amœbae.

amibiforme [amibifɔrm], *a.* amoebiform.

amiboïde [amibɔid], *Biol:* **1.** *a.* amoeboid, amoeba-like. **2.** *s.m.* amoeba.

amical, -aux [amikal, -o], *a.* friendly (advice, tone, etc.); amicable (relations); **être a. avec qn,** to be friendly towards s.o.; **peu a.,** unfriendly; *Sp:* **match a.,** *s.m.* **amical,** friendly match; **association amicale,** *s.f.* **amicale,** association (in defence of common interests).

amicalement [amikalmɑ̃], *adv.* in a friendly way; like a friend; *Corr:* **bien a. à vous,** yours (sincerely).

amict [ami], *s.m. Ecc.Cost:* amice.

amide [amid], *s.m. Ch:* **1.** amide. **2. -amide,** *s.suff.m.* -amide; **acétamide,** acetamide; **cyanamide,** cyanamide.

amidine [amidin], *s.f. Ch:* amidin(e).

amidogène [amidoʒɛn], *s.m. Ch:* amidogen.

amidol [amidɔl], *s.m. Phot:* amidol.

amidon [amidɔ̃], *s.m.* starch; **colle d'a.,** starch paste.

amidonnage [amidɔnaːʒ], *s.m. Laund:* starching.

amidonner [amidɔne], *v.tr. Laund:* to starch.

amidonnerie [amidɔnri], *s.f.* starch factory.

amidonnier [amidɔnje], *s.m.* (*a*) worker in a starch factory; (*b*) starch manufacturer.

amiénois, -oise [amjenwa, -waːz]. **1.** *a.* & *s. Geog:* (native, inhabitant) of Amiens. **2.** *s.m.* **l'Amiénois,** district of ancient France, with capital Amiens.

Amilcar [amilkaːr], *Pr.n.m. A.Hist:* Hamilcar.

aminche [amɛ̃ːʃ], *s.m. A: P:* friend, pal.

amincir [amɛ̃siːr], *v.tr.* (*a*) to make (sth.) thinner; to fine down, thin down (wood); to machine down (metal); **taille amincie,** slender, slim, figure; (*b*) **robe qui amincit,** dress which makes one look slender, that is slimming, *U.S:* slenderizing.

s'amincir, to grow thinner, more slender.

amincissant [amɛ̃sisɑ̃]. **1.** *a. Cost:* giving an effect of slenderness, slimming; *U.S:* slenderizing. **2.** *s.m.* (paint) thinner; *Petroleum Ind:* **a. pour boues,** mud thinner.

amincissement [amɛ̃sismɑ̃], *s.m.* (*a*) thinning down, machining down; (*b*) (*of pers.*) growing thinner, slimmer.

amine [amin], *s.f. Ch:* **1.** amine. **2. -amine,** *s.suff.f.* -amine; **méthylamine,** methylamine; **vitamine,** vitamin.

aminé [amine], *a. Ch:* **acide a.,** amino-acid.

amino(-)acide [aminoasid], *s.m. Ch:* amino-acid; *pl. amino(-)acides.*

aminoplaste [aminɔplast], *s.m. Ch:* aminoplastic, aminoplast.

amique [amik], *a. Ch:* amidic; amic.

amiral, -aux [amiral, -o]. **1.** *s.m.* admiral, flag-officer; **a. de la flotte,** admiral of the fleet; **l'A. Nelson,** Admiral Nelson; **c'est un a. suisse,** he's in the horse-marines, he's never seen the sea. **2.** *a.* (**navire**) **a.** (*m*), (i) (*at sea*) flagship; (ii) (*in port*) guardship. **3.** *s.m. Conch:* admiral shell.

amiralat [amirala], *s.m.* (*rare*) admiralship.

amirale [amiral], *s.f.* admiral's wife.

amiralissime [amiralisim], *s.m. A:* commander-in-chief (of the fleet).

Amirantes [amirɑ̃ːt], *Pr.n.f.pl. Geog:* the Amirante Islands.

amirauté [amirote], *s.f.* **1.** *A:* office of admiral, admiralship. **2.** Admiralty; **conseil d'a.** = (i) Board of Admiralty; (ii) High Court of Admiralty. **3.** *Navy:* residence of the port admiral. **4.** *Geog:* **îles de l'A.,** the Admiralty Islands; **île de l'A.,** Admiralty Island (British Columbia).

amissible [amisibl̩], *a. Jur: Theol:* (*of privilege, etc.*) amissible, losable, liable to be lost.

amissibilité [amisibilite], *s.f. Jur:* amissibility.

amission [amisjɔ̃], *s.f. Jur: Theol:* loss, *A:* amission (of privilege, grace, document).

amitié [amitje], *s.f.* **1.** friendship, friendliness, affection; **une étroite a.,** a close friendship; **être, vivre, en a., sur un pied d'a., avec qn,** to be on friendly terms, on a friendly footing, with s.o.; **concevoir de l'a. pour qn, prendre qn en a.,** to take a liking to s.o., to take to s.o.; **se lier d'a. avec qn, nouer a. avec qn, se prendre d'a. pour qn,** to form, to strike up, a friendship with s.o.; to make friends with s.o.; **par a.,** out of friendship. **2.** (*a*) kindness, favour; **faites-moi l'a. de le lui dire,** do me the favour of telling him so; (*b*) *pl.* **faites, présentez, mes amitiés à votre frère,** remember me kindly, give my compliments, give my love, my kindest regards, to your brother; **(mes) amitiés à tout le monde,** (my) love to all; **avec les sincères amitiés de . . .,** with kind regards from . . .; **il m'a fait mille amitiés,** he was effusively friendly.

amitose [amitoːz], *s.f. Biol:* amitosis.

amixie [amiksi], *s.f. Biol:* amixia.

amman [amɑ̃], *s.m. Adm:* amman; amtman, *pl.* -men.

ammine [amin], *s.f. Ch:* ammine.

ammiolit(h)e [amjɔlit], *s.f. Miner:* ammiolite.

ammobium [amɔbjɔm], *s.m. Bot:* ammobium.

ammocète [ammɔsɛt], *s.m. Ich:* ammoc(o)ete, larval lamprey.

ammodyte [ammɔdit]. **1.** *a. Z:* living in sand. **2.** *s.f.* (*a*) *Ich:* ammodyte, sand-eel; (*b*) *Rept:* ammodyte, sand viper, sand-natter.

ammonal [amɔnal], *s.m. Exp:* ammonal.

ammonées [amɔne], *s.m.pl. Paleont:* Ammonea.

ammoniac, -iaque [amɔnjak], *a. Ch:* **gaz a.,** *s.* **ammoniac,** ammonia; **sel a.,** sal ammoniac; **gomme ammoniaque,** gum ammoniac.

ammoniacal, -aux [amɔnjakal, -o], *a. Ch:* ammoniacal; **eau ammoniacale,** ammonia-liquor, -water; *Ind:* **liqueur ammoniacale de cuivre,** cuprammonium.
ammoniacé [amɔnjase], *a. Pharm: etc:* ammoniated.
ammoniaque [amɔnjak], *s.f.* **1.** *Ch:* ammonia. **2.** (**solution aqueuse d'**)**a.,** ammonium hydrate, ammonia (solution).
ammoniaqué [amɔnjake], *a.* ammoniated; *Pharm:* **teinture de quinquina ammoniaquée,** ammoniated (tincture of) quinine.
ammonié [amɔnje], *a.* containing ammonia.
ammoniémie [amɔnjemi], *s.f. Med:* ammoniaemia.
ammonisation [amɔnizasjɔ̃], *s.f. Ch:* ammonification, ammonization.
ammonite [am(m)ɔnit], *s.f. Paleont:* ammonite.
Ammonites [ammɔnit], *s.m.pl. B.Hist:* Ammonites.
ammonitidés [amɔnitide], *s.m.pl. Paleont:* Ammonitoidea.
ammonium [am(m)ɔnjɔm], *s.m. Ch:* ammonium.
ammoniurie [amɔnjyri], *s.f. Med:* ammoniuria.
ammonoïdés [amɔnɔide], *s.m.pl. Paleont:* Ammonoidea.
ammophile [amɔfil]. **1.** *a.* ammophilous. **2.** *s.f. Bot:* ammophila, sand reed. **3.** *s.m. Ent:* (**guêpe**) **a.,** ammophila, digger wasp.
amnésie [amnezi], *s.f. Med:* amnesia.
amnésique [amnezik], *a. & s. Med:* amnesic; (*patient*) suffering from amnesia.
amniens [amnjɛ̃], *s.m.pl. Z:* Amniota.
amniographie [amniɔgrafi], *s.f. Obst:* amniography.
amniorrhée [amniɔre], *s.f. Obst:* amniorrhea.
amnios [amnjɔs], *s.m.* (*a*) *Obst:* amnion; (*b*) *Bot:* amnios.
amniotes [amniɔt], *s.m.pl. Z:* Amniota.
amniotique [amnjɔtik], *a.* amniotic (liquid, etc.).
amnistiable [amnistjabl], *a.* (*of convicted pers.*) eligible for grant of an amnesty.
amnistie [amnisti], *s.f.* amnesty, general pardon, act of oblivion; **ordonnance d'a.,** amnesty ordinance.
amnistié, -ée [amnistje], *a. & s.* (*person, action*) included in an amnesty; amnestied.
amnistier [amnistje], *v.tr.* (*pr.sub. & p.d.* **n. amnistiions, v. amnistiiez**) to amnesty, pardon.
amocher [amɔʃe], *v.tr. P:* **1.** (*a*) to hit (s.o.) in the face, on the nose; to knock (s.o.) about; (*b*) **patte amochée,** game leg. **2.** to damage (building by bombardment, etc.).
s'amocher, *P:* to become weak, slack; to deteriorate.
amodiataire [amɔdjatɛːr], *s.m. & f.* **1.** lessee (of farm, of fishing). **2.** sub-lessee (of mining concession).
amodiateur, -trice [amɔdjatœːr, -tris], *s.* lessor (of farm, etc.).
amodiation [amɔdjasjɔ̃], *s.f.* **1.** (*a*) leasing (of land for farming, of fishery or fishing rights); (*b*) *F:* dividing, parcelling (of land). **2.** subleasing (of mining rights).
amodier [amɔdje], *v.tr.* **1.** to farm out, lease (land, fishing). **2.** to lease (mining concession).
amoindrir [amwɛ̃driːr]. **1.** *v.tr.* to reduce, decrease, lessen, diminish, belittle; to weaken; **a. un mal,** to mitigate an evil; **a. la puissance de qn,** to curtail s.o.'s power; **a. (le mérite de) qn,** to detract from s.o.'s credit, to belittle s.o.; **a. un contraste,** to lower, soften, a contrast; **il ne faut pas vous a.,** you must not belittle yourself; **pays amoindri dans sa puissance,** country diminished in power; **sa maladie l'a. amoindrie,** her illness has weakened her. **2.** *v.i. & pr.* to diminish, to grow less; **gloire qui va s'amoindrissant,** fading glory.
amoindrissement [amwɛ̃drismɑ̃], *s.m.* reduction, lessening, decrease, diminution; *Fin:* **a. de crédit,** contraction, shortening, of credit.
amoise [amwaːz], *s.f. Const:* binding-piece; tie, brace.
amoitir [amwatiːr], *v.tr.* to damp, moisten (*esp.* the skin, as with perspiration).
amok [amɔk]. **1.** *a.* (running) amok. **2.** *s.m.* amok (frenzy). **3.** *s.m.* person running amok.
amollir [amɔliːr], *v.tr.* **1.** to soften (substance, s.o.'s heart, etc.). **2.** to weaken, enervate (mind, courage, etc.).
s'amollir. 1. to soften, to become soft. **2.** (*a*) to grow weak, effeminate; (*b*) (*of courage, etc.*) to flag, weaken.
amollissant [amɔlisɑ̃], *a.* softening; enervating, weakening.
amollissement [amɔlismɑ̃], *s.m.* **1.** softening (of substance, of the brain, etc.). **2.** loss of vigour (through easy living); weakening, flagging (of courage, etc.).

amome [amɔm], *s.m.,* **amomum** [amɔmɔm], *s.m. Bot:* amomum.
amonceler [amɔ̃sle], *v.tr.* (**j'amoncelle, n. amoncelons; j'amoncellerai**) to pile up, heap up, bank up; to accumulate.
s'amonceler, to pile up; to gather (in a heap); to accumulate; (*of clouds*) to bank up, pile up; **un orage s'amoncelle,** a storm is brewing; **la neige s'amoncelle,** the snow is drifting.
amoncellement [amɔ̃sɛlmɑ̃], *s.m.* **1.** heaping (up), piling (up), banking up, accumulation. **2.** heap, pile; **a. de neige,** snowdrift.
amont [amɔ̃], *s.m.* **1.** (*a*) upper waters (of river); **en allant vers l'a.,** going upstream; **bief d'a.,** head-race (of mill); *adv.phr.* **en a.,** upstream, up-river; **en a. de l'écluse, du pont,** above the lock, above the bridge; **la Seine en a. de Paris,** the Seine above Paris; (*b*) **vent d'a.,** (i) wind from the same direction as the current; (*esp. in Channel & Bay of Biscay*) easterly wind; (ii) off-shore wind. **2.** (*a*) *Tg:* up-side; (*b*) *Rail:* **en a.,** up the line.
amoral, -aux [amɔral, -o], *a.* amoral, non-moral, unmoral.
amoralisme [amɔralism], *s.m.* **1.** amorality. **2.** amoralism.
amoralité [amɔralite], *s.f.* amorality.
amorçage [amɔrsaːʒ], *s.m.* **1.** beginning, setting going (of sth.); priming (of pump, fire-arm, motor, etc.); capping (of shell); *El:* flash-over; *El.E:* starting, excitation (of dynamo); striking (of electric arc); building up (of magnetic field); energizing; *Metalw:* scarfing (of weld); *Med:* **a. du sommeil,** induction of sleep. **2.** baiting (of hook, line); (ground-)baiting (of pool).
amorce [amɔrs], *s.f.* **1.** beginning; **amorces de rhumatisme,** incipient rheumatism; **a. de négociations,** preliminary talks; *Civ.E:* **a. d'une rue, d'un tunnel,** beginning (of the cutting) of a road, of a tunnel; **a. de pont flottant,** shore end, fastening, of pontoon bridge; *Const:* toothing-stone. **2.** (*a*) *Exp:* (i) primer, fuse, detonator; **a. électro-pyrotechnique,** squib; **a. cirée,** pellet primer, wax primer; **a. détonateur,** primer detonator, initiator; **branche d'a.,** fuse lead, wire; (ii) priming; (*b*) *Sm.a:* percussion cap, cartridge cap; *Toys:* toy pistol (snap) cap; **sans brûler une a.,** without firing a shot; (*c*) *El.E:* fuse; **a. à fil discontinu, à étincelles,** high tension fuse; **a. à fil continu,** low tension fuse; (*d*) *Hyd.E:* priming (of pump); (*e*) *Metalw:* scarf (of weld); (*f*) *Electroplating:* starting bath; (*g*) *Ap:* decoy-comb. **3.** bait, lure; **a. de fond,** ground-bait; *F:* **se laisser prendre à l'amorce,** to swallow the bait. **4.** *Cin: Rec:* leader; **a. initiale,** running, start, head, leader; **a. de sortie,** end tail, stop, leader.
amorcement [amɔrs(ə)mɑ̃], *s.m.* = AMORÇAGE.
amorcer [amɔrse], *v.tr.* (**j'amorçai(s); n. amorçons**) **1.** (*a*) to begin, start, prepare (building, road, attack, subject, etc.); **a. des négociations,** to prepare the way for, to initiate, negotiations; *Aut: etc:* **a. un virage,** to (begin to) take a bend; (*b*) to prime, fetch (pump); to cap (shell); *El.E:* to start, excite (dynamo); to strike (arc); *Metalw;* to scarf (weld); to fuse (bomb). **2.** (*a*) to bait (line, trap, etc.); to ground-bait (pool); (*b*) to allure, entice, decoy, inveigle (animal, person).
s'amorcer, (*of pump, dynamo, etc.*) to start; (*of dynamo*) to energize; (*of magnetic field*) to build up; **un virage s'amorce dès la sortie du village,** there is a bend in the road which begins directly one leaves the village.
amorceur, -euse [amɔrsœːr, -øːz], *s.* **1.** (*a*) baiter; (*b*) decoy. **2.** *s.m.* (*a*) *Hyd.E:* priming-cock; (*b*) *I.C.E:* engine primer; (*c*) *Exp:* igniter; **a. à percussion,** push igniter; **a. à tirette,** pull igniter.
amorçoir [amɔrswaːr], *s.m.* **1.** *Tls:* (*a*) auger, twist-bit, boring bit; (*b*) entering tap; (*c*) centre punch. **2.** *Fish:* ground-baiting appliance.
amorite [amɔrit], *s.m. Ling:* Amorite.
amorphe [amɔrf], *a.* **1.** *Ch: Miner: Biol:* amorphous, structureless. **2.** flabby; without personality; without energy; *F:* spineless.
amorphie [amɔrfi], *s.f.,* **amorphisme** [amɔrfism], *s.m.* amorphism, amorphia.
Amorrhéens [amɔreɛ̃], *s.m.pl. B.Hist:* Amorites.
amorti [amɔrti], *a.* **1.** (*a*) *Ph: W.Tel:* damped (wave); **ondes non amorties,** undamped, continuous, waves; (*b*) *Tls:* **marteau a.,** cushioned hammer. **2.** *Nau:* **navire a.,** neaped ship, ship aground. **3.** *Fin:* (bond) due for repayment. **4.** *s.f. Ten: etc:* **amortie,** drop shot. **5.** *s. F:* **les amortis,** the not so young.

amortir [amɔrtiːr], *v.tr.* **1.** (*a*) to deaden, muffle (sound); to allay (fever, pain); to subdue (light, fever, pain); to dull (pain); to damp (ardour); to damp, cool (passion); to tone down, flatten (colour); to break (fall); to absorb, deaden (shock); to break the force of (blow); *Nau:* **a. l'erre d'un bâtiment,** to deaden a ship's way; (*b*) *Ph:* to damp down, damp out (oscillations). **2.** *Const:* to slack, slake (lime). **3.** *Cu:* to tenderize, to make (meat) tender (by beating, hanging, etc.). **4.** (*a*) *Fin:* to redeem, pay off, extinguish, amortize (debt); (*b*) to allow for depreciation of, to write off (plant).
s'amortir. 1. to become deadened, absorbed; (*of passion*) to cool; *Ph:* (*of oscillations*) to grow less, to die away, to damp down; **marais où s'amortit le trop-plein des eaux de crue,** marshes that break the force of flood waters. **2.** (*of debt*) to be gradually paid off, to be redeemed; *F:* **ça s'amortira tout seul,** it will pay for itself.
amortissable [amɔrtisabl], *a. Fin:* redeemable (stock, etc.).
amortissement [amɔrtismɑ̃], *s.m.* **1.** breaking (of fall); absorption (of shock); *Nau:* slackening (of vessel's speed); *Av:* **angle d'a.,** angle of dead rise; *Ph:* damping (of oscillations); **a. du son,** sound-deadening, -damping; sound-proofing (of wall, etc.). **2.** *Arch:* amortizement. **3.** *Const:* slacking, slaking (of lime). **4.** *Fin:* (*a*) redemption, amortization, paying off, liquidation (of debt); **fonds, caisse, d'a.,** sinking fund; (*b*) (*amount written off for*) depreciation. **5.** extinction, absorption (of office).
amortisseur [amɔrtisœːr], *s.m.* **1.** *Mec.E:* damping device; **a. à moulinet,** air brake; **a. pneumatique,** air cushion; **a. de rebondissement,** rebound-check, -stop; *Aut: Av:* shock absorber, *U.S:* snubber; *Av:* **a. de vibrations,** shock mount; *Arms:* **a. de recul,** recoil reducer; *Artil:* **a. de chute** (*gun carriage*), **a. de crosse,** shock absorber. **2.** *El.E:* damper, damping grid. **3.** *Nau:* fender. **4.** *P:* (female) breast.
amouillante [amujɑ̃t], *a. & s.f.* (cow) about to calve.
amouille [amuːj], *s.f. Husb:* beestings.
amouiller [amuːje], *v.i.* (*of cow*) to be about to calve.
amour [amuːr], *s.m. occ. f. in poetry, often f. in pl. in* 1, 2.) **1.** (*a*) love, affection, passion; **a. d'une mère,** a mother's love; **l'a. du prochain,** love of one's neighbour; **dieu, déesse, de l'A.,** god, goddess, of love; **avec a.,** lovingly; **il soigne ses fleurs avec a.,** he tends his flowers lovingly, with loving care; **mal d'a.,** love-sickness; **chagrin d'a.,** unhappy love affair; **elle est morte d'un chagrin d'a.,** she died of a broken heart; **a. platonique,** platonic love; **a. libre,** free love; **a. intéressé,** cupboard love; *F:* **a. vache,** cave-man tactics; **chanson d'a.,** love-song; **enfant de l'a.,** love-child; *s.a.* COTE 4; **s'éprendre d'a. pour qn,** to fall in love with s.o.; **être féru d'a. pour qn,** to be head over heels in love with s.o.; **filer le parfait a.,** to live love's young dream; **l'a. que vous me portez,** the love you bear me, your love for me; **vous savez l'a. que je vous porte,** you know how dearly I love you; **se marier par a.,** to marry for love; **mariage d'a.,** love match; **il vit d'a. et d'eau fraîche,** he lives on love (and fresh air); *P:* **y a plus d'a.,** it just doesn't work any longer; **a. de, envers, pour, qn, qch.,** love of, for, s.o., sth.; **a. de soi,** self-love; **a. du foyer,** love of home; **a. du plaisir,** devotion to pleasure; **faire l'a.,** to make love, to have sexual intercourse (**avec,** with); *P:* **c'est un remède à l'a.,** she's as ugly as sin; **pour l'a. de qn, qch., par a. pour qn,** for the sake of, for love of s.o., sth.; *s.a.* DIEU 2; *Prov:* **heureux au jeu, malheureux en a.,** lucky at cards, unlucky in love; **il n'y a point de laides amours,** beauty is in the eye of the beholder; **l'a. est aveugle,** love is blind; **froides mains, chaudes amours,** cold hands, warm heart; *A:* **au battre, faut l'a.,** come blows, love goes; **tout par a., rien par force,** some can be led who won't be driven; (*b*) *pl.* love-affairs; *Pej:* amours; **les premières amours,** first love, calf-love; **de folles amours,** wanton love; **comment vont les amours?** how is your love life? **à vos amours!** cheers! (*c*) (*of animals*) **être en a.,** to be on heat; **la saison des amours,** the mating season. **2.** (*object of one's love*) **mon a.,** my love, sweetheart; **l'a. de sa famille,** the idol of her family; **une de mes anciennes amours,** an old flame of mine; **les voitures sont ses seul(e)s amours,** cars are his sole passion, the only things he cares about. **3.** Cupid, Eros, the god of Love; *F:* **beau comme l'A.,** handsome as a Greek god; **peindre des**

petits Amours, to paint little Cupids; **quel a. d'enfant!** what a sweet child! what an adorable child! **c'est un petit a.**, he, she, is a little darling; **tu es un a.!** you('re an) angel! **sois un a.!** be a dear, be an angel! **quel a. de bague!** what a lovely, heavenly, divine, ring! what a dream of a ring; *Lit:* **l'A. Médecin**, Doctor Cupid. **4.** *Bot: see* ARBRE 2, HERBE 4, POMME 1.

amouracher [amuraʃe], *v.tr. O: Pej:* **a. qn**, to capture s.o.'s affections.

s'amouracher, *Pej:* to fall head over heels in love (de, with).

amourette [amurɛt], *s.f.* **1.** amourette, love affair, passing fancy (for s.o.). **2.** *Bot:* (*a*) quaking-grass; (*b*) London pride. **3.** *Ent: F:* museum beetle, carpet beetle. **4.** *pl. Cu:* **amourettes**, spinal marrow.

amoureusement [amurøzmɑ̃], *adv.* (*a*) lovingly; (*b*) amorously.

amoureux, -euse [amurø, -øːz]. **1.** *a.* (*a*) loving (care, look, gesture); **cœur a.**, heart full of love; **vie amoureuse**, love life; **être a. de qn, de qch.**, to be in love with s.o.; to be a lover of sth.; **il est a. fou de Lucie**, he's madly in love with Lucy; *Art:* **pinceau a.**, soft, delicate, touch; (*b*) amorous (look, gesture); amatory (letter); (*c*) *Agr:* **terre amoureuse**, rich, well-dressed, soil. **2.** *s.* lover, sweetheart; **les grandes amoureuses**, the great courtesans; *Th:* **l'a.**, the (rejected) lover; **jouer les amoureux**, to play lovers' parts.

amour-propre [amurprɔpr], *s.m.* (*a*) self-respect, (legitimate) pride; **mettre son a.-p. dans son travail**, to take pride in one's work; **blesser l'a.-p. de qn**, to hurt, wound, s.o.'s pride; **stimuler l'a.-p. de qn**, to put s.o. on his mettle; (*b*) amour-propre, vanity, conceit, egotism; **pétri d'a.-p.**, eaten up with conceit; **faire qch. par a.-p.**, to do sth. out of vanity; *pl. amours-propres.*

amovibilité [amɔvibilite], *s.f.* **1.** uncertainty of tenure (of office); liability to be removed (to another post, locality). **2.** *Mec.E:* detachableness, interchangeableness (of machine parts).

amovible [amɔvibl], *a.* **1.** (*a*) (*of office*) revocable at pleasure, held during pleasure; (*b*) removable (official). **2.** (*of parts of machine*) removable, detachable, interchangeable; *Aut:* **jante a.**, detachable rim; **siège a.**, sliding seat.

ampélidacées [ɑ̃pelidase], *s.f.pl. Bot:* Ampelidaceae.

ampélidés [ɑ̃pelide], *s.m.pl. Orn:* Ampelidae.

ampélite [ɑ̃pelit], *s.f. Miner:* ampelite.

ampélographie [ɑ̃pelɔgrafi], *s.f. Vit:* ampelography.

ampélophage [ɑ̃pelɔfaːʒ], *a.* (insect) which attacks the vine.

ampélopsis [ɑ̃pelɔpsis], *s.m. Bot:* ampelopsis.

ampérage [ɑ̃peraːʒ], *s.m. El:* amperage.

ampère [ɑ̃pɛːr], *s.m. El.Meas:* ampere; **intensité en ampères**, amperage; **règle du bonhomme d'A.**, Ampère's rule.

ampère(-)heure [ɑ̃pɛrœːr], *s.m. El.Meas:* ampere-hour; *pl. ampères-heures, ampèreheures.*

ampèremètre [ɑ̃pɛrmɛtr], *s.m. El:* ammeter, amperemeter; **a. thermique**, hot-wire ammeter; **a. apériodique**, dead-beat ammeter; **a. de courant débité**, load ammeter; **a. de courant de charge**, charging ammeter.

ampère(-)tour [ɑ̃pɛrtuːr], *s.m. El:* ampere turn; *pl. ampère(-)tours.*

amphétamine [ɑ̃fetamin], *s.f. Pharm:* amphetamine.

amphi [ɑ̃fi], *s.m. F:* (*a*) *Sch:* lecture-room; (*b*) *Sch:* lecture; (*c*) *Av: Mil:* briefing.

amphi- [ɑ̃fi], *pref.* amphi-.

amphiarthrose [ɑ̃fiartroːz], *s.f. Med:* amphiarthrosis.

amphibie [ɑ̃fibi]. **1.** *a.* (*a*) *Nat.Hist:* amphibious (plant, animal); (**homme**) **a.**, double-faced man; (ii) Jack of all trades; (*b*) *Av:* **appareil a.**, *Aut:* **voiture a.**, amphibian; *Mil: Nav: Av:* **opération a.**, combined operation. **2.** *s.m.* (*a*) *Nat.Hist:* amphibian; (*b*) *Av:* amphibian.

amphibiens [ɑ̃fibjɛ̃], *s.m.pl. Z:* Amphibia.

amphibiotique [ɑ̃fibiɔtik]. *Ent:* **1.** *a.* amphibiotic. **2.** *s.m.pl.* **amphibiotiques**, Amphibiotica.

amphibola [ɑ̃fibɔla], *s.f. Moll:* Amphibola.

amphibole [ɑ̃fibɔl], *s.f. Miner:* amphibole.

amphibolite [ɑ̃fibɔlit], *s.f. Miner:* amphibolite.

amphibologie [ɑ̃fibɔlɔʒi], *s.f. Rh: Log:* amphibology, ambiguity.

amphibologique [ɑ̃fibɔlɔʒik], *a.* amphibological, ambiguous.

amphibraque [ɑ̃fibrak], *s.m. Pros:* amphibrach.

amphictyon [ɑ̃fiktjɔ̃], *s.m. Gr.Hist:* Amphictyon; **le Conseil des Amphictyons**, the Amphictyonic Council.

amphictyonat [ɑ̃fiktjɔna], *s.m. Gr.Hist:* membership of the Amphictyonic Council; status of amphictyon.

amphictyonide [ɑ̃fiktjɔnid], *a. Gr.Hist:* Amphictyonic (town).

amphictyonie [ɑ̃fiktjɔni], *s.f. Gr.Hist:* **1.** Amphictyony, Amphictyonic Council. **2.** right of being represented on the Amphictyonic Council.

amphictyonique [ɑ̃fiktjɔnik], *a. Gr.Hist:* Amphictyonic (council, etc.).

amphigame [ɑ̃figam], *a. Bot:* amphigamous.

amphigène [ɑ̃fiʒɛn]. **1.** *a. Bot: A.Ch:* amphigenous. **2.** *s.m. Miner:* leucite.

amphigouri [ɑ̃figuri], *s.m. Lit:* amphigouri, amphigory, tissue of nonsense, rigmarole.

amphigourique [ɑ̃figurik]. *a. Lit:* amphigoric; **vers amphigouriques**, nonsense-verse; **discours a.**, rambling discourse.

amphigourisme [ɑ̃figurism], *s.m.* incomprehensibility; **tomber dans l'a.**, to lapse into absurdity.

amphimacre [ɑ̃fimakr], *s.m. Pros:* amphimacer, cretic.

amphineures [ɑ̃finœːr], *s.m.pl. Moll:* Amphineura.

amphioxus [ɑ̃fiɔksyːs], *s.m. Ich:* amphioxus, lancelet.

amphipode [ɑ̃fipɔd], *s.m. Crust:* (*a*) amphipod; sand-flea; (*b*) *pl.* **amphipodes**, Amphipoda.

amphisbaenidés, -bénidés [ɑ̃fisbenide], *s.m.pl. Rept:* Amphisbaenidae, Amphisbaenians.

amphisbène [ɑ̃fizbɛn], *s.m. Myth: Her: Rept:* Amphisbaena.

amphisciens [ɑ̃fisjɛ̃], *s.m.pl. Geog:* Amphiscians.

amphithéâtral, -aux [ɑ̃fiteɑtral, -o], *a.* amphitheatrical.

amphithéâtre [ɑ̃fiteɑːtr], *s.m.* **1.** *Archeol: Arch: Th:* amphitheatre; **en a.**, in tiers; tier upon tier. **2.** lecture-room; **a. anatomique**, anatomical theatre.

Amphitrite [ɑ̃fitrit]. **1.** *Pr.n.f. Myth:* Amphitrite. **2.** *Ann:* Amphitrite.

amphitryon [ɑ̃fitrijɔ̃], *s.m.* amphitryon, host, entertainer; (*from Molière's play 'Amphitryon'*); **un aimable a.**, a pleasant host.

amphitype [ɑ̃fitip], *s.m. A: Phot:* ferrotype; tintype.

ampholyte [ɑ̃fɔlit], *s.m. Ch:* ampholyte.

amphore [ɑ̃fɔːr], *s.f.* **1.** *Archeol:* amphora. **2.** jar.

amphorique [ɑ̃fɔrik], *a. Med:* amphoric (resonance, buzzing, breathing).

amphotère [ɑ̃fɔtɛːr], *a. Ch:* amphoteric.

ample [ɑ̃ːpl], *a.* **1.** ample, full (dress, skirt, etc.). **2.** roomy, wide, spacious (shop, theatre, etc.). **3.** full, plentiful, copious (account, supply, etc.); **attendre de plus amples nouvelles**, to await further news; **jusqu'à plus a. informé . . .**, until fuller information is available . .

amplement [ɑ̃pləmɑ̃], *adv.* amply; fully, copiously; **nous avons a. le temps**, we have ample time, plenty of time.

ampleur [ɑ̃plœːr], *s.f.* **1.** width, fullness (of garment); copiousness (of meal); volume (of voice); extent (of damages); **a. de formes**, fullness of figure. **2.** fullness (of account); breadth (of style); generality (of appeal).

amplexicaude [ɑ̃plɛksikoːd], *a. Z:* amplexicaudate.

amplexicaule [ɑ̃plɛksikoːl], *a. Bot:* amplexicaul.

amplexifolié [ɑ̃plɛksifɔlje], *a. Bot:* amplexifoliate.

ampli [ɑ̃pli], *s.m. F:* amplifier.

ampliatif, -ive [ɑ̃pliatif, -iːv], *a.* **1.** *Log:* ampliative, amplifying (proposition). **2.** *Jur:* duplicate (deed, document).

ampliation [ɑ̃pliasjɔ̃], *s.f.* **1.** *Jur:* certified copy (of deed, receipt, etc.); exemplification; **"Pour a."** "true copy"; *U.S:* "authority." **2.** expansion (of the chest).

amplifiant [ɑ̃plifjɑ̃], *a.* **1.** magnifying (lens, etc.); amplifying (power). **2.** *Log:* **induction amplifiante**, ampliative inference.

amplificateur, -trice [ɑ̃plifikatœr, -tris]. **1.** (*a*) *a.* magnifying; (*b*) *s.* magnifier (of trifles, etc.). **2.** *a.* amplifying; *Phot:* (**lentille**) **amplificatrice**, amplifier. **3.** *s.m.* (*a*) *Phot:* enlarger; (*b*) *W.Tel: etc:* amplifier; **a. à réaction**, feed-back amplifier; **a. à résonance**, tuned amplifier; **a. de tension**, voltage amplifier; *Elcs:* **a. de sortie**, final amplifier; (*c*) record-reproducer; (*d*) *Artil:* **a. de couple**, torque amplifier; (*e*) *Av:* **a. d'effacement**, wash-out amplifier; **a. à contre-réaction**, negative feed-back amplifier.

amplificateur-normaliseur [ɑ̃plifikatœːr-nɔrmalizœːr], *s.m. Elcs:* pulse shaper; *pl. amplificateurs-normaliseurs.*

amplificatif, -ive [ɑ̃plifikatif, -iːv], *a.* amplifying, magnifying (lens, etc.).

amplification [ɑ̃plifikasjɔ̃], *s.f.* **1.** (*a*) amplification, development, expansion (of a subject); (*b*) exaggeration. **2.** (*a*) *Opt:* magnification; (*b*) *Phot:* enlarging; (*c*) *W.Tel:* **a.** (**à haute fréquence, etc.**), (high-frequency, etc.) amplification.

amplifier [ɑ̃plifje], *v.tr.* (*p.d. & pr.sub.* **n. amplifiions, v. amplifiiez**) **1.** (*a*) to enlarge, amplify, develop, expand (thought, etc.); (*b*) to embroider (one's adventures); to exaggerate; to magnify (one's danger). **2.** *Opt:* to magnify.

amplitude [ɑ̃plityd], *s.f.* **1.** amplitude, vastness (of space, etc.). **2.** *Astr: Ph:* amplitude (of star, of oscillation); *Artil:* **a. de pointage en direction, en hauteur**, limit of traversing, of elevation; *W.Tel:* **modulation d'a.**, amplitude modulation; *Fin:* **mouvements de capitaux à courte, longue, a.**, short-, long-term movements of capital; *s.a.* OCCASE[1], ORTIVE. **3.** range; **a. thermique**, range of temperature; **a. moyenne annuelle**, mean annual range (of temperature); **a. de la marée**, range of the tide.

ampoule [ɑ̃pul], *s.f.* **1.** ampulla, phial; *Hist:* **la sainte Ampoule**, the (Holy) Ampulla. **2.** (*a*) bulb (of thermometer, electric light); *Phot:* **a. de flash**, flash bulb; (*b*) *Ch:* **a. à décanter**, separating funnel; **a. de Dumas**, Dumas flask; (*c*) container (of vacuum flask); **a. de rechange**, refill; (*d*) *El:* **a. de Crookes**, Crookes's tube; (*e*) *Med:* ampoule. **3.** blister (on foot, metal, photographic plate, etc.); **petite a. (sur la peau)**, bleb, water blister; **j'ai une a. au talon**, I've got a blister on my heel; **il me vient facilement des ampoules**, I blister easily; *F:* **il ne se fait pas d'ampoules aux mains**, he doesn't strain himself.

ampoulé [ɑ̃pule], *a.* inflated, turgid, highfalutin, bombastic (speech, style); **d'un style a.**, bombastically.

ampullacé [ɑ̃pyl(l)ase], *a. Bot:* ampullaceous.

ampullariidés [ɑ̃pylariide], *s.m.pl. Moll:* Ampullariidae.

amputation [ɑ̃pytasjɔ̃], *s.f.* **1.** (*a*) *Surg:* amputation, (of limb, etc.); **a. dans la continuité**, amputation through a bone; **a. dans la contiguïté, dans l'article**, amputation through a joint; **a. à lambeau(x)**, flap-amputation; **faire l'a. d'un membre**, to amputate a limb; (*b*) curtailment, cutting-down (of book, etc.); reduction (of claim). **2.** *F:* cut; **faire des amputations dans un article**, to make cuts in an article, to cut down an article.

amputé, -ée [ɑ̃pyte], *a. & s.* (one) who has lost a limb; amputee; limbless (person); **il est a. du bras gauche**, he has lost his left arm; **homme a. de la cuisse**, man with his leg amputated at the thigh.

amputer [ɑ̃pyte], *v.tr.* **1.** *Surg:* **a. un membre**, to amputate a limb; **a. qn**, to amputate s.o.'s limb; **il fut amputé du bras gauche**, his left arm was amputated. **2.** to cut down, curtail (article, etc.); to cut, reduce (claim) (de, by).

amstellodamois, -oise [amstɛlɔdamwa, -waːz], *a. & s. Geog:* (native, inhabitant) of Amsterdam.

Amsterdam [amstɛrdam], *Pr.n. Geog:* Amsterdam.

amuïr (s') [samɥiːr], *v.pr. Ling:* (*of sound*) to become mute, to disappear.

amuïssement [amɥismɑ̃], *s.m. Ling:* disappearance (of a sound).

amulette [amylɛt], *s.f.* amulet, charm.

amunitionnement [amynisjɔnmɑ̃], *s.m. Mil:* provisioning; supplying with stores.

amunitionner [amynisjɔne], *v.tr. Mil:* to provision; to supply (army, etc.) with provisions, with stores.

Amurat [amyra], *Pr.n.m. Hist:* Murad, Amurath.

amure [amyːr], *s.f. Nau:* (*a*) tack (of sail); (*b*) tack, clew-line (securing sail); **a. de grande voile, grande a.**, main tack; **a. de misaine**, fore-tack; **point d'a.**, tack (of sail); *s.a.* REVERS 1; (*c*) **être bâbord, tribord, amures**, to be on the port, starboard, tack; **courir, faire route, tribord amures**, to sail, run, go, on the starboard tack; **changer d'amures**, to put, go, about; to change tack.

amurer [amyre], *v.tr. Nau:* to board the tack of (sail); to haul, bring, aboard the tack of (sail); *abs.* **a. à tribord**, to tack to starboard.

amusable [amyzabl], *a.* amusable, who can be amused.

amusant [amyzɑ̃], *a.* amusing, diverting, entertaining; funny; **chose amusante à voir**, very amusing thing to see; **ce n'est pas a. d'attendre**, it is not pleasant waiting; there's no fun in waiting.

amuse-gueule [amyːzgœl], *s.m.* cocktail snack; *pl. amuse-gueules.*

amusement [amyzmɑ̃], *s.m.* (*a*) (*action of*) entertaining, amusing; **faire qch. pour son a.,** to do sth. for one's own amusement, for fun; (*b*) amusement, recreation, pastime, diversion; **cela n'est qu'un a. pour lui,** it is mere child's play for him; **amusements innocents,** innocent pleasures.

amuser [amyze], *v.tr.* **1.** to amuse, entertain, divert; **en attendant il faut a. la salle,** meanwhile we must keep the audience amused; *s.a.* TAPIS 1. **2.** *A:* to divert (s.o.'s) attention; to stave off (creditors) by ruse.

s'amuser. **1.** (*a*) to amuse, enjoy, oneself; **bien s'a.,** to have a good time; **on va s'a.,** we're going to have some fun; **je ne me suis jamais aussi bien amusé,** I've had the time of my life; **on s'est bien amusé,** we had a good time; **les enfants s'amusent dans le jardin,** the children are playing in the garden; **amusez-vous bien!** enjoy yourselves! (*b*) **s'a. de qch., (aux dépens) de qn,** to laugh at, make fun of, sth., s.o.; **il s'amusait beaucoup de la voir ivre,** it amused him very much to see her drunk; **faire, dire, qch. pour s'a.,** to do, say, sth. by way of a joke; **s'a. en chemin,** to loiter, dawdle, on the way; **s'a. à faire qch.,** to amuse oneself doing sth., to pass the time doing sth.; *F:* **ne t'amuse pas à recommencer,** don't you dare do that again; **si tu crois que je vais m'amuser à faire ça,** if you think I've nothing better to do than that; **si je dois m'amuser à y aller à pied,** if I'm expected to walk there. **2.** *F:* to see life, to have a good time, to lead a gay life.

amusette [amyzɛt], *s.f.* **1.** toy, plaything; diversion; **ce n'est pour lui qu'une a.,** it's mere child's play for him. **2.** *Artil: A:* amusette.

amuseur, -euse [amyzœːr, -øːz], *s.* amuser, entertainer.

amusie [amyzi], *s.f. Psy:* amusia; **a. (sensorielle),** sensory amusia, tone-deafness; **atteint d'a.,** tone-deaf.

amusique [amyzik], *a.* tone-deaf.

amusoire [amyzwaːr], *s.f. A: F:* = AMUSETTE 1.

amygdale [ami(g)dal], *s.f.* **1.** tonsil; *Med:* **inflammation des amygdales,** tonsillitis; *s.a.* HYPERTROPHIE. **2.** *Geol:* amygdule.

amygdalectomie [ami(g)dalɛktɔmi], *s.f. Surg:* amygdalectomy, tonsillectomy.

amygdalien [ami(g)daljɛ̃], *a.* **angine amygdalienne,** tonsillitis.

amygdalin [ami(g)dalɛ̃], *a. Bot: Ch:* amygdaline, amygdalic; **savon a.,** almond soap.

amygdaline [ami(g)dalin], *s.f. Ch:* amygdalin.

amygdalite [ami(g)dalit], *s.f. Med:* tonsillitis.

amygdaloïde [ami(g)dalɔid], *a. & s.m.* **1.** *Geol:* amygdaloid (rock). **2.** *Med:* **cavité a.,** amygdaloid fossa.

amygdalotome [ami(g)dalɔtɔm], *s.m. Surg:* tonsillotome, amygdalotome; tonsil guillotine.

amygdalotomie [ami(g)dalɔtɔmi], *s.f. Surg:* tonsillotomy, amygdalotomy; cutting of the tonsils.

amylacé [amilase], *a. Ch:* = AMYLOÏDE.

amylacétique [amilasetik], *a. Ch:* **éther a.,** amyl acetate.

amylase [amilaz], *s.f. Bio-Ch:* amylase.

amyle [amil], *s.m. Ch:* amyl.

amylène [amilɛn], *s.m. Ch:* amylene.

amyline [amilin], *s.f. Ch:* amylin(e), starch cellulose.

amylique [amilik], *a. Ch:* amyl(ic); **alcool a.,** amyl alcohol, potato spirit, fusel oil.

amylobacter [amilɔbaktɛr], *s.m. Bac:* amylobacter.

amyloïde [amilɔid], *a. Ch:* starchy, amyloid; amylaceous, amyloidal; *Med:* **maladie a.** = AMYLOSE.

amylolyse [amilɔliːz], *s.f. Ch:* amylolysis, saccharization of starch.

amylose [amiloːz]. **1.** *s.f. Med:* amyloidosis; amyloid, waxy, degeneration (of the liver, of the spleen). **2.** *s.m. Ch:* amylose.

amyotrophie [amiɔtrɔfi], *s.f. Med:* amyotrophy, amyotrophia.

an [ɑ̃], *s.m.* **1.** year; **l'an passé, dernier,** last year; **deux fois l'an, deux fois par an,** twice a year; **tous les ans,** every year; **il y a eu, il y aura, un an en septembre,** a year last, next, September; **avoir dix ans,** to be ten (years old); **il a bientôt seize ans,** he is nearly sixteen (years old); **il pouvait avoir entre quarante et soixante ans,** he might be, may have been, any age between forty and sixty; **un poulain de deux ans,** a two-year-old (colt); **ami de vingt ans,** friend of twenty years' standing; **bon an, mal an,** taking one year with another; **en l'an 1200,** in the year 1200; *s.a.* GRÂCE 3, MOQUER (SE); **le jour de l'an, le nouvel an, le premier de l'an,** New Year's day; *Ecc:* **(service du) bout de l'an,** year's end memorial service (a year after s.o.'s death); *Jur:* **an et jour,** a year and a day. **2.** *pl. Lit:* **les ans ont ralenti sa marche,** the years have slowed his pace; **l'outrage des ans,** the ravages of time, of old age; *s.a.* CHARGÉ 1.

anabantes [anabɑ̃t], *s.m.pl. Ich:* (*a*) (*genus*) Anabas; (*b*) (*family*) Anabantidæ.

anabaptisme [anabatism], *s. Rel.H:* anabaptism.

anabaptiste [anabatist]. *Rel.H:* **1.** *a.* anabaptist(ical) (doctrine, etc.). **2.** *s.m. & f.* anabaptist.

anabas [anabas], *s.m. Ich:* anabas; **a. grimpeur,** climbing perch.

anabase [anabɑːz], *s.f.* **1.** *Med: Bot:* anabasis. **2.** *Gr.Lit:* **l'A.,** the Anabasis.

anabiose [anabjoːz], *s.f. Biol:* anabiosis, reanimation.

anableps [anablɛps], *s.m. Ich:* anableps, four-eyed fish.

anabolique [anabɔlik], *a. Biol:* anabolic.

anabolisme [anabɔlism], *s.m. Biol:* anabolism.

anacarde [anakard], *s.m. Bot:* anacard, cashew-nut.

anacardiacées [anakardjase], *s.f.pl. Bot:* Anacardiaceae.

anacardier [anakardje], *s.m.* anacardium, cashew-tree.

anachorète [anakɔrɛt], *s.m.* anchorite; recluse; **repas d'a.,** frugal meal.

anachorétique [anakɔretik], *a.* anchoretic, austere (life, etc).

anachromatique [anakrɔmatik], *a. Phot:* anachromatic, soft-focus (lens).

anachronique [anakrɔnik], *a.* anachronistic.

anachroniquement [anakrɔnikmɑ̃], *adv.* anachronistically.

anachronisme [anakrɔnism], *s.m.* anachronism.

anaclastique [anaklastik], *a. Opt:* anaclastic (point, curve).

anacoluthe [anakɔlyt], *s.f. Gram:* anacoluthon.

anaconda [anakɔ̃da], *s.m. Z:* anaconda.

Anacréon [anakreɔ̃]. *Pr.n.m. Gr.Lit:* Anacreon.

anacréontique [anakreɔ̃tik], *a. Lit:* Anacreontic, convivial, amatory (verse).

anacréontisme [anakreɔ̃tism], *s.m. Lit:* imitation of Anacreon.

anacrouse [anakruːz], *s.f. Pros: Mus:* anacrusis.

anacycle [anasikl], *s.m. Bot:* anacyclus.

anacyclique [anasiklik], *Poet:* **1.** *s.m.* palindrome; **2.** *a.* palindromic.

anadrome [anadroːm], *a. Ich:* anadromous.

anadromie [anadrɔmi], *s.f. Ich:* anadromous movement (of fish ascending rivers from the sea for spawning).

Anadyomène [anadjɔmɛn]. **1.** *a. Myth:* (Venus) Anadyomene. **2.** *s.f. Bot:* anadyomene.

anaérobie [anaerɔbi]. *Bac:* **1.** *a.* anaerobic. **2.** *s.m.* anaerobe; *pl.* anaerobia.

anaérobiose [anaerɔbioːz], *s.f. Bac:* anaerobiosis.

anagallide [anagal(l)id], *s.f.,* **anagallis** [anagal(l)is], *s.f. Bot:* anagallis, pimpernel; **a. des champs,** scarlet pimpernel.

anagénèse [anaʒenɛːz], *s.f. Physiol:* anagenesis.

anaglyphe [anaglif], *s.m.,* **anaglypte** [anaglipt], *s.m. Art: Pal: Phot:* anaglyph.

anaglyptique [anagliptik], *a.* anaglyptic(al), anaglyphic; **impression a.,** raised print (for the blind); *Opt:* **diapositive a.,** anaglyphic lantern-slide.

anagogie [anagɔʒi], *s.f. Theol:* anagoge, anagogy.

anagogique [anagɔʒik], *a.* anagogic(al).

anagrammatique [anagramatik], *a.* anagrammatic(al).

anagrammatiste [anagramatist], *s.m. & f.* anagrammatist.

anagramme [anagram], *s.f.* anagram.

anagyre [anaʒiːr], *s.m.,* **anagyris** [anaʒiris], *s.m. Bot:* anagyris foetida, bean-trefoil.

anal, -aux [anal, -o], *a. Anat:* anal; **nageoire anale,** *s.f.* **anale,** anal fin.

analcime [analsim], *s.f.,* **analcite** [analsit], *s.f. Miner:* analcime, analcite.

analectes [analɛkt], *s.m.pl. Lit:* analecta, gleanings.

analemme [analɛm], *s.m. Geom: Astr:* analemma.

analeptique [analɛptik], *a. & s.m. Med:* analeptic, building-up (diet).

analgésie [analʒezi], *s.f. Med:* analgesia, analgia.

analgésine [analʒezin], *s.f. Pharm:* analgesine, antipyrine.

analgésique [analʒezik], *a. & s.m.* analgesic, analgic, analgetic.

analgie [analʒi], *s.f.* = ANALGÉSIE.

anallagmatique [analagmatik], *a. & s.f. Mth:* anallagmatic (curve).

anallantoïdiens [anal(l)ɑ̃tɔidjɛ̃], *s.m.pl. Ich: Amph:* anallantoidea.

anallatique [anal(l)atik], *a. Surv:* anallatic (telescope).

analogie [analɔʒi], *s.f.* analogy; **raisonner par a.,** to argue from analogy; **par a. avec . . .,** on the analogy of . . ., by analogy with . . .; **ce texte présente, offre, une certaine a. avec un manuscrit du XV**[e] **siècle,** this text bears some resemblance to a XVth century manuscript.

analogique [analɔʒik], *a.* analogical; *Elcs:* **calculatrice a.,** analogue computer.

analogiquement [analɔʒikmɑ̃], *adv.* analogically.

analogisme [analɔʒism], *s.m. Log:* analogism; reasoning by analogy.

analogue [analɔg]. **1.** *a.* analogous (**à,** to, with); similar (**à,** to). **2.** *s.m.* analogue, parallel, counterpart.

analphabète [analfabɛt], *a. & s.* analphabetic, illiterate.

analphabétisme [analfabetism], *s.m.* illiteracy; **campagne contre l'a.,** literacy campaign, campaign against illiteracy.

analysable [analizabl], *a.* analysable.

analyse [analiːz], *s.f.* analysis. **1.** (*a*) *Log: Gram:* **a. grammaticale,** parsing; **a. logique,** analysis; **faire l'a. d'une phrase,** (i) to parse; (ii) to analyse, a sentence; **en dernière a.,** in the last analysis, to sum up, when all is said and done, all things considered; **roman d'a.,** psychological novel; **esprit d'a.,** analytical mind; (*b*) *Ch:* **a. quantitative,** quantitative analysis; **a. volumétrique,** volumetric analysis; **a. qualitative,** qualitative analysis; **a. par voie humide, sèche,** wet, dry, analysis; **a. contradictoire,** check analysis; **faire l'a. d'une substance,** to analyse a substance; (*c*) *Meteor:* **a. maîtresse,** master analysis; **a. auxiliaire,** advisory analysis; **a. en surface,** surface analysis; **a. en altitude,** upper air analysis; **centre d'a. principal,** main analysis centre; **centre d'a. secondaire, sous-centre d'a.,** subsidiary analysis centre; (*d*) *Miner: etc:* assaying; (*e*) *Mth:* **a. infinitésimale,** (differential and integral) calculus; (*f*) *Med:* **laboratoire d'analyses,** pathology laboratory. **2.** abstract, résumé, précis.

analyser [analize], *v.tr.* to analyse (facts, substance, etc.); to assay (ore); **a. une phrase,** (i) to parse; (ii) to analyse, a sentence; **a. un livre,** to analyse, give an abstract of, a book; **a. un dossier,** to make a précis of a set of documents.

analyseur [analizœːr], *s.m.* **1.** *A: & Pej:* (*pers.*) analyser. **2.** *Opt:* analyser (of polariscope); *Ac:* **a. de son,** sound analyser.

analyste [analist], *s.m. & f. Mth: Ch: etc:* analyst; *Miner:* assayer.

analytique [analitik]. **1.** *a.* analytic(al); **géométrie a.,** analytical geometry; *Meteor:* **bulletin a.,** analysis; **bulletin a. d'orientation,** advisory analysis. **2.** *s.f.* analytics.

analytiquement [analitikmɑ̃], *adv.* analytically.

anamésite [anamesit], *s.f. Miner:* anamesite.

anamnèse [anamnɛːz], *s.f. Med: Ecc:* anamnesis.

anamnésie [anamnezi], *s.f. Med:* anamnesis; return of memory.

anamnien, -ienne [anamnjɛ̃, -jɛn], **anamnié** [anamnje], **anamniote** [anamnjɔt], *a. Ich: Amph:* anamniote, anamniotic.

anamorphose [anamɔrfoz], *s.f. Bot: Opt:* anamorphosis.

anamorphoseur, -euse [anamɔrfozœːr, -øz], **anamorphotique** [anamɔrfotik], *a. Opt:* anamorph(ot)ic.

ananas [anana(s)], *s.m.* (*a*) pineapple; (*b*) ananas, pineapple plant; **serre à a.,** pinery.

anandraire [anɑ̃drɛːr], **anandre** [anɑ̃ːdr], *a. Bot:* anandrous.

Ananias [ananjɑːs], *Pr.n.m. B.Hist:* Ananias.

anapeste [anapɛst], *Pros:* **1.** *a.* anapaestic. **2.** *s.m.* anapaest.

anapestique [anapɛstik], *a. Pros:* anapaestic.

anaphase [anafɑːz], *s.f. Biol:* anaphase.

anaphore [anafɔːr], *s.f. Rh:* anaphora.

anaphorique [anafɔrik], *a. Gram:* anaphoric.

anaphrodisiaque [anafrɔdizjak], *a. & s.m.* anaphrodisiac.

anaphrodisie [anafrɔdizi], *s.f. Med:* anaphrodisia, frigidity.

anaphylactique [anafilaktik], *a. Med:* anaphylactic.

anaphylaxie [anafilaksi], *s.f. Med:* anaphylaxis, anaphylaxy.

anaplasie [anaplazi], *s.f. Med: Biol:* anaplasia.

anaplasmose [anaplazmoːz], *s.f. Vet:* anaplasmosis.

anaplastie [anaplasti], *s.f.* = AUTOPLASTIE.

anar [anar], *s.m. P:* anarchist.

anarchie [anarʃi], *s.f.* (*a*) anarchy; lawless condition; (*b*) state of confusion, of disorder.

anarchique [anarʃik], *a.* anarchic(al); anarchistic.

anarchiquement [anarʃikmɑ̃], *adv.* anarchically.
anarchisant [anarʃizɑ̃], *a.* with anarchist tendencies, leanings.
anarchiser [anarʃize], *v.tr.* to anarchize.
anarchisme [anarʃism], *s.m. Pol:* anarchism.
anarchiste [anarʃist], *a. & s. Pol:* anarchist.
anarcho [anarʃo], *s.m. P:* anarchist.
anarcho-syndicalisme [anarʃosɛ̃dikalism], *s.m. Pol:* anarcho-syndicalism.
anarrhique [anarik], *s.m. Ich:* wolf-fish.
anasarque [anazark], *s.f. Med:* anasarca.
Anastase [anastɑːz], *Pr.n.m.* Anastasius.
Anastasie [anastazi], *Pr.n.f.* 1. Anastasia. 2. *F:* the censorship.
anastatica [anastatika], *s.f.*, **anastatique**[1] [anastatik], *s.f. Bot:* anastatica, rose of Jericho.
anastatique[2], *a. Engr:* anastatic.
anastigmat [anastigma], **anastigmatique** [anastigmatik], *a. Opt: Phot:* anastigmatic (lens); *s.m.* anastigmat.
anastome [anastom], *s.m. Orn:* African open-bill stork.
anastomose [anastomoːz], *s.f. Surg: Anat: Bot:* anastomosis, inosculosis, inosculation.
anastomosé [anastomoze], *a. Geog:* (*of stream*) braided.
anastomoser [anastomoze], *v.tr. Anat: Surg:* to anastomose.
s'anastomoser, *Anat:* to anastomose, inosculate.
anastrophe [anastrɔf], *s.f. Ling:* anastrophe.
anastylose [anastiloz], *s.f. Arch:* anastylosis.
anatase [anatɑːz], *s.f. Miner:* anatase.
anathématisation [anatematizasjɔ̃], *s.f.* anathematization.
anathématiser [anatematize], *v.tr.* to anathematize, curse.
anathème [anatɛm], *s.m.* 1. (*a*) anathema, ban, curse; **frapper qn d'a.,** to anathematize s.o.; (*b*) blame, opprobrium. 2. anathema, person accursed.
anatidés [anatide], *s.m.pl. Orn:* Anatidae.
anatife [anatif], *s.m. Crust:* anatifa, anatifer; barnacle.
anatocisme [anatɔsism], *s.m. Fin:* anatocism, compound interest.
Anatole [anatɔl], *Pr.n.m.* Anatolius.
Anatolie [anatɔli], *Pr.n.f. Geog:* Anatolia.
anatomie [anatɔmi], *s.f.* 1. anatomy; *Med:* **a. pathologique,** morbid anatomy; **a. topographique,** topography; *F:* **une belle a.,** a fine figure. 2. (*a*) **pièce d'a.,** anatomical figure; (*b*) *O:* (detailed) analysis.
anatomique [anatɔmik], *a.* anatomical.
anatomiquement [anatɔmikmɑ̃], *adv.* anatomically.
anatomiser [anatɔmize], *v.tr. A:* to anatomize, dissect, analyse (body, book, etc.).
anatomiste [anatɔmist], *s.m.* anatomist.
anatoxine [anatɔksin], *s.f.* anatoxin, toxoid.
anatrope [anatrɔp], *a. Bot:* (**ovule**) **a.,** anatropous (ovule).
Anaxagore [anaksagoːr], *Pr.n.m. Gr.Phil:* Anaxagoras.
Anaximandre [anaksimɑ̃ːdr], *Pr.n.m. Gr.Phil:* Anaximander.
Anaximène [anaksimɛn], *Pr.n.m. Gr.Phil:* Anaximenes.
-ance [ɑ̃ːs], *s.suff.f.* 1. -ance; **alliance,** alliance; **assistance,** assistance. 2. -ancy; **constance,** constancy; **enfance,** infancy. 3. -ence; **subsistance,** subsistence; **indépendance,** independence. 4. -ency; **persistance,** persistency; **consistance,** consistency.
ancenien, -ienne [ɑ̃sənjɛ̃, -jɛn], *a. & s. Geog:* (native, inhabitant) of Ancenis.
ancestral, -aux [ɑ̃sɛstral, -o], *a.* ancestral.
ancêtre [ɑ̃sɛːtr], *s.m.* ancestor, forefather, forbear; **portraits d'ancêtres,** ancestral, family, portraits; **ses ancêtres,** his ancestors, his ancestry; **culte des ancêtres,** ancestor worship; **la montgolfière est l'a. de l'avion,** Montgolfier's balloon is the ancestor of the aeroplane; **Ader est l'a. de l'aviation,** Ader is the father of aviation.
anche [ɑ̃ːʃ], *s.f.* 1. *Mus:* reed, tongue (of oboe, clarinet, etc.); **jeu d'anches,** reed-stop (of organ); **a. libre,** free reed; **a. battante,** beating reed, striking reed. 2. *Mill: etc:* spout (of hopper). 3. *Const: etc:* (sheer-) leg, sheer (of gin, etc.).
Anchise [ɑ̃ʃiːz], *Pr.n.m. Lt.Lit:* Anchises.
anchois [ɑ̃ʃwa], *s.m.* 1. *Ich: Cu:* anchovy; **a. de Norvège,** sprat; **beurre d'a.,** anchovy paste; **sauce aux a.,** anchovy sauce; *F:* **serrés, tassés, comme des a.,** packed like sardines. 2. *Bot:* **poire d'a.,** anchovy pear.
ancien, -ienne [ɑ̃sjɛ̃, -jɛn], *a.* 1. ancient, old, antique; of long, of old, standing; **monument a.,** ancient monument; **amitié ancienne,** friendship of long standing. 2. ancient, old(en), early, bygone, past; **les anciens auteurs, les auteurs anciens,** ancient authors; **le grec a.,** ancient Greek; **l'A. Testament,** the Old Testament. 3. former, late, old, ex-, (teacher, pupil, etc.); **a. président,** past president; **a. élève,** old pupil, old boy (of a school); *U.S:* alumnus; **anciens combattants,** ex-servicemen, veterans; **a. prêtre de cette paroisse,** sometime, at one time, priest of this parish. 4. senior (captain, officer, etc.); **les élèves anciens, les anciens,** the senior boys (in a school); **il est votre a.,** he is your senior, is senior to you; **moins a.,** junior; **Pline l'A.,** Pliny the Elder. 5. *s.m.* (*a*) *B:* **l'A. des jours,** the Ancient of days, God; (*b*) **les anciens,** the ancients; (*c*) *Ecc: Pol:* elder; (*d*) **les anciens du village,** the older inhabitants of the village; *F:* **l'a.,** the old man, the governor; (*e*) *F: Mil:* veteran; (*f*) *Scouting:* patrol leader.
anciennement [ɑ̃sjɛnmɑ̃], *adv.* anciently; in the old(en) days; formerly, previously.
ancienneté [ɑ̃sjɛnte], *s.f.* 1. oldness, antiquity (of monument, race, etc.); **de toute a.,** from time immemorial. 2. seniority, length of service; **a. de grade,** seniority in rank; **liste à l'a.,** seniority list; **avancer à l'a.,** to be promoted by seniority.
ancillaire [ɑ̃sil(l)ɛːr], *a.* ancillary.
ancipité [ɑ̃sipite], *a. Bot:* ancipital, ancipitous, two-edged (stem, etc.).
ancolie [ɑ̃kɔli], *s.f. Bot:* aquilegia, columbine.
ancon [ɑ̃kɔ̃], *s.m. Anat: Arch:* ancon.
Ancône [ɑ̃koːn], *Pr.n.f. Geog:* Ancona.
anconitain, -aine [ɑ̃kɔnitɛ̃, -ɛn], *a. & s. Geog:* (native, inhabitant) of Ancona.
ancrage [ɑ̃kraːʒ], *s.m.* 1. *Nau:* (*a*) anchoring; (*b*) anchorage; (**droits d'**)**a.,** anchorage dues. 2. *Mec.E: Civ.E: etc:* (*a*) anchoring, anchorage, fixing; (*b*) bracing, staying; (*c*) wall-tie; **plaque, tige, d'a.,** anchor-plate, -tie; **câble d'a.,** anchor-stay (of mast, etc.).
ancre [ɑ̃ːkr], *s.f.* 1. anchor; *Nau:* **grosse a. de bossoir,** bower (anchor); **petite a. de bossoir,** second bower; **a. de veille,** *A:* **a. de miséricorde,** sheet anchor; **a. de grand panneau,** waist anchor; **a. du large, de terre,** sea-, shore-anchor; **a. sans jas,** stockless anchor; **a. flottante, a. de cape,** drag, drogue, deep-sea anchor; **a. de corps mort, a. borgne,** mooring anchor; **a. de toue, de touée, à empenneler, à jet,** kedge anchor; *s.a.* MAÎTRE 3; **mettre les ancres à poste,** to stow anchors; **brider l'a.,** to shoe the anchor; **être à l'a.,** to be, lie, ride, at anchor; **être à l'a. devant Margate,** to lie (at anchor) off Margate; **fatiguer, ne pas fatiguer, l'a.,** to ride hard, easy; **mouiller, jeter, l'a.,** to cast, drop, anchor; to anchor; (*of pers.*) **jeter l'a. dans un lieu,** to settle down somewhere; *Lit:* **a. de salut,** last hope; **lever l'a.,** to weigh anchor; *F:* to leave, to get moving; *Aer:* **a. de ballon,** balloon anchor, grapnel. 2. *Const: etc:* anchor, cramp-iron, tie, tie-plate (of wall, furnace, etc.); brace, stay (of boiler); **a. à fourchette,** forked tie; **affermir qch. par des ancres,** to anchor, brace, stay, sth. 3. anchor (of clock); **montre à a.,** lever-watch.
ancre-chaîne [ɑ̃krəʃɛːn], *s.f. Aer:* balloon anchor; *pl. ancres-chaînes.*
ancrer [ɑ̃kre], *v.tr.* 1. *Nau: Aer:* to anchor (ship, balloon); **idée ancrée dans la tête,** idea deep-rooted in the mind; **il a réussi à lui ancrer dans la tête que . . .,** he managed to sink into his head that . . . 2. *Const: etc:* to brace, tie, stay, anchor (chimney, engine, boiler, etc.); **ancré en place,** tied down, irremovable.
s'ancrer, *F:* to establish oneself, to get a firm footing (in a place, position); to anchor oneself (in a job).
ancrure [ɑ̃kryːr], *s.f.* 1. *Const:* (*a*) cramp-iron, tie, brace; (*b*) eye (of tie-rod). 2. *Tex:* crease.
Ancyre [ɑ̃siːr], *Pr.n.f. A.Geog:* Ancyra.
andaillot [ɑ̃dajo], *s.m. Nau:* cringle.
andain [ɑ̃dɛ̃], *s.m. Agr:* swath, wind-row.
andalou, -ouse [ɑ̃dalu, -uːz]. 1. *a. & s. Geog:* Andalusian. 2. *s.m. Ling:* Andalusian (dialect). 3. *s.m.* Andalusian horse.
Andalousie [ɑ̃daluzi], *Pr.n.f. Geog:* Andalusia.
andalousite [ɑ̃daluzit], *s.f. Miner:* andalusite.
andante [ɑ̃dɑ̃ːt], *adv. & s.m. Mus:* andante.
andantino [ɑ̃dɑ̃tino], *adv. & s.m. Mus:* andantino.
andelysien, -ienne [ɑ̃delizjɛ̃, -jɛn], *a. & s. Geog:* (native, inhabitant) of Les Andelys.
Andes [ɑ̃ːd], *Pr.n.f.pl. Geog:* **les A.,** the Andes; **la Cordillère des A.,** the Andean, the Great Cordillera.
andésite [ɑ̃dezit], *s.f. Miner:* andesite.
andésitique [ɑ̃dezitik], *a.* andesitic.
andin [ɑ̃dɛ̃], *a. Geog:* Andean.
andorite [ɑ̃dɔrit], *s.f. Miner:* andorite.
andorran, -ane [ɑ̃dɔrɑ̃, -an], *a. & s. Geog:* Andorran.
Andorre [ɑ̃dɔːr], *Pr.n.Geog:* **le val, la principauté d'A.,** the Vale, Principality, of Andorra.
andouille [ɑ̃duːj], *s.f.* 1. *Cu:* chitterlings (made into sausages); *F:* **il est ficelé comme une a.,** his clothes are so tight on him he can hardly move; *F:* **s'en aller en brouet d'a.,** to fizzle out. 2. **a. de tabac,** twist of tobacco. 3. (*a*) *P:* idiot, nit; **faire l'a.,** to play the fool; (*b*) **faire son a.,** to swagger, swank.
andouiller [ɑ̃duje], *s.m. Ven:* tine (of antler); **cerf à trois, quatre, andouillers,** three-, four-tined stag; **maître a.,** brow antler; **a. de combat, de massacre,** brow, browtine.
andouillette [ɑ̃dujɛt], *s.f. Cu:* small sausage made of chitterlings.
André [ɑ̃dre], *Pr.n.m.* Andrew.
andrène [ɑ̃drɛn], *s.m. Ent:* andrena.
Andrinople [ɑ̃drinɔpl]. 1. *Pr.n.f. Geog:* Adrianople; **rouge d'A.,** turkey-red. 2. *s.f. Tex:* turkey-red cotton.
andrinopolitain, -aine [ɑ̃drinɔpɔlitɛ̃, -ɛn], *a. & s. Geog:* (native, inhabitant) of Adrianople.
androcée [ɑ̃drɔse], *s.m.*, **andrœcie** [ɑ̃dresi], *s.f. Bot:* androecium.
androcéphale [ɑ̃drɔsefal], *a.* androcephalous.
Androclès [ɑ̃drɔklɛːs], *Pr.n.m.* Androcles.
androconie [ɑ̃drɔkɔni], *s.f. Ent:* androconium, *pl.* androconia.
androgène [ɑ̃drɔʒɛn], (*a*) *a.* androgenic; (*b*) *s.m.* androgen, male hormone.
androgenèse [ɑ̃drɔʒənɛz], *s.f. Biol:* androgenesis.
androgynaire [ɑ̃drɔʒinɛːr], *a. Bot:* androgynary.
androgyne [ɑ̃drɔʒin], 1. *a.* (*a*) *Bot:* androgynous; (*b*) *Z:* hermaphroditic. 2. *s.m.* (*a*) *Bot:* androgyne; (*b*) *Z:* hermaphrodite.
androgynie [ɑ̃drɔʒini], *s.f.* (*a*) *Bot:* androgyny; (*b*) *Biol:* pseudo-hermaphroditism.
androïde [ɑ̃drɔid], *a. & s.m.* android.
Andromaque [ɑ̃drɔmak], *Pr.n.f. Gr.Lit:* Andromache.
andromeda [ɑ̃drɔmeda], *s.m.*, **andromède**[1] [ɑ̃drɔmɛd], *s.f. Bot:* andromeda; stagger-bush; moorwort.
Andromède[2], *Pr.n.f. Myth: Astr:* Andromeda.
andron [ɑ̃drɔ̃], *s.m.* (*a*) *Gr.Ant:* andron; (*b*) *Gr. & R.C.Ch:* side of nave reserved for men.
Andronic [ɑ̃drɔnik], *Pr.n.m. Hist:* Andronicus.
androphobe [ɑ̃drɔfɔb]. 1. *a.* (*a*) misanthropic; (*b*) man-hating. 2. *s.* (*a*) misanthrope; (*b*) man-hater.
andropogon [ɑ̃drɔpɔgɔ̃], *s.m. Bot:* andropogon.
andropogonées [ɑ̃drɔpɔgɔne], *s.f.pl. Bot:* Andropogon (genus of) grasses.
androsème [ɑ̃drɔzɛm], *s.m. Bot:* tutsan.
androsphinx [ɑ̃drɔsfɛ̃ks], *s.m. Archeol:* androsphinx.
androspore [ɑ̃drɔspɔːr], *s.f. Bot:* androspore.
androstérone [ɑ̃drɔsterɔn], *s.f. Physiol:* androsterone.
âne [ɑːn], *s.m.* 1. donkey, ass; **â. mâle,** jack(-ass), jackass; (*a*) **faire une promenade à â., à dos d'â.,** to go for a donkey ride; *F:* **têtu comme un â.,** as stubborn as an ass, a mule, a donkey; **le coup de pied de l'â.,** the most unkindest cut of all; **chercher son â. et être dessus,** to look for sth. which one has in one's hands; **ressembler à l'â. de Buridan,** not to be able to make up one's mind; **contes de Peau-d'â.,** fairy tales; **l'â. du moulin,** the scapegoat; *Prov:* **on ne saurait faire boire un â. qui n'a pas soif,** you may lead a horse to water but you cannot make him drink; **faute d'un point Martin perdit son â.,** for want of a nail the shoe was lost; **il y a plus d'un â. à la foire qui s'appelle Martin,** there are more Jacks than one at the fair; **à laver la tête d'un â. on perd sa lessive, son savon,** it's a waste of time trying to teach stupid people; **personne ne sait mieux que l'â. où le bât le blesse,** everyone knows best where his own shoe pinches; **il n'y a point d'â. plus mal bâté que celui du commun,** everybody's business is nobody's business; **il est méchant comme un â. rouge,** he'd murder his own grandmother; *s.a.* BRIDER 1, DOS-D'ÂNE. 2. *F:* fool, ass, dunce; **mettre un bonnet, les oreilles, d'â. à un enfant,** to put a dunce's cap on a child; **un â. parmi les singes,** a fool among rogues; **l'â. frotte l'â.,** one fool praises another; **faire l'â. pour avoir du son,** to pretend ignorance in order to achieve one's end; **il ne sera jamais qu'un â.,** he'll always be a fool; *s.a.* BÂTER, PONT[1] 1. 3. *Games: A:* **â. salé,** Aunt Sally. 4. *Ich:* **tête d'â.,** bull-head, miller's thumb; *Moll: F:* **â. marin,** octopus; *F:* devil-fish. 5. *Tls:* bench vice; **banc d'â.,** vice bench.

anéantir [aneɑ̃tiːr], *v.tr.* (*a*) to reduce to nothing; to annihilate, destroy (empire, town, etc.); **a. les espérances de qn,** to blast, dash, s.o.'s hopes; **je suis anéanti,** I am exhausted, dead-beat; (*b*) to overwhelm, dumbfound; **anéanti par la douleur,** prostrate with grief.

s'anéantir. 1. to come to nothing, to vanish; to melt into thin air. **2.** to humble, abase, oneself (before God).

anéantissant [aneɑ̃tisɑ̃], *a.* exhausting (work); overwhelming (misfortune).

anéantissement [aneɑ̃tismɑ̃], *s.m.* **1.** destruction, annihilation (of hope, empire, etc.). **2.** (*state of*) prostration, exhaustion; **dans l'a.,** prostrate. **3.** self-humiliation, self-abasement.

anecdote [anɛgdɔt, -kd-], *s.f.* anecdote.

anecdotier, -ière [anɛgdɔtje, -kd-, -jɛːr], *s.* anecdotist, teller of anecdotes.

anecdotique [anɛgdɔtik, -kd-], *a.* anecdotal, anecdotic(al).

anecdotiser [anɛgdɔtize], *v.i.* to tell, collect, anecdotes.

anéchoïde [anekɔid], *a. Ac:* anechoic.

ânée [ɑne], *s.f.* donkey-load.

anémiant [anemjɑ̃], *a. Med:* impoverishing, weakening.

anémie [anemi], *s.f. Med:* anaemia; **a. pernicieuse,** pernicious anaemia; **a. des mineurs,** miners' anaemia, ankylostomiasis, hookworm disease.

anémié [anemje], *a.* anaemic.

anémier [anemje], *v.tr.* **1.** to render (s.o.) anaemic. **2.** to impoverish, weaken (a people, etc.).

s'anémier. 1. to become anaemic. **2.** to grow weak.

anémique [anemik], *a.* **1.** anaemic, bloodless. **2.** feeble; lacking in energy.

anémogramme [anemɔgram], *s.m. Meteor:* anemogram.

anémographe [anemɔgraf], *s.m. Meteor:* anemograph.

anémographique [anemɔgrafik], *a.* anemographic.

anémomètre [anemɔmɛtr], *s.m.* anemometer, wind-gauge; wind indicator; **a. badin,** airspeed indicator; **a. à fil chaud,** hot wire anemometer; **a. transmetteur,** wind direction and wind velocity transmitter.

anémométrie [anemɔmetri], *s.f.* anemometry.

anémométrique [anemɔmetrik], *a.* anemometric.

anémone [anemɔn], *s.f.* **1.** *Bot:* anemone; **a. des Apennins,** blue mountain anemone; **a. couronnée,** poppy anemone; **a. des jardins,** star anemone; **a. pulsatille,** pasque-flower; **a. hépatique,** liver-leaf, hepatica; **a. sylvie,** wood-anemone. **2.** *Coel:* **a. de mer,** sea-anemone.

anémophile [anemɔfil], *a. Bot:* anemophilous.

anémophilie [anemɔfili], *s.f. Bot:* anemophily.

anémoscope [anemɔskɔp], *s.m. Meteor:* anemoscope.

anémotrope [anemɔtrɔp], *s.m. Mec.E:* wind-motor.

anencéphale [anɑ̃sefal]. **1.** *s.m.* anencephalus. **2.** *a.* anencephalous, anencephalic.

anencéphalie [anɑ̃sefali], *s.f.* anencephalia, anencephaly.

anergie [anɛrʒi], *s.f. Med:* anergia, anergy.

ânerie [ɑnri], *s.f. F:* **1.** stupidity, ignorance. **2.** foolish act, remark; **faire des âneries,** to make an ass, a fool, of oneself; **dire des âneries,** to talk a lot of nonsense, tripe.

anéroïde [anerɔid], *a. Meteor:* aneroid (barometer, etc.).

ânesse [ɑnɛs], *s.f.* she-ass, jenny; **lait d'â.,** ass's milk.

anesthésiant [anɛstezjɑ̃], *a. & s.m. Med:* anaesthetic.

anesthésie [anɛstezi], *s.f. Med:* anaesthesia; **a. générale, a. locale,** general, local, anaesthesia; **a. rachidienne,** spinal anaesthesia.

anesthésier [anɛstezje], *v.tr. Med:* to anaesthetize; **se faire a. (chez le dentiste),** *F:* to have gas.

anesthésiologie [anɛstezjɔlɔʒi], *s.f.* anaesthesiology.

anesthésiologiste [anɛstezjɔlɔʒist], *s.m. & f.* anaesthesiologist.

anesthésique [anɛstezik], *a. & s.m. Med:* anaesthetic; **sous l'influence de l'a.,** under the anaesthetic.

anesthésiste [anɛstezist], *s.m. & f. Med:* anaesthetist.

aneth [anɛt], *s.m. Bot:* anethum; **a. odorant,** dill; **a. doux,** fennel; *Pharm:* eau d'a., dill water.

aneurine [anœrin], *s.f.* aneurin, vitamin B.

anévrismal, anévrysmal, -aux [anevrismal, -o], *a. Med:* aneurismal, aneurysmal.

anévrismatique, anévrysmatique [anevrismatik], *a. Med:* aneurismatic, aneurysmatic.

anévrisme, -ysme [anevrism], *s.m. Med:* aneurism, aneurysm; *Med:* **rupture d'a.,** breaking of a blood-vessel.

anfractueux, -euse [ɑ̃fraktɥø, -øːz], *a.* (*a*) *A:* circuitous, sinuous, winding; (*b*) irregular (outline, etc.); craggy (rock, mountain).

anfractuosité [ɑ̃fraktɥozite], *s.f.* **1.** (*a*) *A:* anfractuosity, sinuosity; (*b*) *Anat:* **anfractuosités cérébrales,** anfractuosities of the brain. **2.** *usu. pl.* deep, rugged, cavities, hollows.

angarie [ɑ̃gari], *s.f. Internat. Jur:* angary.

ange [ɑ̃ːʒ], *s.m.* **1.** angel; **a. gardien,** guardian angel; **a. déchu,** fallen angel; *B:* **l'A. de l'abîme,** Apollyon; *Art:* **a. joufflu,** chubby little cherub; **être aux anges,** to be in the seventh heaven (of delight), to walk on air; **parler aux anges,** to talk to oneself; **rire aux anges,** (i) to wear a beatific smile; (ii) to smile in one's sleep; *F:* **faiseuse d'anges,** (i) abortionist; (ii) baby-farmer; *F:* **les anges,** motor-cycle cops; *F:* **un a. passe,** an angel passes; *F:* **voulez-vous être un a. et me passer la salière?** be an angel and pass me the salt; *Swim:* **saut de l'a.,** swallow dive; *U.S:* swan dive; *A.Cost:* **manches d'a.,** angel sleeves; *A.Furn:* **lit d'a.,** angel bed; **cheveux d'a.,** white floss (for Christmas decorations, etc.); *s.a.* MAUVAIS. **2.** *Ich:* (i) **a. (noir, de mer),** (black) angel-fish; (ii) **a. (de mer),** monk-fish, angel-fish, -ray, -shark; (iii) **a. noir du Brésil,** Brazilian angel-fish.

Angèle [ɑ̃ʒɛl], *Pr.n.f.* Angela.

angelet [ɑ̃ʒlɛ], *s.m.* little angel, cherub.

Angéline [ɑ̃ʒelin], *Pr.n.f.* Angelina.

angélique [ɑ̃ʒelik]. **1.** *a.* angelic(al); **la salutation a.,** the Hail Mary. **2.** *s.f. Bot: Cu:* angelica; *Bot:* **a. sauvage,** wild angelica, pig-weed, hogweed, cow-parsnip; **petite a.,** gout-weed, aegopodium, bishop('s)-weed.

angéliquement [ɑ̃ʒelikmɑ̃], *adv.* angelically, like an angel.

angéliser [ɑ̃ʒelize], *v.tr.* to angelize.

angélisme [ɑ̃ʒelism], *s.m. Psy:* abnormal desire to escape from the conditions of bodily existence.

angélolâtrie [ɑ̃ʒelɔlɑtri], *s.f.* angelolatry, angel-worship.

angelot [ɑ̃ʒlo], *s.m.* **1.** = ANGELET. **2.** *Num: Com: Hist:* angelot. **3.** *Ich:* monk-fish, angel-fish, -ray, -shark. **4.** angelot cheese.

angélus [ɑ̃ʒelyːs], *s.m. Ecc:* angelus (-bell).

angevin, -ine [ɑ̃ʒvɛ̃, -in], *a. & s.* angevin(e), (i) of Angers; (ii) *Hist:* of Anjou.

angine [ɑ̃ʒin], *s.f. Med:* **1.** angina; tonsillitis; quinsy; **a. diphtérique, couenneuse,** diphtheria. **2. a. de poitrine,** angina (pectoris).

angineux, -euse [ɑ̃ʒinø, -øːz], *a. Med:* anginous, anginal, anginose (complaint, etc.).

angio- [ɑ̃ʒjɔ], *pref.* angio-; **angiographie,** angiography; **angiologie,** angiology; **angiotomie,** angiotomy.

angiocarpe [ɑ̃ʒjɔkarp], *Bot:* **1.** *a.* angiocarpous. **2.** *s.m.* angiocarp.

angiocarpien, -ienne [ɑ̃ʒjɔkarpjɛ̃, -jɛn], *a. Bot:* angiocarpous.

angiocholite [ɑ̃ʒjɔkɔlit], *s.f. Med:* angiocholitis.

angiologie [ɑ̃ʒjɔlɔʒi], *s.f. Med:* angiology.

angiome [ɑ̃ʒjom], *s.m. Med:* angioma.

angioscope [ɑ̃ʒjɔskɔp], *s.m. Med:* angioscope.

angiosperme [ɑ̃ʒjɔspɛrm], *Bot:* **1.** *a.* angiospermal, angiospermous. **2.** *s.m.pl.* **Angiospermes,** Angiospermae.

angiospore [ɑ̃ʒjɔspɔːr], *a. Bot:* angiosporous.

anglais, -aise [ɑ̃glɛ, -ɛːz]. **1.** *a.* English (language, etc.); British (army, goods, etc.); **métal a.,** Britannia metal; *F:* **s'en aller, filer, à l'anglaise,** to take French leave, to slip away; *s.a.* APPAREIL 4, ASSIETTE 4, BRODERIE 1, CAPOTE 2, CARACTÈRE 1, CLEF 5, ÉPINGLE 1, JARDIN 1, RELIURE 2, SEL 1, SELLE 2, SEMAINE. **2.** *s.* Englishman, Englishwoman, Briton; **les A.,** the English; *F:* **les A. ont débarqué,** she's got the curse. **3.** *s.m.* English (language); **l'a. correct,** the King's, Queen's, English. **4.** *s.f.pl.* **anglaises,** ringlets. **5.** *s.f.* (*box-making*) **anglaise,** batten. **6.** *s.f. Mus: Danc:* anglaise. **7.** *s.f.* (*handwriting*) Italian hand. **8.** *Cu:* **pommes (de terre) à l'anglaise,** boiled potatoes served with melted butter.

anglaisage [ɑ̃glɛzaːʒ], *s.m.* nicking (of horse's tail).

anglaiser [ɑ̃gleze], *v.tr.* **1.** to nick (horse's tail). **2.** to hog (horse's mane).

angle [ɑ̃ːgl], *s.m.* **1.** (*a*) angle; *Geom:* **a. plat,** straight angle; **a. plein,** reflex angle; **a. aigu,** acute angle; **a. droit,** right angle; **à a. droit avec . . .,** at right angles to . . .; **à angles droits,** rectangular; **a. constant,** steady angle; **a. curviligne,** curvilinear angle; **courbes qui se rencontrent sous un a.,** curves which meet at an angle; **angles opposés par le sommet,** vertically opposite angles; (*of house*) **faire a. avec la rue,** to stand at an angle to the street; *Civ.E:* **a. naturel de repos, a. de talus,** angle of repose (of embankment); *Av:* **a. critique,** stalling angle; **a. d'atterrissage,** ground angle; **a. de retard,** angle of lag; **a. de garde,** clearance (of propeller); **a. de levée de pale,** flapping angle (of helicopter); **a. de calage,** blade angle; **a. d'amortissement,** angle of dead rise; **a. de dérapage,** angle of side-slip; **a. de cap,** track course; *Ball: Artil:* **a. de tir,** angle of departure; (*missiles*) quadrantal elevation; **a. au niveau,** quadrant angle, quadrant elevation; *Fort:* **a. mort,** dead angle; *Join: etc:* **abattre les angles de qch.,** to chamfer sth.; *Arch:* **a. arrondi,** half-round fillet; **soudure d'a.,** fillet weld; **arrondir les angles,** to smooth things over; *Mec.E:* **roue d'a.,** bevel wheel, mitre wheel; **engrenage d'a.,** bevel gear; **fer d'a.,** angle iron; *Machine Tls:* **a. de coupe, de taillant,** lip angle; **a. d'incidence, de dépouille,** relief angle; **a. de dégagement,** (*back*) rake angle; **a. d'attaque,** (i) *Machine Tls:* cutting angle; (ii) *Aer:* angle of attack, of incidence; (iii) fleet angle (of cable); **a. d'attaque vis-à-vis d'un problème,** approach to a subject; *El.E:* **conduit d'a.,** elbow duct; *Navy:* **ordre en a. de chasse, de retraite,** order in two quarter-lines, in two bow-lines; (*b*) *Tls:* **a. oblique,** bevel rule, mitre square. **2.** edge (of a tool); **à angles vifs,** with sharp edges. **3.** (*a*) corner, angle (of wall, room, etc.); **armoire d'a.,** corner cupboard; **boutique d'a.,** corner shop; **l'a. de la rue,** the street corner; **à l'a. du chemin,** at the bend of the road; (*b*) *Arch: Const:* quoin (of building); **a. de mur rectangulaire, obtus,** rectangular, obtuse, quoin; **a. de mur aigu,** squint quoin; (*c*) *Dressm:* step (of collar). **4.** *N.Arch:* **a. de couple,** knuckle. **5.** angle, point of view; **discuter un problème sous tous ses angles,** to discuss a problem from every angle.

angledozer [ɑ̃gl(ə)dɔzœːr], *s.m.* angledozer.

Angles [ɑ̃ːgl], *s.m.pl. Ethn: Hist:* Angles.

anglésite [ɑ̃glezit], *s.f. Miner:* anglesite.

anglet [ɑ̃glɛ], *s.m.* **1.** *Arch: Const:* channelled, rebated, joint. **2.** *Typ:* bevel (of a rule).

Angleterre [ɑ̃glətɛːr], *Pr.n.f.* **1.** *Geog:* England; **la bataille d'A.,** the Battle of Britain (1940). **2.** *Lacem:* **point d'A.,** Brussels (bobbin) lace.

anglican, -ane [ɑ̃glikɑ̃, -an], *a. & s. Rel:* Anglican; **l'Église anglicane,** the Church of England, the Anglican Church.

anglicanisme [ɑ̃glikanism], *s.m. Rel:* Anglicanism.

angliche [ɑ̃gliʃ], *a. & s.m. & f. P:* = ANGLAIS.

anglicisant, -ante [ɑ̃glisizɑ̃, -ɑ̃t], *s.* student of English; English scholar; Anglicist.

angliciser [ɑ̃glisize], *v.tr.* to anglicize (word, etc.).

s'angliciser, to adopt English manners, to become English.

anglicisme [ɑ̃glisism], *s.m. Ling:* Anglicism; English idiom, turn of phrase (used in speaking or writing another language).

angliciste [ɑ̃glisist], *s.m. & f.* (i) student of English; (ii) teacher of English; Anglicist.

anglo- [ɑ̃glɔ], *pref.* Anglo-; **anglo-américain,** Anglo-American.

anglo-arabe [ɑ̃glɔarab], *a. & s.m.* anglo-arab (horse).

anglo-catholique [ɑ̃glɔkatɔlik], *a. & s.m. & f. Ecc:* Anglo-Catholic; *occ.* Anglo-Roman.

angloir [ɑ̃glwaːr], *s.m. Tls:* bevel(-square).

anglo-irlandais, -aise [ɑ̃glɔirlɑ̃dɛ, -ɛz], *a. & s. Hist:* Anglo-Irish(man, -woman); **les Anglo-irlandais,** the Anglo-Irish.

anglomane [ɑ̃glɔman], *s.m. & f.* anglomaniac.

anglomanie [ɑ̃glɔmani], *s.f.* anglomania.

anglo-normand, -ande [ɑ̃glɔnɔrmɑ̃, -ɑ̃ːd]. **1.** *Hist:* (*a*) *a. & s.* Anglo-Norman; (*b*) *s.m. Ling:* Anglo-Norman. **2.** *Geog:* **les îles Anglo-Normandes,** the Channel Islands.

anglophile [ɑ̃glɔfil], *a. & s.* anglophil(e), pro-English.

anglophilie [ɑ̃glɔfili], *s.f.* anglophilia, anglophilism, admiration for England.

anglophobe [ɑ̃glɔfɔb]. **1.** *a.* anglophobi(a)c. **2.** *s.* anglophobe.

anglophobie [ɑ̃glɔfɔbi], *s.f.* anglophobia.

anglophone [ɑ̃glɔfɔn], *a. & s.* English-speaking (person).

anglo-saxon, -onne [ɑ̃glɔsaksɔ̃, -ɔn], *a. & s.* Anglo-Saxon; **les pays anglo-saxons,** the English-speaking countries.

angoissant [ɑ̃gwasɑ̃], *a.* alarming, distressing (news); agonizing, heart-rending (spectacle); tense, anxious (moment).

angoisse [ɑ̃gwas], *s.f.* **1.** anguish; distress; agony; **les angoisses de la mort,** the pangs of death; **angoisses de conscience,** qualms of conscience; **poire d'a.,** (i) *Bot:* choke-pear; (ii) *A:* iron gag, choke-pear; **avaler des poires d'a.,** to suffer bitter mortification. **2.** *Med:* anguish, angor; spasm.

angoissé [ɑ̃gwase], *a.* distressed, anxious; anguished; **j'étais a.,** my heart was in my mouth.

angoisser [ɑ̃gwase], *v.tr.* to distress; to cause (s.o.) anguish.

s'angoisser, to become filled with anguish, distress; **sa voix s'angoissa,** his voice broke.

angoisseux, -euse [ɑ̃gwasø, -øːz], *a. A:* fraught with anguish; full of, wrung with, anguish; anxious.

Angola [ɑ̃gɔla], *Pr.n.m. Geog:* Angola.

angolais, -aise [ɑ̃gɔlɛ, -ɛːz], *a. & s.,* **angolan, -ane** [ɑ̃gɔlɑ̃, -an], *a. & s. Geog:* (native, inhabitant) of Angola.

angolar [ɑ̃gɔlar], *s.m. Num:* angolar.

angon [ɑ̃gɔ̃], *s.m.* **1.** *A:* angon, barbed spear (of the Franks). **2.** hook, spear (for catching shellfish).

Angora [ɑ̃gɔra]. **1.** *Pr.n.f. A.Geog:* Ankara; *A:* Angora. **2.** *a. usu. inv.* angora (wool); **poil de chèvre a.,** mohair. **3.** *s.m.* (*a*) angora rabbit; (*b*) Persian cat; (*c*) angora (goat).

angosture [ɑ̃gɔstyːr], *s.f.* = ANGUSTURE.

angoumois, -oise [ɑ̃gumwa, -waːz], *a. & s. Geog:* **1.** (native, inhabitant) of Angoulême. **2.** *s.m. Hist: Geog:* **l'A.,** the Angoumois.

angstrœm, angström [ɑ̃gstrœm], *s.m. Ph.Meas:* angström.

anguiforme [ɑ̃g(ɥ)ifɔrm], *a.* anguiform, anguine, snake-like.

anguille [ɑ̃giːj], *s.f.* **1.** *Ich:* eel; **a. argentée, a. d'avalaison,** silver eel; *Cu:* **matelote d'a.,** eel matelote; stewed eels; **il y a a. sous roche,** (i) there's something in the wind; (ii) there's something fishy going on; **soupçonner a. sous roche,** to smell a rat; **écorcher l'a. par la queue,** to do something back to front; to begin by the most difficult; *Nau:* **nœud d'a.,** timber hitch; (*b*) **a. de mer,** conger-eel; (*c*) **a. de sable, a. plat-bec,** sand-eel, grig; (*d*) *F:* **a. de haie,** grass snake; *s.a.* SOUPLE. **2.** *Ann:* **a. du vinaigre,** vinegar eel. **3.** *pl.* **anguilles.** *Nau:* launching ways, slips.

anguiller [ɑ̃gije], *s.m. Nau:* limber hole; **canal des anguillers,** limber passage.

anguillère [ɑ̃gijɛːr], *s.f.* **1.** eel-pond, eel-preserve. **2.** *Fish:* eel-pot.

anguillette [ɑ̃gijɛt], *s.f.* small eel.

anguillidés [ɑ̃gijide], *s.m.pl. Ich:* Anguillidae.

anguillière [ɑ̃gijɛːr], *s.f.* = ANGUILLÈRE.

anguilliforme [ɑ̃gijifɔrm], *a.* anguilliform.

anguillule [ɑ̃gijyl], *s.f. Ann:* anguillula; eel worm; **a. du blé,** wheat worm.

anguilluline [ɑ̃gijylin], *s.f. Ann:* wheat-worm.

angulaire [ɑ̃gylɛːr]. **1.** *a.* angular; **bride a.,** angle-flange; *Const:* **pierre a.,** corner-stone, head-stone, *s.a.* ARC[1] **2. 2.** *s.m. Phot:* **grand a.,** wide-angle lens.

angulairement [ɑ̃gylɛrmɑ̃], *adv.* angularly.

angularité [ɑ̃gylarite], *s.f.* angularity.

angulé [ɑ̃gyle], *a. Bot:* angulate.

anguleux, -euse [ɑ̃gylø, -øːz], *a.* angular, bony (face, elbows, etc.); rough, rugged (outline, etc.); **caractère a.,** awkward disposition.

angusticlave [ɑ̃gystiklav], *s.m. Rom.Ant: Cost:* angusticlave.

angustie [ɑ̃gysti], *s.f. Med:* constriction (of heart, arteries); narrowness (of pelvis).

angustifolié [ɑ̃gystifɔlje], *a. Bot:* angustifoliate, narrow-leaved.

angustirostre [ɑ̃gystirɔstr], *a. Orn:* angustirostrate.

angustura [ɑ̃gystyra], *s.f.* **angusture** [ɑ̃gystyːr], *s.f. Bot:* angustura bark, angostura bark.

angwangtibo [ɑ̃gwɑ̃tibo], *s.m. Z:* angwantibo.

anharmonique [anarmɔnik], *a. Mth:* anharmonic; **rapport a.,** cross-ratio, anharmonic ratio.

anhélation [anelasjɔ̃], *s.f.* (*rare*) *Med:* anhelation; shortness of breath.

anhéler [anele], *v.i.* (**j'anhèle, n. anhélons j'anhélerai**) (*rare*) to breath with difficulty, to be short of breath; to gasp.

anhéleux, -euse [anelø, -øːz], *a.* (*rare*) *Med:* anhelous, short of breath.

anhinga [anɛ̃ga], *s.m. Orn:* anhinga, darter, snake-bird.

anhydre [anidr], *a. Ch:* anhydrous; **chaux a.,** unsla(c)ked lime.

anhydride [anidrid], *s.m. Ch:* anhydride; **a. sulfureux,** sulphur dioxide; **a. sulfurique,** sulphur trioxide; **a. carbonique,** carbonic acid gas, carbon dioxide; **a. azotique,** nitrogen pentoxide.

anhydrisation [anidrizasjɔ̃], *s.f. Ch:* anhydration, dehydration.

anhydrite [anidrit], *s.f. Miner:* anhydrite.

anicien, -ienne [anisjɛ̃, -jɛn], *a. & s. Geog:* (native) of Le Puy.

anicroche [anikrɔʃ], *s.f. F:* difficulty, hitch, snag, upset, spot of bother, of trouble; **se passer sans a.,** to go off smoothly, without a hitch.

ânier, -ière [ɑnje, -jɛːr], *s.* donkey-, ass-driver; donkey-boy, donkey-girl.

anil [anil], *s.m. Bot:* anil, indigo plant.

aniléine [anilein], *s.f. Ch: Dy:* aniline purple.

anilide [anilid], *s.f. Ch:* anilid(e), phenylamid(e).

aniline [anilin], *s.f. Ch: Dy:* aniline.

anille [aniːj], *s.f.* **1.** *Bot:* tendril. **2.** *Const:* anchor-tie. **3.** *Mil: Her:* mill-rind, moline.

anillé [anije], *a.* **1.** *Bot:* tendrilled. **2.** *Her:* moline (cross).

animadversion [animadvɛrsjɔ̃], *s.f.* **1.** animadversion, censure, blame; **encourir l'a. générale,** to be universally censured. **2.** reproof, reprimand.

animal[1], -aux [animal, -o], *s.m.* animal; **société protectrice des animaux,** society for the prevention of cruelty to animals; **bon envers les animaux,** kind to dumb animals, to dumb beasts; *F:* **quel a.!** what a brute! what a beast! **il en a de la chance, cet a.-là!** what a lucky brute! **espèce d'a.!** you bastard!

animal[2], -aux, *a.* **1.** animal (kingdom, matter, etc.); **alimentation animale,** animal foods; **chaleur animale,** animal warmth. **2.** animal, sensual, brute (instinct, etc.).

animalculaire [animalkylɛːr], *a.* animalcular.

animalcule [animalkyl], *s.m. Biol:* animalcule.

animalerie [animalri], *s.f.* animal house.

animalesque [animalɛsk], *a.* animal(-like).

animalier [animalje], *a. & s.m.* painter, sculptor, of animals; animalist.

animalisation [animalizasjɔ̃], *s.f.* animalization.

animaliser [animalize], *v.tr.* to animalize. **1.** *Physiol:* to convert (food) into animal matter. **2.** to sensualize, brutalize (passion, etc.).

s'animaliser. 1. (*of food*) to become animalized (by absorption). **2.** to become animalized, brutalized; to sink to the level of a beast.

animalisme [animalism], *s.m. Biol:* animalism.

animalité [animalite], *s.f.* **1.** animality, animal nature. **2.** the animal kingdom.

animant [animɑ̃], *a.* animating, inspiriting, enlivening (music); stimulating, exciting (news, music, etc.).

animateur, -trice [animatœːr, -tris]. **1.** *a.* animating, life-giving (power, principle, etc.); stimulating (person). **2.** *s.* (*a*) stimulating person; life (and soul) (of an enterprise); *F:* live wire; (*b*) *T.V: etc.* compère; M.C., *U.S:* emcee; quiz master; question master; **a. de loisirs,** entertainments officer; (*c*) *Cin:* animator. **3.** *s.m. Mec:* prime mover.

animation [animasjɔ̃], *s.f.* **1.** quickening; (i) coming to life; (ii) bringing to life. **2.** animation, liveliness, briskness, vivacity; **l'a. de son teint,** his heightened colour; **l'a. des rues,** the bustle in the streets; **ville pleine d'a.,** town full of life; *Com:* **la demande présente de l'a.,** the demand is brisk; **a. du marché,** buoyancy of the market. **3.** *Cin:* animation.

animé [anime], *a.* animated, spirited, lively (person, discussion, etc.), busy (street); **description animée,** animated description; **un regard a. de haine,** a look full of hatred; **cheval a.,** fresh, frisky, horse; **teint a.,** heightened colour; **tableau a.,** picture full of life; **marché a.,** brisk, buoyant, market; *s.a.* DESSIN.

animer [anime], *v.tr.* **1.** to animate, quicken; to endow with life; to give life to (s.o., sth.); **animé par un nouvel espoir,** buoyed up with new hope. **2.** to actuate; (*a*) to move, propel; **la force qui anime la machine, la balle,** the force which actuates, drives, the machine, which impels the bullet; (*b*) **animé d'un sentiment de jalousie,** prompted, actuated, by feelings of jealousy; **être animé d'un sentiment bienveillant pour qn,** to entertain a kindly feeling for s.o.; **l'esprit qui anime ses œuvres,** the spirit that breathes through his work. **3.** to quicken, enliven (conversation); to stir up (feelings); **a. un cheval,** to urge on, brisk up, a horse; *A:* **a. qn à (faire) qch.,** to incite, encourage, s.o. to (do) sth.; **a. qn contre qn,** to stir up s.o.'s anger against s.o., to set s.o. against s.o.; *Mus:* **"animez," "quicker." 4.** *Th: T.V:* to compère, M.C.; *U.S:* emcee (a show, etc.). **5.** *Cin:* to animate (cartoon).

s'animer. 1. to come to life; to quicken. **2.** to become animated, cheerful, excited, lively; **sa figure s'anima,** his face brightened up, lit up; **la dispute s'animait,** the quarrel was becoming fierce; **s'a. contre qn,** to become angry with, incensed against, s.o.

animisme [animism], *s.m. Rel.H: etc:* animism.

animiste [animist]. **1.** *a.* animistic (belief, etc.). **2.** *s.m. & f.* animist.

animosité [animozite], *s.f.* animosity, animus, spite (**contre,** against); **avoir, garder, de l'a. contre qn,** to nurse a grudge against s.o.; **agir par a.,** to act out of spite.

anion [anjɔ̃], *s.m. Ph: El:* anion.

anionique [anjɔnik], *a.* anionic.

aniridie [aniridi], *s.f. Med:* aniridia.

anis [ani(s)], *s.m.* **1.** (*a*) *Bot:* anise; (*b*) (**graine d')a.,** aniseed; **à l'a.,** aniseed-flavoured; (*c*) aniseed aperitif. **2.** *Bot: Pharm:* **a. étoilé, a. de la Chine,** star anise, Chinese anise.

aniser [anize], *v.tr. Cu: etc:* to flavour with aniseed; to anisate.

anisette [anizɛt], *s.f.* anisette(-cordial).

anisidine [anisidin], *s.f. Ch:* anisidine.

anisique [anizik], *a. Ch:* anisic; **aldéhyde a.,** anisaldehyde.

anisomère [anizɔmɛːr], *a. Bot:* anisomerous; *Ch:* anisomeric.

anisométropie [anizɔmetrɔpi], *s.f. Opt: Med:* anisometropia.

anisopétale [anizɔpetal], *a. Bot:* anisopetalous.

anisophylle [anizɔfil], *a. Bot:* anisophyllous.

anisoptère [anizɔptɛːr], *s.m. Ent:* (*a*) dragonfly; (*b*) *pl.* **anisoptères,** Anisoptera.

anisosthène [anizɔstɛn], *a. Med:* anisosthenic.

anisosthénie [anizɔsteni], *s.f. Med:* anisosthenia.

anisotrope [anizɔtrɔp], *a. Ph:* anisotropic, aeolotropic.

anisotropie [anizɔtrɔpi], *s.f. Ph:* anisotrophy, anisotropism.

Anjou [ɑ̃ʒu], *Pr.n.m. Geog:* Anjou.

ankyloblépharon [ɑ̃kilɔblefarɔ̃], *s.m Med:* ankyloblepharon.

ankyloglossie [ɑ̃kilɔglɔsi], *s.f. Med:* ankyloglossia.

ankylorrhinie [ɑ̃kilɔrini], *s.f. Med:* ankylorrhinia.

ankylose [ɑ̃kiloːz], *s.f. Med:* ankylosis.

ankyloser [ɑ̃kiloze], *v.tr. Med:* to ankylose.

s'ankyloser, to ankylose; to become stiff, ossified; to stiffen; *F:* (*of pers.*) to get stiff.

ankylostome [ɑ̃kilɔstɔm], *s.m. Ann:* ankylostome, hookworm.

ankylostomiase [ɑ̃kilɔstɔmjaːz], *s.f.,* **ankylostomose** [ɑ̃kilɔstɔmoz], *s.f. Med:* ankylostomiasis, hookworm disease, miners' anaemia.

annal, -aux [an(n)al, -o], *a. Jur:* valid, lasting, for one year; **location annale,** yearly letting, let by the year.

annales [an(n)al], *s.f.pl.* annals, (public) records; **les annales du crime,** the annals of crime.

annaliste [an(n)alist], *s.m.* annalist.

annalité [an(n)alite], *s.f. Jur:* yearly nature (of right, tenancy).

Annam [an(n)am], *Pr.n.m. Geog:* Annam.

annamite [an(n)amit], *a. & s. Geog:* Annamese, Annamite; *Ling:* Annamese.

annates [an(n)at], *s.f.pl. Ecc: A:* annates, first-fruits.

Anne [ɑːn]. **1.** *Pr.n.f.* Anna, Ann(e). **2.** *Pr.n.m. B.Hist:* Annas.

anneau, -eaux [ano], *s.m.* **1.** ring; *Bot:* annulus; **a. de rideau,** curtain ring; **a. de fermeture,** pull-ring (of door); **a. nuptial, de mariage,** wedding ring; **a. épiscopal,** episcopal, bishop's, ring; **a. sigillaire,** signet ring; *Gym:* **les anneaux,** the rings; **jeu des anneaux,** hoop-la; *Geom:* **a. sphérique,** annulus. **2.** (*a*) link (of chain); *F:* **l'a. manquant,** the missing link; (*b*) ringlet, curl (of hair); (*c*) coil (of serpent); **enroulé en anneaux,** coiled up; (*d*) bow (of key). **3.** (*a*) *Tchn:* ring, collar; hoop (of hub, etc.); **a. brisé,** key-ring, split ring; **a. à fiche,** ring-bolt, eye-bolt; *Nau:* **a. de retenue,** casing clamp; **a. de corde,** grummet; **a. en fer,** iron cringle, iron hank; **a. mobile,** runner; *Mount:* sling, loop (of rope); (*b*) *Artil:* **a. de pointage,** traverse circle; (*c*) *El:* **a. de Gramme,** ring armature; (*d*) *Ch:* pellet; (*e*) *Av:* **a. d'entrée d'air,** nacelle air-intake ring; **a. d'étanchéité de turbine,** turbine shroud ring; **a. de hissage,** hoisting ring; **a. de levage,** hoisting eye; **a. d'azimut,** outer axis gimbal; **a. de suspension,** axis gimbal. **4.** *Astr:* **l'a. de Saturne,** Saturn's ring. **5.** *Z:* somite, segment.

annécien, -ienne [an(n)esjɛ̃, -jɛn], *a. & s.* (**native**) of Annecy.

année [ane], *s.f.* year; **a. solaire,** solar year; **a. civile,** calendar year; **souhaiter la bonne a. à qn,** to wish s.o. a happy new year; **a. budgétaire, d'exercice, fiscale,** financial, fiscal, year; **a. scolaire,** school, academic, year; **étudiant de troisième a.,** third year student; **payer à l'a.,** to pay by the year; **pendant toute une a.,** for a whole year, a whole twelvemonth; **pendant de longues années,** for many years; **d'un bout de l'a. à l'autre, tout le long de l'a.,** from one year's end to another; **d'a. en a.,** year by year; **d'une a. à l'autre,** from year to year; **une a. après l'autre,** year in year out; **les plus belles années de notre vie,** the best years of our life; **il est dans sa vingtième a.,** he is in his twentieth year; *s.a.* CHARGE 1, CINQUANTE, QUARANTE, TRENTE, VINGT.

année-lumière [anelymjɛːr], *s.f.* light-year; *pl. années-lumière.*

annélation [anelasjɔ̃], *s.f. Arb:* ring-barking.

annelé [anle]. **1.** *a.* ringed (column, worm, etc.); *Nat.Hist:* annulate(d). **2.** *s.m.* = ANNÉLIDE.

anneler [anle], *v.tr.* **(j'annelle, n. annelons; j'annellerai) 1.** to arrange (the hair) in ringlets, in curls. **2.** *Husb:* to ring (pig, etc.).

annelet [anlɛ], *s.m.* small ring; *Arch: Her:* annulet.

annélide [anelid], *s.m. Z:* annelid(e); **les annélides,** the Annelida.

annemassien, -ienne [anəmasjɛ̃, -jɛn], *a. & s.* (native) of Annemasse.

Annette [anɛt], *Pr.n.f. F:* Annie, Nancy, Nan.

annexe [an(n)ɛks], *s.f.* **1.** *(a)* annex(e), outbuilding, outlying building; outlier (of library, etc.); *(b) Ecc:* chapel of ease; *(c) Nau:* tender (of ship). **2.** dependency (of a state). **3.** *(a)* rider (to bill); schedule (to act); supplement, appendix (to book, report); *(b)* enclosure (with letter). **4.** *Anat:* appendant, appendage, accessory part (of an organ). **5.** *a.* **établissement a.,** annex(e); **lettre a.,** covering letter; **industries annexes,** subsidiary industries; **revenus annexes,** supplementary income.

annexer [an(n)ɛkse], *v.tr.* **1.** to annex (territory). **2.** to annex, join, append, attach (document, etc.); **pièces annexées (à une lettre),** enclosures.

annexion [an(n)ɛksjɔ̃], *s.f.* annexation.

annexionniste [an(n)ɛksjɔnist], *a. & s. Pol:* annexationist.

Annibal [an(n)ibal], *Pr.n.m. A.Hist:* Hannibal.

annihilable [an(n)iilabl̩], *a.* **1.** annihilable. **2.** *Jur:* annullable.

annihilant [an(n)iilɑ̃], *a.* annihilating.

annihilateur, -trice [an(n)iilatœːr, -tris]. **1.** *a.* annihilating. **2.** *s.* annihilator.

annihilation [an(n)iilasjɔ̃], *s.f.* **1.** annihilation. **2.** *Jur:* annulment.

annihilation(n)iste [aniilasjɔnist], *s.m. Theol:* annihilationist.

annihiler [an(n)iile], *v.tr.* **1.** to annihilate, destroy (army, will-power, etc.). **2.** *Jur:* to annul, cancel (will, donation).

anniversaire [anivɛrsɛːr]. **1.** *a.* anniversary (festival, ceremony). **2.** *s.m.* anniversary (of victory, birth, death, etc.); **l'a. de mon mariage, mon a. de mariage,** my wedding anniversary; **l'a. de ma naissance, mon a.,** my birthday.

annonacées [anɔnase], *s.f.pl. Bot:* Annonaceae.

annonce [anɔ̃ːs], *s.f.* **1.** *(a)* announcement, notification, notice; **faire l'annonce de qch.,** to give out (a notice); *Ecc:* **faire l'a. d'un mariage,** to publish the banns; **les annonces de la semaine,** the weekly notices; *(b) Cards:* declaration; **a. de trois carreaux,** call of three diamonds; **a. d'indication,** informatory bid; *(c)* sign, indication; **la baisse subite du baromètre est une a. de tempête,** a sudden fall of the barometer is a sign of storm. **2.** advertisement; **petites annonces,** classified advertisements; **demander qch. par voie d'annonces,** to advertise for sth.; **annonces lumineuses,** illuminated signs; **a. de spectacle,** play-bill.

annoncer [anɔ̃se], *v.tr.* **(j'annonçai(s); n. annonçons) 1.** to announce, give notice of, give out (sth.); **a. une mauvaise nouvelle à qn,** to break, impart, bad news, to s.o.; *Aut: Jur:* **a. son approche,** to give audible warning of approach; **a. qch. à son de caisse,** to proclaim sth. from the house-tops; **a. un mariage,** to publish the banns of marriage; **a. l'évangile,** to preach the Gospel; *Cards:* **a. son jeu,** to declare. **2.** to advertise (sale, etc.). **3.** *(a)* to promise, foretell; **tout semble a. le succès,** everything seems to promise, points to, success; **événement qui annonce une époque nouvelle,** event that heralds a new era; **cela n'annonce rien de bon,** it looks unpromising, nothing good will come of that; *(b)* to give proof of (sth.); to show, evince (sth.); **son visage annonçait sa joie,** his face showed his delight; **visage qui annonce l'énergie,** face that reveals energy; **cela annonce de l'intelligence,** it shows intelligence. **4.** to announce (s.o.) to usher (s.o.) in; **se faire a. (chez qn),** to send in one's name to s.o.; to give in one's name (at reception, etc.); **qui dois-je a.?** who, what name, shall I say?

s'annoncer. 1. to give one's name, to introduce oneself. **2.** to give promise; to augur (well, ill); **la moisson s'annonce bien, belle,** the harvest looks promising, is coming on; **le temps s'annonce beau,** the weather promises to be fine; **la tempête se lève sans s'annoncer en montagne,** the storm comes in without warning in the mountains.

annonceur [anɔ̃sœːr], *s.m.* **1.** advertiser. **2.** *(a) Th: A:* spokesman (of company of players); *(b) W.Tel: T.V:* announcer.

annonciateur, -trice [anɔ̃sjatœːr, -tris], *s.* **1.** *(a)* announcer, harbinger; forerunner; *(b) Th: A:* announcer. **2.** *s.m.* *(a) Tp: etc:* indicator board, annunciator (board); **a. à volets,** drop indicator, drop annunciator; **a. de fin,** ring-off signal; *(b) El:* **a. de couplage,** interlocking signal. **3.** *a.* **signes annonciateurs du printemps,** signs which are forerunners of spring.

annonciation [anɔ̃sjasjɔ̃], *s.f. B.Hist:* annunciation; *Ecc:* **fête de l'A.,** Feast of the Annunciation, Lady Day.

annoncier [anɔ̃sje], *s.m. Journ:* **1.** *(a)* publicity editor; *(b)* advertising agent. **2.** advertiser.

annone [anɔn], *s.f. Rom.Hist:* annona.

annotateur, -trice [an(n)ɔtatœːr, -tris], *s.* annotator, commentator (of text, etc.).

annotation [an(n)ɔtasjɔ̃], *s.f.* **1.** annotating, making notes. **2.** annotation, note.

annoter [an(n)ɔte], *v.tr.* to annotate; to write notes on (text).

annuaire [an(n)ɥɛːr], *s.m.* **1.** annual, yearbook. **2.** almanac, calendar; **a. des marées,** tide table. **3.** (yearly) list; **l'A. militaire,** the Army list; *U.S:* the Army Register; **l'A. de la Marine,** the Navy List; **l'A. du téléphone, téléphonique,** the telephone directory; *F:* the phone book; **a. de l'université,** university calendar.

annualité [an(n)ɥalite], *s.f.* yearly recurrence (of tax, meeting, etc.).

annuel, -elle [an(n)ɥɛl]. **1.** *a.* annual, yearly; **plante annuelle,** annual; **rente annuelle,** annuity. **2.** *s.m. Ecc:* *(a)* annual (requiem mass said daily for a year); *(b)* yearly festival.

annuellement [an(n)ɥɛlmɑ̃], *adv.* annually, yearly, every year, year by year.

annuitaire [an(n)ɥitɛːr], *a.* (debt) redeemable by yearly payments.

annuité [an(n)ɥite], *s.f.* **1.** *Fin:* annual instalment (in repayment of debt). **2.** (terminable) annuity; **a. à vie,** life annuity.

annulabilité [an(n)ylabilite], *s.f. Jur:* voidableness.

annulable [an(n)ylabl̩], *a. Jur:* voidable, rescindable, defeasible (contract, etc.); that can be annulled, cancelled, quashed.

annulaire [an(n)ylɛːr], *a.* **1.** *(a)* annular, ring-shaped; **espace a.,** annulus; *El.E:* **aimant a.,** ring-magnet; *Med:* **épreuve a. de la globuline,** globulin ring-test; *(b) Min:* **pression a.,** annulus pressure. **2. le doigt a.,** *s.m.* **l'annulaire,** the ring-finger, the third finger.

annulatif, -ive [an(n)ylatif, -iːv], *a. Jur:* annulling, quashing; (act) of annulment.

annulation [an(n)ylasjɔ̃], *s.f. Jur:* annulment; *(a)* repeal, quashing, setting aside, rescission (of judgment); abatement (of writ); *(b)* voidance (of contract); defeasance (of right); cancelling, cancellation (of contract); setting aside (of will).

annulement [an(n)ylmɑ̃], *s.m. Nau:* **signal d'a.,** annulling signal; *Jur:* **arrêt d'a.,** annulment of judgment.

annuler [an(n)yle], *v.tr.* to annul; *(a)* to render void, repeal, quash, set aside, rescind (law, will, judgment); *(b)* to cancel (contract, etc.); to call off (a deal); **a. un ordre de grève,** to call off a strike; *(c)* to cancel (cheque, etc.); *(d)* **ce catalogue annule les précédents,** this catalogue supersedes, cancels, all previous issues; *Nau: etc:* **a. un signal,** to negative a signal; *(e) Fb:* to disallow (a goal).

s'annuler. *Mth: etc:* *(a)* to reduce to zero; *(b)* to cancel out, to cancel each other; *(c) (of forces)* to counterbalance one another; *(d) Jur:* to abate.

anoa [anɔa], *s.m. Z:* anoa, pigmy buffalo (of the Celebes).

anobie [anɔbi], *s.m.*, **anobion** [anɔbjɔ̃], *s.m. Ent:* anobium, *esp.* death-watch beetle.

anobli, -e [anɔbli]. **1.** *a.* ennobled, raised to the peerage. **2.** *s.* newly created member of the nobility.

anoblir [anɔbliːr], *v.tr.* to ennoble (s.o.), *i.e.* to raise (s.o.) to the nobility; to raise (s.o.) to the peerage.

anoblissement [anɔblismɑ̃], *s.m.* ennoblement (de, of); conferring of a title (de, on); raising to the peerage; *Hist:* **lettres d'a.,** patent of nobility.

anode [anɔd], *s.f. El:* anode, positive pole; **décharge à l'a.,** discharge at anode; **a. réactive, soluble,** sacrificial anode.

anodin [anɔdɛ̃]. **1.** *a.* *(a)* anodyne, pain-alleviating, soothing; *(b)* mild (criticism); tame (poetry); harmless, innocuous (talk, medicine). **2.** *s.m.* palliative, anodyne, pain-killer, analgesic.

anodique [anɔdik], *a. El:* anodic, anodal; **courant a.,** anode current; **courant a. continu,** direct anode current.

anodonte [anɔdɔ̃t]. **1.** *a. Z:* edentate; toothless. **2.** *s.m.pl. Moll:* **anodontes,** Anodonta.

anodontie [anɔdɔ̃ti], *s.f.* anodontia.

anolyte [anɔlit], *s.m. El:* anolyte.

anomal, -aux [anɔmal, -o], *a.* anomalous (verb, motion).

anomalie [anɔmali], *s.f.* *(a)* anomaly; *Ph:* **a. de Bouguer,** Bouguer anomaly; *(b) Biol:* anomaly; aberration; abnormality; deviation.

anomalistique [anɔmalistik], *a. Astr:* anomalistic (year).

anomalure [anɔmalyːr], *s.m. Z:* spiny-tailed squirrel.

anomaluridés [anɔmalyride], *s.m.pl. Z:* Anomaluridae.

anomie[1] [anɔmi], *s.f. Moll:* anomia, beaked cockle, saddle-shell, saddle-oyster.

anomie[2], *s.f.* anomy.

anomocarpe [anɔmɔkarp], *a. Bot:* anomocarpous.

anomophylle [anɔmɔfil], *a. Bot:* anomophyllous.

anomoures [anɔmur], *s.m.pl. Crust:* Anomura.

ânon [ɑnɔ̃], *s.m.* **1.** ass's foal, ass's colt. **2.** dunce, ass. **3.** *Ich: P:* haddock.

anonacé [anɔnase], *a. Bot:* anonaceous.

anone [anɔn], *s.f. Bot:* anona; **a. muriquée, réticulée,** custard-apple, bullock's heart; **a. écailleuse,** sweet-sop.

ânonnement [ɑnɔnmɑ̃], *s.m.* stumbling, unintelligent, delivery; stammering; humming and hawing.

ânonner [ɑnɔne], *v.tr.* to stumble, blunder, through (speech, recitation); to hum and haw; to read, perform, (sth.) in a lame, halting, manner; **a. un sermon,** to mumble, drone, through a sermon.

ânonneur, -euse [ɑnɔnœːr, -øːz]. **1.** *a.* stumbling, hesitating (delivery, etc.). **2.** *s.* mumbler.

anonymat [anɔnima], *s.m.* anonymity; **écrire sous l'a.,** to write anonymously; **garder l'a.,** to remain anonymous, to preserve, retain, one's anonymity.

anonyme [anɔnim]. **1.** *a.* *(a)* anonymous (writer, letter, etc.); unnamed (benefactor); **homme qui restera a.,** man who shall go unnamed; *(b) Com:* **société a. (par actions),** joint-stock company, limited (-liability) company. **2.** *s.m.* anonymous writer. **3.** *s.m.* anonymity.

anonymement [anɔnimmɑ̃], *adv.* anonymously.

anonymographe [anɔnimɔgraf], *s.m. & f.* *(a)* anonymous writer, author; *(b)* writer of anonymous letters.

anonymographie [anɔnimɔgrafi], *s.f.* morbid tendency to write anonymous letters.

anophèle [anɔfɛl], *s.m. Ent:* anopheles.

anophthalme [anɔftalm], *s.m. Ent:* anophthalmus.

anophthalmie [anɔftalmi], *s.f. Ter:* anophthalmia.

anoplothéridés [anɔplɔteride], *s.m.pl. Paleont:* Anoplotheriidae.

anoplothérium [anɔplɔterjɔm], *s.m. Paleont:* anoplotherium.

anoploures [anɔpluːr], *s.m.pl. Ent:* Anopleura, Anoplura.

anopsie [anɔpsi], *s.f. Med:* anopsia.

anorak [anɔrak], *s.m. Cost:* anorak.

anorchidie [anɔrkidi], *s.f. Med:* anorchia.

anordie [anɔrdi], *s.f.* strong and cool northerly breeze.

anordir [anɔrdiːr], *v.i. (of wind)* to veer round to the north.

anorexie [anɔrɛksi], *s.f. Med:* anorexia; loss of appetite.

anorexigène [anɔrɛksiʒɛn], *s.m. Med:* appetite depressant, anoretic, anorexiant.

anormal, -aux [anɔrmal, -o]. **1.** *a.* abnormal, irregular; **quelque chose d'a.,** something out of the ordinary; **caractère a.,** abnormality; **(enfants) anormaux,** mental defectives; *Biol:* **type a.,** sport; **structure anormale,** aberration. **2.** *s.m.* abnormality; the abnormal.

anormalement [anɔrmalmɑ̃], *adv.* abnormally.

anorthite [anɔrtit], *s.f. Miner:* anorthite.

anorthose [anɔrtoz], *s.f. Miner:* anorthose.

anosmatique [anɔzmatik], *a. Z:* anosmatic.

anosmie [anɔzmi], *s.f. Med:* anosmia.

anostracés [anɔstrase], *s.m.pl. Crust:* Anostraca.

anoure [anuːr]. *Z:* **1.** *a.* an(o)urous, tailless; anuran. **2.** *s.m.pl.* **Anoures,** An(o)ura; the tail-less Amphibia.

anoxémie [anɔksemi], *s.f. Med:* anox(a)emia.

anoxie [anɔksi], *s.f. Med:* anoxia.

anse [ɑ̃ːs], *s.f.* **1.** handle (of jug, basket); ear (of bell, pitcher; bow (of watch); shackle (of pad-lock); *Min:* bail; **a. de la tête d'injection,** swivel bail; *A:* dolphin (of cannon); *F:* **faire le pot à deux anses,** to stand with one's arms akimbo; *A:* **faire le panier à deux anses,** to have a girl on each arm; **(***of servant***) faire danser l'anse du panier,** to make a bit on the side; *Arch:* **voûte en a. de panier,** basket-handle arch. **2.** (*a*) loop, bight (of rope, etc.); *Anat:* loop; (*b*) **a. à vis,** screw eye(-bolt). **3.** *Geog:* bight, cove.

ansé [ɑ̃se], *a. Her:* **croix ansée,** crux ansata, ansate(d) cross; ankh.

Anselme [ɑ̃sɛlm], *Pr.n.m.* Anselm.

ansérides [ɑ̃seride], *s.m.pl. Orn:* Anseridae, Anatidae.

ansériformes [ɑ̃seriform], *s.m.pl. Orn:* Anseri-formes.

ansérine [ɑ̃serin]. **1.** *a.f. Med:* **peau a.,** anserine skin; *F:* goose-flesh. **2.** *s.f. Bot:* goose-foot, pigweed, chenopodium; **a. à balais,** belvedere.

ansérinés [ɑ̃serine], *s.m.pl. Orn:* Anserinae.

ansette [ɑ̃sɛt], *s.f.* **1.** small handle (of vase, etc.). **2.** ring (of medal).

anspect [ɑ̃spɛk], *s.m.* **1.** *Nau:* **barre d'a.,** hand-spike. **2.** crowbar; lever (for shifting heavy objects); pinch-bar.

ant- [ɑ̃t], *pref.* anti-; **antéphialtique,** anti-nightmare (draught, etc.).

antagonique [ɑ̃tagɔnik], *a.* antagonistic.

antagonisme [ɑ̃tagɔnism], *s.m.* antagonism; **a. de deux choses,** antagonism between two things; **éveiller l'a. de qn,** to antagonize s.o.

antagoniste [ɑ̃tagɔnist]. **1.** *a.* antagonistic, opposed; *Mec:* **force a.,** (i) antagonistic force; (ii) controlling force, counter-check; **couple a.,** opposing couple. **2.** *s.* antagonist, opponent.

antalgique [ɑ̃talʒik], *a. & s.m. Med:* antalgic; anodyne; *a.* pain-killing; *s.* pain-killer.

antan [ɑ̃tɑ̃], *adv.* (*a*) *A. & Lit:* yesteryear; **où sont les neiges d'a.?** where are the snows of yester-year? (*b*) *Lit:* **il vendit tout, ne voulant pas garder le moindre souvenir d'a.,** he sold every-thing, not wishing to keep the slightest souvenir of the past.

antanaclase [ɑ̃tanaklaz], *s.f. Rh:* antanaclasis.

antarctique [ɑ̃tar(k)tik]. *Geog:* (*a*) *a.* Antarctic; **cercle a.,** Antarctic circle; (*b*) *Pr.n.m.* **l'A.,** Antarctica, the Antarctic.

Antarès [ɑ̃tarɛs], *Pr.n.m. Astr:* Antares, the Scorpion's Heart.

ante¹ [ɑ̃ːt], *s.f. Arch:* anta.

ante², *s.f.* handle (of paintbrush).

anté- [ɑ̃te], *pref.* ante-, pre-; **antédiluvien,** ante-diluvian; **antéoccupation,** ante-occupation.

antebois [ɑ̃tәbwa], *s.m.*, **antébois** [ɑ̃tebwa], *s.m.* chair-rail (round floor of a room).

antécédemment [ɑ̃tesedamɑ̃], *adv.* antece-dently, previously.

antécédence [ɑ̃tesedɑ̃s], *s.f.* antecedence; *Astr:* **en a.,** (planet) in antecedence.

antécédent [ɑ̃tesedɑ̃]. **1.** *a.* antecedent, previous, anterior (**à,** to). **2.** *s.m.* (*a*) *Gram: Mus: Mth: etc:* antecedent; (*b*) *pl.* previous history, past record; antecedents.

antéchrist [ɑ̃tekrist, *A:* -kri], *s.m.* antichrist.

antécime [ɑ̃tesim], *s.f.* (subsidiary) peak.

antéconsonantique [ɑ̃tekɔ̃sɔnɑ̃tik], *a. Ling:* ante-consonantal.

antédiluvien, -ienne [ɑ̃tedilyvjɛ̃, -jɛn], *a.* antedi-luvian.

antédon [ɑ̃tedɔ̃], *s.m. Echin:* antedon.

Antée [ɑ̃te], *Pr.n.m. Gr.Myth:* Antaeus.

antéfixe [ɑ̃tefiks], *s.f. Arch:* antefix.

antéflexion [ɑ̃tefleksjɔ̃], *s.f. Med:* anteflexion.

antenais, -aise [ɑ̃tәnɛ, -ɛːz], *a. Husb:* **agneau a., agnelle antenaise,** teg(g).

antennaire [ɑ̃tɛnɛːr]. **1.** *a. Ent:* antennary. **2.** *s.m. Ich:* antennarius, frog-fish.

antennaria [ɑ̃tɛnaria], *s.f. Bot:* antennaria.

antennates [ɑ̃tɛnat], *s.m.pl. Z:* Antennata.

antenne [ɑ̃tɛn], *s.f.* **1.** *Nau:* lateen yard. **2.** *W.Tel: etc:* (*a*) aerial, antenna; **a. de réception, a. réceptrice,** receiving aerial; **a. d'émission, de transmission,** transmitting, sending, aerial; **a. de télévision,** television aerial; **a. de compensa-tion,** balancing aerial, aerial screen; **a. com-pensée,** screened aerial; **a. à deux fils, à deux brins,** twin (-wire) aerial; **a. directionnelle en arête de poisson,** fish-bone antenna; **a. dirige-able,** directional aerial (for any station); **a. dirigée,** directional aerial (fixed for one station); **a. encastrée,** flush antenna; **a. fermée, en cadre,** loop aerial; **a. d'incidence,** incidence probe; **a. noyée,** built-in, suppressed, antenna; **a. en parapluie,** umbrella aerial; **a. prismatique,** cage aerial; **a. (de) radar,** radar scanner, aerial, antenna, horn antenna; **réglage de circuit d'a.,** antenna alignment; *Av:* **a. pendante,** trailing aerial; (*b*) *F:* **l'a.,** the wireless, radio; **ce pro-gramme passera sur les antennes de . . . ,** this programme will be transmitted by . . . **3.** (*a*) *Z:* antenna; *F:* feeler, horn (of insect, etc.); (*b*) *El:* **coup-circuit à antennes,** horn-fuse; (*c*) *Navy:* horn (of mine); (*d*) branch (of pipe-line); *Rail:* branch line (with sidings); (*e*) *Mil: Med:* **a. chirurgicale,** advanced surgical unit.

antenné [ɑ̃tɛne], *a.* antennate.

antennifère [ɑ̃tɛnifɛr], *a.* antenniferous.

antenniforme [ɑ̃tɛnifɔrm], *a.* antenniform.

antennule [ɑ̃tɛn(n)yl], *s.f. Crust:* antennule, short feeler.

antenois, -oise [ɑ̃tәnwa, -waːz], = ANTENAIS.

anténuptial, -aux [ɑ̃tenypsjal, -o], *a.* ante-nuptial.

antépénultième [ɑ̃tepenyltjɛm]. **1.** *a.* antepenulti-mate, last but two. **2.** *s.f.* antepenultimate, antepenult.

antéphélique [ɑ̃tefelik], *a. Pharm:* freckle-removing (lotion).

antéposition [ɑ̃tepozisjɔ̃], *s.f. Gram:* anteposition.

antérieur, -eure [ɑ̃terjœːr], *a.* **1.** (*a*) anterior (**à,** to); former (period); earlier (date); previous (year) (**à,** to); prior (engagement) (**à,** to); antecedent (**à,** to); **contrat a.,** prior contract; **a. au mariage,** pre-marital; (*b*) *Gram:* **futur a.,** future perfect; **passé a.,** past anterior. **2.** an-terior (muscle); fore-(limb, etc.); front- (wall, vowel, etc.).

antérieurement [ɑ̃terjœrmɑ̃], *adv.* anteriorly, pre-viously, earlier; **son livre a paru a. au vôtre,** his book appeared before yours.

antériorité [ɑ̃terjɔrite], *s.f.* anteriority, priority, antecedence; *Jur:* **droit d'a.,** right of priority.

antérograde [ɑ̃terɔgrad], *a. Med:* anterograde.

antéro(-)inférieur, -eure [ɑ̃teroɛ̃ferjœːr], *a. Anat:* anteroinferior.

antéro(-)interne [ɑ̃teroɛ̃tɛrn], *a. Anat:* antero-internal.

antéropostérieur, -eure [ɑ̃terɔpɔsterjœːr], *a. Anat:* anteroposterior.

antérosupérieur [ɑ̃terosyperjœːr], *a. Anat:* antero-superior.

antéversion [ɑ̃tevɛrsjɔ̃], *s.f. Med:* anteversion.

anthèle [ɑ̃tɛl], *s.f. Bot:* anthela.

anthélie [ɑ̃teli], *s.f. Meteor: Opt:* anthelion, glory, Ulloa's circle.

anthélix [ɑ̃teliks], *s.m. Anat:* ant(i)helix (of ear).

anthelminthique [ɑ̃tɛlmɛ̃tik], *a. & s.m. Pharm:* anthelmint(h)ic; *s.* vermifuge; **poudre a.,** worm-powder.

anthémis [ɑ̃temis], *s.f. Bot:* anthemis.

anthère [ɑ̃tɛːr], *s.f. Bot:* anther.

anthericum [ɑ̃terikɔm], *s.m. Bot:* Anthericum.

anthéridie [ɑ̃teridi], *s.f. Bot:* antheridium.

anthérifère [ɑ̃terifɛːr], *a. Bot:* antheriferous.

anthérozoïde [ɑ̃terɔzɔid], *s.m. Bot:* antherozoid.

anthèse [ɑ̃tɛz], *s.f. Bot:* anthesis, flowering.

anthidie [ɑ̃tidi], *s.f. Ent:* anthidium.

anthocéros [ɑ̃tɔserɔs], *s.m. Bot:* anthoceros.

anthocérotales [ɑ̃tɔserɔtal], *s.f.pl. Bot:* Antho-cerotales.

anthocorides [ɑ̃tɔkɔrid], *s.m.pl. Ent:* Antho-coridae.

anthocyane [ɔ̃tɔsjan], *s.f.*, **anthocyanine** [ɑ̃tɔsjanin], *s.f. Bio-Ch:* anthocyan, anthocyanin.

anthocyanidine [ɑ̃tɔsjanidin], *s.f. Bio-Ch:* antho-cyanidin.

anthogénèse [ɑ̃tɔʒenɛz], *s.f.* anthogenesis.

anthologie [ɑ̃tɔlɔʒi], *s.f. Lit:* anthology.

anthologique [ɑ̃tɔlɔʒik], *a.* anthological.

anthologue [ɑ̃tɔlɔg], *s.m.* anthologist.

anthonome [ɑ̃tɔnɔm], *s.m. Ent:* anthonomus.

anthophage [ɑ̃tɔfaʒ], *a.* anthophagous.

anthophile [ɑ̃tɔfil], *a. Ent:* anthophilous.

anthophores [ɑ̃tɔfɔːr], *s.m.pl. Ent:* Anthophora.

anthore [ɑ̃tɔr], *s.m. Bot:* perennial monkshood.

anthozoaires [ɑ̃tɔzɔɛːr], *s.m.pl. Z:* Anthozoa.

anthracène [ɑ̃trasɛn], *s.m.*, **anthracine** [ɑ̃trasin], *s.f. Ch:* anthracene.

anthracénique [ɑ̃trasenik], *a. Ch: Dy:* anthracene (dye).

anthracifère [ɑ̃trasifɛːr], *a. Geol:* anthraciferous, anthracitic.

anthracite [ɑ̃trasit]. **1.** *s.m. Miner:* anthracite; **a. en morceaux,** checker coal; **équivalence en a.,** hard-coal equivalent. **2.** *a.inv.* charcoal grey.

anthraciteux, -euse [ɑ̃trasitø, -øːz], *a. Geol:* anthracitous, anthracitic.

anthracitifère [ɑ̃trasitifɛr], *a. Miner:* anthraciti-ferous.

anthracnose [ɑ̃traknoːz], *s.f. Bot:* anthracnose, anthracnosis.

anthracose [ɑ̃trakoːz], *s.f. Med:* anthracosis; miner's phthisis.

anthraquinone [ɑ̃trakinɔn], *s.f. Ch:* anthraquin-one.

anthrax [ɑ̃traks], *s.m.* **1.** *Med:* (*a*) carbuncle; (*b*) **a. malin,** anthrax. **2.** *Ent:* anthrax.

anthrène [ɑ̃trɛn], *s.m. Ent:* anthrenus, (i) carpet-beetle; (ii) museum-beetle.

anthribidés [ɑ̃tribide], *s.m.pl. Ent:* Anthribidae.

anthrisque [ɑ̃trisk], *s.f. Bot:* anthriscus.

anthropo- [ɑ̃trɔpɔ], *comb.fm.* anthropo-; **anthro-pobiologie,** anthropobiology; **anthropographie,** anthropography; **anthropogéographie,** anthropo-geography.

anthropocentrique [ɑ̃trɔpɔsɑ̃trik], *a.* anthropo-centric.

anthropocentrisme [ɑ̃trɔpɔsɑ̃trism], *s.m.* anthro-pocentrism, anthropocentricism.

anthropoclimatologie [ɑ̃trɔpɔklimatɔlɔʒi], *s.f.* anthropoclimatology.

anthropogenèse [ɑ̃trɔpɔʒenɛːz], *s.f.*, **anthro-pogénésie** [ɑ̃trɔpɔʒenezi], *s.f.*, **anthropogénie** [ɑ̃trɔpɔʒeni], *s.f.* anthropogenesis, anthropo-geny.

anthropogéographie [ɑ̃trɔpɔʒeɔgrafi], *s.f.* anthro-pogeography.

anthropographie [ɑ̃trɔpɔgrafi], *s.f.* anthropo-graphy.

anthropoïde [ɑ̃trɔpɔid]. **1.** *a.* anthropoid. **2.** *s.m. Z:* anthropoid (ape).

anthropolithe [ɑ̃trɔpɔlit], *s.m. Paleont:* anthropo-lite, anthropolith.

anthropologie [ɑ̃trɔpɔlɔʒi], *s.f.* anthropology.

anthropologique [ɑ̃trɔpɔlɔʒik], *a.* anthropolo-gical.

anthropologiste [ɑ̃trɔpɔlɔʒist], *s.m.*, **anthropo-logue** [ɑ̃trɔpɔlɔg], *s.m.* anthropologist.

anthropomètre [ɑ̃trɔpɔmɛtr], *s.m.* anthropo-meter.

anthropométrie [ɑ̃trɔpɔmetri], *s.f.* anthropometry.

anthropométrique [ɑ̃trɔpɔmetrik], *a.* anthropo-metric(al); *Adm:* **service a.,** criminal anthropo-metry department (= Criminal Records Office); **fiche a.** = (criminal's) dossier.

anthropomorphe [ɑ̃trɔpɔmɔrf]. **1.** *a.* anthropo-morphous. **2.** *s.m.* (*a*) *Bot:* mandragora; (*b*) *Z:* anthropoid (ape); *pl.* **anthropomorphes,** Anthro-pomorpha.

anthropomorphie [ɑ̃trɔpɔmɔrfi], *s.f. Z:* anthro-pomorphousness.

anthropomorphique [ɑ̃trɔpɔmɔrfik], *a.* anthropo-morphic.

anthropomorphiser [ɑ̃trɔpɔmɔrfize], *v.tr.* to anthropomorphize.

anthropomorphisme [ɑ̃trɔpɔmɔrfism], *s.m. Phil:* anthropomorphism.

anthropomorphiste [ɑ̃trɔpɔmɔrfist], *s.m. & f.* anthropomorphist.

anthroponymie [ɑ̃trɔpɔnimi], *s.f.* anthropo-nymy, study of family names.

anthropophage [ɑ̃trɔpɔfaːʒ]. **1.** *a.* anthropo-phagous, cannibalistic, man-eating. **2.** *s.m. & f.* cannibal, man-eater; **les anthropophages,** an-thropophagi.

anthropophagie [ɑ̃trɔpɔfaʒi], *s.f.* anthropophagy, cannibalism.

anthropophobie [ɑ̃trɔpɔfɔbi], *s.f. Med:* anthro-pophobia.

anthropopithèque [ɑ̃trɔpɔpitɛk], *s.m. Paleont:* anthropopithecus, pithecanthropus.

anthroposomatologie [ɑ̃trɔpɔsɔmatɔlɔʒi], *s.f.* an-throposomatology.

anthropozoïque [ɑ̃trɔpɔzɔik], *a. Geol:* anthro-pozoic.

anthure [ɑ̃tyːr], *s.m. Bot:* anthurium.

anthyllide [ɑ̃til(l)id], *s.f.*, **anthyllis** [ɑ̃til(l)is], *s.f. Bot:* anthyllis; **a. barbe-de-Jupiter,** Jupiter's beard; **a. vulnéraire,** lady's fingers, kidney vetch.

anti¹- [ɑ̃ti], *pref.* anti-; **anti-académique,** anti-academical; **anti-réglementaire,** against the regulations; **anti-tout,** anti-everything.

anti²-, *pref.* ante-; **antichambre,** antechamber; **antidater,** to antedate.

antiacide [ɑ̃tiasid], *a. & s.m. Ch:* antiacid, ant-acid; **vernis a.,** acid-proof varnish.

antiadministratif, -ive [ɑ̃tiadministratif, -iːv], *a.* **1.** against, contrary to, office regulations. **2.** **agitation antiadministrative,** anti-red-tape agitation.

antiaérien, -ienne [ɑ̃tiaerjɛ̃, -jɛn], *a.* anti-aircraft (gun, defence).

antialcoolique [ɑ̃tialkɔlik]. **1.** *a.* (*a*) anti-alcohol (league, etc.); (*b*) teetotal. **2.** *s.* (*a*) anti-alcoholist; (*b*) teetotaller.

antialcoolisme [ɑ̃tialkɔlism], *s.m.* antialcoholism; teetotalism.

antiamaril [ɑ̃tiamaril], *a.* **vaccin a.,** yellow fever vaccine.

antiar [ɑ̃tjaːr], *s.m.*, **antiaris** [ɑ̃tjaris], *s.m. Bot: Pharm:* antiar.

antiarcs [ɑ̃tiark], *s.m.pl. El.E:* non-arcing gear.

antiarthritique [ɑ̃tiartritik], *a.* & *s.m. Med:* ant(i)arthritic.

antiasthmatique [ɑ̃tiasmatik], *a.* & *s.m. Med:* antiasthmatic.

antiatomique [ɑ̃tiatɔmik], *a.* antinuclear; anti-atomic; **abri a.,** fall-out shelter; **manifestation a.,** ban-the-bomb demonstration.

anti-aveuglant [ɑ̃tiavœglɑ̃], *a.* anti-dazzling, -dazzle.

antiballes [ɑ̃tibal], *a.inv.* bullet-proof.

antibélier [ɑ̃tibelje], *s.m. Hyd.E:* desurger.

antibiblique [ɑ̃tibiblik], *a.* antiscriptural.

antibilieux, -euse [ɑ̃tibiljø, -øːz], *a. Med:* antibilious.

antibiotique [ɑ̃tibjɔtik], *a.* & *s.m.* antibiotic.

antiblindé [ɑ̃tiblɛ̃de], *a. Mil:* anti-tank.

antiboche [ɑ̃tibɔʃ], *a.* & *s. A: P:* anti-German.

antibois[1] [ɑ̃tibwɑ], *s.m.* = ANTEBOIS.

antibois[2], **-oise** [ɑ̃tibwa, -waːz], *a.* & *s. Geog:* (native, inhabitant) of Antibes.

antibrouillage [ɑ̃tibrujaːʒ], *s.m. W.Tel: etc:* anti-jamming.

antibrouillard [ɑ̃tibrujaːr], *a.* & *s.m. Aut:* **(phare) a.,** fog-lamp.

antibrouilleur [ɑ̃tibrujœːr], *s.m. W.Tel: etc:* anti-jammer.

antibuée [ɑ̃tibɥe], *a.* & *s.m. Aut:* **(dispositif) a.,** demister.

anticalaminant [ɑ̃tikalaminɑ̃], *a.* & *s.m. I.C.E:* **(additif) a.,** anti-carbon additive.

anticalcaire [ɑ̃tikalkɛːr], *s.m. Mch:* scale-preventer, scale-remover, scale-removing composition.

anticancéreux, -euse [ɑ̃tikɑ̃serø, -øːz], *a.* **centre, sérum, a.,** cancer hospital, cancer serum.

anticatarrhal, -aux [ɑ̃tikataral, -o], *a.* & *s.m.* anti-catarrhal.

anticathode [ɑ̃tikatɔd], *s.f. X-rays:* anticathode; target.

anticatholique [ɑ̃tikatɔlik], *a.* & *s.* anticatholic.

antichambre [ɑ̃tiʃɑ̃ːbr], *s.f.* anteroom, waiting-room, antechamber; **faire a. chez qn,** to dance attendance on s.o., to cool one's heels in the waiting-room; **courir les antichambres,** to run after the great; **pilier d'a.,** hanger-on (of minister, etc.); **propos d'a.,** back-stair gossip.

antichar [ɑ̃tiʃaːr]. *Mil:* **1.** *a.* anti-tank. **2.** *s.m.* anti-tank device, appliance.

antichlore [ɑ̃tiklɔːr], *s.m. Tex: etc:* antichlor.

antichoc [ɑ̃tiʃɔk], *a.inv.* shock-proof; *Med:* **traitement a.,** anti-shock treatment.

anticholérique [ɑ̃tikɔlerik], *a.* & *s.m. Pharm:* anticholeraic.

antichrèse [ɑ̃tikrɛːz], *s.f. Jur:* antichresis, pledging of real estate (as security for debt).

antichrétien, -ienne [ɑ̃tikretjɛ̃, -jɛn], *a.* & *s.* antichristian.

antichristianisme [ɑ̃tikristjanism], *s.m.* antichristianism.

anticipatif, -ive [ɑ̃tisipatif, -iːv], *a.* anticipatory anticipative; **paiement a.,** prepayment.

anticipation [ɑ̃tisipasjɔ̃], *s.f.* **1.** (*a*) anticipation; **payer par a.,** to pay in advance; **payement par a.,** advance (payment), prepayment; *Mus:* **note d'a.,** note of anticipation; **littérature d'a.,** (early) science fiction; **film, roman, romancier, d'a.,** (early) science fiction film, novel, writer; (*b*) *Rh:* prolepsis. **2.** encroachment (on s.o.'s rights, etc.).

anticiper [ɑ̃tisipe]. **1.** *v.tr.* to anticipate (sth.), to forestall (s.o.'s action); **plaisir anticipé,** anticipated pleasure; **"avec mes remerciements anticipés,"** "thanking you in anticipation"; *Fin:* **a. un paiement de dix jours,** to anticipate a payment by ten days; **dividende anticipé,** advanced dividend; **remboursement anticipé,** redemption before due date; *Mil:* **évacuation anticipée,** early evacuation (of a region). **2.** *v.i.* to anticipate; (*a*) **a. sur les droits de qn,** to encroach on s.o.'s rights; (*b*) **a. sur les événements,** to anticipate events; **a. sur ses revenus,** to anticipate one's income.

anticivique [ɑ̃tisivik], *a.* anticivic.

Anticlée, *Pr.n.f. Gr.Lit:* Anticlea.

anticlérical, -aux [ɑ̃tiklerikal, -o], *a.* anticlerical.

anticléricalisme [ɑ̃tiklerikalism], *s.m.* anticlericalism.

anticlimax [ɑ̃tiklimaks], *s.m. Rh:* anticlimax.

anticlinal, -aux [ɑ̃tiklinal, -o]. *Geol:* **1.** *a.* anticlinal; **pli, axe, a.,** anticlinal fold, axis. **2.** *s.m.* anticline.

anticlinorium [ɑ̃tiklinɔrjɔm], *s.m. Geol:* anticlinorium.

anticoagulant [ɑ̃tikɔagylɑ̃]. **1.** *a.* anticoagulant. **2.** *s.m.* anticoagulant.

anticolonialisme [ɑ̃tikɔlɔnjalism], *s.m.* anticolonialism.

anticolonialiste [ɑ̃tikɔlɔnjalist], *a.* anticolonialist.

anticombustible [ɑ̃tikɔ̃bystibl]. **1.** *a.* incombustible, fireproof. **2.** *s.m.* fireproof material.

anticonceptionnel, -elle [ɑ̃tikɔ̃sɛpsjɔnɛl], *a.* (*a*) contraceptive; (*b*) birth-control (measures, etc.).

anticonformisme [ɑ̃tikɔ̃fɔrmism], *s.m.* anticonformism.

anticonformiste [ɑ̃tikɔ̃fɔrmist], *a.* & *s.m.* & *f.* anticonformist.

anticonstitutionnel, -elle [ɑ̃tikɔ̃stitysjɔnɛl], *a.* anticonstitutional.

anticonstitutionnellement [ɑ̃tikɔ̃stitysjɔnɛlmɑ̃], *adv.* anticonstitutionally.

anticorps [ɑ̃tikɔːr], *s.m. Physiol:* antibody.

Anticosti [ɑ̃tikɔsti], *Pr.n. Geog:* Anticosti.

anticryptogamique [ɑ̃tikriptɔgamik]. **1.** *a.* fungicidal. **2.** *s.m.* fungicide.

anticyclique [ɑ̃tisiklik], *a.* anticyclic.

anticyclonal [ɑ̃tisiklɔnal], *a. Meteor:* anticyclonic; **aire anticyclonale,** high-pressure area.

anticyclone[1] [ɑ̃tisikloːn], *s.m. Meteor:* anticyclone.

anticyclone[2], *a.* anticyclone; *U.S:* **abri a.,** cyclone cellar.

anticyclonique [ɑ̃tisiklɔnik], *a. Meteor:* anticyclonic.

antidate [ɑ̃tidat], *s.f.* antedate.

antidater [ɑ̃tidate], *v.tr.* to antedate, foredate (contract, etc.).

antidéflagrant [ɑ̃tideflagrɑ̃], *a.* explosion-proof; flame-proof; *Atom.Ph:* **détecteur a.,** flame-proof monitor.

antidémocratique [ɑ̃tidemɔkratik], *a.* antidemocratic.

antidéperditeur, -trice [ɑ̃tidepɛrditœːr, -tris], *a. Physiol:* anti-waste (food, etc.).

antidérapant [ɑ̃tiderapɑ̃], *a. Aut: etc:* non-skid(ding), non-slipping; *s.m.* **(pneu) a.,** non-skid tyre.

antidétonant [ɑ̃tidetɔnɑ̃], *a.* & *s. I.C.E:* anti-knock.

antidiphtérique [ɑ̃tidifterik], *a.* **vaccin a.,** diphtheria vaccine.

antidote [ɑ̃tidɔt], *s.m. Med:* antidote **(de, contre,** for, to, against).

antidramatique [ɑ̃tidramatik], *a.* contrary to the rules of dramatic art, anti-dramatic.

anti-éblouissant [ɑ̃tiebluisɑ̃], *a.* anti-glare, anti-dazzle; **lunettes anti-éblouissantes,** non-glare goggles.

antiémétique [ɑ̃tiemetik], *a.* antiemetic.

antienne [ɑ̃tjɛn], *s.f. Ecc.Mus:* (*a*) antiphon; **chanter toujours la même a.,** to be always harping on the same string; (*b*) anthem.

antiesclavagiste [ɑ̃tiɛsklavaʒist]. **1.** *a.* anti-slavery (society, etc.). **2.** *s.* abolitionist.

anti-étincelles [ɑ̃tietɛ̃sɛl], *a.* anti(-)spark.

antif [ɑ̃tif], *s.m. A: P:* road; **battre l'a.,** to be on the tramp; **batteur d'a.,** tramp.

antifading [ɑ̃tifadiŋ]. *W.Tel:* **a.** antifading; **a.** & *s.inv.* **(dispositif) a.,** automatic volume control.

antifasciste [ɑ̃tifasist, -ʃist], *a.* & *s.m.* & *f. Pol:* anti-fascist.

antifébrile [ɑ̃tifebril], *a.* & *s.m.* = FÉBRIFUGE.

antifébrine [ɑ̃tifebrin], *s.f. Pharm:* antifebrin.

antiféminisme [ɑ̃tifeminism], *s.m.* antifeminism.

antiféministe [ɑ̃tifeminist], *s.m.* antifeminist.

antiferment [ɑ̃tifɛrmɑ̃], *s.m. Ch: Physiol:* antiferment.

antifle [ɑ̃tifl], *s.f. P:* church.

antifler [ɑ̃tifle], *v.i. P:* to barge in.

s'antifler, s'a. de sec, *P:* to get married.

anti-freudisme [ɑ̃tifrødism], *s.m.* anti-Freudism.

antifriction [ɑ̃tifriksjɔ̃], *s.m. Mec.E:* antifriction metal; white metal, Babbitt's metal, babbitt (metal); **emportement d'a.,** wiped bearing.

anti-fuite [ɑ̃tifɥit], *s.m.inv.* leak-preventer (for radiators, etc.).

anti-g [ɑ̃tiʒe], *a.inv. Av:* **vêtement, combinaison, a.-g.,** (anti)G suit.

antigaz [ɑ̃tigaz], *a.* anti-gas.

antigel [ɑ̃tiʒɛl], *s.m.* & *a.inv.* anti-freeze.

antigène [ɑ̃ntiʒɛn], *s.m. Med:* antigen.

antigénique [ɑ̃tiʒenik], *a.* antigenic.

antigivrage [ɑ̃tiʒivraːʒ], *s.m. Av:* anti-icing.

antigivrant [ɑ̃tiʒivrɑ̃], *a.*, **antigivre** [ɑ̃tiʒivr], *a.inv.* anti-icing.

antigivreur, -euse [ɑ̃tiʒivrœːr, -øz]; (*a*) *a. Av:* anti-icing; *Aut:* de-icing; (*b*) *s.m. Av:* anti-icer; *Aut:* de-icer.

Antigone [ɑ̃tigɔn], *Pr.n.f. Gr.Lit:* Antigone.

antigorite [ɑ̃tigɔrit], *s.f. Miner:* antigorite.

anti-gouttes [ɑ̃tigut], *a.inv.* non-spill.

antigouvernemental [ɑ̃tiguvɛrnəmɑ̃tal], *a.* anti-government.

antigréviste [ɑ̃tigrevist]. **1.** *a.* anti-strike (group, etc.). **2.** *s.* anti-striker.

antigrippal [ɑ̃tigripal], *a.* anti-flu.

Antigue [ɑ̃tig], *Pr.n. Geog:* Antigua.

antihalo [ɑ̃tialo]. *Phot:* **1.** *a.inv.* **plaques a.,** anti-halation, non-halation plates; *s.a.* ADHÉSIF 2, ENDUIT 4. **2.** *s.m.* (antihalation) backing.

antihistaminique [ɑ̃tiistaminik], *a.* & *s.m. Med:* antihistamine.

antihygiénique [ɑ̃tiiʒjenik], *a.* unhygienic, insanitary.

anti-incrustant [ɑ̃tiɛ̃krystɑ̃]. *Mch:* **1.** *a.* scale-preventing; **graphite a.-i.,** boiler graphite. **2.** *s.m.* scale-preventer, boiler composition.

antijuif, -ive [ɑ̃tiʒɥif, -iːv], *a.* anti-Jewish.

antilibéral, -aux [ɑ̃tiliberal, -o], *a. Pol:* anti-liberal.

antillais, -aise [ɑ̃tijɛ, -ɛːz], *a.* & *s. Geog:* West-Indian.

Antilles [ɑ̃tij], *Pr.n.f.pl. Geog:* **les A.,** the West Indies, the Antilles; **les Petites A.,** the lesser Antilles; **les Grandes A.,** the Greater Antilles; **la Mer des A.,** the Caribbean (Sea).

antillien, -ienne [ɑ̃tijɛ̃, -jɛn], *a.* & *s.* = ANTILLAIS.

antilocapre [ɑ̃tilɔkapr], *s.f. Z:* antilocapra, pronghorn; **a. nord-américain,** North-American pronghorn.

antilocapridés [ɑ̃tilɔkapride], *s.m.pl. Z:* Antilocapridae.

antilog [ɑ̃tilɔg], *s.m. Mth: F:* antilog.

antilogarithme [ɑ̃tilɔgaritm], *s.m. Mth:* antilogarithm.

antilogie [ɑ̃tilɔʒi], *s.f. Log:* antilogy.

antilogue [ɑ̃tilɔg], *a. El:* antilogous (pole).

antilogique [ɑ̃tilɔʒik], *a.* antilogical.

antilope [ɑ̃tilɔp], *s.f. Z:* antelope; **a. singsing,** jackass deer, sing-sing; **a. chevreuil,** reebok; **a. à sabre,** oryx; **a. naine,** duiker; **a. royale, a. pygmée,** royal antelope; **a. rouane,** roan antelope; **a. cervicapre,** blackbuck; **a. noire géante,** sable antelope; **a. de Bates,** Bates' dwarf antelope; **a. des roseaux,** reedbuck; **a. tétracère,** four-horned antelope, chousingha.

antilopinés [ɑ̃tilɔpine], *s.m.pl. Z:* Antilopinae.

antimaçonnique [ɑ̃timasɔnik], *a.* antimasonic.

antimagnétique [ɑ̃timaɲetik], *a.* antimagnetic (metal).

antimatière [ɑ̃timatjɛːr], *s.f.* antimatter.

antiméphitique [ɑ̃timefitik], *a.* & *s.m. Med:* antimephitic.

antimétabolite [ɑ̃timetabɔlit], *s.m. Med:* antimetabolite.

antimicrobien, -ienne [ɑ̃timikrɔbjɛ̃, -jɛn], *a.* antimicrobic, antimicrobial.

antimilitarisme [ɑ̃timilitarism], *s.m.* antimilitarism.

antimilitariste [ɑ̃timilitarist], *s.* antimilitarist, pacifist.

antiministériel [ɑ̃tiministerjɛl], *a.* antiministerial.

anti-missile *occ.* **antimissile** [ɑ̃timisil], *a.* anti-missile; **missile a.-m.,** anti-missile missile.

antimite(s) [ɑ̃timit], (*a*) *a.* moth-proof; (*b*) *a.* moth-destroying; *s.m.* moth-killer.

antimiter [ɑ̃timite], *v.tr.* to moth-proof.

antimoine [ɑ̃timwan], *s.m. Ch:* antimony; **sel d'antimoine,** antimony salt; **sulfure noir d'a., a. cru, sulfuré,** antimony sulphide, black antimony.

antimonarchique [ɑ̃timɔnarʃik], *a.* antimonarchic(al).

antimonarchisme [ɑ̃timɔnarʃism], *s.m.* antimonarchism.

antimonarchiste [ɑ̃timɔnarʃist], *s.m.* & *f.* antimonarchist.

antimonial, -aux [ɑ̃timɔnjal, -o], *a.* & *s.m. Ch: Pharm:* antimonial.

antimoniate [ɑ̃timɔnjat], *s.m. Ch:* antimon(i)ate.

antimonié [ɑ̃timɔnje], *a.* antimoniated; antimoniuretted (hydrogen).

antimonieux, -euse [ɑ̃timɔnjø, -øːz], *a.* antimonious.

antimonique [ɑ̃timɔnik], *a. Ch:* antimonic.

antimonite [ɑ̃timɔnit], *s.m. Ch:* antimonite.

antimoniure [ɑ̃timɔnjyːr], *s.m. Ch:* antimonide; **a. d'hydrogène,** stibine.

antimoral, -aux [ɑ̃timɔral, -o], *a.* antimoral.
anti-mousse [ɑ̃timus], *a.inv. Ind:* **additif a.-m.,** defoamer; **agent a.-m.,** foam inhibitor.
antinataliste [ɑ̃tinatalist], *a.* = ANTICONCEPTIONNEL.
antinational, -aux [ɑ̃tinasjɔnal, -o], *a.* antinational.
antinazi, -e [ɑ̃tinazi], *a. & s.* anti-nazi.
antinéphrétique [ɑ̃tinefretik], *a. & s.m. Pharm:* antinephritic.
antineutron [ɑ̃tinøtrɔ̃], *s.m.* antineutron.
antinévralgique [ɑ̃tinevralʒik], *a. & s.m. Pharm:* antineuralgic.
antinodal, -aux [ɑ̃tinɔdal, -o], *a. Ph:* antinodal.
antinœud [ɑ̃tinø], *s.m. Ph:* antinode, loop.
antinomie [ɑ̃tinɔmi], *s.f.* (*a*) antinomy, paradox; (*b*) discrepancy.
antinomien [ɑ̃tinɔmjɛ̃], *s.m. Rel.H:* antinomian.
antinomique [ɑ̃tinɔmik], *a.* antinomic, paradoxical.
Antinoüs [ɑ̃tinɔys], *Pr.n.m. Rom.Ant:* Antinous; *A:* **c'est un véritable A.,** he is a regular Adonis.
antiobésique [ɑ̃tiɔbezik], *a. Med:* anti-fat; **régime a.,** banting diet.
Antioche [ɑ̃tjɔʃ], *Pr.n.f. A.Geog:* Antioch.
Antiochus [ɑ̃tjɔkyːs], *Pr.n.m. A.Hist:* Antiochus.
Antiope [ɑ̃tjɔp], *Pr.n.f. Gr.Myth:* Antiope.
antioxydant [ɑ̃tiɔksidɑ̃], *a. & s.m.* antioxydant.
antioxygène [ɑ̃tiɔksiʒɛn], *Ch:* anti-oxygen.
antipaludique [ɑ̃tipalydik]. **1.** *a.* antimalaria(l). **2.** *s.m.* remedy against malaria, antimalarial.
antipape [ɑ̃tipap], *s.m. Rel.H:* antipope.
antipapisme [ɑ̃tipapism], *s.m.* antipopery.
antipapiste [ɑ̃tipapist], *a. & s.m.* antipapist; **émeutes anti-papistes,** no-popery riots.
antiparallèle [ɑ̃tiparalɛl], *a. & s.m. Geom:* antiparallel.
antiparalytique [ɑ̃tiparalitik], *a. Med:* antiparalytic.
antiparasitage [ɑ̃tiparazitaːʒ], *s.m. W.Tel: El:* suppression.
antiparasitaire [ɑ̃tiparazitɛːr]. **1.** *s.m.* pesticide. **2.** *a.* pest-destroying.
antiparasite [ɑ̃tiparazit]. **1.** (*a*) *a.* pesticidal; (*b*) *s.m.* pesticide. **2.** *a. & s.m. W.Tel: Aut: etc:* **(dispositif) a.,** suppressor; **équilibre a.,** noise balance.
antiparasiter [ɑ̃tiparazite], *v.tr. W.Tel: El: etc:* to suppress; to shield.
antiparlementaire [ɑ̃tiparləmɑ̃tɛːr], *a. Pol:* (*a*) antiparliamentary; (*b*) unparliamentary (language, etc.).
antiparti [ɑ̃tiparti], *a. Pol:* **groupe a.,** splinter group.
antiparticule [ɑ̃tipartikyl], *s.f. Atom.Ph:* antiparticule.
antipathie [ɑ̃tipati], *s.f.* **a. pour, contre, qn, qch.,** antipathy to, against, s.o., sth.; repugnance to, against, s.o., sth.; aversion for, from, to, s.o., sth.
antipathique [ɑ̃tipatik], *a.* antipathetic; **elle lui est a.,** he has an aversion to her; **c'est un (bon) homme a.,** he's an unlikeable fellow.
antipatriote [ɑ̃tipatriɔt], *s.m. & f.* antipatriot.
antipatriotique [ɑ̃tipatriɔtik], *a.* **1.** unpatriotic. **2.** antipatriotic.
antipatriotisme [ɑ̃tipatriɔtism], *s.m.* **1.** lack of patriotism. **2.** antipatriotism.
antipéristaltique [ɑ̃tiperistaltik], *a. Physiol:* antiperistaltic, antivermicular (motion); **contraction a.,** antiperistalsis.
antipersonnel [ɑ̃tipɛrsɔnɛl], *a.inv.* **bombe a.,** anti-personnel bomb.
antipesteux, -euse [ɑ̃tipɛstø, -øz], *a.* **sérum a.,** antiplague serum.
antipestilentiel, -elle [ɑ̃tipɛstilɑ̃sjɛl], *a.* antiplague.
antiphilosophique [ɑ̃tifilɔzɔfik], *a.* antiphilosophical.
antiphlogistique [ɑ̃tiflɔʒistik], *a.* antiphlogistic.
antiphonaire [ɑ̃tifɔnɛːr], *s.m. Ecc:* antiphonary.
antiphone[1] [ɑ̃tifɔn], *s.m. Ecc:* antiphon.
antiphone[2], *s.m.* ear-plug.
antiphrase [ɑ̃tifrɑːz], *s.f. Rh:* antiphrasis.
antipied [ɑ̃tipje], *s.m. Z:* forefoot.
antipodal, -aux [ɑ̃tipɔdal, -o], *a. Geog:* antipodal, antipodean.
antipode [ɑ̃tipɔd]. **1.** *a. A:* antipodal. **2.** *s.m.* (*a*) place, person, diametrically opposite to another place or person on the earth's surface; **les antipodes,** the antipodes; **aux antipodes,** at the antipodes; **votre théorie est aux antipodes de la mienne,** our theories are poles apart; (*b*) *Bot:* antipodal cells.
antipodisme [ɑ̃tipɔdism], *s.m.* foot-juggling.
antipodiste [ɑ̃tipɔdist]. **1.** *a.* **exercice a.,** foot-juggling exercise. **2.** *s.m. & f.* foot-juggler.
antipoétique [ɑ̃tipɔetik], *a.* antipoetic.
antipoints [ɑ̃tipwɛ̃], *s.m.pl. Mth:* antipoints.
antipôle [ɑ̃tipoːl], *s.m. Mth:* antipole, reciprocal pole.
antipoliomyélite [ɑ̃tipɔljɔmjelit], *a.* **vaccination a.,** polio vaccination.
antipolitain, -aine [ɑ̃tipɔlitɛ̃, -ɛn], *a. & s. Geog:* = ANTIBOIS[2].
antipolitique [ɑ̃tipɔlitik], *a.* impolitic, ill-advised (measure, etc.).
antipopulaire [ɑ̃tipɔpylɛːr], *a.* antipopular, directed against the people.
anti-poussière [ɑ̃tipusjɛːr], *a.inv.* protecting from dust; **plaque a.-p.,** dust-shield.
antiprogressif, -ive [ɑ̃tiprɔgresif, -iːv], *a.* antiprogressive, reactionary.
antiprogressiste [ɑ̃tiprɔgresist], *a. & s. Pol:* antiprogressionist, reactionary.
antiprohibitionnisme [ɑ̃tiprɔibisjɔnism], *s.m.* antiprohibitionism.
antiprohibitionniste [ɑ̃tiprɔibisjɔnist], *a. & s. Pol:* antiprohibitionist.
antiprotectionniste [ɑ̃tiprɔtɛksjɔnist]. **1.** *a.* free-trade (policy, etc.). **2.** *s.* antiprotectionist; free-trader.
antiproton [ɑ̃tiprɔtɔ̃], *s.m.* antiproton.
antiputride [ɑ̃tipytrid], *a.* antiputrefactive.
antipyrétique [ɑ̃tipiretik], *a. & s.m. Med:* antipyretic.
antipyrine [ɑ̃tipirin], *s.f. Pharm:* antipyrin(e).
antiquaille [ɑ̃tikɑːj], *s.f.* **1.** *A:* antiques. **2.** *Pej:* worthless old stuff, old junk.
antiquaire [ɑ̃tikɛːr], *s.m.* antiquary, antiquarian; antique dealer.
antique [ɑ̃tik]. **1.** *a.* (*a*) ancient, pertaining to classical antiquity; **la Grèce a.,** ancient Greece; (*b*) old, ancient; (*c*) old-fashioned, antiquated; (*d*) *Lit:* former, belonging to the past; long-established; **son a. prouesse,** his former prowess. **2.** *s.f. O:* work of art (of classical antiquity); *s.m. Coll.* the antique, classical antiquity; **dessiner d'après l'a.,** to draw from the antique. **3.** *s.f. Typ:* antique. **4.** *adv.phr.* **à l'a.,** (i) in an old-fashioned style; (ii) after the antique, modelled on classical antiquity.
antiquement [ɑ̃tikmɑ̃], *adv.* antiquely.
antiquer [ɑ̃tike], *v.tr. Bookb:* to antique.
antiquité [ɑ̃tikite], *s.f.* **1.** antiquity, ancientness. **2.** ancient times, antiquity. **3.** **l'a. grecque,** ancient Greek civilization. **4.** *usu. pl.* (*a*) **les antiquités,** the works of art of classical antiquity; (*b*) antiques; **magasin d'antiquités,** antique shop; **amateur d'antiquités,** antiquary.
antirabique [ɑ̃tirabik], *a. Med:* anti-rabic.
antirachitique [ɑ̃ntiraʃitik], *a. Med:* anti-rachitic (vitamin, etc.).
antiracisme [ɑ̃tirasism], *s.m.* antiracialism, antiracism.
antiradar [ɑ̃tiradar], *a. & s.m.* anti-radar (device).
antirationalisme [ɑ̃tirasjɔnalism], *s.m.* antirationalism.
antirationnel [ɑ̃tirasjɔnɛl], *a.* antirational.
antiréalisme [ɑ̃tirealism], *s.m.* antirealism.
antireflet [ɑ̃tirəflɛ], *a. Opt:* anti-reflecting.
antireligieux, -euse [ɑ̃tirəliʒjø, -øːz], *a.* antireligious.
antirépublicain, -aine [ɑ̃tirepyblikɛ̃, -ɛn], *a. & s.* antirepublican.
anti-retour de flamme(s) [ɑ̃tirətuːrdəflɑːm], *s.m. inv. Ind:* flame-damper; *Av: etc:* flame trap.
antirévolutionnaire [ɑ̃tirevɔlysjɔnɛːr], *a. & s.* antirevolutionary.
anti-roman [ɑ̃tirɔmɑ̃], *s.m. Lit:* anti-novel; *pl. anti-romans.*
antirouille [ɑ̃tiruj]. **1.** *s.m.* antirust composition, rust preventive. **2.** *a.inv.* rust-proof, nonrusting; rust-free.
antiroulis [ɑ̃tiruli], *s.m. Nau: Av:* (gyro-) stabilizer.
antirrhinum [ɑ̃tirinɔm], *s.m. Bot:* antirrhinum, snapdragon.
antisalle [ɑ̃tisal], *s.f.* ante(-)room.
antisciens [ɑ̃tisjɛ̃], *s.m.pl. Geog:* antiscians.
antiscorbutique [ɑ̃tiskɔrbytik], *a. & s.m. Pharm:* antiscorbutic.
antiscripturaire [ɑ̃tiskriptyrɛːr], *a.* antiscriptural.
antiscrofuleux, -euse [ɑ̃tiskrɔfylø, -øːz], *a.* antiscrofulous (treatment, etc.).
antisèche [ɑ̃tisɛʃ], *s.f. Sch: F:* crib.
antiségrégationniste [ɑ̃tisegregasjɔnist], *s.m. & f.* antisegregationist.
antisémite [ɑ̃tisemit], *s.m. & f.* anti-Semite.
antisémitique [ɑ̃tisemitik], *a.* anti-Semitic, anti-Semite, anti-Jewish.
antisémitisme [ɑ̃tisemitism], *s.m.* anti-Semitism.
antisepsie [ɑ̃tisɛpsi], *s.f. Med:* antisepsis.
antiseptique [ɑ̃tisɛptik], *a. & s.m. Med:* antiseptic.
antiseptiser [ɑ̃tisɛptize], *v.tr. Med:* to antisepticize.
antisérum [ɑ̃tiserɔm], *s.m. Med:* antiserum.
antisifflement [ɑ̃tisifləmɑ̃], *s.m. W.Tel:* anti-howl.
antisocial, -aux [ɑ̃tisɔsjal, -o], *a.* antisocial.
antisocialiste [ɑ̃tisɔsjalist], *s.m. & f.* antisocialist.
anti-sous-marin [ɑ̃tisumarɛ̃], *a.* anti-submarine.
antisoviétique [ɑ̃tisɔvjetik], *a.* anti-Soviet.
antispasmodique [ɑ̃tispasmɔdik], *a. & s.m. Pharm:* antispasmodic.
antispastique [ɑ̃tispastik], *a.* = ANTISPASMODIQUE.
antisportif, -ive [ɑ̃tispɔrtif, -iːv], *a.* **1.** unsporting, unsportsmanlike. **2.** opposed to sports.
Antisthène [ɑ̃tistɛn], *Pr.n.m. Gr.Phil:* Antisthenes.
antistrophe [ɑ̃tistrɔf], *s.f. Pros:* antistrophe.
antisyphilitique [ɑ̃tisifilitik], *a. & s.m. Med:* antisyphilitic.
antitache [ɑ̃titaʃ], *a.* stain-resisting.
anti-tank [ɑ̃titɑ̃ːk], *a.* anti-tank.
antitétanique [ɑ̃titetanik], *a. & s.m. Med:* antitetanus (serum).
anti-théâtre [ɑ̃titeatr̥], *s.m. Lit:* anti-theatre; *pl. anti-théâtres.*
antithermique [ɑ̃titɛrmik], *a. & s.m. Med:* antithermic, febrifuge.
antithèse [ɑ̃titɛːz], *s.f.* **1.** *Rh:* antithesis. **2.** direct contrary (**de,** to, of).
antithétique [ɑ̃titetik], *a.* antithetic(al); in strong contrast.
antithrombine [ɑ̃titrɔ̃bin], *s.f. Med:* antithrombin.
antithyroïdien, -ienne [ɑ̃titirɔidjɛ̃, -jɛn], *a.* antithyroid.
antitorpilleur [ɑ̃titɔrpijœːr], *a. & s.m. Navy:* anti-torpedo (gun).
antitoxine [ɑ̃titɔksin], *s.f. Med:* antitoxin.
antitoxique [ɑ̃titɔksik], *a. & s.m. Med:* antitoxic.
antitragien, -ienne [ɑ̃titraʒjɛ̃, -jɛn], *a. Anat:* antitragel, antitragic.
antitragus [ɑ̃titragys], *s.m. Anat:* antitragus.
antitrinitaire [ɑ̃titrinitɛːr], *a. & s.,* **antitrinitarien, -ienne** [ɑ̃titrinitarjɛ̃, -jɛn], *a. & s. Theol:* anti-Trinitarian.
antitrope [ɑ̃titrɔp], *a. Biol:* antitropic.
anti-trust [ɑ̃titrœst], *a.inv.* antitrust.
antituberculeux, -euse [ɑ̃titybɛrkylø, -øːz], *a. Med:* antitubercular; **centre a.,** tuberculosis centre.
antitype [ɑ̃titip], *s.m.* antitype.
antivaccinateur, -trice [ɑ̃tivaksinatœːr, -tris], *s.* antivaccinationist.
antivariolique [ɑ̃tivariɔlik], *a. Med:* antivariolar.
antivénéneux, -euse [ɑ̃tivenenø, -øːz]. *Med:* **1.** *a.* alexipharmic, antitoxic, antidotal. **2.** *s.m.* antidote, antipoison.
antivenimeux, -euse [ɑ̃tivənimø, -øz], *a.* antivenomous.
antivésicant [ɑ̃tivezikɑ̃], *a. Med:* anti-vesicant, anti-blistering.
antivibratile [ɑ̃tivibratil], *a.* anti-vibratory; preventing vibration; **isolement a. des fondations des bâtiments,** insulating of the foundations of buildings against vibration.
antivirus [ɑ̃tivirys], *s.m.* antivirus.
antivitamine [ɑ̃tivitamin], *s.f. Med:* antivitamin.
antivivisection(n)isme [ɑ̃tiviviseksjɔnism], *s.m.* antivivisection.
antivivisection(n)iste [ɑ̃tiviviseksjɔnist], *s.m. & f.* antivivisectionist; **société a.,** antivivisection society.
anti-voile [ɑ̃tivwal], *a.inv. Phot:* non-fogging (plate).
antivol [ɑ̃tivɔl], *a.inv. & s.m.* anti-theft, thief-proof (lock, device).
antivrille [ɑ̃tivrij], *a. Av:* anti-spin.
antivrilleur [ɑ̃tivrijœːr]. **1.** *a. Tex:* anti-kink. **2.** *a. & s.m. Av:* anti-spin (device).
antizymique [ɑ̃tizimik], *a. Biol:* antizymic.
antlérite [ɑ̃tlerit], *s.f. Miner:* antlerite.
Antoine [ɑ̃twan], *Pr.n.m.* Ant(h)ony; *s.a.* FEU[1] I. 1.
Antoinette [ɑ̃twanɛt], *Pr.n.f.* Antoinette, Antonia.
antoit [ɑ̃twa], *s.m. N.Arch:* (w)ring-bolt.
Antonin [ɑ̃tɔnɛ̃], *Pr.n.m. Hist:* Antoninus; **les Antonins,** the Antonines; **A. le Pieux,** Antoninus Pius.
antonomase [ɑ̃tɔnɔmɑːz], *s.f. Rh:* antonomasia.
antonyme [ɑ̃tɔnim]. **1.** *a.* antonymous. **2.** *s.m.* antonym.
antonymie [ɑ̃tɔnimi], *s.f.* antonymy, opposition of contrary terms.
antral, -aux [ɑ̃tral, -o], *a. Anat:* antral.
antre [ɑ̃ːtr̥], *s.m.* **1.** (*a*) cave, cavern; (*b*) den, lair, retreat (of animal, brigand, etc.). **2.** *Anat:* antrum; sinus.

antrectomie [ɑ̃trektɔmi], *s.f. Surg:* antroduodenectomy, antrectomy.

antrotomie [ɑ̃trɔtɔmi], *s.f. Surg:* antrotomy.

anucléaire [anykleɛr], *a. Atom.Ph:* anuclear.

anucléé [anyklee], *a. Biol:* anucleate.

anuité [anɥite], *a. Lit:* benighted (traveller, etc.).

anuiter (s') [sanɥite], *v.tr. A:* to be overtaken by the night.

anurèse [anyrɛːz], *s.f.*, **anurie** [anyri], *s.f. Med:* anuresis; anuria.

anus [anyːs], *s.m. Anat: Bot:* anus.

anuscope [anyskɔp], *Med:* anal speculum.

Anvers [ɑ̃vɛːr, ɑ̃vɛrs], *Pr.n.m. Geog:* Antwerp.

anversois, -oise [ɑ̃vɛrswa, -waːz]. **1.** *a. & s.* (native, inhabitant) of Antwerp. **2.** *s. Orn:* Antwerp pigeon.

anxieusement [ɑ̃ksjøzmɑ̃], *adv.* anxiously.

anxiété [ɑ̃ksjete], *s.f.* **1.** anxiety, concern; **un moment d'a.**, an anxious moment; **avec a.**, anxiously. **2.** *Med:* precordial anxiety.

anxieux, -ieuse [ɑ̃ksjø, -jøːz], *a.* anxious, uneasy; concerned; **a. de l'avenir, des siens**, anxious about the future, about one's family; **ils se quittèrent a.**, they parted full of anxiety.

anzinois, -oise [ɑ̃zinwa, -waːz], *a. & s.* (native) of Anzin.

aofien, -enne [aɔfjɛ̃, -jɛn], *a. & s. Hist:* French West African (*from* A.O.F., Afrique occidentale française).

aoriste [aɔrist], *s.m. Gr.Gram:* aorist; **a. sigmatique, premier a.**, sigmatic aorist, weak aorist.

aorte [aɔrt], *s.f. Anat:* aorta.

aortectomie [aɔrtektɔmi], *s.f. Surg:* aortectomy.

aortique [aɔrtik], *a. Anat:* aortic, aortal.

aortite [aɔrtit], *s.f. Med:* aortitis.

aortographie [aɔrtɔgrafi], *s.f. Med:* aortography.

Aoste [ɔst], *Pr.n.f. Geog:* Aosta.

août [u, *Dial:* au(t)], *s.m.* **1.** August; **en a.**, in August; **au mois d'a.**, in the month of August; **le premier, le sept., a.**, (on) the first, the seventh, of August, (on) August (the) first, (the) seventh. **2.** *A:* harvest (time); **faire l'a.**, to harvest, to get in the corn.

aoûtage [utaːʒ], *s.m. A:* harvest season.

aoûtat [uta, auta], *s.m. Arach: F:* harvest-bug, -tick, -mite, -louse; harvester.

aoûté [ute], *a.* ripened by the August sun.

aoûtement [(a)utmɑ̃], *s.m.* **1.** ripening (of fruit). **2.** lignification (of young branch before the winter).

aoûter [(a)ute]. **1.** *v.tr. & i.* to ripen. **2.** *v.i. & pr.* (*of young shoot*) to lignify; to get woody. **3.** *v.i. Dial:* to harvest.

aoûteron [utrɔ̃], *s.m. Husb:* harvester, harvest-hand.

aoûteur [utœːr], *s.m. A:* = AOÛTERON.

aoûtien, -ienne [ausjɛ̃, -jɛn], *s.* August holiday-maker.

apache [apaʃ], *s.m.* **1.** *Ethn:* Apache. **2.** hooligan, rough (of Paris); ruffian, tough.

apagogie [apagɔʒi], *s.f. Log:* apagoge.

apaisant [apɛzɑ̃], *a.* appeasing, quieting, soothing (news, effect, etc.).

apaisement [apɛzmɑ̃], *s.m.* appeasement. **1.** pacifying, appeasing, quieting (of child, crowd, creditor, etc.); assuaging (of pain, grief, etc.); **l'a. de la faim**, the appeasing, allaying, of (the pangs of) hunger; **réclamer des apaisements**, to demand satisfactory assurances (from the Government). **2.** subsiding, abatement, calming (down) (of wind, waves, etc.).

apaiser [apeze], *v.tr.* **1. a. qn**, to appease, pacify, calm, soothe, s.o.; **a. un enfant qui pleure**, to calm a weeping child; **non apaisé**, unappeased. **2.** to allay, alleviate, soothe, assuage (pain); to allay (hunger); to still (fears); to quench, slake (thirst); to quell, still, lull (storm); to put down, quell (revolt).

s'apaiser, to become appeased; to calm down, to grow quiet; to abate; (*of wind*) to die away, die down, to drop; (*of storm, excitement*) to subside; **l'orage s'était apaisé**, the storm had spent itself.

Apalaches [apalaʃ], *Pr.n.m.pl.* (*a*) *Ethn:* **les A.**, the Apalachee(s); (*b*) *Bot:* **thé des A.**, Appalachian tea.

Apalachie [apalaʃi]. *Pr.n.f. Geog:* **baie d'A.**, Apalachee Bay.

apalachine [apalaʃin], *s.f. Bot:* Appalachian tea.

apanage [apanaːʒ], *s.m.* **1.** *Hist:* ap(p)anage. **2.** ap(p)anage, attribute, prerogative (de, of); **les conceptions hardies sont l'a. des élites**, bold conceptions are the prerogative of the élite.

apanager[1] [apanaʒe], *v.tr.* (**j'apanageai(s), n. apanageons**) *Hist:* to endow (prince, etc.) with an ap(p)anage.

apanager[2], **-ère** [apanaʒe, -ɛːr], *a. Hist:* bestowed as an apanage.

apanagiste [apanaʒist], *s.m. & f. Hist:* ap(p)anagist.

apapelardir (s') [sapaplardiːr], *v.pr. A:* to grow sanctimonious.

aparté [aparte], *s.m.* **1.** *Th:* aside, stage-whisper; **en a.**, aside, in a stage-whisper. **2.** private conversation; **de petits apartés se formaient pour discuter la nouvelle**, small groups were forming to discuss the news; **couper l'a. de deux personnes**, to interrupt two people's private conversation.

apartheid [aparteid], *s.m.* (*in S. Africa*) apartheid.

apathie [apati], *s.f.* apathy, listlessness; **sortir de son a.**, to rouse oneself; **faire sortir qn de son a.**, to rouse s.o. (from his listlessness); **il affecta une a. entière**, he affected complete indifference.

apathique [apatik], *a.* apathetic, listless; lackadaisical.

apathiquement [apatikmɑ̃], *adv.* apathetically, listlessly.

apatite [apatit], *s.f. Miner:* apatite.

apatride [apatrid], *a. & s.m. & f. Jur:* stateless (person).

apatridie [apatridi], *s.f.* statelessness.

Apelle [apɛl], *Pr.n.m. Gr.Ant:* Apelles.

Apennins [apɛn(n)ɛ̃], *s.m.pl. Geog:* Apennines.

apens [apɑ̃], *a. A:* premeditated; *now used only in* GUET-APENS.

apepsie [apɛpsi], *s.f. Med:* apepsy, indigestion, dyspepsia.

aperceptible [apɛrsɛptibl], *a. Psy:* perceptible.

aperceptif, -ive [apɛrsɛptif, -iːv], *a. Psy:* apperceptive.

aperception [apɛrsɛpsjɔ̃], *s.f. Psy:* apperception.

apercevable [apɛrsəvabl], *a.* perceivable, perceptible; **a. au microscope**, perceivable under the microscope.

apercevoir [apɛrsəvwaːr], *v.tr.* (*pr.p.* **apercevant**; *p.p.* **aperçu**; *pr.ind.* **j'aperçois, il aperçoit, n. apercevons, ils aperçoivent**, *pr.sub.* **j'aperçoive, n. apercevions, ils aperçoivent**, *p.d.* **j'apercevais**; *p.h.* **j'aperçus**, *fu.* **j'apercevrai**) **1.** to perceive, see; to set eyes upon, to catch sight of, catch a glimpse of (s.o., sth.); **je n'ai fait que l'a.**, I only caught a glimpse of him; **cela ne s'aperçoit pas**, it is not noticeable; **je l'aperçus qui arrivait**, I saw him coming; **enfin nous avons aperçu un hôtel**, at last we saw a hotel. **2.** to perceive (mentally); to see, observe (sth.); *A:* **nous aperçûmes qu'il était aveugle**, we saw, realized, that he was blind.

s'apercevoir de qch., to perceive, realize, notice, sth.; to become aware, conscious, of sth.; **je m'aperçois qu'il est temps de partir**, I see, find, it is time to go; **ne pas s'a. de qch.**, to be, remain, unconscious of sth.; **sans s'en a.**, without being aware of it, without noticing it.

aperçu [apɛrsy], *s.m.* **1.** glimpse, insight; **a. sur la campagne**, glimpse of the country (through an opening); **ouvrage où il y a des aperçus très fins**, work that shows flashes of insight. **2.** general idea, outline, sketch, survey, summary; approximate estimate; **par a.**, at a rough estimate, at a rough guess. **3.** *Nau:* **(Pavillon d')a.**, answering pennant; **faire l'a.**, to acknowledge a signal.

apériodique [aperjɔdik], *a. Mec: El:* aperiodic, dead-beat (galvanometer, etc.).

apériteur [aperitœr], *s.m. Ins:* leading underwriter.

apéritif, -ive [aperitif, -iːv]. **1.** *a. & s.m.* (*a*) *Med:* sudorific, diuretic (medicine); (*b*) aperitive; **vin a.**, aperitif (wine). **2.** *s.m.* aperitif, appetizer; **l'heure de l'a.**, cocktail time; **viens prendre l'a. chez moi demain soir**, come round and have a drink tomorrow evening.

apéro [apero], *s.m. P:* = APÉRITIF 2.

aperture [apɛrtyːr], *s.f. Ling:* aperture.

apesanteur [apəzɑ̃tœr], *s.f.* weightlessness.

apétale [apetal], *a. Bot:* apetalous.

apetir [apətir], *v.tr.* to diminish.

apetissement [aptismɑ̃], *s.m. A:* diminution (in size, extent).

apetisser [aptise], *v.tr. A:* to diminish (sth., s.o.); to make (sth.) smaller.

s'apetisser, to grow smaller, diminish, shrink.

à-peu-près [apøprɛ], *s.m.inv.* **1.** approximation; rough estimate; **je n'aime pas les à-p.-p.**, I don't like loose, vague, answers, slipshod definitions; **calculer une somme par à-p.-p.**, to make a rough reckoning, calculation. **3.** *O:* pun.

apeuré [apœre, -øre], *a.* scared, frightened.

apeurer [apœre], *v.tr.* to frighten, scare.

apex [apɛks], *s.m.* apex.

apexien, -ienne [apɛksjɛ̃, -jɛn], *a. Anat:* relating to the apex of the heart.

apexique [apɛksik], *a.* apical, relating to an apex.

aphaniptères [afaniptɛːr], *s.m.pl. Ent:* Siphonaptera.

aphaniptéroïdes [afanipterɔiːd], *s.m.pl.* Aphaniptera, Siphonapteroidea.

aphasique [afazik], *a. & s. Med:* aphasic, aphasiac.

aphasie [afazi], *s.f. Med:* aphasia.

aphélie [afeli], *Astr:* **1.** *s.m.* aphelion. **2.** *a.* in aphelion.

aphémie [afemi], *s.f. Med:* aphemia.

aphérèse [aferɛːz], *s.f. Ling: Surg:* aph(a)eresis; *Ling:* aphesis.

aphidés [afide], *s.m.pl.*, **aphidiens** [afidjɛ̃], *s.m.pl. Ent:* Aphides, plant-lice, green-fly.

aphididés [afidide], *s.m.pl. Ent:* Aphididae.

aphidiphage [afidifaːʒ], *a. Z:* aphidophagous.

aphis [afis], *s.m. Ent:* aphis, plant-louse, green fly.

aphlogistique [aflɔʒistik], *a. A: Ch:* aphlogistic, uninflammable, non-inflammable.

aphone [afɔn], *a. Med:* voiceless; aphonic, aphonous.

aphonie [afɔni], *s.f. Med:* loss of voice; aphonia, aphony.

aphorisme [afɔrism], *s.m.* aphorism.

aphoristique [afɔristik], *a.* aphoristic.

aphrodisiaque [afrɔdizjak], *a. & s.m. Pharm:* aphrodisiac.

aphrodisie [afrɔdizi], *s.f. Med:* aphrodisia.

Aphrodite [afrɔdit], **1.** *Pr.n.f. Gr.Myth:* Aphrodite. **2.** *s.f. Ann:* Aphrodite; *F:* sea mouse.

aphroditidés [afrɔditide], *s.m.pl.*, **aphroditiens** [afrɔdisjɛ̃], *s.m.pl. Ann:* Aphroditidae.

aphrosidérite [afrɔsiderit], *s.f. Miner:* aphrosiderite.

aphte [aft], *s.m. Med:* aphtha; **aphtes des nouveau-nés**, thrush.

aphteux, -euse [aftø, -øːz], *a. Med:* aphthous; *Vet:* **fièvre aphteuse**, aphthous fever, foot-and-mouth disease.

aphthongie [aftɔ̃ʒi], *s.f. Med:* aphthongia.

aphtoïde [aftɔid], *a. Med:* aphthoid.

aphylle [afil], *a. Bot:* aphyllous, leafless.

api [api], *s.m. Hort:* **(pomme d')a.**, lady-apple.

à-pic [apik], *s.m.* cliff, bluff, steep; *pl. à-pics.*

apical, -aux [apikal, -o], *a. Geom: Bot: etc:* apical.

apiciforme [apisifɔrm], *a. Cryst: etc:* spicate, needle-like; apiculate, spiked.

apicole [apikɔl], *a.* apiarian; **exploitation a.**, bee-keeping.

apicule [apikyl], *s.m. Bot:* apiculus.

apiculé [apikyle], *a. Bot:* apiculate.

apiculteur [apikyltœːr], *s.m.* apiculturist, apiarist, bee-keeper.

apiculture [apikyltyːr], *s.f.* apiculture, bee-keeping, bee-rearing.

apides [apiːd], *s.f.pl.*, **apidés** [apide], *s.m.pl. Ent:* Apidae.

apiéceur, -euse [apjesœːr, -øz], *s. Tail:* piece-worker.

apigénine [apiʒenin], *s.f. Ch:* apigenin.

apiine [apiin], *s.f. Ch:* apiin.

apiol [apjɔl], *s.m. Ch: Pharm:* apiol, apiole.

apion [apjɔ̃], *s.m. Ent:* apion, gorse-weevil, seed-weevil.

apionol [apjɔnɔl], *s.m. Ch:* apionol.

apios [apiɔs], *s.m. Bot:* apios.

apiphile [apifil]. **1.** *a.* bee-loving. **2.** *s.m.* bee-lover.

apiquage [apikaːʒ], *s.m. Nau:* **1.** peaking (of gaff, etc.). **2.** steeve, steeving; angle (of bowsprit).

apiquer [apike], *v.tr.* **1.** to peak, cockbill (yard, etc.); **vergue apiquée**, yard apeak. **2.** to steeve (bowsprit).

apitoiement [apitwamɑ̃], *s.m.* commiseration, pity, compassion; **porté à l'a.**, compassionate.

apitoyant [apitwajɑ̃], *a.* piteous, pitiful (plight, tale).

apitoyer [apitwaje], *v.tr.* (**j'apitoie, n. apitoyons; j'apitoierai**) to move (to pity); to incite to pity.

s'apitoyer sur qch., to feel pity for sth; **s'a. sur qn**, to pity s.o., to feel pity for s.o.; **s'a. sur le sort de qn**, to commiserate with s.o.

apium [apjɔm], *s.m.* apium, (*scientific name for*) celery.

apivore [apivɔr], *a. & s.* apivorous, bee-eating (creature).

aplacentaires [aplasɑ̃tɛːr], *s.m.pl. Z:* aplacentalia, aplacentaria.

aplacophores [aplakɔfɔːr], *s.m.pl. Moll:* Aplacophora.

aplaignage [aplɛɲaːʒ], *s.m. Tex:* raising, teaseling, teazling (of nap).

aplaigner [aplɛɲe], *v.tr. Tex:* to raise, teasel, teazle (the nap).

aplaigneur [aplɛɲœːr], *s.m. Tex:* napper, teaseler, teazler.

aplanat [aplana], *s.m. Phot:* aplanat, aplanatic lens.

aplaner [aplane], *v.tr.* **1.** to plane, smooth (wood with a spokeshave). **2.** *Tex:* = APLAIGNER.

aplanétique [aplanetik], *a. Opt: Phot:* aplanatic (lens).

aplanétisme [aplanetism], *s.m.* aplanatism (of mirror, lens).

aplanir [aplaniːr], *v.tr.* **1.** to flatten, smooth (surface); to plane (wood); to planish (metal); to smooth out (imperfections); to float (plaster); to smooth down, remove, iron out (difficulties); to settle (dispute); **a. les difficultés pour qn,** to iron out the difficulties, to smooth things out for s.o. **2.** to level (road, etc.).

s'aplanir, (*a*) (*of road*) to grow easier, smoother; (*of difficulties*) to disappear, vanish, to be ironed out; (*b*) to become level.

aplanissage [aplanisaːʒ], *s.m.*, **aplanissement** [aplanismɑ̃], *s.m.* **1.** flattening, smoothing (of surface); planing, dressing (of timber); planishing (of metal); floating (of plaster). **2.** (*a*) levelling; (*b*) *Geol:* **aplanissement,** peneplanation.

aplanisseur, -euse [aplanisœːr, -øːz], *s.* **1.** planer, smoother; *Carp:* **a. de parquets,** floor-dresser. **2.** leveller. **3.** *s.f.* (*machine*) **aplanisseuse,** (surface) leveller.

aplasie [aplazi], *s.f. Med:* aplasia.

aplastique [aplastik], *a. Med:* **anémie a.,** aplastic anæmia.

aplat [apla], *s.m.* **1.** *Engr:* flat tint. **2.** *Dressm:* appliqué.

aplater [aplate], *v.tr. Nau:* to mess (crew).

aplati [aplati], *a.* **1.** (*a*) flattened, flat; (*b*) deflated. **2.** oblate (spheroid, etc.).

aplatir [aplatiːr], *v.tr.* **1.** to make (sth.) flat, to bring (sth.) level; to flatten (surface, seam); to flat (metal); to blunt (angle); *Metalw:* to clench (rivet); to hammer down (rivet head); to squash; **a. qch. à coups de marteau,** to beat sth. flat; **s'a. les cheveux,** to plaster down one's hair; **a. un chapeau d'un coup de poing,** to bash in a hat; **a. l'orgueil de qn,** to lower, humble, s.o.'s pride. **2.** *F:* **a. qn,** (i) to knock s.o. down, to lay s.o. out flat, to send s.o. sprawling; (ii) to floor s.o., to strike s.o. all of a heap; to squash s.o. (by piece of news, by rebuff); (iii) to beat s.o. to a frazzle.

s'aplatir. **1.** to become flat, flattened out; (of tube, balloon) to collapse; (*of tyre*) to become deflated, to get flat. **2.** **s'a. par terre,** (i) to lie down flat on the ground; (ii) *F:* to fall down flat, to come a cropper; *F:* **s'a. sur qch.,** to fall squash on sth.; *F:* **s'a. devant qn,** to grovel before s.o.

aplatissage [aplatisaːʒ], *s.m.* **1.** pressing; crushing (down); flattening; flatting (of iron, etc.); hammering down (of rivet). **2.** deflation (of tyre).

aplatissement [aplatismɑ̃], *s.m.* **1.** (*a*) = APLATISSAGE; (*b*) humiliation (of s.o.); (*c*) **a. devant la richesse,** truckling to wealth. **2.** flatness (of the earth); oblateness (of curve).

aplatisseur [aplatisœːr], *s.m.* **1.** *Metall:* (*pers.*) flatter. **2.** *Husb:* grain-crushing mill.

aplatissoir [aplatiswaːr], *s.m.* **aplatissoire** [aplatiswaːr], *s.f. Metall:* **1.** flatting-hammer. **2.** flatting-mill.

aplet [aple], *s.m. Fish:* longline.

aplite [aplit], *s.f. Miner:* aplite.

aplodontidés [aplɔdɔ̃tide], *s.m.pl. Z:* Aplodontiidae.

aplodontie [aplɔdɔ̃ti], *s.f. Z:* aplodontia.

aplomb [aplɔ̃], *s.m.* **1.** (*a*) perpendicularity, equilibrium, uprightness, just poise, balance (of pers., thg); **prendre l'a. d'un mur,** to take the plumb of a wall; **s'assurer un solide a.,** to take a firm stand on one's feet; **d'a.,** upright, vertical(ly), plumb; **marcher d'a.,** to walk steadily; **bien d'a. sur ses pieds,** steady on one's feet; *F:* **je ne suis pas d'a. aujourd'hui,** I am out of sorts, off colour, today; **voilà qui vous remettra d'a.,** that will set you up, revive you; *F:* buck you up; **me revoilà d'a.,** I am all right again; **il me faut dix mille francs pour me remettre d'a.,** I want ten thousand francs to get straight; **hors d'a.,** (i) out of plumb, out of square, out of true; (ii) *F:* wobbly, shaky; *prep.phr.* **à l'a., de qch.,** straight above, below sth.; *Tchn:* plumb with sth; (*b*) set of the legs (of horse); **a. régulier,** good stand; (*of horse*) **avoir de beaux aplombs,** to have a good stand. **2.** (self-)assurance, self-possession, coolness; **il a de l'a.,** he's a cool hand; **perdre son a.,** to lose one's self-possession, one's nerve; **avoir l'a. de dire, de faire, qch.,** to have the cheek, the impudence, to say, do, sth.; to have the nerve to do sth.; **quel a.!** what impudence! **vous en avez de l'a.!** you're a cool customer!

aplome [aplɔm], *s.m. Miner:* aplome.

aplustre [aplystr], *s.m. Rom.Ant:* aplustre (of stern of a ship).

apnée [apne], *s.f. Med:* apnoea.

apnéique [apneik], *a. Ent: Med:* apnœic, apneic.

apocalypse [apɔkalips], *s.f.* **1.** apocalypse, revelation; *B:* **l'A.,** the Book of Revelation, the Apocalypse; **les quatre cavaliers de l'A.,** the four horsemen of the Apocalypse; **style d'A.,** obscure, apocalyptic, style; **parler comme l'A.,** to speak cryptically. **2.** the end of the world; **un ciel d'a.,** a doom-laden sky; **un spectacle d'a.,** a vision out of hell.

apocalyptique [apɔkaliptik], *a.* (*a*) apocalyptic(al); (*b*) cryptic (style).

apocarpé [apɔkarpe], *a. Bot:* apocarpous.

apocarpie [apɔkarpi], *s.f. Bot:* apocarpy.

apochromatique [apɔkrɔmatik], *a. Opt:* apochromatic (lens).

apocope [apɔkɔp], *s.f. Ling:* apocope.

apocopé [apɔkɔpe], *a. Ling:* apocopated, truncated.

apocrites [apɔkrit], *s.m.pl. Ent:* Apocrita.

apocryphe [apɔkrif]. **1.** *a.* (*a*) apocryphal; (*b*) of doubtful authenticity. **2.** *s.m.pl.* **les Apocryphes,** the apocryphal books of the Old and the New Testament.

apocyn [apɔsɛ̃], *s.m. Bot:* apocynum; dog's-bane, dogbane; **a. gobe-mouches,** fly-trap; **a. à ouate,** milkweed, swallow-wort, *U.S:* silk-weed; **a. chanvrin,** Indian hemp.

apocynacées [apɔsinase], *s.f.pl.* **apocynées** [apɔsine], *s.f.pl. Bot:* Apocynaceae.

apocynum [apɔsinɔm], *s.m. Bot:* apocynum.

apode [apɔd]. *Z:* **1.** *a.* (*a*) apodal, apodous, footless; (*b*) *Ich:* without ventral fins. **2.** *s.m.* (*a*) apod, apodal, apodan; (*b*) *pl.* **apodes,** Apoda.

apodème [apɔdɛm], *s.m. Ent: Crust:* apodeme.

apodictique [apɔdiktik], *a. Log: Phil:* apod(e)ictic, clearly demonstrable, indisputable.

apodidés [apɔdide], *s.m.pl. Orn:* Apodidae.

apodie [apɔdi], *s.f. Ter:* apodia.

apodiformes [apɔdifɔrm], *s.m.pl. Orn:* Apodiformes.

apodose [apɔdoːz], *s.f. Gram:* apodosis, the main clause in a conditional sentence.

apogamie [apɔgami], *s.f. Bot:* apogamy.

apogamique [apɔgamik], *a. Biol:* apogamic, apogamous.

apogée [apɔʒe], *s.m.* (*a*) *Astr:* apogee; **la lune est à son a.,** the moon is at apogee; **être à l'a., de sa gloire,** to be at the height, zenith, acme, in the heyday, of one's glory; (*b*) *Mth:* peak (of curve).

apogon [apɔgɔ̃], *s.m. Ich:* apogon.

apographe [apɔgraf], *s.m.* apograph.

apolaire [apɔlɛːr], *a. Biol:* apolar (cell).

apolitique [apɔlitik], *a.* apolitical, outside politics; non-political.

apolitisme [apɔlitism], *s.m.* attitude of a person or organization outside politics.

apollinaire [apɔl(l)inɛːr]. **1.** *a.* apollinarian (games, etc.). **2.** *Pr.n.m.* Apollinarius.

Apollodore [apɔl(l)ɔdɔːr], *Pr.n.m. Gr.Ant:* Apollodorus.

Apollon [apɔl(l)ɔ̃]. **1.** *Pr.n.m. Myth:* Apollo; *Art:* **A. du Belvédère,** Apollo (of the) Belvedere; **c'est un A.,** he's an Adonis, a Greek god. **2.** *s.m. Ent:* Apollo butterfly.

apologétique [apɔlɔʒetik]. **1.** *a.* apologetic(al), vindicatory. **2.** *s.f. Theol:* apologetics.

apologie [apɔlɔʒi], *s.f.* apology, apologia, (de, for); defence, vindication (written) justification (de, of); **faire l'a. de qn, de qch.,** to vindicate, justify, defend, s.o., sth.; NOTE: never = EXCUSE, *q.v.*

apologique [apɔlɔʒik], *a.* apologetic, by way of justification, defence.

apologiste [apɔlɔʒist], *s.m. & f. Lit: Ecc.Hist:* apologist.

apologue [apɔlɔg], *s.m. Lit:* apologue, fable.

apoltronner [apɔltrɔne], **apoltronnir** [apɔltrɔniːr], *v.tr.* **1.** *A: & Lit:* to unman, to make cowardly. **2.** to disarm, to clip the talons (of a bird of prey).

apolyse [apɔliz], *s.f. Ecc:* (*Orthodox Church*) apolysis.

apomixie [apɔmiksi], *s.f. Biol:* apomixis.

apomorphine [apɔmɔrfin], *s.f. Ch:* apomorphine, apomorphia.

aponévrose [apɔnevroːz], *s.f. Anat:* aponeurosis, fascia.

aponévrosite [apɔnevrozit], *s.f. Med:* aponeurositis.

aponévrotique [apɔnevrɔtik], *a. Anat:* aponeurotic, fascial (membrane).

aponévrotomie [apɔnevrɔtɔmi], *s.f. Surg:* aponeurotomy.

aponogéton [apɔnɔʒetɔ̃], *s.m. Bot:* aponogeton.

aponogétonacées [apɔnɔʒetɔnase], *s.f.pl. Bot:* Aponogetonaceae.

apophonie [apɔfɔni], *s.f. Ling:* vowel gradation, ablaut, apophony.

apophtegme [apɔftɛgm], *s.m.* apophthegm.

apophyge [apɔfiːʒ], *s.f. Arch:* apophyge; spring (of column).

apophyllite [apɔfilit], *s.f. Miner:* apophyllite.

apophysaire [apɔfizɛr], *a. Anat:* apophysary.

apophyse [apɔfiːz], *s.f.* apophysis. **1.** *Anat:* process; **a. transverse,** transverse process; **l'a. coracoïde,** the coracoid process; **a. articulaire,** zygapophysis. **2.** *Bot:* offshoot. **3.** *Geol:* apophysis, offshoot.

apophysite [apɔfizit], *s.f. Med:* apophysitis.

apoplectique [apɔplɛktik], *a. & s. Med:* apoplectic.

apoplexie [apɔplɛksi], *s.f. Med:* apoplexy; cerebral haemorrhage; apoplectic seizure; **a. foudroyante,** fatal seizure; **tomber en a., être frappé d'a.,** to have an apoplectic fit; to have a stroke (of apoplexy); to have a seizure.

aporétique [apɔretik], *a. & s. A.Phil:* aporetic.

aporia [apɔria], *s.f. Ent:* black-veined white butterfly.

aporie [apɔri], *s.f. Log:* aporia.

aposématique [apɔzematik], *a. Ent:* aposematic.

aposiopèse [apɔzjɔpɛːz], *s.f. Rh:* aposiopesis.

apostasie [apɔstazi], *s.f.* apostasy.

apostasier [apɔstazje], *v.* (*pr.sub. & p.d.* **n. apostasiions, v. apostasiiez**). **1.** *v.i.* to apostatize, to become an apostate; to renounce one's party, one's principles. **2.** *v.tr.* to apostatize from (faith).

apostat, -ate [apɔsta, -at], *a. & s.* apostate.

aposter [apɔste], *v.tr.* to station, post, set (spy, agent, etc.); **a. un assassin derrière une porte,** to post, station, a murderer behind a door.

a posteriori [apɔsterjɔri], *Lt.adv.phr. Log:* a posteriori; **méthode a p.,** a posteriori method.

apostille [apɔstij], *s.f.* **1.** (marginal) recommendation (on petition, etc.). **2.** (*a*) *Jur:* marginal note (to deed, etc.); apostil, footnote, side-note; (*b*) *Nau:* entry (in log).

apostiller [apɔstije], *v.tr.* **1.** to add a (marginal) recommendation to (petition, etc.). **2.** *Jur:* to add a marginal note to (document).

apostolat [apɔstɔla], *s.m.* apostolate, apostleship.

apostolicité [apɔstɔlisite], *s.f.* apostolicity.

apostolique [apɔstɔlik], *a.* **1.** apostolic (times, Church, etc.). **2.** apostolic, papal; **vicaire a.,** vicar apostolic; **pères apostoliques,** apostolic fathers.

apostoliquement [apɔstɔlikmɑ̃], *adv.* apostolically.

apostrophe[1] [apɔstrɔf], *s.f.* (*a*) *Rh:* apostrophe; (*b*) reproach, reprimand; **adresser une a. à qn,** to reprimand s.o.

apostrophe[2], *s.f. Gram:* apostrophe.

apostropher[1] [apɔstrɔfe], *v.tr.* (*a*) to apostrophize; (*b*) (i) to upbraid (s.o.); **a. qn d'injures,** to abuse s.o.; (ii) to speak peremptorily (to s.o.).

apostropher[2], *v.tr. Gram:* to apostrophize (preposition, article, etc.).

apothèce [apɔtɛs], *s.f.*, **apothécie** [apɔtesi], *s.f. Fung:* apothecium.

apothème [apɔtɛm], *s.m. Geom:* apothem.

apothéose [apɔteoːz], *s.f.* **1.** apotheosis; deification. **2.** *Th:* grand finale, transformation scene (of fairy play, etc.).

apothéoser [apɔteoze], *v.tr.* to apotheosize; to deify.

apothicaire [apɔtikɛːr], *s.m. A:* apothecary; *Pej:* **mémoire, compte, d'a.,** exorbitant bill.

apothicairerie [apɔtikɛr(ə)ri], *s.f. A:* apothecary's shop; pharmacy, dispensary.

apôtre [apoːtr], *s.m.* apostle; **cuiller avec figurine d'a.,** apostle spoon; **se faire l'a. d'une cause,** to become the advocate, apostle, of a cause; **un bon a.,** a sanctimonious rogue; **faire le bon a.,** to sham the honest man, to play the saint.

apôtres [apoːtr], *s.f.pl. N.Arch:* knightheads.

apozème [apɔzɛm], *s.m. Pharm:* apozem; decoction.

Appalaches [apalaʃ], *Pr.n.m.pl. Geog:* **les (monts) Appalaches,** the Appalachian Mountains.

appalachien, -ienne [apalaʃjɛ̃, -jɛn], *a. Geog:* Appalachian; **relief a.,** Appalachian relief, topography.

appaméen, -enne [apameɛ̃, -ɛn], *a. & s. Geog:* (native, inhabitant) of Pamiers.

apparaître [aparɛːtr], *v.i.* (*conj. like* PARAÎTRE; *the auxiliary is usu.* **être,** *occ.* **avoir**) **1.** to appear; to become visible, to come into sight; **une île apparut à l'horizon,** an island loomed up on the

horizon; a. à travers le brouillard, to loom out of the fog; un spectre lui était apparu, a ghost had appeared to him; a. brusquement aux regards, to come suddenly into view; Phot: (of detail) a. distinctement, to come out (clearly). 2. (a) to appear (to one's mind); to become evident; la vérité lui apparut, the truth became apparent to him; (b) le projet lui apparaissait impossible, the plan seemed impossible to him. 3. (= SEMBLER) (a) A: il m'apparaît que . . ., it seems to me that . . .; (b) il apparut bientôt que . . ., it soon became obvious that . . .

apparat [apara], s.m. 1. state, pomp, show, display; dîner d'a., banquet; discours d'a., set speech; lettres d'a., illuminated capitals (in ancient MSS., etc.). 2. (a) A: concordance (of an author); (b) a. critique, critical apparatus, apparatus criticus.

apparaux [aparo], s.m.pl. 1. Nau: tackle, gear; a. des ancres, anchor(ing) gear; les gros a., the purchase; a. de mouillage, ground tackle; a. de chaloupe, launch tackle; Jur: agrès et a., tackle. 2. gymnastic apparatus.

appareil [aparɛj], s.m. 1. (a) Lit: (all that goes to make for) display, magnificence, pomp; (b) mettre en jeu l'a. de la justice, to put the machinery of the law in motion; (c) (i) A: garb, apparel; (ii) dans le plus simple a., in the nude. 2. (a) apparatus; equipment; Ind: (sg. or pl.) plant; Petroleum Ind: still; appareils de laboratoire, laboratory apparatus; a. auxiliaire, de secours, stand-by equipment; a. de pêche, fishing tackle; Min: a. de forage, drilling rig; Anat: a. vocal, vocal apparatus; a. digestif, digestive system; (b) device, appliance, fixture, apparatus (for safety, lubricating, etc.); gear, mechanism; a. à gaz, gas appliance; Mch: etc: a. de mise en marche, starting gear; a. de changement de marche, reversing gear; Rail: a. de voie, switch gear; a. de vissage, screwing tackle; a. de levage, lifting appliance; Nau: a. pour mâter, purchase for masting; (c) machine, instrument; (i) Tp: telephone; qui est à l'a.? who's speaking? gardez l'a.! hold the line! Tg: a. à cadran, dial instrument; (ii) W.Tel: A: a. à galène, a. à lampes, crystal set, valve set; (iii) Av: plane; a. de chasse, fighter; a. d'école, training aircraft, trainer; a. à coussin d'air, hovercraft; (iv) Phot: a. (photographique), a.-photo, camera; a. à plaques, plate camera; a. reflex, reflex camera; a. (à forme rigide), box camera; a. à pied, field camera, stand camera; A: a. à instantané, snapshot camera; O: a. à pellicules, roll-film camera; (v) a. contre la surdité, pour sourds, de correction auditive, hearing aid; a. de prothèse, prosthesis, artificial limb, etc.; Dent: a. (dentaire), brace; (vi) a. à sous, slot machine; fruit machine, one-armed bandit. 3. Surg: dressing (on wound). 4. Const: (a) height (of stones); assise de grand a., course of large stones; (b) bond; a. anglais, old English bond; a. polonais, double Flemish bond; a. croisé, cross-bond; a. de boutisses, heading bond; a. en besace, toothing; s.a. POLYGONAL. 5. Lit: a. critique, critical apparatus; apparatus criticus. 6. Cu: mixture, filling.

appareillade [aparɛjad], s.f. Orn: pairing of partridges.

appareillage[1] [aparɛja:ʒ], s.m. 1. (a) installation, fitting up, preparation, setting up (of wireless receiving station, etc.); (b) Const: (i) drafting (of stones); (ii) bonding (of stones, bricks); (c) Nau: getting under way; weighing; setting sail; (d) fitting (of s.o.) with artificial limbs; Adm: centre d'a., artificial limb supply centre. 2. (a) outfit, fittings, equipment, accessories; instrumentation; a. électrique d'une auto, electrical equipment of a car; (b) Ind: plant.

appareillage[2], s.m., **appareillement** [aparɛjmɑ̃], s.m. 1. matching (of colours, of dinner-service, etc.). 2. pairing, mating (of animals for breeding); pairing (of oxen for the yoke).

appareiller[1] [apareje], v.tr. 1. to install, fit up (workshop, etc.). 2. Const: (a) to draft (stones, for shaping); (b) to bond (stones, bricks); (c) Tex: to tune (a loom). 3. to spread (net). 4. Nau: (a) a. une voile, to trim a sail; a. un vaisseau en voiles latines, to rig a ship with lateen sails; (b) abs. to get under way; to weigh, to set sail; a. à la vapeur, à la voile, to get under steam, under sail.

appareiller[2], v.tr. = APPARIER.

appareilleur [aparɛjœ:r], s.m. (a) trimmer, fitter, dresser (of stone, etc.); (b) Const: (i) house carpenter; (ii) foreman mason; maître a., master bondman; (c) a. à gaz, gas-fitter; (d) Tex: tuner (of looms).

apparemment [aparamɑ̃], adv. 1. apparently, to all appearances; obviously. 2. A: clearly.

apparence [aparɑ̃:s], s.f. 1. (a) appearance, semblance, look; quelque a. de (la) vérité, some semblance of truth; partout il y a une a. de confort, there is an air of comfort everywhere; il y a toute, grande, a. qu'il dit vrai, there is every indication of his speaking the truth; il y a toute a. de beau temps pour demain, it looks as though it will be fine tomorrow; selon toute a., to all appearances; il se manifesta sous l'a. de . . ., he appeared in the guise, in the shape of . . .; (b) (fausse) a., false, fallacious, appearance; s'introduire chez qn sous de fausses apparences, to force one's way in under false pretences; en a., outwardly, on the surface; en a. il vous protège, he makes a show, a pretence, of protecting you; plus difficile en a. qu'en réalité, less difficult than it looks; il venait en a. pour vendre sa marchandise, he came ostensibly to sell his goods. 2. avoir de l'a., (i) (of pers.) to have a good presence; (ii) (of thg) to look well; de belle a., of good appearance; good-looking; sauver les apparences, to keep up appearances; pour sauver les apparences, for the sake of appearances; to save face; faire qch. pour les apparences, to do sth. for show; il ne faut pas se fier aux apparences, one should not, cannot, judge by appearances; s.a. JUGER I. 2. 3. A: likelihood; je n'y vois point d'a., I see no likelihood, no probability, of it; il est hors d'a. que . . ., it is unlikely that . . .

apparent [aparɑ̃], a. 1. (a) visible, conspicuous, apparent; couleur peu apparente, faint, inconspicuous, colour; défaut peu a., hardly noticeable defect; Phot: papier à image apparente, printing-out paper, P.O.P.; (b) obvious, evident. 2. apparent, not real; mouvement a. du soleil, apparent movement of the sun; piété apparente, sham, seeming, piety. 3. Jur: héritier a., heir-apparent.

apparentage [aparɑ̃ta:ʒ], s.m. alliance, connection (by marriage).

apparentement [aparɑ̃tmɑ̃], s.m. political alliance.

apparenté [aparɑ̃te], a. (a) related (by marriage); Jur: affinitive (à, avec, to); bien a., well connected; (b) Ch: éléments apparentés, related, affinitive, elements; (c) Pol: (of lists of candidates) worked in conjunction; (d) closely connected.

apparenter [aparɑ̃te], v.tr. A: to ally, connect (by marriage).

s'apparenter (à). 1. to marry into (the nobility, etc.). 2. to have sth. in common with . . . 3. Pol: to make a political alliance.

appariage [aparia:ʒ], s.m., **appariement** [aparimɑ̃], s.m. 1. Lit: pairing, matching; harmonizing 2. mating, coupling (of birds).

apparié [aparje], a. Atom.Ph: réseaux appariés, paired lattice.

apparier [aparje], v.tr. (p.d. & pr.sub. n. appariions, v. appariiez) 1. to match, pair (socks, horses, etc.); to pair off (opponents). 2. to couple, pair, mate (birds for breeding).

s'apparier, (of birds) to pair, mate.

appariteur [aparitœ:r], s.m. 1. apparitor, beadle, mace-bearer (of university court, of corporation). 2. A: (laboratory) attendant.

apparition [aparisjɔ̃], s.f. 1. appearance, advent; coming out; publication (of book, etc.); emergence (of new state, of new leader, etc.); faire son a., to make one's appearance, F: to turn up; une courte a. de la lune nous permit de nous orienter, a glimpse of the moon allowed us to take our bearings; il a fait une courte a., (i) he put in a brief appearance; (ii) he popped in for a moment. 2. (a) apparition, ghost, spectre; on nous a avertis d'une a. lorsque la cloche sonnera minuit, we have been warned that a ghost will appear on the stroke of twelve; (b) vision (of angels, etc.).

apparoir [aparwa:r], v.i.def. (used only in third pers.sg. pr.ind. il appert, and in inf.); Jur: to appear; comme il appert par jugement du tribunal, as it appears from a judgment of the court; faire apparoir son bon droit, to show, establish, one's right.

appartement [apartəmɑ̃], s.m. 1. (a) flat, U.S: apartment; suite, set of rooms; j'ai un a. en ville, I have a flat in town; a. de passage, pied-à-terre; plantes d'a., indoor plants; (b) (in château, etc.) les grands appartements, l'a. de parade, the state apartments; appartements domestiques, living quarters; appartements de réception, public, reception, rooms: (c) Fr. C: room. 2. A: reception, levée; tenir a., to hold a reception.

appartenance [apartənɑ̃:s], s.f. 1. action of belonging; a. à un parti, adherence to, membership of, a party. 2. Phil: logical relationship between an individual and the class to which he belongs. 3. property. 4. pl. (a) appurtenances (of house, castle); (b) Equit: (saddle) accessories, appurtenances.

appartenant [apartənɑ̃], a. Jur: appurtenant, pertaining; somme d'argent à lui appartenante, sum of money pertaining to him.

appartenir [apartəni:r], v.i. (conj. like TENIR) 1. to belong (à, to); to be owned (à, by); cette maison lui appartient en propre, this house is his own personal property; l'avenir appartient aux audacieux, the future belongs to the bold; cela n'appartient pas à mes fonctions, this does not come within the scope of my duties; navire appartenant au port de Londres, ship hailing from London. 2. v. impers. à tous ceux qu'il appartient, to all whom it may concern; ainsi qu'il appartiendra, as it shall be deemed advisable, as shall seem fit; il lui appartient de . . ., it is part of his functions to . . .; it rests with him to . . ., it falls to him to . . .; il appartient au besoin au conseil de décider, the Council may decide; il ne m'appartient pas de le critiquer, it is not for me to criticize him; il appartient à lui de réussir, he must depend on himself for success; il appartient à lui seul de . . ., it rests with him alone to . . .; Iron: il vous appartient bien de me critiquer, you're a fine one to criticize me.

s'appartenir. 1. to be one's own master; il y a des jours où je ne m'appartiens pas, there are days when my time is not my own. 2. il ne s'appartenait plus, he was beside himself, he had lost control of himself.

appas [apɑ], s.m.pl. 1. (physical) charms, esp. breasts (of woman). 2. lure, attraction (of wealth, etc.).

appât [apɑ], s.m. 1. (a) bait; a. de fond, ground-bait; mettre l'a. à la ligne, to bait the line; mordre à l'a., to rise to the bait; c'est un trop vieux poisson pour mordre à l'a., he is too old a bird to be caught with chaff; a. de vase, mud-worm; (b) lure (of success); attraction, allurement (of pleasure). 2. Husb: soft food (for poultry).

appâter [apɑte], v.tr. 1. to lure (birds, fishes, etc.) with a bait; to entice (pers.). 2. to feed (poultry) forcibly; to cram (geese). 3. to bait (a hook, etc.).

appaumée [apome], a.f. Her: appaumé(e).

appauvrir [apovri:r], v.tr. to impoverish; a. la constitution de qn, to weaken s.o.'s constitution.

s'appauvrir. (a) to grow poor(er), to become impoverished; (b) (of thg) to become impoverished; notre théâtre s'appauvrit en idées, our drama is becoming poorer in ideas; (of soil) to lose its fertility.

appauvrissant [apovrisɑ̃], a. impoverishing.

appauvrissement [apovrismɑ̃], s.m. impoverishment (of country, of health, etc.); degeneration (of race); deterioration (of stock); thinning (of blood).

appeau, -eaux [apo], s.m. 1. Ven: (a) decoy-bird; stool-pigeon; lure; (b) bird-call; se faire prendre à l'a., to be lured into the trap. 2. Clockm: bell striking the quarters; quarter-bell.

appel [apɛl], s.m. 1. appeal; (a) calling; calling in (of specialist, etc.); faire a. à qn, to appeal to s.o., to send for s.o., to call upon s.o.'s help, services; faire a. à un expert, to call in an expert; to send for an expert; faire un a. au peuple, (i) to appeal to the public; (ii) F: to have a whip-round; faire a. à tout son courage, to summon up, call on, call forth, all one's courage; le moteur part au premier a., the engine starts at the first touch of the switch; Cards: faire un a. à trèfle, to ask for a club return; (b) Jur: appeal at law; avis d'a., notice of appeal; cour d'a., Court of Appeal; faire a. (à un tribunal) d'une décision, to appeal (to a court) against a decision; interjeter a., to lodge an appeal; accorder l'a. à qn, to give s.o. liberty to appeal; to grant a new trial to s.o.; juger en a. (d'une décision), to hear an appeal (from a decision); casser un jugement en a., to quash a sentence on appeal; jugement sans a., final judgment; la décision de cette cour est sans a., there is no appeal from this court. 2. call, (vocal) summons; l'a. du printemps, the call of spring; l'a. de la mer, sea fever; l'a. de la conscience, the voice of conscience; on a sonné l'a. au dîner, the dinner-bell has gone; cri d'a., call for help; Equit: a. de langue, click (of the tongue); a. d'incendie, fire alarm; sonnette d'a.,

call bell; *Fin:* **faire un a. de fonds,** to call up capital; **avis d'a. de fonds,** call letter; *Com:* **a. d'offres,** invitation to tender; **faire un a. d'offres,** to invite bids, tenders; *F:* **faire un a. du pied à,** to make advances to; *Mil:* **l'a. aux armes,** the call to arms; **a. de mobilisation,** mobilization order; **a. d'une classe,** calling up, call-up, of a class; *s.a.* DEVANCER 3, ORDRE 5; *Tg: Tp:* **touche d'a.,** call-key; **signe d'a.,** ringing tone; **a. téléphonique,** (tele)phone call; **a. avec préavis,** personal call, *U.S:* person to person call; *Tp: Nau:* **lettres d'a., indicatif d'a.,** call letters; *Av:* **a. particulier,** selective calling; **a. codé,** code tone; *s.a.* PHONIQUE. **3.** roll-call, call-over; **feuille d'a.,** roll; *Nau:* muster-roll; **faire l'a.,** (i) to call the roll, to take the call-over; (ii) (*on ship*) to muster (all hands); *Mil:* **l'a. du soir,** tattoo; **battre, sonner l'a.,** to beat, sound the (fall-in) call; *F:* **battre l'a. (dans les journaux),** to rouse public opinion; **répondre à l'a.,** to answer the roll-call, to answer (to) one's name; **manquant à l'a.,** missing; *F:* **il manque un livre à l'a.,** there is one book missing; *s.a.* NOMINAL I, RÉPONDRE I. **4.** *E:* **a. d'air,** intake of air, in-draught, suction; **vitesse d'a.,** inflow; *Nau:* lead (of a rope); *Magn:* **a. d'un aimant,** pull of a magnet. **5.** reference mark; *Typ:* **a. de note,** footnote reference, superior figure. **6.** *Fenc:* alarm; appel; **un bon coup d'a. sur le tremplin,** a good kick-off from the springboard; *Sp:* take-off.

appelable [aplabl̩], *a. Jur:* appealable (action).

appelant, -ante [aplɑ̃, -ɑ̃:t]. **1.** *Jur: a.* appealing (party, etc.); (*b*) *s.* **a. d'un jugement,** appellant against a judgement; **se porter a.,** to appeal. **2.** *s.m. Ven:* decoy (bird), stool pigeon, call-bird.

appeler [aple], *v.tr.* (**j'appelle, n. appelons, j'appellerai**) **1.** (*a*) to call, call to (s.o.); *abs.* to call out; **il a appelé,** he called (out); **a. au secours,** to call for help; (*b*) to call, hail (taxi); **a. qn de la main, du geste,** to beckon (to) s.o.; (*c*) *Tp:* **a. qn (au téléphone),** to ring s.o. up, *U.S:* to call s.o.; **a. Paris à l'automatique,** to dial Paris; **a. un taxi, un médecin,** to phone for a taxi, a doctor; **a. l'ascenseur,** to ring for the lift, *U.S:* to call the elevator. **2.** (*a*) to call in, send for, summon (s.o.); *Jur:* to summon (s.o.) to attend; **faire a. un médecin,** to call in, send for, a doctor; *Mil:* **a. une classe,** to call up a class; *s.* **les appelés,** the conscripts; *U.S:* draft-ees; **a. qn sous les drapeaux,** to call s.o. to the colours; **le devoir m'appelle,** duty calls (me); **être appelé au trône,** to be called to the throne; **être appelé à une haute fonction,** to be called to high office; **a. qn en duel,** to call s.o. out; *Jur:* **a. qn en justice,** to summon(s) s.o., to sue s.o.; **a. qn à témoin,** to call s.o. to witness; *Fin:* **capital appelé,** called up capital; (*b*) **être appelé à qch.,** to be destined for sth.; **être appelé à faire qch.,** to be bound to do sth.; **industrie appelée à un brillant avenir,** industry marked out for a brilliant future; **les petites exploitations sont appelées à être supprimées,** the small farms are doomed, are bound to be abolished. **3.** to call (by name); to term, name; **nous l'avons appelé Jean,** we have called him John; *F:* **si j'arrive en retard je vais me faire a. Arthur,** if I'm late my name will be mud; **a. les choses par leur nom,** to call a spade a spade; **vous appelez cela danser?** do you call that dancing? **voilà ce que j'appelle une sotte réponse,** I call that a stupid answer; *Cards:* **a. l'atout,** *abs.* **appeler,** to call, declare (a suit, trumps). **4.** (*a*) to appeal to, call on, invoke (s.o., sth.); **a. une bénédiction, la colère du ciel, sur qn,** to invoke, call down, a blessing, the wrath of heaven, upon s.o.; **a. qn à faire qch.,** to call on, invite, s.o. to do sth; (*b*) to call for (sth.); to invite (criticism); **ce problème appelle une solution immédiate,** the problem calls for an immediate solution. **5.** (*a*) to provoke, arouse, attract; **la vanité appelle le mépris des autres,** conceit provokes the contempt of others; *Prov:* **un malheur en appelle un autre,** misfortunes never come singly; **en mécanique le jeu appelle le jeu,** in machinery play begets play; (*b*) **corps appelé par une force,** body pulled, attracted, by a force. **6.** *v.i.* (*a*) *Jur:* **a. d'un jugement,** to appeal against a sentence; **il veut en a. de sa défaite,** he wants to issue a fresh challenge; **j'en appelle de votre décision,** I challenge your decision; (*b*) **en appeler à qn,** to appeal to s.o.; **en a. au Seigneur,** to call on the Lord; **j'en appelle à votre honneur,** I appeal to your honour; **j'en appelle à votre témoignage,** I call you to witness.

s'appeler, to be called, named, termed; **comment vous appelez-vous?** what is your name? **je m'appelle . . .,** my name is . . .; *F:* **voilà qui s'appelle pleuvoir!** that's something like rain! there's rain with a vengeance!

appelet [aple], *s.m. Fish:* longline.

appeleur [aplœ:r], *s.m. Ven:* decoy-bird.

appellatif, -ive [apɛl(l)atif, -i:v], *a. & s.m. Gram: Log:* appellative.

appellation [apɛl(l)asjɔ̃], *s.f.* **1.** appellation; (*a*) name, term; **a. injurieuse,** abusive term; (*b*) way of naming, nomenclature; designation; trade name; (*c*) *Vit:* **a. contrôlée,** guaranteed vintage; **vin sans a.,** non-vintage wine; **des bourgognes d'a.,** vintage burgundies. **2.** *Jur:* appeal at law; *s.a.* NÉANT 1.

appendice [ap(p)ɛ̃dis], *s.m.* **1.** appendix, supplement (of book). **2.** annex(e), appendage (of building). **3.** (*a*) *Anat: Bot:* (i) appendix; (ii) appendage; **a. caudal,** caudal appendage; **l'a. vermiforme,** the vermiform appendix; (*b*) *Hum:* proboscis. **4.** (*a*) neck (of balloon); (*b*) tail (of aircraft).

appendicectomie [apɛ̃disɛktɔmi], *s.f. Med:* append(ic)ectomy.

appendicitaire [ap(p)ɛ̃disitɛ:r], *s.m.* appendicitis patient.

appendicite [ap(p)ɛ̃disit], *s.f. Med:* appendicitis; **a. chronique,** grumbling appendix.

appendicocèle [apɛ̃dikɔsɛl], *s.f. Med:* appendicocele, appendicular hernia.

appendicostomie [apɛ̃dikɔstɔmi], *s.f. Surg:* appendicostomy.

appendiculaire [ap(p)ɛ̃dikylɛ:r]. **1.** *a. Anat: Bot:* appendicular. **2.** *s.m.pl. Z:* Appendicularia.

appendicule [ap(p)ɛ̃dikyl], *s.m. Bot:* appendicle, small appendix, small appendage.

appendiculé [ap(p)ɛ̃dikyle], *a. Bot:* appendiculate.

appendre [apɑ̃:dr̩], *Lit:* **1.** *v.tr.* to hang (up against sth.); to suspend (flag, ex voto, etc.) (on wall, etc.). **2.** *v.i.* to hang; **des trophées appendent aux murs,** trophies hang on the walls.

appension [apɑ̃sjɔ̃], *s.f.* suspension (of a limb by means of a sling).

appentis [apɑ̃ti], *s.m.* **1.** *Const:* (*a*) penthouse; lean-to (building); **toit en a.,** lean-to roof; (*b*) outhouse; shed (built on to main building).

appertisation [apɛrtizasjɔ̃], *s.f.* bottling, preserving (of food).

appesantir [apəzɑ̃ti:r], *v.tr.* **1.** to make (sth.) heavy; to weigh (sth.) down; **yeux appesantis par le sommeil,** eyes heavy with sleep. **2.** to dull; to render (the step, the mind, etc.) less active. **3.** to bring (sth.) down heavily; **a. son autorité sur le peuple,** to lord it more heavily on the people.

s'appesantir. 1. (*of burden, etc.*) to become heavy; **la fatalité s'appesantit sur nous,** fate weighs heavy on us. **2. s'a. (trop) sur un sujet,** to lay (too much) stress, dwell (too long), (over-)insist, on a subject.

appesantissement [apəzɑ̃tismɑ̃], *s.m.* increasing heaviness (of mind, body, etc.); increasing dullness (of mind).

appétence [ap(p)etɑ̃:s], *s.f.* appetency, appetence (**de, pour,** of, for, after); craving, desire (for).

appéter [ap(p)ete], *v.tr.* (**j'appète, n. appétons; j'appéterai**) *A:* to have a craving, to crave, for (sth.).

appétissant [apetisɑ̃], *a.* (*a*) tempting, appetizing; savoury; (*b*) alluring.

appétit [apeti], *s.m.* **1.** appetite; **couper l'a. à qn,** to spoil, take away, s.o.'s appetite; **demeurer, rester, sur son a.,** (i) to eat sparingly, to curb one's appetite; (ii) to remain unsatisfied; **manger de bon a., avec a.,** to eat heartily, with relish, with gusto; **bon a.!** (i) I hope you (will) enjoy your dinner; (ii) fall to! **avoir un a. de loup, de cheval,** to be ravenous; **avoir un a. d'oiseau,** to have a small, poor, appetite; to eat like a bird; **avoir bon a.,** to have a hearty appetite; **je n'ai plus d'a.,** I am off my feed; *Prov:* **l'a. vient en mangeant,** (i) when once you start eating you soon get hungry; (ii) the more a man gets the more he wants; the appetite grows with what it feeds on. **2.** appetite, desire, craving, lust (**de,** for); **mortifier les appétits,** to mortify carnal appetites; **a. du gain,** greed, craving, for money; **mettre qn en a., aiguiser l'a. de qn.,** (i) to give s.o. an appetite, to whet s.o.'s appetite; (ii) to set s.o. agog (for sth.). **3.** *pl. Cu:* (*a*) appetizers, seasoning; (*b*) chives.

appétitif, -ive [apetitif, -i:v], *a. A:* appetitive.

appétition [apetisjɔ̃], *s.f. Phil: etc:* appetition.

appienne [ap(p)jɛn], *a.f.* **la Voie a.,** the Appian Way.

applaudimètre [aplodimɛtr̩], *s.m. T.V: etc:* clapometer.

applaudir [aplodi:r]. **1.** *v.tr.* (*a*) to applaud, clap (s.o., sth.); **a. vivement qn, qch.,** to receive s.o., sth., with loud applause; *F:* to give a big hand to s.o.; *F:* **se faire a. à tout casser,** to bring the house down; (*b*) to applaud, approve, commend (s.o., sth.); **a. qn d'un choix,** to approve s.o.'s choice; **a. qn d'avoir fait qch.,** to commend s.o. for doing sth. **2.** *v.ind.tr.* **a. à qch.,** to approve, commend, sth.

s'applaudir. 1. to have a high opinion of oneself, to pat oneself on the back. **2. s'a. de qch., d'avoir fait qch.,** to congratulate oneself on sth., on having done sth.

applaudissement [aplodismɑ̃], *s.m. usu. pl.* **1.** applause, clapping; **salve d'applaudissements,** round of applause; **soulever les applaudissements,** to be applauded, to be greeted with applause. **2.** approval, commendation, approbation; **couvrir qn d'applaudissements,** to praise s.o. up to the skies.

applaudisseur [aplodisœ:r], *s.m.* applauder; *Th:* **applaudisseurs à gages,** hired applauders; *claque.*

applicabilité [aplikabilite], *s.f.* applicability, appropriateness (**à,** to).

applicable [aplikabl̩], *a.* **1.** that can be applied; **l'or est a. sur certains métaux,** gold can be applied to certain metals. **2.** (*a*) applicable; **loi a. à un cas,** law applicable to a case; **cette règle est a. à tous les cas,** this rule applies to all cases; **règlement a. à partir du premier janvier,** regulation to take effect from the first of January; **mot a.,** appropriate, suitable, word; **traitement a. à une fonction,** salary appropriate to, that goes with, an office; (*b*) chargeable (against sth.); **les dommages-intérêts sont applicables à la partie lésée,** the damages go to the injured party.

applicage [aplika:ʒ], *s.m.* application, applying (of ornaments to pottery, etc.).

applicateur [aplikatœ:r], *s.m.* (*device*) applicator.

application [aplikasjɔ̃], *s.f.* application. **1.** (*a*) **a. de qch. à, sur, qch.,** application, superposition, laying, of sth. (up)on sth.; **a. d'un bandage sur une blessure,** applying of a bandage to a wound; (*b*) **première a. de peinture,** first coat of paint; (*c*) *Needlew:* **a. d'Angleterre,** Honiton lace; **broderie d'a.,** appliqué (work); (*d*) **bois d'a.,** veneer. **2. a. d'une loi à un cas,** application of a law to a case; **une nouvelle a. de cette loi,** a new application of this law; **pour l'a. de la présente convention . . .,** for the purpose of this convention . . .; **a. de la loi,** enforcement of the law; **fonctionnaires chargés de l'a. de la loi,** (law) enforcement officers; **a. d'une règle,** applying, working, of a rule; **mettre une théorie en a.,** to put a theory into practice, to apply a theory; **faire l'a. de qch. à qch., à qn,** to apply sth. to sth., to s.o.; **en a. de ce décret,** in pursuance of this decree; *Jur:* **a. de, d'une, peine,** determination of penalty; *Mil: Navy:* **école d'a.,** school of instruction. **3.** diligence, steadiness, industriousness (in work); **travailler avec a.,** to apply oneself to one's work, to work diligently; **style qui sent l'a.,** laboured style.

applique [aplik], *s.f.* **1.** application (against wall, etc.); **treuil d'a.,** wall-hoist, bracket-crab; **lampe d'a.,** bracket-lamp. **2.** applied ornament; *Needlew:* appliquéd ornament; *Bookb:* (i) paste-on label; (ii) (leather) inlay. **3.** (*a*) (wall-) bracket (for lamps, etc.); (*b*) sconce, bracket-lamp. **4.** *Rail:* = CONTRE-AIGUILLE.

appliqué [aplike], *a.* **1.** studious, diligent (person); **écriture appliquée,** painstaking handwriting. **2. sciences appliquées,** applied sciences. **3.** *Needlew:* appliquéd (trimming).

appliquer [aplike], *v.tr.* to apply. **1. a. qch. sur, à, contre, qch.,** to apply sth. on, to, sth.; **a. une couche de peinture sur qch.,** to apply a coat of paint to sth.; **a. une échelle contre un mur,** to set up, lean, a ladder against a wall; **n'appliquez pas trop le crayon sur le papier,** don't press too hard on the pencil; **a. une gifle à qn,** to slap, smack, s.o.'s face; **a. un coup de pied à qn,** to give s.o. a kick, to kick s.o.; **un coup bien appliqué,** a well-planted blow; **a. des coups de bâton à qn,** to give s.o. a thrashing. **2. a. l'algèbre à la géométrie,** to apply algebra to geometry; **a. une loi à un cas particulier,** to apply the law to, to bring a law to bear upon, a special case; **a. une somme à qch.,** to apply, devote, a sum of money to sth.; **a. une épithète à qn,** to apply an epithet to s.o.; **s'a. un éloge,** to appropriate the praise; **a. (les dispositions de) la loi,** to bring, put, the law into operation; to carry out, enforce, administer, the law; *Jur:* **a. le maximum de la peine,** to impose the

maximum penalty; **les méthodes appliquées actuellement,** the methods now in force. **3. a. son esprit à ses études,** to apply one's mind to one's studies.

s'appliquer. 1. s'a. à qch., to apply oneself, to sth., to take pains over sth., to work hard at sth.; *F:* to put one's back into sth., to buckle to (a task); **s'a. à l'étude,** to apply oneself to study; **s'a. à faire qch.,** to apply oneself to doing sth., to lay oneself out to do sth.; **il s'applique à apprendre le français,** he is making a serious effort to learn French; *abs.* **un enfant qui s'applique,** a studious child; a good pupil. **2.** (*of law, etc.*) to apply (à, to); **à qui s'applique cette remarque?** to whom does this remark apply? to whom are you referring?

appog(g)iature [apɔʒjatyːr], *s.f. Mus:* appoggiatura.

appoint [apwɛ̃], *s.m.* **1.** added portion; (*a*) *Com: Fin:* balance, odd money; **le public, le débiteur, est tenu de faire l'a.,** the public must tender the exact amount, the debtor is bound to make up the even money; "no change given"; (*b*) **ressources d'a.,** means of making up one's income; **eau d'a.,** make-up water (for accumulator, etc.); *Aut:* **faire l'a.,** to top up (battery, engine oil, etc.); **chauffage, éclairage, d'a.,** auxiliary heating, lighting; **siège d'a.,** extra chair. **2.** contribution; **apporter son a. à qch.,** to contribute to sth., to take a part in sth.; **élu avec des appoints de gauche,** elected with help from the left; **les soirées sont animées par le double a. du bridge et de la radio,** bridge and the radio contribute equally to the pleasure of the evenings.

appointage [apwɛ̃taːʒ], *s.m.* **1.** *Leath:* fulling. **2.** pointing, sharpening (of pencil, etc.).

appointé [apwɛ̃te], *a. Her:* appointé.

appointements [apwɛ̃tmɑ̃], *s.m.pl.* salary, emoluments, allowance; *Ecc:* stipend; **toucher ses a.,** to draw one's salary.

appointer[1] [apwɛ̃te], *v.tr.* **1.** *Jur: A:* (*a*) to settle (case) amicably; (*b*) to fix a day for (hearing of a case). **2.** to pay, give, a salary to; **commis appointés,** salaried clerks. **3.** *Mil:* **a. un homme de corvée,** to put a man on extra fatigue.

appointer[2], *v.tr.* to point, sharpen (pencil, etc.).

appointir [apwɛ̃tiːr], *v.tr. Tchn:* to point (needles, stakes, etc.).

appontage [apɔ̃taːʒ], *s.m. Nav: Av:* landing on flight-deck of aircraft carrier; **officier d'a.,** landing officer; **miroir d'a.,** landing mirror; **crosse, crochet, d'a.,** arrester hook.

appontement [apɔ̃tmɑ̃], *s.m. Nau:* **1.** (wooden) staging (of wharf). **2.** (wooden, iron) wharf, pier, quay; landing-stage. **3.** = APPONTAGE.

apponter [apɔ̃te], *v.i. Nav: Av:* to land (on deck of aircraft carrier).

apponteur [apɔ̃tœːr], *s.m. & a. Nav: Av:* **(officier) a.,** landing officer.

apport [apɔːr], *s.m.* **1.** (*action of bringing*) contribution, contributing; (*a*) *Fin:* **a. de capitaux,** contribution of capital; **a. en nature,** contribution in kind; **a. effectif,** conveyance of actual chattels; **capital d'a.,** initial capital; **actions d'a.,** founder's, promoter's, shares; (*b*) *Jur:* **a. de pièces,** deposit(ing) of documents (in a suit); (*c*) *Jur:* **biens d'a.,** estate brought in by husband or wife upon marriage; (*d*) *Mil:* **a. de munitions,** bringing up of munitions; *Civ.E: Fort:* **terres d'a.,** earthworks; (*e*) *Pol.Ec:* inflow; influx; **a. d'argent frais,** injection of new money. **2.** (*thing brought*) (*a*) *Fin:* initial share (in undertaking); (*b*) *Jur:* the contribution of husband or wife to joint resources upon marriage; **a. dotal,** (wife's) dowry; marriage portion; (*c*) *Geol:* alluvial deposits; silt; **a. des glaciers,** glacial drift; (*d*) *Nau:* **a. d'une marée,** (amount of) rise of tide; (*e*) *Tchn:* coating layer, deposit; (*welding*) **métal d'a.,** filler metal; (*f*) *Agr:* **un gros a. de fumier,** a heavy dressing of manure; (*g*) **a. de chaleur, a. calorifique,** heat supply, input; (*h*) admixture (of blood, etc.). **3.** *Psy:* apport.

apporte [apɔrt], *s.f. Ven:* **chien d'a.,** retriever.

apporter [apɔrte], *v.tr.* to bring. **1. a. du charbon, des nouvelles,** to bring coal, news (à, to); **apportez votre raquette,** bring along your racquet; **apportez-le!** bring it along! (*to dog*) **apporte!** fetch! **a. un changement, une modification, à qch.,** to bring about a change in sth., to modify sth.; **apporté par le vent,** wafted by the wind; *P:* **apporte-toi ici!** come here! **2.** to bring to bear, to exercise, to use; **a. du soin, de la précaution, du zèle, à faire qch.,** to exercise care, to use precaution, to show zeal, in doing sth.; **a. des difficultés à qch.,** to put, throw, difficulties in the way of sth.; to raise difficulties. **3.** to bring in, provide, supply; **a. des capitaux dans une affaire,** to bring capital into a business. **4.** to bring forward, adduce (reason, authority); *Jur:* **a. des preuves à l'appui de ce qu'on avance,** to substantiate one's assertion. **5.** to cause, produce; **qui sait ce que l'avenir apportera?** who knows what the future will bring forth?

apporteur, -euse [apɔrtœːr, -øːz], *a. & s.m.* **1.** *a.* which, who, brings; bearing. **2.** *s.m.* **un a. de bonnes nouvelles,** a bearer of good news; *Fin:* **a. de capitaux,** contributor of capital.

apposer [apoze], *v.tr. Adm: Jur:* (*a*) to affix, place, put; **a. une affiche sur un mur,** to stick a bill on a wall; **a. sa signature, son sceau, à un acte,** to set one's hand, one's seal, to append one's seal, one's signature to a deed; **a. sa griffe à une circulaire,** to put one's (stamped) signature to a circular; *s.a.* SCELLÉ 2; (*b*) **a. une clause à un acte,** to insert a clause in, add a clause to, an act.

appositif, -ive [apozitif, -iːv], *a. & s.m. Gram:* appositive (word, complement); (word) in apposition.

apposition [apozisjɔ̃], *s.f.* **1.** *Adm:* affixing, appending (of seal, signature, etc.). **2.** *Gram:* apposition; **mot en a.,** word in apposition. **3.** *Physiol:* accretion.

appréciable [apresjabl̩], *a.* appreciable; **a. aux sens,** perceptible; **à une distance a.,** at an appreciable, a considerable, distance.

appréciateur, -trice [apresjatœːr, -tris]. **1.** *a.* appreciative. **2.** *s.* (*a*) appreciator (de, of); (*b*) *Com: etc:* appraiser, valuer.

appréciatif, -ive [apresjatif, -iːv], *a.* denoting the value; **devis a.,** estimate; **dresser l'état a. d'un mobilier,** to draw up the valuation of, to value, furniture.

appréciation [apresjasjɔ̃], *s.f.* **1.** valuation, estimating, estimation, estimate, appraising, appraisement; judging (of distance); **faire l'a. des marchandises,** to value, appraise, to make an appraisement of, a valuation of, goods; *Jur:* **l'a. du juge,** the judge's comment, summing up; *Sch:* **note d'a.,** mark. **2.** judgement; opinion; appreciation (of work of art, meal, etc.); **une affaire d'a.,** a matter of opinion, of taste; **faire une a. d'un ouvrage,** to give an appreciation of a work; **a. favorable,** favourable criticism; **il a noté ses appréciations en marge,** he noted his comments in the margin. **3.** appreciation, rise in value.

apprécier [apresje], *v.tr.* (*pr.sub. & p.d.* **n. appréciions, v. appréciiez**) **1.** (*a*) to appraise, to estimate the value of (sth.); to value (sth.); to set a value on (sth.); (*b*) to determine, estimate (temperature, distance, sound); to judge (distance); *Artil: etc:* **a. long, court,** to over-, underestimate (distance, range); (*c*) **il faut avoir l'esprit subtil pour apprécier une telle nuance,** it requires great subtlety of mind to appreciate such a distinction. **2.** to appreciate (virtue, good thing); **il apprécie la cuisine française,** he appreciates, enjoys, French cooking; **être apprécié,** to be appreciated, esteemed; **j'apprécie le fait que . . .,** I appreciate, I do not deny, I quite realize the fact that . . .

appréhender [apreɑ̃de], *v.tr.* **1.** *Jur:* **a. qn (au corps),** to seize, arrest, to apprehend, s.o. **2.** to dread, apprehend, fear (sth.); **j'appréhende de le revoir,** I dread (the idea of) seeing him again; **on appréhende qu'il (ne) devienne aveugle,** it is feared he may become blind. **3.** *A: Phil:* to apprehend, to perceive.

appréhensible [apreɑ̃sibl̩], *a.* apprehensible.

appréhensif, -ive [apreɑ̃sif, -iːv], *a.* apprehensive, fearful, timid; **a. du danger,** apprehensive of danger.

appréhension [apreɑ̃sjɔ̃], *s.f.* apprehension. **1.** *Jur:* **a. (au corps),** seizure, arrest. **2.** *A:* understanding. **3.** dread (de, of); **éprouver de l'a. (que (+ ne) +** *sub.*), to be filled with apprehension (lest). **4.** *Phil:* apprehension; **simple a.,** simple apprehension.

apprendre [aprɑ̃ːdr̩], *v.tr.* (*conj. like* PRENDRE) **1.** (*a*) to learn (lesson, trade, etc.); **il a appris la musique,** he was trained in music; **a. (de qn) à faire qch.,** to learn (from s.o.) (how) to do sth.; **j'ai appris à patienter,** I have learnt to be patient; *abs.* **a. facilement,** to be a quick learner; *Prov:* **on apprend à tout âge,** it is never too late to learn; (*b*) to learn, hear (of), come to know of, get to know of (piece of news, etc.); **je l'ai appris de bonne part,** I have it on good authority; **j'ai appris que . . .,** I have heard that . . ., it has come to my knowledge that . . .; **à la gare nous avons appris que le train était parti,** at the station we found that the train had gone. **2. a. qch. à qn** (*a*) to teach s.o. sth; *F:* **qui vous a appris ce truc-là?** who put you up to that dodge? **a. à qn à faire qch.,** to teach, show, s.o. how to do sth.; **la vie seule nous apprend à vivre,** only life can teach, tell, us how to live; **si vous ne le savez pas ce n'est pas moi qui vous l'apprendrai,** if you don't know it already I'm certainly not going to start teaching, telling, you now; *F:* **je vous apprendrai à me parler de la sorte!** I'll teach you to speak to me like that! **ça vous apprendra!** serve(s) you right! (*b*) to inform, s.o. of sth.; to acquaint s.o. with sth., to tell s.o. sth.; *F:* **vous ne m'apprenez rien!** you're telling me!

apprenti, -ie [aprɑ̃ti], *s.* apprentice; *Jur:* articled clerk; **a. menuisier,** carpenter's apprentice; **a. imprimeur,** printer's devil; **a. marin,** *U.S:* apprentice seaman; **a. conducteur,** learner (driver); **je ne suis qu'un a.,** I'm only a beginner, a novice.

apprentissage [aprɑ̃tisaːʒ], *s.m.* (*a*) apprenticeship; (*b*) (*in liberal professions*) articles; **mettre qn en a. chez qn.,** to apprentice, article, s.o. to s.o.; to bind s.o. as an apprentice to s.o.; **être en a. chez qn,** to be apprenticed, articled, to s.o.; **faire son a. chez qn,** to serve one's apprenticeship with s.o.; **il n'est pas encore sorti d'a.,** he is not yet out of his time; **contrat d'a.,** articles, deed, of apprenticeship; indenture; **engager qn par un brevet d'a.,** to indenture s.o.; **taxe d'a.,** (employers') tax levied as a contribution to state technical training schemes; **faire l'a de la vie,** to learn (life) by experience; **faire l'a. de la politique,** to obtain a working knowledge of politics.

apprêt [aprɛ], *s.m.* **1.** *pl.* preparations (for journey, etc.). **2.** affectation, affectedness (of speech, etc.); **parler, écrire, sans a.,** to speak, write, unaffectedly; *F:* without frills; **manifester une satisfaction sans a.,** to show unfeigned satisfaction. **3.** *Cu:* dressing, seasoning, trimming (of food, etc.). **4.** (*a*) (process of) dressing, finishing (fabrics, hides, etc.); mill-finishing (of paper); (*b*) finish, stiffening (of fabrics, etc.); **a. infroissable,** crease-resistant finish. **5.** *Paint:* priming, primer; sizing, size.

apprêtage [apretaːʒ], *s.m. Tchn:* **1.** dressing, finishing (of fabrics). **2.** priming, sizing (of a surface before painting).

appressé [aprɛse], *a. Bot:* = APPRIMÉ.

apprêté [aprete], *a.* (*a*) affected, stiff (style, manner, etc.); (*b*) **papier a.,** glazed, glossy, paper.

apprêter [aprete], *v.tr.* **1.** (*a*) to prepare; to get, make, ready (luggage, meal, dish, etc.); *abs.* **elle apprête à manger,** she is (busy) cooking; **vous vous apprêtez bien des ennuis,** you are laying up trouble for yourself; *Mil:* **a. l'arme,** to come to the "ready"; (*b*) to rig (pack of cards). **2.** to dress, finish, stiffen (fabrics, etc.); to get up (shirt, etc.); finish (leather); *Ind:* **machine** *f.* **à a. (le cuir, le papier, les tissus, etc.),** finishing-machine. **3.** to prime (surface before painting).

s'apprêter. 1. (*a*) to prepare oneself, get ready; **s'a. à sortir,** to get ready to go out; **s'a. à la lutte,** to prepare for the struggle; **s'a. à faire qch.,** to prepare to do sth.; (*b*) to tidy oneself; to titivate. **2.** (*of meal, etc.*) to be in course of preparation; (*of storm, trouble, etc.*) to be brewing.

apprêteur, -euse [apretœːr, -øːz], *s.* **1.** *Ind:* finisher, dresser (of fabrics, metal, etc.). **2.** *s.f.* **apprêteuse,** *Hatm:* trimmer.

apprimé [aprime], *a. Bot:* adpressed; appressed.

appris [apri], *a.* **bien a., mal a.,** well-, ill-bred.

apprivoisable [aprivwazabl̩], *a.* that can be tamed, domesticated; tamable.

apprivoisé [aprivwaze], *a.* tame (animal, etc.).

apprivoisement [aprivwazmɑ̃], *s.m.* taming, domestication.

apprivoiser [aprivwaze], *v.tr.* to tame (animal); to win over (s.o.); to make (child) tractable.

s'apprivoiser, to grow, become, tame; (*of pers.*) to become more sociable, to tame down; **s'a. avec qch.,** to get accustomed to, grow familiar with, sth.

apprivoiseur, -euse [aprivwazœːr, -øz], *s.* tamer.

approbateur, -trice [aprɔbatœːr, -tris]. **1.** *a.* approving (gesture, speech, etc.). **2.** *s.* approver (de, of); applauder (of policy, etc.); assentor (to proposal, etc.); **a. (servile),** yes-man.

approbatif, -ive [aprɔbatif, -iːv], *a.* approving (gesture), (gesture, look, etc.) of approval; **sourire a.,** smile of approval.

approbation [aprɔbasjɔ̃], *s.f.* approval, approbation (de qch., of sth.); (*a*) consent, authorization; **soumettre un projet à l'a. des supérieurs,** to

submit a plan to one's superiors for approval; (*b*) certifying (of accounts, of document); passing (of accounts); (*c*) favourable opinion; **a. tacite,** tacit approval; **conduite qui a obtenu l'a. de . . .,** conduct approved, commended, by . . .; **recevoir l'a. de tous les gens raisonnables,** to be approved by all sensible people; *Com:* **pour a.,** for approval; *Journ:* **"marques d'a.",** "hear, hear!" (*d*) *Publ: A:* censor's authorization, imprimatur; (*e*) *R.C.Ch:* grant of faculties (to priest).

approbativement [aprɔbativmɑ̃], *adv.* approvingly.

approchable [aprɔʃabl̩], *a.* approachable, accessible (place, person).

approchant [aprɔʃɑ̃]. **1.** *a.* (*a*) approximating, akin, similar (**de,** to); **offre approchante,** near offer; **couleur approchante du bleu,** colour approximating to blue; **je n'ai jamais rien vu d'a.,** I never saw anything like it, anything approaching it; **voilà ce qu'il a dit, ou quelque chose d'a.,** that is what he said, or something like it; *s.m.* (i) **a. d'un sens,** approximation to a meaning; (ii) (*at lottery*) near-winner; (*b*) *A:* **calculs très approchants,** closely approximative calculations; (*c*) *s.m.* (*in lottery*) number close to the winning number; *F:* near miss. **2.** *A:* (*a*) *adv.* **deux heures a.,** nearly, about, just on, two; **deux heures ou a.,** two o'clock or thereabouts; (*b*) *prep.* **il y a a. un an,** (it is) well on to a year ago; *prep.phr.* **il est a. de huit heures,** it is nearly, just on, eight.

approche [aprɔʃ], *s.f.* **1.** (*a*) approach, oncoming, drawing near; advance; **l'a. de l'hiver,** the approach of winter; **à son a.,** as he came up; **à leur a. le groupe se dispersa,** when they drew near the group dispersed; **à l'a. des montagnes,** as the mountains came nearer; as I, (s)he, we, they, drew near the mountains; **d'une a. difficile,** difficult of access; **un homme d'a. facile,** an easily approachable man; **il évitait l'a. des humains,** he avoided human contacts; *F:* **c'est une nouvelle a. du problème,** this is a new approach to the problem; (*b*) *Mil:* **marche d'a.,** approach march; **a. couverte,** covered, under cover, march; (*c*) *Av:* **a. à vue,** visual approach; **a. asymptotique,** level approach; **a. basse,** flat approach; **moyens d'a.,** approach aids; (*d*) *Ven:* **chasse (au daim) à l'a.,** deer stalking; (*e*) *Golf:* **a. (piquée, allongée),** (short, long) approach (shot, stroke); (*f*) *Mth:* **approches successives,** successive approximations, continual approach; (*g*) *Z:* mating; (*h*) *Typ:* set; *s.a.* GREFFE 2, LUNETTE 1. **2. approches d'un camp, d'une ville,** approaches of a camp, a town; *Mil:* **travaux d'a.,** approach works, approaches; *F:* ground work. **3.** *Constr:* **les approches,** the ridge course.

approché [aprɔʃe], *a.* approximate (figure, etc.).

approcher [aprɔʃe]. **1.** *v.tr.* (*a*) **a. qch. de qn, de qch.,** to bring, draw, sth. near (to) s.o., sth.; **approchez votre chaise,** draw up, draw in, bring up, your chair; (*b*) to approach, come near (s.o., sth.); to come close to (s.o., sth.); **ne m'approchez pas,** don't come near me; **homme difficile à a.,** man difficult of access; (*c*) *Tex:* to shear (cloth) close. **2.** *v.i.* (*a*) to approach, draw near, come nearer; **l'heure approche,** the hour draws near, is at hand; **la nuit approchait,** night was drawing on; **faire a. qn,** to bring s.o. forward; to beckon s.o.; (*b*) **a. de qn, de qch.,** to approach s.o., sth.; to come, draw, near to s.o., sth.; **nous approchons de Paris,** we are getting near Paris; **a. du but,** to be nearing one's goal; (*c*) **a. de qn, de qch.,** to resemble s.o., sth.; to approximate, be akin, to s.o., to sth.; **la France? il n'y a pas de pays qui en approche,** France? there is no country like it; **sa conduite approche de la folie,** his conduct borders on insanity; (*d*) *Golf:* to approach; (*e*) *Z:* to mate.

s'approcher, to come near; to approach; to come on; **s'a. de qn, de qch.,** to draw, come, near (to) s.o., sth., to come up to s.o., sth.; **la vieillesse s'approche,** old age is creeping on.

approfondi [aprɔfɔ̃di], *a.* elaborate, careful (study); extensive (researches); **enquête approfondie,** thorough, searching, enquiry; **la question a été l'objet d'un débat a.,** the question was thoroughly discussed; **connaissance approfondie du français,** thorough command of French.

approfondir [aprɔfɔ̃diːr], *v.tr.* **1.** (*a*) to deepen, excavate (river-bed, etc.); (*b*) **cela approfondit ma tristesse,** it increases my sadness. **2.** to go deeply, thoroughly, into (sth.); to study (sth.) thoroughly; to sift (sth.); **a. une affaire,** to get to the core of a matter.

s'approfondir, to get, grow, deeper; to deepen.

approfondissement [aprɔfɔ̃dismɑ̃], *s.m.* **1.** deepening, excavating, excavation (of canal, etc.). **2.** investigation, profound study (of question).

appropriable [aprɔpriabl̩], *a.* (*a*) assumable (title); (*b*) appropriable.

appropriation [aprɔpriasjɔ̃], *s.f.* **1.** appropriation (of property, etc.); **a. de fonds,** embezzlement. **2. a. de qch. à qch.,** adaptation, suiting, of sth. to sth.

approprié [aprɔprie], *a.* **1.** appropriate, adapted (**à,** to); proper, suitable (term, measure, etc.). **2.** *Ecc:* **bénéfice a.,** appropriated benefice. **3.** *El: Tp: Tg:* **circuit a.,** composite circuit.

approprier [aprɔprie], *v.tr.* (*pr.sub. & p.d.* **n. appropriions, v. appropriiez**) **1.** to make appropriate; to arrange (sth.) to fit (sth.); to adapt; **a. son langage aux circonstances,** to adapt one's language to the circumstances. **2.** *A:* to clean; to tidy (sth.); to put (house, etc.) to rights.

s'approprier qch., to appropriate sth.; *A:* **s'a. à qch.,** to adapt oneself to, to fall in with, sth.

approuvé [apruve], *s.m.* mark or formula of approval (at foot of document); countersignature.

approuver [apruve], *v.tr.* **1.** (*a*) **a. qch.,** to approve of, be pleased with, *U.S:* to approbate, sth.; **a. de la tête,** to nod approval; **a. que qn fasse qch.,** to approve of s.o.'s doing sth.; **ne pas a. qch.,** to disapprove of sth.; (*b*) **a. qn de faire, d'avoir fait, qch.,** to commend s.o. for doing sth. **2.** to consent to, agree to, to back, sanction (marriage, expenditure, etc.); **a. qch. officiellement,** to agree formally to sth.; **être approuvé,** to receive approval; to meet with (s.o.'s) approval; *Com:* **a. une facture,** to pass an invoice; **a. un contrat,** to ratify a contract; *Adm:* **a. une nomination,** to confirm an appointment; **a. un appel,** to endorse an appeal; **"lu et approuvé,"** "read and approved."

approvisionné [aprɔvizjɔne], *a.* stocked, supplied (**de, en,** with); **bien a.,** well stocked.

approvisionnement [aprɔvizjɔnmɑ̃], *s.m.* **1.** provisioning, supplying, victualling (of town, army); procurement of supplies; catering (for s.o.); stocking (of shop); loading (of firearm); *Nau: O:* **a. de charbon,** coaling. **2.** (*a*) supply, stock, store; **faire un a. de qch.,** to lay in a supply of sth.; **les greniers regorgeaient d'approvisionnements,** the attics were overflowing with supplies, provisions; **approvisionnements de réserve,** reserve stocks; **magasin d'approvisionnements de navires,** marine stores; (*b*) *Mil:* **officier d'a.,** supply officer; (*c*) *Ind:* raw materials, semi-manufactures (used in processing industry).

approvisionner [aprɔvizjɔne], *v.tr.* to supply (**de,** with); to furnish with supplies; to provide with stores; to provision; to victual; to cater for (s.o.); *Mil:* to charge (rifle magazine).

s'approvisionner, to take in, lay in, a stock, a supply (**en, de,** of); to lay in stores; **s'a. chez (qn),** to get one's supplies from (a dealer); **s'a. en charbons étrangers,** to supply oneself with coal from abroad; **les commerçants s'approvisionnent pour Noël,** the shopkeepers are getting in their Christmas goods.

approvisionneur, -euse [aprɔvizjɔnœːr, -øːz], *s.* supplier; furnisher of supplies; purveyor, caterer; *Nau:* marine-store dealer, ship-chandler.

approximatif, -ive [aprɔksimatif, -iːv], *a.* approximate; rough (calculation, estimate); **ces chiffres sont très approximatifs,** these figures are only a rough estimate.

approximation [aprɔksimasjɔ̃], *s.f.* approximation; close estimate; near likeness; *Mth:* **approximations successives,** continual approach; **par a.,** (i) approximately, at a rough guess; (ii) *Mth:* by methods of approximation, by continual approach.

approximativement [aprɔksimativmɑ̃], *adv.* approximately, roughly; **dans une heure a.,** in an hour or so; **trois livres a.,** three pounds or thereabouts, about three pounds.

appui [apɥi], *s.m.* **1.** (*a*) support, prop, stay, shore; **mettre un a. à un mur,** to shore up a wall; (*b*) rest; *Arch:* balustrade; **a. d'un tour,** rest of a lathe; **a. de fenêtre,** (i) window-ledge, -sill; (ii) window-rail; **a. de porte,** door sill; **a. de tir,** firing, aiming, test; **a. d'escalier,** banisters; **appuis d'un pont métallique,** bearings of a steel bridge; **a. à bascule,** roller bearing, tilting bearing; **a. sphérique,** ball bearing; **a. d'un rail,** foot of a rail. **2.** support; (*a*) (*of beam, etc.*) **prendre a. sur qch.,** to rest on, take its bearing on, sth.; **mur d'a.,** supporting, retaining, bearing, wall; **plaque d'a.,** bearing plate; *Veh:* wheel-guard plate; *Plumb:* bed plate; **barre d'a.,** (i) handrail; (ii) window bar; *Nau:* **lisse d'a.,** breast rail; **à hauteur d'a.,** breast-high, elbow-high; **pieu d'a.,** bearing pile; *Mec.E: etc:* **pièce d'a.,** backing piece, backer; *Av:* **a. de cric,** jacking pad; *Min:* **a. simple,** surface bearing; (*b*) **a. moral,** moral support; **a. d'un candidat,** backing up of a candidate; **prêter son a. à qn,** to back s.o. up; **fournir, prêter, à qn un a. efficace,** to give s.o. effectual support; **être sans appui(s),** to be friendless, unprotected; **accusation avec preuves à l'a.,** accusation supported by proofs; **preuves à l'a. d'une cause,** proofs in support of a case, that support a case; **il est venu à l'a. de mon dire,** he supported, endorsed, my statement; **en a. à votre théorie,** in support of your theory; (*c*) *Mil:* **a. direct,** close, *U.S:* direct, support; **a. d'artillerie, d'aviation,** artillery, air, support; **tir d'a.,** covering fire; **poste d'a.,** inlying picket; *s.a.* POINT[1]. **3.** *Equit:* (*a*) appui; **cheval qui a l'a. lourd, qui n'a point d'a.,** hard-, soft-mouthed horse; (*b*) bearing (of the foot). **4.** *Ling: Mus:* **a. de la voix sur une syllabe,** stress on a syllable.

appui-bras [apɥibra], *s.m.* *Aut: Rail:* arm-rest, -loop; *pl. appuis-bras.*

appuie- [apɥi]. *compound nouns of which the first element is* **appui-** *have an alternate form* **appuie-,** *in which case they are invariable.*

appui-jambes [apɥiʒɑ̃ːb], *s.m.* leg-rest; *pl. appuis-jambes.*

appui-livre(s) [apɥilivr̩], *s.m.* (i) book-rest; (ii) book-shoulder; *pl. appuis-livre(s).*

appui-main [apɥimɛ̃], *s.m.* (painter's) maulstick; *pl. appuis-main.*

appui-queue [apɥikø], *s.m.* *Bill:* cue-rest: *F:* jigger; *pl. appuis-queue.*

appui-tête [apɥitɛt], *s.m.* head-rest; *pl. appuis-tête.*

appuyé [apɥije], *a.* laboured, heavy (joke, irony); insistent (stare).

appuyer [apɥije], *v.tr.* (**j'appuie, n. appuyons; j'appuierai**) **1.** to support; (*a*) to prop (up), (joist, wall, etc.); **galerie appuyée sur des colonnes,** gallery supported by pillars; (*b*) **a. une pétition,** to support a petition (**par,** by); **a. une proposition,** to second a proposal; **a. qn (dans une demande, etc.),** to support; back up, s.o. (in a request); **a. une demande, une candidature,** to back a request, a candidature; *Navy:* **a. un signal (par un coup),** to enforce a signal by a gun; **a. son pavillon,** to fire a shot under one's true colours; *cf.* ASSURER; *Mil:* **a. la progression de l'infanterie,** to support the infantry's advance. **2.** (*a*) to lean, rest; **a. qch. contre qch.,** to lean sth., rest sth., against sth.; **a. une maison contre une colline,** to build a house up against a hill; **a. la main sur la table,** to rest one's hand on the table; **tirer avec le fusil appuyé,** to shoot with the rifle rested; **a. son opinion sur qch.,** to base, rest, ground, one's opinion on sth.; **théorie appuyée sur des faits,** theory supported by facts; (*b*) to press; **a. son doigt sur une plaie,** to press one's finger on a wound; **a. un regard sur qn,** to let one's eye dwell on s.o.; *Equit:* **a. l'éperon à son cheval,** to touch, prick, one's horse with the spur, to clap spurs to one's horse; **a. des deux,** to clap both spurs to one's horse; **a. un cheval,** to passage a horse; *Mus:* **a. (sur) une note,** to dwell on, sustain, a note; *Fenc:* **a. la botte,** to dwell on the lunge. **3.** *v.i.* to bear (**sur, on**); (*a*) **poutre qui appuie sur deux montants,** beam resting, bearing, upon two uprights; **cheval qui appuie sur le mors,** horse that hangs on the bit; (*b*) **a. sur sa plume,** to press on one's pen; **a. sur le bouton,** (i) to press the button; (ii) to touch the bell; **a. sur une syllabe,** to lay stress on a syllable; **a. sur un mot,** to dwell on, lay emphasis upon, a word; **a. sur une demande,** to insist on a request; **regard qui appuie au lieu d'effleurer,** prolonged look instead of a casual glance; *Navy:* **a. la chasse,** to keep up a running fight; *Mil:* **appuyez à droite, à gauche!** (i) on the right, left, close! (ii) feel your right! feel your left! **appuyez à droite à la sortie du village,** bear to the right at the end of the village.

s'appuyer. 1. s'a. sur, contre, à, qch., to lean, rest, on, against, sth.; **s'a. sur qn,** (i) to lean on s.o.; (ii) to rely, depend, on s.o.; *F:* **s'a. sur un roseau,** to lean on a broken reed; **appuyé sur sa canne,** leaning on his stick. **2. s'a. d'une autorité,** to found (up)on, to take one's stand on, an authority. **3.** *P:* **s'a. un bon dîner, un gentil petit voyage,** to stand oneself, treat oneself to, a good dinner, a nice little trip; **s'a. une corvée,** to be landed with a thankless job; **je me suis appuyé deux ans de captivité,** I had to put up with two years' captivity; **qu'est-ce que je me suis appuyé (comme travail)!** how I worked!

apraxie [apraksi], *s.f. Med:* apraxia.

apraxique [apraksik], *a. Med:* apraxic.

âpre [ɑːpr], *a.* **1.** rough, harsh; **peau â. au toucher,** skin rough to the touch; **voix â.,** rasping voice; **goût â.,** tart taste; **vin â.,** rough, harsh, wine; **une solennité â.,** a stern solemnity. **2.** bitter, biting, sharp (frost, rebuke); scathing (irony); **temps â.,** raw weather. **3.** keen (competition, etc.); **homme â. au jeu,** ruthless player; **homme â. (au gain),** grasping man; man bent on gain; **il est â. à réclamer son argent,** he is ruthless in claiming his money, he claims his debts to the last farthing.

âprement [ɑprəmɑ̃], *adv.* bitterly. **1.** harshly, roughly, fiercely, with asperity. **2.** keenly, eagerly (fought, etc.).

après [aprɛ]. I. *prep.* **1.** (*order in time, space*) (*a*) after; **il est arrivé a. moi,** he arrived after me; **a. tout . . .,** after all . . .; **jour a. jour,** day after day; **il buvait verre a. verre,** he drank glass after glass; **a. vous, monsieur!** after you, sir! (*in shop*) **et a. cela, madame?** anything else, madam? **a. quoi . . .,** after which . . .; *s.a.* COUP 4; (*b*) **marcher a. un guide,** to walk behind a guide; **je suis, viens, a. lui,** I am, come, next to him. **2.** *F:* (*proximity* = À, CONTRE) **épingler une carte a. le mur,** to pin a card to, against, on, the wall. **3.** *F:* (*pursuit, tendency towards a goal*) **courir a. qn,** to run after s.o.; **jurer, maugréer, a. qn,** to swear, grumble, at s.o.; **a. qui en avez-vous?** who is it you are angry with? *F:* who are you getting at? **nous n'en avons pas a. vous,** our quarrel is not with you; **il est toujours a. moi,** he is always nagging at me; *F:* he is always at me. **4.** *prep.phr.* **d'a.,** according to, after, from; **d'a. ce qu'il a dit,** by, according to, what he said; **d'a. l'horloge il est trois heures,** by the clock it is three; **peint d'a. nature,** painted from nature; **paysage d'a. Turner,** landscape after Turner; **texte d'a. Cicéron,** text adapted from Cicero; **d'a. ce que j'ai entendu dire . . .,** from what I heard . . .; **d'a. ce que l'on dit,** as the story goes; **d'a. l'article 12 . . .,** under article 12 . . .; **une politique d'a. vos instructions,** a policy in conformity with your instructions. **5.** (*a*) **après** + *perf.inf.* **a. avoir dîné, il sortit,** after dining he went out; (*b*) *occ.* **après** + *pr.inf.* **il est d'humeur gaie a. boire,** he is cheerful when he has had a drink; (*c*) **après** + *p.p.* **il revint a. la paix faite,** he came back after peace had been made.

II. **après,** *adv.* **1.** (*a*) afterwards, later; **parlez d'abord, je parlerai a.,** you speak first, I shall speak afterwards; **six semaines a. il mourut,** six weeks later he died; **le jour (d')a.,** the next day, the day after; *Dial:* tomorrow; **l'instant d'a. il tomba,** the next moment he fell; *F:* **eh bien, et puis a.?** well, what of it? what about it? *F:* so what? **et a.?** what then? (*b*) *conj.phr.* **a. que,** after, when; **a. que je fus parti,** after I had gone; **il parlera a. que j'aurai fini,** he will speak when I have finished; **il parla a. que j'eus fini, il a parlé a. que j'ai eu fini,** he spoke when I had finished. **2.** *F:* **tout le monde leur court a.,** everybody runs after them; **la lettre lui courait a. depuis trois mois,** the letter had been chasing him for three months; **portez-lui ce livre, il attend a.,** take this book to him, he is waiting for it.

après-demain [aprɛdmɛ̃], *adv. & s.m.inv.* the day after tomorrow.

après-dîner [aprɛdine], *s.m.* evening; *A:* afternoon (after dinner); **discours d'a.-d.,** after-dinner speech; *pl. après-dîners.*

après-guerre [aprɛgɛːr], *s.m.* post-war period, conditions; aftermath of war; *pl. après-guerres.*

après-midi [aprɛmidi], *s.m. or f.inv. in pl.* afternoon; **à cet a.-m.!** I hope to see you again this afternoon; **trois heures de l'a.-m.,** three (o'clock) in the afternoon, three p.m.

après-rasage [aprɛrɑzaːʒ], *a.inv.* **lotion a.-r.,** aftershave lotion.

après-ski [aprɛski], *s.m.inv.* **tenue d'a.-s.,** après-ski outfit; **des a.-s.,** snow-boots.

après-souper [aprɛsupe], *s.m.* late evening; *pl. après-soupers.*

après-vente [aprɛvɑ̃ːt], *a.inv. Com:* **service a.-v.,** aftersales service.

âpreté [ɑprəte], *s.f.* **1.** roughness, harshness (of wine, voice, etc.); tartness (of fruit); roughness (of path). **2.** asperity (of tone, etc.); sharpness, bitterness (of weather, reproach); **critiquer un projet avec â.,** to criticize a plan with asperity, to be bitter against a plan. **3.** (*a*) **â. à qch.,** keenness for sth.; **â. à faire qch.,** ruthlessness, keenness, in doing sth.; (*b*) greed (for money, etc.).

a priori [apriɔri], *Lt.adv.phr. & a.* a priori; **raisonnement a p.,** a priori reasoning.

apriorisme [aprijɔrism], *s.m.* apriorism.

aprioriste [apriɔrist], *s.m. & f.* a priori reasoner; apriorist.

aprioristique [aprijɔristik], *a.* aprioristic.

aproctie [aprɔksi], *s.f.*, **aproctose** [aprɔktoːz], *s.f., Ter:* aproctia.

à-propos [aprɔpo], *s.m.* **1.** aptness, appropriateness, propriety, suitability, felicity, pertinence, relevance (of an expression, etc.); **le don de (saisir) l'à-p.,** the knack of saying, doing, the right thing; **avec assez d'à-p.,** not unaptly; **votre observation manque d'à-p.,** your remark is not to the point, is irrelevant. **2.** opportuneness, seasonableness, timeliness; **manque d'à-p.,** untimeliness. **3.** play written for a special occasion; occasional poem.

aprosexie [aprɔsɛksi], *s.f. Med:* aprosexia.

apsidal, -aux [apsidal, -o], *a. Astr:* apsidal.

apside [apsid], *s.f.* **1.** *Arch:* = ABSIDE. **2.** *Astr:* apsis.

apte [apt], *a.* **1. a. à faire qch., à qch.,** fit, fitted, suited, qualified, to do sth., for sth.; **il est a. à occuper le poste,** he is fitted for the post; **peu a. (à faire qch.),** unsuitable, ill-equipped (to do sth.); *Nau:* **a. à naviguer,** seaworthy; *Mil:* **a. au service,** fit for military service; *Jur:* **a. à hériter,** entitled to inherit. **2.** apt, suitable (example, etc.); **peu a.,** unsuitable, irrelevant.

aptère [aptɛːr], *Ent:* **1.** *a.* apterous, wingless. **2.** *s.m.pl.* **aptères,** Aptera. **3.** *Sculp:* **victoire aptère,** wingless victory; *Gr.Arch:* **temple aptère,** apteral temple.

aptérisme [apterism], *s.m. Ent:* winglessness, wingless condition (of an insect).

aptérygidés [apteriʒide], *s.m.pl. Orn:* Apterygidae.

aptérygiformes [apteriʒifɔrm], *s.m.pl. Orn:* Apterygiformes.

aptérygotes [apterigɔt], *s.m.pl. Ent:* Apterygota.

aptéryx [apteriks], *s.m. Orn:* apteryx, kiwi.

aptien [aptjɛ̃], *a. & s.m. Geol:* Aptian.

aptitude [aptityd], *s.f.* aptitude, natural disposition, fitness; inclination, tendency (**à, pour,** to); *Jur:* capacity; **avoir une a. à (faire qch.),** to have the capacity (for doing sth.); to have a gift (for (doing) sth.); *Adm: Mil:* **aptitudes physiques,** physique; **brevet d'a. militaire,** military efficiency certificate (obtained before entering the army); *Aut:* **a. à conduire,** fitness to drive; *s.a. abbreviations* C.A., C.A.P., C.A.P.E.S., C.A.P.E.T.

aptyalisme [aptjalism], *s.m. Physiol: Med:* aptyalism.

aptychus [aptikys], *s.m. Paleont:* aptychus.

Apulée [apyle], *Pr.n.m. Lt.Lit:* Apuleius.

Apulie [apyli], *Pr.n.f. A.Geog:* Apulia.

apulien, -ienne [apyljɛ̃, -jɛn], *a. & s. Geog:* Apulian.

apurement [apyrmɑ̃], *s.m.* **1.** auditing, agreeing (of accounts). **2.** discharge (of liability).

apurer [apyre], *v.tr.* **1.** to audit, pass, agree (accounts). **2.** to discharge (liability).

apus [apys], *s.m. Crust:* apus.

apyre [apiːr], *a. Cer: Ch: Miner:* apyrous, fireproof, refractory.

apyrène [apirɛn], *a. Biol:* apyrene.

apyrétique [apiretik], *a.* **1.** *Med:* apyretic, apyrexial, afebrile; free from fever. **2.** *Pharm:* antipyretic.

apyrexie [apirɛksi], *s.f. Med:* apyrexia, abatement of fever.

apyrite [apirit], *s.f. Miner:* rubellite.

apyrogène [apirɔʒɛn], *a.* **1.** apyrogenic; apyrogenetic. **2.** pyrogen-free.

aquabonisme [akwabɔnism], *s.m. F:* what's the use of it all attitude.

aquafortiste [akwafɔrtist], *s.m. & f. Art:* etcher, aquafortist.

aquamanile [akwamanil], *s.m. Ecc:* aquamanile.

aquanaute [akwanot], *s.m. & f.* aquanaut.

aquaplane [akwaplan], *s.m.* (*a*) aquaplane; surf-board; (*b*) aquaplaning; surf-riding.

aquaplaniste [akwaplanist], *s.m. & f.* surf-rider.

aquapuncture [akwapɔ̃ktyr], *s.f. Med:* aquapuncture.

aquarelle [akwarɛl], *s.f. Art:* aquarelle; water-colour (painting); **peindre à l'a.,** to paint in water-colours.

aquareller [akwarɛle], *v.tr.* to colour (engraving) by hand.

aquarelliste [akwarelist], *s.m. & f.* aquarellist, water-colourist, painter in water-colours.

aquariophile [akwariofil], *s.m. & f.* aquarist.

aquariophilie [akwariɔfili], *s.f.* the breeding of fish for aquaria.

aquarium [akwarjɔm], *s.m.* aquarium; **a. d'eau de mer,** oceanarium.

aquastat [akwasta], *s.m.* aquastat.

aquatile [akwatil], *a.* aquatile.

aquatinte [akwatɛ̃ːt], *s.f. Engr:* aquatint.

aquatintiste [akwatɛ̃tist], *s. Engr:* aquatinter.

aquatique [akwatik], *a.* **1.** aquatic (bird, plant, sport). **2.** marshy, watery (land).

aquatiquement [akwatikmɑ̃], *adv.* aquatically.

aquatubulaire [akwatybylɛːr], *a.* **chaudière a.,** water-tube boiler.

aqueduc [ak(ə)dyk], *s.m.* **1.** *Civ.E:* (*a*) aqueduct; (*b*) culvert, conduit. **2.** *Anat:* aqueduct, canal.

aqueux, -euse [akø, -øːz], *a.* **1.** *Anat: Ch: etc:* aqueous, watery; **humeur aqueuse,** aqueous humour. **2.** water-logged (ground); watery, waxy (potato); **couche aqueuse,** water layer.

aquicole [akɥikɔl], *a.* **1.** aquicultural. **2.** aquicolous (plant, animal).

aquiculteur [akɥikyltœːr], *s.m.* aquiculturist.

aquiculture [akɥikyltyːr], *s.f.* **1.** aquiculture, *e.g.* fish-breeding, etc. **2.** hydroponics.

aquifère [akɥifɛːr], *a.* aquiferous, water-bearing (stratum, etc.); *Geol:* **couche, nappe, a.,** *s.f.* **aquifère,** aquifer, aquafer; *Hyd.E:* **tuyau a.,** water conduit; *Echin:* **système a.,** water vascular system; *Bot:* vascular (bundle).

aquifoliacées [akɥifɔljase], *s.f.pl. Bot:* Aquifoliaceae.

aquilain [akilɛ̃], **aquilant** [akilɑ̃], *a. & s.m. Lit:* eagle-, clove-brown (horse).

aquilaria [akɥilarja], *s.m. Bot:* aquilaria.

Aquilée [akile], *Pr.n.f. Geog:* Aquileia, Aquileja.

aquilegia [akɥileʒja], *s.f.*, **aquilégie** [akɥileʒi], *s.f. Bot:* aquilegia; *F:* columbine.

aquilien, -ienne [akɥiljɛ̃, -jɛn], *a.* **1.** *Orn:* aquiline. **2.** *Rom.Jur:* Aquilian.

aquilifer [akɥilifɛr], *s.m. Rom.Mil:* standard-bearer.

aquilin [akilɛ̃], *a.* aquiline (profile, etc.); **nez a.,** Roman nose.

aquilon [akilɔ̃], *s.m. Lit:* aquilon, north wind; *Poet:* icy blast.

Aquin [akɛ̃], *Pr.n.m.* **Saint Thomas d'A.,** St Thomas Aquinas.

aquisextain, -aine [akɥisɛkstɛ̃, -ɛn], *a. & s. Geog:* = AIXOIS.

aquitain, -aine [akitɛ̃, -ɛn]. **1.** *a. & s. Geog: Hist:* Aquitanian. **2.** *s.m. A.Ling:* **l'a.,** Aquitanian.

Aquitaine [akitɛn], *Pr.n.f. Hist:* (province of) Aquitaine; *Geog:* **bassin d'A.,** Basin of Aquitaine.

aquitanien [akitanjɛ̃], *a. & s.m. Geol:* Aquitanian.

aquitubulaire [akɥitybylɛːr], *a.* (*rare*) = AQUATUBULAIRE.

aquosité [akozite], *s.f.* aquosity, aqueousness, wateriness.

ara [ara], *s.m. Orn:* ara, macaw.

araba [araba], *s.m. & f. Veh:* araba.

arabanne [araban], *s.m. Ch:* araban.

arabe [arab]. **1.** *a. & s.* (*a*) Arab (person, horse); **République a. unie,** United Arab Republic; (*b*) *a.* Arabian (customs, etc.); *s.a.* TÉLÉPHONE. **2.** *a. & s.m. Ling: etc:* Arabic (language, numerals, etc.). **3.** *s.m. F: A:* screw, usurer, (regular) Shylock.

Arabelle [arabɛl], *Pr.n.f.* Arabella; *F:* Bella.

arabesque [arabɛsk]. **1.** *a.* arabesque, Arabian (ornament, architecture, etc.). **2.** *s.f. Danc:* arabesque.

arabette [arabɛt], *s.f. Bot:* arabis, wall-cress.

arabidopsis [arabidɔpsis], *s.f. Bot:* arabidopsis.

Arabie [arabi], *Pr.n.f. Geog:* Arabia; **A. séoudite, saoudite,** Saudi Arabia; *A:* **l'A. heureuse,** Arabia Felix; *s.a.* PÉTRÉ.

arabinose [arabinoːz], *s.m. Ch:* arabinose.

arabique [arabik], *a. used in a few phrases, esp.* **le désert a.,** the Arabian desert; *Com:* **gomme a.,** gum arabic.

arabis [arabi], *s.f.* = ARABETTE.

arabisant, -ante [arabizɑ̃, -ɑ̃ːt], *s.* Arabic scholar, Arabist.

arabisation [arabizasjɔ̃], *sf.* Arabization.

arabiser [arabize], *v.i. & tr.* to Arabize; to Arabicize.

arabisme [arabism], *s.m. Ling:* Arab(ic)ism.

arabite [arabit], *s.f.*, **arabitol** [arabitɔl], *s.m. Ch:* arabitol, arabite.

arable [arabl̩], *a.* arable, tillable (land, etc.); **couche a.,** tilth.

arabophone [arabɔfɔn], *a. & s.* Arabic-speaking (person).

aracari [arakari], *s.m. Orn:* aracari.

aracées [arase], *s.f.pl. Bot:* Araceae.

arachide [araʃid], *s.f.* ground-nut, peanut; *F:* monkey-nut; **huile d'a.,** ground-nut, peanut, oil; **beurre d'a.,** peanut butter.

arachique [araʃik], *a. Ch:* arachic, arachidic.

arachnéen, -enne [arakneɛ̃, -ɛn], *a.* arachnoid, arachnean; cobweb-like; gossamer (tissue, etc.).

arachnides [araknid], *s.m.pl. Z:* Arachnida.

arachnitis [araknitis], *s.f. Med:* arachnitis.

arachnodactylie [araknɔdaktili], *s.f. Med:* arachnodactyly, arachnodactilia.

arachnoïde [araknɔid]. **1.** *a. Anat: Bot:* arachnoid. **2.** *s.f. Anat:* arachnoid (membrane). **3.** *s.m. Z:* (*a*) arachnid(an); (*b*) spider monkey.

arachnoïdien, -ienne [araknɔidjɛ̃, -jɛn], *a.* (*a*) arachnoid, cobweb-like; (*b*) *Anat:* arachnoidal.

arachnoïdite [araknɔidit], *s.f. Med:* arachnoiditis, arachnitis.

arachnologie [araknɔlɔʒi], *s.f.* arachnology.

arachnologique [araknɔlɔʒik], *a.* arachnological.

arachnologue [araknɔlɔg], *s.m. & f.* arachnologist.

arack [arak], *s.m. Dist:* arrack, arak.

Aragon [aragɔ̃], *Pr.n.m. Geog:* Aragon.

aragonais, -aise [aragɔnɛ, -ɛːz], *a. & s. Geog:* Aragonese.

aragonite [aragɔnit], *s.f. Miner:* aragonite; **a. confluente,** twin aragonite.

araignée [areɲe], *s.f.* **1.** (*a*) spider; **a. fileuse,** web-making spider; weaver; **a. d'eau,** water spider; **a. domestique,** house spider; **toile d'a.,** cobweb, spider's web; *F:* **avoir une a. au, dans le, plafond,** to have a bee in one's bonnet, to have something wrong in the upper story, to have a screw loose, to have bats in the belfry; *s.a.* FIL 1, PATTE 1; (*b*) *F:* **a. de mer,** (i) *Crust:* sea-spider, spider-crab; (ii) *Ich:* weever (fish); **grande a. de mer,** thornback; (*c*) *Fish:* **(mouche) a. (d'hameçon),** palmer. **2.** (*spider-like object, instrument*) (*a*) grapnel, drag; (*b*) *Aer: etc:* spider-support (of engine); (*c*) *Nau:* crowfoot, clew (of awning, of hammock); (*d*) *A: F: Cy:* penny-farthing; (*e*) *Mec.E:* **patte d'a.,** oil-tracks (of bearing); (*f*) *Tchn:* well-creeper; *Min: F:* spider; (*g*) *Veh:* buggy, spider; (*h*) *Fish:* gill-net; (*i*) *Lacem:* spider stitch, spider wheel; (*j*) *Vet: F:* gangrenous mastitis (of ewe). **3.** *Tex:* floss (silk).

araigner [areɲe], *v.tr.* to brush away the cobwebs from (ceiling, etc.); to clear (ceiling) of cobwebs.

araire [arɛːr], *s.m. Agr:* swing-plough.

arak [arak], *s.m. Dist:* arrack, arak.

aralia [aralja], *s.m. Bot:* Aralia.

araliacées [araljase], *s.f.pl. Bot:* Araliaceae.

araméen, -enne [arameɛ̃, -ɛn]. **1.** *a. & s. B.Hist:* Aramaean. **2.** *s.m. Ling:* Aramaic.

aramon [aramɔ̃], *s.m. Vit:* aramon (vine-stock, wine).

aranéen, -enne [araneɛ̃, -ɛn], *a.* **1.** spider-like. **2.** *Med:* thready, weak, (pulse).

aranéeux, -euse [araneø, -øːz], *a.* araneous; cobweb-like; spider-like.

aranéides [araneid], *s.m.pl. Arach:* Araneida.

aranéiforme [araneifɔrm], *a.* araneiform.

aranéisme [araneism], *s.m. Med:* arachnidism.

aranéologie [araneɔlɔʒi], *s.f.* araneology.

aranéologue [araneɔlɔg], *s.m. & f.* araneologist.

arapaima [arapaima], *s.m. Ich:* arapaima, pirarucu.

arapède [arapɛd], *s.m. Moll:* (*in S. France*) limpet.

araponga [arapɔ̃ga], *s.m. Orn:* arapunga, (*S. American*) bell bird.

araracanga [ararakɑ̃ga], *s.m. Orn:* ara(ra)canga.

arase [arɑːz], *s.f. Const:* **(pierres d')a., les arases,** levelling course (of masonry).

arasé [arɑze], *a.* flush; *Furn:* **armoire arasée,** built-in cupboard.

arasement [arɑzmɑ̃], *s.m. Carp: Const: etc:* **1.** (*a*) (*action of*) levelling (wall); making (wall) even, level, flush; (*b*) cutting to length; cutting off. **2.** (*a*) *Carp:* shoulder cut; shoulder (of tenon); (*b*) *Const:* last course, levelling course (of bricks or stones).

araser [arɑze], *v.tr.* **1.** (*a*) to level (down) (wall, etc.); to make (wall) level, even; to make (two stones, etc.) flush; to wear (surface) flat; to plane (plank) even; (*b*) *Geol:* to raze, to plane. **2.** to saw off (end); to square (plank); to cut off, strike off (heads of piles); to cut (rails, etc.) to length.

s'araser, (*of screw, etc.*) to strip.

aratoire [aratwaːr], *a.* agricultural, farming (implement, etc.).

araucan, -ane [arokɑ̃, -an], *a. & s. Geog:* Araucanian.

Araucanie [arokani], *Pr.n.f. Geog:* Araucania.

araucanien, -ienne [arokanjɛ̃, -jɛn], *a. & s. Geog:* = ARAUCAN.

araucaria [arokarja], *s.m.*, **araucarie** [arokari], *s.f. Bot:* araucaria, Chile pine; *F:* monkey-puzzle.

araucariées [arɔkarie], *s.f.pl. Bot:* Araucariaceae.

arbalète [arbalɛt], *s.f.* **1.** (*a*) *A.Arms:* cross-bow; *A:* arbalest; **a. à jalet,** stone-bow; (*b*) *A: Mil: P:* rifle. **2.** *A:* **attelage en a.,** unicorn team; **cheval en a.,** trace-horse; leader (of unicorn team). **3.** springe, snare (for moles, etc.). **4.** *Const:* hanging-post truss. **5.** *Tls:* bow-handle (of file); file-carrier.

arbalétière [arbaletjɛːr], *s.f. A.Fort:* loophole (for cross-bows).

arbalétrier [arbaletrie], *s.m.* **1.** *A.Mil:* cross-bowman; *A:* arbalester. **2.** *Const:* principal rafter (of roof, centering, etc.); *N.Arch:* awning stretcher. **3.** *Orn: F:* black swift, black martin, black swallow.

arbalétrière [arbaletriɛːr], *s.f. A:* = ARBALÉTIÈRE.

Arbelles [arbɛl], *Pr.n. A.Geog:* Arbela.

arbi [arbi], *s.m.*, **arbico** [arbiko], *s.m. P: Pej:* Arab; wog.

arbitrable [arbitrabl̥], *a.* (*difference, etc.*) submissible to arbitration.

arbitrage [arbitraːʒ], *s.m.* **1.** arbitration, arbitrament; *Sp:* umpiring; refereeing; **s'en tenir à l'a. de qn,** to abide by s.o.'s arbitration; **l'a. de la guerre,** the arbitrament of war; **la cour permanente d'a.,** the Hague tribunal; **conseil d'a.,** conciliation, arbitration, board (in industrial dispute). **2.** *Banking: etc:* arbitrage; **a. de change,** arbitration of exchange; *St.Exch:* **a. en reports,** jobbing in contango(e)s; **faire l'a. de place à place,** to shunt.

arbitragiste [arbitraʒist], *Fin:* **1.** *s.m.* arbitragist. **2.** *a.* **syndicat a.,** arbitrage syndicate.

arbitraire [arbitrɛːr], *a.* **1.** arbitrary (name, choice, etc.); discretionary (punishment, etc.); *s.m.* **laisser qch. à l'a. de qn,** to leave sth. to s.o.'s discretion. **2.** arbitrary, despotic, overbearing, high-handed (government, power, action, etc.). **3.** *Mth:* **quantités arbitraires (d'une équation),** *s.f.* **arbitraires,** arbitrary constants, arbitraries (of an equation). **4.** *s.m.* arbitrariness, high-handedness.

arbitrairement [arbitrɛrmɑ̃], *adv.* arbitrarily. **1.** at will. **2.** despotically, in an overbearing manner, in a high-handed way.

arbitral, -aux [arbitral, -o], *a. Jur:* arbitral; **tribunal a.,** court of arbitration; **solution arbitrale, règlement a.,** settlement by arbitration; **commission arbitrale,** board of referees.

arbitralement [arbitralmɑ̃], *adv.* by arbitration.

arbitre[1] [arbiːtr̥], *s.m.* (*a*) *Jur:* arbitrator, referee, adjudicator; **a. rapporteur,** referee (in commercial suit); *s.a.* TIERS-ARBITRE; (*b*) *Games:* referee, umpire; **a. de lignes,** *Fb:* **a. de touche,** linesman; (*in rugby*) touch-judge; **voulez-vous être a.?** will you referee, umpire, (the match)? (*c*) arbiter, disposer (of s.o.'s lot, of fashion, etc.); **ce ministre était l'a. des faveurs royales,** this minister was the sovereign disposer of royal favours; **a. des élégances,** arbiter of taste.

arbitre[2], *s.m. Phil:* **libre, franc, a.,** free will; **l'homme peut agir selon son libre a.,** man has free agency.

arbois [arbwa], *s.m. Bot:* alpine laburnum.

arbitrer [arbitre], *v.tr.* **1.** *Jur:* to arbitrate; to settle, decide (sth.) as arbitrator. **2.** *Games:* to referee (at), umpire (at) (match).

arborer [arbɔre], *v.tr.* to raise, erect, set up; to hoist (flag); to step (mast); **a. l'étendard de la révolte,** to raise, rear, the standard of revolt; **a. une cravate rouge,** to wear; *F:* sport, a red tie; **a. un sourire,** to wear a set smile.

arborescence [arbɔrɛsɑ̃ːs], *s.f.* **1.** *Bot:* arborescence. **2.** *Tchn:* branched chain.

arborescent [arbɔrɛsɑ̃], *a. Bot:* arborescent; **fougère arborescente,** tree-fern.

arborétum [arbɔretɔm], *s.m.* arboretum.

arboricole [arbɔrikɔl]. **1.** *a.* (*a*) *Z:* tree-dwelling, arboreal, arboricole, arboricolous (animal); (*b*) *Bot:* arboricolous, arboricoline, growing upon trees.

arboricolisme [arbɔrikɔlism], *s.m. Nat.Hist:* tree-dwelling habits.

arboriculteur [arbɔrikyltœːr], *s.m.* arboriculturist, arborist; nurseryman.

arboriculture [arbɔrikyltyːr], *s.f.* arboriculture; **a. fruitière,** orcharding, fruit growing.

arborisation [arbɔrizasjɔ̃], *s.f.* (*a*) *Miner: Ch: etc:* arborization, dendritic marking (of crystals, etc.); **a. (protoplasmique),** dendrite.

arborisé [arbɔrize], *a. Miner:* arborized, dendritic; *s.a.* AGATE.

arbouse [arbuːz], *s.f. Bot:* arbutus-berry.

arbousier [arbuzje], *s.m. Bot:* arbutus, cane-apple; **a. commun,** strawberry-tree.

arbre [arbr̥], *s.m.* **1.** (*a*) tree; **jeune a.,** sapling; **a. à fruit, fruitier,** fruit tree; **a. de plein vent,** standard; **a. en espalier,** espalier (tree); **a. en buisson,** bush; **a. vert,** evergreen (tree); **a. à feuille(s) caduque(s),** deciduous tree; **a. d'ornement, d'agrément,** ornamental tree; **grimper à, monter à, un a.,** to climb a tree; *F: A:* **faire monter qn à l'a.,** to play a hoax on s.o., to have s.o. on; **faire l'a. fourchu,** to walk on one's hands; to do a handstand; **se tenir au gros de l'a.,** to side with the strongest party, with the majority; *Prov:* **entre l'a. et l'écorce il ne faut pas mettre le doigt,** don't interfere in family quarrels; **se trouver entre l'a. et l'écorce,** to be between the devil and the deep blue sea; **l'a. ne tombe pas du premier coup,** Rome was not built in a day; **il ne faut pas juger de l'a. par l'écorce,** one should not judge by appearances; **tel a. tel fruit, au fruit on connaît l'a.,** the tree is known by its fruit; **les arbres cachent la forêt,** you can't see the wood for the trees; (*b*) **a. généalogique,** genealogical tree, family tree; pedigree; **a. de Jessé,** tree of Jesse; (*c*) **l'a. de la Croix,** the Rood; (*d*) **a. de Noël,** (i) Christmas tree; (ii) *Min:* control-manifold, Christmas tree; (*e*) **a. de la liberté,** tree of liberty. **2.** (*a*) *Bot: F:* **a. d'amour, de juda, de Judée,** Judas-tree; **a. à calebasse,** calabash-tree; **a. à caoutchouc,** (Para)rubber tree; **a. de, à, castor,** magnolia (virginiana), sweet-bay, *U.S:* beaver-tree; **a. à chandelle,** candleberry tree; **a. à chapelet(s), a. saint,** bead-tree; **a. de Chypre,** black cypress, bald cypress; **a. du ciel, a. aux quarante écus,** gingko; **a. à cire,** (i) wax-palm; (ii) wax-myrtle, wax-berry, wax-tree; **a. des conseils,** peepul-tree, bo-tree; **a. de dragon,** dragon-tree; **a. à aux, fraises,** strawberry-tree; **a. à la gale, a. à la puce, a. à poison,** poison-ivy; poison-oak; poison sumac; **a. à la glu,** holly; **a. à la gomme,** gum-tree; **a. à grives,** rowan, mountain ash; **a. indécent, impudique,** screw-pine; **a. aux lis, aux tulipes,** tulip-tree; **a. aux mamelles,** mammee; **a. à la manne,** manna ash, manna tree; **a. de Moïse,** pyracanth; **a. de neige,** viburnum; **a. à pain,** bread(fruit)-tree; **a. de paradis, de vie,** thuya, tree of life, arbor vitae; **a. à pauvre homme,** common elm; **a. à la perruque, aux perruques,** wig sumac, Venetian sumac, young fustic, smoke tree; **a. de sagesse,** common birch; **a. à suif,** Chinese tallow-tree; **a. triste,** tree of sadness, sad-tree, night-jasmine; **a. du voyageur,** traveller's tree; (*b*) *Ch:* **a. de Diane,** arbor Dianae, arborescent silver; **a. de Saturne,** arbor Saturni, lead tree; (*c*) *Anat:* **a. de vie,** arbor vitae; **a. respiratoire,** respiratory system. **3.** *Mec.E:* shaft, spindle, axle; *Clockm: etc:* arbor; *Mec.E:* **a. moteur, de couche, d'attaque, de commande,** main shaft, driving shaft, power shaft, engine shaft, drive shaft; **a. moteur,** sail-axle (of windmill); **a. commandé,** driven shaft; **a. d'entraînement,** (i) drive shaft; (ii) quill shaft; **gros a.,** heavy shaft; **a. de, du, tambour,** drum shaft; **a. de synchronisation,** interconnecting shaft; **a. transversal,** cross-drive shaft; **a. suspendu,** overhead shaft; **a. fou,** loose shaft; **a. d'accouplement,** coupling shaft; **a. creux,** hollow spindle; tubular shaft; **a. flexible,** flexible shaft; **a. démultiplié,** reducing shaft; **a. fixe,** stationary shaft; **a. oscillant,** rocker, rocking shaft; **a. à excentrique(s), a. excentré, excentrique,** eccentric shaft; **a. de chariotage,** feed shaft; **a. coudé, a. manivelle, a. vilebrequin,** crankshaft; **a. de renvoi,** counter-shaft, lay shaft, tumbling shaft; **a. de tour,** lathe spindle; mandrel; **a. d'alésage,** cutter bar, boring bar; **a. à cardan, a. de cardan(s),** cardan shaft; **a. à cames,** camshaft; **a. de transmission,** line shaft; *Aut:* propeller-shaft; **arbres (de transmission),** (transmission-)shafting; *Aut:* **a. nu,** open (propeller-)shaft; *Aut:* **a. gainé, à carter,** enclosed propeller-shaft; *Aut:* **a. de roue,** half-shaft, axle-shaft; *Aut:* **a. arrière,** back axle-shaft; *Aut:* **a. primaire, d'entrée (dans la boîte de vitesses),** primary, input, shaft; *Aut:* **a. secondaire, de sortie (dans la boîte de vitesses),** secondary, output, shaft; *Aut:* **a. intermédiaire (dans la boîte de vitesses),** layshaft, jackshaft, offset shaft; *Aut:* **a. (de colonne) de direction,** steering column shaft; *I.C.E:* **a. de culbuteur,** rocker-shaft; *I.C.E:* **a. de distribution d'allumage,** ignition (timing) camshaft; *I.C.E:* **moteur avec a. à cames en tête, en dessus,** overhead camshaft engine; *El.E:* **a. d'induit,** armature shaft; *N.Arch:* **a. de l'hélice, a. porte-hélice,** propeller shaft, screw shaft; *N.Arch:* **a. de butée,** thrust shaft. **4.** (*a*) *A: Nau:* (lateen-rig) mast; **a. de mestre,** mainmast; **a. de trinquet,** foremast; (*b*) stem, (jib-)post (of crane).

arbrisseau, -eaux [arbriso], *s.m.* shrub; **plantation d'arbrisseaux,** shrubbery.

arbuscule [arbyskyl], *s.m.* **1.** *Bot:* arbuscule. **2.** *Z:* arbuscule.

arbuste [arbyst], *s.m.* bush, (arborescent) shrub; **plantation d'arbustes,** shrubbery.

arbustif, -ive [arbystif, -iːv], *a.* pertaining to shrubs; shrubby; **plantations arbustives,** shrubberies.

arc[1] [ark], *s.m.* **1.** bow; *(a)* **tirer de l'a.,** to shoot with a bow; **tir à l'a.,** archery; **à la portée de l'a.,** within bowshot; **corde de l'a.,** bowstring; **fabricant d'arcs,** bowyer; **avoir plus d'une corde à son a.,** to have more than one string to one's bow; **bander, tendre, l'a.,** to brace, string, the bow; **débander, détendre, l'a.,** (i) to unbend the bow; (ii) *F:* to take things easy; to relax; *(b)* *Mec.E:* **ressort à a.,** bow-spring; *Tls:* **scie à a.,** bow-saw. **2.** arch; *(a)* *Arch:* **a. en plein cintre, a. roman,** semicircular arch; **a. brisé, aigu,** pointed, gothic, arch; **a. rampant,** rampant arch; **a. lancéolé,** lancet arch; **a. angulaire,** triangular arch; **a. outre-passé, en fer à cheval,** horseshoe, Moorish arch; **a. surhaussé,** raised arch; **a. surbaissé,** obtuse, depressed arch; **a. ébrasé,** splayed arch; **a. en carène,** Tudor arch; *s.a.* ÂNE 1; *Civ.E:* **a. en treillis,** trussed arch; **ferme, poutre, en a.,** arched girder; *(b)* **a. de triomphe,** triumphal arch; *(c)* **l'a. des sourcils, de l'aorte,** the arch of the eyebrows, of the aorta; **a. dentaire,** dental arch. **3.** *(a)* *Geom:* **a. de cercle,** arc of a circle; *(b)* *Mec.E:* **a. denté,** toothed arc, segmental rack; **a. de roulement,** rolling arc (of gearing); *(c)* *El:* **a. voltaïque,** voltaic arc; **a. électrique,** electric arc; **a. en retour,** arc back; **a. oscillant,** arc converter; **soudure en a.,** arc welding; **lampe à a.,** arc-lamp; **a. à mercure,** mercury arc; **faire jaillir un a.,** to arc; *W.Tel:* **a. chantant,** singing arc; *(d)* *Nau:* sagging (of a yard); hogging (of the keel); **avoir de l'a.,** to sag, to hog; *(e)* *Artil:* **a. privé de flux,** dead arc.

Arc[2], *Pr.n. Hist:* **Jeanne d'A.,** Joan of Arc; *s.a.* JEANNE.

arcade [arkad], *s.f.* **1.** *(a)* archway; **une a. de verdure,** a leafy vault; *(b)* *pl.* **arcades,** arcade. **2.** *(a)* arch (of saddle, etc.); *Anat:* **a. dentaire,** dental arch; **a. orbitaire,** orbital arch; *(b)* bridge (of pair of spectacles); *(c)* horseshoe curve (of double staircase); *(d)* **a. feinte,** blind arch.

arcadé [arkade], *a.* arcaded (court, walk, etc.).

Arcadie [arkadi], *Pr.n.f. A.Geog: Myth:* Arcadia; *s.a.* ROUSSIN[1].

arcadien, -ienne [arkadjɛ̃, -jɛn], *a.* & *s.* Arcadian.

arcane [arkan]. **1.** *a.* *A:* arcane; mysterious. **2.** *s.m.* *(a)* arcanum; *(b)* *pl.* arcana, mysteries; **les arcanes de la science,** the arcana of science.

arcanite [arkanit], *s.m. Miner:* arcanite.

arcanne [arkan], *s.f.* ruddle, red ochre.

arcanseur [arkɑ̃sœːr], *s.m. Tls:* pinch-bar.

arcanson [arkɑ̃sɔ̃], *s.m.* = COLOPHANE.

arcasse [arkas], *s.f.* **1.** *N.Arch:* transom, stern frame, buttock. **2. a. d'une poulie,** pulley-block.

arcature [arkatyːr], *s.f. Arch:* arcature; blind arcade.

arc-boutant [arkbutɑ̃], *s.m.* **1.** *Arch:* *(a)* flying-buttress; **pilier d'a.-b.,** buttress; *(b)* *Civ.E:* abutment pier. **2.** *Const: Carp: etc:* strut, stay, spur; bracket; *Av:* buttress; **arcs-boutants d'un parapluie,** stretchers of an umbrella. **3.** *(a)* *N.Arch:* **a.-b. de soutien,** spur; *(b)* *Nau:* **a.-b. de martingale,** dolphin-striker; *(c)* *Row:* outrigger; *pl. arcs-boutants.*

arc-boutement [arkbutmɑ̃], *s.m.* **1.** staying, buttressing. **2.** jamming, interference (of cogs); *pl. arc-boutements.*

arc-bouter [arkbute], *v.tr.* **1.** to buttress; to support (wall) with flying buttresses. **2.** to prop up, shore up (wall, etc.).

s'arc-bouter contre un mur, to set one's back, to brace oneself, against a wall (in order to resist a shock, etc.); **s'a.-b. sur ses jambes,** to take a firm stand with legs planted wide apart.

arc-de-cloître [arkdəklwatr̥], *s.m. Arch:* **voûte en a.-de-c.,** domical vault; *pl. arcs-de-cloître.*

arc-doubleau [arkdublo], *s.m. Arch:* transverse rib; *pl. arcs-doubleaux.*

arceau, -eaux [arso], *s.m.* **1.** arch (of vault). **2.** ring bow (of padlock); (croquet) hoop; **passer l'a.,** to run the hoop. **3.** *Surg:* (bed)cradle.

arcelle [arsɛl], *s.f. Z:* arcella.

arc-en-ciel [arkɑ̃sjɛl], *s.m.* rainbow; **a.-en-c. marin,** sea rainbow; *pl. arcs-en-ciel* [arkɑ̃sjɛl].

arc-en-terre [arkɑ̃tɛr], *s.m. Meteor:* dew bow; *pl. arcs-en-terre.*

Arcésilas [arsezilas], *Pr.n.m. Gr.Phil:* Arcesilaus.

archæocyathidés [arkeəsiatide], *s.m.pl. Paleont:* Archæocyathidae.

archaïque [arkaik], *a.* archaic (style, etc.); antiquated (appearance, etc.).

archaïsant [arkaizɑ̃]. **1.** *s.* archaist. **2.** *a.* arch-a(ist)ic (style, etc.).

archaïser [arkaize], *v.i.* to archaize, to use archaisms.

archaïsme [arkaism], *s.m.* archaism.

archaïste [arkaist], *s.m.* & *f.* archaist.

archal [arʃal], *s.m.* brass; *used only in* **fil d'a.,** brass wire, binding wire.

Archambaud [arʃɑ̃bo], *Pr.n.m.* Archibald.

archange [arkɑ̃ːʒ], *s.m.* archangel.

archangélique [arkɑ̃ʒelik], *a.* archangelic(al).

arche[1] [arʃ], *s.f.* **1.** ark; **l'a. de Noé,** Noah's ark; **l'a. d'alliance, l'a. sainte,** the Ark of the Covenant; **être hors de l'a.,** to be outside the pale (of the Church). **2.** *Husb:* **a. d'élevage,** coop. **3.** *Furn:* *A:* **a. de mariage,** bridal chest. **4.** *Moll:* arca; ark shell. **5.** *Glassm:* **a. à calciner, à fritter,** calcar.

arche[2], *s.f.* **1.** *(a)* arch (of bridge, etc.); *(b)* *Geol:* **a. de glacier,** glacier cave; **a. naturelle,** natural arch; *(c)* *Mch:* crown (of furnace). **2.** (croquet) hoop.

archée[1] [arʃe], *s.f.* bowshot.

archée[2], *s.m. or f.* **1.** *A.Phil: etc:* arche. **2.** *Alch:* molten core of the earth.

archéen, -enne [arkeɛ̃, -ɛn], *a.* & *s.m. Geol:* archaean.

archégone [arkegɔn], *s.m. Bot:* archegonium.

archégoniates [arkegɔniat], *s.f.pl. Bot:* Archegoniatae.

archégosaure [arkegɔzɔr], *s.m. Paleont:* archegosaurus.

Archélaüs [arkelayːs], *Pr.n.m. Gr.Myth: Hist:* Archelaus.

archencéphale [arkɑ̃sefal], *a. Anthr:* archencephalic.

archentérique [arkɑ̃terik], *a. Biol:* archenteric.

archentéron [arkɑ̃terɔ̃], *s.m. Biol:* archenteron.

archéocètes [arkeɔsɛːt], *s.m.pl. Z: Paleont:* Archæoceti, Zeuglodontia.

archéolithique [arkeɔlitik], *a. Geol:* palaeolithic.

archéologie [arkeɔlɔʒi], *s.f.* archaeology.

archéologique [arkeɔlɔʒik], *a.* archaeological.

archéologiquement [arkeɔlɔʒikmɑ̃], *adv.* archæologically; from an archæological point of view.

archéologue [arkeɔlɔg], *s.m.* & *f.* archaeologist.

archéopteryx [arkeɔpteriks], *s.m. Paleont:* archaeopteryx.

archet [arʃɛ], *s.m.* **1.** *(a)* bow; *Mus:* **instrument à a.,** bow instrument; **a. de violon,** violin bow; **mouvement de l'a.,** bowing; **quels coups d'a. faites-vous dans ce passage?** how do you bow that passage? **l'art de l'a.,** the art of bowing; *Tls:* **a. de foret,** drill-bow; **scie à a.,** bow-saw; *Ethn:* **allume-feu à a.,** fire-drill; *(b)* *Rail:* pantograph. **2.** *Surg:* (bed)cradle.

archer [arʃe], *s.m.* **1.** archer, bowman. **2.** *A:* constable (of the watch); **les archers,** the watch. **3.** *Ich:* archer, darter.

archère [arʃɛːr], *s.f. A. Arch:* arrow-slit, loophole (for shooting arrows).

archétypal, -aux [arketipal, -o], *a.* archetypal.

archétype [arketip], *s.m.* archetype, prototype.

archevêché [arʃəveʃe], *s.m.* **1.** archbishopric, archdiocese, archsee. **2.** archbishop's palace.

archevêque [arʃəvɛk], *s.m.* archbishop.

archi- [arʃi], *pref.* *(a)* **archifou,** stark, staring mad; **archiriche,** tremendously wealthy; **la salle était pleine et archipleine,** the house was packed and more than packed; **c'est faux et archifaux,** that's as false as false can be; **il l'a prouvé et archiprouvé,** he has proved it to the hilt; *(b)* **archichancelier,** arch-chancellor; **archidémon,** archfiend.

archiatre [arkiatr̥], *s.m.* *(a)* *Gr. & Rom. Ant:* archiater; *(b)* a sovereign's doctor.

archichancelier [arʃiʃɑ̃səlje], *s.m. Hist:* archchancellor.

archiconfrérie [arʃikɔ̃freri], *s.f. Ecc:* archconfraternity; **l'a. de la Vierge,** the (head) Guild of the Virgin.

archiconnu [arʃikɔny], *a.* very well known; only too well known.

archicube [arʃikyb], *s.m. Sch: F:* former student of the *École Normale Supérieure.*

archidémon [arʃidemɔ̃], *s.m.* arch-fiend.

archidiaconat [arʃidjakɔna], *s.m. Ecc:* archdeaconship, archdeaconry.

archidiaconé [arʃidjakɔne], *s.m.* archdeaconry.

archidiacre [arʃidjakr̥], *s.m. Ecc:* archdeacon.

archidiocésain [arʃidjɔsezɛ̃], *a. Ecc:* archdiocesan.

archidiocèse [arʃidjɔsɛːz], *s.m. Ecc:* archdiocese; archbishopric.

archiduc [arʃidyk], *s.m.* archduke.

archiducal, -aux [arʃidykal, -o], *a.* archducal.

archiduché [arʃidyʃe], *s.m.* archduchy.

archiduchesse [arʃidyʃɛs], *s.f.* archduchess.

archiépiscopal, -aux [arʃiepiskɔpal, -o], *a.* archiepiscopal.

archiépiscopat [arʃiepiskɔpa], *s.m.* **1.** archiepiscopacy. **2.** archiepiscopate.

archière [arʃiɛːr], *s.f. A.Arch:* arrow-slit, loophole (for shooting arrows).

Archiloque [arʃilɔk], *Pr.n.m. Gr.Lit:* Archilochis.

archiluth [arʃilyːt], *s.m. Mus:* archlute.

archimandritat [arʃimɑ̃drita], *s.m. Ecc:* rank, benefice, of archimandrite.

archimandrite [arʃimɑ̃drit], *s.m. Ecc:* archimandrite.

Archimède [arʃimɛd], *Pr.n.m. Gr.Hist:* Archimedes; *Ph:* **le principe d'A.,** the Archimedean principle, Archimedes' principle; **vis d'A.,** *Hyd:* Archimedean screw; *Ind:* spiral conveyor.

archimédien, -ienne [arʃimedjɛ̃, -jɛn], *a.* Archimedean.

archimillionnaire [arʃimiljɔnɛːr], *a.* & *s. F:* multimillionaire.

archimonastère [arʃimɔnastɛr], *s.m. Ecc:* mother house (of a religious order).

archimycètes [arʃimisɛt], *s.m.pl. Fung:* Archimycetes.

archine [arʃin], *s.f. Russian Meas:* arshine.

archipel [arʃipɛl], *s.m. Geog:* archipelago.

archipompe [arʃipɔ̃ːp], *s.f. Nau:* pump-well.

archipope [arʃipɔp], *s.m. E. Orthodox Ch:* archpriest.

archiprêtre [arʃiprɛtr̥], *s.m. Ecc:* archpriest.

archiptérygie [arkipteriʒi], *s.f. Ich:* archipterygium.

archisec, -sèche [arʃisɛk, -sɛʃ], *a. F:* bone-dry.

archisecret [arʃisɔkrɛ], *a. F:* top secret; *F:* hush-hush.

architecte [arʃitɛkt], *s.m.* architect; **a. de jardins,** garden-designer; **a. paysagiste,** landscape gardener; **a. naval,** naval architect; **a. urbaniste,** town-planner.

architectonique [arʃitɛktɔnik]. **1.** *a.* architectonic. **2.** *s.f.* architectonics, tectonics.

architectural, -aux [arʃitɛktyral, -o], *a.* architectural.

architecture [arʃitɛktyːr], *s.f.* architecture; **a. navale,** naval architecture; **a. de paysage,** landscape design, landscape-architecture.

architecturer [arʃitɛktyre], *v.tr. Art: Lit:* to structure.

architraître [arʃitrɛtr̥], *s.m.* arch-traitor.

architrave [arʃitraːv], *s.f. Arch:* architrave.

architravé [arʃitrave], *a. Arch:* architraved.

archivage [arʃivaːʒ], *s.m.* filing.

archiver [arʃive], *v.tr.* to archive; to file (documents).

archives [arʃiːv], *s.f.pl.* archives. **1.** records; **ajouter un rapport aux archives,** to file a report; *Publ:* **exemplaire des a.,** file-copy. **2. les archives nationales** = the Record Office.

archiviste [arʃivist], *s.m.* & *f.* **1.** archivist; keeper of public records; keeper of the records (of a society, etc.). **2.** *Com: etc:* clerk (in charge of records); filing clerk.

archiviste-paléographe [arʃivistpaleɔgraf], *s.m.* & *f.* palæographer (with diploma of the *École des Chartes*); *pl. archivistes-paléographes.*

archivistique [arʃivistik]. **1.** *a.* archivistic. **2.** *s.f.* the science of keeping archives.

archivolte [arʃivɔlt], *s.f. Arch:* archivolt.

archontat [arkɔ̃ta], *s.m. Gr.Hist:* archonship, archontate.

archonte [arkɔ̃ːt], *s.m. Gr.Hist:* archon.

arcifère [arsifɛːr], *a. Amph:* arciferous.

arcifères [arsifɛr], *s.m.pl. Amph:* Arcifera.

arciforme [arsifɔrm] *a.* arciform.

arçon [arsɔ̃], *s.m.* **1.** *Harn:* saddle-bow, saddletree; **bande d'a.,** side bar (of saddle); **a. de devant,** pommel; **a. de derrière,** hind saddle-bow, cantle; **vider les arçons,** to be unhorsed, thrown; to take a toss; *Gym:* **cheval d'arçons,** (vaulting) horse. **2.** *Tls:* *(a)* *Tex:* (felter's) bow; *(b)* frame (of saw); *(c)* **foret, drille, à a.,** fiddle-drill, bow-drill.

arçonner [arsɔne], *v.tr. Tex:* to card, clean (cotton, wool, etc.) with a (felter's) bow.

arcosolium [arkɔsɔljɔm], *s.m. Archeol:* arcosolium.

arcot [arko], *s.m. Metall:* dross; slag.

arcpincer [arkpɛ̃se], *v.tr. P:* = ARQUEPINCER.

arc-rampant [arkrɑ̃pɑ̃], *s.m.* **1.** *Arch:* rampant arch. **2.** *Tchn:* (*metal*) ramp support.

arctation [arktasjɔ̃], *s.f. Med:* arctation.

arctia [arktia], *s.f. Ent:* arctia; tiger-moth.

arctiidés [arktiide], *s.m.pl. Ent:* Arctiidae.

arctique [arktik], *(a)* *a.* arctic; **cercle a.,** arctic

circle; *F:* **température a.,** arctic temperature; (*b*) *Pr.n.m. Geog:* **l'A.,** the Arctic.

arcure [arkyːr], *s.f. Hort:* bending; *Mec.E:* buckling, bending.

ardéchois, -oise [ardeʃwa, -waːz], *a. & s. Geog:* (native, inhabitant) of the department of Ardèche.

ardéidés [ardeide], *s.m.pl. Orn:* Ardeidae, Ciconiidae.

ardéiformes [ardeifɔrm], *s.m.pl. Orn:* Ciconiiformes.

ardélion [ardeljɔ̃], *s.m. A:* busybody, meddler.

ardemment [ardamɑ̃], *adv.* ardently, warmly, passionately, zealously; eagerly.

ardennais, -aise [ardɛnɛ, -ɛːz], *a. & s. Geog:* (native, inhabitant) of the Ardennes.

Ardennes (les) [lezardɛn], *Pr.n.f.pl. Geog:* the Ardennes; **la Bataille des Ardennes,** the Battle of the Bulge.

ardent [ardɑ̃], *a.* **1.** burning, hot, scorching, blazing (fire, etc.); **soleil a.,** scorching, *F:* broiling, sun; **charbons ardents,** live coals; **fournaise ardente,** fiery furnace; **fièvre ardente,** burning, raging, fever; high fever; **cheveux d'un blond a.,** reddish blond hair; **rouge a.,** fiery red; *A.Ph:* **verre a.,** burning-glass; **miroir a.,** burning mirror; *A.Ch:* **esprits ardents,** ardent spirits; *s.a.* BUISSON 1, CHAPELLE[1] 1, CHARBON 1; *s. A:* **mal des ardents,** ergotism, ergotic poisoning, St Anthony's fire. **2.** ardent, passionate, eager; **prière ardente,** fervent prayer; **cheval a.,** fiery, high-mettled, horse; **a. radical,** red-hot Radical; **a. sportif,** keen sportsman; **a. à la poursuite,** eager in pursuit; **a. à poursuivre l'ennemi,** ardent, eager, in pursuit of the enemy; **a. à s'enrichir,** keen on money-making. **3.** (*a*) *Mill: etc:* keen (millstone); (*b*) *Nau:* (*of boat*) griping; (*of boat*) **être a.,** to gripe; to carry a weather helm. **4.** *s.m.pl. A:* **ardents,** will o' the wisp.

arder [arde], *v.tr.* = ARDRE.

arderelle [ardərɛl], *s.f. Orn: F:* great tit, tomtit.

ardeur [ardœːr], *s.f.* **1.** heat (of sun, fire, etc.). **2.** eagerness, ardour, fervour; mettle; **faire qch. avec a.,** to do sth. fervently, earnestly, with zeal; **cheval plein d'a.,** high-spirited, high-mettled, horse; **a. à faire qch.,** eagerness to do sth., keenness on doing sth.; **a. à poursuivre la gloire,** ardour, eagerness, in the pursuit of glory; **a. de posséder,** eagerness to own. **3.** (*a*) *A: Med:* **ardeur(s) d'estomac,** heartburn; (*b*) *Vet: F:* **ardeurs,** itch.

ardez [arde], *F: A:* = REGARDEZ.

ardillon [ardijɔ̃], *s.m.* **1.** tongue, tang (of buckle). **2.** *Fish:* barb (of hook). **3.** *Typ:* (blanket) pin.

ardoisage [ardwazaːʒ], *s.m.* slating (of roof, etc.).

ardoise [ardwaːz], *s.f.* slate; **(couleur) gris a.,** slate-grey (colour); (*a*) *Const:* **(feuille d')a.,** slate; **couvrir un toit en a.,** to slate a roof; *Nau:* **mettre les sabords en a.,** to slope the ports; *V:* **prendre une a. à l'eau,** *F:* to see a man about a dog, to have a look at the plumbing, to shed a tear for Nelson; (*b*) **a. à écrire,** writing slate; **crayon d'a.,** slate-pencil; *Geol:* **division en crayons d'a.,** prismatic jointing; *F:* **inscrire les consommations à l'a.,** to chalk up the drinks; *P:* **avoir une ardoise,** to be allowed to run up a score (at the pub, etc.); to have credit; to be able to chalk it up.

ardoisé [ardwaze], *a.* slate-colour(ed), bluish-grey.

ardoiser [ardwaze], *v.tr.* to slate (roof).

ardoiserie [ardwazri], *s.f.* slateworks.

ardoiseux, -euse [ardwazø, -øːz], *a.* slaty.

ardoisier, -ière [ardwazje, -jɛːr]. **1.** *a.* slaty; **schiste a.,** slate clay, shale. **2.** *s.m.* (*a*) owner of a slate-quarry; (*b*) slate-worker, slate-quarry-man. **3.** *s.f.* **ardoisière,** slate-quarry.

ardre [ardr], *v.tr. A:* (*p.p.* ars) to burn.

ardu [ardy], *a.* **1.** steep, abrupt, difficult (path, etc.). **2.** arduous, difficult, hard (task, etc.); **travail a.,** uphill work; **question ardue,** difficult, intricate, matter.

arduité [ardyite], *s.f.* arduousness, difficulty.

are [aːr], *s.m. Land Meas:* are (= 100 square metres).

aréage [areaːʒ], *s.m.* land surveying (by measurement in *ares*).

arec [arɛk], *s.m.,* **areca** [areka], *s.m.* **1.** *Bot:* areca palm (tree); **a. cachou,** areca catechu, betel palm. **2. (noix d')a.,** areca-nut, betel-nut.

arécées [arese], *s.f.pl. Bot:* Arecaceae.

arécoline [arekɔlin], *s.f.* arecoline.

aréique [areik], *a. Geog:* **région a.,** region without any (permanent) river system.

aréisme [areism], *s.m. Geog:* areism.

aréna [arena], *s.f. Fr.C:* arena; skating-rink.

arénacé [arenase], *a. Geol:* arenaceous.

arénaire [arenɛːr]. **1.** *a. Nat.Hist:* arenicolous; growing, living, in sandy places. **2.** *s.f. Bot:* arenaria, sandwort.

arenaria [arenarja], *s.f. Bot:* arenaria.

arène [arɛn], *s.f.* **1.** (*a*) *A: & Poet:* sand; (*b*) *Geol:* **a. (granitique),** quartz sand; *Civ.E: Constr:* **a. marine,** sea gravel. **2.** arena; bullring; **les arènes d'Arles,** the amphitheatre of Arles; **descendre dans l'a.,** to enter the lists, the fray.

aréner [arene], *v.i.* (*of building*) to subside, sink. **s'aréner** (*of building*) to subside, sink.

arénicole [arenikɔl]. **1.** *a. Nat.Hist:* arenicolous; growing or living in sand. **2.** *s.f. Ann:* **a. des pêcheurs,** arenicola, lobworm, lugworm.

aréneux, -euse [arenø, -øz], *a. A: Lit:* sandy.

arénière [arenjɛːr], *s.f.* sandpit.

arénifère [arenifɛːr], *a. Geol:* arenaceous (limestone, etc.).

aréniforme [arenifɔrm], *a.* arenoid; sand-like.

aréographie [areɔgrafi], *s.f.* areography.

aréolaire [areɔlɛːr], *a.* **1.** *Nat.Hist:* areolar (tissue, etc.). **2.** *Geol:* **érosion a.,** areal erosion, surface erosion.

aréolation [areɔlasjɔ̃], *s.f.* areolation.

aréole [areɔl], *s.f.* **1.** *Anat: Bot: Med:* areola. **2.** *Meteor:* halo, nimbus, ring (round the moon).

aréolé [areɔle], *a. Nat.Hist:* areolate(d).

aréomètre [areɔmɛtr], *s.m. Ph: etc:* hydrometer, areometer.

aréométrie [areɔmetri], *s.f. Ph:* hydrometry, areometry.

aréométrique [areɔmetrik], *a. Ph:* areometric(al).

Aréopage [areɔpaːʒ], *s.m. Gr.Hist:* **l'A.,** the Areopagus.

aréopagite [areɔpaʒit], *s.m. Gr.Hist:* areopagite.

aréostyle [areɔstil], *s.m. Arch:* ar(a)eostyle.

aréquier [arekje], *s.m. Bot:* areca palm(tree).

Arès [arɛːs], *Pr.n.m. Gr.Myth:* Ares, (*Roman*) Mars.

arête [arɛt], *s.f.* **1.** (*a*) (fish) bone; **poisson plein d'arêtes,** bony fish; **grande a.,** backbone (of fish); **dessin en a. de hareng,** *Arch:* **de poisson,** herringbone pattern; (*b*) ridge, rib (of sword blade, bayonet). **2.** (*a*) *Const: etc:* line; solid angle of intersection (of two surfaces); edge, arris, sharp edge, square edge; **a. mousse,** rounded, blunted, edge; **a. creuse,** hollow chamfer; **a. d'un comble,** hip of a roof; **pierre d'a.,** quoin-stone; *Arch:* **voûte d'arêtes,** groined vault; **a. de voûte,** groin (of an arch); **arêtes d'une colonne,** arrises of a column; (*b*) *Mec.E:* **arêtes d'un boulon,** cants of a bolthead; (*c*) *Hyd.E:* **a. médiane,** splitter (of Pelton wheel); (*d*) *Anat:* **a. du nez,** bridge of the nose; **nez dont l'a. existe à peine,** almost bridgeless nose; (*e*) **a. de dérive,** fin leading edge; **a. dorsale,** *Aer:* turtleback; *Av:* dorsal fin (of fuselage); (*f*) *Ph.Geog:* arête, (serrate) ridge, sharp crest. **3.** beard, awn, arista (of ear of wheat, barley, etc.); *s.a.* VOÛTE.

Aréthuse [aretyːz]. **1.** *Pr.n.f. Gr.Myth:* Arethusa. **2.** *s.f. Bot:* arethusa.

arêtier [aretje], *s.m.* **1.** (*a*) *Const:* hip(-rafter) arris-, corner-rafter; **a. de noue,** valley-rafter; (*b*) hip-beard (of sheet-lead). **2.** *Av:* nose-spar; edge (of wing); **a. avant, arrière,** leading, trailing, edge.

arêtière [arɛtjɛːr], *s.f. Const:* arris tile, hip tile.

Arétin[1] (l') [laretɛ̃], *Pr.n.m. Ital.Lit:* Aretino.

arétin[2], -ine [aretɛ̃, -in], *a. & s. Geog:* A(r)retine; of Arezzo.

argali [argali], *s.m. Z:* argali.

argan [argɑ̃], *s.m. Bot:* argan(-tree).

arganeau [argano], *s.m. Nau:* mooring ring.

arganier [arganje], *s.m. Bot:* argan (tree).

Argand [argɑ̃], *Pr.n.m. A:* **lampe d'A.,** Argand lamp.

argas [argas], *s.m. Arach:* argas.

argémone [arʒemɔn], *s.f. Bot:* argemone; **a. du Mexique,** Mexican poppy.

argent [arʒɑ̃], *s.m.* **1.** silver; **a. corné,** horn silver; **a. orfévré, vaisselle d'a.,** (silver) plate; **a. monnayé,** *A:* **blanc,** silver money; **a. blanc d'Allemagne,** German silver; **a. en feuille,** silver foil, silver leaf; *Geog:* **Côte d'A.,** the Gascony coast; *Prov:* **la parole est d'a., le silence est d'or,** speech is silvern, silence is golden; *Poet:* **l'astre au front d'a.,** the moon; *s.a.* DOUBLÉ 2. **2.** money, cash; **a. de poche,** pocket money; **a. liquide,** ready money, cash (in hand); **gagner de l'a.,** to make money; **a. dormant, mort,** money lying idle, paying no interest; **avoir de l'a. en caisse,** (i) to have cash in hand; (ii) to have money put by; **trouver de l'a.,** to raise money; **faire a. de qch., de tout,** to turn sth., everything into cash; *F:* **avoir un a. fou, être (tout) cousu d'a.,** to be rolling in money; **homme d'a.,** money grubber; **bourreau d'a.,** spendthrift; **manger, dissiper, son a., jeter son a. par la fenêtre,** to squander, run through, one's money, to throw one's money down the drain; **l'a. lui fond entre les mains,** he spends money like water, money just slips through his fingers; **il vous en donne pour votre a.,** he gives (you) good value for money; **en avoir pour son a.,** (i) to have one's money's worth; to have got full, good, value, for one's money; (ii) *F:* to have a run for one's money; **avoir toujours l'a. à la main,** to be always paying out; *A:* (*of servant*) **avoir sa nourriture en a.,** to be on board wages; *Provs:* **point d'a. point de Suisse,** nothing for nothing, no pay, no piper; **l'a. est un bon serviteur et un mauvais maître,** money is a good servant and a bad master; **l'a. ne fait pas le bonheur,** money does not create happiness; **l'a. est le nerf de la guerre,** money is the sinews of war; **l'a. n'a pas d'odeur,** money has no smell, *pecunia non olet*; *s.a.* COMPTANT 1. **3.** *Her:* argent.

argental, -aux [arʒɑ̃tal, -o], *a. Miner:* argental (mercury or gold).

argentan [arʒɑ̃tɑ̃], *s.m. Com:* German silver, nickel silver, argentan.

argentanais, -aise [arʒɑ̃tanɛ, -ɛːz], *a. & s. Geog:* (native, inhabitant) of Argentan.

argentage [arʒɑ̃taːʒ], *s.m.* = ARGENTURE.

argentation [arʒɑ̃tasjɔ̃], *s.f.* **1.** silvering, argentation. **2.** mercury treatment to give a silvery appearance.

argenté [arʒɑ̃te], *a.* **1.** silver(ed), silvery; **gris a.,** silver-grey; *Z:* **renard a.,** silver fox. **2.** silver-plated. **3.** *F:* rich, *F:* flush, *U.S:* well-heeled; **touristes bien argentés,** tourists well provided with money, tourists with well-lined pockets; **se trouver bien a.,** to be very flush (of money).

argenter [arʒɑ̃te], *v.tr.* to silver; **a. par des procédés électrochimiques,** to (electro-)plate; *Lit:* **la lune argentait les flots,** the moon cast a silver shimmer on the waves.

argenterie [arʒɑ̃tri], *s.f.* (silver-)plate; silverware.

argenteur [arʒɑ̃tœːr]. **1.** *a.m.* silvering (salt). **2.** *s.m.* silverer, silver-plater.

argentier [arʒɑ̃tje], *s.m. A:* **1.** (*a*) banker, money-changer, money-lender; (*b*) treasurer (of royal household); *Hum:* **le grand a.,** = the Chancellor of the Exchequer. **2.** silversmith. **3.** *Furn:* (display) cabinet (for silver).

argentifère [arʒɑ̃tifɛːr], *a. Miner:* argentiferous, silver-bearing.

argentin[1], -ine [arʒɑ̃tɛ̃, -in]. **1.** *a.* silvery (waves); silver-toned (voice); tinkling (bell). **2.** *s.f.* **argentine,** (*a*) *Bot:* (i) mouse-ear chickweed; (ii) silver-weed, argentine, goose-grass; (*b*) *Ich:* argentine, silver-fish; (*c*) *Miner:* argentine, slate-spar.

argentin[2], -ine, *a. & s. Geog:* Argentinian; (native, inhabitant) of Argentina, of the Argentine; **la République Argentine,** *s.f.* **l'Argentine,** Argentina, the Argentine (Republic).

argentique [arʒɑ̃tik], *a. Ch:* argentic; silver (compound, etc.); *Phot:* **image a.,** silver image.

argentiste [arʒɑ̃tist], *s.m. Pol.Ec: U.S:* silverite.

argentite [arʒɑ̃tit], *s.f. Miner:* argentite, silver-glance.

argenton [arʒɑ̃tɔ̃], *s.m.* = ARGENTAN.

argenture [arʒɑ̃tyːr], *s.f.* silvering (of mirror); silver-plating (of metal).

argien, -ienne [arʒjɛ̃, -jɛn], *a. & s. A. Geog:* Argive.

argilacé [arʒilase], *a.* argillaceous; clayey; clay-coloured.

argile [arʒil], *s.f.* (*a*) clay; *Coal Min:* (*on wall of working*) muckle; **a. pauvre,** lean clay; **a. grasse,** rich, greasy clay; **a. à blocaux,** boulder clay; **a. schisteuse,** shale; (*b*) **a. cuite,** terra-cotta, earthenware; **a. réfractaire, apyre,** fire-clay, flint clay; **a. figuline,** pottery clay, ball-clay; (*c*) **une statue, un colosse, aux pieds d'a.,** an idol with feet of clay.

argileux, -euse [arʒilø, -øːz], *a.* argillaceous; clayey (soil).

argilière [arʒiljɛːr], *s.f.* clay-pit.

argilifère [arʒilifɛːr], *a.* argilliferous, clay-bearing.

argilisation [arʒilizasjɔ̃], *s.f. Geol:* formation of clay (from rocks).

argilolit(h)e [arʒilɔlit], *s.m. Geol:* clay-stone.

argiope [arʒiɔp], *s.f. Arach:* argiope.

argiopidés [arʒiɔpide], *s.m.pl. Arach:* Argiopidae.

argol [argɔl], *s.m.* argol (yak etc. dung used as fuel).

Argolide [argɔlid], *Pr.n.f. A.Geog:* Argolis.

argon [argɔ̃], *s.m. Ch:* argon.

argonaute [argonoːt], *s.m.* **1.** *Myth:* Argonaut. **2.** *Moll:* argonaut, paper nautilus.

argonide [argɔnid], *s.m. Ch:* **les argonides,** the inert gases.
argot [argo], *s.m.* slang; jargon; **a. des voleurs,** thieves' cant; **a. du milieu,** underworld slang; **a. scolaire,** schoolboy slang; **a. des écoles,** university, students' slang; **cela s'appelle, en a. des coulisses, . . .,** it's called, in stage slang . . .
argoter [argɔte], *v.tr. For: Arb:* to trim, to cut (off the end of) a dead branch.
argoteur, -euse [argɔtœ:r, -ø:z], **argotier, -ière** [argɔtje, -jɛ:r]. **1.** *s.* talker of slang. **2.** *a.* slangy (person).
argotique [argɔtik], *a.* slangy (language); **expression a.,** (i) cant phrase; (ii) piece of slang, slang phrase.
argotisme [argɔtism], *s.m.* tendency to use slang.
argotiste [argɔtist], *s.m. & f.* student of, expert in, slang.
argousier [arguzje], *s.m. Bot:* sallow-thorn, sea-buckthorn, hippophaë.
argousin [arguzɛ̃], *s.m. A:* **1.** warder (in convict prison). **2.** *F: Pej:* copper, bobby, *U.S:* cop.
Argovie [argɔvi], *Pr.n.f. Geog:* Aargau.
argovien, -ienne [argɔvjɛ̃, -jɛn]. **1.** *a. & s. Geog:* (native, inhabitant) of Aargau. **2.** *a. & s.m. Geol:* Argovian.
argue [arg], *s.f. Metalw:* wire-drawing appliance, wire-drawer, drawing frame (for gold, etc.).
arguer[1] [argɥe], *v.* (j'arguë [ʒargy], **n. arguïons** [nuzargyjɔ̃]) **1.** *v.tr.* (*a*) to infer, assert, deduce; **a. qch. d'un fait,** to infer, deduce, sth. from a fact; (*b*) *Jur:* **a. une pièce de faux,** to assert a deed to be forged. **2.** *v.i.* to argue; **a. sur tout,** to argue about everything; **il argua de ma jeunesse pour m'exclure,** he made my youthfulness a reason for excluding me; **il arguë de ses relations et de son nom pour . . .,** *F:* he is plugging his connections and his name in order to . . .; **a. d'un retard dû aux lenteurs de la poste,** to plead postal delays.
arguer[2] [arge], *v.tr. Metalw:* to wire-draw.
arguésienne [argezjɛn], *a. Mth:* **transformation a.,** Arguesian transformation, transformation by isogonal conjugates, focal transformation.
argueur [argɥœ:r], *s.m.* arguer.
argule [argyl], *s.m.* **argulus** [argylys], *s.m. Crust:* argulus; **argule foliacé,** carp louse.
argument [argymɑ̃], *s.m.* **1.** argument; **par manière d'a.,** for argument's sake; **tirer a. de qch.,** to argue from sth.; **réfuter, détruire, une objection à force d'arguments,** to argue away an objection. **2.** outline, summary, plot, argument (of book, etc.); synopsis (of contents). **3.** *Mth: Astr: etc:* (*a*) argument, variable; (*b*) heading (of tables).
argumentaire [argymɑ̃tɛ:r], *a. & s.m. Com:* sales (talk, gambit); **rédiger un a.,** to draw up a list of selling points.
argumentateur, -trice [argymɑ̃tatœ:r, -tris], *Pej:* **1.** *a.* argumentative. **2.** *s.* arguer.
argumentation [argymɑ̃tasjɔ̃], *s.f.* argumentation.
argumenter [argymɑ̃te]. **1.** *v.i.* (*a*) to argue (contre, against); (*b*) *F:* to argufy, to be argumentative. **2.** *v.tr. A:* **a. qn,** to remonstrate, argue with s.o.
argumenteur, -euse [argymɑ̃tœ:r, -ø:z], *s.* arguer.
Argus [argy:s]. **1.** *Pr.n.m. Myth:* Argus; *F:* **aux yeux d'A.,** Argus-eyed. **2.** *s.m.* (*a*) *Orn: Ent:* argus; *Moll:* argus shell; *Ent:* **a. bleu,** holly-blue; (*b*) *A: F:* **a. de la police,** police spy; (*c*) **l'A. (de l'Automobile),** publication giving information on second-hand cars; **l'A. de la Presse,** a press-cutting agency.
argutie [argysi], *s.f.* quibble; cavil(ling).
argutieux, -euse [argysjø, -ø:z], *a.* quibbling, cavilling (speech).
argynne [arʒin], *s.m. Ent:* argynnis (fritillary); **a. tabac d'Espagne,** silver-washed fritillary.
argyrie [arʒiri], *s.f. Med:* argyrism.
argynnides [arʒinid], *s.m.pl. Ent:* Fritillaries.
argyrique [arʒirik], *a. Ch:* argyric (compound, etc.).
argyrisme [arʒirism], *s.m. Med:* argyria, silver poisoning.
argyrite [arʒirit], *s.f.* = ARGYROSE.
argyrodite [arʒirɔdit], *s.f. Miner:* argyrodite.
argyrol [arʒirɔl], *s.m. Pharm:* argyrol.
argyronète [arʒirɔnɛt], *s.f. Arach:* argyroneta, water-spider.
argyrose [arʒiro:z], *s.f.* **1.** *Miner:* argentite, argyrose, argyrite, silver-glance. **2.** *Med:* argyria, silver poisoning.
argyrythrose [arʒiritro:z], *s.f. Miner:* argyrythrose.
aria[1] [arja], *s.m. F:* fuss, bother; **ne faites pas tant d'arias,** don't make so many bones, such a song, about it; **quel a. que de déménager!** a removal is an awful job! **que d'arias!** what a lot of fuss and bother!
aria[2], *s.f. Mus:* aria.
Ariane [arjan], *Pr.n.f. Gr.Myth:* Ariadne; *s.a.* FIL 1.
arianisme [arjanism], *s.m. Ecc.Hist:* arianism.
aride [arid], *a.* arid, dry, barren (country, subject, etc.); **cœur a.,** unfeeling heart.
aridité [aridite], *s.f.* aridity, aridness, dryness, barrenness (of country, of imagination).
ariégeois, -oise [arieʒwa, -wa:z], *a. & s. Geog:* (native, inhabitant) of Ariège.
arien, -ienne [arjɛ̃, -jɛn], *a. & s. Ecc.Hist:* Arian.
ariette [arjɛt], *s.f. Mus:* arietta.
arille [arij], *s.m. Bot:* aril(lus).
arillé [arije], *a. Bot:* arillate, arillated.
arillode [arilɔd], *s.m. Bot:* arillode.
Arimathie [arimati], *Pr.n.f. B.Geog:* Arimathaea.
arion [arjɔ̃], *s.m. Moll:* arion.
arioso [arjozo], *s.m. Mus:* arioso.
Arioste (l') [larjɔst], *Pr.n.m. Lit.Hist:* Ariosto.
Arioviste [arjɔvist], *Pr.n.m. Hist:* Ariovistus.
ariser [arize], *v.tr. Nau:* = ARRISER.
Aristarque [aristark]. **1.** *Pr.n.m. Gr.Ant:* Aristarchus. **2.** *s.m. A:* severe critic.
aristé [ariste], *a. Bot:* aristate, bearded.
Aristée [ariste], *Pr.n.m. Gr.Myth:* Aristaeus.
Aristide[1] [aristid], *Pr.n.m. Gr.Hist:* Aristides.
aristide[2], *s.f. Bot:* aristida.
Aristippe [aristip], *Pr.n.m. Gr.Ant:* Aristippus.
aristo [aristo], *s.m. A: P:* bloated aristocrat; toff, swell.
aristocrate [aristɔkrat], *s.m. & f.* aristocrat.
aristocratie [aristɔkrasi], *s.f.* aristocracy.
aristocratique [aristɔkratik], *a.* aristocratic; **sang a.,** *F:* blue blood.
aristocratiquement [aristɔkratikmɑ̃], *adv.* aristocratically.
aristocratiser [aristɔkratize], *v.tr. A:* **1. a. un État,** to turn a state into an aristocracy. **2. a. qn,** to make an aristocrat of s.o.
s'aristocratiser, to grow aristocratic.
aristogenèse [aristɔʒənɛ:z], *s.f.* aristogenesis.
aristol [aristɔl], *s.m. Pharm:* aristol.
aristoloche [aristɔlɔʃ], *s.f. Bot:* aristolochia, birthwort; **a. serpentaire,** (i) Virginia snakeroot; (ii) *Pharm:* serpentaria; **a. siphon,** Dutchman's-pipe.
aristolochi(ac)ées [aristɔlɔʃi(a)se], *s.f.pl. Bot:* Aristolochiaceae.
Aristophane [aristɔfan], *Pr.n.m. Gr.Lit:* Aristophanes.
aristophanesque [aristɔfanɛsk], *a.* Aristophanic.
Aristote [aristɔt], *Pr.n.m.* (*a*) *Gr.Phil:* Aristotle; **la logique d'A.,** Aristotelian logic; (*b*) *Echin:* **lanterne d'A.,** Aristotle's lantern.
Aristotélicien, -ienne [aristɔtelisjɛ̃, -jɛn], *a. & s.* Aristotelian.
aristotélique [aristɔtelik], *a.* Aristotelian (doctrine).
aristotéliser [aristɔtelize], *v.i.* to Aristotelize.
aristotélisme [aristɔtelism], *s.m.* Aristotelism.
aristotype [aristɔtip], *s.m. Phot:* P.O.P. print.
aristotypique [aristɔtipik], *a. Phot:* **papier a.,** printing-out paper, P.O.P.
Aristoxène [aristɔksɛn], *Pr.n.m. Gr.Hist:* Aristoxenus.
arite [arit], *s.f. Miner:* arite.
arithméticien, -ienne [aritmetisjɛ̃, -jɛn], *s.* arithmetician.
arithmétique [aritmetik]. **1.** *a.* arithmetical; **machine a.,** adding machine, calculating machine. **2.** *s.f.* arithmetic; **faire de l'a.,** (i) (*of young children*) to do sums; (ii) to do arithmetic; *F:* **je vais acheter une a.,** I am going to buy an arithmetic book.
arithmétiquement [aritmetikmɑ̃], *adv.* arithmetically.
arithmographe [aritmɔgraf], *s.m. Mth:* computing machine; type of slide-rule; arithmograph.
arithmographie [aritmɔgrafi], *s.f.* arithmography.
arithmologie [aritmɔlɔʒi], *s.f.* arithmology.
arithmomancie [aritmɔmɑ̃si], *s.f.* arithmomancy.
arithmomanie [aritmɔmani], *s.f.* arithmomania.
arithmomètre [aritmɔmɛtr], *s.m.* **1.** arithmometer, calculating machine. **2.** slide-rule.
arizonite [arizɔnit], *s.f. Miner:* arizonite.
arkansite [arkɑ̃sit], *s.f. Miner:* arkansite.
Arkhangel(sk) [arkɑ̃ʒɛl(sk)], *Pr.n. Geog:* Archangel.
arkose [arko:z], *s.f. Miner:* arkose.
arlequin [arləkɛ̃], *s.m.* **1.** (*a*) *Th:* Harlequin; **habillé en a.,** dressed in motley; **manteau d'a.,** proscenium arch; (*b*) *F:* inconsequent person, weathercock. **2.** *pl. Cu:* left-overs. **3.** (*a*) *Z:* harlequin Dane (dog); (*b*) *Orn:* mule canary. **4.** *Ven:* (camouflaged) punt.
arlequinade [arləkinad], *s.f.* (*a*) *Th:* harlequinade; (*b*) (piece of) buffoonery; **arlequinades,** music-hall slapstick; slapstick comedy.
arlequine [arləkin], *s.f.* harlequina (at fancy-dress ball, etc.).
arlésien, -ienne [arlezjɛ̃, -jɛn], *a. & s. Geog:* Arlesian; of Arles.
armada [armada], *s.f. Hist:* armada; **l'Invincible A.,** the Invincible Armada.
armadille [armadij], *s.f. Crust:* armadillo; wood louse.
Armagnac [armaɲak]. **1.** *s.m. A.Geog:* **L'A.,** a region of France, with capital Auch. **2.** *a.m. & s.m.* (*a*) (native, inhabitant) of Armagnac; (*b*) *pl. Hist:* **Les Armagnacs,** the Armagnac faction, the Armagnacs. **3.** *s.m.* armagnac (brandy).
armangite [armɑ̃ʒit], *s.f. Miner:* armangite.
armateur [armatœ:r], *s.m. Nau:* **1.** (*a*) fitter-out (of ship, expedition); (*b*) (ship-)owner. **2.** *A:* corsair, commander of a privateer; (*b*) privateer (vessel).
armature [armaty:r], *s.f.* **1.** (*a*) frame, brace, armature (of window, etc.); reinforcement (of concrete work); truss (of girder, etc.); **a. en étrier,** (stirrup-)strap; **a. d'une raquette,** frame of a (tennis) racquet; *N.Arch:* **a. de l'étambot,** braces of the sternpost; *Metall:* **a. de noyau,** core frame (for casting); *Mch:* **armatures d'une boîte à feu,** bridge stays; **a. d'un soutien-gorge,** bones of a brassière; (*b*) *F:* backbone (of country); sinews (of undertaking). **2.** coating (of Leyden jar, etc.); armouring, sheathing, (of electric cable). **3.** *El:* (*a*) armature (of magnet, small dynamo, magneto); *cf.* INDUIT 2; (*b*) plate (of condenser). **4.** *E:* **a. de soupape, de pompe,** valve-gear, pump-gear. **5.** *Mus:* key-signature. **6.** *Geol:* (*a*) framework (of volcano); (*b*) **méandre à a. rocheuse,** rock-defended meander.
arme [arm], *s.f.* **1.** arm, weapon; *A:* **homme d'armes,** man-at-arms; *A:* **cheval d'armes,** charger, war-horse; **a. d'escrime,** fencing sword; foil; **faire des armes,** to fence, to go in for fencing; **salle d'armes,** (i) armoury; (ii) fencing-school; **maître d'armes,** fencing-master; **armes blanches,** cutting and thrusting weapons, *armes blanches*; weapons used in hand-to-hand fighting; **se battre à l'a. blanche,** to fight with cold steel; **armes de jet, de trait,** missile weapons; **armes de coup,** weapons of percussion; **armes d'hast,** staff-weapons; **armes de main,** hand weapons; **armes à feu,** fire-arms; **armes portatives,** small arms; **armes de guerre,** military weapons; **armes classiques, traditionnelles, conventionnelles,** conventional weapons; **a. non classique, a. non conventionnelle,** non-conventional weapon; *U.S:* advanced weapon; **a. bactériologique,** bacteriological weapon, germ weapon; **a. biologique,** biological weapon; **a. de destructions massives,** mass destruction weapon; **a. nucléaire,** nuclear weapon; **a. de dissuasion,** deterrent; **hommes en, sous les, armes,** men under arms; **nation en, sous les, armes,** nation in arms; **appeler la réserve sous les armes,** to call up the reserve; **prendre les armes,** (i) to take up arms, to rise up in arms (contre, against); (ii) *Mil:* to parade under arms; **porter les armes,** (i) to bear, carry, arms; (ii) to be a soldier; **mettre bas, poser, déposer, rendre les armes,** to lay down one's arms; *F:* **dans les discussions avec sa femme c'était toujours lui qui le premier rendait les armes,** in arguments with his wife, he was always the one who gave in first; **faire ses premières armes sous qn,** to go through one's first campaign under s.o.; **faire ses premières armes,** to make one's début; **aux armes!** to arms! *Mil:* stand to! guard turn out! **le métier, la carrière, des armes,** the profession of arms, the military profession, soldiering; **suspension d'armes,** cessation of hostilities; **frères d'armes,** brothers in arms; *Mil:* **place d'armes,** (i) parade-ground; (ii) (*tactics*) assembly area; *Mil:* **prise d'armes,** (*special*) ceremonial parade under arms; *Mil:* **portez armes!** shoulder arms! **l'a. au pied,** (arms) at the order; **mettre l'a. à la bretelle,** to sling arms; **l'a. à la bretelle!** sling arms! **l'a. à la main,** trail arms; **l'a. sous le bras,** reverse arms; *s.a.* ÉPAULE 1, PRÉSENTER 1, REPOSER I. 1.; **passer qn par les armes,** to have s.o. (court-martialled and) shot; **passer les habitants d'un village par les armes,** to shoot, execute by shooting, the inhabitants of a village; **sans armes,** unarmed; **à armes égales,** on equal terms; **avec armes et bagages,** (with) bag and baggage; **faire a. de tout,** to use every means at hand; **donner, fournir, des armes contre soi-même,** to make a rod for one's own back; **il les a battus**

avec leurs propres armes, he beat them with their own weapons, at their own game; *s.a.* BAGAGE 1, GAUCHE 4, PORT² 1, RENDRE 4. 2. arm (as a branch of the army); **douze mille hommes de toutes armes,** twelve thousand men of all arms, services; **dans quelle a. comptez-vous servir?** which branch of the service do you expect to enter? 3. *pl. Her:* arms, cognizance; coat of arms; **(peint) aux armes de la ville,** emblazoned with, bearing, the arms of the town; *s.a.* PARLANT.

armé [arme]. 1. *a.* (*a*) armed; **vaisseau a. de gros canons,** ship armed with heavy guns; **troupe armée,** body of troops; **agression à main armée,** hold-up; (*b*) fortified; strengthened; **poutre armée,** trussed beam; **béton a.,** ferro-concrete, reinforced concrete; **verre a.,** wired glass; (*c*) cocked; **pistolet à l'a., avec le chien a.,** pistol at full cock; **pistolet à demi a.,** pistol at half cock. 2. *s.m.* (*fine arms*) full cock, cocking; **a. automatique,** automatic cocking, self-cocking.

armée [arme], *s.f.* 1. *Mil:* (*a*) army, force(s); **a. de métier,** professional army; **a. nationale, levée par conscription,** conscript army; **a. permanente,** standing army; **a. active,** regular army; **l'a. de terre,** the army, the land forces; **l'a. de l'air,** the air force; **l'a. de mer,** the navy, the naval forces; **fournisseur de l'a.,** contractor; **aux armées,** on active service, in the field; (*b*) (field) army; **une a. forte de cent mille hommes,** an army, a field army, a hundred thousand strong; **une a. de secours,** a relieving army; **la 8ième a.,** the 8th army; **un groupe d'a.,** an army group; (*c*) **une a.** (*terre, air ou mer*), a service; **les trois armées sont l'a. de terre, l'aviation et la marine,** the three services are the army, the navy and the air force; *Hist:* **la Grande A.,** the Grande Armée. 2. **le Dieu des armées,** the Lord of Hosts; **les armées célestes,** the heavenly hosts; **l'A. du Salut,** the Salvation Army; **toute une a. de fonctionnaires,** a whole army, a host, of officials; **à lui seul il valait une a.,** he was a host in himself.

armée-cadre [armekɑːdr], *s.f.* skeleton peace-army; *pl. armées-cadres.*

armeline [armәlin], *s.f.* ermine, *A:* armeline.

armement [armәmɑ̃], *s.m.* 1. (*a*) arming; providing (army, etc.) with arms; equipping; *A:* **Ministère de l'Armement,** Ministry of Munitions; Ministry of Supply; (*b*) armament, equipment; **officier d'a.,** ordnance officer; (*c*) *pl.* armaments; *U.S:* weaponry; **course aux armements,** arms, armaments, race; **pousser ses armements,** to step up, increase, one's production of armaments; **nos soldats sont pourvus de l'a. américain,** our troops are provided with American arms. 2. (*a*) *A:* providing, equipping, (of s.o.) with armour; dubbing (of knight); (*b*) fortifying, strengthening, bracing (of girder, etc.); sheathing (of cable, etc.); (*c*) *Const:* slate hanging. 3. *Nau:* (*a*) (i) commissioning, fitting out, outfitting; (ii) equipment, gear, stores; **mettre un navire en a.,** to put a ship in commission, to commission a ship; **port d'a.,** port of registry; home port; (*b*) (i) manning; (ii) crew (of boat, gun, etc.); **canot à a. complet,** fully-manned boat; (*c*) commercial, merchant, shipping; **l'Armement,** the shipping business; the (big) shipowners. 4. (*a*) loading (of gun); arming (of fuse); (*b*) setting (of camera-shutter, etc.); cocking (of loaded fire-arm); (*c*) mounting, fitting up (of machine, etc.). 5. fittings, mounting, gear (of machine).

Arménie [armeni], *Pr.n.f. Geog:* Armenia; **papier d'A.,** paper which burns slowly giving off smell of incense; *F:* **ça ne sent pas le papier d'A.,** it stinks!

arménien, -ienne [armenjɛ̃, -jɛn], *a. & s.* Armenian.

armentiérais, -aise [armɑ̃tjerɛ, -ɛːz], *a. & s. Geog:* (native, inhabitant) of Armentières.

armer [arme]. I. *v.tr.* 1. (*a*) to arm; to provide (s.o., sth.) with arms; **a. qn de qch.,** to arm s.o. with sth.; **vol à main armée,** armed robbery; **l'éléphant est armé de défenses,** the elephant is armed with tusks; **a. une massue de pointes de fer,** to put iron spikes on a club; **armé de pleins pouvoirs,** armed with full powers; *F:* **être armé d'un laissez-passer,** to be armed with a free pass; *s.a.* DENT 1; (*b*) **a. qn contre qn,** to set s.o. against s.o. 2. (*a*) *A:* to provide (s.o.) with armour, to equip (s.o.); **a. qn chevalier,** to dub s.o. a knight; *s.a.* PIÈCE 2; (*b*) **a. une ville,** to fortify a town; (*c*) to fortify, strengthen, brace; **courage armé contre les dangers,** courage fortified against dangers; *Metall:* **a. une hache,** to steel an axe; *El.E:* **a. une dynamo,** to wind a dynamo; **a. un câble,** to sheathe, armour, a cable; **a. un aimant,** to arm, cap, a magnet. 3. *Nau:* (*a*) to equip, fit out, commission (ship); (*b*) to man (boat, prize, winch); to rig (capstan); *s.a.* PIÈCE 1; (*c*) **a. les avirons,** to ship the oars. 4. (*a*) **a. une fusée,** to arm a fuse; (*b*) to set (an apparatus, *e.g.* camera-shutter); to cock (fire-arm); **armé à fond,** at full cock; *Tex:* **a. la lisse,** to draw the warp; (*c*) to mount (machine, battery of guns, etc.); to fit up (machine). 5. *Mus:* **a. la clef,** to put the key-signature (to a piece of music).

II. *v.i.* 1. *Mil:* to arm, prepare for war; **on arme de tous côtés,** they are arming on all sides. 2. *Nau:* (*a*) **le navire arme à Brest,** the ship is being commissioned at Brest; (*b*) **a. sur un navire,** to serve on a vessel.

s'armer. 1. (*a*) **s'a. d'un revolver, etc.,** to arm oneself with a revolver, etc. 2. **s'a. de patience,** to take patience; **s'a. de tout son courage,** to summon up all one's courage, to brace oneself (to a task); (*b*) to arm; to take up arms; **tout le pays s'est armé contre l'envahisseur,** the whole country took up arms against the invader.

armeria [armerja], *s.f.*, **armérie** [armeri], *s.f. Bot:* **a. commune,** thrift; **a. maritime,** sea-thrift.

armet [armɛ], *s.m. A.Arm:* armet.

Armide [armid], *Pr.n.f. Lit:* Armida.

armillaire [armil(l)ɛːr]. 1. *a.* (*a*) armillary (sphere); (*b*) *Bot:* armillate. 2. *s.f.pl.* **armillaires,** *Fung:* Armillaria.

armille [armij], *s.f.* 1. *Archeol:* (*a*) *Astr:* armilla; (*b*) armlet, bracelet. 2. *pl.* **armilles,** *Arch:* annulets.

armillé [armije], *a. Arch:* annulate(d).

arminianisme [arminjanism], *s.m. Rel.H:* Arminianism.

arminien, -ienne [arminjɛ̃, -jɛn], *a. & s. Rel.H:* Arminian.

armistice [armistis], *s.m.* armistice; truce; **journée, anniversaire, de l'A.,** Armistice Day, Remembrance Day.

armoire [armwaːr], *s.f.* (*a*) cupboard, *U.S:* closet; **a. à linge,** linen-cupboard, -press; **a. à provisions,** store-cupboard; **a. de cuisine,** kitchen cupboard; **a. vitrée,** glazed cupboard; **a. de toilette, à pharmacie,** bathroom cabinet, medicine cabinet; **a. à outils,** tool-chest; *Navy:* **a. à sacs,** bag rack; *Nau: Av:* **a. pour gilets de sauvetage,** life-jacket compartment; (*b*) wardrobe; **a. à glace,** mirror wardrobe; *F:* (*of pers.*) **c'est une vraie a. à glace,** he's built like a battleship; **a. normande,** antique (bridal) wardrobe (made in Normandy); **fond d'a.,** cast-off clothes; (*c*) **a. frigorifique,** ice-box; **a. froide,** cold larder; (*d*) **a. à incendie,** fire cabinet; (*e*) *Min:* **a. à boue,** mud screen.

armoire-penderie [armwaːrpɑ̃dri], *s.f.* hanging cupboard.

armoiries [armwari], *s.f.pl. Her:* (coat of) arms, armorial bearings.

armoise [armwaːz], *s.f.* 1. *Bot:* artemisia; *U.S:* sagebrush; **a. commune,** mugwort; **a. absinthe, amère,** wormwood; **a. en épi,** spicate wormwood. 2. = ARMOISIN.

armoisin [armwazɛ̃], *s.m. Tex:* sarcenet, *A:* armozeen.

armon [armɔ̃], *s.m. Veh:* futchel.

armoracia [armɔrasja], *s.f. Bot:* armoracia.

armorial, -aux [armɔrjal, -o]. 1. *a.* armorial, pertaining to heraldry. 2. *s.m.* armorial, book of heraldic arms.

armoricain, -aine [armɔrikɛ̃, -ɛn]. 1. *a. & s. Ethn: Geog:* Armorican; **massif a.,** Armorican chain; *Lit:* **le cycle armoricain,** the Breton cycle. 2. *s.m. Ling:* Armorican; Breton (language).

armorier [armɔrje], *v.tr.* (*pr.sub. & p.d.* **n. armoriions, v. armoriiez**) to (em)blazon; to adorn (sth.) with heraldic bearings.

Armorique [armɔrik], *Pr.n.f. A.Geog:* Armorica.

armoriste [armɔrist], *s.m.* armorist, emblazoner; heraldic designer, engraver, artist.

armure [armyːr], *s.f.* 1. (*a*) armour; **a. complète,** suit of armour; (*b*) **a. d'un navire de guerre,** armour(-plating) of a warship; (*c*) **a. d'un arbre,** tree-guard; **mettre une a. sur une pièce de charpente, etc.,** to reinforce a timber, etc.; (*d*) **a. d'un mât,** fish of a mast; (*e*) defence (of animals). 2. *Tex:* (*a*) cording and healds (of loom); (*b*) draught (of warp); (*c*) weave, pattern, design; **a. fondamentale,** ground weave; **a. toile,** plain weave; **a. satin,** satin-weave. 3. *El.E:* (*a*) pole-piece (of dynamo); (*b*) *occ.* armature (of magnet); (*c*) armouring; sheathing (of cable). 4. *Fish:* **a. à brochet,** trace for pike-fishing. 5. *Mus:* key-signature.

armuré [armyre], *a. Tex:* with self-colour design.

armurerie [armyr(ә)ri], *s.f.* 1. manufacture of arms. 2. arms factory. 3. (*a*) gunsmith's shop; (*b*) (*in barracks*) armoury.

armurier [armyrje], *s.m.* 1. arms manufacturer; gunsmith. 2. *Mil: Navy:* armourer.

arnaque [arnak], *s.f. P:* swindle, trickery.

arnaquer [arnake], *v.tr. P:* to cheat, swindle.

arnaqueur, -euse [arnakœːr, -øːz], *s. P:* cheat, swindler.

Arnaud [arno], *Pr.n.m.* Arnold.

Arnaute [arnoːt], *s.m. Ethn:* Arnaut, Arnaout, Albanian.

arnebia [arnebja], *s.m. Bot:* arnebia.

arnica [arnika], *s.f. Bot: Pharm:* arnica; **a. des montagnes,** mountain tobacco.

Arnoul [arnul], *Pr.n.m.* Arnold.

arobe [arɔb], *s.f.* = ARROBE.

arole, arolle [arɔl], *s.m. Bot:* arolla (pine).

aromate [arɔmat], *s.m.* aromatic; spice.

aromatique [arɔmatik], *a.* 1. aromatic, spicy. 2. *Ch:* **carbures aromatiques,** aromatics; **pétrole non a.,** aromatic-free petróleum.

aromatisation [arɔmatizasjɔ̃], *s.f. Ch:* aromatization.

aromatiser [arɔmatize], *v.tr.* 1. to give aroma to (sth.); *Cu:* to flavour. 2. *Ch:* to aromatize.

arome, arôme [aroːm], *s.m.* aroma; flavour, fragrance; *Cu:* **aromes pour potages,** flavourings for soups.

aronde [arɔ̃ːd], *s.f.* 1. *Orn: A:* swallow. 2. *Carp:* **queue d'a.,** dovetail; **assembler qch. à, en, queue d'a.,** to dovetail sth.; *Fort:* **ouvrage en queue d'a.,** horn-work.

arondelle [arɔ̃dɛl], *s.f. Fish:* (strong, heavy) ground-line.

arpège [arpɛʒ], *s.m. Mus:* arpeggio; spread, broken or arpeggiated chord.

arpègement [arpɛʒmɑ̃], *s.m. Mus:* arpeggiation, playing of arpeggios.

arpéger [arpeʒe], *v.tr.* (**j'arpège, n. arpégeons; j'arpégeai(s); j'arpégerai**); *Mus:* to arpeggiate; **accord arpégé** = ARPÈGE.

arpent [arpɑ̃], *s.m. Meas:* arpent (*an old French measure, roughly = an acre*).

arpentage [arpɑ̃taːʒ], *s.m.* (land-)surveying, land-measuring; **faire l'a. d'un terrain,** to measure a piece of ground; **borne d'a.,** land-mark; *s.a.* CHAÎNE 1.

arpenter [arpɑ̃te], *v.tr.* 1. to survey, measure (land). 2. *F:* **a. le terrain,** to stride over the ground; **il arpentait le quai,** he was tramping, pacing, up and down the platform; he was pacing the platform.

arpenteur [arpɑ̃tœr], *s.m.* 1. (land-)surveyor; *s.a.* CHAÎNE 1. 2. *Orn:* great plover.

arpenteuse [arpɑ̃tøːz], *a. & s.f. Ent:* **(chenille) a.,** span-worm, looper, measuring worm, *U.S:* inch-worm.

arpète, arpette [arpɛt], *s.f. P:* milliner's apprentice, errand-girl.

arpin [arpɛ̃], *s.m. A: F:* (professional) wrestler; strong man (of the fair); *Wr:* **coup d'a.,** head throw.

arpion [arpjɔ̃], *s.m. P:* (*a*) foot; **j'ai mal aux arpions,** my dogs are killing me; (*b*) toe.

arpon [arpɔ̃], *s.m.* pit-saw, cross-cut saw, two-handled saw.

arqué [arke], *a.* arched, curved; cambered (beam, etc.); high-bridged (nose); bandy-legged (horse); cambered, hogged (ship); **jambes arquées,** bow-legs; **plumes arquées,** (cock's) sickle-feathers; *Bot:* **feuille arquée,** fornicate leaf.

arquebusade [arkәbyzad], *s.f. A.Mil:* (h)arquebusade.

arquebuse [arkәbyːz], *s.f. A.Mil:* (h)arquebus.

arquebuserie [arkәbyzri], *s.f. A.Mil:* = ARMURERIE.

arquebusier [arkәbyzje], *s.m. A.Mil:* 1. (h)arquebusier. 2. = ARMURIER.

arquepincer [arkpɛ̃se], *v.tr. P:* to steal, pinch (watch, etc.); se faire a., to get nabbed.

arquer [arke]. 1. *v.tr.* to bend, arch, curve (wood, iron, etc.); to camber (surface); **a. le dos,** to bend, hump, the back; (*of cat*) to arch its back; *Nau:* **a. un mât,** to bow a mast. 2. *v.i.* to bend; to sag; to buckle. 3. *v.i. P:* to walk, *P:* to hoof it.

s'arquer, (of the legs, back, etc.) to bend; to become bent; (*of ship, keel*) to hog.

arquérite [arkerit], *s.f. Miner:* arquerite, silver amalgam.

arqûre [arkyːr], *s.f.* arcuation, incurvation, bending; *Vet:* bandy-legs.

arrachage [araʃaːʒ], *s.m.* pulling up, rooting up, (of plants, etc.); lifting (of potatoes); pulling out, wrenching out, drawing, extraction (of tooth, nail, etc.).

arraché [araʃe]. 1. *a. Her:* erased. 2. *s.m. Sp: Weight-lifting:* snatch; *adv.phr.* **à l'a., gagner à l'a.,** to snatch a win, to win with a terrific effort.

arrache-cartouche [araʃkartuʃ], *s.m. Sm.a:* (cartridge) extractor; *pl. arrache-cartouche(s).*

arrache-chaussures [araʃʃosy:r], *s.m.inv. in pl.* boot-jack.

arrache-clou [araʃklu], *s.m. Tls:* nail-drawer, -claw, -wrench; case-opener; *pl. arrache-clous.*

arrache-douille [araʃdu:j], *s.m. Sm.a:* (cartridge-case) extractor; *pl. arrache-douille(s).*

arrachement [araʃmɑ̃], *s.m.* 1. rooting up, tearing-up (of tree, etc.). 2. (*a*) tearing away from; parting; **ils ne pouvaient se décider à l'a.,** they could not decide to part; (*b*) wrench; **nous ne pouvons rien quitter sans a.,** we can't leave anything without a wrench. 3. *Const:* toothing; **pierre d'a.,** toothing stone. 4. (*a*) *Mec:* tearing, wrenching, stripping; **effort d'a.,** wrenching force; (*b*) *Med: Surg:* evulsion, extraction, wrench. 5. landslide.

arrache-pied (d') [daraʃpje], *adv.phr.* without interruption; **travailler d'a.-p.,** (i) to work steadily, *F:* to hammer away; (ii) to slave away; **parler deux heures d'a.-p.,** to talk for two hours at a stretch, on end.

arrache-pieux [araʃpjø], *s.m.inv.* pile-drawer.

arrache-pointe(s) [araʃpwɛ̃:t], *s.m.inv. in pl. Tls:* tack-drawer.

arracher [araʃe], *v.tr.* to tear (out, up, away); to, pull (up, out, away); to draw (nail); **a. un arbre,** to root up, uproot, a tree; **a. un arbre pour le planter ailleurs,** to take up a tree to plant elsewhere; **a. des souches,** to dig up, grub up, the stumps of trees; **a. des pommes de terre,** to lift potatoes; **a. qch. de qch.,** to pull sth. off, from, out of, sth.; **un obus lui arracha le bras,** a shell blew off his arm; **a. qch. à qn, des mains de qn,** to snatch sth. from s.o., out of s.o.'s hands; **on lui arracha l'enfant des bras,** they tore the child from her arms; **a. un oiseau des griffes d'un chat,** to snatch a bird from a cat's claws; **s'a. de force à l'étreinte de qn,** to wrench oneself free; **a. qn de son foyer,** to drag, uproot, s.o. from his home; **a. le filet d'une vis,** to strip a screw; **a. le papier d'un mur,** to strip a wall; **a. une affiche,** to tear down a poster; **a. une dent à qn,** to pull (out), extract, draw, s.o.'s tooth; **se faire a. une dent,** to have a tooth out; **le chat lui arracha la joue,** the cat tore his cheek; **a. les yeux à qn,** to tear s.o.'s eyes out; **a. un aveu à qn,** to draw a confession from s.o.; **a. de l'argent à qn,** to extort, extract, money from s.o., to squeeze money out of s.o.; **a. un secret à qn,** to drag a secret from s.o.; **a. des promesses à qn,** to extract promises from s.o.; **essayer en vain d'a. qn à ses mauvaises habitudes,** to try in vain to break s.o. of his bad habits; **la douleur lui arracha des gémissements,** pain wrung groans from him; **a. des larmes à qn,** to wring tears from s.o.; **s'a. les cheveux,** to tear one's hair; **a. qn à la mort,** to snatch, rescue, s.o. from the jaws of death, to save s.o. from death; **a. qn à ses réflexions, au sommeil,** to rouse s.o. from his reflections, from his sleep; **la sonnerie du réveil m'arracha du lit,** the ringing of the alarm dragged me out of bed; **je l'ai arraché à un rêve en éternuant,** my sneeze woke him from his dream; **a. qn à son travail,** to tear s.o. away from his work; **a. la victoire à qn,** to snatch victory from s.o.; **pierres arrachées aux falaises,** stones torn from the cliffs; *s.a.* PILOTIS; **s'a. de ses livres,** to tear oneself away from one's books; *F:* **cela lui arrache le cœur de . . .,** it breaks his heart to . . .; *F:* **on se l'arrache,** he, she, is in great demand; *Weight-lifting:* **a. un poids,** to snatch a weight.

arrache-racine(s) [araʃrasin], *s.m. Tls: Hort:* spud; *pl. arrache-racines.*

arrache-tuyau [araʃtɥijo], *s.m.* casing spear, casing dog; *pl. arrache-tuyaux.*

arracheur, -euse [araʃœ:r, -ø:z], *s.* 1. puller; *F:* **a. de dents,** tooth-drawer; **il ment, il est menteur, comme un a. de dents,** he is an arrant liar, he lies like a trooper. 2. (*a*) person who lifts potatoes, beetroot, etc.; (*b*) *s.f. Agr:* **arracheuse,** (i) grubbing-plough, grubber; (ii) potato-lifter, potato-lifting plough; potato-digger, -harvester; **arracheuse de betteraves,** beet puller, beet harvester; **arracheuse-décolleteuse,** topper-harvester; **arracheuse de lin,** flax puller.

arrachis [araʃi], *s.m.* 1. uprooting, rooting up (of trees). 2. piece of cleared ground; clearing. 3. uprooted plant, tree, etc.

arrachoir [araʃwa:r], *s.m. Agr:* = ARRACHEUR 2 (*b*).

arrageois, -oise [araʒwa, -wa:z], *a. & s. Geog:* (native) of Arras.

arraisonnement [arɛzɔnmɑ̃], *s.m. Nau:* 1. boarding (of ship); **officier chargé de l'a.,** boarding officer. 2. **a. de la patente (d'un navire),** examination of the bill of health, sanitary report.

arraisonner [arɛzɔne], *Nau:* 1. *v.tr.* **a. un navire,** (i) to hail, speak, a vessel (as to her destination, health on board, etc.); (ii) to stop and examine a ship. 2. *v.i.* **a. avec les autorités du port,** to report to the port authorities.

arraisonneur [arɛzɔnœ:r], *a.* hailing; **le navire a.,** the hailing, boarding, ship.

arrangeable [arɑ̃ʒabl̩], *a.* arrangeable; repairable; adjustable.

arrangeant [arɑ̃ʒɑ̃], *a.* accommodating, obliging, complaisant, helpful.

arrangement [arɑ̃ʒmɑ̃], *s.m.* arrangement; (*a*) ordering; disposition; order; **a. des mots dans une phrase,** (i) ordering; (ii) order, of the words in a sentence; **mal prendre ses arrangements,** to make bad arrangements, to take faulty measures; *Mth:* **arrangements de dix objets pris quatre à quatre,** permutations of ten things taken four at a time; (*b*) (i) **il a du goût dans l'a. de ses meubles,** he shows good taste in the way he arranges his furniture; (ii) **cet homme manque d'a.,** this man lacks method; (*c*) agreement; *Jur:* settlement; **prendre un a., des arrangements, avec qn,** to make arrangements, come to an arrangement, to terms, with s.o.; **il a fait des arrangements avec son propriétaire,** he has come to terms with his landlord; **sauf a. contraire,** unless otherwise agreed; **ils ont un a.,** they have an agreement, an understanding; **a. avec ses créanciers,** composition with one's creditors; (*d*) *Mus:* **a. pour piano, pour violon,** arrangement, transcription, for the piano, for the violin.

arranger [arɑ̃ʒe], *v.tr.* **(j'arrangeais n. arrangeons)** to arrange. 1. (*a*) to set in order; **a. une bibliothèque,** to arrange a library, to put books in order in a library; **a. les livres dans une bibliothèque,** to place, arrange, books in a bookcase, in a library; **a. une chambre,** (i) to tidy up, clear up, a room, to put a room straight, in order; (ii) to lay out, organize, a room; **a. sa cravate,** to adjust, straighten, one's tie, to put one's tie straight; **s'a. les cheveux,** to tidy one's hair, to put one's hair straight; **bien arrangé,** tidy, *Nau:* shipshape (and Bristol fashion); **elle est mal arrangée,** she is badly turned out; **a. une montre,** to overhaul, mend, a watch; **a. un appareil de radio,** to adjust, put right, fix, a wireless set; *Cards:* **a. ses couleurs,** to sort one's cards; *F:* **je l'ai arrangé de la belle manière,** (i) I gave him a good dressing-down; (ii) *P:* I fixed him; **vous voilà bien arrangé(e)!** you do look a sight! **on vous a arrangé,** you've been had; (*b*) *Mus:* to set, arrange (song for violin, etc.). 2. to contrive; **a. un concert,** to arrange for, organize, a concert; **a. une fête,** to get up an entertainment; **a. qch. d'avance,** to arrange sth. in advance, to plan sth. ahead, to pre-arrange sth.; **tout a. d'avance,** to plan everything in advance; **a. un projet dans sa tête,** to work out a plan in one's head; **a. un complot,** to hatch a plot. 3. to settle (quarrel, matter, etc.); to compose, make up (quarrel); **a. un procès,** to settle a lawsuit amicably; **je vais essayer d'a. les choses,** I will try to put things straight, to straighten things out; *F:* **ce qui n'est pas (fait) pour a. les choses,** which doesn't help matters; **a. un mariage,** to arrange a marriage; **comment arrangez-vous cela avec votre conscience?** how do you square it with your conscience? 4. **faire qch. pour a. qn,** to do sth. to accommodate, to oblige, s.o.; **cela m'arrangera le mieux du monde,** that will suit me excellently, *F:* fine; **il est difficile d'a. tout le monde,** it is hard to please everybody.

s'arranger. 1. (*a*) to manage, contrive; **arrangez-vous comme vous pouvez, arrangez-vous au mieux,** manage as best you can; **arrangez-vous pour être là,** you must arrange to be there; **si vous pouvez vous arranger pour le voir,** if you can manage to see him; **s'a. de ce qu'on a,** to make do, to make shift, with what one has; **qu'il s'arrange!** that's his look-out! *F:* that's his pigeon! **arrange-toi (tout seul)!** *F:* that's your baby! **il s'arrange de tout,** he is easily pleased, very adaptable, he can do, put up, with anything; (*b*) **les idées s'arrangeaient dans ma tête avec la plus incroyable facilité,** my ideas fell into place, in my head with the most incredible ease; *F:* **s'a. dans un fauteuil pour s'endormir,** to settle oneself down in an armchair to go to sleep. 2. (*a*) **s'a. avec qn,** to come to an agreement, to terms with s.o., *F:* to fix things (up) with s.o.; **arrangez-vous,** settle it among(st) yourselves; **s'a. avec ses créanciers,** to compound with one's creditors; (*b*) **cela s'arrangera,** things will turn out all right; **cela s'arrangera tout seul,** it will take care of itself, it will sort itself out; **c'est malheureux que les choses ne se soient pas mieux arrangées,** it is a pity that things did not turn out better. 3. **ce mécanisme peut s'a.,** this machine can be repaired. 4. to dress, to get oneself ready; *F:* **elle est allée s'a.,** she has gone to titivate; *F:* **elle ne s'est pas arrangée,** her appearance has not improved.

arrangeur, -euse [arɑ̃ʒœ:r, -ø:z], *s. esp. Mus:* arranger.

arraphique [arafik], *a.* **reliure a.,** perfect binding.

arrecteur [arɛktœ:r], *a.m. Anat:* **muscle a.,** arrector.

arrentement [ar(r)ɑ̃tmɑ̃], *s.m. A:* 1. (*a*) renting; (*b*) rent. 2. leasing.

arrenter [ar(r)ɑ̃te], *v.tr. A:* 1. to rent (land). 2. to lease (land).

arrérager [arerаʒe], *v.i.* **(arrérageant)** to remain unpaid; **laisser a. ses dividendes,** to allow one's dividends to accumulate.

arrérages [arera:ʒ], *s.m.pl.* 1. arrears (of wages, of pension, etc.); **a. de salaire,** arrears of wages. 2. back interest; **laisser courir les a.,** to allow the back-interest to accumulate; **coupon d'a.,** interest or dividend warrant; **toucher ses a.,** to draw one's pension, dividends.

arrestation [arɛstasjɔ̃], *s.f.* arrest; **opérer une arrestation,** to effect an arrest; **mettre qn en a.,** to take s.o. into custody, to arrest s.o.; **en état d'a.,** under arrest; **arrestations en masse,** wholesale arrests, general round-up; **a. arbitraire,** false arrest.

arrêt [arɛ], *s.m.* 1. (*a*) stop, stoppage; stopping, arrest (of motion); **a. d'un train,** stopping of a train; **a. d'urgence,** emergency stop; **point d'a.,** (i) stopping-place, halt, stopping-point; (ii) *Mus:* pause (over a rest); **faire un a. au cours de son voyage,** to break one's journey, *U.S:* to stop over; **billet avec faculté d'a.,** ticket allowing one to break one's journey, *U.S:* stop-over (ticket); **a. en cours de route,** break of journey, *U.S:* stop-over; **facultés d'arrêts en cours de route,** option of break of journey; **trajet sans a.,** non-stop journey; **combien de temps d'a. à . . .?** how long do we stop at . . .? **dix minutes d'a.,** ten minutes' stop, halt; ten minutes' break; **temps d'a.,** pause, halt; **marquer un temps d'a.,** to pause, halt, mark time; **moment d'a.,** short stop, pause; **elle travaillait sans a.,** she worked unceasingly, without a stop; she was working full tilt; **elle a parlé sans a. pendant deux heures,** she talked for two hours without stopping, non-stop; **a. des affaires commerciales,** stoppage, cessation, of business; **a. de circulation,** traffic hold-up, jam; *Com:* **a. de payement d'un chèque,** stopping of a cheque; **mettre a. à qch.,** to stop sth.; **mettre a. à un chèque,** to stop a cheque; *Jur:* **mettre a. à un procès,** to stop a case; *Phot:* **bain acide pour a. (du développement), bain d'a.,** stop-bath; *Physiol:* **a. de développement,** arrest of development, of growth; *Med:* **a. (du cœur),** acute heart failure; *Tchn:* **appareil, dispositif, d'a.,** stopping device, stop gear; *Atom.Ph:* **a. brusque automatique,** scram; *Av:* shut down; **barrière, dispositif, d'a.,** arresting gear; *Mil:* **bataille d'a.,** holding battle; **ligne d'a.,** holding line; **fort d'a.,** barrier fort; **tir d'a.,** barrage fire; **robinet d'a.,** (i) stop-cock; (ii) stop-valve; **"arrêt," "off"**; **soupape d'a.,** stop-valve; **boulon d'a.,** check-bolt; **saillie d'a.,** stop-shoulder; **ergot d'a.,** stop-piece, stop-pin; **collier, bague, d'a.,** stop-collar; **cheville, goupille, d'a.,** stop-bolt; **blochet d'a. (d'un frein),** stop-block; *Nau:* **cales d'a. (d'un gouvernail),** rudder-stops; *Rail:* **taquet d'a.,** stop-block, stop-buffer; *Mch:* **a. inopiné,** breakdown; *W.Tel: T.V:* **a. d'émission,** breakdown, break in transmission; *Rail:* **signal à l'a.,** signal at danger; **signal d'a.,** stop-signal; *s.a.* DISTANCE; (*b*) (= **point d'arrêt**) stop; **a. d'autobus, de trolleybus,** bus-stop, trolleybus-stop; **a. fixe, obligatoire,** (compulsory, regular) bus-stop; **a. facultatif, sur demande,** request stop; **ne pas descendre avant l'a.,** do not get off before the bus (train, etc.) stops; **parcours à arrêts fréquents,** route with frequent stops; (*c*) stop, catch, check (of door, etc.); tumbler (of a lock); stay (of window); **cran d'a.,** safety-catch; **couteau avec a. de sûreté,** clasp-knife with lock-back; *Mec.E:* **a. de chaîne,** chain-stop; *Cy:* **a. de pied,** toe-clip; (*d*) *Mec.E:* **a. de secours,**

automatic stop motion, knock-off motion (of press, etc.); automatic stop-gear. **2.** (*a*) decree, general order; **les arrêts de la Providence,** the decrees of Providence; (*b*) *Jur:* judgement, adjudication (*delivered by* **Cour d'assises, Cour d'appel,** *or* **Cour de cassation**); **prononcer, rendre, un a.,** to pronounce, deliver, judgment, give an award; **a. par défaut,** judgment by default; **a. de défense,** stay of execution; **a. de mort,** sentence of death, death sentence; *s.a.* SUSPENSION 2. **3.** (*a*) seizure, impounding, attachment; **faire a. sur des marchandises,** to impound, seize, goods; to seize goods in transit; (*b*) *Nau:* detention (of ship); *A:* **a. de prince,** embargo; **mettre a. sur un navire,** (i) to order the detention of a ship; (ii) to put an embargo on a ship. **4.** arrest; (*a*) **ordre, mandat d'a.,** order, warrant of arrest, for the arrest (of s.o.); **décerner, lancer, un mandat d'a. contre qn,** to issue, make out, a warrant for the arrest of s.o.; **maison d'a.,** house of detention; prison; (*b*) *pl.* **mettre un officier aux arrêts,** to put an officer under arrest; *Mil:* **arrêts forcés, de rigueur,** close arrest; **arrêts simples,** open arrest; **arrêts à la chambre, arrêts domestiques,** house-arrest; **arrêts de forteresse,** fortress arrest (of high-ranking officer); **garder les arrêts,** to be, remain, under arrest; **lever les arrêts de qn,** to release s.o. from arrest; **rompre les arrêts,** to break arrest. **5.** *Arm:* **a. (de lance),** rest (for couched lance); **lance en a.,** lance in rest; **mettre sa lance en a.,** to couch one's lance; **courir la lance en a.,** to *Fb:* run a-tilt (sur, at); to tilt (at). **6.** *Sp:* (*a*) (i) *Fb:* tackle; (ii) *Rugby Fb:* **a. de volée,** fair catch; (*b*) **coup d'a.,** *Box:* counter, *Fenc:* stop-thrust; crushing argument. **7.** *Ven:* set; **chien d'a.,** setter, pointer; (*of dog*) **tomber en a. (devant le gibier),** to point (at game); to set; **faire un bel a.,** to make a dead set (**devant,** at); **être à l'a., en a.,** to be at a dead set; *F:* **rester, tomber, en a. devant qn, qch.,** to stop and stare at s.o., sth. **8.** *Cards:* **(carte d')a.,** stop(per).

arrêt-barrage [arɛbaraːʒ], *s.m. Min:* barrier; *pl. arrêts-barrages.*

arrêté [arɛte]. **1.** *a.* (*a*) (*of ideas, etc.*) fixed, decided; **homme aux opinions arrêtées,** dogmatic person, person with set ideas; **dessein a.,** settled design; **plan a.,** preconcerted plan; **avoir des idées bien arrêtées,** to have settled ideas, very decided views; (*b*) *Sp:* **départ a.,** standing start; (*c*) *Paint:* **un dessin a.,** a finished drawing. **2.** *s.m.* (*a*) decision, order, decree; **a. ministériel,** departmental order (signed by a minister); **a. municipal,** by(e)-law; **a. d'exécution,** decree providing for the enforcement of a law; **prendre un a.,** to pass a decree; (*b*) *Com:* **a. de compte(s),** settlement (of an account).

arrête-bœuf [arɛtbœf], *s.m.inv. Bot:* rest-harrow, cammock.

arrêter [arete]. **I.** *v.tr.* **1.** to stop (s.o., sth.); to check (attack); to bring (train) to a standstill; to hinder, impede, hold up; to detain, delay, keep back; to stem (flood, torrent, etc.); **a. un cheval,** to stop, pull up, a horse; **a. qn tout court,** to stop s.o. short; **arrêté en pleine course,** checked in full career; **rien ne l'arrêtera,** nothing will stop him, he will stick at nothing; **cette objection arrêtera les esprits sérieux,** this objection will make serious-minded people stop to, and, think; this objection will prove an obstacle to serious-minded people; **a. un flot de sang,** to stem, stanch, a flow of blood; *Mec: Av: etc:* to shut down; **quel obstacle vous arrête?** what is stopping you? **un seul obstacle m'arrête,** only one thing stands in my way; **obstacle qui arrête nos projets,** obstacle that impedes our plans; **il y a un mur qui arrête la vue,** there is a wall blocking the view; **a. le progrès,** to block, hold up, progress; **cela a tout arrêté,** that put a stop to everything; **a. un mouvement,** to arrest a motion, to check a movement; **a. le vent,** to break (the force of) the wind; **a. une machine,** to stop a machine, to put a machine out of action; *Aut:* **a. le moteur,** to shut off, switch off, the engine; **a. une hémorragie,** to suppress a haemorrhage; **a. le paiement d'un chèque,** to stop (payment of) a cheque; **a. la croissance, le développement,** to arrest growth, development; to stunt; **la flotte était arrêtée par le mauvais temps,** foul weather detained the fleet, the fleet was weather-bound; **le brouillard, la neige, a complètement arrêté toute circulation,** fog, snow, has brought traffic to a standstill, traffic is completely fog-bound, snow-bound; **la voiture de ma tante a été arrêtée par des brigands,** my aunt's car was held up by brigands; *Fb:* **a. un adversaire,** to stop an opponent; **a. un but,** to stop, save, a goal; *Ven:* (*of dog*) **a. le gibier,** to point game; *abs:* **ce chien arrête bien,** this dog points well. **2.** to fix, fasten, secure (shutter, plank, etc.); **a. ses yeux, ses soupçons, sur qn,** to fix one's eyes, one's suspicions, on s.o.; **a. l'attention,** to arrest attention; *Needlew:* **a. un point, un tour de crochet,** to fasten off a stitch, a row; *Knitting:* **a. les mailles,** to cast off. **3.** to arrest, seize (criminal); to seize (contraband, books, etc.); **être arrêté,** to be arrested, taken in charge (by the police); **l'assassin n'est pas encore arrêté,** the murderer is still at large; **faire a. qn,** to have s.o. arrested; to give s.o. in charge. **4.** (*a*) to engage, hire (room, seat, servant, etc.); to retain (s.o.'s services); (*b*) to decide sth.; **a. un jour,** to fix, appoint, settle, a day; **a. un programme,** to draw up a programme; **a. des dispositions générales,** to lay down general rules (of procedure, etc.); **le président a arrêté que . . .,** the president has decreed that . . .; **a. de faire qch.,** to decide to do sth. **5.** *Com:* to make up, close, settle (account).

II. *v.i.* to stop, halt; **dites au chauffeur d'arrêter devant l'hôtel de ville,** tell the driver to stop at, in front of, the town hall; **arrêtez un moment,** stop a moment, *F:* hold on a second; **elle n'arrête jamais de parler,** she never stops talking; *int.* **arrête! arrêtez!** stop (it)! halt! that's enough! *F:* hold on! whoa! don't! *P:* lay off!

s'arrêter. **1.** to stop, to come to a stop, to a standstill; *Mec:* (*of moving body*) to come to rest; **être forcé de s'a.,** to be brought to a stand; **s'a. court,** to stop short; **la voiture s'arrêta,** the car stopped, drew up; **l'auto s'arrêta devant ma porte,** the car pulled up, drew up, at my door; **il sortit de la foule et s'arrêta devant moi,** he emerged from the crowd and stood before me; **s'a. en route,** to break one's journey; **ma montre s'est arrêtée,** my watch has stopped; **s'a. de faire qch.,** to stop, leave off, doing sth; **s'a. à contempler qch.,** to stand looking at sth., to stop in contemplation before sth; **il s'arrêta à la porte pour me dire . . .,** he paused at the door to say to me . . .; **s'a. de fumer,** to give up smoking; **s'a. de parler,** to stop talking; **s'a. chez qn,** to call at s.o.'s; **passer sans s'a.,** to pass by without stopping; **les aliments s'arrêtent dans ma gorge,** food sticks in my throat. **2.** (*a*) **s'a. à, sur, un sujet,** (i) to pay attention to a subject; (ii) to lay stress on, dwell on, insist on, a subject; (*b*) **son regard s'arrêta sur moi,** (i) he eyed me intently; (ii) his eyes fell on me; **mes regards s'arrêtèrent sur la statue,** my eyes fastened on the statue; **son choix s'est arrêté sur . . .,** his choice fell on . . .; **ne pas s'arrêter sur . . .,** to pass over . . .; (*c*) **s'a. à une résolution,** to abide by a resolve.

arrêtiste [aretist], *s.m. Jur:* legal commentator.

arrêtoir [arɛtwaːr], *s.m.* **1.** *Mec.E: etc:* (*a*) stop (of bolt, spring, etc.); lug, catch; keeper (of chain); (*b*) pawl; (*c*) *Nau:* stopper. **2.** *Arch:* shoulder.

arrhement [arəmɑ̃], *s.m.* payment of a deposit; leaving a deposit; giving an earnest.

arrhénotoquie [arenɔtɔki], *s.f. Biol:* arrhenotoky.

arrher [are], *v.tr. A:* (*a*) to give earnest money to (s.o.); (*b*) to pay a deposit on (rented house, etc.), to leave a deposit with (s.o.).

arrhes [aːr], *s.f.pl.* (*a*) deposit, down payment; earnest(-money); **verser des a.,** to pay a deposit; **laisser mille francs d'a.,** to leave a thousand francs as a deposit; (*b*) fine; **stipulation d'a.,** right to annul a sale by paying a fine.

Arrien [arjɛ̃], *Pr.n.m. Gr.Lit:* Arrian.

arriération [arjerasjɔ̃], *s.f. Psy:* retardation; backwardness (of child, etc.); feeble-mindedness.

arrière [arjɛːr]. **1.** *adv.* **(en) arrière** (*a*) behind; **cent ans en a.,** a hundred years back; **la casquette en a.,** with his cap tilted back, on the back of his head; **rester en a.,** to remain, stay behind; to lag behind; **il reste de plus en plus en a.,** he is dropping, falling, behind; *Nau:* **droit a.,** right abaft; **avoir le vent en a.,** to have the wind astern; *s.a.* VENT 1; *prep.phr.* **en a. de qn, de qch.,** behind s.o., sth.; **il est resté en a. de sa classe,** he stayed at the bottom of the class; **en a. de son siècle, de son temps,** behind the times; (*b*) in arrears, behindhand; **locataire en a. pour ses loyers,** tenant behind(hand) with his rent; (*c*) backwards, backward (motion); *int.* **arrière!** (stand) back! *A:* avaunt! *A:* **a. les méchantes langues!** away with evil tongues! **a. la raillerie!** stop joking! *B:* **arrière Satan! get thee behind me, Satan! faire un pas en a.,** to step back a pace; **sauter en a.,** to jump backwards; **revenir en a.,** to come back; **retourner en a.,** to go, turn, back; **aller en a.,** to back; **regard en a.,** backward glance; **regarder en a.,** (i) to look back; (ii) to look into the past; *Nau:* **en a. (à) toute (vitesse)!** full speed astern! **tout le monde en a.!** everybody back! **marche (en) a.,** (i) backing (of engine); reverse motion, action; (ii) *Nau:* motion astern; *Nau:* **turbine de marche a.,** astern turbine; *Aut: Mch:* **pignon de marche a.,** reverse gear; **mettre en marche a.,** (i) to go into reverse; (ii) to back; **entrer dans le, sortir du, garage en marche a.,** to back into, out of, the garage; **faire marche (en) a.,** to back; *Nau:* to go astern; *Aut:* to reverse; *F:* to back down, retract; **faire machine (en) a.,** to reverse the engine(s) (of steam engine, ship, etc.); *F:* to back down, to back-pedal. **2.** *a.inv.* back; **essieu a.,** back-axle, rear-axle; *Aut:* **feu a.,** rear-light; **à moteur a.,** rear-engined; **siège, banquette a.,** back seat (of car); **siège a. (de motocyclette),** pillion-seat; *Needlew:* **point a.,** back-stitch; *Nau:* **cale a.,** after-hold; **vapeur à roue a.,** stern-wheeler, stern-wheel steamer; *Surv:* **coup a.,** back-sight. **3.** *s.m.* (*a*) back, back part, rear (of house, etc.); *Mil:* **les arrières, l'a.,** (i) the rear, the rear area(s); (ii) the back area(s,) the home front, non-operational zone; tail (of ski); **transporter un blessé à l'a.,** to remove a casualty to the rear; **voyager en a., à l'a.,** to travel in the back (of a car); **voyelle d'a.,** back vowel; *Aut:* **un modèle tout à l'a.,** a rear-engined model; (*b*) *Nau:* stern (of ship); stern-sheet (of small boat); **a. de croiseur,** cruiser stern; **a. carré,** flat, square, stern; **a. à voûte, en cul de poule,** counter stern; **vers l'a.,** aft, abaft; **sur l'a.,** astern; **sur l'a. du travers,** abaft the beam; **aller à l'a.,** to go aft; **le plus à l'a.,** aftermost; **chambre de l'a.,** after-cabin; **navire haut de l'a.,** high-sterned ship. **4.** *s.m. Fb:* (full) back; *Rugby Fb:* full back; *Fb:* **a. gauche, droit,** right, left, back.

arriéré [arjere]. **1.** *a.* (*a*) late, behind(hand), in arrears; **paiement a.,** overdue, outstanding, payment; **intérêt a.,** outstanding interest; (*b*) **enfant a.,** backward child; **gens arriérés,** people behind the times; **idées arriérées,** old-fashioned notions, ideas; **il vit dans quelque village a.,** he lives in some benighted village; *Pol.Ec:* **pays arriérés,** under-developed countries; *Mil: F:* **le peloton des arriérés,** the awkward squad. **2.** *s.m.* arrears (of account, correspondence, etc.); backlog; **a. du loyer,** arrears of rent, back rent; **avoir de l'a.,** to be in arrear(s), behindhand; *Mil:* **a. de solde,** back pay; **a. de permissions,** accumulated leave.

arrière-automne [arjɛrotɔn], *s.m.* late autumn; **un soir d'a.-a. . . .,** one evening in late autumn . . .; *pl. arrière-automnes.*

arrière-ban [arjɛrbɑ̃], *s.m. Hist:* whole body of vassals (including the second levy); arrière-ban; *F:* **une équipe d'a.-b.,** a scratch team; **il invita le ban et l'a.-b. de ses parents et amis,** he invited all his friends and relations; *s.a.* BAN 3; *pl. arrière-bans.*

arrière-bassin [arjɛrbasɛ̃], *s.m.* inner dock; *pl. arrière-bassins.*

arrière-bâtiment [arjɛrbɑtimɑ̃], *s.m.* the back part of a building; *pl. arrière-bâtiments.*

arrière-bec [arjɛrbɛk], *s.m. Civ.E:* **1.** downstream cutwater (of bridge pier); starling (downstream). **2.** stern, after-peak (of pontoon boat); *pl. arrière-becs.*

arrière-bief [arjɛrbjɛf], *s.m. Hyd.E:* head-bay; *pl. arrière-biefs.*

arrière-bouche [arjɛrbuʃ], *s.f.* back of the mouth; fauces; *pl. arrière-bouches.*

arrière-boutique [arjɛrbutik], *s.f.* back-shop, *U.S:* back-store; *pl. arrière-boutiques.*

arrière-bras [arjɛrbra], *s.m.inv.* **1.** *Anat:* upper arm. **2.** *Arm:* **a.-b.,** rerebrace. **3.** *Civ.E:* balance-lever (of bascule-bridge).

arrière-caution [arjɛrkosjɔ̃], *s.f. Com:* surety for a surety; *pl. arrière-cautions.*

arrière-cavité [arjɛrkavite], *s.f.* (*a*) *Anat:* **a.-c. des épiploons,** oriental bursa, bursa orientalis; (*b*) *Anat:* **a.-c. des fosses nasales,** pars nasalis pharyngis; *pl. arrière-cavités.*

arrière-cerveau [arjɛrsɛrvo], *s.m. Med:* rhombenecephalon; epencephalon; *pl. arrière-cerveaux.*

arrière-chaîne [arjɛrʃɛn], *s.f. Geog:* lower ridge; *pl. arrière-chaînes.*

arrière-chœur [arjɛrkœːr], *s.m. Ecc:* retrochoir; *pl. arrière-chœurs.*

arrière-corps [arjɛrkɔːr], *s.m.inv.* **1.** retreating part (of building); back premises. **2.** *Join:* sunk panel; coffer. **3.** *Art:* background (of bas-relief).

arrière-cour [arjɛrkuːr], *s.f.* back-yard; *pl. arrière-cours.*

arrière-cousin, -ine [arjɛrkuzɛ̃, -in], *s.* distant cousin; *pl. arrière-cousin(e)s.*

arrière-cuisine [arjɛrkɥizin], *s.f.* scullery, back-kitchen; *pl. arrière-cuisines.*

arrière-défense [arjɛrdefɑ̃ːs], *s.f. Fb:* (the) back-line defence, the backs; *pl. arrière-défenses.*

arrière-faix [arjɛrfɛ], *s.m.inv. Obst:* after-birth, secundines.

arrière-fief [arjɛrfjɛf], *s.m. A: Jur:* sub-fief; *pl. arrière-fiefs.*

arrière-fleur [arjɛrflœːr], *s.f.* (*a*) late flower; (*b*) second efflorescence, flowering; *pl. arrière-fleurs.*

arrière-foin [arjɛrfwɛ̃], *s.m. Agr:* aftermath; *pl. arrière-foins.*

arrière-fond [arjɛrfɔ̃], *s.m.* innermost depth; *pl. arrière-fonds.*

arrière-garde [arjɛrgard], *s.f.* **1.** *Mil:* rear-guard. **2.** *Navy:* rear squadron; *pl. arrière-gardes.*

arrière-gorge [arjɛrgɔrʒ], *s.f.* back of the throat; **voix d'a.-g.,** throaty voice; *pl. arrière-gorges.*

arrière-goût [arjɛrgu], *s.m.* after-taste, faint taste (de, of); *pl. arrière-goûts.*

arrière-grand-mère [arjɛrgrɑ̃mɛːr], *s.f.* great-grandmother; *pl. arrière-grand-mères.*

arrière-grand-père [arjɛrgrɑ̃pɛːr], *s.m.* great-grandfather; *pl. arrière-grands-pères.*

arrière-grands-parents [arjɛrgrɑ̃parɑ̃], *s.m.pl.inv.* great-grandparents.

arrière-main [arjɛrmɛ̃], *s.m. or f.* **1.** (*a*) *A:* back of the hand; (*b*) *Ten: etc:* **(coup d')a.,** back-hand (stroke); **avoir l'a.-m. belle,** to be good on the back-hand. **2.** (hind)quarters (of horse); *pl. arrière-mains.*

arrière-neveu, -nièce [arjɛrnəvø, -njɛs], *s.* grand-nephew, -niece; *Lit:* **nos arrière-neveux,** our children's children.

arrière-pays [arjɛrpei], *s.m.inv.* hinterland; back-country.

arrière-pensée [arjɛrpɑ̃se]. *s.f.* (*a*) mental reservation; (*b*) ulterior motive; **ils n'avaient pas accepté le traité sans une a.-p. de revanche,** they had not accepted the treaty without a lurking thought of revenge; *pl. arrière-pensées.*

arrière-petit-fils, -petite-fille [arjɛrpətifis, -pətitfij], *s.* great-grandson, -grand-daughter; *pl. arrière-petits-fils, -petites-filles.*

arrière-petit-neveu, -petite-nièce [arjɛrpətinvø, -pətitnjɛs], great-grand-nephew, -niece; *pl. arrière-petits-neveux, -petites-nièces.*

arrière-petits-enfants [arjɛrpətizɑ̃fɑ̃], *s.m.pl.* great-grand-children.

arrière-pièce [arjɛrpjɛs], *s.f.* back room; *pl. arrière-pièces.*

arrière-plage [arjɛrplaːʒ], *s.f. Geol:* backshore; *pl. arrière-plages.*

arrière-plan [arjɛrplɑ̃], *s.m.* background; **à l'a.-p.,** in the background; *Th:* up-stage, at the back; **ce projet est passé à l'a.-p.,** this plan has been shelved for the time being; *F:* **se trouver relégué à l'a.-p.,** to be pushed into the background, to be under an eclipse; **les artistes d'a.-p.,** artists not in the front rank; *pl. arrière-plans.*

arrière-point [arjɛrpwɛ̃], *s.m. Needlew:* back-stitch; *pl. arrière-points.*

arrière-pont [arjɛrpɔ̃], *s.m. Nau:* after-deck; *pl. arrière-ponts.*

arrière-port [arjɛrpɔːr], *s.m.* inner harbour; *pl. arrière-ports.*

arriérer [arjere], *v.tr.* **(j'arrière, n. arriérons, j'arriérerai)** to postpone, delay, defer (payment, etc.).

s'arriérer. **1.** to fall behind. **2.** to get, fall, into arrears.

arrière-radier [arjɛrradje], *s.m. Civ.E:* down-stream apron (of dock, basin, etc.); *pl. arrière-radiers.*

arrière-rang [arjɛrrɑ̃], *s.m. Mil:* rear-rank; *pl. arrière-rangs.*

arrière-saison [arjɛrsɛzɔ̃], *s.f.* (*a*) late season, end of autumn, back-end (of the year); **l'a.-s. de la vie,** the autumn, closing years, evening, of life; (*b*) off-season (for fruit, vegetables, etc.); **les pommes de terre sont chères dans l'a.-s.,** potatoes are expensive at the end of the season, in the off-season; *pl. arrière-saisons.*

arrière-salle [arjɛrsal], *s.f.* inner room (of public house); *pl. arrière-salles.*

arrière-scène [arjɛrsɛn], *s.f. Th:* **1.** back of the stage; **à l'a.-s.,** backstage. **2.** back curtain; back-cloth; back-drop; *pl. arrière-scènes.*

arrière-train [arjɛrtrɛ̃], *s.m.* **1.** (hind)quarters (of animal); *P:* (*of pers.*) rump, hindquarters, rear. **2.** *Veh:* waggon-body; hind-carriage; *pl. arrière-trains.*

arrière-vassal, -ale [arjɛrvasal], *s. Hist:* arrière-vassal, rear vassal, under-vassal; *pl. arrière-vassaux, -ales.*

arrière-voussure [arjɛrvusyːr], *s.f. Arch:* rear-vault, arrière-voussure. *pl. arrière-voussures.*

arrimage [arimaːʒ], *s.m. Nau: etc:* (*a*) stowing, trimming, packing (away) (of ship's cargo, waggon-load, etc.); **bois d'a.,** dunnage; (*b*) stowage; **vides d'a.,** broken stowage; **changement d'a.,** cargo shifting, breaking bulk; rummage; (*c*) trim (of ship); (*d*) *Av:* **dispositif d'a., d'aile, de fuselage,** wing, fuselage rack; (*e*) *Space:* docking (of spacecraft).

arrimer [arime], *v.tr.* **1.** *Nau: etc:* (*a*) to stow (away) (cargo, etc.); (*b*) to trim (ship); *Nau: Av:* **a. le chargement,** to trim the cargo. **2.** (*a*) to secure (gun for travelling, etc.); (*b*) *Space:* to dock.

arrimeur [arimœːr], *s.m. Nau:* (*a*) stower, trimmer; (*b*) stevedore.

arriser [arize], *Nau:* **1.** *v.tr. & i.* **(faire) a.,** to touch (a sail). **2.** *v.tr.* to (touch and) reef (topsail); to scandalize.

arrivage [arivaːʒ], *s.m.* arrival; consignment (of goods); *Fin:* **a. de fonds de l'étranger,** accession of funds from abroad.

arrivant, -e [arivɑ̃, -ɑ̃ːt], *s.* person arriving; arrival; **le dernier a.,** the last comer; **les nouveaux arrivants,** the new arrivals, the new-comers. *a.* incoming (letters, etc.).

arrivé, -ée [arive]. I. *s.* (*pers.*) arrival; **un nouvel a.,** a new-comer; a new arrival.

II. *s.f.* **1.** arrival, coming, advent; **on attend son a. pour la semaine prochaine,** he is expected to arrive next week; **à mon a.,** on my arrival; *Rail:* **a. du printemps,** the coming of spring; *Rail:* **a. des voyageurs,** arrival platform; *Trans:* **arrivées,** arrivals; *Post:* **heures d'a.,** times of delivery; *s.a.* ATTENDRE 1; *Com:* **payable sous réserve d'a., à l'heureuse a.,** "to arrive", payable after safe arrival; **"à livrer à l'heureuse a.",** "to be delivered after safe arrival"; **"vente à l'heureuse a.",** "sale subject to safe arrival", "sale to arrive"; *Nau:* **"à livrer à l'a.",** "for arrival"; *Mch: etc:* **tuyau d'a.,** delivery pipe. **2.** *Mch:* inlet (for steam, etc.); intake, admission; *Metall:* **a. d'air chaud,** blast-main; *El.E:* **(câble d')a.,** leading-in cable; *Tchn:* **a. (d'huile),** (oil) feed; *Min:* **a. (d'eau),** break through (of water). **3.** *Sp:* (winning-)post; finish; **juge à l'a., d'a.,** judge; **ligne d'a.,** finishing line; **franchir la ligne d'a.,** to cross the finishing line, to breast the tape. **4.** *Nau:* falling-off, lee lurch (of vessel). **5.** *Ling:* on-glide. **6.** *Ball:* **angle d'a.,** angle of impact.

arriver [arive], *v.i.* (*aux.* **être**). **1.** (*a*) to arrive, come; **il arriva en auto,** he arrived in a car, by car; **il arriva en courant,** he came running up; **il arrive de voyage,** he is just back from a journey; **a. chez soi,** to get home; **a. à temps,** to be in time; **a. en retard,** to be late; **a. en retard pour dîner,** to turn up late for dinner; **il arrive toujours en retard,** he always turns up late; **je pense qu'il arrivera demain,** I think he'll get here tomorrow; **l'avion devait a. à midi,** the plane was due at midday; **les voilà qui arrivent!** here they come! **nous voilà arrivés!** here we are, then! *F:* **arrivez!** come on! **arrivez vite!** hurry up! **il arrive donner sa leçon,** he has come, here he comes, to give his lesson; **la nuit arriva,** night came on; **votre dernière heure est arrivée,** your last hour has come; *Sp:* **il était arrivé le premier,** he had come in first; *F:* **a. en trois bateaux,** to arrive in state, with a great flourish; *F:* **il arrive de son pays,** he's a bit green, he's easily taken in; *s.a.* MARÉE 2, MARS 2; *impers.* **il arriva un soldat qui . . .,** there came a soldier who. . .; **il lui est arrivé des marchandises par le bateau,** he has received goods by the steamer; **il m'est arrivé des nouvelles de Paris,** I have had news from Paris; (*b*) **a. à un endroit,** to reach, get to, a place; **a. à Londres,** to get to, to arrive in, London; **a. à bon port,** (i) to reach a port of safety; (ii) *F:* to arrive safely, duly; **a. jusqu'au ministre,** to manage to see, to obtain an interview with, the minister; **le paquet m'est arrivé trop tard,** the parcel reached me too late; **ma fille m'arrive déjà à l'épaule,** my daughter comes up to my shoulder already; **l'eau était arrivée au deuxième étage,** the water had reached, come up to, the second floor; **aujourd'hui la recette n'est pas arrivée à dix livres,** today the takings didn't come to ten pounds; **a. à la vérité,** to arrive at, get at, the truth; **a. au bonheur,** to attain happiness; **a. à son but, à ses fins,** to attain, compass, achieve, one's ends, one's aim; **a. à une conclusion,** to reach a decision; **a. au fait,** to come to the point; *F:* to come down to brass tacks; **j'y arrive,** I'm coming to that; **a. à l'âge de discrétion,** to reach the age of discretion; **a. à un grand âge, à la perfection,** to attain, reach, a great age, perfection; (*c*) **en arriver: j'en étais arrivé là lorsque . . .,** I had got to that point when . . .; **il en était arrivé à demander l'aumône,** he had been reduced to begging; **il en arriva peu à peu à se montrer plus obéissant,** by degrees he became more obedient; **en a. aux voies de fait, aux coups,** to come to blows; **il faudra bien en a. là,** it must come to that; **comment en êtes-vous arrivé là?** how did you come to this? **2.** to succeed; (*a*) **c'est un homme qui arrivera,** he is a man who will get on, do well; **avec du courage on arrive à tout,** with courage one can get anywhere, one can achieve anything; **il n'arrivera jamais à rien,** he will never come to, achieve, anything, he will never get anywhere; **c'est un (homme) arrivé,** he's a made man, *F:* he's arrived; (*b*) **a. à faire qch.,** to manage to do sth., to succeed in doing sth.; **je n'arrive pas à y croire,** I just can't believe it; **elle n'arrive pas à apprendre,** she simply cannot learn; **il arrivera à être général,** he will be a general one day; **tâchez d'a. à ce que tout se fasse avec ordre,** try and manage to have everything done in an orderly way; **comment y a.?** how can it be done? *F:* **tu y arrives?** can you do, manage, get, make it? **3.** to happen, occur; **aller en France, cela ne m'arrive guère,** I hardly ever go to France; **cela arrive tous les jours,** it happens every day; *Prov:* **un malheur n'arrive jamais seul,** misfortunes never come singly; **cela ne nous arrivera jamais,** that will never be the case with us, it can never happen here; **cela n'arrive qu'à nous!** it would happen to us! just our luck! **cela peut a. à n'importe qui,** it could happen to anyone; **cela ne m'arrivera plus,** I shall never do it again; **que cela ne t'arrive plus!** don't let it happen again! see it doesn't happen again! *Iron:* **que cela t'arrive encore!** just let that happen again! **si le cas arrive,** if the case arises, if the case should arise; *F:* **il croit que c'est arrivé,** (i) he takes it all for gospel truth; (ii) he thinks he's the cat's whiskers; **faire a. qch.,** to bring sth. to pass, to bring sth. about; **faire a. un accident,** to cause, be responsible for, an accident; *impers.* **il lui est arrivé un accident, un malheur,** he has met with an accident, a disaster has befallen him; **il arriva un accident,** an accident happened, took place; **elle était en retard, comme il lui arrive souvent,** she was late, as she often is; **quoi qu'il arrive,** whatever happens, whatever may happen; **s'il m'arrive de gagner,** if I happen to win, if I ever win; **il arrive que je gagne, il m'arrive de gagner,** I sometimes win; **il m'arrive souvent d'oublier,** I often forget, I am apt to forget; **il m'est arrivé de le voir,** I chanced, happened, to see him; **il arriva que l'homme mourut,** it happened, came about, it fell out, that the man died; **il en arrivera ce qu'il pourra,** (i) we shall see what comes of it; (ii) *F:* hang the consequences! *F:* **c'est arrivé,** the penny's dropped. **4.** *Nau:* (*a*) to bear away, to fall off; **laisser a.,** (i) to keep the boat away; (ii) to bear away; **n'arrivons pas!** nothing off! **a. en grand,** to bear round; (*b*) **a. sur qch.,** to bear down on sth.; *F:* **l'autobus arrivait sur les piétons,** the bus was bearing down on the pedestrians; *F:* **ma belle-mère arriva sur moi, le rouleau à pâtisserie à la main,** my mother-in-law bore down on me with a rolling-pin in her hand.

arrivisme [arivism], *s.m.* unscrupulous ambition, go-getting; art of getting on.

arriviste [arivist], *s.m. & f.* man, woman, of unscrupulous ambition; climber, pusher; careerist; go-getter; arrivist(e).

arrobe [arɔb], *s.f. Meas:* arroba.

arroche [arɔʃ], *s.f. Bot:* orach; **a. des jardins,** mountain spinach.

arrogamment [arɔgamɑ̃], *adv.* arrogantly.

arrogance [arɔgɑ̃ːs], *s.f.* arrogance, arrogancy; overbearing manner.

arrogant, -ante [arɔgɑ̃, -ɑ̃t], (*a*) *a.* arrogant, overbearing; (*b*) *s.* arrogant person.

arroger (s') [sarɔʒe], *v.tr.pr.* **(je m'arrogeai(s); n.n. arrogeons); s'a. un droit, un privilège,** to arrogate to oneself, a right, a privilege, to assume a right; *F:* **s'a. la meilleure chambre,** to take the best room as a matter of course.

arroi [arwa], *s.m. A:* array; *F:* **être en mauvais arroi,** to be in a sad, sorry, plight.

arrondi [arɔ̃di]. 1. *a.* (*a*) rounded, round (chin, tool, etc.); **nombres arrondis,** round numbers; (*b*) well-rounded; **une phrase bien arrondie,** a well-rounded sentence; (*c*) (horse) broken in. 2. *s.m.* (*a*) round (of chin, surface, etc.); round-off (of edge, etc.); *Av:* fillet, fillet radius; (*b*) *Av:* flare out; **atterrissage avec a.,** flared landing.

arrondir [arɔ̃diːr], *v.tr.* 1. (*a*) to round (sth.) (off); to make (sth.) round; **a. sa fortune, une somme,** to round off one's fortune, a sum (of money); **a. son champ,** to add to, to round off, one's land; **a. le bras,** to round one's arm; **yeux arrondis, bouche arrondie, par l'étonnement,** eyes round, mouth agape, with astonishment; **a. une lentille,** to nibble a lens; (*b*) **a. ses manières,** to cultivate an easy manner; **a. une période,** to give fullness, roundness, to a sentence; **a. les angles,** to round off the angles; *Ling:* **a. une voyelle,** to round a vowel; (*c*) *Math:* to approximate; **a. un résultat,** to make an approximation, to correct a result (to so many places of decimals); (*d*) *Equit:* to break in (horse). 2. *Nau:* to go round; **a. un cap,** to round, double, a cape. 3. *Av:* to flare out (before touch-down).

s'arrondir. 1. to become round; to fill out; **sa taille s'arrondit,** she's pregnant; **le terrain s'arrondit en colline,** the ground swells into an eminence. 2. *F:* to feather one's nest.

arrondissage [arɔ̃disaːʒ], *s.m. Tchn:* rounding.

arrondissement [arɔ̃dismɑ̃], *s.m.* 1. (*a*) rounding (off) (of sentence, territory, etc.); rounding (of face); (*b*) roundness. 2. *Fr.Adm:* (*a*) (administrative) district; (*b*) one of the main subdivisions of a department; (*in Paris, etc.*) = ward, borough (in London); **ils se sont mariés dans le 21e a.,** they are living together without being married. 3. *Com:* **a. d'une somme,** rounding off of a sum.

arrondisseur [arɔ̃disœːr], *s.m. Tchn:* rounder; *Dressm:* **a. de jupe,** hemline, skirt, marker.

arrondissure [arɔ̃disyːr], *s.f. Bookb:* rounding.

arrosable [arɔzabl], *a.* that can be watered.

arrosage [arozaːʒ], *s.m.,* **arrosement** [arozmɑ̃], *s.m.* 1. (*a*) watering; sprinkling, spraying (of lawn, etc.); wetting, moistening (of dough, etc.); *F:* **un bon a.,** a good soaking; *Mil: F:* systematic shelling (of trenches, etc.); *Mil: F:* **un bon a.** heavy bombing; **un drôle d'a.,** a terrific pasting (severe bombing); *Cu:* **a. du rôti,** basting of the joint; **voiture, tonneau, d'arrosage,** watering-cart; **a. des rues,** watering of the streets; (*b*) *Hyd.E:* **a. d'une prairie,** irrigation of meadow-land; (*c*) watering, diluting (of wine, etc.); (*d*) celebrating (with drinks); (*e*) *Av:* cooling. 2. (*a*) *Games: F:* paying all round (by dealer or players); (*b*) *F:* paying all round of something on account (to one's creditors); (*c*) *F:* handing out of bribes, of hush-money.

arroser [aroze], *v.tr.* 1. (*a*) to water (streets, plants); to sprinkle, spray (lawn); to wet, moisten (food); *Cu:* **a. un rôti,** to baste a joint; *Mil:* **a. une ville,** to bomb, shell, plaster, strafe, paste, a town; **yeux arrosés de larmes,** eyes bathed in tears; *F:* **j'ai été bien arrosé,** I got a (thorough) wetting; **s'a. la gorge,** to wet one's whistle; **bifteck arrosé d'une bouteille de bordeaux,** steak washed down with a bottle of claret; **a. une affaire,** to wet a bargain; **a. ses galons,** to wet one's stripes, to pay one's footing; **a. un client,** to keep in with a customer, to ply him with plenty of drink; **courage arrosé,** Dutch courage; **café arrosé,** laced coffee; **elle arrosait son verre de bière de larmes silencieuses,** she shed silent tears into her glass of beer; **a. son pays de son sang,** to shed one's blood for one's country; **a. la terre de ses sueurs,** to work the land by the sweat of one's brow; **a. de ses larmes,** to bathe with one's tears; to weep over; **a. qn (d'une pluie d'or),** to shower gold, money, on s.o.; (*b*) **a. une prairie,** to irrigate a meadow; **rivière qui arrose une région,** river that waters a district; **la Seine arrose Paris,** the Seine flows through Paris; **la Seine et ses affluents arrosent le bassin parisien,** the Paris basin is drained by the Seine and its tributaries; (*c*) to water, dilute (wine, milk). 2. (*a*) *Gaming:* **a. la banque,** to renew the bank; (*b*) *F:* **a. ses créanciers,** to put off all one's creditors with something on account, to sprinkle a little money among one's creditors.

arroseur, -euse [arozœːr, -øːz], *s.* 1. street orderly, water-cart man or woman. 2. (*a*) *s.f.* **arroseuse,** *Adm:* water(ing)-cart, street sprinkler; (*b*) *Hort: etc:* **a. à poussière d'eau,** sprayer, spray-diffuser, sprinkler; **a. à jet tournant,** sprinkler; (*c*) *s.m. Hort:* **arroseur, a. automatique rotatif,** sprinkler.

arrosoir [arozwaːr], *s.m.* 1. (*a*) watering-can; (*b*) *P* = MITRAILLETTE. 2. *Moll:* watering-pot shell.

arrow-root [arorut], *s.m. Com: Cu:* arrowroot.

arroyo [arɔjo], *s.m.* arroyo.

arrugie [aryʒi], *s.f. Min:* drain, sough.

arsenal, -aux [arsənal, -o], *s.m.* 1. (*a*) arsenal; (*b*) **a. maritime, de la marine,** naval dockyard; (*c*) **a. d'artillerie,** gun factory, gunshop. 2. **il emporta son a. de drogues,** he took his whole store, stock of drugs with him. 3. *Jur:* **l'a. des lois,** the body of the law.

arsénamine [arsenamin], *s.f. Ch:* arsine.

arsenbismuth [arsɛnbismyt], *s.m. Miner:* arsenobismite.

Arsène [arsɛn], *Pr.n.m.* Arsenius.

arséniate [arsenjat], *s.m. Ch:* arsen(i)ate; **a. diplombique, a. acide de plomb,** acid lead arsenate; **a. triplombique, a. basique de plomb,** basic lead arsenate.

arsenic [arsənik], *s.m.* 1. *Ch:* arsenic; **a. sulfuré rouge,** red arsenic. 2. *Com:* **arsenic (blanc),** arsenious oxide, *F:* (white) arsenic, flaky arsenic, flowers of arsenic.

arsenical, -aux [arsənikal, -o], *a. Ch:* arsenical; **pyrite arsenicale, fer a.,** arsenopyrite, arsenical pyrite, mispickel.

arseniciase [arsənisjɑːz], *s.f.,* **arsenicisme** [arsənisism], *s.m. Med:* arsenical poisoning, arseniasis, arsenicism, arsenism.

arsenicophage [arsənikɔfaːʒ], (*a*) *s.m. & f.* arsenic eater; (*b*) *a.* arsenic-eating.

arsénié [arsenje], *a. Ch:* arseniuretted (hydrogen, etc.).

arsénieux, -ieuse [arsenjø, -jøːz], *a. Ch:* arsenious; **acide, anhydride, a.,** arsenious oxide; *Com:* (white) arsenic, flaky arsenic, flowers of arsenic.

arsénifère [arsenifɛːr], *a. Miner:* arseniferous.

arsénique [arsenik], *a. Ch:* arsenic (acid).

arsénite [arsenit], *s.m. Ch:* arsenite.

arséniure [arsenjyːr], *s.m. Miner: Ch:* arsenide, *A:* arseniuret.

arsénopyrite [arsenɔpirit], *s.f. Miner:* arsenopyrite, mispickel.

arsénothérapie [arsenɔterapi], *s.f. Med:* arsenotherapy.

arsin [arsɛ̃], *a. & s. A:* (*now used only in*) *For:* (**bois**) **a.,** (wood) damaged by fire.

arsine [arsin], *s.f. Ch:* arsine.

arsis [arsis], *s.f. Mus: Pros:* arsis.

arsonvalisation (d') [darsɔ̃valizasjɔ̃], *s.f. Med:* arsonvalization; diathermy.

arsouille [arsuj], *P:* 1. *a.* blackguardly. 2. *s.m. & f.* blackguard.

art [aːr], *s.m.* 1. art; (*a*) art, craft, profession; **apprendre un a.,** to learn a craft; **homme de l'a.,** specialist; *F:* doctor; **selon toutes les règles de l'a.** as well as possible; **terme d'a.,** term of art, technical term; **l'a. militaire, l'a. de la guerre,** the art of war; warcraft; **le noble a.,** boxing, the noble art (of self-defence); **l'a. dramatique,** dramatic art; stagecraft; **l'a. de l'ingénieur,** engineering; **l'a. du maçon,** the mason's art; **l'a. de la mécanique,** mechanical engineering; **l'a. de la poésie,** the art of poetry; **l'a. de l'éloquence,** the art of fine speaking; **a. culinaire,** culinary art, the art of cooking; **l'a. de faire qch.,** the art of doing sth.; **l'a. de gouverner,** statesmanship; (*b*) **a. figuratif, non-figuratif,** figurative, non-figurative, art; **a., sacré,** religious art; **a. populaire,** popular art, folk-art; **a. abstrait,** abstract art; **l'a. antique, russe, nègre,** classical, Russian, negro, art; **l'a. pour l'a.,** art for art's sake; **les maîtres de l'a.,** the greatest artists; *F:* **le septième a.,** the cinema; **éditeurs d'a.,** art publishers; **œuvre d'a.,** work of art; **galerie d'a.,** art gallery; **un critique d'a.,** an art-critic; **poterie d'a.,** art pottery; **reliure d'a.,** art binding; **ville d'a.,** city of artistic interest; **beaux-arts,** fine arts; **arts plastiques,** plastic arts; **arts décoratifs,** decorative arts; **arts mécaniques,** useful, applied, arts; **arts graphiques,** graphic arts; **arts industriels,** industrial art; **protecteur des arts,** patron of the arts; **arts d'agrément,** accomplishments, talents; artistic hobbies; *Sch:* extras; *s.a.* MÉNAGER 1, MÉTIER 1; (*c*) **les arts libéraux,** the liberal arts; *Fr.C: Sch:* **maître-ès-arts,** master of arts; *Sch: A:* **faculté des arts,** arts faculty; (*d*) *A:* **le grand a., l'a. sacré, l'a. hermétique,** the hermetic art, alchemy. 2. (*a*) skill, dexterity, knack; artistry; *Civ.E:* **travaux, ouvrages, d'a.,** (*generic term for*) bridges, viaducts, tunnels, etc.; constructive works; **ouvrier d'a.,** skilled workman; (*b*) artfulness, cunning; (*c*) talent; (*d*) artificiality; **sans a.,** natural(ly), without pose, artless, (*e*) method; **l'Art poétique,** the Art of Poetry, *ars poetica*; **l'Art d'aimer,** the Art of Love, *Ars Amatoria, Ars Amoris, Ars Amandi.*

Artaxerxès [artagzɛrsɛs], *Pr.n.m. A.Hist:* Artaxerxes.

Artaban [artabɑ̃], *Pr.n.m.* **fier comme A.,** proud as a peacock, as Lucifer.

artefact [artefakt], *s.m. Biol:* artefact, artifact.

Artémis [artemis], *Pr.n.f. Gr.Myth:* Artemis.

Artémise [artemiːz], *Pr.n.f. A.Hist:* Artemisia.

artémisiées [artemizje], *s.f.pl. Bot:* Artemisias, *F:* sage-brushes, sage-bushes.

artère [artɛːr], *s.f.* 1. *Anat:* artery; **on a l'âge de ses artères,** a man is as old as he feels. 2. (*a*) channel of communication (in country); thoroughfare (in town); **a. de circulation,** traffic artery; (*b*) **a. à gaz,** gas-main; *El.E:* **a. alimentaire,** feeding cable, feeder; **a. secondaire,** sub-feeder.

artérialisation [arterjalizasjɔ̃], *s.f. Physiol:* arterialization (of the blood).

artérialiser [arterjalize], *v.tr. Physiol:* to arterialize (the blood).

s'artérialiser, (*of blood*) to become arterialized.

artériectomie [arterjɛktɔmi], *s.f. Surg:* arter(i)ectomy.

artériel, -ielle [arterjɛl], *a. Physiol:* arterial; **pression, tension, artérielle,** blood-pressure, arterial pressure.

artérieux, -euse [arterjø, -øːz], *a. Anat: A:* arterial.

artériodème [arterjɔdɛm], *s.m. Surg:* artery forceps.

artériographe [arterjɔgraf], *s.m. Med:* arteriograph, sphygmograph.

artériographie [arterjɔgrafi], *s.f. Med:* arteriography, sphygmography.

artériole [arterjɔl], *s.f. Anat:* arteriole, small artery.

artériologie [arterjɔlɔʒi], *s.f.* arteriology.

artériopathie [arterjɔpati], *s.f.* arteriopathy.

artériorragie [arterjɔraʒi], *s.f. Med:* arteriorrhagia, arterial haemorrhage.

artérioscléreux, -euse [arterjosklerø, -øːz], *a. & s.* arteriosclerotic.

artériosclérose [arterjoskleroːz], *s.f. Med:* arteriosclerosis.

artériotome [arterjɔtɔm], *s.m. Surg:* arteriotome.

artériotomie [arterjɔtɔmi], *s.f. Surg:* arteriotomy.

artérite [arterit], *s.f. Med:* arteritis, inflammation of the arteries.

artésien, -ienne [artezjɛ̃, -jɛn], *a. & s.* 1. Artesian; (native) (i) of Artois; (ii) of Arras. 2. **puits artésien,** Artesian well.

arthralgie [artralʒi], *s.f. Med:* arthralgia, pain in the joints.

arthralgique [artralʒik], *a. Med:* arthralgic.

arthrectomie [artrɛktɔmi], *s.f. Surg:* arthrectomy.

arthrite [artrit], *s.f. Med:* arthritis; **a. sèche, déformante,** rheumatoid arthritis.

arthritique [artritik], *a. & s. Med:* arthritic (patient).

arthritisme [artritism], *s.m. Med:* arthritism; arthritic diathesis.

arthro- [artrɔ], *pref.* arthro-; **arthrologie,** arthrology; **arthrozoaire,** arthrozoic.

arthrobranchie [artrɔbrɑ̃ʃi], *s.f. Crust:* arthrobranch(ia);

arthrodèse [artrɔdɛːz], *s.f. Surg:* arthrodesis.

arthrodie [artrɔdi], *s.f. Anat:* arthrodia.

arthrologie [artrɔlɔʒi], *s.f. Anat:* arthrology.

arthroplastie [artrɔplasti], *s.f. Surg:* arthroplasty.

arthropode [artrɔpɔd], *Z:* 1. *a.* arthropodal, arthropodous. 2. *s.m.* arthropod, *pl.* arthropoda.

arthrose [artroːz], *s.f. Path:* arthrosis.

arthrosique [artrɔzik], (*a*) *a.* suffering from arthrosis; (*b*) *s.* arthrosis patient.

arthrospore [artrɔspɔːr], *s.f. Bot:* arthrospore.

arthrotomie [artrɔtɔmi], *s.f. Surg:* arthrotomy.

Arthur [artyːr], *Pr.n.m.* Arthur.

artichaut [artiʃo], *s.m.* 1. *Bot: Hort:* (*a*) globe artichoke, leaf artichoke; *Cu:* **fonds, culs, cœurs, d'artichauts,** artichoke bottoms, hearts; *F:* **avoir un cœur d'a.,** to be fickle-hearted; (*b*) *F:* **artichaut d'hiver,** Jerusalem artichoke; (*c*) *F:* **a. des toits,** house-leek; (*d*) **a. d'Espagne,** squash(-melon); **a. de Jérusalem,** gourd, squash. 2. cluster of spikes (on gate-posts, etc.).

artichautière [artiʃotjɛːr], *s.f. Hort:* globe-artichoke bed.

article [artikl], *s.m.* 1. (*a*) *Bot: Ent:* joint, article; (*b*) (critical point, moment) **être à l'a. de la mort,** to be *A:* in the article of death, *in articulo mortis,* at the point of death. 2. (*a*) article,

clause (of treaty, etc.); **a. de foi,** article of faith; **articles d'un traité,** provisions of a treaty; (*b*) item (of bill, etc.); **articles de dépense,** items of expenditure; **articles divers,** sundries; (*c*) article (in newspaper, etc.); **a. de tête, de fond,** editorial, leader; leading article. **3.** *Com:* article, commodity, *pl.* goods, wares; **a. (en) réclame,** special offer; **article(s) de Paris,** fancy goods; **quel est son a.?** what's his line (of business)? **je ne fais pas cet a.,** I don't deal in that line; **faire l'a.,** to puff one's goods; **faire l'a. d'un produit,** *F:* to boom, boost, plug, a product; **articles de voyage,** travel goods; **articles d'exportation,** exports, export goods; **articles de ménage,** household requisites; **articles de toilette,** toilet requisites, *U.S:* toiletries. **4.** subject, point; **c'est un autre a.,** that's quite another matter; **laissons là cet a.,** enough on this subject. **5.** *Gram:* **article défini, indéfini,** definite, indefinite, article; **a. partitif,** partitive article.

articlier [artiklie, -ije], *s.m. Journ:* columnist.

articulaire [artikylɛːr], *a. Anat:* articular, articulatory, of the joints; *Med:* **rhumatisme a.,** rheumatoid arthritis, rheumatism in the joints.

articulairement [artikylermɑ̃], *adv. A:* article by article, under separate heads.

articulateur [artikylatœːr], *s.m. Dent:* articulator.

articulation [artikylasjɔ̃], *s.f.* **1.** (*a*) *Anat: etc:* articulation, joint; **a. du doigt,** knuckle; *Bot:* node; (*b*) connection, joint, link, hinge; **accouplement à a.,** jointed coupling; **a. à rotule,** ball-and-socket joint; **assemblage par a.,** hinged connection; **a. coulissante,** slip joint; **a. de frein,** brake wedge; (*c*) *Mil:* **a. du commandement,** chain of command; **l'a. du 5ème corps d'armée,** the general deployment of the 5th corps. **2.** articulation, utterance; (manner of) speech. **3.** *Jur:* enumeration (of facts). **4.** *Geol:* dissection.

articulatoire [artikylatwaːr], *a.* articulatory.

articulé [artikyle]. **1.** *a.* (*a*) articulate(d); jointed (limb, coupling, etc.); hinged; *Mec.E:* **courroie articulée,** chain-belt, link-belt; *Av: A:* **ailes articulées,** flapper wings; *Civ.E:* **poutre articulée,** hinged, articulated, girder; **bielle articulée,** articulated connecting-rod; (*b*) articulate (speech); distinct (utterance); (*c*) *Geog:* **plateau a.,** dissected plateau. **2.** *s.m.* (*a*) **a. dentaire,** bite; (*b*) *pl.* **articulés** *Z:* articulata.

articuler [artikyle], *v.tr.* **1.** to articulate, hinge, link, joint; to connect by joints; **bielle articulée sur un maneton,** connecting-rod linked to, taking its bearing upon, a crank-pin. **2.** to articulate; to utter, pronounce, distinctly; **articulez!** speak clearly, distinctly! **mal a.,** to mumble, to swallow one's words; **il n'avait pas la force d'a. une seule parole,** he had not the strength to utter a single word. **3.** *Jur:* (*a*) to enumerate, to set forth (facts); (*b*) to state (fact) clearly, definitely.

s'articuler. 1. (*of bone*) **s'a. avec un autre os,** to be jointed, to hinge, with another bone; **comment s'articulent les fonctions du ministre des Affaires Étrangères et celles du Ministre de l'Intérieur?** how do the functions of the Foreign Secretary tie up with those of the Home Secretary? **2. la côte s'articule,** the coast becomes more and more distinct. **3.** *Mil:* **s'a. en largeur,** to deploy in width; **s'a. en profondeur,** to deploy in depth.

articulet [artikyle], *s.m. F: Journ:* short article.

artifice [artifis], *s.m.* **1.** artifice, artificial means; guile; (guileful) expedient, contrivance, wile; **a. de guerre,** artifice of war; stratagem; **user de tous les artifices pour . . .,** to resort to every trick in order to . . .; **tromper qn par des artifices,** to trick s.o.; **les artifices d'une coquette,** feminine wiles. **2.** (*a*) **feu d'a.,** fireworks, pyrotechnic display; **tirer un feu d'a.,** to let off fireworks; **pièce d'a.,** set piece; **grand feu d'a.,** grand display of fireworks; **son discours est un vrai feu d'a.,** he makes a dazzling speech; *Bot:* **plante au feu d'a.,** artillery plant, burning bush; (*b*) *pl.* **artifices,** *Mil:* light and smoke devices; flares, light signals, etc.

artificialité [artifisjalite], *s.f.* artificiality.

artificiel, -ielle [artifisjɛl], *a.* artificial; imitation (pearl, etc.); false (teeth, etc.); **lumière, glace, prairie, fleur, artificielle,** artificial light, ice, meadow, flower; *Astr:* **horizon a.,** artificial horizon; **jambe artificielle,** artificial leg; **langage a.,** artificial, made-up, language; **classification artificielle,** arbitrary classification, artificial system; **rire a.,** forced laugh; **style a.,** artificial, unnatural, style; **tout en lui est a.,** he is all sham.

artificiellement [artifisjɛlmɑ̃], *adv.* artificially.

artificier [artifisje], *s.m.* **1.** firework-maker, pyrotechnist. **2.** *Mil: Navy: etc:* artificer; armourer; **maître a.,** master artificer. **3.** *Min:* shotfirer.

artificieusement [artifisjøzmɑ̃], *adv.* artfully, craftily, guilefully.

artificieux, -ieuse [artifisjø, -jøːz], *a.* crafty, artful, cunning, guileful, wily.

artiflot [artiflo], *s.m. Mil: P:* artilleryman, gunner.

artillerie [artijri], *s.f.* **1.** artillery, ordnance; **a. de campagne,** field artillery; **a. légère, lourde,** light, heavy artillery; **a. moyenne, de moyen calibre,** medium artillery; **a. à grande puissance,** super-heavy artillery; **a. tractée,** tractor-drawn artillery; **a. automotrice,** self-propelled artillery; **a. hippomobile,** horse-drawn artillery; **a. à cheval,** horse artillery; **a. sur bât,** pack artillery; **a. de montagne,** mountain artillery; **a. sur voie ferrée,** railway artillery; artillery on railway mountings; **a. de forteresse, de place,** fortress artillery; **a. de côte,** coast artillery; **a. de marine,** *A:* **a. coloniale,** marine artillery; **a. navale, de bord,** naval artillery; **a. anti-chars** (*Belgium:* **anti-blindés**) antitank artillery; **a. anti-aérienne,** anti-aircraft artillery; **a. (organique) de corps d'armée,** corps artillery; **a. divisionnaire,** divisional artillery; **a. d'accompagnement,** accompanying artillery; **a. d'appui direct,** artillery covering the infantry; *U.S:* direct support artillery; **a. guidée,** (guided) missile field artillery; **a. d'action d'ensemble,** artillery detailed for general work; *U.S:* general support artillery; **a. d'assaut,** assault artillery, guns; **pièce d'a.,** piece of ordnance, of artillery; **manufacture d'a.,** ordnance factory; *Aut:* **roue type a.,** artillery-type wheel. **2.** gunnery.

artilleur [artijœːr], *s.m.* artilleryman, artillerist, gunner.

artimon [artimɔ̃], *s.m. Nau:* **(mât d')a.,** mizzen-mast; **voile d'a.,** mizzen(-sail); **a. de cape,** storm-mizzen.

artinite [artinit], *s.f. Miner:* artinite.

artiodactyle [artjɔdaktil], *Z:* **1.** *a.* even-toed, artiodactyl(e), artiodactylous. **2.** *s.m.pl.* **artiodactyles,** artiodactyla.

artisan, -ane [artizɑ̃, -an], *s.* **1.** (*a*) artisan, craftsman; (*b*) *esp.* small craftsman (*e.g.* cobbler, watch-maker). **2.** maker, contriver; **il a été l'a. de ses propres malheurs,** he owes his misfortunes to himself; **il a été l'a. de sa fortune,** he is a self-made man, he's the architect of his fortune.

artisanal, -aux [artizanal, -o], *a.* (*a*) relating to crafts, artisanal; (*b*) skilled; (*c*) on a small scale; **production artisanale,** small-scale production (by craftsmen).

artisanat, *s.m.* **1.** craftsmen (as a class); **l'a. indigène,** the native craftsmen. **2.** (*a*) cottage industry; (*b*) **a. d'expression,** arts and crafts, handicrafts; **produits d'a. régional,** products of the local handicrafts.

artison [artizɔ̃], *s.m. Ent:* **1.** wood-worm, (wood-) moth, wood-fretter. **2.** clothes-moth.

artisonné [artizɔne], *a. A:* (*a*) worm-eaten; (*b*) moth-eaten.

artiste [artist]. **1.** *s.m.* & *f.* (*a*) artist (including musician, etc.); **artiste peintre,** painter; *F:* **c'est un a. dans la matière,** he is an artist at it; (*b*) *Th: Mus:* performer; (*c*) *Th:* actor, actress; singer; dancer; entertainer; artiste (of variety stage); **entrée des artistes,** stage entrance. **2.** *a.* artistic (temperament, style); *s.a.* ÉCRITURE 3.

artistement [artistəmɑ̃], *adv.* skilfully, cleverly, with art.

artistique [artistik], *a.* (*a*) **sens, tempérament, a.,** artistic sense, temperament; (*b*) artistic (furniture, arrangement, etc.); (*c*) **cachets artistiques,** fees paid to an artist, artists.

artistiquement [artistikmɑ̃], *adv.* artistically.

artocarpe [artɔkarp], **artocarpus** [artɔkarpys], *s.m. Bot:* artocarpus; bread-fruit tree.

Artois [artwa], *Pr.n.m. Hist: Geog:* Artois.

arum [arɔm], *s.m. Bot:* arum; **a. maculé,** wake-robin, cuckoo-pint, lords-and-ladies.

arundinaria [arɔ̃dinarja], *s.f. Bot:* arundinaria, cane-brake.

arundo [arɔ̃dɔ], *s.m. Bot:* arundo.

aruspice [aryspis], *s.m. Rom.Ant:* haruspex.

arvales [arval], *a.pl. Rom.Ant:* **les frères a.,** the Arval Brethren.

arverne [arvɛrn], *a.* & *s. Hist:* (native, inhabitant) of Arverne (in Gaul, later Auvergne).

arvicole [arvikɔl], *a.* arvicoline.

arvicolinés [arvikɔline], *s.m.pl. Z:* Arvicolinae.

aryanisme [arjanism], *s.m. Ethn: Ling: Pol:* aryanism.

Aryas [arjaːs], *s.m.pl. Ethn:* Aryas, Aryans.

aryen, -enne [arjɛ̃, -ɛn], *a.* & *s. Ethn: Ling: etc:* Aryan, Indo-European.

arylamine [arilamin], *s.f. Ch:* arylamine.

aryle [aril], *s.m. Ch:* aryl.

aryténoïde [aritenɔid], *a.* & *s.m. Anat:* arytenoid.

aryténoïdite [aritenɔidit], *s.f. Path:* arytenoiditis.

arythmie [aritmi], *s.f.* ar(r)hythmia, irregularity (of heart, etc.).

arythmique [aritmik], *a.* ar(r)hythmic (pulse, etc.).

arzel [arzɛl], *s.m. Equit:* horse with white fore-head and white rear feet.

as [ɑːs], *s.m.* **1.** (*a*) *Dice: Cards:* ace; **amener deux as,** to throw two aces; **as de pique,** (i) ace of spades; (ii) *F:* rump (of fowl); *F:* parson's nose; (iii) person of no importance, consequence; *P:* **fichu comme l'as de pique,** misbegotten; dressed like a guy; **as de carreau,** (i) ace of diamonds; (ii) *Mil: P:* knapsack, pack; (iii) *P:* ribbon of the Legion of Honour; **veiller à l'as,** to be on the look-out; *P:* **aller à l'as,** to come a cropper; *P:* **être aux as, plein aux as,** to be rolling (in it); to have plenty of money; **passer qch. à l'as,** to juggle sth. away; *F:* **n'avoir plus d'as dans son jeu,** to be at the end of one's resources; (*b*) *Dominoes:* one; **l'as blanc,** one blank; (*c*) *F:* **l'as,** (table) No. 1 (in restaurants, etc.). **2.** (*a*) *Av:* ace; (*b*) *F:* first-rater; *Games:* crack player, star; **au tennis c'est un as,** *F:* he's an ace at tennis; *Aut:* **as du volant,** crack (racing) driver. **3.** *Row:* single-sculler (skiff). **4.** *Rom.Ant:* as.

asaret [azarɛ], *s.m. Bot:* asarum; **a. d'Europe,** asarabacca.

asbeste [azbɛst, as-], *s.m. Miner:* asbestos.

asbestin [azbɛstɛ̃], *a.* asbestine.

asbestose [azbɛstoːz], *s.f. Path:* asbestosis.

asbolane [azbɔlan, as-], *s.f.* **asbolit(h)e** [azbɔlit, as-], *s.f. Miner:* asbolite; asbolan(e); earthy cobalt; wad; bog manganese.

Ascagne [askaɲ], *Pr.n.m. Rom.Myth:* Ascanius.

ascaride [askarid], *s.m.,* **ascaris** [askaris], *s.m. Med:* ascaris; ascarid; *F:* thread-worm; **a. lombricoïde,** stomach-worm.

ascaridés [askaride], *s.m.pl. Med:* Ascaridae, Ascarides; *F:* thread-worms.

ascaridiose [askaridjoːz], *s.f. Path:* ascariasis, ascaridiasis, ascaridiosis.

ascendance [as(s)ɑ̃dɑ̃ːs], *s.f.* **1.** *Astr:* ascent. **2.** *Genealogy:* ancestry, lineage; **l'une et l'autre famille avait une a. canadienne,** both families were of Canadian ancestry. **3.** *Meteor:* anabatic wind.

ascendant [as(s)ɑ̃dɑ̃]. **1.** *a.* ascending, upward (motion, etc.); *Av:* **vol ascendant,** climbing flight; *Mch:* **course ascendante,** up-stroke (of piston); *Mch: etc:* **tuyau a.,** uptake pipe, riser, stand-pipe; *Meteor:* **courant a.,** ascending current; *Mus:* **gamme ascendante,** ascending scale; *Mth:* **progression ascendante,** ascending series; *Anat: Bot:* ascending; **aorte ascendante,** ascending aorta; *Astr:* **nœud a.,** ascending node; *Hyd:* **eau ascendante,** rising water. **2.** *s.m.* (*a*) *Astr: Astrol: etc:* ascendant, ascendent; **astre qui est à l'a.,** star in the ascendant; (*b*) ascendancy, ascendency, influence; **prendre l'a. sur qn,** to gain the ascendancy over s.o.; **exercer un grand a. sur qn,** to have great influence (up)on s.o.; **subir l'a. de qn,** to be under the spell of s.o.'s personality; (*c*) *pl.* **ascendants,** ancestry (of family); *Adm:* **pension d'ascendants,** pension to parents.

ascenseur [asɑ̃sœːr], *s.m.* lift, *U.S:* elevator; **a. de marchandises,** goods-hoist; **"a. à tous les étages,"** "lift to all floors." *Hyd.E:* **a. à sas,** canal-lift; *F:* **renvoyer l'a.,** to give tit for tat, to throw back the ball.

ascenseur-écluse [asɑ̃sœreklyːz], *s.m.* ship-canal lock; *pl. ascenseurs-écluses.*

ascension [asɑ̃sjɔ̃], *s.f.* (*a*) ascent, ascension; rising (of sap, etc.); *Oil Min:* lift; **a. capillaire,** creep; **faire l'a. d'une montagne,** to make the ascent of, to climb, a mountain; **a. d'un astre,** ascension, rising, of a star; *Astr:* **a. droite,** right ascension; **a. du baromètre,** rising of the barometer; **a. en ballon,** balloon ascent; *Mch:* **a. du piston,** up-stroke of the piston; *Av:* climb; **angle d'a.,** climbing angle; **a. verticale,** (i) *Av:* vertical climb; (ii) *Astr:* right ascension; *Ecc:* **fête, jeudi, de l'A.,** Ascension Day; *Geog:* **l'île de l'A.,** Ascension Island; (*b*) progress, ascent; rise; (i) **son a. à la classe moyenne,** his rise to middle-class status; (ii) **l'a. de l'intelligence,** the progress of intelligence; (iii) **l'a. de Bonaparte,** the rise of Bonaparte.

ascensionnel, -elle [asɑ̃sjɔnɛl], *a.* ascensional; upward (motion); *Aer:* **force ascensionnelle,** lifting power, lift, elevating power, ascending power; **vitesse ascensionnelle,** rate of climb, climbing speed; *Mch:* **mouvement a.,** up-stroke.

ascensionner [asɑ̃sjɔne], *v.i.* **1.** to climb. **2.** to make an (air) ascent.
ascensionniste [asɑ̃sjɔnist], *s.m. & f.* **1.** (mountain) climber, mountaineer, ascensionist; **a. de rochers,** cragsman. **2.** *Aer:* balloonist.
ascèse [as(s)ɛːz], *s.f. Phil:* ascesis.
ascète [as(s)ɛt], *s.m. & f.* ascetic; **vivre en a.,** to live ascetically.
ascétique [as(s)etik]. **1.** *a. & s.* ascetic(al); **une vie a.,** an ascetic life. **2.** *s.m.pl.* **ascétiques,** ascetic books, ascetics. **3.** *s.f.* asceticism, ascetical theology.
ascétiquement [asetikmɑ̃], *adv.* ascetically.
ascétisme [as(s)etism], *s.m.* asceticism; austere life.
ascidiacés [asidjase], *s.m.pl. Z:* Ascidiacea.
ascidie [asidi], *s.f.* **1.** *Bot:* ascidium, vasculum, *F:* pitcher. **2.** *s.f.pl. Z:* Ascidia; *F:* sea-squirts.
ascidien [asidjɛ̃], *a. & s.m. Z:* ascidian; *s. F:* sea-squirt.
ascidiforme [asidifɔrm], *a. Bot:* ascidiform, pitcher-shaped.
Asciens [as(s)jɛ̃], *s.m.pl. Geog:* Ascians.
ascite [as(s)it], *s.f. Med: Vet:* ascites; abdominal dropsy.
ascitique [as(s)itik]. **1.** *a. Med: Vet:* ascitic(al). **2.** *s.* **ascitique,** patient suffering from ascites.
asclépiad(ac)ées [asklepjad(as)e], *s.f.pl. Bot:* Asclepiadaceae.
Asclépiade [asklepjad]. **1.** *Pr.n.m. Gr.Hist:* Asclepiades. **2.** *s.m. Pros:* asclepiad; **le petit a.,** lesser, minor asclepiad; **le grand a.,** greater, major asclepiad. **3.** *s.f. Bot:* asclepias, milkweed; **a. à ouate, de Syrie,** silkweed, swallow-wort; **a. dompte-venin,** white swallow-wort.
asclepias [asklepjas], *s.m. Bot:* = ASCLÉPIADE 3.
ascochyta [askɔkita], *s.m. Fung:* ascochyta.
ascogène [askɔʒɛːn], *a.* ascogenous.
ascogone [askɔgɔn], *s.m. Fung:* ascogonium, ascogone.
ascolichen [askɔlikɛn], *s.m.* ascolichen.
ascomycètes [askɔmisɛt], *s.m.pl. Fung:* Ascomycetes.
ascophylle [askɔfil], *s.f. Algae:* ascophyllum.
ascorbique [askɔrbik], *a.* **acide ascorbique,** ascorbic acid.
ascospore [askɔspɔr], *s.f.* ascospore.
ascothoraciques [askɔtɔrasik], *s.m.pl. Crust:* Ascothoracica.
asdic [asdik], *s.m. Nav:* asdic (*Allied Submarine Detection Investigation Committee*).
ase [az], *s.f. A.Bio.Ch:* enzym(e), ase.
aséismicité [aseismisite], *s.f. Geol:* aseismicity.
aséismique [aseismik], *a. Geol:* aseismic.
aséité [aseite], *s.f. Theol:* aseity, aseitas.
aselle [azɛl], *s.m. Crust:* asellus; **a. aquatique,** water-slater.
asémie [asemi], *s.f. Med:* asemia.
asepsie, aseptie [asɛpsi], *s.f. Med:* asepsis. **1.** aseptic state. **2.** asepticism, aseptic treatment.
aseptique [asɛptik], *a. Med:* aseptic.
aseptisation [asɛptizasjɔ̃], *s.f. Med:* asepticizing.
aseptiser [asɛptize], *v.tr. Med:* to asepticize.
asexué [asɛksɥe], *a.*, **asexuel, -elle** [asɛksɥɛl], *a. Biol:* asexual.
asialie [asjali], *s.f. Med:* asialia, aptyalism.
asianique [azjanik], *a. Ling:* Asianic.
asiarque [asjark], *s.m. Rom.Ant:* Asiarch.
asiate [azjat], *a. & s.m. & f.* Asian.
asiatique [azjatik], *a. & s. Geog:* Asiatic, Asian; **luxe a.,** oriental splendour; *Med:* **grippe a.,** Asian flu.
asidère [azidɛːr], *s.f.*, **asidérite** [aziderit], *s.f. Miner:* asiderite, aerolite, aerolith.
Asie [azi], *Pr.n.f. Geog:* Asia; **l'A. Mineure,** Asia Minor; *Hist:* **L'A. antérieure, occidentale,** Western Asia.
asile[1] [azil], *s.m.* **1.** (*a*) *Jur: A:* sanctuary; **droit d'a.,** right of sanctuary; (*b*) *Pol:* **a. politique, diplomatique,** political, diplomatic, asylum; **donner a. à qn,** to afford asylum to s.o. **2.** shelter, home, refuge, retreat; **lieu d'a.,** (place of) refuge; **sans a.,** homeless; **n'avoir pas d'a.,** to be homeless; **a. des pauvres** = workhouse; **a. de nuit,** night-shelter, *F:* doss-house; **a. d'aliénés,** mental hospital, *O:* lunatic asylum; **a. d'indigents,** alms-house; **a. des marins,** sailors' home; *A:* **salle d'a.,** infant school; **donner a. à qn,** to harbour, shelter, s.o., to take s.o. in; **chercher a.,** to take refuge.
asile[2], *s.m. Ent:* asilus; hornet-, robber-, assassin-fly.
asilidés [azilide], *s.m.pl. Ent:* Asilidae.
asiminier [aziminje], *s.m. Bot:* asimina, (American) papaw.
asine [azin], *a.f.* (*a*) *A.Jur:* **bête a.,** ass; (*b*) *Z:* asinine.
asinien, -ienne [azinjɛ̃, -jɛn], *a. Z:* asinine.
asiphonés [asifɔne], *s.m.pl. Moll:* Asiphonates.
askari [askari], *s.m. Mil:* askari.
asmanite [asmanit], *s.f. Miner:* asmanite.
Asmodée [asmɔde, az-], *Pr.n.m. B:* Asmodeus.
Asmonéens [asmɔneɛ̃], *Pr.n.m.pl. Jew.Hist:* Hasmoneans.
asniérois, -oise [anjerwa, -waːz], *a. & s. Geog:* (native, inhabitant) of Asnières-sur-Seine.
asocial, -ale, -aux [asɔsjal, -o], *a. & s.* asocial (person); (person) maladjusted (to society).
asomatognosie [asɔmatɔgnozi], *s.f. Med:* asomatognosia.
asparagiculteur [asparaʒikyltœːr], *s.m.* asparagus grower.
asparagiculture [asparaʒikyltyːr], *s.f.* asparagus growing.
asparaginase [asparaʒinaːz], *s.f. Bio.Ch:* asparaginase.
asparagine [asparaʒin], *s.f. Ch:* asparagine.
asparaginées [asparaʒine], *s.f.pl. Bot:* asparaginous plants.
asparagolite [asparagɔlit], *s.f. Miner:* asparagus stone.
asparagus [asparagys], *s.m.* **1.** *Bot:* asparagus. **2.** asparagus-fern.
aspartique [aspartik], *a. Ch:* **acide a.,** aspartic acid.
Aspasie [aspazi], *Pr.n.f. Gr.Hist:* Aspasia.
aspe [asp], *s.m. Tex:* winder.
aspect [aspɛ], *s.m.* **1.** sight, aspect; **trembler à l'a. de qn, de qch.,** to tremble at the sight of s.o., of sth.; **à l'a. du danger qu'il court . . . ,** at the thought of the risk he is running . . .; **au premier a.,** at first sight, at a first glance. **2.** (*a*) aspect, appearance, look; facet (of a job, etc.); **être d'un a. repoussant,** to be repulsive-looking; **elle a un a. imposant** [aspɛk ɛ̃pozɑ̃], she has an imposing presence; **prendre l'a. de,** (to come to) look like; **considérer une affaire sous tous ses aspects,** to look at a thing from every angle, from all its angles, from every viewpoint, from all points of view; **je n'aime pas l'a. de l'affaire,** I don't like the look of the thing; **l'affaire prend un fâcheux a.,** the affair is shaping badly; (*b*) get-up (of book, etc.). **3.** *Astrol:* aspect, relative positions (of stars). **4.** *Ling:* aspect (of verb).
aspecter [aspɛkte], *v.tr. Arch:* to face; **a. le nord,** to face North.
aspectuel, -elle [aspɛktyɛl], *a. Gram:* aspectual.
asperge [aspɛrʒ], *s.f.* (*a*) *Bot:* asparagus; **a. plumeuse,** asparagus-fern; *Hort:* **plant d'asperges,** asparagus bed; *Cu:* asparagus; **botte d'asperges,** bundle of asparagus; **une a.,** a stick of asparagus; **pince à asperges,** asparagus tongs; (*b*) *F:* tall person, *F:* bean-pole; gawky young person.
asperger [aspɛrʒe], *v.tr.* (**j'aspergeai(s) n. aspergeons**) to sprinkle (linen, etc.) with water; **a. qn d'eau bénite,** to sprinkle s.o. with holy water; **a. qn d'eau,** to spray s.o. with water; **tous les matins il s'aspergeait la figure d'eau froide,** every morning he used to splash his face with cold water.
aspergeraie [aspɛrʒərɛ], *s.f.*, **aspergerie** [aspɛrʒri], *s.f.* asparagus bed.
aspergès [aspɛrʒɛs], *s.m. Ecc:* **1.** aspergillum, holy-water sprinkler. **2.** asperges, sprinkling.
aspergette [aspɛrʒɛt], *s.f. Bot: Cu:* Bath asparagus.
aspergière [aspɛrʒjɛːr], *s.f.* asparagus bed.
aspergillales [aspɛrʒilal], *s.f.pl. Fung:* Aspergillales.
aspergille [aspɛrʒil], *s.f. Fung:* aspergillus.
aspergilliforme [aspɛrʒilifɔrm], *a. Bot:* aspergilliform.
aspergilline [aspɛrʒilin], *s.f.* aspergillin.
aspergillose [aspɛrʒiloːz], *s.f. Med:* aspergillosis.
aspergillum [aspɛrʒilɔm], *s.m. Moll:* aspergillum; *F:* watering-pot shell, sprinkler.
aspergillus [aspɛrʒilys], *s.m. Fung:* aspergillus.
aspérifolié [asperifɔlje], *a. Bot:* asperifoliate, asperifolious.
aspérité [asperite], *s.f.* asperity. **1.** unevenness, ruggedness, roughness (of surface, etc.). **2.** harshness, sharpness (of character, voice); crabbedness (of style).
aspermatisme [aspɛrmatism], *s.m. Med:* aspermatism.
asperme [aspɛrm], *a. Bot:* aspermous, seedless.
aspermie [aspɛrmi], *s.f.* **1.** *Bot:* aspermatism. **2.** *Med:* aspermia; aspermatism.
aspersion [aspɛrsjɔ̃], *s.f.* aspersion, sprinkling; spraying (of wound, etc.); *Agr:* drench.
aspersoir [aspɛrswaːr], *s.m.* **1.** *Ecc:* aspergillum. **2.** rose (of watering-can).
asperugo [asperygo], *s.m. Bot:* asperugo, German madwort.
aspérula [asperyla], *s.f.*, **aspérule** [asperyl], *s.f. Bot:* asperula; **a. odorante,** woodruff; **a. à esquinancie,** quinsy-wort.
asphaltage [asfaltaːʒ], *s.m. Civ.E: etc:* asphalting; covering, laying, with asphalt.
asphalte [asfalt], *s.m.* (*a*) asphalt; **a. minéral,** pitch, bitumen; *Civ.E: etc:* **revêtement d'a.,** asphalt covering; **a. coulé,** poured asphalt; **mastic d'a.,** mastic asphalt; **a. comprimé, damé,** compressed asphalt; (*b*) road; *P:* **polir l'a.,** to loaf about the streets.
asphaltène [asfaltɛn], *s.m. Civ.E:* asphaltene.
asphalteur [asfaltœːr], *s.m.* asphalter, asphalt worker.
asphalteux, -euse [asfaltø, -øːz], *a.* = ASPHALTIQUE.
asphalter [asfalte], *v.tr.* to asphalt (road, etc.); to cover (road, etc.) with asphalt.
asphaltier [asfaltje], *s.m. Nau:* tanker used for transporting asphalt.
asphaltique [asfaltik], *a.* asphaltic.
asphaltite [asfaltit], *a. & s.m.* **1.** *a. A:* **le lac a.,** the Asphaltic Pool (the Dead Sea). **2.** *s.m. Geol:* asphaltite.
asphérique [asferik], *a. Opt:* aspheric(al).
asphodèle [asfɔdɛl], *s.m. Bot:* asphodel; **a. rameux,** branched lily, king's-rod; **a. blanc,** king's-spear.
asphygmie [asfigmi], *s.f. Med:* asphygmia.
asphyxiant [asfiksjɑ̃], (*a*) asphyxiating, suffocating; **gaz a.,** poison gas; **atteint de gaz asphyxiants,** gassed; (*b*) stifling, suffocating (atmosphere, etc.); *F:* stinking.
asphyxie [asfiksi], *s.f.* asphyxia, asphyxiation, suffocation; *Min: etc:* gassing; **salle d'a. (d'une fourrière),** lethal chamber; **a. économique,** economic strangulation.
asphyxié, -ée [asfiksje], *a. & s.* asphyxiated, suffocated (person); *Min: etc:* gassed.
asphyxier [asfiksje], *v.tr.* (*pr.sub. & p.d.* **n. asphyxiions, v. asphyxiiez**) **1.** to asphyxiate, suffocate; *Min: etc:* to gas. **2.** *P: A:* to astound, to astonish, to flabbergast, to knock endways. **3.** to stifle; **sa personnalité était asphyxiée par celle de son frère,** his personality was stifled by that of his brother.
s'asphyxier, to asphyxiate oneself, to be asphyxiated; to gas oneself.
aspic[1] [aspik], *s.m. Rept:* asp; *Poet:* aspic; *F:* **langue d'a.,** venomous tongue; *A.Artil:* aspic.
aspic[2], *s.m. Cu:* aspic(-jelly).
aspic[3], *s.m. Bot:* aspic, French lavender, great lavender; spike; **huile d'a.** = **essence de spic,** *q.v.* under SPIC.
aspidie [aspidi], *s.f.*, **aspidium** [aspidjɔm], *s.m. Bot:* aspidium, shield-fern.
aspidiote [aspidjɔt], *s.m.*, **aspidiotus** [aspidjɔtys], *s.m. Ent:* aspidiotus.
aspidistra [aspidistra], *s.m. Bot:* aspidistra.
aspidobranches [aspidɔbrɑ̃ʃ], *s.m.pl. Moll:* Aspidobranchia.
aspidosperma [aspidɔspɛrma], *s.m. Bot:* aspidosperma.
aspirail, -aux [aspiraːj, -o], *s.m.* air-hole, -inlet; draught-, vent-hole; vent, flue.
aspirant, -ante [aspirɑ̃, -ɑ̃ːt]. **1.** *a.* sucking; **pompe aspirante,** suction-pump; **ventilateur a.,** exhaust-, suction-fan; air exhauster; *I.C.E:* **course aspirante,** induction stroke, admission stroke. **2.** *s.* (*a*) aspirant (**à,** to); candidate (for degree, etc.); **les aspirants à sa main,** the aspirants to, for, after, her hand; her suitors; (*b*) *Navy: s.m.* midshipman; *Nau:* **a. pilote,** apprentice-pilot; (*c*) (i) (*in Fr. military schools and officer training courses*) = officer candidate; cadet; (ii) (*in wartime in the Fr. army and air force*), a junior probationary officer ranking under second lieutenant or pilot officer. **3.** *s.m.* strainer (of pump).
aspirateur, -trice [aspiratœːr, -tris]. **1.** *a.* aspiratory; suction-(device). **2.** *s.m. Ch: Ind: Med:* (gas-, air-) exhauster; aspirator; **a. à céréales,** grain elevator; *Mec.E: etc:* (i) exhaust-fan, suction-fan; (ii) suction-conveyor; **a. de buées,** extractor fan; **a. de poussières,** (i) *Ind:* dust-exhauster, dust-collector; (ii) *Dom.Ec:* vacuum cleaner, Hoover (*R.t.m*): **passer une pièce à l'a.,** to run the vacuum cleaner over a room, to vacuum-clean, to hoover, a room.
aspiratif, -ive [aspiratif, -iːv], *a. Ling:* **signe a.** sign of aspiration, rough breathing (in classical Greek).

aspiration [aspirasjɔ̃], *s.f.* **1.** aspiration, yearning (**à, vers,** for, after); **aspirations à la scène,** hankering after the stage. **2.** *Ling:* aspiration, rough breathing. **3.** (*a*) inspiration, inhaling (of air into the lungs, etc.); (*b*) suction, sucking-up (of water into pump, etc.); exhaustion; **ventilateur à a.,** exhaust-fan; **installation d'a. des poussières,** dust-exhausting plant; (*c*) *I.C.E:* admission, induction; **clapet d'a.,** intake valve; **temps de l'a.,** suction stroke, induction stroke; *Med:* aspiration.

aspiratoire [aspiratwa:r], *a.* **1.** aspiratory. **2.** (*of breathing*) inspiratory.

aspiré, *a.* (*a*) *Ling:* aspirate(d); (*b*) *Av:* **air a. (réacteur),** intake air (jet).

aspirée, *s.f. Ling:* aspirate.

aspirer [aspire]. **1.** *v.ind.tr.* to aspire (**à,** to, after), to aim at; to long for; to yearn for; **a. à faire qch.,** to aspire to do sth. **2.** *v.tr.* (*a*) to inspire, inhale, breathe (in) (air, scent, etc.); to sniff up (powder, etc.); (*b*) to exhaust, suck up, suck in, draw (up) (water, etc.); (*of sinking ship*) to suck down (boat, etc.); (*c*) *Ling:* to aspirate, breathe (a sound); **l'h est aspirée en allemand,** the h is aspirated, breathed, in German; **ne pas a. les h (en anglais),** to drop one's h's. NOTE: for French people, **"aspirer une h initiale"** means no more than to treat a word beginning with h as if it began with a consonant, *i.e.*, the 'aspiration' merely prevents both elision and liaison: **le héros** [ləero], **les héros** [leero].

aspirine [aspirin], *s.f. Pharm:* aspirin.

asple [aspl], *s.m. Tex:* winder.

asplenium [asplenjɔm], *s.m. Bot:* asplenium.

asporogène [aspɔrɔʒɛ:n], *a. Bot:* asporogenous, asporogenic.

asprède [asprɛd], *s.m. Ich:* aspredo.

asque [ask], *s.m. Fung:* ascus.

assablé [as(s)ɑble], *a.* = ENSABLÉ.

assacu [asaky], *s.m. Bot:* assacu, sandbox tree.

assa-fœtida [asafetida], *s.f. Pharm:* as(s)afoetida.

assagir [asaʒi:r], *v.tr.* to make (s.o.) wiser; to sober (s.o.) (down); **le mariage l'a. assagi,** marriage has made him settle down; **voilà qui l'assagira,** that will knock the nonsense out of him, knock some sense into him.

s'assagir, to become wiser, reasonable; to sober down; to settle down.

assagissement [asaʒismɑ̃], *s.m.* **1.** making wiser, making better behaved. **2.** growing wiser, growing better behaved; sobering down.

assai [asai], *adv. Mus:* assai.

assaillant [asajɑ̃]. **1.** *a.* attacking, assaulting, besetting (force, etc.). **2.** *s.m.* assailant, attacker, assaulter; aggressor, besieger.

assaillir [asaji:r], *v.tr.* (*pr.p.* **assaillant,** *p.p.* **assailli,** *pr. ind.* **j'assaille, n. assaillons, ils assaillent,** *p.d.* **j'assaillais,** *p.h.* **j'assaillis,** *fu.* **j'assaillirai**) to assail, assault, attack, beset; **être assailli de doutes,** to be beset, assailed, by doubts; **l'orage nous assaillit,** we were caught by the storm; **à mon retour de Russie je fus assailli de questions,** when I came back from Russia I was bombarded with questions.

assainir [asɛni:r], *v.tr.* to make (sth.) healthier; to cleanse, purify (atmosphere, etc.); to sweeten (soil, stable, etc.); to drain (marshes); to improve the sanitation of (town); to purge (the drama, literature, etc.); to stabilize (budget, etc.); **a. les finances, l'administration,** to reorganize the finances, the administration, *F:* to set one's house in order; **a. la monnaie,** to stabilize the currency.

s'assainir, to improve, grow healthier, become sounder.

assainissant [asɛnisɑ̃], *a.* cleansing, health-giving.

assainissement [asɛnismɑ̃], *s.m.* cleansing, purifying, purification; drainage (of ground); disinfecting (of goods); sweetening (of soil, etc.); improving of the sanitation (of town); purging (of literature, etc.); *Mil:* mopping-up; *Fin:* stabilization (of budget, etc.); **a. des finances,** reorganization, rehabilitation, of finances.

assainisseur [asɛnisœr], *s.m.* **a. d'air,** air purifier.

assaisonnant [asɛzɔnɑ̃], *a. Cu:* savoury (herbs, etc.).

assaisonnement [asɛzɔnmɑ̃], *s.m.* **1.** (*action of*) seasoning, flavouring (dish); dressing (of salad). **2.** condiment, seasoning, flavouring, relish. **3.** *F:* spice, zest, piquancy.

assaisonner [asɛzɔne], *v.tr.* to season, flavour (**de,** with); to give a relish to (sth.); to dress (salad); *Prov:* **la faim, l'appétit, assaisonne tout,** hunger is the best sauce; **discours assaisonné d'ironie,** speech seasoned, touched, with irony; **a. un récit,** to give spice, zest, to a story; *P:* **se faire a.,** (i) to be given hell, to get hauled over the coals; (ii) to be beaten up.

Assam [asam], *Pr.n.m. Geog:* Assam.

assamais, -aise [asame, -ɛ:z], (*a*) *a. & s. Geog:* Assamese; (*b*) *s.m. Ling:* Assamese.

assarmenter [asarmɑ̃te], *v.tr.* to cut the shoots off (vine).

assassinant [asasinɑ̃], *a. F: A:* deadly dull; wearisome; fulsome (compliments).

assassin, -ine [asasɛ̃, -in]. **1.** *s.* assassin, murderer, *f.* murderess; **crier à l'a.,** to cry murder; **à l'a!** murder! **1.** *a.* (*a*) murderous (horde, etc.); deadly (epigram); (*b*) provocative, bewitching (smile, glance). **3.** *A:* **assassin, (mouche) assassine,** (black silk) patch (worn on face).

assassinat [asasina], *s.m.* assassination, murder; *Jur:* premeditated murder, *U.S:* murder in the first degree; *s.a.* LÉGAL 1.

assassiner [asasine], *v.tr.* **1.** to assassinate, murder. **2.** *F:* (*a*) to murder (song, etc.); (*b*) to worry, pester, bore, (s.o.) to death (**de,** with); **a. qn de compliments,** to shower fulsome compliments on s.o.

assaut [aso], *s.m.* **1.** (*a*) assault, attack, onslaught; charge; **canon d'a.,** assault gun; **pont d'a.,** assault bridge; **troupes d'a.,** storm(ing) troops; storming party; **monter à l'a.,** to storm; to go over the top (trench warfare); **livrer, donner, l'a. à une position,** to storm a position, to make an assault on a position; **a. à la baïonnette,** bayonet charge; **engin d'a.,** assault craft; **piste d'a.,** assault course; **embarcation, bâtiment d'a.,** assault boat, ship; **a. d'aviation,** air attack; **emporter, enlever, d'a. une position,** to carry, to take a position by storm; **prendre d'a.,** to capture by storm; **soutenir un a.,** to withstand an assault; **repousser un a.,** to beat off an assault; *Pol:* **une section d'a.,** a storm troop; **un membre des sections d'a.,** a storm trooper; *F:* **la veille de Noël les grands magasins ont essuyé l'a. de clients de dernière heure,** on Christmas Eve, the big stores were besieged by last-minute customers; *s.a.* CHAR 2; (*b*) **les assauts répétés d'une maladie,** the repeated attacks, onslaughts, of a disease. **2.** match, bout; **a. de lutte,** wrestling bout; **a. de boxe,** sparring match; **a. d'armes,** fencing bout, assault at arms; **faire a. d'esprit avec qn,** to vie in wit with s.o.; **ils faisaient a. de générosité,** they tried to outdo each other, they vied with each other, in generosity; **faire a. de paroles avec qn,** to bandy words with s.o.

assauvagir [asovaʒi:r], *v.i. & pr.* to grow wild; **terres qui (s')assauvagissent faute de culture,** lands growing wild for want of cultivation.

assavoir [asavwa:r], *v.tr. Jur: A:* = SAVOIR now used only in the *inf.*; **je lui ai fait a.,** I let him know.

-asse [as], *suff. Pej:* **1.** *forming adjs;* **blondasse,** insipidly fair; **fadasse,** insipid, sickly; **hommasse,** masculine, mannish; **mollasse,** flabby, indolent. **2.** *forming sbs, f.* **lavasse,** slops, wishy-washy stuff; **paperasse,** waste-paper; **vinasse,** washy wine.

asse [as], *s.f.,* **asseau** [aso], *s.m. Tls:* (cooper's) adze; tiler's hammer.

asséchage [aseʃa:ʒ], *s.m.,* **assèchement** [asɛʃmɑ̃], *s.m.* drying, draining, drainage (of land, road, pond, etc.); **a. d'une mine,** pumping dry, unwatering, de-watering, of a mine; *Min:* **galerie d'a.,** drainage level.

assécher [aseʃe], *v.* (**j'assèche, n. asséchons; j'assècherai**) **1.** *v.tr.* to dry, drain (marsh, etc.); to pump (mine, etc.) dry; to fork, unwater, pump out (mine), to de-water (graving dock). **2.** *v.i. & pr.* (*of land, stream, etc.*) to become dry, to dry up.

assemblage [asɑ̃bla:ʒ], *s.m.* **1.** assemblage, gathering, collection, combination; blending (of wines, etc.); **a. de personnes,** assemblage, aggregation, gathering, of people; **a. de circonstances,** combination of circumstances; **a. de tableaux,** collection of pictures. **2.** assembling, assembly (of parts of machine, etc.); *Bookb:* gathering, collating, assembling (of sheets); **bulletin d'a.,** imperfection note. **3.** (*a*) framework, support, structure; (*b*) *Carp: Metalw: Nau: etc:* joint, jointing, joining, coupling, connection; **a. à queue d'aronde,** dovetail joint; **a. à tenon et mortaise,** mortise-and-tenon joint; **a. à clavettes,** keyed connection; *Metalw:* **a. par recouvrement,** lap-rivetting; **a. par boulons,** bolted joint; **a. à clin,** lap joint; **a. à emboîtement,** faucet joint; **a. à manchon,** sleeve joint; **a. à manchon taraudé,** jump-coupling; *Mec.E:* **tige d'a.,** link; *Carp:* **pièce d'a.,** bond-timber; *Nau:* **mât d'a.** made mast, built mast; (*c*) *El.E:* connection, joining-up; **a. en quantité,** parallel connection; **a. en tension, en série,** joining-up in series. **4.** *Metalw:* bond; **trous d'a. (pour rivets),** bond holes.

assemblé [asɑ̃ble], *s.m. Danc:* assemblé.

assemblée [asɑ̃ble], *s.f.* assembly. **1.** (*a*) meeting; **a. générale d'actionnaires,** general meeting of shareholders; **a. (de village),** village fête; **se réunir en a. publique,** to hold a public meeting; **a. de famille,** family gathering; **a. choisie,** select company; **a. de chasseurs,** meet of hunters; **l'a. des fidèles,** the congregation; (*b*) *Hist:* **L'A. législative,** the Legislative Assembly; **la Haute A.,** the Senate; *Pol:* **A. nationale** = House of Commons, *U.S:* House of Representatives. **2.** *Mil: Navy: O:* **battre, sonner, l'a.,** to beat, sound, the assembly; *Mil:* **quartier d'a.,** assembling point, alarm post.

assembler [asɑ̃ble], *v.tr.* **1.** to assemble; to call (people) together; to convene (committee, etc.); to collect, gather; to blend (wines, etc.); *Nau:* **A. l'équipage,** to muster the crew; **a. des malheurs sur sa tête,** to bring misfortunes on oneself. **2.** to assemble, fit together (machine, dress, etc.); *Bookb:* to collate, gather (sheets of book); *El.E:* to connect, join up (cells); *Carp: Mec.E: etc:* to join (up); to joint; to couple; **a. deux morceaux à plat,** to butt-joint two pieces.

s'assembler. 1. to assemble, meet, gather; to be joined, assembled; *Prov:* **qui se ressemble s'assemble,** birds of a feather flock together. **2. tout s'assemble contre moi,** everything is combining against me.

assembleur, -euse [asɑ̃blœ:r, -ø:z], *s.* **1.** assembler; (*a*) fitter (of machines, etc.); (*b*) **Zeus, l'a. de nuages,** Zeus, the cloud-compeller. **2.** collector, gatherer; *Bookb:* gatherer, collator (of sheets). **3.** *s.f.* **assembleuse,** *Bookb:* (*machine*) gatherer.

assener, asséner [asene], *v.tr.* (**j'assène, n. assenons, n. assénons, j'assènerai, j'asséneraì**) to strike (blow); **coup bien asséné,** telling, well-planted, blow; **a. un coup sur la tête de qn,** to bludgeon s.o., *F:* to bash s.o. on the head; **il lui assena un coup de hache sur la tête,** he brought the axe down on his head.

assentement [asɑ̃tmɑ̃], *s.m. Ven:* scent.

assentiment [asɑ̃timɑ̃], *s.m.* assent, consent, approbation, acquiescence; **avoir l'a. de tous,** to be supported by all; **signe d'a.,** nod; **il fit un signe d'a.,** he nodded assent; **avec un sourire d'a.,** with smiling assent; **il me regarda avec un sourire d'a.,** he looked at me and smiled assent; **donner son a. à,** to assent to.

assentir [asɑ̃ti:r], *v.tr. Ven:* (*of pack*) **a. la voie,** to pick up the scent.

asseoir [aswa:r], *v.tr.* (*pr.p.* **asseyant,** *F:* **assoyant;** *p.p.* **assis;** *pr.ind.* **j'assieds** [asje], **il assied, n. asseyons, ils asseyent,** or **j'assois, il assoit,** *F:* **n. assoyons, ils assoient;** *pr.sub.* **j'asseye, n. asseyions,** or **j'assoie,** *F:* **n. assoyions;** *imp.* **assieds,** *F:* **asseyons, asseyez** or **assois, assoyons, assoyez;** *p.d.* **j'asseyais** or *F:* **j'assoyais;** *p.h.* **j'assis;** *p.sub.* **j'assisse;** *fu.* **j'assiérai,** *O:* **j'asseyerai, j'assoirai**) **1.** (*a*) to set, seat; **asseyez-le sur le gazon,** sit him down on the grass; **a. qn à côté du cocher,** to give s.o. a seat beside the driver; **a. un prince sur le trône,** to put, set a prince on the throne; (*b*) *F:* to sit on (s.o.); to shut s.o. up; to take the wind out of (s.o.'s) sails. **2.** to place lay, establish (foundations, etc.); **a. une pierre,** to bed a stone; **a. une statue sur un piédestal,** to stand a statue on a pedestal; **a. une tente, un camp,** to pitch a tent, a camp; *Golf:* **a. sa crosse sur le sol,** to ground one's club; *Av:* **a. l'appareil,** to pancake (to the ground); **a. son opinion sur le fait que . . .,** to base, ground, found, one's opinion on the fact that . . . **a. son autorité,** to establish one's authority; (*c*) **a. l'impôt sur le revenu,** to base taxation on income. **3.** (*a*) **a. une pension sur qn,** to settle a pension on s.o.; (*b*) **a. un impôt sur les tabacs,** to impose, to lay, to levy, a tax on tobacco.

s'asseoir. 1. (*a*) to sit down; **faire a. qn,** to ask s.o. to sit down; to ask, beg, s.o. to be seated; **asseyez-vous, messieurs,** take your seats, gentlemen; **s'a. (sur son séant),** to sit up; *F:* **s'a. sur qn,** to sit on s.o., to snub s.o.; *P:* **va t'asseoir!** go to blazes! *P:* **les ordres du patron, moi, je m'asseois dessus,** I don't care a damn about the boss's orders! (*b*) **s'a. devant une ville,** to lay siege to a town. **2.** (*of house, gun, etc.*) to settle.

assermenté [asɛrmɑ̃te], *a.* (*a*) sworn (in); **fonctionnaire a.,** sworn official; *Hist:* **(prêtre) non a.,** non-juring (priest); **prêtre a.,** juror; (*b*) (witness, etc.) on oath.

assermenter [asɛrmɑ̃te], *v.tr.* to swear (s.o.) in; to administer the oath to (s.o.).

assertif, -ive [asɛrtif, -iːv], *a. Log:* assertive (proposition).
assertion [asɛrsjɔ̃], *s.f.* assertion.
assertivement [asɛrtivmɑ̃], *adv. Log:* assertively, affirmatively.
assertoire [asɛrtwaːr], **assertorique** [asɛrtɔrik], *a. Phil:* assertoric, assertorial.
asservi [asɛrvi], *a.* **1. être a. à l'étiquette,** to be a slave to, the slave of, etiquette. **2.** *Mec.E:* servo-(appliance); **moteur a.,** servomotor; *W.Tel:* **station asservie,** slave station.
asservir [asɛrviːr], *v.tr.* **1.** (*a*) to enslave, subjugate, subdue (nation, etc.); to reduce (nation) to slavery; **a. ses passions,** to subdue one's passions; (*b*) **a. qn à une tâche,** to tie s.o. down to a task. **2.** to bring (part) under control (of actuating device, etc.).
s'asservir à qch., to submit, become a slave, subject oneself, to sth.
asservissable [asɛrvisabl̩], *a.* that can be subdued, enslaved; **volonté qui n'est pas a.,** indomitable will.
asservissant [asɛrvisɑ̃], *a.* enslaving; **joug a.,** servile yoke.
asservissement [asɛrvismɑ̃], *s.m.* **1.** (*a*) reduction to slavery; (*b*) state of bondage; subjection (**à,** to), enslavement; **a. à la mode,** subservience to fashion. **2.** control (of mechanism); servo-control; **à a.,** pilot-controlled (mechanism).
asservisseur, -euse [asɛrvisœːr, -øːz]. **1.** *a.* enslaving; *Techn:* **organe a.,** controlling element, member. **2.** *s.* enslaver.
assesseur [asɛsœːr], *s.m.* (*a*) *Jur:* (**juge**) **a.,** assessor (to magistrate, etc.); (*b*) **être secondé par ses assesseurs,** to be supported by one's assistants, advisers.
assessoral, -aux [asɛsɔral, -o], *a.* assessorial.
assessorat [asɛsɔra], *s.m.* assessorship.
assessorial, -aux [asɛsɔrjal, -o], *a.* = ASSESSORAL.
assette [asɛt], *s.f.* = ASSE.
assez [ase], *adv.* **1.** enough, sufficient, sufficiently; (*a*) **vous travaillez bien a.,** you work quite enough; **elle parle a. bien l'anglais,** she speaks English quite, fairly, well; **c'est a. parlé!** enough said! that's enough talking! **j'aurais a. de cent francs,** a hundred francs will be enough, I will have enough with a hundred francs; **pour le paysage, c'est a. de six tubes de couleurs,** for landscape work six tubes of paint are plenty; **tu n'es pas a. grand, tu ne marches pas a. vite,** you are not big enough, you don't walk fast enough; (*b*) **assez de** + *s.*; **il y a a. de temps que je l'attends,** I have been waiting for her long enough; **avez-vous a. d'argent?** have you enough money? **oui, j'en ai a.,** yes, I have got enough; **il en avait a. d'elle,** he had had enough of her; *F:* **j'en ai assez!** I have had enough of it, I am sick, tired, of it! I'm fed up; *U.S:* I'm through! **en voilà a. sur ce sujet!** that's enough about that! **c'en est a.!** that's enough of that! **(c'est) a. de discours,** that's enough talking; **a. de larmes!** stop crying! **avoir a. et plus qu'il n'en faut,** to have enough and to spare; *Prov:* **a. vaut festin,** enough is as good as a feast; (*c*) **c'est assez** + *inf.*; **c'est a. parler,** I, you, have said enough; that's enough talking; **c'est a. de lui faire savoir que vous êtes ici,** it is sufficient to let him know that you are here; (*d*) **assez pour** + *inf.*; **assez pour que** + *sub.*; **soyez a. bon pour me diriger,** would you be kind enough to direct me, would you be so kind as to direct me; **être a. près pour voir,** to be near enough to see; **elle ne serait pas a. stupide pour le faire,** she wouldn't be so stupid as to do it; **je n'ai pas a. d'influence pour vous aider,** I have not enough influence to help you; **quel est l'homme a. mesquin pour ne pas l'admirer?** what man would be so mean as not to admire her? **il n'était pas a. grand pour qu'on le laissât seul,** he was not big enough to be left alone; **il n'avait pas a. pour vivre,** he did not have enough to live on; **en voilà a. pour le mettre en fureur,** that is enough to infuriate him; (*e*) *int.* **assez!** that's enough! stop! **2.** rather, fairly, tolerably, passably; **elle est a. jolie,** she is rather pretty, tolerably good-looking; **je suis a. de votre avis,** I am rather inclined to agree with you; **les deux villes sont a. semblables,** the two towns are quite, fairly, similar; **arriver a. tard,** to arrive somewhat late; **avoir a. de bon sens,** to have a fair amount, plenty, of (common) sense; **la maison est a. confortable,** the house is comfortable enough; **il parle a. peu,** he does not talk much; **a. d'autres vous diront la même chose,** plenty of other people will say the same; *Iron:* **il est a. étrange que ce soit moi qui doive faire les excuses,** it is a bit peculiar that I should be the one who has to apologize. **3.** (*intensive*) **est-il a. enfant!** isn't he a baby! how childish of him! **est-il a. grossier!** isn't he rude!
assibilation [asibilasjɔ̃], *s.f. Ling:* (as)sibilation.
assibiler [asibile], *v.tr. Ling:* to (as)sibilate; **mot où le t s'assibile,** word in which the *t* takes a sibilant sound, is assibilated.
assidu [asidy], *a.* assiduous; (*a*) sedulous, diligent, industrious, hard-working, persevering, steady (pupil, workman, etc.); **efforts assidus,** untiring efforts; **être a. à qch., à faire qch.,** to be diligent at sth., in doing sth., to be persevering, assiduous, in (doing) sth.; **a. à son travail,** devoted to his work; **travailleur a.,** hard worker; (*b*) persistent, unremitting, unceasing, constant (care, work, attention, etc.); (*c*) regular, constant (visitor, etc.); **être a. auprès de qn,** to be assiduous in one's attentions to s.o., in one's care of s.o.; **étudiant a. aux cours,** student attending lectures regularly, who is a regular attendant at lectures.
assiduité [asidɥite], *s.f.* assiduousness, assiduity. **1.** (*a*) sedulousness, steadiness; **a. à (faire) qch.,** assiduity, steadiness, in (doing) sth.; **a. à l'étude,** close application to study; **a. au travail,** devotion to work; **à force d'a.,** by dint of perseverance; (*b*) *Sch: etc:* regular attendance; **l'a. à ce cours ne se dément jamais,** the attendance at this class never drops off; **prix d'a.,** attendance prize; **a. au travail,** industriousness. **2.** constant attention(s), constant care; **avoir des assiduités auprès de qn,** to show s.o. unremitting attention.
assidûment [asidymɑ̃], *adv.* assiduously, unremittingly, sedulously, diligently; regularly; **il y travaille a.,** he is hard at work on it.
assiégé, -ée [asjeʒe], *a. & s.* besieged; **les assiégés,** the besieged.
assiégeant [asjeʒɑ̃]. **1.** *a.* besieging (army, etc.). **2.** *s.m.* besieger.
assiéger [asjeʒe], *v.tr.* (**assiégeant, j'assiège, n. assiégeons, j'assiégerai**) **1.** (*a*) to besiege, beleaguer; to lay siege to (s.o., sth.); (*b*) *F:* **a. qn de demandes d'emploi,** to besiege s.o. with requests for employment. **2.** to surround, beset, mob, throng round, crowd round (s.o., sth.); **ils assiègent la porte,** they throng round the door; **être assiégé par ses créanciers,** to be dunned by one's creditors; **être assiégé par des souvenirs,** to be haunted by memories; **il est assiégé d'ennuis,** he is beset with worries.
assiette [asjɛt], *s.f.* **1.** action of giving a firm and stable position to sth., of laying down sth.; (*a*) laying down (of foundations); bedding (of stone); pitching (of camp); laying out (of railway line); (*b*) establishment (of tax, of rates); funding (of annuity). **2.** stable position; (*a*) *A:* sitting position, seat; **rester deux heures dans la même a.,** to remain for two hours in the same position; **le blessé ne pouvait trouver une bonne a.,** the wounded man could not find a comfortable way to sit; (*b*) seat (on horse); trim (of boat); *Av: Nau:* **angle d'a.,** trim angle; **avoir une bonne a.,** (i) to have a good seat (on horseback); (ii) (*of ship*) to be in good trim; **il n'a pas d'a.,** he is very shaky in the saddle; **perdre son a.,** to lose one's seat, to be unseated; *F:* **n'être pas dans son a.,** to be out of sorts, off colour, to feel seedy, not to be up to the mark; (*c*) established position; **avoir une certaine a. dans le monde,** to have, enjoy, a certain position in the world; **a. de pied,** foothold; (*d*) position; situation, site (of building, etc.); disposition (of camp); lie (of land); *Golf:* **a. d'une balle,** lie of a ball; *For:* **a. des coupes,** felling plan; (*e*) set (of stone, beam, etc.); (*of foundation, gun, etc.*) **prendre son a.,** to set, to settle, to bed down. **3.** support, basis; (*a*) **a. d'une chaussée,** foundation, bottom, bed, of a road; *Mch:* **a. d'un cylindre, du moteur,** seat, saddle, of a cylinder, of the engine; (*b*) **a. d'un impôt,** property, income, imports, etc., on which a tax rests, basis of a tax; **a. d'une rente,** property, funds, on which an annuity is secured. **4.** (*a*) plate; **a. plate,** dinner plate; **a. creuse, à soupe,** soup plate; **a. à dessert,** dessert plate; **a. à bouillie,** baby's bowl; porringer; **a. montée,** cake dish; **a. à réchaud, a. chauffante,** (hot) water plate; **manger dans une a.,** to eat from, off, a plate; **manger dans une a. à soupe,** to eat out of a soup plate; *F:* **son a. dîne pour lui,** he pays for his meal whether he is present or not; *F:* **a. au beurre,** cushy job; *s.a.* BEURRE 1, CASSEUR, PIQUER 4; (*b*) = ASSIETTÉE; **a. anglaise,** assorted cold meat, *U.S:* cold cuts; **a. de charcuterie,** plate of assorted delicatessen.
assiettée [asjete], *s.f.* plate(ful); **deux assiettées de soupe,** two platefuls, helpings, plates, of soup.
assignable [asiɲabl̩], *a.* **1.** assignable (cause, etc.) (**à,** to). **2.** *Jur:* liable to be summoned or sued, su(e)able.
assignat [asiɲa], *s.m. Hist:* assignat, promissory note (issued by the French Revolutionary Government, 1790–96).
assignataire [asiɲatɛːr], *a.* **banque a.,** warrant bank.
assignation [asiɲasjɔ̃], *s.f.* **1.** *Fin:* assignment, transfer (of shares, of funds) (**à,** to). **2.** *Jur:* (*a*) serving of a writ, summons, or process; (*b*) writ of summons; subpœna; **signifier, faire, donner, envoyer, une a. à qn,** to serve a writ on s.o., to serve s.o. with a writ; to issue a summons to s.o.; to subpoena (witness); (*c*) **a. à résidence,** placing under forced residence. **3.** *A:* appointment, rendezvous, assignation; **a. amoureuse,** lovers' tryst.
assigné [asiɲe], *a. & s.* (person) served with a writ.
assigner [asiɲe], *v.tr.* **1.** to assign; (*a*) to fix, appoint (hour, meeting, etc.); **a. une tâche à qn,** to assign, allot, a task to s.o.; **a. un programme à qn,** to lay down a programme for s.o.; **a. une cause à un événement,** to assign a cause to an event; **a. des limites à . . .,** to set limits to . . .; (*b*) **a. une somme à un paiement,** to assign, earmark, a sum for a payment, to allocate a sum to a payment; (*c*) **a. une dépense sur le trésor public,** to charge an expense to, to make an expense payable out of, public funds. **2.** *Jur:* (*a*) to summon, subpoena, cite (witness, etc.); (*b*) (i) to issue a writ against (s.o.); (ii) to have a writ issued against (s.o.); (iii) to serve a writ on (s.o.); **a. qn en contrefaçon,** to bring an action for infringement of patent against s.o.; to sue s.o. for infringement of patent; **a. à qn un lieu de séjour,** to assign a forced residence to s.o.
assimilable [asimilabl̩], *a.* **1.** assimilable (food, knowledge, people). **2.** comparable, similar (**à,** to).
assimilateur, -trice [asimilatœːr, -tris]. **1.** *a. Physiol: etc:* assimilative, assimilating, assimilatory. **2.** *s.* assimilator.
assimilatif, -ive [asimilatif, -iːv], *a.* assimilative, assimilatory.
assimilation [asimilasjɔ̃], *s.f.* **1.** (*a*) assimilation (of food, knowledge, etc.); (*b*) assimilation (of racial groups, etc.); **politique d'a.,** policy of assimilation; (*c*) *Hist:* **a. des colonies,** putting the colonies on the same footing as the mother country; (*d*) *Ling:* **a. d'une consonne à celle qui suit,** assimilation of a consonant with the one following it. **2.** *Mil: Navy:* (*a*) correlation (of ranks between various arms); (*b*) relative rank (of non-combatant).
assimilé [asimile]. **1.** *a.* (*a*) *Mil: Navy:* **être a. à . . .,** to rank as, with; ranked as; **a. aux officiers, aux sous-officiers,** ranking with officers, with noncommissioned officers; **a. au grade de capitaine,** ranking, ranked as a captain; (*b*) assimilated (immigrants, etc.). **2.** *s.m.* (*a*) **officiers et assimilés,** officers and equivalent; **cadres et assimilés,** executives and acting executives.
assimiler [as(s)imile], *v.tr.* **1.** (*a*) to assimilate (food, knowledge, etc.); **l'organisme s'assimile facilement ces minéraux,** the system can easily assimilate these minerals; **ces minéraux s'assimilent facilement,** these minerals are easily assimilated; (*b*) to assimilate (immigrants, etc.). **2.** to assimilate; (*a*) to liken, compare (**à,** to, with); **pensez-vous que j'ose m'a. à lui?** do you think I dare compare myself to him? (*b*) **a. deux catégories de fonctionnaires,** to put two classes of civil servants on the same footing (as regards salary, etc.); (*c*) **a. à,** to class as, to put in the same category as.
assiminéidés [asimineide], *s.m.pl. Moll:* Assimineidae.
assis [asi]. **1.** *a.* (*a*) seated; **nous étions a. auprès du feu,** we were sitting, seated, round the fire; **demeurer a.,** to remain seated, to keep one's seat; *F:* **en rester a.,** to be flabbergasted, to be struck all of a heap; *Her:* **lion a.,** lion sejant; **assis!** sit down; (*b*) **danses assises,** dances that one sits out; *Rail: Th: etc:* **places assises,** seats; **il n'y a plus de places assises,** "standing room only"; (*c*) **la maison est assise sur la colline,** the house stands on the hill; **navire bien a. sur l'eau,** well-trimmed ship; **fortune bien assise,** fortune resting on a sound foundation, well-established fortune; **sa gloire est assise sur ses romans,** his fame rests on his novels; *s.a.* MAGISTRATURE 2. **2.** *s.m.* **voter par assis et levé,** to give one's vote by rising or remaining seated.

assise[1] [asiːz], *s.f.* **1.** seating, laying (of foundation). **2.** (*a*) seating, foundation; bed(-plate) (of engine, etc.); **assurer l'a. d'une portée,** to bed a bearing; **ajuster l'a. d'une soupape,** to seat a valve; *F:* **les assises de la société,** the foundations of society; (*b*) *Geol:* bed, stratum. **3.** (*a*) *Const:* course (of masonry); course, row (of brick); layer (of cement); **assises de béton,** bed of concrete; **assises de renforcement,** stretcher course; **assises réglées,** coursed work; **mur sans assises,** rubble wall; (*b*) **la montagne s'élève en assises,** the mountain rises in tiers. **4.** *pl.* (*a*) *Jur:* **les assises,** the assizes; **cour d'assises,** Assize Court; **être renvoyé devant la cour d'assises,** to be committed for trial; **avocat d'assises,** criminal lawyer; (*b*) **assises d'un congrès, etc.,** sittings of a congress, etc.; **assises solennelles de la chrétienté,** solemn conclave of Christendom; **tenir ses assises (en un lieu),** (to meet, hold one's meetings (in a place); (*c*) *Hist:* **les Assises de Jérusalem,** the Assizes of Jerusalem.

Assise[2], *Pr.n.f. Geog:* Assisi.

assistanat [asistana], *s.m. Sch:* assistantship.

assistance [asistɑ̃ːs], *s.f.* **1.** presence, attendance (*esp.* of magistrate or priest). **2.** (*a*) audience, company; *Ecc:* congregation; (*b*) spectators, onlookers; **toute l'a. l'a entendu,** all present heard it. **3.** (*a*) assistance, help, aid; **prêter a. à qn,** to assist s.o.; **faire qch. sans assistance,** to do sth. unaided; **a. sociale,** welfare work; **a. économique à un pays étranger,** foreign aid; *Com:* **a. maritime,** salvage; *s.a.* COMPLICE; (*b*) **procurer a., des assistances, aux pauvres,** to obtain assistance, relief, for the poor; **a. aux vieillards,** relief of old people; *A:* **L'A. publique** = (i) National Assistance Board; (ii) Child Welfare; *Jur:* **a. judiciaire,** legal aid; **intenter une action avec a. judiciaire,** to sue *in forma pauperis.*

assistant, -ante [asistɑ̃, -ɑ̃ːt]. **1.** *s. usu. pl.* (*a*) bystander, onlooker, spectator; (*b*) member of the audience; **quelques-uns d'entre vous, messieurs les assistants,** some of you gentlemen here. **2.** *s.* (*a*) assistant; **l'a. du chirurgien,** the surgeon's assistant; (*b*) foreign assistant (in school); (*c*) *Sch:* demonstrator (of practical work); laboratory assistant; (*d*) **assistante sociale,** welfare worker, welfare officer, caseworker; **assistante sociale d'un hôpital,** medical social worker. **3. médecin a.,** assistant doctor.

assisté, -ée [asiste], *a. & s. Adm:* (person) in receipt of (public) assistance; **enfants assistés,** children in care.

assister [asiste]. **1.** *v.i.* **a. à qch.,** to attend sth., to be (present) at sth., to take part in sth.; **a. à une partie de football,** to attend, to watch, to be a spectator at, a football match; **a. à une rixe,** to witness a brawl; **l'infirmière assista à l'opération sans broncher,** the nurse saw the operation through without wincing. **2.** *v.tr.* (*a*) to help, assist, succour (s.o.); **a. qn de ses conseils,** to help s.o. with advice; **les pauvres sont assistés,** the poor receive State relief; *s.a.* DIRECTION 2; (*b*) to attend (s.o.); **prêtre assisté de deux enfants de chœur,** priest attended by two altar-boys; (*c*) **Dieu vous assiste!** bless you! (when sneezing).

associabilité [asɔsjabilite], *s.f.* associability.

associable [asɔsjabl̩], *a. Rare:* associable (à, with).

associatif, -ive [asɔsjatif, -iːv], *a.* associative. **1. mémoire associative,** associative memory. **2.** *Math:* **loi associative,** associative law.

association [asɔsjasjɔ̃], *s.f.* **1.** (*a*) association (of words, ideas); *Psycho-analysis:* **associations sonores,** clang associations; (*b*) *El:* connecting, grouping, coupling (of cells); (*c*) *Jur:* **a. de malfaiteurs,** conspiracy. **2.** (*a*) society, company; association, fellowship; **a. syndicale,** trade-union; **a. de secours,** friendly society; **a. de bienfaisance,** charity, charitable institution; (*b*) *Com:* partnership; **entrer en a. avec qn,** to enter into partnership with s.o.

associationnisme [asɔsjasjɔnism], *s.m. Phil:* associationism.

associationniste [asɔsjasjɔnist], *a. & s. Phil:* associationist.

associativité [asɔsjativite], *s.f.* associativeness.

associé, -ée [asɔsje]. **1.** *a.* associated; joint-; **porteurs, souscripteurs, associés,** joint-holders (of stock); *Adm:* **territoires associés,** associated territories. **2.** *s.* (*a*) *Com:* partner; **a. principal,** senior partner; **dernier a., a. intéressé,** junior partner; **a. commandité,** responsible, special, acting partner; **a. commanditaire,** dormant, sleeping partner; **prendre qn comme a.,** to take s.o. into partnership; (*b*) associate, honorary member (of learned body, etc.). **3.** *a.* **à,** in conjunction with.

associement [asɔsimɑ̃], *s.m.* association.

associer [asɔsje], *v.tr.* (*pr. sub. & p.d.,* **n. associions, v. associiez**) **1.** (*a*) to associate, unite, join; **a. qn à qch.,** to make s.o. a party to sth., to associate s.o. with sth.; **a. des idées,** to connect, associate, ideas; **elle associe la beauté à l'intelligence,** in her beauty and intelligence are joined; (*b*) *El:* to connect, join up (cells, etc.). **2. s'a. qn, a. qn à sa maison, à ses travaux,** to take s.o. into partnership.

s'associer. 1. s'a. à qch. (*a*) to share in, participate in, join in, sth; **s'a. à un crime,** to be a party to, a participator in a crime; to abet a crime; **s'a. aux vues de qn,** to associate oneself with, to endorse, the opinion of s.o.; (*b*) to join (a corporate body). **2. s'a. à, avec, qn** (*a*) to enter into a combination with s.o., to associate oneself with s.o.; (*b*) to enter into partnership with s.o.; (*c*) to associate with, mix with, keep company with, frequent, s.o. **3.** *abs.* **états qui s'associent,** states which join forces; **idées qui s'associent,** ideas which go well together.

assoiffer [aswafe], *v.tr.* to make thirsty (for, de) (*chiefly used in the p.p.*); **être assoiffé de qch.,** to be thirsty, eager for sth.; **a. de sang,** bloodthirsty; thirsting for blood.

assolement [asɔlmɑ̃], *s.m. Agr:* rotation cropping, course, shift (of crops); **a. triennal,** three-field system, three-course system; *s.a.* QUADRIENNIAL.

assoler [asɔle], *v.tr.* **a. une terre,** to vary, rotate, the crops on a piece of land.

assombrir [asɔ̃briːr], *v.tr.* (*a*) to darken, obscure; **ciel assombri,** cloudy, overcast, sky; (*b*) to render (s.o., sth.) gloomy; to spread, cast, throw, a gloom over (s.o., sth.); **visage assombri,** gloomy face.

s'assombrir, (*a*) (*of the day, the sky, etc.*) to darken, to become dark, to cloud over; **tout s'assombrit,** everything became dark; (*b*) to become gloomy, sad; **son visage s'assombrit,** his face clouded over.

assombrissement [asɔ̃brismɑ̃], *s.m.* **1.** darkening, becoming gloomy; toning down. **2.** gloom, gloominess.

assommant [asɔmɑ̃], *a.* **1.** *O:* overwhelming (heat, argument, etc.); **coup a.,** knock-down blow. **2.** *F:* boring, tedious, weariness, tiresome; **il est a., cet enfant-là!** that child is a fearful bother, an awful nuisance! **bavard a.,** deadly bore; **soirée tout à fait assommante,** thoroughly dull evening; **une besogne assommante,** a deadly dull task.

assommement [asɔmmɑ̃], *s.m.* **1.** = ABATTAGE 3. **2.** boredom.

assommer [asɔme], *v.tr.* **1.** (*a*) **a. un bœuf,** to fell an ox; **a. qn,** to brain s.o.; to knock, *F:* bash, s.o. on, over, the head; **a. qn à coups de massue, à coups de gourdin, de trique,** to club, cudgel, s.o. to death; (*b*) to knock (s.o.) senseless; to stun, to sandbag (s.o.); (*c*) *F: A:* to belabour (s.o.), to beat (s.o.) unmercifully. **2.** *F:* (*a*) to overwhelm, overpower, overcome, stun; **assommé par la chaleur,** overcome with heat; **assommé par l'alcool,** sodden with drink; (*b*) to bore; to tire (s.o.) to death; **a. qn de questions,** to pester s.o. with questions; **vous m'assommez avec vos questions,** you are a nuisance with your questions; (*c*) **a. qn avec des arguments,** to flatten s.o. with arguments.

assommeur, -euse [asɔmœːr, -øːz]. **1.** *s.m.* (*a*) slaughterer, slaughterman; (*b*) ruffian (armed with club), tough. **2.** *s.m. & f. F:* **quel a. que votre ami!** your friend is a terrible bore!

assommoir [asɔmwaːr], *s.m.* **1.** *O:* (*a*) pole-axe; (*b*) *O:* club, bludgeon, cosh; *U.S:* black-jack; *F:* **porter un coup d'a. à qn,** to deal s.o. a staggering blow, *F:* a knock-out blow. **2.** (*a*) *Ven:* deadfall, fall-trap; (*b*) **(piège) a.,** break-back trap. **3.** *A:* low pub.

assomptif, -ive [asɔ̃ptif, -iːv], *a.* **1.** *Log:* assumptive (proposition). **2.** *Her:* **armes assomptives,** assumptive arms, arms of assumption.

assomption [asɔ̃psjɔ̃], *s.f.* **1.** *Log:* assumption. **2.** *Ecc:* **(fête de) l'A. (de la Sainte Vierge),** (feast of) the Assumption (of the Blessed Virgin). **3.** *Geog:* (*a*) **Assomption,** Asuncion; (*b*) *A:* **L'île de l'A.,** Anticosti.

assomptionniste [asɔ̃psjɔnist], *s.m. Ecc:* assumptionist.

assonance [asɔnɑ̃ːs], *s.f. Ling: Pros:* assonance.

assonant [asɔnɑ̃], *a. Ling: Pros:* assonant.

assoner [asɔne], *v.i. Pros:* to assonate.

assorti [asɔrti], *a.* **1.** matched, matching, paired; **bien, mal, a.,** well-, ill- matched; **couple mal a.,** ill-sorted, ill-assorted, couple; **couleurs assorties,** colours to match; **elle porte des souliers assortis à sa robe,** she wears shoes to go with, to match, her dress; **pull-over avec jupe assortie,** sweater with matching skirt. **2.** assorted, mixed (sweets, nails, etc.). **3. bien assorti,** well-stocked, well-furnished (shop, etc.).

assortiment [asɔrtimɑ̃], *s.m.* **1.** matching, suitability; **a. parfait de couleurs,** perfect match(ing) of colours; **ce mariage est un a. parfait,** this union is a perfect match; **un mauvais a.,** a bad match. **2.** (*a*) assortment, variety, diversified collection (of goods, etc., of the same sort); **ample a. d'échantillons,** wide range of patterns; **un a. (de charcuterie),** (slices of) assorted cold meats, assorted delicatessen; **librairie d'a.,** general bookseller; (*b*) set (of tools, etc.); *Typ:* sorts; (*c*) *pl. Mil: etc:* small stores.

assortir [asɔrtiːr], *v.* **(j'assortis, n. assortissons) 1.** *v.tr.* (*a*) to assort, sort, match (colours, type, etc.); **a. son style à la matière,** to suit one's style to the matter; **elle voudrait a. un manteau à sa robe,** she would like a coat to match the colour of her dress; (*b*) to blend (ores, etc.); (*c*) to stock, furnish (shop, etc., with varied goods). **2.** *v.i.* (*of colours, etc.*) to match; to go well together; **a. à, avec qch.,** to go well with sth.

s'assortir. 1. to match, to suit one another, to go well together, to harmonize. **2.** (*a*) *Com:* to stock varied goods; (*b*) **s'a. de livres pour les vacances,** to lay in a stock of books for the holidays.

assortissable [asɔrtisabl̩], *a.* matchable.

assortissant [asɔrtisɑ̃], *a.* that suits, matches; that goes well (à, with); **actions assortissantes à ses principes,** actions in keeping with his principles.

assoter [asɔte], *v.tr. A:* to infatuate (s.o.).

s'assoter de qn, to become foolishly infatuated with, fond of s.o.

Assouan [aswɑ̃], *Pr.n.m. Geog:* Assuan, Aswan.

assouchement [asuʃmɑ̃], *s.m. Arch:* (stone forming the) base of a pediment.

assoupi [asupi], *a.* **1.** dozing; **être a.,** to doze, *F:* to snooze. **2.** dormant (grief, volcano, etc.).

assoupir [asupiːr], *v.tr.* **1.** (*a*) to make (s.o.) drowsy, sleepy, heavy; to send (s.o.) to sleep; (*b*) to assuage, allay, deaden, lull, quiet (pain, the senses). **2.** *A:* to hush up, suppress, stifle (scandal, etc.).

s'assoupir. 1. to drop off to sleep; to doze off; to grow sleepy, drowsy. **2.** (*of pain, etc.*) to wear away; **le bruit s'assoupit,** the sound died away.

assoupissant [asupisɑ̃], *a.* soporific, sleep-inducing; **potion assoupissante,** sleeping-draught; **occupation assoupissante,** dull, humdrum, occupation.

assoupissement [asupismɑ̃], *s.m.* **1.** (*a*) assuaging, allaying, lulling (of pain, etc.); (*b*) *A:* hushing up (of scandal, etc.). **2.** (*a*) drowsiness, somnolence; dozing, slumber; **un court a.,** a short nap; (*b*) *Med:* torpor; (*c*) somnolence of mind; sloth.

assouplir [asupliːr], *v.tr.* to make supple, to supple; to break in (horse); **a. du cuir,** to supple, soften, leather; **peuple assoupli à la servitude,** people broken (in) to servitude; **a. ses manières,** to unbend; **a. le caractère d'un enfant,** to soften, to bend, a child's character, to make a child more tractable; **le gouvernement a assoupli certains règlements,** the Government has relaxed, eased, some regulations.

s'assouplir, to become supple; **s'a. les muscles,** to limber up; to make one's muscles supple, lithe.

assouplissage [asuplisaːʒ], *s.m. Tex:* soupling.

assouplissant [asuplisɑ̃], *a.* suppling.

assouplissement [asuplismɑ̃], *s.m.* (*action of*) making soft, supple, flexible; suppling (of leather, etc.); bending; softening; easing (of regulations); *Agr:* loosening (of soil); **exercices d'a., assouplissements,** limbering-up exercises; **a. d'un cheval,** breaking-in of a horse.

assourdir [asurdiːr], *v.tr.* **1.** to make (s.o.) deaf; to deafen. **2.** (*a*) to deaden, damp, muffle (sound); to muffle (drum, bell, oars); to mute (violin); *Const:* to make (partition) soundproof; *Ling:* to unvoice (consonant); (*b*) to soften, subdue, tone down (light, colour).

s'assourdir, (*of sound*) to grow fainter, to die away; (*of consonant*) to become unvoiced.

assourdissant [asurdisɑ̃], *a.* deafening (noise, etc.).

assourdissement [asurdismɑ̃], *s.m.* **1.** (*a*) deafening; (*b*) deadening (of sound); muffling (of drum, oars); *Ling:* unvoicing (of consonant); (*c*) softening, subduing (of light). **2.** temporary deafness; **mon a. dure encore,** my ears are still ringing.

assouvir [asuviːr], *v.tr.* to satiate, sate, appease, satisfy (hunger, passions); **a. sa soif,** to slake, quench, one's thirst; **a. ses yeux de qch.,** to feast one's eyes on sth.

s'assouvir, to satiate, gorge, glut, oneself; to become sated (**de,** with); **s'assouvir de carnage,** to slake one's thirst for blood.

assouvissement [asuvismɑ̃], *s.m.* satisfying, sating, satisfaction (of hunger, passions, etc.); quenching, slaking (of thirst).

Assuérus [asɥeryːs], *Pr.n.m. B.Hist:* Ahasuerus.

assuétude [asyetyd], *s.f. Med:* addiction, dependence.

assujétir [asyʒetiːr], *v.tr.* = ASSUJETTIR.

assujetti [asyʒeti]. **1.** *a.* (*a*) subject (**à,** to); **dieux assujettis aux passions humaines,** gods subject to human passions; **être a. à son service, être fort a.,** to be tied down to, by, one's duties; **document a. au timbre,** document liable to stamp-duty; (*b*) fixed, fastened. **2.** *s.* **les assujettis à l'impôt,** the tax-payers.

assujettir [asyʒetiːr], *v.tr.* **1.** (*a*) to subdue, subjugate (province, etc.), to bring (province, etc.) into subjection; **a. ses passions,** to govern, curb, one's passions; to master one's passions; (*b*) **a. qn à faire qch.,** to compel, oblige, s.o. to do sth. **2.** to fix, fasten (**à,** to); to make (sth.) secure; *Nau:* to cleat (rope); to batten down (hatches); *Vet:* to secure, immobilize (beast). **3.** to subject, to make liable (**à,** to).

s'assujettir, to subject oneself (**à,** to); **s'a. à un régime de . . .,** to follow a strict diet of . . .

assujettissant [asyʒetisɑ̃], *a.* tying, demanding (work); **mon travail est a.,** I am never off duty, I am tied to my duties, *F:* I always have my nose to the grindstone.

assujettissement [asyʒetismɑ̃], *s.m.* **1.** (*action*) subjection, subjugation. **2.** (*a*) (state); **a. à qn, à qch.,** subjection to s.o., subservience to (etiquette, etc.); (*b*) tie; **la grandeur a ses assujettissements,** greatness has its obligations. **3.** fixing, fastening, securing; **boulons d'a.,** holding-down bolts.

assumer [asyme], *v.tr.* to assume; to take upon oneself (right, responsibility, etc.); **a. de faire qch.,** to take it upon oneself to do sth.; **a. les frais,** to take charge of the expenditure; **a. son service,** to take up one's duties.

assurable [asyrabl̩], *a. Ins:* assurable, insurable.

assurance [asyrɑ̃ːs], *s.f.* **1.** assurance; (*a*) (self-) confidence; **parler avec a.,** to speak with confidence; **perdre son a.,** to lose one's self-assurance; (*b*) **avez-vous la pleine a. de le revoir?** are you perfectly sure you will see him again? **il est parti avec l'a. de revenir un jour,** he left confident that one day he would return; **agréez l'a. de mes sentiments dévoués,** believe me yours faithfully; **donner à qn l'a. de son amitié,** to assure s.o. of one's friendship; to give s.o. proof of one's friendship; (*c*) **vous pouvez l'acheter en toute a.,** you can buy it with complete confidence. **2.** security, pledge; **prendre une montre pour a.,** to take a watch as a pledge; **demander, recevoir, des assurances,** to ask for, receive assurances; *s.a.* AGRÉER 1, CROIRE 2. **3.** (*a*) making sure, safe; *A:* **en lieu d'a.,** in a place of safety; *Mount:* **(point d')a.,** belay; (*b*) *Com:* insurance, assurance; **police d'a.,** insurance policy; *s.a.* CONTRACTER 1; **prime d'a.,** insurance premium; **compagnie, société, d'assurances,** insurance company; **a. sur la vie, a.-vie,** (*pl. assurances-vie*) life-insurance, life-assurance; **a. contre les accidents, a.-accident,** accident insurance; **a. en cas de vie, à terme fixe, à capital différé, à rente différée,** endowment insurance; **a. contre l'incendie, a.-incendie,** fire-insurance; **a. (des patrons) contre les accidents du travail,** employers'-liability insurance, workmen's compensation insurance; **a. contre l'invalidité, a.-invalidité,** disablement insurance; **a. maladie-invalidité,** sickness and disablement insurance; **a. vieillesse,** old-age insurance; **a. maritime,** marine, maritime, insurance; **a. vis-à-vis des tiers, aux tiers,** third-party insurance; **a. maladie,** health, sickness, insurance; **a. collective,** group, collective, insurance; **a. (contre le) vol,** burglary insurance; **a. auto,** car insurance; **a. tous risques,** *Sw. Fr:* **a. casco,** all-in, comprehensive, insurance; all risk(s) insurance; **a. à cotisations,** contributory insurance; **a. facultative,** voluntary insurance; **agent d'assurance(s),** insurance agent; **courtier d'assurance(s),** insurance broker; **il est dans les assurances,** he is in insurance; **il y a a.,** the property is, was, insured; (*c*) *Adm:* **assurances sociales,** social, national, State, insurance; **a. chômage** = unemployment insurance, benefits; **a. invalidité** = disablement pension; **a. vieillesse** = old-age pension; **a. maternité** = maternity benefits; **a. maladie** = sickness benefits; **a. mutuelle,** mutual insurance.

assure [asyːr], *s.f. Tex:* weft (of tapestry).

assuré, -ée [asyre]. **1.** *a.* firm, sure (step, voice, etc.); bold (glance, tone); assured, confident (air, person); certain (cure); secure, safe (retreat); **voix mal assurée,** unsteady, quavering, voice; **d'une main assurée,** with a sure hand; **marcher d'un pas a.,** to walk with a firm step, to tread firmly; **a. de l'avenir,** assured of the future; **a. du succès,** confident of success; **il n'y a encore rien d'a.,** there is nothing fixed yet. **2.** *s. Ins:* (*a*) policy-holder; insurant; insured; (*b*) *Adm:* insured person; **a. social,** member of the National Insurance Scheme.

assurément [asyremɑ̃], *adv.* **1.** *A:* **marcher a.,** to tread boldly. **2.** assuredly, surely, undoubtedly, certainly; **a. non!** certainly not! **oui, a.!** yes, to be sure!

assurer [asyre], *v.tr.* **1.** (*a*) to make (sth.) firm, steady; to fix, secure, fasten, strengthen, steady (sth.); to prop up (wall); to make fast (rope); *Mount:* to belay; to secure; **a. qn sec,** to give s.o. a tight rope; (*b*) to ensure (result), to make (result) sure; **assurer un pays,** to make a country secure; **la paix est assurée par ce traité,** peace is assured by this treaty; **a. sa fortune,** to consolidate one's fortune; **a. la liberté de qn,** to secure s.o.'s liberty; **le vote des ouvriers lui a assuré le retour au pouvoir,** the workers' vote secured his return to power; **a. le service,** to ensure good service; **a. des vivres, des munitions, à une armée,** to ensure the supply of food, munitions, to an army; **a. une rente à qn,** to settle an annuity on s.o.; **a. à qn de quoi vivre,** to ensure s.o. enough to live on; **il m'a assuré tous ses biens,** he bequeathed me all his property; **a. ses arrières,** (i) *Mil:* to protect one's rear; (ii) to protect oneself against any eventuality; **le courrier littéraire sera assuré par M. X,** the literary column will be in the hands of Mr X; **M. X assure les cours de français,** Mr X is looking after, is giving, the French lectures; **un service régulier est assuré entre Paris et Londres,** a regular service is provided between Paris and London; **cette maison assurera notre déménagement,** that firm will handle our removal; **la permanence de nuit sera assurée par M. Y,** the night duty will be carried out by Mr Y; **ce qu'il a fait hier m'assure de l'avenir,** what he did yesterday makes me confident for the future; **a. qch. à qn,** to make s.o. certain, sure, of sth.; **s'a. qch.,** to secure, make certain of, sth.; (*c*) *Lit:* **a. son visage, sa contenance,** to put on a firm countenance; (*d*) *Navy:* **a. son pavillon (par un coup de canon),** to enforce one's colours by a shot; *cf.* APPUYER 1; (*e*) **a. une créance,** to stand security for a debt. **2. a. qch. à qn, a. qn de qch.,** to assure s.o. of sth., to declare, affirm, sth.; to vouch for sth. to s.o.; **a. qn de son affection,** to assure s.o. of one's affection; **je les assurai, leur assurai, que la chose était vraie,** I assured them that it was true; **il m'a assuré qu'il voulait bien le faire,** he assured me of his willingness, that he was willing, to do it; **je lui assurai l'avoir vu,** I assured him that I had seen it; **elle assure qu'elle ne l'a pas fait,** she insists that she didn't do it; **c'est bien vrai, je te l'assure, je t'assure,** it's quite true, I (can) assure you. **3.** *Ins:* **a. qn,** to insure s.o.; **la Compagnie n'assure pas contre les dégâts causés par la pluie,** the Company will not insure against damage caused by rain; **se faire a. sur la vie,** to have one's life insured, to take out a life insurance (policy); **a. un navire pour l'aller et le retour,** to insure a ship out and home; **a. un immeuble contre l'incendie,** to insure a building against fire.

s'assurer. 1. to make oneself firm (in a position); **s'a. sur ses pieds, sur ses jambes,** to adopt a firm stance; **assurez-vous dans cette position,** stand firm in this position; **s'a. sur sa selle,** to steady oneself in the saddle; **il faut s'entraîner pour s'a. la main,** you must practise to steady your hand. **2.** *A:* **s'a. sur qn, dans qch.,** to trust, put one's trust in, s.o., sth. **3. s.a. de qch.,** to make sure, certain, of sth., to ascertain sth.; **s'a. des provisions pour l'hiver,** to lay in, ensure, a supply of provisions for the winter; **je vais m'en assurer,** I will go and see; **s'a. que** + *ind. or sometimes sub.* to make sure, ascertain, satisfy oneself, that . . .; **s'a. que tout est en ordre,** to see that everything is in order. **4. s'a. de qch., de (la personne de) qn,** to lay hold of, to make sure of, to secure, sth., s.o.; to impound sth., to arrest s.o. **5.** *Ins:* to get insured, to take out an insurance (**contre,** against).

assureur [asyrœːr], *s.m. Ins:* (*a*) insurer; (*b*) underwriter.

assurgent, -ente [asyrʒɑ̃, -ɑ̃ːt], *a. Bot:* assurgent.

Assyrie [asiri], *Pr.n.f. A.Geog:* Assyria.

assyrien, -ienne [asirjɛ̃, -jɛn], *a. & s.* Assyrian.

assyriologie [asirjɔlɔʒi], *s.f.* Assyriology.

assyriologue [asirjɔlɔg], *s.m. & f.* Assyriologist.

astacicole [astasikɔl], *a.* pertaining to crayfish breeding.

astaciculteur [astasikyltœːr], *s.m.* crayfish breeder.

astaciculture [astasikyltyːr], *s.f.* crayfish breeding.

astacidés [astaside], *s.m.pl. Crust:* Astacidæ.

astacoures [astakuːr], *s.m.pl. Crust:* Astacura.

astacus [astakys], *s.m. Crust:* astacus (*European*) crayfish.

Astarté [astarte]. **1.** *Pr.n.f. Myth:* Astarte; *s.f. Moll:* astarte.

astasie [astazi], *s.f. Med:* astasia.

astate [astat], *s.m.,* **astatine** [astatin], *s.f. Ch:* astatine.

astatique [astatik]. **1.** *a. Magn: etc:* astatic (system, needle, etc.). **2.** *s.m. & f. Med:* one who suffers from astasia.

astéatose [asteatoːz], *s.f. Med:* asteatosis.

astéisme [asteism], *s.m.* asteism.

asténosphère [astenosfɛːr], *s.f. Geol:* asthenosphere.

aster [astɛːr], *s.m.* **1.** *Biol:* aster. **2.** *Bot:* aster, sea-starwort; **a. de Chine,** China aster; **a. œil-du-Christ,** Michaelmas daisy, *U.S:* aster. **3.** *Gr.Ecc:* asteriskos.

astéréognosie [astereɔgnozi], *s.f. Med:* astereognosis.

astérie [asteri], *s.f.* **1.** *Echin:* asterias, star-fish. **2.** *Cryst:* six-rayed star, asterism. **3.** *Miner:* asteriated opal.

astérinidés [asterinide], *s.m.pl. Zool:* Asterinidae.

astérion [asterjɔ̃], *s.m. Anat:* asterion.

astérique [asterik], *a. Cryst:* **pierre a.,** asteriated stone.

astériser [asterize], *v.tr.* to asterisk, to put an asterisk against . . .

astérisme [asterism], *s.m. Astr: Cryst:* asterism.

astérisque [asterisk], *s.m. Typ:* asterisk.

asternale [astɛrnal], *a.f. Anat:* asternal, not attached to the sternum; **côte asternale,** asternal, false, floating, short rib.

astéroïde [asterɔid], *s.m. Astr:* **1.** asteroid. **2.** planetoid, minor planet.

astéronyme [asterɔnim], *s.m. Typ:* three asterisks in a row (to indicate letters missing).

astérophyllitées [asterɔfilite], *s.f.pl. Paleont:* Asterophyllites.

astérozoaires [asterɔzɔɛːr], *s.m.pl. Echin:* Asterozoa.

asthénie [asteni], *s.f. Med:* asthenia; debility.

asthénique [astenik], *a. & s.m. & f. Med:* asthenic.

asthénopie [astenɔpi], *s.f. Med:* asthenopia.

asthénospermie [astenɔspɛrmi], *s.f. Med:* asthenospermia.

asthmatique [asmatik], *a. & s.m. & f. Med:* asthmatic.

asthme [asm], *s.m. Med:* asthma; **a. d'été, des foins,** hay-fever; **être atteint d'a., avoir de l'a.,** to suffer from, to have asthma; **crise d'a.,** attack of asthma; **a. thymique,** thymic asthma.

asthmogène [asmɔʒɛn], *a.* asthmogenic.

asti[1] [asti], *s.m.* **1.** *Tex:* silk (made at Asti). **2.** (= **vin d'Asti**) Asti (*white wine*).

asti[2], *s.m.,* **astic** [astik], *s.m. Bootm: Mil: etc:* **1.** polishing stick. **2.** polishing paste.

asticot [astiko], *s.m.* maggot; *Fish:* gentle; **plein d'asticots,** maggoty; *F:* **c'est un drôle d'a.!** he's a queer chap!

asticoter [astikɔte], *v.tr.* (*a*) *F:* to tease, worry; *F:* to rag, plague; (*b*) *F:* **j'ai qch. qui m'asticote sous le pied,** I've got an itching under the foot.

astien [astjɛ̃], *a. & s.m. Geol:* astian.

astigmate[1] [astigmat], *s.m. & f. Med:* astigmat.

astigmate[2], **astigmatique** [astigmatik], *a. Med:* astigmatic(al); **œil astigmate,** astigmatic eye.

astigmatisme [astigmatism], *s.m.,* **astigmie** [astigmi], *s.f. Med: Opt:* astigmatism, astigmia.

astigmomètre [astigmɔmɛtr], *s.m. Med:* astigmometer.

astiquage [astikaːʒ], *s.m.* (action of) polishing, furbishing.

astiquer [astike], *v.tr.* **1.** to polish, furbish (belt, brass, etc.); *F:* **homme bien astiqué,** well-groomed man; *P:* to beat, thrash.

s'astiquer. 1. *F:* to tidy oneself up, to tit(t)ivate. **2.** *P:* to fight; to have a set-to (**avec,** with).

astome [astoːm], *a. Nat.Hist:* astomatous.

astomie [astɔmi], *s.f. Ter:* astomia.

astracan [astrakɑ̃], *s.m.* = ASTRAKAN.

astræidés [astreide], *s.m.pl. Z:* Astraeidæ.

astragale [astragal], *s.m.* **1.** *Anat:* astragalus, ankle-bone, talus. **2.** *Mil:* astragal (of canon); *Arch:* astragal (of column, etc.); nosing (of stair tread). **3.** *Bot:* astragalus, milk-vetch, *U.S:* locoweed.

astrakan [astrakɑ̃], *s.m. Com:* astrakhan (fur).

astral, -aux [astral, -o], *a.* (*a*) astral (influence, body, etc.); **esprits astraux,** astral spirits; (*b*) **lampe astrale,** astral lamp, astral.

astrance [astrɑ̃:s], *s.f.*, **astrantia** [astrɑ̃sja], *s.f. Bot:* astrantia, black masterwort, black sanicle.

astraphobie [astrafɔbi], *s.f. Med:* astra(po)-phobia.

astre [astr], *s.m.* heavenly body; luminary; star; *Poet:* **l'a. du jour,** the sun; *F:* **louer qn jusqu'aux astres,** to praise s.o. to the skies; **elle est belle comme un a.,** she is as beautiful as the morning star; **contempler les astres,** (i) to look at the stars; (ii) (*of dreamer*) to star-gaze; **consulter les astres,** to consult the stars; **être né sous un a. favorable,** to be born under a lucky star.

Astrée [astre]. **1.** *Pr.n.f. Myth:* Astraea. **2.** *s.f. Coel:* astraea.

astreignant [astrɛɲɑ̃], *a.* exacting, demanding, (work).

astreindre [astrɛ̃:dr], *v.tr.* (*pr.p.* **astreignant,** *p.p.* **astreint,** *pr.ind.* **j'astreins, il astreint, n. astreignons,** *p.d.* **j'astreignais,** *p.h.* **j'astreignis,** *fu.* **j'astreindrai**) to compel, oblige; to tie down (**à un devoir,** to a duty); **a. qn à un labeur,** to subject s.o. to heavy work; **être astreint à faire qch.,** to be compelled, under compulsion, to do sth.; **astreint au service militaire,** liable to military service.

s'astreindre, to make a strict rule for oneself; **s'a. à faire tous les jours une longue promenade à pied,** to make a strict rule of a long daily walk; **s'a. à un régime sévère,** to keep to a strict diet.

astreinte [astrɛ̃:t], *s.f.* (*a*) *Jur:* daily fine for delay in performance of contract, in payment of debt, etc.; (*b*) obligation; **les astreintes de la vie moderne,** the pressures, the demands of modern life.

astrictif, -ive [astriktif, -i:v], *a. Med:* astrictive.

astriction [astriksjɔ̃], *s.f. Med:* effect of an astringent, astriction.

astrild [astrild], *s.m. Orn:* astrild, a southern African wax-bill.

astringence [astrɛ̃ʒɑ̃:s], *s.f.* astringency.

astringent [astrɛ̃ʒɑ̃], *a.* & *s.m. Med:* astringent, styptic; binding.

astro- [astrɔ], *pref.* astro-; **astroscope,** astroscope; **astrophysique,** astrophysics.

astrobiologie [astrɔbjɔlɔʒi], *s.f.* astrobiology.

astrocarye [astrɔkari], *s.f.*, **astrocaryum** [astrɔkarjɔm], *s.m. Bot:* astrocaryum.

astrocyte [astrɔsit], *s.m. Biol:* astrocyte.

astrodôme [astrɔdo:m], *s.m. Av:* astrodome.

astrodynamique [astrɔdinamik], *s.f.* astrodynamics.

astrographe [astrɔgraf], *s.m.* astrograph.

astroïde [astrɔid]. **1.** *s.f. Math:* astroid. **2.** *a.* astroid, star-shaped.

astroïte [astrɔit], *s.f. Miner:* astroite.

astrolabe [astrɔlab], *s.m. Astr: A:* astrolabe.

astrolâtre [astrɔlɑ:tr], *a.* & *s.* astrolater, star-worshipper.

astrolâtrie [astrɔlatri], *s.f.* astrolatry, star-worship.

astrologie [astrɔlɔʒi], *s.f.* astrology; **a. judiciaire,** judicial astrology; **a. naturelle,** natural astrology.

astrologique [astrɔlɔʒik], *a.* astrologic(al).

astrologiquement [astrɔlɔʒikmɑ̃], *adv.* astrologically.

astrologue [astrɔlɔg], *s.m.* astrologer, *F:* star-gazer.

astromancie [astrɔmɑ̃si], *s.f.* astromancy.

astrométéorologie [astrɔmeteɔrɔlɔʒi], *s.f.* astrometeorology.

astrométéorologique [astrɔmeteɔrɔlɔʒik], *a.* astrometeorological.

astromètre [astrɔmɛtr], *s.m.* astrometer.

astrométrie [astrɔmetri], *s.f.* astrometry.

astrométrique [astrɔmetrik], *a.* astrometrical.

astronaute [astrɔno:t], *s.m.* & *f.* astronaut, *F:* space traveller, spaceman.

astronauticien, -ienne [astrɔnotisjɛ̃, -jɛn], *s.* research worker in the field of astronautics; person interested in astronautics.

astronautique [astrɔnotik], *s.f.* astronautics, *F:* space travel.

astronavigation [astrɔnavigasjɔ̃], *s.f.* astronavigation.

astronef [astrɔnɛf], *s.m. O:* spaceship, spacecraft.

astronome [astrɔnɔm], *s.m.* astronomer.

astronomie [astrɔnɔmi], *s.f.* astronomy.

astronomique [astrɔnɔmik], *a.* astronomic(al); **heure a.,** sidereal time; **unité a.,** astronomical unit; **fractions astronomiques,** astronomical numbers, astronomicals, sexagesimal fractions, sexagesimals; *F:* **la vente atteint aux chiffres astronomiques,** the sales have reached astronomical figures; *s.a.* VISÉE 1.

astronomiquement [astrɔnɔmikmɑ̃], *adv.* astronomically.

astrophotographie [astrɔfɔtɔgrafi], *s.f.* astrophotography.

astrophotographique [astrɔfɔtɔgrafik], *a.* astrophotographic.

astrophyllite [astrɔfilit], *s.f. Miner:* astrophyllite.

astrophysicien, -ienne [astrɔfizisjɛ̃, -jɛn], *s.* astrophysicist.

astrophysique [astrɔfizik]. **1.** *a.* astrophysical. **2.** *s.f.* astrophysics.

astroscope [astrɔskɔp], *s.m.* astroscope.

astuce [astys], *s.f.* **1.** astuteness, artfulness, wiliness, craftiness, guile, *F:* foxiness; **politicien plein d'a.,** tricky politician. **2.** wile; **les astuces du métier,** the tricks of the trade. **3.** *F:* witticism; pun; **je ne saisis pas l'a.,** I don't see the point (of a joke), I don't see it, *F:* I don't get it; *F:* **une a. vaseuse,** a wet joke. **4.** *F:* gadget; gimmick.

astucieusement [astysjøzmɑ̃], *adv.* astutely, artfully, wilily, craftily, guilefully, cunningly, slyly.

astucieux, -ieuse [astysjø, -jø:z], *a.* astute, artful, wily, guileful, deep, crafty, cunning, tricky, *F:* foxy (person, behaviour); **réponse astucieuse,** crafty, clever, answer.

asturien, -ienne [astyrjɛ̃, -jɛn], *a.* & *s. Geog:* Asturian.

Asturies (les) [lezastyri], *Pr.n.f.pl. Geog:* Asturias.

Astyage [astja:ʒ], *Pr.n.m. A.Hist:* Astyages.

asyllabie [asilabi], *s.f. Med:* asyllabia.

asymbolie [asɛ̃bɔli], *s.f. Med:* asymbolia.

asymétrie [asimetri], *s.f.* asymmetry.

asymétrique [asimetrik], *a.* asymmetrical, unsymmetrical; *Ch:* **carbone a.,** asymmetrical carbon.

asymptomatique [asɛ̃ptɔmatik], *a. Med:* asymptomatic.

asymptote [asɛ̃ptɔt], *Mth:* **1.** *a.* asymptotic(al) (line, etc.). **2.** *s.f.* asymptote.

asymptotique [asɛ̃ptɔtik], *a. Mth:* asymptotic(al).

asymptotiquement [asɛ̃ptɔtikmɑ̃], *adv. Mth:* asymptotically.

asynapsis [asinapsis], *s.f.* asynapsis.

asynchrone [asɛ̃kron], *a. Ph:* asynchronous, non-synchronous.

asynchronisme [asɛ̃krɔnism], *s.m. Ph:* asynchronism.

asynclitisme [asɛ̃klitism], *s.m. Obst:* asynclitism.

asyndète [asɛ̃dɛt], *s.m.*, **asyndéton** [asɛ̃detɔ̃], *s.m. Rh:* asyndeton.

asynergie [asinɛrʒi], *s.f. Med:* asynergy, asynergia.

asyntactique [asɛ̃taktik], *a. Gram:* asyntactic.

asystolie [asistɔli], *s.f. Med:* asystolia, asystole, asystolism.

-at [a], *s.suff.m.* **1.** -ate; **syndicat,** syndicate; **acolytat,** acolythate; **califat,** caliphate. **2.** -acy; **célibat,** celibacy; **épiscopat,** episcopacy. **3.** -ate, -ship; **apostolat,** apostolate, apostleship; **cardinalat,** cardinalate, cardinalship; **diaconat,** diaconate, deaconry, deaconship; **professorat,** professoriate, professorship.

atabek [atabɛk], *s.m. Turkish Civ:* atabek, atabeg.

atacamite [atakamit], *s.f. Miner:* atacamite.

Atalante [atalɑ̃:t], *Pr.n.f. Myth:* Atalanta.

ataraxie [ataraksi], *s.f. Phil: Med:* ataraxia, ataraxy.

atavique [atavik], *a.* atavistic; *Biol:* **retour a.,** throw-back.

atavisme [atavism], *s.m.* atavism.

ataxie [ataksi], *s.f. Med:* ataxy, ataxia; tabes; *s.a.* LOCOMOTEUR I.

ataxique [ataksik]. **1.** *a. Med:* ataxic, tabetic. **2.** *s.m.* & *f.* one who suffers from ataxia, ataxic.

ataxite [ataksit], *s.f. Miner:* ataxite.

atchoum [atʃum], *int.* (*sneeze*) atishoo.

atèle [atɛl], *s.m. Z:* Ateles, coaita, spider-monkey.

atélectasie [atelɛktazi], *s.f. Med:* atelectasis.

atélie [ateli], *s.f. Biol:* atelia.

atélinés [ateline], *s.m.pl. Z:* Ateles.

atelier [atəlje], *s.m.* **1.** (*a*) (work)shop, workroom, atelier; loft; **a. de chaudronnerie,** boiler-works; **a. de réparations,** repair shop; *Mec.E: Mil:* **a. de montage, d'assemblage,** assembly shop; **a. d'ajustage,** fitting shop; **a. des machines, a. de constructions mécaniques,** machine-shop; **a. de tissage,** weaving shed; **a. de constructions navales,** shipyard; **il est monté contremaître après cinq ans d'a.,** he became a foreman after five years on the factory floor; **chef d'a.,** shop-head-foreman, overseer; *Mil:* **a. de campagne,** field workshop; **a. de réparation mobile, camion a.,** repair van; **a. du matériel,** ordnance workshop; *Nau:* **a. de bricolage,** hobby shop; (*b*) lodge (of freemasons); (*c*) studio (of artist, sculptor, etc.); *Phot:* **a. (de pose),** studio; **appareil d'atelier,** studio camera. **2.** (*a*) (shop-, workroom-) staff; (printer's) chapel; working party; (repair) gang; (*b*) *Anthr: Pol.Ec:* industrial unit, work-group; (*c*) students (of a studio).

atellanes [atɛllan], *s.f.pl. Rom.Ant:* atellans.

atélomitique [atelɔmitik], *a. Biol:* atelomitic.

atermoiement [atɛrmwamɑ̃], *s.m.* **1.** *Com: Jur:* arrangement with creditors for extension of time for payment; letter of respite; **a. d'une lettre de change,** renewal of a bill. **2.** *pl. F:* delays, excuses; shillyshally(ing).

atermoyer [atɛrmwaje], *v.* (**j'atermoie, n. atermoyons, j'atermoierai**) **1.** *A: v.tr. Com:* (*a*) to put off (payment); (*b*) to grant a respite for (payment). **2.** *v.i. F:* to put things off, to procrastinate.

s'atermoyer avec ses créanciers, *A:* to arrange with one's creditors for an extension of time.

ateuchus [atøkys], *s.m. Ent:* dung-beetle.

-ateur, -atrice [atœ:r, atris], *a.* & *s.suff.* **1.** *forming sbs.* (*a*) -ator, -atrix; **administrateur, -trice,** administrator, administratix; (*b*) -ator, -atress; **spectateur, -trice,** spectator, spectatress; (*c*) -ator; **agitateur,** agitator; **aviateur,** aviator; **cultivateur,** cultivator; **isolateur,** insulator; **régulateur,** regulator; **perforatrice,** perforator; (*d*) -er; **admirateur, -trice,** admirer; **consolateur, -trice,** consoler, comforter; **explorateur, -trice,** explorer. **2.** *forming adjs.* (*a*) -atory; **acclamateur,** acclamatory; **explorateur,** exploratory; (*b*) -ating; **accélérateur,** accelerating; **régulateur,** regulating; (*c*) -ing; **colonisateur,** colonizing.

Athalie [atali], *Pr.n.f. B.Hist:* Athaliah.

Athanase [atanɑ:z], *Pr.n.m. Ecc.Hist:* Athanasius; *Theol:* **le symbole de saint Athanase,** the Athanasian Creed.

athanor [atanɔr], *s.m. Alch:* athanor.

athée [ate]. **1.** *a.* atheistic(al) (person, argument). **2.** *s.* atheist.

athéisme [ateism], *s.m.* atheism.

athéistique [ateistik], *a.* atheistic(al) (philosophy).

athélie [ateli], *s.f. Med:* athelia.

athématique [atematik], *a. Ling:* athematic.

athénée [atene], *s.m.* **1.** athenaeum. **2.** (*in Belgium and Switzerland*) public secondary school.

Athènes [atɛn], *Pr.n.f. Geog:* Athens.

athénien, -ienne [atenjɛ̃, -jɛn], *a.* & *s.* (*a*) *Geog: Gr.Civ:* Athenian; **c'est un vrai a.,** he is a person of refinement and culture; **pureté de lignes athénienne,** Attic purity of line; (*b*) *F:* member of the *École française d'Athènes.*

athénium [atenjɔm], *s.m. Ch:* athenium.

athérine [aterin], *s.f. Ich:* atherine.

athermal, -aux [atɛrmal, -o], *a.* athermal.

athermane [atɛrman], *a. Ph:* athermanous; impervious to radiant heat.

athermanéité [atɛrmaneite], *s.f. Ph:* athermancy.

athermique [atɛrmik], *a. Tchn: Med:* athermic.

athéromateux, -euse [aterɔmatø, -ø:z]. **1.** *a.* atheromatous. **2.** *s.m.* & *f.* one who suffers from atheroma.

athéromatose [aterɔmato:z], *s.f. Med:* atheromatosis.

athérome [aterɔm], *s.m. Med:* atheroma. **1.** *A:* encysted tumour; wen. **2.** degeneration of the arteries, atherosclerosis.

athérosclérose [aterɔsklero:z], *s.f. Med:* atherosclerosis.

athérosperme [aterɔspɛrm], *s.m. Bot:* atherosperma, *F:* plume-nutmeg; **essence d'athérosperme,** Tasmanian sassafras oil.

athérure [atery:r], *s.m. Z:* atherurus; brush-tailed porcupine.

athétèse [atetɛ:z], *s.f. Ling:* athetesis.

athétose [ateto:z], *s.f. Med:* athetosis.

athlète [atlɛt], *s.m.* & *f.* athlete; well-built man; *F:* **les athlètes de la foi,** the martyrs; *Med:* **pied de l'a.,** athlete's foot.

athlétique [atletik]. **1.** *a.* athletic; (*of pers.*) strong, vigorous; *F.* sporty. **2.** *s.f.* athletics.

athlétiquement [atletikmɑ̃], *adv.* athletically.

athlétisme [atletism], *s.m.* athleticism; athletics, **épreuves d'a.,** athletic events, track and field events.

athlétoïde [atletɔid], *a. Med:* **type a.,** athletic type.

athrepsie [atrɛpsi], *s.f. Med:* athrepsia.

athrombasie [atrɔ̃bazi], *s.f. Med:* athrombia.

athyroïdie [atiroidi], *s.f. Med:* athyreosis.

atlante [atlɑ̃:t], *s.m.* **1.** *Arch:* telamon; *pl.* atlantes, telamones (supporting entablature). **2.** *Moll:* atlanta.

Atlantide [atlɑ̃tid]. *Myth:* **1.** *Pr.n.f.* **l'Atlantide,** Atlantis. **2.** *s.f.pl.* **les Atlantides,** the Atlantides, the daughters of Atlas.

atlantique [atlɑ̃tik], *a.* **1. l'océan A.,** *s.m.* **l'A.,** the Atlantic (Ocean); **le littoral a.,** the Atlantic coast-line; *Pol:* **la Charte de l'A.,** the Atlantic Charter; **Organisation du Traité de l'A. Nord,** North Atlantic Treaty Organisation. **2. format a.,** atlas size (of book, etc.).

atlantosaure [atlɑ̃tɔsɔ:r], *s.m. Paleont:* atlantosaurus.

Atlas[1] [atlɑ:s]. **1.** *Pr.n.m. Myth: Geog:* Atlas. **2.** *s.m.* (*a*) *Anat:* the atlas, the first cervical vertebra; (*b*) atlas, book of maps, of plates; **format a.,** atlas or large folio size.

atlas[2], *s.m. Tex: A:* Indian satin, atlas.

atloïdé [atlɔide], *a.* **atloïdien, -ienne** [atlɔidjɛ̃, -jɛn], *a. Anat:* atloid, atloidean, atlantal.

atloïdo-occipital, -ale [atlɔidɔɔksipital], *a. Anat:* occipital atlantal; *pl. atloïdo-occipitaux, -ales.*

atm(id)omètre [atm(id)ɔmɛtr̥], *s.m. Ph:* atmidometer, evaporimeter.

atmolyse [atmɔli:z], *s.f. Ch:* atmolysis.

atmosphère [atmɔsfɛ:r], *s.f.* **1.** (*a*) atmosphere; **la lune n'a pas d'a.,** the moon is not surrounded by atmosphere; **humidité de l'a.,** atmospheric humidity; **un orage pendant la nuit avait rafraîchi l'a.,** a storm during the night had freshened the atmosphere; **une a. de vacances,** a holiday atmosphere, feeling; **chaque être a une a. personnelle qu'il répand autour de lui,** each individual is surrounded by, radiates, his own personal atmosphere; *F:* **il me faut changer d'a.,** I need a change of atmosphere, of air; *s.a.* GAZEUX 1; (*b*) **a. de vice,** atmosphere of vice. **2.** *Ph:* (*pressure of* 760 *mm. of mercury*) atmosphere.

atmosphérique [atmɔsferik], *a.* atmospheric(al); **pression a.,** air pressure; **rocher usé par l'action des agents atmosphériques,** weathered rock; *W.Tel:* **parasites atmosphériques, les atmosphériques,** *s.f.pl.,* strays, statics, atmospherics; **perturbations atmosphériques,** atmospheric disturbances; **conditions atmosphériques,** weather conditions, atmospheric conditions.

atoca [atɔka], *s.m. Fr.C: Bot:* cranberry.

atoll [atɔl], *s.m. Geog:* atoll.

atome [atɔ:m], *s.m.* (*a*) *Ph:* atom; **a. père,** parent atom; **a. mésique,** mesonic atom; **a. marqué,** tagged atom; (*b*) particle; bit; *F:* (*of pers.*) scrap; mite; *F:* = ATOME-GRAMME; **atomes de poussière,** specks of dust; *F:* **pas un a. de vérité,** not a jot, not an atom, of truth; **plus un a. de fièvre,** not the slightest fever left.

atome-gramme [atɔmgram], *s.m. Ph:* atomgramme, gram(me)-atom; *pl. atomes-grammes.*

atomicité [atɔmisite], *s.f. Ch:* atomicity.

atomique [atɔmik], *a. Ch: Ph:* atomic (theory, weight, etc.); **masse a.,** atomic mass; **nombre, numéro a.,** atomic number; **sciences atomiques,** atomics; *Atom.Ph:* **bombe a.,** atom(ic) bomb; **détruire à la bombe a.,** to atom-bomb; **guerre a.,** atomic warfare; **énergie a.,** atomic energy, nuclear power; **sous-marin à propulseur, propulsion, a.,** nuclear(-powered, -propelled) submarine; **pile a.,** atomic reactor, pile; **ère, âge, a.,** Atomic Age; **centre a.,** atomic research station; **usine a.,** atomic energy plant; **Commissariat à l'énergie a.** = Atomic Energy Authority, *U.S:* Atomic Energy Commission.

atomiquement [atɔmikmɑ̃], *adv.* atomically.

atomisation [atɔmizasjɔ̃], *s.f.* atomization; pulverization.

atomisé, -ée [atɔmize], *s.* person subjected to an atom bomb attack; **les atomisés de Hiroshima qui survécurent à l'explosion de la bombe,** the people who survived the atom bomb attack on Hiroshima.

atomiser [atɔmize], *v.tr.* (*a*) to atomize, to spray (liquid); (*b*) *F:* to A-bomb; *F:* to smash to smithereens, to pulverize.

atomiseur [atɔmizœ:r], *s.m.* atomizer, spray; pulverizer.

atomisme [atɔmism], *s.m.* **1.** *Phil:* atomism. **2.** the atomic theory, atomism.

atomiste [atɔmist], *s.m. Phil: Ph:* atomist; *Atom. Ph:* nuclear, atomic, physicist.

atomisticien, -ienne [atɔmistisjɛ̃, -jɛn], *s.* expert in atomistics.

atomistique [atɔmistik], (*a*) *s.f.* atomistics; nucleonics, nuclear engineering; atomics; (*b*) *a.* pertaining to nucleonics; atomic; atomistic; *Com:* **concurrence a.,** atomistic competition.

atonal, -aux [atɔnal, -o], *a. Mus:* atonal.

atonalité [atɔnalite], *s.f. Mus:* atonality.

atone [atɔn], *a.* **1.** dull, vacant, lack-lustre (look, life). **2.** *Ling: Med:* atonic; *Ling:* unstressed, unaccented.

atonie [atɔni], *s.f. Med:* atony, want of tone, low physical condition; **a. du foie,** sluggish liver.

atonique [atɔnik], *a. Med:* atonic; lacking tone.

atopite [atɔpit], *s.f. Miner:* atopite.

atour [atu:r], *s.m. usu. pl. A. & Hum:* finery, attire; *A:* bravery; **parées de tous leurs atours, de leurs plus beaux atours,** in fine array. decked out in all their finery, in all their war-paint; *A:* **dame d'a.,** mistress of the robes.

atout [atu], *s.m.* **1.** *Cards:* trump; **a. maître,** master trump; **jouer a.,** to play a trump, to play trumps; **avoir tous les atouts dans son jeu,** to hold all the winning cards, to have every chance of winning; **M. Dupont est un a. dans notre jeu,** Mr Dupont is an asset, a great asset, to our party. **2.** *F:* **recevoir un a.,** to receive a blow; to get badly hit.

atoxique [atɔksik], *a. Biol:* atoxic, non-poisonous.

atoxyl(e) [atɔksil], *s.m. Ch:* atoxyl.

atrabilaire [atrabilɛ:r], *a.* atrabilious. **1.** melancholy. **2.** acrimonious, irritable; **homme a.,** man of moods.

atrabile [atrabil], *s.f. A: Med:* black bile.

atractaspis [atraktaspis], *s.m. Rept:* atractaspis.

âtre[1] [ɑ:tr̥], *s.m.* **1.** fireplace, hearth(-stone); **le feu dans l'â.,** the fire in the hearth; **coin, manteau, de l'â.,** chimney-corner. **2.** *Ind:* (*a*) hearth (of forge, etc.); (*b*) (blacksmith's) forge.

âtre[2], *a. A:* black; *s.a.* ABEILLE.

Atrée [atre], *Pr.n.m. Gr.Lit:* Atreus.

atremata [atremata], *s.m.pl. Z:* Atremata.

atrésie [atrezi], *s.f. Med:* atresia.

atrésié [atrezje], *a. Med:* atresic, atretic.

atrichie [atriki], *s.f.,* **atrichiasis** [atrikjazis], *s.f. Med:* atrichia, atrichosis.

Atrides [atrid], *s.m.pl. Gr.Lit:* (the) Atridae.

atriplex [atriplɛks], *s.m. Bot:* atriplex.

atrium [atriɔm], *s.m. Rom.Arch:* atrium; *pl. atriums.*

atroce [atrɔs], *a.* (*a*) atrocious, heinous, abominable (crime, etc.); (*b*) **sa douleur était a. à voir,** his grief was terrible, unbearable to see; **douleur a.,** excruciating, agonizing, pain; **mourir dans d'atroces souffrances,** to die in terrible, dreadful, agony; **peur a. de . . .** agonizing dread of . . .; **j'avais une peur a. de le rencontrer,** *F:* I was dead scared of meeting him; (*c*) awful, horrid, ghastly; **une laideur a.,** a hideous ugliness; **un temps a.,** atrocious, *F:* lousy, weather; **un rhume a.,** a shocking cold.

atrocement [atrɔsmɑ̃], *adv.* **1.** atrociously, shockingly. **2.** dreadfully; awfully, horribly, terribly.

atrocité [atrɔsite], *s.f.* **1.** atrociousness, atrocious character (of sth.). **2.** (*a*) atrocious act, atrocity; (*b*) *F:* **on m'a raconté des atrocités sur votre compte,** I have been hearing dreadful things about you; (*c*) *F:* **ce tableau est une a.,** this picture is a real horror, a shocker.

atromarginé [atrɔmarʒine], *a.* black-edged (paper).

atropa [atrɔpa], *s.f.,* **atrope** [atrɔp], *s.f. Bot:* atropa; **a. belladone,** belladonna, deadly nightshade.

atrophie [atrɔfi], *s.f. Med:* (*a*) atrophy (of a limb, of the liver); degeneration; (*b*) wasting (away), emaciation.

atrophié [atrɔfje], *a.* atrophied (liver, intelligence); wasted, withered (arm); emaciated; degenerated.

atrophier [atrɔfje], *v.tr.* to atrophy (limb, intelligence); **l'inaction prolongée atrophie les muscles,** prolonged inactivity atrophies the muscles; **vice qui atrophie l'intelligence,** vice that stunts, dulls, the intelligence; **l'habitude atrophie les sensations,** habit, blunts reactions.

s'atrophier, to atrophy; to waste (away); to become emaciated.

atrophique [atrɔfik]. **1.** *a.* atrophic, atrophous. **2.** person suffering from atrophy.

atropine [atrɔpin], *s.f. Ch:* atropin(e).

atropinisation [atrɔpinizasjɔ̃], *s.f. Med:* atropinization.

atropique [atrɔpik], *a. Ch:* atropic.

atropisme [atrɔpism], *s.m. Med:* atrop(in)ism.

Atropos [atrɔpɔs]. **1.** *Pr.n.f. Myth:* Atropos. **2.** *s.m. Ent:* (*a*) **(sphinx) a.,** death's-head hawk-moth; (*b*) (= PSOQUE) death-watch.

atrypa [atripa], *s.m. Paleont:* atrypa.

attabler [atable], *v.tr.* to seat (s.o.) at table.

s'attabler. 1. to sit down to table; **s'a. pour toute la soirée,** to settle down at the table for the evening; **rester attablé à savourer le cognac,** to sit over the brandy; **ils restèrent attablés toute la soirée,** they spent the rest of the evening sitting round the table. **2.** *P:* (i) to own up (to a crime); to make a clean breast of it; (ii) to squeal.

attachant [ataʃɑ̃], *a.* **1.** that holds the attention; interesting (book); fascinating (spectacle) **2.** engaging, winning, attractive (personality).

attache [ataʃ], *s.f.* **1.** (*action of*) fastening; tying up; sewing on; **prendre des chevaux à l'a.,** to take in horses at livery; **chien d'a.,** house-dog; guard dog; *Civ.E: etc:* **point d'a.,** connection; **pièce d'a.,** fastening; **rivets d'a.,** jointing rivets; *Ind:* **matériel d'a.,** fixtures; *Nau:* **droit d'a.,** mooring right, right of moorage; **droits d'a.,** mooring dues, moorage; **port d'a.,** home port; port of registry; **borne d'a.,** *Nau:* bollard; *El:* terminal. **2.** *A:* (*attached*) assent (to decree, etc.); approbation. **3.** tie, fastener, fastening, attachment; (*a*) head-rope (of horse): lead, leash, chain (of dog); cord, guy(-rope); tether; parchment strip (for attaching seals); **mettre un chien à l'a.,** to put a dog on the lead, on the chain; **tenir qn comme un chien d'a., comme un chien à l'a.,** to keep s.o. on a string; *F:* **être toujours à l'a.,** to be tied down to one's work; to be always at it, always slaving away; **rompre une a.,** to break a tie, a connection (with a friend, etc.); to break off an affair; **nos attaches dans ce pays,** our close ties, links, with this country; **avoir des attaches avec la police,** to be in with the police; **sans attaches,** unattached, unconnected; (*b*) rivet (for mending china); *El:* (wire) clamp; **a. en S,** S-clamp; *Cost:* loop, tab (for hanging up, fastening, coat, etc., pulling on boots); **a. de bureau, a. métallique,** clip, paper-fastener, paper-clip; **a. trombone,** paper-clip, wire-clip, slide-on clip (for papers); **a. de diamants,** diamond clasp; *Rail:* **a. de rail,** rail fastening; (*c*) *Anat:* origin, attachment (of muscle); **a. de la main, du pied,** wrist-joint, ankle-joint; **membres aux fines attaches,** delicately jointed limbs; **a. de la queue,** tail setting; *s.a.* FIN[2] 2; (*d*) *Civ.E: etc:* connection, bond, brace; binder (of reinforced concrete beam); **a. de poutre,** girder connection, cleat; *Av:* **a. d'aile,** wing-support (of aircraft); wing setting; wing-root; **angle d'a. d'aile,** angle of wing setting, dihedral; (*e*) *Bot:* tendril. **4.** *A:* attachment; *A:* **avoir de l'a. à, pour, son chez-soi,** to be greatly attached to, very fond of, one's home.

attaché [ataʃe]. **1.** *a.* (*a*) fastened, tied-up; chained (dog); **yeux attachés au sol,** eyes bent on the ground; **il gardait son regard a. sur moi,** he kept his eyes fixed on me; **parfum qui demeure a.,** (i) clinging perfume; (ii) long-lasting perfume; (*b*) **être a. à qn, à qch.,** to be attached, devoted to s.o., to sth.; **ils sont très attachés l'un à l'autre,** they are very much wrapped up in each other; **a. à une opinion,** wedded to an opinion; **rester a. à une opinion,** to cling to an opinion; (*c*) **il est a. à mes pas,** he dogs my footsteps; **mon bonheur est a. au vôtre,** my happiness is bound up with yours; *A:* **a. près de moi,** at my service; **il reste a. à la maison sans rien faire,** he hangs about (the house) doing nothing; (*d*) **des mains finement attachées,** delicately jointed hands; (*e*) attached; dependent on; **le bonheur n'est pas a. à la richesse,** happiness is not dependent on wealth; (*f*) *St.Exch:* **coupon a.,** cum dividend. **2.** *s.m.* (*a*) *Dipl: etc:* attaché; **a. militaire,** military attaché; **a. commercial,** commercial attaché; **a. de presse,** press attaché; **a. d'administration,** junior civil servant; (*b*) devotee (of cult); adherent (of party, etc.).

attache-capot [ataʃkapo], *s.m. Aut: A:* bonnet fastener; *pl. attache-capots.*

attache-courroie [ataʃkurwɑ], *s.m.inv. Mec.E:* belt-fastener.

attache-fil(s) [ataʃfil], *s.m. inv.* **1.** *Av: A:* wiring-plate (of aeroplane). **2.** *El.E:* clamp; wire coupler; cable connector.

attache-lettre [ataʃlɛtr̥], *s.f.* paper-clip, letter-clip; *pl. attache-lettres.*

attachement [ataʃmɑ̃], *s.m.* **1.** (*a*) **a. pour qn,** attachment, affection, for s.o.; **a. à l'étude,** fondness for study; **avoir de l'a. pour qn, qch.,** to be fond of, have a liking for, s.o., sth.; **a. à ses devoirs,** zeal for, assiduity in, one's duties. (*b*) **rompre un a.,** to break off a liaison. **2. attachements (d'un architecte),** (architect's) daily statement of materials used and work done.

attacher [ataʃe]. **1.** *v.tr.* to attach; (*a*) to fasten, bind; to tie (up), to do up; **a. un cheval,** to tie up, tether, a horse; **a. un chien à une chaîne,** to chain up, tie up, a dog; *F:* **il n'attache pas ses chiens avec des saucisses,** he is an old skinflint; **a. avec une agrafe,** to do up (dress, etc.), hook (up), clip (together); **a. avec une amarre,** to make fast, moor (boat); **a. avec une ancre,** to anchor; **a. avec une boucle,** to buckle; to tie with a bow; **a. avec des boutons,** to button (up); **a. avec des clous,** to nail (on, together); **a. avec une corde,** to rope (together); to tie on, together, with string; **a. avec des épingles,** to pin (on, together); **a. avec un lacet,** to lace (up, together); **a. avec un nœud,** to knot (together), to tie (on, together) with a knot; **a. avec des rivets,** to rivet (on, together); **a. avec des vis,** to screw (on, together); **a. deux feuilles ensemble avec de la colle,** to gum, stick, two sheets of paper together; **a. une étiquette à un colis,** to fasten, tie, stick, a label on a parcel; to label a parcel; **a. un sceau à un acte,** to append a seal to an act; *s.a.* GRELOT 1; (*b*) **a. de l'importance à qch.,** to attach importance to sth.; **a. un sens, une signification, à qch.,** to attach, give, attribute, a meaning to sth.; **a. du prix, de la valeur, à qch.,** to value sth.; to attach (great) value to sth.; **a. son ambition à qch.,** to set one's ambition on sth.; **a. son bonheur, sa gloire, sa réputation, à qch.,** to stake one's happiness, fame, reputation, on sth.; **spectacle qui attache l'attention,** spectacle that rivets the attention; **livre qui attache l'intérêt,** book that captures one's interest; **l'étude des langues l'attachait beaucoup,** the study of languages interested him greatly; *abs.* **c'est une pièce qui attache,** it's a play that captivates one; **a. les yeux, les regards, sur qch.,** to fix one's eyes, one's gaze, on sth.; **il attacha sur elle un regard pénétrant,** he stared at her fixedly; **a. sa haine à qn,** to conceive an aversion for s.o.; (*c*) **a. un nouveau secrétaire à une ambassade,** to attach a new secretary to an embassy; **tout ce qui nous attache à la vie,** all that makes us cling to life; **il s'était attaché les paysans,** he had gained the affections of the peasants. **2.** *v.i. Cu: F:* **les pommes de terre ont attaché,** the potatoes have caught, stuck; **casserole qui n'attache pas,** non-stick saucepan.

s'attacher. 1. (*a*) to attach oneself, to cling, stick (à, to); to fasten (à, on); to be attached, stuck (à, to); to be fastened, tied (à, on, to); **la poix s'attache aux doigts,** pitch sticks to the fingers; **le lierre s'attache aux arbres,** ivy clings to trees; **le capuchon s'attache au manteau avec une fermeture éclair,** the hood is attached, fastened, to the coat by a zip fastener; **collier qui s'attache avec une agrafe,** necklace that fastens with a clip; **ses regards s'attachaient sur sa figure,** his eyes were riveted on her face; **une certaine importance s'y attache,** some importance is attached to it; **les remords s'attachaient au criminel,** the criminal was overcome by remorse; **s'a. au solide,** to keep an eye on the main chance; **s'a. à une indication,** to follow up a clue; **s'a. aux faits,** to stick to the facts; **s'a. à qn, à un parti,** to attach oneself to s.o., to a party; **s'a. au destin, à la fortune, de qn,** to throw in, cast in, one's lot with s.o.; *Lit:* **s'a. au char de qn,** to subject oneself to s.o.; *F:* **s'a. aux pas de qn,** to follow, dog s.o., to dog s.o.'s footsteps; *Mil:* **s'a. au sol,** to hold on to the ground; (*b*) **s'a. à qn,** to become, grow, fond of, attached to, devoted to, s.o. **2. s'a. à une tâche,** to apply oneself to a task; **s'a. à une carrière,** to follow a career; **s'a. à remplir son devoir,** to stick to one's duty; **s'a. (surtout) à qch., à faire qch.,** to pay particular attention to sth.; **il s'attache à ce que tout se fasse avec méthode,** he is very particular about having things done methodically.

attachot [ataʃo], *s.m. Leath:* retaining strap (for lid of suitcase).

attacolite [atakɔlit], *s.f. Miner:* attacolite.

attacus [atakys], *s.m. Ent:* attacus; **a. chinois de l'ailant(h)e,** Chinese Ailanthus moth.

Attale [attal], *Pr.n.m. Hist:* Attalus.

attalée [atale], *s.f. Bot:* attalea; **attalée à cordes,** coquilla-nut.

attapulgite [atapylʒit], *s.f. Miner:* attapulgite.

attaquable [atakabl], *a.* **1.** attackable; open to attack, assailable (town, etc.). **2.** contestable, assailable (fact, opinion, etc.); (codicil, etc.) open to attack. **3.** attackable (metal, etc.).

attaquant, -ante [atakɑ̃, -ɑ̃:t]. **1.** *a.* assailing, attacking. **2.** *s.* assailant, attacker.

attaque [atak], *s.f.* **1.** (*a*) *Mil: etc:* attack, assault, onslaught; **a. mûrement préparée, montée en détail,** deliberate attack; **a. de rencontre,** encounter attack; **a. combinée,** combined attack; **a. concertée,** concerted attack; **a. décousue, non coordonnée,** disconnected attack; **a. enveloppante, d'enveloppement,** roll-up, enveloping attack; **a. par débordement (sur les flancs, sur les ailes),** outflanking attack; **a. de fixation, d'arrêt,** holding attack; **a. dans la nuit, de nuit,** night attack; **a. en rase campagne, en terrain découvert,** attack in the open; **a. simulée,** feigned attack, feint; **a. par gaz, aux gaz,** gas attack; **a. atomique, nucléaire,** atomic, nuclear attack, strike; **a. d'artillerie,** artillery attack; **a. de grande envergure, de grand style,** large scale attack; **a. par petits paquets, fragmentaire,** piecemeal attack; **a. par surprise,** surprise attack; **a. brusquée, inopinée,** rush, sudden attack; **reprise d'a.,** (i) (*conventional warfare*) renewed attack; (ii) (*atomic warfare*) re-strike; **corps d'a.,** attacking party; **formation, dispositif, ordre, d'a.,** attack formation; **passer à l'a.,** to take the offensive; **repasser à l'a.,** to return to the attack; **monter une a.,** to stage an attack; **lancer, déclencher, une a.,** to launch, to deliver an attack; **pousser l'a. à fond,** to push the attack home; **repousser une a.,** to repel, to beat off an attack; **briser, dissocier une a.,** to break up, to disrupt an attack; (*b*) *Av:* **a. à basse altitude, en vol rasant,** low flying attack; **a. aérienne,** air raid, aerial attack; **a. en rase-mottes,** hedgehopping attack; **a. en montée, en piqué,** climbing, dive, diving, attack; **a. par-dessous,** attack from below; **a. par-dessus, par le haut,** attack from above; **a. par-devant, par-derrière,** nose, tail, attack; **a. par vagues successives,** attack in waves; *Av: Nau:* **bord d'a.,** leading edge (of wing, propeller); **angle d'a.,** leading angle; *F:* **son angle d'a. vis-à-vis d'un problème,** his approach to a problem; (*c*) attack, onslaught, assault (**de,** on); onset, onrush; hold-up (**de,** of) (of a car, train, etc.); **a. de front,** direct, frontal, attack; **subir une a.,** to be attacked; **diriger de violentes attaques contre qn,** to attack s.o. violently; **attaques contre le gouvernement,** attacks on the government; **les attaques de la calomnie,** the attacks of calumny; **les attaques de la gelée,** the ravages of frost; (*d*) *Sp:* attack; **ligne d'a.,** attacking line; **fausse a.,** feint; *Rac:* spurt; *Cards:* lead; (*e*) *Row:* beginning of a stroke; catch (as the blade grips the water); *adv.phr. F:* **d'attaque,** vigorously; **il y va d'a.,** he goes at it tooth and nail, hammer and tongs; **être d'a.,** (i) to have plenty of pluck; (ii) *F:* to be full of beans, on top form; (iii) *Mil:* (*of troops*) to be fit; **il est toujours d'a.,** he is still going strong; **ma femme n'est pas d'a.,** my wife is not up to the mark; *s.a.* DÉFENSE 1; (*d*) *Med:* attack (of gout); bout (of fever, influenza); **légère a. de goutte,** touch of gout; **a. d'épilepsie,** epileptic fit; **a. d'apoplexie,** (apoplectic) stroke; **il a eu une a.,** he had a stroke; **a. de nerfs,** fit of hysterics; (*e*) *Metalw:* etching; **a. micro,** micro-etching; **a. électrolytique,** electrolytic corrosion. **2.** (*a*) *Mec.E:* **a. directe,** direct drive (of motor); **a. (d'un organe),** drive; *Aut:* **a. au différentiel (par la transmission),** differential drive; **pignon d'a.,** driving pinion; **a. des soupapes,** valve actuating mechanism; (*b*) *Metall:* gate; feeder; **a. de coulée,** inlet gate, ingate. **3.** *Mus:* (*a*) short fugue theme; (*b*) entry (of instrument); attack (of note); **chef d'a.,** (i) leading first violin, leader (of the orchestra); (ii) chorus leader; (iii) leader of a group. **4.** *Tg:* call. **5.** *Ling:* attack.

attaquer [atake], *v.tr.* **1.** (*a*) to attack, assail (enemy, stronghold, etc.); to set upon, assault (s.o., enemy); *Mil:* **a. de front,** to make, to launch a front(al) attack; **"attaquez!"** engage!; (*b*) to attack, criticize, go for, get at, (s.o., s.o.'s opinions); (*of acid*) to attack, eat into, bite into, corrode (metal); **la rouille attaque le fer,** rust attacks iron; **les doryphores ont attaqué les pommes de terre,** the Colorado beetles attacked the potatoes; **a. qn par le sentiment,** to play on s.o.'s feelings; **a. qn par son côté faible,** to attack s.o.'s weak spot; **a. l'honneur de qn, a. qn dans son honneur,** to impeach, impugn, s.o.'s honour; **a. les opinions, l'action, de qn,** to attack, impugn, s.o.'s opinions, s.o.'s course of action; **a. les abus, les préjugés,** to attack abuses, prejudices; **a. qn dans les journaux,** to attack s.o. in the papers; **on m'attaque de nouveau,** *F:* they're getting at me again; **a. qn sur un sujet,** to tackle s.o. on a subject; *Jur:* **a. (la validité d')un testament,** to contest a will; **a. qn en justice,** to prosecute, take action against, sue, bring an action against, s.o.; **être attaqué d'une maladie,** to be attacked by a disease; **le poumon droit est attaqué,** the right lung is affected; (*b*) *abs.* to attack; to take the offensive. **2.** (*a*) *F:* to tackle, dig into, get to work on (meal, subject, piece of work, etc.); **elle attaque le pâté,** she's tucking into the pâté; **a. le repas,** *F:* to fall to; (*b*) *Mus:* to attack, *F:* to strike up; **à l'arrivée du président l'orchestre attaqua l'hymne national,** on the president's arrival the band struck up the national anthem; **il attaque bien la corde,** he has a fine attack (on the violin); (*of singer*) **bien a. la note,** to hit the note well; *abs.* **a. faux,** to hit the wrong note; (*c*) *Cards:* **a. trèfle, de la reine,** to lead clubs, the queen; (*d*) *Equit:* to spur (horse); (*e*) *Ling:* to attack; (*f*) *Nau:* **a. un cap,** to sail towards a headland; (*g*) (*of acids, etc.*) to corrode; to etch. **3.** (*of piece of mechanism*) to drive, operate, engage with (another piece). **4.** *Tg: etc:* to call; to ring up (the exchange).

s'attaquer à qn, à qch., to attack, make an attack on, tackle, s.o., sth.; **s'a. à plus fort que soi, à son maître,** to meet s.o. who is more than a match for one, to meet one's master; **s'a. à une difficulté, à un problème,** to grapple with a difficulty, a problem; **s'a. à un pâté,** to attack, tuck into, a pâté; **le poumon droit commence à s'a.,** the right lung is becoming affected.

attaqueur [atakœ:r], *s.m.* attacker; leader of an attack.

attardé [atarde], *a.* **1.** belated (traveller, etc.); late; behindhand; *Mil: s.m.* **les attardés,** the laggards. **2.** behind the times; *s.m.* **les attardés,** old fogies, back numbers. **3.** *Sch:* backward, mentally retarded (child); *s.m.* **les attardés,** the mentally retarded.

attarder [atarde], *v.tr.* to keep (s.o.) late, beyond his time; **une crevaison nous a attardés,** a puncture delayed us, we were delayed by a puncture.

s'attarder. 1. (*a*) to be delayed; (*b*) to stay (too) late; to stay up late; to stay beyond one's time; **s'a. à faire qch.,** to stay (up) late doing sth.; **s'a. chez qn,** to stay late at somebody's house; **il s'est vraiment trop attardé hier soir,** he stayed too long, he outstayed his welcome, last night; (*c*) to linger, dally, loiter; lag behind, dawdle; **s'a. en route,** to dawdle, to tarry, on the way. **2. s'a. à qch.,** to waste one's time on, to linger over, sth. **3.** *abs.* to be behind the times.

atte [at], *s.m. Bot:* sweet-sop (fruit), atta; *Ent:* atta, leaf-cutting ant.

atteindre [atɛ̃:dr], *v.* (*pr.p.* **atteignant;** *p.p.* **atteint;** *pr.ind.* **j'atteins, il atteint, n. atteignons;** *p.d.* **j'atteignais;** *p.h.* **j'atteignis;** *fu.* **j'atteindrai**) **1.** *v.tr.* to reach; to overtake; to attain; (*a*) **a. la ville,** to reach, get to, the town; **a. qn,** to catch s.o. up, to overtake s.o.; **l'eau a atteint le premier étage,** the water has reached the first floor; **a. l'ennemi,** to catch up with, to come up to, the enemy; **comment puis-je vous a.?** (i) how can I reach, get to, you? (ii) how can I get in touch with you? **le châtiment atteint quelquefois le criminel,** retribution sometimes catches up with the criminal; **a. son but,** to attain, achieve, one's end; **la pièce a atteint une vogue inouïe,** the play has had an enormous vogue; **a. l'âge de soixante ans,** to reach, attain, the age of sixty; (*b*) **a. une boîte sur un rayon,** to reach, get at, a box on a shelf; **sa taille atteint six pieds,** he is six feet tall; **très peu de montagnes atteignent 8000 mètres,** very few mountains reach a height of 26,200 feet; **a. un prix élevé,** to reach, fetch, a high price; **ce tableau a atteint deux mille livres aux enchères,** this painting fetched, brought in, two thousand pounds at the auction; **dépenses qui atteignent une somme considérable,** expenses which amount to a considerable sum; **il prétend a. Molière,** he thinks he's another Molière; (*c*) **a. le but,** to hit the target, the mark; **ne pas a. le but,** to fall short of the mark; **l'usine a atteint son but pour l'année,** the factory has reached its target for the year; **a. qn d'une pierre,** to hit s.o. with a stone; **le trépan a atteint une couche pétrolifère,** the drill hit an oil deposit, struck oil; **être atteint (d'un coup de feu) au bras, à la jambe,** to be wounded, shot, in the arm, in the leg; **la catastrophe atteignit beaucoup de personnes,** the catastrophe fell on, overtook, many people; **les maux qui pourraient nous a.,** the evils which might assail us, to which we might be subject; **être atteint d'une maladie,** to have caught a disease; to be struck down by a disease; (*of trees, etc.*) to be attacked by a disease; **atteint de fièvre,** stricken with fever; **malade encore légèrement atteint,** early case; **le poumon est atteint,** the lung is affected; **la**

gelée a atteint les fraises, the frost has caught the strawberries; **être atteint par une baisse de prix,** to be affected by a fall in prices; **gravement atteint par une faillite,** heavily hit by a bankruptcy; **atteint dans son honneur,** wounded in his honour; *s.a.* CONVAINCU 2. **2.** *v.ind.tr.* **a. à qch.,** to reach, attain (to), sth. (with difficulty); **a. à la perfection,** to attain (to) perfection; **a. à son but,** to achieve one's aim; **ma vue n'atteint pas jusqu'au château, jusque-là,** I cannot see as far as the castle, as far as that.

atteinte [atɛ̃:t], *s.f.* **1.** reach; **l'a. de la lune,** reaching the moon; **se mettre hors de l'a. de qn,** to get out of s.o.'s reach; **hors d'a.,** beyond reach, out of reach; **sa réputation est hors d'a.,** his reputation is unassailable, beyond suspicion; **se dérober, se soustraire, à l'a. de la loi,** (i) to circumvent, get round, *F:* dodge, the law; (ii) to get out of the clutches of the law. **2.** blow, stroke, attack; **légère a. au bras,** slight blow or wound on the arm; **a. au crédit de qn,** blow to s.o.'s credit; **les atteintes du froid,** the bad effects of cold; **les atteintes de la calomnie,** the attacks of calumny; **a. à l'honneur,** attack on honour; **sa santé n'a jamais eu d'a.,** his health has never been impaired, *F:* he has never had a day's illness; **légère a. de malaria,** touch of malaria; **légère a. de goutte,** twinge of gout; **il ressentait les premières atteintes de la goutte,** he felt the first symptoms of gout, he felt his gout coming on; **porter a. à l'honneur de qn,** to cast a slur on, aspersions on, to reflect on, s.o.'s honour; **porter a. à l'autorité de qn,** to strike a blow at s.o.'s authority; **porter a. à un droit,** to derogate from a right, to prevent the exercise of a right; **a. portée aux privilèges,** breach of privilege; **porter a. aux intérêts de qn,** to interfere with s.o.'s interests, to affect s.o.'s interests.

attélabe [atelab], *s.m. Ent:* vine-weevil.

attelable [atlabl̥], *a.* (*horse, etc.*) fit for harness.

attelage [atla:ʒ], *s.m.* **1.** (*a*) harnessing; yoking (of oxen); **garçon d'a.,** ostler; **crochet d'a.,** tug-hook; (*b*) (*way of harnessing*) draught; **a. à l'allemande, à timon,** pole draught; **a. à quatre,** four-in-hand; *s.a.* ARBALÈTE 2, DAUMONT. **2.** (*a*) team; pair (of horses, of oxen); yoke (of oxen); **a. en file,** tandem team; **l'a. de devant,** the leaders; **l'a. de derrière,** the wheelers; **a. haut-le-pied,** spare team; **marcher en tête de l'a.,** to walk at the head of the team; (*b*) *Veh:* carriage (and horses); **le bel a.!** what a fine turn-out! **3.** *Civ.E: etc:* attachment; (*a*) tying, fastening; hooking on; *Rail:* coupling; **chaîne d'a.,** chain-coupling; (*b*) tie; hook, fastening.

atteler [atle], *v.tr.* (**j'attelle, n. attelons; j'attellerai**) **1.** to harness, put to (horses, etc.); to yoke (oxen); **a. un cheval à une charrette,** to harness a horse to a cart; **dire au cocher qu'il attelle,** to tell the coachman to put to; **être attelé à un travail ingrat,** to be harnessed, tied, to a thankless task; **toujours attelé à son travail,** always hard at it. **2. a. une voiture,** to put horses to a carriage; **voiture attelée de quatre chevaux,** carriage drawn by four horses; *F:* **c'est une charrette mal attelée,** they are an ill-matched pair; *Rac:* **course attelée,** trotting race. **3.** *Rail:* **a. des wagons,** to couple (up) waggons.

s'atteler. ses partisans s'attelèrent à sa voiture et le traînèrent jusqu'à l'hôtel de ville, his supporters harnessed themselves to his carriage and pulled him to the town hall; **s'a. à une tâche,** to settle down to a task; **s'a. au travail,** *F:* to buckle to; **s'a. avec qn,** (i) to join forces with s.o., to associate with s.o.; (ii) to marry s.o.

attelle [atɛl], *s.f.* **1.** *Surg:* splint; **porter des attelles en fer,** to have one's legs in irons. **2.** *Harn:* **les attelles,** the hames. **3.** *Tchn:* handle (of certain tools).

attelle-étrier [atɛletrie], *s.f. Surg:* caliper(-splint) (for fractured leg); *pl. attelles-étriers.*

attellement [atɛlmɑ̃], *s.m.* harnessing; yoking (of oxen); putting the horses to, *F:* hitching up.

attelloire [atɛlwa:r], *s.f.,* **atteloire** [atəlwa:r], *s.f.* **1.** *Veh:* thill-pin, shaft-pin. **2.** handle (of certain tools).

attenance [atnɑ̃:s], *s.f.* dependency (of house, etc.).

attenant [atnɑ̃]. **1.** *a.* contiguous (à, to); abutting (à, on); adjoining; bordering; **jardin a. au mien,** garden next to mine, adjoining mine. **2.** *A: adv.* **tout a.,** close by. **3.** *A: prep.* **prairie a. la rivière,** meadow adjoining the river; **murs a. la rue,** walls (bordering) on the street; *prep.phr. A:* **loger a. de, à, l'école,** to live next door to the school.

attendre [atɑ̃:dr], *v.tr.* **1.** (*a*) to wait for (s.o., sth.), to await (s.o., sth.); **qu'attendez-vous?** what are you waiting for? **on attend la réponse,** (the messenger, etc.) is waiting for the answer; **a. la mort,** to await death; **a. qn au passage,** to lie in wait for s.o.; **j'attends mon heure,** I am biding my time; **a. qn de pied ferme,** (i) to wait for s.o. without budging; (ii) to be ready to face s.o., s.o.'s arguments; **il va écrire aux journaux pour se justifier, et c'est là que je l'attends, c'est où je l'attends,** he is going to write to the papers to justify his action, and that is when I shall go for him, when I shall pounce on him, when I shall get him; **le déjeuner nous attend,** lunch is waiting, is ready; **ne m'attendez pas pour vous mettre à table,** don't wait for me to start dinner, don't wait dinner for me; *abs.* **le train n'attend pas,** the train won't wait; **le sort qui l'attend,** the fate that is in store for him; **l'avenir nous attend,** the future lies before us, we have a great future before us; **aller a. qn à la gare,** to go to meet, to go and meet, s.o. at the station; *s.a.* MESSIE, ORME; **(prière d')a. l'arrivée,** "to be (left till) called for," "please await arrival"; **faire a. qch. à qn,** to keep s.o. waiting for sth., to make s.o. wait for sth.; **il se fait a.,** he is keeping us waiting, we are still waiting for him, he is late; **tu t'es fait a.!** and about time too! **les progrès se font a.,** progress is slow in coming; **sa réponse ne se fit pas a.,** his answer was not long in coming; **a. de faire qch.,** to wait (until it is time) to do sth.; **ils attendaient d'entrer,** they were waiting to go in; **attendez de voir le résultat,** wait until you see the result; *abs. F:* **attendez voir,** (i) just wait; (ii) let me see . . .; **a. d'avoir soixante ans,** to wait till one is sixty; **a. que qn fasse qch.,** to wait for s.o. to do sth., to wait till s.o. does sth.; **il attend pour partir qu'il fasse moins chaud,** he is waiting for it to get cooler before he goes; **nous attendons qu'on nous serve,** we are waiting to be served; **j'attendrai (jusqu'à ce) qu'il soit prêt,** I shall wait until he's ready; (*b*) *abs.* **perdre son temps à a.,** to waste one's time waiting; **faire a. qn,** to keep s.o. waiting; **attendons jusqu'à demain,** let's wait until tomorrow; **attendez (donc)!** wait a bit! just a moment, minute! **sans plus a.,** without waiting any longer; *Prov:* **tout vient à point à qui sait a.** everything comes to him who waits; **cela peut a.,** it can wait, *U.S:* it can lie over; there is no (need to) hurry; **ne rien perdre pour a.,** to lose nothing by waiting; **cette fois vous avez échappé, mais vous ne perdrez rien pour a.!** you may have got away with it for the moment, but I'll be even with you yet!; **il ne perdra rien pour a.,** he's got it coming to him; **un plat qui n'attend pas,** a dish that won't stand keeping; (*c*) *adv.phr.* **en attendant,** meanwhile, in the meantime; *prep.phr.* **en attendant son arrivée,** until he arrives; while waiting for him to arrive; **en attendant l'arrivée du courrier,** pending arrival of the mail; *conj.phr.* **en attendant de + *inf.*,** while waiting to . . .; **en attendant de vous voir,** until I see you; **en attendant que + *sub.*,** till, until; pending the time when . . .; **en attendant qu'il s'en aille,** until he leaves; while waiting for him to leave, pending his departure; (*d*) *v.ind.tr. F:* **a. après qn, qch.,** to wait for, to want, s.o., sth.; **portez-lui ce livre, il attend après,** take that book to him, he is waiting for it; **faire a. qn après son argent,** to keep s.o. waiting for his money. **2.** to expect; **on l'attend la semaine prochaine,** he is expected next week; **on l'attend d'un moment à l'autre,** we expect him, are expecting him, he is expected, at any moment; **femme qui attend un bébé,** expectant mother; **a. fiévreusement qch.,** to be on tiptoe with expectation; **qu'a. d'une fille comme cela?** what can one, you, expect from a girl like that? **a. une vie heureuse,** to look forward to a happy life; *Prov:* **n'attends ton salut que de toi-même,** rely on yourself; be your own salvation; **j'attends de vous aide et protection,** I look to you for assistance and protection. **3.** to keep (fruit, etc., till fit to eat); **a. du mouton,** to hang mutton (till tender).

s'attendre. 1. s'a. à qch., to expect sth.; **on peut s'a. à tout,** one may expect anything; **je m'y attendais,** I expected, anticipated, as much; **attendez-vous à être mal accueilli,** be prepared to be coldly received; **je m'attends à ce que vous viendrez demain,** I expect you to come tomorrow; **je ne m'attendais pas (à ce que) que les choses dussent tourner si mal,** I did not expect things to turn out so badly; **je ne m'attends pas à ce qu'il me réponde,** I do not expect him to answer me; **je ne m'attendais pas à ce que vous ameniez tous vos amis,** *F:* I didn't bargain for your bringing all your friends. **2.** *A:* **ne t'attends qu'à toi seul,** rely only on yourself.

attendri [atɑ̃dri], *a.* **regard a.,** fond, compassionate, look; **yeux attendris,** eyes brimming with tears, full of pity, shining with emotion; **je ne peux le voir sans être a.,** I can't see him without being moved, touched.

attendrir [atɑ̃dri:r], *v.tr.* **1.** to make (meat) tender, to tenderize; to soften (vegetables). **2.** to soften (s.o.'s heart), to move (s.o.) to pity; to touch; **se laisser a. au spectacle de qch.,** to be moved to tears, to be affected, at the sight of sth.; **il ne se laissa pas a.,** he would not relent; **cela attendrirait un cœur de pierre,** it would melt a heart of stone.

s'attendrir. 1. (*of meat, etc.*) to become tender. **2.** to be moved (to pity); **s'a. au spectacle de qch.,** to be softened, touched, moved to tears, at the sight of sth.; **elle s'attendrissait sur leur bébé,** she gushed over their baby; **il s'attendrit facilement,** he is emotional; **s'a. sur soi-même,** to indulge in self-pity.

attendrissable [atɑ̃drisabl̥], *a.* **1.** (*of meat, etc.*) that can be made tender. **2.** that can be moved, touched.

attendrissant [atɑ̃drisɑ̃], *a.* moving, touching, affecting.

attendrissement [atɑ̃drismɑ̃], *s.m.* **1.** (*of meat, etc.*) making or becoming tender; tenderizing. **2.** (feeling of) pity, emotion; **a. sur soi-même** self-pity; **un a. lui serrait la gorge,** the pity of it brought a lump to his throat; **larmes d'a.,** tears of emotion.

attendrisseur [atɑ̃drisœ:r], *s.m.* **a. de viande,** tenderizer.

attendu [atɑ̃dy]. **1.** (*a*) *prep.* considering (the circumstances); owing to (the events); in consideration of (his services); **on l'a. mis à la retraite a. ses infirmités,** he has been retired on the ground of, because of, his infirmities; (*b*) *conj.phr.* **a. que + *ind.*,** considering that . . ., seeing that . . ., *Jur:* whereas . . . **2.** *s.m.* **les attendus (d'un jugement)** the reasons adduced.

attenir [at(ə)ni:r], *v.i.* (*pr.p.* **attenant;** *p.p.* **attenu;** *pr.ind.* **j'attiens, n. attenons, ils attiennent;** *fu.* **j'attiendrai**) *A:* **1.** to adjoin; **le jardin attient à la maison,** the garden adjoins the house. **2.** (*rare*) **a. à une famille illustre,** to be connected with, related to, an illustrious family.

attentat [atɑ̃ta], *s.m.* (criminal) attempt; outrage; **faire, commettre, un a. contre la vie de qn,** to make an attempt on s.o.'s life; **victime d'un a.,** victim of a crime; *Jur:* **a. aux mœurs,** indecent behaviour, immoral offence; **a. à la sûreté de l'État,** high treason; treason-felony; *s.a.* PUDEUR.

attentatoire [atɑ̃tatwa:r], *a. Jur:* **action a. à l'autorité,** action that is a challenge to, in contempt of, authority; **mesure a. à la liberté,** measure that constitutes an attempt upon liberty, measure involving undue restraint of personal liberty; **mesure a. à la propriété,** attack on the rights of property.

attente [atɑ̃:t], *s.f.* **1.** (*a*) wait(ing); **être dans l'a. de qch.,** to be waiting for sth; **salle d'a.,** waiting-room; **rester en a.,** (*of requisitions, etc.*) to be held over; **liste d'a.,** waiting list; *Mil:* **combat d'a.,** delaying action; *Turf:* **faire une course d'a.,** to ride a waiting race; (*b*) *Const:* **pierre d'a.** toothing stone; **matière d'a.,** temporary material; *Her:* **table d'a.,** field; *Surg:* **ligature d'a.,** temporary ligature; (*c*) **circuit d'a.,** (i) *Av:* holding pattern, orbiting; (ii) *Th:* holding circuit. **2.** expectation(s), anticipation; **contre toute a.,** contrary to all expectations; **remplir l'a. de qn, répondre à l'a. de qn,** to come up to, to answer, s.o.'s expectations; **la marchandise ne répond pas à l'a.,** the goods do not come up to, fall short of, expectations, are below the mark; **être dans l'a. de qch.,** to be awaiting sth.; **dans l'a. de la mort,** in the expectation of death; **"dans l'a. de votre réponse,"** "looking forward to your reply," "awaiting your reply." **3.** *Mil:* epaulette loop; shoulder-strap.

attenter [atɑ̃te], *v.ind.tr.* to make an attempt (à, on, against); **a. à la vie de qn, a. sur qn,** to make an attempt on s.o.'s life; **a. à ses jours,** to attempt suicide; **a. à la liberté de qn,** to interfere with s.o.'s liberty; **a. à la réputation de qn,** to cast a slur on s.o.'s reputation; **a. contre l'État,** to attempt treason.

attentif, -ive [atɑ̃tif, -i:v], *a.* **1.** (*a*) attentive (à, to); heedful (à, of); careful; **il n'est pas a.,** he does not pay attention; **il écoutait d'un air a.,** he followed attentively; **à ces mots il devint a.,**

at these words he pricked up his ears; **sois a. à mes paroles,** pay attention to what I say; **a. aux conseils,** heedful of advice; **soyez attentifs!** pay attention! (*b*) **être a. à qch.,** to look after sth., to see to sth., to be careful of, attentive to, sth.; **être a. à sa santé,** to be mindful of one's health, to look after oneself; **"toujours attentifs à vos ordres,"** "assuring you of our prompt attention to your orders"; **il est a. à m'épargner toute peine,** he is careful to spare me all trouble; (*c*) *A:* **être a. auprès d'une femme,** *s.m.* **être l'a. d'une femme,** to pay one's attentions to a woman. **2. examen a.,** careful examination, searching enquiry.

attention [atɑ̃sjɔ̃], *s.f.* attention, care; (*a*) **appliquer toute son a. à qch.,** to give one's whole mind to sth.; to devote one's whole attention to sth.; **a. suivie,** close attention; **donner une a. suivie à un raisonnement,** to follow an argument closely; **manque d'a., défaut d'a.,** inattentiveness, inattention; **faute d'a., il a eu une mauvaise note en chimie,** through not paying attention he got a bad mark in chemistry; **écouter avec a.,** to listen attentively; *Com:* **je vous remercie de votre a.,** thank you for your kind attention; *Com:* **à l'a. de M. X,** (for the) attention of Mr X; **son a. à ne nous laisser manquer de rien,** his care that we should not lack anything; **indigne de son a.,** beneath his notice; **porter, tourner, diriger, son a. vers, sur, qch.,** to turn one's attention to sth.; to bring one's mind to bear on sth.; **appeler, porter, attirer, l'a. de qn sur qch., qn, signaler, désigner, recommander, qch., qn, à l'a. de qn,** to call, draw, s.o.'s attention to sth., s.o.; to point out sth., s.o., to s.o.; to bring sth., s.o., before s.o., to s.o.'s notice; **question qui s'impose à l'a. du Parlement,** question that commands, demands, the attention of Parliament, that must be faced by Parliament; (*of object or fact*) **arrêter, retenir, l'a.,** to arrest, hold, engage, the attention; **attirer l'a.,** to catch the eye, to be conspicuous; **attirer l'a. de qn,** to be noticed by s.o., to catch s.o.'s eye; to draw, catch, s.o.'s attention; **faire a., prêter (son) a., à qn, à qch.,** to pay attention to, pay heed to, take heed of, take notice of, beware of, to mind, s.o., sth.; **faire a. à sa santé,** to take care of one's health; **ne faire aucune a., ne pas prêter la moindre a., à qch.,** to take no, not the least, notice of sth.; **je n'y ai pas fait particulièrement a.,** I did not take any particular notice; **faites a.!** (i) take care! mind out! watch out! *U.S:* watch it! (ii) *Sch:* pay attention! **faire bien a.,** *F:* to mind one's p's and q's; **a.!** (i) look out! (ii) *Nau: etc:* stand by! **a. à la peinture,** mind the paint, wet paint; **a. au départ!,** (i) *Rail:* = stand clear of the doors! mind the doors! (ii) *Bus:* = hold tight! *P.N:* **"a. aux portes,"** "stand clear of the gates!" **"a. au train,"** "beware of (the) trains"; **"a., descente rapide,"** "caution, steep hill"; **"a. aux travaux,"** "danger!" "road up," "road works ahead"; **faire a. à, de,** + *inf.*; to be careful to + *inf.*, to take (good) care to + *inf*; **faites a. à, de, ne pas vous perdre,** be careful not to get lost; mind you don't get lost; **faire a. que,** *F:* **faire a. à ce que,** + *sub.*, to be careful that (sth. is done); **faites a. (à ce) que personne ne sorte,** take care, be sure, that no one leaves the house; **faire a. que** + *ind.*, to note (a fact); **faites a. qu'il n'a que dix ans,** remember, don't forget, that he is only ten years old; (*b*) **être plein d'attention(s) pour qn,** to show s.o. much attention; (*c*) **il a eu l'a. de m'avertir,** he was thoughtful enough to notify me.

attentionné [atɑ̃sjɔne], *a.* attentive; (*a*) careful (pupil, workman, etc.); (*b*) **être a. pour qn,** to be considerate to s.o.; to be attentive to s.o.

attentisme [atɑ̃tism], *s.m.* wait-and-see policy.

attentiste [atɑ̃tist]. **1.** *s.m. & f.* one who follows or advocates a wait-and-see policy. **2.** *a.* **une tactique a.,** a waiting policy.

attentivement [atɑ̃tivmɑ̃], *adv.* attentively, carefully; closely.

atténuant [atenɥɑ̃]. **1.** *a. Jur:* mitigating, extenuating, extenuatory, palliating (circumstances). **2.** *a. & s.m. A.Med:* attenuant.

atténuateur [atenɥatœːr], *s.m. W.Tel:* attenuator, fader; **a. à résistance,** pad; *Av:* damper.

atténuation [atenɥasjɔ̃], *s.f.* **1.** (*a*) attenuation, lessening, abatement, diminishing, reducing; dimming, subduing (of light); toning down (of colour); breaking (of fall); mitigation, reduction (of punishment, sentence); *Med:* **a. d'un virus par inoculation,** attenuation of a virus by inoculation; (*b*) emaciation, wasting (of body); (*c*) *Phot:* reduction (of negative), softening (of contrasts). **2.** extenuation, palliation (of crime).

atténué [atenɥe], *a.* **1.** attenuated, diminished; *Jur:* **responsabilité atténuée,** diminished responsibility. **2.** *Bot:* **feuille atténuée,** attenuate leaf. **3.** *Med:* **virus a.,** attenuated virus.

atténuer [atenɥe], *v.tr.* **1.** (*a*) to attenuate, lessen, diminish, reduce; to tone down (colour); to dim, subdue (light); to mitigate (punishment, sentence, consequences); **a. les cahots d'un wagon,** to lessen the jolting of a cart; **a. une chute,** to break a fall; *Med:* **a. un virus,** to attenuate a virus; (*b*) to emaciate, waste; to make (s.o.) thin; (*c*) *Phot:* to reduce (negative, etc.), to soften, tone down (contrasts). **2.** to extenuate, palliate (offence); to render (crime, etc.) less grave; **circonstances qui atténuent sa faute,** circumstances in extenuation of his fault.

s'atténuer. **1.** to lessen; (*of light*) to grow dimmer, softer; (*of sound*) to diminish, to grow softer; **son chagrin s'atténue rapidement,** his sorrow fades quickly. **2.** to become thin(ner), wasted, emaciated.

atterrage [atɛraːʒ], *s.m. Nau:* **1.** (*a*) approach (to land), shoaling; (*b*) landing-place. **2.** landfall.

atterrant [atɛrɑ̃], *a. Lit:* overwhelming; shattering, crushing, staggering (news); startling, astounding.

atterré [atere], (*a*) utterly crushed (by news); *F:* struck all of a heap; **ils se contemplèrent atterrés,** they looked at each other in consternation; (*b*) horror-stricken, -struck.

atterrement [atɛrmɑ̃], *s.m.* **1.** *A:* throwing (of an opponent). **2.** (*a*) stupefaction, consternation; (*b*) state of prostration.

atterrer [atere], *v.tr.* **1.** to throw (to the ground); to strike down, to fell; to bring down (opponent); **a. la puissance d'un empire,** to bring an empire low. **2.** to overwhelm, astound, stupefy, shatter.

atterrir [ateriːr]. **1.** *v.i.* (*a*) *Nau:* to make, sight, land; to make a landfall; (*b*) (*of boat*) to ground, to run ashore; (*c*) *Av:* to alight, to land; **a. sans heurts, normalement,** to soft-land; **a. en vol plané,** to glide in for a landing; **a. trop court,** to undershoot; **a. trop long,** to overshoot; **a. brutalement,** to crash (land); *F:* **a. sur son derrière,** to land on one's behind; *F:* **a. finalement dans un bar,** to land up in a bar. **2.** *v.tr. Nau:* to bring (boat) to land, to ground (boat), to run (boat) ashore. **3.** *A: v.tr.* to choke up, silt up (canal, etc.).

atterrissage [aterisaːʒ], *s.m.* **1.** *Nau:* (*a*) making (the) land; landfall; (*b*) grounding (of ship); running ashore. **2.** *Av:* landing; touch-down; **a. forcé,** forced landing; **a. trop long,** overshoot; **a. trop court,** undershoot; *Space:* **a. en douceur,** soft landing; **a. à vue,** visual landing; **a. aux instruments,** instrument landing; **a. sans visibilité,** blind landing; **a. par contrôle au sol,** ground control approach; **a. normal,** smooth landing; **a. de précision,** spot landing; **a. de fortune,** emergency landing; **a. train rentré, sur le ventre,** wheels-up landing, belly landing; *F:* **a. dans les choux,** landing in the rough; **a. dur,** bumpy landing; **a. brutal,** crash landing; **a. à plat,** pancake landing; **a. plané,** glide landing; **a. sur les roues,** level landing; **a. sur la queue,** tail down landing; **a. sur trois points,** three-point landing; **a. à hélice calée,** deadstick landing; **a. à moteur calé,** stall landing; landing with engine cut off; **a. contre le vent,** landing against the wind; **a. vent arrière,** down-wind landing; **a. vent de travers, de côté,** cross-wind landing; **terrain d'a.,** landing ground, field; **pont d'a.,** landing deck (of aircraft carrier); **feu d'a.,** landing (direction) light; landing flare; **longueur d'a.,** landing distance; **amortisseur d'a.,** bumper bag; **châssis d'a.,** undercarriage; *s.a.* TRAIN. **3.** *Tg:* (*a*) landing (of machine cable); (*b*) point of emergence of cable (from the sea); **bout d'a.,** shore end (of cable).

atterrissement [atɛrismɑ̃], *s.m.* **1.** alluvium, alluvial deposit. **2. a. de câble,** landing of a cable.

atterrisseur [atɛrisœːr], *s.m. Av:* undercarriage; landing-gear.

attestation [atɛstasjɔ̃], *s.f.* attestation; (*a*) **a. du médecin,** doctor's certificate; *Jur:* **a. du titre,** warranty of title; **a. sous serment, sur l'honneur,** affidavit; (*b*) testimonial, certificate; **a. de bonne vie et mœurs,** certificate of good character.

attester [atɛste], *v.tr.* **1. a. qch.,** to attest, certify, sth.; to bear testimony, bear witness, testify, to sth.; to warrant, to vouch for, sth.; **a. que qch. est vrai,** to attest, certify that sth. is true; **a. avoir fait qch.,** to testify, bear witness, to having done sth.; **les ruines de la ville attestent sa splendeur,** the ruins of the town bear witness to its former glory; **son regard atteste la maturité,** his expression reveals his maturity. **2. a. qn (de qch.),** to call s.o. to witness (to sth.); **j'en atteste les cieux,** as heaven is my witness; **a. l'autorité de qn en faveur d'une affirmation,** to advance a statement on the authority of s.o.

atticisme [at(t)isism], *s.m.* **1.** *Lit:* atticism. **2.** attic salt.

atticiste [at(t)isist], *s.m. Lit:* atticist.

attiédir [atjediːr], *v.tr.* to make tepid, lukewarm; (i) to cool (hot water, etc., s.o.'s ardour); (ii) to warm, to take the chill off (cold water).

s'attiédir, to grow, become, lukewarm, tepid; **son intérêt s'est attiédi,** his interest has cooled off, has waned.

attiédissement [atjedismɑ̃], *s.m.* cooling (of sth. hot, of s.o.'s ardour); warming, cooling off (of passion).

attier [atje], *s.m. Bot:* sweet-sop, custard apple (plant).

attifage [atifaːʒ], *s.m.,* **attifement** [atifmɑ̃], *s.m.* *A: usu. Pej:* **1.** dressing up, rigging out. **2.** get-up, rig-out.

attifer [atife], *v.tr. usu. Pej:* to dress (s.o.) up, to get (s.o.) up, to deck (s.o.) out (de, in); **qui t'a attifée ainsi?** whoever got you up like that?

s'attifer, to dress, get, oneself up; to deck oneself out; **comme la voilà attifée!** what a sight, fright, she looks! **attifée d'un grand chapeau à plumes,** decked out, bedecked, in a large feathered hat; **attifée de pierreries,** smothered in jewels.

attifet [atife], *s.m. A.Cost:* (French) hood.

attiger [atiʒe], *v.* (**j'attigeais, n. attigeons**) *P:* **1.** *v.tr.* (*a*) to hit, wound; to damage; **il s'est fait a.,** he got it, *P:* he copped it; (*b*) *V:* to infect with venereal disease. **2.** *v.i.* (*a*) to receive a wound; to be, get, wounded; *P:* to cop it; **il a attigé au beau milieu de la poitrine,** he caught it right in the chest; (*b*) to exaggerate, *F:* to spin a yarn, to shoot a line; **tu attiges, mon vieux,** come off it, old chap.

attignole [atiɲɔl], *s.f. Cu:* faggot; rissole.

attillon [atijɔ̃], *s.m.* small log (cut from upper part of root of tree).

attinage [atinaːʒ], *s.m. N.Arch:* stocks, blocking.

attique [attik]. **1.** *a.* Attic, Athenian; **sel attique,** Attic salt. **2.** *s.m. Arch:* attic (storey). **3.** *Pr.n.f. A.Geog:* **L'A.,** Attica.

attiquement [attikmɑ̃], *adv.* **écrire a.,** to write in the Attic style, purely, classically.

attirable [atirabl̥], *a.* attractable.

attirail [atiraːj], *s.m.* **1.** apparatus, gear; outfit; set (of tools, etc.); appliances, utensils; implements; **a. de pêche,** fishing tackle; **l'a. de la guerre,** the apparatus of war. **2.** *F:* (*a*) paraphernalia; (*b*) pomp, show; finery.

attirance [atirɑ̃ːs], *s.f.* attraction (vers, to); lure (of pleasure, etc.); **a. pour un aliment,** natural liking for a food; **l'a. du gouffre,** the fascination, spell, of the abyss, the temptation to jump from a height; **exercer une a. sur qn,** to allure s.o.

attirant [atirɑ̃], *a.* attractive; drawing (force, etc.); alluring, engaging, winning (manners, etc.); fetching (smile).

attirer [atire], *v.tr.* **1.** (*a*) (*of magnet, sun, etc.*) to attract, draw; **tourbillon qui attire les canots au fond,** whirlpool that sucks down boats; **sa pièce attire un grand public,** his play is a great draw; (*b*) **a. qch. à, sur, qn,** to bring sth. on s.o.; **cette action attira sur lui la haine du peuple,** this action drew upon him the hatred of the people; **les malheurs que cela m'a attirés,** the misfortunes that it brought me; **a. la colère de qn sur qn,** to bring down s.o.'s wrath upon s.o.; **a. à soi, s'a., l'attention publique,** to attract public attention; **s'a. un blâme,** to incur a reprimand; **s'a. des critiques, des éloges,** to come in for criticism, praise; **s'a. la haine universelle,** to incur universal hatred, odium; **vous vous l'êtes attiré vous-même,** you have brought it on yourself; **sa fortune attire l'envie,** his fortune provokes, excites, envy. **2.** to entice, lure; **a. qn dans un piège,** to lure s.o. into a trap; **a. qn par des promesses,** to entice s.o. with promises; *Jur:* **a. une mineure,** to decoy a girl under age; **affiche qui attire les regards,** poster that attracts attention, that draws the eye; **a. l'imagination,** to appeal to the imagination; **a. tous les cœurs,** to win all hearts; **a. qn à son parti,** to win s.o. over, bring s.o. over, to one's side.

attisage [atizaːʒ], *s.m.,* **attisement** [atizmɑ̃], *s.m.* **1.** stirring (up), poking (of fire). **2.** fanning into flame.

attisée [atize], *s.f.* armful of firewood; *Fr.C:* good fire, good blaze.

attiser [atize], *v.tr.* **1.** to stir (up), poke (up) (fire); *Mch: etc:* to stoke (fire); **a. les haines,** to stir up hatred. **2.** to fan (fire, discontent); **a. le feu d'une passion,** to fan the ardour of a passion.

attisoir [atizwa:r], *s.m.*, **attisonnoir** [atizɔnwa:r], *s.m.* (*a*) poker; (*b*) fire-rake (for furnaces), prick-bar, pricker.

attitré [atitre], *a.* **1.** regular, appointed, recognized; ordinary (agent); **fournisseurs attitrés de sa Majesté,** purveyors by appointment to his, her, Majesty; **mon marchand de légumes a.,** my usual, regular, greengrocer. **2.** *A:* hired, paid, bribed (assassin, witness).

attitrer [atitre], *v.tr.* **1.** *Dipl:* to appoint (ambassador, etc.). **2.** *Ven:* to lay (hounds) on.

attitude [atityd], *s.f.* **1.** attitude, posture; **être toujours en a.,** to be always striking attitudes, posing; **prendre une a. histrionique,** to strike a theatrical attitude; **a. hostile, intransigeante,** hostile, uncompromising, attitude (**envers, à l'égard de, pour, en face de,** towards). **2.** behaviour.

attoll [atɔl], *s.m.* = ATOLL.

attouchement [atuʃmɑ̃], *s.m.* touching, contact; *A:* **guerir les écrouelles par a.,** to touch for King's Evil; **a. maçonnique,** mason's grip or token; *Geom:* **point d'a.,** point of contact, of osculation.

attracteur, -trice [atraktœ:r, -tris], *a.* attractile (force, etc.).

attractif, -ive [atraktif, -i:v], *a.* attractive, drawing (power, force of magnet); gravitational (force); *Biol:* **sphère attractive,** attraction sphere.

attraction [atraksjɔ̃], *s.f.* **1.** (*a*) attraction, pull (of magnet, etc.); *Ph:* **a. universelle,** gravitation; **a. moléculaire,** molecular attraction, cohesive force, adhesive attraction; (*b*) attraction, attractiveness (of resort, person, etc.); **la grande a. du jour,** the great attraction of the day; **exercer une a. sur qn,** to attract s.o.; (*c*) number (in cabaret). **2.** *pl.* **attractions,** attractions; sideshows; *Th:* varieties; cabaret show; *s.a.* PARC 2.

attractivement [atraktivmɑ̃], *adv. Ph:* attractively.

attractivité [atraktivite], *s.f. Ph:* attractivity, attractive power.

attraire [atrɛ:r], *v.tr. def. conj. like* **traire,** *but rarely used except in infin.* **1.** *A: Jur:* to institute proceedings against (s.o.). **2.** *A: & Lit:* to attract, charm.

attrait [atrɛ], *s.m.* **1.** (*a*) attraction, lure; attractiveness, allurement; charm (of youth, etc.); **l'a. de la mer,** the lure of the sea; **les attraits d'une carrière dans le commerce,** the inducements of a business career; **plein d'attraits,** most attractive; **dépourvu d'a.,** unattractive (face, etc.); **carrière qui n'a pas d'a. pour moi,** career for which I have no taste, no liking; (*b*) inclination; **se sentir de l'a. pour qn,** to feel drawn towards s.o., to feel a liking, a sympathy, for s.o.; **suivre son a.,** to follow one's bent; (*c*) *pl.* **attraits,** charms (of woman). **2.** *Fish:* bait.

attrapade [atrapad], *s.f.*, **attrapage** [atrapa:ʒ], *s.m. F:* **1.** quarrel, set-to. **2.** ticking-off, dressing-down.

attrape [atrap], *s.f.* **1.** (*a*) trap, gin, snare (for birds, etc.); (*b*) trick, hoax, catch; **faire une a. à qn,** to play a trick, a practical joke, on s.o.; to take s.o. in; **c'est une a.,** there's a catch in it; *s.a.* FARCE 2. **2.** *Nau:* (*a*) life-line; **ligne d'a.,** heaving, hauling, line; (*b*) relieving tackle.

attrape-gouttes [atrapgut], *s.m.inv. Mec.E: etc:* drip-pan.

attrape-lourdaud [atraplurdo], *s.m.* = ATTRAPE-NIAIS; *pl. attrape-lourdauds.*

attrape-marteau [atrapmarto], *s.m. Mus:* check-action, check (of piano); *pl. attrape-marteaux.*

attrape-minon [atrapminɔ̃], *s.m.* trickster; *pl. attrape-minon(s).*

attrape-mouche(s) [atrapmuʃ], *s.m.inv.* **1.** fly-trap, fly-paper. **2.** *Bot:* fly-catcher; catch-fly; Carolina catch-fly; Venus' fly-trap, dionaea; lychnis viscaria.

attrape-niais [atrapniɛ], *s.m.inv.*; **attrape-nigaud** [atrapnigo], *s.m.* trick; booby-trap; *pl. attrape-nigaud(s).*

attrape-poussières [atrappusjɛ:r], *s.m.inv.* **1.** air-strainer, dust-trap. **2.** *F:* white elephant, unused object that collects dust.

attraper [atrape], *v.tr.* to catch. **1.** (*a*) to (en)trap, (en)snare (animal); (*b*) **a. qn,** to trick, cheat, s.o., to take s.o. in, *F:* to have s.o.; **je suis bien attrapé,** I've been properly had; **attrapé!** caught! (*c*) **on m'a attrapé mon argent,** I have been cheated, *F:* done, out of my money. **2.** (*a*) to seize (ball, thief, idea, etc.); **a. un autobus,** to catch a bus; **elles se sont attrapées aux cheveux,** they grabbed each other by the hair; **vous avez bien attrapé la ressemblance,** you have caught the likeness; **attrape!** take that! *F:* **a. le bout de l'année,** to hold on till the end of the year, to make both ends meet; **en a. pour dix ans,** to get ten years' imprisonment, *F:* to get ten years; (*b*) to hit; **une pierre l'a attrapé au front,** a stone hit him, caught him, on the forehead; (*c*) **a. froid,** to catch a chill; **a. un rhume,** to catch cold; (*d*) **a. qn à faire qch.,** to catch s.o. doing sth.; **a. qn sur le fait,** to catch s.o. in the act, red-handed; (*e*) *F:* **a. qn,** to scold s.o., to give s.o. a good talking to, *F:* to come down on s.o. like a ton of bricks; **on va vous a.,** you'll catch it, get it in the neck; *Aut: etc:* **a. une contravention,** to get a ticket; **se faire a.,** (i) to get hauled over the coals, to get into a row, to catch it; (ii) to let oneself be cheated, taken in.

s'attraper. 1. s'a. à qch. (*a*) to hit against, to be caught by, on, sth.; **s'a. à la jambe,** (i) to knock, hit, one's leg; (ii) to get one's leg caught; (*b*) (*of burs, etc.*) to stick, cling (to sth.). **2. s'a. à qn,** to tackle, attack, s.o.; **s'a. avec qn,** to have a row, a quarrel, with s.o. **3.** (*of horse*) to overreach. **4. est-ce que cette maladie s'attrape?** is this illness catching?

attrape-touristes [atrapturist], *s.m.inv. F:* tourist trap.

attrapeur, -euse [atrapœ:r, -ø:z], *s.* **1.** (*a*) deceiver, trickster; (*b*) grabber, cadger, sponger. **2.** *s.m. Sp:* catcher (at base-ball).

attrayant [atrɛjɑ̃], *a.* attractive, engaging, alluring, enticing, winning; **de manière attrayante,** attractively; **peu a.,** unattractive; **ce projet est a. pour les esprits positifs,** this plan appeals to practical minds.

attremper [atrɑ̃pe], *v.tr. A:* to temper (steel, etc.).

attribuable [atribɥabl̩], *a.* attributable, assignable, ascribable, (**à,** to); **erreur attribuable à . . .** error due to . . .

attribuer [atribɥe], *v.tr.* **1.** to assign, allot (**à,** to); to confer, bestow (**à,** upon); to award; **a. des rôles, des fonctions,** to allocate parts, duties (**à,** to); *Th:* **a. un rôle à qn,** to cast s.o. for a part; **a. un traitement à un emploi,** to assign a salary to a post. **2.** to attribute, ascribe (fact, book, etc.) (**à,** to); to impute (crime, mistake) (**à,** to); to put down, set down, ascribe (sth. to a cause); to attach (importance to sth.); **a. un projet à qn,** to credit s.o. with a design; **on lui attribue du génie,** he is credited with genius; **un tableau attribué à Hogarth,** a reputed Hogarth; **je sais qu'on m'a attribué cet article,** I know this article has been attributed to me, fathered on me; **a. un malheur à qch.,** to blame sth. for a misfortune. **3. s'a. qch.,** to assume, claim, lay claim to, sth.; to arrogate sth. to oneself; to take (duty, etc.) upon oneself.

attribut [atriby], *s.m.* attribute. **1.** (*a*) essential characteristic, inherent property; (*b*) symbol, emblem; *Mil:* badge. **2.** *Log:* predicate; *Gram:* complement; **adjectif a.,** predicative adjective.

attributaire [atribytɛ:r], *s.m. & f. Jur:* assign; *Fin:* allottee.

attributif, -ive [atribytif, -i:v], *a.* **1.** *Jur:* (act, etc.) of assignment. **2.** *Gram:* predicative (clause, adjective).

attribution [atribysjɔ̃], *s.f.* **1.** (*a*) assigning, attribution, attributing, ascription (**à,** to); allocation, allocating (of duties); awarding (of scholarships, etc.); *Th:* casting (of parts); *Gram:* **complément d'a.,** indirect object; *St.Exch:* **actions d'a.,** bonus shares; **avis d'a.,** letter of allotment; (*b*) **a. (d'essence, de sucre),** (i) quota; (ii) ration (of petrol, sugar). **2.** *usu. pl.* (*a*) prerogative, competence, powers; **cela entre dans ses attributions,** this lies within his competence, his province, his powers, his attributions; (*b*) duties, functions, responsibilities.

attristant [atristɑ̃], *a.* saddening (news, etc.); sad (news, memory); **temps a.,** gloomy, depressing, weather; **attristante médiocrité,** depressing mediocrity.

attristé [atriste], *a.* sad (face); sorrowful (look); **contempler qch. d'un œil a.,** to gaze sadly at sth.

attrister [atriste], *v.tr.* (*a*) to sadden, grieve; **cela m'attriste d'entendre . . .,** it makes me sad to hear . . .; (*b*) to give a gloomy appearance to (sth.).

s'attrister, to grow sad; **s'a. de voir qch.,** to grieve to see sth.; **en hiver le paysage s'attriste,** winter casts a gloom over the landscape.

attrition [atrisjɔ̃], *s.f.* **1.** attrition; abrasion; wearing away, down; wear due to friction. **2.** *Theol:* attrition.

attroupement [atrupmɑ̃], *s.m. Jur:* unlawful, riotous, assembly; *F:* mob; **la loi contre les attroupements** = the Riot Act; **il se forma un grand a.,** a great crowd gathered.

attrouper [atrupe], *v.tr.* to gather (mob, etc.) together.

s'attrouper, to gather into a mob, to form a mob; to crowd together; (*of birds, etc.*) to flock together.

aturien [atyrjɛ̃], *a. & s.m. Geol:* aturian.

atypique [atipik], *a. Med: etc:* atypic(al).

aubade [obad], *s.f.* **1.** *Mus:* (*a*) aubade; morning concert; short instrumental piece in song style; (*b*) *A:* hunt's up. **2.** *F: Iron:* (*a*) cat-calling, cat-calls; rag; noisy disturbance; hot reception; (*b*) *Mil:* surprise at dawn.

aubage [oba:ʒ], *s.m.* **1.** *Carp:* thin wood (for panels); panelling. **2.** *Turb:* blading; *Av:* **a. de tourbillonnement,** flame-holder.

aubain [obɛ̃], *s.m. A.Jur:* aubain.

aubaine [obɛn], *s.f.* (*a*) *Jur: A:* (**droit d'**)**a.,** aubaine, right of escheat, escheatage, reversion to the Crown of the estate of a non-naturalized alien; (*b*) windfall, godsend; (*c*) *Fr.C:* bargain, good buy.

aubanien, -ienne [obanjɛ̃, -jɛn], *a. & s. Geog:* (native, inhabitant) of Aubagne.

aube[1] [o:b], *s.f.* **1.** dawn; **à l'a. (du jour),** at dawn, at break of day, at daybreak, at cock-crow; *Mil:* at first light; **l'a. de la civilisation,** the dawn of civilization. **2.** *Ecc:* alb.

aube[2], *s.f.* **1.** *Harn:* side-bar (of saddle). **2.** (*a*) *Nau: Hyd.E:* paddle, blade, float(-board) (of wheel); **a. articulée,** feathering paddle; **roue à aubes,** paddle(-wheel); **vapeur à roue à aubes,** paddle-boat; (*b*) *Mch: etc:* blade, vane (of turbine); vane (of fan).

aubépine [obepin], *s.f. Bot:* hawthorn, white thorn, *F:* may (tree); **fleurs d'a.,** may (blossom).

aubère [obɛ:r], *a. & s.m.* red-roan (horse).

auberge [obɛrʒ], *s.f.* inn; **tenir a.,** (i) to keep an inn; (ii) *F:* to keep open house; **auberges de jeunesse,** youth hostels; **il prend notre maison pour une a.,** he treats our house like a hotel; *F:* **on n'est pas sorti de l'a.,** now we'll be here all day, all night.

aubergine [obɛrʒin]. **1.** *s.f.Bot:* aubergine, egg-plant. **2.** *a.inv.* aubergine-coloured.

aubergiste [obɛrʒist], *s.m. & f.* innkeeper; landlord, landlady, host, hostess (of inn).

auberon [obrɔ̃], *s.m.* **1.** (bolt-)staple (of chest-lock). **2.** catch, keeper (of bolt).

auberonnière [obrɔnjɛ:r]. **1.** *s.f.* (*a*) catch-plate (of chest-lock, of bolt); (*b*) staple-plate. **2.** *a.* **serrure a.,** chest-lock, box-lock.

auber(t) [obɛ:r], *s.m. P:* money; *P:* dough, lolly.

aubette [obɛt], *s.f.* **1.** (*in Belgium, Alsace*) newspaper kiosk. **2.** *Mil.Hist:* post to which the non-commissioned officers of a garrison went to receive the orders of the day.

aubevigne [obviɲ], *s.f. Bot: F:* traveller's joy, old man's beard.

aubier [obje], *s.m.* **1.** *Bot: Ind:* alburn(um), sapwood; **faux a.,** false sap. **2.** *Dial:* willow(-tree).

aubifoin [obifwɛ̃], *s.m. Bot: F:* cornflower.

aubiner [obine], *v.tr. Rail:* to put (a signal) automatically at stop.

aubois, -oise [obwa, -wa:z], *a. & s. Geog:* (native, inhabitant) of the department of Aube.

aubour [obu:r], *s.m.* **1.** *Bot:* (*a*) Laburnum; (*b*) wild guelder rose. **2.** = AUBIER 1.

aubriétie [obriesi], *s.f.*, **aubrietia** [obriesja], *s.f. Bot:* aubrietia.

auburn [obœrn], *a.inv.* auburn.

aubussonnais, -aise [obysɔnɛ, -ɛ:z], *a. & s. Geog:* (native, inhabitant) of Aubusson.

aucuba [okyba], *s.m. Bot:* Aucuba.

aucun, -une [okœ̃, -yn]. **1.** *pron.* (*a*) anyone, any; **il travaille plus qu'a.,** he works more than anyone (else); (*b*) *with implied negation:* **de tous vos soi-disant amis, a. interviendra-t-il?** will any of all your so-called friends intervene? (*c*) *with negation expressed or understood, accompanied by* **ne** *or* **sans** (i) no one, no man, nobody; (ii) none, not any; **je ne me fie à a. d'entre eux,** I trust none of them, I don't trust any of them; **j'attendis deux heures, sans qu'a. d'entre eux arrivât,** I waited for two hours but none of them came; **nous avons des quantités de fruits, mais aucun (de) mûr,** we have masses of fruit, but none ripe; **a. (des deux) ne viendra,** neither (of them) will come; (iii) not one; **de tous ces élèves a. n'a répondu,** not one of all these boys answered; **"Connaissez-vous quelqu'un de ses parents?" "Aucun,"** "Do you know any of her

relations?" "None"; (*d*) *pl. Lit:* some, some people; **d'aucuns,** *A:* **aucuns, prétendent qu'il est encore en vie,** some (people) maintain, there are some who maintain, that he is still alive. **2.** *a.* (*a*) any; **un des plus beaux livres qui aient été écrits sur a. sujet,** one of the finest books that have been written on any subject; (*b*) *with implied negation:* **avez-vous aucune intention de le faire?** have you any intention of doing it? *Lit:* **avez-vous fait aucune observation?** did you say anything at all? (*c*) *with negation expressed or understood, accompanied by* **ne** *or preceded by* **sans vendre qch. sans a. bénéfice,** to sell sth. without any profit; **sans aucune exception,** without any exception; **tous, sans aucune exception, sans exception aucune,** all without exception; **le fait n'a aucune importance,** the fact is of no importance; **il n'a absolument a. talent pour la musique,** he has no talent whatsoever for music; **sans mentionner a. nom,** without mentioning any names; **on ne voyait plus a. bateau,** you could no longer see any boats; **il n'a jamais fait a. mal à personne,** he never did anyone any harm; **ne faites aucuns frais, aucunes dépenses, à mon intention,** do not go to any expense on my account; (*d*) *pl. Lit:* **d'aucunes fois . . .,** now and again.

aucunement [okynmɑ̃], *adv.* **1.** *A:* (*with implied negation*) in any way, at all; **le connaissez-vous a.?** do you know him at all? **2.** (*with negation expressed or understood*) in no way, in no wise, not at all, by no means, not in the slightest, not in the least; **je n'en suis a. étonné,** I am not at all, in no way, astonished; **le tenez-vous pour responsable?—a.,** do you hold him responsible?—by no means; **je ne le connais a.,** I don't know him at all, in the slightest (degree), *F:* from Adam; **je ne m'attendais a. à ce qu'il vînt,** I never expected his coming; **sans a. vouloir critiquer . . .,** without in any way wishing to criticize . . .; **il ne s'en porte a. mieux,** he is not a whit the better for it.

audace [odas], *s.f.* audacity, audaciousness. **1.** boldness, daring; **son a. à attaquer,** his boldness in attacking, in attack; **n'ayez pas l'a. de le toucher!** don't you dare touch him! *s.a.* COUP 2, PAYER. **2.** impudence; **excusez mon a.,** forgive my presumption; **vous avez l'a. de me dire cela!** you have the cheek, nerve, to tell me that! **son a. à mentir, dans le mensonge,** his brazen lying.

audacieusement [odasjøzmɑ̃], *adv.* audaciously. **1.** boldly, daringly. **2.** impudently, brazenly; *F:* cheekily.

audacieux, -euse [odasjø, -øːz], *a.* audacious. **1.** bold, daring; *A:* **homme a. à faire qch.,** man bold to do sth. **2.** impudent; brazen (lie, etc.); **vêtement a.,** daring costume.

au-deçà [odsa]. *A:* (*a*) *adv.* on this side; (*b*) *prep. phr.* **a.-d. de,** on this side of; without going as far as.

au-dedans [od(ə)dɑ̃], (*a*) *adv.* inside; within; (*b*) *prep.phr.* **a.-d. de,** inside; within.

au-dehors [odəɔːr], (*a*) *adv.* outside; (*b*) *prep.phr.* **a.-d. de,** outside, beyond.

au-delà [odla], (*a*) *adv.* beyond; (*b*) *s.m.* **l'a.-d.,** the next world, the hereafter; (*c*) *prep.phr.* **a.-d. de,** beyond, on the other side of; **n'allez pas a.-d. de cent francs,** don't go above, beyond, a hundred francs.

au-dessous [odsu], *adv.* **1.** (*a*) below (it); **sur la table et a.-d.,** on the table and below it; **le château est en haut de la colline, le village est a.-d.,** the castle is at the top of the hill, with the village below (it); (*b*) below, underneath; **les locataires a.-d.,** the tenants below, underneath, downstairs; (*c*) **les enfants âgés de sept ans et a.-d.,** children of seven years old and under; (*d*) **musique transposée deux tons a.-d.,** music transposed two tones lower, two tones down. **2.** *prep.phr.* **a.-d. de** (*a*) below, under; **le village est a.-d. du château,** the village lies below the castle; **sur la Seine, cinquante kilomètres au-d. de Paris,** on the Seine, fifty kilometres below, down river from, Paris; **a.-d. du genou,** below the knee; (*b*) **les locataires a.-d. de nous,** the tenants below us, under(neath) us; **quinze degrés a.-d. de zéro,** fifteen degrees below zero; **a.-d. de la moyenne, du pair,** below the average, below par; *Sch:* **compositions au-d. de la moyenne,** papers below pass mark; **il reste a.-d. de lui-même,** he does not do himself justice; **il est a.-d. de lui de se plaindre,** it is beneath him to complain; (*c*) **épouser qn a.-d. de soi,** to marry beneath one; (*d*) **a.-d. de cinq ans,** under five (years of age); **quantités a.-d. de 30 kilos,** quantities of less than 30 kilos; **acheter qch. au-d. de sa valeur,** to buy sth. for less than it is worth; (*e*) **son travail était a.-d. de mon attente,** his work fell short of my expectation; **il est a.-d. de ses affaires,** his business is not paying; **être a.-d. de sa tâche,** to be unequal to one's task, not up to one's job; **être a.-d. de tout,** to be worse than useless.

au-dessus [odsy], *adv.* **1.** (*a*) above (it); **le village est en bas de la colline, le château a.-d.,** the village is at the foot of the hill, with the castle above (it); (*b*) **une terrasse avec une marquise a.-d.,** a terrace with an awning over it, above; **la salle de bains est a.-d.,** the bathroom is upstairs; (*c*) **mille francs et a.-d.,** a thousand francs and upwards; **pour les enfants de cinq ans et a.-d.,** for children of five years and upwards; *Post:* **a.-d., par 50 gr.,** for each additional 50 gr.; (*d*) **musique transposée un ton a.-d.,** music transposed a tone higher, a tone up; (*e*) **il n'a rien fait qui soit a.-d.,** he has done nothing better. **2.** *prep.phr.* **au-dessus de;** (*a*) above; **le château est situé a.-d. du village,** the castle stands above the village; (*b*) **il a son nom a.-d. de la porte,** his name is above the door, over the door; **nous demeurons l'un a.-d. de l'autre,** we live one above the other; **les avions volaient a.-d. de nos têtes,** the planes were flying overhead; **l'eau leur montait jusqu'a.-d. des genoux,** the water came up to above their knees; **deux degrés a.-d. de zéro,** two degrees above zero; **surtout, ne payez pas a.-d. de cinquante francs,** above all, don't pay more than fifty francs; **sur la Seine, cinquante kilomètres a.-d. de Paris,** on the Seine, fifty kilometres above, up-river from, Paris; *Sch:* **compositions a.-d. de la moyenne,** papers above pass mark; *A:* **être a.-d. de sa condition,** to be intellectually above one's social class, position in life; *A:* **épouser qn a.-d. de soi, se marier a.-d. de sa condition,** to marry above one's station; **il n'est guère a.-d. d'un paysan,** he is no better, little better, than a peasant; **le colonel est a.-d. du commandant,** a colonel is higher than a major; **les amateurs s'estiment a.-d. des professionnels,** *F:* amateurs consider themselves a cut above professionals; *A:* **avoir une mise a.-d. de son état,** to dress above one's position; **être a.-d. de sa place,** to be too good for one's job; **il est a.-d. de cela,** he is above doing such a thing, he is above it; **être a.-d. de la flatterie,** to be superior to, above, flattery; **vous avez été a.-d. de vous-même,** you have surpassed yourself; (*c*) **a.-d. de cinq ans,** over five (years of age); **elle a une sagesse a.-d. de son âge,** she is wise beyond her years; (*d*) **a.-d. de tout éloge,** beyond all praise; **courage a.-d. de toute discussion,** courage beyond question; **travail a.-d. de ses capacités,** work beyond his powers, beyond him; **la tâche est a.-d. de leurs forces,** the task is too much for them, beyond them; **a.-d. de la calomnie,** beyond the reach of calumny; *F:* **être a.-d. du vent,** to have nothing to fear; **vivre a.-d. de ses moyens,** to live beyond one's means.

au-devant [odvɑ̃], *adv. used only in such phrases as* **aller, courir, se jeter, se précipiter, a.-d. 1.** (*a*) **quand il y a du danger, je vais a.-d.,** when there is danger ahead, I go to meet it; (*b*) **quand je prévois une objection je vais a.-d.,** when I foresee an objection, I anticipate it. **2.** *prep.phr.* **a.-d. de;** (*a*) **aller, courir, a.-d. de qn,** to go, run, to meet s.o.; **aller a.-d. des désirs de qn,** to anticipate s.o.'s wishes, to meet s.o.'s wishes half-way; (*b*) **aller a.-d. d'un danger,** to anticipate, provide against, a danger; **aller a.-d. d'un complot,** to forestall a plot; (*c*) **aller a.-d. du danger, d'une défaite,** to court danger, failure.

audibilité [odibilite], *s.f.* audibility.

audible [odibl̩], *a.* audible.

audience [odjɑ̃ːs], *s.f.* **1.** audience, hearing; (*a*) *A:* **vous avez a.,** I am ready to hear you; **recevoir qn sur lettre d'a.,** to interview s.o. by appointment; (*b*) (*of king*) **tenir une a.,** to hold an audience; (*c*) *Jur:* (i) hearing (by the court); sitting, session, court; **plaider en pleine a., en a. publique,** to plead in open court; **a. à huis clos,** hearing in camera; **tenir a.,** to hold a court, a sitting; **lever, fermer, l'a.,** to close the session, the sitting; **l'a. est reprise,** the case is resumed; **feuille d'a.,** record of a court; (ii) court (room); **mettre qn hors d'a.,** to put s.o. out of court; (iii) public; **l'a. fut scandalisée par les révélations du témoin,** the court room was shocked by the revelations of the witness; (*d*) interest, attention, favourable reception. **2.** = AUDITOIRE.

audiencer [odjɑ̃se], *v.tr.* (**j'audiençai(s); n. audiençons**) *Jur:* to put (case) down for hearing.

audiencier [odjɑ̃sje]. **1.** *a. & s.m. Jur:* (**huissier**) **a.,** court crier; usher. **2.** *s.m. F:* frequenter of law-courts.

audimètre [odimɛtr̩], *s.m.* = AUDIOMÈTRE.

audiodétection [odjodetɛksjɔ̃], *s.f. Z:* echo-location (of bats).

audiofréquence [odjofrekɑ̃ːs], *s.f. W.Tel:* audio-frequency.

audiogramme [odjogram], *s.m.* audiogram.

audiologie [odjɔlɔʒi], *s.f. Med:* audiology.

audiomètre [odjomɛːtr̩], *s.m.* audiometer.

audiométrie [odjometri], *s.f.* audiometry.

audion [odjɔ̃], *s.m. W.Tel: A:* audion, vacuum-tube; **lampe a.,** (vacuum-) valve.

audiophone [odiɔfɔn], *s.m.* = AUDIPHONE.

audio(-)visuel, -elle [odjovizɥɛl], *a.* audio-visual.

audiphone [odifɔn], *s.m.* audiphone.

auditeur, -trice [oditœːr, -tris], *s.* **1.** hearer, listener; **les auditeurs,** the audience; *W.Tel: T.V:* **programme des auditeurs,** request programme. **2.** student (merely attending lectures). **3.** *Adm:* **a. à la Cour des comptes** = Commissioner of Audit. **4.** *Mil.Jur: A:* public prosecutor (before court martial).

auditif, -ive [oditif, -iːv]. **1.** *a.* auditory (nerve, meatus); auditive; **prothèse auditive, appareil de correction auditive, aide auditif,** hearing aid; **mémoire auditive,** aural memory. **2.** *s.* audile.

audition [odisjɔ̃], *s.f.* **1.** (*a*) *Physiol:* hearing (of sounds); audition; *Psy:* **a. colorée,** coloured hearing; (*b*) **juger d'un opéra à la première a.,** to judge an opera at the first hearing; *s.a.* CABINE. **2.** (*a*) **a. de piano,** (private) piano recital; *W.Tel: A:* **auditions musicales,** wireless concerts; **auditions du jour,** today's broadcasting; (*b*) audition (of singer, etc.); (*c*) *Jur:* **a. des témoins,** hearing, examination, of the witnesses; **nouvelle a.,** rehearing.

auditionner [odisjɔne]. **1.** *v.tr. F:* to audition (s.o.). **2.** *v.i. F:* to have an audition, to audition (for a part).

auditoire [oditwaːr], *s.m.* **1.** (*a*) auditorium, auditory; (*b*) court (of tribunal). **2.** (*a*) audience (assembly of listeners); (*b*) *Ecc:* congregation.

auditorat [oditɔra], *s.m.,* **auditoriat** [oditɔrja], *s.m. Adm:* office, function, of *auditeur.*

auditorium [oditɔrjɔm], *s.m.* (*a*) auditorium; (*b*) (broadcasting, television) studio.

audomarois, -oise [odɔmarwa, -waːz], *a. & s. Geog:* (native, inhabitant) of Saint-Omer.

audonien, -ienne [odɔnjɛ̃, -jɛn], *a. & s. Geog:* (native, inhabitant) of Saint-Ouen.

auge [oːʒ], *s.f.* **1.** trough; (*a*) feeding trough; water trough; *P:* plate; *A: F:* **c'est un cochon à l'a.,** he eats like a pig; **a. d'écurie,** manger; (*b*) *El:* **a. galvanique, pile à a.,** trough-battery; *Const:* **a. à mortier,** mortar-trough; *Gold Min:* **a. à laver,** sluice-box; *Nau: etc:* **a. à goudron,** tar-bucket. **2.** *Hyd.E:* (*a*) = AUGET 3; (*b*) flume, channel (for leading water to mill). **3.** *Z:* hollow space within the lower jaw (of horse); **abcès dans l'a.,** abscess in the lower jaw. **4.** *Geol:* (*a*) glacial valley; (*b*) (*rare*) syncline.

augée [oʒe], *s.f. A:* troughful, mangerful; hodful.

augélite [oʒelit], *s.f. Miner:* augelite.

augelot [oʒəlo], *s.m. Vit:* small trench (for planting vine).

Auger [oʒe], *Pr.n. Atom.Ph:* **effet A.,** Auger effect.

augeron, -onne [oʒərɔ̃, -ɔn], *a. & s. Geog:* (native, inhabitant) of the pays d'Auge.

auget [oʒɛ], *s.m.* **1.** (small) trough; **a. d'une cage,** seed-trough, water-trough, of a bird-cage; *El:* **accumulateur à augets,** trough-accumulator; *Sm.a:* **a. de répétition,** feed-trough (of magazine rifle); cartridge loader. **2.** (*washerwoman's*) kneeling-box. **3.** *Hyd.E:* bucket (of water-wheel); **roue à augets,** bucket-wheel, overshot wheel.

augette [oʒɛt], *s.f.* **1.** small trough; *Gold Min:* small pan, small sluice-box, abacus major. **2.** (mason's) hod.

Augias [oʒjaːs], *Pr.n.m. Gr.Myth:* Augeas; *Lit:* **nettoyer les écuries d'A.,** to cleanse the Augean stables.

augite [oʒit], *s.f. Miner:* augite.

augment [ɔgmɑ̃], *s.m. Ling:* augment.

augmentable [ɔgmɑ̃tabl̩], *a.* augmentable.

augmentateur, -trice [ɔgmɑ̃tatœːr, -tris], *s.* augmenter (of book, etc.).

augmentatif, -ive [ɔgmɑ̃tatif, -iːv], *a. & s.m. Ling:* augmentative (suffix, etc.).

augmentation [ɔgmɑ̃tasjɔ̃], *s.f.* **1.** increase, augmentation, enlargement; *Mth:* increase (of function, etc.); *Adm:* increment; **a. de gages, de paie,** rise, increase, in wages, *U.S:* raise; **a. de prix,** increase in prices; **être en a.,** to be on the rise, on the increase; **chiffre d'affaires en a. sur**

l'année dernière, turnover showing an increase on last year('s); **a. du stock monétaire,** expansion of the currency. **2.** *Mus:* augmentation. **3.** *Knitting:* **faire une a.,** to make a stitch, to make one. **4.** *Her:* augmentation.

augmenter [ɔgmɑ̃te]. **1.** *v.tr.* to increase, augment, enlarge; **a. sa maison,** to enlarge one's establishment; **a. ses terres,** to extend, add to, one's estate; **édition augmentée,** enlarged edition; **a. une douleur,** to aggravate a pain; **a. le prix de qch.,** to raise, put up, the price of sth.; **a. l'intérêt pour qch.,** to heighten the interest in sth.; **a. la difficulté,** to make sth. still more difficult; **a. qn,** to raise, increase, s.o.'s (i) salary, wages; (ii) rent; *Mus:* **en augmentant,** crescendo. **2.** *v.i.* to increase (*a*) **le crime augmente beaucoup,** crime is on the increase; **la rivière a augmenté,** the river has risen; **empêcher les frais d'a.,** to keep expenses down; **elle augmente en beauté,** she grows in beauty; **tout a, est, augmenté de prix,** everything has risen, advanced, in price; **la valeur a augmenté de 10% par rapport à l'année dernière,** the value is 10% up on last year; (*b*) *Nau:* **a. de toile,** to crowd on sail, to make more sail; (*c*) *Knitting:* to make a stitch, to make one; **a. de deux points au commencement du rang suivant,** increase two at the beginning of the next row.

s'augmenter, to increase.

Augsbourg [ɔgzbuːr], *Pr.n.m. Geog:* Augsburg; *s.a.* CONFESSION 2.

augnathe [ɔgnat], *s.m. Ter:* two-headed monster.

augural, -aux [ogyral, -o], *a. Rom.Ant:* augural (staff, etc.).

augurat [ogyra], *s.m. Rom.Ant:* augurship, augurate.

augure¹ [ogyːr], *s.m. Rom.Ant:* augur; **le Collège des augures,** the College of Augurs.

augure², *s.m.* augury, omen; **prendre les augures,** to take the auguries; **prendre qch. à bon a.,** to take sth. as a good omen; **de bon a.,** auspicious; **de mauvais a.,** ominous; **oiseau de mauvais a.,** bird of ill omen; **agitation de mauvais a.,** agitation that bodes no good; **j'en accepte l'a.,** I expect success.

augurer [ogyre], *v.tr.* to augur, foresee, forecast; **a. l'avenir d'après le passé,** to forecast the future, according to, from the past; **a. bien de qch.,** to augur well of sth., to feel optimistic about sth.; **a. mal de qch.,** to augur ill of sth., to feel pessimistic about sth.; **qu'en augurez-vous?** what do you think (will come) of it?

Augusta [ogysta], *Pr.n.f.* Augusta.

augustal, -aux [ogystal, -o]. **1.** *a. Rom.Hist:* Augustan; **jeux augustaux,** Augustalia. **2.** *s.f. Num:* **augustale,** augustal(e).

Augustales [ogystal], *s.m.pl. Rom.Hist:* Augustales.

Auguste¹ [ogyst]. **1.** *Pr.n.m.* Augustus; *Lit:* **le siècle d'A.,** the Augustan Age. **2.** *s.m.* **l'a.,** the "funny man" (at circus).

auguste² [ogyst], *a.* august, majestic.

augustement [ogystəmɑ̃], *adv.* augustly, majestically.

Augustin [ogystɛ̃]. **1.** *Pr.n.m.* Augustine. **2.** *a. & s.m. Ecc:* **(religieux) a.,** Augustinian (friar); **les Augustins,** the Austin friars.

Augustine [ogystin]. **1.** *Pr.n.m.* Augusta. **2.** *a. & s.f. Ecc:* **(religieuse) a.,** Augustinian (nun). **3.** *s.f.* (*a*) *A: F:* foot warmer (heated by spirit lamp); (*b*) *A: F:* razor paste.

augustinien, -ienne [ogystinjɛ̃, -jɛn], *a. Ecc:* Augustinian (monk, doctrine).

augustinisme [ogystinism], *s.m. Ecc: Phil:* Augustinianism.

aujourd'hui [oʒurdɥi], today; (*a*) *adv.* **il arrive a.,** he arrives today; *F:* **c'est quel jour a.?** what day is it today? what is it today? **c'est a. le cinq, c'est a. dimanche,** today is the fifth, today is Sunday; **a. que les avions raccourcissent les distances entre les pays . . .** today when planes shorten distances between countries . . .; **cela ne se pratique plus a.,** this is not done nowadays; **les jeunes gens d'a.,** the young people of today, of the present day; **le journal d'a.,** today's paper; **(d')a. en huit, en quinze,** today week, today fortnight; a week today, a fortnight today; *F:* **à a. en huit, alors,** till a week today, then; **il y a a. huit jours,** a week ago today; **je l'ai différé jusqu'à a., jusqu'a.,** I put it off till today; **je ne l'ai pas vue d'a.,** I have not set eyes on her today; I have not seen her all day; **ce n'est pas d'a. que je la connais,** I have known her for a long time; *P:* **au jour d'a.,** nowadays; *F:* **c'est pour a. ou pour demain?** hurry up! (*b*) *s.* **a. passé, on ne pourra plus y aller,** after today we shall no longer be able to go there.

Aulide [olid], *Pr.n.f. Lit:* Aulis.

aulique [olik], *a. Hist:* Aulic (Council, etc.).

aulnaie [onɛ], *s.f.* alder plantation, alder grove.

aulne [oːn], *s.m. Bot:* alder; **a. grisâtre,** silver-leaved alder, common alder.

aulnée [one], *s.f. Bot:* Inula; **a. hélène,** elecampane, horse-heal, scab-wort.

aulof(f)ée [olɔfe], *s.f. Nau:* luffing; **faire une a.,** to luff.

Aulu-Gelle [olyʒɛl], *Pr.n.m. Lt.Lit:* Aulus Gellius.

Aululaire (l') [lolylɛːr], *s.f. Lt.Lit:* The Aulularia (of Plautus).

aulx [o]; *see* AIL 2.

aumaille [omaj], *s.f. A:* cattle.

aumalois, -oise [omalwa, -waːz], *a. & s. Geog:* (native, inhabitant) of Aumale.

aumône [omoːn], *s.f.* alms; **faire l'a. à qn,** to give alms to s.o.; **donner qch. en a. à qn,** to give s.o. sth. out of charity; **réduit à l'a.,** reduced to beggary; **vivre d'aumônes,** to live by begging, on charity; *F:* **elle m'a fait l'a. d'un sourire,** she favoured me with a smile.

aumônerie [omonri], *s.f.* **1.** *A:* (*a*) almonership; (*b*) almonry. **2.** (*a*) chaplaincy, chaplainship; (*b*) chaplain's residence, headquarters.

aumônier [omonje], *s.m.* **1.** almoner. **2.** chaplain; **aumônier militaire,** army chaplain, *F:* padre.

aumônière [omonjɛːr], *s.f.* **1.** *A:* alms-purse, -bag. **2.** chain-purse, mesh-bag; Dorothy-bag.

aumuce, aumusse [omys], *s.f. Ecc:* amice.

aunage [onaːʒ], *s.m. A:* **1.** measuring by the ell; *A:* alnage. **2.** measure (of piece of cloth).

aunaie [onɛ], *s.f.* alder plantation, grove.

aune¹ [oːn], *s.m. Bot:* alder; **a. grisâtre,** silver-leaved alder.

aune², *s.f. A:* ell (*Meas.:* 1ᵐ.188); *F:* **figure longue d'une aune,** face as long as a fiddle; **vocable long d'une a.,** sesquipedalian word; **mesurer les autres à son aune,** to judge others by oneself, by one's own yard-stick; **les hommes ne se mesurent pas à l'a.,** you must not measure a man with a yard-stick, judge a man by his stature; **elle sait ce qu'en vaut l'a.,** she knows it through bitter experience; *Prov:* **au bout de l'a. faut le drap,** all things have an end; *cf.* FAILLIR 1.

aunée¹ [one], *s.f. A:* ell (of cloth, etc.).

aunée², *s.f. Bot:* inula; **a. hélène,** elecampane, horse-heal, scabwort.

auner [one], *v.tr. A:* to measure (with an ell, by the ell); **il a. les autres à sa mesure,** he judges others by his own yard-stick.

aunisien, -ienne [onizjɛ̃, -jɛn], *a. & s. Geog:* (native, inhabitant) of Aunis.

auparavant [oparavɑ̃], *adv.* before(hand), previously; **a. il faut s'assurer de . . .,** first we must make sure of . . .; **l'année d'a.,** the preceding year, the year before; **un moment a., le moment d'a.,** a moment before; **comme a.,** as before.

auprès [oprɛ], *adv.* **1.** (*a*) close to, near to; **voilà l'église, la maison est tout a.,** there is the church; the house is close to it; (*b*) **œuvre magnifique, il n'y a rien à mettre a.,** a magnificent piece of work, there is nothing to be compared with it. **2.** *prep.phr.* **a. de,** (*a*) close to, by, close by, beside, near; **tout a. de qn, de qch.,** close beside s.o., sth.; **il a toujours une garde-malade a. de lui,** he always has a nurse with him, at hand, in his service; **ambassadeur a. du roi de Suède,** ambassador to the King of Sweden, at the Court of Sweden; **avocat a. du tribunal,** advocate attached to the tribunal; **il vit a. de ses parents,** he lives with his parents; (*b*) *indicating a moral relation;* **agir a. de qn,** to use one's influence with s.o.; **être bien a. de qn,** to be in favour with s.o., to be in s.o.'s good books; **il cherche à me nuire a. de vous,** he is trying to set you against me; **trouver grâce a. de qn,** to find favour in s.o.'s sight; (*c*) *with motion,* **admettre qn a. de qn,** to admit s.o. into s.o.'s presence; to show s.o. in to s.o.; (*d*) compared with, in comparison with; **nous ne sommes rien a. de lui,** we are (as) nothing beside him, *F:* we can't hold a candle to him.

aura [ɔra], *s.f. Med: etc:* aura; **a. épileptique,** epileptic aura.

auramine [ɔramin], *s.f. Ch: Dy:* auramine.

aurantia [ɔrɑ̃sja], *s.f. Phot:* aurantia.

aurantiacées [ɔrɑ̃tjase], *s.f.pl.,* **aurantiées** [ɔrɑ̃tje], *s.f.pl. Bot:* Auranti(ac)eae.

aurate [ɔrat], *s.m. Ch:* aurate.

Aurèle [ɔrɛl], *Pr.n.m.* Aurelius; *s.a.* MARC-AURÈLE.

aurelia [ɔrelja], *s.f. Coel:* Aurelia.

Aurélie [ɔreli], *Pr.n.f.* Aurelia.

Aurélien [ɔreljɛ̃], *Pr.n.m. Rom.Hist:* Aurelian.

auréole [ɔreɔl], *s.f.* **1.** (*a*) aureola, aureole, glory, halo (of saint); **a. elliptique,** vesica piscis; **a. de gloire,** radiance of glory; **détachant qui ne laisse pas d'a.,** stain-remover which leaves no ring; (*b*) halo (of moon); corona (of sun); (*c*) *Min:* gas-cap, blue cap (of safety lamp). **2.** *Phot:* halation.

auréolé [ɔreɔle], *a.* haloed (martyr, etc.).

auréoler [ɔreɔle], *v.tr.* (*a*) to surround with a halo; (*b*) to exalt, glorify; **a. qn de toutes les vertus,** to crown s.o. with all the virtues.

auréomycine [ɔreɔmisin], *s.f. Med:* aureomycin.

aureus [ɔreys], *s.m. Rom.Hist: Num:* aureus.

aureux [ɔrø], *a.m. Ch:* aurous.

auric(h)alcite [ɔrikalsit], *s.m. Miner:* aurichalcite.

auriculaire [ɔrikylɛːr], *a.* auricular (confession, etc.); **témoin a.,** auricular witness, ear-witness; **le doigt a.,** *s.m.* **l'a.,** the little finger; *Artil: etc:* **protecteur a.,** ear-protector.

auricularia¹ [ɔrikylarja], *s.f. Echin:* auricularia.

auricularia², *s.m. Fung:* auricularia.

auriculariales [ɔrikylarjal], *s.f.pl. Fung:* Auriculariales.

auricule [ɔrikyl], *s.f.* **1.** *Anat: Bot:* auricle (of the heart, of a petal); **a. de l'oreille,** lower lobe of the ear. **2.** *Bot:* auricula. **3.** *Echin:* auricula, auricle. **4.** *Moll:* auricula.

auriculé [ɔrikyle], *a.* auriculate, auricled, eared (leaf, shell).

auriculidés [ɔrikylide], *s.m.pl. Moll:* Auriculidae.

auriculiste [ɔrikylist], *s.m. Med:* ear specialist; aural surgeon.

auriculo-temporal, -aux [ɔrikylotɑ̃pɔral, -o], *a. Anat:* auriculo-temporal.

auriculo-ventriculaire [ɔrikylovɑ̃trikylɛːr], *a. Anat:* auriculo-ventricular.

auride [ɔrid], *s.m. Miner:* auride.

aurifère [ɔrifɛːr], *a.* auriferous, gold-bearing; **champ a.,** gold-field.

aurification [ɔrifikasjɔ̃], *s.f. Dent:* stopping, filling, (of teeth) with gold; aurification.

aurifier [ɔrifje], *v.tr.* (*pr.sub. & p.d.* **n. aurifiions, v. aurifiiez**) *Dent:* to stop, fill, (teeth) with gold.

aurifique [ɔrifik], *a.* aurific.

auriforme [ɔrifɔrm], *a.* auriform, ear-shaped.

Auriga [ɔriga], *s.m.,* **Aurige** [ɔriːʒ], *s.m.* **1.** *Astr:* the Wag(g)oner, Auriga. **2.** *Rom.Ant:* **aurige,** auriga, charioteer.

aurignacien, -ienne [ɔriɲasjɛ̃, -jɛn], *a. & s.m. Prehist:* aurignacian.

Aurigny [ɔriɲi], *Pr.n.m. Geog:* Alderney; *Husb:* **vache d'A.,** Alderney cow.

aurillacois, -oise [ɔrijakwa, -waːz], **aurillaquais, -aise** [ɔrijakɛ, -ɛːz], *Geog:* (native, inhabitant) of Aurillac.

aurine [ɔrin], *s.f. Ch:* aurin.

auriol [ɔriɔl], *s.m. Or:* oriole.

aurique¹ [ɔrik], *a. & s.f. Nau:* fore-and-aft (sail, rig).

aurique², *a. Ch:* auric.

auriste [ɔrist], *s.m. Med:* aurist; ear specialist; aural surgeon.

aurochs [ɔrɔks], *s.m. Z:* aurochs, urus, wild ox.

auron(n)e [ɔrɔn], *s.f. Bot:* southernwood, abrotanum, old-man; **a. femelle,** santolina, lavender-cotton.

auroral, -aux [ɔrɔral, -o], *a.* auroral; *Ecc:* **messe aurorale,** mass for the aurora.

aurore [ɔrɔːr]. **1.** *s.f.* (*a*) dawn, daybreak; break of day; *Lit: Ecc:* aurora; **l'a. commence à paraître, à poindre,** the dawn is breaking; *Poet:* **éveiller l'a.,** to rise before dawn; *Poet:* **l'a. aux doigts de rose,** the rosy-fingered dawn; **beauté à, dans, son aurore,** budding beauty; **du couchant à l'a.,** from west to east; **l'a. de la civilisation,** the dawn of civilization; (*b*) **a. australe,** aurora australis; **a. boréale,** aurora borealis, northern lights; **a. polaire,** aurora polaris, polar light. **2.** (*a*) *a.inv.* (saffron, golden) yellow; (*b*) *s.f. Ent:* orange tip (butterfly). **3.** *Pr.n.f. Myth: etc:* Aurora.

auscitain, -aine [ositɛ̃, -ɛn], *a. & s. Geog:* (native, inhabitant) of Auch [oʃ].

auscultateur [ɔskyltatœːr], *s.m.* auscultator.

auscultation [ɔskyltasjɔ̃], *s.f. Med:* auscultation; sounding.

ausculter [ɔskylte], *v.tr. Med:* to auscultate, to examine (s.o.) by auscultation; to sound (patient, the chest).

Ausone [ozɔn], *Pr.n.m. Lt.Lit:* Ausonius.

auspice [ɔspis], *s.m. usu. pl.* (*a*) *Rom.Ant:* auspice; **prendre les auspices,** to take the auspices; (*b*) auspice, omen, presage, prognostic; **mauvais a.,** ill omen; **faire qch. sous des auspices favorables,** to do sth. in favourable circumstances, under favourable auspices; **l'année commence sous d'heureux, de fâcheux, auspices,** the year begins auspiciously, inauspiciously; **faire qch. sous les auspices de qn,** to do sth. under s.o.'s patronage, under the auspices of s.o.

aussi [osi]. **1.** *adv.* (*a*) as (*in comparative sentences*) **pas a.,** not so, not as; **il est a. grand que son frère,** he is as tall as his brother; **ce tableau est deux fois a. grand que celui-là,** this painting is twice as big as that one; **elle était a. bonne que vertueuse,** she was as kind as she was virtuous; **il avait l'air a. à son aise que vous,** he seemed as much at his ease as you; **tout a. au sud, à l'est, que Paris,** as far south, east, as Paris; **il n'est pas a. grand que vous,** he is not as tall as you; **vous ne le connaissez pas a. bien que moi,** you don't know him as well as I do; **ma méthode est tout a. bonne que la vôtre,** my method is quite as good, *F:* every bit as good, as yours; **je le connais a. peu que son frère,** I don't know him any better than I know his brother; **elle n'est pas a. belle que l'on m'avait dit,** she is not as beautiful as they said, as she was made out to be; **a. longtemps que vous serez riches, vous aurez des amis,** as long as you are rich you will have friends; (*b*) so; **après avoir attendu a. longtemps . . .,** after waiting so long, for such a long time; **un homme a. travailleur que vous,** such an industrious man as yourself; a man as industrious as you are; **ce n'est pas facile de juger d'a. loin,** it isn't easy to tell from this distance, from as far as this; **avez-vous jamais entendu une symphonie a. bizarre?** have you ever heard such a peculiar symphony? (*c*) (i) also, too; **vous venez a.,** you are coming too; **gardez a. ceux-là,** you may keep those as well; **je prends mon imper et mon parapluie a.,** I am taking my mac and my umbrella as well; (ii) so; **moi a.** so am I, so can I, so do I, so shall I, so did I, so was I, *etc.*; **et moi a. je suis peintre,** and I too am a painter; **"J'ai froid"—"Moi a.",** "I'm cold"—"So am I"; **il a refusé et son associé a.,** he declined and so did his partner; **"Je reviendrai"—"Moi a.",** "I shall come back"—"So shall I"; (iii) *F:* **a. sec,** like a flash; **il vit le lapin et a. sec il tira,** he saw the rabbit and fired immediately; (*d*) *conj.phr.* **a. bien que,** as well as, (both) . . . and . . .; **Aristote, a. bien que Platon, affirme que . . .,** Aristotle, as well as Plato, asserts that . . .; **le paysan a. bien que sa femme se frottaient les mains,** (both) the peasant and his wife rubbed their hands; (*e*) **a. léger qu'il soit . . .,** however light it may be; **a. bizarre que cela me semblât . . .,** although it seemed to me very peculiar . . . **2.** *conj.* (*a*) therefore, consequently, so; **la vie est chère ici, a. nous devons, devons-nous, économiser,** the cost of living is dear here, so (that), consequently, we have to economize; **c'est une belle étoffe, a. coûte-t-elle cher,** it is a fine material, but then it is expensive; (*b*) *F:* **a., c'est ta faute,** after all, it's your fault; (*c*) **a. bien,** moreover, for that matter, in any case, besides, and as a matter of fact, though; *A:* **elle est pauvre, a. bien elle ne lui plaît pas,** she is poor, moreover he is not attracted by her; **venez comme vous êtes, a. bien personne ne fait de toilette,** come as you are, indeed no one is dressing (up); **il faut patienter un peu, a. bien n'avez-vous que vingt ans,** you must have patience, after all, you are only twenty.

aussière [osjɛːr], *s.f. Nau:* hawser; **a. de halage,** warp; **a. de touée,** stream-cable; **cordage commis en a.,** hawser-laid rope.

aussitôt [osito]. **1.** *adv.* (*a*) immediately, directly, at once, forthwith; **a. dit, a. fait,** no sooner said than done; **a. après,** immediately after; **a. après son retour je suis parti,** as soon as, the minute, he returned I left; (*b*) *conj.phr.* **a. que** + *ind.*, as soon as; **il se repentit de ses paroles a. qu'il les eut prononcées,** he repented (of) his words as soon as he had uttered them; (*c*) **a.** + *p.p.* **a. l'argent reçu je vous paierai,** as soon as I get the money I will pay you. **2.** *F: prep.* **a. son départ, je reviens,** as soon as, the minute, he is gone I shall come back; **a. son retour je lui ai écrit,** immediately on his return I wrote to him.

austénite [ostenit], *s.f. Metall:* austenite.

austénitique [ostenitik], *a. Metall:* austenitic.

auster [ostɛr], *s.m. Poet:* auster, south wind.

austère [ostɛːr], *a.* austere (life); strict (fast); severe (style); stern (countenance).

austèrement [ostɛrmɑ̃], *adv.* austerely, in an austere manner; with austerity.

austérité [osterite], *s.f.* austerity. **1.** austereness, strictness, sternness; **la période d'a.,** the days of austerity; *Pol.Ec: etc:* **mesures d'a.,** austerity measures. **2.** *usu. pl.* asceticism, strict abstinence, mortification of the flesh; **pratiquer des austérités,** to practise austerities.

austral, -als, -aux [ostral, -o], *a.* austral, southern (hemisphere, etc.); **aurore australe,** aurora australis, southern lights.

Australasie [ostralazi], *Pr.n.f. Geog:* Australasia.

australasien, -ienne [ostralazjɛ̃, -jɛn], *a. & s. Geog:* Australasian.

Australie [ostrali], *Pr.n.f. Geog:* Australia; **l'A. méridionale,** South Australia; **l'A. occidentale,** Western Australia; *A:* **L'A. septentrionale,** the Northern Territory.

australien, -ienne [ostraljɛ̃, -jɛn], *a. & s.* **1.** *Geog:* Australian; **la faune, la région, australienne,** the Notog(a)ean fauna, region. **2.** *Ethn:* Australian (aborigine).

australoïde [ostralɔid], *a. Ethn:* Australoid.

australopithèque [ostralɔpitɛk], *s.m. Paleont:* australopithecus.

Austrasie [ostrazi], *Pr.n.f. A.Geog: Hist:* Austrasia (in the east of Gaul, with capital Metz).

austrasien, -ienne [ostrazjɛ̃, -jɛn], *a. & s. Hist:* Austrasian.

austro-hongrois, -oise [ostroɔ̃grwa, -waːz], *a. & s. Hist:* Austro-Hungarian.

austro-italien, -ienne [ostroitaljɛ̃, -jɛn], *a. & s. Hist:* Austro-Italian.

autacoïde [otakɔid], *Physiol:* **1.** *a.* autacoidal. **2.** *s.m.* autacoid.

autan [otɑ̃], *s.m.* (*a*) (*in S. of Fr.*) southerly wind bringing thunderstorms; (*b*) *Poet:* boisterous wind; **braver les autans,** to brave the elements.

autant [otɑ̃], *adv.* **1.** (*a*) as much, so much; as many; so many; **je ne le savais pas a. respecté,** I did not know he was so much respected; (*of promises, etc.*) **a. en emporte le vent,** it's all idle talk, it's all gone with the wind; *s.a.* NEZ 1, OREILLE 1; **on ne peut pas en dire a. de tout le monde,** one cannot say as much for everybody; **vous avez été heureuse, mais moi je n'en puis dire a.,** you have been happy, but I cannot say as much for myself; **il a cinq voitures, tout le monde n'en a pas a.,** he has five cars, not everyone has so many; **je consens, mais à charge d'a.,** I consent, but on condition that I do the same for you; **a. vous l'aimez, a. il vous hait,** he hates you as much as you love him; **tout a.,** quite as much, quite as many; **encore a., une fois a.,** twice as much, as much again, as many again; **deux fois a.,** twice as much; **rendre à qn six fois a.,** to repay s.o. sixfold; *F:* **cela vaut a.,** it's just as well; **j'aimerais a. aller au cinéma,** I would just as soon go to the cinema; **il se leva, j'en fis a.,** he got up, and I did the same, and I followed suit; **j'en ai fait a. pour elle,** I did as much, the same, for her; (*b*) **a. vaut,** (i) **le travail est fini ou a. vaut,** the work is as good as finished; **a. vaut rester ici,** we may as well stay here; **a. vaudrait dire que . . .,** one might as well say that . . .; (ii) (*with ellipsis of* **valoir**) **ils ont a. dire accepté,** they have practically accepted; **cela vous coûtera neuf cent quatre-vingt-dix-sept francs, a. dire mille,** that will cost you nine hundred and ninety-seven francs, let us say a thousand, we might as well say a thousand, (that is) to all intents and purposes a thousand; **la bataille était a. dire perdue,** the battle was as good as lost; **a. le faire tout de suite que de le différer,** better do it straightaway than put it off; **a. ne rien faire du tout,** we might as well do nothing at all; *s.a.* AIMER 1. **2. a. que,** (*a*) as much as, as many as; **a. que possible,** as much as possible; **a. que de besoin,** as much as is necessary; **faites a. que vous pourrez,** do as much as you can; **j'en sais a. que toi,** your guess is as good as mine; **cette voiture vaut a. que celle-ci,** that car is worth as much as this one; **c'est a. ta faute que la mienne,** it is as much your fault as mine; **il est libéral a. que riche,** he is as generous as he is wealthy; **il est a. à craindre qu'elle,** he is as much to be feared as she is; **l'homme n'est responsable qu'a. qu'il est libre, que pour a. qu'il est, soit, libre,** man is responsible only in as much as he is free; **venez tous, a. que vous soyez,** come all of you, however many you may be, however many of you there are; **tous a. que nous sommes,** all of us; *F:* **a. ça qu'autre chose,** it's all the same to me; I don't really care which; it's no worse, better, than anything else; (*b*) as far as, as near as; **a. qu'il est possible, a. que faire se peut,** as far as it is possible; **a. que j'en puis(se) juger,** as far as I can judge; **(pour) a. que, d'a. que, je puisse m'en souvenir, a. qu'il m'en souvienne, qu'il m'en souvient, que je m'en souviens,** as far, as near, as I can remember . . ., to the best of my recollection . . .; *s.a.* SAVOIR I. 2; **cela n'a d'utilité qu'a. qu'on sache comment le faire fonctionner,** it's of no use unless one knows how to operate it; **elle n'a d'intérêt qu'a. qu'elle est riche,** she is interesting only in so far as she is well-off; **pour a. qu'il est en mon pouvoir . . .,** within the limits of my power, my authority . . .; (*c*) **a. qu'il ait plu, la rivière ne déborde pas,** however much it has rained the river doesn't overflow; **a. que nous désirions vous aider . . .,** much as we would like to help you . . . **3. a. de,** as much, as many, so much, so many; (*a*) **ils ont a. de terrain, a. d'amis, que vous,** they have as much land, as many friends, as you; **il n'y a pas a. de messieurs que de dames,** there are not as many gentlemen as (there are) ladies; *Prov:* **a. de têtes a. d'avis,** so many men, so many minds; **ce sont a. de (voleurs,** *etc.*), they are nothing better than (a pack of thieves, etc.); they are just so many (thieves, etc.); **se battre avec a. d'audace que d'habileté,** to fight with no less daring than skill; **les garçons grimpent comme a. de singes,** the boys climb like so many monkeys; (*b*) **ce sera a. de moins à payer,** it will be so much the less to pay; **c'est a. de gagné,** it is so much gained, so much to the good; **c'est a. de fait,** it is so much done, so much accomplished; *s.a.* PRENDRE I. 2. **4. d'autant,** (*a*) *A:* **nous mangeâmes comme quatre et bûmes d'a.,** we ate copiously and drank likewise, in proportion; *A:* **boire d'a.,** to drink copiously; **cela augmente d'a. nos rentes,** that increases our incomes accordingly, proportionately; (*b*) **en voyageant pendant quelques mois vous vous soustrairez d'a. à vos soucis journaliers,** if you travel for a few months you will to that extent escape your day-to-day worries; *conj.phr.* **d'a. que . . ., d'a. plus que . . .,** more especially as . . .; **vous devriez faire un grand voyage, d'a. (plus) que vous êtes riche,** you ought to go for a long trip, (more) especially, particularly, as you are well-off; (*c*) **d'a. plus, moins,** (all, so much) the more, the less; **s'il a le courage de ses convictions je l'en aime d'a. plus,** if he has the courage of his convictions I like him (all) the better, the more, for it; **ses défauts me le rendent d'a. plus cher,** I love him all the better, the more, for his faults; **avoir d'a. moins à faire,** to have (so much) the less to do; (*d*) (i) **d'a. plus, moins, . . . que . . .,** (all) the more, the less, . . . as . . .; **je le conçois d'a. mieux que . . .,** I can understand it all the better because . . .; **la chaleur se conserve d'a. mieux que vous laissez les fenêtres fermées,** you keep the heat in better if you leave the windows shut; **je suis d'a. plus surpris que . . .,** I am all the more surprised because . . .; **j'en suis surpris, d'a. plus qu'au fond il est honnête,** I am surprised, all the more so because basically he is honest; **cela vous sera d'a. plus facile que vous êtes jeune,** it will be all the easier for you as you are young; (ii) **les aiguilles sont d'a. meilleures que leur pointe est fine,** the sharper the point, the better the needle; **on attache d'a. plus de prix aux joies de la vie qu'elles sont moins nombreuses,** the fewer the joys of life, the more we value them. **5.** *Golf:* **a.,** the like. **6. pour a.,** for all that; **elle ne s'en fait pas pour a.,** she doesn't worry for all that.

autarchie [otarʃi], *s.f. Pol:* **1.** autarchy, despotism. **2.** self-government.

autarcie [otarsi], *s.f.* national economic self-sufficiency; autarky.

autarcique [otarsik], *a.* autarkic(al).

autécologie [ɛtekɔlɔʒi], *s.f. Biol:* autecology.

autel [otɛl], *s.m.* **1.** altar; **maître a.,** high altar; **a. latéral,** side altar; **a. improvisé,** table altar; **nappe d'a.,** altar cloth; **pierre d'a.,** altar stone, altar table; **tableau d'a.,** altarpiece; **s'approcher de l'a.,** (i) to celebrate Mass; (ii) to take communion; **conduire qn à l'a.,** (i) to give s.o. away (in marriage); (ii) to marry s.o., to lead s.o. to the altar; **qui sert à l'a. doit vivre de l'a.,** a man lives by his profession; **il mérite des autels,** he deserves every honour; **élever qn sur les autels,** to canonize s.o.; **dresser un a.,** to set up an altar; **dresser des autels à qn,** to make a god of s.o.; **le Trône et l'A.,** the monarchy and the church; **parée comme l'a. de la Vierge,** decked out in all her finery; *A:* **il prendrait sur l'a.,** he would rob even a church. **2.** *Metall: Mch:* furnace bridge, fire bridge; fire stop. **3.** *Astr:* **l'A.,** Ara, the Altar.

auteur [otœːr], *s.m.* **1.** (*a*) author, maker, originator; founder (of race); perpetrator (of crime); contriver, promoter, sponsor (of scheme); *Lit:* **l'a. de ses jours,** his father; **a. d'un procédé,** inventor, originator of a process; **a. d'une commande,** giver of a (trade) order; **a. d'un accident,** party at fault in an accident; **a. d'une prise, d'une capture,** capturer; **être l'a. de la ruine de qn,** to be the cause of s.o.'s downfall; **les auteurs de nos jours,** our progenitors, the fathers that begat us; (*b*) *Jur:* principal; **a. principal,** principal in the first degree. **2.** (*a*)

author, writer (of book); composer (of song); painter (of picture); femme a., woman writer, authoress; **droit d'a.**, copyright; **droits d'a.**, royalties; **un droit d'a. de 10%**, a royalty of 10%; (*b*) **citer ses auteurs**, to quote one's authorities; *s.a.* COMPTE.

authente [otɑ̃:t], *a. A.Mus:* authentic.

authenticité [otɑ̃tisite], *s.f.* authenticity, genuineness.

authentification [otɑ̃tifikasjɔ̃], *s.f.* authentication; **cachet d'a.**, approved stamp.

authentifier [otɑ̃tifje], *v.tr.* (*pr.sub. & p.d.* **n. authentifiions, v. authentifiiez**) = AUTHENTIQUER.

authentique [otɑ̃tik], *a.* authentic, genuine; *Mus:* authentic (cadence, mode); **c'est un fait a.**, it's a positive fact; **bourgogne a.**, genuine burgundy; *Jur:* **acte a.**, instrument drawn up by a solicitor; **copie a.**, certified copy, exemplified copy, exemplification; *Fin:* **cours a.**, official quotation.

authentiquement [otɑ̃tikmɑ̃], *adv.* authentically, genuinely.

authentiquer [otɑ̃tike], *v.tr.* to authenticate, certify, legalize (document, etc.).

authigène [otiʒɛn], *a. Geol:* authigenic, authigenous.

autisme [otism], *s.m. Psy:* autism.

autiste [otist], *a. Psy:* autist.

autistique [otistik], *a, Psy:* autistic.

auto [oto, ɔto], *s.f. F:* (= AUTOMOBILE) (motor) car; **aller en a. jusqu'à Paris**, to drive, motor, to Paris.

auto- [oto, ɔto], *pref.* **1.** auto-; **autocéphale**, autocephalous (bishop, etc.); **autogamie**, autogamy. **2.** self-; **auto-accusateur**, self-accuser; **auto-équilibrant**, self-balancing. **3.** motor; **autoroute**, motorway.

auto-accusateur [otoakyzatœ:r, ɔto-], *s.m. Psy:* self-accuser.

auto-accusation [otoakyzasjɔ̃, ɔto-], *s.f.* self-accusation.

auto-alarme [otoalarm, ɔto-], *s.m. W.Tel:* auto-alarm.

auto-alimentation [otoalimɑ̃tasjɔ̃], *s.f. Tchn:* self-feed.

auto-allumage [otoalyma:ʒ, ɔto-], *s.m. I.C.E:* **1.** self-ignition, spontaneous ignition, auto-ignition. **2.** pre-ignition, *F:* pinking; *pl. des auto-allumages.*

auto-amorçage [otoamɔrsa:ʒ, ɔto-], *s.m.* automatic priming (of pump engine, etc.).

auto-amorceur, -euse [otoamɔrsœ:r, -øz, ɔto-], *a.* self-priming.

auto-amputation [otoɑ̃pytasjɔ̃, ɔto-], *s.f. Z:* autotomy, self-amputation.

autobiographe [otobjɔgraf, ɔto-], *s.m. & f.* autobiographer.

autobiographie [otobjɔgrafi, ɔto-], *s.f.* autobiography.

autobiographique [otobjɔgrafik, ɔto-], *a.* autobiographic(al).

autobus [ɔtɔbys, oto-], *s.m. Aut:* (motor) bus; **a. à étage**, double-decker bus; **nous y sommes allés en a.**, we went there by bus.

autocar [ɔtɔka:r, oto-], *s.m.* (*a*) (motor) coach; **a. de luxe**, luxury coach; (*b*) (country) bus.

autocatalyse [otokataliz, ɔto-], *s.f. Ch:* autocatalysis.

autocensure [otosɑ̃syr, ɔt-], *s.f. F:* self-criticism.

autocéphale [otosefal, ɔt-], *Ecc:* (*Gr. orthodox Ch:*) **1.** *a.* autocephalous. **2.** *s.m.* autocephalous church, bishop, etc.

autocéphalie [otosefali, ɔto-], *s.f. Ecc:* (*Gr. orthodox Ch:*) autocephaly.

autochenille [otoʃnij, ɔt-], *s.f.* caterpillar-tractor; half-track vehicle.

autochrome [otokro:m, ɔt-], *a. & s.f. A.Phot:* autochrome (plate).

autochromie [otokrɔmi, ɔt-], *s.f. A.Phot:* autochromy.

autochtone [ɔtɔktɔn, otokto:n]. **1.** *a.* autochthonal, autochthonous; aboriginal (race, plant, etc.). **2.** *s.* autochthon.

autochtonie [ɔtɔktɔni], *s.f. Geol:* autochtony.

autochtonisme [ɔtɔktɔnism], *s.m.* autochtonism.

autocinésie [otosinezi, ɔt-], *s.f. Physiol:* autokinesis.

autoclave [ɔtɔkla:v, ot-]. **1.** *a.* hermetically-sealed, pressure-sealed. **2.** *s.m.* (*a*) *Ch: Ind:* (**marmite**) **a.**, autoclave, digester; **a. à blanchiment**, kier, keir; *Sug.-R:* **a. à vide**, vacuum-pan; (*b*) *Bac: Med:* sterilizer; (*c*) *O: Cu:* pressure cooker. **3.** *s.m. Mch:* **a. d'un trou d'homme**, manhole lid, door.

autocoat [otoko:t], *s.m.* motoring, driving, coat.

autocollant [otokɔlɑ̃, ɔt-], *a.* self-adhesive.

autoconsommation [otokɔ̃sɔmasjɔ̃, ɔt-], *s.f. Pol.Ec:* subsistence farming.

autocopie [otokɔpi, ɔt-], *s.f.* **1.** duplicating, manifolding (of documents). **2.** (duplicated) copy.

autocopier [otokɔpje, ɔt-], *v.tr.* (*pr.sub. & p.d.* **n. autocopiions, v. autocopiiez**) to duplicate, manifold (document).

autocopiste [otokɔpist, ɔt-], *s.m.* duplicator; manifolding, copying machine; *s.a.* PAPIER.

autocrate, -trice [ɔtɔkrat, -tris, ot-]. **1.** *s.* autocrat, *A: f.* autocratix. **2.** *a.m. & f.* **autocrate,** autocratic.

autocratie [ɔtɔkrasi, ot-], *s.f.* autocracy.

autocratique [ɔtɔkratik, ot-], *a.* autocratic.

autocratiquement [ɔtɔkratikmɑ̃, ot-], *adv.* autocratically.

autocratrice. *See* AUTOCRATE 1.

autocritique [otokritik, ɔt-], *s.f.* self-criticism.

autocuiseur [otokɥizœ:r, ɔt-], *s.m. Dom.Ec:* pressure-cooker.

autocycle [otosikl, ɔt-], *s.m. A. & Adm:* motor bicycle, tricycle.

autodafé [otodafe, ɔt-], *s.m. Hist:* auto-da-fé; **faire un a. de ses manuscrits,** to commit one's manuscripts to the flames.

autodébrayage [otodebrɛja:ʒ, ɔt-], *s.m. Aut:* automatic clutch.

autodéfense [otodefɑ̃:s, ɔt-], *s.f.* self-defence.

auto-démarrage [otodemara:ʒ, ɔt-], *s.m. Mch: I.C.E: etc:* self-starting.

autodémarreur [otodemarœ:r, ɔt-]. *A:* **1.** *a.m.* self-starting (device). **2.** *s.m.* self-starter.

autodestructeur [otodɛstryktœ:r], *a.* self-destroying.

autodestruction [otodɛstryksjɔ̃, ɔt-], *s.f.* self-destruction.

autodétermination [otodeterminasjɔ̃, ɔt-], *s.f. Pol:* self-determination.

autodidacte [otodidakt, ɔt-]. **1.** *a.* (*a*) self-taught, self-educated; (*b*) intuitive, innate (idea). **2.** *s.* autodidact, self-educated person.

autodidaxie [otodidaksi, ɔt-], *s.f.* self-culture.

autodigestion [otodiʒɛstjɔ̃, ɔt-], *s.f. Med:* autodigestion, autopepsia.

autodrome [otodro:m, ɔt-], *s.m.* motor-racing track; car-testing track.

autodyne [otodin, ɔt-], *s.m. W.Tel:* autodyne.

auto-école [otoekɔl, ɔt-], *s.f.* school of motoring, driving school; *pl. auto-écoles.*

auto-érotique [otoerɔtik, ɔt-], *a. Psy:* autoerotic.

auto-érotisme [otoerɔtism, ɔt-], *s.m. Psy:* autoeroti(ci)sm.

autoexcitateur, -trice [otoɛksitatœ:r, -tris, ɔt-], *a. El.E:* self-exciting (dynamo, etc.).

autoexcitation [otoɛksitasjɔ̃, ɔt-], *s.f. El.E:* self-excitation, self-excitement; **dynamo à a.,** self-exciting dynamo.

autofécondation [otofekɔ̃dasjɔ̃, ɔt-], *s.f. Z: Bot:* self-fertilization; autogamy, autofecundation.

autofertile [otofɛrtil, ɔt-], *a.* self-fertile; self-fertilizing.

autofinancement [otofinɑ̃smɑ̃, ɔt-], *s.m. Fin:* ploughing back of profits.

autofondant [otofɔ̃dɑ̃, ɔt-], *a. Metalw:* **soudure autofondante,** self-fluxing welding.

autofrettage [otofrɛta:ʒ, ɔt-], *s.m. Mec.E:* autofrettage.

autogamie [ɔtɔgami, ot-], *s.f. Biol:* autogamy; self-fertilization.

autogare [otoga:r, ɔt-], *s.f.* coach station; bus station.

autogène [ɔtɔʒɛn, oto-], *a.* autogenous; *s.a.* SOUDER 1, SOUDURE 1.

autogénèse [ɔtɔʒenɛ:z, oto-], *s.f. Biol:* autogenesis.

autogénie [ɔtɔʒeni, oto-], *s.f. Biol:* autogeny.

autogérer [otoʒere], *v.tr:* to self-manage.

autogestion [otoʒɛstjɔ̃], *s.f.* self-management.

autogire [ɔtɔʒi:r, oto-], *s.m. Av:* autogiro.

autognose [otognoz, ɔto-], *s.f.* **autognosie** [otognozi, ɔt-], *s.f. Phil:* autognosis.

autograissage [otogrɛsa:ʒ, ɔto-], *s.m. Mec.E:* self-lubrication.

autograisseur, -euse [otogrɛsœ:r, -ø:z, ɔt-], *a. Mec.E:* self-lubricating (bearing, etc.).

autographe [ɔtɔgraf, ot-]. **1.** *a.* autograph; handwritten (letter, etc.). **2.** *s.m.* (*a*) autograph; (*b*) *A:* copying machine.

autographie [ɔtɔgrafi, ot-], *s.f.* autolithography.

autographier [ɔtɔgrafje, ot-], *v.tr.* (*pr.sub. & p.d.* **n. autographiions, v. autographiiez**) to autograph; (*a*) to write (sth.) in one's own hand; (*b*) to make a facsimile of (letter, etc.).

autographique [ɔtɔgrafik, oto-], *a.* autographic; *Lith:* **encre a.,** transfer-ink.

autographisme [ɔtɔgrafism, oto-], *s.m. Med:* autographism.

autogreffe [otogrɛf, ɔt-], *s.f. Surg:* autograft.

autoguidage [otogida:ʒ, ɔt-], *s.m.* (**retour par**) **a.,** homing; **cellule d'a.,** homing eye.

autoguidé [otogide, ɔt-], *a.* self-guided, self-directional, homing (missile).

autogyre [ɔtɔʒi:r, oto-], *s.m. Av:* autogyro.

auto-hémorrhée [otoemɔre], *s.f. Ent:* bleeding reflexes (in insects).

autohémothérapie [otoemɔterapi, ɔt-], *s.f. Med:* autohemotherapy.

auto-inductance [otoɛ̃dyktɑ̃:s, ɔt-], *s.f. El:* self-inductance; **bobine d'a.-i.,** self-inductance coil.

auto-induction [otoɛ̃dyksjɔ̃, ɔt-], *s.f. El:* self-induction.

auto-infection [otoɛ̃fɛksjɔ̃, ɔto-], *s.f. Med:* auto-infection.

auto-intoxication [otoɛ̃tɔksikasjɔ̃, ɔt-], *s.f. Med:* auto-intoxication.

autojustification [otozystifikasjɔ̃], *s.f.* self-justification.

autolubrifiant [otolybrifjɑ̃, ɔto-], *a. Mec.E:* self-lubricating.

autolubrification [otolybrifikasjɔ̃, ɔto-], *s.f. Mec.E:* self-lubrication.

autolyse [ɔtɔli:z, oto-], *s.f. Physiol:* autolysis.

autolytique [ɔtɔlitik, oto-], *a. Physiol:* autolytic (process).

auto-marché [otomarʃe, ɔto-], *s.m.* car mart; *pl. auto-marchés.*

automate [ɔtɔmat, otɔ-], *s.m.* automaton, robot; **n'être qu'un a.,** to be a mere machine, an automaton.

automaticité [ɔtɔmatisite, ot-], *s.f.* automatic working.

automation [ɔtɔmasjɔ̃, ot-], *s.f.* automation.

automatique [ɔtɔmatik, ot-]. **1.** *a.* automatic (action); self-acting (apparatus); **à mise en marche a.,** self-starting; *A:* **plume à remplissage a.,** self-filling pen; *s.a.* DISTRIBUTEUR 2. **2.** *s.m.* (*a*) automatic (telephone); (*b*) automatic (pistol). **3.** *s.f. Tchn:* (*a*) automatics; (*b*) automation.

automatiquement [ɔtɔmatikmɑ̃, ot-], *adv.* automatically; **système (de tenue de livres) contrôlé a.,** self-checking system (of book-keeping).

automatisation [ɔtɔmatizasjɔ̃, ot-], *s.f.* automatization; automation.

automatiser [ɔtɔmatize, ot-], *v.tr.* to automatize, to automate.

automatisme [ɔtɔmatism, ot-], *s.m.* **1.** *Physiol: Med:* automatism. **2.** *Tchn:* (*a*) automatic working; **à a. poussé,** highly automatized, automated; (*b*) automatic device.

automatiste [ɔtɔmatist, ot-], *s.m. & f.* automatist.

Automédon [otomedɔ̃, ɔt-]. **1.** *Pr.n.m. Gr.Myth:* Automedon. **2.** *s.m. Hum: A:* **un a.,** a cabby, a (regular) Jehu.

auto-mitrailleur [otomitrajœ:r, ɔt-], *s.m. Mil:* member of an armoured car crew; *pl. auto-mitrailleurs.*

auto-mitrailleuse [otomitrajø:z, ɔt-], *s.f. Mil:* armoured car; *pl. auto-mitrailleuses.*

automnal, -aux [otɔ(m)nal, ɔt-, -o], *a.* autumnal.

automne [otɔn, ɔt-], *s.m. occ. f.* autumn, *U.S:* fall; **l'équinoxe d'a.,** the autumnal equinox; **en a., à l'a.,** in autumn; **à l'a. de 1694,** in the autumn of 1694; **une soirée d'a.,** an autumn evening; **l'a. de la vie,** the autumn of life.

automobile [ɔtɔmɔbil, ot-]. **1.** *a.* (*a*) self-propelling; **voiture a.,** motor vehicle; **canot a.,** motor boat; (*b*) **club a.,** automobile club; **assurance a.,** car, motor, insurance; **accessoires automobiles,** car accessories; *s.a.* FIACRE, INDUSTRIE. **2.** *s.f.* (motor) car, *U.S:* automobile; *Mil:* **a. blindée,** armoured car; **salon de l'a.,** motor show; **termes techniques de l'a.,** technical motoring terms.

automobilisme [ɔtɔmɔbilism, ot-], *s.m.* motoring.

automobiliste [ɔtɔmɔbilist, ot-], *s.m. & f.* motorist.

automolite [ɔtɔmɔlit, ot-], *s.f. Miner:* automolite.

automorphe [ɔtɔmɔrf, ot-], *a. Miner:* idiomorphic, automorphic.

automoteur, -trice [otomɔtœ:r, -tris, ɔt-]. **1.** *a.* self-propelling (vehicle); self-acting (valve, etc.); **train a.,** multiple-unit Diesel train; **canon a.,** self-propelled gun; *s.a.* PLAN[1] 2. **2.** *s.f.* **automotrice,** self-propelling railway coach, railcar. **3.** *s.m. Nau:* self-propelled barge.

automutilation [otomytilasjɔ̃, ɔt-], *s.f.* self-mutilation.

auto-neige [otonɛ:ʒ, ɔt-], *s.f. Fr.C:* snowmobile.

autonome [ɔtɔnɔm, otono:m], *a.* autonomous, self-governing; independent (state, army, etc.); self-contained (apparatus); *s.a.* SCAPHANDRE 2, PLONGEUR 2.

autonomie [ɔtɔnɔmi, ot-], *s.f.* (*a*) autonomy; self-government; independence; (*b*) self-sufficiency; (*c*) *Tchn:* cruising radius, range; (*d*) *Av:* endurance.

autonomisme [ɔtɔnɔmism, ot-], *s.m.* autonomism.

autonomiste [ɔtɔnɔmist, ot-], (*a*) *s.m.* autonomist; (*b*) *a.* with autonomist tendencies.

autonyme [ɔtɔnim, ot-], *a.* autonymous; **ouvrage a.**, autonym.

autopatin [otopatɛ̃, ɔt-], *s.m. A:* motor trolley.

autophagie [ɔtɔfaʒi, ot-], *s.f. Med: Biol:* autophagy; autophagia.

autophagique [ɔtɔfaʒik, oto-], *a.* autophagous.

autoplastie [ɔtɔplasti, oto-], *s.f. Surg:* autoplasty, anaplasty; plastic surgery.

autoplastique [ɔtɔplastik, oto-], *a. Surg:* autoplastic, anaplastic.

autopompe [otopɔ̃p, ɔt-], *s.f.* fire-engine.

autoportant [otopɔrtɑ̃, ɔt-], *a.*, **autoporteur, -euse** [otopɔrtœːr, -øːz, ɔt-], *a. Aut:* **coque autoporteuse**, integral all-steel welded body, monopiece body; *Arch:* **voûte autoportante**, self-supporting vault.

auto-portrait [otopɔrtrɛ, ɔt-], *s.m.* self-portrait; *pl. auto-portraits.*

autopropulsé [otoprɔpylse, ɔt-], *a.* self-propelled, -propelling.

autopropulsion [otoprɔpylsjɔ̃, ɔt-], *s.f.* self-propulsion; **à a.**, self-propelled, -propelling.

auto-protection [otoprɔtɛksjɔ̃, ɔt-], *s.f.* self-protection.

autopsie [ɔtɔpsi, ot-], *s.f.* autopsy; **a. (cadavérique)**, post-mortem (examination).

autopsier [ɔtɔpsje, ot-], *v.tr.* to perform a post-mortem (examination) upon; *U.S:* to autopsy.

autoptique [ɔtɔptik, ot-], *a.* autoptic.

autopunition [otopynisjɔ̃, ɔt-], *s.f. Psy:* self-punishment.

autor [ɔtɔːr, ot-], *s.m. P:* = AUTORITÉ; *used only in the phrases* **faire qch. d'a.**, to do sth. on one's own (responsibility), off one's own bat; **travailler d'a. et d'achar**, to work like a nigger (**à qch.**, at sth.); to put one's back into it.

autoradiogramme [otoradjɔgram, ɔt-], *s.m.* autoradiogram, autoradiograph.

autoradiographie [otoradjɔgrafi, ɔt-], *s.f.* **1.** autoradiography. **2.** autoradiograph, autoradiogram.

autorail [otorɑːj, ɔtoraj], *s.m.* rail-car.

auto-régénérateur, -trice [otoregeneratœːr, -tris, ɔt-], *a. Atom.Ph:* breeder (reactor, etc.).

autoréglage [otoreglaːʒ, ɔt-], *s.m. Tchn:* automatic regulating.

autorégulateur, -trice [otoregylatœr, -tris, ɔt-], *Mec.E:* **1.** *a.* self-regulating. **2.** *s.m.* self-acting regulator.

autorégulation [otoregylasjɔ̃, ɔt-], *s.f.* automatic regulation; **à a.**, self-regulating, self-regulatory.

auto-relieur [otorəljœːr, ɔt-], *s.m.* spring-back binder; *pl. auto-relieurs.*

autorisable [ɔtɔrizabl̩, ot-], *a. Jur:* authorizable, allowable.

autorisation [ɔtɔrizasjɔ̃, ot-], *s.f.* **1.** (*a*) authorization, authority; permission; permit; **donner à qn une a. pour faire qch.**, to authorize s.o. to do sth.; **a. spéciale**, special permit; **a. d'exporter**, export permit; (*b*) *Av:* **a. de vol**, flight clearance. **2.** licence; **a. de colportage**, pedlar's licence; **avoir l'a. de vendre qch.**, to be licensed to sell sth.; **avec l'a. de l'auteur**, with the author's sanction, under licence from the author.

autorisé [ɔtɔrize, ot-], *a.* **1.** authorized, authoritative; of approved authority; **tenir qch. d'une source autorisée**, to have sth. from an authoritative source; *F:* from the horse's mouth. **2.** *Breed:* approved (stallion, etc.).

autoriser [ɔtɔrize, ot-], *v.tr.* **1.** to invest (s.o.) with authority; **a. qn à faire qch.**, to authorize, empower, s.o. to do sth., to give s.o. authority to do sth.; **il faut que le projet soit autorisé par le conseil municipal**, the plan must be passed by the town council. **2.** to justify, authorize, sanction (an action); **ces découvertes autorisent à penser que . . .**, these discoveries entitle us to believe that . . .; **la comédie autorise une certaine familiarité**, comedy allows of a certain familiarity. **3.** to allow, permit, give permission, leave, (to do sth.); **la pêche est autorisée**, fishing is free.

s'autoriser. **1.** to establish one's authority; to become authorized. **2. s'a. de qn, de qch.**, to act on the authority of s.o., sth.; **il s'autorise de votre exemple**, he cites your example as his authority.

autoritaire [ɔtɔritɛːr, ot-]. **1.** *a.* authoritative, dictatorial, overbearing, self-assertive, *F:* bossy. **2.** *s.m.* authoritarian.

autoritairement [ɔtɔritɛrmɑ̃, ot-], *adv.* authoritatively; in an overbearing, dictatorial, manner.

autoritarisme [ɔtɔritarism, ot-], *s.m.* **1.** authoritarianism. **2.** *F:* bossiness.

autorité [ɔtɔrite, ot-], *s.f.* **1.** (*a*) authority; **avoir a. sur qn**, to have authority over s.o.; **exercer son a. sur qn**, to exercise authority over s.o.; **a. paternelle**, parental authority; **régime d'a.**, autocratic régime; **coup d'a.**, decisive blow; **il veut tout emporter d'a.**, he wants his own way in everything, *F:* he wants to run the whole show; **agir de pleine a.**, to act with full powers; **faire acte d'a.**, to bring one's authority to bear; **faire qch. de son a. privée, de sa propre a.**, to do sth. on one's own authority; **faire qch. d'a.**, to do sth. on one's own (responsibility), off one's own bat, to take it upon oneself to do sth.; **agir sur l'a. de qn**, to act on s.o.'s authority; **territoire soumis à l'a. de . . .**, area within the jurisdiction of . . .; **échapper à toute a.**, to break loose from all control; **corps doué de l'a. suffisante pour . . .**, body sufficiently authoritative to . . .; *Cards:* **jouer d'a.**, to stand pat; (*b*) **l'a. de l'âge, de l'expérience**, the authority of age, of experience; **avoir de l'a. sur qn**, to have influence, authority, over s.o.; **faire a., être une a., en matière de faïence**, to be an authority on china; *Jur:* **cas d'espèce qui font a.**, leading cases; **cette édition de Shakespeare fait a.**, this edition of Shakespeare is the authoritative one; **ton d'a.**, imperious, authoritative, tone; **parler avec a.**, to speak authoritatively, with authority; **sa parole a de l'a.**, his word carries weight. **2.** (*a*) **l'a. fiscale**, the (income) tax people; **les agents de l'a.**, the police force; **intervention de l'a.**, intervention of the armed forces; **les autorités (d'une ville, etc.)** the authorities (of a town, etc.); **les autorités constituées**, the powers that be; **les autorités militaires**, the military authorities; (*b*) **citer une a.**, to quote an authority; to quote chapter and verse. **3.** control (**sur**, over); **ce professeur n'a pas d'a. sur ses élèves**, this teacher has no control over his pupils, cannot keep order.

autorotation [otorɔtasjɔ̃, ɔt-], *s.f. Aer:* autorotation; (*d'un réacteur*) **tourner en a.**, to windmill; **a. du réacteur**, engine windmilling.

autoroute [otorut, -ɔt], *s.f.* motorway, *U.S:* freeway, superhighway; **a. à péage**, toll motorway, *U.S:* turnpike road.

autoroutier, -ière [otorutje, -jɛːr, ɔt-], *a.* **système a.**, motorway system, network.

autorupteur [otoryptœːr, ɔt-], *s.m. El.E:* make-and-break device.

autoscooter [otoskutɛːr, ɔt-, -œːr], *s.m.* light three-wheeled delivery van.

autoscopie [ɔtɔskɔpi, oto-], *s.f. Psy:* autoscopy.

autosérothérapie [otoserɔterapi, ɔt-], *s.f. Med:* autoserotherapy.

autosome [otozoːm, ɔt-], *s.m. Biol:* autosome.

autosomique [otozɔmik, ɔt-], *a. Med:* autosomal.

autostable [otostabl̩, ɔt-], *a. Aer:* self-stabilizing.

autostérile [otosteril, ɔt-], *a. Bot:* self-sterile.

autostérilité [otosterilite, ɔt-], *s.f. Bot:* self-sterility.

auto-stop [otostɔp, ɔt-], *s.m.* hitch-hiking; **faire de l'a.**, to hitch-hike, *F:* to thumb a lift.

auto-stoppeur, -euse [otostɔpœːr, -øːz, ɔt-], *s.* hitch-hiker; *pl. auto-stoppeurs, auto-stoppeuses.*

autostrade [ɔtɔstrad, oto-], *s.f.* = AUTOROUTE.

autosuffisant [otosyfizɑ̃, ɔt-], *a.* self-sufficing.

autosuggestion [otosygʒɛstjɔ̃, ɔt-], *s.f.* autosuggestion.

auto-supportant [otosypɔrtɑ̃, ɔt-], *a.* free-standing.

auto-taxi [ototaksi, ɔt-], *s.m. A:* taxi(-cab); *pl. autos-taxis.*

autotest [ototest, ɔt-], *s.m. Psy: etc:* self-administered test.

autotomie [ɔtɔtɔmi, oto-], *s.f. Z:* autotomy.

autotoxine [ototɔksin, ɔt-], *s.f. Med: Physiol:* autotoxin.

auto-tracteur, -trice [ototraktœːr, -tris, ɔt-], *a.* self-propelled.

auto-transformateur [ototrɑ̃sfɔrmatœːr, ɔt-], *s.m. El.E:* autotransformer; *pl. auto-transformateurs.*

auto-trembleur [ototrɑ̃blœːr, ɔt-], *s.m. El.E:* contact-breaker; buzzer; *pl. auto-trembleurs.*

auto-trempant [ototrɑ̃pɑ̃, ɔt-], *a.* self-hardening (steel); *pl. auto-trempants.*

autotrophe [otɔtrɔf, -ɔt]. *Bot:* **1.** *a.* autotrophic (plant). **2.** *s.m.* autotroph.

autour[1] [otuːr], *adv.* **1.** round (it, them), about (it, them); **une vieille ville avec des murs tout a.**, an old town with walls all around (it); **il demeure ici a.**, he lives hereabouts; *Prov:* **il ne faut pas confondre a. avec alentour**, we must not mistake one thing for another. **2.** *prep.phr.* **a. de**, round, about; **nous nous assîmes a. de la table**, we sat down round the table; **ce qui se passe a. de nous**, what takes place round about us, around us; *F:* **il a a. de cinquante ans**, he is (somewhere) about fifty; **tourner a. de la question, a. du pot**, to beat about the bush.

autour[2], *s.m. Orn:* **a. (des palombes)**, goshawk; **a. des chauves-souris**, bat-eating buzzard.

autourserie [otursəri], *s.f. Ven:* (the art of) training goshawks.

autoursier [otursje], *s.m. Ven:* ostreger, ostringer.

autovaccin [otovaksɛ̃, ɔt-], *s.m. Med:* autovaccine.

autovaccination [otovaksinasjɔ̃, ɔt-], *s.f. Med:* autovaccination.

auto-vireur [otovirœːr, ɔt-], *a.m. Phot:* self-toning; *pl. auto-vireurs.*

autoxydable [otɔksidabl̩, ɔt-], *a. Ch:* autoxidizable.

autoyacht [otojak, -otojɔt], *s.m.* motor yacht.

autre [oːtr̥], *a. & pron.* **1.** (*a*) other, further; **les deux cents autres francs**, the other two hundred francs; **tous les autres verbes que ceux en -er**, all verbs other than those in *-er*; **je ne pourrai pas y aller; entre autres raisons je suis à court d'argent**, I can't go; for one thing I'm short of funds; **une a. semaine, un a. jour**, another week, another day; **un a. jour, une a. fois**, later; **à un a. jour, à une a. fois**, see you soon, see you later; **un jour ou l'a.**, some time or other; **les défauts des autres**, the failings of others; **d'autres vous diront que . . .**, others, other people, will tell you that . . .; **tous les autres sont là**, all the others are there; **on vous préfère à tous autres**, they prefer you to all others, to anyone else; **il y en a d'autres que lui**, there are others besides him; **encore un a.**, one more; another (one); **encore bien d'autres**, many more besides; **eh bien, et les autres?** what about the others? *F:* **les autres**, the other half; *F:* **regarde-moi ce qu'il fait, cet a.**, just look what that man over there's doing; **en voici un a. exemple**, here is another example; **c'est un a. moi-même**, he is my *alter ego;* **il se croit un a. Napoléon**, he thinks he is a second, another, Napoleon; **toute a. femme aurait agi de la même façon**, any other woman would have acted in the same way; **j'ai reçu trois cents autres francs**, I have received another three hundred francs; **les choux et autres légumes**, cabbages and (all) other vegetables; **les choux et d'autres légumes**, cabbages and some other vegetables; **de l'a. côté du champ**, on the other, farther, side of the field, across the field; **l'a. monde**, the next world, the beyond; **sans faire d'a. observation**, without making any further observation; **les autres recommendations de . . .**, the further recommendations of . . .; **sans a. perte de temps**, without further loss of time; **je n'ai pas eu d'a. mère qu'elle**, she was the only mother I ever had; **la science est une chose, l'art en est une a.**, science is one thing, art is another; **il parle d'une façon et agit d'une a.**, he says one thing and does another; **parler d'une chose et d'une a., de chose(s) et d'autre(s)**, to talk about one thing and another, about various things, about this and that, about this, that and the other; **je l'ai vu l'a. jour**, I saw him the other day; **c'était un touriste comme un a.**, he was just an ordinary tourist; **c'est une raison comme une a.**, it's as good a reason as any, it's a good enough reason, quite a plausible reason; **c'est un homme pas comme les autres**, he is an exceptional man; *F:* **je reste jusqu'à l'a. lundi**, I'm staying until Monday week; *F:* **comme dit l'a.**, as the saying goes, as they say; (*b*) (*stressing the pers. pron.*) **vous autres hommes (vous) êtes seuls coupables**, it is you men who are alone to blame; **nous autres Anglais**, we English (people); **vous autres**, you fellows, all of you; *F:* **ils n'en savent rien, eux autres**, *they* don't know anything about it; (*c*) (i) **cela peut arriver d'un jour à l'a.**, it may happen any day; **je l'attends d'un moment à l'a.**, I expect him any moment; **je le vois de temps à a.**, I see him now and again, now and then; (ii) **sa réputation grandit d'une année à l'a.**, his fame is increasing from year to year; (*d*) **l'un et l'a.**, both; **les uns et les autres**, (i) all (and sundry), one and all; (ii) both parties; **il a parlé aux uns et aux autres**, he spoke to them all, every one of them; **l'un et l'a. a été puni, ont été punis**, both were punished; (*e*) **l'un ou l'a.**, either; **ni l'un ni l'a.**, neither; **comme l'une ou l'a. me rendrait heureux!** how happy could I be with either! **ni l'un ni l'a. ne sont venus**, neither of them came; (*occ. with sg. concord*) **jamais ni l'un ni l'a. n'en parle**, neither of them ever speaks of it; **je ne les connais ni l'un ni l'a.**, I don't know either of them; **je n'ai vu ni les uns ni les autres**, I didn't see any of them; **est-elle heureuse ou seulement contente?—ni l'un ni l'a.**, is she happy or merely satisfied?—neither (the one nor the other); (*f*) **l'un . . ., l'a. . . .**, one . . ., the other . . .; **l'un dit ceci, l'a. dit cela**, one says this and the other says that; **les uns**

. . ., **les autres, . . .,** some . . ., others . . .; some . . ., some . . .; **ils s'en allèrent les uns par ci les autres par là,** they went off some one way, some another; **sans prendre parti pour les uns ni pour les autres,** without taking either side; **le dimanche il va toujours chez l'un ou chez l'a.,** on Sundays he always goes out visiting; **l'un ne va pas sans l'a.,** you can't have one without the other; **qui voit l'un voit l'a.,** there's no difference between them, you can't tell the two apart; **l'un vaut l'a.,** there's no difference between them, the one's just as bad as the other; (*g*) **l'un l'a.,** each other, one another; **lui et sa femme s'admirent l'un l'a.,** he and his wife admire each other, one another; **elles se moquent les unes des autres,** they make fun of each other; **on va les uns chez les autres,** we call on each other; **l'un auprès de l'a., auprès l'un de l'a.,** near each other, near one another; (*h*) **l'un dans l'a., l'un portant l'a., on se fait trente francs,** one thing with another, on an average, we earn thirty francs; **une année dans l'a.,** taking one year with another; (i) *A:* **l'a.,** (i) the devil; (ii) Napoleon. **2.** (*a*) other, different; **j'ai maintenant une a. maison,** I have got a new house, different house, now; *Prov:* **autres temps autres mœurs,** other days other ways; manners change with the times; **quand je le revis je le trouvai (tout) a.,** when I saw him again I found him (quite) different, altered; **il est a. que je ne le pensais,** he is different from what I thought; **cela a fait de lui un a. homme,** it made a new man of him; it reformed him; **une tout a. femme,** quite a different woman; **le père était un tout, bien, a. homme que son fils,** the son could not hold a candle to, could not be compared to, his father; **j'ai des idées autres,** I have different ideas, my ideas are different; **elle a de bien autres idées,** she has very different ideas; **être d'une a. opinion,** to think otherwise; **c'est tout (l')un ou tout (l')a.,** there is no happy medium, it's either one thing or the other; *F:* **en voilà bien d'une a.!** here we go again! **j'en sais d'autres,** I can do better than that; **"Que penses-tu de ce café?—J'en ai eu d'autre,"** "What do you think of this coffee?" "I've had better"; **j'en ai vu bien d'autres,** that's nothing, I've been through worse than that; **il n'en fait jamais d'autres!** that's just like him! he always makes the same mistakes! (*b*) (someone, something) else; **adressez-vous à un a., à quelqu'un d'a.,** ask someone else, somebody else; **je l'ai pris pour un a.,** I mistook him for s.o. else; **il n'est pas plus bête qu'un a.,** he is no more stupid than anyone else; **nul a., personne (d') a., ne l'a vu,** no one else, nobody else, saw him; **je ne demande rien d'a.,** I don't ask for anything more; I ask for nothing more; **que pouvait-il faire d'a.?** what else could he do? **que pouvaient-ils faire d'a. que de l'inviter?** what could they do but invite him? **qui d'a. que lui aurait pu le faire?** who else could have done it (apart from him)? **(dites cela) à d'autres!** nonsense! don't tell me! I know better! tell that to the marines! (*c*) *indef. pron. m.* (i) **a. chose,** something else; something different; **j'ai a. chose d'important à vous dire,** I have something else of importance to tell you; **avez-vous a. chose à faire?** have you anything else to do? **c'est a. chose que je n'avais d'abord pensé,** it is different from what I had first thought; (ii) **a. chose, ma mère est partie hier,** and another thing, not only that, but, my mother left yesterday; **c'est tout a. chose!** that's quite a different thing! *F:* that's quite a different kettle of fish! **a. chose est de parler, a. chose d'agir,** it's one thing to talk, it's another to act; *s.a.* PART[1] 3.

autrefois [otrəfwa], *adv.* formerly, in the past; **il y avait a. un roi,** once upon a time there was a king; **c'était l'usage a.,** it was the custom formerly, in times past, in olden days; **je vous crus a.; cet a. n'est plus,** I believed you in the past; that past is no longer; **livre a. si populaire,** book once, at one time, so popular; **d'a.,** of long ago; **sa vie d'a.,** his former way of living; **les hommes d'a.,** the men of old, of olden times; **des chants d'a.,** old-time songs; **des mœurs d'a.,** bygone customs.

autrement [otrəmɑ̃], *adv.* otherwise. **1.** (*a*) differently; **il agit a., qu'il ne parle,** he acts differently from the way he talks; **il parle a. que vous,** he speaks differently from you; **faisons a.,** let us set about it in another way; **il ne put faire a. que d'obéir,** he had no alternative but to obey; (*b*) **c'est bien a. sérieux,** that is far more serious; *F:* **il n'est pas a. riche,** he is not particularly rich. **2.** or (else); **venez demain, a. il sera trop tard,** come tomorrow, otherwise, or (else) it will be too late.

Autriche [otriʃ], *Pr.n.f. Geog:* Austria.

Autriche-Hongrie [otriʃɔ̃gri], *Pr.n.f. Hist:* Austria-Hungary.

autrichien, -ienne [otriʃjɛ̃, -jɛn], *a. & s. Geog:* Austrian.

autruche [otryʃ], *s.f. Orn:* ostrich; **plumes d'a.,** ostrich feathers, ostrich plumes; **élevage des autruches,** ostrich farming; *F:* **avoir un estomac d'a.,** to have the digestion of an ostrich, a cast-iron stomach; *F:* **pratiquer une politique d'a.,** to bury one's head in the sand.

autrucherie [otryʃri], *s.f.* ostrich-farm.

autruchon [otryʃɔ̃], *s.m.* young ostrich.

autrui [otrɥi], *pron.indef.* others, other people; **convoiter le bien d'a.,** to covet one's neighbour's property; *Com:* **pour le compte d'a.,** for account of a third party; **ne fais pas à a. ce que tu ne voudrais pas qu'on te fît,** do as you would be done by; **juger a. d'après soi-même,** to judge others by one's own standards; **il est beau d'appuyer l'opinion d'a. quand a. a raison,** it is all right to uphold the opinion of another when that other is right; **là où a. vous croit coupable,** where others think you guilty.

autunien [otynjɛ̃], *a. & s.m. Geol:* Autunian.

autunite [otynit], *s.f. Miner:* autunite.

autunois, -oise [otynwa, -wa:z], *a. & s.* (native, inhabitant) of Autun.

auvent [ovɑ̃], *s.m.* **1.** (*a*) penthouse; open shed; (*b*) porch roof; window roof; (*c*) canopy (of tent); (*d*) *Av:* **a. d'éclairage,** glare shield (of instrument panel). **2.** *Ch: Ind:* hood (over hearth, part of laboratory). **3.** *Hort:* screen, matting. **4.** (*a*) *Const:* weather-board; (*b*) *Nau:* **a. de sabord,** weather-board. **5.** (*a*) *A.Veh:* dash; *Aut:* scuttle; (*b*) *Aut:* **auvents de capot,** bonnet louvres. **6.** visor (of helmet).

auvergnat, -ate [ovɛrɲa, -at]. (*a*) *a.* of Auvergne; (*b*) *s.* Auvergnat; (native, inhabitant) of Auvergne; (*c*) *s.m.* Auvergnat dialect.

Auvergne[1] [ovɛrɲ], *Pr.n.f. Geog:* Auvergne.

auvergne[2], *s.f. Leath:* tannin solution.

auvergner [ovɛrɲe], *v.tr. Leath:* to steep in tannin solution.

auverpin [ovɛrpɛ̃], *s.m. P:* (*a*) Auvergnat; (*b*) (i) coalman; (ii) commissionaire, doorman.

auvert [ovɛ:r]. *See* DIABLE 1.

auxanomètre [oksanɔmɛtr], *s.m. Bot:* auxanometer.

auxerrois, -oise [ɔserwa, -wa:z], *a. & s. Geog:* (native, inhabitant) of Auxerre.

auxiliaire [ɔksiljɛ:r, o-]. **1.** *a.* auxiliary (verb, troops, etc.); **machine a.,** auxiliary engine; feed engine; *Mch:* **lumière a.,** additional port; **bureau a.,** sub-office; **services auxiliaires de l'armée,** non-combatant services; *Mth:* **variable a.,** auxiliary (variable). **2.** *s.* auxiliary; (*a*) helper, assistant; **a. familiale** = mother's help; *Adm:* temporary civil servant; **c'est un a. précieux,** he's a valuable helper; **s'associer un a.,** to secure the help of a collaborator; (*b*) *s.m.pl. Mil:* **auxiliaires,** auxiliaries; (*c*) *s.m. Nau:* auxiliary cruiser; (*d*) *Av:* **auxiliaires d'atterrissage,** landing aids; *Av: Nau:* **les auxiliaires,** the auxiliary engines.

auxiliairement [ɔksiljɛrmɑ̃, o-], *adv.* in an auxiliary way; as an auxiliary.

auxiliariser [ɔksiljarize], *v.tr. & i.* to make an auxiliary.

auxiliateur, -trice [ɔksiljatœ:r, -tris], *a. & s.* (one) who helps.

auxine [ɔksin, o-], *s.f. Bot: Ch:* auxin.

auxochrome [ɔksɔkrom, o-], *s.m. Ch:* auxochrome.

auxocyte [ɔksɔsit, o-], *s.m. Biol:* auxocyte.

auxonnois, -oise [osɔnwa, -wa:z], *a. & s. Geog:* (native, inhabitant) of Auxonne [osɔn].

auxospore [ɔksɔspɔ:r, o-], *s.f. Algae:* auxospore.

ava [ava], *s.m. Bot:* ava, kava.

avachi [avaʃi], *a.* **1.** (*a*) (*of boots, etc.*) out of shape (through much use); (*b*) flabby, sloppy (figure). **2. c'est un homme a.,** he has gone to seed; he will never be any good again.

avachir [avaʃi:r], *v.tr.* **1.** to soften (leather, etc.). **2.** to enervate, to make flabby.

s'avachir. 1. to lose shape; (of leather, etc.) to perish; **elle s'est avachie,** she has got flabby, sloppy, she has gone to seed. **2. s'a. à ne rien faire,** to let oneself go.

avachissement [avaʃismɑ̃], *s.m.* **1.** (*a*) deterioration, perishing (of leather); (*b*) *Mec:* **a. des ressorts,** slackening of springs; (*c*) flabbiness, sloppiness (of figure). **2. a. de l'esprit,** decay of intellectual power.

avahi [avai], *s.m. Z:* woolly avahi, woolly lemur.

aval[1] [aval], *s.m. Fin:* endorsement (on bill); **donner son a. à un billet,** to endorse, back, a bill; **donneur d'a.,** guarantor, backer (of bill); *pl. avals.*

aval[2], *s.m.* **1.** downstream side; **eau d'a.,** downstream water; tail-water (below water-wheel); **les villages d'a.,** the villages down (the) stream; **canal d'a.,** tail-race (of lock); **porte d'a.,** tailgate, aft-gate; **en a.,** downstream; *Rail:* down the line; **en a. de l'aqueduc,** below the aqueduct, downstream from the aqueduct. **2. vent d'a.,** (i) wind from the opposite direction to the current; *esp.* (*in Channel and Bay of Biscay*) westerly wind; (ii) sea-breeze. **3.** *Tg:* down-side.

avalage [avala:ʒ], *s.m.* **1.** (*a*) going downstream (of barges, etc.); (*b*) downstream migration (of fish). **2. a. du vin,** (i) cellaring of wine; (ii) leakage of wine (from cask).

avalaison [avalɛzɔ̃], *s.f.* **1.** (*a*) spate, freshet; (*b*) heap of stones (deposited by a torrent). **2.** *Nau:* (*a*) steady westerly winds; (*b*) backing (of wind). **3.** downstream migration (of fish).

avalanche [avalɑ̃:ʃ], *s.f.* avalanche; **a. de pierres,** avalanche of stones, stone slide; *Geol:* **a. sèche,** slip (in volcanic ash); **a. boueuse,** mud avalanche, mud stream; **a. électronique, ionique,** avalanche of electrons, ions; **a. d'injures,** shower of insults; **ce fut une a. de lettres,** letters came pouring in, arrived in shoals.

avalant [avalɑ̃], *a.* going, on its way, downstream.

avalasse [avalas], *s.f.* = AVALAISON 1(*a*).

avalé [avale], *a.* **1.** drooping (shoulders, croup of horse, etc.); flabby (cheeks); **lapin à oreilles avalées,** lop-eared rabbit; **chien à oreilles avalées,** dog with floppy, hanging ears. **2. aller à bride avalée,** to ride full tilt.

avalement [avalmɑ̃], *s.m.* **1.** lowering (of cask into cellar, etc.). **2.** deglutition, swallowing.

avalent [avalɑ̃], *a. Ch:* avalent.

avaler [avale]. **1.** *v.tr.* (*a*) *A:* to lower (cask into cellar, etc.); (*b*) **a. une branche,** to lop off a bough; *s.a.* BOTTE[2] 2; (*c*) *Min:* **a. un puits,** to sink a shaft. **2.** *v.i. Nau: A:* (*of ship, etc.*) to sail or drift downstream. **3.** *v.tr.* to swallow (down); to drink up; to devour; **a. son repas,** to bolt one's meal; **a. son dîner à grosses bouchées,** to wolf one's dinner; **a. son vin à grandes gorgées,** to gulp down one's wine; **je ne pouvais pas l'a.,** I could not get it down; **a. la fumée,** to inhale; **cheval qui avale de l'air,** wind-sucker; *F:* **a. qn, qch., des yeux,** to devour s.o. with one's eyes, to eye sth. greedily; **a. un héritage,** to squander, run through, an inheritance; **c'est dur à a.,** I can hardly take that; **a. une couleuvre, une insulte,** to pocket an affront; **a. une bourde,** to swallow a lie; to let oneself be taken in; **celle-là est dure à a.,** that's a tall story, I can hardly swallow that; **il avale ça doux comme (le) lait,** he takes it all in; **j'ai avalé de travers,** it went down the wrong way; **a. ses mots,** to swallow one's words, to mumble; **il veut tout a.,** he wants to rule the roost; **a. le morceau, la pilule, la médecine, le calice,** to take one's medicine, one's punishment; **tu auras du mal à leur faire a. ça,** you will have a job to make them believe that; *F:* **a. les kilomètres,** to eat up the miles; *F:* **tu as avalé ta langue?** have you lost your tongue? *P:* **a. son acte, extrait, de naissance, avaler sa langue, sa chique, l'avaler,** to kick the bucket, conk out, turn up one's toes; *s.a.* CANNÉ[1] 2, PARAPLUIE 1. **4.** *v.tr.* = AVALISER.

s'avaler. 1. cheval dont le ventre s'avale, low-bellied horse. **2. ces pilules s'avalent facilement,** these pills are easy to swallow.

avale-tout [avaltu], *s.m.inv. P:* glutton.

avale-tout-cru [avaltukry], *s.m.inv. P:* boaster, fire-eater.

avaleur, -euse [avalœ:r, -ø:z], *s.* swallower; **a. de viande,** great eater of meat; **a. de sabre,** sword-swallower; *F:* **a. de gens, de charrettes (ferrées),** fire-eater, braggart, boaster.

avalies [avali], *s.f.pl.* pelt wool.

avaliser [avalise], *v.tr. Com:* to endorse, guarantee, back (bill).

avaliste [avalist], *s.m. Com:* surety, guarantor, backer.

avallonnais, -aise [avalɔnɛ, -ɛ:z], *a. & s. Geog:* (native, inhabitant) of Avallon.

avaloir [avalwa:r], *s.m.* **1.** head (of drain pipe); hood (over fireplace, etc.). **2.** fish trap. **3.** *P:* throat, gullet.

à-valoir [avalwa:r], *s.m.inv.* advance (payment).

avaloire [avalwa:r], *s.f.* **1.** *P:* throat, gullet. **2.** fish-weir. **3.** *Geol:* swallow-hole, swallet. **4.** *Harn:* breeching.

avalure [avalyːr], *s.f.* **1.** (*a*) *Farr:* regular growth of horse's hoof; (*b*) *Vet:* sloughing, cracking off (of hoof). **2.** crack, cleft, crevice (in cliff, etc.).

avançage [avɑ̃saːʒ], *s.m. Adm:* special stand for one taxi.

avance [avɑ̃ːs], *s.f.* **1.** advance, lead; **mouvement d'a. et de recul,** backward and forward movement; *Pol.Ec:* **l'a. rapide de l'indice du coût de la vie,** the rapid rise, climb, of the cost of living index; **a. et recul,** move and counter-move; **avoir de l'a. sur qn,** to be ahead, in advance, of s.o., to have the start of s.o.; **garder son a. sur qn,** to maintain one's lead over s.o.; **prendre de l'a. sur un concurrent,** to draw away from, take a lead over, get the start of, a competitor; to steal a march on a competitor; to overtake a competitor; **il avait une a. de douze mètres, de deux secondes, il avait douze mètres, deux secondes d'a., sur les autres coureurs,** he had a lead of thirteen yards, two seconds, he had thirteen yards' lead, two seconds' lead, he had a thirteen yard lead, a two second lead, over the other runners; **avoir une grande a. sur qn,** to have a good, substantial, lead over s.o.; **c'est une grande a. quand on part en voyage, que d'avoir ses billets tout prêts,** when going on a journey, it is a great help to have your tickets ready; **ma montre prend de l'a.,** my watch gains; **ma montre a dix minutes d'a.,** my watch is ten minutes fast; **arriver avec cinq minutes d'a.,** to arrive five minutes too soon, too early; **(prendre un train) avec cinq minutes d'a.,** (to catch a train) with five minutes in hand, to spare; *F:* **la belle a.!** much good that will do you! *Mil:* progression, advance; **ralentir l'a. de l'ennemi,** to slow down the enemy advance; *Sp:* **donner de l'a. à qn,** to give s.o. a (head) start; **donner à qn soixante mètres d'a.,** to give s.o. a sixty-five yard start; *Golf:* **tant de trous d'a.,** so many holes up; *El.E:* **a. d'une magnéto,** magneto-lead; *I.C.E:* **a. à l'allumage,** ignition advance; **mettre de l'a. à l'allumage,** to advance the ignition; *F:* to get a move on; **mettre toute l'a.,** to advance the ignition fully; **réduire l'a.,** to retard the ignition; **dispositif automatique d'a.,** automatic advance mechanism; **a. automatique à dépression,** vacuum spark control; **levier d'a.,** ignition lever; **graphique d'a.,** advance diagram; *Mch:* **a. à l'échappement,** exhaust lead; **a. (du tiroir),** (slide-valve) lead. **2.** *Mec.E:* feed movement, travel (of tool); **mécanisme d'a.,** feed mechanism, feeding gear; **a. en plongée,** in-feed; **a. longitudinale,** traverse feed; **a. transversale,** cross feed. **3.** projection; (*a*) **l'a. d'un toit,** the projecting part, eaves, of a roof; **balcon qui forme a.,** balcony that juts out; (*b*) *Arm:* peak (of some helmets). **4.** (*a*) **a. (de fonds),** advance, loan; advance loan, imprest (*to a government contractor for travelling expenses, etc.*); **a. permanente,** standing advance; *Fin:* **par a., à titre d'a.,** by way of advance, as an advance; **faire une a. de mille francs à qn,** to advance s.o. a thousand francs; **faire les avances d'une entreprise,** to advance funds for an enterprise; **compte d'avances,** working capital fund; **être en a. avec qn de mille francs,** to be s.o.'s creditor to the sum of a thousand francs; *s.a.* HOIRIE, RENTRER I. 1; (*b*) *pl.* **faire des avances à qn,** to make approaches, advances, overtures, to s.o., to make up to s.o.; **faire la moitié des avances,** to meet s.o. half-way; **faire les premières avances (pour une réconciliation),** to make the first move, to hold out the olive-branch. **5.** *adv.phr.* (*a*) **d'a., à l'a., par a.,** in advance, beforehand; **il faut vous dire d'a. que . . .,** I must tell you beforehand that . . .; **je jouis d'a. de ce bon repas,** I am looking forward to this good meal; **savourer un plaisir d'a.,** to anticipate a pleasure; **tous mes remerciements par a.,** all my thanks in advance; **c'était entendu d'a.,** it was agreed beforehand; **payer qn d'a., à l'a.,** to pay s.o. in advance; **payé d'a.,** prepaid; **payable à l'a.,** payable in advance; **arranger d'a.,** to prearrange; **prévenir qn six mois d'a.,** to give s.o. six months' notice, to warn s.o., let s.o. know, six months in advance; **préparer qch. d'a., à l'a.,** to prepare sth. beforehand; **se réjouir d'a., à l'a., par a.,** to rejoice beforehand; **je me réjouis d'a. de vous revoir,** I'm looking forward to seeing you again; *Aut:* **avec cette boîte de vitesses on peut passer d'a. en seconde,** with this gear-box you can pre-engage second gear; **retenir, louer, une place huit jours à l'a.,** to book a seat a week in advance; **retenir ses places trois mois d'a., à l'a.,** to book three months ahead; **chose décidée à l'a.,** foregone conclusion; (*b*) **l'horloge est en a.,** the clock is fast; **partir en a.,** to go off in advance (of the party); **arriver en a.,** to arrive in advance; **je suis en a. d'une demi-heure,** I am half an hour early; **être en a. sur l'horaire prévu,** to be ahead of schedule; **il est en a. sur sa classe,** he is ahead of his class; **être en a. sur son temps,** to be ahead, in advance, of one's time; **tout est en a. cette année,** everything is in advance, forward, this year.

avancé [avɑ̃se], *a.* advanced; (*a*) **position avancée,** advanced, forward, position; *Mil:* **les éléments avancés de la cinquième division,** the advanced, leading, elements of the fifth division; **le plus a.,** foremost; *Mec.E:* **excentrique a. sur une manivelle,** eccentric in front of a crank; *Rail:* **signal a.,** distant signal; *Fort:* **ouvrage a.,** advanced work; (*b*) **opinions avancées,** advanced, progressive, left-wing, ideas; **c'est un esprit a.,** he's a progressive; (*c*) **élève a.,** forward pupil; **peu a.,** backward; **les pommiers sont bien avancés cette année,** the apple trees are well forward this year; (*d*) **la nuit est fort avancée,** the night is far spent; **à une heure avancée de la nuit,** at a late hour of the night, late in the night, well on in the night; **à une heure peu avancée,** quite early on; **l'été est bien a.,** summer is nearly over; (*e*) **a. en âge,** elderly, getting on (in years); **à un âge a.,** late in life, at an advanced age; (*f*) (*of fruit*) overripe; **viande avancée,** high, tainted, meat; (*g*) *F:* **vous voilà bien a.!** a lot of good that's done you! **vous n'en êtes pas plus a.,** you're no further forward for it, no better for it.

avancée [avɑ̃se], *s.f.* **1.** (*a*) *Mil:* advanced post; (*b*) *Min:* head, heading (of level driven into a seam); (*c*) prominence, bulge, projection, protuberance; *Const:* **a. du toit,** eaves. **2.** advance (of sea, ice, etc.). **3.** *Geol:* **a. en profondeur,** underthrust. **4.** *Fish:* trace, cast.

avancement [avɑ̃smɑ̃], *s.m.* **1.** (*a*) advancing, putting forward; **a. d'un pied après l'autre,** moving forward of one foot after another; *Mec.E:* **a. automatique,** automatic feed; **a. de l'outil à la pièce,** feeding of the tool to the workpiece; **mouvements d'a.,** feed motions; (*b*) putting forward (of dinner hour, etc.); hastening (of event, etc.); (*c*) furtherance (of plan); (*d*) promotion, preferment; **a. à l'ancienneté,** promotion by seniority; **a. au choix,** promotion by selection; **proposition d'a.,** recommendation for promotion; **recevoir de l'a.,** to be promoted; (*e*) *A:* advancing of funds; *s.a.* HOIRIE. **2.** advance(ment), progress; going ahead; **peu d'a.,** backwardness (of a pupil); **l'a. des sciences,** the progress of science; **où en est l'a. du travail?** how is the work progressing? **3.** projection, jutting out (of wall, etc.). **4.** *Min:* = AVANCÉE 1 (*b*). **5.** pitch (of screw).

avancer [avɑ̃se], *v.* (j'avançai(s); n. avançons) **I.** *v.tr.* **1.** (*a*) to advance, put forward; to stretch out, hold out (one's hand, etc.); **il avança la tête hors de la voiture,** he stuck, poked, thrust, his head out of the car; **a. des chaises,** to set out chairs (for the company); *Chess:* **a. un pion,** to advance a pawn; *Mec.E:* **a. un outil à la pièce,** to feed a tool to the work; *Min:* **a. une galerie,** to drive a gallery; (*b*) **a. une proposition,** to put forward, advance, a proposal; **a. une théorie,** to put forward a theory; **a. ses raisons,** to produce, set out, adduce, give, one's reasons; **il n'avance rien sur lui-même,** he advances, gives, no details about himself. **2.** to make (sth.) earlier; to hasten (sth.); to hurry (sth.) on; **la réunion a été avancée du 14 au 7,** the meeting has been brought forward from the 14th to the 7th; **a. l'heure du dîner,** to put dinner forward; **a. la mort de qn,** to hasten s.o.'s death; **a. une montre,** (i) to make a watch go faster; (ii) to put a watch on, forward; **a. son travail,** to advance one's work; *Hort:* **a. une plante,** to bring on, force, a plant. **3.** **a. de l'argent à qn,** to advance money to s.o., to lend s.o. money; **a. un mois d'appointements à qn,** to advance s.o. a month's salary, to pay s.o. a month's salary in advance. **4.** to promote, forward, further, advance, (science, s.o.'s interests, etc.); **a. qn,** to promote s.o.; *F:* **à quoi cela vous avancera-t-il?** what good will that do you? what good will it be to you? how much better (off) will you be for it? *F:* **cela ne va pas nous a. beaucoup,** it won't get us much further forward.

II. *v.i.* **1.** to advance; (*a*) to move, go, step, forward; (*of ship*) to make headway; (*of watch*) (i) to be fast; (ii) to gain; **a. à grands pas,** to take, make, rapid strides, to stride along; **a. à pas de loup, à tâtons,** to creep along, feel, grope, one's way; **a. avec difficulté,** to trudge along, to plod along, forward; **a. à bicyclette,** to ride, cycle, on, ahead; **a. d'un pas,** to take one step forward; *Mil:* **"avance à l'ordre, au ralliement,"** "advance and give the countersign"; **chaque année la mer avance un peu plus sur notre terrain,** each year the sea encroaches a little further on our land; **faire a. qn,** to bring s.o. forward; **faire a. un âne à coups de bâton,** to drive a donkey along with a stick; **faire a. les troupes,** to advance the troops, to move the troops forward; **faire a. des renforts,** to bring up reinforcements; **faire a. sa voiture jusqu'à la porte,** to drive one's car up to the door; **faire a. un taxi,** to hail a taxi; **a. en âge,** to be getting on, to get on, in years; **montre qui avance d'une minute par jour,** watch that gains a minute a day; **la nuit avance,** the night is getting on; **l'été avance,** summer is almost over; (*b*) to progress, to get on, to make headway; **le travail avance,** the work is going forward; **elle se tue de travail mais n'avance pas,** she kills herself working but doesn't get any further forward; **les choses n'avancent plus,** things are at a standstill; **a. en sagesse,** to grow in wisdom; **la lune avance,** the moon is waxing; *Prov:* **plus on se hâte moins on avance,** more haste less speed; (*c*) *Min:* to head; (*d*) to advance, be promoted (in a service); **a. en grade,** to advance in rank; *s.a.* ANCIENNETÉ 2, CHOIX. **2.** (*a*) to be ahead of time; **l'horloge avance,** the clock is fast; **vous avancez de dix minutes,** your watch is ten minutes fast; **a. sur son époque,** to be ahead, in advance, of one's time; (*b*) (*of promontory, roof, etc.*) to jut out, to project, to protrude; **les figures n'avancent pas dans ce tableau,** the figures do not stand out sufficiently in this picture.

s'avancer. 1. to move forward, to advance; **s'a. vers qch.,** to make one's way, to head, towards sth.; **le bâtiment s'avançait,** the ship drew on; **l'aiguille du compteur s'avança lentement jusqu'à 80,** the speedometer needle crept up to 80; **s'a. d'un pas,** to take a, one, step forward; **s'a. péniblement,** to drag oneself along. **2.** to progress; **la nuit s'avance,** the night is getting on, is wearing on, is far advanced; **il s'est trop avancé pour reculer,** he has gone too far to withdraw; *F:* **vous vous avancez beaucoup,** you're sticking your neck out. **3.** (*of promontory, etc.*) to jut out; **une langue de terre s'avance dans la mer,** a strip of land runs out into the sea.

avanceur [avɑ̃sœːr], *s.m.* **a. de fonds,** advancer of funds; *El.E:* **a. de phase,** phase advancer.

avançon [avɑ̃sɔ̃], *s.m. Fish:* snood; leader, cast (of fishing line).

avanie [avani], *s.f.* **1.** *Hist:* avania (extorted by Turks). **2.** (*a*) insult, affront; (*b*) snub; **faire une a. à qn,** (i) to let s.o. down, to play a dirty trick on s.o., (ii) to snub s.o.; **essuyer une a. (de la part de qn),** to suffer an affront (at the hands of s.o.).

avant [avɑ̃]. **I. 1.** *prep.* before; **a. le temps,** too soon, prematurely; **venez a. midi,** come before twelve o'clock; **a. J.-C.,** B.C.; **il sera ici a. une heure,** he will be here, (i) by one o'clock; (ii) within an hour; **a. sa nomination,** prior to his appointment; **je le verrai a. quinze jours (d'ici),** I shall see him within, in less than, a fortnight; **pas a. lundi,** not before, not until, Monday; **il n'arrivera pas a. un quart d'heure,** he won't be here for a quarter of an hour (yet); **pas a. de nombreuses années,** not for many years to come; **l'article se place a. le nom,** the article is placed before the noun; **la maison est a. l'église,** the house comes before the church; **les dames a. les messieurs,** ladies before gentlemen, ladies first; **(surtout et) a. tout,** first of all, above all; **a. toute chose,** in the first place; **en ce qui concerne l'intelligence je mettrais Jean a. Georges,** as far as intelligence goes, I would put John above, before, George. **2.** (*a*) *prep.phr.* **a. de,** *A. & Lit:* **a. que de,** + *inf.* **je vous reverrai a. de partir,** I shall see you before I leave, before leaving; (*b*) *conj.phr.* **a. que** + *sub.* **je vous reverrai a. que vous (ne) partiez,** I shall see you again before you leave; **a. que vous ayez fini je serai parti,** by the time (that) you have finished I shall be gone; (*c*) **pas a. de, que,** not before, not until; **ne partez pas a. d'en recevoir l'ordre, a. qu'on vous le dise,** don't go until, till, you are told; (*d*) *Jur:* **a. faire droit, avant dire droit,** *s.m.inv.,* injunction, interim order. **3.** *adv.* (*a*) (= AUPARAVANT) **il était arrivé quelques mois a.,** he had arrived some months before; **a., il y en avait assez pour tout le monde; maintenant il n'en reste plus,** formerly there was enough for everyone, but now there is none left; (*b*) **réfléchis a., tu parleras après,** think first, speak later; (*c*) **n'allez pas**

jusqu'à l'église, sa maison est a., do not go as far as the church, his house is before (you come to) it; **les dames passent a.,** ladies take precedence; **il l'a mentionné a. dans la préface,** he mentioned it before, earlier, in the preface. 4. *adv.* (*a*) far, deep; **pénétrer très a. dans les terres,** to penetrate far inland; **le harpon pénétra très a. dans les chairs,** the harpoon sank deep into the flesh; **entrer plus a. dans une question,** to go further, more deeply, into a question; **il est mêlé bien a. dans l'affaire,** he is very deeply involved in the affair; **comme nous l'avons vu plus a.,** as we saw earlier on; (*b*) far, late; **bien a., fort a., très a., dans la nuit,** far into the night, very late at night, well on into the small hours; **très a. dans la journée,** very late in the day. 5. *adv.phr.* **en a.,** in front, before, forward, ahead; **en a.!** forward! *Mil:* **en a., (marche)!** quick march! **envoyer qn en a.,** to send s.o. on (in front); *F:* **aller en a.,** to push ahead, press on; *F:* **regarder en a.,** to look ahead, into the future; **mouvement en a.,** motion forward, *Mil:* advance steps; **faire deux pas en a.,** to advance two steps; **"numéros impairs, un pas en a."** "odd numbers, one pace forward"; **le plus en a.,** the foremost; **être le plus en a.,** to stand foremost; **mettre, jeter, qn en a.,** to bring s.o. forward, quote s.o. (as an authority), to name s.o. (as a guarantee); **mettre en a. une raison,** to advance, urge, produce, a reason; **mettre en a. un candidat,** to put a candidate forward; **il veut se mettre en a.,** he tries to push himself forward; **mettre en a. une question,** to bring up a question; *Nau:* **en a. (à) toute (vitesse),** full (steam) ahead; *Cr:* **coup en a. à gauche, à droite,** on-drive, off-drive; *prep.phr.* **il est bien en a. de son siècle,** he is well ahead, in front, in advance, of his time; **il est à quelques mètres en a. de nous,** he is a few metres in front of us. 6. *in adj. relation to sb.* (*a*) fore, forward, front; **la partie a. du navire,** the fore-part of the ship; **essieu a.,** fore-axle, leading axle (of engine); **roue a.,** front wheel; *Aut:* **à traction a.,** with front-wheel drive; *Aut:* **marche a.,** going forward, forward motion, forward ratios, forward gears; **excentrique de marche a.,** forward eccentric; (*b*) **d'a.,** previous, before; **la nuit d'a.,** the night before; *Dial:* **le jour d'a.,** yesterday; (*c*) *Ling:* **voyelle d'a.,** front vowel; *Nau:* **cabine d'a.,** fore-cabin.

II. *s.m.* 1. (*a*) *Nau:* **a. d'un vaisseau,** (i) bow, head (of a ship); (ii) eyes (of a ship); (iii) the steerage; **a. fin,** lean bow; **a. à guibre,** clipper bow; **a. à bulbe,** bulbous bow; **a. renflé,** bluff bow; **présenter l'a. à la lame,** to be head to sea; **le logement de l'équipage est à l'a.,** the crew's quarters are forward; **par tribord a.,** on the starboard bow; **vaisseau trop sur l'a.,** ship too much by the head; **aborder un navire par l'a.,** to collide with a ship head on; **sur, à, l'a. du mât,** before the mast; *Nau:* **sur l'a. du travers,** forward of the beam; **de l'a. à l'arrière,** fore-and-aft; **gagner l'a. d'un autre vaisseau,** to get ahead of another ship; *Nau: F:* **aller de l'a., pousser de l'a., marcher de l'a.,** to go, forge, ahead; *Row:* **a. partout!** give way! **retourner sur l'a.,** to come forward; *Aut:* **un modèle tout à l'a.,** a front-wheel-drive model; *s.a.* RETOUR 2; (*b*) front (of camera, carriage, etc.); nose (of plane); *Mch:* crank-end (of piston); head-end (of locomotive piston). 2. *Fb: etc.* forward. 3. *Mil:* **l'a.,** the front; the forward area(s).

avantage [avɑ̃taːʒ], *s.m.* 1. advantage; **a. pécuniaire,** monetary gain; **faire à qn tous les avantages possibles,** to give s.o. every (possible) advantage; **a. en nature,** perquisite; **octroyer certains avantages à qn,** to grant s.o. certain privileges; **il ne m'en revient aucun a.,** I reap no benefit from it; **tout l'a. est d'un côté,** it is rather a one-sided bargain; **être à l'a. de qn,** to turn out to s.o.'s advantage; **plan qui offre les plus grands avantages,** most suitable, profitable, plan; **le grand a. c'est qu'il est déjà sur les lieux,** the great thing is that he is already on the spot; **sa connaissance du français lui est un a. précieux,** his knowledge of French is a great asset to him; **tirer a. de qch.,** to turn sth. to account; to benefit, profit, from sth., to derive (an) advantage from sth.; **prendre a. de qch.,** to take advantage of sth.; **s'habiller à son a.,** to dress to the best advantage; **il est à son a. en uniforme,** he looks his best in uniform; **elle n'est pas à son a. le matin,** she doesn't look her best in the morning; **il a changé à son a.,** he has changed for the better; **parler à l'a. de qn,** to speak in s.o.'s favour; *P:* **fais moi un a.,** do me a favour; **je n'ai pas l'a. de le connaître,** I have not the pleasure, privilege, of knowing him; *F:* **à qui ai-je l'a.?,** to whom have I the privilege of speaking? **j'ai l'a. de vous informer que . . .,** I have much pleasure in informing you that . . ., I am pleased to inform you that . . .; **à l'a. (de vous revoir)!** (hope to) see you again soon! **avoir l'a. du nombre,** to have the advantage in numbers; *Nau:* **avoir l'a. du vent,** to have the weather-gauge (of another ship), to have the advantage of being to windward; *Jur:* gift, donation; **à titre d'a.,** as a gift. 2. (*a*) *Sp:* **donner l'a. à qn,** to give s.o. odds; **accorder, concéder, donner un a. à qn,** to give s.o. points; **il a l'a.,** the odds are in his favour; (*b*) *Ten:* (ad)vantage; **a. dedans, a. au servant,** (ad)vantage in, (ad)vantage server; **a. dehors, a. au relanceur,** (ad)vantage out, (ad)vantage striker; **a. détruit,** deuce; (*c*) **prendre l'a. sur qn,** to get an advantage over s.o.; **avoir l'a. sur qn,** to have the advantage of, over, s.o.; **remporter l'a. sur qn,** to get the better, best, of, s.o.; to gain the advantage over s.o.; **garder l'a.,** to retain the advantage, to keep the upper hand; **trouver de l'a. à faire qch.,** to find it an advantage to do sth.; **il y a a. à** + *inf.*, it is best to, it comes cheaper to, + *inf.*; **il y aura a. à ce que vous soyez présent,** it will be a good thing, just as well, if you are present; **avoir l'a.,** to have the best of it, to come off best.

avantagé [avɑ̃taʒe], *a.* 1. **être fort a. par rapport aux autres,** to enjoy many advantages over others; **a. par la nature,** well endowed; *A: F:* **femme avantagée,** woman with a fine bust. 2. *Sp:* **joueur a.,** player who has been given a start, been given odds.

avantager [avɑ̃taʒe], *v.tr.* **(j'avantageai(s); n. avantageons)** (*a*) to favour (s.o.); to give (s.o.) an advantage; (*b*) **l'uniforme l'avantage,** he looks his best in uniform; **cette robe ne l'avantage pas,** this dress doesn't do her justice; she doesn't look her best in this dress.

avantageur [avɑ̃taʒœːr], *s.m. Sp:* scratch player.

avantageusement [avɑ̃taʒøzmɑ̃], *adv.* advantageously, to advantage, favourably; **s'habiller a.,** to dress to the best advantage; **se marier a.,** to make a good match.

avantageux, -euse [avɑ̃taʒø, -øːz], *a.* 1. (*a*) advantageous, favourable; *Com:* **prix a.,** reasonable, popular, prices; **cet article est très a.,** this article is very good value; (*b*) **robe avantageuse,** becoming dress; (*c*) **poitrine avantageuse,** well-developed bust. 2. conceited, vain; **prendre un ton, un air, a.,** to adopt a superior tone, attitude; **prendre une attitude avantageuse,** *O:* **faire l'a.,** to act in a superior manner.

avant-bassin [avɑ̃basɛ̃], *s.m. Nau:* outer basin, dock; *pl. avant-bassins.*

avant-bec [avɑ̃bɛk], *s.m. Civ.E:* (upstream) starling, upstream-cutwater; pier-head (of bridge); *pl. avant-becs.*

avant-bouche [avɑ̃buʃ], *s.f. Anat:* vestibule of the mouth; *pl. avant-bouches.*

avant-bras [avɑ̃bra], *s.m.inv.* 1. *Anat:* (*a*) forearm; (*b*) "arm" (of horse). 2. *Arm:* vambrace. 3. *Civ.E:* front armlever (of bascule-bridge).

avant-cale [avɑ̃kal], *s.f.* 1. *Nau:* fore-hold. 2. *N.Arch:* ways-end; lower end of slipway, of slip-dock; *pl. avant-cales.*

avant-carré [avɑ̃kare], *s.m. Navy:* steerage; *pl. avant-carrés.*

avant-centre [avɑ̃sɑ̃ːtr], *s.m. Fb:* centre-forward; *pl. avant-centres.*

avant-chœur [avɑ̃kœːr], *s.m. Ecc.Arch:* choir and chancel, presbytery; *pl. avant-choeurs.*

avant-clou [avɑ̃klu], *s.m. Tls:* (fine) gimlet; *pl. avant-clous.*

avant-contrat [avɑ̃kɔ̃tra], *s.m.* preliminary contract; *pl. avant-contrats.*

avant-corps [avɑ̃kɔːr], *s.m.inv. Arch: etc:* avant-corps, fore-part, projecting part (of building); *Tchn:* projection.

avant-cour [avɑ̃kuːr], *s.f. Arch:* forecourt; *pl. avant-cours.*

avant-coureur [avɑ̃kurœːr]. 1. *s.m.* forerunner, harbinger, precursor; *Mil:* scout; *pl. avant-coureurs.* 2. *a.m.* precursory, premonitory (symptom); **signes avant-coureurs,** premonitory signs (of storm, etc.); **choc a.-c. (de séisme),** preliminary tremor.

avant-courrier, -ière [avɑ̃kurje, -jɛːr], *s.* 1. forerunner, precursor, harbinger, herald; *Poet:* **l'avant-courrière du jour,** the harbinger of day. 2. *s.m.* (*a*) *A:* messenger (riding a stage ahead of carriage); (*b*) advance publicity manager (of circus); *pl. avant-courriers, -ières.*

avant-creuset [avɑ̃krøzɛ], *s.m. Metall:* fore-hearth (of blast furnace); *pl. avant-creusets.*

avant-dernier, -ière [avɑ̃dɛrnje, -jɛːr], *a. & s.* last but one, next to last, penultimate; **l'avant-dernière fois,** the time before last; *pl. avant-derniers, -ières.*

avant-deux [avɑ̃dø], *s.m.inv. Danc:* second figure of the quadrille; *l'Été.*

avant dire droit [avɑ̃dirdrwa], *s.m. See* AVANT 2 (*d*).

avant-duc [avɑ̃dyk], *s.m. Civ.E:* protective piling (of river bank, etc.); *pl. avant-ducs.*

avant faire droit [avɑ̃ferdrwa], *s.m. See* AVANT 2 (*d*).

avant-foyer [avɑ̃fwaje], *s.m. Metall:* = AVANT-CREUSET; *pl. avant-foyers.*

avant-garde [avɑ̃gard], *s.f.* (*a*) *Mil:* advance(d) guard; **détachement d'a.-g.,** advance(d) party; **pointe de l'a.-g.,** leading elements, point, of the advance(d) guard; **tête de l'a.-g.,** head of the advance(d) guard; vanguard; **gros de l'a.-g.,** main guard; main body of the advanc(d) guard; *U.S:* support of the advance(d) guard; (*b*) **hommes d'a.-g.,** men in the van (of reform, etc.); pioneers; *Pol:* **les éléments d'a.-g.,** the avant-garde party; (*c*) **un livre d'a.-g.,** an advanced book, an avant-garde book; **une technique d'a.-g.,** a technique ahead of its time; (*d*) *Navy:* van (of fleet); *pl. avant-gardes.*

avant-gardisme [avɑ̃gardism], *s.m. usu. sing. Lit: Art: etc:* avant-gardism.

avant-gardiste [avɑ̃gardist]. *Lit: Art: etc:* 1. *a.* avant-garde; **un film a.-g.,** an avant-garde film. 2. *s.m. & f.* avant-garde writer, etc.; avant-gardist(e); *pl. avant-gardistes.*

avant-goût [avɑ̃gu], *s.m.* foretaste; anticipation; first impression; *pl. avant-goûts.*

avant-guerre [avɑ̃gɛːr], *s.m. or f.* pre-war period; **prix d'a.-g.,** pre-war prices; *pl. avant-guerres.*

avant-hier [avɑ̃tjɛːr], *adv.* the day before yesterday; **la nuit d'a.-h.,** the night before last; **a.-h. au soir,** the night, evening, before last.

avant-la-lettre [avɑ̃lalɛtr̥], *a. & s.f.inv. Engr:* **(épreuve) a.-la-l.,** proof before (all) letters, before the letter.

avant-ligne [avɑ̃liɲ], *s.f. Mil:* advanced line; *pl. avant-lignes.*

avant-main [avɑ̃mɛ̃], *s.m.* 1. *Anat:* flat of the hand. 2. *Z:* forequarters, forehand (of horse). 3. *Cards:* **avoir l'a.-m.,** to have the lead. 4. *Ten:* **coup d'a.-m.,** forehand stroke; *pl. avant-mains.*

avant-métré [avɑ̃metre], *s.m. Const:* specification; *pl. avant-métrés.*

avant-molaire [avɑ̃mɔlɛːr], *s.f. A: Anat:* premolar; *pl. avant-molaires.*

avant-mont [avɑ̃mɔ̃], *s.m. Geog: usu.pl.* foothill(s); *pl. avant-monts.*

avant-mur [avɑ̃myr], *s.m. Anat:* claustrum; *pl.* claustra; *pl. avant-murs.*

avant-nef [avɑ̃nɛf], *s.f. Gr.Ant: Arch:* pronaos; *pl. avant-nefs.*

avant-pied [avɑ̃pje], *s.m.* 1. *Anat:* = MÉTATARSE. 2. *Bootm:* upper (of boot), vamp; *pl. avant-pieds.*

avant-pieu [avɑ̃pjø], *s.m. Civ.E:* pile-helmet; dolly; *pl. avant-pieux.*

avant-plage [avɑ̃plaːʒ], *s.f. Geog:* offshore; *pl. avant-plages.*

avant-plan [avɑ̃plɑ̃], *s.m. Art: Phot: etc:* foreground; *pl. avant-plans.*

avant-poignet [avɑ̃pwaɲɛ], *s.m. Anat:* = MÉTACARPE; *pl. avant-poignets.*

avant-pont [avɑ̃pɔ̃], *s.m. Nau:* foredeck; *pl. avant-ponts.*

avant-port [avɑ̃pɔːr], *s.m. Nau:* outer harbour; outport; *pl. avant-ports.*

avant-portail [avɑ̃pɔrtaːj], *s.m. Arch:* outer portal; *pl. avant-portails.*

avant-porte [avɑ̃pɔrt], *s.f. Arch:* outer door; *pl. avant-portes.*

avant-poste [avɑ̃pɔst], *s.m. Mil:* outpost; **réseau d'a.-p.,** outpost screen, system; *pl. avant-postes.*

avant-première [avɑ̃prəmjɛːr], *s.f.* (*a*) private view, preview (of art exhibition, etc.); *Th:* dress rehearsal; (*b*) *Journ:* pre-performance write-up; *pl. avant-premières.*

avant-projet [avɑ̃prɔʒɛ], *s.m.* (rough) draft, estimate, preliminary plan (of works, etc.); draft (of treaty); *pl. avant-projets.*

avant-propos [avɑ̃propo], *s.m.inv.* 1. preface, foreword, avant-propos (to book). 2. **après quelques a.-p.,** after some preliminary remarks, after a short preamble.

avant-puits [avɑ̃pɥi], *s.m.inv. Min:* foreshaft.

avant-quart [avɑ̃kaːr], *s.m.* warning stroke (given by clock before striking).

avant-scène [avɑ̃sɛn], *s.f. Th:* 1. (*a*) proscenium, apron, forestage; (*b*) **(loge d')a.-s.,** stage-box; (*c*) *P:* woman's breasts; **il y a du monde à l'a.-s.,** she's well stacked, well endowed. 2. events leading to the situation given (at the beginning of a play); *pl. avant-scènes.*

avant-solier [avɑ̃sɔlje], *s.m. Arch:* overhang (of upper storey of house); *pl. avant-soliers.*

avant-terrain [avɑ̃tɛrɛ̃], *s.m. Mil:* foreground; *pl. avant-terrains.*

avant-terre [avɑ̃tɛr], *s.f.inv. Civ.E:* **arche a.-t.,** end arch (of bridge).

avant-titre [avɑ̃tiːtr̥], *s.m.* half-title (of book); *pl. avant-titres.*

avant-toit [avɑ̃twa], *s.m.* eaves (of roof); **comble avec a.-t.,** umbrella-roof; *pl. avant-toits.*

avant-train [avɑ̃trɛ̃], *s.m.* **1.** (*a*) *Veh:* fore-, front-carriage; *Aut:* front-axle unit; (*b*) wheels (of plough); (*c*) *Artil:* limber; **mettre, décrocher l'a.-t.,** to limber up, to unlimber. **2.** = AVANT-MAIN 2; *pl. avant-trains.*

avant-veille [avɑ̃vɛːj], *s.f.* two days before; **l'a.-v. de Noël,** two days before Christmas; *pl. avant-veilles.*

avare [avaːr]. **1.** *a.* (*a*) miserly; (*b*) **il n'est pas a. de son argent,** he is generous with his money; **être a. de (ses) paroles,** to be sparing of one's words; **a. de louanges,** chary of praise. **2.** *s.m. & f.* miser; *F:* skinflint.

avarement [avarmɑ̃], *adv.* avariciously, stingily.

avariable [avarjabl̥], *a. Com: Ins:* damageable (goods); liable to be damaged, liable to spoil.

avarice [avaris], *s.f.* avarice; stinginess, niggardliness.

avaricieusement [avarisjøzmɑ̃], *adv.* avariciously.

avaricieux, -ieuse [avarisjø, -jøːz], *a.* avaricious, stingy, miserly, grasping; *s.* **un vieil a.,** an old miser, skinflint.

avarie [avari], *s.f.* **1.** (*a*) damage, injury (to ship, engine, etc.); **subir une a.,** to be damaged, to break down; **faire subir une a. à qch.,** to damage sth.; **avec des avaries un navire avance lentement,** when disabled a ship makes little headway; (*b*) *A: Med: F:* syphilitic infection; **souffrir une a.,** to get "damaged." **2.** *M.Ins:* (*a*) **déclaration d'avaries,** (ship's) protest; **avaries matérielles de mer,** damage done by sea water; (*b*) **avaries-frais,** average; **avaries communes, grosses avaries,** general average; **avaries simples, particulières,** particular average; **franc d'avaries,** free from average; **compromis d'a.,** average bond; **règlement d'avaries,** adjustment of average; **répartiteur d'avaries,** average-adjuster.

avarié, *a.* **1.** damaged, spoiled (goods, etc.). **2.** (*a*) wounded, injured (arm, etc.); (*b*) *A:* "damaged" (in one's constitution); syphilitic.

avarier [avarje], *v.tr.* (*pr.sub. & p.d.* **n. avariions, v. avariiez**) to damage; injure, spoil (goods, etc.).

s'avarier, to deteriorate, go bad.

avaro [avaro], *s.m. P:* accident.

avasculaire [avaskylɛːr], *a. Med:* avascular.

avatar [avataːr], *s.m.* (*a*) *Hindu Rel:* avatar; (*b*) transformation, change; phase; *esp. in pl.* **avatars,** (varied) experiences; ups and downs (of political life, etc.); (*c*) mishap, misadventure.

à vau-l'eau [avolo], *adv.phr. See* VAU.

Ave [ɑve], *s.m.*, **avé** [ɑve], *s.m.* **1. Ave,** Ave; **L'Ave Maria,** *inv.* the Hail Mary. **2. avé,** Ave Maria (bead).

avec [avɛk]. **I.** *prep.* (*denoting concomitance and various derived ideas*) with. **1.** (*a*) (*accompaniment, collaboration*) **je vous ai vu a. lui,** I saw you with him, in his company; **déjeuner a. qn,** to lunch with s.o.; **collaborer a. qn,** to collaborate with s.o.; **je crois a. vous que . . .,** like you, I believe that . . .; **dans cette affaire, je suis a. les Français,** in this matter, I am on the side of the French; **le public est a. nous,** the public is behind us; *P:* **nous l'avons fait a. mon frère,** my brother and I did it; (*b*) (*indicating an adjunct or special feature*) **il est sorti a. son parapluie,** he has gone out with his umbrella; **le petit Martin a. sa figure d'ange,** little Martin with his angel face; **elle ressemble à sa sœur, a. des traits plus réguliers,** she is like her sister, but with more regular features; **leur maison a. ses murs nouvellement blanchis,** their house with its newly whitewashed walls; *Com:* **et a. cela, madame?** anything else, madam? (*c*) (*contemporaneity*) **il se lève a. le soleil,** he gets up at sunrise, he rises with the sun; **il est arrivé a. la nuit,** he arrived at nightfall; **le paysage change a. les saisons,** the countryside changes with, according to, the seasons. **2.** (*denoting an attendant circumstance*) (*a*) (*suggesting cause*) **on n'y arrive plus, a. cette vie chère,** it is becoming impossible to manage with the cost of living as high as it is; (*b*) (*equivalent to* **malgré**) **a. tous ses défauts, je l'aime cependant,** with, in spite of, all his faults, I still love him; **a. tout le respect que je vous dois,** with all due respect. **3.** (*manner*) **combattre a. courage,** to fight with courage; **servir son maître a. dévouement, a. un sincère dévouement,** to serve one's master devotedly, with sincere devotion; **ce mot s'écrit a. un seul "t,"** this word is written with one "t." **4.** (*means, instrument, material*) **cela viendra a. le temps,** that will come in time; **faire qch. a. l'aide de qn,** to do sth. with s.o.'s help; **ouvrir une porte a. une clef,** to open a door with a key; **cabane construite a. quelques planches,** hut built out of a few planks; **marcher a. des béquilles,** to walk with (the help of) crutches. **5.** (*union, association*) **un métal qui se combine a. un acide,** a metal which combines with an acid; **se marier a. qn,** to marry s.o., to get married to s.o.; **lier conversation a. qn,** to get into conversation with s.o. **6.** (*conformity*) **être d'accord a. qn,** to agree with s.o.; **s'harmoniser a. qch.,** to harmonize, be in keeping, with sth.; **mot qui rime a. un autre,** word that rhymes with another. **7.** (*comparison*) **soutenir la comparaison a. qch.,** to stand, bear, comparison with sth. **8.** (*opposition: equivalent to* **contre**) **lutter a. qn,** to struggle with s.o.; **se battre a. qn,** fight s.o.; **la guerre a. l'Allemagne,** the war with Germany. **9.** (*in expressing personal relationship*) **être en relations d'amitié a. qn,** to be on friendly terms with s.o.; **être bien, mal, a. qn,** to be on good, bad, terms with s.o.; *F:* (*with an adj., equivalent to* **envers, pour,** *etc.*) **être gentil, aimable, a. qn,** to be kind, nice, to s.o.; **être poli, impoli, a. qn,** to be polite, impolite, to s.o.; **être sévère a. qn,** to be hard on s.o.; **être franc a. qn,** to be frank with s.o.; **elle est froide a. lui,** she is cold towards him. **10.** (*equivalent to* **en ce qui concerne . . .**) **a. elle on ne sait jamais,** with her you never can tell; **c'est une idée qui ne me viendrait jamais a. vous,** it is an idea which would never occur to me as far as you are concerned. **11.** *F:* **a. cela, a. ça (que): elle est grande et a. ça mince,** she is tall, and slender too, and, what's more, slim; **a. ça qu'elle ne savait rien faire,** besides which she was quite untrained; *P:* **a. ça!** nonsense! **a. ça que . . .,** as if . . .; **a. ça qu'on vous le permettrait!** as if they would let you! do you suppose they would let you? **a. ça qu'il n'a pas triché!** don't say he didn't cheat!

II. **d'avec,** *prep.phr.* from; **distinguer, séparer, le bon d'a. le mauvais,** to distinguish, to separate, (the) good from (the) bad; **se désolidariser d'a. ses collègues,** to break with one's colleagues, to go one's own way; **divorcer (d')a. sa femme,** to divorce one's wife.

III. **avec,** *adv.* with it, with them; *F:* **il a pris mon chapeau et s'est sauvé a.,** he took my hat and ran off with it; *P:* (*of pers.*) **vous nous ferez tuer, et vous a.,** you will get us killed, and yourself too.

avecque(s) [avɛk], *prep. A:* = AVEC.

aveindre [avɛ̃ːdr], *v.tr. Dial:* To reach, to pull out.

aveinière [avenjɛr], *s.f.* oat-field.

avelanède [avlanɛd], *s.f. Com: Tan: etc:* val(l)onia.

aveline [avlin], *s.f. Bot:* **1.** filbert, hazel-nut, cob(-nut). **2. a. purgative,** coral-plant.

avelinier [avlinje], *s.m.*, **avellanier** [avelanje], *s.m. Bot:* filbert-tree, hazel-tree.

avelle [avɛl], *s.f. Ich:* bleak.

aven [avɛn], *s.m. Geol:* aven; swallow-hole.

avena [avena], *s.f. Bot:* Avena.

avénacé [avenase], *a. Bot:* avenaceous.

avenage [avənaːʒ], *s.m. A.Jur:* avenage.

avenant [avnɑ̃], *a.* **1.** comely, pleasing, prepossessing (person, manners, etc.); **mal a.,** unseemly, uncouth (manner, etc.). **2. à l'a.,** in keeping, in conformity, correspondingly; *adv.phr.* **ils se sont conduits à l'a.,** they acted accordingly, their action was in keeping; *adj.phr.* **et un chapeau à l'a.,** and a hat to match, to suit; **le bâtiment est beau et le jardin est à l'a.,** the building is beautiful and the garden is in keeping with it; *prep.phr.* **mœurs à l'avenant de leurs croyances,** morals in keeping with their beliefs. **3.** *s.m.* **avenant** (*a*) codicil (to treaty); (*b*) endorsement, additional clause (to insurance policy); (*c*) rider (to verdict).

avénéine [avenein], *s.f. Ch:* = AVÉNINE.

avènement [avɛnmɑ̃], *s.m.* (*a*) advent (of Christ, etc.); coming (of Messiah); **l'a. d'un art nouveau,** the advent of a new art; **depuis l'a. de l'automobile,** since the advent of the motor car; (*b*) **a. au trône,** accession to the throne.

avéneron [avenrɔ̃], *s.m. Bot:* wild oats.

avénière [avenjɛːr], *s.f.* = AVEINIÈRE.

avénine [avenin], *s.f. Ch:* avenin(e).

avenir[1] [avniːr], *v.i. A:* = ADVENIR.

avenir[2], *s.m.* future; **l'a. nous jugera,** the future will judge us; **qu'est-ce que l'a. nous réserve?** what has the future in store for us? **prédire l'a.,** to predict the future; **avoir un bel a. devant soi,** to have a fine future, fine prospects, before one; **jeune homme d'un grand a., de beaucoup d'a.,** young man of great promise; **c'est un homme d'a.,** he's a coming man, a man with a future; *Sp:* **un joueur d'a.,** a coming player; **situation sans a.,** job with no future, dead-end occupation; **situation d'a.,** job with a future, with prospects; **assurer l'a. de qn,** to make provision for s.o.; **dans l'a.,** at some future date; **dans un a. très prochain,** in the very near future; **à l'a.,** in (the) future, hereafter; **à l'a. je serai plus circonspect,** in future I shall be more cautious.

à-venir [avniːr], *s.m.inv. Jur:* writ of summons (to opposing counsel); **signifier un à-v. à la partie adverse,** to serve a writ on the other party.

Avent [avɑ̃], *s.m. Ecc:* Advent; *s.a.* PRÊCHER.

aventer [avɑ̃te], *v.tr. Nau:* **a. une voile,** to set a sail to the wind.

Aventin [avɑ̃tɛ̃], *Pr.n.m. Geog:* **le mont A.,** the Aventine; **se retirer sur l'A.,** to secede; to refuse to consult others.

aventure [avɑ̃tyːr], *s.f.* **1.** (*a*) adventure; **homme d'aventures,** adventurous man, adventurer; **vie d'a.,** life of adventure; **a. effrayante,** terrifying experience; (*b*) intrigue, (love) affair. **2.** (*a*) chance, luck, venture; **tenter l'a.,** to try one's luck; **l'a. est au coin de la rue,** the unexpected is always round the corner; **avoir part en une a.,** to have a share in a venture; *adv.phr.* **à l'a.,** at random, at a venture; **aller, errer, à l'a.,** to wander about aimlessly; **vivre à l'a.,** to live haphazardly, in a happy-go-lucky fashion; **mettre tout à l'a.,** to leave everything to chance; *s.a.* NAVIGUER 1; **par a., d'a.,** by chance, *A:* perchance, *A:* peradventure; (*b*) *Com:* **prêt à l'a., à la grosse a.,** bottomry. **3. dire, tirer, la bonne a. (à qn),** to tell fortunes; to tell (s.o.'s) fortune; **diseuse de bonne a.,** fortune-teller. **4.** *F:* **mal d'a.,** whitlow.

aventuré [avɑ̃tyre], *a.* risky, chancy.

aventurer [avɑ̃tyre], *v.tr.* to venture, hazard, risk (life, etc.).

s'aventurer, (*a*) to venture; **s'a. en pays inconnu,** to venture into an unknown country; (*b*) to expose oneself; **prenez garde de trop vous a.,** mind you don't take too many risks, chances.

aventureusement [avɑ̃tyrøzmɑ̃], *adv.* adventurously, venturesomely; in an adventurous manner.

aventureux, -euse [avɑ̃tyrø, -øːz], *a.* adventurous, venturesome; overbold (hypothesis, etc.); **homme a. au jeu,** reckless gambler; **projet a.,** hazardous, risky, plan; *s.* **jeune a.,** rash, venturesome, youth.

aventurier, -ière [avɑ̃tyrje, -jɛːr]. **1.** *a. A:* adventurous (life, person, etc.). **2.** *s.* adventurer; (*a*) *A:* soldier of fortune; privateer; **marchand a.,** merchant adventurer; (*b*) **a. politique,** political adventurer; **c'est un a.,** he lives by his wits; **c'est une aventurière,** she's an adventuress.

aventurine [avɑ̃tyrin], *s.f.* **1.** *Glassm:* aventurine (glass); gold flux. **2.** *Miner:* **a. naturelle,** aventurine, sunstone.

aventurisme [avɑ̃tyrism], *s.m.* (political) adventurism.

avenu [avny], *a.* (*a*) *A:* **choses avenues,** things which occurred, did not occur; (*b*) *now used only in the phr.* **nul et non a.,** null and void; as if it had never occurred.

avenue [avny], *s.f.* (*in town*) avenue; (*leading to house*) (carriage) drive; **les avenues du pouvoir,** the paths to power.

avérage [averaːʒ], *s.m.* **1.** smaller livestock. **2.** *Fb:* goal average.

avéré [avere], *a.* authenticated, established (fact, etc.); (fact) beyond doubt; **prendre qch. pour a.,** to take sth. for granted; **crime a.,** patent and established crime; **ennemi a.,** avowed enemy; **voleur a.,** known thief; **marxistes avérés,** professed Marxists.

avérer [avere], *v.tr.* (**j'avère, n. avérons; j'avérerai**) *A:* to establish; *Jur:* to aver (fact).

s'avérer. 1. to turn out to be correct; (*of news, etc.*) to be confirmed. **2. s'a. +** *adj.* to turn out, to prove; **la science s'est avérée impuissante,** science has shown itself powerless; **l'entreprise s'avère improductive,** the undertaking is proving unproductive; *F:* **la nouvelle s'est avérée fausse,** the news proved false.

Averne [avɛrn], *Pr.n.m.* (*a*) *A.Geog:* **le lac A.,** Lake Avernus; (*b*) *Poet:* **L'A.,** the infernal regions, Hades.

averrhoa [avɛr(r)ɔa], *s.m. Bot:* Averrhoa.

Averr(h)oès [avɛr(r)ɔɛːs], *Pr.n.m. Hist: Phil:* Averr(h)oes.

averr(h)oïsme [avɛr(r)ɔism], s.m. Phil: averr(h)o-ism.

avers [avɛːr], s.m. Num: obverse (of coin).

averse [avɛrs], s.f. sudden shower, downpour; essuyer une a., to be caught in a shower; une a. de félicitations, a flood, flow, stream, of congratulations.

aversion [avɛrsjɔ̃], s.f. aversion (pour, to, for); dislike (pour, to, for, of); avoir une a., de l'a., pour qch., pour, contre qn, to have an aversion to, for, sth., s.o., a distaste for sth., a dislike for s.o.; prendre qn en a., to take, conceive, a dislike to s.o.; (of pers.) ma bête d'a., my pet aversion.

averti [avɛrti], a. (a) experienced, wide-awake (observer, etc.); un homme a., an experienced man, an expert; un homme a., A: un bon a., en vaut deux, qui dit a. dit muni, forewarned is forearmed; (b) a. de qch., aware, warned, of sth.; se tenir pour a., to be on one's guard; to take the hint; vous voilà a.! I give you fair warning!

avertin [avɛrtɛ̃], s.m. 1. A: madness. 2. Vet: staggers.

avertir [avɛrtiːr], v.tr. 1. a. qn de qch., to warn, notify, advise, inform, s.o. of sth., to give s.o. notice, warning, of sth.; je l'en avais averti, I had warned him of it, against it; F: je vous en avertis! I give you fair warning; avertissez-le de venir, tell him to come; Equit: a. un cheval, (i) to "wake up"; (ii) to gather, a horse. 2. Aut: to signal (intention to turn, stop, etc.).

avertissement [avɛrtismɑ̃], s.m. 1. (a) warning, notice; renvoyer qn sans a. préalable, to discharge s.o. at a moment's notice; (b) reprimand; Sp: warning (by the referee); lettre envoyée à titre d'a., (i) letter sent as a reminder; (ii) warning letter, admonitory letter; (c) danger signal, danger sign; warning signal; a. de tempête, gale warning; (d) a. (au lecteur), prefatory note, foreword (to book); (e) Jur: billet d'a., summons to appear before a magistrate. 2. Adm: demand note.

avertisseur [avɛrtisœːr], s.m. 1. warner; Th: call-boy. 2. (a) warning signal, call-bell, alarm; Tp: annunciator; Aut: warning device, horn; P.N: avertisseurs sonores interdits, no hooting; Ind: hooter; Rail: signal; a. d'incendie, fire alarm; Av: a. de décrochage, stall warning indicator; a. de marge d'altitude, terrain clearance warning indicator; (b) a. signal a., warning signal.

avesnois, -oise [avɛnwa, -waːz], a. & s. Geog: (native, inhabitant) of Avesnes.

avette [avɛt], s.f. A: Lit: bee.

aveu, -eux [avø], s.m. 1. Hist: recognition between a vassal and his overlord; homme sans a., vagabond, vagrant. 2. Jur: consent, authorization; obtenir l'a. de qn pour faire qch., to obtain s.o.'s consent to do sth. 3. avowal, confession; Jur: admission; acknowledgment by record; faire l'a. d'une erreur, to own up to, admit, a mistake; faire des aveux complets, to make a full confession; de l'a. de tout le monde . . ., by common consent . . .; il est certain, de l'a. de tout le monde, que . . ., all the world, everyone, agrees, admits, that . . .; de leur propre a. . . ., on their own confession . . .; il est socialiste de son plein a., he is a self-confessed socialist.

aveuglant [avœglɑ̃], a. blinding; dazzling; glaring (sun).

aveugle [avœgl], a. blind, sightless. 1. (a) devenir a., to go blind; a. d'un œil, blind in one eye; Opt: point a., blind spot; F: a. comme une taupe, as blind as a bat; (b) s. un, une, a., a blind man, woman; les aveugles, the blind; aveugles de guerre, blinded ex-servicemen; il est a. de guerre, he lost his sight in the war; c'est un a. qui en conduit un autre, it's a case of the blind leading the blind; au royaume des aveugles les borgnes sont rois, in the country of the blind the one-eyed man is king. 2. Arch: fenêtre a., arcade a., blind window, arch; mur a., blind wall; Tchn: écrou a., blind nut; trou a., dead hole; bout a. (d'un tuyau), blind end. 3. blind, unreasoning (hatred); implicit (confidence, etc.); avoir une confiance a. en qn, to trust s.o. implicitly, unreservedly; obéissance a., blind, unquestioning, obedience; être a. aux défauts, pour, devant, sur les défauts, de qn, to be blind to, to shut one's eyes to, s.o.'s faults; suivre qn en a., to follow s.o. blindly, unreasoningly; aller à l'a., to grope one's way; to go blindly on; sujet auquel les savants travaillent encore à l'a., subject at which scientists are still working in the dark.

aveuglement [avœgləmɑ̃], s.m. 1. (a) A: blinding; depuis son a., since he was blinded; (b) Nau: stopping (of leak). 2. (moral, mental) blindness; infatuation; cf. CÉCITÉ.

aveuglément [avœglemɑ̃], adv. blindly, blindfold; obéir a., to obey implicitly, blindly, without question.

aveugle-né, -née [avœglǝne], a. & s. (man, woman) blind from birth; pl. aveugles-né(e)s.

aveugler [avœgle, -vø-], v.tr. 1. (a) to blind (s.o.); to put (s.o.'s) eyes out; (b) to dazzle, blind; les éclairs nous aveuglaient, the lightning blinded us; (c) a. l'entendement, to obscure the understanding; aveuglé par la passion, blinded by passion; aveuglé par la colère, blind with rage. 2. Nau: (a) a. une voie d'eau, to stop a leak; (b) a. une couture, to parcel a seam; (c) a. une fenêtre, to wall up, block, a window.

s'aveugler sur les défauts de qn, to blind oneself, to shut one's eyes to, s.o.'s faults.

aveuglette (à l') [alavœglɛt], adv.phr. blindly; aller à l'a., to go blindly on; avancer à l'a. vers qch., to feel, grope, one's way to sth.; choisir qch. à l'a., to choose sth. at random; lancer des coups à l'a., to hit out blindly; Av: voler à l'a., to fly "blind."

aveulir [avœliːr], v.tr. to enervate; to render (s.o.) indifferent, blasé; to deaden (feelings, etc.).

s'aveulir, to become enervated, limp; to become indifferent to everything; to go to pieces.

aveulissant [avœlisɑ̃], a. enervating, deadening.

aveulissement [avœlismɑ̃], s.m. enervation, limpness; atony; lack of will-power.

aveyronnais, -aise [avɛrɔnɛ, -ɛːz], a. & s. Geog: (native, inhabitant) of the department of Aveyron.

aviaire [avjɛːr], a. peste a., fowl plague, fowl pest; s.a. DIPHTÉRIE 2.

aviateur, -trice [avjatœːr, -tris]. 1. a. A: flying (machine, etc.). 2. s. aviator; airman, -woman; mal des aviateurs, altitude sickness, altitude anoxia.

aviation [avjasjɔ̃], s.f. aviation; air force; a. civile, commerciale, militaire, civil, commercial, military aviation; compagnie d'a., air company; a. de tourisme, private aviation; a. tactique, stratégique, tactical, strategic aviation; commandement de l'a. tactique, de l'a. stratégique, tactical, strategic air command; a. de bombardement, bomber command; bomber forces; U.S: bomber aviation; a. de chasse, fighter command; fighter forces; U.S: fighter aviation; notre a. de chasse a abattu 20 appareils ennemis, our fighters shot down 20 enemy planes; a. d'interception, interceptor aircraft; a. de reconnaissance, reconnaissance aviation; a. de transport, transport command; U.S: transport aviation; champ, terrain d'a., airfield; flying ground; base d'a., air base; centre d'a., air station; usine d'a., aircraft factory; enthousiaste de l'a., air-minded; s.a. EMBARQUÉ.

Avicenne [avisɛn], Pr.n.m. Hist: Phil: Avicenna.

avicennia [avisɛnia], s.m. Bot: Avicennia.

avicole [avikɔl], a. 1. avicolous, parasitic on birds. 2. élevage a., (i) poultry farming; (ii) poultry farm.

avicula [avikyla], s.f., **avicule** [avikyl], s.f. Moll: avicula, wing-shell.

aviculaire [avikylɛːr]. 1. a. (a) eaten by birds; (b) bird-eating; mygale a., bird(-eating) spider; (c) avicolous, living on birds. 2. s.m. (a) Arach: Avicularia, bird-spider; (b) Moll: avicularium.

aviculidés [avikylide], s.m.pl. Moll: Aviculidae.

aviculteur [avikyltœːr], s.m. 1. bird-fancier. 2. poultry farmer, U.S: poultryman.

aviculture [avikyltyːr], s.f. aviculture. 1. bird-fancying. 2. poultry farming; établissement d'a., poultry farm; concours d'a., poultry show.

avide [avid], a. 1. greedy; a. de qch., (i) greedy, avid, for sth.; (ii) eager for sth.; espérances avides, eager hopes; a. d'aventures romanesques, hungering for romance; a. de sang, thirsting for blood, bloodthirsty; a. de tout savoir, eager for knowledge; Ch: etc: a. d'eau, absorbent of water; (of plant) thirsty for water. 2. covetous (de, of); grasping (hands, nature).

avidement [avidmɑ̃], adv. greedily, hungrily, with avidity; covetously; écouter a., to listen eagerly.

avidité [avidite], s.f. avidity, greed(iness); voracity (for food); greed(iness), graspingness (for money); keenness, eagerness, voracity (for learning); manger avec a., to eat with avidity, greedily; a. du gain, greed for gain; écouter avec a., to listen eagerly.

avien, -ienne [avjɛ̃, -jɛn], a. avian, birdlike.

aviette [avjɛt], s.f. = AVIONNETTE.

avifaune [avifoːn], s.f. avifauna.

avignonnais, -aise [aviɲɔnɛ, -ɛːz], a. & s. Geog: (native, inhabitant) of Avignon.

avilir [aviliːr], v.tr. 1. to render vile; to degrade, debase, lower; avili aux yeux du public, degraded in the eyes of the people. 2. Com: to depreciate, lower, bring down (currency prices, etc.).

s'avilir. 1. to debase, lower, demean, oneself; s'a. à faire qch., to lower oneself to the point of doing sth., to stoop to do(ing) sth. 2. to lose value; to fall, to come down (in value, in price); to depreciate.

avilissant [avilisɑ̃], a. debasing, degrading.

avilissement [avilismɑ̃], s.m. 1. debasement, degradation; tomber dans l'a., to fall into (a state of) degradation. 2. depreciation; fall (in price).

avilisseur, -euse [avilisœːr, -øːz]. 1. a. defamatory, vilifying. 2. s. detractor, defamer, traducer, vilifier.

avillon [avijɔ̃], s.m. Orn: hallux (of bird of prey).

avinage [avinaːʒ], s.m. seasoning (of casks).

aviné [avine], a. intoxicated, inebriated, (with wine); in liquor, drunk; d'une voix avinée, in a drunken voice.

aviner [avine], v.tr. to season (cask).

s'aviner, to drink (to excess), F: to soak, to booze.

avion [avjɔ̃], s.m. aircraft, aeroplane, F: plane, U.S: airplane; en a., by air, by plane; j'ai fait une partie du trajet en a., I flew part of the way; "par a.", "(by) air mail"; embarquer, monter en a., to board a plane, to emplane; débarquer, descendre, d'a., to get off a plane, to deplane; mal d'a., air-sickness; a. commercial, commercial aircraft; a. de ligne, airliner; a. de transport de marchandises, freight plane; a. transbordeur, air-ferry; A: a. postal, mail plane; a. de tourisme, private aircraft; a. à une place, monoplace, single-seater (aircraft); a. à deux places, biplace, two-seater (aircraft); a. bimoteur, twin-engine aircraft; a. à hélice arrière, pusher; a. à hélice avant, tractor; a. à ailes hautes, surélevées, high-wing aircraft; a. à ailes mi-surélevées, semi-high-wing aircraft; a. à ailes surbaissées, low-wing aircraft; a. militaire, military aircraft; a. de combat, fighter; fighter-bomber; a. de bombardement, bomber; a. de chasse, fighter; a. de chasse et de bombardement = CHASSEUR-BOMBARDIER; a. d'interception = INTERCEPTEUR; a. de chasse et d'interception = CHASSEUR INTERCEPTEUR; a. d'assaut, (ground) strike aircraft; a. d'attaque au sol, ground-attack aircraft; a. de pénétration, intruder; a. (de repérage) d'artillerie, artillery-reconnaissance aircraft; a. de réglage de tir, artillery co-operation aircraft, F: spotter; a. d'observation, observation aircraft; a. de reconnaissance, reconnaissance, F: recce, aircraft; (Fleet Air Arm) scout plane; a. éclaireur, pathfinder; a. estafette, messenger, courier, aircraft; a. de liaison, liaison aircraft; a. toutes fins, general purpose, utility, aircraft; a. transporteur de troupe, de transport de troupe, troop carrier plane; transport plane; a. transporteur de matériel, de transport de matériel, cargo plane; a. sanitaire, ambulance aircraft, plane; a. ravitailleur, tanker; a. gros, moyen, petit porteur, heavy-, medium-, light-transport aircraft; a. à grand, à moyen, à petit rayon d'action, long-, medium-, short-range aircraft; a. d'entraînement au sol, ground trainer; a. d'entraînement élémentaire, supérieur, primary, advanced trainer; a. d'entraînement aerobatique, aerobatic-training aircraft, aerobatic trainer (aircraft); a. télécommandé, radio-controlled aircraft; a. télécommandé à partir d'un avion mère, drone; a. sans pilote, a.-robot, pilotless aircraft; robot-plane; a. piloté, manned aircraft; a. de l'aéronavale, naval aircraft; a. marin, seaplane; a. embarqué, carrier-based aircraft; a. basé à terre, land-based aircraft; a. torpilleur, torpedo-aircraft; pièce contre-avions, anti-aircraft gun; a. à géometrie, à flèche, variable, variable geometry aircraft; a. à ailes variables, swing-wing aircraft; a. de, en, papier, paper dart; s.a. RAYON[1] 2, RÉACTION 2, STRATOSPHÉRIQUE.

avion-canard [avjɔ̃kanar], s.m. Av.Hist: canard; pl. avions-canards.

avion-cargo [avjɔ̃kargo], s.m. Av: freighter, cargo plane, freight plane; pl. avions-cargos.

avion-cible [avjɔ̃sibl], s.m. Mil.Av: target-practice aircraft; drone; pl. avions-cibles.

avion-citerne [avjɔ̃sitɛrn], s.m. Av: tanker (aircraft); pl. avions-citernes.

avion-école [avjɔ̃ekɔl], s.m. trainer, training aircraft; pl. avions-écoles.

avion-fusée [avjɔ̃fyze], s.m. rocket (aircraft); pl. avions-fusées.

avionique [avjɔnik], s.f. Av: avionics.

avion-maquette [avjɔnmakɛt], s.m. Mil: model aircraft (for aircraft recognition); pl. avions-maquette.

avionnette [avjɔnɛt], s.f. light, low-powered aircraft.

avionneur [avjɔnœːr], s.m. (a) airframe designer; (b) airframe manufacturer.

avion-robot [avjɔ̃rɔbɔ], s.m. robot-plane, pilotless aircraft; pl. avions-robots.

avion-suicide [avjɔ̃sɥisid], s.m. Av.Hist: suicide plane; pl. avions-suicides.

avion-taxi [avjɔ̃taksi], s.m. charter aircraft; pl. avions-taxis.

aviophone [avjɔfɔn], s.m. Av: voice-pipe, speaking tube.

avir [aviːr], v.tr. Tchn: to flange (sheet of metal); to beat over the edges (of a sheet of metal).

aviron [avirɔ̃], s.m. 1. oar; Fr.C: (canoe) paddle; a. de couple, scull; a. de nage, rowing oar; avirons de couple, accouplés, double-banked oars; avirons de, en, pointe, single-banked oars; à quatre, huit, avirons, four-, eight-oared; a. de galère, sweep; armer, border, les avirons, to ship the oars; les avirons dans l'eau! hold water! engager son a., to catch a crab; coup d'a., stroke; a. de l'arrière, du chef de nage, stroke-oar; a. de l'avant, du brigadier, bow-oar; a. de queue, stern-oar. 2. l'a., rowing; cercles d'a., rowing clubs; faire de l'a., to row, to go in for rowing; après mon travail je fais de l'a., after my work I go rowing, go for a row.

avironner [avirɔne], v.i. Fr.C: to paddle (a canoe).

avis [avi], s.m. 1. (a) opinion, judgment, decision; avis d'expert, expert advice, opinion; dire son a., to speak one's mind; exprimer, émettre, un a., to express a view, an opinion; émettre l'a. que . . ., to express the opinion that . . .; ne pas être du même a. que qn, to disagree with s.o.; à mon a., c'est le jeu qui l'a perdu, if you ask me, gambling was his ruin; il exprima, A: ouvrit, l'a. que l'on marchât sur Rome, he put forward the view, he proposed, that they should march on Rome; sauf meilleur avis je crois que . . ., with all due deference I think that . . .; A: aller aux a., to put the question to the vote; Prov: deux a. valent mieux qu'un, two heads are better than one; s.a. TÊTE 2; à, selon, mon a. . . ., in my opinion . . ., to my mind . . ., as it strikes me . . .; I consider that . . .; à mon humble a., in my humble opinion; de l'a. de tous, in the opinion, judgment, of all; être du même a. que qn, to be of the same mind, of the same opinion, as s.o.; je suis tout à fait de votre a., I am quite of your way of thinking, F: I'm with you; j'ai changé d'a., I have changed my mind; je suis d'a., il m'est a., F: m'est a., qu'il viendra, I rather think, my impression is, that he will come; je suis d'a. qu'il vienne, in my opinion he ought to come, my advice is that he should come; c'est mon a., that's my opinion; êtes-vous d'a. de rester ici? are you for staying here? (b) advice, counsel; un a. paternel, a piece of fatherly advice; donner des a. à qn sur qch., to advise s.o. on sth.; rendre un a., to make a recommendation; prendre, demander, l'a. de qn, to ask s.o.'s advice; se conformer à l'a. de qn, to take s.o.'s advice. 2. Notice, notification, intimation, warning, announcement; a. (au public), notice (to the public), "take notice!" donner a. de qch., to give notice of sth.; donner a. de qch. six mois d'avance, to give six months' notice of sth.; donner a. à qn de qch., to advise s.o. of sth., to give s.o. intelligence of sth.; donner a. que . . ., to give notice that . . .; a. par écrit, notice in writing; a. peu voilé, broad hint; a. au lecteur, (i) foreword, prefatory note (to book); (ii) A: F: a word to the wise; jusqu'à nouvel a., until further notice, until further orders; until you hear further; à moins d'a. contraire, unless I (you) hear to the contrary; Journ: a. divers, miscellaneous column; Com: note, lettre, d'a., advice note, notification of dispatch; a. de livraison, delivery note; suivant a., as per advice; St.Exch: a. d'exécution, contract note.

avisé [avize], a. prudent, circumspect; far-seeing; intelligent, sagacious; shrewd; être trop a. pour faire qch., to be too cautious, wary, to do sth.; il est trop a. pour . . ., he knows better than to . . .; acheteur a., discriminating purchaser; bien a., well-advised; vous serez bien a. de le faire, you will be well-advised to do so; mesures mal avisées, ill-advised, thoughtless, measures; s. c'est un mal a., he is thoughtless; s.a. MALAVISÉ.

aviser [avize]. 1. v.tr. (a) to perceive, to catch a glimpse of (sth., s.o.); F: to spot (s.o.); (b) a. qn de qch., to inform, warn, Com: advise, s.o. of sth.; a. qn de faire qch., to give s.o. notice to do sth.; a. qn que + ind., to warn s.o. that . . . 2. v.i. a. à qch., to decide what to do about (situation, etc.), to see about sth.; a. à un cas, to take such steps as are required by a case; vous ferez bien d'y a., you had better look into it; a. à faire qch., to see about doing sth.; a. à ce que qch. se fasse, to see to it that sth. is done; to take steps to have sth. done; abs. il est temps d'a., it is time to decide, to make up one's mind.

s'aviser. 1. s'a. de qch., to think of sth.; il ne s'avise de rien, he never thinks of anything; s'a. de faire qch., (i) to take it into one's head to do sth.; (ii) to take it upon oneself to do sth.; ne vous en avisez pas! don't dare to do such a thing! you'd better not! A: Prov: de tout s'avise à qui pain fault, necessity is the mother of invention. 2. s'aviser que, to notice, to realize.

aviso [avizo], s.m. aviso, sloop, despatch-boat, A: advice-boat; a.-torpilleur, torpedo-gunboat; a. d'escorte, corvette; canonnière-aviso, gunboat; A: a. de première classe, a. colonial, sloop; U.S: Navy: a. de croisière, cruising cutter.

avissure [avisyr], s.f. = AVISURE.

avis-train [avitrɛ̃], s.m. Rail: warning notice (sent to stations, etc.) of the running of an extra train; pl. avis-trains.

avisure [avizyr], s.f. Tchn: (a) flange (of sheet of metal); (b) flanging.

avitailler [avitaje], v.tr. (a) A: to victual (town, ship); (b) Nau: Av: to (re)fuel (ship, aircraft).

avitaillement [avitajmɑ̃], s.m. (a) A: ordnance and supplies (of town, ship); (b) Nau: Av: (re)-fuelling; a. par poste fixe, hydrant fuelling.

avitailleur [avitajœːr], s.m.Nau: refuelling tanker.

avitaminose [avitaminoːz], s.f. Med: avitaminosis, vitamin deficiency.

avivage [avivaːʒ], s.m. quickening, brightening; reviving (of colours, fire, etc.); touching up (of colour, picture).

avivé [avive], s.m. sawn timber.

avivement [avivmɑ̃], s.m. Surg: refreshing (of edges of a wound).

aviver [avive], v.tr. 1. (a) to quicken; to revive, brighten (colours, etc.); to touch up (colour, picture); to irritate (wound, sore); to excite, stir up (passion); to fan, revive, stir up (fire); to sharpen (appetite); a. d'anciennes rancunes, to revive ancient grudges; (b) to burnish (metalwork); to polish (marble); (c) Metalw: to clean up, to tin (surfaces for soldering). 2. to put a keen edge on (tool, etc.). 3. Surg: a. les bords d'une plaie, to refresh a wound.

s'aviver, (a) (of nature, etc.) to quicken, revive; (b) (of anxiety, etc.) to become more acute, to become keener.

avives [aviːv], s.f.pl. Vet: vives.

aviveur [avivœːr], s.m. brightener (of colour, etc.).

avivoir [avivwaːr], s.m. Tls: burnisher.

avocaillon [avɔkajɔ̃], s.m. Pej: F: briefless barrister, petty lawyer.

avocasser [avɔkase], v.i. F: Pej: to pettifog; (b) to carry on a business as a pettifogging lawyer.

avocasserie [avɔkasri], s.f. Pej: F: pettifoggery, pettifogging, quibbling; chicanery.

avocassier, -ière [avɔkasje, -jɛːr]. Pej: 1. a. F: pettifogging. 2. s.m. pettifogger; pettifogging lawyer.

avocat[1], -ate [avɔka, -at], s. 1. Jur: barrister(-at-law), counsel; Scot: advocate; a. consultant, a. (-)conseil, counsel in chambers, chamber-counsel, consulting barrister; a. général, assistant public prosecutor (in a court of appeal); plaider par a., to be represented by counsel; être reçu a., to be called to the bar; avant d'être a., before going to the bar, before being called to the bar; entendre les avocats des deux parties, to hear counsel on both sides. 2. pleader, advocate, intercessor; Ecc: a. du diable, devil's advocate.

avocat[2], s.m. Bot: avocado(-pear), alligator-pear.

avocat-avoué [avɔkaavwe], s.m. = attorney; pl. avocats-avoués.

avocatier [avɔkatje], s.m. Bot: avocado (tree).

avocatoire [avɔkatwaːr], a. Dipl: lettres avocatoires, letters avocatory.

avocette [avɔsɛt], s.f. Orn: a. (à manteau noir), avocet.

avoi [avwa], s.m. Brew: donner un a., to run off the wort.

avoine [avwan], s.f. oat(s); a. commune, common oat; a. stérile, folle a., wild oats; a. nue, naked, Chinese, oat; pilcorn; a. de Tartarie, Tartarian oat; a. élevée, false oat; farine d'a., oatmeal; flocons d'a., porridge oats; bouillie d'a., (oatmeal) porridge; galette d'a., oat-cake; F: A: semer sa folle a., to sow one's wild oats; F: il a bien gagné son a., he has thoroughly earned his pay; s.a. FILER 7.

avoir [avwaːr]. I. v.tr. (pr.p. ayant; p.p. eu; pr.ind. j'ai, tu as, il a, n. avons, v. avez, ils ont.; pr.sub: j'aie, tu aies, il ait, n. ayons, v. ayez, ils aient; imp. aie, ayons, ayez; p.d. j'avais; p.h. j'eus, tu eus, il eut, n. eûmes, v. eûtes, ils eurent; p.sub. j'eusse; fu. j'aurai; avoir is the auxiliary of all transitive and of many intransitive verbs). 1. (a) to have, possess; a. beaucoup d'amis, to have many friends; a. une grande fortune, to be in possession of a large fortune; a. mille livres de rente(s), to have a thousand pounds a year; il a deux voitures, he runs two cars; il a des poulets, une maîtresse, he keeps chickens, a mistress; la porte n'a pas de clef, the door has no key (to it), there is no key to the door; il a pour lui sa jeunesse, he has (his) youth on his side; il a encore son père, his father is still alive; ce frêle petit homme qu'elle a pour mari, that mousy little husband of hers; il n'a pas de savoir-faire, he lacks savoir-faire; a. une opinion, to hold an opinion; abs: B: à tout homme qui a l'on donnera, unto every one that hath shall be given; (b) elle avait une robe bleue, she had on, was wearing, was in, a blue dress; qu'est-ce que vous avez là? what have you got there? a. une querelle avec qn, to (have a) quarrel with s.o.; a. des amis à dîner, to have friends to dinner; en juin nous avons eu du beau temps, in June we had some fine weather; enfants qui ont de leur mère, children who take after their mother; Dieu ait son âme, God rest his, her, soul; (c) a. les yeux bleus, to have blue eyes; a. les mains pleines, les poches vides, les yeux ouverts, to have one's hands full, one's pockets empty, one's eyes open; il a les bras longs, he has long arms, is long in the arm, is long-armed, has a long reach; F: il a le bras long, he is very influential; a. qn, qch., en horreur, to have a horror of s.o., sth.; a. qn, qch., en haute estime, to hold s.o., sth., in high esteem; to think highly of s.o., sth.; (d) a. dix ans, to be ten years old; mur qui a dix pieds de haut, wall that is ten feet high; (e) for the verbal phrases avoir affaire, faim, froid, pitié, raison, etc., see under these words. 2. (a) to get, obtain, to come into possession of (sth.); il a eu le prix, he got the prize; j'ai eu ce cheval à bon marché, I got, bought, this horse cheap; il m'aura ce poste, he will get me this post; F: j'ai bien eu mon train ce matin, I caught my train all right this morning; F: je l'ai eu, I passed (my exam.); la propriété qu'il a eue de son père, the property which he inherited from his father; j'ai eu sa réponse ce matin, I got his answer this morning; P: a. une femme, to have a woman; Tp: j'ai eu du mal à vous a. (au téléphone), I have had some trouble getting you (on the phone); Tp: vous l'avez, you're through, U.S: you're connected; (b) a. un enfant, to have, bear, a child; combien d'enfants a-t-elle eus? how many children has she had? (c) il avait eu d'elle deux enfants, he had had two children by her; (d) W.Tel: a. Paris, to tune in to, get, pick up, Paris. 3. F: to get the better of (s.o.), to pull a fast one (on s.o.); je l'aurai au tournant! I'll get him yet! comment on les a eus, how we got the better of them; P: on l'a eu! he's been had! U.S: he's been taken for a ride! P: il a été bien eu! he's been properly, well and truly, had! he's been had good and proper! on ne m'a pas comme ça, you can't fool me. 4. avoir = FAIRE, etc., chiefly in p.h.; elle eut une exclamation, she uttered an exclamation; il eut un mouvement brusque, he made a sudden gesture; il eut un sourire dédaigneux, he smiled disdainfully. 5. to be ill, to ail; qu'avez-vous? qu'est-ce que vous avez? what is the matter with you? F: j'ai que je suis furieux, the matter is that I am furious; il a quelque chose, there is something the matter with him; a. la rougeole, to have measles; a. une quinte de toux, to have a fit of coughing. 6. en avoir; (a) nous en avons pour deux heures, it will take us two hours; we'll be two hours; j'en ai assez, I've had enough (of it), I am tired, sick, of it, esp. U.S: I'm through; j'en ai pour la vie, it will last me a lifetime; tu en as pour dix francs, (i) you'll have to pay ten francs; (ii) you've got ten francs' worth; F: vous en aurez, you've got it coming to you; (b) en a. à, contre, qn, to have a grudge against s.o., to be angry with s.o.; est-ce à moi que vous en avez? are you annoyed with, getting at, me? à qui en avez-vous? who are you cross with? who are you getting at? quoi qu'il en ait, whatever he may say, feel; (c) il en a., (i) he's been hard hit; (ii) he's smitten (with love). 7. (a) a. qch. à faire, to have sth. to do, to be obliged to do sth.; je n'ai rien à faire, I have nothing to do;

j'ai à travailler, j'ai un devoir à finir, I have work to do, an exercise to finish; **vous n'avez pas à vous inquiéter,** you have no need to feel anxious; **j'ai à me plaindre de . . .,** I have cause to complain of . . .; **moi, je n'ai pas à travailler,** I don't have to work, I haven't got to work; **après cela je n'ai plus qu'à me taire,** after that I may as well hold my tongue; **je n'ai plus qu'à me retirer,** it only remains for me to withdraw; the only thing for me to do now is to withdraw; (*b*) **je n'ai que faire de cela,** I don't need that. **8.** *impers.* **y avoir;** (*a*) **qu'est-ce qu'il peut y a. dans ce tiroir?** what can there be in this drawer? **il n'y avait rien dans le porte-monnaie,** there was nothing in the purse, the purse had nothing in it, the purse was empty; **combien y a-t-il de blessés?** how many wounded are there? **il n'y en a qu'un,** there is only one; **il n'y a eu qu'eux de tués,** they were the only ones killed; **un homme comme il y en a peu,** a man in a thousand; **il y en a qui disent que . . .,** there are some, those, who say that . . .; **il y en a un qui va être surpris,** someone is in for a surprise; **il n'y a qu'à donner le signal,** (i) the only thing left to do is to give the signal; (ii) you have only to give the signal; **il n'y a pas de quoi,** don't mention it; **il y aurait de l'impertinence à moi de le démentir,** it would be out of place for me to deny it; **qu'est-ce qu'il y a à voir?** what is there to see? **il n'y a pas de village qui n'ait son église,** there is no village without its church; (*b*) **il doit y a. quelque chose,** something must be the matter; **il y a quelque chose,** there is something the matter; **qu'est-ce qu'il y a?** what's the matter? *F:* what's up? **qu'y a-t-il à présent?** what now? *A:* **tant (il) y a qu'elle l'a quitté,** to cut a long story short, she left him; *F:* **personne ne sait si ç'avait été la polio, tant y a qu'il en est mort,** no one knows if it was polio, anyway he died of it; (*c*) **il y a deux ans,** two years ago; **il y a deux ans aujourd'hui que je suis arrivé,** it is two years today since I arrived; **il y avait six mois que j'attendais,** I had been waiting for six months; **elle était venue il y avait deux ans,** she had come two years previously, before; **il y a une dizaine d'années,** some ten years ago, back; *F:* **combien y a-t-il qu'ils sont partis?** how long (ago) is it since they left? **il doit y a. au moins trois ans,** it must be at least three years ago; **il y a de cela trente ans,** that was thirty years ago; (*d*) **combien y a-t-il d'ici (à) Londres?** how far is it (from here) to London? **il y a bien dix milles d'ici (à) Londres,** it is a good ten miles (from here) to London. **9.** *aux. use;* **j'ai fini,** I have finished; **attendez que nous ayons fini,** wait till we have finished; **je l'ai déjà vu, je les ai déjà vus,** I have already seen him, I have seen them, before; **je l'ai vu, vue, hier,** I saw him, her, yesterday; **j'ai eu vingt ans hier,** I was twenty yesterday; **je l'avais vu la veille,** I had seen him the day before; **j'eus, j'ai eu, bientôt fini de m'habiller,** I (had) soon finished dressing, I was not long dressing; **quand il eut fini de parler, il vint à moi, quand il a eu fini de parler, il est venu à moi,** when he had finished speaking, he came to me; **j'aurai bientôt fini,** I shall soon have finished.

II. **avoir,** *s.m.* property, what is possessed; **tout mon a.,** all I possess, all I am worth; my all; **hériter d'un joli a.,** to inherit a substantial amount of money, *F:* to come in for a pretty penny; *Com:* **doit et a.,** debit and credit.

avoirdupois [avwardypwa], *s.m. Meas:* avoirdupois.

avoisinant [avwazinɑ̃], *a.* neighbouring; close by, near by.

avoisiné [avwazine], *a. A:* **être bien a.,** (i) to have good neighbours; (ii) to be in a good neighbourhood.

avoisiner [avwazine], *v.tr.* **a. qch.,** to be near sth., close, adjacent, to sth., to border (up)on sth.; **des idées qui avoisinent la folie,** ideas bordering on, next door to, madness.

s'avoisiner, *O:* (*of season, event*) to approach, draw near.

avortement [avɔrtəmɑ̃], *s.m.* **1.** (*a*) **a. spontané,** miscarriage; (*b*) **a. provoqué,** (procured) abortion; (*c*) (*of animal*) slipping, slinking, casting (of young); **a. épizootique,** infectious abortion; **2.** *Bot:* non-formation, incompletion (of a part). **3.** failure, miscarriage, falling through (of plan, etc.).

avorter [avɔrte], *v.i.* **1.** to miscarry, to abort; **faire a. (qn),** to procure abortion; to bring on a miscarriage. **2.** (*of animals*) to slip, slink, cast (young). **3.** *Bot:* to develop imperfectly; to fail to ripen; to abort; **arbres avortés,** stunted trees. **4. entreprise qui a avorté,** venture that has miscarried, proved abortive, gone wrong, come to nothing, fallen through; **faire a. un dessein,** to frustrate a plan, to bring a plan to nought.

avorteur, -euse [avɔrtœːr, -øːz], *F:* **1.** *a.* **médecin a.,** abortionist. **2.** *s.f.* **avorteuse,** abortionist.

avorton [avɔrtɔ̃], *s.m.* abortion; (*a*) *A:* child, animal, born prematurely; (*b*) abortion, monster, freak; deformed, undeveloped, plant, animal; (*c*) puny, undersized, stunted, *Pej:* man, child; *F:* a shrimp; *P:* little squit.

avouable [avwabl̩], *a.* avowable (fact, motive); **c'est un métier plus a.,** as a trade it sounds better, it's a more respectable trade.

avoué[1] [avwe], *s.m. Jur:* = solicitor, *U.S:* attorney.

avoué[2], *a.* **1.** (*a*) acknowledged, admitted (fact); (*b*) confessed (author of . . .). **2.** ostensible (purpose, object).

avouer [avwe], *v.tr.* **1.** (*a*) to acknowledge, recognize (s.o., debt, etc.); (*b*) **a. qn pour frère,** to acknowledge, own, s.o. as one's brother; **s'a. coupable,** to admit one's guilt; **s'a. vaincu,** to acknowledge oneself beaten, to acknowledge defeat; *F:* to throw in one's cards, one's hand; (*c*) to take responsibility for, to endorse (an action); **j'avoue tout ce que vous avez fait,** I endorse all you have done. **2.** to confess, admit, own (fault, etc.); **avouez tout!** make a clean breast of it! **elle avoue trente-cinq ans,** she admits to being thirty-five; **ceci me surprend, je l'avoue,** this surprises me, I confess, I must say; **a. avoir fait qch.,** to confess, own (up), to having done sth.

avoyer[1] [avwaje], *s.m. Jur:* avoyer, senior magistrate (in some Swiss cantons).

avoyer[2], *v.tr. conj. like* **aboyer;** *Carp:* to swage (a saw).

avranchin, -ine [avrɑ̃ʃɛ̃, -in], *a. & s.* (i) *Geog:* (native, inhabitant) of Avranches; (ii) *Hist:* the Avranchin region.

avranchinais, -aise [avrɑ̃ʃinɛ, -ɛːz], *a. & s. Geog:* (native, inhabitant) of Avranches.

avril [avril], *s.m.* April; **en a.,** in April; **au mois d'a.,** in the month of April; **pluie d'a.,** April showers; **le sept a.,** (on) the seventh of April, (on) April (the) seventh; **le premier a.,** (i) the first of April; (ii) All Fools' Day, April Fools' Day; **faire un poisson d'a. à qn,** to make an April fool of s.o.; **poisson d'a.!** April fool! *Prov:* **en a. ne te découvre pas d'un fil,** cast not a clout ere May is out.

avrilé [avrile], *a. Agr:* sown in April.

avulsion [avylsjɔ̃], *s.f.* **1.** *Jur:* avulsion (of land). **2.** extraction (of tooth).

avunculaire [avɔ̃kylɛːr], *a.* avuncular.

axe [aks], *s.m.* **1.** axis (*pl.* axes) (of plant, the earth, ellipse, etc.); **grand a., petit a.,** major, minor, axis; *Civ.E:* **a. d'une route, d'un pont,** centre line of a road, of a bridge; **a. de circulation,** major route; **conduire sur l'a. de la chaussée,** to drive on the crown of the road; **en plein dans l'a. de la tradition française,** following the direct line, main stream, of French tradition; *Mth:* **a. des** *x*, **des** *y*, *x*-axis, *y*-axis; **axes de coordonnées,** co-ordinate axes; *Mec:* **axes principaux d'un corps,** principal axes of a body; *Mec:* **a. neutre,** zero-line (of stresses); **cristal à deux axes,** biaxial crystal. **2.** *Mch: Mec.E: etc:* axle, spindle, pin; **a. d'une meule,** spindle, axle, arbor, of a grindstone; **a. de pompe,** pump spindle; **a. démultiplié,** reducing axle, shaft; **a. d'une grue,** pin of a crane; **a. tournant d'une voiture,** axle(-tree) of a vehicle; **a. de chape,** yoke pin; *I.C.E: etc:* **a. du piston,** gudgeon pin; **a. mobile,** floating gudgeon pin; **a. de tête de biellette,** wrist, knuckle, pin. **3.** *Hist:* axis; **les Puissances de l'A.,** the Axis powers. **4.** (*a*) *Mil:* **a. de progression,** axis of advance; main direction of advance; **a. de marche,** direction, axis of march; **a. (principal) de ravitaillement,** axis of supply; main line of supply (MLS); *U.S:* main supply route (MSR); **a. (principal) des transmissions,** axis of signal communication, main signal artery; *U.S:* main axis, line, of communications; (*b*) *Av:* **a. de sustentation,** lift axis; **a. de descente,** glide-path, line of descent; **a. balisé,** radio range course; **a. balisé d'atterrissage,** radio landing beam; **a. de référence,** datum line.

axer [akse], *v.tr.* **1.** *Mch:* to centre; **être axé sur, autour de,** to follow (a tendency, etc.), to centre on; **elle axait sa vie autour de son mari,** she centred her life around her husband. **2.** *F:* to direct, guide.

axial, -aux [aksjal, -o], *a.* axial (line, plane); *Mec:* **effort de compression axiale,** collapsible load; *Navy:* **pièce axiale,** gun firing all round; **éclairage a.,** central overhead lighting (of streets).

axifère [aksifɛːr], *a. Bot:* bearing an axis.

axile [aksil], *a. Bot:* axile.

axilé [aksile], *a. Bot:* having, growing round, an axis.

axillaire [aksil(l)ɛːr], *a. Anat: Bot:* axillary.

axille [aksil], *s.f. Orn:* axilla.

axilliflore [aksiliflɔr], *a. Bot:* having axillary flowers.

axinite [aksinit], *s.f. Miner:* axinite.

axiolite [aksjɔlit], *s.m. Miner:* axiolite.

axiologie [aksjɔlɔʒi], *s.f. Phil:* axiology.

axiologique [aksjɔlɔʒik], *a. Phil:* axiological.

axiomatique [aksjɔmatik], *a.* axiomatic(al).

axiomatisation [aksjɔmatizasjɔ̃], *s.f.* axiomatization.

axiomatiser [aksjɔmatize], *v.tr.* to axiomatize.

axiome [aksjoːm], *s.m.* (*a*) *Mth: Phil:* axiom; (*b*) axiom, truism.

axiomètre [aksjɔmɛtr̩], *s.m. Nau:* helm indicator, steering indicator; tell-tale.

axis[1] [aksis], *s.m. Anat:* axis (second vertebra).

axis[2], *s.m. Z:* axis (deer).

axoïdien, -ienne [aksɔidjɛ̃, -jɛn], *a. Anat:* axoidean.

axolotl [aksɔlɔtl̩], *s.m. Amph:* axolotl.

axone [aksɔn], *s.m. Anat:* axon.

axonge [aksɔ̃ːʒ], *s.f. Pharm: etc:* lard, hog's fat; *Mil:* rifle grease; axle grease.

axonométrique [aksɔnɔmetrik], *a. Mch.Draw:* **perspective a.,** axonometric projection.

axoplasma [aksɔplasma], *s.m.* axoplasm.

axopode [aksɔpɔd], *s.m. Z:* axopodium, axopod.

axuel, -elle [aksɥɛl], *a.* = AXIAL.

ayant [ɛjɑ̃]. **1.** *See* AVOIR. **2.** *s.m. Jur:* **a. cause,** assign, trustee, executor; *pl.* **ayants cause; a. droit,** rightful claimant or owner; interested party; beneficiary; *pl.* **ayants droit.**

aye-aye [ajaj], *s.m. Z:* aye-aye; *pl. ayes-ayes.*

azalée [azale], *s.f. Bot:* azalea.

azaline [azalin], *s.f. Ch: Phot:* azaline.

Azarias [azarias], *Pr.n.m. B:* Azariah.

azarolier [azarɔlje], *s.m. Bot:* = AZEROLIER.

azédarac(h) [azedarak], *s.m. Bot:* azedarach; bead-tree.

azéotrope [azeɔtrɔp], *a. Ch:* **mélange a.,** azeotropic mixture.

Azerbaïdjan [azɛrbaidʒɑ̃], *Pr.n.m. Geog:* Azerbaijan.

azerbaïdjanais, -aise [azɛrbaidʒanɛ, -ɛz], *a. & s.* Azerbaijani.

azerole [azrɔl], *s.f. Bot:* azarole, (*fruit of*) Neapolitan medlar.

azerolier [azrɔlje], *s.m. Bot:* azarole, Neapolitan medlar.

azide [azid], *s.m. Ch:* azide.

azimide [azimid], *s.m. Ch:* azimino compound.

azimidé [azimide], *a. Ch:* azimido-, azimino-.

azimut [azimyt], *s.m.* **1.** *Astr: etc:* azimuth; *Nau: Surv: etc:* **prendre un a.,** to take a bearing; **a. magnétique,** magnetic azimuth; **a. vrai,** true azimuth; **a. inverse,** reverse azimuth; *Mil:* **défense tous azimuts,** all-directional, all-round, perimeter defence; *F:* **dans tous les azimuts,** everywhere, all over the place; *F:* **direction tous azimuts,** facing all ways, all directions. **2.** *Arch:* **a. d'un mur,** inclination of a wall to the meridian.

azimutal, -aux [azimytal, -o]. **1.** *a.* azimuth(al); **cercle a.,** azimuth circle; **cadran a.,** azimuth dial; *Ph:* **nombre quantique a.,** azimuthal quantum number. **2.** *s.m.* azimuth compass.

azimuté [azimyte], *a. P:* crazy, batty, bonkers.

Azincourt [azɛ̃kuːr], *Pr.n.m. Geog: Hist:* Agincourt.

azine [azin], *s.f. Ch:* azine.

azoamidé [azɔamide], **azoaminé** [azɔamine], *a. Ch:* aminoazo (dye, etc.).

azobenzène [azɔbɛ̃zɛn], *s.m. Ch:* azobenzene.

azobenzoïque [azɔbɛ̃zɔik], *a. Ch:* azobenzoic.

azoïque[1] [azɔik], *a. Geol:* azoic.

azoïque[2], *a. Ch: Ind:* **colorants azoïques,** azo dyes; aniline dyes; **composés azoïques,** azo compounds.

azol(e) [azɔl], *s.m. Ch:* azol(e).

azolla [azɔla], *s.f.,* **azolle** [azɔl], *s.f. Bot:* Azolla.

azonal, -aux [azɔnal, -o], *a.* azonal, azonic.

azoospermie [azɔɔspɛrmi], *s.f. Med: Physiol:* azoospermia, azoospermatism.

Azor [azɔːr], *A:* **1.** *Pr.n.m.* (*name given to dogs*) = Fido. **2.** *s.m.* (*a*) *F:* **voilà Arthur et son a.,** here comes Arthur with his dog; (*b*) *Mil: P:* knapsack; (*c*) *P:* pistol, barker.

azorelle [azɔrɛl], *s.f. Bot:* azorella.

azotate [azɔtat], *s.m. Ch:* nitrate; **a. de potasse,** nitre, saltpetre.

azotation [azɔtasjɔ̃], *s.f. Ch:* nitrogenization.

azote [azɔt], *s.m. Ch:* nitrogen.

azoté [azɔte], *a.* nitrogenous; *Agr:* engrais azotés, nitrate fertilizers, *F:* nitrates; *Exp:* poudre azotée, nitrogen powder; aliment a., nitrogenous food.

azotémie [azɔtemi], *s.f. Med:* azot(a)emia.

azotémique [azɔtemik], *a. Med:* azot(a)emic.

azoter [azɔte], *v.tr.* to nitrogenize, azotize.

azoteux, -euse [azɔtø, -øːz], *a. Ch:* nitrous.

azoth [azɔt], *s.m. A: Alch:* azoth.

azothydrique [azɔtidrik], *a. Ch:* hydrazoic.

azotimètre [azɔtimɛtr], *s.m. Ch:* azotometer.

azotine [azɔtin], *s.f. Agr:* shoddy, nitrate fertilizer.

azotique [azɔtik], *a. Ch:* nitric.

azotisation [azɔtizasjɔ̃], *s.f.* = AZOTATION.

azotite [azɔtit], *s.m. Ch:* nitrite.

azotobacter [azɔtɔbaktɛr], *s.m. Bac:* azotobacter.

azotorrhée [azɔtɔr(r)e], *s.f. Med:* azotorrhea.

azoture [azɔtyːr], *s.m. Ch:* hydrazoate, azide.

azoturie [azɔtyri], *s.f. Med:* azoturia.

azotyle [azɔtil], *s.m. Ch:* nitryl.

Azov [azɔv], *Pr.n.m. Geog:* mer d'A., Sea of Azov.

azoxy- [azɔksi-], *comb. fm. Ch:* azoxy-.

azoxybenzène [azɔksibɛ̃zɛn], *s.m. Ch:* azoxybenzene.

azoxyque [azɔksik], *a. & s.m. Ch:* azoxy(-compound).

aztèque [aztɛk]. **1.** *a. & s. Ethn: Hist:* Aztec. **2.** *s.m. P:* little shrimp of a man, little squit.

azulène [azylɛn], *s.m. Ch:* azulene.

azuline [azylin], *s.f. Ch:* azulin.

azulmine [azylmin], *s.f. Ch:* azulmin.

azur [azyːr], *s.m.* **1.** azure, blue; ciel d'a., azure sky; *Geog:* la Côte d'Azur, the Riviera; *Her:* azure; champ d'a., field azure; *Poet:* s'envoler dans l'a., to fly off into the sky, the blue; *Miner:* pierre d'a., (i) lapis lazuli; (ii) lazulite; *Glassm:* smalt; *Dy: Paint:* azure blue. **2.** *Com:* blue (for washing, etc.).

azurable [azyrabl], *a. Dom.Ec: Ind:* which can be blued, tinged with blue.

azurage [azyraːʒ], *s.m. Dom.Ec: Ind:* blu(e)ing (of linen, paper, etc.).

azural, -aux [azyral, -o], *a.* azure, azurean.

azuré, *a.* **1.** (sky-)blue, azure; *Poet:* la plaine azurée, the sea; la voûte azurée, the sky. **2.** tinged with blue. **3.** covered with close parallel lines; *Bookb:* azure.

azuréen, -éenne [azyreɛ̃, -ɛɛn], *a. F:* of, from, the Côte d'Azur.

azurer [azyre], *v.tr.* **1.** *Dom.Ec: Ind:* to blue (linen, etc.). **2.** to tinge with blue.

azurescent [azyrɛs(s)ɑ̃], *a.* bluish.

azurin [azyrɛ̃], *a.* azurine, pale (grey) blue.

azurine [azyrin], *s.f. Dy:* azurin(e).

azurite [azyrit], *s.f. Miner:* azurite.

azuror, -e [azyrɔːr], *a.* blue shot with gold.

azygos [azigos, -os]. *Anat:* **1.** a.inv. azygous, unpaired (vein). **2.** *s.f.* azygous vein.

azygospore [azigɔspɔːr], *s.f. Fung:* azygospore.

azyme [azim]. **1.** *a.* azymous, unleavened; pain a., unleavened bread, *Pharm:* wafer. **2.** *s.m.* azyme; *Jew.Rel:* fête des azymes, feast of unleavened bread.

azymique [azimik], *a.* unfermentable.

azymite [azimit], *s.m. Rel.Hist:* azymite.

B

B, b [be], *s.m.* (the letter) B, b, *F: A:* être marqué au B (bancal, bête, bigle, boiteux, borgne, bossu), (i) to be a poor specimen of humanity; (ii) to be an underhand, suspicious, sort of character; *F: A:* ne parler que par B. et par F. (bougre et foutre), to be foul-mouthed, never to open one's mouth without swearing; **B. . . .** = BOUGRE; *Tp:* B comme Berthe, B for Bertie; *Geol:* horizon B, B-horizon.

Baal [baal], *Pr.n.m. Rel.H:* Baal, *pl.* Baals *or* Baalim.

baba¹ [baba], *s.m. Cu:* (rum) baba.

baba², *a.inv. F:* dumbfounded, flabbergasted; **en rester b.**, to stand in open-mouthed astonishment; *s.m. V:* fanny; *P:* **l'avoir dans le b.**, to be badly let down, to have one's hopes dashed.

B.A. ba [beaba], *s.m.* ce livre vous donne le B.A. ba de la philosophie, this book gives you the ABC, the rudiments, of philosophy.

Babel [babɛl], *Pr.n.f.* Babel; **la tour de B.**, the Tower of Babel; **c'est une vraie tour de B.**, it's a perfect Babel, it's pandemonium.

babélique [babelik], *a.* of, pertaining to, the Tower of Babel; (a) gigantic, immense (building, etc.); (b) confused, discordant (voices, etc.).

babélisme [babelism], *s.m.*

Babet, Babette [babɛ, babɛt], *Pr.n.f. F:* Betty.

babeurre¹ [babœ:r], *s.m.* buttermilk.

babeurre², *s.m.* dasher (of churn).

babiche [babiʃ], *s.f.*, **babichon** [babiʃɔ̃], *s.m.* lapdog.

babichonner [babiʃɔne], *v.tr. F:* to clean up, tidy up, comb the hair of (child).

babil [babi(l)], *s.m.* **1.** prattling (of child); twittering (of birds); babbling (of a brook). **2.** prattle (of children); *F:* il n'a que du b., his talk is all twaddle.

babilan [babilɑ̃], *s.m.* impotent man.

babillage [babijaʒ], *s.m.* = BABIL.

babillan [babijɑ̃], *s.m.* = BABILAN.

babillant [babijɑ̃], *a.* prattling (child); babbling (stream).

babillard, -arde [babija:r, -ard]. **1.** *a.* garrulous, talkative; **cours d'eau b.**, babbling brook. **2.** *s.* (a) tattler, chatter box; (b) *Ven:* (of hound) babbler. **3.** *s.m. F:* notice board. **4.** *s.f. P:* babillarde, letter, missive.

babillement [babijmɑ̃], *s.m.* = BABIL.

babiller [babije], *v.i.* to prattle; to chatter; (of brook, hound) to babble; **b. sur qn**, to chatter, gossip, about s.o.

babines [babin], *s.f.pl. Z:* pendulous lips (of monkey); chops (of ruminants); *F:* lips (of pers.); **s'essuyer les b.**, to wipe one's lips; **vous vous en lécherez les b.**, you'll lick your chops, smack your lips, over it; **se caler les b.**, to have a good blow-out, a good tuck-in.

Babinski [babɛ̃ski], *Pr.n.m. Med:* signe de B., Babinski's reflex.

babiole [babjɔl], *s.f.* **1.** *A:* bauble, toy. **2.** curio, knick-knack; trifle.

babiroussa [babirusa], *s.m. Z:* horned hog; babirussa.

babisme [babism], *s.m. Rel.H:* Babism, Babiism.

bablad, bablah [babla], *s.m. Bot:* bablah.

bâbord [babɔ:r], *s.m. Nau:* port (side), *A:* larboard; **la barre toute à b.! toute! b. la barre!** hard a-port! venez sur b.! starboard (the helm)! **la terre par b.!** land on the port side! **par b. devant**, on the port bow; *Row:* aviron de b.,

stroke-side oar; **courir, faire route, b. amures**, to sail, to run, on the port tack; **être b. amures**, to be on the port tack.

bâbordais [babɔrdɛ], *s.m. Nau:* man of the port watch; **les b.**, the port watch.

babouche [babuʃ], *s.f.* Turkish slipper; babouche.

babouin [babwɛ̃], *s.m.* **1.** (a) *Z:* baboon; (b) *F: A:* c'est un petit b., f. une petite babouine, he, she, is a young monkey, a little imp. **2.** *F:* pimple (on the lip).

babouines [babwin], *s.f.pl. F:* (= BABINES) mouth, lips.

babouvisme [babuvism], *s.m. Pol.Ec:* babouvism.

baby [babi, bebi], *s.m.* **1.** *F:* baby, tiny tot. **2.** *pl. A:* ankle-strap shoes; *pl.* babys.

baby-foot [bebifut], *s.m. F:* pin-table football.

Babylone [babilɔn], *Pr.n.f. A.Geog:* Babylon; *B:* **la Captivité de B.**, the Babylonian Captivity.

Babylonie [babilɔni], *Pr.n.f. A.Geog:* Babylonia.

babylonien, -ienne [babilɔnjɛ̃, -jen], *a. & s.* Babylonian; *F:* **hôtel b.**, huge hotel.

babylonisme [babilɔnism], *s.m.* cult of the huge (*esp.* in building).

baby-sitting [bebisitiŋ], *s.m. F:* **faire du b.-s.**, to baby-sit.

bac¹ [bak], *s.m.* **1.** (a) ferry; ferry boat; pontoon; emplacement, points d'accostage de b., ferry site; **b. à traille**, trail ferry; **b. à chaîne**, chain ferry; **b. à piétons**, passenger ferry; **b. à voitures**, car ferry; **b. transbordeur**, train ferry; **passer qn dans un b.**, to ferry s.o. across; **passer le b.**, to cross the ferry; (b) *Jur:* **droit de b.**, ferry (right). **2.** tank, vat; pot (of electric cell); jar, box, container (of accumulator); box, container (for food, etc.); (miner's) truck or tub; hopper (of dredger, etc.); **b. à ordures**, dustbin; **b. à laver**, wash tub; *Ind:* **b. de lavage**, washer; *Min:* **b. à boue**, mud pit.

bac², *s.m. F:* (= BACCARA(T)) **tailler un b.**, to have a game of baccarat.

bac³, *s.m. F:* = BACCALAURÉAT.

bacaliau [bakaljo], *Dial: Nau:* stock-fish, dried cod.

baccalauréat [bakalɔrea], *s.m.* **1.** b. (de l'enseignement secondaire) = General Certificate of Education (A Level); *Scot:* Scottish Certificate of Education; *Eire:* School Leaving Certificate. **2.** b. en droit, degree granted when a student has passed his first two examinations for the *Licence en Droit*.

baccara(t)¹ [bakara], *s.m. Cards:* baccara(t).

baccarat², *s.m. Glassm:* crystal (made at Baccarat).

bacchanal [bakanal], *s.m. no pl. F:* uproar, racket, row; **faire un b. de tous les diables**, to make, kick up, the dickens, the hell, of a row, to raise Cain.

bacchanale [bakanal], *s.f.* **1.** *Rom.Ant:* les bacchanales, the bacchanalia. **2.** (a) drinking song; (b) *F: O:* noisy dance, uproarious dance; (c) *F: O:* orgy, drunken revel.

bacchanaliser [bakanalize], *v.i. F: O:* to revel.

bacchante [bakɑ̃:t], *s.f.* **1.** *Ant:* bacchante, maenad. **2.** *pl. P:* moustache.

baccharis [bakaris], *s.m. Bot:* Baccharis.

bacchie [baki], *s.f.* red flush (on nose of drunkard).

Bacchus [bakys], *Pr.n.m. Rom.Myth:* Bacchus; adorateur, disciple, enfant, de B., son of Bacchus.

baccien [baksjɛ̃], *a. Bot:* fruit b., berry.

bacciforme [baksifɔrm], *a. Bot:* bacciform, baccate, berry-shaped.

baccifère [baksifɛ:r], *a. Bot:* bacciferous, baccate, berry-producing.

baccivore [baksivɔ:r], *a. Nat.Hist:* baccivorous, berry-eating.

bâchage [baʃaʒ], *s.m.* (*action of*) covering with tarpaulin, awning, etc.

bachal, -s [baʃal], *s.m. Dial:* water-trough.

bâche [baːʃ], *s.f.* **1.** (a) tank, cistern; *Mch:* b. de condenseur, hot well of a condenser; b. d'alimentation, feed-tank; (b) pool (left at low tide); (c) *Fish:* b. volante, traînante, bag-net, drag-net. **2.** *Hort:* forcing frame. **3.** (a) (*coarse canvas*) cover (for hayricks, etc.); tilt (for carts, boats, etc.); awning; b. goudronnée, tarpaulin; b. de campement, ground sheet; *P:* se mettre dans les bâches, to get between the sheets; (b) casing (of turbine, etc.). **4.** canvas band (of conveyor). **5.** *P:* cap, *P:* titfer.

bachelette [baʃlɛt], *s.f. A:* maid, lass.

bachelier¹ [baʃəlje], *s.m. A:* **1.** (a) bachelor, novice in arms; (b) young man, youth. **2.** (a) *Sch:* b. (formé), student who had completed a course in theology; (b) b. d'église, minor canon.

bachelier², -ière [baʃəlje, -jɛːr], *s. Sch:* (a) b., bachelière, en droit, student who has passed the first two examinations for the *Licence en Droit*; (b) student who has passed the *baccalauréat, q.v.*

bâcher [baʃe], *v.tr.* to sheet (sth.) over; to cover (sth.) with a tarpaulin; to tilt, to put a tilt on (cart, etc.); to case (turbine, etc.).

se bâcher, *P:* (a) to go to bed, to turn in; (b) to dress.

bachi-bouzouk [baʃibuzuk], *s.m. Turk.Hist:* bashi-bazouk; *pl.* bachi-bouzouks.

bachique [baʃik], *a.* bacchic; **scène b.**, bacchanalian scene; **chanson b.**, drinking song.

Bachkirs [baʃkir], *s.m.pl. Ethn:* Bashkirs.

bacholle [baʃɔl], *s.f.* small barrel; large wooden bucket.

bachon [baʃɔ̃], *s.m.* (small) pine log (used for consolidating mountain paths).

bachonnage [baʃɔnaʒ], *s.m.* consolidation of mountain paths (with pine logs).

bachot¹ [baʃo], *s.m.* **1.** wherry, punt. **2.** *Ind:* sieve.

bachot², *s.m. F:* = BACCALAURÉAT 1; *A:* b. complet, both parts of the *baccalauréat*; **four, boîte, à b.**, crammer's, cramming school.

bachotage [baʃota:ʒ], *s.m. Sch: F:* cramming.

bachoter [baʃɔte], *Sch: F:* **1.** *v.tr.* to cram (up) (a subject) for the *baccalauréat*. **2.** *v.i.* (a) to cram, grind; (b) to sit the *baccalauréat* examination.

bachoteur¹ [baʃotœːr], *s.m.* wherryman.

bachoteur², -euse [baʃotœːr, -øz], *s.*, **bachotier, -ière** [baʃotje, -jɛːr], *s. F:* student cramming, swotting up, for an exam., *esp.* the *baccalauréat*.

bachotte [baʃɔt], *s.f.* barrel (used for the transport of live fish).

bacile [basil], *s.m. Bot: F:* samphire.

bacillaire [basilɛːr]. **1.** *a.* bacillar(y). **2.** *s.m. & f. F:* tubercular person. **3.** *s.f. Algae:* bacillaria.

bacille [basil], *s.m.* **1.** *Biol:* bacillus; **b. de Koch**, tubercle bacillus; *Med:* **porteur de bacilles**, germ-carrier. **2.** *Ent:* bacillus, stick-insect, walking-stick; *s.a.* VIRGULE 1.

bacillémie [basil(l)emi], *s.f. Med:* **1.** bacillemia. **2.** bacillary septicaemia. **3.** (*incorrect use*) generalized tubercular infection.

bacilliforme [basil(l)ifɔrm], *a.* bacilliform, rodshaped.

bacillisation [basil(l)izasjɔ̃], *s.f. Med:* bacillus infection.
bacillose [basil(l)oːz], *s.f. Med:* bacillosis; bacillus infection; *esp.* pulmonary tuberculosis.
bacillurie [basil(l)yri], *s.f. Med:* bacilluria.
bacilloscopie [basilɔskɔpi], *s.f. Med:* bacilloscopy.
bacitracine [basitrasin], *s.f. Med:* bacitracin.
backer [bake], *v.tr. & i. F:* to back (train, steamer).
bâclage [bɑklaːʒ], *s.m.* **1.** *Nau:* (*a*) closing, blocking (of a harbour or port); (*b*) gathering, arrangements, of boats in port; (*c*) order of loading or unloading (of ships). **2.** *F:* doing (sth.) perfunctorily; scamping (of work).
bâcle [bɑːkl], *s.f.* bar (of door).
bâclé [bɑkle], *a.* **1.** blocked (harbour, etc.). **2.** slap-dash (work, etc.); **un travail b.,** a botched job.
bâcler [bɑkle], *v.tr.* **1.** (*a*) *O:* to bar, bolt (door, etc.); **b. une maison,** to lock up a house; (*b*) *F:* to slam (door). **2.** *Nau:* (*a*) to block up, close (port, harbour); (*b*) **b. des bateaux,** (i) to gather boats; (ii) to lash boats side by side (alongside quay). **3.** *F:* to do (sth.) perfunctorily; to scamp, skimp, botch (work); to hurry over (one's toilet, etc.).
bâcleur, -euse [bɑklœːr, -øːz], *s. F:* **1. b. de besogne,** man who scamps his work. **2. b. d'affaires, de besogne,** hustler.
bacon [bakɔ̃, bekœn], *s.m.* bacon.
bacon(n)er [bakɔne], *v.tr.* to preserve (fish) in brine.
baconien, -ienne [bakɔnjɛ̃, -jɛn], *a. Phil:* Baconian; **induction baconienne,** inductive method, philosophical induction, Baconian method.
baconisme [bakɔnism], *s.m. Phil:* Baconianism.
bactériacées [bakterjase], *s.f.pl. Biol:* Bacteriaceae.
bactéricide [bakterisid]. **1.** *a.* bactericidal. **2.** *s.m.* bactericide.
bactérie [bakteri], *s.f.* **1.** *Biol:* bacterium, *pl.* -ia. **2.** *Ent:* bacteria, *F:* stick-insect.
bactérien, -ienne [bakterjɛ̃, -jɛn], *a.* bacterial.
bactériologie [bakterjɔlɔʒi], *s.f.* bacteriology.
bactériologique [bakterjɔlɔʒik], *a.* bacteriological; **guerre b.,** bacteriological, germ, warfare.
bactériologiste [bakterjɔlɔʒist], **bactériologue** [bakterjɔlɔg], *s.m. or f. Biol:* bacteriologist.
bactériolyse [bakterjɔliz], *s.f. Med:* bacteriolysis.
bactériolysine [bakterjɔlizin], *s.f. Med:* bacteriolysin.
bactériophage [bakterjɔfaːʒ], *s.m. Biol:* bacteriophage (virus).
bactérioscopie [bakterjɔskɔpi], *s.f.* bacterioscopy.
bactériose [bakterjoz], *s.f. Bot:* bacteriosis.
bactériostase [bakterjɔstɑz], *s.m.* bacteriostasis.
bactériostatique [bakterjɔstatik], *a.* bacteriostatic.
bactériothérapie [bakterjɔterapi], *s.f.* bacteriotherapy.
bactériurie [bakterjyri], *s.f. Med:* bacteriuria.
Bactres [baktr̥], *Pr.n.f. A.Geog:* (town of) Bactria.
Bactriane [baktrian], *Pr.n.f. A.Geog:* (province of) Bactria.
bactrien, -enne [baktriɛ̃, -ɛn], *a. & s. A.Geog:* Bactrian.
bactrioles [baktriɔl], *s.f.pl.* trimmings (from gold leaf).
bacul [baky], *s.m. Harn:* swingle-bar, whipple tree.
baculiforme [bakylifɔrm], *a.* baculiform.
baculite [bakylit], *s.f. Paleont:* baculite.
badaud, -aude [bado, -oːd], *a. & s.* (*the s. is rarely f.*) idler; person who stands and stares (in the streets); *U.S: F:* rubberneck; **faire le b.,** *F:* to gape, gawp; **le Parisien est b.,** Parisians are full of idle curiosity, like to stand and stare.
badaudage [badodaːʒ], *s.m.* sauntering, strolling; **b. devant les étalages,** window-shopping.
badauder [badode], *v.i.* to stroll about (full of idle curiosity); *F:* to gape, gawp.
badauderie [badodri], *s.f.* **1.** sauntering, lounging. **2.** *pl. A:* puerilities, absurdities.
badaudier, -ière [badodje, -jeːr], *a.* given to idling, fond of gazing at shop windows.
Bade [bad], *Pr.n.f. Geog:* Baden.
badelaire [badəlɛːr], *s.m. A.Arm:* falchion.
baderne [badɛrn], *s.f.* **1.** *A: Nau:* (*a*) thrummed mat; (*b*) (boat-)fender, pudd(en)ing, dolphin; (*c*) *Mec.E:* (packing-)gasket. **2.** *F: Pej:* **une (vieille) b.,** an old fogey, an old fossil, an old stick-in-the-mud, *Mil:* a blimp.
badernisme [badɛrnism], *s.m. F: Pej:* stick-in-the-mud attitude, blimpishness.
badge [badʒ], *s.m. Scouting:* badge.
badiane [badjan], *s.f.*, **badianier** [badjanje], *s.m. Bot:* Chinese anise-(tree).

badigeon [badiʒɔ̃], *s.m.* **1.** (*a*) (colour-)wash, distemper (for walls, etc.); **b. à la chaux,** whitewash; (*b*) *F:* coat of paint (to renovate old furniture, etc.); (*c*) *F:* make-up, *F:* paint (for the face); (*d*) badigeon (for making good defects in woodwork, sculpture, etc.). **2.** whitewash brush, distempering brush.
badigeonnage [badiʒɔnaːʒ], *s.m.* **1.** (*a*) whitewashing; (*b*) colour-washing, distempering; (*c*) *Med:* painting (with iodine, etc.). **2.** (*a*) wash (of distemper, etc.); (*b*) application (of iodine, etc.).
badigeonner [badiʒɔne], *v.tr.* **1.** (*a*) **b. une surface de qch.,** to brush over a surface with sth.; **b. un mur en blanc, en couleur,** to whitewash, to colour-wash, distemper a wall; (*b*) *F:* to paint, touch up (old piece of furniture, etc.); to make up, *F:* paint (one's face); (*c*) *Med:* to paint **(d'iode, à l'iode,** with iodine). **2.** *Sculp: etc:* to stop, plaster up, (defects) with badigeon.
badigeonneur [badiʒɔnœːr], *s.m.* **1.** (*a*) whitewasher; (*b*) *Art: F: Pej:* dauber. **2.** patcher-up (of furniture, etc.).
badigoinces [badigwɛ̃ːs], *s.f.pl. P:* = BABOUINES.
badin[1], **-ine**[1] [badɛ̃, -in]. **1.** *a.* merry, playful; **style b.,** light, playful, style. **2.** *s.* joker, banterer.
badin[2], *s.m. Av:* air-speed indicator.
badinage [badinaːʒ], *s.m.* (*a*) trifling, joking, jesting; **l'élégant b. de Musset,** Musset's elegant trifling; **je l'ai dit par b.,** I said it as a joke; (*b*) banter, badinage.
badine[2] [badin], *s.f.* **1.** cane, switch. **2.** *sg. or pl.* (blacksmith's) elbow-tongs.
badiner [badine]. **1.** *v.i.* (*a*) to jest, trifle; **b. de tout,** to make sport of everything, to turn everything into a joke; **on ne badine pas avec l'amour,** do not trifle with love; **il ne badine pas,** he's not joking; **on ne badine pas avec la loi,** the law is not to be trifled with; (*b*) **b. avec sa canne,** to play, toy, with one's stick; **cheval qui badine avec son mors,** horse that champs the bit; (*c*) **ruban qui badine,** fluttering, waving, ribbon. **2.** *v.tr. O:* to tease (s.o.).
badinerie [badinri], *s.f.* (*a*) jest, piece of fun; (*b*) *esp. pl.* banter, jesting.
Badinguet [badɛ̃gɛ], *Pr.n.m. Pol: F:* Napoleon III.
bad-lands [badlɑ̃ːd], *s.m. pl. Geog:* badlands.
badminton [badmintɔn], *s.m.* badminton.
badoche [badɔʃ], *s.f.* salt cod.
badois, -oise [badwa, -waːz], *a. & s. Geog:* (native, inhabitant) of Baden.
bâdrage [bɑdraːʒ], *s.m. Fr.C: P:* nuisance, annoyance.
bâdrant [bɑdrɑ̃], *a. Fr.C:* bothersome.
bâdrer [bɑdre], *v.tr. Fr.C: P:* to bother, to annoy.
baffe [baːf], *s.f.*, **baffre, bâfre** [bɑːfr̥], *s.f. P:* slap, blow, cuff.
Baffin [bafɛ̃], *Pr.n.m. Geog:* **la terre de B.,** Baffin Island.
baffle [bafl̥], *s.m. W.Tel: etc:* baffle(-board) (of loud-speaker, etc.).
bafouer [bafwe], *v.tr.* to ridicule, scoff at, jeer at, (s.o.); to flout (regulations); **amoureux bafoué,** rejected lover.
bafouage [bafwaʒ], *s.m.* ridiculing; hoaxing.
bafouillage [bafujaːʒ], *s.m. F:* (*a*) unintelligible speech; stammering, spluttering; (*b*) nonsense; (*c*) *Aut: Mch:* bad running, spluttering (of engine, motor).
bafouille [bafuj], *s.f. P:* letter.
bafouillement [bafujmɑ̃], *s.m. F:* = BAFOUILLAGE.
bafouiller [bafuje], *v.tr. & i. F:* (*a*) to splutter, stammer; **b. quelque chose,** to stammer out something; (*b*) to talk incoherently, to sputter, babble; (*c*) (*of engine*) to run badly; to miss, to misfire; to splutter.
bafouilleur, -euse [bafujœːr, -øːz], *s. F:* (*a*) stammerer; (*b*) talker of nonsense.
bafouillis [bafuji], *s.m. F:* = BAFOUILLAGE.
bâfre [bɑːfr̥], *s.f. P:* **1.** feasting, gorging, guzzling. **2.** = BÂFRÉE.
bâfrée [bɑfre], *s.f. P:* feed, tuck-in, blow-out.
bâfrer [bɑfre], *P:* **1.** *v.i.* to stuff oneself, to guzzle. **2.** *v.tr.* to wolf (one's food).
se bâfrer, to stuff, cram, oneself.
bâfrerie [bɑfrəri], *s.f. P:* gluttony.
bâfreur, -euse [bɑfrœːr, -øːz], *s. P:* glutton, guzzler; *P:* greedy-guts, gutsy.
bagage [bagaːʒ], *s.m.* **1.** baggage, impedimenta; **plier b.,** (i) to pack up one's bags, *Mil:* one's kit; (ii) *F:* to do a bunk, to decamp; to pack up, clear out; (iii) *F:* to die, kick the bucket; *F:* **j'ai reçu cent francs pour tout b.,** I got a hundred francs all told out of it; **avec armes et b.,** with all one's belongings, *Mil:* with all one's equipment; **b. d'un auteur,** an author's works, writings; **quitter l'école avec un mince b.,** to leave school with a small amount of knowledge. **2.** *also pl.* luggage, *U.S:* baggage; **faire enregistrer ses bagages,** to have one's luggage registered; **bagages accompagnés,** personal luggage, luggage travelling with the passenger; **bagages non accompagnés,** luggage in advance; **bagages à main,** hand-luggage; **gros bagage(s),** heavy luggage; **menu(s) bagage(s),** light luggage; (*on ship*) **bagages de cale,** luggage not wanted on the voyage; **bagages de cabine,** cabin luggage; **fourgon à bagages,** luggage van, *U.S:* baggage car; **voyager avec peu de b.,** to travel light.
bagagerie [bagaʒəri], *s.f.* travel goods shop.
bagagiste [bagaʒist], *s.m.* (luggage) porter.
bagarre [bagaːr], *s.f.* **1.** scuffle; brawl; free fight; free-for-all; roughhouse. **2.** *A:* crowd, crush.
bagarrer [bagare], *v.i. F:* to fight, to battle **(pour,** for).
se bagarrer, to fight, to quarrel, to brawl.
bagarreur, -euse [bagarœːr, -øz], *a. & s. F:* rowdy.
bagasse [bagas], *s.f. Sug.-R: etc:* bagasse, megass, cane-trash.
bagatelle [bagatɛl], *s.f.* **1.** trifle, bagatelle; **se fâcher pour une b.,** to take offence at a (mere) trifle; **traiter une affaire de b.,** to make light of a matter; **acheter qch. pour une b.,** to buy sth. for next to nothing, for a song; **il a dépensé en une soirée la b. de 10.000 francs,** he spent in a single evening a cool 10,000 francs, the trifling sum of 10,000 francs. **2.** *Mus:* bagatelle. **3.** *A: F:* **être porté sur la b.,** to be of an amorous disposition, to be a bit of a Lothario. **4.** *int. A:* (stuff and) nonsense! fudge!
bagnard [baɲaːr], *s.m.* convict.
bagne [baɲ], *s.m.* (*a*) *A:* convict prison; **b. flottant,** hulks; (*b*) *F:* penal servitude; **il a été condamné à cinq ans de b.,** he was sentenced to five years' penal servitude; **le b. de la bureaucratie,** the chains of bureaucracy; **quel b.!** it's sheer slavery!
bagnérais, -aise [baɲerɛ, -ɛːz], *a. & s. Geog:* (native, inhabitant) of Bagnères-de-Bigorre.
bagnole [baɲɔl], *s.f.* **1.** *Rail: F:* horse-box; cattle-truck. **2.** *P: Aut:* (*a*) (i) dud car, *U.S:* lemon; (ii) old crock, *U.S:* jalopy, heap; (*b*) car; **c'est une belle b.,** she's a nice job.
bagnolet[1] [baɲɔlɛ], *s.m. Nau:* tarpaulin; *Mil:* gun-cover.
bagnolet[2], *s.m.*, **bagnolette** [baɲɔlɛt], *s.f. A.Cost:* (type of) woman's headdress.
bagot [bago], *s.m. P:* = BAGAGE.
bagoter [bagɔte], *v.i. P:* **1.** to handle luggage. **2.** (*a*) *Mil:* to drill; to go on a march; (*b*) to walk, *P:* to hoof it. **3. "Comment vont les affaires?"—"Ça bagote,"** "How's business?"—"Not so bad."
bagotier [bagɔtje], *s.m. F: A:* **1.** cab-runner, cab-tout. **2.** (station) porter, *U.S: P:* baggage smasher.
bagou(t) [bagu], *s.m. F:* glibness (of tongue); **avoir du b.,** to have the gift of the gab; **il a un b. de commis-voyageur,** he is as glib as a commercial traveller.
bagre [bagr̥], *s.m. Ich:* = PAGRE.
baguage [bagaʒ], *s.m.* **1.** *Arb:* ringing, ring barking. **2.** *Orn:* ringing (of pigeon, etc.). **3.** *Tchn:* bushing (of bearing); packing (of piston).
bague [bag], *s.f.* **1.** (*a*) (jewelled) ring; **b. de sûreté,** keeper (*ring worn to prevent another from slipping off*); *F:* **sa place est une b. au doigt,** his post is a sinecure, *F:* he's got a cushy job; (*b*) **b. (d'un cigare),** band (round a cigar); **b. de stylo,** clip; (*c*) *Nau:* **b. en corde,** hank ring, grommet, grummet; *El.E:* **b. en charbon,** carbon ring; (*d*) **courir la b.,** to ride, run, tilt, at the ring; **jeu de bagues,** tilting at the ring; (*e*) ring, band, (for marking birds); (*f*) **b. d'un champignon,** annulus of a fungus. **2.** (*a*) *Mec.E:* **b. d'assemblage,** collar, sleeve; thimble-coupling, -joint; **b. de butée,** thrust collar ring; **b. de centrage,** centring ring, band; **b. de serrage,** set collar, ring; clamping collar, ring; **b. d'arrêt, de fixation,** retainer (ring); lock ring; **b. d'amortissement,** buffer ring; **b. coulissante,** slip ring; **b. de réglage,** adjusting ring, collar; setting ring, collar; **b. de retenue,** (plunger) retainer; **b. d'espacement,** sleeve; **b. d'étanchéité,** seal ring; **b. de sertissage,** seating collar, clamp; band-setter; **b. à bride,** adapter; **b. à ressort,** snap-ring; spring-clip; **b. entretoise,** spacer (ring); **b.-guide,** guide bushing; **b. pivotante,** swivel ring; **b. écrou,** assembling nut; **b. molletée,** knurled ring; **b. filetée,** threaded

ring; **demi-b.**, split ring; **b. de roulement**, ball race; bearing race; *Av:* **b. d'entraînement**, coupling ring; **b. de calage**, lock ring; **b. de projection**, slinger ring; (*b*) *Mch:* **b. de tube de chaudière**, thimble, ferrule, of a boiler-tube; (*c*) **b. d'un excentrique**, strap of an eccentric; (*d*) *Arch:* band. 3. *Mch:* (*a*) **b. (de garniture) de piston**, piston ring, packing ring; *I.C.E:* **b. de fond**, packing ring (of cylinder); **b. large**, sleeve; (*b*) **b. d'appui**, washer; (*c*) **b. d'étoupe**, grommet, gland (of stuffing-box); (*d*) bushing; **b. borgne**, blind bushing; *Av:* **b. de guidage**, guide bush; (*e*) **b. en bronze (de pied de bielle, etc.)**, bronze bush (of small end, etc.); (*f*) **b. filetée**, screw ring gauge; **b. lisse**, plain ring gauge.

bague-agrafe [bagagraf], *s.f.* (fountain-pen) clip; *pl. bagues-agrafes.*

baguenaudage [bagnoda:ʒ], *s.m. F:* idling; fooling about; loafing.

baguenaude [bagno:d], *s.f.* 1. *Bot:* bladder-nut, bladder-senna pod. 2. *A:* trifle, puerile nonsense. 3. *P:* pocket.

baguenauder [bagnode], *v.i. & pr. F:* to fool around, to mooch about, to loaf; to fiddle-faddle, to waste time on trifles.

baguenauderie [bagnodri], *s.f. F:* 1. fooling around, loafing. 2. frivolous chatter, small talk.

baguenaudier [bagnodje], *s.m.* 1. *F:* (*a*) trifler, loafer; (*b*) gossip. 2. ring-puzzle, tiring-irons. 3. *Bot:* bladder-senna, bladder-nut (-tree).

baguer[1] [bage], *v.tr.* 1. to put rings on (one's fingers). 2. (*a*) to ring, *U.S:* band (bird); to ring (tree); to ferrule (tube); **cigare bagué d'or**, cigar with a gold band; (*b*) *Tchn:* to bush (bearing); to pack (piston).

baguer[2], *v.tr.* 1. *Needlew:* to tack, baste (pleats, etc.). 2. *Com:* to pack (highly perishable goods).

baguettage [bagɛta:ʒ], *s.m.* 1. (*cartography*) striping. 2. stretching (of gloves).

baguette [bagɛt], *s.f.* 1. rod, wand, stick; long thin loaf of French bread; *pl.* **baguettes**, chop-sticks; **b. de fée**, fairy's wand; **b. magique**, magic wand; **b. de coudrier**, **b. divinatoire**, (dowser's) hazel-twig, wand, diviner's rod; **b. de démonstration, de laboratoire**, pointer; **b. de verre**, glass rod; **b. de peintre**, maul-stick; **baguettes de tambour**, (i) drum-sticks; (ii) *F:* spindle-shanks; *F:* **cheveux raides comme des baguettes de tambour**, hair straight as a poker, as a yard of pump water, dead straight hair; **b. de timbale**, kettledrum stick; *Mus:* stick (of bow); **b. de chef d'orchestre**, baton; **orchestre placé sous la b. de . . .**, orchestra conducted by . . .; **b. à encoches**, tally; **b. à gants**, glove stretcher; *El:* **b. de charbon**, carbon-stick, -rod; *Mil:* **b. de fusil**, cleaning-rod, *A:* ramrod; *F:* **commander, mener, faire marcher, qn à la b.**, to rule s.o. with a rod of iron; **passer par les baguettes**, to run the gauntlet; *Pyr:* **b. de direction (d'une fusée)**, **b. de fusée (volante)**, rocket-stick; *Nau:* **b. de senau**, trysail mast; *Metall:* **b. de coulée**, sprue. 2. *Bot:* **b. d'or**, wall-flower. 3. (*a*) *Join:* moulding, beading, fillet, reed; **b. demi-ronde**, half-round batten; **appliquer une b. sur un cadre**, to bead a frame; (*b*) *Bootm:* foxing; (*c*) piping (on trousers); (*d*) stitching (on gloves); (*e*) **baguettes à jour**, open-work clocks (on socks, etc.); (*f*) black border (on writing paper).

baguettisant [bagetizɑ̃], *s.m.* dowser, water-diviner.

bagueur [bagœ:r], *s.m. Hort:* knife for ringing trees.

baguier [bagje], *s.m.* 1. ring-case; ring-casket; ring-stand. 2. ring gauge.

bah [bɑ], *int.* 1. nonsense! fiddlesticks! pooh! rubbish! 2. you don't say so! 3. who cares!

Bahamas [baama], *Pr.n.f.pl. Geog:* **les îles B., l'archipel des B.**, the Bahamas.

Bahrain [barɛ̃], **Bahreïn** [bareɛ̃], *Pr.n.m. Geog:* **les îles B.**, Bahrain, Bahrein.

bahut [bay], *s.m.* 1. (*a*) *A.Furn:* round-topped chest, travelling box; **en b.**, convex, (i) *Mec.E: etc:* dished (outwards); (ii) *Arch:* vaulted; (*b*) (low) cupboard, buffet, sideboard; (*c*) *Mil:* kit-box; (*d*) *P:* school; (*e*) *P:* taxi, crate; **griffer un b.**, to grab a cab. 2. *Arch:* **b. d'un parapet**, saddle-backed coping of a breast-wall.

bahutage [bayta:ʒ], *s.m. Sch: P:* (*a*) row, din, uproar; (*b*) ragging.

bahuté [bayte], *a. P:* (of uniform, at the *École polytechnique*) of a fancy cut; extra-smart.

bahuter [bayte], *v.i. Sch: P:* (*a*) to make a din; (*b*) to rag.

bahuteur, -euse [baytœ:r, -ø:z], *s. Sch: P:* rowdy pupil

bahutier [baytje], *s.m. A:* casket-maker, trunk-maker.

bai [bɛ], (*a*) *a.* bay (horse); **b. châtain**, chestnut-bay; **b. doré**, yellow-dun; **jument baie**, bay mare; **cheval b. lavé**, light bay horse. (*b*) *s.m.* bay (colour); **un bai**, a bay (horse).

baie[1] [bɛ], *s.f. Geog:* bay; **la B. d'Hudson**, Hudson Bay; **la grande B. de l'Australie, la grande B. australienne**, the Great Australian Bight.

baie[2], *s.f. A:* 1. (*a*) *Arch:* bay, opening; **fenêtre en b.**, bay-window; (*b*) *Nau: A:* hatch. 2. *F: A:* tall story; piece of humbug.

baie[3], *s.f. Bot:* berry; (*of shrub*) **se garnir de baies**, to berry; **à baies**, berried; **b. de laurier**, bay berry.

Baïes [baj], *Pr.n.f. A.Geog:* Baiae.

baignade [bɛɲad], *s.f.* 1. (*a*) bathe, *F:* dip; **b. mortelle**, fatal bathing accident; (*b*) *A:* watering (of horses). 2. bathing-place.

baignage [bɛɲa:ʒ], *s.m.* 1. (*action of*) bathing, soaking, dipping. 2. *Agr:* irrigation (of meadows, etc.).

baigner [beɲe]. 1. *v.tr.* (*a*) to bathe, steep; to dip; **b. ses pieds dans le ruisseau**, to dip one's feet in the stream; **yeux baignés de larmes**, eyes bathed in tears; **baigné de soleil**, bathed in sunlight; **il était baigné de sueur**, he was in a bath of perspiration, dripping with sweat; (*b*) (*of sea*) to wash (coast, etc.); (*of river*) to water (a district); (*c*) to bath, give a bath to (dog, baby, etc.). 2. *v.i.* to soak, steep (in sth.); **le riz en culture baigne dans l'eau**, rice under cultivation lies under water; **il baignait dans son sang**, he was weltering in his own blood; **b. dans une atmosphère de vice**, to be steeped in an atmosphere of vice; *P:* **envoyer qn b.**, to send s.o. packing.

se baigner. 1. to take a bath. 2. (*a*) to bathe, to have a bathe, a dip; (*b*) **faire b. des chevaux**, to take horses to water.

baigneur, -euse [bɛɲœ:r, -ø:z], *s.* 1. (*a*) bather; (*b*) holiday visitor (at seaside resort). 2. (*a*) *A:* bath attendant, bathing attendant; (*b*) *O:* (*on beach*) lifeguard; (*c*) (i) small china doll (*occ.* put in Twelfth-night cake); (ii) small (naked) (china, plastic) doll. 3. *s.f. A:* **baigneuse**, (i) bathing costume; (ii) bathing wrap; (iii) bathing cap; (iv) *pl.* bathing shoes.

baignoire [bɛɲwa:r], *s.f.* 1. bath; (bath-)tub; **b. de zinc**, zinc bath. 2. *Th:* baignoire, ground-floor box. 3. *Av: F:* dustbin. 4. *Nau:* upper part of submarine's conning tower.

baïkalite [baikalit], *s.f. Miner:* baikalite.

baïkérite [baikerit], *s.f. Miner:* baikerite.

bail, baux [bɑ:j, bo], *s.m.* lease (by landlord to tenant); (real) agreement; **b. à ferme**, farming lease; **b. à loyer**, house-letting lease; **b. à long terme**, long lease; **louer une ferme à b.**, to lease out a farm; **prendre une maison à b.**, to take a lease of a house, to take a house on lease, to lease a house; **passer un b.**, to draw up, to sign, an agreement; **renouveler son b. de vie**, to take on a new lease of life; *F:* **Ça fait un b. que je l'ai vu**, I haven't seen him for ages; *s.a.* EMPHYTÉOTIQUE.

baile[1] [bɛl], *s.m. A.Fort:* bailey.

baile[2] [bɑjl], *s.m.* 1. *Hist:* bailo. 2. *A.Jur:* (*a*) guardian (of minor, etc.); (*b*) guardianship.

baïle [bail], *s.m. Dial:* shepherd (in charge of flocks for transhumance).

Bailey [beli], *Pr.n.m.* **pont B.**, Bailey bridge.

bâillatif, -ive [bɑjatif, -i:v], *a.* yawn-provoking.

bâillant [bɑjɑ̃], *a.* 1. gaping (blouse); yawning (chasm); (door) ajar. 2. *Bot:* dehiscent.

baille [bɑ:j], *s.f. Nau:* (*a*) tub, bucket, pail; **b. à brai**, tar pail; **b. à incendie**, fire bucket; *F:* **la B.**, the *École navale*; *P:* **la (grande) B.**, the sea, *F:* the drink; (*b*) dilapidated ship, old tub.

bâille-bec [bɑjbɛk], *s.m.inv. Husb: F:* gape-worm.

bâillement [bɑjmɑ̃], *s.m.* 1. (*a*) yawn, yawning; **étouffer un b.**, to stifle a yawn; **avec un b. de sommeil**, with a sleepy yawn; (*b*) *Husb:* gapes (of birds). 2. gaping (of seam, etc.); fissure, crack (in woodwork, etc.); **b. des rideaux**, gap between the curtains.

bailler [bɑje], *v.tr.* (*a*) *A:* (= DONNER) **b. un coup à qn**, to deal s.o. a blow; **b. à ferme**, to farm out; (*b*) *F:* **vous me la baillez belle!** tell that to the marines!

bâiller [bɑje], *v.i.* 1. to yawn; *F:* **b. à se décrocher la mâchoire, b. comme une carpe**, to yawn one's head off; **b. sa vie**, to yawn one's life away. 2. (*of seams, etc.*) to gape; to fit badly; (*of door*) to be ajar, to stand ajar.

baillet [bɑjɛ], *a.m.* sorrel (horse).

bailleulois, -oise [bɑjœlwa, -wa:z], *a. & s. Geog:* (native, inhabitant) of Bailleul.

bailleur, -eresse [bɑjœ:r, bɑjrɛs], *s.* 1. (*a*) *A:* giver; (*b*) *Jur:* lessor. 2. **b. de fonds**, (i) *Com:* sleeping partner; (ii) money-lender; (iii) financial backer.

bâilleur, -euse [bɑjœ:r, -ø:z], *s.* yawner.

bailli [baji], *s.m. A:* bailli, bailiff, magistrate, judge.

bailliage [baja:ʒ], *s.m. A:* 1. bailiwick; (*in Fr. or Switz.*) bailliage. 2. bailiff's court.

baillie[1] [baji], *s.f. A.Jur:* bailiwick; bailiffry.

baillie[2] [baji], *s.f.*, **baillive** [baji:v], *s.f. A:* bailiff's wife.

bâillon [bɑjɔ̃], *s.m.* (*a*) gag; **mettre un b. à qn**, to gag s.o.; **mettre un b. d'or à qn**, to stop s.o.'s mouth with a bribe; (*b*) muzzle (for horse).

baillonné [bɑjɔne], *a. Her:* bailloné.

baillonnella [bɑjɔnɛla], *s.m. Bot:* baillonnella.

bâillonnement [bɑjɔnmɑ̃], *s.m.* gagging.

bâillonner [bɑjɔne], *v.tr.* to gag; **b. la presse**, to muzzle the press.

bain [bɛ̃], *s.m.* 1. bath; (*a*) (i) bath, (*action of*) bathing; (ii) bath(-water); (iii) bath(-tub); **salle de bain(s)**, (i) bathroom; (ii) *Furn:* bath-room suite; **prendre un b.**, to take, have a bath, to bath; **donner un b. à qn**, to bath s.o.; **b. chaud, froid**, hot, cold, bath; **sels pour bain(s)**, bath salts; **remplir, vider, le b.**, to fill (up), empty, the bath; *s.a.* CHAUFFER 3; **b. de pieds**, (i) foot-bath; (ii) *P:* coffee, etc., slopped in the saucer; *P:* **prendre un b. de pieds**, to be sent to a penal colony; **demi-b.**, hip-bath; short bath; **b. maure, b. turc**, Turkish bath; **b. russe**, Russian bath; **b. de vapeur**, steam-bath, vapour-bath; **b. de mousse**, bubble-bath; **b. de soleil**, sun-bath; **bains de soleil**, sun-bathing; **prendre un b. de soleil, des bains de soleil**, *F:* **prendre un b. de lézard**, to sunbathe; *Cost:* sun-suit; **décolleté, encolure, b.-de-soleil**, halter neck; **corsage, haut b.-de-soleil**, halter top, sun top, *U.S:* halter; *Med:* **b. d'œil**, eye-bath; **b. de bouche**, mouth-wash; **b. de boue**, mud-bath; **b. de moutarde, b. sinapisé**, mustard bath; *Cost:* **peignoir, sortie, de b.**, bath(ing)-wrap, bath-robe; **serviette de b.**, bath towel; **l'Ordre du Bain**, the Order of the Bath; *F:* **envoyer qn au b.**, to send s.o. about his business, to send s.o. packing, to send s.o. away with a flea in his ear, to tell s.o. where he gets off; *F:* **il a pris tout le b.**, he has been blamed for the lot, for everything; *F:* **être dans le b.**, (i) to be implicated in sth.; (ii) to be in the know, to be in the swing of things; (iii) to be in the mood; **se mettre dans le b.**, (i) to get down to it; to get to the heart of things; (ii) to get into the swing of things; (iii) to get into the mood, to get warmed up; *s.a.* TREMPER 2; (*b*) **bains publics, établissement de bains**, public baths, bathing establishment, *U.S:* bath-house; **b. de natation**, swimming-bath(s); **garçon de bains**, bath attendant; (*c*) *pl.* baths, watering-place, spa; (*d*) bathe (in sea, etc.); bathing; **bains de mer**, (i) sea-bathing; (ii) seaside resort; **saison des bains**, bathing season; *Cost:* **costume, maillot, de b.**, bathing-, swimming-, bathing-costume, swimsuit, *U.S:* bathing-suit; **caleçon, culotte, slip, de b.**, bathing trunks, slip; **bonnet de b.**, bathing-cap; **cabine de b.**, bathing-hut; **b. de minuit**, midnight bathe, dip (in the nude), *U.S:* skin dip. 2. (*a*) *Husb:* (sheep-)dip; *Tan: etc:* soak; *Ch: etc:* solution; *Phot:* **b. révélateur, de développement**, developing bath; **b. de fixage, fixateur**, fixing-bath; **b. clarifiant, clarificateur**, clearing bath; **b. de coagulation**, coagulation bath; **b. d'alunage, b. aluné**, hardening bath, alum bath; **b. d'arrêt**, stop-bath; *Ind: Mec.E: Dy:* **b. d'huile**, oil bath, white bath; *El.-Ch:* **b. de cuivrage**, copper bath; **b. acide**, acid bath; **b. électrolytique**, electrolytic bath; (*b*) *Const:* bed (of mortar); *Ch:* **b. de sable**, sand-bath. 3. *Bot:* **b. de Vénus**, Venus's bath, wild teazel.

bain-de-mer [bɛ̃dmɛr], *s.m. Cost:* beach sandal; *pl. bains-de-mer.*

bain-de-siège [bɛ̃dsjɛ:ʒ], *s.m.* sitz-bath, short bath (in which one bathes in sitting position); *pl. bains-de-siège.*

bain-douche [bɛ̃duʃ], *s.m.* shower-bath; *pl. bains-douches.*

bain-marie [bɛ̃mari], *s.m.* 1. *Ch:* water bath. 2. (*a*) *Dom.Ec:* bain-marie, double saucepan; *Cu:* **faire cuire au b.-m.**, cook in a double saucepan; (*b*) kitchen range boiler; *pl. bains-marie.*

bainite [bɛnit], *s.f. Ch: Metalw:* bainite.

bainitique [bɛnitik], *a.* bainitic.

baïonnette [bajɔnɛt], *s.f.* 1. bayonet; **b. à douille**, socket bayonet; **arrêtoir de b.**, bayonet stop; **tenon de b.**, bayonet stud; **piste d'assaut à la b.**, bayonet assault course; **escrime à la b.**, bayonet drill, exercise; **mettre, remettre, la b.**, to fix.

unfix, bayonets; **b. au canon!** fix bayonets! **avancer la b. en avant, la b. au canon,** to advance with fixed bayonets; **charge à la b.,** bayonet charge; **emporter une tranchée à la b.,** to carry a trench at the point of the bayonet; *Mec.E: etc:* **joint en b.,** bayonet joint; *El:* **douille, culot, à b.,** bayonet socket or base (of bulb, etc.). **2.** *Nau:* **b. de clinfoc,** flying jib-boom.

baisemain [bɛzmɛ̃], *s.m.* hand-kissing, kissing of hands; *A:* **envoyer ses baisemains à qn,** to send one's respects to s.o.

baisement [bɛzmɑ̃], *s.m.* kissing (*esp. Ecc:* (i) of the Pope's slipper; (ii) of the feet on Maundy Thursday).

baiser [beze]. I. *v.tr.* **1.** (*a*) *Lit:* **b. qn sur, à, la joue,** to kiss s.o. on the cheek; **b. la mule du Pape,** to kiss the Pope's slipper; **b. la croix,** to kiss the cross; (*b*) *Poet:* to touch lightly; (*c*) **il baise la trace de ses pas,** he worships the very ground she treads on; **b. les pieds, la poussière des pieds de qn,** to humble oneself before s.o.; (*c*) *A:* **je vous baise les mains,** (i) (*in letter*) so bidding you farewell, I remain . . .; (ii) (*usu. iron.*) farewell; (*d*) **b. la main qui vous frappe,** to return good for evil; (*e*) *V:* to have sexual intercourse with (s.o.); (*f*) *P:* **se faire b.,** (i) to be done, swindled; (ii) to get arrested. **2.** *Mth:* (*of curve*) to osculate with (line, etc.).

se baiser, (*of loaves in oven*) to touch; *Mth:* (*of curves*) to osculate.

II. **baiser,** *s.m.* (*a*) kiss; **b. de paix,** kiss of peace; **b. d'adieu,** parting kiss; **un gros b.,** a smack(er); **donner un b. à qn,** to give s.o. a kiss; **dérober un b. à qn,** to steal a kiss from s.o.; **couvrir qn de baisers,** to smother s.o. with kisses. **aux jolis minois les baisers,** kissing goes by favour; **avec quelques baisers j'eus bientôt fait de sécher ses larmes,** I soon kissed away her tears, kissed her tears away; (*b*) *Poet:* caress; *s.a.* JUDAS.

baiser-de-paix [bezedəpɛ], *s.m. Ecc: Art:* pax.

baiseur, -euse [bɛzœːr, -øz], *s. P:* one who kisses, *P:* necker, *U.S:* smoocher.

baisoter [bɛzɔte], *v.tr. O: F:* to peck at (s.o.); to neck.

baissage [bɛsaːʒ], *s.m. Phot:* reduction.

baissant [bɛsɑ̃]. **1.** *a.* declining, diminishing; **soleil b.,** setting sun; **vue baissante,** failing sight. **2.** *s.m.* **b. de l'eau,** ebbing of the tide; ebb-tide.

baisse [bɛs], *s.f.* **1.** fall, falling, subsidence, going down (of water, of ground, etc.); ebb (of tide); **ma santé est dans une de ses baisses,** this is one of my low periods, one of the times when I am rather down, when I am below the mark; **température en b.,** falling temperature; *El.E:* **b. de la charge,** falling off of the load; **b. de courant,** decrease in current; *Av:* **b. de régime,** losing revs; **mouvement de monte et b.,** up and down movement. **2.** decline, failing (of eyesight, etc.). **3.** *Com: Fin:* **b. (de prix),** fall, drop, decline (in prices); **marché orienté à la b.,** falling market; **spéculations à la b.,** bear speculations; **prendre position à la b.,** to bear; **actions en b.,** shares that are falling; **ses actions sont en baisse,** he is losing his credit, his influence; he is going downhill; *s.a.* JOUEUR 2, SPÉCULER 2. **4.** = BAISSIÈRE.

baissement [bɛsmɑ̃], *s.m.* lowering; **b. de tête,** nod.

baisser [bese]. I. *v.* **1.** *v.tr.* (*a*) to lower (a curtain, a blind); to shut down (window, etc.); to let down, to open (car window); *Aut:* to dip (headlights); **b. son chapeau sur ses yeux,** to pull down, to tip, one's hat over one's eyes; **b. le col de son pardessus,** to turn down one's coat collar; **b. une lampe,** to turn down a lamp; *Th: etc:* **b. les lumières,** to dim the lights; **le régisseur a fait b. le rideau,** the stage-manager had the curtain brought down, lowered; **le store est baissé,** the blind is drawn, down; **b. la tête, le front,** (i) to bend one's head; (ii) to hang one's head; **b. brusquement la tête,** *F:* to duck; to bob down; **faire qch. tête baissée,** to do sth., (i) resolutely, fearlessly, (ii) blindly, thoughtlessly; **donner tête baissée dans un piège,** to fall headlong into a trap; *F:* **y aller tête baissée,** to go at it bald-headed, like a bull at a gate; **b. les yeux,** to cast down one's eyes, to look down; **faire b. les yeux à qn,** to outstare s.o.; to stare s.o. out (of countenance); **yeux baissés,** downcast eyes; **b. le nez,** to hide one's blushes; to look crestfallen; *s.a.* OREILLE 1; *Equit:* **b. la main à un cheval,** to give full rein to a horse; **b. la voix,** to lower one's voice; *F:* **b. la radio,** to turn down the radio; *Mus:* **b. un morceau d'un demi-ton,** to lower a piece one semitone; **b. le ton de sa voix,** to pitch one's voice lower; **b. un instrument,** to tune an instrument to a lower pitch; *F:* **b. le ton,** to climb down (a little); *F:* **faire b. qn d'un ton, faire b. le ton à qn,** to take s.o. down a peg; *s.a.* PAVILLON 3; **b. le prix de qch.,** to lower, reduce, cut, bring down, the price of sth.; **faire b. le prix à qn,** to beat s.o. down; **b. les loyers,** to lower, bring down, the rents; *Phot:* **b. un cliché,** to reduce a negative; (*b*) **b. un mur,** to lower a wall, to make a wall lower, to reduce the height of a wall; *Hort:* **b. un cep,** to cut back a vine. **2.** *v.i.* (*a*) to go, come, down; to be on the decline, on the wane; (*of tide*) to ebb; (*of flood*) to abate, go down, subside; (*of fire*) to sink, to get low; (*of lamp, fire*) to burn low, burn down; *Th:* **les lumières baissent,** the lights are going down; **la rivière baisse,** the river is going down; **le vent baissa,** the wind dropped; **le baromètre baisse,** the glass is falling, the barometer is going down; **la température baisse,** it is getting colder; **nos provisions baissent,** our provisions, stores, are running low; **le soleil baisse,** the sun is sinking; **le rideau baisse entre les actes,** the curtain is lowered between the acts; **le jour baisse,** the light is going, night is falling; it's getting dark; **sa vue, sa mémoire, baisse,** his sight, memory, is failing, going; **le malade baisse,** the patient is sinking, losing his strength; **il baisse,** (i) he is failing; (ii) he is sinking; **b. dans l'estime de qn,** to go down, sink in s.o.'s estimation; (*b*) (*of prices*) to fall, to come, go, down, *U.S:* to dip; **le thé a baissé,** tea has come down in price, the price of tea has come down; **la valeur de ces maisons a baissé,** the value of these houses has gone down, these houses have gone down in value; **la concurrence fait b. les prix,** competition brings prices down; **le dollar a baissé,** the dollar has weakened; **ses actions baissent,** (i) his shares are going down; (ii) *F:* his influence is on the decline, his stock is falling.

se baisser, to stoop; to bend down, to bow down; **se b. subitement,** to bob down, to duck; *F:* **il pense qu'il n'y a qu'à se b. et à prendre,** he expects everything just to fall into his lap; *F:* **vous n'avez qu'à vous b.,** you have the ball at your feet, you have success in your grasp.

II. **baisser,** *s.m.* **b. du soleil,** sunset, sundown; *Th:* **b. du rideau,** fall of the curtain.

baissier [besje], *s.m.* **1.** *St.Exch:* bear. **2.** *pl.* **baissiers,** shoals, banks (on river bed).

baissière [bɛsjɛːr], *s.f.* **1.** *Agr:* depression, dip (where rain collects). **2.** *Wine-m:* lee.

baissoir [bɛswar], *s.m.* (*in salt industry*) brine pan.

baisure [bɛzyːr], *s.f.* kissing-crust (of loaf).

bajocien, -ienne [baʒɔsjɛ̃, -jɛn], *a. & s.m. Geol:* Bajocian.

bajoue [baʒu], *s.f.* **1.** *pl.* (*of pig, etc.*) cheeks, chaps, chops; *Pej:* (*of pers.*) flabby, pendulous, cheeks. **2.** *Aut:* inside valance; wing-flange.

bajoyer [baʒwaje]. **1.** *a. & s.m. Civ.E: etc:* **(mur) b.,** chamber wall, side-wall, lateral wall (of a lock); (*b*) quay wall; river wall; (*c*) wing-wall (of abutment). **2.** *s.m. Fish:* side (of fish ladder).

bak(h)chich [bakʃiʃ], *s.m.* baksheesh; *P:* tip.

bakéliser [bakelize], *v.tr.* to bakelize.

bakélite [bakelit], *s.f. R.t.m:* bakelite.

Bakou [baku], *Pr.n.m. Geog:* Baku.

bal [bal], *s.m.* **1.** ball; dance; **b. travesti, costumé,** fancy-dress ball; **b. masqué,** masked ball; **b. public,** public dance; **b. privé,** private dance; *A:* **b. blanc,** young ladies' dance (to which no men are invited); **robe de b.,** dance dress, ball dress, evening dress; **la reine du b.,** (i) the belle of the ball; (ii) the lady in whose honour the ball is given; **ouvrir le b., mettre le b. en train,** (i) to open the ball; (ii) to start a topic, to set the ball rolling; *Mil: P: A:* **le b.,** the defaulters' squad; **faire le b.,** to do punishment drill; *F: A:* **donner le b. à qn,** to give s.o. a good talking to, a good dressing-down. **2. salle de b.,** ballroom; **b. public, populaire,** dance hall; *pl.* **bals.**

Balaam [balaam], *Pr.n.m. B.Hist:* Balaam.

baladage [baladaːʒ], *s.m. Aut:* **fourchette de b.,** (gear-change) selector-fork.

balade [balad], *s.f. F:* stroll; excursion, ramble, jaunt; **être en b.,** to be out walking, out for the day; **faire une b.,** (i) to go for a ramble; (ii) to go on an excursion; to go for a run in the car, etc.

balader [balade], *F:* **1.** *v.i. & pr.* to stroll, saunter, knock about; **se b. en auto,** to be, go, out for a spin, run; *P:* **envoyer b. qn,** to send s.o. packing; to give s.o. the brush-off; **envoyer b. qch.,** to chuck sth. (up). **2.** *v.tr.* (*a*) to take (s.o.) out, to take (dog, etc.) for a walk; (*b*) to trot (s.o.) round; **je les ai baladés toute la matinée,** I trotted them round the whole morning.

baladeur, -euse [baladœːr, -øːz]. **1.** *F:* (*a*) wandering, strolling; **avoir des mains baladeuses,** to have wandering hands; (*b*) *s.* wanderer, saunterer. **2.** *s.m. Mec.E:* sliding collar, clutch; *Aut:* selector rod; **(train) b.,** sliding gear, throw-over gear. **3.** *s.f.* **baladeuse,** (*a*) trailer (of tramcar, motor car, etc.); (*b*) costermonger's barrow; hand-cart; (*c*) portable lamp, inspection lamp (of garage, etc.).

baladin, -ine [baladɛ̃, -in], *s.* **1.** *A:* ballet dancer. **2.** *A: Th:* (*a*) buffoon; (*b*) mountebank. **3.** (*a*) indifferent, second-rate comedian, comic; (*b*) tiresome joker, buffoon.

baladinage [baladinaːʒ], *s.m.* foolery, buffoonery.

baladiner [baladine], *v.i.* to play the fool.

balæniceps, baléniceps [baleniseps], *s.m. Orn:* shoe-bill, whale-head.

balafo [balafo], *s.m.*, **balafon** [balafɔ̃], *s.m. Mus:* balafo, balaphon.

balafre [balafr, -ɑːfr], *s.f.* **1.** cut, slash, gash (*esp.* in face); sabre-cut. **2.** scar.

balafrer [balafre], *v.tr.* **1.** to cut, gash, slash (*esp.* the face). **2. visage balafré,** scarred face; **le vieux sergent balafré,** the old sergeant with the sabre-cut; old Scarface; *Hist:* **le Balafré,** the Balafré (Henri de Guise).

balai [balɛ], *s.m.* **1.** (*a*) broom; (long-handled) brush; **b. de crin,** hair broom; **b. de jonc,** carpet-broom; **b. de bruyère,** brushwood besom; **b. en caoutchouc,** squeegee; **b. de nettoyage, b. à franges, b. à laver,** mop; **b. tue-mouches,** fly-whisk; **b. mécanique,** carpet sweeper; *F:* **b. électrique,** vacuum cleaner; **manche à b.,** (i) broomstick; (ii) *Av:* joy-stick; (iii) *F:* thin, lanky person, *F:* bean-pole; **donner un coup de b. à une pièce,** to sweep out a room, to give a room a sweep; *F:* **donner un coup de b.,** to make a clean sweep (of one's staff); *F:* **faire b. neuf,** to start off well (in a new job, etc.); **il fait b. neuf,** a new broom sweeps clean; **rôtir le b.,** (i) *A:* to drudge in obscurity; (ii) to lead a fast life, to live it up; *Nau: F:* **ramasser les balais,** to allow oneself to be overtaken (by another ship); *F:* **b. de l'estomac,** spinach; (*b*) *F:* last bus, underground train, etc. (at night); (*c*) *Mil: F:* miss (at target practice). **2.** (*a*) tail (of hawk); (*b*) feather (of dog's tail). **3.** *El.E:* (*a*) brush (of commutator); **b. de régulation,** shunt-brush (of three-brush dynamo); **b. rotatif (du distributeur),** distributor arm, rotor; **b. en charbon,** carbon brush; **b. collecteur,** slip-ring brush; **ajustage des balais,** brush setting; (*b*) shoe (of tramcar); (*c*) *Computers:* **b. de lecture,** read(ing) brush. **4.** *Aut:* blade (of windscreen-wiper); **double b.,** twin blades. **5.** *Bot:* (*a*) broom; (*b*) **b. de sorcière,** witches'-broom.

balais [balɛ], *a.m.* **rubis b.,** balas ruby.

Balaklava [balaklava], *Pr.n. Geog:* Balaclava.

balalaïka [balalaika], *s.f. Mus:* balalaika.

balançant [balɑ̃sɑ̃], *a.* swinging (gait, etc.).

balance [balɑ̃ːs], *s.f.* **1.** (*a*) (*occ. pl.* **balances**) balance, (pair of) scales; weighing machine; **b. ordinaire, à plateaux,** household scales, kitchen scales, shop scales; **b. automatique,** (automatic) shop scales, weighing machine; **b. à fléau,** beam-scales; **b. à bascule,** weighbridge; **b. à ressort,** spring balance; **b. à levier, b. romaine,** Roman balance, steelyard; **b. chimique, de précision,** chemical balance, analytical balance, precision balance; **b. (de) Roberval,** Roberval's balance; **mettre, jeter, qch. dans la b.,** to throw sth. into the scale; **mettre deux choses en b.,** to weigh two things one against the other, to weigh one thing against another; **faire entrer en b.,** to take into account; **(main)tenir la b. égale,** to be impartial; **égaliser la b. entre le beau et l'utile,** to strike a balance between the beautiful and the useful; **faire pencher la b., incliner la b., emporter la b.,** to turn the scale, the balance; *Turf:* **enceinte des balances,** weighing enclosure; (*b*) scale(-pan); (*c*) *El:* **b. d'induction,** induction bridge; **b. de courant,** current balance, current weigher; **b. de torsion,** torsion balance; (*d*) *Astr:* **la B.,** Libra, the Scales. **2.** (state of) balance, indecision; **être en b.,** to be undecided; **être en b. entre deux projets,** to waver between two plans; **tenir qn en balance,** to keep s.o. in suspense; **être, rester, en b.,** to be, hang, in the balance; **la victoire était, restait, en b.,** victory hung in the balance; *Sp:* **partir en b.,** to jump the gun. **3.** (*a*) *Com:* **b. d'un compte,** balance, balancing, of an account; **b. de vérification,** trial balance, rough balance; **b. d'inventaire,** balance-sheet; **faire la b.,** to make up the balance (-sheet); **compte en b.,** account that balances; *Pol.Ec:* **b. du commerce, b. commerciale,** trade balance, balance of trade; **b. générale des**

comptes, **b. des paiements,** balance of payments; (*b*) **b. des forces au pouvoir,** balance of power; **b. politique,** (i) balance of parties; (ii) *Hist:* balance of power. **4.** *Fish:* dipping net; **b. à écrevisses,** crayfish net.

balancé, *a.* **1.** well-balanced, well-poised; **garçon bien b.,** well set up boy; *F:* **elle est bien balancée,** she's well-proportioned, *P:* she comes out in the right places. **2.** *Box:* **coup b.,** swing; *s.m.* **b. du droit,** swing in with the right.

balance-cuvette [balɑ̃skyvɛt], *s.m. Phot:* rocker (for dishes); *pl. balance-cuvettes.*

balancelle [balɑ̃sɛl], *s.f. Nau:* balancelle.

balancement [balɑ̃smɑ̃], *s.m.* **1.** (*a*) balance (of figures in picture, etc.); (*b*) balancing; *Nau:* trimming (of weight, of sails). **2.** (*a*) swinging, rocking (of lamp, boat, etc.); swaying (of trees, etc.); *Nau:* **b. de la machine,** swinging, trying, of the engines; **appareils de b.,** balancing gear (of torpedo); (*b*) *A:* hesitation, wavering; (*c*) *Mus:* tremolo.

balancer [balɑ̃se], *v.* (**je balançai(s) n. balançons**) **I.** *v.tr.* **1.** to balance; (*a*) **b. le mal par le bien,** to (counter)balance evil with good; *Com:* **b. un compte,** to balance, settle, an account; **b. les livres,** to close, make up, the books; **un discours bien balancé,** a well-balanced speech; (*b*) to poise (javelin, etc.); **b. son corps,** to balance one's body; (*c*) *Nau:* to trim (weight, sails). **2.** (= PESER) to weigh (the pros and cons, etc.). **b. si l'on fera qch.,** to be in two minds about doing sth. **3.** to swing, rock (s.o. in a hammock, etc.); **b. un enfant sur ses genoux,** to rock a child on one's knees; *A:* **b. son esprit entre deux idées,** to waver, hesitate, between two ideas; *Nau:* **b. la machine,** to swing, try, the engines; *N.Arch:* **b. les couples,** to horn (the frame). **4.** *F:* (*a*) to throw, heave, chuck (stones, etc.); **b. un coup de pied à qn,** to kick out at s.o.; (*b*) to dismiss, fire (employee); to give (s.o.) the sack; to throw (s.o.) out; to throw (sth.) away; **il y a des moments où j'ai envie de b. le dictionnaire,** there are times when I feel like giving up the dictionary work; (*c*) to swindle (s.o.).

II. **balancer,** *v.i.* **1.** (*a*) to swing, to dangle; (*b*) *Danc:* **balancez!** set to partners! **2.** (*a*) *Lit:* to waver, hesitate; **il ne balança pas à accepter cette offre,** he did not hesitate to accept this offer; (*b*) **longtemps la victoire balança,** for a long time victory hung in the balance.

se balancer. 1. (*a*) to swing; to sway, rock, to dangle; *Nau:* (*of ship*) **se b. sur ses ancres,** to ride at anchor; **se b. sur sa chaise,** to rock backwards and forwards on one's chair; (*b*) to seesaw, *U.S:* to teeter; (*c*) *P:* **je m'en balance!** I don't care a damn! **2.** (*of bird, etc.*) to poise, hover. **3.** *Com:* to balance; **compte qui se balance de tant au passif,** account that leaves a debit balance of so much.

balancerie [balɑ̃sri], *s.f.* **1.** scale-making. **2.** scale-maker's factory.

balance-trébuchet [balɑ̃streby∫ɛ], *s.f. Ph: Ch:* precision balance; *pl. balances-trébuchets.*

balancier[1] [balɑ̃sje], *s.m.* scale-maker; dealer in scales, balances.

balancier[2], *s.m.* **1.** (*a*) balancing pole (of tight-rope walker); (*b*) *pl. Ent:* balancers, poisers (of diptera); (*c*) *pl.* outriggers (of boat). **2.** (*a*) *Clockm: etc:* (i) pendulum(-bob); (ii) balance-wheel (of watch); (*b*) handle (of pump, of smith's bellows); *Hyd.E:* balance-bar, balance-beam, sweep, swipe (of lock-gate); (*c*) *Mch:* (i) beam, walking-beam (of beam-engine); (ii) rocking lever (of marine engine); (*d*) *Mec.E:* (i) fly; (ii) fly-press, screw-press; *Bookb: etc:* die-stamp; **b. monétaire,** coining-press; **b. découpoir,** cutting-press; (iii) flyer (of roasting-jack, etc.); (*e*) *Civ.E:* saddle (of vertical girder); (*f*) *Aut:* **b. du vilebrequin,** crank-shaft balancer; (*g*) backfall (in organ). **3.** *pl. Nau:* gimbals (of compass).

balancine [balɑ̃sin], *s.f.* **1.** *Nau:* (topping-)lift; **fausse b.,** preventer lift; **b. de gui,** spanker-boom topping-lift. **2.** *pl.* (*a*) *Aer:* (wire) car supports (of dirigible); (*b*) *Av:* (small) wing tip wheels (for lateral support).

balancier-compensateur [balɑ̃sjekɔ̃pɑ̃satœ:r], *s.m.* (*a*) *Mec.E:* equalizer, equalizing spring; (*b*) *Clockm:* compensation balance wheel; *pl. balanciers-compensateurs.*

balançoire [balɑ̃swa:r], *s.f.* **1.** (*a*) seesaw, *U.S:* teeter; (*b*) (child's) swing; (*c*) (*at fairs*) swing-boat. **2.** *F:* (*a*) *A:* hoax, take-in; **tout ça c'est de la b., des balançoires,** that's all humbug; (*b*) **envoyer qn à la b.,** to leave s.o. in the lurch.

balandre [balɑ̃:dr], *s.f.* canal barge; narrow boat.

balane [balan], *s.f. Crust:* balanus, acorn-shell, barnacle.

balanin [balanɛ̃], *s.m. Ent:* balaninus, nut-weevil.

balanite [balanit], *s.f. Med:* balanitis.

balanites [balanit], *s.m. Bot:* Balanites.

balanoglosse [balanɔglɔs], **balanoglossus** [balanɔglɔsys], *s.m. Z:* Balanoglossus.

balanophage [balanɔfa:ʒ], *a.* acorn-eating.

balanophoracées [balanɔfɔrase], *s.f.pl. Bot:* Balanophoraceae.

balanophore [balanɔfɔ:r], *Bot:* **1.** *a.* balaniferous, acorn-bearing. **2.** *s.f.* Balanophora.

balano-posthite [balanopɔstit], *s.f. Med:* balanoposthitis.

balant [balɑ̃], *a. & s.m.* = BALLANT.

balanus [balanys], *s.m. Crust:* = BALANE.

balantidium [balɑ̃tidjɔm], *s.m. Z:* Balantidium.

balaou [balau], *s.m. Ich:* needlefish.

balata [balata]. **1.** *s.m. Bot:* balata-tree, bully-tree. **2.** *s.f.* balata (gum); *Mec.E:* **courroie (en) b.,** balata belt.

balayage [balɛja:ʒ], *s.m.* **1.** sweeping (out) (of room, etc.); scavenging, scavengering, sweeping (of roads); sweeping up (of dirt, etc.); *Mil: Av:* sweep; *Mch:* **soupape de balayage,** scavenging valve. **2.** (*of beam of light*) sweeping (across) an area; *Radar: Elcs: T.V:* scan(ning), sweep, exploration; **b. horizontal,** horizontal scan(ning), sweep; **b. vertical,** vertical scan(ning), sweep; **zone de b.,** scanning area; **circuit de b.,** sweep circuit; **fréquence de b.,** sweep frequency; **générateur de b.,** sweep generator; **organe de b.,** scanner, scanning unit; **disque de b.,** scanning disc; *Elcs:* **vitesse de b.,** drum speed; *T.V:* **transformateur de b.,** frame output transformer.

balayer [baleje], *v.tr.* (**je balaie, je balaye, je balaierai, je balayerai**) **1.** to sweep; to sweep out (room, etc.); to sweep up (dirt, etc.); **le vent a balayé les nuages,** the wind has swept away the clouds; **b. la mer,** to scour the sea; *F:* **b. tout le personnel,** to make a clean sweep of the staff, the personnel; **b. un ministre,** to get rid of a minister; **b. l'ennemi,** to drive away the enemy; *Th: F:* **b. les planches,** to act in the curtain-raiser. **2.** *Mch:* to scavenge. **3.** (*of beam of light*) to sweep, sweep across (an area); *Radar: Elcs: T.V:* to scan, to explore, to sweep.

balayette [balɛjɛt], *s.f.* **1.** small broom; (hearth-) brush; whisk. **2.** *A.Cost:* piping, binding (used on hem of dress).

balayeur, -euse [balɛjœ:r, -ø:z]. **1.** *a.* that sweeps; *Nau:* **câble b.,** sweep, trawl (for mines). **2.** *s.m.* (*a*) (*pers.*) sweeper; *A:* **b. de rues,** crossing sweeper; **b. municipal, de rues,** street sweeper; (*b*) *F: A:* hack, *pl.* small fry (of certain professions). **3.** *s.f.* **balayeuse,** (*a*) **b. automatique, mécanique,** (i) carpet sweeper; (ii) street sweeper; (*b*) *A.Cost:* **balayeuse,** dust ruffle (round hem of skirt); (*c*) *Agr:* bush-harrow.

balayures [balɛjy:r], *s.f.pl.* sweepings; **b. de mer,** sea-wrack.

balbusard [balbyza:r], *s.m.* = BALBUZARD.

balbutiant [balbysjɑ̃], *a.* stuttering; inarticulate (in speech).

balbutie [balbysi], *s.f.* inarticulateness of speech, stuttering.

balbutiement [balbysimɑ̃], *s.m.* (*a*) stuttering, stammering; mumbling; (*b*) **cette science n'était alors qu'à ses premiers balbutiements,** this science was then only in its infancy.

balbutier [balbysje], *v.* (*pr.sub. & p.d.*, **n. balbutiions, v. balbutiiez**) **1.** *v.i.* to stammer; mumble. **2.** *v.tr.* to mumble, stammer out (sth.); to falter out (an excuse).

balbutieur, -euse [balbysjœ:r, -ø:z], *s.* mumbler; stammerer.

balbuzard [balbyza:r], *s.m. Orn:* **b. pêcheur, fluviatile,** osprey, bald buzzard.

balcon [balkɔ̃], *s.m.* **1.** (*a*) *Arch:* balcony, *U.S:* gallery; **en b.,** overhanging; **concours de balcons fleuris,** window-box competition; (*b*) *N. Arch:* pulpit; **b. arrière,** quarter gallery. **2.** *Th:* dress circle; *P:* **y a du monde au b.!** she's well stacked!

balconnet [balkɔnɛ], *s.m. R.t.m:* (i) half-cup brassière; (ii) strapless brassière.

baldaquin [baldakɛ̃], *s.m.* baldachin, balda-c(c)hino, canopy; tester (of bed).

bale [bal], *s.f. Bot: etc:* = BALLE[3].

Bâle [ba:l], *Pr.n.f. Geog:* Basel, Basle.

baléare [balea:r], *Geog:* **1.** *a.* Balearic; **les (îles) Baléares,** the Balearic Islands. **2.** *s.* native, inhabitant, of the Balearic Islands.

baléarique [balearik], *s.f. Orn:* Balearica.

baleinage [balɛna:ʒ], *s.m. Dressm:* whaleboning.

baleine [balɛn], *s.f.* **1.** whale; **b. bleue,** blue whale; **b. franche, du Groënland,** right, bowhead, arctic, great polar, whale; **b. de Biscaye,** Basque whale, black whale, North Atlantic right whale, northcaper, scrag whale, southern right whale; **b. franche naine,** pigmy right whale; **b. à bosse,** hump-backed whale; **blanc de b.,** spermaceti; *Nau:* **pont en dos de b.,** whale-back(ed) deck; *P:* **se tordre, rire, comme une b.,** to split one's sides with laughter; *Nau: F:* **embarquer une b.,** to ship a green sea. **2.** (*a*) whalebone, baleen; (*b*) steel, bone (of a corset); **garnir de baleines,** to bone (corset); (*c*) **baleines d'un parapluie,** ribs of an umbrella.

baleiné [balene], *a.* (whale)boned; stiffened (with whalebone or steels).

baleineau, -eaux [balɛno], *s.m.* whale-calf.

baleiner [balene], *v.tr.* to (whale)bone; to stiffen (garment); to rib (umbrella); to steel, bone (corset).

baleinier, -ière [balenje, -jɛ:r]. **1.** *a.* whaling (vessel, industry). **2.** *s.m.* whaler (whale-fisher or ship); whaleman. **3.** *s.f.* **baleinière,** whale-boat; **b. de sauvetage,** lifeboat.

baleinon [balenɔ̃], *s.m. Z:* whale-calf.

balénidés [balenide], *s.m.pl. Z:* Balaenidae.

balénoptère [balenɔptɛ:r], *s.m. Z:* balaenoptera, rorqual; *F:* furrow-throated whale; **b. à bec,** piked whale.

balès [balɛs], *a. & s.m. P:* (great) strapping (fellow).

baleston [balɛstɔ̃], *s.f. Nau:* (*in the Mediterranean*) sprit; **voile à b.,** sprit-sail.

balêtre [balɛ:tr̥], *s.m. Metall:* fin (of casting).

balèvre [balɛ:vr̥], *s.f.* **1.** (*a*) *A:* under-lip; (*b*) *Pej: pl.* pouting lips. **2.** *Const:* overplus, lip (in course of stone work). **3.** *Metall:* burr, scale.

balèze [balɛz], *a. & s.m. P:* (great) strapping (fellow).

balinais, -aise [balinɛ, -ɛz], *a. & s. Geog:* Balinese.

balisage [baliza:ʒ], *s.m.* **1.** (*a*) *Nau:* buoyage; *Nau: Av:* **feu de b.,** beacon (light); **droite de b.,** beacon course; **projecteur de b.,** direction beacon; (*b*) *Nau:* beaconing, buoying, setting of buoys; *Av:* ground lighting (of airfield, etc.); signalling, marking out (with beacons); (*c*) *Surv:* setting up of survey poles. **2.** (**droits de**) **b.,** beaconage.

balise[1] [bali:z], *s.f.* **1.** (*a*) *Nau:* beacon; staff-and-ball; sea-mark; **b. flottante,** buoy; (*b*) *Av:* ground-light, marker; (radio) beacon; **b. d'aéroport,** airport beacon; approach light; **b. lumineuse,** marker light; **b. de délimitation d'aérodrome, de délimitation de terrain,** boundary beacon, marker; (*c*) *Radar:* **b. radar,** radar beacon; **b. répondeuse,** responder beacon. **2.** (survey) pole.

balise[2], *s.f. Bot:* canna-seed.

balisement [balizmɑ̃], *s.m.* = BALISAGE 1.

baliser [balize], *v.tr.* (*a*) *Nau:* to beacon, buoy, mark out (channel); (*b*) *Av:* to equip (airport) with ground lights, approach lights; (*c*) *Aut:* to signal; (*d*) to mark out (course) with beacons; (*e*) to set up survey poles (along road, etc.).

baliseur [balizœ:r], *s.m.* (*a*) (**bateau**) **b.** = Trinity House boat; (*b*) (*pers.*) = Trinity (House) buoy-keeper.

balisier [balizje], *s.m. Bot:* canna, Indian shot.

baliste [balist]. **1.** *s.f. Rom.Ant:* bal(l)ista. **2.** *Ich:* triggerfish; filefish.

balistique [balistik]. **1.** *a.* ballistic; **engin b.,** ballistic missile; **trajectoire b.,** aerodynamic trajectory; **véhicule mi-b., mi-planeur,** boost-glide vehicle; **onde b.,** ballistic wave. **2.** *s.f.* ballistics; **b. intérieure, extérieure,** interior, exterior, ballistics.

balistite [balistit], *s.f. Exp:* ballistite.

balistocardiographe [balistɔkardjɔgraf], *s.m.* ballistocardiograph.

balistocardiographie [balistɔkardjɔgrafi], *s.f.* ballistocardiography.

balivage [baliva:ʒ], *s.m. For:* staddling.

baliveau, -eaux [balivo], *s.m.* **1.** (*a*) *For:* staddle; (*b*) *Hort:* sapling. **2.** *Const:* scaffold-pole; standard.

baliver [balive], *v.tr. For:* to staddle (cutting).

baliverne [balivɛrn], *s.f.* (*a*) futile remark; **débiter des balivernes,** to talk twaddle, nonsense; (*b*) futile occupation; **perdre son temps à des balivernes,** to waste one's time on trifles.

baliverner [balivɛrne], *v.i. A:* (*a*) to talk twaddle, nonsense; (*b*) to exchange banter.

balkanique [balkanik], *a. Geog:* Balkan (state, etc.).

balkaniser [balkanize], *v.tr. A:* to Balkanize.

Balkans [balkɑ̃], *a. & s.m.pl. Geog:* **la Péninsule des B.,** the Balkan Peninsula; **les (Monts) B.,** the Balkan Mountains, the Balkans.

ballade [balad], *s.f. Lit: Mus:* (*a*) ballade; **les ballades de Villon,** Villon's ballades; (*b*) ballad.

ballage [balaːʒ], *s.m. Metall:* balling up (of iron, etc.).

ballant [balɑ̃]. **1.** *a.* (*a*) swinging, dangling (arms, etc.); **assis les pieds ballants,** seated with (his) feet dangling; (*b*) slack (rope). **2.** *s.m.* (*a*) swing, rocking motion; *Golf:* **b. horizontal,** flat swing; **b. ascendant, b. descendant,** upward, downward, swing; **plein b.,** full swing; (*b*) *Nau:* bight, slack (in rope).

ballast [balast], *s.m.* **1.** *Civ.E: etc:* ballast, bottom (of road, railway track). **2.** *Nau:* (*a*) ballast-tank (of submarine, etc.); **chasser aux ballasts,** to blow the tanks; (*b*) ballast.

ballastage [balastaːʒ], *s.m.* **1.** *Civ.E: etc:* ballasting (of railway track, etc.); boxing, ballast bed. **2.** *Nau:* (i) ballasting; (ii) unballasting.

ballaster [balaste], *v.tr.* **1.** *Civ.E: etc:* to ballast (track, etc.). **2.** *Nau:* (i) to ballast; (ii) to unballast.

ballastière [balastjɛːr], *s.f.* ballast-pit: gravel-pit; borrow(-pit).

balle[1] [bal], *s.f.* **1.** ball; (*a*) **b. de golf, de tennis,** golf ball, tennis ball; **jouer à la b.,** to play ball; **avoir la b.,** to have first shot, first go; **avoir la b. belle,** (i) to be in a good position (for playing a ball); (ii) *F:* to have a good opportunity; *F:* **vous avez la b. belle,** the ball is at your feet; now's your chance; **renvoyer la b. à qn,** (i) to return the ball to s.o.; (ii) *F:* to give s.o. tit for tat, to let s.o. have it back; *s.a.* BOND 2; **mettre la b. en mouvement,** to start the ball rolling; **à vous la b.,** (i) it's your turn (to play); (ii) *F:* it's your turn (to speak, etc.); (iii) *F:* that (remark, etc.) was aimed at you; *P:* **c'est ma b.,** that's my affair; *P:* **ça fait ma b.,** that just suits me; *F:* **faire (la) b.,** to score a bull's-eye; *Games:* **b. au camp,** boundary ball, *U.S:* catch ball; **b. au chasseur,** ball tag; **b. simple,** ball-bouncing (against a wall); **b. nommée,** call ball; **b. au mur** = fives; *Cr:* **b. nulle, fausse b.,** no ball; **b. passée,** bye; **b. écartée,** wide; *Ten:* **faire des, quelques, balles,** to have a knock-up; **b. de filet,** let (ball); **une b.,** one point; **être à une b. du jeu,** to want one point for game; **une belle b.,** a beautiful shot; **b. de match,** (i) match(-winning) shot; (ii) match point; **b. de set,** set point; *Range-shooting:* **b. à la volée,** trap-ball; *F:* **enfant de la b.,** (i) *A:* son of a keeper of a *jeu de paume* (*q.v. under* PAUME 2), *hence:* person expert in his profession; (ii) person following in his father's footsteps, person born into a profession, *esp.* actor brought up on the boards; (*b*) *P:* (i) head, *P:* block; (ii) face, *P:* dial, mug; (*c*) *P:* franc; **dix balles,** ten francs; (*d*) *Typ: A:* inking-pad. **2.** (*a*) bullet, shot; **b. de fusil,** rifle bullet; **b. blindée, à enveloppe,** jacketed bullet; **b. morte,** spent bullet; **b. perdue,** (i) stray bullet; (ii) wasted shot, *F:* wasted effort; **b. d'obus,** shrapnel (bullet); **b. pleine,** solid bullet; **ogive de b.,** bullet nose; **b. traçante,** tracer bullet; **b. d'expansion, b. dum-dum,** expanding bullet, dumdum bullet; **tirer à b.,** to fire ball-cartridge; **b. d'essai,** sighting shot; **criblé de balles,** riddled with bullets; **à l'épreuve des balles,** bullet-proof; *V:* **trou de b.,** arse-hole; *s.a.* CARTOUCHE[1] 2, RAIDE 1; (*b*) *Fish:* plumb, sinker, bullet. **3.** *Metall:* (puddle-)ball; loupe.

balle[2], *s.f. Com:* (*a*) bale (of cotton, etc.); *Paperm:* parcel of ten reams; **mise en b.,** baling; **marchandises en balles,** bale goods; *Nau:* **capacité balles,** bale capacity; *A:* **porter la b.,** to peddle, to be a pedlar; **marchandises de b.,** pack goods, goods of small value; *A:* **écrivain de b.,** trashy writer; *P:* **peau de b.,** nothing at all, *P:* nix, damn all.

balle[3], *s.f.* husk, chaff (of corn); *Bot:* glume (of flower).

baller[1] [bale], *v.tr. Metall:* to ball (up) (iron, etc.)

baller[2], *v.i.* **1.** *A:* to dance; *P:* **envoyer b. qn,** to send s.o. packing. **2. laisser b. ses bras,** to let one's arms dangle.

baller[3], *v.tr. Husb:* to hull (corn).

baller[4] [bolœr], *s.m. Cr:* bowler.

ballerine [balrin], *s.f.* **1.** *Th:* ballerina, ballet-dancer; danseuse. **2.** *Bootm:* ballerina (shoe).

ballet [balɛ], *s.m. Th:* ballet; **le corps de b.,** the corps de ballet; the ballet; **maître de b.,** ballet-master.

balletomane [balɛtɔman], *s.m. & f.* balletomane.

balletomanie [balɛtɔmani], *s.f.* balletomania.

ballon [balɔ̃], *s.m.* **1.** (*a*) balloon; **b. déformable, indéformable,** flexible, rigid, balloon; **b. dirigeable,** airship, dirigible; **b. captif,** captive-, kite-balloon; **b. libre,** free balloon; **b. d'observation,** observation balloon; **b. de protection, de barrage,** barrage balloon; **b. de sondage,** pilot-balloon, sounding-balloon; **b. cerf-volant,** kite-balloon; **b. d'essai, b. pilote,** pilot-balloon; **envoyer, lancer, un b. d'essai,** (i) to send up a pilot-balloon; (ii) to put out a feeler; **monter en b.,** to go up in a balloon; to go ballooning; **b. d'enfant,** toy balloon; *Aut:* **pneu b.,** balloon tyre; *P:* **enlever le b. à qn,** to kick s.o.'s bottom, behind; *F:* **enflé, gonflé, comme un b.,** conceited; self-satisfied; full of one's own importance; *P:* **se remplir le b.,** to have a good blow-out, tuck in; *P:* **avoir le b.,** to be in the family way, *P:* to have a bun in the oven; *P:* **attraper le b.,** to get in the family way; *P:* **faire b.,** to do without, to tighten one's belt; (*b*) **b. à gaz,** gas-bag (for oxygen, etc.). **2.** (*a*) (child's large) india-rubber ball; (*b*) football; **s'amuser avec le b.,** to kick the ball about; (*c*) **b. d'entraînement (pour boxeurs, à boxer,** punch-ball; (*d*) paper hoop (in circus). **3.** (*a*) *Ch:* balloon-flask; bulb; **b. de distillation,** distillation flask, still; (*b*) *Ind:* carboy; (*c*) **(verre) b.,** barrel-shaped glass; brandy glass, balloon glass; (*d*) **b. d'eau chaude, b. réchauffeur,** hot water reservoir (for central heating system). **4.** *Nau:* (*a*) ball-signal; **b. de marée,** tide ball; (*b*) **b. de défense,** fender. **5.** *Geog:* (*in the Vosges*) ballon. **6.** *Min:* pocket (of fire-damp). **7.** *P:* prison, *P:* quod; **faire du b.,** to do time. **8.** *Dressm:* **manches b.,** puff(ed) sleeves.

ballonnant [balɔnɑ̃], *a.* distended, bulging (stomach, etc.); puffed, full (sleeve).

ballonné [balɔne], *a.* distended, swollen; puffed out.

ballonnement [balɔnmɑ̃], *s.m.* (*a*) swelling, bulging; standing out (of skirts, etc.); (*b*) *Med:* distension (of stomach); flatulence; *Vet:* hoove, bloat.

ballonner [balɔne]. **1.** *v.tr.* to swell, distend (the stomach). **2.** *v.i. & pr.* (*a*) to swell (out), to become distended; (of skirt, etc.) to balloon out; **faire b. une manche,** to puff (out) a sleeve; (*b*) (*of wall*) to bulge (out).

ballonnet [balɔnɛ], *s.m.* **1.** *Aer:* (*a*) small balloon; (*b*) *pl.* gas-bags, gas-cells (of dirigible); (*c*) **b. compensateur,** ballonet. **2.** *Av:* wing-float (of hydroplane); **b. de bout d'aile,** stub wing stabilizer.

ballonnier [balɔnje], *s.m. A: F:* balloonist.

ballon-observatoire [balɔ̃ɔpservatwaːr], *s.m. A: Mil:* observation balloon; *pl. ballons-observatoires.*

ballon-panier [balɔ̃panje], *s.m.inv. Fr.C: Sp:* basket-ball.

ballon-pilote [balɔ̃pilɔt], *s.m. Meteor:* pilot-balloon; *pl. ballons-pilotes.*

ballon-sonde [balɔ̃sɔ̃ːd], *s.m. Meteor:* sounding balloon; *pl. ballons-sondes.*

ballot [balo], *s.m.* **1.** bundle, package, bale; *A:* (pedlar's) pack; *Mil:* kit-bag; *F:* **voilà votre b.,** that's just the thing for you, there you are! **2.** *P:* nit(wit), clot; *a.* **t'es pas b.?** are you mad?

ballota [balɔta], *s.f.,* **ballote** [balɔt], *s.f. Bot:* ballota, black horehound.

ballot(t)ade [balɔtad], *s.f. A.Equit:* ballotade.

ballottage [balɔtaːʒ], *s.m.* **1.** shaking, jolting. **2.** (*a*) *A:* voting (by white or black balls); (*b*) *Pol: etc:* failure to gain absolute majority; **scrutin de b.,** second ballot, *U.S:* run off election; **élection sans b.,** single ballot.

ballotté [balɔte], *a. Pol: etc:* (candidate) eliminated in the first ballot.

ballottement [balɔtmɑ̃], *s.m.* tossing (of ship); shaking, rattling (of goods, etc.); *Obst:* ballottement (of fœtus).

ballotter [balɔte]. **1.** *v.tr.* (*a*) to toss (about), shake (about); to hesitate; **ballotté par la tempête,** storm-tossed; **ballotter qn (de l'un à l'autre),** to drive, chase, s.o. from pillar to post; (*b*) *Pol:* to subject (candidates) to a second ballot. **2.** *v.i.* (*a*) (*of door, etc.*) to rattle, shake; to wobble; to swing to and fro; *Nau:* (*of mast, etc.*) to fetch way; (*b*) to toss (on the water).

ballottin [balɔtɛ̃], *s.m.* small bundle.

ballottine [balɔtin], *s.f. Cu:* meat roll, (kind of) galantine (served hot or cold).

ball-trap [baltrap, bol-], *s.m.* (clay pigeon) shooting trap; *pl. ball-traps.*

balluche [balyʃ], *s.f. F:* nit(wit), clot.

balluchon, *s.m.* = BALUCHON 2.

balme [balm], *s.f.* (*in Provence*) cave.

balnéable [balneabl̩], *a.* (*of water*) suitable for (medicinal) baths.

balnéaire [balneɛːr], *a.* of, pertaining to, baths; balneal; **station b.,** (i) seaside resort; (ii) spa.

balnéation [balneasjɔ̃], *s.f.* taking of (medicinal) baths.

balnéatoire [balneatwaːr], *a.* of a spa; hydropathic.

balnéothérapie [balneɔterapi], *s.f.* balneotherapy.

balochard [balɔʃaːr], *s.m.* (*a*) *P:* reveller; dissipated person; (*b*) *Dial:* lazy, lifeless, person.

bâlois, -oise [bɑlwa, -waːz], *a. & s. Geog:* (native, inhabitant) of Basel, Basle.

balourd, -ourde [baluːr, -urd]. **1.** *a.* (*a*) awkward, lumpish; (*b*) stupid. **2.** *s.* (*a*) awkward person; lout; **un grand b.,** a great hulking fellow; (*b*) stupid person. **3.** *s.m. Mec.E:* want of balance; unbalance; (*of flywheel, etc.*) **tourner à b., avoir du b.,** to run untrue; **tourner sans b.,** to run true.

balourdise [balurdiːz], *s.f.* **1.** (*a*) awkwardness, lumpishness; (*b*) stupidity. **2.** stupid blunder; *F:* bloomer; **commettre une b.,** to put one's foot in it.

baloutchi, -e [balutʃi], *a. & s.,* **baloutche** [balutʃ], *a. & s. Geog:* Baluchi.

Baloutchistan [balutʃistɑ̃], *Pr.n.m. Geog:* Baluchistan.

balsa [balza], *s.m. Bot:* balsa (wood), *U.S:* cork-wood.

balsamier [balzamje], *s.m.* = BAUMIER.

balsamifère [balzamifɛːr], *a. Bot:* balsamiferous.

balsaminacées [balzaminase], *s.f.pl. Bot:* Balsaminaceae.

balsamine [balzamin], *s.f. Bot:* impatiens, balsamine, garden balsam, yellow balsam; *F:* busy Lizzie, jumping-betty, touch-me-not.

balsamique [balzamik]. **1.** *a.* balsamic (syrup, etc.); balmy (air); aromatic (perfume). **2.** *s.m. Pharm:* balsamic.

balte [balt], *a. Hist:* **les Pays baltes,** the Baltic States (Estonia, Latvia, Lithuania).

Balthazar [baltazaːr]. **1.** *Pr.n.m. B.Hist:* Belshazzar; **le festin de B.,** Belshazzar's Feast. **2.** *s.m.* (*a*) *A: P:* blowout; feast; (*b*) (*wine bottle*) balthazar.

baltique [baltik], *Geog:* **1.** *a.* Baltic; **la mer B.,** the Baltic (Sea); *A:* **les provinces baltiques,** the Baltic States. **2.** *Pr.n.f.* **la B.,** the Baltic (Sea). **3.** *s.m. Ling:* Baltic.

Baluchistan [balykistan], *Pr.n.m. Geog:* = BALOUTCHISTAN.

baluchon [balyʃɔ̃], *s.m.* **1.** (*a*) refuse-box; (*b*) miner's bucket; (*c*) dredge bucket. **2.** bundle (*esp.* of clothes); **faire son b.,** to pack up.

balustrade [balystrad], *s.f.* **1.** balustrade. **2.** (hand-)rail; railing.

balustre [balystr̥], *s.m.* **1.** (*a*) baluster; (*b*) *pl.* banisters (of stairs). **2.** (*in King's chamber*) = BALUSTRADE.

balustrer [balystre], *v.tr.* (*rare*) to balustrade (balcony, etc.).

balzacien, -ienne [balzasjɛ̃, -jɛn]. *Lit:* (*a*) *a.* like, after the manner of Balzac; **il a fait des études balzaciennes,** he has made a special study of Balzac; (*b*) *s.* student of Balzac.

balzan [balzɑ̃], *a.* **cheval b.,** (black, bay) horse with white stockings.

balzane [balzan], *s.f.* white stocking (of horse).

bambin, -ine [bɑ̃bɛ̃, -in], *s. F:* little child; tiny tot.

bambochade [bɑ̃bɔʃad], *s.f.* **1.** *Art: A:* bambocciade, humorous, rustic, *genre,* picture. **2.** *F:* (little) spree.

bambochard [bɑ̃bɔʃar], *s.m.* = BAMBOCHEUR.

bamboche[1] [bɑ̃bɔʃ], *s.f.* **1.** (*a*) (large) marionette, puppet; (*b*) *F:* stunted, ill-formed, person; *F:* freak. **2.** *F:* spree, lark; **faire (une) bamboche,** to go on the spree, to live it up; *a. F:* **étudiants bamboches,** wild students.

bamboche[2], *s.f.* rattan (cane).

bambocher [bɑ̃bɔʃe], *v.i.* **1.** *F:* to go, to be constantly, on the spree, to live it up. **2.** *Typ:* (*of matter*) to be badly imposed, to lie squint on the page.

bambocheur, -euse [bɑ̃bɔʃœːr, -øːz], *s. F:* reveller; rake, dissipated person; **air de b.,** rakish appearance.

bambou [bɑ̃bu], *s.m. Bot:* bamboo (cane); *Cu:* **pousses de b.,** bamboo shoots; *Pol.Hist:* **le rideau de b.,** the Bamboo Curtain; *F:* (*in tropical areas*) **coup de b.,** (i) sunstroke; (ii) barefaced overcharging; *P:* **il a (reçu) le coup de b.,** (i) he's mad, crackers, nuts; (ii) he's tired out, whacked.

bamboula [bɑ̃bula]. **1.** *s.m.* (*a*) bamboula, bamboo drum; (*b*) *P:* negro, *P:* nigger. **2.** *s.f.* (*a*) bamboula, negro dance; (*b*) *F:* = BAMBOCHE[1] 2.

bambouseraie [bɑ̃buzrɛ], *s.f.* bamboo plantation.

bambusées [bɑ̃byze], *s.f.pl. Bot:* Bambuseae.

ban[1] [bɑ̃], *s.m.* **1.** (*a*) *A:* royal proclamation; (*b*) (public) proclamation; official crying (of event); (*c*) roll of drum, bugle call (before and after proclamation); (*d*) round of (rhythmical) applause; **accorder un b. à qn** = to give three cheers for s.o.; (*e*) *pl.* banns (of marriage); **dispense de bans** = marriage licence; **acheter des bans** = to get a marriage licence; **publier les**

bans, to publish the banns. **2.** *Hist:* (proclamation of) banishment; sentence of outlawry; ban; **mettre qn au b.,** (i) to banish s.o.; (ii) *F:* to send s.o. to Coventry; **être au b. de l'opinion publique,** to be outlawed by public opinion; **être au b. de la société,** to be beyond the pale; **rompre son b.,** (i) *Hist:* to break one's ban; (ii) *Jur:* to break one's ticket-of-leave, one's parole; to break an *interdiction de séjour, q.v.* under INTERDICTION 1; **rupture de ban,** (i) *Hist:* breaking of one's ban; (ii) *Jur:* breaking of one's ticket-of-leave, one's parole; **être en rupture de b.,** (i) to have broken bounds; (ii) *F:* to be on the loose, on the spree. **3. le b. et l'arrière-ban,** (i) *Hist:* the ban and the arrière-ban; (ii) all one's supporters; (iii) *Mil:* the regulars and reserves; **le b. et l'arrière-ban des actionnaires,** the whole crowd of shareholders; **il a invité le b. et l'arrière-ban de ses parents et amis,** he invited all his friends and relations.

ban[2], *s.m. Hist:* (*in Croatia*) ban.

ban[3], *s.m. Num:* ban; *pl. bani.*

banal [banal], *a.* **1.** *m.pl.* **banaux** *A:* banal, communal (mill, bakehouse). **2.** *m.pl.* **banals** (*a*) commonplace, banal, trite; **parler de choses banales,** to engage in small talk; (*b*) of little account; innocuous (microbe, etc.); (*c*) ordinary; normal; *Med:* **rhume b.,** simple cold; **de petites choses qui nous semblent banales,** little things we take for granted.

banalement [banalmã], *adv.* in a banal, commonplace, manner.

banalisation [banalizasjɔ̃], *s.f.* **1.** vulgarizing (of sth.); standardizing, standardization (of sth.). **2.** *Rail:* (*a*) signalling (of track) for two-way working; (*b*) use of engine by several crews.

banaliser [banalize], *v.tr.* **1.** to vulgarize; to render, make, (sth.) commonplace. **2.** *Rail:* (*a*) to signal (track) for two-way working; (*b*) **b. une locomotive,** to have an engine manned by several crews; (*c*) **b. un train,** to use a train for two-way working.

banalité [banalite], *s.f.* **1.** banality, triteness. **2.** *pl.* (*a*) small talk; (*b*) **écrire des banalités,** to write commonplaces, platitudes. **3.** *Rail:* **(locomotive) conduite en b.,** common user (engine). **4.** *A.Jur:* **droit de b.,** right of banality.

banane [banan], *s.f.* **1.** (*a*) *Bot:* banana; **b. d'Abyssinie,** ensete; **b. de Chine, des Canaries,** Canary banana; **b. des Antilles,** plantain; **figue b.,** banana (as opposed to plantain); (*b*) *Ich:* **b. de mer,** albula. **2.** *P:* campaign medal, *F:* gong. **3.** *Aut: F:* overrider. **4.** *El:* **fiche b.,** banana plug. **5.** *Haird:* (French) pleat. **6.** *Mil: P:* (big) helicopter.

bananeraie [bananrɛ], *s.f.,* **bananerie** [bananri], *s.f.* banana plantation.

bananier [bananje], *s.m.* **1.** *Bot:* banana tree; **b. des sages,** banana tree (proper); **b. du paradis,** plantain tree; **b. textile,** abaca, Manila hemp. **2.** *Nau:* banana boat.

bananifère [bananifɛːr], *a.* banana-producing.

banaste [banast], *s.f.* (wicker) fruit basket.

banban [bãbã], *P: Pej:* **1.** *s.m. & f.* lame, gamelegged, person. **2.** *adv.* with a limp.

banc [bã], *s.m.* **1.** bench, seat, form; **b. à dossier,** settle; *Arch:* **b. continu au socle,** bench-table; *F:* **il faut vous remettre sur les bancs,** you'd better go back to school; **s'asseoir sur un b. de derrière,** to take a back seat; **b. d'église,** pew; **le b. d'œuvre, de l'œuvre,** the churchwardens' pew; *Pol:* **le b. ministériel, le b. des ministres** = the Treasury bench, the government front bench; *Nau:* **b. de nage,** thwart (of boat); *Row:* **b. à coulisses,** sliding seat; *Nau:* **b. de voilier,** sailmaker's bench; **b. de quart,** bridge (deck); *Hist:* **b. de rameurs,** bank of galley-slaves; *Jur:* **b. des magistrats,** magistrates' bench; *Jur:* (*in Eng.*) **cour du b. de la reine, du roi,** the Queen's, King's, Bench Division (of the High Court of Justice); **b. des prévenus, des accusés,** dock; **b. des témoins,** witness box; **b. du jury, des jurés,** jury box. **2.** (*carpenter's, engineer's*) bench; *Mec.E:* bed (of lathe); table (of drilling machine); **b. d'épreuve,** testing stand (for firearms); **b. d'essai,** testing bench, test-bed (for engines); *Techn:* **b. d'étirage, à tirer,** drawing-bench; **b. de montage,** assembly bench; *Carp:* **b. d'âne,** shaving-horse; *Opt:* **b. optique,** optical bench; *s.a.* ROMPU 1. **3.** *Tex:* **b. à broches,** roving frame, fly-frame. **4.** (*a*) layer, bed (of stone, etc.); *Min:* seam (of coal); (*b*) **b. de sable,** sand-bank, shoal; **b. de vase,** mud-bank; **b. de gazon,** grass(y) bank, turf bank; **b. de glace,** ice-floe, -field; **b. de roches,** reef; **b. de corail,** bank of coral, coral-reef; **b. d'huîtres,** oyster-bed; *Geog:* **b. continental,** continental shelf; **le Banc, les Bancs, de Terre-Neuve,** the Banks (of Newfoundland); *Nau:* **toucher au b.,** to run aground, to touch (bottom); *Fr.C:* **b. de neige,** snowbank, heap of snow; (*c*) **b. de brouillard,** bank of fog, fog-bank; **b. de nuages,** bank of clouds, cloud-bank. **5.** shoal, school (of fish, whales, etc.).

bancable [bãkabl̩], *a. Fin:* bankable, negotiable.

bancaire [bãkɛːr], *a.* pertaining to banking; **opérations bancaires,** banking operations, transactions; **chèque b.,** banker's draft, bank cheque; **monnaie b.,** bank or other forms of financial credit; *s.a.* FOURGON[2].

bancal, -als [bãkal]. **1.** (*a*) *a. & s.* bandy-legged (person); **jambes bancales,** bandy legs; (*b*) *a.* wobbly, rickety (furniture, etc.); **raisonnement b.,** ill-supported, lame, argument. **2.** *s.m. A: & F:* light (curved) cavalry sword, bancal.

bancbrocheur, -euse [bãbrɔʃœːr, -øːz], *s. Tex:* rover; fly-frame tenter.

bancelle [bãsɛl], *s.f. Dial:* long and narrow bench.

banchage [bãʃaːʒ], *s.m. Const:* moulding of concrete with forms or shutters.

banche [bãːʃ], *s.f. Const:* form, shutter (for moulding concrete).

banchée [bãːʃe], *s.f. Const:* concrete slab (moulded in a shutter).

bancher [bãʃe], *v.tr.* to build in concrete using shutters or forms; **béton banché,** concrete moulded with timber or steel forms.

banco [bãko]. **1.** *a. & s.m. Fin: A:* banco, bank value. **2.** *Cards:* banco; **faire b.,** to go banco; **b.! banco! un joli b.!** a fine scoop!

bancocratie [bãkɔkrasi], *s.f.* **1.** rule, sway, of high finance. **2.** world of high finance.

bancoul [bãkul], *s.m. Bot:* **(noix de) b.,** candleberry, candlenut.

bancoulier [bãkulje], *s.m. Bot:* candleberry tree, candlenut (tree).

bancroche [bãkrɔʃ], *a. & s. A: F:* = BANCAL 1.

Banda [bãda], *Pr.n. Geog:* Banda; *s.a.* NOIX 2.

bandage [bãdaːʒ], *s.m.* **1.** *Surg: Hyg:* (*a*) bandaging, binding up (of wound); (*b*) bandage; **b. de corps,** binder; **b. herniaire (sans pelote),** truss; **b. (herniaire) avec pelote,** scrotal truss with rat-tail pad. **2.** (steel, rubber) tyre, *esp.* solid tyre; **b. à talons,** beaded tyre; **b. à tringles,** wired tyre; **b. plein,** solid tyre; *Rail:* **b. à boudin,** flanged tyre; **b. sans boudin,** blank tyre. **3.** (*a*) hooping, binding (of beam, etc.); (*b*) hoop, band; (*c*) *Hyd.E:* shrouding (of wheel). **4.** tightening, winding (up) (of spring, etc.); stringing or bending (of bow).

bandagiste [bãdaʒist], *a. & s.m. Med:* truss manufacturer; truss supplier.

bandar [bãdar], *s.m. Z:* bandar.

bande[1] [bãːd], *s.f.* **1.** (*a*) band, strip (of cloth, paper, metal, etc.); stretch (of ground); belt (of land); (trouser) stripe; *Astr:* belt; **mettre un journal sous b.,** to put a newspaper in a wrapper; **envoyer qch. sous b.,** to send sth. by book post; *Phot:* **b. gommée,** gummed binding strip (for lantern slides, etc.); *Journ:* **b. publicitaire,** advertising streamer; *Hyg:* **b. hygiénique,** sanitary towel; *Nau:* **b. de ris,** reef-band; *Opt:* **bandes du spectre,** bands of the spectrum; **bandes d'absorption,** absorption bands; *Ph: Meteor:* **b. de la pluie (dans le spectre),** rain-band; *Agr:* **b. de délimitation,** balk (between fields); **culture en bandes de niveau,** strip contour farming; *Adm: Aut:* **b. de stationnement,** lay-by; (*on road*) **b. médiane,** white line; *Av:* **b. d'envol,** airstrip, landing-strip; *s.a.* MOLLETIÈRE, ROULEMENT 1; (*b*) (surgical) bandage; **b. adhésive,** adhesive tape, *Surg:* dressing strip; *Vet:* **b. jambière,** horse bandage; (*c*) *Civ.E:* **b. (de recouvrement),** (butt-) strap; *Arch:* **bandes lombardes,** Lombard bands, pilaster strip, arched corbel table; *Tchn:* **b. de frein,** brake band, strap; **b. courroie transporteuse,** travelling apron; *El:* **b. omnibus,** busbar; *Harn:* **b. d'arçon,** saddle-bar; (*d*) *Bookb: etc:* off-cut; (*e*) *Cin:* reel (of film); film; **b. des images,** picture strip (of film); **bandes vierges,** (film)-stock; **bandes ininflammables,** non-flam stock; **tourner une b. d'essai,** to have a film test; **b. sonore,** sound track; **b. magnétique, de Magnétophone,** recording tape; **b. de base,** master tape; **b. enregistrée,** pre-recorded tape; (*f*) *Tg:* **b. du récepteur,** tape; **b. (de téléimprimeur),** tickertape; (*g*) (*steel*) tire, tyre (of wheel); (*h*) *Bill:* cushion; **coller la bille sous b.,** to play the ball close to the cushion; *F:* **par la b.,** in a roundabout way, indirectly; **prendre qn par la b.,** to make an indirect approach to s.o.; (*i*) = BANDE-CHARGEUR; (*j*) *W.Tel:* **b. de fréquences,** frequency band; **largeur de b.,** band width; **b. latérale,** side band; **filtre de b.,** band filter; **dans la b. des 19 mètres,** in the 19 metre band; **b. passante,** transmission band; (*k*) *Elcs:* **b. passante (d'un filtre),** (filter) pass band; **b. d'atténuation (d'un filtre),** (filter) stop band; (*l*) **b. dessinée, illustrée,** strip cartoon, comic strip. **2.** *Mec.E:* set, compression (of spring). **3.** *Her:* bend. **4.** *Nau:* (*a*) side (of ship); **faire passer l'équipage à la b.,** to man ship; **mettre un navire à la b.,** to cant a ship; (*b*) heel, list(ing); **donner de la b. (à bâbord),** (of ship) to heel (over), to careen, to have a list, take a list (to port).

bande[2], *s.f.* **1.** (*a*) band, party, troop; **b. de voleurs,** set, gang, of thieves; **petite b. de disciples,** little body of disciples; **être de la b. de qn,** to belong to s.o.'s party; **toute la b.,** the whole gang, *P:* the whole caboodle, shoot; **faire b. à part,** to keep to oneself; *P:* **b. d'imbéciles!** you (pack of) idiots! **b. noire,** (i) *Com:* ring, knockout; (ii) gang of swindlers; (iii) gang of terrorists; (*b*) *Mil.Hist:* unit of 500 mercenaries; **la vieille b.,** the old gang. **2.** *Mus:* (*a*) *A:* special orchestra; **la Grande B.,** orchestra of 24 violins; (*b*) military band; (*c*) *Th:* group of wind instruments (playing on the stage). **3.** flight, flock (of birds); pack (of wolves); herd (of buffaloes); school, shoal (of porpoises); pride (of lions).

bandé [bãde]. **1.** *a.* (*a*) taut, fully set; (*b*) *Mec.E:* (*of spring*) loaded; (*c*) *Her:* bendy. **2.** *s.m.* = BANDE[1] 2; **pistolet au b.,** pistol at full-cock.

bande-annonce [bãdanɔ̃ːs], *s.f. Cin:* trailer, *U.S:* preview.

bandeau, -eaux [bãdo], *s.m.* **1.** (*a*) bandeau, head-band; *Mil:* cap-band; **mettre un b. sur ses cheveux,** to wear a bandeau round one's hair; (*b*) **elle porte les cheveux en bandeaux,** she wears her hair parted down the middle; (*c*) **b. royal,** diadem. **2.** bandage (over the eyes, the jaw); **mettre un b. à qn,** (i) to blindfold s.o.; (ii) *F:* to hoodwink s.o. **3.** *Arch:* string-course. **4.** *N.Arch:* curtain, frieze, plate. **5.** *Tex:* (*in knit goods*) band of defective colour. **6.** *Typ:* band.

bande-chargeur [bãdʃarʒœːr], *s.f. Mil:* **b.-c. souple,** (feeding) belt (of machine-gun); **b.-c. rigide,** (feeding) strip; **b.-c. articulée,** link belt; *pl. bandes-chargeurs.*

bande-culotte [bãdkylɔt], *s.f. Cost:* loin cloth; *pl. bandes-culottes.*

bande-gouttière [bãdgutjɛːr], *s.f. Av:* drip flag; *pl. bandes-gouttières.*

bandeler [bãdle], *v.tr.* **b. un pneu,** to wrap a tyre.

bandelette [bãdlɛt], *s.f.* **1.** (*a*) narrow band, strip, bandage; (*b*) *pl.* bandages, wrappings (of mummies). **2.** *Anat:* **bandelettes optiques,** optic tracts. **3.** *A.Cost:* fillet (round the head). **4.** *Arch:* bandelet.

bander[1] [bãde]. **I.** *v.tr.* **1.** to bandage, bind (up), tie up (wound); to put a bandage on (s.o., sth.); **b. les yeux à, de, qn,** (i) to blindfold s.o.; (ii) *F:* to hoodwink s.o.; **il avait la tête bandée d'un mouchoir,** his head was bound up in a handkerchief. **2.** to put bands on, to band (sth.); **b. une roue,** to put a tyre on, to shoe, tyre, a wheel. **3.** (*a*) to tighten, stretch, wind up (spring, cable, etc.); **b. un arc,** (i) to bend; (ii) to string, a bow; **b. un tambour,** to brace a drum; (*b*) *Const:* to key (in) (an arch).

II. bander, *v.i.* **1.** to strain; to be tight; *V:* to have an erection. **2.** *Bill:* (*a*) (*of ball*) to touch the cushion; (*b*) to play off the cushion.

se bander contre qn, contre qch., *A:* to oppose, resist, s.o., sth.

bandereau, -eaux [bãdro], *s.m.* (trumpet or bugle) cord.

banderille [bãdrij], *s.f. Bull-fighting:* banderilla.

banderillero [bãderijero], *s.m. Bull-fighting:* banderillero.

banderole [bãdrɔl], *s.f.* **1.** banderole, streamer; *Mil:* lance-pennon; *Agr:* **b. à lapins,** rabbit scarer. **2.** *O:* shoulder-belt; *O:* **b. de fusil,** rifle-sling. **3.** balloon (in comic strips, etc.). **4.** *Sp:* **b. d'arrivée,** tape.

bandière [bãdjɛːr], *s.f. A:* banner, flag; *Mil: A:* **front de b.,** colour-line of the camp; front of the army.

bandine [bãdin], *s.f.* (*a*) buckwheat flour; (*b*) buckwheat.

bandingue [bãdɛ̃g], *s.f. Fish:* guy-rope (of a fishing net).

bandit [bãdi], *s.m.* (*a*) bandit, brigand, highwayman; gangster; (*b*) ruffian, villain; **c'est un tour de mon b. de neveu,** that's one of my rascally nephew's tricks.

banditisme [bãditism], *s.m.* banditry, banditism.

bandolier [bãdɔlje], *s.m.,* **bandoulier** [bãdulje], *s.m. A:* **1.** (Pyrenean) smuggler; bandit; adventurer. **2.** (forest) guard (armed with bow and arrow).

bandoline [bãdəlin], s.f. Hairdr: A: bandoline.
bandonéon [bãdəneõ], s.m. Mus: bandonion, bandoneon.
bandoulière [bãduljɛːr], s.f. **1.** shoulder-strap, (carbine) shoulder-belt; **passer la b. d'une harpe sur son épaule,** to sling a harp over one's shoulder; **porter, mettre, qch. en b.,** to carry, sling, sth. across one's shoulder; **mettre le fusil en b.,** to sling one's rifle (crosswise). **2.** bandoleer, U.S: cross-belt; **b. à cartouches,** (cartridge) bandolier.
bandoura [bãdura], s.f. Mus: bandore.
bandure [bãdyːr], s.f. Bot: pitcher-plant.
bang [bãg], s.m. Av: double bang.
bang(h) [bã(ːg)], s.m. Bot: B(h)ang; Indian hemp; hashish.
banian [banjã], s.m. **1.** banian, banyan, Hindu trader. **2.** Bot: banyan (tree).
banjo [bãʒo, -dʒo], s.m. **1.** Mus: banjo. **2.** Av: banjo (of rotary motor). **3.** Aut: banjo; **pont b.,** banjo axle.
bank [bãk], s.f. Paperm: banknote paper.
Bankiva [bãkiva], Pr.n. Husb: **race de B.,** Bankiva jungle-fowl.
banksie [bãksi], s.f. Bot: banksia.
banlieue [bãljø], s.f. suburbs, outskirts (of a town); **la b.,** suburbia, the commuter belt; **il habite en b.,** he lives in the suburbs; Rail: **ligne, gare, de b.,** suburban line, station.
banlieusard, -arde [bãljøzaːr, -ard], F: (a) s. suburbanite, esp. = commuter; (b) a. suburban.
banne [ban], s.f. **1.** coal cart. **2.** hamper, large basket, skep; basket-trunk. **3.** (a) tarpaulin; tilt (of cart); (b) awning (of shop, etc.); shop-blind (over pavement). **4.** = BENNE.
banneau, -eaux [bano], s.m. fruit-basket, hamper.
bannelle [banɛl], s.f. small wicker basket (for corks).
banner [bane], v.tr. to cover (with tarpaulin); to tilt, to put a tilt over (cart).
banneret [banrɛ], s.m. A: banneret; **chevalier b.,** knight-banneret.
banneton [bantõ], s.m. **1.** (baker's) bread-basket. **2.** Fish: corf.
bannette [banɛt], s.f. small hamper, basket.
banni, -e [bani]. **1.** a. banished, outlawed. **2.** s. exile, outlaw.
bannière [banjɛːr], s.f. banner; **se ranger sous la b. de qn,** to fall in under s.o.'s banner, to join s.o.'s party; **la b. étoilée,** the star-spangled banner (of the U.S.A.); Nau: **hisser un pavillon en b.,** to hoist a flag flying; P: **être en b.,** to be in one's shirt tails; s.a. CROIX 1.
bannir [baniːr], v.tr. to banish (s.o. from the kingdom); **b. qn d'une société,** to exclude, expel, s.o. from a society; **b. une mauvaise pensée de son esprit,** to put an unpleasant thought out of one's mind; **il a banni complètement le café,** he has completely given up drinking coffee.
bannissable [banisabl], a. deserving, punishable by, banishment; that should be banished.
bannissement [banismã], s.m. banishment, (i) banishing (of s.o.); (ii) exile; **b. à vie,** banishment for life; **b. d'une habitude,** the giving up of a habit.
bannisseur [banisœːr], s.m. banisher.
banquable [bãkabl], a. = BANCABLE.
banquais [bãkɛ]. **1.** a. engaged in the Newfoundland fisheries. **2.** s.m. Fish: banker (fisherman or boat).
banque [bãːk], s.f. **1.** (a) bank; **la B. Mondiale,** the World Bank; (b) banking; **la haute b.,** high finance; **maisons de haute b.,** big banking houses; **b. anonyme, b. par actions,** joint-stock bank; **b. de placement, d'émission,** bank of issue; issuing house; **b. d'affaires,** merchant bank; **affaires de b.,** (i) banking; (ii) outside broking; **papier hors b.,** unbankable paper; **billet de b.,** banknote; **carnet, livret, de b.,** bank-book, pass-book; **avoir un compte de, en, b. chez . . .,** to have a banking account with . . ., to bank with . . .; **crédit en b.,** bank credit; **employé de b.,** bank clerk; P: **(jour de) b.,** pay-day; (c) Med: **b. de, du sang,** blood bank; **b. d'yeux, des yeux,** eye bank. **2.** Cards: bank; **tenir la b.,** to hold the bank; **faire sauter la b.,** to break the bank. **3.** F: (a) (mountebank's) patter; **faire de la b.,** to puff one's goods; (b) **la b.,** the circus world; (c) travelling show. **4.** (work)bench.
banquer [bãke]. **1.** v.tr. Nau: to seat (a boat). **2.** v.i. Nau: to fish on the Newfoundland banks, to bank. **3.** v.i. P: to pay, to cough up.
banqueroute [bãkrut], s.f. Jur: **b. simple,** bankruptcy (with irregularities amounting to a breach of the law); **b. frauduleuse,** fraudulent bankruptcy (amounting to crime); **faire b.,** to go bankrupt; cf. FAILLITE; **faire b. à l'honneur,** to fling away one's honour, to stand dishonoured.

banqueroutier, -ière [bãkrutje, -jɛːr], a. & s. bankrupt (usu. fraudulent).
banquet [bãkɛ], s.m. banquet, feast; **salle de b.,** banqueting hall; **b. nuptial, de noces** = wedding breakfast; **le banquet sacré, eucharistique,** holy communion; Gr.Lit: **le B. (de Platon),** (Plato's) Symposium, the Banquet.
banqueter [bãk(ə)te], v.i. (je banquette, n. banquetons; je banquetterai) to banquet, feast.
banqueteur, -euse [bãk(ə)tœːr, -øːz], s.m. banqueter, feaster.
banquette [bãkɛt], s.f. **1.** (a) bench, seat, form; wall-sofa (in restaurant, etc.); **b. de piano,** duet stool; Sp: (of reserve player) **faire b.,** to sit out the game; Th: **jouer devant les banquettes, devant des banquettes vides,** to play to empty benches, to an empty house; Aut: **b. à coussins,** frame to support squabs; (b) A: **banquette,** outside-seat (of coach), knifeboard seat (of bus, tram); **voyager sur la b.,** to ride on the outside, on top. **2.** Civ.E: etc: banquette, bank (of earth, etc.), berm, verge; Min: spoil-bank; Golf: bunker; Turf: **b. (irlandaise),** bank. **3.** footway, banquette; Civ.E: service-path (of bridge, tunnel, etc.); **b. de halage,** tow(ing)-path. **4.** (a) platform, ledge; **b. de fenêtre,** window-ledge; (b) Fort: banquette; **b. de tir,** firing step (of trench); (c) pl. steps (of graving dock).
banquette-lit [bãkɛtli], s.f. Furn: studio couch; pl. des banquettes-lits.
banquier¹, -ière [bãkje, -jɛːr]. **1.** a. banking (house, etc.). **2.** s. Fin: Cards: banker; **la banquière,** the banker's wife; **être le b. de qn,** to supply s.o. with money; to lend s.o. money.
banquier², s.m. Newfoundland fishing boat; banker.
banquise [bãkiːz], s.f. **1.** ice-floe, ice-pack, ice-bank. **2.** barrier ice; **la B.,** the Great Ice Barrier.
banquiste [bãkist], s.m. charlatan, quack (at a fair).
Bantam [bãtam], Pr.n. Geog: Bantam; Husb: **coq, poule, de B.,** bantam (-cock, -hen); Box: **poids b.,** bantam-weight.
banteng [bãtɛ̃], s.m. Z: banteng.
Bantou, -e [bãtu], a. & s. Ethn: Bantu.
banyulais, -aise [banjulɛ, -ɛːz], a. & s., **banyulen, -enne** [banjulɛ̃, -ɛn], **banyulenque** [banjulɛ̃k], a. & s. Geog: (native, inhabitant) of Banyuls-sur-Mer [banjulssyrmɛːr].
baobab [baɔbab], s.m. Bot: baobab (tree).
bapaumois, -oise [bapomwa, -waːz], a. & s. Geog: (native, inhabitant) of Bapaume.
baphia [bafja], **baphier** [bafje], s.m. Bot: baphia.
baptême [batɛm], s.m. **1.** baptism, christening; **administrer le b. à qn,** to baptize s.o.; **recevoir le b.,** to receive baptism, to be baptized; **nom de b.,** Christian name, baptismal name; **être invité à un b.,** to be invited to a christening (party). **2.** blessing (of a bell); naming (of a ship); **b. du sang,** baptism of blood; **b. de l'air,** first flight; Nau: **b. de la ligne, des tropiques,** (ducking on) crossing the line.
baptisé, -ée [batize], a. & s. baptized (person).
baptiser [batize], v.tr. to baptize (s.o.), to christen (s.o., ship, etc.); to bless (bell, etc.); (a) **b. un enfant sous le nom de Georges,** to christen a child George; F: **baptiser son vin,** (i) to water down one's wine; (ii) to water down one's language, one's claims, etc.; **il fut baptisé catholique,** he was baptized a Roman Catholic; (b) to christen, nickname, dub; **on l'avait baptisé "le Balafré"** they had nicknamed him "Scarface"; **b. son chien du nom de Toutou,** to call one's dog Toutou.
baptiseur [batizœːr], s.m. baptizer.
baptismal, -aux [batismal, -o], a. baptismal; s.a. FONTS.
baptisme [batism], s.m. Rel: Hist: the Baptist doctrine.
baptistaire [batistɛːr], a. **registre b.,** register of baptisms; **extrait b.,** certificate of baptism.
Baptiste [batist]. **1.** Pr.n.m. Baptist; F: **tranquille comme B.,** (i) as quiet as a mouse; (ii) as cool as a cucumber. **2.** s.m. A: **un b.,** a clown, a simpleton. **3.** a. & s. Ecc: (member of the) Baptist (community).
baptistère [batistɛːr], s.m. Ecc: baptist(e)ry.
baquet [bakɛ], s.m. **1.** tub, bucket. **2.** Aut: **(siège en) b.,** bucket seat.
baqueter [bakte], v.tr. (je baquette, n. baquetons, je baquetterai) to bale out, scoop out (liquid).
baquettes [bakɛt], s.f.pl. Metalw: draw-tongs.
baquoi(s) [bakwa], s.m. **1.** Bot: screw-pine. **2.** vacoa fibre.
bar¹ [baːr], s.m. Ich: bass; **b. commun,** sea-perch, sea-dace, sea-wolf; **b. rayé,** striped bass.

bar², s.m. (public) bar; bar (counter); **prendre une consommation au b.,** to have a drink at the bar; **b. tabacs,** bar with tobacco licence.
bar³, s.m. = BARD.
bar⁴, s.m. Meas. (Meteor): bar.
barachois [baraʃwa], s.m. Fr.C: sand-bar (in a river).
baragouin [baragwɛ̃], s.m. F: **1.** gibberish, jargon, jabber. **2.** lingo.
baragouinage [baragwinaːʒ], s.m. **1.** jabbering. **2.** = BARAGOUIN.
baragouiner [baragwine], v.tr. & i. F: (a) to speak a language badly; **b. l'anglais,** to talk broken English; **je baragouine un peu l'anglais,** I can (manage to) speak a little English; (b) to talk unintelligibly; to talk gibberish; **ces étrangers qui baragouinent entre eux,** these foreigners jabbering to each other.
baragouineur, -euse [baragwinœːr, -øːz], s. jabberer.
baraka [baraka], s.m. (a) (in N. Africa) blessing, favourable influence (of saint, relic); (b) F: (good) luck.
baralipton [baraliptõ], s.m. Log: baralipton; bramantip.
barandage [barãdaʒ], s.m. Fish: fishing by means of a net stretched right across a river.
baraque [barak], s.f. (a) hut, shanty; pl. Mil: huts, hutments; **b. de pêcheur,** fisherman's shanty; **b. d'outils,** tool shed; P: **toute la b.,** the whole outfit; (b) F: hovel, hole (of a place); Pej: house; (c) booth (at fair, etc.); (d) Sch: P: cupboard; locker.
baraqué [barake], a. P: (of pers.) **bien b.,** well-built.
baraquement [barakmã], s.m. **1.** lodging (of troops) in huts; hutting. **2.** usu. pl. (a) Mil: camp of huts; hutments; (b) (workmen's) living quarters (while road-making, etc.); **loger dans un b.,** to live in (i) a (wooden) shack; (ii) a temporary dwelling-unit; (iii) a hovel.
baraquer [barake]. **1.** v.tr. to lodge (troops, etc.) in huts; to hut. **2.** v.i. & pr. to house oneself; **le bataillon va (se) b.,** the battalion is going into huts. **3.** v.i. (of camel) to kneel down.
baraquette [barakɛt], s.f. **1.** small hut. **2.** Nau: sister-block.
baraquiste [barakist], s.m. Mil: hut-builder.
barate [barat], s.f. Nau: strain-band.
baraterie [baratri], s.f. Marine Jur: barratry.
baratin [baratɛ̃], s.m. P: (a) (cheapjack's) patter; (b) line-shooting; blah; **faire du b.,** to spin a yarn, to shoot a line; (c) sweet talk.
baratiner [baratine], v.tr. & i. P: (a) to patter (like a cheapjack); (b) to shoot a line, to spin a yarn; (c) to chat up (a girl).
baratineur, -euse [baratinœːr, -øz], s.m. & f. P: (a) tout; (b) smooth talker.
barattage [barataːʒ], s.m. churning (of milk).
baratte [barat], s.f. churn; **b. ordinaire,** plunger churn; **b. circulaire,** barrel churn.
baratter [barate], v.tr. to churn (milk).
barattin [baratɛ̃], s.m., **barattiner** [baratine], v.tr. & i., **barattineur, -euse** [baratinœːr, -øz], s. P: = BARATIN, BARATINER, BARATINEUR, -EUSE.
barat(t)on [baratõ], s.m. plunger, dasher (of churn).
barbacane [barbakan], s.f. **1.** A.Fort: (a) barbican, outwork; (b) loop(-hole). **2.** Civ.E: draining channel (of bridge); weep hole (of retaining wall).
barbacole [barbakɔl], s.m. A: schoolmaster; bearded pedant.
barbacou [barbaku], s.m. Orn: barbacou.
Barbade (la) [labarbad], Pr.n.f. Geog: Barbados; Dist: **eau des Barbades,** Barbados water.
barbant [barbã], a. F: boring.
barbaque [barbak], s.f. P: meat (of poor quality).
barbara [barbara], s.m. Log: barbara.
barbarasse [barbaras], s.f. Nau: dog-stopper.
barbare [barbaːr]. **1.** a. (a) barbaric (people, art, etc.); uncouth; (b) O: barbarous, cruel, inhuman; **être b. envers les animaux,** to be cruel, brutal, to animals. **2.** s.m. & f. barbarian.
barbarée [barbare], s.f. Bot: barbarea, winter-cress.
barbarement [barbarmã], adv. **1.** barbarically. **2.** barbarously, cruelly, inhumanly.
barbaresque [barbarɛsk]. **1.** a. (a) Barbaresque, Berber; (b) les États barbaresques, the Barbary States; **les pirates barbaresques,** Barbary pirates. **2.** s.m. & f. Berber.
barbarie¹ [barbari], s.f. **1.** barbarism. **2.** barbarousness, barbarity, cruelty.
Barbarie², Pr.n.f. (a) Geog: the Barbary States, A: Barbary; (b) Orn: **canard de B.,** Barbary duck; s.a. FIGUIER.

barbarin [barbarɛ̃], *a. Z:* Barbary (sheep).
barbariser [barbarize]. **1.** *v.tr.* to barbarize (people, one's style). **2.** *v.i.* to use barbarous expressions, barbarisms (in writing, speaking).
barbarisme [barbarism], *s.m. Gram:* barbarism.
barbastelle [barbastɛl], *s.f. Z:* barbastelle.
barbe[1] [barb], *s.f.* **1.** beard (of man, goat, etc.) (*a*) **homme portant b.,** bearded man; **homme portant toute sa b.,** full-bearded man; **longue b., b. de fleuve, flottante,** flowing beard; *Lit:* **du côté de la b.,** on the male side; *A:* **par ma b.!** gadzooks! **rire dans sa b.,** to laugh up one's sleeve; **faire qch. (au nez et) à la b. de qn, de tous,** to do sth. to s.o.'s face, in the face of all; to do sth. under s.o.'s nose; **faire la b. à qn,** (i) to shave s.o.; (ii) *F:* to be one up on s.o.; **se faire la b.,** to shave; **il avait une b. de huit jours,** he had a week's beard, a week's growth; **mon jour de b.,** my shaving day; **brosse à b.,** shaving brush; **combien prenez-vous pour la b.?** how much do you charge for a shave? **"Pour la b. ou les cheveux?"** "shave or hair-cut?" *F:* **c'était la b. et les cheveux,** it was no end of a bore, a never-ending job; *F:* **quelle b.!** what a nuisance! **ce qu'il est b.!** he's an awful bore, he bores me stiff; **la b. avec,** to hell with; **prendre une b.,** to get drunk; **la b.!** (i) heck! (ii) not so much of it! shut up! *Nau:* **mouiller en b.,** to moor with two anchors ahead; *Comest:* **b. à papa,** candy floss, *U.S:* cotton candy; (*b*) **vieille b., b. grise,** grey-beard; **jeune b.,** beardless youth; (*c*) *Moss:* **b. de vieillard,** long-beard; (*d*) whiskers (of cat); barbel, wattle (of fish); beard, wattle (of bird); barb (of feather, fish-hook); beard (of wheat); *Meteor: F:* **barbes de chat,** mare's tail. **2.** mildew; **prendre de la b.,** to go mouldy. **3.** *Tchn:* (*a*) notch (in lock bolt); (*b*) barb (of metal); bur(r) (on casting, engraved plate); (*c*) *pl.* deckle edge (of paper); (*d*) butt-end (of plank); *N.Arch:* hood-end (of strake). **4.** *A.Cost:* pinner (of coif).
barbe[2], *a. & s.m.* barb, Barbary horse.
Barbe[3], *Pr.n.f.* Barbara; *s.a.* SAINTE-BARBE.
barbeau[1], **-eaux** [barbo], *s.m.* **1.** *Ich:* **b. commun,** barbel; **b. de mer,** red mullet. **2.** *P:* pimp.
barbeau[2]. **1.** *s.m. Bot:* bluebottle; cornflower. **2.** *a.inv.* **(bleu) b.,** cornflower blue, light blue.
Barbe-Bleue [barbəblø], *Pr.n.m.* Bluebeard.
barbecue [barbəkju], *s.m.* barbecue.
barbe-de-bouc [barbdəbuk], *s.f.* **1.** *Bot: F:* salsify, goat's-beard. **2.** *Fung: F:* (*a*) goat's beard; (*b*) hydnum repandum, *F:* teeth-bearing fungus; *pl. barbes-de-bouc.*
barbe-de-capucin [barbdəkapysɛ̃], *s.f. Bot: Cu:* wild chicory; *pl. barbes-de-capucin.*
barbe-de-Jupiter [barbdəʒypitɛːr], *s.f. Bot:* red valerian, spur valerian, Jupiter's-beard; *pl. barbes-de-Jupiter.*
barbe-de-moine [barbdəmwan], *s.f. Bot:* dodder; *pl. barbes-de-moine.*
barbe-de-vache [barbdəvaʃ], *s.f. Fung: F:* hydnum repandum, *F:* teeth-bearing fungus; *pl. barbes-de-vache.*
barbelé [barbəle], *a.* barbed (arrow, hook); **fil de fer b.,** *s.m.* **barbelé,** barbed wire; *Mil:* **des barbelés,** barbed-wire entanglement; **pose des barbelés,** wiring, setting, of barbed wire entanglements.
barbelure [barbəlyːr], *s.f.* **1.** *Bot:* beard, awn (of wheat). **2.** barb (of arrow).
barber [barbe], *F:* **1.** *v.tr.* to bore (s.o.). **2.** *v.pr.* to be bored.
Barberousse [barbərus], *Pr.n.m. Hist:* Barbarossa.
barbet, -ette[1] [barbɛ, -ɛt], *s.* **1.** *Z:* barbet (spaniel); *s.a.* CROTTÉ. **2.** *s.m. Ich:* barbel.
barbeyer [barbeje], *v.i. Nau:* (*of sails*) to shiver.
barbette[2], *s.f.* **1.** *Ecc.Cost:* barb (of nun's head-dress). **2.** *Fort:* barbette; **batterie (à) b.,** barbette battery; **tirer à b.,** to fire in barbette, over the parapet; **tir en b.,** *Infantry:* fire over the parapet, *Artil:* over-bank fire; **pièce en b.,** barbette-gun; *F:* **officier de b.** = sapper. **3.** *P:* **coucher à b.,** to sleep (on a mattress) on the floor.
barbezilien, -ienne [barbəziljɛ̃, -jɛn], *a. & s. Geog:* (native, inhabitant) of Barbezieux.
barbican [barbikɑ̃], *s.m. Orn:* barbican.
barbiche [barbiʃ], *s.f.* **1.** (*a*) short beard (on the chin); (*b*) goatee. **2.** *Bot:* bishop's-wort, love-in-a-mist. **3.** young barbet (spaniel).
barbichet [barbiʃɛ], *s.m.,* **barbichon** [barbiʃɔ̃], *s.m.* young barbet (spaniel).
barbichu [barbiʃy], *a. F:* **un petit bonhomme b.,** a little man with a goatee (beard).
barbier [barbje], *s.m.* **1.** barber; *Fr.C:* **salon de b.,** barber's, *U.S:* barber shop; men's hairdresser. **2.** *Ich:* (lepadogaster) sucker.
barbifère [barbifɛːr], *a. Nat.Hist:* barbate, barbigerous.
barbifier [barbifje], *v.tr.* (*pr.sub. & p.d.* **n. barbifiions, v. barbifiiez**) *F:* to shave.
se barbifier. 1. to shave. **2.** *F:* to be bored.
barbillon [barbijɔ̃], *s.m.* **1.** (*a*) wattle (of cock, fish); barb, barbel (of fish); palp (of insect); *pl.* barbels (of horse, cattle); (*b*) barb, beard (of fish-hook, arrow); **relever le b. d'un hameçon,** to barb a hook. **2.** *Ich:* = BARBEAU[1] 1. **3.** *P:* pimp.
barbiste [barbist], *a. & s.m.* (old boy, scholar) of the college of Sainte-Barbe (in Paris).
barbital [barbital]. **1.** *s.m. Pharm:* barbital. **2.** *a.* barbituric.
barbiturate [barbityrat], *s.m.* **barbiturique** [barbityrik], *a. & s.m. Ch:* barbiturate.
barbiturisme [barbityrism], *s.m. Med:* barbiturism, barbiturate habit.
barboche [barbɔʃ], *s.f.* half round file (used for sharpening saws).
barbon [barbɔ̃], *s.m.* **1.** *A: & Hum:* greybeard, old fog(e)y; **faire le b., s'ériger en b.,** to put on the airs of an old man. **2.** *Bot:* Andropogon.
barbot [barbo], *s.m.* **1.** *Ich:* eel-pout, burbot; **petit barbot,** (common) loach. **2.** *P:* pimp.
barbotage [barbɔtaːʒ], *s.m.* **1.** (*a*) paddling, splashing; *Mch:* **graissage par b.,** splash lubrication; (*b*) bubbling (of gas through liquid); stirring, mixing (of liquids); (*c*) *F:* mumbling, floundering; (*d*) *P:* stealing, filching, *P:* scrounging, pinching. **2.** (*a*) mess, mud (stirred up by paddling); (*b*) bran mash (for horses).
barbot(t)e [barbɔt], *s.f.* **1.** = BARBOT 1. **2.** *P:* frisking (of person, taken into custody).
barbotement [barbɔtmɑ̃], *s.m.* = BARBOTAGE 1.
barboter [barbɔte]. **1.** *v.i.* (*a*) to paddle, splash (about); to dabble (like a duck); (*b*) (*of gases*) to bubble; (*c*) *F:* to become confused, muddled; to flounder. **2.** *v.tr.* (*a*) *Laund:* **b. le linge dans la lessive,** to work the linen about in the suds; (*b*) to mumble, mutter (sth.); (*c*) *P:* to steal, filch, *P:* to scrounge, pinch, sneak, bone (sth.); *U.S:* to corral (sth.); *abs.* to pick pockets.
barboteur, -euse [barbɔtœːr, -øːz], *s.* **1.** (*a*) paddler, *F:* mudlark; (*b*) *F:* muddler, flounderer. **2.** *P:* thief, scrounger. **3.** *s.m.* tame duck. **4.** *s.m.* (*a*) *Ind:* bubbler, blower; **b. à gaz,** gas scrubber; *Ch:* **b. pour lavage,** wash-bottle; (*b*) *Ind:* mixer, stirrer; (*c*) *Laund:* washing machine. **5.** *s.f.* **barboteuse,** (*a*) (*child's*) (i) play-suit; (ii) crawlers, rompers; (*b*) *Laund:* washing machine.
barbotier [barbɔtje], *s.m. P:* officer who searches persons taken into custody.
barbotière [barbɔtjɛːr], *s.f.* **1.** duck-pond. **2.** *Husb:* mash-tub.
barbotin [barbɔtɛ̃], *s.m. Mec.E:* **1.** sprocket-wheel; *Nau:* cable wheel. **2.** chain-pulley. **3.** = BARBOT 1.
barbotine [barbɔtin], *s.f.* **1.** *Cer:* barbotine, slip, slop. **2.** *Bot:* (*a*) (common) mugwort; (*b*) tansy.
barbottage [barbɔtaːʒ], *s.m.,* **barbottement** [barbɔtmɑ̃], *s.m.,* **barbotter** [barbɔte], *v.i. & tr.,* **barbotteur, -euse** [barbɔtœːr, -øːz], *s.* = BARBOTAGE, BARBOTEMENT, BARBOTER, etc.
barbouillage [barbujaːʒ], *s.m.* **1.** (*a*) daubing, smearing; blurring (of print); (*b*) scrawling, scribbling; (*c*) *A:* confusing, bungling. **2.** (*a*) bad picture, daub; (*b*) blur (in print, etc.); (*c*) scrawl, scribble.
barbouillé [barbuje]. **1.** *a.* (*a*) dirty; **b. d'encre,** ink-stained; (*b*) *F:* **avoir le cœur b.,** to feel sick, squeamish; **avoir l'estomac b.,** to have an upset stomach. **2.** *s.m. Th.Hist:* **le B.,** the Clown (in old farces).
barbouiller [barbuje], *v.tr.* **1.** (*a*) to daub; to smear (de, with); (*b*) to smear, dirty (one's face, etc.); to blot, soil (paper); to blur (printing, etc.); **visage barbouillé de larmes,** tear-stained face. **2.** to scribble, scrawl; **b. un article,** to scribble off an article. **3.** *A:* to mumble, stammer out (sth.). **4.** *F:* **b. une affaire,** to bungle, make a botch of, tangle up, a piece of business; **mets qui (vous) barbouille le cœur,** dish that turns one's stomach.
se barbouiller. 1. to get dirty. **2.** *A:* **se b. de grec et de latin,** to dabble in Greek and Latin. **3. le temps se barbouille,** the weather's turning bad.
barbouilleur, -euse [barbujœːr, -øːz], *s.* **1.** dauber, inferior artist. **2. b. (de papier),** scribbler, penny-a-liner, hack.
barbouillis [barbuji], *s.m.* = BARBOUILLAGE 2.
barbouse, barbouze [barbuz], *s.f. P:* **1.** (*a*) beard; *P:* beaver; (*b*) bearded man; *P:* **beaver. 2.** secret agent; member of secret police.
barbu, -ue [barby]. **1.** *a.* (*a*) bearded (man); (*b*) *Nat.Hist:* barbate; *Bot:* bearded, aristate; (*c*) mouldy, mildewed. **2.** *s.m. Orn:* barbet. **3.** *s.f. Ich:* **barbue,** brill.
barbule [barbyl], *s.f.* **1.** *Orn:* barbule (of feather). **2.** *Moss:* Barbula.
barbure [barbyːr], *s.f. Metall:* beard, burr, scale (on casting).
barca [barka], *int. P:* that's enough! cut it out!
barcarolle [barkarɔl], *s.f. Mus:* barcarol(l)e, boat-song.
barcasse [barkas], *s.f. Nau:* **1.** *A:* large barque. **2.** *F:* old tub (of a boat); dull ship. **3.** lighter.
barcelonais, -aise [barsəlɔnɛ, -ɛːz], *a. & s. Geog:* (native, inhabitant) of Barcelona.
Barcelone [barsəlɔn], *Pr.n.f. Geog:* Barcelona.
barcelonnettain, -aine [barsəlɔnɛtɛ̃, -ɛn], *a. & s. Geog:* (native, inhabitant) of Barcelonnette.
barcelonnette [barsəlɔnɛt], *s.f.* = BERCELONNETTE.
barcous [barkus], *s.m. Dial:* reservoir (in the pine forests of the Landes).
bard [baːr], *s.m.* **1.** (wheelless) hand-barrow, stone-barrow, two-man tray. **2.** (wheeled) hand-trolley.
barda [barda], *s.m. Mil: P:* pack, kit; luggage.
bardage [bardaːʒ], *s.m.* **1.** hand transport (of heavy materials); stone carrying. **2.** shifting (of heavy material) on rollers. **3.** *Constr:* boarding.
bardane [bardan], *s.f. Bot:* burdock; **petite b.,** burweed.
barde[1] [bard], *s.f.* **1.** *Harn:* pack-saddle. **2.** *Arm:* (*a*) bard (protecting war-horse); (*b*) *pl.* bards (of 16th cent. armour); (*c*) *F:* **à toute b.,** at full speed. **3.** *Cu:* **b. (de lard),** slice of bacon (used to cover fowl, etc.), bard.
barde[2], *s.m.* bard, poet.
bardeau, -eaux [bardo], *s.m.* **1.** *Const:* (*a*) shingle (-board); (*b*) lath. **2.** small raft (of floated timber). **3.** *Typ:* extra-fount case. **4.** = BARDOT 1. **5.** *Ich: F:* cod.
bardée[1] [barde], *s.f. Cu:* bard (covering of thin bacon over a fowl or joint).
bardée[2], *s.f.* (hand-barrow) load.
barder[1] [barde], *v.tr.* **1.** to remove, carry (stones, etc., on hand-barrow). **2.** *abs. F:* to work hard; (*of storm or fight*) to rage; **aujourd'hui ça barde,** to-day we're hard at it; *P:* **Ça va b.!** look out for squalls! **c'est là que ça a commencé à b.!** and then the fun began!
barder[2], *v.tr.* **1.** *A:* to bard; to arm (man or horse) with bards; **chevalier bardé de fer,** knight cased in steel; steel-clad knight. **2.** *Cu:* to bard (fowl, etc., with bacon); *F:* **il était bardé de croix,** he was covered, blazing, with decorations; **malle bardée d'étiquettes,** trunk stuck all over with labels.
bardeur [bardœːr], *s.m.* **1.** hand-barrowman, stone-barrowman. **2.** *Civ.E:* truck.
bardis [bardi], *s.m. Nau:* shifting boards (for stowing cargo).
bardit [bardi], *s.m.* bardic song.
bardot [bardo], *s.m.* **1.** (*a*) hinny; (*b*) pack-mule; *F:* **être le b. de tout le pays,** to be a butt for everyone's jokes; **passer pour b.,** to be admitted, entertained scot free (with the rest of the party); "to go in with the crowd." **2.** *Typ:* waste paper.
barège [barɛːʒ], *s.m. A: Tex:* barege.
barégine [bareʒin], *s.f. Med:* glairin.
barème [barɛːm], *s.m.* **1.** ready-reckoner; calculator. **2.** scale (of marks, of salaries); scheme of marking (examination papers); **b. graphique,** graph. **3.** (printed) table, schedule (of prices, etc.); (price) list; *Trans:* **b. mondial des taux de fret nominaux,** intascale.
baresthésie [barɛstezi], *s.f. Med:* baresthesia.
baréter [barete], *v.i.* **(il barète, il barétera)** (*of elephant, rhinoceros*) to trumpet, roar.
barette[1] [barɛt], *s.f.* = BARRETTE[2].
barette[2], *s.f. Fb:* rugby without tackling (as played by young boys).
barge[1] [barʒ], *s.f.* **1.** (*a*) barge, lighter; (*b*) state barge. **2.** (*rectangular*) haystack.
barge[2], *s.f. Orn:* godwit; **b. rousse,** bar-tailed godwit; **b. à queue noire, b. égocéphale,** black-tailed godwit.
bargette [barʒɛt], *s.f. Orn:* **b. de Terek,** Terek sandpiper.
barguette [barɡɛt], *s.f.* flat-bottomed river ferry.
barguignage [barɡiɲaːʒ], *s.m. F:* humming and hawing, hesitating, shilly-shally.
barguigner [barɡiɲe], *v.i. F:* to hum and haw, to hesitate, to shilly-shally; **jamais il ne barguigne à choisir le morceau le plus succulent,** he is always ready to choose the best bit; *A:* **b. pour dire son opinions,** to beat about the bush.

barguigneur, -euse [bargiɲœːr, -øːz], *s. F:* hummer and hawer, shilly-shallier.

baribal, -aux [baribal, -o], *s.m. Z:* American black bear.

baricaut [bariko], *s.m.* keg.

barigoule [barigul], *s.f. Cu:* **artichauts à la b.,** artichokes stuffed in the Provençal manner.

baril [bari(l)], *s.m.* **1.** (*a*) barrel, keg, cask; *Nau:* **b. de galère,** breaker, water cask (of boat); **mettre qch. en b.,** to barrel sth.; (*b*) barrelful, kegful, caskful; **un b. de poudre,** a keg of powder; (*c*) *Meas:* (i) *A:* barrel (18 bushels); (ii) *Petroleum Ind:* barrel (42 gallons); **b. par mille,** barrel-mile. **2.** socket (of carpenter's brace).

barilite [barilit], *s.f. Miner:* barylite.

barillage [barijaːʒ], *s.m.* **1.** cooperage, coopering. **2.** barrelling. **3.** *Nau:* cargo in barrels.

barille [barij], *s.f. Bot: Ind:* barilla.

barillet [barijɛ], *s.m.* **1.** small barrel, keg. **2.** *Anat:* middle-ear. **3.** drum (of pressure indicator); barrel piston-chamber (of pump); cylinder (of revolver); *Opt:* (body-)tube (of lens); *Gasm:* exit tube (of coke-oven); *Clockm: etc:* **b. (de ressort),** spring-box, spring-drum; *Mec.E:* **b. porte-outils,** turret of lathe.

barilleur [barijœːr], *s.m.* cooper.

barine [barin], *s.m. Russian Lit:* barine; (i) lord, master; (ii) gentleman; (iii) sir; my lord.

bariolage [barjɔlaːʒ], *s.m.* **1.** variegation, ((i) variegating; (ii) variegated condition). **2.** medley (of colours); gaudy colour scheme; splashes of colour; motley (of ideas); *Mil:* (*camouflage*) disruptive painting.

bariolé [barjɔle], *a.* gaudy, motley; of many colours, parti-coloured; splashed with colour; **poule bariolée,** speckled hen.

barioler [barjɔle], *v.tr.* to variegate; to paint (sth.) in many colours, in gaudy colours.

bariolure [barjɔlyːr], *s.f.* = BARIOLAGE.

barisien, -ienne [barizjɛ̃, -jɛn], *a. & s. Geog:* (native or inhabitant) of Bar-le-Duc.

barjaquer [barʒake], *v.i. S. of Fr. Dial:* to chatter.

barkhane [barkan], *s.f. Geog:* barchan(e), barkhan.

barle [barl], *s.f. Min:* fault.

barlong, -longue [barlɔ̃, -lɔ̃ːg], *a.* having the shape of an unequal-sided quadrilateral; lopsided, oblong.

barlotière [barlɔtjɛːr], *s.f.* iron window-bar, saddle-bar (of stained-glass window).

Barlow[1] [bɑrlo], *Pr.n. Ph:* **roue de B.,** Barlow's wheel.

Barlow[2], *Pr.n. Med:* **maladie de B.,** Barlow's disease, infantile scurvy.

barmaid [barmɛd], *s.f.* barmaid.

barman [barman], *s.m.* barman; *pl. barmen, barmans.*

Barmécide [barmesid], *s.m. Hist: Lit:* Barmecide; **festin de B.,** Barmecide feast.

barn [barn], *s.m. Atom.Ph.Meas:* barn (10^{-24} cm^2).

Barnabé [barnabe], *Pr.n.m.* Barnabas, Barnaby.

barnabite [barnabit], *s.m. Ecc:* Barnabite.

barnum [barnɔm], *s.m.* showman.

baro- [barɔ-], *pref. Ph:* baro-.

baroco [barɔko], *s.m. Log:* baroco.

Barodet (le) [ləbarɔdɛ], *s.m.* the French Political Directory.

barogramme [barɔgram], *s.m.* barogram.

barographe [barɔgraf], *s.m. Meteor:* barograph; altigraph.

barologie [barɔlɔʒi], *s.f.* (*rare*) barology.

baromètre [barɔmɛtr], *s.m.* **1.** (*a*) barometer, *F:* glass; **b. à cadran,** wheel-barometer; **b. à cuvette,** cistern barometer; **b. enregistreur,** recording barometer; barograph altigraph; **b. à siphon,** siphon barometer; **b. anticyclonal,** barocyclonometer; **le b. est à la pluie, au beau,** the barometer points to rain, to set fair; *s.a.* BAISSER I. 2; (*b*) *Mch:* vacuum-gauge. **2.** *Bot:* **b. du pauvre homme,** pimpernel.

barométrie [barɔmetri], *s.f.* barometry.

barométrique [barɔmetrik], *a.* barometric; baric; **hauteur b.,** barometer reading.

barométriquement [barɔmetrikmɑ̃], *adv.* barometrically.

barométrographe [barɔmetrɔgraf], *s.m. O:* barograph, reading barometer.

baron[1] [bɑrɔ̃, ba-], *s.m.* **1.** baron; **les (hauts) barons de la finance, de l'industrie,** the financial tycoons, the captains, leaders, of industry. **2.** *P:* (*a*) street hawker's assistant, *U.S:* shill; (*b*) protector (of prostitute), *P:* daddy, *U.S:* John.

baron[2], *s.m. Cu:* **b. d'agneau,** cut consisting of the saddle and both hind legs of a lamb.

baronarcose [barɔnarkoz], *s.f. Med:* baronarcosis.

baronnage [bɑrɔnaːʒ, ba-], *s.m.* **1.** baronage. **2.** barony.

baronne[1] [bɑrɔn, ba-], *s.f.* **1.** baroness; **madame la b.,** (i) my lady; (ii) her ladyship. **2.** *P:* **la b.,** the missus, my better half.

baronne[2], *s.f. Cu:* **(aiguillette) b.,** thick flank (of beef).

baronner [bɑrɔne, ba-], *v.i. P:* to act as a decoy.

baronnet [bɑrɔnɛ, ba-], *s.m.* (*in Eng.*) baronet.

baronnial, -iaux [bɑrɔnjal, ba-, -jo], *a.* baronial.

baronnie [bɑrɔni, ba-], *s.f. A:* **1.** barony. **2.** baronage.

baroque [barɔk]. **1.** *a.* (*a*) *A:* baroque (pearl, etc.); (*b*) quaint, odd, baroque. **2.** *s.m. Arch:* **le b.,** the baroque (style).

baroquisme [barɔkism], *s.m. Arch:* baroque character; flamboyancy.

baroscope [barɔskɔp], *s.m.* baroscope.

baroséisme [barɔseism], *s.m. Meteor:* earth tremor.

barosma [barɔsma], *s.m. Bot:* Barosma.

barostat [barɔsta], *s.m.* barostat.

barot [barɔ, bɑ-], *s.m. N.Arch:* = BARROT.

barotaxie [barɔtaksi], *s.f. Biol:* barotaxis, barotaxy.

baroter [barɔte, bɑ-], *v.tr. Nau:* = BARROTER.

barothérapie [barɔterapi], *s.f. Med:* hyperbaric therapy.

barotin [barɔtɛ̃], *s.m. Nau:* = BARROTIN.

barothermographe [barɔtɛrmɔgraf], *s.m.* barothermograph.

baroud [barud], *s.m. P: Mil:* fighting.

barouder [barude], *v.i. P: Mil:* to fight.

baroudeur [barudœːr], *s.m. F:* scrapper, fighter.

barouf(le) [baruf(l)], *s.m. P:* noise, din, row, racket.

barque [bark], *s.f. Nau:* **1.** boat; *Pej:* (*of large ship*) **quelle b.!** what an old tub! **b. de pêcheur,** fishing-boat, fishing-smack; **patron de b.,** skipper; **b. de cérémonie,** state barge; *Lit:* **la b. fatale, de Charon,** Charon's bark, Charon's ferry; **bien mener, bien conduire, sa b.,** to manage one's affairs well; to play one's cards well; **conduire seul sa b.,** to paddle one's own canoe; *F:* **mener (qn) en b.,** to lead s.o. astray. **2. trois-mâts b.,** barque, bark; **gréé en trois-mâts b.,** barque-rigged; **b. goélette,** barkentine, barquentine. **3.** (*a*) *Dy:* vat; (*b*) *For:* (cemented) ditch (dug in pine forests to collect the resin).

barquée [barke], *s.f.* boatload, boatful.

barquentin [barkɑ̃tɛ̃], *s.m. Nau:* barquentine.

barquerolle [barkərɔl], *s.f.* **1.** (*in the Mediterranean*) small sculling boat. **2.** pleasure-boat.

barquette [barkɛt], *s.f.* **1.** small craft, skiff. **2.** boat-shaped pastry. **3.** *Ind:* (any small boat-shaped) receptacle, trough.

Bar(r)abbas [barabɑːs], *Pr.n.m. B.Hist:* Barabbas.

barracuda [barakyda], *s.m. Ich:* barracuda.

barradeau [barado], *s.m. Agr:* land drain.

barrage [baraːʒ], *s.m.* **1.** (*a*) barring, stopping (of road, etc.); blocking (of harbour); damming (of valley); closing (of street); **faire b. à (qch.),** to obstruct; to be obstructive; (*b*) *Com:* crossing (of cheque); (*c*) *Sp:* playing off (of tie); **troisième après b.,** third after tying; **match de b.,** deciding match, game, *Fb:* replay; *U.S:* play-off match, run-off match, tie-breaker. **2.** (*a*) barrier, obstruction; (harbour) boom; **b. routier, de route,** road block; *Adm:* toll gate; *Sp:* hurdle; *Hyd.E:* **b. (de retenue),** barrage, dam; weir; **b. criblant,** filter dam; **b. au fil de l'eau,** river dam, low head dam; **b. poids,** gravity dam; **b. voûte,** arch(ed) dam; **b. voûte-poids,** arch gravity dam; **b. en enrochements,** rock fill dam; **b. en terre,** earth dam; *Mil:* **b. d'obstacles, de mines atomiques, etc.,** obstacle, atomic demolition mine, etc., barrage, barrier; **b. antichar,** anti-tank barrage, barrier; **établir un b. (d'obstacles),** to lay down a barrier, a barrage; **établir un b. flottant sur un cours d'eau,** to boom (off) part of a river; (*b*) *Mil:* **b. aérien,** anti-aircraft barrage; **b. de ballons,** balloon barrage; **b. de mines,** minefield; *Artil:* **(tir de) barrage,** barrage (fire); **b. fixe,** standing barrage; **b. mobile,** moving barrage; curtain fire; **b. roulant,** creeping, rolling, barrage; **établir un b.,** to lay down a barrage; **lever un b.,** to lift a barrage; **bonds et horaire d'un b.,** lifts and timing of a barrage; **l'infanterie doit coller au b.,** infantry must follow close to the barrage. **3.** *Mus:* (*guitar playing*) barrage.

barrage-réservoir [baraʒrezɛrvwar], *s.m. Hyd.E:* storage dam.

barragiste [baraʒist], *s.m. & f.* weir-keeper.

barranco [barɑ̃ko], *s.m. Ph.Geog:* barranco.

barras [barɑːs], *s.m.* barras (resin).

barre [bɑːr], *s.f.* **1.** (*a*) bar, rod, rail (of metal, wood, etc.); (wooden) batten; **b. de chocolat,** bar, stick, of chocolate; *Mus:* **b. de mesure,** bar (line); **b. d'harmonie,** bass-bar (of violin); *Gym:* **b. fixe,** horizontal bar; **barres parallèles,** parallel bars; **b. à disques, à sphères,** bar-bell; *Fb:* **b. transversale (du but),** cross-bar (of the goal); *Com:* **fer en barres,** bar iron; **b. à T,** T-iron; **b. à U,** channel-iron; *Mch:* **b. d'excentrique,** eccentric rod; *Rail:* **b. d'attelage,** draw-bar; *Aut:* **b. de connexion,** cross-bar, tie-rod (of steering gear); *Mch: Aut:* **b. de torsion,** torsion bar; *Atom.Ph:* **b. de réglage, de contrôle,** control rod; *s.a.* ACCOUPLEMENT 1, OMNIBUS 2; *Harn:* **b. de mors,** bar of the bit; *Min:* **b. à mine,** miner's bar, jumper bar; (*b*) bar, barrier, obstacle; **b. d'appui,** hand-rail; *Jur:* **b. d'un tribunal,** bar of a court of justice; **b. des témoins** = witness box, *U.S:* witness stand; **paraître à la b.,** to appear before the Court, at the bar; (*c*) *Nau:* (harbour) boom; (*d*) bar (of river or harbour); *Geol:* **b. glaciaire,** glacial threshold; **b. de travertin,** rimstone bar; **port obstrué d'une b. de sable,** barred harbour; **b. d'eau,** (tidal) bore; **b. de flot,** tidal wave; **b. de plage,** surf; (*e*) *Mus:* capo tasto (of guitar, etc.). **2.** *Nau:* (*a*) bar, tiller (of boat); helm (of ship); **b. à main,** hand steering-gear; **b. franche,** (hand) tiller; **b. à bras,** hand-wheel; **b. de plongée,** diving rudder, diving plane, hydroplane; (*of ship*) **sentir la barre,** to answer the helm; **homme de b.,** man at the wheel, helmsman; **kiosque de la b.,** wheelhouse; **être à la b., tenir la b.,** to be at the helm, to steer; **mettre la b. en grand,** to put the helm hard over; **tenir b. à la vague,** to steady the ship against a sea; **tenir b. à un abus,** to make a stand against an abuse; **donner un brusque coup de b.,** to put the tiller hard over; *F:* **coup de b.,** barefaced overcharging, racket; *F:* **donner un brusque coup de b. à la conversation,** to change the subject abruptly; **mettre moins de b.,** to ease the helm; (*of ship*) **passer sur sa b.,** to gripe; (*b*) **b. de nage des pieds (d'un canot),** stretcher; **b. à tire-veilles,** yoke (of rudder); (*c*) **barres de hune,** cross-trees; **b. de cacatois,** jack cross-tree; (*d*) *N.Arch:* **b. d'arcasse,** transom; **b. de pont,** deck-transom; **b. sèche,** hold-beam. **3.** *pl.* (*horse's*) bars, (i) of mouth; (ii) of hoof. **4.** (*a*) line, dash, stroke, bar; *Typ:* **b. transversale, b. de fraction,** oblique (stroke); **b. d'un t,** cross(-bar, -stroke) of a t; **la barre est tirée,** the list is closed; (*b*) *Mus:* bar(-line); **double barre,** double bar; *Her:* bend sinister. **5.** stripe; **étoffe à barres,** striped cloth. **6.** *Games:* **jeu de barres,** prisoners' base; *F:* **je ne fais que toucher barres,** I am not stopping a moment; **avoir barres, b., sur qn,** to have an advantage over s.o.; to have a hold over s.o.

barré [bare, bɑ-], *a.* **1.** obstructed; *P.N:* **route barrée,** road closed; no thoroughfare; *Golf:* **trou b.,** stymie. **2.** (*a*) **chèque b.,** crossed cheque; *Mus:* C b., barred C; (*b*) *Her:* bendy sinister. **3.** *Dent:* **dent barrée,** impacted, malformed, locked, tooth. **4.** *Row:* coxed, **un deux b.,** a coxed pair. **5.** *Geol:* **couche barrée,** mixed stratum.

barreau, -eaux [baro], *s.m.* **1.** (*a*) small bar, rail; **fenêtre garnie de barreaux,** barred window; **être derrière les barreaux,** to be behind prison bars; **barreaux d'une échelle,** rungs of a ladder; **b. de chaise,** (i) (cross-)bar, stretcher, of a chair; (ii) *P:* cigar; **b. de côtière,** hinge-post (of iron railings); (*b*) grate-bar, fire-bar; (*c*) handspike; (*d*) *Mec.E:* **b. d'essai,** test-bar. **2.** *Jur:* bar; **être reçu, admis, au b., se faire inscrire au b.,** to be called to the bar; **entrée au b.,** call to the bar; **rayer qn du b.,** to disbar s.o.

barrême [barɛm], *s.m.* = BARÈME.

barrement [barmɑ̃], *s.m.* crossing (of cheque).

barrémien [baremjɛ̃], *a. & s.m. Geol:* Barremian.

barrer [bare, bɑ-], *v.tr.* **1.** to strengthen (sth.) by means of a bar or bars. **2.** (*a*) to fasten (sth.) with a bar; to bar (door, etc.); *Fr.C:* to lock (a window, etc.); **b. la porte à, contre, qn,** to bar the door against s.o., to bar, lock, s.o. out; (*b*) to bar, obstruct (the way); to dam (stream); to block (up), close (road); *Surg:* to ligature, bar (vein); **b. le chemin à qn,** (i) to obstruct s.o.'s path; (ii) to thwart s.o.; **b. la route à la réaction,** to bar the way to reaction. **3.** to cross (a *t*, an *A*); *Com:* **b. un chèque,** to cross a cheque; **un pli dur barrait son front,** there was a hard line across his forehead; *s.a.* T. **4.** to cross out, strike out (word, etc.); to blue-pencil (article). **5.** *Nau:* to steer; **yacht qui se barre lui-même,** yacht that steers itself; automatic steering yacht; *Row:* to cox.

se barrer, *P:* to make off, skedaddle, to beat it, to scram.

barrette[1] [barɛt], *s.f.* (*a*) *Ecc:* biretta; (cardinal's) cap; (*b*) *Sch:* doctor's cap; (*c*) *Dial:* (*N. France*) miner's helmet; (*d*) *A: F:* **parler à la b. de qn,** to knock s.o.'s hat, cap, off.

barrette[2] [barɛt], *s.f.* **1.** (small) bar; *Clockm:* axle (of spring-box); *El.E:* connecting strip; **b. à barres,** terminal bar; **b. de connection,** jumper; **b. de masse,** grounding strip; *Aut:* **b. (verticale),** overrider; *Cr:* bail; **faire tomber les barrettes,** to break the wicket; *Cost:* soft-collar pin; **b. d'entrée de tête,** bandeau (of woman's hat); **b. de chaîne de montre,** watch-chain toggle; **b. (pour les cheveux),** hair-slide; **b. de médaille,** bar of medal; **barrettes de souliers,** bars, ankle-straps; *Mec.E:* **b. d'essai,** test-piece, test-bar; *Sm.a:* **b. de revolver,** rotating pawl of a revolver. **2.** (*a*) *Ind:* damper (of furnace); (*b*) *Mch:* **b. du tiroir,** valve-face, port-bridge. **3.** *Tls:* cant-file.

barrette-verrou [barɛtvɛru], *s.f.* locking bar; *pl. barrettes-verrous.*

barreur [barœːr], *s.m.* **1.** *Nau:* man at the wheel, steersman, helmsman, man at the helm. **2.** *Row:* coxswain, *F:* cox; **deux de pointe sans b.,** pair oar; **sans b.,** coxless; **un deux sans b.,** a coxless pair.

barricade [barikad], *s.f.* barricade; **forcer toutes les barricades,** to break down all opposition; **de l'autre côté de la b.,** on the opposing side; on the other side of the fence; **se mettre du mauvais côté de la b.,** to come down on the wrong side of the hedge; *Mil:* **b. (de route),** road block; **b. (de rue),** street barricade.

barricader [barikade], *v.tr.* to barricade (street, etc.); **se b. dans une chambre,** (i) to barricade oneself in a room (**contre,** against); (ii) to shut, lock, oneself up in one's room (so as not to be disturbed).

barrière [barjɛːr, bɑ-], *s.f.* **1.** barrier; *Geog:* **b. naturelle,** natural frontier; *Rail:* (ticket collectors') gate, barrier; **mettre une b. à un passage,** to put a barrier across a passage; **mettre une b. entre deux personnes,** to raise a barrier between two persons; *Aut:* **b. de dégel,** barrier closing road to heavy traffic during a thaw; *Rail:* **barrières d'un passage à niveau,** level-crossing gates; **b. pivotante,** swing gate; **b. à bascule,** drop-arm barrier; **b. oscillante,** lift gate; **b. roulante,** sliding gate; *Av:* **b. de décrochage,** wing fence; **b. antisouffle,** blast wall; anti-blast barrier; *Geog:* **la Grande B.,** the Great Barrier Reef; *s.a.* DOUANIER 1. **2.** gate (of town, castle, etc.); toll-gate, turnpike; *A:* (*in Paris*) **rôdeur de barrière,** suspicious character, loafer (who haunted the *boulevards extérieurs* and the gates); *s.a.* PÉAGE. **3.** *Sp:* starting post. **4.** (*a*) *Anat: A:* **b. des apothicaires,** ileo-caecal valve; (*b*) **b. placentaire,** placental barrier; (*c*) *Med:* **b. hépatique,** blockage of the hepatic duct. **5.** *Ph:* **b. de potentiel,** potential barrier.

barriquaut [bariko], *s.m.* = BARICAUT.

barrique [barik], *s.f.* large barrel (*usu.* 225 litres); cask, butt, hogshead; **vin qui a trois ans de b.,** wine three years in the wood.

barrir [bariːr], *v.i.* (*of elephant*) to trumpet.

barrissement [barismɑ̃], *s.m.,* **barrit** [bari], *s.m.* trumpeting (of elephant).

barriste [barist], *s.m. & f. Gym:* specialist in exercises on horizontal or parallel bars.

barrois, -oise [barwa, -waːz], *a. & s. Geog:* (native, inhabitant) of Bar-sur-Seine, Bar-le Duc.

barrot [baro, bɑ-], *s.m. N.Arch:* (deck-)beam; **b. de coqueron,** panting-beam; **sous barrots,** 'tween-decks.

barroter [barɔte, bɑ-], *v.tr.* to load (vessel) up to the beams.

barrotin [barɔtɛ̃], *s.m. N.Arch:* half-beam, cross-beam, cross-carling.

barrottage [barɔtaːʒ], *s.m. Husb:* small-mesh wire netting.

barsacais, -aise [barsakɛ, -ɛːz], *a. & s.* (native) of Barsac.

barse [bars], *s.f. Com:* tea-chest.

bartavelle [bartavɛl], *s.f.* (**perdrix**) **b.,** rock partridge.

Barthélemy [bartelmi; bartel(e)mi], *Pr.n.m.* Bartholomew.

barthite [bartit], *s.f. Miner:* barthite.

bartholinite [bartɔlinit], *s.f. Med:* bartholinitis.

bartonien [bartɔnjɛ̃], *a. & s.m. Geol:* Bartonian.

bartramie [bartrami], *s.f. Orn:* **b. à longue queue,** Bartram's, upland, sandpiper, *U.S:* upland plover.

barycentre [barisɑ̃tr], *s.m. Mth:* barycentre.

barycentrique [barisɑ̃trik], *a. Geom:* barycentric (co-ordinates).

barye [bari], *s.f. Ph.Meas:* barye.

barylithe [barilit], *s.f.* = BARILITE.

barysphère [barisfɛr], *s.f. Geol:* barysphere.

baryte [barit], *s.f. Ch: Miner:* baryta, barium oxide.

baryté [barite], *a.* **papier b.,** baryta paper, art paper; chalk-overlay; *Med:* **bouillie barytée,** barium meal.

barytifère [baritifɛːr], *a. Geol:* barytic (chalk, etc.).

barytine [baritin], *s.f. Miner:* barytes, heavy spar, barytine.

barytique [baritik], *a.* **1.** *Miner:* barytic. **2.** *Ch:* baric.

barytite [baritit], *s.f. Miner:* = BARYTINE.

barytocalcite [baritɔkalsit], *s.f. Miner:* barytocalcite.

baryton [baritɔ̃], *a. & s.m.* (*a*) *Mus:* baritone, barytone (voice, saxhorn); (*b*) *Ling:* barytone.

baryton(n)er [baritɔne], *v.i.* **1.** to sing, talk, in a baritone voice. **2.** to hum (tune).

baryum [barjɔm], *s.m. Ch: Miner:* barium.

barzoï [barzɔi], *s.m. Z:* borzoi.

bas, basse [bɑ, bɑːs]. I. *a.* **1.** low; **maison basse de toit, à toit b.,** low-roofed house, house with a low roof; **homme de basse stature,** man of short stature; **b. sur pattes, b. sur, de, jambes,** short-legged, with short legs; *Box:* **coup b.,** blow below the belt, foul (blow); **enfant en b. âge,** child of tender years, infant; **avoir la vue basse,** to be short-sighted, near-sighted; **voix basse,** low, deep, voice; **parler à voix basse,** to speak under one's breath; **conversation à voix basse,** muttered, whispered, conversation, conversation in low tones; *F:* **faire parler qn d'un ton plus b.,** to make s.o. climb down; **maintenir les prix b.,** to keep prices down, low; **prix les plus b.,** rock-bottom prices; **les prix sont au plus b.,** prices have touched bottom; **le change est b.,** the rate of exchange is low; **le soleil est b.,** the sun is low (down); **le jour est b.,** the day is drawing to its close; **temps, ciel, b.,** weather with much low-lying cloud; *Meteor:* **plafond b.,** low ceiling (of clouds); **mer basse,** low water, low tide; **la marée est basse,** the tide, the sea, is out; **la rivière est basse,** the river is low; *F:* **les eaux sont basses chez lui,** (i) he is, has fallen, out of favour; (ii) he is hard up; **marcher la tête basse,** to walk along with a hang-dog look; **le front b.,** shamefacedly; **le moral est très b.,** morale is very low; *s.a.* BOUT[1] 1, MAIN 1, OREILLE 1. **2.** mean, base, low; **homme de basse extraction,** man of low birth; **à l'âme basse,** base-minded; **motif b.,** base, mean, contemptible, motive; **basses pensées,** vile, contemptible, thoughts; **terme, genre, style, b.,** vulgar term, manner, style; **basses fonctions,** servile, degrading, functions; **maître des basses œuvres,** scavenger (of cesspools); **basse littérature,** cheap writing, pulp fiction; **3.** low(er); **les basses classes,** (i) the lower classes (of society); (ii) *Sch:* the lower forms, *U.S:* the lower grades; *Cu:* **b. morceaux,** cheap cuts; *Cards:* **les basses cartes,** the small, low, cards; **le b. clergé,** the lower clergy; *Pol:* **la Chambre basse,** the Lower House; **les notes basses,** the low notes; **la partie basse d'une ville, la basse ville, les bas quartiers,** (i) the lower (part of a) town; (ii) the poor districts (of a town); **terres, régions, basses,** lowlands; **le b. Rhin,** the lower Rhine; **la basse Normandie,** Lower Normandy; *Ling:* **b. allemand,** low German; *Rom.Hist:* **le B.-Empire,** the Lower, Later, Byzantine, Empire; *Ling:* **b. latin,** low Latin; **en ce b. monde,** here below; **au b. mot,** at the lowest estimate, valuation; **cela lui a coûté cent livres au b. mot,** it cost him at least a hundred pounds.

II. **bas,** *adv.* **1.** low (down); **être assis trop b.,** to be sitting too low down; **quelques marches plus b.,** a few steps further down, lower down; **dix lignes plus b.,** ten lines (further) down; **les hirondelles volent b.,** the swallows are flying low; **voir plus b.,** see below; **mettre qn plus b. que terre,** to humiliate s.o.; **est-il possible de tomber si b.?** is it possible to fall so low? **le thermomètre est tombé très b.,** the thermometer has dropped very low; *St.Exch:* **les cours sont tombés très b.,** prices have fallen very low; **porter b. l'oreille,** to be humiliated, to be ashamed; (*of a horse*) **porter b.,** to keep its head down; *Nau:* **couler b.,** to sink; **le malade est bien b.,** the patient is very low, at death's door; **il est trop b. pour parler,** he is too low, too far gone, to speak. **2.** (*a*) **jeter b. une maison,** to pull a house down; **chapeaux b.!** hats off!; **chapeau b.,** (i) hat in hand; (ii) I take my hat off to you; *F:* **b. les mains, les pattes!** hands off! keep your paws off! (*to dog*) **b. les pattes!** paws (down)! *Nau:* **mettre b. une voile,** to haul down a sail; **mettre pavillon b.,** (i) *Nau:* to lower, strike, the colours; (ii) *F:* to climb down; (*b*) (*of animals*) **mettre b.,** to give birth to, drop, throw (young); (*of mare*) to foal; (*of sheep*) to lamb; (*of goat*) to kid; (*of bitch*) to pup, to whelp; (*of sow*) to pig, to farrow; **mettre b. avant terme,** to cast, slip, its young; *s.a.* MISE 1; (*c*) **mettre b. les armes,** (i) *Mil:* to lay down one's arms; (ii) to give up (arguing); **mettre b. les outils,** to down tools; (*d*) *Nau:* **mettre b. les feux,** to draw the fires. **3. vous chantez trop b.,** (i) you are singing in too low a key; (ii) you are singing too softly; **parler (tout) b.,** to speak in a whisper, to whisper; **rire tout b.,** to laugh to oneself; **entre haut et b.,** half aloud.

III. **bas,** *s.m.* **1.** lower part (of sth.); (*a*) **b. d'une échelle, d'une page,** foot, bottom, of a ladder, of a page; **au b. de la côte,** at the bottom, foot, of the hill; **veuillez noter au b.,** please state below; **l'étage du b.,** the lower storey; **tirer son chandail vers le b.,** to pull one's sweater down; **les pieds de cette table sont recourbés par le b.,** the legs of this table are bent at the bottom; **la voix de ce chanteur est belle dans le b.,** this singer's voice is beautiful in the lower register; **b. du dos,** small of the back; **le b. du pavé,** the outside of the pavement; *Nau:* **le, les, b. du navire,** the ship's bottom; *Fish:* **b. de canne à pêche,** butt of a fishing-rod; *Fish:* **b. de ligne,** trace, cast; *Tail:* **b. américains,** turn-ups (of trousers), *U.S:* cuffs; **pantalon à b. américains,** turn-up trousers; *Typ:* **b. de casse,** (i) lower case; (ii) small letters; *Astrol:* **b. du ciel,** part of the sky covered by the third and fourth houses; **de haut en b.,** from top to bottom, from head to toe; **regarder qn de haut en b.,** to look s.o. up and down; (*b*) *adv.phr.* **en b.,** (down) below; **il loge en b.,** he lives downstairs; **les gens d'en b.,** the people downstairs, (down) below; **dents d'en b.,** bottom teeth; **la tête en b.,** upside down, head down; **tomber la tête en b.,** to fall head first, head foremost; *s.a.* HAUT III. 3; **ce vase s'élargit par en b.,** this vase is wider at the bottom; **aller en b.,** to go downstairs; *Nau:* **tout le monde en b.!** all hands below! *prep.phr.* **en b. de, au b. de,** at the foot of, at the bottom of; **au b. de, en b. de, l'escalier,** downstairs; at the foot, bottom, of the stairs; *adv.phr.* **à b.,** down; **mettre, jeter, à b.,** to pull down (tree); to demolish, pull down (house); to overthrow (s.o.), to bring (s.o.) low; to lay low, overthrow (empire); **excès qui mettent à b. la résistance,** excesses that ruin, destroy, (one's, a person's) resistance; **à b. les étudiants!** down with the students! *prep.phr.* **tomber à b. de son cheval,** to fall off one's horse; **sauter à b. de son lit,** to jump out of bed. **2.** low state (of sth.); **b. de l'eau,** low water; **les hauts et les b.,** the ups and downs (of life, illness, etc.); **tomber dans le b. et le ridicule,** to lapse into triviality and ridiculousness. **3.** stocking; **b. à baguettes, à coins, à grisotte,** clock(ed) stocking; **b. à côtes,** ribbed stocking; **b. sans couture,** seamless stocking; **b. diminué, proportionné,** fully-fashioned stocking; **b. extensible,** stretch nylons; **b. filet,** mesh stocking; **b. fin, de jauge fine,** fine gauge stocking, sheer stocking; **b. de grosse jauge,** heavy gauge stocking; **b. indémaillable,** ladder-proof stocking, *U.S:* non-run stocking; **b. à jour,** open-work stocking; **b. de soie extra fin,** sheer silk stocking; *Med:* **b. à varices, b. élastique,** elastic stocking; *F:* **b. de laine,** savings; *F:* **un b. de laine bien garni,** a well-lined stocking, a nice little nest-egg.

IV. **basse,** *s.f.* **1.** *Mus:* (*a*) bass part; **basse d'Alberti,** Alberti bass; **basse chiffrée, continue, figurée,** figured bass, thorough bass, basso continuo; **basse contrainte, obstinée,** ground-bass; **basse fondamentale,** root, generator (of chord); (*b*) bass (voice, singer); **basse chantante, basse-taille,** basso cantante, singing bass; **basse profonde, basse-contre, basse noble,** basso profundo; (*c*) (*instrument*) (i) 'cello; (ii) bass saxhorn, euphonium; *A:* **basse de hautbois,** bassoon; **basse de viole,** bass-viol; (*d*) bass strings (of instrument). **2.** *Nau:* shoal, flat, sandbank; (*b*) (sunken) reef.

basal, -aux [bazal, -o], *a.* basal (growth, cell); **membrane basale,** *s.f.* **basale,** basement membrane.

basalte [bazalt], *s.m.* **1.** *Geol: Miner:* basalt; **b. vitreux,** basalt glass. **2.** *El:* dark-glazed porcelain.

basaltiforme [bazaltifɔrm], *a. Geol:* basaltiform.

basaltique [bazaltik], *a. Miner:* basaltic.

Basan [bazɑ̃], *Pr.n.m. B:* Bashan.

basane [bazan], *s.f.* **1.** *Leath:* basan, basil, sheepskin, roan; *Mil: P:* (human) skin, *F:* hide; **tanner la b. à qn,** to give s.o. a tanning, a hiding. **2.** *pl. A: Mil:* false boots (of cavalryman's overalls); *F:* **être dans la b.,** to be in the cavalry.

basané [bazane], *a.* sunburnt, tanned, swarthy (complexion, etc.).

basaner [bazane], *v.tr.* to bronze, tan; to make sunburnt.

se basaner, to tan, bronze, become sunburnt.

basanite [bazanit], *s.f. Miner:* basanite.

bas-alpin, -ine [bɑzalpɛ̃, -in], *a. & s. Geog:* (native, inhabitant) of the department of Basses-Alpes.

bas-bleu [bɑblø], *s.m.* bluestocking; *pl. bas-bleus.*

bas-bleuisme [bɑbløism], *s.m.* bluestockingism.

bas-breton, -onne [bɑbrətɔ̃, -ɔn], *a. & s.* (*a*) (native, inhabitant) of Western, Lower, Brittany; *pl. Bas-Bretons, -onnes;* (*b*) *s.* the language of Lower Brittany.

bas-côté [bɑkote], *s.m.* **1.** (side-)aisle (of church). **2.** shoulder, side (of road, etc.); **défense de stationner sur les bas-côtés,** no parking on the verge.

basculage [baskyla:ʒ], *s.m.* **1.** (*a*) rocking; (*b*) seesawing, *U.S:* teetering. **2.** tilting, tipping.

basculaire [baskylɛ:r], *a.* rocking, seesaw, tilting (motion, etc.).

basculant [baskylɑ̃], *a.* rocking, tilting; **wagon b.,** tip-wagon; **pont b.,** drawbridge; **siège b.,** tip-up seat.

bascule [baskyl], *s.f.* **1.** (*a*) rocker; seesaw, bascule, scale; *U.S: F:* teeter; **mouvement de b.,** rocking motion; **faire la b.,** (i) to seesaw; to rock; (ii) *F:* to overbalance, tip over; **chaise, cheval, à b.,** rocking-chair, -horse; **miroir, porte, à b.,** swing-glass, -door; **plate-forme à b.,** tipping platform; **(balance à) b.,** weigh-bridge, weighing machine; **b. romaine,** platform scales, (with steelyard); **wagon à b.,** tip-wagon; *s.a.* PONT[1] 1; (*b*) sweep, swipe (for drawing water); (*c*) *Phot:* **b. avant, b. antérieure,** swing-front; **b. (arrière),** swing-back (of camera). **2.** (*a*) lever (of lock, etc.); **b. d'une sonnette,** bell-crank (-lever); (*b*) *pl. I.C.E:* toggle-levers (of carburettor float); (*c*) *Elcs:* **(montage en) b.,** bistable trigger circuit, flip-flop circuit; (*d*) lever-handle (of car door, etc.). **3.** *Swim:* jack-knife dive.

basculement [baskylmɑ̃], *s.m.* = BASCULAGE.

basculer [baskyle], *v.tr. & i.* **1.** (*a*) to rock, swing; to seesaw, *U.S:* to teeter; to throw (a switch); **b. sur un pivot,** to rotate on a pivot; **(faire) b. un creuset,** to rotate a crucible; **levier basculé par une came,** lever rocked by a cam; **b. de la richesse à la pauvreté,** to alternate, fluctuate, between riches and poverty; (*b*) to tip (up), tilt; **(faire) b. une charrette,** to tip a cart. **2.** to topple over; **tout a basculé,** the whole lot toppled over, came down.

basculeur [baskylœ:r], *s.m.* **1.** swing part, rocker; *Mec.E: etc:* rocking-lever, tappet-lever; *Av:* **b. de train principal,** main gear axle beam. **2. b. à charbon,** coal-tip.

base [bɑ:z], *s.f.* **1.** (*a*) lower part, foot, bottom, base (of mountain, etc.); foundations (of building); **jeter les bases,** to lay the foundations; (*b*) *Anat: Bot:* base; (*c*) *Geom:* base (of triangle, etc.); (*d*) *Surv:* base (line); (*e*) *Nau:* measured mile; *Av:* **b. de vitesse,** speed course; (*f*) *Mec.E:* base-plate, bed-plate (of machine); (*g*) *Hyd.E:* (downstream) toe. **2.** *Mil:* **b. d'opérations,** base of operations; **b. avancée,** advanced base; **b. de ravitaillement,** supply base; **b. de réparation et d'entretien,** repair and maintenance base; **atelier de b.,** base shop; **zone de (la) b.,** base area; *Av:* **b. aérienne, b. d'aviation,** air base; **b. école,** training base; *Missiles:* **b. de lancement (d'engins),** launching site, base; *Navy:* **b. navale,** naval base; *Mil:* (*tactics*) **b. de feu,** covering fire unit(s), supporting weapons; *U.S:* base of fire; fire support; **b. de départ,** start(ing) line; *U.S:* line of departure; *Mil:* (*drill*) **homme de b.,** guide; *Artil:* **pièce de b.,** directing gun. **3.** basis, foundation; grounds (of suspicion, etc.); *Pol:* officials of a trade-union; **les bases de la musique,** the foundations of music; **argument qui pèche par la b.,** fundamentally unsound argument; **sans b.,** without foundation; ungrounded (suspicions, etc.); **prendre la justice pour b.,** to found upon justice; *Ling:* **vocabulaire de b.,** basic vocabulary; **l'anglais de b.,** basic English; **traitement de b.,** basic salary; **produits à b. d'amidon,** starch products; **boisson à b. de gin,** drink with a gin basis; (*welding*) **métal de b.,** parent metal; (*computers*) **documents de b.,** source documents; *Toil:* **b. de maquillage,** make-up foundation. **4.** (*a*) *Rail:* **b. kilométrique,** standard rate per mile; (*b*) *Mth:* base, radix (of system of notation); radix root, basis (of logarithm). **5.** *Ch:* base; **b. oxygénée,** basyl(e).

base-ball [bɛzbo:l], *s.m. Sp:* baseball.

baseballeur [bɛzbɔlœ:r], *s.m. Sp:* baseball player.

Basedow [baz(ə)do:v], *Pr.n. Med:* **maladie de B.,** Basedow's disease.

baselle [bazɛl], *s.f. Bot:* Basella, Malabar nightshade.

Bas-Empire (le) [ləbazɑ̃pi:r], *s.m. Hist:* the Lower, Later, Byzantine, Empire.

baser [baze], *v.tr.* to base, ground, found (opinion, etc.) (sur, on); **b. de vaines espérances sur qch.,** to build vain hopes on sth.; *Av:* **un avion américain basé en Grande Bretagne,** an American aircraft based in Great Britain; **aviation basée à terre,** ground-based air force.

se baser sur qch., to take one's stand on sth., to take (principle, etc.) as a basis.

bas-fond [bafɔ̃], *s.m.* **1.** low ground, hollow; swamp; flat; *U.S:* bottom-land; **les bas-fonds de la société,** the lowest strata of society, the underworld; **les bas-fonds du journalisme,** the gutter-press. **2.** (*a*) (= HAUT-FOND) shallow, shoal (in sea or river); (*b*) deep bottom; deep hole, pool (in river); *pl. bas-fonds.*

bas-foyer [bafwaje], *s.m. Metall: A:* low hearth; *pl. bas-foyers.*

basial, -aux [bɑzjal, -o], *a. Anat:* basal.

basicité [bazisite], *s.f. Ch:* basicity.

baside [bɑzid], *s.m. Fung:* basidium.

basidiomycètes [bɑzidjɔmisɛt], *s.m.pl. Fung:* Basidiomycetes.

basidiospore [bɑzidjɔspɔr], *s.f. Fung:* basidiospore.

basification [bɑzifikasjɔ̃], *s.f. Ch:* basification.

basifixe [bɑzifiks], *a. Bot:* basifixed.

basigame [bɑzigam], *a. Bot:* basigamous.

basifuge [bɑzifyʒ], *a. Bot:* basifugal.

basilaire [bazilɛ:r], *a. Anat: Bot:* basilar (groove, placenta).

Basile[1] [bazil], *Pr.n.m.* Basil.

basile[2], *s.m. Tls:* pitch (of plane-iron).

basilic[1] [bazilik], *s.m. Bot:* basil; **b. commun,** sweet basil; **b. noir, à petites feuilles,** bush basil, lesser basil.

basilic[2], *s.m.* **1.** *Myth:* basilisk; **regarder qn d'un œil, avec des yeux, de b.,** to cast a withering glance at s.o., to look daggers at s.o. **2.** *Rept:* Basiliscus, basilisk. **3.** *Her:* basilisk.

basilical, -aux [bazilikal, -o], *a. Arch:* basilical, basilican.

basilicon [bazilikɔ̃], **basilicum** [bazilikɔm], *s.m. A: Pharm:* basilicon.

basilien, -ienne [baziljɛ̃, -jɛn], *a. Ecc:* Basilian.

basilique[1] [bazilik], *a. & s.f. Anat:* basilic (vein).

basilique[2], *s.f. Arch:* basilica.

basin [bazɛ̃], *s.m. Tex:* (*a*) *A:* dimity; (*b*) cotton damask.

basion [bɑzjɔ̃], *s.m. Anat:* basion.

basique [bazik], *a.* **1.** *Ch: Metall:* basic (salt, process, etc.); **scorie b.,** basic slag. **2.** *Cryst:* basal (cleavage). **3.** *Ling: A:* basic.

bas-jointé [bɑʒwɛ̃te], *a.* low-pasterned (horse); *pl. bas-jointé(e)s.*

basket(-ball) [baskɛt(-bo:l)], *s.m. Games: F:* basket-ball.

basketteur, -euse [baskɛtœ:r, -ø:z], *s.* basket-ball player, *U.S:* basketeer.

Baskirs [baskir], *s.m.pl. Ethn:* Bashkirs.

bas-mât [bɑma], *s.m. Nau:* lower mast; *pl. bas-mâts.*

bas-métier [bɑmetje], *s.m. Tex: A:* small hand loom; *pl. bas-métiers.*

basoche [bazɔʃ], *s.f.* (*a*) *Jur: Hist:* body of clerks attached to the courts of justice; (*b*) *usu. Pej:* the legal fraternity, the legal gang; attorneydom; **termes de b.,** legal jargon.

basochien, -ienne [bazɔʃjɛ̃, -jɛn]. *Jur: Hist:* **1.** *a.* belonging, pertaining to the law courts. **2.** *s.m.* clerk, official, attached to the law courts.

bas-officier [bazɔfisje], *s.m. A.Mil:* non-commissioned officer; *pl. bas-officiers.*

basommatophores [bazɔmatɔfɔr], *s.m.pl. Moll:* Basommatophora.

basophile [bazɔfil], *a. Biol:* basophilic, basophile.

basquais, -aise [baskɛ, -ɛ:z], *a.* Basque; of the Basque country; *Cu:* **à la basquaise,** served with casseroled potatoes, boletus and chopped Bayonne ham.

basque[1] [bask]. **1.** *a. & s.* Basque; **le Pays b.,** the Basque country; **courir comme un B.,** to run like a hare; *s.a.* TAMBOUR. **2.** *s.m. Ling:* Basque.

basque[2], *s.f.* (*a*) skirt, tail (of coat, etc.); **ne pas quitter les basques de qn, être toujours pendu aux basques de qn.,** to be always following s.o. about, to be always at s.o.'s heels; (*b*) **soutien-gorge à b.,** long-line brassière.

basquet [baskɛ], *s.m.* crate.

basquine [baskin], *s.f. Cost:* basquine.

bas-relief [bɑrəljɛf], *s.m.* bas(s)-relief, low-relief; *pl. bas-reliefs.*

bass [bɑs], *s.m. Ich:* bass.

bassage [bɑsa:ʒ], *s.m. Tan:* plumping (of hides).

basse. See BAS.

basse-cor [bɑskɔr], *s.f. Mus:* tenor clarinet in F, basset-horn; *pl. basses-cors.*

basse-contre [bɑskɔ̃:tr], *s.f. Mus:* basso profundo; *pl. basses-contre.*

basse-cour [bɑsku:r], *s.f.* (*a*) *A.Arch:* bail, bailey (of fortified castle); (*b*) farmyard, poultry yard; **se charger de la b.-c.,** to look after the poultry; *pl. basses-cours.*

basse-courier, -ière [bɑskurje, -jɛ:r], *s.* (*rare*) poultry hand; *pl. basses-couriers, -ières.*

basse-court [bɑskur], *s.f. A.Fort:* passage between a postern gate and a barbican tower; *pl. basses-courts.*

Basse-Écosse (la) [labɑsekɔs], *Pr.n.f. Geog:* the Lowlands (of Scotland).

basse-étoffe [bɑsetɔf], *s.f. Metall:* base metal (*esp.* alloy of lead and tin); *pl. basses-étoffes.*

basse-fosse [bɑsfo:s], *s.f.* dungeon; **cul de b.-f.,** deepest dungeon, oubliette; *pl. basses-fosses.*

basse-lice, -lisse [bɑslis], *s.f. See* LICE[3] 2; *pl. basses-lices, -lisses.*

bassement[1] [bɑsmɑ̃], *adv.* basely, meanly, contemptibly; **agir b.,** to act in a low, mean, way.

bassement[2] [basmɑ̃], *s.m.*, **basserie** [basri], *s.f. Tan:* plumping (of hides).

basser [base], *v.tr. Tex:* to dress, size (the warp).

bassesse [bɑsɛs], *s.f.* **1.** baseness, lowness (of birth, expression, action, etc.). **2.** low, mean, contemptible, action; **homme prêt à toutes les bassesses,** man who would stoop to anything.

basset,[1] **-ette**[1] [bɑsɛ, ba-, -ɛt]. **1.** *a.* short, low; **chien b.,** *s.m.* **basset,** basset hound, badger-dog; **b. allemand,** dachshund. **2.** *s.m. P:* revolver, *P:* barker.

basset[2], *s.m. Mus:* **cor de b.,** tenor clarinet in F, basset-horn.

basse-taille [bɑstɑ:j], *s.f.* **1.** *Mus: A:* basso cantante; singing bass. **2.** (*a*) *Sculp: A:* bas-relief; (*b*) **(émail de) b.-t.,** basse-taille enamel(ling); *pl. basses-tailles.*

bassetite [basetit], *s.f. Miner:* bassetite.

bassette[2], *s.f. A.Cards:* basset.

basse-vergue [bɑsvɛrg], *s.f. Nau:* lower yard; *pl. basses-vergues.*

basse-voile [bɑsvwal], *s.f. Nau:* lower sail; *pl. basses-voiles.*

bassia [basja], *s.f. Bot:* Bassia; **b. butyracée,** shea(tree), butter-tree.

bassicot [basiko], *s.m.* wooden bucket (for aerial ropeway).

bassier [bɑsje], *s.m.* **1.** (amateur) shrimper, crab fisherman, clam digger, etc. (who fishes for shellfish at low tide). **2.** *pl. bassiers,* sandbanks (in a river).

bassin [bɑsɛ̃], *s.m.* **1.** basin, bowl, pan; *Ecc: A:* **b. (à aumône),** alms dish; *Med:* **b. (de lit),** bedpan, slipper; **b. oculaire,** eye-bath; **bassins de balance,** scale pans, **b. à cracher,** spitoon; (*of pers.*) *P:* **quel b.! ce qu'il est b.!** what a bore! *s.a.* CRACHER 1. **2.** (*a*) ornamental lake, pond; basin (of a fountain); (*b*) *Hyd.E:* reservoir, tank; **b. filtrant,** filter bed; **b. de chasse,** flush pond; **b. de mise en charge,** forebay; (*c*) *Hyd.E:* coffer (of lock); *N.Arch:* **b. d'essai des carènes,** experimental tank, ship-testing tank, test tank; (*d*) salt pan. **3.** dock, basin; **b. à flot,** wet dock, flooding dock; **b. de desserte,** docking basin; **b. d'évitage,** turning basin; **b. d'échouage,** tidal dock; **b. de carénage,** careening basin; **b. de radoub,** dry dock, graving dock; **faire passer un navire au b.,** to dock a ship; **entrer au b.,** to be docked, to dock; **sortir du b.,** to undock. **4.** (*a*) *Geol:* basin; *Oc:* depression; **b. sédimentaire,** basin of deposition; **b. fermé,** inland drainage basin; **le b. parisien,** the Paris basin; (*b*) **b. (hydrographique),** river basin; **b. de réception, b. versant,** catchment area, basin; **le b. de la Tamise,** the Thames basin; (*c*) **b. houiller,** coal basin; **le b. de la Sarre,** the Saar basin; (*d*) *Min:* **b. à boue,** mud pit; (*e*) *Metall:* **b. de coulée,** pouring basin. **5.** *Anat:* pelvis; **os du b.,** pelvic bone; *Obst:* **b. barré,** pelvis obtecta.

bassinage [basina:ʒ], *s.m.* (*rare*) (*a*) *Med:* bathing (of wound, etc.); (*b*) *Hort:* spraying, sprinkling, syringing (of seedlings, etc.).

bassinant [basinɑ̃], *a. P:* boring, importunate.
bassine [basin], *s.f.* (*a*) Pan; **b. à confitures,** preserving pan; **b. à vaisselle,** washing-up bowl, basin; (*b*) vat (for cheese making).
bassinée [basine], *s.f.* (*rare*) panful, basinful.
bassinement [basinmɑ̃], *s.m.* **1.** sprinkling, spraying (with water). **2.** warming (of bed with pan).
bassiner [basine], *v.tr.* **1.** (*a*) to bathe (wound, etc.); (*b*) to spray, sprinkle, syringe (seedlings, etc.); to moisten (dough, etc.). **2. b. un lit,** to warm a bed (with a warming-pan). **3.** *P:* to bore, plague (s.o.).
bassinet [basinɛ], *s.m.* **1.** (*a*) small (metal) basin; (*b*) spittoon; *s.a.* CRACHER 1; (*c*) *A:* pan (of flintlock gun). **2.** *Arm:* basinet, basnet. **3.** *Bot: F:* buttercup. **4.** *Anat:* pelvis renalis, pelvis (of the kidney).
bassinoire [basinwa:r], *s.f.* **1.** warming-pan; *F:* **c'est une vraie b.,** he's an awful bore. **2.** *P:* large watch, *P:* turnip.
bassiste [bɑsist], *s.m. Mus:* **1.** euphonium player. **2.** 'cellist. **3.** tuba player; saxhorn player.
bas-slip [bɑslip], *s.m. Cost:* (nylon) tights, panty-hose.
basson [bɑsɔ̃], *s.m. Mus:* **1.** bassoon. **2.** bassoonist.
bassoniste [bɑsɔnist], *s.m.* bassoonist.
Bassouto [basuto], *s.m.& f. Ethn:* Basuto (native).
bastague [bastag], *s.f.,* **bastaque** [bastak], *s.f. Nau:* runner and tackle.
bastaing [bastɛ̃], *s.m. Carp:* plank (10 in. × $2\frac{1}{2}$ in.)
baste[1] [bast], *int.* **1.** (*a*) enough of that! (*b*) *Nau:* hold hard! avast! **2.** pooh! nonsense!
baste[2], *s.f.* (*a*) *Vit:* wooden tub (for transporting grapes); (*b*) pannier (of donkey, etc.).
baste[3], *s.m. Cards:* basto (ace of clubs in quadrille and ombre).
bastiais, -aise [bastjɛ, -ɛ:z], *a. & s. Geog:* (native, inhabitant) of Bastia.
bastide [bastid], *s.f.* **1.** *Mil: A:* blockhouse. **2.** *Dial:* (*S. of Fr.*) country farm.
bastidon [bastidɔ̃], *s.m. Dial:* (*S. of Fr.*) small country house, farm.
bastille [bastij], *s.f. Fort:* small fortress, bastille; *Hist:* **La Bastille,** the Bastille (State prison in Paris; destroyed 1789).
bastillé [bastije], *a. Her:* **bande bastillée,** bend (em)battled.
bastillon [bastijɔ̃], *s.m.* small fortress.
bastin [bastɛ̃], *s.m. Nau:* **1.** coir. **2.** bass(-rope).
basting [bastɛ̃], *s.m.* = BASTAING.
bastingage [bastɛ̃ga:ʒ], *s.m. Nau:* **1.** *A:* hammock netting; **toiles de b.,** hammock cloths. **2.** *pl.* (*a*) bulwarks, topsides; (*b*) rails; **accoudé aux bastingages,** leaning over the rails.
bastion [bastjɔ̃], *s.m.* (*a*) *Fort:* bastion; (*b*) bulwark, stronghold (of liberty, etc.).
bastionné [bastjɔne], *a.* bastioned (front, etc.).
bastionner [bastjɔne], *v.tr.* to fortify with bastions.
bastir [basti:r], *v.tr. Hatm:* to bason (felt).
bastissage [bastisa:ʒ], *s.m. Hatm:* basoning (of felt).
bastisseur [bastisœ:r], *s.m. Hatm:* felt worker.
bastisseuse [bastisøz], *s.f. Hatm:* basoning equipment.
bastite [bastit], *s.f. Miner:* bastite.
bastnaésite [bastnaezit], *s.f. Miner:* bastnasite.
Bastoche (la) [la bastɔʃ], *Pr.n.f. P:* The Bastille.
bastonnade [bastɔnad], *s.f.* **1.** *A:* beating, flogging. **2.** bastinado; **donner la b. à qn,** to bastinado s.o.
bastos [bastɔs], *s.m. P:* bullet, *P:* slug.
bastringue [bastrɛ̃:g], *s.m. P:* **1.** (*a*) low dance hall; (*b*) = pub. **2.** noise, din, shindy. **3.** luggage; kit; paraphernalia; **tout le b.,** the whole bag, box, of tricks, the whole shooting-match.
bastringuer [bastrɛ̃ge], *v.i. P:* **1.** to frequent low dance halls. **2.** to make a row, a din.
bastude [bastyd], *s.f. Fish: Dial:* fishing net used in salt-water lagoons.
Basutoland [basytɔlɑ̃d], *Pr.n.m.* Basutoland.
bas-ventre [bɑvɑ̃:tr], *s.m.* lower part of the abdomen; *pl. bas-ventres.*
bas-voler [bɑvɔle], *s.m.* **oiseaux de b.-v.,** low-flying birds.
bas-volet [bɑvɔlɛ], *s.m. Av:* tab; *pl. bas-volets.*
bat [ba], *s.m.* **1.** *A:* tail (of fish). **2.** *Fish:* length (of fish, from snout to tail).
bât [bɑ], *s.m.* **1.** pack(-saddle); **animal de b.,** pack animal; **cheval de b.,** pack horse; *F:* drudge; **artillerie de b.,** pack artillery; **b. de pièce,** gun pack; **b. porte-munitions,** ammunition pack; **être blessé par le b.,** to be galled by the pack (-saddle); **c'est là que le b. (le) blesse,** that's where the shoe pinches; *s.a.* ÂNE 1. **2.** pack; **porter le b.,** to do all the drudgery, all the dirty work.
bataclan [bataklɑ̃], *s.m. F:* belongings, traps, paraphernalia; **ils ont un yacht, une Rolls-Royce, des laquais, et tout le b.,** they have a yacht, a Rolls-Royce, footmen, and all the rest of it; **vendez tout le b.!** sell the whole lot, the whole shoot!
bataillard [batɑjar], *a.* quarrelsome.
bataille [batɑ:j, -aj], *s.f.* **1.** (*a*) battle, fight, action, engagement; **b. terrestre, aérienne, navale,** land, air, naval, battle; **b. aéro-terrestre,** land-air, ground-air, battle; **b. aéro-navale,** sea-air battle; **b. de rencontre,** encounter battle; **b. offensive, défensive,** offensive, defensive battle; **b. d'arrêt,** holding battle; **b. de fixation,** containing battle; **b. d'interdiction,** interdiction battle; **b. rangée,** pitched, set, battle; **b. de vaincu,** losing battle; **b. indécise,** indecisive battle; **le fort de la b.,** the thick, the brunt of the fight, battle; **champ de b.,** battlefield; **zone de b.,** battle area; **livrer b. à,** to give battle to, to join battle with; **engager la b.,** to begin the battle, action; to engage in combat; to bring on the action; **une b. fut livrée, (eut lieu), à Verdun,** a battle was fought at Verdun; **ranger en b.,** (i) to draw up in battle order, in battle formation; (ii) *A:* to draw up in battle array, in line; **ordre de b.,** (i) battle formation, battle order; (ii) troop precedence; (iii) order of battle (*list of troops composing a major unit*); **corps de b.,** field forces; (*b*) *Art:* battle piece. **2.** (*a*) *Nau:* **pousser, mettre une vergue en b.,** to rig a derrick with a yard; (*b*) *A:* **chapeau en b.,** cocked hat worn broadside on (*as opposed to a fore-and-after*); (*c*) **cheveux en b.,** dishevelled hair. **3.** *Cards:* beggar-my-neighbour.
batailler [batɑje, -aje], *v.i.* **1.** (*a*) *Mil: A:* to engage in small-scale actions; to skirmish; (*b*) **il est toujours prêt à b.,** he's always spoiling for a fight; (*c*) **b. pour faire entendre raison,** to struggle to make s.o. see reason; **b. pour l'augmentation des salaires,** to fight, battle, for a wage increase; *F:* **j'ai dû b. pendant une heure pour ouvrir la porte,** I had to battle for an hour to open the door. **2.** *Nau:* to beat.
batailleur, -euse [batajœ:r, -ø:z], **1.** *a.* fighting, quarrelsome, pugnacious. **2.** *s.* (*a*) fighter, controversialist; (*b*) *Box:* battler.
bataillon [batajɔ̃], *s.m.* (*a*) *Mil:* battalion; *A:* **b. scolaire** = cadet corps; **commandant de b.,** battalion commander; **b. d'instruction,** training battalion; **b. d'Afrique,** French disciplinary battalion (formerly stationed in North Africa); **b. de travailleurs auxiliaires,** labour battalion; **b. de pionniers,** pioneer battalion; **b. formant corps,** independent, separate, battalion; (*b*) *Pol:* **s'assurer le vote des gros bataillons,** to make sure of a mass, massive, vote; **elle a un b. d'enfants,** she has a whole swarm of children; *F: Hum:* **inconnu au b.,** never heard of him.
bataillon-école [batajɔ̃ekɔl], *s.m. Mil:* instruction battalion; *pl. bataillons-écoles.*
bataillonnaire [batajɔnɛ:r], *s.m.* young criminal serving in a *bataillon d'Afrique.*
batara [batara], *s.m. Orn:* batara, (Central American) ant-shrike.
bâtard, -arde [bɑta:r, -ard], *a. & s.* **1.** bastard; (*a*) **des enfants bâtards,** bastard children; *Fr. Hist:* **le B. d'Orléans,** the Bastard of Orleans; (*b*) (*not pure, mixed*) **chien b.,** mongrel, crossbred; **écriture bâtarde,** *s.f.* **bâtarde,** bastard hand; **porte bâtarde,** medium-sized door; **(lime) bâtarde,** bastard file; *Typ:* **format b.,** bastard size (*c*) (*degenerate, of inferior quality*) **race bâtarde,** degenerate, bastard, race; **sucre b.,** *s.m.* **bâtard,** bastard sugar; **laine bâtarde,** wool from the second shearing, wether wool; **peau bâtarde,** bastard skin; **marée bâtarde,** neap tide; (*d*) *s.m.* (small) loaf of bread; (*e*) *Nau:* **hauban b.,** swifter (of shrouds). **2.** *Nau:* alike; **deux canots bâtards,** two boats alike. **3.** *s.f. Nau:* **bâtarde de racage,** parrel rope.
bâtardé [bɑtarde], *a.* bastard, bastardized.
bâtardeau, batardeau, -eaux [bɑtardo], *s.m.* **1.** *Fort:* batardeau. **2.** *Hyd.E:* (coffer-)dam, caisson; **b. mobile,** movable dam, flash(ing)-board.
bâtardise [bɑtardi:z], *s.f.* **1.** bastardy. **2.** *F:* spuriousness.
batate [batat], *s.f.* = PATATE.
Bataves [bata:v], *s.m.pl. A.Hist:* **les B.,** the Batavi: **les îles des B.,** the Batavian Islands.
bataviole [batavjɔl], *s.f.,* **batayole** [batajɔl], *s.f. Nau:* stanchion.
batavique [batavik], *a.f. Ph:* **larme batavique,** Prince Rupert's drop.
bat-beurre [babœ:r], *s.m.inv. in pl. Husb:* dasher (of churn).
bat-cul [baky], *s.m. Harn: A:* = BACUL; *pl. bat-culs.*
bat' d'Af [batdaf], *s.m. P:* **1.** = *Bataillon d'Afrique, q.v.* under BATAILLON. **2.** = BATAILLONNAIRE.
bateau, -eaux [bato], *s.m.* **1.** (*a*) boat; merchant vessel; **grands, petits, bateaux,** large, small, craft; **b. à voiles,** sailing boat; **b. à vapeur,** steamboat, steamer; **b. automobile, b. à moteur,** motor boat, motor launch; **b. plat,** flat-bottomed boat, (i) barge; (ii) punt; **b. pneumatique,** rubber boat; *Mil:* **b. d'assaut,** storm, assault, boat; **b. pliant,** collapsible boat; **b. conduit à la perche,** pole boat; **b. ponté,** decked boat; **b. non ponté,** open boat; **b. à rames,** rowing-boat; **b. d'agrément, de plaisance,** pleasure boat; **b. de passage,** ferry-boat, wherry; **b. (dé)lesteur,** (ballast) lighter; **b. à provisions,** bumboat; **b. charbonnier,** collier; **b. de pêche,** fishing-boat, -smack; **b. de sauvetage,** lifeboat, rescue boat; **pont de bateaux,** pontoon-bridge; **faire une partie de b.,** to go boating; *Rail:* **le train du b.,** the boat-train; **je suis venu sur le, par, b.,** I came by boat; **aller, se promener, en b.,** to go boating, to boat; *F:* **arriver en trois, quatre, bateaux,** to arrive in state, with much pomp and ceremony; **être du dernier b.,** to be in the height of fashion, to be up to date; **c'est du dernier b.,** it is the latest thing; **ils sont du même bateau,** they are of the same class, they are tarred with the same brush; *P:* **monter un b. à qn,** to have s.o. on, pull s.o.'s leg; **mener qn en b.,** to take s.o. in, to fool s.o., to hoax s.o.; **c'est un b.,** it's a have, a take-in; *s.a.* FOND 1; (*b*) shipload, boatload; shipment. **2.** *A:* (*a*) car (of a balloon); (*b*) body (of a carriage). **3.** *pl. P:* boots (of a large size), *P:* beetle-crushers, boats.
bateau-chasseur [batoʃasœ:r], *s.m.* whaling-boat, whale-catcher, whale-hunter, whaler (as opposed to the factory ship); *pl. bateaux-chasseurs.*
bateau-citerne [batositɛrn], *s.m.* tanker, water-boat; *pl. bateaux-citernes.*
bateau-feu [batofø], *s.m. Nau:* lightship; *pl. bateaux-feux.*
bateau-grue [batogry], *s.m.* crane-boat; *pl. bateaux-grues.*
bateau-lavoir [batolavwar], *s.m. A:* (*boat*) wash-house (on the Seine); *pl. bateaux-lavoirs.*
bateau-mouche [batomuʃ], *s.m.* river passenger boat (in Paris, etc.); water-bus; *pl. bateaux-mouches.*
bateau-pêcheur [batopɛʃœ:r], *s.m.* fishing-smack, -boat; *pl. bateaux-pêcheurs.*
bateau-phare [batofa:r], *s.m.* lightship; *pl. bateaux-phares.*
bateau-piège [batopjɛ:ʒ], *s.m. Nav:* decoy-ship, mystery-ship, Q-ship, boat; *pl. bateaux-pièges.*
bateau-pilote [batopilɔt], *s.m.* pilot boat; *pl. bateaux-pilotes.*
bateau-pompe [batopɔ̃:p], *s.m.* fire-float, fire-boat; *pl. bateaux-pompes.*
bateau-porte [batopɔrt], *s.m. Nau:* caisson (of dry dock); *pl. bateaux-portes.*
batée [bate], *s.f.* = BATTÉE 3.
batelage[1] [batla:ʒ], *s.m.* loading, unloading, (of ships) with boats; lighterage, waterage; **(frais de) b.,** lighterage (charges).
batelage[2], *s.m.* mountebank's tricks; juggling.
batelée [batle], *s.f.* **1.** boatload; barge-load. **2.** *Adm:* maximum load (of boat). **3.** large quantity; large number (of people, etc.).
bateler[1] [batle], *v.tr.* (**je batelle, n. batelons, je batellerai**) to carry, convey (sth.) in boats; to lighter.
bateler[2], *v.i.* to juggle.
batelerie [batɔlri], *s.f.* mountebank's trick.
batelet [batlɛ], *s.m.* small boat, skiff.
bateleur, -euse [batlœ:r, -ø:z], *s.* (*a*) *A:* mountebank, juggler, tumbler; (*b*) knock-about comedian; *A: Pej:* actor; (*c*) *Pej:* **quel b.!** what a buffoon!
batelier, -ière [batɔlje, -jɛ:r]. **1.** *s.* boatman, -woman; waterman; ferryman, -woman; **b. de chaland,** bargeman, bargee, lighterman. **2.** *a.* pertaining to inland, river, navigation.
batellerie [batɛlri], *s.f.* **1.** transport, carriage, of goods by boat; inland water transport; lighterage. **2.** small craft (taken collectively); **b. fluviale,** river fleet; **la b. du Rhin, de la Seine,** the Rhine, the Seine shipping.
bâter [bɑte], *v.tr.* **b. un mulet,** to put a pack-saddle, a load, on a mule; *F:* **c'est un âne bâté,** he's a perfect ass, an unmitigated ass, a dunderhead.
bat-flanc [baflɑ̃], *s.m.inv.* **1.** (*a*) swinging bail (of horse-stall); (*b*) wooden partition (in a dormitory). **2.** *Mil:* wooden platform on which to sleep.

bath [bat], *a.inv. P:* first-class, first-rate, super; **t'es b.**, you're a good sort, *U.S:* a great guy; **un b. pantalon**, snazzy trousers; **quatre jours de congé, c'est bien b.!** four days off, that's something like!
bathoïdes [batɔid], *s.m.pl. Ich:* Batoidei.
batholit(h)e [batɔlit], *s.m. Geol:* batholith.
bathomètre [batɔmɛtr̥], *s.m.*, **bathymètre** [batimɛtr̥], *s.m. Oc:* bathometer, bathymeter.
bathonien, -ienne [batɔnjɛ̃, -jɛn]. **1.** *a. Geol: etc:* Bathonian, of the city of Bath; **pierre à bâtir de la grande oolithe bathonienne**, Bath-stone. **2.** *s.m. Geol:* Bathonian.
bathyal, -aux [batjal, -o], *a. Oc:* bathyal.
bathybius [batibiys], *s.m. Nat.Hist:* bathybius.
bathydrique [batidrik], *a.* bathybic, bathybial.
bathyergidés [batjɛrʒide], *s.m.pl. Z:* Bathyergidae.
bathymètre [batimɛtr̥], *s.m.* bathymeter.
bathymétrie [batimetri], *s.f. Oc:* bathymetry.
bathymétrique [batimetrik], *a. Oc:* bathymetric(al).
bathypélagique [batipelaʒik], *a.* bathypelagic.
bathyplancton [batiplɑ̃ktɔ̃], *s.m.* bathyplankton.
bathyscaphe [batiskaf], *s.m.* bathyscaph(e).
bathysphère [batisfɛːr], *s.f.* bathysphere.
bathythermographe [batitɛrmɔgraf], *s.m. Oc:* bathythermograph.
bâti[1] [bɑti], *s.m.* frame(-work), structure, support, stand; *Mch:* bed-plate; **b. de fenêtre**, window frame; **b. d'un moteur**, frame, body, of a motor; **b. moteur**, engine mounting; **b. d'assemblage**, assembly jig; *Nau:* **b. de la machine**, engine-columns; *Typ:* **b. de la presse**, bed of the press.
bâti[2], *s.m.* **1. b. (d'un vêtement)**, garment basted, tacked, together (for trying on). **2.** basting-, tacking- thread.
bâtière [bɑtjɛːr], *s.f.* **1.** *Dial:* pack-saddle. **2.** *Arch:* (toit en) **b.**, (pack-)saddle roof, saddle-back roof.
batifolage [batifɔlaːʒ], *s.m. F:* **1.** romping, larking, playing around. **2.** flirting; necking.
batifoler [batifɔle], *v.i. F:* **1.** to romp, lark about, play around. **2. b. avec une jeune fille**, to flirt with a young woman.
batifoleur, -euse [batifɔlœːr, -øːz], *s. F:* **1.** person who likes larking about. **2.** flirt.
batifouiller [batifuje], *v.i. P:* to fumble and mumble; to get muddled.
batik [batik], *s.m. Tex:* batik.
batiker [batike], *v.tr.* to ornament (silk, etc.) with batik work.
batillage [batijaʒ], *s.m.* wake (of boat).
batillement [batijmɑ̃], *s.m.* lapping (of water against bank).
batiller [batije], *v.i.* (*of water*) to lap.
bâtiment [bɑtimɑ̃], *s.m.* **1.** building (trade); **entrepreneur de, en, b.**, builder; *s.a.* PEINTRE 2; **quand le b. va tout va**, activity in the building trade is a sign of prosperity. **2.** building, edifice, structure; **bâtiments de ferme**, farm buildings; **b. des machines**, engine-house, -room; *Min:* **b. d'extraction**, shaft house; **usine en trois corps de b.**, factory (contained) in three main buildings; *O: F:* **il n'est pas médecin mais son père est du b.**, he is not a doctor but his father's in that line; **il est du b.**, (i) he's in the same line of business; (ii) he's one of us. **3.** ship, vessel; **b. de guerre**, warship, *A:* man-of-war; **b. de ligne cuirassé**, capital ship; **b. marchand**, merchant ship, merchantman; **petits bâtiments**, small craft; **b. d'assaut**, assault ship; **b. de ligne**, battleship; **b. auxiliaire**, auxiliary vessel or ship; **b. armé en course**, privateer; **b. piquet radar, de veille aérienne**, radar picket ship; **b. de débarquement**, landing-craft.
bâtiment-caserne [bɑtimɑ̃kazɛrn], *s.m.* barrack-ship; *pl. bâtiments-casernes.*
bâtiment-école [bɑtimɑ̃ekɔl], *s.m. Nau:* training ship; *pl. bâtiments-écoles.*
bâtiment-grue [bɑtimɑ̃gry], *s.m.* crane-ship.
bâtimoteur [bɑtimɔtœːr], *s.m. Av:* engine-bearers.
bâtir[1] [bɑtiːr], *v.tr.* to build. **1.** to erect, construct; **b. une maison**, to build a house; **faire b. une maison**, to have a house built; **la maison se bâtit**, the house is being built; **b. une fortune**, to build up a fortune; **b. sur le sable**, to build on sand, to be engaged in an undertaking that has no solid foundation; **b. en l'air**, to build castles in the air; **homme bien bâti**, well-built man; **gaillard bien bâti**, strapping fellow; **un homme bâti comme moi**, a man of my build; **voilà comme il est bâti**, that's the sort of man he is; *O:* **il commence à b. sur le devant**, he's beginning to grow stout, to show a corporation. **2. b. un vaste terrain**, to build over, upon, an extensive site; **terrain à b.**, building site.
bâtir[2], *v.tr.* to baste, tack (garment) together; **coton à b.**, tacking thread.
bâtissable [bɑtisabl̥], *a.* **1.** that may be built. **2.** that may be built upon; **terrain b.**, building land.
bâtissage [bɑtisaːʒ], *s.m.* basting, tacking together (of garment).
bâtisse [bɑtis], *s.f.* **1.** (*a*) masonry, bricks and mortar; (*b*) *F:* **la b.**, the mania for building. **2.** (*a*) *F:* **ce n'est qu'une grande b.**, it's a great (ugly) barracks of a place; (*b*) **b. de bois**, frame building. **3.** *Ap:* (= RAYON) comb.
bâtisseur, -euse [bɑtisœːr, -øz], *s.* builder; building maniac; **b. d'empires**, empire builder, founder of empires.
batiste [batist], *s.f. Tex:* batiste, cambric; **b. de France**, French cambric.
batoïdes [batɔid], *s.m.pl. Ich:* Batoidei.
bâton[1] [bɑtɔ̃], *s.m.* **1.** stick, staff, rod; (*a*) **b. épineux**, thorny stick; **c'est un b. épineux**, he, she, is very touchy, a regular porcupine, prickly to handle; **b. ferré**, iron-shod pole, alpenstock; **b. (à deux bouts)**, quarter-staff; **jouer du b.**, to fence with quarter-staffs; **b. (d'agent de police)**, truncheon; **bâtons de ski**, ski sticks; *Fenc:* singlestick; *Her:* baton; **martin b.**, (i) donkey driver (armed with thick stick); (ii) thick stick, cudgel; **b. d'une chaise**, stretcher, rung, of a chair; *F:* **vie de b. de chaise**, life of pleasure, fast life; **b. de cage**, perch; **b. de perroquet**, parrot's perch; **b. de route**, ash plant; **b. de vieillesse**, support, prop, of old age; **le b. blanc du pèlerin**, the white staff of the pilgrim; *A:* **il est venu à Paris le b. blanc à la main**, he came to Paris in poverty, without a penny in his pocket; **coup de b.**, blow, hit, with a stick; **donner des coups de b. à qn**, to beat s.o.; **battre l'eau avec un b.**, to beat the air, to strike to no purpose; **faire mourir qn sous le b.**, to beat s.o. to death; **mener qn le b. haut**, to rule s.o. with a high hand; **sauter le b.**, (i) (*of circus-dog*) to jump over the stick; (ii) *F:* (*of pers.*) to go through the hoop; **mettre des bâtons dans les roues**, to put a spoke in s.o.'s wheel; to throw a spanner in the works; *Toil:* **b. d'oranger**, orange-stick; (*b*) *Arch:* **bâtons rompus**, zigzag moulding; **travailler à bâtons rompus**, to work without method, by fits and starts; **conversation à bâtons rompus**, desultory, rambling, conversation; *s.a.* PARQUET 3; (*c*) staff, pole; **b. d'une croix**, staff of a cross; **b. de pavillon**, flagstaff, flagpole; *Nau:* **b. de pavillon de beaupré**, jack-staff; **b. de foc**, jib-boom; *Rail:* **b. pilote**, (train-)staff; (*d*) (*wand of office*) **b. pastoral**, pastoral staff, crozier; **b. de maréchal**, field-marshal's baton; **il a son b. de maréchal**, he's got as far as he will ever get; he has reached the height of his career; **b. de magicien, de Jacob**, conjurer's wand; **b. de chef d'orchestre**, conductor's baton; *F:* **savoir le tour du b.**, to know how to conjure things away, how to filch; **tour de b.**, (i) conjuring trick; (ii) perquisites, illicit gains, pickings. **2.** stick, roll; **b. de cire à cacheter**, stick of sealing wax; **b. à barbe**, shaving-stick; **b. de cannelle**, roll of cinnamon; **b. de soufre**, stick, cane, of sulphur. **3.** stroke (of the pen, etc.); **apprendre à un enfant à faire des bâtons**, to teach a child to write; **bâtons et jambages**, pothooks and hangers; *Typ:* **capitale b.**, block letter; *Mus:* **b. de reprise**, repeat (bar). **4.** *Bot:* **b. de Jacob**, yellow asphodel; **b. de Saint-Jacques**, hollyhock; **b. d'or**, wallflower; **b. royal**, white asphodel, king's spear.
bâton[2], *s.m. P:* = BATAILLON.
bâtonnade [bɑtɔnad], *s.f.* = BASTONNADE.
bâtonnat [bɑtɔna], *s.m.* office, function, of president of the barristers attached to a French law court.
bâtonner [bɑtɔne], *v.tr.* **1.** to beat, cudgel, cane. **2.** to cross out (written words or figures). **3.** to pleat (linen).
bâtonnet [bɑtɔnɛ], *s.m.* small stick; **b. de dynamite**, stick of dynamite; (*a*) square ruler; (*b*) *Games:* tip-cat; (*c*) *Toil:* orange-stick; (*d*) *Biol:* rod-bacterium; (*e*) *Anat:* (i) rod-like cell; (ii) *pl.* rods (of retina); (*f*) *Ch:* pellet; (*g*) *Geol:* **division en bâtonnets**, prismatic jointing; (*h*) chopstick.
bâtonnier [bɑtɔnje], *s.m.* **1.** leader, president, of the barristers attached to a French law court. **2. b. en chaises**, chair-rung maker, chair-stick maker.
bâtonniste [bɑtɔnist], *s.m.* (*a*) singlestick player, fencer; (*b*) juggler (with a stick).
Batoum [batum], *Pr.n.m. Geog:* Batum.
batracien [batrasjɛ̃], *s.m. Z:* (*a*) batrachian; (*b*) *pl.* **batraciens**, Batrachia.
battable [batabl̥], *a.* which can be beaten, overcome, beatable.
battage [bataːʒ], *s.m.* **1.** (*a*) beating (of carpet, etc.); churning (of butter); threshing (of corn); *Ser:* loosening of cocoons; ramming (of earth); **b. d'or**, gold beating; *Min:* **b. au câble**, spudding; **b. des pieux**, pile-driving; *Min:* **levier, bascule, balancier, de b.**, walking-beam (of boring-machine); (*b*) *Artil:* field of fire (of gun). **2.** *F:* blatant publicity, boosting, booming; **faire du b. autour d'un livre**, to push, boost, a book.
battant [batɑ̃]. I. *a.* **1.** *Nau:* **vaisseau bien b.**, ship in good fighting trim, good fighting ship. **2.** (*a*) beating; **pluie battante**, beating, driving, pelting, rain; downpour; **porte battante**, (i) hanging door; (ii) swing-door, self-closing door; (iii) folding-door; **tambour b.**, with drums beating, with beat of drum; *F:* **mener qn tambour b.**, to treat s.o. high-handedly; **les armées alliées semblent marcher tambour b.**, the allied armies seem to be going great guns; **mener les choses tambour b.**, to hustle things on; *A:* **mener b. l'ennemi**, to keep the enemy on the run; *F:* **(tout) b. neuf**, brand-new (*Note:* **tout b. neuf** *sometimes remains inv. & sometimes* **battant** *agrees with the noun it qualifies*); (*b*) striking; **à onze heures b., battantes**, on the stroke of eleven. **3.** (*of signal, flag*) **être b.**, to be flying. **4.** *Tex:* **métier b.**, working loom, loom at work.
II. **battant**, *s.m.* **1.** (*a*) clapper, tongue (of bell); (*b*) lift (of latch); (*c*) fly (of flag); slab (of sail); (*d*) *Tex:* batten, lathe, lay (of loom); (*e*) *Mill:* clapper (of hopper). **2.** (*a*) leaf, flap (of table, counter, etc.); leaf (of door, shutter); **porte à deux battants**, double door, folding doors; **ouvrir les portes à deux battants**, to fling the gates wide open; (*b*) door (of cupboard, etc.); (*c*) rabbet (at junction of double doors or windows). **3.** (*a*) snap-over fastener; (*b*) swivel. **4.** *Nau:* adequate free-board. **5.** (*a*) **un b. de 10 cm.**, 10 cm clearance; (*b*) *Com:* **nous avons un b. de 200.000 francs**, we have a margin of 200,000 francs.
bat-tapis [batapi], *s.m.inv.* carpet-switch, carpet-beater.
batte[1] [bat], *s.f.* **1.** beating; **b. de l'or**, gold beating. **2.** (*a*) beater, mallet; **b. de blanchisseuse**, washerwoman's beater, beetle; **b. de terrassier**, turf-beetle; **b. à bourrer**, earth rammer, tamper; **b. à beurre**, dasher, plunger (of churn); **b. de plombier**, plumber's dresser; *For:* **b. à feu**, fire beater; (*b*) **b. (à cricket)**, (cricket) bat; **la b. d'Arlequin**, Harlequin's bat, lath; slapstick.
batte[2], *s.f.* fore-peak (of saddle).
battée [bate], *s.f.* **1.** amount (of wool, etc.) beaten at one time. **2.** *Const:* jamb (of door, window). **3.** *Gold-min:* wash-trough.
battellement [batɛlmɑ̃], *s.m. Const:* eaves.
battement [batmɑ̃], *s.m.* **1.** (*a*) beat(ing) (of drum); stamp(ing), tap(ping) (of feet); clapping (of hands); flutter(ing) (of wings, of eyelids); flapping (of sails); banging (of door); whipping (of machine belting); **b. de paupières**, blink(ing); quivering (of the eyelids); **regarder qn avec un b. de paupières**, to blink at s.o.; (*b*) *Ph:* (i) beating, pulsation (of oscillations); (ii) (interference) beat; (*c*) *Mus: Pros:* beat; (*d*) beat(ing), throb(bing), pulsation; **chaque b. de cœur**, every heartbeat, throb; **avoir des battements de cœur**, (i) to suffer from palpitations; (ii) to be in, *F:* to be all of, a flutter; **b. des tempes**, throbbing of the temples; (*e*) jarring, hammering (of machinery); *Aut:* **b. dans les cahots**, bouncing; (*f*) swing(ing) (of pendulum); tick-tock (of clock); *Danc:* high kick; (*g*) *Cards:* shuffling. **2.** interval (between two events, two duties, etc.); **on vous accorde deux heures de b.**, you are allowed two clear hours (before starting); *Rail:* **b. de vingt minutes**, wait of twenty minutes between trains (at junction, etc.). **3.** (*a*) shutter catch; (*b*) heel (of jack-knife).
batte-queue [batkø], *s.f. Orn:* wagtail; *pl. batte-queue(s).*
batterand [batrɑ̃], *s.m.* (*a*) (stonebreaker's) hammer; (*b*) (quarryman's) beetle, maul, sledge-hammer.
batterie [batri], *s.f.* **1.** *A:* fight, scuffle, rough-and-tumble. **2.** *Mus:* (*a*) beat (of drum); roll (on side-drum); (*b*) quick succession of notes; broken chords; (*c*) **la b.**, (i) the percussion instruments, the drums; (ii) *Mil:* the (drum and bugle) band. **3.** *Civ.E:* **b. pour pilotis**, pile-driver. **4.** (*a*) *Artil:* (i) (*unit*) troop; *A: & U.S:* battery; (ii) (*any number of guns*) battery; **b. de campagne**, (i) field troop; (ii) field battery; **b. anti-aérienne**, anti-aircraft battery; *A:* **b. à cheval, b. volante**, horse, mounted, battery; **b. de commandement et des services**, headquarters battery; *U.S:* headquarters and service

battery; **b. tractée,** tractor-drawn battery; **b. enterrée,** sunken battery; **b. de projecteurs,** searchlight battery; **b. de repérage par le son et les lueurs,** sound and flash battery; **b. d'instruction,** training battery; **fausse b.,** dummy battery; (*b*) *Artil:* **pièces en b.,** guns in firing position, in action; **"en b.!"** "action!"; **retour en b.** (*of the tube after a shot*), run-up, counter-recoil; (*c*) *Navy:* **pont de b.,** battery deck; **feu de b.,** broadside fire; (*d*) **dresser ses batteries,** to lay one's plans; **dévoiler ses batteries,** to show one's hand; **démonter les batteries de qn,** to demolish s.o.'s arguments. **5.** (*a*) set, collection; **b. de turbines,** turbine set, unit; **b. de chaudières, de fours à coke,** battery, range, bank, of boilers, of coke ovens; **b. de laminoirs,** train of rolling-mills; **b. de cuisine,** (i) (set of) kitchen utensils; (ii) *F:* one's whole set of medals, *F:* all one's gongs; (iii) *P:* percussion instruments; percussion band; (*b*) *Husb:* battery (for raising chicks); *Cu:* **poulet de b.,** battery (-reared) chicken; (*c*) **b. électrique,** electric battery; **b. au plomb,** lead-acid battery; **b. de rechange,** refill (for torch, etc.); *s.a.* STATIONNEMENT 2.

batterie-tampon [batritɑ̃pɔ̃], *s.f. El.E:* balancing, equalizing, battery; buffer battery; floating battery; *pl. batteries-tampons.*

batteur, -euse [batœːr, -øːz], *s.* **1.** *s.m.* beater; (*a*) *Tchn:* **b. d'or,** gold beater; **b. de coton,** cotton breaker, shaker; **b. de chaudières,** boiler scaler; **b. de pieux,** pile driver; **b. en grange,** thresher; (*b*) *Ven:* beater; (*c*) *F:* **b. de pavé,** loafer, idler; **b. de grève,** beach-comber; **b. de fer,** swash-buckler; *s.a.* ESTRADE[1]; (*d*) *Cr:* batsman; *Baseball:* batter; (*e*) *Mus:* (*jazz*) drummer. **2.** *s.m. Cu:* **b. à œufs,** egg-beater, whisk. **3.** (*a*) *s.f.* **batteuse;** *Husb:* threshing-machine, thresher; (*b*) *s.m.* **b.,** beater-drum (of thresher); (*c*) *Mec.E:* **entraînement à b.,** dog movement; (*d*) *Tchn:* damper; *Aut:* **b. à inertie,** inertia damper.

batteur-broyeur [batœːrbrwajœːr], *s.m. Dom.Ec:* coffee (etc.) grinder; (electric) mixer.

batteur-mélangeur [batœːrmelɑ̃ʒœːr], *s.m. Dom.Ec:* (electric) mixer.

battitures [batityːr], *s.f.pl. Metall:* (hammer-) scales, anvil-dross.

battoir [batwaːr], *s.m.* beater (instrument). **1.** (*a*) washerwoman's beetle, paddle or battledore; (*b*) *P:* (large) hand, *P:* ham. **2.** *Husb:* swingle, swipple (of flail). **3.** (whale's) flipper, fin.

battologie [batɔlɔʒi], *s.f.* battology.

battre [batr], *v.* (*pr.p.* **battant,** *p.p.* **battu,** *pr.ind.* **je bats** [ba], **tu bats, il bat, n. battons, ils battent;** *p.h.* **je battis,** *fu.* **je battrai**) to beat. **1.** *v.tr.* (*a*) to beat, thrash, flog, s.o.; **b. qn avec les poings, avec une canne,** to pommel, to cane, s.o.; **b. qn comme plâtre,** to beat s.o. to a jelly, to thrash s.o. within an inch of his life; **b. un tapis, un tambour,** to beat a carpet, a drum; **b. un pieu,** to drive a pile; **b. du blé,** to thresh corn; *abs.* **b. des bras,** to beat oneself to keep warm; *Swim:* **b. l'eau (avec les jambes),** to thrash the water; **b. une faux,** to hammer a scythe sharp; **b. le beurre,** to churn butter; (*b*) *Mil: A:* **b. les murs avec un bélier,** to batter the walls with a ram; **b. le fer (avec un marteau),** to hammer iron; **b. le fer à froid,** to cold-hammer iron; *Prov:* **il faut b. le fer pendant qu'il est chaud,** we must strike while the iron is hot; *Artil:* **b. un objectif,** to engage, to cover a target; to fire on a target; **b. par le feu,** to take under fire, to engage with fire, to fire on; **b. une position,** to fire on a position; **b. une zone,** to fire over a zone, an area; **b. de front,** to engage with frontal fire; **b. en écharpe,** to engage with oblique fire; to fire obliquely (on); **b. à revers,** to engage with reverse fire; to take in reverse; **zone battue,** beaten zone (of fire); (*c*) to beat, defeat, *F:* lick (s.o.); **b. qn au tennis,** to beat s.o. at tennis; **battre qn à plate(s) couture(s),** to beat s.o. hollow; *s.a:* BRÈCHE 1, COUTURE 2, MONNAIE 1; (*d*) **b. la campagne,** (i) *Mil:* to scour the country-side; (ii) *F:* to be delirious, to wander (in one's mind), to be all at sea; (iii) to beat about the bush; **b. la campagne à la recherche de qn,** to scour the country for s.o.; **b. son quart,** (*of policeman, etc.*) to be on one's beat; *s.a.* PAVÉ 2, PAYS[1]; *Ven:* **b. un bois,** to beat a wood; **b. les buissons,** (i) *Ven:* to beat for game; (ii) (of police) to make a thorough comb-out of criminal haunts; *s.a.* EAU 2; (*e*) *Nau:* **b. un pavillon,** to fly a flag; **navire qui bat (le) pavillon anglais,** ship carrying the British ensign; (*f*) **b. les cartes,** (i) to shuffle, *U.S:* to mix, the cards; (ii) *computers:* to joggle the cards. **2.** *v.tr. & i.* (*a*) **b. la mesure,** to beat time; **la montre bat,** the watch ticks; (*b*) **b. l'alarme,** to beat the alarm; **le tambour bat,** the drum is beating; **b. le réveil,** to beat, sound, the reveille; *s.a.* RETRAITE[1] 2; **le cœur lui battait,** his heart was beating, was going pit-a-pat; **son cœur battait à se rompre, battait à grands coups,** his heart was thumping (fit to break), was beating like mad; **la nouvelle nous fit b. le cœur,** we thrilled at the news, the news thrilled us; *s.a.* CHAMADE; **ses tempes battent la fièvre,** his temples throb with fever; **sentir b. une machine,** to feel a machine throbbing; (*c*) **la pluie bat (contre) les carreaux,** the rain beats, lashes, against the panes; **la mer bat les rochers,** the sea breaks against the rocks; **île battue par les flots,** island washed by the waves; **vaisseau battu (rudement) par les vagues,** ship buffeted by the waves; **sa robe de chambre lui battait sur les talons,** his dressing-gown flapped round his heels; **porte qui bat,** banging door; **voile qui bat dans le vent,** sail that flaps in the wind; (*d*) **b. des mains,** to clap one's hands, to applaud; **b. du pied,** (i) to stamp one's foot; (ii) to tap with one's foot; **b. des paupières,** to blink; *s.a.* AILE 1, ENTRECHAT, ŒIL 1, SEMELLE 1; (*e*) *Mch:* **b. contre vapeur,** to reverse steam; *Nau:* **b. en arrière,** to reverse, back; (*f*) *Tex:* (*of loom*) to be working; (*g*) **b. sa coulpe,** to admit one's guilt; *s.a.* PLEIN[1] 2.

se battre, to fight; **se b. avec qn,** to fight (with) s.o.; **se b. contre qn,** to fight against s.o.; **se b. en duel,** to fight a duel; **il s'est bien battu,** he fought well; **se b. avec qn pour qch.,** to battle with s.o. for sth.

battu [baty], *a.* **1.** (*a*) beaten; **enfant b.,** child who has had a beating; **avoir l'air d'un chien b.,** to look cowed; **avoir les yeux battus,** to have rings, circles, round one's eyes; (*b*) **armée battue,** defeated army. **2.** *Metalw:* **fer b.,** wrought iron; **sol en terre battue,** floor of beaten earth; mud floor; **or b.,** beaten gold. **3. chemin b.,** trodden path; **suivre les sentiers battus, le chemin b.,** to follow the beaten track; *s.a.* SENTIER. **4.** *Nau:* **mer battue,** broken sea. **5.** *s.m.* beaten, vanquished, person; **les battus,** the defeated; *s.a.* AMENDE 1.

battude [batyd], *s.f.* = BASTUDE.

battue [baty], *s.f.* **1.** (*a*) *Ven:* battue, beat; *Nau:* **b. en mer,** scouting cruise; (*b*) round-up (by police). **2.** beat, tramp, clatter (of horses' hoofs). **3.** *Ser:* batch of silkworms (ready for loosening of cocoons before reeling the silk).

batture [batyːr], *s.f.* **1.** gold lacquer. **2.** (*a*) **b. de roches,** reef; (*b*) *Fr.C:* sandbank.

bau, -aux [bo], *s.m. N.Arch:* beam; **b. du faux-pont,** orlop beam; **maître b.,** midship beam; **b. composé,** trussed beam; **navire à larges baux,** beamy, broad-beamed, ship.

Baucis [bosis], *Pr.n.f. Gr.Lit:* Baucis; **ils sont comme Philémon et B.,** they are like Darby and Joan.

baud [bo], *s.m. Tg.Meas:* baud.

baudelaire [bodəlɛːr], *s.m.* = BADELAIRE.

baudelairien, -ienne [bodəlɛrjɛ̃, -jɛn], *a.* imitating, pertaining to, Baudelaire.

bauder [bode], *v.i. Ven:* (*of hounds*) to give tongue, to bay.

baudequin [bodəkɛ̃], *s.m. Furn: A:* baldaquin, baldachin.

baudet [bodɛ], *s.m.* **1.** (i) (he-)ass, donkey, *U.S:* burro; (ii) stallion (ass). **2.** *F:* (jack)ass, dolt, idiot. **3.** *Carp:* sawyer's trestle, saw-pit horse.

baudir [bodiːr], *v.tr. Ven:* to urge on (hounds, etc.).

Baudouin [bodwɛ̃], *Pr.n.m.* Baldwin.

baudrier [bodri(j)e], *s.m.* cross-belt, shoulder-belt, *A:* baldrick (for drum, etc.); *Astr:* **le B. d'Orion,** Orion's belt; *Algae:* **B. de Neptune,** sugar-wrack, sea-belt, sweet tangle.

baudroie [bodrwa], *s.f. Ich:* Lophius, angler; **b. commune,** angler(-fish), frog-fish, toad-fish, sea-devil, fishing frog.

baudruche [bodryʃ], *s.f.* (*a*) gold-beater's skin; **b. gommée,** artificial gold-beater's skin; (*b*) *F:* (i) balloon; (ii) windbag; *F:* **se dégonfler comme une b.,** to get into a funk; **c'est une b.,** he's all façade.

bauère [boɛr], *s.f. Bot:* Bauera.

bauge [boːʒ], *s.f.* **1.** (*a*) lair, wallow (of wild boar); (*b*) *F:* pigsty; **c'est une vraie b.,** the place is a pigsty; (*c*) squirrel's drey. **2.** *Tex:* bauge, coarse drugget. **3.** *Const:* clay and straw mortar.

baugeois, -oise [boʒwa, -waːz], *a. & s.* (native) of Baugé.

bauger (se) [səboʒe], *v.pr.* (**baugeant; il baugea(it)**) (*of boar*) to lair, to retire to its lair.

baugue [boːg], *s.f.* = ZOSTÈRE.

bauhinia [boinia], *s.m. Bot:* Bauhinia.

baume[1] [boːm], *s.m.* **1.** (*a*) balm, balsam; **b. de, du, Canada,** Canada balsam; **b. de Copahu,** gurjun (balsam); *Pharm:* **b. de benjoin,** compound tincture of benzoin, friar's balsam; **b. vert des Antilles, b. Marie,** calaba balsam, tacamahac; **b. de la Mecque,** balsam of Mecca, balm of Gilead; *s.a.* TOLU; **fleurer comme b.,** to smell sweet; *Iron:* **sa réputation fleure comme b.,** he is in very good odour; (*b*) consolation; **mettre du b. dans le cœur de qn,** to pour balm into, upon, a wounded heart; *F:* **je n'ai pas de foi dans son b.,** I have no faith in his promises, in his remedy. **2.** *Bot:* **b. des jardins,** costmary; **b. sauvage, des champs,** wild mint; **b. vert,** garden mint, spear-mint. **3.** *A:* **b. de momie,** bitumen of Judaea.

baume[2], *s.f.* (*in Provence*) cave.

Baumé [bome], *Pr.n. Ph:* **aéromètre de B.,** Baume hydrometer; **degrés B.,** degrees Bé.

baumhauérite [bomoerit], *s.f. Miner:* baum-hauerite.

baumier [bomje], *s.m. Bot:* balsam(-tree); balm; *Com:* **b. de la Jamaïque,** Jamaica rosewood.

baumois, -oise [bomwa, -waːz], *a. & s. Geog:* (native, inhabitant) of Baume-les-Dames.

bauque [boːk], *s.f.* = ZOSTÈRE.

bauquière [bokjɛːr], *s.f. N.Arch:* beam-shelf; shelf (-piece).

bauquin [bokɛ̃], *s.m. Glassm:* mouthpiece (of glassblower's tube).

baux[1,2]. *See* BAIL, BAU.

bauxite [boksit], *s.f. Miner:* bauxite.

bauxitique [boksitik], *a.* bauxitic; (*a*) pertaining to bauxite; (*b*) containing bauxite.

bavard, -arde [bavaːr, -ard]. **1.** *a.* (*a*) talkative, loquacious, garrulous, *U.S: F:* gabby; *F:* **il est b. comme une pie,** he'd talk the hind-leg off a donkey; (*b*) tale-bearing, gossiping; (*c*) *Ven:* **chien b.,** babbler. **2.** *s.* (*a*) chatterer, chatterbox, prater; **c'est un b. assommant,** he's a deadly bore; (*b*) telltale, gossipmonger. **3.** *s.f.* **bavarde,** *P:* (*a*) mouth; (*b*) letter. **4.** *s.m. P:* (*a*) lawyer; *P:* mouthpiece; (*b*) *Mil:* = *livret militaire.*

bavardage [bavardaːʒ], *s.m.* chatter(ing), chit-chat; **leur conversation n'est que du b.,** their talk is mere chit-chat, mere twaddle; **bavardages de commères,** gossip, tittle-tattle.

bavarder [bavarde], *v.i.* **1.** to chatter. **2.** to gossip, chat. **3.** to blab, to tell tales.

bavarderie [bavard(ə)ri], *s.f.* **1.** talkativeness. **2.** = BAVARDAGE.

bavardise [bavardiːz], *s.f. A:* talk, idle, gossip.

bavarois, -oise [bavarwa, -waːz]. **1.** *a. & s. Geog:* Bavarian. **2.** *s.f.* **Bavaroise;** *Cu:* (*a*) Bavarian cream; (*b*) Bavarian sauce.

bavasser [bavɑse], *v.i. F:* (*a*) to talk without thinking; to talk nonsense; **b. comme un perroquet,** to chatter away like a parrot; (*b*) to sling mud.

bave [baːv], *s.f.* (*a*) slaver, dribble; slobber (of dog); slime (of snail); froth, foam (of horse, of mad dog); spittle (of toad); **couvert de b.,** beslavered; (*b*) spiteful talk, *F:* mud-slinging.

baver [bave], *v.i.* (*a*) to slaver; to drivel, dribble (at the mouth), to slobber; (*of blood*) to ooze; **b. de colère,** to foam at the mouth; **b. sur l'honneur de qn,** to cast a slur on s.o.'s honour; **en b.,** to have a hard, rough, time of it; to have a rough passage, to sweat blood; (*b*) *v.tr. & i. P:* to talk too much; to talk drivel; **en b. des ronds de chapeau,** to be flabbergasted, *P:* to be struck all of a heap; (*c*) (*of dog, etc.*) to foam at the mouth; (*d*) (*of pen*) to run; (*of ink*) to smudge.

baverette [bavrɛt], *s.f. A:* bib (of apron).

bavette [bavɛt], *s.f.* **1.** bib; **être encore à la bavette,** to be still a child; *F:* **tailler une b., des bavettes, avec une vieille connaissance,** to have a chat with an old crony. **2.** (*a*) *Av: etc:* drip-flap; *Cy:* **b. garde-boue,** mud-flap; (*b*) *Const:* hip-lead, -sheet. **3.** *Cu:* **b. d'aloyau,** top of the sirloin.

baveur, -euse[1] [bavœːr, -øːz]. **1.** *a.* drivelling, slobbering. **2.** *s.* dribbler, slobberer. **3.** *s.f.* **baveuse;** *Ich:* blenny.

baveux, -euse[2] [bavø, -øːz]. **1.** *a.* (*a*) slobbery (mouth); (*b*) moist, sloppy; **omelette baveuse,** moist, runny omelette; **plaie baveuse,** weeping wound; *Typ:* **lettres baveuses,** slutted, blurred letters. **2.** *s.m. Mil: P:* newspaper. **3.** *s.m. P:* soap.

Bavière [bavjɛːr], *Pr.n.f. Geog:* Bavaria.

bavoché [bavɔʃe], *a.* smeared, blurred, mackled (proof, letter, etc.).

bavocher [bavɔʃe]. **1.** *v.tr.* to blur, smear (picture, proof, etc.); to mackle. **2.** *v.i.* (*of type, etc.*) to spread; to give a blurred impression; to mackle.

bavocheux, -euse [bavɔʃø, -øːz], *a.* blurry, blurred, mackled.

bavochure [bavɔʃyːr], *s.f.* blur, smear; *Typ:* mackle.

bavoir [bavwa:r], *s.m.* (baby's) bib.

bavolet [bavɔlɛ], *s.m. Cost:* **1.** (peasant's) bonnet. **2.** *A:* curtain (of woman's bonnet). **3.** *Aut: A:* valance, side-apron.

bavure [bavy:r], *s.f.* **1.** (*a*) *Metall:* fin, beard, bur(r) (of casting, etc.); fash (on bullet); flash, barb (of metal); (*b*) wire-edge, bur(r). **2.** **bavures de plume,** pen smudges; *F:* **sans bavure(s),** (i) *adv.phr.* clearly, precisely; (ii) *adj.phr:* precise; impeccable.

bayadère [bajadɛ:r], *s.f.* **1.** (*a*) (Indian) dancing-girl, nautch-girl; (*b*) *Th:* dancer. **2.** *Tex:* bayadere, barré.

bayart [baja:r], *s.m.* = BARD.

bayer [bɑje], *v.* (**je baye, baie, n. bayons; je bayerai, baierai**) **1.** *v.i. A:* to stand gaping; *still used in a few phrases, esp.* **bayer aux corneilles,** to gape at the moon, to catch flies, to star-gaze. **2.** *v.tr.* **odeur bayée par le puits,** smell rising from the (gaping) well.

bayeur, -euse [bɑjœ:r, -ø:z], *s. A:* gaper, gazer.

bayeusain, -aine [bajøzɛ̃, -ɛn], *a. & s. Geog:* (native, inhabitant) of Bayeux.

bayle [bɛl], *s.m. Dial:* farm hand.

baylero [bɛlerɔ], *s.m.* shepherd's song (from Auvergne).

bayonnais, -aise [bajɔnɛ, -ɛ:z], *a. & s. Geog:* (native, inhabitant) of Bayonne.

bayonnette [bajɔnɛt], *s.f. A:* = BAÏONNETTE.

bayou [baju], *s.m. Geog:* (*in Louisiana*) bayou.

baz' [baz], *s.m. A: P: Sch:* the school.

bazadais, -aise, -ois, -oise [bazadɛ, -ɛ:z; -wa, -wa:z], *a. & s. Geog:* (native, inhabitant) of Bazas.

bazar [baza:r], *s.m.* **1.** (oriental) bazaar. **2.** (*a*) cheap stores; **article de b.,** cheap, shoddy, object, idea, etc.; *A: Sch: P:* **le b.,** the school, the *lycée*; (*b*) *occ.* (= **vente de charité**) charity bazaar, sale of work; (*c*) *P:* **on avait invité le maire, le curé, et tout le b.,** they had invited the mayor, the priest, and the whole lot of them; **j'aurais vendu maison, champs, tout le b., pour les acquérir,** I would have sold my house and land and everything I possessed to get them; (*d*) *P:* untidy room, etc.; **quel b.!** what a mess! (*e*) *P:* **il a tout son b. dans sa valise,** he's got all his clobber stuffed in his suitcase.

bazarder [bazarde], *v.tr. P:* (*a*) to sell off (one's effects); to get rid of (sth.); to turn (sth.) into money; to flog (sth.); **b. un employé,** to give an employee the sack; (*b*) to denounce (s.o.), *P:* to sell out on (s.o.).

bazenne [bazɛn], *s.f. Dial:* (*at Dunkirk*) fishwife, fish-seller.

bazooka [bazuka], *s.m. Artil:* bazooka.

bdellaire [bdɛllɛ:r]. **1.** *a. Z:* suctorial. **2.** *s.m.pl.* **bdellaires;** *Ann:* leeches.

bdellium [bdɛljɔm], *s.m. Bot:* bdellium, gum-resin.

bdelloïdes [bdɛlɔid], *s.m.pl. Z:* Bdelloidea.

bdellostome [bdɛlɔstɔm], *s.m. Ich:* bdellostoma.

bé [be], *s.m.* (the letter) b.

bê [bɛ], *Onomat:* baa.

beagle [bigl], *s.m.* beagle.

béal [beal], *s.m. Dial:* irrigation ditch.

béance [beɑ̃:s], *s.f.* (*a*) gaping (of wound, etc.); (*b*) *Dent:* gap (between the incisors and the canine teeth).

béant [beɑ̃], *a.* open, gaping (wound); yawning (chasm); **regarder qch. bouche béante,** to stare open-mouthed, agape, at sth.

béarnais, -aise [bearnɛ, -ɛ:z], *a. & s.* (*a*) *Geog:* (native, inhabitant) of Béarn; *Hist:* **le B.,** Henry IV (of France); (*b*) *a. Cu:* **sauce béarnaise,** béarnaise sauce (containing vinegar, chervil, shallots, tarragon, egg yolks and butter).

béat, -ate [bea, -at], *a. & s.* **1.** (*a*) *Ecc: A:* beatified (person); (*b*) *s. Ecc: A:* monk; (*c*) *A:* blissful, happy (person); (*d*) **optimisme b.,** complacent, smug, optimism. **2.** sanctimonious, smug, self-satisfied (person). **3.** stupid.

béatement [beatmɑ̃], *adv.* **1.** *A:* blissfully, complacently. **2.** sanctimoniously, smugly. **3.** stupidly.

béatification [beatifikasjɔ̃], *s.f.* beatification (of martyr, etc.).

béatifier [beatifje], *v.tr.* (*pr.sub. & p.d.*, **n. béatifiions, v. béatifiiez**) *Ecc:* to beatify (s.o.).

béatifique [beatifik], *a.* beatific (vision).

béatilles [beatij], *s.f.pl.* **1.** pious odds and ends. **2.** *Cu:* beatilles, filling (for vol-au-vent, etc.).

béatitude [beatityd], *s.f.* **1.** beatitude; (*a*) bliss; (*b*) **les huit béatitudes,** the eight beatitudes; (*c*) **sa B. l'évêque de Smyrne,** his Beatitude the Bishop of Smyrna. **2.** smugness, complacency.

beatnik [bitnik], *s.m. F:* beatnik.

Béatrice [beatris], *Pr.n.f.*, **Béatrix** [beatriks], *Pr.n.f.*, Beatrice, Beatrix.

beau [bo], **bel** [bɛl], *f.* **belle** [bɛl], *pl.* **beaux** [bo], **belles.** (*The form* **bel** *is used* (i) *before m.sg. sbs. or a mute* **h**; (ii) *in the two expressions* **bel et bon** *and* **bel et bien;** (iii) *in* **Charles le Bel** *and* **Philippe le Bel; bel** *is also sometimes used instead of* **beau** *when a phrase consisting of this adjective linked to another adjective by* **et** *immediately precedes a m.sg.s. beginning with a vowel or mute* **h,** *as in* **un bel et charmant enfant.**) I. *a.* **1.** beautiful handsome, good-looking; **un bel homme,** (i) a handsome, good-looking man; (ii) a tall, fine-looking man; **il est bel homme,** he's good-looking; **une belle femme,** (i) a beautiful woman; (ii) a fine-looking woman; **ma belle amie, ma belle enfant,** my dear; **le b. sexe,** the fair sex; **un fort b. visage,** a very beautiful face, a face of great beauty; **un b. corps,** a beautiful body; **belle jambe,** shapely leg; *s.a.* JAMBE 1; **une belle tête,** handsome features; **un b. chien,** a fine(-looking) dog; **de beaux arbres,** beautiful, fine, trees; **b. paysage,** beautiful landscape; **la mer est belle,** the sea is (i) beautiful; (ii) calm; **l'eau est plus belle en amont,** the water is clearer upstream; *Hist:* **Philippe le Bel,** Philip the Fair; **b. comme un astre, comme le jour,** as beautiful as the morning star, divinely beautiful; **porter b.,** (i) to have a noble bearing; (ii) *F:* to think no small beer of oneself; **il était b. d'indignation,** he was magnificent in his indignation. **2.** fine; (*a*) **de beaux sentiments,** fine, noble, lofty, feelings; **belle pensée,** lofty thought; **belle âme,** noble, generous, soul; **belle action,** fine deed; **une belle vie,** a full life; **il a fait une belle mort,** he died with his mind at peace; **mourir de sa belle mort,** to die a natural death; **trouver une belle mort,** to die a glorious death; **un b. nom,** an honoured, a glorious name; **cela n'est pas b. de votre part,** that was unworthy of you, that was a mean trick; *F:* **ce n'est pas b. de parler la bouche pleine,** it's not polite to speak with one's mouth full; **il est b. de pardonner,** it is generous to forgive; (*b*) **b. danseur,** fine dancer; **bel esprit,** (i) (pretty) wit; (ii) (*person*) wit; **faire le bel esprit,** (i) to make a show of being witty; (ii) to make a show of one's knowledge; *Prov:* **les beaux esprits se rencontrent,** great minds think alike; **c'est un b. parleur,** he has a smooth tongue, he is a glib talker; **c'est une belle intelligence,** he, she, has a brilliant mind; **une belle invention,** a great invention; **un b. talent,** a promising artist, writer, etc.; **b. discours,** fine speech; **le bel âge, les beaux jours de la jeunesse,** (the days of) youth; **dans ses beaux jours,** in his heyday; **un bel âge,** a ripe old age; **belle santé,** good health; **belle humeur,** happy disposition; **belle vieillesse,** robust old age; **belle occasion,** a grand, fine, opportunity; **l'avoir belle,** *A:* **l'avoir b.,** to have a good opportunity; to be in a good position (to do sth.); **personne de belle position,** person in a good, high, position; **il a une belle situation,** he has a good, high, position; **belle fortune,** handsome, large, comfortable, fortune; **b. poulet,** large, sizeable chicken; *Cards:* **avoir (un) b. jeu,** to have good cards; *F:* **il avait b. jeu à faire cela,** (i) it was easy for him to do this; (ii) he had every opportunity to do this, of doing this; **il est b. joueur,** he is a good loser, *F:* a sport; *adv.phr.* **en b.,** favourably; **voir les choses en b.,** to see things through rose-coloured spectacles; **vous lui ressemblez, mais en plus b.,** you are like him but better-looking; **voir tout du b. côté,** to see the bright, sunny, side of everything; **présenter une chose sous un b. jour,** to show sth. in a good light; (*c*) smart, spruce; *F:* **un b. monsieur,** a smartly, stylishly, dressed man; **le b. monde,** society, the fashionable set; **belle robe,** beautiful, smart, dress; **ma belle robe,** my best, my party, dress; **se faire b.,** to smarten oneself up, to dress up, to titivate; **vous voilà b.!** you do look smart! (*d*) **b. temps,** fine, fair, weather; **ami des beaux jours,** fair-weather friend; **un (de ces) beau(x), jour(s),** one (of these) fine day(s); **les beaux jours, la belle saison,** spring and summer days; (*e*) *Iron:* **le bel avantage, ma foi!** well, that's a fine advantage! **tout cela est fort b. mais . . .,** that's all very fine, well, but . . .; **tout cela est bel et bon mais . . .,** that's all well and good but . . .; *F:* **il en a fait de belles,** pretty things, he's been up to! **vous avez fait du b. travail!** you've done some fine work! **en conter, dire, de belles,** to say outrageous things; **en conter, dire, de belles sur qn,** to spread unpleasant reports about s.o.; **j'en ai entendu de belles sur votre compte,** I have heard some pretty tales about you! *F:* **vous en avez fait une belle!** you *have* put your foot in it! *P:* you've (been and) gone and done it! *A: F:* **en voici (d') une belle!** here's a fine how-d'ye-do! *F:* **en faire voir de belles à qn,** to give s.o. an unholy time of it, to put s.o. through it; *s.a.* DRAP 2; **belles paroles,** fine words; **c'est un b. monsieur, votre ami!** he's a fine rogue, your friend! *s.a.* AFFAIRE 1, MANIÈRE 1; (*f*) (*intensive*) **j'ai eu une belle peur,** I had an awful fright! **au b. milieu de la rue,** in the very middle, right in the middle, of the road; **il y a beaux jours, beau temps, bel âge, qu'il est parti,** it's many a long day, a long time, ages, since he went away; **une belle congestion pulmonaire,** a first-class attack of pneumonia; **belle correction;** good thrashing; **b. tapage,** (terrific) din, racket; **son bras n'est pas b. à voir, est dans un bel état,** his arm is a frightful sight, in an awful state; *P:* **un b. salaud,** a proper, regular, bastard; **il se démène comme un b. diable,** he is like a cat on hot bricks, *U.S:* on a hot tin roof; *s.a.* DENT 1, TEMPS 1. **3.** *adv.phrs.* **bel et bien,** entirely, fairly, quite, well and truly; **il est bel et bien venu,** he did indeed come; **vous voilà bel et bien grand-père!** so you've actually become a grandfather! **il a été bel et bien attrapé,** he was well and truly caught; **on le mit bel et bien à la porte,** they threw him out and made no bones about it; **tout b.!** steady! gently! stop! **de plus belle,** more, worse, than ever; **il recommença de plus belle,** he began again (i) with renewed vigour, harder than ever; (ii) worse than ever. **4.** *v.phrs.* (*a*) **l'échapper belle,** to have a narrow escape, a close shave; **la manquer belle,** (i) to miss a brilliant opportunity; (ii) *occ.* to have a narrow escape; **ce sera b. s'il n'est pas condamné à mort,** he will be lucky if he is not sentenced to death; (*b*) *F:* **il ferait b. voir cela,** that would be a fine thing to see; **il fait b. voir un pareil dévouement,** it is heartening to see such devotion; *F:* **il ferait b. voir qu'il se soumette à cette exigence,** it would be strange if he submitted to this demand; (*c*) (*of weather*) **il fait b. (temps),** it is fine; the weather is fine; *F:* **il fera b. quand j'y retournerai!** it will be a long time before I go there again! (*d*) **avoir b. faire qch.,** (i) to be able to do sth. with impunity; (ii) to do sth. in vain; *Prov:* **a b. mentir qui vient de loin,** travellers have leave to lie; **j'avais b. chercher, je ne trouvais rien,** search as I might, I found nothing; **il avait b. crier,** it was no use his shouting, no matter how much he shouted . . .; **vous avez b. courir, vous ne le rattraperez pas,** you won't catch him no matter how fast you run, run as you may, you won't catch him; **il eut b. dire . . .,** in spite of his assertions . . .; **vous avez b. parler,** *F:* you can talk till you are blue in the face.

II. **beau, belle,** *s.* **1.** (*a*) **une belle,** (i) a beauty, a beautiful woman; (ii) *F:* the woman whom one loves, *F:* one's girl friend; **ma belle,** my dear; *F:* beautiful; **les belles,** women, the fair sex; **courtiser les belles,** to run after women; **la Belle et la Bête,** Beauty and the Beast; **la Belle au bois dormant,** the Sleeping Beauty; (*b*) *A:* **un b.,** a dandy, a beau; **un vieux b.,** an old beau; **faire le b.,** (i) to strut, swagger, show off; (ii) (*of dog*) to sit and beg. **2.** *s.m.* (*a*) **le b.,** the beautiful; **l'amour du b.,** the love of beauty; (*b*) **le b. de l'histoire c'est que . . .,** the best part of the story is that . . .; (*c*) fine weather; **le temps est au b. (fixe),** the weather is set fair; **le temps a l'air d'être au b.,** it looks as if it's going to be fine; (*d*) **acheter du b.,** to buy things of the best quality. **3.** *s.f.* **belle;** (*a*) **jouer la belle,** to play (i) (*at tennis*) the deciding game or set; (ii) the odd trick; (iii) (*at cards*) the rubber game; (*b*) *Nau:* waist (of ship); **en belle,** abeam; (*c*) **faire la belle,** (i) (*of woman*) to parade her beauty; (ii) *P:* to break out of prison; (*d*) *Bot:* **belle d'onze heures,** star of Bethlehem.

beaucairien, -ienne [bokɛrjɛ̃, -jɛn], **beaucairois, -oise** [bokɛrwa, -wa:z], *a. & s. Geog:* (native, inhabitant) of Beaucaire.

beauceron, -onne [bosrɔ̃, -ɔn], *a. & s. Geog:* (native, inhabitant) of the Beauce region.

beaucoup [boku]. **1.** *s.m.inv.* (*a*) much, a great deal, *F:* a lot; **il reste encore b. à faire,** much still remains to be done; **il sait b.,** he knows a great deal; **cela compte pour b.,** that counts for much, for a good deal; **c'est déjà b., s'il veut bien, qu'il veuille bien, vous parler,** it is a great thing that he condescends to speak to you; (*b*) (a great) many, *F:* a lot; **b. pensent que . . .,** many are of the opinion that, many people think that . . .; **b. de,** much; (a great) many; a great deal of, *F:* lots of; **avoir b. d'argent,** to have a great deal, plenty, a lot, of money; **b. de**

gens, a great many people, a lot of people, *F:* no end of people; **avec b. de soin,** with much care, with a great deal of care; **il en est arrivé b. ce matin,** a great many, a lot, arrived this morning; **il y est pour b.,** he has had a great deal to do with it; **b. d'entre nous, d'entre vous,** many of us, of you; **b. d'entre eux se firent tuer,** many of them fought to the death; (*c*) *adv.phr.* **de b.,** much, by far, by a great deal; **c'est de b. le meilleur,** it is far and away the best, the best by a long way; *F:* the best by a long chalk; **cela dépasse de b. mon attente,** this much exceeds my expectations; **je préférerais de b. . . .,** I'd much rather . . .; **il s'en faut de b. que je sois riche,** I'm far from being rich; *s.a.* PRÈS 2. **2.** *adv.* much; **il vous aime b.,** he is very fond of you; **elle parle b.,** she talks a great deal, she is a great talker; **elle parle b. trop,** she talks a great deal too much, far too much; **il est b. plus âgé que sa femme,** he is much older than his wife; **il a b. voyagé,** he has travelled widely; **se servir b. de qch.,** to use sth. extensively, a great deal, to make great, much, use of sth.; *F:* **un peu b.,** a bit, rather, much.

beau-fils [bofis], *s.m.* **1.** stepson. **2.** (= GENDRE) son-in-law; *pl. beaux-fils.*

Beaufort [bofɔr], *Pr.n. Meteor:* **échelle de B.,** Beaufort scale.

beaufortain, -aine [bofɔrtɛ̃, -ɛn], *a. & s. Geog:* (native, inhabitant) of Beaufort.

beau-frère [bofrɛːr], *s.m.* brother-in-law; *pl. beaux-frères.*

beaujolais, -aise [boʒɔlɛ, -ɛːz]. **1.** *Pr.n. Geog:* **le B.,** the Beaujolais (region). **2.** *a. & s.* (native, inhabitant) of (i) the Beaujolais; (ii) Beaujeu. **3.** *s.m.* beaujolais (wine).

beaune [boːn], *s.m.* beaune (wine).

beaunois, -oise [bonwa, -waːz], *a. & s. Geog:* (native, inhabitant) of Beaune.

beau-père [bopɛːr], *s.m.* **1.** father-in-law. **2.** stepfather; *pl. beaux-pères.*

beau-petit-fils [bopətifis], *s.m.* stepgrandson; *pl. beaux-petits-fils.*

beaupré [bopre], *s.m.* **1.** *Nau:* bowsprit; **b. fixe,** standing bowsprit; **b. rentrant,** running bowsprit; **rentrer le b.,** to run in the bowsprit; **naviguer b. sur poupe,** to sail in close order astern. **2.** = BIGUE.

beauté [bote], *s.f.* **1.** beauty, handsomeness, loveliness; **conserver, perdre, sa b.,** to preserve, lose, one's beauty, one's good looks; **être dans toute sa b.,** to be in one's prime, in the flower of one's beauty; **être en b.,** to be looking one's best; **vous êtes en b. ce soir,** you're looking very beautiful, lovely, this evening; you *are* looking well this evening! **elle n'était pas en b. hier soir,** she was not looking her best last night; **vieillir en b.,** to keep one's beauty in old age; **mourir en b.,** to make a good end; *F:* **finir en b.,** to end in a blaze of glory; **grain, tache, de b.,** mole, beauty spot; **la b. du diable,** the bloom, freshness, of youth (in the face of a woman not otherwise beautiful); **de toute b.,** extremely beautiful; **des bijoux de toute b.,** magnificent jewels; **institut de b.,** beauty parlour; **produits de b.,** beauty preparations, cosmetics; **crème de b.,** face, beauty, cream; **soins de b.,** beauty treatment; *F:* **se refaire une b.,** to make up, *F:* to do one's face. **2.** beauty, beautiful woman; **la b. du bal,** the belle of the ball. **3. les beautés artistiques de l'Italie,** the art treasures of Italy; **les beautés touristiques,** the sights; **les beautés du style de Racine,** the beauty of Racine's style.

beauvaisien, -ienne [bovɛzjɛ̃, -jɛn], *a. & s.,* **beauvaisin, -ine** [bovɛzɛ̃, -in], *a. & s. Geog:* (native, inhabitant) of Beauvais.

Beauvaisis [bovɛzi], *Pr.n.m. Geog:* = the Beauvais region.

beaux-arts [bozaːr], *s.m.pl.* fine arts; **école des b.-a.,** *F:* **les B.-A.,** art school (of university standing).

beaux-parents [boparɑ̃], *s.m.pl.* parents-in-law.

bébé [bebe], *s.m.* **1.** baby; **faire le b.,** to behave childishly, like a baby. **2.** *Com:* (baby-)doll. **3.** *attrib.* (*used sometimes for the young of animals*) **b. gazelle,** baby gazelle. **4.** *Furn:* small (upholstered) armchair.

bébé-éprouvette [bebeepruvɛt], *s.m. Med. F:* test-tube baby; *pl. bébés-éprouvette.*

bébête [bebɛːt, bɛ-], *a. F:* silly, babyish, childish; **rire b.,** giggle; **je ne suis pas si b.,** I am not such a fool, such an idiot.

be-bop [bibɔp], *s.m. Mus: Danc:* be-bop.

bec [bɛk], *s.m.* **1.** beak; (*a*) bill (of bird); **au bec long, court, jaune,** long-, short-, yellow-billed; **coup de b.,** peck; **donner un coup de b. à qn,** (i) to peck s.o.; (ii) *F:* to have a dig, a poke at s.o.; **l'oiseau se fait le bec,** the bird is sharpening its beak, its bill; *F:* **faire le b. à qn,** to prime s.o. (with what he is to say); **il a b. et ongles,** he can defend, look after, himself; **attaquer qn du b. et des ongles,** to go for s.o. tooth and nail; (*b*) snout, beak (of certain fishes). **2.** *F:* (i) mouth; (ii) nose; **ils se rencontrèrent b. à b.,** they met face to face; *P:* **se rincer le b.,** to have a drink, *P:* to wet one's whistle; **il a le b. salé,** he's a thirsty customer; **claquer du b.,** to be hungry, starved; **se refaire le b.,** to have a good meal, *F:* to stoke up; **se coucher le morceau au b.,** to go to bed on a full stomach; **fin b.,** gourmet; **pincer le b.,** to purse up one's mouth; to pout; **mener qn par le b.,** to lead s.o. by the nose; **tenir qn le b. dans l'eau,** to keep s.o. in suspense. on the end of a string; **laisser qn le b. dans l'eau,** to leave s.o. in the lurch; **rester le b. dans l'eau,** to be stranded, left in the lurch; **ferme ton b.!** shut up! **river, clouer, clore, le b. à qn,** to reduce s.o. to silence, to shut s.o. up; **être fort en b., avoir bon b.,** to have the gift of the gab; *s.a.* CAQUET 2; **avoir le b. bien affilé,** to have a sharp tongue; **se prendre de b. avec qn, avoir une prise de b. avec qn,** to exchange (sharp) words with s.o.; to bicker with s.o.; **donner un coup de b.,** to make a stinging remark, to come out with a stinger; **donner du b.,** to kiss. **3.** (*a*) nose (of tool); nozzle, nose-piece (of tube); **b. de lance,** water-hose nozzle; spout (of coffee-pot); peak (of bicycle saddle); mouth-piece (of clarinet); beak, horn, beak-iron (of anvil); catch, nose (of latch); prow (of boat); bill (of anchor); cutwater (of bridge pier); jib (of crane); **b. élastique,** flexible jib (of cable crane); toe (of butt of rifle); tip (of aircraft wing); *Av:* **b. d'attaque,** leading edge; (*b*) **b. de plume,** pen-nib; (*c*) **b. de lampe,** lamp burner; **b. de gaz,** (i) gas burner; (ii) *F:* lamp-post; **b. Bunsen,** Bunsen burner; **b. en queue de poisson,** fish-tail burner; **b. en ailes de chauve-souris,** bat's-wing burner; **b. Auer,** incandescent burner; **b. allumeur,** bypass jet; *P:* **tomber sur un b. (de gaz),** to come up against a difficulty; to come a cropper; (*d*) *Geog:* (*in place names*) bill; **le B. de Portland,** Portland Bill; (ii) spit (at confluence of two rivers). **4.** *Med:* **b. de perroquet,** osteophyte.

bécabunga [bekabœ̃ga], *s.m. Bot:* brooklime.

bec-à-cuiller [bɛkakɥijɛːr], *s.m. Orn:* spoonbill; *pl. becs-à-cuiller.*

bécane [bekan], *s.f. F:* **1.** *Rail: A:* old shunting engine. **2.** bicycle, *F:* bike.

bécard [bekar], *s.m. Ich:* (*a*) grilse; male salmon (coming up to spawn); (*b*) adult pike.

bécarde [bekard], *s.f. Orn:* becard.

bécarre [bekaːr]. **1.** *a. & s.m. Mus:* natural (sign); *F: A:* **fou (par nature et) par b.,** perfect fool. **2.** *s.m. P: A:* dandy.

bécasse [bekas], *s.f.* (*a*) *Orn:* **b. (des bois),** woodcock; **b. d'arbre, perchante,** hoopoe; **b. de mer,** oyster-catcher; *F:* **ils ont bridé la b.,** they've caught their bird; (*b*) **c'est une petite b.,** she's a little idiot; (*c*) *Ich:* **b. de mer,** trumpet fish.

bécasseau, -eaux [bekaso], *s.m. Orn:* sandpiper; **b. de Baird,** Baird's sandpiper; **b. falcinelle,** broad-billed sandpiper; **b. minuscule,** least sandpiper, American stint; **b. semi-palmé,** semipalmated sandpiper; **b. à queue pointue,** sharp-tailed sandpiper; **b. de Bonaparte,** white-rumped, Bonaparte's, sandpiper; **b. variable,** dunlin, *U.S:* red-backed sandpiper; **b. échasse, minute,** little stint; **b. rousset,** buff-breasted sandpiper; **b. cocorli,** curlew-sandpiper; **b. maubèche,** knot; **b. sanderling,** sanderling; **b. tacheté,** pectoral sandpiper; **b. violet,** purple sandpiper; **b. de Temminck,** Temminck's stint.

bécassin [bekasɛ̃], *s.m. Orn:* jack-snipe, judcock.

bécassine [bekasin], *s.f.* **1.** (*a*) *Orn:* snipe; **b. sourde,** jack-snipe; **b. des marais,** common, *U.S:* Wilson's, snipe; **b. double,** great snipe; **b. rousse (du Canada),** red-breasted snipe, robin snipe; (*b*) *F:* naïve (country) girl. **2.** *Ich:* **b. de mer,** snipe-eel.

bécat [beka], *s.m. Agr:* two-pronged fork.

bécau, -aux [beko], *s.m. Orn:* young snipe.

beccard [bekar], *s.m.* = BÉCARD.

bec-courbe [bɛkkurb], *s.m.,* **bec-courbé** [bɛkkurbe], *s.m.* **1.** *Orn: F:* avocet. **2.** caulker's tool; *pl. becs-courbes, -courbés.*

bec-croisé [bɛkkrwaze, -aze], *s.m. Orn:* crossbill; **b.-c. des sapins,** *U.S:* red crossbill; **b.-c. perroquet,** parrot crossbill; **b.-c. bifascié,** two-barred, *U.S:* white-winged, crossbill; *pl. becs-croisés.*

bec-d'âne [bɛkdɑːn], *s.m.* = BÉDANE; *pl. becs-d'âne.*

bec-de-canard [bɛkdəkanar], *s.m. Ich: F:* pike; *pl. becs-de-canard.*

bec-de-cane [bɛkdəkan], *s.m.* **1.** *Bot:* tongue-shaped aloe. **2.** (*a*) spring lock; (*b*) slide-bolt; (*c*) lever handle (of shop door). **3.** (*a*) *Tls:* flat-nosed pliers; (*b*) *Surg:* crowbill, crow's bill; *pl. becs-de-cane.*

bec-de-cire [bɛkdəsiːr], *s.m. Orn:* wax-bill; *pl. becs-de-cire.*

bec-de-corbeau [bɛkdəkɔrbo], *s.m.* **1.** *Surg:* curved dressing-forceps. **2.** *Tls:* (*a*) rave-hook; (*b*) (long-nose) wire nippers. *pl. becs-de-corbeau.*

bec-de-corbin [bɛkdəkɔrbɛ̃], *s.m.* (*name of various bill-headed instruments, e.g.*) claw (for drawing nails); (caulker's) rave-hook, ripping-iron; *A.Arms:* **hallebarde en b.-de-c.,** halberd; *F:* **canne à b.-de-c.,** crutch-handled walking-stick; **nez en b.-de-c.,** hooked nose; *pl. becs-de-corbin.*

bec-de-faucon [bɛkdəfokɔ̃], *s.m.* **1.** *A.Arms:* halberd. **2.** *Z:* hawksbill turtle; *pl. becs-de-faucon.*

bec-de-grue [bɛkdəgry], *s.m. Bot: F:* geranium, crane's-bill, stork's-bill; *pl. des becs-de-grue.*

bec-de-hache [bɛkdəaʃ], *s.m. Orn: F:* oyster-catcher; *pl. becs-de-hache.*

bec-de-jar [bɛkdəʒar], *s.m. Moll:* soft clam, long clam; *pl. becs-de-jar.*

bec-de-lièvre [bɛkdəljɛːvr], *s.m.* **1.** harelip. **2.** harelipped person; *pl. becs-de-lièvre.*

bec-de-perroquet [bɛkdəpɛrɔkɛ], *s.m.* **1.** *Ich:* parrot fish. **2.** *Med:* osteophyte. **3.** (*a*) double fishhook; (*b*) *Surg:* crowbill; crow's bill; *pl. becs-de-perroquet.*

bec-d'oie [bɛkdwa], *s.m. Z: F:* common dolphin, *F:* porpoise; *pl. becs-d'oie.*

bec-dur [bɛkdyːr], *s.m. Orn: F:* common grosbeak, hawfinch; *pl. becs-durs.*

bec-en-ciseaux [bɛkɑ̃sizo], *s.m. Orn:* scissor-bill; *pl. becs-en-ciseaux.*

bec-en-croix [bɛkɑ̃krwa, -ɑ], *s.m. Orn:* common cross-bill; *pl. becs-en-croix.*

bec-en-cuiller [bɛkɑ̃kɥijɛːr], *s.m. Orn:* boat-bill; *pl. becs-en-cuiller.*

bec-en-fourreau [bɛkɑ̃furo], *s.m. Orn: F:* sheath-bill; *pl. becs-en-fourreau.*

bec-en-sabot [bɛkɑ̃sabo], *s.m. Orn:* shoe-bill, whale-head; *pl. becs-en-sabot.*

bec-en-scie [bɛkɑ̃si], *s.m. Orn:* flycatcher; *pl. becs-en-scie.*

becfigue [bɛkfig], *s.m. Orn:* (i) the garden warbler; (ii) the blackcap; (iii) the waxwing; (iv) the pipit; *Cu:* beccafico.

bec-fin [bɛkfɛ̃], *s.m. Orn:* warbler; *pl. becs-fins.*

bêchage [bɛʃaːʒ], *s.m.* **1.** digging (up). **2.** *F:* disparagement, running down (of s.o.).

béchamel(le) [beʃamɛl], *a.f. & s.f. Cu:* **(sauce (à la)) b.,** béchamel sauce, white cream sauce.

bêchard [bɛʃaːr], *s.m. Agr:* double-headed hoe.

bêche [bɛʃ], *s.f.* **1.** (*a*) spade; **labour à la b.,** digging; **profondeur de fer de b.,** graft, spit; **labourer à deux fers de b.,** to dig two spits deep; **donner des coups de b. dans l'édifice social,** to undermine the social structure; *P:* **faire de la b. sur qn,** to run s.o. down, pick s.o. to pieces; to turn up one's nose at s.o.; (*b*) *Artil:* **b. de crosse,** trail spade. **2.** *Ent: F:* Eumolpus vitis, common vine-grub.

bêche-de-mer [bɛʃdəmɛːr]. **1.** *s.f. Echin: F:* sea-slug, trepang, sea-cucumber, bêche-de-mer. **2.** *s.m. Ling:* bêche-de-mer (English), beach-la-mar.

bêchelon [bɛʃlɔ̃], *s.m.* small hoe.

becher [beʃɛr], *s.m. Ch:* beaker.

bêcher [beʃe], *v.tr.* **1.** to dig. **2.** *F:* to run (s.o.) down, to pull (s.o.) to pieces.

bêcheton [bɛʃtɔ̃], *s.m.* small narrow spade.

bêchette [bɛʃɛt], *s.f.* small spade.

bêcheur,-euse [bɛʃœːr, -øːz], *s.* **1.** digger (of the soil). **2.** *F:* depreciator, detractor, carping critic; *P:* **(l'avocat) b.,** the public prosecutor.

béchique [beʃik], *a. & s.m. A: Pharm:* cough-(mixture, syrup, etc.); antitussive.

bêchoir [bɛʃwaːr], *s.m. Agr:* broad hoe.

bêchon [bɛʃɔ̃], *s.f.* small hoe.

bêchot [bɛʃo], *s.m.* small spade.

bec-jaune [be(k)ʒon], *s.m.* = BÉJAUNE; *pl. becs-jaunes.*

bécot [beko], *s.m.* **1.** *Orn:* jacksnipe. **2.** *F:* little kiss; peck; **donner un gros b. à qn,** to give s.o. a big kiss.

bécoter [bekɔte], *v.tr. F:* to give (s.o.) a little kiss, a peck; **ils étaient en train de se b.,** they were kissing away; *F:* they were necking.

bec-ouvert [bɛkuvɛːr], *s.m. Orn:* gaper, clapper-bill, openbill; *pl. becs-ouverts.*

bec-plat [bɛkplɑ], *s.m. Orn: F:* spoonbill, duck, shoveller; *pl. becs-plats.*

bec-pointu [bɛkpwɛ̃ty], *s.m. Ich: F:* white skate; *pl. becs-pointus.*

becqué [beke], *a.* **1.** *Her:* beaked. **2.** *Husb:* **Œuf b.,** egg through the shell of which the beak of the chick can be seen.

becquée [beke], *s.f.* **1.** beakful, billful; *F:* **encore une b.!** another little mouthful! another little bite! **2. l'oiseau donne la b. à ses petits,** the bird feeds its young; **donner la b. à un enfant, à un malade,** to feed a child, a sick person.

becquefleur [bɛkflœːr], *s.m. Orn: F:* humming-bird.

becquerélite [bɛkərelit], *s.f. Miner:* becquerelite.

becquet [bɛkɛ], *s.m.* = BÉQUET.

becquetage [bɛktaːʒ], *s.m.* pecking, peck.

becquetance [bɛktɑ̃ːs], *s.f. P:* food, *P:* grub.

becqueter [bɛkte], *v.tr.* **(je becquète, n. becquetons; je becquèterai)** **1.** *(of birds)* *(a)* to pick up (crumbs, etc.); *(b)* to peck at (sth.); *(c) abs.* *(of pers.)* to eat, feed, *P:* to stoke up; *P:* **b. des clarinettes,** to do without one's rations, to fast. **2.** *(a)* *(of bird)* to caress (another) with the beak, to bill; *(b) F:* *(of pers.)* to kiss.

bec-rond [bɛkrɔ̃], *s.m. Orn: F:* bullfinch; *pl. becs-ronds.*

bectance [bɛktɑ̃ːs], *s.f. P:* food, *P:* grub.

becter [bɛkte], *v.i. P:* to eat, *P:* to stoke up.

bécu [beky], *a. Ven:* *(bird)* with a long or strong beak.

bécune [bekyn], *s.f. Ich:* barracuda, becuna.

bedaine [bədɛn], *s.f. F:* stomach, belly; paunch, corporation.

bedame [bədam], *int.* = DAME[2].

bédane [bedan], *s.m. Tls:* mortise, chisel, heading chisel; *Metalw:* cold chisel, cross-cut chisel.

bédaner [bedane], *v.tr.* to mortise.

bédaricien, -ienne [bedarisjɛ̃, -jɛn], *a. & s. Geog:* (native, inhabitant) of Bédarieux.

bedeau, -eaux [bədo], *s.m.* **1.** *A:* beadle. **2.** *Ecc:* verger.

bédégar, bédéguar [bedegaːr], *s.m. Hort:* bedeg(u)ar, rose-gall.

beder [bəde], *v.i.* to go back to square one (when playing "snakes and ladders," etc.).

bedford [bɛdfɔːr, -d], *s.m. Tex:* Bedford cord.

bedole [bədɔl], *a. P: O:* idiotic.

bedon [bədɔ̃], *s.m.* **1.** *A:* kettle-drum. **2.** *F:* belly, corporation; **un gros b.,** a big fat man.

bedonnant [bədɔnɑ̃], *a. F:* corpulent, pot-bellied.

bedonner [bədɔne], *v.i. F:* to get stout; to acquire a corporation.

bédouin, -ouine [bedwɛ̃, -win], *a. & s.* bedouin.

bed-rock [bɛdrɔk], *s.m. Geol:* bed-rock.

bée[1] [be], *s.f.* **1.** *Const:* opening (for door, window); doorway. **2.** *Hyd.E:* *(a)* mill-leet, -leat, *U.S:* flume; *(b)* penstock (of mill).

bée[2], *a.f.* open, gaping; *used in* **bouche b.,** agape; **rester bouche b. devant qch.,** to stand gaping, open-mouthed, before sth.; **regarder qch. bouche b.,** to gape at sth.

beefsteak [bifstɛk], *s.m.* = BIFTECK.

béer [bee], *v.i. Lit:* *(a)* *(of thg.)* to be wide open; **la valise béait à ses pieds,** the case lay wide open at his feet; *(b)* *(of pers.)* (i) to stand open-mouthed (in astonishment, etc.); (ii) to day-dream.

beffroi [bɛfrwa], *s.m.* **1.** belfry. **2.** alarm-bell (hung in belfry). **3.** *Hyd.E:* gantry (of dredge).

bégaiement [begɛmɑ̃], *s.m.* **1.** stammering, stuttering. **2.** lispings (of baby). **3.** early attempts, tentative beginnings.

bégayant [begɛjɑ̃], *a.* *(a)* stuttering, stammering; *(b)* *(of child)* lisping.

bégayement [begɛmɑ̃], *s.m. A:* = BÉGAIEMENT.

bégayer [begeje], *v.* **(je bégaye, bégaie, n. bégayons; je bégayerai, bégaierai)** **1.** *v.i.* *(a)* to stutter, stammer; **homme qui bégaie,** man with a stammer; *(b)* *(of babies)* to lisp. **2.** *v.tr.* **b. une excuse,** to stammer out an excuse; **il ne sait que le turc, mais il bégaie aussi quelques mots français,** he knows only Turkish, but can manage to stammer out a few French words.

bégayeur, -euse [begɛjœːr, -øːz]. **1.** *a.* stuttering, stammering. **2.** *s.* stutterer, stammerer.

bégonia [begɔnja], *s.m.,* **bégonie** [begɔni], *s.f.,* **bégone** [begɔn], *s.f. Bot:* begonia; *P:* **cherrer, charrier, dans les bégonias,** to lay it on with a trowel.

bégoniacées [begɔnjase], *s.f.pl. Bot:* Begoniaceae.

bégu, -uë [begy], *a.* (horse) that has not lost mark of mouth.

bègue [bɛg]. **1.** *a.* *(a)* stuttering, stammering; *(b)* clumsy. **2.** *s.* stutterer, stammerer.

béguètement [begɛtmɑ̃], *s.m.* bleating (of goat).

bégueter [beg(ə)te], *v.i.* **(elle béguète; elle béguètera)** *(of goat)* to bleat.

bégueule [begœl]. **1.** *s.f.* prude. **2.** *a.* prudish, strait-laced.

bégueulerie [begœlri], *s.f. F:* prudishness, prudery, squeamishness.

bégueulisme [begœlism], *s.m. A:* = BÉGUEULERIE.

béguin [begɛ̃], *s.m.* **1.** *(a)* hood (of beguine nun); *(b)* (baby's) bonnet; *(c) Artil:* ear protector; *(d) Min:* *(in N.Fr.)* cloth cap (worn under miner's helmet); *(e)* hood (for horse); *(f) A: P:* **laver le b. à qn,** to give s.o. a good talking to. **2.** *(a) F:* **avoir un, le, b. pour qn,** to have an infatuation for s.o.; to be in love with s.o.; *(of schoolgirl)* to have a crush on s.o.; *(b) P:* **c'est mon b.,** I've got a thing on him, her.

béguinage [beginaːʒ], *s.m.* **1.** (beguine) convent. **2.** *F:* excessive devotion, excessive piety.

béguine [begin], *s.f.* **1.** *Ecc:* beguin(e). **2.** *F: Pej:* very devout woman.

bégum [begɔm], *s.f.* begum.

behavio(u)risme [beavjurism], *s.m. Psy:* behaviourism.

behavio(u)riste [beavjurist], *a. & s.m. Psy:* behaviourist.

béhémot [beemɔt], *s.m.* behemoth.

béhen [beɛn], *s.m. Bot:* *(a)* behen, behn; **b. blanc,** white behen, frothy poppy, bladder-campion; **b. rouge,** red behen; *(b)* ben.

béhénique [beenik], *a. Ch:* behenic (acid).

béhénolique [beenɔlik], *a. Ch:* behenolic (acid).

Behist(o)un [beistun], *Pr.n.m. Geog:* Behistun, Bisitun.

behourdis [bəurdi], *s.m. Ecc: Dial:* *(in Picardy)* first Sunday in Lent.

beige [bɛːʒ]. **1.** *a.* beige; natural, raw (wool); **un manteau b.,** a beige coat. **2.** *s.f.* unbleached serge; **étoffe en beige,** cloth in natural colour, undyed cloth.

beigne[1] [bɛɲ], *s.f.* **1.** *A:* bruise; bump, lump (on the head). **2.** *P:* blow, clout, *P:* sock, bash; **donner, flanquer, une b. à qn,** to give s.o. a sock (in the face); to beat s.o. up.

beigne[2], *s.m. Fr.C: Cu:* doughnut.

beignet [bɛɲɛ], *s.m.* **1.** *A:* small bump, lump (on the head). **2.** *Cu:* fritter; **b. de, aux, pommes,** apple fritter.

béjaune [beʒoːn], *s.m.* **1.** *(a)* yellow, beak (of young bird); *(b)* young bird, nestling; *Ven:* eyas, nias (hawk). **2.** *(a) A:* (i) novice; (ii) fool, simpleton; *(b)* **montrer son b.,** to reveal one's ignorance, one's stupidity.

bel[1] [bɛl], *s.m. Ph.Meas:* bel (unit of sound).

bel[2]. *See* BEAU.

bélandre [belɑ̃ːdr], *s.f.* canal-barge, bilander.

bélandrier [belɑ̃dri(j)e], *s.m.* canal bargeman.

bêlant [bɛlɑ̃], *a.* bleating.

bêlement [bɛlmɑ̃], *s.m.* bleating, bleat.

bélemnite [belɛmnit], *s.f. Paleont:* belemnite.

bélemnitidés [belɛmnitide], *s.m.pl. Paleont:* Belemnitidae.

bélemnoïdes [belɛmnɔid], *s.m.pl. Paleont:* Belemnoidea.

bêler [bele]. **1.** *v.i.* *(a)* to bleat, *F:* *(of sheep)* to baa; *(b) F:* *(of pers.)* to complain, to wail; **qu'est-ce que vous avez à b. comme ça?** what on earth are you bleating, bellyaching, about? **2.** *v.tr.* **b. une chanson, un discours,** to bleat out a song, a speech.

belette [bəlɛt], *s.f.* **1.** *Z:* weasel; **b. pygmée,** least weasel. **2.** *Metall:* puddle-ball.

belfortain, -aine [bɛfɔrtɛ̃, -ɛn], **belfortin, -ine** [bɛfɔrtɛ̃, -in], *a. & s. Geog:* (native, inhabitant) of Belfort.

belga [bɛlga], *s.m. A: Fin:* belga.

belge [bɛlʒ], *a. & s.* **1.** *Geog:* Belgian. **2.** *Civ.E:* **méthode b.,** Belgian system (of tunnelling).

belgicisme [bɛlʒisism], *s.m.* Belgian turn of phrase.

belgique [bɛlʒik]. **1.** *a. Hist:* Belgic (Gaul, etc.). **2.** *Pr.n.f.* **la B.,** Belgium, *A: P:* **filer en B.,** (of financier) to bolt.

belgo- [bɛlgo-], *pref.* Belgo-; **belgo-luxembourgeois,** Belgo-Luxemburg(er).

bélier [belje], *s.m.* **1.** *Z:* ram, *U.S:* buck. **2.** *(a) Mil: A:* battering ram; *(b) Civ.E:* **b. à pilotage,** pile-driver, rammer, ram; **b. mécanique,** bulldozer; *(c) Hyd.E:* (i) **b. hydraulique,** hydraulic ram, water-ram; (ii) **coup de b.,** (water-)hammering; *(d) Wr:* **coup de b.,** (i) flying head butt; (ii) body check. **3.** *Astr:* **le B.,** the Ram, Aries.

bélière[1] [beljɛːr], *s.f.* sheep-bell (of the bell-wether).

bélière[2], *s.f.* *(a)* ring (of watch, etc.); clapper-ring (of bell); shackle (of knife); *(b)* (sword-)sling; *(c) a. A.Mil:* **tour bélière,** ram penthouse.

béliner [beline], *v.i. Breed:* *(of ram, or ewe),* to tup.

bélinogramme [belinɔgram], *s.m.* telephotograph; phototelegraph (transmitted on the Belin system).

bélinographe [belinɔgraf], *s.m.* phototelegraphic apparatus (Belin system).

Bélisaire [belizɛːr]. *Pr.n.m. Hist:* Belisarius.

bélître [belitr̥], *s.m.* **1.** *A:* beggar. **2.** *A:* good-for-nothing.

bellachon, -onne [bɛlaʃɔ̃, -ɔn], *a. & s.,* **bellacquais, -aise** [bɛlakɛ, -ɛːz], *a. & s. Geog:* (native, inhabitant) of Bellac.

belladone [bɛladɔn], *s.f. Bot:* belladonna, *F:* deadly nightshade, great morel.

bellâtre [bɛlɑːtr̥]. **1.** *a.* foppish, dandified. **2.** *s.m.* fop.

belle. *See* BEAU.

belle-à-voir [bɛlavwaːr], *s.f. Bot:* belvedere; *pl. belles-à-voir.*

belle-dame [bɛldam], *s.f.* **1.** *Bot:* *(a)* garden orach; *(b)* deadly nightshade. **2.** *Ent:* painted lady (butterfly); *pl. belles-dames.*

belle-de-jour [bɛldəʒuːr], *s.f. Bot:* convolvulus; *pl. belles-de-jour.*

belle-de-nuit [bɛldənɥi], *s.f.* **1.** *Bot:* marvel of Peru, *U.S:* pretty-by-night. **2.** *Orn:* sedge-warbler. **3.** *F:* prostitute; *pl. belles-de-nuit.*

belle-d'onze-heures [bɛldɔ̃zœːr], *s.f. Bot:* Star of Bethlehem; *pl. belles-d'onze-heures.*

belle-d'un-jour [bɛldœ̃ʒuːr], *s.f. Bot:* day-lily; *pl. belles-d'un-jour.*

belle-face [bɛlfas], *a. & s.m.inv.* white-faced, bald (horse).

belle-famille [bɛlfamij], *s.f.* wife's family; husband's family; *F:* the "in-laws"; *pl. belles-familles.*

belle-fille [bɛlfij], *s.f.* **1.** stepdaughter. **2.** daughter-in-law; *pl. belles-filles.*

belle-maman [bɛlmamɑ̃], *s.f. F:* = BELLE-MÈRE; *pl. belles-mamans.*

bellement [bɛlmɑ̃]. **1.** *adv.* *(a) O:* beautifully, finely; *(b)* well and truly; **il est b. en prison,** he's well and truly in prison. **2.** *int. Dial: A:* gently! softly!

belle-mère [bɛlmɛːr], *s.f.* **1.** stepmother. **2.** mother-in-law; *F:* **vous cherchez une b.-m.?** your slip is showing, Charley's dead, it's snowing down south; *pl. belles-mères.*

belle-petite-fille [bɛlpətitfij], *s.f.* stepgranddaughter; *pl. belles-petites-filles.*

bellérophon [belerɔfɔ̃], *s.m. Paleont:* bellerophon.

belles-lettres [bɛllɛtr̥], *s.f.pl.* humanities, belles-lettres.

belle-sœur [bɛlsœːr], *s.f.* sister-in-law; *pl. belles-sœurs.*

bellevillois, -oise [bɛlvilwa, -waːz], *a. & s. Geog:* (native, inhabitant) of Belleville.

belleysan, -ane [bɛlezɑ̃, -an], *a. & s. Geog:* (native, inhabitant) of Belley.

bellicisme [bɛl(l)isism], *s.m.* warmongering.

belliciste [bɛl(l)isist], *s.m. & f.* warmonger.

bellicosité [bɛl(l)ikozite], *s.f.* bellicosity.

bellifontain, -aine [bɛl(l)ifɔ̃tɛ̃, -ɛn], *a. & s. Geog:* (native, inhabitant) of Fontainebleau.

belligérance [bɛl(l)iʒerɑ̃ːs], *s.f.* belligerency.

belligérant [bɛl(l)iʒerɑ̃], *a. & s.* belligerent.

bellîlois, -oise [bɛlilwa, -waːz], *a. & s. Geog:* (native, inhabitant) of Belle-Ile-en-Mer.

belliqueux, -euse [bɛl(l)ikø, -øːz], *a.* warlike, bellicose; quarrelsome.

bellis [bɛl(l)is], *s.f. Bot:* Bellis; daisy.

bellissime [bɛllisim], *a. F: Iron:* splendid, superb.

bellite [bɛllit], *s.f. Exp:* bellite.

bellon[1] [bɛlɔ̃], *s.m. Med:* lead colic.

bellon[2], *s.m.* *(a) Vit:* trolley with vat for collecting grape harvest; *(b)* vat used in cider-making.

Bellone [bɛllɔn]. *Pr.n.f. Myth:* Bellona.

bellot, -otte [bɛlo, -ɔt], *a.* **1.** *F:* pretty. **2.** dandified. **3.** *s.* **mon b., ma bellotte,** my little cherub.

belluaire [bɛl(l)ɥɛːr], *s.m.* **1.** *Rom.Ant:* beast-fighter. **2.** wild-beast tamer.

béloce [belɔs], *s.f. Bot: F:* bullace.

bélocier [belɔsje], *s.m. Bot: F:* bullace(-tree).

belon [bəlɔ̃], *s.m.* oyster (from the estuary of the river Belon).

belone [belɔn], *s.f. Ich:* Belone; garfish, needlefish.

bélonite [belɔnit], *s.f. Miner:* belonite.

belote [bəlɔt], *s.f. Cards:* card game similar to pinocle; **faire une b.,** to play a game of *belote.*

beloter [bəlɔte], *v.i.* to play *belote.*

beloteur, -euse [bəlɔtœːr, -øːz], *s. belote* player.

bélostomatidés [belɔstɔmatide], *s.m.pl. Ent:* Belostomatidae.

bélostome [belɔstɔm], *s.m. Ent:* Belostoma.

bélouga [beluga], *s.m. Z:* Beluga, white whale.

béloutche [belutʃ], *a. & s.* = BALOUTCHI.

Bélou(t)chistan [belu(t)ʃistɑ̃]. *Pr.n.m.* = BALOUTCHISTAN.

bel-outil [bɛluti], *s.m.* (jeweller's) anvil; *pl. beaux-outils.*

béluga [belyga], *s.m.* = BÉLOUGA.

belvédère, *A:* **belvéder** [bɛlvedɛːr], *s.m.* **1.** belvedere, gazebo. **2.** summer-house. **3.** view-point (at beauty spot). **4.** *Bot:* belvedere.

Belzébuth [bɛlzebyt], *Pr.n.m. B.Hist:* Beelzebub.
bembex [bɛmbɛks, bɛ̃-], *s.m. Ent:* bembex; bembix.
bémentite [bemɑ̃tit], *s.f. Miner:* bementite.
bémol [bemɔl], *s.m. Mus:* flat; **clarinette en si b.,** B-flat clarinet; **mettre un b. à la clef,** to soften one's tone and manners.
bémoliser [bemɔlize], *v.tr. Mus:* to flatten; to mark (note) with a flat; *U.S:* to flat (note).
ben [bɛ̃], *adv. P:* = BIEN. **b. oui!** why, yes!
ben [bɛn], *s.m. Bot:* ben; **noix de ben,** ben-nut; **huile de ben,** oil of ben.
bénard [benaːr], *s.m. P:* trousers, pants.
bénarde [bɛnard], *a.f. & s.f.* **(serrure) b.,** pin-key lock, double-sided lock; **clef b.,** pin-key.
bénédicité [benedisite], *s.m.* grace (before meat). **Dire le b.,** to say grace; to ask a blessing.
Benedicite omnia [benedisite ɔmnia], *s.m.inv. Ecc:* Benedicite (omnia opera).
bénédictin, -ine [benediktɛ̃, -in], *a. & s.* **1.** Benedictine (monk, nun); **un vrai b.,** a learned man, a scholar; **les Bénédictins,** the Benedictines, the Black Friars; **un travail de b.,** a prodigious work of painstaking scholarship. **2.** *s.f. R.t.m:* **Bénédictine,** Benedictine (liqueur).
bénédiction [benediksjɔ̃], *s.f. O:* blessing, benediction; consecration (of colours); *O:* **donner des bénédictions à qn,** to bestow blessings on s.o.; **recueillir les bénédictions des pauvres,** to be blessed by the poor; **donner la b.,** to give, pronounce, the blessing; **il a donné sa b. au projet,** he gave the plan his blessing; **la b. nuptiale sera donnée à . . .,** the marriage will be celebrated at . . .; **pays de b.,** land of plenty; **il a plu; (que) c'est une b.,** the rain has come as a real blessing; *Iron:* **il neige que c'est une b.,** it is snowing with a vengeance; **quelle b.!** what a blessing! what a godsend!
bénédictionnaire [benediksjɔnɛːr], *s.m. Ecc:* benedictional, benedictionary.
benedictus [benediktys], *s.m. Ecc:* benedictus.
bénef [benɛf], *s.m. P:* **petits bénefs,** perks.
bénéfice [benefis], *s.m.* **1.** profit, gain; **réaliser de gros bénéfices,** to make large, handsome profits; *Fin:* **vendre qch. à b.,** to sell sth. at a profit, at a premium; **participation aux bénéfices, compensation des bénéfices,** profit-sharing; **part de b.,** bonus; **petits bénéfices,** perquisites; **je suis en b.,** I am in pocket; **affaire qui donne un b.,** firm that shows a profit. **2.** benefit; (*a*) **faire qch. au b. de qn,** to do sth. for s.o.'s benefit; *Th: Sp:* **représentation, match, à b.,** benefit performance, match; **sous le b. de cette observation . . .,** (i) having made this point . . .; (ii) with this reservation . . .; *Jur:* **b. du doute,** benefit of the doubt; *Jur:* **b. de discussion,** benefit of discussion; **b. de division,** right of sureties to go bail each for his own part only; *s.a.* CLERGIE, INVENTAIRE; (*b*) *Com:* **b. d'aunage,** allowance for cutting (cloth, etc.). **3.** *Ecc:* living, benefice; **il faut prendre le bénéfice avec les charges,** one must take the rough with the smooth.
bénéficiaire [benefisjɛːr]. **1.** *a. Com:* **solde b.,** profit balance; **compte b.,** account showing a credit balance; **marge b.,** profit margin. **2.** *s.* (*a*) recipient, payee (of cheque, money order); (*b*) *Ecc: Ins: Jur: Th: etc:* beneficiary.
bénéficial, -aux [benefisjal, -o], *a. Ecc:* beneficiary.
bénéficier[1], **-ière** [benefisje, -jɛːr]. *Ecc:* **1.** *a.* beneficiary (privilege, etc.). **2.** *s.m.* beneficiary; beneficed clergyman; incumbent.
bénéficier[2], *v.* (*p.d. & pr.sub.* **n. bénéficiions, v. bénéficiiez**) **1.** *v.i.* (*a*) to profit (de, by); **faire b. qn d'une expérience,** to give s.o. the benefit of one's experience; *Jur:* **il a bénéficié d'une ordonnance de non-lieu,** he was discharged; **bénéficiant d'une remise de dix pour cent,** subject to a discount of ten per cent; **faire b. qn d'une remise,** to allow s.o. a discount; (*b*) to make a profit (sur, on). **2.** *v.tr.* to work (mine, etc.) at a profit.
bénéfique [benefik], *a.* (*a*) *Astrol:* benefic, beneficent (planet); *s.a.* PIERRE[1]; (*b*) favourable, beneficial (à, to).
Bénélux [benelyks], *Pr.n.m.* Benelux.
benêt [bənɛ]. **1.** *a. m.* silly, stupid, simple-minded. **2.** *s.m.* simpleton.
Bénévent [benevɑ̃], *Pr.n.m. Geog:* Benevento, (which occupies the site of ancient Beneventum).
bénéventin, -ine [benevɑ̃tɛ̃, -in], *a. & s. Geog:* (native, inhabitant) of Benevento.
bénévole [benevɔl], *a.* **1.** benevolent; kindly (reader, etc.); indulgent. **2.** gratuitous (service); **organisation b.,** voluntary organization; **mandataire b.,** agent unpaid; **infirmière b.,** voluntary nurse. **3.** *Sch:* **auditeur bénévole (à un cours),** non-matriculated person privileged to attend lectures.
bénévolement [benevɔlmɑ̃], *adv.* **1.** kindly, benevolently, out of kindness. **2.** gratuitously, voluntarily.
bénévolence [benevɔlɑ̃ːs], *s.f. A:* goodwill.
bengalais, -aise [bɛ̃galɛ, -ɛz]. **1.** *a. & s.* Bengali, Bengalese. **2.** *s.m. Ling:* Bengali.
Bengale [bɛ̃gal], *Pr.n.m.* **1.** *Geog:* Bengal. **2.** *Pyr:* **feu de B.,** (i) Bengal light; blue fire; (ii) light signal; flare.
Bengali[1] [bɛ̃gali]. **1.** *s.m.* Bengali, Bengalese. **2.** *a.inv. in f.* **la race b.,** the Bengalese race.
bengali[2], *s.m. Orn:* bengali.
bengaline [bɛ̃galin], *s.f. Tex:* bengaline.
béni bouffe-tout, béni-bouftou [benibuftu], *s.m.inv. P:* glutton, *F:* greedy hog.
béni-coco [benikoko], *s.m.inv. P:* idiot, *P:* nit.
bénigne. *See* BÉNIN.
bénignement [beniɲmɑ̃], *adv.* benignly, benignantly, kindly.
bénignité [beniɲite], *s.f.* (*a*) benignity, kindness; (*b*) mildness (of climate, of a disease).
bénin, -igne [benɛ̃, -iɲ], *a.* (*a*) benign, kindly, indulgent, favourable; **astre b.,** benignant star; (*b*) **remède b.,** mild, gentle, remedy; **hiver b.,** mild winter; **fièvre, tumeur, bénigne,** benign fever; benign, non-malignant, tumour; **forme bénigne de (la) rougeole,** mild form of measles.
bénincase [benɛ̃kaːz], *s.f. Bot:* gourd-melon.
béni-oui-oui [beniwiwi], *s.m.inv. F:* yes-man.
bénir [beniːr], *v.tr.* (*p.p.* **béni, bénit;** *the latter used chiefly as an adj.*) **1.** (*a*) to bless, to grant blessings to (s.o.); **(que) Dieu vous bénisse!** (i) (may) God bless you! (ii) *F:* (*to s.o. who has just sneezed*) (God) bless you! **être béni des dieux,** to have been born under a lucky star; (*b*) to bless, ask God's blessing on (s.o.); to pronounce a blessing on (s.o.); **b. un mariage,** to solemnize a marriage; (*c*) to glorify, to render thanks to (God); **le ciel en soit béni!** heaven be thanked for it! **2.** to consecrate (church, bread, water, etc.); **quand le prêtre a béni le pain . . .,** when the priest has blessed the bread. . .
bénissage [benisaːʒ], *s.m. F:* blarney, soft sawder.
bénissant [benisɑ̃], *a.* blessing, that confers blessings.
bénisseur, -euse [benisœːr, -øːz], *a. & s.* (*a*) (one) who blesses, gives a blessing; (*b*) (one) who pays empty compliments.
bénit [beni], *a.* consecrated, blessed; **pain b.,** consecrated bread, holy bread; *F:* **c'est pain b.,** it serves him, them, right; **eau bénite,** holy water; *F:* **eau bénite de cour,** fair promises, empty words; **cierge b.,** consecrated taper; **médailles et chapelets bénits,** holy objects of piety.
bénitier [benitje], *s.m.* **1.** *Ecc:* holy-water basin, stoop, stoup; **b. portatif,** aspersorium. *s.a.* DÉMENER (SE) 1. **2.** *Conch:* giant clam. **3.** *Geol:* pool (in cave).
Benjamin [bɛ̃ʒamɛ̃]. **1.** *Pr.n.m.* Benjamin. **2.** *s.m. & f.* **benjamin, -ine**[1], benjamin, youngest child.
benjamine[2] [bɛ̃ʒamin], *s.f. Nau:* main try-sail.
Benjaminites [bɛ̃ʒaminit], *s.m.pl. Jew.Hist:* the tribe of Benjamin.
benjoin [bɛ̃ʒwɛ̃], *s.m.* **1.** *Com:* gum benzoin, *F:* benjamin; *see* also BAUME 1. **2.** *Bot: F:* = BENZOIN.
benne [bɛn], *s.f.* **1.** flat hamper, basket; pannier (for grape harvest). **2.** *Min: etc:* (*a*) skip, tub, hutch, corf, bucket, truck; (*b*) (shaft) cage. **3.** (*a*) bucket (of dredger, etc.); **b. piocheuse,** grab (bucket); **b. preneuse,** clam-shell bucket; **b. roulante,** wheeled kibble; (*b*) **(camion à) b. basculante,** tip-lorry, tip-wagon.
benne-drague [bɛndrag], *s.f. Civ.E:* earth grab; *pl. bennes-dragues.*
Benoist, Benoît[1] [bənwa], *Pr.n.m.* Benedict.
benoît[2], *a.* (*a*) *A:* blessed, kind, gentle; *Lit:* **b. lecteur,** gentle reader; (*b*) sanctimonious.
benoite [bənwat], *s.f. Bot:* **b. commune,** herb bennet, common avens; **b. des ruisseaux,** water avens.
benoîtement [bənwatmɑ̃], *adv.* (*a*) gently; (*b*) in a mealy-mouthed, soft-spoken, manner, sanctimoniously.
benthamisme [bɛ̃tamism], *s.m.* Benthamism.
benthique [bɛ̃tik], *a.*, **benthonique** [bɛ̃tɔnik], *a.* benthic, benthonic (fauna, etc.).
benthos [bɛ̃tɔs], *s.m. Oc:* (*a*) benthos; (*b*) benthos, benthic flora and fauna.
bentonite [bɛ̃tɔnit], *s.f. Miner:* bentonite.
benzaldéhyde [bɛ̃zaldeid], *s.m. Ch:* benzaldehyde.
benzamide [bɛ̃zamid], *s.m. Ch:* benzamide.
benzanilide [bɛ̃zanilid], *s.f. Ch:* benzanilide.
benzanthrone [bɛ̃zɑ̃trɔn], *s.f. Ch:* benzanthrone.
benzazide [bɛ̃zazid], *s.f. Ch:* benzazide.
benzazimide [bɛ̃zazimid], *s.m. Ch:* benzazimide.
benzédrine [bɛ̃zedrin], *s.f. R.t.m:* benzedrine.
benzéine [bɛ̃zein], *s.f. Ch:* benzein.
benzène [bɛ̃zɛn], *s.m. Ch:* benzene.
benzénique [bɛ̃zenik], *a. Ch:* benzene (hydrocarbons, etc.).
benzénisme [bɛ̃zenism], *s.m. Med:* benzolism.
benzhydrol [bɛ̃zidrɔl], *s.m. Ch:* benz(o)hydrol.
benzine [bɛ̃zin], *s.f.* **1.** benzine. **2.** (*in Switz.*) petrol.
benzinier [bɛ̃zinje], *s.m. Nau:* benzine tanker.
benz(o)- [bɛ̃z(o)], *pref. Ch:* benz(o)-.
benzoate [bɛ̃zɔat], *s.m. Ch:* benzoate.
benzoin [bɛ̃zwɛ̃], *s.m. Bot:* **(styrax) b.,** benzoin laurel; *F:* benjamin-tree.
benzoïque [bɛ̃zɔik], *a. Ch:* benzoic.
benzol [bɛ̃zɔl], *s.m. Ch:* benzol.
benzoline [bɛ̃zɔlin], *s.f.* benzoline.
benzolisme [bɛ̃zɔlism], *s.m. Med:* benzolism.
benzonaphtol [bɛ̃zɔnaftɔl], *s.m.* benzonaphtol.
benzonitrile [bɛ̃zɔnitril], *s.m. Ch:* benzonitrile.
benzophénone [bɛ̃zɔfenɔn], *s.f.* benzophenone.
benzoyle [bɛ̃zɔil], *s.m. Ch:* benzoyl.
benzyle [bɛ̃zil], *s.m. Ch:* benzyl.
Béotie [beɔsi], *Pr.n.f. A.Geog:* Boeotia.
béotien, -ienne [beɔsjɛ̃, -jɛn], *a. & s.* **1.** (*a*) *a. & s. A.Geog:* Boeotian; (*b*) *s.m. A.Ling:* **le b.,** Boeotian. **2.** (*a*) *a.* (i) philistine; (ii) unintelligent, ignorant, dull-witted; (*b*) *s.* layman; **je suis un b. en cette matière,** I'm a complete layman in that field.
béotisme [beɔtism], *s.m.* dullness of mind, stupidity.
béquée [beke], *s.f.* = BECQUÉE.
bèque(-)bois [bɛkbwa], *s.m. Orn:* = PIC-VERT.
béquet [bekɛ], *s.m.* **1.** *Typ:* (*a*) paste-on (to proof); (*b*) overlay (on press cylinder). **2.** *Bootm:* (*a*) middle-sole; (*b*) hobnail. **3.** *Ich:* (*a*) grilse; male salmon (coming up to spawn); (*b*) adult pike.
béqueter [bɛkte], *v.tr.* = BECQUETER.
béquillage [bekijaːʒ], *s.m. Nau:* shoring up.
béquillard, -arde [bekijaːr, -ard], *s.* (*a*) person who walks with crutches; cripple; (*b*) one-legged man.
béquille [bekij], *s.f.* **1.** crutch; **s'appuyer sur des béquilles,** to walk on crutches; **parapluie à b.,** crutch-handled umbrella; *F:* **vieille b.,** dotard, driveller. **2.** (*a*) *Veh: etc:* prop; (*b*) *Aut:* sprag; crutch, stand (of motor cycle); (*c*) *Av:* tail-skid; (*d*) *Nau:* (i) leg, shore, prop; (ii) tiller (of rudder); (*e*) *Sm.a:* **b. de crosse,** butt leg, rest; stock rest. **3.** *Agr:* spud, grubbing hoe. **4.** lever (door-) handle, crutch-handle; **(clef à) b.,** crutch-key (of cock).
béquiller [bekije]. **1.** *v.i. F:* to walk on crutches. **2.** *v.tr.* (*a*) *Agr:* to spud (a plot); (*b*) *Nau:* to shore up, prop up (ship); (*c*) to prop up (the branches of a tree).
béquillon [bekijɔ̃], *s.m.* **1.** crutch-handled walking-stick. **2.** *Agr:* spud.
ber(s) [bɛːr], *s.m.* **1.** *N.Arch:* (launching) cradle. **2.** (boiler) seatings. **3.** *Veh:* rave.
berbère [bɛrbɛːr]. **1.** *a. & s. Ethn:* Berber. **2.** *s.m. Ling:* Berber.
berbéridacées [bɛrberidase], *s.f.pl. Bot:* Berberidaceae.
berbéride [bɛrberid], *s.m. Bot:* berberis, barberry.
berbérine [bɛrberin], *s.f. Ch: Physiol:* berberine.
berbéris [bɛrberis], *s.m. Bot:* berberis; **b. commun,** barberry.
bercail [bɛrkaːj], *s.m. not used in the pl.* (*a*) *Husb:* (sheep-)fold; (*b*) the fold (of the Church); **ramener au b. la brebis égarée,** to bring the lost sheep back to the fold; (*c*) (family) home; **l'enfant prodigue revint au b.,** the prodigal son returned home.
berçant [bɛrsɑ̃], *a. Fr.C:* **chaise berçante,** rocking-chair.
berce [bɛrs], *s.f. Bot:* heracleum; **b. commune, b. branc-ursine,** cow-parsnip, hogweed, pigweed.
berceau, -eaux [bɛrso], *s.m.* **1.** (*a*) cradle, (swing-)cot; **b. alsacien,** basket cot on wheels; **j'ai appris cela au b.,** I have known this from my cradle, from my infancy; **étouffer le mal au b.,** to strangle evil at its birth; **le b. d'un mouvement populaire,** the birthplace of a popular movement; (*b*) *Gold-Min:* (cradle-)rocker. **2.** (*a*) *Aut: Min: N.Arch: Typ: etc:* cradle, bed, support; *Artil:* cradle (of gun); *Artil:* **b. de pointage,** elevating carriage; *Aut: Av:* **b. (du) moteur,** engine mounting; (*b*) *Arch:* **voûte en b.,** barrel-vault; (*c*) *Hort:* arbour, bower; *Orn:* **oiseaux à berceaux,** bower-birds; (*d*) *Av:* **b. à bombes,** bomb-rack. **3.** *Bot: F:* **b. de la Vierge,** Virgin's bower, traveller's joy, old man's beard.

bercelonnette [bɛrsələnɛt], *s.f.* bassinet, (swing-)cot.

bercement [bɛrsəmɑ̃], *s.m.* **1.** rocking, lulling. **2.** swaying.

bercer [bɛrse], *v.tr.* **(je berçai(s); n. berçons) 1.** to rock; **b. un bébé,** (i) to rock a baby (in a cradle); (ii) to dandle a baby (in one's arms); **j'ai été bercé là-dedans,** I was brought up to it from my cradle. **2.** to lull, (i) to send (s.o.) to sleep; (ii) to soften, soothe (grief), to soothe (s.o.); **b. qn de promesses,** to delude, beguile, s.o. with promises. **3.** *v.i.* (*of horse*) to sway from side to side (when walking).

se bercer. 1. to rock, swing, sway. **2. se b. d'une illusion, d'un espoir,** to cherish, indulge in, an illusion, a hope; to delude oneself.

berceur, -euse [bɛrsœːr, -øːz], *s.* **1.** cradle-rocker. **2.** *s.f.* **berceuse:** (*a*) swing-cot; (*b*) rocking-chair; (*c*) *Mus:* (i) lullaby, cradle-song; (ii) berceuse. **3.** *a.* soothing; lulling.

Bérenger [berɑ̃ʒe], *Pr.n.m. Hist:* Berengarius.

Bérénice [berenis], *Pr.n.f.* Berenice, Bernice.

béret [berɛ], *s.m.* beret; **b. (de marin),** (sailor's) cap; **b. écossais,** tam-o'-shanter; *Mil:* **les bérets rouges,** the parachutists; *Pol:* **les bérets bleus,** UNO's police force.

bergamasque [bɛrgamask], *a. & s.* **1.** *a. Geog:* Bergamask. **2.** *a. & s.f. Danc: Mus:* bergamask. **3. berger b.,** Italian sheepdog (of N. Italy).

Bergame [bɛrgam]. **1.** *Pr.n.f. Geog:* Bergamo. **2.** *s.f. Tex:* Bergamot (tapestry).

bergamote [bɛrgamɔt], *s.f.* **1.** *Hort:* (*a*) bergamot (orange); **essence de b.,** bergamot oil; (*b*) bergamot (pear). **2.** (*a*) sweet-box, comfit-box (lined with bergamot bark); (*b*) sweet (flavoured with bergamot, made at Nancy). **3.** = BERGAMOTIER.

bergamotier [bɛrgamɔtje], *s.m.* bergamot (tree).

berge[1] [bɛrʒ], *s.f.* (steep) bank (of river); banked edge (of railway track, of road); slope, side (of valley); flank (of mountain); *Mil:* rampart, parapet.

berge[2], *s.f. Orn:* (= BARGE[2]) godwit.

berge[3], *s.f. Nau:* barge; lighter.

berge[4], *s.f. P:* (*usu. pl.*) year.

berger, -ère [bɛrʒe, -ɛːr], *s.* **1.** (*a*) shepherd, shepherdess; herdsman; **chien de b.,** sheepdog; **b. allemand,** Alsatian (dog); *P:* **ma bergère,** my old woman, the missus; **l'étoile du B.,** the Evening Star; *Dial:* the Shepherd's Lamp; **l'heure du b.,** the auspicious hour (for lovers); the gloaming; *Chess:* **coup du b.,** fool's mate; (*b*) shepherd, (spiritual) pastor. **2.** *s.f.* **bergère;** (*a*) *Furn:* bergère; *s.a.* OREILLE 3; (*b*) *Bot: F:* larger periwinkle; (*c*) *Orn:* wagtail; (*d*) *F:* last card in the pack.

bergerette [bɛrʒərɛt], *s.f.* **1.** *Poet:* young shepherdess, shepherd-maid. **2.** honey-wine, winemead. **3.** *Mus:* bergerette, pastoral song. **4.** *Orn:* wagtail.

bergerie [bɛrʒəri], *s.f.* **1.** (*a*) *Husb:* sheep-fold, pen; sheep-run; **enfermer le loup dans la b.,** to set the fox to mind the geese; (*b*) *Rail:* cattle-truck. **2.** *Art: Lit: etc:* pastoral (poem, painting, tapestry, etc.).

bergeronnette [bɛrʒərɔnɛt], *s.f.* **1.** *A:* young shepherdess. **2.** *Orn:* wagtail; **b. des ruisseaux, jaune,** grey wagtail; **b. (printanière) flavéole,** yellow wagtail; **b. (printanière) à tête cendrée, à tête noire, nordique, d'Espagne,** ashy-headed, black-headed, grey-headed, Spanish, wagtail; **b. citrine,** yellow-headed wagtail; **b. printanière,** blue-headed wagtail; **b. de Yarrell,** pied wagtail; **b. grise,** white wagtail.

berginisation [bɛrʒinizasjɔ̃], *s.f. Ind:* berginization (of fuel oils); hydrogenation under pressure and heat.

bergsonien, -ienne [bɛrksɔnjɛ̃, -jɛn], *a. Phil:* Bergsonian.

bergsonisme [bɛrksɔnism], *s.m. Phil:* Bergsonism.

berguois, -oise [bɛrgwa, -waːz], *a. & s. Geog:* (native, inhabitant) of Bergues.

bergusien, -ienne [bɛrgyzjɛ̃, -jɛn], *a. & s. Geog:* (native, inhabitant) of Bourgoin.

béribéri [beriberi], *s.m. Med:* beriberi.

béril [beril], *s.m.* = BÉRYL.

berkélium [bɛrkeljɔm], *s.m. Ch:* berkelium.

berkois, -oise [bɛrkwa, -waːz], *a. & s.* (native) of Berck.

berlander [bɛrlɑ̃de], *v.i. Fr.C:* to dawdle, to fool around.

berle [bɛrl], *s.f. Bot:* **1.** water-parsnip; **b. des potagers,** skirret. **2.** ferula.

berline [bɛrlin], *s.f.* (*a*) *A:* berlin(e) (coach); (*b*) *Aut:* four-door saloon, *U.S:* four-door sedan; (*c*) *Min:* truck, tram, corf; (*d*) *A:* **(avion-)b.,** saloon air-liner.

berlingot[1] [bɛrlɛ̃go], *s.m. A:* (*a*) single-seated berline; (*b*) *F:* rickety old carriage.

berlingot[2], *s.m.* **1.** *Comest:* (*a*) burnt-sugar sweet; caramel; (*b*) humbug. **2.** (*a*) *F:* carton (of milk); sachet (of shampoo, etc.); (*b*) *Atom. Ph:* **champ magnétique en forme de b.,** humbug-shaped magnetic field.

berlinite [bɛrlinit], *s.f. Miner:* berlinite.

berlinois, -oise [bɛrlinwa, -waːz], *Geog:* **1.** *a.* of Berlin. **2.** *s.* Berliner.

berloque [bɛrlɔk], *s.f. P:* = BRELOQUE 2.

berlue [bɛrly], *s.f. Med:* metamorphopsia, false vision, *F:* **avoir la b.,** to be blind to the facts, to see things wrong; to be mistaken; **j'ai cru avoir la b. en voyant tous ces changements,** I thought my eyes were deceiving me when I saw all those changes.

berme [bɛrm], *s.f.* **1.** *Fort:* berm, foreland. **2.** *Civ.E:* set-off, bench (with foot-path); (*on road*) **b. centrale,** central reservation.

bermuda [bɛrmyda], *s.m. Cost:* (pair of) Bermuda shorts.

Bermudes [bɛrmyd], *Pr.n.f.pl. Geog:* **les (îles) B.,** the Bermudas, the Bermuda Islands.

bermudien, -ienne [bɛrmydjɛ̃, -jɛn]. **1.** *a. & s. Geog:* Bermudian. **2.** *Nau:* (*a*) *s.m.* Bermuda-rigged sloop; (*b*) *a.* Bermuda (rig). **3.** *Bot:* **bermudienne,** *s.f.* Bermuda lily.

bernable [bɛrnabl̩], *a.* easily taken in, easily hoaxed.

bernache [bɛrnaʃ], *s.f.,* **bernacle** [bɛrnakl̩], *s.f.* **1.** *Crust:* barnacle; *Moll:* goose-barnacle. **2.** *Orn:* **b. nonnette,** barnacle goose; **b. cravant,** brent goose, *U.S:* American brant; **b. du Canada,** Canada goose; **b. à cou roux,** red-breasted goose.

Bernard[1] [bɛrnaːr], *Pr.n.m.* Bernard.

bernard[2], *s.m. Anat: P:* backside, bum, fanny.

bernardin, -ine [bɛrnardɛ̃, -in], *s.* Bernardine (monk, nun).

bernard-l'(h)ermite [bɛrnarlɛrmit], *s.m. Crust:* hermit-crab, soldier-crab.

bernayen, -enne [bɛrnɛjɛ̃, -ɛn], *a. & s. Geog:* (native, inhabitant) of Bernay.

berne[1] [bɛrn], *s.f. A:* **1.** (*a*) woollen blanket; (*b*) woollen cloak. **2.** tossing in a blanket, blanketing.

berne[2], *s.f. used only in the following:* **1.** *Nau:* **pavillon en b.,** flag at half-mast, (*in Brit. marine*) union down; **mettre en b.,** to half-mast the flag. **2.** *Mil:* **drapeau en b.,** flag furled and craped.

Berne[3], *Pr.n. Geog:* Bern(e).

berne[4], *s.m. A:* large cauldron for water (with lip and handles).

bernement [bɛrnəmɑ̃], *s.m. A:* tossing (in a blanket), blanketing.

berner [bɛrne], *v.tr.* **1.** *A:* to toss (s.o.) in a blanket, to blanket (s.o.). **2.** (*a*) to ridicule (s.o.); to laugh at (s.o.); (*b*) to hoax (s.o.); **b. qn d'une excuse,** to put s.o. off with an excuse.

berneur, -euse [bɛrnœːr, -øːz], *s.* **1.** *A:* tosser. **2.** deceiver, joker.

bernicle [bɛrnikl̩], *s.f.,* **bernique**[1] [bɛrnik], *s.f. Moll: F:* limpet.

bernique[2], *int. F:* not a bit of use! no go! nothing doing!

bernois, -oise [bɛrnwa, -waːz], *a. & s. Geog:* Bernese.

Bernoulli [bɛrnuli], *Pr.n. Mth: etc:* **théorème de B.,** Bernoulli's theorem.

bernoullien [bɛrnuljɛ̃], *a. Mth:* **nombres bernoulliens,** Bernoullian coefficients.

berquinade [bɛrkinad], *s.f.* child's book after the manner of those of Berquin (1747-91); puerile, insipid, piece of literature.

berratin, -ine [bɛratɛ̃, -in], *a. & s. Geog:* (native, inhabitant) of Berre-l'Etang.

berriasien [bɛriazjɛ̃], *a. & s.m. Geol:* Berriasian.

berrichon, -onne [bɛriʃɔ̃, -ɔn]. **1.** *a.* of Berry; *Cu:* **à la berrichonne,** served with cabbage braised with small onions and bacon. **2.** *s.m. & f.* native, inhabitant, of Berry. **3.** *s.m. Ling:* **le b.,** the patois of Berry.

berriot, -ote [bɛrjo, -ɔt], *a. & s.* (native, inhabitant) of Berry.

berruyer, -ère [bɛrɥ(i)je, -ɛːr], *a. & s.* (native, inhabitant) of Bourges.

Berry (le) [ləbɛri], *Pr.n.m. Geog:* Berry.

bers[1] [bɛːr], *s.m.pl. Husb:* (cart-)rack, cart-ladder; (floating) raves.

bers[2], *s.m.* = BER.

Bersabée [bɛrsabe], *Pr.n. A.Geog:* Beersheba.

bersaglier [bɛrsalje, -agli(j)e], *s.m. Mil:* Bersagliere, (Italian) sharpshooter, light-infantryman; *pl. bersagliers, bersaglieri.*

berserk [bɛrsɛrk], *s.m. Scand.Hist:* berserk(er).

berteroa [bɛrtərɔa], *s.m. Bot:* Berteroa.

Bertha [bɛrta], *s.f. A.Artil: F:* **la grosse B.,** Big Bertha (1914-18 war).

Berthe [bɛrt]. **1.** *Pr.n.f.* Bertha; *Lit:* **du temps où B. filait** (with reference to Berthe de Bourgogne, Xth cent.), in olden times; in the days of yore. **2.** *s.f.* (*a*) *Cost:* bertha (collar); (*b*) flat band of false hair; (*c*) (dairy-man's) milk-can.

berthollétie [bɛrtɔleti], *s.f. Bot:* Bertholletia; brazil-nut tree.

berthon [bɛrtɔ̃], *s.m. Nau:* **(canot)b.,** berthon boat, collapsible dinghy; foldboat, faltboat.

bertillonnage [bɛrtijɔnaʒ], *s.m.* bertillonnage, the Bertillon system of anthropometry.

Bertrand [bɛrtrɑ̃]. **1.** *Pr.n.m.* Bertram, Bertrand. *Lit:* **B. et Raton,** the schemer and the cat's-paw (from La Fontaine's fable *Le Singe et le Chat*). **2.** *s.m. A: F:* rogue, pickpocket's accomplice and victim (from the character in Antier's melodrama *L'Auberge des Adrets*).

béryl [beril], *s.m. Miner:* beryl; **b. noble,** aquamarine.

beryllium [beriljɔm], *s.m. Ch:* beryllium, glucin(i)um.

béryllonite [berijɔnit], *s.f. Miner:* beryllonite.

béryx [beriks], *s.m. Ich:* beryx; *F:* coral fish.

berzélianite [bɛrzeljanit], *s.f. Miner:* berzelianite.

berzélite [bɛrzelit], *s.f. Miner:* berzelite.

besace [bəzas], *s.f. A:* double sack, double bag (closed at both ends, with opening in the centre, carried over the shoulder by beggars and mendicant monks); scrip; **porter la b.,** to beg, to be very poor; **mettre, réduire, qn à la b.,** to reduce s.o. to beggary, to poverty; *s.a.* APPAREIL 4.

besacier, -ière [bəzasje, -jɛr], *a. & s.* (person) who carries a *besace*; beggar, tramp.

besaigre [bəzɛːgr], *a. & s.m. A:* **(vin) b.,** sour, tart, wine; (*of wine*) **tourner au b.,** to sour, to turn sour; **son caractère tourne au b.,** he is becoming soured.

besaiguë [bəzegy], *s.f. Tls:* **1.** mortising axe, twibill. **2.** glazier's hammer.

besant [bəzɑ̃], *s.m. Num: Arch: Her:* besant, bezant; *Num:* **b. d'argent,** white bezant.

besas [bəzɑːs], *s.m.* ambsace, double ace (at backgammon, etc.).

bésef [bezɛf], *adv. P:* = BÉZEF.

beset [bəzɛ], *s.m.,* **besetet** [bəzətɛ], *s.m.,* **beseton** [bəzətɔ̃], *s.m.* = BESAS.

bésau [bezo], *s.m. Dial:* (*in Provence*) irrigation ditch.

besicles [bəzikl̩], *s.f.pl.* **1.** *F:* spectacles. **2.** *Surg: Tchn:* goggles.

bésigue [bezig], *s.m. Cards:* bezique.

besoche [bəzɔʃ], *s.f.* spade (for planting trees).

besogne [bəzɔɲ], *s.f.* work; task, job, piece of work; **se mettre en, à la, b.,** to set to work; **mourir à la b.,** to die in harness; **une grosse, une rude, b.,** a hard task or job; a stiff piece of work; **il a une rude b. à faire,** he has his work cut out (for him); *F:* **tailler de la b. à qn,** to make work for s.o.; **aller vite en b.,** to despatch work quickly, to act quickly, *F:* to be a bit of a hustler; **abattre de la b.,** to get through a lot of work, a lot of business; **pousser la b.,** (i) to put one's best foot forward; (ii) to urge on the work; **aimer la b. faite,** to dislike work, to be work-shy; **vous n'avez pas b. faite,** you're not at the end of your troubles, of your difficulties; **en voilà une belle b.! voilà de la belle b.!** here's a pretty kettle of fish!

besogner [bəzɔɲe]. **1.** *v.i.* to work hard, to slave. **2.** *v.tr.* **b. mal tout ce qu'on fait,** to work badly, to do everything badly.

besogneux, -euse [bəzɔɲø, -øːz], *a. & s.* necessitous, needy, impecunious; *F:* hard up (person); **un petit employé b.,** a poor, scruffy little clerk.

besoin [bəzwɛ̃], *s.m.* want, need. **1.** necessity, requirement; urge (to do sth.); craving (for sth.); (*a*) **pourvoir aux besoins de qn,** to provide for s.o.'s wants; **les besoins en professeurs,** the need for teachers; **faire connaître ses besoins,** to make one's requirements known; **je le ferais si le b. s'en faisait sentir,** I should do it if the necessity arose; **pour le b. de la cause,** for the sake of the cause; *F:* **faire ses (petits) besoins,** to relieve oneself, *F:* to spend a penny; **être pris d'un b. pressant,** to be taken short; *adv.phr.* **au b., en cas de b.,** in case of need, of emergency, of necessity; if necessary; when required, *F:* at a pinch; *s.m.inv. Com:* **un au b.,** a surety (for bill, etc.); (*b*) **avoir b. de qch.,** to need, require, want, sth.; **avoir b. de qn,** to need, want, s.o.; **j'ai grand b. de son aide,** I am, I stand, in great need of, I badly want, his assistance; **je n'ai aucun b. de son aide,** I have no need, no occasion, for his help; **je n'ai plus b. de vos services,** I have no further use for your services; **il n'a pas b. de**

venir lundi, he need not come, there is no need, no necessity, for him to come, on Monday; **j'ai b. que vous me disiez toute la vérité,** I want you to tell me, I must know, the whole truth; **je n'avais pas b. qu'on me le rappelât,** I did not need to be reminded of it; **aujourd'hui nous avons b. de lui,** today we cannot spare him; **vous aviez bien b. d'aller lui parler de cela!** you *would* go and tell him about that! (*c*) *impers.* **il n'est pas b.,** there is no need; **est-il b.?** is there any necessity? **il n'est pas, n'y a pas, b. de vous dire, que je vous dise, combien je vous suis reconnaissant,** I need hardly tell you how grateful I am; **point n'est b. d'insister,** no need to insist; **s'il (en) est b., si b. (en) est,** if need(s) be; (*d*) *A:* **faire b. à qn,** to be necessary to s.o. **2.** poverty, indigence; **être dans le b.,** to be in want, in straitened circumstances; **vieillards dans le b.,** needy old people; **cela vous mettra à l'abri du b.,** that will keep the wolf from your door; *Prov:* **c'est dans le b. que l'on connaît les vrais amis, au b. on connaît l'ami,** a friend in need is a friend indeed.

Bessarabie [bɛsarabi], *Pr.n.f.* Bessarabia.

bessemer [bɛsmɛr], *s.m. Metall:* **(convertisseur) b.,** Bessemer converter.

bessemérisation [bɛsmerizasjɔ̃], *s.f. Metall:* bessemerizing.

bessin, -ine [bɛsɛ̃, -in], *a. & s. Geog.* (native, inhabitant) of the Bessin region of Normandy.

besson, -onne [bɛsɔ̃, -ɔn], *a. & s. Dial:* (*used by sheep farmers*) twin.

bessonnière [bɛsɔnjɛːr], *a.f. & s.f. Husb:* (ewe) which has dropped twin lambs.

bestiaire [bɛstjɛːr], *s.m.* **1.** *Rom.Ant:* bestiarius, bestiary, beast-fighter. **2.** *Lit.Hist:* bestiary, book of beasts.

bestial, -aux[1] [bɛstjal, -o], *a.* (*a*) bestial, beastly, brutish; (*b*) theroid (idiot).

bestialement [bɛstjalmɑ̃], *adv.* bestially, brutishly, brutally.

bestialiser [bɛstjalize], *v.tr.* to bestialize, brutify. **se bestialiser,** to become bestial, brutish.

bestialité [bɛstjalite], *s.f.* bestiality.

bestiaux[2] [bɛstjo], *s.m.pl.* cattle, beasts, livestock; **cinquante b.,** fifty head of cattle; **parc à bestiaux,** stock-yard.

bestiole [bɛstjɔl], *s.f.*, **bestion** [bɛstjɔ̃], *s.m.* small, tiny, beast, insect; *Scot:* beastie; *A: & F:* **bestioles,** small deer.

best-seller [bɛstsɛlœːr, -sɛlɛːr], *s.m.* best-seller; *pl. best-sellers.*

beta [beta], *s.f. Bot:* beta.

bêta[1], **-asse** [bɛta, -as], *s. F:* stupid, blockhead, numskull, *P:* nit; *a.* **elle est jolie mais bêtasse,** she is pretty but rather silly, *F:* she's a dumb blonde.

bêta[2] [bɛta], *s.m.* **1.** *Gr.Alph:* beta. **2.** *Atom.Ph:* **particule b.,** beta particle; **rayons b.,** beta rays.

bêtafite [betafit], *s.f. Miner:* betafite.

bétail [betaːj], *s.m.* **1.** *Coll.* no *pl.* cattle, live-stock, grazing stock; **gros b.,** cattle (including horses, asses, mules); heavy beasts; **menu b.,** smaller live-stock; light beasts. **2.** *Occ.* **élever des bétails,** to breed (different breeds of) cattle.

bétaillère [betajɛːr], *s.f.* cattle-float.

bétaïne [betain], *s.f. Ch:* betain(e).

bêtathérapie [bɛtaterapi], *s.f.* beta ray therapy.

bêtatron [bɛtatrɔ̃], *s.m. Atom.Ph:* betatron.

Betchouana(land) [bɛtʃwana(lɑ̃ːd)], *Hist:* **1.** *Pr.n.m.* Bechuanaland. **2.** *s.m.* **les Betchouanas,** the Bechuanas.

bête [bɛt], *s.f.* **1.** beast, animal; dumb creature; (*a*) **b. à quatre pieds,** four-footed beast; **b. à cornes,** (i) horned beast; (ii) *F:* two-pronged fork; **b. à laine,** sheep; **b. brute,** brute beast; **b. de trait,** draught-animal; *F:* **c'est une mauvaise b., une fine b.,** he is a spiteful fellow, a shrewd fellow; **mourir comme une b.,** to die (i) like a beast; (ii) without the sacraments, *F:* **reprendre du poil de la b.,** (i) to take a hair of the dog that bit one; (ii) to perk up; *F:* **b. à concours,** examination fiend; **remonter sur sa b.,** to get on one's legs again, to recover one's health, one's position; *Prov:* **morte la b., mort le venin,** dead men tell no tales; *s.a.* NOIR 1, SOMME[1]; (*b*) **petites bêtes,** (i) insects, vermin; (ii) *Fish:* fresh-water shrimps; (iii) *A: & F:* small deer; *F:* **chercher la petite b.,** to be over-critical; **b. à bon Dieu,** (i) ladybird, (ii) *F:* harmless individual; **b. à feu,** glow-worm; **b. de la mort,** churchyard beetle; (*c*) *Ich: F:* **b. à sept trous,** river lamprey; (*d*) *Ven:* quarry; (*e*) *Cards:* **b. hombrée,** loo. **2.** *F:* (*a*) fool, idiot, *P:* nit(wit); **faire la b.,** (i) to affect stupidity; (ii) to act like a fool; **c'est une bonne b., une b. du bon Dieu,** he's a good-natured ass; (*b*) *a.* stupid, foolish, unintelligent; **il est plus b. que méchant,** he's more of a fool than a knave; **que je suis b.!** how silly, stupid, of me! **pas si b.!** I am not such a fool (as all that)! not if I know it! not likely! **il n'est pas si b. qu'il en a l'air,** he's not such a fool as he looks; **c'est b. comme chou, à en pleurer,** (i) it's simplicity itself; (ii) it's idiotic; **il est b. comme un pot, comme un panier, b. comme tout, b. à manger du foin, à couper au couteau, comme un âne, comme ses pieds, à en pleurer,** he has nothing between his ears, he's a real idiot, he's wood from the neck up, as stupid as an owl, a downright fool; **sourire b.,** idiotic smile; **rire b.,** haw-haw; **pourquoi as-tu fait ce b. de voyage?** why did you go on that stupid, senseless, journey? **ses bêtes d'idées,** his silly, idiotic, ideas.

bétel [betɛl], *s.m. Bot:* betel.

Bételgeuse [betɛlgøːz], *Pr.n. Astr:* Betelgeuse.

bêtement [bɛtmɑ̃], *adv.* stupidly, like a fool; **sourire b.,** to smile idiotically; **rire b.,** to give a stupid laugh; **tout b.,** purely and simply.

Béthanie [betani], *Pr.n.f. B.Hist:* Bethany.

Bethléem [betleɛm], *Pr.n.m. B.Hist:* Bethlehem.

Bethsabée [bɛtsabe], *Pr.n.f. B.Hist:* Bathsheba.

béthunois, -oise [betynwa, -waːz], *a. & s. Geog:* (native, inhabitant) of Béthune.

bêtifier [betifje]. **1.** *v.tr. F:* (*pr.sub. & p.d.* **n. bêtifiions, v. bêtifiiez**) to stupefy, dull; to make (s.o.) stupid. **2.** *v.i.* (*a*) to talk stupidly; (*b*) to play the fool.

bétille [betij], *s.f. Tex:* betille.

Bétique [betik]. **1.** *Pr.n.f. A.Geog:* Baetica. **2.** *a. Geog:* **la chaîne b.,** the Betic Cordillera.

bêtise [betiːz], *s.f.* **1.** stupidity, folly, silliness; **être d'une b. extrême,** to be exceedingly stupid. **2.** nonsense, absurdity; **dire des bêtises,** to talk nonsense; **quelle b.!** what nonsense! *P:* what bosh! **faire des bêtises,** to play the fool. **3.** blunder, foolish action, error of judgment; piece of stupidity; **faire une grande b.,** to make a bad blunder; to act foolishly. **4.** trifle; **dépenser tout son argent en bêtises,** to fritter away one's money; **cinq mille francs, une b.!** five thousand francs, a mere trifle! a mere nothing! **5. bêtises de Cambrai** = mint humbugs.

bêtiser [betize], *v.i.* to talk stupidly.

bêtisier [betizje], *s.m.* collection of howlers.

bétoine [betwan], *s.f. Bot:* betony; **b. d'eau,** water betony; **b. des montagnards, des Vosges,** arnica.

bétoire [betwaːr], *s.m.* **1.** *Geol:* (small) swallow (-hole), sink-hole; (limestone) cavern. **2.** *Dial:* pond.

bétol [betɔl], *s.m. Ch:* naphthol salicylate.

béton [betɔ̃], *s.m.* **1.** *Const:* **b. (de ciment),** concrete, beton; **b. armé,** ferro-concrete, reinforced concrete; **bloc en b.,** concrete block. **2.** *Fb:* **faire le b.,** to pack the defence.

betonica [betɔnika], *s.f. Bot:* Betonica.

bétonnage [betɔnaːʒ], *s.m. Const:* concreting, concrete work.

bétonner [betɔne], *v.tr.* **1.** to concrete; to construct (building, etc.) with concrete; **b. une paroi,** to face a wall with concrete. **2.** *Fb:* to form a "bolt" defence, to pack the defence.

bétonneur [betɔnœːr], *s.m. Fb:* forward who packs the defence.

bétonneuse [betɔnøːz], *s.f.* concrete spreader; *F:* concrete-mixer.

bétonnière [betɔnjɛːr], *s.f.* concrete-mixer, cement-mixer.

bétoure [betur], *s.f. Dial:* = BÉTOIRE 2.

bette[1] [bɛt], *s.f. Nau:* lighter barge; **b. à escarbilles,** ash-boat.

bette[2], *s.f. Bot:* beet; **b. poirée,** white beet; **b. à couper,** perpetual spinach, spinach-beet; *Cu:* **b. à carde (blanche), b. à côtes,** sea-kale beet, Swiss chard.

betterave [bɛtraːv], *s.f. Bot:* beet(root); **b., sucrière, à sucre,** sugar-beet; **b. fourragère,** fodder beet; **b. longue,** tap-rooted beet; **b. ronde,** turnip-rooted beet.

betteraverie [bɛtravri], *s.f.* sugar-beet factory.

betteravier, -ière [bɛtravje, -jɛːr]. **1.** *a.* **l'industrie betteravière,** the beet industry. **2.** *s.* (*a*) worker in a beet-sugar factory; (*b*) grower of beet.

bétula [betyla], *s.f. Bot:* Betula.

bétulacées [betylase], *s.f.pl. Bot:* Betulaceae.

bétulaie [betylɛ], *s.f.* birch forest.

bétuline [betylin], *s.f. Ch:* betulin(ol).

bétyle [betil], *s.m. Archeol:* baetyl, baetulus.

beudantine [bødɑ̃tin], *s.f.*, **beudantite** [bødɑ̃tit], *s.f. Miner:* beudantine, beudantite.

beuglant [bøglɑ̃], *s.m. P:* low-class music-hall.

beugle [bœgl], *s.f.* = BURE.

beuglement [bøgləmɑ̃], *s.m.* **1.** lowing (of cattle); bellowing (of bull); *F:* (*of pers.*) bawling. **2.** bellow.

beugler [bøgle], *v.i.* (*of cattle*) to low; (*of a bull*) to bellow; *F:* (*of pers.*) to bawl; *v.tr.* **b. une chanson,** to bawl, bellow out, a song.

beuh [bœ], *int.* ugh!

beurre [bœːr], *s.m.* **1.** butter; **b. frais, salé,** fresh butter, salt butter; **b. fondu,** melted, run, butter; **b. clarifié,** clarified butter; *Cu:* **au b.,** with melted butter, cooked in butter; **b. d'anchois,** anchovy butter; **au b. noir,** with browned butter sauce; *P:* **avoir un œil au b. noir,** to have a black eye; **rond de b.,** pat of butter; **pot à b.,** butter-jar; **pot de b.,** jar of butter; *a.inv.* **des gants b. (frais),** butter-colour gloves; *F:* **comme dans du b.,** with the greatest ease; **nous sommes entrés dedans comme dans du beurre,** it, they, offered no resistance; *F:* **c'est un (vrai) beurre,** (i) it is very easy to do; *F:* it's a soft job; (ii) it's first-rate, first-class, the goods; **compter pour du b.,** (i) (*of small child playing with older ones*) to be allowed to play without being penalized according to the rules of the game; (ii) to count for nothing; *F:* **il a fait son b.,** he has feathered his nest; **ça fait mon b.,** that's the very thing (I wanted), that just suits my book; *F:* **assiette au b.,** cushy job, soft job, *U.S:* pork barrel, gravy train; **tenir l'assiette au b.,** (i) to have one's hand in the till; (ii) to have a nice fat job in the Government; **ça mettra du b. dans les épinards,** that will make our life more comfortable, will ease the situation; **les belles paroles ne mettent pas de b. dans les épinards,** fine words, fair words, butter no parsnips; **promettre plus de b. que de pain,** to be lavish of promises; **maintenant ils peuvent mettre du b. sur leur pain,** now they are better off; **avoir les mains en b.,** to be butter-fingered; *s.a.* FERMIER, LAITIER. **2. b. de Galam,** Galam butter, shea-butter. **3.** *Miner:* **b. de montagne,** stone-butter; **b. des tourbières,** bog-butter.

beurré[1] [bœre], *s.m. Hort:* butter-pear, beurré.

beurré[2], *a. P:* **être b.,** to be canned.

beurrée [bœre], *s.f.* slice of bread and butter.

beurre-œufs-fromage [bœːrøfrɔmaːʒ], *s.m. O: P:* spiv, black marketeer.

beurrer [bœre], *v.tr.* to butter, add butter to; **b. des tartines,** to cut slices of bread and butter; *F:* **savoir de quel côté son pain est beurré,** to know on which side one's bread is buttered.

beurrerie [bœrri], *s.f.* **1.** butter-dairy, butter-room, butter-factory. **2.** butter industry.

beurret [bœrɛ], *s.m. O:* butter pat; butter sample.

beurrier, -ière [bœrje, -jɛːr]. **1.** *a.* **l'industrie beurrière,** the butter industry; **région beurrière,** butter-producing district. **2.** *A: s.* butter-man, -woman; butter-dealer; dairy-man, -maid. **3.** *s.m.* butter-dish; **b. rafraîchisseur,** butter-cooler. **4.** *s.f.* **beurrière;** (*a*) *Husb:* (i) butter-tub; (ii) churn; (*b*) *Tex:* butter-muslin, cheese-cloth.

beurtia(t) [bœrtja], *s.m. Min:* winze, blind gallery.

beuveau, -eaux [bøvo], *s.m.* = BIVEAU.

beuverie [bøvri], *s.f.* drinking; *F:* carouse, drinking bout, drinking session.

bévatron [bevatrɔ̃], *s.m. Atom.Ph:* bevatron.

béveau, -eaux [bevo], *s.m.* = BIVEAU.

béverage [bevəraːʒ], *s.m. W.Tel:* wave antenna, beverage antenna.

bévue [bevy], *s.f.* blunder, mistake, slip; *F:* bloomer; **commettre une b.,** to make a blunder, to blunder.

bey [bɛ], *s.m.* bey.

beylical, -aux [belikal, -o], *a.* beylical.

beylicat [belika], *s.m.*, **beylik** [belik], *s.m.* beylic.

beylisme [belism, bɛ-], *s.m.* attitude of a Stendhalian hero.

Beyrouth [berut], *Pr.n. Geog:* Beirut.

bézef [bezɛf], *adv. P:* much; **il n'y en a pas b.,** there's not much of it.

bezel [bəzɛl], *s.m. Jewel:* bezel (of gem).

bezet [bəzɛ], *s.m.* = BESAS.

bézoard [bezɔaːr], *s.m.* bezoar.

bharal [baral], *s.m. Z:* bharal.

Bhoutan (le) [ləbutɑ̃], *Pr.n. Geog:* Bhutan.

bi [bi], *s.m. F: A:* (= BICYCLE); **(grand) bi,** penny-farthing.

bi(s)- [bi(z)], *pref.* (*a*) bi(s)-; **biocellé,** biocellate; **bilobé,** bilobate; **bisalterne,** bisalternate; (*b*) *Ch:* bi-, di-; **biacétyle,** biacetyl; **bicalcique,** dicalcic; (*c*) **bimoteur,** twin-engine(d).

biacide [biasid], *a. Ch:* biacid, diacid.

biacromial, -aux [biakromjal, -o], *a. Anat:* biacromial.

biacuminé [biakymine], *a. Bot:* biacuminate, double-pointed.

Biafra [biafra, bja-], *Pr.n.m. Geog:* Biafra.

biafrais, -aise [biafrɛ, -ɛːz, bja-], *a. & s.* (native, inhabitant) of Biafra, Biafran.

biais, -aise [bjɛ, -ɛːz]. **1.** *a.* oblique, sloping, slanting, bevelled; **voûte biaise,** skew(ed) arch. **2.** *s.m.* (*a*) skew (of tool, of arch); slant (of wall); slanting, obliquity; bias (of bowl); **le b., l'angle du b., d'un pont,** the angle of skew of a bridge; **il y a du b. dans ce bâtiment,** that building is out of the straight; **en b.,** on the slant, slantwise, obliquely, on the skew; aslant, askew; **tailler un tissu en b., de b.,** to cut material (on the) bias, on the cross; **regarder qn de b.,** to look sideways, askance, at s.o.; **marcher de b.,** to walk crabwise; (*b*) indirect manner or means; expedient; **aborder de b. une personne, une question,** to approach a person, a question, in a roundabout way, indirectly; **prendre l'affaire du bon b., du mauvais b.,** to go about it the right, the wrong way; **chercher un b. pour faire qch.,** to look for a roundabout way of doing sth.; (*c*) **par plus d'un b.,** in more ways than one. **3.** *s.m. Dressm:* (*a*) false tuck; band cut on the cross (for trimming); (*b*) **b. de corsage,** bias front seam, dart, on a bodice.

biaisement [bjɛzmɑ̃], *s.m.* **1.** (*a*) skewing, sloping; (*b*) oblique motion. **2.** shift, evasion, shirking.

biaiser [bjeze], *v.i.* **1.** to skew, slant; to be on the slant; to lean over. **2.** to use shifts, evasions; to shuffle.

biarrot, -ote [bjaro, -ɔt], *a. & s. Geog:* (native, inhabitant) of Biarritz.

biathlon [biatlɔ̃], *s.m.Sp:* biathlon.

biatomique [biatɔmik], *a. O: Ch:* diatomic.

biauriculaire [biɔrikylɛːr], *a.* biauricular, binauricular, biaural, binaural; *s.a.* STÉTHOSCOPE.

biaxe [biaks], *a. Cryst:* biaxal, biaxiate, biaxial.

bibace [bibas], *s.f.* = BIBASSE.

bibacier [bibasje], *s.m.* = BIBASSIER.

bibasique [bibɑzik, -ba-], *a. Ch:* bibasic, dibasic.

bibasse [bibas], *s.f. Bot:* loquat, Japanese medlar.

bibassier [bibasje], *s.m. Bot:* loquat, Japanese medlar.

bibelot [biblo], *s.m.* **1.** curio, knick-knack, trinket. **2.** *pl.* odds and ends, sundries, belongings.

bibelotage [biblɔtaːʒ], *s.m.* curio-hunting, -collecting; **faire du bibelotage** = BIBELOTER 1.

bibeloter [biblɔte]. **1.** *v.i. F:* (*a*) (i) to collect curios; (ii) to deal in curios; (*b*) to do odd, trifling, small jobs; to potter. **2.** *v.tr.* **je ne sais ce qu'ils bibelotent,** I don't know what they are fiddling around like that for.

bibeloteur, -euse [biblɔtœːr, -øːz], *s.* curio-hunter, -collector.

bibelotier, -ière [biblɔtje, -jɛːr], *s.* **1.** *A:* dealer in knick-knacks. **2.** = BIBELOTEUR.

biberon¹, -onne [bibrɔ̃, -ɔn], *F:* **1.** *a.* tippling, boozing. **2.** *s.* tippler, boozer, soak.

biberon², *s.m.* (*a*) *Med:* feeding-cup; (*b*) (feeding-) bottle (for infants); **nourrir, élever, un enfant au b.,** to bring up a child by hand, on the bottle; **nourri au b.,** bottle-fed; *F:* **service b.,** baby-sitting; *F:* **tu les prends au b.!** cradle-snatcher! baby snatcher! **je ne les prends pas au b.,** I don't go in for cradle-snatching.

biberonner [bibrɔne], *v.i. F:* to soak, to booze, to tipple.

bibi [bibi], *s.m.* **1.** *F:* **mon b.,** my darling, my pet (*esp. to children*). **2.** *P:* I, me, myself, *F:* yours truly; **ça c'est pour b.,** that's for myself, for number one. **3.** *F:* (woman's) hat. **4.** *Fish:* sipunculid (worm for bait).

bibiche [bibiʃ], *s.f. P:* (*term of affection addressed to a woman*) ducky.

bibine [bibin], *s.f. P:* **1.** low tavern, pub. **2.** tasteless drink, slops; swipes.

bibion [bibjɔ̃], *s.m. Ent:* bibio.

bibionidés [bibjɔnide], *s.m.pl. Ent:* Bibionidae; the March flies.

bibite [bibit], *s.f. Fr.C: P:* bug, insect.

Bible [bibl̩], *s.f.* **la B.,** the Bible; **une B.,** a Bible; **il a fait de ce dictionnaire sa b.,** this dictionary is his bible; *s.a.* JURER 1.

biblio- [bibliɔ], *pref.* biblio-; **bibliolâtre,** bibliolater; **bibliophage,** bibliophagous.

bibliobus [bibliɔbys], *s.m.* mobile library, library van; *U.S:* = bookmobile.

bibliographe [bibliɔgraf], *s.m. & f.* bibliographer.

bibliographie [bibliɔgrafi], *s.f.* **1.** bibliography; **b. sommaire,** short bibliography. **2.** book column (of periodical), list of recent publications.

bibliographique [bibliɔgrafik], *a.* bibliographical.

bibliolâtre [bibliɔlɑːtr]. **1.** *a.* bibliolatrous. **2.** *s.* bibliolater.

bibliologie [bibliɔlɔʒi], *s.f.* bibliology.

bibliologique [bibliɔlɔʒik], *a.* bibliological.

bibliomancie [bibliɔmɑ̃si], *s.f.* bibliomancy.

bibliomane [bibliɔman], *a. & s.m. & f.* bibliomaniac, book collector.

bibliomaniaque [bibliɔmanjak], *a.* bibliomaniac(al).

bibliomanie [bibliɔmani], *s.f.* bibliomania, book collecting.

bibliophage [bibliɔfaːʒ], *a.* bibliophagous.

bibliophile [bibliɔfil], *s.m. & f.* bibliophile, bibliophilist, book-lover; *attrib.* **édition b.,** collector's edition.

bibliophilie [bibliɔfili], *s.f.* love of books, bibliophily, bibliophilism.

bibliotechnie [bibliɔtɛkni], *s.f.* (*technique of*) book-production, book making.

bibliothécaire [bibliɔtekɛːr], *s.m. & f.* (*a*) librarian; (*b*) *Rail:* bookstall attendant.

bibliothèque [bibliɔtɛk], *s.f.* **1.** (*a*) library (building); (*b*) library (room), reading-room; (*c*) **b. de prêt, de location de livres,** lending library; **b. circulante,** circulating library; (*d*) *Rail:* bookstall. **2.** book-case, book-stand; **b. d'appui,** dwarf book-case; **b. tournante,** revolving book-case. **3.** library, collection of books; *F:* **c'est une b. ambulante, vivante,** he is a walking encyclopaedia. **4.** series (of children's books, etc.); *s.a.* BLEU 1.

biblique [biblik], *a.* biblical; **société b.,** Bible Society.

bibliste [biblist], *s.* biblist; biblical scholar.

biblorhapte [biblɔrapt], *s.m.* loose-leaf binder, office-binder; *a.* **grand-livre b.,** loose-leaf ledger.

bibus [bibys], *s.m. O:* trifle.

bica [bika], *s.m. Sch: P:* = BICARRÉ 2.

bicâble [bikɑːbl̩], *s.m. Min: Civ.E:* bi-cable.

bicaméral, -aux [bikameral, -o], *a. Pol:* bicameral, double-chamber (system, etc.).

bicaméralisme [bikameralism], **bicamérisme** [bikamerism], *s.m. Pol:* bicameralism, bicameral system.

bicapsulaire [bikapsylɛːr], *a. Bot:* bicapsular.

bicarbonate [bikarbɔnat], *s.m. Ch:* bicarbonate.

bicarbonaté [bikarbɔnate], *a. Pharm:* **eau bicarbonatée,** (*solution of*) bicarbonate of soda.

bicarboné [bikarbɔne], *a. A.Ch:* **hydrogène b.,** (bi)carburetted hydrogen.

bicarré [bikɑre]. **1.** *a. Mth:* biquadratic. **2.** *s.m. Sch: F:* fourth-year student in a class preparing for the *grandes écoles* or in a *grande école.*

bicentenaire [bisɑ̃tnɛːr], *s.m.* bicentenary; *U.S:* bicentennial.

bicéphale [bisefal]. **1.** *a.* bicephalous, double-, two-, headed. **2.** *s.m.* bicephalous animal.

biceps [bisɛps], *a. & s.m. Anat:* biceps (muscle); *F:* **avoir du, des, biceps,** to be strong in the arm, to be muscular.

Bicêtre [bisɛtr̩], *Pr.n.m.* village near Paris, known especially for its mental hospital; hence *F:* **c'est un échappé de B.,** he's mad, he's an absolute lunatic; *cf.* CHARENTON.

biche [biʃ], *s.f.* **1.** *Z:* hind, doe; *a.inv.* **ventre de biche,** reddish-white; **table à pieds de biche,** table with cabriole legs; **aux yeux de b.,** doe-eyed. **2.** (*a*) *F:* (*term of endearment*) **ma biche,** my darling, dear; (*b*) *A:* mistress, kept woman. **3.** *Ent:* female stag-beetle.

biche-cochon [biʃkɔʃɔ̃], *s.f. Z: F:* duiker, bush-buck.

biche-de-mer [biʃdəmɛːr], *s.f.* = BÊCHE-DE-MER¹ *pl. biches-de-mer.*

bicher [biʃe], *v.i.* **1.** *F:* (*used only in third pers.*) **ça biche?** how goes it? **ça biche, les affaires?** how's business? **ça biche entre eux,** they hit it off well, they are getting very friendly, very thick (with one another). **2.** *P:* to be delighted; **ça me fait b.,** that does me good.

bicherie [biʃri], *s.f. A:* **la haute bicherie,** the higher prostitution.

bichet [biʃɛ], *s.m. A.Meas:* **1.** measure for wheat [varying from approx. ½ bushel to one bushel]. **2.** land-measure [approx. one acre].

bichette [biʃɛt], *s.f.* **1.** *Z:* young hind, small hind. **2.** *F:* = BICHE 2 (*a*). **3.** *Fish:* shrimping net. **4.** *A.Meas:* (*a*) (*for wheat*) half of bichet; (*b*) (*for land*) approx. one-sixth of *bichet.*

bichir [biʃir], *s.m. Ich:* bichir.

bichlamar [biʃlamaːr], *s.m.* = BÊCHE-DE-MER 2.

bichlorure [biklɔryːr], *s.m. Ch:* bichloride, dichloride.

bicho [biʃo], *s.m.* = BÊCHE DE-MER 1.

bichof [biʃɔf], *s.m.* mulled wine, bishop.

bichon, -onne [biʃɔ̃, -ɔn], *s.* **1.** Maltese dog, lapdog. **2.** *F:* darling, little dear; *P:* ducky. **3.** *s.m.* (velvet) pad (for brushing silk hats).

bichonner [biʃɔne], *v.tr.* **1.** to curl, frizz (hair). **2.** to make (s.o.) spruce, smart; to titivate (s.o.); to doll (s.o.) up. **3.** to pet (s.o.). **4.** to brush (hat).

se bichonner, to smarten, spruce, doll, oneself up; to titivate.

bichromate [bikrɔmat], *s.m. Ch:* bichromate, dichromate.

bichromaté [bikrɔmate], *a. Phot:* **gomme bichromatée,** gum dichromate.

bichromie [bikrɔmi], *s.f. Typ:* two-colour printing.

Bickford [bikfɔrd], *s.m.* **(cordeau) B.,** Bickford fuse, Bickford match.

bicolore [bikɔlɔːr], *a.* bicoloured, of two colours; *Typewr:* **ruban b.,** two-colour ribbon.

biconcave [bikɔ̃kaːv], *a.* biconcave, double-concave.

biconique [bikɔnik], *a.* biconical.

biconjugué [bikɔ̃ʒyge], *a. Bot:* biconjugate.

biconvexe [bikɔ̃vɛks], *a.* biconvex, double-convex.

bicoq, bicocq [bikɔk], *s.m. Techn:* = PIED-DE-CHÈVRE.

bicoque [bikɔk], *s.f. F:* poky little house; shanty; **nous avons une b. à la campagne,** we have a little place in the country.

bicorne [bikɔrn]. **1.** *a.* (*a*) *Nat.Hist: Anat:* bicornuate, bicornate, bicornuous; (*b*) two-pointed (hat). **2.** *s.m.* two-pointed hat, bicorne.

bicot [biko], *s.m.* **1.** *Z:* kid. **2.** *P: Pej.* Arab, wog.

bicoudé [bikude], *a.* doubly bent, having two bends; *Mch:* cranked.

biculturalisme [bikyltyralism], *s.m.* bicultural tradition, etc.

bicuspidé [bikyspide], *a.* bicuspid, bicuspidate.

bicycle [bisikl̩], *s.m.* **1.** *A:* velocipede; *F:* penny-farthing. **2.** *pl. Adm:* bicycles (in general).

bicyclette [bisiklet], *s.f.* bicycle, cycle; **b. de route,** roadster, **b. de course,** racer; **b. à moteur,** motorized bicycle; **b. à moteur auxiliaire,** motor-assisted bicycle, bicycle with motor attachment; **je sais aller en b.,** I can ride a bicycle; **aller à b. chez le boucher,** to cycle to the butcher's; **faire de la b.,** to cycle (as a sport).

bicycliste [bisiklist], *s.m. & f. A:* cyclist.

bidard [bidaːr], *s.m. A: P:* lucky fellow (at games, at gambling, from the name of the winner of the first prize at the State lottery of 1878).

bidasse [bidas], *s.m. P: Mil:* private; *U.S:* G.I.

bide [bid], *s.m.* **1.** *P:* belly; *cf.* BIDON. **2.** *F: esp. Th:* **faire un b.,** to be a flop.

bident¹, bidens [bidɑ̃], *s.m. Bot:* bidens; **bident à calice feuillé,** water-hemp.

bident², *s.m.* (two-pronged) (i) pitch-fork; (ii) carving-fork.

bidenté [bidɑ̃te], *a. Anat: Bot:* bidentate, double-toothed.

bidet [bidɛ], *s.m.* **1.** pony, nag, small horse; *O: F:* **pousser son bidet,** to do well in one's business, to forge ahead. **2.** *Hyg:* **bidet (de toilette),** bidet. **3.** *Carp: etc:* (*a*) sawing-horse, trestle; (*b*) (ungeared) lathe.

bidoche [bidɔʃ], *s.f. P:* meat (*esp. of inferior quality*).

bidon [bidɔ̃]. **1.** *s.m.* (*a*) can, drum (for oil, etc.); **b. à lait,** milk-churn; *Aut:* **b. à essence,** petrol-tin, -can; **b. d'essence, d'huile,** tin of petrol, of oil; **b. de secours,** spare tin; *P:* **se remplir le bidon,** to fill one's belly; (*b*) *Mil:* water-bottle, canteen; (*c*) *Nau:* (wooden) grog-tub; (*d*) *P:* **c'est du b.,** it's a load of rubbish, cod's wallop; *P:* **c'est pas du b.,** it's gospel truth. **2.** *a. P:* false, fake, phoney.

bidonnant [bidɔnɑ̃], *a. P:* comical, screamingly funny; **c'est b.,** it's a scream.

bidonner (se) [səbidɔne], *P:* to laugh one's head off, to split one's sides.

bidonville [bidɔ̃vil], *s.m.* shantytown, suburbs built out of old tin cans and boxes.

bidule [bidyl], *s.m. P:* thing, gadget; gimmick; (*pers.*) thingammy; someone or other; **quel b.!** what a (queer) type!

biebérite [biberit], *s.f. Miner:* red vitriol, bieberite.

bief [bjɛf], *s.m. Hyd.E:* **1.** (canal) reach, level; **b. d'amont,** head-bay; **b. d'aval, de fuite,** tail-bay, aft-bay. **2.** mill-course, -race; *Scot:* -lade. **3.** *Geol:* **b. à silex,** clay with flints.

Biélides [bjelid], *s.f.pl. Astr:* Bielids, Andromedes.

bielle [bjɛl], *s.f.* **1.** (*a*) (tie-)rod; (*in compression*) push-rod; crankarm; *I.C.E:* **b. de soupape,** valve push-rod; *Aut:* **b. d'accouplement (des roues avant),** track-link; **b. de commande de direction,** drag-link; (*b*) *Mch:* **b. articulée sur un maneton,** connecting-rod taking its bearing on a crank-pin; **tête de bielle;** *Mch:* crank-head; *I.C.E:* big end; **pied de bielle,** *Mch:* crosshead; *I.C.E:* small end; **b. à fourche, fourchue,** forked connecting-rod; **b. à talon,** slipper connecting-rod; **b. à rotule,** spherical head rod; **b. de commande,** push

and pull rod, control rod; *Av:* control rod; **b. de poussée,** thrust rod; **b. motrice, principale, directrice, maîtresse,** main (connecting-)rod; driving-rod; **système b.-manivelle,** crank-connecting rod system; **b. de va-et-vient,** push-pull rod; **b. d'interdiction de commande de gaz,** throttle override rod; *s.a.* COULER 1, RENVERSÉ 1. **2.** *Const:* strut, brace (of iron roof); *Av: etc:* **b. de triangulation,** bracing truss. **3.** *Civ.E:* rocker-bar (of steel bridge).

biellette [bjɛlɛt], *s.f. Mec.E:* **1.** small rod; *Av:* **b. double,** fork rod. **2.** link.

biélorusse [bjelorys]. **1.** *a. & s.* Byelorussian, Bielorussian, Belorussian, White Russian. **2.** *s.m. Ling:* Belorussian.

Biélorussie [bjelorysi], *Pr.n.f. Geog:* Byelorussia, Bielorussia, Belorussia.

bien [bjɛ̃]. I. *adv.* **1.** well; **livre b. écrit,** well-written book; **homme b. bâti,** well-built man; **femme b. faite,** woman with a good figure; **b. reçu,** duly received; **b. balayé,** swept clean; **manteau b. doublé,** well-lined coat; **tout lui va, sied, b.,** everything suits him, he wears everything well; **il danse b.,** he dances well, is a good dancer; **il parle b.,** he is a good speaker; **homme b. né,** man of gentle birth, of good family; **une âme b. née,** a noble soul; **être b. vu de ses chefs,** to be well thought of by one's superiors, to be in good standing with one's superiors; **b. se rappeler,** to remember exactly, clearly, well; **écoutez b. ceci,** now, listen to this; **agir b.,** to act rightly; **se conduire b.,** to behave (well); **il travaille aussi b. que vous,** he works as well as you (do); **il faut b. les soigner, les soigner b.,** they must be well looked after; **il faut b. faire les choses,** we must do things in style, properly; **pour b. faire,** by right(s), to have everything as it should be; **vous avez b. fait,** you did right, acted rightly; **vous auriez b. fait de ne pas y aller,** you might just as well not have gone; **vous faites b. d'être sur vos gardes,** you do well, are right, to be on your guard; **vous feriez aussi b. de prendre votre parapluie,** you might as well, had better, take your umbrella; **c'est b. fait, b. mérité,** it serves you, him, etc., right; **ceux-là feront très b. l'affaire,** those will do very nicely; **aller, se porter, b.,** to be well, in good health; **ma montre va b.,** (i) my watch goes well, keeps good time; (ii) my watch is right; **tout va b.,** all's well, *F:* everything is O.K.; **tout se passe b.,** everything is going well, everything is turning out right; **tout est b. qui finit b.,** all's well that ends well; *Iron:* **voilà qui commence b.,** that's a fine start! **l'affaire a b. tourné,** it turned out all right; **bien!** (i) good! (ii) that's enough! that will do! (iii) all right! **très b.! fort b.!** very good! well done! (*in speech*) hear, hear! *Nau:* aye, aye! **vous arrivez joliment b.,** you have come opportunely, just in the nick of time. **2.** (*predicatively with* **être**) (*a*) right, proper; **c'est b.!** all right! **comme c'est b. à vous d'être venu!** how nice of you to come! **c'est b. à eux de l'avoir secouru,** they did a good deed in helping him; **ce n'est pas b. de vous moquer de lui,** it's not kind of you to make fun of him; **ce n'est pas b. de sa part,** it's too bad of him; **voilà qui est b.,** that's nicely done, said; (*b*) comfortable; **êtes-vous b. dans ce fauteuil?** are you comfortable in that arm-chair? **il est b. partout où il se trouve,** he is happy, feels at home, wherever he may be; **vous ne savez pas quand vous êtes b.,** you don't know when you are well off; *F:* **vous voilà b.!** now you're in a fine fix, in a fine pickle! **on est très b. à cet hôtel,** they do you very well at this hotel; (*c*) (*of health*) **je ne me sens pas très b.,** I don't feel very well; *F:* **je me sens rudement b.,** I feel marvellous; **se trouver b. de qch.,** to derive benefit from sth.; **se trouver b. d'avoir fait qch.,** to be the better for doing sth.; (*d*) on good terms; **être b. avec qn,** to be on good terms with s.o.; **être b. auprès de ses chefs,** to be well in with one's superiors; **être b. en cour,** to have friends at court; (*e*) of good appearance, position, quality, etc.; **elle est b. de figure,** she has a nice face, is good-looking; **il est très b., fort b.,** he is very gentlemanly; **il est b. de sa personne,** he is a personable man; **elle est b. de sa personne,** (i) she is attractive; (ii) she looks well-bred, like a lady; **ce sont des gens très b.,** (i) they are very respectable people; (ii) they are people of a good social position; (iii) they are people it's a pleasure to meet; **tu es très b. dans cette robe-là,** you look very nice in that dress; **suis-je b. ainsi?** do I look all right? **donnez-moi quelque chose de b.,** give me something good, of good quality. **3.** (*emphatic*) (*a*) indeed, really, quite; **c'est b. cela,** that's right; **il y a b. deux ans que je ne l'ai vue,** it is fully, at least, two years since I saw her; **cela vaut b. mille francs,** (i) it is well worth a thousand francs; (ii) it is worth at least a thousand francs; **je l'ai regardé b. en face,** I looked him full in the face; **être b. d'accord,** to agree entirely, thoroughly, to be entirely, thoroughly, in agreement; **nous sommes b. d'accord là-dessus,** we are quite agreed on that; **b. à vous,** yours (sincerely); **je veux b. le croire,** I can quite believe it, him; **croyez-vous b. cela?** do you really believe that? **croyez b. que nous ne pouvons pas faire autrement,** you must understand that we can't do anything else, you will appreciate that we cannot do otherwise; **est-ce b. vous?** is it really you? it *is* you, is it? **qu'est-ce que ça peut b. être?** what ever can it be? **voilà b. les femmes!** that's just like a woman! **cela est b. de lui,** it's just like him; **j'ai oublié!—c'est b. de vous (d'avoir oublié)!** I quite forgot!—you would (forget)! *F:* **c'est b. de lui!** trust him (to say, do, that)! *F:* **c'est b. à moi, ça?** you're sure that's mine? **est-ce b. le train pour Paris?** is this the right train for Paris? **je l'avais b. dit!** didn't I say so? **j'espère b. qu'il viendra,** I do hope he will come; **remarquez b. qu'il a réussi son examen,** he passed his exam, mind you; **je sais b. que vous avez des ennuis,** I am well aware of your difficulties; **on voit b. que vous ne payez pas l'électricité,** it's easy to see that you don't pay the electricity bill; **nous arriverons b. à le convaincre,** we shall convince him yet; **voulez-vous b. vous taire!** (i) what a thing to say! (ii) will you hold your tongue! **il est b. entendu que . . .,** it is quite understood that . . .; **b. entendu,** of course; **je m'en doutais b.,** I thought as much; **de quoi vous mêlez-vous? je peux b. m'amuser si cela me plaît!** why are you butting in? surely I can enjoy myself if I like! **il est b. venu, mais j'étais occupé,** he did come, but I was busy; **je ne veux pas que tu fasses cela.—mais vous le faites b., vous!** I don't want you to do that.—Well, *you* do it, don't you? *Iron:* **c'est b. le moment de parler comme ça!** a fine time to, what a time to, speak like that! **c'est b. à vous à dire cela!** you're a fine one to say that! listen who's talking! that comes very well from you! (*b*) (= TRÈS) very; **b. malheureux,** very unhappy; **vous venez b. tard,** you are very late (in) coming; **il est b. mal,** he is in a very bad way; **b. loin de, que,** far from; **b. loin d'en demeurer d'accord,** far from being in agreement (about it); **b. loin qu'il vous serve, il vous nuit,** far from helping you he does you harm; **c'est b. simple,** it is quite, very, simple; **b. avancé pour son âge,** very advanced for his, her, age; **des résultats b. autres,** very different results; (*c*) (= BEAUCOUP) much, many, a great deal, a great many; (i) **b. moins, b. plus,** much more, much less; a lot more, a lot less; **j'ai b. souffert,** I have suffered, been through, a great deal; **j'ai b. envie de lui écrire,** I have a good mind to write to him; **ce qui est b. pis,** which is much worse, far worse, a good deal worse; **les temps ont b. changé,** times have changed a lot, have certainly changed; **il s'en faut b.,** far from it; (ii) (*with partitive article*) **j'ai eu b. de la peine, b. du mal, à la convaincre,** I (have) had a great deal of, much, trouble in convincing her; **je l'ai vu b. des fois,** I have seen him many times, many a time, scores of times; **b. des hommes,** many men; **b. des choses,** many things; *F:* lots of things, heaps of things; **b. d'autres,** many others; *F:* lots of others; **il en a vu b. d'autres,** he has seen worse in his time; (*d*) **il faut b. continuer à vivre,** one still has to go on living; **j'y suis b. obligé,** I just have to. **4.** *adv. phr.* (*a*) **aussi b.,** in any case, after all, anyway, when all's said and done; **aussi b. votre frère aurait-il pu vous avertir,** indeed your brother might have warned you; (*b*) **bel et b.,** *see* BEAU I. 3; (*c*) **tant b. que mal,** somehow (or other), after a fashion; **je l'ai fait tant b. que mal, et plutôt mal que b.,** I did it after a fashion and not a very good fashion at that! **je m'en suis acquitté tant b. que mal,** I muddled through; (*d*) **b. plus,** moreover, besides, furthermore; **il m'offrit la place; b. plus il m'avança de l'argent,** he offered me the post; he went even further and advanced me some money, he even went as far as advancing me some money; (*e*) *Iron:* **un peu b.,** somewhat; **elle est un peu b. mûre,** she's on the ripe side. **5.** *conj.phr.* (*a*) **aussi b. que** (=AINSI QUE), as well as, besides; **Dieu jugera les bons aussi b. que les méchants,** God will judge both the righteous and the wicked; (*b*) **b. que,** though, although; (i) (*with sub.*) **je le respecte, b. qu'il ne me soit pas sympathique,** I respect him though I don't like him; (ii) (*occ. with ind.*) **il faudra rester auprès d'elle, b. que vous n'aurez rien à faire,** you will have to stay by her, although there will be nothing for you to do; (*c*) **si b. que** +*ind.*, so that, and so, with the result that; **il ne reparut plus, si b. qu'on le crut mort,** he failed to reappear, so that, and so, he was thought dead; (*d*) **ou b.,** or else, otherwise. **6.** *int.* **eh b.!** well! **eh b. donc!** well then! **eh b. ça alors!** well, I'm blowed! **ses titres? eh b. oui! parlons-en,** his titles, what a joke!

bien, II. *s.m.* **1.** good; (*a*) **la science du b. et du mal,** the knowledge of good and evil; **l'idée du b.,** the notion of good; **la pratique du b.,** well-doing; **faire le b.,** to engage in good works, to do good; **trouver son plaisir à faire le b.,** to find pleasure in well-doing, in doing good; **homme de b.,** good, upright, man; **imputer qch. à b.,** to put sth. down to good intentions; **quel b. attendre d'un pareil régime?** what good can one expect from such a régime? **le b. de la patrie, le b. public,** the public weal, the commonweal; **c'est pour votre b.,** it is for your own good; **je l'ai fait pour votre b.,** I did it for your benefit; **cela me fit beaucoup de b.,** it was very beneficial to me, it did me a lot of good; **grand b. vous fasse!** much good may it do you! **vouloir du b. à qn, vouloir le b. de qn,** to wish s.o. well; **une personne qui vous veut du b.,** your well-wisher; **tout le monde dit du b., parle en b., de lui,** everyone gives him a good character, speaks well of him; **que ce soit un b. ou un mal, nous avons . . .** for good or ill we have . . .; **c'est peut-être un b. pour un mal,** it is perhaps a blessing in disguise; **b. lui a pris de,** he did well to; (*b*) **ils sont du dernier b.,** they are on most intimate terms, on a most friendly footing; *F:* as thick as thieves. **2.** (*a*) possession, property, assets, wealth, goods (and chattels); **les biens du ciel,** heavenly possessions; **les biens de ce monde, temporels, de la terre,** earthly possessions; **il a du b., de grands biens,** he is well-to-do, wealthy; **réclamer, reprendre son b.,** to claim, take back, one's own; **prendre son b. où on le trouve,** not to be too particular where you get your material from; **manger son b.,** to run through one's property, one's possessions; **nul b. sans peine,** no rose without a thorn; *F:* **avoir du b. au soleil,** to own land, to be a man of property; (*b*) *Jur:* **biens meubles, mobiliers,** personal property, personal estate, personalty, chattels, movables; **biens immeubles, immobiliers,** real estate; **biens fonciers,** landed property; **biens propres** (husband's, wife's) separate property; **biens communs, de communauté,** communal estate, joint estate of husband and wife; *U.S:* community property; **biens de famille insaisissables,** homestead immune from attachment; **biens corporels,** tangible property; **biens incorporels,** intangible property; **biens dotaux,** dowry; **biens successoraux,** hereditaments; **biens de main-morte,** property in mortmain; **confiscation de biens,** confiscation, seizure, of real property; **biens vacants,** ownerless property, derelict; *Pol.Ec:* **biens de consommation,** consumer('s) goods; **biens de production,** producer's goods, capital goods; **biens d'équipement, permanents,** durable goods, hard goods. **3.** (*a*) **prendre qch. en b.,** to take sth. in good part; **il y a ce matin un changement en b.,** there is a change for the better this morning; (*b*) **mener une affaire à b.,** to bring a matter to a successful issue, to a satisfactory conclusion; to bring off a piece of business; **mener à b. une mission,** to carry out a mission; (*c*) **il a agi en tout b. (et) tout honneur,** he acted with the best and most honourable intentions.

bien-aimé, -ée [bjɛ̃nɛme, bjɛn-], *a. & s.* beloved, darling, favourite, well-beloved; *Hist:* **(Louis) le Bien-Aimé,** Louis XV; *pl. bien-aimé(e)s.*

bien-dire [bjɛ̃diːr], *s.m.* no *pl.*; elegance of speech, fine words, eloquence; *A:* **être, se mettre, sur son b.-d.,** to speak carefully, to pick one's words carefully.

bien-disant [bjɛ̃dizɑ̃], *a. & s. A:* eloquent, well-spoken (person); *pl. bien-disant(e)s.*

bien-être [bjɛ̃nɛtr̥, bjɛn-], *s.m.* no *pl.*; (*a*) well-being, comfort; **sentiment de b.-ê.,** feeling of well-being, of comfort; **chambre qui donne une impression de b.-ê.,** room that gives an impression of snugness; (*b*) welfare (of population, etc.); (*c*) **jouir d'un b.-ê. suffisant,** to be reasonably well-off, comfortably off.

bien-faire [bjɛ̃fɛːr], *s.m.* well-doing.

bienfaisance [bjɛ̃fəzɑ̃ːs], *s.f.* beneficence, benevolence, charity; **bureau de b.,** charitable board, relief committee; **société de b.,** benevolence society; **bal de b.,** charity ball; *Jur:* **contrat de b.,** charitable contract (securing to s.o. a gratuitous benefit).

bienfaisant [bjɛ̃fəzɑ̃], *a.* **1.** beneficent, benevolent, charitable, kindly; bountiful. **2.** beneficial, salutary (remedy, etc.); grateful (warmth).

bienfait [bjɛ̃fɛ], *s.m.* **1.** benefit, kindness, service, good turn. **2.** gift, blessing, boon, mercy; **un b. du ciel,** a godsend; **b. insoupçonné,** blessing in disguise.

bienfaiteur, -trice [bjɛ̃fetœːr, -tris], *s.* benefactor, benefactress; **un b. des pauvres,** a friend of the poor; *a.* **divinité bienfaitrice,** beneficent deity.

bien-fondé [bjɛ̃fɔ̃de], *s.m.* no *pl.*; *Jur:* cogency, justice, merits, validity (of case, claim); **prouver, établir, le b.-f. de sa réclamation,** to substantiate, make good, one's claims; **maintenir le b.-f. de son jugement,** to stick to one's verdict; **le b.-f. d'une opinion,** the reasonableness of an opinion.

bien-fonds [bjɛ̃fɔ̃], *s.m.* real estate, landed property; *pl.* *biens-fonds.*

bienheureux, -euse [bjɛ̃nœrø, bjɛ̃nørø, -øːz], *a.* **1.** blissful, happy. **2.** *Ecc:* blessed; **b. sont les miséricordieux,** blessed are the merciful; **le b. Urbain II,** the blessed Urban II; *s.* **les bienheureux,** the blessed, the blest; *Myth:* **les îles des Bienheureux,** the Islands of the Blest; *F:* **avoir l'air d'un b.,** to look blissfully happy.

bien-jugé [bjɛ̃ʒyʒe], *s.m.* no *pl.*; *Jur:* just and lawful decision, sentence, or verdict.

biennal, -aux [bien(n)al, -o]. **1.** *a.* biennial, two-yearly. **2.** *s.f.* **biennale,** biennial festival, etc.; **la b. de Venise,** the Venice Biennale.

bien-pensant, -e [bjɛ̃pɑ̃sɑ̃(t)], *a.* & *s.* *usu. Pej:* **1.** *a.* (*a*) right-minded, right-thinking; (*b*) self-righteous. **2.** *s.* right-minded person.

bien-portant, -e [bjɛ̃pɔrtɑ̃(t)], *a.* & *s.* (*person*) in good health.

bienséance [bjɛ̃seɑ̃ːs], *s.f.* **1.** propriety, decency, seemliness; **observer les bienséances,** to observe the proprieties; **manquer aux bienséances,** to fail in good breeding; *A:* **il est de la b. de (faire qch.),** it is seemly to (do sth.); *O:* **laisser un morceau par b.,** *F:* to leave a piece for manners. **2.** *A:* **cela est à ma b.,** that suits me.

bienséant [bjɛ̃seɑ̃], *a.* seemly, decorous, proper; **il est b. aux jeunes gens de respecter la vieillesse,** it is right and proper for young people to respect old age.

bientôt [bjɛ̃to], *adv.* (very) soon, before long; **à b.!** good-bye, see you again soon! *F:* so long! **il eut b. fait de dresser une échelle,** he was not long in putting up a ladder; **on a b. fait de céder à la tentation,** it is only too easy to yield to temptation; **c'est b. dit!** it is easier said than done! **b. après,** soon, after(wards) shortly after(wards).

bien-trouvé [bjɛ̃truve], *s.m.* no *pl.* **1.** *Lit:* felicity (of a phrase, etc.). **2.** *Bank:* interest on bank deposit.

bienveillamment [bjɛ̃vɛjamɑ̃], *adv.* kindly, benignantly.

bienveillance [bjɛ̃vɛjɑ̃ːs], *s.f.* **1.** benevolence; kindness (**envers, pour,** to); good-will; benignancy; **faire qch. par b.,** to do sth. out of kindness; **parler avec b. de qn,** to speak favourably of s.o.; *s.a.* CULTIVER 3. **2.** *pl. Eng.Hist:* benevolences.

bienveillant [bjɛ̃vɛjɑ̃], *a.* kind, kindly, benevolent (**envers, pour,** to); **examinateur b.,** kindly-disposed, benignant, lenient, examiner.

bienvenir [bjɛ̃vniːr], *v.i.* used only in **se faire b. de qn,** to ingratiate oneself with s.o.

bienvenu, -e [bjɛ̃vny], *a.* & *s.* welcome; **soyez le b., la b.!** welcome! **vos lettres sont toujours les bien-venues,** your letters are always welcome, always acceptable; **l'horaire prévoit une nuit entière d'arrêt, qui est assez b.,** the time-table allows for a whole night's rest which is rather welcome; *s.a.* VENIR I. 1.

bienvenue [bjɛ̃vny], *s.f.* welcome; **souhaiter la b. à qn, exprimer des veux de b. à qn,** to welcome s.o., to bid s.o. welcome, to address a warm welcome to s.o.; **quelques mots de b.,** a few words of welcome; *A:* **payer sa b.,** to pay one's footing.

bière[1] [bjɛːr], *s.f.* beer; **b. blanche, blonde,** light ale, pale ale; **b. brune,** brown ale; **b. piquante, b. amère,** bitter beer; *F:* bitter; **petite b.,** small beer; *F:* **ce n'est pas de la petite b.,** (i) he's a big shot; (ii) it's not to be sneezed at; **ne pas se prendre pour de la petite b.,** to think no small beer of oneself.

bière[2], *s.f.* coffin; **mettre un corps en b.,** to coffin a body; **mise en b.,** coffining.

Biermer [birmɛːr], *Pr.n. Med:* **maladie de B.,** Biermer's anaemia, pernicious anaemia.

bièvre [bjɛːvr], *s.m.* **1.** *A:* beaver. **2.** *Orn:* **harle b.,** goosander; *U.S:* American merganser.

biez [bje], *s.m.* = BIEF.

biface [bifas], *s.m. Prehist:* biface.

bifère [bifɛːr], *a. Hort:* remontant (rose, etc.).

biffage [bifaːʒ], *s.m.* crossing-out, striking-out, erasure (of word).

biffe[1] [bif], *s.f.* **1.** cancelling stamp. **2.** cancelling mark (made by stamp).

biffe[2], *s.f. P:* infantry.

biffement [bifmɑ̃], *s.m.* = BIFFAGE.

biffer [bife], *v.tr.* to cross out, strike out, put a stroke through, cancel (word, etc.); *Jur:* to strike (action) off the roll.

biffeton [biftɔ̃], *s.m. P:* **1.** (*railway, theatre*) ticket. **2.** letter.

biffin [bifɛ̃], *s.m.* **1.** *P:* ragman, rag-picker. **2.** *P:* infantryman, foot-slogger.

biffure [bifyːr], *s.f.* erasure, cancelling stroke; *Jur:* striking off the roll (of an action to be heard).

bifide [bifid], *a. Nat.Hist:* bifid, bifidate(d).

bifilaire [bifilɛːr], *a.* bifilar (suspension); two-wire (system); *W.Tel:* **antenne b.,** two-wire aerial.

biflèche [biflɛʃ], *s.m. Mil:* double trail, bipod.

biflore [biflɔːr], *a. Bot:* biflorous, biflorate.

bifocal, -aux [bifɔkal, -o], *a.* bifocal (lens, etc.).

bifolié [bifɔlje], *a. Bot:* bifoliate.

bifoliolé [bifɔljɔle], *a. Bot:* bifoliolate.

biforme [bifɔrm], *a.* biform.

bifrons [bifrɔ̃s], *a.* & *s.m. Arch:* two-faced (statue); **Janus b.,** Janus bifrons.

bifteck [biftɛk], *s.m.* **1.** beefsteak; *F:* **faire du b.,** to become sore with riding, to get saddle-sore, to lose leather; *P:* **gagner son b.,** to earn one's living; **défendre son b.,** (i) to look after one's own bread and butter; (ii) to guard one's own domain; **la lutte, la course, au b.,** the rat-race. **2. b. de veau, de cheval, d'ours,** veal steak, horse steak, bear steak.

bifurcation [bifyrkasjɔ̃], *s.f.* bifurcation, fork, branching (of road, tree-trunk, etc.); road fork; *El:* shunt, branch(ing) (of a current); *Rail:* **(gare de) b.,** branching station, junction; *Sch:* **b. des études,** streaming.

bifurqué [bifyrke], *a. Nat.Hist:* bifurcate; *I.C.E:* **échappement b.,** divided exhaust.

bifurquer [bifyrke], *v.tr.* & *i.* to fork, bifurcate, divide; to branch off; *El:* **b. un courant,** to shunt, branch off, a current; **la route bifurque à Noyon,** the road forks at Noyon; **b. sur Lausanne,** to turn off towards Lausanne; **b. vers la politique,** to go into politics, to take up a political career.

se bifurquer, *O:* to fork, divide, bifurcate; **c'est ici que la route se bifurque,** the road forks here.

bigaille [bigɑːj], *s.f. F:* (*in tropics*) winged insect pest.

bigame [bigam]. **1.** *a.* bigamous. **2.** *s.* bigamist.

bigamie [bigami], *s.f.* bigamy.

bigarade [bigarad], *s.f.* bitter orange, Seville orange.

bigaradier [bigaradje], *s.m.* Seville orange-tree, bitter orange-tree.

bigarré [bigare], *a.* variegated, mottled, streaked, parti-coloured, motley; **foule bigarrée,** motley crowd.

bigarreau, -eaux [bigaro], *s.m.* whiteheart cherry, bigaroon, bigarreau (cherry).

bigarreautier [bigarotje], *s.m.* bigaroon (cherry-tree).

bigarrer [bigare], *v.tr.* to variegate, mottle; to make a medley, a motley, of (sth.); **robe bigarrée de rouge,** dress slashed with red.

bigarrure [bigaryːr], *s.f.* (*a*) medley, mixture (of colours); (*b*) slash (of colour); (*c*) *Bot:* mosaic (disease).

bigaut [bigo], *s.m.* = BIGOT[2].

bige [biːʒ], *s.m. Rom.Ant:* biga.

bigéminé [biʒemine], *a.* **1.** *Bot:* bigeminate. **2.** *Anat: Med:* bigeminal (organ, pulse, etc.).

bigéminisme [biʒeminism], *s.m. Med:* bigeminy.

bighorn [bigɔrn], *s.m. Z:* bighorn (sheep).

bigle, *A:* **-esse** [bigl, -ɛs], *a.* & *s.* squint-eyed; *F:* cock-eyed (person).

bigler [bigle]. **1.** *v.i.* to squint. **2.** *v.tr. P:* (*a*) to squint (at); (*b*) to have a squint at sth.

bigleton [biglətɔ̃], *s.m. Cards:* doubleton.

bigleux, -euse [biglø, -øːz], *a.* & *s.* **1.** *P:* = BIGLE-, -ESSE. **2.** *P:* short-sighted.

bignone [biɲɔn], *s.f.*, **bignonia** [biɲɔnja], *s.m. Bot:* bignonia.

bignoniacées [biɲɔnjase], *s.f.pl. Bot:* Bignoniaceae.

bigophone [bigɔfɔn], *s.m.* **1.** toy musical instrument with vibrating paper membrane. **2.** *F:* telephone; *P:* blower.

bigornage [bigɔrnaːʒ], *s.m.* shaping (sth.) on a *bigorne.*

bigorne [bigɔrn], *s.f.* **1.** two-beaked anvil, two-horned anvil; beak-iron, stake; *Metalw:* **b. de pliage,** creasing stake. **2.** beak, horn (of anvil).

bigorneau, -eaux [bigɔrno], *s.m.* **1.** *Metalw:* small beak-iron, small anvil. **2.** *Moll:* periwinkle; *F:* winkle; **b. noir,** common periwinkle; **petit b.,** small periwinkle; **b. rugueux,** rough periwinkle; **b. jaune,** dwarf periwinkle. **3.** *F:* telephone. **4.** *Navy: F:* naval gunner.

bigorner [bigɔrne], *v.tr.* **1.** *Metalw:* to work, shape, round, (sth.) on a beak-iron. **2.** *P:* to bash; to damage.

se bigorner, *P:* to fight.

bigornette [bigɔrnɛt], *s.f. P:* cocaine; *P:* snow.

bigot[1], **-ote** [bigo, -ɔt]. **1.** *a.* (over-)devout; *F:* churchy; priest-ridden (country). **2.** *s.* zealous church-goer, religious bigot; **une vieille bigote,** a narrow-minded, sanctimonious, old woman; *F:* an old "church hen."

bigot[2], *s.m. Tls:* mattock.

bigot[3], *s.m. Nau:* rib (of parrel).

bigoterie [bigɔtri], *s.f.* **1.** religious bigotry; *F:* churchiness. **2. se livrer à un tas de bigoteries,** to be always bowing and scraping before the altar. **3. la b. de la ville,** all the bigots in the town, place.

bigotisme [bigɔtism], *s.m.* bigoted outlook; bigotry.

bigouden [bigudɛn]. **1.** *s.m.* woman's head-dress worn in the region of Pont-l'Abbé (Brittany). **2.** *s.f.* woman wearing this head-dress.

bigoudène [bigudɛn], *s.f.* = BIGOUDEN 2.

bigoudi [bigudi], *s.m.* hair-curler; roller.

bigre [bigr], *int. F:* (mild form of BOUGRE) **bigre! qu'il fait froid!** my God, it is cold!

bigrement [bigrəmɑ̃], *adv. F:* (mild form of BOUGREMENT) **vous avez b. raison!** you are dead right! **il fait b. froid,** it is awfully cold; **c'est b. embêtant!** it's a blessed nuisance!

bigrille [bigriːj], *a. W.Tel:* **lampe b.,** double-grid valve.

biguanide [bigwanid], *s.f. Ch:* biguanide.

bigue [big], *s.f.* **1.** (*a*) hoisting-gin, sheers; (*b*) *pl.* sheer-legs. **2.** *Nau:* mast-crane, jumbo derrick, heavy lift derrick.

biguine [bigin], *s.f. Danc:* beguine.

bihebdomadaire [biɛbdɔmadɛːr], *a.* appearing, happening, twice a week; twice-weekly; bi-weekly.

bihoreau, -eaux [biɔro], *s.m. Orn:* **(Héron) bihoreau,** night heron.

bihydrate [biidrat], *s.m. Ch:* double hydrate.

bijon [biʒɔ̃], *s.m. Pharm:* pine-resin.

bijou, -oux [biʒu], *s.m.* piece of jewel(le)ry; jewel, gem; **coffret à bijoux,** jewel-case; **quel b. d'enfant!** what a gem of a child! *F:* **mon b.!** my precious! my pet!

bijouterie [biʒutri], *s.f.* **1.** jeweller's trade, business, or shop. **2.** jewel(le)ry, jewels; **b. fine,** fine jewellery; **b. fausse,** imitation jewellery; paste.

bijoutier, -ière [biʒutje, -jɛːr], *s.* jeweller.

bijugué [biʒyge], *a. Bot:* bijugate.

bijumeau, -eaux [biʒymo], *a. Anat:* **muscles bijumeaux,** biceps muscles.

bikini [bikini], *s.m. Cost:* bikini.

bilabiale [bilabjal], *a.f.* & *s.f. Ling:* bilabial (consonant).

bilabié [bilabje], *a. Bot:* bilabiate.

bilame [bilam], *s.f.* bimetallic strip; *Av:* thermal switch.

bilan [bilɑ̃], *s.m.* **1.** (*a*) *Fin:* balance-sheet; **faire un b.,** to draw up a balance-sheet; **dresser le b.,** to strike the balance; **dresser le b. de ses pertes,** to reckon up one's losses; **le b. hebdomadaire,** the weekly bank return; (*b*) evaluation; **b. d'une opération militaire,** results of an operation (with regard to achievement and losses); **faire le b. de la situation,** to take stock of the situation; (*c*) **faire le b. de santé de qn,** to give s.o. a complete (medical) check-up; *Surg:* **b. préopératoire,** preoperative assessment (of patient's condition). **2.** *Fin:* schedule (of assets and liabilities); **déposer son b.,** to file one's petition (in bankruptcy). **3.** (*a*) *Fin:* balance (of an account); (*b*) balance; total amount; *Physiol:* **b. nutritif,** nutritional balance.

bilatéral, -aux [bilateral, -o], *a.* **1.** bilateral, two-sided (paralysis, contract, etc.); **symétrie bilatérale,** bilateral symmetry. **2.** *Telecom:* **téléphone b.,** sending and receiving telephone; **communication bilatérale,** two-way communication.

bilatéralement [bilateralmɑ̃], *adv.* bilaterally.

bilbaude [bilboːd], *s.f.* = BILLEBAUDE.

bilbauder [bilbode], *v.i.* = BILLEBAUDER.

bilboquet [bilbɔkɛ], *s.m.* **1.** *Toys:* (*a*) cup-and-ball; (*b*) tumbler (weighted figure). **2.** *Typ:* (piece of) job work. **3.** *Geol:* ball joint. **4.** *Const:* rubblestone.

bildstein [bildʃtain], *s.m. Miner:* agalmatolite, figure-stone, pagodite.

bile [bil], *s.f.* 1. bile, gall; *F: O:* **b. répandue,** jaundice. 2. bad temper; **allumer, remuer, la b. de, à, qn,** to rouse s.o.'s anger, to rile s.o.; **s'échauffer la b.,** to worry, fret, get excited, angry; *F:* **ne te fais pas de b.!** don't worry! **à force de se faire de la b. il se donna la fièvre,** he fretted himself into a fever; **épancher sa b. contre qn,** to rail at s.o.; **épanchement de b.,** (i) *Med:* bilious attack; (ii) fit of bad temper.

biler (se) [səbile], *v.pr. F:* to get worked up, all hot and bothered; **ne te bile pas!** (i) easy does it! (ii) don't worry!

bileux, -euse [bilø, -øːz], *a. F:* given to worrying, easily upset; **il n'est pas b.,** he's a cool one; **quel b.!** what a worryguts!

bilharzia [bilarzia], *s.f.,* **bilharzie** [bilarzi], *s.f., Ann:* bilharzia.

bilharzieux, -euse [bilarziø, -øz], *a. & s. Med:* bilharziosis (patient).

bilharziose [bilarzioz], *s.f. Med:* bilharziosis.

biliaire [biljɛːr], *a. Anat:* biliary; **conduits biliaires,** bile vessels; **acides biliaires,** bile acids; *Med:* **calcul b.,** biliary calculus, gallstone; **cirrhose b.,** cirrhosis (of the liver).

bilieux, -ieuse [biljø, -jøːz], *a. & s.* 1. bilious (person). 2. (*a*) choleric, irascible, cross, testy (person); (*b*) morose (person).

biligénèse [biliʒenɛːz], *s.f.* **biligénie** [biliʒeni], *s.f. Physiol:* biligenesis, bilification.

biligénique [biliʒenik], *a. Physiol:* **fonction b.,** biligenesis, bilification.

bilimbi [bilɛ̃bi], *s.m. Bot:* bilimbi.

bilinéaire [bilineɛːr], *a. Mth:* bilinear.

bilingue [bilɛ̃ːg], *a.* bilingual, diglot.

bilinguisme [bilɛ̃gɥism], *s.m.* bilingualism.

bilinite [bilinit], *s.f. Miner:* bilinite.

bilirubine [bilirybin], *s.f. Physiol:* bilirubin.

bilirubinémie [bilirybinemi], *s.f. Med:* bilirubinaemia.

bilitère [bilitɛːr], *a.* biliteral.

biliverdine [biliverdin], *s.f. Physiol:* biliverdin.

bill [bil], *s.m. Pol:* bill.

billage [bijaːʒ], *s.m. Metalw:* ball testing (for hardness).

billard [bijaːr], *s.m.* 1. (*a*) (game of) billiards; **jouer une partie de b. en cinquante points,** to play fifty up at billiards; (*b*) **billard Nicolas,** puff billiards; **b. russe,** bar billiards; **b. électrique,** pinball; **billard chinois,** pin-table. 2. (*a*) billiard-table; *P:* **dévisser son billard,** to die; *P:* to peg out; *F:* **c'est du b.,** it's all plain sailing; it's a pushover; *P:* **c'est pas du b.,** it takes a lot of doing, it's no pushover; **cette route est un véritable b.,** this road is smooth as a bowling-green; (*b*) *F:* operating-table; **monter, passer, sur le billard,** to undergo an operation. 3. (*a*) billiard-room; (*b*) billiard-saloon. 4. *A:* cue (with curved head).

billarder [bijarde], *v.i.* **bœuf dont les cornes billardent,** ox whose horns arch away; *cf.* BILLARD 4.

bille[1] [biːj], *s.f.* (small) ball. 1. *F:* (*a*) billiard-ball; **faire une bille,** to pocket a ball; (*b*) *F:* (i) head; *F:* nut; **il a une b. de billard,** he's as bald as a coot; (ii) face; *F:* mug; **il a une bonne b.,** he looks pleasant enough. 2. marble, taw, alley; *F:* **être à billes égales,** to be level, even (with one another). 3. *Mec.E:* ball; **roulement à, sur, billes, coussinet(s) à billes,** ball bearing(s); **essai de dureté à la b.,** ball test for hardness; **b. d'arrêt,** ball-check; *Hyd.E:* **b. clapet, clapet à b.,** ball-valve; *Toil:* **flacon (à) b.,** roll-on (bottle); **stylo (à) b.,** ball-point (pen).

bille[2], *s.f.* 1. (saw-)log, billet (of timber); *Rail:* sleeper. 2. rack-stick. 3. steel ingot. 4. *Cu:* rolling pin.

billebarrer [bijbɑre], *v.tr. O: F:* to streak, stripe, (sth.) with gaudy, glaring colours.

billebaude [bijboːd], *s.f. A:* confusion, disorder; **chasser à la b.,** to pot away at anything that offers; *Mil: A:* **tir à la b.,** individual fire.

billebauder [bijbode], *v.i. Ven: A:* (*of hounds*) to lose the scent, to cast about.

biller[1] [bije], *v.tr.* 1. to strain (on sth.) with a stick; **b. un ballot,** to bind, strain, a pack; **b. une peau,** to wring a skin. 2. *Cu:* to roll out (paste).

biller[2], *v.tr. Mec.E:* to ball-test (metal); **b. une barre d'acier,** to put a bar through the ball test.

billet [bije], *s.m.* 1. note, short letter; **b. doux,** love-letter. 2. notice, invitation-card, circular; **b. de faire part,** notice announcing a family event (birth, marriage, death); **faire courir le b.,** to send round a notice or circular; to circularize people; *s.a.* AVERTISSEMENT 1. 3. ticket; *Rail: etc:* **b. simple, b. d'aller,** single ticket; **b. de retour, d'aller et retour,** return ticket; **b. d'abonnement,** season ticket; **b. de correspondance,** transfer ticket; **b. de déclassement,** excess ticket; **b. de quai,** platform ticket; **b. circulaire,** tourist ticket; **b. direct,** through ticket; **prendre un b. direct pour Paris,** to book through to Paris; (*in lottery*) **tirer un b. blanc,** to draw a blank; **b. d'entrée,** admission ticket or card; *Th: etc:* **b. de faveur,** complimentary ticket, free ticket; *F:* **prendre un b. de parterre,** to fall flat on one's face; *s.a.* ARRÊT 1. 4. *Com: Fin: Jur:* (*a*) note, promissory note, bill; **b. simple,** note of hand, promissory note; *F:* I.O.U.; *F:* **je vous donne, fiche, mon b. que,** you take my word for it that, I'll swear that; *P:* **je te fous mon b. que (c'est vrai),** I'll bet you (it bloody well is true); **b. au porteur,** bill payable to bearer; **b. à vue,** bill payable at sight, sight-bill; **b. à présentation,** bill payable on demand; **b. du Trésor,** Treasury-bill; *s.a.* CIRCULAIRE 1, ORDRE 5, VOLONTÉ 1; (*b*) **b. de banque,** banknote; *U.S:* bank-bill; **billets émis à l'intérieur du pays,** home currency issues; (*c*) *F:* ten-franc note. 5. **b. de santé,** certificate, bill, of health; *Navy:* **b. d'hôpital,** sick voucher; (*in hospital*) **b. d'entrée,** admission order; **b. de sortie,** order of discharge. 6. permit, permission; *Sch: etc:* **b. de sortie,** pass, exeat. 7. **b. de vote,** voting paper. 8. *Mil:* **b. de logement,** billeting order.

billeté [bij(ə)te], *a. Her:* billety.

billeter [bij(ə)te], *v.tr.* (**je billette, n. billetons; je billetterai**) 1. *O:* to ticket, label. 2. *A: Mil:* to allot billets to, to billet (soldiers).

billette[1] [bijɛt], *s.f.* 1. *Adm:* custom-house receipt. 2. *A: Com:* ticket, label (indicating price, etc., of goods).

billette[2], *s.f.* 1. billet (of firewood, of metal); **b. de réglisse,** stick of licorice. 2. *Arch:* billet (-moulding). 3. *Her:* billet.

billevesée [bilvəze, bij-], *s.f.* crack-brained notion, (piece of) nonsense.

billion [biljɔ̃], *s.m.* 1. (*since 1948*) billion (10^{12}); *U.S:* trillion. 2. (*before 1948*) milliard, one thousand million (10^9), *U.S:* billion.

billon [bijɔ̃], *s.m.* 1. (*a*) balk (of squared timber); (*b*) *Vit:* vine-plant (cut very short); (*c*) *Agr:* ridge of earth (formed by two plough furrows); **b. de délimitation (entre deux champs),** balk; **labourer en billons,** to rafter (field). 2. (*a*) alloy (of precious metal with copper); (*b*) **(monnaie de) b.,** copper or nickel coinage; (*c*) base, defective, coinage.

billonnage[1] [bijɔnaːʒ], *s.m. Jur:* uttering of base coin.

billonnage[2], **billonnement** [bijɔnmɑ̃], *s.m.* 1. *Agr:* ridging (of field). 2. *For:* sawing (of trees) into balks.

billonner[1] [bijɔne], *v.tr.* 1. *Agr:* to ridge (field). 2. *For:* to saw (trees) into balks. 3. to traffic in base coin.

billonner[2], *v.tr. Husb:* to castrate, geld.

billonnette [bijɔnɛt], *s.f.* branch of timber-tree (used for charcoal-making or firewood).

billonneur [bijɔnœr], *s.m. Jur:* utterer of base coin.

billot [bijo], *s.m.* (*a*) block (of wood); chopping-log, -block; **b. de boucher,** butcher's block, meat-block; (*b*) executioner's block; *F:* **j'en mettrais ma tête, ma main, sur le b.,** I would stake my life on it; (*c*) **b. d'enclume,** anvil-block, -stock; (*d*) wheel drag; (*e*) clog (to tether cattle); **b. de longe,** toggle (of a halter); (*f*) **b. à pâtée pour poussins,** wooden feeding trough for chicks.

bilobé [bilɔbe], *a. Arch: Biol:* bilobate, bilobed.

bilocation [bilɔkasjɔ̃], *s.f. Psy:* bilocation.

biloculaire [bilɔkylɛːr], *a.* bilocular (anthers, etc.).

biloquer [bilɔke], *v.tr. Agr:* to plough deeply.

bimane [biman], *Z:* 1. *a.* bimanous, bimanal, bimane, two-handed. 2. *s.m.* bimane.

bimarginé [bimarʒine], *a. Nat.Hist:* bimarginate.

bimastoïdien-ienne [bimastɔidjɛ̃, -jɛn], *a. Anat:* bimastoid.

bimbelot [bɛ̃blo], *s.m.* 1. *O:* toy. 2. trumpery article, bauble.

bimbeloterie [bɛ̃blɔtri], *s.f.* 1. toy business or trade; cheap "bazaar" trade. 2. toys, knick-knacks, odds and ends.

bimbelotier [bɛ̃blɔtje], *s.m.* maker of, dealer in, toys or fancy articles.

bimensuel, -elle [bimɑ̃sɥɛl], *a. & s.m.* fortnightly, semi-monthly (periodical).

bimensuellement [bimɑ̃sɥɛlmɑ̃], *adv.* twice a month, every fortnight.

bimestre [bimɛstr], *s.m.* period of two months.

bimestriel, -elle [bimɛstriɛl], *a.* bi-monthly, two-monthly, in alternate months.

bimétallique [bimetalik], *a.* bimetallic.

bimétallisme [bimetalism], *s.m. Pol.Ec:* bimetallism.

bimétalliste [bimetalist], *s.m. & a. Pol.Ec:* bimetallist.

bimillénaire [bimil(l)enɛːr], *s.m.* bimillenary.

bimoléculaire [bimolekylɛːr], *a.* bimolecular.

bimorphe [bimɔrf], *a.* = DIMORPHE.

bimoteur [bimɔtœːr], *a. & s.m.* twin-engine, bimotored (aircraft).

binage [binaːʒ], *s.m.* 1. *Agr:* second dressing, harrowing, hoeing (of land, etc.). 2. *Ecc:* celebration of two masses on the same day; duplication.

binaire [binɛːr], *a.* binary; *Mth:* **numération b.,** binary numeration; **système b.,** binary number system.

binard, binart [binaːr], *s.m.* (low) dray, lorry (for carting stone).

binauralité [binoralite], *s.f. Med:* **un test de b.,** a test for binaural hearing.

binder [bajndər], *s.m. Civ.E:* binding course.

bine [bin], *s.f. A: Agr: Hort:* hoe.

biné [bine'] *a. Bot:* binate (leaves).

biner [bine]. 1. *v.tr.* (*a*) *Agr:* to dig, harrow, dress, (ground) for a second time; (*b*) to hoe. 2. *v.i. Ecc:* to celebrate mass twice in one day, to duplicate, to binate.

binervé [binɛrve], *a. Nat.Hist:* binervate.

binette[1] [binɛt], *s.f. Agr: Hort:* hoe.

binette[2], *s.f. A.Cost:* 1. full-bottomed wig. 2. *F:* face; *P:* phiz, mug.

bineur [binœr], *s.m.,* **bineuse** [binøz], *s.f.* 1. hoer. 2. (*machine*) = BINOT.

biniou [binju], *s.m.* (i) Breton (bag-)pipes; (ii) *P: Mus:* musical instrument.

binoche [binɔʃ], *s.f. Agr:* two-pronged hoe.

binocher [binɔʃe], *v.tr. Agr: Hort:* to hoe.

binochon [binɔʃɔ̃], *s.m. Agr:* small (two-pronged) hoe.

binoclard, -arde [binɔklaːr, -ard], *s.m. & f. F:* person who wears glasses.

binocle [binɔkl], *s.m.* 1. eye-glasses, pince-nez, folders. 2. *O:* (*handled*) lorgnette.

binoculaire [binɔkylɛːr], *a.* 1. binocular (vision, etc.). 2. *Opt:* two-eyed, binocular.

binodal, -aux [binɔdal, -o], *a. Mth:* **quartique binodale,** binodal quartic (curve).

binode [binɔd], *s.f. Elcs:* binode.

binoir [binwaːr], *s.m. Hort:* = BINOT.

binôme [binoːm], *Mth:* 1. *a.* binomial (factor, etc.). 2. *s.m.* (*a*) binomial; **le binôme de Newton,** the binomial theorem; (*b*) *F: Sch:* room-mate.

binomial, -aux [binɔmjal, -o], *a. Statistics:* **distribution binomiale,** binomial distribution.

binominal, -aux [binɔminal, -o], *a. Nat.Hist:* binominal, binomial.

binormale [binɔrmal], *s.f. Mth:* binormal.

binot [bino], *s.m. Agr:* 1. cultivator, light plough. 2. hoe.

binotage [binɔtaːʒ], *s.m. Agr: Hort:* preparing, dressing, of the soil (with a *binot*).

binoter [binɔte], *v.tr. Agr: Hort:* to prepare, dress (the soil, with a *binot*).

binturong [binty:rɔ̃g], *s.m. Z:* binturong.

binucléaire [binykleɛːr], *a. Ph:* binuclear.

bio- [bjɔ], *pref.* bio-; **bioblaste,** bioblast.

biobibliographie [bjɔbiblijɔgrafi], *s.f.* biobibliography.

biobibliographique [bjɔbiblijɔgrafik], *a.* biobibliographical.

biocatalyseur [bjɔkatalizœːr], *s.m. Bio.Ch:* biocatalyst.

biocénose [bjɔsenoːz], *s.f.* bioc(o)enosis, bioc(o)enose.

biochimie [bjɔʃimi], *s.f.* biochemistry.

biochimique [bjɔʃimik], *a.* biochemic(al).

bioclimatologie [bjɔklimatɔlɔʒi], *s.f.* bioclimatology.

biocœnose [bjɔsenoːz], *s.f. Nat.Hist:* bioc(o)enosis, bioc(o)enose.

biodynamique [bjɔdinamik], *s.f.* biodynamics.

bioénergétique [bjɔenɛrʒetik], *s.f.* bioenergetics.

biogène [bjɔʒɛn], *s.m. Biol:* biogen.

biogénèse [bjɔʒenɛːz], *s.f. Biol:* biogenesis.

biogénétique [bjɔʒenetik], *a.* biogenetic.

biogéographie [bjɔʒeɔgrafi], *s.f.* biogeography.

biogéographique [bjɔʒeɔgrafik], *a.* biogeographic.

biographe [bjɔgraf]. 1. *s.m. & f.* biographer. 2. *s.m. Phot: A:* biograph.

biographie [bjɔgrafi], *s.f.* biography.

biographique [bjɔgrafik], *a.* biographic(al).

biologie [bjɔlɔʒi], *s.f.* biology.

biologique [bjɔlɔʒik], *a.* biologic(al).

biologiste [biɔlɔʒist], **biologue** [biɔlɔg], *s.m. & f.* biologist.

bioluminescence [bjɔlyminesɑ̃:s], *s.f.* bioluminescence.

bioluminescent [bjɔlyminesɑ̃], *a.* bioluminescent.

biomécanique [bjɔmekanik], *s.f.* biomechanics.

biométrie [bjɔmetri], *s.f.* biometry, biometrics.

biométrique [bjɔmetrik]. 1. *a.* biometric(al). 2. *s.f.* biometrics, biometry.

biomicroscope [bjɔmikrɔskɔp], *s.m. Opt:* biomicroscope.

bion [bjɔ̃], *s.m. Bot:* shoot, sucker.

bionique [bjɔnik], *s.f.* bionics.

bionner [bjɔne], *v.tr.* to plant the suckers of (artichoke, etc.).

bionomie [bjɔnɔmi], *s.f.* bionomics, bionomy; (o)ecology.

bionomique [bjɔnɔmik], *a.* bionomic, ecological; **niveaux bionomiques**, bionomic levels.

biophysicien, -ienne [bjɔfizisjɛ̃, -jɛn], *s.* biophysicist.

biophysique [bjɔfizik], *s.f.* biophysics.

bioplasme [bjɔplasm], *s.m.* bioplasm.

biopsie [biɔpsi], *s.f. Surg:* biopsy.

biosatellite [bjɔsatɛllit], *s.m. Astr:* biosatellite.

bioscope [bjɔskɔp], *s.m. A:* bioscope.

biosphère [biɔsfɛ:r], *s.f.* biosphere.

biosynthèse [bjɔsɛ̃tɛ:z], *s.f.* biosynthesis.

biothérapie [bjɔterapi], *s.f. Med:* biotherapy.

biotique [bjɔtik], *a. Biol:* biotic(al).

biotite [bjɔtit], *s.f. Miner:* biotite.

biotope [bjɔtɔp], *s.m. Biol: Bot: Geog: etc:* biotope, habitat (of plant or animal life).

biotropisme [bjɔtrɔpism], *s.m. Bot:* biotropism.

biotype [bjɔtip], *s.m. Biol:* biotype.

biotypologie [bjɔtipɔlɔʒi], *s.f.* biotypology.

biovulaire [bjɔvylɛ:r], *a.* biovular.

biovulé [bjɔvyle], *a. Bot:* biovulate.

bioxyde [biɔksid], *s.m. Ch:* dioxide.

bipale [bipal], *a. Av:* two-bladed (propellor).

bipare [bipa:r], *a. Bot: Z:* biparous.

bipariétal, -aux [biparjetal, -o], *a.* biparietal.

biparti, -ie [biparti], *a.* **bipartite** [bipartit], *a.* (*a*) *Nat.Hist:* bipartite; (*b*) *Pol: etc:* bipartisan.

bipartisme [bipartism], *s.m. Pol:* coalition government (formed by association of two parties).

bipartition [bipartisjɔ̃], *s.f.* bipartition.

bip-bip [bip bip], *s.m. W.Tel:* bleep-bleep (of a satellite).

bipède [bipɛd]. 1. *a.* two-footed, two-legged, biped(al). 2. *s.m.* biped; *F:* man. 3. *s.m.* (*any*) two feet, two legs (of a horse); **le b. antérieur**, the fore-feet; **le b. postérieur**, the hind feet; **le b. latéral gauche**, the near feet.

bipenne[1] [bipɛn], *a.*, **bipenné** [bipɛn(n)e], *a. Nat. Hist:* bipennate.

bipenne[2], *s.f. Rom.Hist: etc:* double axe.

biphasé [bifɑze], *a. El:* two-phase (current, etc.).

bipied [bipje], *s.m. Mil:* **bipied (de fusil mitrailleur)**, bipod.

bipinnaria [bipinarja], *s.f. Echin:* bipinnaria.

bipinné [bipinne], *a. Bot:* bipinnate(d), doubly pinnate.

biplace [biplas], *a. & s.m. Aut: Av:* two-seater.

biplan [biplɑ̃], *a. & s.m. Av:* biplane.

biplanaire [biplanɛ:r], *a. Mth:* biplanar; *El:* **lampe à filament b.**, biplane filament lamp.

bipolaire [bipɔlɛ:r], *a. El: Ph: etc:* bipolar, two-pole; **interrupteur b.**, double-pole switch.

bipolarité [bipɔlarite], *s.f.* bipolarity.

bipontin, -ine [bipɔ̃tɛ̃, -in], *a. Typ.Hist:* bipont(ine) (edition).

bipoutre [biputr̥], *s.m. & a. Av:* twin-boom (aircraft).

biprisme [biprism], *s.m. Opt:* biprism.

biquadratique [bikwadratik], *a. Mth:* biquadratic (equation).

biquartz [bikwarts], *s.m. Opt:* biquartz.

bique [bik], *s.f.* 1. *F:* she-goat, nanny-goat; **peau de b.**, goatskin. 2. *P:* (*a*) old horse, nag; (*b*) (*of woman*) old bag, old trout, old cow.

biquet, -ette [bikɛ, -ɛt], *s.* 1. *Z:* (*a*) *F:* kid; (*b*) *F:* fawn. 2. *F: s.m.* **mon biquet**, my pet.

biqueter [bikte], *v.i.* (**elle biquette; elle biquettera**) (*of goat*) to kid.

biquotidien, -ienne [bikɔtidjɛ̃, -jɛn], *a.* occurring, published, twice a day, twice-daily.

biramé [birame], *a. Ent: Crust:* biramous, biramose, double-branched (antennae, etc.).

birbe [birb], *s.m.*, **birbon** [birbɔ̃], *s.m. P:* old man; **vieux b.**, old dotard.

biréacteur [bireaktœ:r], *s.m.* twin-jet aircraft.

biréfringence [birefrɛ̃ʒɑ̃:s], *s.f. Opt:* double refraction, birefringence, birefraction.

biréfringent [birefrɛ̃ʒɑ̃], *a. Opt:* doubly-refractive, birefringent, birefractive.

birème [birɛ:m], *s.f. A.Hist:* bireme.

birgue [birg], *s.m. Crust:* birgus.

biribi [biribi], *s.m. Mil: P:* = **Compagnies de discipline**, *q.v.* under DISCIPLINE 2.

birkenia [birkenja], *s.m. Paleont:* birkenia.

birloir [birlwa:r], *s.m.* window-catch, sash-bolt.

birman, -ane [birmɑ̃, -an]. 1. *a. & s.m. & f. Geog:* Burmese. 2. *s.m. Ling:* Burmese.

Birmanie [birmani], *Pr.n.f. Geog:* Burma.

biroue [biru], *a.* two-wheeled.

biroute [birut], *s.f. F: Av: Meteor:* wind cone, *F:* (wind-)sock, (wind-)sleeve.

biroutier [birutje], *s.m. Av:* (i) target-towing aircraft; (ii) pilot (of such aircraft).

Birshéba [birʃeba], *Pr.n.f. Geog:* Beersheba.

bis[1], **bise** [bi, bi:z], *a.* greyish-brown, brownish-grey; **teint b.**, dark, swarthy complexion; **toile bise**, unbleached linen; **pain b.**, whole-meal bread; *F:* **changer son pain blanc en pain b.**, to make a poor bargain; **faire qch. à b. ou à blanc**, to do sth. anyhow.

bis[2] [bis], (*a*) *adv.* (i) **No. 10b.**, No. 10A (of street); (ii) *Mus:* repeat; (*b*) *int.* encore; **crier b.**, to encore (a song); (*c*) *s.m.* **chanter un b.**, to sing an encore.

bisaïeul, -eule [bizajœl], *s.* great-grandfather, great-grandmother; *pl. bisaïeul(e)s.*

bisaiguë [bizegy], *s.f.* = BESAIGUË.

bisaille [bizɑ:j], *s.f.* 1. *Mill:* coarse flour, whole (wheat-)meal. 2. *Husb:* mixed peas and vetches (for feeding animals, etc.).

bisannuel, -elle [bizanɥɛl], *a.* biennial.

bisbille [bisbij], *s.f. F:* petty quarrel, tiff, bickering; **être en bisbille avec qn**, to be at variance, at loggerheads, with s.o.; **il y a eu de la b.**, there has been unpleasantness.

biscaïen, -ïenne [biskajɛ̃, -jɛn]. 1. (*a*) *a. & s.m. & f. Geog:* Biscayan; (*b*) *s.m. Ling:* Biscayan. 2. *s.m. A:* (*a*) bullet (of case-shot); (*b*) *Arms:* biscayen. 3. *s.f. A.Nau:* biscayner.

Biscaye [biskaj], *Pr.n. Geog:* Biscay; *A:* **le golfe de Biscaye**, the Bay of Biscay.

biscayen, -enne [biskajɛ̃, -jɛn], *a. & s.m. & f.* = BISCAÏEN, -ÏENNE.

biscornu [biskɔrny], *a.* 1. mis-shapen, knocked out of shape, crooked. 2. irregular, ill-proportioned (building), etc.). 3. *F:* distorted, bizarre, queer (ideas); crotchety, cranky (mind); inconsequent, illogical (argument).

biscotin [biskɔtɛ̃], *s.m.*, **biscotine** [biskɔtin], *s.f.* 1. crisp biscuit. 2. ship's biscuit.

biscotte [biskɔt], *s.f.* 1. rusk. 2. dry sponge-finger.

biscuit [biskɥi], *s.m.* 1. (*a*) biscuit or plain cake; cracker; **b. à la cuiller**, lady('s)-finger, finger-biscuit, sponge-finger; **b. de savoie**, sponge-cake; **b. de mer**, (i) ship's biscuit, sea-bread, hard-tack, pilot-bread; (ii) *F:* cuttle(-fish) bone; **b. pour chiens**, dog-biscuit; *s.a.* EMBARQUER 2. *Husb:* **b. de fourrage**, cake (of oats, peas, etc.); (*b*) *P:* money, brass, dibs. 2. *Cer:* unglazed porcelain, biscuit-ware, bisque; *Miner:* streak-plate.

biscuiter [biskɥite], *v.tr.* 1. *Mil:* **pain biscuité**, biscuit. 2. *abs. Cer:* to make biscuit.

biscuiterie [biskɥitri], *s.f.* (*a*) biscuit factory; (*b*) biscuit trade.

bise[1] [bi:z], *s.f.* (*a*) north wind; (*b*) *Lit:* (the) icy blast of winter.

bise[2], *s.f. F:* kiss; **faire, donner, une b. à qn**, to kiss s.o.; **se faire la b.**, to kiss (each other) on both cheeks.

bise[3], *s.f. Ich:* bonito.

biseau, -eaux [bizo], *s.m.* 1. (*a*) chamfered edge, feather edge, chamfer, bevel; **planche taillée en b.**, bevel-edged, bevelled, chamfered, board; **glace (taillée) en b.**, bevelled mirror; **b. d'un pain**, overlapping crust of the slash in a loaf; (*b*) *Crust:* bevelment; *Lap:* bezel; *Clockm:* bezel (of watch or clock case); *Mus:* lip (of a recorder). 2. *Typ:* side-stick. 3. *Tls:* (*a*) skew (turning-)chisel; (*b*) (**fer à**) **b.**, (*joiner's*) chamfering iron; *s.a.* LIME[1] 1.

biseautage [bizota:ʒ], *s.m.* 1. bevelling, chamfering; *Lap: etc:* bezelling. 2. marking, nicking (of playing cards).

biseauter [bizote], *v.tr.* 1. to bevel, chamfer; *Lap: etc:* to bezel. 2. to mark, nick, fake (cards).

biseauteur, -euse [bizotœ:r, -ø:z]. 1. *s. Glassm: etc:* (*pers.*) beveller. 2. **biseauteuse**, *s.f.* bevelling-machine, beveller. 3. *s.m. & f.* cardsharper (who marks the cards).

biseautoir [bizotwa:r], *s.m. Bookb:* bevelling-machine.

bisegmentation [bisɛgmɑ̃tasjɔ̃], *s.f.* bisegmentation.

bisegmenter [bisɛgmɑ̃te], *v.tr.* to divide into two.

bisel [bizɛl], *s.m. Ch:* dibasic salt.

biser[1] [bize], *v.tr.* to re-dye (cloth).

biser[2], *v.i. Agr:* (*of grain*) to darken, deteriorate.

biser[3], *v.tr. F:* to kiss.

bisérié [biserje], *a. Nat.Hist:* biserial, biseriate.

biset [bizɛ], *s.m. Orn:* rock-pigeon, carrier pigeon.

bisette[1] [bizɛt], *s.f.* 1. *A:* gold lace. 2. narrow lace, footing; bisette.

bisette[2], *s.f. Orn:* sea-duck, scoter.

bisexué [bisɛksɥe], **bisexuel, -elle** [bisɛksɥɛl], *a. Nat.Hist:* bisexual, bisexed.

bismite [bismit], *s.f. Min:* bismite, bismuth ocre.

bismuth [bismyt], *s.m. Ch: Miner:* bismuth; *Ch: F:* subnitrate.

bismuthine [bismytin], *s.f. Ch:* bismuthinite; bismuthine; bismuth hydride.

bismuthisme [bismytism], *s.m. Med:* bismuth poisoning.

bismuthite [bismytit], *s.f. Min:* bismuthite.

bismuthocre [bismytɔkr], *s.m. Min:* bismuth ocre.

bisness [bis(z)nɛs], *s.m. P: Pej:* business; job.

bisnessman [bis(z)nɛsman], *s.m. P: Pej:* business-man.

bisoc [bisɔk], *s.m.* = BISSOC.

bison [bizɔ̃], *s.m. Z:* bison; *U.S: F:* buffalo.

bisonne [bizɔn], *s.f. Bookb:* grey cloth.

bisontin, -ine [bizɔ̃tɛ̃, -in], *a. & s. Geog:* (native, inhabitant) of Besançon.

Bisoutoun [bizutun], *Pr.n.m. Geog:* Behistun.

bisquain [biskɛ̃], *s.m* sheepskin dressed with the wool on; *esp.* sheepskin pad of a horse's collar.

bisquant [biskɑ̃], *a. P:* annoying; vexing, irritating; **ce que c'est b.!** what a nuisance! what a bother!

bisque[1] [bisk], *s.f.* 1. *A: Sp:* bisque, odds; **donner une b. à qn**, to give s.o. odds; *F:* **prendre sa b.**, (i) *A:* to seize one's opportunity; (ii) to leave one's work and go off on the spree. 2. *P:* vexation, ill-humour; **avoir la b.**, to be riled, out of temper, in a pet; **prendre la b.**, to take umbrage.

bisque[2], *s.f. Cu:* (*a*) shell-fish soup; bisque, bisk; **b. d'écrevisses**, crayfish soup; (*b*) **b. à la reine** (thick white) chicken soup.

bisquer [biske], *v.i. P:* to be vexed, in a pet; to be riled; to sulk; **faire b. qn**, to rile s.o.; **bisque! bisque! rage!** yah! yah!

bisquin [biskɛ̃], *s.m.* = BISQUAIN.

bisquine [biskin], *s.f. Nau:* fishing smack (from Cancale and Channel ports).

bissac [bisak], *s.m.* double wallet, sack, or bag; *F:* **être au b.**, to be reduced to beggary; *s.a.* TOUR[2] 5.

bisse [bis], *s.f. Her:* bisse, snake erect and knotted.

bissecter [bisɛkte], *v.tr. Geom:* to bisect.

bissecteur, -trice [bisɛktœ:r, -tris], *Geom:* 1. *a.* bisecting (line, etc.). 2. *s.f.* **bissectrice**, bisectrix, *occ.* bisector.

bissection [bisɛksjɔ̃], *s.f. Geom:* bisection.

bissel [bisɛl], *s.m. Rail:* pony-truck (of engine); (*from the name of the inventor.*)

bisséqué [biseke], *a.* bisected.

bisser [bise]. 1. *v.tr. & i.* to encore (song, etc.). 2. *v.tr.* (*a*) to repeat, to sing (sth.) twice over; (*b*) to give an encore of (song, etc.).

bissexte [bisɛkst], *s.m. A:* odd day (of leap year), 29th of February.

bissextile [bisɛkstil], *a.f.* bissextile; *used only in* **année bissextile**, leap year.

bissexué [bisɛksɥe], **bissexuel, -elle** [bisɛksɥɛl], *a. Nat.Hist:* bisexual, bisexed.

bissoc [bisɔk], *s.m. Agr:* double-furrow plough.

bistoquet [bistɔkɛ], *s.m.* 1. *Games:* cat (in tip-cat). 2. *Ind:* wire-nail cutting machine.

bistorte [bistɔrt], *s.f. Bot:* (dock) bistort, snake-weed, adderwort.

bistortier [bistɔrtje], *s.m.* pharmacist's pestle.

bistouille [bistuj], *s.f. P:* 1. raw spirits, rot-gut. 2. (*Dial: in N. of Fr.*) coffee laced with spirits. 3. nonsense, bosh.

bistouri [bisturi], *s.m. Surg:* bistoury, lancet, (surgical) knife.

bistouriser [bisturize], *v.tr. A: F:* to lance, to open (abscess, etc.).

bistournage [bisturna:ʒ], *s.m. Husb:* castration (by twisting of the cord).

bistourner [bisturne], *v.tr.* 1. to wring, wrench (sword-blade, etc.). 2. *Husb:* to castrate (by twisting the cord).

bistre [bistr̥]. 1. *s.m.* bistre; *s.a.* CERCLÉ 1. 2. *a.* (*a*) blackish-brown, swarthy, browned; (*b*) *Phot:* **papier b.**, sepia paper.

bistré [bistre], *a.* browned, swarthy.

bistrer [bistre], *v.tr.* to darken (complexion, etc.).

bistro(t) [bistro], *s.m. P:* 1. *A:* keeper of a public-house, bar-keeper. 2. wine merchant. 3. public-house; *F:* pub; eating-house; bar; **le b. du coin**, the local.

bistrouillage [bistruja:ʒ], *s.m. P:* manufacture of bogus wine.

bistrouille [bistruj], *s.f. P:* **1.** = BISTOUILLE. **2.** bogus wine.

bistrouiller [bistruje], *v.i. P:* to manufacture bogus wine.

bisulce [bisyls], *a.* = BISULQUE.

bisulfate [bisylfat], *s.m. Ch:* bisulphate.

bisulfite [bisylfit], *s.m. Ch:* bisulphite, acid sulphite.

bisulfure [bisylfy:r], *s.m. Ch:* disulphide, bisulphide.

bisulque [bisylk]. **1.** *a. Z:* bisulcate, cloven-hoofed. **2.** *s.m.pl.* **bisulques;** *Z:* ruminants.

bit [bit], *s.m. Min:* bit.

bitangent [bitɑ̃ʒɑ̃], *a. Geom:* bitangential (**à**, to).

bitartrate [bitartrat], *s.m. Ch:* bitartrate; **b. de potasse,** cream of tartar.

bitemporal, -aux [bitɑ̃pɔral, -o], *a. Anat:* bitemporal.

bitemps [bitɑ̃], *a.inv. & s.m. I.C.E: A:* **(moteur) bitemps,** two-stroke engine.

biterné [bitɛrne], *a. Bot:* biternate.

biterrois, -oise [bitɛrwa, -wa:z], *a. & s. Geog:* (native, inhabitant) of Béziers.

Bithynie [bitini], *Pr.n.f. Geog:* Bithynia.

bithynien, -ienne [bitinjɛ̃, -jɛn], *a. & s. Geog:* Bithynian.

bitis [bitis], *s.m. Rept:* bitis.

bitonal, -als [bitɔnal, -al], *a. Mus:* bitonal.

bitord [bitɔ:r], *s.m. Nau:* spun-yarn; **b. en trois,** three-yarn spun-yarn.

bitos [bitɔs], *s.m. P:* hat, *P:* titfer.

bittacidés [bitaside], *s.m.pl. Ent:* Bittacidæ.

bitte [bit], *s.f. Nau:* bitt; bollard (on ship); **bittes de remorque,** towing bitts; **b. en croix,** cruciform bitt, staghorn.

bitter[1] [bite], *v.tr. Nau:* to bitt (cable).

bitter[2] [bitɛ:r], *s.m.* appetizer, bitters.

bitton [bitɔ̃], *s.m. Nau:* small bitt, kevel-head, mooring-post, bollard.

bitture [bity:r], *s.f.* **1.** *Nau:* range of cable. **2.** *P:* (*a*) *Nau:* stiff glass of grog; (*b*) **se donner, se flanquer, une b. de qch.,** to have a rare tuck-in of sth.; (*c*) **prendre une b.,** to get drunk.

bitturer [bityre], *v.tr. P:* to make (s.o.) drunk.

se bitturer, *P:* **1.** to tuck in, to do oneself well. **2.** to get drunk.

bitumacadam [bitymakadam], *s.m.* asphalt macadam.

bitumage [bityma:ʒ], *s.m. Civ.E:* **1.** asphalting. **2.** tarring.

bitumastic [bitymastik], *s.m. Tchn:* bitumastic (*R.t.m.*).

bitume [bitym], *s.m. Miner:* **1.** bitumen, asphalt; **b. de Judée,** Judean bitumen, Jew's pitch. **2.** (*mineral*) pitch, tar; **bitume glutineux,** maltha.

bitumier [bitymje], *s.m.* (*a*) *Nau:* asphalt-tanker; (*b*) asphalt paviour.

bitum(in)er [bitym(in)e], *v.tr.* **1.** to bituminize; to cover (road, etc.) with bitumen; to asphalt. **2.** to tar; **carton bitumé,** tarred felt.

bitum(in)eux, -euse [bitym(in)ø, -ø:z], *a. Miner:* **1.** bituminous, asphaltic. **2.** tarry.

bituminifère [bityminifɛ:r], *a. Miner:* bituminiferous.

bituminisation [bityminizasjɔ̃], *s.f.* bituminization.

bituminiser [bityminize], *v.tr.* to bituminize.

biture [bity:r], *s.f.* = BITTURE.

biturer [bityre], *v.tr. P:* = BITTURER.

biuret [biyrɛ], *s.m. Ch:* biuret; **réaction du b.,** biuret reaction.

bivac [bivak], *s.m. A:* = BIVOUAC.

bivalence [bivalɑ̃:s], *s.f. Ch:* bivalence, bivalency.

bivalent [bivalɑ̃], *a. Ch:* bivalent, divalent.

bivalve [bivalv], *Nat.Hist:* **1.** *a.* bivalvular. **2.** *s.m.* bivalve.

bivalvulaire [bivalvylɛ:r], *a.* bivalved, bivalvular.

bivaquer [bivake], *v.i. A:* = BIVOUAQUER.

biveau, -eaux [bivo], *s.m.* **1.** *Const:* bevel(-angle). **2.** *Tls:* bevel-rule, mitre-rule; bevel-square.

bivium [bivjɔm], *s.m. Echin:* bivium.

bivoie [bivwa], *s.f.* (*a*) *A:* junction (of two roads), fork; (*b*) *Rail:* splitting the point.

bivoltin [bivɔltɛ̃], *a. Ent:* bivoltine.

bivoltinisme [bivɔltinism], *s.m. Ent:* bivoltinism.

bivouac [bivwak], *s.m. Mil:* bivouac; **feu de bivouac,** watch-fire.

bivouaquer [bivwake], *v.i.* (*a*) to bivouac; (*b*) *F:* to sleep in the open.

bixacées [biksase], *s.f.pl. Bot:* Bixaceae.

bizarre [biza:r], *a.* peculiar, singular, eccentric, odd, strange, queer, outlandish, bizarre, whimsical; *s.m.* **le b.,** the bizarre; **le b. de l'affaire, c'est que . . .,** the strange part of the business is that . . .

bizarrement [bizarmɑ̃], *adv.* peculiarly, whimsically, queerly, oddly.

bizarrerie [bizarri], *s.f.* **1.** peculiarity, particularity, oddness. **2.** whimsicalness; extravagance; eccentricity, oddity; **on lui pardonne ses bizarreries,** people forgive his oddities.

bize [bi:z], *s.f. Ich:* bonito.

bizé [bize], *s.m. Bootm:* burnishing-iron.

Bizerte [bizɛrt], *Pr.n.f. Geog:* Bizerta.

bizertin, -ine [bizɛrtɛ̃, -in], *a. & s. Geog:* (native) of Bizerta.

bizonal, -aux [bizɔnal, -o], *a.* bizonal.

bizone [bizɔ:n], *s.f. Hist:* bizone.

bizontin, -ine [bizɔ̃tɛ̃, -in], *a. & s. Geog:* = BISONTIN.

bizut(h) [bizy], *s.m. Sch: F:* freshman, fresher, *esp.* first-year student in preparatory class for the *grandes écoles*, or in the *grandes écoles* themselves.

bizut(h)age [bizyta:ʒ], *s.m. Sch: F:* initiation (of freshmen); ragging.

bizut(h)er [bizyte], *v.tr. Sch: F:* to rag (a freshman).

bla-bla-bla [blablabla], *s.m. F:* blah; claptrap, boloney; padding (of a speech, etc.).

black-bass [blakbas], *s.m. Ich:* black-bass.

blackboulage [blakbula:ʒ], *s.m. F:* blackballing, rejection.

blackbouler [blakbule], *v.tr.* to blackball, reject; *F:* turn down (candidate).

black-out [blakaut], *s.m.* black-out; **faire le b.-o.,** (i) to black-out; (ii) to suppress news, etc.; *F:* **faire le b.-o. sur un scandale,** to hush up a scandal.

black-rot [blakrɔt], *s.m. Vit: etc:* black-rot.

blafard, -arde [blafa:r, -ard], *a.* **1.** pallid, wan, pale (moon, light, etc.); lambent (light, flame). **2.** *P:* (*a*) *s.m. A:* silver coin; (*b*) *s.f.* **la blafarde,** (i) death; (ii) the moon.

blague [blag], *s.f.* **1. b. à tabac,** tobacco-pouch. **2.** *F:* (*a*) tall story, humbug, bunkum, hoax; **tout ça c'est de la b.,** that's all bosh, all tosh, all flummery, all bunkum; **ne racontez pas de blagues!** don't tell cock-and-bull stories! **sans b.?** really? no joking? no kidding? (*b*) joke; **quelle b.!** what a joke! **il m'a joué une sale b.,** he played me a dirty trick; **b. à part, dans le coin,** joking apart; (*c*) scoffing, banter; **il prend tout à la b.,** he is never serious about anything, he always has his tongue in his cheek.

blaguer [blage], *F:* **1.** *v.i.* (*a*) to talk through one's hat, with one's tongue in one's cheek; (*b*) to joke; **c'est assez b.!** enough of that! **2.** *v.tr.* to chaff, banter (s.o.); to make fun of (s.o., sth.).

blagueur, -euse [blagœ:r, -ø:z], *F:* **1.** *s.* (*a*) humbug, teller of tall stories; (*b*) joker; (*c*) scoffer, cynic. **2.** *a.* bantering, ironical, scoffing, mocking, cynical.

blair [blɛ:r], *s.m. P:* nose; **je l'ai dans le b.,** I can't stand him at any price.

blaireau, -eaux [blɛro], *s.m.* **1.** *Z:* badger. **2.** (*a*) (badger-hair) shaving-brush; (*b*) *Art:* (badger-hair) brush; softener, blender; **b. pied de biche,** (*de doreur, etc.*) badger.

blaireau-furet [blɛrofyrɛ], *s.m. Z:* ferret-badger; *pl. blaireaux-furets.*

blaireauter [blɛrote], *v.tr. Art: F:* **1.** to scumble, to soften down. **2.** to paint with excessive care, to niggle at (picture).

blairer [blɛre]. **1.** *v.tr. P:* to sniff at (sth.); **je ne peux pas le b.,** I can't stand him at any price. **2.** *v.i. P:* to smell bad; *P:* to hum.

blakéite [blakeit], *s.f. Miner:* blakeite.

blâmable [blɑmabl̩], *a.* blamable, blameworthy; **être b. de qch.,** to be to blame for sth.

blâme [blɑ:m], *s.m.* **1.** blame, disapprobation; **rejeter, faire tomber, le b. de qch. sur qn,** to lay, cast, throw, all the blame for sth. on s.o.; **encourir le b. public,** to come under public obloquy; **digne de b.,** blameworthy. **2.** *Adm:* reprimand; **infliger un b. à un fonctionnaire,** to reprimand an official; **s'attirer un b.,** to incur a reprimand, to incur censure.

blâmer [blɑme], *v.tr.* **1.** to blame (pers. or action); to find fault with (s.o.); to pass censure on (Government, etc.); **b. qn de qch.,** to blame s.o. for sth.; **b. qn de faire, d'avoir fait, qch.,** to blame s.o. for doing sth; *s.a.* PLAINDRE 1. **2.** *Adm:* to reprimand.

blanc, blanche [blɑ̃, blɑ̃:ʃ]. **I.** *a.* **1.** white; **b. comme (la) neige,** white as snow, snow-white; **barbe blanche,** white, grey, beard; **vieillard à cheveux blancs,** white-haired, *Lit:* hoary-headed, old man; *F:* **dire tantôt b. tantôt noir,** to say first one thing and then another; *Parl:* **livre b.,** white paper; *s.a.* BAL 1, DRAPEAU 1. **2.** light-coloured, pale; **la race blanche,** the white race; *s.* **un blanc,** a white man; *s.* **pauvres blancs, petits blancs,** poor whites (in colonies, etc.); **vin b.,** white wine; *s. F:* **un verre de b.,** a glass of white wine; *Winem:* **b. de b.,** white wine made with white grapes; **bière blanche,** pale ale; **b. de peur,** white with fear; **b. comme un linge,** as white as a sheet; **se mettre dans une colère blanche,** to become livid with anger; **verre b.,** colourless glass; **porcelaine blanche,** unpainted china; **monnaie blanche,** (small) silver change; *Cu:* **sauce blanche,** white sauce, melted butter; *Dist:* clear; **eau de lavande blanche,** clear lavender water; **alcool b.,** spirit of raspberry, pear, etc. **3.** clean, white, pure, stainless; **linge b.,** clean, unsoiled, linen; **sortir d'une accusation b. comme neige,** to leave the court without a stain on one's character; *F:* **je ne le vois pas b.,** he's anything but the snow-white lamb; *P:* he's for it; *F:* **c'est bonnet b. et b. bonnet,** it is six of one and half a dozen of the other; it's as broad as it's long; **montrer patte blanche,** to show one's credentials, to give the countersign. **4.** blank (paper, page, etc.); **affaire blanche,** profitless, break-even, deal; **nuit blanche,** sleepless, wakeful, night; **examen b.,** mock examination; **mariage b.,** unconsummated marriage; **voix blanche,** toneless voice; **vers blancs,** blank verse; *Ten:* **jeu b.,** love game; **gagner son service b.,** to win one's service to love. **5.** (*a*) *Mil: s.a.* ARME 1; (*b*) *Nau:* **cordage b.,** untarred, white, rope; *s.a.* FER-BLANC.

II. blanc, *s.m.* white. **1. b. mat,** dead white; **robe d'un b. sale,** dingy white dress; **aller, passer, du blanc au noir,** to go from one extreme to the other; **être habillé de b., être en b.,** to be dressed in white, to be in white; **mariage en b.,** white wedding; *Hist:* **les Blancs,** the Royalist armies (French Revolution); *Nau:* **tenue en b., les blancs,** white uniform, whites; **voir tout en b.,** to see everything on the bright side; **je vous l'écris noir sur b.,** I'm putting it in black and white; *Bookb:* **exemplaire en b.,** copy in sheets; *Typ:* **tirer en b.,** to print only on one side of the paper; *s.a.* MACHINE 1. **2.** (*white part*) (*a*) **le b. des yeux,** the white of the eyes; **regarder qn dans le b. des yeux,** to look s.o. straight in the face; **rougir jusqu'au b. des yeux,** to blush to the roots of one's hair; *F:* **se manger le b. des yeux,** to have a terrific row; (*b*) **b. d'une cible,** bull's-eye of a target; **donner, mettre, dans le b.,** to hit the bull's eye; *s.a.* BUT 4; (*c*) blank; **b. d'une lettre, d'un livre,** blank space, margin of a letter, of a book; **laisser des blancs,** to leave blanks; **signer un document en b.,** to sign an uncompleted document; **chèque en b.,** blank cheque; **acceptation en b.,** blank acceptance; *Telecomm:* **b. des chiffres, des lettres,** figures, letters, blank; *Rec:* **b. sonore,** pause; (*d*) *Typ:* (i) spacing; (ii) margin, blank (space); white line; **les blancs,** the whites; (iii) space (quad, etc.); (*e*) *Dominoes:* **double b.,** double blank. **3.** *adv.phr.* **à b.** (*a*) **saigner qn à b., jusqu'au b.,** to bleed s.o. white; **il gèle (à) b.,** there is a white frost; *Metalw:* **chauffer un métal à b.,** to bring a metal to a white heat; **chauffé à b.,** white hot; *F:* **chauffer qn à b.,** to work s.o. up, to bring s.o. up to the scratch; *For:* **coupe à b.,** complete clearing of woodland; **chevalier armé à b.,** knight armed from head to toe; (*b*) **cartouche à b.,** blank cartridge; *s.a.* TIRER I 6; *Mec.E:* (*of machine*) **marche à b.,** running light, on no load; *Mch: I.C.E:* **course à b.,** idle stroke. **4.** (*white substance*) (*a*) **b. de volaille,** breast of chicken; **b. d'œuf,** (i) white of egg; (ii) *Bookb:* glair; **un b. d'œuf,** the white of an egg; *s.a.* BALEINE 1, CHAMPIGNON 1; (*b*) **b. de craie, d'Espagne, de Meudon,** whiting; **b. de Paris,** Paris white; **b. de Briançon,** French chalk; **b. de Chine,** Chinese white (porcelain), blanc de chine; **b. de bismuth, de fard,** Spanish white; **b. de baryum, b. fixe,** barium sulphate; **b. d'antimoine,** antimony sesquioxide; **b. de billard,** billiard chalk; *Bill:* **mettre du b. au procédé,** to chalk one's cue; **b. de chaux,** whitewash; **b. de terre à pipe,** pipe-clay; (*c*) *Paint:* **b. de zinc, de neige,** zinc white, oxide of zinc; **b. de céruse, d'argent, de plomb, de Gênes, de Hambourg, de Venise,** white lead; **b. de charge,** filler, extender; (*d*) **(articles de) b.,** linen, white goods; **magasin, maison, de b.,** linen draper's; **(mise en) vente de b.,** white sale. **5.** *A: P:* one-franc piece. **6.** *Hort:* **(maladie du) b.,** = OÏDIUM; **b. du rosier,** rose mildew.

III. blanche, *s.f.* **1.** *Bill: Voting: etc:* white ball. **2.** *Mus:* minim; half-note.

IV. Blanche, *Pr.n.f.* Blanche.

blanc-aune [blɑ̃o:n], *s.m. Bot:* service-tree; *pl. blancs-aunes.*

blanc-bec [blɑ̃bɛk], *s.m. F:* callow youth, greenhorn, sucker; *pl. blancs-becs.*

blanc-bourgeois [blɑ̃burʒwa], *s.m. A: Mill:* best white flour; *pl. blancs-bourgeois.*

blanc-cul [blɑ̃ky], *s.m. Orn: F:* bullfinch; *pl. blancs-culs.*

blanc-étoc, blanc-estoc [blɑ̃etɔk], *s.m. For:* complete clearing of woodland; *pl. blancs-étocs, blancs-estocs.*

blanchaille [blɑ̃ʃɑ:j], *s.f.* **1.** *Fish:* small fry, bait. **2.** *Cu:* whitebait.

blanchâtre [blɑ̃ʃɑ:tr̥], *a.* whitish, whity.

Blanche-Neige [blɑ̃ʃnɛ:ʒ], *Pr.n.f. Lit:* Snow-White.

blanche-queue [blɑ̃ʃkø], *s.f. Orn:* harrier-eagle; *pl. blanches-queues.*

blancherie [blɑ̃ʃri], *s.f. Tan:* **1.** tawing, dressing (of light skins). **2.** tawery.

blanchet[1], **-ette** [blɑ̃ʃɛ, -ɛt], *a.* of a pretty white colour, nice and clean.

blanchet[2], *s.m.* **1.** (*a*) *A:* white woollen stuff; (*b*) *Pharm: etc:* cloth filter; strainer; (*c*) *Typ:* (press-)blanket. **2.** *Harn: etc:* strengthening strap; strengthening piece (on strap). **3.** *Bot: F:* (*a*) (*variety of*) agaric; fairy-ring mushroom; (*b*) lamb's lettuce. **4.** *Med:* (= MUGUET) thrush.

blancheur [blɑ̃ʃœ:r], *s.f.* **1.** whiteness, paleness; **d'une b. de perle,** pearl-white; **les premières blancheurs de l'aube,** the first light of dawn. **2.** purity, spotlessness (of soul).

blanchi [blɑ̃ʃi], *s.m. For:* blaze, mark (on tree to be felled).

blanchiment [blɑ̃ʃimɑ̃], *s.m.* **1.** (*a*) whitening; (*b*) whitewashing; (*c*) *Cu:* scalding (of meat, etc.); blanching (of almonds). **2.** *Metall:* (*a*) blanching, washing (of silver); (*b*) whitening, refining (of pig-iron); deblooming. **3.** *Tex:* bleaching; **b. sur, au, pré,** grassing.

blanchir [blɑ̃ʃi:r]. **1.** *v.tr.* (*a*) to whiten, to make (sth.) white; **se b. les cheveux, la figure,** to powder one's hair, one's face; **la colère blanchissait ses lèvres,** rage blanched, whitened, his lips; *Typ:* **b. la composition,** to space out, lead out, the matter; (*b*) *Tex:* to bleach; **b. sur, au, pré,** to grass; (*c*) to wash, launder; **donner du linge à b.,** to send clothes to the wash; **qui est-ce qui vous blanchit? chez qui vous blanchissez-vous?** who washes for you, does your washing, your laundry? *abs.* **on blanchit aujourd'hui chez nous,** it is our washing day; *F:* **b. un manuscrit,** to touch up, revise, a manuscript (belonging to someone else); *F:* **b. un failli,** to whitewash a bankrupt; **il est arrivé à se b.,** he managed to clear his character, to exculpate himself; (*d*) to whitewash, limewash, *U.S:* calcimine (ceiling, wall, etc.); *A: Med:* **b. une maladie,** to cover up the symptoms of a disease, to mask a disease; *B. & F:* **sépulcre blanchi,** whited sepulchre; (*e*) *Cu:* to scald (cabbage, meat); to blanch (almonds); (*f*) *Metall:* to blanch (silver); to refine (pig-iron); (*g*) to polish (surface); to plane, trim, clean up, smooth (board); (*h*) *For:* to blaze (tree to be felled). **2.** *v.i.* (*a*) to whiten, to turn white; **il commence à b.,** he is turning grey, going white; *s.a.* HARNAIS 2; **l'eau blanchit sous nos rames,** the water turns to spray under our oars; (*b*) (*of colours*) to fade; (*c*) to blanch, to turn pale.

blanchis [blɑ̃ʃi], *s.m.* = BLANCHI.

blanchissage [blɑ̃ʃisa:ʒ], *s.m.* **1.** washing, laundering (of linen, etc.); **b. non calandré,** dry-wash; **b. de fin,** fine laundering; **liste du b.,** laundry list; **elle fait le b.,** she takes in washing. **2.** white-washing, lime-washing (of wall, etc.). **3.** *Ind:* refining (of sugar). **4.** *occ.* = BLANCHIMENT.

blanchissant [blɑ̃ʃisɑ̃], *a.* (*a*) whitening, growing white; greying (hair); **l'aube blanchissante,** the brightening dawn; **produits blanchissants,** bleaching agents; (*b*) paling.

blanchisserie [blɑ̃ʃisri], *s.f.* **1.** (*a*) laundering; **b. de fin,** fine laundering; (*b*) laundry, laundry-works; **b. automatique,** launderette. **2.** *Tex:* (*a*) bleachery, bleaching-house, -ground; (*b*) bleaching trade.

blanchisseur, -euse [blɑ̃ʃisœ:r, -ø:z], *s.* **1.** (*a*) laundryman, *f.* laundress; **blanchisseuse de fin,** fine laundress; (*b*) washerwoman; *F:* **porter le deuil de sa blanchisseuse,** to wear grubby, dingy, linen; (*c*) launderer. **2.** (*a*) *Tex:* bleacher; (*b*) *Tan:* whitener. **3.** *P:* (prisoner's) counsel; *cp.* BLANCHIR 1 (*c*). **4. blanchisseuse automatique,** electric washing-machine.

blanchoyer [blɑ̃ʃwaje], *v.i.* (**il blanchoie; il blanchoiera**) **1.** (*of sky, etc.*) to begin to whiten, to grow bright. **2.** *Metall:* (*of metal*) to go white-hot.

blanc-manger [blɑ̃mɑ̃ʒe], *s.m. Cu:* = blancmange; *pl. blancs-mangers.*

blanc-manteau [blɑ̃mɑ̃to], *s.m. A: Ecc:* Servite; *pl. blancs-manteaux.*

blanc-nez [blɑ̃ne], *s.m.* white-nosed monkey; *pl. blancs-nez.*

blanc-poudré, -ée [blɑ̃pudre], *a.* powdered (hair, etc.); *pl. blanc-poudré(s).*

blanc-russe [blɑ̃rys], *a. & s. A:* White Russian; *pl. blancs-russes.*

blanc-seing [blɑ̃sɛ̃], *s.m.* (*a*) signature to a blank document; (*b*) paper signed in blank; *F:* **donner b.-s. à qn,** to give s.o. a free hand, full power; *pl. blancs-seings.*

blanc-soudant [blɑ̃sudɑ̃], *s.m. Metalw:* white heat, welding heat.

blandices [blɑ̃dis], *s.f.pl. Lit:* blandishments; allurement, lure.

blanque [blɑ̃:k], *s.f. A:* raffle, draw; *A: F:* **faire b.,** to draw a blank.

blanquette [blɑ̃kɛt], *s.f.* **1.** (*a*) (*variety of*) white grape; (*b*) **b. de Limoux,** blanquette (*light sparkling white wine made in the South of France*); (*c*) (*variety of*) pale ale. **2.** *Cu:* blanquette (*stew of white meat, esp. veal, with white sauce*). **3.** *Hort:* (*variety of whitish*) (i) fig; (ii) pear.

blaps [blaps], *s.m. Ent:* blaps, black-beetle, churchyard beetle.

blasé [blɑze], *a.* blasé, indifferent; surfeited (with pleasures).

blasement [blɑzmɑ̃], *s.m.* (*state of*) satiety, surfeit, boredom.

blaser[1] [blɑze], *v.tr.* to blunt, cloy (the palate, etc.); to surfeit (s.o.).

se blaser, to become blasé, indifferent; **se b. des, sur les, plaisirs,** to become indifferent to enjoyment; **on se blase de ces plaisirs,** these pleasures pall; **on s'en blase vite,** it soon palls.

blaser[2] [blazœ:r], *s.m. Cost:* blazer.

blason [blɑzɔ̃], *s.m. Her:* (*a*) coat of arms, armorial bearings, blazon; *F:* **ternir, salir, son b.,** to sully, besmirch, one's escutcheon; **redorer son b.,** to restore the fortunes of one's house; (*b*) blazon(ry), heraldry, armory.

blasonnement [blɑzɔnmɑ̃], *s.m. Her:* blazoning, blazonry.

blasonner [blɑzɔne], *v.tr. Her:* **b. un écu,** to blazon an escutcheon; (i) to paint, (ii) to describe, trick, an escutcheon heraldically.

blasonneur, -euse [blɑzɔnœ:r, -ø:z], *s. Her:* blazoner.

blasphémateur, -trice [blasfematœ:r, -tris]. **1.** *s.* blasphemer. **2.** *a.* blaspheming, blasphemous, profane.

blasphématoire [blasfematwa:r], *a.* blasphemous.

blasphème [blasfɛm], *s.m.* blasphemy; **proférer des blasphèmes,** to blaspheme.

blasphémer [blasfeme], *v.tr. & i.* (**je blasphème, n. blasphémons; je blasphémerai**) to blaspheme; to swear; **b. le saint nom de Dieu,** to profane, blaspheme, the name of God.

blaste [blast], *s.m. Bot:* blastus, plumule.

blastématique [blastematik], *a. Biol:* blastemal, blastematic, rudimentary.

blastème [blastɛ:m], *s.m. Biol:* blastema.

blastocarpe [blastɔkarp], *a. Bot:* blastocarpous.

blastocœle [blastɔsɛl], *s.m. Biol:* blastocoel.

blastocolle [blastɔkɔl], *s.f. Bot:* blastocolla.

blastoderme [blastɔdɛrm], *s.m. Biol:* blastoderm.

blastodermique [blastɔdɛrmik], *a. Biol:* blastodermic.

blastogenèse [blastɔʒ(ə)nɛ:z], *s.f. Biol:* blastogenesis.

blastoïdes [blastɔid], *s.m.pl. Paleont:* blastoidea.

blastomère [blastɔmɛ:r], *s.m. Z:* blastomere.

blastomycètes [blastɔmisɛt], *s.m.pl. Bot:* blastomycetes.

blastomycose [blastɔmiko:z], *s.f. Med:* blastomycosis.

blastopore [blastɔpɔ:r], *s.m. Biol:* blastopore.

blastosphère [blastɔsfɛ:r], *s.m. Biol:* blastosphere.

blastospore [blastɔspɔ:r], *s.f. Bot:* blastospore.

blastozoïde [blastɔzɔid], *s.m. Biol:* blastozooid.

blastula [blastyla], *s.f.*, **blastule** [blastyl], *s.f., Biol:* blastula, blastule.

blatérer [blatere], *v.i.* (**il blatère; il blatérera**) (*of camels*) to roar; (*of rams*) to bleat.

blatier [blatje], *s.m.* corn-chandler.

blattaire [blat(t)ɛ:r]. **1.** *a. Ent:* blattid. **2.** *s.m.pl. Ent:* **blattaires,** Blattidae. **3.** *s.f. Bot:* (**molène**) **b.,** moth mullein.

blatte [blat], *s.f. Ent:* cockroach.

blattides [blatid], **blattidés** [blatide], *s.m.pl. Ent:* Blattidae.

blattoptéroïdes [blatɔpterɔi:d], *s.m.pl. Ent:* Blattopteroidea.

blaude [blod], *s.f. Dial:* Smock.

blazer [blazœ:r], *s.m. Cost:* blazer.

blé [ble], *s.m.* **1.** (*a*) corn; **champ de b.,** corn-field; **faire les blés,** to harvest the corn; **grenier à b.,** granary; **halle aux blés,** corn-exchange; **b. en herbe,** corn in the blade; *F:* **manger son b. en herbe, en vert,** to anticipate one's income, to spend one's money before one gets it; *F:* **c'est du b. en grenier,** it's like money in the bank; *P:* **avoir du b.,** to have money; (*b*) corn-field; *F:* **être pris comme dans un b.,** to be caught like a rat in a trap. **2. b. (froment),** wheat; **mettre une terre en b.,** to crop land with wheat; **terre à b.,** wheat-growing land; **b. noir,** buck-wheat; Saracen corn; **b. poulard,** duck-bill; **b. de Turquie, d'Espagne,** *Fr.C:* **b. d'Inde,** maize, Indian corn, *U.S:* corn; **b.-seigle,** rye; **b. d'Égypte, de mai,** barley; **grands blés,** wheat and rye; **petits blés,** oats and barley; **b. dur,** hard wheat; *U.S:* durum wheat; **b. vitreux,** (*in England and U.S.*) hard wheat; **b. barbu,** bearded-wheat; **b. à moudre,** grist; **b. tendre, b. farineux,** soft wheat.

bléchard [bleʃa:r], *P:* **1.** *a.* ugly, deformed. **2.** *s.m.* quill-driver.

blêche [blɛʃ], *a. P: A:* **1.** weak (in character), unreliable. **2.** ugly; **elle est rien b.!** isn't she a fright! **3.** = BLET[1].

bléchir [bleʃi:r], *v.i.* **1.** to become weak, flabby (in character). **2.** (*of fruit*) to become sleepy, woolly.

blechne [blɛkn], **blechnum** [blɛknɔm], *s.m. Ferns:* blechnum.

bled [blɛd], *s.m.* (*in Northern Africa*) inland country; **dans le b.,** up country; *F:* **en plein b.,** at the back of beyond; *F:* **un sale b.,** a rotten place; **quel b.!** what a dump! *Mil: P:* **monter sur le b.,** to go over the top.

blédard [bleda:r], *s.m. F:* colonist, settler (*living far away from other white men*).

bleime [blɛm], *s.f. Vet:* corn, sore (on horse's foot).

blême [blɛm], *a.* **1.** (*a*) livid, ghastly; deathly pale; (*b*) cadaverous (face). **2.** pale, colourless; wan (light).

blêmir [blemi:r], *v.* **1.** *v.i.* to turn pale, livid; to blanch; to turn ghastly pale. **2.** *v.i.* (*of light, etc.*) to grow dim, faint, wan. **3.** *v.tr.* to turn sth. pale, to blanch.

blêmissant [blemisɑ̃], *a.* paling, turning pale, livid.

blêmissement [blemismɑ̃], *s.m.* turning pale, paleness.

blende [blɛ̃d], *s.f. Miner:* blende, sphalerite; *F:* black-jack, mock-lead.

blenheim [blɛnaim, blɛnɛm], *s.m.* blenheim spaniel.

blennie [blɛni], *s.f. Ich:* blenny; **b. ocellée,** ocellated blenny.

blennorr(h)agie [blɛnɔraʒi], *s.f. Med:* blennorrhagia, gonorrhoea.

blennorr(h)agique [blɛnɔraʒik], *a. Med:* blennorrhagic.

blennorr(h)ée [blɛnɔre], *s.f. Med:* blennorrhoea.

blépharite [blefarit], *s.f. Med:* blepharitis; **b. ciliaire,** ciliary, marginal, blepharitis.

blépharo-blennorr(h)ée [blefarɔblɛnɔre], *s.f. Med:* blepharoblennorrhoea.

blépharo-conjonctivite [blefarɔkɔ̃ʒɔ̃ktivit], *s.f. Med:* blepharoconjunctivitis.

blépharoplastie [blefarɔplasti], *s.f. Med:* blepharoplasty.

blépharoptose [blefarɔpto:z], *s.f. Med:* blepharoptosis.

blèse [blɛ:z]. **1.** *a.* lisping; **être b.,** to lisp. **2.** *s.m. & f.* lisper.

blèsement [blɛzmɑ̃], *s.m.* lisping, lisp.

bléser [bleze], *v.i.* (**je blèse, n. blésons; je bléserai**) to lisp.

blésité [blezite], *s.f.* lisping.

blésois, -oise [blezwa, -wa:z]. **1.** *a. & s.* (native, inhabitant) of Blois. **2.** *s.m.* **le Blésois,** region of ancient France, capital Blois.

blessant [blɛsɑ̃], *a.* offensive, stinging, cutting (remark, etc.).

blessé, -ée [blese], *s.* wounded, injured, person; *Mil:* casualty; **les blessés,** (i) *Mil:* the wounded, the casualties; (ii) (*in an accident*) the injured; **les grands blessés,** (i) *Mil:* the severely wounded, the serious cases; (ii) the severely disabled; **b. assis,** sitting case; **b. couché, ne pouvant pas marcher,** stretcher, lying, case; *U.S:* litter case; **b. pouvant marcher,** walking case; **b. récupérable,** short-duration case; **b. intransportable, unévacuable,** non-transportable, unevacuable, case.

blesser [blese], *v.tr.* **1.** (*a*) to wound, injure, hurt; **b. qn d'un coup d'épée,** to wound s.o. with a sword(-thrust); **blessé à mort,** mortally wounded, fatally injured; **ces souliers me blessent,** these shoes hurt, pinch, me; (*b*) (*of saddle, etc.*) to gall (*horse*). **2.** to offend (s.o.); to wound the feelings

of (s.o.); to give offence to (s.o.); **b. les yeux, l'oreille,** to offend the eye, to shock, grate upon, the ear; **b. qn dans son orgueil,** to wound s.o.'s pride; **blessé dans son orgueil,** wounded, hurt, in his pride; **cette suspicion de ta part me blesse,** I resent this suspiciousness on your part; **être blessé de qch.,** to be offended at sth.; to feel (oneself) aggrieved at, by, sth.; **il n'y a que la vérité qui blesse,** truth alone wounds. **3.** to hurt (s.o.'s interests), to wrong, do wrong to (s.o.), to be prejudicial to (s.o.); **b. l'honneur de qn,** to wound s.o.'s honour; **b. les convenances,** to offend, sin against, propriety; **b. la loi,** to violate the law.

se blesser. 1. to injure, wound, hurt, oneself (**avec,** with). **2.** to take offence (**de,** at); **se b. d'un rien,** to take offence at trifles.

blessir [blesi:r], *v.i.* = BLETTIR.

blessure [blesy:r], *s.f.* (*a*) wound, hurt, injury; **faire une b. à qn,** to inflict a wound on s.o., to wound s.o.; **sans b.,** unwounded, unhurt; **les blessures de l'amour,** the pangs of love; *Jur:* **coups et blessures,** assault and battery; *Mil: P:* **la bonne b.,** a blighty; **b. légère,** flesh wound; **b. par balle,** bullet wound; (*b*) (rub-) sore, gall.

blet, blette[1] [blɛ, blɛt], *a.* (*a*) over-ripe, sleepy, soft (fruit); (*b*) *F:* yellowish; *P:* drunk.

blette[2], **blète** [blɛt], *s.f. Bot:* white-beet, spinach-beet; **b. à tête,** strawberry-blite.

blettir [blɛti:r], *v.i.* (*of fruit*) to become over-ripe, sleepy; to blet.

blettissement [blɛtismɑ̃], *s.m.* softening, bletting (of fruit).

blettissure [blɛtisy:r], *s.f.* **1.** over-ripeness, softness, sleepiness (of fruit). **2.** over-ripe portion (of fruit).

bleu, *pl.* **bleus** [blø]. **1.** *a.* blue; **enfant aux yeux bleus,** blue-eyed child; *A:* **la Bibliothèque bleue,** collection of mediaeval tales of adventure (with blue covers); hence **conte b.,** fairy-tale; **lèvres bleues de froid,** lips blue with cold; **battre qn tout b.,** to beat s.o. black and blue; *F:* **colère bleue,** towering rage; **cela m'a donné une peur bleue,** it put me in a blue funk; **j'en suis resté b.,** I was flabbergasted; **il en a vu de bleues,** he has had a rough time of it, has had some queer experiences; **il m'en a fait voir de bleues,** he has led me a fine dance; *Med:* **maladie bleue,** blue disease; cyanosis; **enfant b.,** blue baby; *s.a.* CORDON BLEU, **2.** *s.m.* (*a*) (i) blue (colour); **b. clair,** light blue; **b. foncé,** dark blue, navy blue; **robes b. de ciel,** sky-blue dresses; *Mil:* **b. horizon,** horizon blue, (*French*) field-service colour (*c.* 1915-*c.* 1935); **le b. de la mort,** the livid hue of death; *F:* **mon bras est couvert de bleus,** my arm is all black and blue; **j'ai un b.,** I've got a bruise; *Cu:* **b. (d'Auvergne, etc.),** blue cheese; **poisson au b.,** fish cooked in a mixture of water, wine and vinegar; (ii) blue (pigment, dye); **b. de Prusse, de Berlin,** Prussian blue; **b. marine,** navy blue; **b. (de) roi, (de) France,** royal blue; **b. d'outremer,** ultramarine (blue); (iii) (laundry-)blue; **passer du linge au b.,** to blue linen; (*b*) **le b. (du ciel),** the blue, the air; **le pays du b.,** the land of dreams; **se perdre dans le b.,** to lose oneself in day-dreams; *Artil:* **tirer dans le bleu,** to fire at random; *F:* **tout cet argent a passé au b.,** all this money has disappeared into thin air, has vanished; **passer qch. au b.,** to conceal, hush up, sth; **n'y voir que du b.,** (i) to be puzzled, all at sea; (ii) to allow oneself to be hoodwinked; to remain blissfully unconscious of sth.; to be unaware of sth., blind to sth. **3.** *s. F:* tyro, greenhorn; raw hand; *Mil:* recruit, conscript; *P:* rookie; **les bleus,** the awkward squad; *Hist:* **les Bleus,** the French Republican armies (of the Revolution). **4.** *s.m.* (*a*) *Tchn:* blue print; (*b*) *F:* **petit b.,** (i) light red wine; (ii) express letter transmitted by pneumatic tube, in Paris; (*c*) *F:* **un paquet de b.,** a packet of cheap pipe tobacco; (*d*) **un b., des bleus, (de travail, de chauffe),** dungarees, boiler-suit, overalls; *Navy:* number eight (uniform). **5.** *s.f.* (*a*) *A: P:* **bleue,** absinthe; (*b*) **la Grande Bleue,** the Mediterranean.

bleuâtre [bløɑ:tr], *a.* bluish.

bleuet [bløɛ], *s.m. F:* **1.** *Orn:* kingfisher. **2.** = BLUET. **3.** *Fr.C: Bot:* blueberry.

bleuir [bløi:r]. **1.** *v.tr.* to blue; to make (sth.) blue; **acier bleui,** blued steel. **2.** *v.i.* (*a*) to become, turn, blue; (*b*) to become discoloured.

bleuissage [bløisa:ʒ], *s.m. Metalw:* blueing, *U.S: Cer:* reduction firing.

bleuissant [bløisɑ̃], *a.* turning blue.

bleuissement [bløismɑ̃], *s.m.* **1.** (*a*) blueing, turning blue; (*b*) discoloration. **2.** *Arb:* blue-rot. **3.** *Metalw:* **b. par échauffement,** burning (of metal).

bleusaille [bløzɑ:j], *s.f. Mil: P:* **1.** young recruit. **2.** *coll.* young recruits.

bleutage [bløta:ʒ], *s.m.* (slight) blueing (of body-linen).

bleuté [bløte], *a.* steely blue (swallow's wings, etc.); blued (spectacles, etc.); bluish (hue); *Phot:* **objectif b.,** coated lens.

bleuter [bløte], *v.tr.* to blue (linen, etc.) slightly; to give a blue tinge to (glass, steel, etc.).

blin [blɛ̃], *s.m.* **1.** beetle, paving-rammer, earth-rammer. **2.** *Nau:* boom-iron, clamp.

blindage [blɛ̃da:ʒ], *s.m.* **1.** *Civ.E: Min:* timbering, poling, sheeting. **2.** (*a*) *Mil:* blindage, shielding. (*b*) *Mil: Navy:* armour, (armour-)plate, (armour-)plating; **plaque de b.,** armour plate; plate of armour; **b. avant,** front plating, armour; **b. arrière,** rear plating, armour; **b. de flanc, b. latéral,** side plating, armour; **b. à l'épreuve des bombes, des obus, des balles,** bomb-proof, shell-proof, bullet-proof, plating, armour. **3.** metal casing. **4.** *W.Tel: El:* (*a*) (i) screening, (ii) screen (of valve); (*b*) shrouding (of transformer, etc.).

blinde [blɛ̃:d], *s.f. Mil: Fort:* **1.** piece of wood for a blindage; blind. **2.** *pl.* wooden frame (to support planks, fascines, etc.), blindage frame.

blindé [blɛ̃de], *a.* **1.** timbered (shaft, trench); iron-clad (shaft), metal-clad (motor, etc.). **2.** *Mil: Navy:* armoured, armour-plated; *Mil:* **abri b.,** bomb-proof shelter, dug-out; **train b.,** armoured train; *Navy: A:* **vaisseaux blindés,** armoured ships; **pont b.,** armoured deck, protective deck; *Mil:* **l'arme blindée,** The Royal Tank Corps, *U.S:* The Armored Corps; **infanterie, cavalerie blindée,** armoured infantry; cavalry; **groupement b.,** armoured brigade group, *U.S:* combat command; **division blindée,** armoured division; **engin b.,** armoured fighting, combat, vehicle; **véhicule b. de transport de troupe,** armoured personnel carrier, APC; **engin b. de reconnaissance,** armoured car; **véhicule non blindé,** soft-skinned vehicle; **légèrement, fortement, b.,** lightly, heavily, armoured; *F:* **être b. (contre le danger),** to be proof against danger; *P:* **être b.,** to be drunk; *P:* blotto. **3.** *Mil:* (*a*) *s.f.* **blindée,** armoured car; (*b*) *s.m.pl.* **les blindés,** the armour. **4.** *El.E: W.Tel:* **panneau b.,** armoured, ironclad, panel; **lampe blindée,** screened valve; **transformateur b.,** shrouded, screened, transformer.

blinder [blɛ̃de], *v.tr.* **1.** *Civ.E: Min:* to sheet, case, pole, timber, line (trench, mine-shaft, etc.). **2.** *Mil: Navy:* to armour, to protect with armour plating, to armour-plate (ship), to plate, to make bomb-proof. **3.** *El.E:* to screen, shroud (parts).

bliner [bline], *v.tr.* **1.** *Civ.E:* to ram (paving-stones, etc.); to tamp (earth). **2.** *Nau:* to clamp.

blitz [blits], *s.m.* blitz.

blizzard [bliza:r], *s.m.* blizzard.

bloc [blɔk], *s.m.* **1.** (*a*) block, lump (of wood, stone, metal, etc.); *Metall:* rough forging; **b. de maisons,** block (of houses); *Ind:* **b. technique,** design department (in a factory); **gros b. de pierre,** *Geol:* **b. erratique,** boulder; **b. de béton,** concrete block; *Sp:* **b. de départ,** starting block; **b. de marchandises,** job lot of goods; **acheter qch. en b.,** to buy the whole stock of sth., to buy sth. in the lump; **démonter qch. en b.,** to remove sth. as an assembly, as a unit; **acquérir des droits (de traduction, etc.) en b.,** to buy rights outright; **coulé en b.,** cast in one piece; **tout d'un b.,** all of a piece; **faire b. avec qch.,** to form one unit with sth.; *Aut:* **b. moteur,** engine block, motor unit; *Cin:* **b. sonore,** sound unit; *Computers:* **b. fonctionnel,** hardware; *W.Tel:* **condensateur à deux blocs,** two-gang condenser; *Typ:* **b. d'empreinte,** impression block; *Mch:* **b. de serrage,** wrench adapter; *adv.phr:* **à b.,** tight, home; *Nau:* chock-a-block, chock up; **visser, serrer, qch. à b.,** to screw sth. home; **serrer les freins à b.,** to jam on the brakes hard; **enfoncer une cartouche à b.,** to push a cartridge home; **hisser un pavillon à b.,** to hoist a flag right up; *Nau:* **mettre les amures à b.,** to haul the tacks aboard; *F:* **je suis tout à fait à b..** I am absolutely exhausted; *F:* **gonflé à b.,** (i) full of beans; (ii) a bit above oneself; (iii) sure of oneself; (*b*) *Rail:* block-system. **2.** *Pol:* coalition (of parties), bloc; **b. du centre,** the centre; **faire b.,** to unite (**contre,** against); **le b. occidental,** the Western bloc. **3.** *P:* prison, quod; *Mil:* guard-room, cells, clink; **fourrer, mettre, qn au b.,** to put s.o. in quod. **4.** pad (of paper), *U.S:* tablet; **b. à dessin,** drawing block.

blocage [blɔka:ʒ], *s.m.* **1.** (*a*) clamping, blocking-up (of machine, etc.); locking (of part); *Av:* **b. des gyros,** gyro caging; **vis de b.,** locking screw; *Aut:* **sièges à dispositif de b.,** seats with locking device; *s.a.* TOUCHE 2; (*b*) jamming on (of brakes). **2.** *Civ.E: Const:* (*a*) filling-in, packing (of wall, etc.); (*b*) rubble(-work); (*c*) cement block foundation. **3.** (*a*) *El:* blocking (of current); (*b*) *Mch:* sticking, seizing, jamming (of valve, piston). **4.** *Rail:* **section de b.,** block-section. **5.** *Typ:* turning (of letter); blank. **6.** *Pol.Ec:* pegging; *Fin:* freezing; **b. des prix et des salaires,** price and wage freeze; **le b. de la dette brittannique,** the freezing of the British debt.

blocaille [blɔkɑ:j], *s.f. Civ.E:* **1.** rubble(-stone), broken bricks. **2.** ballast; hardcore.

bloc-bain [blɔkbɛ̃], *s.m.* bathroom-unit; *pl. blocs-bains.*

bloc-buvard [blɔkbyva:r], *s.m.* blotting-pad; *pl. blocs-buvards.*

bloc-correspondance [blɔkkɔrɛspɔ̃dɑ̃:s], *s.m.* writing-pad; *pl. blocs-correspondance.*

bloc-cuisine [blɔkkyizin], *s.m. Furn:* kitchen unit; *pl. blocs-cuisines.*

bloc-cylindres [blɔksilɛ̃:dr], *s.m. Aut:* engine block, cylinder block; *pl. blocs-cylindres.*

bloc-diagramme [blɔkdjagram], *s.m. Geol: Geog:* (block-)diagram; *pl. blocs-diagrammes.*

bloc-douche [blɔkduʃ], *s.m.* shower-unit; *pl. blocs-douches.*

bloc-eau [blɔko], *s.m. Hyd.E: Plumb:* hydraulic system; waterwork(s); plumbing; *pl. blocs-eaux.*

bloc-évier [blɔkevje], *s.m.* sink-unit; *pl. blocs-éviers.*

bloc-film [blɔkfilm], *s.m. Phot:* film-pack; *pl. blocs-films.*

blochet [blɔʃɛ], *s.m.* **1.** (small) block; **b. d'arrêt d'un frein,** stop-block of a brake; *s.a.* PALIER 3. **2.** *Const:* tie-beam, -piece; brace, strut (of roof); **charpente à blochets** = hammer-beam roof.

blockhaus [blɔko:s], *s.m.* **1.** *Fort:* blockhouse; *O:* sconce; *F:* pill-box. **2.** *Navy:* armoured tower; **b. de commandement,** conning tower.

bloc-moteur [blɔkmɔtœ:r], *s.m. Aut:* engine-block, motor unit; *pl. blocs-moteurs.*

bloc(k)-notes [blɔknɔt], *s.m.* memorandum-block, writing-pad; *U.S:* scratch-pad; *pl. bloc(k)s-notes.*

blockship [blɔkʃip], *s.m. Nau:* blockship.

bloc-système [blɔksistɛm], *s.m. Rail:* block-system.

blocus [blɔkys], *s.m.* blockade; investment; **b. effectif,** effective blockade; **b. fictif,** paper blockade; **b. rigoureux,** close blockade; **b. maritime,** sea blockade; **faire le b. d'un port,** to blockade a port; **lever le b.,** to raise the blockade; **forcer le b.,** to run the blockade; **forcement de b.,** blockade running; *s.a.* FORCEUR; *Hist:* **le B. continental,** the Continental System.

blœdite [bledit], *s.f. Miner:* blœdite, blodite.

blond, -onde [blɔ̃, -ɔ̃:d]. **1.** *a.* (*a*) fair, flaxen (hair); blond (person); **bière blonde,** pale ale; *F:* **bouteille de blonde,** bottle of pale ale; *Poet:* **les blonds épis,** the golden, yellow, ears of corn; (*b*) *Tex:* beige. **2.** *s.* fair(-haired) man, woman; blond(e); *F:* **il va voir sa blonde,** he's off to see his sweetheart, his girl. **3.** *s.m.* (*a*) blond, flaxen (colour); **cheveux (d'un) b. doré,** golden hair; **b. ardent,** auburn; **blond vénitien,** Titian red; **b. platine,** platinum blonde; **b. cendré,** light, silvery (hair); ash-blond(e); **b. tendre,** very fair; **aux cheveux b. filasse,** tow-headed; (*b*) *Cu:* meat stock. **4.** *s.f.* **blonde,** blond-lace.

blondasse [blɔ̃das], *a.* flaxen-haired (person); insipidly fair, washed out (hair).

blondeur [blɔ̃dœ:r], *s.f.* blondness, fairness; golden hue (of corn).

blondier, -ière [blɔ̃dje, -jɛ:r], *s.* maker of blond lace.

blondin,[1] **-ine** [blɔ̃dɛ̃, -in]. **1.** *a. & s.* fair-haired (person). **2.** *s.m. A:* beau, fop.

blondin[2], *s.m.* cableway.

blondinet, -ette [blɔ̃dinɛ, -ɛt], *a. & s.* (person) with rather fair hair; **une petite blondinette,** a fair-haired little girl.

blondir [blɔ̃di:r]. **1.** *v.i.* (*esp. of corn*) to turn yellow, golden; (*of hair*) to go blond. **2.** *v.tr.* (*a*) to bleach (linen); (*b*) to dye or bleach (hair) blond; (*c*) *Cu:* to brown (slightly).

blondissant [blɔ̃disɑ̃], *a.* (*of corn*) yellowing.

blondoiement [blɔ̃dwamɑ̃], *s.m.* yellow reflection, gleam, sheen (of ripe corn).

blondoyer [blɔ̃dwaje], *v.i.* (**il blondoie; il blondoiera**) to have a yellow reflection, to gleam yellow.

blongios [blɔ̃ʒios], *s.m. Orn:* **b. nain,** little bittern.

bloom [blum], *s.m. Metall:* bloom.

bloomerie [blumri], *s.f. Metall:* **1.** bloomery, finery, puddling-furnace. **2.** catalan forge.

blooming [blumiŋ], *s.m. Metall:* blooming-mill.

bloquer [blɔke], *v.tr.* **1.** *Const:* (*a*) to block up, fill up, (wall) with rubble; (*b*) to point (wall). **2.** to lock, clamp (piece of machinery, etc.); to jam on (brake); **b. les roues,** to lock the wheels; *Bill:* **b. la bille de son adversaire,** to pocket one's opponent's ball; **b. les billes,** to jam the balls; **b. un écrou à refus,** to screw up a nut (spanner-) tight; *F:* **rouler klaxon bloqué,** to drive with one's thumb on the horn. **3.** *Typ:* **b. une lettre,** to turn a letter; **b. une page,** to build up a page (leaving space for a block). **4.** (*a*) to block, obstruct (road, measure, etc.); to stop (cheque); to block (account); **b. les salaires,** to freeze wages; **b. le chemin à qn,** to block s.o.'s way; *Rail:* **b. une section,** to close a section; (*b*) to blockade (a port); to invest (a place); *F:* **me voilà bloqué à l'hôpital pour six semaines,** here I am stuck in hospital for six weeks; **si nous ne sommes pas bloqués par la neige,** if we are not snowbound; **bloqué dans une grotte,** trapped in a cave; (*c*) *Sp:* to stop, block (blow, ball). **5.** to combine to form a block; *Com:* *F:* **b. une commande,** to make one's orders *en bloc*.

se bloquer. 1. to jam; to get jammed; to seize. **2.** *Ven:* (*of hawk*) to poise (in mid-air).

bloquet [blɔkɛ], *s.m.* bobbin (for pillow lace).

bloquette [blɔkɛt], *s.f.* **1.** hole, pit, dug in the ground (for playing marbles). **2.** (game of) pits.

bloqueur, -euse [blɔkœːr, -øːz]. **1.** *s.m.* blockader; *Rail:* signalman. **2.** *a.* blockading (ship, etc.); *Rail:* **dispositif b.,** blocking device.

blot[1] [blo], *s.m. Com:* job lot (of goods); *F:* **acheter qch. à bas b.,** to buy sth. on the cheap; *P:* **c'est mon b.,** that's my affair; **ça fait mon b.,** that suits me.

blot[2], *s.m. A: Nau:* log.

blotch [blɔtʃ], *s.m. Arb: Fung:* blotch.

blottir (se) [səblɔtiːr], *v.pr.* to cower, crouch, squat, hide; **se b. dans le fond d'une campagne,** to bury oneself in the country; **village blotti au fond de la vallée,** village tucked away in the valley; **se b. dans son lit,** to curl up, snuggle down, in bed; **blotti dans un coin, huddled,** huddling, in a corner.

bloum [blum], *s.m. A: P:* **1.** hat, opera hat. **2.** reservist.

bloumard [bluma:r], *s.m. A: P:* hat.

blouse[1] [bluːz], *s.f. Bill: A:* pocket; **mettre une bille dans la b.,** to pocket a ball.

blouse[2], *s.f.* **1.** *a.* loose protecting over-garment; (*artist's*) overall, smock; (*peasant's*) blouse; (*b*) *A: F:* **les blouses,** the proletariat. **2.** blouse; **b. qui rentre dans la jupe,** tuck-in blouse; **b. qui va, se porte, par-dessus la jupe,** overblouse.

blouser [bluze], *v.tr.* **1.** *Bill: A:* to pocket (ball). **2.** *F:* to cheat, deceive, mislead; to take (s.o.) in. **3.** *Cost:* to blouse; to drape loosely; to gather in (the waistline).

se blouser, *F:* to be wide of the mark, to be mistaken, to make a blunder.

blouson [bluzɔ̃], *s.m.* (lumber-)jacket; *Sp:* sweat shirt; **b. de golf,** windcheater, golfing-jacket; *U.S:* windbreaker; *F:* **b. noir,** teddy-boy.

blousse [blus], *s.f. Tex:* noil, combings.

blue-jean [blu(d)ʒin], *s.m. Cost:* jeans.

blues [bluːz], *s.m. Mus:* blues.

bluet [blyɛ], *s.m. Bot:* **1.** corn-flower, bluebottle. **2.** bilberry, whortleberry; **b. du Canada** (Canada) blueberry.

bluette [blyɛt], *s.f.* (*a*) (short-lived) spark; (*b*) flash, sparkle (of precious stones, etc.); *F:* **bluettes d'esprit,** flashes, sparks, of wit; **composer des bluettes,** to write sparkling trifles; (*c*) *Orn:* guinea-fowl.

bluff [blœf], *s.m. F:* bluff; **coup de b.,** piece of bluff.

bluffer [blœfe]. **1.** *v.tr. F:* to bluff (s.o.). **2.** *v.i.* to try it on.

bluffeur, -euse [blœfœːr, -øːz], *s.* bluffer.

blutage [blytaːʒ], *s.m. Mill: etc:* bolting, sifting, screening; **taux de b. (de la farine),** extraction rate (of flour).

bluteau, -eaux [blyto], *s.m. Mill: etc:* **1.** (*a*) bolter-sieve; (*b*) bolting-machine, -mill; bolter. **2.** bolting-cloth.

bluter [blyte], *v.tr. Mill: etc:* to bolt, sift.

bluterie [blytri], *s.f. Mill: etc:* **1.** bolting-mill, bolter. **2.** bolting-reel. **3.** bolting-room, -house.

bluteur [blytœːr], *s.m.* worker in bolting-mill; sifter.

blutoir [blytwaːr], *s.m.* = BLUTEAU.

boa [bɔa], *s.m.* **1.** *Rept:* boa; **b. constricteur,** boa-constrictor. **2.** *Cost:* (feather-)boa.

Boadicée [bɔadise], *Pr.n.f. Hist:* Boadicea.

boarmie [bɔarmi], *s.f. Ent:* boarmia (moth); **b. du chêne,** great oak-beauty.

bob [bɔb], *s.m. F:* = BOBSLEIGH.

bobard [bɔbaːr], *s.m. P:* tall story; **tout ça c'est des bobards,** that's all rubbish, boloney; **monter un b.,** to spin a yarn, to shoot a line.

bobe [bɔb], *s.f. A: F:* **faire la b.,** to pout.

bobèche [bɔbɛʃ], *s.f.* **1.** (*a*) socket, sconce (of candlestick); (*b*) candle-ring, candle-drip, drip-glass. **2.** *P:* head, nut; **se monter la b.,** to kid oneself.

bobéchon [bɔbeʃɔ̃], *s.m.* **1.** candle-holder (*with spike for fixing into wood-work, etc.*). **2.** *P:* = BOBÈCHE 2.

bobinage [bɔbinaːʒ], *s.m.* **1.** *Tex:* winding, spooling, reeling. **2.** *El.E:* winding, coiling.

bobinard [bɔbinaːr], *s.m. P:* brothel.

bobine [bɔbin], *s.f.* **1.** (*a*) *Tex: etc:* bobbin, spool, reel; **b. de papier,** reel, roll, of paper; **b. de coton,** reel of cotton; *U.S:* spool of thread; *Typewr:* **bobines du ruban,** ribbon spools; (*b*) reel, drum (for rope, wire, etc.); *Phot:* spool, roll of film, roll-film; *Cin:* spool, reel; (*c*) *El:* (i) **(corps de) b.,** bobbin, spool; (ii) (induction or resistance) coil; **b. à rupteur,** make-and-break coil; **b. de couplage,** coupling coil; **b. d'allumage,** ignition coil; **b. de Ruhmkorff,** Ruhmkorff coil; **b. de réaction, de réactance,** choking-coil, reaction coil; *F:* choke; *Magn:* **b. d'essai, d'exploration,** search coil; *s.a.* ABEILLE; (*d*) *Av:* **b. entretoise,** spacer; **b. de polarisation,** bias coil. **2.** *P:* face; **il a une drôle de b.,** I don't like his face.

bobiner [bɔbine], *v.tr.* to wind, spool, reel (silk, etc., on bobbin); to wind, coil (cable, etc., on drum); **machine à b.,** winding machine; *El: etc:* **bobiné,** wire-wound; **induit bobiné en, de, cuivre,** copper-wound armature.

bobinette [bɔbinɛt], *s.f.* **1.** *A:* wooden (door-) latch, bobbin(-latch). **2.** *Aut: Adm:* Denver shoe.

bobineur, -euse [bɔbinœːr, -øːz], *s. El.E: Tex:* **1.** winder (i.e. operative). **2.** *s.f.* **bobineuse,** winding-machine, winder.

bobinier [bɔbinje], *s.m. El.E:* coil winder (person or machine).

bobinoir [bɔbinwaːr], *s.m.* (*a*) *Tex:* winding-machine, roving-frame, bobbin-frame; (*b*) *El.E:* *Cin: etc:* winding-bench.

bobo [bobo], *s.m. F:* (*a*) (*nursery*) pain, hurt, sore; **avoir du bobo,** to have a bump, a bruise, etc.; **est-ce que ça fait bobo?** does it hurt? (*b*) *F:* **avoir un b. au doigt,** to have a sore on one's finger, a gathered finger.

bobonne [bɔbɔn], *s.f.* **1.** *A: F:* (*a*) (*nursery*) nurse, nanny; (*b*) **petites bobonnes en sortie,** little housemaids out for the day. **2.** *P:* (*term of affection*) my dear, my pet, duckie.

bobsleigh [bɔbslɛ], *s.m.* bob-sleigh.

bocage[1] [bɔkaːʒ], *s.m.* **1.** *Lit:* grove, copse. **2.** *Geog:* mixed woodland and pasture-land; bocage.

bocage[2], *s.m. Metalw: Com:* scrap(-metal) (recovered on crushing the slag).

bocager, -ère [bɔkaʒe, -ɛːr], *a. Lit: A:* of the woodlands.

bocain, -aine [bɔkɛ̃, -ɛn], *a. & s. Geog:* (native, inhabitant) of the *Bocage normand*.

bocal, -aux [bɔkal, -o], *s.m.* **1.** (*a*) (wide-mouthed, short-necked) bottle or jar (used for drugs, sweets, pickles, etc.); **mettre des fruits en b.,** to bottle fruit; (*b*) (glass) globe; **b. (à poissons rouges)** goldfish bowl; (*c*) (chemist's) show-bottle; (*d*) jarful. **2.** *Mus:* **(embouchure en) b.,** (bell-shaped) mouthpiece (of trumpet, cornet, etc.).

bocard[1] [bɔkaːr], *s.m. Metall:* ore-crusher, stamp, stamping-mill.

bocard[2], *s.m. P:* brothel.

bocardage [bɔkardaːʒ], *s.m. Metall:* crushing, stamping (of ore).

bocarder [bɔkarde], *v.tr. Metall:* to crush, stamp (ore).

Boccace [bɔkas], *Pr.n.m.* Boccaccio.

boccage [bɔkaːʒ], *s.m.* = BOCAGE[2].

bocfil [bɔkfil], *s.m. Tls:* piercing-saw frame; fret-saw.

boche [bɔʃ], *a. & s. P: Pej:* German, jerry, kraut.

Bochie [bɔʃi], *Pr.n.f. P: Pej:* Germany.

Bochiman [bɔʃimɑ̃], *s.m.* = BOSCHIMAN.

bock [bɔk], *s.m.* **1.** (*a*) beer-glass; (*b*) (small) glass of beer. **2.** *Hyg:* irrigator, douche, enema.

bodo [bɔdo], *s.m. Prot:* bodo.

Boèce [bɔɛs], *Pr.n.m. A.Hist:* Boëthius.

Boer [buːr, bɔɛːr], *s.m.* Boer.

boësse [bwɛs], *s.f.* **1.** (*chasing*) chisel. **2.** *Engr:* wire brush, burnishing brush.

boësser [bwese], *v.tr.* **1.** to beard off, clean (chased or cast metal). **2.** *Engr:* to scrape, burnish.

boette, boëte [bwɛt]. *s.f. Fish:* bait.

boetter [bwɛte], *v.i. & tr.* to bait.

bœuf, *pl.* **bœufs** [bœf, bø], *s.m.* **1.** ox, bullock; **jeune b.,** steer; **paire de bœufs,** yoke of oxen; **accoupler, découpler, les bœufs,** to yoke, unyoke, the oxen; **troupeau de bœufs,** drove of oxen; **bœufs à l'engrais,** beeves, *U.S:* beefs; **b. gras** [bøgrɑ], fatted ox, prize ox; **bœufs de boucherie,** beef cattle, animals; *F:* **lourd comme un b.,** stupid, loutish; **travailler comme un b.,** to work like a cart-horse; **fort comme un b.,** as strong as a horse; **c'est un b. pour le travail,** he's a glutton for work; **avoir un b. sur la langue,** to (have been paid to) keep one's mouth shut; *s.a.* CHARRUE 1, ŒUF 1; *Z:* **b. musqué,** musk-ox; **b. à bosse,** zebu. **2.** beef; **b. (à la) mode,** stewed beef; *P:* **faire du b. à la mode,** to get saddle-sore; **b. salé,** salt beef; **conserve de b., b. de conserve,** corned beef, *Mil: Nau: F:* bully beef; *Nau:* (salt) junk. **3.** *a. P:* (*f. occ.* **bœuve** [bœːv]) colossal, tremendous, great; **c'est bœuf,** it's astounding, fine, tip-top, *U.S:* bully; **il a une chance b., bœuve,** he has the devil's own luck. **4.** *Orn:* **b. des marais,** bittern.

bœutier [bøtje], *s.m.* beef butcher.

bog [bɔg], *s.m. Cards:* card game (similar to Pope Joan).

Bogarmiles [bɔgarmil], *s.m.pl. Rel.H:* Bogomils.

boggie [bɔʒi], *s.m.* = BOGIE.

boggy [bɔge], *s.m.* = BOGUET.

boghead [bɔgɛd], *s.m. Miner:* boghead coal.

boghei [bɔge], *s.m.* = BOGUET.

bogie [bɔʒi], *s.m. Rail: etc:* bogie(-truck), radial truck; **b. avant, b. directeur,** pilot-truck, leading bogie; **b. arrière,** trailing truck.

Bogomiles [bɔgɔmil], *s.m.pl.* = BOGARMILES.

bogue[1] [bɔg], *s.m. Ich:* boöps.

bogue[2], *s.f. Bot:* chestnut-bur, -husk, *U.S:* -shuck.

bogue[3], *s.f.* **1.** mud shovel. **2.** helve-ring (of forge hammer).

boguet [bɔgɛ], *s.m.* buggy, light gig.

bohé [bɔe], *s.m.* Bohea (tea).

Bohême [bɔɛm], *Pr.n.f. Geog:* Bohemia.

bohème, 1. *a. & s.* Bohemian; **mener une vie de b.,** to lead a Bohemian, an unconventional, a free and easy, life; **foi de b.,** honour among thieves. **2.** *s.f.* **bohème;** (*a*) Bohemia (of the artistic world); (*b*) bohemianism.

bohémianisme [bɔemjanism], *s.m.* bohemianism.

bohémien, -ienne [bɔemjɛ̃, -jɛn], *a. & s.* **1.** *Geog:* Bohemian. **2.** gipsy.

boïar(d) [bɔjaːr], *s.m.* boyar.

boïdés [bɔide], *s.m.pl. Rept:* Boidae.

boire [bwaːr]. **I.** *v.tr.* (*pr.p.* **buvant;** *p.p.* **bu, bue;** *pr.ind.* **je bois** [bwa], **tu bois, il boit, n. buvons, v. buvez, ils boivent;** *pr.sub.* **je boive, n. buvions, ils boivent;** *imp.* **bois, buvons, buvez;** *p.d.* **je buvais;** *p.h.* **je bus, n. bûmes, v. bûtes, ils burent;** *fu.* **je boirai**) **1.** to drink; **b. qch. à petites gorgées, à petits coups,** to sip sth; **b. qch. d'un (seul) trait, d'un seul coup,** to drink sth. at one gulp, at a draught; to swig off (a glass); **b. un verre jusqu'à la dernière goutte,** to drain a glass; **b. un coup,** to have a drink; *F:* a wet; **b. un bon coup,** to have a long drink; **boire un affront,** to swallow, pocket, an insult; **ce vin se laisse b.,** this wine is palatable, goes down well; **faire b. qn,** to give s.o. a drink; *F:* **b. la, une, tasse,** to get a mouthful (when swimming); *F:* **b. à la grande tasse,** to drown; **ce n'est pas la mer à b.,** it is not so very difficult (to do); **il n'y a pas de l'eau à b. à ce métier,** there's nothing to be made out of that business; **croyez ça et buvez de l'eau!** don't you believe it! *F:* **b. du lait,** to take it in eagerly, to lap it up; *Th:* to be applauded; **b. à la bouteille,** to drink from the bottle; **b. à sa soif,** to drink one's fill; **faire b. les chevaux,** to water the horses; *F:* **il y a à b. et à manger,** it's like the curate's egg; **b. les paroles de qn,** to drink in someone's every word; *s.a.* BOUILLON 2, FONTAINE 1, GOUTTE 3, MÊME 4, SANTÉ, SOIF, VIN 1. **2.** (*of plants, porous substances, etc.*) to absorb, imbibe, drink up, soak up, suck in (moisture); (*of boots, etc.*) to take in water. **3.** to drink (alcoholic beverages); **il boit trop,** he drinks too freely; **il a trop bu, il a bu un coup (de trop),** he is the worse for drink, he has had a drop; **il a bu,** he's had one too many, one over the eight, he's been drinking; **b. sa fortune,** to drink away one's fortune, to spend one's fortune in drink; *abs.* **il boit,** he drinks, is a drunkard; **c'est est un homme qui boit,** he drinks too much; **se tuer à force de b.,** to drink oneself to death; *F:* **il boit comme un trou, il boirait la mer et ses poissons,** he drinks like a fish; **payer à b. à qn,** to stand s.o. a drink, to treat s.o.; **commander à b.,** to order a drink, drinks; **b. avidement,** to swill; **b. une bouteille,** *F:* to crack, drain, a bottle; **il est gai après b.,** he is lively when he's been drinking; *Prov:* **qui a bu boira,** once a drunkard always a drunkard. **4.**

to drink in (with one's eyes, ears); **b. qn des yeux,** to devour s.o. with one's eyes; to look at s.o. with rapture; to gloat over the sight of (victim, etc.). **5.** *Aut:* **roues qui boivent l'obstacle,** wheels that absorb the shock of an obstacle.

II. **boire,** *s.m.* drink, drinking; **le b. et le manger,** food and drink, eating and drinking; **il est amoureux à en perdre le b. et le manger,** he is head over heels in love.

bois [bwɑ], *s.m.* **1.** wood, forest; **petit b.,** spinney, grove, thicket; **b. taillis,** copse, coppice, underwood; **pays de b.,** woodland, wooded country; **homme des b.,** (i) rough, boorish, man; (ii) *F:* orang-utan; *F:* **le Bois,** the Bois de Boulogne (*outskirts of Paris*); **nous étions déjà sous b.,** we were already in the woods. **2.** timber (-tree); **b. en état, b. debout,** standing timber (-tree); **abattre, couper, le b.,** to cut down, fell, timber; *F:* **abattre du b.,** to work hard, to slog away. **3.** wood, timber, lumber; **faire du b.,** to cut timber; to timber; **b. de chauffage,** firewood; **(aller) faire du b.,** to gather sticks; **menu b.,** brushwood; **b. de service, b. d'œuvre, b. à ouvrer,** timber, lumber; **chantier de b.,** timber-yard; **jambe de b., en b.,** wooden leg; *Fr.C:* **maison en b. rond,** log house; *Min:* **b. de mine,** pit-props; **travail du b.,** wood-working; **construction en b.,** timber-work; **fil, veine du b.,** grain of the wood; **b. de fil,** wood split with the grain; **b. de bout, debout,** wood cut against the grain; **train de b.,** float, raft, of timber; **b. dur,** *Fr.C:* **b. franc,** hardwood; **b. tendre,** soft-wood; **b. de sapin, b. blanc,** deal; **b. d'ébène,** ebony; *Com:* **b. du nord,** Baltic timber; **sciure de b.,** sawdust; **gravure sur b.,** (i) engraving on wood, (ii) woodcut; *s.a.* FLÈCHE[1] 1, GUEULE 1, SOUTÈNEMENT 1; *F:* **homme de b.,** dull, lifeless man; **n'être pas de b.,** to be more sensitive than one looks; **je leur ferai voir de quel b. je me chauffe,** I'll show them what stuff I'm made of; **ils ne se chauffent pas du même b.,** they have nothing in common; **être du b. dont on fait les héros,** to be the stuff of which heroes are made; **il est du b. dont on fait les flûtes,** he is a man of pliable temper, you can twist him round your little finger; *Sp:* **abattre du bois,** to knock skittles down; *Av:* **casser du b.,** to crash (in landing); *Th:* **avoir du b.,** to have friends in the audience (to lead the clapping); **donner à qn une volée de b.,** to give s.o. a good thrashing; **touchez du b.!** touch wood! keep your fingers crossed; *s.a.* VISAGE. **4.** (*a*) *Typ:* wood-block; (*b*) *Engr:* wood-cut. **5.** *Bot:* **b. d'absinthe, de quassier,** quassia-wood; **b. d'aigle, d'aloès,** eagle-wood, aloes-wood; **b. de mai,** hawthorn; **b. gentil,** mezereon, spurge olive, **b. punais,** dogwood; **b. satiné,** snake-wood; **b. des îles,** West-Indian hardwood, marquetry wood; **b. de Pernambouc, b. brazil,** braziletto, brazilwood; **b. de fer,** ironwood; **b. de violette,** Brazilian rosewood; **b. de rose,** rose-wood. **6.** *pl.* **b. de cerf, de daim,** horns, antlers, of a stag, deer; *P:* **il lui pousse du b.,** (*of cuckold*) his horns are sprouting. **7. b. de lit,** bedstead; **b. de chaise,** framework (of a chair); **les b. de justice,** the scaffold (guillotine or gallows); **b. de fusil,** stock of a rifle; **b. de selle,** saddle-tree; *Tls:* **b. de rabot,** plane-stock; **b. de drapeau,** flagstaff; **b. de lance,** spear shaft; *Mus:* **les bois,** the wood-wind instruments; *F:* the wood-wind.

boisage [bwɑzaːʒ], *s.m.* **1.** *Const: Min: etc:* (*a*) timbering; casing (of shaft, gallery, etc.) with timber; tubbing, cribbing (of mine-shaft); (*b*) (i) scaffold(ing) timbering, framing; (ii) frame, framework; (*c*) = BOISERIE 2. **2.** (*a*) timbering, afforestation; (*b*) young trees, saplings.

boisé [bwɑze], *a.* **1.** wooded, well-wooded, well-timbered (country); **pays b.,** woodland, wooded country. **2.** wainscoted, panelled (room).

boisement [bwɑzmɑ̃], *s.m.* timbering, afforestation, tree-planting.

boiser [bwɑze], *v.tr.* **1.** (*a*) to panel, wainscot (wall, room); (*b*) to timber, prop (mine); to tub (shaft). **2.** *For:* to afforest; to put (region) under timber.

boiserie [bwɑzri], *s.f.* **1.** joiner's work. **2.** *Const:* woodwork, wainscot(ing), panelling; **murs revêtus de boiseries,** walls lined with wooden panelling.

boiseur [bwɑzœːr], *s.m. Min:* timberman.

boiseux, -euse [bwɑzø, -øːz], *a.* (= LIGNEUX) woody, of the nature of wood.

boisseau, -eaux [bwaso], *s.m.* **1.** (*a*) *A:* bushel, *Agr: F:* = approx. 13 litres; **mettre (la lumière, la lampe) sous le b.,** to hide one's light under a bushel; *s.a.* LAMPE 1; (*b*) *Mil: P:* shako. **2.** (*a*) drain-tile or chimney-flue tile; (*b*) faucet-pipe; **b. de robinet,** cock-casing, -shell; (*c*) *Mch: I.C.E:* throttle-chamber.

boisselée [bwasle], *s.f. A:* bushel(ful).

boisselier [bwasəlje], *s.m.* bushel-maker; (white, dry) cooper.

boisselière [bwasəljɛːr], *s.f. Orn:* great grey shrike.

boissellerie [bwasɛlri], *s.f.* **1.** bushel making; (white) cooperage. **2.** cooper's wares, hollow-ware.

bois-sent-bon [bwɑsɑ̃bɔ̃], *s.m.inv. in pl. Bot:* bog-myrtle.

boisson [bwasɔ̃], *s.f.* **1.** (*a*) beverage, drink; (*b*) **boissons fermentées,** fermented liquors (malt liquors, wine, cider); **impôt sur les boissons,** tax on fermented liquors; (*c*) *Fr.C:* hard liquor, spirits; (*d*) *F:* **adonné à la b.,** addicted to drink, to drunkenness; **pris de b.,** the worse for drink, for liquor; in liquor. **2.** rape-wine or water-cider; (*in Normandy*) *F:* cider.

boissonner [bwasɔne], *v.i. F:* to tipple; *P:* booze.

boîtard [bwataːr], *s.m. Mec.E:* vertical floor-bearing.

boite[1] [bwat], *s.f. F:* **avoir la b.,** to walk lame (after a march).

boite[2], *s.f.* **1.** *A:* maturity (of wine); **vin en b., de bonne b.,** matured wine. **2.** = BOISSON 2.

boîte [bwat], *s.* **1.** box; *Phot: F: O:* box camera; **b. de, en, fer blanc,** tin box, can, canister, tin; **b. à conserves,** tin, can; **conserves en b.,** tinned, canned, foods; **b. à lait,** milk-can; **b. à pain,** bread bin; **b. de secours,** first-aid box; **b. à gants,** glove-box; *Aut:* glove-compartment; *Atom.Ph: etc:* glove box; **en b.,** boxed; **mettre en b.,** to box (goods); to tin (sardines); *F:* **mettre qn en b.,** to pull s.o.'s leg, to take s.o. off; **b. aux lettres,** letter-box, pillar-box, posting-box, *U.S:* mailbox; **b. postale 260,** Post-Office box 260; **b. de montre,** watch-case; **b. d'allumettes,** box of matches; **b. à allumettes,** matchbox; **b. de cubes,** box of bricks; **b. de construction,** constructional kit; **b. à outils,** tool-chest, -box; **b. à musique,** musical-box, *U.S:* music-box; **b. à violon,** violin case; **b. à documents,** dispatch-box; **b. à malice, à surprise,** jack-in-the-box; *F:* **b. de singe,** tin of bully-beef; *P:* **ferme ta b.,** shut your trap! *F:* **elle a l'air de sortir d'une b.,** she looks as if she had just stepped out of a bandbox; **élevé dans une b.,** brought up in cotton-wool; *s.a.* THÉ 1; *Anat:* **b. du crâne, crânienne,** brain-pan. **2.** *Tchn:* **b. d'une serrure,** case of a lock; **b. à billes,** ball-bearing case; *Mch:* **b. à feu,** fire-box; **b. à fumée,** smoke-box; **b. à vapeur,** steam-chest; *Aut: etc:* **b. d'allumage,** ignition unit; *Aut:* **b. de vitesses,** gear-box, *U.S:* transmission; **b. de l'embrayage,** clutch-casing; *Rail:* **b. de l'essieu,** axle-box; **b. à graisse,** grease-box; *El.E:* **b. à fusible,** fuse-box; **b. de jonction, de raccordement,** junction box; *Artil: Mil:* **b. d'amorce,** primer box; **b. de culasse,** breech casing; *Clockm:* **b. à ressort,** spring-barrel, spring box; *Metall:* **b. à vent (du cubilot),** air-chamber; *Av: etc:* **b. de claquage,** flash tester; **b. d'écoute,** audio control panel; **b. de commande,** control-box; **b. de démarrage réacteur,** engine starting unit; *Organ:* **b. d'expression,** swell-box. **3.** *P:* (*a*) uncomfortable, poky, little room; (*b*) one's office, shop, school, etc.; **sale b.,** rotten hole (of a school, shop, boarding-house, etc.); *Sch:* **entrer en b.,** to become a boarder; *s.a.* BACHOT[2]; (*c*) **b. de nuit,** night-club, cabaret, joint; (*d*) *Mil:* guard-room, cells, clink.

boîte-chargeur [bwatʃarʒœːr], *s.f. Mil:* magazine pocket, loader; *pl. boîtes-chargeurs.*

boitement [bwatmɑ̃], *s.m.* **1.** limp(ing), halt(ing). **2.** irregular action (of machine).

boiter [bwate], *v.i.* to limp, halt; to be or walk lame; to hobble; **b. d'un pied,** to be lame in one foot; **homme qui boite,** lame man, *F:* man with a game leg; **b. bas,** to limp badly; **passer en boitant,** to hobble by; *Lit:* **vers qui boitent,** halting verse.

boiterie [bwatri], *s.f.* lameness.

boiteux, -euse [bwatø, -øːz]. **1.** *a.* (*a*) lame, halt, limping; **jambe boiteuse,** lame, *F:* game, leg; **vers b.,** halting verse; **esprit b.,** halting, slow-working, mind; (*b*) wobbly, rickety, gimcrack, ramshackle, insecure (furniture, etc.); **union boiteuse,** ill-assorted match; **paix boiteuse,** patched-up, unsatisfactory, peace. **2.** *s.m. or f.* **un boiteux, une boiteuse,** a cripple, lame, man, woman.

boîtier[1] [bwatje], *s.m.* case; **b. de montre,** watch-case; **b. pour lampe électrique,** electric-torch case; **b. de chirurgien,** surgeon's instrument-case; *Aut: etc:* box, case, housing; **b. de direction,** steering box, gear; **b. de frein,** brake housing; *Av: etc:* **b. de crépine,** filter housing; *s.a.* MONTRE 2.

boîtier[2], *s.m.* **1.** (*a*) box-, case-maker; (*b*) watch-case maker. **2.** postman who clears the letter-boxes.

boitillement [bwatijmɑ̃], *s.m.* slight limp, hobble.

boitiller [bwatije], *v.i.* to hobble; **s'avancer en boitillant,** to hobble along, up.

boitout [bwatu], *s.m.* = BOIT-TOUT 2, 3.

boitte [bwat], *s.f. Fish:* bait.

boit-tout [bwatu], *s.m.inv. in pl.* **1.** *Hyg:* leaching cesspool. **2.** wine-glass without foot. **3.** *P:* drunkard (who drinks all his earnings).

bol[1] [bɔl], *s.m.* **1.** (*a*) *Physiol:* **b. alimentaire,** alimentary bolus; gastric contents; (*b*) *Pharm: Vet:* bolus, pellet. **2.** *Miner:* bole; *Pharm: A:* **bol d'Arménie,** bole (Armeniac).

bol[2], *s.m.* **1.** (*a*) bowl, basin; *Cu:* **b. à mélanger,** mixing-bowl; (*b*) finger-bowl; (*c*) *P:* luck; **manque de b.,** bad luck! **2.** bowl(ful); *F:* **prendre un b. d'air,** to get a lungful of air.

bolaire [bɔlɛːr], *a. Miner:* bolar, clayey; **terre bolaire,** bole.

bolbécais, -aise [bɔlbekɛ, -ɛːz], *a. & s. Geog:* (native, inhabitant) of Bolbec.

bolchevik, bolchevique [bɔlʃəvik], *s.m. & f.* Bolshevik, Bolshevist.

bolchevisation [bɔlʃəvizasjɔ̃], *s.f.* Bolshevization.

bolcheviser [bɔlʃəvize], *v.tr.* to Bolshevize.

bolchevisme [bɔlʃəvism], *s.m.* Bolshevism.

bolcheviste [bɔlʃəvist], *a. & s.* Bolshevist.

boldine [bɔldin], *s.f. Pharm:* boldine.

boldo [bɔldo], *s.m. Bot:* boldo.

bolduc [bɔldyk], *s.m.* (*a*) (thin) coloured ribbon (for tying up boxes of chocolates, etc.); (*b*) red tape.

bolée [bɔle], *s.f.* bowl(ful), basin(ful) (of soup, etc.).

bôler [bole], *v.tr. Cr:* to bowl (a ball, s.o.).

boléro [bɔlero], *s.m. Danc: Cost:* bolero.

bolet [bɔlɛ], *s.m. Bot:* boletus.

bôleur [bolœːr], *s.m. Cr:* bowler.

bolide [bɔlid], *s.m.* (*a*) *O: Meteor:* bolide, fire-ball, meteor; *F:* thunderbolt; (*b*) *F:* racing car; *F:* **lancé comme un b. sur la route,** hurtling along the road.

bolier [bɔlje], *s.m. Fish:* bag-net, wing-net.

bolivar [bɔlivaːr], *s.m. Cost:* **1.** *A:* tall, bell-shaped hat (as worn by Bolivar, *c.* 1820). **2.** *Num:* bolivar.

Bolivie [bɔlivi], *Pr.n.f. Geog:* Bolivia.

bolivien, -ienne [bɔlivjɛ̃, -jɛn], *a. & s. Geog:* Bolivian.

bollandiste [bɔlɑ̃dist], *s.m. Ecc.Hist:* Bollandist.

bollard [bɔlaːr], *s.m. Nau:* bitt, bollard.

bollénois, -oise [bɔlenwa, -waːz], *a. & s. Geog:* (native, inhabitant) of Bollène.

Bologne [bɔlɔɲ]. *Pr.n.f. Geog:* Bologna.

bolomètre [bɔlɔmɛtr̥], *s.m. Ph:* bolometer, thermic balance.

bolonais, -aise [bɔlɔnɛ, -ɛːz], *a. & s. Geog:* Bolognian, Bolognese.

bolson [bɔlsɔn], *s.m. Geog: Geol:* bolson.

bolténie [bɔlteni], *s.f. Echin:* sea-pear.

bolus [bɔlys], *s.m.* = BOL[1] 1.

bombaçacées [bɔ̃basase], *s.f.pl.,* **bombacées** [bɔ̃base], *s.f.pl. Bot:* Bombacaceae.

bombage [bɔ̃baːʒ], *s.m.* **1.** *Tchn:* bending (of glass into convex shape); dishing (of metal plate). **2.** bulging (of tins containing preserves).

bombance [bɔ̃bɑ̃ːs], *s.f. F:* feast(ing); carousing, carouse; junket(ing); **faire b.,** to feast; *F:* to have a good blow-out.

bombarde [bɔ̃bard], *s.f.* **1.** *Artil: A:* bombard, mortar. **2.** *Organ:* bombardon (stop).

bombardement [bɔ̃bardəmɑ̃], *s.m.* **1.** *Artil:* bombardment, shelling, gun-fire; **b. massif,** heavy bombardment, shelling. **2.** *Av:* bombing; **b. aérien,** air, aerial, bombing; **effectuer, exécuter un b.,** to make, to execute, to carry out, a bomb attack, a bombing raid; **angle de b.,** range, dropping angle; **viseur, collimateur, de b.,** bomb-sight; **ligne de sécurité de b.,** bomb-line, bomb-safety line; **b. en piqué,** dive bombing; **b. en plané, b. avec bombes planantes,** glide bombing; **b. en traînée,** trail bombing; **b. par vagues (d'avions) successives,** carpet bombing; **b. systématique,** pattern bombing; **b. par ricochet en vol rasant,** skip bombing; **b. sur zone,** area bombing; **b. sur objectif ponctuel,** pin-point bombing; **b. de précision,** spot bombing; **l'aviation de b.,** Bomber Command, *U.S:* bombardment aviation; **avion de b.,** bombing plane, bomber. **3.** *Ph:* bombardment; **b. par électrons, par ions, par neutrons, par deutons, etc.,** bombardment with electrons, with ions,

with neutrons, with deutons, etc.; **b. électronique,** bombardment of the electrons; **b. par particules alpha,** bombardment with alpha-particles.

bombarder [bɔ̃barde], *v.tr.* **1.** (*a*) to bombard, shell; *Av:* to bomb; **maison bombardée,** (i) shelled house; (ii) bombed house; (*b*) *Ph:* to bombard (with neutrons, etc.); (*c*) *F:* **b. qn de pierres,** to pelt s.o. with stones; **b. qn de questions,** to fire questions at s.o., to assail s.o. with questions; **b. qn de demandes d'argent,** to pester s.o. (with requests) for money. **2.** (*with object and complement*) *F:* to appoint, nominate, (s.o.) suddenly to some post; **on l'a bombardé ministre,** he has been made a minister out of the blue.

bombardier [bɔ̃bardje], *s.m. Mil:* **1.** *A:* bombardier. **2.** bomber, trench-mortarman. **3.** *Av:* (i) bomber; *O:* bombing plane; (ii) *Pers:* bomb-aimer; *U.S:* bombardier; **b. lourd, moyen, léger,** heavy, medium, light bomber; **b. en piqué,** dive-bomber; **b. en plané,** glide-bomber; **b. de jour, de nuit,** day, night bomber; **b. à grand rayon d'action,** long-range bomber. **4.** *Ent:* bombardier beetle.

bombardon [bɔ̃bardɔ̃], *s.m. Mus:* bombardon.

bombasin [bɔ̃bazɛ̃], *s.m. Tex:* bombazine.

bombax [bɔ̃baks], *s.m. Bot:* bombax, silk-cotton tree.

bombe [bɔ̃:b], *s.f.* **1.** (*a*) *Mil: Av:* bomb; **b. aérienne, b. d'avion,** air, aerial, bomb; **b. empennée, à empennage,** winged bomb; **b. à fragmentation,** fragmentation, scatter, bomb; **b. à pénétration,** earthquake bomb; **b. à retardement,** delayed-action bomb, time-bomb; **b. dirigée, b. planante,** glide(r) bomb; **b. volante,** flying-bomb; *F:* doodle-bug; **b. de destruction,** demolition bomb; **b. de rupture,** armour-piercing bomb; **b. au napalm,** napalm bomb; **b. incendiaire,** incendiary bomb; **b. lacrymogène,** tear-gas bomb; **b. fumigène,** smoke bomb; **b. chimique, b. à gaz,** chemical bomb; **b. éclairante,** illuminating, flash-, bomb; **b. (aérienne) photographique,** photo-flash bomb; **b. sous-marine,** depth bomb; **b. nucléaire,** nuclear bomb; **b. à l'uranium,** uranium bomb, U-bomb; **b. atomique, b. A.,** atom(ic) bomb, A-bomb; **b. à(l')-hydrogène, b. H.,** hydrogen bomb, H-bomb; **b. de ravitaillement,** supply container (containing food or ammunition); (*b*) **attaque à la b.,** bomb attack, bombing raid; **abri à l'épreuve des b.,** bomb-proof shelter; **jeter, lâcher, larguer, une b.,** to release, to drop, to deliver a bomb; **ligne, cercle, point, de largage des bombes,** bomb release line, circle, point; *F:* **entrer en, comme une, b.,** to come bursting in; **faire l'effet d'une b.,** to have an effect like a bombshell; *s.a.* GARE[1]; (*c*) *Ph:* **b. calorimétrique,** bomb calorimeter; (*d*) *Med:* **b. au cobalt,** cobalt bomb. **2.** (*a*) *Cu:* **b. glacée,** *bombe glacée;* (*b*) *Geol:* bomb; **b. volcanique,** bomb; **b. spiralée, fusiforme, en fuseau,** spindle bomb; **b. craquelée,** cracked bomb; **b. en croûte de pain,** bread-crust bomb; (*c*) *Nau:* **b. de signaux,** signal-, tide-ball; (*d*) *Com:* aerosol; **b. à peinture,** paint-spray. **3.** (*a*) huntsman's cap; (*b*) body (of helmet); (*c*) *P:* billycock (hat). **4.** *P:* feast, spree; **s'offrir une vraie b.,** to have a rare old beano; **être en b., faire la b.,** to be on the spree, on the binge.

bombé [bɔ̃be], (*a*) *a.* convex, curved, dished, bulging; **fenêtre bombée,** bay-window; **avoir le dos b.,** to be round-shouldered; *Civ.E:* **chaussée bombée,** cambered road; *Cu:* **une cuiller bombée (de sucre),** a heaped spoonful (of sugar); (*b*) *s.m.* **le b. d'une route,** the camber(ing) of a road.

bombement [bɔ̃bmɑ̃], *s.m.* bulge, bulging, swelling, convexity; camber, cambering (of road).

bomber [bɔ̃be]. **1.** *v.tr.* (*a*) to cause (sth.) to bulge, belly; **b. la poitrine,** to throw out one's chest; **b. le torse,** (i) to throw out one's chest; (ii) *F:* to swagger; (*b*) to dish (metal plate); (*c*) to bend, curve, arch; *F:* hump (one's back); (*d*) *Civ.E:* to camber (road). **2.** *v.i.* (*of wall, etc.*) to bulge (out); (*of sail*) to belly (out).

se bomber, (*a*) to become convex, to bulge; (*b*) to swell out; (*c*) *P:* **tu peux te b.!** don't you wish you may get it!

bombidés [bɔ̃bide], *s.m.pl. Ent:* Bombidae.

bombinateur [bɔ̃binatœ:r], **bombinator** [bɔ̃binatɔr], *s.m. Amph:* bombinator; *F:* fire-belly toad.

bombonne [bɔ̃bɔn], *s.f.* = BONBONNE.

bombycidés [bɔ̃biside], **bombyciens** [bɔ̃bisjɛ̃], *s.m.pl. Ent:* Bombycidae.

bombyle [bɔ̃bil], *s.m. Ent:* hover-fly; bee fly.

bombylidés [bɔ̃bilide], *s.m.pl. Ent:* Bombyliidae.

bombyx [bɔ̃biks], *s.m. Ent:* bombyx; **b. mori, du mûrier,** silkworm moth; **b. du chêne,** processionary moth, oak eggar-moth; **b. gâte-bois,** goat-moth; **b. livrée,** lackey-moth.

bôme [bo:m], *s.f. Nau:* (spanker-)boom.

bômerie [bomri], *s.f. Com:* bottomry.

bon[1], bonne[1] [bɔ̃, bɔn]. **I.** *a.* **1.** good, virtuous, upright, honest (person, etc.); **le b. M. Seguin,** good old M. Seguin; **mon b. monsieur,** (i) *Iron:* my dear sir, my good man; (ii) *F:* (*old servant to employer*) my dear Mr (John, etc.); **bonne action,** good deed. **2.** good, nice, pleasing (book, smell, etc.); **bonne histoire,** good story; **bonne soirée,** pleasant evening; **bonne nourriture,** good food; **j'ai trouvé le rôti b.,** I enjoyed the roast; **la bonne société,** polite society; **ça ne se fait pas en bonne société,** it isn't done in polite society; **jeune fille de bonne famille,** girl of good family; **avoir b. air,** (i) to look well; (ii) to look distinguished; **prendre qn pour les bons comme pour les mauvais jours,** to take s.o. for better (or) for worse; *Prov:* **à b. jour bonne œuvre,** the better the day, the better the deed; **homme b. à vivre,** man easy to get on with; **c'est si b. de (faire qch.),** it is such a delight to (do sth.); *F:* **cela est b. à dire,** it's easier said than done. **3.** (*of person*) clever, capable, good (at one's work, etc.); **b. en anglais,** good at English. **4.** good, right, correct, proper, sound; **si j'ai bonne mémoire . . .,** if my memory is correct . . .; **b. fonctionnement d'une machine,** efficient working of a machine; **en b. état,** sound, in working order; **la bonne voie, route,** the right path, track; **suis-je dans le b. train pour . . .?** am I on the right train for . . .? **faire bonne garde,** to keep a close watch; **en b. français,** (i) in good French; (ii) = in plain English; **un b. Normand,** a real Norman; *Ten:* **la balle est bonne,** the ball is in; *Typ:* **b.,** stet. **5.** good, kind (-hearted) **(pour, envers,** to); **b. fils,** good, dutiful, son; **c'est un b. garçon;** *F:* **un b. type, un b. gars,** he's a good sort, a decent fellow, he's all right; **une bonne âme,** a simple, artless, soul; **il est trop b.,** he is too kind-hearted; *F:* **elle est bonne fille,** she is rather naïve; **il se montre b. pour sa mère,** he is kind to his mother; **vous êtes bien b. de m'inviter,** it is very good, kind, of you to invite me; *s.a.* PAIN 1. **6.** good, profitable, advantageous (investment, etc.); **bonne affaire,** good deal, good speculation; good bargain; **acheter qch. à b. marché,** to buy sth. cheap; **n'est-ce pas que c'est b. marché?** isn't it cheap? **c'est b. à savoir, à se rappeler,** it is worth knowing, worth remembering; **c'est toujours b. à avoir,** it's always worth having, no point in not having it; **ce qui est b. à prendre est b. à garder,** what is worth picking up is worth keeping; **à quoi b.?** what's the good of it? what's the use? **à quoi b. se plaindre?** what is the use, the good, of complaining? **à quoi b. courir ces risques?** what object is there in running these risks? **à quoi b. sa richesse?** what good is his wealth to him? **puis-je vous être b. à quelque chose?** can I do anything for you, be of any service to you? **7.** good, fit, suitable, proper; **b. à manger,** (i) good to eat; (ii) ready to eat; (iii) fit to eat; *Mil:* **b. pour le service,** fit for duty; **être b. à qch.,** to be good for sth.; **à quoi êtes-vous b.?** what can you turn your hand to? **il n'est b. qu'à cela,** that is all he is fit for; **être b. pour l'asile,** to be ripe for the asylum; **si b. vous semble,** if you think proper; if you think it advisable; **je ferai comme b. me semblera,** I shall do as I think fit, as I please; **faites comme b. vous semblera,** have it your own way; **il est b. que vous sachiez,** it is fit and proper, well, that you should know; **il n'est pas toujours b. de . . .,** it is not always good, advisable to . . .; **si vous jugez b. d'attendre,** if you think it advisable to wait; **trouver b. de faire qch.,** to think fit, think it advisable, to do sth.; **je ne trouve pas b. que vous sortiez seule,** I do not approve of your going out alone; **trouvez b. que je +** *sub.*, allow me to . . .; **remède b. contre les piqûres,** medicine that is good for stings; **l'eucalyptus est b. en fumigation,** eucalyptus is a good fumigator. **8.** good, happy, favourable (omen, etc.); **souhaiter une, la, bonne année à qn,** to wish s.o. a happy New Year; **b. week-end, dimanche!** have a good week-end, Sunday! **bonne chasse!** good hunting! *Nau:* **b. vent,** fair wind. **9.** good, sound, safe (security, credit, etc.); **il est b. pour 25.000 frs.,** he is good for 25,000 frs.; **billet b. pour trois mois,** ticket good, available, valid, for three months; **être du b. côté,** to be on the safe side; **son affaire est bonne, son compte est b.!** he's in for it! *P:* **être b.,** (i) to be in for it; (ii) to be done, had; *F:* **on est b. pour rentrer à pied,** (i) we are in for walking home; (ii) we are game for walking home. **10.** *F:* good, full, considerable; **b. baiser,** hearty kiss; **un b. rhume,** a bad cold; **de b. matin,** in the early morning; **j'ai attendu deux bonnes heures,** I waited a full, a good, two hours, (for) two solid hours; **arriver b. premier,** to come in an easy first; **arriver b. dernier,** to finish a long way behind the others; **prendre une bonne moitié de qch.,** to take a good half of sth.; **une bonne centaine,** over a hundred; **donner bonne mesure,** to give full measure; *s.a.* FOIS 1. **11.** *Miscellaneous phrs:* **pour de b., tout de b.,** *F:* **pour tout de b.,** (i) for good, (ii) seriously speaking, in earnest, really; **est-ce pour de b.?** are you in earnest? **il pleut pour de b.,** it is raining in real earnest; *A:* **la faire courte et bonne,** to have a short life and a merry one; *A: F:* **la garder bonne à qn,** to have a grudge against s.o.; *F:* **prendre qch. à la bonne,** to take sth. in good part; *P:* **avoir qn à la bonne,** to like, to have a soft spot for, s.o.; *int.* **c'est b.!** that will do! *F:* enough said! *F:* **(prendre un train) avec cinq minutes de b.,** (to catch a train) with five minutes to spare, in hand. **12.** *int.* **bon!** right! good! **b., je viendrai,** all right, I'll come.

II. **bon,** *adv.* **tenir b.,** to stand fast, to hold one's own; **tenez b.!** *F:* hold tight! hold on (tight)! **tenir b. sur qch.,** to be firm about sth.; **sentir b.** (*of flower*) to smell nice; (*of food*) to smell good; **il fait b. vivre,** it's good to be alive; **il ne fait pas b. se promener dans ce quartier,** it's not safe to walk in this district; (*of weather*) **il fait b.,** it's nice and warm.

III. **bon,** *s.* **les bons,** the righteous, the good; *F:* **mon b.,** my dear fellow, my dear chap; **ma bonne,** my dear; *F:* **c'est un b.,** he's a sound, reliable, man; *P:* **c'est du b.,** that's the stuff; **il a du b.,** there is some good in him; **cela a du b.,** there is some good in it; **il y a du b. dans ce livre,** there are some good parts in this book; **le b. de l'histoire,** (i) the most important part of the story; (ii) the best part, the cream, of the story; **en dire de bonnes,** (i) to tell good stories; (ii) to tell tall stories; (iii) to spread some fine tales; **en voilà une (bien) bonne!** I like that! that's a good one! that's a good joke; **il en a de (bien) bonnes (de faire cela)!** he's got a nerve (doing that)!

bon[2], *s.m.* **1.** order, voucher, ticket; **b. de caisse,** cash voucher; *Com:* **b. de livraison,** delivery order; **b. de commande,** purchase order; **b. d'achat,** gift voucher; **b. de commission,** commission note; *Mil:* **b. de vivres,** ration indent; **b. de distribution, de sortie,** issue voucher; **b. de réintégration,** return voucher; *Adm:* **b. d'essence,** petrol coupon. **2.** *Fin:* (*a*) bond, bill, draught; **b. au porteur,** bearer bond; **b. nominatif,** registered bond; **b. du trésor,** treasury bond, exchequer bill; **b. à vue,** sight draft; (*b*) I.O.U., note of hand; **donner un b. pour une somme,** to give an I.O.U. for an amount.

bonace [bɔnas], *s.f.* lull, calm (before or after a storm).

bonanza [bɔnɑ̃za], *s.m. Geol:* bonanza.

bonapartisme [bɔnapartism], *s.m.* Bonapartism.

bonapartiste [bɔnapartist], *s. & a.* Bonapartist.

bon-à-rien [bɔ̃arjɛ̃], *s. F:* good-for-nothing; *P:* rotter; blighter; bad egg; *pl. bons-à-rien* [bɔ̃arjɛ̃].

bonasse [bɔnas], *a. F:* simple-minded, innocent.

bonassement [bɔnasmɑ̃], *adv.* innocently.

bonasserie [bɔnasri], *s.f.* simple-mindedness, innocence, innocent good-nature.

Bonaventure [bɔnavɑ̃ty:r], *Pr.n.m. Ecc.Hist:* Bonaventura.

bon-bec [bɔ̃bɛk], *s.f.* (*a*) gossip; (*b*) person who can hold his own; *pl. bons-becs.*

bonbon [bɔ̃bɔ̃], *s.m.* (*a*) sweetmeat, comfit, bonbon; *F:* sweet, *U.S:* candy; **bonbons anglais,** acid drops; (*b*) (*in Belgium*) biscuit.

bonbonne [bɔ̃bɔn], *s.f.* (*a*) *Ind:* carboy; (*b*) demijohn; (*c*) *Ch:* **b. à gaz,** gas-bottle.

bonbonnerie [bɔ̃bɔnri], *s.f.* sweetmeat (i) factory; (ii) trade.

bonbonneuse [bɔ̃bɔnø:z], *s.f.* sweetmeat-maker.

bonbonnière [bɔ̃bɔnjɛ:r], *s.f.* **1.** bonbonnière, *U.S:* candy box. **2.** daintily furnished, neat, little house or flat.

bon-chrétien [bɔ̃kretjɛ̃], *s.m. Hort:* bon chrétien (pear); *pl. bons-chrétiens.*

bond [bɔ̃], *s.m.* **1.** bound, leap, jump, spring; **faire un b.,** to leap, spring; *F:* **les loyers ont fait un b.,** rents have soared; **franchir qch. d'un bond,** to clear sth. at one bound; **il s'échappa d'un b.,** he leapt away; **se lever d'un b.,** to spring to one's feet, to stand up with a start; **du**

premier b., right away, immediately; *Mil:* **progresser, se déplacer, par bonds,** to advance, to move, by bounds, by rushes; *Artil:* **b. en portée,** range-jump; **b. en direction,** deflection shift; *Tchn: etc:* **b. en avant,** break-through; *s.a.* SAUT 1. **2.** (*of ball, etc.*) bound, bounce, rebound; **second b.**, rebound; **prendre, saisir, la balle au b.**, (i) to catch the ball on the bounce, at the rebound; (ii) *F:* to seize the opportunity; **faire faux b.**, (*of ball*) to break; *F:* **faire faux b. à qn,** to fail in one's promise to s.o.; to fail to turn up; to leave s.o. in the lurch, to let s.o. down; *s.a.* VOLÉE 1.

bonde [bɔ̃:d], *s.f.* **1.** (*a*) bung (of cask); (*b*) plug (of sink, bath); (*c*) *Hyd.E:* sluice-gate, shut-off (of pond); **lâcher la b.**, to open the sluice; *F:* **lâcher la b. à sa colère,** to let loose one's anger, to pour out the vials of one's wrath. **2.** (*a*) bunghole (of cask); plug-hole (of bath, etc.); (*b*) drainage-hole, -opening; outlet (of pond, etc.).

bondé [bɔ̃de], *a.* chock-full, crammed, packed (bus, etc.); **des trains bondés de vacanciers,** trains chock-a-block, crammed, with holidaymakers; *Th:* **salle bondée,** packed house; house filled to capacity.

bonder [bɔ̃de], *v.tr.* to fill (sth.) chock-full, to cram.

bondérisation [bɔ̃derizasjɔ̃], *s.f. Metall:* bonderization.

bondériser [bɔ̃derize], *v.tr. Metall:* to bonderize.

bondieu [bɔ̃djø]. **1.** *s.m. & int. P: See* DIEU 2(*c*), 3 (*b*), in which meanings this spelling is also found for *bon Dieu.* **2.** *s.m. Tls:* wedge.

bondieusard, -arde [bɔ̃djøza:r, -ard]. **1.** *a. P:* churchy, sanctimonious. **2.** *s.* sanctimonious person.

bondieuserie [bɔ̃djøzri], *s.f. F:* **1.** churchiness; **je déteste la b.**, I can't stick all this religiosity. **2.** *Pej: pl.* church ornaments, devotional objects (in bad taste).

bondir [bɔ̃di:r], *v.i.* **1.** (*a*) to leap, bound; to spring up; **b. sur qch.**, to spring at, pounce on, sth.; **b. à l'assaut,** to spring to the attack; **il bondit de colère,** he flew into a rage; **son cœur bondit,** his heart gave a leap; **cela me fait bondir,** it infuriates me, it makes me wild to hear it; **ce spectacle fait b. le cœur,** this scene makes one's heart leap; (*b*) to gambol, skip, caper. **2.** (*of ball, etc.*) to bounce, bound.

bondissant [bɔ̃disɑ̃], *a.* (*a*) bounding, leaping; (*b*) skipping, frisking; (*c*) **sein b.**, heaving, panting, bosom.

bondissement [bɔ̃dismɑ̃], *s.m.* (*a*) bounding, leaping; **il eut un bondissement de cœur, de joie,** his heart gave a leap; (*b*) skipping, frisking.

bondon [bɔ̃dɔ̃], *s.m.* **1.** bung, plug. **2.** (bung-shaped) cheese from Neufchâtel-en-Bray. **3.** bar of soap.

bondonner [bɔ̃dɔne], *v.tr.* to bung, to plug up (cask, etc.).

bondonnière [bɔ̃dɔnjɛ:r], *s.f. Tls:* bung-, tap-borer; auger.

bondrée [bɔ̃dre], *s.f. Orn:* pern; **b. apivore,** honey-buzzard.

bonduc [bɔ̃dyk], *s.m. Bot:* **bonduc jaune,** bonduc.

bongo [bɔ̃gɔ], *s.m. Z:* bongo (antelope).

bon-henri [bɔ̃ɑ̃ri, bɔnɑ̃ri], *s.m.inv. Bot: F:* = **blette à tête,** *q.v.* under BLETTE².

bonheur [bɔnœ:r], *s.m.* **1.** good fortune, good luck, success; **avoir du b.**, to be lucky; **être en b.**, to be in luck; **j'ai eu le b. de le connaître,** I had the good fortune, it was my good fortune, I was fortunate enough, to know him; **avoir le b. de posséder qch.**, to be blest with sth.; **Dieu leur accorda le b. d'avoir des enfants,** God blessed them with children; **porter b.**, to bring (good) luck (**à**, to); **coup de b.**, stroke, piece, of luck; **quel b.!** what a blessing! **par b.**, luckily, fortunately, by good fortune, as luck would have it; **jouer de b.**, to be lucky despite unfavourable odds; **au petit b.**, in a haphazard manner, as chance directs; **faire qch. au petit b.**, to do sth. hit or miss, to have a shot at sth., to do sth. in a happy-go-lucky manner; *F:* **au petit b. la chance,** trusting to luck; **écrire avec b.**, to have a felicitous style of writing. **2.** happiness, bliss; **faire le b. de qn,** to make s.o. happy, to delight s.o., to be the source of s.o.'s happiness; **si vous voulez faire mon b. . . .**, if you want to make me supremely happy . . .; **avoir à cœur le b. de qn,** to have s.o.'s welfare at heart; **trouver son b. à faire le bien,** to delight in doing good; **marchand de b.**, fortune-teller.

bonheur-du-jour [bɔnœrdyʒu:r], *s.m. Furn: A:* escritoire; cabinet; *pl. bonheurs-du-jour.*

bonhomie [bɔnɔmi], *s.f.* **1.** simple good-heartedness; good nature; **avec bonhomie,** good-naturedly. **2.** simplicity, guilelessness, bonhomie.

bonhomme [bɔnɔm], *s.m.*, **bonne femme** [bɔnfam], *s.f.* **1.** (*a*) simple, good-natured, man, woman; **faux b.**, sly, shifty, customer; **il fait le b.**, his simplicity is all put on; **le b. Corneille,** good old Corneille; **bonne femme,** *F:* old woman; *F:* **une petite bonne femme,** a little old woman; **un vilain b.**, a nasty fellow; **quelle sale bonne femme!** what an unpleasant woman! **contes, remèdes, de bonne femme,** old wives' tales, remedies; **pourquoi pleures-tu, mon b.?** why are you crying, my little man? **il va son petit b. de chemin,** he is jogging quietly along, is successful in a small way; (*in car*) he potters along, tootles along; *F:* **nom d'un petit bonhomme!** by jingo! *s.a.* NOËL 1; *a.* **prendre un air b.**, to put on an air of simplicity, of good-nature, a bland appearance; **rideaux, vitrages, bonne femme,** draped curtains; (*b*) *A:* **Jacques B., le B. Misère,** Hodge; (*c*) *Mil: P:* soldier; (*d*) **dessiner des bonshommes,** to draw funny figures; **b. de, en, pain d'épice,** gingerbread man; *s.a.* NEIGE; *Th: F:* **entrer dans la peau du b.**, to get into the skin of the character; **tenir son b.**, to fill the part well. **2.** *Mec.E:* (bolt-)catch; pin; **b. à ressort,** spring catch or stud; *pl. des bonshommes* [bɔ̃zɔm].

boni [bɔni], *s.m.* **1.** *Fin:* surplus, balance in hand; *Mil:* ration savings. **2.** bonus, profit; *esp.* margin of profit due to pawner on sale of pledged article; **avoir cinq livres de b.**, to be five pounds to the good.

boniche [bɔniʃ], *s.f.* = BONNICHE.

bonichon [bɔniʃɔ̃], *s.m. P:* woman's or child's cap.

boniface [bɔnifas], *a. & s. P:* simple, artless, silly (person).

bonifacien, -ienne [bɔnifasjɛ̃, -jɛn], *a. & s. Geog:* (native, inhabitant) of Bonifacio.

bonification [bɔnifikasjɔ̃], *s.f.* **1.** improvement, amelioration (of land, etc.). **2.** (*a*) *Com:* allowance, rebate, reduction, bonus; (*b*) *Bank:* payment, transfer; (*c*) *Ins:* **b. pour non sinistre,** no claim bonus; (*d*) *Sp:* time bonus.

bonifier [bɔnifje], *v.tr.* (*pr.sub. & p.d.* **n. bonifiions, v. bonifiiez**) **1.** to improve, ameliorate (field, one's character, etc.). **2.** *Com:* (*a*) to make up, make good (shortage, etc.); (*b*) **b. qn d'une remise,** to allow s.o. a discount; (*c*) **b. qch. à qn,** to allow, credit, sth. to s.o.; (*d*) *Bank:* to pay, to transfer.

se bonifier, (*of wine*) to improve; to get, become, better.

boniment [bɔnimɑ̃], *s.m.* (*a*) (quack's) patter, puff; (*b*) sales talk; **faire du b. à qn,** to try to coax s.o.; *F:* **tout ça c'est du b.**, that's all flummery, hanky-panky, claptrap; *s.a.* GRAISSE 1.

bonimenter [bɔnimɑ̃te], *v.i. P:* to kid.

bonimenteur, -euse [bɔnimɑ̃tœ:r, -ø:z], *a. & s. P:* barker.

bonir [bɔni:r], *v.i. P:* to talk, to disclose, to reveal.

bonisseur [bɔnisœ:r], *s.m. P:* tout, barker, (for shop, show, etc.).

bonite [bɔnit], *s.f. Ich:* bonito.

bonjour [bɔ̃ʒu:r], *s.m.* good-day, good-morning, good-afternoon; **souhaiter le b., dire b., à qn,** to greet s.o., to pass the time of day with s.o.; **envoyer le b. à qn,** to send s.o. greetings, one's kind regards; **(dites) b. à Madame votre mère (de ma part),** my kind regards to your mother; **bien le b. à tout le monde,** (i) good day, everybody; (ii) remember me to everybody; **vous avez le b. de Paul,** Paul says good-morning, etc.; *F:* (*to dismiss s.o.*) **je vous souhaite bien le b.**, good-day to you, sir; *s.a.* SIMPLE 2.

bonnard [bɔna:r], *a. P:* simple-minded, soft.

bonne², *s.f.* (*a*) maid(-servant), servant; **b. à tout faire,** maid of all work; (*b*) **b. d'enfants,** nursery-maid, nurse; (*c*) waitress.

bonne-dame [bɔndam], *s.f. Bot: F:* = ARROCHE; *pl. bonnes-dames.*

Bonne-Espérance [bɔnɛsperɑ̃:s], *Pr.n. Geog:* **le Cap de Bonne-Espérance,** the Cape of Good Hope.

bonne femme, *s.f. see* BONHOMME.

bonne-maman [bɔnmamɑ̃, -mɑ̃mɑ̃], *s.f. F:* grandma(mma), granny; *pl. bonnes-mamans.*

bonnement [bɔnmɑ̃], *adv. A:* still in use in adv.phr; **tout b.**, simply, plainly, without guile, frankly; **je lui ai dit tout b. que . . .**, I just, simply, told him that . . . .

bonnet [bɔnɛ], *s.m.* **1.** (close-fitting and brimless) cap; (*woman's, child's*) bonnet; (*sailor's*) cap; *Cost:* cup (of brassière); (*a*) **donner un coup de b. à qn,** to touch one's hat, one's cap, to s.o.; *F:* **avoir la tête près du b.**, to be hot-tempered, hot-headed, of a fiery disposition; **ce sont deux têtes sous le même b.**, (i) in everything they are alike; (ii) they are as thick as thieves; *F:* **parler à son b.**, to talk to oneself; *A:* **j'y jette mon b.!** I give it up! **prendre qch. sous son b.**, (i) to imagine sth.; (ii) to do sth. off one's own bat; **prendre sous son b. de faire qch.**, to take (it) upon oneself to do sth.; **avoir mis son b. de travers,** to be in an ill-humour; **b. de coton, de nuit,** (*man's*) night-cap; **b. de nuit,** (*woman's*) slumber cap; **histoire triste comme un b. de nuit,** tale as dull as ditch-water; **être triste comme un b. de nuit,** to be as cheerful as the grave; **b. grec,** smoking cap, fez; *s.a.* ÂNE 2, BLANC I. 3; *Hist:* **bonnets rouges,** revolutionaries; *A:* **le b. de Gessler,** Gessler's hat; *Mil:* **b. de police,** fatigue cap, forage cap; **b. à poil,** busby, bear-skin; **b. de canonnier, b. parasouffle,** ear-, blast-, protector; *s.a.:* HUSSARD 1; (*b*) **b. carré,** (i) doctor's cap; (ii) *F: A:* doctor; *A:* **prendre le b.**, to be capped (as a doctor); *F:* **gros b.**, big shot, bigwig, *U.S:* big wheel; **opiner du b.**, (i) *A:* to signify one's assent by lifting one's cap; (ii) *F:* to say ditto to s.o.; to vote with the crowd; to nod approval, to nod assent; *A:* **passer au b., à volée de b.**, (*of a resolution*) to be carried unanimously; **b. d'évêque,** (i) bishop's mitre; (ii) *Cu: F:* parson's nose (of fowl); (iii) *Nau:* horseshoe plate; (*c*) (*woman's head-dress*) **b. de nourrice,** nurse's cap; *F:* **elle a jeté son b. par-dessus les moulins,** she has kicked over the traces, she has thrown propriety to the winds, flung her cap over the windmill; **b. de bain,** bathing-cap; (*d*) *Cost:* cup (of brassiere). **2.** *Hort: F:* **b. de prêtre,** squash(-melon); *Bot:* **b. carré, b. de prêtre,** spindletree, prick-wood. **3.** *Physiol:* honeycomb stomach, second stomach (of ruminant); *Z:* bonnet (of the black whale). **4.** *Z:* **b. chinois,** bonnet macaque.

bonneteau, -eaux [bɔnto], *s.m.* **1.** three-card trick. **2.** three-card set.

bonneter [bɔnte], *v.tr.* (**je bonnette, n. bonnetons; je bonnetterai**) *Pyr:* to cap (fuse, etc.).

bonneterie [bɔntri], *s.f.* **1.** hosiery, knitted goods; **b. de corps,** woollen undergarments. **2.** hosiery trade.

bonneteur [bɔntœ:r], *s.m.* (*a*) card sharper (who works the three-card trick); (*b*) cheat.

bonnetier, -ière [bɔntje, -jɛ:r], *s.* **1.** hosier. **2.** **bonnetière,** *s.f. Furn:* press, cupboard.

bonnette [bɔnɛt], *s.f.* **1.** (baby's) cap, (child's) bonnet. **2.** *Fort:* bonnet(te). **3.** *Nau:* (*a*) studding-sail; **b. de tapecul, de brigantine, de sous-gui,** ring-tail; (*b*) **b. lardée,** collision mat; (*c*) **b. de hublot,** wind-catcher, wind-scoop. **4.** *Opt:* eye-glass shade (of telescope, etc.). **5.** *Phot:* **b. d'approche, de mise au point,** supplementary lens; **b. à portrait,** portrait attachment.

bonniche [bɔniʃ], *s.f. P: Pej:* young maid-servant, maid.

bon-papa [bɔ̃papa], *s.m. F:* grandpa(pa), grandad; *pl. bons-papas.*

bon-prime [bɔ̃prim], *s.m. Com:* free-gift coupon; *pl. bons-primes.*

bonsoir [bɔ̃swa:r], *s.m.* good-evening, good-night; **dire b., souhaiter le b., à qn,** to wish, bid, s.o. good-night; *P:* **dire b. aux amis, aux voisins,** to die; *F:* **tout est dit, b.!** there is nothing more to be said! there's an end of it!

bonté [bɔ̃te], *s.f.* **1.** (*a*) goodness, kindness; kindly feeling; benignancy; **avoir de la b. pour qn,** to be kind to s.o.; **sourire plein de b.**, kindly, benevolent, smile; **ayez la b. de me faire savoir . . .**, (will you) be so kind as, be good enough, to let me know . . . ; **b. du ciel!** good heavens! (*b*) *pl.* kindnesses, kind actions; **avoir des bontés pour qn,** to do s.o. kindnesses; **elle a eu des bontés pour lui,** she has been his mistress. **2.** goodness, good quality, excellence (of things). **3.** righteousness, justice (of cause, etc.).

bonze [bɔ̃:z], *s.m.* **1.** bonze, Buddhist priest; *F:* high-priest (of political party, etc.). **2.** *P:* **vieux b.**, old dodderer; *P: Sch:* supervisor (in a *lycée*).

bonzerie [bɔ̃zri], *s.f.* bonze monastery.

bonzesse [bɔ̃zɛs], *s.f.* Buddhist nun.

boogie-woogie [bugiwugi], *s.m. Mus: Danc:* boogie-woogie.

bookmaker [bukmɛkœ:r, -make:r], *s.m.*, *F:* **book** [buk], *s.m.* bookmaker, *F:* bookie; **b. marron,** welsher.

boom [bum], *s.m.* **1.** *Com: Fin:* boom. **2.** *F:* young people's party.

boomerang [bumrɑ̃:g], *s.m.* boomerang.

boort [bort], *s.m.* bort, diamond fragments.

booster [buster], *s.m. Atom.Ph:* booster-rocket.

boosting [bustiŋ], *s.m. Tch:* booster pump.

Booz [bɔɔːz], *Pr.n.m. B.Hist:* Boaz.
bop [bɔp], *s.m. Mus:* bop, bebop.
bopyre [bɔpiːr], *s.m. Crust:* bopyrus.
boqueteau, -eaux [bɔkto], *s.m.* small wood, copse, spinney.
bora [bɔra], *s.f.* bora.
boracique [bɔrasik], *a. Ch: A:* = BORIQUE.
boracite [bɔrasit], *s.f. Miner:* boracite.
borain, -aine [bɔrɛ̃, -ɛn], *a. & s.* = BORIN.
borasse [bɔras], **borassus** [bɔrasys], *Bot: s.m.* borassus.
borate [bɔrat], *s.m. Ch:* borate.
boraté [bɔrate], *a. Ch:* borated.
borax [bɔraks], *s.m. Ch: Metall:* borax.
borborygme [bɔrbɔrigm], *s.m. usu. pl. Med:* rumbling(s) (in the bowels); **avoir des borborygmes,** *F:* to have the collywobbles.
bord [bɔːr], *s.m.* **1.** *Nau:* (*a*) board, side (of ship); **par dessus le b.,** outboard; **jeter qch. hors du b., par-dessus (le) b.,** to throw sth. overboard; **tomber par-dessus b.,** to fall overboard; (*of mast*) to go by the board; **moteur hors b.,** outboard motor; **le b. du vent,** the weather side; **le b. sous le vent,** the lee side; **de quel b. dépend le vent?** from what quarter is the wind blowing? **rouler bord sur b.,** (*of ship*) to roll gunwale under; **faux b.,** list; **le long du bord,** alongside; **b. à b. avec un navire,** close alongside a ship, yard-arms touching; **être b. à quai,** to be alongside the quay; **franc b.,** carvel (work); **bordé, construit, à franc b.,** carvel-built; **joint à franc b.,** carvel-joint; *s.a.* FRANC-BORD; **navire de haut b.,** rated ship; (*b*) tack, leg; **courir un b.,** to make a tack, a board; **être à bout de b.,** to be at the end of the tack; **courir un b. à terre,** to stand inshore; **courir un b. au large,** to stand off; (*c*) **les hommes du b.,** the ship's company; **être de tel ou tel b.,** to belong to such and such a ship; **avec les moyens du b.,** with the means at one's disposal; *F:* **être du b. de qn,** to be in the same boat, the same party, as s.o.; **il est seul de son b.,** he stands alone (in his opinions); **être du même b.,** to be of the same opinion; **journal de b.,** ship's log; **papiers de b.,** ship's papers; *adv.phr.* **à b. d'un vaisseau,** on board, aboard, a ship; *adv. phr.* **à b.,** on board (ship), aboard; **la vie à b.,** life afloat; **mettre des marchandises à b.,** to ship goods; **mise à b.,** shipment; **à mon b.,** on board my ship; **avoir qn à son b.,** to have s.o. aboard. **2.** edge (of table, etc.); border, hem (of garment); brink, verge (of precipice, of the grave); rim, brim (of hat, vase, etc.); lip (of cup, wound); limb (of sun, moon); **au b. de l'abîme,** at the edge of the abyss; *Pol:* **diplomatie, politique, du b. du gouffre, de l'abîme,** brinkmanship; **être au b. du tombeau,** to be at death's door; **j'avais le mot au b. des lèvres,** I had the word on the tip of my tongue; **avoir l'âme sur le b. des lèvres,** to be at one's last gasp; **au b. des larmes,** on the verge of tears; **au b. de la route,** (i) at the road-side; (ii) on the side of the road; **auberge sur le b. de la route,** wayside inn; **chapeau à larges bords,** broad-brimmed hat; **chapeau sans bord(s),** brimless hat; **b. de pierre,** stone border, edging; **b. à b.,** edge to edge; **verser du vin b. à b. du verre,** to fill one's glass to the brim; **remplir les verres à pleins bords,** to fill the glasses brim-full; *F:* **il est un peu mystique, un peu chauvin, sur les bords,** he's a bit of a mystic, a bit of a chauvinist; *Metalw:* **tomber un b.,** to crease, flange, an edge; *Av:* **b. d'attaque,** leading edge (of wing); **b. d'attaque articulé,** slat; **b. de sortie, de fuite,** trailing edge, following edge; **b. relevé,** flange. **3.** shore, strand (of sea); bank (of river); margin (of fountain); **aller au b. de la mer,** to go to the seaside; **maison au b. de la mer,** house at the seaside; **maison sur le b. de la mer,** house right on the shore; **Marseille par b. de mer,** Marseilles by the coast road; **la rivière est pleine jusqu'aux bords,** the river is full to the brim.
Borda (le) [ləbɔrda], *Pr.n.m.* the French training-ship for naval cadets (up to 1913).
bordache [bɔrdaʃ], **bordachien** [bɔrdaʃjɛ̃], *s.m. A: F:* naval cadet (from the Borda training-ship).
bordage¹ [bɔrdaːʒ], *s.m.* **1.** (*a*) *Nau:* plank(ing), sheathing (of vessel); **b. à clin,** clinker-, clincher-work; **b. franc,** carvel-work. **2.** (*a*) border(ing); **b. de pierres,** stone kerb; (*b*) *Const:* frame-work, framing, form (for concrete); (*c*) bordering, edging, taping (of dress, etc.); *Mec.E:* flanging; (*d*) **b. d'un lit,** tucking in of the bedclothes. **3.** petty coasting trade.
bordage², *s.m. A:* = MÉTAYAGE.
bordaille [bɔrdɑːj], *s.f. Nau:* plank.
bordant [bɔrdɑ̃], *s.m. Nau:* foot(-rope) (of sail).
borde [bɔrd], *s.f. A. & Dial:* = MÉTAIRIE.
bordé [bɔrde]. **1.** *a.* (*a*) edged, fringed (**de,** with); **tapis b. d'une frange rouge,** carpet edged with a red fringe; **yeux bordés de cils noirs,** eyes fringed with black lashes; *Ch:* (*glass tube*) with rolled edge; (*b*) *Her:* bordered. **2.** *s.m.* (*a*) edging, border, braid (of garment, etc.); (*b*) *Nau:* (i) planking, planks; (ii) plating (of ship); (iii) side (of ship); **b. de pont,** deck flat, plank; **b. extérieur d'un canot,** skin of a rowing boat.
bordeaux [bɔrdo], *s.m.* Bordeaux (wine); **b. rouge,** claret; *a.inv.* claret-coloured.
bordée [bɔrde], *s.f. Nau:* **1.** broadside (guns, fire); **feu de b.,** broadside (firing); **lâcher une b.,** to let fly a broadside; *F:* **lâcher une b. de jurons,** to let fly a volley of oaths; *Fr.C:* **b. (de neige),** heavy snowfall. **2.** board, tack; **courir une b.,** to make a board, a tack; **tirer des bordées,** to tack, to fetch about, to beat up to windward; *F:* **tirer, courir, une b.,** to overstay one's leave; to go on the spree; *F:* on a binge; **être en b.,** to be on the spree. **3.** watch; **b. de tribord, de bâbord,** starboard watch, port watch; **petite b.,** dog-watch; **grande b.,** full watch of four hours.
bordel [bɔrdɛl], *s.m.* brothel, bordello; *A. & Lit:* bawdy-house; *P:* **quel b.!** what a mess! what a bloody shambles! what an orgy! **tout le b.,** the whole bloody lot, the whole bang shoot.
bordelais, -aise [bɔrdəlɛ, -ɛːz]. **1.** *a. & s.* (native, inhabitant) of Bordeaux. **2.** *s.f.* **bordelaise;** (*a*) Bordeaux cask of about 225 litres; (*b*) Bordeaux bottle of about ¾ litre.
border [bɔrde], *v.tr.* **1.** (*a*) to border, bound; **un fossé borde le jardin,** a ditch runs along, forms a boundary to, the garden; (*b*) **b. qch. de qch., avec qch.,** to edge, fringe, sth. with sth., to put a border of sth. on sth.; **b. une allée de peupliers,** to edge, line, a walk with poplars; **b. un tissu d'un lacet,** to bind a material with a piece of braid; **b. un puits,** to curb a well; *Nau:* **navire qui borde la côte,** ship skirting the coast; (*c*) **b. un lit,** to tuck in the bedclothes; **b. qn dans son lit,** to tuck s.o. in; (*d*) *Mec.E:* to edge, flange; *Mec.E:* **machine, presse, à b.,** flanging machine, press. **2.** *Nau:* to plank (ship); **b. un navire en fer,** to plate a ship; **b. un pont,** to lay a deck. **3.** to ship (oars). **4. b. une voile,** to haul the sheets taut.
bordereau, -eaux [bɔrdəro], *s.m.* memorandum, (detailed) statement; invoice, account, docket (of goods, cash, etc.); consignment note; abstract, schedule; bordereau; **b. de(s) prix,** price-list; **b. d'expédition,** (i) *Com:* dispatch note; (ii) *Banking:* list of securities forwarded; **b. de paye,** wages docket; **b. de livraison,** issue voucher; **b. d'expédition,** consignment, dispatch, note; **b. d'escompte,** list of bills for discount; *St.Exch:* **b. d'achat, de vente,** contract note; *Banking:* **b. de crédit, de débit,** credit note, debit note.
bordeur, -euse [bɔrdœːr, -øːz]. **1.** *s.* binder (of shoes, etc.). **2.** *s.m.* binder (of sewing machine).
bordier¹, -ière [bɔrdje, -jɛːr], *a. & s.m.* **1. (navire) b.,** lop-sided ship, lopsider. **2.** *Geol: etc:* **mer bordière,** epicontinental sea, bordering sea, marginal sea; shelf-sea.
bordier², -ière, *s.* **1.** *A:* = MÉTAYER. **2.** *Jur: Sw.Fr:* = RIVERAIN 2.
bordigue [bɔrdig], *s.f. Fish: Pisc:* crawl.
bordj [bɔr(d)ʒ], *s.m.* (*North Africa*) blockhouse, small isolated fort.
bordoyer [bɔrdwaje], *v.tr.* (**je bordoie, n. bordoyons; je bordoierai**) *Art:* **b. les figures,** to border, encircle, the faces (in a picture).
bordure [bɔrdyːr], *s.f.* **1.** (*a*) border, rim; fringe, edging, edge (of shawl, etc.); curb, kerb (of pavement, etc.); skirt (of a wood); *Typ:* ornamental border; *Her:* bordure; **papier à b. noire,** black-edged note-paper; **grille en b. de la rue,** railing running along the side of the street; **chaises en b. du trottoir,** chairs drawn up along the pavement; **pays en b. de la Méditerranée,** countries bordering on the Mediterranean; **récif en b.,** fringing reef; (*b*) binding (of hat, etc.); welt (of glove); (*c*) *Nau:* foot-band, foot (of sail); (*d*) *Ch:* **b. réactionnelle,** reaction rim. **2.** frame (of mirror, etc.).
bordurer [bɔrdyre], *v.tr.* **1.** to border, edge (material, etc.). **2.** to bind (hat, etc.); to welt (glove).
bore [bɔːr], *s.m. Ch:* boron.
boréal, -aux [bɔreal, -o], *a.* boreal, north(ern); **le pôle b.,** the North Pole; *s.a.* AURORE.
Borée [bɔre], *Pr.n.m. Myth:* Boreas; *Poet:* The North Wind.
borgne [bɔrɲ], *a.* **1.** (*a*) one-eyed, blind in one eye; *s.* **un(e) b.,** one-eyed man, woman; *F:* **changer un cheval b. contre un aveugle,** to make a bad bargain; *s.a.* JASER; (*b*) **rue b.,** blind alley; *Med:* **fistule b.,** blind fistula; *Mec.E:* **trou b.,** recessed hole; (*c*) *Nau:* **ancre b.,** (i) anchor with only one fluke; (ii) unbuoyed anchor. **2.** suspicious, evil-looking (house, etc.); disreputable, shady (public house, etc.); **café b.,** low dive; **compte b.,** fishy account.
borgnesse [bɔrɲɛs], *s.f. Pej: P:* one-eyed woman or girl.
borin, -ine [bɔrɛ̃, -in], *s. Dial: Min:* miner or colliery worker (of the Borinage district of Belgium, or of N. Fr.).
borinage [bɔrinaːʒ], *s.m.* (*in Belgium and N. France*) *Min:* (i) coal-mining; (ii) *coll.* colliery workers.
borique [bɔrik], *a. Ch:* boric; *F:* boracic (acid).
boriqué [bɔrike], *a. Pharm:* treated with, containing, boric acid; **pommade boriquée,** boracic ointment; **compresse en coton b.,** boracic-lint compress.
bornage [bɔrnaːʒ], *s.m.* **1.** (*a*) *Surv:* demarcation, marking out (of land); pegging out, staking (of claim); (*b*) boundary (of staked claim, etc.) **pierre de bornage,** boundary stone. **2.** *Nau: A:* limited coastal navigation, home-trade navigation.
borne [bɔrn], *s.f.* **1.** (*a*) landmark, boundary-mark, -stone, -post; *A:* merestone; (*b*) *F:* kilometre; **b. routière, kilométrique** = milestone; *F:* **il était planté là comme une b.,** he stood there like a post; **b. d'incendie,** fire hydrant; *Av:* **b. de balisage,** boundary light, marker; (*c*) *pl.* boundaries, limits, bounds, confines (of kingdom, etc.); *F:* **(dé)passer toutes les bornes, n'avoir pas de bornes,** to go beyond all bounds, to pass all bounds, to know no bounds; **cela passe les bornes,** that is going too far, beyond a joke; **sans bornes,** boundless, unbounded; **la plaine s'étend sans bornes,** the plain stretches endlessly (on). **2.** (*a*) (stone) corner-post, fender; *Nau:* **b. d'amarrage,** bollard (on wharf); *F:* **orateur de b.,** soap-box, stump, orator; (*b*) *Rom.Ant:* turning-post, goal (in circus). **3.** *El:* terminal, (binding-)post; **b. à vis,** binding screw; **b. d'entrée,** input terminal; **b. de sortie,** output terminal; **b. de jonction,** connecting, binding, terminal; **b. de dérivation, de branchement,** branch terminal; **plaque à bornes,** terminal plate; **b. de mise à la terre, b.-terre, b. de masse,** earth terminal; *U.S:* ground terminal; **tension aux bornes,** terminal voltage.
borné [bɔrne], *a.* limited, restricted (intelligence, fortune, etc.); **homme (d'un esprit) b.,** narrow-minded man; **gens bornés dans leurs vues,** people of limited views.
bornéen, -enne [bɔrneɛ̃, -ɛn], *a. & s. Geog:* Bornean.
bornéène [bɔrneɛn], *s.m.,* **bornéol** [bɔrneɔl], *s.m. Pharm:* borneene, borneol, Borneo camphor.
borne-fontaine [bɔrn(ə)fɔ̃tɛn], *s.f.* (*a*) public street fountain (shaped like a milestone); (*b*) *Fr.C:* fire hydrant; *pl. bornes-fontaines.*
Bornéo [bɔrneo], *Pr.n.m. Geog:* Borneo.
bornéol [bɔrneɔl], *s.m. Pharm:* = BORNÉÈNE.
borner [bɔrne], *v.tr.* **1.** (*a*) to set landmarks to, to mark out, to mark the boundary of (field, vineyard, etc.); to peg out, stake (claim); **b. une route,** to set up milestones along a road; (*b*) to bound, to form the boundary of (country, etc.). **2.** to limit, restrict (s.o.'s view, power, the meaning of a word, etc.); to set limits, bounds, to (ambition, desires).
se borner. 1. to restrict oneself, to exercise self-restraint; **je me borne au strict nécessaire,** I confine myself to, content myself with, strict necessaries; **se b. à faire qch.,** to content oneself with doing sth.; **je me suis borné à (vous) faire remarquer que . . .,** I merely, simply, observed that . . . . **2.** (*of things*) (**à,** to) (*a*) to be confined; *F:* to stop; **toute leur science se borne à cela,** all their knowledge is confined to this; *F:* stops there; (*b*) to amount, come down; *F:* to boil down; **voici à quoi se borne son raisonnement,** this is what his argument amounts to, comes down to; *F:* boils down to.
borne-repère [bɔrnrəpɛːr], *s.f. Surv:* bench-mark; *pl. bornes-repères.*
borne-signal, -aux [bɔrnsiɲal, -o], *s.f. Surv:* triangulation point; *pl. bornes-signaux.*
bornière [bɔrnjɛːr], *s.f.* angle-iron.
bornite [bɔrnit], *s.f. Miner:* bornite, erubescite.
bornoyer [bɔrnwaje], *v.tr.* (**je bornoie, n. bornoyons; je bornoierai**) **1.** to look at, along, (an edge or surface) with one eye closed (so as to judge of its straightness or levelness); to test (an edge). **2.** *Surv:* to stake off, mark off (line, etc.).
bornyle [bɔrnil], *s.m. Ch:* bornyl; **acétate de b.,** bornyl acetate.

borosilicate [bɔrɔsilikat], *s.m. Ch:* borosilicate, silicoborate.
borraginacées [bɔraʒinase], *A:* **borraginées** [bɔraʒine], *s.f.pl. Bot:* Bor(r)aginaceae.
borren, -enne [bɔrɛ̃, -ɛn], *a. & s.*, **borrin, -ine** [bɔrɛ̃, -in], *a. & s. Geog:* (native, inhabitant) of Bourg-Saint-Maurice.
Borromées [bɔrɔme], *Pr.n.f.pl. Geog:* **les îles Borromées,** the Borromean Islands.
bort [bɔrt], *s.m.* = BOORT.
borure [bɔryːr], *s.m. Ch:* boride.
Borysthène (le) [ləbɔristɛn], *Pr.n.m. A.Geog:* the Borysthenes (now the Dnieper).
Boschiman [bɔʃimɑ̃], *s.m.* (South African) bushman.
bosco [bɔsko], *s.m. Navy: F:* bosun.
bosco(t), -otte [bɔsko, -ɔt], *A: F:* **1.** *a.* hunchbacked. **2.** *s.* hunchback.
bosniaque [bɔsnjak], **bosnien, -ienne** [bɔsnjɛ̃, -jɛn], *a. & s. Geog:* Bosniac, Bosnian.
Bosnie [bɔsni], *Pr.n.f. Geog:* Bosnia.
Bosphore (le) [ləbɔsfɔːr], *Pr.n.m. Geog:* the Bosphorus.
bosquet [bɔskɛ], *s.m.* grove, thicket, shrubbery; clump of trees.
bossage [bɔsaːʒ], *s.m.* **1.** embossing. **2.** *(a)* boss; *I.C.E:* **bossages du piston,** (gudgeon-pin) bosses, lugs of the piston; *(b)* (strengthening) swell (of gun-barrel, etc.); *(c) Const:* bossage (of building-stone); *(d)* **soudure par b.,** projection welding; *(e) Av:* **b. de montage,** mounting pad.
bossant [bɔsɑ̃], *a. A: P:* (screamingly) funny.
bosse [bɔs], *s.f.* **1.** hump (of hunchback, camel, etc.); *Med: F:* **b. de bison,** dowager's hump; *F:* **rouler sa b.,** to knock about the world; **il a roulé sa b. partout,** he's been a regular rolling stone; *P:* **allons, roule ta b.!** now then, get a move on, *U.S:* hump yourself! **tomber sur la b. de qn,** to assail s.o.; **il lui est tombé sur la bosse,** he went for him; *(of trousers)* **faire b. aux genoux,** to bag at the knees; *P:* **s'en donner une b.,** (i) to have a jolly good tuck-in; (ii) to have a spree, to go on the spree; **se payer une b. de rire,** to laugh uproariously. **2.** *(a)* bump, bruise, swelling, lump; *s.a.* PLAIE 1; *(b)* unevenness, bump (in the ground); *Rail: F:* hump; *(c) Phrenology:* bump; *F:* **avoir la b. de la musique,** to have a gift for music; *(d) Bill:* kiss. **3.** dent (in tea-pot, etc.). **4.** boss, embossment, swell; **en b.,** in relief, in the round; *Art:* **dessiner d'après la b.,** to draw from the round; *s.a.* RONDE-BOSSE. **5.** *Nau:* *(a)* stopper, keeper (of cable, etc.); **b. de bout,** cathead stopper; **b. de ris,** reef pendant; *(b)* painter (of boat); **fausse b.,** lazy painter; **larguer la b.,** to cast off the painter.
bosselage [bɔslaːʒ], *s.m.* embossing.
bosseler [bɔsle], *v.tr.* **(je bosselle, n. bosselons; je bossellerai) 1.** to emboss (plate, etc.). **2.** *(a)* to dent, bruise (things); **théière toute bosselée,** battered tea-pot; *(b) F:* **collines qui bossellent la surface du pays,** hillocks that break up the country.
bosselle [bɔsɛl], *s.f.* eel-pot.
bossellement [bɔsɛlmɑ̃], *s.m.* **1.** denting, bruising. **2.** = BOSSELURE 1.
bosselure [bɔslyːr], *s.f.* **1.** *(a)* dent, bruise; *(b)* inequality, unevenness (of surface). **2.** *occ.* = BOSSELAGE.
bosser [bɔse], **1.** *v.tr. Nau:* to stopper (cable, etc.). **2.** *v.i. P:* to work hard; to slave; slog.
bossetier [bɔstje], *s.m.* *(a) Glassm:* glass-blower; *(b)* embosser.
bossette [bɔsɛt], *s.f. Harn:* **1.** boss (of bit). **2.** blinker. **3.** *Sm.a:* swell, boss (of trigger-piece). **4.** *Av: etc:* **b. d'entrée d'air,** air scoop.
bosseur [bɔsœːr], *s.m. P:* hard worker, swot; plodder; slogger.
bosseyer [bɔsɛje], *v.tr. Min:* to drill, bore (rock, etc.); to plug and feather.
bosseyeuse [bɔsɛjøːz], *s.f. Min:* rock-drill, plug-and-feathering machine.
bossoir [bɔswaːr], *s.m. Nau:* **1.** *(a)* cathead; *(b)* bow (of ship); **par le b. du bâbord,** on the port bow; **ancre de b.,** bower(-anchor); **homme de b.,** look-out (man). **2.** davit; **les bras de b.,** the davit guys.
bossu, -ue [bɔsy]. **1.** *a.* hunch-backed, hump-backed (person); humped (animal); **b. par devant,** pigeon-chested; *F:* **terrain b.,** hummocky, uneven, ground. **2.** *s.* hunchback; *s.a.* RIRE I. 1.
bossué [bɔsɥe], *a.* battered (kettle, etc.).
bossuer [bɔsɥe], *v.tr.* = BOSSELER 2.
se bossuer, to bulge out of shape.
boston [bɔstɔ̃], *s.m.* **1.** *Cards:* boston. **2.** *Danc:* boston.
bostonien, -ienne [bɔstɔnjɛ̃, -jɛn], *a. & s. Geog:* (native, inhabitant) of Boston (U.S.A.).
bostonner [bɔstɔne], *v.i.* (i) *Cards:* to play boston; (ii) *Dance:* to dance the boston.
bostryche [bɔstriʃ], *s.m. Ent:* bark-beetle.
bot [bo], *a.* **pied b.,** (i) club-foot; (ii) club-footed person; **main bote,** club-hand; **cheval pied b.,** club-footed horse.
botanique [bɔtanik]. **1.** *a.* botanical. **2.** *s.f.* botany.
botaniser [bɔtanize], *v.i.* to botanize.
botaniste [bɔtanist], *s.m. & f.* botanist.
Bot(h)nie [bɔtni], *Pr.n.f. Geog:* Bothnia.
bothrops [bɔtrɔps], *s.m. Rept:* Bothrops, Lachesis, the pit vipers.
botrychion, -ium [bɔtrikjɔ̃, -jɔm], *s.m. Bot:* botrychium; **b. lunaire,** moonwort.
botrylle [bɔtril], *s.m. Biol:* Botryllus.
botryoïde [bɔtrijɔid], *a. Miner:* botryoidal.
botrytis [bɔtritis], *s.m. Bot:* botrytis.
botte[1] [bɔt], *s.f.* *(a)* bunch, bundle (of carrots, etc.); truss, bundle (of hay); bale (of hemp, etc.); coil (of wire); *F:* **j'ai reçu une b. de lettres ce matin,** I had a whole sheaf, budget, of letters this morning; *F:* **il y en a des bottes,** there are heaps of them; *s.a.* FUTAILLE; *(b) Mil: F:* **la b.,** (i) horses' feed; (ii) (horses') feeding time.
botte[2], *s.f.* **1.** *(a)* (high) boot; **bottes à l'écuyère,** riding boots; **bottes de mer,** sea-boots, jack-boots; **bottes d'égoutier, bottes cuissardes imperméables,** waders; **bottes à revers, retroussées,** top-boots; **bottes à la Souvarov,** Hessian boots; *F:* Hessians; **bottes de, en, caoutchouc,** Wellingtons, rubber-boots, gum-boots; **b. de vol,** flying boot; **sous la b. de l'envahisseur,** under the heel of the invader; *Geog: F:* **la b. de l'Italie,** the boot of Italy; **le talon de la b.,** the heel of Italy; **le bout de la b.,** the toe of Italy; **l'éperon de la b.,** the spur of Italy; *s.a.* DEMI-BOTTE; *Mil:* **charger b. à b.,** to charge boot to boot; **coup de b.,** kick; *F:* **à propos de bottes,** apropos of nothing at all, without rhyme or reason; **chercher querelle à qn à propos de bottes,** to pick a quarrel with s.o. over nothing; **il y laissa ses bottes,** he left his boots, he died, there; **il était haut comme ma b.,** he was quite a little mite; *P:* **ça fait ma b.,** that suits me to a T; *P:* **en avoir plein les bottes,** to be fed up with sth.; *s.a.* FOIN[1] 1, GRAISSER 1; *(b)* **bottes de cheval,** foot-guards (for horse that interferes, etc.). **2.** slip (for dog); **avaler la b. aux limiers,** to slip the hounds. **3.** *Mil:* bucket (for carbine, colour); **carabine à la b.,** carbine carried in the bucket.
botte[3], *s.f. Fenc:* pass, lunge, hit; **porter, pousser, allonger, une b. à qn,** (i) to lunge, make a thrust, at s.o., to thrust at s.o.; (ii) *F:* to play a nasty trick on s.o., to deal s.o. a nasty blow (in debate, etc.); to have a tilt at s.o.; *s.a.* APPUYER 2.
botte[4], *s.f. Sch:* the students who leave the *École Polytechnique* with the highest marks.
botte[5], *s.f. Ent: F:* fly-weevil.
bottelage [bɔtlaːʒ], *s.m.* trussing, tying up (of hay, straw, etc.).
botteler [bɔtle], *v.tr.* **(je bottelle, n. bottelons; je bottellerai)** to bundle, tie up, truss (hay, etc.); to bunch (radishes, etc.).
bottelette [bɔtlɛt], *s.f.* bunch (of carrots, etc.); small truss, bundle (of hay, etc.).
botteleur, -euse [bɔtlœːr, -øːz], *s. Agr: Hort:* **1.** binder *(pers.).* **2.** *s.f.* **botteleuse,** binding-machine, binder.
botteloir [bɔtlwaːr], *s.m. Agr: Hort:* bundling-machine (for asparagus).
botter [bɔte]. **1.** *v.tr.* *(a)* to put boots, shoes, on (s.o.); **le Chat botté,** Puss in Boots; *(b)* to supply (s.o.) with boots; **être bien botté,** to be well-shod; **ces chaussures me bottent mal,** these shoes do not fit, suit, my foot; *F:* **vos conditions me bottent,** your terms suit me fine; *s.a.* SINGE 1. **2.** *v.tr.* to kick; *Fb:* **b. le ballon,** to kick, *F:* boot, the ball; *F:* **b. qn,** to kick s.o.'s bottom. **3.** *v.i. (of shoes, etc.)* to become caked with snow, with mud.
se botter. 1. to put on one's boots. **2.** to get one's shoes caked with snow, with mud.
botterie [bɔtri], *s.f.* **1.** *(a)* boot-, shoemaker's workshop, boot factory; *(b)* boot-shop. **2.** boot trade.
bottier [bɔtje], *s.m.* bootmaker, shoemaker.
bottillon[1] [bɔtijɔ̃], *s.m. Husb:* bunch, small bundle (of herbs, etc.).
bottillon[2], *s.m.* bootee; ankle-boot.
Bottin [bɔtɛ̃], *Pr.n.m.* trade mark applied to the well-known French street and trade directory from the name of the original compiler of the work; **le Bottin mondain,** French equivalent of "Who's Who."
bottine [bɔtin], *s.f.* **1.** *(a) O:* (half-)boot, ankle-boot; **bottines à boutons, à lacets, à élastiques,** button boots, lace boots, elastic-sided boots; *(b)* infant's bootee. **2.** *Mil:* Wellington (boot). **3. bottines de cheval = bottes de cheval,** *q.v.* under BOTTE[2] 1.
botulique [bɔtylik], *a.* botulinal, botulinic; **bacille b.,** bacillus botulinus.
botulisme [bɔtylism], *s.m. Med:* botulism.
boubouler [bubule], *v.i.* = ULULER.
bouc [buk], *s.m.* **1.** he-goat; *F:* billy-goat; **(barbe de) b.,** goatee (beard); **b. émissaire,** scapegoat; *F:* **puer comme un b., puer le b.,** to stink like an old goat; *P:* **c'est un bouc,** he's a dirty, lousy, fellow; *s.a.* HERBE 4. **2.** *(a) Leath:* goat-skin; *(b)* goat-skin (bottle). **3. porter le b.,** to wear a goatee. **4.** *(a) Hyd.E:* hydraulic ram; *(b) Mec.E:* sprocket-wheel (of pulley).
boucage [bukaːʒ], *s.m. Bot:* pimpinella; **b. anis,** anise, aniseed.
boucan[1] [bukɑ̃], *s.m.* **1.** (Caribs') buc(c)an. **2.** (Caribs') smoked meat.
boucan[2], *s.m. P:* hullabaloo, row, din, uproar, shindy; **faire du b., faire un b. de tous les diables,** to make the devil of a row, to raise Cain.
boucanage [bukanaːʒ], *s.m.* smoking (of meat, fish, etc.).
boucane [bukan], *s.f. Fr.C:* smoke.
boucané [bukane], *a.* swarthy (complexion).
boucaner[1] [bukane]. **1.** *v.i.* *(a)* to hunt wild animals (for their hides); *(b)* to buccaneer, lead the life of a buccaneer. **2.** *(a) v.tr.* to smoke-dry, cure (meat, fish, etc.); *(b) v.i.* to be smoke-dried, cured.
boucaner[2], *v.i. P:* to make, kick up, a row; to raise a shindy.
boucaner[3], *v.i. P:* to stink.
boucanier, -ière [bukanje, -jɛːr]. **1.** *s.m.* *(a)* buccaneer, pirate; *(b)* (buccaneer's) gun. **2.** *a.* buccaneerish; *adv.phr:* **à la boucanière,** like a buccaneer.
boucau [buko], *s.m. Dial:* harbour entrance.
boucaud [buko], *s.m.* shrimp.
boucaut [buko], *s.m.* barrel, cask (for dry goods).
bouchage [buʃaːʒ], *s.m.* **1.** *(a)* stopping, corking, plugging, stoppering; *(b)* sealing (of passage, etc.); *(c)* damping down (of furnace). **2.** stopper, cork; *Metall:* clay plug (of blast furnace).
bouchain [buʃɛ̃], *s.m. N.Arch:* bilge; **accores de b.,** bilge shores; **b. vif,** hard, sharp, bilge.
Bouchaïr [buʃaiːr], *Pr.n.m. Geog:* Bushire.
bouchardage [buʃardaːʒ], *s.m. Stonew:* roughening.
boucharde [buʃard], *s.f. Stonew:* bush-hammer.
boucharder [buʃarde], *v.tr. Stonew:* to roughen.
bouche [buʃ], *s.f.* mouth. **1.** *(of pers.)* *(a)* **regarder qn la b. entr'ouverte,** to look at s.o. with parted lips; **faire la b. en cœur,** to screw up one's mouth, to simper; *(b)* **avoir la b. pleine,** to have one's mouth full; **une pipe à la bouche,** with a pipe in his mouth; **avoir bonne, mauvaise, b.,** to have a pleasant, a disagreeable, taste in one's mouth; **garder qch. pour la bonne b.,** to keep something as a titbit; **laisser qn sur la bonne b.,** to leave s.o. after making a good impression; **être porté sur la b.,** to make a god of one's belly; **cela fait venir l'eau à la b.,** it makes one's mouth water; **faire la petite b.,** (i) to pick at one's food; (ii) to be dainty, fastidious; **en avoir à b. que veux-tu,** to have enough (food) to cut and come again, enough and to spare; **louer qn à b. que veux-tu,** to praise s.o. unstintingly; **s'embrasser à pleine b., à b. que veux-tu,** to kiss passionately; **manger à pleine b.,** to eat greedily, to gobble one's food; **provisions de b.,** victuals, food; **dépense de b.,** amount spent on food, housekeeping expenses; **avoir une douzaine de bouches à nourrir,** to have a dozen mouths to feed; **c'est une fine b.,** he is a gourmet; **faire la fine b.,** to be a gourmet; to have a sweet tooth; *Prov:* **il arrive beaucoup de choses entre la b. et le verre,** there's many a slip 'twixt the cup and the lip; *(b)* **les bouches inutiles,** those unable to bear arms; women, children and old people; *Med:* **à prendre par la b.,** to be taken internally; **administration par la b.,** oral administration (of a drug); *Poet:* **la déesse aux cent bouches,** Fame; *(c)* **elle n'osait pas ouvrir la b.,** she dared not open her mouth (to speak); **je l'ai appris de sa propre b.,** I had it from her own lips; **son nom est dans toutes les bouches,** his name is on every tongue, is a household word; **avoir qch. constamment à la b.,** to keep on repeating sth.; **homme fort en b.,** tremendous talker; **demeurer b. close,** to remain silent, to hold one's tongue; **b. close!** not a word! mum's the word! *P:* **ta b.!**

shut up! dry up! *F:* **il en avait la b. pleine, plein la b.**, he was full of it, he could talk of nothing else; **faire la petite b. sur qch.**, to be reticent about sth.; *adv.phr:* **de b. à oreille,** (i) by word of mouth, verbally; (ii) off the record, unofficially; **parler à qn à b.**, to speak to s.o. face to face. **2.** mouth (of horse, ass, cattle, elephant, fish; NOTE: of carnivorous animals *gueule* is used); **cheval qui a la b. faite,** horse that has all its teeth; **cheval sans b., qui n'a pas de b., fort en b.,** hard-mouthed horse; **cheval à la b. chatouilleuse,** tender-mouthed horse. **3.** mouth, opening, aperture (of crater, well, etc.); muzzle (of gun); slot (of money-box, etc.); nozzle; **b. à feu,** gun, piece of ordnance, of artillery; **b. de métro,** underground entrance, *U.S:* subway entrance; *Civ.E: etc:* **b. d'accès,** manhole (of sewer); **b. d'eau,** (i) hydrant; (ii) *Rail:* watercrane; **b. d'incendie,** hydrant, fire-plug; **b. de chaleur,** hot-air vent, *U.S:* (heat-)register; **b. d'aération,** air vent; **b. d'égout,** gully-hole; *Geog: pl.* **les Bouches du Gange,** the mouths of the Ganges; *cf.* EMBOUCHURE 2.

bouché [buʃe], *a.* **1.** plugged up, blocked, choked (pipe, etc.); *Mus:* **son b.**, closed note (on horn); *F:* **avoir l'esprit b., être b.**, to be dull-witted, dense, to be a blockhead, a duffer; **être b. à l'émeri,** to be a crass idiot, a complete moron; **temps b.**, thick weather. **2. flacon b. à l'émeri,** (ground glass) stoppered flask. **cidre b.**, bottled cider.

bouche-à-bouche [buʃabuʃ], *s.m.* mouth-to-mouth artificial respiration; *F:* kiss of life.

bouche-bouteilles [buʃbutɛj], *s.m.inv. in pl.* bottle-corking machine.

bouchée [buʃe], *s.f.* **1.** mouthful; **mangez-en une b.**, take a bite; **mettre les bouchées doubles,** (i) to eat quickly, to gobble up one's food; (ii) to do a job in double quick time; *F:* **ne faire qu'une b. d'un mets,** to eat a dish quickly, greedily, to gobble it up in no time; **ne faire qu'une b. de qn, de qch.**, to make short work of s.o., sth.; *s.a.* PAIN 1. **2.** *Cu:* small patty, pasty; **b. aux huîtres,** oyster patty; **b. à la reine,** chicken vol-au-vent.

bouche-porage [buʃpɔraːʒ], *s.m. Tchn: Furn: Paint:* filling in; *pl. bouche-porages.*

bouche-porer [buʃpɔre], *v.tr. Tchn: Furn: Paint:* to fill in.

bouche-pores [buʃpɔːr], *s.m.inv. Tchn: Furn: Paint:* filler.

boucher[1] [buʃe], *v.tr.* (*a*) to occlude, stop, fill up (gap, etc.); **b. un trou,** to stop (up), to plug, block up, a hole; **cela servira à b. un trou,** (i) it will serve as a stop-gap; (ii) *Fin: F:* it will tide us over; **b. les trous d'une flûte,** to stop a flute; **b. un tonneau,** to bung a barrel; **b. une carafe,** to put the stopper in a decanter; **b. une bouteille,** to cork a bottle; **b. une fenêtre,** to wall up, build in, a window; **pluie qui bouche la vue,** rain that curtails vision, limits the view; **b. la vue d'un voisin,** to obstruct, block (out), a neighbour's view; **se b. le nez,** to hold one's nose; **se b. les oreilles,** to stop one's ears, to refuse to listen; *P:* **en boucher un coin à qn,** to astound s.o., make a smart retort on s.o., to take the wind out of s.o.'s sails; (*b*) to choke (up) (pipe).

boucher[2], *s.m.* (*a*) butcher; **garçon b.**, butcher's boy; *s.a.* GROS 2; (*b*) *F:* butcher, (i) cruel man; (ii) bad surgeon.

bouchère [buʃɛːr], *s.f.* **1.** butcher's wife, butcher-woman. **2.** *Cu:* **côtelette à la b.**, undressed grilled cutlet.

boucherie [buʃri], *s.f.* **1.** (*a*) butcher's shop; (*b*) butcher's trade; *s.a.* BOEUF 1. **2.** butchery, slaughter; **ce ne fut pas un combat, ce fut une b.**, it was not a fight, it was sheer butchery.

bouche-sous-trottoir [buʃsutrɔtwaːr], *s.f. Civ.E:* sewer aperture, gully-hole, under the kerb; *pl. bouches-sous-trottoir.*

boucheton (à) [abuʃtɔ̃], *adv.phr.* stacked.

bouche-trou [buʃtru], *s.m.* stop-gap, substitute; makeshift; **un ministère b.-t.,** a stop-gap ministry; *pl. bouche-trous.*

Bouchir [buʃiːr], *Pr.n.m. Geog:* Bushire.

bouchoir [buʃwaːr], *s.m.* iron door (of furnace, oven, etc.).

boucholeur [buʃɔlœːr], *s.m.* = BOUCHOT(T)EUR.

bouchon [buʃɔ̃], *s.m.* **1.** (*a*) *A:* bush, sign, ale-post (of tavern); *Prov:* **à bon vin il ne faut point de b.,** good wine needs no bush; (*b*) tavern, public house. **2.** wisp, handful (of straw); hank (of wool); bundle (of linen); knot, inequality (in raw-silk yarn). **3.** (*a*) stopper, plug, bung (of cask); *F:* traffic-jam; large lorry, bus, holding up traffic; *Metall:* clay plug (of furnace); **b. de liège,** cork; **vin qui sent le b.,** corked wine; **b. verseur,** (*bottle*) pourer; **se noircir le visage au b.,** to cork one's face; **b. de verre,** glass stopper; **b. à l'émeri,** ground (glass) stopper; **b. stilli-goutte,** dropper; *I.C.E:* **b. de radiateur,** radiator cap; **b. de cylindre, de clapet, de soupape,** valve-cap; *Phot: etc:* **b. d'objectif,** lens cap; *El:* **b. de contact, de prise,** wall-plug; **b. de raccord,** adaptor plug; *Mch:* **b. fusible,** safety plug; **b. atomiseur;** swirl plug; *Mec.E:* **b. de graissage,** lubricating plug; **b. de remplissage,** filling filler, plug; filler cap; **b. de vidange, de trop-plein,** drain(ing) plug, tap; **b. de presse-étoupe,** packing gland; **b. fileté, b.-écrou,** screw-plug; *Artil:* threaded fuse-plug; **b. extensible,** expansion plug; *Artil:* **b. d'œil de projectile, b. d'obus,** adapter plug; *Mil:* **b. allumeur,** igniter set, fuse-plug, fuse assembly; **b. d'amorce,** primer-plug, fuse-plug; **b. de canon,** tampion; **b. de caoutchouc,** rubber stopper; *P:* **ramasser un b.,** to meet with failure, to come a cropper; **mets-y un b.!** put a sock in it! dry up! *F:* **b. de carafe,** large diamond; *s.a.* CIRCUIT 3; (*b*) *Hyd.E: Mch: etc:* **b. d'air,** airlock (in pipe); (*c*) *Physiol:* **b. de cérumen,** earwax; (*d*) (**jeu de**) **b.,** (game of) cork-penny; *F:* **c'est plus fort que de jouer au b.,** that beats everything. **4.** *Fish:* float, bob (of line).

bouchonnage [buʃɔnaːʒ], *s.m.*, **bouchonnement** [buʃɔnmɑ̃], *s.m.* rubbing down (of horse) (with a wisp of straw).

bouchonner [buʃɔne], *v.tr.* **1.** *v.tr.* **b. du linge,** (i) to roll up linen into bundles; (ii) to twist linen (when wringing out). **2.** *v.tr.* (*a*) to rub down; wisp down (horse); (*b*) to coddle (child). **3.** *v.i. Nau:* to be buoyant as a cork.

se bouchonner, (*of stuff*) to crumple, get crumpled.

bouchonnier [buʃɔnje], *s.m.* cork-cutter; maker of, dealer in, corks.

bouchot [buʃo], *s.m.* **1.** crawl, fishing-hurdles. **2.** oyster- or mussel-farm.

bouchot(t)eur [buʃɔtœːr], *s.m.* mussel-farmer.

bouchure [buʃyːr], *s.f.* (quickset) hedge.

bouclage [buklaːʒ], *s.m.* **1.** (action of) buckling; looping. **2.** *Hairdr:* curling. **3.** *W.Tel:* **b. de batterie,** battery loop. **4.** (*a*) *A: P:* imprisonment; (*b*) *Mil:* cordoning off (of area); *Pol:* **b. des frontières,** closing of the frontiers.

boucle [bukl], *s.f.* **1.** buckle, shackle; **b. de ceinture,** belt-buckle; *F:* **se serrer la b.,** to tighten one's belt (when hungry). **2.** (*a*) loop, bow (of ribbon, string, etc.); **b. à nœud coulant,** running loop; (*b*) *Nau:* bight, loop, eye (of rope); (*c*) loop, sweep (of river); bend (of river, road); (*of river*) **décrire de nombreuses boucles,** to meander; *Rail:* **b. d'évitement,** loop (at terminus); (*d*) *El:* **b. de couplage,** coupling loop; (*e*) *Atom.Ph: etc:* loop (in a reactor, etc.). **3.** ring; **b. de rideau,** curtain ring; **b. de porte,** ring door-knocker; **b. d'amarrage,** ring-bolt; **boucles d'oreilles,** ear-rings. **4.** curl, ringlet, lock (of hair); **grandes boucles éparses,** large loose curls. **5.** *Tex:* kink, snarl. **6.** *Sp:* lap.

bouclé [bukle]. **1.** *a.* **cheveux bouclés,** curly hair; *Tex:* **velours bouclé,** uncut velvet, terry; **laine bouclée,** knop wool. **2.** *s.m. Tex:* bouclé.

bouclement [bukləmɑ̃], *s.m. Husb:* ringing (of cattle, pigs).

boucler [bukle]. **1.** *v.tr.* (*a*) to buckle (belt, portmanteau, etc.); to fasten (strap); *F:* **se b. la ceinture,** *P:* **se la boucler,** to tighten one's belt, to go on short commons; **boucle-la! la boucle!** belt up! shut up! *F:* **b. une affaire,** to settle, clinch, a matter (for good and all); **c'est une affaire bouclée,** it's all settled and done with; *Book-k:* **b. les comptes,** to close the books; *s.a.* BUDGET; *F:* **il n'y a plus qu'à b.,** we'll have to close down, to shut up shop; **b. sa porte,** to shut one's door to all comers; **b. sa valise, ses malles,** (i) to get ready to go (on a journey), (ii) to prepare for death; (*b*) to loop, tie up, knot (ribbon, cord, etc.); *W.Tel:* to loop; *Av:* **b. la boucle,** to loop the loop; **b. son tour de qch.,** to circle (round) sth.; (*c*) *Husb:* to ring ((i) pig, bull, etc., (ii) mare, etc.); (*d*) *P:* (i) to lock up, imprison (s.o.); to put (s.o.) in irons; (ii) to cordon off; (*e*) *A:* **b. (les cheveux de) qn,** to curl s.o.'s hair; **elle se boucle,** she curls her hair; (*f*) *Sp:* to lap (competitor). **2.** *v.i.* (*a*) (*of wall*) to bulge; (*of metal*) to buckle; (*b*) (*of hair*) to curl, to be curly.

bouclerie [bukləri], *s.f.* (*a*) buckle-making; buckle-trade; (*b*) buckle factory.

boucleteau, -eaux [bukləto], *s.m. Harn:* **1.** tug. **2.** buckling-piece (of the crupper).

bouclette [buklɛt], *s.f.* **1.** small buckle. **2.** small ring. **3.** small curl. **4.** *attrib. Tex:* **laine b.,** knop wool.

bouclier [bukli(j)e], *s.m.* **1.** buckler, shield; curtain (of bullets, etc.); *A:* **levée de boucliers,** armed rising; *F:* **faire une levée de boucliers,** to organize a public protest; **faire un b. de son corps à qn,** to shield s.o. with one's body; **servir de b. à qn,** to protect, shield, s.o.; *Artil:* **b. articulé,** apron shield. **2.** (*a*) *Civ.E:* shield; **b. de creusement,** umbrella; (*b*) *A: Aut:* scuttle; (*c*) *Geol:* shield; *s.a.* CANADIEN. **3.** *Crust:* carapace. **4.** *Ent:* silpha, carrion beetle.

boucot [buko], *s.m.* = BOUCAUD.

Bouddha [buda], *Pr.n.m.* Buddha; **b. vivant,** living Buddha.

bouddhique [budik], *a.* Buddhist, Buddhistic(al); **art b.,** Buddhist art.

bouddhisme [budism], *s.m.* Buddhism.

bouddhiste [budist], *a.& s.m.& f.* Buddhist; **prêtre b.,** Buddhist priest.

bouder [bude]. **1.** *v.i.* to sulk, to be sullen; **b. contre qn,** to be sulky, in the sulks, with s.o.; **b. à la besogne,** to be afraid of work, to be work-shy, a shirker; **b. contre son ventre,** to cut off one's nose to spite one's face; *Dominoes:* "**je boude,**" "pass!" "go!" "I can't play."; **jeunes arbres qui boudent,** young trees that are doing badly; **cheval qui boude sur son avoine,** horse off its feed. **2.** *v.tr.* (*a*) **b. qn,** to be sulky, in the sulks, with s.o.; **ils se boudent depuis longtemps,** there has been a coolness, bad feeling, between them for a long time; (*b*) **b. le gouvernement du jour,** to stand, hold, aloof from the Government of the day; **b. la vie,** to reject the pleasures of life.

bouderie [budri], *s.f.* sulkiness; (fit of the) sulks.

boudeur, -euse [budœːr, -øːz]. **1.** *a.* & *s.* sulky, sullen (person). **2.** *s.f.* **boudeuse,** double back-to-back settee.

boudin [budɛ̃], *s.m.* **1.** (*a*) *Cu:* **b.** (**noir**), black pudding, *U.S:* blood sausage; **b. blanc,** white pudding; *F:* (*of undertaking*) **s'en aller, tourner, finir, en eau de b.,** to fail, to fizzle out; *F:* **c'est clair comme de l'eau de b.,** it's as clear as mud; (*b*) *F:* **boudins,** fat, podgy, fingers. **2.** (*a*) cork-screw curl; roll, twist (of tobacco); *Tex:* slub (of wool, etc.); *Min: etc:* sausage (of explosive); *Av: etc:* **b. d'étanchéité,** seal tube; *El:* **b. de résistance,** resistance coil; *s.a.* RESSORT[1] 1; (*b*) *Arch:* torus, ovolo; *Mec.E: etc:* fillet, beading; flange (on wheel, etc.); *Com:* **fer à b.,** bulb-iron; *s.a.* BANDAGE 2; (*c*) *Nau:* puddening. **3.** *Echin:* **b. de mer,** holothurian, sea cucumber. **4.** *F:* **faire du boudin,** to sulk.

boudinage [budinaːʒ], *s.m. Tex:* roving, slubbing.

boudine [budin], *s.f.* bull's-eye (in blown sheet-glass); **verre à b.,** (i) *A:* bull's-eye glass; (ii) crown-glass.

boudiné, -ée [budine], *F:* **1.** *a.* (*a*) dressed in skin-tight, in close-fitting, garments; crammed into (a tight garment); (*b*) podgy (fingers, etc.); (*c*) *El:* spiral-wound (filament). **2.** *s.m. A:* young dandy (whose clothes are absurdly tight). **3.** *s.f.* **boudinée,** *Cu:* making of *boudins*; (stock of) *boudins.*

boudiner [budine], *v.tr.* **1.** (*a*) *Tex:* to rove, slub; (*b*) *Tch:* to plasticize. **2.** *F:* **cette robe me boudine car elle est trop juste,** this dress is too tight and makes me bulge.

boudineur, -euse [budinœːr, -øːz], *s. Tex:* **1.** slubber, rover (employee). **2.** *s.f.* **boudineuse,** (*a*) slubbing machine; slubber; rover; (*b*) plasticizing machine.

boudinoir [budinwaːr], *s.m.* = BOUDINEUSE.

boudoir [budwaːr], *s.m.* boudoir; *A. & Poet:* bower; **diplomatie de b.,** drawing-room diplomacy; **avoir des succès de b.,** to be a success with the ladies.

boue [bu], *s.f.* **1.** mud, mire, ooze, slush; filth, dirt; **tas de b.,** mud-heap; *F:* **il me considère comme la b. de ses souliers,** he treats me like dirt; **tirer qn de la b.,** to raise s.o. from the gutter; **couvrir qn de b.,** to throw, fling, mud at s.o., to tarnish s.o.'s reputation; *s.a.* TRAÎNER 1. **2.** (*a*) (*building*) mud, clay; *F:* **maison faite de b. et de crachat,** jerry-built house. **3.** sediment, mud, deposit; *Oc:* ooze; *Mch:* sludge, mud; *Min:* **b. de forage,** drilling mud; *Med:* **b. urinaire,** urinary sediment; **b. d'un abcès,** pus of an abscess; **boues minérales,** mineral muds, mud-baths; **bain de boues,** mud-bath; **boues activées,** *Med:* radioactive mud; *Hyg:* activated sludge; **b. de meule, d'émoulage,** swarf, sludge, slurry; *Mch:* **robinet à b.,** sludge-cock; *s.a.* BASSIN 4.(*d*)

bouée [bwe], *s.f.* **1.** *Nau:* buoy; **b. à cloche,** bell-buoy; **b. en olive,** nun-buoy; **b. à fuseau,** spar-buoy; **b. conique,** can-buoy; **b. d'amarrage, de corps-mort,** mooring-buoy; **b. sonore,** sonobuoy; **b. à sifflet,** whistling-buoy; **b. sonore directionnelle, omnidirectionnelle,** directional, omnidirectional, sonobuoy; **b. couronne,** ringbuoy; **b. lumineuse,** light buoy, floating light; **b. de balisage,** marking buoy; **b. de pêcheur,** dan buoy;

s'amarrer à, sur, une b., to make fast to a buoy; *Av:* **b. d'amerrissage,** alighting buoy; *A: F:* **je suis au vent de ma b.,** I have weathered the storm. **2. b. de sauvetage,** life-buoy; **b. culotte,** breeches-buoy; **s'accrocher à une idée comme un naufragé à une b.,** to cling to, hang on to, an idea like grim death.

bouée-tonne [bwetɔn], *s.f.* barrel-buoy; *pl. bouées-tonnes.*

bouette [buɛt], *s.f. Fish:* bait.

boueur [buœːr], *s.m.* dustman, *U.S:* garbage man, garbage collector.

boueux, -euse [buø, -øːz]. **1.** *a.* (*a*) muddy, miry (road, boots, etc.); *s.a.* SOURCE; (*b*) smudgy, thick (writing, print, etc.); **maçonnerie boueuse,** badly executed brickwork. **2.** *s.m.* = BOUEUR.

bouffant [bufɑ̃]. **1.** *a.* puffed (sleeve, etc.); full (skirt); baggy (trousers); **cheveux bouffants,** (i) (man's) wavy hair; (ii) (woman's) bouffant hair-do; *A:* padded hair; *Paperm:* **papier b.,** feather-weight paper, bulking paper. **2.** *s.m.* puff (of sleeve).

bouffarde [bufard], *s.f. F:* (tobacco-)pipe.

bouffarder [bufarde], *v.tr. F:* to smoke (pipe).

bouffe[1] [buf]. **1.** *a.* **opéra b.,** opera bouffe, comic opera, musical comedy; **(chanteur) b.,** singer in comic opera. **2.** *s.m.pl. A:* **les Bouffes,** the Italian opera (in Paris).

bouffe[2], *s.f. P:* **1.** food, grub. **2.** gorging.

bouffée [bufe], *s.f.* **1.** (*a*) puff (of smoke); whiff (of scent); **lancer des bouffées de fumée,** to puff out smoke; **tirer une b. de sa pipe,** to take a puff at one's pipe; **b. d'air,** gust; blast, puff, of air; **b. de vent,** gust of wind; *Nau: F:* capful of wind; **b. de chaleur,** blast of hot air; **b. de musique apportée par le vent,** snatch of music brought by the wind; (*b*) *Med:* sudden onset (of fever); **b. de chaleur,** sudden flush, hot flush; **avoir des bouffées de chaleur,** to feel suddenly hot all over. **2.** (out)burst, gust (of eloquence, anger, etc.); **travailler par bouffées,** to work by fits and starts.

bouffer [bufe]. I. *v.i.* **1.** (*of dress, etc.*) to puff (out), swell out; (*with puff of wind*) to balloon out; (*of bread*) to rise; (*of plaster*) to blister, swell; *F:* **b. de colère,** to puff, snort, with anger. **2.** *Nau: F:* **ça bouffe,** it is blowing hard.

II. **bouffer,** *v.tr.* **1. b. les joues,** to puff out one's cheeks. **2. b. un veau, un mouton,** to blow up a calf, a sheep (before skinning). **3.** *P:* (*a*) (i) to eat (sth.) greedily; to guzzle; *abs.* **j'ai bien bouffé,** that was a bloody good meal; **il a bouffé du lion aujourd'hui,** he is like a raging lion today; **b. de la vache enragée,** to go through the mill; **b. de la boîte, de la case,** to be gaoled; *Sch:* to be a boarder; (*of car*) **b. de l'essence,** to be heavy on petrol; **b. du kilomètre,** to be a compulsive motorist; *s.a.* BRIQUE; (ii) **b. le blair à qn,** to bash s.o. on the snout; **ils se sont bouffé le nez,** they pitched into one another; (*b*) to blue (money); **b. un million en six mois,** to run through a million in six months.

bouffe-la-balle [buflabal], *s.m.inv. P:* greedy-guts.

bouffetance [buftɑ̃s], *s.f. P:* **1.** food, grub. **2.** gorging.

bouffette [bufɛt], *s.f.* (*a*) (ribbon) rosette; (*b*) tassel.

bouffi [bufi], *a.* puffy, puffed, swollen (eyes, cheeks, etc.); bloated (face, etc.); **enfant à la face bouffie,** puffy-faced child; **être b. d'orgueil,** to be puffed up with pride; **style b.,** inflated, turgid, style; *Com:* **hareng b.,** bloater.

bouffir [bufiːr]. **1.** *v.tr.* (*a*) to swell, blow out, inflate, bloat; (*b*) to bloat (herrings). **2.** *v.i.* to become swollen, puffed up, bloated, inflated.

bouffissure [bufisyːr], *s.f.* **1.** swelling; puffiness (of the face, etc.); **b. des yeux,** puffiness round the eyes. **2.** inflation, turgidity (of style). **3.** *A:* vanity, self-importance.

bouffon [bufɔ̃]. **1.** *s.m.* (*a*) buffoon, clown, fool, jester; **il leur servait de b.,** they made him their laughing-stock, the butt of their jokes; (*b*) *Ich:* **b. des mers,** frogfish, sea-clown. **2.** *a.* (*f.* **bouffonne** [bufɔn]) (*a*) farcical, (broadly) comical; ludicrous; (*b*) fond of buffoonery.

bouffonner [bufɔne]. **1.** *v.i.* to play, act, the buffoon. **2.** *v.tr.* to imitate, burlesque, travesty.

bouffonnerie [bufɔnri], *s.f.* buffoonery; clownery; **dire, faire, des bouffonneries,** to indulge in buffoonery, to play the fool; to perform one's antics.

bougainvillea [bugɛ̃vilea], *s.f.* = BOUGAINVILLÉE 1.

bougainvillée [bugɛ̃vile], *s.f.* **1.** *Bot:* bougainvillea. **2.** *Z:* bougainvillia.

bouge [buːʒ], *s.m.* **1.** (*a*) bilge (of cask); bulge (of wall); swell (of wheel-nave); (*b*) *Nau:* round up, camber (of deck, beam, etc.); *Metalw:* **marteau à bouges,** repoussé hammer. **2.** (*a*) *A:* apse, recess (in a room); (*b*) den, slum, hovel; **ils habitent dans des bouges mortels,** they live in foul slums; **sa cuisine est un b.,** her kitchen is a regular pigsty; (*c*) brothel. **3.** (*jeweller's*) chasing-chisel. **4.** tub, vat (for carrying grapes).

bougeoir [buʒwaːr], *s.m.* **1.** flat candlestick. **2.** *Ecc:* taper-stand.

bougeonnier [buʒɔnje], *s.m. Orn:* bull-finch.

bougeotte [buʒɔt], *s.f. F:* **avoir la b.,** to be restless, to be always on the move.

bouger [buʒe], *v.* (**je bougeai(s); n. bougeons**) **1.** *v.i.* to budge, stir, move; **rester sans b.,** to stand, remain, quite still; **ne pas b. de sa place,** to sit tight; **ne bougez pas!** don't move! stand fast! *Phot:* **ne bougeons plus!** hold it! *F: Pol:* **ça bouge,** things are stirring. **2.** *v.tr. F:* **il ne faut rien b.,** you must not move, shift, anything; **b. son pied,** to move one's foot (out of the way).

bougette [buʒɛt], *s.f. A:* (small leather) bag, wallet.

bougie [buʒi], *s.f.* **1.** (*a*) candle; **b. de cire,** wax-candle, wax-light; **b. stéarique,** stearic candle, composite candle; *Com:* composite; **à la b., aux bougies,** by candlelight; (*b*) (i) *A:* **b. électrique,** electric, Jablochkoff, candle; (ii) **b. à incandescence électrique,** candle-shaped glow-lamp. **2.** *Ph.Meas:* candle-power; **intensité (d'éclairage) en bougies,** candle-power; *Ph:* **b. nouvelle,** new candle, candela. **3.** *I.C.E:* **b. (d'allumage),** sparking-plug; *U.S:* spark-plug; igniter (for jet-engine); **b. incandescente,** glow plug (of Diesel); **b. blindée, non blindée,** shielded, unshielded plug; **axe de (la) b.,** plug core; **culot de (la) b.,** plug body or shell; *W.Tel:* **b. antiparasites,** radio shielded plug. **4.** *Surg:* bougie. **5.** (candle-shaped) filter, bougie; **b. Chamberland,** Chamberland filter.

bougier [buʒje], *v.tr.* (*p.d.* & *pr.sub.* **n. bougiions, v. bougiiez**) *Dressm:* to wax (the raw edge of cloth, silk).

bougn(i)at [buɲa], *s.m. F:* (*a*) retailer of charcoal (*esp.* in Paris); (*b*) coalman.

bougniou [buɲju], *s.m. Min:* sump.

bougnou(le) [buɲu(l)], *s.m. P: Pej:* **1.** nigger, **2.** wog.

bougon, -onne [bugɔ̃, -ɔn], *F:* **1.** *s.* grumbler, grouser. **2.** *a.* grumpy.

bougonner [bugɔne], *F:* **1.** *v.i.* to grumble, grouse. **2.** *A: v.tr.* to scold; to grumble, nag, at (s.o.).

bougran [bugrɑ̃], *s.m. Tex:* buckram; *Dressm:* foundation.

bougraner [bugrane], *v.tr.* **1.** *Tex:* to stiffen (linen, etc.). **2.** to line (material) with buckram; to buckram.

bougre, bougresse [bugr, bugrɛs], *s.m. & f. P:* **1. mauvais b.,** ugly customer; **b. de temps,** brute, of a day; **b. d'imbécile!** you bloody fool! **2.** fellow, chap; **c'est un bon b.,** he's not a bad sort. **3.** *int.* **b. que ça fait mal!** that hurts like blazes. **4.** *s.f.* **bougresse,** strapping great woman.

bougrement [bugrəmɑ̃], *adv.* damn(ed); **il fait b. chaud,** it's damn hot.

boui-boui [bwibwi], *s.m. P:* low theatre or music-hall; low dive; *pl. bouis-bouis.*

bouif [bwif], *s.m. P: A:* cobbler.

bouillabaisse [bujabɛs], *s.f. Cu:* Provençal fish soup or chowder; bouillabaisse.

bouillage [bujaːʒ], *s.m.* **1.** *Laund:* boil(ing) (of clothes). **2.** = BOUILLAISON.

bouillaison [bujɛzɔ̃], *s.f.* fermentation (of beer, cider, etc.).

bouillant [bujɑ̃], *a.* **1.** boiling; **de l'eau bouillante,** boiling water; **boire du thé b.,** to drink scalding hot tea; **le café était b.,** the coffee was piping hot; **b. de colère,** boiling with anger; **b. d'impatience,** bursting with impatience. **2.** fiery, hot-headed, impetuous. **3.** *s.f.* **bouillante,** *A: Mil: P:* soup.

bouillasse [bujas], *s.f. P:* mud.

Bouillaud [bujo], *Pr.n. Med:* **maladie de B.,** rheumatic fever.

bouille[1] [buj], *s.f. Fish:* (fisherman's) pole for driving fish into net.

bouille[2], *s.f.* **1.** *P:* face, mug. **2.** (*a*) *A:* (dairy man's) milk-can; (*b*) (wooden) tub for collecting grapes.

bouiller [buje], *v.i. Fish:* to beat water with pole to drive fish into net.

bouillerie [bujri], *s.f.* brandy distillery.

bouilleur [bujœːr], *s.m.* **1.** (brandy) distiller; **b. de cru,** farmer, etc., who distils privately, for his own consumption; home distiller. **2.** *Mch:* (*a*) water-space, water-room (of a ship's boiler); (*b*) **(tube) b.,** subsidiary shell, heater (of boiler). **3.** (*a*) water-distilling apparatus (on board ship); (*b*) *Ind:* evaporator. **4.** *Atom.Ph:* (small) nuclear reactor.

bouilli [buji], *Cu:* **1.** *a.* boiled. **2.** *s.m.* boiled meat.

bouillie [buji], *s.f.* **1.** pap (for infants), gruel, porridge; **mettre de la farine en b.,** to make flour into a thick paste; *F:* **être comme de la b.,** to have no backbone; **c'est de la b. pour les chats,** that's just fit for the cat; it is a worthless jumble; **faire de la b. pour les chats,** to take, unnecessary, useless, trouble; **les malheureux voyageurs ont été réduits en b.,** the unfortunate passengers were crushed to a pulp. **2.** *Paperm:* pulp. **3.** *Mec.E:* **b. de graphite,** non-freezing graphite compound (for lubrication); *Metall:* slurry. **4.** *Vit:* wash, spraying mixture (against mildew, etc.); **b. bordelaise, cuprique, cupro-calcique,** Bordeaux mixture; *Hort:* **b. soufrée, sulfocalcique,** lime sulphur.

bouillir [bujiːr], *v.* (*pr.p.* **bouillant;** *p.p.* **bouilli;** *pr.ind.* **je bous** [bu], **tu bous, il bout, n. bouillons, v. bouillez, ils bouillent;** *pr.sub.* **je bouille, n. bouillions;** *imp.* **bous, bouillons, bouillez;** *p.d.* **je bouillais;** *p.h.* **je bouillis;** *p.sub.* **je bouillisse;** *fu.* **je bouillirai**) **1.** *v.i.* to boil; **l'eau bout,** the water is on the boil, is boiling; **commencer à b.,** to come to the boil; **cesser de b.,** to go off the boil; **faire b. qch.,** to boil sth.; **faire b. qch. à demi,** to par-boil sth.; *F:* **cela fera b. la marmite,** that will keep the pot boiling; **b. de colère,** to boil with anger. **2.** *v.tr. F:* (= **faire bouillir**) to bring (milk, etc.) to the boil; *Dial:* to distil.

bouilloire [bujwaːr], *s.f.* kettle.

bouillon [bujɔ̃], *s.m.* **1.** (*a*) bubble (given off by boiling liquid); **bouillir à gros bouillons,** to boil fast; **cuire à petits bouillons,** to boil gently, to simmer; **faire jeter un b. à qch.,** to bring sth. to the boil; *A:* **dans les premiers bouillons de sa colère,** in the first ebullition, outburst, of his wrath; **le sang sortait à gros bouillons,** the blood was gushing out, welling out; (*b*) bleb, air-bubble (in glass); blowhole (in metal); (*c*) *Cost:* puff, gauging; **manches à bouillons,** puffed, gauged, sleeves; (*d*) *Mil:* bullion fringe (of epaulet); (*e*) *Arch: Furn:* swag, festoon; (*f*) *Surg:* proud flesh. **2.** (*a*) *Cu:* bouillon; stock; **b. gras,** clear (meat) soup, beef-tea, meat-stock; **b. maigre, de légumes,** vegetable soup, vegetable stock; **b. en tablette,** soup tablet; **être (réduit) au b.,** to be on a liquid diet, on slops; *F:* **b. pointu,** enema (contents of the syringe); **b. d'onze heures,** poisoned draught; **avaler, boire, un b.,** (i) to get a mouthful (when swimming); (ii) to come to grief, to suffer a heavy loss (in business); *F:* **nous allons avoir du b.,** we are in for a heavy shower; *P:* **tomber dans le, au, b.,** to fall into the water; *P:* into the drink; (*b*) *Biol:* **b. de culture,** culture medium; gelatine meatbroth; (*c*) *Hort: F:* liquid manure. **3.** *O:* **b. (Duval),** (Duval) restaurant. **4.** *pl. Com:* returns, remainders, unsold copies (of book or daily papers).

bouillon-blanc [bujɔ̃blɑ̃], *s.m. Bot:* great mullein, common mullein, Aaron's rod; *pl. bouillons-blancs.*

bouillonnage [bujɔnaːʒ], *s.m.* **1.** *Ch:* slugging. **2.** *Publ: Journ:* return of unsold copies.

bouillonnant [bujɔnɑ̃], *a.* bubbling, seething, boiling; *F:* **enfants bouillonnants de vie,** children bubbling over with life.

bouillonné [bujɔne], *s.m. Dressm:* ruffle, ruffled border, inset.

bouillonnement [bujɔnmɑ̃], *s.m.* (*a*) bubbling; boiling; seethe, seething; *El.E:* gassing (of accumulator); (*b*) boiling over; **b. des vagues,** foaming of the waves; *F:* **b. de la jeunesse,** effervescence, impetuousness, of youth.

bouillonner [bujɔne]. **1.** *v.i.* (*a*) to bubble, boil up, seethe, froth up; **la colère bouillonne dans son âme,** his soul seethes with anger; (*b*) to boil over; *F:* **b. de colère,** to boil, seethe, with anger. **2.** *v.tr. Dressm:* to gauge; to gather (material) into puffs. **3.** *Com:* (*of newspaper, magazine*), to remain unsold; **le journal bouillonne à 20% de son tirage,** 20% of the newspaper remains unsold.

bouillotte [bujɔt], *s.f.* **1.** (*a*) *Rail: A:* foot-warmer; (*b*) hot-water bottle; (*c*) *O:* boiler (in kitchener); (*d*) *F:* head, nut; face; *P:* mug. **2.** *occ.* = BOUILLOIRE. **3.** *Cards:* bouillotte.

bouillottement [bujɔtmɑ̃], *s.m.* simmering.

bouillotter [bujɔte], *v.i.* to boil gently, to simmer.

bouisbouis [bwibwi], *s.m.* = BOUI-BOUI.

bouisse [buis], *s.f. Bootm:* lapstone.

boujaron [buʒarɔ̃], *s.m. A: Nau:* **1.** tot, ration (of rum). **2.** dungarees.

Boukhara [bukara], *Pr.n.f. Geog:* Bokhara, Bukhara; **tapis de B.,** Bokhara (carpet).

boukhare [bukaːr], *a. & s.m. & f. Geog:* Bokharian.

Boukharie [bukari], *Pr.n.f. Hist: Geog:* Khanate of Bokhara; Bukharia.

boukharien, -ienne [bukarjɛ̃, -jɛn], *a. & s. Geog:* = BOUKHARE.

boulage [bulaːʒ], *s.m.* **1.** *Tex:* boiling (of linen in order to bleach it). **2.** *Sug-R:* crushing (of sugar beet). **3.** *Bullfighting:* buttoning, padding, (of bull's horns). **4.** *Fish:* stirring up of the bottom (with a *bouloir*).

boulaie [bulɛ], *s.f.* **1.** birch plantation. **2.** *A:* mace (of *huissier*).

boulange [bulɑ̃ːʒ], *s.f. O:* bread-making.

boulanger¹, -ère [bulɑ̃ʒe, -ɛːr]. **1.** *s.* baker; *f.* baker's wife, bakeress, or (*in convent*) nun in charge of the bakery. **2.** *s.f.* **boulangère;** (*a*) *A: Aut:* farmer's market van; (*b*) children's round dance (and song); fifth figure of the quadrille; Paul Jones. **3.** *a.* **blé de grande valeur boulangère,** wheat of high milling value. **4.** *s.m. F:* **le B.,** old Nick.

boulanger², *v.tr.* (**je boulangeai(s); n. boulangeons**) (*a*) to knead (the flour, in bread-making); to make (bread); (*b*) *abs.* to bake.

boulangerie [bulɑ̃ʒri], *s.f.* **1.** (*a*) bread-making, baking; (*b*) baker's business. **2.** (*a*) bakery, bakehouse; (*b*) baker's shop; (*c*) *Nau:* bread-locker.

boulangérite [bulɑ̃ʒerit], *s.f. Miner:* boulangerite.

boulangisme [bulɑ̃ʒism], *s.m. Fr.Hist:* Boulangism, adherence to the party of General Boulanger.

boulangiste [bulɑ̃ʒist], *s.m. Fr.Hist:* Boulangist, follower of General Boulanger.

boulant [bulɑ̃]. **1.** *Orn: a. & s.m.* **(pigeon) b.,** pouter (pigeon). **2.** *Min: Civ.E:* (*a*) **sables boulants,** quicksand.

boule¹ [bul], *s.f.* **1.** (*a*) ball, sphere, globe; **b. de croquet, de hockey,** croquet ball, hockey ball; **b. à thé,** tea egg; **foudre en b.,** globular lightning, ball-lightning; *F:* **la b. terrestre,** the terrestrial sphere, the globe; *A: F:* **laisser rouler la b.,** to let things go, slide; **arbre en b.,** bushy-topped tree; *F:* **b. de feu, b. de fer,** cross my heart; être **rond comme une b.,** to be short and fat, podgy; *F:* **c'est une petite b. de suif,** she's a regular little dumpling; (*of hedge-hog, etc.*) **se rouler, se pelotonner, se mettre, en b.,** to curl (itself) up; *F:* **se mettre en b.,** to get angry; *F:* **il me met en b.,** he gets my back up; *F:* **j'ai les nerfs en b.,** my nerves are all on edge; *F:* **b. dans la gorge,** lump in one's throat; *Med:* **b. hystérique,** *globus hystericus; s.a.* GOMME 1, NEIGE, PUANT; (*b*) *P:* face; *P:* mug, dial; head, *P:* nut; **perdre la b.,** to go off one's head, to go dotty, to go round the bend, *U.S: F:* to go nuts; (*c*) *Mch:* **boules du régulateur,** governor fly-balls; *Nau: etc:* **b. horaire, d'observatoire,** hour-ball, time-ball; *Nav:* **b. de signaux,** (red or black) ball; (*d*) **b. de scrutin,** ballot(-ball), voting-ball; **b. blanche,** favourable vote; **b. noire,** black ball; *F:* **la b. noire lui tombe toujours,** ill-luck follows him, nothing ever turns out well for him; (*e*) **b. de balustre,** banister knob; (*f*) **b. à gibecière,** gate-catch (with counterpoise). **2.** (*a*) hot-water bottle; (*b*) bulb (of thermometer, etc.); (*c*) *Tls:* tinman's dome-head stake; (*d*) *Mil:* ration loaf; **b. de son,** (i) *P:* ration loaf; (ii) *F:* freckled face. **3.** (*a*) *Games:* (any form of) bowl or game of bowls; **jouer aux boules,** to play bowls; **jeu de boules,** (i) (game of) bowls; (ii) bowling green or (*in France*) alley; **partie de boules,** a game of bowls, bowling match; **lancer la b.,** to bowl; *F:* **tenir pied à b.,** to stand firm; **juger qch. à b. vue,** to judge sth. hastily, without proper consideration; (*b*) *Gaming:* **la b.,** (i) the ball (thrown into the cup); (ii) (the game of) boule; *s.a.* LOTO. **4.** *Vet:* rot (in sheep).

boule², *s.m.* = BOULLE.

bouleau, -eaux [bulo], *s.m. Bot: Com:* birch (-tree); birch-wood; **b. blanc,** silver, lady, white, common, birch; **b. pubescent,** pubescent birch; **b. pleureur,** weeping, drooping, birch; **b. nain,** dwarf birch; **balai de b.,** birch broom; **essence d'écorce de b.,** birch oil; *Orn:* **poule des bouleaux,** grey-hen.

boule-chaufferette [bulʃofrɛt], *s.f.* hot-water bottle; *A:* foot-warmer; *pl. boules-chaufferettes.*

boule-de-neige [buldənɛːʒ], *s.f. Bot:* guelder-rose, snowball-tree; *pl. boules-de-neige.*

bouledogue [buldɔg], *s.m.* bulldog; **chienne b.,** bull-bitch; *F:* **être aimable comme un b.,** to be (permanently) ill-tempered.

boule-d'or [buldɔːr], *s.f. Bot:* globe-flower; *pl. boules-d'or.*

bouler [bule]. **1.** *v.tr.* (*a*) *F:* to send (s.o.) rolling, to roll (s.o.) on the ground; *F:* **envoyer b. qn,** to tell s.o. to go to blazes, to send s.o. packing; (*b*) *F:* to make a failure of (sth.): *F:* to mess (sth.) up; *Th:* **b. son rôle, son entrée,** to fluff one's part, one's entrance; *abs.* to fluff; (*c*) *Fish:* to stir up the bottom; (*d*) *Husb:* **b. les cornes d'un taureau,** to pad a bull's horns; (*e*) *v.i.* to roll, go rolling. **2.** *v.i.* (*of seed, bread, etc.*) to swell; (*of pigeon*) to pout. **3.** *v.i. & tr. Games:* (*a*) to measure (distance of opposing bowls); (*b*) to scatter one's opponent's bowls.

boulet [bulɛ], *s.m.* **1.** (*a*) *Artil:* **b. de canon,** cannon-ball, round shot; **b. plein, massif,** solid shot; **tirer sur qn à boulet(s) rouge(s),** to go for s.o. hammer and tongs; **passer, débouler, comme un b. (de canon),** to hurtle past, by; (*b*) *Jur: A:* chain-and-ball punishment; *F:* **traîner le b.,** to be tied down to an uncongenial occupation, to have one's nose to the grindstone; **c'est un b. qu'il traînera toute sa vie,** it, he, she, will be a millstone round his neck all his life. (*c*) *Bot:* **b. de canon,** cannon-ball. **2.** (*a*) *Mec.E:* **b. de soupape,** ball of a valve; **joint à b.,** ball-and-socket joint; (*b*) *Civ.E:* **moulin à boulets,** ball-mill; (*c*) *Com:* **boulets (de charbon),** ovoids. **3.** fetlock-joint, pastern-joint (of horse); *F:* **mettre qn sur les boulets,** to wear s.o. out.

bouleté [bulte], *a. Vet:* (horse) with overshot fetlock.

boulette [bulɛt], *s.f.* **1.** small ball, pellet (of paper, etc.); *Metall: Ch:* pellet. **2.** (*a*) *Cu:* forcemeat ball; meat ball; **b. de poisson,** fish-ball; (*b*) *Vet: etc:* (poison) ball; bolus; *Turf:* **donner une b. à un cheval,** to tamper with; *P:* nobble, a horse. **3.** *F:* **faire une b.,** to make a blunder, a bloomer; to drop a brick.

bouleture [bultyːr], *s.f. Vet:* overshot fetlock.

bouleur [bulœːr], *s.m. Gaming:* (*at boule*) thrower-in (of the ball).

bouleux, -euse [bulø, -øːz], *a. & s.* **1.** stocky, cobby (mare, horse); *s.m.* cob. **2.** *F:* hard-working, plodding (person); **un bon b.,** a plodder.

boulevard [bulvaːr], *s.m.* **1.** *A:* bulwark, rampart. **2.** boulevard; **théâtre de b.** = variety theatre; **le b.,** variety; *F:* **les événements du b.,** life in town; **les boulevards extérieurs,** (*in Paris*) the boulevards following the line of the old fortifications.

boulevarder [bulvarde], *v.i. A:* to stroll along the boulevards (of Paris).

boulevardier, -ière [bulvardje, -jɛːr]. **1.** *a.* (*in Paris*) **argot b.,** slang of the boulevards; **esprit b.,** facile humour. **2.** *s. O:* frequenter of the boulevards; man about town.

bouleversant [bulvɛrsɑ̃], *a.* upsetting, staggering, bewildering; **une femme bouleversante,** a stunning woman.

bouleversé [bulvɛrse], *a.* disordered, upset; **avoir l'esprit b.,** to be completely upset; *F:* knocked, struck, all of a heap, bowled over; **figure bouleversée,** distressed, distracted, distraught, face; **terrain b.,** disrupted ground.

bouleversement [bulvɛrsəmɑ̃], *s.m.* (*a*) overthrow, overturning, upsetting; (*b*) disorder, confusion, upheaval; (*c*) disruption.

bouleverser [bulvɛrse], *v.tr.* (*a*) to upset, overturn, overthrow; to turn (sth.) topsy-turvy; to throw (sth.) into confusion; (*b*) to unsettle, upset, discompose (s.o.); to overwhelm; **la nouvelle l'a complètement bouleversé,** *F:* the news bowled him over; **cela m'a tout bouleversé;** *F:* it gave me quite a turn; **événement qui bouleversa le monde,** event that convulsed the world; **la moindre chose le bouleverse,** the least thing upsets him.

se bouleverser, to become perturbed; to get flurried, upset.

boulier [bulje], *s.m.* **1.** (*a*) **b. compteur,** abacus, counting-frame; (*b*) billiard scoring-board. **2.** *Dial:* earthenware jar. **3.** *Fish:* bag-net, wing-net.

boulimie [bulimi], *s.f. Med:* bulimia, bulimy, boulimia, morbid hunger.

boulimique [bulimik], *a. & s.* bulimic (subject).

boulin [bulɛ̃], *s.m.* **1.** pigeon-hole. **2.** *Const:* (*a*) putlog-hole; (*b*) putlog.

boulinage [bulinaːʒ], *s.m. Nau:* sailing close-hauled.

bouline [bulin], *s.f. Nau:* bowline; **naviguer, aller, à la b.,** to sail close-hauled, close to the wind; **nœud de b.,** bowline-knot; *A:* **courir la b.,** to run the gauntlet.

bouliner [buline], *Nau:* (*a*) *v.tr.* **b. une voile,** to haul a sail to windward; (*b*) *v.i.* to sail close to the wind.

boulingrin [bulɛ̃grɛ̃], *s.m.* lawn, grass-plot.

boulinier [bulinje], *Nau:* **1.** *a.* weatherly (ship); **navire mauvais b.,** leewardly ship. **2.** *s.m. A:* ship that sails well to windward.

boulisme [bulism], *s.m.* playing bowls (of any sort), bowling.

bouliste [bulist], *s.m.* **1.** bowls player. **2.** *Adm:* interdepartmental messenger.

boulisterie [bulistəri], *s.f. Adm:* interdepartmental messenger service.

boulle [bul], *s. Furn:* boule, buhl; **cabinet de b.,** buhl, boule, cabinet.

Boul'Mich' (le) [ləbulmiʃ], *s.m. F:* = **le Boulevard Saint-Michel** (in Paris).

boulocher [bulɔʃe], *v.i. F:* (*of wool garment*) to go into lumps, *U.S:* to pill.

boulodrome [bulodroːm], *s.m.* bowling-alley; bowling-green.

bouloir [bulwaːr], *s.m. Tls:* **1.** *Constr:* larry. **2.** tanner's hook. **3.** *Fish:* stick (to stir the bottom).

boulon [bulɔ̃], *s.m. Mec.E: Const: etc:* bolt, pin; **b. à écrou,** screw-bolt; **b. à œil,** eye-bolt; **b. d'assemblage,** through-bolt; pole bolt; **b. à oreilles,** wing-bolt; **b. de charnière,** hinge-pin; *Const:* **b. barbelé,** rag-bolt, barb-bolt; **b. de scellement,** expansion bolt; **b. à queue de carpe,** Lewis bolt; **b. de suspension,** hanger pin; **b. mécanique,** machine bolt; **b. à chapeau,** cap bolt; **b. à ressort,** spring bolt; **b. d'accouplement,** tie bolt; **b. à tête ronde,** round-head bolt; **b. à tête carrée,** square-head bolt; **b. à tête creuse,** socket-head bolt; **b. à tête fraisée,** countersunk-head bolt; **b. à tête noyée,** flush bolt; **b. décolleté,** machine (-made) bolt; **b. de fixation,** securing, hold(ing)-down bolt; **b. taraudé,** threaded, tap-, bolt; *Rail:* **b. d'éclisse,** fish-bolt; **b. d'attelage,** coupling pin.

boulonnage [bulɔnaːʒ], *s.m. Mec.E:* bolting.

boulonnais, -aise [bulɔnɛ, -ɛz]. **1.** *a. & s.* (*a*) *Geog:* (native, inhabitant) of (i) Boulogne-sur-Mer; (ii) Boulogne-sur-Seine; (*b*) heavy draught-horse (of the Boulogne region). **2.** *Pr.n.m. Hist: Geog:* **le Boulonnais,** the Boulonnais.

boulonner [bulɔne]. **1.** *v.tr.* to bolt (down); to secure (door, etc.) with bolts. **2.** *v.i. P:* to work hard.

boulonnerie [bulɔnri], *s.f.* **1.** nut-and-bolt, (i) works, (ii) trade. **2.** *Coll:* nuts and bolts.

boulonnière [bulɔnjɛːr], *s.f.* bolt-hole borer.

boulot, -otte [bulo, -ɔt]. **1.** (*a*) *a. & s. F:* fat, dumpy, plump, chubby (person); **petit b. (d'enfant),** little dumpling; **gros b.,** fat podge (of a boy); (*b*) *a.inv. P:* hard-working. **2.** *s.m.* (*a*) *P:* work; **quel est son b.?** what's his job? (*b*) *A: P:* meal, food, grub; **un bon b.,** a square meal; (*c*) large crusty loaf; (*d*) *P:* workman.

boulottage [bulɔtaːʒ], *s.m. A: P:* food, grub, feeding.

boulotter [bulɔte], *P:* **1.** *v.i.* to jog along, scrape along; **comment ça va-t-il?—ça boulotte,** how are you?—I'm getting along nicely, I'm going strong. **2.** *v.tr.* to eat.

boum¹ [bum], *int.* **1.** bang! boom! **2.** *A:* (answer from café waiter) coming, sir!

boum², **1.** *s.m.* (*a*) *Com: Fin:* boom; *P:* **en plein b.,** in full spate; (*b*) **sa déclaration a fait un b.,** his statement caused a sensation. **2.** *s.f. F:* young people's party.

boumer [bume], *v.i. P:* **ça boume!** it's going fine! **ça boume?** how goes it?

boumerang [bumrɑ̃(ːg)], *s.m.* boomerang, throw-stick.

bouque [buk], *s.f. A: Nau:* (*a*) strait, sound; (*b*) channel, mouth.

bouquer [buke], *v.i.* **1.** *Ven:* **faire b. le renard,** to unearth the fox. **2.** *Nau: P:* to give it up (as a bad job); to cry off (an undertaking).

bouquet¹ [bukɛ], *s.m.* **1.** (*a*) bunch of flowers, nosegay, posy, bouquet; *Cu:* **b. garni,** (bunch of) mixed herbs, bouquet garni; (*b*) (*at fairs*) wisp of straw (fastened to animals for sale); **avoir, porter, le b. sur l'oreille,** to be for sale; *A: F:* **elle avait trois filles avec le b. sur l'oreille,** she had three daughters to marry off; (*c*) cluster, clump (of trees, of electric lamps); plume, tuft (of feathers); **b. de pierreries,** cluster, knot, of precious stones; (*d*) *Nau:* set of three blocks; **b. de basse voile,** tack, sheet and clew-garnet block of the lower course. **2.** *A:* (*a*) birthday present; (*b*) birthday ode. **3.** aroma (of wine, cigar); bouquet, nose (of wine). **4.** *Pyr:* crowning-, finishing-piece (of display of fireworks); wind-up; *F:* **réserver qch. pour le b.,** to keep sth. for the last, for the grand finale; **pour le b. . . .,** last, but not least . . .; **comme b. de la fête . . .,** as a climax to the entertainment . . .; *F:* **ça, c'est le b.!** that takes the biscuit! that's the last straw!

bouquet², *s.m. Med: Vet:* scab, tetter.
bouquet³, *s.m.* **1.** *Ven:* (*a*) hare; (*b*) buck-rabbit. **2.** *Crust:* prawn.
bouquetier, -ière [buktje, -jɛːr]. **1.** *s.* flower-seller, *esp.f.* flower-girl, -woman. **2.** *s.m.* flower vase.
bouquetin [buktɛ̃], *s.m. Z:* ibex; **b. de l'Himalaya,** Siberian ibex.
bouquin¹ [bukɛ̃], *s.m.* (*a*) old book, book of no value; (*b*) *F:* book.
bouquin², *s.m.* (*a*) old he-goat; (*b*) old hare; (*c*) *Ven:* buck-hare, -rabbit; (*d*) *A: F:* old rake, old buck, roué.
bouquin³, *s.m.* **1.** mouthpiece (of pipe, etc.). **2.** *Vet:* = BOUQUET².
bouquinage [bukinaːʒ], *s.m.* **1.** book-hunting. **2.** rut (of hares and rabbits).
bouquiner¹ [bukine], *v.i.* **1.** to hunt after, to collect, old books; to browse in bookshops. **2.** (*a*) to read, consult, pore over, old books; (*b*) *F:* to read (for pleasure).
bouquiner², *v.i.* (*of rabbit, hare*) to cover the doe.
bouquinerie [bukinri], *s.f.* second-hand (i) book-trade; (ii) book-shop.
bouquineur [bukinœːr], *s.m.* lover of old books; book-hunter.
bouquiniste [bukinist], *s.m.* second-hand book-seller; (*in Paris*) bouquiniste.
bourache [buraʃ], *s.f. A. & Dial:* (leather) wine-bottle.
bourbe [burb], *s.f.* mud (of pond, etc.); mire.
bourbeux, -euse [burbø, -øːz], *a.* **1.** muddy, miry. **2.** *Rept:* **(tortue) bourbeuse,** mud-turtle, -tortoise.
bourbier [burbje], *s.m.* slough, mire, mud-pit; *F:* **se tirer d'un b.,** to get out of a scrape, out of a mess; *s.a.* VICE 1.
bourbillon [burbijɔ̃], *s.m.* **1.** clot, lump, of mud. **2.** *Med: Vet:* core (of boil, abscess, ulcer).
Bourbon [burbɔ̃], *Pr.n.m. Fr.Hist:* Bourbon; **les Bourbons,** the Bourbon dynasty, the Bourbons; **nez à la B.,** Bourbon nose (large and aquiline).
bourbonnais, -aise [burbɔnɛ, -ɛːz]. **1.** *a. & s. Geog:* (native, inhabitant) of the Bourbonnais. **2.** *Pr.n.m.* **le Bourbonnais,** old province of France, with capital Moulins.
bourbonien, -ienne [burbɔnjɛ̃, -jɛn], *a.* Bourbon (party, etc.); **nez b.,** Bourbon nose.
bourbonniste [burbɔnist], *s.m. Hist:* Bourbonist.
bourbouil [burbuːj], *s.m.*, **bourbouille** [burbuːj], *s.f. F:* prickly heat.
bourboulien, -ienne [burbuljɛ̃, -jɛn], *a. & s. Geog:* (native, inhabitant) of La Bourboule.
bourcet [bursɛ], *s.m. Nau:* **(voile à) b.,** lug-sail.
bourcette [bursɛt], *s.f. F:* corn salad, lamb's-lettuce.
bourdaine [burdɛn], *s.f. Bot:* alder buckthorn, black alder; *Pharm:* **écorce de b.,** frangula.
bourdalou [burdalu], *s.m.* **1.** (*a*) hat-band; (*b*) leather edging (round the base of a shako). **2.** *A:* bed-pan.
bourdaloue [burdalu], *s.m. Surv:* bench-mark (on certain Paris houses, indicating height above sea-level).
bourde [burd], *s.f. F:* **1.** fib, falsehood; *F:* thumper; **débiter des bourdes,** to tell fibs; *O:* **faire avaler des bourdes à qn,** to take s.o. in; to stuff s.o. up with, get s.o. to swallow, tall stories. **2.** blunder, bloomer; (schoolboy's) howler; **faire une b.,** to put one's foot in it, to drop a brick. **3.** *Cu:* apple turnover.
bourdelot [burdlo], *s.m. Cu:* **petit b.,** apple dumpling.
bourdillon [burdijɔ̃], *s.m. Coop:* cask wood, stave-wood.
bourdon¹ [burdɔ], *s.m.* **1.** (*a*) bourdon, pilgrim's staff; *F:* **planter (son) b. dans un lieu,** to pitch one's tent, to settle down, in a place; (*b*) *A. Arms:* = BOURDONNASSE; (*c*) *Fish:* seine-staff, net-staff. **2.** *Bookb:* **reliure à bourdons,** studded binding. **3.** *Lacem:* **point de b.,** bourdon lace.
bourdon², *s.m.* **1.** *Mus:* (*a*) drone (of bagpipes, etc.); (*b*) drone bass; (*c*) bourdon stop (of organ); (*d*) *P:* **avoir le b.,** to have the blues. **2.** great bell, tenor (bell). **3.** *Ent:* (*a*) humble bee, bumble bee; (*b*) *F:* drone; (*c*) **b. des mousses,** carder bee. **4.** *P:* old horse.
bourdon³, *s.m. Typ:* omission, "out."
bourdonnant [burdɔnɑ̃], *a.* humming, buzzing (insects, etc.); booming (bell).
bourdonnasse [burdɔnas], *s.f. A.Arms:* bourdonasse (tilting lance).
bourdonné [burdɔne], *a.* **1.** crinkled (paper). **2.** *Her:* bourdonné.
bourdonnement [burdɔnmɑ̃], *s.m.* hum(ming), buzz(ing) (of insects); booming (of bell), low roar, murmur (of crowd); *Tp:* buzzing; *Med:* buzzing in the ears; head-noises.
bourdonner [burdɔne]. **1.** *v.i.* (*of insects*) to buzz, hum, boom; (*of crowd, etc.*) to murmur; *Tp:* to buzz. **2.** *v.tr.* to hum (tune, song); *F:* **b. qch. à qn,** to din sth. into s.o.'s ears. **3.** *v.tr.* to sound (bell).
bourdonnet [burdɔnɛ], *s.m. Surg:* pledget, dossil; (antiseptic) plug.
bourdonneur, -euse [burdɔnœːr, -øːz]. **1.** *a.* humming (insect, etc.). **2.** *s.m. Orn:* humming-bird. **3.** *s.f. Ap:* **bourdonneuse,** drone layer (of hive).
bourdonnière¹ [burdɔnjɛːr], *s.f. Ap:* drone-trap.
bourdonnière², *s.f. Tchn:* eye of gate hinge.
bourg [buːr], *s.m.* **1.** small market-town. **2.** *Eng. Hist:* borough; **b. pourri,** rotten borough.
bourgade [burgad], *s.f.* (*a*) straggling village; (*b*) important village.
bourgène [burʒɛn], *s.f. Bot:* = BOURDAINE.
bourgeois, -oise¹ [burʒwa, -waːz]. I. *s.* **1.** (*a*) *A:* burgess, burgher, citizen; (*b*) commoner; (*c*) civilian, townsman; **en b.,** in plain clothes; *F:* in mufti, in civies; *O:* **agent de police en b.,** plain-clothes detective. **2.** middle-class man, woman; *Pej:* bourgeois; capitalist; **un honnête b.,** a man of independent means; **les petits bourgeois,** the lower middle class; trades-people, small shopkeepers. **3.** *F:* (*in art circles*) philistine, bourgeois. **4.** *O: P:* (as used by workmen, etc.); (*a*) governor, boss, master, mistress; **et le pourboire, mon b.?** what about something for myself, governor? (*b*) **la bourgeoise,** the missis.
II. **bourgeois, -oise,** *a.* **1.** middle-class (family, etc.); **quartier b.,** residential area; **caution bourgeoise,** security given by a solid, solvent, man; *s.a.* COMÉDIE 1. **2.** homely, simple, plain (cooking, tastes, etc.); **pension bourgeoise,** private boarding-house; **chambre à louer dans (une) maison bourgeoise,** room to let in a private house; **journées bourgeoises,** needle-work, etc., done by a woman who goes out by the day. **3.** vulgar; bourgeois; philistine; *s.m.* **c'est du dernier b.!** it's horribly middle-class! **4.** *Adm:* **en tenue bourgeoise = en b.**
bourgeois, -oise², *a. & s. Geog:* (native, inhabitant) of Bourg-en-Bresse.
bourgeoisement [burʒwazmɑ̃], *adv.* **1.** in a homely, plain, way. **2.** in a bourgeois, middle-class, way; vulgarly. **3. vivre b.,** to live comfortably, to be comfortably off. **4.** *Adm:* **occuper b. un local,** to occupy premises for residential, for non-commercial, purposes.
bourgeoisie [burʒwazi], *s.f.* **1.** burgesses, citizens, freemen (of a city); **droit de b.,** freedom of a city. **2.** the middle class; the bourgeoisie; **la haute b.,** the upper middle class; **la petite b.,** the lower middle class, the small shopkeeper class; **de bonne b.,** of good social standing; *Iron:* genteel.
bourgeoisisme [burʒwazism], *s.m. O:* **1.** middle-class condition. **2.** manners, way of thinking, of the middle class.
bourgeon [burʒɔ̃], *s.m.* **1.** *Bot: Z:* bud; **petit b.,** budlet; **b. à fleur,** flower-bud; **couvert de bourgeons,** budded; **sans bourgeons,** budless. **2.** *O: F:* pimple (on the nose, etc.); grog-blossom. **3.** *Anat:* **b. gustatif,** gustatory, taste, bud; *Med:* **b. conjonctif,** granulation tissue, cicatricial tissue.
bourgeonné [burʒɔne], *a.* **1.** *Bot:* (*of plants*) in bud. **2.** *F:* **nez, visage b.,** pimply nose, face; grog-blossomed nose.
bourgeonnement [burʒɔnmɑ̃], *s.m.* **1.** *Bot:* (*a*) budding, sprouting; (*b*) budding-time. **2.** budding (of yeast, etc.). **3.** *F:* breaking out into pimples. **4.** *Med:* granulation.
bourgeonner [burʒɔne], *v.i.* **1.** *Bot:* to bud, shoot; to come out (in bud). **2.** *F:* (*of the nose, etc.*) to become pimply, to break out into pimples. **3.** *Med:* (*of wound*) to granulate.
bourgeron [burʒərɔ̃], *s.m. O:* (workman's) blouse, overall; *Mil:* fatigue coat; *Nau:* jumper.
bourgmestre [burgmɛstr], *s.m.* burgomaster.
Bourgogne [burgɔɲ]. **1.** *Pr.n.f. Hist: Geog:* (province of) Burgundy. **2.** *s.m.* also **vin de B.,** burgundy (wine).
bourgot [burgo], *s.m. Fr.C:* moose-caller.
bourguignon, -onne [burgiɲɔ̃, -ɔn], *a. & s.* **1.** Burgundian; *Cu:* **bœuf b.,** bœuf bourguignon (stewed in red wine). **2.** *s.m.pl. A:* **bourguignons,** *Nau:* brash (ice). **3.** *s.m. P:* sun.
bourguignotte [burgiɲɔt], *s.f.* **1.** *A.Arms:* burgonet (helmet). **2.** *Mil: F:* steel helmet; tin hat.
bouriate [burjat], *s.m. Ethn:* Buriat, Buryat.
bourlinguer [burlɛ̃ge], *v.* **1.** (*a*) *v.i. Nau:* (*of ship*) to labour, toil, strain (in a seaway); to make heavy weather; (*b*) *F:* to live a hard life, to rough it; (*c*) *F:* **il a bourlingué dans les mers de Chine,** he has sailed the China Seas; **b. de par le monde,** to knock about the world. **2.** *v.tr.* to ill-treat.
bourlingueur, -euse [burlɛ̃gœːr, -øːz], *s.* adventurer; **un vieux b.,** an old salt.
bourrache [buraʃ], *s.f. Bot:* borage; **petite b.,** Venus's navelwort.
bourrade [burad], *s.f.* **1.** *Ven: A:* (*of dog*) **donner une b. (à un lièvre),** to snap off some fur (from chased hare). **2.** (*a*) blow; thrust; rough word; **on ne reçoit de lui que des bourrades,** he is always biting our heads off; (*b*) kick (of gun, rifle); thump (in the back, etc.).
bourrage [buraːʒ], *s.m.* **1.** stuffing, padding (of chair, etc.); filling up (of holes in wall, etc.); tamping (of fire-arms, mines, etc.); packing, stuffing (of stuffing-box); cramming, packing tight (of stove with coal, etc.); *Sch:* cramming; *Min:* **b. (d'un trou de mine),** bulling; **boîte à b.,** stuffing-box; *Computers:* **b. (de cartes),** card jam, card wreck; *F:* **b. de crâne,** optimistic news fed to the public; eye-wash, bluff. **2.** (*material used*) stuffing, filling, packing.
bourras [burɑ], *s.m.* coarse grey cloth; frieze.
bourrasque [burask], *s.f.* **1.** squall, gust, of wind; (snow) flurry. **2.** gust, outbreak, attack, fit (of temper, fever, etc.)
bourratif [buratif], *a. F:* stodgy, filling.
bourre¹ [buːr], *s.f.* **1.** (*a*) flock (for stuffing or padding); waste, fluff (of cotton, etc.); linters; *Bot:* (i) bud (of vine); (ii) down, floss (of buds); *Tex: etc:* **b. de soie,** floss silk, silk waste; **b. de laine,** tag-wool, flock; (*b*) stuffing (of saddle, etc.). **2.** (*a*) plug, wad (of fire-arm); (*b*) tamping (of blast-hole). **3.** *Furs:* under-fur.
bourre², *s.m. P:* policeman.
bourré [bure], *a. P:* drunk; *P:* stoned, sloshed.
bourreau, -eaux [buro], *s.m.* **1.** executioner; hangman; *F:* **b. que vous êtes!** unfeeling, brute, inhuman wretch, that you are! **2.** tormentor, torturer, plague; **être le b. de qn,** to torment, torture, s.o.; **c'est un b. de travail,** he's a glutton for work; **b. des cœurs,** lady-killer; *s.a.* ARGENT 2. **3.** *Bot:* **b. des arbres,** climbing bitter-sweet; waxwork.
bourrée¹ [bure], *s.f.* faggot, bundle of sticks, of fire-wood; *Prov:* **fagot cherche b.,** like will to like.
bourrée², *s.f. Danc: Mus:* old French dance in $\frac{3}{4}$ time, *bourrée.*
bourrel [burɛl], *s.m. Orn:* buzzard.
bourrèlement [burɛlmɑ̃], *s.m.* anguish, (tormenting) pain; pangs (of remorse, etc.).
bourreler¹ [burle], *v.tr.* (**je bourrelle, n. bourrelons; je bourrellerai**) to torment, rack, torture (s.o. mentally); **bourrelé de remords,** tortured by remorse; conscience-stricken.
bourreler², *v.tr.* **b. une porte,** to fit draught-preventers, -tubes, -excluders, to a door.
bourrelet [burlɛ], *s.m.* **1.** (*a*) pad, wad, cushion; *Nau:* rubbing strake; puddening; *Nau:* **b. de défense,** fender; **b. de porteur,** porter's pad; **b. de porte,** draught-tube, -preventer, -excluder, weather-strip; (*b*) *Harn:* (horse-)collar. **2.** (*a*) *Bot:* excrescence (round tree trunk); *Med:* (dropsical) swelling; **b. de terrain,** fold in the ground; *F:* **b. de graisse,** roll, fold, of fat (round the neck, etc.); *F:* spare tyre (round the waist); (*b*) coronary cushion, coronary ring (of horse's foot). **3.** (*a*) rim, flange, shoulder (of pipe, wheel, railhead); fillet; **b. de cartouche,** cartridge rim; (*b*) bead (of tyre); **pneu à bourrelets,** beaded tyre.
bourrelier [burəlje], *s.m.* harness-maker, saddler.
bourrellerie [burɛlri], *s.f.* **1.** harness-maker's business, trade. **2.** harness-maker's shop.
bourre-pipe [burpip], *s.m.* pipe-stopper; *pl. bourre-pipes.*
bourrer [bure], *v.tr.* **1.** to stuff, pad (cushion, etc., with hair, etc.); to cram, pack tight (cupboard with linen, etc.); to fill (pipe with tobacco); *F:* **poches bien bourrées,** well-lined pockets; *F:* **b. un élève de latin,** to cram, stuff, a pupil with Latin; *F:* **il est bourré de complexes,** he's one mass of complexes; *F:* **b. le crâne;** *V:* **le mou, à qn,** to stuff s.o. with false stories; *F:* to stuff s.o. up; **se b. de gâteaux,** to stodge oneself with cakes; **aliment qui bourre,** stodgy food; **bourré à craquer,** full to busting. **2.** (*a*) *Mil: Min:* to ram (charge) home; to stem, tamp (blast-hole, mine); (*b*) *Mch:* to pack (piston, stuffing-box); **b. de graisse,** to pack with grease; (*c*) *v.i.* (*of plane*) to choke (with shavings). **3.** (*a*) *Mil:* to strike (opponent) with the butt of the rifle; (*b*) *F:* **b. qn (de coups),** to pummel, trounce, s.o.; to give s.o. a pummelling, a drubbing, a trouncing; *Box:* **il le bourrait de coups du gauche,** he was plugging

at him with his left; (*c*) *F: A:* to abuse, rate, insult (s.o.); **comme ils se sont bourrés!** how they slanged one another! **4.** (*a*) *Equit:* (*of horse*) to bore; *v.i.* **b. sur l'obstacle,** to bolt at a jump; (*b*) *F:* to jib (**sur,** at). **5.** *Ven:* (*of dog*) to snap at (hare); to bite off some fur.

bourrette [burɛt], *s.f. Tex:* (*a*) floss (silk); (*b*) bourette.

bourreur [burœːr], *s.m.* **1.** stuffer, padder; *F:* **b. de crâne,** one who crams, stuffs, people up with false stories (of victory); dispenser of eye-wash. **2.** *Min:* tamper.

bourriche [buriʃ], *s.f.* **1.** basket, hamper, pad, bass (for conveying oysters, game, etc.). **2.** basketful, hamperful.

bourrichon [buriʃɔ̃], *s.m. P:* head; *used only in* **se monter le b.,** to get excited, to work oneself up into a state.

bourricot [buriko], *s.m. Dial:* (small) donkey, burro.

bourride [burid], *s.f. Cu:* provençal fish-soup.

bourrin [burɛ̃], *s.m. P:* (*a*) horse, nag; (*b*) old screw (of a horse).

bourrique [burik], *s.f.* **1.** (*a*) she-ass; (*b*) *F:* dunce, duffer, ignoramus; **faire tourner qn en b.,** to drive s.o. crazy. **2.** *P:* sorry horse, screw. **3.** *P:* police-spy; *P:* copper's nark; *P:* **soûl comme une b.,** dead-drunk.

bourriquet [burikɛ], *s.m.* **1.** ass's colt. **2.** windlass, winch.

bourriquier [burikje], *s.m. F:* donkey-driver.

bourriquot [buriko], *s.m.* = BOURRICOT.

bourroir [burwaːr], *s.m. Min:* tamping-bar, tamper.

bourron [burɔ̃], *s.m.* tag-wool.

bourru [bury], *a.* **1.** rough, rude, surly, churlish (person, etc.); shaggy (material, fabric); rough (thread); *s.* **un bourru,** a churlish lout; a bear, a curmudgeon; **b. bienfaisant,** rough diamond. **2.** *Const:* **pierre bourrue,** ragstone, roughstone. **3.** **vin b.,** (i) (new) unfermented wine; (ii) wine clouded by a large quantity of lees; *Dial:* **lait b.,** milk fresh from the cow.

bourse [burs], *s.f.* **1.** (*a*) purse, bag, pouch; *Ecc:* **b. de quête,** offertory bag; **b. des corporaux,** burse; **b. ronde, bien garnie,** well-lined purse, long purse; **la b. ou la vie!** your money or your life! **tenir les cordons de la b.,** to hold the purse-strings, to look after the cash; **sans b. délier,** without spending a penny, without any expense; **des prix à la portée de votre b.,** prices to suit your pocket; *F:* **ami jusqu'à la b.,** fair-weather friend; **faire b. à part,** to keep separate accounts; **faire b. commune,** to share expenses, to pool resources; **payer qch de sa b.,** to pay for sth. out of one's own pocket; **faire une b.,** to make up a purse (for a presentation); *F:* **loger le diable dans sa b.,** to have an empty purse; *Prov:* **selon ta b. gouverne ta bouche,** cut your coat according to your cloth; (*b*) *Ven:* rabbit-net, bag-net; (*c*) *Anat:* bursa; **bourses synoviales,** synovial bursae; **bourses testiculaires,** scrotum; (*d*) *Z:* pouch (of marsupial) (*e*) *Fung:* volva. **2.** *Sch:* **b. d'études,** exhibition, scholarship; *Scot:* bursary; **b. de voyage,** travelling scholarship; **b. d'entretien,** maintenance grant. **3.** stock exchange, money market; **à la B., en B.,** on 'Change; **jouer à la B.,** to speculate; **coup de B.,** deal on the Stock Exchange, speculation; **b. de commerce,** commodities exchange; **b. du travail** = (*in large cities*) Labour Exchange.

bourse-à-berger [bursabɛrʒe], *s.f.,* **bourse-à-pasteur** [bursapastœːr], *s.f. Bot: F:* shepherd's-purse; *pl. bourses-à-berger, bourses-à-pasteur.*

bourset [bursɛ], *s.m. Nau:* (**voile à**) **b.,** lug-sail.

boursette [bursɛt], *s.f. F:* corn salad, lamb's-lettuce.

boursicaut, boursicot [bursiko], *s.m. F:* **1.** *A:* purse. **2.** small hoard (of money); savings, nest-egg.

boursicotage [bursikɔtaːʒ], *s.m.* (Stock Exchange) dabbling.

boursicoter [bursikɔte], *v.i.* **1.** to save little by little. **2.** to speculate in a small way, to dabble on the Stock Exchange.

boursicoteur, -euse [bursikɔtœːr, -øːz], *s.,* **boursicotier, -ière** [bursikɔtje, -jɛːr], *s.* speculator in a small way.

boursier, -ière [bursje, -jɛːr]. **1.** *a.* (*a*) (scholar) holding a bursary; (*b*) **opérations boursières,** Stock Exchange transactions. **2.** *s.* (*a*) holder of a bursary, scholarship; exhibitioner; (*b*) (i) *F:* stock-broker; (ii) speculator, gambler (on the Stock Exchange); (*c*) pursemaker.

boursiller [bursije], *v.i. A: F:* **1.** to club together; to pool expenses. **2.** to keep on paying out (small sums).

boursouflage [bursuflaːʒ], *s.m.* (*a*) swelling; (*b*) bombast.

boursouflé [bursufle], *a.* swollen; bloated; **style b.,** inflated, turgid, flatulent, style.

boursouflement [bursufləmɑ̃], *s.m.* swelling, puffing-up (of flesh, etc.); blistering (of paint); *Min:* heaving (of floor).

boursoufler [bursufle], *v.tr.* to puff up, swell (flesh, etc.); to bloat (the face, etc.); to blister (paint).

se boursoufler, to rise, swell; to increase in volume; (*of paint*) to blister; *Min:* (*of floor*) to heave.

boursouflure [bursuflyːr], *s.f.* **1.** swelling, puffiness (of face, etc.); turgidity, inflation, flatulence (of style). **2.** blister (on paint).

bousage [buzaːʒ], *s.m. Dy:* dunging (of cloth).

bousard [buzaːr], *s.m. Ven:* deer's dropping.

bouscaille [buskɑːj], *s.f. A: P:* mud.

bouscailleur [buskɑjœːr], *s.m. A: P:* crossing-sweeper.

bouscarle [buskarl], *s.f. Orn:* **b. de Cetti,** Cetti's warbler.

bouscatier [buskatje], *s.m. Dial:* woodman.

bousculade [buskylad], *s.f.* scrimmage; scuffle, hustle; **recevoir une b.,** to be jostled, hustled about; **une b. vers la porte,** a rush for, a general scurry towards, the door; **l'heure de la b.,** the rush-hour; **vol à la b.,** method of stealing used by pickpockets who purposely bump into their victims.

bousculement [buskylmɑ̃], *s.m.* **1.** knocking over, knocking about (of articles). **2.** jostling, shouldering.

bousculer [buskyle], *v.tr.* **1.** **b. des objets,** to knock things over, upset things, turn everything upside down; **b. les traditions,** to upset established rules. **2.** **b. qn,** to jostle, hustle, s.o.; *F:* to barge into s.o.; to knock s.o. about; **b. l'ennemi,** to hustle the enemy out of their positions. **3.** **b. qn,** to rush s.o.; **il est toujours bousculé,** he is always in a rush.

bouse [buːz], *s.f.* **b. (de vache),** cow-dung; *Dy:* **bain de b.,** dung-bath; **gâteau de b.,** cow-pat(ch).

bouser [buze]. **1.** *v.tr.* (*a*) to floor (farm-building) with earth and dung; (*b*) *Dy:* to dung (cloth). **2.** *v.i.* (*of animal*) to dung.

bousier [buzje], *s.m. Ent: F:* dung-beetle, dor (-beetle).

bousillage [buzijaːʒ], *s.m.* **1.** *Const:* (*a*) mud-walling; (*b*) = TORCHIS. **2.** *F:* bungled, scamped, botched, piece of work; bungle.

bousiller [buzije], *v.tr.* **1.** = TORCHER[1] 3. **2.** *F:* **b. un ouvrage,** to bungle, botch, scamp, a piece of work; **travail bousillé,** botch; *Av: P:* **b. son appareil,** to crash one's plane; **b. une voiture,** to wreck, smash, a car; **b. qn,** to bump s.o. off; *Mil: P:* **se faire bousiller,** to get killed, *P:* done in.

bousilleur, -euse [buzijœːr, -øːz], *s.* **1.** *Const:* mud-wall builder. **2.** *F:* botcher, bungler.

bousin[1] [buzɛ̃], *s.m. A: P:* **1.** low drinking house, pot-house; brothel. **2.** uproar, great noise, rumpus.

bousin[2], *s.m.* **1.** low-grade peat. **2.** dirt, earth (clinging to quarried stone).

bousiner [buzine], *v.i. A: P:* to make a row, kick up a shindy; to run round the brothels.

bousineur [buzinœːr], *s.m. A: P:* rowdy, roisterer.

bousingot [buzɛ̃go], *s.m. A:* **1.** sailor's glazed hat. **2.** demagogue, agitator.

boussole [busɔl], *s.f.* **1.** compass; **b. marine,** mariner's compass; **b. de poche,** pocket compass; **b. d'inclinaison,** inclination, dipping, compass; inclinometer; **b. de déclinaison,** declination compass; declinometer; **b. directrice,** marching compass; **b. d'arpenteur, topographique,** surveyor's compass; **b. à pinnules,** sight-compass; **b. à prisme,** prismatic compass; **b. affolée,** erroneous, defective, compass; **marcher à la b.,** to march on a compass bearing; **vos conseils me serviront de b.,** I shall be guided by your advice; *F:* **perdre la boussole,** (i) to be all at sea; (ii) to go dotty; to lose one's head; *s.a.* EMBARQUER 2. **2.** *El:* **b. des sinus, des tangentes,** sine-, tangent-galvanometer.

boustifaille [bustifɑːj], *s.f. P:* **1.** *A:* blow-out, tuck-in. **2.** food, grub.

boustifailler [bustifɑje], *v.i. P:* to eat and drink greedily and often; to eat and swill; to stuff oneself.

boustrophédon [bustrɔfedɔ̃], *s.m. Pal:* **inscriptions en boustrophédon,** boustrophedon inscriptions.

bout [bu], *s.m.* **1.** (*a*) extremity, end; **le gros b.,** the butt end (of billiard cue, etc.); **voir les choses par le gros b., par le petit b., de la lorgnette,** to minimize, magnify, events; **le haut b. de la table,** the head, top (end), of the table; **tenir le haut b.,** to have the upper hand, the whip-hand; **le bas b. de la table,** the foot, bottom, of the table; **b. d'un navire,** bows, stem, head, of a ship; *Nau:* **avoir le vent de b.,** to have a head wind; **b. au vent,** head to wind; *Nau:* **aborder un navire de b. en plein,** to ram a ship broadside on, to run square into a ship; *Carp:* **cheville à b. perdu,** pin not passing through, short pin; **joint b. à b.,** butt(-and-butt) joint; **assembler deux planches b. à b.,** to join two planks end to end, end on; to butt-joint two planks; *s.a.* BOIS 3; *Const:* **assise de b.,** brick-on-end course; *Mec.E:* **jeu en b.,** end play; **je n'en vois pas le b.,** I am nowhere near the end of it; *F:* **joindre les deux bouts,** to make (both) ends meet; **manger son bien par les deux bouts,** to go through one's fortune; **de b. en b.,** from beginning to end, from end to end; *Nau:* from stem to stern; **je connais Paris de b. en b.,** I know Paris through and through, inside out; **d'un b. à l'autre,** from end to end, from beginning to end; **lire un livre d'un b. à l'autre,** to read a book through from cover to cover; **d'un b. à l'autre du pays,** from one end of the country to the other; **d'un b. de la semaine, de l'année, à l'autre,** week in week out, year in year out; **au b. du compte,** after all; *F:* **au b. le b.,** we'll see the end when it comes; **tout au b.,** at the very end; **au b. de la rue,** at the end, bottom, top, of the street; **au b. d'une heure, de quelques jours,** at the end of, after, an hour, a few days; when an hour, a few days, had passed; **au b. d'une seconde,** a second later; the next second; **vous n'êtes pas encore au b. avec moi,** you haven't done with me yet; **nous ne sommes pas encore au b.,** we are not yet out of the wood; **jusqu'au b.,** to the very end; **écouter, entendre, qn jusqu'au b.,** to hear s.o. through, to hear s.o. out; **aller jusqu'au b.,** (i) to go the whole way; (ii) to go on to the bitter end, to fight (it out) to the finish, to see a thing through; to go the whole hog; **j'irai jusqu'au b.,** I mean to go through with it; **je désire assister à la scène jusqu'au b.,** I want to see it through; **se battre jusqu'au b.,** to fight to the bitter end; **lire la lettre jusqu'au b.,** to read the letter right through; **aller jusqu'au b. d'une affaire,** to carry a deal through, to go through with a deal; **aller jusqu'au b. de ses idées,** to follow one's ideas to their logical conclusion; **accompagner qn jusqu'au b. de la route,** to accompany s.o. to the end, turn, of the road; **disparaître au b. de l'horizon,** to disappear over the horizon; **aller au b. du monde,** to go to the ends of the earth; *F:* **c'est le b. du monde,** (i) (*of town, village*) it's a God-forsaken hole, it's a dump; (ii) it's as much as I, he, she, can do; *F:* **s'il a cinq mille francs, c'est le b. du monde,** (i) he gets five thousand francs at the outside; (ii) he's lucky if he has five thousand francs to his name; **parcourir les deux bouts de la terre,** to travel the four corners of the earth; **être à b.,** to be exhausted; to give out; **pousser, mettre, qn à b.,** to aggravate s.o. to a degree, to drive s.o. to extremities; **pousser à b. la patience de qn,** to exhaust s.o.'s patience, to try s.o.'s patience to breaking-point; **poussé à b., le peuple se souleva,** the people rose in desperation; **à b. de patience,** at the end of one's patience, one's tether; **vieillard à b. de forces,** old man at the end of his tether; **être au b. de son rouleau, de ses écus, à b. de course,** to be at the end of one's resources; **à b. de ressources,** with no courage, no money, left; **nous sommes à b. d'essence,** we have run out of petrol; **venir à b. de la résistance de qn,** to break down s.o.'s resistance; **venir à b. d'une épidémie,** to stamp out an epidemic; **sa fermeté vint à b. de toute opposition,** his firmness bore down all opposition; **ils n'en viendront jamais à b.,** they will never manage it; **venir à b. de qch., de faire qch.,** to succeed in doing sth., to contrive, manage, to do sth.; **venir péniblement à b. d'une masse de chiffres,** to wade through a mass of figures; (*b*) *Ecc:* (**messe, service, du**) **b. de l'an, b. d'an,** year's mind; mass, memorial service (held on the anniversary of s.o.'s death); (*c*) **b. de table,** (table) candelabra. **2.** end, tip, end-piece; **b. du doigt, du nez, de la langue,** tip of one's finger, nose, tongue; **avoir un mot sur le b. de la langue, de la plume,** to have a word on, at, the tip of one's tongue; *F:* **ne pas remuer le b. du petit doigt,** (i) to be motionless; (ii) not to lift a finger; **b. de sein,** nipple, teat; *Bootm:* **b. de pied, b. rapporté,** toe-cap; **souliers à bouts carrés,** square-toed shoes; *Furn:* **b. de pied,** foot-rest; **b. de pipe,** mouthpiece of a pipe; **b. de l'archet (d'un violon),** point of the bow; **b. ferré, b. de canne,** ferrule (of walking-stick); **b. d'un**

fusil, muzzle of a gun; **à b. portant,** point-blank; *Mil:* with open sights; *Fb:* **marquer un but à b. portant,** to score from the goal-mouth; *Rail.E:* **b. de rail,** rail-head; *El:* **b. mort,** dead-end (of coil); *Mec.E: etc:* **b. d'arbre,** tail shaft; **b. mâle,** spigot; *Nau:* **(bon) b.,** hauling end (of rope); *F:* **tenir le bon b.,** to have the best of it, to be on the right tack, to have the right end of the stick; *F:* **prendre qn, qch., par le bon b.,** to tackle s.o., sth., the right way; *F:* **on ne sait jamais par quel b. le prendre,** one never knows how to approach, tackle, him; *P:* **mettre les bouts (de bois),** to run away; *P:* to do a bunk, to scarper. **3.** bit, fragment, scrap; **b. de papier,** scrap of paper; **b. de fil,** bit of cotton; **b. de ficelle,** piece of string; **b. de pain,** hunk, bit, scrap, of bread; **b. de chandelle,** candle-end; **b. de cigarette,** cigarette butt, end; **b. de cigare,** stub, butt, of a cigar; **nous avons un b. de jardin,** we have a bit of a garden, a scrap of garden; **faire un b. de lecture,** to do a bit of reading; **écrivez-moi un b. de lettre,** write me a note, a line or two; **garder tous les petits bouts,** to save up all the odds and ends; *F:* **un petit b. d'homme,** (i) a short little man, a little wisp of a man; (ii) a slip, bit, of a boy; *F:* **un tout petit b. de femme,** a tiny little woman; *F:* **un (gentil) petit b. de chou,** a little darling; **un petit b. de temps,** a little while; **un bon b. de temps,** quite a while; **nous avons fait un b. de chemin ensemble,** we went a short way, part of the way, together; **nous avons fait un bon b. de chemin,** we have come, we went, a good way; **c'est un bon b. de chemin,** it's a good step; *Cin: T.V:* **b. d'essai,** screen test.

boutade [butad], *s.f.* **1.** whim, caprice; **travailler par boutades,** to work by fits and starts. **2.** sudden outburst (of ill-temper); tirade. **3.** sally, flash of wit.

boutargue [butarg], *s.f. Cu:* botargo.

boutasse [butas], *s.f. Dial:* small pond.

bout-dehors [budəɔːr], *s.m. Nau:* boom; **b.-d. de foc,** jib-boom; **b.-d. de tapecul,** boomkin, bumkin; *pl. bouts-dehors.*

boutée [bute], *s.f. Arch: Civ.E:* abutment (of bridge, etc.).

boute-en-train [butɑ̃trɛ̃], *s.m.inv. in pl.* **1.** *Breed:* teaser. **2.** *F:* exhilarating companion; **le b.-en-t. d'une société,** the life and soul of the party; **c'est un b.-en-t.,** he is full of fun.

boutefeu, -eux [butfø], *s.m.* **1.** *(a) Artil: A:* linstock; *(b) Min: etc:* portfire, igniter. **2.** *(a) Min:* shot-firer, blaster; *(b) F:* (social) fire-brand.

bouteille [butɛj], *s.f.* **1.** *(a)* bottle; **nous allons boire une b.,** we'll have a bottle (of wine) together; **b. d'eau,** bottle(ful) of water; **b. carrée,** case-bottle; **b. isolante,** vacuum flask; **mettre du vin en bouteilles,** to bottle wine; **mise en bouteilles,** bottling; **vin qui a plusieurs années de b.,** wine that has been in bottle for several years; *F:* **aimer, caresser, la b.,** to be fond of the bottle; *F:* **plaisanterie qui a de la b.,** vintage joke, fine old crusted joke; *F:* **prendre, avoir, de la b.,** to be, get, long in the tooth; **c'est du Proust de la bonne b.,** it's vintage Proust; **tenir qn loin de la tentation de la b.,** to keep s.o. from the bottle; *A:* **elle n'a rien vu que par le trou d'une b.,** she knows nothing of the world; *A:* **être dans la b.,** to be in the secret; *s.a.* ENCRE; *(b) El:* **b. de Leyde,** Leyden jar, electric jar; *Ind:* **b. à gaz,** gas cylinder; *Mch:* **b. de purge,** steam-trap; *Gym:* **bouteilles en bois,** Indian clubs. **2.** *Bot:* bottle-gourd. **3.** *Nau:* *(a) A:* quarter-gallery, round-house; **fausse b.,** quarter-badge; *(b) pl.* (officers') water-closets; *F:* the heads. **4.** *Vet:* core (of sheep-rot).

bouteiller [butɛje], *s.m. A:* (king's) butler, cup-bearer.

bouteillerie [butɛjri], *s.f.* **1.** *(a)* bottle-works; *(b)* bottle-trade, -making. **2.** *A:* office of cupbearer, butlership (to a king).

bouteillon [butɛjɔ̃], *s.m. Mil:* dixie.

bouteloue [butlu], *s.m. Bot:* **1.** gram(m)a (-grass). **2.** mesquite-grass.

bouter [bute]. **1.** *v.tr. A. & Dial:* *(a)* to put; *(b)* **b. l'ennemi hors de France,** to drive the enemy out of France. **2.** *v.i. (of wine)* to turn ropy. **3.** *v.tr. Leath:* to pare (skin).

bouterolle [butrɔl], *s.f.* **1.** *Sm.a:* chape (of scabbard). **2.** ward, snap (of lock); ward (in key). **3.** *Tls:* rivet-set, rivet-snap, riveting-die, cup-set. **4.** shrimping-net.

bouteroller [butrɔle], *v.tr. Metalw:* to snap (rivet); to rivet over (the head of a rivet); **rivet bouterollé,** snap-head rivet; *s.a.* RIVURE 2.

bouteroue [butru], *s.f.* guard-stone, -pile, -post; fender; spur-stone (at corners of buildings, etc.); guard-rail (on roadway of bridge).

boute-selle [butsɛl], *s.m.inv. in pl. Mil: A:* boot-and-saddle (trumpet call).

boutillier [butije], *s.m.* = BOUTEILLER.

boutiquaillerie [butikajri], *s.f.* petty shopkeepers.

boutique [butik], *s.f.* **1.** *(a)* shop, *U.S:* store; boutique; **tenir b., avoir b.,** to keep, run, a shop; **se mettre en b.,** to set up shop; **fermer b.,** (i) to shut up shop, to close down; (ii) to give up one's shop; *F:* **parler b.,** to talk shop; **prendre garde à la b.,** to mind one's own concerns; **cela vient de sa b.,** that's (some of) his doing; *F:* **j'en ai assez de cette sale b.!** I am sick of the whole beastly place, of the whole show! *F:* **toute la b.,** the whole caboodle, the whole works; *A:* **b. à treize sous,** sixpenny-ha'penny bazaar or stores; *(b)* **boutique (en plein vent),** (market) stall. **2. b. d'artisan,** artisan's set of tools, of implements; workshop. **3.** *Fish:* *(a)* cage (for keeping live fish in stream, etc.); *(b)* tank (on boat, for keeping fish alive).

boutiquier, -ière [butikje, -jɛːr], *s.* shopkeeper, tradesman, tradeswoman; **un petit b.,** a small man; *a.* **nation boutiquière,** nation of shopkeepers.

boutisse [butis], *s.f. Const:* header, bonder, bond-stone; **assise de boutisses,** heading(-course); *s.a.* APPAREIL 4.

boutoir [butwaːr], *s.m.* **1.** *Ven:* groin, snout (of a boar); *F:* **coup de b.,** (i) rough, cutting, aggressive, remark; thrust (at s.o.); (ii) staggering blow. **2.** *(a) Farr:* paring-iron, butteris; *(b) Leath:* (currier's) paring-knife.

bouton [butɔ̃], *s.m.* **1.** bud; **b. de rose,** rose-bud; **en b.,** budding, in bud; *Com:* **champignon en b.,** button mushroom. **2.** button; **b. boule,** ball-button; **b. à freluche,** tufted button; **b. d'étoffe,** cloth button, self-button; **b. à queue,** shank button; **b. sans queue,** shankless button; **b. de plastron de chemise,** stud; **b. de col,** collar-stud; **boutons de manchette (jumelés),** sleeve-links, cuff-links; **b. (à) pression,** press-stud; *F:* popper; **b. (à) pression femelle,** snap-fastener socket; **b. (à) pression mâle,** snap-fastener stud; **b. mécanique, automatique, mobile,** bachelor's button; *F:* **ne tenir qu'à un b.,** to hang by a thread. **3.** *(a)* knob, handle (of door, lock, etc.); button (of foil); peg (of harp-string, etc.); button, tail-pin (of violin, etc.); nipple (of breast); *A: Nau:* mouse (in rope); *Ch:* button (in crucible); *W.Tel:* knob (of dial); **b. de mise en marche,** motor switch (of record-player); **b. électrique,** switch; **b. poussoir,** push button; *W.Tel:* **b. d'accord,** tuning knob; **b. de puissance,** volume control; *T.V:* **b. de cadrage,** centring knob; *El:* **b. d'appel,** bell push-button; *Sm.a:* **b. de mire,** fore-sight; *(b)* thumb-piece; lug; head; **b. quadrillé,** roughened thumb-piece; **b. moleté,** milled head; knurled knob; **b. à index, à flèche,** pointer-knob; **b. de commande,** control knob; **b. de réglage,** (i) *Mec:* control knob; (ii) *W.Tel:* setting, tuning knob; (iii) *Opt:* focusing knob; **tourner le b.,** to switch (the wireless, etc.) on, off; *(c) Mec.E:* **b. de manivelle, de bielle,** crank-pin, wrist-pin; *(d)* **b. de sonnerie, de sonnette, d'appel,** push button, bell-push, call-button; **"appuyez sur le b.,"** "press the button"; **b. de signalisation,** signal knob; **b. d'arrêt,** stop-button; **b. de blocage,** clamping knob, wedge knob; **b. de déblocage,** releasing knob. **4.** *Harn:* **b. mobile, coulant,** running, sliding, button or loop; **mettre un cheval sous le b.,** to rein a horse in tightly; *O: F:* **serrer le b. à qn,** to keep a tight hand over s.o. **5.** pimple, pustule (on face, etc.); pock (of smallpox); bleb; **couvert de boutons,** pimpled, pimply; *Med:* **b. d'Alep, b. d'Orient,** endemic ulcer; *F:* Aleppo ulcer, boil, or gall; Biskra button; Delhi sore. **6.** *Bot:* **b. d'argent,** (i) sneezewort; (ii) button mushroom; **b. d'or,** buttercup, bachelor's button; *F:* **b. de pompier,** bur (of burdock).

boutonnage [butɔnaːʒ], *s.m.* buttoning.

boutonnant [butɔnɑ̃], *a. (of frock, etc.)* that buttons up.

boutonné [butɔne], *a.* **1.** = BOURGEONNÉ. **2.** *F:* close, reticent (person). **3.** *Her:* botoné, botonée, botony, bottony. **4.** *Tex:* **laine boutonnée,** knop wool.

boutonnement [butɔnmɑ̃], *s.m.* = BOURGEONNEMENT.

boutonner [butɔne]. **1.** *v.i.* *(a) Bot:* to bud; *(b) (of nose, etc.)* to come out in pimples; *(c)* **(se) b. par derrière,** to button up at the back. **2.** *v.tr.* *(a)* to button (up) (coat, dress, etc.); *(b) Fenc:* (i) to put a button on (sword); (ii) to touch (opponent).

se boutonner, to fasten (up) one's buttons.

boutonnerie [butɔnri], *s.f.* **1.** button manufacture, button trade. **2.** button factory.

boutonneux, -euse [butɔnø, -øːz], *a.* **1.** pustulous, pimply (eruption, etc.). **2.** uneven (paper, cloth, etc.).

boutonnier, -ière[1] [butɔnje, -jɛːr], *s.* *(a)* button manufacturer, button maker; *(b)* button-dealer.

boutonnière[2] [butɔnjɛːr], *s.f.* **1.** *(a)* buttonhole; **porter une fleur à la b.,** to wear a buttonhole; **attraper qn par la b.,** to buttonhole s.o.; *s.a.* FLEURI 1, FLEURIR 2; *(b)* (flower worn in one's) buttonhole; *(c)* stud-hole. **2.** *Surg:* incision; buttonhole; *F:* **faire une b. à qn,** to pink s.o. (with rapier). **3.** rosette (of Legion of Honour, etc.). **4.** *Geol: Geog:* weald.

bouton-poussoir [butɔ̃puswaːr], *s.m. W.Tel: etc:* push-button; *pl. boutons-poussoirs.*

bouton-pression [butɔ̃prɛsjɔ̃], *s.m.* snap-fastener, press-stud; *F:* popper; *pl. boutons-pression.*

boutre [butr̥], *s.m. N.Arch:* d(h)ow.

bout-saigneux [busɛɲø], *s.m. Cu:* scrag(-end) of the neck *(of mutton, veal)*; *pl. bouts-saigneux.*

bouts-rimés [burime], *s.m.pl.* (composing verses to) set rhymes.

bouturage [butyraːʒ], *s.m.* propagation (of plants) by cuttings; piping (of carnations).

bouture [butyːr], *s.f. Hort:* **1.** slip, cutting; **b. d'œillet,** piping. **2.** stem sucker.

bouturer [butyre]. **1.** *v.i. (of plants)* to shoot suckers. **2.** *v.tr.* to propagate (plants) by cuttings; to pipe (carnations).

bouvard, bouvart [buvɑːr], *s.m.,* **bouveau, -eaux** [buvo], *s.m.,* **bouvelet** [buvlɛ], *s.m.* steer, young bullock.

bouvement [buvmɑ̃], *s.m. Tls:* ogee plane.

bouveret [buvrɛ], *s.m. Orn: F:* bullfinch.

bouverie [buvri], *s.f.* byre, cowshed.

bouvet [buvɛ], *s.m. Tls:* **b. à joindre,** match-plane; **b. femelle, à rainure,** grooving-plane; **b. mâle, à languette,** tonguing-plane; **b. à approfondir,** plough(-plane).

bouvetage [buvtaːʒ], *s.m. Join:* tonguing (and grooving).

bouveter [buvte], *v.tr.* **(je bouvette, n. bouvetons; je bouvetterai)** *Join:* **1.** to groove and tongue (boards); to join (boards) by groove and tongue, to match (boards). **2.** to plough; *s.a.* PLANCHE 1.

bouvier, -ière [buvje, -jɛːr], *s.* **1.** *(a)* cowherd, cow-girl; cowman, herdsman; *(b)* drover, cattleman; *(c) F:* boor. **2.** *Husb:* **b. des Flandres,** bouvier des Flandres (sheep-dog). **3.** *Astr:* **le B.,** Boötes; the Waggoner. **4.** *s.f. Ich:* **bouvière,** bitterling.

bouvillon [buvijɔ̃], *s.m.* = BOUVARD.

bouvret [buvrɛ], *s.m. Orn: F:* bullfinch.

bouvreuil [buvrœːj], *s.m. Orn:* **b. (pivoine),** bullfinch; **b. ponceau,** Northern bullfinch; **b. githagine,** trumpeter bullfinch.

bouvril [buvril], *s.m. (in a slaughterhouse)* lair.

bouzin [buzɛ̃], *s.m.* dirt, earth (clinging to quarried stone).

bovaryser [bɔvarize], *v.tr.* to live in a romantic dream, divorced from reality; (from Madame Bovary, the heroine of Flaubert's famous novel).

bovette [bɔvɛt], *s.f. Min:* (cross-)cut.

bovidés [bɔvide], *s.m.pl. Z:* Bovidae.

bovin, -ine [bɔvɛ̃, -in]. **1.** *a.* bovine; **bêtes bovines,** horned cattle. **2.** *s.m.pl. Z:* **bovins,** bovines.

bovinés [bɔvine], *s.m.pl. Z:* bovines.

bowden [bodɛn], *s.m. Mec.E:* Bowden wire.

bowette [bɔvɛt], *s.f. Min:* (cross-)cut.

bowling [boliŋ], *s.m.* **1.** bowling; (American) tenpin bowling. **2.** bowling alley.

bowstring [bostriŋ], *s.m. Civ.E:* bowstring beam, bowstring girder.

bow-window [bowindo], *s.m.* bow-window; *pl. bow-windows.*

box[1] [bɔks], *s.m.* **1.** horse-box, loose box (in stable). **2.** *(a)* cubicle (in dormitory, etc.); *(b) Jur:* **être dans le b. des accusés,** to be in the dock. **3.** *Aut:* lock-up (garage); *pl. boxes.*

box[2], *s.m. F:* box-calf.

box-calf [bɔkskalf], *s.m.* box-calf.

boxe [bɔks], *s.f.* boxing; **b. française,** foot boxing, French boxing.

boxer[1] [bɔkse], *v.i. & tr.* to box, spar; **b. qn,** to box, spar, with s.o.

boxer[2] [bɔksɛːr], *s.m. (dog)* boxer.

boxeur [bɔksœːr], *s.m.* boxer, prize-fighter.

boxon [bɔksɔ̃], *s.m. P:* = BORDEL.

boy [bɔj], *s.m.* **1.** groom. **2.** *(in the former colonies)* boy, native servant.

boyard [bɔjaːr], *s.m.* boyar.

boyau, -aux [bwajo], *s.m.* **1.** *(a) F:* bowel, gut; *F:* **les petits boyaux,** the small intestine; *P:* **aimer qn comme ses petits b.,** to love s.o. dearly, tenderly; **descente de b.,** hernia; **corde à, de, b.,**

(cat)gut; (*b*) (sausage) casing. **2.** (*a*) hose(-pipe); (*b*) *Cy:* tubular tyre. **3.** narrow thoroughfare, alley(way); *Mil:* communication trench; **b. d'approche,** approach trench; **b. d'évacuation,** evacuation trench. **4.** *Algae:* sea-whipcord.
boyauderie [bwajodri], *s.f.* gut-dressing works.
boyaudier [bwajodje], *s.m.* gut-dresser.
boyautant [bwajotɑ̃], *a. P:* screamingly funny, side-splitting.
boyauter (se) [səbwajote], *v.pr. P:* to shake, split, one's sides with laughter.
boycottage [bɔjkɔta:ʒ], *s.m.* boycotting.
boycotter [bɔjkɔte], *v.tr.* to boycott; *F:* to freeze (s.o.) out.
boycotteur, -euse [bɔjkɔtœ:r, -ø:z], *s.* boycotter.
boy-scout [bɔjskaut, -skut], *s.m.* boy-scout; *pl. boy-scouts.*
brabançon, -onne [brabɑ̃sɔ̃, -ɔn], *a. & s.* Brabantine, Belgian; **la Brabançonne,** the Belgian national anthem.
Brabant [brabɑ̃]. **1.** *Pr.n.m. Geog:* Brabant. **2.** *s.m.* (*a*) *Agr:* all-metal wheel plough; **b. double,** turn-wrest plough, one-way plough; (*b*) metal band or strap; **b. à patte,** holdfast, clip.
brabantin, -ine [brabɑ̃tɛ̃, -in], *a. & s.* = BRABANÇON.
brac [brak], *s.m. See* BRIC.
bracelet [braslɛ], *s.m.* **1.** (*a*) bracelet, bangle; **b. esclave,** slave-bangle; **b. en cuir pour montre,** wrist-watch strap; **b. de montre (en métal),** watchband; *Gym:* **b.** de force, leather wrist-band; (*b*) arm-garter; (*c*) *P:* **bracelets,** handcuffs, bracelets. **2.** (*a*) metal band, ring; **b. de fourreau,** scabbard-band; locket; (*b*) *Bot:* node, knot (in stem of grasses).
bracelet-montre [braslɛmɔ̃:tr], *s.m.* wrist-watch; *pl. bracelets-montres.*
brachial, -iaux [brakjal, -jo], *a. Anat:* brachial (artery, etc.).
brachialgie [brakialʒi], *s.f. Med:* brachialgia, brachionalgia.
brachiation [brakjasjɔ̃], *s.f. Z:* (*of monkey*) swinging by the arms, brachiation.
brachiocéphalique [brakjɔsefalik], *a. Anat:* brachiocephalic.
brachiopode [brakjɔpɔd], *s.m. Moll:* brachiopod.
brachistochrone [brakistɔkrɔn, -on]. *Mth:* **1.** *a.* brachistochronic (curve). **2.** *s.f.* brachistochrone; *Av:* least-time track.
brachy- [braki], *pref.* brachy-; **brachydactyle,** brachydactylous; **brachylogie,** brachylogy.
brachycéphale [brakisefal], *a.* brachycephalic, short-headed.
brachycéphalidés [brakisefalide], *s.m.pl. Amph:* Brachycephalidae.
brachycéphalie [brakisefali], *s.f.* brachycephalism, brachycephaly.
brachycère [brakisɛ:r]. *Ent: Paleont:* **1. brachycères,** *s.m.pl.* Brachycera. **2.** *a.* brachycerous.
brachylogie [brakilɔʒi], *s.f.* brachylogy.
brachyne [brakin], *s.m.* **b. tirailleur, b. crépitant,** bombardier beetle.
brachyoures [brakju:r], **brachyures** [brakjy:r], *s.m.pl. Crust:* Brachyura.
brachyptère [brakiptɛ:r], *a. Orn: Ent:* brachypterous, small-winged (insects, birds).
bracon[1] [brakɔ̃], *s.m.* (*a*) *Const:* brace, strut; (*b*) *Hyd.E:* diagonal brace (of lock-gate).
bracon[2], *s.m. Ent:* bracon.
braconides [brakɔnid], **braconidés** [brakɔnide], *s.m.pl. Ent:* Braconidae.
braconnage [brakɔna:ʒ], *s.m.* poaching.
braconner [brakɔne], *v.i.* **1.** to poach; *F:* **b. dans la chasse de qn,** to poach on s.o.'s preserves. **2.** to shoot in close time.
braconnier, -ière [brakɔnje, -jɛ:r]. **1.** *a.* poaching (mood, etc.). **2.** *s.m.* poacher.
bractéaire [brakteɛ:r], **bractéal, -aux** [brakteal, -o], *a. Bot:* bracteal.
bractéate [brakteat], *a. & s.f. Num:* bracteate.
bractée [brakte], *s.f. Bot:* bract.
bractéifère [brakteifɛ:r], *a. Bot:* bracteiferous.
bractéole [brakteɔl], *s.f.* (*a*) *Bot:* bracteole; (*b*) faulty gold leaf.
bractéolé [brakteɔle], *a. Bot:* bracteolate.
bractété [braktete], *a. Bot:* bracteate.
bradage [brada:ʒ], *s.m. F: Com:* cut-price selling.
bradel [bradɛl], *s.m. or f.* **(reliure) b.,** cloth binding.
brader [brade], *v.tr.* (*a*) to sell off (old stock, wardrobe articles, etc.) on the pavement (in front of shop, of private house) at the annual BRADERIE, *q.b.* (*b*) *F:* to sell off dirt cheap; *F:* **le gouvernement a bradé nos colonies,** the government has sold off our colonies.
braderie [bradri], *s.f.* annual sale, *usu.* in September, of old stock, cast-off clothing, etc., on the pavement; (yearly) jumble-sale; rummage sale.
bradeur [bradœ:r], *s.m.* surplus stores merchant.
bradipodidés [bradipɔdide], *s.m.pl. Z:* Bradipodidae.
brady- [bradi], *pref.* brady-; **bradypepsie,** bradypepsia; **bradyurie,** bradyuria; **bradycardie,** bradycardia.
bradype [bradip], *s.m. Z:* bradypod; *F:* three-toed sloth.
Bragance [bragɑ̃:s], *Pr.n.f. Geog:* Braganza.
bragard, -arde [braga:r, -ard], *a. & s. Geog:* (native, inhabitant) of Saint-Dizier.
brague [brag], *s.f. A:* **1.** *usu. pl.* breeches. **2.** *Nau: A:* breech-tackle, breeching (of gun).
braguet [bragɛ], *s.m. Nau:* top-tackle pendant.
braguette [bragɛt], *s.f.* **1.** (front) slit, fly (of trousers); **votre b. est déboutonnée,** *F:* you're showing your medals. **2.** *A.Cost:* cod-piece.
brahma [brama], *s.m. & f. Husb:* = BRAHMAPOUTRE 2.
brahmane [braman], *s.m.* Brahmin, Brahman.
brahmanique [bramanik], *a.* Brahminic(al), Brahmanic(al).
brahmanisme [bramanism], *s.m.* Brahminism, Brahmanism.
Brahmapoutre [bramaputr]. **1.** *Pr.n.m. Geog:* Brahmaputra. **2.** *s.m. & f. Husb:* brahma (pootra) fowl.
brahme [brɑ:m], *s.m.* = BRAHMANE.
brahmine [bramin], *s.f.* Brahmanee.
brai [brɛ], *s.m.* **1.** pitch, tar; **b. sec,** dry pitch, resin, rosin; **b. de pétrole fluxé,** cutback. **2.** *Brew:* grist, bruised barley.
braie [brɛ], *s.f.* **1.** *pl. Cost: A:* breeches; *F:* **se tirer d'une affaire les braies nettes,** to get off unharmed, scot-free. **2.** *Nau:* coat, sheeting (of the rudder, of the pump).
braillage [brɑja:ʒ], *s.m. Fish:* stowing (of herrings) in salt.
braillard, -arde [brɑja:r, -ard]. **1.** *a. F:* (*a*) vociferous, clamorous, uproarious, bawling, noisy; squalling (child); **luxe b.,** blatant display of wealth; (*b*) *Ven:* babbling (hound). **2.** *s.m.* (*a*) bawler, shouter, vociferator; brawler; **petit b.,** noisy brat; (*b*) *Ven:* (*of hound*) babbler.
braille [brɑ:j], *s.m.* Braille; *a.inv.* **alphabet b.,** Braille alphabet; **caractères b.,** Braille type.
braillement [brɑjmɑ̃], *s.m. F:* bawling, squalling; uproar, brawling.
brailler[1] [brɑje]. **1.** *v.i. F:* (*a*) to bawl, shout; (*of child*) to squall; to brawl; **faire b. la radio,** to turn, have, the wireless on full blast; (*b*) *Ven:* (*of hound*) to babble. **2.** *v.tr.* **b. une chanson,** to bawl (out) a song.
brailler[2], *v.tr. Fish:* to stow (herrings) in salt.
braillerie [brɑjri], *s.f. F:* shouting, vociferation, bawling; squalling.
brailleur, -euse [brɑjœ:r, -ø:z], *a. & s. F:* = BRAILLARD.
braiment [brɛmɑ̃], *s.m.* bray(ing) (of an ass).
brainstorming [brɛnstɔrmiŋ], *s.m.* brainstorming; **pratiquer le b.,** to brainstorm.
brain-trust [brɛntrœst], *s.m.* brains trust; *pl. brain-trusts.*
braire [brɛ:r], *v.i.def.* (*pr.ind.* **il brait, ils braient;** *fu.* **il braira, ils brairont;** *condit.* **il brairait, ils brairaient**) to bray. **2.** *F:* to cry, bawl; *F:* to boo-hoo. **3.** *v.tr.* **b. une chanson,** to bray a song.
braise [brɛ:z], *s.f.* **1.** (*a*) (glowing) embers; live charcoal; cinders of wood; *F:* **des yeux de b.,** glowing eyes; **être sur la b., avoir les pieds sur la b.,** to be on tenter-hooks; **comme chat sur b.,** like a cat on hot bricks; **passer sur une chose comme un chat sur la b.,** to skim over a subject; **tomber de la poêle sur la b.,** to fall out of the frying pan into the fire; *Cu:* **bœuf à la b.,** braised beef; (*b*) *P:* cash, oof. **2.** small cinders, breeze. **3. b. chimique,** artificial fuel (*esp. for* CHAUFFERETTES, *q.v.*).
braiser [brɛze], *v.tr. Cu:* to braise.
braisette [brɛzɛt], *s.f.* (i) small (glowing) embers; (ii) (small pieces of) charcoal.
braisier [brɛzje], *s.m.* extinguishing box (for charcoal).
braisière [brɛzjɛ:r], *s.f.* **1.** *Cu:* braising-pan, stew-pan. **2.** = BRAISIER.
braisille [brɛzi:j], *s.f.* flying ember, spark (from blazing building, etc.).
braisillon [brɛzijɔ̃], *s.m.* glowing end (of a match).
Bramah [brama], *Pr.n.m.* **serrure de B.,** Bramah lock; **presse de B.,** Bramah press.
brame[1] [brɑ:m], *s.m.* = BRAHMANE.
brame[2] [bram], *s.f. Metall:* (iron) slab, bloom.
brame[3] [bram], *s.m. Ich:* brama, ray's bream.
brame[4], *s.m. Ven:* = BRAMEMENT; **le temps du b.,** the rutting season.
bramement [brammɑ̃], *s.m.* troating (of stag).
bramer [brame]. **1.** (*a*) *v.i.* (*of stag*) to troat; (*b*) *F:* to sing. **2.** *v.tr. F:* to sing a song.
bramine [brɑmin, bra-], *s.f.* = BRAHMINE.
bran [brɑ̃], *s.m.* **1.** (*a*) bran; *s.a.* JUDAS 1; (*b*) **b. de scie,** sawdust. **2.** *P:* shit, muck; *Nau: F:* **un temps de b.,** foul weather, dirty weather. **3. b. d'agace,** cherry-tree gum.
brancard [brɑ̃ka:r], *s.m.* **1.** *Veh:* (*a*) shaft (of carriage); **ruer dans les brancards,** (i) to kick when between the shafts; (ii) to kick, to jib; to strain at the leash; *F:* to kick over the traces; *s.a.* CHEVAL 1; *P:* **les brancards,** the legs; *F:* pins; (*b*) side-sill (of railway-wagon); *Aut:* **brancards de caisse,** lowest members of body-framework. **2.** (*a*) stretcher, *U.S:* litter; **b. roulant,** wheeled stretcher; **b. à bretelles,** sling stretcher; **b. de bât,** mule stretcher; (*b*) hand-barrow, barrow-truck; (*c*) (hand-)bier; (*d*) wooden pole; (carrying) handspike.
brancardage [brɑ̃karda:ʒ], *s.m.* carrying (of sick and wounded) on stretchers.
brancarder [brɑ̃karde], *v.tr.* to convey (s.o.) on a stretcher.
brancardier [brɑ̃kardje], *s.m.* stretcher-bearer; *U.S:* litter-bearer.
branchage [brɑ̃ʃa:ʒ], *s.m.* (*a*) *Coll.* branches, boughs (of trees); (*b*) **cabane de branchages,** hut made of branches.
branche [brɑ̃:ʃ], *s.f.* **1.** (*a*) branch, limb, bough (of tree); *F:* **sauter de b. en b.,** to flit from flower to flower, from subject to subject; **s'accrocher à toutes les branches,** to clutch at every straw; *P:* **vieille b.,** old friend, old pal; **avoir de la b.,** to look distinguished, aristocratic, to have an air about one; (*b*) **notre b. de la famille,** our branch of the family; **la b. maternelle,** the maternal line (of ascent); (*c*) *Anat:* **b. (collatérale, terminale),** (collateral, terminal) branch; (*of primary division*) ramus, *pl.* rami; (*d*) **b. d'un fleuve,** branch of a river; (*e*) **branches du bois d'un cerf,** tines of a stag's antlers; (*f*) **les différentes branches des sciences, de l'industrie,** the various branches, divisions, of learning, of industry. **2.** (*a*) leg (of compasses, dividers); cheek (of bit); side (of spectacle frame); arm (of tool); prong (of pitch-fork, tuning-fork); blade (of propeller); shank (of key); bow (of padlock); arm (of horseshoe); **b. à coulisse,** telescopic leg (of tripod); **b. inférieure d'un siphon,** lower limb of a siphon; **chandelier à plusieurs branches,** branched candlestick; (*b*) *Nau:* bridle (of bow-line, of moorings); (*c*) *Mth:* branch (of curve).
branché [brɑ̃ʃe], *a. F:* **être b.,** to be with it, up-to-date.
branchée [brɑ̃ʃe], *s.f.* branchful, boughful (of fruit, etc.).
branchement [brɑ̃ʃmɑ̃], *s.m.* **1.** *El: Tp:* junction, branch(ing), branch-circuit, *U.S:* tap; *Computers:* make and break; **ligne de b.,** branch-line, spur; **borne de b.,** branch terminal; **point de b.,** branch point; **b. d'abonné,** (i) *El:* (service) lead; (ii) *Tp:* drop(-wire). **2.** *Hyd.E: Pipelines: etc:* tapping (of main), connection, branch(ing); **(tube de) b.,** branch-pipe. **3.** *Rail:* turn-out; **b. double,** three-throw switch (or points); **b. simple à droite, à gauche,** right-hand, left-hand turn-out; **b. symétrique,** split switch.
brancher [brɑ̃ʃe]. **1.** *v.i. & v.pr.* (*of bird*) (*a*) to perch (on a branch); (*b*) to roost; *F:* **il était branché sur une vergue,** he was perched on one of the yard-arms. **2.** *v.tr.* (*a*) to branch; *El:* to plug in (connection); *Tp:* to put through (**sur,** to); **on vous a mal branché,** you have been given the wrong connection, the wrong line; **b. une conduite de gaz,** to tap a gas main; *El.E:* **b. une sonnerie sur le circuit de lumière,** to run a bell off the light circuit; **b. un fer électrique,** to plug in an electric iron; **se b. sur le secteur urbain,** to connect up with the town supply; (*b*) *Min:* to break out (a new gallery); (*c*) *A:* to string up, hang (murderer).
branchette [brɑ̃ʃɛt], *s.f.* small branch, branchet, twig.
branche-ursine [brɑ̃ʃyrsin], *s.f. Bot:* brank-ursine, bear's-breech; *pl. branches-ursines.*
branchial, -iaux [brɑ̃ʃjal, -jo], *a. Z:* branchial.
branchié [brɑ̃ʃje], *a.* branchiate(d).
branchies [brɑ̃ʃi], *s.f.pl. Z:* branchiae, gills (of fish); **sans b.,** abranchial.
branchillon [brɑ̃ʃijɔ̃], *s.m.* branchlet; twig.
branchiopode [brɑ̃kjɔpɔd], *s.m. Crust:* branchiopod.
branchiostomes [brɑ̃kjɔstɔm], *s.m.pl. Ich:* Branchiostomidae, Acrania.
branchu [brɑ̃ʃy], *a.* branchy, branching, ramifying.
branchure [brɑ̃ʃy:r], *s.f.* (*in centre of France*) = BRANCHAGE.

branc-ursine [brɑ̃kyrsin], *s.f. Bot.* = BRANCHE-URSINE; *pl. brancs-ursines.*
brandade [brɑ̃dad], *s.f. Cu:* salt cod pounded with garlic, oil, and cream.
brande [brɑ̃:d], *s.f.* **1.** heather. **2.** heath.
Brandebourg [brɑ̃dbu:r]. **1.** *Pr.n.m. Geog:* Brandenburg. **2.** (*a*) *s.m.pl. Cost:* Brandenburgs, frogs and loops; **orné de brandebourgs,** frogged; (*b*) *s.m.* long-sleeved pelisse.
brandebourgeois, -oise [brɑ̃dburʒwa, -wa:z]. **1.** *a.* (of) Brandenburg. **2.** *s.* Brandenburger.
brandevin [brɑ̃dvɛ̃], *s.m.* brandy.
brandevinier [brɑ̃dvinje], *s.m.* travelling brandy-distiller.
brandillement [brɑ̃dijmɑ̃], *s.m.* wagging, dangling, swinging.
brandiller [brɑ̃dije], *v.tr. & i.* to swing; to wag; to dangle; to shake to and fro; to flap (in the wind); **il commence à b. (de) la tête,** he is beginning to dodder.
se brandiller, to rock oneself (in one's chair); to swing (on a swing).
brandillon [brɑ̃dijɔ̃], *s.m. P:* arm.
brandir [brɑ̃di:r], *v.tr.* to brandish, flourish (weapon, etc.); **b. un journal,** to hold up, wave about, a newspaper; **il brandit devant moi la perspective du renvoi,** he threatened to sack me.
brandissement [brɑ̃dismɑ̃], *s.m.* brandishing, flourishing (of weapon, etc.).
brandon [brɑ̃dɔ̃], *s.m.* **1.** (fire-)brand; torch (of twisted straw); **dimanche des brandons,** first Sunday in Lent; *F:* **jeter des brandons de discorde parmi les citoyens,** to sow seeds of discord among the citizens; **c'est un b. de discorde,** he is a fire-brand. **2.** wisp of straw (stuck on pole in a field to indicate that the crops have been seized for debt).
branlant [brɑ̃lɑ̃]. **1.** *a.* shaky; loose (tooth, etc.); tottery, unsteady; **chaise branlante,** rickety, crazy, chair; **toit, escalier, b.,** ramshackle roof, stair; **chef b.,** doddering head; *s.a.* ROCHER[1] 1. **2.** *s.f.pl. P:* **branlantes,** teeth.
branle [brɑ̃:l], *s.m.* **1.** (*a*) oscillation, swing (motion); (*b*) impulse, impetus; **donner le b. à qch.,** to give an impetus to sth.; **donner le b. à un mouvement,** to set a movement on foot; **donner le b. à tout le pays,** to wake up the country; **donner le b. à la mémoire de qn,** to jog s.o.'s memory; **mettre qch. en b.,** to set sth. going, in action; **mettre une cloche, une sonnerie, en b.,** to set a bell, or bells, swinging or ringing; **mettre les choses en b.,** *F:* to open the ball; to start the ball rolling. **2.** *Danc: Mus: A:* branle, brawl; **mener le b.,** (i) to lead the dance, to take the lead; (ii) *F:* to set the ball rolling. **3.** *Nau: A:* hammock. **4.** *pl. Tls:* jaws (of vice).
branle-bas [brɑ̃lbɑ], *s.m.inv. in pl.* **1.** *Navy:* (*a*) (beat, pipe to) quarters; **b.-b. de combat,** general quarters, clearing for action; **faire le b.-b. de combat,** to clear (the decks) for action; (*b*) **b.-b.!** show a leg! **2.** *F:* bustle, commotion; **toute la ville était en b.-b.,** the whole town was in a turmoil; **il met toute la maison en b.-b. parce qu'il a perdu sa cravate,** he's turning the house upside down because he's lost his tie.
branlement [brɑ̃lmɑ̃], *s.m.* oscillation, shaking, swinging (of bell, etc.); wagging (of one's head).
branle-queue [brɑ̃lkø], *s.m. Orn: F:* wagtail; *pl. branle-queues.*
branler [brɑ̃le]. **1.** *v.tr.* to swing, shake (one's legs, etc.); to wag (one's head). **2.** *v.i.* (*a*) to shake, move, rock,; to be loose; **dent qui branle,** loose tooth; *s.a.* NEZ 1; **b. dans le manche,** (*of tool*) to be loose in the handle; *F:* **il branle dans le manche,** he is in jeopardy, his position is insecure, shaky, precarious; *Prov:* **tout ce qui branle ne tombe pas,** a creaking gate hangs long; (*b*) *A:* (*of pers.*) to move, stir; (*of troops*) to waver.
se branler, *P:* to masturbate.
branle-tête [brɑ̃ltɛt], *s.m.inv. in pl. Toys:* (nodding) mandarin.
branlette [brɑ̃lɛt], *s.m.* centre section (of three-piece fishing-rod).
branleur [brɑ̃lœ:r], *s.m. Metall:* wobbler (of rolling-mill).
branloire [brɑ̃lwa:r], *s.f.* **1.** seesaw, *U.S:* teeter. **2.** pump or bellows handle; rock-staff. **3.** hanging box (under cart).
branque-ursine [brɑ̃kyrsin], *s.f. Bot:* = BRANCHE-URSINE.
brante [brɑ̃:t], *s.f. Orn:* **b. roussâtre,** red-crested pochard.
brantômais, -aise [brɑ̃tomɛ, -ɛ:z], *a. & s. Geog:* (native, inhabitant) of Brantôme.
braquage [braka:ʒ], *s.m.* **1.** aiming, levelling, pointing (of gun, telescope, etc.). **2.** changing the direction, deflexion (of road wheels, of aeroplane, etc.); steering; *Aut:* **angle de b.,** (steering) lock (of car); **cercle de b.,** turning circle; **b. (au) maximum,** full lock; *Av:* **angle de b.,** helm, steering, angle; **angle de b. d'aileron,** aileron angle; **angle de b. de gouvernail de direction, de gouvernail de profondeur,** rudder, elevator, angle; **rayon de b.,** radius of turning circle.
braque [brak]. **1.** *s.m. Ven:* pointer. **2.** *s.m. & a. F:* hare-brained fellow, feather-brain, mad-cap; *a.* **air b.,** daft appearance.
braquement [brakmɑ̃], *s.m.* = BRAQUAGE 1.
braquer [brake], *v.tr.* **1.** (*a*) **b. un fusil sur qn, qch.,** to aim, level, point, a gun at s.o., sth.; **b. une lunette sur qn, qch.,** to fix, direct, train, a telescope on sth., to bring a telescope to bear on sth.; (*b*) **b. les yeux sur qn,** to fix one's eye(s) on s.o., to stare steadily at s.o.; **il a toujours l'œil braqué sur nous,** he keeps a close watch on us, his eye is always on us; *F:* **b. son attention (sur qch.),** to fix one's attention (on sth.); **2.** *Aut: Av:* to change the direction of (car, etc.); *Aut:* to put the wheel over; **b. à gauche, à droite,** to lock over to the left, to the right; **auto qui braque à** 30°, car with a lock of 30°; **b. au maximum, jusqu'à la limite,** to apply full lock. **3.** *F:* to antagonize; **être braqué contre,** to be stubbornly opposed to.
se braquer, (*a*) *Equit:* (*of horse*) to pull; **se b. sur le mors,** to bore on the bit; **cheval braqué,** pulling horse; (*b*) to oppose stubbornly (**contre,** to).
braquet [brakɛ], *s.m. Cy:* gear-ratio; **changer de b.,** to change gear.
bras [bra], *s.m.* arm. **1.** (*a*) **il a le(s) bras long(s),** he is long in the arm; *F:* **avoir le b. long,** to have a wide influence; **allonger le b. vers qch.,** to make a long arm for sth.; **arrêter le b. à qn,** to stay s.o.'s hand; **offrir le b. à qn,** to offer s.o. one's arm; **offrir le b. à une dame pour passer à la salle à manger,** to take a lady in to dinner; **avoir qn à son b.,** to have s.o. on one's arm; **faire les beaux b.,** to affect refined manners; **les b. m'en tombent,** I am dumbfounded, I don't know whether I am (standing) on my head or my heels; **les b. lui sont tombés,** she was utterly discouraged; **cette nouvelle m'a cassé b. et jambes,** this piece of news bowled me over, stunned me; **avoir les b. rompus,** to be worn out, dead beat; **il m'appelait Monsieur gros comme le b.,** he was sirring me all the time; **rester les b. croisés,** to twiddle, twirl, one's thumbs; **tout cède à son b.,** everything, everyone, gives way to him; **vivre de ses b.,** to make a living as a manual worker; *Ten:* **jouer petit b.,** to be afraid to hit out; *s.a.* RETOURNER 1; **ouvrir, tendre, les b. à qn,** to receive s.o. with open arms; *s.a.* OUVERT 1; **tendre les b. vers, à, qn,** to ask s.o. for help; **être sur les b. de qn,** (i) to be maintained by s.o., (ii) to be a nuisance to s.o.; **avoir qn, qch., sur les b.,** to have s.o., sth., on one's hands; **se mettre, s'attirer, qch. sur les b.,** to bring sth. on oneself; *F:* **être le b. droit de qn,** to be s.o.'s right hand; *Mec.E:* **la force des b.,** man-power, hand-power; *adv.phr:* **à b. (d'hommes), à force de b.,** by hand; **voiture à b.,** hand-cart; **tenir qch. à b. tendu(s), à bout de b.,** to hold sth. at arm's length; **prendre qch. à pleins b.,** to take sth. with both arms, to fill one's arms with sth.; **prendre qn à pleins b.,** to hug s.o.; **b. dessus b. dessous,** arm in arm; **en b. de chemise,** in one's shirt sleeves; *s.a.* RACCOURCI 1, SÉCULIER 1, TOUR[2] 3; (*b*) *pl.* hands (= workmen); **manquer de b.,** to be short-handed; (*c*) *Z:* (i) arm (of vertebrates); (ii) arm (of brachiopods). **2.** leg (of sheers); arm (of lever, of anchor); jib (of crane); limb (of cross); sail arm (of windmill); **b. d'aile,** wing-spar (of aeroplane); **b. de pompe,** pump-handle; **b. d'élévateur,** elevator link; **b. de balancier,** cam lever; **b. d'un fauteuil,** arm of a chair; *Gramophones:* **b. (acoustique),** tone-arm; **b. de lecture,** pick-up arm; **b. de mer,** arm of the sea, sound; **b. d'un fleuve,** arm, branch, of a river; **b. mort (d'un cours d'eau),** ox-bow (lake), cut-off; **b. de décharge (d'une rivière),** backwater; *Nau:* **b. d'une vergue,** brace of a yard; **b. de bossoir,** davit guys; *Mch:* **b. de manivelle,** crank-arm; *I.C.E:* **les b. de manivelle du vilebrequin,** the crank-webs, the throws, of the crankshaft; *s.a.* BOSSOIR 2; RAPPEL 5.
brasage [braza:ʒ], **brasement** [brazmɑ̃], *s.m.* brazing, hard-soldering; **b. à l'arc,** arc brazing.
braser [braze], *v.tr. Metallw:* to braze, to hard-solder; **b. au cuivre,** to copper-solder.
brasero [brazero], *s.m.* brazier, charcoal-pan, fire-pan, fire-basket, fire-devil; **b. de boutique, de cuisine,** chafing-dish.
brasier [brazje, bra-], *s.m.* **1.** = BRASERO. **2.** (*a*) clear glowing fire; fire of live coals; (*b*) source of intense heat; **l'auto n'était plus qu'un b.,** the car was reduced to a blazing mass; **son cœur était un b.,** his heart was afire, was burning with a fierce passion; *F:* **son corps est un b.,** he has got a high temperature.
brasillement [brazijmɑ̃], *s.m.* broiling heat.
brasiller [brazije, bra-]. **1.** (*a*) *v.tr.* to grill, broil (meat, etc.); (*b*) *v.i.* (*of meat, etc.*) to sputter, sizzle (in the pan). **2.** *v.i.* (*of sea*) to glitter, gleam, sparkle.
bras-le-corps (**à**) [abraləkɔ:r], *adv.phr.* **saisir qn à b.-le-c.,** to seize s.o. round the waist, to grapple with s.o.
brasque [brask], *s.f. Metall:* brasque, lute, luting (of crucible).
brasquer [braske], *v.tr.* to brasque, lute (crucible, etc.).
brassage [brasa:ʒ], *s.m.* **1.** brewing, mashing. **2.** (*a*) mixing, stirring; *F:* **le b. des classes sociales,** the mixing of social classes; (*b*) *I.C.E:* **b. d'air et d'essence,** mixing of air and petrol; (*c*) *F:* **b. des affaires,** handling of big business; (*d*) *Nau:* **b. de l'hélice,** propeller wake; (*e*) *Metall:* rabbling.
brassard [brasa:r], *s.m.* **1.** *Archeol:* brassard, arm-guard. **2.** armlet; **b. de deuil,** mourning-band, arm-band; **b. de la Croix Rouge,** Red-Cross badge. **3.** *Med:* **b. à tension artérielle,** blood-pressure cuff.
brasse [bras], *s.f.* **1.** span (of the arms); *Nau:* fathom; **être sur les brasses,** to touch bottom. **2.** *Swim:* stroke; **nager (à) la b.,** to swim breast stroke; **b. (coulée, française, sur le ventre),** breast stroke; **b. papillon,** butterfly stroke; **b. sur le dos,** inverted breast stroke. **3.** *Tls:* pitch-stirrer.
brassée [brase], *s.f.* **1.** armful; **saisir qn à la b.,** to fling one's arms round s.o., to hug s.o.; to grapple with s.o. **2.** *Swim:* stroke.
brassement [brasmɑ̃], *s.m.* **1.** brewing. **2.** *F:* mixing, mingling (of nations, etc.).
brasser[1] [brase], *v.tr.* **1.** to brew, mash (beer, etc.); *F:* **b. une intrigue,** to brew, hatch, a plot. **2.** (*a*) to mix, stir (up); **b. une paillasse,** to shake up a palliasse; *F:* **b. des affaires,** to handle a lot of business; **b. des écus,** to turn over a lot of money; **b. les cartes,** to shuffle the cards; *Nau:* **b. l'écume,** (*of a ship's propeller*), to churn up the foam; (*b*) *Metall:* to puddle, rabble, work (pig-iron).
brasser[2], *v.tr.* **1.** *Nau:* to brace (yard); *abs.* **b. au vent,** to brace in, haul in; **b. sous le vent,** to brace forward, up; **b. à culer,** to brace aback; **b. carré,** to square the yards. **2.** *Av:* **b. l'hélice,** to swing the propeller.
se brasser, *F:* to slap oneself (to keep warm); to beat the goose (to warm oneself up).
brasserie [brasri], *s.f.* **1.** brewery. **2.** brewing, beer-making; **fortune faite dans la b.,** fortune made in beer. **3.** brasserie.
brasseur, -euse [brasœ:r, -ø:z], *s.* **1.** brewer. **2.** *Metall:* mixer, puddler; *F:* **b. d'affaires,** (i) man who handles a lot of business, big-business man; *F:* tycoon; live wire; (ii) shady financier. **3.** *s.m.* agitator (for mixing). **4.** (breast-stroke) swimmer.
brasseyage [brasɛja:ʒ], *s.m. Nau:* bracing (of yard).
brasseyer [brasɛje, -eje], *v.i. Nau:* = BRASSER[2] 1.
brassiage [brasja:ʒ], *s.m. Nau:* **1.** fathoming, sounding. **2.** depth in fathoms, soundings.
brassicaire [brasikɛ:r]. **1.** *a.* of, pertaining to, cabbages. **2.** *s.f. Ent:* cabbage-moth.
brassicourt [brasiku:r], *a. & s.m.* knee-sprung (horse); (horse) over at the knees.
brassière [brasjɛ:r], *s.f.* **1.** (*a*) child's sleeved vest; (*b*) **b. de sauvetage,** life-jacket; (*c*) *Fr.C:* brassière. **2.** *pl.* (*a*) leading-strings (for infants); *F:* **être en brassières,** to be in leading-strings; (*b*) shoulder-straps, slings (of knapsack, etc.). **3.** *Veh:* arm-sling.
brassin [brasɛ̃], *s.m. Brew:* **1.** gyle, brew. **2.** mash-tub.
brassure [brasy:r], *s.f.* spider (of wheel).
brasure [brazy:r, bra-], *s.f.* **1.** (brazed) seam, joint. **2.** (*a*) hard-soldering, brazing; (*b*) hard solder, brazant.
bravache [bravaʃ]. **1.** *s.m.* blusterer, bully. **2.** *a.* swaggering, blustering, raffish, bullying; **d'un air b.,** blusteringly, raffishly.
bravacherie [bravaʃri], *s.f. A:* bluster, swagger.
bravade [bravad], *s.f.* bravado, bluster; *A:* **faire b. à qn,** to brave, defy, s.o.; **faire qch. par b.,** to do sth. out of bravado.
bravader [bravade], *v.i. A:* to bluster.

brave [bra:v], *a.* **1.** brave, bold, gallant; *s.m.* **un (homme) b.,** a brave, courageous, man; **vieux b.,** veteran; **b. à trois poils,** hard, proven, fighter; **se conduire en b.,** to acquit oneself bravely, gallantly; **faire le b.,** to bluster, to brag. **2.** (*preceding the noun*) good, honest, worthy; **c'est un b. homme,** *F:* **un b. type,** he's a decent sort, a good chap; **ma b. femme de nourrice,** my good old nurse; *s.m.* **je vous félicite, mon b.,** I congratulate you, my good man; *Nau:* **allons, mes braves!** now then, my hearties! **3.** *A: F:* smart, spruce, fine; **comme vous voilà b.!** you do look smart! **4.** *s.m. A:* hired assassin; bravo, cut-throat.

bravement [bravmɑ̃], *adv.* **1.** bravely, stoutly, boldly. **2.** *A: F:* skilfully; finely.

braver [brave], *v.tr.* to brave. **1.** to face (sth.) bravely; **toujours prêt à b. le danger,** always ready to face danger. **2.** to defy, dare (s.o.); to set (s.o.) at defiance; to beard (s.o.); **b. qn avec insolence,** to be insolently defiant to s.o.

braverie [bravri], *s.f.* **1.** boldness. **2.** ostentation.

bravo[1] [bravo]. **1.** *int.* bravo! good! well done! hear, hear! **2.** *s.m.pl.* **des bravos,** applause, cheers.

bravo[2], *s.m.* bravo, hired assassin, cut-throat; *pl. bravi.*

bravoure [bravu:r], *s.f.* **1.** bravery, gallantry. **2.** *pl.* exploits, deeds of valour, of daring, of derring-do. **3.** *Mus:* **air de b.,** bravura; *Lit:* **morceau de b.,** purple passage.

brayage [brɛja:ʒ], *s.m.* roping (of load for hoisting).

braye [brɛ(j)], *s.f. Const:* **1.** sling, strap (for hoisting load). **2.** pulley, tackle.

brayer[1] [brɛje], *v.tr.* **(je braie, je braye, n. brayons; je brayerai, je braierai)** *Nau:* to pitch, tar, pay (boat).

brayer[2], *v.tr. Const:* to sling (burden for hoisting).

brayer[3], *s.m.* **1.** *Surg: A:* truss, belt. **2.** thong (of bell-clapper). **3.** *Mil:* (flag-bearer's) colour belt; bucket (for stave of lance). **4.** = BRAYE.

brayette [brajɛt], *s.f. A: Dial:* = BRAGUETTE.

break[1] [brɛk], *s.m. Veh:* break; station-wagon; **b. de chasse,** shooting-brake.

break[2], *s.m.* **1.** *Mus:* break. **2.** *Box:* **b.!** break!

bréant [breɑ̃], *s.m. Orn:* = BRUANT.

brebis [brəbi], *s.f.* **1.** ewe. **2.** sheep; **b. égarée,** lost sheep; **b. noire,** black sheep; *s.a.* GALEUX; *F:* **faire un repas de b.,** to eat a meal without drinking; *Prov:* **à b. tondue Dieu mesure le vent,** God tempers the wind to the shorn lamb; **qui se fait b., le loup le mange,** mugs are always fleeced; **brebis comptées, le loup les mange,** the best laid plans may fail.

brèche [brɛʃ], *s.f.* **1.** breach, opening, gap, break (in wall, hedge, etc.); hole (in ship's side); notch (in blade); *Mil:* **monter sur la b.,** to stand in the breach; **être toujours sur la b.,** to be hard at it, to be always on the go; *Mil:* **mourir sur la b.,** to be killed in action; **colmater une b.,** to stop, to close, a gap; **battre en b. une forteresse,** to batter a fortress for breaching; *F:* **battre qn en b.,** to attack, disparage, s.o.; to run s.o. down; **batterie de b.,** breaching battery; *s.a.* TIR 2. **faire une b. dans un mur,** to break through a wall; **faire b. à un rempart,** to breach a rampart; *F:* **faire une b. à la fortune de qn,** to make a hole, a dent, in s.o.'s fortune; **faire une b. à un pâté,** to cut into a pie. **2.** *Geol:* breccia; **marbre b.,** breccia marble.

brèche-dent [brɛʃdɑ̃], *a. & s.* gap-toothed (person); **elle est b.-d.,** she has a gap in her teeth; *pl. brèche-dent(s).*

brechet, bréchet [brəʃɛ, bre-], *s.m. Anat: F:* breast-bone, sternum; *esp.* carina (of fowl).

bréchiforme [breʃifɔrm], *a. Geol:* brecciated.

bréchite [breʃit], *s.m. Moll:* watering-pot shell.

Bréda [breda], *Pr.n.* **1.** *Geog:* Breda. **2.** *A:* **le quartier B.,** the Breda quarter (in Paris, at one time the home of the *demi-monde*).

bredi-breda [brədibrəda], *adv.phr: F:* in a hasty, slap-dash, manner; **dire une messe b.-b.,** to gabble through a mass.

bredindin [brədɛ̃dɛ̃], *s.m. Nau:* garnet, Spanish burton.

bredouillage [brəduja:ʒ], *s.m.,* **bredouillement** [brədujmɑ̃], *s.m.,* jabbering, mumbling.

bredouille [brədu:j]. **1.** *s.f.* (*a*) (*at backgammon*) lurch, gammon; (*b*) *Th: F:* **il n'a à dire que quelques bredouilles,** he has got only a few words to mumble. **2.** *a.inv.* (*a*) **être b.,,** (i) to be gammoned; (ii) *F:* to have failed completely (in sth.); (*b*) *F:* **rentrer, revenir, b.,** to come home (from a day's shooting) with an empty bag, empty-handed.

bredouiller [brəduje]. **1.** *v.i.* to jabber, mumble. **2.** *v.tr.* **b. une excuse,** to stammer out, mumble, an excuse.

bredouilleur, -euse [brədujœ:r, -ø:z], *F:* **1.** *a.* jabbering, mumbling. **2.** *s.* jabberer, mumbler.

breeder [bridœ:r], *s.m. Atom.Ph:* breeder (reactor).

bref, brève [brɛf, brɛv]. **1.** *a.* (*a*) brief, short; **soyez b.!** be brief! *F:* make it short! **répondre d'un ton b.,** to give a curt answer; **raconter qch. en b.,** to relate sth. in a few words, briefly; (*b*) *A:* of small stature; *Hist:* **Pépin le B.,** Pepin the Short. **2.** *adv.* briefly, in a word, in short; **b., il accepte,** in short, the long and the short of it is, to make a long story short, he accepts; **parler bref,** to speak curtly. **3.** *s.m.* (*a*) *Ecc:* (Papal) brief; (*b*) *Ecc:* ordo; (*c*) *Jur:* briefs, summary (of facts). **4.** *s.f.* **brève;** (*a*) short syllable; *s.a.* LONG 3; (*b*) *Mus:* (*plainsong*) breve; (*c*) *Tg:* **brèves et longues,** dots and dashes; (*d*) *Orn:* short-tail; **b. à ceinture bleue,** blue-banded pitta; **b. de Nouvelle-Guinée,** New Guinea black-headed pitta.

bregma [brɛgma], *s.m. Anat:* bregma.

bregmatique [brɛgmatik], *a. Anat:* bregmatic.

bréhaigne [breɛɲ], *a. O:* (*of mare, etc.*) barren, sterile.

breitschwanz [brɛtʃvɑ̃ts], *s.m.* broadtail.

brêlage [brɛla:ʒ], *s.m. Mil.E:* lashing; **corde de b.,** lashing (rope); **courroie de b.,** lashing strap.

brelan [brəlɑ̃], *s.m.* **1.** *Cards:* (*a*) brelan; (*b*) pair royal, threes, three of a kind; **avoir brelan d'as,** to have three aces. **2.** *A:* gaming house, gambling den.

brelau [brəlo], *s.m. Cost: A:* head-dress (of women in Bresse).

brêle [brɛl], *s.m Mil: P:* mule.

brêler [brɛle], *v.tr. Mil.E: etc:* to lash; to bind (sth.) fast; to rack-lash.

brelique-breloque [brəlikbrəlɔk], *adv.phr. A: F:* higgledy-piggledy, any way.

brelle [brɛl], *s.f.* (small) raft; float (of timber).

breller [brɛle], *v.tr.* = BRÊLER.

breloque [brəlɔk], *s.f.* **1.** charm, trinket; *esp.* watch-charm. **2.** (*a*) *Mil:* break-off; (drum-, bugle-call to) dismiss; **battre la b.,** (i) to sound the dismiss; (ii) to sound the "all clear" (after air-raid, etc.); (iii) *F:* to wander, ramble (in one's mind); (iv) *F:* (*of watch*) to go erratically; **mon cœur bat la b.,** my heart is (i) racing, (ii) giving out, (iii) playing me up; (*b*) *Navy:* "Disperse" (after action).

brelot [brəlo], *s.m.* = BRELAU.

breluche [brəlyʃ], *s.f.,* **breluchet** [brəlyʃɛ], *s.m. Tex: A:* drugget, linsey-woolsey, wincey.

brème [brɛm], *s.f.* **1.** *Ich:* bream; **b. de mer,** pomfret, Ray's bream, sea-tench, sea-bream. **2.** *P:* playing card.

Brême [brɛm], *Pr.n.f. Geog:* Bremen.

brémois, -oise [bremwa, -wa:z], *a. & s. Geog:* (native, inhabitant) of Bremen.

breneux, -euse [brənø, -ø:z], *a. P:* (*of linen*) soiled (with fecal matter).

brent(h)e [brɛ̃:t], *s.m. Ent:* brentid.

brenthides [brɛ̃ti:d], *s.m.pl. Ent:* Brent(h)idae.

brescian, -ane [brɛsjɑ̃, -an], *a. & s. Geog:* (native, inhabitant) of Brescia.

Brésil [brezil], *Pr.n.m. Geog:* Brazil; **bois de B.,** *s.m.* **b.,** Brazil wood, logwood, red dye-wood.

brésilien, -ienne [breziljɛ̃, -jɛn], *a. & s.* Brazilian.

brésiline [brezilin], *s.f. Ch:* brazilin.

brésiller [brezije]. **1.** *v.tr.* to break (sth.) into small pieces; to crumble; *F:* **à tout b.,** at top speed. **2.** *v.i. & pr.* to crumble.

brésillet [brezijɛ], *s.m. Bot: Com:* braziletto, Jamaica wood; **b. des Indes,** sapan-wood.

bressan, -ane [brɛsɑ̃, -an], *a. & s. Geog:* (native, inhabitant) of the Bresse region.

bressant [brɛsɑ̃], *s.f. Hairdr:* crew-cut.

bressuirais, -aise [brɛsɥirɛ, -ɛ:z], *a. & s. Geog:* (native, inhabitant) of Bressuire.

brestois, -oise [brɛstwa, -wa:z], *a. & s. Geog:* (native, inhabitant) of Brest.

Bretagne [brətaɲ], *Pr.n.f. Geog:* **1.** Brittany; **Basse-Bretagne,** Lower, Western, Brittany; **Haute-Bretagne,** Upper, Eastern, Brittany; *s.a.* NEVEU, NIÈCE, ONCLE, TANTE. **2.** Britain (in GRANDE-BRETAGNE, NOUVELLE-BRETAGNE, *q.v.*).

bretailler [brətɑje], *v.i. F:* **1.** to draw one's sword on the slightest provocation. **2.** to go in for fencing.

bretailleur [brətɑjœ:r], *s.m. F:* swashbuckler, fire-eater.

bretauder [brətode], *v.tr. Vet:* to castrate.

bretèche [brətɛʃ], *s.f.* **1.** *A: Fort: Arch:* (*a*) brattice; (*b*) bartizan. **2.** bay-, bow-window. **3.** *Arm:* nasal (of basinet).

bretelle [brətɛl], *s.f.* **1.** strap, brace, sling, suspender; **b. de fusil,** rifle-sling; *Mil:* **l'arme à la b.!** sling arms! *Av:* **bretelles,** shoulder harness; *A:* **passer par les bretelles,** to run the gauntlet. **2.** *Cost:* (*a*) shoulder-strap (of lady's garment); (*b*) **(paire de) bretelles,** (pair of) braces, *U.S:* suspenders; *F:* **en avoir jusqu'aux bretelles, par-dessus les bretelles,** (i) to be head over ears in trouble; (ii) to be very drunk. **3.** (*a*) *Rail:* scissors cross-over; (*b*) *Civ.E:* transversal road, oblique road; **b. de raccordement,** feeder road; (*c*) *Mil:* lateral position, transversal position, transversal trench.

bretellerie [brətɛlri], *s.f.* manufacture of or factory for braces, belts, etc.

bretellier, -ière [brətɛlje, -jɛ:r], *s.* maker of braces, belts, etc.

bretesse [brətɛs], *s.f.* = BRETÈCHE.

bretessé [brətese], *a. Her:* bretessé, crenellated on both sides.

breton, -onne [brətɔ̃, -ɔn]. **1.** *a. & s. Ethn: Ling: Geog:* Breton; *Lit:* **le cycle b.,** the Arthurian cycle of romance. **2.** *adv.phr. Nau:* **arrimé en b.,** stowed aburton. **3.** *s.f. Orn: F:* **(fauvette) bretonne,** warbler.

bretonnant [brətɔnɑ̃], *a.* of, pertaining to, Lower Britanny; **Breton b.,** Breton-speaking Breton.

brette [brɛt], *s.f. A:* long sword, rapier.

bretteler [brɛtle], *v.tr.* **(je brettelle** [brɛtɛl], **n. brettelons** [brɛtlɔ̃]; **je brettellerai)** to tool, tooth (stone, etc.); to hatch, chase (jewellery).

brettelure [brɛtly:r], *s.f.* (fine) hatching, chasing (on gold and silver plate).

bretter[1] [brɛte], *v.i. A:* to act the BRETTEUR, *q.v.*

bretter[2], *v.tr.* = BRETTELER.

bretteur [brɛtœ:r], *s.m. A:* swashbuckler, duelling bravo; **vie de b.,** swashbuckling life.

bretture [brɛty:r], *s.f.* **1.** notching, toothing, tooling (of stone with the gradine, etc.). **2.** notched-, toothed-work. **3.** *pl.* teeth (of notching implements).

bretzel [brɛtsɛl, -dzɛl], *s.m. Cu:* pretzel.

breuil [brœ:j], *s.m. Ven:* copse, brake, spinney.

breuvage [brœva:ʒ], *s.m.* **1.** beverage, drink. **2.** *Med:* draught, potion; *Vet:* drench.

brève. *See* BREF.

brevet [brəvɛ], *s.m.* **1.** (*a*) *A:* (letters) patent, (royal) warrant; *Mil: A:* **b. d'officier,** (King's, Queen's) commission; (*b*) **b. d'inventeur, b. d'invention,** (letters) patent; **bureau des brevets,** patent office; **prendre un b.,** to take out a patent; **possesseur du b.,** patentee. **2.** diploma, certificate; *Scouting:* badge; *Sch: A:* **b. élémentaire, de capacité** = school certificate; *A:* **b. supérieur,** higher school certificate; *Mil:* **b. d'état-major** = staff college certificate; *Nau:* **b. de capitaine,** master's certificate; **b. de capitaine au long cours,** certificate of competency as master of a foreign-going ship; **passer son b. de capitaine,** to obtain one's certificate; *F:* to get one's "ticket"; *Av:* **b. de pilote,** pilot's certificate; **passer son b. de pilote,** to qualify as a pilot. **3.** *Jur:* (*a*) **b. d'apprentissage,** indentures, articles; (*b*) **acte en b.,** contract delivered by notary in original.

brevetable [brəvtabl̩], *a.* patentable.

brevetaire [brəvtɛ:r], *s.m. A:* (*in ancien régime*) patentee.

breveté, -ée [brəvte]. **1.** (*a*) *s.* (i) patentee; (ii) person with a diploma; (*b*) *a.* (i) **fournisseur b. de sa Majesté,** (tradesman) by appointment to His, Her, Majesty; (ii) patented (invention); **b. sans garantie du Gouvernement,** patent without Government warranty (of quality); (iii) **inventeur b.,** inventor holding letters patent. **2.** *a.* certificated, qualified; **officier b. (d'état-major)** = officer holding a Staff College certificate, "passed Staff College."

breveter [brəvte], *v.tr.* **(je brevète, je brevette, n. brevetons; je brevèterai, je brevetterai) 1.** (*a*) *A:* to grant a (royal) warrant, letters patent, to (s.o.); (*b*) to grant a patent to (s.o.); (*c*) **se faire b. capitaine de vaisseau,** to qualify as captain of a ship; *F:* to get one's "ticket." **2.** to patent (invention); **faire b. une invention,** to take out a patent for an invention.

brévi- [brevi], *comb.fm.* brevi-; **brévifolié,** brevifoliate.

bréviaire [brevjɛ:r], *s.m. Ecc:* breviary.

brévicaude [breviko:d], *a. Z:* brevicaudate, short-tailed.

brévicaule [breviko:l], *a. Bot:* short-stemmed.

brévicipitidés [brevisipitide], *s.m.pl. Amph:* Brevicipitidae.

brévicorne [brevikɔrn], *a. Z:* short-horned.

bréviligne [breviliɲ], *a. & s.* short, squat, thick-set (person).

brévipède [brevipɛd], *a. Z:* breviped, short-footed, -legged.

brévipenne [brevipɛn], *a. Orn:* brevipennate.

brévirostre [breviroʃtr], *a. Orn:* brevirostrate, short-billed.

brévistyle [brevistil], *a. Bot:* short-styled, thrum-eyed (flower).

brévité [brevite], *s.f.* shortness (of vowel, speech, life).

brezel [brezɛl], *s. Cu:* = BRETZEL.

briançonnais, -aise [briɑ̃sɔnɛ, -ɛːz], *a. & s. Geog:* (native, inhabitant) of Briançon.

briard, -arde [briaːr, -ard]. **1.** *a. & s. Geog:* (native, inhabitant) of the Brie region. **2.** sheep-dog of the Brie region.

Briarée [briare], *Pr.n.m. Myth:* Briareus.

briarois, -oise [briarwa, -waːz], *a. & s. Geog:* (native, inhabitant) of Briare.

bribe [brib], *s.f.* **1.** *A:* hunch, chunk (of bread). **2.** *pl.* scraps, fragments, odds and ends; **ramasser des bribes de connaissances,** to pick up scraps of knowledge; **bribes de conversation,** snatches, scraps, of conversation; **apprendre qch. par bribes,** to learn sth. piecemeal, from scraps of conversation.

bric [brik], *s.m.* used only in BRIC-À-BRAC, *q.v.*, and in the adv.phrs: **de b. et de broc** [brɔk], from one source and another, here a little and there a little, haphazardly, when the opportunity occurs; **de b. ou de broc,** some way or other.

bric-à-brac [brikabrak], *s.m.* no *pl.*; odds and ends, curios, bric-à-brac; mess, jumble; **marchand de b.-à-b.,** dealer in old furniture, in curios, in old pictures; **boutique de b.-à-b.,** curiosity shop.

bricheton [briʃtɔ̃], *s.m. P:* **1.** loaf (of bread). **2.** *A:* food, *P:* grub.

brichetonner [briʃtɔne], *v.i. A: P:* to have a meal; *F:* to feed, grub.

brick [brik], *s.m. Nau:* brig; **brick-goélette,** schooner-brig.

bricolage [brikɔlaːʒ], *s.m. F:* pottering about, doing odd jobs; **du beau b.!** a nice bit of do-it-yourself! **un mordu, un passionné, du b.,** a do-it-yourself enthusiast.

bricole [brikɔl], *s.f.* **1.** strap; (*a*) breast-strap (for barrows, etc.); (*b*) breast-harness (of horse, etc.); (*c*) axle drag-rope (of gun); (*d*) *Mil: F:* Sam Browne (belt); (*e*) **b. de voiture,** carriage window-strap. **2.** (*a*) rebound, ricochet; **toucher le but par b.,** to make an indirect hit; (*b*) *Bill: Ten:* stroke off the cushion or off the wall; bricole; *Bill:* **jouer la b.,** to play off the cushion. **3.** *pl. Ven:* toils (for deer, etc.). **4.** *Fish:* (*a*) pair of hooks mounted back to back, double-hook; (*b*) ledger-line. **5.** *usu. pl. F:* odd jobs, piffling jobs, trifles, odds and ends; **s'occuper à des bricoles,** to potter about the house, to do odd jobs.

bricoler [brikɔle]. **1.** *v.tr.* to put the breast-harness on (horse). **2.** *F:* (*a*) *v.tr.* **b. une affaire** to arrange a piece of (often shady) business; **c'est une affaire bricolée,** it's a put-up job; **il a bricolé une table,** he's knocked together a table; **il a bricolé le moteur,** he's tinkered up the engine; **il a bricolé le compteur,** he's fiddled the meter; (*b*) *v.i.* to do odd jobs; **b. à la maison,** to potter, tinker, about the house. **3.** (*a*) *v.i. Ven:* (*of hound*) to quarter the ground; *v.tr. F:* (*of intoxicated pers.*) **b. le chemin,** to zigzag, tack, lurch, along the road; (*b*) *Bill:* to play off the cushion.

bricoleur, -euse [brikɔlœːr, -øːz], *F:* **1.** *a.* (*a*) handy (person); (*b*) pottering (person). **2.** *s.* (*a*) Jack-of-all-trades, handyman; (*b*) potterer; do-it-yourself man.

bricolier [brikɔlje], *s.m.* side (trace-)horse; off horse.

bridable [bridabl̩], *a.* (horse) that can be bridled.

bridage [bridaːʒ], *s.m.* **1,** (*a*) bridling; (*b*) curbing, checking; (*c*) trussing (of fowls); (*d*) clamping, fastening together. **2. b. de sauvetage,** rescue sling (for use in sewers, etc.).

bride [brid], *s.f.* **1.** (*a*) bridle; **mettre la b. à un cheval,** to bridle, put the bridle on, a horse; *Prov:* **à cheval donné on ne regarde pas à la b.,** one does not look a gift-horse in the mouth; (*b*) rein(s); **aller b. en main, mener un cheval par la b.,** to lead a horse; *F:* **aller b. en main dans une affaire,** to proceed cautiously, warily, in a business; **aller à b. abattue, à b. avalée, à toute b.,** to ride at full speed, to ride full tilt; *F:* to ride hell for leather; **accourir à b. abattue,** to gallop up; **la voiture nous emporta à toute b.,** the carriage drove off at full speed; *s.a.* TOURNER 1; **lâcher la b.,** to slacken the rein; **lâcher la b. à un cheval,** *F:* **à qn,** to give rein to a horse; *F:* to s.o.; to give a horse, s.o., his head; to give s.o. more liberty (than usual); **lâcher la b. à sa colère,** to give full rein, full vent, to one's anger; **laisser à un cheval,** *F:* **à qn, la b. sur le cou,** (i) to ride with loose rein, to give a horse his head; (ii) *F:* to give s.o. full liberty, to let s.o. have his own way; **tenir un cheval en b.,** to curb, check, a horse; *F:* **tenir qn en b.,** to keep s.o. within bounds, to keep a tight hand over s.o.; *F:* **tenir la b. haute à qn,** (i) to keep a tight rein on s.o.; (ii) to be high-handed with s.o.; **fureur sans b.,** unbridled fury. **2.** (*a*) string (of bonnet, etc.); *Cu:* trussing string; *Aer:* **b. d'amarrage,** mooring bridle; (*b*) *Needlew:* bar (of buttonhole, in embroidery, etc.); *Crochet:* treble; (*c*) *Mil:* **b. d'épaulette,** epaulette loop. **3.** *Mec.E: etc:* (*a*) strap, tie; **b. de bielle,** connecting-rod strap; **b. de serrage,** clamp, cramp; **b. à capote,** G cramp; **b. de ressort,** stirrup-piece, clip (of leaf-spring); (*b*) flange, collar (of cylinder, pipe, etc.); **b. d'échappement,** exhaust-flange; **b. d'obturation,** blank, blind, flange; **b. mobile,** loose flange; **b. de fermeture,** cover-band; **joint** *m*, **raccordement** *m*, **à b.,** flange-assembly, -connection, -coupling, -joint; **tuyau à brides,** flanged pipe; **façonnage de brides,** flanging; (*c*) thimble (joining two pipes); (*d*) *Surg: Path:* adhesion; bridle.

bridé [bride], *a.* **1.** bridled (horse, etc.). **2.** tied up, constricted; **avoir les yeux bridés,** to have slit eyes; **sourire b.,** constrained smile. **3.** *Mec.E: etc:* flanged.

bridement [bridmɑ̃], *s.m.* = BRIDAGE.

brider [bride], *v.tr.* **1.** (*a*) to bridle (horse); *F:* **b. son cheval, son âne, par la queue,** to start at the wrong end; **chacun bridera sa bête,** everyone will act as he thinks best; (*b*) **b. ses passions,** to check, restrain, curb, one's passions; (*c*) *Husb:* **b. une oie,** to pass a feather or a twig through the beak of a goose (to prevent it from straying); *F:* **c'est une oie bridée,** he, she, is a regular goose, a fool of fools. **2.** (*a*) to tie up, fasten (up); *Cu:* to truss (fowl); **b. son casque,** to tighten (up), the chin-strap of one's helmet; **mon habit me b. trop,** my coat is too tight for me; *Needlew:* **b. une boutonnière,** to bind a buttonhole, to finish off a buttonhole with a bar; (*b*) to lash, seize, frap (cable, etc.); to rack (two ropes); **b. un hauban,** to swift(er) a shroud; (*c*) to rack-lash (load); (*d*) to flange (tube, pipe); (*e*) to clamp (pipes).

bridge [bridʒ], *s.m.* **1.** *Cards:* bridge; **b. aux enchères,** auction bridge; **b. plafond, b. contrat,** contract bridge; **faire un b.,** to have a hand of bridge. **2.** *Dent:* bridge.

bridger [bridʒe], *v.i.* (**je bridgeai(s); n. bridgeons**) to play bridge.

bridgeur, -euse [bridʒœːr, -øːz], *s.* bridge-player.

bridon [bridɔ̃], *s.m.* snaffle(-bridle), bridoon; **conduire un cheval sur le b.,** to ride a horse on the snaffle.

bridonner [bridɔne], *v.tr.* to put a bridoon on (horse).

bridure [bridyːr], *s.f.* **1.** *Nau:* frapping, racking, seizing. **2.** *Cu:* trussing (of fowl).

Brie [bri]. **1.** *Pr.n.f. Geog:* district bordering on Champagne, with chief town Meaux. **2.** *s.m.* soft, flat cheese of the Brie district, brie.

brief, -ève [briɛf, -ɛːv], *a. A:* = BREF.

briefer [brife], *v.tr.* to brief.

briefing [brifiŋ], *s.m.* briefing.

brièvement [briɛvmɑ̃], *adv.* briefly, succinctly.

brièveté [briɛvte], *s.f.* **1.** shortness, brevity (of time). **2.** brevity, briefness, conciseness; **pour plus de b.,** for brevity's sake.

brif(f)e [brif], *s.f. F:* **1.** (*a*) **b. de pain,** chunk of bread; (*b*) food; *F:* grub. **2.** *P:* **avoir une fameuse b.,** to be as hungry as a hunter.

brif(f)ée [brife], *s.f. P:* square meal, blow-out.

brif(f)er [brife], *v.tr. F:* **1.** to devour, gobble, bolt (food); *Abs.* to eat, feed. **2.** *A:* to crumple, spoil, ruin (clothes).

brif(f)eton [briftɔ̃], *s.m. P:* bread.

brif(f)eur, -euse [brifœːr, -øːz], *s. P:* glutton, ravenous eater.

brigade [brigad], *s.f.* **1.** *Mil:* brigade; **être de b. avec qn, faire b. avec qn,** to be brigaded with s.o.; *Av:* **b. aérienne,** group, *U.S:* wing. **2.** (*a*) squad, body, party, detachment (of gendarmes, etc.); (*b*) gang, party (of workmen, etc.); **chef de b.,** foreman.

brigadier [brigadje], *s.m.* **1.** (*a*) *Mil:* (i) corporal (of mounted arms); (ii) *F:* brigadier-general; (*b*) **b. de police,** police sergeant; (*c*) *Civ.E:* (i) overseer; (ii) foreman. **2.** *Nau:* bowman, bow-oar(sman); *Row:* bow(-oar).

brigadier-chef [brigadjeʃɛf], *s.m. Mil:* lance-sergeant (mounted arms); *pl. brigadiers-chefs.*

brigand [brigɑ̃], *s.m.* (*a*) brigand, bandit; *A:* highwayman; **conter des histoires de brigands,** to tell fantastic lies, improbable stories; **extérieur de b.,** ruffianly appearance; (*b*) crook; *F:* **oh le b.!** oh, the rascal!

brigandage [brigɑ̃daːʒ], *s.m.* brigandage, highway robbery.

brigandeau, -eaux [brigɑ̃do], *s.m. F:* cheat, rascal, rogue; petty crook; (*esp. of lawyer*) shark.

brigander [brigɑ̃de], *v.i. F:* to rob, plunder.

briganderie [brigɑ̃dri], *s.f.* (act of) brigandage.

brigandine [brigɑ̃din], *s.f. A.Arms:* brigandine, brigantine.

brigantin [brigɑ̃tɛ̃], *s.m.* **1.** *Nau:* brigantine. **2.** camp-bed.

brigantine [brigɑ̃tin], *s.f. Nau:* spanker (sail); driver.

Bright [brait], *Pr.n. Med:* **mal de B.,** Bright's disease.

brightique [braitik]. **1.** *a.* pertaining to Bright's disease. **2.** *s.m.* & *f.* sufferer from Bright's disease.

brightisme [braitism], *s.m. Med:* Bright's disease.

bright stock [braitstɔk], *s.m. no pl. Petroleum Ind:* bright stock.

Brigitte [briʒit], *Pr.n.f.* Bridget.

brigittin, -ine [briʒitɛ̃, -in], *a. & s. Ecc:* brigitine, bridgetine (monk, nun).

brignolais, -aise [briɲɔlɛ, -ɛːz], *a. & s. Geog:* (native, inhabitant) of Brignoles.

brignole [briɲɔl], *s.f.* (Brignoles) plum or prune.

brigue [brig], *s.f.* **1.** intrigue; underhand work; corrupt practices. **2.** cabal.

briguer [brige], *v.tr.* **1.** to solicit, to canvass for, cast about for (sth.); to court (s.o.'s favour); **b. des voix dans une région,** to canvass (for votes) in a district, to canvass a district for votes. **2.** to try to obtain (a post, etc.) by intrigue, by underhand manœuvring.

brigueur, -euse [brigœːr, -øːz], *s.m. & f.* (*a*) intriguer, schemer; (*b*) **b. d'éloges,** person who fishes for praise.

brillamment [brijamɑ̃], *adv.* brilliantly.

brillance [brijɑ̃ːs], *s.f.* brilliance; *Opt:* brilliancy (of image, of source of light); *T.V:* brightness (of image, screen); *Mus:* brightness of tone.

brillant [brijɑ̃]. **1.** *a.* brilliant; (*a*) sparkling, glittering, bright (light, gem, colour, etc.); sparkling (conversation); **yeux brillants,** sparkling eyes; **acier b.,** bright steel; *F:* **b. comme un sou neuf,** as bright as a button; *s.a.* PAPIER 1; (*b*) splendid, striking; **b. orateur,** brilliant speaker; **spectacle b.,** splendid sight; **d'une intelligence brillante,** brilliantly intelligent; **il est le plus b. de la classe,** he is the brightest boy in the class; (*c*) **b. de jeunesse,** radiant with youth; **je ne suis pas b.,** I'm not over-grand, not feeling too well; **la situation n'est pas brillante,** the situation is far from brilliant. **2.** *s.m.* (*a*) brilliancy, brilliance, brightness, lustre, glitter (of gem, metal, etc.); glossiness (of paper, material); (*b*) polish, shine (on boots, buttons, etc.); (*c*) *O:* **b. pour les ongles,** nail-polish. **3.** *s.m.* brilliant (diamond); **faux b.,** (piece of) paste, imitation diamond; **pierre montée en b.,** stone mounted as a brilliant.

brillantage [brijɑ̃taːʒ], *s.m.* polishing (of leather, steel, jewels, etc.).

brillanté [brijɑ̃te]. **1.** *a.* glossed, glossy; **fil b.,** bright-silk (thread); **style b.,** showy, glossy, style. **2.** *s.m.* (*a*) *Tex:* dimity, (glazed) jaconet; (*b*) machine-made lace, artificial lace.

brillanter [brijɑ̃te], *v.tr.* **1.** to impart brilliancy, glitter, to (sth.); to polish; *Tex:* to gloss (thread); **b. son style,** to write in a showy style. **2.** to cut (diamond) into a brilliant.

se brillanter, to acquire brilliancy, to begin to sparkle.

brillanteur [brijɑ̃tœːr]. *Metalw:* **1.** *a.* **agent b.,** brightener. **2.** *s.m.* brightener.

brillantine [brijɑ̃tin], *s.f.* **1.** brilliantine (cosmetic). **2.** *Dressm:* glazed lining.

brillantiner [brijɑ̃tine], *v.tr.* to brilliantine, put brilliantine on (s.o.'s hair).

se brillantiner, to brilliantine one's hair.

brillement [brijmɑ̃], *s.m. A:* brilliance, sparkle; shining.

briller [brije], *v.i.* to shine. **1.** (*of steel*) to glisten, to glint; (*of candle, water*) to glimmer; (*of stars*) to glitter, sparkle, twinkle; (*of moon, satin*) to shimmer; (*of gold*) to glitter, to glisten; (*of headlights*) to glare; (*of sunrise*) to gleam; (*of embers*) to glow; **b. par moments, çà et là,** to glint. **2.** *F:* **b. dans la, par sa, conversation,** to shine in conversation; **faire b. qch.,** to set off, enhance, sth. (by contrast); **faire b. ses invités,** to draw out one's guests; **faire b. sa fille,** to show off one's daughter; **b. par son absence,** to be conspicuous by one's absence; *Prov:* **tout ce qui brille n'est pas or,** all that glitters, glistens, is not gold.

brillot(t)er [brijɔte], *v.i. F:* to shine, glitter, faintly; to glimmer, to shimmer.

brimade [brimad], *s.f.* **1.** rough joke (played on freshmen, recruits, or new boys). **2.** *pl.* (*a*) ragging, *U.S:* hazing; (*b*) persecution, bullying, victimization.

brimbale [brɛ̃bal], *s.f. Mec.E:* **1.** balance; rocker-arm; rocking-lever, -shaft. **2.** handle, lever (of pump); (pump-)brake.

brimbalement [brɛ̃bal(ə)mã], *s.m.* (*a*) swinging (to and fro), dangling; (*b*) wobbling (of wheel).

brimbaler [brɛ̃bale]. **1.** *v.i.* (*a*) to swing (to and fro), to dangle; (*b*) (*of wheel*) to wobble. **2.** *v.tr. F:* to carry, cart, (sth.) about.

brimbelle [brɛ̃bɛl], *s.f. F:* whortleberry, bilberry, *U.S:* huckleberry.

brimbellier [brɛ̃bɛlje], *s.m. F:* whortleberry, bilberry, *U.S:* huckleberry (bush).

brimborion [brɛ̃bɔrjɔ̃], *s.m.* (*a*) knick-knack; (*b*) trifle; (*c*) small child, mite.

brimer [brime], *v.tr.* (*a*) to rag, *U.S:* haze (recruit, freshman, new boy); (*b*) to persecute; to bully; to victimize; **il se croyait brimé,** he felt he was being victimized, picked on, got at.

brimeur [brimœ:r], *s.m.* bully (at school).

brin [brɛ̃], *s.m.* **1.** (*a*) shoot (of tree); **arbre de b.,** tree with a single straight stem; sapling; *Com:* **bois de b.,** timber in the log; *F:* **un beau b. de fille,** a fine strapping girl, a handsome girl; (*b*) blade (of grass, corn); sprig, twig (of myrtle, etc.); spray (of mimosa); wisp (of straw). **2.** *F:* bit, jot, fragment; **pas un b. de pain,** not a scrap of bread, not a crumb of bread; **un b. d'air,** a breath of air; **aller prendre un b. d'air,** to go for a breather; **avec un b. d'envie,** with a touch of envy; **b. de consolation,** grain, crumb, of comfort; **b. à b.,** little by little, bit by bit; *F:* **un b. de toilette,** (i) a lick and a promise; (ii) a quick wash and brush up; **un b. de regret,** a shade of regret; **un b. de causette,** a bit of a chat. **3.** staple (of wool, flax, etc.); ply (of wool); strand (of rope, wire, etc.); *Tex:* **cordage de premier b.,** ropes made of the finest hemp; **laine en trois brins,** three-ply wool. **4.** (*a*) **b. d'éventail,** stick, rib, of a fan; **canne à pêche à trois brins,** three-piece fishing rod; **gros b.,** butt (of rod); (*b*) *W.Tel:* **brins d'une antenne,** wires of an aerial; *Mec.E:* **b. tendu, conducteur,** driving side (of belt); **b. mou, conduit,** slack side; *Nau: etc:* **b. libre d'une corde,** free end of a rope; **b. mort,** dead end. **5.** *adv.* **il est un b. ennuyeux,** he is a trifle boring, a bit of a bore.

brinde [brɛ̃:d], *s.f. A:* toast; *P:* **être dans les brindes,** to be in one's cups; *P:* to be squiffy.

brindezingue [brɛ̃dzɛ̃:g], *s.f. P:* **être (en) b., être dans les brindezingues,** to be in one's cups; *P:* to be squiffy; to be three sheets in the wind.

brindille [brɛ̃di:j], *s.f.* (*a*) sprig, twig; (*b*) *pl.* brushwood.

Brinell [brinel], *s.m. Metall:* Brinell machine.

bringé [brɛ̃ʒe], *a.* brindled (cow, etc.).

bringue¹ [brɛ̃:g], *s.f. F:* **1.** piece, bit; **en bringues,** (i) in bits, in rags and tatters; (ii) at sixes and sevens. **2.** raw-boned horse; **grande b. de femme,** big gawk of a woman.

bringue², *s.f. P:* spree; **faire la b.,** to be, go, on the spree.

bringuebale [brɛ̃gbal], *s.f.* = BRIMBALE.

bringuebaler [brɛ̃gbale], **brinquebal(l)er** [brɛ̃kbale], *v.* = BRIMBALER.

brinvillière [brɛ̃vilje:r], *s.f. Bot:* demerara pink-root.

brio [bri(j)o], *s.m. Mus:* **con b.,** con brio; **parler avec b.,** to talk brilliantly, with spirit.

briochain, -aine [briɔʃɛ̃, -ɛn], *a. & s. Geog:* (native, inhabitant) of Saint-Brieuc.

brioche [briɔʃ, -ijɔʃ], *s.f.* **1.** *Cu:* brioche; *F:* **faire une b.,** to make a blunder, a bloomer. **2.** *F:* droppings of horses, mules, etc. **3.** *F:* stomach; **prendre de la b.,** to develop a paunch.

brioché [briɔʃe], *a. Bak:* **pain b.** = milk bread.

briochin, -ine [briɔʃɛ̃, -in], *a. & s.* = BRIOCHAIN.

briolette [briɔlɛt], *s.f. Lap:* briolette.

brion¹ [briɔ̃], *s.m. N.Arch:* fore-foot, gripe (of ship's stem).

brion², *s.m. Moss:* Bryum.

briotin, -ine [briɔtɛ̃, -in], *a. & s.* (native, inhabitant) of Briey.

briquage [brika:ʒ], *s.m. Nau:* holystoning.

briquaillon [brikajɔ̃], *s.m.* brickbat.

brique [brik], *s.f.* **1.** (*a*) brick; **b. crue,** sun-dried, air-dried, brick; **b. cuite,** burnt brick; **b. vernissée,** glazed brick; **b. à four, hollandaise,** clinker; **b. tubulaire, creuse,** hollow brick; **b. tendre,** rubber; **b. de verre,** glass brick; **terre à b.,** brick-clay; **poussière de b.,** brick-dust; **maison de, en, briques,** brick house; **lancer des**

bouts de b. à qn, to shy brickbats at s.o.; *P:* **bouffer des briques,** to live on air; (*b*) **b. à paver,** flag, tile. **2.** (*a*) **b. anglaise,** Bath brick; (*b*) *Nau:* **b. à pont, à briquer,** holystone. **3.** **b. de savon,** bar of soap. **4.** *P:* million (old) francs. **5.** *a.* brick-red.

briquer [brike], *v.tr. Nau:* to holystone (deck); *F:* to scrub.

se briquer, *F:* to polish oneself up.

briquet¹ [brike], *s.m.* **1.** (*a*) flint and steel, strike-a-light, tinder-box; **pierre à b.,** flint; **battre le b.,** (i) to strike a light; (ii) *F:* to knock one's ankles (in walking); (*b*) gas-lighter; **b. (à gaz, à essence),** (pipe)lighter, (cigarette-)lighter; (*c*) *Ph:* **b. pneumatique, b. à air,** fire syringe. **2.** *Mil: A:* short curved (infantry) sword. **3.** *Join:* flap-hinge.

briquet², *s.m.* beagle.

briquet³, *s.m. Min:* (*in N. France, Belgium*) snack.

briquetage [brikta:ʒ], *s.m.* **1.** (*a*) brickwork; (*b*) imitation brickwork. **2.** (*a*) *Const:* bricking; (*b*) *Metall:* briquetting.

briqueter [brikte], *v.tr.* (**je briquette, n. briquetons;** **je briquetterai**) (*a*) to brick (sth.); to pave or face (sth.) with bricks; (*b*) to face (wall) in imitation brickwork; (*c*) to briquette (coal dust, metal powders).

briqueterie [briktri], *s.f.* **1.** brick-field, -works, brickyard. **2.** brick-kiln. **3.** brick-making.

briqueteur [briktœ:r], *s.m.* bricklayer, brick-setter.

briquetier [briktje], *s.m.* brick-maker.

briqueton [briktɔ̃], *s.m.* brickbat; half-brick.

briquette [brikɛt], *s.f.* briquette; compressed block of patent fuel; compressed slack.

bris [bri], *s.m.* **1.** breaking (of seals, glass, etc.); breaking, breakage (of piston-rod, etc.); break-up (of ship, etc.); *Jur:* (*a*) smashing of, wilful damage to (anything of value); (*b*) **b. de prison,** prison breaking; **b. de clôture,** breach of close. **2.** *A: Nau:* (fragments of) wreckage.

brisable [brizabl], *a.* breakable.

brisance [brizɑ̃:s], *s.f. Exp:* brisance; shattering properties.

brisant [brizɑ̃]. **1.** *a.* (*a*) **explosif b.,** high explosive; **obus b.,** high-explosive shell; (*b*) *Nau:* **lame brisante,** breaker. **2.** *s.m.* (*a*) half-submerged rock; reef, shoal; (*b*) *pl.* **brisants,** broken water, breakers; **des brisants devant!** breakers ahead! (*c*) = BRISE-LAMES.

briscard [briska:r], *s.m.* = BRISQUARD.

brise [bri:z], *s.f.* (*a*) breeze; **b. de mer, de terre,** on-shore, off-shore, breeze; **jolie b.,** moderate breeze; *Nau:* **bonne b.,** fresh breeze; **forte b.,** stiff breeze.

brisé¹ [brize], *a.* **1.** broken; (*a*) *F:* **être tout b.,** to be sore, aching, all over; **b. de fatigue,** tired out; (*b*) *Her:* brisé. **2.** (*a*) folding (door, shutter, bedstead, etc.); (*b*) *Bookb:* **dos b.,** round back; *s.a.* COMBLE¹ 2, LIGNE 1.

brisé², *s.m. Danc:* brisé.

brise-arcs [brizark], *a.inv. El.E:* non-arcing (device, etc.).

brise-bise [brizbi:z], *s.m.inv.* **1.** draught excluder (for doors and windows). **2.** short window curtain, brise-bise.

brise-circuit [brizsirkɥi], *s.m.inv. O: El.E:* **1.** make and break key, circuit-breaker. **2.** cut-out; fuse-box.

brise-copeau [brizkɔpo], *s. Tchn:* chip breaker; *pl.* **brise-copeaux.**

brisées [brize], *s.f.pl.* **1.** *Ven:* (*a*) broken boughs (to mark, track, run, of deer in wood); (*b*) track (of deer, etc.); *F:* **suivre les b. de qn,** to follow in s.o.'s footsteps, to follow s.o.'s lead or example; **aller, courir, sur les b. de qn,** to rival s.o., to compete with s.o.; **revenir sur ses b.,** to retrace one's steps. **2.** (forester's) marks (to indicate limits of cutting).

brise-fer [brizfɛ:r], *s.m. or f. inv.* = BRISE-TOUT.

brise-glace [brizglas], *s.m.* **1.** (*a*) ice-fender, starling, ice-apron (of a bridge pier); (*b*) ice-beam (of ship). **2.** ice-breaker (ship); *pl.* **brise-glace(s).**

brise-jet [brizʒɛ], *s.m.inv.* (ajutage) b.-jet, anti-splash (tap)-nozzle.

brise-lames [brizlam, -ɑ:m], *s.m.inv.* **1.** break-water, mole. **2.** groyne (across beach).

brisement [brizmã], *s.m.* **1.** breaking (of waves, of images, etc.); shattering; **b. de cœur,** heart-break. **2.** *Aut:* rear panel.

brise-mottes [brizmɔt], *s.m.inv. Agr:* clod-crusher, brake-harrow.

briser [brize], *v.tr.* to break, smash, shatter; (*a*) **se b. une jambe,** to break one's leg; **se b. la santé,** to ruin one's health; **b. une porte,** to break open, burst open, a door; **b. une glace en mille morceaux,** to shiver, shatter, a mirror; **b. qch. en**

éclats, to smash sth. to fragments; *F:* into smithereens; to break sth. to shivers; to splinter sth.; (*b*) to break up (clods of earth, ship, etc.); to pound up, crush (ore, etc.); *Tex:* to brake (hemp); **b. un mot en syllabes,** to break up a word into syllables; **brisé par la douleur,** crushed by grief; (*c*) to break (treaty, s.o.'s will, s.o.'s heart, etc.); to crush (opposition); to suppress (revolt); **b. ses liens,** *Lit:* to burst one's bonds asunder; **b. ses fers,** to break one's chains; *F:* **b. les fers de qn,** to free s.o., set s.o. free; **b. toute résistance,** to break down all resistance; **b. la résistance de qn,** to break down s.o.'s resistance, to wear s.o. down; **b. les espérances de qn,** to blight s.o.'s hopes; **b. le courage de qn,** to break s.o.'s courage, spirit; **une existence brisée,** a wrecked life; **j'ai le cœur brisé,** my heart is broken; (*d*) to break off (conversation, speech, etc.); *abs.* **brisons là,** enough said, let us say no more about it; *Box:* **b. un corps-à-corps,** to break a clinch, to make boxers break away; (*e*) *abs.* **b. avec qn,** to break with s.o.; (*f*) *Ph:* to refract (ray).

se briser. 1. (*of china, glass, heart, etc.*) to break; **cela se brise comme du verre,** it is as brittle as glass; **son cœur se brisait,** her heart was breaking. **2.** to break up, to be shattered, dashed to pieces; (*of mast, etc.*) to shiver; **le navire s'est brisé en deux,** the ship broke her back. **3.** *A:* (*of bedstead, shutter, etc.*) to fold up. **4.** *Ph:* (*of rays*) to be or become refracted.

brise-reins [brizrɛ̃], *s.m.inv. Wr:* back-breaker.

brise-roc [brizrok], *s.m.inv. Civ.E:* rock-breaker.

brise-soleil [brizsɔlɛ:j], *s.m.inv. Const:* brise-soleil.

brise-tout [briztu], *s.m. or f. inv.* person, child, who breaks everything; destructive child; **c'est un b.-t.,** he's like a bull in a china-shop.

briseur, -euse [brizœ:r, -ø:z], *s.* breaker, shatterer; **b. d'idoles,** breaker of images, icono-clast; **b. de grève,** strike breaker.

brise-vent [brizvã], *s.m.inv. Hort: etc:* windbreak, windscreen, shelter belt.

Brisgau [brizgo], *Pr.n.m. Geog:* Breisgau.

brisis [brizi], *s.m. Const:* break, lower slope (of mansard roof).

briska [briska], *s.m. Veh:* britzska.

brisoir [brizwa:r], *s.m. Tex:* brake, breaker (for hemp or flax).

brisquard [briska:r], *s.m. O: P:* old soldier, veteran.

brisque [brisk], *s.f.* **1.** *Cards:* (*a*) (*in bezique*) ace or ten; (*b*) (*game*) brisque, matrimony. **2.** *Mil: F:* (*a*) long-service badge; stripe; war-service chevron; (*b*) *P:* **une vieille b.,** an old soldier, a veteran.

Bristol [bristɔl]. **1.** *Pr.n.m. Geog:* Bristol. **2.** *s.m.* (*a*) Bristol-board; *F: O:* **déposer un b. chez qn,** to leave one's visiting card on s.o.; (*b*) *Needlew:* perforated cardboard (for embroidery).

brisure [brizy:r], *s.f.* **1.** break, crack, fissure, flaw. **2.** break (of hinge); folding-joint (of shutter); *O:* **porte à brisures,** folding door. **3.** *Her:* difference, mark of cadency; brisure; **b. déshonorante,** abatement. **4.** fragment (of shell, etc.); **brisures de riz,** broken rice. **5.** *F:* long-firm trickery, fraud.

britannique [britanik], (*a*) *a.* British; **les Iles Britanniques,** the British Isles; **Sa Majesté Britannique,** His, Her, Britannic Majesty; (*b*) *s.m. & f.* Briton, British subject, *U.S:* Britisher; *pl.* the British.

brittonique [britɔnik], *a. & s.m. Ling:* Brythonic.

brivadois, -oise [brivadwa, -wa:z], *a. & s. Geog:* (native, inhabitant) of Brioude.

briviste [brivist], *a. & s.m. & f.,* **brivois, -oise** [brivwa, -wa:z], *a. & s., Geog:* (native, inhabitant) of Brive.

brize [bri:z], *s.f.,* **briza** [briza], *s.f. Bot:* briza; quaking-grass.

broc¹ [bro], *s.m.* pitcher, (large) jug; **b. de tonnelier,** cellar jug (for drawing wine); **b. (de toilette),** (porcelain or enamelled) water jug or can.

broc² [brɔk], used only in the adv.phr.; **de bric ou (or et) de b.,** *s.a.* BRIC.

broc³ [brɔk], *s.m.* (*a*) *A:* spit; **manger qch. de b. en bouche,** to eat sth. straight off the spit; (*b*) **faire qch. de b. en bouche,** to do sth. straight off, right off.

broc⁴ [brɔk], *s.f. P:* **ça ne vaut pas une b.,** it's not worth a brass farthing.

brocage [broka:ʒ], *s.m.,* **brocaille** [brokaj], *s.f. Civ. E:* rubble, waste stones (for road making).

brocantage [brokɑ̃ta:ʒ], *s.m.* dealing in second-hand goods; **faire le b.,** to buy and sell.

brocante [brɔkɑ̃:t], *s.f. F:* **1.** general dealing in second-hand goods. **2.** trifling deal, small bargain. **3.** *O:* odd job, extra work (done in spare time).

brocanter [brɔkɑ̃te]. **1.** *v.i.* to deal in second-hand goods, in curios; to buy and sell. **2.** *v.tr. F:* (*a*) **b. ses bijoux, ses effets,** to sell one's jewels, one's effects (to a second-hand dealer); (*b*) to barter, exchange (goods).

brocanteur, -euse [brɔkɑ̃tœ:r, -ø:z], *s.m. & f.* second-hand dealer; broker; **magasin de b.,** second-hand shop; junk shop.

brocard[1] [brɔka:r], *s.m.* gibe, lampoon, squib; **lancer des brocards contre qn,** to lampoon s.o.; **lancer des brocards à qn,** to gibe at s.o.; **il est l'objet de brocards de la part de tout le quartier,** he is the butt of the whole place.

brocard[2], *s.m. Ven:* yearling (male) roe-deer, pricket; brocket.

brocard[3], *s.m. Metall:* ore-crushing mill plant.

brocarder [brɔkarde], *v.tr. F:* to gibe at (s.o.); to lampoon (s.o.); to launch squibs at (s.o.).

brocart[1] [brɔka:r], *s.m. Tex:* brocade.

brocart[2], *s.m. Ven:* = BROCARD[2].

brocatelle [brɔkatɛl], *s.f.* **1.** *Tex:* brocatelle; coarse brocade. **2.** brocatel(lo), clouded marble.

Brocéliande [brɔseljɑ̃:d], *Pr.n. Lit:* Broceliande (in Brittany).

brochage [brɔʃa:ʒ], *s.m.* **1.** *Bookb:* stitching, sewing; **b. au fil de fer,** wire-stitching; stapling. **2.** *Tex:* brocading, figuring, figure-weaving (of stuffs). **3.** *Metalw:* drifting (of rivet-hole, etc.). **4.** *Mec.E:* broaching.

brochant [brɔʃɑ̃], *a. Her:* brochant, brouchant; overlying; *F:* **et b. sur le tout . . .,** and to crown all . . ., to cap it all. . . .

brochantite [brɔʃɑ̃tit], *s.f. Miner:* brochantite.

broche [brɔʃ], *s.f.* **1.** *Cu:* (*a*) spit; **mettre un poulet à la b.,** to spit a chicken; (*b*) **b. de boucher,** meat skewer. **2.** *Tchn:* (*a*) peg, pin; **b. de tente,** tent-peg; **b. de charnière,** hinge-pin; **b. de tour,** lathe spindle; **b. d'une roue,** wedge, key, of a wheel; **b. d'une serrure,** brooch, gudgeon, of a lock; key-pin; **b. d'un tonneau,** spile, spigot, of a cask; *El:* **fiche à deux broches,** two-pin plug; *Metall:* **b. (de moule en terre),** prod; (*b*) drift (-pin); tommy(-bar, -rod); (*c*) *A: Sm.a:* **cartouche, fusil, à b.,** pin-fire cartridge, gun. **3.** *Tex:* spindle; *s.a.* BANC 3. **4.** *Cost:* brooch; **queue de b.,** brooch-pin. **5.** *Fin:* (*a*) sheaf of small bills pinned together; (*b*) bill of exchange (for a small amount). **6.** (*a*) *pl. Ven:* tusks (of boar); (*b*) pricket, dag (of roe-deer). **7.** *Mec.E:* cutting tool (of a broaching machine). **8.** *Dent:* broach; *Surg:* pin. **9.** knitting-needle, -pin.

broché [brɔʃe]. **1.** *a.* brocaded, broché; **b. d'or,** brocaded in gold. **2.** *s.m.* (*a*) brocading (of stuffs); (*b*) brocaded stuff, figured stuff, broché; (*c*) figure, pattern (on brocaded stuff).

brochée [brɔʃe], *s.f. Cu:* spitful (of meat, fowls).

brocher [brɔʃe], *v.tr.* **1.** *Tex:* to brocade, figure (stuffs). **2.** *Bookb:* to stitch, sew (book); **b. au fil de fer,** to wire-stitch, to staple; **livre broché,** paper-backed, paper-covered, book; paperback; *F:* **b. un travail,** to scamp a piece of work. **3.** (*a*) to peg (skins, heels of boots, etc.); to drive (nails in horse-shoeing); (*b*) to drift (rivet-hole). **4.** *v.i. Her:* **pièce qui broche sur une autre,** charge overlying another; *F:* **pour brocher sur le tout . . .,** to crown all . . ., to cap it all. . . . **5.** *Mec.E:* to broach.

se brocher, se b. sur le tout, to come on top of everything else.

brochet [brɔʃɛ], *s.m. Ich:* pike; **b. de mer,** sea-pike, snook.

brocheter [brɔʃte], *v.tr.* **(je brochette, n. brochetons; je brochetterai) 1.** to skewer (fowl, etc.). **2.** to fix (roast) to the spit. **3.** to pin, peg (skin on the ground, clothes on a line, etc.).

brocheton [brɔʃtɔ̃], *s.m. Fish:* pickerel, young pike; jack.

brochette [brɔʃɛt], *s.f.* **1.** *Cu:* skewer; small spit, brochette; **rognons à la b.,** broiled kidneys. **2.** (*a*) brochette (for medals, etc.); **b. de décorations,** row of decorations; (*b*) row (of people, etc.). **3.** stick (for feeding young birds); **élever des oiseaux à la b.,** to feed birds by hand; *O:* **enfant élevé à la b.,** daintily reared child.

brocheur, -euse [brɔʃœ:r, -ø:z], *s.* **1.** *s.m. & f.* (*a*) *Bookb:* (i) stitcher, sewer; (ii) stitching-room foreman; (*b*) *Tex:* brocade weaver. **2.** *s.f.* **brocheuse** (*a*) *Bookb:* (i) stitching-machine; (ii) staple press; stapler; (*b*) *Mec.E:* broaching machine, broacher. **3.** *s.m. Tex:* brocade loom.

brochoir [brɔʃwa:r], *s.m. Farr:* shoeing-hammer.

brochure [brɔʃy:r], *s.f.* **1.** *Bookb:* (*a*) stitching, sewing (of books); (*b*) book-stitching trade. **2.** booklet, brochure. **3.** *Tex:* inwoven, brocaded, pattern.

brocoli [brɔkɔli], *s.m. Hort:* (sprouting) broc(c)oli.

brodequin [brɔdkɛ̃], *s.m.* **1.** (stout) laced boot, ankle-boot; *A:* brodekin, brodequin; (woman's) half-boot; *Mil:* ammunition boot, service shoe. **2.** the sock (in the drama of the ancients); *Lit:* **chausser le b.,** to put on the sock, to take to comedy; *cf.* COTHURNE. **3.** *pl. Hist:* (the torture of) the boot.

broder [brɔde], *v.tr.* to embroider; **b. un mouchoir,** to embroider a handkerchief; **b. des fleurs sur un tissu,** to embroider flowers on a material; **un mouchoir brodé main,** a hand-embroidered handkerchief; *F:* **b. une histoire,** to embroider, embellish, a story; **donner les faits sans b.,** to state the bare facts; *s.a.* CANEVAS.

broderie [brɔdri], *s.f.* **1.** (*a*) embroidery, (i) piece of embroidery; (ii) embroidery work, embroidering; tambour-work; tapestry-work, gros-point; **broderies d'or,** gold-lace embroidery; **b. anglaise,** broderie Anglaise; **b. blanche,** fancy needlework (on lingerie, etc.); (*b*) *F:* embellishment, embroidery (in narrative); **ajouter des broderies au canevas,** to embellish a bare narrative; *Mus:* **broderies,** graces. **2.** embroidery shop. **3.** *Hort:* box edging (to bed).

brodeur, -euse [brɔdœ:r, -ø:z], *s.* **1.** (*a*) embroiderer, embroideress; (*b*) *F:* embellisher (of story); exaggerator. **2. b. mécanique,** *s.f.* **brodeuse,** embroidering-machine.

brodoir [brɔdwa:r], *s.m.* frame for braid-making.

brogue [brɔg], *s.f. Cost:* brogue.

broie [brwɑ], *s.f.* **1.** *Tex:* brake (for hemp and flax). **2.** *Agr:* brake-harrow.

broiement, broîment [brwamɑ̃], *s.m.* grinding, crushing, pounding, pulverizing; *Tex:* braking, hackling (of hemp); *Med:* **syndrome de b.,** crush syndrome.

broigne [brwaɲ], *s.f. A.Arms:* broigne, byrnie.

bromacétique [brɔmasetik], *a. Ch:* bromacetic, bromoacetic.

bromacétone [brɔmasetɔn], *s.f. Ch:* bromacetone, bromoacetone.

bromal [brɔmal], *s.m. Ch:* bromal.

bromargyre [brɔmarʒir], *s.f.,* **bromargyrite** [brɔmarʒirit], *s.f. Miner:* bromargyrite, bromyrite.

bromate [brɔmat], *s.m. Ch:* bromate.

bromation [brɔmasjɔ̃], *s.f. Ch:* bromination.

brome[1] [bro:m], *s.m. Ch:* bromine.

brome[2], *s.m. Bot:* Bromus, brome-grass.

bromé [brome], *a. Ch:* brominated.

bromélia [brɔmelja], *s.m.,* **bromélie** [brɔmeli], *s.f. Bot:* Bromelia.

broméliacées [brɔmeljase], *s.f.pl. Bot:* Bromeliaceae.

bromer [brome], *v.tr. Ch:* to brominate.

bromhydrate [brɔmidrat], *s.m. Ch:* hydrobromide.

bromhydrique [brɔmidrik], *a. Ch:* hydrobromic (acid).

bromidrose [brɔmidro:z], *s.f.* bromhidrosis; *Med:* bromidrosis.

bromique [brɔmik], *a. Ch:* bromic (acid).

bromisme [brɔmism], *s.m. Med:* bromism, brominism, bromidism.

bromite [brɔmit], *s.f. Miner:* bromargyrite, bromyrite.

bromlite [brɔmlit], *s.f. Miner:* bromlite.

bromobenzène [brɔmɔbɛ̃zɛn], *s.m. Ch:* bromobenzene.

bromoforme [brɔmɔfɔrm], *s.m. Med:* bromoform.

bromoïl [brɔmɔil], *s.m. A.Phot:* **procédé b.,** bromoil process.

bromuration [brɔmyrasjɔ̃], *s.f.* **1.** *Phot:* bromide process. **2.** *Ch:* = HALOGÉNATION.

bromure [brɔmy:r], *s.m. Ch:* bromide; *Phot:* **papier au b.,** bromide paper; *F:* **bromure,** print (on bromide paper).

bromurer [brɔmyre], *v.tr. Ch:* to bromize; *Phot:* **b. le révélateur,** to add bromide to the developer.

bromus [brɔmys], *s.m.* = BROME[2].

bromyrite [brɔmirit], *s.f. Miner:* bromyrite, bromargyrite.

bronchade [brɔ̃ʃad], *s.f. Equit: A:* flounder (of horse); stumble.

bronche [brɔ̃:ʃ], *s.f. Anat:* bronchus, *pl.* bronchi; **b. souche,** (right or left) bronchus; **b. lobaire,** lobe; **b. extra-lobulaire,** bronchium, branch; **b. intralobulaire,** bronchiole.

bronchectasie [brɔ̃ʃɛktazi], *s.f. Med:* bronchiectasis.

bronchement [bfɔ̃ʃmɑ̃], *s.m.* (*rare*) (*a*) stumbling (of horse); (*b*) shying.

broncher [brɔ̃ʃe], *v.i.* **1.** (*of horse*) (*a*) to stumble, to flounder; *Prov:* **il n'y a si bon cheval qui ne bronche,** it's a good horse that never stumbles; (*b*) to shy. **2.** *F:* (*a*) to falter, waver, flinch; **sans b.,** without flinching, without wincing, without turning a hair; **il n'a pas bronché,** he didn't turn a hair, he never blenched; (*b*) to budge, move, stir.

bronchial, -aux [brɔ̃ʃjal, -o], *a. O:* = BRONCHIQUE.

bronchiectasie [brɔ̃ʃjɛktazi], *s.f. Med:* bronchiectasis.

bronchiole [brɔ̃ʃjɔl], *s.f. Anat:* bronchiole.

bronchique [brɔ̃ʃik], *a. Anat:* bronchial.

bronchite [brɔ̃ʃit], *s.f. Med:* bronchitis; **b. à répétition,** recurrent bronchial catarrh; **b. capillaire,** capillary bronchitis, broncho-pneumonia.

bronchitique [brɔ̃ʃitik], *a. & s. Med:* bronchitic.

bronchocèle [brɔ̃kɔsɛl], *s.f. Med:* bronchocele.

bronchographie [brɔ̃kɔgrafi], *s.f. Med:* **1.** bronchogram. **2.** bronchography.

broncho-pleurésie [brɔ̃kɔplœrezi], *s.f. Med:* bronchopleurisy; *pl. broncho-pleurésies.*

broncho-pneumonie [brɔ̃kɔpnømɔni], *s.f. Med:* broncho-pneumonia; *pl. broncho-pneumonies.*

bronchorrhée [brɔ̃kɔre], *s.f. Med:* bronchorrhea.

bronchoscope [brɔ̃kɔskɔp], *s.m. Med:* bronchoscope.

bronchoscopie [brɔ̃kɔskɔpi], *s.f. Med:* bronchoscopy.

bronchospasme [brɔ̃kɔspasm], *s.m. Med:* bronchospasm.

bronchospirométrie [brɔ̃kɔspirɔmetri], *s.f. Med:* bronchospirometry.

bronchosténose [brɔ̃kɔsteno:z], *s.f.Med:* bronchostenosis.

bronchotome [brɔ̃kɔtɔm], *s.m. Surg:* bronchotome.

bronchotomie [brɔ̃kɔtɔmi], *s.f. Surg:* bronchotomy.

brondir [brɔ̃di:r], *v.i. O:* (*of top*) to hum; (*of stove*) to roar.

brondissement [brɔ̃dismɑ̃], *s.m. O:* humming (of top); roaring (of stove).

brontomètre [brɔ̃tɔmɛtr̥], *s.m. Meteor:* brontometer.

brontosaure [brɔ̃tɔzɔ:r], *s.m.,* **brontosaurus** [brɔ̃tɔzɔrys], *s.m. Paleont:* brontosaurus, brontosaur.

brontothéridés [brɔ̃tɔteride], *s.m.pl. Paleont:* Brontotheriidae.

bronzage [brɔ̃za:ʒ], *s.m.* **1.** (*a*) bronzing; (*b*) suntanning. **2.** *Metall:* browning, blueing (of rifle and gun barrels).

bronze [brɔ̃:z], *s.m.* **1.** bronze; **b. d'aluminium,** aluminium bronze; **b. de rodage,** break-in bronze; **statue, médaille, de b.,** bronze statue, medal; **un beau b.,** fine bronze (statue); *F:* **cœur de b.,** heart of stone, of flint; *s.a.* ÂGE 3, PHOSPHOREUX, VOIX 1. **2. b. à canon, b. industriel,** gun-metal.

bronzé [brɔ̃ze], *a.* bronze, bronzed; **dindon b. d'Amérique,** bronze, bronze-turkey; *Med:* **diabète b.,** bronze diabetes; **maladie bronzée,** Addison's disease.

bronzer [brɔ̃ze]. **1.** *v.tr.* (*a*) to bronze (statue, etc.); **peinture bronzée,** bronze paint; (*b*) to brown, blue (gun-barrels, etc.); (*c*) to tan, sunburn; **teint bronzé,** sunburnt, tanned, bronzed, complexion; **que vous êtes bronzé!** you are brown! (*d*) *F:* **l'égoïsme lui a bronzé le cœur,** selfishness has hardened his heart. **2.** *v.i.* **je bronze, j'ai une peau qui bronze, facilement,** I tan, have a skin that tans, easily.

se bronzer. 1. (*of skin,* etc.) to tan, to bronze. **2.** *O:* (*of heart*) to harden.

bronzerie [brɔ̃zri], *s.f.* **1.** art of working in bronze. **2.** *usu. Pej:* bronzes (in general).

bronzeur [brɔ̃zœ:r], *s.m.* **1.** maker of bronzes. **2.** bronzer; bronze colourer.

bronzeuse [brɔ̃zø:z], *s.f. Typ:* bronzing-machine.

bronzier [brɔ̃zje], *s.m.* **1.** bronze-founder. **2.** maker of bronzes. **3.** bronzesmith.

bronzite [brɔ̃zit], *s.f. Miner:* bronzite.

brook [bruk], *s.m. Rac:* water-jump.

brookite [brukit], *s.f. Miner:* brookite.

broquard, broquart[1] [brɔka:r], *s.m.* = BROCARD[2].

broquart[2], **broqué** [brɔke], *s.m.* = BROQUETTE.

broque [brɔk], *s.m. Hort:* = BROCOLI.

broqueteur [brɔktœ:r], *s.m. Agr:* pitcher (of sheaves).

broquette [brɔkɛt], *s.f.* **1.** tack, tin-tack. **2.** *Coll:* tacks; **clouer qch. avec de la b.,** to tack sth. down.

broquille [brɔki:j], *s.f. P:* minute.

broquillon [brɔkijɔ̃], *s.m.* bung (of barrel).

brosimum [brɔzimɔm], *s.m. Bot:* Brosimum.

brossage [brɔsa:ʒ], *s.m.* brushing.

brosse [brɔs], *s.f.* **1.** brush; (*a*) **b. à cheveux, à habits,** hair-brush, clothes-brush; **b. de cuisine,** scrubbing-brush; **b. à cirer,** blacking-brush; **b. à dents,** (i) tooth-brush; (ii) *Mil: P:* moustache; **donner un coup de b. à qch., à qn,** to give sth. a brush, to give s.o. a brush (down); **enlever la boue d'un coup de b.,** to brush off the mud; **b. à reluire,** polishing-brush; **b. de nettoyage, b. à poussière,** cleaning brush; **b.-écouvillon,** duct cleaner; **b. à graisse,** oiling brush; **b. à décrotter,** hard brush (for shoes); *Hairdr:* **cheveux (taillés) en b.,** crew cut; **b. métallique,** wire brush; *Mch:* **b. à tubes,** scaling-brush; *s.a.* CHIENDENT; (*b*) (artist's) brush, (child's) paint-brush; **peintre qui a la b. légère,** artist who has a light touch (in painting); **passer la b. sur qch.,** to paint sth. out; *F:* **passons la b. sur ces souvenirs,** let us wipe out these recollections; (*c*) **b. à coller (de peintre en bâtiment),** sweep-brush; **b. à peinture,** paint-scrubber. **2.** *Ent:* scopa (on bee's leg, etc.). **3.** *pl.* brushwood (skirting forest, etc.). **4.** *Ven:* brush (of fox).

brossée [brɔse], *s.f.* (*a*) brushing, brush (given to garment, etc.); (*b*) *Leath:* staining, brush-dyeing; (*c*) *O:* drubbing, thrashing.

brosser [brɔse], *v.tr.* **1.** to brush; to clean (s.o., sth.) with a brush; to scrub (floor, deck); **se b. les cheveux,** to brush one's hair; **b. de l'argenterie,** to brush up silverware; **b. un cheval,** to brush down a horse; **b. qn,** (i) to brush s.o.'s clothes; (ii) *O:* to dust s.o.'s jacket, to give s.o. a good thrashing; (iii) to beat (opponent) hollow; *P:* **se b. le ventre,** to have an empty belly; **se b.,** to go without sth.; **tu peux te b.!** don't you wish you may get it! you can whistle for it; (*in Belgium*) **b. un cours,** to cut a lecture. **2.** to paint (boldly); **b. les décors d'une pièce,** to paint the scenery for a play; **b. un tableau général de la situation,** to outline, give a general picture of, the situation. **3.** *Sp:* to cut (ball).

brosserie [brɔsri], *s.f.* (*a*) brush-factory; (*b*) brush-trade; (*c*) brush-ware.

brosseur [brɔsœːr], *s.m.* **1.** (*a*) *Tchn:* brusher, cleaner, polisher; (*b*) *A: Mil:* officer's servant. **2. b. de décors,** scene-painter.

brosseuse [brɔsøːz], *s.f. Tex:* brushing-machine, brushing-mill.

brossier [brɔsje], *s.m.* brushmaker, dealer in brushes.

brotulidés, -ides [brɔtylide, -id], *s.m.pl. Ich:* Brotulidae.

brou [bru], *s.m.* **1.** husk, hull, *U.S:* shuck (of walnut, almond, etc.). **2. b. de noix,** (i) walnut cordial; (ii) walnut stain.

broue [bru], *s.f. Fr.C: P:* froth; **faire de la b.,** to talk big, to show off.

brouelle [bruɛl], *s.f. Tex:* homespun (woollen cloth).

brouet [bruɛ], *s.m.* (*thin*) gruel, broth; *F:* skilly; **b. noir,** (i) *Gr.Hist:* black broth (of Spartans); (ii) *F:* dubious, nasty-looking, stew or soup; *A:* **b. de l'accouchée, de l'épousée,** posset (for woman in childbirth, for bride).

brouettage [bruɛtaːʒ], *s.m.* conveyance by wheel-barrow; barrowing.

brouette [bruɛt], *s.f.* **1.** *A:* sedan chair (on two wheels). **2.** wheelbarrow; **b. à deux roues,** hand-cart.

brouettée [bruete, -ete], *s.f.* barrowful, barrow-load.

brouetter [bruete, -ete], *v.tr.* **1.** to carry, convey, wheel, (sth.) in a wheelbarrow; to barrow. **2.** *F:* to pull (s.o.) in a bath-chair.

brouetteur [bruɛtœːr], *s.m.* barrow-man; wheeler.

brouettier [bruɛtje], *s.m.* **1.** = BROUETTEUR. **2.** wheelbarrow maker. **3.** *A:* chair-man.

brougham [bruəm, brugam], *s.m. Veh:* brougham.

brouhaha [bruaa], *s.m.* (*a*) *A:* applause; (*b*) hub-bub, uproar, commotion; hullabaloo; **b. de conversation,** hum of conversation.

brouillade [brujad], *s.f. Cu:* (*in Provence*) scrambled eggs.

brouillage [brujaːʒ], *s.m.* **1.** (*a*) *W.Tel: Elcs:* (i) jamming, interference; (ii) **b. par parasites** = Watson effect; clutter; **b. aléatoire,** noise jamming; **b. de barrage,** barrage jamming; **b. étroit,** spot jamming; **station de b.,** jamming-station; *Radar:* **zone de b.,** interference area, mush area; (*b*) (i) *W.Tel: Elcs:* **b. (par altération systématique de la modulation),** scramble, scrambling; (ii) *Tp:* **b. (par inversion du spectre de fréquence),** scramble, scrambling; (iii) *Ciphering:* **b. (d'un texte codé),** scramble, scrambling. **2.** (*a*) *Geol:* jumbling; (*b*) *Hort:* mulching.

brouillamini [brujamini], *s.m.* **1.** *Pharm: A:* = **bol d'Arménie,** *q.v.* under BOL[1] 2. **2.** *F:* confusion, disorder, tangle.

brouillard [brujaːr], *s.m.* **1.** fog, mist, haze; **il fait du b.,** it is foggy; *F:* **b. à couper au couteau,** dense fog; *F:* pea-souper; **arrêté par le b., pris dans le b.,** fog-bound; **je n'y vois que du b.,** I can't make head or tail of it, I am very hazy about it; *P:* **être dans le b., dans les brouillards,** to be tipsy, fuddled, sozzled; *P:* **abattre le b.,** to have a morning drink to brush away the cobwebs; *T.V:* **b. de fond,** background mush. **2.** *Com:* day-book, waste-book; counter cash-book. **3.** *A:* **(papier) b.,** (i) blotting-paper; (ii) filter-paper.

brouillasse [brujas], *s.f.* (*a*) *Nau:* mist; (*b*) wet fog, Scotch mist.

brouillasser [brujase], *v.impers. F:* **il brouillasse,** (i) it is foggy; (ii) it is mizzling, drizzling.

brouille [bruːj], *s.f.* quarrel, estrangement; **être en b. avec qn,** to be on bad terms, at loggerheads, with s.o.; **jeter la b. dans une famille,** to set off a family feud, to split a family; **b. de ménage,** domestic quarrel; **il y a de la b.,** they've been quarrelling.

brouillé [bruje], *a.* **1.** jumbled, mixed, confused; blurred (photography, etc.); murky (sky); **œufs brouillés,** scrambled eggs; **teint b.,** blotchy complexion. **2.** être **b. avec qn,** to be on bad terms with s.o., to have fallen out with s.o.; *F:* **être b. avec les chiffres,** to be hopeless at figures.

brouillement [brujmɑ̃], *s.m.* **1.** mixing up, jumbling. **2.** jumble, medley.

brouiller [bruje], *v.tr.* **1.** to mix up, jumble, embroil; to throw (sth.) into confusion; **b. qn,** to confuse, embarrass, s.o.; **b. des œufs,** to scramble eggs; **b. les cartes,** (i) to shuffle the cards; (ii) *F:* to spread confusion, sow discord; **b. une serrure,** to spoil, hamper, a lock; **b. ses papiers,** to mix up one's papers; *A: Lit:* **b. du papier,** to scribble; **la pluie brouille les fenêtres,** the rain blurs the windows. **2.** to set (people) at variance, at loggerheads; to cause a misunderstanding between (people). **3.** (*a*) *W.Tel: Elcs:* **b. (une émission d'un autre poste),** to jam (a transmission of another station); (*b*) (i) *W.Tel: Elcs:* **b. (une émission par altération systématique de la modulation),** to scramble; (ii) *Tp:* **b. (une communication téléphonique par inversion du spectre de fréquence),** to scramble; (iii) *Ciphering:* to scramble.

se brouiller. 1. (*a*) to become mixed, confused; **le temps se brouille,** (i) the weather is breaking up; (ii) *F:* affairs are looking black; *F:* **les cartes se brouillent,** (i) there's trouble brewing; (ii) things are going wrong; (*b*) (*of eyes*) to grow dim; **yeux brouillés de larmes,** eyes blurred with tears. **2.** to quarrel, to fall out (**avec,** with); to fall foul (**avec,** of).

brouillerie [brujri], *s.f.* misunderstanding, disagreement; **il s'éleva une b. entre eux,** a coolness arose between them.

brouilleur [brujœːr]. **1.** *a. W.Tel: Elcs:* (*a*) jamming; **émetteur b.,** jamming station; (*b*) scrambling. **2.** *s.m.* (*a*) *W.Tel: Elcs:* jammer, jamming transmitter; (*b*) *W.Tel: Elcs: Tp:* **(circuit) b.,** scrambler; (*c*) *Ciphering:* scrambler.

brouillon, -onne [brujɔ̃, -ɔn]. **1.** *a.* blundering, unmethodical; muddle-headed; **caractère b.,** muddle-headed nature. **2.** *s.* muddler. **3.** *s.m.* (*a*) (rough) draft, rough copy; scrap, *U.S:* scratch-paper; *Sch:* rough work; **(cahier de) b.,** rough note-book; **faire le b. d'un document,** to draft a document; (*b*) = BROUILLARD 2.

brouillonner [brujɔne], *v.tr.* **1.** to botch (exercise, etc.). **2.** to draft, make a rough copy of (letter, etc.).

brouir [bruiːr], *v.tr. Agr: Hort:* (*of sun*) to blight, nip (plants after frost).

brouissure [bruisyːr], *s.f. Agr: Hort:* blight, frost-nip.

broussaille [brusɑːj], *s.f. usu. pl.* brushwood, underwood, scrub, bush(es); **épaisses broussailles,** dense undergrowth; **cheveux en b.,** (i) thick, bushy, shaggy, (ii) tousled, unkempt, hair; **sourcils en b.,** shaggy eyebrows.

broussailler [brusɑje]. **1.** *v.tr.* to cover, fill up, (opening, etc.) with brushwood. **2.** *v.i.* to wander through the scrub.

broussailleux, -euse [brusɑjø, -øːz], *a.* bushy (country, hair, eyebrows); covered with bushes, with scrub; **terrain b.,** scrubland.

broussard [brusaːr], *s.m.* bushman.

brousse[1] [brus], *s.f.* (*in Australia, etc.*) (i) the bush; (ii) *F:* back of beyond; *s.a.* BRÛLER I. 1.

Brousse[2], *Pr.n.f. Geog:* Brusa.

brousse[3], *s.f.* fresh goat cheese.

broussin [brusɛ̃], *s.m.* gnarl (on tree).

broussiné [brusine], *a.* choked with brushwood.

broussonetia [brusɔnesja], *s.m.* **broussonétie** [brusɔneti], *s.f. Bot:* broussonetia; **b. à papier,** paper mulberry.

brout [bru], *s.m.* browse(-wood), tender shoots (of shrubs, etc.).

broutage [brutaːʒ], *s.m.*, **broutement** [brutmɑ̃], *s.m.* **1.** browsing. **2.** *Mec.E:* chatter(ing), jarring, (of brake, of tool); *Aut:* **b. des freins,** brake chatter. **3.** *pl.* indentations, "utters" (caused by chattering tool).

brouter [brute]. **1.** *v.tr.* **b. l'herbe,** to browse on the grass, to graze; *Prov:* **où la chèvre est attachée il faut qu'elle broute,** one must make the best of things. **2.** *v.i.* (*of brake, tool*) to chatter, jump.

broutille [brutiːj], *s.f. usu. pl.* sprigs, twigs; *F:* trifles, things or matters of no importance, *esp.* the morass of law technicalities.

brouture [brutyːr], *s.f.* shoots nibbled by browsing animals.

brownien, -ienne [braunjɛ̃, -jɛn; bron-], *a. Ph:* Brownian, molecular (motion).

browning [brauniŋ, bron-], *s.m. Sm.a:* Browning (pistol), automatic pistol.

broyage [brwajaːʒ], *s.m.* pounding; powdering, pulverizing (of coal, etc.); crushing (of stone, ore); milling; grinding (of colours); *Tex:* breaking, braking, hackling (of hemp); **b. primaire,** pre-crushing; **b. secondaire,** regrinding; **b. à l'eau, par voie humide,** wet crushing, grinding; **b. à sec, par voie sèche,** dry crushing, grinding; **b. fin, moyen, grossier,** fine, medium, coarse crushing, grinding.

broyer [brwaje], *v.tr.* **(je broie, n. broyons; je broierai)** to pound, pulverize, crush; to mill; to crunch (food); *Tex:* to break, brake, hackle (hemp, etc.); **b. des couleurs,** to grind, bray, colours; *F:* **b. du noir,** to be (down) in the dumps, to have the blues, to brood.

broyeur, -euse [brwajœːr, -øːz]. **1.** *a.* crushing, grinding (mill, etc.). **2.** *s.* (*a*) **b. de couleurs,** colour grinder; (*b*) *Tex:* hemp-breaker, dresser. **3.** *s.m.* crusher, grinder, disintegrator; crushing machine; (coal) pulverizer; grinding mill; **b. à boulets,** ball-mill; **b. à cylindres,** crushing rolls; **b. à meules horizontales,** roller-mill; **b. à meules verticales,** edge-runner; edge-mill; **b. à mâchoires,** jaw crusher; **b. des fins, des mixtes, des gros,** fine, medium, coarse crusher; **b. à marteaux,** hammer mill; **b. tamiseur,** combined grinder and sieve; **b. malaxeur, b. mélangeur,** (i) mixing-mill; (ii) (paint-, oil-)mill; *Dom.Ec:* **b. à ordures,** waste, *U.S:* garbage, disposal unit. **4. b. de noir,** worryguts. **5.** *s.f.* **broyeuse** = BROIE.

broyon [brwajɔ̃], *s.m. Const:* **b. à mortier,** mortar larry.

brrr [brrr], *int.* brr . . . !

bru [bry], *s.f.* daughter-in-law.

bruant [bryɑ̃], *s.m. Orn:* bunting; **b. jaune,** yellow-hammer; **b. mélanocéphale, crocote, à tête noire,** black-headed bunting; **b. cendré,** cinereous bunting; **b. zizi,** cirl bunting; **b. cendrillard,** Cretzchmar's bunting; **b. lapon,** Lapland bunting; **b. nain,** little bunting; **b. masqué,** masked bunting; **b. ortolan,** ortolan bunting; **b. à calotte blanche,** pine bunting; **b. à tête rousse,** red-headed bunting; **b. des roseaux,** reed-bunting; **b. fou,** rock bunting; **b. roux,** rufous bunting; **b. rustique,** rustic bunting; **b. des prés,** Siberian meadow bunting; **b. auréole,** yellow-breasted bunting; **b. à sourcils jaunes,** yellow-browed bunting; **b. des neiges,** snow-bunting; **b. proyer,** corn-bunting; **b. ardoisé,** slate-coloured junco; **b. renard,** fox sparrow; **b. à col blanc,** white-throated sparrow.

brucella [brysɛla], *s.f. Bac:* brucella.

brucelles [brysɛl], *s.f.pl.* tweezers, spring nippers.

brucellose [bryselοːz], *s.f.* (*a*) *Med:* brucellosis; undulant fever; (*b*) *Vet:* Bang's disease; brucellosis; infectious abortion.

bruche [bryʃ], *s.m., occ. f. Ent:* bruchus; **b. des pois,** pea-beetle, -weevil.

brucine [brysin], *s.f. Ch:* brucine.

Bruegel [brœgɛl], *Pr.n. Hist. of Art:* Breughel.

brugeois, -oise [bryʒwa, -waːz], *a. & s.* (native) of Bruges.

brugnon [bryɲɔ̃], *s.m. Hort:* nectarine.

brugnonier [bryɲɔnje], *s.m.* nectarine(-tree).

bruine[1] [brɥin], *s.f.* **1.** fine drizzling rain; drizzle, mizzle. **2.** thin paint (for spraying); **peinture à la b.,** spatter-work.

bruine[2], *s.f. Agr:* stinking smut, bunt.

bruinement [brɥinmɑ̃], *s.m.* **1.** drizzling, mizzling. **2.** = BRUINE[1] 1.

bruiner [brɥine], *v.impers.* to drizzle, mizzle.

bruineux, -euse [brɥinø, -ø:z], *a.* drizzly, mizzly; *s.a.* SERINGUE 1.

bruire [brɥi:r], *v.i.def.* (*pr.p.* **bruissant;** *pr.ind.* **il bruit, ils bruissent;** *p.d.* **il bruyait, il bruissait;** *perf.* **il a bruit;** *fu.* **il bruira,** the *pr.p.* **bruyant** is now used only as an adj.); to make a continuous noise; to rustle, rumble; (*of machinery*) to hum; (*of brook*) to murmur, to plash; (*of sea*) to sough.

bruissant [brɥisɑ̃], *a.* rumbling, humming; murmuring, babbling (brook); sounding, surging; soughing (sea).

bruissement [brɥismɑ̃], *s.m.* rumbling; humming (of machinery, etc.); murmuring, bubbling (of brook); rustling (of leaves); buzzing (of bees); hissing (of arc-lamp); burr (of milling cutter); *W.Tel:* **bruissements parasites,** strays; *Gramophones:* **b. de l'aiguille,** surface noise (of the needle).

bruit [brɥi], *s.m.* **1.** (*a*) noise; sound; din; snap (of press-button); **campagne contre le b.,** noise abatement campaign; **b. de vaisselle,** clatter of dishes; **le b. de la guerre,** the din of war; **b. d'un coup de feu,** report of a gun; **le b. métallique d'une grille de jardin,** the clang of a garden gate; **le b. des marteaux sur l'enclume,** the clang of the hammers on the anvil; **quelque chose tomba avec un b. sourd,** something fell with a thud, with a thump; **faire du b.,** to make a noise; *s.a.* MAL[2] 1; *F:* **faire un b. de tous les diables,** to kick up the dickens, the devil, of a row, an awful din; **b. à tout casser, à tout rompre,** noise fit to wake the dead; **quel b.!** what a row! *F:* what a racket! **vivre loin du b.,** to live far from the madding crowd; **ne faites pas de b.!** don't make a noise! **b. de bouchons qui sautent,** popping of corks; **b. de branches qu'on casse,** noise of cracking branches; **b. de friture,** sizzle, sizzling; **b. de pas,** sound of footsteps; **b. de pas marqués, lourds,** noise of tramping; **b. de surface,** surface noise (of a gramophone); **le b. des flots qui passent,** the wash of the waves; **il amena le phoque à terre avec un grand b. d'eau,** he landed the seal with a swash; *Aut:* **le capot fait du b.,** the bonnet rattles; *W.Tel: Elcs: T.V:* **b. atmosphérique,** atmospherics; **b. parasite,** parasitic, spurious; noise; **b. de fond,** background noise; **b. de salle, b. ambiant,** room noise; **b. de scintillation,** flicker noise; **niveau de b.,** noise level; **réduction des bruits,** noise reduction; **appareil, dispositif, limiteur de b.,** noise limiter; **b. blanc,** white noise; *Tp:* **b. de ligne,** line, circuit, noise, line scratches; (*b*) noise, fuss, ado; **beaucoup de b. pour rien,** much ado about nothing; **beaucoup de b. et peu de besogne,** much cry and little wool; **faire beaucoup de b. au sujet de qch., faire grand b. de qch.,** to make a great to-do, a great fuss, about sth.; **son livre a fait du b.,** his book made a stir; **ce succès fut célébré à grand b.,** this success was noised abroad, trumpeted abroad; there was a great to-do about it; **sans b., à petit b.,** noiselessly, silently, without any fuss, quietly; **propagande faite sans b.,** silent propaganda; (*c*) *Med:* (cardiac, respiratory) murmur. **2.** rumour, report; **le b. court que . . .,** rumour has it that . . ., it is rumoured that . . .; **faire courir un b.,** to set a rumour afloat; **faire courir le b. de qch.,** *A. & Lit:* to bruit sth. abroad; **il n'est b. que de cela,** it is the talk of the town; **le b. se répandit de tous côtés que . . .,** it was noised on all sides that . . .; *A: Prov:* **le b. pend l'homme,** give a dog a bad name and hang him.

bruitage [brɥita:ʒ], *s.m. Th: Cin: T.V:* sound-effects.

bruiter [brɥite], *v.tr. & v.i.Th: Cin: T.V:* to produce sound-effects.

bruiteur [brɥitœ:r], **bruitiste** [brɥitist], *s.m. Th: Cin: T.V:* (*pers.*) noises off; sound-effects man.

brûlable [brylabl̩], *a.* burnable.

brûlage [bryla:ʒ], *s.m.* **1.** (*a*) burning (of weeds, etc.); burning-off (of paint); (*b*) *Agr:* sod-burning; burn-baiting, -beating; denshiring (of moorland, etc.); (*c*) **b. de cheveux,** singeing of the hair; **faire un b. à qn,** to singe s.o.'s hair. **2.** scorching (of clothes, etc.); roasting (of coffee). **3.** *Petroleum Ind:* **b. des gaz (inutilisés sur le chantier),** popping.

brûlant [brylɑ̃], *a.* burning, on fire, flaming; glowing (style, etc.); *Med:* feverish; *Bot:* stinging; **café b.,** steaming-, piping-, boiling-, hot coffee; **il a les mains brûlantes,** his hands are (burning-)hot; **larmes brûlantes,** scalding tears; **soleil b.,** scorching, blazing, fiery, sun; *F:* broiling sun; **cœur b. d'amour,** heart afire with love; **un sujet b.,** a ticklish subject; *s.a.* PAPIER 2.

brûlé [bryle]. **1.** *a.* burnt; *Mch:* **tube b.,** burnt-out tube; *Cu:* **crème brûlée,** caramel custard; **vin b.,** mulled wine; *F:* **cerveau b., tête brûlée,** fanatic, dare-devil; **homme b.,** man who has lost his reputation, credit, influence; **c'est un homme b.,** he is done for. **2.** *s.m.* (*a*) **odeur, goût, de b.,** smell, taste, of burning; burnt smell, burnt taste; *F:* **sentir le b.,** (*of opinions*) to smack of heresy; (*of business, etc.*) (i) to look fishy; (ii) to look bad; (*b*) *Fr.C:* burnt-out woodland area, *U.S:* brûlé(e); (*c*) **crier comme un b.,** to scream like a madman.

brûle-bout [brylbu], *s.m.* save-all; *pl. brûle-bout(s).*

brûlée [bryle], *s.f. P:* thrashing; **flanquer une b. à qn,** to thrash s.o., give s.o. a good licking.

brûle-gueule [brylgœl], *s.m.inv.* short clay pipe; cutty; *P:* nose-warmer.

brûlement [brylmɑ̃], *s.m.* **1.** burning, consuming by fire. **2.** burning sensation.

brûle-parfum(s) [brylparfœ̃], *s.m.inv.* perfume-pan, -brazier.

brûle-pourpoint (à) [abrylpurpwɛ̃], *adv.phr.* point-blank; *A:* **tirer sur qn à b.-p.,** to fire at s.o. at close range, point-blank; **dire qch. à qn à b.-p.,** (i) to tell s.o. sth. point-blank, to his face; (ii) to spring sth. on s.o.

brûler [bryle]. I. *v.tr.* to burn. **1.** (*a*) to burn (down) (house, etc.); to burn (up) (rubbish, etc.); to burn away (metal); to burn out (s.o.'s eyes, electrical resistance, etc.); **b. une maison de fond en comble,** to burn a house to the ground; **b. de la peinture,** to burn off paint; **elle fut brûlée vive,** (i) she was burnt alive; (ii) she was burnt at the stake; *s.a.* FEU I. 2; **se b. les doigts,** to burn one's fingers; *F:* **se b. à la chandelle,** to singe one's wings; **b. la cervelle à qn,** to blow s.o.'s brains out; *Med:* **b. une plaie,** to cauterize a wound; *s.a.* VAISSEAU 2; (*b*) *Agr:* **b. le terrain, la brousse,** to burn the ground; to burn-bait, -beat, to denshire (moorland, etc.); (*c*) **b. de la bougie,** to burn candles; **huile à b.,** burning-oil; **la chandelle était brûlée jusqu'au bout,** the candle had burnt itself out; (*d*) to use, consume (fuel, electricity); (*e*) **prendre une ville sans b. une cartouche,** to take a town without firing a shot; (*f*) *Physiol:* to destroy (tissue) by oxidation; (*g*) (*of acid*) to corrode; (*h*) *Distill: O:* to distil. **2.** to scorch; (*a*) **b. le pain,** to burn, scorch, the bread; **le lait est brûlé,** the milk has caught; **b. du café,** to roast coffee; **b. les cheveux, un porc,** to singe the hair, a pig; **se b. la langue,** to burn, scald, blister, one's tongue; **l'argent lui brûle la poche,** money burns a hole in his pocket; **terre brûlée par le soleil,** sun-scorched earth; *F:* **b. la route, le pavé,** to go along the road at full speed, to scorch, tear, along the road; *s.a.* PLANCHE 1; (*b*) **train qui brûle toutes les petites stations,** train that does not stop at any of the small stations, train passing small stations; **b. un signal,** to run past, overrun, a signal; *Aut:* **b. les signaux,** to shoot, jump, the traffic lights, to crash the lights; *U.S:* to run through a red light; *Rac:* **b. un concurrent,** to race past a competitor; *F:* to leave a competitor standing; *s.a.* ÉTAPE 2, POLITESSE; (*c*) **la gelée brûle les feuilles,** frost bites the leaves; **la gelée a brûlé les bourgeons,** the frost has nipped the buds; **la fumée me brûlait les yeux,** the smoke made my eyes smart. **3.** *F:* (*a*) **b. qn,** to ruin s.o.'s credit, reputation; (*b*) **b. un agent, un espion,** to spot a (disguised) policeman, a spy.

II. **brûler,** *v.i.* **1.** to burn, to be on fire, to be alight; *Med:* to be feverish; (*of wound*) to smart; **b. lentement, sans flamme,** to smoulder; **b. sec,** to burn like tinder; **laisser b. la lumière,** to leave the light on; *F:* **on brûle ici,** it is unbearably hot here; *F:* **nous brûlons par cette chaleur,** we are baking in this heat; *Games:* **tu brûles,** you are getting hot; *s.a.* TORCHON 1. **2. b. de curiosité,** to be consumed with curiosity; **b. de soif,** to have a burning thirst; **b. du désir de savoir . . .,** to be consumed, with a desire to know . . .; **b. d'indignation,** to burn with indignation; **b. d'amour pour qn,** to be consumed with passion for s.o.; **b. de faire qch.,** to be eager, impatient, to do sth.; **il brûle de prendre la parole, de se venger,** he is burning to speak, to take his revenge; **elle brûle de se faire actrice,** she is dying to go on the stage; **les mains lui brûlent,** (i) his hands are hot; (ii) *F:* he is all impatience to be up and doing. *F:* **les pieds lui brûlent,** he is itching to be off. **3.** (*of meat*) to burn; (*of milk*) to catch.

brûlerie [brylri], *s.f.* (*a*) (brandy) distillery; (*b*) coffee-roasting plant.

brûle-tout [bryltu], *s.m.inv.* = BRÛLE-BOUT.

brûleur, -euse [brylœ:r, -ø:z], *s.* burner. **1.** (*a*) **grand b. de sorcières,** great burner of witches; **b. de maisons,** incendiary, fire-raiser; **b. de café,** coffee-roaster; *F:* **b. de planches,** actor who puts plenty of life into his part; (*b*) brandy distiller. **2.** *s.m.* (*a*) burner (of gas-cooker, etc.); **b. à allumage automatique, à allumage électrique,** flash-burner; **b. à gaz,** (i) Bunsen burner; (ii) gas-jet; **b. à couronne,** gas-ring; rose burner; **b. à mazout,** oil-fired furnace; **b. à flamme filiforme,** rat-tail, pinhole, burner; (*b*) sprayer, jet (for oil fuel); (*c*) *Av:* **b. à retour,** spill burner.

brûlis [bryli], *s.m. Agr:* patch of burnt, denshired, burn-baited, land.

brûloir [brylwa:r], *s.m.* **1.** (coffee-)burner, roaster (machine). **2.** singer (for horse's tails, fleeces, etc.). **3.** (painter's) blowlamp.

brûlot [brylo], *s.m.* **1.** *Naval Hist:* fire-ship; *F:* **brûlot d'un parti,** fire-brand of a party. **2.** burnt brandy (brandy burnt with sugar). **3.** *F:* = BRÛLE-GUEULE. **4.** *Dial:* (*Centre of Fr.*) bonfire. **5.** *Av:* flare. **6.** *Fr.C:* kind of gnat.

brûlure [bryly:r], *s.f.* **1.** (*a*) burn, scald; **se faire une b. à la main,** to burn one's hand; (*b*) **(sensation de) b.,** smarting; (*c*) **b. d'estomac,** heartburn. **2.** *Agr: Hort:* (*a*) frost-nip; (*b*) blight; smut (on corn).

brumaille [brymɑ:j], *s.f. Nau:* slight fog or haze; mist.

brumailleux, -euse [brymɑjø, -ø:z], *a.* misty.

brumaire [brymɛ:r], *s.m. Fr.Hist:* second month of the Fr. Republican calendar (22 October-21 November).

brumal [brymal], *a*, no *masc. pl.* wintry, brumous.

brumasse [brymas], *s.f. Nau:* = BRUMAILLE.

brumasser [brymase], *v.impers. Nau:* to be rather misty, foggy; **il brumasse,** there is a haze.

brume [brym], *s.f.* **1.** thick fog, haze, or mist (*esp.* at sea); **banc de b.,** fog-bank; **signal de b.,** fog-signal; **cornet, trompe, de b.,** fog-horn. **2.** *Mil: Navy:* **b. artificielle,** smoke-screen.

brumer [bryme], *v.impers. Nau:* to be foggy, hazy.

brumeux, -euse [brymø, -ø:z], *a.* (*a*) foggy; misty, hazy; (*b*) melancholic; (*c*) obscure; vague.

brumisage [brymiza:ʒ], *s.m. Ind:* fogging.

brumiser [brymize], *v.tr. Ind:* to fog.

brumiseur [brymizœ:r], *s.m. Ind:* fogger.

brun, brune [brœ̃, bryn]. **1.** *a.* brown (cloth, hair, etc.); dark, dusky, swarthy; sunburnt, tanned (complexion); **un (homme) b., une (femme) brune,** a dark(-haired, -skinned) man, woman; **une belle brune,** a handsome brunette; *s.a.* COURTISER; **(bière) brune,** (i) brown (ale); (ii) mild (beer). **2.** *s.m.* (*a*) brown (colour); **b. foncé,** dark brown; **rubans (d'un) b. clair,** light brown ribbons; (*b*) *Lit:* **Brun,** Bruin (the Bear). **3.** *s.f.* **la brune,** dusk, nightfall; **à la brune,** at dusk, in the dusk of the evening.

brunante [brynɑ̃t], *s.f. Fr.C:* dusk, **à la b.,** at dusk.

brunâtre [brynɑ:tr], *a.* brownish.

Brunehaut [brynəo], *Pr.n.f.* Brunhild.

brunelle [brynɛl], *s.f. Bot:* prunella, self-heal.

brunet, -ette [brynɛ, -ɛt]. **1.** *a.* brownish. **2.** *s.f.* (*usu.* young) brunette. **3.** *s.f. A.Mus:* **brunette,** simple little air; love-song.

bruni [bryni], *s.m.* (*a*) burnish; (*b*) burnished, polished, part (on metal, etc.).

brunir [bryni:r]. **1.** *v.i. & pr.* to become dark, tanned; to brown. **2.** *v.tr.* (*a*) to brown, darken, tan; **le soleil l'a bruni,** the sun has tanned, bronzed, his complexion; (*b*) to burnish (gold, edges of book, etc.); (*c*) to polish, planish (metal).

brunissage [brynisa:ʒ], *s.m.* (*a*) burnishing; (*b*) polishing, planishing.

brunissement [brynismɑ̃], *s.m.* (*a*) browning; (*b*) darkening; (*c*) polishing, planishing.

brunisseur, -euse [brynisœ:r, -ø:z], *s.* burnisher.

brunissoir [bryniswa:r], *s.m. Tls:* burnisher, polisher, polishing-tool; polishing file.

brunissure [brynisy:r], *s.f.* **1.** burnish, polish (of metals). **2.** (potato-)blight or rot.

brunswickois, -oise [brœ̃zvikwa, -wa:z], *a. & s. Geog:* (native, inhabitant) of Brunswick.

brusque [brysk], *a.* **1.** abrupt, blunt, off-hand(ed), brusque, bluff (person, manner); **il s'est montré très b.,** he was very short with me. **2.** sudden (happening); **geste b.,** quick, sudden, gesture; *Aut:* **tournant b.,** sudden turning, "sharp turn"; "sharp bend."

brusquement [bryskəmɑ̃], *adv.* **1.** abruptly, bluntly, brusquely; **parler b.,** to speak bluntly, discourteously; **ouvrir b. la porte,** to burst the door open. **2.** suddenly; **la porte s'ouvrit b.,** the door was flung open; **la route plonge b.,** the

road dips sharply; **b. il reconnut l'endroit,** in a flash he recognized the spot; **la soirée s'acheva b.,** the evening came to an abrupt end.

brusquer [bryske], *v.tr.* **1. b. qn,** to be sharp, rude, abrupt, uncivil, with s.o., to speak harshly to s.o., to treat s.o. with scant courtesy. **2. b. les choses,** to precipitate matters; **il voulut b. la fortune,** *F:* he tried to get rich quick, to force the hand of fortune, to rush fortune; *Th: etc:* **b. le dénouement,** to hurry, rush, the ending; *Mil:* **b. un poste,** to attempt to seize a post by sudden assault; **attaque brusquée,** rush attack, surprise attack. **3.** *Nau:* to bream (ship).

brusquerie [brysk(ə)ri], *s.f.* **1.** abruptness, bluntness, brusqueness, bluffness (of action, manner, language). **2.** abrupt, off-hand(ed), words or action.

brut [bryt], *a.* **1.** brutish; **force brute,** brute force; **bête brute,** brute beast; **faits bruts,** bald, hard, facts. **2.** (*a*) raw, unmanufactured (material); unpolished (marble, etc.); undressed (timber, skin); (statue, literary work) in the rough; unrefined (sugar); crude (acid, oil, etc.); rough, uncut (diamond); extra-dry (champagne); **produit b.,** primary product; **fer b.,** crude iron; **fonte brute,** pig-iron; **corps bruts,** inorganic bodies; **or b.,** gold in nuggets; *Const:* **joint b. de truelle,** joint rough from the trowel; **briquetage à joints bruts de truelle,** unpointed brickwork; *Metall:* **b. de fonte, de coulée,** rough-cast; *Metalw:* **b. d'estampage,** rough-stamped; **pièce brute d'estampage,** rough stamping; (*b*) *A:* uncultured, unrefined, rude (life, nation). **3.** (*a*) *Com:* gross (profit, value, weight, etc.); *adv.* **affaire qui produit mille francs b.,** business which produces a thousand francs gross; (*b*) *Ph: etc:* **résultat b.,** result uncorrected for temperature, pressure, etc.; *Pol.Ec:* **chiffres bruts,** unweighted figures. **4.** *s.m.* crude (oil); **b. corrosif,** sour crude; **b. lourd,** low gravity, crude. **5.** *s.f.* **brute,** (*a*) brute beast; **les brutes,** brutes, brute beasts; (*b*) ruffian; **quelle brute!** isn't he a brute! a beast! (*c*) boor, clod; *F:* **travailler comme une b.,** to work like a black.

brutage [bryta:ʒ], *s.m.* rough cutting (of diamond).

brutal, -aux [brytal, -o]. **1.** *a* (*a*) brutal, brutish, savage, ruffianly; (*b*) ruthless; (*c*) coarse, rough, churlish; **force brutale,** brute force; **coup b.,** brutal, savage, blow; **esprit b.,** coarse mind; **le fait b.,** the hard, blunt, fact; **bon sens b.,** hard common sense; **vérité brutale,** plain, unvarnished, truth; **être b. avec qn,** to be very rough, very plain-spoken, with s.o.; **arrêt b.,** sudden stop; *Veh: etc:* **frein, embrayage, b.,** fierce brake, clutch; (*d*) harsh (of colour); (*e*) **il n'y a aucune limite brutale entre maturité et sénilité,** there is no clear-cut dividing line between maturity and senility. **2.** *s.m.* (*a*) *P:* heady wine; (*b*) *P:* gun.

brutalement [brytalmɑ̃], *adv.* (*a*) brutally, brutishly, savagely, coarsely, churlishly; (*b*) bluntly; (*c*) abruptly, suddenly; **freiner b.,** to brake suddenly.

brutaliser [brytalize], *v.tr.* to ill-treat, maltreat; to treat (s.o.) in a brutal, unkind, manner; to bully.

brutalité [brytalite], *s.f.* **1.** (*a*) brutality, brutishness (of appetites, etc.); (*b*) brutality, savagery, savage cruelty, ruffianism; (*c*) coarseness, lack of civility. **2.** (*a*) brutal act, piece of brutality; (*b*) **dire des brutalités à qn,** to be coarsely uncivil, to say grossly discourteous things, to s.o.

Bruxelles [brysɛl], *Pr.n.f. Geog:* Brussels; *A: F:* **filer à B.,** (*of financier*) to bolt.

bruxellois, -oise [brysɛlwa, -wa:z], *a. & s. Geog:* (native, inhabitant) of Brussels.

bruyamment [bryjamɑ̃, brɥijamɑ̃], *adv.* **1.** noisily, loudly; **rire b.,** to laugh boisterously; **la voiture passa b. à travers le village,** the carriage clattered, rumbled, through the village. **2.** clamorously.

bruyance [bryjɑ̃:s, brɥijɑ̃:s], *s.f.* noise, noisy clamour.

bruyant [bryjɑ̃, brɥijɑ̃], *a.* **1.** noisy (street, company, etc.); **succès b.,** resounding success. **2.** loud, clamorous (applause); boisterous, rollicking (laughter); uproarious (game); **homme b.,** loud-talking man.

bruyère [bryɛ:r], *s.f.* **1.** (*a*) heather, heath; (*b*) heath(-land); moor(land); **terre de b.,** heath-mould; *s.a.* COQ[1] 1. **2. b. arborescente,** white heath, brier, briar; **racine de b.,** briar root; **pipe (en) b.,** briar pipe; **b. des marais,** cross-leaved heath; **b. cendrée,** fine-leaved heath.

bryacées [briase], *s.f.pl. Bot:* Bryaceae.

bryologie [briɔlɔʒi], *s.f. Bot:* bryology.

bryologiste [briɔlɔʒist], *s.* bryologist.

bryon [bri(j)ɔ̃], *s.m. Bot:* bryum (moss).

bryone [bri(j)ɔn], *s.f. Bot:* bryony.

bryophytes [bri(j)ɔfit], *s.f.pl. Bot:* Bryophyta.

bryozoaires [bri(j)ɔzɔɛ:r], *s.m.pl. Biol:* bryozoa, polyzoa, sea-mosses.

bryum [bri(j)ɔm], *s.m. Bot:* bryum (moss).

bu [by], *a. P:* **il est bu,** he's drunk, tipsy.

buanderie [bɥɑ̃dri], *s.f.* wash-house, laundry-room.

buandier, -ière [bɥɑ̃dje, -jɛ:r], *s.* **1.** bleacher (of new linen). **2.** laundry-man, -woman; washer-woman.

bubale [bybal], **bubalis** [bybalis], *s.m. Z:* bubal, bubale, bubalis; hart(e)beest.

bube [byb], *s.f. A:* pimple.

bubon [bybɔ̃], *s.m. Med:* bubo.

bubonique [bybɔnik], *a. Med:* bubonic (tumour, plague); **peste b.,** bubonic plague.

bucarde [bykard], *s.f. Moll:* cockle.

Bucarest [bykarɛst], *Pr.n.f. Geog:* Bucharest.

buccal, -aux [bykal, -o], *a. Anat:* buccal (cavity, etc.); *Med:* **vaccin b.,** oral vaccine; **par voie buccale,** orally.

buccin [byksɛ̃], *s.m.* **1.** *Moll:* whelk. **2.** trumpet, buccin(a).

buccinateur [byksinatœ:r], *s.m. Anat:* buccinator (muscle).

buccine [byksin], *s.f. Cl.Ant:* trumpet, buccin(a).

buccinidés [byksinide], *s.m. Moll:* Buccinidae.

bucconidés [bykɔnide], *s.m.pl. Orn:* Bucconidae, the puff(-)birds.

bucentaure [bysɑ̃tɔ:r], *s.m.* bucentaur.

Bucéphale [bysefal]. **1.** *Pr.n.m. A.Hist:* Bucephalus; *F:* **monté sur son Bucéphale,** mounted on his charger; *Iron:* on his old hack. **2.** *s.m. Ent:* buff-tip (moth).

bucérotidés [byserɔtide], *s.m. pl. Orn:* Bucerotidae, the hornbills.

bûche[1] [byʃ], *s.f.* (*a*) (fire-)log; billet (of firewood); **b. de Noël,** yule-log; **ne pas se remuer plus qu'une b.,** not to stir a finger; **b. économique,** (coal) briquette; *F:* **ramasser, prendre, une b.,** to fall, to have a spill, to come a cropper; **gare la b.!** mind you don't fall, you don't come a cropper! *Cards: P:* **tirer, amener, une b.,** to draw a court card or a ten (at baccarat); (*b*) *Cu:* Swiss roll, log cake; (*c*) *F:* dolt, duffer, blockhead, thick-head.

bûche[2], *s.f. A: F:* hard work, swot(ting); **temps de b.,** work-time, working hours.

bûcher[1] [byʃe], *s.m.* **1.** (fire-) wood-house, wood-shed. **2.** (*a*) pile of faggots, stake; **monter, mourir, sur le b.,** to be burnt at the stake; (*b*) funeral-pile, -pyre.

bûcher[2], *v.tr.* **1.** *Tchn:* to rough-hew (wood, stone). **2.** *P:* to belabour, thrash (s.o.). **3.** *F:* **b. son latin,** to work hard at, swot up, grind (away) at, mug up, one's Latin; **b. un examen,** to swot, grind, mug up, for an examination; **il faut tout le temps b.,** it's a constant grind; **b. toute la journée,** to slave away all day.

se bûcher, *P:* to fight, to have a set-to.

bûcheron [byʃrɔ̃], *s.m.* (*a*) woodcutter, woodman; logger; (*b*) lumberman, lumberer, *U.S:* lumber-jack.

bûcheronne [byʃrɔn], *s.f.* woodcutter's wife.

bûchette [byʃɛt], *s.f.* stick, bit of dry wood; *A:* **tirer à la b.,** to draw lots.

bûcheur, -euse [byʃœ:r, -ø:z], *s. F:* hard worker, swot(ter), *U.S:* grind.

bûchille [byʃi:j], *s.f.* **1.** small log. **2.** *pl. Metalw:* turnings.

bucoliaste [bykɔljast], *s.m.* bucolic (poet), writer of bucolics.

bucolique [bykɔlik]. **1.** *a.* bucolic, pastoral (song, etc.); **poète b.,** bucolic (poet). **2.** *s.m.* bucolic style. **3.** *s.f.pl.* (*a*) **les Bucoliques,** the Bucolics (of Virgil, etc.); (*b*) *F: A:* odds and ends (of personal property).

bucrâne, bucrane [bykrɑ:n], *s.m. Arch:* bucranium, bucrane.

budget [bydʒɛ], *s.m.* budget; **b. de la marine, de la guerre,** navy, army, estimates; **inscrire qch. au b.,** to budget for sth.; **présenter le b.,** to introduce, open, the budget; **b. extraordinaire,** emergency budget; **b. type,** average living expenditure according to which the minimum official wage is established; *s.a.* COMMISSION 6; **b. de ménage,** household budget; *F:* **arriver à boucler le b.,** to make both ends meet; **b. bien garni,** ample funds.

budgétaire [bydʒetɛ:r], *a.* budgetary; fiscal (year); financial (period); **situation b. de l'année,** budget statement for the year.

budgétairement [bydʒetɛrmɑ̃], *adv.* from the point of view of the budget; economically.

budgéter [bydʒete], *v.tr.* **(je budgète, n. budgétons; je budgéterai),** to include (sth.) in the budget, to budget for (sth.).

budgétisation [bydʒetizasjɔ̃], *s.f.* inclusion (of item) in budget; budgeting.

budgétiser [bydʒetize], *v.tr.* = BUDGÉTER.

budgétivore [bydʒetivɔ:r], *Iron:* **1.** *a.* parasitic (on the state). **2.** *s.* parasite (on the state).

buée [bɥe], *s.f.* **1.** *Dom.Ec: A:* lye. **2.** steam, reek, vapour (on window-panes, in wash-house); blur (of breath on mirror); mist, moisture (on mirror); *Nau:* **b. de cale,** sweat.

buénos-airien, -ienne [bɥenozɛrjɛ̃, -jɛn], *a. & s. Geog:* Buenos-Airean.

buer [bɥe], *v.i.* (*of hot bread, pastry, etc.*) to steam.

buffet [byfɛ], *s.m.* **1.** (*a*) sideboard; **b. de cuisine,** (kitchen) dresser; **b. glacière,** ice-chest; *F:* **danser devant le b.,** to have a bare cupboard; *P:* **n'avoir rien dans le b.,** to have an empty belly; (*b*) **b. (d'argenterie),** set of cutlery; (*c*) **b. d'orgue,** organ-chest. **2.** (*a*) buffet (in hotel, restaurant, etc.); *Rail:* **b. de gare,** buffet, refreshment room, station restaurant; (*b*) buffet, refreshment table (at ball, etc.); (*c*) **b. froid,** cold buffet (meal).

buffetier, -ière [byftje, -jɛ:r], *s.* refreshment-room manager or manageress.

buffeting [byfɛtiŋ], *s.m. Aer:* buffeting.

buffiage [byfla:ʒ], *s.m. E: Metalw:* buffing.

buffle [byfl], *s.m.* **1.** *Z:* buffalo; **b. de Cafrerie,** Cape buffalo; **b. commun, d'Asie,** Indian, Asiatic, buffalo; **b. pygmée, des Célèbes,** pygmy buffalo of the Celebes, anoa; **(cuir de) b.,** buffalo hide; buff (-leather); *F:* **tête de b.,** blockhead, duffer. **2.** (buff) strop. **3.** *Metalw:* buff-stick. **4.** *A:* (buff-) jerkin.

bufflesse [byflɛs], *s.f.* cow-buffalo.

buffleterie [byflətri, -lɛ-], *s.f. Mil:* leather equipment.

buffletin [byflətɛ̃], *s.m.* **1.** *Z:* buffalo calf. **2.** *Leath:* buffalo-calf hide. **3.** *A:* jerkin.

bufflette [byflɛt], *s.f. Z:* cow-buffalo.

bufflon [byflɔ̃], *s.m.* young buffalo.

bufflonne [byflɔn], *s.f. Z:* cow-buffalo.

bufonidés [byfɔnide], *s.m.pl. Amph:* Bufonidae, the common toads, the true toads.

bugalet [bygalɛ], *s.m.* (*a*) *Navy:* ammunition lighter; (*b*) hoy.

buggy [bygi, bœge], *s.m. Veh:* buggy.

bugle[1] [bygl], *s.m. Mus:* flugelhorn; key(ed) bugle; **petit b.,** soprano cornet (in E flat); *Rail: U.S:* whistle.

bugle[2], *s.f. Bot:* bugle; **b. rampante,** common bugle.

buglosse [byglɔs], *s.f. Bot:* bugloss, alkanet.

bugrane [bygran], *s.f. Bot:* rest-harrow, cammock.

bugule [bygyl], *s.f. Biol:* Bugula.

bugulidés [bygylide], *s.m.pl. Biol:* Bugulidae.

building [bildiŋ], *s.m.* large modern block (of flats, offices).

buire [bɥi:r], *s.f.* (*a*) (*brass or silver*) ewer, flagon; (*b*) *Dial:* milk can.

buirette [bɥirɛt], *s.f. Dial:* haycock.

buis [bɥi], *s.m.* **1.** *Bot:* (*a*) box(-tree); **b. nain, commun, des forêts,** ground-box; (*b*) **faux b., b. piquant,** butcher's-broom, knee-holly; (*c*) *Ecc:* **b. béni,** (blessed) palm. **2.** (*a*) box(-wood); (*b*) *Bootm: etc:* sleeking tool.

buissaie [bɥisɛ], *s.f.,* **buissière** [bɥisjɛ:r], *s.f.* box-shrubbery.

buisse [bɥis], *s.f. Bootm:* lapstone.

buisson [bɥisɔ̃], *s.m.* **1.** bush; **b. ardent,** (i) *Bot:* evergreen thorn, fire-thorn; (ii) *B:* burning-bush; **b. épineux,** briar. **2.** thicket, brake, spinney; *Ven. & F:* **trouver, faire, b. creux,** to draw a blank; to find the bird flown; *F:* **se sauver à travers les buissons,** to run away from, shirk, the issue; *s.a.* BATTRE 1. **3.** *Cu:* **b. (d'écrevisses, etc.),** buisson.

buissonnant [bɥisɔnɑ̃], *a.* growing in the shape of a bush; bushy.

buissonner [bɥisɔne], *v.i.* **1.** to grow into a bush, to grow like bushes. **2.** *Ven:* (*a*) (*of stag*) to take to the bush; (*b*) to beat for game.

buissonnet [bɥisɔnɛ], *s.m.* small bush.

buissonneux, -euse [bɥisɔnø, -ø:z], *a.* bushy (country, etc.).

buissonnier, -ière [bɥisɔnje, -jɛ:r]. **1.** *a.* that lives, lurks, in the bush; **lapin b.,** thicket-rabbit; *A:* **école buissonnière,** hedge-school; *F:* **faire l'école buissonnière,** to play truant, *U.S:* to play hook(e)y. **2.** *s.m.* (*a*) shrub, tree, trained in the shape of a bush; (*b*) shrubbery.

Bukovine [bykɔvin], *Pr.n.f. Geog:* Bukovina.

bulb [bœlb], *s.m. Nau:* bulge, bulb.

bulbaire [bylbɛ:r], *a.* bulbar.

bulbe [bylb]. **1.** *s.m. or f. Bot:* bulb, corm. **2.** *s.m. Anat:* bulb; **b. pileux,** root of a hair; **b. rachidien,** *medulla oblongata*; **b. aortique,** bulb of the aorta, *bulbus aortae, bulbus arteriosus*; *Algae:* hold-fast. **3.** *Nau:* bulb; **étrave en b.,** bulb-keel.

bulbeux, -euse [bylbø, -ø:z], *a.* bulbous; bulbed (plant); nodular; *Aut: etc:* **formes bulbeuses,** rounded lines.
bulbiculteur [bylbikyltœ:r], *s.m. Hort:* bulb-grower.
bulbiculture [bylbikylty:r], *s.f. Hort:* bulb-growing.
bulbifère [bylbifɛ:r], *a.* bulbiferous.
bulbiforme [bylbifɔrm], *a.* bulbiform.
bulbille [bylbij], *s.f. Bot:* bulbil, bulblet.
bulbul [bylbyl], *s.m. Orn:* bulbul.
bulgare [bylga:r], *a. & s. Geog:* Bulgarian; *Bac:* **bacille b.,** *lactobacillus acidophilus* (used for making yoghourt).
Bulgarie [bylgari], *Pr.n.f. Geog:* Bulgaria.
bulge [bœlʒ], *s.m. N.Arch:* bulge.
bulime [bylim], *s.m. Moll:* bulimus.
bullaire[1] [bylɛ:r], *s.m.* **1.** bullary, bullarium, collection of papal bulls. **2.** engrosser of papal bulls.
bullaire[2], *a. Bot: etc:* bullate; (of) blistered (appearance).
bulldog [buldɔg], *s.m. Z:* = BOULEDOGUE.
bulldozer [byldɔzɛ:r], *s.m.* bulldozer.
bulle [byl], *s.f.* **1.** *Rom.Ant:* bulla, locket (of Roman children). **2.** *Hist: esp. Ecc.Hist:* (*a*) bull, bulla (seal of official document); (*b*) bull (document); **la B. d'or,** the Golden Bull. **3.** (*a*) bubble (of air, water, etc.); **b. de savon,** soap-bubble; **faire des bulles de savon,** to blow soap-bubbles; *F: Mil:* **coincer la b.,** to hit the hay; (*b*) *Med:* blister, bleb, bulla; (*c*) *Metall:* blister, air-hole (in casting); (*d*) balloon (in comic strips, etc.); (*e*) *Ph:* **chambre à b.,** bubble chamber. **4.** *Com:* **(papier) b.,** *s.m.* **du b.,** manila (paper); cap-paper. **5.** *Arch: Furn:* bullen-nail.
bullé [byle], *a.* bullate (leaf); blistered (paper, etc.).
buller [byle], *v.tr. Ecc:* to affix the papal seal to (document); **bénéfice bullé,** benefice conferred by a bull.
bulletin [byltɛ̃], *s.m.* **1.** bulletin; (*a*) official report, summary (of news, information, etc.); **b. météorologique,** weather report; **b. d'actualités,** news bulletin; *Sch:* **b. hebdomadaire, trimestriel,** weekly, quarterly, report (to parents); *Mil:* **b. de renseignement,** intelligence summary; (*b*) periodical publication (of a body, firm, etc.); *Fin:* **b. des cours,** official (Stock Exchange) price-list. **2.** ticket, receipt, certificate; (telegraph) form; **b. de paie,** pay (advice) slip; *Com:* **b. de commande,** order form; **b. d'expédition,** way-bill; *Rail:* **b. (d'enregistrement) de bagages,** luggage-ticket, -check; **b. de consigne,** cloak-room ticket; **b. de correspondance,** train and bus ticket; **b. de vote,** ballot, voting, paper; **b. blanc,** blank voting paper; (a blank ballot paper returned by a person who does not wish to vote for any candidate but desires it to be known that he has gone to the polling station.) *s.a.* ASSEMBLAGE 2, SOUSCRIPTION 2.
bulletinier [byltinje], *s.m.* writer of bulletins, of reports.
bulleux, -euse [bylø, -ø:z], *a.* **1.** (*of water, etc.*) covered with bubbles, bubbly; *Geol: Med:* vesicular (rock, fever); *Med:* **râle b.,** bubbling râle. **2.** *Bot:* = BULLÉ.
bull-finch [bulfinʃ], *s.m. Equit:* bullfinch.
bullionisme [byljɔnism], *s.m. Pol.Ec:* bullionism.
bull-terrier [bultɛrje], *s.m.* bull-terrier.
bulot [bylo], *s.m. Moll: F:* whelk.
Buna [byna], *s.m. R.t.m:* Buna (rubber).
bungalow [bœ̃galo], *s.m.* **1.** (*in India*) bungalow. **2.** one-storied country cottage.
bungare [bœ̃ga:r], *s.m. Rept:* Bungarus, the Kraits.
bunion [bynjɔ̃], *s.m. Bot:* **bunion bulbeux,** pignut, earthnut.
bunker [bunkɛr], *s.m.* (*a*) *Mil:* bunker; (*b*) *Golf:* bunker.
bunodonte [bynɔdɔ̃t], *a. Z:* bunodont.
Bunsen [bɛ̃zɛn], *a. Ch:* **bec B.,** Bunsen burner; *F:* **un B.,** a Bunsen.
buphtalme [byftalm], *s.m. Bot:* ox-eye.
buphtalmie [byftalmi], *s.f. Med:* buphthalmia, buphthalmos.
buplèvre [byplɛ:vr̥], *s.m. Bot:* hare's-ear, thorough-wax.
bupreste [byprɛst], *s.m. Ent:* buprestis (beetle).
buprestidés [byprɛstide], *s.m.pl. Ent:* Buprestidae.
buraliste [byralist], *s.m. & f.* (*a*) clerk (in post office, etc.); (*b*) receiver of taxes in charge of office; (*c*) tobacconist (in country districts); *a.* **recette b.,** licensed tobacconist's.
burat [byra], *s.m. Tex:* frieze.
burdigalien[byrdigaljɛ̃], *a.&s.m.Geol:* Burdigalian.
bure[1] [by:r], *s.f.* (*a*) *Tex:* frieze; rough homespun; (*b*) sackcloth; **couleur de b.,** of a brownish colour (like sackcloth); (*c*) *Ecc:* frock.
bure[2], *s.f. Min:* blind shaft, bore-hole.
bure[3], *s.f.* = BUIRE.
bureau, -eaux [byro], *s.m.* **1.** *A:* coarse woollen cloth, frieze. **2.** (*a*) *A:* table covered with *bureau;* (*b*) writing-table, -desk; bureau; **b. américain, à rideau, b. à cylindre,** roll-top desk; **b. ministre,** knee-hole writing-table; **b. ministre, b. à deux corps de tiroirs, à deux caissons,** double-pedestal desk; **b. demi-ministre, à un caisson,** single-pedestal desk; *Pol:* **déposer un projet de loi sur le b.,** to lay a bill on the table, to table a bill; (*c*) **b. du caissier,** pay-desk; *A:* **payer à b. ouvert,** to pay on the nail. **3.** (*a*) office; study; **b. personnel,** private office; **ceci fera d'excellents bureaux,** this will be very good office space; **b. d'études,** design, planning department, office; **b. de poste,** post office; **b. central (des postes),** head post office; **b. de quartier,** district post office; **"b. restant,"** "to be called for"; **b. téléphonique,** telephone call-office; *Tp:* **b. central,** exchange; **b. de police,** police station; **b. des objets trouvés,** lost-property office; **b. de banque,** bank; **b. d'expédition,** forwarding office; **b. de douane,** custom-house; *Th:* **b. de location,** box-office; *Th:* **représentation à bureaux fermés,** performance (i) before an invited audience, with admission by invitation; (ii) with all seats reserved in advance, to capacity; (iii) open to members only; **représentation à b. ouvert,** performance open to general public; *s.a.* MACHINE 1; (*b*) (office) staff; (*c*) **b. de tabac,** tobacconist's shop (licensed by the State), *U.S:* cigar store. **4.** (*a*) *A:* bench (of judges); *F:* **prendre l'air du b.,** (i) to see how one's case stands, how the wind blows; (ii) (*through confusion with* 3(*a*)) to look in at the office; (*b*) board, committee, governing body, executive; **constituer le b. (d'une société, etc.),** to elect, appoint, a committee, a board; *Pol:* **b. électoral,** returning, polling, officers. **5.** (*a*) department; **les différents bureaux (d'une administration),** the different departments (of the civil service, etc.); (*b*) *Mil: Navy:* **b. (d'état-major),** branch, department, division; **Premier B.,** (i) *Mil:* A Branch, Department; *U.S:* G1 (division); (ii) *Navy:* Naval Personnel Department; **Deuxième B.,** (i) *Mil:* I Branch, Department; *U.S:* G2 (Division); (ii) *Navy:* Naval Intelligence Division; **Troisième B.,** (i) *Mil:* G Branch, Department; *U.S:* G3 (Division); (ii) *Navy:* Plans and Operations Division; **Quatrième B.,** (i) *Mil:* Q Branch, Department, *U.S:* G4 (Division); (ii) *Navy:* Administrative Planning Department.
bureaucrate [byrɔkrat], *s.m. Pej:* **1.** bureaucrat. **2.** *P:* black-coated clerk.
bureaucratie [byrɔkrasi], *s.f.* bureaucracy, officialdom; *F:* red tape, bumbledom.
bureaucratique [byrɔkratik], *a.* bureaucratic; **style b.,** formal, official, style; officialese, *U.S: F:* gobbledygook.
bureaucratiser [byrɔkratize], *v.tr.* to bring (charity, etc.) under official control; to bureaucratize; **aujourd'hui tout est bureaucratisé,** to-day red tape reigns supreme.
burelage [byrla:ʒ], *s.m. Philately:* burelé, burelage.
burèle, burelle [byrɛl], *s.f. Her:* barrulet.
burelé [byrle], *a.* **1.** *Her:* barry; **b. de dix pièces,** barry of ten pieces. **2.** *Philately:* burelé.
burette [byrɛt], *s.f.* **1.** cruet; *Ecc:* altar-cruet; burette. **2.** *Ch:* burette. **3.** oil-can, oiler, oil-feeder; **b. à pompe,** oil-squirt.
burgau, burgo [byrgo], *s.m. Moll:* burgau, burgao.
Burgondes, Burgundes [byrgɔ̃:d], *s.m.pl. Hist:* Burgundians (in the Vth cent.).
burgos [byrgos], *s.m. Cer:* lustre.
burgrave [byrgra:v], *s.m. Hist:* burgrave.
burgraviat [byrgravja], *s.m. Hist:* burgraviate.
burhinidés [byrinide], *s.m.pl. Orn:* Burhinidae.
burin [byrɛ̃], *s.m.* **1.** (*a*) graver, graving tool, etcher's needle, burin; (*b*) *F:* engraving, print. **2.** *Mec.E: Tls:* (*a*) (cold-)chisel, cutter; (*b*) *Dent:* burr-drill. **3.** *Nau:* (*a*) caulking iron; (*b*) toggle; (*c*) fid.
burinage [byrina:ʒ], *s.m.* **1.** graving. **2.** (*a*) chisel-work, chiselling, chipping; (*b*) *Dent:* burring; *F:* bishoping (of horse's teeth).
buriner [byrine], *v.tr.* **1.** to engrave (copper-plate); *F:* **un visage buriné,** (i) a seamed face; (ii) chiselled features; *F:* **b. l'histoire,** to relate history in incisive, trenchant, terms. **2.** (*a*) *Tchn:* to chisel, to work (sth.) with a chisel; to chip, score; *abs. P:* to work hard, to swot; (*b*) *Dent:* to burr (tooth); *F:* **b. les dents d'un cheval,** to bishop a horse, a horse's teeth.
burineur [byrinœ:r], *s.m.* **1.** (*of pers.*) (*a*) engraver; (*b*) chipper, trimmer, chiseller; *P:* hard worker, swot. **2.** chiselling-, chipping-tool.
burlesque [byrlɛsk], *a.* **1.** burlesque, mock-heroic (poem, etc.). **2.** comical, ludicrous, ridiculous (appearance, etc.).
burlesquement [byrlɛskəmɑ̃], *adv.* in a burlesque manner, comically, ridiculously.
burnous [byrnus, -nu], *s.m.* Arab cloak, burnouse.
buron [byrɔ̃], *s.m. Dial:* shepherd's hut (in Auvergne) where cheese is made.
bursite [byrsit], *s.f. Med:* bursitis.
bus [bys], *s.m. F:* = AUTOBUS.
busard [byza:r], *s.m.* **1.** *Orn:* harrier; **b. pâle, blafard,** pallid harrier; **b. St Martin,** hen-harrier, *U.S:* marsh-hawk; **b. harpaye, des roseaux,** marsh-harrier; **b. de Montagu, b. cendré,** Montagu's harrier. **2.** *Const: etc:* wooden gutter.
busc [bysk], *s.m.* **1.** *Cost:* (corset-)busk, steel; *Dressm:* whalebone. **2.** *Hyd.E:* locksill; mitre-sill (of lock). **3.** *Sm.a:* shoulder (of rifle-butt).
buse[1] [by:z], *s.* **1.** *Orn:* buzzard; **b. féroce,** long-legged buzzard; **b. pattue,** rough-legged buzzard; *U.S:* rough-legged hawk; **b. variable,** common buzzard; **b. des déserts,** desert buzzard; **b. des coquillages,** (American) snail hawk. **2.** *F:* block-head, dolt, fool; *Prov:* **on ne saurait faire d'une b. un épervier,** you cannot make a silk purse out of a sow's ear.
buse[2], *s.f.* channel, tube, pipe. **1.** nose-piece, nozzle (of bellows, tuyère); *Metall:* blast-pipe; **b. aspiratrice,** suction nozzle (of vacuum cleaner, etc.); **b. d'injecteur,** injector spray tip; *Av: etc:* **b. d'entrée d'air,** air scoop; *I.C.E:* **b. du carburateur,** carburettor choke-tube. **2.** *Min:* **b. d'aérage,** air-channel, -pipe, -shaft. **3.** *Hyd.E:* penstock, flume, leat (of water-wheel).
buselure [byzly:r], *s.f. Mec.E:* bush.
busette [byzɛt], *s.f. Gasm:* gas-nozzle (of coke-oven).
business [biznɛs], *s.m.* business; job.
businessman [biznɛsman], *s.m.* businessman; *pl. businessmen.*
busqué [byske], *a.* **1. nez b.,** aquiline nose, Roman nose; hooked nose. **2.** *Hyd.E:* **portes busquées,** mitre-gates (of lock).
busquer [byske], *v.tr.* **1.** to busk (corset); *A:* **b. une petite fille,** to put a little girl into stays. **2.** to curve.
se busquer, (*of nose*) to curve.
busserole [bysrɔl], *s.f. Bot:* **b. raisin d'ours,** bear-berry; **b. des Alpes,** Alpine bearberry.
buste [byst], *s.m.* bust; **b. en, de, marbre,** marble bust; **se faire peindre en b.,** to have a half-length portrait painted of oneself; *Nau:* **b. de proue,** figurehead.
bustier [bystje], *s.m.* long-line (strapless) brassière.
but [by(t)], *s.m.* **1.** mark (to aim at); target, objective; **un coup au b.,** a direct hit; *Artil:* **b. auxiliaire, b. témoin,** auxiliary target; **b. à battre,** target; **b. fixe,** stationary target; **b. mobile,** moving target; **b. à éclipse,** disappearing target; **b. fictif,** hypothetical target; **b. flottant,** floating target, target ship; *F:* **aller au-delà du b.,** to succeed beyond one's expectations. **2.** (*a*) *Rac:* goal, winning post; **aller droit au b.,** to go straight to the point; (*b*) *Fb:* goal, goal-posts; **ligne de b.,** goal-line; **entrée du b.,** goal-mouth; **marquer le premier b.,** to open the score; **b. de transformation,** converted goal, goal from a try; **b. égalisateur, d'égalisation,** equalizer; **b. sur coup franc,** goal from a free kick; (*c*) *Curling:* tee. **3.** object, end, aim, purpose, design; **mesure ayant pour b. d'assurer . . .,** measure intended to ensure . . .; **avec,** *F:* **dans, le b. de faire qch.,** with the object of, intention of, with a view to, doing sth.; *F:* **dans le b. de frauder,** with intent to defraud; **j'ai pour b. de . . .,** my (aim and) object is to . . .; *F:* **dans ce b. . . .,** with this object . . ., to this end . . .; **mon b. est de réformer le monde,** *F:* I am out to reform the world; **cette loi vise un double b.,** this law has two objects, two aims, in view; **je manquerais mon b. si . . .,** I should be defeating my object if . . .; **quel est le b. de votre voyage?** (i) what is the purpose of your journey? (ii) what is your objective? **le b. suprême,** the be-all and end-all; **errer sans b.,** to wander about aimlessly; **je n'ai pas de b. ce soir,** I have nothing particular in view this evening. **4.** *adv.phr.* (*a*) **b. à b.,** even, without any advantage to either party; **jouer b. à b.,** to play without giving or taking odds; (*b*) *Artil:* **tirer de b. en blanc,** to fire direct, point-blank; *F:* **faire une offre de b. en blanc,** to make an offer point-blank; **faire qch. de b. en blanc,** to do sth. on the spur of the moment; **il raconta l'affaire de b. en blanc,** he blurted out the whole story.
butadiène [bytadiɛn], *s.m. Ch:* butadiene.

butane [bytan], *s.m. Ch:* butane.

butanier [bytanje], *s.m. Nau:* tanker.

butanol [bytanɔl], *s.m. Ch:* butanol.

buté [byte], *a.* fixed, set; **caractère b.**, obstinate nature; **être b. à qch., à faire qch.**, to be dead set on sth., on doing sth.

butea [bytea], *s.f. Bot:* butea.

butée [byte], *s.f.* 1. thrust (of ground, etc.); (*b*) butting, striking (of two parts, etc.); *Mec.E:* thrust; **palier de b.**, thrust-block, -bearing; **collet (du palier) de b., collier de b.**, thrust-collar; **arbre de b.**, thrust-shaft; **plaque de b.**, thrust-plate; **b. à billes**, ball thrust-bearing. 2. abutment, buttress, prop; *Civ.E:* abutment(-pier) (of bridge). 3. *Mec.E:* (*a*) **b. (d'arrêt)** stop; **vis de b.**, stop-screw, adjusting screw; **b. mécanique**, mechanical stop unit; **b. mobile**, movable stop; **b. réglable**, adjustable stop; **b. de ressort**, spring stop; **b. d'aiguille (d'un cadran)**, hand stop (on a dial); *s.a.* BAGUE 2; (*b*) knock-off (cam, etc.); (*c*) footstep (bearing).

butène [byten], *s.m. Ch:* butylene.

buter [byte]. **1.** *v.i.* (*a*) (*of thg*) to butt, strike, knock (**contre, sur,** against); (*b*) (*of pers.*) to knock (**contre,** against); to stumble (**contre, over**); (*c*) (*of beams, etc.*) to abut, rest (**contre,** against). **2.** *v.tr.* (*a*) to prop up; **b. un mur,** to buttress, shore up, a wall; (*b*) **b. qn,** to cross, oppose, s.o. **3.** *v.tr. P:* to kill, bump (s.o.) off.

se buter. 1. (*a*) **se b. contre qch.,** to prop oneself firmly against sth.; (*b*) **se b. à un obstacle,** to come up against an obstacle; (*c*) **se b. à qch., à faire qch.,** to be obstinately set on sth., on doing sth.; **se b. à une difficulté invincible,** *F:* to run one's head against a wall. **2.** *P:* to commit suicide.

buteur [bytœːr], *s.m. Sp:* (goal-)scorer.

butin [bytɛ̃], *s.m.* 1. booty, spoils, plunder; *F:* loot; *F:* **faire son b. dans une affaire,** to make a handsome profit out of a deal. 2. *A: F:* goods and chattels.

butinement [bytinmɑ̃], *s.m.* 1. *A:* plundering; *F:* looting. 2. (*of bees*) honey-gathering.

butiner [bytine], *v.tr. & i.* 1. *A:* to loot, plunder; *b.* **dans les ouvrages de qn,** to pilfer, *F:* to lift, thoughts, facts, from s.o.'s works. 2. (*of bees, etc.*) *b.* (sur) **les fleurs,** to gather honey from the flowers.

butineur, -euse [bytinœːr, -øːz]. 1. *a.* honey-gathering (insect); industrious (bee). 2. *s.f.* **butineuse;** *Ap:* foraging bee, forager, field bee.

butique [bytik], *a. Ch:* butic, arachic (acid).

butoir [bytwaːr], *s.m.* 1. stop, check; buffer; stop-pin. *Rail:* buffer-stop, terminal buffer; **b. d'une porte,** door-stop. 2. catch, tappet; *Nau:* pawl-head (of capstan). 3. *Geol:* horst.

butôme [bytom], *s.m. Bot:* butomus; **b. à ombelles** flowering rush, water-gladiole.

butor [bytɔːr]. 1. *s.m. Orn:* bittern; *F:* bull-of-the-bog; **b. étoilé, grand b.,** bittern (*Botaurus stellaris*); **b. blongios,** little bittern; **b. d'Amérique,** American bittern. 2. *F: f.* (*rare*) **butorde** [bytɔrd]) churl, lout; clod; *f.* dull, clumsy, woman.

butorderie [bytɔrdri], *s.f.* stupidity, dullness, loutishness.

buttage [bytaːʒ], *s.m.* (*a*) *Agr:* ridging (of earth); (*b*) *Hort:* earthing up (of plants); (*c*) *P:* murder.

butte [byt], *s.f.* 1. rising ground, knoll, hillock, mound; *Geol:* **b. témoin,** (flat-topped) outlier; *butte témoin; Rail:* **b. de triage, de gravité,** hump. 2. *Mil:* stop-butt, butts (of range); *F:* **être en b. à qch.,** to be exposed to sth.; **être en b. au ridicule,** to be an object of ridicule, a butt for ridicule; **mettre qn en b. aux rires,** to raise a laugh at s.o.'s expense. 3. *Min:* prop, shore.

buttée [byte], *s.f.* = BUTÉE.

butter [byte], *v.tr.* (*a*) *Agr:* to ridge (ground for draining purposes); (*b*) *Hort:* to earth up (plants); (*c*) *P:* to kill.

se butter, take shelter under a mound.

butteur [bytœːr], *s.m.* (*a*) *Agr:* ridge-plough, ridging-plough; (*b*) *P:* murderer.

buttoir [bytwaːr], *s.m.* 1. *Agr:* ridge-plough, ridging-plough, ridger. 2. = BUTOIR.

butylcaoutchouc [bytilkautʃu], *s.m.* butylrubber.

butyle [bytil], *s.m. Ch:* butyl; **caoutchouc b.,** butylrubber.

butylène [bytilɛn], *s.m. Ch:* butylene.

butylique [bytilik], *a.* butylic (alcohol, etc.).

butyracé [bytirase], *a.* butyraceous.

butyrate [bytirat], *s.m. Ch:* butyrate.

butyreux, -euse [bytirø, -øːz], *a.* 1. buttery. 2. *Ch:* butyrous.

butyrine [bytirin], *s.f. Ch:* butyrin(e).

butyrique [bytirik], *a.* butyric (acid).

butyromètre [bytirɔmɛtr], *s.m.* butyrometer.

buvable [byvabl], *a.* (*a*) drinkable, fit to drink; (*b*) *Med:* to be taken orally.

buvant [byvɑ̃], *s.m.* edge of a (drinking) glass.

buvard [byvaːr]. 1. *a.* **papier b.,** (i) blotting-paper; (ii) filter-paper. 2. *s.m.* blotter, blotting-pad; **passer le b. sur l'encre,** to blot the ink.

buvée [byve], *s.f. Vet:* drench.

buverie [byvri], *s.f. F:* = BEUVERIE.

buvetier, -ière [byvtje, -jɛːr], *s.* tavern-keeper, bar-keeper, -maid.

buvette [byvɛt], *s.f.* 1. (*a*) refreshment bar (at railway station, etc.); (*b*) small bar, *U.S:* soda-fountain. 2. pump-room (at watering-place).

buveur, -euse [byvœːr, -øːz], *s.* 1. drinker; **b. d'eau,** water-drinker, teetotaller; *s.a.* SANG 1. 2. toper, drunkard, wine-bibber.

buvoter [byvɔte], *v.i. F:* to tipple.

buxacées [byksase], *s.f.pl. Bot:* Buxaceae, the box family.

buzançaïen, -enne [byzɑ̃sajɛ̃, -jɛn], *a. & s. Geog:* (native, inhabitant) of Buzançais.

by-pass [bipas, bajpas], *s.m.* (*a*) *F:* (*road*) by-pass; (*b*) *Plumb:* by-pass.

by-passer [bipase, bajpase], *v.tr.* to by-pass.

byronien, -ienne [birɔnjɛ̃, -jɛn], *a. Lit:* Byronic (gloom, outlook); Byronian (verse).

byrrhe [biːr], *s.m. Ent:* pill-beetle.

byssinose [bisinoːz], *s.f. Med:* byssinosis.

byssus [bisys], *s.m. Ant: Conch:* byssus.

Byzance [bizɑ̃ːs], *Pr.n. A.Geog:* Byzantium.

byzantin, -ine [bizɑ̃tɛ̃, -in], *a. & s.* 1. Byzantine. 2. ill-timed and beside the point; **discussions byzantines,** futile and ill-timed discussions.

byzantinisme [bizɑ̃tinism], *s.m.* (*a*) byzantinism; (*b*) *F:* logic-chopping.

byzantiniste [bizɑ̃tinist], *s.m. & f.* Byzantinist.

C

C, c [se], *s.m.* (the letter) C, c; **c cédille**, c with a cedilla, ç; **fer en C**, C-shaped bar iron; *Tp:* **C comme Célestin**, C for Charlie.

c'. *See* CE[1].

çà [sa]. **1.** *adv.* hither; **çà et là**, this way and that; hither and thither; here and there; **jambe de çà, jambe de là**, astride, astraddle. **2.** *int.* (*a*) *A:* **çà, répondez!** now then, come now, answer! (*b*) **ah çà!** now then!

ça [sa], *dem.pron.neut.* **1.** *F:* = CELA. **2.** *Psy:* **le ça**, the id.

Caaba (la) [laka:ba], *s.f. Rel.H:* the Kaaba.

caama [ka:ma], *s.m. Z:* kaama, hart(e)beest.

cab [kab], *s.m. A:* hansom(-cab).

cabale [kabal], *s.f.* **1.** *Jew.Rel.H:* cab(b)ala. **2.** cabal; (*a*) intrigue, scheme, plot; **monter une c. contre qn**, to work up an intrigue against s.o.; (*b*) faction, junto, clique, caucus.

cabaler [kabale], *v.i.* to cabal, plot, intrigue (**contre**, against); to work for the overthrow of (s.o.).

cabaleur, -euse [kabalœ:r, -ø:z], **1.** *a.* caballing, intriguing, plotting. **2.** *s.* (*a*) caballer, plotter, intriguer; (*b*) *Fr.C: Pol:* canvasser.

cabaliste [kabalist], *s.* **1.** *Jew.Rel.H:* cab(b)alist. **2.** caballer, plotter, intriguer.

cabalistique [kabalistik], *a.* cab(b)alistic.

caballin [kabal(l)ɛ̃], *a.* caballine; *Z:* equine; *Gr.Myth:* **fontaine caballine**, caballine fountain; *Bot:* **aloès c.**, caballine aloe.

caban [kabã], *s.m.* **1.** *Nau:* (*a*) (sailor's) pea-jacket; (*b*) pilot-coat; (*c*) (officer's) hooded overcoat; (*d*) oilskins. **2.** (hooded) cloak.

cabanage [kabana:ʒ], *s.m.* **1.** (*a*) camping (in huts); (*b*) camping ground, hutments. **2.** *Nau:* capsizing, canting (of boat).

cabane [kaban], *s.f.* **1.** (*a*) hut, shanty; *Scot:* bothy, bothie; (dog-)kennel; (rabbit-)hutch; *Fr.C:* **c. à sucre**, sap-house; (*b*) cabin (on river barge, etc.); (*c*) *P:* jail, clink; (*d*) *P:* brothel. **2.** *Av: A:* cabane, central unit (of aeroplane); **mât de c.**, king-post.

cabanement [kabanmã], *s.m. Nau:* tipping.

cabaner [kabane]. **1.** *v.i.* (*of boat*) to capsize. **2.** *v.tr.* to cant (boat), to turn (boat) over (for repairs).

cabanon [kabanɔ̃], *s.m.* **1.** (*a*) small hut; (*b*) *Dial:* (i) small country, seaside, house; (ii) shooting-box. **2.** (*a*) dark cell (of prison); (*b*) (lunatic's) padded cell; *F:* lunatic asylum; **il est bon pour le c.**, he is ripe for the nut-house.

cabaret [kabarɛ], *s.m.* **1.** (*a*) = public-house, tavern, wine-shop; *F:* pub; (*b*) inn, eating-house; (*c*) (small fashionable) restaurant; night-club, cabaret. **2.** (*a*) liqueur-stand; (*b*) (tea-, coffee-, chocolate-) set, service (with its tray); cabaret; (*c*) *Nau:* fiddle; (*d*) *Fr.C:* tray. **3.** *Bot:* (*a*) asarabacca; (*b*) **c. des murailles**, Venus's navelwort; (*c*) **c. des oiseaux**, fuller's teasel. **4.** *Orn:* (North-European) linnet.

cabaretier, -ière [kabartje, -jɛ:r], *s.* (*a*) publican, tavern-keeper; (*b*) inn-keeper.

cabas [kaba], *s.m.* **1.** (*a*) frail, basket; **c. à figues**, tapnet; *F:* tap, frail; (*b*) (plaited two-handled) (i) shopping basket; (ii) tool-basket, bass. **2.** *Cost:* poke-bonnet. **3.** *A:* wicker-work carriage.

cabasson [kabasɔ̃], *s.m. F: A:* old-fashioned bonnet.

cabèche [kabɛʃ], *s.f. P:* head, nut.

cabère [kabɛ:r], *s.f. Ent:* cabera; *F:* wave (moth).

cabernet [kabɛrnɛ], *s.m. Vit:* cabernet.

cabestan [kabɛstã], *s.m. Nau: etc:* capstan, windlass, winch; *Oil Min:* cathead; **c. à vapeur**, steam-capstan, -winch; **c. à bras**, hand capstan; **c. volant**, crab (-capstan); **grand c.**, main capstan; **petit c.**, jeer-capstan; **armer un c.**, (i) to rig a winch; (ii) to man a capstan; **virez au c.!** heave! *Min:* **c. à cheval**, (horse-)whim; gin.

cabiai [kabie], *s.m. Z:* capybara, water-cavy, water-hog, -pig.

cabillau(d) [kabijo], *s.m.* codfish, fresh cod.

cabillot [kabijo], *s.m. Nau:* **c. d'amarrage**, toggle (-pin); **c. de tournage**, belaying pin.

cabilloter [kabijɔte], *v.tr. Nau:* to toggle (rope).

cabine [kabin], *s.f.* cabin; cubicle; (*a*) *Nau:* **la c.**, the saloon; **c. intérieure, extérieure**, inside, outside, cabin; **c. individuelle**, single(-berth) cabin; **c. de luxe**, stateroom; *Av:* (passenger) cabin; **c. étanche**, pressure cabin; **c. de navigation**, navigator's cabin; **c. de pilotage**, cockpit; *Space:* **c. (spatiale)**, (space) capsule; (*c*) hut; **c. de bains**, cabin, (bathing) hut; **c. de douche**, shower cubicle; **c. (téléphonique)**, phone-box, (telephone) call-box, (tele)phone booth; **c. d'écoute**, listening booth; acoustic hood; *Rail:* **c. d'aiguillage**, signal-box; (*d*) cab, house (of crane); cab (of locomotive, lorry); cage, car (of lift); **camion à c. avancée**, lorry with cab over engine.

cabinet [kabinɛ], *s.m.* **1.** (*a*) closet, small room; **c. de toilette**, dressing-room (with basin); small bathroom; **c. (d'aisances)**; *F:* **les cabinets**, lavatory; **c. de travail**, study; **c. noir**, (i) box-room; (ii) *Phot:* dark-room; (*in restaurant*) **c. particulier**, private dining-room; (*b*) **c. de verdure**, arbour. **2.** (*a*) office, room; chambers (of judge, barrister); (doctor's) consulting room; **c. dentaire**, dental surgery; *Hist:* **le C. noir**, the postal censorship office (*esp.* under Louis XV), the *Cabinet noir*; (*b*) practice (of professional man); **accroître son c.**, to increase one's connection. **3.** (*a*) collection (of works of art, etc.); **c. d'histoire naturelle**, private natural history collection; **c. de physique**, collection of physical apparatus, physical laboratory; **c. d'estampes**, print-room (in museum); **c. de lecture**, reading-room. **4.** *Pol:* *Foreign Pol:* **renverser le c.**, to overthrow the government; **le c. de Paris**, the French government; (*b*) *Home Pol:* cabinet; **question de c.**, ministerial question; (*c*) **c. d'un ministre**, minister's departmental staff; **chef de c.** = principal private secretary. **5.** *Antique Furn:* cabinet.

cabinier [kabinje], *s.m.* cable-car conductor.

câblage [kabla:ʒ], *s.m.* **1.** *Tex:* twisting, cabling (of yarn). **2.** *El.E:* connecting up; cabling, wiring, twisting (of wire); **schéma de c.**, wiring diagram; **c. coaxial**, coaxial wiring; **c. par paires**, pairing; **c. par paires torsadées**, twisted pair lay-up. **3.** *Av:* rigging.

câble [ka:bl], *s.m.* **1.** (*a*) cable, rope; *Nau:* **c. d'amarrage**, mooring cable; **c. de remorque**, towing line, tow; **filer le c.**, to pay out the cable; **filer son c. par le bout**, (i) to slip one's cable; (ii) *F:* to die; (*b*) **c. métallique**, (i) wire-rope; (ii) stranded wire; **c. aérien**, aerial ropeway, wire-way; **c. (de) Bowden**, Bowden wire; *Av:* **c. de commande**, control wire; **c. d'acier**, steel-wire cable. **2.** *El.E:* (i) cable; (ii) (*in apparatus*) wiring lead; (iii) flex, cord; (*b*) **c. aérien**, overhead cable; **c. enterré, souterrain**, underground cable; **c. sous-marin**, submarine cable; **c. des** grandes profondeurs, deep-sea cable; **c. à deux conducteurs**, twin-wire, -lead; -cable; **c. à paires câblées en étoile**, **c. à quartes**, quad(ded) cable; quad pair cable; **c. à paires**, paired, non-quadded cable; **c. à courant porteur**, carrier cable; **c. coaxial**, coaxial cable; **c. armé, c. blindé**, **c. sous gaine**, armoured cable; **c. sous plomb**, lead-covered cable; **c. isolé au caoutchouc**, **c. sous caoutchouc**, rubber-covered, -sheathed, -insulated, cable; rubber cable; **gaine de c.**, cable tube; **c. à huile, à gaz**, oil-filled, gas-filled, cable; **c. entre centraux interurbains**, trunk cable; **c. de répartition, de distribution**, distribution cable; **c. d'alimentation (force)**, power cable; **c. d'arrivée, de sortie**, inlet, outlet cable; **c. de ceinture, de rocade**, ring cable; **c. d'évitement, de contournement**, by-pass cable; **c. de commande à distance**, remote control cable; **c. de télécommande, de télémanipulation**, keying cable; **c. de raccordement**, sub-cable; **tronçon de c. (de raccordement)**, cable stub; **tête de c.**, cable terminal; **poser un c.**, to lay a cable; **pose de c.**, cable laying; **dénuder un c.**, to strip a cable; (*b*) *Telecom:* cable; **aviser qn par c.**, to cable to s.o.; (*c*) *Elcs:* **c. hertzien**, radio link. **3.** *Nau: A:* (= ENCABLURE) cable's length. **4.** *Arch:* cable moulding.

câblé [kable]. **1.** *a.* (*a*) *Arch:* cabled (moulding); (*b*) *Tex:* spun. **2.** *s.m.* (*a*) (twisted) cord (for looping curtains, etc.); (*b*) **c. six-fils**, six-cord sewing-machine cotton; cable-cord; **c. d'Alsace**, Alsatian crochet-cotton.

câbleau, -eaux [kablo], *s.m. Nau:* (*a*) cablet, small cable; (*b*) mooring-rope, painter; (*c*) tow-rope (for barges); (*d*) *Rail:* electric cable (connecting two carriages).

câble-chaîne [kabləʃɛn], *s.m. Mec.E:* chain cable; *pl.* **câbles-chaînes**.

câblée [kable], *s.f.* = ENCABLURE.

câblegramme [kabləgram], *s.m.* = CÂBLOGRAMME.

câbler [kable], *v.tr.* **1.** to twist, lay (strands into cable). **2.** to cable (message); *abs.* **câbler à qn.**, to cable (to) s.o.; to wire; **machine câblée selon schéma B**, machine wired to wiring diagram B.

câblerie [kabləri], *s.f.* (*a*) cable-making; (*b*) cable-manufacturing plant; (*c*) cable trade.

câbliau, -iaux [kablijo], *s.m.* = CABILLAUD.

câblier [kablije], *s.m.* **1.** cable-ship. **2.** cable-maker.

câblogramme [kabləgram], *s.m.* cablegram; *F:* cable (message).

câblot [kablo], *s.m.* = CÂBLEAU.

cabochard, -arde [kabɔʃa:r, -ard], (*a*) *a.* stubborn; (*b*) *s.* stubborn person.

caboche [kabɔʃ], *s.f.* **1.** *F:* head, nut, noddle; **avoir la c. dure**, (i) to be thick-headed; (ii) to be obstinate. **2.** **(clou) c.**, (i) heavy-headed nail, clout-nail; *Bootm:* hobnail; (ii) = CABOCHON 2.

caboché [kabɔʃe], *a. Her:* caboched, cabossed, cabossed.

cabochon [kabɔʃɔ̃], *s.m.* **1.** (*a*) *Lap:* cabochon; **émeraude en c.**, tallow-drop emerald, emerald *en cabochon*; (*b*) *Cy:* **c. rouge**, red reflector. **2.** *Furn:* (fancy) brass-nail, stud-nail. **3.** *P:* (*a*) = CABOCHE 1; (*b*) *A:* blow, smack. **4.** *Av: etc:* dimmer cap.

cabosse [kabɔs], *s.f.* **1.** *F:* bruise, bump; **se faire une c.**, to raise a bump. **2.** *Bot:* cacao-pod; *F:* chocolate-nut.

cabosser [kabɔse], *v.tr. F:* **1.** to bump, bruise. **2.** to dent (silverware); to bash in (hat); **vieux chapeau cabossé,** battered old hat.
cabot[1] [kabo], *s.m. P:* **1.** = CABOTIN. **2.** *(a)* dog; *F:* pooch; *(b) Mil:* corporal.
cabot[2], *s.m. Ich: F:* miller's-thumb, bull-head.
cabotage [kabɔtaːʒ], *s.m. Nau:* coasting; coastal trade; cabotage; **grand c., petit c.,** offshore, inshore, coastal traffic; *A:* **capitaine, maître, patron, au c.,** master, skipper, of a coasting vessel.
caboter [kabɔte], *v.i. Nau:* to coast.
caboteur [kabɔtœːr], *Nau:* **1.** *s.m.* coaster, (i) coast sailor; (ii) coasting vessel. **2.** *a.m.* coasting, coastwise, coastal (trade).
cabotier [kabɔtje], *s.m. O:* = CABOTEUR.
cabotin, -ine [kabɔtɛ̃, -in], *s. F:* *(a)* (third-rate) play-actor, -actress, ham actor; *(b) A:* strolling player; *F:* barn-stormer; *(c) F:* show-off; **c. de la politique,** histrionic politician.
cabotinage [kabɔtinaːʒ], *s.m.* **1.** (third-rate) acting. **2.** *A:* life of a strolling player; *F:* barn-storming. **3.** *(a)* looseness of conduct, low bohemianism; *(b)* quackery; histrionics (in politics, etc.).
cabotiner [kabɔtine], *v.i.* **1.** *A:* to lead the life of a strolling player; *F:* to busk. **2.** to play to the gallery. **3.** to lead a bohemian life.
Caboul [kabul], *Pr.n.m.* = KABOUL.
caboulot [kabulo], *s.m. F:* low pub, dive.
cabourgeois, -oise [kaburʒwa, -waːz], *a. & s. Geog:* (native, inhabitant) of Cabourg.
cabrade [kɑbrad], *s.f.* *(of horse)* **faire une c.,** to rear.
cabrage [kɑbraːʒ], *s.m.* rearing; *Av:* nose-lift; elevating (of plane).
cabre [kɑːbr̥], *s.f. Nau:* sheer(-legs); gin.
cabré [kabre], *a.* **1.** *(of horse)* rearing. **2.** *Av:* tail down, *cabré.*
cabrement [kɑbrəmɑ̃], *s.m.* *(of horse)* rearing.
cabrer [kɑbre]. **1.** *v.tr. Av:* to pull up, *F:* to hoick (aircraft). **2.** *v.pr.* *(a)* *(of horse, etc.)* to rear; *F:* *(of pers.)* **se c. contre qch.,** to jib at sth., to rise in protest against sth.; to rebel against; *F:* to kick at (one's fate); *(b) Av:* to rear, buck; to nose up; *(c) Mil:* **faire c. un char,** to belly a tank; *(d) Artil:* *(of gun)* to jump.
cabrette [kabrɛt], *s.f.* *(in Auvergne)* bagpipe.
cabri [kabri], *s.m.* kid; *F:* **faire des sauts de c.,** to caper about.
cabriole [kabri(j)ɔl], *s.f.* *(a)* leap, caper; **faire des cabrioles,** to cut capers, to caper about; *(b) Equit:* capriole, goat's leap; *(c)* tumble, somersault; *F:* **faire une c.,** to come a cropper.
cabrioler [kabri(j)ɔle], *v.i.* to cut capers, to caper (about).
cabriolet [kabri(j)ɔlɛ], *s.m.* **1.** *Veh:* *(a) A:* cab(riolet); *(b)* gig; *(c) Aut:* cabriolet. **2.** *(a) Cost: A:* poke-bonnet (under the Directoire); *(b) Furn: A:* small armchair. **3.** *A:* (policeman's) twister.
cabrioleur, -euse [kabri(j)ɔlœːr, -øːz], *s.* caperer.
cabrion [kabri(j)ɔ̃], *s.m.* **1.** *N.Arch:* ba(u)lk. **2.** *Nau:* chock (for cask, etc.); **c. d'arrêt,** skid, cleat; **c. d'arrimage,** ba(u)lk.
cabron [karbrɔ̃], *s.m.* **1.** *Leath:* kid(-skin). **2.** *Mec.E: Clockm:* buff-stick.
cabrouet [kabrue], *s.m.* hand-truck.
cabus [kaby]. **1.** *a.* **chou c.,** headed cabbage. **2.** *s.m. Sw.Fr:* lettuce; *pl. des cabusses.*
caca [kaka], *s.m. F:* *(nursery):* excrement; *F:* big job; *(to child)* **as-tu fait c.?** *F:* have you done your duty? **jette ça, c'est du c.,** throw that away, it's nasty, dirty; **c. d'oie,** gosling green.
cacade [kakad], *s.f. P:* **1.** *A:* copious evacuation; *P:* squitters. **2.** mess, failure. **3.** funk, climb-down.
cacafouiller [kakafuje], *v.i. P: A:* = CAFOUILLER.
cacahouète, *s.f.,* **cacahouet(t)e,** *s.f.,* **cacahuète** [kakawɛt], *s.f.* peanut, monkey-nut.
cacao [kakao], *s.m. Bot:* cacao; *Com:* cocoa; **beurre de c.,** cocoa-butter.
cacaoté [kakaɔte], *a.* containing cocoa, cocoa-flavoured.
cacaotier [kakaɔtje], *s.m.* = CACAOYER.
cacaotière [kakaɔtjɛːr], *s.f.* = CACAOYÈRE.
cacaouette [kakawɛt], *s.f.* = CACAHOUÈTE.
cacaoyer [kakaɔje], *s.m. Bot:* cacao-tree.
cacaoyère [kakaɔjɛːr], *s.f.* cacao-plantation.
cacarder [kakarde], *v.i.* *(of goose)* to cackle, to gabble.
cacatoès [kakatɔɛs], *s.m. Orn:* cockatoo.
cacatois [kakatwa], *s.m.* **1.** *Orn:* = CACATOÈS. **2.** *Nau:* royal(-sail); **grand c., petit c.,** main-, fore-royal; **c. de perruche,** mizzen-royal.
cachalot [kaʃalo], *s.m. Z:* cachalot, sperm-whale.
cachalotier, -ière [kaʃalɔtje, -jɛːr], *a.* of, pertaining to (the catching of) cachalots; *s.m.* **(navire) cachalotier,** (sperm-)whaler.
cache[1] [kaʃ]. **1.** *s.f.* hiding-place, (i) cache (of explorer, etc.); (ii) *F:* hidie-hole (of child, etc.). **2.** *s.m.* *(a) Phot:* mask (for printing); **c. flou,** soft mask; **c. net,** sharp mask; *(b) Typ:* frisket; *(c) Draw:* overlay; *(d) Av: etc:* cover, guard.
cache[2], *s.m.inv. Chinese Num:* cash.
cache-cache [kaʃkaʃ], *s.m.* hide-and-seek.
cache-carte [kaʃkart], *s.m. Mil:* map-cover, -case; *pl. cache-carte(s).*
cache-ceinture [kaʃsɛ̃tyːr], *s.m.inv. Artil:* band-guard (of shell).
cache-col [kaʃkɔl], *s.m.,* **cache-cou** [kaʃku], *s.m. Cost:* (man's) scarf; *pl. cache-col(s), -cou(s).*
cache-corset [kaʃkɔrsɛ], *s.m.inv. Cost:* camisole, under-bodice.
cache-couture [kaʃkutyːr], *s.m.inv. Dressm:* selvage, selvedge, tape.
cachectique [kaʃɛktik], *a. & s. Med:* cachectic (patient).
cache-entrée [kaʃɑ̃tre], *s.m.inv.* drop, guard, sheave, curtain (of key-hole).
cache-éperon [kaʃeprɔ̃], *s.m.* spur-hood, -cover; *pl. cache-éperon(s).*
cache-flamme [kaʃflɑːm], *s.m.,* **cache-lueur** [kaʃlɥœːr], *s.m. Artil:* flash-concealer, -eliminator, -screen; *pl. cache-flamme(s), -lueur(s).*
cache-lumière [kaʃlymjɛːr], *s.m.* **1.** *Artil: A:* vent-cover, -apron. **2.** sunshade (of telescope); *pl. cache-lumière(s).*
cache-maillot [kaʃmajo], *s.m.* **1.** (baby's) long clothes. **2.** beach tunic, beach shirt; *pl. cache-maillots.*
cachement [kaʃmɑ̃], *s.m. A:* hiding, concealing.
Cachemire [kaʃmiːr]. **1.** *Pr.n.m. Geog:* Cashmere, Kashmir. **2.** *s.m.* *(a) Tex:* (i) cashmere; (ii) (imitation) Paisley pattern; *(b) Cost:* cashmere shawl.
cachemirette [kaʃmirɛt], *s.f. Tex:* cashmerette.
cachemirien, -ienne [kaʃmirjɛ̃, -jɛn], *a. & s. Geog:* Cashmerian, Kashmirian.
cache-misère [kaʃmizɛːr], *s.m.inv. in pl. F:* coat or wrap (hiding the shabbiness underneath).
cache-mouchoir [kaʃmuʃwaːr], *s.m.inv.* (game of) hide-the-handkerchief, hunt-the-slipper.
cache-nez [kaʃne], *s.m.inv.* **1.** muffler, comforter, scarf. **2.** nose-band (of bridle).
cache-peigne [kaʃpɛɲ], *s.m.inv. Cost:* ornament (used to conceal back-comb).
cache-platine [kaʃplatin], *s.m.inv. Sm.a: A:* lock cover.
cache-pot [kaʃpo], *s.m.inv.* flower-pot case, cover; (flower) pot holder; *adv.phr:* **faire qch. à c.-p.,** to do sth. secretly, *sub rosa*; *esp.* **vendre à c.-p.,** to sell drink secretly; to shebeen.
cache-poussière [kaʃpusjɛːr], *s.m.inv.* *(a) A:* dust-coat; *(b) Av:* **c.-p. souple,** dust boot; **c.-p. rigide,** dust cover.
cacher [kaʃe], *v.tr.* *(a)* to hide, conceal, secrete (s.o., sth.); *(b)* to conceal: to hide (one's face, etc.) from view; to cover up (picture, etc.); to mask, dissemble (one's feelings, etc.); **se c. la figure dans ses mains,** to bury one's face in one's hands; **sentiers cachés,** by-paths; **douleur cachée,** secret grief; **c. qch. à qn,** to hide, conceal, keep back, withhold, sth. from s.o.; **c. sa vie,** to live in retirement, secluded from the world; **esprit caché,** (i) reserved, (ii) sly, person; **n'avoir rien de caché pour qn,** to have no secrets from s.o.; **il n'y a rien de caché dans cette affaire,** all is open and above-board in this transaction; **il ne cache pas que . . .,** he makes no secret of the fact that . . .; **il n'a pas caché qu'il était très mécontent,** he made it plain that he was very displeased; **défaut caché,** latent defect; *s.a.* JEU 4.
se cacher. 1. to hide, lie in hiding; to skulk; **les périls qui se cachent dans ces montagnes,** the perils that lurk in these mountains; *Av:* **se c. dans le soleil,** to dodge into the sun. **2.** *(a)* **se c. à qn, au monde,** (i) to hide from, (ii) to shun, avoid, s.o., the world; **se c. de qn,** (i) to keep out of s.o.'s way; (ii) to conceal one's feelings, actions, from s.o.; *(b)* **se c. de qch.,** *O:* **de faire qch.,** to make a secret of sth., of doing sth.; **je ne m'en cache pas,** I make no secret of it; **en se cachant,** secretly, on the sly; **sans se c.,** openly, overtly.
cache-radiateur [kaʃradjatœːr], *s.m.inv.* radiator cover.
cachereau, -eaux [kaʃ(ə)ro], *s.m.* file of deeds (of property).
cacherie [kaʃri], *s.f.* hiding, concealing; **pas de cacheries!** no underhand work!
cache-sexe [kaʃsɛks], *s.m.inv. cache-sexe,* G-string.
cache-soupape(s) [kaʃsupap], *s.m. I.C.E: etc:* valve-casing, -cover; dust guard.
cachet [kaʃɛ], *s.m.* **1.** *(a)* seal, stamp (on letter, document); **mettre un c. sur la bouche de qn,** to seal s.o.'s lips; *Hist:* **lettre de c.,** order under the King's private seal; *(b)* mark, stamp, impress; **c. d'oblitération, de la poste,** postmark; **c. d'un fabricant,** maker's trade-mark; **le c. du génie,** the stamp, hall-mark, of genius; **il a dans toute sa personne un c. de distinction,** his whole personality carries the stamp of distinction; **il a beaucoup de c.,** he has an air about him, he has style; **œuvre qui manque de c.,** work that lacks character, distinctive style; **monument empreint d'un c. de noblesse,** monument of noble appearance. **2.** *(a)* stamp, seal (implement); *(b)* signet (-ring). **3.** *(a)* ticket (issued in sets, *e.g.* at swimming-baths, restaurants); *A:* voucher (for lessons); **donner des leçons à dix francs le c.,** to give tuition at ten francs a lesson; **courir le c.,** to give private lessons (in the pupils' homes); to eke out a living by tutoring; *(b)* fee (of artiste, counsel, consulting physician, etc.); **son c. est de 500 frs,** his fee is 500 francs; *(c) Th: Cin:* **les cachets,** the crowd. **4.** *Pharm:* cachet; wafer; tablet.
cachetage [kaʃtaːʒ], *s.m.* **1.** sealing (of letters, etc.). **2.** *Civ.E:* reinforcement (of slow hardening concrete with a quick hardening layer).
cache-tampon [kaʃtɑ̃pɔ̃], *s.m.inv.* (game of) hide-the-handkerchief, hunt-the-slipper.
cacheter [kaʃte], *v.tr.* **(je cachette, n. cachetons; je cachetterai)** to seal (up) (letter, bottle, etc.); **cire à c.,** sealing-wax; *s.a.* PAIN 3; **vin cacheté,** vintage wine.
cachette [kaʃɛt], *s.f.* hiding-place; *adv.phr:* **en c.,** secretly, on the sly, on the quiet, *sub rosa*; in an underhand manner; **vendre en c.,** to sell under the counter.
cachexie [kaʃɛksi], *s.f.* cachexy, general debility; *Vet:* rot.
cachiman, cachiment [kaʃimɑ̃], *s.m. Bot:* soursop, custard-apple.
cachimentier [kaʃimɑ̃tje], *s.m. Bot:* soursop (-tree).
cachot [kaʃo], *s.m.* **1.** dungeon, dark cell; *Navy:* cell; **c. en basse-fosse,** bottle-dungeon. **2.** *(a)* prison, gaol, jail; *A:* **être aux cachots,** to be in prison; *(b)* solitary confinement.
cachotter [kaʃɔte], *v.tr.* to make a mystery of (unimportant trifles).
cachotterie [kaʃɔtri], *s.f. F:* affectation of mystery; **faire des cachotteries à qn,** to keep things back from s.o.
cachottier, -ière [kaʃɔtje, -jɛːr], *F:* **1.** *a.* secretive, reticent, close. **2.** *s.* secretive person, mystery-maker.
cachou [kaʃu]. **1.** *s.m.* *(a) Com:* catechu; cutch; *Pharm: Dy:* **c. pâle,** pale catechu, gambier; *Bot:* **acacia c.,** catechu acacia, catechu tree; *(b)* cachou. **2.** *a.inv.* snuff-coloured.
cachucha [katʃytʃa], *s.f. Danc:* cachucha.
caciquat [kasika], *s.m.* dignity, rank, of cacique.
cacique [kasik], *s.m.* *(a)* cacique, Indian chief; *(b) Sch: F:* candidate who has obtained first place in a competitive examination (*esp.* for entrance to the *École normale supérieure*); *(c) F: O:* (i) landowner; boss; big shot; *F:* the old man; (ii) (the) headmaster.
caco- [kakɔ], *pref.* caco-; **cacochylie,** cacochylia; **cacothymie,** cacothymia.
cacochyme [kakɔʃim], *a. & s. A. & Hum:* cacochymic, dyspeptic (person).
cacochymie [kakɔʃimi], *s.f. Med:* cacochymia, cacochymy.
cacodémon [kakɔdemɔ̃], *s.m. Myth:* cacodemon.
cacodylate [kakɔdilat], *s.m. Pharm:* **c. de soude,** sodium cacodylate.
cacodyle [kakɔdil], *s.m. Ch:* cacodyl(e).
cacodylique [kakɔdilik], *a. Ch:* cacodylic.
cacographe [kakɔgraf], *s.m.* cacographer.
cacographie [kakɔgrafi], *s.f.* cacography, (i) bad handwriting; (ii) faulty spelling, mis-spelling; (iii) ungrammatical language; poor style.
cacographique [kakɔgrafik], *a.* cacographic(al).
cacolet [kakɔlɛ], *s.m. Mil: & Dial:* mule-litter, pack-saddle (for wounded men); **mulet de c.,** pack-mule.
cacologie [kakɔlɔʒi], *s.f.* cacology.
cacologique [kakɔlɔʒik], *a.* cacological.
cacophonie [kakɔfɔni], *s.f.* cacophony.
cacophonique [kakɔfɔnik], *a.* cacophonous, harsh-sounding; jangling.
cacosmie [kakɔzmi], *s.f. Med:* cacosmia.
cacostomie [kakɔstɔmi], *s.f. Med:* halitosis.
cacotrophie [kakɔtrɔfi], *s.f.* cacotrophy, wrong dieting.

cacoxène [kakɔksɛn], *s.m. Miner:* cacoxene, cacoxenite.

cactacées [kaktase], *s.f.pl.*, **cactées** [kakte], *s.f. pl. Bot:* Cactaceae.

cactier [kaktje], *s.m.* = CACTUS.

cactiforme [kaktifɔrm], *a.*, **cactoïde** [kaktɔid], *a. Bot:* cactaceous.

cactus [kaktys], *s.m. Bot:* cactus.

cacuminal, -aux [kakyminal, -o], *a. O: Ling:* **l'r c.,** point r, dental r, cerebral r.

cadastrage [kadastra:ʒ], *s.m.* land registration.

cadastral, -aux [kadastral, -o], *a.* cadastral (register, survey).

cadastre [kadastr̥], *s.m. Adm:* **1.** cadastral survey; plan (of commune); land register; cadastre. **2.** survey (staff, operations).

cadastrer [kadastre], *v.tr. Adm:* **1.** to survey and value (parish). **2.** to register (property) in the land register.

cadastreur [kadastrœ:r], *s.m.* (land) surveyor (and valuer).

cadavéreux, -euse [kadaverø, -ø:z], *a.* cadaverous, death-like; deadly pale.

cadavérine [kadaverin], *s.f. Bio-Ch:* cadaverine.

cadavérique [kadaverik], *a.* cadaveric; **aliments cadavériques,** flesh of dead animals taken as food; **rigidité c.,** *rigor mortis; s.a.* AUTOPSIE.

cadavre [kadɑ:vr̥], *s.m. (a)* corpse, dead body, *U.S:* cadaver; carcase (of dead animal); *(b)* **c'est un c. ambulant,** he's a walking corpse; *F:* **il y a un c. entre eux,** they are linked by a crime; *Lit:* **ce n'était plus que le c. d'une grande ville,** it was only the ghost, the shadow, of a great city; *(c) P:* chap, type; *(d) P:* empty (wine) bottle; *F:* dead man; *(e)* **jeu du c. exquis** = game of consequences.

caddie [kadi], *s.m. Golf:* caddie.

cade[1] [kad], *s.m. Bot:* cade, Spanish juniper; **huile de c.,** cade oil.

cade[2], *s.m. Meas:* cade; barrel ((i) *Gr.Ant:* of about 32 litres; (ii) of 1,000 litres).

cadeau, -eaux [kado], *s.m.* **1.** present, gift; **envoyer qch. à qn en c.,** to send s.o. sth. as a present; **faire un c. à qn,** to make s.o. a present; **faire c. à qn de qch.,** to make s.o. a present of sth., to give sth. to s.o. as a present, to present s.o. with sth.; **j'aimerais mieux en faire c.,** I'd rather give it away; *F:* **il ne lui a pas fait de c.,** (i) he didn't spare him; (ii) he didn't help him much, he was a fat lot of use to him. **2.** *A:* entertainment (given to friends). **3.** *Pal:* **lettres cadeaux,** ornate capitals (as used in XVth century).

cadédiou [kadedju], **cadédis** [kadedi(s)], *int. A:* (*in Gascony*) faith! upon my word!

cadenas [kadna, -ɑ], *s.m.* **1.** padlock; **c. à chiffre, à combinaison,** combination lock; **fermer la porte au c.,** to padlock the door; **mettre un c. aux lèvres de qn,** to seal s.o.'s lips. **2.** clasp, snap (of bracelet, etc.).

cadenasser [kadnase], *v.tr.* **1.** to padlock (door, etc.); to fasten, clasp (bracelet, etc.). **2. c. qn,** to put s.o. under lock and key.

cadence [kadɑ̃:s], *s.f.* **1.** cadence, rhythm (of verse, motion); **en c.,** rhythmically; **danser en c.,** to keep time (in dancing); **c. de travail,** rhythm of work; **marcher en c.,** to march, walk, in step; **tenir la c.,** to keep step; *Ten:* **casser la c. à un adversaire,** to break up an opponent's game; *Row:* **donner la c.,** to set the stroke; **à la c. de . . .,** at the rate of . . .; *Artil: etc:* **c. du tir,** rate of fire; **ralentir la c.,** to slacken the rate of fire. **2.** *(a) Mus:* (i) cadence; **c. parfaite,** perfect cadence; **c. rompue, interrompue,** interrupted cadence; **c. évitée,** avoided, interrupted, cadence; (ii) *A:* **c. brisée,** trilled cadence, trill, shake; *(b)* intonation (of voice).

cadencé [kadɑ̃se], *a.* rhythmical; measured (step, blows); **rythme bien c.,** well-marked rhythm; **prendre le pas c.,** (i) to fall into step; (ii) to break into quick time; **pas c., marche!** quick march! **marcher au pas c.,** to march, walk, in step.

cadencer [kadɑ̃se], *v.tr.* **(je cadençai(s); n. cadençons) 1.** to give rhythm to (one's style, etc.); **c. son pas,** (i) to get into step; (ii) to adopt a rhythmical pace. **2.** *Mus:* to lead up to a cadence.

cadène [kadɛn], *s.f.* **1.** *A:* (convict's) chain. **2.** *Nau:* chainplate, channel-plate.

cadenelle [kad(ə)nɛl], *s.f. Bot:* cade berry, Spanish juniper berry.

cadenette [kad(ə)nɛt], *s.f. A:* long love-lock; tress (of hair); *cadenette.*

cadenza [kadɛnza], *s.f. Mus:* cadenza.

cadet, -ette [kadɛ, -ɛt], *s.* **1.** *(a)* (the) younger, junior; **il est mon c. de deux ans,** he is my junior by two years, he is two years younger than I am; *a.* **avoir trois frères cadets,** to have three younger brothers. *Sp:* **épreuve des cadets** = junior event; *(b)* junior (in position, rank); *(c)* the youngest (of a family); *F:* **c'est le c. de mes soucis,** that's the least of my worries. **2.** *(a) Hist:* cadet; *(b) Mil:* cadet; *(c) F: O:* young fellow, chap. **3.** *Golf:* caddie. **4.** *s.f.* **cadette;** *(a) Bill:* half-butt (cue); *(b)* paving-stone, flagstone.

cadi [kadi], *s.m.* cadi (Mohammedan judge).

cadichonne [kadiʃɔn], *s.f. (a) A.Cost:* white coiffe (worn by laundrywomen, dressmakers, etc. in Bordeaux); *(b) A:* working girl (of the Bordeaux region).

cadis [kadi], *s.m. Tex: A: (a)* caddis; *(b)* **c. ras, foulé,** milled shalloon.

Cadix [kadis, -iks], *Pr.n.f. Geog:* Cadiz.

cadméen, -enne [kadmeɛ̃, -ɛn], *a.* Cadmean (victory, etc.).

cadmiage [kadmja:ʒ], *s.m. Tchn:* cadmium-coating.

cadmie [kadmi], *s.f. Metall:* **c. des fourneaux,** sublimated oxide of zinc, tutty, cadmia.

cadmié [kadmje], *a.* cadmium-coated; cadmium-plated, cadmiated.

cadmier [kadmje], *v.tr. Tchn:* to coat with cadmium.

cadmifère [kadmifɛ:r], *a.* cadmiferous.

cadmique [kadmik], *a. Ch:* cadmic.

cadmium [kadmjɔm], *s.m. Ch:* cadmium; **sulfure (naturel) de c.,** cadmium blende, cadmium ochre, greenockite.

cadmiumage [kadmjɔma:ʒ], *s.m. Tchn:* = CADMIAGE.

cadogan [kadɔgɑ̃], *s.m.* = CATOGAN.

cadole [kadɔl], *s.f. Dial:* latch (of door).

cadrage [kadra:ʒ], *s.m.* **1.** *(a) Print:* registering; *(b) Cin:* (i) centring (of film image); (ii) frame line. **2.** *Min:* casing.

cadran [kadrɑ̃], *s.m.* **1.** *(a) (of clock, barometer, etc.)* face, dial (-plate); *(b)* **c. solaire,** sundial; **faire le tour du c.,** (i) *(of hands of clock)* to go right round the clock; (ii) *F: (of pers.)* to sleep the clock round. **2.** dial (of instrument); **c. à aiguille,** needle dial; **c. gradué,** (i) graduated, calibrated dial (of scientific instrument); (ii) graduated, calibrated, index disc (of machine-tool); **c. démultiplicateur,** vernier dial; **c. démultiplié,** slow-motion dial; *Tp:* **c. (d'appel, d'abonné),** dial; *F:* **appeler qn au c.,** to dial s.o.; *Nau:* **c. de transmission d'ordres,** engine-room telegraph; *Artil:* **c. de pointage,** range dial. **3.** *Moll:* solarium.

cadrané [kadrane], *a. (of wood)* heart-shaken.

cadran(n)erie [kadranri], *s.f.* **1.** dial-making. **2.** dial-works.

cadran(n)ier [kadranje], *s.m.* maker of dials and compasses.

cadran(n)ure [kadrany:r], *s.f.* heart-shake, star-shake (in timber).

cadrat [kadra], *s.m. Typ:* quadrat; *F:* quad.

cadratin [kadratɛ̃], *s.m. Typ:* em quadrat, em quad; **demi-c.,** en quad.

cadrature [kadraty:r], *s.f.* train, dial-work (of watch, clock).

cadre [kɑ:dr̥], *s.m.* **1.** *(a)* frame (of picture, door, car chassis, hive, mine-shaft, etc.) *(in Switzerland)* notice-board; casing (of ship's screw, etc.); *W.Tel:* **c. (de réception),** frame aerial, loop aerial; **c. radiogoniométrique,** directional loop; *Min:* **c. coffrant,** mine-shaft case; *Phot:* **c. arrière réversible,** reversing back; **cadres intermédiaires,** plate adapters; *(b) (on form, etc.)* space, box; **c. réservé à l'administration** = for office use only; *(c)* border (of map, etc.); *(d)* setting (of scene); surroundings; *(e)* compass, limits, bounds, framework; **renfermer un sujet dans un c. étroit,** to confine a subject to narrow limits; **sortir du c. de ses fonctions,** to go beyond one's duties; **dans le c. des Nations Unies,** within the framework of the United Nations; **dans le c. de ce programme d'expansion,** as part of this expansion programme; **ces produits n'entrent pas dans le c. de notre fabrication,** these products do not come within the scope of our manufacture; **l'étude de ce sujet n'entre pas dans le c. de ce manuel,** the study of this subject is outside the scope of this manual; *(f) Paperm:* **c. volant (de la forme),** deckle; *(g) Trans:* **c. d'emballage,** packing-crate; **c. de fret, de transport, de déménagement,** container; **transports maritimes par cadres,** container-shipping; **navire porte-cadres,** container-ship; **poste à quai pour navire porte-cadres,** container-berth; *Av:* **avion porte-cadres,** container-aircraft, -plane; *Rail:* **wagon porte-cadres,** container-wagon, *U.S:* container-truck. **2.** *(a)* frame(work) (of bicycle, etc.); *(b) Lit:* outline, skeleton, plan (of book, etc.). **3.** *Mil: Navy: (a)* **les cadres** *pl,* (i) commissioned and non-commissioned officers; officers and N.C.O.'s; (ii) cadre, staff (of a skeleton unit, of a school); **les cadres de l'Armée,** the Army commissioned and non-commissioned officers, the Army list; **les cadres de la Marine,** the Navy officers and petty officers, the Navy list; **les cadres actifs, de l'armée active,** the regular officers and N.C.O.'s, the active list; *U.S:* officers and N.C.O.'s on active duty; **les cadres de réserve,** the commissioned and non-commissioned officers of the reserve; the officers and N.C.O.'s of the reserve; *U.S:* the reserve officers and N.C.O.'s; **c. noir,** officers and N.C.O.'s who teach horsemanship in French Army (*from colour of their uniforms*); *(b)* **le c. de réserve** (French organization), special reserve of general, flag, officers; **rajeunir les cadres,** to reduce the age of retirement (of commissioned and non-commissioned officers); **renouvellement des cadres,** replacement of commissioned and non-commissioned officers; **figurer sur les cadres,** to be on the muster-roll; **rayer qn des cadres,** to strike s.o. off the strength; **hors c.,** not on the roll of an organic unit or service; specially employed; **être mis hors c.,** to be seconded; **unité c.,** skeleton unit; **exercice de cadres,** skeleton exercises, exercise without men, without troops, *U.S:* command post exercise; *(c) Ind: Com:* salaried staff, executives; **cadres moyens,** lower-salaried staff, trained personnel; **cadres supérieurs,** higher-salaried staff, managerial staff; **c. de maîtrise,** supervisory staff; *(d) Pol:* (i) cadre, cell; (ii) cadre, member of a cell. **4.** *Nau: (a)* cot; *(b)* berth; *(c)* **c. d'hôpital,** cradle; *Navy:* **être sur les cadres,** to be on the sick-list.

cadrer [kɑdre]. **1.** *v.i.* to tally, agree, fall in, square (**avec,** with); **faire c. un compte,** (i) to agree an account; (ii) to doctor an account; *F:* to cook an account; **projet qui ne cadre pas bien avec la disposition prévue,** scheme that does not conform, fit in, with the other arrangements; **cela ne cadre pas avec mes opinions,** that does not go with my opinions. **2.** *v.tr. Cin: Phot: etc:* to centre (a photograph).

caduc, -uque [kadyk], *a.* **1.** *(a)* decaying, crumbling (house, etc.); **l'âge c.,** declining age; *(b)* decrepit, broken down, worn out, frail. **2.** *Nat. Hist:* deciduous, caducous (membrane, leaf, etc.). **3.** *Jur:* **legs c.,** null and void legacy; **contrat déclaré c.,** agreement declared to have lapsed; **dette caduque,** debt barred by the Statute of Limitations. **4.** *F:* **mal c.,** falling sickness, epilepsy. **5.** *s.f.* **caduque;** *Obst:* deciduous membrane; decidua.

caducée [kadyse], *s.m. Myth:* **1.** caduceus, Mercury's wand. **2.** = Aesculapius's staff (*esp.* as a badge).

caducité [kadysite], *s.f.* **1.** *A: (a)* decayed state, dilapidated state (of building, etc.); *(b)* senility, decrepitude, senile decay; *(c) Nat.Hist:* caducity, deciduousness. **2.** *Jur:* lapsing, nullity (of legacy, etc.).

cadurcien, -ienne [kadyrsjɛ̃, -jɛn], *a. & s. Geog:* (native, inhabitant) of Cahors.

cæcal, -aux [sekal, -o], *a. Anat:* caecal (appendage, etc.).

cæciforme [sesifɔrm], *a.* caeciform.

cæcum [sekɔm], *s.m. Anat:* caecum.

caennais, -aise [kanɛ, -ɛ:z], *a. & s. Geog:* (native, inhabitant) of Caen.

cænogénèse [senɔʒenɛ:z], *s.f. Biol:* caenogenesis, cenogenesis.

cænozoïque [senɔzɔik], *a. Geol:* cainozoic.

cæruleum [seryleɔm], *s.m.* ceruleum.

cæsalpinacées [sezalpinace], *s.f.pl. Bot:* Caesalpiniaceae.

cæsium [sezjɔm], *s.m. Ch:* caesium; *Med:* **bombe au c.,** caesium bomb.

cafard, -arde [kafa:r, -ard]. **1.** *s. (a) A:* canting humbug, canter; **faire le c.,** to cant; *a.* **air c.,** sanctimonious air; **parler de qch d'un ton c.,** to cant about sth.; *(b) Mil: P:* spy; *(c) Sch:* sneak, tale-bearer. **2.** *s.m. (a) Ent: F:* cockroach; *(b) F:* **avoir le c.,** to be bored stiff; to have the hump, the blues; *P:* the pip; to be fed up; **cela me donne le c.,** it gives me the blues; it makes me fed up; **vous donnez le c. à tout le monde,** you make everybody miserable.

cafardage [kafarda:ʒ], *s.m. (a) A:* playing the hypocrite; *(b)* tale-bearing.

cafarder [kafarde], *v.i. (a) A:* to affect sanctity; *(b)* to sneak, peach; to carry tales; to split on s.o.; *P:* to let on; *(c) P:* to spy.

cafarderie [kafardri], *s.f. A:* cant, sanctimoniousness.

cafardeux, -euse [kafardø, -øːz]. **1.** *a.* depressed; *F:* in the dumps, cheesed off, browned off; **temps c.,** depressing weather. **2.** *s.* dismal, gloomy, miserable person.

cafardise [kafardiːz], *s.f. A:* **1.** (*a*) piece of hypocrisy; (*b*) sneaky action. **2.** = CAFARDERIE.

caf'conc' [kafkɔ̃ːs], *s.m. P: A:* = CAFÉ-CONCERT.

café [kafe], *s.m.* **1.** coffee; (*a*) **grain de c.,** coffee-bean; **c. vert,** unroasted coffee; **c. torréfié,** roasted coffee; **brûler, torréfier, du c.,** to roast coffee; **moudre du c.,** to grind coffee; **c. moulu,** ground coffee; **c. en poudre,** instant coffee; (*b*) **c. noir,** black coffee; (*in Switzerland*) **c. nature,** black coffee (without spirits); **c. au lait,** white coffee; **c. crème** (i) coffee with cream; (ii) white coffee; **garçon, un c. crème!** waiter, a cup of (white) coffee! **c. complet,** coffee, hot milk, rolls and butter; *s.a.* FILTRE 1, FORT I. 1; (*c*) *a.inv.* coffee-coloured (material, etc.); **c. au lait,** *café-au-lait.* **2.** (*a*) *A:* coffee-house; (*b*) bar; (*c*) café; **garçon de c.,** waiter.

café-brasserie [kafebrasri], *s.f.* café which makes a speciality of its beers; *pl. cafés-brasseries.*

café-chantant [kafeʃɑ̃tɑ̃], *s.m.,* **café-concert** [kafekɔ̃sɛːr], *s.m. A:* café providing evening entertainment by artistes; *pl. cafés-chantants, cafés-concerts.*

caféier [kafeje], *s.m. Bot:* coffee-shrub, coffee-tree.

caféière [kafejɛːr], *s.f.* coffee-plantation.

caféine [kafein], *s.f. Ch:* caffein(e).

caféique [kafeik], *a. Ch:* caffeic (acid).

caféisme [kafeism], *s.m. Med:* caffe(in)ism.

café-restaurant [kaferɛstɔrɑ̃], *s.m.* bar with restaurant; *pl. cafés-restaurants.*

cafetan [kaftɑ̃], *s.m. Cost:* caftan, kaftan.

caféteria, caféterie [kafeterja, kafetri], *s.f.* cafeteria.

cafetier, -ière [kaftje, -jɛːr]. **1.** *s.* owner of a café; **il est c.,** he keeps a café. **2.** *s.f.* **cafetière;** (*a*) coffee-pot; (*b*) coffee machine, coffee maker; **c. automatique, c. russe,** percolator; **c. à pression,** espresso (machine).

caffût [kafy], *s.m. A:* (piece of) cast-iron scrap.

cafier [kafje], *s.m.* = CAFÉIER.

cafiot [kafjo], *s.m. A: P:* weak coffee, slops.

cafouillage [kafujaːʒ], *s.m. F:* getting into a mess, floundering; missing, misfiring, (of car engine); *W.Tel:* "mush"; **les cafouillages de la loi,** the blunderings of the law.

cafouiller [kafuje], *v.i.* **1.** *F:* to get into a mess, to muddle, flounder; (*of rowing crew, etc.*) to be (all) at sixes and sevens; (*of car engine*) to miss, to misfire. **2.** *P:* = BAFOUILLER.

cafouilleur, -euse [kafujœr, -øz], *s. F:* ham-fisted person; muddler.

cafouillis [kafuji], *s.m. F:* muddle.

cafre [kafr], *a. & s. Ethn:* kaf(f)ir.

Cafrerie [kafrəri], *Pr.n.f. Geog: A:* Kaffraria.

caftan [kaftɑ̃], *s.m.* = CAFETAN.

cage [kaːʒ], *s.f.* **1.** (*a*) (bird-)cage, (hen-)coop; cage (of lions, monkeys, etc.); **c. à lapins,** hutch; **mettre un oiseau,** *F:* **qn, en c.,** to cage a bird, to put s.o. in prison; *A: Av: P:* **c. à poules,** Farman aeroplane; *Prov:* **la belle c. ne nourrit pas l'oiseau,** gold plate does not fill your belly; *F:* **habiter une c. à mouches,** to live in a real doll's house; (*b*) cage (of mine-shaft); (*c*) shell, carcass (of house). **2.** cover, case (for protection); **c. protectrice d'un moteur,** engine casing; *s.a.* THORACIQUE. **3.** well(-hole) (of stairs), stairway; shaft; (of lift); *Nau:* **c. de l'hélice,** screw aperture; *Metalw:* **c. de laminoir,** housing of a rolling-mill. **4.** *Mec.E:* **c. à billes,** ball-race, -cage; **c. de roulement,** bearing cage; **c. de roue,** wheel-race. **5.** *El:* **c. de Faraday,** cage, electrostatic screen.

cagée [kaʒe], *s.f.* cageful; *P:* vanful (of prisoners).

cageot [kaʒo], *s.m.,* **cageotte** [kaʒɔt], *s.f.* **1.** *A:* small cage; *Husb:* **c. d'engraissement,** fattening-coop. **2.** (*a*) hamper; (*b*) crate.

cagerotte [kaʒrɔt], *s.f.* cheese-basket, -drainer.

caget [kaʒe], *s.m.* cheese-basket, -drainer.

cagette [kaʒɛt], *s.f.* **1.** small cage. **2.** bird-trap. **3.** = CAGEOT 2.

cagibi [kaʒibi], *s.m. F:* **1.** hut, shelter. **2.** small room, lumber-room.

cagna [kaɲa], *s.f. P:* **1.** *Mil:* hut; dug-out. **2.** digs.

cagnard, -arde [kaɲaːr, -ard]. **1.** *a. F: O:* lazy, idle. **2.** *s. O:* lazy-bones, *m.* **3.** *s.m. Dial:* sunny, sheltered, corner (among rocks, etc.). **4.** *s.m. Nau:* (*a*) weather cloth; (*b*) weather board.

cagnarder [kaɲarde], *v.i. F: O:* to laze.

cagnarderie [kaɲardri], *s.f. F: O:* laziness.

cagnardise [kaɲardiːz], *s.f. F: O:* laziness.

cagne[1] [kaɲ], *s.f. P:* **1.** useless individual or animal; (*of horse*) crock; (*of woman*) slut. **2. avoir la c.,** to feel lazy.

cagne[2], *s.f. P: Sch:* second-year class preparing to compete for entrance to the *École normale supérieure.*

cagner [kaɲe], *v.i. P:* to scrimshank.

cagneux, -euse [kaɲø, -øːz]. **1.** *a. & s.* (*a*) knock-kneed, baker-legged (person); (*b*) (*of the legs*) crooked; (*c*) (*of horse*) (i) **(de devant)** pigeon-toed; (ii) **(par derrière)** with sickle-shaped legs. **2.** *P:* pupil of the CAGNE[2].

cagnot [kaɲo], *s.m. Ich:* dog-fish, miller's dog, blue shark.

cagnotte[1] [kaɲɔt], *s.f. Games:* pool, kitty, pot; *F:* **manger la c.,** to blue the pool.

cagnotte[2], *s.f. Ich:* blenny.

cagoler [kagɔle], *v.tr. Nau:* to let (boat) drift (with the current).

cagot, -ote [kago, -ɔt], *s.* **1.** *A:* **les cagots,** outcasts, cretins (of the Western Pyrenees). **2.** (*a*) (canting) hypocrite; (*b*) *a.* sanctimonious.

cagoterie [kagɔtri], *s.f.* **1.** cant, sanctimoniousness. **2.** act of hypocrisy; piece of cant.

cagotisme [kagɔtism], *s.m.* false piety.

cagouille [kaguːj], *s.f. Dial:* snail.

cagoulard [kagulaːr], *s.m.* (*a*) *Ecc:* person wearing a penitent's hood; (*b*) *Hist: Pol:* cagoulard (*member of the* Cagoule *q.v.*); (*c*) *F:* conspirator.

cagoule [kagul], *s.f.* **1.** *Ecc:* (*a*) cowl; (*b*) penitent's hood. **2.** *Hist: Pol: the* Cagoule (*an extreme right-wing organization in the 1930's*).

cague [kag], *s.m.* Dutch barge.

cahier [kaje], *s.m.* (*a*) exercise book; **c. d'écriture,** copy-book; *Nau: etc:* **c. de punitions,** defaulters' book; **mettre un homme sur le c.,** to enter a man in the defaulters' book; *s.a.* CHARGE 6; (*b*) **c. de papier à lettres,** six sheets, quarter of a quire, of note paper; (*c*) *Typ:* signature, section.

cahin-caha [kaɛ̃kaa], *adv. F:* **se porter c.-c.,** to be so-so; **aller c.-c.,** to limp along; **le vieillard avançait c.-c.,** the old man was going along as best he could; **devoir fait c.-c.,** exercise done without method, anyhow; **ses affaires vont c.-c.,** his business is struggling along; **les affaires vont c.-c.,** business is slow, slack; **après avoir vécu c.-c. pendant quelques années,** after some years of muddling on, along; **leur ménage va c.-c.,** they are getting along somehow.

cahorsain, -aine [kaɔrsɛ̃, -ɛn], *a. & s.,* **cahorsin, -ine** [kaɔrsɛ̃, -in], *a. & s. Geog:* = CADURCIEN.

cahot [kao], *s.m.* **1.** jolt, road shock, bump (of vehicle); **la voiture avait des cahots terribles,** the carriage jolted terribly; **d'un c. nous franchîmes la pierre,** we jolted, jerked, over the stone; *F:* **les cahots de la vie,** the vicissitudes of life; life's ups and downs. **2.** bump (of road).

cahotage [kaɔtaːʒ], *s.m.* jolting, bumping.

cahotant [kaɔtɑ̃], *a.* **1.** jolting (carriage). **2.** jolty, bumpy (road).

cahotement [kaɔtmɑ̃], *s.m.* jolting, bumping.

cahoter [kaɔte], *v.tr. & i.* to jolt, shake, bump along (in cart, etc.); **nous avons été pas mal cahotés,** we got a good shaking up; *F:* **cahoté par la fortune,** tossed about, buffeted, by fortune; **vie cahotée,** life full of ups and downs.

cahoteux, -euse [kaɔtø, -øːz], *a.* rough, jolty, bumpy (road).

cahute [kayt], *s.f.* **1.** hut, shanty. **2.** cabin (on river barge, etc.).

caïc [kaik], *s.m. Nau:* caïque.

caiche [kɛʃ], *s.f. Nau:* ketch.

caïd [kaid], *s.m.* (*a*) kaid, (i) Arab chief (in Algeria); (ii) magistrate (in Turkey, etc.); (*b*) *P:* gang-leader; (*c*) *F:* **c'est le gros c. en maths,** he's our great maths expert.

caïeu, -eux [kajø], *s.m. Hort:* off-set bulb (of tulip etc.); clove (of garlic).

caïl-cédra, cailcédrat [kailsedra], *s.m. Bot:* **(bois) c.-c.,** bastard mahogany.

caillage [kajaːʒ], *s.m.* curdling, clotting (of milk).

caillasse [kajas], *s.f.* **1.** *Geol:* (gravelly) marl; soft bed of chalk (under tilth). **2.** road-metal.

caille[1] [kaːj], *s.f. Orn:* **c. (des blés),** quail; *F:* **ma petite c.,** my pet; **dodu comme une c.,** as plump as a partridge.

caille[2], *s.f. P:* **l'avoir à la c.,** to be put out; **avoir qn à la c.,** to hate s.o.'s guts.

caillé [kaje], *s.m.* curdled milk, curds; cottage cheese.

caillebot [kajbo], *s.m. Bot:* guelder rose, snow-ball-tree.

caillebotage [kajbɔtaːʒ], *s.m.* = CAILLEBOTTAGE.

caillebotis [kajbɔti], *s.m.* **1.** *Nau: etc:* grating. **2.** *Mil:* duckboard(s).

caillebottage [kajbɔtaːʒ], *s.m.* curdling.

caillebotte [kajbɔt], *s.f.* curds.

caillebotté [kajbɔte], *a.* curdled; *Ch:* **précipité c.,** curdy precipitate.

caillebotter [kajbɔte], *v.tr.* to curdle, clot, coagulate.

se caillebotter, to curdle.

caillebottis [kajbɔti], *s.m.* = CAILLEBOTIS.

caille-lait [kajlɛ], *s.m.inv.* **1.** *Bot:* = GAILLET. **2.** rennet.

caillement [kajmɑ̃], *s.m.* curdling, clotting.

cailler [kaje], *v.tr., i., & pr.* **1.** to clot, curdle; (*of blood*) to cake, to congeal; **faire c. du lait,** to curdle milk; **crème caillée au citron,** lemon-curd. **2.** *P:* **ça caille, on se caille,** it's bloody cold; *V:* **on se les caille,** it's cold enough to freeze the balls off a brass monkey; *F:* **se c. les sangs,** to worry.

cailletage [kajtaːʒ], *s.m. A:* chatter; idle, vacuous, talk.

cailleteau, -eaux [kajto], *s.m.* young quail.

cailleter [kajte], *v.i.* **(je caillette, n. cailletons; je cailletterai)** *A:* to chatter, prate.

caillette[1] [kajɛt], *s.f. Orn:* petrel.

caillette[2], *s.f. F:* **1.** *A:* (*of man or woman*) empty-headed individual, tittle-tattler, frivolous person; (*from Caillette, a buffoon of the XVIth cent.*). **2.** *A:* young woman of easy virtue.

caillette[3], *s.f.* **1.** rennet. **2.** fourth stomach, reed, rennet stomach, abomasum, (of ruminants).

caillot [kajo], *s.m.* clot (of blood, milk, etc.); *Med:* **c. (de fibrine),** clump.

caillot-rosat [kajoroza], *s.m. Hort:* rose-water pear; *pl. caillots-rosats.*

caillou, -oux [kaju], *s.m.* **1.** (*a*) pebble; *F:* **avoir le cœur dur comme un c.,** to have a heart of flint; *P:* **casser des cailloux,** to break stones (in a penal quarry), = to pick oakum; **on avançait lentement sur le c.,** we got on slowly over the cobblestones; (*b*) boulder; *Nau: P:* rocks; **cailloux roulés,** drift boulders; (*c*) *Lap:* **c. d'Égypte,** Egyptian pebble. **2.** *P:* (*a*) head, pate; **avoir le c. déplumé, n'avoir plus de mousse sur le c.,** to be bald, to have lost one's thatch; **il a un c. à caler les roues d'un corbillard,** (i) he's an ugly customer; (ii) he has a funereal, woe-begone, look; **se sucer le c.,** *P:* (*of couple*) to neck; (*b*) dupe, gull.

cailloutage [kajutaːʒ], *s.m.* **1.** (*a*) *Const:* pebble-(work)dash; rough-cast(ing); (*b*) *Civ.E:* road-metal(ling); *Rail:* gravel(ling), ballast(ing); (*c*) pebble paving. **2.** *Cer:* fine stoneware.

cailloute [kajut], *s.f. Med: F:* silicosis, stone-mason's disease.

caillouté [kajute]. **1.** *a. Tex: etc:* pebbled; (*b*) *Cer:* **faïence cailloutée,** fine stoneware. **2. caillouté,** *s.m.,* **cailloutée,** *s.f.* (*a*) ornamental pebble-work (in garden); (*b*) = CAILLOUTAGE 2.

caillouter [kajute], *v.tr.* (*a*) to ballast, metal (road, track); (*b*) to pave (road) with pebbles.

caillouteur [kajutœr], *s.m.* roadman.

caillouteux, -euse [kajutø, -øːz], *a.* flinty, stony (road, etc.); pebbly, shingly (beach).

cailloutis [kajuti], *s.m.* **1.** (*a*) broken stones, gravel; *Civ.E:* road metal; (*b*) (*of beach*) shingle. **2.** pebble-work surface (of yard, etc.); cobble-stone pavement.

caïman [kaimɑ̃], *s.m.* **1.** *Rept:* cayman, caiman; **c. à lunettes,** spectacled cayman. **2.** *Sch: F:* director of studies at the *École normale supérieure.*

Caïn [kaɛ̃], *Pr.n.m.* Cain.

caïnite [kainit], *s.f. Ch:* kainite.

Caïphe [kaif], *Pr.n.m. B.Hist:* Caiaphas; *s.a.* RENVOYER 1.

caïque [kaik], *s.m. Nau:* caïque.

caire[1] [kɛːr], *s.m.* coir, cocoanut fibre.

Caire[2] **(le),** *Pr.n.m. Geog:* Cairo.

cairn [kɛrn], *s.m.* cairn.

cairote [kɛrɔt], *a. & s.* (native, inhabitant) of Cairo.

caisse [kɛs], *s.f.* **1.** (*a*) (packing-)case; **c. de marchandises,** case of goods; **c. à claire-voie, en voliges,** crate; **mettre des marchandises en c.,** to case goods; **c. en carton,** cardboard box; **c. à rabats,** slotted box; *P:* **n'avoir rien au fond de la c.,** to feel very empty; to be starving; (*b*) box, chest (of tea, tools, medicines); tub (for shrub); tank, cistern (for oil, water); **c. à bagages,** trunk; *Nau:* **c. à eau douce,** freshwater-tank; **c. d'assiette,** trimming-tank; **c. de roue,** paddle-box; *Aut:* **c. de l'embrayage,** casing of the clutch; (*c*) **c. de plomb,** lead shell (of coffin); (*d*) *Min:* ore buddle; (*e*) *P:* chest; **il s'en va de la caisse,** he's got T.B. very badly. **2.** (*a*) case (of piano, clock); body (of vehicle); **c. en toile,** fabric body; (*b*) *Mch:* **c. de piston,** piston-body; **c. à feu,** fire-box; (*c*) shell (of pulley). **3.** *Com: Fin:* (*a*) cash-box, till; **c. automatique enregistreuse,** cash-register; check-till; **les caisses de l'État,** the coffers of the

State; *Adm:* **c. centrale,** central treasury; (*b*) (i) pay-desk, cashier's desk; **payez à la c.,** please pay at the desk; (ii) counting-house; cashier's office; pay-office; **tenir la c.,** to be in charge of the cash, of the counting-house; *F:* **passer à la c.,** (i) to be paid; (ii) to be paid off; (*c*) (i) cash (in hand); (ii) takings; **petite c.,** petty cash; **livre de c.,** cash book; **faire la, sa, c.,** to balance (up) one's cash; *F:* **faire la c.,** to rob the till; **avoir tant d'argent en c.,** to have so much money in hand; (*d*) fund; **c. contre le chômage,** unemployment fund; **c. d'amortissement,** sinking-fund; **c. de défense,** fighting fund (of an association, etc.); *Pol:* **c. noire,** bribery fund, *U.S:* boodle, graft; (*e*) bank; **c. (nationale) d'épargne (postale),** (post-office) savings-bank; **c. hypothécaire,** mortgage loan office. **4.** (*a*) *Mus:* drum; **c. roulante,** side-drum, long-drum, tenor drum; **c. claire,** high-pitched side-drum, snare drum; **c. plate,** shallow side-drum; **grosse c.,** (i) bass drum; *F:* big drum; (ii) *s.m. or f.* bass drummer; *F:* **battre la grosse c.,** to advertise, to bang the big drum; (iii) *Mil: P:* prison, clink; (*b*) *Anat:* **c. du tympan,** drum of the ear. **5.** *Nau:* heel (of mast).

caisserie [kɛsri], *s.f.* (wooden) box factory.

caissette [kɛsɛt], *s.f.* small case, box.

caissier, -ière [kesje, kesjɛːr], *s.* **1.** (*a*) cashier, cash clerk; (*b*) *Banks:* cashier, teller; (*c*) collecting clerk. **2.** case-maker; **c. en pianos,** piano-case maker.

caissier-comptable [kesjekɔ̃tabl], *s.m.* cashier and book-keeper; *pl. caissiers-comptables.*

caisson [kɛsɔ̃], *s.m.* box. **1.** *Mil:* (*a*) coffer, chest; **c. à poudre,** powder-chest; (*b*) **c. à munitions,** ammunition wagon, caisson; (*c*) *F:* head; **se faire sauter le c.,** to blow one's brains out; (*d*) *Civ.E:* **poutre à c.,** box-girder; (*e*) *Min:* **c. à minerai,** ore bin, ore bunker. **2.** boot, seat-box (of carriage). **3.** (*a*) *Nau:* locker, bin; **caissons de l'équipage, à sacs,** bag-racks; (*b*) *Av:* **c. du train avant,** nose gear, nose wheel, well; **c. de dérive,** fin spar box; **c. de voilure,** wing spar. **4.** *Arch:* **plafond en caissons,** panelled, coffered, ceiling. **5.** (*a*) *Civ.E:* caisson; **c. hydraulique,** caisson, coffer-dam; *Med:* **mal des caissons,** caisson disease, decompression sickness; diver's paralysis, aero(-)embolism; *F:* the bends; (*b*) air-tank (of life-boat).

cajeput [kaʒpyt], *s.m. Bot:* cajeput; paper-bark.

cajet [kaʒɛ], *s.m.* cheese-basket, -drainer.

cajoler [kaʒɔle]. **1.** *v.tr.* to cajole, coax, wheedle; *F:* to blarney, carney. **2.** *v.i.* (*of jay*) to scream.

cajolerie [kaʒɔlri], *s.f.* cajolery, coaxing, wheedling; *F:* blarney.

cajoleur, -euse [kaʒɔlœːr, -øːz]. **1.** *a.* cajoling, wheedling. **2.** *s.* cajoler, wheedler.

cake [kɛk], *s.m.* fruit cake.

cake-walk [kɛkwoːk], *s.m.inv. Danc: A:* cake-walk.

cal [kal], *s.m.* **1.** callosity. **2.** *Bot: Surg:* callus; *pl. cals.*

Calabar [kalabaːr], *Pr.n.m. Geog:* Calabar; *Bot:* **fève de C.,** Calabar bean, ordeal bean.

calabousse [kalabus], *s.f. Nau: P:* prison cell (on board ship).

calabrais, -aise [kalabrɛ, -ɛːz], *a. & s.* **1.** *Geog:* Calabrian. **2.** *s.m.* liquorice sweet.

Calabre [kalɑːbr]. **1.** *Pr.n.f. Geog:* Calabria. **2.** *s.f.* (*a*) liquorice sweet; (*b*) liquorice powder.

calade [kalad], *s.f. Equit:* calade, exercising ground.

caladium [kaladjɔm], *s.m. Bot:* caladium.

calage[1] [kalaːʒ], *s.m.* **1.** (*a*) chocking (up), wedging (up), steadying (of piece of furniture, etc.); scotching (of wheels of vehicle); clamping (of telescope, etc.); (*b*) propping (up); (*c*) ramming home (of projectile). **2.** *Mec.E: etc:* wedging, keying, cottering (of crank to spindle, etc.); fixing (of wheel on axle, etc.); **c. à la presse,** pressed-on fit; **c. à retrait,** shrunk-on fit; **c. juste,** exact fit. **3.** adjustment; setting; *Mch:* timing, tuning (of valve, engine); *El:* **c. des balais,** (i) setting, adjustment; (ii) lead, of the brushes; **angle de c.,** angle of lead; angle of brush displacement; *Cin:* **c. de l'obturateur,** shutter setting. **4.** *Mch: etc:* jamming (of machinery, of piston); stalling (of engine).

calage[2], *s.m. Nau:* housing (of mast); lowering, striking (of sail).

calais [kalɛ], *s.m.* (*a*) (vegetable) basket, hamper; (*b*) twelve head (of cabbage, salad, etc.).

calaisien, -ienne [kalɛzjɛ̃, -jɛn], *a. & s. Geog:* (native, inhabitant) of Calais or of Saint-Calais.

calaison [kalɛzɔ̃], *s.f. Nau:* **1.** load water-line. **2.** load-draught.

calamandre [kalamɑ̃ːdr], *s.m.* calamander (wood).

calamandrie [kalamɑ̃dri], *s.f. Bot:* germander.

calamar [kalamaːr], *s.m.* = CALMAR.

calambac [kalɑ̃bak], *s.m.*, **calambouc** [kalɑ̃buk], *s.m.*, **calambour** [kalɑ̃buːr], *s.m. Com:* agalloch, agalwood, eaglewood.

calame [kalam], *s.m.* **1.** *Bot:* calamus. **2.** *Archeol:* reed pen, calamus.

calament [kalamɑ̃], *s.m. Bot:* calamint.

calamiforme [kalamifɔrm], *a.* calamiform, reed-like.

calaminage [kalaminaːʒ], *s.m. I.C.E:* carbonizing.

calaminaire [kalaminɛːr], *a. Miner:* calamine-bearing.

calamine [kalamin], *s.f.* **1.** *Miner:* calamine; (*a*) (electric, siliceous) calamine; (*b*) *occ.* zinc-spar, smithsonite. **2.** (*a*) *I.C.E:* carbon (deposit); **gratter la c.,** to decarbonize the engine; (*b*) *Metall:* scale (on casting).

calamistrer [kalamistre], *v.tr.* to curl, to wave.

calamite[1] [kalamit], *s.f.* **1.** *Paleont:* (*fossil*) calamite. **2.** *Com: A:* liquid amber. **3.** *Rept:* natter-jack.

calamite[2], *s.f.* **1.** *A:* loadstone, lodestone. **2.** *Miner:* calamite, white hornblende.

calamité [kalamite], *s.f.* (*a*) calamity, disaster; (*b*) great misfortune.

calamiteusement [kalamitøzmɑ̃], *adv.* calamitously.

calamiteux, -euse [kalamitø, -øːz], *a.* **1.** calamitous, disastrous. **2.** *F:* broken-down.

calamus [kalamys], *s.m. Bot:* **1.** calamus, rattan (-palm). **2.** (= ROSEAU) reed. **3.** *Anat:* calamus; **c. scriptorius,** *calamus scriptorius.*

calanche [kalɑ̃ʃ], *s.f. Geog:* (*in the Mediterranean*) (deep) creek.

calandrage [kalɑ̃draːʒ], *s.m.* (*a*) *Tex: Paperm:* calendering, hot-pressing, surfacing; (*b*) *Laund: O:* mangling.

calandre[1] [kalɑ̃ːdr], *s.f.* **1.** (*a*) *Tex: Paperm:* calender, roller; (*b*) *O: Laund:* mangle. **2.** trough(-shaped part); *Aut:* **c. de radiateur,** radiator grille; *Min:* **c. de bocard,** ore-chest of crusher.

calandre[2], *s.f. Orn:* calandra; **c. nègre,** black lark.

calandre[3], *s.f. Ent:* Calandra; *F:* grain-weevil.

calandrelle [kalɑ̃drɛl], *s.f. Orn:* **(alouette) c.,** calandrelle, short-toed lark.

calandrer [kalɑ̃dre], *v.tr.* (*a*) *Tex: Paperm: etc:* to calender, roll, press; to surface; (*b*) *Laund: O:* to mangle.

calandrette [kalɑ̃drɛt], *s.f. Orn:* song-thrush.

calandreur, -euse [kalɑ̃drœːr, -øːz], *s.m. & f.* (*a*) *Tex: etc:* calenderer; (*b*) *Laund: O:* mangler.

calandrinia [kalɑ̃drinja], *s.f. Bot:* Calandrinia.

calane [kalan], **calanus** [kalanys], *s.m. Crust:* calanus.

calanque [kalɑ̃ːk], *s.f. Nau:* (*in the Mediterranean*) deep creek.

calanthe [kalɑ̃t], *s.m. Bot:* calanthe.

calao [kalao], *s.m. Orn:* calao, hornbill.

calathea [kalatea], *s.m. Bot:* calathea.

calathos [kalatɔs], *s.m. Gr.Ant:* calathos, calathus.

calavérite [kalaverit], *s.f. Miner:* calaverite.

calcaire [kalkɛːr]. **1.** *a.* calcareous (rock, etc.); **spath c.,** lime-spar; **sol c.,** chalky soil; **eau c.,** hard water. **2.** *s.m.* (*a*) limestone; **c. oolithique,** oolitic limestone; **c. organogène,** organic limestone; **c. corallien,** coral limestone; **c. jurassique,** Jurassic limestone; **c. dolomitique,** dolomitic limestone; **c. carbonifère,** carboniferous limestone; **c. crayeux,** chalk; (*b*) *F:* fur (in kettle).

calcanéen [kalkaneɛ̃], *a. Anat:* calcaneal, calcanean.

calcanéum [kalkaneɔm], *s.m. Anat:* calcaneus, calcaneum; *F:* heel-bone.

calcar [kalkaːr], *s.m. Ent:* calcar.

calcaréo-argileux, -euse [kalkareoarʒilø, -øːz], *a.* calcareo-argillaceous.

calcarifère[1] [kalkarifɛːr], *a. Miner:* calciferous, lime-bearing.

calcarifère[2], *a. Nat.Hist:* spurred, calcarate(d).

calcariforme [kalkarifɔrm], *a. Nat.Hist:* calcariform, spur-like.

calcédoine [kalsedwan], *s.f. Miner:* chalcedony.

calcéiforme [kalseifɔrm], *a. Bot:* calceiform, calceolate.

calcéolaire [kalseɔlɛːr], *s.f. Bot:* calceolaria; *F:* slipperwort.

calcet [kalsɛ], *s.m. Nau:* (lateen) mast-head; **mât de c.,** lateen-mast.

calcifère [kalsifɛːr], *a. Miner:* calciferous, lime-bearing.

calciférol [kalsiferɔl], *s.m. Ch:* calciferol.

calcification [kalsifikasjɔ̃], *s.f.* calcification (of organic tissues).

calcifier [kalsifje], *v.tr.* to calcify.

se calcifier, to calcify.

calcifuge [kalsifyːʒ], *a. Bot:* calcifuge, calcifugous.

calcimètre [kalsimɛtr], *s.m. Ch:* calcimeter.

calcimorphe [kalsimɔrf], *a. Geol: Ch:* of high calcium content.

calcin [kalsɛ̃], *s.m.* **1.** *Glassm:* cullet. **2.** *Mch:* fur(ring), boiler-scale. **3.** *Geol:* hard-pan.

calcinable [kalsinabl], *a.* calcinable.

calcinage [kalsinaːʒ], *s.m. Ind:* calcination, calcining.

calcinateur [kalsinatœːr], *s.m. Ind:* calciner.

calcination [kalsinasjɔ̃], *s.f.* **1.** calcination. **2.** *Metall:* (i) oxidation; (ii) roasting (of ores); **résidu de c.,** calx.

calciner [kalsine], *v.tr.* **1.** (*a*) to char; *F:* **rôti calciné,** joint burnt to a cinder; *F:* **désert calciné par le soleil,** sun-baked desert; (*b*) **être calciné,** to be burnt to death. **2.** *Ch: Ind:* to calcine; *Metall:* (i) to oxidize; (ii) to roast (ores).

calcineur [kalsinœːr], *s.m. Ind:* calciner.

calciphobe [kalsifɔb], *a. Bot:* calcifuge, calciphobe.

calcique [kalsik], *a. Ch:* calcic; **chlorure c.,** calcium chloride; *Med:* **dépôts calciques,** chalky deposits.

calcite [kalsit], *s.f. Miner:* calcite, calc-spar.

calcium [kalsjɔm], *s.m. Ch:* calcium.

calcul[1] [kalkyl], *s.m.* (*a*) calculation, reckoning, computation; **faux c.,** miscalculation, mistake in reckoning; **règle à calcul,** slide-rule; **cercle à calcul,** watch-calculator; **faire, effectuer, un c.,** to do a sum, to work out a calculation; *F:* **faire son c.,** to lay one's plans; **agir par c.,** to act from selfish motives; **tout c. fait,** taking everything into account; **déranger le c. de qn,** to upset s.o.'s calculations; **cela ne rentre pas dans mes calculs,** *F:* that does not suit my book; **prêter de bas calculs à qn,** to impute low motives to s.o.; (*b*) arithmetic; *s.a.* TÊTE 2; (*c*) *Mth:* **c. infinitésimal,** (differential and integral) calculus; **c. des probabilités,** theory of probabilities; (*d*) *Mec: etc:* **c. de résistance,** stress analysis.

calcul[2], *s.m. Med:* calculus, stone (in the bladder, etc.).

calculable [kalkylabl], *a.* calculable, computable.

calculateur, -trice [kalkylatœːr, -tris]. **1.** *Pers.* (*a*) *s.m. & f.* reckoner, computer, calculator; *F:* level head, one who looks ahead; (*b*) *a.* far-sighted (person, policy). **2.** *s.m.* **calculateur (électronique),** (electronic) computer; **c. de données, d'éléments,** data computer; **c. numérique, c. arithmétique,** digital computer; *Av:* **c. de cap et de distance,** course and distance computer; **c. de vol,** flight computer. **3.** *s.f.* (*a*) **calculatrice (électronique),** (electronic) computer; (*b*) (desk) calculator.

calculatoire [kalkylatwaːr], *a.* calculative.

calculé [kalkyle], *a.* premeditated (malice); deliberate (insolence); **générosité calculée,** interested (act of) generosity.

calculer [kalkyle], *v.tr.* to calculate, compute, reckon; *Hyd.El: etc:* to design; **c. de tête,** to reckon in one's head; **l'impôt se calcule sur . . .,** the tax is calculated on . . .; **c. un prix,** to arrive at, work out, a price; **tout bien calculé,** taking everything into account; **c. son élan,** to judge one's spring; **c. ses dépenses,** to regulate one's expenditure; **c. vite et bien,** to be quick and accurate at figures; **machine à c.,** calculating machine, desk calculator.

calculeux, -euse [kalkylø, -øːz], *Med:* **1.** *a.* calculous (affection). **2.** *s.m. & f.* patient suffering from stone.

calculiforme [kalkylifɔrm], *a.* calculiform, pebble-shaped, pebble-like.

caldeira [kaldɛra], *s.f.*, **caldère** [kaldɛːr], *s.f. Geol:* caldera.

cale[1] [kal], *s.f. Nau:* **1.** (*a*) hold (of ship); **c. avant, arrière,** forehold, after-hold; **eau de c.,** bilge water; **fond de c.,** bilge; **à fond de c.,** down in the hold; *F:* **être à fond de c.,** to be down on one's uppers, down and out, on the rocks, on one's last legs; **passager de c., de fond de c.,** stowaway; *Nav: Av:* **c. à bagages,** luggage hold, room, *U.S:* baggage compartment; (*b*) **c. à eau,** water-tank. **2.** (*a*) slope, slip (of quay); slipway; (*b*) **c. de construction, de lancement,** slip(way), (ship-building) stocks; slip-dock, building-slip, -berth; **c. couverte,** covered slip, way; building-shed; **mettre un navire sur c.,** to lay down a ship; **navire sur c.,** ship on the slips, on the stocks; (*c*) **c. sèche,** dry dock; **entrer, passer, en c. sèche,** to go into dry dock, to dry-dock; **c. sèche flottante,** floating (dry) dock; **c. de radoub,** graving-dock, -slip; (*d*) **c. d'échouage,** graving beach. **3. supplice, peine, de la c.,** (i) ducking; (ii) keel-hauling; **donner la grande c. (à un matelot),** to keelhaul.

cale², *s.f.* **1.** (*a*) wedge, chock, block (to steady furniture, scotch wheel, etc.); **mettre une voiture sur cales**, to put a car on blocks; *Av: etc:* **enlever les cales**, to remove the chocks; **enlevez les cales!** chocks away! *Aut:* **c. de fer**, skid shoe; (*b*) (i) prop, strut, (ii) needle; (*c*) packing-piece, shim; rail-key; (*d*) *Mec.E:* (i) (shaft-)key, tightening-key; (ii) **c. d'épaisseur**, liner, shim; (*e*) *Typ:* quoin. **2.** *pl. Const:* garreting. **3.** *Carp:* (*a*) sandpaper block; (*b*) caul.

calé [kale], *a.* **1.** *Mch:* **piston c.**, (i) jammed piston; (ii) piston at one of the dead points; *Av:* **hélice calée**, dead airscrew. **2.** *F:* (*a*) *A:* **homme c.**, man of substance, of property; (*b*) **être c. sur, en, qch.**, to be well up in, know all about, sth.; *F:* **c'est un type c.**, he's (i) well-read, well-informed, (ii) handy; (*c*) *F:* difficult, complicated; (*d*) *F:* **ça c'est c.!** that's cunning, clever!

calebas [kalbɑ], *s.m.* = HALE-BAS.

calebasse [kalbɑːs], *s.f.* **1.** (*a*) calabash, gourd, water-bottle; (*b*) *Bot: F:* **vraie c.**, bottle-gourd; **c. à colin**, cannon-ball fruit. **2.** *P:* (*a*) head, nut; (*b*) big gawk (of a woman); (*c*) *pl.* drooping, udder-like, breasts. **3.** *Metall:* small lathe.

calebassier [kalbɑsje], *s.m. Bot:* calabash-(tree), gourd-tree.

calèche [kalɛʃ], *s.f.* (*a*) *A.Veh:* barouche, calash; (*b*) *A.Cost:* calash.

caléchier [kaleʃje], *s.m. A:* **1.** carriage builder. **2.** jobmaster.

caleçon [kalsɔ̃], *s.m.* pants, *U.S:* underpants; **c. long**, long (under)pants; *Sp:* (*wrestler's, etc.*) shorts; **c. de bain**, bathing trunks.

Calédonie [kaledɔni], *Pr.n.f. A.Geog: Poet:* Caledonia.

calédonien, -ienne [kaledɔnjɛ̃, -jɛn], *a. & s. Geog:* Caledonian.

calédonite [kaledɔnit], *s.f. Miner:* caledonite.

cale-étalon [caletalɔ̃], *s.f. Metalw:* stop measure; *pl. cales-étalons.*

caléfaction [kalefaksjɔ̃], *s.f.* **1.** heating, warming, calefaction. **2.** *Ph:* spheroidal condition (of liquid).

calembour [kalɑ̃buːr], *s.m.* pun, play on words; **faire un c.**, to make a pun (**sur**, upon); **faire des calembours**, to pun.

calembouriste [kalɑ̃burist], *s.m.* punster.

calembredaine [kalɑ̃brədɛn], *s.f.* foolish utterance or action; joke, absurdity; **dire, débiter, des calembredaines**, to talk nonsense, to make jokes; **faire des calembredaines**, to play the fool, behave preposterously.

calendaire [kalɑ̃dɛːr], *s.m. Ecc:* obituary; obit-book.

calendes [kalɑ̃ːd], *s.f.pl.* **1.** *Rom.Ant:* kalends, calends; *F:* **renvoyer qn, qch., aux c. grecques**, to put s.o., sth., off indefinitely. **2.** *Ecc: A:* convocation (of clergy of diocese).

calendrier [kalɑ̃dri(j)e], *s.m.* **1.** calendar, almanac; **le c. julien, le vieux c.**, the Julian, old-style calendar; **le c. grégorien, le nouveau c.**, the Gregorian, new-style, calendar; **bloc c.**, desk diary; **c. bloc, c. à effeuiller**, block calendar, tear-off calendar; **c. perpétuel**, perpetual calendar; *F:* **figurer sur le c. de qn**, to be in s.o.'s good books. **2.** (*a*) diary; (*b*) time-table; **mon c. ne le permet pas**, my time-table does not allow it.

calendule [kalɑ̃dyl], *s.f. Bot:* Calendula.

calenture [kalɑ̃tyːr], *s.f. Med: A:* calenture.

cale-pied(s) [kalpje], *s.m. Cy:* toe-clip; *pl. cale-pieds.*

calepin [kalpɛ̃], *s.m.* note-book, memorandum-book; *F:* **mettez ça sur votre c.!** let this be a lesson to you!

cale-porte [kalpɔrt], *s.m.* door-stop; *pl. cale-portes.*

caler¹ [kale], *v.tr.* **1.** (*a*) to chock (up), wedge (up), pack, steady (piece of furniture); to scotch (wheel); to clamp (telescope, etc.); *P:* **se c. les joues, se les c.**, to stuff, to have a good feed; **j'avais besoin de me les c.**, I wanted a good feed; (*b*) to prop up; *F:* **c. un malade sur des coussins**, to prop up a patient on cushions; (*c*) to ram home (projectile). **2.** (*a*) *Mec.E: etc:* to wedge, key, cotter (crank to shaft, etc.); to shim (rail, etc.); to drive in (cotter, etc.); to fix (wheel on axle, etc.); to jam (valve); **c. une frette à la presse**, to force on a collar; **c. une frette à chaud**, to shrink on a collar; (*b*) *Aut:* to stall (the engine); *v.i.* (*of engine*) to stall; *F:* **je cale**, I give up; **Voltaire calait devant l'expression "histoire universelle,"** Voltaire jibbed at, shied at, the words "*histoire universelle.*" **3.** to adjust; to time, tune (valve, engine, etc.); *El.E:* **c. les balais**, to adjust, set, the brushes (of dynamo). **4.** *Fish:* **c. les filets**, to set the nets. **5.** *Cin:* **c. l'obturateur**, to set the shutter. **6.** *Games:* **c. une bille**, to shoot, knuckle, a marble.

se caler. 1. (*a*) (*of piston, etc.*) to stick, jam; (*b*) (*of engine*) to stall. **2.** (*of bridge*) **se c. dans la terre**, to bed (down). **3.** *F:* to settle (oneself) comfortably (in armchair).

caler², *v.i. Nau:* **navire qui cale vingt pieds**, ship that draws, whose draught is, twenty feet of water; **navire qui cale trop**, ship that is too deep in the water.

caler³, *v.tr.* to house (mast); to strike (sail).

caleter (se) [(sə)kalte], *v.i.* = (SE) CALTER.

caleur, -euse [kalœːr, -øːz], *s. P:* **1.** loafer, idler, shirker. **2.** funk.

calfait [kalfɛ], *s.m. Tls:* caulking-chisel, -iron, -tool.

calfat [kalfa], *s.m.* **1.** caulker; **chaise de c.**, bosun's chair. **2.** *Orn:* Java sparrow.

calfatage [kalfataːʒ], *s.m.* caulking; **c. par soudure**, caulk welding.

calfater [kalfate], *v.tr.* to caulk.

calfateur [kalfatœːr], *s.m.* caulker.

calfeutrage [kalføtraːʒ], *s.m.*, **calfeutrement** [kalføtrəmɑ̃], *s.m.* stopping-up (of chinks); listing, weather-stripping (of door, etc.).

calfeutrer [kalføtre], *v.tr.* to block up, stop (up) (chinks); to make air-tight, to weather-strip; to list (door, etc.); **c. une chambre**, to make a room draught-proof; *F:* **se c. dans sa chambre**, (i) to make oneself snug; (ii) to shut oneself up, in one's room.

caliborgne [kalibɔrɲ], *a. A: P:* **1.** = BORGNE. **2.** near-sighted, dim-sighted, purblind. **3.** cross-eyed.

calibrage [kalibraːʒ], *s.m.* **1.** *Mec.E:* (*a*) gauging, callipering, sizing; (*b*) calibration (of thermometer, etc.). **2.** *Cer:* turning (of clay) with a profile. **3.** *Phot:* trimming (of print). **4.** *Typ:* (*a*) casting-off (of copy); (*b*) cast-off. **5.** *Com:* grading (of eggs, etc.).

calibre [kalibr̥], *s.m.* **1.** (*a*) calibre, bore (of fire-arm, pipe, etc.); gauge (of sporting gun); **fusil de c. 8 mm**, (i) *Mil:* 8-mm calibre rifle; (ii) *Sp:* 8-mm gauge gun; **canon de gros c.**, heavy gun; **vérifier le c. d'un canon, d'un thermomètre**, to calibrate a gun, a thermometer; (*b*) size, diameter, calibre, (of bullet, etc.); **il n'est pas de ce c.-là**, he's not a man of that calibre; he's not as good, as bad, as that; **une sottise d'un tel c.**, a stupidity of such enormity. **2.** (*a*) *Tls:* gauge, gage, measuring tool; **c. d'épaisseur**, thickness-gauge; **c. de profondeur**, depth-gauge; **c. de tolérance**, limit-, clearance-gauge; **c. étalon**, reference-gauge; **c. mère**, master-gauge; **c. de filetage**, thread, screw-gauge; **c. à bague**, ring-gauge; **c. à bouchon**, plug-gauge; **c. à lames**, feeler-gauge; **c. à coulisse**, sliding, slide callipers; calliper-gauge; **c. à cadran**, dial gauge; **c. à curseur**, slide gauge, sliding gauge; **c. à vis micrométrique**, micrometer gauge, micrometer caliper(s); **c. de pas, c. à vis**, screw(-pitch) gauge; **c. de référence, c. étalon**, reference gauge; **c. "entre," go gauge; c. "n'entre pas,"** no-go gauge; **c. pour fil métallique**, wire-gauge; **c. pour tôles**, (i) (**épaisses**), plate gauge; (ii) (**minces**), plate gauge; **c. réglable**, adjustable gauge; (*b*) (*for reproduction*) template, pattern, mould; (*c*) *Machine Tls:* jig, former; **c. de montage**, jig; **c. de forage, de fraisage**, drilling-, milling-jig; (*d*) *Cer:* (turner's) profile; **tour à c.**, jigger-machine; (*e*) cutting shape (for photographic prints, etc.). **3.** *P:* revolver; rod, gun.

calibrer [kalibre], *v.tr.* **1.** *Mec.E:* (*a*) to gauge, calliper; to measure; (*b*) to calibrate (thermometer, etc.); (*c*) *Mil:* to tertiate (gun-barrel); (*d*) *Com:* to grade (eggs, etc.). **2.** *Cer:* to turn (clay) with a profile; to jigger. **3.** *Phot:* to trim (print). **4.** *Typ:* to cast off (copy).

calibreur [kalibrœːr], *s.m.* **1.** calibrator; *Mec.E:* tube-gauge, tube caliper. **2.** *Cer:* jiggerer.

calice¹ [kalis], *s.m.* (*a*) *A:* drinking cup; (*b*) *Ecc:* chalice; **boire, avaler, le c.** (**d'amertume**), to drain the cup (of bitterness); **boire le c. jusqu'à la lie**, to drain the cup to its dregs; **vider un c. amer**, to drink a bitter cup.

calice², *s.m.* **1.** *Bot:* calyx. **2.** *Anat:* calix.

calicé [kalise], *a. Bot:* having a calyx; sepalled.

caliche [kaliʃ], *s.m. Miner:* caliche, Chile salt-petre.

caliciflore [kalisiflɔːr], *a.* calycifloral, calyciflorate, calyciflorous.

caliciforme [kalisifɔrm], *a. Bot: Med:* caliciform, cup-shaped.

calicin, -ine [kalisɛ̃, -in], *a.*, **calicinaire** [kalisinɛːr], **calicinal, -aux** [kalisinal, -o], *a. Bot:* calycinal, calycine.

calicot [kaliko], *s.m.* **1.** (*a*) *Tex:* calico; (*b*) strip of calico, streamer (bearing advertisement, etc.). **2.** *O: F:* draper's assistant, counter-jumper.

caliculaire [kalikyleːr], *a. Bot:* calicular (leaf, etc.).

calicule [kalikyl], *s.m. Bot:* calicle, caliculus.

caliculé [kalikyle], *a. Bot:* caliculate.

calier [kalje], *s.m. Nau:* holder.

califat [kalifa], *s.m.* caliphate.

calife [kalif], *s.m.* caliph.

Californie [kalifɔrni], *Pr.n.f. Geog:* California; **la Basse, Haute, C.**, Lower, Upper, California.

californien, -ienne [kalifɔrnjɛ̃, -jɛn], *a. & s.* Californian.

californium [kalifɔrnjɔm], *s.m. Ch:* californium.

califourchon [kalifurʃɔ̃]. **1.** *adv.phr.* **à c.**, astride, astraddle; **se mettre à c. sur qch., qn**, to sit astride (on), to bestride, sth., s.o. **2.** *s.m. Fr.C:* bottom, backside, behind.

calige [kaliːʒ], *s.m.*, **caligus** [kaligys], *s.m. Crust:* sea-louse.

caligineux, -euse [kaliʒinø, -øːz], *a.* caliginous, hazy, misty.

caligo [kaligo], *s.m. Ent:* caligo.

calimande [kalimɑ̃ːd], *s.f. Ich:* dab.

calimbé [kalɛ̃be], *s.m. Cost:* breech-clout; lap (of natives of Guiana).

calin [kalɛ̃], *s.m. Metall:* calin.

câlin [kɑlɛ̃], *a.* coaxing, winning (child, ways, etc.); **prendre un ton c.**, to speak caressingly; *F:* (*of child*) **faire c. à qn**, to caress s.o.; *s.m. & f.* **un petit câlin**, a little wheedler.

calinage [kalinaːʒ], *s.m.* (*in Far East*) manufacture of tea-canisters (of calin).

câlinage [kɑlinaːʒ], *s.m.* caressing, fondling, wheedling, coaxing.

câlinement [kɑlin(ə)mɑ̃], *adv.* coaxingly.

câliner [kɑline], *v.tr.* to caress, fondle; to make much of, to pet (s.o.); to wheedle, to coax.

se câliner. 1. *A:* to coddle oneself, be self-indulgent; **se c. dans un fauteuil**, to take one's ease in an armchair. **2.** to fondle each other.

câlinerie [kɑlinri], *s.f.* **1.** caressing, fondling; wheedling, coaxing. **2.** caress.

calino [kalino], *s.m. A: F:* (traditional type of) inconsequential fool (*from a character in a XIXth century vaudeville*).

calinotade [kalinɔtad], *s.f.* stupid, naïve, remark.

caliorne [kaljɔrn], *s.f. Nau:* (heavy) purchase tackle; main purchase.

caliptriforme [kaliptrifɔrm], *a.* calyptriform.

calisson [kalisɔ̃], *s.m. Comest:* (diamond-shaped) marzipan sweet.

Calixte [kalikst], *Pr.n.m.* Calixtus.

calla [kala], **calle** [kal], *s.f. Bot:* Calla, water arum; **c. des marais**, bog arum.

calleux, -euse [kalø, -øːz], *a.* **1.** callous, horny (hand, etc.); **forgeron aux mains calleuses**, horny-handed blacksmith. **2.** *Anat:* **corps c.**, *corpus callosum*, callosum.

call-girl [kɔlgœrl], *s.f.* call-girl; *pl. call-girls.*

calli- [kali-], *Gr. comb.form.* calli-; colli-; cali-; calo-.

callianasse [kaljanas], *s.f. Crust:* Callianassa, *F:* burrowing prawns.

callicarpa [kalikarpa], *s.m. Bot:* callicarpa.

callicèbe [kalisɛb], *s.m. Z:* callicebus.

Callicrate [kallikrat], *Pr.n.m. Gr.Hist:* Callicrates.

callidie [kalidi], *s.f. Ent:* long-horned beetle.

callidulidés [kalidylid], *s.m.pl. Ent:* Callidulidae.

calligramme [kaligram], *s.m.* picture-poem.

calligraphe [kaligraf], *s.m. & f.* calligrapher.

calligraphie [kaligrafi], *s.f.* calligraphy, penmanship.

calligraphier [kaligrafje], *v.tr.* (*pr. sub. & p.d.* **n. calligraphiions, v. calligraphiiez**) to write (letter, etc.) beautifully and ornamentally; to calligraph.

calligraphique [kaligrafik], *a.* calligraphic.

Callimaque [kal(l)imak], *Pr.n.m. Gr.Lit:* Callimachus.

callimorphides [kalimɔrfid], *s.m.pl. Ent:* Callimorphidae.

callionyme [kaljɔnim], *s.m. Ich:* callionymus, sculpin; *F:* dragonet; **c. lyre**, yellow gurnard.

Calliope [kaljɔp]. **1.** *Pr.n.f. Gr.Myth:* Calliope. **2.** *Orn:* **c. sibérienne**, ruby throat.

callipédie [kal(l)ipedi], *s.f. A:* eugenics.

calliphore [kalifɔːr], *s.m. Ent:* calliphora.

calliphoridés [kalifɔride], *s.m.pl. Ent:* Calliphoridae.

callipyge [kal(l)ipiːʒ], *a.* callipygian, callipygous; **La Vénus Callipyge**, the Callipygian Venus.

Callisthène [kal(l)istɛn], *Pr.n.m. Gr.Hist:* Callisthenes.

callisthénie [kal(l)isteni], *s.f.* callisthenics.

callisthénique [kal(l)istenik], *a.* callisthenic.

callitriche [kal(l)itriʃ], *s.m.* **1.** *Z:* callithrix, green monkey. **2.** *Bot:* Callitriche, water starwort.

callitrich(ac)ées [kal(l)itrik(as)e], *s.f.pl.* **callitrichinées** [kal(l)itrikine], *s.f.pl. Bot:* Callitrichaceae.

callitypie [kal(l)itipi], *s.f. Phot:* kallitype (process).
callorhynque [kalɔrɛ̃k], *s.m. Ich:* Callorhynchus.
callose [kaloːz], *s.f. Bot:* callose.
callosité [kallɔzite], *s.f.* callosity, callus.
callot [kalo], *s.m.* = CALOT.[1]
callovien [kalɔvjɛ̃], *a. & s.m. Geol:* Callovian.
calluna [kalyna], *s.m.*, **callune** [kalyn], *s.f. Bot:* Calluna, the genus Ling.
calmage [kalmaːʒ], *s.m. Metall:* killing (of steel).
calmande [kalmɑ̃ːd], *s.f. A: Tex:* calamanco.
calmant [kalmɑ̃]. **1.** *a.* calming; soothing, sedative (draught, etc.). **2.** *s.m. Med:* sedative; calmative; pain-killer.
calmar [kalmaːr], *s.m.*, **calmaret** [kalmarɛ], *s.m. Moll:* calamary, calamar, sleeve-fish; *F:* squid; **c. flèche,** sea-arrow.
calme[1] [kalm], *s.m.* **1.** calm, calmness; stillness (of air, night, etc.); peace (of mind, etc.); peace and quiet; quiet(ness), hush; peacefulness; self-possession, coolness, placidity; **agir avec c.,** to act coolly, with composure; **il a du calme,** he keeps cool, unruffled, he does not get flurried; **retrouver son c.,** to recover one's equanimity; **le c. est rétabli,** everything is back in order; *Nau:* **pris par le c.,** becalmed; **c. plat,** dead calm; **zones des calmes,** calm-belts; the doldrums. **2.** pool.
calme[2], *a.* calm; still, quiet (air, night, etc.); untroubled, unruffled, cool, composed (person, manner); steady (horse); **journée c.,** unexciting day; **rester c.,** to keep calm; *Com:* **marché c.,** flat, quiet, dull, market; *Nau:* **temps presque c.,** light airs.
calmement [kalməmɑ̃], *adv.* calmly, coolly.
calmer [kalme], *v.tr.* **1.** to calm, quiet, still, allay (tempest, fears); to soothe (pain, nerves, conscience); to set at rest (mind); to quench (thirst); **c. sa faim,** to appease one's hunger. **2.** *Metall:* **acier calmé,** calmed, killed, steel.
se calmer, to become, calm; to compose oneself, to recover one's composure; to calm down; (*of storm*) to abate; **calmez-vous!** gently! compose yourself! **le vent se calme,** the wind is dropping, subsiding, abating; **la tempête s'est calmée,** the storm has blown over; **l'agitation se calme,** the unrest is dying down, things are calming down.
calmir [kalmiːr], *v.i. Nau:* (*of sea*) to calm (down); (*of wind*) to drop, abate; to fall calm.
caloger, -ère [kalɔʒe, -ɛːr], *s.m. & f. Ecc:* = CALOYER.
calomel [kalɔmɛl], *s.m. Ch: Pharm: Ph:* calomel.
calomniateur, -trice [kalɔmnjatœːr, -tris]. **1.** *s.* calumniator, slanderer, back-biter. **2.** *a.* slanderous, libellous.
calomnie [kalɔmni], *s.f.* calumny, slander, libel; **répandre des calomnies sur qn,** to cast aspersions on s.o.
calomnier [kalɔmnje], *v.tr.* (*pr.sub. & p.d.* **n. calomniions, v. calomniiez**) to calumniate, slander, libel (s.o.); to misrepresent (s.o.'s motives, etc.).
calomnieusement [kalɔmnjøzmɑ̃], *adv.* slanderously, libellously.
calomnieux, -ieuse [kalɔmnjø, -jøːz], *a.* slanderous, libellous.
calorescence [kalɔrɛs(s)ɑ̃ːs], *s.f. Ph:* calorescence.
caloricité [kalɔrisite], *s.f. Physiol:* caloricity.
calorie [kalɔri], *s.f. Ph.Meas:* calorie, calory; **grande c.,** (kilogram, large, great) calory; **petite c., calorie-gramme,** small calory, lesser calory, gramme-calory.
calorifère [kalɔrifɛːr]. **1.** *a.* heat-conveying; **tuyaux calorifères,** heating pipes. **2.** *s.m.* (*a*) (central) heating installation; *Fr.C:* radiator; (*b*) *F:* slow-combustion stove; (*c*) **c. à pétrole, à mazout,** oil heater.
calorifiant [kalɔrifjɑ̃], *a.* heating, calorific, calorifacient.
calorification [kalɔrifikasjɔ̃], *s.f. Physiol:* calorification.
calorifique [kalɔrifik], *a. Ph:* calorific, heating, thermal; **spectre c.,** heat-spectrum; **capacité c.,** heat capacity.
calorifuge [kalɔrifyːʒ]. **1.** *a.* (*a*) non-conducting (composition, etc.); (heat-)insulating; **enveloppe c.,** insulating lagging, cleading (of pipe, etc.); (*b*) (*of varnish, etc.*) heat-proof. **2.** *s.m.* heat-insulator.
calorifugeage [kalɔrifyʒaːʒ], *s.m.* heat insulation, lagging.
calorifuger [kalɔrifyʒe], *v.tr.* to insulate, lag (steam-pipe, etc.).
calorimètre [kalɔrimɛtr], *s.m. Ph:* calorimeter.
calorimétrie [kalɔrimetri], *s.f. Ph:* calorimetry.
calorimétrique [kalɔrimetrik], *a. Ph:* calorimetric(al) (unit, etc.).
calorique [kalɔrik]. **1.** *s.m. A: Ph:* heat, caloric; **c. spécifique,** specific heat; **c. latent,** latent heat. **2.** *a. Physiol: etc:* **rendement c.,** heating power; **valeur c.,** heat value.
calorisation [kalɔrizasjɔ̃], *s.f. Metalw:* calorizing, calorization, aluminium plating.
caloriser [kalɔrize], *v.tr. Metalw:* to calorize, to plate with aluminium.
calosome [kalɔzɔm], *s.m. Ent:* calosoma (beetle).
calot[1] [kalo], *s.m.* **1.** rough block of slate, of stone (from the quarry). **2.** small wedge. **3.** *Games:* (large) taw, marble; ally. **4.** *P:* eye.
calot[2], *s.m.* **1.** *Mil:* (*a*) body (of kepi); (*b*) *F:* forage cap. **2.** = glengarry.
calotin [kalɔtɛ̃], *s.m. F: Pej:* **1.** priest. **2.** church-goer.
calotte [kalɔt], *s.f.* **1.** skull-cap; **c. grecque,** smoking cap; (*b*) *Ecc:* calotte, zucchetto; *F:* **porter la c.,** to be in Holy Orders; *P: Pej:* **la c.,** (i) the priests, the clergy, the cloth, parsondom; (ii) *Pol:* the clerical party; **influence de la c.,** influence of the Church, clerical influence; (*c*) *Hatm:* crown; tip; (*d*) *Bak:* **c. bretonne** = cottage loaf. **2.** (*a*) **c. (sphérique),** portion of a sphere; *Arch:* calotte, flattened dome; *Geol:* **c. glaciaire,** ice-cap; ice sheet; *Anat:* **c. du crâne,** brain-pan; *Mec.E:* **(joint à) c. sphérique,** ball-and-socket joint; *Lit:* **la c. des cieux,** the vault, canopy, of heaven; **c. à souris,** round wire mouse-trap; **c. d'un bouton,** dome of a (metal) button; **c. d'une pompe,** cover, cap, of a pump; *Radar:* **c. de protection,** radar dome, radome; *Tchn:* **c. de barbotage,** bubble cap; *Petroleum Ind:* **c. gonflable,** vapour dome; (*b*) (watch-)case, dome. **3.** *F:* cuff, box on the ears; **flanquer une c. à qn,** to cuff s.o.
calotter [kalɔte], *v.tr.* **1.** *F:* to cuff (s.o.). **2.** *Golf:* to top (the ball). **3.** *P:* to steal.
calottier [kalɔtje], *s.m.* calotte-, cap-maker.
calotype [kalɔtip], *s.m. A.Phot:* calotype.
caloyer, -ère [kalɔje, -ɛːr], *s. Ecc:* Caloyer, Basilian monk, nun.
calquage [kalkaːʒ], *s.m.* **1.** tracing. **2.** *F:* imitating (of work of art, etc.).
calque [kalk], *s.m.* (*a*) tracing, traced design, counterdrawing; **c. par frottement,** (taking a) rubbing (of a pattern); **toile à c.,** tracing-cloth; **prendre un c.,** to make, take, a tracing; (*b*) *F:* servile copy; (*c*) **(papier) c.,** tracing paper; (*d*) **elle est le c. de sa mère,** she's the dead spit of her mother; (*e*) *Ling:* calque.
calquer [kalke], *v.tr.* **1.** to trace (sur, from); to make a tracing of (drawing); *Needlew:* to transfer (design); **dessin calqué,** tracing; **c. une inscription par frottement,** to take a rubbing of an inscription; **toile à c.,** tracing-cloth. **2.** to copy (sth.) (sur, from); **c. une robe sur un modèle de Paris,** to copy a Paris model; **expression calquée sur l'anglais,** expression copied from the English. **3.** to imitate, to copy.
se calquer sur qn, to copy, model oneself on, ape, s.o.
calqueur, -euse [kalkœːr, -øːz], *s.* tracer.
calquoir [kalkwaːr], *s.m.* tracing point; tracer.
calter (se) [(sə) kalte], *v.i. & pr. P:* to run away, make off; **je suis pressé, je calte,** I'm in a hurry, I'll be off.
caltha [kalta], *s.m. Bot:* marsh marigold.
calumet [kalymɛ], *s.m.* calumet. **1.** *Bot:* reed. **2.** (Red Indian's) pipe; **fumer le c. de la paix avec qn,** to smoke the pipe of peace with s.o.
calus [kalys], *s.m. Nat.Hist: Med:* callus.
calutron [kalytrɔ̃], *s.m. Atom.Ph:* calutron.
calvados [kalvados], *s.m.* cider-brandy, apple-brandy (originally of Calvados in Normandy).
calvadosien, -ienne [kalvadɔsjɛ̃, -jɛn], *a. & s.* (native, inhabitant) of Calvados.
calvaire [kalvɛːr], *s.m.* **1. Le Calvaire,** (Mount) Calvary; *F:* **sa vie fut un long c.,** his life was one long martyrdom, tribulation. **2.** *R.C.Ch:* (*a*) Calvary; wayside cross; (*b*) stations, way, of the Cross; calvary.
calvanier [kalvanje], **calvarnier** [kalvarnje], *s.m. Dial:* stacker, harvest hand.
calville [kalvil], *s.m. or f.* calville apple, queening apple.
calvinisme [kalvinism], *s.m.* Calvinism.
calviniste [kalvinist]. **1.** *a.* Calvinistic(al). **2.** *s.* Calvinist.
calvitie [kalvisi], *s.f.* baldness; **c. naissante,** incipient baldness.
calycanthe [kalikɑ̃ːt], *s.m. Bot:* calycanthus.
calyciflore [kalisiflɔːr], *a.* = CALICIFLORE.
Calypso[1] [kalipso], *Pr.n.f. Gr.Lit:* Calypso; *A: F:* **faire sa C.,** to lay oneself out to please, tempt (men).
calypso[2], *s.m. Poet: Mus: Danc:* calypso.
calyptre [kaliptr], *s.f. Bot:* calyptra, calypter, coif (of mosses).
calyptré [kaliptre], *a .Bot:* calyptrate.
cam [kɑ̃], *s.m. Bot: Com:* **bois de c.,** camwood, barwood.
camaïeu, -eux [kamajø], *s.m.* (*a*) camaieu, monochrome painting; *Engr:* tint-drawing; **c. en grisaille,** painting executed in grey; (*b*) *F:* colourless painting or literary composition; (*c*) cameo.
camail [kamaj], *s.m.* **1.** camail; (*a*) *Archeol:* hood or collar of mail; (*b*) *R.C.Ch:* cape (worn over the surplice). **2.** *Cost:* cape, cloak. **3.** *Harn:* hood. **4.** *Orn:* neck feathers, cape, hackles (of fowl).
camaldule [kamaldyl], *s.m. Ecc:* camaldolite.
camarade [kamarad], *s.m. & f.* comrade; fellow, mate, *F:* chum, pal; (*as term of address*) comrade; **c. de pension, d'école, de collège,** school-fellow, school chum; **c. de classe, de promotion,** class-mate; **c. de jeu,** playmate, playfellow; **c. de lit,** bedfellow; *Nav:* **c. de plat,** messmate; **c. de bord,** shipmate; **c. de régiment,** army pal; **c. de chambrée,** room-mate; **c. de bouteille,** boon companion; (*of horse*) **c. d'écurie,** stable companion; **faire un, une, c. de qn,** to make a *F:* chum, a pal, of s.o.; *F: O:* **faire c.!** to put one's hands up and cry "Kamerad!", to surrender.
camaraderie [kamaradri], *s.f.* **1.** (*a*) comradeship, close friendship, good-fellowship; **c. de longue date,** long-standing fellowship; (*b*) spirit of mutual co-operation, camaraderie; (*c*) cliquishness, clannishness. **2.** clique, set.
camard, -arde [kamaːr, -ard], *a.* **1.** (*of pers. or nose*) = CAMUS; *F:* **la Camarde,** (grim) death. **2.** *Nau:* bluff-headed (ship); *s.a.* SERRURE.
camarguais, -aise [kamargɛ, -ɛːz], *a. & s.*, **camarguen, -enne** [kamargɛ̃, -ɛn], *a. & s.*, **camarguin, -ine** [kamargɛ̃, -in], *a. & s.* **1.** *Geog:* (native, inhabitant) of the Camargue delta. **2.** *s.* **camarguais, -aise,** cattle from Camargue.
Camargue [kamarg], *Pr.n.f.* **1.** *Geog:* **la C.,** the Camargue. **2.** *s. & a.* = CAMARGUAIS 2.
camarilla [kamarilla, -ija], *s.f.* camarilla, court clique.
camarin [kamarɛ̃], *s.m. Orn:* (red-throated) diver.
camarine [kamarin], *s.f. Bot:* crowberry, heath-berry.
camaro [kamaro], *s.m. P: A:* comrade, pal.
cambial[1], **-aux** [kɑ̃bjal, -o], *a. Fin:* relating to exchange.
cambial[2], **-aux,** *a. Bot:* cambial (tissue, etc.).
cambiste [kɑ̃bist]. **1.** *s.m. Fin:* exchange broker, money-changer. **2.** *a.* **marché c.,** exchange market.
cambium [kɑ̃bjɔm], *s.m. Bot:* cambium.
Cambodge [kɑ̃bɔdʒ], *Pr.n.m. Geog:* Cambodia.
cambodgien, -ienne [kɑ̃bɔdʒjɛ̃, -jɛn], *a. & s. Geog:* Cambodian.
cambouis [kɑ̃bwi], *s.m.* **1.** *Mec.E: etc:* dirty oil or grease. **2.** *Vet:* smegma.
cambouisé [kɑ̃bwize], *a.* (*of fire-arm, etc.*) foul, clogged.
cambrage [kɑ̃braːʒ], *s.m.* cambering, bending (of wood, etc.).
cambrai [kɑ̃brɛ], *s.m. Tex:* **1.** cambric. **2.** machine-made lace.
cambré [kɑ̃bre], *a.* **1.** cambered, arched; **pied très c.,** highly arched foot, foot with a high instep; **personne à la taille cambrée,** well set-up person. **2.** (*a*) bent, warped, crooked; (*b*) bow-legged (horse, etc.); **jambes cambrées,** bow-legs.
cambrement [kɑ̃brəmɑ̃], *s.m.* = CAMBRAGE.
cambrer [kɑ̃bre], *v.tr.* to bend; (*a*) to arch (one's foot, etc.); **c. la taille, les reins,** to throw out, stick out, one's chest; to straighten one's back; (*b*) to camber, curve (wood, etc.); **c. la forme d'un soulier,** to block a shoe.
se cambrer, (*a*) (*of pers.*) (to curve in the small of the back, hence) to throw out one's chest; to draw oneself up or back; (*b*) (*of beam, etc.*) to warp.
cambrésien, -ienne [kɑ̃brezjɛ̃, -jɛn], *a. & s. Geog:* (native, inhabitant) of (i) Cambrai, (ii) the Cambrésis region.
Cambrésis [kɑ̃brezi], *Pr.n.m. Geog:* the Cambrésis region (of Northern France).
cambrien, -enne [kɑ̃bri(j)ɛ̃, -ɛn], *a. & s.m. Geol:* Cambrian.
cambrillon [kɑ̃brijɔ̃], *s.m. Bootm:* shank.
cambriolage [kɑ̃briɔlaːʒ], *s.m.* house-breaking; burglary; burgling.
cambrioler [kɑ̃briɔle], *v.tr.* to break into (house); to burgle.
cambrioleur, -euse [kɑ̃briɔlœːr, -øːz], *s.* house-breaker; burglar; **c. acrobate,** cat burglar.

cambrique [kɑ̃brik]. 1. *a.* Cambrian, Welsh. 2. *s.m. Ling:* Welsh, Cymric.

Cambronne [kɑ̃brɔn], *Pr.n.m. F:* **le mot de C.** = MERDE!

cambrousard, -arde [kɑ̃bruzaːr, -ard]. *P:* 1. *a.* countrified, slow, awkward. 2. *s.m.* yokel; peasant; *s.f.* peasant woman.

cambrous(s)e [kɑ̃bruːz, -us], *s.f. P:* 1. country (as opposed to town); *esp. U.S:* backwoods. 2. servant girl (fresh from the country).

cambrure [kɑ̃bryːr], *s.f.* 1. camber, curve (of wood, etc.); arch (of foot); instep; **c. de la taille,** curve of the back. 2. **c. orthopédique, pour chaussures,** arch-support; instep raiser.

cambuse [kɑ̃byːz], *s.f.* 1. *Nau:* steward's room, store-room; *Navy:* issuing room. 2. canteen (in shipyard). 3. *P:* (*a*) house, hovel, *esp.* poor lodging; (*b*) glory-hole; (*c*) low public house.

cambusier [kɑ̃byzje], *s.m. Nau:* 1. steward, purser. 2. (*a*) canteen-keeper (in shipyard, etc.); (*b*) store-keeper.

Cambyse [kɑ̃biːz], *Pr.n.m. A.Hist:* Cambyses.

came[1] [kam], *s.f. Mec.E:* cam, lifter, wiper; **c. à profil brusque,** quick-action cam; **arbre à cames,** cam-shaft, wobbler-shaft; **c. de butée,** knock-off cam; **levée de la c.,** cam-lift; **roue à cames,** sprocket wheel; **c. à cylindre, à tambour,** drum-cam; **c. fixe,** stationary cam; **c. double,** two-lobe cam; **c. à levée rapide,** quick action cam; *I.C.E:* **distribution à came(s),** cam gear; **moteur avec arbre à cames en tête,** overhead camshaft engine.

came[2], *s. P:* dope, junk; snow.

camé [kame], *s. P:* drug addict; *P:* junkie, junky.

camée [kame], *s.m.* (*a*) cameo; (*b*) painting executed in grey.

caméléon [kameleɔ̃], *s.m.* 1. (*a*) *Rept: Astr: Miner:* chameleon; (*b*) *F:* (*of pers.*) turncoat. 2. *Tex:* **c. de soie,** shot silk; *a.* **taffetas c.,** changeable taffeta.

caméléonisme [kameleɔnism], *s.m. Z:* faculty of changing colour.

caméléontidés [kameleɔ̃tide], *s.m.pl. Rept:* Chamaeleonidae.

caméléopard [kameleɔpaːr], *s.m.* 1. *A:* camelopard, giraffe. 2. *Astr:* Camelopard(alis), Giraffe.

camélia [kamelja], *s.m. Bot:* Camellia; *O:* **dame aux camélias,** courtesan.

camélidés [kamelide], *s.m.pl. Z:* Camelidae.

caméliforme [kameliform], *a.* camel-shaped.

camelin [kamlɛ̃], *s.m. Tex:* cameline.

cameline [kamlin], **caméline** [kamelin], *s.f. Bot:* camelina, gold-of-pleasure.

camelle [kamɛl], *s.f. Dial:* salt-pile (in open-air saltworks).

camellia [kamelja], *s.m.* = CAMÉLIA.

camelot [kamlo], *s.m.* 1. *Tex:* camlet. 2. *F:* (*a*) cheapjack, street hawker; (*b*) *O:* newsvendor; *Fr.Pol:* **les camelots du roi,** young royalists grouped round the royalist paper *L'Action française.*

camelote [kamlɔt], *s.f.* (*a*) *F:* cheap goods, shoddy goods, trash, junk; **meubles de c.,** rubbishy, trumpery, gimcrack, furniture; **maison de c.,** jerry-built house; (*b*) *P:* goods; **fais voir ta c.!** let's have a look at your stuff.

cameloter [kamlɔte]. 1. *v.tr.* to camlet (cloth). 2. *v.i. F:* (*a*) to deal in or manufacture cheap goods; (*b*) to produce botched, trashy, scamped work.

camelotier, -ière [kamlɔtje, -jɛːr]. 1. *s.m. & f.* (i) dealer in, (ii) maker of, cheap or trashy goods. 2. *s.m. Com:* coarse paper.

camembert [kamɑ̃bɛːr], *s.m.* Camembert (cheese).

camera, caméra [kamera], *s.f.* film, *U.S:* movie, camera; cinecamera; *T.V:* camera; **c. (T.V.) d'exploration,** survey T.V. camera.

caméral, -aux [kameral, -o], *a.* fiscal, *U.S:* cameral.

cameraman [kameraman], *s.m. Cin:* cameraman; *pl. cameramen.*

camérier [kamerje], *s.m.* chamberlain (to Pope, to cardinal).

camérière [kamɛrjɛːr], *s.f.* 1. *A:* maid of honour. 2. (*a*) lady's maid; (*b*) chambermaid.

caméristat [kamerista], *s.m. A: Adm: Sch:* lodging (of pupils who supply their own board).

caméristes [kamerist]. 1. *s.f.* = CAMÉRIÈRE. 2. *A: s.m. & f. Adm: Sch:* pupil who is granted lodging (but not board) by the State.

camerlingat [kamɛrlɛ̃ga], *s.m.* camerlingate.

camerlingue [kamɛrlɛ̃ːg], *s.m.* cardinal camerlingo.

caméronien, -ienne [kamerɔnjɛ̃, -jɛn], *a. & s. Hist:* Cameronian.

Cameroun (le) [ləkamrun], *Pr.n.m. Geog:* the Cameroons.

camerounais, -aise [kamrunɛ, -ɛːz], *a. & s.* (native, inhabitant) of the Cameroons.

Camille [kamːj]. 1. *Pr.n.m.* Camillus. 2. *Pr.n.f.* Camilla.

camion[1] [kamjɔ̃], *s.m.* 1. (*a*) *Veh:* dray, wag(g)on; *Cin:* **c. de son, d'enregistrement,** sound-truck, recording van; (*b*) *Aut:* lorry, *U.S:* truck; **c. de déménagement,** removal van; **c. de dépannage, c. dépanneur,** breakdown lorry, -van, *U.S:* wrecking truck, wrecker; **c. plateau,** flat truck; **c. bétonnière,** mobile concrete mixer. 2. (painter's) kettle.

camion[2], *s.m.* minikin (pin).

camion-atelier [kamjɔ̃atəlje], *s.m.* mobile workshop; *pl. camions-ateliers.*

camion-benne [kamjɔ̃bɛn], *s.m.* Tip(ping) lorry, tipper, *U.S:* dump(ing)-truck; *pl. camions-bennes.*

camion-citerne [kamjɔ̃sitɛrn], *s.m.* tank-lorry, tanker (lorry), *U.S:* tank-wagon, tank truck; (*petrol supply*) petrol (tank-)lorry, *U.S:* petrol (tank) truck; *pl. camions-citernes.*

camion-grue [kamjɔ̃gry], *s.m. Aut:* breakdown-van, -lorry; *Civ.E:* travelling crane; *pl. camions-grues.*

camionnage [kamjɔnaːʒ], *s.m.* cartage, carting, haulage, carriage, *U.S:* truckage; carrying, *U.S:* trucking (trade).

camionner [kamjɔne], *v.tr.* to cart, carry, convey, haul, *U.S:* truck (goods).

camionnette [kamjɔnɛt], *s.f.* (delivery) van, *U.S:* light truck; delivery truck; **c. de police,** (loud-speaker) van.

camionnette-boutique [kamjɔnɛtbutik], *s.f.* travelling, mobile, shop; *pl. camionnettes-boutiques.*

camionneur [kamjɔnœːr], *s.m.* 1. (*a*) carrier, carman; (*b*) van-, lorry-driver; *U.S:* truck-driver, trucker, teamster. 2. *A:* vanner, van-horse.

camisade [kamizad], *s.f. A.Mil:* camisado, camisade.

camisard [kamizaːr], *s.m. Hist:* Camisard; *a.* **la révolution camisarde,** the Camisard rebellion.

camisole [kamizɔl], *s.f.* 1. (*a*) (woman's) dressing jacket; (*b*) sleeved vest, spencer; (*c*) *Fr.C:* vest, *U.S:* undershirt. 2. **c. de force,** strait-waistcoat, -jacket.

camomille [kamɔmːj], *s.f. Bot:* (*a*) camomile; **tisane de c.,** camomile tea; (*b*) **c. puante,** stinking camomile, dog-fennel, mayweed.

camorra [kamɔra], *s.f. Hist:* camorra.

camouflage [kamuflaːʒ], *s.m.* camouflage; *Mil:* **filet de c.,** camouflage net; **c. des lumières,** blackout; **peinture de c.,** dazzle painting.

camoufle [kamufl], *s.f. P:* candle, lamp; *P:* glim.

camouflement [kamufləmɑ̃], *s.m. F:* disguise, make-up.

camoufler [kamufle], *v.tr.* to camouflage; to disguise; to hide; **c. les lumières,** to black out; **organisation camouflée,** blind, front, cover; **article camouflé,** faked article.

se camoufler, *v.pr. F:* to hide.

camouflet [kamuflɛ], *s.m.* 1. (*a*) *A:* whiff of smoke (puffed into s.o.'s face); (*b*) affront, insult, snub; *F:* slap in the face. 2. *Mil.Min:* camouflet, stifler.

camoufleur [kamuflœːr], *s.m.* camouflager.

camp [kɑ̃], *s.m.* 1. camp; (*a*) **établir,** (*Mil: O:* **dresser, asseoir**) **un c.,** to pitch (a) camp; **lever le c.,** to strike camp; **tracer le, un, c.,** to lay out (a) camp; *Mil:* **c. de tentes, de toile,** camp under canvas; **c. de baraquements, de baraques,** hutment, hutted, camp; **c. d'instruction,** training, *U.S:* practice, camp; **c. de passage,** transit camp; *O:* **c. volant,** (i) flying, temporary camp; (ii) flying column; *F:* **être en c. volant,** to be somewhere temporarily; **c. de repos, de loisirs,** rest camp; recreation camp; **lit de c.,** (i) camp bed; (ii) *Mil:* guardroom bed; **c. de vacances,** holiday camp; *Fr.C:* **c. d'été,** summer cottage; *Pol:* **c. de concentration,** concentration camp; **c. d'internement,** internment, detention, camp; (*b*) *Hist:* **le C. du Drap d'or,** the Field of the Cloth of Gold. 2. (*a*) *A:* arena (of single combat); lists; **demander le c.,** to demand a decision by single combat; **prendre le c.,** to accept combat, to enter the lists; (*b*) *F:* **fiche(r),** *V:* **foutre le c.,** to decamp, to clear off, to clear out, to scram. 3. (*a*) party, faction; **changer de c.,** to change sides; (*b*) *Games:* side; **se constituer en deux camps,** to form two sides; **tirer les camps,** to pick sides; *Fb:* **changer de c.,** to change ends.

campagnard, -arde [kɑ̃paɲaːr, -ard]. 1. *a.* country (gentleman, accent, etc.); rustic (simplicity, etc.); **gentilhomme c.,** gentleman farmer. 2. *s.* countryman, countrywoman; rustic.

campagne [kɑ̃paɲ], *s.f.* 1. (*a*) plain; open country; **en rase c., en pleine c.,** (i) in the open (country); (ii) openly, without disguise; *Geog:* **la C. romaine,** the Campagna; *s.a.* BATTRE 1; (*b*) country(side), fields (as opposed to town); **à la c.,** in the country; **vie de c.,** country life; **partie de c.,** (i) country outing; (ii) *O:* picnic; *P:* **aller à la c.,** to go to prison; *P:* to clink, to jug; *P:* **emmener qn à la c.,** to lead s.o. up the garden path; (*c*) **(maison de) c.,** small estate, little place in the country. 2. (*a*) *Mil:* (the) field; **en c.,** in the field; on active service; **mettre trois armées en c.,** to put three armies into the field; **matériel, artillerie, de c.,** field equipment, artillery; **manuel de service en c.,** field (service) manual; **entrer en c.,** (i) to begin military operations, *O:* to take the field; (ii) (*of soldier*) to join an active unit; **indemnité d'entrée en c.,** field outfit allowance; **tenue de c.,** field dress; heavy marching order; **chargement de c.,** full pack; (*b*) **se mettre en c. pour qn,** (i) to start campaigning for s.o.; (ii) to take action on behalf of s.o., to take up s.o.'s cause; **se mettre en c. pour qch.,** to set about doing sth. 3. (*a*) *Mil: Pol: etc:* campaign; *Mil:* **faire c.,** to campaign, to go through a campaign, to see active service; *Pol:* **faire c. pour qn,** to campaign on s.o.'s behalf; **faire c. contre qch.,** to campaign against sth.; **c. de presse,** press campaign; **c. publicitaire, de publicité,** advertising campaign; publicity drive; **c. de calomnies,** smear campaign; **mener une c. contre qn, qch.,** to lead, conduct, a campaign against s.o., sth.; *Com:* **faire une bonne c.,** to have a good year, a good season, a good run of business; (*b*) *Navy:* (i) cruise, (ii) (naval) campaign; (*c*) *Ind:* run (of kiln, furnace); run of work; mill-run; campaign.

campagnol [kɑ̃paɲɔl], *s.m. Z:* (field-)vole, meadow mouse; **c. roussâtre,** bank vole; **c. des champs,** field vole; **c. agreste,** short-tailed field vole; **c. souterrain,** pine vole; **c. à douze côtes,** Mediterranean pine vole; **c. de Crespan, des neiges,** snow vole; **grand c.,** large water-vole.

campanaire [kɑ̃panɛːr], *a.* campanological; **art c.,** campanology.

campane [kɑ̃pan], *s.f.* 1. (*a*) *A:* bell; (*b*) *Arch:* campana (of Corinthian capital, etc.); (*c*) *Furn: etc:* tasselled fringe. 2. *Bot:* pasque flower. 3. *Vet:* capped hock.

campanelle [kɑ̃panɛl], *s.f.* 1. *A:* campanella, bells (on tourney-horse, etc.). 2. *Bot:* bindweed.

Campanie [kɑ̃pani], *Pr.n.f. Geog:* Campania.

campanien, -ienne [kɑ̃panjɛ̃, -jɛn]. 1. *a. & s. Geog:* Campanian. 2. *s.m. Ling:* Campanian (dialect). 3. *s.m. Geol:* Campanian.

campaniflore [kɑ̃paniflɔːr], *a. Bot:* having bell-shaped flowers.

campaniforme [kɑ̃panifɔrm], *a. Arch:* campaniform, bell-shaped.

campanile[1] [kɑ̃panil], *s.m. Arch:* campanile, bell-tower.

campanile,[2] *s.f. Bot:* = CAMPANULE.

campanulacées [kɑ̃panylase], *s.f.pl. Bot:* Campanulaceae.

campanulales [kɑ̃panylal], *s.f.pl. Bot:* Campanulales.

campanularia [kɑ̃panylarja], *s.f. Biol:* campanularia.

campanulariidés [kɑ̃panylariide], *s.m.pl. Biol:* Campanulariidae.

campanule [kɑ̃panyl], *s.f. Bot:* campanula, bell-flower, bellwort; **c. à feuilles rondes,** harebell, bluebell; **c. gantelée,** nettle-leaved bell-flower, throat-wort; **c. doucette,** Venus's looking-glass; *Hort:* **c. (à grosses fleurs),** giant bell-flower, Canterbury bell(s).

campanulé [kɑ̃panyle], *Bot:* 1. *a.* campanulate, bell-shaped. 2. *s.f.pl. O:* **campanulées,** Campanulaceae.

campanuliflore [kɑ̃panyliflɔːr], **campanuliforme** [kɑ̃panylifɔrm], *a. Bot:* campanulate.

campé [kɑ̃pe], *a.* (well) established, poised; (*of pers.*) **bien c.,** well built, well set-up; **portrait bien c.,** well-sketched portrait; **récit bien c.,** well-constructed, well-told, story; **bien c. sur ses jambes,** standing firmly on his feet, firmly planted; **homme solidement c. dans ses idées,** man firmly fixed in his opinions.

Campêche [kɑ̃pɛʃ]. 1. *Pr.n.* **bois de C.,** *s.m.* **c.,** Campeachy wood, logwood. 2. *s.m. P: A:* wine.

campement [kɑ̃pmɑ̃], *s.m.* 1. *Mil: etc:* (*a*) encamping, camping; (*b*) encampment, camp; **établir un c.,** to camp, to pitch camp; **replier le c.,** to strike camp; **matériel de c.,** camp equipment; (*c*) camping ground. 2. *Mil:* advanced camp detachment, advanced billeting party, *U.S:* quartering party. 3. *Aer: A:* (i) bringing out (of dirigible) from shed and into a favourable position; (ii) balloon field.

camper [kɑ̃pe]. **1.** *v.i.* (*a*) to (en)camp, to pitch camp; to camp out; **c. sous la tente, dans des baraquements,** to camp under canvas, in huts; (*b*) to install oneself provisionally (somewhere), to camp out. **2.** *v.tr.* (*a*) to encamp (troops); to put (troops) under canvas; (*b*) *Aer: A:* to bring (balloon) into a sheltered position; (*c*) *F:* to place, fix, put; **il campa son chapeau sur sa tête,** he stuck, clapped, his hat on his head; **c. là qn,** to leave s.o. in the lurch; (*of painter*) **c. ses personnages,** to arrange, pose, the subjects of the picture; **écrivain qui campe bien ses personnages,** writer who is good at presenting his characters; **voilà votre homme campé en peu de mots,** there you have your man in a nutshell; *Th:* **c. un personnage,** to play a part effectively.

se camper. 1. to encamp, to pitch one's camp. **2. se c. solidement sur ses jambes,** to take up a firm stance; *F:* **se c. devant qn,** to plant oneself in front of s.o.; **ne te campe pas là!** don't plant yourself there! **se c. sur un banc,** to plank, plonk, oneself down on a seat.

campeur, -euse [kɑ̃pœːr, -øːz], *s.* camper.

camphène [kɑ̃fɛn], *s.m. Ch:* camphene.

camphol [kɑ̃fɔl], *s.m. Ch:* camphol, borneol.

campholide [kɑ̃fɔlid], *s.f. Ch:* campholide.

campholique [kɑ̃fɔlik], *a.* campholic (acid).

camphorate [kɑ̃fɔrat], *s.m. Ch:* camphorate.

camphorique [kɑ̃fɔrik], *a. Ch:* camphoric (acid).

camphre [kɑ̃ːfr̥], *s.m. Ch: Ind:* camphor; **essence de c.,** camphor oil.

camphré [kɑ̃fre], *a.* camphorated (oil, etc.); **d'odeur camphrée,** smelling of camphor.

camphrer [kɑ̃fre], *v.tr.* to camphorate; to treat (sth.) with camphor.

camphrier [kɑ̃fri(j)e], *s.m. Bot:* camphor tree.

camphrique [kɑ̃frik], *a. Ch:* camphoric.

campignien [kɑ̃piɲjɛ̃], *a.* & *s.m. Prehist:* Campignian.

campimètre [kɑ̃pimɛtr̥], *s.m.* (oculist's) campimeter.

Campine [kɑ̃pin]. **1.** *Pr.n.f. Geog:* the Campine. **2.** *s.f. Husb:* campine (fowl).

camping [kɑ̃piŋ], *s.m.* **1.** camping; **faire du c.,** to go camping; **l'art du c.,** camp craft. **2.** camping ground, site. **3.** (holiday) camp.

campisme [kɑ̃pism], *s.m.* = CAMPING 1.

campo [kɑ̃po], *s.m. Geog:* campo (of Brazil).

campode [kɑ̃pɔd], *s.m. Ent:* Campodea.

campodéidés [kɑ̃pɔdeide], *s.m.pl. Ent:* Campodeidae.

campodéiforme [kɑ̃pɔdeifɔrm], *a. Ent:* campodeiform.

camponote [kɑ̃pɔnɔt], *s.m. Ent:* camponotus.

campos [kɑ̃po], *s.m. Sch: F:* holiday, rest; **donner c. à son personnel,** to give the staff a day off, an afternoon off; **avoir c.,** to have a holiday, a day off.

campus [kɑ̃pys], *s.m.* campus.

campylographe [kɑ̃pilɔgraf], *s.m. Geom: etc:* harmonic-curve tracer.

campylomètre [kɑ̃pilɔmɛtr̥], *s.m. Surv:* campylometer.

campylotrope [kɑ̃pilɔtrɔp], *a. Bot:* campylotropous.

camus [kamy], *a.* **1.** (*a*) flat-, snub-nosed (person); pug-nosed (dog); (*b*) broad-nosed (tool). **2.** flat, snub (nose).

can [kɑ̃], *s.m.* edge (of board, of armour-plate, etc.); **sur c., de c.,** on edge, edgewise.

Canaan [kanaɑ̃], *Pr.n.m.* = CHANAAN.

Canada [kanada], *Pr.n.m. Geog:* Canada; **au C.,** in Canada; **chat du C.,** Canada lynx.

canadien, -ienne [kanadjɛ̃, -jɛn]. **1.** *a.* & *s.* Canadian; *Geog:* **le bouclier c.,** the Laurentian shield; *Aut:* **(carrosserie) canadienne,** shooting-brake, station-wag(g)on (body). **2.** *s.f.* **canadienne;** (*a*) sheepskin jacket, waistcoat; fur-collared lumberman's jacket, lumber-jacket; (*b*) Canadian canoe.

canadite [kanadit], *s.f. Miner:* canadite.

canaille [kanɑːj, -aːj]. **1.** *s.f.* (*a*) *coll.* rabble, scum, riff-raff; rag-tag and bobtail; (*b*) scoundrel, bad lot. **2.** *a.* low, dirty, crooked (action, etc.); vulgar, coarse, smutty (song, etc.); **il a l'air c.,** he has a wicked twinkle in his eye.

canaillerie [kanɑjri, -ajri], *s.f.* **1.** (*a*) low-down trick; piece of blackguardism; (*b*) smutty remark. **2.** (*a*) low-down mind; (*b*) vulgarity (of song, etc.).

canal, -aux [kanal, -o], *s.m.* **1.** (*a*) channel (of river); **par le c. de la poste,** through (the medium of) the post; (*b*) **le C. de Mozambique,** the Mozambique Channel; (*c*) *Nau:* passage (between rocks); (*d*) *Hyd.E:* (i) culvert; **c. à ciel ouvert, couvert,** open, closed(-in), culvert; (ii) (mill) race; **c. de prise, d'amenée,** head race, feeder, penstock, inlet channel; **c. de décharge, de fuite,** way-gate, tail race, discharge channel; **c. de dérivation,** diversion, bypass, channel; **c. d'évacuation, de trop plein,** spillway channel. **2.** *Civ.E:* canal; **c. à point de partage,** summit canal; **c. de dérivation,** branch canal; **c. maritime, de navigation,** ship canal; **le C. de Suez,** the Suez Canal; **la Zone du C. (de Panama),** the Canal Zone; **c. d'irrigation,** irrigation canal, ditch; **c. d'assèchement, d'écoulement, de drainage,** drainage canal, drain. **3.** (*a*) pipe, spout, conduit, tube; *Av:* duct (of ducted propeller); **c. à air, d'aérage,** air passage, duct, flue; **c. de fuite,** waste pipe; (*b*) *Anat: Bot:* canal, duct, meatus; **c. alimentaire,** alimentary canal; **c. biliaire,** bile duct; **c. thoracique,** thoracic duct; **c. déférent,** *vas deferens, pl. vasa deferentia;* **c. de Wirsung,** canal of Wirsung; **canaux de Havers,** Haversian canals; (*c*) *Artil:* **c. de lumière,** vent; (*d*) groove; **c. de graissage,** oil groove; (*e*) *Arch:* flute, fluting; (*f*) *T.V:* channel, *U.S:* airway.

canaliculaire [kanalikylɛːr], *a. Nat.Hist:* canalicular, canal-shaped.

canalicule [kanalikyl], *s.m. Nat.Hist: Arch:* canaliculus, small channel, small pipe.

canaliculé [kanalikyle], *a. Nat.Hist:* canaliculate(d), channelled, grooved.

canalifère [kanalifɛːr], *a. Anat:* canaliferous.

canaliforme [kanalifɔrm], *a.* canaliform; channelled.

canalisable [kanalizabl̥], *a.* which may be canalized, suitable for canalization.

canalisateur, -trice [kanalizatœːr, -tris], *a.* canalizing, canalization (project).

canalisation [kanalizasjɔ̃], *s.f.* **1.** *Civ.E:* (*a*) canalization (of river, etc.); (*b*) draining (of plain); (*c*) piping. **2.** (*a*) (*system of*) pipes, pipework, mains, distribution system; ducting; **c. d'électricité,** electric conduits, wiring; **établir une c. dans un bâtiment,** to pipe a building; (*b*) pipeline (for mineral oils, etc.).

canaliser [kanalize], *v.tr.* **1.** to canalize (region, river, etc.). **2.** *A:* to lay down pipes, mains; to pipe (oil, etc.). **3.** *F:* **la police a canalisé les manifestants vers . . .,** the police shepherded the demonstrators in the direction of . . .; **bureau qui canalise les correspondances,** office which channels the correspondence.

canal-tunnel [kanaltynɛl], *s.m. Civ.E:* underground canal; *pl. canaux-tunnels.*

canamelle [kanamɛl], *s.f.* sugar-cane.

cananéen[1], **-enne** [kananeɛ̃, -ɛn], *a.* & *s.* = CHANANÉEN.

cananéen[2], **-enne,** *a.* & *s. A.Geog:* (native, inhabitant) of Cana (of Galilee).

canapé [kanape], *s.m.* **1.** *Furn:* sofa, couch, settee, *U.S:* chesterfield, davenport. **2.** *Cu:* (*a*) slice of bread fried in butter (on which quails, etc. are served); (*b*) (cocktail) canapé. **3.** *Cards:* canapé (system).

canapé-lit [kanapeli], *s.m.* bed-settee; *pl. canapés-lits.*

canaque [kanak], *a.* & *s. Ethn:* Kanaka.

canard [kanaːr], *s.m.* **1.** duck; (*of the male bird*) drake; **c. turc, c. de Barbarie, c. musqué,** Muscovy duck, musk duck; **c. d'Amérique,** canvas-back(ed duck); **c. marchand,** surf-scoter; **c. de Miquelon,** long-tailed duck, *U.S: F:* old squaw; **c. milouinan,** scaup-duck; **c. morillon,** tufted duck; **c. à tête blanche,** white-headed duck; **c. col-vert, c. sauvage,** mallard; **c. milouin,** pochard; **c. nyroca,** white-eyed pochard, ferruginous duck; **c. siffleur,** wi(d)geon; **c. siffleur d'Amérique,** American wi(d)geon, *U.S:* baldpate; **chasse aux canards,** duck shooting; *A:* **c. privé,** decoy duck, stool-pigeon; *F:* **mon petit c.,** darling, *P:* ducky; **marcher comme un c.,** to waddle. **2.** (*a*) *A:* broadsheet; *hence* (*b*) *F:* false report, hoax, *canard; hence* (*c*) newspaper; *F:* rag. **3.** *P:* horse; *F:* nag. **4.** *F:* lump of sugar dipped in coffee, in brandy. **5.** *Med:* feeding-cup. **6.** *Mus:* false note (on reed instrument, etc.). **7.** *a.* (*a*) *Nau:* **bâtiment c.,** pitching ship; *F:* pile-driver; (*b*) **chien c.,** water spaniel; (*c*) **bois c.,** log that has come loose from the raft.

canardeau, -eaux [kanardo], *s.m.* duckling.

canarder [kanarde]. **1.** *v.i.* (*a*) *Nau:* (*of ship*) to pitch, to bury her nose; (*b*) *F:* **c. sur le compte de qn,** to publish false reports about s.o.; (*c*) *Mus:* to play, sing, a false note. **2.** *v.tr. F:* **c. qn,** to fire at s.o. from behind cover, to snipe at s.o.; to take pot shots at s.o.; **ils canardaient les fuyards,** they were sniping away at the fugitives.

canarderie [kanardri], *s.f.* duck farm.

canardeur [kanardœːr], *s.m. F:* **1.** *Nau:* ship that labours heavily; bruise-water. **2.** sniper.

canard-faisan [kanaːrfəzɑ̃], *s.m. Orn:* pintail duck; *pl. canards-faisans.*

canardier [kanardje], *s.m.* **1.** *F:* spreader of false news. **2.** *P:* newspaper boy.

canardière [kanardjɛːr], *s.f.* **1.** (*a*) duck-pond; (*b*) decoy-pond. **2.** (*a*) screen (for duck-shooting); (*b*) *Mil:* loop-hole. **3.** duck-gun, punt-gun, swivel gun.

canari [kanari], *s.m. Orn:* canary; *a.inv.* **jaune c.,** canary (yellow).

canarien, -ienne [kanarjɛ̃, -jɛn], *a.* & *s. Geog:* Canarian.

Canaries [kanari], *Pr.n.f.pl. Geog:* **les (îles) Canaries,** the Canary Islands.

canarium [kanarjɔm], *s.m. Bot:* canarium.

canasse [kanas], *s.m. Com:* **1.** tea chest. **2.** (*a*) canaster (for importing tobacco); (*b*) canaster (-tobacco).

canasson [kanasɔ̃], *s.m. P:* (*a*) broken-down horse; hack, jade; (*b*) horse; *F:* nag.

canasta [kanasta], *s.f. Cards:* canasta.

canastre [kanastr̥], *s.m.* = CANASSE 1.

cancalais, -aise [kɑ̃kalɛ, -ɛːz]. **1.** *a.* & *s. Geog:* (native, inhabitant) of Cancale. **2.** *a. Cu:* **à la cancalaise,** (fish) served with a sauce containing oysters and shrimps.

cancale [kɑ̃kal], *s.f.* Cancale oyster.

cancan [kɑ̃kɑ̃], *s.m. F:* **1.** (*a*) (piece of) ill-natured gossip; (*b*) *pl.* tittle-tattle, gossip; **faire des cancans,** to tattle, to "talk" **(sur,** about). **2.** (*a*) cancan (dance); (*b*) boisterous dance. **3.** quacking (of ducks).

cancaner [kɑ̃kane], *v.i.* **1.** *F:* to tittle-tattle, gossip; to talk scandal. **2.** (*of ducks*) to quack.

cancanier, -ière [kɑ̃kanje, -jɛːr]. *F:* **1.** *a.* fond of tittle-tattle; tale-bearing. **2.** *s.* gossip, scandalmonger, (tittle-)tattler.

cancel [kɑ̃sɛl], *s.m. A:* chancel (of church).

cancellaire [kɑ̃sɛl(l)ɛːr], *s.f.*, **cancellaria** [kɑ̃sɛl(l)-aria], *s.f. Moll:* Cancellaria.

cancellariat [kɑ̃sɛl(l)arja], *s.m.* chancellorship.

cancellation [kɑ̃sɛl(l)asjɔ̃], *s.f. A.Jur:* annulment, cancellation.

cancellé [kɑ̃sele], *a. Bot:* cancellate, reticulate, lattice-like.

canceller [kɑ̃sele], *v.tr. Jur: A:* to cancel, to annul.

cancer [kɑ̃sɛːr], *s.m.* **1.** *Astr:* **le C.,** the Crab; Cancer; **le tropique du C.,** the Tropic of Cancer. **2.** *Med:* cancer, malignant growth; **c. du sang,** leukaemia; **c. des ramoneurs,** soot-cancer, soot-wart.

cancéreux, -euse [kɑ̃serø, -øːz]. **1.** *a.* cancerous (tumour, etc.). **2.** *s.* cancer patient.

cancériforme [kɑ̃serifɔrm], *a. Med:* cancriform, cancroid.

cancérigène [kɑ̃seriʒɛn], (*a*) *a.* cancerigenic, cancerogenic, carcinogenic; (*b*) *s.m.* carcinogen.

cancérigénèse [kɑ̃seriʒenɛz], *s.f.* carcinogenesis.

cancérisable [kɑ̃serizabl̥], *a.* cancer-prone.

cancérisation [kɑ̃serizasjɔ̃], *s.f. Med:* canceration.

cancérisé [kɑ̃serize], *a. Med:* cancerated, cancered.

cancériser [kɑ̃serize], *v.tr. Med:* to cancerate.

cancérogène [kɑ̃serɔʒɛn], (*a*) *a.* cancerogenic, cancerigenic, carcinogenic; (*b*) *s.m.* carcinogen.

cancérologie [kɑ̃serɔlɔʒi], *s.f.* cancerology.

cancérologue [kɑ̃serɔlɔg], *s.m.f.* cancer specialist, cancerologist.

canche [kɑ̃ːʃ], *s.f. Bot:* hair-grass; **c. touffue,** tussock(-grass).

cancoillotte [kɑ̃kwajɔt], *s.f.* cream cheese made in Franche-Comté.

cancre [kɑ̃ːkr̥], *s.m.* **1.** *Crust:* crab. **2.** (*a*) *a.* & *s.m. F:* dunce, duffer, dud; (*b*) *A: P:* miser, old hunks; (*c*) *A:* beggar, starveling.

cancrelas, cancrelat [kɑ̃krəlɑ, -la], *s.m.* cockroach.

cancrinite [kɑ̃krinit], *s.f. Miner:* cancrinite.

cancroïde [kɑ̃krɔid], *s.m. Med:* cancroid (ulcer).

candale [kɑ̃dal], *s.f.* cotton skirt worn in Senegal.

candéfaction [kɑ̃defaksjɔ̃], *s.f. Metall:* white heat.

candéla [kɑ̃dela], *s.f. Ph: Meas:* candela.

candélabre [kɑ̃delaːbr̥], *s.m.* **1.** (*a*) candelabrum, branched candlestick, cluster-candlestick; (*b*) street lamp-post (with branched lamps). **2.** *Hort:* pyramidal or espalier fruit-tree.

candelette [kɑ̃dlɛt], *s.f. A: Nau:* fish-tackle; top-tackle, -purchase, -burton.

candeur [kɑ̃dœːr], *s.f.* **1.** *A:* frankness, candour. **2.** ingenuousness, simplicity, guilelessness, artlessness; **elle est d'une c. de nouveau-né,** she is as guileless as a new-born babe.

candi [kɑ̃di], *a.m.* candied; **fruits candis, fruits au c.,** *s.m.pl.* **des candis,** crystallized fruit; **sucre c.,** (sugar) candy.

candidat, -ate [kɑ̃dida, -at], *s.* candidate; applicant (**à une place,** for a place); examinee; **c. au doctorat,** candidate for a doctorate; **se porter c. à la députation,** to stand for Parliament; **il est c. à Bordeaux,** he is standing for Bordeaux; **un c. à la tuberculose,** a probable case of tuberculosis.
candidature [kɑ̃didatyːr], *s.f.* candidature, *U.S:* candidacy; **poser sa c. à un poste,** to apply for a post; **retirer sa c.,** to withdraw one's candidature, to stand down; **présenter la c. de qn,** to nominate s.o.
candide [kɑ̃did], *a.* **1.** *A:* candid, frank. **2.** ingenuous, guileless, simple, artless.
candidement [kɑ̃didmɑ̃], *adv.* **1.** *A:* frankly, candidly. **2.** guilelessly, artlessly, ingenuously.
Candie [kɑ̃di], *Pr.n.f.* **1.** *A: Geog:* **(l'île de) C.,** Crete, Candia. **2.** *Bot:* **fleur de C.,** resurrection fern, plant.
candir (se) [səkɑ̃diːr], *v.pr.* (*of sugar*) to candy, to crystallize; **faire c. du sucre,** to candy, crystallize, sugar.
candisation [kɑ̃dizasjɔ̃], *s.f.* crystallizing, candying (of sugar, etc.).
candite [kɑ̃dit], *s.f. Miner:* spinel.
cane [kan], *s.f.* duck (as opposed to drake); **c. du Caire, de Guinée,** musk duck; **c. de mer à collier blanc,** brent-goose; **c. à collier,** bernicle-goose; **c. à tête rousse,** pochard; **marcher comme une c.,** to waddle; *P:* **faire la c.** = CANER.
canebière [kanbjɛːr], *s.f. Dial:* (*S.E. France*) = CHÈNEVIÈRE.
canéfice [kanefis], *s.f. Bot:* cassia.
canéficier [kanefisje], *s.m. Bot:* cassia(tree).
canela [kanela], *s.m.* canela wood.
canepetière [kanpətjɛːr], *s.f. Orn:* (little) bustard, field-duck.
canéphore [kanefɔːr], *s.f. Gr.Ant: Arch:* canephoros, *pl.* canephoroi; canephorus, *pl.* canephori; canephora, *pl.* canephorae.
caner [kane], *v.i. P:* (*a*) to be afraid, to have the jitters; (*b*) to funk, *U.S: P:* to chicken out; (*c*) to die; *P:* to kick the bucket, to pass in one's chips, to pass out.
caneteau, -eaux [kanəto], *s.m.* = CANETON.
canetière [kantjɛːr], *s.f. Tex:* spooler, (spool-, pirn-, cop-)winder (person and machine).
caneton [kantɔ̃], *s.m. Orn:* young (male) duck, young drake, duckling; *Cu:* duckling, duck.
canette[1] [kanɛt], *s.f. Orn:* (*a*) young (female) duck, duckling; (*b*) young teal.
canette[2], *s.f.* = CANNETTE 2, 3.
caneur, -euse [kanœːr, -øːz]. *P:* **1.** *a.* cowardly, funky. **2.** *s.m.* funk.
canevas [kanva], *s.m.* **1.** *Tex:* canvas; *F:* **broder le c.,** to embroider the story. **2.** (*a*) *Art: Lit: Mus:* groundwork, sketch, outline, skeleton (of drawing, novel, etc.); (*b*) *Surv:* (i) skeleton map; (ii) skeleton triangulation; **c. d'ensemble,** general triangulation. **3.** *Box:* **le c.,** the floor of the ring. **4.** *Artil:* **c. de tir,** (i) fire plan; (ii) artillery triangulation.
canezou [kanzu], *s.m. A.Cost:* canezou.
canfieldite [kɑ̃fildit], *s.f. Miner:* canfieldite.
cange [kɑ̃ːʒ], *s.f. Nau:* cangia.
cangue [kɑ̃ːg], *s.f.* cang(ue).
cani [kani], *a.* (*of timber*) beginning to rot, unsound.
caniche [kaniʃ], *s.m. & f.* poodle (dog, bitch).
canichon[1] [kaniʃɔ̃], *s.m.* small poodle.
canichon[2], *s.m.* (unfledged) duckling.
caniculaire [kanikylɛːr], *a.* **1.** canicular; **les jours caniculaires,** the dog-days. **2.** sultry (heat, day, etc.).
canicule [kanikyl]. **1.** *Pr.n.f. Astr:* **la C.,** (i) the Dog-star; (ii) the Dog. **2.** *s.f.* the dog-days.
canidés [kanide], *s.m.pl. Z:* Canidae.
canif [kanif], *s.m.* penknife; **c. à deux lames,** two-bladed penknife; *F:* **donner des coups de c. dans le contrat,** (i) to be unfaithful (to one's husband, wife); (ii) *Com:* to fail to respect an agreement.
canillée [kanije], *s.f. Bot:* duckweed.
canillon [kanijɔ̃], *s.m.* plug (of cock, tap).
canin [kanɛ̃]. **1.** *a.* canine; *F:* **avoir une faim canine,** to be ravenously hungry, to be as hungry as a wolf; **société canine,** dog-club; **exposition canine,** dog-show; *Anat:* **fosse canine,** canine fossa. **2.** *s.f.* **(dent) canine,** canine (tooth), eye-tooth.
canitie [kanisi], *s.f. Med:* canities.
caniveau, -eaux [kanivo], *s.m.* **1.** *Civ.E:* (*a*) kennel-stone, gutter-stone; (*b*) gutter, gully. **2.** *El.E:* trough, conduit (for cables); main, duct. **3.** dip (in road).
canna[1] [kan(n)a], *s.m. Bot:* canna, Indian shot.
canna[2], *s.m. Z:* eland.
cannabin [kan(n)abɛ̃], *a. Bot:* cannabic.
cannabinacées [kan(n)abinase], *s.f.pl.*, **cannabinées** [kan(n)abine], *s.f.pl. Bot:* Cannabinaceae; *F:* hempworts.
cannabis [kanabis], *s.m. Bot:* cannabis.
cannabisme [kan(n)abism], *s.m.* cannabism.
cannacées [kan(n)ase], *s.f.pl. Bot:* Cann(ac)eae.
cannage [kanaːʒ], *s.m.* **1.** cane-bottoming (of chairs). **2.** cane bottom.
cannaie [kanɛ], *s.f.* cane-brake, -field, -plantation.
cannais, -aise [kanɛ, -ɛːz], *a. & s. Geog:* (native) of Cannes.
cannamelle [kanamɛl], *s.f.* = CANAMELLE.
canne[1] [kan], *s.f.* **1.** cane, reed; **c. à sucre,** sugar-cane; **c. de Provence,** great reed, donax (-reed); **sucre de c.,** cane sugar; **sièges en c.,** cane seats. **2.** (*a*) walking-stick, cane; **c. plombée,** loaded stick; **c. armée, à épée,** sword-stick, -cane; **(escrime à) la c.,** singlestick (play); **donner des coups de c. à qn,** to whack s.o. (with one's stick); **c. blanche,** (i) blind man's stick; (ii) blind man, woman; *F:* **il a l'air d'avoir avalé sa c.,** he's stiff and starchy; *P:* **casser sa c.,** to die, to pass out, peg out; (*b*) golf-club. **3. c. à pêche,** fishing rod; **c. à lancer,** casting rod; **c. à fouetter,** fly-rod. **4.** *El.E: Ind:* **c. thermo-électrique,** thermo-couple thermometer, pyrometer. **5.** *Glassm:* blowing-iron, blowpipe.
canne[2], *s.f. Dial:* milk churn.
canne[3], *s.f.* stopcock (on water main).
canné [kane], *a.* cane-seated (chair).
canneau, -eaux [kano], *s.m. Arch:* godroon, gadroon.
canneberge [kanbɛrʒ], *s.f. Bot:* cranberry, moor-berry.
cannebière [kanbjɛːr], *s.f. Dial:* (*S.E. France*) = CHÈNEVIÈRE.
canne-fusil [kanfyzi], *s.f.* cane-gun; *pl. cannes-fusils.*
cannelas [kanlɑ], *s.m.* candied cinnamon.
cannel-coal [kanlkol], *s.m. Min:* cannel coal.
cannelé [kanle]. **1.** *a.* (*a*) fluted, channelled; striated; **pneu c.,** grooved tyre; *Mec.E:* **arbre c.,** splined shaft; *s.a.* TRANCHE 3; (*b*) corrugated; (*c*) ribbed, corded (material); (*d*) *Her:* invected; (*e*) (*of coin*) with a milled edge. **2.** *s.m. Tex:* rep(p), reps.
canneler [kanle], *v.tr.* **(je cannelle, n. cannelons; je cannellerai)** (*a*) to flute, channel; to groove; (*b*) to corrugate.
cannelier [kanəlje], *s.m. Bot:* cinnamon tree.
cannelle[1] [kanɛl], *s.f.* **1.** cinnamon (bark); **c. bâtarde, c. fausse,** bastard cinnamon; **c. blanche, c. poivrée,** wild cinnamon; *A: F:* **mettre qch., qn, en c.,** to break sth. up into small pieces, to reduce sth. to matchwood; to pull s.o. to pieces; to pulverize s.o. **2.** *Furn:* whitewood. **3.** *a.* cinnamon-coloured.
cannelle[2], *s.f.* spigot, faucet, tap.
cannellé [kanele], *a.* cinnamon-coloured.
cannellier [kanelje], *s.m. Bot:* cinnamon-tree.
cannelloni [kanelɔni], *s.m. Cu:* cannelloni.
cannelure [kanlyːr], *s.f.* **1.** (*a*) groove, channel, key-way, slot; *Arch:* flute, (of column); *Mec.E:* spline; *Tls:* **alésoir à cannelures droites,** straight-fluted reamer; *I.C.E:* **cannelures des pistons,** (ring-) grooves in the pistons; (*b*) corrugation; (*c*) *Metall:* pass (of rolling-mill); **c. à poutrelles, à rails,** girder-, rail-pass. **2.** *pl. Bot: etc:* striae. **3.** *pl. Tex:* ribs (of material). **4.** *Geol:* fault fissure.
canner [kane], *v.tr.* to cane(-bottom) (chair).
Cannes [kan], *Pr.n.f.* **1.** *Hist:* **la bataille de C.,** the battle of Cannae. **2.** *Geog:* Cannes (in France).
canne-siège [kansjɛːʒ], *s.f. Ven:* shooting-stick; *pl. cannes-sièges.*
cannetière [kantjɛːr], *s.f.* = CANETIÈRE.
cannetille [kantiːj], *s.f.* **1.** (gold, silver) purl. **2.** flat twisted braid (of gold or silver); bullion (fringe). **3.** covering wire (of violin strings, etc.).
cannetiller [kantije], *v.tr.* to work (embroidery) with gold or silver thread.
cannette [kanɛt], *s.f.* **1.** = CANNELLE[2]. **2. c. à bière,** beer-bottle (with patent stopper); **c. de bière,** bottle of beer; *Fr.C:* can of beer; **bière en c.,** bottled beer; **c. en métal,** can (for preserved goods). **3.** (*a*) *Tex:* cop, spool, pirn; quill (or loom); (*b*) spool (of sewing-machine).
canneur, -euse [kanœːr, -øːz], *s.* chair-caner, cane-worker.
canneux, -euse [kanø, -øːz], *a.* reedy, reed-like.
cannibale [kanibal]. **1.** *s.m. & f.* cannibal. **2.** *a.* cannibal (tribe, etc.); cannibalistic (propensities, etc.).
cannibalisation [kanibalizasjɔ̃], *s.f. Mec.E: etc:* cannibalization.
cannibaliser [kanibalize], *v.tr. F:* to cannibalize.
cannibalisme [kanibalism], *s.m.* cannibalism.
cannier, -ière [kanje, -jɛːr], *s.* = CANNEUR.
cannisse [kanis], *s.f.* (*in S. of France*) screen (or tray) made of (split) canes.
cannois, -oise [kanwa, -waːz], *a. & s.* = CANNAIS.
canoë [kanɔe], *s.m.* canoe; **faire du c.,** to canoe.
canoéisme [kanɔeism], *s.m.* canoeing.
canoéiste [kanɔeist], *s.m. & f.* canoeist.
canon[1] [kanɔ̃], *s.m.* **1.** *Mil: Navy:* gun, cannon; (*a*) **c. à âme lisse,** smooth-bore gun; **c. rayé,** rifled gun; **c. se chargeant par la bouche, par la culasse,** muzzle-, breech-loading gun; **c. de 13 livres,** thirteen-pounder; **c. de 105 mm, de 280 mm,** 105 mm gun, 280 mm gun; **c. court,** howitzer, short gun; **c. hexatube,** six-barrelled gun; **c. classique,** conventional gun; **c. atomique,** atomic gun; **c. pouvant lancer des projectiles à ogive atomique,** gun with atomic capability; **c. de campagne,** field gun; **c. d'accompagnement,** accompanying gun; **c. de tranchée,** trench gun; **c. antichar,** anti-tank gun; **c. antiaérien,** anti-aircraft gun; **c. automoteur,** self-propelled gun; **c. tracté,** tractor-drawn, motorized, gun; **c. de char,** tank gun; **c. d'assaut,** assault gun; **c. sans recul,** recoilless gun, *U.S:* recoilless rifle; **c. sous-calibré,** subcaliber gun; **c. à longue portée,** long-range gun; **c. lourd, moyen, léger; c. de gros, de moyen, de petit calibre,** heavy, medium, light gun; **c. monté sur pivot,** swivel gun; **c. de marine, de bord,** naval gun; **c. de chasse,** bow-chaser; **c. de retraite,** stern-chaser; **canons jumelés,** guns in pairs; **tirer un coup de c.,** to fire a gun (a gun-shot, a shot); **démolir un pont à coups de c., au c.,** to destroy a bridge by gunfire, by artillery fire; **à portée de c.,** within gun-range; **marcher au c.,** to march to the sound of guns; **poudre à c.,** gunpowder; *F:* **chair à c.,** cannon fodder; (*b*) *Coll.* artillery, the guns; **le gros c.,** the heavy guns; (*c*) *Nau:* **c. lance-amarre,** lifeline-throwing gun; **c. porte-amarre,** rocket, life-saving, gun; **c. d'amarrage,** bollard (on quay, on wharf); (*d*) *Min:* (*of shot*) **faire c.,** to blow out; *s.a.* COUP 1. **2.** (*a*) barrel (i) of rifle; (ii) of watch; (iii) of lathe headstock; (iv) of carriage-lamp; (v) of pen; **fusil à deux canons,** double-barrelled gun; (*b*) barrel, pipe (of key, of lock); (*c*) spout (of watering-can); *Const:* spout, pipe; (*d*) body (of syringe, etc.); (*e*) stick (of sulphur); **soufre en canons,** stick sulphur; (*f*) *Harn:* beam (of bit); (*g*) *Laund:* **c. de repasseuse,** goffering tongs; (*h*) **c. de centrage, de guidage,** guide bush. **3.** (*a*) *A:* wine-measure of one-sixteenth of a litre; (*b*) *P:* **boire un c.,** to drink a glass of wine; (*c*) *Pharm:* measuring-glass. **4.** *Vet:* cannon (-bone), shin, shank (of horse). **5.** *pl* (*a*) *Cost: A:* can(n)ions, canons (worn below the knees); (*b*) *Arm:* **c. d'avant-bras,** vambrace. **6.** *T.V: X rays:* **c. à électrons,** electron gun; *s.a.* SERVICE 2.
canon[2], *s.m.* **1.** *Ecc:* (= *Church decree, rule*) canon (of an order, of the Mass, etc.); *a.* **droit c.,** canon law. **2.** (*a*) table, list, canon (of festivals, saints); **le c. pascal,** the Paschal canon; (*b*) (general) formula, rule, canon. **3.** *Mus:* canon, round, catch. **4.** *Typ:* **gros c.,** canon, 48-point type; **petit c.,** 28-point type. **5.** *Art:* canon.
cañon [kaɲɔ̃], *s.m. Geog:* canyon, cañon.
canon-harpon [kanɔ̃arpɔ̃], *s.m.* harpoon gun; *pl. canons-harpons.*
canonial, -iaux [kanɔnjal, -jo], *a. Ecc:* **1.** canonic(al) (hours, etc.). **2.** pertaining to a canon (*chanoine*); **maison canoniale,** canon's residence.
canonialement [kanɔnjalmɑ̃], *adv.* canonically.
canonicat [kanɔnika], *s.m.* canonry; *F:* **c'est un vrai c.,** it's a sinecure.
canonicité [kanɔnisite], *s.f.* canonicity.
canonique [kanɔnik], *a.* canonical (book, etc.); **droit c.,** canon law; **âge c.,** (i) canonical age (for priest's housekeeper); (ii) *F:* respectable age; *F:* **ce n'est pas c.,** it's not conventional; *F:* not the thing.
canoniquement [kanɔnikmɑ̃], *adv.* (*a*) canonically; (*b*) *F:* conventionally.
canonisable [kanɔnizabl̩], *a. Ecc:* that merits canonization.
canonisation [kanɔnizasjɔ̃], *s.f. Ecc:* canonization.
canoniser [kanɔnize], *v.tr. Ecc:* to canonize.
canoniste [kanɔnist], *s.m.* canonist, specialist in canon law.
canon-mitrailleuse [kanɔ̃mitrajøːz], *s.m.* pom-pom; *pl. canons-mitrailleuses.*
canonnade [kanɔnad], *s.f.* cannonade, cannonading; gunfire.
canonnage [kanɔnaːʒ], *s.m. Navy:* (*a*) (art of) gunnery; (*b*) shelling, cannonading (of port, etc.).
canonner [kanɔne], *v.tr.* to cannonade, to shell (enemy); to batter (fort).

canonnerie [kanɔnri], *s.f.* gun-foundry.

canonnier [kanɔnje], *s.m.* gunner.

canonnière [kanɔnjɛːr], *s.f.* 1. *Navy:* gunboat. 2. *Fort:* loophole (for gun). 3. (*a*) *Const:* drain-hole; (*b*) *Hyd.E:* water outlet (of lock, etc.). 4. *Toys:* pop-gun. 5. *A:* bell-tent.

canonnière-aviso [kanɔnjɛravizo], *s.f. Navy:* gun-vessel; *pl. canonnières-avisos.*

canon-obusier [kanɔ̃obyzje], *s.m. Artil:* howitzer; *pl. canons-obusiers.*

canon-revolver [kanɔ̃revɔlvɛːr], *s.m. Artil:* revolving gun, pompom; *pl. canons-revolvers.*

Canope[1] [kanɔp], *Pr.n.f. A.Geog:* Canopus.

canope[2], *a. & s.m.* canopic (jar, vase).

Canopus [kanɔpys], *s.m. Astr:* Canopus.

Canossa [kanɔsa], *Pr.n.* Canossa; **aller à C.,** to go to Canossa, to eat humble pie.

canot [kano], *s.m.* (open) boat; dinghy; **faire une partie de c.,** to go boating; *Nau:* **grand c.,** long-boat, pinnace; *Navy:* **c. amiral,** admiral's barge; **c. major,** officers' boat; **petit c.,** jollyboat, gig; **c. à l'aviron,** rowing boat, pulling-boat, *U.S:* rowboat; **c. à vapeur,** steam launch; **c. automobile, à moteur,** motorboat, motor launch; **c. automobile (de course),** speedboat; *s.a.* PNEUMATIQUE 1, SAUVETAGE.

canotage [kanɔtaːʒ], *s.m. Sp:* boating, rowing; (dinghy) sailing; *Fr.C:* canoeing; **faire du c.,** to row, to go in for rowing.

canoter [kanɔte], *v.i.* to go (in for) boating, rowing, (dinghy) sailing; to row, to sail; *Fr.C:* to canoe.

canoteur [kanɔtœːr], *s.m. Fr.C:* canoeist, paddler.

canotier, -ière [kanɔtje, -jɛːr], *s.* 1. rower; oarsman, oarswoman; boatman. 2. *s.m.* (man or woman's) sailor-hat, straw-hat, boater.

canqueter [kɑ̃kəte], *v.i.* (**elle canquette; elle canquettera**), (*of duck*) to quack.

canquoillote [kɑ̃kwajɔt], *s.f.* cream cheese made in Franche-Comté.

canson [kɑ̃sɔ̃], *s.m.* canson (drawing paper).

cant[1] [kɑ̃], *s.m.* = CAN.

cant[2] [kɑ̃t], *s.m. Lit:* cant, hypocritical prudishness.

cantabile [kɑ̃tabile], *adv. & s.m. Mus:* cantabile.

Cantabres [kɑ̃tabr̥], *s.m.pl.* 1. *Hist:* Cantabri. 2. *Geog:* **les monts C.,** the Cantabrian Mountains.

cantabrique [kɑ̃tabrik], *a.* Cantabrian; **les monts Cantabriques,** the Cantabrian Mountains.

cantal [kɑ̃tal], *s.m.* cantal cheese; *pl. cantals.*

cantalien, -ienne [kɑ̃taljɛ̃, -jɛn], *a. & s. Geog:* (native, inhabitant) of the department of Cantal.

cantaloup [kɑ̃talu], *s.m. Hort:* cantaloup (melon).

cantate [kɑ̃tat], *s.f. Mus:* cantata.

Cantate Domino [kɑ̃tatedɔmino], *s.m.inv. Ecc:* Cantate (Domino).

cantatrice [kɑ̃tatris], *s.f.* cantatrice, vocalist, professional singer.

canter[1] [kɑ̃te], *v.tr.* to lay (piece of metal, etc.) edgeways, on edge.

canter[2] [kɑ̃tɛːr], *s.m. Sp:* canter.

canthare [kɑ̃taːr], *s.m. Ant:* cantharus; *pl.* canthari.

cantharide [kɑ̃tarid], *s.f. Ent:* cantharis, Spanish fly, blister-fly; *Pharm:* **poudre de cantharide,** cantharides.

cantharidine [kɑ̃taridin], *s.f. Ch: Pharm:* cantharidin(e).

canthère [kɑ̃tɛːr], *s.m. Ich:* sea-bream.

canthoplastie [kɑ̃tɔplasti], *s.f. Surg:* canthoplasty.

canthus [kɑ̃tys], *s.m. Anat: Ent:* canthus; **grand, petit, c.,** greater, lesser, canthus.

cantilène [kɑ̃tilɛn], *s.f. Mus:* cantilena.

cantilever [kɑ̃tilevɛːr], *s.m. & a.inv. Civ.E:* cantilever; **pont c.,** cantilever bridge; *Aut:* **suspension c.,** cantilever-spring suspension.

cantine [kɑ̃tin], *s.f.* 1. (*a*) *Mil: etc:* canteen; **c. mobile,** mobile canteen, *U.S: P:* chow wagon; (*b*) soup-kitchen. 2. *Mil:* **c. à bagages,** (officer's) uniform-case, -chest; tin trunk; **c. à vivres,** (officer's) mess-chest, canteen; **c. médicale,** field medical chest.

cantinier, -ière [kɑ̃tinje, -jɛːr], *s.* canteen-keeper, -attendant.

cantique [kɑ̃tik], *s.m. Ecc:* (*a*) canticle, song of praise; **le C. des cantiques,** the Song of Songs; (*b*) hymn; (*c*) hymn tune, choral.

canton [kɑ̃tɔ̃], *s.m.* 1. (*a*) *Adm:* (*in Switz., Fr.*) canton; (*b*) *Geog: Fr.C:* **les Cantons de l'Est,** the Eastern Townships. 2. (*a*) *A:* district, region; (*b*) *Civ.E:* section (of road; railway, etc.); **chef de c.,** ganger; (*c*) *Rail:* block (in block-system); (*d*) forest range; **c. en défens,** area in which grazing is forbidden; (*e*) (*in slate industry*) stockage area, zone; (*f*) *Arch:* cell (of vault). 3. *Her:* canton.

cantonade [kɑ̃tɔnad], *s.f. Th:* (the) wings; **parler à la c.,** (i) so speak (to s.o.) behind the scenes, to speak off; (ii) to address one's remarks to nobody in particular, to speak to the company at large.

cantonais, -aise [kɑ̃tɔnɛ, -ɛːz], *a. & s. Geog:* Cantonese.

cantonal, -aux [kɑ̃tɔnal, -o], *a.* cantonal, of the canton.

cantonalisme [kɑ̃tɔnalism], *s.m.* cantonalism.

cantonaliste [kɑ̃tɔnalist], *s.m.* (*in Switz.*) federalist.

cantonné [kɑ̃tɔne], *a.* 1. *Arch: Her:* cantoned. 2. *Mil:* **troupes cantonnées,** billeted troops. 3. *Geol:* **gisement c.,** limited deposit.

cantonnement [kɑ̃tɔnmɑ̃], *s.m.* 1. (*a*) dividing into sections; (*b*) confining, isolating (of sick animals, etc.); (*c*) *Mil:* cantonment, billeting, quartering; **zone, officier, de c.,** billeting area, officer; **état de c.,** billeting distribution list. 2. (*a*) section (of forest, etc.), forest range; stretch of river (with fishing rights); *Rail:* block-section; (*b*) *Mil:* billets, quarters, cantonment; **c. d'alerte,** emergency, stand-by, close billets; **répartir, occuper, le c.,** to allot, to go into, billets; (*c*) *Hyd.E: etc:* **c. d'air,** airlock, airpocket (in pipe, etc.).

cantonner [kɑ̃tɔne]. 1. *v.tr.* (*a*) to divide (district, etc.) into sections; (*b*) to confine (within circumscribed area); to isolate (sick animals, etc.); *Mil:* to quarter, billet, (troops); **ces faits ne sont pas cantonnés dans la chimie,** these facts are not limited to the field of chemistry; **se c. dans la philologie,** to confine oneself to philology; (*c*) *Jur:* to pay (sum of money) into court. 2. *v.i.* (*of troops*) to be billeted, quartered.

cantonnier [kɑ̃tɔnje]. 1. *s.m.* (*a*) *Civ.E:* roadman, roadmender; (*b*) district road-surveyor; (*c*) *Rail:* line(s)man; **chef c., c. chef,** ganger. 2. *a.* **maison cantonnière,** roadman's hutment.

cantonnière [kɑ̃tɔnjɛːr], *s.f.* 1. *Furn:* (*a*) valance; (*b*) window drapery. 2. metal corner-piece (on trunk).

Cantorbéry [kɑ̃tɔrberi], *Pr.n.f. Geog:* Canterbury.

canulant [kanylɑ̃], *a. F:* boring, troublesome, a nuisance.

canular(d) [kanylaːr], *s.m. Sch: F:* (*a*) tall story; (*b*) hoax, practical joke, leg-pull; rag.

canularesque [kanylaresk], *a. F:* faked (information, etc.).

canule [kanyl], *s.f. Med:* (*a*) nozzle (of syringe, enema); *F:* (*of pers.*) **quelle c.!** what a bore! (*b*) *Surg:* cannula.

canulé [kanyle], *a.* nozzle-shaped.

canuler [kanyle], *v.tr. F:* (*a*) to bore; to be a nuisance to (s.o.); (*b*) *Sch:* to play a practical joke on, to hoax (s.o.).

canus [kany], *a.* of, pertaining to, the silk weavers of Lyons.

canut[1], **-use** [kany, -yːz], *s.* (*in Lyons*) silk-weaver.

Canut[2] [kany(t)], *Pr.n.m. Hist:* Canute, Cnut.

canut[3], *s.m. Orn:* knot.

canyon [kaɲɔ̃], *s.m.* = CAÑON.

canzone [kantsone], *s.f. Lit: Mus:* canzone; *pl. canzones, canzoni* [kantsoni].

canzonette [kɑ̃dzɔnet], *s.f. Lit: Mus:* canzonet.

caodaïsme [kaɔdaism], *s.m. Rel:* Caodaism.

caolin [kaɔlɛ̃], *s.m.* = KAOLIN.

caoua [kawa], *s.m. Mil: P:* coffee, *U.S: P:* java.

caouan(n)e [kawan], *s.f. Rept:* loggerhead (turtle).

caoutchouc [kautʃu], *s.m.* 1. rubber, caoutchouc; **c. durci,** hard rubber; **c. synthétique,** synthetic rubber; **c. mousse** (*R.t.m.*), foam rubber; sponge rubber; **bottes de c.,** rubber boots, gumboots; **fil sous (gaine de) c.,** rubber-covered wire; **rondelle de c. de pompe,** pump rubber; *St.Exch:* **caoutchoucs,** rubber shares, rubbers. 2. (*a*) (i) waterproof, mackintosh; (ii) *pl.* (= **chaussures en c.**) galoshes, rubber overshoes, *U.S:* rubbers; (*b*) tyre (of car, cycle); **c. plein,** solid tyre; (*c*) rubber ring, band; (*d*) *Tex:* elastic. 3. **c. minéral,** elaterite, elastic bitumen, mineral caoutchouc.

caoutchoutage [kautʃutaːʒ], *s.m.* treating with rubber, rubberizing.

caoutchouter [kautʃute], *v.tr.* to treat (sth.) with rubber, to rubberize (silk, cotton); **roue caoutchoutée,** rubber-tyred, -shod, wheel; **ruban caoutchouté,** shirr, elastic ribbon.

caoutchouteux, -euse [kautʃutø, -øːz], *a.* rubbery.

caoutchoutier, -ière [kautʃutje, -jɛːr]. 1. *a.* pertaining to rubber; rubber (shares, industry, etc.). 2. *s.m. Bot:* rubber-plant.

caoutchoutifère [kautʃutifɛːr], *a.* rubber-bearing.

cap [kap], *s.m.* 1. (*a*) *A:* head; **se trouver c. à c. avec qn,** to come face to face with s.o.; **de pied en c.,** *see* PIED 1; (*b*) (*S. of Fr.*) foreman, man in charge; (*c*) *Nau:* **c. de mouton,** dead-eye. 2. *Geog:* cape, headland, foreland; **le C. Beachy,** Beachy Head; **le C.,** (i) the Cape of Good Hope; (ii) Cape Horn; (iii) Capetown; **le c. Vert,** Cape Verde; *Hist:* **la Colonie du C.,** Cape Colony; **franchir, doubler, un c.,** (i) to weather, (ii) to round, a cape; **quand on a franchi le c. de la quarantaine,** when one has turned forty; **elle a franchi le c. de la quarantaine,** she's on the wrong side of forty; *s.a.* PIC[1] 3. 3. *Nau: Av:* course, heading, head, direction; **mettre le c. sur . . .,** to head for, to steer for, to direct one's course to . . .; *Nau:* to stand in for . . .; **mettre le c. au large,** to stand out to sea; **c. au vent, au large,** head (on) to the wind, to sea; **suivre un c.,** to steer a course; **suivre le c. fixé,** to be on the course; **dévier du c. fixé,** to veer off one's course; **quel c. suivons-nous? quel est le c.?** what course are we steering? how does she head? what is her head? **c. de collision,** collision course; *Av:* **indicateur de c.,** course indicator; **conservateur de c.,** directional gyro; **information de c.,** heading information; *s.a.* VIRER 1.

capable [kapabl̥], *a.* capable. 1. (*a*) **salle c. de contenir . . .,** hall big enough to hold . . ., capable of holding . . .; *Mth:* **segment c. d'un angle donné,** segment containing a given angle; (*b*) fit; **c. de qch.,** capable of sth.; **être c. de faire qch.,** to be capable of doing sth.; to be fit, able, to do sth.; to be equal to doing sth.; **il est même c. de tuer sa grand-mère,** he is quite capable of killing his own grandmother; **cette maladie est c. de le tuer,** this illness might well, may be enough to, kill him; (*c*) *Jur:* entitled, qualified, competent (to do sth.); **rendre qn c. de . . .,** to entitle, empower, s.o. to . . . . 2. capable, able, efficient, competent, business-like; **homme très c.,** very able man; *F:* **faire le c.,** to be bossy, bumptious.

capablement [kapabləmɑ̃], *adv.* capably, ably.

capace [kapas], *a.* capacious.

capacimètre [kapasimɛtr̥], *s.m. El:* faradmeter.

capacitaire[1] [kapasitɛːr], *s.m. & f. Jur:* holder of the *Capacité en droit* diploma.

capacitaire[2], *a. El:* capacitive, capacitative.

capacitance [kapasitɑ̃ːs], *s.f. El:* capacitance.

capacité [kapasite], *s.f.* 1. capacity (of vase, accumulator, etc.); *Nau:* **c. de chargement,** tonnage (of ship); *El:* **c. électrostatique,** capacitance; **c. limite,** load capacity, cut-out capacity; *Med:* **c. vitale,** vital capacity; *s.a.* MESURE 2. 2. (*a*) capacity, ability; capability; talent; **c. manœuvrière,** manœuvrability; **homme de haute c.,** very capable man; **avoir les capacités pour faire qch.,** to be qualified to do sth.; **c. pour les affaires,** business ability; **c. de travail, d'aimer,** capacity for work, for love; **je ne m'en sens pas la c.,** I don't feel equal to it; *F:* **faire appel aux capacités,** to call for men of ability; *Jur:* **certificat de C. en droit,** certificate entitling holder to practise in some branches of the legal profession; (*b*) *Jur:* capacity, legal competency, ability (**de faire qch.,** to do sth.); **avoir c. pour faire qch.,** to be (legally) entitled, qualified, to do sth.; **priver qn de c. légale,** to incapacitate s.o.

capacitif, -ive [kapasitif, -iːv], *a. El:* capacitive; **couplage c.,** capacitive coupling.

capage [kapaːʒ], *s.m.* wrapping (of cigars).

caparaçon [kaparasɔ̃], *s.m. Harn:* caparison, housings, trappings.

caparaçonner [kaparasɔne], *v.tr.* to caparison (horse); *F:* **se c.,** to deck oneself out, get oneself up, ridiculously.

caparaçonnier [kaparasɔnje], *s.m.* maker of trappings.

cape [kap], *s.f.* 1. (*a*) (hooded) cape, cloak; **n'avoir que la c. et l'épée,** to have nothing but one's name and sword, to be fortuneless; **roman de c. et d'épée,** historical romance of the cape and rapier period; cloak-and-dagger story; *Lit:* **quitter la c. pour l'épée,** to give up the gown for the sword; **sous c.,** secretly, on the sly; **rire sous c.,** to laugh up one's sleeve; to chuckle; (*b*) hood; (*c*) wrapper, outer leaf (of cigar). 2. *Cost:* bowler-hat, *U.S:* derby. 3. *Nau:* **à la c.,** hove to; **à la c. sèche,** ahull; **être à la c. courante,** to try (under topsails); **être à la c., tenir la c.,** to lie to, to be hove to; **mettre à la c., prendre la c.,** to heave to; **voile de c.,** trysail, storm-sail; **abandonner la c.,** to cast off the tiller-lashing (in yachting). 2. *Sp:* (football) cap.

capéer [kapee], *v.i. Nau:* to lie to.

capelage [kaplaːʒ], *s.m. Nau:* 1. rigging (of mast). 2. masthead (under rigging); hounds.

capelan [kaplɑ̃], *s.m.* 1. *Dial: F:* (*S. of Fr.*) priest. 2. *Dial:* (*S. of Fr.*) glow-worm. 3. *Ich:* cap(e)lin.

capelanier [kaplanje], *s.m.* fisherman ((i) who fishes for cap(e)lins; (ii) who uses cap(e)lins as bait (for cod fishing)).

capeler [kaple], *v.tr.* **(je capelle, n. capelons; je capellerai)** *Nau:* 1. to rig (mast, spar, etc.); **c. le gréement,** to send up the rigging. 2. **c. une lame,** to take a green sea; **le canot fut capelé par une lame,** the boat was swamped by a sea. 3. **voile capelée sur une vergue,** sail blown over a yard. 4. *Navy:* **c. les masques,** to put on the gas-masks.

capelet [kaplɛ], *s.m. Vet:* capped hock.

capeline [kaplin], *s.f.* 1. *A.Cost:* (*a*) capeline, woman's riding-hood; (*b*) (lady's) hooded cape; sun-bonnet; (*c*) *Mil:* capeline; **homme de c.,** soldier. 2. *Surg:* capeline (bandage).

capendu [kapɑ̃dy], *s.m. Hort:* short-start, -shank (apple).

caper [kape], *v.tr.* 1. *Sp:* to cap (a football player, etc.). 2. to wrap (cigar).

capésien, -ienne, *s. Sch: F:* student reading for the C.A.P.E.S. (*Certificat d'Aptitude pédogogique à l'Enseignement secondaire*).

capétien, -ienne [kapesjɛ̃, -jɛn], *a. & s. Hist:* Capetian.

capeyer [kapeje], *v.i.* = CAPÉER.

Capharnaüm [kafarnaɔm]. 1. *Pr.n.m. B.Hist:* Capernaum. 2. *s.m.* lumber-room; *F:* glory-hole; **un véritable c.,** a regular jumble, chaos.

cap-hornier [kapɔrnje], *s.m. A.Nau:* Cape-Horner.

capilitium [kapilisjɔm], *s.m. Bot:* capillitium.

capillacé [kapil(l)ase], *a. Nat.Hist:* capillaceous.

capillaire [kapil(l)ɛːr]. 1. *a.* (*a*) capillary (tube, attraction); *Anat:* **les vaisseaux capillaires,** *s.* **les capillaires,** the capillary blood vessels, the capillaries; *Civ.E:* **réseau c.,** network of feeders (to the arterial roads); (*b*) **lotion c.,** hair lotion, hair tonic; **artiste c.,** hairdresser, coiffeur. 2. *s.m. Bot:* maidenhair (fern), adiantum. 3. *s.f.pl. Typ:* **capillaires,** hair-line type.

capillarimètre [kapil(l)arimɛtr̥], *s.m. Ph:* capillarimeter.

capillarite [kapil(l)arit], *s.f. Med:* capillaritis.

capillarité [kapil(l)arite], *s.f. Ph:* capillarity, capillary attraction.

capilliculture [kapil(l)ikyltyːr], *s.f.* capilliculture.

capillifolié [kapil(l)ifɔlje], *a. Bot:* capillifolious.

capilliforme [kapil(l)ifɔrm], *a.* capilliform.

capilotade [kapilɔtad], *s.f. Cu:* hash; *F:* **mettre qn en c.,** (i) to beat s.o. to a jelly, black and blue, to make mincemeat of s.o.; (ii) to pull s.o. to pieces; **j'ai le dos en c.,** my back is bruised, sore, all over; **avoir le bras réduit en c.,** to have one's arm crushed to pulp; **mettre qch. en c.,** to smash sth. to pieces.

capiston [kapistɔ̃], *s.m. Mil: Nau: P:* captain.

capitainat [kapitɛna], *s.m. A:* captaincy.

capitaine [kapitɛn], *s.m.* 1. (*a*) captain; *Mil:* **c. adjudant-major,** adjutant; **c. trésorier,** (regimental) paymaster; *U.S:* pay officer; *A:* **c. d'habillement,** quartermaster; *Mil.Av:* **c. (d'aviation)** = flight-lieutenant; *U.S:* (air) captain; *Navy:* **c. de corvette,** lieutenant-commander; **c. de frégate,** commander; **c. de vaisseau,** captain; **c. de pavillon,** commander of a flagship, flag-captain; **c. d'armes,** master-at-arms; *Nau:* **c. marchand,** (ship)master; skipper (of small vessel); **c. de port,** harbour master; **c. au long cours,** master of an ocean-going, foreign-going, vessel; master mariner; **c. au cabotage,** master, skipper, of a coasting vessel, of a coaster; **brevet de c. (de la marine marchande),** master's certificate; **c. d'armement,** ship's husband; marine superintendent; **passer c.,** (i) *Mil:* to be promoted captain; *O:* to obtain one's captaincy; (ii) *Mil.Av:* to be promoted flight-lieutenant; (iii) (*merchant navy*) to obtain one's master's certificate; *F:* to get one's ticket; (*b*) *Hist:* **c. des chasses,** captain of the royal hunt. 2. chief, head, leader (of band, gang, team, etc.); *Mil:* **un grand c.,** a great (military) leader; *Ind:* **les capitaines de l'industrie,** the captains of industry; **il a l'étoffe d'un grand c.,** he is cut out for a leader (of men). 3. *Ich:* thread-fin.

capitainerie [kapitɛnri], *s.f.* 1. *Hist:* office of captain of the royal hunt. 2. **c. (de port),** harbour master's office.

capital, -aux [kapital, -o]. 1. *a.* (*a*) *A:* **taille capitale,** poll tax; (*b*) capital (crime, punishment); **la peine capitale,** the death penalty; **condamné c.,** man under sentence of death; **procès c.,** capital case; (*c*) fundamental, essential, chief, principal; **le (point) c.,** the essential point; **il est c. que . . .,** it is essential, of first importance, of capital importance, that . . .; **une décision capitale,** a major decision; **les sept péchés capitaux,** the seven deadly sins; **son défaut c.,** his greatest fault; **la ville capitale,** *s.f.* **la capitale,** the chief town, the capital; **jouer un rôle c. dans qch.,** to play a chief part in sth.; **d'une importance capitale,** of paramount importance; **affaire d'importance capitale,** matter of cardinal importance; (*d*) *Typ:* **lettre capitale,** *s.f.* **une capitale,** capital (letter); **capitales penchées,** italic capitals; **grandes, petites, capitales,** large, small, capitals; **(écrire en) capitales d'imprimerie** (write in) block capitals. 2. *s.m.* (*a*) *Fin:* capital, assets; **c. et intérêt,** principal and interest; **mettre des capitaux dans une affaire,** to put capital into a business; **avoir des capitaux dans une affaire,** to have vested interests in a business; **faire un appel de c.,** to call for funds; **c. d'apport,** initial capital; **c. engagé,** tied-up capital; **c. de roulement,** trading capital, working capital; **c. souscrit,** subscribed capital; **c. versé, appelé, réel, effectif,** paid-up, called-up, capital; **c. social,** registered capital; **société au c. de . . .,** company with a capital of . . .; **procéder à une nouvelle augmentation de c.,** to make a new issue of capital; **capitaux de circulation,** circulating capital; **les capitaux abondent,** money is plentiful; **capitaux flottants, errants,** hot money; (*b*) *Pol.Ec:* **c. réel,** capital assets; **c. technique,** (technical) equipment; **association c.-travail,** profit-sharing scheme.

capitalisable [kapitalizabl̥], *a.* capitalizable (interest, etc.).

capitalisation [kapitalizasjɔ̃], *s.f.* capitalization (of interest, etc.).

capitaliser [kapitalize], *v.tr.* to capitalize (interest, etc.); *abs.* to save; to put money by.

capitalisme [kapitalism], *s.m.* capitalism.

capitaliste [kapitalist]. 1. *a.* capitalist, capitalistic. 2. *s.m. & f.* (*a*) capitalist; (*b*) investor.

capital-ship [kapitalʃip], *s.m. Navy:* capital ship.

capitan [kapitɑ̃], *s.m. A.Th:* swashbuckler, bully, braggadocio; **faire le c.,** to swagger; bluster; to play the bully.

capitane [kapitan], *s.f. A.Nau:* capitana.

capitan-pacha [kapitɑ̃paʃa], *s.m. Hist:* captain pasha (of Turkey); *pl. capitans-pachas.*

capitation [kapitasjɔ̃], *s.f. A.Adm:* capitation, poll-tax, head-money.

capité [kapite], *a. Bot:* capitate.

capiteux, -euse [kapitø, -øːz], *a.* (*a*) (*of wines*) heady, strong, exhilarating; (*b*) sensuous (charm, etc.); exciting, alluring, sexy (woman).

Capitole (le) [ləkapitɔl], *s.m.* the Capitol (of ancient Rome, of Toulouse, and of Washington).

capitolin [kapitɔlɛ̃], *a. Rom.Ant:* Capitoline (hill, games, etc.).

capiton [kapitɔ̃], *s.m.* 1. *Com:* cappadine, silk waste. 2. *Furn:* (*a*) cap, boss (between tufts or buttons); (*b*) cushion back (of seat).

capitonnage [kapitɔnaːʒ], *s.m.* 1. (*a*) upholstering; (*b*) upholstery padding. 2. quilting. 3. = CAPITON 2.

capitonner [kapitɔne], *v.tr.* 1. to upholster, pad (furniture). 2. to quilt (garment, etc.).

capitoul [kapitul], *s.m. Hist:* municipal magistrate (of Toulouse), *capitoul.*

capitoulat [kapitula], *s.m. Hist:* dignity, office, of *capitoul.*

capitulaire [kapitylɛːr]. 1. *a.* capitular(y) (act, letter); **salle c.,** chapter-house. 2. *s.m. A.Jur:* capitulary (of Charlemagne).

capitulairement [kapitylɛrmɑ̃], *adv. Ecc:* in chapter.

capitulant [kapitylɑ̃]. 1. *a. & s.m.* (canon, monk) with a voice in chapter. 2. *a. Swiss Hist:* **cantons capitulants,** cantons supplying mercenaries.

capitulard, -arde [kapitylaːr, -ard]. 1. *s. F:* (*a*) *Hist:* partisan of capitulation (of Paris in 1871); (*b*) funk, coward. 2. *a.* cowardly.

capitulation [kapitylasjɔ̃], *s.f.* 1. (*a*) *A:* convention; *pl. Hist:* **les capitulations,** the capitulations (drawn up with Turkey). 2. capitulation, surrender (on stipulated terms); **c. sans conditions,** unconditional surrender; **c. de conscience,** compromise with one's conscience; *s.a.* SE RENDRE 2.

capitule [kapityl], *s.m.* 1. *Bot:* capitulum, flower-head; **en c.,** capitate(d). 2. *Ecc:* capitulum.

capitulé [kapityle], *a. Bot:* capitular, capitate.

capituler [kapityle], *v.i.* to capitulate **(devant,** to); *Mil:* to surrender (on stipulated terms); **forcer qn à c.,** to bring s.o. to terms; **c. avec sa conscience,** to compromise, compound, with one's conscience.

capituliforme [kapitylifɔrm], *a. Bot:* capituliform.

capnofuge [kapnɔfyːʒ], *a.* smoke-preventing.

capodastre [kapɔdastr̥], *s.m. Mus:* capo tasto; *F:* capo (of guitar, banjo, etc.).

capok [kapɔk], *s.m. Com:* kapok.

capon¹, -onne [kapɔ̃, -ɔn]. 1. *a. F:* (*a*) afraid, cowardly; *F:* funky, *U.S:* yellow; (*b*) crest-fallen. 2. *s. F:* (*a*) coward, funk, sneak; (*b*) *Sch:* sneak; (*c*) *A:* (*at games*) cheat, swindler.

capon², *s.m. Nau:* cat(-purchase, -tackle); **bossoir de c.,** cat-head.

caponner¹ [kapɔne], *v.i.* (*a*) to funk; to show the white feather; (*b*) *Sch:* to sneak; to tell tales; (*c*) *A:* (*at games*) to cheat, swindle.

caponner², *v.tr. Nau:* to cat (anchor).

capon(n)ière [kapɔnjɛːr], *s.f.* shelter, refuge; *Fort:* caponier(e); *Mil:* **en c.,** in a masked flanking emplacement.

capoquier [kapɔkje], *s.m. Bot:* kapok-tree.

caporal, -aux [kapɔral, -o], *s.m.* 1. *Mil:* corporal (of unmounted troops; *cf.* BRIGADIER); *Av:* leading aircraftman; **c. d'ordinaire,** mess corporal; **c. de garde,** corporal of the guard; **c. de chambrée,** corporal in charge of squad room; *Hist: F:* **le Petit C.,** Napoleon. 2. caporal, standard tobacco (as issued by the French State factories).

caporal-chef [kapɔralʃɛf], *s.m. Mil:* lance-sergeant; senior corporal; *Mil.Av:* corporal; *pl. caporaux-chefs.*

caporaliser [kapɔralize]. 1. *v.tr.* to militarize, Prussianize. 2. *v.i.* to attach too much importance to petty drill.

caporalisme [kapɔralism], *s.m.* militarism.

caporal-tambour [kapɔraltɑ̃buːr], *s.m. Mil:* drum-corporal; *pl. caporaux-tambours.*

capot¹ [kapo], *s.m.* 1. *A: Mil: Nau:* hooded great-coat. 2. (*a*) cover, hood, casing (of arc-lamp, accumulator-charger, etc.); cap (over sth.), *e.g.:* end-cap (of torpedo-tube); cowl (of funnel); *Aut:* bonnet, *U.S:* hood (of car); *Av:* cowl(ing) (of aircraft engine); **c. de carénage,** fairing; **c. inférieur,** undershield; *Aut:* **c. d'essieu,** axle-cap; (*b*) *Nau:* tarpaulin. 3. *Nau:* companion(-hatch); **c. en bois,** booby-hatch; **entrée de c.,** companion-way. 4. *Navy:* look-out hood (of gun turret).

capot², *s.m.* **faire c.** = CAPOTER².

capot³, *s.m. Cards:* (*at piquet*) Capot; **faire c.,** to take all the tricks; *a.inv.* **rester, être, c.,** (i) not to take a single trick; (ii) *F:* to be nonplussed, to be taken aback; *F:* to be struck all of a heap.

capotage¹ [kapɔtaːʒ], *s.m.* 1. hooding (of gig, motor car, etc.); *Av:* cowling. 2. folding (of hood).

capotage², *s.m.* 1. capsizing (of boat). 2. *Aut: Av:* overturning; somersault (on landing); **faire un c.** = CAPOTER².

capote [kapɔt], *s.f.* 1. *Cost:* (*a*) *A:* capote; (*b*) *Mil:* greatcoat, overcoat; *Mil: Navy:* **c. de faction, de guérite,** watchcoat; (*c*) (lady's, baby's) bonnet. 2. *Veh:* (adjustable) hood (convertible) top; *Aut:* **coupé avec c. pliante,** drop-head coupé. 3. cowl, hood (of chimney). 4. *P:* **c. anglaise,** contraceptive sheath; *P:* French letter, *U.S:* French safe.

capoter¹ [kapɔte], *v.tr.* to hood, put a hood on (vehicle).

capoter², *v.i.* 1. *Nau:* to capsize, to turn turtle. 2. *Aut: Av:* to turn a somersault (on landing); to capsize, overturn.

capouan, -ane [kapwɑ̃, -an], *a. & s. A.Geog:* Capuan.

Capoue [kapu], *Pr.n.f. A.Geog:* Capua; **les délices de C.,** voluptuous idleness.

capout [kaput], *s.m. A: Mil: P:* **faire c. (à) qn,** to kill s.o.

Cappadoce [kapadɔs], *Pr.n.f. A.Geog:* Cappadocia.

cappadocien, -ienne [kapadɔsjɛ̃, -jɛn], *a. & s.* Cappadocian.

capparidacées [kaparidase], *s.f.pl. Bot:* Capparidaceae.

cappelénite [kap(ə)lenit], *s.f. Miner:* cappelenite.

câpre [kɑːpr̥], *s.f. Bot:* caper; *s.a.* CAPUCINE 2.

caprella [kaprɛla], *s.f.,* **caprelle** [kaprɛl], *s.f. Crust:* Caprella, the skeleton shrimp.

caprellidés [kaprɛlide], *s.m.pl. Crust:* Caprellidae.

capréolaire [kapreɔlɛːr], *a. Anat:* capreolar, pampiniform.

capréolé [kapreɔle], *a. Bot:* capreolate.

capricant [kaprikɑ̃], *a.* (*a*) *Med:* caprizant (pulse); (*b*) *Lit:* bounding, leaping (motion).

caprice [kapris], *s.m.* 1. caprice, whim, freak; **elle s'en va à Nice, revient à Paris, selon son c.,** she is off to Nice, back in Paris, as the whim, as the notion, takes her; *A:* **il travaille de c.,** he works when the fit is on him; **faire qch. par c.,** to do sth. on a sudden impulse; **les caprices de la mode,** the vagaries of fashion; **les caprices du sort,** the whims of fate; **avoir un c. pour qn,** to take a passing fancy to s.o. 2. *Mus:* capriccio, caprice. 3. *Geol:* offshoot (of vein).

capricieusement [kaprisjøzmɑ̃], *adv.* capriciously, whimsically.
capricieux, -ieuse [kaprisjø, -jøːz], *a.* capricious, freakish, whimsical; temperamental (woman); **enfant c.**, capricious, unruly, child; **temps c.**, changeable weather.
capricorne [kaprikɔrn], *s.m.* **1.** *Astr:* Capricorn; *Geog:* **le Tropique du C.**, the Tropic of Capricorn. **2.** *Ent:* capricorn beetle. **3.** *Z:* serow.
capridés [kapride], *s.m.pl. Z:* Capridae.
câprier [kɑpri(j)e], *s.m. Bot:* caper bush, plant.
câprière [kɑpri(j)ɛːr], *s.f.* **1.** *Agr:* caper plantation, field. **2.** caper jar, pot.
caprification [kaprifikasjɔ̃], *s.f. Hort:* caprification.
caprifigue [kaprifig], *s.f. Bot:* caprifig.
caprifiguier [kaprifigje], *s.m. Bot:* caprifig (tree).
caprifoliacées [kaprifɔljase], *s.f.pl. Bot:* Caprifoliaceae.
caprimulgidés [kaprimylʒide], *s.m.pl. Orn:* Caprimulgidae.
caprimulgiformes [kaprimylʒifɔrm], *s.m.pl. Orn:* Caprimulgiformes.
caprin, -ine [kaprɛ̃, -in], *a. Z:* caprine.
caprinés [kaprine], *s.m.pl. Z:* Caprinae.
capriote [kapri(j)ɔt], *a. & s. Geog:* (native, inhabitant) of (i) Capri, (ii) *A:* Capreae.
capripède [kapripɛd], *a. & s.* capriped, goat-footed (faun, etc.).
caprique [kaprik], *a. Ch:* capric (acid).
caprisant, caprizant [kaprizɑ̃], *a. Med:* = CAPRICANT.
caproïne [kaprɔin], *s.f. Ch:* caproin.
caproïque [kaprɔik], *a. Ch:* caproic (acid).
caprolactame [kaprɔlaktam], *s.m. Ch:* caprolactam.
capromys [kaprɔmis], *s.m. Z:* capromys, hutia.
capron [kaprɔ̃], *s.m. Bot:* hautboy strawberry.
capron(n)ier [kaprɔnje], *s.m. Bot:* hautboy strawberry (plant).
caproyle [kaprɔil], *s.m. Ch:* caproyl.
capryle [kapril], *s.m. Ch:* capryl.
caprylique [kaprilik], *a. Ch:* caprylic (acid).
capselle [kapsɛl], *s.f. Bot:* cassweed, shepherd's purse.
capsidés [kapside], *s.m.pl. Ent:* Capsidae.
capsien, -ienne [kapsjɛ̃, -jɛn], *a. Prehist:* Capsian.
capsulage [kapsylaːʒ], *s.m.* capsuling, capping (of bottles, etc.).
capsulaire [kapsylɛːr], *a. Bot: Anat:* capsular.
capsulateur [kapsylatœːr], *s.m.* bottle-capping machine, capper.
capsule [kapsyl], *s.f.* **1.** *Anat: Bot: Pharm:* capsule; **c. de lin**, boll. **2.** *Ch:* **c. d'évaporation**, evaporating dish; *s.a.* INCINÉRATION. **3.** *Mil: Sm.a: Min:* (firing) cap, primer. **4.** (*a*) (metallic) capsule, cap, crown-cork (of bottle); (*b*) seal (of bottle); (*c*) diaphragm case (of telephone). **5.** (*a*) *W.Tel:* **c. de la galène**, cup of the crystal; (*b*) *El.E:* **électrode à c.**, dished electrode. **6. c. (spatiale)**, (space) capsule.
capsuler [kapsyle]. **1.** *v.tr.* to seal, capsule, cap (bottle); **électrode capsulée**, dished electrode. **2.** *v.i. Sm.a:* to miss fire.
capsulerie [kapsylri], *s.f. Sm.a:* (*a*) manufacture of (firing) caps; (*b*) plant for the manufacture of (firing) caps.
capsuleur, -euse [kapsylœr, -øːz], *s.* (*pers.*) (bottle) capper.
capsulifère [kapsylifɛːr], *a. Bot:* capsuliferous.
capsulite [kapsylit], *s.f. Med:* capsulitis.
capsulorraphie [kapsylɔrafi], *s.f. Surg:* capsulorrhaphy.
capsulotomie [kapsylɔtɔmi], *s.f. Surg:* capsulotomy.
capsus [kapsys], *s.m. Ent:* capsus.
captage [kaptaːʒ], *s.m. Hyd.E:* **1.** (*a*) collecting, piping (of waters, etc.); *El.E:* picking up (of current by tram, etc.); (*b*) *Ind:* recovery (of waste products, of by-products). **2.** water-catchment. **3.** *Med:* uptake.
captal [kaptal], *s.m. A:* (*in Gascony*) chief, lord; *pl. captals.*
captateur, -trice [kaptatœːr, -tris], *s. Jur:* inveigler; **c. de successions**, legacy-hunter.
captation [kaptasjɔ̃], *s.f.* **1.** *Jur:* captation, inveigling; **c. d'héritage**, captation of an inheritance. **2.** *El:* collecting (of current); *Geog: Hyd.E:* **surface de c. des eaux**, catchment basin. **3.** *Tg:* scanning; *Tp:* intercepting (of messages); *F:* tapping (of line).
captatoire [kaptatwaːr], *a.* inveigling, insidious (means of obtaining sth.).
capter [kapte], *v.tr.* **1.** *usu. Pej:* (*a*) to obtain (sth.) by undue influence, by insidious means; **c. les suffrages de . . .**, *F:* to nobble the votes of . . .; (*b*) to captivate; to win (s.o.) over (by ingratiating means); **c. l'attention de qn**, to rivet s.o.'s attention. **2.** (*a*) to collect, pick up (electric current, etc.); to catch, impound, pipe (waters); (*b*) *Ind:* to recover, save (by-product). **3.** *Tg:* to scan; *Tp:* to intercept (messages); *F:* to tap (a line). **4.** *W.Tel:* **c. un poste**, to pick up a station.
capte-suies [kaptsɥi], *s.m.inv.* smoke washer.
capteur [kaptœːr], *s.m.* **1.** *Navy:* captor; *a.* **navire c.**, captor ship. **2.** *El: Elcs:* pick-up; pick-off; **c. de pression**, pressure pick-up; **c. piézo électrique**, piezo electric pressure gauge; **c. d'impulsions**, pulse chamber.
captieusement [kapsjøzmɑ̃], *adv.* speciously, deceitfully, insidiously.
captieux, -ieuse [kapsjø, -jøːz], *a.* fallacious, sophistical, specious, misleading, captious (argument, etc.).
captif, -ive [kaptif, -iːv], *a. & s.* **1.** captive, *s.* prisoner; **emmener qn c.**, to lead s.o. away captive, into captivity; **tenir qn c.**, to hold s.o. prisoner; **être c. du plaisir**, to be a slave to pleasure. **2.** *s.m.* captive balloon.
captivant [kaptivɑ̃], *a.* captivating; enthralling.
captiver [kaptive], *v.tr.* **1.** *A:* to capture, to take prisoner. **2.** to captivate, enthral, charm (s.o.); **c. l'attention de qn,** to win s.o.'s attention. **3.** *O:* to subjugate, master (one's passions, etc.).
captivité [kaptivite], *s.f.* captivity; **tenir qn en c.**, (i) to hold s.o. in captivity; (ii) to keep (child, etc.) under great restraint, in subjection.
capture [kaptyːr], *s.f.* **1.** (*a*) capture, seizure (of ship, etc.); confiscation (by customs officer); arrest (of deserter, etc.); *Mil: Nau:* **esquive à la c.**, evasion; (*b*) capture, prize; (*c*) *Geog:* (river) capture. **2.** stopping (of escape of gas, etc.).
capturer [kaptyre], *v.tr.* **1.** to capture, take (ship, etc.); to seize; to arrest (deserter); to catch (whale, etc.). **2.** (*a*) to collect (steam, gases, etc.); (*b*) to stop, check (leak).
capuce [kapys], *s.m.* (monk's) hood, cowl; *Bot:* **c. de moine**, monkshood.
capuche [kapyʃ], *s.f.* (woman's) hood.
capuchon [kapyʃɔ̃], *s.m.* **1.** *Cost:* (*a*) hood; (*b*) *Ecc:* cowl; **prendre le c.**, to take the cowl; *Bot:* **c. de moine**, monkshood; (*c*) *Orn:* cap (of a bird); (*d*) *Nat.Hist:* **à c.**, hooded (seal, etc.). **2.** cap, cover, hood (of lamp, etc.); muzzle-cover (of rifle); cap (of fountain pen); whipping (of handle); **c. de cheminée**, chimney-cowl; **c. de valve**, valve-cap (of tyre valve); **c. de pipe**, (tobacco-)pipe cover.
capuchonné [kapyʃɔne], *a.* (*a*) (*of pers.*) hooded; cowled; (*b*) *Bot:* capped, hooded.
capuchonnement [kapyʃɔnmɑ̃], *s.m.* putting a cowl, a hood, a cap (on sth.); **c. d'une cheminée**, cowling of a chimney.
capuchonner [kapyʃɔne], *v.tr.* to cover (sth.) with a cowl, a hood; to cowl (chimney, etc.).
capucin [kapysɛ̃], *s.m.* **1.** Capuchin friar, mendicant friar; *F:* **barbe de c.**, very long beard; *s.a.* BARBE-DE-CAPUCIN; *A:* **parler comme un c.**, to speak through one's nose; *A:* **capucins de cartes**, friars cut out of playing cards (by children); *F:* **tomber comme des capucins de cartes**, to go down, topple over, like a row of tin soldiers, like ninepins. **2.** *Meteor: F:* **c. hygrométrique**, weather box. **3.** (*a*) *Husb:* **(pigeon) c.**, capuchin; (*b*) *Z:* hooded seal; (*c*) *Z:* capuchin monkey; (*d*) *Ven: F:* hare.
capucinade [kapysinad], *s.f. F:* (*a*) dull sermon, address; (*b*) assumed, affected, piety.
capucine [kapysin], *s.f.* **1.** Capuchin nun. **2.** *Bot:* nasturtium; **câpres capucines**, nasturtium seeds, English capers; **c. jaune canari**, canary creeper. **3.** *A:* pipkin, porringer (with handle). **4.** *Sm.a: A:* band (of rifle); **première c.**, lower band. **5.** *Arch:* drip-stone. **6.** *Veh:* hood (of gig, etc.). **7.** children's dance.
capucinière [kapysinjɛːr], *s.f. F:* (*a*) Capuchin convent; friary; (*b*) sanctimonious household.
capulet [kapyle], *s.m.* hood (worn by women in the Pyrenees).
Cap-Vert [kapvɛr], *Pr.n. Geog:* **Iles du C.-V.**, Cape Verde Islands.
capvirade [kapvirad], *s.f. Agr:* headland (at end of field).
capybara [kapibara], *s.m. Z:* = CABIAI.
caquage [kakaːʒ], *s.m.* **1.** curing and barrelling (of herrings). **2.** barrelling (of gunpowder, etc.).
caque [kak], *s.f.* keg; herring-barrel; *F:* **pressés, serrés, comme (des) harengs en c.**, packed together like sardines, packed like sardines in a tin; *Prov:* **la c. sent toujours le hareng**, what's bred in the bone will come out in the flesh.
caquelon [kaklɔ̃], *s.m. Cu:* dish for fondue.
caquer [kake], *v.tr.* **1.** to cure and barrel (herrings). **2.** to barrel (gunpowder, etc.).
caquerolle [kakrɔl], *s.f.* copper saucepan (with three legs and a long handle).
caquet [kakɛ], *s.m.* **1.** cackle, cackling (of hens, etc.); chatter (of magpies). **2.** *F:* (noisy) chatter, cackle, idle gossip, tittle-tattle; **elle lui a rabattu, rabaissé, le c.**, she shut him up, made him sing small, took him down a peg (or two); **c. bon bec**, (i) magpie (in La Fontaine's fables); (ii) chatterbox.
caquetage [kak(ə)taːʒ], *s.m.* **1.** cackling (of hens, etc.). **2.** *F:* chatter(ing), gossip(ing).
caqueter [kak(ə)te], *v.i.* (**je caquette, n. caquetons; je caquetterai**) **1.** (*of hen, etc.*) to cackle. **2.** *F:* to gossip, chatter; **elle continua à c.**, she went on chattering.
caqueterie [kak(ə)tri], *s.f.* = CAQUETAGE.
caqueteur, -euse [kak(ə)tœːr, -øːz], *s.* chatterer, tattler, gossip.
caqueur, -euse [kakœːr, -øːz], *s.* **1.** (*a*) (i) curer; (ii) packer, of herrings; (*b*) barreller (of gunpowder, etc.). **2.** *s.m.* herring-curer's knife.
caquilier [kakije], *s.m. Bot:* sea-rocket.
car[1] [kaːr], *conj.* for, because; *s.m.inv.* **mettre des si et des c. dans une affaire**, to ask too many whys and wherefores.
car[2], *s.m.* **1.** (railway-, tram-)car. **2.** (*a*) (motor) coach; (country) bus; (*b*) **c. de police**, police van; **c. de radio-reportage, des émissions extérieures**, outside broadcasting van, mobile broadcasting unit; **c. sonore**, mobile sound unit.
Carabas[1] [karabɑ], *Pr.n.* (*a*) **le marquis de Carabas**, the Marquis of Carabas (in *Puss-in-boots*); (*b*) *F:* **un marquis de C.**, man of doubtful pedigree; adventurer.
carabas[2], *s.m. A:* public conveyance (in the region round Paris).
carabe [karab], *s.m. Ent:* carabus, carabid (beetle); **c. doré**, ground beetle.
carabidés [karabide], *s.m.pl. Ent:* Carabidae; carabids.
carabin [karabɛ̃], *s.m.* **1.** *A:* mounted skirmisher, carabineer. **2.** *F:* (*a*) (i) (*occ. f. Hum:* **carabine**), medical student; *F:* medico; (ii) *Fr.C:* (any) student (at university); (*b*) *Gaming:* occasional punter; cautious player.
carabinade [karabinad], *s.f. Sch: F:* medical students' rag.
carabinage [karabinaːʒ], *s.m.* rifling (of gun-barrel).
carabine [karabin], *s.f. Sm.a:* (cavalry) carbine; rifle; **c. de salon**, gallery rifle; **c. à air comprimé**, air-gun.
carabiné [karabine], *a. Nau:* **vent c.**, strong, stiff, gale; *F:* **rhume c.**, heavy cold; **fièvre carabinée**, violent fever; **guigne carabinée**, extraordinary run of bad luck.
carabiner [karabine]. **1.** *v.tr.* to rifle (gun-barrel). **2.** *v.i.* (*a*) *A:* to skirmish; (*b*) *F: Gaming:* to lay an occasional stake; to play timidly.
se carabiner, *Nau:* (*of gale*) to stiffen.
carabinier [karabinje], *s.m.* **1.** (*a*) *A:* car(a)bineer; heavy-cavalryman; (*b*) *F:* **arriver comme les carabiniers**, to arrive too late. **2.** (*in Italy*) member of the State police; (*in Spain*) frontier guard.
carabiques [karabik], *s.m.pl.* = CARIBIDÉS.
Carabosse [karabɔs], *Pr.n.* (*a*) **la fée C.**, the wicked (hunch-backed) fairy; (*b*) *hence* **une fée C.**, an old hag.
caracal, *pl.* **-als** [karakal], *s.m. Z:* caracal, Persian lynx.
caraco [karako], *s.m. Cost:* (woman's) loose (working) jacket.
caracole [karakɔl], *s.f.* **1.** (*a*) *Equit:* caracol(e), half-turn; (*b*) **faire des caracoles**, to cut capers. **2.** *Arch:* caracol(e); **escalier en c.**, winding, spiral, staircase.
caracoler [karakɔle], *v.i.* (*a*) *Equit:* to caracol(e); (*b*) to gambol, caper.
caracolite [karakɔlit], *s.f. Miner:* caracolite.
caracore [karakɔːr], *s.m. Nau:* caracore, caracora.
caractère [karaktɛːr], *s.m.* **1.** character, letter graphic sign; *Mth: etc:* symbol; *Typ:* (metal) type; **écrire en petits caractères**, to write in a small hand; **écrivez en caractères d'imprimerie**, use block letters, capitals, *U.S:* please print; **imprimer en petits, gros, caractères**, to print in small, large, type; *Typ:* **c. anglais**, light-faced type; *Tp:* **caractères**, codes and numbers. **2.** (*a*) characteristic, feature, stamp; **c. d'un style**, characteristics of a style; **l'affaire a pris un c. grave**, the matter has taken a serious turn; **publication de c. officiel**, publication of an official nature; *Biol:* **c. héréditaire, acquis**, hereditary, acquired, character; *Lit.Hist:* **comédie de c.**,

comedy of character; *Danc:* **danse de c.,** character dance; (*b*) *Phil:* distinguishing mark; (*c*) *A:* official capacity (of ambassador, etc.); **avoir c. pour faire qch.,** to be entitled to do sth; **agir en c. de . . .,** to act in the capacity, in the quality of. . . . **3.** (*a*) nature, disposition; **homme d'un, au, c. emporté,** hot-tempered man; **gai de c.,** gay by nature; **d'un c. facile,** easy-going; **d'un c. jaloux,** of a jealous disposition; **sortir de son c.,** to lose one's temper; **avoir mauvais c., avoir le c. mal fait,** to be bad-tempered, to be cantankerous; **avoir bon c.,** to be good-natured; (*b*) personality, character; **avoir du c.,** to have character, grit, backbone; **montrer du c.,** to show character, spirit; **manquer de c.,** to lack strength of character, of mind, of will; to have no backbone; **homme sans c.,** spineless individual; **cette maison a beaucoup de c.,** this house has plenty of character.

caractériel, -ielle [karakterjɛl]. **1.** *a.* characterial, of or pertaining to character; temperamental; *Psy:* **trouble c.,** psychopathic disorder; **enfant c.,** psycho-neurotic, *F:* problem, child. **2.** *s.m. & f.* (*a*) psycho-neurotic; (*b*) psychopath.

caractérisant [karakterizɑ̃], *a.* characterizing, characteristic.

caractérisation [karakterizasjɔ̃], *s.f.* characterizing, characterization.

caractérisé [karakterize], *a.* characterized; **physionomie caractérisée,** face full of character; **une rougeole caractérisée,** a clear, typical, unmistakable, case of measles; **la maladie n'est pas nettement caractérisée,** the illness is difficult to diagnose.

caractériser [karakterize], *v.tr.* to characterize; (i) to set forth the character of (nation, etc.); (ii) to mark, distinguish, to be peculiar to (sth.); **symptômes qui caractérisent une maladie,** symptoms characteristic of an illness, which indicate an illness.

se caractériser. 1. to assume, take on, character; (*of symptoms*) to become clearly marked. **2.** to be characterized, distinguished (**par,** by).

caractéristique [karakteristik]. **1.** *a.* characteristic, distinctive, typical; **la cordialité qui a été c. de nos débats,** the cordiality which has marked our proceedings; **opinions caractéristiques de la bourgeoisie,** opinions typical of the middle classes. **2.** *s.f.* characteristic; feature; (*a*) *Metall:* **caractéristiques des métaux non-ferreux,** properties of non-ferrous metals; *E:* **caractéristiques du fonctionnement,** operating features; *Av:* **caractéristiques de stabilité,** surge characteristics; *Surv:* **c. du terrain,** character of the terrain; (*b*) **c. (imposée),** specification; **caractéristiques du moteur, de la coque,** engine, hull, specifications; (*c*) *pl.* **caractéristiques,** particulars; **caractéristiques des ponts suspendus,** particulars of suspension bridges; **caractéristiques techniques,** data; (*d*) *Mth:* characteristic (of logarithm, series of curves); (*e*) *El:* distinctive wave-length.

caractérologie [karakterɔlɔʒi], *s.f.* characterology.

caractérologue [karakterɔlɔg], *s.m.* characterologist.

caracul [karakyl, -kul], *s.m. Com:* caracul, karakul (fur).

carafe [karaf], *s.f.* **1.** (*a*) (glass) decanter; water-bottle, carafe; **vin en c.** = wine by the glass; (*b*) **boire une c. de vin,** to drink a carafe (full) of wine; (*b*) *Fish:* (bottle-shaped) gudgeon trap; (*c*) *P:* head; *P:* nut. **2.** *F:* **rester en c.,** (i) to be left in the lurch; (ii) to be left out of it, out in the cold; (*of car, etc.*) **tomber en c.,** to break down.

carafée [karafe], *s.f. Bot:* wallflower.

carafon [karafɔ̃], *s.m.* **1.** small carafe (= ½ bottle). **2.** (wine-)cooler, ice-pail. **3.** *P:* head; *P:* nut.

caraïbe [karaib]. *Ethn:* **1.** *a.* Caribbean. **2.** *s.m.* Carib, Caribbee; *Geog:* **la mer des Caraïbes,** the Caribbean Sea; **les îles Caraïbes,** the Caribbean Islands.

Caraïte [karait], *s.m. Rel.H:* Karaite.

caraman [karamɑ̃], *s.m. Ich:* red gurnard.

caramanage [karamana:ʒ], *s.m. Mec.E:* mandrelling.

Caramanie [karamani], *Pr.n.f. Geog:* Kerman.

carambolage [karɑ̃bɔla:ʒ], *s.m.* (*a*) *Bill:* cannon, *U.S:* carom; **série, suite, de carambolages,** break; (*b*) *F: Aut:* pile-up.

carambole [karɑ̃bɔl], *s.f.* **1.** *Bill: O:* red ball. **2.** *Bot:* carambola, Chinese gooseberry, Coromandel gooseberry.

caramboler [karɑ̃bɔle]. **1.** *v.i. Bill:* to cannon, *U.S:* to carom; **c. par la rouge,** to cannon off the red. **2.** *v.tr. F:* (*a*) **c. les billes,** to knock the balls about; (*b*) **c. une voiture,** to run into a car; **plusieurs voitures se sont carambolées sur l'autoroute,** several cars ran into each other, piled up, on the motorway.

caramboleur [karɑ̃bɔlœ:r], *s.m.* billiard player.

carambolier [karɑ̃bɔlje], *s.m. Bot:* carambola (tree); **c. cylindrique,** cucumber-tree.

carambouillage [karɑ̃buja:ʒ], *s.m.,* **carambouille** [karɑ̃bu:j], *s.f. F:* fraudulent conversion; larceny by a bailee.

carambouiller [karɑ̃buje], *v.i. F:* to convert fraudulently.

carambouilleur [karɑ̃bujœ:r], *s.m. F:* one who converts fraudulently.

caramel [karamɛl], *s.m. Cu:* (*a*) caramel, burnt sugar; **bonbons au c., des caramels,** caramels; **c. au beurre,** butterscotch, toffee; (*b*) browning (for gravy).

caramélé [karamele], *a.* (like) caramel (in taste, appearance); caramel-flavoured.

caramélisation [karamelizasjɔ̃], *s.f. Cu:* caramelization.

caraméliser [karamelize], *v.tr.* **1.** to caramel(ize) (sugar). **2.** to mix caramel with (sth.). **3.** to coat (bowl, mould) with caramel.

se caraméliser, (*esp. of roast*) to brown (well); to caramelize.

carange [karɑ̃:ʒ], *s.f.* = CARANGUE.

carangidés [karɑ̃ʒide], *s.m.pl. Ich:* Carangidae.

carangue [karɑ̃:g], *s.f.,* **caranx** [karɑ̃:ks], *s.m. Ich:* caranx, scad, horse-mackerel, *U.S:* cavally.

caranguer [karɑ̃ge], *v.i. Nau:* to heave to (in gale).

carapace [karapas], *s.f.* **1.** carapace, shell (of lobster, etc.); *s.a.* TORTUE 1. **2.** *Geol:* hardpan.

carapata [karapata], *s.m. A: Mil: P:* infantryman, foot-slogger.

carapater (se) [səkarapate], *v.pr. P:* to decamp, bolt, scram.

caraque[1] [karak], *s.f.* **1.** *A.Nau:* car(r)ack, argosy. **2.** *a.* **porcelaine c.,** fine Chinese porcelain.

caraque[2], *a. & s.m.* (**cacao**) **c.,** Caracas, Venezuelan, cacao.

carassin [karasɛ̃], *s.m. Ich:* crucian carp; **c. doré,** goldfish.

carat [kara], *s.m.* **1.** *Meas:* carat; (*a*) **or à dix-huit carats (de fin),** eighteen-carat gold; *A: F:* **sot à vingt-quatre carats,** out-and-out fool; (*b*) *Lap:* carat (weight) (0·2 gr.). **2.** small diamond.

caraté [karate], *s.m. Med:* carate, pinta, pinto.

carature [karaty:r], *s.f.* **1.** alloying (of gold). **2.** gold alloy.

Caravage (le) [ləkarava:ʒ], *Pr.n.m.* Caravaggio.

caravane [karavan], *s.f.* **1.** (*a*) caravan, desert convoy; (*b*) conducted tour; conducted party (of tourists, school-children, etc.). **2.** *Veh:* caravan, *U.S:* trailer.

caravanier [karavanje], *s.m. & a.* **1.** (*in desert*) (*a*) *s.m.* caravaneer; (*b*) *a.* **chemin c.,** caravan route, track. **2.** *Aut:* *s.m.* caravaner.

caravan(n)ing [karavaniŋ], *s.m.,* **caravanisme** [karavanism], *s.m.* **faire du c.,** to go caravan(n)ing, to caravan.

caravaniste [karavanist], *s.m.* caravanist, caravaner.

caravansérail [karavɑ̃sera:j], *s.m.* caravanserai.

caravelle [karavɛl], *s.f.* **1.** *A: Nau:* caravel, carvel. **2.** (square-headed) ship-nail.

carbamate [karbamat], *s.m. Ch:* carbamate.

carbamide [karbamid], *s.f. Ch:* carbamide.

carbamique [karbamik], *a. Ch:* carbamic (acid).

carbamyle [karbamil], *s.m. Ch:* carbamyl(e).

carbanile [karbanil], *s.m. Ch:* carbanil.

carbatine [karbatin], *s.f. Tan:* green hide, green skin.

carbazole [karbazɔl], *s.m. Ch:* carbazol(e).

carbène [karbɛn], *s.m. Ch:* carbene.

carbénium [karbenjɔm], *s.m. Ch:* carbonium.

carbinol [karbinɔl], *s.m. Ch:* carbinol.

carbochimie [karbɔʃimi], *s.f.* (*a*) the chemistry of coal derivatives and by-products; (*b*) the coal by-products industry.

carbodiimide [karbɔdiimid], *s.m. Ch:* carbodiimide.

carbogène [karbɔʒɛ:n], *s.m.* **1.** seltzogene powder. **2.** *Petroleum Ind:* carbogen.

carboglace [karbɔglas], *s.f. R.t.m:* dry ice.

carbohémoglobine [karbɔemɔglɔbin], *s.f. Bio-Ch:* carbohæmoglobin.

carbol [karbɔl], *s.m. Ch:* carbolic acid.

carbolique [karbɔlik], *a.* **acide c.,** (i) *Ch:* carbolic acid; (ii) *Com:* coal-tar creosote.

carboloy [karbɔlɔ:j], *s.m. Metall:* carboloy.

carbonade [karbɔnad], *s.f. Cu* = CARBONNADE.

carbonado [karbɔnado], *s.m. Miner:* carbonado, carbon diamond, black diamond.

carbonage [karbɔna:ʒ], *s.m. Typ:* carbon process.

carbonarisme [karbɔnarism], *s.m. Italian Hist:* carbonarism.

carbonaro, *pl.* **-i** [karbɔnaro, -i], *s.m. Italian Hist:* carbonaro.

carbonatation [karbɔnatasjɔ̃], *s.f.* carbonatation, carbonation.

carbonate [karbɔnat], *s.m. Ch:* carbonate; **c. de soude,** carbonate of soda; *Com:* washing soda.

carbonater [karbɔnate], *v.tr. Ch:* to carbonate.

carbone [karbɔn], *s.m. Ch:* carbon; *Com:* **(papier) c.,** carbon paper; **copie au (papier) c.,** *F:* **carbone,** carbon copy.

carboné [karbɔne], *a. Ch:* carbonaceous, carburetted.

carbonifère [karbɔnifɛ:r], *a. & s.m.* carboniferous.

carbonifèrien [karbɔniferjɛ̃], *a. & s.m. Geol:* = CARBONIFÈRE.

carbonique [karbɔnik], *a. Ch:* carbonic (anhydride, etc.); **acide c.,** carbonic acid; *Organic Ch:* carboxylic; *s.a.* NEIGE.

carbonisateur [karbɔnizatœ:r], *s.m. Ind:* charcoal furnace.

carbonisation [karbɔnizasjɔ̃], *s.f.* carbonization, charring.

carboniser [karbɔnize], *v.tr.* (*a*) to carbonize (bones, etc.); to char (wood); (*b*) **être carbonisé,** to be burnt to death (in house fire, accident); **c. la viande,** to burn the meat to a cinder.

carbonite [karbɔnit], *s.f.* **1.** *Exp:* carbonite. **2.** *Ind:* carbonite, mineral coke.

carbonitruration [karbɔnitryrasjɔ̃], *s.f. Ch:* carbonitriding.

carbonitrurer [karbɔnitryre], *v.tr. Metall:* to carbonitride.

carbonium [karbɔnjɔm], *s.m. Ch:* = CARBÉNIUM.

carbonnade [karbɔnad], *s.f. Cu:* meat grilled on charcoal.

carbonylage [karbɔnila:ʒ], *s.m.* creosoting (of wood).

carbonyle [karbɔnil], *s.m. Ch:* carbonyl; **(bois) passé au c.,** creosoted (wood).

carborundum [karbɔrɔ̃dɔm], *s.m.* carborundum, silicon carbide.

carbostyryle [karbɔstiril], *s.m. Ch:* carbostyril.

carbosulfure [karbɔsylfy:r], *s.m. Ch:* carbon disulphide.

carboxyhémoglobine [karbɔksiemɔglɔbin], *s.f. Bio-Ch:* carboxyhæmoglobin.

carboxylase [karbɔksila:z], *s.f. Biol:* carboxylase.

carboxyle [karbɔksil], *s.m. Ch:* carboxyl (group).

carburant [karbyrɑ̃]. **1.** *s.m.* (motor) fuel. **2.** *a.* containing hydrocarbon; **alcool c.,** motor spirit.

carburateur, -trice [karbyratœ:r, -tris]. **1.** *a. Ch: A:* carbonizing, carburizing, carburet(t)ing (apparatus). **2.** *s.m. I.C.E:* carburettor, carburetter, *U.S:* carburetor; **c. à niveau constant,** constant level, float, carburettor; **c. double, jumelé,** twin, dual, carburettor; **c. inversé,** down-draught carburettor; **c. à gicleur, à ajutage,** jet-carburettor; **c. alimenté par gravité, par différence de niveau,** gravity-fed carburettor; **c. alimenté par pompe,** pump-fed carburettor; **c. alimenté sous pression,** pressure-fed carburettor; **c. à dépression,** suction-carburettor; **c. à pulvérisation,** spray-carburettor; **c. à deux phases,** two-stage carburettor; **c. à pointeau de dosage,** metering-pin carburettor; **c. noyé,** flooded carburettor.

carburation [karbyrasjɔ̃], *s.f.* **1.** *Ch:* carburetting. **2.** *El:* flashing (of filament). **3.** *Metall:* carburization. **4.** *I.C.E:* carburation, carburating, carburetting; **moteur à c.,** internal combustion engine; **c. double, jumelée,** dual carburation; **c. inversée,** down-draught carburation; **c. riche,** rich mixture; **chambre de c.,** carburettor-, mixing- chamber.

carbure [karby:r], *s.m. Ch:* **1.** carbide; **c. d'hydrogène,** hydrocarbon; **carbures saturés,** methane series. **2. c. (de calcium)** (calcium) carbide; **c. fritté,** sintered carbide.

carburé [karbyre], *a. I.C.E:* **air c.,** carburetted air; *Ch:* **hydrogène c.,** carburetted hydrogen.

carburéacteur [karbyreaktœ:r], *s.m. Av:* jet fuel.

carburer [karbyre], *v.tr.* **1.** *Ch:* to carburet. **2.** *El:* to flash (filament). **3.** *Metall:* to carburize. **4.** *I.C.E:* to vaporize (fuel). **5.** *F:* to work, to go strong; **ça carbure,** it's going fine, it's going like a bomb.

carcailler [karkaje], *v.i.* (*of quail*) to call.

carcajou [karkaʒu], *s.m. Z:* carcajou, North American badger.

carcan [karkɑ̃], *s.m.* **1.** (*a*) *A:* carcan, iron-collar; (*b*) *Cost: Jewelry:* choker; (*c*) *Husb:* yoke (to prevent animals passing through hedge, etc.); (*d*) **le c. de la discipline,** the yoke, restraint, of discipline. **2.** *P:* (*a*) (*of horse*) jade, screw; (*b*) big ungainly shrew of a woman.

carcas [karka], *s.m. Metall:* salamander, shadrach.

carcasse [karkas], *s.f.* **1.** carcass, carcase; dead body (of animal); *F:* body (of living person). **2.** framework, frame (of umbrella, piece of scenery, airship, etc.); shell, skeleton (of house, ship, etc.); carcase (of ship); body, shape (of hat, etc.); carcase (of electric motor); casing (of pneumatic tyre).

carcassier [karkasje], *s.m.* frame-maker (for scenery, umbrellas).

carcassonnais, -aise [karkasɔnɛ, -ɛːz], *a. & s. Geog:* (native, inhabitant) of Carcassonne.

carcel [karsɛl], *s.m.* **1.** carcel lamp. **2.** *Ph.Meas: A:* carcel (unit of light, = 9·5 candles).

carcharhinides [karkarinid], *s.m.pl. Ich:* Carchar(h)inidae.

carcharias [karkarjas], *s.m. Ich:* carcharias.

carcharinus [karkarinys], *s.m. Ich:* carcharinus.

carcharodon [karkarɔdɔ̃], *s.m. Ich:* Carcharodon.

carcin [karsɛ̃], *s.m. Crust:* green crab, shore-crab.

carcinogène [karsinɔʒɛːn], *Med:* (*a*) *a.* carcinogenic; **substance c.,** carcinogen; (*b*) *s.m.* carcinogen.

carcinoïde [karsinɔid], *s.m. Med:* carcinoid (tumor).

carcinologie [karsinɔlɔʒi], *s.f.* **1.** *Z:* carcinology. **2.** *Med:* = CANCÉROLOGIE.

carcinologique [karsinɔlɔʒik], *a. Z:* carcinological.

carcinologiste [karsinɔlɔʒist], *s.m. & f. Z:* carcinologist.

carcinologue [karsinɔlɔg], *s.m.* (*a*) carcinologist; (*b*) cancer specialist.

carcinomateux, -euse [karsinɔmatø, -øːz], *a. Med:* carcinomatous.

carcinome [karsinoːm, -ɔm], *s.m. Med:* carcinoma.

carcinose [karsinoːz], *s.f. Med:* carcinosis.

carcinus [karsinys], *s.m. Crust:* Carcinus, the common crabs.

cardage [kardaːʒ], *s.m. Tex:* **1.** carding, combing (of wool, etc.). **2.** teaseling, raising (of cloth).

cardamine [kardamin], *s.f. Bot:* cardamine; **c. des prés,** lady's-smock, mayflower.

cardamome [kardamoːm, -ɔm], *s.m. Bot:* cardamom.

Cardan [kardɑ̃], *Pr.n.m. & s.m. Mec.E:* **c., joint de C.,** universal joint, Cardan joint; **arbre à C.,** propeller shaft, Cardan shaft; **suspendu à la C.,** hung on gimbals.

carde [kard], *s.f.* **1.** *Cu:* chard. **2.** *Tex:* card, carding brush, teasel (frame). **3.** *Ind: etc:* **c. métallique,** wire brush.

cardée [karde], *s.f. Tex:* cardful (of wool).

carder [karde], *v.tr. Tex:* **1.** to card (wool, etc.); **laines cardées,** woollens. **2.** to teasel, raise (cloth); to comb out (mattress). **3.** *P:* (*a*) to scratch (s.o.); (*b*) **c. le cuir à qn,** to give s.o. a thrashing.

cardère [kardɛːr], *s.f. Bot:* teasel; fuller's teasel; **c. poilue,** shepherd's-rod.

carderie [kard(ə)ri], *s.f. Tex:* carding-room, -house.

cardeur, -euse [kardœːr, -øːz], *s. Tex:* **1.** carder, card-tenter, teaseler. **2.** *s.f.* **cardeuse,** carding-machine, carder.

cardia [kardja], *s.m. Anat:* cardia (of œsophagus).

cardiaire [kardjɛːr]. **1.** *a. Anat:* cardiac. **2.** *s.f. Bot:* motherwort.

cardiale [kardjal], *a.f. Anat:* cardiac (glands).

cardialgie [kardjalʒi], *s.f. Med:* (*a*) cardialgia; *F:* heartburn; (*b*) gastralgia.

cardialgique [kardjalʒik], *a. & s. Med:* (*a*) cardialgic; (*b*) gastralgic.

cardiaque [kardjak]. **1.** *a.* cardiac (nerves, murmur, etc.); **orifice c.,** cardiac orifice; **crise c.,** heart attack; **excitation c. artificielle,** pacemaking. **2.** *s.m. & f.* cardiac; *F:* heart case. **3.** *s.m.* cardiac stimulant. **4.** *s.f. Bot:* motherwort.

cardiectasie [kardjɛktazi], *s.f. Med:* cardiectasis, enlarged heart; athletic heart.

cardiff [kardif], *s.m. F:* anthracite.

cardigan [kardigɑ̃], *s.m. Cost:* cardigan.

cardiidés [kardiide], *s.m.pl. Moll:* Cardiidae.

cardinal, -aux [kardinal, -o]. **1.** *a.* (*a*) cardinal (point, wind, virtue); chief (altar, etc.); **nombres cardinaux,** cardinal numbers; (*b*) *Moll:* **ligne cardinale,** hinge-line (of bivalve). **2.** *s.m. R.C. Ch:* cardinal. **3.** *s.m. Orn:* **c. d'Amérique,** cardinal tanager; **c. du Cap,** cardinal bird. **4.** *s.f.* **cardinale;** *Bot:* cardinal flower.

cardinalat [kardinala], *s.m.* cardinalate, cardinalship.

cardinalesque [kardinalɛsk], *a. F: Iron:* cardinal-like (dignity).

cardinalice [kardinalis], *a.* pertaining to a cardinal; **revêtir la pourpre c.,** (*of ecclesiastic*) to don the scarlet; **élever qn à la dignité c.,** to make s.o. a cardinal.

cardinaliser [kardinalize], *v.tr. F:* to create (s.o.) a cardinal.

se cardinaliser, *F:* (*of nose, etc.*) to become red.

cardinaliste [kardinalist], *s.m. Hist:* cardinalist, partisan of Richelieu or of Mazarin.

cardine [kardiːn], *s.f. Ich:* top knot.

cardinifère [kardinifɛːr], *a. Moll:* hinge-jointed.

cardiocèle [kardjɔsɛl], *s.f. Med:* cardiocele.

cardiogramme [kardjɔgram], *s.m. Med:* cardiogram.

cardiographe [kardjɔgraf], *s.m.* **1.** cardiographer. **2.** *Med:* cardiograph.

cardiographie [kardjɔgrafi], *s.f. Med:* cardiography.

cardiographique [kardjɔgrafik], *a.* cardiographic.

cardioïde [kardjɔid], *s.f. Mth:* cardioid.

cardiologie [kardjɔlɔʒi], *s.f.* cardiology.

cardiologique [kardjɔlɔʒik], *a.* cardiologic(al).

cardiologue [kardjɔlɔg], *s.m.* cardiologist.

cardiolyse [kardjɔliːz], *s.f. Surg:* cardiolysis.

cardiomégalie [kardjɔmegali], *s.f. Med:* cardiomegaly, cardiomegalia.

cardiopathie [kardjɔpati], *s.f. Med:* cardiopathy.

cardiopéricardite [kardjɔperikardit], *s.f. Med:* cardiopericarditis.

cardioplastie [kardjɔplasti], *s.f. Surg:* cardioplasty.

cardiopneumographe [kardjɔpnømɔgraf], *s.m.* cardiopneumograph.

cardio-pulmonaire [kardjɔpylmɔnɛːr], *a. Med:* cardiopulmonary; *pl. cardio-pulmonaires.*

cardio-rénal, -aux [kardjɔrenal, -o], *a.* cardiorenal.

cardiorhexie [kardjɔrɛksi], *s.f. Med:* cardiorrhexis.

cardiorraphie [kardjɔrafi], *s.f. Surg:* cardiorrhaphy.

cardiosclérose [kardjɔskleroːz], *s.f. Med:* cardiosclerosis.

cardioscope [kardjɔskɔp], *s.m.* cardioscope.

cardiospasme [kardjɔspasm], *s.m.* cardiospasm.

cardiosperme [kardjɔspɛrm], *s.m. Bot:* cardiospermum.

cardiotomie [kardjɔtɔmi], *s.f. Surg:* cardiotomy.

cardiotonique [kardjɔtɔnik], *a. & s.m.* cardiotonic.

cardiotrophie [kardjɔtrɔfi], *s.f.* cardiotrophia.

cardio-vasculaire [kardjɔvaskylɛːr], *a. Anat: Med:* cardiovascular.

cardite [kardit], *s.f. Med:* carditis.

cardium [kardjɔm], *s.m. Moll:* Cardium.

cardo [kardo], *s.m. Ent:* cardo.

cardon [kardɔ̃], *s.m.* **1.** *Bot:* cardoon, edible thistle. **2.** *Crust: F:* shrimp; prawn.

cardonnette [kardɔnɛt], *s.f.* = CHARDONNETTE.

carélien, -ienne [kareljɛ̃, -jɛn]. **1.** *a. & s. Geog:* Karelian. **2.** *s.m. Ling:* Karelian.

carémage [karemaːʒ], *s.m. Agr:* (*in E. of Fr.*) March sowing.

carême [karɛm], *s.m.* **1.** Lent; **viandes de c.,** Lenten fare; *s.a.* MARÉE 2, MARS 2. **2.** (Lenten) fast(ing); **faire (son) c.,** to keep Lent, to fast; *F:* **figure, face, de c.,** thin, dismal, face. **3.** (course of) Lenten sermons.

carême-prenant [karɛmprənɑ̃], *s.m. A:* **1.** Shrovetide. **2.** Shrovetide revels. **3.** (*a*) Shrovetide reveller; (*b*) figure of fun; *pl. carêmes-prenants.*

carénage [karenaːʒ], *s.m.* **1.** *Nau:* (*a*) careening, careenage (of ship); (*b*) careening-place, -beach; careenage; (*c*) docking (for graving). **2.** *Av: Aut:* streamlining; fairing (of the lines); *Av:* **c. d'emplanture d'aile,** wing fillet; **c. de roue,** wheel spat.

carence [karɑ̃ːs], *s.f.* **1.** *Jur:* lack of assets; insolvency; *Adm:* **délai de c.,** period (of three days) for which unemployment or sickness benefit is not paid. **2.** default(ing); shirking of one's obligations; **la c. des pouvoirs publics,** the inefficiency, indifference, of public authorities. **3.** *Med:* deficiency (de, in, of); **maladies de, par, c.,** deficiency diseases, *esp.* diseases due to lack of vitamins.

carencer [karɑ̃se], *v.tr.* (**je carençai(s), n. carençons**) **1.** to record, note, s.o.'s defaulting, absence (in a match, etc.). **2.** *Med:* **c. en vitamines,** to deprive of vitamins.

carène[1] [karɛn], *s.f.* **1.** *N.Arch:* bottom, (underwater) hull (of ship); **centre de c.,** centre of buoyancy; **abattre un navire en c.,** to careen a ship, to heave a ship down, over; **abattage en c.,** careening, heaving over. **2.** *Nat.Hist:* carina, keel. **3.** *Anat:* carina fornicis. **4.** *Av:* body, hull.

carène[2], *s.m. Ch:* carene.

caréné [karene], *a.* **1.** *Nat.Hist:* carinate, keeled. **2.** *Av: Aut: N.Arch:* streamlined, faired (body, etc.).

caréner [karene], *v.tr.* (**je carène, n. carénons; je carénerai**) **1.** *Nau:* to careen (ship); **navire caréné,** ship hove down. **2.** *Av: Aut:* to streamline, to fair the lines of (fuselage, etc.).

carentiel, -ielle [karɑ̃sjɛl], *a.* pertaining to, due to, deficiency; **maladie carentielle,** deficiency disease.

carentinois, -oise [karɑ̃tinwa, -waːz], *a. & s. Geog:* (native, inhabitant) of Carentan.

carer [kare], *v.tr. P:* **1.** to hide, stash away. **2.** to steal, pinch (sth.).

caressant [karɛsɑ̃], *a.* (child, etc.) who shows affection; tender, fond, affectionate (word, look, etc.); soft, gentle (wind).

caresse [karɛs], *s.f.* caress, (act of) endearment; **faire des caresses à un chien,** to pat, stroke, make much of, a dog.

caresser [karɛse], *v.tr.* **1.** to caress, fondle, stroke; **c. un cheval,** to pat, make much of, a horse; **le chat se caresse à mes jambes,** the cat is rubbing itself against my legs; **c. qn du regard,** to look fondly at s.o.; **c. la vanité de qn,** to flatter s.o.'s vanity. **2.** to cherish (hope, etc.); **c. une idée,** to toy with an idea; **c. des projets sans espoir,** to indulge in hopeless plans; **ses désirs les plus longtemps caressés,** his most cherished desires; **3. travail trop caressé,** niggling work.

caresseur, -euse [karɛsœːr, -øːz], (*a*) *a.* coaxing, wheedling; (*b*) *s.* coaxer, wheedler.

caret[1] [kare], *s.m.* (rope-maker's) reel; **fil de c.,** rope-yarn.

caret[2], *s.m. Rept:* (*a*) loggerhead (turtle); (*b*) hawkbill (turtle).

carex [karɛks], *s.m. Bot:* carex, sedge.

cargaison [kargɛzɔ̃], *s.f. Nau:* **1.** (*a*) cargo, freight; **c. mixte,** general cargo; **c. d'aller, de retour,** outward, homeward, cargo; (*b*) *F:* load. **2.** shipping, lading (of cargo).

cargue [karg], *s.f. Nau:* brail (of sail); **c. basse,** foot-brail; **fausse c.,** slabline.

cargo [kargo], *s.m.* (*a*) *Nau:* (i) cargo-boat, -ship; freighter; (ii) tramp; **c. mixte,** mixed cargo and passenger vessel; (*b*) **c. aérien, avion c.,** cargo-plane, (air) freighter; (*c*) **camion c.,** lorry; *U.S:* cargo truck.

cargue-bouline [karg(ə)bulin], *s.f. Nau:* leechline; *pl. cargues-boulines.*

cargue-fond [karg(ə)fɔ̃], *s.f. Nau:* bunt-line; *pl. cargues-fonds.*

cargue-point [karg(ə)pwɛ̃], *s.f. Nau:* clew-line; *pl. cargues-points.*

carguer [karge], *v.tr. Nau:* to take in, clew (up), brail (up) (sail).

cargueur [kargœːr], *s.m. Nau:* reefer.

carhaisien, -ienne [karɛzjɛ̃, -jɛn], *a. & s. Geog:* (native, inhabitant) of Carhaix.

cari [kari], *s.m.* = CURRY.

cariacou [karjaku], *s.m. Z:* Virginia deer.

cariatide [karjatid], *s.f. Arch:* caryatid.

caribe [karib], *a. & s.* = CARAÏBE.

caribou [karibu], *s.m. Z:* caribou; *Geog:* **le lac, la rivière, C.,** Reindeer Lake, River.

caricacées [karikase], *s.f.pl. Bot:* Caricaceae.

caricatural, -aux [karikatyral, -o], *a.* caricatural.

caricature [karikatyːr], *s.f.* (*a*) caricature; cartoon; (*b*) *F:* figure of fun; **quelle c. que cette femme!** what a fright that woman is!

caricaturer [karikatyre], *v.tr.* to caricature (s.o.); *F:* to take (s.o.) off.

caricaturiste [karikatyrist], *s.* caricaturist; cartoonist.

caricoïde [karikɔid], *a.* caricous, fig-shaped.

carididés [karidide], *s.m.pl. Crust:* Carides, Carid(e)a.

carie[1] [kari], *s.f.* (*a*) *Med:* caries, decay (of bone); **c. dentaire,** dental decay; (*b*) blight (of trees); stinking smut, bunt (of corn); (*c*) **c. sèche, humide,** dry, wet, rot (in timber).

Carie[2], *Pr.n.f. A.Geog:* Caria.

carié [karje], *a.* decayed, carious, bad (tooth); blighted (tree); smutty (corn); rotted (wood).

carien, -ienne [karjɛ̃, -jɛn], *a. & s. A.Geog:* Carian.

carier [karje], *v.tr.* to rot; decay; to smut (corn).

se carier, to rot, decay, grow carious; (*of corn*) to smut.

carieux, -ieuse [karjø, -jøːz], *a. Med:* carious (bone, etc.).

carillon [karijɔ̃], *s.m.* **1.** (*a*) chime(s), carillon; (**horloge à**) **c.,** chiming clock; (*b*) full peal of bells, bob; *F:* **faire du c.,** to kick up a row; **un c. d'enfer,** an infernal row; **le c. des verres,** the jingling of glasses; (*c*) (*in orchestra*) tubular bells, chimes; (*b*) melody for bells. **2.** rod (of iron), chimes. **3.** *Bot:* Canterbury bells.

carillonnement [karijɔnmɑ̃], *s.m. F:* **1.** (*a*) chiming; (*b*) bell-ringing; (*c*) change-ringing. **2.** *F:* jingling.

carillonner [karijɔne]. **1.** *v.i.* (*a*) to play on the carillon; to chime the bells; to ring a peal; to ring the changes; (*b*) (*of bells*) to chime; (*c*) to jingle; clang; **c. à la porte,** to ring the (door) bell loudly. **2.** *v.tr.* to chime (air); to announce (church festival) with a full peal; **fête carillonnée,** high festival; *F:* **aux fêtes carillonnées,** on special occasions, on high days and holidays; **c. une victoire,** to proclaim a victory.

carillonneur [karijɔnœːr], *s.m.* (*a*) carillonneur, carillon player; (*b*) *pl.* bell-ringers, change-ringers.

carinaire [karinɛːr], *s.f. Moll:* carinaria.

carinates [karinat], *s.m.pl. Orn:* Carinatae, Carinates.

cariniana [karinjana], *s.m. Bot:* cariniana.

Carinthie [karɛ̃ti], *Pr.n.f. Geog:* Carinthia.

carinthien, -ienne [karɛ̃tjɛ̃, -jɛn], *a. & s. Geog:* Carinthian.

cariopse [karjɔps], *s.m.* = CARYOPSE.

Carioque [kariɔk], *s.m. & f.* inhabitant of Rio de Janeiro.

carique [karik], *s.f.* (*in Provence*) wild fig.

cariqueux, -euse [karikø, -øːz], *a. Med:* caricous (tumour, etc.).

cariste [karist], *s.m.* driver of mechanical equipment (*esp.* fork-lift trucks).

carité [karite], *s.m. Bot:* = KARITÉ.

caritif [karitif], *s.m. Gram:* caritive.

carlin, -ine[1] [karlɛ̃, -in], *a. & s.* pug(-dog, -bitch); *F:* **nez c.,** pug-nose; turned-up nose.

carline[2] [karlin], *s.f. Bot:* carlina, carline; **c. vulgaire,** carline thistle.

carlingage [karlɛ̃gaːʒ], *s.m. N.Arch: Av:* engine-bed, engine seating, engine-bearers.

carlingue [karlɛ̃ːg], *s.f.* **1.** *Nau:* keelson. **2.** *Av:* (*a*) fuselage; (*b*) engine undershield, engine-bed, -bearers; (*c*) cockpit; cabin.

carlisme [karlism], *s.m. Hist:* Carlism.

carliste [karlist], *s.m. Hist:* Carlist.

carlovingien, -ienne [karlɔvɛ̃ʒjɛ̃, -jɛn], *a. & s. A:* = CAROLINGIEN.

carmagnole [karmaɲɔl]. **1.** *s.f. Hist:* carmagnole; (*a*) jacket (worn by Revolutionaries in 1793); (*b*) revolutionary speech; (*c*) revolutionary dance and song. **2.** *s.m. A:* ultra-Jacobin.

Carmanie [karmani], *Pr.n.f.* **1.** *A.Geog:* Carmania. **2.** CARAMANIE.

carmausin, -ine [karmozɛ̃, -in], *a. & s. Geog:* (native, inhabitant) of Carmaux.

carme [karm]. **1.** *a. & s.m.* **(frère) c.,** Carmelite friar, White friar; **carmes déchaux, déchaussés,** discalced Carmelites. **2.** *s.m. P:* money.

Carmel [karmɛl], *Pr.n. Geog:* **le Mont C.,** Mount Carmel; *Ecc:* **l'ordre du C.,** the Carmelite order.

carmeline [karməlin], *s.f. Tex:* carmelite.

carmélite [karmelit]. **1.** *s.f.* Carmelite (nun). **2.** *s.m. & a.inv.* light brown (colour).

carmer [karme], *v.i. P:* to pay; *F:* to stump up.

carmin [karmɛ̃], *s.m.* **1.** carmine (colour); *Lit:* **lèvres de c.,** ruby lips; *a.inv.* **étoffe carmin,** carmine material. **2.** *Toil: O:* rouge.

carminatif, -ive [karminatif, -iːv], *a. & s.m. Med:* carminative.

carminé [karmine], *a.* carmine-coloured, ruby.

carminer [karmine], *v.tr.* to paint, colour, dye, (sth.) with carmine; **se c. les lèvres,** to rouge one's lips.

Carnac [karnak], *Pr.n.m. Geog:* **1.** Karnak (Egypt). **2.** Carnac (Brittany).

carnacois, -oise [karnakwa, -waːz], *a. & s.* (native, inhabitant) of Carnac.

carnage [karnaːʒ], *s.m.* **1.** carnage, slaughter. **2.** *A:* (*a*) *Ven:* flesh of animals killed, that is given to the hounds; (*b*) raw meat (for feeding lions, etc.).

carnaire [karnɛːr], *a.* (*of flies*) living on flesh.

carnallite [karnalit], *s.f. Miner:* carnallite.

carnasse [karnas], *s.f. Ind:* glue stock.

carnassier, -ière [karnasje, -jɛːr]. **1.** *a.* carnivorous, flesh-eating (animal); *Z:* **dent carnassière,** carnassial (tooth). **2.** *s.m.* carnivore; *pl.* **les carnassiers,** the Carnivora. **3.** *s.f.* **carnassière,** game-bag.

carnation [karnasjɔ̃], *s.f. Art:* (*a*) flesh tint, carnation; (*b*) rendering of flesh-tints.

carnau, -aux [karno], *s.m.* = CARNEAU.

carnauba [karnoba], *s.m. Bot:* (*a*) carnauba, wax palm; (*b*) carnauba wax, palm wax.

carnaval, -als [karnaval], *s.m.* **1.** (*a*) Shrovetide; (*b*) carnival. **2.** King Carnival; **c'est un vrai c.,** he's a regular figure of fun.

carnavalesque [karnavalesk], *a.* (*a*) carnivalesque; carnival-like; (*b*) grotesque.

car-navette [karnavet], *s.m. Min:* shuttle wagon; tub; *pl. cars-navettes.*

carne[1] [karn], *s.f.* corner, edge, salient angle (of stone, etc.).

carne[2], *s.f.* **1.** *P:* (*a*) tough meat; (*b*) old horse; screw. **2.** (*a*) bad-tempered person; (*of man*) cantankerous brute; (*of woman*) bitch; (*b*) wastrel, bad egg; (*of woman*) slut.

carné [karne], *a.* **1.** flesh-coloured. **2.** *Med:* **régime c.,** meat diet.

carneau, -eaux [karno], *s.m.* (boiler) flue; **c. de descente,** down-take flue.

carnèle, carnelle [karnɛl], *s.f. Num:* border, rim (of coin).

carnet [karnɛ], *s.m.* **1.** (*a*) notebook; memorandum book; **c. multicopiste,** duplicating book; *Com:* **c. de commandes,** order book; **c. de dépenses,** account book, housekeeping book; *Sch:* **c. de notes,** mark book; *Min:* **c. de sondage,** driller's log book; *W.Tel:* **c. d'écoute,** log book; *Mil:* **c. de tir,** firing record; *Bank:* **c. de banque,** pass book; *s.a.* ÉCHÉANCE 1; (*b*) *O:* **c. de bal,** dance card, programme; (*c*) **c. à souche(s),** counterfoil book, *U.S:* stub book; **c. de chèques,** cheque book; **c. de timbres(-poste),** book of stamps; *Trans:* **c. (de tickets d'autobus, etc.),** book of tickets; (*d*) *Aut: etc:* **c. de route, de bord,** log book; **c. (de passage en douane),** (international customs') carnet; (*e*) *Journ:* **c. mondain,** diary of social events; **c. rose,** births (column); **c. blanc,** marriages (column). **2.** *Min:* airway; **c. d'aérage,** cross hole.

carnet-bloc [karnɛblɔk], *s.m. Cards:* (bridge) marker, scoring-block; *pl. carnets-blocs.*

carnet-répertoire [karnɛrepɛrtwaːr], *s.m.* address-book; *pl. carnets-répertoires.*

carnier [karnje], *s.m.* game-bag.

carnification [karnifikasjɔ̃], *s.f. Med:* carnification.

carnifier (se) [səkarnifje], *v.pr. Med:* to carnify.

Carniole [karnjɔl], *Pr.n.f. Geog:* Carniola.

carniolien, -ienne [karnjɔljɛ̃, -jɛn], *a. & s. Geog:* Carniolan.

Carnique [karnik], *a. Geog:* **les Alpes Carniques,** the Carnic Alps.

carnisation [karnizasjɔ̃], *s.f. Med:* carnification.

carnivore [karnivɔːr], *Z:* **1.** *a.* carnivorous, flesh-eating (animal). **2.** *s.m.pl.* **carnivores,** Carnivora.

carnotite [karnɔtit], *s.f. Miner:* carnotite.

Carnutes [karnyt], *s.m.pl. Hist:* Carnutes.

carogne [karɔɲ], *s.f.* (*a*) *Dial:* = CHAROGNE; (*b*) *P:* (i) horse, screw; (ii) (*of woman*) slut; bitch.

carole [karɔl], *s.f.* **1.** *A:* round dance. **2.** *Arch:* ambulatory.

carolin [karɔlɛ̃]. **1.** *a.* (*a*) Carolingian; (*b*) appertaining to (the Emperor) Charles V. **2.** *s.m. Orn:* Carolina duck, wood duck. **3.** *s.m. A.Num:* carolin.

Caroline [karɔlin], *Pr.n.f.* **1.** Caroline. **2.** *Geog:* (*a*) Carolina; (*b*) **l'archipel des Carolines,** the Caroline Islands.

carolingien, -ienne [karɔlɛ̃ʒjɛ̃, -jɛn], *a. Hist:* Carolingian, Carlovingian.

carolinien, -ienne [karɔlinjɛ̃, -jɛn], *a. & s. Geog:* Carolinian.

carolopolitain, -aine [karɔlɔpɔlitɛ̃, -ɛn], *a. & s. Geog:* (native, inhabitant) of Charleville.

carolorégien, -ienne [karɔlɔreʒjɛ̃, -jɛn], *a. & s. Geog:* (native, inhabitant) of Charleroi.

carolus [karɔlys], *s.m. A.Num:* carolus.

Caron [karɔ̃, ka-], *Pr.n.m. Myth:* Charon.

caronade [karɔnad], *s.f. A.Artil:* carronade.

caroncule [karɔ̃kyl], *s.f.* (*a*) *Anat:* caruncula, caruncle; **c. lacrymale,** lacrymal papilla; (*b*) *Bot: Z:* caruncle; *usu. pl.* wattles (of turkey); dewlap (of bloodhound).

caronculé [karɔ̃kyle], *a. Nat.Hist:* caruncúlate(d); (*of bird*) wattled.

caronculeux, -euse [karɔ̃kylø, -øːz], *a.* caruncular, carunculous.

carone [karɔn], *s.f. Ch:* carone.

caronien, -ienne [karɔnjɛ̃, -jɛn], *a. Myth:* Charonian, pertaining to Charon; **la barque caronienne,** Charon's barque.

caronnade [karɔnad], *s.f.* = CARONADE.

carotène [karɔtɛn], *s.m. Ch:* carotene.

caroténoïde [karɔtenɔid], *a. & s. Bot:* carotenoid.

carotide [karɔtid], *a. & s.f. Anat:* carotid (artery).

carotidien, -ienne [karɔtidjɛ̃, -jɛn], *a. Anat:* carotid (ganglion).

carotinémie [karɔtinemi], *s.f. Med:* carotinæmia.

carotique [karɔtik], *a.* carotic.

carottage [karɔtaːʒ], *s.m.* **1.** *F:* swindling, cheating; *Mil:* malingering; wangling; *St.Exch:* overcharging. **2.** *Min:* coring, core drilling, taking of a core sample.

carotte [karɔt], *s.f.* **1.** (*a*) *Bot: Hort:* carrot; *F:* **Poil de c.,** Ginger; *a.inv. F:* **cheveux (rouge) c.,** carroty, ginger, hair; *F:* **ses carottes sont cuites,** he's cooked his goose, he's done for; **les carottes sont cuites,** it's as good as settled; (*b*) *Bot:* **c. sauvage,** Queen Anne's lace. **2.** (*a*) (i) plug, carrot (of tobacco); (ii) tobacconist's sign (in France); (*b*) *Min:* core (sample). **3.** *F:* (*a*) trick, sell; *St.Exch:* fraudulent overcharge; **tirer une c. à qn,** (i) to wangle money out of s.o.; (ii) to try to pull the wool over s.o.'s eyes; *Bill:* **jouer, tirer, la c.,** to leave nothing on the table; (*b*) *Ten:* drop shot.

carotter [karɔte]. **1.** *v.tr. P:* (*a*) to steal, pinch; (*b*) **c. qch. à qn,** to do s.o. out of sth.; *St.Exch:* **c. qn,** to overcharge s.o.; (*c*) *Mil:* **c. le service,** to shirk, dodge, duty; to malinger; **c. une permission,** to wangle leave. **2.** *v.tr. Min:* to core; **échantillon carotté,** core sample. **3.** *v.i. P:* (*a*) *Cards: etc:* to play for trifling stakes; to play a piddling game; (*b*) to jump the queue, to queue-barge.

carotteur, -euse [karɔtœːr, -øːz], *s.,* **carottier,**[1] **-ière** [karɔtje, -jɛːr], *s.* **1.** diddler, trickster; wangler. **2.** shirker, malingerer. **3.** queue-barger, queue-jumper.

carottier[2] [karɔtje], *s.m. Min:* **(tube) c.,** core barrel; **trépan c.,** core bit.

caroube [karub]. **1.** *s.f. Bot:* carob(-bean), locust-bean. **2.** *s.m.* (timber) acacia.

caroubier [karubje], *s.m. Bot:* carob tree; locust tree.

carouble [karubl], *s.f. P:* duplicate key (used for robbery); skeleton key.

caroubler [karuble], *v.tr. P:* to break into (house, etc.) with a duplicate key.

caroubleur [karublœːr], *s.m. P:* (*pers.*) picklock.

carouge[1] [karuːʒ], *s.f.* = CAROUBE.

carouge[2], *s.m. Orn:* cowbird, cow blackbird.

Carpates [karpat], *Pr.n.f.pl. Geog:* the Carpathian Mountains, the Carpathians.

carpe[1] [karp], *s.m. Anat:* carpus, wrist; **os du c.,** wrist-bone, carpal (bone).

carpe[2], *s.f. Ich:* carp; **c. cuir,** leather carp; **c. miroir,** mirror carp; **c. de mer,** ballan wrasse; *Swim:* **saut de c.,** jack-knife (dive); *F:* **faire des sauts de carpe,** to flop about, to somersault; **faire des yeux de c. pâmée,** to show the whites of one's eyes; **regarder qn avec des yeux de c.,** to make sheep's eyes at s.o.; **muet comme une c.,** as dumb as a an oyster; **bâiller comme une c.,** to yawn one's head off; *s.a.* S'ENNUYER.

carpé [karpe], *a. Swim:* **saut c.,** jack-knife (dive).

carpeau, -eaux [karpo], *s.m.* young carp.

carpellaire [karpɛl(l)ɛːr], *a. Bot:* carpellary.

carpelle [karpɛl], *s.m. Bot:* carpel.

Carpentarie [karpɑ̃tari], *Pr.n.f. Geog:* **le Golfe de C.,** the Gulf of Carpentaria.

carpentrassien, -ienne [karpɑ̃trasjɛ̃, -jɛn], *a. & s. Geog:* (native, inhabitant) of Carpentras.

carpette[1] [karpɛt], *s.f.* rug; **tapis de c.,** (floor) rug; **c. de foyer,** hearth-rug.

carpette[2], *s.f. Ich:* young carp.

carpholite [karfɔlit], *s.f. Miner:* carpholite.

carpiculture [karpikyltyr], *s.f.* carp breeding.

carpien, -ienne [karpjɛ̃, -jɛn], *a. Anat:* carpal (bone, etc.).

carpier [karpje], *s.m.,* **carpière** [karpjɛːr], *s.f.* carp-pond.

carpillon [karpijɔ̃], *s.m.* (very) small carp.

carpocapse [karpɔkaps], *s.f. Ent:* carpocapsa; **c. des pommes,** codling moth.

carpogone [karpɔgɔn], *s.f. Bot:* carpogonium.

carpologie [karpɔlɔʒi], *s.f. Bot:* carpology.

carpologique [karpɔlɔʒik], *a.* carpological.

carpo-métacarpien, -ienne [karpɔmetakarpjɛ̃, -jɛn], *a. Anat:* carpometacarpal.

carpomorphe [karpɔmɔrf], *a. Bot:* fructiform.

carpophage [karpɔfaːʒ]. **1.** *a.* carpophagous, fruit-eating. **2.** *s.m.pl.* (*a*) *Z: A:* Carpophaga; (*b*) *Orn:* Carpophaga, fruit pigeons.

carpophore [karpɔfɔːr], *s.m. Bot:* carpophore.

carpophylle [karpɔfil], *s.m. Bot:* carpophyl, carpel.

carquois [karkwa], *s.m.* quiver; **il a vidé son c.,** he has shot all his bolts, he has nothing to fall back upon; *Furn:* **pied en c.,** fluted leg.

carrable [kɑrabl], *a. Geom:* squarable.

Carrache [karaʃ], *Pr.n.m. Hist. of Art:* Carracci.

carragheen [karageɛ̃], *s.m. Algae:* carrag(h)een, pearl moss, Irish moss.

Carrare [karaːr]. **1.** *Pr.n. Geog:* Carrara. **2.** *s.m.* Carrara marble.

carrassin [karasɛ̃], *s.m. Ich:* crucian (carp).

carre [kɑːr], *s.f.* **1.** (*a*) cross-section (of board, etc.); (*b*) corner (of field, book, etc.); (*c*) crown (of hat); (*d*) square-toe (of boot); (*e*) edge (of skate, of ski). *Skiing:* **lâcher les carres,** to flatten, take the edge off, the skis; (*f*) cut (in pine trunk for tapping resin). **2.** *A:* = CARRURE.

carré, -ée [kare]. **1.** *a.* (*a*) square (figure, garden, etc.); square, broad (shoulders); squared (stone); *Mth:* **nombre c.,** square number; **dix mètres carrés,** ten square metres; **mots carrés,** word square; *Nau:* **trois-mâts c.,** square-rigged three-masted vessel; **partie carrée,** foursome, party of two men and two women, *U.S:* double date; **tête carrée,** (i) level-headed man; (ii) stubborn man; (iii) *P:* German, square head; *s.a.* HERBE 4, RACINE 1; (*b*) perpendicular, square (with another line); **trait c.,** perpendicular; (*c*) *F:* plain, straightforward, blunt (answer, person, etc.); plain-spoken, outspoken (person); **être c. en affaires,** to be downright in business. **2.** *s.m.* (*a*) *Mth:* square; **élever au c.,** to square; **trois pieds en c.,** three foot square; **c. d'un nombre,** square of a number; *s.a.* MOINDRE 2; (*b*) **c. long,** rectangle; **c. de papier,** slip of paper; **le c. des halles,** the market square; **c. d'un escalier,** landing of a staircase; **c. de choux,** cabbage patch; *A: Mil:* **c. creux, vide,** hollow square; **former le c.,** to form square; **c. des officiers,** *Nau:* mess-room; *Navy:* wardroom; (*c*) *Cost:* (silk) square; (*d*) *Cu:* loin (of mutton, etc.); (*e*) *Anat:* **(muscle) c.,** quadrate muscle; (*f*) *Paperm:* **(format) c.,** demy; (*g*) (*skiing*) **c. amont, aval,** upper, lower edge (of ski); **c. extérieur, intérieur,** outer, inner, edge; **prendre plus de c.,** to edge more; (*h*) *Sch: P:* second-year student preparing for entry into a *grande école* or in a *grande école*; (*i*) *Cards:* (*at poker*) **c. de valets,** four jacks. **3.** *s.f.* **carrée;** (*a*) *A:* tester (of bed); tester-frame; (*b*) *Mus: A:* square note; breve; (*c*) *F:* room, *esp.* furnished apartment; *F:* digs; *Mil: P:* barrack room.

carreau, -eaux [karo], *s.m.* **1.** small square; **étoffe à carreaux,** check material; *Surv:* **carreaux de réduction,** reducing squares; *Art:* **mettre un croquis au c.,** to square up a sketch (for enlargement on canvas); **mise au c.,** squaring. **2.** (*a*) (flooring) tile, flag; (flooring) quarry; **c. de pierre,** flagstone; **c. de revêtement,** wall-tile; *P:* **mettre le cœur sur les carreaux,** to puke, to throw up; (*b*) **c. (de vitre);** (i) window-pane; **regarder aux carreaux,** to look in at the window; (ii) *P:* monocle, "glass-eye"; (iii) *P:* eye; (*c*) **c. de fulmicoton, etc.,** slab of gun-cotton, etc. **3.** (*a*) floor (of room); **coucher sur le c.,** to sleep on the ground; *F:* **coucher qn sur le c.,** to lay s.o. out; **rester sur le c.,** (i) to be killed on the spot; (ii) to be left high and dry, to be left out of the running; (*b*) (*in Paris*) **le c. des Halles,** the (floor of the) market; (*c*) *Min:* **c. de mine,** pit head. **4.** *Cards:* diamonds; **jouer (du) c.,** to play diamonds; *F:* **se garder, se tenir, à c.,** to take every precaution; to keep one's weather eye open; *s.a.* AS 1. **5.** *Const:* stretcher (stone). **6.** *Lacemaking:* pillow. **7.** *Nau:* sheer-strake. **8.** (tailor's) goose, seam-presser. **9.** *A:* **c. (d'arbalète),** bolt, quarrel. **10.** *Med:* carreau.

carreau-module [karomɔdyl], *s.m.* *Surv:* (reference-)square (on map); *pl. carreaux-modules.*

carreautage [karota:ʒ], *s.m.* *Tex:* squaring (of design).

carrefour [karfu:r], *s.m.* (*a*) cross-roads, *esp. U.S:* intersection; (*in town usu. Pr.n.*) square, circus; **c. en as de trèfle,** clover-leaf intersection; **tête de c.,** T-junction; **musicien de c.,** street musician; *F:* **être au c.,** to be at the parting of the ways; (*b*) symposium.

carréger [kareʒe], *v.i.* **(je carrège, n. carrégeons; je carrégeai(s); je carrégerai)** *Nau:* (*in Mediterranean*) **1.** to sail under heavy canvas. **2.** to beat.

carrelage [karla:ʒ], *s.m.* **1.** tiling; laying (of floor) with tiles; **salle de bain revêtue de c.,** tiled bathroom. **2.** tiling; tile-, flagstone-pavement or floor(ing); **c. en briques,** brick pavement.

carreler [karle], *v.tr.* **(je carrelle, n. carrelons; je carrellerai) 1.** to tile (floor, walls); to lay (floor) with tiles, flags; to floor (kitchen); to pave (yard). **2.** to draw squares on, to square (sheet of paper, etc.); **étoffe carrelée,** check material. **3.** *A:* to cobble (old shoes).

carrelet [karlɛ], *s.m.* **1.** (*a*) square ruler; (*b*) (locksmith's) square file. **2.** large needle; sail needle; *Bootm:* sewing awl; **c. d'emballeur,** packing needle. **3.** *Fish:* square dipping-net. **4.** *Ich:* (*a*) plaice; (*b*) brill.

carrelette [karlɛt], *s.f.* (locksmith's) square polishing file.

carreleur [karlœ:r], *s.m.* **1.** tile-layer, paviour, paver. **2.** *A:* itinerant cobbler.

carrelier [karlje], *s.m.* worker in a tile factory.

carrelure [karly:r], *s.f.* *Bootm: A:* **1.** re-soling. **2.** pair of new soles.

carrément [karemɑ̃], *adv.* square(ly); **pièce coupée c.,** square-cut piece; **se tenir c. sur ses jambes,** to stand firmly, squarely, on one's legs; **agir c.,** to act (i) on the square, (ii) without beating about the bush; **il y est allé c.,** he made no bones about it; **dire c. qch. à qn,** to tell s.o. sth. (i) straightforwardly, (ii) bluntly, flat; **pour parler c. . . .,** not to put too fine a point on it . . .; **je vais lui parler c.,** I'll give him a piece of my mind; **je lui ai dit c. ce que je pensais,** I told him straight (out), in no uncertain terms, what I thought.

carrer [kare], *v.tr.* **1.** to square (plank, number, etc.); **c. les épaules,** to square one's shoulders. **2.** *P:* to hide away, stash away.

se carrer, (*a*) *A:* to swank, put on airs; (*b*) **se c. en marchant,** to strut, swagger, along; **le maire se carrait dans son fauteuil,** the mayor was sitting in his chair looking very important.

carrick [karik], *s.m.* *A.Cost:* coachman's heavy coat; box-coat.

carrier[1] [karje], *s.m.* **1.** quarryman, quarrier. **2.** **(maître) c.,** quarry-owner.

carrier[2], *s.m.* carrier pigeon.

carrière[1] [karjɛ:r], *s.f.* **1.** (*a*) *A:* race-course, arena; **bout de la c.,** winning post; (*b*) course (of life); **être au bout de sa c.,** to be at the end of one's life; **il a eu une longue c.,** *F:* he had a long innings; *s.a.* FOURNIR 1; *Lit:* **la c. de la gloire,** the path of glory; **la c. du succès,** the road to success. **2.** *Equit:* track, ground; **donner c. à un cheval,** to give free rein to a horse; **sujet qui donne c. à l'éloquence,** subject that gives scope for eloquence; **donner libre c. à son imagination,** to give free play, full scope, full swing, to one's fancy; **donner c. à ses sentiments, à ses opinions, se donner c.,** to let oneself go; **donner libre c. à ses goûts,** to indulge one's tastes to the full. **3.** career; **la c. des armes,** the military career; **militaire de c.,** regular (soldier); **diplomate de c.,** professional, *U.S:* career, diplomat; **il est de la c.,** he is in the diplomatic service; **embrasser une c.,** to take up a career; **se faire une c.,** to carve out a career for oneself; **dans ma c. . . .,** in my walk of life . . .; **ouvrir une belle c. à qn,** to open up possibilities, a career, for s.o.

carrière[2], *s.f.* **1.** (stone-)pit, quarry. **2.** grit (in pear).

carriérisme [karjerism], *s.m.* careerism.

carriériste [karjerist], *s.m. & f.* careerist.

carriole [karjɔl], *s.f.* *Veh:* **1.** light cart, carriole. **2.** *Fr.C:* (horsedrawn) sled, sleigh.

carrossable [karɔsabl̩], *a.* **route c.,** road suitable for motor vehicles.

carrossage [karɔsa:ʒ], *s.m.* *Veh:* set, rake (of the axle pin).

carrosse [karɔs], *s.m.* **1.** (*a*) coach; four-wheeled carriage; **c. d'apparat,** state coach; *F:* **rouler c.,** (i) *A:* to have one's own carriage; (ii) to live in great style; **cheval de c.,** (i) carriage horse; (ii) *A: F:* stupid fellow, lubberly fellow; *s.a.* ROUE; (*b*) *Fr.C:* perambulator, *F:* pram. **2.** (wheeled) wine basket (for the table). **3.** *Nau: A:* deck saloon.

carrossée [karɔse], *s.f.* *F:* coachful, carriageful.

carrosser [karɔse], *v.tr.* **1.** to convey (sth., s.o.) in a coach, in a carriage. **2.** *Aut:* to fit the body to (chassis); **châssis carrossé,** chassis with body complete. **3.** *P:* **elle est bien carrossée,** she comes out in the right places.

carrosserie [karɔsri], *s.f.* **1.** coach-building, body-building. **2.** body, coachwork, *U.S:* panel body (of car, etc.); **c. coque (tout acier),** integral all-steel welded body; **c. de série,** standard body; **c. hors série, spéciale,** custom-built body; *s.a.* CANADIEN.

carrossier [karɔsje], *s.m.* **1.** *Veh: Aut:* coach-, carriage-, body-builder. **2.** coach-horse, draught-horse.

carrousel [karuzɛl], *s.m.* **1.** *A:* (*a*) tilting-match, tournament; (*b*) tilt-yard. **2.** (*a*) **c. militaire,** military tattoo; (*b*) tattoo ground. **3.** merry-go-round, roundabout. **4.** *Mil.Av: F:* dog-fight.

carroyage [karwaja:ʒ], *s.m.* *Surv:* squaring (of map, etc.).

carroyer [karwaje], *v.tr.* to square (a map).

carrure [kary:r], *s.f.* **1.** breadth (*of pers.,* of coat) across the shoulders; **homme d'une belle c.,** well-built man; **homme d'une forte c.,** broad-shouldered man. **2.** breadth, straight-forwardness (of thought, of style).

carry [kari], *s.m.* = CURRY.

cartable [kartabl̩], *s.m.* **1.** blotting-pad, blotting-book, blotter. **2.** (cardboard) portfolio. **3.** school satchel.

cartahu [kartay], *s.m.* *Nau:* **1.** whip, gantline. **2.** purchase. **3.** clothes-line.

cartayer [karteje], *v.i.* to avoid the ruts (in driving).

carte [kart], *s.f.* **1.** *A:* sheet of paper; **c. blanche,** blank paper (bearing signature) (i) given to anyone on which to write his own conditions, (ii) conferring full discretionary powers; full warrant to act for the best; **donner, laisser, c. blanche à qn,** to give s.o. carte blanche, a free hand, unlimited powers, *F:* a blank cheque; **avoir c. blanche,** to have a free hand, full liberty **(pour,** to). **2.** map; chart; **c. d'état-major** = ordnance (survey) map; **c. aéronautique,** air, aeronautical, chart, **c. de navigation aérienne,** air-navigation chart; **c. marine,** (nautical, sea-) chart; **c. hydrographique,** hydrographic chart; **c. type,** standard map; **c. en relief,** relief model; **c. murale,** wall map; **c. carroyée, quadrillée,** grid(ded), squared, map; **c. muette,** outline, skeleton, map; **c. photographique,** photo-map; **c. géologique,** geological map; **c. physique,** relief, physical, map; **c. politique,** political map; **c. cadastrale,** cadastral map; **c. routière,** (i) road map; (ii) *Nau:* track chart; **c. urbaine, c. des agglomérations,** town plan; *Mil:* **c. d'objectif(s),** target map; **c. astronomique, céleste, c. du ciel,** astronomic map, chart, star map; **c. météorologique,** meteorological, *F:* weather, map; **c. de visibilité,** visibility chart; **c. synoptique,** weather, *U.S:* synoptic, chart; **c. prévue,** weather forecast map; **lecture de la c.,** map reading; **dresser la c. d'une région,** to map (out) an area, a region; **porter (une île, etc.) sur la c.,** to chart (an island, etc.); **c. au 500.000ème,** map to the scale of 1:500,000 (one in 500,000); 1:500,000 map; **c. au millionième, au deux-millionième,** one in a million, one in two million map; *A:* **savoir la c.,** to know the ropes; *F:* **perdre la c.,** (i) to lose one's bearings; (ii) *F:* to get flustered, to lose one's presence of mind. **3.** (piece of) pasteboard or cardboard; (*a*) **c. de moulage,** cartridge paper; *Art:* **c. grattage,** scraperboard; (*b*) **c. (à jouer),** playing card; **jouer aux cartes,** to play cards; **c. peinte,** court card; **fausse c.,** (i) card of the wrong suit; (ii) card thrown away; **faire les cartes,** to deal; **faire, perdre, la c.,** to take, lose, the odd trick; **jeter, jouer, cartes sur table,** to put one's cards on the table; **jouer sa dernière c.,** to play one's last card; **aller aux cartes,** to take, draw, cards from the stock pile; **premier, dernier, en cartes,** first, fourth, hand; *F:* **c'était la c. forcée,** it was Hobson's choice; *F:* **connaître, voir, le dessous des cartes,** to be in the know, to know the inside story; **cacher ses cartes,** to play a close game; **brouiller les cartes,** to complicate matters; to confuse the issue; **on ne sait jamais avec lui de quelle c. il retourne,** you never know where you are with him; *s.a.* TIRER 4; (*c*) **c. de visite,** visiting card, *U.S:* calling card; **faire passer sa c. à qn,** to send in one's card; **mettre des cartes chez qn,** to leave cards on s.o.; **c. d'affaires, d'adresse,** business card; **c. d'invitation,** invitation card; **c. d'entrée,** admission card; **c. postale,** postcard; **c. postale illustrée,** picture postcard; **c. d'abonnement,** season ticket; **c. de lecteur,** reader's ticket; *Adm:* **c. de commerce,** trading licence; **c. d'identité,** identity card; *A:* **c. de fille soumise,** prostitute's police card; **femme en c.,** registered prostitute; *Rail: etc:* **carte de circulation,** free pass; *Aut:* **c. grise** = car licence; *A:* **c. rose** = driving licence; *War Adm:* **c. d'alimentation, c. de ravitaillement** = ration-book; **c. d'habillement** = clothing book; **c. de priorité,** card given to expectant and nursing mothers and badly disabled ex-servicemen entitling them to priority in queues, public transport, etc.; (*d*) *Computers: etc:* **c. perforée,** punched card; (*e*) **c. (de restaurant),** menu; **c. du jour,** menu for the day; **c. des vins,** wine list; **manger, dîner, à la c.,** to eat, dine, à la carte; **restaurant de grande c.,** first-class restaurant; (*f*) *Tex:* point paper; **mise en c.,** designing; **metteur en c.,** designer; (*g*) **c. de boutons, de coton, de laine,** card of buttons, of cotton, of wool; *Com:* **c. d'échantillons,** sample card.

carte-fiche [kart(ə)fiʃ], *s.f.* index card, loose card (for card index); *pl. cartes-fiches.*

cartel[1] [kartɛl], *s.m.* **1.** (*a*) *A:* cartel, challenge; (*b*) *Mil: Navy:* agreement, cartel (for exchange of prisoners). **2.** (*a*) dial-case (of clock); (*b*) hanging wall-clock. **3.** *Her:* **c. d'armoiries,** shield, escutcheon.

cartel[2], *s.m.* **1.** *Com:* cartel, trust; combine; ring; **c. horizontal,** horizontal combine. **2.** *Pol:* coalition; *Fr.Hist:* **le C.,** the Coalition (of 1924).

carte-lettre [kart(ə)lɛtr̩], *s.f.* letter-card; *pl. cartes-lettres.*

cartellisation [kartɛlizasjɔ̃], *s.f.* *Ind:* cartel(l)ization.

cartelliser [kartɛlize], *v.tr.* to cartel(l)ize.

cartellisme [kartɛlism], *s.m.* cartel(l)ism; *Pol:* (i) government by coalition; (ii) favouring of a coalition.

cartelliste [kartɛlist], *s.m. Ind:* cartel(l)ist; *Pol. Hist:* upholder of the *Cartel.*

carter [kartɛːr], *s.m.* (*a*) *Mch:* case, casing, housing (of crank, chain, gear, etc.); cover (of small machines, etc.); **c. d'engrenage,** gear-case, gear-housing, gear-guard, gear-box; **c. de moteur,** motor-housing; **c. à huile,** oil-pan; *Cin:* spool-box; (*b*) *Aut: I.C.E:* **c. du moteur,** crank-case; **c. inférieur,** lower crank-case, underpan; **c. supérieur,** upper crank-case, upper gear-case; **fond de c.,** sump; **c. à bain d'huile,** wet sump; **c. sec,** dry sump; **c. du différentiel,** differential-case, -casing, -housing; **c. d'embrayage,** clutch-casing, -housing; **c. du tambour de frein,** brake-drum housing; **c. du pont arrière,** rear-axle housing; **c. de l'arbre moteur,** drive-shaft, jack-shaft, housing; **c. de distribution,** timing case, chain, gear.

carte-réponse [kartrepɔ̃ːs], *s.f. Post:* reply card, *pl. cartes-réponse(s).*

carterie [kartəri], *s.f.* playing-card factory.

carteron[1], **-onne** [kart(ə)rɔ̃, -ɔn], *a. & s.* = QUARTERON[1].

carteron,[2] *s.m. Meas:* = QUARTERON.[2]

cartésianisme [kartezjanism], *s.m. Phil:* cartesianism.

cartésien, -ienne [kartezjɛ̃, -jɛn]. **1.** *a. & s. Phil: Mth:* Cartesian; **esprit c.,** clear, logical, mind; *Mth:* **coordonnées cartésiennes,** Cartesian coordinates. **2.** *s.f.* **cartésienne;** *Mth:* Cartesian oval.

carteux, -euse [kartø, -øːz]. **1.** *a. Tex:* substantial (material). **2.** *s.m.* stiffness (of paper, cardboard).

Carthage [kartaːʒ], *Pr.n.f. Hist: Geog:* Carthage.

Carthagène [kartaʒɛn], *Pr.n.f. Geog:* Cartagena.

carthaginois, -oise [kartaʒinwa, -waːz], *a. & s. Hist: Geog:* Carthaginian; **foi carthaginoise,** Punic faith, treachery.

carthame [kartam], *s.m. Bot:* safflower, bastard saffron.

cartier [kartje], *s.m.* **1.** *A:* paper used in manufacture of playing cards. **2.** playing-card manufacturer.

cartilage [kartilaːʒ], *s.m. Anat:* cartilage; *Cu:* gristle; *Med:* **c. d'ossification,** temporary cartilage.

cartilagineux, -euse [kartilaʒinø, -øːz], *a. Anat: Ich:* cartilaginous; *Cu:* gristly; *Bot:* hard, tough.

cartogramme [kartɔgram], *s.m.* cartogram.

cartographe [kartɔgraf], *s.m. & f.* cartographer.

cartographie [kartɔgrafi], *s.f.* cartography; map-making, mapping; **c. aérienne,** aero-charting, photo-charting; **c. photographique,** photo-mapping, photographic mapping.

cartographique [kartɔgrafik], *a.* cartographic(al); **service c.** = ordnance survey.

cartomancie [kartɔmɑ̃si], *s.f.* cartomancy, fortune-telling (by cards).

cartomancien, -ienne [kartɔmɑ̃sjɛ̃, -jɛn], *s.* fortune-teller (by cards).

cartomètre [kartɔmɛtr̥], *s.m.* chartometer; opisometer; map-measurer.

carton [kartɔ̃], *s.m.* **1.** (*a*) cardboard; **c. ondulé,** corrugated paper, cardboard; **c. gris,** chipboard; **c. d'amiante,** asbestos millboard; **c. de collage,** pasteboard; **c. épais,** millboard; **c. paille,** strawboard; **reliure de c.,** binding in boards; **c. bitumé, asphalté, goudronné,** roofing felt; **c. dur,** hardboard; *F:* **homme de c.,** man of straw; **maison de c.,** jerry-built house; *F:* **déposer son c. chez qn,** to leave one's card on s.o.; (*b*) papier mâché, pasteboard; **poupée, moulure, de c.,** papier mâché doll, moulding; **nez en c.,** papier mâché nose; (*c*) *P:* playing card; **battre, manier, taper, graisser, le c.,** to play cards. **2.** card-board box; carton; **c. à chapeau(x),** hatbox; **c. à dessins,** portfolio; **c. de bureau** (cardboard) filing case; *F:* **ma demande est restée, dort, dans les cartons,** my request has been pigeon-holed, shelved. **3.** (*a*) *Art:* cartoon, sketch (for a canvas, a tapestry); (*b*) *Geog:* inset (map). **4.** (*a*) *Phot: etc:* mount; (*b*) carton (at shooting-range, -gallery); **faire un carton,** to fill a target; *F:* to shoot at the enemy, etc.; **faire un bon c.,** to make a good score. **5.** *Bookb:* (*a*) off-cut, cut out; (*b*) **c. de 8 pages,** 8-page cancel, inset; **c. deux pages,** single leaf; **livre en c.,** book in portfolio form. **6.** (*a*) *Tex:* = CARTE 3 (*f*); (*b*) *Mus:* **c. perforé,** perforated music roll. **7.** *Miner:* **c. de montagne, fossile, minéral,** mountain paper.

carton-bois [kartɔ̃bwa], *s.m.* pulp board; *pl. cartons-bois.*

carton-cuir [kartɔ̃kɥir], *s.m.* leather-board; *pl. cartons-cuirs.*

carton-feutre [kartɔ̃føtr̥], *s.m.* carpet felt; *pl. cartons-feutres.*

cartonnage [kartɔnaːʒ], *s.m.* **1.** (*a*) making of pasteboard articles; (*b*) *coll.* (cardboard) boxes, cases (etc.). **2.** *Bookb:* (binding in) paper boards, boarding, casing; **c. pleine toile,** (binding in) cloth boards, full cloth binding; **c. souple,** limp boards.

cartonner [kartɔne], *v.tr.* **1.** to bind (book) in boards, to case (book). **2.** *Bookb:* to put in the cancels, the insets. **3.** *abs. P:* (*a*) to be an inveterate card-player; (*b*) to play (cards) badly.

cartonnerie [kartɔnri], *s.f.* **1.** cardboard factory. **2.** cardboard trade.

cartonnette [kartɔnɛt], *s.f.* light cardboard (used in the manufacture of corrugated paper).

cartonneur, -euse [kartɔnœːr, -øːz], *s.* binder (in boards); boarder (of books).

cartonneux, -euse [kartɔnø, -øːz], *a.* resembling cardboard.

cartonnier, -ière [kartɔnje, -jɛːr], *s.* **1.** cardboard-maker, -seller. **2.** *s.m.* filing cabinet (for files). **3.** *s.f. Ent:* **(guêpe) cartonnière,** paper-wasp. **4.** card sharper. **5.** *Art:* artist who paints cartoons for tapestries and carpets.

carton-paille [kartɔ̃pɑj], *s.m.* strawboard; *pl. cartons-pailles.*

carton-pâte [kartɔ̃pɑːt], *s.m.* papier mâché; paste board; *F:* **empire de c.-p.,** cardboard empire; *pl. cartons-pâtes.*

carton-pierre [kartɔ̃pjɛr], *s.m.* carton pierre; *pl. cartons-pierres.*

cartoon [kartun], *s.m. Cin: etc:* cartoon; comic strip.

cartooniste [kartunist], *s.m.* cartoonist.

cartophilie [kartɔfili], *s.f.* (the hobby of) collecting postcards.

cartothèque [kartɔtɛk], *s.f.* map library.

cartouche[1] [kartuʃ]. **1.** *s.m.* (*a*) *Arch: etc:* cartouche, tablet; (*b*) scroll (round title, etc.); (*c*) inset. **2.** *s.f.* (*a*) cartridge; **cent cartouches,** a hundred rounds (of ammunition); **c. à balle, à blanc,** ball cartridge, blank cartridge; **c. de chasse,** sporting cartridge; **c. à percussion centrale,** central-fire cartridge; *A:* **c. à broche,** pin-fire cartridge; **c. amorce,** primer; **fausse c., c. inerte, c. d'instruction,** dummy cartridge; **bandoulière, collier, à cartouches,** bandolier, bandoleer; **brûler ses dernières cartouches,** to use up one's last reserves (of ammunition, money, etc.); (*b*) (*in Paris*) carrier (for express letter); (*c*) *Phot:* cartridge; (*d*) *Com:* carton (of cigarettes); (*e*) *Com:* refill; (*f*) **c. d'ammoniaque,** ammonia canister.

cartouche[2], *s.m. A:* highwayman, robber (from Cartouche, the XVIIIth-c. highwayman).

cartoucherie [kartuʃri], *s.f.* cartridge factory.

cartouchier [kartuʃje], *s.m. Navy:* ammunition pouch, cartridge pouch.

cartouchière [kartuʃjɛːr], *s.f. Mil:* **1.** (i) cartridge pouch; (ii) cartridge belt. **2. c. d'infirmier,** first-aid case.

cartulaire [kartylɛːr], *s.m. Ecc.Hist:* c(h)artulary.

carus [karys], *s.m. Med:* carus, deep coma.

carvelle [karvɛl], *s.f. Nau:* **(clou à) c.,** weight-nail, deck-nail.

carvi [karvi], *s.m. Bot:* **1. c. des prés,** caraway; **graines de c.,** caraway seeds. **2. c. noix de terre,** earth-nut, pig-nut.

carvinois, -oise [karvinwa, -waːz], *a. & s. Geog:* (native, inhabitant) of Carvin.

carvone [karvɔn], *s.f. Ch:* carvone.

cary [kari], *s.m.* = CURRY.

caryatide [karjatid], *s.f. Arch:* caryatid.

caryocar [karjɔkaːr], *s.m. Bot:* caryocar.

caryocinèse [karjɔsinɛːz], **caryokinèse** [karjɔkinɛːz], *s.f. Biol:* karyokinesis; mitosis.

caryogamie [karjɔgami], *s.f. Biol:* karyogamy.

caryogamique [karjɔgamik], *a.* karyogamic.

caryolymphe [karjɔlɛ̃ːf], *s.f. Biol:* karyolymph.

caryolyse [karjɔliːz], *s.f. Med: Biol:* karyolysis.

caryolytique [karjɔlitik], *a.* karyolytic.

caryophyllacées [karjɔfilase], *s.f.pl. Bot:* Caryophyllaceæ, the pink family.

caryophyllé [karjɔfil(l)e], *a. Bot:* caryophyll(ac)eous.

caryophyllène [karjɔfil(l)ɛn], *s.m. Ch:* caryophyllene.

caryophyllia [karjɔfil(l)ja], **caryophyllie** [karjɔfil(l)i], *s.f.* caryophyllia, cup coral.

caryopse [karjɔps], *s.m. Bot:* caryopsis.

caryorrhexis [karjɔrɛksis], *s.f.* karyorrhexis.

caryosome [karjɔzoːm], *s.m. Biol:* karyosome.

caryota [karjɔta], *s.m. Bot:* Caryota.

caryotype [karjɔtip], *s.m. Biol:* chromosomic chart.

cas [kɑ], *s.m.* **1.** (*a*) case, instance, circumstance; **c. limite, indéterminé,** borderline case; **c. imprévu,** unforeseen event; emergency; *Ins:* act of God; **dans le premier c.,** in the first instance; **c'est votre c.,** that's how it is with you; **être dans un mauvais c.,** to be in a sorry plight; *F:* **c'est bien le c. de le dire,** there's no mistake about it; . . . and no mistake; **c'est le c. ou jamais de . . .,** now if ever, now or never, is the time to . . .; it's (a case of) now or never; **être dans le c. de faire qch.,** to be in a position to do sth.; *F:* **il est dans le c. de le faire,** he is quite likely to do it; **être tous dans le même c.,** to be all in the same case; *F:* in the same boat; (*b*) **c. juridique,** legal case, cause; *Jur:* **c. d'espèce,** concrete case, case in point; **c'est un c. d'espèce,** it depends upon the particular circumstances; **c. de divorce,** grounds for divorce; **citer un c. analogue,** to quote a similar case; (*c*) **c. médical,** medical case; **c. de rougeole,** case of measles. **2.** case, matter, affair, business; **cela change le c.,** that alters the case, the matter; **ce n'est pas le c.,** this is not the case; **c. de conscience,** matter of conscience; **se faire un c. de conscience de faire qch.,** to make a point of doing sth.; *P: A:* **faire son c.,** to relieve nature. **3. faire c. de qn, de qch.,** to value s.o., sth.; **faire peu de c. de qch.,** to set little value on, little store by, to make light of, sth.; **je fais peu de cas des médecins,** I have no faith in doctors; **faire peu de c. de la vie humaine,** to have little regard for human life; **faire grand c. de qn, qch.,** to have a high opinion of s.o., to set great store by sth., to set a high value upon sth.; **je ne fais pas grand c. de votre ami, de vos conseils,** I don't think much of your friend, of your advice; **ne faire aucun c. de qch.,** to leave sth. out of account, to take no account of sth. **4.** *Gram:* case; **au c. nominatif,** in the nominative case. **5.** (*a*) *adv.phr.* **en, dans, ce c.,** in that case, if that is the case, if so, under those circumstances; **dans, en, aucun c.,** in no case, under no circumstances, on no account, not on any account; **en tout c., dans tous les c.,** in any case, at all events; **dans tous les c. il est trop tard,** it is too late now, anyhow; **le c. échéant,** should the occasion arise, in case of need, should it so happen; **selon le c.,** as the case may be; (*b*) *prep.phr.* **en c. de nécessité,** in case of need, of necessity; **hors le c. de . . .,** barring the case of . . .; (*c*) *conj.phr.* **au c. où, dans le c. où, il viendrait,** if he comes; **je laisserai la porte ouverte pour le c. où vous désireriez quelque chose,** I will leave the door open in case you should want anything; **au c. où il serait exact que . . .,** should it prove correct that . . .; *O:* **au, en, c. qu'il n'y soit pas,** in case he should not be there.

casanier, -ière [kazanje, -jɛːr], *a. & s.* stay-at-home; *s.* home-bird, *U.S:* homebody.

casaque [kazak], *s.f.* **1.** *A:* (*a*) cassock, cloak; (*b*) *F:* **tourner casaque,** to turn round (in one's opinions, etc.); to desert one's party, turn one's coat; *F:* to rat. **2.** (*a*) coat, jacket (of jockey, liveried servant, etc.); *Th:* **grande c.,** leading manservant's part; (*b*) *O:* (woman's) over-blouse; loose jacket.

casaquin [kazakɛ̃], *s.m.* (*a*) *Cost: A:* jacket, blouse; (*b*) *P:* (human) body; **tomber, donner, sur le c. à qn,** to set about s.o., to beat s.o. up; **avoir qch. dans le c.,** to be ill; (*of wine*) **donner sur le c.,** to go to one's head.

casarca [kazarka], *s.m. Orn:* **tadorne c. (roux),** ruddy sheldrake.

casba(h) [kazba], *s.f.* **1.** kasba(h); (Berber ruler's) fortified palace. **2.** *P:* house.

cascabelle [kaskabɛl], *s.f. Rept:* cascabel. **1.** rattle (of snake). **2.** rattlesnake.

cascade [kaskad], *s.f.* **1.** cascade, waterfall, falls; **c. d'un glacier, de glace,** ice fall; **cascades de rires,** peals of laughter; **une c. de belles draperies,** a cascade of fine draperies; *El:* **batterie en c.,** battery in series; **couplage en c.,** cascade connection. **2.** lack of cohesion, non-sequitur (in speech, etc.). **3.** (*a*) *F: O:* loose, disorderly, conduct, way of life; **faire des cascades,** to go the pace; (*b*) *Th:* **A:** gag; **prendre un rôle à la c.,** to caricature, guy, a part; (*c*) *Cin: F:* stunt; (*in circus*) pratfall.

cascader [kaskade], *v.i.* **1.** to fall in cascades, to cascade. **2.** *F:* (*a*) *O:* to live a wild life, to act the fool; (*b*) *Th: A:* to gag or guy one's part.

cascadeur, -euse [kaskadœːr, -øːz]. *F:* **1.** *a.* wild, loose, disorderly, fast, rakish. **2.** *s.* (*a*) *O:* reveller, roisterer; (*b*) *Th: A:* actor, actress, who guys, gags, his, her, part; (*c*) *s.m. Th: Cin:* (i) stunt man; (ii) clown specializing in pratfalls; (iii) trapeze artist (who executes a whole series of leaps).

cascalho [kaskajo], *s.m. Miner:* cascalho.
cascara sagrada [kaskarasagrada], *s.f. Pharm:* cascara sagrada (bark).
cascaret [kaskarɛ], *s.m. A: P:* puny individual.
cascarille [kaskariːj], *s.f. Bot:* cascarilla.
cascatelle [kaskatɛl], *s.f.* small cascade.
case [kɑːz], *s.f.* **1.** (*a*) small dwelling; (native) hut, cabin; (*b*) *P: O:* prison, clink. **2.** (*a*) compartment, division (of drawer, etc.); locker; pigeonhole; **c. postale,** Post Office box, P.O. box; *Computers:* **c. d'organigramme,** box of flow-chart; (*b*) bunker, bin; (*c*) division, space to be filled in (on printed form); *Typ: Journ:* box; (*d*) *Games:* (i) point (of blackgammon board); (ii) square (of chessboard); (*e*) cell (of honeycomb); (*f*) *Anat: A:* division (of the brain); *P:* **il lui manque une c., il a une c. vide, une c. en moins,** he's got something missing in the upper storey, he's got a screw loose; (*g*) (sub)division (of classification).
caséate [kazeat], *s.m. Ch:* caseate.
caséation [kazeasjɔ̃], *s.f.* **1.** caseation, transformation into cheese. **2.** *Med:* caseation, caseous degeneration.
caséeux, -euse [kazeø, -øːz], *a.* **1.** caseous, cheesy. **2.** *Med:* **lésion caséeuse,** caseous lesion.
caséification [kazeifikasjɔ̃], *s.f.* **1.** (*a*) *Ch:* (action of) precipitating casein; (*b*) caseation, transformation into cheese. **2.** *Med:* caseation, caseous degeneration.
caséifier [kazeifje], *v.tr. Ch:* to precipitate the casein in, to casefy (milk).
caséiforme [kazeifɔrm], *a.* cheese-like, cheesy.
caséine [kazein], *s.f. Ch:* casein.
caséinerie [kazeinri], *s.f.* casein factory.
caséique [kazeik], *a. Ch:* caseic, lactic (acid).
casemate [kazmat], *s.f. Fort:* casemate; pillbox.
casemater [kazmate], *v.tr. Fort:* to casemate.
caser [kɑze], *v.tr.* to put, stow, (sth.) away; **c. des papiers,** to file, pigeon-hole, papers; **caser qch. dans sa mémoire,** to make a mental note of sth.; *F:* **c. qn,** to find employment, a job, for s.o.; *F:* **il est bien casé,** he has a good billet, a good job; *F:* **elle a trois filles à c.,** she has three daughters to marry off; **la voilà casée,** now she is fixed up for life, is settled, married.
se caser, to settle down; to find a home (**chez qn,** with s.o.); to find a job; to get married.
caserel [kɑzrɛl], **caseret** [kɑzrɛ], *s.m.*, **caserette** [kɑzrɛt], *s.f.* cheese-sieve.
caserne [kazɛrn], *s.f.* (*a*) *Mil:* barracks; *Pej:* large (ill-designed) building; *F:* a barrack of a place; **c. maritime,** naval barracks; **quand tu seras à la c.,** when you are in barracks; when you are a soldier; **plaisanteries de c.,** coarse jokes, barrack-room jokes; (*b*) **c. de pompiers,** fire station; (*c*) **c. flottante, bâtiment-c.,** barrack ship, receiving ship, receiving hulk.
casernement [kazɛrnəmɑ̃], *s.m.* **1.** barracking, quartering (of troops). **2.** barrack accommodation; **officier de c.,** barrack-master.
caserner [kazɛrne]. **1.** *v.tr.* to quarter (troops) in barracks, to barrack; *F:* **j'ai été caserné toute la semaine,** I was kept indoors all the week. **2.** *v.i.* to live in barracks.
casernet [kazɛrnɛ], *s.m. A: Navy:* entry-book, register; **c. d'appel,** muster-roll; **c. de la timonerie,** log-book.
casernier, -ière [kazɛrnje, -jɛːr]. **1.** *a.* (*manners, etc.*) of the barracks; **la promiscuité casernière,** the promiscuity of barrack life. **2.** *s.m.* barrack-warden.
caset [kɑzɛ], *s.m. Fish:* case-worm, caddis worm.
casette [kɑzɛt], *s.f.* **1.** *A:* little house, hut. **2.** *Cer:* sagger, seggar.
caséum [kazeɔm], *s.m. Ch:* casein.
cash[1] [kaʃ], *adv. F:* **payer c.,** to pay cash (down).
cash[2], *s.m.inv. Chinese Num:* cash.
casher, -ère [kaʃɛːr], *a. Jew.Rel:* kosher.
casier [kɑzje], *s.m.* **1.** (*a*) set of pigeon-holes; (*b*) **c. judiciaire,** (i) registry where police records are kept; (ii) records of punishments (of convict); **inscrit au c. judiciaire,** entered in the police record; **son c. judiciaire est vierge,** he has a clean record; **il a un c. judiciaire chargé,** he has had many previous convictions. **2.** (*a*) (wine)bin, rack; **c. à bouteilles,** bottle-rack; **c. d'un porte-habits, d'une malle,** tray of a suit-case, of a trunk; **c. à monnaie,** till; (*b*) **c. à musique,** music cabinet, canterbury; (*c*) *Fish:* **c. à homards,** lobster-pot; (*d*) tool cabinet.
casilleux, -euse [kazijø, -øːz], *a.* brittle (glass, etc.).
casimir [kazimiːr], *s.m.* **1.** *Tex: A:* kerseymere. **2.** *P:* waistcoat.
casing [kasiŋ], *s.m.* **1.** *Min:* casing, piping (of oil-well). **2.** (boiler) casing.
casino [kazino], *s.m.* casino.
casoar [kazɔaːr], *s.m.* **1.** *Orn:* cassowary. **2.** plume (of shako worn by the cadets at Saint-Cyr).
caspien, -ienne [kaspjɛ̃, -jɛn], *a. Geog:* Caspian; **la (mer) Caspienne,** the Caspian (Sea).
casque [kask], *s.m.* **1.** (*a*) helmet (of soldier, fireman, astronaut, diver, etc.); hood (of welder, etc.); *Ind:* **c. de sécurité,** safety hat, cap; *Mil: etc:* **c. (métallique),** (steel) helmet; *F:* tin hat; *O:* **c. de tranchée,** shrapnel helmet; *Aut: Cy:* **c. protecteur, c. blindé,** crash helmet; **c. respiratoire,** smoke helmet; **c. colonial,** tropical helmet, sun helmet; *F: O:* **c. à mèche,** cotton nightcap; *F:* **Casques bleus,** United Nations troops; *German Hist:* **Casques d'Acier,** the Stahlhelm; (*b*) *Her:* helmet (surmounting shield); (*c*) *W.Tel: Tp:* **c. d'écoute, c. téléphonique,** headphone(s), headset; **écouter au c.,** to listen in with headphones; (*d*) upswept hair style; *F:* **un c. de cheveux blonds,** a crown of fair, golden, hair; (*e*) *P:* **avoir le, son, c.,** to have a thick head (after drinking); **il en a dans le c.,** he's a bit fuddled; **s'en donner dans le c.,** to get drunk; *P:* to get tanked up. **2.** (*a*) *Nat.Hist:* galea, hood, casque; (*b*) *Bot:* **c. de Jupiter,** monkshood; (*c*) *Conch:* helmet shell; (*d*) *Cu:* forequarters (of mutton, etc.). **3.** (*a*) *Civ.E:* **c. de battage,** pile helmet; (*b*) *Hairdr:* (hair) dryer.
casqué [kaske], *a.* (*a*) helmeted; **c. d'un bonnet de coton,** wearing a cotton nightcap; (*b*) *Nat.Hist:* galeate(d); (*c*) *F:* wearing headphones.
casquer[1] [kaske], *v.i. P:* to pay (up), fork out, shell out; to foot the bill; **faire c. qn de cinq francs,** to touch s.o. for five francs; to get five francs out of s.o.
casquer[2], *v.tr. F:* (*of hair*) to frame (the face).
casquette [kaskɛt], *s.f.* (peaked) cap (of schoolboy, sailor, jockey, etc.); **c. de skieur,** ski cap; *Mil:* **c. d'ordonnance, c. militaire,** service cap; **c. de grande tenue,** dress cap; **une pleine c. de . . .,** a capful of . . .; *A:* **c. à (trois) ponts,** "three-decker" cap (as worn by prostitute's bullies, apaches); *A: P:* **être c.,** to have had a couple, to be high, merry, mellow.
casquet(t)ier, -ière [kasketje, -jɛːr], *s.* maker of caps.
casqueur, -euse [kaskœːr, -øːz], *a. & s. P:* (the person) who pays, *F:* forks out.
cassable [kɑsabl̥], *a.* (*a*) breakable; (*b*) annullable, (agreement, etc.), that can be annulled.
cassade [kɑsad], *s.f.* **1.** *A:* evasion, fib. **2.** *Cards:* bluff; **faire c.,** to bluff.
cassage [kɑsaːʒ], *s.m.* breaking; *Civ.E:* crushing (of stones, ore).
Cassandre [kasɑ̃dr̥]. **1.** *Pr.n.f. Gr.Lit:* Cassandra. **2.** *Pr.n.m.* (*a*) *Gr.Hist:* Cassander; (*b*) *Th:* Pantaloon; (*c*) *s.m. F: A:* old grey-beard. **3.** *s.m. & f.* defeatist, Cassandra.
cassant [kɑsɑ̃], *a.* **1.** (*a*) brittle (china, etc.); **chemise cassante,** stiffly starched shirt; **pantalon au pli c.,** trousers with a knife-edge crease; (*b*) crisp (biscuit, etc.); (*c*) *Metall:* short (steel, etc.); **fer c. à chaud,** red-short iron. **2.** curt, abrupt, imperious (tone of voice); **être c. avec qn,** to be short with s.o.; *s.m.* **il a du c. dans le caractère,** he does not suffer fools gladly.
cassate [kasat], *s.f. Cu:* cassata.
cassation [kasasjɔ̃], *s.f.* **1.** *Jur:* cassation, annulment, reversing, reversal, quashing, setting aside (of sentence, will, etc.); **Cour de c.,** supreme court of appeal; *s.a.* RECOURIR 2, RECOURS. **2.** *Mil:* reduction (of N.C.O. to the ranks).
cassation[2], *s.f. A.Mus:* cassation.
cassave [kasaːv], *s.f.* (*a*) *Bot: Com:* cassava; **farine de c.,** cassava(-flour); (*b*) cassava bread.
casse[1] [kɑːs], *s.f.* **1.** (glassmaker's) ladle, scoop. **2.** *Metall:* crucible.
casse[2], *s.f. Typ:* case; **bas, haut, de c.,** lower case, upper case; **mettre en c.,** to distribute (type); **mise en c.,** distribution.
casse[3], *s.f.* **1.** *Bot:* cassia **2.** *Pharm:* senna; **c. en bâton(s),** senna pods; *Prov:* **passe-moi la c. et je te passerai le séné,** you scratch my back and I'll scratch yours.
casse[4], *s.f.* **1.** (*a*) (action of) breaking; breakage, damage; **payer la c.,** to pay for the breakage, the damage; **il y aura de la c.,** (i) something will get broken; (ii) *F:* there will be trouble, a row; *F:* **faire de la c.,** to smash the place up; (*b*) things broken, breakages; (*c*) *Com:* **vendre à la c.,** to sell for scrap; (*d*) **c. nette,** clean break; (*e*) *Mil: F:* casualties, losses. **3.** (*a*) *Mil:* cashiering (of officer); (*b*) *F:* **donner la c. à qn,** to sack s.o.
casse[5], *s.m. P:* burglary.
casse[6], *s.f. Wine-m:* casse.
cassé[1] [kɑse], *a.* **1.** broken, worn out (person, etc.); cracked (voice); **c. de vieillesse,** worn out, broken-down, with age. **2.** *Paperm:* **papier c.,** *s.m.(pl.),* **cassé(s),** damaged paper, casse-paper.
cassé[2], *a. Wine-m:* attacked by casse.
casseau, -eaux [kɑso], *s.m. Typ:* (*a*) half-case; (*b*) (spare) fount-case.
casse-chaîne [kɑsʃɛn], *s.m.inv. Tex:* warp-protector.
casse-cœur [kɑskœːr], *s.m.inv. F:* lady-killer.
casse-coke [kɑskɔk], *s.m.inv.* coke-breaker.
casse-cou [kɑsku], *s.m.inv.* **1.** (*a*) danger spot; death-trap; dangerous corner; *F:* **aller au c.-c.,** to ride at a break-neck pace; to ride for a fall; **crier c.-c. à qn,** (i) to shout a warning to s.o.; (ii) to warn s.o. (of a danger); (*b*) rickety step-ladder. **2.** (*a*) *F:* dare-devil, reckless individual; (*b*) *Cin: etc:* stunt man; (*c*) *Equit:* rough-rider; (*d*) acrobat (performing dangerous acts).
casse-croûte [kɑskrut], *s.m.inv.* **1.** snack (meal). **2.** = snack counter (in public house); café serving snack meals.
casse-cul [kɑsky]. **1.** *s.m.inv. A: F:* **faire un c.-c.,** to sit down unexpectedly, with a bump. **2.** *a. & s.inv. P:* annoying, boring, unbearable (person, thing).
casse-fer [kɑsfɛːr], *s.m.inv.* (blacksmith's) steel wedge.
casse-gueule [kɑsgœl], *s.m.inv. P:* **1.** raw spirit; *P:* rot-gut. **2.** dangerous spot, joint. **3.** *a. & s.* break-neck, dare-devil, reckless (undertaking).
casse-lunette(s) [kɑslynɛt], *s.m. Bot:* **1.** eye-bright, eyewort. **2.** cornflower.
cassement [kɑsmɑ̃], *s.m.* **1.** breaking; **c. de tête,** (i) worry, anxiety; (ii) splitting headache. **2.** *P:* burglary.
casse-motte(s) [kɑsmɔt], *s.m. Agr:* clod-breaker.
casse-museau [kɑsmyzo], *s.m.* **1.** *A: P:* punch in the face. **2.** *Cu:* small cream bun; *pl. casse-museaux.*
casse-noisettes [kɑsnwazɛt], *s.m.inv.* **1.** (pair of) nut-crackers; **menton en c.-n.,** nut-cracker chin. **2.** *Orn:* nut-hatch.
casse-noix [kɑsnwa], *s.m.inv.* **1.** (pair of) nut-crackers. **2.** *Orn:* nut-cracker; **c.-n. de Sibérie,** slender-billed nut-cracker; **c.-n. moucheté,** thick-billed nut-cracker.
casse-noyau [kɑsnwajo], *s.m. Orn:* hawfinch; *pl. casse-noyaux.*
casse-os [kɑso, -ɔs], *s.m.inv.* bone-crusher.
casse-pattes [kɑspat], *s.m.inv. P:* **1.** raw spirit; *F:* rot-gut. **2.** *Cy:* break-neck descent.
casse-pieds [kɑspje]. **1.** *s.m.inv. F:* society bore, nuisance (of a man); *F:* pain in the neck. **2.** *a.inv.* boring, tiresome; pestering.
casse-pierre(s) [kɑspjɛːr], *s.m.* **1.** (*a*) stone-breaker's hammer; (*b*) *Civ.E:* stone-breaker, stone-crusher (machine); disintegrator. **2.** *Bot:* (*a*) (white, meadow) saxifrage; (*b*) samphire; (*c*) pellitory.
casse-pipes [kɑspip], *s.m.inv.* (*a*) shooting-gallery; (*b*) *P:* war; *F:* (violent) death (in war); **il est reparti au c.-p.,** he has gone back to the front line.
casse-poitrine [kɑspwatrin], *s.m.inv. P: A:* raw spirit; *P:* rot-gut.
casser [kɑse], *v.tr.* **1.** (*a*) to break (plate, etc.); to snap (twigs); to crack (nuts, etc.); to crush (stones); to fracture (bone); **c. du bois,** (i) to chop wood; (ii) *Av: F:* to smash up one's plane; *F:* **c. les oreilles à qn,** to bother, importune, s.o.; *P:* **c. les pieds (à qn),** to plague (s.o.); **c. la tête à qn,** (i) *O:* to crack s.o.'s skull; (ii) to bother, annoy, importune s.o.; **se c. la tête,** (i) *O:* to crack one's skull; (ii) to rack one's brains; *P: Iron:* **ne te casse pas la tête,** don't overdo it! *F:* **il ne se cassera pas les reins à travailler,** he won't kill himself working; *F:* **il s'est cassé le nez,** he's failed, he's come a cropper; **se c. le nez à la porte de qn,** to find nobody at home, to find the door shut in one's face; *F:* **tu vas te c. les yeux à lire,** you'll wear your eyes out reading; *F:* **c. le cou, la figure,** *P.* **la gueule, à qn,** to give s.o. a (good) thrashing, to give s.o. a punch on the head, on the nose; *F:* **se c. la figure,** (i) to fall flat on one's face, to come a cropper; (ii) to meet with an accident; (iii) to kill oneself; *P:* **c. sa pipe, sa canne,** to die, to go west, to kick the bucket; *P:* **se (la) c.,** to do a bunk; *F:* **c. le morceau,** (i) to confess, to come clean; (ii) to denounce s.o.; *F:* **ça ne casse rien, ça ne casse pas trois pattes à un canard,** it's not up to much, it's nothing to write home about, there's nothing extraordinary about that; *F:* **il ne casse rien,** he's no great shakes; **qu'est-ce qu'il y a encore de cassé?** what's the trouble now? *A: P:* **je t'en casse,** don't you wish you may get it? *St.Exch:* **c. les**

cours, to bang the market; *F:* **vouloir tout c.,** to go all out; *P:* (*of a girl*) **c. sa cruche,** to lose her virginity; *P:* **c. ses œufs,** to have a miscarriage; (*b*) *adv.phr.* **à tout c.,** at full speed, without restraint; **applaudir à tout c.,** to raise the roof (with applause); **se faire applaudir à tout c.,** to bring the house down; *F:* **(une attaque) à tout c.,** (an) all-out (attack); **cet objet vaut 1,000 francs à tout c.,** this article is worth 1,000 francs at the very most; *s.a.* BRAS 1, CROÛTE 1, GRAINE 1, MARMITE 1, POT 1, RAGE 2, SUCRE. **2.** (*a*) to cashier (officer); to degrade, demote (civil servant, etc.); **c. un sous-officier (de son grade),** to reduce an N.C.O. (to the ranks); *Navy:* **cassé de son grade,** dismissed his ship. **3.** *Jur:* to annul, quash, set aside (verdict, etc.). **4.** *Nau:* **c. l'erre d'un navire,** to check, slacken, a ship's way; **(navire)cassé,** broken-backed (ship). **5.** *v.i.* **l'assiette a cassé en tombant,** the plate broke as it fell; **cela casse comme du verre,** it breaks like glass; *Lit:* **tout passe, tout lasse, tout casse,** all is vanity and vexation of spirit.

se casser. **1.** to break, snap, give way, part; *Prov:* **quand la corde est usée, trop tendue, elle se casse,** everything has its breaking point. **2.** (*of pers.*) to break up. **3.** *Nau:* (*of ship*) to break her back.

casserole [kasrɔl], *s.f.* **1.** (*a*) saucepan, (stew)pan; **veau en c.,** braised veal; (*b*) *P:* **passer qn à la c.,** (i) to bump s.o. off; (ii) to knock s.o. flat; **passer à la c.,** (i) to get bumped off; (ii) to go through a tough time; (iii) to be raped. **2.** *P:* (*a*) *A:* large watch, *F:* turnip; (*b*) tinny piano; (*c*) police spy, *P:* nark; (*d*) (*woman*) tart.

casserolée [kasrɔle], *s.f.* (sauce)panful.

casse-sucre [kɑssykr̥], *s.m.inv.* *Sug.-R:* sugar-cutting machine.

cassetée [kɑste], *s.f.* caseful.

casse-tête [kɑstɛt], *s.m.inv.* **1.** (*a*) (war-)club, tomahawk; (*b*) loaded stick, life-preserver; (*c*) truncheon; **la police a chargé la foule à coups de c.-t.,** the police made a baton charge on the crowd. **2.** (*a*) puzzling, brain-racking, task; *F:* headache; **ceci est l'un des plus colossaux c.-t. de tout le problème de la main-d'œuvre,** this is one of the greatest headaches of the whole manpower problem; (*b*) **c.-t. chinois,** Chinese puzzle, tangram. **3.** din, ear-splitting noise, racket. **4.** *F:* heady wine.

cassetin [kɑstɛ̃], *s.m.* **1.** *Typ:* box (of type case). **2.** *Metall:* crucible (of furnace).

casse-trame [kɑstram], *s.m.inv.* *Tex:* **(fourchette) c.-t.,** weft-fork.

cassette [kasɛt], *s.f.* (*a*) casket (for jewels, etc.); case (for instruments); (*b*) money-box; *A:* **c. du roi,** King's privy purse; **biens de la c.,** crown estates; (*c*) *Tchn:* cassette.

casseur, -euse [kɑsœːr, -øːz]. **1.** *s.* (*a*) breaker; **c. de pierres,** stone-breaker; (*b*) smasher (of crockery, etc.); **c. d'assiettes,** rowdy person; (*c*) scrap merchant; **dépôt de c.,** breaker's yard; **c. de voitures,** (car) breaker; (*d*) *P:* burglar. **2.** *a.* (*a*) *F:* **domestique casseuse,** maid who smashes everything; (*b*) aggressive (look, etc.). **3.** *s.f.* **casseuse,** sugar-cutting machine, sugar chopper.

casside [kasid], *s.f.* *Ent:* cassida, tortoise-beetle.

cassididés [kasidide], *s.m.pl.* *Moll:* Cassididae.

cassidien, -ienne [kasidjɛ̃, -jɛn], *a & s.* (native, inhabitant) of Cassis.

cassie [kasi], *s.f.*, **cassier**[1] [kasje], *s.m.* *Bot:* sponge tree, huisache; cassia-tree.

cassier[2] [kɑsje], *s.m.* *Typ:* case-rack.

Cassin [kasɛ̃], *Pr.n.m.* *Geog:* **le mont C.,** Monte Cassino.

cassine [kasin], *s.f.* **1.** *O:* (*a*) cottage; (*b*) *F:* hovel, hut. **2.** *Mil:* small defensive post; blockhouse.

cassinoïde [kasinɔid], *s.f.* *Mth:* Cassinian ellipse.

Cassiodore [kasjɔdɔːr], *Pr.n.m.* *Lt.Lit:* Cassiodorus.

cassiope [kasjɔp], *s.m.* *Bot:* cassiope.

Cassiopée [kasjɔpe], *Pr.n.f.* *Myth:* *Astr:* Cassiopeia.

cassis[1] [kasis], *s.m.* **1.** blackcurrant. **2.** blackcurrant bush. **3.** blackcurrant liqueur.

cassis[2] [kɑsi], *s.m.* *Civ.E:* cross-drain, open gutter (across road).

cassis[3] [kasis], *s.m.* *Moll:* Cassis.

cassis[4] [kasis], *s.m.* *P:* head; *P:* nut, block.

cassitérides [kasiterid]. **1.** *s.m.pl.* tin-bearing ores. **2.** *Pr.n.f.pl.* *A.Geog:* **Les C.,** the Cassiterides (i.e. the Scilly Islands).

cassitérite [kasiterit], *s.f.* *Miner:* cassiterite; tinstone.

cassolette [kasɔlɛt], *s.f.* **1.** (*a*) cassolette; incense-burner; (*b*) *Poet:* perfume; *Iron:* bad smell, stink; (*c*) *Arch:* flame ornament, (stone) fire pot; (*d*) *Cu:* ramekin. **2.** *Bot:* garden rocket.

casson [kɑsɔ̃], *s.m.* (*a*) piece of broken glass; (*b*) (rough) lump of sugar.

cassonade [kasɔnad], *s.f.* brown sugar, moist sugar; cassonade, muscovado.

cassot [kasɔ], *s.m.* *Fr.C:* (cardboard) cornet; punnet.

cassotte [kasɔt], *s.f.* **1.** *A:* artificial flower (made of red wool). **2.** long-handled saucepan. **3.** (type of) long-handled ladle for drawing water.

cassoulet [kasulɛ], *s.m.* (*a*) earthenware dish; (*b*) *Cu:* sort of stew made in Languedoc.

cassure [kɑsyːr], *s.f.* **1.** (*a*) break, fracture, crack, broken place; *Geol:* **c. (avec rejet),** fault; (*b*) fractured edge; (*c*) fold mark (in linen), crease. **2.** broken fragment; **cassures de pâtisserie,** broken cakes, biscuits. **3.** *Wine-m:* casse.

castagnette [kastaɲɛt], *s.f.* castanet.

castagneux [kastaɲø], *s.m.* *Orn:* **grèbe c.,** little grebe, dabchick.

castagnole [kastaɲɔl], *s.f.* *Ich:* **1.** pomfret, sea-bream. **2.** Ray's bream.

Castalie [kastali], *Pr.n.f.* *Gr.Lit:* (fountain of) Castalia.

castanopsis [kastanɔpsis], *s.m.* *Bot:* castanopsis.

caste [kast], *s.f.* caste; **esprit de c.,** class consciousness; **hors c.,** outcaste.

castel [kastɛl], *s.m.* (*in S. of Fr.*) manor house.

castelbriantais, -aise [kastɛlbriɑ̃tɛ, -ɛːz], *a. & s.* *Geog:* (native, inhabitant) of Châteaubriant.

castelet [kastəlɛ], *s.m.* puppet-theatre.

castellinois, -oise [kastɛlinwa, -waːz], *a. & s.* (native, inhabitant) of Châteaulin.

castelnaudarien, -ienne [kastɛlnodarjɛ̃, -jɛn], *a. & s.* *Geog:* (native, inhabitant) of Castelnaudary.

castelroussin, -ine [kastɛlrusɛ̃, -in], *a. & s.* *Geog:* (native, inhabitant) of Châteauroux.

castelsarrasinois, -oise [kastɛlsarazinwa, -waːz], *a. & s.* *Geog:* (native, inhabitant) of Castelsarrasin.

castelthéodoricien, -ienne [kastɛlteɔdɔrisjɛ̃, -jɛn], *a. & s.* *Geog:* (native, inhabitant) of Château-Thierry.

castillan, -ane [kastijɑ̃, -an], *a. & s.* *Geog:* *etc:* Castilian.

Castille[1] [kastiːj], *Pr.n.f.* *Geog:* Castile.

castille[2], *s.f.* *A:* bickering, altercation; **chercher c. à qn,** to pick a quarrel with s.o.; **être en c.,** to be at loggerheads.

castine [kastin], *s.f.* *Metall:* limestone flux.

castniides [kastniid], *s.m.pl.* *Ent:* Castniidae.

castor[1] [kastɔːr], *s.m.* **1.** (*a*) *Z:* beaver; **c. de montagne nord-américain,** North-American mountain-beaver, sewellel; *s.a.* ARBRE 2; (*b*) (i) *F:* *O:* stay-at-home officer or sailor; (ii) *F:* ship's boy; (*c*) *O:* person of dubious morals; (*d*) *F:* person who builds his own house. **2.** *Com:* (*a*) beaver fur; (*b*) **c. du Chili,** *Z:* coypu; *Com:* nutria; (*c*) **c. du Canada,** musquash (fur); (*d*) *A:* beaver (-hat); (*e*) *Leath:* castor (goatskin for gloves); (*f*) *Tex:* **drap c.,** beaver cloth; beaverette.

Castor[2], *Pr.n.m.* *Myth:* *etc:* **C. et Pollux,** Castor and Pollux.

castoréum [kastɔreɔm], *s.m.* *A.Pharm:* *Perfume Ind:* castor(eum).

castoridés [kastɔride], *s.m.pl.* *Z:* Castoridae, the beavers.

castorine [kastɔrin], *s.f.* **1.** *Ch:* castorin. **2.** *Tex:* beaver, castor.

castrais, -aise [kastrɛ, -ɛːz], *a. & s.* *Geog:* (native, inhabitant) of (i) Castres; (ii) La Châtre.

castramétation [kastrametasjɔ̃], *s.f.* *A.Mil:* castrametation.

castrat [kastra], *s.m.* castrated man, eunuch; *Mus:* castrato; *pl. castrati.*

castration [kastrasjɔ̃], *s.f.* castration; gelding (of horse, etc.).

castrer [kastre], *v.tr.* to castrate, geld.

castreur [kastrœːr], *s.m.* = CHÂTREUR.

castrogontérien, -ienne [kastrɔgɔ̃terjɛ̃, -jɛn], *a. & s.* *Geog:* (native, inhabitant) of Château-Gontier.

castrothéodoricien, -ienne [kastroteɔdɔrisjɛ̃, -jɛn], *a. & s.* *Geog:* (native, inhabitant) of Château-Thierry.

casualisme [kazɥalism], *s.m.* *Phil:* casualism.

casualiste [kazɥalist], *s.m.* *Phil:* casualist.

casualité [kazɥalite], *s.f.* fortuitousness.

casuaridés [kazyaride], *s.m.pl.* *Orn:* Casuariidae.

casuel, -elle [kazɥɛl]. **1.** *a.* (*a*) fortuitous, accidental, casual; *Jur:* **condition casuelle,** contingent condition; (*b*) *Gram:* **flexions casuelles,** case-endings; (*c*) inherent in the case; **les difficultés casuelles qui s'opposent à la réalisation du projet,** the difficulties that are inherent in the case, that derive from the nature of the case and that go against it. **2.** *s.m.* perquisites, fees (in addition to fixed salary); *Ecc:* surplice fees.

casuellement [kazɥɛlmɑ̃], *adv.* *A:* *Lit:* fortuitously, accidentally.

casuiste [kazɥist], *s.m.* *Theol:* casuist.

casuistique [kazɥistik], *s.f.* (*a*) *Theol:* casuistry; (*b*) sophistry.

cata- [kata], **cath-** [kat], *pref.* cata-, cath-; **catadrome,** catadromous; **cathérétique,** catheretic.

catabolique [katabɔlik], *a.* *Biol:* catabolic (change, etc.).

catabolisme [katabɔlism], *s.m.* *Biol:* catabolism, katabolism.

catacaustique [katakostik], *a. & s.f.* *Opt:* catacaustic (curve).

catachrèse [katakrɛːz], *s.f.* *Rh:* catachresis.

cataclastique [kataklastik], *a.* *Geol:* cataclastic.

cataclinal, -aux [kataklinal, -o], *a.* *Geog:* cataclinal.

cataclysme [kataklism], *s.m.* cataclysm, disaster.

cataclysmique [kataklismik], *a.* cataclysmic, cataclysmal.

cataclyste [kataklist], *s.f.* *Ent:* cataclysta.

catacombes [katakɔ̃ːb], *s.f.pl.* catacombs; *occ. sg.* **la catacombe de saint Calixte,** the catacomb of Saint Calixtus.

catacoustique [katakustik], *s.f.* *Ph:* catacoustics.

catadioptre [katadiɔptr̥], *s.m.* reflector; (*in middle of road*) cat's-eye.

catadioptrique [katadjɔptrik], *Ph:* **1.** *a.* catadioptric(al). **2.** *s.f.* *O:* catadioptrics.

catadrome [katadrɔm], *a.* *Ich:* catadromous.

catadromie [katadrɔmi], *s.f.* *Ich:* catadromous migration (of fish leaving fresh water to spawn in the sea.)

catafalque [katafalk], *s.m.* catafalque.

catagenèse [kataʒenɛːz], *s.f.* *Biol:* catagenesis.

catagénétique [kataʒenetik], *a.* *Biol:* catagenetic.

cataire [katɛːr]. **1.** *a.* *Med:* **frémissement c.,** purring tremor (of the heart). **2.** *s.f.* *Bot:* catmint, *U.S:* catnip.

catalan, -ane [katalɑ̃, -an], *a. & s.* *Geog:* Catalan, Catalonian; *Metall:* **feu c.,** Catalan forge, bloomery fire.

catalanisme [katalanism], *s.m.* *Pol:* Catalanism.

catalaniste [katalanist], *s.m. & f. & a.* *Pol:* Catalanist.

catalauniens [katalonjɛ̃], **catalauniques** [katalonik], *a.m.pl.* *Hist:* Catalaunian (fields).

catalectes [katalɛkt], *s.m.pl.* *A.Lit:* catalects.

catalectique [katalɛktik], *a.* *Pros:* catalectic.

catalepsie [katalɛpsi], *s.f.* *Med:* catalepsy.

cataleptiforme [katalɛptifɔrm], *a.* *Med:* cataleptiform.

cataleptique [katalɛptik], *a. & s.* *Med:* cataleptic (patient, etc.).

Catalogne [katalɔɲ]. **1.** *Pr.n.f.* *Geog:* Catalonia. **2.** *s.m.* *Tex:* **couvertures de, en, c.,** Barcelona rugs (of rough wool).

cataloguage [katalɔgɑːʒ], *s.m.* cataloguing.

catalogue [katalɔg], *s.m.* catalogue; list; **c. raisonné,** descriptive catalogue; **c. méthodique, c. matière,** subject catalogue; **faire le c. des qualités de qn,** to run over s.o.'s good points; *Com:* **achat, vente, sur c.,** mail order.

cataloguer [katalɔge], *v.tr.* (*a*) to catalogue, list; to make a catalogue of (things); (*b*) *F:* *Pej:* to size (s.o.) up.

catalogueur [katalɔgœːr], *s.m.* cataloguer.

catalpa [katalpa], *s.m.* *Bot:* catalpa.

catalyse [kataliːz], *s.f.* *Ch:* catalysis.

catalyser [katalize], *v.tr.* *Ch:* to catalyse.

catalyseur [katalizœːr], *Ch:* *etc:* **1.** *a.* catalytic. **2.** *s.m.* catalyst.

catalytique [katalitik], *a.* *Ch:* catalytic.

catalytiquement [katalitikmɑ̃], *adv.* catalytically.

catamaran [katamarɑ̃], *s.m.* *Nau:* catamaran; *Av:* **flotteurs disposés en c.,** parallel, paired, floats.

cataménial, -aux [katamenjal, -o], *a.* *Physiol:* catamenial, menstrual.

catanais, -aise [katanɛ, -ɛːz], *a. & s.* *Geog:* (native, inhabitant) of Catania.

catananche [katanɑ̃ːʃ], *s.f.* *Bot:* catananche.

Catane [katan], *Pr.n.f.* *Geog:* Catania.

catapétale [katapetal], *a.* *Bot:* catapetalous.

cataphasie [katafazi], *s.f.* *Med:* cataphasia.

cataphonique [katafɔnik], *s.f.* *Ph:* cataphonics, catacoustics.

cataphora [katafɔːra], *s.f.* *Med:* cataphora.

cataphorèse [katafɔrɛːz], *s.f.* *Ph:* *Med:* cataphoresis.

cataphorétique [katafɔretik], *a.* cataphoretic.

cataphorique [katafɔrik], *a.* *El:* **action c.,** electro-osmosis, electrical endosmosis.

cataphote [katafɔt], *s.m.* *R.t.m:* cat's-eye (reflector).

cataplasme [kataplasm], *s.m. Med:* poultice, cataplasm; **c. sinapisé, à la farine de moutarde,** mustard plaster; **c. à mie de pain,** bread poultice; **c. électrique,** electric pad; *F:* **c'est un bon c. pour l'estomac,** it's a good lining for the stomach.
cataplectique [kataplɛktik], *a. Med:* cataplectic.
catapléite [katapleit], *s.f. Miner:* catapleiite.
cataplexie [katapl ɛksi], *s.f. Med:* cataplexy.
catapultable [katapyltabl], *a.* **(avion) c.,** catapult-launched (aircraft).
catapultage [katapyltaːʒ], *s.m. Av:* catapult-launching, catapulting; **crochet de c.,** catapulting hook.
catapultaire [katapyltɛːr], *s.m. Mil: Hist:* catapultier.
catapulte [katapylt], *s.f.* catapult; *Av:* **catapulte (de lancement),** (launching) catapult; **lancer par c.,** to catapult off.
catapulter [katapylte], *v.tr.* (*a*) *Av:* to catapult; (*b*) to send (sth.) hurtling off; **on l'a catapulté à Tokyo,** he was sent flying off, he was packed off, to Tokyo at a moment's notice.
cataracte [katarakt], *s.f.* **1.** (*a*) cataract, falls; *Poet:* **les cataractes du ciel sont ouvertes,** the sluice-gates of heaven have opened; *F:* **lâcher les cataractes,** to give full vent to one's anger; (*b*) *Hyd.E:* difference in level (above and below bridge). **2.** *Med:* cataract; **enlever une c.,** to extract a cataract.
cataracté [katarakte], *a. Med:* cataractous, affected with cataract.
catarhiniens [katarinjɛ̃], *s.m.pl. Z:* Catarrhina.
catarrhal, -aux [kataral, -o], *a. Med:* catarrhal.
catarrhe [kataːr], *s.m. Med:* catarrh; **c. nasal,** nasal catarrh; **c. vésical,** cystitis.
catarrheux, -euse [katarø, -øːz], *a. & s.* catarrhous (person).
catasetum [katasetɔm], *s.m. Bot:* catasetum.
catastase [katastɑːz], *s.f. Lit:* catastasis.
catastrophe [katastrɔf], *s.f.* catastrophe. **1.** denouement (of tragedy, etc.). **2.** disaster; **c. financière,** crash; **c'est la c.!** the worst has happened.
catastrophé [katastrɔfe], *a. F:* (*a*) wrecked, come to grief; (*b*) overwhelmed, dumbfounded.
catastropher [katastrɔfe], *v.tr. F:* (*a*) to wreck; (*b*) to overwhelm, dumbfound.
catastrophique [katastrɔfik], *a.* catastrophic.
catastrophisme [katastrɔfism], *s.m. A.Geol:* catastrophism.
catathermomètre [katatɛrmɔmɛtr], *s.m.* catathermometer.
catatonie [katatɔni], *s.f. Med:* catatonia, catatonic schizophrenia.
catatypie [katatipi], *s.f. Phot:* catatype.
catau [kato], *s.f. F:* (*a*) farm girl; (*b*) slut; (*c*) tart.
catazone [katazon], *s.f. Geol:* katazone.
cat-boat [katbot], *s.m. Nau:* catboat; *pl. cat-boats.*
catch [katʃ], *s.m.* catch-as-catch-can, all-in wrestling; **c. à quatre,** tag wrestling.
catcher[1] [katʃɛːr], *s.m.* **1.** *Cr:* wicket keeper. **2.** (*baseball*) catcher.
catcher[2] [katʃe], *v.i.* to practice, go in for, all-in wrestling.
catcheur [katʃœːr], *s.m.* catch-as-catch-can, all-in, wrestler.
catéchèse [kateʃɛːz], *s.f. Ecc: A:* catechesis.
catéchète [kateʃɛt], *s.m. Ecc: A:* catechist.
catéchétique [kateʃetik], *Ecc: A:* **1.** *a.* catechetic(al). **2.** *s.f.* catechetics.
catéchisation [kateʃizasjɔ̃], *s.f. A:* catechization, catechizing.
catéchiser [kateʃize], *v.tr.* **1.** (*a*) *Ecc:* to catechize; (*b*) *F:* to tell s.o. what to say. **2.** (*a*) to reason with, to try to persuade (s.o.), to try to win (s.o.) over; (*b*) to reprove, lecture (s.o.).
catéchisme [kateʃism], *s.m.* catechism; **le petit c.,** the shorter catechism; **aller au c.,** to go to a catechism class; *F:* **faire le c. à qn,** to coach s.o. up; to put s.o. up to what he has to say or do.
catéchiste [kateʃist], *s.m.&f.* catechist, catechizer.
catéchistique [kateʃistik], *a.* catechistic(al).
catéchuménat [katekymena], *s.m. Ecc:* catechumenate.
catéchumène [katekymɛn], *s.m. Ecc:* catechumen.
catégorématique [kategɔrematik], *a. Log:* categorematic.
catégorème [kategɔrɛm], *s.m. Phil:* **1.** category, predicament. **2.** categorematic word.
catégorie [kategɔri], *s.f.* (*a*) category; (i) *Log:* predicament; (ii) class, order; department; **dans la même c.,** under the same head; **différentes catégories de marchandises,** different types of goods; **de la même c.,** of the same quality; **de dernière c.,** of poor quality; (*b*) (*women's services*) **première c.,** regimental sergeant-major (W.R.A.C.); **deuxième c.,** (i) company sergeant-major (W.R.A.C.); (ii) Warrant officer (W.R.A.F.); **troisième c.,** quarter-master sergeant (W.R.A.C.); **quatrième c.,** (i) sergeant-major (W.R.A.C.); (ii) Flight sergeant (W.R.A.F.); **cinquième c.,** sergeant (W.R.A.C. and W.R.A.F.); **sixième c.,** corporal (W.R.A.C. and W.R.A.F.).
catégorique [kategɔrik], *a.* (*a*) categorical (proposition, imperative); (*b*) categorical, explicit, clear (answer, etc.); **expression d'opinion c.,** definite opinion; **refus c.,** categorical refusal, flat refusal; **affirmation c.,** unqualified statement.
catégoriquement [kategɔrikmɑ̃], *adv.* (*a*) categorically; (*b*) clearly, explicitly, positively.
catégorisation [kategɔrizasjɔ̃], *s.f.* categorization, classification.
catégoriser [kategɔrize], *v.tr. A:* to categorize, classify.
catélectrotonus [katelɛktrotɔnys], *s.f. Physiol:* catelectrotonus.
caténaire [katenɛːr], *a.* **1.** (*a*) catenary (suspension of bridge, etc.); (*b*) *s.f. Rail: etc:* overhead contact wire, overhead line; trolley wire (with catenary suspension). **2.** *Ch:* **réactions caténaires,** series, chain, of reactions.
caténation [katenasjɔ̃], *s.f.* (con)catenation, series.
caténoïde [katenɔid], *s.f. Mth:* catenoid.
catérail [katerɑːj], *s.m. Rail:* overhead monorail system.
caterpillar [katɛrpilaːr], *s.m. Veh: Mec.E:* caterpillar track.
catésien, -ienne [katezjɛ̃, -jɛn], *a. & s. Geog:* (native, inhabitant) of Le Cateau.
catgut [katgyt], *s.m.* catgut.
cath-. *See* CATA-.
cathare [kataːr], *a. & s.m.f. Rel.H:* Cathar, Catharist, Catharian.
catharsis [katarsis], *s.f. Gr.Lit: Med:* catharsis.
cathartique [katartik]. **1.** *a. Ch:* cathartic (acid). **2.** *a. & s.m. Med:* cathartic, laxative.
Cathay [katɛ], *Pr.n.m. A.Geog:* Cathay.
cathédral [katedral]. **1.** *a.* cathedral (authority, etc.). **2.** *a. & s.m.* **(chanoine) c.,** canon (of a cathedral); *the plural cathédraux is rarely used.*
cathédrale [katedral], *s.f.* cathedral.
Catherine [katrin], *Pr.n.f.* Catherine, Catharine, Katherine, Kathleen; *Hist:* **la grande C.,** Catherine the Great; **coiffer sainte C.,** (*of woman*) to have reached one's twenty-fifth birthday without marrying.
catherinette [katrinɛt], *s.f. F:* **1.** (*a*) young unmarried woman (*esp. milliner*) who has reached her twenty-fifth birthday; (*b*) *Publ:* book no longer quite recent. **2.** *Bot:* (*a*) spurge; (*b*) bramble. **3.** *Ent: F:* ladybird.
cathéter [katetɛːr], *s.m. Surg:* catheter.
cathétériser [kateterize], *v.tr. Surg:* to catheterize; to sound with a catheter.
cathétérisme [kateterism], *s.m. Med:* catheterization, sounding with a catheter.
cathétomètre [katetɔmɛtr], *s.m.* cathetometer.
cathion [katjɔ̃], *s.m.* = CATION.
cathode [katɔd], *s.f.* (*a*) *El:* cathode; **c. à bain, à liquide,** pool cathode; **c. à bain de mercure,** mercury-pool cathode; **c. à oxydes,** oxide (-coated) cathode; **c. à chauffage direct, indirect,** directly-, indirectly-, heated cathode; **c. photoélectrique,** photo(-electric) cathode; **c. équipotentielle,** unipotential, equipotential, cathode; **c. asservie, suiveuse,** cathode follower; **polarisation de c.,** cathode bias; **revêtement de c.,** cathode coating; (*b*) (*electrolysis*) starting-sheet; **c. non traitée,** starting-sheet blank; **support de c.,** plating-rack.
cathodique [katɔdik], *a. El:* cathodic; **courant c.,** cathode current; **rayons cathodiques,** cathode rays; **lampe à luminescence c.,** cathode-ray glow-lamp, **tube à rayons cathodiques, tube c.,** cathode-ray tube; **faisceau c.,** (cathode) beam.
catholicisant [katɔlisizɑ̃], *a.* inclined to Roman Catholicism.
catholiciser [katɔlisize], *v.tr.* to convert to Roman Catholicism.
catholicisme [katɔlisism], *s.m.* Catholicism, *esp.* Roman Catholicism.
catholicité [katɔlisite], *s.f.* **1.** catholicity; *F:* orthodoxy. **2.** the (Roman) Catholic Church; the (whole body of) Roman Catholics.
catholique [katɔlik], *a.* **1.** (*a*) catholic, universal; (*b*) *F:* orthodox; in order, straight; **c'est un peu plus c.,** it's a bit more shipshape, a bit straighter; **ce n'est pas c.,** I don't like the look, the sound, of it; it looks, sounds, fishy; **il n'est pas c.,** he's a bit phoney; he's not quite straight; **cognac peu c.,** doubtful, dubious, brandy. **2.** *a. & s.* (Roman) catholic; *Hist:* **les Rois Catholiques,** Ferdinand and Isabella (of Spain).
catholiquement [katɔlikmɑ̃], *adv.* according to (Roman) Catholic doctrine.
catholyte [katɔlit], *s.m. El:* catholyte.
cati [kati], *s.m. Tex:* (*a*) gloss, lustre; (*b*) dressing (solution).
Catilina [katilina], *Pr.n.m. Rom.Hist:* Catiline.
catilinaire [katilinɛːr], *s.f.* (*a*) Catilinarian oration (of Cicero); (*b*) diatribe, outburst.
catillac [katijak], **catillard** [katijaːr], *s.m. Hort: Cu:* warden(-pear).
catimaron [katimarɔ̃], *s.m. Nau:* = CATAMARAN.
catimini (en) [ɑ̃katimini], *adv.phr. F:* stealthily, on the sly; **entrer, sortir, en c.,** to steal in, out.
catin [katɛ̃], *s.f.* (*a*) *A:* farm-wench; (*b*) *A. & Dial:* doll; (*c*) *P:* prostitute, whore.
cation [katjɔ̃], *s.m. El:* cation.
cationique [katjɔnik], *a. El:* cationic.
catir [katiːr], *v.tr. Tex:* to press, gloss, give lustre to (material); **c. une étoffe à chaud, à froid,** to hot-press, cold-press, material.
catissage [katisaːʒ], *s.m. Tex:* glossing, pressing.
catisseur, -euse [katisœːr, -øːz], *s. Tex:* (piece-) presser, glosser.
cativo [kativo], *s.m. Bot:* cativo.
catmarin [katmarɛ̃], *s.m. Orn:* **(plongeon) c.,** red-throated diver; loom.
catoblépas [katɔblepɑs], *s.m. Z: Myth:* catoblepas.
catocala [katɔkala], *s.f. Ent:* catocala, catocalid.
catocale [katɔkal], *s.f. Ent:* catocala.
catogan [katɔgɑ̃], *s.m.* (*a*) *A.Hairdr:* cadogan; hair tied back in a bunch; (*b*) ribbon used for tying back hair in this style.
Caton [katɔ̃], *Pr.n.m. Rom.Hist:* Cato.
catonien, -ienne [katɔnjɛ̃, -jɛn], *a.* **1.** *A:* Catonian, stern, austere. **2.** *A.Jur:* **règle catonienne,** Catonian law of inheritance.
catoptrique [katɔptrik]. *Ph:* **1.** *a.* catoptric(al), reflecting. **2.** *s.f.* catoptrics; (study of) reflection.
catoptromancie [katɔptrɔmɑ̃si], *s.f.* catoptromancy.
catostome [katɔstoːm], *s.m. Ich:* catostomus.
catostomidés [katɔstɔmide], *s.m.pl. Ich:* Catostomidae.
Cattégat (le) [ləkategat], *Pr.n. Geog:* the Kattegat.
cattiche [katiʃ], *s.f.* otter's burrow, holt.
cattleya [katleja], *s.m. Bot:* cattleya.
Catulle [katyl], *Pr.n.m. Rom.Lit:* Catullus.
Caucase (le) [ləkokaːz], *Pr.n. Geog:* the Caucasus.
caucasien, -ienne [kokazjɛ̃, -jɛn], *a. & s. Geog:* Caucasian.
caucasique [kokazik], *a.* = CAUCASIEN.
cauchemar [kɔʃmaːr, ko-], *s.m.* (*a*) nightmare; *Med:* incubus; **avoir le c.,** to have a nightmare, to be troubled with nightmares; (*b*) *F:* bugbear, pet aversion.
cauchemardant [kɔʃmardɑ̃, ko-], *a. O: P:* boring, wearisome; that gets on your nerves.
cauchemarder [kɔʃmarde, ko-], *F:* **1.** *v.i.* to have nightmares. **2.** *v.tr.* (*a*) to bore (s.o.) stiff, to get on (s.o.'s) nerves; (*b*) **ça me cauchemardait, cette perspective,** this prospect was a nightmare to me.
cauchemardesque [kɔʃmardɛsk], **cauchemardeux, -euse** [kɔʃmardø, -øːz], *a.* nightmarish.
cauchois, -oise [koʃwa, -waːz], *a. & s.* (native, inhabitant) of the Pays de Caux (in Normandy).
caudal, -aux [kodal, -o], *Z:* **1.** *a.* caudal. **2.** *s.f.* **caudale,** caudal fin.
caudataire [kodatɛːr], *s.m.* (*a*) train-bearer (to Pope, etc.); (*b*) *F:* toady, flatterer.
caudé [kode]. **1.** *a. Nat.Hist:* caudate, tailed. **2.** *s.m. Dial:* (*Beauce*) soup made with milk.
caudebec [kodbɛk], *s.m. A:* felt hat.
caudex [kodɛks], *s.m. Bot:* caudex, stock, stem (of tree).
caudicule [kodikyl], *s.f. Bot:* caudicle.
caudifère [kodifɛːr], **caudigère** [kodiʒɛːr], *a. Nat. Hist:* tailed, caudate.
caudimane [kodiman], *Z:* **1.** *a.* caudimanous, prehensile-tailed (monkey). **2.** *s.m.* caudimane.
Caudine [kodin], *a.f. Rom.Hist:* **les Fourches Caudines,** the Caudine Forks; **passer sous les Fourches Caudines,** to be forced to accept humiliating terms.
caudrette [kodrɛt], *s.f. Fish:* lobster-net; bow-net.
caule [kol], *s.f. Bot:* caulis.
caulerpe [kolɛrp], *s.f. Algae:* caulerpa.
caulescent [kolɛsɑ̃], *a. Bot:* caulescent.
caulicole [kolikɔl]. **1.** *a. Nat.Hist:* caulicolous. **2.** *s.f.pl. Arch:* **caulicoles,** caulicoli.
caulicule [kolikyl], *s.f. Bot:* caulic(u)le.
caulifère [kolifɛːr], *a. Bot:* cauliferous.
cauliflore [kolifl ɔre], *a. Bot:* cauliflorous.
cauliflorie [kolifl ɔri], *s.f. Bot:* cauliflory.

cauliforme [koliform], *a. Bot:* cauliform.

caulinaire [koline:r], *a. Bot:* cauline, caulinary.

caulocarpe [kolɔkarp], **caulocarpien, -ienne,** [kolɔkarpjɛ̃, -jɛn], **caulocarpique** [kolɔkarpik], *a. Bot:* caulocarpic, caulocarpous.

caulosarque [kolɔsa:rk], *s.m. Bot:* caulosarc.

caurale [koral], *s.m. Orn:* caurale.

cauri(s) [kori], *s.m.* cowrie.

causailler [kozaje], *v.i. F:* to chatter, to indulge in small talk.

causal [kozal], *a. no m.pl. Gram:* causal.

causalgie [kozalʒi], *s.f. Med:* causalgia.

causalisme [kozalism], *s.m. Phil:* doctrine of causality.

causalité [kozalite], *s.f. Phil:* causality.

causant [kozɑ̃], *a. F:* 1. chatty, talkative (person). 2. dîner très c., chatty dinner, dinner with plenty of conversation.

causateur, -trice [kozatœ:r, -tris], *a.* effective, causal (energy, etc.).

causatif, -ive [kozatif, -i:v], *a. Gram:* causative (voice, etc.).

causation [kozasjɔ̃], *s.f. Phil:* causation.

cause [ko:z], *s.f.* 1. cause; c. de défiance, cause for distrust; c. première, prime cause; c. seconde, secondary cause; être c. de qch., to be the cause of sth.; c'est vous qui êtes la c. de cet ennui, it is you who have brought this trouble on us; c'est elle qui en est c., it is her fault; pour quelle c.? for what reason? on what grounds? il ne viendra pas et pour c., he will not come and for a very good reason; il est en colère et pour c., he's annoyed, and with good reason, and well he may be; maison à céder pour c. de faillite, house for sale on account of bankruptcy; absent pour c. de santé, absent for reasons of health; absent on medical grounds; *prep.phr.* à c. de, on account of; (i) through . . ., owing to . . .; (ii) for the sake of . . .; je renonce au voyage à c. de la dépense, I am giving up the journey owing to the expense; relâcher à c. d'une panne de la machine, to put into port by reason of a breakdown; c'est à c. de moi qu'il a manqué le train, it was through me that he lost his train; je me tais à c. de lui, I keep silent for his sake; c'est à c. de toi! it's all because of you! *F:* à c. de quoi? why? *F:* sa timidité est c. qu'il n'est pas venu me voir, his shyness is the reason for his not having come to see me; *A: & P:* à c. que + *ind.* (= PARCE QUE), because; *Jur:* à ces causes, for these reasons, wherefore. 2. (a) *Jur:* cause, suit, action; causes célèbres, famous trials; c. sommaire, summary proceedings; avocat sans c., briefless barrister; être chargé d'une c., to hold a brief; confier une c. à un avocat, to brief a barrister; affaire en c., case before the court; c. qui a établi un précédent, leading case; entendre une c., to hear a case; *F:* la c. est entendue, there's nothing more to add; sans que je sois en c., through no fault of mine; être en c., (i) to be party to a suit; (ii) *F:* to be concerned in sth.; véhicule en c., vehicle involved (in an accident); mettre qn en c., (i) to summon, sue, s.o.; (ii) to implicate s.o.; mettre en c. la probité de qn, to question s.o.'s honesty; questions hors de c., irrelevant questions; cela est hors de c., that is beside the point, the question; mettre qn, qch., hors de c., (i) to rule (plaintiff, argument) out of court; (ii) to exonerate s.o.; sa probité reste hors c., his honesty has never been in question; en tout état de c., at all events, in any case; agir en connaissance de c., to act with full knowledge of the case; condamner qn sans connaissance de c., to condemn s.o. without a hearing; (b) cause, interest; c'est pour une bonne c., it is for a good cause; pour la c. de la justice, in the cause of justice; souffrir pour une c., to suffer in a cause; faire c. commune avec qn, to make common cause with s.o., to side with, stand by, s.o.; *s.a.* AYANT 2, FAIT² 2, GAIN 2. 3. *Jur:* consideration (given by contracting parties); *Com:* c. d'un billet, consideration given for a bill of exchange.

causer¹ [koze], *v.tr.* 1. to cause, be the cause of (sth.); c. de l'anxiété à qn, to cause s.o. anxiety; c. un changement, to bring about a change; la dévastation causée par l'incendie, the havoc wrought by the fire. 2. *Com:* c. un billet, to state the consideration for a bill; billet causé en valeur reçue en marchandises, bill issued for value received in goods.

causer², *v.i.* (a) to talk, chat (de, about); c. avec, *F:* à, qn, to have a chat, a talk, with s.o.; la vieille dame aime à c., she's a talkative old lady; c. de choses et d'autres, de la pluie et du beau temps, to talk about one thing and another, about nothing in particular, to talk about the weather, to indulge in small talk; c. musique, to

talk (about) music; (c'est) assez causé! that's enough talking! we're, you've, been talking long enough! je vous dis ça pour c., histoire de c., I'm telling you this just for something to say; *F:* causez toujours, you can talk as much as you like (I'm not listening); (b) to blab, to give the show away; faire c. qn, to pump s.o.; (c) (of magpie) to chatter.

causerie [kozri], *s.f.* (a) talk, chat; (b) causerie, chatty lecture, chatty article.

causette [kozet], *s.f. F:* little chat; faire la c., faire un bout, un brin, de c., avec qn, to have a bit of a chat, a natter, with s.o.

causeur, -euse [kozœ:r, -ø:z]. 1. *a.* talkative, chatty. 2. *s.* (a) talker, conversationalist; (b) *F:* blabber. 3. *s.f. Furn:* causeuse, sociable, causeuse, courting chair, *U.S:* love seat.

causse [kos], *s.m. Geog:* causse.

caussenard, -arde [kosnar, -ard], *a. & s.* (native, inhabitant) of the Causses region.

causticité [kostisite], *s.f.* (a) *Ch:* causticity; (b) causticity, caustic humour; biting, stinging, nature (of remark, etc.).

caustifier [kostif je], *v.tr. (pr.sub. & p.d. n.* caustifiions, v. caustifiiez) *Ch:* to causticize; to make (sth.) caustic.

caustique [kostik]. 1. *a.* (a) *Ch:* caustic; (b) biting, caustic, cutting (remark, etc.). 2. *s.m. Ch: Pharm:* caustic. 3. *s.f. Opt:* caustic (curve).

caustiquement [kostikmɑ̃], *adv.* caustically, bitingly.

cautèle [kotɛl], *s.f.* (a) *Lit:* wile, cunning; (b) wariness, caution; *Ecc:* absolution à c., conditional absolution.

cauteleusement [kotløzmɑ̃], *adv.* 1. cunningly, slily. 2. warily, cautiously.

cauteleux, -euse [kotlø, -ø:z], *a.* 1. cunning, wily, sly. 2. wary, cautious.

cautère [kote:r], *s.m.* 1. *Med:* (a) cautery; c. actuel, searing-, cauterizing-iron; actual cautery; c. potentiel, potential cautery; pierre à c., common caustic; c. sur (une) jambe de bois, useless act or remedy; (b) issue, ulcer (produced by cauterizing). 2. rowel (of spur).

cautérisant [koterizɑ̃], *a. Surg:* cauterizing.

cautérisation [koterizasjɔ̃], *s.f.* cauterization, cauterizing, cautery.

cautériser [koterize], *v.tr.* to cauterize, sear (wound, etc.).

caution [kosjɔ̃], *s.f.* 1. security, guarantee, bail-bond; donner c. pour qn, to go bail for s.o., to be surety for s.o.; admettre une c., to grant bail; mettre qn en liberté sous c., to admit s.o. to bail, to let s.o. out on bail; c. judiciaire, c. judicatum solvi, security for costs (given by plaintiff in lawsuit); *Com:* verser une c., to pay a deposit; c. bonne et solvable, sufficient security; sujet à caution, unreliable, unconfirmed (news, etc.). 2. surety, guaranty, bail(-bondsman); se rendre c. de qn, se porter c. pour qn, (i) to go bail for s.o.; (ii) *Com:* to stand, go, become, surety for s.o.; je vous suis c. que . . ., I will answer for it that . . .

cautionnaire [kosjone:r], *a.* pertaining to bail, to security.

cautionnement [kosjonmɑ̃], *s.m. Com:* 1. surety-ship. 2. (a) surety-bond, guarantee; s'engager par c., to enter into a surety-bond; (b) security, caution-money, guarantee, guaranty; c. judiciaire, bail.

cautionner [kosjone], *v.tr.* (a) to stand surety for (s.o.); *Jur:* to go bail for (s.o.); to bail (s.o.) out; (b) to answer for, guarantee (sth.); *Cust:* c. les droits, to deposit the duty (repayable).

cavage [kava:ʒ], *s.m.* 1. excavation. 2. storage (of goods) in a cellar. 3. cellarage.

cavaille [kava:j], *s.f. Ich:* jack crevalle, amber(-)jack.

cavaillon [kavajɔ̃], *s.m.* balk (between rows of vine).

cavaillonnais, -aise [kavajone, -e:z], *a. & s. Geog:* (native, inhabitant) of Cavaillon.

cavalcade [kavalkad], *s.f.* 1. *A:* calvalcade, expedition on horseback. 2. cavalcade, procession; pageant. 3. *F:* une c. d'enfants qui dégringolent l'escalier, an unruly group of children rushing down the stairs.

cavalcader [kavalkade], *v.i.* 1. *A:* to cavalcade; to ride (in a cavalcade). 2. *F:* les étudiants cavalcadaient dans les rues, unruly bands of students swarmed the streets.

cavalcadour [kavalkadu:r], *s.m. A:* equerry, master of the horse.

cavale [kaval], *s.f.* 1. *Lit:* mare. 2. *P:* big, lanky, woman. 3. *P:* escape.

cavaler [kavale], *v.i.* (a) *A:* to ride (on horseback); (b) *F:* to run (at full speed). 2. *v.tr. P:* c. qn, to plague, pester, s.o.

se cavaler, *P:* to run away, scoot, make tracks, do a bunk.

cavalerie [kavalri], *s.f.* 1. *Mil:* cavalry; c. montée, à cheval, horse cavalry; mounted cavalry; c. motorisée, mécanisée, motorized, mechanized, cavalry; c. blindée, armoured cavalry; *Mil.Hist:* c. légère, lourde, light, heavy, cavalry. 2. stable (of circus horses, etc.). 3. *Com:* billet, papier, de c., effets, traites, de c., accommodation bill, note. 4. la C. de Saint-Georges, English money.

cavaleur, -euse [kavalœ:r, -ø:z], *a. & s.* 1. *s.m.* (man) wolf. 2. *s.f.* girl, woman, of loose morals.

cavalier, -ière [kavalje, -jɛ:r]. 1. (a) *s.* rider; horseman, horsewoman; habit de c., riding costume; *B:* les cavaliers de l'Apocalypse, the (four) Horsemen of the Apocalypse; (b) *a.* piste cavalière, (i) riding track, (ii) bridle path; (in forest, etc.) allée cavalière, ride. 2. (a) *s.m. Mil:* trooper; (b) *s.m. Chess:* knight; (c) *s.m. A:* gentleman, gallant; beau c., dashing young spark; *Hist:* Cavaliers et Têtes-rondes, Cavaliers and Roundheads; (d) *s.m.* escort (to a lady); *A:* c. servant, mounted attendant (on a lady); faire le c. servant auprès d'une dame, to dance attendance on a lady; (e) *s.m. & f.* partner (at dance); faire c. seul, (i) to perform the *cavalier seul* (in quadrille, etc.); (ii) to act alone; (iii) *Turf:* to leave the field standing, to win in a canter; (iv) to go it alone. 3. *s.m. Tchn:* (a) staple; (b) rider (of balance); (c) *Civ.E:* side-piling, spoil-bank (of road); (d) *Mec.E:* quadrant (plate), tangent plate (of lathe); (e) *Fort:* cavalier. 4. *a.* (a) cavalier, free and easy; offhand (manner, etc.); rakish, jaunty (appearance); *adv.phr.* à la cavalière, in a cavalier, offhand, manner; (b) vue cavalière, bird's-eye view; *Geom:* perspective cavalière, isometric projection; *s.a.* PLAN².

cavalièrement [kavaljɛrmɑ̃], *adv.* cavalierly, off-handedly.

cavatine [kavatin], *s.f. Mus:* cavatina.

cave¹ [ka:v], *a.* 1. hollow, sunken (cheeks, eyes). 2. *Anat:* veine c., vena cava. 3. *A.Chr:* (a) deficient (month, year); (b) incomplete (year).

cave², *s.f.* 1. (a) cellar, vault; (cheesemaking) cellar, cave; avoir une bonne c., to keep a good cellar (of wine); je n'ai plus de vin en c., I am at the end of my stock of wine; c. à charbon, coal-cellar; c. forte, strong room; aller de la c. au grenier, du grenier à la c., (i) to skip from one subject to another; (ii) to go from one extreme to the other; (b) cellar night-club; (c) *A:* sepulchral vault. 2. c. à liqueurs, cellaret, liqueur cabinet. 3. *Ind:* c. à coke, wharf (of coke-oven). 4. *Veh: A:* boot (of carriage). 5. *Aut:* foot-well (of car).

cave³, *s.f. Cards:* money put up by each player (at beginning of game); stock of money or counters put up; stake.

cave⁴, *s.m. P:* 1. outsider (*as opposed to a member of the underworld*). 2. clot, dupe; sucker; *a.* ce qu'elle est c.! what a sucker!

caveau, -eaux [kavo], *s.m.* 1. (a) small (wine-)cellar, vault; (b) understair cupboard, cupboard under the stairs; (c) *Mus.Hist:* cave of harmony (after the one formed in 1729). 2. burial vault.

caveautier [kavotje], *s.m.* worker in a firm of monumental masons.

caveçon [kavsɔ̃], *s.m. Horse-training:* cavesson; *Lit:* donner un coup de c. à qn, to humiliate s.o.

cavée [kave], *s.f.* hollow road, sunken road.

caver¹ [kave], *v.tr. A: & Lit:* to hollow (out), dig (out), excavate, undermine; c. les fondations de la société, to undermine the foundations of society; yeux cavés par les veilles, eyes hollowed by late hours; *Prov:* l'eau qui tombe goutte à goutte cave la pierre, constant dripping wears away the stone.

se caver, (a) to become hollow; (b) to wear away.

caver², *Cards:* 1. *v.tr.* to put up (so many counters or so much money). 2. *v.i.* to put up a sum of money (on beginning game); c. au plus fort, (i) to put up an amount equal to the highest on the table; (ii) to carry things to extremes; c. sur la bêtise humaine, to count upon, bank on, human foolishness.

se caver, (a) se c. de deux cents francs, to put up two hundred francs; (b) to ruin oneself.

cavernaire [kaverne:r], *a.* of, relating to, caves; cavernal.

caverne [kavern], *s.f.* (a) cave, cavern; *Prehist:* l'homme des cavernes, cave-man; l'âge des cavernes, the age of the cave-man; (b) deep cellar; (c) den (of thieves); (d) *Med:* cavity (in lungs, etc.); (e) *Mil:* logement c., casemated barrack (in fort).

caverneux, -euse [kavɛrnø, -øːz], *a.* **1.** (*a*) cavernous, caverned (mountain, rock); (*b*) *Anat:* cavern(ul)ous; spongy (tissue). **2.** hollow, sepulchral (voice).
cavernicole [kavɛrnikɔl], (*a*) *a. Nat.Hist:* cavernicolous, cave-dwelling, cave-loving (animal, etc.); (*b*) *s.m. & f.* cavernicole.
cavesson [kavsɔ̃], *s.m.* = CAVEÇON.
cavet [kavɛ], *s.m. Arch:* cavetto, hollowed moulding.
caviar [kavjaːr], *s.m.* **1.** caviar; **c. rouge,** salmon caviar; *Lit:* **c'est du c. pour le peuple,** it is caviar to the general. **2.** ink for obliterating censored passage; **passer au c.,** to censor.
caviarder [kavjarde], *v.tr.* to suppress, block out, censor (passage in paper, etc.).
cavicorne [kavikɔrn], *Z:* **1.** *a.* cavicorn, hollow-horned. **2.** *s.m.pl.* **cavicornes,** Cavicornia.
cavin [kavɛ̃], *s.m.* hollow (in ground).
caviste [kavist], *s.m.* cellarman (at hotel, etc.).
cavitaire [kaviteːr], *a.* cavitary.
cavitation [kavitasjɔ̃], *s.f. Av: Nau: etc:* cavitation (behind propeller blades, etc.).
cavité [kavite], *s.f.* cavity, hollow; pit (in metal); *Anat:* **c. articulaire,** socket (of bone).
cawcher, -ère [kaʃɛːr], *a. Jew.Rel:* kosher.
caye [kaːj], *s.f. Geog:* key, (coral) reef.
Cayenne [kajɛn]. **1.** *Pr.n.f. Geog:* Cayenne (Island); **poivre de C.,** *s.m.* **cayenne,** cayenne pepper. **2.** *s.f. A:* (*a*) floating barracks; (*b*) floating prison; (*c*) place, factory, etc., "off the map"; (*d*) cook-house, canteen (in ship-building yards).
cayeu, -eux [kajø], *s.m.* = CAÏEU.
cazette [kazɛt], *s.f. Cer:* = CASETTE 2.
ce¹ [s(ə)], *dem. pron. neut.* (**c'** *before parts of* **être** *beginning with a vowel;* **ç'** *before* **a**) it, that; **1.** (*used as neut. subject real or temporary to* **être, devoir être, pouvoir être,** *etc.*) (*a*) (*with adj. or adv. complement*) **c'est faux!** it's not true! it's untrue! **ce doit être faux,** it is probably untrue; **c'est bien!** good! very well! **le voilà, ce n'est pas trop tôt!** there he is, and about time too! **est-ce** [ɛs] **assez?** is that enough? (*b*) (*with sb. or pron. as complement—with 3rd pers. pl. complement the verb should be in the plural, but colloquial usage allows the singular*) **qui est là?—c'est moi, c'est nous, ce sont eux,** *F:* **c'est eux,** who is there?—it is I, we, they; *F:* it's me, us, them; **est-ce vous, Jean?** is that you, John? *F:* **c'est vous, Jean?** that you, John? **est-ce bien eux?** is it really them? **ce peut être eux,** it may be they; *F:* them; **c'est peut-être eux,** perhaps it's them; **ce n'est pas eux,** it isn't them; **ce doivent,** *F:* **doit, être eux,** it must be them; **qui l'a fait?—c'est lui,** who did it?—he did; **ce sont ceux qui viennent d'arriver,** it is those who have just arrived; **c'est un brave type,** he's a good chap; **ce sont mes amis,** they are my friends; **c'est un bon soldat,** he's a good soldier; NOTE: *Cp. il est soldat, il est vicomte* (*he is a soldier, a viscount*), (*but colloquially and in a disparaging sense*) **c'est vicomte, on ne sait comment!** he's a viscount, no one knows how! **ce n'est pas mon parapluie,** it, that, is not my umbrella; **ce ne sont pas mes souliers,** they, these, are not my shoes; **si ce n'est,** except, unless (*this phr. is usually invariable*); **personne si ce n'est vos parents,** no one with the (possible) exception of your parents; (*c*) (*with inf. as complement*) **ce serait jeter de l'argent par la fenêtre,** it would be throwing money down the drain; (*d*) **ce . . . ici** = CECI; **ce n'est pas ici une auberge!** this is not an inn! **c'est ici le moment de parler,** now is the time to speak; *A:* **c'est ici mon fils,** this is my son; (*e*) **ce . . . là** = CELA; **ce n'est pas là mon parapluie,** that is not my umbrella; **est-ce que ce sont là vos enfants?** are these your children? **était-ce là le grand homme?** was that the great man? *s.a.* CELA (*b*); (*f*) (*representing a subject which has been isolated in order to stress it*) **Paris, c'est bien loin! c'est bien loin, Paris!** it's a long way to Paris! Paris is a long way off; **le retrouver, ce pourra être bien difficile!** finding him may prove very difficult; **le temps, c'est de l'argent,** time is money; (*g*) (*anticipating the subject*) **c'est demain dimanche,** tomorrow is Sunday; **c'est vous le maître,** you are the master; **c'était lui l'imprudent,** it was he who was imprudent; (*h*) (i) *F:* (*as temporary subject when an adj. is followed by a sb. clause or an inf. subject—careful speech requires* **il**); **c'était inutile de sonner,** you need not have rung; **c'est heureux que tu sois là,** it is a good thing that you are here; (ii) **c'est assez qu'il veuille bien pardonner, oublier,** it is enough that he is willing to forgive, forget; **c'est à vous de vous en occuper,** it is for you to see to it; **allez le voir, ne fût-ce que pour me faire plaisir,** go and see him, if only to please me; (*i*) **c'est . . . qui, c'est . . . que** (*used to bring a word into prominence*); *F:* **c'est une fameuse idée que vous avez là!** that's a wonderful idea you've got there! **c'est un bon petit garçon que Jean!** what a fine little chap John is! **ce serait imprudence que d'y aller,** it would be unwise to go (there); **c'est un péché que de mentir,** it is a sin to lie; **c'est moi qui lui ai écrit,** it was I who wrote to him; **est-ce à moi que vous parlez?** are you speaking to me? (*j*) (i) **c'est que** (*introducing a statement*) **c'est que . . .,** you see . . ., the point is . . .; **c'est qu'il fait froid!** it is cold and no mistake! **s'il n'est pas des nôtres c'est qu'il est malade,** if he is not with us today he must be ill, it must be because he is ill; **c'est que je n'ai rien à me mettre,** the truth is that I have nothing to put on; (ii) **ce n'est pas que je veuille y aller,** it is not that I want to go; **ce n'est pas qu'il n'y tienne pas,** it is not that he isn't keen on it; (iii) **est-ce que** [ɛskə] (*introducing a question*) **est-ce que je peux entrer?** may I come in? **est-ce qu'il est là?** is he there? *s.a.* QUI EST-CE QUI, QUI EST-CE QUE, QU'EST-CE QUI, QU'EST-CE QUE, N'EST-CE PAS. **2.** *literary use, always* [sə] (*a*) (*used as subject to* **devenir, laisser, sembler, venir**) **ce lui devint un plaisir de la voir,** it became a pleasure to him to see her; **ce ne laissa pas de m'amuser,** I couldn't help being rather amused at it; *A:* **ce semble,** it seems; **voilà, ce me semble, un avis excellent,** that, to my mind, is excellent advice; *A:* **quand ce vint à mon tour,** when it came to my turn; (*b*) (*used as object to* **faire, dire, etc.**) **pour ce faire . . .,** in order to do this . . ., with this intention . . .; **ce faisant . . .,** doing which . . .; **ce disant . . .,** saying which . . ., so saying . . ., with these words . . .. **3.** *used as neut. antecedent to a rel. pron.* (*a*) **ce qui, ce que,** *etc.* = what; **je sais ce qui est arrivé,** I know what has happened; **voilà ce que j'ai répondu,** this is what I answered; **savez-vous ce que ça vaut?** do you know what that's worth? **il sait ce qu'est la vie,** he knows what life is; **je sais ce que c'est que la pauvreté,** I know what poverty is; **savez-vous ce que c'est que les anthropophages?** do you know what anthropophagi are? **si vous saviez ce que c'est que de vivre seul!** if you knew what it means, what it's like, to live alone! **voilà ce que c'est que faire l'idiot!** that's what comes of playing the fool! **c'est ce que je lui dis,** so I tell him; **je vais vous dire ce que c'est,** I'll tell you all about it; **voici ce dont il s'agit,** this is the point; this is what it's all about; **ce qu'il y a de plus remarquable, c'est que . . .,** what is most remarkable is that . . .; **ce qui me plaît, ce sont ses idées,** what I like about him is his ideas; **à ce qu'il me semble,** as it seems to me; **à ce qu'on dit,** by, according to, what they say; **voici ce à quoi** [seakwa], **j'avais pensé,** this is what I had thought of; **il nous conseille d'attendre, ce en quoi il a raison,** he advises us to wait, and he's quite, absolutely, right; (*b*) **ce qui, ce que,** *etc.* = which; **on dit qu'il est déjà parti, ce que je ne savais pas,** they say he has gone already, (a fact) which I did not know; **il faudrait qu'il soit grand, ce qu'il n'est pas,** he ought to be tall, which he is not; **il veut employer la force, ce à quoi je m'opposerai toujours,** he wants to use force, something which I shall always be against; (*c*) **tout ce qui, que,** everything, all (that); **voici tout ce que j'ai d'argent,** here is all the money I have; **faites tout ce que vous voudrez,** do whatever you like; (*d*) *F:* **ce que . . .!** how . . .! **ce qu'elle a changé!** how she has changed! *F:* **ce qu'il en a écrit de livres!** the number of books he has written! *F:* **c'est formidable ce que tu es belle aujourd'hui!** how devastatingly beautiful you are today! *F:* **c'est inouï ce qu'il boit,** it is extraordinary the amount he drinks. **4.** (= CELA) **on l'a attaqué et ce** [sə] **en plein jour,** he was attacked, and in broad daylight; **registre à ce destiné,** book kept for the purpose; **sur ce . . .,** thereupon . . .; *A:* **depuis ce . . .,** since then; *s.a.* NONOBSTANT. **5.** *conj.phr.* **tenez-vous beaucoup à ce qu'il vienne?** are you very anxious for him to come? **quoi d'étonnant à ce qu'il soit marié?** what's so extraordinary about his being married? **il profita de ce que j'avais le dos tourné,** he took advantage of my having my back turned to him; **différer en ce que . . .,** to differ in that . . .; **6.** *prep.phr.* **pour ce qui est de la qualité et du prix,** with regard to, as regards, quality and price, as far as quality and price are concerned; **pour ce qui est de cela,** for that matter, for the matter of that; **pour ce qui est d'elle,** for her part, as for her.
ce² (**cet**), **cette, ces** [sə (sɛt), sɛt, se or sɛ], unstressed *dem.a.* (*The form* **cet** *is used before a sb. or adj. beginning with a vowel or h 'mute.'*) This, that, *pl.* these, those. **1. un de ces jours,** one of these days; **il fera de l'orage cette nuit,** there will be a storm tonight; **j'ai mal dormi cette nuit,** I slept badly last night; **je l'ai vu, je le verrai, ce matin, cet été,** I saw him, I shall see him, this morning, during the summer; **à ce moment,** (i) at the moment; (ii) at that moment; at the time. **2.** *Determining a sb. qualified by a defining clause.* (*a*) that, these; **mon père, ce héros au sourire si doux,** my father, that hero with the gentle smile; **il y a de ces gens qui . . .,** there are those who, people who . . .; (*b*) the; **cette idée lui vint que . . .,** the idea occurred to him that . . .; **il eut cette sensation que . . .,** he experienced the feeling that . . .; **rien de ce genre,** nothing of the kind. **3.** *Determining a sb. previously referred to;* (*a*) **elle avait une poupée; cette poupée était en . . .,** she had a doll; this doll was made of . . .; **j'ai lu votre livre; j'ai eu cette patience,** I read your book; I had the patience, patience enough, to do so; (*b*) **ce dernier,** the latter; (*c*) *F:* **mais laissez-la donc, cette enfant!** do leave the child alone! **4.** *pl. Deferential use.* **que prendront ces messieurs?** what will you take, gentlemen? **ces dames sont au salon,** the ladies are in the drawing-room. **5.** *stressed forms;* **ce . . . -ci,** this; **ce . . . -là,** that; **prenez cette tasse-ci,** take this cup; **je n'oublierai jamais ce jour-là,** I shall never forget that day; **je l'ai vu, je le verrai, ces jours-ci,** I have seen him, shall see him, during the last, the next, few days. **6.** *F:* (*a*) **eh bien, et cette jambe?** well, how's that leg of yours? **et ce café, garçon?** what about that coffee, waiter? **ce bon Martin! ce cher Martin!** good old Martin! **cette question!** what an absurd question! **cette raison!** what a reason to give! (*b*) **je lui ai écrit une de ces lettres!** I wrote him such a letter! **vous avez de ces expressions!** you do use such expressions! **j'ai une de ces faims!** I'm ravenous!
cé [se], *s.m.* (the letter) c.
céans [seɑ̃], *adv. A:* (here) within, in this house; **elle n'est pas c.,** she is not within, not at home; **sortez de c.,** leave this house; **le maître de c.,** the master of this house.
cébidés [sebide], *s.m.pl. Z:* Cebidae.
céboïdes [sebɔid], *s.m.pl. Z:* (*super family*) Ceboidea, Platyrrhina.
cebus [sebys], *s.m. Z:* cebus.
ceci [səsi], *dem. pron. neut. inv.* this (thing, fact, etc.); **c. est mon testament,** this is my last will and testament; **écoutez bien c.,** listen to this; **tout c. rejaillit sur moi,** all this sort of thing is a reflexion on me; **le cas offre c. de particulier, que . . .,** the case is peculiar in this, that . . .; *s.a.* CE¹ 1 (*d*), CELA.
cécidie [sesidi], *s.f. Bot:* cecidium, gall.
cécidogène [sesidɔʒɛn], *a.* cecidogenous.
cécidomyidés [sesidɔmiide], *s.m.pl. Ent:* Cecidomyiidae.
cécidomyie [sesidɔmii], *s.f. Ent:* cecidomyia; gall-gnat; **c. destructrice,** Hessian fly; **c. des poirettes,** pear midge.
Cécile [sesil], *Pr.n.f.* Cecilia, Cecily, Cicely.
cécité [sesite], *s.f.* blindness, cecity; **c. des neiges,** snow-blindness; **c. verbale,** word-blindness, alexia.
cecropia [sekrɔpja], *s.m. Bot:* cecropia.
Cécrops [sekrɔps]. **1.** *Pr.n.m. Myth:* Cecrops. **2.** *s.m. Crust:* cecrops.
cédant, -ante [sedɑ̃, -ɑ̃ːt], *Com: Jur:* **1.** *a.* granting, assigning, transferring (party). **2.** *s.* (*a*) grantor, assignor, transferor, transfer(r)er (of shares, etc.); (*b*) preceding party (to bill).
cédarite [sedarit], *s.f. Miner:* chemawinite.
céder [sede], *v.* (**je cède, n. cédons; je céderai**) **1.** *v.tr.* (*a*) (i) to give up, part with, yield, cede (**à,** to); to surrender (right); **les droits à eux cédés,** the rights granted to them; **c. sa place à qn,** to give up one's seat to s.o.; **c. le passage,** to give way; **c. la priorité à qn,** to give s.o. the right of way; **c. le pas à d'autres,** to take a back seat; *Nau:* **c. la place,** to give way (to a ship); **le théâtre est en train de c. la place au cinéma,** the theatre is losing ground to the cinema; *s.a.* PAS 1, PAVÉ 2; (ii) to transfer, make over, assign (**à,** to); to dispose of, sell (lease); **maison à c.,** business for sale; **je vous le céderai pour cent francs,** I will let you have it for a hundred francs; (*b*) **ne le c. en rien à qn,** to be s.o.'s equal, to be in no way inferior to s.o.; **le c. à qn en qch.,** to yield to s.o. in sth., to be inferior to s.o. in sth.; **pour l'intelligence elle ne (le) cède à personne,** in intelligence she is second to none.

2. *v.i.* to yield, give way (under pressure); (*a*) **c. sous le pied,** to give beneath the foot; **le câble céda sous l'effort,** the rope gave way, parted, under the strain; **si la porte cède, vous allez tomber,** if the door gives, you will fall; **tout cède devant lui,** he carries everything before him; **c. au sommeil,** to succumb to sleep; **c. aux circonstances,** to yield to circumstances; **forcer qn à c.,** to bring s.o. to terms; *Mus:* **cédez,** (i) diminuendo; (ii) rallentando; (*b*) to give in, submit (**à,** to); *F:* to knuckle under; **il a cédé à nos désirs,** he gave in to us.

cédille [sediːj], *s.f. Gram:* cedilla.

cédiller [sedije], *v.tr.* to put a cedilla under (the letter c).

cédraie [sedrɛ], *s.f.* cedar plantation.

cédrat [sedra], *s.m. Bot:* (*a*) citron tree; (*b*) citron.

cédraterie [sedratri], *s.f.* citron plantation.

cédratier [sedratje], *s.m. Bot:* citron (tree).

cèdre [sɛːdr̥], *s.m.* (*a*) cedar(-tree); **c. acajou,** Barbadoes bastard cedar; (*b*) cedar-wood; **c. de Virginie,** red, pencil, cedar.

cédrel(a) [sedrɛl(a)], *s.m. Bot:* cedrela; **c. odorant,** Barbadoes bastard cedar.

cédréléon [sedreleɔ̃], *s.m.* oil of cedar.

cédrène [sedrɛn], *s.m. Ch:* cedrene.

cédrie [sedri], *s.f.* cedar-resin, -pitch.

cédrol [sedrɔl], *s.m. Ch:* cedrol.

Cédron [sedrɔ̃], *Pr.n.m. B.Hist:* **Le C.,** the (brook) Cedron; Kidron.

cédulaire [sedylɛːr], *a.* pertaining to income-tax schedules; *A:* **impôts cédulaires,** scheduled taxes.

cédule [sedyl], *s.f.* **1.** *Jur:* (*a*) *A:* note of hand, promise to pay; **plaider contre sa c.,** (i) to deny an agreement; (ii) to fly in the face of evidence; (*b*) *A:* **c. de citation,** authority given by the *juge de paix* to issue a summons. **2.** (*a*) *Adm:* (*classification of taxes*) schedule; **c. d'impôts,** tax bracket; (*b*) *Fin:* (Argentine) cedula.

cégétiste [seʒetist]. **1.** *s.m. & f.* member of the C.G.T. (*Confédération générale du travail*). **2.** *a.* connected with the C.G.T.; **les délégués cégétistes,** the C.G.T. delegates.

ceince [sɛ̃s], *s.f.* floorcloth.

ceindre [sɛ̃ːdr̥], *v.tr.* (*pr.p.* **ceignant;** *p.p.* **ceint;** *pr. ind.* **je ceins, il ceint, n. ceignons, ils ceignent;** *p.d.* **je ceignais;** *p.h.* **je ceignis;** *fu.* **je ceindrai**) *Lit:* **1.** to gird; (*a*) **c. une épée,** to gird on, buckle on, a sword; **c. l'écharpe municipale,** to put on, assume, one's sash of office; **c. la couronne,** to put on, assume, the crown; (*b*) **c. qch. à qn,** to gird sth. on s.o.; (*c*) **c. qn de qch.,** to gird, encircle, s.o. with sth.; **se c. les reins, c. ses reins,** to gird up one's loins. **2.** (*of a wreath, etc.*) to encircle (s.o.'s head, etc.); **tête ceinte d'une couronne de lauriers,** head wreathed with laurels. **3. c. une ville de murailles,** to encompass, encircle, surround, a town with walls.

ceinte [sɛ̃ːt], *s.f. N.Arch:* (= PRÉCEINTE) wale, bend.

ceintrage [sɛ̃traːʒ], *s.m.* **1.** *Nau: A:* swifting, frapping (of ship at sea). **2.** = CINTRAGE.

ceintre [sɛ̃ːtr̥], *s.m.* **1.** *Nau:* swifter (of launch). **2.** *Arch:* = CINTRE 2.

ceintrer [sɛ̃tre], *v.tr.* **1.** *Nau: A:* to frap, swift (vessel). **2.** = CINTRER.

ceinturage [sɛ̃tyraːʒ], *s.m.* **1.** banding (of shell, etc.). **2.** ringing (of trees for felling).

ceinture [sɛ̃tyːr], *s.f.* **1.** (*a*) girdle (leather, etc.) belt; waistband (of skirt, trousers); **c. (-écharpe),** silk sash; **c. de grossesse,** maternity corset; *Med:* **c. orthopédique,** surgical corset, belt; *A:* **c. de flanelle,** colic-, cholera-belt; *A:* **c. de chasteté,** chastity belt; **c. de sauvetage,** lifebelt; *Fb: etc:* **c. protectrice abdominale,** abdominal guard; **c. de parachute,** parachute harness; *Aut: Av:* **c. de sécurité,** seat belt, safety belt; *F:* **se serrer, se boucler, se mettre, la c., faire c.,** to tighten one's belt; to go without (sth.); *P:* **tu peux te mettre la c., mon vieux!** you've had it, chum! *P:* **je peux me mettre la c. pour la Légion d'Honneur,** I can say goodbye to the Legion of Honour; **être toujours pendu à la c. de qn,** to be always dogging s.o.'s footsteps, to be always on s.o.'s heels; **il ne vous arrive pas à la c.,** (i) he's not nearly as tall as you (are); (ii) he can't hold a candle to you; (*Judo*) **la c. blanche, marron, noire,** the white, brown, black, belt; (*b*) waist, middle (of the body); **coup au-dessous de la c.,** blow below the belt; *P:* **s'en mettre plein la c.,** to stuff oneself, to tuck in, to have a good blow-out; *P:* **femme grosse à pleine c.,** woman in an advanced stage of pregnancy; (*c*) *Algae:* **c. de Neptune,** tangle; (*d*) *Ich:* **c. d'argent,** hair-tail, trichiurid, cutlass fish, *U.S:* silver eel; (*e*) *Med: F:* shingles; (*f*) *Wr:* hold round the waist; **c. de devant,** Cornish hug; (*g*) *Anat:* **c. pelvienne,** pelvic girdle; **c. scapulaire,** pectoral, scapular, arch, girdle. **2.** enclosure; circle (of walls); belt (of hills); *Adm:* **c. de verdure,** green belt; *Fort:* **c. d'ouvrages,** ring of forts, of works. **3.** *Arch:* cincture (of column). **4.** *Artil:* **c. d'obus, de forcement,** driving band (of shell); **c. de bouche de canon,** muzzle ring. **5.** *Nau:* rubbing strake, swifter; **c. de hamac,** hammock girtline. **6.** *N.Arch:* (*a*) armour belt; (*b*) **c. de cloison,** bulk-head stringer; (*c*) **c. d'accostage,** fender. **7.** (*a*) *Rail:* **chemin de fer de c.,** (railway) line encircling a town; **la grande, la petite, C.,** lines encircling Paris outside and inside the former fortifications; (*b*) **route de c.,** orbital road, ring road.

ceinturer [sɛ̃tyre], *v.tr.* **1.** to girdle, surround; **c. un enfant,** to put a belt on a child; **ville ceinturée de murs,** town surrounded, girdled, with walls. **2.** *Wr:* to grip round the waist; *Rugby Fb:* **c. un joueur,** to tackle a player, to collar a player low.

ceinturier [sɛ̃tyrje], *s.m.* = CEINTURONNIER.

ceinturon [sɛ̃tyrɔ̃], *s.m. Mil:* belt, sword-belt; **c.-baudrier d'officier** = Sam Browne (belt).

ceinturonnier [sɛ̃tyrɔnje], *s.m.* belt-maker.

cel [sɛl], *s.m. Jur:* concealment (of chattels).

cela [səla, sla], *F:* **ça** [sa] (*occ. before* **avoir, ç'**), *dem. pron. neut.* (*a*) that (thing, fact, etc.); **et c. d'une façon telle que . . .,** and this in such a way that . . .; **qu'est-ce que c'est que c.,** *F:* **que ça?** what's that? **il y a deux ans de c.,** that was two years ago; **c'est pour c. que je viens,** that is what I have come for, why I have come; **il ne manquait plus que ça!** that's the last straw! **sans c. je ne serais pas venu,** but for that, otherwise, I should not have come; **à c. près nous sommes d'accord,** we are agreed, with that one exception, except on that point; **s'il n'y a que c. de nouveau,** if that is all that is new; **vous n'emportez que ça de bagages?** is that all the luggage you're taking? (*b*) that, it (**cela** *is the pron. used as neut. subject to all verbs other than* **être,** *and may be used with* **être** *as more emphatic than* **ce**); **c. ne vous regarde pas,** that, it, is no business of yours; **c. ne se paye pas,** it is invaluable, money cannot buy it; **la voir si malheureuse, c. m'est pénible,** to see her so unhappy is very painful to me; **tout c. coûte très cher,** all that is very expensive; **ça y est!** that's that! that's it! (*c*) *F:* (*disparagingly of people and things*) **c'est ça les hommes!** that's what men are like! **c'est ça ta voiture?** is that your car? **les femmes, il faut que ça jase!** women will chatter! **ça arrive en retard et ça veut qu'on l'attende,** she, he, comes late, and then expects me, us, to wait for her, him; (*d*) *F:* **ceci . . . cela; il m'a dit ceci et c.,** he told me this, that and the other; **c'est ceci, c'est c.,** it's first one thing, then another, it's one thing after another; **comment allez-vous?—comme (ci comme) ça,** how are you?—so-so, middling; (*e*) (*idiomatic uses*) **ça alors!** you don't say! well I'm damned! *P:* cor! **c'est ça!** that's it! that's right! **ce n'est pas ça!** that's not it! that's not right! **c'est comme ça!** that's how it is! that's how things are! **ce n'est plus c.,** it's no longer what it was, no longer the same thing; **c'est c. même!** the very thing! **n'est-ce que c.?** is that all? **il n'y a que c. pour me tenir éveillé,** it's the only thing that will keep me awake; **par c. même . . ., pour c. même . . .,** for that very reason . . .; **ah, pour cela, oui!** yes, indeed! yes, of course! **il y a trop de grands immeubles dans la ville, mais nous ne nous arrêterons pas de construire pour c.,** there are too many large blocks of flats in the town, but we shall not stop building on that account, because of that; *P:* **avec ça!** tell that to the marines! get along with you! **et avec c.,** and besides all that; *Com:* **et avec c., madame?** anything else, madam? **après c.,** next, after that; **après c. il a peut-être raison,** after all he may be right; **une petite femme haute comme ça,** a little woman no taller than that, only so high (*indication of height shown by gesture*); **un poisson long comme ça,** a fish so long (*span shown by two hands*); **je suis comme ça,** that's how I am, I'm like that; **il est comme ça,** he's like that; **comme ça vous déménagez?** so you are moving, are you? *P:* **il a dit comme ça qu'il regrettait bien,** he said he was very sorry; *F:* **il a de ça,** he's got what it takes (*intelligence, money, grit, etc.*); *P:* **elle a de ça,** she's got *it,* what it takes; *F:* **allons, pas de ça!** hey! none of that! **ce n'est pas si facile que ça,** it isn't as easy as all that; **ce n'est pas si difficile que ça,** it isn't so very difficult; **je n'en suis pas si sûr que ça,** I'm not as sure as all that; **et nos invités avec tout ça?** and what about our guests? **et où est-ce que nous déjeunerons avec tout ça?** that's all very well, but where are we going to (have) lunch? (*f*) (*added to an interrogative, etc., to give it more "body"*) **je l'ai vu hier—où ça?** I saw him yesterday—where? *F:* **on m'a flanqué à la porte—comment ça?** I've been sacked—how so? how come? **ça oui!** yes indeed! **ça non!** no indeed! never!

céladon [seladɔ̃], *s.m.* **1.** *A: Lit:* sentimental lover; (*from* Céladon, *the shepherd in L'Astrée, by* Honoré d'Urfé.) **2.** *s.m. & a.inv.,* willow-green.

céladonique [seladɔnik], *a. Lit:* sentimental; platonic; lackadaisical.

céladonisme [seladɔnism], *s.m. Lit:* affected sentimentality.

céladonite [seladɔnit], *s.f. Miner:* celadonite.

célan [selɑ̃], *s.m. Ich:* pilchard.

célastracées [selastrase], *s.f.pl. Bot:* Celastraceae.

célastre [selastr̥], *s.m.,* **celastrus** [selastrys], *s.m. Bot:* celastrus; **c. grimpant,** climbing bitter-sweet; waxwork.

célation [selasjɔ̃], *s.f. Jur:* concealment (of birth, etc.).

célébéen, -enne [selebeɛ̃, -ɛn], *a. & s. Geog:* Celebesian.

Célèbes [selɛb], *Pr.n.f. Geog:* **L'île de C.,** the island of Celebes.

célébrant [selebrɑ̃], *a. & s.m. Ecc:* celebrant.

célébrateur [selebratœːr], *s.m. A:* celebrator (**de,** of).

célébration [selebrasjɔ̃], *s.f.* celebration.

célèbre [selɛbr̥], *a.* celebrated, famous; **c. par ses vertus,** famous for his virtues; **devenir c. du jour au lendemain,** to become famous overnight; **un certain Charles Dickens, mais non pas le c. Charles Dickens,** a certain Charles Dickens—not *the* Charles Dickens; **il est c. pour ses erreurs,** he is famous for his errors.

célébrer [selebre], *v.tr.* (**je célèbre, n. célébrons; je célébrerai**) **1.** to celebrate, (i) to solemnize (rite); (ii) to observe, keep (feast); **c. la messe,** to celebrate mass; **c. des funérailles,** to hold a funeral; **c. un concile,** to hold a council. **2.** to extol (s.o.); **c. les louanges de qn,** to sing s.o.'s praises.

célébrité [selebrite], *s.f.* **1.** celebrity; (*a*) renown, fame; (*b*) celebrated person. **2.** *A:* pomp, ceremony.

celer [səle], *v.tr.* (**je cèle, n. celons; je cèlerai**) *Lit:* to conceal, keep secret; **c. qch. à qn,** to hide sth. from s.o.; *A:* **se faire c.,** to refuse to see visitors.

se celer, *Lit:* to hide.

célérette [selerɛt], *s.f. A:* hobby-horse.

céleri [selri, -sɛ], *s.m.* celery; **pied de c.,** head of celery; **morceau de c., branche de c.,** stick of celery.

célérifère [selerifɛːr], *s.m. A:* celeripede.

célerin [selrɛ̃; sɛ-], *s.m. Ich:* pilchard.

céleri-rave [selrirav; sɛ-], *s.m. Hort:* celeriac; *pl. céleris-raves.*

célérité [selerite], *s.f.* (*a*) speed, rapidity, *Lit:* celerity, dispatch; **avec une étonnante c.,** with astonishing speed, at an astonishing rate; **cette affaire demande de la c.,** this matter demands immediate action; (*b*) *Ph:* velocity of propagation (of a sound wave, etc.); *Ch:* speed (of a reaction).

célesta [selɛsta], *s.m. Mus:* celesta.

céleste [selɛst, sɛ-], *a.* **1.** celestial, heavenly; *Lit:* **la voûte c.,** the vault of heaven; **bleu c.,** sky blue; **don c.,** divine gift, gift from heaven; **le royaume c.,** the heavenly kingdom; *Organ:* **voix c.,** vox angelica (stop); *s.a.* EAU 3. **2.** *A:* (*a*) **le C. Empire,** the Celestial Empire; (*b*) *s.* Celestial, Chinaman.

célestement [selɛstmɑ̃, sɛ-], *adv. Lit:* celestially.

Célestin[1], **-ine**[1] [selɛstɛ̃, -in; sɛ-]. **1.** *Pr.n.* Celestine. **2.** *s. Ecc:* Celestine (monk, nun).

célestin[2], *s.m.,* **célestine,**[2] *s.f. Miner:* celestine.

céliaque [seljak], *a.* = CŒLIAQUE.

célibat [seliba], *s.m.* (*a*) celibacy, single life; (*b*) abstinence from marital intercourse.

célibataire [selibatɛːr], *a. & s.* unmarried, single, celibate (man, woman); *s.m.* bachelor; *s.f.* spinster; **c'est un c. endurci,** he's a confirmed bachelor; *s.a.* FEMME 1.

célimène [selimɛn], *s.f. Lit:* (witty but heartless) coquette; flirt, jilt. (*From the character of that name in* Molière's *Le Misanthrope*).

cella [sɛ(l)la], *s.f. Arch:* cella.

celle, celle-ci, celle-là, *pron. See* CELUI.

cellepora [sɛlɔpɔra], *s.f. Biol:* Cellepora.

cellérier, -ière [sɛlerje, -jɛːr], *s. Ecc:* cellarer; *f.* cellaress.

cellier [sɛlje], *s.m.* storeroom (for wine, etc.); store-cupboard (on ground floor); stillroom.

cellite [sɛl(l)it], *s.f. Ch: Cin:* cellulose acetate.

cellobiose [sɛlɔbjoːz], *s.f. Ch:* cellobiose.

celloïdin, -ine [sɛl(l)oidɛ̃, -in]. **1.** *a. Phot:* collodion-coated. **2.** *s.f.* **celloïdine,** celloidin; *A:* **papier c., à la celloïdine,** collodion-coated P.O.P.

Cellophane [sɛlɔfan], *s.f. Com: R.t.m:* Cellophane.

cellulaire [sɛlylɛːr], *a.* **1.** cellular (tissue, girder, etc.); *Av: O:* **gouvernail c.,** box-tail. **2.** *Adm:* **voiture c.,** police-van, *F:* Black Maria; **emprisonnement c., prison c.,** solitary confinement.

cellular [sɛlylaːr], *s.m. Tex:* cellular linen.

cellule [sɛlyl], *s.f.* **1.** (*a*) cell (of prison, convent, honeycomb, etc.); *Mil:* **dix jours de c.,** ten days' confinement in the cells; *F:* ten days' cells; (*b*) *F:* den. **2.** *Biol:* cell; **lignée de cellules,** cellular line. **3.** *Av:* airframe, (aircraft) structure. **4. c. photoélectrique,** photoelectric cell; photo-cell, -tube, -valve; *T.V:* electric eye; **c. de filtrage,** filter-cell; filter section; *El:* **c. de couplage,** coupling stage (of transmitter).

cellulé [sɛlyle], *a.* **1.** *Biol:* cellulate(d), celled, cellate(d). **2.** imprisoned in a cell, celled.

celluleux, -euse [sɛlylø, -øːz], *a. Nat.Hist:* cellate(d), cell(at)ed; cellulous.

celluliforme [sɛlylifɔrm], *a.* celliform.

cellulifuge [sɛlylifyʒ], *a. Physiol:* cellulifugal.

cellulipète [sɛlylipɛt], *a. Physiol:* cellulipetal.

cellulite [sɛlylit], *s.f. Med:* cellulitis.

celluloïd [sɛlylɔid], *s.m. Ind:* celluloid.

cellulose [sɛlyloːz], *s.f. Ch: Com:* cellulose.

cellulosique [sɛlylozik], *a.* cellulose; **vernis c.,** cellulose varnish.

cellulosité [sɛlylozite], *s.f.* cellulosity.

célosie [selɔzi], *s.f. Bot:* celosia; **c. à crête,** cockscomb.

Célotex [sɛlɔteks], *s.m. R.t.m:* Celotex.

celsia [sɛlsja], *s.m. Bot:* celsia.

celsiane [sɛlsjan], *s.f. Miner:* celsian.

celte [sɛlt]. **1.** *Ling: etc: a. & s.m.* = CELTIQUE. **2.** *Ethn: s.m. & f.* Celt.

celt(o)-[sɛlt(ə)], *pref.* celt(o)-; **celticisme,** Celticism; **celtomanie,** Celtomania; **celtophile,** Celtophil.

Celtibères [sɛltibɛːr], *s.m.pl. Hist:* Celtiberi.

Celtibérie [sɛltiberi], *Pr.n.f. A.Geog:* Celtiberia.

celtibérien, -ienne [sɛltiberjɛ̃, -jɛn], *a.* Celtiberian.

celtique [sɛltik]. **1.** *a.* Celtic. **2.** *s.m.* Celtic (language).

celtisant [sɛltizɑ̃], *s.m.,* **celtiste** [sɛltist], *s.m.* celtist, celtologist, Celtic scholar.

celtium [sɛltjɔm], *s.m. Miner:* celtium.

celtomanie [sɛltɔmani], *s.f.* celtomania.

celui [səlɥi], **celle** [sɛl], *pl.* **ceux** [sø], **celles** [sɛl], *dem.pron.* **1.** (*completed by an adj. clause*) the one, *pl.* those; he, she, *pl.* those; **c. qui était parti le dernier arriva le premier,** the one who started last arrived first; **c. qui mange peu dort bien,** he who eats little sleeps well; *F:* **elle faisait celle qui ne sait rien,** she pretended to know nothing; **celui dont j'ai parlé,** the one, the man, I spoke about; **celle à qui j'ai écrit,** the one, the woman, I wrote to, to whom I wrote; **c. de ces livres que je déteste le moins,** the book out of these (that) I dislike the least; **est-ce que tu as déjà entendu celle du chien qui entre dans un bar . . .?** have you heard the one about the dog which goes into a pub . . .? **2.** (*completed by a sb. adv., inf. governed by* de) **mes livres et ceux de Jean,** my books and John's; **s'il nous faut une ambition, ayons celle de faire le bien,** if we must have an ambition, let it be that of doing good, let it be to do good; **les hommes d'aujourd'hui et ceux d'autrefois,** the men of today and those of former times; **il néglige ses affaires pour s'occuper de celles des autres,** he neglects his own business to look after other people's; **les maisons de briques et celles de bois,** brick houses and wooden ones. **3.** (*completed by an adj. equivalent, not introduced by* de) **les rails en acier et ceux en fer,** steel rails and iron ones; **entre ma chaise et celle occupée par la jeune fille il y avait malheureusement dix places,** there were unfortunately ten seats between mine and the one occupied by the girl, the one in which the girl was sitting; **tous ceux ayant la même idée,** all those with the same idea; **tous ceux porteurs d'arme à feu,** all those carrying fire-arms; **les lettres distribuées et celles à expédier,** the letters delivered and those to be dispatched; **toutes les maisons sont en bois sauf celles voisines de l'église,** all the houses are built of wood except those near the church. **4.** (*completed by* -ci, -là) (*a*) **celui-ci, ceux-ci,** this (one), these; **celui-là, ceux-là,** that (one), those; **ceux-ci coûtent plus cher que ceux-là,** these cost more that those; **ah, celui-là! quel idiot!** oh him! that idiot! **autre exemple, plus technique c.-là . . .,** another example, a more technical one this time; (*b*) **celui (ceux) -ci . . ., celui (ceux) -là . . .,** the latter . . ., the former . . . **5. celui-là** *is used for* CELUI 1, *when the rel. pron. does not follow at once;* **celui-là est heureux qui . . .,** he is happy who . . ., happy the man who . . ..

cembro [sɛ̃bro], *s.m. Bot:* cembra pine, stone pine.

cément [semɑ̃], *s.m.* **1.** *Anat:* cement (of tooth, fang). **2.** *Metall: Cer:* cement, cementation powder, powdered carbon.

cémentation [semɑ̃tasjɔ̃], *s.f. Metall:* cementation, case-hardening.

cémentatoire [semɑ̃tatwaːr], *a. Metall:* cementatory.

cémenter [semɑ̃te], *v.tr. Metall:* to case-harden, face-harden (steel); to cement (armour-plate).

cémenteux, -euse [semɑ̃tø, -øːz], *a.* cemental.

cémentite [semɑ̃tit], *s.f. Metall:* cementite.

cémentoblaste [semɑ̃tɔblast], *s.m. Anat:* cementoblast.

cénacle [senakl̥], *s.m.* **1.** *Ant:* cenacle; dining, supping room; *esp. B:* upper room (of the Last Supper). **2. c. littéraire,** literary club, group, coterie.

cendre [sɑ̃ːdr̥], *s.f.* (*a*) ash(es), cinders; *in pl.* **cendres,** (mortal) remains, ashes; **fosse aux cendres,** ash-pit; **laisser tomber de la c. sur son pantalon,** to drop (cigarette) ash on one's trousers; **mettre, réduire, une ville en cendres,** to reduce a town to ashes; *Lit:* **les cendres d'une passion mourante,** the embers of a dying passion; **tisonner les cendres du passé,** to rake over the ashes of the past; **le mercredi des Cendres,** Ash-Wednesday; **son visage devint couleur de cendre,** his face turned ashen; *Lit:* **troubler la c. des morts,** to speak ill of the dead; *s.a.* SAC[1] 2, (*b*) *Miner:* **c. verte,** (green) malachite; **c. bleue (native),** azurite; **c. noire,** lignite; *Geol:* **cendres volcaniques,** volcanic ash.

cendré [sɑ̃dre], *a.* ash-grey, ashy; *Anat:* **substance cendrée du cerveau,** grey matter of the brain; *s.a.* BLOND 3, LUMIÈRE 1, VERT 1.

cendrée [sɑ̃dre], *s.f.* **1.** (*a*) *Ch:* lead ashes; (*b*) *Sp:* cinders (for track, etc.); **piste en c.,** (i) cinder-track; (ii) dirt-track; **course sur c.,** cinder-track race; **moto sur c.,** dirt-track racing; (*c*) *Constr:* **brique de c.,** breeze block. **2.** *Ven:* dust-shot, *U.S:* mustard-seed.

cendrer [sɑ̃dre], *v.tr.* **1.** to colour (wall, etc.) ash-grey. **2.** *Metall:* to ash (mould). **3.** to cinder (path, track).

cendreux, -euse [sɑ̃drø, -øːz], *a.* **1.** ashy, ash-grey. **2.** full of ashes; gritty; soiled with ashes; *Metall:* **acier c.,** flawy, brittle, steel.

cendrier [sɑ̃drije], *s.m.* (*a*) ash-pan (of stove); ash-pit, ash-hole (of furnace); ash-box (of locomotive); (*b*) ashtray.

cendrière [sɑ̃drijɛːr], *s.f.* (*a*) peat; (*b*) field of peat or lignite.

Cendrillon [sɑ̃drijɔ̃]. **1.** *Pr.n.f.* Cinderella. **2.** *s.f. F:* (*a*) (household) drudge, slavey; (*b*) stay-at-home; (*c*) slut.

cendrure [sɑ̃dryːr], *s.f.* ash-spot (in iron, steel).

cène [sɛn], *s.f.* (*a*) **La (Sainte) C.,** the Last Supper; (*b*) *Ecc:* (*in Protestant Church*) Holy Communion, the Lord's Supper; **faire la C.,** to take Communion.

cenelle [sənɛl], *s.f. Bot:* haw (of hawthorn).

cenellier [sənɛlje], *s.m. Fr.C: Bot:* hawthorn.

cénesthésie [senɛstezi], *s.f. Physiol:* cœn(a)esthesis.

cénesthésique [senɛstezik], *a.* cœn(a)esthetic.

cénobite [senɔbit], *s.m.* (*a*) c(o)enobite (monk); (*b*) ascetic.

cénobitique [senɔbitik], *a.* c(o)enobitic, monastic; austere (life).

cénobitisme [senɔbitism], *s.m. Ecc.Hist:* c(o)enobitism.

cénogénèse [senɔʒenɛːz], *s.f. Biol:* cenogenesis, kenogenesis.

cénomanien [senɔmanjɛ̃], *a. & s.m. Geol:* cenomanian.

cénosite [senɔzit], *s.f. Miner:* cenosite.

cénotaphe [senɔtaf], *s.m.* cenotaph.

cénotoxine [senɔtɔksin], *s.f. Physiol:* kenotoxin.

cénozoïque [senɔzɔik], *a. & s.m. Geol:* cenozoic.

cens [sɑ̃ːs], *s.m. Hist:* **1.** *Rom.Ant:* census. **2.** *Jur:* (*a*) *Feudal:* (quit-)rent; (*b*) *Adm:* quota (of taxes payable); rating; **c. électoral,** property qualification (for the franchise).

censé [sɑ̃se], *a.* considered, supposed, reputed; **il est c. juge infaillible,** he is reputed to be, regarded as, an infallible judge; **je ne suis pas c. le savoir,** I am not supposed to know; **il est c. être mort,** he is presumed to be dead; **nul n'est c. ignorer la loi,** ignorance of the law is no excuse; **tous les chemins sont censés mener à Rome,** all roads are assumed to lead to Rome; **il est c. faire de la peinture,** he is by way of being a painter.

censément [sɑ̃semɑ̃], *adv. F:* (i) supposedly; (ii) practically; **il est c. le maître,** (i) he is supposed to be the master; (ii) to all intents and purposes he is the master; **il sortit c. pour s'acheter du tabac,** he went out ostensibly to buy tobacco.

censeur [sɑ̃sœːr], *s.m.* **1.** *Rom.Ant:* censor. **2.** censor, censurer, critic, fault-finder; *Lit:* **de téméraires censeurs des conseils de Dieu,** rash censurers of the counsels of God; *a.* **esprit c.,** carping spirit. **3.** (*a*) *Adm: Mil:* censor; (*b*) *Fin:* auditor. **4.** *Sch:* vice-principal (of *lycée*).

censitaire [sɑ̃sitɛːr], *s.m.* **1.** *A:* copyholder (of land). **2.** *a. & s.m. Hist:* **(électeur) c.,** elector qualified by property, by his assessment.

censive [sɑ̃siːv], *s.f. Mediev: Jur:* sort of fief, manor.

censorat [sɑ̃sɔra], *s.m.* **1.** censorship. **2.** (*a*) vice-principalship (of *lycée*); (*b*) term of office as vice-principal.

censorial, -iaux [sɑ̃sɔrjal, -jo], *a.* censorial.

censuel, -elle [sɑ̃sɥɛl], *a.* **1.** *A: Adm:* relating to money qualification for franchise, relating to rating. **2.** *A:* copyhold (tenure).

censurable [sɑ̃syrabl̥], *a.* censurable, open to censure.

censure [sɑ̃syːr], *s.f.* **1.** (*a*) *Rom.Ant:* censorship; (*b*) censorship (of the press, etc.); (*c*) *Cin: etc:* board of censors; (*d*) *Com: Fin:* audit (of accounts); (*e*) *Psy:* (the) censor. **2.** censure, blame; reprehension, condemnation; **motion de c.,** vote of censure; **encourir les censures de l'Église,** to incur the censure of the Church.

censurer [sɑ̃syre], *v.tr.* (*a*) to censure, find fault with, criticize (s.o., sth.); to pass a vote of censure on (s.o.); (*b*) to censor (film).

cent[1] [sɑ̃]. **1.** (*a*) *num.a.* (*takes a plural* s *when multiplied by a preceding numeral but not followed by another numeral. Does not vary when used with ordinal function.*) (A, one) hundred; **deux cents hommes,** two hundred men; **deux cent cinquante hommes,** two hundred and fifty men; **la page deux cent,** page two hundred; **l'an trois cent,** the year three hundred; **cent un** [sɑ̃ œ̃], one hundred and one; **je vous l'ai dit c. fois,** I have told you (so) a hundred times, again and again; **vous avez c. fois raison,** you are absolutely right; **déjà elle se sentait c. fois mieux,** *F:* she felt a hundred times better already; *F:* **je ne vais pas t'attendre (pendant) c. sept ans,** I'm not going to wait for you for ever; **faire les c. pas,** to pace up and down; *F:* **faire les quatre cents coups,** (i) to kick up no end of a racket, of a shindy; (ii) to paint the town red; (iii) to be up to all sorts of tricks; *F:* **être aux c. coups,** to be in desperation; *F:* **mettre qn aux c. coups,** to drive s.o. to distraction; *F:* **mettre une maison aux c. coups,** to throw a house into utter confusion; **il y en avait c. sans compter le premier,** if there was one there were a hundred; **il est à c. pieds au-dessus des autres,** he is far and away above the rest; *F:* **je vous le donne en c.,** I'll give you a hundred guesses; *F:* (*in hotels*) **le numéro c.,** the w.c.; (*b*) *s.m.inv.* a hundred; **sept pour c. d'intérêt,** seven per cent interest; *Bill: etc:* **partie en c.,** game of a hundred up; *F:* **il y a c. à parier contre un que . . .,** it's a hundred to one that . . .; *Ch:* **solution à trente pour c.,** thirty per cent solution; *adv.phr.* **c. pour c.,** a hundred per cent. **2.** *s.m.var.* **un c. d'œufs,** a hundred eggs; **le grand c.,** the great hundred, long hundred; *A:* **un c. pesant,** a hundredweight; *F:* **il a des mille et des cents,** he has pots of money; *Sp:* **le c. mètres,** the hundred metre race, the hundred metres.

cent[2] [sɛn(t)], *s.m. esp. Fr.C:* (*coin*) cent.

centaine [sɑ̃tɛn], *s.f.* **1.** (approximate) hundred; **une c. de francs,** about a hundred francs, a hundred francs or so; **quelques centaines de francs,** a few hundred francs; **atteindre la c.,** to live to be a hundred; **des prisonniers par centaines de mille,** hundreds of thousands of prisoners; **les gens moururent par centaines, par centaines de mille,** people died in hundreds, in thousands. **2.** tie, end of thread which binds a skein. **3.** *Hist:* (*Frankish Kingdom*) centenary.

centaure [sɑ̃tɔːr], *s.m.* **1.** *Myth:* centaur. **2.** *Astr:* Centaurus.

centaurée [sɑ̃tɔre], *s.f. Bot:* **1.** centaurea, centaury; **grande c.,** great centaury; **c. noire,** knapweed; **c. bleuet,** blue bottle, cornflower; **c. musquée** (purple, yellow) sweet sultan. **2. petite c.,** lesser centaury, erythraea, gall of the earth; **c. du solstice,** Barnaby's thistle.

centauresse [sɑ̃tɔrɛs], *s.f. Myth:* centauress.

centauromachie [sɑ̃tɔrɔmaʃi], *s.f. Myth:* centauromachy.

centavo [sɛntavo], *s.m. Num:* centavo.

centenaire [sɑ̃tnɛːr]. **1.** *a.* of a hundred years' standing; age-old; **chêne c.,** ancient oak; **plusieurs fois c.,** hundreds of years old. **2.** *s.m. & f.* centenarian. **3.** *s.m.* centenary (anniversary).

centenier [sɑ̃tənje], *s.m.* **1.** *Rom.Hist:* centurion. **2.** *Hist:* (*Frankish Kingdom*) centenar.
centenille [sɑ̃tniːj], *s.f. Bot:* bastard pimpernel, chaff-weed.
centennal, -aux [sɑ̃tɛn(n)al, -o], *a.* centennial (celebration, etc.).
centésimal, -aux [sɑ̃tezimal, -o], *a.* centesimal (fraction, scale, etc.); **composition centésimale d'un produit,** composition of a product expressed in percentages.
centésime [sɑ̃tezim], *s.m. Fin:* interest of one per cent per month.
centète [sɑ̃tɛt], *s.m. Z:* centetid.
centétidés [sɑ̃tetide], *s.m.pl. Z:* Centetidae.
cent-garde [sɑ̃gard], *s.m. Hist:* member of Napoleon III's household cavalry; **les cent-gardes,** the household cavalry.
centi- [sɑ̃ti], *pref.* centi-.
centiare [sɑ̃tjaːr], *s.m. Meas:* centiare (one sq. metre, or about 1¼ square yard).
centibar [sɑ̃tibaːr], *s.m. Meteor:* centibar.
centième [sɑ̃tjɛm]. **1.** *num. a. & s.* hundredth; **être le c. sur une liste,** to be placed (the) hundredth on a list; **c'est la c. fois que je vous le dis,** if I've told you once I've told you a hundred times. **2.** *s.m.* hundredth (part); **trois centièmes de la somme globale,** three hundredths ($\frac{3}{100}$), of the total sum; **sept trois-centièmes de la somme globale,** seven three-hundredths of the total sum; **je ne vous dis même pas le c. de ce qu'il m'a raconté,** I'm not telling you a fraction of what he told me. **3.** *s.f. Th:* hundredth performance.
centièmement [sɑ̃tjɛmmɑ̃], *adv.* in the hundredth place.
centigrade [sɑ̃tigrad], *s.m.* centigrade; *s.a.* THERMOMÈTRE.
centigramme [sɑ̃tigram], *s.m.* centigram(me).
centile [sɑ̃til], *s.m.* (*statistics*) centile.
centilitre [sɑ̃tilitṛ], *s.m.* centilitre.
centime [sɑ̃tim], *s.m.* (*a*) *Num:* centime; **ne pas avoir un c.,** to be hard up; **cela ne vaut pas un c.,** it's not worth anything, a cent; (*b*) *Adm:* **centimes additionnels,** special surtax.
centimètre [sɑ̃timɛtṛ], *s.m.* **1.** *Meas:* centimetre; **c. carré,** square centimetre; **c. cube,** cubic centimetre; *Mec:* **c.-gramme,** gramme-centimetre. **2.** tape-measure.
centinode [sɑ̃tinɔd], *s.f. Bot:* knotgrass, hogweed.
centinormal, -aux [sɑ̃tinɔrmal, -o], *a. Ch: etc:* centinormal.
centipoise [sɑ̃tipwaːz], *s.m. Meas:* centipoise.
Cent-Jours (les) [lesɑ̃ʒuːr], *s.m.pl. Fr.Hist:* The Hundred Days (March 20th to June 28th, 1815).
centon [sɑ̃tɔ̃], *s.m. Lit:* cento.
centrafricain [sɑ̃trafrikɛ̃], *a. & s. Geog:* Central African; **République centrafricaine,** Central African Republic.
centrage [sɑ̃traːʒ], *s.m.* centring, centering, adjusting (of work in lathe, etc.); *Aer:* trim; *Tchn:* concentricity; *Mec.E:* **à c. automatique,** self-centering; **assurer le parfait c. d'une roue,** to centre a wheel dead true; *Aut: Av:* **c. des disques de freins,** brake disc alignment.
central, -aux [sɑ̃tral, -o]. **1.** *a.* central; (*a*) middle (point, etc.); **quartier c. de la ville,** town centre; **Amérique centrale,** Central America; (*b*) principal. head (office. etc.); **maison, prison, centrale** = county gaol; **École centrale,** (university level) State school of engineering; **chauffage c.,** central heating; *Computers:* **unité centrale,** central processing unit, central processor, main frame. **2.** *s.m.* (*a*) *Tp:* **c. téléphonique,** telephone exchange; **c. automatique,** automatic exchange; **c. d'arrivée,** called exchange, *U.S:* terminating office; **chef de c.,** chief, head, supervisor; (*b*) **c. dactylographique,** typing pool; (*c*) *F:* student of the *École centrale.* **3.** *s.f.* **centrale (électrique),** power station, generating station; **c. hydraulique, thermique, atomique, nucléaire, marémotrice,** hydro-electric, thermal, atomic, nuclear, tidal, power station; **centrale de chauffage urbain,** central heating station (serving district of town); *Const:* **centrale à béton,** concrete batching and mixing plant; (*b*) **centrale** (**syndicale**), group of affiliated trade unions.
centralement [sɑ̃tralmɑ̃], *adv.* centrally; in the centre.
centralisateur, -trice [sɑ̃tralizatœːr, -tris]. **1.** *a.* centralizing (force, etc.). **2.** *s.* (*a*) centralizer; (*b*) *Pol:* centralist.
centralisation [sɑ̃tralizasjɔ̃], *s.f.* centralization, centralizing.
centraliser [sɑ̃tralize], *v.tr.* to centralize.
centralisme [sɑ̃tralism], *s.m. Pol:* centralism.
centraliste [sɑ̃tralist], *a. & s. Pol:* centralist.
centralité [sɑ̃tralite], *s.f. Physiol:* centricity, centrality; *Pol: etc:* centre of action (of a movement).
centranthe [sɑ̃trɑ̃ːt], *s.m.,* **centranthus** [sɑ̃trɑ̃tys], *s.m. Bot:* centranthus, valerian; **c. rouge,** red valerian.
centrarchidés [sɑ̃trarkide], *s.m.pl. Ich:* Centrarchidae.
centre [sɑ̃ːtṛ], *s.m.* **1.** (*a*) centre, central point; middle, midst; **c. politique,** political centre; **c. commercial,** (i) business centre; (ii) shopping precinct, shopping centre; **c. industriel,** industrial centre; **c. civique, social,** civic, community, centre; **c. de villégiature,** holiday resort; **c. d'intérêt,** centre of interest; **il se croit le c. de l'univers,** he thinks that the world revolves round him; *Sch:* **c. d'études secondaires** = comprehensive school; **vocabulaire arrangé par centres d'intérêt,** classified vocabulary; *Rail:* **c. de triage,** shunting yard; *Pol:* **les membres du C.,** the centre; **le c. droit, gauche,** the centre right, left; *Computers:* **c. de calcul,** data (processing) centre; (*b*) *Fb: etc:* (i) centre (player); (ii) centre (pass). **2.** *Mec: etc:* **c. d'un levier,** fulcrum of a lever; **c. des masses centrifuges ou excentriques,** centre of gyration; **c. de gravité,** centre of gravity; *Ph:* **c. d'attraction, de gravitation,** centre of attraction; *Anat: Opt:* **c. optique,** optical centre; *Meteor:* **c. d'action,** centre of action; **c. de dépression,** storm centre. **3.** *Geol:* centrum (of an earthquake).
centre-africain [sɑ̃trafrikɛ̃], *a.* = CENTRAFRICAIN.
centrer [sɑ̃tre], *v.tr.* (*a*) to centre, adjust (wheel, tool, lens, etc.); **photo mal centrée,** badly centred photograph; (*b*) to centre (**sur,** on); **c. l'attention du lecteur sur qch.,** to focus the reader's attention on sth.; **discussion centrée autour de . . .,** discussion centred round . . .; (*c*) *Fb: etc:* **c. le ballon,** to centre the ball.
centreur [sɑ̃trœːr], *s.m.* (*a*) *Tls:* centering tool; (i) centre punch; (ii) centre-finder; (*b*) *Rec:* adaptor (for 45 r.p.m. records).
centrifugation [sɑ̃trifygasjɔ̃], *s.f. Ind:* centrifugation, centrifuging; **bol de c.,** centrifugal bowl; *Metall:* **mouler, couler, par c.,** to cast centrifugally.
centrifuge [sɑ̃trifyːʒ], *a.* centrifugal (force, etc., *Bot:* inflorescence); **essoreuse c.,** spin dryer; *s.a.* TURBINE 1.
centrifugé [sɑ̃trifyʒe], *a.* centrifugal (cream, etc.).
centrifuger [sɑ̃trifyʒe], *v.tr. Ind:* to centrifuge (liquid); to separate (cream).
centrifugeur [sɑ̃trifyʒœːr], *s.m.,* **centrifugeuse** [sɑ̃trifyʒøːz], *s.f.* centrifugal machine; centrifuge; (cream) separator; **c. d'huile,** lubricating oil purifier.
centriole [sɑ̃triɔl], *s.m. Biol:* centriole.
centripète [sɑ̃tripɛt], *a.* centripetal (force; *Bot:* inflorescence); *s.a.* TURBINE 1.
centrisque [sɑ̃trisk], *s.m. Ich:* centriscus, trumpet-fish.
centriste [sɑ̃trist], *Pol:* **1.** *a.* (of the) centre. **2.** *s.m. & f.* member of the centre (group), centrist; les **centristes,** the centre.
centro- [sɑ̃tro], *pref.* centro-.
centrocerque [sɑ̃trosɛrk], *s.m. Orn:* centrocercus; **c. des montagnes Rocheuses,** sage-cock, -grouse.
centrolécithe [sɑ̃trolesit], *a. Biol:* centrolecithal.
centronote [sɑ̃tronɔt], *s.m. Ich:* butterfly blenny.
centrosome [sɑ̃trozɔm], *s.m. Biol:* centrosome.
centrosphere [sɑ̃trosfɛːr], *s.f.* centrosphere.
centrote [sɑ̃trɔt], *s.m. Ent:* centrotus.
cent-Suisse [sɑ̃sɥis], *s.m. Fr.Mil.Hist:* member of the Swiss Guards; **les cent-Suisses,** the Swiss Guards.
centumvir [sɛ̃tɔmviːr-sɑ̃-], *s.m. Rom.Ant:* centumvir.
centunculus [sɑ̃tɔ̃kylys], *s.m. Bot:* centunculus.
centuple [sɑ̃typḷ], *a. & s.m.* centuple, centuplicate, hundredfold; **être payé au c.,** to be repaid a hundredfold; **mille est (le) c. de dix,** a thousand is a hundred times as much as ten.
centupler [sɑ̃typle], *v.tr. & i.* to centuple, centuplicate; to increase a hundredfold.
centuriate [sɑ̃tyrjat], *a. Rom.Ant:* centuriate.
centuriation [sɑ̃tyrjasjɔ̃], *s.f. Rom.Ant:* centuriation.
centurie [sɑ̃tyri], *s.f.* **1.** *Rom.Ant:* century. **2.** *Rel: Hist:* **Centuries de Magdebourg,** the Magdebourg Centuries.
centurion [sɑ̃tyrjɔ̃], *s.m. Rom.Ant:* centurion.
cénure [senyːr], *s.m. Vet:* coenure, many-headed bladder-worm.
cep [sɛp], *s.m.* **1.** (*a*) *Hort:* **c. de vigne** [sɛdviɲ, sɛpdəviɲ], vinestock, -plant; (*b*) stem (of artificial flower). **2.** *Agr:* sole, slade (of plough). **3.** *pl.* **ceps;** *A:* (*a*) stocks, pillory; (*b*) fetters, shackles.
cépacé [sepase], *a.* cepaceous.
cépage [sepaːʒ], *s.m.* (*a*) vine-plant; (*b*) (variety of) vine.
cèpe [sɛp], *s.m. Fung:* boletus, cepe, *F:* penny bun (mushroom).
cépée [sepe], *s.f. For:* (*a*) clump of shoots (from stool of copse-wood); (*b*) young wood, coppice.
cependant [s(ə)pɑ̃dɑ̃]. **1.** *adv.* meanwhile, in the meantime. **2.** *conj.* yet, still, nevertheless, for all that; though. **3.** *conj.phr. Lit:* **c. que,** while, whilst.
céphalalgie [sefalalʒi], *s.f. Med:* cephalalgia.
céphalanthe [sefalɑ̃ːt], *s.m. Bot:* cephalanthus.
céphalaspis [sɛfalaspis], *s.m. Paleont:* cephalaspis.
céphalé [sefale], *a. Ent: Moll:* cephalate.
céphalée [sefale], *s.f. Med:* cephalalgia, headache.
céphalématome [sefalematɔm], *s.m. Med:* cephalhaematoma.
céphaline [sefalin], *s.f. Bio-Ch:* cephalin.
céphalique [sefalik], *a.* cephalic; *Biol:* **bouton c.,** acrosome.
céphalisation [sefalizasjɔ̃], *s.f.* cephalization.
céphalo- [sefalɔ], *pref.* cephalo-.
céphalocordés [sefalɔkɔrde], *s.m.pl. Z:* Cephalochorda(ta).
céphalogénèse [sefalɔgeneːz], *s.f.* cephalogenesis.
céphalographe [sefalɔgraf], *s.m. Anthr:* cephalograph.
céphaloïde [sefalɔid], *a. Nat.Hist:* cephaloid.
céphalomètre [sefalɔmɛtṛ], *s.m. Anthr:* cephalometer.
céphalométrie [sefalɔmetri], *s.f. Anthr:* cephalometry, craniometry.
céphalométrique [sefalɔmetrik], *a. Anthr:* cephalometric.
céphalon [sefalɔ̃], *s.m. Z:* cephalon.
Céphalonie [sefalɔni], *Pr.n.f. Geog:* Cephalonia.
céphalopage [sefalɔpaːʒ], *s.m. Ter:* cephalopagus.
céphalopagie [sefalɔpaʒi], *s.f. Ter:* cephalopagy.
céphalophe [sefalɔf], *s.m. Z:* cephalophus, duiker(bok); **c. à dos jaune,** yellow-backed duiker; **c. à front noir,** black-fronted duiker; **c. bleu,** blue duiker; **c. de Grimm,** Cape duiker, duikerbok.
céphalopode [sefalɔpɔd], *s.m. Moll:* cephalopod; *pl.* cephalopoda.
céphaloptère [sefalɔptɛːr], *s.m. Orn:* cephalopterus; umbrella-bird.
céphalo-rachidien, -ienne [sefaloraʃidjɛ̃, -jɛn], *a.* cephalo-r(h)achidian.
céphalo-spinal [sefalɔspinal], *a.* cephalo-spinal.
céphalosporium [sefalɔspɔrjɔm], *s.m. Fung:* cephalosporium.
céphalotaxus [sefalotaksys], *s.m. Bot:* cephalotaxus.
céphalote [sefalɔt], *s.m. Bot:* cephalotus.
céphalothorax [sefalɔtɔraks], *s.m. Ent:* cephalothorax.
céphalotribe [sefalɔtrib], *s.m. Obst:* cephalotribe.
céphalotroque [sefalɔtrɔk], *a.* **larve c.,** cephalotroca.
céphe [sɛf], *s.m. Ent:* cephid, cephus, sawfly.
céphéide [sefeid], *s.f. Astr:* Cepheid.
Céphise [sefiːz], *Pr.n.m. A.Geog:* (the river) Cephis(s)us.
Céphisodote [sefizɔdɔt], *Pr.n.m. Gr.Ant:* Cephisodotus.
cépole [sepɔl], *s.m. Ich:* cepola; red band-fish, snake-fish; ribbon-fish.
ceps [sɛp], *s.m.* = CÈPE.
céraiste [serest], *s.m. Bot:* cerastium; (mouse-ear) chickweed.
cérambycides [serɑ̃bisid], *s.m.pl. Ent:* cerambycids.
cérambycidés [serɑ̃biside], *s.m.pl. Ent:* Cerambycidae.
cérame [seram]. **1.** *s.m. Gr.Archeol:* earthenware vase. **2.** *a.* **grès c.,** stoneware.
céramique [seramik]. **1.** *a.* ceramic (arts, etc.); **industries céramiques,** pottery industry. **2.** *s.f.* (*a*) ceramics, (art of) pottery; (*b*) piece of pottery; (*c*) tiles; **salle de bains en c.,** tiled bathroom.
céramiste [seramist], *s.m.* ceramist.
céramium [seramjɔm], *s.m. Algae:* Ceramium, the rose tangles.
céramographie [seramɔgrafi], *s.f.* ceramography.
céramographique [seramɔgrafik], *a.* ceramographic.
cérargyre [serarʒiːr], *s.m.,* **cérargyrite** [serarʒirit], *s.f. Miner:* cerargyrite.

cérasine [serazin], *s.f. Ch:* cerasin.
céraste [serast], *s.m. Rept:* cerastes, horned viper.
cerastium [serastjɔm], *s.m. Bot:* cerastium.
cérat [sera], *s.m. Pharm:* cerate, ointment.
cératias [seratjas], *s.m. Ich:* ceratias.
cératides [seratid], **cératidés** [seratide], *s.m.pl. Ich:* Ceratiidae.
cératite [seratit], *s.m. Paleont:* ceratites.
ceratitis [seratitis], *s.f. Ent:* ceratitis.
cération [seratjɔ̃], *s.m.*, **ceratium** [seratjɔm], *s.m. Algae:* ceratium.
ceratocampides [seratɔkɑ̃pid], *s.m.pl. Ent:* Ceratocampidae.
ceratodus [seratodys], *s.m. Ich:* ceratodus.
cératoglosse [seratɔglɔs], *s.m. Anat:* ceratoglossus.
ceratonia [seratɔnja], *s.m. Bot:* ceratonia.
cératophyll(ac)ées [seratɔfil(as)e], *s.f.pl. Bot:* Ceratophyllaceae.
cératopsidés [seratɔpside], *s.m.pl. Paleont:* ceratopsidae.
cératosaure [seratɔzɔːr], *s.m.*, **ceratosaurus** [seratɔzɔrys], *s.m. Paleont:* Ceratosaurus.
ceratostomella [seratɔstɔmɛla], *s.m. Fung:* ceratostomella.
ceratozamia [seratɔzamja], *s.m. Bot:* ceratozamia.
céraunies [seroni], *s.f.pl.* ceraunia.
Cerbère [sɛrbɛːr]. **1.** *Pr.n.m. Myth:* Cerberus. **2.** *s.m. F:* ill-tempered hall porter, etc.; **c'est un vrai c.,** he's a regular old cross-patch.
cercaire [sɛrkɛːr], *s.f. Ann:* cercaria.
cerce [sɛrs], *s.f.* **1.** curved template (*esp.* in road-making). **2.** hoop, frame (of sieve, etc.); *Av: A:* hoop (of fuselage).
cerceau, -eaux [sɛrso], *s.m.* **1.** hoop; **c. de baril,** barrel hoop; **faire courir un c.,** to bowl, trundle, a hoop; *F:* **avoir le dos en c.,** to be round-backed. **2.** (*a*) half hoop, round-frame, bail (of cart-tilt); (*b*) cradle (over bed); (*c*) (type of) net to catch birds. **3.** *pl.* **cerceaux,** primaries (of bird of prey).
cercelle [sɛrsɛl], *s.f. Orn:* teal.
cerche [sɛrʃ], *s.f.* = CERCE 2.
cercis [sɛrsis], *s.m. Bot:* cercis; Judas-tree.
cerclage [sɛrklaːʒ], *s.m.* **1.** (*a*) hooping (of casks, etc.); (*b*) binding, tyring (of wheel). **2.** *Veh:* tyre (of wheel). **3.** *Surg:* wiring (of fractured bone).
cercle [sɛrkl̩], *s.m.* **1.** circle; (*a*) **faire c., former c.,** to lie, stand, in a circle, in a ring; **on fait c. autour d'elle,** she has her circle of admirers; **les avions décrivent des cercles au-dessus de nos têtes,** the planes circle overhead; **c. d'activités,** circle, sphere, range, of activities; *Log:* **c. vicieux,** vicious circle; **tourner dans un c. (vicieux),** to reason, argue, in a circle; *Geog:* **c. polaire,** polar circle; **c. (polaire) arctique,** Arctic Circle; *Geog:* **c. de feu (du Pacifique),** (Pacific) ring of fire; *Astr:* **c. de déclinaison,** declination circle; *Nav:* **(arc de) grand c.,** great circle; *Fb:* **c. d'envoi,** centre circle; *s.a.* ROUTE 2; (*b*) circle, set (of friends, etc.); **c. littéraire,** literary circle, society; (*c*) club; **c. militaire, des officiers,** officers' club; **aller au c.,** to go to the club. **2.** (*a*) (binding-)hoop, ring; **cercles d'un tonneau,** hoops of a cask; **vin en cercles,** wine in the wood; **c. d'une roue,** tyre of a wheel; *Mch:* **c. de piston, d'étoupe,** packing ring; *s.a.* PRIMITIF 1; (*b*) *Mus:* flesh-hoop (of drum); **grand c.,** snare-hoop. **3.** (*a*) dial, circle; *Artil:* **c. de pointage,** dial (of dial-sight); *Surv:* **c. de visée,** goniometer; *Mth:* **c. à calculer,** circular slide-rule; (*b*) **quart de c.,** quadrant.
cerclé [sɛrkle]. **1.** *a.* ringed; **lunettes cerclées d'or,** gold-rimmed spectacles; **yeux cerclés de bistre,** eyes with dark rings round them. **2.** *s.m. Com: F:* cask, barrel.
cercler [sɛrkle], *v.tr.* **1.** to encircle, to ring; **les arbres qui cerclent le lac,** the trees bordering the lake. **2.** to hoop (barrel, mast, gun); to tyre (wheel); **cerclé de fer,** iron-bound.
cercleux [sɛrklø], *s.m. F:* club-man; man about town.
cerclier [sɛrkli(j)e], *s.m.* hoop-maker, cooper.
cercocèbe [sɛrkɔsɛːb], *s.m. Z:* cercocebus; **c. à collier blanc,** white-collared mangabey; **c. à gorge blanche,** grey-cheeked mangabey.
cercope [sɛrkɔp], *s.f. Ent:* frog-hopper.
cercopids [sɛrkɔpid], *s.m.pl. Ent:* Cercopids.
cercopidés [sɛrkɔpide], *s.m.pl. Ent:* Cercopidae.
cercopithécidés [sɛrkɔpiteside], *s.m.pl. Z:* Cercopithecidae.
cercopithèque [sɛrkɔpitɛk], *s.m. Z:* cercopithecus, guenon.
cercospora [sɛrkɔspɔra], *s.m. Fung:* cercospora.
cercosporella [sɛrkɔspɔrɛla], *s.m. Fung:* cercosporella.
cercueil [sɛrkœːj], *s.m.* **1.** coffin, *U.S:* casket; **c. de chêne,** oak coffin; **c. de plomb,** leaden shell. **2.** *Com:* egg-crate.
cerdagnol, -ole [sɛrdaɲɔl], *a. & s.*, **cerdan, -ane** [sɛrdɑ̃, -an], *a. & s. Geog:* (native, inhabitant) of the Cerdagne valley.
céréale [sereal], *a.f. & s.f.* cereal; **plantes céréales,** *s.f.pl.* **céréales,** cereals; **céréales en flocons,** cereals, breakfast foods; **commerce des céréales,** the corn, grain, trade; *Hist:* **lois céréales,** corn laws.
céréaliculture [serealikyltyːr], *s.f.* cultivation of cereals.
céréalier, -ière [serealje, -jɛːr]. **1.** *a.* **la production céréalière,** the cereal production. **les cultures céréalières,** cereal crops; **2.** *s.* cereal grower.
céréaline [serealin], *s.f. Ch:* cerealin, aleurone, diastase.
céréaliste [serealist], *s.m.* **1.** *Hist:* advocate of protective corn-laws. **2.** wholesale dealer in cereals. **3.** cerealist, specialist in the study of cereals.
céréalose [serealoːz], *s.f.* cerealose.
cérébelleux, -euse [serebɛllø, -øːz], *a. Anat:* cerebellar (artery, vein, etc.).
cérébellite [serebɛlit], *s.f. Med:* inflammation of the cerebellum.
Cérébos [serebɔs], *Pr.n.m. R.t.m:* sel **C.,** free-running salt.
cérébral, -ale, -aux [serebral, -o]. **1.** *a.* (*a*) cerebral (artery; *Ling:* consonant, etc.); (*b*) **travail c.,** intellectual work; **surmenage c., fatigue cérébrale,** mental exhaustion; *Med:* **ramollissement c.,** softening of the brain. **2.** *s.* intellectual.
cérébralité [serebralite], *s.f.* mental ability.
cérébration [serebrasjɔ̃], *s.f. Psy:* cerebration.
cérébratule [serebratyl], *s.m.*, **cerebratulus** [serebratylys], *s.m. Ann:* cerebratulus.
cérébriforme [serebrifɔrm], *a.* cerebriform.
cérébrite [serebrit], *s.f. Med: A:* cerebritis, encephalitis.
cérébro-cardiaque [serebrɔkardjak], *a. Med:* cerebro-cardiac (neuropathy, etc.); *pl. cerebro-cardiaques.*
cérébroïde [serebrɔid], *a.* cerebroid.
cérébrologie [serebrɔlɔʒi], *s.f.* cerebrology.
cérébro-malacie [serebrɔmalasi], *s.f. Med:* cerebro-malacia, softening of the brain.
cérébro-rachidien, -ienne [serebrɔraʃidjɛ̃, -jɛn], *a.* cerebro-r(h)achidian; *pl. cérébro-rachidiens, -iennes.*
cérébrosclérose [serebrɔskleroz], *s.f.* cerebrosclerosis.
cérébro-spinal [serebrɔspinal], *a. Anat: Med:* cerebro-spinal; **méningite cérébro-spinale,** cerebro-spinal meningitis; *pl. cérébro-spinaux.*
cérémoniaire [seremɔnjɛːr], *s.m. Ecc:* ceremoniarius.
cérémonial, -aux [seremɔnjal, -o]. **1.** *A: a.* ceremonial. **2.** *s.m. no pl.* ceremonial; **c. de l'Église,** Church ceremonial, ceremonies; **c. de la cour,** court etiquette.
cérémonialisme [seremɔnjalism], *s.m.* ceremonialism, ritualism.
cérémonie [seremɔni], *s.f.* ceremony; (*a*) **escorter un prince en grande c.,** to escort a prince in state, with great pomp; **faire une visite de c.,** to pay a ceremonial, formal, call (**à, on**); **tenue de c.,** full dress; **complet, habit, de c.,** dress suit; **sans c.,** without ceremony, unceremoniously; **homme sans c.,** plain man; **faire des cérémonies,** to stand on ceremony; to make a fuss; **sans plus de c.,** without (any) more ado; **maître des cérémonies,** master of ceremonies; (*b*) proceedings, function.
cérémoniel, -ielle [seremɔnjɛl], *a.* **1.** ceremonial. **2.** formal.
cérémonieusement [seremɔnjøzmɑ̃], *adv.* ceremoniously.
cérémonieux, -ieuse [seremɔnjø, -jøːz], *a.* ceremonious, formal; **homme très c.,** stickler for etiquette.
Cérès [serɛːs], *Pr.n.f. Myth:* Ceres.
cérésine [serezin], *s.f. Ch:* ceresin(e).
céreux, -euse [serø, -øːz], *a. Ch:* cerous (oxide).
cerf [sɛːr, sɛrf, *pl. always* sɛːr], *s.m.* (*a*) *Z:* stag, hart; **c. commun,** red deer; **c. à queue noire,** mule deer; **c. du Kashmir,** Szechwan deer; **c. andin,** Andean deer, guemal; **c. d'Aristote,** sambur; *Ven:* **c. dix cors,** hart of ten; *s.a.* ENCOLURE 1; *A.Pharm: etc:* **corne de c.,** hartshorn; **c'est un c. à la course,** he runs like a deer; *Vet:* **mal de c.,** stag-evil, lock-jaw; (*b*) *Cu:* venison; (*c*) *F:* good horseman; athletic type; **courir comme un c.,** to run like a hare.
cerf-cochon [sɛrkɔʃɔ̃], *s.m.* hog deer; *pl. cerfs-cochons.*
cerfeuil [sɛrfœːj], *s.m. Bot:* chervil; **c. d'Espagne, odorant, musqué,** sweet cicely, myrrh; **c. à aiguillettes,** shepherd's needle, scandix.
cerf-volant [sɛrvɔlɑ̃], *s.m.* **1.** *Ent:* stag-beetle. **2.** kite; **c.-v. cellulaire,** box-kite; **ballon c.-v.,** kite-balloon. **3.** *Com: F:* accommodation bill; *F:* kite; *pl. cerfs-volants.*
cérianthe [seriɑ̃ːt], *s.m.*, **cerianthus** [seriɑ̃tys], *s.m. Coel:* cerianthus, cerianthid (anemone).
céride [serid], *s.f. Bio-Ch:* cerid(e).
cérifère[1] [serifɛːr], *a. Bot: Ent:* ceriferous, wax-bearing.
cérifère[2], *a. Miner:* cerium-bearing.
cérificateur [serifikatœːr], *s.m. Ap:* wax extractor.
cérigène [seriʒɛn], *a.* that produces wax.
cérigère [seriʒɛːr], *a. Orn:* cerigerous, cerate.
cérinthe [serɛ̃ːt], *s.m. Bot:* cerinthe; honey-wort.
cérique [serik], *a. Ch:* ceric (oxide, etc.).
cerisaie [s(ə)rizɛ], *s.f.* cherry orchard.
cerise [s(ə)riːz]. **1.** *s.f.* (*a*) *Bot:* cherry; **c. des Antilles,** Barbados cherry; **c. en cœur,** heart-cherry; **cerises jumelées,** cherry bob, bob-cherry; **c. gommeuse,** China berry; **c. de juif, de suif, d'hiver, en chemise,** winter-cherry; **c. d'ours,** bearberry; *A:* **faire deux morceaux d'une c.,** to take two bites at a cherry; **bouche en c.,** rosebud mouth; **rouge comme une c.,** as red as a turkey cock; **eau-de-vie de cerises,** cherry brandy; **cerises à l'eau-de-vie,** brandied cherries; *P:* **avoir la c.,** to have a run of bad luck; *P:* **ficher la c.,** to bring bad luck; (*b*) **c. de caféier,** coffee-berry; (*c*) *Orn: F:* **oiseau aux cerises,** golden oriole; (*d*) *P:* face, mug; head, nut. **2.** *s.m. & a.inv.* cherry-red; *Tex:* cerise.
cerisette [s(ə)rizɛt], *s.f.* **1.** dried cherry. **2.** *Bot:* winter-cherry. **3.** cherry drink.
cerisier [s(ə)rizje], *s.m.* **1.** (*a*) *Hort:* cherry tree; (*b*) *Bot:* **c. d'amour, petit c. d'hiver,** winter-cherry (tree); **c. à grappes,** bird-cherry (tree), hagberry tree. **2.** cherrywood.
cérite [serit], *s.f. Min:* cerite.
cérithe [serit], *s.m.*, **cerithium** [seritjɔm], *s.m. Moll:* cerithium.
cérithiidés [seritiide], *s.m.pl. Moll:* Cerithiidae.
cérium [serjɔm], *s.m. Ch:* cerium; **oxyde de c.,** ceria.
cermet [sɛrmɛ], *s.m.* ceramal, cermet.
cerne [sɛrn], *s.m.* **1.** ring, circle (round moon, eyes, wound). **2.** age-ring (of tree).
cerneau, -eaux [sɛrno], *s.m.* green walnut.
cernement [sɛrnəmɑ̃], *s.m.* **1.** surrounding, encircling (of army); investing (of town, etc.). **2.** *For:* girdling, ringing (of tree).
cerner [sɛrne], *v.tr.* **1.** (*a*) to encircle, surround, close in upon, beset (army, etc.); **c. une ville,** to invest, beleaguer, a town; **cerné par les flammes,** trapped by the flames; (*b*) to harass; **les soucis le cernent de toutes parts,** worries harass him on all sides; (*c*) **le bleu de la mort cernait ses lèvres,** her lips were ringed with the livid tinge of death; **avoir les yeux cernés,** to have rings round one's eyes; (*d*) to grasp; to determine. **2. c. des noix,** to shell, husk, walnuts. **3.** *For:* (*a*) to dig round (tree); (*b*) to girdle, ring (tree).
cernier [sɛrnje], *s.m. Ich:* stone-bass, wreckfish.
cernure [sɛrnyːr], *s.f.* dark ring (round the eyes).
céroféraire [serɔferɛːr], *s.m. Ecc:* candle-bearer.
cérolite [serɔlit], *s.f. Miner:* cerolite.
céroplastique [serɔplastik], *s.f.* ceroplastics, wax modelling.
cérotique [serɔtik], *a. Ch:* cerotic.
céroxyle [serɔksil], *s.m.*, **ceroxylon** [serɔksilɔ̃], *s.m. Bot:* ceroxylon, wax-palm.
cerque [sɛrk], *s.m. usu. pl. Ent:* (*a*) cercus; *pl.* cerci; anal appendages; (*b*) seta.
cers [sɛːr], *s.m.* (*in Languedoc*) violent wind from W. or S.W.
certain, -aine [sɛrtɛ̃, -ɛn]. **1.** *a.* (*a*) certain, sure, unquestionable (proof, news, etc.); **il est c. qu'il viendra,** it is certain that he will come; **tenir qch. pour c., pour chose certaine,** to look on sth. as a certainty; **vous pouvez tenir pour c. que . . .,** you may rest assured that . . .; *F:* **c'est sûr et c.,** it's absolutely certain; **il le fait avec une facilité certaine,** he does it with unquestionable facility; (*b*) **il est c. de réussir,** he is certain to succeed; **j'en suis c.,** I am sure, certain, of it; **moi, je n'en suis pas bien c.,** I'm not so sure myself; **soyez c. que je dis la vérité,** you may depend upon it that what I say is true; (*c*) fixed, stated (date, price, etc.); (*d*) *s.m.* certainty, sure thing; *Fin:* fixed, direct, exchange; **donner le c.,** to quote certain, in home currency. **2.** *indef. a. & pron.*

(*a*) some, certain; **certains, (de) certaines gens, affirment que . . .,** some (people) maintain that . . ., there are those who maintain that . . .; **après un c. temps,** after a certain time, after some time; **jusqu'à un c. point,** in some measure; up to a point; **d'un c. âge,** (i) of a certain age; (ii) elderly; **il le fait avec une certaine facilité,** he does it with a certain facility; **dans un c. sens, d'un c. point de vue,** in a sense, in a manner; **tous ou certains d'entre eux,** some or all (of them); (*b*) *often Pej:* **un c. M. Martin,** a certain Mr Martin, a Mr Martin.

certainement [sɛrtɛnmɑ̃], *adv.* certainly, assuredly, undoubtedly; **il réussira c.,** he is sure to succeed; **c.!** of course! by all means!

certes [sɛrt], *adv.* (*a*) *O:* most certainly; **oui c.!** yes indeed! to be sure! (*b*) (*indicating a concession*) **c. je n'irais pas jusqu'à dire que . . .,** I certainly wouldn't go as far as to say that . . ..

certificat [sɛrtifika], *s.m.* (*a*) certificate; (i) **c. de bonne conduite,** good conduct certificate; **c. de bonne vie et mœurs,** certificate of good character; *Mil:* **c. de bien vivre,** certificate of good behaviour (on leaving billets); **c. d'aptitude physique,** certificate of fitness; **donner un c. à un domestique,** to give a servant a reference, a character; **montrer ses certificats,** to show one's testimonials; *O:* **je vous en donne mon c.!** take my word for it! *Adm.Mil:* **c. d'origine de blessure,** certificate that wound was received in action, was an injury in the course of duty; *Mil:* **c. de cessation de paiement,** last pay certificate; (ii) *Nau:* **c. de jauge,** tonnage certificate; **c. de chargement,** certificate of receipt; **c. de mise à terre,** landing certificate; **c. de navigabilité,** *Nau:* certificate of seaworthiness; *Aer:* certificate of airworthiness; (iii) *Com:* **c. d'origine,** certificate of origin; **c. d'homologation,** certificate of approval; **c. de conformité,** certificate of compliance; *Fin:* **c. provisoire,** share certificate, (provisional) scrip; *Cust:* **c. d'entrepôt,** warrant; (iv) *Sch:* **c. de licence, d'études supérieures,** (i) each of the four examinations for the *licence*; (ii) certificate so obtained; **c. d'aptitude professionnelle,** certificate of education for those who have received vocational training; **c. d'aptitude pédagogique à l'enseignement secondaire** (C.A.P.E.S.) = teacher's training diploma (for graduates); *A:* **c. d'études (primaires),** certificate given after an examination at the end of an elementary course of studies; *F:* **il a son c.,** he has a sound elementary education; (v) *Breed:* **c. d'origine,** pedigree (of dog, etc.); *s.a.* CAPACITÉ 2, MÉDICAL 2; (*b*) guarantee; **votre constitution est un c. de longue vie,** your constitution is a guarantee of long life.

certificateur [sɛrtifikatœːr], *s.m.* (*a*) certifier, guarantor; (*b*) attestor.

certificatif, -ive [sɛrtifikatif, -iːv], *a.* certifying, attesting, certificatory (document, etc.).

certification [sɛrtifikasjɔ̃], *s.f. Jur: Com:* certification, authentication; **c. d'une signature,** witnessing of a signature.

certifié, -ée [sɛrtifje], *a. & s. Sch:* **(professeur) c.,** teacher who holds the C.A.P.E.S.

certifier [sɛrtifje], *v.tr.* (*pr.sub. & p.d.* **n. certifiions, v. certifiiez**) to certify, attest, assure; **c. qch. à qn,** to assure s.o. of sth.; **c. une signature,** to witness, authenticate, a signature; *Jur:* **copie certifiée,** attested, certified, copy; **c. une caution,** to guarantee a surety.

certitude [sɛrtityd], *s.f.* **1.** certainty, certitude; **j'en ai la c.,** I am sure of it; **dire qch. avec c.,** to speak with assurance; **quand nous eûmes acquis la c. qu'il n'y avait pas de blessés . . .,** when we had ascertained that there were no casualties . . .; **la c. qu'il n'était pas venu,** the knowledge that he hadn't come; *Turf:* **une c.,** a certainty; *F:* **c'est une c. absolue,** it's a dead cert. **2. dessin tracé avec c.,** drawing executed with a sure hand.

cérulé [seryle], **céruléen, -enne** [seryleɛ̃, -ɛn], *a. Lit:* cerulean, azure; **bleu c.,** cerulean blue.

cérulescent [serylɛsɑ̃], *a.* cerulescent.

céruléum [seryleɔm], *s.m. Paint:* ceruleum.

cérumen [serymɛn], *s.m. Physiol:* cerumen, earwax.

cérumineux, -euse [seryminø, -øːz], *a. Physiol:* ceruminous (gland, etc.).

céruse [seryːz], *s.f.* (*a*) white-lead; **joint à la c.,** white-lead joint; **c. en lamelles,** flake-white; (*b*) *Th: etc:* ceruse (for making-up).

cérus(s)ite [seryzit, -ysit], *s.f. Miner:* cerus(s)ite.

cervaison [sɛrvɛzɔ̃], *s.f. Ven:* stag(-hunting) season.

cervantesque [sɛrvɑ̃tɛsk], *a.* Cervantic (style, etc.).

cervantite [sɛrvɑ̃tit], *s.f. Min:* cervantite.

cerveau, -eaux [sɛrvo], *s.m.* **1.** (*a*) brain; *Anat:* **c. antérieur** = forebrain; **c. moyen** = midbrain; **c. postérieur** = hindbrain; **rhume de c.,** cold in the head; *F:* **être pris du c.,** to have a cold in the head; *F:* **vous me rompez le c.,** you give me a headache, make me tired; **vin qui monte au c.,** wine that goes to the head, heady wine; (*b*) mind, intellect, brains; **homme à c. étroit, vide,** shallow-brained, empty-headed, man; *F:* **avoir le c. dérangé, fêlé,** to be mad, *F:* cracked, bats; **se creuser le c.,** to rack one's brains; (*c*) person of intellectual ability, brain; **c. brûlé,** hothead; **c. creux,** dreamer; (*d*) **c. électronique,** electronic brain; (*e*) *Coel:* **c. de Jupiter,** meandrine coral; **2.** cannon (of a bell).

cervelas [sɛrvəla], *s.m. Cu:* saveloy, cervelat.

cervelet [sɛrvəlɛ], *s.m. Anat:* cerebellum.

cervelière [sɛrvəljɛːr], *s.f. A.Arm:* cervelière.

cervelle [sɛrvɛl], *s.f.* **1.** (*a*) *Anat:* brain(s) (as matter); **brûler, faire sauter, la c. à qn,** to blow s.o.'s brains out; *Cu:* **c. de veau,** calves' brains; (*b*) mind, brains, intelligence; **se creuser la c. pour . . .,** to rack one's brains to . . .; **se mettre qch. dans la c.,** to get an idea fixed in one's mind; *F:* **idée qui me trotte dans la c.,** idea running through my head; (*of pers.*) **sans c.,** brainless, dim-witted; **avoir une c. de lièvre,** to have a memory like a sieve; **elle a une c. de moineau,** she has the brains of a canary, she's completely feather-brained; *F:* **il a la c. à l'envers,** he's not quite right in his mind, in the head. **2. cervelle de palmier,** palm-tree pith. **3.** *N.Arch:* drop-bolt (of rudderhead, etc.); deck-bolt.

cervical, -aux [sɛrvikal, -o], *a. Anat:* cervical (artery, vertebra).

cervicapre [sɛrvikapr̩], *s.m. Z:* (*a*) reedbuck, rietbok; (*b*) black buck, sasin, Indian antelope.

cervicite [sɛrvisit], *s.f. Med:* cervicitis.

cervico-brachial, -aux [sɛrvikɔbrakjal, -o], *a. Anat:* cervico-brachial.

cervico-bregmatique [sɛrvikɔbrɛgmatik], *a. Anat:* cervicobregmatic; *pl. cervico-bregmatiques.*

cervidés [sɛrvide], *s.m.pl. Z:* Cervidae, the deer tribe.

cervier [sɛrvje], *a. Z: see* LOUP-CERVIER.

cervin, -ine [sɛrvɛ̃, -in]. **1.** *a. Z:* cervine. **2.** *Pr.n.m. Geog:* **le Mont C.,** the Matterhorn.

cervoise [sɛrvwaːz], *s.f. A:* cervisia, barley beer.

cervule [sɛrvyl], *s.m. Z:* cervulus; **c. de Malaisie,** muntjac.

cérylique [serilik], *a. Ch:* ceryl (alcohol).

Césaire [sezɛːr], *Pr.n.m.* Caesarius.

césalpiniacées [sezalpinjase], *s.f.pl.,* **césalpin(i)ées** [sezalpin(j)e], *s.f.pl. Bot:* Caesalpiniaceae.

César [sezaːr], *Pr.n.m. Rom.Hist:* Caesar; **Jules C.,** Julius Caesar.

Césarée [sezare], *Pr.n.f. A.Geog:* Caesarea.

césaréwitch [sezarevitʃ], *s.m.* = TSARÉVITCH.

césarien, -ienne [sezarjɛ̃, -jɛn]. **1.** *a. Hist:* Caesarean, Caesarian. **2.** *a.f. & s.f. Obst:* **(opération) césarienne,** Caesarean (operation, section).

césarisée [sezarize], *a.f. & s.f. Med:* (woman) who has had a Caesarean operation; *F:* Caesarean.

césariser [sezarize], *v.tr. Obst:* to perform a Caesarean operation, section, on (s.o.).

césarisme [sezarism], *s.m.* caesarism; imperialism.

césariste [sezarist], *s.m.* caesarist; imperialist.

césarolite [sezarɔlit], *s.f. Miner:* cesarolite.

césium [sezjɔm], *s.m. Ch:* caesium.

cespiteux, -euse [sɛspitø, -øːz], *a. Bot:* cespitose.

cessant [sɛsɑ̃], *a.* ceasing; **toute(s) chose(s), affaire(s), cessante(s),** to the exclusion of all other business; immediately.

cessation [sɛsasjɔ̃], *s.f.* cessation, ceasing, discontinuance, stoppage; **c. des hostilités, de paiements,** suspension of hostilities, of payments; **c. de relations d'affaires,** termination of business relations; **c. d'un contrat,** closure of a contract; *P.N:* **c. de commerce,** closing down.

cesse [sɛs], *s.f.* cease, ceasing; (*always used without article and usu. with neg.*) **sans c.,** without cease, unceasingly; constantly; **elle parle sans c.,** she never stops talking; **il n'aura (pas) de c. qu'il n'ait réussi,** he will not stop, will not rest, until he has succeeded; **il n'eut pas de c. de prouver sa force et son intelligence,** he never gave up trying to prove his strength and intelligence.

cesser [sese, se-], *v.* to cease, leave off, stop. **1.** *v.i.* **les collines cessent à. . . .,** the hills fall away at . . .; **cette mode a cessé tout doucement,** this fashion died a natural death; **faire c. qch.,** to put a stop to sth., to put down (abuse, etc.); **c. de faire qch.,** to cease (from), stop, doing sth; **cesse de pleurer!** stop crying! **c. de fumer,** to give up smoking; **il n'a pas cessé de nous observer,** he has been watching us all this time; **elle ne cesse (pas) de parler,** she never stops talking. **2.** *v.tr.* **c. le travail,** to cease, leave off, work; **c. les affaires,** to give up business; **c. toutes relations avec qn,** to break off all relations with s.o.; **c. les paiements,** to stop, suspend, discontinue, payment(s); *Mil:* **cessez le feu!** cease fire!

cessez-le-feu [sɛselfø, se-], *s.m.inv.* cease-fire.

cessibilité [sɛsibilite], *s.f. Jur:* transferability, assignability (of estate, etc.); negotiability (of pension).

cessible [sɛsibl̩], *a. Jur:* transferable, assignable; (*of pension, etc.*) negotiable.

cession [sɛsjɔ̃], *s.f.* **1.** *Jur:* transfer, assignment; **c. d'une créance,** transfer of a debt; **faire c. de qch. à qn,** to transfer, surrender, sth. to s.o.; **(acte de) cession,** deed of transfer, of assignment; **cession de biens,** assignment of property (to creditors), cessio bonorum; **c. (d'un territoire),** cession (of a territory). **2.** (*a*) *Mch:* delivery (of heat); supply (of power); (*b*) issue, delivery (of shares, etc.).

cessionnaire [sɛsjɔnɛːr]. **1.** *s.m. Com:* (*a*) transferee, assignee; holder (of bill); *Jur:* cessionary; (*b*) endorser (of cheque). **2.** *a. Jur:* cessionary.

cession-transport [sɛsjɔ̃trɑ̃spɔːr], *s.f. Jur:* assignment of chose in action; *pl. cessions-transports.*

c'est-à-dire [sɛtadiːr], *conj.phr.* **1.** that is (to say); *i.e.*; in other words; **la Ville éternelle, c.-à-d. Rome,** the Eternal City, that is to say Rome; **le roi, c.-à-d. Richelieu, avait ordonné que . . .,** the King, in other words Richelieu, had decreed that . . .. **2. c.-à-d. que** + *ind.,* the fact is that . . ., indeed . . .; **vous l'avez prévenu?—c.-à-d. que non,** you sent him word?—well, no, I'm afraid I didn't.

ceste[1] [sɛst], *s.m. Rom.Ant:* c(a)estus (of pugilist).

ceste[2], *s.m.* **1.** *Rom.Ant:* cestus, girdle (of Venus or Juno). **2.** *Z:* cestus; Venus's girdle.

cestodes [sɛstɔd], *s.m.pl. Nat.Hist:* Cestoda, tapeworms.

cestoïde [sɛstɔid], *a. & s.m. Nat.Hist:* cestoid; **(vers) cestoïdes,** tapeworms.

cestrum [sɛstrɔm], *s.m. Bot:* cestrum.

cestus [sɛstys], *s.m. Z:* cestus, Venus's girdle.

césure [sezyːr], *s.f. Pros:* caesura.

cétacé [setase], *Z:* **1.** *a.* cetacean, cetaceous. **2.** *s.m.* cetacean; **les cétacés,** the Cetacea.

cétane [setan], *s.m. Ch:* cetane; **indice de c.,** cetane number.

cétazine [setazin], *s.f. Ch:* ketazine.

cétène [setɛn, sɛ-], *s.m. Ch:* cetene, ketene.

cétéosaure [seteozɔːr], *s.m. Paleont:* ceteosaur(us).

cétérac(h) [seterak], *s.m. Bot:* ceterach, finger-fern.

cétimine [setimin], *s.f. Ch:* ketimine.

cétine [setin], *s.f. Ch:* cetin(e).

cétogène [setɔʒɛn], *a. Bio-Ch:* ketogenetic.

cétogenèse [setɔʒ(ə)nɛːz], *s.f. Bio-Ch:* ketogenesis.

cétographie [setɔgrafi], *s.f. Z:* cetology.

cétoine [setwan], *s.f. Ent:* cetonia; **c. dorée,** rose-beetle, rose-chafer, goldsmith-beetle.

cétologue [setɔlɔg], *s.m.* cetologist.

cétone [setɔn], *s.f. Ch:* ketone.

cétonique [setɔnik], *a. Ch:* ketonic.

cétorhinidés [setɔrinide], *s.m.pl. Ich:* Cetorhinidae.

cetorhinus [setɔrinys], *s.m. Ich:* cetorhinus.

cétose [setoːz]. **1.** *s.m. Bio-Ch:* ketose. **2.** *s.f. Med:* ketosis.

cétoxime [setɔksim], *s.f. Ch:* ketoxime.

cetraria [setrarja], *s.m. Moss:* cetraria.

cétyle [setil], *s.m. Ch:* cetyl.

cétylique [setilik], *a. Ch:* cetyl (alcohol).

cévadille [sevadiːj], *s.f. Bot:* sabadilla, cevadilla.

Cévennes (les) [lesevɛn], *Pr.n.f.pl.* the Cevennes.

cévenol, -ole [sevnɔl], *a. & s. Geog:* (native, inhabitant) of the Cevennes region.

Ceylan [sɛlɑ̃], *Pr.n.m. Geog:* Ceylon.

ceylanais, -aise [sɛlanɛ, -ɛːz], *a. & s.* = CING(H)ALAIS.

ceylanite [selanit], *s.f.* **ceylonite** [selɔnit], *s.f. Miner:* ceylanite, ceylonite.

ceyssatite [sesatit], *s.f. Miner:* ceyssatite.

chabacite [ʃabasit], *s.f. Miner:* chabasie, chabasite, chabazite.

chabanais [ʃabanɛ], *s.m. A: P:* noise, din, racket.

chabasie [ʃabazi], *s.f. Miner:* chabasie, chabasite, chabazite.

chabichou [ʃabiʃu], *s.m.* goat's milk cheese (made in Poitou).

chablaisien, -ienne [ʃablɛzjɛ̃, -jɛn], *a. & s. Geog:* (native, inhabitant) of the Chablais region.

chable [ʃɑːbl], *s.m. Mec.E:* hoisting cable, tackle.

chableau, -eaux [ʃablo], *s.m.* tow-line, warp.

chabler[1] [ʃɑble], *v.tr.* **1.** *A:* to twist (a cable). **2.** to hoist (load). **3.** to tow (boat).

chabler[2], *v.tr.* to beat (walnut-tree).

chablis[1] [ʃɑbli], *s.m. For:* windfallen wood; *a.* **bois c.,** dead wood.

chablis[2], *s.m.* Chablis (wine).

chabot [ʃabo], *s.m.* **1.** *Ich:* (*a*) bullhead, lasher; **c. de mer,** marine miller's thumb; (*b*) chub, miller's thumb. **2.** *Her:* chabot.

chabotte [ʃabɔt], *s.f. Metall:* anvil-bed, -block (of power-hammer).

chabraque [ʃabrak], *s.f.* **1.** *Mil:* shabrack (under saddle). **2.** *a. & s.f. P: Dial:* (i) ugly; (ii) loose(-living); (iii) scatter-brained (girl, woman).

chabreteire [ʃabrətejr], *s.m. Dial:* (*Limousin*) piper.

chabrette [ʃabrɛt], *s.f. Dial:* (*Limousin*) bagpipes.

chabrol [ʃabrɔl], *s.m.* **chabrot** [ʃabro], *s.m. Dial:* (*S.W. France*) **faire c.,** to mix wine with one's soup.

chacal [ʃakal], *s.m.* (*a*) *Z:* jackal; (*b*) *Mil: P:* zouave; *pl. chacals.*

chacma [ʃakma], *s.m. Z:* chacma.

chacon(n)e [ʃakɔn], *s.f. Mus:* chaconne.

Chactas [ʃaktɑːs, -as], *s.m.pl. Ethn:* Choctaws.

chacun, -une [ʃakœ̃, -yn], *indef.pron.* **1.** each, every one, each one; **trois groupes de c. dix hommes,** three groups of ten men each; **chacune d'elles a refusé,** each (one), every one, of them has refused; **trois francs c.,** three francs each; **après avoir avalé c. une tasse de café, nous partîmes,** after each of us had swallowed a cup of coffee, we set out; *F:* **c. avait sa chacune,** every Jack had his Jill; **ils ont pris c. son, leur, chapeau,** each of them took his hat; **nous avons pris c. notre chapeau,** each of us took his hat; **ils causaient c. de leur côté,** they each carried on their conversations; **ils s'en allèrent c. de son côté, c. de leur côté,** they went their several ways. **2.** everybody, everyone; **c. en rit,** everyone is laughing about it; **c. pour soi (et Dieu pour tous),** every man for himself (and the devil take the hindmost); **dans une petite ville c. se connaît,** in a small town everyone knows everybody else; **pour c. et pour tous,** for each and every one, for all and sundry; **c. (à) son goût,** every man to his taste; **c. son métier,** let every man stick to his trade; **c. son tour** (each in (his) turn, turn and turn about; **c. est d'accord (pour déclarer) que . . .,** all agree that . . .; *F:* **un c., tout (un) chacun,** any and everybody; **il le racontait à un c.,** he told all and sundry about it; **tout (un) c. lui faisait la cour,** she was courted by every Tom, Dick, and Harry.

chacunière [ʃakynjɛːr], *s.f. A: F:* (*used after* **chacun**) **on s'en alla chacun à sa c.,** they all departed for their respective homes.

chadburn [ʃadbœrn], *s.m. Nau:* chadburn telegraph, engine-room telegraph.

chadouf [ʃaduf], *s.m.* well-sweep (in Egypt, etc.); shadoof.

chætodontidés [ketɔdɔ̃tide], *s.m.pl. Ich:* Chaetodontidae.

chæture [ketyːr], *s.f.,* **chætura** [ketyra], *s.f. Orn:* chætura.

chafaud [ʃafo], *s.m.* **1.** *A:* = ÉCHAFAUD. **2.** (*a*) *Fish:* (cod) drying-platform (on the banks); (*b*) *A:* hay-loft.

chafouin, -ine [ʃafwɛ̃, -in], *a. & s. F:* weasel-faced, foxy-looking, sly-looking (person).

chagrin[1] [ʃagrɛ̃]. **1.** *a.* (*a*) *A:* grieved, afflicted; distressed; (*b*) sad, melancholy; morose; **c'est un esprit c.,** he is embittered. **2.** *s.m.* (*a*) grief, sorrow, affliction, trouble; **j'ai du c. de vous voir si changé,** I am grieved to see you so altered; **faire du c. à qn,** to grieve s.o., to distress s.o.; **laisser échapper son c.,** to give vent to one's grief; **usé par le c.,** care-worn; **mourir de c.,** to die of a broken heart; (*b*) vexation, chagrin, annoyance; **chagrins domestiques,** domestic worries.

chagrin[2], *s.m. Leath:* shagreen, grained leather, grain(-leather).

chagrinant [ʃagrinɑ̃], *a.* (*a*) distressing, melancholy, sad; (*b*) provoking, vexing.

chagrinement [ʃagrinmɑ̃], *adv. A:* (*a*) sadly; (*b*) peevishly, fretfully.

chagriner[1] [ʃagrine], *v.tr.* **1.** to grieve, distress, afflict; **cela me chagrine lorsque je vois que . . .,** I feel aggrieved when I see that . . .. **2.** *A:* to vex, provoke, annoy; to ruffle (s.o.'s) temper.

se chagriner, to grieve; to fret.

chagriner[2], *v.tr. Leath:* to shagreen, grain (leather); **papier chagriné,** pebbled, granulated, paper; **gélatine à surface chagrinée,** frosted gelatine.

chah [ʃa], *s.m.* shah.

chahut [ʃay], *s.m.* (*a*) *A:* rowdy dance; (*b*) *F:* noise, din; **faire du c.,** to make, *F:* kick up, a din, a racket; to make an uproar; (*c*) *Sch: F:* rag; uproar (in class).

chahutage [ʃaytaːʒ], *s.m. F:* (*a*) rowdyism; *Sch:* ragging (of teacher); (*b*) booing (at a play, etc.); *Sp:* barracking.

chahuter [ʃayte]. **1.** *v.i.* (*a*) *A:* to dance the *chahut;* (*b*) *F:* to make, *F:* kick up, a din, a racket; to rag; to lark about; (*c*) *F:* to boo; to give (s.o.) the bird; to barrack; (*d*) *F:* **vol chahuté,** bumpy flight. **2.** *v.tr. F:* (*a*) to knock (things) about, to send (things) flying; to bump into (s.o.); (*b*) to rag (schoolmaster, etc.).

chahuteur, -euse [ʃaytœːr, -øːz], *a. & s.* (*a*) *A:* (one) who dances the *chahut;* (*b*) *F:* rowdy, disorderly (student, etc.).

chahutoir [ʃaytwaːr], *s.m. A: P:* low-class dancing saloon.

chai [ʃɛ], *s.m.* **1.** wine and spirits store(house). **2.** wine-making plant (attached to a vineyard).

chail [ʃɑːj], *s.m.,* **chaille** [ʃɑːj], *s.f.* **1.** flint (in Jurassic limestone). **2.** road metal.

chaînage [ʃɛnaːʒ], *s.m.* **1.** *Surv:* chaining, chain-measuring. **2.** *Const:* (*a*) tying, clamping (of walls); (*b*) tie-irons, (series of) clamps, ties. **3.** *Const:* = CHAÎNE 3.

chaîne [ʃɛn], *s.f.* **1.** chain (of iron, gold, etc.); chain (of order of chivalry); *Nau:* cable; (*a*) **c. de cou,** necklace; **c. de montre, de gilet,** watch-chain, -guard; **c. de porte, de sûreté,** door-chain, safety-chain; **c. de bicyclette,** (i) bicycle chain; (ii) *see* 1(*b*); **c. d'huissier,** usher's chain of office; *Clockm:* **c. de montre,** fusee chain; *Rail: etc:* **c. d'attelage,** coupling-, drag-, chain; *Aut:* **c. antidérapante,** non-skid chain, tyre-chain; **c. à neige,** snow chain; (*b*) *Tchn: Mec.E:* chain; **c. calibrée,** pitch(ed) chain; **c. à maillons pleins, à blocs,** *F:* **de bicyclette,** block-chain; **c. à galets,** roller-chain; **c. à barbotins, c. de Galle, de Gallo,** sprocket-chain; **pignon de c.,** sprocket; **c. de, à la, Vaucanson,** ladder-chain; **c. à augets, à godets,** bucket-chain; **c. à étais,** stud-link chain; **c. sans fin,** endless chain; **relâchement de la c.,** chain slack; **tendeur de c.,** chain adjuster; **guide-c.,** chain-guide; *Tls:* **c. coupante, scie à c.,** chain saw; (*c*) chains, shackles, fetters, bonds; **mettre un chien à la c.,** to chain up a dog; **mettre qn à la c.,** to clap s.o. in irons, to put s.o. in chains; to fetter s.o.; **être à la c.,** to be in chains, in fetters, in irons; to be chained, fettered; *A:* **condamner qn à la c.,** to send s.o. to the galleys; *A:* **c. (de forçats), forçats à la c.,** chain-gang; **être rivé à la c.,** (i) to be in hopeless bondage; (ii) to be tied to one's work; **rompre, briser sa c., ses chaînes,** to burst one's fetters, one's chains; to escape from bondage; (*d*) *Surv:* **c. d'arpentage, d'arpenteur,** surveying, measuring chain; surveyor's, engineer's, chain; land-(measuring) chain; Gunter's, Ramsden's chain; **c. à ruban (d'acier)** (steel) band-chain; (*e*) *Nau:* cable; **c. de bossoir,** bower cable; **c. de veille,** sheet cable; **tour(s) de c.,** foul cable(s), foul hawse; **les chaînes,** the hawse, the chains; **c. du gouvernail,** rudder-chain; **le navire a cassé sa chaîne,** the ship has parted her cable; **c. flottante,** boom; **c. de port,** harbour (chain-) boom; (*f*) **commande, transmission, par c.,** chain-drive; **c. de transmission,** drive, transmission, chain; **c. de distribution,** timing chain; **roue à c.,** chain-wheel; **engrenage à c.,** chain gear; **transporteur à c.,** chain conveyor; (*g*) **former la c.,** (*of pers.*), to form a chain; **c. de montage,** (assembly) conveyor, assembly line; **c. de fabrication, de production en série,** production line; **travail à la c.,** (i) conveyor-work; assembly-line, production-line, work; (ii) chain-work, work in a (human) chain; (iii) *F:* monotonous work; *F:* grind; **travailler à la c.,** (i) to work on an assembly line, on a production line; (ii) to pass from hand to hand; to work in a (human) chain; *Butchery:* **c. d'abattage,** killing line, killing rail. **2.** chain, succession, sequence, series; (*a*) **c. de montagnes, de collines,** mountain, hill, range; chain of mountains, of hills; **c. de chalands,** string of barges; **c. d'idées,** train of thoughts; *Mil:* **c. d'agents de transmission, c. de liaison, c. de coureurs,** line of messengers, of runners, of despatch-riders; **c. de tirailleurs,** line of skirmishers; **c. du commandement,** chain of command; **c. de combat,** firing line; (*b*) chain-letter; **ne rompez pas la c.,** don't break the chain; (*c*) *Danc:* **c. anglaise,** grand chain, right and left. **3.** *Const:* **c. de liaison,** (i) tie-iron; (ii) stone pier (in brickwork), brick pier (in rubble-work); **c. d'encoignure,** corner-stone, quoins (of brick-work, etc.); **c. d'ancrage,** anchor-chain. **4.** *Ph: Ch: El: Elcs:* chain; **c. de désintégration,** disintegration, decay, chain; **c. fermée d'atomes,** closed chain of atoms; *s.a.* RÉACTION 1; **c. ramifiée,** branched chain; **c. de stations radio,** radio link; *T.V:* channel; *W.Tel:* **c. nationale,** = B.B.C. Home Service. **5.** (*a*) *Tex:* warp; *Paperm:* **toile triple c.,** triple warp; (*b*) *Knitting:* **faire une c. de mailles,** to cast on (a row of stitches).

chaîné [ʃɛne, ʃe-], *a.* linked, joined end-to-end.

chaînée [ʃɛne, ʃe-], *s.f. Surv:* chain(-length) (= 1 decametre).

chaîner [ʃɛne, ʃe-], *v.tr.* **1.** *Surv:* to chain, to measure (land) with a chain. **2.** *Const:* to chain, tie (walls, etc.).

chaînetier [ʃɛntje, ʃe-], *s.m. Jewel:* chain maker.

chaînette [ʃɛnɛt, ʃe-], *s.f.* **1.** small chain; **c. de sûreté,** safety-chain (of bracelet, etc.); *Cy: etc:* **c. antivol,** chain-lock. **2.** *Geom: etc:* **(arc en) c.,** catenary (curve); (*of trolley-line, etc.*) **faire la c., (entre les supports),** to sag. **3.** *Needlew:* **point de c.,** chain-stitch.

chaîneur [ʃɛnœːr, ʃe-], *s.m.* **1.** *Surv:* chainman. **2.** one of a line of men forming a chain.

chaînier [ʃɛnje, ʃe-], *s.m. Tchn: etc:* chain maker, chainsmith.

chaîniste [ʃɛnist, ʃe-], *s.m. Jewel:* chain maker.

chaînon [ʃɛnɔ̃, ʃe-], *s.m.* (*a*) link (of chain); *Mch: etc:* **grille à chaînons,** chain grate; *Biol:* **c. manquant,** missing link; (*b*) *Ph.Geog:* secondary chain (of mountains).

chaintre [ʃɛ̃ːtr], *s.m. or f.* (*a*) *Agr:* headland; (*b*) *Vit:* trailing method of planting vines; (*c*) path bordering a woodland area or marsh.

chair [ʃɛːr], *s.f.* flesh. **1.** (*a*) **blessure dans les chairs,** flesh wound; **le harpon pénétra dans les chairs de la baleine,** the harpoon went deep into the whale's flesh; *Med:* **c. baveuse,** proud flesh; **c. vive,** raw flesh; **voir qn en c. et en os,** to see s.o. in the flesh; **c'est lui en c. et en os,** it's him in person; **être (bien) en c.,** (i) (*of chicken*) to be nice and plump; (ii) (*of pers.*) to be in (good) condition, well-developed; (iii) (*of pers.*) to be fat, plump, fleshy, *F:* tubby, well-covered; **c'est une (grosse) masse de c.,** she's a great mound of flesh; **ce n'est qu'une masse de c.,** he's all brawn and no brains; **le saumon a une c. rose,** salmon has pink flesh; **marchand de c. humaine,** (i) slave trader; (ii) *F:* white slaver; **c. à canon,** cannon fodder; (*b*) *Leath:* flesh-side (of hide). **2.** (*a*) (i) *A:* meat (as opposed to fish); **c. de boucherie,** butcher's meat; (ii) **c. blanche, rouge,** white, red, meat; **c. noire,** game; **c. à saucisse,** sausage-meat; **c. à pâté,** minced meat; *F:* **hacher qn menu comme c. à pâté, battre qn en c. à pâté,** (i) to make mincemeat of s.o.; (ii) to beat s.o. within an inch of his life; **faire c. à pâté d'une pièce,** to tear a play to pieces; **n'être ni c. ni poisson,** to be neither fish nor fowl, neither fish nor flesh (nor good red herring), neither fish, flesh, nor fowl; (*b*) flesh, pulp (of peach, melon, etc.); flesh (of mushroom); *Metall:* fibre (of iron). **3.** (*a*) skin, outer surface of flesh; **avoir la c. fraîche,** to have a rosy complexion; **entre cuir et c.,** under the skin; *s.a.* CUIR 1; **c. de poule,** goose-flesh; **cela vous donne la c. de poule,** it makes your flesh creep; **j'en ai la c. de poule,** I shudder at the thought of it; *F:* it gives me the creeps; *a.inv.* **(couleur) c.,** flesh-coloured; **bas c.,** flesh-coloured stockings; **maillot c.,** flesh tights; (*b*) *pl. Art:* flesh-parts; *Paint:* carnations, flesh tints; *Sculp:* nude parts. **4.** body; **la résurrection de la c.,** the resurrection of the body; *B:* **le Verbe s'est fait c.,** the Word was made flesh; **c. de sa c.,** his, her, own flesh and blood; **le monde, le démon et la c.,** the world, the flesh and the devil; **les plaisirs de la c.,** the pleasures of the flesh; **le péché de la c.,** the sins of the flesh; **œuvre de c.,** sexual intercourse; **être de c.,** to be of the flesh, to be only human; *B: etc:* **l'esprit est prompt mais la c. est faible,** the spirit is willing but the flesh is weak.

chaire [ʃɛːr], *s.f.* **1.** chair, throne; **la c. de saint-Pierre, la c. apostolique, pontificale,** the Chair of St. Peter, the Holy See; **c. d'un évêque,** bishop's throne. **2. c. du prédicateur,** pulpit; **exprimer une opinion en pleine c.,** to express an opinion from the pulpit; **vocation pour la c.,** vocation for preaching; **monter en c.,** to ascend the pulpit. **3.** (*a*) chair, desk, rostrum (of lecturer, professor); (*b*) (*at university*) chair, professorship; **il a été nommé à la c. d'anglais,** he has been appointed professor of English; (*c*) (*at lycée*) **professeur de première c. d'anglais,** senior English master. **4.** *A.Furn:* box settle.

chairfaix [ʃɛrfɛ], *s.m. Fish:* caddis bait.

chais [ʃɛ], *s.m.* = CHAI.

chaise [ʃɛːz], *s.f.* **1.** (*a*) chair, seat; **c. de paille, c. cannée,** straw-, cane-bottomed chair; *A:* **c. à bras,** armchair; **c. pliante,** folding chair; **c. haute, c. d'enfant,** high chair; *A:* **c. curule,** curule chair; **c. longue,** reclining chair; *chaise-longue,* couch; **elle est obligée de faire de la c. longue,** she has to lie down every day; **c. à bascule,** *Fr.C:* **c. berçante,** rocking-chair; **c. à dos,** high-backed chair; **être assis entre deux chaises,** to be in an awkward position; *F:* **s'asseoir entre deux chaises (le cul par terre),** to fall between two stools; **porter qn en c., faire la c. à qn,** to carry s.o. in a bandy-chair, to give s.o. a bandy-chair; *Games:* **le jeu, la polka, des chaises,** musical chairs; *Ecc:* **c. de chœur,** (choir-)stall; (*b*) **c. chirurgicale,** operating chair; **c. roulante,** Bath chair, wheel-chair; **c. percée,** (night-)commode; *A:* close-stool; (*c*) *Jur: U.S:* **c. électrique,** (electric) chair. **2.** (*a*) *A:* **c. à porteurs,** sedan-chair; **c. (de poste),** (post-)chaise; (*b*) **c. à roulettes,** (child's) go-cart. **3.** *Const:* frame, timber-work (of windmill, tower, etc.). **4.** *Mec.E:* support, bracket; hanger; **c. de coussinet,** pedestal block, plummer block; seat (of bearing); **c. de, au, sol,** standard (hanger); **c. console,** bracket-hanger; **c. suspendue, c. pendante,** hanger, bearing-bracket; *Rail:* **c. de rail,** (rail) chair; *N.Arch:* **c. d'hélice,** "A" bracket; *Artil:* **c. de route,** gun (travelling) support. **5.** *Nau: Const: etc:* rope sling; **c. de gabier, de mâture, de calfat,** bosun's chair, seat, cradle; **nœud de c.,** bowline hitch; **nœud de c. double,** bowline on a bight.

chaise-lit [ʃɛːzli], *s.f.* bed-chair; *pl. chaises-lits.*

Chaix [ʃɛ(ks)], *s.m.* French railway time-table.

chaisier, -ière [ʃɛzje-, ʃe-; ʃɛzjɛːr], *s.* **1.** chair-maker. **2.** (*a*) chair attendant (in park, etc.); (*b*) = pew opener (in church).

chako [ʃako], *s.m.* = SHAKO.

chalade [ʃalad], *s.f. Equit:* calade; exercising ground.

chaland[1] [ʃalɑ̃], *s.m.* barge, lighter, scow; **c. à moteur,** motor barge; **c. à clapets,** hopper barge; **c. transporteur de tanks, c. porte-chars,** tank landing-craft; **c. à vase,** mud-scow, hopper; **transport par chalands,** lighterage; **frais de chalands,** lighterage.

chaland[2], **-ande** [ʃalɑ̃, -ɑ̃ːd], *s.* (*a*) *A:* customer, purchaser; (*b*) *F:* **c'est un drôle de chaland,** he's a queer customer; *A:* **c'est un fameux c.!** he's a great chap!

chaland-citerne [ʃalɑ̃sitɛrn], *s.m.* tanker barge; *pl. chalands-citernes.*

chalandeau, -eaux [ʃalɑ̃do], *s.m. often Pej:* bargeman, bargee, lighterman.

chalandier [ʃalɑ̃dje], *s.m.* bargee; bargemaster.

chalandise [ʃalɑ̃diːz], *s.f.* **1.** *A:* clientele (of shop, etc.). **2.** *Com:* **région de c.,** market radius (of main shopping town).

chalaze [kalɑːz], *s.f.* **1.** *Biol: Bot:* chalaza. **2.** *Med:* = CHALAZION.

chalazie [ʃalazi], *s.f.,* **chalazion** [ʃalazjɔ̃], *s.m. Med:* chalazion; stye (on the eyelid).

chalazogame [kalazɔgam], *a. Bot:* chalazogamic.

chalazogamie [kalazɔgami], *s.f. Bot:* chalazogamy.

chalcanthite [kalkɑ̃tit], *s.f. Miner:* chalcanthite.

Chalcédoine [kalsedwan]. **1.** *Pr.n.f. A.Geog:* Chalcedon. **2.** *s.f. Miner:* chalcedony.

chalcédonien, -ienne [kalsedɔnjɛ̃, -jɛn], *a.* & *s. A.Geog:* Chalcedonian.

chalcide [kalsid], *s.m. Rept:* **c. européen,** Southern European eyed skink.

chalcidides [kalsidid], *s.m.pl.,* **chalcididés** [kalsidide], *s.m.pl.,* **chalcidiens** [kalsidjɛ̃], *s.m.pl. Ent:* Chalcididae, chalcidids.

Chalcidique (la) [lakalsidik], *Pr.n.f. A.Geog:* Chalcidicum.

chalcis [kalsis], *s.m. Ent:* chalcid (fly).

chalcosiides [kalkɔsiid], *s.m.pl. Ent:* Chalcosiidae, the chalcosiid moths.

chalcocite [kalkɔsit], *s.f. Miner:* chalcocite.

chalcographe [kalkɔgraf], *s.m.* chalcographer, engraver on copper.

chalcographie [kalkɔgrafi], *s.f.* **1.** chalcography, engraving on copper. **2.** engraving studio.

chalcographier [kalkɔgrafje], *v.tr.* (*p.d.* & *pr.sub.* **n. chalcographiions, v. chalcographiiez**) to engrave (on copper).

chalcographique [kalkɔgrafik], *a.* chalcographic.

chalcolite [kalkɔlit], *s.f. Miner:* chalcolite, torbernite.

chalcolithique [kalkɔlitik], *a. Prehist:* chalcolithic.

chalcoménite [kalkɔmenit], *s.f. Miner:* chalcomenite.

chalcone [kalkɔn], *s.f. Ch:* chalcone.

chalcophanite [kalkɔfanit], *s.f. Miner:* chalcophanite.

chalcophyllite [kalkɔfilit], *s.f. Miner:* chalcophyllite.

chalcopyrite [kalkɔpirit], *s.f. Min:* chalcopyrite, copper pyrites.

chalcosidérite [kalkɔsiderit], *s.f. Miner:* chalcosiderite.

chalcosine [kalkɔzin], *s.f.,* **chalcosite** [kalkɔzit], *s.f. Miner:* chalcocite, chalcosine, glance-copper.

chalcosome [kalkɔsɔm], *s.m. Ent:* chalcosoma; Atlas beetle.

chalcostibite [kalkɔstibit], *s.f. Miner:* chalcostibite, wolfsbergite.

chaldaïque [kaldaik], *a.* & *s.* = CHALDÉEN.

Chaldée [kalde], *Pr.n.f. A.Geog:* Chaldea.

chaldéen, -enne [kaldeɛ̃, -ɛn], *a.* & *s.* Chaldean.

châle [ʃɑːl], *s.m.* shawl.

chalet [ʃɑlɛ, ʃa-], *s.m.* **1.** (*a*) (Swiss, etc.) chalet; (*b*) country cottage. **2.** *A:* **c. de nécessité,** public convenience.

chaleur [ʃalœːr], *s.f.* **1.** (*a*) heat, warmth; **il fait une grande c.,** it is very hot; **vague de c.,** heat-wave; **c. étouffante,** sultry weather; *Com:* **craint la c.,** store in a cool place; *Ph:* **c. spécifique, c. latente,** specific, latent, heat; *Med:* **éprouver des chaleurs,** to flush; **sensation de c.,** (i) glow (after cold bath, etc.); (ii) burning sensation; *Med: Vet:* **coup de c.,** heat-stroke, heat apoplexy; *Metall:* **c. suante,** welding heat; (*b*) *pl.* **les chaleurs,** the hot weather; **dans les grandes chaleurs,** during the hot season; (*c*) *Art:* **c. de coloris,** warmth of colour; (*d*) ardour, zeal; **dans la c. du combat,** in the heat of the strife; **parler avec c.,** to speak warmly, enthusiastically; **la c. de la jeunesse,** the fire, glow, of youth. **2. en c.,** (*of bitch, etc.*) on heat; (*of deer*) in rut.

chaleureusement [ʃalørøzmɑ̃], *adv.* warmly, cordially, effusively.

chaleureux, -euse [ʃalørø, -øːz], *a.* warm, ardent (friend, thanks, etc.); cordial (welcome, etc.); glowing (colour, terms); **remercier qn en termes c.,** to thank s.o. warmly; **applaudissements c.,** enthusiastic applause.

chalicodome [kalikɔdɔm], *s.f. Ent:* **c. (des hangars),** wall bee, mason bee.

chalicose [kalikoːz], *s.f. Med:* silicosis; chalicosis, stonemason's disease.

chalicothéridés [kalikɔteride], *s.m.pl. Paleont:* Chalicotheriidae.

chalina [kalina], *s.f. Spong:* Chalina.

châlit [ʃɑli], *s.m.* (*a*) *A:* bed; (*b*) bedstead.

chalking [tʃɔːkiŋ], *s.m. Paint: F:* chalking.

challenge [ʃalɑ̃ːʒ], *s.m. Sp:* challenge match, tournament.

challenger[1] [ʃalɑ̃ʒɛːr], *s.m. Sp:* challenger.

challenger[2] [ʃalɑ̃ʒe], *v.tr.* to challenge.

chaloir [ʃalwaːr], *v.impers. A:* to matter; *used only in* **il ne m'en chaut, il ne m'en chalait, guère,** it matters, mattered, not to me; **peu m'en chaut,** I don't care (a rap); *Lit:* I care not; **non qu'il m'en chaille,** not that I care.

chalon [ʃalɔ̃], *s.m.* **1.** *Fish:* drag-, trawl-net. **2.** *Tex: A:* shalloon.

chalonnais, -aise [ʃalɔnɛ, -ɛːz], *a.* & *s. Geog:* (native, inhabitant) of (i) the Chalonnais; (ii) Chalon-sur-Saône.

châlonnais, -aise [ʃɑlɔne, -ɛːz], *a.* & *s. Geog:* (native, inhabitant) of (i) Châlons-sur-Marne; (ii) Châlonnes-sur-Loire.

chaloupe [ʃalup], *s.f.* **1.** *Nau:* launch, longboat; *Fr.C:* rowing boat, *U.S:* rowboat; **c. à vapeur,** steam-launch. **2.** *Moll:* **c. cannelée,** paper nautilus.

chaloupé [ʃalupe]. **1.** *a.* swaying, swinging, rocking (dance, walk). **2.** *s.f.* **chaloupée,** swaying, rocking, dance.

chalouper [ʃalupe], *v.i.* to sway, swing, rock (like a boat, in dancing, walking).

chaloupier [ʃalupje], *s.m. Nau:* longboatman.

chalumeau, -eaux [ʃalymo], *s.m.* **1.** (drinking) straw; **c. de roseau,** reed. **2.** *Mus:* (*a*) pipe; *A:* shawm; (*b*) chalumeau, lowest register (of clarinet). **3.** *Ch: Ind:* blowpipe, blowlamp, (oxyacetylene) burner; **c. de découpage,** oxyacetylene cutting torch; **découpage au c.,** oxyacetylene cutting-out; **c. à découper,** flame-cutter; **c. soudeur,** welding torch, burner. **4.** *Fr.C:* spout (for collecting sap of maple tree).

chalumet [ʃalymɛ], *s.m.* mouthpiece (of a pipe).

chalut [ʃaly], *s.m.* drag-net; trawl.

chalutage [ʃalytaːʒ], *s.m.* trawling.

chalut-bois [ʃalybwa], *s.m. Fish:* caddis bait; *pl. chaluts-bois.*

chaluter [ʃalyte], *v.i.* to trawl.

chalutier, -ière [ʃalytje, -jɛːr]. **1.** *a.* **pêche chalutière,** trawling. **2.** *s.m.* (*boat or fisherman*) trawler; **c. à vapeur,** steam-trawler; **c. congélateur,** freeze(r) trawler.

chalybé [kalibe], *a. Pharm:* chalybeate.

Cham[1] [kam], *Pr.n.m. B.Hist:* Ham.

cham[2] [tʃam], *a. Geog:* Cham (tribe, language).

chama [kama], *s.f. Moll:* chama.

chamade [ʃamad], *s.f.* (*a*) *Mil: A:* signal (with drum or trumpet) for a parley; chamade; **battre, sonner la c.,** (i) to sound a parley; (ii) to capitulate, surrender; (iii) to bang the drum (in front of booth, etc.); (*b*) **battre la c.,** to be in a panic; **son cœur battait la c.,** his, her, heart was beating wildly.

chamæcéphale [kamesefal], *s.m.* = CHAMÉCÉPHALE.

chamæcyparis [kamesiparis], *s.m. Bot:* chamæcyparis.

chamæléonidés [kameleɔnide], *s.m.pl. Rept:* Chamaeleonidae.

chamærops [kamerɔps], *s.m. Bot:* chamærops, palmetto.

chamaillage [ʃamɑjaːʒ], *s.m. F:* bickering.

chamaillard [ʃamɑjaːr]. **1.** *a.* quarrelsome, argumentative. **2.** *s.m.* wrangler, squabbler.

chamaille [ʃamɑːj], *s.f. F:* squabble.

chamailler [ʃamɑje], *v.i. A: F:* to bicker, squabble.

se chamailler, *F:* to bicker, quarrel, squabble; **se c. avec qn,** to come to loggerheads with s.o., to be at loggerheads with s.o., to squabble with s.o., to bandy words with s.o.

chamaillerie [ʃamɑjri], *s.f. F:* **1.** bickering, quarrelling, squabbling, wrangling. **2.** squabble, wrangle.

chamailleur, -euse [ʃamɑjœːr, -øːz], *a.* & *s.* quarrelsome (person).

chamaillis [ʃamɑji], *s.m. A: Lit:* fray, scuffle, brawl; squabble.

chaman [ʃamɑ̃], *s.m.* shaman, medicine-man.

chamanisme [ʃamanism], *s.m.* shamanism.

chamaniste [ʃamanist], *a.* & *s.* shamanist.

chamarrage [ʃamaraːʒ], *s.m. A:* bedizenment; gaudy display (**de,** of).

chamarre [ʃamaːr], *s.f.* **1.** *A.Cost:* long robe, gown. **2.** *A:* trimmings, gaudy trappings.

chamarrer [ʃamare], *v.tr. A:* to bedizen, bedeck; *now used mainly in p.p.* **général tout chamarré d'ordres étrangers,** general plastered over with foreign orders; **c. un récit,** to embroider a tale; *Lit:* **montagne chamarrée de fleurs,** mountainside decked, spangled, with flowers.

se chamarrer, *A:* to bedizen oneself, to over-dress.

chamarrure [ʃamaryːr], *s.f. usu. pl.* (*a*) *Lit:* **une chapelle toute or et chamarrures,** a chapel all in gold and heavily decorated; (*b*) *A: Pej:* bedizenment; tawdry ornamentation.

chambard [ʃɑ̃baːr], *s.m. F:* (*a*) disorder, shambles; (*b*) din, racket.

chambardement [ʃɑ̃bardəmɑ̃], *s.m. F:* upset, upheaval; general re-shuffle; smashing of everything; **un grand c. général,** a major upheaval, revolution.

chambarder [ʃɑ̃barde], *F:* **1.** *v.tr.* (*a*) to sack, rifle (room, etc.); (*b*) to upset, smash up (furniture, etc.); **tout c.,** to turn everything upside down; **c. les plans de qn,** to upset s.o.'s apple cart; (*c*) to re-arrange, reorganize. **2.** *v.i.* (*a*) to reorganize everything, to have a general reshuffle; (*b*) to kick up a racket.

chambardeur, -euse [ʃɑ̃bardœːr, -øz], *s. F:* rowdy, hooligan; general disrupter; revolutionary.

chambart [ʃɑ̃baːr], *s.m.* = CHAMBARD.

chambellan [ʃɑ̃bɛlɑ̃], *s.m.* chamberlain.

chambérien, -ienne [ʃɑ̃berjɛ̃, -jɛn], *a.* & *s. Geog:* (native, inhabitant) of Chambéry.

chambouler [ʃɑ̃bule]. **1.** *v.i. P: O:* to be shaky on one's pins. **2.** *v.tr. F:* **tout c.,** to disturb everything; to turn everything topsy-turvy, upside down; **ça m'a chamboulé,** it gave me quite a turn.

chambourin [ʃɑ̃burɛ̃], *s.m.* **1.** white sand used in the manufacture of strass or paste (for imitation jewellery). **2.** common green glass.

chambrage [ʃɑ̃braːʒ], *s.m. Tchn:* recessing.

chambranle [ʃɑ̃brɑ̃ːl], *s.m. Arch:* frame-lining, casing (of door, window); jamb-lining (of door); (standing) window-frame; **c. de cheminée,** mantelpiece.

chambre [ʃɑ̃ːbr], *s.f.* **1.** room; (*a*) **c. à coucher,** (i) bedroom; (ii) bedroom suite; **c. à grand lit, c. à deux (personnes),** double room; **c. à deux lits,** room with twin beds; **c. à un lit,** single room; **c. d'amis,** spare (bed)room, guest room; **c. d'enfants,** nursery; **c. de débarras,** box-room;

c. d'apparat, state-room; **c. garnie, meublée,** bed-sitting-room; *F:* bed-sitter; **chambres meublées, garnies, à louer,** furnished rooms to let; **c. sur la rue,** front room; **c. sur la cour,** back-room; **faire c. à part,** (*of married couple*) to sleep in separate rooms; **garder la c.,** to keep, stay in, one's room; **faire, nettoyer, une c.,** to clean (out), tidy (up), do, a room; *s.a.* FEMME 3, POT 1; **c. blindée,** strong room; **c. forte,** safety vault; **c. froide, frigorifique,** cold (storage) room; **travailler en c.,** to work at home; **ouvrier en c.,** workman who works at home; home-worker; worker in cottage industry; **stratège en c.,** armchair strategist; *A:* **mettre une femme en c.,** to set up a woman in a flat; *s.a.* GENTILHOMME, ROBE 1; **musique de c.,** chamber music; (*b*) *Nau:* **c. des cartes, c. de veille,** chart-house, -room; (*c*) *Navy:* cabin; **c. du capitaine,** captain's cabin; **envoyer un officier à sa c.,** to put an officer under arrest; **passer à la c.,** to go before the promotion board; (*d*) **c. des machines,** engine-room; **c. de chauffe,** boiler-room, *Nau:* stokehold; **c. des pompes,** pump-room; (*e*) *Nau:* **c. (d'embarcation),** sternsheets (of boat); (*f*) **c. de torture,** torture-chamber; **c. à gaz,** gas-chamber. **2.** *Adm: Jur: etc:* chamber, house; **c. de commerce,** chamber of commerce, *U.S:* Board of Trade; **c. de justice,** division of a court of justice; *s.a.* SPONTANÉ; *A:* **c. des Députés** = House of Commons; *U.S:* = House of Representatives; *Pol:* **convoquer les Chambres,** to summon Parliament; **siéger à la C.,** to sit in Parliament; **C. basse,** Lower House, Lower Chamber; **C. haute,** Upper House, Upper Chamber; *Fin:* **c. de compensation, de liquidation,** clearing house; *Jur:* **en c. du conseil,** in chambers; *s.a.* CRIÉE. **3.** *Tchn:* chamber, room cavity, box space; *Physiol:* chamber (of the eye); (*a*) *Aut: Cy:* **c. à air,** inner tube (of tyre); **(pneu) sans c.,** tubeless tyre; *Sm.a.:* **c. d'un fusil,** chamber of a rifle, of a gun; **c. d'alimentation (d'arme automatique),** feed block (of automatic weapon); *Artil:* **c. à poudre,** gun chamber, powder chamber; *Hyd.E:* **c. d'écluse,** lock-chamber; **c. de mise en charge, c. d'eau,** forebay; turbine-chamber, -pit; **c. des pompes,** pump-room; *Metalw:* **c. de fonderie,** defect, cavity, in a casting; (*b*) *I.C.E: Mec.E:* **c. de combustion, d'explosion,** combustion chamber; (*of jet engine*) **c. de combustion,** combustion chamber, flame-tube; **c. de carburation,** mixing chamber; **c. de compression,** compression chamber; **c. d'aspiration,** suction-box, -chamber; **c. à air,** (i) air-chamber (of pump); (ii) *Ind:* wind-box (of blast-furnace); **c. à niveau constant,** float-chamber (of carburettor); **c. de soupape,** pocket (for a valve); *Ind:* **c. de plomb,** lead chamber; *Petroleum Ind:* **c. d'équilibre, de tranquillisation,** surge chamber; (*c*) *Mch:* **c. à feu,** fire-chamber; **c. à eau, d'eau,** water-space (of boiler); water-jacket; **c. de vapeur (d'une chaudière),** steam-space (of boiler); **c. de distribution,** steam-chest, -chamber; (*d*) *Min:* **exploitation par chambres,** panel-working; **c. d'envoyage,** shaft-, landing-, station; (*e*) *Ph:* **c. à condensation, c. de Wilson,** cloud chamber, Wilson's expansion chamber; **c. barométrique,** Torricellian vacuum; *Atom.Ph:* **c. d'ionisation, à détente,** ionization-, fog-, cloud-, expansion-chamber; **c. à bulles,** bubble-chamber. **4.** *Phot:* **c. noire,** (i) camera obscura; (ii) camera (body); (iii) dark room; **c. claire,** camera lucida; **c. d'atelier,** studio camera; **c. à soufflet,** bellows camera; **c. pliante,** folding camera.

chambré [ʃɑ̃bre], *a.* **1.** chambered (shell, etc.). **2.** *A:* honeycombed, pitted (gun, etc.). **3.** (*of wine*) at room temperature.

chambrée [ʃɑ̃bre], *s.f.* **1.** roomful (of people sharing a room). **2.** *Mil:* barrack room; **chef de c.,** corporal in charge of a barrack room. **3.** *Th:* house; audience.

chambrer [ʃɑ̃bre]. **1.** *v.i. A:* to share a room, lodge together, to room, **(avec,** with). **2.** *v.tr.* (*a*) to confine, lock up (s.o.) in a room; (*b*) to take the chill off (wine), to bring (wine) to room temperature; (*c*) *Sm.a:* to chamber (gun); (*d*) *P:* to tease (s.o.).

se chambrer, *A:* (of gun) to become pitted, to wear.

chambrette [ʃɑ̃brɛt], *s.f. F:* little room; garret.

chambrière [ʃɑ̃bri(j)ɛːr], *s.f.* **1.** *A:* chambermaid. **2.** long whip, lungeing whip. **3.** (cart-)prop; drag (of truck, etc.); *Mec.E:* (safety-)dog. **4.** *Nau:* furling gasket.

chame [kam], *s.f. Moll:* chama.

chameau, -eaux [ʃamo], *s.m.* **1.** (*a*) camel; **c. (à deux bosses),** Bactrian, two-humped, camel; **transport à dos de c.,** camel transport; **corps de chameaux,** camelry; **rejeter le moucheron et avaler le c.,** to strain at a gnat and swallow a camel; (*b*) *Bot:* **épine de c.,** camel-thorn; (*c*) *P:* (*of man*) beast, brute; (*of woman*) (old) cow, bitch, cat; *occ.* **la c.!** the bitch! *a.* **ce qu'il, qu'elle, est c.!** what a brute he is! what a bitch she is! **2.** *Nau:* camel (for raising ships). **3.** *Rail:* dolly, shunting engine. **4.** *F:* impurity (in chemical solution).

chamécéphale [kamesefal], *a. Anthr:* chamecephalic, chamecephalous.

chamécéphalie [kamesefali], *s.f. Anthr:* chamecephaly.

chamelée [ʃamle], *s.f.* camel-load.

chamelier [ʃaməlje], *s.m.* camel-driver, cameleer.

chamelet [ʃamlɛ], *s.m.* young camel, camel colt.

chamelle [ʃamɛl], *s.f.* she-camel.

chamelon [ʃamlɔ̃], *s.m.* young camel, camel colt.

chaméphyte [kamefit], *s.f. Bot:* chamephyte.

chamite [kamit], *s.m. B.Hist:* Hamite.

chamitique [kamitik], *a. B.Hist:* Hamitic.

chamito-sémitique [kamitosemitik], *a.* hamito-semitic.

chamois [ʃamwa]. **1.** *s.m. Z:* chamois; **c. du cap,** gemsbok; *Leath:* **(peau de) c.,** wash-leather, chamois leather, shammy (leather). **2.** *a.inv.* buff-coloured.

chamoisage [ʃamwazaːʒ], *s.m. Leath:* chamoising, tawing, dressing (of leather).

chamoiser [ʃamwaze], *v.tr. Leath:* to chamois, dress, taw; **cuir chamoisé,** wash-leather, shammy leather.

chamoiserie [ʃamwazri], *s.f.* (*a*) chamois-leather factory; (*b*) chamois-leather industry, trade; (*c*) *coll.* chamois leather.

chamoiseur [ʃamwazœːr], *s.m. Leath:* chamois-leather dresser, tawer, chamoiser.

chamoisine [ʃamwazin], *s.f.* soft (yellow) duster.

chamoisite [ʃamwazit], *s.f. Miner:* chamoisite, chamosite.

chamoniard, -iarde [ʃamɔnjaːr, -jard], *a. & s. Geog:* (native, inhabitant) of Chamonix.

chamosite [ʃamɔzit], *s.f. Miner:* = CHAMOISITE.

chamotte [ʃamɔt], *s.f.* chamotte, grog; fire-clay.

champ[1] [ʃɑ̃], *s.m.* field. **1.** (*a*) **c. de blé,** field of corn, of wheat, cornfield; **fleur des champs,** wild flower; *B:* **les lis des champs,** the lilies of the field; **courir les champs,** to wander about the country; **aux champs,** in the fields; **mener les vaches aux champs,** to drive the cows into the fields; **aller aux champs,** to go into the country; **prendre, couper, à travers champs,** to go, cut, across country; *F:* **se sauver à travers champs,** to dodge a question, an issue, to change the conversation; *F:* **avoir la clef des champs,** to be free to roam; **donner la clef des champs à qn,** to give s.o. his liberty; **prendre la clef des champs,** (i) to decamp, abscond; to run off; (ii) to take a day off in the country; *F:* **fou à courir les champs,** mad as a hatter; *A:* **être aux champs,** (i) to be all at sea; (ii) to be furious; *A:* **mettre qn aux champs,** (i) to muddle s.o., to put s.o. off; (ii) to drive s.o. wild; *adv.phr. A:* **semer à c.,** to scatter broadcast; **en plein(s) champ(s),** in the open (fields); **à tout bout de c.,** repeatedly, at every turn, at every available opportunity; (*b*) **c. de foire,** fair ground; **c. d'aviation,** airfield; **c. d'atterrissage,** landing ground; **c. de course(s),** race-course, *U.S:* race-track; *Turf:* **le c.,** the field; **c. fourni,** big field (of starters); **parier contre le c.,** to lay against the field; **prendre du c.,** to draw ahead; **c. de neige,** snowfield; *Nau:* **c. de glace,** ice-field; **c. pétrolifère,** oil field; **c. diamantifère,** diamond field; **c. aurifère,** goldfield; (*c*) *Mil:* **c. de bataille,** battlefield; **rester maître du c. de bataille,** to be left in possession of the field; **le c. d'honneur,** the battlefield; the field of honour; **mort au c. d'honneur,** killed in action; **c. de manœuvres,** drill, exercise, ground; **c. de tir,** (firing, shooting) range; *Artil:* practice ground; **c. de tir au fusil,** rifle-range; **c. de tir réduit,** miniature range; **c. de tir anti-aérien,** anti-aircraft range; **c. de mines,** minefield; **battre aux champs,** to beat (i) the general salute; (ii) a ruffle; *s.a.* MARS 1; (*d*) *A:* **c. clos,** lists; **combat en c. clos,** trial by battle, by combat; **livrer c.,** to order a trial by battle; **ouvrir le c.,** to open the lists (for a tournament); *s.a.* ÉLYSÉE 2, REPOS 1. **2.** (*a*) field of action; range, scope; **prendre du c. (pour sauter, tourner sa voiture, etc.),** to give oneself ample room, plenty of room (to jump, turn one's car, etc.); **donnez-moi du c.,** give me (some) elbow-room; *Nau:* **c. d'evitage,** swinging circle; **laisser le c. libre à qn,** to leave s.o. a clear field; *F:* **le c. est libre,** the coast is clear; **avoir le c. libre,** to have a clear field before one; **donner (un) libre c. à son imagination, à sa colère,** to give free rein, full scope, to one's imagination, full vent to one's anger; **ouvrir le c. aux conjectures,** to open up a wide field for conjecture; **ses lectures embrassent un c. très étendu,** his reading covers a very wide range, embraces a very wide range of subjects; **vaste c. d'hypothèses,** wide field, range, of speculation; **élargir le c. de son activité,** to extend the scope of one's activities; **c. de recherches,** field of research; (*b*) *Artil: etc:* **c. de tir (d'une pièce),** (i) (*on ground*) field of fire; (ii) (*traversing and elevation*) arc of fire; **c. de tir horizontal, latéral,** lateral arc of fire; traversing arc; arc of training; **c. de tir vertical, en hauteur,** vertical arc of fire; elevating arc; **dégager le c. de tir,** to clear the field of fire; **c. de tir dégagé,** cleared, unobstructed, field of fire; (*c*) *Cin: etc:* shot, picture; *Opt:* **c. d'une lunette,** field of a telescope; **c. optique, c. visuel, c. de vision, c. d'observation,** field of view; **c. de vision dégagé,** clear field of view; **c. de vision étendu,** long field of view; **c. de netteté,** focal field; **c. de couverture,** (lens) coverage; **c. de visibilité,** field of vision, visibility; **c. de visibilité vers l'avant, vers l'arrière,** forward, rear, visibility; **angle de c.,** angle of view, of field; *T.V:* **en c.,** on camera; **hors c.,** off camera; *Phot:* **c. corrigé,** flat field; (*d*) *Cin: etc:* shot, picture. **3.** *El: Elcs:* field; **c. électrique, électro-statique,** electric (electro)-static, field; **c. d'induit,** armature field; **c. excité en dérivation, c. de shunt,** shunt-field; **c. excité en série, c. de série,** series-field; **c. magnétique,** magnetic field; **c. magnétique tors, tordu, déformé,** distorted field; **c. magnétique perturbateur,** disturbing magnetic field; **c. tournant,** rotating field; **bobine de c.,** field(-coil); **intensité de c.,** field intensity; (electric, magnetic) field, strength; **microscope à c. émissif,** field emission microscope; **énergie du c. magnétique,** field energy; *Radar:* **c. d'exploration, de balayage, de lecture,** scanning field. **4.** (*a*) *Her:* field (*of coat of arms*); (*b*) *Art:* field, ground (*of picture*); *Num:* field (*of a medal*); (*c*) *Surg:* **c. opératoire,** operative field.

champ[2], *s.m. O:* edge, side; **pierres (posées) de c., sur c.,** stones set on edge, edgewise; **assise de c.,** brick-on-edge course; **roue de c.,** crown-wheel, face-wheel; *s.a.* CHANT[2].

Champagne [ʃɑ̃paɲ]. **1.** *Pr.n.f. Geog:* Champagne; **C. humide,** wet Champagne; **C. pouilleuse,** dry Champagne. **2.** *s.m.* (*also* **vin de C.**) champagne; **c. brut,** dry champagne; **c. nature,** still champagne; *s.a.* ORIGINE 3. **3.** *s.f.* **fine c.,** liqueur brandy (from the Champagne de Saintonge).

champagnisation [ʃɑ̃paɲizasjɔ̃], *s.f. Wine-m:* champagnization.

champagniser [ʃɑ̃paɲize], *v.tr.* to champagnize, give a sparkle to (wine).

champart [ʃɑ̃paːr], *s.m.* **1.** *Hist:* champart. **2.** *Husb:* cereal fodder.

champbord [ʃɑ̃bɔːr], *s.m. Civ.E:* spoil-bank.

champelure [ʃɑ̃plyːr], *s.f.* frost-bite (of fruit-trees, etc.).

champenois, -oise [ʃɑ̃pənwa, -waːz]. **1.** *a. & s.* (native, inhabitant) of Champagne. **2.** *s.m. Ling: Hist:* Champagne dialect. **3.** *Wine-m:* (*a*) *a.* **méthode champenoise,** (natural) champagnization method; (*b*) *s.f.* **champenoise,** champagne bottle.

champêtre [ʃɑ̃pɛːtr], *a.* rustic, rural, pastoral; **vie c.,** country life; **garde c.,** country policeman.

champi(s), -is(s)e [ʃɑ̃pi, -iːz, -is], *s. A: Dial:* foundling, waif.

champignon [ʃɑ̃piɲɔ̃], *s.m.* **1.** (*a*) **c. (comestible),** (i) mushroom; (ii) edible fungus; **c. de couche,** cultivated mushroom; **blanc de c.,** mushroom spawn; *F:* **pousser comme un c.,** to (spring up like a) mushroom; **ville c.,** mushroom town, boom town; (*of dumdum bullet*) **faire c.,** to set up, to mushroom; **c. atomique,** mushroom cloud; (*b*) **c. vénéneux,** poisonous fungus; (*c*) *Med:* fungoid growth; (*d*) *F:* **le c.,** dry rot. **2.** (*a*) wig stand; **c. de modiste,** milliner's hatstand; (*b*) cowl (of chimney); (*c*) collar (of axle); (*d*) round head (of bolt); *Tls:* **fraise c.,** rose countersink bit; (*e*) *Rail:* head (of rail); **rail à double c.,** double-headed rail; bull-head rail; (*f*) *I.C.E:* (i) atomizing cone (of carburettor); (ii) **(soupape à) c.,** mushroom valve, poppet valve; (*g*) *Nau:* mushroom anchor; (*h*) *F:* thief, stranger (in candle); (*i*) *Aut: F:* accelerator pedal; **appuyer sur, écraser, le c.,** to step on the gas. **3.** low mound, tumulus.

champignonner [ʃɑ̃piɲɔne], *v.i. F:* to mushroom.

champignonnier [ʃɑ̃piɲɔnje], *s.m.* mushroom grower.

champignonnière [ʃɑ̃piɲɔnjɛːr], *s.f.* mushroom bed.
champignonniste [ʃɑ̃piɲɔnist], *s.m.* mushroom grower; *s.a.* FOURMI.
champigny [ʃɑ̃piɲi], *s.m. Cu:* apricot millefeuille.
champion, -ionne [ʃɑ̃pjɔ̃, -jɔn], *s.* (*a*) champion; *Golf:* scratch player; (*b*) champion (of), fighter (for), partisan (of) (a cause, etc.); (*c*) *a. F:* champion; **c'est c.!** it's first-rate!
championnat [ʃɑ̃pjɔna], *s.m.* championship.
champlé [ʃɑ̃ple], *a.* (*of fruit-trees, etc.*) frost-bitten; nipped (by the frost).
champlevage [ʃɑ̃ləvaːʒ], *s.m.* chasing (of enamel).
champlevé [ʃɑ̃ləve]. **1.** *a. & s.m.* champlevé enamel. **2.** *s.f.* **champlevée,** chasing (of enamel).
champlever [ʃɑ̃l(ə)ve], *v.tr.* (**je champlève, n. champlevons; je champlèverai**); (*a*) to chase out (ground of enamel); (*b*) to cut away (wood-engraving).
champlure [ʃɑ̃plyːr], *s.f.* = CHAMPELURE.
champoreau, -eaux [ʃɑ̃pɔro], *s.m.* **1.** (hot) coffee with wine, rum, or brandy (as first drunk in Algeria). **2.** American drink of mixed liqueurs.
chamsin [kamsin], *s.m. Meteor:* chamsin, k(h)amsin.
Chanaan [kanaɑ̃], *Pr.n.m. B.Hist:* **la terre, le pays, de C.,** the land of Canaan.
chananéen, -éenne [kananeɛ̃, -eɛn], *B.Hist:* **1.** *a.* Canaanitish. **2.** *s.* Canaanite.
chançard, -arde [ʃɑ̃saːr, -ard], *a. & s. P:* lucky (chap, woman).
chance [ʃɑ̃ːs], *s.f.* **1.** (*a*) chance, likelihood; **les chances sont contre lui,** the chances, the odds, are against him; **il a toutes les chances contre lui,** he has all the odds, heavy odds, against him; **il n'a pas la moindre c., l'ombre d'une c., de réussir,** he hasn't the slightest chance, hasn't the ghost of a chance, *F:* hasn't an earthly chance, of succeeding; **vous avez toutes les chances d'être accusé, il y a toutes les chances pour que vous soyez accusé,** there is every likelihood that you will be charged; **donner une c. à qn,** to give s.o. a chance; **il a peu de chances de réussir, il y a peu de chances qu'il réussisse,** he has little chance of succeeding; **il y a peu de chances (pour) qu'il pleuve,** it's not likely, it's unlikely, to rain; **il a des chances égales d'être nommé,** he has an even, a fifty-fifty, chance of being appointed; **les chances sont à peu près égales,** it's about fifty-fifty, there's not much in it; **il y a des chances, beaucoup de chances, que . . .,** the chances are that . . .; **il a des chances d'être choisi,** he stands a good chance of being chosen; **vous avez des chances d'y gagner,** you stand to gain; **candidats qui ont des chances,** candidates in the running; **projet qui offre des chances de succès,** plan likely to succeed; **il y a une c.,** it's just possible; **il y avait toujours la c. que,** it was always possible, *F:* on the cards, that; **courir la c.,** to run the risk; **risquer les chances,** to take a chance; **c. aléatoire, douteuse,** off-chance; **donner une bonne c. à qn,** to give a good opening to s.o., to give s.o. a chance; (*b*) *Mth:* **théorie des chances,** calculus of probabilities. **2.** luck, fortune; **la c. lui sourit,** fortune smiles on him; **tenter la c.,** to try one's luck, to chance it; **souhaiter bonne c. à qn,** to wish s.o. good luck; **bonne c.!** good luck! **quelle c.!** what a bit of luck! what a blessing! **quelle c. que vous soyez venu!** how lucky you came! **avoir de la c.,** to be lucky, in luck's way; **vous avez de la c. de pouvoir faire ce qui vous plaît,** you are lucky to be able to do what you like; **il n'a pas eu de c.,** he had no luck, was unlucky; **décidément, je n'ai pas de c. aujourd'hui,** there's no doubt about it, it's not my lucky day; **j'ai eu la c. de ne pas être remarqué,** luckily for me, I was not noticed; **j'eus la c. de réussir,** I had the good fortune to succeed; **la c. m'a toujours été favorable,** I always had the best of luck, luck was always on my side; **porter c. à qn,** to bring s.o. luck; **c'est bien ma c.!** just my luck! **pas de c.!** hard luck! **par c.,** luckily, by good fortune, by a stroke of luck; **par une c. heureuse,** by a lucky, happy, chance; **rompre la c.,** (i) to break a run of luck; (ii) to make sth. misfire; **la c. a tourné,** my, your, his, etc., luck has turned.
chancelant [ʃɑ̃slɑ̃], *a.* staggering, wavering, unsteady; **pas chancelants,** staggering, tottering, unsteady, footsteps; **santé chancelante,** (i) delicate (state of) health; (ii) delicate constitution; **sa santé devient chancelante,** his health is failing; **empire c.,** tottering empire.
chancelariat [ʃɑ̃sələrja], *s.m.* chancellorship.
chanceler [ʃɑ̃sle], *v.i.* (**je chancelle, n. chancelons; je chancellerai**) to stagger, totter; to be unsteady (on one's legs); **avancer, reculer, entrer, sortir, en chancelant,** to stagger, reel, forward, back, in, out; **traverser la pièce en chancelant,** to stagger across the room; **descendre la rue en chancelant,** to go staggering down the street; **trône qui chancelle,** tottering throne; **c. dans sa résolution,** to waver in one's resolution.
chancelier [ʃɑ̃səlje], *s.m.* **1.** chancellor; (*in Britain*) **Grand C.,** Lord Chancellor; **C. de l'Échiquier,** Chancellor of the Exchequer. **2.** *Dipl:* head of chance(lle)ry (in an embassy).
chancelière [ʃɑ̃səljɛːr], *s.f.* **1.** chancellor's wife. **2.** footmuff.
chancellement [ʃɑ̃sɛlmɑ̃], *s.m.* staggering, tottering.
chancellerie [ʃɑ̃sɛlri], *s.f.* **1.** chancellory, -ery; (*in Fr.*) **Grande Chancellerie,** Chancellery of the Legion of Honour. **2.** *Dipl:* chance(lle)ry (of an embassy); **style de c.,** diplomatic jargon.
chanceux, -euse [ʃɑ̃sø, -øːz], *a.* **1.** *O:* dependent upon chance, hazardous, chancy; **une affaire chanceuse,** a matter of chance, a risky business. **2.** lucky, fortunate; **vous voilà bien c.!** you're lucky! you're in luck!
chanci [ʃɑ̃si]. **1.** *a.* mouldy, mildewed (bread, ham, etc.). **2.** *s.m.* (*a*) dunghill covered with mushroom spawn; (*b*) mould(iness), mildew.
chancir [ʃɑ̃siːr], *v.i. & pr.* to go mouldy, to become mildewed.
chancissure [ʃɑ̃sisyːr], *s.f.* mould, mildew.
chancre [ʃɑ̃ːkr], *s.m.* **1.** *Bot:* canker; **c. du mélèze,** larch blister. **2.** *Med:* (*a*) *A:* ulcer; (*b*) **c. (vénérien),** chancre; **c. induré,** hard chancre; **c. syphilitique, mou,** soft chancre; (*c*) *Vet:* canker; (*d*) *F:* **manger comme un c.,** to eat enormously.
chancrelle [ʃɑ̃krɛl], *s.m. Med:* soft chancre.
chancreux, -euse [ʃɑ̃krø, -øːz], *a.* **1.** (*of growth, etc.*); (*a*) cankerous; (*b*) (i) ulcerous; (ii) chancrous. **2.** (*of part or organ*) (*a*) cankered; (*b*) (i) ulcerated; (ii) infected with chancre.
chancroïde [ʃɑ̃krɔid], *s.m. Med:* chancroid, soft chancre.
'chand [ʃɑ̃], *s.m. A: P:* (= MARCHAND) **'chand de vin,** tavern-keeper; **"'chand d'habits!"** "old clo'!"
chandail [ʃɑ̃daːj], *s.m. Cost:* sweater, pullover.
Chandeleur (la) [laʃɑ̃dlœːr], *s.f. Ecc:* Candlemas.
chandelier, -ière [ʃɑ̃dəlje, -jɛːr], *s.* **1.** tallow chandler; candle-maker. **2.** *s.m.* (*a*) candlestick; **mettre la lumière sur le c.,** to reveal the truth (about sth.); to make no secret (of sth.); *F:* **mettre qn sur le c.,** to put s.o. in the limelight; **être sur le c.,** to be in a prominent position; (*b*) *A: F:* (male friend used as) decoy (to screen real lover); (*c*) *Mch:* pedestal (of boiler); *Nau:* stanchion; **c. à fourche,** crutch; (*d*) water tap with a long bend; (*e*) stump (of a tree); (*f*) *P:* nose, conk; (*g*) *Ven:* **porter le c.,** (i) (*of stag*) to have large hollow antlers; (ii) (*of hare*) to be sitting on the watch for the hounds.
chandelle [ʃɑ̃dɛl], *s.f.* **1.** (*a*) (tallow) candle; **c. à la baguette, c. plongée,** dip (candle); **c. moulée,** mould-candle; **fabricant de chandelles, marchand de chandelles,** tallow-chandler; **bout de c.,** candle-end; **économies de bouts de c.,** cheese-paring economy; **c'est une économie de bouts de c.,** that's being penny-wise (and pound-foolish); **travailler à la c.,** to work by candle-light; **brûler la c. par les deux bouts,** to burn the candle at both ends; **se brûler à la c.,** to singe one's wings; *F:* **souffler sa c.,** to die; *P:* to snuff it; *F:* **s'en aller comme une c.,** to die, to fade out; **le jeu n'en vaut pas la c.,** the game is not worth the candle; **tenir la c.,** to pander, to act as go-between in a love-affair; **(en) voir trente-six chandelles,** to see stars; *A:* **vente à c. éteinte,** candle auction, auction by inch of candle; *F:* **allons, la c. brûle,** come along, there's no time to lose; (*b*) (church) candle, taper; *F:* **je vous dois une fière c.,** I owe you more than I can (ever) repay, you've saved my life. **2.** (*a*) *P:* snot; **une c. lui pend au nez,** his nose is running; (*b*) *F:* dandelion clock; (*c*) *P:* bottle. **3.** (*a*) *Pyr:* **c. romaine,** Roman candle; (*of partridge, aircraft*) **monter en c.,** to rocket; (*of aircraft*) to zoom; **les prix ont monté en c.,** prices have soared, rocketed; *Av:* **(montée en) c.,** zoom, chandelle; (*b*) *Ten: Cr: etc:* lob, skyer; *Fb:* high kick, balloon; **faire une c.,** to sky, lob, loft, a ball; (*c*) *Fb:* bouncing of ball by umpire (to re-start game); (*d*) *Gym:* shoulder stand. **4.** *Const: etc:* stay, prop, shore, pillar, upright. **5.** *Bot:* **arbre à c.,** candleberry tree.
chandeller [ʃɑ̃dɛle, -d(ə)-], *v.tr. Const: etc:* to prop up, shore up.
chandellerie [ʃɑ̃dɛlri], *s.f.* **1.** candle-works. **2.** candle trade.
chane[1] [kan], *s.f. Dial:* large milk can.
chane[2] [ʃan], *s.m.* soldering iron.
chanfraindre [ʃɑ̃frɛ̃ːdr], *v.tr.* to chamfer, bevel.
chanfrein[1] [ʃɑ̃frɛ̃], *s.m.* **1.** (*a*) *Arm:* chamfron, chamfrain; (*b*) plume (on horse's head). **2.** nose (of horse).
chanfrein[2], *s.m.* chamfered edge, chamfer, bevelled edge; **bord en c.,** bevel(led) edge.
chanfreinage [ʃɑ̃frɛnaːʒ], *s.m.* bevelling, chamfering.
chanfreindre [ʃɑ̃frɛ̃ːdr], **chanfreiner** [ʃɑ̃frene], *v.tr.* to chamfer, bevel.
chanfreineuse [ʃɑ̃frɛnøːz], *s.f.* edge-planing machine.
chanfrer [ʃɑ̃fre], *v.tr.* = CHAMPLEVER.
change [ʃɑ̃ːʒ], *s.m.* **1.** *A. & Lit:* = CHANGEMENT. **2.** *Fin:* (*a*) *A:* change; **demander le c. d'une pièce de monnaie,** to ask for change for a coin; **rendre le c. à qn,** to pay s.o. back in his own coin; (*b*) (i) exchange; **gagner, ne pas perdre, au c.,** to gain on, by, the exchange, to lose nothing on a deal; **c. réel, effectif,** real exchange; **lettre de c.,** bill of exchange; **lettre de c. sur l'intérieur, sur l'extérieur,** inland, foreign, bill; **première, seconde, de c.,** first, second, of exchange; **bureau de c.,** foreign exchange office; **opérations de c.,** (foreign) exchange transactions; **devise à c. élevé,** hard currency; **pays à c. élevé,** countries with hard currencies; **cours du c.,** rate of exchange; **au c. du jour,** at the current rate of exchange; (ii) agio; *s.a.* AGENT 2, CONTRÔLE 3. **3.** *F:* **avoir un c. de chaussures,** to have a change of shoes, a spare pair of shoes. **4.** *Ven:* **donner le c. aux chiens,** to put hounds on the wrong scent; **donner le c. à qn,** to put s.o. on a false scent, to put s.o. off, to side-track s.o.; *A:* **je ne prends point le c.,** I am not deceived.
changeable [ʃɑ̃ʒabl], *a.* **1.** changeable, alterable. **2.** exchangeable.
changeant [ʃɑ̃ʒɑ̃], *a.* changing, altering; fitful, changeable, variable; **caractère changeant,** changeable, fickle, disposition; **d'humeur changeante,** fitful; **teintes changeantes,** shimmering tints; **taffetas c.,** shot silk; **temps c.,** unsettled weather.
changement [ʃɑ̃ʒmɑ̃], *s.m.* change (of air, of residence, of condition, etc.); alteration; *Sch:* **c. (de section, de classe),** transfer; **il vous faudrait un c. d'air, d'occupation,** you need a change; **il y a eu c. de propriétaire,** the hotel, etc., has changed hands; *P.N:* **c. de propriétaire,** under new ownership; under new management; **opérer un c.,** to bring about a change; **un grand c. s'était opéré en lui,** a great change had come over him; **c. de marée,** turn of the tide; **c. de vent,** shift of wind; **c. de pente,** break of slope; *Ph:* **c. d'état,** change of state; **c. en mal, en mieux,** change for the worse, for the better; **c. à une clause,** alteration, change, in a clause; **faire quelques changements à une robe,** to make a few alterations to a dress; *Nau:* **c. de route,** alteration of course; *Mch:* **c. de marche,** (i) reversing; (ii) reversing gear (of locomotive, etc.); **c. de vitesse,** (i) change of gear; (ii) change-speed gear; *Rail:* **c. de voie,** points, turn-off; *Th:* **c. à vue,** transformation scene.
changer [ʃɑ̃ʒe], *v.* (**je changeai(s); n. changeons**) **1.** *v.tr.* to change; to exchange; **c. un billet de banque,** to change a (bank-)note; **c. des dollars contre des francs, en francs,** to change dollars into francs; **c. des meubles contre des tableaux,** to exchange furniture for pictures; **j'ai changé mes gants pour une paire plus grande,** I changed my gloves for a larger pair; **c. les draps,** to change the bed(clothes); **on lui a changé son parapluie dans le train,** he got the wrong umbrella on the train; *Th:* **c. le décor,** to shift the scenery; **c. un bébé,** to change a baby's nappy, *U.S:* diaper; *F:* to change a baby; *s.a.* NOURRICE 2. **2.** *v.tr.* (*a*) to change, alter; **c. sa manière de vivre,** to change one's way of life; **cette robe vous change,** that dress makes you look different, changes you completely; **c. une défaite en déroute,** to turn a defeat into a rout; **le magicien le changea en cochon,** the magician changed, turned, him into a pig; **homme changé en bête,** man turned, changed, into a beast; **c. sa chaise de place,** to change the position of, to move, shift, one's chair; *Nau:* **c. la barre,** to shift the helm; *Nau:* **c. une voile,** to shift a sail; (*b*) **la campagne me changera,** the country will be a nice change for me; it will be a change for me to stay in the country; **ça doit vous c. ici,** things must seem very different to you here, you must find things very different here; **une promenade me changera les idées,** a walk will make a change for me, will take my mind off things; *abs.* **ça change des livres mal écrits,** it

makes a change from badly written books; **ça ne le change pas,** it's just like him. 3. *v.i.* to change; (*a*) to undergo a change; **le temps a changé depuis hier,** the weather has changed since yesterday; **le temps est changé aujourd'hui,** the weather is different today; **c. de couleur, de visage,** to change colour; **c. du tout au tout,** to change completely; *Iron:* **pour c.,** (just) for a change; **plus ça change, plus c'est la même chose,** *plus ça change . . .*; (*b*) **c. de train,** to change (trains); **c. de main,** to change hands, to use the other hand; **c. de mains,** to change hands, to pass into the possession of s.o. else; **c. de place,** to change one's seat; **c. de place avec qn,** to change seats with s.o.; **c. de places,** to change places; **c. de maison,** to move (to, into, a new house); **c. de logis,** *F:* to shift one's quarters; **la rue a changé de nom,** the name of the street has been changed, the street has been renamed; **le magasin a changé de propriétaire,** the shop is under new management, ownership; *s.a.* DISQUE 2, FACE 1; **c. d'habits,** *abs:* **c.,** to change (one's clothes); **c. de robe,** to change one's dress; (*of snake*) **c. de peau,** to change, slough, its skin; **c. d'avis,** to change one's mind, one's opinion; **c. de sujet,** to change the subject (of a conversation); **c. d'air,** to go somewhere for a change of air; **c. de route,** (i) to take another road; (ii) *Nau:* to alter course; **la rivière a changé de cours,** the river has shifted its course; *Nau:* **changez!** let go and haul! *Mil:* **c. de pas,** to change step; **c. de ton,** (i) to change one's tune; (ii) to improve one's manner.

se changer, to change (one's clothes); **je n'ai pas de quoi me c.,** I've nothing to change into, I haven't a change of clothes with me.

changeur, -euse [ʃɑ̃ʒœːr, -øːz], *s.* 1. money changer. 2. *s.m. W.Tel:* **c. de fréquence,** frequency changer. 3. *s.m. Rec:* **c. de disques,** record changer.

Changhaï [ʃɑ̃gaj], *Pr.n.m. Geog:* Shanghai.

chanlat(t)e [ʃɑ̃lat], *s.f. Const:* eaves-board; chantlate.

channe [ʃan], *s.m.* soldering iron.

chanoine [ʃanwan], *s.m. Ecc:* canon; *F:* **vie de c.** easy life.

chanoinesse [ʃanwanɛs], *s.f. Ecc:* canoness.

chanoinie [ʃanwani], *s.f. Ecc:* canonry.

Chan-si [ʃɑ̃si], *Pr.n.m. Geog:* Shansi.

chanson [ʃɑ̃sɔ̃], *s.f.* 1. song, ditty, ballad; **c. à boire,** drinking song; **c. de route,** marching song; **c. de bord, de marins,** sea-shanty; **c. à hisser,** hauling song; **c. à virer,** capstan song; **c. réaliste,** cabaret song, music-hall song; **mettre qn en chansons,** to write satirical songs about s.o., to lampoon s.o.; **la c. du vent dans les feuilles,** the song of the wind in the leaves; *F:* **c'est toujours la même c.!** it's the same old story! **voilà bien une autre c.!** that's quite another matter! **chansons (que tout cela)!** nonsense! **il ne se paie pas de chansons,** he is not to be put off with words; *s.a.* AIR III. 2. song, lay, verse chronicle; **la c. de Roland,** the Song of Roland.

chansonner [ʃɑ̃sɔne], *v.tr. & i.* to write satirical songs (about s.o.); to lampoon (s.o.).

chansonnette [ʃɑ̃sɔnɛt], *s.f.* (*a*) comic song with patter; **diseur, diseuse, de chansonnettes,** humorist (at concert); entertainer; (*b*) *F: Jur:* harsh questioning by police.

chansonneur [ʃɑ̃sɔnœːr], *s.m. O:* writer of satirical songs.

chansonnier, -ière [ʃɑ̃sɔnje, -jɛːr], *s.* 1. (*a*) *O:* song-writer; (*b*) chansonnier (who sings in the *cabarets artistiques*). 2. *s.m.* song-book.

chant[1] [ʃɑ̃], *s.m.* 1. singing, song; **leçon, maître, de c.,** singing lesson, master; **le c. des oiseaux,** the song of the birds; **c'était son c. du cygne,** it was his swan song; **c. du grillon,** chirping of the cricket; **c. du coq,** (i) crowing of the cock; (ii) whoop(ing) (of whooping-cough); **au (premier) c. du coq,** at cock-crow. 2. (*a*) song; **c. de victoire,** song of victory; **c. de guerre,** war-song; **c. de Noël,** Christmas carol; (*b*) melody, air; **c. repris par les clarinettes,** melody taken up by the clarinets; (*c*) *Ecc:* **c. grégorien,** Gregorian chant; (*d*) *Mus:* canto (in harmony). 3. *Lit:* (*a*) song, lyric; (*b*) canto (of long poem).

chant[2], *s.m.* edge, side; **pierres (posées) de c., sur c.,** stones set on edge, edgewise; **assise de c.,** brick-on-edge course; **roue de c.,** crown-wheel, face-wheel.

chantable [ʃɑ̃tabl], *a.* singable.

chantage [ʃɑ̃taːʒ], *s.m.* blackmail, extortion of hush-money; **faire du c.,** to blackmail.

chantant [ʃɑ̃tɑ̃], *a.* (*a*) singing; **accent c.,** sing-song accent; lilting accent; **vers chantants,** musical, melodious, verse; **l'italien est une langue chantante,** Italian is a musical language; *s.a.* ARC[1] 3; (*b*) singable; **air c.,** catchy tune; (*c*) **soirée chantante,** musical evening.

chanteau, -eaux [ʃɑ̃to], *s.m.* 1. hunk (of bread). 2. cutting (of cloth); *Tail:* gore. 3. felly, felloe (of wheel).

chanteclair, chantecler [ʃɑ̃tklɛːr], *s.m. Lit:* Chanticleer.

chantefable [ʃɑ̃tfɑːbl], *s.f. Lit:* chantefable.

chantepleure [ʃɑ̃tplœːr], *s.f.* 1. (*a*) wine funnel (pierced with holes); *Ind:* colander; (*b*) long-spouted watering-can, sprayer; (*c*) tap (of cask); (*d*) *Fr.C:* tap. 2. *Const:* (*a*) weep-hole (in wall); (*b*) spout (of gutter).

chanter [ʃɑ̃te], *v.* to sing. 1. *v.tr.* **c. un air, une chanson,** to sing a melody, a song; **chante-moi une chanson,** sing me a song; *abs.* **chante pour moi!** sing to me, for me! **je chante l'homme et les armes,** I sing of arms and the man; **c. qch. sur l'air de . . .,** to sing sth. to the tune of . . .; *Nau:* **c. le fond,** to call the soundings; **c. victoire,** to exult; **c. victoire sur qn,** to crow over s.o.; *Ecc:* **c. la messe,** to sing mass; **pain à c.,** (unconsecrated) host, wafer; **c. toujours la même chanson, la même antienne,** to be always harping on the same string; **c. l'an neuf,** to sing the new year in; *F:* **qu'est-ce que vous me chantez là?** what's this fairy tale you're telling me? 2. *v.i.* (*a*) (*of bird, pers.*) to sing; (*of cock*) to crow; (*of cricket*) to chirp; (*of butter*) to sizzle; **la porte chante,** the door's creaking (on its hinges); **la bouilloire chante,** the kettle's singing; **c'est comme si je chantais,** I'm wasting my breath; *F:* **faire c. qn,** (i) to compel s.o. to do sth.; (ii) to blackmail s.o.; *P:* **il a chanté,** he coughed up; **faire c. qn sur un autre ton,** to make s.o. sing another tune; **c. plus haut,** to offer a better price, to go a bit higher; (*b*) *F:* **est-ce que cela vous chante?** do you like the idea (of it)? does it appeal to you? **je le ferai si ça me chante,** I'll do it if I choose, if it suits me; (*c*) *P:* to give away one's accomplices, to squeal, to grass.

chanterelle[1] [ʃɑ̃trɛl], *s.f.* 1. (*a*) decoy (bird), stool pigeon; (*b*) bird call. 2. *Mus:* first, highest string (of violin); chanterelle; *F:* **appuyer sur la c.,** to hammer a point home, to rub it in.

chanterelle[2], *s.f. Bot:* cantharellus (mushroom); *Cu:* chanterelle.

chanterie [ʃɑ̃tri], *s.f.* = CHANTRERIE.

chanteur, -euse [ʃɑ̃tœːr, -øːz], (*a*) *s.* singer, vocalist; **c. des rues,** street singer; **c. de charme,** crooner; **maître chanteur,** (i) *Mus.Hist:* mastersinger, meistersinger; (ii) *F:* blackmailer; (*b*) *a.* **oiseau c.,** song-bird, songster.

chantier [ʃɑ̃tje], *s.m.* 1. (*a*) gantry, stilling, stillage, stand (for barrels); barrel-horse; **je n'ai plus de vin en c.,** I am at the end of my stock of wine; (*b*) *Nau:* boat chock, cradle. 2. (*a*) yard, depot, site; **c. (de travail),** working site, place; **c. (de construction),** (i) building site, works site; (ii) builder's yard; *For: etc:* **c. (de forêt, de bois),** forest, timber, depot; timber-, lumber-, yard; **travailler au c.,** to work on the site; **mettre un travail en c.,** to lay out a piece of (building) work; **mettre des hommes en c.,** to set men to work; **avoir une œuvre en c., sur le c.,** to have a piece of work in hand, on the stocks; **quel c.!** what a mess! what a shambles! *P.N:* **c.,** men at work, work in progress, road up, works, *U.S:* work zone; **fin de c.,** end of road works; **c. interdit au public,** no admittance except on business; (*b*) *Min:* **c. d'exploitation,** working(s); **c. d'abat(t)age,** stope; **c. de lavage,** washings, placers; (*c*) *Ind:* floor (of foundry, etc.); **c. de versage,** tip, dump; (*d*) (*in Canada*) lumber camp; shanty; **faire c.,** to lumber; **monter, aller, aux chantiers,** to go out into bush; (*e*) **c. de jeunesse, de travail (1940-44),** work camp, agricultural camp. 3. *Nau: Navy:* **c. maritime, c. de construction navale, c. de construction maritime,** (i) shipyard, shipbuilding yard; (ii) slipway, (building) slip; **c. de l'État,** naval (dock)yard, navy yard; **c. à flot,** floating dock; **vaisseau sur le c.,** vessel on the slips; **mettre un navire en c.,** to lay down a ship; to lay a ship on the stocks; **mise en c. (d'un navire),** laying down (of ship); *Av: etc:* **mise en c.,** setting up; *s.a.* RADOUB 1. 4. *Rail:* **c. de voies de garage et de triage,** shunting yard; *Mil:* **c. d'embarquement,** (i) *Rail:* entraining point, yard; (ii) (*on road*) embussing point; **c. de débarquement,** (i) *Rail:* detraining point, yard; (ii) (*on road*) debussing point.

chantignol(l)e [ʃɑ̃tiɲɔl], *s.f. Const:* purlin-cleat, bracket.

Chantilly [ʃɑ̃tiji], *Pr.n.m. Geog:* Chantilly; *Cu:* **crème C.,** crème Chantilly, whipped cream.

chantonné [ʃɑ̃tɔne], *a. Paperm:* (*of paper*) lumpy.

chantonnement [ʃɑ̃tɔnmɑ̃], *s.m.* humming (of tune, etc.).

chantonner [ʃɑ̃tɔne], *v.tr. & i.* to hum; to sing softly.

Chantoung [ʃɑ̃tung, -tuŋ]. 1. *Pr.n.m. Geog:* Shantung. 2. *s.m. Tex:* shantung.

chantournage [ʃɑ̃turnaːʒ], *s.m.* cutting, sawing (of a piece of wood) round a curved outline; jig-sawing.

chantournement [ʃɑ̃turnəmɑ̃], *s.m. Carp:* 1. = CHANTOURNAGE. 2. pattern, profile.

chantourner [ʃɑ̃turne], *v.tr.* to cut, saw (sth.) round a curved outline, to jig-saw; **scie à c.,** (i) (*hand*) bow-saw, turning-saw, sweep-saw; (ii) (*machine*) jig-saw, scroll-saw.

chantre [ʃɑːtr̥]. 1. *s.m. Ecc:* cantor; succentor; chorister; **grand c.,** precentor; *F:* **ronfler comme un c.,** to snore one's head off, to snore like a (drunken) pig; *s.a.* HERBE. 2. *s.f. Ecc:* precentress, precentrix. 3. *s.m. Lit:* (*a*) poet; (*b*) songster; **les chantres des bois,** the woodland chorus.

chantrerie [ʃɑ̃trəri], *s.f. Ecc:* 1. (*a*) (i) cantorship; (ii) precentorship; (*b*) choir school. 2. chantry (chapel).

chanvre [ʃɑ̃ːvr̥], *s.m. Bot: Ind:* hemp; **c. d'eau,** (i) water agrimony; (ii) lycopus, gipsy-wort; water horehound; **c. bâtard, c. sauvage,** hemp-nettle; **c. d'Afrique,** African hemp, bowstring hemp; **c. du Bengale,** Bengal hemp; **c. du Canada,** Canada hemp, Indian hemp; **c. indien,** Indian hemp, hashish; **c. de Gombo,** ambari; brown Indian hemp; **c. de Manille,** Manila hemp; **c. de la Nouvelle-Zélande,** New Zealand flax, flax lily; **c. du Yucatan,** sisal-hemp, -grass; **cordage en c.,** hemp rope; **cheveux couleur de c.,** flaxen hair; *A: F:* **cravate de c.,** hangman's noose; *F:* hempen collar.

chanvreux, -euse [ʃɑ̃vrø, -øːz], *a.* hemp-like.

chanvrier, -ière [ʃɑ̃vri(j)e, -(j)ɛːr]. 1. *a.* hemp-(industry, etc.). 2. *s.* hemp grower. 3. *s.f.* **chanvrière,** hemp-field.

chanvrin [ʃɑ̃vrɛ̃], *s.m. Bot:* hemp-nettle.

chaos [kao], *s.m.* chaos, confusion; **tout est dans le c.,** everything is in confusion, in a state of chaos.

chaotique [kaɔtik], *a.* chaotic, confused.

chapardage [ʃapardaːʒ], *s.m. P:* theft, scrounging, pinching, boning; **menus chapardages,** pilfering.

chaparder [ʃaparde], *v.tr. P:* to steal, scrounge, pinch, filch, bone.

chapardeur, -euse [ʃapardœːr, -øːz], *P:* 1. *a.* thieving, scrounging, pinching. 2. *s.* thief, scrounger.

chape [ʃap], *s.f.* 1. *Ecc:* cope; *A: F:* **disputer de la c. de l'évêque,** to dispute about matters that do not concern the disputants. 2. covering; (*a*) *Aut: etc:* tread (of tyre); (*b*) coping (of bridge); *Const: etc:* **chapes d'une plate-forme en charpente,** cappings of a timber platform; (*c*) *A: Dom.Ec:* dish cover; (*d*) *Mec.E: etc:* cover, cap, lid; **c. protectrice,** protection cover. 3. (*a*) *Mec.E:* fork-joint, yoke, clevis; **c. de cardan,** cardan fork; **c. à queue,** turnbuckle, fork; **c. de bielle,** strap of connecting-rod; **chapes d'un moufle,** straps of a pulley-block; (*b*) cap (of compass-needle); (*c*) bearings (of balance); (*d*) shell (of pulley); (*e*) flange (of roller); (*f*) *Mil:* chape (of scabbard); (*g*) *Nau:* gin-block; (*h*) *Nav:* boss, cap (of compass card).

chapé [ʃape], *a. Ecc:* robed in a cope, coped.

chapeau, -eaux [ʃapo], *s.m.* 1. hat; (*a*) **c. mou, c. souple,** soft felt hat, trilby, *U.S:* crush-hat, fedora; **grand c. mou,** slouch-hat; **ruban de c.,** hat-band; **c. Gibus, c. claque,** opera-hat, *F:* crush-hat; *F:* top-hat; **c. de paille,** straw hat; **c. de paille d'Italie,** Leghorn (hat); **c. de soleil,** sun-hat; **c. pointu,** witch's hat; sugar-loaf hat; **c. Gainsborough,** picture-hat; **c. de fleurs,** (bride's) head-dress of flowers; **c. à cornes, de gendarme,** cocked hat; **c. de chasse (en drap et à petits bords),** deer-stalker (hat); **c. de brousse,** bush hat; *Ecc:* **c. de cardinal, le c. rouge,** cardinal's hat, the red hat; *F:* **recevoir le c.,** to be made (a) cardinal; **c. d'ecclésiastique, c. romain,** shovel-hat; *s.a.* BATAILLE 1, FORME 3; **coup de c.,** bow; **saluer qn d'un coup de c., donner un coup de c. à qn, ôter son c. à qn,** to raise, lift, one's hat to s.o.; **après un coup de c. vers la France . . .,** after a nod in the direction of France, after a few polite remarks addressed to France . . .; **tirer son c. à qn,** to take off one's hat to s.o.; *int.* **c.!** bravo! well done! I take my hat off to you; **porter, mettre, la main à son c.,** to touch one's hat; **chapeaux bas!** hats off! **c. bas,** hat in hand; **parler à qn c. bas,** to talk to s.o. very respectfully; **mettre son c. de travers,** (i) to cock one's hat, to

put one's hat on crooked; (ii) *F:* to assume a threatening attitude; **enfoncer son c.,** (i) to jam one's hat firmly on one's head; (ii) to square up (to a task, to s.o. etc.), to take the bull by the horns; **faire passer le c. (pour recevoir les cotisations),** to pass the hat round; *P:* **t'occupe pas du c. de la gamine,** mind your own business; *P:* **il travaille du c.,** he's bats; (*b*) *F:* big chief, boss (of firm, etc.); (*c*) *Orn:* cap (of bird); *Bot:* pileus, cap (of mushroom); (*d*) *Nau: Com:* **c. (du capitaine, de mérite),** primage, *F:* hat money; (*e*) *Mus:* **c. chinois,** Chinese pavilion, jingling Johnnie; (*f*) *Bot:* **c. d'évêque,** alpine barrenwort; (*g*) *Nau:* bunt whip (of sail); (*h*) *Ch: Brew:* head (on fermenting liquid); *Dist:* marc (left in still). **2.** cover; (*a*) *Cu:* pie-crust; hat, lid, top (of vol-au-vent, etc.); (*b*) cap (of fountain-pen, tyre-valve, etc.); cap(ping); drum-head, trundle-head (of capstan); *Hort:* shade (for protecting plants from sun); **c. à poussière,** dust-cap; **c. graisseur,** lubricator cap; **c. de palier,** bearing-cap, cover, keep (of plummer block); **c. de presse-étoupe** (stuffing-box) gland; **c. de scie,** saw guard; *Aut:* **c. de roue,** hub-cap; *F:* **prendre un virage sur les chapeaux de roues,** to scorch round a corner; *Civ.E:* **c. de pieu,** cap, hood, of a pile; *I.C.E:* **c. incandescent,** hot-bulb; (*c*) *Const:* hood, cowl (of chimney); *Nau:* funnel bonnet; (*d*) *Civ.E:* capping, cross-beam (of row of piles, etc.); bolster (on top of post); *Hyd.E:* cap-sill (of sluice-gate); *Const:* **c. de montant,** corbel block; (*e*) *Tex:* headstock (of loom); (*f*) *Geol: Miner:* **c. de fer, c. ferrugineux (d'une couche métallifère),** iron cap, gossan. **3.** *Typ: Journ:* (*a*) heading; caption; (*b*) introductory paragraph. **4.** *Surv:* triangle of error.

chapeauter [ʃapote], *v.tr. F:* (*a*) to put a hat on (s.o.); to fit (s.o.) with a hat; **elle est bien chapeautée,** she has a nice, smart, hat; (*b*) to be in charge of (of); **M. X chapeaute les trois services,** Mr X is in charge of the three departments; (*c*) *Journ:* to write an introductory paragraph to (an article); (*d*) to give (s.o.) a helping hand; to put in a word for (s.o.).

chape-chute [ʃapʃyt], *s.f. A:* godsend, windfall.

chapelain [ʃaplɛ̃], *s.m. Ecc:* chaplain (attached to private chapel).

chapeler [ʃaple], *v.tr.* **(je chapelle, n. chapelons; je chapellerai) c. du pain,** to cut, rasp, the crust off bread.

chapelet [ʃaple], *s.m.* **1.** (*a*) (lesser) rosary (of fifty-five beads), chaplet; (string of) beads; **c. bouddhique,** Buddhist rosary; **égrener, dire, son c.,** to tell one's beads; *F:* **il n'a pas gagné cela en disant son c.,** he didn't get that saying his prayers; **défiler son c.,** to have one's say, to speak one's mind; *F:* **il me lança tout un c. d'invectives,** he fired, let off, a regular string of abuse at me; (*b*) bead (of wine); **c. de bombes,** stick of bombs; **c. de péniches, d'outils,** string of barges, of tools; **c. d'oignons,** string, rope, of onions; *El:* **c. d'isolateurs,** chain of insulators; **réservoirs en c.,** reservoirs arranged in series; **c. d'îles,** archipelago; *s.a.* ARBRE 2. **2.** *Arch:* astragal. **3.** *Hyd.E:* **(pompe à) c.,** chain-pump, Jacob's ladder. **4.** *Med:* **c. rachitique,** rachitic rosary. **5.** *Vet:* cradle (to stop horse from licking itself).

chapelier, -ière [ʃapəlje, -jɛːr]. **1.** *a.* hat-making, hat-(trade, etc.). **2.** *s.* hatter, hat maker. **3.** *s.f. A:* **chapelière,** Saratoga trunk, dress trunk.

chapelle[1] [ʃapɛl], *s.f.* **1.** (*a*) chapel (in private house, hospital, etc.); (side-)chapel (of church); chapel of ease (of parish); **c. de la (sainte) Vierge,** Lady Chapel; **c. ardente,** *chapelle ardente*; mortuary chapel (lit with tapers); (*of Pope, bishops*) **tenir c.,** to hear (but not celebrate) Mass; (*b*) *Lit: Art:* **(petite) c.,** clique, coterie; (*c*) *esp. Ecc:* choir and/or orchestra; **maître de c.,** musical director, choir master; (*d*) *Ecc:* ornaments and plate (for the celebration of mass). **2.** *Const:* vault (of baking oven). **3.** *Mch:* (*a*) cylinder casing, steam jacket; (*b*) **c. du tiroir,** valve-chest, -case, steam-chest; **c. de pompe,** pump-case; **c. de soupape,** (i) *Hyd.E:* clack-box, valve-box; (ii) *I.C.E:* pocket for valve; *I.C.E:* **soupapes en c.,** side-valves.

chapelle[2], *s.f.* **faire c.,** (i) *Nau:* to be taken aback; to be in irons; to broach to, to chapel; (ii) *A:* (of woman) to tuck up one's skirts in front of the fire.

chapellenie [ʃapɛlni], *s.f.* chaplaincy.

chapellerie [ʃapɛlri], *s.f.* **1.** hat trade, hat industry. **2.** hat shop.

chapelure [ʃaplyːr], *s.f. Cu:* breadcrumbs.

chaperon [ʃaprɔ̃], *s.m.* **1.** (*a*) hood; **le Petit C. rouge,** Little Red Riding Hood; (*b*) *Sch:* = (graduate's) hood. **2.** chaperon; **servir de c. à qn,** to act as chaperon to s.o. **3.** (*a*) *Const:* coping (of wall); cap-stone (of roof); (*b*) (types of) protecting lid or cover; (*c*) *Ent:* clypeus.

chaperonner [ʃaprɔne], *v.tr.* **1.** to put a hood on, to hood (falcon, etc.). **2.** to chaperon (young woman). **3.** *Const:* (*a*) to cope, put the coping on (wall); (*b*) to flash (joint), to lap (joint) with sheet-metal.

chaperonnier, -ière [ʃaprɔnje, -jɛːr], *a.* hooded (falcon, etc.).

chapier [ʃapje], *s.m. Ecc:* **1.** (*a*) *A:* cantor wearing a cope; (*b*) cope-maker. **2.** cope chest.

chapiteau, -eaux [ʃapito], *s.m.* **1.** (*a*) *Arch:* capital (of column); (*b*) cornice (of wardrobe, etc.). **2.** cap(ping) (of bridge-pier). **3.** head (of still, rocket); roof (of beehive); cap (of windmill); apron (of cannon). **4.** big top (of circus).

chapitral, -aux [ʃapitral, -o], *a. Ecc:* pertaining to the chapter; **maison chapitrale,** chapter-house.

chapitre [ʃapitr̥], *s.m.* **1.** (*a*) *Ecc:* chapter (of canons); **salle du c.,** chapter-house, audit-room; **tenir c.,** to meet in council, hold a meeting; to deliberate **(sur,** on); **avoir voix au c.,** to have a say in the matter; (*b*) chapter (of free-masons). **2.** (*a*) chapter (of book); (*b*) head(ing), item (of expenditure, etc.); **nous traiterons demain ce c.,** we will deal with this subject, matter, to-morrow; **elle est sévère sur le c. de la discipline,** she is strict as regards, in the matter of, discipline; **en voilà assez sur ce c.,** that's enough about that.

chapitrer [ʃapitre], *v.tr.* (*a*) *Ecc:* to rebuke in chapter; (*b*) to reprimand (s.o.).

chaploir [ʃaplwaːr], *s.m.* (small) anvil.

chapon [ʃapɔ̃], *s.m.* (*a*) *Cu: etc:* capon; **c. de Gascogne, c. à l'ail,** crust rubbed with garlic (in salad); **c. de Normandie,** crust in soup; **c. du Limousin,** chestnut; *Prov:* **qui c. mange, c. lui vient,** he that hath, to him shall be given; (*b*) *Vit:* young vine which has not yet borne fruit.

chaponnage [ʃapɔnaːʒ], *s.m.* caponizing, caponization, castration (of cockerel).

chaponneau, -eaux [ʃapɔno], *s.m.* young capon.

chaponner [ʃapɔne], *v.tr.* to caponize, castrate (cockerel).

chaponnière [ʃapɔnjɛːr], *s.f. A:* stewpan (for cooking fowl).

chapoter [ʃapɔte], *v.tr.* (*a*) to smooth, trim, (wood) with a drawing knife; (*b*) *Cer:* to remove loose particles (from sagger).

chapska [ʃapska], *s.m. A.Mil.Cost:* lancer cap.

chaptalisation [ʃaptalizasjɔ̃], *s.f. Wine-m:* chaptalization.

chaptaliser [ʃaptalize], *v.tr. Wine-m:* to chaptalize.

chaque [ʃak]. **1.** *a.* each, every; **une place pour c. chose, c. chose à sa place,** a place for everything and everything in its place; *B:* **à c. jour suffit sa peine,** sufficient unto the day is the evil thereof; **c. fois qu'il vient,** whenever, every time, he comes; **c. cinq ou six pas,** every five or six paces; **entre c. plat on danse,** between courses, *F:* between each course, we dance; *F:* **c. deux jours,** every other day; **de c. côté de . . .,** on either side of . . .. NOTE. *The concords are in the sg. or pl.* **c. année et c. jour nous rapproche(nt) de la tombe,** every year, every day, brings us nearer to the grave. **2.** *pron. F:* (= CHACUN) **ces volumes coûtent cinq francs c.,** these books cost five francs each.

char [ʃaːr], *s.m.* **1.** (*a*) *A.Veh:* chariot; **c. romain,** Roman chariot; (*b*) waggon; **c. à bœufs,** ox-cart, bullock-cart; **c. à échelle,** hay-cart; **c. funèbre,** hearse; *A:* **c. à bancs,** (horse) charabanc; (*c*) **c. (de carnaval),** float; (*d*) *Lit:* **le c. de l'État,** the Ship of State; (*e*) **s'attacher au c. de qn,** to devote oneself to s.o., to s.o.'s cause; (*f*) *Fr.C:* car, *U.S:* automobile. **2.** *Mil:* **c. (de combat),** *O:* **c. d'assaut,** tank; **c. léger, moyen, lourd,** light, medium, heavy, tank; **les chars,** the armour; **c. d'accompagnement,** close support tank; assault tank; accompanying tank; **c. de bataille,** cruiser tank; **c. amphibie,** amphibious tank; **c. poseur de pont,** bridge-laying tank; **chasseur de chars,** tank destroyer; **remorque, plateforme porte-c.,** tank-trailer, tank-carrier; **faire cabrer un c.,** to belly a tank; **groupe de chars,** armoured sub-troop; *U.S:* tank section; **peloton de chars,** armoured troop; *U.S:* tank platoon; **escadron de chars,** armoured squadron; *U.S:* tank company; **régiment de chars,** armoured regiment; *U.S:* tank battalion. **3.** *Bot: F:* **c. de Vénus,** monkshood, helmet-flower, Venus's chariot, aconite.

chara [kara], *s.f. Bot:* chara, stonewort.

charabia [ʃarabja], *s.m. F:* (*a*) Auvergnat patois; (*b*) jargon, gibberish; nonsense.

characées [karase], *s.f.pl. Bot:* Characeae.

characinidés [karasinide], **characins** [karasɛ̃], *s.m.pl. Ich:* Characinidae, characinids.

charade [ʃarad], *s.f.* charade; **c'est une c.!** I can't make head or tail of it!

charadriidés [karadriide], *s.m.pl. Orn:* Charadriidae.

charadriiformes [karadriifɔrm], *s.m.pl. Orn:* Charadriiformes.

charagne [karaɲ], *s.f. Bot:* chara, stonewort.

charançon [ʃarɑ̃sɔ̃], *s.m. Ent:* weevil.

charançonné [ʃarɑ̃sɔne], *a.* weevil(l)ed, weevil(l)y; **avoine charançonnée,** weevil-eaten oats.

charasse [ʃaras], *s.f.* crate (for packing china).

charbon [ʃarbɔ̃], *s.m.* **1.** (*a*) **c. (de bois),** charcoal; **c. animal,** animal charcoal; **c. activé,** activated charcoal; **c. à dessiner,** drawing charcoal; **c. ardent,** glowing embers, live coals; **amasser des charbons ardents sur la tête de qn,** to heap coals of fire on s.o.'s head; **être sur des charbons ardents,** to be on tenter-hooks; **ses yeux brillaient comme des charbons,** his eyes were like glowing embers; *Cu: F:* **rôti en c.,** joint done to death, to a cinder; (*b*) coal dust; **avoir un c. dans l'œil,** to have a bit of grit in one's eye; (*c*) *Ch:* carbon; **c. de cornue,** gas carbon; **filtre à c.,** carbon filter; *El:* **lampe à filament de c.,** carbon filament lamp; **balai de c.,** carbon brush; *Phot:* **procédé au c.,** carbon-printing, -process; **papier au c.,** carbon tissue, autotype tissue; (*d*) **c. (de terre),** (mineral) coal; **c. à vapeur,** steam coal; **c. à coke,** coking coal; **c. sans fumée,** smokeless coal; **c. en morceaux,** cobbles; **c. de Paris,** briquettes; **caisse à c.,** coal-box; *Nau: O:* **faire le c.,** to coal; **approvisionner un navire de c.,** to coal a ship. **2.** (*a*) *Agr:* smut (of cereal, etc.); (*b*) *Med: Vet:* anthrax; *Med:* carbuncle; **bactéridie du c.,** anthrax bacillus.

charbonnage [ʃarbɔnaːʒ], *s.m.* **1.** coal mining. **2.** *usu. pl.* collieries, coal-field; **les charbonnages de France,** (French) National Coal Board. **3.** coal depot. **4.** *Nau: O:* bunkering.

charbonnaille [ʃarbɔnaːj], *s.f.* (*a*) Small (coal); smalls, slack; (*b*) coal cinders, breeze.

charbonné [ʃarbɔne], *a.* (*of cereals*) smutty.

charbonnée [ʃarbɔne], *s.f.* **1.** *Cu:* (charcoal-) grilled steak. **2.** *Art:* charcoal sketch. **3.** *Tchn:* layer of charcoal (in a kiln).

charbonner [ʃarbɔne], *v.tr.* **1.** to reduce to carbon; to carbonize, char; **c. du bois,** to char wood (for charcoal); *Cu:* **viande charbonnée,** joint that is burnt, done to death; *v.i.* **la lampe charbonne,** the lamp is smoking. **2.** (*a*) to blacken (sth.) with charcoal; to make a charcoal sketch, drawing, on (sth.); **se c. le visage,** to black one's face; (*b*) to make a charcoal sketch of (sth.). **3.** *abs. Nau: O:* to coal ship; to bunker, take bunkers.

charbonnerie [ʃarbɔnri], *s.f.* **1.** coal depot. **2.** *Hist:* **la C.,** the Carbonari.

charbonneux, -euse [ʃarbɔnø, -øːz], *a.* **1.** coaly, carbonaceous; **dépôt c.,** sooty deposit, carbon deposit. **2.** *Med:* anthracic, anthracoid, carbuncular; **mouches charbonneuses,** anthrax-carrying flies; **bactéridie charbonneuse,** anthrax bacillus; **fièvre charbonneuse,** anthrax.

charbonnier, -ière [ʃarbɔnje, -jɛːr]. **1.** *a.* (*a*) charcoal(-trade, etc.); (*b*) coal-mining (industry, etc.), coal(-trade, etc.); **(navire) c.,** collier, coaler. **2.** *s.* (*a*) charcoal-burner; *Prov:* **c. est maître dans sa maison, chez soi, chez lui,** a man's house is his castle; **la foi du c.,** simple faith; (*b*) coal-merchant; coalman; (*c*) *Hist:* carbonaro. **3.** *s.m.* (*a*) coal-hole, coal-cellar; (*b*) *Ich:* coal-fish, black cod, green pollack. **4.** *s.f.* **charbonnière,** (*a*) coal(-scuttle, coal-box; (*b*) charcoal kiln; (*c*) *Nau:* coal lighter; (*d*) *Orn:* (tom-)tit; great tit; **petite charbonnière,** coal-tit. **5.** *s.m. & f. Fung:* russula cyanoxantha, blue and yellow russula.

charcuter [ʃarkyte], *v.tr.* to cut up (meat) into small pieces; *F:* **c. son menton en se rasant,** to gash one's chin shaving; **c. un malade,** to operate clumsily upon, to slash, hack, butcher, a patient; **c. un poulet,** to mangle a chicken (in carving).

charcuterie [ʃarkytri], *s.f.* **1.** pork-butchery; delicatessen trade. **2.** pork-butcher's business, shop; delicatessen (shop). **3.** pork-butcher's meat; delicatessen; **assiette de c.,** plateful of cold meats, of delicatessen.

charcutier, -ière [ʃarkytje, -jɛːr], *s.* **1.** pork-butcher. **2.** *P:* (*a*) surgeon, *P:* saw-bones; (*implying ruthlessness*) butcher; (*b*) bungler.

chardon [ʃardɔ̃], *s.m.* **1.** thistle; **c. étoilé,** star-thistle; **c. bleu,** alpine sea-holly; **c. argenté, c.-Marie,** milk-thistle; **c. aux ânes,** cotton-thistle; **c. doré,** carline thistle; **c. laineux,** woolly thistle; **faux c.,** false cardoon; **c. bonnetier, à foulon,** fuller's teasel; **c. des champs,** corn-, creeping-thistle, cursed thistle, *U.S:* Canada thistle; **c. bénit,** knapweed; *F:* **bête à manger du c.,** as stupid as a donkey; **aimable comme un c.,**

prickly as a porcupine. **2.** *pl.* clustered spikes (on iron railing, etc.).
chardonner [ʃardɔne], *v.tr. Tex:* to bur(r), teasel (cloth).
chardonneret [ʃardɔnrɛ], *s.m. Orn:* goldfinch.
chardonnet [ʃardɔnɛ], *s.m. Hyd.E: etc:* hanging-post (of lock-gate or farm-gate).
chardonnette [ʃardɔnɛt], *s.f. Bot:* **1.** cotton-thistle. **2.** teasel. **3.** cardoon, prickly artichoke.
chardonnière [ʃardɔnjɛːr], *s.f.* teasel plantation.
charentais, -aise [ʃarɑ̃tɛ, -ɛːz], *a. & s.* (native, inhabitant) of Charente; **(pantoufle) charentaise,** black felt and leather slipper; **(faïences) charentaises,** pottery from Charente.
Charenton [ʃarɑ̃tɔ̃], *Pr.n.m.* Charenton (town near Paris, with a mental hospital); *F:* **c'est un pensionnaire de C., il faut l'envoyer à C.,** he's mad, he ought to be locked up; **on se croirait à C.,** it's absolute Bedlam, an absolute madhouse.
charentonesque [ʃarɑ̃tɔnɛsk], *a. F:* mad, worthy of a madman.
charentonnais, -aise [ʃarɑ̃tɔnɛ, -ɛːz], *a. & s. Geog:* (native, inhabitant) of Charenton.
charge [ʃarʒ], *s.f.* **1.** *(a)* load, burden; **animal, bête de c.,** beast of burden, pack-animal; **cheval, mulet, de c.,** pack-horse, -mule; **j'ai acheté cinq charges de bois,** I bought five loads of wood; *F:* **il a reçu une c. de coups de bâton,** he got a thrashing; *(b)* *(of vehicle)* (i) load, cargo, capacity; (ii) loading, charging; **c. d'un camion,** lorry-load; *U.S:* truck-load; *Rail:* **c. d'un wagon,** waggon-, car-, truck-, load; **c. d'essieu, des roues,** axle-, wheel-, load; **c. normale,** normal load, capacity; **c. admise, limite,** maximum load, capacity; **c. utile,** (i) carrying capacity; (ii) live weight, load; (iii) pay(-)load; *Av:* commercial load; **c. payante, commerciale, utile,** pay(-)load; *Av:* **c. en vol,** flight-load; **c. d'essai,** proof load; **c. alaire,** wing loading; **c. maximum (de rupture),** ultimate, breaking, load; **c. imposée à l'impact,** touch-down load; *Mil:* **c. de bombes,** bomb-load; **rompre (la) c.,** to break bulk, to transfer cargo, to tran(s)ship; **rupture de c.,** transfer of cargo, tran(s)shipment; **point de rupture de c.,** transfer point; *Nau:* **navire de c.,** cargo ship, freighter; **c. d'un navire,** shipload, burden of a ship; **navire en pleine c.,** fully laden ship; **ligne de c.,** load-line; **tirant d'eau en c.,** load-draught; **mât de c.,** derrick, cargo-boom; **navire en c.,** ship loading; **en c. pour Bombay,** loading for Bombay; **déplacement en c.,** load displacement, displacement loaded; **prendre c.,** to load (up), to take in cargo; **rompre c.,** to unload cargo; **on a donné trop de c. à ce navire,** this ship has been overloaded; *(of taxi)* **prendre (un client) en c.,** to pick up (a fare); **prise en c.,** minimum fare; *(c)* *Const: Min:* weight(ing), pressure (on pillar, wall, etc.); *(d)* **être à c. à qn,** to be a burden to, a drag on, s.o.; **la vie lui est à c.,** life is a burden to him; *F:* **il en a sa c.,** (i) he's had as much as he can take; (ii) he's very fat. **2.** *Tchn:* *(a)* (i) load; (ii) stress; **c. d'essai, d'épreuve,** test-load; **c. de sécurité, admissible,** safe load; **c. de rupture,** breaking-load; breaking-stress; **c. à vide,** weight empty; **c. constante,** dead load; **c. de travail, c. pratique,** working-load; working stress; **courbe de c.,** load curve; **c. d'une soupape,** load of a valve; **c. du palier,** bearing stress; **lit de c.,** boxing, ballast, bed; **c. de sécurité,** safe-stress; **taux de c.,** load per unit; **facteur de c.,** load factor; *(b)* *Mch:* *(of motor, machine-tool, etc.)* **en c.,** under load; **mettre le moteur en c.,** to put the motor under load; **démarrage en c.,** starting under load; *(c)* *Metall:* **c. d'un fourneau,** charge, stock, of a furnace; **c. d'allumage,** bed-charge; *(d)* *Hyd.E: etc:* **c. d'eau,** head of water; **perte de c.,** loss of head, of pressure; **c. de la vitesse (d'écoulement),** velocity-head (of flow); *Hyd.E: Mec.E:* **alimentation en c.,** gravity feed; *Mch:* **huile en c. sur le filtre,** head of oil on the filter; *s.a.* RÉSERVOIR 2; *(e)* *Ind: Roadm:* filler; *Paperm:* (clay) loading; *Paint:* extender; *Plastics:* filler; *Tex:* filling; *(f)* *Vet:* poultice. **3.** *(a)* *El.E:* charge (of battery, of electrical body, etc.); load (of circuit, of line); power load (of network); capacitance (of capacitor); **c. minimum (d'un générateur),** base load; **c. limite,** ultimate load; **c. maximum, de pointe,** peak load; **c. d'entretien,** trickle charge; **c. équilibrée,** balanced load; **c. d'espace, spatiale,** space charge; **coefficient de c.,** load factor; **c. résiduelle,** residual charge; **montage à c. cathodique,** cathode-loaded circuit; **conducteur en c.,** live conductor; **perte de c.,** loss of charge; **courant de c.,** charting current; **c. de régime,** rated load; **c. normale,** normal, operating, load; **c. résistante,** resistive load; **c. capacitive,** condenser load; **c. cathodique,** cathode follower; **c. d'anode,** anode load; **c. inductive,** inductive, inductance, load; **groupe de c.,** charging set (of accumulator); **tension de c.,** charging voltage; **tableau de c.,** charging panel; *(b)* *Atom.Ph:* fuel element (for charging reactors). **4.** *(a)* *Exp:* **c. explosive (de mine),** blasting charge (of mine); **c. d'amorçage,** priming charge; **c. d'amorce,** primer charge; **c. de détonation (de mine),** booster-charge (of mine); *(b)* *Artil: Ammunition:* **c. d'un projectile,** charge, filler, of a projectile; **c. amorce,** priming charge; **c. de mise de feu,** percussion charge; **c. propulsive,** propelling, propellant, charge; **c. explosive,** bursting charge; **c. creuse,** hollow-shaped charge; **c. de combat,** full charge, service charge; **c. d'exercice,** drill-charge, practice charge; **c. fractionnée,** fractional charge; **c. de salut,** blank charge; **c. pleine,** battering charge; **il reçut toute la c. en pleine poitrine,** he caught the whole charge full in the chest. **5.** *(a)* charge, responsibility, trust; **prendre qch. en c., à sa c.,** to take charge of sth., assume, take, responsibility for sth.; **prise en c.,** taking charge; **prendre en c. les recettes et dépenses,** to take over the receipts and expenditure; **avoir c. de qch.,** to be in charge of sth.; *Ecc:* **avoir c. d'âmes,** to have the cure of souls; **avoir la c. de faire qch.,** to have the onus of doing sth.; **cela est à votre c.,** that is part of your duty; **enfants confiés à ma c.,** children entrusted to me, in my charge, in my care; **femme de c.,** housekeeper; **aller au-delà de sa c.,** to go beyond one's instructions; to exceed one's duty; *Jur:* **c. de la preuve,** burden of proof, *onus probandi*; *Jur:* **fait de c.,** breach of trust; *s.a.* PRENDRE I. 1; *(b)* office; **haute c.,** high, important, office; **charges publiques,** public offices; **être en c.,** to hold office; **entrer en c.,** to take office, to take up one's duties; **entrée en c.,** taking office, taking up of one's duties; **se démettre de sa c.,** to resign one's office; **c. d'avoué,** solicitor's practice; **c. de notaire,** notary's office and goodwill. **6.** charge, expense; **les frais de transport sont à notre c.,** the cost of transport is borne by, payable by, chargeable to, us; **les réparations sont à la c. du locataire,** the repairs are to be paid for by the tenant; **charges sociales,** social insurance contributions (paid by employer); **être à la c. de qn,** to be dependent on s.o., to be supported by s.o.; **charges de famille,** dependents; **deux enfants à c.,** two dependent children; **tomber à la c. de qn,** to become a burden to s.o.; **il est à ma c.,** I have him on my hands; *Jur:* **frais à la c. de . . .,** costs taxable to . . ., to be paid by . . .; **charges fiscales,** tax burden; **j'ai payé mes charges,** I have paid my taxes; **prendre le bénéfice avec les charges,** to take the rough with the smooth; **loyer plus les charges,** rent plus service charge; **libre de toute c.,** free from all encumbrances; *Ind:* **charges d'exploitation,** working expenses; **livre de charges,** cost book; **cahier des charges,** (i) specifications; (ii) articles and conditions (of sale, etc.); **conditions imposées par le cahier des charges,** specification conditions; *prep.phr.* **à (la) c. de,** on condition that, provided that; **j'accepte, mais à c. de revanche,** I accept, but on condition that you let me do the same for you some other time; **à c. pour vous de payer,** on condition, provided, that you pay. **7.** exaggeration (of story); tall story; *Th:* overacting (of part); *(genre)* skit; *Lit: Paint:* caricature (of character, portrait); burlesque; **il joue tous ses rôles en c.,** he hams all his parts; **c. d'atelier,** hoax; *F:* **faire une c. à qn,** to play a nasty trick on s.o.; **il a fait la c. de son professeur,** he guyed, took off, his teacher; he caricatured his teacher. **8.** *(a)* *Mil:* charge; **c. de cavalerie,** cavalry charge; **c. à la baïonnette,** bayonet charge; **sonner la c.,** to sound the charge; *(of cavalry)* **c. en ligne (de bataille),** charge in close order, in line; **c. en fourrageurs,** charge in extended order; **faire une c. à fond,** to drive a charge home; **revenir, retourner, à la c.,** to return to the charge, to make a fresh attempt; *(b)* *Fb:* (shoulder) charge. **9.** *Jur:* charge, indictment; **relever des charges contre qn,** to bring charges against s.o.; **il y a de fortes charges contre lui,** there are serious charges against him; **témoin à c.,** witness for the prosecution. **10.** *Her:* charge.
chargé [ʃarʒe]. **1.** *a.* loaded, laden, charged; *Nau:* **bateau c.,** ship carrying too much sail; **bateau fortement c.,** heavily laden ship; **train très c.,** crowded train; **avoir la conscience chargée,** to have a guilty conscience; **langue chargée,** coated, furred, tongue; **urine chargée,** cloudy urine; **jour c.,** full, busy, day; **regard c. de reconnaissance,** look full of gratitude; **mots chargés de sens,** meaningful words, words pregnant with, full of, meaning; *Lit:* **c. d'ans, d'années,** stricken in years; **mourir c. d'ans,** to die at a ripe old age; *Lit:* to die full of years; **temps c.,** heavy, overcast, weather; **peinture trop chargée,** paint laid on too thick; **dès chargés,** loaded dice; **hérédité chargée,** tainted heredity; *Paperm:* **papier c.,** loaded paper; *Typ:* **impression peu chargée,** clean impression; *Artil:* **obus c.,** live shell. **2.** **lettre chargée** = registered letter (value declared). **3.** *(a)* *s.m. Dipl:* **c. d'affaires,** chargé d'affaires; *(b)* *s. Sch:* **chargé(e) de cours** = assistant lecturer (at university); **c. de travaux,** demonstrator.
chargebot [ʃarʒəbo], *s.m. A:* cargo boat.
chargement [ʃarʒəmɑ̃], *s.m.* **1.** *(a)* loading(-up) (of lorry, cart, waggon, etc.); lading (of ship); shipping (of cargo); loading (of camera); *Nau:* **navire en c.,** ship loading; **c. par élingues,** slinging; *Rail:* **voie de c.,** goods siding; **endroit de c.,** loading, entraining, point; **c. en bout, en enfilade,** end-on loading; *(b)* *Artil: Sm.a:* loading (of gun, rifle, pistol, etc.); filling (of cartridge, shell, bomb, etc.); **c. à la main, à bras,** loading by hand; **c. automatique,** self-loading; **(à) c. par la bouche,** muzzle-loading; **(à) c. par la culasse,** breech-loading; **(à) c. par bandes,** belt-loading; **plateau, planchette, de c.,** loading-tray; **c. coup par coup,** single loading; *(c)* *El.E:* charging (of battery, accumulator); **c. par filtrage,** trickle charging; *(d)* registration (of letter, packet). **2.** *(a)* load, bulk, cargo, freight; **c. complet,** (i) full load; (ii) *Mil:* full pack (on man, animal); **c. réglementaire,** prescribed load; *Nau:* **prendre c.,** to embark cargo; **c. endommagé** *(dont la valeur est exonérée)*, exception cargo; *(b)* registered letter, parcel.
charger [ʃarʒe], *v.tr.* **(je chargeai(s); n. chargeons)** **1.** to load, to fill, to charge; *(a)* **c. un camion, un wagonnet,** to load, to fill, a lorry, a truck; **c. une voiture de foin,** to load (up) a cart with hay; **c. une table de plats,** to spread, to load, a table with dishes; **c. un navire,** to load a ship; **navire chargé de blé,** ship laden with wheat; **c. qch. sur son dos,** to take sth. on one's back; **c. une valise sur son épaule,** to hoist a case on to one's shoulder; *(of taxi driver)* **c. un client,** to pick up a fare; **c. des marchandises, des véhicules, sur un train,** to entrain goods, vehicles; to load goods, vehicles, on a train; **c. des marchandises, une cargaison, sur un paquebot,** to ship goods, a cargo, on a steamer; *abs:* **navire qui charge pour Londres,** ship taking in freight for London; *(b)* to weight (down); **c. un couvercle (avec des poids) pour l'empêcher de se soulever,** to weight (down) a lid to prevent lifting; **toiture qui charge trop les murs,** roof that bears too heavily on the walls, that overloads the walls; *abs:* **toit qui charge,** roof undergoing squeeze; *Const:* **c. une voûte,** to weight an arch; **mets qui chargent l'estomac,** food that lies heavy on the stomach; *(c)* **c. le peuple d'impôts,** to burden the people with taxes; **c. sa mémoire de dates inutiles,** to burden one's memory, to clutter up one's mind, with useless dates; **c. son style d'ornements,** to over-elaborate one's style; **c. qn de reproches,** to load s.o. with reproaches; to heap reproaches on s.o.; **c. un compte de certains frais,** to charge certain expenses to an account; **l'air est chargé du parfum des fleurs,** the air is heavy with the scent of flowers; *(d)* **c. le feu,** to feed, to make up, to stoke, the fire; *Min:* **c. un trou de mine,** to charge a shot-hole; **c. une chaudière,** to fire a boiler; **c. un fourneau avec du coke,** to charge a furnace with coke; **c. un stylo d'une cartouche,** to put a refill in a pen; **c. une pipe (à tabac),** to fill a pipe; **c. une bobine de soie,** to wind silk on to a reel; *(e)* **c. un canon,** etc., to load a gun, etc.; **c. un canon à blanc,** to load a gun with blank ammunition; **c. un fusil avec des balles réelles, un canon avec des obus réels,** to load a rifle, a gun, with live ammunition; *Phot:* **c. un appareil, un châssis,** to load a camera, a slide; *(f)* *El.E:* **c. une batterie, un accumulateur,** to charge a battery, an accumulator; **batterie chargée, accumulateur chargé, à fond, à refus,** fully charged battery, accumulator; *(g)* *Paperm:* to load; *Tex:* to load, weight (cloth). **2.** to entrust; **c. qn de qch., de faire qch.,** to entrust, charge, s.o. with sth., with doing sth., to instruct s.o. to do sth.; **il fut chargé de** + *inf.*, he was commissioned, instructed, to . . .; **personne chargée de l'entretien,** maintenance man, worker. **3.** *(a)* to turn (portrait) into a caricature; to caricature (s.o.); *Th:* (i) to overact, overdo (a part); (ii) to gag (one's part); **c. (un récit),** to embroider (a story); *(b)* *Com:* **c. un compte,** to inflate an accoun t; *Typ*

c. une couleur, to strengthen a colour, to increase the inking. **4.** (*of troops, bull, etc.*) to charge; *Fb:* to (shoulder) charge; **chargez!** at them! **c. à la baïonnette,** to charge with fixed bayonets, with bayonet; **c. la baïonnette haute,** to charge at the high part; **c. en tirailleurs, en fourrageurs,** to charge in extended order. **5.** *Jur:* to charge, accuse, indict (s.o.); **c. qn d'un crime,** to charge s.o. with a crime. **6.** *Her:* to charge; **c. son écu d'un lion rampant,** to charge a lion rampant.

se charger. 1. le temps se charge, the weather is becoming overcast. **2.** (*a*) **se c. d'un fardeau,** to shoulder a burden; (*b*) **se c. de qch., de faire qch.,** to undertake sth.; to undertake, take it upon oneself, to do sth.; **se c. d'une affaire,** to take a matter in hand; **je m'en chargerai,** I will attend to it; **je me charge de le faire venir,** I shall see to it that he comes; (*of commercial traveller*) **se c. d'une série d'articles,** to take up a line. **3.** *P:* to get drunk, loaded.

chargette [ʃarʒɛt], *s.f.* powder measure (for making cartridges).

chargeur [ʃarʒœːr], *s.m.* **1.** loader. *Nau:* shipper, lader; **commissionnaire c.,** shipping agent. **2.** (*a*) stoker, fireman; **c. mécanique,** (i) mechanical stoker, feeder; (ii) charging machine (at gasworks, etc.); (*b*) *Artil:* loading number (of men serving gun); loader (of machine-gun etc.); **3.** (*a*) *Sm.a:* magazine; (cartridge-, loading-) clip; charger; **c. de 20 coups,** twenty-round clip, magazine; **c. à main,** hand-loader; **c. automatique,** self-loader; (*b*) *Phot:* cassette, (loading-) magazine; (*c*) *El:* **c. de batterie, d'accumulateur,** battery, accumulator, charger; **c. à régime lent,** trickle-charger; (*d*) *Min: Ind:* **c. de benne,** kibble filler; **c. de wagon,** trimmer.

chargeure [ʃarʒyːr], *s.f. Her:* charge.

chargeuse [ʃarʒøːz], *s.f. Ind:* charging machine, charger; (mechanical) loader; **c. à godets,** bucket loader.

charibotée [ʃaribɔte], *s.f. P:* **une c. de . . .,** heaps, loads, piles, of . . .; **une c. d'injures,** a string of abuse.

chariboter [ʃaribɔte], *v.i. P:* **1.** (*a*) to work unmethodically, to muddle through one's work; (*b*) to create disorder, to make a mess. **2.** to exaggerate; *P:* to spread it on thick.

chariolle [ʃarjɔl], *s.f. A.Furn:* truckle bed.

chariot [ʃarjo], *s.m.* **1.** (*a*) (four-wheeled) waggon, cart; **c. bâché,** covered waggon; **c. de foin,** hay-waggon; *Mil:* **c. de parc,** transport waggon; *Astr:* **le Grand C., le C. de David,** the Great Bear, Charles's Wain; *U.S:* the (Big) Dipper; **le petit C.,** the little Bear; *U.S:* the little Dipper; (*b*) (child's) go-cart, *U.S:* baby-walker; **c. alsacien,** basket cot on wheels; (*c*) *A:* chariot; **c. de guerre,** war chariot; *Lit:* **le c. de Thespis,** the car of Thespis; (*d*) *Cin:* dolly. **2.** *Tchn: Min: Civ.E:* truck, waggon, trolley; (*a*) **c. de manutention,** handling trolley; dolly; **c. élévateur à fourche, c. gerbeur,** fork-lift truck; *Rail:* **c. à bagages,** luggage-trolley; *Med:* **c. porte-brancard,** stretcher carrier, *U.S:* litter-carrier; *Ind:* **c. à charbon,** coal-car; *El.E: Tp:* **c. dérouleur,** wheeled cable-drum carriage, *U.S:* cable-reel trailer; (*b*) *Artil:* **c. de chargement,** shell-truck; **c. porte-affût,** carriage-truck; **c. porte-canon,** gun carriage, *U.S:* gun-truck; (*c*) *Rail:* **c. de service, c. transbordeur,** traverser, travelling platform; railway-slide; **c. porteur,** bogie (of engine, car, etc.); (*d*) *Av:* **c. d'atterrissage,** landing gear, undercarriage; **c. de piste,** handling trolley; **c. de sortie, de manœuvre,** docking trolley; **c. de manutention de bombes,** bomb-carrying trolley; **c. de transport d'hydravion,** seaplane (handling) trolley. **3.** *Mec.E: Ind:* trolley, truck; *Mch:* carriage, carrier; (*a*) **c. à palan,** telpherage trolley; **c. à poutre de plafond,** ceiling-crab; **c. de pont roulant,** crane-crab, traveller, (travelling) runner, trolley, truck; **c. tendeur, c. tenseur,** tension carriage; (*b*) **chariot (de tour),** slide, carriage (of lathe); **c. transversal (de tour),** cross-slide (of lathe); **c. porte-tourelle (de tour revolver),** turret-slide (of turret-lathe); **c. porte-outil,** tool-carriage; **c. porte-broche (de fraiseuse),** spindle-carriage (of milling machine); **c. porte-meule (de machine à meuler),** wheel-carriage (of grinding machine); (*c*) *El.E:* **c. de prise (de courant),** plough-collector (of tram, etc.). **4.** *Av: Navy:* **c. de lancement,** (i) starting cradle (for launching aircraft by catapult); (ii) launching carriage (of torpedo). **5.** *Phot:* baseboard (of camera); **c. à charnière,** folding baseboard (of camera).

chariotage [ʃarjɔtaːʒ], *s.m. Mec.E: Ind:* (i) (*lathework*) traverse, traversing; (ii) (*machine-tool*) turning; **c. longitudinal,** sliding; **c. transversal,** cross-traverse; **barre de c.,** feed-rod (of lathe); **rectification par c.,** traverse grinding.

charioter [ʃarjɔte], *v.tr. Mec.E:* **c. une pièce,** to traverse a piece on the lathe; **tour à c.,** slide-lathe.

charioteur [ʃarjɔtœːr], *s.m. Mec.E:* **outil c.,** traversing tool.

chariot-grue [ʃarjogry], *s.m.* mobile crane; *pl. chariots-grues.*

charismatique [karismatik], *a. Theol:* charismatic.

charisme [karism], *s.m. Theol:* charism(a).

charitable [ʃaritabl̩], *a.* charitable, benevolent (envers, to, towards); **œuvres charitables,** charities.

charitablement [ʃaritabləmɑ̃], *adv.* charitably.

charité [ʃarite], *s.f.* **1.** charity, love; **faire qch. par c.,** to do sth. out of, for, charity; *A:* **dame de c.,** district visitor; *Ecc:* **les Filles de la C.,** the Sisters of Charity; **sœur de la C.,** Sister of Charity; *Prov:* **c. bien ordonnée commence par soi-même,** charity begins at home. **2.** act of charity; alms (giving); *A:* **maison de c.,** almshouse; **faire la c. à qn,** to give alms to s.o.; **vivre de charités, être à la c.,** to live on charity.

charitois, -oise [ʃaritwa, -waːz], *a. & s. Geog:* (native, inhabitant) of La Charité-sur-Loire.

charivari [ʃarivari], *s.m.* (*a*) charivari, tin-kettle music, mock serenade; (*b*) din, row, racket; **faire un c. de tous les diables,** to kick up no end of a din, no end of a racket.

charivariser [ʃarivarize], *F:* **1.** *v.tr.* to treat (s.o.) to a serenade on tin kettles, to a charivari. **2.** *v.i.* to kick up a din, a racket.

charlatan, -ane [ʃarlatɑ̃, -an], *s.* charlatan, quack, mountebank, **remède de c.,** quack remedy.

charlatanerie [ʃarlatanri], *s.f.* charlatanry, quackery, imposture; *F:* **tout ça c'est de la c.,** that's all eye-wash.

charlatanesque [ʃarlatanɛsk], *a.* charlatanic(al), quackish.

charlatanisme [ʃarlatanism], *s.m.* charlatanism, quackery.

Charlemagne [ʃarləmaɲ], *Pr.n.m. Hist:* Charlemagne; **faire C.,** to leave the game, the gaming table, when one is in pocket.

Charles [ʃarl], *Pr.n.m.* Charles; *Hist:* **C. le Téméraire,** Charles the Bold (of Burgundy); **C. le Mauvais,** Charles the Bad (of Navarre); *s.a.* QUINT 1.

charleston [ʃarlɛstɔn], *s.m. Danc:* charleston.

charliandin, -ine [ʃarljɑ̃dɛ̃, -in], *a. & s. Geog:* (native, inhabitant) of Charlieu.

Charlot [ʃarlo]. **1.** *Pr.n.m. F:* (*a*) Charley, Charlie; *Cin:* Charlie Chaplin; (*b*) *A:* public executioner, = Jack Ketch; *F:* **la bascule à C.** = the guillotine. **2.** *s.m. Orn:* (*a*) curlew; (*b*) **c. de plage,** summer-snipe, red-backed sand-piper.

Charlotte [ʃarlɔt]. **1.** *Pr.n.f.* Charlotte. **2.** *s.f. Cu:* (*a*) apple-charlotte; (*b*) **c. russe,** charlotte russe. **3.** *A.Cost:* mob cap.

charmant [ʃarmɑ̃], *a.* charming, fascinating, delightful (person, thing); **ça a été c. de me trouver avec vous,** it's been lovely being with you; *Lit:* **Le Prince C.,** Prince Charming.

charme[1] [ʃarm], *s.m.* **1.** charm, spell; **cette musique exerce un c. mystérieux,** this music exerts a mysterious spell; **demeurer, être, sous le c.,** to be under the spell; **tenir ses auditeurs sous le c.,** to hold one's audience spell-bound; **rompre le c.,** to break the spell; *Med:* **état de c.,** hypnotic state, hypnosis; **porter un c. sur soi,** to wear a lucky charm, a mascot; *F:* **se porter comme un c.,** to be in the best of health, to be as fit as a fiddle. **2.** (*a*) charm, attraction; seductiveness; **elle n'a pas de c.,** she is devoid of charm; **cela donne du c. au paysage,** it lends a charm, a beauty, to the landscape; **c'est ce qui en fait le c.,** that's what makes it so attractive; *F:* **faire du c.,** to make oneself pleasant, charming; *F:* to turn on the charm; **chanteur de c.,** crooner; (*b*) *pl.* (physical) attractions (of a woman); **vivre de ses charmes,** to be a prostitute; **3.** *Jur:* **délit de c.,** infliction of wilful damage to a tree trunk (in order to kill the tree).

charme[2], *s.m. Bot:* hornbeam, yoke-elm.

charme-houblon [ʃarmublɔ̃], *s.m. Arb:* hop hornbeam; *pl. charmes-houblon.*

charmer [ʃarme], *v.tr.* **1.** to charm, bewitch, fascinate; **c. un serpent,** to charm a snake; *A:* **c. les ennuis de qn,** to charm s.o.'s cares away. **2.** to charm, please, delight; **tableau qui charme les yeux,** picture that delights, charms, the eye; **être charmé de faire qch.,** to be delighted to do sth.; **c. l'imagination,** to appeal to the imagination. **3. c. un arbre,** to inflict wilful damage on a tree-trunk (in order to kill the tree).

charmeur, -euse [ʃarmœːr, -øːz], *s. A:* **charmeresse** [ʃarmərɛs], *s.f.* **1.** (*a*) *O:* magician, sorcerer; (*b*) **c. de serpents,** snake charmer; (*c*) charming, attractive, person; **impossible à résister à ce c.,** you can't resist his charm; *a.* **d'un air c.,** in an attractive, appealing, manner. **2.** *s.f.* **charmeuse,** (*a*) *Tex:* charmeuse; (*b*) *pl. P:* moustache.

charmille [ʃarmiːj], *s.f.* (*a*) hedge(-row) (of hornbeams and other trees); (*b*) bower, arbour.

charmoie [ʃarmwa], *s.f. A:* hornbeam plantation.

charmot [ʃarmo], *s.m. Cer:* grog.

charnel, -elle [ʃarnɛl], *a. & s.* (*a*) *a.* carnal, fleshly (desires, etc.); *a. & s.* sensual (person); (*b*) *a.* worldly (goods, etc.).

charnellement [ʃarnɛlmɑ̃], *adv.* carnally, sensually.

charnier [ʃarnje], *s.m.* **1.** (*a*) *A:* larder, store-room; (*b*) *Nau:* scuttle-butt; drinking-tank; **c. au lard,** steep-tub. **2.** (*a*) *A:* cemetery; (*b*) charnel-house, ossuary; **un vrai c.,** a regular charnel-house.

charnière [ʃarnjɛːr], *s.f.* **1.** *Tchn: Mec.E: etc:* hinge, butt-hinge, joint; (*a*) **couvercle à charnière(s),** hinged lid; **assemblage, joint, à c.,** hinge-joint, knuckle-joint; **c. universelle,** universal joint, cardan joint; **axe, broche, de c.,** hinge-pin; **c. à fiche, à broche,** pin hinge; **c. à rotule,** ball-joint hinge; (*b*) *Av:* **c. d'aileron, de gouvernail de profondeur,** aileron-, elevator-, hinge; (*c*) *Mil:* **attaquer à la c. des 1ère et 6ème armées,** to attack at the (point of) junction of the 1st and 6th armies; (*d*) *Anat:* hinge-joint; (*e*) *Moll:* hinge (of bivalve); (*f*) *F:* **nom à c.,** double-barrelled name; (*g*) *F:* **l'une des grandes charnières de l'histoire,** one of the great turning-points of history; **voici la c. de l'affaire,** the whole affair hinges on this. **2.** (*a*) *Geol:* crest, bend, axis (of fold); **c. inférieure,** synclinal fold; **c. supérieure,** anticlinal fold; (*b*) *Geom:* axis.

charnigue [ʃarnig], *s.m. Z:* Ibizan hound.

charnon [ʃarnɔ̃], *s.m.* knuckle (of hinge).

charnu [ʃarny], *a.* fleshy, plump; *F:* well-covered; **bras c.,** plump arm; **lèvres charnues,** fleshy lips; *F:* **atteint d'une balle dans les parties charnues (de son individu),** shot through the buttocks; **feuille charnue,** fleshy leaf; **fruits charnus,** fleshy, pulpy, succulent, fruit; **perdrix charnue,** plump partridge; **vin c.,** wine that has substance (but a low alcohol content).

charnure [ʃarnyːr], *s.f.* (body) flesh (as a whole); **avoir une c. sèche, ferme, molle,** to be sparely built, firm-fleshed, flabby.

charognard [ʃarɔɲaːr], *s.m.* **1.** *Orn:* griffon vulture. **2.** *Pisc:* kelt. **3.** *P:* butcher who sells tainted meat. **4.** *P:* (*pers.*) heel, skunk.

charogne [ʃarɔɲ], *s.f.* **1.** (*a*) carrion, decaying carcass; (*b*) (human) corpse; (*c*) *F:* tainted meat, meat unfit to eat. **2.** *P:* (*pers.*) (*a*) louse, swine; (*b*) slut.

charol(l)ais, -aise [ʃarɔlɛ, -ɛːz]. **1.** *a. & s. Geog:* (native, inhabitant) of the Charolais region (of Burgundy). **2.** (*a*) *a. & s.m.* **(bœuf) c.,** Charolais steer; (*b*) *s.f.* **charolaise,** Charolais cow; (*c*) *s.f. Cu:* knuckle (of beef).

Charon [karɔ̃], *Pr.n.m. Myth:* Charon.

charophytes [karɔfit], *s.m.pl. Bot:* Charophyta.

charpe [ʃarp], *s.m.*, **charpenne** [ʃarpɛn], *s.m. Bot: F:* hornbeam, yoke elm.

charpentage [ʃarpɑ̃taːʒ], *s.m.* carpentry; *Civ.E: etc:* constructional work.

charpente [ʃarpɑ̃ːt], *s.f.* frame(work), framing, skeleton; basic structure; (*a*) **c. en bois,** woodwork, timber work; **bois de c.,** constructional timber; **c. en acier,** steelwork; steel structural, constructional, work; **c. en fer,** ironwork; iron structural, constructional, work; **c. métallique,** ironwork, steelwork; iron and steel structural, constructional, work; metal frame; (*b*) **c. de comble, de toiture,** roof frame; **c. de pont,** bridge frame(work); *Av:* **c. d'aile,** wing truss; (*c*) framework (of body), bones, skeleton; (*of pers.*) **avoir la c. solide,** to be solidly built; **c. d'un arbre fruitier,** main branches of a fruit tree; **c. d'un roman, d'un scénario,** (i) framework, skeleton, (ii) structure, of a novel, a scenario.

charpenté [ʃarpɑ̃te], *a.* built, constructed; **homme solidement c.,** well-built man; **pièce de théâtre bien charpentée,** well-constructed play; **personnage bien c.,** well-portrayed character.

charpenter [ʃarpɑ̃te], *v.tr.* **1.** to cut (timber) into shape (for framework, etc.). **2.** to frame (up) (roof, etc.); **c. un drame, un roman,** to construct, a drama, a novel. **3.** *abs.* to carpenter; **il aime c.,** he likes doing carpentry.

charpenterie [ʃarpɑ̃tri], *s.f.* **1.** (*a*) carpentry, carpenter's work; **faire de la c.,** to carpenter; (*b*) **c. en fer,** ironworking; ironwork. **2.** (*a*) carpenter's (work)shop; (*b*) timber-yard.

charpentier [ʃarpɑ̃tje], *s.m.* **1.** worker in heavy timber; carpenter; **matelot c.,** ship's carpenter; **c. de vaisseau,** shipwright. **2. c. en fer,** constructional ironworker. **3. c. de baleine,** flenser.

charpi [ʃarpi], *s.m.* cooper's block.

charpie [ʃarpi], *s.f.* (*a*) *A:* lint; shredded linen; **mettre de la toile en charpie,** to shred linen; (*b*) **mettre qch. en c.,** to tear sth. to pieces; **il vous mettra en c.,** he will make mincemeat of you; **viande en c.,** meat cooked to shreds.

charque [ʃark], *s.f.*, **charqui** [ʃarki], *s.f.* charqui; jerked beef.

charquer [ʃarke], *v.tr.* to dry, desiccate (meat for preserving); to jerk (meat).

charras [ʃaras], *s.m.* charas, resin of Indian hemp.

charrée [ʃare], *s.f. Agr: Glassm: etc:* buck ashes, lye ashes.

charretée [ʃarte], *s.f.* cart-load, cartful; **c. de briques,** load of bricks.

charretier, -ière [ʃartje, -jɛːr]. **1.** *s.* (*a*) carter, carrier, carman; *Prov:* **il n'y a si bon c. qui ne verse,** even Homer sometimes nods; **langage de c.,** coarse language; *s.a.* JURER 4; (*b*) *s.m.* cart-horse. **2.** *a.* **porte charretière,** carriage gate(way); **chemin c., voie charretière,** cart track.

charretin [ʃartɛ̃], *s.m., Dial:* **charreton** [ʃartɔ̃], *s.m.* flat cart.

charrette [ʃarɛt], *s.f.* cart; **c. anglaise,** dog-cart, trap; **c. à bras,** hand-cart, barrow; **c. d'enfant,** go-cart, *U.S:* baby-walker; *Hist:* **c. (des condamnés),** tumbril; *A: F:* **monter dans la c.,** to go to the scaffold; *F:* **rencontrer une c.,** to be buttonholed by a bore; *s.a.* VALEUR, RENVERSEMENT 2.

charretterie [ʃarɛtri], *s.f.* cart-shed.

charriable [ʃarjabl̩], *a.* cartable, transportable.

charriage [ʃarjaːʒ], *s.m.* **1.** (*a*) cartage, carting, haulage, carriage, conveyance; (*b*) drifting (of ice, of alluvial deposit); (*c*) *Geol:* thrusting; overthrust; **c. de cisaillement,** shear thrust. **2.** *P:* (*a*) confidence trick; (*b*) chaffing (of s.o.); (*c*) exaggeration; *F:* line-shooting; (*d*) **c. à la mécanique,** throttling, garrotting.

charrier [ʃarje], *v.tr.* (*p.d. & pr.sub.* **n. charriions, v. charriiez**) **1.** (*a*) to cart, carry, transport; *F:* **c. droit avec qn,** to be straight, to deal squarely, with s.o.; (*b*) to carry along, wash down, drift; **rivière qui charrie du sable,** river that carries, brings down, sand; *abs.* **le fleuve charrie,** the river is full of drift-ice; **nuages charriés par le vent,** wind-driven clouds. **2.** *P:* (*a*) to poke fun at (s.o.); **sans c.,** joking aside; (*b*) *A:* to swindle (s.o.) (by a confidence trick); (*c*) *v.i. F:* to exaggerate; *F:* to shoot a line; *F:* to pile it on; **il charrie vraiment!** he's laying it on with a trowel! *s.a.* BÉGONIA.

charrière [ʃarjɛːr], *s.f.* cart-track.

charrieur, -ieuse [ʃarjœːr, -jøːz], *s.* **1.** carrier, carter. **2.** *P:* (*a*) *A:* swindler; (*b*) scoffer; (*c*) sneak thief.

charroi [ʃarwa], *s.m.* (*a*) cartage; transport (by horse-drawn vehicle); **chemin de c.,** cart track; (*b*) *pl. A.Mil:* transport, convoy, baggage train.

charron [ʃarɔ̃], *s.m.* cartwright (and plough-wright); wheelwright.

charronnage [ʃarɔnaːʒ], *s.m.* cartwright's, wheelwright's (i) work, (ii) trade.

charronnerie [ʃarɔnri], *s.f.* **1.** cartwright's, wheelwright's, trade. **2.** cartwright's, wheelwright's, workshop.

charroyer [ʃarwaje], *v.tr.* (**je charroie, n. charroyons; je charroierai**) (*a*) to transport (sth.) in a cart, to cart (sth.); (*b*) **l'idée de c. tous ces livres m'effraie,** the idea of having to move; *F:* to cart, all these books frightens me.

charroyeur [ʃarwajœːr], *s.m.* carter, carrier.

charruage [ʃarɥaːʒ], *s.f.* (*a*) ploughland, area which can be cultivated with a single plough; (*b*) ploughing.

charrue [ʃary], *s.f.* (*a*) plough, *U.S:* plow; **c. (à) balance,** balance plough; **c. tilbury,** sulky plough; **c. vigneronne,** vineyard plough; **c. à disques,** disc plough; **c. défonceuse,** rooter (plough); trenching plough; **mener, pousser, la c.,** to drive the plough; **faire passer la c. dans, sur, un champ,** to plough a field; *F:* **faire passer la c. sur une mauvaise affaire,** to remove all traces of an unfortunate affair; *F:* **tirer la c.,** to have a hard life; **cheval de c.,** (i) plough horse; (ii) *F:* bumpkin, lout; **il a conduit la c.,** he was bred at the plough (tail), he has followed the plough (tail); *F:* **mettre la c. devant les bœufs,** to put the cart before the horse; **mettre la main à la c.,** to put one's hand to the plough; (*b*) (i) ploughing; (ii) agriculture, the land.

charruer [ʃarɥe]. **1.** *v.tr.* to plough. **2.** *v.i.* to (drive a) plough.

charrue-semoir [ʃarysəmwaːr], *s.f.* seeding plough; *pl. charrues-semoirs.*

charruyer [ʃarɥje], *s.m. Dial:* ploughman.

charte [ʃart], *s.f.* **1.** charter; **compagnie à c.,** chartered company; *Eng.Hist:* **la Grande C.,** Magna Carta; *Pol: Hist:* **la C. de l'Atlantique,** the Atlantic Charter. **2.** (ancient) deed; title; **l'École des chartes,** the School of Palaeography and Librarianship (in Paris).

charte-partie [ʃartəparti], *s.f. Nau:* charter-party; *pl. chartes-parties.*

chartier [ʃartje], *s.m. A:* carter.

chartil [ʃarti], *s.m. A:* **1.** harvesting-waggon, wain. **2.** cart-shed.

chartisme [ʃartism], *s.m. Eng.Hist:* chartism.

chartiste [ʃartist], *s.m.* **1.** student, former student, of the *École des chartes.* **2.** *Eng.Hist:* chartist.

chartrain, -aine [ʃartrɛ̃, -ɛn], *a. & s. Geog:* (native, inhabitant) of (i) Chartres; (ii) la Chartre-sur-le-Loir.

chartre[1] [ʃartr̩], *s.f. A:* = CHARTE.

chartre[2], *s.f. A:* prison; **tenir qn en c. privée,** to detain s.o. illegally.

chartré [ʃartre], *a.* chartered (company, association, etc.).

chartreux, -euse [ʃartrø, -øːz]. **1.** *s.* (*a*) Carthusian (monk, nun); (*b*) **(chat) c.,** = British blue (cat). **2.** *s.f.* **chartreuse.** (*a*) Carthusian monastery, charterhouse; (*b*) *A:* country cottage; **vivre retiré dans une chartreuse,** to live in retirement, far from the world; (*c*) *R.t.m:* Chartreuse (liqueur); (*d*) *Cu:* chartreuse (of vegetables and poultry).

chartrier [ʃartri(j)e], *s.m.* **1.** custodian of charters. **2.** (*a*) cartulary, collection of charters; (*b*) charter-room.

Charybde [karibd], *Pr.n.m. Gr.Myth:* Charybdis; **tomber de C. en Scylla,** to fall from Scylla into Charybdis; *F:* to fall out of the frying pan into the fire.

chas[1] [ʃɑ], *s.m.* eye (of needle).

chas[2], *s.m. Tex:* starch paste; dressing.

chasement [ʃɑzmɑ̃], *s.m. A.Jur:* (*feudal system*) fief; fee; feud; precarium.

chasme [kasm], *s.m. A: & Lit:* chasm.

chasmogame [kasmɔgam], *a. Bot:* chasmogamous.

chasmogamie [kasmɔgami], *s.f. Bot:* chasmogamy.

chasmophyte [kasmɔfit], *a. & s.f. Bot:* chasmophyte.

chassage [ʃasaːʒ], *s.m. Min:* drivage.

chasse [ʃas], *s.f.* **1.** (*a*) pursuit, quest, of game; (i) hunting, the hunt, *A:* chase; game shooting; (ii) a hunt, a shoot; **c. à courre, c. à cor et à cri,** (i) (stag, fox)hunting; (ii) (stag, fox)hunt; **c. à tir,** (i) (game) shooting; (ii) shoot; **c. aux pièges,** trapping; **c. au faucon, au vol,** hawking; **c. au furet,** ferreting; **c. au lévrier,** coursing; **c. au renard,** (i) foxhunting; (ii) foxhunt; **c. aux perdrix,** (i) partridge shooting; (ii) partridge shoot; **c. aux oiseaux,** fowling; **c. au lapin,** rabbiting; rabbit shooting; **c. au daim,** deer-stalking; **c. au blaireau,** badger baiting, drawing; **c. au gibier d'eau, à la sauvagine, au marais,** wild-fowling; **c. au sanglier,** (i) boar hunting; (ii) boar hunt; **c. au sanglier (à l'épieu),** pig-sticking; **c. aux rats,** rat catching; ratting; **c. aux souris,** mousing; **c. à la baleine,** whaling; **c. à l'homme,** manhunt; *F:* **c. au mari,** husband hunting; **c. aux soldes,** bargain hunting; **c. aux appartements,** flat hunting; **c. sous-marine,** underwater fishing; **c. en barque,** punt shooting; **aller à la c.,** to go hunting, shooting; **partir à la c.,** to go hunting, shooting; **partir en c.,** (i) (*of lion, etc.*) to go on the prowl, (ii) *F:* (*of collector, etc.*) to go off looking for bargains, bargain hunting; (*of animal*) **être en c.,** (i) to be after its prey; (ii) to be on heat; **la c. est ouverte, fermée,** the shooting season has begun, ended; **ouverture, fermeture, de la c.,** opening, closing, of the shooting season; *Prov:* **qui va à la c. perd sa place,** he who leaves his place loses it; **étiez-vous de la c.?** were you among the field? **la c. a passé par ici,** the hunt, the field, went past here; **fusil de c.,** (i) sporting gun; (ii) fowling piece; **couteau, habit, de c.,** hunting knife, coat; **chien de c.,** (i) hound; (ii) gun dog; **terrain de c.,** hunting ground, hunt; **cor de c.,** hunting horn; **cheval de c.,** hunter; **droit de c.,** (i) hunting rights; (ii) licence to kill game; *s.a.* CHIEN 1, PERMIS 2; **c. réservée,** private shooting; **faire bonne c.,** to have good sport, make a good bag; *Mil: P:* **peloton de c.,** punishment squad, *P:* jankers brigade; (*b*) **c. gardée,** (game) preserves; **louer une c.,** to rent a shoot; (*c*) chase; **donner la c. à qch., à qn, prendre qch., qn, en c.,** to chase, pursue, give chase to, sth., s.o.; **faire la c. à qch.,** to hunt down sth.; to root out (abuses, etc.); (*d*) *Nau:* **donner c. à un navire, prendre un navire en c.,** to give chase to a ship; **prendre c., soutenir la c.,** to stand away; **abandonner la c.,** to give up the chase; **pièce de c.,** bow chaser; (*e*) drive (*of horse's hind legs*); (*f*) *Mil.Av:* **la c.,** the fighter forces; Fighter command; the fighters; **couverture de c.,** fighter cover; **escadrille de c.,** fighter squadron; **pilote de c.,** fighter pilot; *s.a.* ANGLE 1, AVIATION, AVION; (*g*) *Court Ten:* chase; **marquer une c.,** to make a chase. **2.** *Mus:* hunting-song. **3.** *Civ.E: etc:* (*a*) **c. (d'eau),** flush, scour; (*in W.C.*) **c. d'eau,** flushing system, flush; *F:* **tirer la c. (d'eau),** to pull the (lavatory) chain; **chambre de c.,** flushing chamber (of sewer); **réservoir de c.,** flushing cistern; **écluse de c.,** scouring sluice; (*b*) **c. d'air,** rush of air, air-blast; *Artil:* blow through. **4.** *Mec.E:* play (of wheels, etc.); set (of saw teeth); *Aut:* trail (of front wheels); **c. axiale,** end play; **angle de c.,** rake; *Aut:* **c. de l'essieu,** castor action of front wheels. **5.** *Typ:* overrun (of page); *Bookb:* **chasses (des plats),** squares. **6.** *Tls:* (*a*) drift, (key-)driver; punch, snap; (*b*) *Metalw:* **c. à parer,** flatt(en)er; **c. ronde,** (top) fuller; **c. carrée,** set hammer. **7.** *Tex:* (*a*) batten, lathe (of loom); (*b*) shot, pick.

châsse [ʃɑːs], *s.f.* **1.** *Ecc:* reliquary, shrine; *s.a.* PARÉ 2. **2.** mounting; (*a*) frame, rims (of pair of spectacles); (*b*) scales (of lancet, etc.). **3.** *P:* eye.

chassé [ʃase], *s.m. Danc:* chassé.

chasse-avant [ʃasavɑ̃], *s.m.inv. A: Ind:* foreman, overseer, superintendent.

chasse-bestiaux [ʃasbɛstjo], *s.m.inv. Rail:* cow-catcher.

chasse-bondieu [ʃasbɔ̃djø], *s.m.inv.* punch for driving a wedge into a log.

chasse-boulon(s) [ʃasbulɔ̃], *s.m. Tls:* drift-bolt; *pl. chasse-boulons.*

chasse-clavette [ʃasklavɛt], *s.m.*, **chasse-clef** [ʃaskle], *s.m. Tls:* drift(-punch), cotter-driver; *pl. chasse-clavettes, -clefs.*

chasse-clou(s) [ʃasklu], *s.m. Tls:* (nail-)set, punch; brad punch; *pl. chasse-clous.*

chasse-coin(s) [ʃaskwɛ̃], *s.m. Rail: Tls:* wedge-hammer, keying-hammer; *pl. chasse-coins.*

chasse-coquin [ʃaskɔkɛ̃], *s.m. P:* verger; *pl. chasse-coquins.*

chasse-corps [ʃaskɔːr], *s.m.inv.* = CHASSE-BESTIAUX.

chasse-cousin(s) [ʃaskuzɛ̃], *s.m.* no pl. **1.** meagre, inhospitable, fare; cheap wine; **donner du c.-c. à qn,** to show s.o. scant hospitality. **2.** *Fenc:* stiff foil.

chassé-croisé [ʃasekrwaze], *s.m.* (*a*) *Danc:* set to partners, *chassé-croisé;* (*b*) (i) re-arrangement of personnel, etc.; *F:* general post; (ii) **faire c.-c.,** to play Box and Cox; *pl. chassés-croisés.*

chasse-goupille(s) [ʃasgupiːj], *s.m. Tls:* pin-drift, -punch; *pl. chasse-goupilles.*

chasselas [ʃaslɑ], *s.m. Vit:* chasselas (*esp.* of the Fontainebleau region).

chasse-marée [ʃasmare], *s.m.inv.* **1.** (*a*) fish-cart, -waggon; (*b*) driver of a fish cart. **2.** coasting lugger.

chasse-mouches [ʃasmuʃ], *s.m.inv.* **1.** fly-whisk. **2.** fly-net (for horse's head).

chasse-navettes [ʃasnavɛt], *s.m.inv. Tex:* picker (of loom).

chasse-neige [ʃasnɛːʒ], *s.m.inv.* **1.** snow-plough; **c.-n. rotatif,** rotary snow-plough. **2.** *Skiing:* stem; snow-plough; **virage (en) c.-n.,** snow-plough turn. **3.** strong wind (which forms snowdrifts).

chasse-pierres [ʃaspjɛːr], *s.m. Rail: etc:* rail-guard; *pl. des chasse-pierres.*

chasse-pointe(s) [ʃaspwɛ̃ːt], *s.m.* = CHASSE-CLOU(S); *pl. chasse-pointes.*

chassepot [ʃaspo], *s.m. A:* chassepot (rifle) (*from name of designer*).

chasse-punaise [ʃaspynɛːz], *s.m. Bot: F:* (*a*) bug-bane, bugwort; (*b*) baneberry, herb St. Christopher; *pl. chasse-punaise(s).*

chasser [ʃase]. **1.** *v.tr* (*a*) to chase, pursue, hunt; **c. le renard, la perdrix,** to go fox-hunting, partridge shooting; **c. les souris,** to mouse, go mousing; **c. les papillons,** to chase butterflies; **c. à courre, au chien courant,** to ride to hounds; to hunt, go hunting; **c. au fusil,** to shoot; **c. au collet, au lacet,** to snare; **c. au faucon,** to hawk; **c. au furet,** to ferret; **c. devant soi,** to go rough-shooting; **passer la journée à c.,** to spend the day out hunting, shooting; *F:* **c. sur les terres de qn,** to poach on s.o.'s preserves; **c. plusieurs lièvres à la fois,** to have several irons in the fire; *s.a.* COR 2, RACE 2; *Nau:* **c. un navire ennemi,** to chase an enemy ship; **c. la terre,** to reconnoitre

land; *St.Exch:* **c. le découvert,** to raid the shorts, the bears; (*b*) to drive (s.o.) out, away; to turn (s.o.) out (of doors); to expel (s.o. from school, club, etc.); to dismiss (servant); *B:* to cast out (devils); to drive (cattle to graze); **c. qn du pays,** to drive, expel s.o. from the country; **il fut chassé de (la) France par l'indignation publique,** he was hounded out of France; **c. l'ennemi de sa position,** to drive the enemy out of his position; **c. qn de la maison,** to chase s.o. out of the house; *F:* **pardon si je te chasse, mais je dois partir,** sorry to push you out, but I must be going; **les peintres m'ont chassé de chez moi,** I have been driven out of the house by the decorators; **c. qn de son esprit,** to dismiss s.o. from one's mind, from one's thoughts; **c. un chien,** to chase away a dog; **c. une mouche (du revers de la main),** to brush away a fly; **c. des guêpes,** to swat wasps; **aérosol qui chasse les mites,** aerosol that gets rid of moths; **le vent chasse la pluie contre les vitres,** the wind drives the rain against the window-panes; **les nuages ont été chassés par le vent,** the clouds have been blown away, driven away, cleared, by the wind; **nuages chassés par le vent,** wind-driven clouds; **c. la fumée d'une chambre,** to drive, clear, the smoke out of a room; **c. le mauvais air d'une chambre,** to ventilate a room; **c. une mauvaise odeur,** to get rid of a nasty smell; *P:* **c. le brouillard,** to clear one's head, wake onself up (with a glass of wine or brandy first thing in the morning); *P:* to take a hair of the dog that bit you; *Mch:* **c. l'air,** to blow out the air; **c. un clou,** to drive a nail in or out; **un clou chasse l'autre,** one person, passion, event, etc., drives out the memory of another; one fire burns out another's burning; **c. une goupille,** to drive out, knock out, punch out, a pin; **marteau à c.,** chasing hammer; *N.Arch:* **c. l'étoupe,** to drive oakum into the seams; *Mth:* **c. les dénominateurs d'une équation,** to clear an equation of fractions; *F:* to multiply up; *Ten:* **c. une balle,** to drive a ball; *Prov:* **chassez le naturel, il revient au galop,** what's bred in the bone will come out in the flesh; *s.a.* FAIM. **2.** *v.i.* (*a*) to hunt, go hunting, go shooting; (*of animal*) to hunt, go hunting, to go, be, on the hunt; **c. au lion,** to hunt lions; **c. au lièvre,** to course, go coursing; **c. au lapin,** to rabbit, to go rabbiting; **c. aux souris,** to mouse, to go mousing; *F:* **elle chasse au mari,** she's after a husband, on the hunt for a husband; *F:* **il aime à c. au plat,** he has a hearty appetite; (*b*) to drive; (*of ship*) to run; **nuages qui chassent du nord,** clouds that are driving from the north; *Nau:* **navire qui chasse sur ses ancres,** *abs.* **qui chasse,** ship that is dragging her anchors; **c. à la côte, sur un autre navire,** to drive ashore, to drive on to another ship; (*c*) *Equit:* **c. en avant,** to urge one's horse forward; (*d*) *Danc:* to chassé (to the right); *cf.* DÉCHASSER); (*e*) *Aut:* to skid; (*of wheels*) to spin; *Nau:* (*of anchor*) to come home; to drag; (*f*) *Typ:* (i) (*of type*) to drive out; to space out (too much); (ii) (*of matter*) to overrun; (*g*) *Hyd.E:* to scour; *Nau:* (*of submarine*) to run ballasts, to blow the tanks; (*h*) *Min:* **c. par palplanches,** to forepole; (*i*) *Ch:* **c. par ébullition,** to boil (sth.) off; **c. par évaporation,** to evaporate (sth.) off.

chasseresse [ʃasrɛs], *s.f. Lit:* huntress; **Diane c.,** Diana the Huntress.

chasse-rivet(s) [ʃasrivɛ], *s.m. Tls:* **1.** rivet snap, snaphead. **2.** drift; *pl. chasse-rivets.*

chasse-rond(s) [ʃasrɔ̃], *s.m. Tls:* beading plane, tool.

chasse-roue(s) [ʃasru], *s.m.* spur stone, guard stone, (metal) barrier (to protect wall, etc. from impact of vehicles); *pl. chasse-roues.*

chasse-tampon(s) [ʃastɑ̃pɔ̃], *s.m. Tls:* plugging-bar; *pl. chasse-tampons.*

chasse-taupe [ʃasto:p], *s.m. Bot:* thorn-apple, *U.S:* jimson weed, *A:* Jamestown weed; *pl. chasse-taupes.*

chasseur, -euse [ʃasœ:r, -ø:z], *s.* **1.** (*a*) hunter, huntress; huntsman; **c. de sauvagine,** water-fowler; **c. de baleines,** whale catcher; **c. de tête,** head-hunter; *F:* **c. d'images,** keen photographer; **c. d'autographes,** autograph hunter; **ce chien est bon c.,** this is a good gun-dog; (*b*) sportsman with a gun. **2.** *s.m.* (*a*) *A:* footman, lackey; (*b*) (*in hotel, etc.*) commissionaire; porter; messenger (boy); page (boy), *U.S:* bell boy, bell hop. **3.** *s.m.* (*a*) *A: Mil:* rifleman, light infantryman, chasseur; **les chasseurs (à pied),** the light infantry; **chasseurs à cheval,** light cavalry; **c. à cheval,** light cavalryman; **chasseurs d'Afrique,** light cavalry for service in North Africa; (*b*) **les chasseurs alpins,** the mountain light infantry,

---

the Alpine chasseurs. **4.** *s.m.* (*a*) *Mil:* **c. de chars,** tank destroyer; (*b*) *Mil.Av:* fighter; **c. de pénétration,** intruder; **c. léger de reconnaissance,** light fighter reconnaissance aircraft; (*c*) *Navy:* (bâtiment) **chasseur,** chaser; **c. de sous-marins,** submarine chaser. **5.** *Nau:* fast-sailing carrier (between fishing-ground and port).

chasseur-bombardier [ʃasœ:rbɔ̃bardje], *s.m.* fighter-bomber; *pl. chasseurs-bombardiers.*

chasseur-fusée [ʃasœ:rfyze], *s.m.* rocket fighter; *pl. chasseurs-fusées.*

chasseur-intercepteur [ʃasœ:rɛ̃tɛrsɛptœ:r], *s.m. Av:* fighter-interceptor; interceptor-fighter; **c.-i. de jour,** interceptor day fighter; **c.-i. de nuit,** interceptor night fighter; *pl. chasseurs-intercepteurs.*

chasse-vase [ʃasva:z], *s.m.inv. Civ.E:* scour.

Chassidiens [ʃasidjɛ̃], *s.m.pl. Jew.Rel:* Chasidim, Hasidim.

chassie [ʃasi], *s.f.* rheum, matter, gum (in the eyes).

chassieux, -euse [ʃasjø, -ø:z], *a.* rheumy (eyes); **aux yeux c.,** rheumy-eyed.

châssis [ʃasi], *s.m.* (*a*) frame; **c. d'un tableau,** stretcher of a canvas; **c. de malle,** tray of a trunk; **c. d'une scie,** frame of a saw; **c. de porte,** door-frame; **c. de fenêtre,** window-sash, -frame; **c. mobile,** sash; **c. dormant,** sash-frame; **c. à guillotine,** sash-window; **c. vitré,** skylight; *Civ. E:* **c. de fondation,** foundation raft; *Phot:* **c. (négatif),** dark slide, (plate-)sheath, plate-holder; **c. à brisures,** roller-blind slide; **c. à charnière,** book-form slide; **c. (positif),** printing frame; **c. à glace dépolie,** focusing screen, back; (*b*) *Hort:* frame; **culture sous c.,** forcing; (*c*) *Th:* flat; (*d*) *Aut:* chassis, frame; **c. avancé,** chassis with forward control cab; *Rail:* frame (of engine); under-frame (of carriage); *Artil:* chassis, slide (of gun); *Av:* undercarriage; *Aut:* **faux c.,** sub-frame; *Av:* **c. d'atterrissage,** landing gear; **c. d'amerrissage,** alighting gear; (*e*) *Metall:* **c. à mouler,** moulding box, box-mould; (*f*) *Typ:* chase.

châssis-grille [ʃasigri:j], *s.m.* ciphering grid, square; *pl. châssis-grilles.*

châssis-magasin [ʃasimagazɛ̃], *s.m. Phot:* changing-box (for plates); *pl. châssis-magasins.*

châssis-presse [ʃasiprɛs], *s.m. Phot:* printing frame; *pl. châssis-presses.*

châssis-truc [ʃasitryk], *s.m. Rail:* (long steel) truck; *pl. châssis-trucs.*

chassoir [ʃaswa:r], *s.m. Coop:* hoop driver.

chaste [ʃast], *a.* chaste, pure.

chastement [ʃastəmɑ̃], *adv.* chastely, purely.

chasteté [ʃastəte], *s.f.* chastity; purity.

chasuble [ʃazybl], *s.f. Cost:* (*a*) *Ecc:* chasuble; (*b*) **robe c.,** pinafore dress, *U.S:* jumper.

chasublerie [ʃazyblǝri], *s.f. Ecc:* (*a*) art of vestment-making; (*b*) church vestment factory; (*c*) clerical outfitters.

chasublier, -ère [ʃazyblie, -ɛ:r], *s.* (*a*) (church) vestment maker; (*b*) clerical outfitter.

chat, chatte [ʃa, ʃat], *s.* **1.** (*a*) cat; *m.* tom(cat); *f.* queen, she-cat; **c. marsupial australien,** Australian native cat; **c. doré,** (African) golden cat; **le C. botté,** Puss in Boots; **petit c.,** kitten; *F:* **mon petit c.,** my dear, my pet; **sabbat, musique, de chats,** caterwauling, cats' chorus; *Pej:* **c. fourré,** judge; *F:* **arriver dès les chats,** to arrive (home) with the milk; **écriture de c.,** illegible scrawl; **il écrit comme un c.,** his writing is a scrawl; **être comme c. sur braise,** to be (like) a cat on hot bricks, *U.S:* on a hot tin roof; **guetter qn comme le c. (fait de) la souris,** to watch s.o. like a cat watching a mouse; **il n'y avait pas un c. dans la rue,** there wasn't a soul in the street; **donner sa langue aux chats,** to give up (trying to guess sth.); **appeler un c. un c.,** to call a spade a spade; **acheter un c. en poche,** to buy a pig in a poke; **avoir un c. dans la gorge, dans le gosier,** to have a frog in one's throat; **se servir de la patte du c. pour tirer les marrons du feu,** to make a cat's paw of s.o.; *Prov:* **ne réveillez pas le c. qui dort,** let sleeping dogs lie, let well alone; **à bon c. bon rat,** tit for tat; **c. échaudé craint l'eau (froide),** once bitten twice shy; **quand le c. est parti, dort, n'est pas là, les souris dansent,** when the cat's away the mice will play; **il n'y a si petit c. qui n'égratigne,** even a worm will turn; *s.a.* ANGORA, CANADA, CHIEN 1, FOUETTER 1, GOUTTIÈRE 1, HARET, HERBE 4, MUSQUÉ 2, NUIT, PERSAN 1, SAUVAGE 1, SIAMOIS 1; (*b*) *a. F:* caressing, feline (manner, etc.). **2.** **c. à neuf queues,** cat-(o'-nine-tails). **3.** *Games:* (*a*) jeu du **c.,** tag, tig, "he"; **jouer au c.,** to play tag, "he"; **c. perché,** "off-ground (he)"; **c. coupé,** cross tag; (*b*) tagger, "it," "he." **4.** *Nau:* trou du **c.,**

---

lubber's hole. **5.** *s.f.* **chatte;** *Nau:* (*a*) creeper, drag; (*b*) flat-bottomed coasting boat; lighter. **6.** *Min:* **c. sauvage,** wildcat.

châtaigne [ʃatɛɲ], *s.f.* **1.** (*a*) *Bot:* (sweet) chestnut; *F:* **c. amère,** horse chestnut; **c. d'eau,** water caltrop(s), water chestnut; **c. du Brésil,** Brazil nut; *O:* **c. de terre,** ground nut; (*b*) *P:* blow, biff; (*c*) *P:* electric shock. **2.** castor, chestnut (of horse). **3.** *Echin:* **c. de mer,** sea urchin.

châtaigner [ʃatɛɲe], *v.tr. P:* to hit, punch (s.o.).

châtaigneraie [ʃatɛɲrɛ], *s.f.* chestnut grove, plantation.

châtaignier [ʃatɛɲe], *s.m.* chestnut (tree or wood).

châtain [ʃatɛ̃], (*a*) *a.* (*usu. inv. in fem., but occ. has fem. in -aine.*) (chestnut-)brown; **une femme châtain,** a brown-haired woman; **cheveux châtains,** brown, chestnut, hair; **cheveux châtain clair,** light brown hair; **cheveux châtain roux,** auburn hair; (*b*) *s.m.* chestnut brown; **c. clair,** light brown; **un c.,** a brown-haired man.

chataire [ʃatɛ:r], *s.f. Bot:* catmint, *U.S:* catnip.

chat-cervier [ʃaservje], *s.m. Z: A:* lynx; *pl. chats-cerviers.*

château, -eaux [ʃato], *s.m.* **1.** castle; stronghold; (*a*) **c. fort,** (fortified) castle; **bâtir des châteaux en Espagne,** to build castles in the air; **c. de cartes,** house of cards; *F:* **c. branlant,** rickety old thing; (*b*) *Her:* castle; (*c*) (*as viticultural term in the names of many wines, e.g.:* Château-Lafite, Château-Yquem) **vin mis en bouteille au c.,** château-bottled wine; *P:* **c.-la-pompe,** (drinking) water, Adam's ale. **2.** (*a*) country seat; mansion; manor; hall; **vie de c.,** gracious living; **mener la vie de c.,** to live like a lord; **lettre de c.,** bread-and-butter letter; (*b*) (royal) palace; **le c. de Versailles,** the palace of Versailles; **les châteaux de la Loire,** the châteaux of the Loire. **3.** *Hyd.E:* **c. d'eau,** water tower; *Rail:* tank. **4.** *N.Arch:* superstructure; *A:* **c. d'avant, de proue,** forecastle, fo'c's'le; **c. d'arrière, de poupe,** aftercastle. **5.** *Atom.Ph:* **c. (de plomb),** (lead) cask, castle.

châteaubriand, châteaubriant [ʃatobrijɑ̃], *s.m. Cu:* double tenderloin; porterhouse steak.

châteaubriantais, -aise [ʃatobrijɑ̃tɛ, -ɛ:z], *a. & s. Geog:* (native, inhabitant) of Châteaubriant.

châteaulinois, -oise [ʃatolinwa, -wa:z], *a. & s. Geog:* (native, inhabitant) of Châteaulin.

châteauroussin, -ine [ʃatorusɛ̃, -in], *a. & s. Geog:* (native, inhabitant) of Châteauroux.

châtelain [ʃatlɛ̃], *s.m.* **1.** *Hist:* (*a*) castellan, governor, constable (of castle); (*b*) lord (of manor). **2.** (i) owner; (ii) tenant, of a *château.*

châtelaine [ʃatlɛn], *s.f.* **1.** *Hist:* (*a*) castellan's wife, chatelaine; (*b*) lady (of manor). **2.** (*a*) (woman) (i) owner, (ii) tenant, of a *château;* wife of (i) owner, (ii) tenant, of a *château.* **3.** *Cost:* chatelaine (for keys, etc.).

châtelard [ʃatla:r], *s.m.* castle mound (with vestiges of ancient fortifications).

châtelet [ʃatlɛ], *s.m.* **1.** (*a*) small castle; (*b*) *Hist:* **le (Grand) C.,** a court of justice in Paris; (*c*) **théâtre du C.,** Paris theatre devoted to spectacular plays. **2.** *A:* fort (defending road or bridgehead).

châtellenie [ʃatɛlni], *s.f. Hist:* castellany.

châtelleraudais, -aise [ʃatelrodɛ, -ɛ:z], *a. & s. Geog:* (native, inhabitant) of Châtellerault.

chathamite [ʃatamit], *s.f. Miner:* chathamite.

chat-huant [ʃaɥɑ̃], *s.m. Orn:* tawny owl, brown owl, wood owl; *pl. chats-huants.*

chati [ʃati], *s.m. Z:* chati.

châtiable [ʃatjabl], *a.* punishable, chastisable.

châtié [ʃatje], *a.* pure, polished (style, verse).

châtier [ʃatje], *v.tr.* (*p.d. & pr.sub.* **n. châtiions, v. châtiiez**) to punish, chastise, castigate (child, etc.); to polish (style); **c. son corps,** to mortify the body; **c. l'impudence de qn,** to punish s.o. for his impudence; *Prov:* **qui aime bien châtie bien,** spare the rod and spoil the child.

chatière [ʃatjɛ:r], *s.f.* **1.** (*a*) cat door; (*b*) spy-hole; (*c*) ventilation hole (in roof); (*d*) *Hyd.E:* outlet channel (for fountain, etc.); (*e*) narrow underground passage. **2.** cat trap.

châtieur [ʃatjœ:r], *s.m.* punisher; chastiser; *Lit:* chastener; scourger.

châtillonnais, -aise [ʃatijɔnɛ, ʃa-, -ɛ:z], *a. & s. Geog:* (native, inhabitant) of Châtillon.

châtiment [ʃatimɑ̃], *s.m.* punishment, chastisement, castigation; retribution; **c. corporel,** corporal punishment.

chatoiement, *A:* **chatoiment** [ʃatwamɑ̃], *s.m.* (*a*) variable lustre (of colours); shimmer, iridescence, sheen; (*b*) glistening; **c. d'un bijou,** play of light on a jewel.

chaton¹, -onne [ʃatɔ̃, -ɔn], *s.* **1.** kitten. **2.** *s.m. Bot:* catkin.

chaton², *s.m. Lap:* **1.** bezel, setting (of stone). **2.** stone (in its setting).

chatonner¹ [ʃatɔne], *v.i.* **1.** to kitten, to have kittens. **2.** *Bot:* to grow catkins.

chatonner², *v.tr. Lap:* to set (a stone) in a bezel.

chatouillant [ʃatujɑ̃], *a. A:* tickling, thrilling, flattering; **chatouillantes approbations**, gratifying praise.

chatouille [ʃatuj], *s.f.* **1.** *F:* **faire des chatouilles à qn,** to tickle s.o.; **craindre les chatouilles,** to be ticklish. **2.** *Z: F:* larval lamprey, ammoc(o)ete.

chatouiller [ʃatuje], *v.tr.* to tickle; **c. un cheval de l'éperon,** to prick up a horse with one's spur; **c. les côtes à qn,** (i) to tickle, poke, s.o. in the ribs; (ii) *F:* to give s.o. a thrashing; **vin qui chatouille le palais,** wine that tickles, pleases, the palate; **c. la curiosité,** to excite, arouse, curiosity; **c. l'amour-propre de qn,** to flatter s.o.'s vanity; *F:* **c. un nid de guêpes,** to stir up a wasp's nest.

chatouillement [ʃatujmɑ̃], *s.m.* tickling; **éprouver un c. dans la gorge,** to have a tickle in one's throat; **être sensible au moindre c.,** to be extremely ticklish; **musique qui cause un c. de l'oreille,** music, that tickles, flatters, the ear.

chatouilleux, -euse [ʃatujø, -øːz], *a.* **1.** (*of pers.*) (*a*) ticklish; (*b*) sensitive, touchy; **cheval à la bouche chatouilleuse,** horse with a sensitive, tender, mouth; **c. sur le point d'honneur,** touchy where honour is concerned, touchy on a point of honour. **2.** delicate, sore (point, question, etc.).

chatoyant [ʃatwajɑ̃], *a.* iridescent, chatoyant; **tissu aux effets chatoyants,** iridescent fabric, fabric with shot silk effects; **soie chatoyante,** shot silk; *Miner:* **pierre chatoyante,** chatoyant stone; **imagination chatoyante,** sparkling imagination.

chatoyé [ʃatwaje], *a.* shot (silk, etc.).

chatoyer [ʃatwaje], *v.i.* (**il chatoie; il chatoyait; il chatoiera**) (*a*) to change colour (with position); to shimmer; (*b*) to glisten, sparkle; **style qui chatoie,** sparkling, colourful style.

chat-pard [ʃapaːr], *s.m. Z:* leopard cat; *pl. chats-pards.*

châtré [ʃɑtre]. **1.** *s.m.* eunuch, castrated man; *F:* **voix de c.,** high-pitched, falsetto, voice. **2.** *a. P:* weak, spineless.

châtrer [ʃɑtre], *v.tr.* (*a*) to castrate, emasculate; to geld (stallion); to neuter; *F:* to doctor (cat); to spay (bitch, etc.); (*b*) (i) to bowdlerize, expurgate; (ii) to cut, mutilate (literary work); to mutilate (building); (*c*) *Ap:* **c. une ruche,** to remove some of the combs from a hive; (*d*) *Hort:* (i) to cut back (plant); (ii) to castrate (flower).

châtreur, -euse [ʃɑtrœːr, -øːz], *s.* (*a*) castrator; gelder; (*b*) *F:* mutilator (of literary work, etc.).

châtrillon [ʃɑtrijɔ̃], *s.m.* young castrated animal.

chat-rochier [ʃarɔʃje], *s.m. Ich:* spotted dogfish; *pl. chats-rochiers.*

châtron [ʃɑtrɔ̃], *s.m.* young bullock.

chattée [ʃate], *s.f.* litter (of kittens).

chattemite [ʃatmit], *s.f.* (*a*) sanctimonious hypocrite; **faire la c.,** *F:* to look as though butter would not melt in one's mouth; (*b*) ingratiating, *F:* smarmy, person; **faire la c. auprès de qn,** to toady to s.o., to smarm over s.o.

chattepeleuse [ʃatpəløːz], *s.f.*, **chattep(e)louse** [ʃatp(ə)luːz], *s.f. Ent:* processionary caterpillar.

chatter [ʃate], *v.i.* to kitten, have kittens.

chatterie [ʃatri], *s.f.* **1.** *usu. pl.* wheedling ways, coaxing. **2.** (*a*) *pl.* delicacies, dainties; (*b*) **être d'une incroyable c.,** to have an incredibly sweet tooth. **3.** cat-breeding establishment, cattery.

chatterton [ʃatertɔ̃, -tɔn], *s.m. El.E: etc:* (i) insulating, adhesive, splicing, tape; (ii) *O:* Chatterton's compound.

chattertonné [ʃatertɔne], *a.* insulated; **ruban c.,** insulating, adhesive, tape.

chat-tigre [ʃatigr], *s.m. Z:* tiger-cat; *pl. chats-tigres.*

chaud, chaude [ʃo, ʃoːd]. **1.** *a.* (*a*) warm; hot; **eau chaude,** warm, hot, water; **temps c.,** hot, warm, weather; **son corps était encore c.,** his body was still warm; **galettes toutes chaudes,** piping-hot, sizzling-hot, cakes; **soupe toute chaude,** steaming-hot soup; **air c.,** hot air; **moteur, machine, à air c.,** hot-air engine; **séchoir à air c.,** hot-air dryer; *Metall:* **courant d'air c.,** hot-air blast; **allure, marche, chaude,** hot working; *Hort:* **serre chaude,** hothouse; **couche chaude,** hotbed; **avoir les pieds chauds,** to have warm feet; *F:* **tenir les pieds chauds à qn,** to keep s.o. on the hop, on the go; *A:* **être c. de vin,** to be heated, flushed, with wine; *F:* **avoir le sang c.,** to be hot-blooded; **avoir la tête chaude,** to be hot-headed, quick to anger, quick to flare up; **une tête chaude,** a hot-head; *Games:* **jouer à main chaude,** to play hot cockles; *F:* **avoir la main chaude,** to have a run of luck (at a game); **affaire chaude,** sharp tussle, brisk engagement; *F:* **guerre chaude,** shooting war; **chaude dispute,** warm, animated, heated, discussion; **chaude amitié,** warm friendship; **personne au cœur c.,** warm-hearted person; *Z:* **animal à sang c.,** warm-blooded animal; **pleurer à chaudes larmes,** to weep hot tears, bitter tears, to cry one's eyes out; **c. partisan de qn,** warm partisan of s.o.; *F:* **il n'est pas c. pour le projet,** he's not keen, hot, on, over-enthusiastic about, the project; *F:* **il n'est ni c. ni froid,** he is hesitating (between two alternatives); *A:* **la donner chaude à qn,** to cause great consternation to s.o.; **servir qch. c.,** to serve up sth. hot; **nouvelle toute chaude,** (piece of) really hot news; **porter une nouvelle toute chaude** (*or adv.phr.* **tout c.**) **à qn,** to take a piece of news straight away to s.o.; **il me l'a rendu tout c.,** he returned (the insult, etc.) immediately; **tout c. de . . .,** straight from . . .; **n'avoir rien de plus c. que de . . .,** to have nothing more pressing than to . . .; *Ven:* **fuite chaude, voie chaude,** hot trail; **piste chaude,** warm scent; *Art:* **tons chauds,** warm tints; **rouges chauds,** warm reds; **voix chaude,** sultry voice; **parfum c.,** heady, strong, scent; *Atom.Ph: F:* **laboratoire c.,** hot laboratory; *Prov:* **il faut battre le fer pendant qu'il est c.,** strike while the iron is hot, make hay while the sun shines; *adv. A:* **c.! c.!** come along, be quick! **j'aime à manger c.,** I like (to eat) my food hot; *F:* **ça a dû coûter c.,** it must have cost a pretty penny; *v.phr.* **il fait chaud aujourd'hui, ici,** it is warm, hot, today, here; *F:* **il fera c. quand elle commencera à travailler!** that'll be the day when she starts working! (*b*) warm, warming; **couverture chaude,** warm blanket; **vin c.,** mulled wine; **fièvre chaude,** high fever with delirium; *A:* **c. mal,** raging fever; *A:* **tomber de fièvre en c. mal,** to fall out of the frying-pan into the fire, to go from bad to worse; (*c*) *P:* lustful, *P:* hot; (*of female animal*) **être chaude,** to be on heat; *P:* (*of pers.*) **être c.,** to be highly sexed; **c'est un c. lapin,** he's a sexy devil. **2.** *s.m.* heat, warmth; hot, warm, state; **le c. du jour était passé,** the heat of the day was over; **il est au c. dans sa maison,** he is snug and warm, nice and warm, at home; **tenir qch. au c.,** to keep sth. hot; (*on label*) **tenir au c.,** to be kept in a warm place; *F:* **avoir les pieds au c.,** to have a cushy job; to be in clover; **ce gilet lui tiendra c.,** this waistcoat will keep him warm; **cela ne fait ni c. ni froid,** it makes no difference, it doesn't alter matters in any way, it is neither here nor there; **cela ne me fait ni c. ni froid,** it is all the same, all one, a matter of complete indifference, to me; *s.a.* DONNER 2; **souffler le c. et le froid,** to blow hot and cold; *F:* **attraper un c. et froid,** to catch a chill; *adv.phr.* **soluble à c.,** soluble when heated, when hot; **marqué à c.,** branded; *Paperm:* **blanchiment à c.,** warm bleach; *Ind:* **laminage à c.,** hot rolling; *s.a.* OPÉRATION 2, OPÉRER 2; *v.phr.* **avoir c.,** (*of pers.*) to be, feel, warm, hot; **j'ai trop c.,** I'm too hot; *F:* **je crève de c.,** I'm baking, boiling; *F:* **il a eu c.,** (i) he was scared stiff; (ii) he had a narrow escape; **prendre c.,** (*of pers.*) to get over-heated. **3.** *s.f.* **chaude,** brisk fire (for warming); *Metall:* heat; **fer à cheval qui exige deux chaudes,** horseshoe that requires two heats; **chaude blanche, grasse,** white heat; **chaude blanc-soudant,** welding heat; **chaude rouge,** (i) red heat; (ii) bringing to red heat; **chaude sombre,** dark red heat; **chaude suante** welding glow; *Num:* **battre la chaude,** to roll ingots (before coining).

chaudeau, -eaux [ʃodo], *s.m. A:* hot drink (egg-flip, basin of hot soup, etc.); caudle.

chaudefonnier, -ière [ʃodfɔnje, -jɛːr], *a. & s. Geog:* (native, inhabitant) of La Chaux-de-Fonds.

chaude-lance [ʃodlɑ̃ːs], *s.f. Med: P:* V.D., *P:* clap; *pl. chaudes-lances.*

chaudement [ʃodmɑ̃], *adv.* **1.** warmly; **se tenir c.,** to keep oneself warm; **être vêtu c.,** to be warmly clad, dressed; **défendre qn c.,** to defend s.o. warmly, with warmth; **protester c.,** to protest hotly. **2.** *A: F:* immediately.

chaude-pisse [ʃodpis], *s.f. Med: P:* V.D., *P:* clap; *pl. chaudes-pisses.*

chaud-froid [ʃofrwɑ], *s.m. Cu:* chaud-froid; **c.-f. de poulet,** cold jellied chicken; *pl. chauds-froids.*

chaudière [ʃodjɛːr], *s.f.* **1.** (*a*) *Dom.Ec:* copper (for washing, etc.); **c. de cuisine,** range boiler; *Brew:* **c. à houblon,** hop copper, wort boiler; (*b*) *Fr.C:* bucket. **2.** (*a*) boiler; **c. à charbon, à mazout,** solid fuel oil-fired, boiler; *Mch:* **c. à vapeur,** steam boiler, steam generator; **c. à bouilleurs,** French boiler; **c. de détente,** flash boiler; **c. à foyer, à chauffage, extérieur,** externally-, outside-, fired boiler; **c. à foyer, à chauffage, intérieur,** internally-, inside-, fired boiler; **c. à flamme directe,** direct-draught boiler; **c. à flamme en retour, à retour de flamme,** return-flue, return-tube, boiler; **c. tubulaire,** (multi-)tubular boiler; multi-flue boiler; **c. aquatubulaire,** water-tube boiler; **c. ignitubulaire,** fire-tube boiler; **c. à vaporisation instantanée,** flash-(steam) boiler; **c. à chaleur perdue,** exhaust-heat boiler; **c. à tombeau,** wag(g)on boiler; **c. principale, grande c.,** main boiler; **c. auxiliaire, petite c.,** donkey boiler; **c. (de) marine,** marine boiler; **c. terrestre,** land-boiler; (*b*) *Rail:* **c. de locomotive,** engine-, locomotive-, boiler; **enveloppe de c.,** boiler cleading, lagging; **lit dec.,** bedding (of boiler); (*c*) *Ind:* **c. à vide,** vacuum pan; *Roadm:* **c. à bitume, de bitumier,** asphalt-, tar-, boiler. **3.** *Geol:* **c. de géant,** giant's kettle.

chaudrée [ʃodre], *s.f.* (type of) fish soup.

chaudron [ʃodrɔ̃], *s.m.* **1.** (*a*) ca(u)ldron; *Soapm:* vat; *s.a.* MÂCHURER¹; (*b*) ca(u)ldronful; (*c*) *F:* worn-out musical instrument; tinny old piano. **2.** *Bot:* (wild) daffodil. **3.** *a.inv. Dy:* dark reddish brown. **4.** *Cost:* bucket top (of boot). **5.** swelling (on tree trunk caused by fungus).

chaudronnée [ʃodrɔne], *s.f.* ca(u)ldronful.

chaudronnerie [ʃodrɔnri], *s.f.* **1.** (*a*) boiler making; hollow-ware manufacture; (*b*) boiler trade; hollow-ware trade. **2. grosse c.,** boilers and industrial hollow-ware; **petite c.,** domestic hollow-ware. **3.** (*a*) boiler works; coppersmith's, tinsmith's works; hollow-ware factory; (*b*) = ironmongery, hardware, store.

chaudronnier, -ière [ʃodrɔnje, -jɛːr]. **1.** *s.* (*a*) boiler maker; coppersmith; tinsmith; hollow-ware maker; (*b*) = ironmonger; *O:* **c. ambulant, au sifflet,** tinker. **2.** *a.* **industrie chaudronnière,** hollow-ware industry.

chauffage [ʃofaːʒ], *s.m.* **1.** (*a*) heating; **c. central,** central heating; **c. urbain,** district heating; **c. à l'électricité, au gaz, à la vapeur, au mazout,** electric, gas, steam, oil, heating; **c. par rayonnement,** radiant heating; **bois de c.,** firewood; *Adm: etc:* **allocation de c.,** fuel allowance; *Metalw:* **c. par arc électrique,** arc heating; **c. à blanc, au rouge,** white-, red-, heating; (*b*) stoking (of boiler); firing (of furnace); **c. mécanique,** mechanical stoking, firing; (*c*) *F:* heating apparatus; *Aut:* (car) heater; **le c. est détraqué,** the boiler, the heater, has gone wrong; (*d*) *Sch: P:* cramming. **2.** *Mec.E:* overheating (of bearing, etc.).

chauffant [ʃofɑ̃], *a.* heating, warming; **couverture chauffante,** electric blanket; **plaque chauffante,** hot plate; *El:* **résistance chauffante,** heating resistance; *Tchn:* **élément c.,** heating unit.

chauffard [ʃofaːr], *s.m. Aut: F:* (*a*) road hog; speed merchant; (*b*) hit-and-run driver.

chauffe [ʃoːf], *s.f.* **1.** (*a*) heating; **c. à blanc,** white heat; **donner une c. à qch.,** to warm sth. up; (*b*) distilling. **2.** *Mch:* firing, stoking; **c. au charbon,** coal firing; **c. au mazout,** oil firing; **porte de c.,** fire-door, fire-hole; **surface de c.,** heating surface; **activer la c.,** to fire up; **chef de c.,** head stoker; *Nau:* leading stoker; *Nau:* **chambre de c.,** stokehold. **3.** overheating (of bearings, etc.). **4.** *Metall:* fire-chamber of furnace.

chauffe-assiette(s) [ʃofasjɛt], *s.m.* plate warmer, hot plate; *pl. chauffe-assiettes.*

chauffe-bain [ʃofbɛ̃], *s.m.* bath heater, water heater; geyser; *pl. chauffe-bains.*

chauffe-cire [ʃofsiːr], *s.m.inv. Hist:* chafewax, chaffwax.

chauffe-eau [ʃofo], *s.m.inv.* water-heater; **c.-e. à accumulation,** storage (water) heater; **c.-e. à immersion,** immersion heater.

chauffe-linge [ʃoflɛ̃ːʒ], *s.m.inv.* (*a*) airing cupboard; (*b*) apparatus for airing linen.

chauffe-liquides [ʃoflikid], *s.m.inv.* (electric) immersion heater.

chauffe-lit [ʃofli], *s.m.* (i) bed-warmer; (ii) warming-pan; *pl. chauffe-lit(s).*

chauffe-pieds [ʃofpje], *s.m.inv.* footwarmer; foot muff.

chauffe-plat(s) [ʃofpla], *s.m.* chafing dish; **c.-p. (électrique),** (electric) hot plate; *pl. chauffe-plats.*

chauffer [ʃofe]. **I.** *v.tr.* **1.** (*a*) *Dom.Ec:* to heat, to warm; **c. une maison au charbon, au gaz, au mazout,** to heat a house with coal, gas, oil; **c. une pièce au bois,** to have a wood fire in a room; **c. de l'eau dans une casserole,** to heat, to warm, water in a pan; **c. du linge,** to air linen; **se c. les mains,** to warm one's hands; (*b*) *Hort:* **c. une plante,** to force a plant; (*c*) *Ind: Mch:* to fire, to stoke (a furnace, a boiler, an engine); *Metalw:*

to heat; **c. un four au coke,** to fire, to stoke, a furnace with coke; **c. le fer à blanc, au rouge,** to bring, to make, iron white-hot, red-hot; **chauffé à blanc, au rouge,** white-hot, red-hot; **c. une locomotive au charbon, au mazout,** to fire, to stoke, an engine, a locomotive, with coal, with oil; **chauffé au pétrole, au mazout,** oil-fired, oil-fuelled; **c. une chaudière, une locomotive,** (i) to fire up, to stoke up, a boiler, an engine; (ii) to tend, to serve, a boiler, an engine; (iii) to raise steam; (*d*) *Nau: A:* **c. un navire,** to bream a ship; (*e*) *F:* **c. qn en vue d'un examen,** to cram, to stuff, to coach, s.o. for an examination; **c. un examen,** to work hard, swot, for an examination; **c. une affaire,** to lose no time over a piece of business; **il faut c. l'affaire,** we must strike while the iron is hot; **c. un livre, un écrivain,** to praise up, to boost, a book, a writer; **c. ses électeurs,** to nurse one's constituency; **c. qn (à blanc),** (i) to excite s.o., to get s.o. worked up; (ii) to incite, exhort s.o.; **c. qn,** to reprimand s.o.; *F:* to give s.o. a rocket; *F:* **c. une femme,** to make hot love to a woman; *Th:* **c. une scène,** to put some go into a scene; *F:* to ginger up a scene. **2.** *P:* (*a*) to steal; **on m'a chauffé mes allumettes,** s.o. has pinched my matches; (*b*) to pinch (s.o.), to run (s.o.) in; **c. qn,** to catch s.o. red-handed; **se faire c.,** to get pinched, nabbed.

II. *v.i.* (*a*) *Dom.Ec:* to get, become, hot, warm; **l'eau chauffe sur la cuisinière,** the water is heating on the cooker; **le potage chauffe lentement,** the soup is heating slowly; **le bain chauffe,** the bath is heating; (*b*) *Ind: Mch: etc:* (i) to get, become, hot; (ii) to burn, to be heated (with); (iii) to get up steam (of steam engine, etc., in order to start); **le four chauffe,** the furnace is getting hot; **c. au charbon, au mazout,** to burn coal, oil; **la chaudière chauffe au gaz, au mazout,** the boiler is heated with gas, with oil; **la locomotive, le navire, chauffe,** the engine, the ship, is getting up steam; (*c*) *P:* **ça chauffe, ça va c.,** things are getting hot, are beginning to hum; we are in for a hot, exciting, time; *F:* **ce n'est pas pour vous que le four chauffe,** this is not for you; *F:* **c'est un bain,** *P:* **un bouillon, qui chauffe,** a storm is brewing. **2.** *Mec.E:* **le moteur, le palier, chauffe,** the engine, the bearing, is running hot, is (over-) heating.

se chauffer. **1. se c. au soleil,** to warm oneself in the sun. **2.** to heat one's house; **se c. au charbon,** to use coal, solid fuel, for heating; **nous nous chauffons au mazout,** we have oil-fired central heating; *s.a.* BOIS 3.

chaufferette [ʃofrɛt], *s.f.* **1.** footwarmer. **2.** chafing dish.

chaufferettier [ʃofrɛtje], *s.m. Rail: A:* footwarmer attendant.

chaufferie [ʃofri], *s.f.* **1.** *Metall:* (*a*) reheating furnace, chafery; (*b*) (smith's) hearth, forge. **2.** *Ind:* boiler-room; *Nau:* stokehold, boiler-room.

chauffe-théière [ʃoftejɛːr], *s.m.* tea-cosy; *pl. chauffe-théières.*

chauffeur, -euse [ʃofœːr, -øːz], *s.* **1.** (*a*) stoker, fireman (of steam engine, etc.); *Navy:* **c. breveté,** leading stoker; (*b*) *Ind:* furnace man; boiler man; (*pers.*) **c. de rivets,** rivet-heater; (*c*) *Sch: P:* crammer, coach. **2.** *Aut:* (*a*) (i) *O:* driver; (ii) **les chauffeurs du dimanche,** weekend drivers; (*b*) *s.m.* chauffeur, *f.* chauffeuse; **c. de camion,** lorry driver; **elle est c. de taxi,** she's a taxi driver. **3.** *s.f.* **chauffeuse,** low fireside chair.

chauffeur-mécanicien [ʃofœːrmekanisjɛ̃], *s.m. Mch:* engine-man; *Aut:* driver-mechanic; *pl. chauffeurs-mécaniciens.*

chauffoir [ʃofwaːr], *s.m.* **1.** heated public rest room; calefactory (in monastery). **2.** *Med:* hot cloth (for covering or rubbing down a patient).

chaufour [ʃofuːr], *s.m.* limekiln.

chaufournerie [ʃofurnəri], *s.f.* lime-burning (industry).

chaufournier [ʃofurnje], *s.m.* lime-burner.

chaulage [ʃolaːʒ], *s.m.* liming (of ground, trees, hides, etc.).

chauler [ʃole], *v.tr.* to lime; to treat (ground, etc.) with lime; to limewash (fruit-trees, etc.).

chauleuse [ʃoløːz], *s.f. Agr:* lime-spreader.

chaulier¹ [ʃolje], *s.m.* lime-burner.

chaulier², **-ière** [ʃolje, -jɛːr], *a. & s. Geog:* (native, inhabitant) of La Chaux-de-Fonds.

chaulmoogra, chaulmugra [ʃolmugra], *s.m.* chaulmoogra (oil).

chaulmoogrique [ʃolmugrik], *a. Ch:* chaulmoogric.

chaumage [ʃomaːʒ], *s.m. Agr:* (i) digging in; (ii) cutting, of stubble.

chaumard [ʃomaːr], *s.m. Nau:* **1.** fairlead(er). **2.** fixed block; sheave-hole, warping chock.

chaume [ʃoːm], *s.m.* **1.** *Agr:* (*a*) straw (of corn), haulm; **c. de blé,** wheat-straw; (*b*) thatch; **couvrir un toit en c.,** to thatch a roof; **toit de c.,** thatched roof; (*c*) (i) stubble; (ii) stubble-field. **2.** *Bot:* culm, haulm (of grasses).

chaumer [ʃome], *v.tr. Agr:* **c. un champ,** to cut, dig in, the stubble in a field, to clear a field of stubble, to stubble a field.

chaumette [ʃomɛt], *s.f.* long-handled sickle.

chaumeur [ʃomœːr], *s.m.* (*a*) thatcher; (*b*) stubble-clearer.

chaumier [ʃomje], *s.m.* **1.** *O:* (*a*) stubble-digger, stubble-clearer; (*b*) thatcher. **2.** *A:* heap of straw, of stubble.

chaumière [ʃomjɛːr], *s.f.* thatched cottage; **une c. et un cœur,** love in a cottage.

chaumine [ʃomin], *s.f. A: & Poet:* tiny (thatched) cottage; cot.

chaumontais, -aise [ʃomɔ̃tɛ, -ɛːz], *a. & s.,* **chaumontois, -oise** [ʃomɔ̃twa, -waːz], *a. & s. Geog:* (native, inhabitant) of Chaumont.

chaunois, -oise [ʃonwa, -waːz], *a. & s. Geog:* (native, inhabitant) of Chauny.

chaurien, -ienne [ʃorjɛ̃, -jɛn], *a. & s. Geog:* (native, inhabitant) of Castelnaudary.

chaussant [ʃosɑ̃]. **1.** *a.* (shoe) that fits well; comfortable (shoe). **2.** *s.m.* fit (of shoe).

chausse [ʃoːs], *s.f.* **1.** *pl. A:* **des chausses, une paire de chausses,** hose, breeches; *F:* **n'avoir pas de chausses,** not to have a shirt to one's back; **tirer ses chausses,** to take to one's heels; **il y laissa ses chausses,** he died there; **c'est la femme qui porte les chausses,** it's the wife who wears the breeches; **être après les chausses, aboyer aux chausses, après les chausses, de qn,** to be always worrying s.o., to badger s.o. **2.** straining-bag (for wine, etc.). **3.** *Const:* **c. d'aisances,** soil-pipe (of water closet). **3.** *Sch:* = (graduate's) hood.

chaussée [ʃose], *s.f.* **1.** (*a*) dyke, embankment; (*b*) causeway (across marsh, etc.); *Geog:* **la C. des Géants,** the Giant's Causeway. **2.** (*a*) roadway, *U.S:* pavement; **c. bombée,** cambered road; **c. déformée,** road in poor condition, *on P.N:* temporary road surface; (*b*) road, high road; (*c*) (*on motorway*) carriageway; *s.a.* PONT¹ 1. **3.** reef, line of rocks.

chausse-pied [ʃospje], *s.m.* shoehorn; *pl. chausse-pieds.*

chausser [ʃose], *v.tr.* **1. c. ses bas, ses souliers,** to put on one's stockings, one's shoes; **chaussé de pantoufles,** wearing (his) slippers; **c. des bottines à qn,** to put s.o.'s boots on (for him); **c. des éperons,** to put on spurs; **chaussé de ses bottes et de ses éperons,** booted and spurred; **c. les étriers,** to put one's feet into the stirrups; **c. son habit, ses lunettes,** to put on one's coat, one's spectacles. **2.** (*a*) to put shoes, boots, stockings, on (s.o.); **se c.,** to put on one's shoes, boots; **se c. (la tête) de qch.,** to get sth. into one's head; **être chaussé d'une opinion,** to be fixed in an opinion; (*b*) to supply, fit, (s.o.) with footwear, to make footwear for (s.o.); **le cordonnier qui me chausse,** the shoemaker who makes my boots, shoes; **se faire c. chez B.,** to buy, get, one's shoes at B.'s; **être bien chaussé,** to be well-shod; **souliers qui chaussent bien,** shoes that fit, look, well; *F:* **cela me chausse (bien),** that suits me (down to the ground); **être difficile à c.,** to be hard to please; **c. du 38,** to take 38 in shoes, to take 38's, size 38 (*Fr. sizes*); *Prov:* **les cordonniers sont les plus mal chaussés,** the shoemaker's wife is always the worst shod. **3.** *Hort:* **c. un arbre,** to earth up a tree. **4.** *Aut:* to tyre; **voiture non chaussée,** car without tyres.

chaussetier [ʃostje], *s.m. A:* hosier.

chausse-trape [ʃostrap], *s.f.* **1.** *Ven:* trap (for wolves, etc.); *F:* trick, trap, ruse. **2.** *Mil: A:* caltrop crow's foot. **3.** *Bot:* star-thistle. caltrops; *pl. chausse-trapes.*

chaussette [ʃosɛt], *s.f.* **1.** sock; *pl. Com:* half-hose; **marcher en chaussettes,** to walk about in one's stockinged feet; *Mil: etc:* **c. russe,** foot-cloth; *P:* **chaussettes à clous,** hobnailed boots; *P:* **jus de chaussette,** bad coffee. **2.** *Fr.C:* slipper.

chausseur [ʃosœːr], *s.m.* footwear specialist.

chaussier [ʃosje], *s.m. A:* hosier.

chausson [ʃosɔ̃], *s.m.* **1.** (*a*) (heel-less) slipper; (*b*) **c. (de danse),** ballet shoe; (*c*) gym shoe; boxing shoe; (*d*) **c. (tricoté) de bébé,** bootee; (*e*) **c. de nuit,** bedsock; (*f*) *Fr.C:* thick (woollen) sock; (*g*) foot bandage. **2.** *Needlew:* **point de c.,** herringbone stitch. **3.** French boxing, foot boxing, savate. **4.** *Cu:* **c. aux pommes,** apple turnover.

chaussonnier [ʃosɔnje], *s.m.* maker of, dealer in, slippers.

chaussure [ʃosyːr], *s.f.* **1.** (*a*) footwear; (*b*) (boot and) shoe industry; **il travaille dans la c.,** he's in the shoe industry, trade. **2.** shoe; **une paire de chaussures,** a pair of shoes; **chaussures montantes,** boots; **chaussures de montagne, d'escalade,** climbing boots; **chaussures de marche,** walking shoes; **chaussures de ski,** ski boots; *F:* **une c. à tout pied,** sth. completely ordinary; a commonplace; *F:* **trouver c. à son pied,** (i) to find what one is looking for, what one wants, *esp.* to find a wife, a husband; (ii) to find one's equal, one's match; *F:* **avoir un pied dans deux chaussures,** to have two strings to one's bow

chaut [ʃo], *see* CHALOIR.

chauve [ʃoːv]. **1.** *a.* (*a*) bald; **à tête c.,** bald-headed; *F:* **c. comme un genou, comme un œuf, comme une bille,** as bald as a coot; (*b*) bare, denuded (mountain, etc.). **2.** *s.m.* bald person, bald-head.

chauve-souris [ʃovsuri], *s.f.* **1.** *Z:* bat. **2.** awning (to protect workmen from the sun). **3.** *N.Arch:* wing-shaped brace-iron of rudder-post; *pl. chauves-souris.*

chauvin, -ine [ʃovɛ̃, -in]. **1.** *s.* chauvinist, jingo-(ist). **2.** *a.* chauvinist(ic), jingoist(ic).

chauvinique [ʃovinik], *a.* chauvinistic, jingoistic.

chauvinisme [ʃovinism], *s.m.* chauvinism, exaggerated patriotism, jingoism.

chauviniste [ʃovinist], *a.* chauvinist(ic), jingoist(ic).

chauvir [ʃoviːr], *v.i. A:* (*of horse, ass, mule*) **c. des oreilles,** to prick up its ears.

chaux [ʃo], *s.f* lime; **c. vive, c. anhydre,** quick-lime, unslaked, unslacked, lime; **c. carbonatée, sulfatée,** carbonate, sulphate, of lime; **c. grasse,** fat lime; **c. maigre,** quiet lime; **c. éteinte,** slaked, slack(ed), lime; **c. fusée, c. éteinte à l'air,** air-slaked lime; **c. hydraulique,** hydraulic lime; **pierre à c.,** limestone; **eau de c.,** limewater; **lait, blanc, de c.,** limewash, whitewash; **blanchir un mur à la c.,** to limewash, whitewash, a wall; **bâtir à c. et à sable, à c. et à ciment,** to build firmly, solidly; **être bâti à c. et à sable,** to have an iron constitution; *s.a.* BADIGEON 1, MORTIER 2.

chavibétol [ʃavibetɔl], *s.m. Ch:* chavibetol.

chavicol [ʃavikɔl], *s.m. Ch:* chavicol.

chavillot [ʃavijo], *s.m. Nau:* toggle.

chavirabilité [ʃavirabilite], *s.f. Nau: A:* liability to capsize; crankness (of ship).

chavirable [ʃavirabl̩], *a. Nau:* crank(-sided) (ship); (ship) liable to capsize.

chavirage [ʃaviraːʒ], *s.m.* turning (of sth.) upside down, inverting; upset(ting) (of boat).

chavirement [ʃavirmɑ̃], *s.m.* **1.** capsizing, upsetting, turning turtle (of boat). **2.** *O:* tipping, dumping (of refuse, etc.).

chavirer [ʃavire], *v.* **1.** *v.i.* (*a*) (*of boat, etc.*) to capsize, turn turtle, overturn; (*b*) (*of pers.*) to be overcome; **son cœur chavira de douleur,** his heart was overwhelmed with grief; **les nations les plus grandes chavirent,** (even) the greatest nations collapse; (*c*) to sway, reel, stagger, spin (round); **tout semblait c. autour de lui,** everything round him seemed to be spinning; **la tête lui chavirait,** his head was spinning; **ses yeux chavirèrent,** he showed the whites of his eyes, he rolled his eyes back. **2.** *v.tr.* (*a*) to upset, capsize (a boat); **c. un canot pour le réparer,** to cant a boat for repairs; (*b*) to turn (sth.) upside down, to overturn (sth.); to knock (sth.) over; (*c*) *F:* **j'en suis tout chaviré,** it's completely upset me; **elle a l'air toute chavirée,** she looks completely overcome; **avoir le cœur chaviré,** to feel queasy.

chayère [ʃɛːr], *s.f. A.Furn:* box settle.

chayote, chayotte [ʃajɔt], *s.f. Hort:* chayote.

chébec, chebek [ʃebɛk], *s.m. Nau:* xebec, chebec(k).

chéchia [ʃeʃja], *s.f. Cost:* chechia.

chèche, cheich [ʃɛʃ], *s.m.* silk or cotton scarf (worn by North-African troops).

check-list [tʃɛklist], *s.f. Aer: F:* checklist; *pl. check-lists.*

cheddite [ʃedit], *s.f. Exp:* cheddite.

chef [ʃɛf], *s.m.* **1.** (*a*) *A: Lit: Hum:* (= TÊTE) head; *A:* **venir à c. de son dessein,** to achieve one's end; *A:* **il pense de son c.,** he thinks for himself; (*still used in*) **branler du c.,** to wag one's head; **opiner du c.,** to nod (one's head); *Ecc: Art:* **c.** (reliquaire), head reliquary; (*b*) *Miner:* head (of slate); *Tex:* **c. d'une pièce de drap,** (piece) heading, show-end of a web; *Surg:* **c. d'une bande,** end of a bandage; (*c*) *Her:* chief (of shield). **2.** (*F: occ. with f.* **chef(f)esse** [ʃɛfɛs]) (*a*) head (of family, etc.); chief, chieftain, leader (of tribe, clan, etc.); leader (of political party); principal, head, chief (of business); foreman (of jury); conductor (of orchestra); founder (of family, of religious order, school of thought, etc.); **c. de**

famille, de maison, householder; c. d'état, head of state; être c. dans un parti, le c. d'un parti, to be the leader, at the head, of a party; c. de bande, de complot, ringleader; c. (de cuisine), head cook, chef; c. de réception, head receptionist (in hotel); U.S: chief reception clerk; Cin: c. opérateur, (chief cameraman; Th: c. d'emploi, principal; c. du chant, chorus master; Row: c. de nage, stroke (oar); Scouting: c. éclaireur, c. de troupe, scoutmaster; c. de patrouille, patrol-leader; c. d'équipe, (i) Sp: team-leader, captain; (ii) Ind: ganger, foreman; charge hand; c. de piste, ring master; Rel.H: (abbaye) c. d'ordre, head house (of monastic order); (b) Adm: c. de bureau, head clerk, chief clerk; office manager; executive officer; c. de service, head of department, departmental manager, officer in charge; executive officer; c. du personnel, personnel, staff, manager; c. de cabinet = (minister's) principal private secretary; (c) Com: Ind: principal, head, chief (of business); c. d'atelier (shop-)foreman; c. du service (des ateliers) works' manager; c. d'équipe, d'escouade, de brigade, de file, de poste, (shift-)foreman, U.S: (shift-)boss; chargeman; chargehand; c. de chaîne de montage, assembly-line supervisor; c. de chauffe, chief-, head-, stoker; c. de fonderie, foundry-foreman; ingénieur en c., chief engineer; c. arrimeur, foreman stevedore, shipworker; c. opérateur, chief operator; c. de rang, head waiter; c. de rayon, (i) head of department, department manager; (ii) shop-walker, U.S: floor walker; les chefs d'industrie, the captains of industry; (d) Rail: c. de gare, station-master; c. de gare adjoint, assistant station-master; sous-c. de gare, inspector; c. de train, guard, U.S: conductor; c. de l'exploitation, traffic manager; c. du mouvement, superintendent of the line; c. régional, district superintendent; c. de manœuvre, shunting foreman; c. de pose (de rails), track-foreman; c. du service des signaux, signal superintendent. 3. Mil: Navy: Av: c. de service, head of service, of administrative branch; c. du génie, district officer of engineers; c. mécanicien, chief engineer; c. du service de santé, chief medical officer; c. des transmissions, chief signal officer; Navy: c. de timonerie, chief yeoman of signals; Av: c. de bord, captain; Nau: c. de quart, officer of the watch; c. de musique, de fanfare, bandmaster; commandant en c., commander-in-chief; commander une armée en c., to be commander-in-chief of an army; c. de corps, commanding officer, U.S: commander of a self-administrating unit; c. de bataillon, major; Artil: c. d'escadron, major; Cav: c. d'escadrons, major; c. de peloton, troop commander; c. de section, platoon leader, platoon commander; c. de groupe, squad, section, leader, commander; c. d'équipe, crew, section, commander, U.S: team leader; Artil: c. de pièce, gun commander, chief of piece; number one, U.S: chief of section; c. de patrouille, patrol leader; c. de char, tank commander; c. de véhicule, vehicle commander; c. de poste, (i) picket commander; (ii) officer, non-commissioned officer, of the guard; c. de file, (i) Mil: leading man (of a file); file leader; (ii) Navy: leading ship; F: les chefs, the officers and non-commissioned officers; les grands chefs, the generals, F: the top brass; F: bien, c.! Navy: (i) aye, aye, P.O.! (ii) aye, aye, chief! Mil: Av: O.K., sarge! s.a. ATTAQUE 3, CHAUFFE 2, FILE, POSTE 2, PUPITRE 3, ÉTAT-MAJOR. 4. authority, right; faire qch. de son (propre, plein) c., to do sth. on one's own authority; F: off one's own bat; intervenir de son propre c., to intervene personally; posséder qch. de son c., to possess sth. in one's own right; avoir une terre du c. de sa femme, to own an estate in one's wife's right. 5. head(ing); arranger les matières sous plusieurs chefs, to arrange the matter under several heads; Jur: c. d'accusation, count of an indictment, charge; poursuivi sous le c. de . . ., prosecuted on account of . . .; le premier c., the most important count; adv.phr. au premier c., essentially; eminently (worthy, etc.), (worthy) in the highest degree; il importe au premier c. que . . ., it is of the highest importance, is essential, that . . .

chef-d'œuvre [ʃɛdœːvr̥], s.m. masterpiece, chef-d'œuvre; un petit c.-d'œ., a minor masterpiece; Iron: vous avez fait là un beau c.-d'œ., a fine mess you've made of it; pl. chefs-d'œuvre.

chefferie [ʃɛfri], s.f. Mil: A: 1. district under a district officer of engineers. 2. district officer's staff. 3. chieftainry.

chef-lieu [ʃɛfljø], s.m. chief town (of department) (= county town, U.S: county seat); c.-l. judiciaire, seat of the highest judicial authorities; pl. chefs-lieux.

cheftaine [ʃɛftɛn], s.f. Scouting: c. de compagnie, de guides, captain; c. de ronde, de Jeannettes, Brown owl; c. de meute, (woman) cubmaster.

chégros [ʃegro], s.m. Bootm: wax end, shoemaker's end.

cheik(h) [ʃɛk], s.m. sheik(h).

chéilalgie [keilalʒi], s.f. Med: ch(e)ilalgia.

chéilite [keilit], s.f. Med: ch(e)ilitis.

chéiloplastie [keiloplasti], s.f. Surg: ch(e)iloplasty.

chéimatobia [keimatobja], **chéimatobie** [keimatobi], s.f. Ent: winter moth.

cheintre [ʃɛ̃ːtr̥], s.m. = CHAINTRE.

cheire [ʃɛr], s.f. Geol: (in Auvergne) solidified lava with rugged surface.

chéiro- [keiro, -kero], pref. chir(o)-, cheir(o)-.

chéirogale [keirogal], s.m. Z: Cheirogaleus.

chéiromys [keiromis], s.m. Z: chiromys, aye-aye.

chéiroptères [keiroptɛːr], s.m.pl. Z: Ch(e)iroptera.

chélate [kelat], s.m. 1. Crust: chela. 2. Ch: chelate.

chélaté [kelate], a. Ch: etc: chelated.

chélateur [kelatœːr], a. & s.m. Ch: etc: chelate(d); agent c., chelating, sequestering agent.

chélation [kelasjɔ̃], s.f. Ch: etc: chelation.

chelem [ʃlɛm], s.m. Cards: slam; grand c., grand slam; (at solo whist) abundance déclarée, declared; petit c., little slam.

chélicérates [keliseraːt], s.m.pl. Arach: Chelicerata.

chélicère [keliseːr], s.m. Arach: chelicera; pl. -ae; chelicer, pl. chelicer(e)s.

chélidés [kelide], s.m.pl. Rept: Chelidae.

chélidoine [kelidwan], s.f. Bot: chelidonium; (grande) c., greater celandine, F: tetterwort, devil's milk; petite c., lesser celandine, pilewort, figwort.

chélidonique [kelidonik], a. Ch: chelidonic.

chélifère [kelifɛːr], s.m. Arach: chelifer, false scorpion; c. cancroïde, book scorpion.

chéliforme [keliform], a. Z: cheliform.

chelinguer [ʃlɛ̃ge], v.i. P: to stink.

chelléen [ʃɛl(l)eɛ̃], a. & s.m. Geol: Prehist: Chellean.

chellois, -oise [ʃɛl(l)wa, -waːz], a. & s. Geog: (native, inhabitant) of Chelles.

chéloïde [keloid], s.f. Med: cheloid, keloid, cheloma.

chélone [kelon], s.f. 1. Ent: Rept: chelone. 2. Bot: chelone, turtlehead, shell-flower.

chélonée [kelone], s.f. Rept: Chelone; c. franche, green turtle.

chélonidés [kelonide], s.m.pl. Rept: Cheloni(i)dae.

chéloniens [kelonjɛ̃], s.f.pl. Rept: Chelonians.

chélydridés [kelidride], s.m.pl. Rept: Chelydridae.

chémawinite [ʃemavinit], s.f. Miner: chemawinite.

chemin [ʃ(ə)mɛ̃], s.m. 1. (a) way, road; ce c. mène à la gare, this road leads to the station; la ligne droite est le plus court c. d'un point à un autre, a straight line is the shortest distance between two points; c. détourné, F: c. des écoliers, roundabout way, by-road; longest way round; demander son c., to ask one's way; c'est sur mon c., it's on my way; nous avons beaucoup de c. à faire, we've a long way to go; il y a dix minutes de c., it is ten minutes away; faire la moitié du c., to meet s.o. half-way; F: il fera son c., he will get on, will make his way, in the world; faire brillamment son c., to carry all before one, to have a brilliant career; cette idée fait son c., this idea is gaining ground; aller (toujours) son c., to jog alone nicely, to be successful in a small way; c. faisant, on the way, as we went along; faire un bout de c. avec qn, to accompany s.o., to go with s.o., a little way; tout le long du c., all the way; montrer le c., to lead the way; to show the way; faire voir bien du c. à qn, to lead s.o. a dance; être en bon c., to be getting on well, to do well for oneself; nous sommes dans le bon c., we are on the right road; rentrer dans le bon c., to turn over a new leaf; suivre, aller, le droit c., to live honestly, virtuously; to go straight; s'écarter du droit c., to go off the rails; à moitié c., à mi-c., half-way; nous ne sommes pas encore à moitié c., we are not half-way there yet; se mettre en c. pour, prendre le c. de, la France, to set out, make, for France; articles qui prennent le c. de la France, articles that find their way into France; ces marchandises prendront le c. de l'étranger, these good are intended for abroad, for export; F: vous pouvez prendre le c. de la porte, out you go! you can clear out! demeurer en (beau) c., to stop in mid-career; être dans, sur, le c. de qn, to be, stand, in s.o.'s way; le c. de la gare, the way to the station; trouver le c. du cœur de qn, to find the way to s.o.'s heart; le c. du crime, the (high) road, highway, to crime; Lit: c. de velours, c. de fleurs, c. fleuri, the primrose path, the easy way; ne pas y aller par quatre chemins, par trente-six chemins, to go straight to the point, not to beat about the bush; not to pull one's punches; il n'y a pas été par quatre chemins, he made no bones about it; on vous cherche par les quatre chemins, they are looking for you all over the place; s'arrêter en c., to stop on the way, en route; on ne s'arrête pas en si beau c., it would be a pity to stop after such a good start; Prov: qui trop se hâte reste en c., more haste, less speed; slow and steady wins the race; s.a. CROIX 1, PASSER I. 1, ROME, RONDE II, SABBAT 1; (b) Nau: (head)way; faire du c., to make headway; c. est, easting; c. est et ouest, departure; c. nord et sud, difference of latitude; c. direct, day's run; (c) road, path, track; route; vieux comme les chemins, as old as the hills; c. piéton, footpath; c. pour les voitures, drive, carriage-drive; c. muletier, mule track, pack-road; c. ferré, metalled road; A: grand c., highway, high road, main road; voleur de grand c., highwayman, highway robber; c. de traverse, side-road; c. de grande communication = B road; c. vicinal, by-road, minor road; c. de terre, de moisson, d'exploitation, de desserte, accommodation road; cart track; c. creux, sunken road; lane (between high banks); c. battu, beaten track, beaten path; c. forestier, drive; c. de halage, tow-path; Fort: c. couvert, covered way; F: le Chemin de Saint Jacques, the Milky Way; F: être toujours sur les chemins, par voie et par c., to gad about, be always gadding about, be always on the go; Mec.E: c. de roulement pour billes, ball-race; c. de glissement, guide-path; Cin: c. du film, c. de défilement, film-channel, film run, film-track. 2. (a) c. de fer, railway, U.S: railroad; F: aller, voyager, en c. de fer, to go, travel, by rail, by train; prendre le c. de fer, to take the train; envoi par c. de fer, dispatch by rail; c. de fer à voie étroite, narrow-gauge line; c. de fer d'intérêt local, local line; c. de fer souterrain, underground (railway), U.S: subway; St.Exch: chemins (de fer), railway stock; F: rails, U.S: railroads; (b) Nau: c. de fer de gui, tramway, jack-line, jack-stay (up the mast or along the boom of a yacht); (c) Gaming: c. de fer, chemin de fer; F: shemmy, chemmy. 3. Dom.Ec: runner (carpet); c. de table, (table) runner; c. d'escalier, stair-carpet.

chemineau, -eaux [ʃ(ə)mino], s.m. 1. (a) A: itinerant workman; (b) tramp, vagrant. 2. A: Nau: (ocean) tramp, tramp steamer.

cheminée [ʃ(ə)mine], s.f. 1. (a) fireplace; rassemblés autour de la c., gathered round the fire(side); pierre de la c., hearthstone; (b) c. prussienne, slow combustion stove (usu. of enamelled iron); (c) (manteau de) c., chimneypiece, mantelpiece; garniture de c., mantelpiece ornaments; F: sous (le manteau de) la c., secretly, sub rosa. 2. (a) chimney (flue, stack); c. d'usine, factory chimney, chimney stalk; feu de c., chimney on fire; (b) funnel, smoke stack (of locomotive, steamer); c. à rabattement, rabattable, hinged funnel; (c) chimney (of lamp); (d) Aer: vent (of parachute). 3. (a) c. d'appel, d'aération, air shaft, ventilating shaft; (b) Hyd.E: c. d'équilibre, surge tank, shaft. 4. Nau: c. de mât, mast hole. 5. Sm.a: (a) barrel sleeve; (b) nipple (of cap and hammer gun). 6. Geol: (a) c. volcanique, vent (of a volcano); (b) c. des fées, (capped) earth pillar; (c) c. diamantifère diamond pipe; (d) Mount: chimney.

cheminement [ʃ(ə)minmɑ̃], s.m. 1. (a) tramping, walking; trudging (along); (b) creeping (of rails, etc.); (c) le c. des eaux, the advance of the water(s). 2. Mil: (a) advancing, approach(ing) (to position), esp. under cover; (b) pl. (siege) approaches. 3. c. de la pensée, (i) advance, progress, march, of thought; (ii) the processes of thought. 4. Surv: plane-table traversing; c. d'angles, taking of angles in traverse. 5. Ind: progress; c. des pièces à travers les différents services, progress of the work through the different departments.

cheminer [ʃ(ə)mine], v.i. 1. (a) to continue on one's way; to tramp along; to walk on; il cheminait seul, d'un pas lent, he was walking on alone, slowly; c. sous la pluie, to trudge along in the rain; l'eau chemine dans le lit de la rivière, the water flows slowly, trickles, along the river bed; F: c. droit, to keep to the straight and narrow; (b) (of rails) to creep. 2. Mil: to advance (towards position, esp. under cover). 3. l'esprit chemine par induction et par déduction, the mind proceeds by induction and deduction. 4. Surv: to traverse.

cheminot [ʃ(ə)mino], *s.m.* railway employee, railwayman; *esp.* permanent-way man, plate-layer; grève des cheminots, railway strike.

chemisage [ʃəmizaːʒ], *s.m.* (*a*) *Min:* (action of) lining (walls of gallery); (*b*) *Mec.E:* lining (of cylinder, gun-barrel, etc.).

chemise [ʃ(ə)miːz], *s.f.* **1.** (*a*) (*for men*) shirt; c. molle, souple, soft shirt; c. empesée, stiff shirt; toile à c., shirting; (nu) en c., (dressed) in nothing but one's shirt; en bras, en manches, de c., in one's shirt sleeves; *F:* donner jusqu'à sa dernière c., to give the very shirt off one's back; *P:* compter ses chemises, to be seasick; *Prov:* la c. est plus proche que le pourpoint, plus près est la chair que la c., close sits my shirt but closer my skin; *F:* penser à qn, à qch., comme à sa première c., s'en soucier comme de sa première c., not to care a hang about s.o., sth.; (*b*) *Hist:* Chemises rouges, Red Shirts; Chemises noires, Black Shirts, (Italian) Fascists; Chemises brunes, Brown Shirts; (*c*) *A.Arm:* c. de mailles, shirt of mail; (*d*) c. de nuit, (i) (man's) nightshirt; (ii) (woman's) nightdress; (*e*) c. américaine, (woman's) vest; (*f*) *Nau:* (sailor's) jersey. **2.** (*a*) folder (for keeping papers); c. (de carton), (cardboard) portfolio, (envelope) file; (*b*) paper wrapper, dust jacket (of book); c. couvre-livre, book cover; (*c*) jacket(ing), case, casing, sheathing, lagging (of boiler, cylinder, etc.); c. de vapeur, steam jacket; c. d'eau, de circulation, water jacket; à c. d'air, air-lagged; (*d*) facing (of wall); *Fort:* chemise; *Civ.E:* mur de c., revetment wall; (*e*) lining (of cylinder, pump, blast furnace, etc.); (*f*) *I.C.E:* c. (de cylindre), (cylinder) liner, sleeve (of sleeve-valve engine); c. de distribution, sleeve valve; c. (extérieure) de cylindre, cylinder casing, jacket; cylindre à c. d'eau, water-jacketed cylinder head; (*g*) *Nau:* skin (of sail); faire la c., to skin up a sail; (*h*) *Sm.a:* envelope (of bullet).

chemise-culotte [ʃ(ə)mizkylɔt], *s.f. O:* cami-knickers; *pl. chemises-culottes.*

chemiser [ʃ(ə)mize], *v.tr.* **1.** (*a*) to jacket, case (boiler, cylinder, etc.); *El.E:* to cover (cable); (*b*) *Cu:* to coat. **2.** to line (gun, cylinder, etc.); chemisé d'acier, steel-lined.

chemiserie [ʃ(ə)mizri], *s.f.* (*a*) shirt making; manufacture of (men's) underwear and ties; (*b*) shirts, underwear and ties; (*c*) shirt factory; (men's) underwear factory; (*d*) shirt (and underwear) shop.

chemisette [ʃ(ə)mizɛt], *s.f. Cost:* **1.** (*a*) dicky; (*b*) *A:* chemisette, tucker. **2.** (light short-sleeved or sleeveless) blouse. **3.** (man's) sports shirt.

chemisier, -ière [ʃ(ə)mizje, -jɛːr]. **1.** *s.* shirt-maker, -seller. **2.** *s.m.* (*a*) (woman's) shirt (blouse); long-sleeved blouse; robe c., shirt-waister (dress); (*b*) sports blouse.

chémosis [kemozis], *s.m. Med:* chemosis.

chênaie [ʃɛnɛ], *s.f.* oak grove; oak plantation.

chenal, -aux [ʃ(ə)nal, -o], *s.m.* **1.** channel, fairway (of river, harbour, etc.); c. d'accès, channel entrance; au milieu du c., in mid-channel; *Fr.C:* poissons des chenaux, smelts. **2.** *Hyd.E:* mill-race; *A: Mec.E:* chenaux à huile, oil-channels; *Metall:* c. de coulée, runner. **3.** gutter (of roof). **4.** *Geol:* c. pro-glaciaire, glacier carved valley.

chenapan [ʃ(ə)napɑ̃], *s.m. Pej: Hum:* rogue, scoundrel; mon c. de fils, my scamp of a son.

chêne [ʃɛn], *s.m.* **1.** oak; c. rouvre, common oak; c. vert, evergreen oak, holm-oak; c. kermès, kermes oak; c. pubescent, c. blanc, durmast (-oak); c. chevelu, c. de Bourgogne, Turkey oak, moss-capped oak; c. à la noix de galle, gall-oak; c. à glands sessiles, à fleurs sessiles, chestnut oak; c. tinctorial, des teinturiers, black oak, dyer's oak; pomme de c., oak apple. **2.** c. des Indes, teak.

chéneau, -eaux [ʃeno], *s.m.* **1.** gutter (of roof); channel. *Const:* ardoise de c., eaves slate. **2.** *Aut:* drip-moulding (of roof).

chêneau, -eaux [ʃeno], *s.m.* **1.** oak sapling. **2.** *Bot:* (*a*) mountain avens; (*b*) wall germander; (*c*) (germander) speedwell.

chêne-liège [ʃɛnljɛːʒ], *s.m. Bot:* cork-oak; *pl. chênes-lièges.*

chenet [ʃ(ə)nɛ], *s.m.* fire-dog, andiron; vivre les pieds sur les chenets, to live a lazy and comfortable life.

chênette [ʃɛnɛt], *s.f.* = CHÊNEAU 2.

chènevière [ʃɛnvjɛːr], *s.f.* hemp field.

chènevis [ʃɛnvi], *s.m.* hemp seed.

chenevixite [ʃɛnviksit], *s.f. Miner:* chenevixite.

chènevotte [ʃɛnvɔt], *s.f.* **1.** (*a*) boon, shove, stalk (of peeled hemp); (*b*) *A:* spill, match. **2.** *Nau:* rope-ends, junk.

chènevotter [ʃɛnvɔte], *v.i.* (*of vine*) to grow weak, straggly, shoots.

chenil [ʃ(ə)ni(l)], *s.m.* (*a*) kennels; valet de c., kennel-man; (*b*) *coll. Ven:* the hounds; (*c*) *F:* logé dans un c., living in a dog-hole, a pigsty; (*c*) *Sw.Fr: F:* mess.

chenille [ʃ(ə)niːj], *s.f.* **1.** (*a*) caterpillar; *F:* c'est une c., you can't shake him (or her) off; he's a regular pest; (*b*) band (of caterpillar tractor); à chenilles, (*of vehicle*) tracked; (*c*) crest (of helmet). **2.** *Tex:* chenille. **3.** *Bot:* scorpiurus; *F:* caterpillar.

chenillé [ʃ(ə)nije], *a. Veh:* tracked.

chenillère [ʃ(ə)nijɛːr], *s.f.* **1.** caterpillars' nest. **2.** *Bot:* = CHENILLETTE.

chenillette [ʃ(ə)nijɛt], *s.f.* **1.** *Bot:* scorpiurus, *F:* caterpillar. **2.** *Mil:* Bren-gun carrier.

chenillon [ʃ(ə)nijɔ̃], *s.m.* **1.** *Agr:* haycock. **2.** *P:* ugly girl, woman; slut.

chénopode [kenɔpɔd], *s.m.*, **chenopodium** [kenɔpodjɔm], *s.m. Bot:* chenopodium; *F:* goosefoot.

chénopodiacées [kenɔpɔdjase], *s.f.pl. Bot:* Chenopodiaceae.

chénopodiales [kenɔpodjal], *s.f.pl. Bot:* Chenopodiales.

chenu [ʃ(ə)ny], *a.* **1.** *A. & Lit:* (*a*) (*of hair, pers.*) bleached, whitened (with age); hoary; (*b*) snow-capped (mountain); (*c*) arbres chenus, (ancient) trees that are dying back. **2.** *a. & s.m.* (*a*) *A:* (vin) c., old (matured) wine; (*b*) *P:* first-rate.

cheptel [ʃ(ə)tɛl, ʃɛptɛl], *s.m.* **1.** *Jur: Husb:* (*a*) bail à c., lease of livestock; c. simple, lease under which profits and losses are divided equally between lessee and lessor; c. à moitié, contract for a joint herd half of which is owned by the farmer; (*b*) c. (vif), livestock leased; c. mort, farm equipment leased. **2.** livestock; c. ovin d'une région, sheep population of a region; *Pej:* dans certains pays communistes on traite les travailleurs comme un c. humain, in some communist countries, workers are treated like cattle.

cheptelier [ʃ(ə)telje], *s.m.* grazier.

chéquard [ʃekaːr], *s.m. Pol: etc: F: Pej:* bribed backer (of undertaking), *U.S:* influence peddler.

chèque [ʃɛk], *s.m. Fin:* cheque, *U.S:* check; c. bancaire, de banque, banker's draft; c. de £60, cheque for £60; c. au porteur, bearer cheque; c. à ordre, cheque to order; c. barré, crossed cheque; c. ouvert, non barré, open, uncrossed, cheque; c. prescrit, stale cheque; toucher un c., to cash a cheque; donner un c. à l'encaissement, encaisser un c., to pay a cheque into the bank; to pay in a cheque; c. en blanc, blank cheque; c. sans provision, sans contrepartie, cheque without cover, dud cheque, N.S.F. (not sufficient funds) cheque; *F:* stumer, bouncer, *U.S:* rubber check; c. visé (pour provision), c. certifié, certified cheque; c. postal, cheque drawn on French Post Office Bank; service de chèques postaux; Giro bank system; c. de voyage, traveller's cheque.

chèque-dividende [ʃɛkdividɑ̃ːd], *s.m. Fin:* dividend-warrant; *pl. chèques-dividendes.*

chèque-fleurs [ʃɛkflœːr], *s.m.* flower token; *pl. chèques-fleurs.*

chèque-repas [ʃɛkrəpɑ], *s.m.*, **chèque-restaurant** [ʃɛkrestɔrɑ̃], *s.m.* luncheon voucher; *pl. chèques-repas, chèques-restaurant.*

chéquier [ʃekje], *s.m.* cheque book, *U.S:* check book.

cher, chère [ʃɛːr], *a. & adv.* **1.** *a.* dear, beloved; être c. à qn, to be dear to s.o.; il sait se rendre c. à tous, he knows how to endear himself to everyone, how to find his way to people's hearts; la vie m'est chère, I hold life dear; tout ce qui m'est c., all that I hold dear; il était ce qu'elle avait de plus c., he was all in all to her; *A:* c. lecteur, gentle reader; *Corr:* C. Monsieur, Dear Mr X; s. mon c., my dear fellow; ma chère, my dear. **2.** (*a*) *a.* dear, expensive, costly; une voiture chère, an expensive car; la vie chère, the high cost of living; c'est trop c. pour moi, I can't afford it; (*b*) *adv.* cela se vendit c., it reached, fetched, a very high price; il fait c. vivre à Paris, the cost of living is high in Paris; cela ne vaut pas c., it's not worth much; comme acteur il ne vaut pas c., as an actor he's not up to much, he's no great shakes; on paie très c. ses services, his services are very highly paid; vendre c. sa vie, to sell one's life dearly; il me le payera c., I'll make him pay for it; *F:* je l'ai eu pour pas c., I got it (on the) cheap; *F:* je ne donne pas c. de sa peau, I wouldn't give much for his chances; je donnerais c. pour + *inf.*, I would give anything to . . .; je donnerais c. pour que cela ne se fût jamais produit, I would give anything for it never to have happened.

cherbourgeois, -oise [ʃɛrburʒwa, -waːz], *a. & s. Geog:* (native, inhabitant) of Cherbourg.

chérant [ʃerɑ̃], *a. Fr.C: F:* (*of shopkeeper*) expensive.

cherche [ʃɛrʃ], *s.f.* **1.** *A:* used in the phr. être en c. de qch., de qn, to be looking for, seeking, sth., s.o. **2.** *Stonew:* template.

cherché [ʃɛrʃe], *a.* artificial, affected, over-elaborate (pose, style).

cherche-fuites [ʃɛrʃofɥit], *s.m.inv.* (gas fitter's) leak-detector.

cherche-pôles [ʃɛrʃəpoːl], *s.m.inv. El:* pole-finding device; papier c.-p., pole paper.

chercher [ʃɛrʃe], *v.tr.* **1.** to search for, look for (s.o., sth.); to seek; c. qn dans une foule, to search, hunt, for s.o. in a crowd; je l'ai cherché partout, I searched, looked, for it high and low; I have hunted for it everywhere; l'aveugle cherchait sa canne, the blind man was feeling for his stick; c. un mot au dictionnaire, look up a word in the dictionary; il cherchait des moyens de s'évader, he looked around for means of escape; c. un emploi, to look for a job; *B:* cherchez, et vous trouverez, seek, and ye shall find; c. son chemin, to try to find one's way; c. son chemin dans l'obscurité, to fumble, grope, about in the dark; c. la solution d'un problème, to try to find the solution of a problem; c. des remèdes nouveaux, to search for new remedies; c. qch. dans satête, to rack one's brains for sth.; c. s'il n'y a pas d'autres moyens (de faire qch.), to try to find other ways (to do sth.); c. sa ruine, to court one's own ruin; c. aventure, to seek adventure; *F:* je l'ai cherché, I've stuck my neck out, I've asked for it; *P:* tu me cherches? are you looking for trouble? *s.a.* BÊTE 1, MIDI 1. **2.** aller c. qn, qch., to (go and) fetch s.o., sth.; allez c. le médecin, go for the doctor; envoyer c. qn, qch., to send for s.o., sth.; j'allai le c. à la gare, I went to meet him at the station; à laisser jusqu'à ce qu'on vienne le c., to be left until called for; ayez la bonté d'envoyer, de venir, le c., kindly send, call, for it; *F:* cela va c. dans les 10.000 francs, this will fetch about 10,000 francs; *F:* ça ne va pas c. loin, it won't come to much. **3.** c. à faire qch., to try, endeavour, attempt, to do sth.; c. à ce que soient conservées les vieilles maisons, to try to save old houses; c. à se sauver, to try to escape; sans c. à se cacher, without any attempt at concealment; c. à découvrir qch., to hunt about for sth.; c. à se faire bien voir, to court popularity.

se chercher, to feel one's way.

chercheur, -euse [ʃɛrʃœːr, -øːz], *a. & s.* **1.** *a.* (*a*) esprit c., enquiring mind; (*b*) tête chercheuse, (i) *Ball:* homing head; (ii) *Rec:* selector. **2.** (*a*) *s.* seeker, searcher, investigator; research worker; c. de vérité, seeker after truth; (*b*) *s.m. Min:* c. d'or, gold digger; c. de grisou, fireman, *U.S:* fire boss. **3.** *s.m.* (*a*) *Opt:* finder (of telescope); *Phot:* c. focimétrique, viewmeter; *Artil: etc:* c. (-collimateur), (open) sight, collimating sight; (*b*) *El:* c. de pôles, pole detector; c. de court-circuit, short-circuit finder; (*c*) *Tp:* (i) (*pour sondage électrique*) testing spike; *U.S:* test pick; (ii) (*téléphone automatique*) c. (de ligne), line finder, line selector; c. primaire, primary, first, line finder; c secondaire, secondary, second, line finder; c. d'appel, call finder.

chère [ʃɛːr], *s.f.* **1.** *A:* (*a*) countenance, expression; (*b*) welcome, entertainment (at one's board); faire bonne c. à qn, to welcome s.o. **2.** cheer, fare, living; faire maigre c., to fare badly, to go short; to be on short commons; faire bonne c., (i) to have a good meal, *F:* to do oneself well; (ii) to live well, fare sumptuously; aimer la bonne c., to be fond of good living.

chèrement [ʃɛrmɑ̃], *adv.* **1.** dearly, lovingly. **2.** dearly, at a high price; vendre c. sa vie, to sell one's life dearly, to die hard; payer c. un plaisir, to pay dear(ly) for a pleasure.

chérer [ʃere], *v.i. P:* = CHERRER.

cherfaix [ʃɛrfɛ], *s.m. Fish:* caddis bait.

chéri, -ie [ʃeri]. **1.** *a.* cherished, dear; c. des dieux, beloved of the gods; c. de tout le monde, everybody's favourite. **2.** *s.* darling; mon c., ma chérie, darling; (*to a woman*) mon chéri, my darling.

chérif [ʃerif], *s.m.* (Mohammedan) sherif.

chérifat [ʃerifa], *s.m.* sherifate.

chérif(f)ien, -ienne [ʃerifjɛ̃, -jɛn], *a.* of, pertaining to, the sherifs; l'empire c., Morocco.

chérimolier [ʃerimɔlje], *s.m. Bot:* cherimoya (tree).

chérir [ʃeriːr], *v.tr.* to cherish (s.o.), to love (s.o.) dearly; je chérissais ma sœur d'avoir eu cette pensée, I loved my sister for having had this thought; c. qch., to attach great value to sth., to be deeply attached to sth.; c. la mémoire de qn, to cherish, keep green, s.o.'s memory; *s.a.* PRUNELLE 2.

chérissable [ʃerisabl̩], *a.* cherishable.

chermes, chermès [kɛrmɛs], *s.m. Ent:* chermes, pine gall louse.

chéromanie [kerɔmani], *s.f. Med:* delusion of grandeur.

Chéronée [kerɔne], *Pr.n.f. A.Geog:* Chaeronea.

chérot [ʃero], *a.m. P:* too dear; *F:* pricey.

chéroub [ʃerub], *s.m.* **1.** *Assyrian Art:* winged bull. **2.** *B:* **les chéroubim** d'or, the golden cherubim; *pl. chéroubim.*

cherre [ʃɛːr], *s.m. Ich:* Norway haddock, rosefish.

cherrer [ʃere], *v.i. P:* **1.** to exaggerate, to pile it on; to boast, to talk big. **2.** *Box:* to press, to attack violently; *s.a.* BÉGONIA.

cherry(-brandy) [ʃeri(brɑ̃di)], *s.m.* cherry brandy.

Chersonèse [kɛrsɔnɛːz], *Pr.n.f. A.Geog:* Chersonesus, Chersonese; **la C. de Thrace,** the Thracian Chersonesus.

chert [ʃɛr], *s.m. Geol:* chert.

cherté [ʃɛrte], *s.f.* dearness, expensiveness; **c. de la vie,** high cost of living; **période de c.,** period of high prices; expensive period.

chérub [ʃeryb], *s.m.* = CHÉROUB; *pl. chérubim.*

chérubin [ʃerybɛ̃]. **1.** *s.m.* cherub; *F:* **un petit c.,** a little cherub (of a boy); **des chérubins,** cherubs, cherubim. **2.** *Pr.n.m. Lit:* Cherubino.

chérubique [ʃerybik], *a.* cherubic, cherub-like; *Gr. orthodox Ch:* **hymne c.,** cherubic hymn.

chervi(s) [ʃɛrvi], *s.m. Bot:* (*a*) caraway; (*b*) skirret; (*c*) **faux c.,** wild carrot.

chester [ʃɛstɛːr], *s.m.* Cheshire cheese.

chétif, -ive [ʃetif, -iːv], *a.* **1.** weak, puny, sickly (person); **arbuste c.,** stunted, puny, shrub. **2.** poor, miserable, wretched; **existence chétive,** squalid existence; **raison chétive,** paltry reason.

chétivement [ʃetivmɑ̃], *adv.* **1.** punily, weakly. **2.** poorly, miserably.

chétiveté, chétivité [ʃetiv(i)te], *s.f.* **1.** puniness, sickliness, weakness. **2.** poorness, wretchedness.

chétivisme [ʃetivism], *s.m. Med:* = INFANTILISME.

chétodon [ketɔdɔ̃], *s.m. Ich:* chaetodon.

chétodontidés [ketɔdɔ̃tide], *s.m.pl. Ich:* Chaetodontidae.

chétoptère [ketɔptɛːr], **chætopterus** [ketɔpterys], *s.m. Ann:* Chætopterus.

chevaine [ʃ(ə)vɛn], *s.m. Ich:* chub.

cheval, -aux [ʃəval, ʃfal, -o], *s.m.* **1.** horse; (*a*) **viande de c.,** horsemeat; **chair de c.,** horseflesh; **c. d'attelage, de voiture,** carriage-horse; **c. de trait, de tirage, de roulage; c. de harnais, de collier;** draught-horse; **c. de trait léger,** light draught-horse. van-horse; **c. de trait lourd,** heavy draught-horse; **c. de charrette,** cart-horse. dray-horse; **c. de diligence, c. de carrosse,** coach-horse; **voiture à un c., à deux chevaux,** one-horse, two-horse, carriage; **voiture à deux chevaux,** carriage and pair; **voiture à quatre chevaux,** four-in-hand; *Aut: A:* **voiture sans chevaux,** horseless carriage; **c. de brancard,** shaft-horse; **c. de ferme, de charrue, de labour, de labeur,** plough-horse; **c. de selle,** saddle-horse; **c. d'école, de manège,** school horse; **c. de promenade,** hack; **c. de chasse,** hunter; *Ven:* **c. d'abri,** stalking-horse; **homme de c.,** horse lover, lover of horses, born horseman; **parler chevaux,** to talk horses; **c. à deux fins,** saddle and draught horse; **c. de course,** race-horse, racer; **c. d'obstacle, de concours,** show-jumper; *Turf:* **c. à réclamer,** plater; **c. de bât,** (i) pack-horse; (ii) *F:* lout, bumpkin; drudge; **c. pur sang,** thoroughbred (horse); **c. entier, mâle** (entire) horse, stallion; **c. hongre,** gelding; **c. de bataille,** war-horse; charger; *F:* **c'est son c. de bataille,** he rides this subject to death; it's his stock answer, argument; **c. de cavalerie,** troop-horse, cavalry horse; *Mil:* **un régiment de cinq cents chevaux,** a regiment of five hundred horse; *F:* **être bon c. de trompette,** to be steady under fire, not easily stampeded; **à c.,** on horseback; **gendarme à c.,** mounted policeman; **à c.!** to horse! **aller à c.,** to go on horseback, to ride; **monter à c.,** (i) to mount, get on, one's horse; (ii) to go in for riding; **l'art de monter à c.,** horsemanship; **montez-vous à c.?** do you ride? **faire du c.,** to ride, go in for riding; **se tenir bien, mal, à c.,** to have a good, poor, seat; **tomber de c., faire une chute de c.,** to fall off one's horse, to have a fall, take a toss; **être à c. sur qch.,** to sit astride sth., to straddle sth.; **l'armée était à c. sur le fleuve,** the army held both sides of the river, straddled the river; **être à c. sur l'étiquette,** to be a stickler for etiquette; **il reste à c. sur ses principes,** he clings tightly to his principles; **écrire à qn une lettre à c.,** to write in strong terms to s.o., to write a stiff letter to s.o.; **monter sur ses grands chevaux,** to get on one's high horse, to ride the high horse; *F:* **c'est un c. à l'ouvrage,** he's a glutton for work; *s.a.* TRAVAILLER 2; **cela ne se trouve pas sous, dans, le pas d'un c., sous le sabot d'un c.,** it is not easily come by, it does not grow on every hedge; *Prov:* **à c. donné on ne regarde pas à la bride,** (you must) never look a gift-horse in the mouth; *Prov:* **c'est en vain qu'on mène à l'abreuvoir un c. qui n'a pas soif,** you can lead a horse to water, but you can't make him drink; **médecine, remède, de cheval,** *F:* horse medicine; tough cure; **fièvre de c.,** raging fever; *P:* **c. de retour,** (i) old offender, old lag; (ii) ancient beauty; (*b*) *Myth: Ich:* **c. marin,** (i) sea-horse, hippocampus; (ii) *A:* walrus. **2. c. de bois,** wooden horse; hobby-horse; *Gym:* (vaulting-) box; *Gym:* **c. d'arçons,** (vaulting-) horse; **c. à bascule,** rocking horse; **petits chevaux,** petits chevaux (*gambling game*); **chevaux de bois,** roundabout, merry-go-round; *P:* **dîner avec les chevaux de bois,** to go dinnerless; *F:* to dine with Duke Humphrey; *Av:* **faire c. de bois,** to slew round (in taxiing), to make a grand-loop; *s.a.* TROIE; **c. frou** = hobby-horse (*in morris-dance, etc.*). **3.** *Games:* **c. fondu,** high-cockalorum. **4.** *Mch:* **petit c.,** donkey engine, auxiliary engine; **petit c. alimentaire,** donkey (feed-) pump. **5.** *Mec:* (= CHEVAL-VAPEUR) horse-power; **c. nominal,** nominal horse-power, rating; **automobile de vingt chevaux,** *F:* **une vingt chevaux,** twenty horse-power car; **chevaux effectifs, au frein,** actual horse-power, brake horse-power. **6. chevaux de frise,** *see* FRISE[3]. **7.** (*a*) *Min: Geol:* **c. de terre,** horse; (*b*) *Nau:* **c. de vergue,** horse (footrope).

cheval-arçons [ʃəvalarsɔ̃, ʃfal-], *s.m. Gym:* vaulting-horse; *pl. des chevaux-arçons.*

chevalement [ʃəvalmɑ̃, ʃfal-], *s.m.* **1.** shoring, props (of wall, etc.). **2.** (pit-)head frame, head-stock, head-gear, gallows frame (of mine shaft); winding plant. **3. c. du sondage,** (oil-well) derrick.

chevaler [ʃəvale, ʃfale], *v.tr.* **1.** *Ind:* (*a*) to put (sth.) on a trestle; **c. du bois,** to put wood on a saw-horse; (*b*) to beam (skins). **2.** *Const:* to shore up, prop (up) (wall, etc.).

chevaleresque [ʃəvalrɛsk, ʃfal-], *a.* chivalrous, knightly.

chevaleresquement [ʃəvalrɛskəmɑ̃, ʃfal-], *adv.* chivalrously.

chevalerie [ʃəvalri, ʃfal-], *s.f.* **1.** knighthood; **conférer la c. à qn,** to confer a knighthood on s.o. **2.** (*a*) chivalry; *Lit:* **roman de c.,** romance of chivalry; **c. errante,** knight-errantry; **fleur de (la) c.,** flower of chivalry; (*b*) chivalrousness. **3.** *A:* body of mounted knights; cavalry (of nobles).

chevalet [ʃəvalɛ, ʃfalɛ], *s.m.* **1.** *A:* **c. (de torture),** (i) *Mil: etc:* wooden horse (for punishment); (ii) rack. **2.** rest, stand, support; (*a*) *Dom.Ec:* **c. à linge,** clothes-horse; **c. porte-serviettes,** towel-horse; **c. porte-couteau,** knife-rest; (*b*) **c. de peintre,** easel; *Phot:* **c. d'agrandissement,** enlarging easel; (*c*) *Mil:* **c. de pointage,** aiming rest; aiming tripod, rifle rest; **c. de tir,** firing stand, firing trestle, rifle rest; (*d*) *Bill:* rest; *F:* jigger; (*e*) *Mus:* bridge (of violin); **sur le c.,** sul ponticello; (*f*) *Veh:* wheel-jack. **3.** (*a*) *Civ.E: Mil.E:* **pont de chevalets,** trestle-bridge; **étai de c.,** trestle bracing-strut; **semelle de c.,** trestle-shoe; **traverse de c.,** (trestle-) transom; **travée de c.,** trestle-span; (*b*) *Mec.E:* pedestal (of bearing); **palier à c. isolé,** outboard-bearing; **c. de levage,** gantry; (*c*) *Min:* **c. d'extraction,** head-frame; (*d*) *Carp:* **c. de scieur,** saw-bench, -horse; jack; (*e*) *Leath:* (currier's) beam, tree.

cheval-heure [ʃəvalœr, ʃfal-], *s.m. Mec:* metric horse-power-hour; *pl. des chevaux-heures.*

chevalier [ʃəvalje, ʃfal-], *s.m.* **1.** (*a*) knight; **c. banneret,** knight-banneret; **c. bachelier,** knight bachelor; **c. errant,** knight-errant; *Span.Lit:* **le C. de la Triste-Figure,** the Knight of the Sorrowful Countenance; *Mus:* **le C. à la rose,** the Rosenkavalier; **créer qn c.,** to knight s.o.; **armer qn c.,** to dub s.o. knight; *F:* **se faire le c. de qn,** to champion s.o.'s cause; *F:* **c. de fortune,** soldier of fortune; **c. d'industrie,** man who lives by his wits, adventurer, sharper, swindler, crook; *A: Hum:* **c. de . . .,** knight of . . .; **c. servant,** faithful admirer; (*b*) Chevalier (of the Legion of Honour, etc.); (*c*) rider; *B.Lit:* **Les Quatre chevaliers de l'Apocalypse,** the Four Horsemen of the Apocalypse; *A:* **c. du guet,** (mounted) captain of the watch. **2.** *Ich:* horseman; *s.a.* OMBRE[3]. **3.** *Orn:* sandpiper; **c. à pieds courts,** grey-rumped sandpiper, *U.S:* wandering tattler; **c. stagnatile,** marsh sandpiper; **c. solitaire,** solitary sandpiper; **grand c. à pattes jaunes,** greater yellowlegs; **petit c. à pattes jaunes,** lesser yellowlegs; **c. à pattes vertes, c. aboyeur,** greenshank; **c. combattant,** ruff; **c. combattant femelle,** reeve; **c. guignette,** common sandpiper; **c. grivelé,** spotted sandpiper; **c. sylvain,** wood-sandpiper; **c. gambette,** redshank; **c. arlequin, brun,** spotted redshank; **c. cul-blanc,** green sandpiper.

chevalière [ʃəvaljɛːr, ʃfal-], *s.f.* **1.** knight's lady. **2. (bague à la) c.,** signet-ring; seal-ring.

chevalin, -ine [ʃəvalɛ̃, ʃfalɛ̃, -in], *a.* equine; **boucherie chevaline,** (i) horsemeat, horseflesh; (ii) horse-butcher's shop; **figure chevaline,** horsy face.

chevalis [ʃ(ə)vali], *s.m. Civ.E:* stepping-stones (across a stream).

cheval-jupon [ʃəvalʒypɔ̃], *s.m. Th: etc:* property horse, hobby-horse; *pl. chevaux-jupons.*

cheval-vapeur [ʃəvalvapœːr, ʃfal-], *s.m. Mec:* (French) horsepower (= 32,549 foot-pounds per minute); **machine de vingt chevaux(-vapeur),** twenty horse-power engine; *pl. chevaux-vapeur.*

chevauchable [ʃəvoʃabl̩], *a.* (track) fit for horse traffic; **chemin c.,** bridle-path.

chevauchage [ʃ(ə)voʃaːʒ], *s.m.* **1.** riding (on a horse); **un long c.,** a long ride. **2.** *Typ:* dropping, falling out of alignment (of type).

chevauchant [ʃ(ə)voʃɑ̃], *a.* **1.** overlapping (teeth, slates, etc.). **2.** *Bot:* equitant (leaves).

chevauchée [ʃ(ə)voʃe], *s.f.* **1.** ride; (*a*) *Lit:* **la c. des Valkyries,** the ride of the Valkyries; (*b*) **faire dix lieues d'une c.,** to ride ten leagues at a stretch; (*c*) **c. à la mort,** death ride (of cavalry). **2.** cavalcade.

chevauchement [ʃ(ə)voʃmɑ̃], *s.m.* **1.** (*a*) *A:* riding (on horse, etc.); (*b*) sitting astride; (*c*) *Civ.E: etc:* spanning, straddling; **le c. du canal par la grue portique,** the spanning of the canal by the gantry. **2.** (*a*) overlap(ping) (of tiles, etc.); (*b*) *Mec.E:* overlapping, lap, interlocking; *I.C.E: etc:* **c. des courses motrices,** overlapping, lap, of power-strokes; **c. des explosions,** overlapping of the explosions; **c. des soupapes,** valve-lap; **c. négatif, positif, des soupapes,** minus, plus, valve-lap; (*c*) crossing (of wires, etc.); (*d*) *Surg:* riding (of fractured bone); (*e*) *Typ:* falling, dropping, out of place (of type); (*f*) *Geol:* (over)thrust (of folds); **pli de c.,** overthrust fold; **faille de c.,** overthrust fault; (*g*) overlapping (of subjects, authority, etc.).

chevaucher [ʃ(ə)voʃe]. **1.** *v.i.* (*a*) to ride (on horse, bicycle, etc.); **c. long, court,** to ride with a long, short, stirrup; **les sorcières chevauchent nuitamment,** the witches ride by night; (*b*) **c. sur un mur,** to sit astride a wall; (*c*) to overlap; **dents qui chevauchent,** overlapping teeth; *Carp:* **joint chevauché,** lapped joint; (*d*) (*of wires, etc.*) to cross; (*e*) *Surg:* (*of fractured bones*) to ride; *Geol:* to overthrust; (*f*) *Typ:* (*of type*) to fall, drop, out of place; **lettres qui chevauchent,** squabbled type. **2.** *v.tr.* (*a*) to ride (on), straddle, to be astride (donkey, etc.); (*b*) to span; *Rail:* **portique chevauchant quatre voies,** gantry spanning four sets of rails.

se chevaucher, (*of categories, etc.*) to overlap.

chevaucheur [ʃ(ə)voʃœːr], *s.m. Lit:* horseman, rider; **c. de ressac,** surf-rider.

chevauchure [ʃ(ə)voʃyːr], *s.f.* overlapping (of teeth, etc.).

chevau-léger [ʃ(ə)voleʒe], *s.m. Hist:* light horseman; **les chevau-légers,** the light horse, light cavalry.

chevêche [ʃəvɛʃ], *s.f. Orn:* (little, sparrow-)owl.

chevêchette [ʃəvɛʃɛt], *s.f. Orn:* pygmy owl.

chevelu [ʃəvly], *a.* **1.** long-haired. **2.** (*a*) hairy; **cuir c.,** scalp; *Hist:* **les rois chevelus,** the Merovingian kings; *Astr:* **comète chevelue,** bearded comet; (*b*) *Bot:* comose, comate (seed); *s.m.* **le c.,** the root-hairs.

chevelure [ʃəvlyːr], *s.f.* **1.** (head of) hair; **belle c.,** fine head of hair; **il est revenu avec cinq chevelures à sa ceinture,** he came back with five scalps hanging from his belt; *Astr:* **C. de Bérénice,** Coma Berenices. **2.** (*a*) *Astr:* tail (of comet); (*b*) *Bot:* coma (of seed, of pine-apple).

chever [ʃəve], *v.tr. Tchn:* to groove out (a piece of metal, etc.).

chevesne, chevenne [ʃ(ə)vɛn], *s.m. Ich:* chub.

chevet [ʃ(ə)vɛ], *s.m.* **1.** (*a*) bed-head; **livre, lampe, table, de c.,** bedside book, lamp, table; **veiller toute la nuit au c. de qn,** to watch all night by s.o.'s bedside; (*b*) bolster; *F:* **c'est son épée de c.,** he always falls back on that; *A:* **vous avez trouvé cela sous votre c.,** you must have dreamt it; *s.a.* CONSULTER 1. **2.** *Arch:* apse (of church). **3.** *Min:* ledger(-wall) (of lode).

chevêtre [ʃ(ə)vɛtr̩], *s.m.* **1.** *Surg:* bandage (for the jaw). **2.** *Const:* trimmer joist (of floor).

chevêtrier [ʃəvɛtri(j)e], *s.m. Const:* trimming-joist.

cheveu, -eux [ʃ(ə)vø], *s.m.* **1.** (*a*) (a single) hair; *F:* **il s'en faut de l'épaisseur d'un c.,** it is only a hair's-breadth short; **être à un c. de la ruine,** to be within a hair's-breadth of disaster; **à un c. près,** by a narrow margin; **fendre, couper, un c., les cheveux, en quatre,** to split hairs; **comme un c., des cheveux, sur la soupe,** out of place, very inappropriately; **arriver comme un c. sur la soupe,** to arrive at an awkward moment; **voilà le c.!** there's the rub; *F:* that's the snag; **il y a un c.,** there is a fly in the ointment; (*b*) *Cer:* crack. **2. les cheveux,** the hair; (*of woman*) **en cheveux,** without a hat (on), hatless; **s'arracher les cheveux,** to tear one's hair; *F:* **elles se sont prises aux cheveux,** they had a regular tussle, a set-to; **argument tiré par les cheveux,** far-fetched argument; **se faire des cheveux (blancs),** to worry oneself grey; *P:* **avoir mal aux cheveux;** (i) to have a bad head; (ii) to have a hang-over; **cheveux d'ange,** (i) tinsel (Christmas decoration); (ii) type of vermicelli; (iii) finely shredded crystallized orange peel; (*occ. in sg.*) **il a le c. gris,** his hair is grey; *P: s.a.* BARBE[1] 1, SE DRESSER, OCCASION 1. **3.** *Bot:* **cheveux du diable,** dodder; *s.a.* VÉNUS.

chevillage [ʃ(ə)vijaːʒ], *s.m. Const: etc:* **1.** pegging, fastening, bolting. **2.** plugging.

chevillard [ʃ(ə)vijaːr], *s.m.* wholesale butcher.

cheville [ʃ(ə)viːj], *s.f.* **1.** peg, pin; (i) *Nau:* trenail; (ii) pintle (of hinge); **c. en bois,** peg, dowel(-pin); **c. de violon,** peg of a violin; **c. en fer,** bolt; **c. barbelée,** rag-bolt; **c. d'assemblage,** shackle-bolt; **c. à œillet,** eye-bolt; **c. d'arrêt,** stop-bolt, -pin (of axle); **c. ouvrière,** (i) king-bolt, -pin (of vehicle); (ii) (any sort of) main bolt; (iii) *F:* mainspring, king-pin (of enterprise, etc.); *Rail:* **c. d'attelage,** coupling-pin; *Veh:* **cheval attelé en c.,** middle horse (between shaft-horse and leader of tandem team); *Com:* **vente à la c.,** wholesale butchery trade; *P:* **être en c. avec qn,** to be in cahoots with s.o.; to play ball with s.o. **2.** (*a*) peg, plug (for filling up hole); *El:* **interrupteur en c.,** plug switch; *Mch:* **c. fusible,** fusible plug; (*b*) *Lit:* expletive (word), padding (in line of verse); make-rhyme. **3.** *Anat:* ankle; **robe à la c.,** ankle-length dress; *F:* **il ne vous arrive, vient, monte, pas à la c.,** he can't hold a candle to you; *F:* **se donner des coups de pied dans les chevilles,** to blow one's own trumpet.

cheviller [ʃ(ə)vije], *v.tr.* **1.** to pin, bolt, peg, (sth.) together; **avoir l'âme chevillée au, dans le, corps,** to be hard to kill; **cheval chevillé, aux épaules chevillées,** shoulder-pegged horse. **2.** to peg, plug (up); *Lit:* **c. (un vers),** to pad, tag, a line of verse.

chevillette [ʃ(ə)vijɛt], *s.f.* **1.** small peg, pin. **2.** iron pin, spike. **3.** latch (of door).

chevilleur [ʃ(ə)vijœːr], *s.m.* wholesale butcher.

chevillier [ʃ(ə)vilje], *s.m. Mus:* peg-box (of violin, etc.).

chevillière [ʃ(ə)viljɛːr], *s.f.* ankle support.

chevillon [ʃ(ə)vijɔ̃], *s.m.* turned rod (of back of chair).

chevillot [ʃ(ə)vijo], *s.m. Nau:* (*a*) belaying pin; (*b*) toggle.

chevillure [ʃəvijyːr], *s.f.* tray(-antler) (of stag).

Cheviot [ʃəvjo, -vjɔt]. **1.** *Pr.n.m. Geog:* les **(monts) Cheviot**(s), the Cheviot Hills. **2.** *s.m.* (*a*) *Husb:* Cheviot sheep; (*b*) Cheviot wool. **3.** *a. Husb:* **mouton c.,** Cheviot sheep.

chevio(t)te [ʃəvjɔt], *s.f. Tex:* Cheviot (cloth); **c. écossaise,** tweed.

chevir [ʃəviːr], *v.i. A:* to be master of a situation.

chèvre [ʃɛːvr], *s.f.* **1.** (*a*) goat, *esp.* she-goat, nanny-goat; **c. égagre,** wild goat; **barbe de c.,** goatee; *F:* **ménager la c. et le chou,** (i) to sit on the fence; (ii) to run with the hare and hunt with the hounds; **il serait amoureux d'une c. coiffée,** he runs after every petticoat, *P:* bit of skirt, he sees; *A: F:* **prendre la c.,** to lose one's temper; (*b*) *Astr:* **la C.,** Capella. **2.** (*a*) *Mec.E: Const: etc:* gin, crab, derrick; **c. à haubans,** sheer legs; **c. à trois pieds,** tripod sheers; (*b*) *Veh:* jack; (*c*) saw-horse, trestle, jack.

chevreau, -eaux [ʃəvro], *s.m.* kid, young goat; **gants de c.,** kid gloves.

chèvrefeuille [ʃɛvrəfœːj], *s.m. Bot:* honeysuckle, woodbine; **c. des buissons,** fly honeysuckle.

chèvre-pied(s) [ʃɛvrəpje]. **1.** *a.* goat-footed (faun, etc.). **2.** *s.m.* goat-footed being; faun; satyr; *pl. chèvre-pieds.*

chèvrerie [ʃɛvrəri], *s.f.* goat fold.

chevreter [ʃəvrəte], **chevretter** [ʃəvrete], *v.i.* = CHEVROTER 1.

chevrette [ʃəvrɛt], *s.f.* **1.** (*a*) kid, young (she-) goat; (*b*) (female) roe-deer. **2.** (*a*) tripod, trivet; (*b*) carriage-jack; (*c*) fire-dog, andiron. **3.** *Crust: F:* shrimp or prawn. **4.** *A: Mus:* musette.

chevreuil [ʃəvrœːj], *s.m.* (*a*) roe-deer (*male*) roe-buck; **c. à queue blanche,** Virginian white-tailed deer; **peau de c.,** buckskin, deerskin; (*b*) venison; **quartier de c.,** haunch of venison.

chevrier, -ère [ʃəvrie, -ɛːr], *s.* **1.** goatherd; *f.* goat-girl. **2.** *s.m.* (small green) kidney bean.

chevrillard [ʃəvrijaːr], *s.m. Ven:* roe-buck, chamois-buck, in its first year.

chevron [ʃəvrɔ̃], *s.m.* **1.** *Const:* (*a*) (common) rafter (of roof); **c. d'arête,** hip-rafter; **c. de croupe,** jack-rafter; (*b*) **bois à chevrons, c.,** squared timber (*esp.* 8 cm. × 8 cm.), = quartering. **2.** (*a*) *Her:* chevron; **c. couché,** chevron couched; *Tex:* **en c.,** in herring-bone pattern; **un tissu à chevrons,** a herring-bone patterned material; *Mec.E:* **engrenage à chevrons,** double helical gear(ing); (*b*) *Mil: etc:* chevron, (service) stripe; **c. de campagne(s),** war (service) stripe.

chevronnage [ʃəvrɔnaːʒ], *s.m. Const:* **1.** raftering. **2.** rafters (of roof).

chevronné [ʃəvrɔne], *a.* **1.** *Her:* chevronny. **2.** (i) *Mil:* wearing chevrons, (service) stripes; (ii) *F:* senior, experienced. **3.** *Mec.E:* **dents chevronnées,** herring-bone teeth (of wheel).

chevronner [ʃəvrɔne], *v.tr. Const:* to rafter (roof).

chevrotain [ʃəvrɔtɛ̃], *s.m. Z:* chevrotain, mouse deer, musk deer; **c. aquatique,** water chevrotain; (*occ.*) **c. porte-musc,** musk-deer; **c. tacheté (de l'Inde),** (Indian) spotted chevrotain.

chevrotant [ʃəvrɔtɑ̃], *a.* quavering, tremulous (voice); **protester d'une voix chevrotante,** to bleat out protestations.

chevrotement [ʃəvrɔtmɑ̃], *s.m.* quaver(ing), tremulousness (of voice).

chevroter [ʃəvrɔte], *v.i.* **1.** (*of goat*) to kid. **2.** (*a*) (*of goat, old man, etc.*) to bleat; (*b*) *v.tr. & i.* to sing, speak, say (sth.) in a quavering voice, to quaver.

chevrotin [ʃəvrɔtɛ̃], *s.m.* **1.** = CHEVROTAIN. **2.** fawn (of roe-deer). **3.** kid (leather). **4.** kind of goat's-milk cheese.

chevrotine [ʃəvrɔtin], *s.f.* (*a*) (pellet of) buck-shot; (*b*) *pl.* buck-shot.

chewing-gum [ʃwiŋgɔm], *s.m.* chewing-gum.

chez [ʃe], *prep.* **1.** (*a*) **c. qn,** at s.o.'s house, home, *F:* place; **il est rentré c. lui,** he has gone home; **je l'ai reconduit c. lui,** I took him home; **en rentrant, en revenant, c. lui,** on his way home; **je vais c. moi,** I am going home; **venez c. nous,** come home with us, come to our place; **venez tous déjeuner c. nous,** you can all come and (have) lunch at our place; **il demeure c. nous,** he lives with us; **comment ça va c. vous?** how is everybody at home? how are they all at home? how is the family? how are things at home? **recevoir qn c. soi,** (i) to give s.o. a home; (ii) to put s.o. up; **c. mon grand-père,** at my grandfather's; **ramener un enfant c. ses parents,** to take a child home; **acheter qch. c. l'épicier,** to buy sth. at the grocer's; **c. tous les épiciers,** stocked by all grocers; **c. tous les libraires,** of all booksellers; obtainable at all booksellers', at all bookshops; **la nouvelle collection de c. Dior,** the new collection from Dior; **200 francs c. Marie-Lou,** 200 francs from "Marie-Lou"; **"Chez Paul,"** "Paul's" (restaurant, café, etc.); (*on letters*) **chez . . .,** care of . . ., c/o . . .; **faire comme c. soi,** to make oneself at home; **faites comme c. vous,** make yourself at home; **il est, se sent, partout c. lui,** he is at home anywhere, he makes himself at home everywhere; **on y est comme c. soi,** it's a home from home, it's just like home; **elle est femme de chambre c. la comtesse,** she is lady's maid to, in the service of, the countess; **porter la guerre c. l'ennemi,** to carry the war into the enemy's country; **il est exilé, et il veut rentrer c. lui,** he is in exile, and he wants to return home; (*of Frenchman*) **c. nous,** at home, in my, our, country, in France; (*b*) **son chez-soi,** one's home, one's house; **c'est un second chez-soi,** it's a home from home; **j'aime mon chez-moi,** I love my home; **dans l'intimité du chez-soi,** in the privacy of the home; **il n'y a pas de petit chez-soi, rien ne vaut un chez-soi,** (be it ever so humble) there's no place like home; **avoir un chez-soi,** to have a home of one's own; **vous avez un chez-vous,** you have a home (of your own); **je pars pour c. ma sœur,** I am off to my sister's (house); *F:* **devant c. la modiste,** in front of the milliner's; **derrière c. moi,** behind my house; **il habite près de c. son ami,** he lives near his friend; **les quelques maisons voisines de c. lui,** the few houses near his home; **je viens de c. moi,** I've come from my place, I've come straight from home; *F:* **(par) c. moi,** in my part of the world; **ils sont passés par c. nous,** (i) they passed through our town, street, etc., they passed through where we live; (ii) they dropped in to see us on their way; **ils ne sont pas de c. nous,** they're not from our part of the world, they're strangers. **2.** with; **c'est devenu une habitude c. moi,** it has become a habit with me; **ce que j'admire c. cet homme c'est . . .,** what I admire about that man is . . .; **c. les Français,** in France; among Frenchmen; **il en est ainsi c. les Français,** it is like that with, in the case of, Frenchmen; **c. les Grecs,** in Ancient Greece; **nous ne sommes pas c. des, les, sauvages,** we are not among savages; **cette expression est courante c. les jeunes,** this expression is current among young people; **je présume c. le locataire une intention de fraude,** I presume an intention of fraud on the part of the tenant; **c. Molière on trouve . . .,** in (the works of) Molière one finds . . .; **il y a c. le cheval un je ne sais quoi qui . . .,** there's something about a horse that . . .; **c. les animaux,** in the animal kingdom.

chez-soi [ʃeswa], *s.m.inv. s.a.* CHEZ 1 (*b*).

chiader [ʃjade], *P:* **1.** *v.i.* (*a*) to swot; (*b*) **j'ai chiadé en latin,** I made a good job of the Latin paper, I did well in Latin. **2.** *v.tr.* **j'ai chiadé mon thème,** I made a good job of my prose.

chialer [ʃjale], *v.i. F:* to snivel, blub(ber); **se mettre à c.,** to turn on the waterworks.

chialeur, -euse [ʃjalœːr, -øːz], *s. F:* cry-baby.

chiant [ʃjɑ̃], *a. V:* annoying, irritating.

chianti [kjɑ̃ti], *s.m.* Chianti (wine).

chiard [ʃjaːr], *s.m. P:* brat.

chiasma [kjasma], **chiasme** [kjasm], *s.m.* **1.** *Anat:* chiasm(a), optic commissure. **2.** *Rh:* **chiasme,** chiasmus.

chiasmatique [kjasmatik], *a. Med:* chiasmatic.

chiasse [ʃjas], *s.f.* **1.** insect dirt; **c. de mouche,** fly-specks; *P:* **avoir la c.,** (i) to have the colic; (ii) to have diarrhœa; *P:* the squitters; (iii) *F:* to have the wind up. **2.** (*a*) rubbish, muck; (*b*) dross, scum (of molten metal).

chiasser [ʃjase], *v.i. V:* to have the wind up.

chiasseur, -euse [ʃjasœːr, -øːz], *s. V:* funk.

chiastolite [kjastɔlit], *s.f. Miner:* chiastolite, macle.

Chibcha [ʃibʃa], *Ethn:* (*a*) *s.* Chibcha; (*b*) *a.* Chibchan.

chibouque [ʃibuk], *s.f.*, **chibouk** [ʃibuk], *s.m.* chibouque, chibouk, Turkish pipe.

chic [ʃik]. **1.** *s.m.* (*a*) skill, knack; **il a le c. pour (faire) cela,** he has the knack of doing it; **c'est un c. à lui,** it's a trick of his; (*b*) smartness, stylishness; **il a du c.,** he has style; **femme, chapeau, qui a du c.,** smart, stylish, woman, hat; **porter un monocle pour faire c.,** to wear a monocle for effect, *F:* for swank; **c'est le grand c. à l'heure actuelle,** it's all the rage at the moment; (*c*) *Art:* **peindre, dessiner, de c.,** to paint, draw, without a model; **écrire un article de c.,** to dash off an article; (*d*) *Sch: F:* cheer. **2.** *a. inv. in f., var. in pl.;* (*a*) smart, stylish, chic; **dîner c.,** fashionable, *F:* posh, dinner; **les gens chics,** the smart set; (*b*) nice, pleasant; **on a passé une c. soirée,** we had a really nice evening; (*c*) **c'est un c. type,** he's a good sort, *U.S:* a swell guy; **(voyons) sois c.!** (come on), be an angel! be a sport! **c'est c. de ta part,** that's very sporting of you, very nice of you; **elle a été très c. dans cette affaire,** she was a perfect angel over this business. **3.** *int. F:* **c. (alors)!** fine!

chicanage [ʃikanaːʒ], *s.m. Tchn:* (set of) baffles; *Mil:* system of zigzag trenches.

chicane [ʃikan], *s.f.* **1.** (*a*) chicanery, pettifoggery; **un suppôt de c.,** a pettifogger; (*b*) quibbling, wrangling; **chercher c. à qn,** to cavil at sth. (s.o. has said, done, etc.), to try to pick a quarrel with s.o.; (*c*) (*at bridge*) chicane. **2.** *A:* pettifoggers, pettifogging lawyers. **3.** obstacle (to progress, to flow of water, etc.); (*a*) *Mec.E:* baffle, baffle-plate, deflector; **c. transversale,** cross baffle; **joints en c.,** staggered joints; (*b*) *Mil:* zigzag trench; (*c*) *Sp:* obstacle, chicane; *Mil:* tank trap.

chicaneau, -eaux [ʃikano], *s.m. F:* = CHICANEUR.

chicaner [ʃikane]. **1.** *v.i.* to chicane, pettifog; **c. sur les frais,** to haggle, quibble, over the expense, to cavil at, about, the expense. **2.** *v.tr.* **c. qn,** to wrangle with s.o. (**sur,** about); to find fault with s.o.; **c. qch.,** to dispute sth.; to haggle over, cavil at, sth.; *Mil:* **c. le terrain à l'ennemi,** to dispute every inch of the ground with the enemy; *Nau:* **c. le vent,** *abs.* **c.,** to hug the wind, to pinch.

se chicaner, to squabble (**avec,** with).

chicanerie [ʃikanri], *s.f.* chicanery, quibbling; captiousness.

chicaneur, -euse [ʃikanœːr, -øːz]. **1.** *s.* (*a*) person fond of lawsuits, barrator; (*b*) quibbler, haggler, caviller. **2.** *a.* = CHICANIER 1.

chicanier, -ière [ʃikanje, -jɛːr]. **1.** *a.* (*a*) fond of lawsuits; (*b*) quibbling, haggling, captious, cavilling. **2.** *s.* = CHICANEUR 1.

chicard [ʃikaːr]. **1.** *a. P:* = CHIC 2 (*a*). **2.** *s.m. A:* fantastically got up reveller and dancer at carnival.

chiche[1] [ʃiʃ], *a.* **1.** (*a*) (*of thg*) scanty, poor; (*b*) (*of pers.*) stingy, niggardly, parsimonious; *F:* **être c. de louanges**, to be chary, sparing, of praise; to be sparing in one's praise; **c. de (ses) paroles**, taciturn; *s.a.* DÉPENSER 1. **2.** *F:* **c. (que tu ne le feras pas)!** I bet you don't! **c. (que je le fais)!** bet you I will! *F:* **c.!** (i) try it! I dare you! (ii) rats!

chiche[2], *s.m. Bot:* **(pois) c.**, chick-pea, gram.

chiche-kebab [ʃiʃkebab], *s.m. Cu:* (shish) kebab; *pl. chiche-kebabs.*

chichement [ʃiʃmɑ̃], *adv.* stingily, meanly; **rue c. éclairée**, scantily lighted street.

chichi [ʃiʃi], *s.m. F:* **1.** (*a*) *O:* piece of false hair (in short curls); (*b*) frill, ruffle (of gauze, etc.). **2.** *pl. F:* affected manners; **gens à chichis**, overpolite, gushing, people; **un type à chichis**, a poseur, a prig; **faire des chichis**, (i) to put on airs; (ii) to make a fuss, a bother; (iii) to put difficulties in the way; **il y a toutes sortes de chichis**, there are all sorts of little snags.

chichiteux, -euse [ʃiʃitø, -øːz], *F:* **1.** *a.* prissy. **2.** *s.* fuss-pot.

chiclé [ʃikle], *s.m.* chicle gum.

chicon [ʃikɔ̃], *s.m. Hort: F:* (*a*) cos lettuce; (*b*) chicory.

chicoracées [ʃikɔrase], *s.f.pl. Bot:* cichoraceae, liguliflorae.

chicorée [ʃikɔre], *s.f.* **1.** *Hort:* **c. sauvage**, chicory, succory; **c. frisée**, endive. **2. (poudre de) c.**, (ground) chicory; **café à la c.**, coffee with chicory.

chicot [ʃiko], *s.m.* **1.** stump (of tree, *F:* of tooth); nog (on tree); **c. de pain**, hunch, hunk, of bread. **2.** *Bot:* bonduc (tree).

chicote [tʃikɔte], *s.f.* chicote.

chicoter [ʃikɔte], *v.i. F:* to wrangle, haggle, over trifles, to split hairs.

chicotin [ʃikɔtɛ̃], *s.m. Pharm: O:* sap of aloes; *s.a.* AMER[1] 1.

chiée [ʃje], *s.f. V:* lashings (**de**, of).

chie-en-lit [ʃiɑ̃li], *s.m. & f. inv. F:* **1.** person who soils his bed. **2.** (*a*) masker, carnival mask; masquerade; (*b*) (i) scarecrow, freak; **à la c.-en-l.!** what a scarecrow! (ii) rabble.

chien, *f.* **chienne** [ʃjɛ̃, ʃjɛn], *s.* **1.** (*a*) dog; *f.* bitch (*when sex is insisted upon*); **jeune c.**, pup, puppy; **c. de berger**, sheep-dog; **c. d'attache**, guard-dog, watch-dog; **c. de garde**, guard-dog, watch-dog; house-dog; **tenir qn comme un c. d'attache**, to keep s.o. under one's thumb; *F:* **être comme un c. à l'attache**, to be tied hand and foot; **c. de bonne garde, de bon guet**, good watch-dog; **c. de chasse (à tir)**, gun-dog; *Ven:* **c. de meute, c. courant**, hound; **c. d'arrêt**, gun-dog; pointer; setter; **c. couchant**, (i) setter; (ii) *F:* bootlicker; *F:* **faire le c. couchant auprès de qn**, to cringe to, fawn on, s.o.; **c. de salon, c. d'appartement, c. de manchon, de luxe**, lap-dog; **c. policier**, police-dog, tracker dog; *Mil:* **c. sanitaire**, ambulance dog; *P.N:* **"c. méchant,"** "Beware of the dog"; **qui m'aime, aime mon c.**, love me love my dog; **c'est saint Roch et son c.**, they're inseparable; *Swim:* **nager à la c., faire le petit c.**, to dog-paddle; **faire le c. après qn**, to follow s.o. like a dog; *F: Journ:* **faire la chronique des chiens écrasés, faire les chiens écrasés**, to write "fillers"; **ils s'entendent, vivent, comme c. et chat**, they lead a cat-and-dog life; **être las comme un c.**, to be dog-tired; **il est, il fait, comme le c. du jardinier (qui ne mange pas de choux et ne laisse pas les autres en manger)**, he is a dog in the manger; **se regarder en chiens de faïence**, to stare rudely, glare defiantly, at one another, to look at one another like stuck pigs; **un c. regarde bien un évêque**, a cat may look at a king; **il est fait à cela comme un c. à aller à pied**, it has become second nature to him; **rompre les chiens**, (i) *Ven:* to call off the hounds; (ii) to break up a meeting; (iii) to change the subject (of a conversation); *F:* **ce n'est pas fait pour les chiens**, it's there to be used; **agir comme un c. fouetté**, to do sth. ungraciously; **leurs chiens ne chassent plus ensemble**, they are no longer friendly, they no longer hit it off; **garder à qn un c. de sa chienne**, to have a rod in pickle for s.o.; to have it in for s.o., to have a grudge against s.o.; **entre c. et loup**, in the dusk of the evening, in the twilight; *Prov:* **qui veut noyer son c. l'accuse de la rage**, give a dog a bad name (and hang him); **bon c. chasse de race**, like father, like son; **autant vaut être mordu d'un c. que d'une chienne**, it's a toss-up which is the worse (course to follow, etc.); it's six of one and half-a-dozen of the other; **c. mort ne mord pas**, dead men tell no tales; **c. qui aboie ne mord pas**, barking dogs don't, seldom, bite; **mieux vaut un c. vivant qu'un lion mort**, a live dog is better than a dead lion; **il n'est pas bon à jeter aux chiens**, hanging is too good for him; *F:* **avoir un mal de c.**, (i) to be in great pain; (ii) to have a lot of difficulty, a devil of a job, (to do sth.); **métier, travail, de c.**, drudgery; *F:* **vie de c.**, dog's life; **mener une vie de c.**, to lead a dog's life; **elle m'a fait mener une vie de c.**, she led me a dog's life; **quelle chienne de vie!** what a miserable life! what a misery! **il a un caractère de c.**, he is bad-tempered; **il est d'une humeur de c.**, he's in a foul mood, in a vile temper; *F:* **il fait un temps, de c., à ne pas mettre un c. dehors**, it's filthy weather; **quel temps de c.!** what awful, ghastly, beastly, foul, filthy, weather! *F:* **coup de c.**, squall; **mourir comme un c.**, to die (i) forsaken, like a dog; (ii) without the sacraments of the church; **être enterré comme un c.**, to be buried unceremoniously, to be thrown into the grave; **tuer qn comme un c.**, to kill s.o. in cold blood; **nom d'un c.!** heavens! hell! *P:* **cette chienne de musique!** that bloody music! *s.a.* BATTU, QUILLE 1; (*b*) *P:* subordinate, underling, dogsbody; **elle en a fait son c.**, she had him on a string, running after her; **le c. du commissaire**, the police-station clerk; *Mil:* **c. de quartier, de caserne** = ADJUDANT 1 (*a*); *Nau: F:* **c. du bord**, second officer. **2.** *F:* (*a*) **avoir du c.**, (i) to have charm, fascination; (ii) to have pluck, plenty of go; **artiste qui a du c.**, artist full of dash; **elle a du c.**, she is attractive; *F:* she has "it," she's sexy; (*b*) **avoir un c. pour qn**, to be gone on, in love with, s.o.; (*c*) **piquer un, son, c.**, to take a nap; (*d*) **être coiffée à la c., porter des chiens**, to wear a fringe; (*e*) *a.* **être c.**, to be mean, stingy; *P:* **cela n'est pas tant c.**, it isn't that bad. **3.** *Tchn:* (*a*) hammer (of gun); **fusil sans c.**, hammerless gun; **armer, bander, le c.**, to cock a gun; *F:* **se coucher en c. de fusil**, to curl up in one's bed; (*b*) *Mec.E:* **c. (d'arrêt)**, pawl, latch, catch, detent; (*c*) trolley (for carrying mineral); (*d*) *Nau:* towing block. **4.** (*a*) *Z:* **c. de prairie**, prairie dog; **c. forestier sud-américain**, forest wild dog, bush dog; (*b*) *Ich:* **c. de mer**, dog-fish; tope; sea dog; **c. d'eau, de fleuve**, (*African*) tiger-fish, hydrocyon; (*c*) *Astr:* **le Grand, le Petit, C.**, the Greater, Lesser, Dog; **l'étoile du Grand C.**, the Dog-Star.

chien-chien [ʃjɛ̃ʃjɛ̃], *s.m. F:* doggie.

chien-dauphin [ʃjɛ̃dofɛ̃], *s.m. Ich:* porbeagle, mackerel-shark; *pl. chiens-dauphins.*

chiendent [ʃjɛ̃dɑ̃], *s.m. Bot:* **c. (officinal, des boutiques)**, couch-grass, creeping wheat-grass, twitch; **c. pied-de-poule**, dog's-tooth grass; **c. queue-de-renard, hunger-grass, -weed**; *P:* **voilà le c.!** there's the snag, the difficulty, the fly in the ointment! **brosse en, de, c.**, scrubbing-brush.

chienlit [ʃjɑ̃li], *s.m. & f. F:* = CHIE-EN-LIT.

chien-loup [ʃjɛ̃lu], *s.m.* wolf-dog, Alsatian; *pl. chiens-loups.*

chiennaille [ʃjɛnaːj], *s.f. F:* **1.** = CANAILLE 1 (*a*). **2.** pack, group, of dogs.

chiennée [ʃjene], *s.f.* litter (of pups).

chienner [ʃjene], *v.i.* to whelp, pup.

chiennerie [ʃjɛnri], *s.f.* **1.** *A:* pack, group, of dogs. **2.** *Coll:* rabble. **3.** *P:* (*a*) beastliness, nastiness; (*b*) sordidness; (*c*) meanness, tightfistedness. **4.** *P:* (*a*) filthy trick; (*b*) shameless act.

chier [ʃje], *v.i. V:* to shit; **va c.!** get stuffed! get knotted! **tu me fais c.**, you make me sick; you're a pain in the neck; **ça va c.**, that will make a stink!

chierie [ʃiri], *s.f. V:* sth. that gets one down, gets one's goat; **quelle c.!** what a bloody mess!

chiffe [ʃif], *s.f.* (*a*) rag, flimsy stuff; *F:* **se sentir mou comme une c.**, to feel as limp as a rag; **c'est une c. (molle)**, he is spineless; *F:* he's a drip; (*b*) *F:* rag-picking trade.

chiffon [ʃifɔ̃], *s.m.* **1.** (*a*) rag; **chiffons de nettoyage**, cotton waste; **papier de c.**, rag paper; (*b*) piece of lace, of ribbon, etc.; **aimer les chiffons**, to be fond of frills and furbelows; *F:* **causer, parler, chiffons**, to talk dress. **2.** scrap; *Hist:* **le c. de papier**, the scrap of paper; *A: F:* **un c. d'enfant**, a little chit of a child. **3.** *Tex:* chiffon.

chiffonnade [ʃifɔnad], *s.f. Cu:* chiffonade.

chiffonnage [ʃifɔnaːʒ], *s.m.* **1.** rumpling, crushing, crumpling. **2.** (mass of) rumpled, crushed, material. **3.** *O: F:* slight annoyance or mortification; snub.

chiffonne [ʃifɔn], *s.f. Hort:* slender branch of peach tree with flower-buds all along it.

chiffonné [ʃifɔne], *a.* **1.** rumpled, creased (dress, etc.); crumpled (paper, etc.). **2.** (*a*) tired, worried; (*b*) **minois c.**, (i) nice, pleasing, but irregular features; (ii) drawn face.

chiffonnement [ʃifɔn(ə)mɑ̃], *s.m.* = CHIFFONNAGE.

chiffonner [ʃifɔne]. **1.** *v.tr.* (*a*) to rumple, disarrange (dress, etc.); to crumple (piece of paper, etc.); (*b*) to annoy, vex, rile; to worry. **2.** *v.i.* (*a*) to do a bit of dressmaking; (*b*) to pick rags, to rake through dustbins.

chiffonnerie [ʃifɔnri], *s.f. A:* **1.** (*a*) rag-picking; (*b*) *coll.* rag-pickers. **2.** (*a*) (small) worry; (*b*) *pl.* trifles, odds and ends.

chiffonnier, -ière [ʃifɔnje, -jɛːr]. **1.** *s.* (*a*) ragman, rag-and-bone man, rag-picker, dustbin raker; *F:* **se battre comme des chiffonniers**, to fight like ragamuffins; (*b*) *Paperm:* rag-sorter. **2.** *Furn:* (*a*) *s.m.* chiffonier; (*b*) (*rare*) *s.f.* **chiffonnière** (smaller) chiffonier.

chiffrable [ʃifrabl], *a.* calculable.

chiffrage [ʃifraːʒ], *s.m.* **1.** calculating, reckoning, figuring out. **2.** numbering, figuring. **3.** (*a*) *Mus:* figuring (of bass); (*b*) = CHIFFREMENT.

chiffre [ʃifr], *s.m.* **1.** (*a*) figure, number, numeral, digit; **chiffres arabes**, Arabic numerals; **nombre de trois chiffres**, three-figure number; *Ar:* **c. des unités, des dizaines, des centaines**, units, tens, hundreds; *Com:* **marqué en chiffres connus**, marked in plain figures; (*b*) amount, total; **le c. de ma dépense**, the total (amount) of my expenses; *Com:* **c. d'affaires**, turnover; *Typ:* **c. de tirage**, printing number. **2.** (*a*) cipher, code; **écriture en c.**, cipher, writing in cipher; **clef de c.**, cipher key; **officier du c.**, cipher officer; **le (service du) C.**, the coding department, cipher department (in service ministries, etc.); **bureau du c.**, cipher office; **personnel du c.**, cipher, cryptographic, personnel; (*b*) combination (for lock of safe). **3.** (*a*) monogram, mark; (*b*) figure stamp; (*c*) (regimental, etc.) badge; (*d*) *Typ:* colophon.

chiffrement [ʃifrəmɑ̃], *s.m.* coding, ciphering (of message, text, etc.); **carnet de c.**, cipher book; code book; **clé de c.**, cipher key; keying elements; **sécurité du c.**, cipher, cryptographic, security.

chiffrer [ʃifre]. **1.** *v.i.* (*a*) to calculate, reckon; (*b*) *F:* **ça doit c.**, that must add up to a lot. **2.** *v.tr.* (*a*) to number (pages of book, etc.); to page (account book, etc.); (*b*) to figure out, work out (amount, etc.); **à combien cela se chiffre-t-il?** how much does it work out at? **opérations qui se chiffrent par plusieurs millions de livres**, transactions amounting to several million pounds; **leur nombre se chiffre par milliers**, their numbers run into thousands; **détails chiffrés**, figures (of scheme, etc.); (*c*) to cipher; to write (dispatch, etc.) in cipher, in code; to code, encode, encipher (a message); **mot chiffré**, code word; **machine à c.**, converter; **message chiffré**, cipher, code, message; message in code; *U.S:* codress message; **texte chiffré**, coded text; (*d*) to mark (linen, etc.); (*e*) *Mus:* **c. la basse**, to figure the bass; (*f*) *Tp:* to dial (a number).

chiffre-taxe [ʃifrətaks], *s.m. Adm:* postage-due stamp or mark; *pl. chiffres-taxes.*

chiffreur, -euse [ʃifrœːr, -øːz], *s.* **1.** calculator, reckoner. **2.** cipher clerk, cryptographer.

chiffrier [ʃifri(j)e], **chiffrier-balance** [ʃifri(j)e-balɑ̃ːs], *s.m. Com: etc:* day-book, waste-book, counter cash-book.

chignard, -arde [ʃiɲaːr, -ard], *O: F:* **1.** *a.* (*a*) grousing, grumbling; (*b*) snivelling, blubbering. **2.** *s.* (*a*) grouser, grumbler; (*b*) sniveller, cry-baby.

chigner [ʃiɲe], *v.i. O: F:* **1.** to grouse, grumble. **2.** to snivel, blubber.

chignol(l)e [ʃiɲɔl], *s.f.* **1.** *P:* (old) car; **ma vieille c.**, my old bus. **2.** *Tls:* hand-drill; breast-drill; portable electric drill.

chignon [ʃiɲɔ̃], *s.m.* **1.** *A:* nape (of the neck). **2.** coil of hair, knot of hair, chignon, bun; **cheveux tordus en c.**, coiled (up) hair; **se faire un c. à la hâte**, to bundle up one's hair; **défaire son c.**, to let down one's back-hair; **peigne c.**, back-comb. **3.** *Pej:* old frump; *s.a.* CRÊPER (SE).

chiite [ʃiit], *s.m. Rel.H:* Shiah, Shiite.

chilalgie [kilalʒi], *s.f. Med:* ch(e)ilalgia.

Chili [ʃili], *Pr.n.m. Geog:* Chile.

chiliarque [kiljark], *s.m. Gr.Mil:* chiliarch.

chiliasme [kiljasm], *s.m. Rel:* chiliasm.

chiliaste [kiljast], *s.m. & f. Rel:* chiliast.
chilien, -ienne [ʃiljɛ̃, -jɛn], *a. & s. Geog:* Chilean.
chilopode [kilɔpɔd]. *Ent:* 1. *a.* chilopodan, chilopodous. 2. *s.m.pl.* Chilopoda.
chimère [ʃimɛːr], *s.f.* 1. *Gr.Myth:* chimera. 2. chimera, dream; **le pays des chimères,** the land of fancy, of imagination; **chimères que tout cela!** these are all idle dreams; **courir après des chimères,** to chase moonbeams. 3. *Biol:* chimera, chimaera. 4. *Ich:* chimaera.
chimérique [ʃimerik], *a.* 1. visionary, fanciful (person). 2. chimerical (idea, thing).
chimériquement [ʃimerikmɑ̃], *adv.* chimerically.
chimiatrie [ʃimjatri], *s.f. A.Med:* chemiatry, iatrochemistry.
chimico-légal [ʃimikɔlegal], *a.* chemico-legal; *pl. chimico-légaux.*
chimico-physique [ʃimikɔfizik], *a.* chemico-physical; *pl. chimico-physiques.*
chimie [ʃimi], *s.f.* chemistry; **c. appliquée,** applied, practical, chemistry; **c. biologique,** biochemistry; **c. minérale,** inorganic chemistry; **c. organique,** organic chemistry; **c. physique,** physical chemistry; **c. industrielle,** industrial, technical, chemistry; **c. nucléaire,** nuclear chemistry; **c. du fer,** chemistry of iron; **c. radioactive,** radiochemistry; **c. sous radiations,** radiation chemistry.
chimi(o)luminescence [ʃimilyminesɑ̃ːs, ʃimjɔ-], *s.f.* chemiluminescence, chemoluminescence.
chimiosynthèse [ʃimjɔsɛ̃tɛːz], *s.f.* chemosynthesis.
chimiotactisme [ʃimjɔtaktism], *s.m. Biol:* chemotactism.
chimiotaxie [ʃimjɔtaksi], *s.f. Biol:* chemotaxis, chemotaxy.
chimiothérapie [ʃimjɔterapi], *s.f. Med:* chemotherapy.
chimiotropisme [ʃimjɔtrɔpism], *s.m. Bot:* chemotropism.
chimique [ʃimik], *a.* chemical; **composition c.,** chemical constitution; **un produit c.,** a chemical; **génie c.,** chemical engineering; **allumettes chimiques,** phosphorus matches; *F:* **mal c.,** necrosis of the jaw, phosphorus-necrosis; *P:* phossy jaw; *Ph:* **rayons chimiques,** actinic rays.
chimiquement [ʃimikmɑ̃], *adv.* chemically.
chimisme [ʃimism], *s.m. Biol:* chemism.
chimiste [ʃimist], *s.m.* chemist, chemical research worker; **c. analyste, c. expert,** analytical chemist; **ingénieur c.,** chemical engineer.
chimiurgie [ʃimiyrʒi], *s.f.* chemurgy.
chimpanzé [ʃɛ̃pɑ̃ze], *s.m. Z:* chimpanzee; *F:* chimp.
china [kina], *s.m. Bot: Pharm:* china-root.
china-clay [tʃainakle], *s.m.* china-clay; porcelain-clay.
chinage[1] [ʃinaːʒ], *s.m.* 1. *Tex:* yarn clouding; dyeing or printing of the warp to obtain the chiné or shadow effect; mottling. 2. *Engr:* (*a*) tinting (of the paper); (*b*) tint.
chinage[2], *s.m. F:* 1. carping, ill-natured criticism; running down (of s.o.). 2. practical joking, ragging. 3. begging, cadging. 4. palming off (of worthless articles).
chinchilla [ʃɛ̃ʃil(l)a], *s.m.* chinchilla.
Chine[1] [ʃin]. 1. *Pr.n.f.* (*a*) *Geog:* China; (*b*) *Com:* encre de C., Indian ink; **papier de C.,** *s.m.* **chine,** China paper, rice paper. 2. *s.m. or f.* Chinese porcelain.
chine[2], *s.f. P:* 1. cadging; scrounging; **tabac de c.,** cadged tobacco. 2. peddling; **marchand à la c.,** street hawker.
chine[3], *s.f. F:* ragging; leg-pulling.
chiné [ʃine], *s.m.* 1. *Engr:* tint (given to paper). 2. shadow(ed) cretonne, chiné.
chiner[1] [ʃine], *v.tr. Tex:* to cloud, shadow, mottle (fabric).
chiner[2]. 1. (*a*) *v.i. O:* to work hard; (*b*) *v.tr. Dial:* **c. un fardeau,** to carry a heavy load. 2. *v.tr.* (*a*) *F:* to run (s.o.) down; to pull (s.o.) to pieces; (*b*) *F:* to make fun of (s.o.); to pull (s.o.'s) leg; (*c*) *P:* to cadge (sth.); (*d*) *P:* **c. une montre,** to palm off a (worthless) watch on s.o.
chinetoque [ʃintɔk], *s.m.* 1. *F: Pej:* Chinaman, *F:* Chink. 2. *P:* bungler.
chineur[1], **-euse** [ʃinœːr, -øːz], *s. Tex:* (*a*) yarn cloud printer; (*b*) shadow-cloth weaver.
chineur[2], **-euse,** *s.* 1. *F:* ill-natured critic, scandal-monger. 2. *F:* practical joker, ragger. 3. *P:* cadger (of tobacco, etc.). 4. second-hand dealer.
chinois, -oise [ʃinwa, -waːz]. 1. *a.* (*a*) Chinese; (*b*) *F:* involved, complicated, over-elaborate; tortuous; **quand il se met à être c.,** when he starts being difficult. 2. *s.* (*a*) Chinaman, Chinese woman; *pl.* Chinese; (*b*) *Mil: P: A:* civilian; (*c*) *s.m. Ling:* Chinese (language); *F:* **c'est du (vrai) c.,** it's all Greek to me. 3. *s.m.* (*a*) small green orange preserved in brandy; (*b*) *F:* stranger, stray, tea-leaf (that has got through the strainer); (*c*) *Cu:* conical strainer; (*d*) *F:* guy, bloke.
chinoiser [ʃinwaze]. 1. *v.tr.* to make (sth.) Chinese-looking, to give a Chinese look to (sth.); 2. *v.i. F:* to be difficult; to split hairs.
chinoiserie [ʃinwazri], *s.f.* 1. (*a*) chinoiserie, Chinese curio; (*b*) chinoiserie, cult of Chinese curios. 2. *F:* (*a*) unnecessary complication; **chinoiseries administratives,** red tape; (*b*) **faire une c. à qn,** to play a dirty trick on s.o.; **chercher des chinoiseries à qn,** to make pernickety difficulties for s.o.
chinonais, -aise [ʃinɔnɛ, -ɛːz], *a. & s. Geog:* (native, inhabitant) of Chinon.
chinone [kinɔn], *s.f. Ch:* quinone.
chinook [ʃinuk], *s.m. Meteor:* chinook.
chintz [ʃints], *s.m. Tex: Furn:* chintz.
chinure [ʃinyːr], *s.f. Tex:* mottled effect, shadowing.
chio[1] [kio], *s.m. Metall: etc:* tap-hole; **c. de décrassage,** scumming-hole.
Chio[2] [kio], *Pr.n.m.* **(l'île de) C.,** (the island of) Khios, Chios.
chiolite [kjɔlit], *s.f. Miner:* chiolite.
chione [kjon], *s.f. Moll:* chione.
chionis [kjonis], *s.m. Orn:* sheathbill.
chionidés [kjonide], *s.m.pl. Orn:* Chionidae, the sheathbills.
chionophile [kjonɔfil], *a. Bot:* (plant) that can live in the snow.
chiot [ʃjo], *s.m.* pup(py) (*esp.* young hound).
chiote [kjɔt], *a. & s. Geog:* Sciot, of Chios.
chiottes [ʃjɔt], *s.f.pl. P:* latrines, *P:* bog, *U.S:* john; *int.* **aux c.!** (i) go to blazes! (ii) chuck it away!
chiourme [ʃjurm], *s.f.* 1. *A:* galley-slaves. 2. gang of convicts.
chip [tʃip], *s.m.* (potato) crisp.
chipage[1] [ʃipaːʒ], *s.m. Leath:* puring, bating (of skins).
chipage[2], *s.m. F:* scrounging.
chipeau, -eaux [ʃipo], *s.m. Orn:* **(canard) c.,** gadwall.
chiper[1] [ʃipe], *v.tr. Leath:* to pure, bate (skins).
chiper[2], *v.tr. F:* 1. to pinch, swipe, sneak, scrounge (**qch. à qn,** sth. from s.o.); to help oneself to (sth.); *Ten:* **c. une balle,** to poach a ball; **c. un rhume,** to catch a cold. 2. **être chipé pour qn,** to be in love with, *P:* nuts on, s.o.
chipette [ʃipɛt], *s.f. P:* **ne pas valoir c.,** not to be worth tuppence.
chipeur, -euse [ʃipœːr, -øːz], *F:* 1. *s.* petty thief, filcher, scrounger. 2. *a.* thieving, scrounging.
chipie [ʃipi], (*a*) *s.f. F:* ill-natured woman; **vieille c.,** old cat; (*b*) *a.f.* catty (woman, etc.).
chipiron [ʃipirɔ̃], *s.m. Dial:* cuttle-fish.
chipmunk [ʃipmœnk], *s.m. Z:* chipmunk.
chipolain, chipolin, chipollin [ʃipɔlɛ̃], *s.m. O:* distemper.
chipolata [ʃipɔlata], *s.f.* 1. *O:* onion stew. 2. small sausage, chipolata.
chipotage [ʃipɔtaːʒ], *s.m.* 1. wasting time; fiddling about; dawdling. 2. haggling, quibbling.
chipoter [ʃipɔte]. 1. *v.i.* (*a*) to nibble, peck, at one's food; **c. sur, dans,** to peck at (a dish); (*b*) to waste time, to fiddle-faddle; (*c*) to haggle, quibble (over trifles). 2. *v.tr.* (*a*) **c. des comptes,** to haggle over accounts; (*b*) *F:* **ça me chipote,** it bothers me.
chipoterie [ʃipɔtri], *s.f.* (useless) haggling, quibbling.
chipoteur, -euse [ʃipɔtœːr, -øːz], **chipotier, -ière** [ʃipɔtje, -jɛːr]. 1. *a.* (*a*) pottering, time-wasting, fiddle-faddling; (*b*) haggling, quibbling. 2. *s.* (*a*) potterer, time-waster, fiddle-faddler; (*b*) haggler, quibbler.
chippes [ʃip], *s.f.pl. P:* scraps, shreds (of cloth, etc.).
chips [ʃip(s)], *s.m.pl. Cu:* potato crisps; **pommes c.,** potato crisps.
chique[1] [ʃik], *s.f.* (*a*) quid (of tobacco); *P:* **il est mou comme une c.,** he's a drip; **couper la c. à qn,** to interrupt s.o. abruptly, to cut s.o. short; **poser, avaler, sa c.,** (i) to keep quiet; *F:* to keep mum; *F:* to shut up; (ii) to die; *F:* to turn up one's toes, *U.S:* to hand in one's checks; **avoir une c.,** to be drunk, *F:* tight; **ça ne vaut pas une c.,** it's not worth a brass farthing; *P:* **c'est clair comme du jus de c.,** *F:* it's clear as mud; (*b*) (*in Belgium*) sweetmeat.
chique[2], *s.f. Ent:* chigoe, jigger.
chiqué, *s.m. F:* sham, pretence, affectation; **c'est du c.,** it's make-believe, it's all a put-up job, a fake; that's all eye-wash; **faire du c., la faire au c.,** to sham, to put on an act; to swank; **faiseur de c.,** swank.
chiquement [ʃikmɑ̃], *adv. F:* 1. smartly, stylishly. 2. splendidly.
chiquenaude [ʃiknoːd], *s.f.* (*a*) flick (of the finger); (*b*) gentle push.
chiquenauder [ʃiknode], *v.tr.* to flick, flip (with the finger).
chiquer[1] [ʃike], (*a*) *v.i.* to chew tobacco; (*b*) *v.tr. P:* to eat, guzzle, gorge.
chiquer[2], *v.tr.* 1. *A: Art: F:* to draw, paint, from memory, without a model. 2. *P:* to make-believe, pretend, sham.
chiquet [ʃikɛ], *s.m.* 1. *A: P:* scrap, morsel, bit (of solids); drop (of liquid). 2. *Nau:* small gore (of sail).
chiquetage [ʃiktaːʒ], *s.m.* 1. shredding, tearing into shreds. 2. pinking out (of pastry, pottery, etc.).
chiqueter [ʃikte], *v.tr.* **(je chiquette, n. chiquetons; je chiquetterai)** 1. to tear (sth.) into shreds, to shred; to card (wool). 2. to pink out (pastry, pottery, etc.).
chiquette [ʃikɛːt], *s.f.* tiny scrap.
chiqueur[1], **-euse** [ʃikœːr, -øːz], *s.* (*a*) tobacco-chewer; (*b*) *P:* guzzler, greedy-guts.
chiqueur[2], **-euse,** *s. A:* 1. *F:* artist who works from memory, without a model. 2. *P:* shammer, pretender.
chiragre [kiragr], *s. Med:* 1. *s.f.* chiragra. 2. *s.m. & f.* person suffering from chiragra, chiragric person.
chiralgie [kiralʒi], *s.f. Med:* cheiralgia.
Chiraz [ʃiraːz], *Pr.n.m. Geog:* Shiraz.
chiro- [kirɔ], *pref.* chiro-; **chirognomie,** chirognomy; **chirogymnaste,** chirogymnast.
chirocentre [kirɔsɑ̃ːtr], *s.m. Ich:* Chirocentrus.
chirogale [kirɔgal], *s.m. Z:* mouse-lemur.
chirognomonie [kirɔgnɔmɔni], *s.f.* chirognomy.
chirographaire [kirɔgrafɛːr], *a.* 1. *Jur:* depending on a simple contract; chirographary; **créance, créditeur, c.,** unsecured debt, creditor; simple-contract creditor; **obligation c.,** simple contract. 2. (document) bearing the autograph signature of the monarch.
chirographe [kirɔgraf], *s.m.* chirograph.
chirographie [kirɔgrafi], *s.f.* chirography.
chirologie [kirɔlɔʒi], *s.f.* science of determining character by a person's hand.
chiromancie [kirɔmɑ̃si], *s.f.* chiromancy, palmistry.
chiromancien, -ienne [kirɔmɑ̃sjɛ̃, -jɛn], *s.* palmist.
chiromégalie [kirɔmegali], *s.f. Med:* cheiromegaly.
chiromètre [kirɔmɛtr], *s.m.* instrument used by glovemakers for measuring the hand; *Med:* cheirometer.
Chiron [ʃirɔ̃, kirɔ̃], *Pr.n.m. Gr.Myth:* Ch(e)iron.
chironecte [kirɔnɛkt], *s.m. Z:* water opossum.
chironome [kirɔnɔm], *s.m. Ent:* *often pl.* chironomid; *F:* midge.
chironomidés [kirɔnɔmide], *s.m.pl. Ent:* Chironomidae.
chiropracteur [kirɔpraktœːr], *s.m.* chiropractor.
chiropractie, chiropraxie [kirɔpraksi], *s.f.* chiropractic.
chiropractor [kirɔpraktɔːr], *s.m.* chiropractor.
chiroptères [kirɔptɛːr], *s.m.pl. Z:* Chiroptera, bats.
chirotonie [kirɔtɔni], *s.f. Ecc:* chirotony.
chirurgical, -aux [ʃiryrʒikal, -o], *a.* surgical; *s.a.* INTERVENTION.
chirurgicalement [ʃiryrʒikalmɑ̃], *adv.* surgically.
chirurgie [ʃiryrʒi], *s.f.* (*a*) surgery; **c. plastique, esthétique,** plastic, cosmetic, surgery; **c. du cœur,** heart surgery; **grande, petite, c.,** major, minor, surgery; **c. buccale,** oral surgery; **c. osseuse,** bone surgery; **c. végétale, arboricole,** tree surgery; (*b*) the whole body of surgeons.
chirurgien, -ienne [ʃiryrʒjɛ̃, -jɛn], *s.* 1. surgeon; *A:* chirurgeon; **c. esthétique,** plastic surgeon; **chirurgien dentiste,** dental surgeon. 2. *Ich:* surgeon-fish.
chirurgique [ʃiryrʒik], *a.* surgical; **l'art c.,** the art of surgery.
chistera [tʃistera], *s.f. Games:* chistera (kind of racket used for pelota).
chital [ʃital], *s.m. Z:* **(cerf) chital (de l'Inde),** (Indian) chital, axis deer.
chite [ʃit], *s.f. Tex:* chintz.
chitine [kitin], *s.f. Ch: Z:* chitin.
chitineux, -euse [kitinø, -øːz], *a.* chitinous.
chiton [kitɔ̃], *s.m.* 1. *Gr.Ant:* chiton. 2. *Moll:* chiton, mail shell.
chitonidés [kitɔnide], *s.m.pl. Moll:* Chitonidae.
chiure [ʃjyːr], *s.f.* fly-speck, -mark; **couvert de chiures de mouches,** fly-blown.
chiviatite [kivjatiːt], *s.f. Miner:* chiviatite.
chiyte [ʃiit], *s.m.* = CHIITE.
chladnite [kladniːt], *s.f. Miner:* chladnite.

chlamyde [klamid], *s.f. Gr.Ant:* chlamys.
chlamydé [klamide], *a. Bot:* chlamidate.
chlamydobactériales [klamidɔbakterjal], *s.f.pl. Bac:* Chlamidobacteriales.
chlamydomonade [klamidɔmɔnad], **chlamydomonas** [klamidɔmɔnas], *s.f. Bac:* chlamydomonas.
chlamydomonadidés [klamidɔmɔnadide], *s.m.pl. Bac:* Chlamydomonadaceae.
chlamydosaure [klamidɔsɔ:r], *s.m.* chlamydosaurus, frilled lizard.
chlamydospore [klamidɔspɔ:r], *s.f. Fung:* chlamydospore.
chlamys [klamis], *s.m. Moll:* Chlamys.
chleuh [ʃlø]. **1.** *s.m.* Chleuh (Moroccan tribesman). **2.** *a. & s. P:* German (1939-1945 war).
chloanthite [klɔɑ̃tit], *s.f. Miner:* chloanthite.
chloasma [klɔasma], **chloasme** [klɔasm], *s.m. Med:* chloasma.
Chloé [klɔe], *Pr.n.f. A.Lit:* Chloe.
chlor(o)- [klɔr(ɔ)], *pref.* chlor(o); **chloracétate**, chloracetate; **chlorochromique**, chlorochromic; **chloréthane**, chloroethane.
chloracétique [klɔrasetik], *a. Ch:* chlor(o)acetic.
chlorage [klɔra:ʒ], *s.m. Ind:* chloring, chlorination, (of wool, etc.).
chloral [klɔral], *s.m. Ch:* chloral; *Pharm:* **hydrate de c.,** chloral (hydrate); *pl.* chlorals.
chloralisme [klɔralism], *s.m. Med:* chloralism.
chloramphénicol [klɔrãfenikɔl], *s.m. R.t.m: Pharm:* chloramphenicol.
chlorate [klɔrat], *s.m. Ch:* chlorate; **c. de potasse**, potassium chlorate.
chloration [klɔrasjɔ̃], *s.f. Hyg:* chlorination (of water).
chlore [klɔ:r], *s.m.* **1.** *Ch:* chlorine. **2.** *F:* calcium chloride.
chloré [klɔre], *a.* chlorinated.
chlorelle [klɔrɛl], *s.f. Algae:* chlorella.
chlorémie [klɔremi], *s.f. Med:* chloræmia, chloremia.
chlorer [klɔre], *v.tr. Ind:* to chlore, chlorinate (wool, etc.).
chloreux, -euse [klɔrø, -ø:z], *a. Ch:* chlorous.
chlorhydrate [klɔridrat], *s.m. Ch:* hydrochlorate, chlorhydrate.
chlorhydraté [klɔridrate], *a. Ch: Ind:* muriated.
chlorhydrine [klɔridrin], *s.f. Ch:* chlor(o)-hydrin.
chlorhydrique [klɔridrik], *a. Ch:* **acide chlorhydrique**, hydrochloric acid; *A:* spirit(s) of salt(s), muriatic acid.
chlorinité [klɔrinite], *s.f.* the amount of chlorine contained in a kilogram of sea water.
chlorique [klɔrik], *a.* chloric (acid).
chlorite [klɔrit], *s.m. Ch:* chlorite.
chlorité [klɔrite], *a. Miner:* containing chlorite.
chloro-anémie [klɔrɔanemi], *s.f. Med:* chloro-anaemia.
chlorobenzène [klɔrɔbɛ̃zɛn], *s.m.* chlorobenzene.
chlorobromure [klɔrɔbrɔmy:r], *s.m. Phot:* **papier au chlorobromure**, chloro-bromide paper.
chlorobutadiène [klɔrɔbytadjɛn], *s.m. Ch:* chloroprene.
chlorocalcite [klɔrɔkalsit], *s.f. Miner:* chlorocalcite.
chlorocarbonique [klɔrɔkarbɔnik], *a.* **acide c.,** carbonyl chloride, phosgene.
chlorofibre [klɔrɔfibr], *s.f. Ch:* polyvinyl.
chloroformation [klɔrɔfɔrmasjɔ̃], *s.f. Med:* chloroforming.
chloroforme [klɔrɔfɔrm], *s.m. Ch: Pharm:* chloroform; *Obst: A:* **c. à la reine**, twilight sleep.
chloroformé [klɔrɔfɔrme], *a.* **1.** *Pharm:* containing chloroform; **eau chloroformée**, chloroform water. **2.** *F:* slow-witted (person).
chloroformer [klɔrɔfɔrme], *v.tr.* **1.** *Med:* to chloroform (s.o.). **2.** *Pharm:* to add chloroform to (sth.).
chloroformique [klɔrɔfɔrmik], *a.* chloroformic (inhalations, etc.).
chloroformisation [klɔrɔfɔrmizasjɔ̃], *s.f. Med:* chloroforming.
chloroformiser [klɔrɔfɔrmize], *v.tr. Med:* to chloroform (s.o.).
chloromètre [klɔrɔmɛtr], *s.m.* chlorometer.
chlorométrie [klɔrɔmetri], *s.f.* chlorometry.
chlorométrique [klɔrɔmetrik], *a. Ch:* chlorometric.
chloromycétine [klɔrɔmisetin], *s.f. Pharm:* chloramphenicol; *R.t.m:* chloromycetin.
chlorophæite [klɔrɔfeit], *s.f. Miner:* chlorophaeite.
chlorophane[1] [klɔrɔfan], *s.f. Miner:* chlorophane.
chlorophane[2], *s.m.* green weevil, *chlorophanus viridis.*

chlorophazite [klɔrɔfazit], *s.f. Miner:* chlorophaeite.
chlorophénol [klɔrɔfenɔl], *s.m. Ch:* chlor(o)-phenol.
chlorophora [klɔrɔfɔra], *s.m. Arb:* chlorophora.
chlorophycées [klɔrɔfise], *s.f.pl. Alg:* Chlorophyceae.
chlorophylle [klɔrɔfil], *s.f.* chlorophyl; *F:* leaf-green.
chlorophyllien, -ienne [klɔrɔfiljɛ̃, -jɛn], *a. Biol:* chlorophyllian (function, etc.).
chlorophyllite [klɔrɔfilit], *s.f. Miner:* chlorophyllite.
chloropicrine [klɔrɔpikrin], *s.f. Ch:* chloropicrin.
chloropidés [klɔrɔpide], *s.m.pl. Ent:* Chloropidae.
chloroplaste [klɔrɔplast], *s.m. Biol:* chloroplast.
chlorose [klɔrɔ:z], *s.f.* **1.** *Med:* chlorosis; *F:* greensickness. **2.** *Bot:* chlorosis, etiolation.
chlorotique [klɔrɔtik]. **1.** *a. Med:* chlorotic. **2.** *s.* chlorotic person.
chlorurage [klɔryra:ʒ], *s.m.,* **chloruration** [klɔryrasjɔ̃], *s.f.* chlorination, chlorinating.
chlorure [klɔry:r], *s.m. Ch:* chloride; **c. stanneux**, stannous chloride; **c. mercurique**, mercuric chloride, corrosive sublimate; **c. de chaux**, bleaching powder; *Ch:* chloride of lime; **c. de calcium, de potassium, de sodium**, calcium, potassium, sodium chloride; **c. d'argent, d'or**, silver, gold, chloride; **c. de cuivre**, cupric chloride; *Phot: F:* **bain de c.,** (gold) toning bath.
chloruré [klɔryre], *a.* chlorinized, chlorinated.
chlorurémie [klɔryremi], *s.f. Med:* chlorœmia, chloremia.
chlorurer [klɔryre], *v.tr.* to chlorinize, chlorinate, chloridize.
chlorurie [klɔryri], *s.f. Med:* chloruria.
chnouf [ʃnuf], *s.f. P:* narcotic, *esp.* heroin; *F:* dope; *P:* junk.
chnouffé, -ée [ʃnufe], *s. P:* junkie, junky.
choane [kɔan], *s.m. Physiol:* choana.
choanocyte [kɔanɔsit], *s.m. Biol:* choanocyte.
choanoflagellés [kɔanɔflaʒele], *s.m.pl. Biol:* Choanoflagellata.
choc [ʃɔk], *s.m.* **1.** shock, jar, bump, collision; **protégé contre les chocs**, shock-proof, shock-resistant; **c. des verres**, clink of glasses; **c. des opinions**, clash, conflict, of opinions; *Rail: etc:* **tampon de c.,** buffer; *Mil:* **troupes de c.,** shock-troops; **tactique de c.,** shock tactics; **c. avec l'ennemi**, collision with the enemy; **soutenir le c. de l'ennemi**, to withstand the onslaught, onset, of the enemy; **to bear the brunt of the enemy's attack; résister au c.,** to stand the shock; *N. Arch: A:* **cloison de c.,** collision bulkhead; *F: Com:* **prix choc!** drastic reductions! **programme c.,** crash programme; **sujet c.,** subject likely to shock people. **2.** (a) *Mec:* shock, impact (of two bodies), percussion, concussion; **c. d'un corps contre un autre**, impact of one body on, against, another; **énergie au c.,** striking energy; **c. en retour**, (i) return-shock, -stroke; reper-cussion; (ii) *El:* reverse power; *Mec.E:* **essai (de résistance) au c.,** essai par c., impact test; *Ball:* **vitesse au c.,** impact, striking, velocity; *Av:* **c. d'atterrissage**, impact load; (b) *Ph: Ch:* collision, impact, shock; **c. acoustique**, acoustic shock; **c. électronique**, electron impact; **c. moléculaire**, molecule collision; **c. des noyaux**, nuclear collision; **ionisation par chocs**, ionization by collisions; (c) *El:* **c. électrique**, electric shock; **excitation par c.,** impact, shock, excitation; **tension de c.,** surge voltage; (d) *Mch:* (i) knocking, hammering (of engine); (ii) surging (of capstan). **3.** shock (to mental faculties, to nervous system); **se remettre d'un c.,** to recover from a shock; **attendez-vous à encaisser un c.,** be prepared for a shock; *Med:* **c. opératoire**, post-operative shock.
chocard [ʃɔka:r], *s.m. Orn:* **c. à bec jaune, c. des Alpes**, Alpine chough.
chochotte [ʃɔʃɔt], *s.f. P:* hypocritically prudish woman.
chocolat [ʃɔkɔla]. **1.** *s.m.* chocolate; **c. à cuire**, cooking chocolate; **c. fondant**, fondant chocolate; **c. à croquer**, plain (eating) chocolate. **2.** *a.inv.* chocolate-coloured; *P:* **être c.,** to have been swindled, rooked, had.
chocolaté [ʃɔkɔlate], *a.* containing, flavoured with, chocolate; **crème chocolatée**, chocolate cream.
chocolaterie [ʃɔkɔlatri], *s.f.* chocolate-factory, -trade.
chocolatier, -ière [ʃɔkɔlatje, -jɛ:r]. **1.** *a.* chocolate (industry, etc.). **2.** *s.* chocolate-maker, -seller. **3.** *s.f.* (i) **chocolatière**, chocolate pot; (ii) box for chocolates.
chocottes [ʃɔkɔt], *s.f.pl. P:* **1.** ivories, teeth. **2.** **avoir les c.,** to have the jitters, to be jittery.

choéphore [kɔefɔ:r], *s.m. & f. Gr.Ant:* libation bearer; *Gr.Lit:* **les Choéphores**, the Choephori; Choephoroe (of Aeschylus).
chœur [kœ:r], *s.m.* **1.** (a) *Gr.Lit:* chorus; (b) **rire, chanter, s'écrier, en chœur**, to laugh, sing, cry out, in chorus; **faire chœur au refrain**, to join in the chorus; **tous en c.!** all together! **2.** (a) choir (of singers); **enfant de c.,** (i) altar-boy; (ii) *F:* naïve person; *Arch:* choir, chancel; (c) (*musical composition*) chorus, concerted vocal piece.
chogramme [ʃɔgram], *s.m. Tchn:* secret combination lock.
choir [ʃwa:r], *v.i.def.* (*p.p.* chu; *pr.ind.* je chois, tu chois, il choit; *p.h.* je chus; *fu.* je choirai, je cherrai; *the aux. is* être); *A:* except *inf. & p.p.;* **se laisser c.** (dans un fauteuil, etc.), to drop, flop, sink (into an armchair, etc.); *F:* **laisser c., qn, qch.,** to drop s.o., to give up sth.
choisi [ʃwazi], *a.* **1.** selected; **morceaux choisis de . .,** selected passages from . . .; **hommes choisis**, picked men. **2.** select, choice; **société choisie**, select company; **s'adresser à quelques auditeurs choisis**, to address a chosen few; *s.* **on lui servait du c.,** he was served with choice food.
choisir [ʃwazi:r], *v.tr.* to choose, select, pick, elect; **c. qn en raison de sa compétence**, to choose s.o. for his ability; **c. entre, parmi, plusieurs choses**, to choose from several things; **c. entre deux maux**, to choose between two evils; **c. une carrière**, to adopt a career; **c. d'une chose ou d'une autre**, to choose between one thing and another; **il fut choisi comme directeur du collège d'Eton**, he was appointed headmaster of Eton College; **c. de partir ou de rester, c. si l'on part ou si l'on reste**, to choose whether one will leave or stay; **nom bien choisi**, appropriate name; **c. ses mots**, to pick one's words; *Sp:* **c. les camps**, to toss for sides; *s.a.* EMPRUNTER.
choix [ʃwa], *s.m.* choice, choosing, selection; **l'embarras du c.,** the difficulty of choosing; **faites votre c.,** take your choice; **je vous laisse le c.,** choose for yourself; **porter son c. sur qch.,** to choose sth.; **faire c. entre deux choses**, to choose between two things; **avoir le c. entre deux maux**, to have the choice of two evils; **avoir le c. de faire qch. ou non**, to have the choice of doing sth. or not; **avoir le c. entre faire qch. et faire qch. d'autre**, to have the choice between doing sth. and doing sth. else; **sans c.,** indiscriminately; **vous n'avez pas le c.,** you have no choice in the matter; **nous n'avons pas d'autre c. que de . . .,** we have no option, choice, but to . . .; **vous n'avez pas de c. dans ce magasin**, you haven't a large choice, selection, in this shop; (*on a menu*) **au c. viande ou poisson**, choice of meat or fish; **article de c.,** choice article; **de tout premier c.,** (of the) best quality, first-class, high-grade; **morceaux de viande de c.,** prime cuts; **hommes de c.,** picked men; *Adm:* **avancer au c.,** to be promoted by selection; *Com:* **"Au c.",** "all at the same price."
choke-bore [tʃɔkbɔr], *s.m. Sm.a:* chokebore; *pl.* **choke-bores.**
cholagogue [kɔlagɔg], *a. & s. Med:* **1.** *s.m.* cholagogue. **2.** *a.* cholagogic.
cholangiographie [kɔlɑ̃ʒjɔgrafi], *s.f. Med:* cholangiography.
chol(é)- [kɔl(e)], **chol(o)-** [kɔl(ɔ)], *pref.* chol(e)-; *Ch: Med:* **cholécyste**, cholecyst.
cholécystectomie [kɔlesistɛktɔmi], *s.f. Med:* cholecystectomy.
cholécystite [kɔlesistit], *s.f. Med:* cholecystitis.
cholécystographie [kɔlesistɔgrafi], *s.f. Med:* cholecystography.
cholécystostomie [kɔlesistɔstɔmi], *Med:* cholecystostomy.
cholédochotomie [kɔledɔkɔtɔmi], *s.f. Surg:* choledochotomy.
cholédoque [kɔledɔk], *a. Anat:* **le canal c.,** the choledoch (duct).
choléine [kɔlein], *s.f. Ch:* cholein.
cholémie [kɔlemi], *s.f. Med:* chol(a)emia.
cholèpe [kɔlɛp], *s.m. Z:* two-toed sloth.
choléra [kɔlera], *s.m. Med:* cholera; **c. asiatique, c. morbus**, Asiatic cholera, *cholera morbus;* **c. sec**, dry cholera, *cholera sicca;* **c. nostras** [nɔstraːs], *cholera nostras;* **c. infantile**, *cholera infantum; Vet:* **c. aviaire, des poules, des oiseaux de basse-cour**, chicken cholera; **c. du porc**, hog, swine cholera; *P:* **cette personne est un c.,** he's, she's, a poisonous character.
cholérétique [kɔleretik], *a. & s.m.* choleretic.
cholériforme [kɔlerifɔrm], *a. Med:* choleriform.
cholérine [kɔlerin], *s.f. Med:* cholerine.
cholérique[1] [kɔlerik], *Med:* **1.** *a.* choleraic. **2.** *s.* cholera patient.

cholérique[2], *a.* bilious (disposition, constitution).
cholestérine [kɔlɛsterin], *s.f. Med:* cholesterol.
cholestérinémie [kɔlɛsterinemi], *s.f. Med:* cholester(a)emia, cholesterol(a)emia.
cholestérol [kɔlɛsterɔl], *s.m. Med:* cholesterol.
cholestérolémie [kɔlɛsterɔlemi], *s.f. Med:* cholester(a)emia, cholesterol(a)emia.
cholet [ʃɔle], *s.m.* material (for handkerchiefs) made in Cholet.
choletais, -aise [ʃɔltɛ, -ɛːz], *a. & s. Geog:* (native, inhabitant) of Cholet.
choliambe [kɔljɑ̃ːb], *s.m. Pros:* choliamb.
choline [kɔlin], *s.f. Ch: Med:* choline.
cholinergique [kɔlinɛrʒik], *a. Ch:* cholinergic.
cholinestérase [kɔlinɛsterɑːz], *s.f. Ch:* cholinesterase, choline esterase.
cholurie [kɔlyri], *s.f. Med:* choluria.
chômable [ʃomabl], *a.* **jour c.**, day to be kept as a holiday.
chômage [ʃomaːʒ], *s.m.* **1.** *O:* abstention from work (on feast days, etc.); **c. du dimanche,** Sunday closing (of factories, shops, etc.). **2.** unemployment; idleness; **ouvriers en c.,** men out of work; **réduire qn au c.,** to throw s.o. out of work; **allocation, indemnité, secours, de c.,** unemployment benefit; *F:* dole; **c. d'une usine,** shutting down of a works; **c. d'une mine,** standing idle of a mine; **c. d'une chaudière,** laying off of a boiler; *F:* **s'inscrire au c.,** to go on the dole; **c. saisonnier,** seasonal unemployment; **c. partiel,** short-time working; **être en c. partiel,** to work short time, to be on short time.
chômer [ʃome], *v.i.* **1.** *O:* to abstain from work, to take a holiday (on feast days, etc.); hence *v.tr.* **c. (la fête d')un saint,** to keep a saint's day; **fête chômée,** public holiday. **2.** *(a)* to be, lie, idle; to be unemployed; not to be working; *(of field)* to lie fallow; **c. une semaine sur deux,** to go off work, knock off work, one week out of two; **les usines chôment,** the works are at a standstill, are standing idle, have shut down; **laisser c. son argent,** to let one's money lie idle; *Journ:* **l'époque où la politique chôme;** *F:* the silly season; *s.a.* MOINE 1, POUR I. 1 (i); *(b) A:* **c. de qch.,** to want, need, sth.
chômeur, -euse [ʃomœːr, -øːz], *s.* (i) unemployed, (ii) idle, workman; **les chômeurs,** the unemployed; **c. partiel,** short-time worker.
chon [ʃɔ̃], *s.m. Num:* chon.
chondre [kɔ̃dr̥], *s.m. Geol:* chondre, chondrule.
chondrilla [kɔ̃drija], *s.f. Bot:* chondrilla.
chondrine [kɔ̃drin], *s.f. Ch:* chondrin.
chondrioconte [kɔ̃drijɔkɔ̃t], *s.m. Biol:* chondriocont.
chondriome [kɔ̃drijɔm], *s.m. Biol: Physiol:* chondriome, chondrioma.
chondriosome [kɔ̃drijɔzoːm], *s.m. Biol: Physiol:* chondriosome.
chondrite [kɔ̃drit], *s.f. Min:* chondrite.
chondro- [kɔ̃drɔ], *pref.* chondr(i)-, chondro-.
chondroblaste [kɔ̃drɔblast], *s.m. Anat:* chondroblast.
chondrocostal, -aux [kɔ̃drɔkɔstal, -o], *a. Anat:* chrondrocostal.
chondrodite [kɔ̃drɔdit], *s.f. Miner:* chondrodite.
chondrogénèse [kɔ̃drɔʒenɛːz], *s.f. Biol:* chondrogenesis.
chondroïde [kɔ̃drɔid], *a. Anat:* chondroid, cartilaginous.
chondrologie [kɔ̃drɔlɔʒi], *s.f. Med:* chondrology.
chondrome [kɔ̃drɔm, -droːm], *s.m. Med:* chondroma.
chondroplaste [kɔ̃drɔplast], *s.m. Anat:* chondroplast.
chondro-sarcome, chondrosarcome [kɔ̃drɔsarkoːm], *s.m. Med:* chondrosarcoma.
chondrostome [kɔ̃drɔstoːm], *s.m. Ich:* chondrostoma.
chondrus [kɔ̃drys], *s.m. Bot:* chondrus, *pl.* -dri, carrag(h)een, Irish moss.
chop [tʃɔp], *s.m. Ten:* chop, slice.
chope [ʃɔp], *s.f. (a)* beer mug, tankard; *(b)* mugful.
choper[1] [ʃɔpe], *v.tr. P:* **1.** to steal, pinch. **2.** to arrest; **se faire c.,** to get nabbed. **3.** to catch.
choper[2] [tʃɔpe], *v.tr. Ten:* to chop, to slice.
chopin [ʃɔpɛ̃], *O: P:* **1.** piece of luck. **2.** easy mark (for rogues).
chopine [ʃɔpin], *s.f.* **1.** half-litre bottle, mug; *Fr.C: Meas:* pint; *F:* **tu viens boire une c.?** come and have a drink. **2.** lower box, plunger, bucket (of pump).
chopiner [ʃɔpine], *v.i. P:* to swill, booze.
chopinette [ʃɔpinɛt], *s.f. F:* small bottle, mug; small mugful.
chopper [ʃɔpe], *v.i.* **1.** *A: Lit:* to trip, stumble. **2.** to make a mistake, to be mistaken.
choquable [ʃɔkabl], *a. (of pers.)* easily shocked; **peu c.,** not easily shocked.
choquant [ʃɔkɑ̃], *a.* shocking, displeasing, disagreeable, offensive; **un abus c.,** a gross, glaring, abuse.
choquard, choquart [ʃɔkaːr], *s.m. Orn:* = CHOCARD.
choquer[1] [ʃɔke], *v.tr.* **1.** to strike, knock, bump (sth. against sth.); **nous choquâmes nos verres,** we clinked glasses. **2.** to shock; *(a)* to displease, offend; **être choqué de qch.,** to be scandalized, shocked, at, by, sth.; **sons qui choquent l'oreille,** sounds that shock, grate on, the ear; **idée qui choque le bon sens,** idea that offends, is contrary to, common sense; *(b)* to distress; **je fus choqué de le voir tellement changé,** I was shocked, it gave me a shock, to see such a change in him; *(c) Med:* to shock.
se choquer. **1.** *O:* to come into collision (**contre,** with). **2.** to be shocked, scandalized; to take offence (**de,** at); to take exception (**de,** to).
choquer[2], *Nau:* **1.** *v.tr. (a)* (i) to ease (off), to slack (rope); (ii) **c. brusquement une amarre au cabestan,** to surge a rope round the capstan; *(b)* **c. les écoutes,** (i) to check the sheets; (ii) to haul in the sheets, to close-haul. **2.** *v.i. (of rope) (a)* to slip; *(b)* **c. brusquement,** to surge; *(c) Nau:* **c. à la demande,** to snub.
choral [kɔral]. **1.** *a.* choral; **société chorale,** choral society; *m.pl. chorals, choraux.* **2.** *s.m. (a)* choral(e); *(b) Ecc:* the body of CHANTRES; *pl. chorals.* **3.** *s.f.* **chorale,** choral society.
chorda [kɔrda], *s.m. Biol:* chorda.
chordotonal, -aux [kɔrdɔtɔnal, -o], *a. Biol: Ent:* **(organe) chordotonal,** chordotonal organ, scolopidium.
chorea [kɔrea], *s.f. Arch:* ambulatory chapels.
chorédrame [kɔredram], *s.m.* choreodrama.
chorée[1] [kɔre], *s.m. Pros:* trochee, choree.
chorée[2], *s.f. Med:* chorea; *F:* Saint Vitus's dance; *s.a.* SALTATOIRE.
chorège [kɔrɛːʒ], *s.m. Gr.Ant:* choragus.
chorégie [kɔreʒi], *s.f. Gr.Ant:* choregy.
chorégique [kɔreʒik], *a. Gr.Ant:* choregic.
chorégraphe [kɔregraf], *s.m. or f.* choreographer.
chorégraphie [kɔregrafi], *s.f.* choreography.
chorégraphique [kɔregrafik], *a.* choreographic.
choréiforme [kɔreifɔrm], *a. Med:* choreiform.
choréique [kɔreik], *a. Med:* choreic.
choreute [kɔrøt], *s.m. Gr.Ant:* chorist, member of the chorus in ancient Greek drama.
chorevêque [kɔrevɛːk], *s.m. Ecc:* chorepiscopus.
choriambe [kɔrjɑ̃ːb], *s.m. Pros:* choriamb(us).
choriambique [kɔrjɑ̃bik], *a. Pros:* choriambic.
chorion [kɔrjɔ̃], *s.m.* **1.** *Anat:* corium (of skin). **2.** *Biol: Obst:* chorion.
chorique [kɔrik], *a.* choric.
choriso [tʃɔriso], *s.m. Cu:* choriso, chorizo.
choriste [kɔrist], *s.m.* chorister (in church); chorus-singer (in opera).
chorizo [tʃɔriso], *s.m. Cu:* = CHORISO.
chorographie [kɔrɔgrafi], *s.f. A:* chorography.
chorographique [kɔrɔgrafik], *a.* chorographic, chorographical.
choroïde [kɔrɔid], *a. Anat:* choroid; **membrane c.,** *s.f.* **c.,** choroid coat, choroid (of the eye).
choroïdien, -ienne [kɔrɔidjɛ̃, -jɛn], *a.* choroid, choroidal.
choroïdite [kɔrɔidit], *s.f. Med:* choroiditis.
chorus [kɔryːs], *s.m.* chorus; *(a)* **faire c.,** to chorus s.o.'s words; to express approval or repeat a request in chorus; *(b) (of jazz musician, etc.)* **prendre un c.,** to take a chorus.
chose [ʃoːz]. **1.** *s.f.* thing; *(a)* **un tas de choses,** a pile of things; **j'ai un tas de choses à faire,** I've masses of things to do; **il y a de bonnes choses dans cet article,** there are some good things in this article; **aller où va toute c.,** to go the way of all flesh; **les choses de la terre,** the things of this world; **c'est de deux choses l'une,** you have the choice of two things; **dire le mot et la c.,** to call a spade a spade *s.a.* APPELER 3; **dites bien des choses (aimables) de ma part à . . .,** remember me kindly to . . .; **j'ai bien des choses à vous raconter,** I have a lot (of things), many things, to tell you; **la c. en question,** the case in point; **la c. parle d'elle-même,** it is self-evident; **je vais vous expliquer la c.,** I'll explain it, the matter, to you; **vous prenez la c. trop sérieusement,** you take the thing too seriously; **cela n'est plus la même c.,** that alters the case; **je vois la c.,** I see how things stand, I understand; **si la c. est vraie,** it is is true, if that is so; **c'est une c. qu'on n'aurait pas dû faire,** that was a silly thing to do; **c. curieuse, personne n'en savait rien,** curiously enough nobody knew anything about it; **avant toute c.,** first of all; **toutes choses égales d'ailleurs,** all things being equal; **aller au fond des choses,** to get to the bottom of things; **dans l'état actuel des choses,** as things are, stand; **les choses vont mal,** things are going badly; **je vous recommande sur toute c. de . . .,** above all, I advise you to . . .; **ce n'est pas c. aisée de . . .,** it is no easy matter to . . .; **le plus mauvais de la c. c'est que . . .,** the worst of it is that . . .; **il fait bien les choses,** he does things in style; **ne pas faire les choses à demi, à moitié,** not to do things by halves; *Jur:* **c. jugée,** res judicata; *F:* matter which is not worth discussing; **décision passée en force de c. jugée,** judgment at law; **choses de flot, de la mer,** flotsam and jetsam; *s.a.* AUTRE 1, 2, GRAND'CHOSE, LEÇON 2, PEU 1, QUELQUE 1, QUELQUE CHOSE, SUR 1, TEMPS 1 *(b)* and *(c)*; *(b)* property, goods; **le serf était la c. du seigneur,** the serf was the property, chattel, of the squire; *Adm:* **c. commune** = *domaine public, q.v. under* DOMAINE 1; *s.a.* PUBLIC 1. **2.** *(a) s.m. & f. F:* **Monsieur Chose, Madame Chose,** Mr, Mrs, What-d'ye-call-him, -her, Mr, Mrs, Thingummy, Thingumabob; **le petit Chose,** little What's-his-name; *(b) s.m. P: (replacing vulgar words)* **je vais te botter le c.,** I'll kick you on the you-know-what. **3.** *a.inv. F:* **être, se sentir, tout c.,** to feel funny, queer, under the weather; **vous avez l'air tout c.,** you look upset, out of sorts, you look as if something had gone wrong.
chosette [ʃozɛt], *s.f.* small thing, trifle.
chosisme [ʃozism], *s.m. Phil:* concretism.
chott [ʃɔt], *s.m. Geog:* saline lake, chott (in North Africa).
chou, -oux [ʃu], *s.m.* **1.** cabbage **c. pommé, c. cabus,** garden cabbage; **c. frisé,** borecole, kale; **c. à jets, de Bruxelles,** Brussels sprouts; **c. de Milan,** Savoy cabbage; **c. rouge, c. roquette,** red cabbage; **c. marin,** sea-kale; *F:* **planter ses choux,** to live retired in the country; **faire ses choux gras,** to feather one's nest; **faire ses choux gras de qch.,** to thrive on sth.; **faites-en des choux et des raves,** do what you like with it; **faire c. blanc,** *(at games)* to fail to score, to make a duck; *F:* to draw a blank; **mon petit c.,** darling, dear; **c. pour c.,** taking one thing with another; **répondre à qn c. pour c.,** to answer s.o. pat; *Typ:* **composer c. pour c.,** to set up a facsimile of the original; **c'est c. vert et vert c.,** it is as broad as it's long, much of a muchness; *P:* **être dans les choux,** (i) to be in a fix, in a pickle, in a mess; *Rac:* to lose; (ii) to have fainted, to be unconscious; **être bête comme c.,** (i) to be stupid, dopey; (ii) to be as easy as pie; *Rac:* **arriver dans les choux,** to be, come in, nowhere, to be an also-ran; **manger les choux par les trognons,** to be pushing up the daisies; **rentrer dans le c. à qn,** to attack, go for, s.o.; **feuille de c.,** newspaper of no standing; *F:* rag; *s.a.* CHÈVRE 1. **2.** *Bot: F:* **c. de chien,** dog's mercury; **c. de mer,** sea-bell. **3.** *Cost:* cabbage-bow, -knot; rosette (of ribbon). **4.** *Cu:* **c. à la crème,** chou; **pâte à choux,** chou(x) pastry.
chouan, -anne [ʃwɑ̃, -an], *s. Fr.Hist:* Chouan, Royalist insurgent in Brittany and the West.
chouanner [ʃwane], *v.i. Fr.Hist:* to engage in guerrilla warfare.
chouannerie [ʃwanri], *s.f. Fr.Hist:* *(a)* body of Royalist insurgents; *(b)* **la C.,** the Chouan rising.
chouc [ʃuk], *s.m. F:* jackdaw.
choucalcyon [ʃukalsjɔ̃], *s.m. Orn:* laughing jackass.
choucas [ʃukɑ], *s.m.,* **chouchette** [ʃuʃɛt], *s.f.* **c. des tours,** jackdaw; **c. de Russie,** East European jackdaw.
chouchou, -oute, chou-chou, chou-choute [ʃuʃu, -ut], *s. F:* pet, darling; **le c. de maman,** mother's blue-eyed boy; **la chouchoute de papa,** daddy's darling; **le c. du professeur,** teacher's pet; *pl. chouchous, choux-choux.*
chouchouter [ʃuʃute], *v.tr. F: (a)* to pet, caress, fondle; *A:* to cosset; *(b)* to coddle (child); *(c) v.pr. P:* **se c.,** to have a cushy time.
choucroute [ʃukrut], *s.f. Cu:* sauerkraut, pickled cabbage.
chouette[1] [ʃwɛt], *s.f.* **1.** *Orn:* **c. des clochers,** screech-owl, *esp.* barn-owl, church-owl; **c. des bois,** wood-owl, brown owl; **c. lapone,** Lapland, great grey, owl; **c. de l'Oural,** Ural owl; **c. effraie,** barn-owl; **c. épervière,** hawk-owl; **c. hulotte,** tawny owl; **c. chevêche,** little owl; **c. chevêchette,** pygmy owl; **c. harfang,** snowy owl; **c. de Tengmalm,** Tengmalm's owl; **c. fouisseuse,** burrowing owl. **2.** *Cards:* **faire la c.,** to play a lone hand.
chouette[2], *a. & int. F:* fine, stunning; **une c. casquette,** a natty cap; **c., papa!** capital! **c. alors!** good show! splendid!

chouettement [ʃwɛtmɑ̃], *adv. P:* splendidly.

chou-fleur [ʃuflœːr], *s.m.* cauliflower; **c.-f. d'hiver,** (purple) sprouting; *Box:* **oreille en c.-f.,** cauliflower ear; *pl. choux-fleurs.*

chouleur [ʃulœːr], *s.m. Civ.E:* front-end loader.

chou-navet [ʃunavɛ], *s.m. Agr:* swede; *pl. choux-navets.*

chou-palmiste [ʃupalmist], *s.m. Bot:* palm-cabbage; *pl. choux-palmistes.*

choupette [ʃupɛt], *s.f. F:* **1.** tuft of baby's hair tied with a bow. **2.** special bow for baby's hair.

chouque [ʃuk], *s.m.*, **chouquet**[1] [ʃukɛ], *s.m. Nau:* cap (of mast).

chouquet[2], *s.m. Metalw:* block used in the drawing of metals.

chou-rave [ʃuraːv], *s.m. Agr:* kohl-rabi, turnip cabbage; *pl. choux-raves.*

chourin [ʃurɛ̃], *s.m. P:* (apache's) knife, dagger.

chouriner [ʃurine], *v.tr. P:* to knife (s.o.); to do (s.o.) in.

chourineur [ʃurinœːr], *s.m. P:* murderer.

chow-chow [tʃoutʃou, ʃuʃu, ʃawʃaw], *s.m.* chow (dog); *pl. chow-chows.*

choyer [ʃwaje], *v.tr.* (**je choie, n. choyons; je choierai**) to pet, coddle, make much of, fondle (s.o.); **c. un espoir,** to entertain, cherish, a hope; **c. un préjugé,** to hug a prejudice.

chrématistique [krematistik]. **1.** *a.* chrematistic. **2.** *s.f.* chrematistics.

chrême [krɛm], *s.m. Ecc:* chrism, consecrated oil.

chrémeau, -eaux [kremo], *s.m. Ecc:* chrisom (-cloth, -robe); chrismal.

chrestomathie [krɛstɔmati, -masi], *s.f.* chrestomathy, anthology.

chrétien, -ienne [kretjɛ̃, -jɛn], *a. & s.* Christian; *F:* **parler (un langage) c.,** to speak (i) in simple language, (ii) in decent language; *F:* **s'enrichir par des moyens peu chrétiens,** to get rich by means not over-scrupulous.

chrétien-démocrate [kretjɛ̃demɔkrat], *a. & s. Pol:* Christian Democrat; *pl. chrétiens-démocrates.*

chrétiennement [kretjɛnmɑ̃], *adv.* Christianly, in a Christian manner, like a Christian.

chrétienté [kretjɛ̃te], *s.f.* Christendom; **la c. de l'Orient,** the Eastern Churches.

chrismal, -aux [krismal, -o], *s.m. Ecc: A:* **1.** chrismal, chrism vessel. **2.** reliquary.

chrismation [krismasjɔ̃], *s.f. Ecc:* **1.** chrismation. **2.** chrismatory.

chrismatoire [krismatwaːr], *s.m. Ecc:* chrismatory.

chrisme [krism], *s.m. Ecc:* chrisma, labarum.

Christ [krist], *s.m.* **1. le Christ** [ləkrist], Christ; **Jésus-Christ** [ʒezykri], Jesus Christ. **2. un c. d'ivoire,** an ivory crucifix.

christadelphe [kristadɛlf], *a. & s.m. Ecc:* Christadelphian.

christe-marine [krist(ə)marin], *s.f. Bot:* = CRISTE-MARINE; *pl. christes-marines.*

christian [kristjɑ̃], *s.m. Num:* christian d'or.

christiania [kristjanja], *s.m. Skiing:* christiania (turn).

christianisation [kristjanizasjɔ̃], *s.f.* christianization.

christianiser [kristjanize], *v.tr.* to christianize.

se christianiser, to become (a) Christian.

christianisme [kristjanism], *s.m.* Christianity.

Christine [kristin], *Pr.n.f.* Christina, Christine.

christologie [kristɔlɔʒi], *s.f.* Christology.

christologique [kristɔlɔʒik], *a.* Christological.

christophanie [kristɔfani], *s.f. Rel:* christophany.

Christophe [kristɔf], *Pr.n.m.* Christopher.

chromaffine [krɔmafin], *a. Biol:* chromaffine.

chromage [krɔmaːʒ], *s.m.* chromium plating.

chromate [krɔmat], *s.m. Ch:* chromate.

chromaté [krɔmate], *a. A:* = CHROMÉ.

chromater [krɔmate], *v.tr. A:* = CHROMER.

chromatie [krɔmati], *s.f. Opt:* chromatism, chromatic aberration.

chromatine [krɔmatin], *s.f. Biol:* chromatin.

chromatinien [krɔmatinjɛ̃], *a. Biol:* **sexe c.,** nuclear sex.

chromatique [krɔmatik]. **1.** *a. Mus: Opt: etc:* chromatic (scale, aberration). **2.** *s.f. Opt: Paint:* chromatics.

chromatiquement [krɔmatikmɑ̃], *adv.* chromatically.

chromatiser [krɔmatize], *v.tr.* **1.** *Mus:* to make (scale) chromatic. **2.** to chromate.

se chromatiser, to become iridescent.

chromatisme [krɔmatism], *s.m. Opt:* chromatism, chromatic aberration.

chromatocyte [krɔmatɔsit], *s.m.* chromatocyte.

chromatographie [krɔmatɔgrafi], *s.f. Ch:* chromatography.

chromatomètre [krɔmatɔmɛtr̥], *s.m.* chromatometer.

chromatophore [krɔmatɔfɔːr], *s.m. Nat.Hist:* chromatophore, pigment-bearing cell.

chromatoscope [krɔmatɔskɔp], *s.m. Opt:* chromatoscope.

chrome [kroːm], *s.m.* **1.** (*a*) *Ch:* chromium; (*b*) chromium fitting; **faire (briller) les chromes,** to polish the chromium (of cars, bicycles, etc.). **2.** *Com:* chrome; **jaune de c.,** chrome yellow.

chromé, *a.* **1.** treated with chromium, chrome; **cuir c.,** chrome(-tanned) leather; **manteau en cuir c.,** chrome-leather overcoat; **veau c.,** box calf; *Metall:* **acier c.,** chrome steel. **2.** chromium-plated.

chromer [krome], *v.tr. Ind:* to chrome, to chromatize, to chromate.

chrome-tungstène [kromtœ̃kstɛn], *s.m.* chromium-tungsten; *pl. chromes-tungstènes.*

chromifère [krɔmifɛːr], *a. Miner:* chromiferous.

chromique [krɔmik, kro-], *a. Ch:* chromic (acid).

chromisation [krɔmizasjɔ̃], *s.f. Metall:* chromizing.

chromiser [krɔmize], *v.tr. Metall:* to chromize.

chromite [krɔmit, kro-], *s.f. Miner:* chromite, chrome iron.

chromo- [krɔmɔ, kromo], *pref.* chromo-; **chromoblaste,** chromoblast; **chromosome,** chromosome; **chromothérapie,** chromotherapy.

chromo [kromo], *s.m. F:* chromo(lithograph), (*usu.* bad) colour-print.

chromogène [krɔmɔʒɛn], *a. Biol:* chromogenous, colour-producing.

chromographe [kromograf], *s.m.* chromograph.

chromolithographe [kromolitɔgraf], *s.m.* chromolithographer.

chromolithographie [kromolitɔgrafi], *s.f.* **1.** chromolithography. **2.** chromo(lithograph).

chromolithographique [kromolitɔgrafik], *a.* chromolithographic.

chromomètre [kromomɛtr̥], *s.m.* chromometer.

chromophile [kromofil], *a. & s.* chrom(at)ophil(e).

chromophore [kromofɔːr]. **1.** *a.* chromophoric; chromophorous. **2.** *s.m.* chromophor(e).

chromophotographie [kromofɔtɔgrafi], *s.f.* chromophotography, colour-photography.

chromoprotéide [kromoprɔteid], *s.f. Biol:* chromoprotein.

chromoscope [kromoskɔp], *s.m. Phot:* chromoscope.

chromosensible [kromosɑ̃sibl̥], *a. Phot:* colour-sensitive.

chromosome [kromozoːm], *s.m. Biol:* chromosome.

chromosomique [kromozomik], *a. Biol:* chromosomal, of or relating to chromosomes.

chromosphère [kromosfɛːr], *s.f. Astr:* chrom(at)osphere, colour sphere (round the sun).

chromosphérique [kromosferik], *a.* chromospheric.

chromothérapie [kromoterapi], *s.f. Med:* chromotherapy.

chromotypographie [kromotipɔgrafi], *s.f.*, **chromotypie** [kromotipi], *s.f.* **1.** chromotype, chromotypography. **2.** chromotype (picture).

chronaxie [krɔnaksi], *s.f. Biol: Physiol:* chronaxia, chronaxy.

chronicité [krɔnisite], *s.f.* chronicity (of disease, etc.).

chronique[1] [krɔnik], *a.* (*a*) *Med:* chronic (disease, etc.); (*b*) **fumeur, joueur, c.,** compulsive smoker, gambler.

chronique[2], *s.f.* **1.** chronicle. **2.** *Journ:* news, reports, "column," essay; **c. financière, musicale,** financial, musical, news; **c. littéraire,** literary column; **c. des tribunaux,** law reports; *F:* **c. scandaleuse,** tittle-tattle of the day; scandalous gossip.

chroniquement [krɔnikmɑ̃], *adv.* chronically.

chroniquer [krɔnike], *v.i.* to write newspaper reports; to write up the news of the day.

chroniqueur, -euse [krɔnikœːr, -øːz], *s.* **1.** chronicler. **2.** *Journ:* writer of news pars; columnist; reporter. **3.** *W.Tel:* broadcaster.

chrono-[1] [krɔnɔ, krono], *pref.* chrono-; **chronoscopique,** chronoscopic; **chronostiche,** chronostichon.

chrono[2] [krɔnɔ], *s.m. F:* = CHRONOMÈTRE; **du 220 c.** (= **au chronomètre**), recorded speed of 220 km.h.

chronogramme [krɔnɔgram], *s.m.* chronogram.

chronographe [krɔnɔgraf], *s.m.* (*a*) *Ph: etc:* chronograph; (*b*) stop-watch.

chronographique [krɔnɔgrafik], *a.* chronographic.

chronologie [krɔnɔlɔʒi], *s.f.* chronology.

chronologique [krɔnɔlɔʒik], *a.* chronological.

chronologiquement [krɔnɔlɔʒikmɑ̃], *adv.* chronologically.

chronologiste [krɔnɔlɔʒist], *s.m.* chronologist, chronologer.

chronométrage [krɔnɔmetraːʒ], *s.m.* time-keeping; timing; chronometric measurement.

chronomètre [krɔnɔmɛtr̥], *s.m.* **1.** chronometer; **c. de bord,** ship's chronometer; **c. étalon,** standard chronometer. **2.** stop-watch.

chronométrer [krɔnɔmetre], *v.tr.* (**je chronomètre, n. chronométrons; je chronométrerai**) *Sp:* to keep the time; to time (race, etc.).

chronométreur [krɔnɔmetrœːr], *s.m.* **1.** *Sp:* timekeeper. **2.** *Ind:* time-clerk; time (and motion) study expert.

chronométrie [krɔnɔmetri], *s.f.* **1.** chronometry, time-measurement. **2.** chronometer-making.

chronométrique [krɔnɔmetrik], *a.* chronometric(al).

chronophotographe [krɔnɔfɔtɔgraf], *s.m. A:* photochronograph (apparatus).

chronophotographie [krɔnɔfɔtɔgrafi], *s.f.* chronophotography, motion-analysis.

chronoscope [krɔnɔskɔp], *s.m. Ph: etc:* chronoscope.

chronotachymètre [krɔnɔtakimɛtr̥], *s.m.* speed-recorder.

chronotrope [krɔnɔtrɔp], *a.* chronotropic.

Chrysale [krizal], *Pr.n.m.* character in Molière's *Femmes Savantes* embodying the common-sense, matter-of-fact, type of man.

chrysalide [krizalid], *s.f. Ent:* chrysalis, pupa, aurelia; *F:* **sortir de sa c.,** to come out of one's obscurity, *F:* out of one's shell.

chrysalider (se) [səkrizalide], *v.pr. Ent:* to pupate; to become a pupa, a chrysalis.

chrysanthème [krizɑ̃tɛm], *s.m. Bot:* chrysanthemum; **c. des jardins, à couronne,** (yellow or white) garden chrysanthemum; **c. frutescent,** marguerite, Paris daisy; **c. des prés,** ox-eye daisy; **c. matricaire,** feverfew.

chrysanthémiste [krizɑ̃temist], *s.m.* chrysanthemum grower.

chryséléphantin [krizelefɑ̃tɛ̃], *a.* chryselephantine.

chrysène [krizɛn], *s.m. Ch:* chrysene.

chrysididés [krizidide], *s.m.pl. Ent:* Chrysididae.

chrysine [krizin], *s.f. Ch: Bot:* chrysin.

chrysis [krizis], *s.f. Ent:* chrysis.

chrys(o)- [kriz(ɔ)], *pref.* chrys(o)-; **chrysochlore,** chrysochlorous; **chrysophylle,** chrysophyll; **chrysamine,** chrysamine.

chrysobéryl [krizɔberil], *s.m. Miner:* chrysoberyl, cymophane.

chrysocal(e) [krizɔkal], **chrysoc(h)alque** [krizɔkalk], *s.m.* pinchbeck.

chrysochlore [krizɔklɔːr], *s.m. Z:* chrysochlore, African golden mole.

chrysocol(l)e [krizɔkɔl], *s.f. Miner:* chrysocolla.

chrysogène [krizɔʒɛn], *a.* **un aristocrate c.,** an aristocrat born with a silver spoon in his mouth.

chrysographe [krizɔgraf], *s.m.* (*a*) copyist who wrote manuscripts in gold lettering; (*b*) craftsman who did embroidery and decorative work in gold.

chrysographie [krizɔgrafi], *s.f.* chrysography.

chrysoïdine [krizɔidin], *s.f. Ch:* chrysoidine.

chrysol [krizɔl], *s.m.* chrysin.

chrysolit(h)e [krizɔlit], *s.f. Miner:* chrysolite, olivin(e).

chrysomèle [krizɔmɛl], *s.f. Ent:* chrysomelid beetle.

chrysomélidés [krizɔmelide], *s.m. pl. Ent:* Chrysomelidae.

chrysope [krizɔp], *s.f. Ent:* chrysopa; *F:* green lace-wing.

chrysopélée [krizɔpele], *s.m. Z:* flying snake.

chrysoprase [krizɔpraːz], *s.f. Miner:* chrysoprase.

Chrysostome [krizɔstoːm], *Pr.n.m.* Chrysostom.

chrysotile [krizɔtil], *s.f. Miner:* chrysotile.

chtonien, -ienne [ktɔnjɛ̃, -jɛn], *a. Gr.Myth:* chthonian, chthonic.

chuchotage [ʃyʃɔtaːʒ], *s.m.* whispering.

chuchotant [ʃyʃɔtɑ̃], *a.* whispering; rustling (silk, etc.).

chuchotement [ʃyʃɔtmɑ̃], *s.m.* whispering, whisper.

chuchoter [ʃyʃɔte]. **1.** *v.i.* to whisper; **parler en chuchotant,** to speak in a whisper. **2.** *v.tr.* **c. quelques mots à l'oreille de qn,** to whisper a few words in s.o.'s ear.

chuchoterie [ʃyʃɔtri], *s.f.* whisper(ing); whispered gossip(ing).

chuchoteur, -euse [ʃyʃɔtœːr, -øːz], *s.* whisperer.

chuchotis [ʃyʃɔti], *s.m.* whispering.

chuintant [ʃɥɛ̃tɑ̃], **chuinté** [ʃɥɛ̃te], *a. Ling:* tongue-and-after-gum (consonant); **sons chuintants,** "hushing" sounds (*e.g.* ʃ, ʒ).

chuintement [ʃɥɛ̃tmɑ̃], *s.m.* hissing, sizzle.

chuinter [ʃɥɛ̃te], *v.i.* **1.** (*of owl*) to hoot. **2.** (*a*) *Ling:* to make a "hushing" sound (in speaking); (*b*) (*of gas*) to hiss, sizzle.

chut [ʃyt,], *int.* hush, sh; *s.m.inv.* **des chut réitérés,** repeated cries of "hush," calls for silence.

chute [ʃyt], *s.f.* **1.** (*a*) *Ph: etc:* fall (of heavy body, of barometer, etc.); **c. de montagne,** landslide; **c. des corps dans le vide, dans les fluides,** fall of bodies in vacuum, in fluids; **corps en c.,** falling body; **c. libre,** free fall; *Av:* **largage de colis, de matériel, en c. libre,** free drop of bundles, of equipment; **point de c.,** point of fall; *Ball:* **angle de c.,** angle of fall; *P.N:* **c. de pierres,** danger! falling stones; (*b*) **faire une c.,** to have a fall, a spill, a tumble; *F:* to come a cropper; *Th:* **c. du rideau,** fall of the curtain; *Meteor:* **c. de pluie, de neige,** rainfall, snowfall; **c. du jour,** nightfall; *Lit:* eventide; *Poet:* **la c. des feuilles,** autumn, *U.S:* the fall; *Com:* **c. des prix,** fall, drop, in prices; collapse of prices; (*c*) (down)fall (of ministry, etc.); **la c. de l'homme,** the fall; **c. d'une femme,** ruin, downfall, of a woman; **il m'a entraîné dans sa c.,** he has dragged me down with him; *Th:* **c. d'une pièce,** failure, *F:* flop, of a play; *Cards:* **avoir deux levées de c.,** to be two tricks down; (*d*) *Med:* prolapsus (of rectum, etc.). **2. c. d'eau,** (i) *Geog:* waterfall; (ii) *Hyd.E:* head of water; **les Chutes du Niagara,** the Niagara Falls; **les Chutes Victoria,** the Victoria Falls; **les Chutes du Nil,** the Falls of the Nile; **c. d'un bief,** drop, lift, of a lock; **c. effective,** working fall, head; **hauteur de c.,** (i) fall, head, (of water); (ii) drop (of pile-ram). **3.** *El.E: Mch:* drop, fall; *El.E:* **c. de potentiel** *m*, **de tension** *f*, voltage drop, fall; **c. anodique, cathodique,** anode, cathode, fall; **c. de tension d'arc,** arc stream voltage; *Mch:* **c. de pression,** pressure drop. **4.** (*a*) (*sth. which falls, slopes down*) **c. d'un toit,** pitch of a roof; **c. d'une robe,** hang of a dress; **c. des reins,** small of the back; **c. de la voix,** fall, cadence of the voice; *Lit:* **c. de la phrase,** round-off of the sentence; (*b*) *F:* punch-line (of a joke). **5.** (*a*) *Min: Ind:* shoot; (*b*) *Fr.C: Post: U.S:* chute (post box). **6.** (*a*) *Tchn:* off-cut (of wood); (*b*) snippets, trimmings (of cloth, etc.); (*c*) scrap (of metal). **7.** *Nau:* **c. d'une voile,** drop of a sail; **c. arrière,** leech (of sail); **c. avant,** luff (of sail); **ralingue de c.,** leech rope. **8.** *Needlew:* **c. de fleurs,** spray of flowers.

chuter[1] [ʃyte]. **1.** *v.i.* to say hush. **2.** *v.tr.* to hiss (an actor).

chuter[2], *v.i. F:* to fall, tumble, down, come to grief; *esp. Th:* (*of play*) to fail, to be a failure; *Cards:* **c. de deux levées,** to be two tricks down.

chutney [tʃœtni], *s.m. Cu:* chutney.

chylaire [ʃilɛːr], *a. Physiol:* chylous, chylaceous.

chyle [ʃil], *s.m. Physiol:* chyle.

chyleux, -euse [ʃilø, -øːz], *a. Physiol:* chylous, chylaceous.

chylifère [ʃilifɛːr], *a. & s.m. Physiol:* chyliferous (vessel).

chylification [ʃilifikasjɔ̃], *s.f. Physiol:* chylification, chylosis.

chylifier [ʃilifje], *v.tr. Physiol:* to chylify.

chyliforme [ʃiliform], *a. Physiol:* chyliform.

chyl(o)- [ʃil(ɔ)], *pref.* chyl(o)-; **chylopoïèse,** chylopoiesis; **chylurie,** chyluria.

chyme [ʃim], *s.m. Physiol:* chyme.

chymification [ʃimifikasjɔ̃], *s.f. Physiol:* chymification.

chymifier [ʃimifje], *v.tr. Physiol:* to chymify.

Chypre [ʃipr̥]. **1.** *Pr.n.f. Geog:* **l'île de C.,** Cyprus; *s.a.* ARBRE 2. **2.** *s.m.* Cyprian wine.

Chypriote [ʃipriɔt], *a. & s. Geog:* Cypriot(e).

chytridiales [kitridjal], *s.f.pl. Fung:* Chytridiales.

ci[1] [si], *adv.* (*a*) *A:* here; (*b*) **par-ci par-là,** here and there; **de-ci, de-là,** here and there, on all sides, in every direction; **ci-annexé,** annexed hereto; *s.a.* CE[2] 5, CECI, CELUI 4, GÉSIR.

ci[2], *dem. pron. neut. inv. A:* still used in *F:* **faire ci et ça,** to do this, that, and the other, odd jobs; **comment ça va-t-il?—comme ci, comme ça,** how are you getting on?—so so.

ci-après [siaprɛ], *adv.* here(in)after; later, further on, below (in the book, etc.); **la résolution énoncée ci-après,** the following resolution.

ci-bas [siba], *adv.* **signature apposée ci-bas,** signature affixed below.

cibiche [sibiʃ], *s.f. P:* cigarette, *P:* fag, gasper.

cible [sibl̥], *s.f.* target, mark; **tir à la c.,** target shooting, target practice; **c.-silhouette,** figure-target; **c. panoramique,** landscape-target; **c. fixe,** stationary, static, target; **c. mobile, mouvante,** moving, fleeting, target; **c. à éclipse,** disappearing, vanishing, collapsible, target; *Navy:* **c. flottante,** floating target; *Av:* **avion-c.,** target-plane; drone; **c. aérienne,** air, aerial, target; *Av: Navy: etc:* **c. remorquée,** towed target; **avion, bâtiment, remorqueur de c.,** target tug; **c.-fusée,** rocket-target; **c. télécommandée, téléguidée,** remote-controlled target; *Av:* drone; **c. à signaux automatiques,** indicator-target; **servir de c. aux railleries de qn,** to be a butt for s.o.'s jests; **son nez énorme fait de lui une c. facile pour les caricaturistes,** his enormous nose makes him a sitting target for caricaturists.

ciboire [sibwaːr], *s.m. Ecc:* pyx, ciborium.

ciborium [sibɔrjɔm], *s.m. Ecc.Arch:* ciborium, baldachin (of basilica).

ciboule [sibul], *s.f. Bot: Cu:* **1.** Welsh onion, scallion, stone-leek. **2.** spring onion.

ciboulette [sibulɛt], *s.f. Bot: Cu:* chive(s).

ciboulot [sibulo], *s.m. P:* head, *F:* noddle, nut.

cicadelles [sikadɛl], *s.f.pl.* **cicadellides** [sikadelid], *s.m.pl. Ent:* Cicadellidae, the leafhoppers.

cicadidés [sikadide], *s.m.pl. Ent:* Cicadidae (family); the crickets.

cicatrice [sikatris], *s.f.* scar; *Surg:* cicatrice (of wound, etc.); *Bot:* cicatrice; mark or scar of attachment (of leaf, fruit, etc.).

cicatriciel, -ielle [sikatrisjɛl], *a.* cicatricial (mark, etc.); **tissu c.,** scar tissue.

cicatricule [sikatrikyl], *s.f.* **1.** *Biol:* cicatricule, tread (of egg). **2.** *Bot:* (*a*) cicatric(u)le, scar; (*b*) hilum.

cicatrisant [sikatrizɑ̃]. **1.** *a.* healing, cicatrizing (lotion, etc.). **2.** *s.m.* cicatrizant.

cicatrisation [sikatrizasjɔ̃], *s.f.* cicatrization, healing, closing (up) (of wound, etc.).

cicatriser [sikatrize], *v.* to cicatrize. **1.** *v.tr.* (*a*) to heal (wound, etc.); **le temps cicatrise toutes les douleurs,** time heals all sorrows. **2.** *v.pr.* (*of wound, etc.*) to heal (up), skin over, scar over.

cicer [siseːr], *s.m. Bot:* cicer; *F:* chick-pea.

cicerelle [sisərɛl], *s.f. Ich:* Mediterranean sand-eel.

cicéro [sisero], *s.m. Typ:* pica, twelve-point type.

cicérole [siserɔl], *s.f. Bot:* cicer; *F:* chick-pea.

Cicéron [siserɔ̃], *Pr.n.m. Cl.Lit:* Cicero.

cicerone [siserɔn, tʃitʃerɔne], *s.m.,* **cicérone** [siserɔn], *s.m.* guide, cicerone; *pl. cicerones, ciceroni.*

cicéronien, -ienne [siserɔnjɛ̃, -jɛn], *a. & s. Lit:* Ciceronian.

cicéroniser [siserɔnize], *v.i.* to affect a Ciceronian style.

cichlides [siklid], **cichlidés** [siklide], *s.m.pl. Ich:* Cichlids, Cichlidæ.

cicindèle [sisɛ̃dɛl], *s.f. Ent:* cicindela, tiger-beetle.

ciconiidés [sikɔniide], *s.m.pl. Orn:* Ciconiidæ.

ciconiiformes [sikɔniifɔrm], *s.m.pl. Orn:* Ciconiiformes.

ci-contre [sikɔ̃ːtr̥], *adv.* (*a*) opposite, in the margin; *Book-k:* **porté ci-contre,** as per contra; (*b*) annexed (circular, etc.); (*c*) on the other side (of the sheet).

cicuta [sikyta], *s.f. Bot:* cicuta.

cicutaire [sikytɛːr], *s.f.* cicuta; **c. (aquatique),** water-hemlock, cowbane.

cicuté [sikyte], *a. Pharm:* containing hemlock.

cicutine [sikytin], *s.f. Pharm:* cicutoxin.

Cid [sid], *s.m. Hist: Lit:* **le Cid,** the Cid.

cidaris [sidaris]. **1.** *s.f. Hist:* cidaris. **2.** *s.m. Biol:* cidaris.

cidaridés [sidaride], *s.m.pl. Biol:* Cidaridæ.

-cide[1] [sid]. **1.** *s.suff.* -cide; (*a*) *m. & f.* (*murderer*) **parricide,** parricide; **liberticide,** liberticide; (*b*) *m.* (*killing agent*) **insecticide,** insecticide; **raticide,** rat-killer, -poison. **2.** *a.suff.* -cidal; **insecticide,** insecticidal; **liberticide,** liberticidal; **raticide,** rat-killing.

-cide[2], *s.suff.m.* -cide; **parricide,** (*crime of*) parricide; **fratricide,** fratricide.

ci-dessous [sidsu], *adv.* hereunder, below, under-mentioned; *Jur:* hereinunder.

ci-dessus [sidsy], *adv.* above(-mentioned); *Jur:* hereinabove, hereinbefore; **dans l'article ci-dessus,** in the preceding article.

ci-devant [sidvɑ̃]. **1.** *adv.* previously, formerly; *Com:* **Jones et Cie, ci-devant Brown,** Jones and Co., late Brown. **2.** *s.m. & f. inv. in pl.* (*a*) *Fr. Hist:* ci-devant, aristocrat; (*b*) *F:* old fogey, back number, has-been.

cidre [sidr̥], *s.m.* cider; **c. sec,** rough cider; **c. bouché,** champagne cider; *F:* **c. de poire,** perry.

cidrerie [sidrəri], *s.f.* **1.** cider-house. **2.** cider-making.

cidricole [sidrikɔl], *a.* cider-producing.

ciel, cieux [sjɛl, sjø], *s.m.* **1.** (*a*) sky, firmament, heaven; **carte du c.,** map of the heavens; **les oiseaux des cieux,** the fowl of the air; **à c. ouvert,** in the open air, out of doors; **agir à c. ouvert,** to act openly; **couleur bleu de c.,** sky-blue; **élever qn jusqu'au c.,** to laud s.o. to the skies; **acrobaties en plein c.,** stunts in mid-air; **Londres vu du c.,** London seen from the air; **être suspendu entre c. et terre,** to hang in mid-air; **il est toujours entre (le) c. et (la) terre,** he is always in the clouds; **le pont sauta jusqu'aux cieux,** the bridge was blown sky-high; (*b*) (*pl. often* **ciels**) climate, clime, sky; **c. doux,** mild, temperate, climate; **les ciels de l'Italie,** the skies of Italy; **vivre sous un c. étranger,** to live in foreign climes; *Art:* **les ciels de Turner,** Turner's skies; **étude de c.,** skyscape. **2.** heaven; **du c., dans le c.,** in heaven; **notre Père qui êtes aux cieux,** our Father which art, *U.S:* who art, in Heaven; **le royaume des cieux,** the Kingdom of Heaven; **gagner le c.,** to go (up) to Heaven; *F:* **tomber du c.,** (i) to come as a godsend; (ii) not to know what is going on; to look blank; **(juste) c.!** (good) heavens! heavens above! **voir les cieux ouverts,** to have a foretaste of Heaven; *F:* **il ne l'emportera pas au c.,** he won't get away with it; *s.a.* REMUER 1. **3.** (*pl.* **ciels**) (*a*) *Ecc:* baldachin, canopy, altar-roof; (*b*) *Furn:* (bed-)tester; (*c*) *Mch: etc:* crown, top, roof (of fire-box, furnace, etc.); (*d*) *Min: Mil:* roof (of quarry, of shelter, etc.); **c. protecteur, protection en c.,** overhead cover; **carrière à c. ouvert,** open(-cast) quarry; **tranchée à c. ouvert,** surface drain; **canal à c. couvert,** closed-in culvert; (*e*) *Nau:* **c. (de chalut),** square.

cierge [sjɛrʒ], *s.m.* **1.** *Ecc:* wax candle, taper; **c. pascal,** Paschal candle; **brûler un c. à un saint,** to burn a candle to a saint; *F:* **devoir à qn un beau c.,** to have reason to be grateful to s.o.; **chat avec la queue en c.,** cat with its tail in the air; *s.a.* DROIT[1]. **2.** *Bot:* (*a*) cereus; **c. géant,** giant cactus; **c. du Pérou,** great torch-thistle; (*b*) verbascum; **c. de Notre-Dame,** white mullein; **c. maudit,** Aaron's rod; **c. de nuit,** evening primrose; (*c*) euphorbia, spurge. **3. c. d'eau,** (vertical) water-jet (in fountain). **4.** *Pyr:* **c. merveilleux,** sparkler.

ciergé [sjɛrʒe], *a. Nau:* upright (mast).

cierger [sjɛrʒe], *v.tr.* **(je ciergeai(s); n. ciergeons)** *O:* to wax the edges of (piece of cloth).

cifran [sifrɑ̃], *s.m. Tail:* sleeve-board.

cigale [sigal], *s.f.* **1.** *Ent:* cicada, balm-cricket; **c. de rivière,** water-grasshopper. **2.** *Crust:* **c. de mer,** squill(-fish). **3.** *Nau:* anchor-ring, shackle; Jew's harp.

cigalon, cigalou [sigalɔ̃, sigalu], *s.m. Dial:* cicada.

cigare [sigaːr], *s.m.* **1.** cigar; *F:* weed. **2.** *P:* head, block, nut. **3.** *Fish:* artificial bait in the shape of a cigar.

cigarette [sigarɛt], *s.f.* **1.** cigarette. **2.** *Cu:* kind of sweet biscuit rolled in the shape of a cigarette.

cigaretteuse [sigarɛtøːz], *s.f.* cigarette-maker.

cigarière [sigarjɛːr], *s.f.* cigar-maker.

cigarillo [sigarijo], *s.m.* cigarillo, whiff.

ci-gisent [siʒiːz], **ci-gît** [siʒi]. *See* GÉSIR.

cigogne [sigɔɲ], *s.f.* **1.** *Orn:* (*a*) stork, white stork; *F:* (*of girl, woman*) beanpole; (*b*) **c. des serpents,** cariama. **2.** *Mch: etc:* (*a*) crank-lever; (*b*) handle, crank (of grindstone).

cigogneau, -eaux [sigɔɲo], *s.m. Orn:* young stork.

ciguë [sigy], *s.f.* **1.** *Bot:* conium, *F:* hemlock; **c. aquatique, c. vireuse,** water hemlock, water dropwort, cowbane; **petite c., c. des jardins,** fool's parsley. **2.** *Med:* hemlock (poison).

ci-inclus [siɛ̃kly], *s.* (*is usu. taken as adverbial and inv. when it precedes the noun*) **la copie ci-incluse,** the enclosed copy; **ci-inclus copie de votre lettre,** herewith a copy of your letter.

ci-joint [siʒwɛ̃], *a.* (*is usu. taken as adverbial and inv. when it precedes the noun*) attached, herewith, hereto (annexed); **les pièces ci-jointes,** the sub-joined documents; **vous trouverez ci-joint quittance,** please find receipt attached.

cil [sil], *s.m.* **1.** (eye)lash. **2.** *Nat.Hist:* cilium, hair, filament.

ciliaire [siljɛːr], *a. Anat: Nat.Hist:* ciliary; **glande c.,** lenticel; *s.a.* BLÉPHARITE.

ciliarotomie [siljarɔtɔmi], *s.f. Surg:* ciliarotomy.

ciliates [siljat], *s.m.pl. Biol:* Ciliata.

cilice [silis], *s.m.* cilice, hair-shirt, shirt of hair.

Cilicie [silisi], *Pr.n.f. Geog:* Cilicia.

cilicien, -ienne [silisjɛ̃, -jɛn], *a. & s. Geog:* Cilician.

cilié [silje], *a. Biol: Nat.Hist:* ciliate(d).

cilifère [silifɛːr], **ciligère** [siliʒɛːr], *a. Biol: Nat. Hist:* ciliferous, ciliated.

ciliforme [silifɔrm], *a.* ciliform.

ciliophores [siljɔfɔːr], *s.m.pl.* Ciliophora.

cillement [sijmɑ̃], *s.m.* nic(ti)tation, blinking.

ciller [sije]. **1.** *v.tr. & i.* (*a*) to blink; to nic(ti)tate; *abs.* **personne n'ose c. devant lui,** no one dares move an eyelid in his presence; **sans c.,** without the least flicker of emotion; without batting an eyelid; (*b*) *v.tr. Ven:* to seel (falcon, etc.). **2.** *v.i.* (*of horse*) to show signs of age (over the eyes).

cimaise [simɛːz], *s.f. Arch:* cyma, ogee moulding, dado; *Art:* **tableau pendu sur, accroché à, la c.,** picture hung on the line.

Cimbres [sɛ̃ːbr̥], *s.m.pl. Hist:* Cimbri, Cimbrians.

cimbrien, -enne [sɛ̃briɛ̃, -ɛn], *a.* = CIMBRIQUE 1.

cimbrique [sɛ̃brik], *a.* **1.** Cimbric, Cimbrian. **2.** *Ling:* Kymric, Cymric.

cime [sim], *s.f.* **1.** summit (of hill, etc.); top (of tree, mast, etc.); **arbre à c. peu développée,** small-crowned tree; **mont à double c.,** two-peaked mountain; *Carp:* **c. d'un poteau,** small end of a pole. **2.** *Bot:* cyme.

ciment [simɑ̃], *s.m.* cement; **c. Portland,** Portland cement; **c. armé,** reinforced cement or concrete; **mettre une surface en c.,** to cement a surface; **c. à prise lente, à prise rapide,** slow-setting, quick-setting, cement; **c. non broyé, non calciné,** clinker; *Path:* **gale du c.,** bricklayer's itch; *s.a.* BÉTON, CHAUX.

cimentage [simɑ̃taːʒ], *s.m. Jewel:* cementing.

cimentaire [simɑ̃tɛːr], *a.* cementing (clay).

cimentation [simɑ̃tasjɔ̃], *s.f.* **1.** *Const: etc:* cementing; injection of cement. **2.** *Min:* cementation.

cimenter [simɑ̃te], *v.tr. Const: etc:* to cement; **c. des moellons,** to cement stones together; **c. un bassin,** to render a reservoir (with cement); **c. une alliance,** to cement, consolidate, an alliance.

cimenterie [simɑ̃tri], *s.f.* cement factory.

cimentier [simɑ̃tje], *s.m. & a.* (*a*) cement-manufacturer; (*b*) worker in cement.

cimeterre [simtɛːr], *s.m.* scimitar.

cimetière [simtjɛːr], *s.m.* (*a*) cemetery, graveyard, burial-ground; *occ.* churchyard, God's-acre; (*b*) garden of remembrance (of crematorium); (*c*) **c. de voitures,** graveyard for cars.

cimicaire [simikɛːr], *s.f. Bot:* cimicifuga, bugbane, bugwort.

cimi(ci)cide [simi(si)sid], *a.* bug-destroying (powder, etc.).

cimicidés [simiside], *s.m.pl. Ent:* Cimicidæ.

cimicifuge [simisifyːʒ]. **1.** *a.* bug-expelling (process, etc.). **2.** *s.m. Bot:* cimicifuga, bugbane, bugwort.

cimier[1] [simje], *s.m.* crest (of helmet); *Her:* crest.

cimier[2], *s.m.* haunch (of venison); rump, buttock (of beef).

ciminite [siminit], *s.f. Miner:* ciminite.

cimmérien, -ienne [sim(m)erjɛ̃, -jɛn], *a. & s. Hist:* Cimmerian; *F:* **ténèbres cimmériennes,** Cimmerian darkness.

cimolite [simɔlit], *s.f. Miner:* cimolite.

cinabre [sinabr̥], *s.m.* (*a*) *Miner: Ch: etc:* cinnabar, red mercuric sulphide; (*b*) *Art: etc:* vermilion.

cincenelle [sɛ̃snɛl], *s.f. Nau:* tow-rope, tow-line.

cinchoméronique [sɛ̃komerɔnik], *a. Ch:* **acide c.,** cinchomeronic acid.

cinchona [sɛ̃kɔna], *s.m. Bot: Ch:* cinchona.

cinchonine [sɛ̃kɔnin], *s.f. Ch:* cinchonia, cinchonin(e).

cinchonique [sɛ̃kɔnik], *a. Ch:* cinchonic, quinic (acid).

cinchophène [sɛ̃kɔfɛn], *s.m. Pharm:* cinchophen.

cincle [sɛ̃ːkl̥], *s.m. Orn:* cinclus; **c. (plongeur),** water-ouzel, dipper.

ciné [sine], *s.m. F: A:* = CINÉMA.

ciné-actualités [sineaktɥalite], *O:* news theatre; *pl. ciné-actualités.*

cinéaste [sineast], *s.m. Cin:* (*a*) person who works in the cinema world; (*b*) film director; (*c*) scenario-writer.

ciné-club [sineklœb], *s.m.* film club, cine-club; *pl. ciné-clubs.*

ciné-comédie [sinekɔmedi], *s.f.* comedy film; *pl. ciné-comédies.*

cinéfier [sinefje], *v.tr.* (*pr. sub. & p.d.* **n. cinéfiions, v. cinéfiiez**) to incinerate, to reduce (body, etc.) to ashes.

cinégramme [sinegram], *s.m. T.V:* kinescope.

cinégraphie [sinegrafi], *s.f.* cinematography.

cinégraphique [sinegrafik], *a.* cinematographic.

cinégraphiste [sinegrafist], *s.m. A: Cin:* scenario-writer.

ciné-journal [sineʒurnal], *s.m. not used in pl.* news-reel.

cinelle [sinɛl], *s.f. Bot:* oak-gall; *F:* oak-apple.

cinéma [sinema], *s.m.* cinema. **1.** pictures, *U.S:* movies; **faire du c.,** to act for the films; to be a cinema actor, *U.S:* a movie actor; **gens qui font du c.,** film people; *F:* people who are in films; **critique de c.,** film critic; **acteur, actrice, de c., artiste de c.,** film actor, film actress; **c. muet,** silent films; **c. parlant, c. sonore,** talking films, sound films; **industrie du c.,** film industry; **amateur de c., client, habitué des salles de c.,** film goer; **engoué, entiché du c.; fanatique,** *F:* **fana, mordu de c.,** film fan; *F:* **tout ca, c'est du c.,** that's all baloney; **c'est du c.,** it's all an act. **2.** (*theatre*) cinema.

cinémascope [sinemaskɔp], *s.m. R.t.m:* cinemascope.

cinémathèque [sinematɛk], *s.f.* **1.** *A:* film-tin, -box. **2.** film-store or library.

cinématique [sinematik]. **1.** *a.* (*a*) *Mec:* kinematic(al); (*b*) *Surg:* **amputation c.,** cineplasty. **2.** *s.f.* kinematics.

cinématiquement [sinematikmɑ̃], *adv.* kinematically.

cinématisation [sinematizasjɔ̃], *s.f. Surg:* cineplastics.

cinématographe [sinematɔgraf], *s.m.* (*a*) cinematograph, projector; (*b*) *A:* cinema, films; **c. sonore,** sound films.

cinématographie [sinematɔgrafi], *s.f.* cinematography.

cinématographier [sinematɔgrafje], *v.tr.* (*pr.sub. & p.d.* **n. cinématographiions, v. cinématographiiez**) to film.

cinématographique [sinematɔgrafik], *a.* cinematographic; cinematic; film (production, etc.); **droits d'adaptation c.,** film rights.

cinématographiquement [sinematɔgrafikmɑ̃], *adv.* cinematographically.

cinémitrailleuse [sinemitrajøːz], *s.f.* camera-gun; ciné-gun; camera machine-gun.

cinémomètre [sinemɔmɛtr̥], *s.m. Mec.E:* tachometer, speedometer.

cinéphile [sinefil], *s.m. & f.* film enthusiast.

cinéprojecteur [sineprɔʒɛktœːr], *s.m. O:* cinematograph projector, (film) projecting apparatus.

cinéraire [sinerɛːr]. **1.** *a.* cinerary (urn, etc.). **2.** *s.m. Archeol:* cinerarium. **3.** *s.f. Bot:* cineraria.

cinérama [sinerama], *s.m. R.t.m:* cinerama.

cinération [sinerasjɔ̃], *s.f.* = INCINÉRATION.

cinérite [sinerit], *s.f. Geol:* ash tuff, vitric tuff.

cinéritique [sineritik], *a.* cinereous.

ciné(-)roman [sinerɔmɑ̃], *s.m.* **1.** film story. **2.** *A:* serial film; *pl. ciné-romans.*

cinéscope [cineskɔp], *s.m. T.V:* kinescope.

cinésialgie [sinezjalʒi], *s.f. Med:* kinesalgia.

cinésithérapeute [sineziterapøt], *s.m. & f.* kinesipath(ist).

cinésithérapie [sineziterapi], *s.f.* kinesitherapy.

cinesthésique [sinɛstezik], *a.* kinesthetic, kinesic.

cinétique [sinetik]. **1.** *a.* kinetic, motive (energy, etc.); **art c.,** kinetic art; **échauffement c.,** aerodynamic heating; *s.a.* MOMENT. **2.** *s.f.* kinetics.

cinétiquement [sinetikmɑ̃], *adv.* kinetically.

cinétochore [sinetɔkɔːr], *s.m. Biol:* kinetochore.

cinétogenèse [sinetɔʒənɛːz], *s.f. Biol:* kinetogenesis.

cing(h)alais, -aise [sɛ̃galɛ, -ɛːz]. **1.** *a. & s. Geog:* Sin(g)halese. **2.** *s.m. Ling:* Sin(g)halese.

cinglage[1] [sɛ̃glaːʒ], *s.m. Nau: O:* (*a*) sailing; (*b*) (ship's) run, sailing (in twenty-four hours); day's run.

cinglage[2], *s.m. Metall:* shingling.

cinglant [sɛ̃glɑ̃], *a.* lashing (rain, etc.); cutting, biting (wind, etc.); bitter (cold); stinging, cutting (rejoinder); slashing (criticism); **il sait être très c.,** he can be very scathing.

cinglé [sɛ̃gle], *a. P:* cracked, daft; *P:* **il est complètement c.,** he's nuts, crackers.

cinglement [sɛ̃gləmɑ̃], *s.m.* lashing (with or of whip, etc.); stinging, biting (of cold).

cingler[1] [sɛ̃gle], *v.i. Nau: O:* (*a*) to sail (before the wind), to scud along; (*b*) to steer a given course.

cingler[2], *v.tr.* **1.** (*a*) to lash, cut (horse, etc.) with a whip; **la grêle lui cinglait le visage,** the hail stung his face; *abs.* **le vent, la pluie, cingle,** it is a cutting, biting, wind, a slashing rain; **le froid cinglait,** it was bitterly cold; **langue qui cingle,** tongue like a whiplash, lashing, scathing, tongue; **cette réponse lui cingla le sang,** this answer sent the blood rushing through him; (*b*) *Carp:* to line out (board, etc.). **2.** *Metall:* to shingle, forge (bloom); *s.a.* MACHINE 1, PRESSE 1.

cingleur [sɛ̃glœːr], *s.m. Metall:* **1.** shingler, squeezer-man. **2. c. (rotatif),** shingling roller, squeezer.

cingleuse [sɛ̃gløːz], *s.f. Metall:* shingling machine, shingler, squeezer.

cinglon [sɛ̃glɔ̃], *s.m.* (*a*) lash (given with whip, etc.); cut; (*b*) stinging, cutting, remark.

cinglure [sɛ̃glyːr], *s.f.* sting, smart (of lash, insult, etc.).

cini [sini], *s.m. Orn:* serin.

cinnamate [sinnamat], *s.m. Ch:* cinnamate.

cinname [sinnam], *s.m. Bot:* = CINNAMOME.

cinnamique [sinnamik], *a. Ch:* cinnamic (acid); **aldéhyde c.,** cinnamaldehyde.

cinnamome [sinnamɔm], *s.m. Bot:* cinnamomum.

cinnamyle [sinnamil], *s.m. Ch:* cinnamyl.

cinnoline [sinnɔlin], *s.f. Ch:* cinnoline.

cinosternon [sinɔstɛrnɔ̃], *s.m. Rept:* kinosternon.

cinq [sɛ̃ːk], *num.a.inv. & s.m.inv.* (*as card. a. before a noun or adj. beginning with a consonant sound* [sɛ̃], *otherwise* [sɛ̃(ː)k]) five; (*a*) **c. (petits) garçons** [sɛ̃ (pti) garsɔ̃], five (little) boys; **c. hommes** [sɛ̃kɔm], five men; **j'en ai c.** [sɛ̃ːk], I have five; **Henri V.,** Henry the Fifth; **le c. mars** [sɛ̃(k)mars], March the fifth; **page c.,** page five; **au chapitre c. de . . .,** in the fifth chapter of . . .; **il est arrivé c. ou sixième,** he arrived fifth or sixth; **cinquante-cinq s'écrit avec deux c.,** fifty-five is represented by two fives; **c. pour cent,** five per cent; **le c. de cœur,** the five of hearts; **c. et trois font huit,** five and three are eight; *F:* **faire c. et trois font huit,** to limp; *F:* to dot and carry one; **il était moins c.,** it was a near thing, a close shave; **le mot de c. lettres** = MERDE *q.v.*; **je lui ai répondu en c. lettres,** (*i.e.* I said "*merde*" to him), I told him to go to blazes, to go to hell; *s.a.* COMPTER 1, SEC I. 2 (*e*); (*b*) (*in dicing*) cinque.

cinq-à-sept [sɛ̃kasɛt], *s.m.inv. F:* reception, party (from 5 p.m. to 7 p.m.).

cinqcentiste [sɛ̃(k)sɑ̃tist], *a. & s.m. & f. Art: Lit:* cinquecentist.

cinq-feuilles [sɛ̃fœj], *s.m.inv. Arch: etc:* cinq(ue)-foil.

cinq-mâts [sɛ̃(k)mɑ], *s.m. Nau:* five-master.

cinq-quatre [sɛ̃katr̥], *s.m.inv. Mus:* five four time.

cinq-six [sɛ̃ksis], *s.m.* brandy 10% above proof.

cinquain [sɛ̃kɛ̃], *s.m. Mil: Hist:* cinquain.

cinquantaine [sɛ̃kɑ̃tɛn], *s.f.* (approximate) fifty; **une c. de personnes,** about, some, fifty people; **une c. de francs,** fifty francs or so; **atteindre la c.,** to reach the age of fifty; **approcher de la c.,** to be getting on for fifty; **avoir passé la c.,** to be in the fifties; *A:* **célébrer la c.,** to celebrate one's golden wedding, one's jubilee.

cinquante [sɛ̃kɑ̃ːt], *num.a.inv. & s.m.inv.* fifty; **billet de c. francs,** fifty-franc note; **page c.,** page fifty; **au chapitre c. de . . .,** in the fiftieth chapter of . . .; **demeurer au numéro c.,** to live at number fifty; **les années c.,** the fifties (1950-1959).

cinquantenaire [sɛ̃kɑ̃tnɛːr]. **1.** *s.m.* fiftieth anniversary, jubilee. **2.** *a.* fifty years old.

cinquantième [sɛ̃kɑ̃tjɛm]. **1.** *num.a. & s.* fiftieth. **2.** *s.m.* fiftieth (part).

cinquécentiste [sɛ̃kesɑ̃tist], *a. & s.m. & f. Art: Lit:* cinquecentist.

Cinque Ports (les) [lesɛ̃(k)pɔːr], *Pr.n.m.pl. Eng. Hist:* the Cinque Ports.

cinquième [sɛ̃kjɛm]. **1.** *num. a. & s.m. & f.* fifth; **loger au c.,** to live on the fifth floor, *U.S:* the sixth floor. **2.** *s.m.* fifth (part); **quatre cinquièmes,** four fifths. **3.** *s.f. Sch:* **(classe de) c.,** (approx.) =) second form (of secondary school).

cinquièmement [sɛ̃kjɛmmɑ̃], *adv.* fifthly, in the fifth place.

cintrage [sɛ̃traːʒ], *s.m.* **1.** bend(ing), deflection (of sheet-iron, pipes, etc.). **2.** centering (of arches). **3.** *Nau:* = CEINTRAGE 1.

cintre [sɛ̃ːtr̥], *s.m.* **1.** curve, bend (of armour-plating of ship, etc.); **c. de charron,** wheel-wright's mould, gauge. **2.** *Arch:* (*a*) arch (of tunnel, etc.); (*b*) soffit (of arch); **arc (en) plein c.,** semicircular arch. **3.** *Const:* centre, centering, truss, template (for arch). **4.** *Cy:* bend (of handle-bar). **5.** *Dom.Ec:* dress-, coat-hanger. **6.** *Mec.E:* bow-piece (for bending machine). **7.** *Th:* rigging loft (above stage); **les cintres,** the flies; **loges du c.,** highest tier of boxes.

cintré [sɛ̃tre], *a.* (*a*) arched (window, etc.); **toit c.,** barrel-roof; (*b*) bent, curved (timber, crank, etc.); **tuyau c.,** angle-pipe; (*c*) **manteau c.,** fitted coat; **taille cintrée,** nipped-in waist; *Dressm:* **robe mi-cintrée,** semi-fitting dress; (*d*) *F:* **il est complètement c.,** he's nuts, crackers.

cintrement [sɛ̃trəmɑ̃], *s.m.* **1.** *Const:* centering (of arches). **2.** cambering (of timber). **3.** sagging (of beam, etc.).

cintrer [sɛ̃tre]. **1.** *v.tr.* (*a*) to bend, curve, (bar, pipe, rail, etc.) to the desired shape; to camber (timber); **latte cintrée à la vapeur,** steam-bent lath; *Metalw:* **presse à c.,** bending-press; **machine à c.,** bulldozer; pipe-bending machine; (*b*) to arch (window); (*c*) to take in (jacket, etc.) at the waist; (*d*) *Const:* to centre (arch); (*e*) *Nau:* = CEINTRER 1. **2.** *v.i.* (*of line of troops, beam, etc.*) to sag; (*of furnace tube, etc.*) to hog.

cintreur [sɛ̃trœːr], *s.m. Metall: etc:* bender.

cintreuse [sɛ̃trøːz], *s.f. Metall: etc:* bending machine, bender.

cionite [sjɔnit], *s.f. Med:* cionitis.

cionotome [sjɔnɔtoːm], *s.m. Surg:* cionotome.

ciotaden, -enne [sjɔtadɛ̃, -ɛn], *a. & s. Geog:* (native, inhabitant) of La Ciotat.

ciota(t) [sjɔta], *s.m.*, **cioutat** [sjuta], *s.m. Vit:* chasselas.

cipahi, cipaïe [sipai], *s.m.* = CIPAYE.

cipal, -aux [sipal, -o], *s.m. P: A:* municipal guard (of Paris).

cipaye [sipa:j], *a. & s.m.* sepoy; **la révolte des cipayes,** the Indian Mutiny.

cipolin [sipɔlɛ̃], *a. & s.m.* cipolin (marble), onion marble.

cippe [sip], *s.m. Arch: Archeol:* cippus.

cirage [sira:ʒ], *s.m.* **1.** (*a*) waxing, polishing (of floors, etc.); **c. du fil,** waxing of thread; **c. de chaussures,** polishing of shoes; (*b*) *Art:* **tableau de c.,** yellow camaieu, yellow monochrome. **2.** (*a*) wax polish; (*b*) shoe polish; (*c*) **être dans le c.,** (i) *Av: F:* to be flying blind; (ii) *F:* to be completely at sea; (iii) *P:* to be drunk, to have passed out. **3.** *Nau:* (suit of) oilskins.

circadien [sirkadjɛ̃], *a. Biol:* circadian; **rythme c.,** circadian rhythm.

circaète [sirkaɛt], *s.m. Orn:* circaëtus; **c. Jean-le-blanc,** short-toed eagle.

Circassie [sirkasi], *Pr.n.f. A.Geog:* Circassia.

circassien, -ienne [sirkasjɛ̃, -jɛn]. **1.** *a. & s. Geog:* Circassian. **2.** *s.f. Tex:* **circassienne,** circassian, circassienne. **3.** *s.m.* circus enthusiast, fan.

Circé [sirse], *Pr.n.f. Gr.Lit:* Circe.

circée [sirse], *s.f. Bot:* circaea, enchanter's nightshade.

circinal, -aux [sirsinal, -o], *a. Nat.Hist:* circinate, circinal, gyrate.

circiné [sirsine], *a.* **1.** *Bot:* circinate, circinal. **2.** *Med:* **herpès c.,** ringworm.

circlip [sirklip], *s.m. Av:* circlip.

circompolaire [sirkɔ̃pɔlɛ:r], *a.* circumpolar.

circon- [sirkɔ̃], *pref.* circum-; **circonvolant,** circumvolant.

circoncire [sirkɔ̃si:r], *v.tr.* (*pr.p.* **circoncisant;** *p.p.* **circoncis;** *pr.ind.* **je circoncis, n. circoncisons;** *pr.sub.* **je circoncise;** *p.h.* **je circoncis;** *fu.* **je circoncirai**) **1.** to circumcise. **2.** to ring (fruit tree).

circoncis [sirkɔ̃si]. **1.** *a. & s.m.* circumcised (person). **2.** *a. Bot:* circumscissile (dehiscence).

circoncision [sirkɔ̃sizjɔ̃], *s.f.* **1.** circumcision. **2.** *Arb:* ringing (of fruit trees).

circonférence [sirkɔ̃ferɑ̃:s], *s.f.* **1.** (*a*) circumference (of circle, ellipse, sphere); **la tour a trente mètres de c.,** the tower is thirty metres in circumference; (*b*) girth (of tree); (*c*) felloe (of wheel). **2.** (*a*) perimeter, boundaries (of town, etc.); (*b*) outer surface.

circonférentiel, -ielle [sirkɔ̃ferɑ̃sjɛl], *a.* circumferential; outer.

circonflexe [sirkɔ̃flɛks], *a.* circumflex (accent, nerve); *s.* **un c.,** a circumflex accent.

circonjacent [sirkɔ̃ʒasɑ̃], *a.* circumjacent, surrounding (region).

circonlocution [sirkɔ̃lɔkysjɔ̃], *s.f.* circumlocution; **parler par circonlocutions,** to speak in a roundabout way; *F:* to beat about the bush; **après de longues circonlocutions,** after much beating about the bush.

circonscriptible [sirkɔ̃skriptibl], *a.* circumscribable.

circonscription [sirkɔ̃skripsjɔ̃], *s.f.* **1.** circumscription, circumscribing; **c. d'un cercle à un triangle,** circumscribing of a circle about a triangle. **2.** *Adm: etc:* division, district, area; **c. électorale,** electoral district; electoral ward; parliamentary division, constituency; **c. de remise gratuite,** radius of free delivery (of telegrams, etc.).

circonscrire [sirkɔ̃skri:r], *v.tr.* (*pr.p.* **circonscrivant;** *p.p.* **circonscrit;** *pr.ind.* **je circonscris, n. circonscrivons;** *p.d.* **je circonscrivais;** *p.h.* **je circonscrivis;** *fu.* **je circonscrirai**) to circumscribe. **1.** to draw a line round (sth.); **c. un cercle à un polygone,** to describe a circle about a polygon. **2.** to surround, encircle (**par,** with, by); **la ville est circonscrite par des fortifications,** the town is encircled with fortifications. **3.** to limit, bound; **c. son sujet,** to define the scope of one's subject; *El.E:* **c. un dérangement,** to locate a fault; **c. un incendie,** to bring a fire under control.

se circonscrire, to be bounded, limited; to centre; **tout le débat se circonscrit autour d'une seule idée,** the whole debate centres on one idea, round one idea.

circonscrit [sirkɔ̃skri], *a.* circumscribed. **1.** *Geom:* **courbe circonscrite à un polygone,** curve circumscribed to, about, described about, a polygon. **2.** limited, restricted (space, outlook, etc.).

circonspect [sirkɔ̃spɛ, -spɛk, -spɛkt], *a.* circumspect, prudent, cautious, wary, guarded.

circonspectement [sirkɔ̃spɛktəmɑ̃], *adv.* (*rare*) circumspectly, cautiously, warily, guardedly.

circonspection [sirkɔ̃spɛksjɔ̃], *s.f.* circumspection, circumspectness, caution, wariness, *Scot:* canniness; **avec c.,** circumspectly, warily, cautiously; *Scot:* cannily; **sans c.,** heedless(ly), incautious(ly).

circonstance [sirkɔ̃stɑ̃:s], *s.f.* **1.** circumstance, incident, event, case, occasion; **dans cette c.,** (i) in this instance; (ii) in this emergency; **en pareille c.,** under such circumstances, in such a case; **à la hauteur des circonstances,** equal to the occasion; **quand les circonstances le demandent,** as occasion requires; **eu égard aux circonstances,** all things considered, *Jur:* **circonstances aggravantes, atténuantes,** aggravating, extenuating circumstances, **selon les circonstances,** as the case may be, may require; **profiter de la c.,** to make the most of the opportunity; **l'homme de la c.,** the very man we want; **de c.,** (play, etc.) for the occasion; **vers de c.,** occasional verse; **loi de c.,** law made for the occasion; **mot de c.,** nonce word, word coined for the occasion; **paroles de c.,** words suited to the occasion; **il a toujours le mot de c.,** he always says the right thing; **faire une toilette de c.,** to dress suitably for the occasion, appropriately; **soldat de c.,** temporary soldier. **2.** *Jur:* **circonstances et dépendances,** appurtenances.

circonstancié [sirkɔ̃stɑ̃sje], *a.* circumstantial, detailed (account).

circonstanciel, -ielle [sirkɔ̃stɑ̃sjɛl], *a.* circumstantial; **supériorité circonstancielle,** superiority due to circumstances; **des mesures rigoureusement circonstantielles,** measures strictly due to the emergency, to exceptional circumstances; *Gram:* **complément c.,** adverbial complement.

circonstancier [sirkɔ̃stɑ̃sje], *v.tr.* (*p.d. & pr.sub.* **n. circonstanciions, v. circonstanciiez**), to give a circumstantial account, full details, of (affair, etc.).

circonvallation [sirkɔ̃valasjɔ̃], *s.f.* circumvallation.

circonvenir [sirkɔ̃vni:r], *v.tr.* (*conj. like* VENIR) **1.** to circumvent, thwart (s.o., a plan); to outwit (s.o.); *F:* to steal a march on (s.o.), to be more than a match for (s.o.). **2.** *A:* to impose on (s.o.).

circonvention [sirkɔ̃vɑ̃sjɔ̃], *s.f.* circumvention, fraud, imposture.

circonvenu [sirkɔ̃vny], *a.* circumvented, thwarted.

circonvoisin [sirkɔ̃vwazɛ̃], *a.* surrounding, neighbouring (district, etc.).

circonvolutif, -ive [sirkɔ̃vɔlytif, -i:v], *a. Anat:* convolutionary; convoluted.

circonvolution [sirkɔ̃vɔlysjɔ̃], *s.f. Anat: Arch:* convolution; *Arch:* circumvolution (of volute, etc.); **les circonvolutions cérébrales, intestinales,** the convolutions of the cerebrum, of the intestines; **parler en usant de circonvolutions,** to speak round one's subject, to fail to come to the point.

circonvolutionnaire [sirkɔ̃vɔlysjɔnɛ:r], *a.* convoluted.

circuit [sirkɥi], *s.m.* circuit. **1.** (*a*) circumference, compass (of town, etc.); **avoir quatre kilomètres de c.,** to be four kilometres round, in circumference; (*b*) *Sp:* round, lap; **boucler le c. en cinq minutes,** to do the lap in five minutes; *Fr.C:* (*basket ball*) **coup de c.,** home run; (*c*) *Sp:* circuit (for motor racing, air race, etc.); (*toy*) **c. automobile,** road racing set; (*d*) **c. touristique,** organized tour; (*e*) **les circuits commerciaux,** commercial, trading, channels; *F:* **être dans le c.,** to be in the same line of business; **enlever des capitaux à leur c. naturel,** to withdraw capital from its natural channels of circulation. **2.** deviation, indirect course, circuitous route; *Av:* **c. d'attente,** holding pattern. **3.** (*a*) *El:* **en c.,** in circuit, connected, switched on; **mettre en c.,** to connect, to switch on; **couper le c.,** to switch off; **rétablir le c.,** to switch on (again); **mise en c.,** connecting (up); **hors c.,** out of circuit, disconnected, switched off, off-circuit; **mettre (une lampe, etc.) hors c.,** to switch (a lamp, etc.) off; **mettre une ligne en court c.,** to short-circuit a line; **mettre l'accu hors c.,** to cut out the battery; **mise hors c.,** disconnecting; **c. fermé,** closed, complete, circuit; **c. ouvert,** open, broken, circuit; **c. sous tension,** live circuit; **c. total,** full circuit; **c. unifilaire,** single-wire circuit; **c. bifilaire,** loop-circuit; metallic circuit; **c. anodique, c. de plaque,** anode, plate, circuit; **c. bouchon,** tank circuit; **c. fantôme,** phantom circuit; **c. en dérivation,** shunt circuit; **c. passe-bande,** band-pass circuit; **c. en parallèle,** parallel circuit; **c. en série,** series circuit; **c. d'entrée,** input circuit; **c. de sortie,** output circuit; **c. de charge,** load circuit; **c. de départ,** outgoing circuit; **c. à action en retour, c. à réaction, c. à rétroaction,** feedback circuit; **c. de retour,** return circuit; **c. mis à la terre, à la masse,** earthed, grounded, circuit; **c. de retour par la terre,** earth-return, ground-return, circuit; **c. de la terre,** earth, ground, circuit; **c. sans retour à la terre,** unearthed circuit; **c. magnétique,** magnetic circuit; *s.a.* DEPART 2 (*a*); *Rail:* **c. de retour par la voie, par les essieux,** track-return, axle-return, circuit; (*b*) *Tp:* **c. interurbain, c. entre centraux,** trunk circuit; **c. auxiliaire,** ancillary, auxiliary, circuit; **c. intermédiaire,** transfer circuit; **c. supplémentaire,** superposed circuit; **c. de transit,** through circuit; **c. spécialisé,** unidirectional, one-way, circuit; **c. exploité dans les deux sens,** two-way circuit; **c. de service,** order-wire circuit; **c. privé,** tie-trunk; **c. de fiche,** cord circuit; *T.V:* **télévision à c. fermé,** closed-circuit television; (*c*) *Elcs:* **c. de balayage,** sweep(ing) circuit; **c. de silence,** squelch (circuit); *Elcs: Tp:* **c. brouilleur,** scrambler; **c. de doublage, de secours,** backup circuit; *W.Tel:* **c. imprimé,** printed, sprayed, circuit; **c. métallique imprimé,** printed-foil circuit; *Computers:* **c. intégrateur,** integrating, differentiating circuit. **4.** *Ph:* **c. fermé, ouvert,** closed, open, cycle; **c. à vide,** vacuum line. **5.** (*a*) *Civ.E: Mch:* **c. d'air,** air-flow (system); **c. d'alimentation,** supply circuit, feeding system; *Min:* **c. d'aérage,** ventilation circuit; *I.C.E:* **c. à deux carburants,** bi-fuel system; **c. de refroidissement,** cooling system; (*b*) *Rail:* **c. d'ouverture des signaux,** clearing circuit.

circulaire [sirkylɛ:r]. **1.** *a.* (*a*) circular (line, movement, letter, etc.); **billet c.,** (i) tourist ticket; (ii) *Com:* circular note; **promener un regard c. sur la salle,** to cast one's eye round the room, to sweep the room with a glance; (*b*) *Tchn: Carp:* **scie c.,** circular saw; *Const:* **brique c.,** compass brick; *Mch:* **soupape c.,** mushroom valve; *Mec.E:* **mouvement c.,** (i) rotary motion; (ii) rocking motion; *El.E:* **aimant c.,** ring magnet; (*c*) *Mth:* circular (function); **permutations circulaires,** cyclic permutations. **2.** *s.f.* (*a*) *Adm: Com: etc:* circular (letter); (administrative) memorandum; service instruction; (*b*) *Artil:* **c. de tir,** racer; base-ring, swivel-ring; **c. dentée,** cog-racer.

circulairement [sirkylɛrmɑ̃], *adv.* circularly, in a circle.

circulant [sirkylɑ̃], *a.* circulating (library, etc.); *Fin:* **billets circulants,** notes in circulation.

circularité [sirkylarite], *s.f.* circularity.

circulateur [sirkylatœ:r], *s.m.* accelerator pump (for central heating system, etc.).

circulation [sirkylasjɔ̃], *s.f.* **1.** circulation (of air, water, blood, news, etc.); *Physiol:* **c. générale,** systemic circulation; **c. pulmonaire,** pulmonary circulation; **troubles de la c.,** circulatory troubles; *Civ.E:* **c. par gravité,** gravity circulation; **c. par pompe,** pump circulation; **c. sous pression,** force-feed circulation; **mettre un livre en c.,** to put a book into circulation, to circulate a book; **retirer un livre de la c.,** to withdraw a book from circulation, to call in a book; **mettre un bruit en c.,** to set a rumour afloat, afoot; to circulate a rumour. **2.** traffic; **c. diurne, nocturne,** day, night, traffic; **c. aérienne,** air traffic; **courant, débit de la c.,** traffic flow; **c. à sens unique, à deux sens,** one-way, two-way, traffic; **c. en sens inverse,** traffic in the opposite direction; **livrer, ouvrir une route à la c.,** to open a road to traffic; **route à grande c.,** main (traffic) road; busy road; **route à simple courant, à une voie, de c.,** one-lane, one-stream, road; **route à double courant, à deux voies, de c.,** two-lane, two-stream, double-track, road; **route à c. libre,** open road; **route à c. réglementée,** supervised road; **régulation de la c.,** traffic control; *Mil:* **bureau des mouvements et de la c.,** traffic head-quarters; **feux, signaux, de c.,** traffic-lights, traffic-signs; *P.N:* **c. interdite,** no thoroughfare; **dévier la c.,** to divert the traffic; **arrêt de c.,** traffic block; **accident de la c.,** road accident; **technique de la c. (routière),** traffic engineering; **technicien de la c. (routière),** traffic engineer. **3.** *Rail:* **c. des trains,** running, working, of trains; **c. à voie unique, à double voie,** single-line, double-line, working; **c. à voie ouverte, à voie fermée,** permissive, absolute, block-signal system. **4.** (*a*) *Fin:* currency, circulation (of bank-notes, etc.); (*b*) *Adm:* **droit de c.,** tax on the transport of alcoholic drinks; *s.a.* MISE 1. **5.** *Pol.Ec:* **libre c. des travailleurs,** free movement of workers.

circulatoire [sirkylatwa:r], *a. Anat:* circulatory; **l'appareil c.,** the circulatory system.

circuler [sirkyle], *v.i.* **1.** (*of blood, air, electric current, etc.*) to circulate, flow; **dans ses veines circule un feu dévorant,** a consuming fire runs, flows, in his veins; **faire c. l'air,** to circulate the air; **faire c. la bouteille,** to pass the bottle round, to hand round the bottle. **2.** to circulate, move about; *Fin:* (*of currency*) to be in circulation; *P.N:* **défense de c. sur l'herbe!** please keep off the grass! **"Circulez!"** "move on! keep moving! pass along!" **M. X a été renversé en circulant à bicyclette,** Mr X was knocked down while riding a bicycle; **les autobus circulent jour et nuit,** the buses run day and night; **il circule beaucoup de fausses pièces,** many false coins are in circulation; **des bruits circulent,** rumours are afloat, are going about, are going round, are circulating, are in the air; **faire c. une nouvelle,** to circulate a piece of news; *Com:* **faire c. des effets,** to keep bills afloat.

circum- [sirkɔm], *pref.* circum-; **circumsolaire,** circumsolar; **circumterrestre,** circumterrestrial; **circumzénithal,** circumzenithal.

circumduction [sirkɔmdyksjɔ̃], *s.f. Physiol:* circumduction.

circumlunaire [sirkɔmlynɛːr], *a.* circumlunar.

circumméridien, -ienne [sirkɔmmeridjɛ̃, -jɛn], *a.* **1.** *Astr:* circummeridian. **2.** *s.f. Nau: Surv:* **prendre plusieurs circumméridiennes,** to take several exmeridians.

circumnavigateur [sirkɔmnavigatœr], *s.m.* circumnavigator.

circumnavigation [sirkɔmnavigasjɔ̃], *s.f.* circumnavigation; **voyage de c.,** voyage round the world.

circumnaviguer [sirkɔmnavige], *v.tr.* to circumnavigate.

circumnutation [sirkɔmnytasjɔ̃], *s.f. Bot:* circumnutation.

circumpolaire [sirkɔmpɔlɛːr], *a.* = CIRCOMPOLAIRE.

circumterrestre [sirkɔmtɛrɛstr̥], *a.* circumterrestrial.

circumzénithal, -aux [sirkɔmzenital, -o], *a. Astr:* circumzenithal.

cire [siːr], *s.f.* **1.** wax; **c. d'abeilles,** beeswax; **c. vierge,** virgin wax; **c. microcristalline,** petroleum ceresin; **c. à cacheter, d'Espagne,** sealing wax; **c. grasse,** cobbler's wax; *Ecc:* **une c.,** a taper; *Art:* **fonte à c. perdue,** cire perdue casting, lost wax process; **caractère de c.,** pliable, easily moulded, character; *s.a.* ARBRE 2, MOULAGE² 1. **2.** *Orn:* cere (of beak).

ciré [sire]. **1.** *a.* waxed, polished; **toile cirée,** oilcloth, American cloth. **2.** *s.m. Nau:* (suit of) oilskins.

cirement [sirmɑ̃], *s.m.* waxing (of thread, etc.); wax polishing (of floor, etc.).

cirer [sire], *v.tr.* to wax (thread, etc.); to polish, to wax (floors, etc.); **c. des chaussures,** to polish shoes; *F:* **c. les bottes à qn,** to lick s.o.'s boots; *Tex:* **c. du drap,** to waterproof cloth.

cireur, -euse¹ [sirœːr, -øːz]. **1.** *s.* (*pers.*) polisher. **2.** *s.m.* **c. de bottes,** shoeblack. **3.** *s.f.* **cireuse,** (*machine*) (electric) polisher.

cireux, -euse² [sirø, -øːz], *a.* waxy; **pommes de terre cireuses,** waxy, soapy, potatoes; **visage c.,** pasty face; *Med:* **dégénérescence cireuse,** waxy degeneration.

cirier, -ière [sirje, -jɛːr]. **1.** *a.* wax-producing, wax-(tree, bee, etc.). **2.** *s.m.* (*a*) wax chandler, wax-taper maker; worker in wax; (*b*) *Hist:* **C. de la grande chancellerie,** chafewax, chaffwax; (*c*) *Bot:* wax-myrtle, candleberry-tree, *U.S:* bayberry. **3.** *s.f.* **cirière,** (*a*) wax-making bee; (*b*) candle-seller (in church).

ciron [sirɔ̃], *s.m. Arach:* (cheese-, sugar-, itch-) mite.

cirque [sirk], *s.m.* **1.** circus, amphitheatre. **2.** *Geol:* cirque, amphitheatre (of mountains); corrie; cwm.

cirral, -aux [sirral, -o], *a. Bot:* cirr(h)ose, cirr(h)ous.

cirratule [sirratyl], *s.m. Ann:* cirratulus.

cirr(h)e [siːr], *s.m.* **1.** *Bot:* cirrus, tendril. **2.** *Ich:* barbel. **3.** *Z:* tentacle.

cirré [sir(r)e], *a.* cirrate, cirriferous (antenna); tendrilled (plant).

cirreux, -euse [sir(r)ø, -øːz], *a.* cirrous, cirrate, (leaf, etc.); barbellate (fish); tentacled (animal).

cirrhal, -aux [sirral, -o], *a. Bot:* cirr(h)ose, cirr(h)ous.

cirrhopetalum [siropetalɔm], *s.m. Bot:* cirrhopetalum.

cirrhose [siroːz], *s.f. Med:* cirrhosis; **c. hypertrophique,** hypertrophic, enlarged, cirrhosis; **c. atrophique,** atrophic cirrhosis.

cirrhotique [sirɔtik], *a. & s. Med:* cirrhotic.

cirri- [sir(r)i], *pref.* cirri-; **cirriflore,** cirriflorous.

cirrifère [sir(r)ifɛːr], *a. Nat.Hist:* cirriferous.

cirriforme [sir(r)ifɔrm], *a. Nat.Hist:* cirriform.

cirr(h)ipèdes [sir(r)ipɛd], *s.m.pl. Crust:* Cirripedia.

cirro-cumulus [sir(r)ɔkymylyːs], *s.m.inv. Meteor:* cirrocumulus (cloud); **ciel couvert de c.-c.,** mackerel sky.

cirro-stratus [sir(r)ɔstratys], *s.m.inv. Meteor:* cirro-stratus.

cirrus [sir(r)yːs], *s.m. Meteor:* cirrus; *F:* mare's tail.

cirsium [sirsjɔm], *s.m. Bot:* cirsium.

cirsoïde [sirsɔid], *a. Med:* cirsoid.

cirure [siryːr], *s.f.* wax polish.

cis- [sis, siz], *pref.* cis-; **cisleithan,** cisleithan, cis-leithan.

cisaillage [sizɑjaːʒ], *s.m. Metalw:* shearing, cutting. **2.** *Laund:* quilling, fluting (of caps, etc.).

cisaille [sizɑːj], *s.f.* **1.** parings, cuttings (of metal); scissel. **2.** (*a*) *Mec.E:* shearing machine; **c. à guillotine,** guillotine-shears, guillotine shearing machine, crocodile-, alligator-shears; *Boobk:* cutting press; **c. (à carton),** guillotine; *Phot: etc:* print trimmer; (*b*) *sg. or pl.* shears, nippers; wire-cutter; **c. à main,** hand-shears; **c. à levier,** lever-shears; *Hort:* **c. à haies,** hedge-clipper; **c. à bordures,** edging-shears; *Metalw:* **cisailles à barres,** bar-cutter; **cisailles circulaires,** rotary shears; **c. à chantourner,** scroll-shears; **cisailles chanfreineuses,** bevelling shears; (*c*) *Rail:* **voies en cisailles,** intersecting tracks.

cisaillement [sizɑjmɑ̃], *s.m.* **1.** (*a*) cutting, shearing (of metal); (*b*) clipping (of coins); (*c*) nipping (of tyres). **2.** (*a*) *Mec:* shearing (stress), shear; **effort de c.,** shearing stress; (*b*) *Geol:* shearing; **zone de c.,** shear zone; **c. du vent,** wind shear.

cisailler [sizɑje], *v.tr.* **1.** (*a*) to shear (metal); to clip (coins); (*b*) **chambre à air cisaillée,** nipped inner tube; *Geol:* **structure cisaillée,** shear structure. **2.** *Laund:* to quill, flute, goffer.

cisailleur [sizɑjœːr], *s.m. Metalw:* shearer, shearman, clipper.

cisailleuse [sizɑjøːz], *s.f. Metalw:* shearing machine, shearer, cropper; **c. à guillotine,** guillotine-shears, guillotine shearing-machine; crocodile-shears; **c. mécanique,** mechanical shears, power shears.

cisalpin [sizalpɛ̃], *a. A.Hist: A.Geog:* on the Roman side of the Alps; Cisalpine; *Hist:* **la République cisalpine,** the Cisalpine Republic.

ciseau, -eaux [sizo], *s.m.* **1.** (*a*) chisel; *Carp: Join: etc:* **c. à biseau, à chanfrein,** bevelled-edge chisel; **c. bédane, c. à mortaiser,** mortise-chisel; **c. fort, c. à panne, c. à planche,** ripping-chisel, firmer-chisel; **c. à gouge,** gouge; **c. long,** paring-chisel; **c. triangulaire,** burr (-chisel); **c. à dégrossir,** roughing-chisel, -tool; **c. à déballer,** case-opener; **creuser une rainure au c.,** to chisel (out) a groove; *Metalw:* **c. à froid,** cold chisel; **c. emmanché,** blacksmith's hardy; **c. à pierre, c. de maçon,** stone chisel, mason's chisel; *Nau:* **c. de calfat,** caulking-chisel, -iron; *Art:* **ouvrage du c.,** sculpture; (*b*) *A.Arms:* quarrel (of cross-bow). **2.** *pl.* (*a*) scissors; *Hort: etc:* shears, clippers; **ciseaux à tondre,** sheep shears; **coup de ciseaux,** snip (of the scissors); **enlever qch. d'un coup de ciseaux,** to snip sth. off; *Journ:* **travailler à coups de ciseaux,** to work with scissors and paste; *Lit:* **les ciseaux de la Parque,** the shears of Atropos; *Dressm:* **ciseaux à denteler,** pinking shears; (*b*) *Gym: Wr: Judo:* scissors; *Wr:* **ciseaux de jambes, de tête,** leg, head, scissors; **ciseaux de volée,** flying scissors; *Swim:* **(coup de) ciseaux,** scissors (kick); *Skiing:* **arrêt en ciseaux,** scissors stop; (*c*) *Danc:* ciseaux; (*d*) *Nau:* **mettre les voiles en ciseaux,** to boom the sails out.

ciselage [sizlaːʒ], *s.m.* **1.** chiselling (of wood); chipping (of metal), chasing (en)graving (of precious metals); tooling, embossing (of leather); cutting (of velvet). **2.** *Vit:* pruning (bunch of grapes).

ciselé [sizle], *a.* **1.** incised (bill of bird). **2.** *Bookb:* **tranche ciselée,** tooled edge. **3.** *Tex:* **velours c.,** cut velvet.

ciseler [sizle], *v.tr.* **(je cisèle, n. ciselons; je ciselerai) 1.** to chase, engrave (gold, silver); to chisel, carve (wood); to tool, emboss (leather); to cut, shear (velvet); **c. une statue,** to hew out a statue; **visage délicatement ciselé,** finely chiselled features. **2.** *Cu:* to slit, cut (sausages, fish, etc., before cooking). **3.** *Vit:* to thin (grapes).

ciselet [sizlɛ], *s.m. Tls:* graver, small chisel, chasing tool.

ciseleur [sizlœːr], *s.m.* **1.** chisel(l)er. **2.** chaser, engraver; tooler.

cisellement [sizɛlmɑ̃], *s.m.* **1.** chiselling (of wood); chipping (of metal); chasing (of precious metals); tooling, embossing (of leather); cutting (of velvet). **2.** *Vit:* thinning (of grapes).

cisellerie [sizɛlri], *s.f.* (*a*) manufacturing of chisels, of scissors; (*b*) *Coll.* chisels; scissors.

ciselure [sizlyːr], *s.f.* **1.** chisel(l)ing. **2.** chasing, embossing, tooling.

ciseron [sizrɔ̃], *s.m. Bot: F:* chick-pea.

cisjuran [sisʒyrɑ̃], *a. Hist:* cisjuran; **la Cisjurane,** Cisjuran Burgundy.

cismontain [sismɔ̃tɛ̃], *a. Hist: Rel.H:* cismontane.

cisoir [sizwaːr], *s.m.* goldsmith's chisel.

cisoires [sizwaːr], *s.f.pl.* bench shears.

cispadan [sispadɑ̃], *a. Hist:* cispadane.

cisrhénan [sisrenɑ̃], *a. Hist:* on the French side of the Rhine, cisrhenane.

cissampélos [sisɑ̃pelɔs, -os], *s.m. Bot:* cissampelos.

cissoïde [sis(s)ɔid], *s.f. Mth:* cissoid (curve).

cissus [sisys], *s.m. Bot:* cissus.

cistacées [sistase], *s.f.pl. Bot:* Cistaceae.

ciste¹ [sist], *s.f. Gr. & Rom.Ant: Prehist:* cist.

ciste², *s.m. Bot:* cistus; **c. de Crète,** rock-rose.

cistercien, -ienne [sistɛrsjɛ̃, -jɛn], *a. & s.* **1.** *Geog:* (native, inhabitant) of Cîteaux. **2.** *Ecc:* Cistercian.

cisticole [sistikɔl], *s.f. Orn:* **c. des joncs, couturière,** fan-tailed warbler.

cistophore [sistɔfɔːr], *s.m. Num:* cistophorus.

cistre¹ [sistr̥], *s.m. Mus:* (*a*) *A:* cittern, cither; (*b*) (Japanese) samisen.

cistre², *s.f. Bot:* Alpine fennel.

cistude [sistyd], *s.f. Rept:* cistudo, box tortoise, European pond tortoise.

citable [sitabl̥], *a.* quotable, fit for quotation, citable.

citadelle [sitadɛl], *s.f.* citadel; stronghold.

citadin, -ine [sitadɛ̃, -in]. **1.** *s.* citizen, townsman, *f.* townswoman. **2.** *a.* **les joies citadines,** the pleasures of town life; **la civilisation citadine,** the civilization of the cities. **3.** *s.f. A:* **citadine,** hackney-coach.

citateur, -trice [sitatœːr, -tris]. **1.** *s.* (*pers.*) quoter, citer. **2.** *s.m.* book of quotations.

citation [sitasjɔ̃], *s.f.* **1.** (*a*) quoting, citing; (*b*) quotation, citation; **c. banale,** tag; **début de c. . . ., fin de c.,** quote . . ., unquote. **2.** *Jur:* citation, writ of summons; **c. des témoins,** subpoena of witnesses; **notifier une c. à qn,** (i) to serve a summons on s.o.; (ii) to subpoena s.o. **3.** *Mil:* **c. (à l'ordre du jour)** = mention in dispatches; **être l'objet d'une c.,** to be mentioned in dispatches.

cité [site], *s.f.* **1.** (*a*) city; (large) town; **c. linéaire,** town with ribbon development; **droit de c.,** freedom of the city; **avoir, gagner droit de c.,** to be accepted; (*b*) **c. (ouvrière),** housing estate; *Sch:* **c. universitaire** = students' hall(s) of residence; (*c*) *Rel:* **c. céleste, c. sainte, c. de Dieu,** holy city, new Jerusalem; **c. future,** paradise; **c. sainte,** holy city (Jerusalem, Rome, Mecca, etc.). **2.** the (ancient) nucleus of a town (*e.g.* l'Ile de la Cité in Paris); **la C. de Carcassonne,** the old city of Carcassonne (within the walls); **la C. (de Londres),** the City (of London).

Cîteaux [sito], *Pr.n.m. Geog:* Cîteaux; *Ecc:* **L'ordre de C.,** the Cistercian Order.

cité-dortoir [sitedɔrtwar], *s.f.* dormitory town; *pl. cités-dortoirs.*

cité-jardin [siteʒardɛ̃], *s.f.* garden city; *pl. cités-jardins.*

citer [site], *v.tr.* **1.** (*a*) to quote, cite; **c. qn pour, en, exemple,** to quote s.o. as an example; **c. qn comme modèle,** to hold s.o. up as a model; **auteur cité,** author quoted above; (*b*) to make mention of. **2.** *Jur:* to summon (s.o. before the court), to subpoena (witness); (*patents*) to cite; **c. un débiteur,** to summons a debtor. **3.** *Mil:* **c. qn (à l'ordre du jour)** = to mention s.o. in dispatches.

citérieur [siterjœːr], *a. A.Geog:* on this side; **la Gaule citérieure,** Hither Gaul.

citerne [sitɛrn], *s.f.* (*a*) cistern, tank, reservoir; *Nau:* **c. de cargaison,** cargo tank, oil tank; **(bateau-, navire-)c.,** *A:* **c. flottante,** tanker; **caboteur c.,** coastal tanker; **(chaland-, péniche-) c.,** tank barge; *Aut:* **(remorque-)c.,** tank trailer; *Rail:* **(wagon-)c.,** tank waggon, *U.S:* tank car; (*b*) *Mch:* **c. de condenseur,** hot well of condenser; (*c*) *Anat:* **c. lombaire,** lumbar cistern; **c. de Pecquet,** cistern of Pecquet.

citerné [siterne], *a.* cistern shaped.

citerneau, -eaux [siterno], *s.m. Hyd.E:* fore-cistern.

cithare [sitaːr], *s.f. Mus:* **1.** *Gr.Ant:* cithara, cither(n). **2.** zither(n).

citharède [sitarɛd], *s.m. Gr.Ant:* citharœdus; **Apollon c.,** Apollo Citherœdus.
citharexylum [sitareksiləm], *s.m. Bot:* Citharexylum.
cithariste [sitarist], *s.* zitherist; *A:* citharist.
cithéroniides [siterəniid], *s.m.pl. Ent:* Citheroniidae.
citole [sitɔl], *s.f. A.Mus:* citole.
citoyen, -enne [sitwajɛ̃, -ɛn], *s.* (*a*) citizen; **droits de c.,** civic rights, citizenship; **de simples citoyens,** ordinary people; **c. d'honneur** = freeman of a city; *Poet:* **citoyens de l'air,** denizens, inhabitants, of the air; *F:* **c'est un drôle de c.!** he's a queer customer! (*b*) *Fr.Hist:* (*Revolution*): (*courtesy title*) citizen, *f.* citizeness.
citoyenneté [sitwajɛnte], *s.f.* citizenship; **c. d'honneur d'une ville** = freedom of a city.
citraconique [sitrakɔnik], *a. Ch:* citraconic.
citragon [sitragɔ̃], *s.m. Bot:* garden balm.
citral [sitral], *s.m. Ch:* citral.
citrange [sitrɑ̃:ʒ], *s.m. Bot:* citrange.
citrate [sitrat], *s.m. Ch:* citrate; *Phot:* **papier au c.** (**d'argent**), P.O.P. paper.
citré [sitre], *a. Pharm:* **potion citrée,** draught flavoured with lemon.
citrène [sitrɛn], *s.m. Ch:* citrene.
citrin, -ine [sitrɛ̃, -in]. **1.** *a. Lit:* lemon-yellow; *Pharm:* **onguent c.,** citrine ointment; *s.a.* HYACINTHE 2. **2.** *s.m. or f. Miner:* false topaz; citrine; (*b*) *s.f. Ch:* **citrine,** lemon oil.
citrique [sitrik], *a. Ch:* citric (acid).
citron [sitrɔ̃], *s.m.* **1.** *Bot:* (*generic term including*) lemon, lime, citron; **bois de c.,** citrus wood. **2.** (*a*) lemon; **c. doux,** (sweet) lime; **c. pressé,** fresh lemon juice; **essence de c.,** lemon oil; **écorce de c.,** lemon peel; (*b*) *a.inv.* lemon-yellow; (*c*) *P:* head, nut; **se presser le c.,** to rack one's brains; (*d*) *Ent:* brimstone butterfly.
citronellal [sitrɔnɛlal], *s.m. Ch:* citronellal.
citronellol [sitrɔnɛlɔl], *s.m. Ch:* citronellol.
citronnade [sitrɔnad], *s.f.* (cold or hot) lemon drink.
citronnat [sitrɔna], *s.m.* **1.** lemon marmalade. **2.** candied lemon-peel.
citronné [sitrɔne], *a.* (*a*) lemon-scented; (*b*) flavoured with lemon juice.
citronnelle [sitrɔnɛl], *s.f.* **1.** *Bot:* (*a*) citronella; (*b*) name of various plants smelling of lemon, *e.g.* lemon balm, melissa, southernwood, three-leafed verbena. **2.** *Dist:* Barbados water.
citronner [sitrɔne], *v.tr. Cu:* to serve (fish, etc.) with lemon juice.
citronnier [sitrɔnje], *s.m.* (*a*) *Bot:* citrus (tree); *usu.* lemon tree; (*b*) citron wood.
citronyle [sitrɔnil], *s.f. Ch:* citronyl.
citrouillard [sitrujaːr], *s.m. A.Mil: P:* dragoon.
citrouille [sitruj], *s.f.* **1.** *Bot:* pumpkin, gourd. **2.** *P:* (*a*) head, nut; (*b*) idiot, fathead.
citrus [sitrys], *s.m. Bot:* Citrus.
Civa [siva], *Pr.n.m. Hindu Rel:* Siva.
civadière [sivadjɛːr], *s.f. Nau:* spritsail.
çivaïsme [sivaism], *s.m. Hindu Rel:* Sivaism, Saivism.
çivaïte [sivait], *a. & s. Hindu Rel:* Sivaite, Saivite.
cive [siːv], *s.f.* chive(s).
civelle [sivɛl], *s.f. Ich:* glass-eel, elver.
civelot [sivlo], *s.m. A: P:* civilian; **en c.,** in civ(v)ies.
civet [sivɛ], *s.m. Cu:* stew (of venison, etc.); **c. de lièvre** = jugged hare.
civette[1] [sivɛt], *s.f.* **1.** *Z:* civet (cat); **c. des palmiers,** Celebes palm civet; **c. arboricole malaise,** small-toothed palm civet. **2.** *Com:* civet (perfume).
civette[2], *s.f. Bot:* chives.
civettone [sivɛtɔn], *s.f. Ch:* civetone.
civière [sivjɛːr], *s.f.* **1.** hand-barrow. **2.** stretcher. **3.** bier (for coffin).
civil [sivil], *a.* civil. **1.** (*a*) civic (rights, life, etc.); **guerre civile,** civil war; *Jur:* **mort civile,** civil death; **fruits civils,** civil fruits; *s.a.* ÉTAT 2; (*b*) *Jur:* **droit c.,** civil law; *s.a.* PARTIE 3; (*c*) **la liste civile,** the civil list; (*d*) lay, secular (as opposed to ecclesiastical); civilian (as opposed to military); **ingénieur c.,** civil engineer; *s.m.* **un c.,** (i) a layman; (ii) a civilian; **main d'œuvre civile,** civilian labour; *Mil:* (**bureau des**) **affaires civiles,** civil affairs; **militaire rendu à la vie civile,** demobilized soldier; **la vie c.,** *F:* **le c.,** private life; **dans le c. je suis jardinier,** in private, civilian, life I'm a gardener; **en c.,** (i) (*of police*) in plain clothes; (ii) *Mil:* in mufti, in civilian clothes; *F:* in civvies. **2.** *A:* polite, courteous (**à l'égard de,** to, towards).
civilement [sivilmɑ̃], *adv.* civilly. **1.** *Jur:* (*a*) **se marier c.,** to contract a civil marriage, to be married at a registry office; **enterré c.,** buried without religious ceremony; (*b*) **poursuivre qn c.,** to bring a civil action against s.o.; **c. responsable,** liable for damages (in respect of crime committed by third party); (*c*) **mort c.,** dead in law, *civiliter mortuus.* **2.** *A:* politely, courteously.
civilisable [sivilizabl], *a.* civilizable.
civilisant [sivilizɑ̃], *a.* civilizing (influence, etc.).
civilisateur, -trice [sivilizatœːr, -tris]. **1.** *a.* civilizing. **2.** *s.* civilizer.
civilisation [sivilizasjɔ̃], *s.f.* civilization.
civilisé [sivilize], *a.* civilized.
civiliser [sivilize], *v.tr.* **1.** (*a*) to civilize; (*b*) *F:* to polish up (s.o.'s manners); *F:* to civilize (s.o.). **2.** *Jur:* to transfer (criminal action) to civil court.
se civiliser, (*a*) to become civilized; (*b*) *F:* to become more polished (in manners), *F:* more civilized.
civiliste [sivilist], *s.m. & f.* = common lawyer; civilist; specialist, expert, in civil law.
civilité [sivilite], *s.f.* **1.** civility, politeness, courtesy; *Iron:* **la c. puérile et honnête,** common courtesy. **2. faire des civilités à qn,** to show s.o. courteous attention; **présenter ses civilités à qn,** to present one's compliments to s.o.
civique [sivik], *a.* civic (duties, virtues, guard); civil, *U.S:* citizen (rights); **chant c.,** patriotic song; *Sch:* **instruction c.,** civics; *Town P:* **centre c.,** civic centre.
civisme [sivism], *s.m.* good citizenship.
clabaud [klabo], *s.m.* **1.** *Ven:* (long-eared) hound (that is constantly giving tongue); babbler. **2.** *F:* (*a*) *A:* idle talker; chatterer; (*b*) ill-natured gossip; scandalmonger.
clabaudage [klaboda:ʒ], *s.m., A:* **clabaudement** [klabodmɑ̃], *s.m.* **1.** *Ven:* babbling, yelping, baying. **2.** *F:* ill-natured talk, spiteful gossip, backbiting.
clabauder [klabode], *v.i.* **1.** *Ven:* (*of hound*) to give tongue falsely. **2.** *F:* **c. sur, contre, qn,** to say ill-natured things about s.o.; **on clabauda,** people talked.
clabauderie [klabodri], *s.f. F:* ill-natured talk, (spiteful) gossip.
clabaudeur, -euse [klabodœːr, -øːz], *a. & s.* **1.** yelping, baying (hound). **2.** *a.* gossiping; *s.* (ill-natured) gossip, scandalmonger.
clabot [klabo], *s.m. Mec.E: Aut:* dog (clutch).
clabotage [klabɔta:ʒ], *s.m. Mec.E: Aut:* **1.** engagement by, of, dog clutch. **2.** dog clutch.
claboter [klabɔte]. **1.** *v.tr. Mec.E:* to assemble with dog clutch. **2.** *v.i. P:* to die, to peg out.
clac [klak], *s.m. & int.* crack(!); **clic-c. d'un fouet, des machines,** crack of a whip, clanking of machinery.
clactonien [klaktɔnjɛ̃], *a. & s.m. Geol: Prehist:* Clactonian.
cladocères [kladɔsɛːr], *s.m.pl. Crust:* Cladocera.
cladode [kladɔd], *s.m. Bot:* cladode.
cladonie [kladɔni], *s.f. Moss:* cladonia; **c. des rennes,** reindeer moss.
cladosporium [kladɔspɔrjɔm], *s.m. Fung:* Cladosporium.
clafoutis [klafuti], *s.m. Cu:* **c. aux pommes, limousin,** apples, (black) cherries, baked in batter.
claie [klɛ], *s.f.* **1.** (*a*) wattle, hurdle; **garnir, entourer, un terrain de claies,** to hurdle a piece of ground; *Mil: etc:* **revêtement en c.,** hurdle revetment; **traîner qn sur la c.,** (i) *A:* to drag s.o. to execution; (ii) *F:* to drag s.o. through the mire, to vilify s.o.; (*b*) **c. à fruits,** (wicker) fruit-tray; *Hort:* **c. à ombrer,** shading mat. **2.** (*a*) screen, riddle; **c. à (passer le) sable,** sand-screen; **passer du minerai à la c.,** to screen, riddle, mineral ore; (*b*) *Hyd.E:* (i) grid; (ii) mattress. **3.** fence (round field, etc.).
clair [klɛːr]. **1.** *a.* clear; (*a*) unclouded, limpid (water, eyes, etc.); **vitres claires,** transparent window panes; **teint c.,** clear complexion; **ciel c.,** cloudless sky; **voix, note, claire,** clear voice, note; **esprit c.,** clear mind; **œuf c.,** unfertile egg; **lait c.,** whey; (*b*) obvious, manifest, plain, explicit (meaning, terms, etc.); **explication claire,** lucid explanation; **il est c. qu'elle a tort,** she is obviously wrong; **voilà qui est c.!** that's clear (enough)! now I understand! **avis assez c.,** broad hint; **règle peu claire,** ambiguously worded rule; **c. comme deux et deux font quatre,** as plain as a pikestaff; **c. comme le jour,** crystal clear, as clear as daylight, as crystal; as plain as a pikestaff; **sa conduite n'est pas claire,** his behaviour is suspicious; *F:* fishy; **argent c.,** ready money; **profit tout c.,** clear profit; **le plus c. de ses économies,** the best part of his savings; **il passe le plus c. de son temps à . . .,** he spends most of his time in . . .; **le plus c. de l'affaire, c'est que . . .,** the one certain thing is that . . .; (*c*) bright, light (room, dress, etc.); **parquet c.,** brightly polished floor; **il fait c.,** (i) it is day (light); (ii) there is plenty of light; **il ne faisait pas encore c.,** it was not yet light; **il ne fait pas c. ici,** you can't see here; **il faisait c. comme en plein jour,** it was as light as day; *Phot: Cin:* **photographie claire et lumineuse,** picture in a high key; (*d*) light, pale (colour); **robe bleu c.,** pale blue dress; (*e*) thin (material, soup); **bois c.,** thinly planted wood. **2.** *adv.* (*a*) plainly, clearly; **parler c.,** to speak clearly; **entendre c.,** (i) to hear distinctly; (ii) to understand clearly; **voir c. dans l'esprit de qn,** to read s.o.'s mind; to see through s.o.; **voir c. dans une affaire,** to understand a matter; **je commence à (y) voir c.,** I am beginning to understand, to get to the bottom of it; **y voir c.,** (i) to be clear-sighted; (ii) to be able to see; **on dit que les chats y voient c. la nuit,** cats are said to see in the dark; (*b*) **avoine semée c.,** thinly sown oats. **3.** *s.m.* (*a*) light; **c. de lune,** moonlight; **au c. de (la) lune,** in the moonlight; **les clairs d'une peinture,** the (high) lights in a painting; (*b*) clearing (in wood, etc.); thin place (in stocking, etc.); (*c*) **message en c.,** message in plain language, in clear (*i.e.* not in cypher); **prendre une lettre en c.,** to take (down) a letter in longhand; (*d*) **tirer du vin au c.,** to decant wine; *F:* **tirer une affaire, les faits, au c.,** to clear a matter up, to elicit the facts, the truth of a matter; **mettre la situation au c.,** to clear the situation; **sabre au c.,** with drawn sword.
clairçage [klɛrsa:ʒ], *s.m.* fining, purging, clarifying (of sugar).
claircer [klɛrse], *v.tr.* (**je clairçai(s); n. clairçons**) to fine, purge, clarify (sugar).
claircière [klɛrsjɛːr], *s.f. Tex:* flaw, thin patch (in fabric).
claire[1] [klɛːr], *s.f.* **1.** (= CLAIR 3 (*b*)) flaw, thin place (in garment, etc.). **2.** clear pool; *Ost:* fattening pond, claire. **3.** *Ch:* **c. de coupelle,** bone-ash. **4.** *Sug.-R:* boiler, clearing-pan, clarifier.
Claire[2], *Pr.n.f.* Clara, Claire, Clare.
claire-étoffe [klɛretɔf], *s.f. Plumb:* soft solder.
clairement [klɛrmɑ̃], *adv.* clearly, plainly, distinctly; *F:* **c'était parler c.,** that was a sufficiently broad hint.
claire-soudure [klɛrsudyːr], *s.f.* soft solder.
clairet, -ette [klɛrɛ, -ɛt]. **1.** *a.* pale, light-coloured; (**vin**) **c.,** light-red wine, locally grown; **voix clairette,** thin, high-pitched, voice. **2.** *s.f.* **clairette;** (*a*) *Bot:* lamb's-lettuce, corn-salad; (*b*) (i) white grape of Languedoc, Drôme; (ii) light sparkling wine (of Die, etc.). **3.** *s.f.* **Clairette,** *Ecc:* nun of a reformed branch of the order of St. Clare.
claire-voie [klɛrvwa], *s.f.* **1.** open-work, lattice (-work), grating; (*a*) **porte à c.-v.,** wicket gate; **clôture à c.-v.,** fence, paling; **cloison à c.-v.,** grating; **caisse à c.-v.,** crate; skeleton case; **rayon à c.-v.,** skeleton shelf; **siège à c.-v.,** lath-seat; **digue à c.-v.,** skeleton pier; **tissu à c.-v.,** loose open(-weave) material; (*b*) clearance (between bars of grate, etc.). **2.** (*a*) *Const:* skylight; *Nau:* deadlight; **panneau de c.-v.,** deadlight; (*b*) *Arch:* bay (of joists). **3.** *Agr:* **semer à c.-v.,** to sow thinly; *pl. claires-voies.*
clairière [klɛrjɛːr], *s.f.* **1.** clearing, glade. **2.** *Tex:* thin place.
clair-obscur [klɛrɔpskyːr], *s.m. Art:* chiaroscuro, light and shade; *pl. clairs-obscurs.*
clair-obscuriste [klɛrɔpskyrist], *s. Art:* chiaroscurist; *pl. clair-obscuristes.*
clairon [klɛrɔ̃], *s.m.* **1.** (*a*) bugle; **sonnerie de c.,** bugle call; (*b*) bugler; **c. major,** bugle major. **2.** (*a*) clarion stop (of organ); (*b*) upper register (of clarinet).
claironnant [klɛrɔnɑ̃], *a.* loud, brassy (sound); **voix claironnante,** loud and metallic voice.
claironner [klɛrɔne], *v.i. & tr.* (*a*) *v.i.* to sound the bugle, the clarion; (*b*) *v.tr.* **c. une nouvelle,** to trumpet a piece of news abroad.
clairsemé [klɛrsəme], *a.* scattered, sparse, (population, vegetation, etc.); thinly sown (corn); thin (hair); **région à population clairsemée,** thinly inhabited district.
clairsemer (se) [səklɛrsəme], *v.pr.* (*conj. like* SEMER) to become scattered, to thin out; **la foule se clairsema,** the crowd thinned away.
clairure [klɛryːr], *s.f. Tex:* flaw, thin patch (in fabric).
clairvoyance [klɛrvwajɑ̃ːs], *s.f.* **1.** perspicacity, penetration, clearsightedness, shrewdness, acumen, vision. **2.** second-sight, clairvoyance.
clairvoyant, -ante [klɛrvwajɑ̃, -ɑ̃ːt]. **1.** *a.* penetrating, perspicacious, clear-sighted, shrewd. **2.** *a. & s.* clairvoyant.
clam [klam], *s.m. Moll:* clam.

clamariot, -ote [klamarjo, -ɔt], *a. & s.*, **clamartois, -oise** [klamartwa, -wa:z], *a. & s. Geog:* (native, inhabitant) of Clamart.
clamatores [klamatɔres], *s.m.pl. Orn:* Clamatores.
clameau, -eaux [klamo], *s.m. Tls:* cramp(-iron), holdfast; (timber) dog.
clamecer [klamse], *v.i. P:* to die; *P:* to peg out.
clamecycois, -oise [klamsikwa, -wa:z], *a. & s. Geog:* (native, inhabitant) of Clamecy.
clamer [klɑme], *v.tr.* (*a*) **c. son innocence,** to protest one's innocence; **c. son indignation, son mécontentement,** to voice loudly one's indignation, one's discontent; (*b*) *A.Jur:* to summon (s.o.).
clameur [klɑmœ:r], *s.f.* **1.** (*a*) clamour, outcry, uproar, hubbub; **pousser une c.,** to shout; *Jur:* **c. publique,** hue and cry; (*b*) **les clameurs du vent, de la tempête,** the howling, roaring, shrieking, of the wind, of the storm. **2.** *A.Jur:* (*a*) execution (by sale of debtor's chattels); (*b*) **c. de haro,** crying haro; (*c*) summons to appear in court.
clamp [klɑ̃p], *s.m.* **1.** *Nau:* clamp, fish (of mast). **2.** *Surg:* clamp, forceps.
clampage [klɑ̃pa:ʒ], *s.m. Surg:* clamping.
clampe [klɑ̃:p], *s.f.* = CLAMEAU.
clamper [klɑ̃pe], *v.tr. Surg:* to clamp.
clampin, -ine [klɑ̃pɛ̃, -in]. *F:* **1.** *a. A:* slow, halting, lame, limping. **2.** *s. F:* laggard; slacker; slowcoach; *Mil:* straggler. **3.** young braggart.
clampiner [klɑ̃pine], *v.i. F:* to loiter, lag, idle, slack.
clam(p)ser [klɑ̃mse], *v.i. P:* to die, *P:* to peg out.
clan[1] [klɑ̃], *s.m.* **1.** clan; (*in Ireland*) sept; **le chef de c.,** the head of the clan. **2.** set, clique.
clan[2], *s.m. Nau:* sheave-hole.
clanche [klɑ̃:ʃ], *s.f.* = CLENCHE.
clandestin, -ine [klɑ̃dɛstɛ̃, -in]. **1.** *a.* clandestine, secret; underground; illicit (betting, etc.); **armée clandestine,** underground forces; **démarche clandestine,** underhand proceeding; *Nau: etc:* **passager, voyageur, c.,** stowaway; **débit c.,** (*in Ireland*) shebeen; *U.S:* speakeasy. **2.** *s.f. Bot:* **clandestine,** broomrape.
clandestinement [klɑ̃dɛstinmɑ̃], *adv.* clandestinely; in a secret, underhand, manner; secretly.
clandestinité [klɑ̃dɛstinite], *s.f.* clandestinity, clandestineness; **passer dans la c.,** to go underground.
clangor [klɑ̃gɔ:r], *s.m. Med:* metallic second heart sound.
clangoreux [klɑ̃gɔrø], *a.m.* metallic (heart sound).
clangueur [klɑ̃gœ:r], *s.f. Orn:* booming cry, boom (of bittern, etc.).
clanique [klanik], *a.* clannish.
clanque [klɑ̃k], *s.f. Moll:* soft clam, long clam.
clapée [klape], *s.f.* trowelful.
claper [klape], *v.i. P:* to eat; *P:* to go to the trough, *U.S:* to hit the chow.
clapet [klapɛ], *s.m.* **1.** *Mec.E: Hyd.E: Civ.E:* valve; clack(-valve); clapper(-valve); (*a*) **c. d'admission,** inlet-valve, -flap; **c. d'échappement,** exhaust-valve; **c. d'aspiration,** suction-valve; **c. de soupape,** valve-flap; **c. de décharge, d'excès de pression, de sécurité, de sûreté,** relief-valve, outlet-valve; **c. de fermeture,** shut-off valve; **c. d'intercommunication,** cross-feed valve; **c. de refoulement,** delivery-valve; **c. de freinage, de retenue, de non-retour,** check-valve, non-return valve; **c. de trop-plein,** overflow-valve; **boîte à c.,** (i) clack-box; (ii) valve-chest; (*b*) **c. à bille, c. sphérique,** ball-valve; **c. à charnière,** hinged valve, leaf-valve; **c. à piston plongeur,** plunger-valve; (*c*) *Aer:* **c. (d'isolement),** crab-pot (valve); (*d*) *I.C.E:* poppet-valve, mushroom-valve; (*e*) **c. de cheminée,** chimney-trap; (*f*) **c. de ventilation,** (air) damper; (*g*) **c. à air (d'un caisson),** air-lock; (*h*) *Av:* **c. de drainage,** dump valve. **2.** *El.E:* rectifier. **3.** *P:* **elle a un de ces clapets!** she never stops (talking)!
clapier [klapje], *s.m.* **1.** rabbit burrow. **2.** rabbit hutch; **lapin de c.,** tame rabbit, hutch rabbit. **3.** *A: F:* brothel. **4.** *Med:* deep-seated source of ulceration. **5.** *Geol:* (*in the Alps*) scree.
clapir [klapi:r], *v.i.* (*of rabbit*) to squeal.
se clapir, (*of rabbit*) to hide, squat, cower (in the burrow).
clapotage [klapɔta:ʒ], *s.m.* **1.** (*rare*) splashing, lapping (of waves). **2.** *Med:* clapotage, clapotement.
clapotant [klapɔtɑ̃], *a.* lapping (waves).
clapoter [klapɔte], *v.i.* **1.** (*of waves*) to lap; **mer qui clapote,** choppy sea. **2.** *P:* to die, *P:* to peg out.
clapotement [klapɔtmɑ̃], *s.m.* splashing, lapping (of waves).
clapoteux, -euse [klapɔtø, -ø:z], *a.* choppy (sea).
clapotis [klapɔti], *s.m.* splash(ing), lap(ping) (of waves); **c. de marée,** tide-rip.
clap(p)ement [klapmɑ̃], *s.m.* **1.** smacking (of tongue). **2.** *Ling:* click (of Kaffirs, etc.).
clap(p)er [klape], *v.i.* **1. c. de la langue,** to smack one's tongue; to give a chuck. **2.** *Ling:* to click (with the tongue).
claps [klaps], *s.m. Glovem:* press-stud.
clapser [klapse], *v.i. P:* to die, *P:* to peg out.
claquage [klaka:ʒ], *s.m.* **1.** strain (of a muscle); **c. sportif,** strained, athletic, heart. **2.** *El:* breakdown; **essai de c.,** breakdown test; **tension de c.,** breakdown voltage; **c. d'un condensateur,** puncture, breakdown, of a condenser.
claquant [klakɑ̃], *a.* **1.** clapping (hands, etc.); cracking (whip, etc.), slamming (door, etc.). **2.** *P:* exhausting.
claque [klak]. I. *s.f.* **1.** smack, slap (on face, etc.); *F:* **tête à claques,** unpleasing, unprepossessing, face. **2.** (*a*) (i) vamp; (ii) golosh, of boot; (*b*) *pl.* (i) *A:* overshoes, pattens; (ii) *Fr.C:* galoshes, *U.S:* rubbers; *F:* **prendre ses cliques et ses claques,** to go off quickly; *F:* to scram. **3.** *Th: A:* hired clappers; *claque.* **4.** *P:* death (*cf.* CLAQUER 1 (*b*)); **il en a sa c.,** (i) he's on his last legs; (ii) he's fed up with it, he's had enough of it.
II. **claque,** *s.m.* **1.** (*a*) opera hat, crush hat; (*b*) **(chapeau) c.,** cocked hat (*the pl. of* **chapeau claque** *is* **chapeaux claques**). **2.** *P:* (*a*) brothel; (*b*) gambling den.
claqué [klake], *a.* **1.** (*a*) (*of horse*) having a strained tendon; **tendon c.,** snapped tendon; (*b*) fagged out, dog-tired; (*c*) *P:* dead; (*d*) *Med:* **cœur c.,** strained, athletic, heart. **2.** vamped (boot).
claquebois [klakbwa], *s.m. Mus:* xylophone.
claquedent [klakdɑ̃], *s.m. P:* **1.** starveling, miserable wretch. **2.** low pothouse, disorderly house; brothel, gambling den.
claquefaim [klakfɛ̃], *s.m. P:* = CLAQUEDENT 1.
claquement [klakmɑ̃], *s.m.* clapping (of hands); slam(ming), bang(ing) (of a door); chattering (of teeth); crack(ing), smack (of whip); smack (of bullet); rattling, chattering (of machine); *Tg:* click (of Morse key); *I.C.E: Mch:* **c. des pistons,** slapping of the pistons, piston-slap.
claquemurer [klakmyre], *v.tr.* to immure, mew up, coop up; **se c.,** to shut oneself up (*e.g.* in order to study); to see nobody.
claquer [klake]. **1.** *v.i.* (*a*) to clap; (*of door*) to bang; (*of clogs, etc.*) to clatter; (*of piston, etc.*) to slap; **c. des mains,** to clap, applaud; **il claque des dents,** his teeth are chattering; **une balle claqua contre le mur,** a bullet smacked against the wall; **le drapeau claque au vent,** the flag is flapping in the wind; **un baiser qui claque,** a smacker; *F:* **c. du bec,** to be hungry; (*b*) *P:* (i) die; *P:* to peg out, to kick the bucket; (ii) (*of business*) to go to pieces; *F:* to go bust; (*of machinery*), to give up; *P:* to go phut; **le moteur m'a claqué dans les mains,** the engine died on me; (*c*) (*of electric lamp*) to burn out; (*d*) *F:* **se c.,** to tire oneself out, to knock oneself up; **je suis claqué,** I'm worn out, I'm all in. **2.** *v.tr. & i.* **(faire) c. la porte,** to slam, bang, the door; *F:* **c. le téléphone,** to bang the receiver down; **faire c. ses lèvres, se c. les lèvres,** to smack one's lips; **faire c. son fouet,** to crack, one's whip; *s.a.* FOUET 2; **faire c. ses doigts,** to snap one's fingers; **faire c. sa langue,** to cluck; **(faire) c. ses talons,** to click one's heels. **3.** *v.tr.* (*a*) to slap, smack (child, etc.); (*b*) *Th:* **c. un acteur,** to clap, applaud, an actor; (*c*) to burst (tyre, etc.); to rupture, tear (ligament, etc.); (*d*) *F:* to squander; *F:* to blue (legacy, etc.); to sell (one's furniture for what it will fetch).
claquet [klakɛ], *s.m.* clapper (of mill-hopper); *F:* **sa langue va comme le c. d'un moulin,** she talks nineteen to the dozen, she'd talk the hind leg off a donkey.
claquètement [klakɛtmɑ̃], *s.m.* (*of stork*) clappering.
claqueter [klakte], *v.i.* (**elle claquette; elle claquettera**) **1.** (*of stork*) to clapper. **2.** (*of hen*) to cackle, cluck.
claquette [klakɛt], *s.f.* **1.** (*a*) *Ecc:* clapper; *Cin:* clapper-board; (*b*) *F:* chatterbox. **2.** folding card-case. **3.** *Tex:* **battant à c.,** spring-batten (of a loom). **4. danse à claquettes,** tap dance. **5.** heel-less sandal; mule.
claqueur [klakœ:r], *s.m.* **1.** *Th:* hired clapper. **2.** *Bootm:* vamper.
claquoir [klakwa:r], *s.m.* clapper; *Cin:* clap-stick.
clarain [klarɛ̃], *s.m. Miner:* clarain.
clarien, -ienne [klarjɛ̃, -jɛn], *a. & s. A.Geog:* (native, inhabitant) of Claros, Clarus.
clarifiant [klarifjɑ̃]. **1.** *a.* clarifying. **2.** *s.m.* clarifier.
clarificateur, -trice [klarifikatœ:r, -tris]. **1.** *a.* clarifying. **2.** *s.m.* clarifier; clarifying substance.
clarification [klarifikasjɔ̃], *s.f.* **1.** clarification (of liquids). **2.** clarification, enlightenment.
clarifier [klarifje], *v.tr.* (*p.d. & pr.sub.* **n. clarifiions, v. clarifiiez**) **1.** to clarify, clear (wine, etc.). **2.** to clarify, enlighten; to clear (the mind).
se clarifier, (*of liquid*) to become clear; to clear.
clarin [klarɛ̃], *s.m. Bot:* cross-leaved heath.
clarine [klarin], *s.f.* cattle bell, cow bell.
clariné [klarine], *a.* **1.** (*of cows, etc.*) wearing bells. **2.** *Her:* clariné.
clarinette [klarinɛt], *s.f.* **1.** (*a*) clarinet; (*b*) clarinettist; (*c*) clarinet stop (of organ); (*d*) *P:* **bouffer, becqueter, des clarinettes,** to go hungry. **2.** *Mil: P:* rifle. **3.** *Tchn:* manifold.
clarinetter [klarinɛte], *v.i. F:* to play the clarinet.
clarinettiste [klarinɛtist], *s.m.* clarinettist.
Clarisse [klaris]. **1.** *Pr.n.f.* Clarissa. **2.** *s.f. Ecc:* (sœur) c., nun of the order of St Clare; Clarisse; **les pauvres clarisses,** the Poor Clares, Clarisses.
clarkéite [klarkeit], *s.f. Miner:* clarkeite.
clarkia [klarkja], *s.f.*, **clarkie** [klarki], *s.m. Bot:* clarkia.
Claros [klarɔs, -os], *Pr.n. A.Geog:* Claros, Clarus; **le dieu de C., Apollon C.,** Apollo Clarius; **l'oracle de C.,** the Colophon oracle.
clarté [klarte], *s.f.* **1.** clearness, clarity; (*a*) limpidity (of water, etc.); transparency (of glass, etc.); **c. du teint,** clearness of the complexion; (*b*) lucidity, perspicuity (of style, etc.); **avoir de la c. d'esprit,** to be clear-minded; (*c*) **avoir des clartés sur un sujet,** to have some knowledge of a subject. **2.** light, brightness (of sun, etc.); **à la c. de la lune, des flambeaux,** by the light of the moon, of the torches; by moonlight, by torchlight; **les premières clartés du soleil,** the first gleams of the sun; *Nau:* **c. des glaces,** ice-blink.
classe [klas], *s.f.* **1.** class, division, category, order; *Adm: etc:* rank; grade; **classes de la société,** classes of society; **les classes dirigeantes,** the governing classes; **les hautes classes,** the upper classes; **la c. moyenne,** the middle class(es); **la c. ouvrière,** the working class(es); **la c. laborieuse,** the working population; **produits de première c.,** top quality goods; *Rail: Nau: etc:* **c. touriste,** tourist class; **c. cabine,** cabin class; **c. économique,** economy class; **billet, voyageur, de première, deuxième c.,** first-, second-class ticket, passenger; *Nau:* **voyager en dernière c.,** to travel steerage; *F:* **avoir de la c.,** to have class, style. **2.** *Sch:* (*a*) class; form; *U.S:* grade; **les hautes classes, les classes supérieures,** the upper, top, forms; **la petite classe,** the infants; **c. de français,** French class; **c. de neige,** class of children sent to winter sports centre (for lessons and skiing); (*b*) **aller en c.,** to go to school; **être en c.,** to be in school; **faire ses classes,** to be at school; **faire la c.,** to teach; **livre de c.,** school-book; **(salle de) c.,** classroom, formroom, schoolroom; **en sortant de c.,** on coming out of school. **3.** *Mil:* (*a*) (*conscription*) class, age-group; annual contingent (of recruits); **c. creuse,** annual contingent corresponding to a low birth-rate period; **la c. 1965,** the 1965 class, the 1965 levy; the young men liable to be called up in 1965; (*b*) (*training*) **faire ses classes,** to be drilled; to undergo basic training; to pass the recruit stage; *F:* **c'est bientôt la c.!** it'll soon be over! (*c*) **c. d'instruction,** squad, men, at drill; (*d*) *Adm:* **c. d'âge,** age group; **il fait partie de la c. des 15 à 20 ans,** he comes into the 15 to 20 age group, bracket; **c. de revenu,** income bracket. **4.** *Mil:* (*Rank*) **un soldat de deuxième c.,** *F:* **un deuxième c.,** a private; **un soldat de première c.,** *F:* **un première c.,** a lance-corporal; *U.S:* a private first class; (*Women's Services*) **hors classe** = (i) Squadron officer (W.R.A.F.); (ii) Major (W.R.A.C.); **première classe** = (i) Flight officer (W.R.A.F.); (ii) Captain (W.R.A.C.); **deuxième classe** = (i) Flying Officer (W.R.A.F.); (ii) Lieutenant (W.R.A.C.); **troisième classe** = (i) Pilot Officer (W.R.A.F.); (ii) Second-lieutenant (W.R.A.C.).
classe-lettres [klɑslɛtr̥], *s.m.inv.* letter-file.
classement [klɑsmɑ̃], *s.m.* **1.** classification, classing (of plants, etc.); rating (of seaman, engine, etc.); docketing (of letter); *Adm:* position on the promotion roster; *Sch: etc:* **c. de sortie,** passing-out list; **numéro de c.,** press-mark (of book in a library); **je ne connais pas son c. de sortie,** I don't know how he was placed in the final result; **donner le c.,** to give the results (of a competition). **2.** (*a*) sorting out; *Min:* grading (of ore); *Rail:* marshalling (of trucks); **c. volumétrique,** sizing; *Min:* **appareil de c.,** separator; (*b*) filing, pigeon-holing (of documents).

classer [klɑse], *v.tr.* **1.** to class(ify) (animal, plant, etc.); to rate (seaman, engine, etc.); to docket (letter, etc.); **ces faits se classent dans une autre catégorie,** these facts fall into another category; **tableau classé comme chef-d'œuvre,** picture which ranks as a masterpiece; **c. comme monument historique,** to schedule as an ancient monument; **romans classés,** standard novels; *Fin:* **valeurs classées,** investment stock; *Nau:* **navire classé suivant cote A1,** ship classed A1; *Sp: etc:* **se c. troisième,** to be placed third; *Turf:* **non classés,** also ran; **classés par pays,** classified according to country; *F:* **c'est un homme classé,** he has been sized up. **2.** *(a)* to sort out (articles); *Min:* to grade (ore); *Rail:* to marshal (trucks); *(b)* to file, pigeon-hole (documents); **c. une question,** to shelve a question; **affaire classée,** criminal case, etc., definitely filed and disposed of (although unsolved).

classeur [klɑsœːr], *s.m.* **1.** *(a)* rack (for letters, music, etc.); *(b) Com: etc:* (index-)file; jacket-file; filing cabinet; **tiroir c.,** filing drawer; *Adm:* **c. des entrées et sorties,** tally file; *(c)* index-book; *(d) Min: etc:* **c. (-trieur),** classifier, sizer, (ore-) separator; *(e) Ind:* **c. centrifuge,** centrifugal strainer; **c. de copeaux,** chip screen. **2.** *(a) Ind:* sorter (of letters, coal, etc.); *(b) Rail:* **c. de trains,** shunter.

classicisme [klasisism], *s.m.* *(a)* classicism; *(b)* perfection, refinement.

classier, -ière [klɑsje, -jɛːr], *s.* filing clerk, *U.S:* file clerk.

classificateur, -trice [klasifikatœːr, -tris]. **1.** *s.* *(a)* classifier. **2.** *a.* classifying. **3.** *s.m. Min:* classifier, sizer, (ore) separator.

classification [klasifikasjɔ̃], *s.f.* **1.** classification, classifying (of plant, animal, etc.); rating (of engine, etc.). **2.** classification, sorting out, arranging in classes; *(in library)* **c. décimale,** Dewey decimal system.

classificatoire [klasifikatwaːr], *a.* classifying (index, etc.).

classifié [klasifje], *a.* **1.** classified. **2.** *Mil:* classified (document).

classifier [klasifje], *v.tr.* (*p.d. & pr.sub.* **n. classifiions, v. classifiiez**) **1.** to classify (plant, etc.); to rate (engine, etc.). **2.** to sort (out) (articles); to arrange (articles) in classes. **3.** *Mil: etc:* to classify (document).

classique [klasik], *a.* **1.** *Sch:* academical, for school use; **livres classiques,** school books. **2.** *(a)* classical (period, author, music); classic (beauty); **études classiques,** classical studies, education; *(b)* standard (work, model, etc.); conventional; stereotyped, recognized, most approved (manner, etc.); standing (custom, excuse, joke); **doctrine devenue c.,** doctrine which has become universally accepted; **guerre c., armes classiques,** conventional warfare, weapons; **c'est un coup c.,** that's an old dodge; *(c) Swim:* **plongeon c.,** straight dive. **3.** *s.m.* *(a)* **les classiques grecs, français,** the Greek, French, classics; *(b)* **les classiques et les romantiques,** the classicists and the romanticists; *(c)* **elle ne joue que du c.,** she only plays classical music.

classiquement [klasikmɑ̃], *adv.* classically.

clastique [klastik], *a.* **1.** *Geol:* clastic; fragmentary. **2.** *Anat: Sch:* *(of skeleton)* that can be taken to pieces.

clathre [klatʀ], *s.m. Fung:* clathrus.

clatir [klatiːr], *v.i.* *(of hounds)* to bay.

clatissement [klatismɑ̃], *s.m.* baying (of hounds).

Claude [kloːd]. **1.** *(a) Pr.n.m.* Claudius, Claud(e); *(b) s.m. F: O:* dolt, simpleton. **2.** *Pr.n.f.* Claudia.

claudétite [klodetit], *s.f. Miner:* claudetite.

claudicant [klodikɑ̃], *a.* limping.

claudication [klodikasjɔ̃], *s.f.* limp(ing), claudication.

claudien¹, -ienne [klodjɛ̃, -jɛn], *a. Rom.Hist:* Claudian (letters, aqueduct, etc.).

Claudien². *Pr.n.m. Rom.Lit:* Claudian.

claudiquement [klodikmɑ̃], *s.m.* clumping (of wooden leg).

claudiquer [klodike], *v.i. Lit:* to limp, to claudicate.

clause [kloːz], *s.f.* *(a) Jur:* clause; **c. additionnelle,** additional clause; rider; **c. pénale,** penalty clause; **c. compromissoire,** arbitration clause; **c. de style,** formal clause; **c. restrictive,** saving clause; *(b) Av: etc:* **clauses techniques,** type specifications.

clausoir [klozwaːr], *s.m. Arch:* keystone (of arch).

clausthalite [klostalit], *s.f. Miner:* clausthalite.

claustral, -aux [klostral, -o], *a.* claustral; monastic; **le silence c. de la ville,** the cloister-like silence of the town.

claustration [klostrasjɔ̃], *s.f.* **1.** cloistering. **2.** (close) confinement; **la monotonie de la c. scolaire,** the monotony of the closed community of scholastic life.

claustre [klostʀ], *s.m. Constr:* semi-cylindrical tile used for ornamentation of wall, balustrade.

claustrer [klostre], *v.tr.* to confine; to shut up, in; to cloister; to hold (s.o.) prisoner.

se claustrer, to shut oneself up; **le jeune homme se claustra en un farouche mutisme,** the young man took refuge in a stubborn silence.

claustrophobie [klostrɔfɔbi], *s.f. Med:* claustrophobia.

claustrum, -a [klostrɔm, -a], *s.m. Arch:* *(a)* traceried window; *(b)* openwork partition (made of concrete or ceramics).

clavage [klavaːʒ], *s.m. Const:* keying up, laying the keystone (of arch).

clavaire [klavɛːr], *s.f. Fung:* clavaria, *F:* coral fungus.

clavé [klave], *a. Bot: Ent:* clavate, club-shaped.

claveau¹, -eaux [klavo], *s.m. Const: Arch:* arch-stone, voussoir; **c. droit,** keystone.

claveau², *s.m. Vet:* *(a)* pus occurring in sheep-pox; *(b)* sheep-pox.

clavecin [klavsɛ̃], *s.m. Mus:* **1.** harpsichord. **2.** keyboard (of carillon).

claveciniste [klavsinist], *s. Mus:* harpsichord player, harpsichordist.

clavelade [klavlad], *s.f. Vet:* sheep pox.

clavelé [klavle], *a. Vet:* *(of sheep)* attacked by sheep-pox.

clavelée [klavle], *s.f. Vet:* sheep-pox.

claveleux, -euse [klavlø, -øːz], *a. Vet:* (i) attacked by, (ii) pertaining to, sheep-pox.

clavelisation [klavlizasjɔ̃], *s.f.* inoculation against sheep-pox.

claveliser [klavlize], *v.tr. Vet:* to inoculate (sheep) against sheep-pox.

clavet(t)age [klavtaːʒ], *s.m. Mec.E:* **1.** keying, wedging, cottering (of machine parts, etc.). **2.** key(s), wedge(s), cotter(s).

clavet(t)er [klavte], *v.tr.* (**je clavette, n. clavetons; je clavetterai**) *Mec.E:* to key, wedge, cotter; **c. une poulie sur un arbre,** to key a pulley on to a shaft.

clavette [klavɛt], *s.f. Mec.E:* key, pin, cotter, forelock; **c. et contre-c.,** gib and key; **c.-axe,** axis pin; **c. Woodruff,** Woodruff key; **c. linguiforme,** feather (key); spline; **c. plate,** flat key; **c. conique,** taper pin; **c. creuse, c. évidée,** hollow key, saddle-key; **c. fendue, c. à ressort,** split key, split pin, split cotter-pin; spring-cotter, spring key; **c. encastrée, c. noyée,** sunk key; **c. à mentonnet, à talon, à tête,** gib-head(ed) key; **rainure, logement, de c.,** keyway; **c. d'assemblage,** body locking pin; **c. de calage,** steady pin; **c. de commande,** actuating pin; **c. d'entraînement,** drivekey, driving dog; **c. de fixation,** retaining pin; **c. filetée de fixation,** screw-cotter; **c. de verrouillage,** locking pin, locking key; **c. d'arbre,** shaft key; **c. d'essieu,** axle-pin, linchpin; *Artil:* **c. de culasse,** breech key; **c. de bloc de culasse,** breech-block key; *Exp:* **c. de sûreté,** safety-pin (of fuse); *I.C.E:* **c. de soupape,** collar (on valve stem); **c. du ressort de soupape,** cotter of the valve spring.

claviceps [klaviseps], *s.m. Fung:* claviceps.

clavicorde [klavikɔrd], *s.m. Mus: A:* clavichord.

clavicornes [klavikɔrn], *s.m.pl. Ent:* Clavicornes.

claviculaire [klavikylɛːr], *a. Anat:* clavicular.

clavicule [klavikyl], *s.f. Anat:* clavicle; *F:* collar-bone; **se fracturer la c.,** to break one's collar-bone.

claviculé [klavikyle], *a. Nat.Hist:* claviculate (shell, leaf, etc.).

clavier [klavje], *s.m.* **1.** key-ring, -chain. **2.** keyboard (of piano, typewriter, etc.); manual (of organ); **c. de récit,** swell manual (of organ); **c. des pédales,** pedal keyboard; **c. expressif,** swell organ; *Typewr:* **c. à quatre rangées de touches,** four-bank keyboard. **3.** range, compass (of clarinet, etc.).

clavifolié [klavifɔlje], *a. Bot:* bearing clavate leaves.

claviforme [klavifɔrm], *a. Bot:* clavate, claviform, club-shaped.

clavin [klavɛ̃], *s.m. Vet:* sheep-pox.

claviste [klavist], *s.m. & f. Typ:* machine compositor.

claxon [klaksɔ̃], *s.m. Aut:* hooter.

claxonner [klaksɔne], *v.i. Aut:* to hoot.

clayère [klɛjɛːr], *s.f.* oyster park.

clayette [klɛjɛt], *s.f.* *(a) Winem:* (grape-sorting) hurdle; *(b) Dom.Ec:* (small) sieve; *(c) Pisc:* tray (made of) glass rods and used for incubation); *(d) (artificial flower industry)* wire tray (used for drying the painted petals).

clayon [klɛjɔ̃], *s.m.* **1.** wicker tray (for draining cheeses, etc.); **c. pour pâtisseries,** wire pastry-stand. **2.** wattle enclosure. **3.** wire netting for protecting windows.

clayonnage [klɛjɔnaːʒ], *s.m.* **1.** wicker-work, wattle fencing, wattling; basket-work; **c. d'un gabion,** waling of a gabion. **2.** *Hyd.E:* mat, mattress (of canal bank, etc.).

clayonner [klɛjɔne], *v.tr.* **1. c. le talus d'une rivière,** to protect a river bank with wattle fencing; to mat a river bank. **2. c. un gabion,** to wale a gabion.

clé [kle], *s.f.* = CLEF.

cleaner [klinœːr], *s.m. Toil:* face cleanser.

Cléanthe [kleɑ̃ːt], *Pr.n.m. Gr.Phil:* Cleanthes.

clearance [klirɑ̃ːs], *s.f. Physiol:* clearance.

clearing [kliriŋ], *s.m. Fin:* clearing-house; **accord de c.,** clearing agreement.

Cléarque [kleark], *Pr.n.m. Gr.Hist:* Clearchus.

clébard [klebaːr], **cleb(s)** [klɛb, klɛps], *s.m. P:* dog, pooch, tyke.

clef [kle], *s.f.* **1.** key; *(a)* **c. de maison,** latch-key; **c. forée,** piped key; **c. bénarde,** pin-key; **fausse c.,** skeleton key; **porte à c.,** door that locks; **fermer une porte à c.,** to lock a door; **donner un tour de c. à la porte,** to turn the key in the lock, to lock the door; **tenir qch. sous c.,** to keep sth. under lock and key; **mettre ses papiers sous c.,** to lock up one's papers; **la c. est sur la porte,** the key is in the lock; **louer une maison clefs en main,** to rent a house with immediate, vacant, possession; **construction livrée c. en main,** turnkey construction; **mettre la c. sous la porte,** to do a moonlight flit, to shoot the moon; *s.a.* CHAMP¹ 1, PAILLASSON 1; *(b)* **c. d'une position,** key to a position; **position c.,** key position; **poste c.,** key post; **Orléans, c. de la vallée de la Loire,** Orléans, gateway to the Loire Valley; *Pol.Ec:* **industrie c.,** key industry; *(c)* **c. d'un chiffre,** key to a cipher; **c. d'une énigme,** clue to a puzzle; **la c. du mystère,** the key to the mystery; **roman à c.,** novel introducing real characters under fictitious names. **2.** *Mus:* *(a)* clef; **c. de sol,** treble clef; *(b)* key-signature; **instrument facile à jouer avec des dièses à la c.,** instrument easy to play in sharp keys; *P:* **dîner avec du champagne à la clef,** dinner with champagne thrown in. **3.** *Arch: Const:* *(a)* **c. (de voûte),** keystone, crown, centre voussoir (of arch); **l'agriculture est la c. de voûte de l'économie,** agriculture is the backbone of the economy; **c. pendante,** pendant, hanging keystone; **c. pendante latérale,** queen post; *(b)* reinforce, reinforcing piece (of beam). **4.** *N.Arch: Nau:* *(a)* shore; *(b)* chock (of bowsprit, etc.); *(c)* hitch; *s.a.* DEMI-CLEF; *(d)* fid (of mast). **5.** *(a) Tls:* key, wrench, spanner; **c. anglaise,** adjustable spanner, shifting-spanner, *U.S:* monkey wrench; **c. universelle,** adjustable spanner, adjustable wrench; **c. à crémaillère,** rack-spanner; **c. à douille, à tire-fonds,** box-spanner, -wrench; socket-spanner, -wrench; **c. pour, à, tubes, pour tuyaux,** tube-wrench, pipe-wrench; **c. à chaîne,** chain wrench; **c. à fourche,** fork wrench, gap-spanner; **c. à ergot, à griffe,** hook-spanner, pin-wrench; **c. à cliquet, à rochet,** ratchet-spanner, -wrench; **c. à six pans,** hexagonal wrench; spanner for hexagonal nuts; **c. à douze pans,** twelve-point wrench; **c. à retour automatique,** non-locking key; **c. coudée,** bent spanner, elbowed spanner, skew spanner; **c. à écrou,** nut-wrench, screw-wrench; **c. crocodile, c. à mâchoires dentées,** alligator wrench, crocodile spanner; **c. fermée,** ring-spanner; **c. plate,** (open) end wrench; **c. simple (à fourche), double (à fourches),** single-ended, double-ended, spanner; *s.a.* ACCORDEUR, DYNAMOMÉTRIQUE, MOLETTE 2; *(b) Carp:* wedge (of marking gauge); *(c) Mec.E:* toggle, hook (at end of chain); **c. de frein,** brake-toggle; *(d) Plumb:* handle (of tap); plug (of cock); **c. de robinet,** cock key; *(e) Aut:* **c. pour roues,** wheel-brace; *Veh:* **c. pour essieux,** axle-spanner, -wrench; *(f) Civ.E:* **c. (de tuyau de poêle),** damper; *(g) Mus:* peg (of stringed instrument). **6.** *(a) El: Aut:* **c. de contact,** ignition key; *(b) Tp:* **c. d'appel, de conversation, de parole,** call(ing)-key; call-button; call-circuit key; speaking key; **c. de rappel,** re-calling key; **c. de réponse,** reply-key; **c. d'écoute, de surveillance,** listening key, monitoring key; **c. de commutation à bascule, à poussoir,** lever key, press-button switch; **c. de rupture,** interruption key; *(c) Tg:* **c. Morse,** Morse key, Morse sender; *(d) W.Tel:* **c. d'écoute,** audio switch. **7.** *Wr:* lock; **c. de bras,** arm(-)lock.

cléidorrhexie [kleidɔrɛksi], *s.f. Obst:* cleidorrhexis.

cléidotomie [kleidɔtɔmi], *s.f. Obst:* cleidotomy.

cléistocarpe [kleistɔkarp], **cléistocarpique** [kleistɔkarpik], *a. Bot:* cleistocarpous.

cléistogame [kleistɔgam], *a. Bot:* cleistogamic.

clématite [klematit], *s.f. Bot:* clematis; **c. des haies,** travellers' joy, old man's beard.

clémence[1] [klemɑ̃ːs], *s.f.* **1.** clemency, mercy, leniency (**pour, envers,** to, towards). **2. c. du temps,** clemency, mildness, of the weather.

Clémence[2]. *Pr.n.f.* Clemence, Clemency.

clément[1] [klemɑ̃], *a.* **1.** clement, merciful, lenient (**pour, envers,** to, towards); forbearing. **2.** mild (disease, temperature, etc.); *Lit:* **ciel c.,** mild climate.

Clément[2]. *Pr.n.m.* Clement, Clemens.

Clémentine [klemɑ̃tin]. **1.** *Pr.n.f.* Clementina, Clementine. **2.** *s.f.pl. Ecc.Hist:* **les Clémentines,** the Clementine Constitutions (of Pope Clement V). **3.** *s.f. Hort:* clementine.

clenche [klɑ̃ːʃ], *s.f.,* **clenchette** [klɑ̃ʃɛt], *s.f.* latch (of door-lock); **porte fermée à la c.,** door on the latch.

cléome [kleɔm], *s.m. Bot:* cleome.

Cléopâtre [kleɔpɑːtr̥], *Pr.n.f. A.Hist:* Cleopatra.

clephte [klɛft], *s.m.* klepht, Greek brigand.

clepsydre [klɛpsidr̥], *s.f. Archeol:* clepsydra, water-clock.

cleptomane [klɛptɔman], *s.m. & f.* kleptomaniac.

cleptomanie [klɛptɔmani], *s.f.* kleptomania.

clerc [klɛːr], *s.m.* **1.** *A:* (*a*) *Ecc:* clerk, cleric; (*b*) learned man, scholar; *still used in:* **point n'est besoin d'être grand c. pour . . .,** one doesn't have to be a genius in order to . . . **2.** clerk (in lawyer's office); **petit c.,** junior clerk, message-boy; *F:* **faire un pas de c.,** (i) to make a blunder; (ii) to take a false step.

clercelière [klɛrsəljɛːr], *s.f. A:* key-ring.

clergé [klɛrʒe], *s.m.* (the) clergy, priests, priesthood; **le respect dû au clergé,** the respect due to the cloth.

clergeon [klɛrʒɔ̃], *s.m.* **1.** *A.Jur:* young clerk. **2.** *F:* altar-boy.

clergesse [klɛrʒɛːs], *s.f. A:* bluestocking.

clergie [klɛrʒi], *s.f. A:* learning, scholarship; **bénéfice de c.,** benefit of clergy.

clergyman [klœrdʒiman], *s.m. Ecc:* (English or American) clergyman; *pl. clergymen.*

clérical, -aux [klerikal, -o], *a. Ecc:* clerical; (*costume, etc.*) **peu c.,** unclerical; **les journaux cléricaux,** (i) the Church papers, press; (ii) *Pol:* the clerical press; *s. Pol: Pej:* **les cléricaux,** the clericals.

cléricalement [klerikalmɑ̃], *adv.* clerically.

cléricaliser [klerikalize], *v.tr. Pol:* to clericalize (the schools, etc.).

cléricalisme [klerikalism], *s.m. Pej:* clericalism.

cléricaliste [klerikalist], *s.m. & f.* clericalist.

cléricature [klerikatyːr], *s.f.* **1.** *Ecc:* priesthood, ministry; **entrer dans la c.,** to take holy orders. **2.** (*a*) clerkship (in lawyer's office); (*b*) clerical staff (of lawyer's office).

clermontois, -oise [klɛrmɔ̃twa, -waːz], *a. & s. Geog:* (native, inhabitant) of Clermont.

clérouchie [kleruʃi], **clérouquie** [kleruki], *s.f. Gr.Hist:* cleruchy.

clérouque [kleruk], *s.m. Gr.Hist:* cleruch.

clèthre [klɛtr̥], *s.m. Bot:* clethra, white alder.

clévéite [kleveit], *s.f. Miner:* cleveite.

clévois, -oise [klevwa, -waːz], *a. & s. Geog:* (native, inhabitant) of Clèves.

clic [klik], (*a*) *s.m. & int.* click; (*b*) *s.m. Ling:* click.

clic-clac [kli(k)klak], *s.m.* cracking (of whip, etc.); clatter (of sabots, etc.); clanking (of machinery).

clichage [kliʃaːʒ], *s.m.* **1.** *Typ:* (*a*) stereotyping; (*b*) electro-typing. **2.** *Min:* (*a*) caging, setting (of hutches); (*b*) *pl.* (landing-)dogs (of shaft); keeps.

cliche [kliʃ], *s.f. P:* (*a*) colic; (*b*) funk, fright; **avoir la c.,** (i) to have diarrhoea; (ii) to have the wind up, to be in a blue funk.

cliché [kliʃe], *s.m.* **1.** *Typ:* (*a*) plate (of type); block (of illustration); **c. trait,** line block; (*b*) (stereotyped) plate, stereotype; *F:* stereo; (*c*) **c. galvano,** electrotype; *F:* electro; **c. à demi-teintes,** process-block; **c. de zinc,** *F:* zinco; (*d*) *Typewr:* **préparation de clichés au stencil,** cutting of wax stencils. **2.** *Phot:* negative; **prendre un c.,** to take a photograph; **c. sur pellicule,** film negative. **3.** *Lit:* cliché, stock phrase, stereotyped phrase, hackneyed expression; tag.

clicher [kliʃe], *v.tr.* **1.** *Typ:* (i) to stereotype; (ii) to take electros of (pages of book, etc.); **discours cliché,** stereotyped speech. **2.** *Min:* to cage (hutches).

clicherie [kliʃri], *s.f. Typ:* stereotyping and electrotyping shop, foundry; stereotype room (of newspaper).

clicheur [kliʃœːr], *s.m.* **1.** *Typ:* stereotyper, electrotyper, blockmaker. **2.** *Min:* cager, (on-)setter (of hutches).

clichien, -ienne [kliʃjɛ̃, -jɛn], *a. & s.* **1.** *Geog:* (native, inhabitant) of Clichy. **2.** *Hist:* **Clichiens, Clichyens,** the Clichy royalist party (1795–97).

client, -ente [kliɑ̃, -ijɑ̃; -ɑ̃ːt], *s.* **1.** *Rom.Ant:* client, dependent. **2.** (lawyer's) client; (tradesman's) customer; (doctor's) patient; (portrait painter's) sitter; (cabman's) fare; (hotel) visitor; (second's) principal (in duel); *F:* **c'est un drôle de c.,** he's a queer customer.

clientèle [kliɑ̃tɛl], *s.f.* **1.** *Rom.Ant:* (*a*) protection, patronage; (*b*) train of clients, of dependents; clientele, clientage. **2.** (*a*) practice (of barrister or doctor); **faire de la c.,** to practise; (*b*) *Com:* (i) custom; (ii) customers; (iii) connection; (iv) goodwill; **belle c.,** (i) fine practice; (ii) wide connection; **accorder sa c. à . . .,** to patronize.

cliff-dwellers [klifdwelœːr], *s.m.pl. Prehist:* cliff-dwellers.

clifoire [klifwaːr], *s.f.* (toy) squirt.

clignement [kliɲmɑ̃], *s.m.* blink(ing), wink(ing); flicker of the eyelids; **regarder qn avec un c. d'yeux, de paupières,** to blink at s.o.; **lancer un c. d'œil à qn,** to wink at s.o.

cligner [kliɲe], *v.tr. & i.* **1.** (*a*) **c. les yeux (pour mieux voir),** to screw up one's eyes; (*b*) **c. les yeux, les paupières,** to blink; **il n'a pas cligné,** he didn't wince, he never made a sign. **2.** (*a*) **c. (de) l'œil à qn,** to wink at s.o.; **c. l'œil droit,** to wink one's right eye; (*b*) **c. des yeux,** to signify assent with a flicker of the eyelids.

clignotant [kliɲɔtɑ̃]. **1.** *a.* blinking (eyes); twitching (eyelid); twinkling (star); *Nau: etc:* **signal c.,** intermittent signal; **feu c.,** (i) occulting light (of lighthouse); (ii) *Adm:* flashing (amber) traffic light. **2.** *a. Z:* **membrane clignotante,** nictitating membrane. **3.** *s.m. Aut:* winker, winking-light (direction) indicator, flashing indicator; *U.S:* flasher, blinker; *Pol.Ec: F:* **clignotants,** indicators.

clignotement [kliɲɔtmɑ̃], *s.m.* blinking (of eyes); twinkling (of star); twitching (of eyelid); flickering (of arc-lamp).

clignoter [kliɲɔte], *v.i.* (*a*) **c. des yeux,** to blink; (*b*) (*of star*) to twinkle; (*c*) (*of eyelid*) to twitch; (*d*) (*of arc-lamp*) to flicker; (*e*) (*of signal light*) to flash.

clignoteur [kliɲɔtœːr], *s.m.* intermittent light signal; flashing indicator.

climacique [klimasik], *a.* of, relating to, a climax.

climat [klima], *s.m.* **1.** climate. **2.** region, climate. **3.** *Lit:* atmosphere. **4.** *Vit:* (*in Burgundy*) = CRU[2].

climatérique[1] [klimaterik]. *A.Med: etc:* **1.** *a.* climacteric (year, etc.). **2.** *s.f.* **la grande c.,** the grand climacteric.

climatérique[2], **climatique** [klimatik], *a.* climatic (conditions, etc.); **station c.,** health-resort.

climatisation [klimatizasjɔ̃], *s.f.* air-conditioning.

climatisé [klimatize], *a. Ind:* air-conditioned.

climatiser [klimatize], *v.tr.* to air-condition.

climatiseur [klimatizœːr], *s.m.* air-conditioner.

climatisme [klimatism], *s.m.* problems and organization of health-resorts.

climatologie [klimatɔlɔʒi], *s.f.* climatology, climatography.

climatologique [klimatɔlɔʒik], *a.* climatological.

climatologue [klimatɔlɔg], *s.m. & f.* climatologist.

climatothérapeutique [klimatɔterapøtik], **climatothérapique** [klimatɔterapik], *a.* climatotherapeutic.

climatothérapie [klimatɔterapi], *s.f.* climatotherapy.

climature [klimatyːr], *s.f.* climature, climatic conditions.

climax [klimaks], *s.m. Bot: Lit:* climax.

clin[1] [klɛ̃], *s.m. Mec.E:* (**joint à**) **c.,** lap-joint, covering joint; **soudure à c.,** fillet weld; *N.Arch:* (**bordé**) **à clin(s),** clinker-built; *s.a.* PLANCHE 1.

clinandre [klinɑ̃dr̥], *s.m. Bot:* clinandrium.

clinch [klinʃ], *s.m. Box:* clinch.

clinche [klɛ̃ːʃ], *s.f.* = CLENCHE.

clin[2] **d'œil** [klɛ̃dœːj], *s.m.* wink; **faire un c. d'œ. à qn,** to give s.o. a wink, to wink at s.o.; **en un c. d'œ.,** in the twinkling of an eye, in a split second.

cline [klin], *s.m. Biol:* cline.

clinfoc [klɛ̃fɔk], *s.m. Nau:* flying jib.

clinicien [klinisjɛ̃], *a. & s.m.* (**médecin**) **c.,** clinician.

clinique [klinik]. *Med:* **1.** *a.* clinical (lecture, etc.); **assister aux leçons cliniques,** to walk the wards. **2.** *s.f.* (*a*) clinical lecture, bedside instruction; **suivre la c. d'un hôpital,** to walk the wards; (*b*) nursing home; **c. d'accouchement,** maternity home; (*c*) teaching hospital.

clinker [kliŋkəːr], *s.m.* (*cement-making*) clinker.

clinocéphalie [klinɔsefali], *s.f. Ter:* clinocephaly.

clinochlore [klinɔklɔːr], *s.m. Miner:* clinochlore.

clinoclase [klinɔklɑːz], **clinoclasite** [klinɔklazit], *s.f. Miner:* clinoclase, clinoclasite.

clinoédrite [klinɔedrit], *s.f. Miner:* clino(h)edrite.

clinohumite [klinɔymit], *s.f. Miner:* clinohumite.

clinoïde [klinɔid], *a. Anat:* clinoid (apophysis).

clinomanie [klinɔmani], *s.f. Med:* the obsession of wanting to lie down.

clinomètre [klinɔmɛtr̥], *s.m. Surv: etc:* clinometer; gradient indicator; *Av: Navy:* inclinometer; *Anthr:* clinometer; **c. à bulle,** bead clinometer.

clinopode [klinɔpɔd], *s.m. Bot:* clinopodium.

clinorhombique [klinɔrɔ̃bik], *a. Cryst:* clinorhombic.

clinostat [klinɔsta], *s.m. Bot:* clinostat.

clinostatique [klinɔstatik], *a. Med:* resulting from a recumbent position.

clinquaille [klɛ̃kɑːj], *s.f. P:* cash, *P:* chink.

clinquant [klɛ̃kɑ̃], *s.m.* **1.** tinsel; **vers pleins de c.,** flashy verse; **c. du style,** meretriciousness, showiness, of style; **tout cela n'est que du c.,** that's all frippery. **2.** *Tchn:* foil; *Bookb: etc:* Dutch foil; *El.E:* **balai de c.,** foil brush. **3.** *a.* flashy, tawdry.

clinquanter [klɛ̃kɑ̃te], *v.tr.* to trim (clothes, etc.) with tinsel.

clintonite [klɛ̃tɔnit], *s.f. Miner:* clintonite.

Clio [klio]. **1.** *Pr.n.f. Gr.Myth:* Clio. **2.** *s.f. Moll:* clio.

clip [klip], *s.m.* (*jewel, fountain-pen*) clip.

clipper [klipœːr], *s.m.* **1.** *A.Nau:* clipper. **2.** *Sp:* small (fast) sailing-boat. **3.** *Av:* clipper.

cliquart [klikaːr], *s.m.* (*a*) *Geol:* (i) (*in Paris Basin*) stratum of limestone or gypsum; (ii) fine-grained sandstone (used in the manufacture of mosaics); (*b*) (*type of*) building stone.

clique[1] [klik], *s.f.* **1.** *Pej:* clique, gang, set. **2.** *Mil: F:* (drum and bugle) band.

clique[2], *s.f. A:* thumb-piece (of latch, etc.).

cliquer [klike], *v.i. A:* to click; **faire c. le loquet de la porte,** to rattle the latch of the door.

cliques [klik], *s.f.pl. A:* wooden shoes, pattens; *F:* **prendre ses c. et ses claques,** to take oneself off smartly; to pack up; to go off bag and baggage; *F:* to scram.

cliquet [klikɛ], *s.m.* **1.** *Mec.E:* catch, pawl (of winch, etc.), click, dog, ratchet, catch-wheel; **c. d'arrêt, c. de retenue,** detent, holding-dog, holding-pawl, stop-pawl, retaining-catch; **c. d'arrêt de frein,** brake-dog, brake-pawl; **c. de déclenchement,** release-pawl; **c. d'entraînement, c. de progression,** driving-pawl; **c. de fermeture, c. de verrouillage,** locking-pawl; **c. de serrure,** locking catch. **2. c. (-fermoir),** catch (of bracelet, etc.). **3.** *Tls:* **c. à canon, c. à percer, c. porte-foret,** ratchet-brace, ratchet-drill; **c. à manchon court,** short-head ratchet-brace; **c. simple,** ratchet-spanner, ratchet-wrench.

cliquetant [kliktɑ̃], *a.* rattling, clanking (chains, etc.); jingling (keys, etc.).

cliquètement [klikɛtmɑ̃], *s.m.* = CLIQUETIS.

cliqueter [klikte], *v.i.* (**il cliquette, il cliquettera**) (*of chains, etc.*) to rattle, clank; (*of swords, etc.*) to click; (*of glasses, etc.*) to clink, chink; (*of keys, etc.*) to jingle; *Aut:* to pink.

cliquetis [klikti], *s.m.* rattling, rattle (of chain); clank(ing) (of fetters, etc.); click(ing), clash (of swords, etc.); clink(ing), chinking (of glasses, etc.); jingling, jingle (of keys, etc.); *Aut:* pinking.

cliquette [klikɛt], *s.f.* **1.** (*a*) (pair of) castanets; (*b*) (minstrels') bones; (*c*) nonsense rhyme, nursery rhyme; (*d*) = CLIQUE[2]; (*e*) (i) *A:* clapper (of leper's rattle); (ii) *Ecc:* **c. ecclésiastique,** clapper (to tell the congregation when to kneel, etc.); (*f*) *A:* bell for matins.

cliquettement [klikɛtmɑ̃], *s.m.* = CLIQUETIS.

clisiade [klizjad]. **1.** *a. Ant:* **porte c.,** chariot entrance (to hippodrome). **2.** *s.f. Civ.E:* lock gate.

clissage [klisaːʒ], *s.m.* **1.** (*a*) wickering (of bottles, etc.); (*b*) wicker-work. **2.** *Surg:* (*a*) splinting, setting (of fractured limb, etc.); (*b*) splint.

clisse [klis], *s.f.* **1.** (*a*) wicker covering (of bottle); (*b*) cheese-drainer. **2.** *Surg:* (= ÉCLISSE) splint.

clisser [klise], *v.tr.* **1.** to wicker (bottles); **bouteille clissée,** demijohn; **tourie clissée,** carboy. **2.** *Surg:* to put (limb) in splints, to splint (limb).

clitocybe [klitɔsib], *s.m. Fung:* clitocybe.

clitocybine [klitɔsibin], *s.f. Med:* clitocybin(e).

clitographe [klitɔgraf], *s.m.* (in)clinometer.

clitoridectomie [klitɔridɛktɔmi], *s.f. Surg:* clitoridectomy.

clitoris [klitɔris], *s.m. Anat:* clitoris.

clitorisme [klitɔrism], *s.m. Med:* clitorism.
clivable [klivabl], *a.* cleavable (rock, crystal, etc.).
clivage [kliva:ʒ], *s.m.* **1.** cleaving (of diamonds, etc.). **2.** cleavage (of rocks, etc.); **à c. net,** cleaving readily, distinctly; **plan de c.,** (i) cleavage plane; (ii) *Surg:* excision line. **3. le c. des, entre les, couches sociales,** the gulf that separates the social strata.
cliver [klive], *v.tr.* **1.** to cleave, split (diamonds, etc.); to chip (stones). **2.** *Surg:* to excise (tumour, etc.).
se cliver, (*of rock, etc.*) to split, cleave.
clivia [klivja], *s.m.*, **clivie** [klivi], *s.f. Bot:* clivia.
cloacal, -aux [klɔakal, -o], *a. Anat:* cloacal (sac).
cloaque [klɔak]. **1.** *s.f. Rom.Ant:* **la grande C.,** the *Cloaca Maxima,* the Great Sewer. **2.** *s.m.* (*a*) cesspool; **c. de vices,** sink of iniquity; (*b*) *Anat: Z:* cloaca.
clochage [klɔʃa:ʒ], *s.m. Hort:* putting (of plant) under a cloche.
clochard [klɔʃa:r], *s.m. F:* tramp, *U.S:* hobo.
clochardiser [klɔʃardize], *v.tr.* to reduce (s.o.) to beggary.
cloche [klɔʃ], *s.f.* **1.** bell; (*a*) **sonner les cloches,** to ring, chime, the bells; *P:* **sonner les cloches à qn,** to haul s.o. over the coals; **tinter la c.,** to toll the bell; **la c. du dîner,** the dinner-bell; **le premier coup de c.,** the first bell; *Ind:* **heures hors c.,** overtime; **fleurs en c.,** bell-shaped flowers; **trajectoire en c.,** looping trajectory; *F:* **déménager à la c. de bois,** to do a moonlight flit, to shoot the moon; *Prov:* **qui n'entend qu'une c. n'entend qu'un son,** one should hear both sides of a question; **voilà un tout autre son de c.,** that's quite a different way of looking at things; *Nau:* **c. flottante,** bell-buoy; **la c. "feu,"** the fire gong; *Coel:* **c. natatoire,** swimming bell (of siphonophore); *s.a.* SONNER 2; (*b*) *Bot:* **c. de bruyère,** heath-bell. **2.** (*a*) bell (of gasometer); *Ch:* bell-jar; receiver; *Ch: Ph:* **c. à vide,** vacuum bell-jar; (*b*) *Hort:* bell-glass, cloche; **c. tente,** tent cloche; **c. tunnel, continue,** continuous cloche; *F:* **mettre qch. sous c.,** to keep sth. in a glass case; (*c*) *Dom.Ec:* (i) dish-cover; (ii) wire dish-cover; **c. à fromage,** cheese-cover; (*d*) *Med:* cup (for blistering); (*e*) *El.E:* petticoat, hood (of insulator); *Petroleum Ind:* **c. à barbotage,** bubbling hood; *Hyd.E:* **c. à plongeur,** diving-bell; **c. d'air,** air-chamber, receiver (of pump); *Mch:* **soupape à c.,** cup-valve; *Metall:* **c. de haut fourneau,** cone, bell, of a blast furnace; *Mec.E:* **c. de cardan,** universal-joint bell-housing; (*f*) *Nau:* barrel, drum (of capstan); (*g*) *Cost:* cloche hat. **3.** (*a*) *Cer:* blister, bubble, bleb; (*b*) *F:* **avoir des cloches aux mains,** to have blistered hands. **4.** *Min:* opening (of quarry). **5.** *Geol:* subsidence, pothole. **6.** *O: P:* head; *P:* **se taper la c.,** to nosh, guzzle. **7.** *P:* ignoramus; clumsy person; **ça fait c.,** that looks idiotic; **avoir un air c.,** to look stupid. **8.** *F:* **la c.,** tramps and beggars (in general); **qn de la c.,** a beggar.
clochement [klɔʃmɑ̃], *s.m.* (*a*) limp(ing); (*b*) (mechanical) defect.
cloche-pied [klɔʃpje], *s.m.* (*no pl.*) *Games:* hopscotch; **sauter à c.-p.,** to hop (on one foot); **s'éloigner à c.-p.,** to hop away.
clocher[1] [klɔʃe], *s.m.* belfry, bell-tower; church tower, steeple; **il n'a vu que le c. de son village,** he knows nothing of the world; **disputes de c.,** petty local quarrels; **esprit de c.,** parochial spirit, parochialism, localism; **politique de c.,** parish-pump politics; *Sp:* **course au c.,** point-to-point race.
clocher[2], *v.i.* to limp, hobble; **c. du pied droit,** to be lame in the right foot; *F:* **vers qui cloche,** halting, lame, verse; **il y a quelque chose qui cloche,** there is something wrong, a hitch, somewhere.
clocher[3]. **1.** *v.tr. Hort:* to cloche; to put (melons, etc.) under a cloche. **2.** (*a*) *v.tr. Rail:* to signal (arrival of train) with a bell; (*b*) *v.i. Dial:* (*of hour*) to strike; (*of bell*) to ring. **3.** *Dressm:* **jupe clochée,** flared skirt.
clocher-mur [klɔʃemy:r], *s.m. Ecc.Arch:* wall-belfry; *pl. clochers-murs.*
clocheton [klɔʃtɔ̃], *s.m. Arch:* pinnacle turret.
clochette [klɔʃɛt], *s.f.* **1.** small bell, hand-bell; **c. de troupeaux,** sheep-bell. **2.** *Bot:* (any) small bell-flower (of the convolulus or campanula families); **c. d'hiver,** snowdrop.
clodo [klɔdo], *s.m. P:* tramp, *U.S:* hobo.
clodoaldien, -ienne [klɔdɔaldjɛ̃, -jɛn], *a. & s. Geog:* (native, inhabitant) of Saint-Cloud.
cloison [klwazɔ̃], *s.f.* **1.** partition, division; **mur de c.,** dividing wall; **c. de bois,** wooden partition; **c. en briques,** parpen wall; **séparer qch. par une c.,** to partition sth. off. **2.** *Nat.Hist:* septum, dissepiment. **3.** (*a*) *Aut:* baffle plate (of silencer); (*b*) *Mch:* **c. d'eau,** water space; (*c*) *Min:* **c. d'aérage,** brattice; (*d*) *Nau: Av:* bulkhead; *Nau:* **c. d'abordage,** collision bulkhead; **c. étanche,** (i) *Nau:* watertight bulkhead; (ii) *Av:* pressure bulkhead; **c. étanche au pétrole, aux gaz,** oil-tight, gas-tight, bulkhead; **c. d'incendie, c. pare-feu,** fire-resisting, fireproof, bulkhead; fire wall; **c. coupe-feu,** fire-retarding bulkhead; *Av:* **c. de décrochage,** wing fence; *F:* **il y a des cloisons étanches entre les différents services,** each department is kept in a watertight compartment; (*e*) *Sm.a:* land (between rifling grooves); (*f*) *Exp:* **c. de grain de poudre,** web.
cloisonnage [klwazɔna:ʒ], *s.m.* **1.** partitioning; baffle-plating; isolation; compartmentalization; *Min:* bratticing; *N.Arch:* bulkheading. **2. construction en c.,** framework.
cloisonné [klwazɔne], *a.* **1.** *Nat.Hist:* septate(d). **2.** *Aer:* cellular (construction). **3.** *Ind: Art:* cloisonné (enamel). **4.** *Mch:* **chaudière cloisonnée,** tube-plate boiler.
cloisonnement [klwazɔnmɑ̃], *s.m.* **1.** partitioning; baffle-plating; *Min:* bratticing; *N.Arch:* bulkheading; **pont de c.,** bulkhead deck. **2.** *Nat.Hist:* septation. **3.** *Aer:* cellular construction. **4.** *Surg:* **c. du vagin,** vaginoplasty.
cloisonner [klwazɔne], *v.tr.* to partition (off) room; *N.Arch:* to bulkhead (off); *Min:* to brattice.
cloître [klwatr̥], *s.m.* **1.** cloister(s) (of monastery, etc.). **2.** cloister, monastery, convent; **vie de c.,** cloistered life. **3.** *A:* close, precincts (of cathedral).
cloîtrer [klwatre], *v.tr.* to cloister (s.o.); to shut (s.o.) up in a convent; **nonne cloîtrée,** enclosed nun.
se cloîtrer. 1. to enter a convent, a monastery. **2.** to live the life of a recluse.
cloîtrier, -ère [klwatri(j)e, -ɛ:r], *a. & s.* enclosed (monk, nun); cloisterer.
clone [klɔn], *s.m. Biol:* clone.
clonique [klɔnik], *a. Med:* clonic (spasm).
clonisme [klɔnism], *s.m. Med:* clonism.
clonus [klɔny:s], *s.m. Med:* clonus, clonic spasm.
clope [klɔp], *s.m. P:* cigarette stub, fag end.
clopin-clopant [klɔpɛ̃klɔpɑ̃], *adv. F:* **aller c.-c.,** to limp along, hobble about; **entrer, sortir, avancer, c.-c.,** to hobble in, out, on; **commerce qui va c.-c.,** business that has its ups and downs.
clopiner [klɔpine], *v.i.* to hobble, limp; (*of one-legged man*) to stump along; **entrer, sortir, en clopinant,** to stump in, out; **il arriva en clopinant,** he limped up.
clopinettes [klɔpinet], *s.f.pl. P:* nothing; **des c.!** nothing doing! **qu'est-ce qu'on vous paie?—des c.!** what do they pay you?—damn all!
cloporte [klɔpɔrt], *s.m.* **1.** *Crust:* wood-louse, slater, *U.S:* sowbug; **c. de mer,** sea-louse. **2.** *P:* (*pun on* **clos-porte**) door-keeper, hall porter, janitor.
cloquage [klɔka:ʒ], *s.m.* (*a*) blistering (of paint); (*b*) formation of bubbles (in soap manufacture).
cloque[1] [klɔk], *s.f.* **1.** (*a*) lump, swelling (from insect bite, etc.); (*b*) blister (on hand, paint, etc.). **2.** *Agr:* rust (of corn); *Arb:* blight; exoascales, curl (of peach-tree, etc.). **3.** *Bot:* **herbe à cloques,** bladder-herb, winter-cherry.
cloque[2], *s.f. P:* (*a*) breaking of wind, fart; (*b*) **être en c.,** to be in the family way.
cloqué [klɔke]. **1.** *a. Agr:* rusty (wheat); *Arb:* blighted, curled (leaf). **2.** *s.m. Tex:* **c. de soie,** ripple silk (fabric).
cloquer[1] [klɔke], *v.i. & pr.* (*of paint, skin, etc.*) to blister.
cloquer[2], *v.i. P:* to break wind, to fart.
clore [klɔ:r], *v.def.* (= FERMER, *which has taken its place in most uses*) (*p.p.* **clos**; *pr.ind.* **je clos, il clôt, ils closent**; *pr.sub.* **je close**; *fu.* **je clorai**). **1.** *v.tr.* (*a*) to close (up), shut (up) (shop, eye, mouth, etc.); (*b*) to enclose (park, garden, etc.); **jardin clos de murs,** walled-in garden; (*c*) to end, finish (discussion, etc.); to conclude (bargain); to close (account); **c. les débats,** to close the meeting; to adjourn; **le registre d'inscriptions sera clos le . . .,** the closing date for applications is . . . . **2.** *v.i.* (*a*) (*of doors, etc.*) to close, shut; **aucune porte ne clôt bien,** there is not one door which shuts properly; (*b*) (*of day, etc.*) to draw to its close.
se clore, (*of meeting, etc.*) to come to an end.
clos [klo]. **1.** *a.* (*a*) closed, shut up; **bouche close!** not a word! **à la nuit close,** after dark; *Jur:* **tenir son locataire c. et couvert,** to keep one's tenant's house in habitable repair; **c. et coi,** snug and cosy at home; *Jur:* **à huis c.,** in camera; **c'est lettre close pour moi,** it's a mystery to me; (*b*) finished; *Ecc:* **Pâques closes,** Low Sunday; (*c*) **cheval c. de derrière,** cow-hocked horse; **jarrets c.,** cow-hocks. **2.** *s.m.* enclosure, enclosed ground (under cultivation); close; **c. (de vigne),** vineyard.
closage [kloza:ʒ], *s.m. Dial:* (*W.Fr.*) orchard (surrounded by hedges).
closeau, -eaux [klozo], *s.m.* small enclosure; cottage garden.
closerie [klozri], *s.f.* **1.** (*a*) small (enclosed) estate; (*b*) smallholding. **2.** *A:* pleasure garden (in Paris).
closier, -ière [klozje, -jɛ:r], *s.m. & f.* (*a*) smallholder; (*b*) farm labourer; worker in orchard, vineyard.
clostre [klostr̥], *s.m.* semi-cylindrical tile (used for decorating balustrade, wall).
clostridium [klostridjɔm], *s.m.inv.*, **clostridion** [klostridjɔ̃], *s.m. Bac:* clostridium.
Clotilde [klɔtild], *Pr.n.f.* Clotilda.
clôture [kloty:r], *s.f.* **1.** (*a*) enclosure, fence, fencing; *Jur:* close; **c. en planches,** hoarding; **c. de fer,** iron railing; **c. en fil métallique,** wire fence; **mur de c.,** (party) fence wall, enclosing wall; cloister wall; *Ecc.Arch:* **c. de chœur,** choir screen; *Jur:* **bris de c.,** breach of close; (*b*) *Mec.E: Hyd.E:* **c. à eau,** water seal; **c. à siphon,** siphon trap; (*c*) *Ecc:* **faire vœu de c.,** to take vows of enclosure. **2.** (*a*) closing, closure (of offices, theatre, etc.); *Ven:* **c. de la chasse,** close of season; *P.N: Th:* **c.,** closed for the season; (*b*) conclusion, end (of sitting, of sittings, etc.); **séance de c.,** closing session; **demander la c. (d'une discussion),** to move the closure (of a debate); **prononcer la c. des débats,** to declare the discussion closed; *St.Exch:* **cours, prix, de, en, c.,** closing, price. **3.** *Com:* closing, winding up (of account); making up, balancing (of books).
clôturer [klotyre], *v.tr.* **1.** to enclose, shut in (field, etc.). **2.** (*a*) to close down (factory, etc.); (*b*) to terminate, conclude (session); to bring (session, etc.) to a close; **ce discours clôtura la séance,** with this speech the meeting came to an end; *Pol:* **c. les débats,** to closure the debate. **3.** *Com:* to wind up, close (accounts, etc.); *Jur:* **c. une faillite,** to close a bankruptcy.
clou [klu], *s.m.* **1.** (*a*) nail; *Surg:* pin; **c. à tête de diamant,** clout nail, spike-nail; **c. à tête perdue, c. étêté,** brad; **c. de bouche, de soufflet,** tack; **c. découpé, étampé,** cut nail; **c. doré,** brass-headed nail; stud; **cuir garni de clous dorés,** studded leather; *Furn:* **c. de tapissier,** bullen-nail; **c. de Paris,** wire nail; **c. à glace,** frost nail, calkin; **c. de vitrier,** glazing sprig; **souliers à gros clous,** hob-nailed boots; *Nau:* **c. de carvelle,** deck nail; **c. à maugère,** scupper nail; **attacher qch. avec un c.,** to nail sth. up (or down); **maigre comme un c.,** as thin as a rake; *Typ:* **tête de c.,** batter; *F:* **poser ses clous,** to down tools; **ça ne vaut pas un c.,** it's not worth a tinker's cuss; *P:* **ne pas en fiche un c.,** to do damn all; *P:* **bouffer des clous,** to have nothing to eat; *s.a.* CHASSER 1, RIVER; *P:* **des clous!** nothing doing! no fear! (*b*) stud (of pedestrian crossing); **traverser dans les clous,** to cross at a pedestrian crossing; (*c*) **c. cavalier,** staple; **c. à crochet,** hook; **c. barbelé,** spike; (*d*) *F:* star-turn, chief attraction (of entertainment); (*e*) *P:* **mettre qch. au c.,** to pawn sth., *P:* to put sth. up the spout; (*f*) *Mil: P:* cells, clink; **au c.,** in clink. **2.** *Arch:* nailhead. **3.** *Med:* (*a*) boil, carbuncle; *Vet:* **c. de rue,** inflammation (due to picked-up nail); (*b*) stab of pain; stitch. **4.** *Cu:* **c. de girofle,** clove. **5. (vieux) c.,** (i) ancient car, old crock; (ii) *Cy:* boneshaker.
clouage [klua:ʒ], *s.m.* nailing.
clou-boule [klubul], *s.m.* round-headed stud; *pl. clous-boules.*
cloué [klue]. **1.** *a.* (*a*) nailed; riveted; (*b*) *Her:* cloué. **2.** *s.m. Bootm:* riveted boot.
clouement [klumɑ̃], *s.m.* nailing.
clou-épingle [kluepɛ̃:gl], *s.m.* brad; *pl. clous-épingles.*
clouer [klue], *v.tr.* **1.** to nail (sth.) (up, down); to fasten (sth.) with nails; **tapis cloué,** fitted carpet; **c. son pavillon,** to nail one's colours to the mast; *F:* **c. le bec à qn,** to silence s.o., to shut s.o. up. **2.** to pin (sth.) down; to rivet; to hold (sth.) fast; **c. qn contre un mur,** to pin s.o. against a wall; **rester cloué sur place,** to stand stock-still, rooted to the spot; **être cloué à son lit,** to be tied to one's bed (by illness); to be bedridden; **être cloué sur place par des affaires urgentes,** to be tied to the spot by urgent business; *Chess:* **c. une pièce,** to pin a piece; *Mil:* **c. au sol,** to pin down.

cloueur [kluœːr], *s.m.* nailer.
cloutage [klutaːʒ], *s.m.* **1.** studding (of box, etc.). **2.** shoeing (of horse); fixing (of horseshoe).
clouté [klute], *a.* studded, bradded (shoes); **passage c.**, pedestrian, zebra, crossing, *U.S:* crosswalk; **ciel c. d'étoiles**, sky studded with stars.
clouter [klute], *v.tr.* **1.** to stud; to ornament (box) with nails. **2.** to fix (horseshoe).
clouterie [klutri], *s.f.* **1.** (*a*) nail-making; (*b*) the nail trade. **2.** nail works, factory; nailery.
cloutier, -ière [klutje, -jɛːr]. **1.** *s.m.* (*a*) nailer, nailsmith; (*b*) nail dealer. **2.** *a.* **machine cloutière**, nail-making machine. **3.** *s.f.* **cloutière**, nail-box.
clouure [kluyːr], *s.f.* **1.** nailing (of cases, etc.); riveting (of plates). **2.** nail-hole.
Clovis [klɔvis], *Pr.n.m. Hist:* Clovis.
clovisse [klɔvis], *s.f. Moll:* carpet-shell; clam.
clown [klun], *s.m.* clown; buffoon.
clownerie [klunri], *s.f.* **1.** (*a*) clownishness; (*b*) clownish trick; piece of clownery. **2.** the clowns (taken collectively).
clownesque [klunɛsk], *a.* clownish.
cloyère [klwajɛːr, klɔ-], *s.f.* **1.** oyster basket; fish hamper. **2.** *Com:* basket of 25 dozen oysters.
club [klyb, klœb], *s.m.* **1.** (*society*) (political, sporting) club; **c. du livre**, book club; *F:* **(fauteuil) c.**, club chair. **2.** (*implement*) (golf) club.
clubionidés [klybjɔnide], *s.m.pl. Arach:* Clubionidae.
clubiste [klybist], *s.m. A:* **clubman** [klœbman], *s.m.* clubman; *pl. clubmen* [klœbmɛn].
clunisien, -ienne [klynizjɛ̃, -jɛn], *a. Ecc:* Cluniac (order, building).
clunisois, -oise [klynizwa, -waːz], *a. & s. Geog:* (native, inhabitant) of Cluny.
cluniste [klynist], *s.m.* Cluniac (monk), Clunist.
clupe [klyp], *s.f. Ich:* clupeid; alose.
clupéa [klypea], *s.f. Ich:* clupea.
clupéidés [klypeide], *s.m.pl. Ich:* Clupeidae.
cluse [klyːz], *s.f. Geol:* cluse; transverse valley (*esp. in* Jura Mountains).
clusiacées [klyzjase], *s.f.pl. Bot:* Clusiaceae.
clyménie [klimeni], **clymenia** [klimenja], *s.f. Paleont:* clymenia.
clypéaster [klipeastɛːr], **clypéastre** [klipeastr̥], *s.m. Echin:* clypeaster, shield-urchin.
clypéastroïdes [klipeastrɔid], *s.m.pl. Echin:* Clypeastroida.
clypéiforme [klipeiform], *a. Nat.Hist:* clypeiform, shield-shaped.
clysmien, -ienne [klismjɛ̃, -jɛn], *a. Geol:* clysmian.
clysoir [klizwaːr], *s.m. Med:* enema(-tube).
clystère [klistɛːr], *s.m. A.Med:* clyster, enema.
Clytemnestre [klitɛmnɛstr̥], *Pr.n.f. Gr.Lit:* Clytemnestra.
cnémide [knemid], *s.f. Gr.Ant:* greave.
cnidaires [knidɛːr], *s.m.pl. Coel:* Cnidaria.
Cnide [knid], *Pr.n.m. A.Geog:* Cnidus.
cnidien, -ienne [knidjɛ̃, -jɛn], *a. & s. A.Geog:* Cnidian.
cnidoblaste [knidɔblast], *s.m. Biol:* cnidoblast.
cnidocil [knidɔsil], *s.m. Biol:* cnidocil.
cnidose [knidoːz], *s.f. Med:* urticaria, cnidosis, *F:* nettle-rash.
Cnossos [knɔsɔs], *Pr.n.m. A.Geog:* Cnossus, Cnossos, Knossos.
co- [kɔ], *pref.* co-. **1. coassurance**, coassurance, co-insurance, mutual assurance. **2. cocaution**, co-surety, joint-surety; **codonataires**, co-donors, fellow-donors; **covariation de deux espèces**, co-variation of two species.
coaccusation [kɔakyzasjɔ̃], *s.f.* joint accusation.
coaccusé, -ée [kɔakyze], *s. Jur:* co-defendant.
coacervat [kɔasɛrva], *s.m. Ch:* coacervate.
coacervation [kɔasɛrvasjɔ̃], *s.f. Ch:* coacervation.
coach [kɔtʃ], *s.m. Aut:* two-door saloon.
coacquéreur [kɔakerœːr], *s.m.* joint purchaser.
coacquisition [kɔakizisjɔ̃], *s.f.* joint purchase.
coactif, -ive [kɔaktif, -iːv], *a.* coercive, compulsory (power, etc.).
coaction [kɔaksjɔ̃], *s.f.* coercion, compulsion.
coactivité [kɔaktivite], *s.f.* coerciveness.
coadapter [kɔadapte], *v.tr.* to adapt (two things) to each other.
coadjuteur [kɔadʒytœːr], *s.m. Ecc:* coadjutor (to bishop).
coadjutorerie [kɔadʒytɔrəri], *s.f. Ecc:* coadjutorship.
coadjutrice [kɔadʒytris], *s.f. Ecc:* coadjutrix (to abbess).
coadjuvant [kɔadʒyvɑ̃], *a.* assisting, contributory (cause, etc.).
coadministrateur [kɔadministratœːr], *s.m.* co-director; *Jur:* co-trustee.
coadné [kɔadne], *a. Bot:* (co)adnate, coadunate, connate.
coagulabilité [kɔagylabilite], *s.f.* coagulability.
coagulable [kɔagylabl], *a.* coagulable.
coagulant [kɔagylɑ̃], *a. & s.m.* coagulant.
coagulateur, -trice [kɔagylatœːr, -tris], *a. Ch: Ph:* coagulative, coagulatory.
coagulation [kɔagylasjɔ̃], *s.f. Ch: Ph: etc:* coagulation, coagulating.
coaguler [kɔagyle], *v.tr.* to coagulate, congeal (albumen, etc.); to curdle (milk).
se coaguler, (*of blood, etc.*) to coagulate, congeal, clot; (*of milk*) to curdle.
coagulum [kɔagylɔm], *s.m.* **1.** coagulum; (*of the blood*) clot. **2.** coagulant; *pl. coagulums.*
coalescence [kɔalɛs(s)ɑ̃ːs], *s.f.* coalescence; coalescing; blending (of ideas, etc.).
coalescent [kɔalɛs(s)ɑ̃], *a.* coalescent.
coalisé, -ée [kɔalize], *a. & s.* allied; belonging to a coalition; **les coalisés envahirent le pays**, the allies invaded the country.
coaliser [kɔalize], *v.tr.* to unite, combine, (powers, etc.) in a coalition.
se coaliser, to form a coalition, to unite; **les nations coalisées**, the allied nations.
coalite [kolit], *s.m.* coalite.
coalition [kɔalisjɔ̃], *s.f.* **1.** coalition, union, league; **ministère de c.**, coalition ministry. **2.** (hostile) combination, conspiracy.
coalitionniste [kɔalisjɔnist], *s.m.* coalitionist.
coallié [kɔalje]. **1.** *a.* (co)allied. **2.** *s.m.pl.* allied forces; allies.
coaltar [koltaːr], *s.m.* coal tar; gas tar.
coaltarer [koltare], *v.tr.* to tar.
coaltariser [koltarize], *v.tr.* to tar, pay (ship).
coaptation [kɔaptasjɔ̃], *s.f.* **1.** *Surg:* setting (of bones); coaptation. **2.** *Biol:* coadapted, co-adjusted, structure.
coapteur [kɔaptœːr], *s.m. Surg:* fixator (for fractured bone).
coarctation [kɔarktasjɔ̃], *s.f. Med:* coarctation.
coarcté [kɔarkte], *a.* coarctate.
coassant [kɔasɑ̃], *a.* croaking (frog).
coassement [kɔasmɑ̃], *s.m.* croak(ing) (of frog).
coasser [kɔase], *v.i.* (*of frog*) to croak.
coassociation [kɔasɔsjasjɔ̃], *s.f.* copartnership, joint partnership.
coassocié, -ée [kɔasɔsje], *s.* copartner, joint partner.
coassurance [kɔasyrɑ̃ːs], *s.f.* mutual assurance; co-insurance, coassurance.
coati [kɔati], *s.m. Z:* coati.
coauteur [kɔotœːr], *s.m.* **1.** collaborator, joint author, co-author. **2.** accomplice (in crime).
coaxial, -aux [kɔaksjal, -o], *a.* coaxial.
cob[1] [kɔb], *s.m.* cob, pony.
cob[2], *s.m. Z:* kobus, water buck; **c. des roseaux**, reed buck; **c. onctueux**, (kind of) water buck.
cobalt [kɔbalt], *s.m.* cobalt; **c. d'outremer**, cobalt blue; *Miner:* **c. gris**, cobaltite, cobalt-glance; **c. arséniaté**, red cobalt; **c. radio-actif**, radio-cobalt; cobalt 60; **bombe au c.**, cobalt bomb.
cobaltage [kɔbaltaːʒ], *s.m.* cobalt plating.
cobalteux, -euse [kɔbaltø, -øːz], *a.* cobaltous.
cobaltammine [kɔbaltamin], *s.f.*, **cobaltiammine** [kɔbaltjamin], cobaltammine.
cobaltides [kɔbaltid], *s.m.pl.* the cobalt group.
cobaltifère [kɔbaltifɛːr], *a.* cobaltiferous, cobalt-bearing (ore).
cobaltine [kɔbaltin], *s.f. Miner:* cobaltine.
cobaltinitrite [kɔbaltinitrit], *s.m.* cobaltinitrite.
cobaltique [kɔbaltik], *a. Ch:* cobaltic.
cobaltiser [kɔbaltize], *v.tr.* to cover, plate, (sth.) with cobalt.
cobaltoammine [kɔbaltɔamin], *s.f.* cobaltammine.
cobaltocre [kɔbaltɔkr̥], *s.m. Miner:* erythrine, erythrite.
cobaye [kɔbaj], *s.m. Z:* guinea-pig; cavy; **servir de c.**, to be a guinea-pig.
cobéa [kɔbea], *s.m.*, **cobée** [kɔbe], *s.f. Bot:* cobaea, Mexican ivy.
cobelligérant [cɔbeliʒerɑ̃], *a. & s.m.* cobelligerent.
cobitidés [cɔbitide], *s.m.pl. Ich:* Cobitidae.
Coblence [kɔblɑ̃ːs], *Pr.n.f. Geog:* Coblentz, Koblentz.
coblencien, -zien [kɔblɑ̃sjɛ̃, -zjɛ̃], *a. & s.m. Geol:* Coblenzian, Koblenzian.
Cobourg [kɔbuːr], *Pr.n.m. Geog:* Coburg.
cobra [kɔbra], *s.m. Rept:* cobra; **c. à cou noir**, black-necked cobra, spitting cobra; **c. royal**, king cobra.
coca [kɔka]. **1.** *s.m. Bot:* coca. **2.** *s.f. Pharm:* coca.
cocagne [kɔkaɲ], *s.f.* **1.** *A:* feast, treat. **2. mât de c.**, greasy pole; **pays de c.**, land of milk and honey; land of plenty.
cocaïer [kɔkaje], *s.m. Bot:* coca (shrub).
cocaïne [kɔkain], *s.f. Pharm:* cocaine.
cocaïnisation [kɔkainizasjɔ̃], *s.f. Med:* cocainization.
cocaïnisme [kɔkainism], *s.m.*, **cocaïsme** [kɔkaism], *s.m.* cocainism.
cocaïnomanie [kɔkainɔmani], *s.f.* the cocaine habit, cocaine addiction.
cocaïnomane [kɔkainɔman], *s.m. & f.* cocaine addict.
cocarboxylase [kɔkarbɔksilɑːz], *s.f. Bio-Ch:* cocarboxylase.
cocarde [kɔkard], *s.f.* **1.** (*a*) cockade; rosette; (*b*) *Av:* roundel; fuselage marking; company crest (on aircraft); (*c*) **prendre la c.**, to enlist, to become a soldier. **2.** *P:* head, nut; **avoir sa c.**, to be drunk; **ce vin vous tape sur la c.**, this wine goes to your head.
cocardeau [kɔkardo], *s.m. Bot:* (common) stock.
cocarder (se) [sɔkɔkarde], *v.pr. P:* to get tipsy.
cocardier, -ière [kɔkardje, -jɛːr], *a.* fond of uniform(s), of all things military; chauvinistic, jingoistic; **esprit c.**, jingoism.
cocasse[1] [kɔkas], *a. F:* comical, laughable (person, sight, etc.); **c'était tout ce qu'il y a de plus c.**, it was a perfect scream.
cocasse[2], *s.f. A:* copper pot.
cocasserie [kɔkasri], *s.f. F:* **1.** oddity. **2.** *pl.* antics (of clown, etc.).
cocassier [kɔkasje], *s.m.* dealer in eggs and poultry (who buys from farms for sale in towns).
cocatris [kɔkatris], *s.m. Myth: Her:* cockatrice.
coccacées [kɔkase], *s.f.pl. Bac:* Coccaceae.
coccidés [kɔkside], *s.m.pl. Ent:* Coccidae.
coccidie [kɔksidi], *s.f.* **1.** *Algae:* cystocarp. **2.** *pl. Z:* coccidies, Coccidia.
coccidien, -ienne [kɔksidjɛ̃, -jɛn], *a. Z:* coccidian.
coccidiose [kɔksidjoːz], *s.f. Vet:* coccidiosis.
coccinelle [kɔksinɛl], *s.f. Ent:* coccinella; **c. à sept points, ladybird.**
coccinellidés [kɔksinɛlide], *s.m.pl. Ent:* Coccinellidae.
coccobacille [kɔk(k)ɔbasil], *s.m. Bac:* coccobacillus.
coccolite [kɔk(k)ɔlit], *s.f.* **1.** *Miner:* coccolite. **2.** *Geol:* coccolith.
coccolithophoridés [kɔk(k)ɔlitɔfɔride], *s.m.pl. Z:* Coccolithophoridae.
coccus [kɔk(k)ys], *s.m. Bac:* coccus.
coccygien, -ienne [kɔksiʒjɛ̃, -jɛn], *a. Anat:* coccygeal (bones, etc.).
coccyx [kɔksis], *s.m. Anat:* coccyx.
coche[1] [kɔʃ], *s.m.* (*a*) *A.Veh:* stage coach; *F:* **faire la mouche du c.**, to buzz around, to be a busybody; *F:* **manquer, rater, louper, le c.**, to miss the bus, to let an opportunity slip by; (*b*) *A.Nau:* **c. (d'eau)**, (type of) passenger barge.
coche[2], *s.f. Z:* sow.
coche[3], *s.f.* (*a*) notch, nick; score (on tally-stick); **c. d'une flèche**, notch, nock, of an arrow; **faire une c. à une taille**, to score, notch, nick, a tally; (*b*) tick; (*c*) *Carp:* gauge-mark, -notch (on timber); (*d*) *Mec.E:* **ressort à coches**, catch-spring; (*e*) *Nau:* **vergue en c.**, yard chock-a-block.
coché, côché [kɔʃe, ko-], *a.* fertile (egg).
cochelet [kɔʃlɛ], *s.m.* **1.** cockerel. **2.** *Dial:* (*in Champagne*) harvest supper.
cochène [kɔʃɛn], *s.m. Bot:* mountain ash; rowan (tree).
cochenillage [kɔʃnijaːʒ], *s.m.* cochineal dye bath.
cochenille [kɔʃniːj], *s.f. Ent: Com:* cochineal.
cocheniller [kɔʃnije], *v.tr.* to dye (material) with cochineal.
cochenillier [kɔʃnijje], *s.m. Bot:* cochineal-fig, nopal.
cocher[1] [kɔʃe], *s.m.* **1.** coachman, driver (of horse-drawn vehicle); **c. de fiacre**, cabman, *F:* cabby; **le siège du c.**, the box; *s.a.* FOUETTER 1; *Astr:* **(constellation du) C.**, the Wag(g)oner, the Charioteer. **2.** *Ich:* whip-fish.
cocher[2], *v.tr.* (*a*) to nick, notch; to mark off; to score (tally); (*b*) to tick; **c. des marchandises, des noms (sur une liste)**, to keep tally of, to check, goods, names; to tick off names on a list.
cocher[3], **côcher** [kɔʃe, ko-], *v.tr.* (*of cock*) to tread (hen).
cochère [kɔʃɛːr], *a.f.* **porte c.**, carriage gateway, main entrance.
cochet [kɔʃɛ], *s.m.* cockerel.
cochette [kɔʃɛt], *s.f. Z:* gilt, young sow.
cochevis [kɔʃvi], *s.m. Orn:* **c. huppé**, crested lark, **c. de Thekla**, Thekla, shortbilled, crested, lark.
Cochinchine [kɔʃɛ̃ʃin], *Pr.n.f. Geog:* Cochin-China.
cochinchinois, -oise [kɔʃɛ̃ʃinwa, -waːz], *a. & s.* **1.** *Geog:* Cochin-Chinese. **2.** *s. Husb:* Cochin-China fowl.

cochléaire[1] [kɔkleɛːr], *a. Anat:* (*a*) cochleate, cochleiform, spiral; (*b*) **nerf c.,** cochlear nerve.

cochléaire[2], *a. Nat.Hist:* cochlear(iform), spoon-shaped.

cochléaria [kɔklearja], *s.m. Bot:* cochlearia; **c. officinal,** scurvy-grass; **c. de Bretagne,** wild horse-radish.

cochlée [kɔkle], *s.f. Anat: Arch:* cochlea.

cochléiforme [kɔkleifɔrm], *a.* cochleiform, cochleate, spiral.

cochlidiidés [kɔklidiide], *s.m.pl. Ent:* Cochlidiidae.

cochoir [kɔʃwaːr], *s.m. Tls:* cooper's adze.

cochon [kɔʃɔ̃]. I. *s.m.* 1. (*a*) pig, hog, porker; **c. de lait,** suck(l)ing pig; **troupeau de cochons,** herd of swine; **gardeur de cochons,** swineherd; **étable à cochons,** pigsty, piggery; *F:* **aux yeux de c.,** pig-eyed; *F:* **sale comme un c.,** as filthy as a pig; *F:* (*in reproof of familiarity*) **nous n'avons pas gardé les cochons ensemble,** not so much of your "all pals together"! *F:* **amis comme cochons,** as thick as thieves; *F:* **un c. n'y retrouverait pas ses petits,** what a pigsty! (*b*) *occ. Cu:* pork; **fromage de c.,** brawn. 2. *Metall:* dross, slag, (old)horse, salamander, sow. 3. *Z:* **c. de mer,** porpoise, seahog; **c. cuirassé,** armadillo; **c. de fer,** porcupine; **c. d'Inde,** guinea-pig; **c. noir, c. des bois, c. d'Amérique,** peccary; **c. d'eau,** capybara; *Crust: F:* **c. de St-Antoine,** sow(-bug), woodlouse.

II. **cochon, -onne,** *P:* 1. *a.* swinish, indecent, foul, beastly; **histoires cochonnes,** smutty stories; **ça, c'est c.!** that's a dirty trick, a foul trick; **dix mille francs, ce n'est pas c.!** ten thousand francs, that's pretty good! **le c. de payant,** the sucker, the mug, who pays; **cochonne de tâche,** brute, swine, of a job; **c. qui s'en dédit,** it's a deal. 2. *s.m.* dirty pig; swine (of a man); **quel c.!** what a swine! **jouer un tour de c. à qn,** to play s.o. a dirty trick. 3. *s.f.* **cochonne,** slut.

cochonnaille [kɔʃɔnaːj], *s.f. F:* (i) pork, (ii) cooked meats bought at a pork butcher's, a delicatessen, shop.

cochonnée [kɔʃɔne], *s.f.* 1. litter (of pigs); farrow. 2. *Bot:* knotgrass.

cochonner [kɔʃɔne]. 1. *v.i.* (*of sow*) to farrow, to pig. 2. *v.tr. F:* to bungle, botch, muck up (piece of work, etc.).

cochonnerie [kɔʃɔnri], *s.f. P:* 1. (*a*) filthiness, beastliness; (*b*) **dire des cochonneries,** to talk smut, obscenities. 2. (*a*) trashy stuff, rubbish; (*b*) vile food, regular pigwash. 3. foul trick, *P:* lousy trick.

cochonnet [kɔʃɔnɛ], *s.m.* 1. young pig. 2. (*a*) *Games:* (*at bowls*) jack; (*b*) die with twelve faces; teetotum. 3. *Tex:* cylinder (for printing calico).

cochouan [kɔʃuɑ̃], **cochuan** [kɔʃyɑ̃], *s.m. Orn:* water-rail.

cochylis [kɔkilis], *s.f. Ent:* cochylis (moth).

cocker [kɔkɛːr], *s.m.* cocker (spaniel).

cockpit [kɔkpit], *s.m. Av: etc:* cockpit.

cocktail [kɔktɛl], *s.m.* (*a*) cocktail; (*b*) cocktail party; (*c*) *F:* mixture; (*d*) *Med:* **c. lytique,** lytic cocktail; (*e*) *Exp:* **c. Molotov,** Molotov cocktail.

coco[1] [koko, kɔ-], *s.m.* 1. (*a*) **noix de c.,** coconut; **huile de c.,** coconut oil; **beurre de c.,** coconut butter; **c. de mer, des Maldives, des Seychelles,** double coconut, sea coco; **fibre de c.,** coir (fibre); **tapis (en fibre) de c.,** coconut matting; (*b*) *P:* head, nut; **avoir le c. fêlé,** to be cracked, off one's nut; (*c*) *P:* stomach; **se remplir le c.,** to have a good blow out; **en avoir plein le c.,** to have a bellyful. 2. (*a*) liquorice water; (*b*) *P:* **mettre le c.,** to step on the gas.

coco[2], *s.m.* 1. (*child's word*) (*a*) cock-a-doodle, cock, hen; (*b*) egg; (*c*) *pl.* shoes. 2. *Mil: P: A:* horse. 3. *F:* (*a*) (poor) type; **drôle de c.,** queer stick; **vilain c.,** nasty type; *Iron:* **c'est un gentil, joli, c.!** he's a nice fellow! (*b*) **mon petit c.,** my pet.

coco[3], *s.f. P:* cocaine, *P:* snow.

coco[4], *a. & s.m. F:* **les cocos,** the commies, the reds.

coco[5], *a. F:* old-fashioned, out of date.

cocochet [kɔkɔʃɛ], *s.m.* (child's game of) horse and rider.

cocodès [kɔkɔdɛs], *s.m. A: F:* dandy, fop.

cocodette [kɔkɔdɛt], *s.f. A:* light woman.

cocon [kɔkɔ̃], *s.m.* (*a*) cocoon (of silkworm, spider, etc.); **s'enfermer dans son c.,** to retire into one's shell; (*b*) *Mil:* cocoon; **matériel en c.,** equipment in cocoon; *Navy: F:* **mettre en c.,** to mothball (a ship).

coconnage [kɔkɔnaːʒ], *s.m.* the spinning of a cocoon.

coconner [kɔkɔne], *v.i.* (*of caterpillar*) to cocoon.

coconnier, -ière [kɔkɔnje, -jɛːr]. 1. *a.* cocoon-(trade, etc.). 2. *s.f.* **coconnière,** *Ser:* cocoonery, silkworm nursery.

cocontractant, -ante [kɔkɔ̃traktɑ̃, -ɑ̃ːt], *a. & s. Jur:* contracting (partner).

cocorico [kɔkɔriko], *Onomat. & s.m.* cock-a-doodle-doo!

cocorli [kɔkɔrli], *s.m. Orn:* sanderling.

cocoter [kɔkɔte], *v.i. P:* to stink.

cocoteraie [kɔkɔtrɛ], *s.f.* coconut grove.

cocotier [kɔkɔtje], *s.m. Bot:* coconut palm; *F:* **radio c.,** bush telegraph.

cocotte [kɔkɔt], *s.f.* 1. (*a*) (*child's word*) hen, chicken, chickabiddy; (*b*) bird made out of folded paper. 2. *F:* (*a*) **ma c.,** darling; (*b*) light woman, *F:* tart. 3. *Cu:* (*a*) stewpan; **rôtir à la c.,** to pot-roast; (*b*) casserole. 4. *F:* (*a*) inflammation of the eyelids; (*b*) gonorrhoea; (*c*) foot-and-mouth disease. 5. *F:* horse; **hue, c.!** gee up! 6. *Mus: F:* **cocottes,** high staccato notes (of soprano).

cocotte-minute [kɔkɔtminyt], *s.f. R.t.m:* pressure-cooker; *pl. cocottes-minute.*

cocotter [kɔkɔte], *v.i. P:* 1. to stink. 2. *A:* (*of woman*) to lead a fast life.

cocquard [kɔkaːr], *s.m. Orn:* pero.

cocréancier, -ière [kɔkreɑ̃sje, -jɛːr], *s.* co-creditor, joint creditor.

coction [kɔksjɔ̃], *s.f.* 1. cooking; *Soapm:* boiling (of soap). 2. *Physiol: A:* digestion (of food).

cocu, -e [kɔky], *P:* 1. *s.* deceived husband, wife, cuckold; **avoir une chance, une veine, de c.,** to have the devil's own luck. 2. *a.* deceived.

cocuage [kɔkɥaːʒ], *s.m. P:* cuckoldry; (the state of) being deceived by one's wife.

cocufier [kɔkyfje], *v.tr. P:* 1. to be unfaithful to, to cuckold (one's husband). 2. to seduce the wife of, to cuckold, s.o.

Cocyte [kɔsit], *Pr.n.m. Myth:* (the river) Cocytus.

coda [kɔda], *s.f. Mus:* coda.

codage [kɔdaːʒ], *s.m.* coding.

codamine [kɔdamin], *s.f. Ch:* codamine.

code [kɔd], *s.m.* 1. collection, system, of laws; statute book; **c. civil** = Common Law; **c. pénal,** penal code; **c. d'instruction criminelle,** code of criminal procedure; **c. de justice militaire,** military law; **c. de commerce,** commercial law; **le c. maritime,** the navigation laws; **se tenir dans les marges du c.,** to keep just within the law; **c. de la morale,** moral code; **c. de la politesse,** code of good manners; *Aut:* **c. de la route,** (i) the Highway Code; (ii) the rule of the road; *Aut:* **se mettre en c.,** to dip one's headlights. 2. (*a*) **c. télégraphique,** telegraphic code; **c. de signaux, c. de signalisation, c. de transmissions,** signal-, signalling-, code; *Nau:* **c. international de signaux,** International Code; (*b*) *Mil: etc:* **c. de chiffrement,** code, cipher-book; **c. de déchiffrement,** cipher-key, code-book; **c. abrégé,** brevity code; **c. de coordonnées cartographiques,** co-ordinate code, map-reference code; **c. de signalisation par panneaux,** panel-code; **c. d'identification par panneaux,** identification-panel code; *Av:* **c. (de liaison) air-sol,** air-ground (liaison) code.

codébiteur, -trice [kɔdebitœːr, -tris], *s. Jur:* joint-debtor.

codéfendeur [kɔdefɑ̃dœːr], *s.m. Jur:* co-defendant, co-respondent.

codéine [kɔdein], *s.f. Ch:* codeine.

codéinomanie [kɔdeinɔmani], *s.f.* codeine addiction.

codemandeur, -eresse [kɔdmɑ̃dœːr, -ərɛs], *s. Jur:* co-plaintiff, joint plaintiff.

codéputé [kɔdepyte], *s.m.* 1. joint-envoy, -delegate; fellow-envoy, -delegate. 2. (*in Fr.*) fellow-member of the *Assemblée nationale.*

coder [kɔde], *v.tr.* to code (message).

codétenteur, -trice [kɔdetɑ̃tœːr, -tris], *s. Jur:* joint-holder; **c. d'un héritage,** joint heir.

codétenu, -ue [kɔdetny], *s. Jur:* fellow-prisoner.

codeur [kɔdœːr], *s.m. Elcs:* 1. **(dispositif) c.,** coder. 2. (*pers.*) programmer (who makes coded programmes for a computer).

codex [kɔdɛks], *s.m.* codex; **c. pharmaceutique,** pharmacopoeia.

codicillaire [kɔdisilɛːr], *a. Jur:* codicillary.

codicille [kɔdisil], *s.m. Jur:* codicil.

codificateur, -trice [kɔdifikatœːr, -tris]. 1. *a.* codifying. 2. *s.* codifier.

codification [kɔdifikasjɔ̃], *s.f.* 1. (*a*) codification, classification (of laws); (*b*) coding (of message). 2. digest (of the law).

codifier [kɔdifje], *v.tr.* (*p.d. & pr.sub.* **n. codifiions, v. codifiiez**) 1. to codify (laws, etc.). 2. to code (message).

codirecteur, -trice [kɔdirɛktœːr, -tris], *s.* co-director, -directress; joint manager, manageress.

codirection [kɔdirɛksjɔ̃], *s.f.* 1. joint directorship. 2. joint management.

coéchangiste [kɔeʃɑ̃ʒist], *s.* party to an exchange.

cæcum [sekɔm], *s.m.* = CÆCUM.

coéducation [kɔedykasjɔ̃], *s.f.* coeducation.

coéducationnel, -elle [kɔedykasjɔnɛl], *a.* coeducational.

coefficient [kɔefisjɑ̃], *s.m.* coefficient, factor; *Sch: U.S:* regularizing factor; **c. d'âge mental,** intelligence quotient, I.Q.; *Mth:* **c. littéral, c. numérique,** literal, numerical, coefficient; **c. multiplicateur,** multiplying factor; *Ph:* **c. d'absorption,** coefficient of absorption; **c. de dilatation,** coefficient of expansion; **c. de saturation,** saturation factor; *Mec:* **c. d'écrasement, c. d'élasticité,** modulus of compression, of elasticity; **c. d'effet utile, c. de rendement,** coefficient of efficiency; **c. de rupture,** modulus of rupture; **c. de sécurité, c. de sûreté,** safety factor; **c. de constante,** constant; *El:* **c. d'amplification,** amplification factor; *U.S:* Mu (factor); **c. de réactance,** reactive factor; **c. de réduction,** reduction factor; *Tp:* **c. d'occupation (d'un circuit),** percentage circuit occupation; *U.S:* circuit usage; *Av:* **c. de charge,** load factor; **c. de force ascensionnelle, c. de portance, c. de sustentation,** lift coefficient; **c. de traction,** thrust coefficient; **c. de traînée, c. de traînage,** drag coefficient; **c. de recul,** slip-value; **c. d'atténuation de rafales,** gust alleviation factor; (*petrol*) **c. d'octane,** octane rating; *Com: Ind: etc:* **c. d'amortissement,** damping factor, decay factor; decrement; **c. d'encombrement,** space factor; **c. d'exploitation,** operating ratio; **c. d'utilisation,** (i) duty cycle, duty factor; (ii) plant (capacity) factor; **c. de qualité,** figure of merit.

coégal, -aux [kɔegal, -o], *a.* coequal.

coégalité [kɔegalite], *sf.* coequality.

cœlacanthe [selakɑ̃ːt], *s.m. Ich:* coelacanth.

cœlacanthidés [selakɑ̃tide], *s.m.pl. Ich:* Coelacanthidae.

cœlentérés [selɑ̃tere], *s.m.pl. Z:* Coelenterata.

cœlialgie [seljalʒi], *s.f. Med:* coelialgia.

cœliaque [seljak], *a. Anat:* coeliac (artery, etc.).

cœlioscopie [seljɔskɔpi], *s.f. Med:* coelioscopy.

cœliotomie [seljɔtɔmi], *s.f. Surg:* coeliotomy.

cœloblastula [seloblastyla], *s.m. Z:* coeloblastula.

cœloglossum [seloglɔsɔm], *s.m. Bot:* coeloglossum.

cœlogyne [selɔʒin], *s.m. Bot:* coelogyne.

cœlomates [selomat], *s.m.pl. Z:* Coelomata.

cœlome [selɔm], *s.m. Z:* coelom(e).

coemption [kɔɑ̃psjɔ̃], *s.f.* coemption.

coendou [kɔɛ̃du], *s.m. Z:* coendou, tree porcupine.

cœnenchyme [senɑ̃ʃim], *s.m. Z:* coenenchyma.

cœnesthésie [senɛstezi], *s.f.* cœnaesthesis.

cœnobe [senɔb], *s.m. Biol:* coenobium.

cœnocyte [senosit], *s.m. Biol:* coenocyte.

cœnogamète [senogamɛt], *s.m. Bot:* coenogamete.

cœnosarc, cœnosarque [senosark], *s.m. Z:* coenosarc.

cœnure [senyːr], *s.m. Ann:* coenurus.

coéquation [kɔekwasjɔ̃], *s.f. Adm:* proportional assessment.

coéquipier [kɔekipje], *s.m. Sp:* fellow-member (of team, crew, etc.).

coercibilité [kɔɛrsibilite], *s.f. Ph:* coercibility (of gas, etc.).

coercible [kɔɛrsibl̩], *a. Ph:* coercible (gas, etc.).

coercitif, -ive [kɔɛrsitif, -iːv], *a. Jur: Magn:* coercive (measure, force of magnet).

coercition [kɔɛrsisjɔ̃], *s.f.* coercion.

coercitivité [kɔɛrsitivite], *s.f. Magn:* coercitivity; **c. (d'un aimant),** magnetic retentivity.

cœrébidés [serebide], *s.m.pl. Orn:* Coerebidae.

coéternel, -elle [kɔetɛrnɛl], *a. Theol:* coeternal.

coéternité [kɔetɛrnite], *s.f. Theol:* coeternity.

cœur [kœːr], *s.m.* heart. 1. (*a*) **maladie de c.,** heart disease; **arrêt de c.,** heart failure; **c. gras, adipeux,** fatty heart; **c. artificiel,** heart-lung machine; **greffe du c., de c.,** heart transplant; **opération à c. ouvert,** open-heart surgery; **tué d'une balle au c.,** killed by a bullet in the heart; **je lui mangerai le c.,** I'll have his blood; **serrer qn contre, sur, son c.,** to clasp s.o. to one's bosom; **en c.,** heart-shaped; **faire la bouche en c.,** to put on airs (and graces); **joli comme un c.,** as pretty as a picture; *F:* **joli c.,** (i) sissy; (ii) poodle-faker; *s.a.* HERBE 4, TROU 1; (*b*) **avoir mal au c., avoir le c. barbouillé, avoir le c. sur les lèvres,** to feel sick; **cela soulève le c., porte sur le c.,** it's nauseating, sickening; it makes one's gorge rise, it turns one's stomach; **cela me soulève le c. de voir . . .,** it makes me sick

to see . . .; **mon déjeuner m'est resté sur le c.,** my lunch lies heavy on my stomach; *F:* **avoir le c. bien accroché,** to have a strong stomach; *s.a.* BOURREAU. **2.** soul, feelings, mind; (*a*) **avoir qch. sur le c.,** to have sth. rankling in one's mind; **en avoir le c. net,** to get to the bottom of it, know the rights of it, to clear the matter up; **en avoir le c. net avec qn,** to have it out with s.o.; **avoir la rage au c.,** to be raging with (suppressed) anger; **au fond du c., au fond de son c.,** in one's heart of hearts; **français jusqu'au fond du c.,** French to the core; **parler à c. ouvert,** to speak freely, with open heart; **mot qui part du c.,** heartfelt word, word from the heart; **remercier qn de tout c., du fond de son c.,** to thank s.o. whole-heartedly, from the bottom of one's heart; **il me portait dans son c.,** he was very fond of me; **mettre tout son c. dans son plaidoyer,** to make a heartfelt appeal; **spectacle qui vous fend le c.,** sight that rends your heart, heart-rending sight; **il mourut le c. brisé,** he died of a broken heart; **partir le c. léger,** to set off with a light heart; **ruiner autrui de gaieté de c.,** to ruin others with a light heart; **avoir le c. gros, serré,** to be heavy-hearted, sad at heart; **il avait le c. gros,** his heart was sad, heavy; **faire qch. le c. gros,** to do sth. with a heavy heart; **avoir la mort dans le c.,** to be heart-sick, sick at heart; **la chose qui lui tient au c.,** (i) the thing he has set his heart on, (ii) the thing that hurts him most, *F:* that sticks in his gullet; **ce reproche lui tient au c.,** he has taken this reproach to heart; **avoir le c. sur la main,** to be very generous, to be open-handed; **avoir le c. sur les lèvres,** to be frank, sincere (*s.a.* **1.** (*b*)); **il est plein de c.,** his heart is in the right place; **avoir trop de c.,** to be too soft-hearted, too tender-hearted; **homme de c.,** great-hearted man; **manque de c.,** heartlessness; **je serai de c. avec vous,** I shall be with you in spirit; **si le c. vous en dit,** if you feel like it, if it appeals to you, if you fancy it; **je n'ai pas le c. à faire cela,** I am not in the mood to do that; **je n'ai pas le c. à rire,** I am in no mood for laughing; **vous n'aurez pas le c. de faire cela,** you will not be so heartless as to do that, you would not find it in your heart to do that; **des gens selon mon c.,** people after my own heart; **avoir qch. à c.,** to have sth. at heart; **avoir à c. de faire qch.,** to be bent, to have one's heart set, on doing sth.; **prendre qch. à c.,** to take sth. to heart; **il avait à c. qu'on vous nommât,** he was set on your being appointed; **cela lui pèse sur le c.,** he has taken it to heart; **prendre à c. de faire qch.,** to set one's heart on doing sth; (*b*) **apprendre, savoir, qch. par c.,** to learn, know, sth. by heart, by rote; *F:* **dîner par c.,** to go without dinner, *A:* to dine with Duke Humphrey. **3.** courage, spirit, pluck; **donner du c. à qn,** to put s.o. in good heart; to give s.o. courage, put (fresh) heart into s.o.; to hearten s.o., *F:* buck s.o. up; *F:* **avoir du c. au ventre,** to have plenty of guts; **remettre du c. au ventre à qn,** to put some fight, guts, into s.o.; **ça vous remettra du c. au ventre,** that will buck you up; **avoir un c. de lion, de poule,** to be lion-, chicken-hearted; **faire contre mauvaise fortune bon c.,** to make the best of a bad job, to put a brave face on things, to keep a stiff upper lip. **4.** (*a*) **avoir le c. à l'ouvrage,** to have one's heart in one's work; **faire qch. de bon c., de grand c.,** to do sth. whole-heartedly, (very) willingly, gladly, with pleasure; **faire qch. de mauvais c.,** to do sth. reluctantly, unwillingly; **rire de bon c.,** to laugh heartily; **travailler, y aller, de bon c., de grand c., avec c., de tout son c.,** to work heartily, with a will; to put one's back into it; **il y va de tout c.,** he puts his heart into it; **entrer de tout son c. dans qch.,** to put one's heart and soul into sth.; **le c. n'y est pas,** his, my, heart isn't in it; *s.a.* JOIE 1; (*b*) **donner son c. à qn,** to lose one's heart to s.o.; **gagner le c. de qn,** to win s.o.'s heart, s.o.'s affection, love; **aimer qn de tout son c.,** to love s.o. with all one's heart; **à vous de tout c.,** yours affectionately; *Lit:* **mon (cher) c.,** dear heart; *Prov:* **loin des yeux loin du c.,** out of sight, out of mind; *s.a.* AFFAIRE 1; (*c*) **avoir un grand c.,** to be great-hearted; **c'est un bon c.,** he is a kind-hearted, good-hearted, good-natured, sort; **il a le c. bien placé,** his heart is in the right place; **n'avoir point de c.,** to be heartless, to have no feelings. **5.** middle, midst; core; **au c. de la ville,** in the heart of the town; **au c. de la mêlée,** in the thick of the fight; **c. d'un fruit,** core of a fruit; **c. d'un chou, d'un artichaut,** heart of a cabbage, of an artichoke; *F:* **avoir un c. d'artichaut,** to fall in love with every pretty girl, handsome boy, one meets; **fromage fait à c.,** ripe cheese; **au c. de l'hiver, de l'été,** in the depth of winter, in the height of summer; *Arb:* **c. du bois,** heart-wood; **c. de chêne,** heart of oak; **pourri au c.,** red-rotted; *Her:* **c. de l'écu,** heart; heart-point; *Atom.Ph:* **c. (d'une pile),** core (of an atomic pile), reactor core; active lattice. **6.** *Cards:* heart(s); **jouer (du) c.,** to play hearts; **avez-vous du c.?** have you any hearts? **7.** (*a*) *Mec.E:* **came, excentrique, en c.,** heart; **c. de tour,** heart-shaped driver, carrier; **c. de renversement,** tumbler frame (of lathe); (*b*) *Rail:* **c. de croisement,** point of crossing, frog-point; (*c*) *Ten:* wedge, throat-piece (of racquet). **8.** *Bot:* heart-cherry.

cœur-de-bœuf [kœːrdəbœf], *s.m.* **1.** *Bot:* bullock's heart. **2.** *Moll:* isocardia; heart shell. *pl. cœurs-de-bœuf.*

cœur-de-Jeannette [kœːrdʒanɛt], *s.m. pl. cœurs-de-Jeannette.* **cœur-de-Marie** [kœːrdəmari], *s.m. pl. cœurs-de-Marie. Bot:* lyre-flower; bleeding heart.

cœur-rouge [kœrruːʒ], *s.m. Arb:* false heart-wood.

coexécuteur, -trice [kɔɛgzekytœːr, -tris], *s.* co-executor; *f.* coexecutrix.

coexistant [kɔɛgzistɑ̃], *a.* coexistent, coexisting (**avec,** with).

coexistence [kɔɛgzistɑ̃s], *s.f.* coexistence (**avec,** with); *Pol:* **c. pacifique,** peaceful coexistence.

coexister [kɔɛgziste], *v.i.* to coexist (**avec,** with).

cofferdam [kɔfɛrdam], *s.m. Hyd.E: N.Arch:* cofferdam.

coffin [kɔfɛ̃], *s.m. Agr:* whetstone sheath.

coffrage [kɔfraːʒ], *s.m.* **1.** *Min: etc:* coffering, planking, lining (of shaft, trench, etc.); **planches de c.,** plank lining. **2.** frame-work, framing, shuttering, formwork, casing (for concrete work).

coffrant [kɔfrɑ̃], *a.* coffering; *Min:* **cadre c.,** mine-shaft case.

coffre [kɔfr̥], *s.m.* **1.** (*a*) chest, coffer, bin; *Artil:* ammunition-box; *W.Tel:* cabinet; **c. à outils,** tool-chest, box; **c. de voyage,** trunk; **c. à linge,** linen chest; **c. à avoine,** (i) corn bin; (ii) *F:* (*horse*) heavy eater; *Nau:* **c. de bord,** sea-chest; **c. à pavillons,** signal locker, flag locker; *Min:* **c. à minerai,** ore bin, bunker; (*b*) *Anat:* *F:* chest; **avoir du c.,** to have plenty of chest; *F:* **avoir le c. bon,** to be sound in wind and limb; (*c*) **c. de sûreté,** safe; **les coffres de l'État,** the coffers of the State, the Treasury; (*d*) boot, *U.S:* trunk (of car). **2.** (*a*) case (of lock, etc.); **c. d'un piano,** body, case, of a piano; *Mch:* **c. à vapeur,** steam-chest, -chamber, -dome; (*b*) *Conc:* form, box; (*c*) *Hyd.E:* cofferdam; **c. d'écluse,** lock chamber. **3.** *Nau:* (*a*) **c. d'amarrage,** mooring-buoy, anchor-buoy, trunk-buoy; (*b*) moorings; **prendre son c.,** to pick up one's moorings. **4.** *Nau:* well-deck; **navire à coffre,** well-decker. **5.** *Rail:* ballast-bed (of track). **6.** *Ich:* ostracion; trunk-, coffer-, fish; **c. triangulaire,** triangular box-fish; **c. cornu,** horned box-fish, cow-fish. **7.** *Fort:* **c. de contrescarpe,** casemate in counterscarp.

coffre-fort [kɔfrəfɔːr], *s.m.* safe; strong-box; *pl. coffres-forts.*

coffrer [kɔfre], *v.tr.* **1.** *F:* to put (s.o.) in prison, *F:* in jug. **2.** *Min: Civ.E:* to coffer, plank, line (shaft, gallery).

coffret [kɔfrɛ], *s.m.* small box; tool box, tool chest; cabinet; locker; casket; **c. d'ivoire,** ivory casket; **c. à bijoux,** jewel case; **c. à documents,** deed box; **c. à, de, pharmacie,** medicine chest; *El:* **c. d'interrupteur,** switch box; *Mil: Nau:* **c. de manœuvre,** control unit.

coffretier [kɔfrətje], *s.m.* (*a*) box maker, casket maker; (*b*) dealer in boxes, caskets.

cofidéjusseur [kofideʒysœːr], *s.m. Rom.Jur:* co-surety.

cofondateur, -trice [kofɔ̃datœːr, -tris], *s.* co-founder.

cogérance [koʒerɑ̃ːs], *s.f.* joint management, co-administration.

cogérant, -ante [koʒɛrɑ̃, -ɑ̃ːt], *s.* joint manager, joint manageress; co-administrator, co-administratrix.

cogérer [koʒere], *v.tr.* to manage jointly.

co(-)gestion [koʒɛstjɔ̃], *s.f.* joint management.

cogitation [kɔʒitasjɔ̃], *s.f.* cogitation, reflection.

cogiter [kɔʒite], *v.i. usu. Iron:* to cogitate, to think.

cognac [kɔɲak], *s.m.* cognac.

cognaçais, -aise [kɔɲasɛ, ɛːz], *a.* & *s. Geog:* (native, inhabitant) of Cognac.

cognage [kɔɲaːʒ], *s.m. A:* **1.** *P:* fisticuffs, brawl. **2.** *Aut:* knocking (of engine).

cognasse [kɔɲas], *s.f. Bot:* wild quince.

cognassier [kɔɲasje], *s.m.* (*a*) *Bot:* wild quince tree; **c. du Japon,** japonica; (*b*) *Hort:* quince (tree).

cognat [kɔgna], *s.m. Jur:* cognate (relative), relation on the mother's side.

cognation [kɔgnasjɔ̃], *s.f. Rom.Jur:* cognation; kinship, *esp.* on the mother's side.

cognatique [kɔgnatik], *a. Jur:* cognatic.

cogne [kɔɲ], *s.m. P:* policeman, *F:* cop.

cognée [kɔɲe], *s.f.* axe; hatchet; **c. de bûcheron,** felling axe, woodman's axe; **mettre la c. à l'arbre,** to set the axe (i) to the tree, (ii) to the root of an evil. *s.a.* MANCHE[2] 1.

cogne-fétu [kɔɲfety], *s.m. A: F:* fussy person; *pl. cogne-fétu(s).*

cognement [kɔɲmɑ̃], *s.m. Mec.E:* knocking, knock (of machinery); thump(ing), hammering (of loose brasses, etc.).

cogner [kɔɲe]. **1.** *v.tr.* (*a*) to drive in, hammer in (wedge, nail, etc.); (*b*) to knock, beat, thump, bump; *Sp:* to hit (the ball) hard; **c. qn en passant,** to bump up against s.o. (in passing); **c. qn du coude,** to dig s.o. in the ribs; *F:* **c. un enfant,** to whack, whop, a child; *abs. F:* **il cogne dur,** he is a hard hitter; *F:* **ils se sont cognés,** they had a stand-up fight; *Fr.C: F:* **c. des clous,** to drop off to sleep. **2.** *v.i.* (*a*) to knock, rap, thump (**sur, on**); to bump (**contre,** against); **c. du poing sur la table,** to bang (one's fist) on the table; (*b*) (*of engine, etc.*) to knock, to hammer; (*c*) *P:* to stink.

se cogner à, contre, qch., to knock, come up, against sth.; *F:* **se c. la tête contre les murs,** to bang one's head against a brick wall.

cogneur, -euse [kɔɲœːr, -øːz]. **1.** *a.* & *s.m. Box:* hard-hitting (opponent, etc.); hard hitter, bruiser, battler. **2.** *a. Ven:* (hound) that is always giving tongue; babbler.

cognitif, -ive [kɔgnitif, -iːv], *a. Phil:* cognitive.

cognition [kɔgnisjɔ̃], *s.f. Phil:* cognition.

cognomen [kɔgnomɛn], *s.m. Rom.Hist:* cognomen.

cognoscibilité [kɔgnɔs(s)ibilite], *s.f. Phil:* cognoscibility.

cognoscible [kɔgnɔs(s)ibl̥], *a. Phil:* cognoscible, perceptible.

cohabitant, -ante [kɔabitɑ̃, -ɑ̃ːt], *a.* & *s.* cohabitant, cohabiter.

cohabitation [kɔabitasjɔ̃], *s.f.* cohabitation; *Jur:* **le refus de c. est considéré comme une injure grave, justifiant le divorce,** refusal to cohabit is considered a serious offence, justifying divorce.

cohabiter [kɔabite]. **1.** *v.i.* to cohabit (**avec,** with); to live together. **2.** *v.tr.* **c. une maison,** to live in the same house.

cohénite [kɔenit], *s.f. Miner:* cohenite.

cohérence [kɔerɑ̃ːs], *s.f.* coherence; consistency; **avec c.,** coherently.

cohérent [kɔerɑ̃], *a.* coherent; consistent; **d'une manière cohérente,** coherently; *Ph:* **lumière cohérente,** phased light; *Psy:* **structure mentale cohérente,** self, internal, consistency.

cohéreur [kɔerœːr], *s.m. El: W.Tg:* coherer.

cohériter [kɔerite], *v.i. Jur:* to inherit conjointly; to be included among the heirs.

cohéritier, -ière [kɔeritje, -jɛːr], *s.* co-heir, -heiress; joint heir(ess).

cohésif, -ive [kɔezif, -iːv], *a.* cohesive.

cohésion [kɔezjɔ̃], *s.f.* cohesion, cohesiveness; *Ph:* **force de c.,** cohesive force.

cohésionner [kɔezjɔne], *v.tr. Bot: Ch: etc:* to cause (molecules, etc.) to cohere.

cohésivement [kɔezivmɑ̃], *adv.* cohesively.

cohibition [kɔibisjɔ̃], *s.f.* cohibition, hindrance, restraint.

cohobation [kɔɔbasjɔ̃], *s.f. Dist:* redistillation, cohobation.

cohober [kɔɔbe], *v.tr. Dist:* to cohobate, redistil.

cohorte [kɔɔrt], *s.f.* **1.** *Rom.Mil:* cohort. **2.** (*a*) *A:* & *Lit:* band of soldiers, cohort; **les célestes cohortes,** the heavenly host; (*b*) *F:* **la c. des invités,** the mob of guests; **c. joyeuse de noceurs,** band of revellers. **3. la c. des femmes nées en 1930,** the women of the 1930 age group.

cohue [kɔy], *s.f.* crowd, press, mob, throng; **c. de voitures,** solid mass of traffic; **quelle c.!** (i) what a mob! (ii) what a mix-up!

coi, coite [kwa, kwat], *a. A:* quiet, peaceful; *still used in* **se tenir c.,** to keep quiet, to lie low; **demeurer, rester, (clos et) c.,** to stay quietly at home; **en rester c.,** to be flabbergasted; *Ven:* **chien c.,** hound that never gives tongue.

coiffage [kwafaːʒ], *s.m.* **1.** *Artil:* fuse-cap. **2.** *Dent:* crowning.

coiffant [kwafɑ̃]. **1.** *a.* (*of hairstyle*) becoming; **un chapeau bien c.,** (i) a very attractive hat; (ii) a hat which fits very well. **2.** *a.* **crème coiffante,** hair cream. **3.** *s.m.* way of wearing one's hat.

coiffe [kwaf], *s.f.* **1.** *Cost:* coiffe; *A:* **c. de nuit,** nightcap. **2.** lining (of hat). **3.** cover; (*a*) sun curtain (attached to *képi*); *Nau:* **c. blanche,** white cap cover; (*b*) *Artil:* breech cover; **c. de fusée,** fuse cap; **obus à c.,** capped shell; **c. de rupture,** armour-piercing cap; (*c*) *Bookb:* head (of the back); (*d*) *A.Aer:* nose cap (of dirigible); (*e*) *Civ.E:* **c. de pieu,** pile helmet; (*f*) *I.C.E:* **c. à capuchon du carburateur,** carburettor dome cap; **c. de bougie,** sparking-plug cover; **c. de clapet,** valve retainer; (*g*) *Av:* **c. mobile (pour le train),** sliding sleeve. **4.** (*a*) caul (i) *Obst:* of new-born child, (ii) *Cu:* of sheep, pig; (*b*) *Bot:* (i) calyptra, coif (of mosses); (ii) pileorhiza.

coiffé [kwafe], *a.* **1. être c. d'un chapeau,** to be wearing a hat; **coiffée en paysanne,** wearing a peasant's head-dress; **il est né c.,** (i) he was born with a caul, (ii) *F:* he was born lucky, he was born with a silver spoon in his mouth. **2.** (*a*) **être bien c.,** to have one's hair well dressed; **je ne suis pas encore coiffée,** I haven't done my hair yet; *O:* **être coiffée à la Ninon,** to have bobbed hair; *s.a.* COIFFURE 2; (*b*) **cheval bien c.,** horse with small, well-placed ears; **chien bien c.,** dog with long, drooping ears; *F:* **chien c., chèvre coiffée,** exceptionally ugly person. **3. être c. de qn,** to be infatuated with s.o. **4.** *Chess:* **pion c.,** ringed pawn. **5.** *Nau:* **voile coiffée,** sail aback. **6.** *Tex:* **drap bien c.,** cloth with good selvedge. **7.** *Civ.E: etc:* capped (pile).

coiffer [kwafe], *v.tr.* **1.** (*a*) to cover (the head); to cap (bottle, pile, etc.); *Chess:* to ring (a pawn); **un grand chapeau coiffait sa tête,** he was wearing a large hat; **ce chapeau vous coiffe bien,** this hat suits you; **c. qn, qch., de qch.,** to cover s.o., sth., with sth.; **c. qn d'un chapeau,** to put a hat on s.o.; *F:* **c. qn d'un seau d'eau,** to throw a bucketful of water over s.o.; to souse s.o. (from a window); **montagne coiffée de neige,** snow-capped mountain; *F:* **c. son mari,** to be unfaithful to one's husband; *s.a.* CATHERINE; *Ven:* (*of hound*) **c. le sanglier,** to seize the boar by the ears; (*b*) **c. un chapeau,** to put on a hat; **du combien coiffez-vous?** what is your size (in hats)? **2. c. qn,** to dress, do, s.o.'s hair; *abs.* **il coiffe bien,** he is a good hairdresser. **3.** *A:* to intoxicate (s.o.); *abs.* **vin qui coiffe,** wine that goes to one's head. **4.** *Nau:* to gybe (the sail); **c. et servir une voile,** to back and fill a sail. **5.** *Ten:* **c. la balle,** to cover the ball. **6.** *Sp: F:* to beat; *Rac: Sp:* **c. d'une courte tête,** to beat by a short head; **se faire c. au, sur le, poteau,** to allow oneself to be beaten at the post. **7.** *Artill:* to cover; to bracket (a target); *Mil:* to reach, take (an objective). **8.** *F:* to control, direct (an organization, etc.).

se coiffer. 1. to put one's hat on; **se c. d'une casquette,** to put on or wear a cap; **se c. en cheveux,** to go without a hat. **2.** to do, dress, one's hair. **3.** *F:* **se c. de qn, de qch.,** to become infatuated with s.o., with sth.

coiffeur, -euse [kwafœːr, -øːz], *s.* **1.** hairdresser, hair stylist, coiffeur; *F:* **ce que vous appelez minute est une minute de c.!** your minute lasts a month of Sundays! **2.** *s.f.* **coiffeuse,** (small) dressing table.

coiffure [kwafyːr], *s.f.* **1.** head-dress; headgear; **c. de mariée,** bridal head-dress. **2.** hairstyle; coiffure; **c. à la grecque,** Greek style of hair-dressing; *O:* **c. à la Ninon, à la Jeanne d'Arc,** bobbed hair; **c. en garçon, à la garçonne,** Eton crop. **3.** hairdressing; **salon de c.,** hairdresser's shop, establishment, *occ.* (*for men*) saloon; (*on shop*) **c. d'art,** hair stylist.

coignassier [kɔɲasje], *s.m.* (wild) quince tree.

coignet [kwaɲɛ], *s.m.* small wedge.

Coïmbre [kɔɛ̃ːbr], *Pr.n.f. Geog:* Coimbra.

coin [kwɛ̃], *s.m.* **1.** (*a*) corner (of street, room, etc.); **maison du c., qui fait le c.,** corner house; **l'épicier du c.,** (i) the grocer round the corner; (ii) any (old) grocer you like to name; **place de c.,** corner seat (in a train); **mettre un enfant au c.,** to put a child in the corner (in disgrace); **c. (des) repas, c. salle à manger,** dining area, dining recess; **coins de la bouche,** corners of the mouth; **regard en c.,** side glance; **regarder qn du c. de l'œil,** to look at s.o. out of the corner of one's eye; **il a visité les quatre coins du monde,** he has travelled all over the world; **on venait des quatre coins du monde,** people came from far and near, from everywhere; *Games:* **jouer aux quatre coins,** to play at puss in the corner; *Bookb:* **reliure avec coins,** binding with leather corners; **demi-reliure à petits coins,** half binding; *F:* **blague dans le c.,** joking apart; *F:* **en boucher un c. à qn.,** to knock s.o. all of a heap, to flabbergast s.o.; *F:* **est-ce que Martin est dans le c.?** is Martin around? (*b*) (retired) spot, place, nook; **petit c. rustique,** small country place; **un petit c. pas cher,** a cheap, inexpensive, little place; *F:* **le petit c.,** the smallest room (in the house), the loo; **coins et recoins,** nooks and crannies; **chercher qch. dans tous les coins et recoins,** to look high and low for sth., to look for sth. all over the place; *F:* **connaître qch. dans les coins,** to know the ins and outs of sth.; *F:* **il la connaît dans les coins,** he's all there, he knows how to look after himself; **mourir au c. d'un bois, d'une haie,** to die abandoned; (*c*) *Furn:* corner cupboard; **c. d'évier,** sink tidy; (*d*) **c. de feu,** (i) *O:* smoking jacket; (ii) corner chair; fireside chair; **c. du feu,** inglenook, chimney corner; **au c. du feu,** by the fireside; **il ne bouge pas du c. du feu,** he's a stay-at-home; **il n'a jamais quitté le c. de son feu,** he has never travelled; **causerie au c. du feu,** fireside chat; (*e*) small piece, patch; **posséder un c. de terre,** to own a small plot of land; (*in a garden*) **le c. des légumes,** the vegetable plot; **voilà un c. de ciel bleu,** there's a patch of blue sky; (*f*) **tenir son c.,** (i) *Games:* to hold one's own, to keep one's end up; (ii) *F:* to shine (in company); (*g*) *Lap:* **c. de table, de culasse,** main facet. **2.** (*a*) wedge, key, quoin, chock; **en c.,** wedge-shaped; *Tls: etc:* **c. à fendre,** wood-splitting wedge; **tranchant du c.,** thin edge of the wedge; **c. de rabot,** plane-wedge; **c. demi-rond,** plug; **c. de verrouillage,** locking-pin; **c. de calage,** key wedge; **c. de centrage,** centering wedge; **c. de serrage, de dressage,** tightening, loosening, wedge; **c. prisonnier,** set key; **courroie en forme de c.,** V-shaped belt; *Mil:* **c. à canon,** gun chock; **c. d'arrêt,** quoin; *Nau:* **c. d'arrimage,** stowing-wedge; **c. de calfat,** reaming-iron; *Rail:* **c. de rail,** key; *Typ:* **c. de serrage,** quoin; (*b*) *Cost: A:* (i) false side-curl; (ii) clock (on stocking). **3.** *Num:* (*a*) stamp, die (for striking coins); **monnaie à fleur de c.,** unworn coin(s); (*b*) (= POINÇON) hallmark; **ouvrage marqué au c. du génie,** work bearing the stamp, the hallmark, of genius; **marqué au bon c.,** of the right stamp. **4.** *Vet:* corner tooth (of horse's mouth). **5.** *Opt:* **c. optique,** photometric wedge.

coinçage [kwɛ̃saːʒ], *s.m.* **1.** wedging, keying, cottering; *Rail:* **c. des rails,** keying, wedging (up) of the rails. **2.** = COINCEMENT.

coincement [kwɛ̃smɑ̃], *s.m.* (*a*) *Carp: Mec.E:* jamming (of valve, etc.); choking up (of saw blade, etc.); (*b*) wedging, keying; *Mec.E:* **c. de l'arbre,** canting of the shaft.

coincer [kwɛ̃se], *v.* (**je coinçai(s); n. coinçons**). **1.** *v.tr.* to wedge (up), chock (up) (rails, etc.); to quoin, chock (cask, etc.); *F:* **c. qn,** (i) to corner s.o., (ii) to arrest, *P:* pinch, s.o.; to run s.o. in; *Rac:* (*of horse*) **être coincé à la corde,** to be driven on the rails; *F:* **vous êtes coincé,** you're stymied; **l'auto a été coincée entre deux tramways,** the car was caught between two trams; *Nau:* **c. les panneaux,** to batten down the hatches. **2.** *v.i. & pr.* (*of machine parts, etc.*) to jam, to stick; to bind.

coincetot [kwɛ̃sto], *s.m. F:* corner.

coïncidence [kɔɛ̃sidɑ̃ːs], *s.f.* coincidence; **fait de pure c.,** entirely coincidental occurrence; **c. curieuse . . .,** by a strange coincidence . . .; **par c.,** by coincidence, by chance; *El.E:* **c. d'oscillations,** surging.

coïncident [kɔɛ̃sidɑ̃], *a.* coincident, coinciding (avec, with).

coïncider [kɔɛ̃side], *v.i.* to coincide (avec, with); **faire c. le coût avec le prix marginal,** to equate price with marginal cost.

coin-coin [kwɛ̃kwɛ̃], *s.m. & int.* (*of ducks*) quacking; quack! quack! *F: Aut:* honk! honk!

co-inculpé, -ée, coïnculpé, -ée [kɔɛ̃kylpe], *s. Jur:* fellow delinquent.

coing [kwɛ̃], *s.m. Bot:* quince; **pâte de coing(s),** quince cheese.

coinsteau, -eaux [kwɛ̃sto], *s.m. P:* sheltered corner, spot.

coïntéresser [kɔɛ̃terese], *v.tr.* **c. qn dans une affaire,** to give s.o. a joint interest in an affair.

cointéressés [kɔɛ̃terese], *s.m.pl.* partners, sharers (à, in).

coir [kwaːr], *s.m.* coir, coconut fibre.

Coire [kwaːr], *Pr.n.f. Geog:* Coire, Chur.

coït [kɔit], *s.m.* coition, copulation; *Vet:* **maladie du c.,** dourine.

coite, *see* COI.

coïter [kɔite], *v.i.* to copulate.

coittes [kwat, kwɛt], *s.f.pl. N.Arch:* **c. dormantes, de lancement,** slipway; **c. courantes,** bilgeways.

coix [kɔiks], *s.m. Bot:* coix.

cojouissance [kɔʒwisɑ̃ːs], *s.f. Jur:* joint use, joint user.

cokage [kɔkaːʒ], *s.m. Petroleum Ind:* coking.

coke [kɔk], *s.m.* coke; **c. de cornue,** retort coke; **c. de gaz,** gas coke; **c. métallurgique,** furnace, foundry, coke; **c. naturel,** native coke; **petit c.,** breeze; **se transformer en c.,** to coke; **four à c.,** coke oven; **gaz de c.,** coke-oven gas; **chariot à c.,** coke car.

cokéfaction [kɔkefaksjɔ̃], *s.f. Coal Ind:* coking.

cokéfiable [kɔkefjabl], **cokéfiant** [kɔkefjɑ̃], *a. Ind:* coking; **charbon cokéfiant,** coking coal.

cokéfier [kɔkefje], *v.tr.* (*pr.sub. & p.d.* **n. cokéfiions**), to coke.

cokéite [kɔkeit], *s.f. Miner:* carbonite.

cokerie [kɔkri], *s.f.* coking plant.

coketier [kɔktje], *s.m.* (*a*) coke merchant; (*b*) coke maker; cokeman.

col [kɔl], *s.m.* **1.** (*a*) *Anat: A:* neck; *still used in certain phrases,* **homme au c. court,** short-necked man; *F:* **se pousser du c.,** to carry one's head high; *F:* to swank, to put on side; to strut; *Min:* **travailler à c. tordu,** to work lying on one's side; *Dressm:* **tour de c.,** collar (of dress); **tour de c. en fourrure,** fur collar; (*b*) neck (of bottle, retort, etc., *Anat:* of bone); *Com:* bottle; *Anat:* cervix (of bladder, uterus, tooth, etc.); *Mec.E:* **c. de cygne, d'oie,** swan-neck, goose-neck, throat; *Rail: Civ.E:* **c. de bouteille,** bottleneck. **2.** *Cost:* collar; **faux(-)col,** (i) detachable collar, (ii) *F:* head (of froth on glass of beer); **c. raide, mou,** stiff, soft, collar; **c. montant, droit,** stand-up collar; **c. rabattu,** turn-down collar, double collar; **c. cassé,** butterfly, wing collar; **c. tailleur,** tailored collar, collar with revers; **c. de dentelle,** lace collar; **c. Claudine,** Peter Pan collar; **c. romain,** clerical collar, *F:* dog collar; **c. haut, montant,** high neck; **chemise à c. tenant,** shirt with collar attached; **c. (à la) Danton,** Byron collar; **chemise à c. Danton,** open-necked shirt. **3.** *F:* **c. bleu,** sailor; *Fr.C:* **les cols bleus,** the blue collar workers, *U.S:* the blue collars; *s.a.* ROULER 1. **4.** *Geog:* col, pass, saddle.

cola [kɔla], *s.m. Bot:* cola, kola.

colapte [kɔlapt], *s.m. Orn:* **c. doré,** flicker.

colarin [kɔlarɛ̃], *s.m. Arch:* colarin, neck, frieze (of Tuscan and Doric column).

Colas [kɔlɑ]. **1.** *Pr.n.m. F:* = NICOLAS; *Hist: F:* **être de la vache à C.,** to be a Huguenot. **2.** *s.m. A: F:* booby, duffer.

colateur [kɔlatœːr], *s.m. Hyd.E:* outlet drain, pipe; irrigation channel.

colatier [kɔlatje], *s.m. Bot:* kola (tree), cola (tree).

colatitude [kɔlatityd], *s.f. Astr:* colatitude.

colature [kɔlatyːr], *s.f. Pharm:* **1.** filtration, straining. **2.** strained, filtered, liquid. **3.** *Agr:* surplus irrigation water (drained back into the channels).

colback [kɔlbak], *s.m. A.Mil.Cost:* kalpak; (Napoleonic) busby.

col-blanc [kɔlblɑ̃], *s.m.* white-collar worker; *pl. cols-blancs.*

col-bleu [kɔlblø], *s.m. Navy: F:* bluejacket; *pl. cols-bleus.*

col-bretelle [kɔlbrətɛl], *s.m. Cost:* halter neck; *pl. cols-bretelles.*

colchicine [kɔlʃisin], *s.f. Pharm:* colchicine.

Colchide [kɔlʃid], *Pr.n.f. A.Geog:* Colchis.

colchique[1] [kɔlʃik], *a. Myth:* **le Dragon c.,** the Dragon of Colchis.

colchique[2], *s.m. Bot: Ch:* colchicum; **c. d'automne,** meadow-saffron; autumn crocus.

colcotar [kɔlkɔtaːr], *s.m. Ch:* colcothar, red peroxide of iron; (jewellers') rouge.

col-cravate [kɔlkravat], *s.m. Cost:* stock; *pl. cols-cravates.*

cold-cream [kɔl(d)krɛm, kɔldkrim], *s.m.* cold cream.

col-de-cygne [kɔldəsiɲ], *s.m. Mec.E:* swan-neck; *pl. cols-de-cygne.*

colectomie [kɔlɛktɔmi], *s.f. Surg:* colectomy.

colégataire [kɔlegatɛːr], *s.m. & f. Jur:* co-legatee, joint legatee.

coléophorides [kɔleɔfɔrid], *s.m.pl. Ent:* Coleophoridae.

coléoptère [kɔleɔptɛːr], *Ent:* **1.** *a.* coleopterous, sheath-winged. **2.** *s.m.* coleopter, beetle; **les coléoptères,** the Coleoptera.

coléoptériste [kɔleɔpterist], *s.m. & f. Ent:* coleopterist.

coléoptéroïdes [kɔleɔpterɔid], *s.m.pl. Ent:* Coleopteroidea.

coléoptile [kɔleɔptil], *s.m. Bot:* coleoptile.

coléorhize [kɔleɔriːz], *s.f. Bot:* coleorhiza.

coléorhynches [kɔleɔrɛ̃ːʃ], *s.m.pl. Ent:* Coleorhyncha.

colère [kɔlɛːr]. 1. *s.f.* (*a*) anger; *Lit:* wrath; **bouffée de c.,** gust of anger; **c. bleue,** towering rage; **être en c.,** to be angry, in a temper; **ressentir de la c.,** to feel angry; **mettre qn en c.,** to make s.o. angry, to get s.o.'s temper up; **se mettre, entrer, en c.,** to get angry (**contre qn,** with, *U.S:* at, s.o.); to flare up; to lose one's temper; **entrer dans une violente c.,** to fly into a violent temper; **elle était dans une c. folle,** she was in a blind rage; **la c. l'emportait,** he was beside himself with rage; **décharger, passer, sa c. sur qn,** to vent one's anger on s.o.; **parler avec c.,** to speak angrily; to speak in anger; *s.a.* BLANC I, 2; *B:* **enfants de c.,** children of wrath; (*b*) **il avait des colères terribles,** he was subject to terrible fits of anger. 2. *a.* angry (voice); irascible, bad-tempered (person).

coléreux, -euse [kɔlerø, -øːz], *a.* quick-tempered, irascible (person).

colérique [kɔlerik], *a.* irritable (disposition).

colériquement [kɔlerikmɑ̃], *adv.* irritably, angrily.

coliade [kɔljad], *s.f.,* **colias** [kɔljas], *s.m. Ent:* sulphur butterfly; **colias géant,** giant arctic sulphur.

coliart [kɔljaːr], *s.m. Ich: F:* skate.

colibacille [kɔlibasil], *s.m. Bac:* colon bacillus.

colibacillose [kɔlibasiloːz], *s.f. Med:* colibacillosis.

colibri [kɔlibri], *s.m. Orn:* colibri, humming-bird.

colichemarde [kɔliʃmard], *a. & s.f. A:* (**lame**) **c.,** colichemarde, rapier.

colicitant [kɔlisitɑ̃], *a. & s.m. Jur:* co-vendor.

colifichet [kɔlifiʃɛ], *s.m.* 1. (*a*) trinket, bauble, gew-gaw; **colifichets de femme,** women's frippery; *Com:* **rayon des colifichets,** fancy goods department; (*b*) *pl.* rubbish, trash. 2. bird-cake.

coliidés [kɔliide], *s.m.pl. Orn:* Coliidae.

coliiformes [kɔliifɔrm], *s.m.pl. Orn:* Coliiformes.

colimaçon [kɔlimasɔ̃], *s.m.* snail; **escalier en c.,** spiral staircase.

Colin [kɔlɛ̃]. 1. *Pr.n.m. F:* = NICOLAS; Colin, Nick(y). 2. *s.m.* (*a*) *Th:* **jouer les colins,** to play the parts of village swains; (*b*) *Orn:* American partridge, bob white partridge, quail; (*c*) *Ich:* (i) coalfish, green pollack; (ii) *F:* hake; (iii) *F:* coalie.

Colinette [kɔlinet]. 1. *Pr.n.f.* = NICOLETTE. 2. *s.f. A:* mob-cap.

colin-maillard [kɔlɛ̃majaːr], *s.m. Games:* 1. blind-man's buff. 2. blind man (in blind-man's buff); *F:* **chercher qch. en c.-m.,** to grope for sth.

colin-tampon [kɔlɛ̃tɑ̃pɔ̃], *s.m. Mil: A:* Swiss march (on the drum); *A:* **se moquer, se soucier, de qn, de qch., comme de c.-t.,** not to care a brass farthing, a damn, about s.o., sth.

coliou [kɔliu], *s.m. Orn:* coly, *pl.* colies, mousebird; **c. à nuque bleue,** blue-naped mousebird.

colique [kɔlik]. 1. *a. Anat:* colic (artery, etc.). 2. *s.f. Med:* colic, *F:* stomach-ache; **c. métallique, saturnine, de plomb,** lead colic, painter's colic; *s.a.* MISÉRÉRÉ; **avoir la c.,** (i) to have an attack of colic, (ii) *F:* to have the wind up, to be in a blue funk; *F:* **quelle c.!** what a bore! what a bind!

coliqueux, -euse [kɔlikø, -øːz], *a.* 1. (*of patient, etc.*) suffering from colic. 2. (*of medicine, etc.*) inducing colic.

coliquidateur [kolikidatœːr], *s.m. Jur:* co-liquidator.

colis [kɔli], *s.m.* 1. parcel, packet, package; case of goods; **c. postal,** postal packet; **par c. postal,** by parcel post; **je peux l'envoyer comme c. postal?** can I send it by parcel post? *Rail:* **le service des c.,** the parcels office; **c. restant,** (parcel) to be called for. 2. *O:* (article of) luggage. 3. *Nau:* (**manœuvre en**) **c. volant,** union purchase, yard and stay, married gear.

colisage [kɔlizaːʒ], *s.m. Com:* packing; **liste de c.,** packing list.

Colisée (le) [ləkɔlize], *s.m. Rom.Ant:* the Colosseum, the Coliseum.

colistier [kɔlistje], *s.m. Pol: etc:* fellow-candidate.

colite [kɔlit], *s.f. Med:* colitis.

collaber [kɔlabe], *v.tr. Med:* **c. un poumon,** to collapse a lung.

collaborateur, -trice [kɔ(l)labɔratœːr, -tris], *s.* (*a*) collaborator; fellow-worker; associate; **collaborateurs d'un livre,** joint authors of a book; **collaborateurs d'une revue,** contributors to a magazine; (*b*) assistant; (*c*) *Pol: Pej:* collaborator.

collaboration[kɔ(l)labɔrasjɔ̃], *s.f.* (*a*) collaboration (**avec,** with); joint authorship; co-operation; contributing (**à,** to); (*b*) *Pol: Pej:* collaboration.

collaborationniste [kɔ(l)labɔrasjɔnist], *s.m. Pol: Hist: Pej:* collaborationist.

collaborer [kɔ(l)labɔre], *v.i.* (*a*) to collaborate, cooperate (**avec,** with); **c. à un journal,** to contribute to a newspaper, to write for a paper; (*b*) *Pol:* to collaborate (with the enemy).

collage [kɔlaːʒ], *s.m.* 1. (*a*) gluing, sticking (of wood, etc.); pasting (of paper, etc.); *Art:* collage; **c. d'affiches,** bill-sticking; **c. du papier (peint),** paper-hanging; *Bookb:* **c. et endossage,** forwarding; *Phot:* **c. à sec,** dry mounting; (*b*) *F:* cohabitation (of unmarried couple); living in sin; *P:* **il a un c.,** he has a mistress. 2. *Paperm:* sizing. 3. fining, clarifying, clearing (of wine). 4. *Metalw:* **c. des métaux,** bonding.

collagène [kɔlaʒɛn], *Biol:* 1. *a.* collagenous, collagenic. 2. *s.m.* collagen.

collaire [kɔllɛːr], *a. Z:* pertaining to the neck; **plumes collaires,** neck feathers.

collant [kɔlɑ̃]. 1. *a.* (*a*) sticky, adhesive; tacky; **papier c.,** gummed paper, sticky paper; **houille collante,** caking coal; *F:* **personne collante,** person who cannot be got rid of; sticker; (*b*) tight-, close-, fitting; skin-tight (garment); **draperies collantes,** clinging draperies; *A:* **pantalon c., culotte collante,** small-clothes. 2. *s.m. Th: etc:* (pair of) tights; pantie-hose.

collante [kɔlɑ̃ːt], *s.f. Sch: F:* letter giving notice of the date and place of an examination.

collapsothérapie [kɔ(l)lapsoterapi], *s.f. Med:* collapse therapy.

collapsus [kɔ(l)lapsyːs], *s.m. Med:* 1. collapse (of patient). 2. **c. d'un poumon,** collapsing of a lung.

collargol [kɔlargɔl], *s.m. Ch:* collargol.

collatéral, -aux [kɔ(l)lateral, -o], *a.* collateral (mountain chain, artery, etc.); **rues collatérales au boulevard,** streets running parallel to the boulevard; **nef collatérale,** *s.m.* **collatéral,** (side) aisle; **points collatéraux,** intermediate points (of the compass); *Jur:* **héritier c.,** collateral heir; (**parents**) **collatéraux,** collaterals; relatives.

collatéralement [kɔ(l)lateralmɑ̃], *adv. Jur:* collaterally.

collateur [kɔ(l)latœːr], *s.m. Ecc: A:* patron (of a living).

collatif, -ive [kɔ(l)latif, -iːv], *a. Ecc:* collative.

collation [kɔ(l)lasjɔ̃], *s.f.* 1. (*a*) granting, conferment, conferring (of title, degree, etc.); (*b*) *A: Ecc:* advowson. 2. collation, collating, comparison (of documents, etc.); *Typ:* checking (of proofs with copy). 3. light meal; snack.

collationnement [kɔ(l)lasjɔnmɑ̃], *s.m.* 1. collating (of documents, proofs). 2. *Tg:* repeating (back) (of message).

collationner [kɔ(l)lasjɔne]. 1. *v.tr.* (*a*) to collate, compare (two written documents); **c. une copie à, avec, sur, l'original,** to check, verify, a copy with the original; **faire c. un télégramme,** to have a telegram repeated; **télégramme collationné,** repetition-paid telegram; (*b*) to check (documents). 2. *v.i.* to have a snack; to have light refreshments.

colle [kɔl], *s.f.* 1. adhesive; (i) paste; (ii) glue; (iii) size; **c. de, en, pâte, c. blanche,** (flour) paste; *F:* **teint c. de pâte,** pasty complexion; **c. animale, c. forte,** glue; **c. à bois,** wood glue; **c. à bouche,** lip glue, mouth glue; **c. de poisson,** fish glue, isinglass; **pot à c.,** (i) paste-pot; (ii) glue-pot; **fabricant de c. forte,** glue boiler; **c. au caoutchouc,** rubber solution; **c. végétale,** vegetable size; **c. de peau, de Flandre,** glue size; **c. au baquet,** builder's size; **papier sans c.,** unsized paper; *P:* **faites chauffer la c.!** that's right, break up the happy home! *F:* **lui, c'est la c.! quel pot de c.!** he sticks around like glue! he's a limpet! you just can't get rid of him! *s.a.* PEINTURE 3. 2. *F:* (*a*) *O:* falsehood, fib, whopper; (*b*) *Sch:* (i) poser; (ii) oral test; (iii) detention; **poser une c. à un candidat,** to ask a candidate a sticky question; (*c*) **quelle c.!** what a bore! what a bind! 3. *P: P:* cohabitation, concubinage; **vivre à la c.,** to live in sin, *U.S:* to shack up.

collé [kɔle], *a. Cy:* (racer) keeping close in the wake of the pacer.

collectage [kɔ(l)lɛktaːʒ], *s.m.* collecting.

collectaire [kɔ(l)lɛktɛːr], *s.m.* book of collects, collectarium.

collecte [kɔ(l)lɛkt], *s.f.* 1. (*a*) *Ecc:* collection (for the poor, etc.); (*b*) collecting; **faire une c.,** to pass the hat round, to have a whip round; **faire une c. de vieux vêtements,** to make a collection of old clothes; **tournée de c. du lait dans les fermes,** milk-collecting round from the farms; **c. des œufs,** collecting, gathering, of eggs; (*c*) (*Computers*) **c. des données,** data gathering. 2. *Ecc:* collect.

collecter [kɔ(l)lɛkte]. 1. *v.tr.* to collect. 2. *v.i. Ecc:* to make a collection.

se collecter, *Med:* (*of pus*) to gather.

collecteur, -trice [kɔ(l)lɛktœːr, -tris]. 1. *a.* (i) collecting; (ii) main; **bac c.,** collecting vat; **puits c.,** collecting pit; **égout c.,** main sewer; *El.E:* **bague collectrice,** collector-ring, slip-ring (of dynamo, etc.); **électrode collectrice,** collecting electrode; *Bot:* **poil c.,** collecting hair. 2. *s.m.* collector; main; (*a*) *Civ.E:* **grand c.,** main sewer; **c. d'évacuation, c. de purge,** drain manifold; **c. d'escarbilles,** cinder catcher (over funnel); **c. de poussières,** dust collector; *Hyd.E:* **c. à air,** air-pocket, air-trap; *Min:* **c. d'eau,** sump, sink-hole; (*b*) *Nau:* **c. d'incendie,** fire main; **c. d'assèchement,** stripping line; **c. d'aspiration,** main suction line; **c. de refoulement,** main discharge line; (*c*) *El.E:* collector (-ring), slip-ring, commutator (of dynamo, etc.); electron-collector (of microwave-valve); **c. d'électricité statique,** comb; **balai de c.,** commutator brush; **lame de c.,** commutator bar; **moteur à c.,** commutator motor; **c. de terre,** main earth lead; *F:* earth; *W.Tel:* **c. d'ondes,** wave collector (of aerial); (*d*) *Mch:* (i) steam-collector, steam-drum (of tubular boiler); (ii) header (of superheater); **c. d'huile,** oil cup; **c. inférieur,** water drum (of boiler); **c. supérieur,** steam drum; (*e*) *I.C.E:* manifold; **c. d'échappement,** exhaust manifold; **c. à carburation inversée,** down-draught manifold; **c. d'admission,** (i) inlet, intake, manifold; (ii) blower-rim (of radial engine); **c. d'admission, d'entrée, d'air,** air manifold, entrance, cone; (*f*) (*ostreiculture*) cultch; collector (for oyster spat).

collectif, -ive [kɔ(l)lɛktif, -iːv]. 1. *a.* collective, joint (action, report, etc.); **ferme collective,** collective farm; **voyages collectifs,** group travel; package tours; **billet c.,** party ticket; **tombe collective,** mass grave; **radiographie collective,** mass radiography. 2. *s.m.* (*a*) *Gram:* collective noun; (*b*) *Adm:* block of flats; (*c*) *Fin:* extra-ordinary credits in the national budget.

collection [kɔ(l)lɛksjɔ̃], *s.f.* 1. collecting; *Med:* **c. purulente,** gathering of pus. 2. (*a*) collection; **faire c. de,** to collect; **c. de papillons,** collection, cabinet, of butterflies; **pièce de c.,** collector's piece; **c. de journaux,** file of newspapers; **la c. du** *Punch,* the back volumes of *Punch; Dressm:* **présentation de la c. de printemps,** showing of the spring collection, spring dress show; *Com:* **c. d'échantillons,** line of samples; (*b*) *Publ:* series.

collectionnement [kɔ(l)lɛksjɔnmɑ̃], *s.m.* collecting (of curios, etc.).

collectionner [kɔ(l)lɛksjɔne], *v.tr.* (*a*) to collect (stamps, curios, etc.); (*b*) **elle collectionnait autour d'elle beaucoup de jeunes gens,** she used to gather a great many young people round her; *F: Aut:* **il collectionne les contraventions,** he's always getting tickets.

collectionneur, -euse [kɔ(l)lɛksjɔnœːr, -øːz], *s.* collector (of curios, stamps, etc.).

collectivement [kɔ(l)lɛktivmɑ̃], *adv.* collectively.

collectivisation [kɔ(l)lɛktivizasjɔ̃], *s.f.* collectivization.

collectiviser [kɔ(l)lɛktivize], *v.tr.* to collectivize.

collectivisme [kɔ(l)lɛktivism], *s.m.* collectivism.

collectiviste [kɔ(l)lɛktivist], *s.* collectivist.

collectivité [kɔ(l)lɛktivite], *s.f.* collectivity. 1. community; **collectivités nationales,** national organizations. 2. common ownership.

collectorat [kɔlɛktɔra], *s.m.* (*in India*) (*a*) collectorate; (*b*) collectorship.

collège [kɔlɛːʒ], *s.m.* 1. college; (*a*) (*corporate body*) **le Sacré C.,** the Sacred College, the College of Cardinals; **c. électoral,** body of electors, electoral body, constituency; (*b*) college buildings. 2. school; **c. d'enseignement secondaire,** secondary modern school; **c. d'enseignement technique,** technical college; **c. libre,** private (secondary) school; **du temps que j'étais au c.,** in my schooldays; **sentir le c.,** to be pedantic; **sentir son c.,** to be fresh from, to smack of, the classroom.

collégial, -iaux [kɔleʒjal, -jo]. 1. *a.* collegial, collegiate. 2. *s.f.* **collégiale,** collegiate church.

collégialité [kɔleʒjalite], *s.f.* collegial structure (of a society, etc.).

collégien, -ienne [kɔleʒjɛ̃, -jɛn]. 1. *s.* schoolboy, schoolgirl. 2. *a.* **argot c.,** school(boy) slang.

collègue [kɔ(l)lɛg], *s.m. & f.* colleague; fellow-worker, -officer, -practitioner, etc.; brother-writer, -teacher, etc.

collemboles [kɔlɑ̃bɔl], *s.m.pl. Ent:* Collembola.

collement [kɔlmɑ̃], *s.m.* adhesion, sticking together.

collenchymateux, -euse [kɔlɑ̃ʃimatø, -øːz], *a. Bot:* collenchymatous.

collenchyme [kɔlɑ̃ʃim], *s.m. Bot:* collenchyma, collenchyme.

coller [kɔle]. **1.** *v.tr.* (*a*) to paste, stick, glue (**à, sur,** to, on); **c. du papier peint sur un mur,** to paper a wall; **cheveux que le sang collait,** hair matted with blood; **c. son visage à, contre, la vitre,** to press, glue, one's face to the window-pane; **être collé sur ses livres,** to pore over one's books; *Bill:* **c. une bille sous bande,** to play a ball close to the cushion; *F:* **c. son poing dans la figure de qn,** to bash s.o. in the face; *Cin:* **presse à c.,** (film) splicer; *Opt: Phot:* **lentille non collée,** uncemented lens; (*b*) (i) *F:* to put, give; **collez ça dans un coin,** stick it in a corner; **c. un élève,** to keep a pupil in; (ii) *F:* to stump, floor (s.o.); **c. un candidat,** to pluck, plough, a candidate; (iii) *P:* **être collé avec une femme,** to keep house with, live with, *U.S:* shack up with, a woman; (*c*) to size (paper); (*d*) to clarify, fine (wine); (*e*) *Typ:* to close up (letters). **2.** *v.i.* to stick, adhere, cling (**à,** to); *Lit:* to cleave (to); **vêtement qui colle,** clinging, tight-fitting, garment; **l'aiguille (du manomètre, etc.) reste collée,** the pointer's sticking; *Cy:* (racer) to keep close in the wake of the pacer; *F:* (*of car*) **c. derrière,** to fall in line in the rear; *F:* **elle colle à lui,** she tags on to him; *F:* **ça ne colle pas tous les deux,** they don't hit it off; *P:* **ça colle?** how are things? **ça colle, Anatole?** how's it go, Joe? **bon, ça colle!** right-ho! *F:* **ça ne colle pas,** it doesn't work; I can't get my figures right; *P:* **ça colle,** that's O.K.; that makes sense, *U.S:* that figures; *Mil:* **l'infanterie colle au barrage (d'artillerie), colle aux chars,** infantry keeps, follows, sticks, close to the (artillery) barrage, to the tanks; **c. au sol,** to hug the ground.

se coller. 1. to stick, adhere closely; **se c. contre un mur,** to stand close to a wall; **elle se colla contre lui,** she clung close to him. **2.** *P:* **se c. avec qn,** to keep house with s.o. (as man and wife), to live (in sin) with s.o., *U.S:* to shack up with s.o.

collerette [kɔlrɛt], *s.f.* **1.** (*a*) collarette, collar, ruff; (*b*) *A.Arm:* neckpiece (of armour). **2.** *Bot:* (*a*) involucre (of umbelliferae); (*b*) annulus (of mushroom). **3.** *Mec.E: etc:* flange (of pipe, joint, etc.); **c. d'assemblage, de raccordement,** coupling flange; *N.Arch:* **c. de pont, de bordé,** deck shell, flange; *s.a.* RONDELLE 2. **4.** *Bot:* **c. de la vierge,** stitchwort.

collet [kɔlɛ], *s.m.* **1.** (*a*) collar (of coat, dress, etc.); **saisir qn par le c., au collet,** to collar s.o., to seize s.o. by the scruff of the neck; *F:* **un c. monté,** a stiff-necked, strait-laced, person; *a.inv.* **elle est très c. monté,** she is very prim (and proper), very formal; (*b*) cape, *A:* tippet (of coat, etc.); (*c*) *A:* **c. de buffle,** buff jerkin; (*d*) *Fr.C:* head (on beer). **2.** neck (of tooth, screw, chisel, cartridge case, violin, etc.); shoulder (of racquet, etc.); *Leath:* shoulder (of hide); *Bot:* neck, collar (of mushroom, etc.); *Cu:* **c. de mouton,** neck, scrag, of mutton. **3.** *Mch: Mec.E: etc:* flange, collar, fillet (of pipe, etc.); journal (of shaft, etc.); bolster (of rolling-mill, etc.); **c. de butée,** thrust collar; **c. tournant,** swivel neck; **c. de la broche,** spindle flange; **c. de boîte à bourrage,** packing-ring. **4.** *Nau:* throat, crown (of anchor); eye (of stay); step (of mast); shaft, loom (of oar). **5.** snare, springe, noose (for trapping small animals); **chasser, prendre, des lapins au c.,** to snare rabbits.

colletage [kɔltaːʒ], *s.m.* **1.** wrestling, grappling; scuffle. **2.** *Tex:* cording.

collet-blanc [kɔlɛblɑ̃], *s.m. Fr.C:* white-collar worker; *pl. collets-blancs.*

colleté [kɔlte], *a. Her:* collared.

collète [kɔlɛt], *s.m. Ent:* Colletes.

colleter [kɔlte], *v.* (**je collette, n. colletons; je colletterai**). **1.** *v.tr.* (*a*) to collar (s.o.); to seize (s.o.) by the collar; (*b*) to grapple, wrestle, scuffle, with (s.o.); **se c.,** to come to grips; **se c. avec (les vices, la misère),** to come to grips with, to grapple with (vice, poverty); *F:* **c. qn,** to embrace, hug, s.o. **2.** *v.i.* to set snares.

collétère [kɔletɛːr], *s.m. Bot:* colleter.

colleteur [kɔltœːr], *s.m.* **1.** snare-setter. **2.** *F: O:* roisterer.

colleteuse [kɔltøːz], *s.f.* collar hand (in clothing factory).

collétie [kɔlesi], *s.f. Bot:* colletia.

colletin [kɔltɛ̃], *s.m. A.Arm:* colletin, neck-piece (of armour).

colletotrichum [kɔlɛtɔtrikɔm], *s.m. Fung:* colletotrichum.

colleur, -euse [kɔlœːr, -øːz], *s.* **1.** (*a*) gluer, paster; **c. de papier de tenture,** paperer, paper hanger; **c. d'affiches,** billsticker; (*b*) sizer (of paper, etc.); (*c*) *Cin:* (*pers.*) (film) splicer. **2.** *F:* (*a*) *O:* liar; (*b*) bore, pest, sticker; (*c*) *Sch:* examiner (who asks sticky questions). **3.** *s.f. Cin:* **colleuse,** film splicer, splicing unit.

colley [kɔlɛ], *s.m. Z:* collie (dog).

collidine [kɔlidin], *s.f. Ch:* collidin(e).

collier [kɔlje], *s.m.* **1.** (*a*) necklace, necklet; (*b*) carcanet. **2.** (*a*) collar (of order, etc.); (*b*) **c. de chien, de cheval,** dog-collar, horse-collar; **cheval de c.,** draught horse; **être franc du c.,** (i) (*of horse*) to be a good puller, to be willing, (ii) *F:* (*of pers.*) to be a hard worker, no shirker; **tirer à plein c.,** (i) (*of horse*) to put its full weight into the collar, (ii) (*of pers.*) to put one's back into it; **coup de c.,** sudden effort, tug (by horse); *El: etc:* sudden overload; *F:* **donner un coup de c.,** to put one's back into it, to make a special effort; **aider qn d'un coup de c.,** to help s.o. through; *F:* **reprendre le c.,** to get back into harness; *s.a.* MISÈRE 1; (*c*) **c. de barbe,** *F:* Newgate frill; (*d*) *Mil:* **c. à cartouches,** (cartridge) bandolier. **3.** (*a*) *Mec.E:* collar, ring; **c. coulissant,** sliding collar; **c. d'appui,** supporting collar; **c. d'arbre,** shaft collar; **c. d'arrêt,** stop, set, collar; **c. d'attache,** securing ring, hitching collar; **c. de blocage, de serrage,** clamping ring, (fastening) clamp; tightening band; **c. de butée, de poussée,** thrust collar; **c. de câble,** cable clamp, clip; **c. d'écartement, d'espacement,** spacer(-collar); **c. d'embrayage,** clutch collar; **c. d'étanchéité,** seal collar; **c. d'excentrique,** eccentric collar, strap; **c. de fixation,** bracket, clip; **c. de frein,** brake band; **c. de palier,** bearing collar; **c. d'obturation,** band clamp; **c. de retenue,** (i) locking ring; (ii) *Min:* casing clamp, pipe clamp (for lowering pipe in well); **c. de support,** seat ring; **c. de tube, de tuyau,** pipe collar, clip; **c. de verrouillage,** lock ring; *Aut:* **embrayage à c.,** expansion clutch; *Opt:* **c. de lunette,** telescope clamp; *Artil:* **c. de pointage,** trunnion ring; *Sm.a:* **c. de percuteur,** striker clip; (*b*) *Nau:* collar (of bowsprit stay, etc.); necklace (of mast); (*c*) *Tchn:* clip; **c. tournant,** swivel clip; **c. ressort,** spring clip; *El:* **c. de masse,** bonding clip; (*d*) bow (of spur). **4.** (*a*) *Z:* collar, ring (on birds, etc.); **pigeon à c., au c.,** ringed, ring-necked, pigeon; (*b*) *Ent:* **c. argenté,** pearl-bordered fritillary. **5.** *Wr:* **c. de force,** head lock. **6.** *Cu:* neck (of beef).

collier-écrou [kɔljeekru], *s.m. Mch:* screw-collar; *pl. colliers-écrous.*

colligatif, -ive [kɔ(l)ligatif, -iv], *a. Ch:* colligative.

colliger [kɔ(l)liʒe], *v.tr.* (**je colligeai(s); n. colligeons**), to collect (and compare, reports, etc.); to make a collection of (extracts); to make extracts from; **c. les livres rares,** to collect rare books.

collignon [kɔliɲɔ̃], *s.m. Pej: P: A:* **1.** cabby, Jehu (*from the name of a cabman executed for murder*). **2.** cab, growler.

collimater [kɔ(l)limate], *v.tr. Opt: etc:* to collimate; to collineate.

collimateur, -trice [kɔ(l)limatœːr, -tris]. **1.** *a.* collimating. **2.** *s.m. Astr: Surv:* collimator, laying prism; *Opt:* collimating lens; *Artil: Av:* gonio-sight.

collimation [kɔ(l)limasjɔ̃], *s.f.* collimation.

colline [kɔlin], *s.f.* hill; **petite c.,** hillock; **haut, penchant, d'une c.,** hilltop, hillside; **c. en dos d'âne,** hog's back (ridge).

colliquation [kɔ(l)likwasjɔ̃], *s.f. Med:* colliquation.

collision [kɔ(l)lizjɔ̃], *s.f.* collision; impact; **entrer en c. avec qch.,** to collide with sth.; to run into (ship, car, etc.); to run aboard, to fall foul of (ship); **entrer en c. avec qn,** to come to loggerheads with s.o., to come up against s.o.; **c. aérienne,** air collision; **c. d'intérêts, de doctrines,** clash of interests, of doctrines; **c. frontale,** head-on collision; *Av: etc:* **cap de c.,** collision course; **interception à cap de c.,** collision course interception; **vecteur de c.,** collision vector; *Atom.Ph:* **c. de neutrons,** knock-on; **c. nucléaire,** nuclear collision; **c. ionisante,** ionizing collision.

colloblaste [kɔ(l)lɔblast], *s.m. Z:* colloblast.

collocation [kɔ(l)lɔkasjɔ̃], *s.f. Jur:* (establishing the) order of priority of creditors (in bankruptcy) and sum due to them; **c. utile,** ranking (of creditor).

collodion [kɔ(l)lɔdjɔ̃], *s.m. Ch: etc:* collodion.

collodionner [kɔ(l)lɔdjɔne], *v.tr. Phot:* to collodionize; to treat (plate) with collodion.

colloïdal, -aux [kɔ(l)lɔidal, -o], *a. Ch: etc:* colloidal; **solution colloïdale,** sol.

colloïde [kɔl(l)ɔid], *a. & s.m. Ch: etc:* colloid, gel; **c. soluble, insoluble,** reversible, irreversible, gel; *Med:* **dégénérescence c., tumeur c.,** colloid degeneration, colloid cancer.

colloque [kɔ(l)lɔk], *s.m.* (*a*) *Rel.H:* colloquy; (*b*) discussion; conference, conversation; symposium.

colloquer [kɔ(l)lɔke], *v.tr.* **1.** *Jur:* (*a*) to collocate (creditors); (*b*) (*in Belgium*) to imprison (s.o.). **2.** *F:* (*a*) **c. qn au bout de la table,** to relegate s.o. to the end of the table; **c. qn entre deux étrangers,** to plump s.o. down between two strangers; (*b*) **c. qch. à qn,** to foist, to palm off, sth. on s.o.

collotypie [kɔ(l)lɔtipi], *s.f. Typ:* collotypy.

colloxyline [kɔ(l)lɔksilin], *s.f. Ch:* colloxylin.

colluder [kɔ(l)lyde], *v.i. Jur: A:* to collude, conspire.

collure [kɔ(l)lyːr], *s.f. Bookb:* gluing.

collusion [kɔ(l)lyzjɔ̃], *s.f. Jur: etc:* collusion.

collusoire [kɔ(l)lyzwaːr], *a. Jur:* collusive.

collusoirement [kɔ(l)lyzwarmɑ̃], *adv. Jur:* collusively, by collusion.

collutoire [kɔ(l)lytwaːr], *s.m. Pharm:* mouthwash.

colluviaire [kɔ(l)lyvjɛːr], *s.f.* inspection hole (in an aqueduct).

colluvion [kɔ(l)lyvjɔ̃], *s.f. Geog:* colluvium, colluvial deposits.

colluvionnement [kɔ(l)lyvjɔnmɑ̃], *s.m. Geog:* colluvial deposition.

collybie [kɔ(l)libi], *s.f. Fung:* collybia.

collyre [kɔ(l)liːr], *s.m. Pharm:* eyewash; eye lotion; **c. mou,** eye salve.

collyrite [kɔ(l)lirit], *s.m. Miner:* collyrite.

colmar [kɔlmaːr], *s.f. Hort:* colmar pear.

colmarien, -ienne [kɔlmarjɛ̃, -jɛn], *a. & s. Geog:* (native, inhabitant) of Colmar.

colmatage [kɔlmataːʒ], *s.m.* **1.** *Agr:* warping (of land). **2.** (*a*) filling in (of pot-holes in road, etc.); (*b*) plugging; (*c*) *Mil:* consolidation (of position). **3.** siltation; clogging (up) (of filter, sieve, etc.); choking, blocking (of pipe, drain). **4.** *Ind:* **bassin de c.,** settling tank.

colmatant [kɔlmatɑ̃], *s.m.* **c. (pour boues de forage),** plugging agent.

colmate [kɔlmat], *s.f. Agr:* **1.** warped land. **2.** warp.

colmater [kɔlmate], *v.tr.* **1.** *Agr:* to warp (land). **2.** (*a*) to fill in (pot-holes in road, etc.); (*b*) *Mil:* to consolidate (position). **3.** to clog (up) (filter, sieve); to choke (up) (pipe, drain, etc.).

se colmater, to clog up; to become choked, to choke up.

colobe [kɔlɔb], *s.m. Z:* colobus; *pl.* colobi; **c. à manteau blanc,** white-mantled colobus, guereza; **c. noir,** black colobus.

colobome [kɔlɔbom], *s.m. Med:* coloboma.

colocase [kɔlɔkaːz], *s.f. Bot:* cush-cush.

colocataire [kɔlɔkatɛːr], *s.m. & f.* joint tenant, co-tenant.

colog [kɔlɔg], *s.m. Mth: F:* colog.

cologarithme [kɔlɔgaritm], *s.m. Mth:* cologarithm.

Cologne [kɔlɔɲ], *Pr.n.f. Geog:* Cologne; *Toil:* **eau de C.,** eau de Cologne.

Colomb [kɔlɔ̃], *Pr.n.m.* **Christophe C.,** Christopher Columbus; **c'est comme l'œuf de C.,** it's easy once you've thought of it.

Colomba [kɔlɔ̃ba], *Pr.n.m.* **Saint C.,** St. Columba.

colombage [kɔlɔ̃baːʒ], *s.m. Const:* half-timbering; frame(-wall), stud-work; **maison en c.,** half-timbered house.

colombaire [kɔlɔ̃bɛːr], *s.m. Rom.Ant: etc:* columbarium.

Colomban [kɔlɔ̃bɑ̃], *Pr.n.m.* **Saint C.,** St. Columban.

colombe[1] [kɔlɔ̃ːb], *s.f. Orn:* dove; **c. biset,** rock pigeon; **c. porphyre,** pink-necked fruit dove.

colombe[2], *s.f.* **1.** *Const:* scantling, stud, upright. **2.** *Tls:* (cooper's) chime-plane.

colombeau, -eaux [kɔlɔ̃bo], *s.m. Orn: A:* little pigeon.

colombelle [kɔlɔ̃bɛl], *s.f.* **1.** *Orn:* young dove. **2.** *Moll:* columbella.

colombia [kɔlɔ̃bja], *s.f. Com:* coney seal; **c. électrique,** electric seal.

colombiculteur [kɔlɔ̃bikyltœːr], *s.m.* pigeon breeder.

colombiculture [kɔlɔ̃bikyltyːr] *s.f.* pigeon breeding.

Colombie [kɔlɔ̃bi], *Pr.n.f. Geog:* **1.** Colombia. **2. la C. britannique,** British Columbia.

colombien, -ienne [kɔlɔ̃bjɛ̃, -jɛn], *a. & s. Geog:* Columbian.

colombier [kɔlɔ̃bje], *s.m.* **1.** (*a*) dovecot(e), pigeon-house, columbarium; *F:* **revenir au c.,** to come back home; (*b*) *Th: F:* the gods. **2.** *Nau:* poppet. **3.** *Paperm:* **format c.,** columbier, colombier.

colombin, -ine[1] [kɔlɔ̃bɛ̃, -in]. **1.** *a.* (*a*) columbine, dove-like; (*b*) dove-coloured. **2.** *s.m.* (*a*) *Orn:* stock-dove; (*b*) *Min:* lead ore; (*c*) *P:* shit. **3.** *s.f.* **colombine,** (*a*) *Agr:* pigeon-dung (manure); (*b*) *Bot:* columbine, aquilegia; (*c*) *Th:* Columbine.

colombine[2], *s.f. Pharm:* columbin.

colombite [kɔlɔ̃bit], *s.f. Miner:* columbite.

colombium [kɔlɔ̃bjɔm], *s.m. Ch:* columbium.

colombo [kɔlɔ̃bo], *s.m. Bot: Pharm:* calumba, colombo.

colombophile [kɔlɔ̃bɔfil]. **1.** *a.* pigeon-fancying (club). **2.** *s.* pigeon-fancier, -breeder.

colombophilie [kɔlɔ̃bɔfili], *s.f.* pigeon-fancying, -breeding.

colomnaire [kɔlɔmnɛːr], *a.* columnar.

colomnifère [kɔlɔmnifɛːr], *a. Bot:* columniferous.

colon[1] [kɔlɔ̃], *s.m.* **1.** (*a*) *Rom.Ant:* colonus, colonist; (*b*) farmer, smallholder; **c. partiaire,** share-cropper. **2.** (*a*) colonist, settler; (*b*) *F:* colonial. **3.** child at a holiday camp.

colon[2], *s.m. Mil: P:* colonel; *P:* "the old man"; **ben, mon colon!** well, I'm damned!

côlon [kolɔ̃, kɔ-], *s.m. Anat:* colon.

colonage [kɔlɔnaːʒ], *s.m. Agr:* **bail à c. partiaire,** share-cropping lease.

colonais, -aise [kɔlɔnɛ, -ɛːz], *a. & s.* (native) of Cologne.

colonat [kɔlɔna], *s.m. Hist:* colonate; **c. partiaire,** share-cropping.

Colone [kɔlɔn], *Pr.n.f. A.Geog:* Colonus; *s.a.* Œdipe.

colonel [kɔlɔnɛl], *s.m. Mil:* colonel; *Mil.Av:* group captain.

colonelle [kɔlɔnɛl], *s.f.* **1.** *F:* colonel's wife. **2. la reine Élisabeth, c. en chef des . . .,** Queen Elizabeth, colonel-in-chief of the . . ..

colonial, -iaux [kɔlɔnjal, -jo]. **1.** *a.* colonial. **2.** *s.m.* (*a*) colonial; (*b*) *Pol:* colonialist. **3.** *s.f. Mil: F: A:* **coloniale,** (the) marines; colonial troops.

colonialisme [kɔlɔnjalism], *s.m. Pol:* (*a*) imperialism; (*b*) colonialism.

colonialiste [kɔlɔnjalist], *Pol:* (*a*) *a.* imperialistic; (*b*) *s.m. or f.* imperialist.

colonie [kɔlɔni], *s.f.* **1.** (*a*) colony; settlement; **vivre aux colonies,** to live in the colonies; (*b*) *Jur: A:* **c. pénitentiaire,** (i) penal settlement; (ii) reformatory (for young offenders); (*c*) **c. de vacances,** children's holiday camp; *F:* **les enfants sont en c.,** the children are at a holiday camp; (*d*) **la c. anglaise à Paris,** the English colony in Paris. **2.** (*a*) *Z:* colony; **c. de manchots,** penguin rookery, penguin(e)ry; (*b*) **c. de cristaux,** colony of crystals.

colonisable [kɔlɔnizabl], *a.* colonizable; that can be colonized; fit for colonization.

colonisateur, -trice [kɔlɔnizatœːr, -tris]. **1.** *a.* colonizing (nation, etc.). **2.** *s.* colonizer.

colonisation [kɔlɔnizasjɔ̃], *s.f.* colonization, settling.

coloniser [kɔlɔnize], *v.tr.* to colonize, settle (region).

coloniste [kɔlɔnist], *a. & s.m. & f. A:* colonizationist.

colonnade [kɔlɔnad], *s.f. Arch:* colonnade.

colonnaire[1] [kɔlɔnɛːr], *a. Bot:* **pin c.,** monkey-puzzle (tree).

colonnaire,[2] *s.m. Ant:* quarry where marble was cut in columns.

colonne [kɔlɔn], *s.f.* **1.** column, pillar; (*a*) *Arch:* **c. dorique, corinthienne,** Doric, Corinthian, pillar; **colonnes accouplées,** grouped columns; **c. cannelée,** fluted column, pillar; **c. lisse,** plain column, pillar; **c. de l'Église,** pillar, mainstay, of the Church; (*b*) **lit à colonnes,** four-poster bed; **c. milliaire,** milestone; **colonne Morris,** Morris pillar (in Paris) (exhibiting play-bills and cinema advertisements); *Geol:* **c. coiffée,** earth pillar; **c. de chiffres,** column of figures; **c. d'un journal,** column of a newspaper; *Anat:* **c. vertébrale,** spinal column, spine, backbone; (*c*) **c. de mercure,** column of mercury; **c. d'eau,** waterspout; **c. de feu,** pillar of fire; **c. de fumée,** column of smoke; (*d*) *Mec.E:* **c. d'une fraiseuse,** column of a milling-machine; **c. d'un laminoir,** bearer, standard, of a rolling-mill; *Aut:* **c. de direction,** steering column; *Artil:* **c. d'affût,** pedestal; *Nau:* **c. d'habitacle,** binnacle-stand, -pillar; **c. à signaux,** Christmas tree; (*e*) *Ind:* **c. à plateau,** plate-column, plate-tower; **c. de lavage,** scrubbing tower. **2.** (*a*) *Hyd.E:* **c. d'eau,** head, fall, of water; **c. ascendante, montante,** (i) *Hyd.E:* stand-pipe; (ii) *Plumb: Ind:* rising-main, riser(-pipe); **c. descendante,** down-pipe; *Rail:* **c. d'alimentation, c. (d'eau) alimentaire,** water-crane, stand-pipe; (*b*) *El.E:* **c. montante,** service-cable, service-conductor, riser; **c. thermo-électrique,** thermo-electric battery; (*c*) *Min:* **c. d'exhaure,** rising-main; **c. de richesse,** shoot, chimney, of ore; **c. de tubage,** tube-column, casing-line; (*d*) *Petroleum Ind:* **c. à chicanes,** baffle column; **c. de détente,** flash column; **c. à cloches,** bulb fractioning column; (*e*) *Av:* **c. manométrique,** pressure head. **3.** *Mil:* column; (*a*) **c. par un,** single file; column of files; **c. par deux, par trois, par quatre,** column of twos, of threes, of fours; **(en) c. par quatre!** form fours! **marcher en c., en c. par un, en c. par quatre,** to march in column, in single file, in column of fours; **marcher en deux colonnes,** to march, move, in two columns; **en c. diluée,** in extended column; **en c. de route,** in route column; **c. en marche,** column on the march, on the move; **c. de marche,** (i) marching column; (ii) march formation (of battalion, brigade, etc.); **c. de tête,** leading column; **tête de c.,** head of a column; **c. de queue,** rear column; **queue de c.,** rear of a column; **(se) former en colonne(s),** to break into column(s); **faire éclater une c.,** to open out a column; **couper, traverser une c.,** to cross, intersect, a column; (*b*) **c. d'assaut, d'attaque,** assaulting, attacking, storming, column; **c. de ravitaillement,** supply column; **c. de secours,** relief (column); **c. de véhicules en marche,** column of moving vehicles; **c. mobile, volante,** flying column; **c. motorisée,** mechanized, motorized, column; (*c*) *Navy:* **en c.,** line ahead; (*d*) *Pol:* **cinquième c.,** fifth column; **un homme, un membre, de la cinquième c.,** a fifth-columnist; **l'emploi, l'action de la cinquième c.,** fifth-columnism; (*e*) *A:* **chapeau porté en c.,** cocked hat worn fore and aft; fore-and-after.

colonnette [kɔlɔnɛt], *s.f.* little column; colonnette.

colopexie [kɔlɔpɛksi], *s.f. Surg:* colopexia, colopexy.

colophane [kɔlɔfan], *s.f.* rosin, colophony.

colophaner [kɔlɔfane], *v.tr.* to rosin (violin-bow).

colophène [kɔlɔfɛn], *s.m. Ch:* colophene.

colophon [kɔlɔfɔ̃], *s.m. Typ:* colophon.

coloquinte [kɔlɔkɛ̃ːt], *s.f.* **1.** *Bot:* colocynth, bitter-apple. **2.** *P:* head, nut.

colorable [kɔlɔrabl], *a.* colourable.

Colorado [kɔlɔrado], *Pr.n.m. Geog:* Colorado; *Ent: F:* **bête du C.,** Colorado beetle.

colorage [kɔlɔraːʒ], *s.m.* colo(u)ration (of sweets, etc.).

colorant [kɔlɔrɑ̃]. **1.** *a.* colouring (matter, etc.); **bain c.,** dye solution. **2.** *s.m.* colouring (matter); colorant; dye.

coloration [kɔlɔrasjɔ̃], *s.f.* **1.** colouring, colo(u)ration; **c. du bois,** wood staining; *Hairdr:* **se faire faire une c.,** to have one's hair tinted. **2.** colour; (*of pers.*) **avoir de la c.,** to have a high colour.

coloratur [kɔlɔratyːr], *a. & s.f. Mus:* coloratura.

coloré [kɔlɔre], *a.* coloured; **vin c.,** dark-red wine; **teint c.,** florid complexion; **récit c.,** highly coloured narrative; **style c.,** style full of colour.

colorectite [kɔlɔrɛktit], *s.f. Med:* colorectitis.

colorement [kɔlɔrmɑ̃], *s.m. Draw:* shading.

colorer [kɔlɔre], *v.tr.* to colour, stain, tinge, tint; **c. qch. en vert,** to colour sth. green; **l'indignation colorait ses joues,** indignation brought the colour to his cheeks; **c. un récit,** to lend colour to a tale; **c. ses préjugés,** to disguise one's prejudices.

se colorer, (*of fruit, etc.*) to colour; to assume a colour, a tinge; (*of complexion*) to grow florid; **les pommes commencent à se c. (en rouge),** the apples are turning red.

coloriage [kɔlɔrjaːʒ], *s.m.* colouring, illuminating (of maps, drawings, by hand).

colorier [kɔlɔrje], *v.tr.* (*p.d. & pr.sub.* **n. coloriions, v. coloriiez**) to colour, lay colour on (map, drawing); **colorié à la main,** hand-coloured; **c. son style,** to embellish one's style; *abs.* **l'enfant a passé sa matinée à colorier,** the child spent his morning painting.

coloricur [kɔlɔrjœːr], *s.m.* **1.** colourer (on china, etc.). **2.** *Tex:* print(ing) roll.

colorifique [kɔlɔrifik], *a.* colorific.

colorimètre [kɔlɔrimɛtr], *s.m.* colorimeter, chromometer.

colorimétrie [kɔlɔrimetri], *s.f.* colorimetry, colorimetrics; **c. trichromatique,** tristimulus colorimetry.

colorimétrique [kɔlɔrimetrik], *a.* colorimetric; **diagramme c.,** chromaticity diagram; **équilibrage c.,** colour matching.

coloris [kɔlɔri], *s.m.* colour(ing) (of painting, fruit, etc.); **pensées d'un c. sombre,** thoughts tinged with gloom; **c. du style,** brilliance, richness, of style; *Com:* **carte de c.,** shade card.

colorisation [kɔlɔrizasjɔ̃], *s.f.* (*a*) *Tchn:* application of colour; (*b*) change of colour (of certain substances).

coloriste [kɔlɔrist], *s.m. & f.* **1.** *Art:* colourist. **2.** *Ind:* colourer, painter (of post-cards, toys, etc.).

coloristique [kɔlɔristik], *a.* colo(u)ristic.

colorraphie [kɔlɔrafi], *s.f. Surg:* colorrhaphy.

colossal, -aux [kɔlɔsal, -o]. **1.** *a.* colossal, gigantic, huge; tremendous. **2.** *s.m.* **le goût du c.,** the taste, liking, for the colossal.

colossalement [kɔlɔsalmɑ̃], *adv.* colossally, enormously; **homme c. riche,** stupendously rich man.

colosse [kɔlɔs], *s.m.* colossus; giant; **le c. de Rhodes,** the Colossus of Rhodes; **femme colosse,** giant-woman (at show).

Colosses [kɔlɔs], *Pr.n. A.Geog:* Colossae.

colossien, -ienne [kɔlɔsjɛ̃, -jɛn], *a. & s. A.Geog:* Colossian; *B:* **l'Épître aux Colossiens,** the Epistle to the Colossians.

colostomie [kɔlɔstɔmi], *s.f. Surg:* colostomy; **effectuer une c.,** to perform a colostomy on, to colostomize (s.o.).

colostomique [kɔlɔstɔmik], *a. Surg:* colostomic; **poche c.,** colostomy bag, pouch; **ceinture c.,** colostomy belt.

colostrum [kɔlɔstrɔm], *s.m. Physiol:* colostrum; *Vet:* beestings.

colotomie [kɔlɔtɔmi], *s.f. Surg:* colotomy.

colpocèle [kɔlpɔsɛl], *s.f. Med:* colpocele.

colpo-hystérectomie [kɔlpɔisterɛktɔmi], *s.f. Surg:* colpo-hysterectomy.

colpopérinéoplastie [kɔlpɔperineɔplasti], *s.f. Surg:* colpoperineoplasty.

colpopérinéorraphie [kɔlpɔperineɔrafi], *s.f. Surg:* colpoperineorrhaphy.

colpoplastie [kɔlpɔplasti], *s.f. Surg:* colpoplasty.

colpo(r)raphie [kɔlpɔrafi], *s.f. Surg:* colporrhaphy.

colportage [kɔlpɔrtaːʒ], *s.m.* (*a*) hawking, peddling (of goods); colportage (of religious books); (*b*) **c. de fausses nouvelles,** rumour-mongering.

colporter [kɔlpɔrte], *v.tr.* (*a*) to hawk, peddle (goods); (*b*) to retail, spread abroad (news).

colporteur, -euse [kɔlpɔrtœːr, -øːz], *s.* (*a*) door-to-door salesman; *A:* packman, pedlar; **c. de livres religieux,** colporteur; (*b*) **c. de nouvelles, d'histoires scandaleuses,** newsmonger, scandalmonger; **c. de fausses nouvelles,** rumour-monger.

colposcopie [kɔlpɔskɔpi], *s.f. Surg:* colposcopy.

colpotomie [kɔlpɔtɔmi], *s.f. Surg:* colpotomy.

colt [kɔlt], *s.m. Sm.a:* Colt.

coltin [kɔltɛ̃], *s.m.* leather hat, *esp.* coal-heaver's hat.

coltinage [kɔltinaːʒ], *s.m.* porterage, carrying (of heavy loads on one's back).

coltiner [kɔltine], *v.tr.* to carry (heavy loads) on one's back.

se coltiner, *F:* to take on (a disagreeable job); **c'est moi qui vais me c. toute cette vaisselle?** have I got to take on all that washing up? *P:* **se c. avec qn,** to have a fight with s.o.

coltineur [kɔltinœːr], *s.m.* porter (who carries heavy loads); lumper; **c. de charbon,** coal-heaver.

coltis [kɔlti], *s.m. Nau:* beak-head frame.

colubridés [kɔlybride], *s.m.pl. Rept:* Colubridae.

colubriforme [kɔlybrifɔrm], *a. Rept:* colubriform.

colubrin [kɔlybrɛ̃], *a. Rept:* colubrine.

columbarium [kɔlɔ̃barjɔm], *s.m. Rom.Ant:* columbarium; *pl. columbaria.*

columbidés [kɔlɔ̃bide], *s.m.pl. Orn:* Columbidae.

columbiformes [kɔlɔ̃bifɔrm], *s.m.pl. Orn:* Columbiformes.

columbite [kɔlɔ̃bit], *s.f. Miner:* columbite.

columbium [kɔlɔ̃bjɔm], *s.m. Miner:* columbium.

columellaire [kɔlymɛlɛːr], *a. Nat.Hist:* columellar.

columelle[1] [kɔlymɛl], *s.f.* **1.** *Archeol:* columel. **2.** *Nat.Hist:* columella.

Columelle[2]. *Pr.n.m. Rom.Lit:* Columella.

columellé, -ée [kɔlymɛle], *a. Nat.Hist:* columellate.

columelliacé, -ée [kɔlymɛljase], *Bot:* **1.** *a.* columelliaceous. **2.** *s.f.pl.* **columelliacées,** Columelliaceae.

columellie [kɔlymɛli], *s.f. Bot:* columellia.

columérien, -ienne [kɔlymerjɛ̃, -jɛn], *a. & s. Geog:* (native, inhabitant) of Coulommiers.

columnaire [kɔlɔmnɛːr], *a. Bot:* columnar.

columnisation [kɔlɔmnizasjɔ̃], *s.f. Med:* columnization, columnizing.

colure [kɔlyːr], *s.m. Astr:* colure.

col-vert [kɔlvɛːr], *s.m. Orn:* mallard; *pl. cols-verts.*

colymbidés [kɔlɛ̃bide], *s.m.pl. Orn:* Colymbidae.

colza [kɔlza], *s.m.* **1.** *Bot:* (summer) rape, colza. **2.** rapeseed, coleseed; **huile de c.,** colza oil.

coma [kɔma]. **1.** *s.m.* coma. **2.** *s.f. Opt:* coma.

comagmatique [komagmatik], *a. Geol:* comagmatic.

Comanche [kɔmɑ̃:ʃ], *s.m. Ethn:* Comanche.

comandant, -ante [komɑ̃dɑ̃, -ɑ̃:t], *s.m. & f. Jur:* joint mandator.

comandataire [komɑ̃datɛ:r], *s.m. & f. Jur:* joint mandatory, joint proxy.

comanique [komanik], *a. Ch:* **acide c.**, comanic acid.

cômasque [komask], *a. & s. Geog:* (native, inhabitant) of Como.

comateux, -euse [kɔmatø, -ø:z], *a. Med:* comatose, comatous.

comatule [kɔmatyl], *s.f. Z:* comatula, *pl.* -ae, comatulid, feather star.

comatulidés [kɔmatylide], *s.m.pl. Z:* Comatulidae.

combat [kɔ̃ba], *s.m.* **1.** *Mil:* combat, fight, battle, engagement, action, encounter, affair; *(a)* **c. défensif**, defensive battle, action; **c. offensif**, offensive battle, action; **c. de rencontre**, encounter-action, -fight; **c. corps à corps**, hand-to-hand fight(ing); **véhicule de c.**, assault vehicle; field craft; **c. rapproché**, close combat; fight at close quarters; **c. d'avant-garde**, advanced-guard fighting, action; **c. d'arrière-garde**, rear-guard fighting, action; **c. en retraite**, combat of retreating troops; running fight, *U.S:* retrograde operation, action; **c. retardateur**, delaying action; **c. en vue de jalonner l'avance de l'ennemi**, screening action; **c. par le choc**, shock action; **c. par le feu**, fire fight; **c. aérien**, **c. dans les airs**, air-fight(ing), air-combat; aerial combat; **c. naval**, **c. sur mer**, battle at sea, sea-fight(ing); naval engagement, action; **c. sur terre**, ground fighting; land operation; **c. de rues**, street fight(ing); **c. sous bois**, bush fighting; **dispositif de c.**, combat, attack, lay-out, set-up; combat, attack, dispositions; **dispositions de c.**, preparations for action; **prendre les dispositions de c.**, to prepare for action; **formation de c.**, combat, attack, formation; **chargement de c.**, combat load; **réserves de c.**, battle reserves; **train de c.**, first line transport, *U.S:* combat train; **zone de c.**, combat zone; **partie arrière de la zone de c.**, rear combat zone; **c. acharné, furieux**, desperate, savage, fighting; **c. à outrance**, fight to the death, to the finish; **c. décousu**, desultory fight; **c. d'usure**, attrition fighting; wearing-down action; **c. inégal**, unequal combat; **c. indécis**, drawn battle; **c. décisif**, decisive battle; **c. simulé**, sham fight; **c. singulier**, single combat; *Av:* dogfight; **dans l'ardeur, dans la fureur, du c.**, in the heat of the battle, the action; **au fort du c.**, in the thick of the fight, of the action; **aller au c.**, to get ready for action; **engager le c.**, to go into action (avec, with); **envoyer au c.**, to order, send, into action; **livrer c. à l'ennemi**, to give battle to the enemy; **offrir le c.**, to offer battle (à, to); **mettre hors de c.**, to disable, to put out of action, to cripple; **hors de c.**, (i) (*of pers.*) hors de combat; disabled; (ii) (*of equipment*) out of action; *(b) Box:* **c. de près**, in-fighting; **c. au finish**, fight to a finish; **maître de c.**, ringmaster; *(c)* **c. de taureaux, de coqs**, bullfight; cockfight; *s.a.* OURS 1. **2.** conflict, struggle; contest (of wits, etc.); **il se livrait entre eux un c. de générosité**, they vied with each other in generosity; **c. d'intérêts**, clash of interests.

combatif, -ive [kɔ̃batif, -i:v], *a.* combative, pugnacious; **il n'a rien de c.**, he's no fighter.

combativité [kɔ̃bativite], *s.f.* combativeness, pugnacity.

combattable [kɔ̃batabl̩], *a.* combatable, disputable (argument, etc.).

combattant [kɔ̃batɑ̃]. **1.** *a. Mil:* **unité combattante**, combatant, fighting, unit; **officier non-c.**, non-combatant officer. **2.** *s.m.* *(a)* combatant, fighter; *Mil:* soldier, (i) on active service; (ii) in a fighting unit; **les combattants**, the contending forces; **anciens combattants**, ex-servicemen, *U.S:* veterans; **combattants pour la cause commune**, fighters for the common cause; *(b)* fighter, brawler. **3.** *s.m.* *(a)* game cock, fowl; *(b) Orn:* ruff; *(c) Ich:* fighting fish.

combattre [kɔ̃batr̥], *v.* (*conj. like* BATTRE) **1.** *v.tr.* to combat, to fight (against), to contend, battle, with (enemy, disease, temptation, opinion, etc.); **partis qui se combattent**, parties in opposition, contending parties. **2.** *v.i.* to fight, strive, struggle; **c. pour, contre, qn, qch.**, to fight for, against, s.o., sth.; (*of ships of war*) **c. bord à bord**, to engage at close quarters; **je n'ai pas combattu**, I did not do any fighting; **c. de politesse avec qn**, to vie with s.o. in politeness.

combe [kɔ̃:b], *s.f. Geog:* (*in the Jura*) anticlinal valley; combe.

combien [kɔ̃bjɛ̃], *adv.* (*& conj. when introducing a clause*) **1.** (*exclamative*) *(a)* how (much)! **si vous saviez c. je l'aime!** if you knew how much I love him! **c. je regrette de vous déranger!** how sorry I am to disturb you! **c. peu vous me comprenez!** how little you understand me! **vous ne savez pas c. vous dites vrai**, you don't know how right you are; **c. de peine cela m'a coûté!** what trouble it has given me! **j'ai regretté, ô c., votre absence!** I regretted—oh, how I regretted!—your absence! how very sorry I was you did not come! *Lit:* **c. rares sont les gens sans ambition!** how few are the people without ambition! *(b)* how (many)! **c. se sont ruinés!** how many have been ruined! **c. de gens!** what a lot of people! **2.** (*interrogative*) *(a)* how much? **c. vous faut-il de temps? c. de temps vous faut-il?** how much time do you need? **c. vous dois-je?** how much do I owe you? **c'est c.?** *F:* **ça fait c.?** how much is it? **à c. évaluez-vous ce cheval?** how much do you think this horse is worth? **depuis c. de temps est-il ici?** how long has he been here? **c. y a-t-il d'ici à Londres?** how far is it (from here) to London? **à c. sommes-nous de Paris?** how far are we from Paris? **c. vous a-t-il fallu pour venir?** how long did it take you to come? **c'est arrivé il y a je ne sais c. de temps**, it happened such a long time ago, I don't know how long ago; *(b)* how many? **c. de livres avez-vous?** how many books have you? **c. de fois?** how many times? how often? **je ne sais c. de gens**, so many people, such a lot of people; *(c) s.m.inv. F:* **le c. sommes-nous?** what's the date? **il y a un car tous les c.?** how often does the bus run? **le c. êtes-vous?** where did you come (in your exam)? **3. c. je voudrais qu'il fût encore en vie!** how I wish he were still alive! **c. d'argent qu'il se fasse il n'en aura jamais assez**, however much money he makes he will never have enough.

combientième [kɔ̃bjɛ̃tjɛm], *a. & s. F:* **nous sommes le c. aujourd'hui?** what's the date today? **tu as été reçu (le) c. à l'examen?** where did you come in the exam?

combinable [kɔ̃binabl̩], *a.* combinable.

combinaise [kɔ̃binɛ:z], *s.f. A: P:* = COMBINE.

combinaison [kɔ̃binɛzɔ̃], *s.f.* **1.** *(a)* combination, arrangement, grouping (of letters, ideas, etc.); **coffre à combinaisons**, safe with combination lock; **c. de couleurs**, colour scheme; **c. financière**, combine; *Mth:* **combinaisons de n objets r à r**, combinations of n things r at a time (n C r); *(b)* plan, contrivance, scheme; *F:* **c. louche**, shady, fishy, scheme; **déranger les combinaisons de qn**, to upset s.o.'s plans; *(c) Ch:* combination; compound. **2.** *(a)* (mechanic's) overalls, dungarees, boiler-suit; *Av:* one-piece flying suit; **c. insubmersible**, exposure suit; *(b) O:* (pair of) combinations; *(c) Cost:* slip.

combinaison-culotte [kɔ̃binɛzɔ̃kylɔt], *s.f. Cost:* *(a)* combinations; *(b)* (pair of) cami-knickers; *pl. combinaisons-culottes.*

combinaison-jupon [kɔ̃binɛzɔ̃ʒypɔ̃], *s.f. Cost: A:* princess petticoat, slip; *pl. des combinaisons-jupons.*

combinard, -arde [kɔ̃bina:r, -ard], *a. & s. P:* grafter; racketeer.

combinat [kɔ̃bina], *s.m.* (*in U.S.S.R.*) *Ind:* combine.

combinateur, -trice [kɔ̃binatœ:r, -tris]. **1.** *(a) s.* combiner, contriver; *(b) a.* combining, scheming. **2.** *s.m. Gasm:* compounder; *El:* selector switch; *El.E:* **c. de couplage**, controller (on electric railway or tram).

combinatoire [kɔ̃binatwa:r], *a. Mth: etc:* combinative.

combine [kɔ̃bin], *s.f. P:* scheme, arrangement, trick; fiddle; **une bonne c.**, a good scheme, wheeze; **on peut gagner beaucoup d'argent au moyen de la c.**, one can make a lot of money by fiddling; **pour faire marcher ma radio, il faut savoir la c.**, to get my radio to work, you must know the trick; **je ne donne pas dans tes combines**, I'm not falling for that, I won't be taken in by that.

combiné [kɔ̃bine]. **1.** *a.* combined, joint (action, etc.); *Mil: etc:* **opérations combinées**, joint operations; *Cin:* **impression combinée**, composite shot. **2.** *s.m.* *(a) Ch:* compound; combination; *(b) Tp:* **c. (téléphonique)**, receiver; *(c)* radiogram; *(d) Skiing:* all-round test; *(e) Cost:* corselette.

combiner [kɔ̃bine], *v.tr.* **1.** *(a)* to combine, unite (forces, etc.); to arrange, group (numbers, ideas, etc.); *(b) Ch:* to combine. **2.** to contrive, devise, think out, concoct (plan, etc.); **c. de faire qch.**, to work out a scheme to do sth.; *F:* **qu'est-ce que tu as combiné?** what have you dreamed up?

se combiner, to combine, unite; *Ch:* **se c. à, avec, qch.**, to combine with sth., to enter into combination with sth.

comble[1] [kɔ̃:bl̩], *s.m.* **1.** *(a) O:* heaped measure, overmeasure; *(b)* **pour c. de malheur**, as a crowning misfortune; to crown all; **pour (y mettre le) c.**, to add the last straw; to add insult to injury; *F:* **ça c'est le c., un c.!** that beats all! that's the limit, the last straw! that takes the cake! **2.** *(a)* roof (timbers); roofing; **faux c.**, deck (of Mansard roof); **c. en appentis**, lean-to roof, pent roof, penthouse roof; **c. sur pignon(s)**, gable-roof; **c. à deux pentes, à deux versants**, span-roof; **c. brisé**, curb-roof; **loger sous les combles**, to live in the attics, in the garret, at the top of the house; **de fond en c.**, from top to bottom; *F:* **ruiné de fond en c.**, utterly ruined; *(b)* highest point; height (of happiness, insolence); depth (of despair); acme, summit (of fame, etc.); **porter qch. à son c.**, to raise sth. to the highest pitch, to a climax.

comble[2], *a.* *(a)* (*of measure, etc.*) heaped up, piled up; full to bursting, to overflowing; **la mesure est c.**, that's the limit, the last straw; *(b)* (*of hall, etc.*) packed; **le parterre est c.**, the pit is crowded, packed; **salle c.**, house filled to capacity; **la pièce fait salle c.**, the play is drawing full houses; the show is playing to capacity, *U.S:* the play is a sellout; *(c) Vet:* **pied c.**, pumiced foot.

comblé [kɔ̃ble], *a.* *(a)* full; *(b)* fortunate; *(c)* happy, pleased; **il est c.**, he is entirely happy.

combleau, -eaux [kɔ̃blo], *s.m. Artil:* drag-rope.

comblement [kɔ̃bləmɑ̃], *s.m.* filling (up, in) (of well, ditch, etc.).

combler [kɔ̃ble], *v.tr.* **1.** to fill (up), fill in (well, ditch, etc.); **c. une perte**, to make up, make good, a loss; **c. une lacune**, to fill a gap; *Mil:* **c. les vides**, to fill the gaps; to make good the casualties. **2.** to fill (measure, etc.) to overflowing; to overload, overwhelm (s.o., sth.; **train comblé de matelots**, train crowded with, chock full of, sailors; **c. qn de bénédictions, de bienfaits**, to shower blessings, to heap kindness, on s.o.; **comblé de douleur, d'honneurs**, laden with grief, with honours; **c. les vœux de qn**, to gratify s.o.'s wishes to the full.

se combler, (*of valley*) to fill up; (*of lake, etc.*) to silt up.

combourgeois, -oise [kɔ̃burʒwa, -wa:z], *a. & s. Geog:* (native, inhabitant) of Combourg.

combrétacées [kɔ̃bretase], *s.f.pl. Bot:* Combretaceae.

combretum [kɔ̃bretɔm], *s.m. Bot:* combretum.

combrière [kɔ̃bri(j)ɛ:r], *s.f. Fish:* (large) fishing-net, tunny-net.

combuger [kɔ̃byʒe], *v.tr.* to soak (cask).

comburable [kɔ̃byrabl̩], *a. Ch:* combustible.

comburant [kɔ̃byrɑ̃]. **1.** *a. Ch: etc:* combustive. **2.** *s.m.* (*rockets*) oxidant.

combustibilité [kɔ̃bystibilite], *s.f.* combustibility, inflammability.

combustible [kɔ̃bystibl̩]. **1.** *a.* combustible, inflammable; **gaz c.**, fuel gas; *Atom.Ph:* **élément c.**, fuel element. **2.** *s.m.* fuel; firing; combustible; (*rockets*) propellant; **c. liquide, solide**, liquid, solid, fuel; **combustibles fossiles**, fossil fuels; **c. pulvérulent**, powdered, pulverized, fuel; **c. atomique, nucléaire**; atomic, nuclear, fuel; **c. de ménage**, household fuel; **c. anti-détonant**, anti-knock fuel; **combustibles à base de charbon**, fuels manufactured from coal; **le feu s'était éteint faute de c.**, the fire had burnt out, gone out, for lack of fuel; **s'alimenter en c.**, to stock up with fuel, to get in one's fuel supplies; *Nau: etc:* **refaire sa provision de c., se réapprovisionner en c.**, to refuel; **consommation de c.**, fuel consumption.

combustion [kɔ̃bystjɔ̃], *s.f.* combustion, burning; **c. lente**, (i) slow combustion; (ii) smouldering; **poêle à c. lente**, slow-combustion stove; **c. des morts**, burning of the dead; **mettre qch. en c.**, to set sth. on fire, *Lit:* aflame; **moteur à c. interne**, internal combustion engine; **chambre de c.**, combustion chamber; **c. vive**, quick combustion; **taux, vitesse, de c.**, rate of combustion; **retard de c.**, combustion lag.

Côme [ko:m], *Pr.n.f. Geog:* Como; **le lac de C.**, lake Como.

comédie [kɔmedi], *s.f.* **1.** *(a)* comedy; **préférer la c. à la tragédie**, to prefer comedy to tragedy; **c. de mœurs**, comedy of manners, social comedy; **c. de salon**, private theatricals; **c. bourgeoise**, (i) middle-class comedy; (ii) amateur theatricals;

c. épisodique, à tiroirs, episodic play; **c. musicale,** musical comedy; **c. de boulevard,** light comedy; **c. attendrissante, larmoyante,** sentimental domestic drama (of the XVIIIth century); **c. dramatique,** sentimental comedy; *A:* **c. lyrique,** comic opera; **c'était une vraie c.!** it was as good as a play! (*b*) **jouer la c.,** (i) to act in a play; (ii) to play a part, to stage a scene, to put on an act; **toute cette cordialité n'est qu'une c.,** all this cordiality is sham, make-believe; **donner la c. aux gens,** to make a laughing-stock of oneself; (*to children*) **allons! pas de c.!** come along! behave yourselves! *F:* **c'est toujours la même c. pour garer sa voiture,** it's always a business trying to park your car. **2.** *A:* (*a*) play; **aller à la c.,** to go to the play; *P:* **envoyer un ouvrier à la c.,** to stand a workman off; (*b*) the drama.

Comédie-Française (la) [lakɔmedifrɑ̃sɛːz], *s.f.* the Comédie Française (one of the State-aided theatres in Paris and the home of French Classical drama).

Comédie-Italienne (la) [lakɔmediitaljɛn], *s.f. Lit.Hist:* the Commedia dell' Arte players (who played in France in the XVIth and XVIIth centuries).

comédien, -ienne [kɔmedjɛ̃, -jɛn], *s.* (*a*) comedian, actor, *f.* actress; player; **comédiens ambulants,** strolling players; *a.* **manières comédiennes,** theatrical, affected, manners; **c'est un(e) comédien(ne),** he, she, is always putting on an act; (*b*) exhibitionist; (*child*) show-off.

comédon [kɔmedɔ̃], *s.m. Med:* comedo, *F:* blackhead.

coménique [kɔmenik], *a. Ch:* comenic.

coméphoridés [kɔmefɔride], *s.m.pl. Ich:* Comephoridae.

comestibilité [kɔmɛstibilite], *s.f.* edibility.

comestible [kɔmɛstibl̩]. **1.** *a.* edible; **champignon c.,** edible fungus; **denrées comestibles,** comestibles, eatables, edibles, food. **2.** *s.m.* (*a*) article of food; (*b*) *pl.* eatables, food; **magasin de comestibles,** food shop, store; **marchand de comestibles,** food retailer.

cométaire [kɔmetɛːr], *a. Astr:* cometary, cometic.

comète [kɔmɛt], *s.f.* **1.** *Astr:* comet; *Pyr:* skyrocket; *Her:* blazing star; *F:* **filer la c.,** to sleep in the open air; *F:* **tirer des plans sur la c.,** (i) to dream up wild schemes; to build castles in the air; (ii) to try to get money; (iii) to try to get somewhere; *Vit:* **l'année de la C.,** the Comet year (1811); *F:* **c'est comme le vin de la c.,** it happens once in a blue moon. **2.** (*a*) *Bookb:* (book-cloth) headband; (*b*) **ruban comète,** baby ribbon.

comice [kɔmis], *s.m.* **1.** *pl.* **comices,** (*a*) *Rom.Ant:* comitia; (*b*) *Fr.Hist:* (*during the Revolution*); electoral meeting. **2. c. agricole,** agricultural association; **comices agricoles,** agricultural show, cattle show; **c. industriel,** industrial gathering, conference. **3.** *a. Hort:* **poire c.,** comice.

comicial, -iaux [kɔmisjal, -jo], *a.* **1.** *Rom.Ant:* comitial. **2.** *Med:* **mal c.,** epilepsy.

comics [kɔmik(s)], *s.m.pl.* strip cartoon, comic strip, *U.S:* the funnies; comic.

comien, -ienne [kɔmjɛ̃, -jɛn], *a. & s. Geog:* (native, inhabitant) of Como.

comifère [kɔmifɛːr], *a. Bot:* criniferous.

coministre [kɔminist̩r], *s.m.* fellow minister.

cominois, -oise [kɔminwa, -waːz], *a. & s.* (native) of Comines.

Comintern [kɔmɛ̃tɛrn, -intɛrn], *s.m. Pol.Hist:* Comintern.

comique [kɔmik]. **1.** *Th: Lit:* (*a*) *a.* comic (actor, author, part, etc.); **le genre c.,** comedy; **opéra c.,** comic opera; (*b*) *s.m.* (i) comedy; **le bas c.,** low comedy, farce; **scène d'un haut c.,** highly comical scene; (ii) comedy-writer; (iii) comic actor; comic; comedian, humorist; **c'est lui le c.,** he's the funny man (of the show). **2.** (*a*) *a.* comic(al), funny, ludicrous (story, face, etc.); (*b*) *s.m.* **le c. de l'histoire c'est que . . .,** the funny part, the joke, is that . . .; **avoir du c. dans l'esprit,** to have a comical turn of mind.

comiquement [kɔmikmɑ̃], *adv.* comically, ludicrously.

comitadji [kɔmitadʒi], *s.m. Hist:* comitadji.

comitard [kɔmitaːr], *s.m. Pol: F:* **1.** member of (opponent's) election party committee, member of a caucus; committee man; **groupe de comitards,** caucus. **2.** upholder of caucus government.

comité [kɔmite], *s.m.* committee, board; **c. consultatif,** advisory board, commission; *Adm:* **c. de censure,** audit committee; **c. d'enquête,** board of enquiry, of investigation; **c. interministériel,** interdepartmental committee; **c. permanent,** standing committtee; *Ind:* **c. d'entreprise,** joint production committee; *Th: Lit:* **c. de lecture,** reading committee, selection committee; *Pol:* (*of the House*) **se constituer en c.,** to go into committee; **se former en c. secret,** to go into secret session; **gouvernement par les comités,** government by caucus; **être en petit c.,** to be a select party, an informal gathering; **dîner en petit c.,** to have a small dinner party.

comité-directeur [kɔmitedirɛktœːr], *s.m.* steering committee; *pl. comités-directeurs.*

comitial, -iaux [kɔmisjal, -jo], *a.* **1.** *Rom.Ant:* comitial. **2. mal c.,** epilepsy.

comitialité [kɔmisjalite], *s.f. Med:* epilepsy.

comma [kɔm(m)a], *s.m.* **1.** *Mus:* comma. **2.** *Typ: occ.* colon; *pl. comma(s).*

command [kɔmɑ̃], *s.m. Com: Jur:* principal (in purchase); **déclaration de c.,** declaration by buyer (in sale of land by auction) that he is acting for a third party.

commandant [kɔmɑ̃dɑ̃]. **1.** *a.* (*a*) commanding, in command of; **général c. la première armée,** general commanding the first army, G.O.C. first army; (*b*) *F:* authoritarian; *F:* bossy. **2.** *s.m.* (*a*) (*function*) commander, commanding officer (of unit, etc.); commandant (of camp, base, etc.); *Nau:* captain (of ship) (whatever his rank); **c. en chef,** commander-in-chief; **c. supérieur,** senior, supreme, commander; **c. adjoint,** deputy commander; **c. en second,** second-in-command; *U.S:* executive; *Navy:* executive officer; **c. subalterne, c. subordonné, c. en sous-ordre,** subordinate commander; **c. par intérim,** temporary commander; **c. d'armes,** *A:* **c. de place,** town-major, *U.S:* post, station, commander, commandant; **c. (à bord d'un navire, etc.),** troop commander, officer commanding troops (on board); *U.S:* commanding officer of troops; **c. d'unité,** unit commander; **c. de compagnie, de bataillon, de division,** company, battalion, divisional, commander; **un c. de bataillon n'est pas nécessairement un chef de bataillon,** a battalion commander is not necessarily a major; *Civil Av:* **c. de bord,** captain; (*b*) (*rank*) *Mil:* major; *Nau:* commander; *Mil. Av:* squadron leader; **c. en chef des forces aériennes** = Marshal of the Royal Air Force; **le C. Martin,** (i) *Mil:* Major Martin; (ii) *Nau:* Commander Martin; (iii) *Mil.Av:* Squadron-Leader Martin; (iv) *Civil Av:* Captain Martin. (NOTE: in the French Navy, the officer in command of a ship is always addressed as "*Commandant,*" whatever his rank; in the Eng. Navy as "Sir"). **3.** *s.f. F:* **commandante,** wife of a *commandant.*

commande [kɔmɑ̃ːd], *s.f.* **1.** (*a*) *Com:* order; **c. pour l'exportation,** export order; **faire, placer, une c.,** to place an order; **mettre un article en c.,** to order an article; **livre, carnet, de commandes,** order book; **bon, bulletin de c.,** order form; **fait sur c.,** made to order; **complet sur c.,** suit made to measure, bespoke suit; **ouvrage écrit sur la c. de l'éditeur,** work commissioned by the publisher; **ouvrages écrits sur c.,** books written to order; **payable à la c.,** cash with order; **représentation de c.,** command performance; (*b*) (*goods ordered*) **livrer une c.,** to deliver an order; (*c*) *Ecc:* **fête de c.,** (holi)day of obligation; **la prudence est de c.,** prudence is essential; **sourire de c.,** feigned, forced, smile; **larmes de c.,** crocodile tears. **2.** *Mec.E:* (*a*) control, operation; **les commandes, les organes de c.,** the controls; **roue de c.,** control wheel; **bouton de c.,** control knob; **c. à distance,** remote control; **c. automatique,** automatic control; **c. par thermostat,** thermostat control; **c. gyroscopique,** gyro-control; **c. hydraulique,** hydraulic drive; hydraulic gear; **c. manuelle, c. à main,** hand, manual, control, operation; **c. mécanique,** mechanical control, operation; **dispositif de c.,** control device, control system; **dispositif de c. à main,** hand-operated device; **levier de c.,** (i) control lever, operating lever; (ii) *Av:* control column; *F:* joy-stick; **c. de postcombustion,** retreat actuation; *Rail:* **bielle de c.,** operating rod; *Mil:* **c. de tir par radar,** radar fire control; **poste de c.,** (i) control post, room, station; (ii) *Ind: etc:* managerial position; (*b*) lever; *Av:* **commandes de vol,** flying controls; **avion à double c.,** dual-control plane; **c. altimétrique,** altitude control; **c. d'aileron,** aileron control; **c. du carburateur, c. des gaz,** throttle (control); **c. du changement de vitesse,** gear lever; *I.C.E:* **distributeur et c. (d'allumage),** ignition tower; (*c*) drive, driving (gear); **c. à mouvement lent,** slow-motion drive; **c. directe,** direct drive; **à c. directe,** direct-driven; **c. électrique,** electric drive; **machine à c. électrique,** electrically-driven machine; **c. par câble, par chaîne,** rope, chain, drive; **c. par cône,** cone drive; **c. par courroie, par poulies,** belt drive; **c. par engrenage(s),** gear drive; **c. par excentrique,** eccentric drive; **arbre de c.,** driving shaft, *U.S:* drive-shaft; *Mec.E: Aut:* **c. (des roues arrière) par le différentiel,** differential drive; *I.C.E:* **c. d'échappement,** exhaust gear; **c. de la pompe d'essence,** fuel-pump drive. **3.** (*a*) *Nau:* (i) fox, knittle (-stuff), nettle(-stuff); (ii) tow(ing) -line, -rope; (*b*) *Mil: etc:* lashing (of pontoons).

commandement [kɔmɑ̃dmɑ̃], *s.m.* **1.** command, order, instructions; (*a*) *Rel:* **les Commandements de Dieu, les Dix Commandements,** the Ten Commandments; (*b*) *Com: Jur:* **agir en vertu d'un c.,** to act (in a purchase) as agent, under instructions, by procuration; (*c*) *Jur:* summons to pay before execution, order to pay; (*d*) *F:* **obéir au c.,** to obey with military promptness; *F:* to do sth. pronto. **2.** authority; command; **avoir le c. sur . . .,** to have authority over . . ., to take precedence of . . .; **avoir le c. d'une province,** to govern a province; **avoir plusieurs langues à son c.,** to have several languages at one's command. **3.** *Mil: Navy:* (*a*) order, (word of) command; **c. à la voix,** command by word of mouth; **c. au clairon,** bugle command; **c. au sifflet,** whistle signal; *Navy:* piping; **c. préparatoire,** cautionary, preparatory, command; warning command; **c. d'exécution,** command of execution; *Nau:* **c. à la machine,** engine-room orders; (*b*) (*authority*) **c. en chef,** command-in-chief; **c. supérieur, haut c.,** (i) higher command (of British forces); (ii) high command (of French, German, etc. forces); **c. suprême,** supreme command; **c. subalterne, subordonné,** subordinate command; **c. par intérim,** temporary command; **aptitude au c.,** leadership; **unité de c.,** unity of command; **organe de c.,** organ, element, of command, *U.S:* command agency; *Navy:* **blockhaus de, poste de, c.,** conning tower; **c. à la mer,** sea-going command; **prendre le c.,** to assume, take (over), command; **recevoir le c.,** to take over command; **reprendre le c.,** to resume command; **transmettre, remettre, le c.,** to hand over, turn over, command; **se démettre de son c.,** to resign command; **avoir le c. d'un bataillon, d'un navire,** to be in command of a battalion, of a ship; (*c*) **c. territorial,** (territorial) command; **le c. territorial de l'Est,** the Eastern command. **4.** *Mil: Navy: etc:* (*power to see from a higher position*): command; **fort de faible c.,** fort with low command.

commandé [kɔmɑ̃de], *a.* **1.** *Mec.E:* (*a*) controlled, operated (motion, valve, etc.); **machine commandée hydrauliquement,** hydraulically operated machine; (*b*) driven (shaft, etc.); **c. par chaîne, par moteur,** chain-, motor-, driven. **2.** *Mil:* **en service c.,** on special duty.

commander [kɔmɑ̃de]. I. *v.tr.* **1.** to command, order (sth.); (*a*) **c. à qn de faire qch.,** to command, order, s.o. to do sth.; **c. qch à qn,** to give s.o. an order for sth., to order sth. from s.o.; **je lui commandai le silence, de se taire,** I told him to be quiet; **c. qu'on serve le dîner,** to give orders for dinner to be served; *abs:* **Monsieur a-t-il commandé?** have you given your order, sir? **il aime à c.,** he is fond of ordering people about; *F:* he is (rather) bossy; *O: F:* **commandez à vos valets!** who do you think you are talking to? (*b*) **c. des marchandises, un dîner, un nouveau costume,** to order goods, a dinner, a new suit; **c. une peinture,** to commission a painting; (*c*) **ces choses-là ne se commandent pas,** these things are beyond our control; **les larmes ne se commandent pas,** one cannot shed tears at will; **il faut apprendre à vous c.,** you must learn to control yourself; (*d*) **c. le respect,** to command, compel, respect. **2.** *Mil: Navy:* to command, to order; to be in charge, in command (of); **c. en chef,** to be commander-in-chief (of); **c. en premier,** to be commander, commanding officer, senior officer, head (of); **c. en second,** to be second-in-command; **c. un bataillon, une flotte, un navire,** to command, to be in command of, a battalion, a fleet, a ship; **c. le feu,** to give the order to fire; **c. l'exercice,** to be in command, in charge, at drill; *Nau:* **c. la manœuvre d'un navire,** to con a ship. **3.** (*a*) *Mil: Navy: etc:* to command, dominate; **la cote 340, le fort, commande la vallée, la ville,** hill 340, the fort, commands, dominates, the valley, the town; (*b*) to give access to; **la salle à manger commande le salon,** access to the drawing-room is through the dining-room; **les pièces de cet appartement**

se commandent, the rooms of this flat communicate with each other. **4.** *Mec.E:* (*a*) to control, operate (motion, valve, etc.); **c. à distance,** to control, operate, from a distance; (*b*) to drive (machine, shaft, etc.); **le piston commande l'axe de manivelle,** the piston drives the crank-axle.

II. **commander,** *v.ind.tr.* **c. à qn, à qch.,** to command, govern, control, s.o., sth.; **c. à son impatience, à ses passions,** to control, curb, one's impatience, one's passions.

commanderie [kɔmɑ̃dri], *s.f. Hist:* commandery.

commandeur [kɔmɑ̃dœːr], *s.m.* **1.** *Hist:* commander (of order of knighthood, *Légion d'Honneur*). **2.** *Orn:* red-winged troupial.

commanditaire [kɔmɑ̃ditɛːr], *a. & s.m. Com:* **(associé) c.** = sleeping partner.

commandite [kɔmɑ̃dit], *s.f.* **1.** *Com:* (*a*) **(société en) c.,** mixed liability company; limited partnership, *U.S:* (*in Louisiana*) commandite; **c. par actions,** liability limited to the extent of holdings, partnership limited by shares; (*b*) interest of, capital invested by, sleeping partner(s). **2.** *Typ:* companionship.

commandité [kɔmɑ̃dite], *a. & s.m. Com:* **(associé) c.,** active partner.

commanditer [kɔmɑ̃dite], *v.tr. Com:* to subscribe capital (to firm, etc.) as sleeping partner; to finance (enterprise, etc.).

commando [kɔmɑ̃do], *s.m.* (*a*) *Mil:* commando (unit); (*b*) team of specialized workmen ready for emergencies, emergency squad.

comme[1] [kɔm], *adv.* **1.** (*in a similar manner*) (*a*) as; **faites c. moi,** do as I do; *Pred:* **je vous dis cela c. ami,** I tell you this as a friend; **adopter qn c. fils,** to adopt s.o. as a son; **je l'ai eu c. maître,** I had him for, as, a master; **il fut vendu c. esclave,** he was sold as a slave; (*b*) like; **faites c. moi,** do like me; **se conduire c. un fou,** to behave like a madman; **tout c. un autre,** (just) like anyone else; **tout c. vous,** like you; **sortir tous les jours, été c. hiver,** to go out every day, summer and winter alike; *F:* **j'ai c. une idée que . . .,** I have a sort of idea that . . .; *F:* **c. ci c. ça,** so so; **c. ça vous venez de Paris?** and so you come from Paris? *Nau:* **c. ça!** so! steady (as you go)! *F:* **il est c. ça,** he's like that, he's made that way, he's given that way; *s.a.* QUOI[1] 4; (*c*) (*in intensifying similes*) (as . . .) as . . .; **doux c. un agneau,** (as) gentle as a lamb; **blanc c. un linge,** (as) white as a sheet; **blanc c. neige,** snow-white; **un chien trois fois gros c. lui,** a dog three times as big as himself; **l'Alaska est grand c. trois fois la France,** Alaska is three times as big as France; *F:* **drôle c. tout,** awfully funny; **rire c. tout,** to laugh like anything, like a drain; (*d*) **comme** (si) (si *is expressed only before a finite verb*), as if, as though; **il travaille c. s'il avait vingt ans,** he works as if he were twenty; **ils faisaient c. si rien ne s'était passé,** they pretended that nothing had happened; **c. si je le permettrais!** as if I would allow it! **ce n'est pas c. si je partais demain,** it isn't as if I were going tomorrow; **il resta c. pétrifié,** he stood as if, as though, petrified; **échapper c. par miracle,** to escape as (if) by a miracle; **il leva la main c. pour me frapper,** he lifted his hand as if to strike me; **c'est un peu c. vivre à la campagne,** it's a bit like living in the country; **décrire qn c. ayant un talent exceptionnel,** to describe s.o as having exceptional talent; *F:* **à ce moment j'ai c. perdu la tête,** at that moment I sort of lost my head; *F:* **c'est c. fait,** it's all but done; **nous considérons l'incident c. clos,** we consider the incident (as) closed; *F:* **c'est tout c.,** it amounts to the same thing; *F:* **est-elle nommée?—non, mais c'est tout c.,** is she appointed? no, but as good as; (*e*) such as; **les bois durs c. le chêne et le noyer,** hard woods such as oak and walnut; **un drap c. on n'en fait plus, c. on n'en voit plus,** a cloth the like of which is not made, not seen, to-day; (*f*) *Tp:* **L comme Lazare,** L for Lucy; (*g*) **il ne recule devant aucune perfidie, comme devant aucune cruauté,** he sticks at no act of treachery, nor at any act of cruelty; (*h*) *F:* **ce n'est pas mal c. film,** it's not a bad film. **2.** (*immediately before finite verbs*) as; (*a*) **faites c. il vous plaira,** do as you please; **je descendais c. je pouvais,** I was coming down as best I could; **c'est arrivé à peu près, tout à fait, c. je l'avais prédit,** it happened much, exactly, as I said it would; (*b*) *adj. & adv. phr.* **c. de juste, de raison,** as is only just, reasonable; **c. il faut,** proper(ly); *F:* (*of pers.*) **être c. il faut,** (i) to be well-bred; (ii) to be prim and proper. **3.** as, in the way of; **qu'est-ce que vous avez c. légumes?** what have you (got) in the way of vegetables? **4.** *excl.* how! **voyez c. elles courent!** see how they run! **c. vous avez grandi!** how you have grown! **c. il est grand!** how tall he is! **qu'est-ce que vous avez c. chance!** how lucky you are! **c. je suis content de vous voir!** how glad I am to see you! *U.S:* am I glad to see you! **5.** *F:* (= COMMENT); how; **il y est arrivé Dieu sait c.,** he managed it, the Lord knows how; **voilà c. il est,** that's just like him; that's his way.

comme[2], *conj.* **1.** as, seeing that; **c. vous êtes mon ami je vous dirai tout,** since you are my friend I will tell you all. **2.** (just) as; **c. il allait frapper on l'arrêta,** (just) as he was about to strike he was arrested; **c. il avançait, je reculais,** as he came forward, I drew back.

commélynacées [kɔmelinase], *s.f.pl. Bot:* Commelinaceae.

commélyne [kɔmelin], *s.f. Bot:* commelina, spiderwort.

commémorable [kɔm(m)emɔrabl̥], *a.* commemorable.

commémoraison [kɔm(m)emɔrɛzɔ̃], *s.f. Ecc:* commemoration, commemorative prayer.

commémoratif, -ive [kɔm(m)emɔratif, -iːv], *a.* commemorative (**de,** of); memorial (service, etc.); (festival) of remembrance; **monument c.,** memorial (monument); *Mil:* **médaille commémorative,** campaign medal; *U.S:* service medal; *Med:* **antécédents commémoratifs,** *s.m.pl.* **commémoratifs,** case history.

commémoration [kɔm(m)emɔrasjɔ̃], *s.f.* commemoration (of events); **en c. de . . .,** in commemoration of . . .; **la c. des morts, de tous les défunts,** the Commemoration of the Faithful Departed.

commémorer [kɔm(m)emɔre], *v.tr.* to commemorate.

commençant, -ante [kɔmɑ̃sɑ̃, -ɑ̃ːt]. **1.** *a.* beginning, early; **passion commençante,** budding passion. **2.** *s.* beginner, tyro.

commencement [kɔmɑ̃smɑ̃], *s.m.* (*a*) beginning, start, commencement; **au c.,** at the outset; *Lit: B:* in the beginning; **au c. de . . .,** at the beginning of . . .; **au c. de mars,** early in March, in early March; **dès, depuis, le c.,** from the start, from the outset; all along; (*of disease, etc.*) **prendre son c.,** to begin, start; **avoir de bons commencements dans qch.,** to have a good grounding in sth.; **il y a c. à tout,** everything has a beginning; **du c. jusqu'à la fin,** from beginning to end, from start to finish; (*b*) set-in, setting-in (of rains, winter, night, etc.).

commencer [kɔmɑ̃se], *v.* (**je commençai(s); n. commençons**) to begin, commence, start. **1.** (*a*) *v.tr.* **c. la leçon,** to begin the lesson; **c. une entreprise,** to embark on an undertaking; **c. un voyage,** to start on a journey; **c. qn dans qch.,** to start s.o. in sth.; **c. un élève,** to ground a pupil; **il a été bien commencé,** he has had a good grounding; **c. un cheval, un chien,** to begin training a horse, a dog; *Mil:* **c. le feu,** to open fire; **c. des poursuites contre une maison,** to institute proceedings against a firm; *abs.* **pour c., je dois vous dire . . .,** to begin with, first of all, I must tell you . . .; *Prov:* **à moitié fait qui commence bien,** well begun is half done; **laissez-moi c. par le commencement,** let me begin at the beginning; (*b*) *v.i.* **c. à, de, faire qch.,** to begin to do sth., to begin doing sth.; **c. à avoir conscience de qch.,** to begin to be aware of sth.; **il commence à pleuvoir,** it is beginning, starting, to rain; it is coming on to rain; **c. par faire qch.,** to begin by doing sth.; **commencez par oublier que . . .,** first forget that . . .; **on commençait à attaquer ce système d'enseignement,** this system of education was beginning to be attacked; **commencez!** fire away! *F:* **je commence à en avoir assez!** I've had just about enough! **2.** *v.i.* (*a*) to begin; **le poème commence par une invocation,** the poem begins, opens, with an invocation; **la pluie vient de c.,** the rain has just come on; **l'année commence le 1er janvier;** the year begins on January 1st; *Prov:* **qui commence mal finit mal,** a bad beginning makes a bad ending; *Games:* **la partie commence à deux heures,** play begins, starts, at two o'clock; *Fb:* kick-off at two o'clock; **la partie avait commencé,** the game had started; **le football est fini et le tennis n'a pas encore commencé,** football is over and tennis hasn't started; (*b*) (*of weather, darkness, etc.*) to set in.

commendataire [kɔmɑ̃datɛːr], *a. & s.m. Ecc:* commendatory (abbot, etc.).

commende [kɔmɑ̃ːd], *s.f. Ecc:* commendam; **abbaye en c.,** abbey (held) in commendam.

commender [kɔmɑ̃de], *v.tr. Ecc:* to give (benefice) in commendam.

commensal, -ale, -aux [kɔm(m)ɑ̃sal, -o], *s.* **1.** (*a*) *Lit:* commensal, table companion; (*b*) habitual guest. **2.** *Biol:* commensal.

commensalisme [kɔm(m)ɑ̃salism], *s.m. Biol:* commensalism, symbiosis.

commensalité [kɔm(m)ɑ̃salite], *s.f. Lit:* commensality, fellowship in eating.

commensurabilité [kɔm(m)ɑ̃syrabilite], *s.f. Mth:* commensurability, commensurableness (**avec,** with, to).

commensurable [kɔm(m)ɑ̃syrabl̥], *a. Mth:* commensurable (**avec,** with, to).

commensuration [kɔm(m)ɑ̃syrasjɔ̃], *s.f. Mth:* commensuration.

comment [kɔmɑ̃], *adv.* **1.** *interr.* how; **c. allez-vous?** how are you? **c. trouvez-vous ce chapeau?** how do you like this hat? **c. cela?** how so? **c. (dites-vous)?** what (did you say)? I beg your pardon? **c. faire?** what is to be done? **c. s'appelle-t-il?** what is his name? **vous vous appelez monsieur c.?** Mr who, did you say? **c. est-il, ce garçon?** what sort of a young man is he? what is this young man like? **je ne sais c. cela se fit,** I don't know how it happened; **je me sens je ne sais c.,** I don't know what's the matter with me; **faire qch. n'importe c.,** to do sth. no matter how, anyhow. **2.** *excl.* (*a*) what! why! **c.! vous n'êtes pas encore parti!** what, haven't you gone yet! **puis-je entrer?—mais c. donc!** may I come in?—why, of course! by all means! to be sure! (*b*) *P:* **ils les ont battus, et c.!** they licked them, and how! **3.** *s.m.inv.* **les pourquoi et les c.,** the whys and the wherefores.

commentaire [kɔ(m)mɑ̃tɛːr], *s.m.* **1.** (*a*) commentary (**sur,** on); annotations (**sur,** on); **faire le c. d'un texte,** to comment on a text; **texte avec c.,** annotated text; (*b*) **les Commentaires de César,** Caesar's Commentaries. **2.** comment; **commentaires de presse,** press commentaries; *F:* **cette action se passe de c.,** this action speaks for itself, is self-explanatory; *F:* **voilà qui se passe de c., sans c.!** enough said! *F:* no comment! **faire des commentaires sur qn, qch.,** to make, pass, remarks about s.o., sth.; *F:* (*to a subordinate*) **point, pas, de c.!** that's final! I don't want any comments from you!

commentateur, -trice [kɔ(m)mɑ̃tatœːr, -tris]. **1.** *s.m. Lit:* commentator, annotator. **2.** *s.m. & f. W.Tel: T.V:* (news) commentator.

commenter [kɔ(m)mɑ̃te], *v.tr.* **1.** to comment on, annotate (text, etc.). **2.** **c. (sur) qn, qch.,** to comment (up)on, criticize (adversely), pass remarks about, s.o., sth.; *W.Tel: T.V:* **journaliste qui commente l'actualité,** journalist who makes a news commentary.

commérage [kɔmeraːʒ], *s.m.* (*a*) piece of (ill-natured) gossip; (*b*) *pl.* gossip(ing); tittle-tattle.

commerçable [kɔmɛrsabl̥], *a. A: Com:* negotiable; marketable.

commerçant, -ante [kɔmɛrsɑ̃, -ɑ̃ːt]. **1.** *a.* commercial, mercantile; business (district, etc.); **rue commerçante,** shopping street; **rue très commerçante,** busy shopping street; **être c.,** to have a good head for business; **peu c.,** (i) bad at business; (ii) (town, etc.) that does little trade; **peuple c.,** trading nation. **2.** *s.* merchant; dealer; tradesman; shopkeeper; **c. en gros,** wholesaler; **nous nous fournissons chez le même c.,** we deal at the same shop; **être c.,** to be in business; to be a shopkeeper; **les commerçants,** the tradespeople.

commerce [kɔmɛrs], *s.m.* **1.** commerce, trade; (transaction of) business; **c. de gros, de détail,** wholesale, retail, trade; **c. par opérations compensées,** barter trade; **c. intérieur, extérieur,** home, foreign, trade; **marchandises destinées au c. intérieur,** goods for the home market; **traité de c.,** commercial treaty; *Jur:* **acte de c.,** act of merchant; **maison de c.,** business house; firm; **marine de c.,** mercantile marine, merchant service; **navire de c.,** merchant ship, merchantman; **chambre de c.,** chamber of commerce; **voyageur de c.,** (commercial) traveller, representative; **le c.,** (i) trade; (ii) the commercial world; **le gros c.,** big business, large-scale business; **le petit c.,** (i) small traders; (ii) shopkeeping; **est-ce que cela se trouve dans le c.?** is this on sale (generally)? **cela fait marcher le c.,** it's good for trade; **hors c.,** not for (general) sale; **édition hors c.,** edition for private circulation only; **exercer un c.,** to carry on a business, a trade; **faire le c. du thé,** to be in the tea trade, to deal in tea; **faire un gros c. de vin,** (i) to deal in wine on a large scale; (ii) to do a large, *F:* a roaring, trade in wine; **il a un petit c. de sucreries,** he has a small sweet-shop; **il fait**

un petit c. de sucreries, he sells sweets on a small scale; he sells a few sweets; **le c. des boissons et spiritueux,** the liquor trade, the wine and spirit trade; **le c. des esclaves,** the slave trade; **c. des chevaux,** horse dealing; **fonds de c.,** stock in trade; **vendre un fonds de c.,** to sell a business as a going concern. **2.** intercourse, dealings; **c. du monde,** human intercourse; **avoir, être en, c. avec qn,** to be in touch, in relationship, with s.o.; **être en c. de lettres avec qn,** to be in correspondence with s.o.; **être d'un c. agréable,** to be easy to get on with, pleasant to deal with; **homme d'un c. agréable,** pleasant man; **rompre tout c. avec qn,** to break off all communication, dealings, connection, with s.o.; **le c. des livres élargit l'esprit,** reading broadens the mind. **3.** (sexual) commerce, intercourse; **c. adultère,** adulterous intercourse.

commercer [kɔmɛrse], *v.i.* (**je commerçai(s); n. commerçons**) **1.** to trade, deal (avec, with). **2. c. avec qn,** to hold intercourse, have dealings, with s.o.

commercial, -iaux [kɔmɛrsjal, -jo]. **1.** *a.* commercial, trading, business (relations, etc.); **foire commerciale,** trade fair; **perspectives commerciales,** trading prospects; **tendances commerciales,** trade trends; **les conditions commerciales sont soumises à la concurrence,** business, trading, conditions are competitive; **entretenir des relations commerciales avec qn,** to trade with s.o.; **service c.,** sales department. **2.** *s.f. Aut:* **commerciale,** estate car.

commercialement [kɔmɛrsjalmɑ̃], *adv.* commercially; by way of trade; from the commercial point of view.

commercialisation [kɔmɛrsjalizasjɔ̃], *s.f.* **1.** commercialization. **2.** marketing.

commercialiser [kɔmɛrsjalize], *v.tr.* **1.** *Fin:* to negotiate (a bill). **2.** to commercialize (art, etc.); to exploit (invention, etc.); **produit non encore commercialisé,** product not yet on sale to the public, not yet marketed.

commercialité [kɔmɛrsjalite], *s.f.* negotiability (of bill, etc.).

commère [kɔmɛːr], *s.f.* **1.** *Ecc: A: & Dial:* godmother; fellow-sponsor (in relation to godfather). **2.** (*a*) gossip, busybody; **c'est une vrai c.,** he's, she's, a dreadful gossip; (*b*) crony. **3.** *A: F:* **ma c.,** gossip, goodwife. **4.** *Th: A:* commère (in music hall).

commérer [kɔmere], *v.i.* (**je commère, n. commérons; je commérerai**) to gossip, to (tittle-)tattle.

commettage [kɔmetaːʒ], *s.m. Ropem:* **1.** laying, stranding (of rope). **2.** lay (of rope).

commettant [kɔmetɑ̃], *s.m.* **1.** *Com: Jur:* principal (to a deal), actual purchaser, actual vendor (when represented by agent); employer; **c. et préposé,** principal and agent. **2.** *pl. Pol:* constituents.

commetteur, -euse [kɔmetœːr, -øːz], *s. Ropem:* ropelayer.

commettre [kɔmɛtr], *v.tr.* (*conj. like* METTRE) **1.** (*a*) *Ropem:* to lay, twist (rope); (*b*) *A:* **c. qn avec qn,** to embroil s.o. with s.o.; to set s.o. at variance with s.o. **2.** (*a*) *A:* (= COMPROMETTRE) to expose; **c. sa réputation,** to risk one's reputation; **se c. aux périls de la mer,** to commit, expose, oneself to the perils of the sea; **il eut soin de ne pas se c.,** he was careful not to commit himself; *Pej:* **se c. avec qn,** to throw in one's lot with s.o.; (*b*) *A:* **c. qch. à qn,** to commit, entrust, sth. to s.o., to s.o.'s keeping; to entrust s.o. with sth.; **il m'a commis son sort,** he has put his fate in my hands; **c. qch. à la garde de qn,** to entrust, commit, sth. to s.o.'s keeping; (*c*) *Jur:* **c. qn à qch.,** to appoint s.o. to sth.; to place s.o. in charge of sth. **3.** to commit, perpetrate (crime, sin, injustice); **c. une erreur,** to make a mistake, a slip.

commination [kɔminasjɔ̃], *s.f. Ecc:* commination.

comminatoire [kɔminatwaːr], *a. Jur:* (*a*) comminatory (decree, etc.); (*b*) threatening (letter); denunciatory (speech, etc.).

comminuer [kɔminɥe], *v.tr. Surg:* to comminute.

comminutif, -ive [kɔminytif, -iːv], *a. Surg:* comminute(d) (fracture).

comminution [kɔminysjɔ̃], *s.f. Surg:* (*a*) comminution; (*b*) comminuted fracture.

commiphora [kɔmifɔra], *s.m. Bot:* commiphora.

commis[1] [kɔmi], *a. Ropem:* **c. de droite à gauche,** back-laid, left-handed; **c. de gauche à droite,** right-handed; **c. en aussière,** hawser-laid; **c. en câble, en grelin,** cable-laid, water-laid; **c. en quatre,** four-stranded; **c. en quatre avec mèche,** shroud-laid; **c. en trois,** three-stranded; **c. serré,** short-laid, hard-laid.

commis[2], *s.m.* **1.** (*a*) clerk, book-keeper; **c. principal, premier c.,** head, chief, clerk; **les grands c.,** the higher civil servants; **c. en douane,** custom broker's clerk; **c. des douanes,** customs clerk; (*b*) *Mil:* **c. d'administration,** administrative clerk; **c. du service de santé,** medical clerk; (*c*) *Nau:* **c. aux vivres,** ship's steward; purser. **2.** (*a*) (*occ. with f.* **commise**) shop assistant; salesman; (*b*) *O. & Pej:* **c. voyageur,** commercial traveller; *F:* **il a un bagout de c. voyageur,** he's as glib as a commercial traveller; he'd talk you into buying anything. **3.** *Jur:* agent (of merchant).

commis-débarrasseur [kɔmidebarasœːr], *s.m.* (*in restaurant*) busboy; *pl. commis-débarrasseurs.*

commise [kɔmiːz], *s.f. A.Jur:* forfeiture.

commisération [kɔm(m)izerasjɔ̃], *s.f.* commiseration, pity; **témoigner de la c. à qn,** to commiserate with s.o.

commissaire [kɔmisɛːr], *s.m.* **1.** (*a*) member of a commission, commissioner; commissary; **c. du gouvernement,** government representative; **juge c.,** judge sitting in a bankruptcy case; (*b*) **c. de police** = police inspector; **c. central** = police superintendent; (*c*) *Mil: etc:* (i) **c. du gouvernement,** prosecutor (at court-martial); (ii) **c. de gare,** railway transport officer (R.T.O.); **c. de réseau,** traffic control officer; (*d*) *Navy:* **c. de la Marine,** paymaster, *U.S:* supply officer; *Nau:* **c. du bord,** purser; (*e*) *Adm:* **c. des naufrages,** wreck commissioner; *Fin:* **c. aux comptes,** auditor; *Com:* **c. de transport,** forwarding agent; (*f*) *Fr.C:* **c. d'école,** school commissioner; (*g*) *Sp: etc:* steward; **commissaires d'un bal, d'une fête,** dance stewards, organisers of a fête; *Rac:* **c. des courses,** race steward; **c. à l'arrivée,** judge; **c. de la piste,** clerk of the course. **2.** *U.S.S.R. Adm:* commissar.

commissaire-priseur [kɔmisɛːrprizœːr], *s.m.* **1.** appraiser, valuer. **2.** auctioneer; *pl. commissaires-priseurs.*

commissariat [kɔmisarja], *s.m.* **1.** (*a*) commissionership, commissaryship; **c. des comptes,** auditorship; (*b*) *Nau:* pursership. **2.** (*a*) commissary or commissioner's office; *Nau:* purser's office; (*b*) **c. (de police),** police station. **3. c. de la marine, de l'air** = naval, air, department (of Ministry of Defence); **c. à l'énergie atomique,** Atomic Energy Commission.

commission [kɔmisjɔ̃], *s.f.* commission. **1.** *Theol:* **péchés d'omission et de c.,** sins of omission and commission. **2.** (*a*) *Jur: etc.* charge, warrant; **avoir la c. de faire qch.,** to be commissioned, empowered, to do sth.; (*b*) *Com:* **donner à qn une c. pour acheter qch.,** to give s.o. an order, to commission s.o., to buy sth.; (*c*) *Com:* factorage, commission business; **maison de c.,** firm of commission agents, commission agency; **vente à c.,** sale on commission; **représentant à la c.,** commission agent; **droits de c.,** commission factorage. **3.** (*a*) *Com:* commission, allowance; **c. de deux pour cent,** commission of two per cent; **3% de c.,** 3% commission; **prendre une c. de 5%,** to charge a 5% commission; (*b*) *Fin:* brokerage, factorage. **4.** (*a*) message, errand; **faire, exécuter, une c.,** (i) to deliver a message; (ii) to do an errand, to go on an errand; **faire des c.,** to run errands; **j'ai fait toutes mes commissions,** I've done all my shopping; *F:* **faire une petite c.,** to spend a penny, to pee, to wee-wee; *F:* **faire une grosse c.,** to do one's duty; (*b*) *Navy:* **hommes de c.,** duty men; **navire en c.,** ship being put into commission. **5.** *Com:* order. **6.** committee, board; **c. exécutive,** executive committee; **c. permanente,** standing committee; **c. médicale,** medical board; **c. d'enquête,** (i) fact-finding commission; board of inquiry, *Scot:* panel; (ii) court of enquiry; **c. du budget,** Budget Committee (= Committee of Ways and Means, and Committee of Supply); *Sch:* **c. d'examen,** board of examiners; *Pol:* (r)envoyer **un projet de loi à une c.,** to commit a bill; **renvoi à une c.,** committal (of a bill); **c. de contrôle,** Control Commission; *Mil.Trans:* **c. régulatrice des chemins de fer,** railway traffic control commission; **c. régulatrice routière,** (road, *U.S:* highway) traffic control commission.

commissionnaire [kɔmisjɔnɛːr], *s.m.* **1.** (*a*) *Com:* mercantile agent, commission agent; **c. en gros,** factor; **c. d'achat,** buyer; *Fin:* **c. en banque,** outside broker; **c. en douane(s),** customs broker; **c. exportateur, importateur,** export, import, agent; **c. expéditeur, de transport, de roulage,** forwarding agent, carrier; *Adm:* **c. au Crédit Municipal** = pawnbroker. **2.** messenger, street-porter; (*in hotels, theatres*) commissionaire; **petit c.,** errand boy; *Rail:* **c. messager,** outside porter.

commissionné [kɔmisjɔne], *s.m. Mil:* re-engaged soldier or N.C.O.

commissionnement [kɔmisjɔnmɑ̃], *s.m.* (act of) commissioning, appointing.

commissionner [kɔmisjɔne], *v.tr.* **1.** (*a*) to commission; to appoint (s.o.) as buyer on commission; (*b*) *Mil:* **c. un soldat,** to allow a soldier (*esp.* N.C.O.) to continue in the service. **2.** *Com:* to order (goods).

commissoire [kɔmiswaːr], *a. Jur:* **clause, pacte, c.,** *commissoria lex.*

commissural, -aux [kɔmisyral, -o], *a. Anat: Bot:* commissural.

commissurant [kɔmisyrɑ̃], *a. Anat:* **les fibres commissurantes du cerveau,** the commissures of the brain.

commissure [kɔmisyːr], *s.f. Anat: Bot: Arch: etc:* commissure; corner (of the lips, etc.); line of junction; *Anat:* **la grande c. cérébrale,** the great commissure (uniting the hemispheres of the brain); **c. des paupières,** canthus.

commodat [kɔm(m)ɔda], *s.m. Jur:* free loan (of sth. to be returned in unimpaired condition); *Scot: commodatum,* commodate.

commodataire [kɔmɔdatɛːr], *s.m. Jur:* commodatary.

commode[1] [kɔmɔd]. **1.** *a.* (*a*) convenient, suitable, opportune (moment, etc.); handy, easily handled (tool, etc.); (*b*) convenient, comfortable (house, etc.); **habit c.,** comfortable, easy-fitting, coat; **voiture c.,** roomy, commodious, carriage; (*c*) **c. à faire,** easy to do, easily done; **ce que vous me demandez là n'est pas c.,** what you are asking me isn't very easy; *F:* that's a large order; (*d*) accommodating, easy, adaptable (disposition, etc.); **personne c.,** easy-going, good-natured, person; **c. à vivre,** easy to live with; **être peu c.,** (i) to be hard, difficult, to deal with; (ii) to be hard to please; **il n'est pas c., il est peu c.,** *F:* he's a tough customer, he takes some handling, he's a hard nut to crack; **mari c.,** complaisant husband; **morale c.,** loose moral standards, permissive morals; **mère c.,** indulgent mother. **2.** *s.f. Furn:* chest of drawers, commode. **3.** *s.f. A.Cost:* commode.

Commode[2]. *Pr.n.m. Rom.Hist:* Commodus.

commodément [kɔmɔdemɑ̃], *adv.* conveniently; comfortably.

commodité [kɔmɔdite], *s.f.* **1.** convenience; (*a*) comfort; **les commodités de la vie,** the conveniences, comforts, of life; **vivre dans la c.,** to live in comfort; **faire qch. à sa c.,** to do sth. at one's convenience; **pour plus de c.,** for convenience sake; (*b*) commodiousness (of carriage, etc.); (*c*) *pl. O:* **commodités,** lavatory. **2.** *A:* (= OCCASION) opportunity; **profiter de la première c. pour faire qch.,** to take the earliest opportunity of doing sth.

commodo [komodo], *s.m. Jur:* **enquête de commodo et incommodo,** public, administrative, inquiry.

commonwealth [kɔmœnwelθ], *s.m.* commonwealth; **le C. britannique,** the British Commonwealth of Nations.

commotion [kɔmosjɔ̃], *s.f.* **1.** commotion, disturbance; **c. électrique,** electric shock; **c. mentale,** mental shock; **c. politique,** political upheaval. **2.** *Med:* (*a*) shell-shock; (*b*) concussion.

commotionné [kɔmosjɔne], *a. Med:* suffering (i) from shell-shock, (ii) from concussion.

commotionner [kɔmosjɔne], *v.tr.* (*a*) *Med:* to cause a state of shock; **une décharge électrique l'avait commotionné,** he had received a severe electric shock; (*b*) **cette nouvelle m'a commotionné,** this news has given me a terrible shock, upset me terribly.

commuabilité [kɔm(m)ɥabilite], *s.f. Jur:* commutability.

commuable [kɔm(m)ɥabl̩], *a. Jur:* commutable (sentence, etc.) (en, to).

commuer [kɔm(m)ɥe], *v.tr. Jur:* to commute (penalty) (en, to); (*for death penalty*) **c. une peine capitale,** to reprieve a condemned man.

commun [kɔmœ̃]. **1.** *a.* (*a*) common (to two or more); **escalier c. à deux appartements,** staircase shared by two flats; **choses communes,** common property; *Jur:* **époux communs en biens,** couple married under the joint property system; **champs communs,** common (land); **salle commune,** (i) common room; (ii) (*in hospital*) public ward; **maison commune,** town hall, municipal buildings; **avoir des intérêts communs,** to have interests in common, to have common interests; **créer une société en c. avec . . .,** to start a company jointly with . . .; **amis communs,** mutual friends; **n'avoir rien de c. avec qn,**

to have nothing in common with s.o.; **cela n'a rien de c. avec ceci**, that has nothing to do with this; **faire bourse commune**, to share expenses, to pool resources; **faire cause commune**, to make common cause (**avec**, with); **vie commune**, community life; **faire vie commune**, to live together; **d'un c. accord**, with one accord; **d'une commune voix**, with one voice; *Mth:* **facteur, dénominateur, c.**, common factor, denominator; *adv.phr.* **en commun**, in common; **mettre son argent en c. pour . . .**, to club together to . . .; **étude en c.**, joint study; **mise en c. de fonds**, pooling of funds; **agir en c. pour atteindre un résultat**, to co-operate in attaining an end; **jeu en c.**, round game; (*b*) common; (i) universal, general (custom, opinion, etc.); **le sens c.**, common sense; **le bien c.**, the public weal; *Gram:* **nom c.**, common noun; (ii) usual, ordinary, everyday (occurrence, etc.); **la manière commune de s'y prendre**, the ordinary, *F:* common or garden, way of setting about it; **lieu c.**, commonplace; **expression peu commune**, out-of-the-way, unusual, uncommon, expression; **situation hors de l'ordre c.**, situation out of the common; *Com:* **tare commune**, average tare, mean tare; (iii) common(place), mediocre; **étoffe commune**, common, poor, material; (iv) vulgar; **terme c.**, vulgar, common, expression. 2. *s.m.* (*a*) *Ecc:* (*R.C. Liturgy*) **le c. des martyrs**, the common of martyrs; (*b*) common run, generality (of persons, etc.); **le c. des hommes**, the majority of men, the (great) bulk of mankind; *A:* **homme du c.**, man of common extraction; **le c. des mortels**, the ordinary, average, man, the common run of mankind; **le c. des lecteurs**, the general reader; **œuvre au-dessus, hors, du c.**, work above the average, out of the common; **gens au-dessus du c.**, people out of the ordinary run; **cela tombe dans le c.**, it is becoming commonplace; **it is being done, worn, by everybody**; (*c*) common fund(s); **vivre sur le c.**, to live at the common expense; (*d*) *A:* **le c.**, the servants (of large household); (*e*) *pl.* **les communs**, (i) offices and outhouses; outbuildings; (ii) *A:* conveniences, water-closets.

communal, -aux [kɔmynal, -o], *a.* 1. common (land, property); *s.m.pl.* **les communaux**, the common (land). 2. (*a*) communal (council, etc.); *A:* **école communale**, *s.f.* **communale =** elementary school; (*b*) parochial, parish (property, feast); *Hist:* **milices communales**, militia; **forêt communale**, communal forest.

communalement [kɔmynalmɑ̃], *adv.* communally.

communalisation [kɔmynalizasjɔ̃], *s.f.* communalization.

communaliser [kɔmynalize], *v.tr.* to communalize.

communaliste [kɔmynalist], *Fr.Pol:* 1. *a.* communalistic. 2. *s.* communalist.

communard [kɔmynaːr], *s.m. Fr.Hist: F:* communard, communist (of 1871).

communautaire [kɔmynotɛːr], *a.* communal; **centre c.**, community centre.

communauté [kɔmynote], *s.f.* 1. (*a*) community (of interests, ideas, etc.); **c. de vues**, like-mindedness; **c. de destin**, common, joint, destiny; **vivre en c. de biens**, to have everything in common; (*b*) *Jur:* joint estate (of husband and wife). 2. (*a*) community, corporation, society, commonalty; (*b*) (religious) community, order, sisterhood; (*c*) *Pol:* commonwealth; community; (*d*) **c. linguistique**, group speaking the same language.

commune [kɔmyn], *s.f.* 1. (*a*) *Fr.Hist:* free town; **les communes**, (i) the commoners, the commons; (ii) the militia; (*b*) (*In Engl.*) **la Chambre des Communes**, the House of Commons; **les Communes**, the Commons. 2. *Fr.Adm:* (*smallest territorial division*) commune, approx. = parish. 3. *Fr.Hist:* **la C.**, (in 1789 and in 1871), the Commune (= municipality of Paris).

communément [kɔmynemɑ̃], *adv.* commonly, ordinarily, generally.

communiant, -ante [kɔmynjɑ̃, -ɑ̃ːt], *s. Ecc:* communicant; **premier c., première communiante**, person taking communion for the first time.

communicabilité [kɔmynikabilite], *s.f.* communicability, communicableness.

communicable [kɔmynikabl], *a.* 1. (*a*) communicable (disease, etc.); *Jur:* transferable (right); (*b*) **cause c.**, case that should be brought to the cognizance of the public prosecutor. 2. *A:* communicating (rooms, etc.). 3. *F: A:* **homme c.**, man of easy access.

communicant [kɔmynikɑ̃], *a.* communicating (vessels, rooms, etc.); communicant (arteries, etc.).

communicateur, -trice [kɔmynikatœːr, -tris]. 1. *a.* connecting (wire, etc.); transmitting (shaft, etc.). 2. *s.m. Mec.E:* organ of transmission; *Tg:* communicator.

communicatif, -ive [kɔmynikatif, -iːv], *a.* 1. communicative, talkative; **personne peu communicative**, uncommunicative, *F:* stand-offish, person. 2. catching, infectious (laughter, gaiety).

communication [kɔmynikasjɔ̃], *s.f.* communication. 1. communicating; (*a*) **c. d'une nouvelle à qn**, communication of a piece of news to s.o.; **donner, faire, c. de qch. à qn**, to communicate sth. to s.o.; to inform s.o. of sth.; **faire une c. (à une société savante)**, to read a paper (to a learned society); **livre envoyé en c.**, book sent on approval; **en c.**, for perusal; (*in library*) **c. de livres**, issue of books; **demander à prendre c. des livres d'une société**, to demand access to the books of a company; *Jur:* **donner c. des pièces**, to give discovery of documents; (*b*) **c. réciproque**, intercommunication; **en c. réciproque**, inter-connected, interrelated; **c. d'idées**, interchange of ideas; **c. entre prisonniers**, communication between prisoners; **entrer, se mettre, en c. avec qn**, to get into communication, into touch, with s.o.; to communicate with (the police, etc.); **mettre deux personnes en c.**, to put two people in touch with each other; **communications de masse**, mass media; **portes de c.**, communicating doors; *Med:* **c. inter-ventriculaire, inter-auriculaire**, (abnormal) interventricular, interauricular, communication; *F:* hole in the heart; *Tchn:* **tuyau de c.**, conduit pipe; **tuyau de c. avec l'échappement**, pipe connected up with exhaust; **mettre en c.**, to connect up (boilers, etc.); *Mil:* **boyau de c.**, communication trench; **ligne de c.**, line of communication; **zone de communications**, communications zone; (*c*) *El:* connection, circuit; **c. électrique**, electrical connection; **c. avec la terre**, ground circuit; *Tp:* **c. téléphonique**, call; *U.S:* connection; **c. à grande distance**, long-distance call, *U.S:* connection; **c. interurbaine**, trunk call, *U.S:* connection; **c. urbaine**, local call, *U.S:* connection; **c. en P.C.V.**, payable à l'arrivée, à la charge du destinataire, reverse, transferred, charge call, *U.S:* collect call; **c. d'arrivée**, à l'arrivée, incoming call; **c. en instance**, call on hand; **c. multiplex**, multiplex working; **mettez-moi en c. avec M. Martin**, put me through to Mr Martin; **donner la c.**, to put a call through; **vous avez la c.**, you're through; **la c. est mauvaise**, the line is bad; *W.Tel:* **nous vous mettons en c. avec Rome**, we take you over to Rome. 2. message; **transmettre une c. à qn**, to pass on, convey, a message to s.o.; **lire une c.**, to read out a notice; *Jur:* **c. au ministère public**, order of court submitting case to public prosecutor. 3. rhetorical question.

communicativement [kɔmynikativmɑ̃], *adv.* communicatively.

communié, -ée [kɔmynje], *s.* one who has received Holy Communion.

communier [kɔmynje], *v.* (*p.d. & pr.sub.* n. **communiions, v. communiiez**) 1. *v.i.* (*a*) *Ecc:* to communicate, to receive Holy Communion, to partake of the sacrament; (*b*) to be, live, in communion. 2. *v.tr. Ecc:* **c. qn**, to administer Holy Communion to s.o., to communicate s.o.

communion [kɔmynjɔ̃], *s.f.* 1. communion; **appartenir à la même c.**, to belong to the same persuasion or faith; **vivre en c. d'idées avec qn**, to live in intellectual fellowship with s.o. 2. *Ecc:* (Holy) Communion, the sacrament, the Lord's Supper; *s.a.* ESPÈCE 3.

communiqué [kɔmynike], *s.m.* communiqué; official statement; press release; *Mil:* (daily) bulletin; **c. publié conjointement**, joint communiqué.

communiquer [kɔmynike], *v.* to communicate. 1. *v.tr.* (*a*) to impart, convey (information, heat, ideas, etc.); **c. qch. par écrit à qn**, to report in writing to s.o. about sth.; to give s.o. a written report about sth.; **c. un mouvement**, to transmit a motion; **c. une maladie à qn**, to pass on an illness to s.o.; (*b*) (*in library*) to issue (a book). 2. *v.i.* to be in communication; **porte qui communique au, avec le, jardin**, door that communicates with, leads into, the garden; **canal qui fait c. deux rivières**, canal that connects two rivers; *Sch:* **défense de c.**, no communication between candidates; **je n'arrive pas à c. avec . . .**, I cannot get into touch with . . ..

se communiquer. 1. *O:* to be communicative; **vous vous communiquez trop**, you talk too much, you are too expansive. 2. **l'incendie se communiqua aux maisons voisines**, the fire spread to the neighbouring houses.

communisant, -ante [kɔmynizɑ̃, -ɑ̃ːt], *F:* (*a*) *a.* communistic; (*b*) *s.* fellow-traveller.

communiser [kɔmynize], *v.tr. usu. Pej:* to subject (country) to Communist rule.

communisme [kɔmynism], *s.m.* Communism.

communiste [kɔmynist]. 1. *s.m. & f. Jur:* joint-owner. 2. *Pol:* (*a*) *s.m. & f.* Communist; *F:* Red; (*b*) *a.* Communist; **la Chine c.**, Communist, *F:* Red, China.

communité [kɔmynite], *s.f.* community (of possessions, etc.).

commutable [kɔmytabl], *a. Jur:* commutable.

commutateur [kɔmytatœːr], *s.m.* 1. commutator (of dynamo, induction coil, etc.). 2. switch; change-over switch; **commutateur sélecteur**, selector switch; **c. à une direction, à une voie**, single-throw switch, one-way switch; **c. à plusieurs directions, à plusieurs voies**, multiway switch; **c. à galettes**, wafer switch; **c. à touche(s)**, piano key switch; **c. à zéro**, zero cut-out, circuit breaker; **c. d'antenne**, aerial switch; **c. de champ**, field switch; **c. de gamme d'ondes**, wave-band switch; **c. de mise à la terre**, ground switch, earthing switch; **c. de direction**, channelling switch; **c. à prises de réglage**, tap changer; *Expl: etc:* **c. de tir, de mise à feu**, firing switch; 3. *a.* **tableau c.**, switchboard.

commutateur-sectionneur [kɔmytatœːrsɛksjɔnœːr], *s.m. El:* isolating switch; *pl.* **commutateurs-sectionneurs**.

commutatif, -ive [kɔmytatif, -iːv], *a. Jur:* commutative (contract, etc.).

commutation [kɔmytasjɔ̃], *s.f.* 1. (*a*) *Jur:* commutation (of penalty); (*b*) *Gram:* replacement, substitution. 2. *Tp: Tg:* switching, switch-over, change-over; **appareillage, appareils, de c.**, switch gear, *U.S:* switcher gear; **armoire de c.**, switch-gear cubicle; **c. automatique**, automatic switching, automatic change-over.

commutatrice [kɔmytatris], *s.f. El.E:* rotary converter, rotary transformer, inverter.

commuter [kɔmyte], *v.tr.* 1. *Jur:* to commute (penalty). 2. *El:* to commutate, to switch over, change over (current). 3. to interchange; **les deux expressions peuvent se c.**, the two expressions are interchangeable.

Comnène [kɔmnɛn], *s. Hist:* **les Comnènes**, the Comneni; **Isaac C.**, Isaac Comnenus; **Anna C.**, Anna Comnena.

Comores [kɔmɔːr], *Pr.n. Geog:* **les îles C.**, the Comoro Islands.

comorien, -ienne [kɔmɔrjɛ̃, -jɛn], *a. & s.*, **comorois, -oise** [kɔmɔrwa, -waːz], *a. & s. Geog:* (native, inhabitant) of the Comoro Islands.

co-mourants [komurɑ̃], *s.m.pl. Jur:* commorientes.

compacité [kɔ̃pasite], *s.f.* compactness, closeness (of mortar, etc.); density (of metal).

compact [kɔ̃pakt], *a.* (*a*) compact, close, dense (mass, formation, etc.); **métaux compacts**, dense metals; *Typ:* composition compacte, solid composition; **foule compacte**, dense crowd; **majorité compacte**, large, solid, majority; (*b*) **voiture compacte**, small car, *U.S:* compact.

compactage [kɔ̃paktaːʒ], *s.m. Civ.E:* compaction.

compacter [kɔ̃pakte], *v.tr. Civ.E:* to compact (earth fill, etc.).

compacteur [kɔ̃paktœːr], *a. Civ.E:* **rouleau c.**, earth roller.

compagne [kɔ̃paɲ], *s.f.* 1. (female) companion; **c'était ma c. de pension, de jeu**, I was at school with her, I used to play with her. 2. partner (in life); wife; (*of animals*) mate. 3. *Lit:* **l'envie, c. de l'ambition**, envy, the attendant upon ambition.

compagnie [kɔ̃paɲi], *s.f.* 1. company, companionship; **tenir c. à qn**, to keep s.o. company; **être une c. pour qn**, to be company for s.o.; **fausser c. à qn**, to give s.o. the slip; **être en c. de qn**, to be in s.o.'s company; **un animal de c.**, a pet; **dame de c.**, (i) companion; (ii) chaperon; **leur c. me manque**, I miss their companionship. 2. company, party, society; **il y avait nombreuse c.**, there was a large gathering, a large party; **ces gens-là et c.**, these people and others like them; **fréquenter la bonne, la mauvaise, c.**, to keep good, bad, company; **être en c.**, to have visitors; **être de bonne, de mauvaise, c.**, to be well-, ill-bred; *O:* **la bonne c.**, (high) society; *Prov:* **il n'est si bonne c. qui ne se sépare**, se **quitte**, the best of friends must part. 3. (*a*) *Com: Th: etc:* company; **c. de navigation**, shipping company; **c. républicaine de sécurité (C.R.S.)**,

state security police (in France); **c. aérienne,** air line; (*b*) *Com:* **la maison Thomas et Compagnie** (*usu.* **et Cie**), the firm of Thomas and Company (*usu.* and Co.); (*c*) *Ecc:* **la C. de Jésus,** the Society of Jesus. **4.** (*a*) *Mil:* company; **c. autonome,** separate company; **c. cadre,** skeleton company; **c. d'accompagnement,** support company; *U.S:* heavy weapons company; **c. de ravitaillement,** supply company; **c. sanitaire auto(mobile),** ambulance company; **c. de triage,** clearing company; **c. de transmissions,** signal(s) squadron, signals company; **c. colombophile,** (signals) pigeon company; **c. de sapeurs-mineurs,** tunnelling company; **c. de pont, de pontage, d'équipage de pont,** bridge company; *U.S:* pontoon company; **c. de pontonniers,** bridging company; **c. du matériel,** ordnance company; **c. de récupération,** salvage company; **c. de réparation, c. d'échelon,** maintenance company; **c. de (fusiliers) voltigeurs,** rifle company; *A:* **c. hors-rang,** headquarters company; **c. du génie de combat,** field company; *U.S:* combat engineer company; (*b*) *Nav:* division; (*c*) *Scouting:* (girl guide, *U.S:* girl scout) company; (*d*) party; **c. de débarquement,** landing party. **5.** *Ven:* herd (of roe deer); bevy (of quails); covey (of partridges).

compagnon [kɔ̃paɲɔ̃], *s.m.* **1.** (*a*) companion, comrade, associate, mate, fellow; **c. d'école,** schoolfellow, -mate; **c. de voyage,** travelling companion; **c. de route,** (i) travelling companion; (ii) *Pol:* fellow-traveller; **c. de bord,** shipmate; **c'était mon c. de jeu,** I used to play with him; **c. d'infortune,** companion in misfortune, fellow-sufferer; **c. d'armes, d'exil,** comrade in arms, in exile; **vivre en compagnons,** to live together as equals; **bon c.,** good (drinking) companion; *s.a.* PAIR 2; (*b*) *Ind:* (workman's) mate; fellow-workman. **2.** *A:* journeyman, workman; **c. tailleur,** journeyman tailor; *A:* **c. d'une société,** member of a trade-guild; *F: A:* **un petit c.,** an insignificant man, a little nobody; *A:* **faire le c.,** to pretend to be very knowing; *s.a.* DÉPÊCHER 1. **3.** *Bot: F:* **c. blanc, rouge,** white, red, campion.

compagnonnage [kɔ̃paɲɔnaːʒ], *s.m. A:* combination of workmen, trade-guild.

compagnonne [kɔ̃paɲɔn], *s.f. found occ. in the sense of* "strapping woman" (of the working class); **c'était une forte c. qui n'avait pas peur de l'ouvrage,** she was a strapping great woman, not afraid of work; *often Pej:* **une horrible c.,** an old battle-axe.

compair [kɔ̃pɛːr], *s.m. Hist:* compeer.

compal [kɔ̃pal], *s.m. P: Sch:* exam.

comparabilité [kɔ̃parabilite], *s.f.* comparability.

comparable [kɔ̃parabl̩], *a.* comparable; **c. à, avec, qch., à, avec, qn,** comparable to, with, worthy to be compared, to, with, sth., s.o.; **il ne vous est pas c.,** he can't compare with you.

comparablement [kɔ̃parabləmɑ̃], *adv.* comparably; **c. à qn,** compared with, in comparison with, s.o.

comparaison [kɔ̃parɛzɔ̃], *s.f.* **1.** comparison; **établir une, la, c. entre deux choses, faire la c. de deux choses,** to make a comparison, draw a parallel, between two things; **soutenir la c., faire c., avec qch.,** to bear, stand, comparison with sth. **hors de toute c.,** beyond compare; **il est sans c. le plus intelligent,** he is far and away the cleverest; **par c.,** comparatively (speaking), by comparison; *Gram:* **les trois degrés de c.,** the three degrees of comparison; *prep.phr.* **en c. de qch., par c. à qch.,** in, by, comparison with, in comparison to, sth., as compared with sth.; **cela n'est rien en c. de ce que j'ai vu,** that is nothing to what I have seen; **c. n'est pas raison,** comparisons are odious. **2.** simile.

comparaître [kɔ̃parɛːtr̩], *v.i.* (*conj. like* PARAÎTRE) *Jur:* **c. (en justice),** to appear before a court of justice; **c. par avoué,** to be represented by counsel; **être appelé à c.,** to be summoned to appear; **on le fit c. devant le commissaire de police** = he was brought before the magistrate.

comparant, -ante [kɔ̃parɑ̃, -ɑ̃ːt], *a. & s. Jur:* (person) appearing (before the court, etc.); *s.* appearer.

comparateur, -trice [kɔ̃paratœːr, -tris]. **1.** *a.* (*of mind, etc.*) given to comparison. **2.** *s.m. Meas:* comparator; *Elcs:* **c. traducteur,** comparator-translator.

comparatif, -ive [kɔ̃paratif, -iːv]. **1.** *a.* comparatively; **c. à qch.,** compared with, to, sth.; in, by, comparison with, in comparison to, sth.

comparatiste [kɔ̃paratist], *s.m. & f.* comparatist; **un livre indispensable à tout c.,** a book indispensable to all students of comparative literature.

comparativement [kɔ̃parativmɑ̃], *adv.* comparatively; **c. à qch.,** compared, to, with, sth.; in, by, comparison with, in comparison to, sth.

comparé [kɔ̃pare], *a.* comparative (anatomy, history, etc.).

comparer [kɔ̃pare], *v.tr.* to compare (**à, avec,** to, with); **c. la vie à une aventure,** to compare, liken, life to an adventure; **on ne saurait les c.,** they cannot be compared, they are not to be mentioned in the same breath.

comparoir [kɔ̃parwaːr], *v.i.* (*used only in inf. and pr.p.* **comparant**) *Jur: A:* to appear (in court, etc.).

comparse [kɔ̃pars], *s.m. & f.* (*a*) *Th:* (i) supernumerary; *F:* super; *Cin:* extra; (ii) **rôle de c.,** walking-on part; (*b*) (conjuror's) assistant, stooge; (*c*) person playing a minor role in an undertaking; **ce n'est qu'un c.,** he's only a stooge.

compartiment [kɔ̃partimɑ̃], *s.m.* compartment (of ceiling, railway-carriage, etc.); partition (of box, drawer, etc.); division; square (of chess-board, etc.); repeat (of decorative design); *Rail:* **c. pour fumeurs,** smoking compartment; **c. de première classe,** first-class compartment; *Arms:* **c. des munitions,** ammunition compartment; **c. pour 10 cartouches,** 10-round compartment; *Nau:* **les compartiments du double fond,** the double-bottom tanks; *Av:* **c. de logement de train,** landing-gear well.

compartimentage [kɔ̃partimɑ̃taːʒ], *s.m.* division into compartments (of ceiling, etc.); partitioning; compartmentation; departmentalization (of knowledge).

compartimenter [kɔ̃partimɑ̃te], *v.tr.* (*a*) to compart, to divide into compartments; (*b*) to compartmentalize.

comparuit [kɔ̃parɥit], *s.m.inv. Jur:* (act of) appearing (before the court).

comparution [kɔ̃parysjɔ̃], *s.f. Jur:* appearance (before the court); **mandat de c.,** summons; **non-c.,** non-appearance; default.

compas [kɔ̃pɑ], *s.m.* **1.** (*a*) (pair of) compasses; **c. à pointes sèches,** dividers; **c. de précision,** callipers with regulating screw; **c. quart de cercle,** wing compasses; **c. à cheveu,** hair compasses; **c. à verge, à trusquin,** beam compass, trammel; **c. d'ellipse, elliptique,** trammel, elliptic compasses; **c. balustre à pointes sèches,** bow dividers; **c. à ressort,** spring dividers; **c. à tire-ligne,** pen-compasses; **c. de proportion,** proportional compasses; **c. de réduction,** reduction compasses; **c. porte-crayon, c. porte-mine,** pencil compasses; **tout faire au c.,** to do everything by rule; *F:* **allonger le, son, c.,** to step out, to quicken one's pace; (*b*) *Mec.E: etc:* **c. d'épaisseur, à calibrer, c. d'intérieur,** inside callipers; **c. d'épaisseur, d'extérieur,** outside callipers; **c. d'épaisseur à ressort,** outside spring callipers; **c. maître à danser, c. maître de danse,** outside and inside callipers; **c. à coulisse,** slide callipers, sliding callipers; **c. de cordonnier,** size stick; **c. forestier,** diameter gauge; (*c*) *Aut: O:* arms (of folding hood); *Phot:* struts (of folding camera). **2.** *Nau: etc:* **c. (de mer),** (mariner's) compass; **c. de route,** steering compass; **c. liquide,** liquid, fluid, compass; *Av:* immersed compass; **c. à répétition, optique,** projector, reflector, compass; **c. renversé,** hanging compass; **c. de relèvement, c. azimutal,** azimuth compass; **c. d'avion, de bord,** air(craft) compass; **c. astronomique,** astro-compass; **c. céleste,** sky compass; **c. gyroscopique,** gyrocompass; **c. magnétique,** magnetic compass; **se diriger au c.,** to march, fly, sail, by compass; **prendre un relèvement au c.,** to take a compass bearing; **répéter le c.,** to box the compass. **3.** standard, scale (of measurement); **avoir le c. dans l'œil,** to have an accurate eye; **asservir les autres à son c.,** to force others to conform to one's own standards. **4.** *Astr:* Circinus, the Compasses.

compascuité [kɔ̃paskɥite], *s.f. A.Jur:* common of pasture.

compas-étalon [kɔ̃pɑetalɔ̃], *s.m. Nau:* standard compass; *pl. compas-étalons.*

compassage [kɔ̃pɑsaːʒ], *s.m.* **1.** measuring with compasses. **2.** considering, studying (in minute detail) (one's actions, words, etc.).

compassé [kɔ̃pɑse], *a.* **1.** stiff, formal, starched (manner, etc.); academic (style). **2.** regular, set (life, etc.).

compassement [kɔ̃pɑsmɑ̃], *s.m.* **1.** measuring (with compasses); *Nau:* pricking (of chart); *Min:* proportioning (of fuses). **2.** formality, setness, stiffness (of manner, etc.).

compasser [kɔ̃pɑse], *v.tr.* **1.** to measure (distances on map, etc.) with compasses; *Nau:* to prick (chart); *Min:* to proportion (firing of fuses). **2.** to gauge (bore of gun, etc.); to regulate, consider one's actions, etc.); to weigh (one's words); **il compasse tous ses gestes,** all his gestures are studied; **il compasse tous ses discours,** he always speaks like a book.

compassier [kɔ̃pɑsje], *s.m.* mechanic specializing in precision instruments (*esp.* compasses).

compassion [kɔ̃pɑsjɔ̃], *s.f.* compassion, pity; **avoir c. de qn, des souffrances de qn,** to have, take, compassion on s.o., on s.o.'s suffering; **faire c.,** to arouse compassion; **par c.,** out of compassion; **avec c.,** compassionately.

compaternité [kɔ̃patɛrnite], *s.f. Ecc:* spiritual relationship (between godparents and god-child), compaternity.

compatibilité [kɔ̃patibilite], *s.f.* compatibility.

compatible [kɔ̃patibl̩], *a.* compatible (**avec,** with); **décision c. avec la justice,** decision consistent with justice.

compatir [kɔ̃patiːr], *v.i.* **1. c. au chagrin de qn,** to sympathize with, feel for, s.o. in his grief. **2. c. aux défauts de qn,** to be indulgent towards, to bear with, s.o.'s faults. **3.** *A:* to be compatible (**avec,** with).

compatissant [kɔ̃patisɑ̃], *a.* **1.** compassionate (**pour,** to, towards); tender(-hearted). **2.** indulgent (**pour,** to); sympathetic.

compatriote [kɔ̃patriɔt], *s.m. & f.* compatriot, fellow-countryman, -countrywoman.

compendieusement [kɔ̃pɑ̃djøzmɑ̃], *adv.* **1.** *A:* compendiously, concisely, in brief. **2.** *F:* at great length.

compendieux, -ieuse [kɔ̃pɑ̃djø, -jøːz], *a. A:* concise, succinct, summarized (report, etc.).

compendium [kɔ̃pɛ̃djɔm], *s.m.* compendium.

compensable [kɔ̃pɑ̃sabl̩], *a.* that can be made up for; that can be counterbalanced, compensated.

compensant [kɔ̃pɑ̃sɑ̃], *a.* compensatory, compensative.

compensateur, -trice [kɔ̃pɑ̃satœːr, -tris]. **1.** *a.* compensating (spring, magnet, etc.); *El:* equalizing (current); balancing (dynamo); *Mch: Mec.E:* equilibrium (ring), expansion (joint, stuffing-box); *Ph:* **balancier c.,** compensation pendulum; *Opt:* **écran, filtre, c.,** correction, compensation, screen, filter. **2.** *s.m.* compensator, balancer (of arc-lamp, of compass, etc.); (pressure) equalizer; *Av:* trimming tab, trimmer; *I.C.E:* **c. de carburateur,** compensator jet; *Turb:* **c. différentiel,** balance gear, differential gear; *El:* **c. de phase,** phase equalizer; **c. de voltage,** line drop, voltage, compensator.

compensatif, -ive [kɔ̃pɑ̃satif, -iːv], *a.* compensative, compensatory.

compensation [kɔ̃pɑ̃sasjɔ̃], *s.f.* (*a*) compensation (of loss); set-off; counterbalancing (of good and evil, etc.); *Psy:* compensation; **en c. de mes pertes,** as an offset to my losses; **entrer en c. de qch.,** to compensate, make amends, for sth.; **cela fait c.,** that makes up for it; (*b*) *Jur:* settlement *per contra*; *Scot:* set-off; *Adm:* **caisse de c.,** equalization fund (for family allowances, etc.); *Fin:* **chambre de c.,** clearing-house; *Fin:* **accord de c.,** clearing agreement; *St.Exch:* **cours de c.,** making-up price; (*c*) *Mec: El: etc:* equalization, balancing (of forces, etc.); compensation; **c. des phases,** phase correction; *W.Tel:* **antenne de c.,** balancing aerial; *Mec.E: Mch:* **tube de c.,** compensation pipe, expansion pipe; **soupape de c.,** compensating valve; **c. des températures,** temperature compensation; **c. statique,** static balance; *Av:* trim; **c. des gouvernes,** (aerodynamic) balancing of control surfaces; **c. de gauchissement,** lateral trim; (*d*) *Nau:* adjustment (of compass); (*e*) *Mec.E: etc:* **c. de l'usure,** taking up of the wear; (*f*) *Mth:* **c. par la méthode des moindres carrés,** least square adjustment; (*g*) *Sp:* handicapping.

compensatoire [kɔ̃pɑ̃satwaːr], *a.* compensatory; **demande c.,** counterclaim.

compensé [kɔ̃pɑ̃se], *a.* balanced, compensated; equalized; adjusted; *Av:* **commandes compensées,** balanced controls; **gouvernes compensées,** balanced (control) surfaces; **gouvernail de direction c.,** compensated rudder; **gouvernail de profondeur c.,** balanced elevator; **hélice compensée,** compensated propeller; *Nau:* **gouvernail c.,** balanced rudder; *Ph:* **pendule c.,** compensation pendulum; *El: Elcs: W.Tel:* **cadre c. (de radiogoniomètre),** compensated loop (of direction-finder); **connexion compensée,** compensated lead; **moteur (électrique) c.,** compensated-winding motor; **transformateur différentiel c.,** balanced differential transformer; **transformateur d'intensité c.,** compensated-current transformer; *Mth:* **valeur compensée,** adjusted value; *Bootm:* **semelle compensée,** wedge heel.

compenser [kɔ̃pɑ̃se], *v.tr.* (*a*) to compensate, counterbalance, to make up for (sth.); to offset (fault, etc.); **ses bonnes qualités compensent ses défauts,** his good qualities compensate for his shortcomings; **c. une perte,** to make good a loss; (*b*) *Jur: etc:* to compensate, balance, set off (debts); *Fin:* to clear (cheques); **c. une dette avec une autre,** to set off one debt against another, to settle a debt *per contra*; **c. les dépens,** to divide out the costs; (*c*) *Mec.E:* **c. une machine,** to balance an engine; (*d*) *Nau:* to adjust (compass); (*e*) *Mec.E: etc:* **c. l'usure,** to take up the wear; (*f*) *Sp:* to handicap (race).

compérage [kɔ̃pera:ʒ], *s.m.* **1.** compaternity, spiritual relationship between godparents and (i) godchild, (ii) his, her, parents. **2.** conspiracy (between instigators of a swindle).

compère [kɔ̃pɛ:r], *s.m.* **1.** *A: or Dial:* godfather; fellow-sponsor (in relation to godmother). **2.** accomplice, confederate, decoy (of conjuror, card-sharper, etc.); *pl.* associates (in a trick); *Th:* compère, announcer (in a revue); *F:* **tout se fait par c. et commère,** it's all a put-up job. **3.** *F: O:* comrade, crony; **un bon c.,** a pleasant companion.

compère-loriot [kɔ̃pɛrlɔrjo], *s.m.* **1.** *Orn:* golden oriole. **2.** sty(e) (on the eyelid); *pl. compères-loriots.*

compétemment [kɔ̃petamɑ̃], *adv.* competently.

compétence [kɔ̃petɑ̃:s], *s.f.* **1.** *Jur:* competence, competency, jurisdiction, powers (of court of justice, etc.); **rentrer dans la c. d'un tribunal,** to fall within the competence, jurisdiction, of a court; **cela ne rentre pas dans sa c., cela n'est pas de sa c.,** that does not come within his province, that is outside his scope; **sortir de sa c.,** to exceed one's powers. **2.** (*a*) competence, ability, proficiency, skill (**pour faire qch.,** to do sth.); **degré de c.,** standard of efficiency; (*b*) **c'est une c. en la matière,** he's the authority on the subject; (*c*) **c. d'un cours d'eau,** competence of a stream.

compétent [kɔ̃petɑ̃], *a. Jur: etc:* competent (tribunal, authority, etc.); **commis c.,** competent, qualified, clerk; **c. en matière de finance,** conversant with finance; **il est d'un âge c. pour signer,** he is of a suitable, proper, age to sign; **en lieu c. on dit . . .,** in well-informed quarters it is said . . .; **je ne suis pas c. dans la matière,** I am not competent to speak on the matter; *Com:* **transmettre au service c.,** to pass on to the department concerned.

compéter [kɔ̃pete], *v.i.* (**je compète, n. compétons; je compéterai**) *Jur:* **1. c. (au tribunal, etc.),** to come within the competence, competency (of the tribunal, etc.). **2. c. à qn,** to belong to s.o. by right.

compétiteur, -trice [kɔ̃petitœ:r, -tris]. **1.** *s.* competitor, candidate (à, for). **2.** *a.* competing, rival.

compétitif, -ive [kɔ̃petitif, -i:v], *a.* **1.** rival (intrigues, etc.). **2.** *Com:* competitive; **prix compétitifs,** competitive prices.

compétition [kɔ̃petisjɔ̃], *s.f.* (*a*) competition, rivalry; **c. entre partis politiques,** political rivalry; **c. ardente,** intense rivalry; (*b*) *Sp:* race; contest.

compétitivité [kɔ̃petitivite], *s.f.* competitiveness.

compiégnois, -oise [kɔ̃pjeɲwa, -wa:z], *a. & s. Geog:* (native, inhabitant) of Compiègne.

compilateur, -trice [kɔ̃pilatœ:r, -tris], *s.* compiler.

compilation [kɔ̃pilasjɔ̃], *s.f.* **1.** compiling, compilation; **théorie fondée sur la c. des données de l'expérience,** theory based on the compilation of experimental data. **2.** *usu. Pej:* compilation; hash-up (of the work of others).

compiler [kɔ̃pile], *v.tr.* **1.** *v.tr. & abs.* to compile. **2.** *Pej:* to plagiarize.

complaignant, -ante [kɔ̃plɛɲɑ̃, -ɑ̃:t], *s. Jur: A:* plaintiff (in matter of possession); complainant.

complaindre [kɔ̃plɛ̃:dr], *v.tr.* (*conj. like* PLAINDRE) *A:* to pity, to have compassion on (s.o.).

se complaindre, *A:* to complain.

complainte [kɔ̃plɛ̃:t], *s.f.* **1.** *Jur: A:* complaint. **2.** (*a*) *A:* plaint, lament; (*b*) *Lit:* (plaintive) ballad, lay; lament.

complaire [kɔ̃plɛ:r], *v.ind.tr.* (*conj. like* PLAIRE) *Lit:* **c. à qn,** to please, humour, gratify, s.o.

se complaire en, dans, qch., à faire qch., to take pleasure, to delight, in sth., in doing sth.

complaisamment [kɔ̃plɛzamɑ̃], *adv.* **1.** obligingly, willingly. **2.** complacently, with satisfaction.

complaisance [kɔ̃plɛzɑ̃:s], *s.f.* **1.** complaisance, obligingness, willingness; **faire qch. par c.,** to do sth. out of kindness; **faire qch. par c. pour qn,** to do sth. to oblige s.o., in compliance with s.o.'s wishes; **auriez-vous la c. de** + *inf.*, would you be so good, so kind, as to + *inf.*; **c'est par trop de c.!** you are too kind! **merci de votre c.,** thank you for your kindness; **avoir une c. basse pour, envers, ses supérieurs,** to truckle, toady, to one's superiors; *Com:* **billet, effet, de c.,** accommodation bill; *Nau:* **pavillon de c.,** flag of convenience. **2.** complacence, complacency, (self-)satisfaction. **3.** *A: & B:* love; *B:* **mon fils bien-aimé en qui j'ai mis toutes mes complaisances,** my beloved Son in whom I am well pleased.

complaisant, -ante [kɔ̃plɛzɑ̃, -ɑ̃:t]. **1.** *a.* (*a*) obliging, accommodating (**envers, pour, à,** towards); willing (person, character, etc.); **prêter une oreille complaisante aux prières de qn,** to lend a sympathetic ear, a ready ear, to s.o.'s requests; (*b*) **mari c.,** complaisant husband; **jeter un voile c. sur des atrocités,** to gloss over atrocities; (*c*) complacent, self-satisfied (smile, etc.). **2.** *s.* flatterer, time-server.

complanter [kɔ̃plɑ̃te], *v.tr.* to plant with trees.

complectif, -ive [kɔ̃plɛktif, -i:v], *a. Bot:* complected.

complément [kɔ̃plemɑ̃], *s.m.* (*a*) complement; rest, remainder; **faire le c. de . . .** to complement . . .; (*b*) *Gram:* complement; extension (of the subject, of the predicate); **c. (d'objet),** object (of verb); **c. circonstanciel,** adjunct; (*c*) *Mil:* full complement (of regiment, etc.); **officier, hommes, de c.,** army-reserve officer, men; (*d*) *Bio-Ch:* complement; **déviation du c. (d'un sérum),** complement deviation; (*e*) *Geom:* complement (of angle).

complémentaire [kɔ̃plemɑ̃tɛ:r], *a.* (*a*) complementary (angle, colour, etc.); (*b*) **pour renseignements complémentaires s'adresser à . . .** for fuller, further, information apply to . . .; (*c*) *Book-k:* **écriture c.,** supplementary, subsequent, entry; (*d*) *Sch:* *A:* **cours c.** = secondary modern school.

complémentarité [kɔ̃plemɑ̃tarite], *s.f.* complementarity.

complet, -ète [kɔ̃plɛ, -ɛt]. **1.** *a.* (*a*) complete, entire, whole (outfit, works, etc.); **ruine complète,** complete, total, ruin; **manque c. de . . .,** utter lack of . . .; **rapport très c.,** very full, comprehensive, report; **programme c. et détaillé,** comprehensive programme; **c'est loin d'être c.,** it's a long way, far, from being complete; **athlète c.,** all-round athlete; **il vous faut un changement c.,** you must have a thorough change; *F:* **ça serait c.!** that would be the last straw! that would put the lid on it! **pain c.,** wholemeal bread; **café c., thé c.,** continental breakfast; (*b*) full (bus, *Th:* house, etc.); *P.N:* **complet!** full (up)! (*outside boarding house*) no vacancies! **2.** *s.m.* (*a*) suit (of clothes); **c. veston,** lounge suit; **c. de bureau,** business suit; (*b*) *adj. phr.* **au c.,** complete, full; **la salle est au c.,** the hall is full; **bataillon au grand c.,** battalion at full strength; **navire au grand c.,** ship that has her full complement; *F:* **nous étions présents au grand c.,** we turned out in full force; *F:* **voilà votre trousseau au grand c.,** now you're quite set up, fitted out.

complètement [kɔ̃plɛtmɑ̃], *adv.* completely, wholly, totally, fully; utterly (ruined, callous); stark (mad, naked).

complètement [kɔ̃plɛtmɑ̃], *s.m.* completion, filling up; *Mil: etc:* bringing up to (full) strength; *Psy:* **tests de c.,** completion tests.

compléter [kɔ̃plete], *v.tr.* (**je complète, n. complétons; je compléterai**) to complete; to make (sth.) complete; **c. un volume,** to perfect, to fill in the gaps in, a volume; **c. une somme,** to make up a sum (of money); **c. les vivres d'un navire,** to replenish a ship's stores; **c. un bataillon,** to bring a battalion up to strength; *Aut:* **c. le niveau de la batterie,** to top up the battery; **les deux volumes se complètent,** the two volumes are complementary to one another.

complétif, -ive [kɔ̃pletif, -i:v], *a. Gram:* **proposition complétive,** noun clause.

complétion [kɔ̃plesjɔ̃], *s.f. Petroleum Ind:* completion.

complexant [kɔ̃plɛksɑ̃], *a. Ch:* **agent c.,** chelating, sequestering, agent.

complexe [kɔ̃plɛks]. **1.** *a.* complex (character, etc.); complicated (question); intricate, many-sided (problem); *Gram:* **sujet c.,** compound subject; **phrase c.,** complex sentence; *Mth:* **nombre c.,** compound number; **quantité c.,** complex number. **2.** *s.m.* complex; (*a*) **le c. industriel de la vallée du Rhône,** the Rhone valley industrial complex; (*b*) *Ch:* complex; (*c*) *Psy:* **c. d'Œdipe,** Oedipus complex; **c. d'infériorité,** inferiority complex; *F:* **avoir des complexes,** to be inhibited, to have complexes; **être bourré de complexes,** to be one mass of complexes.

complexé [kɔ̃plɛkse], *a. F:* inhibited, full of complexes; *F:* mixed-up.

complexer [kɔ̃plɛkse], *v.tr. & i. Ch:* to chelate, to sequester.

complexion [kɔ̃plɛksjɔ̃], *s.f. A:* constitution, disposition, temperament; *O:* **enfant de c. délicate,** child with a delicate constitution.

complexité [kɔ̃plɛksite], *s.f.* complexity.

complexuel, -elle [kɔ̃plɛksɥɛl], *a. Psy:* relating to a complex.

complexus [kɔ̃plɛksys], *s.m. Anat:* complexus.

compliance [kɔ̃pliɑ̃:s], *s.f. Mec: Elcs:* compliance.

complication [kɔ̃plikasjɔ̃], *s.f.* **1.** complication; thickening (of plot); **éviter les complications,** to avoid complications; **complications sentimentales,** emotional entanglements. **2.** complexity, intricacy. **3.** *Med:* complication(s); **s'il ne survient pas de complications,** if no complications set in; **c. méningée,** meningeal involvement.

complice [kɔ̃plis], *a. & s.m. & f.* accessary, accessory (de, to); accomplice, abettor (**de,** of); *Jur:* **c. par assistance,** accessary after the fact; **c. par instigation,** accessary before the fact; **être c. d'une crime,** to be party to, accessary to, a crime; **il fut vendu par un de ses complices,** he was betrayed by an accomplice; **c. en adultère,** co-respondent; *s.a.* FAUTEUR.

complicité [kɔ̃plisite], *s.f.* complicity; *Jur:* aiding and abetting; **complicités dans l'administration,** administrative collusion; **agir de c. avec qn,** to act in collusion, in complicity, with s.o.

complié [kɔ̃plie], *a. Bot:* involute, complicate, conduplicate (leaf).

complies [kɔ̃pli], *s.f.pl. Ecc:* compline.

compliment [kɔ̃plimɑ̃], *s.m.* **1.** compliment; **faire des compliments à qn,** to pay s.o. compliments; **les compliments que vous avez bien voulu m'adresser,** your complimentary remarks; **sans c.,** sincerely, without flattery. **2.** *pl.* compliments, greetings; **"Mes compliments à . . .,"** "Remember me to . . .," "My kind regards to . . ."; **faire des compliments de condoléance à qn,** to offer s.o. one's condolences. **3.** congratulation; **faire, adresser, des compliments, à qn de, sur, qch.,** to offer s.o. one's congratulations on sth.; **(je vous fais) mes compliments, I** congratulate you; *Iron:* **mes compliments!** a nice mess you've made of it! **rengainer son c.,** to stop short (in what one was going to say to s.o.). **4.** speech of congratulation.

complimenter [kɔ̃plimɑ̃te], *v.tr.* (*a*) to compliment (de, sur, on); to pay (s.o.) a compliment; *A:* to deliver a complimentary address to (s.o.); to congratulate (de, sur, on); (*b*) *abs.* **perdre le temps à c.,** to waste one's time exchanging compliments.

complimenteur, -euse [kɔ̃plimɑ̃tœ:r, -ø:z], *a. & s.* obsequious (person); *s.* flatterer; **discours c.,** flattering speech.

compliqué [kɔ̃plike], *a.* complicated, elaborate, intricate (mechanism, etc.); involved, tangled (style); **une personne compliquée,** a difficult person; *Med:* **fracture compliquée,** compound fracture.

compliquer [kɔ̃plike], *v.tr.* to complicate.

se compliquer, to become complicated (de, with); to become involved; (of plot) to thicken; **la maladie se complique,** complications are setting in.

complot [kɔ̃plo], *s.m.* plot, conspiracy, scheme; **tramer un c.,** to weave a plot; **faire (le) c. de . . .,** to plot to (do sth.); **chef de c.,** ringleader; **mettre qn dans le c.,** to let s.o. into the secret; *Jur:* **c. contre la sûreté de l'État,** treason-felony; *Mil: Jur:* **c. militaire,** conspiracy.

comploter [kɔ̃plɔte], *v.tr.* to plot, conspire; to scheme; **c. la ruine de qn,** to plot s.o.'s ruin; **c. de faire qch.,** to plot to do sth.; *F:* **qu'est-ce que vous complotez là?** what are you up to now? **nous avons comploté de vous offrir un voyage en Espagne,** we've thought up a scheme to give you a holiday in Spain.

comploteur [kɔ̃plɔtœ:r], *s.m.* plotter, schemer.

compo [kɔ̃po], *s.f. Sch: P:* test; exam.

componction [kɔ̃pɔ̃ksjɔ̃], *s.f.* **1.** compunction; **sans c.,** without compunction. **2.** *Iron:* **avec c.,** gravely, solemnly.

compon(n)é [kɔ̃pɔne], *a. & s.m. Her:* compony, componé.

comporte [kɔ̃pɔrt], *s.f. Vit: etc:* tub, vat.

comportement [kɔ̃pɔrtəmɑ̃], *s.m.* behaviour; *Psy:* **psychologie du comportement,** behaviourism.

comportemental [kɔ̃pɔrtəmɑ̃tal], *a. Psy:* behavioural.

comporter [kɔ̃pɔrte], *v.tr.* **1.** to allow, allow of; to admit of (sth.); **action qui ne comporte aucune excuse,** action that admits of no excuse; **règle qui comporte des exceptions,** rule not without exceptions. **2.** to call for, require (sth.); **l'appareillage que comporte cette industrie,** the plant required for this industry; **les précautions que comporte la situation,** the care which the situation demands, the care called for by the situation. **3.** to comprise, include (sth.); **objectif qui comporte quatre éléments,** lens that comprises, is made up of, four elements; **régime qui comporte une certaine rigueur,** regime that implies a certain severity; **méthode qui comporte de grandes difficultés,** method which involves great difficulties; **les inconvénients que cela comporterait,** the difficulties which this would involve, entail; **les fatigues que comporte un voyage,** the fatigue incidental to a journey; **profession enviable malgré les soucis qu'elle comporte,** enviable profession in spite of the cares, worries, that go with it; **les avantages que comporte la position,** the advantages attaching to the position.

se comporter, to behave, act (**vis-à-vis de, envers,** towards); **se bien c.,** to behave (oneself); **se c. mal,** to misbehave; **se c. en lâche, comme un lâche,** to act, behave, like a coward; **façon de se c.,** behaviour; **je n'aime pas sa manière de se c.,** I don't like the way she carries on.

composacées [kɔ̃pɔzase], *s.f.pl. Bot:* Compositae.

composant, -ante [kɔ̃pozɑ̃, -ɑ̃:t]. **1.** *a. & s.m.* component, constituent (part). **2.** *s.f.* **composante;** *El: Mec:* component (of voltage, force, velocity, etc.); *El:* **composante wattée, en phase,** watt component.

composé [kɔ̃poze]. **1.** *a.* (*a*) compound (pendulum, beam, interest, etc.); **poutre composée,** built-up girder; *Ch:* **corps c.,** compound; *Mec: etc:* **résistance composée,** combined strength; *Gram:* **mot c.,** compound word; **temps c.,** compound tense; **passé c.,** perfect tense; *Mus:* **mesure composée,** compound time; *Fin:* **intérêt c.,** compound interest; (*b*) *Bot:* composite (flower); *s.f.pl.* **composées,** Compositae; (*c*) composed (demeanour, etc.); set, impassive (countenance). **2.** *s.m. Ch: Gram: etc:* compound.

composer [kɔ̃poze]. **1.** *v.tr.* (*a*) to compose (poem, symphony, etc.); to form (ministry, etc.); *Pharm:* to make up (prescription); *abs. Mus:* to compose; *abs. Sch:* to sit an examination; **c. en thème espagnol,** to sit a Spanish prose paper; *Th:* **cet acteur a vraiment bien composé le personnage de Tartuffe,** this actor portrayed Tartuffe extremely well; *Dom.Ec:* **c. le menu,** to choose the menu; (*b*) *Typ:* to set (type); **c. une ligne,** to compose, set, a line; **machine à c.,** type-setting machine; *Tp:* **c. un numéro,** to dial a number; (*c*) **les personnes qui composent notre famille,** the people of whom our family consists; all the members of our family; (*d*) to compose, arrange, settle (one's life, etc.); **c. son visage,** to compose one's features; **se c. une figure,** to put on an expression suitable to the occasion; (*e*) *Mec:* **c. trois forces,** to find the resultant of three forces. **2.** *v.i.* to compound, compromise, come to terms (**avec,** with); to make a composition (with creditors, etc.).

se composer. 1. se c. (**de**), to be made up (of), to consist (of); **appartement composé de cinq pièces,** flat consisting of five rooms. **2.** to take shape, to take form. **3.** *O:* to compose oneself.

composeuse [kɔ̃pozø:z], *s.f. Typ:* type-setting machine.

composite [kɔ̃pɔzit]. **1.** *a. & s.m. Arch:* composite (order). **2.** *a.* **mobilier des plus composites,** heterogeneous collection of furniture; *Rockets:* **fusée c.,** multi-stage rocket.

compositeur, -trice [kɔ̃pozitœ:r, -tris], *s.* **1.** *Mus:* composer. **2.** *Jur:* **amiable c.,** arbitrator. **3.** *Typ:* compositor, type-setter. **4.** *s.m.* (*a*) *Tg:* keyboard perforator; (*b*) *Typ:* type-setting machine.

composition [kɔ̃pozisjɔ̃], *s.f.* **1.** (*a*) composing, composition (of sonata, poem, etc.); constructing, construction (of machine, novel, etc.); composition (of water, etc.); making up (of prescription, etc.); **ingrédients qui entrent dans la c. de . . .,** ingredients that go to the making of . . .; **la c. de l'assemblée était la suivante . . .,** the assembly was composed of the following members . . .; **c. sociale d'un pays,** social structure, make-up, of a country; (*b*) *Typ:* setting, composing (of type); type-setting. **2.** (*a*) composition, compound, mixture; (*b*) *Lit: Mus: etc:* composition; *Sch:* (i) essay; (ii) test; paper; **c. d'histoire,** history paper; **compositions de fin d'année,** end-of-year examination; (*c*) *Typ:* **paquet de c.,** packet of type; **c. en plein,** plain matter; **c. lardée,** mixed matter. **3.** arrangement, settlement, compromise; **entrer en c. avec qn,** to come to terms with s.o., to compound with s.o.; **amener qn à c.,** to bring s.o. to terms; **homme de bonne c.,** man easy to deal with. **4.** *Jur:* compensation.

compost [kɔ̃pɔst], *s.m. Agr:* compost.

compostage [kɔ̃pɔsta:ʒ], *s.m.* dating (of ticket, etc.).

composter[1] [kɔ̃pɔste], *v.tr. Agr:* to treat (land) with compost, to compost (land).

composter[2], *v.tr.* **1.** *Typ:* to compose (type) (with composing-stick). **2.** to date, perforate (ticket, etc.).

composteur [kɔ̃pɔstœ:r], *s.m.* **1.** *Typ:* (*a*) setting-stick, composing-stick; (*b*) **c. d'apprêt,** dressing-stick. **2.** dating and numbering machine; dating stamp; dater.

compote[1] [kɔ̃pɔt], *s.f.* (*a*) *Cu:* compote (of fruit), stewed fruit; **faire cuire des fruits en c.,** to stew fruit; (*b*) *Cu: A:* **c. de pigeons,** stewed pigeons; (*c*) *F:* **mettre, réduire, qn en c.,** to pound s.o. to a jelly; **avoir les pieds en c.,** to have sore feet; **avoir la tête en c.,** to have one's head in a whirl.

compote[2], *s.f. Sch: P:* test; exam.

compotier [kɔ̃pɔtje], *s.m.* fruit dish, compote dish.

compound [kɔ̃pund]. **1.** *a.inv. El.E: Mch:* compound (engine, winding, motor); *s.f.* **une c.,** compound steam engine; *Metall:* **acier c.,** compound steel, alloy steel. **2.** *s.m. El.E:* insulating compound; **c. de fermeture,** sealing compound (of accumulator).

compoundage [kɔ̃punda:ʒ], *s.m.* **1.** *El.E:* compounding (of motor). **2.** *Ind:* incorporating of an animal or vegetable fat in a lubricating oil (of mineral origin).

compounder [kɔ̃punde], *v.tr.* **1.** *El.E:* to compound (motor). **2.** *Ind:* to incorporate an animal or vegetable fat in a lubricating oil (of mineral origin).

comprador [kɔ̃pradɔ:r], *s.m. Com: A:* (*in China*) middleman, comprador; *pl.* *compradores* [kɔ̃pradɔrɛs].

compréhensibilité [kɔ̃preɑ̃sibilite], *s.f.* comprehensibility.

compréhensible [kɔ̃preɑ̃sibl], *a.* comprehensible, understandable.

compréhensif, -ive [kɔ̃preɑ̃sif, -i:v], *a.* **1.** comprehensive, inclusive (statement, etc.). **2.** (*a*) intelligent, understanding (mind, etc.); (*b*) (*pers.*) understanding; **des parents compréhensifs,** understanding parents.

compréhension [kɔ̃preɑ̃sjɔ̃], *s.f.* **1.** *Phil:* (i) connotation; (ii) intensive quantity; **c. et extension,** intension and extension. **2.** understanding; comprehension; **avoir la c. facile,** to have a ready intelligence, to be quick to understand; *F:* to be quick in the uptake.

compréhensivité [kɔ̃preɑ̃sivite], *s.f.* faculty of comprehending.

comprendre [kɔ̃prɑ̃:dr], *v.tr.* (*conj. like* PRENDRE) **1.** to comprise, include, embrace, cover; *Geom:* to intercept (space); **famille de plantes qui comprend plusieurs genres,** family of plants that includes, comprises, a number of genera; **c. qn, qch., dans qch.,** to include, reckon, s.o., sth., in sth.; **tout est compris,** everything is included; **six cents francs par mois tout compris,** six hundred francs a month inclusive, "all in"; **emballage non compris, non compris l'emballage,** exclusive of, excluding, packing; **êtes-vous compris dans la faillite?** are you involved in the bankruptcy? **y compris . . .,** including . . .; **jusqu'à et y compris le 31 décembre,** up to and including December 31st. **2.** (*a*) to understand; **je ne comprends pas le français,** I don't understand French; **il ne comprend pas l'anglais quand on le lui parle,** he doesn't understand plain English; **je ne comprends pas ce que vous voulez dire,** I don't understand what you mean; *F:* I don't get you; **comme on peut le c.,** understandably; **que ce soit bien entendu et bien compris!** let this be a fair warning! **pour bien comprendre ce passage,** to understand this passage fully, completely; **je n'arrive pas à c. cette phrase,** I can't make sense of this sentence; **ai-je bien compris que . . .?** am I to understand, do you mean to say, that . . .? **vous la comprenez mal,** you misunderstand her; **vous m'avez mal compris,** you have taken me up wrongly; **si je vous ai bien compris,** if I have not misunderstood you; **il a ajouté quelque chose que je n'ai pas pu c.,** he added something which I didn't catch; **je ne comprends rien à l'algèbre,** I don't know a thing about algebra; **comprenez-vous quelque chose à ce qu'il raconte?** do you understand what he is talking about? **je n'y comprends rien,** I can't make it out, make head or tail of it, I can make nothing of it, I am at a loss to understand it, I cannot account for it; **c'est à n'y rien comprendre,** I can't understand it, it is beyond me; *F:* **allez donc y c. qch.!** just try and make sth. out of that! **je lui ai fait c. que** + *ind.*; (i) I gave him to understand that . . .; (ii) I made it clear to him that . . .; **se faire c.,** to make oneself understood; **cela se comprend,** of course, naturally; that's understandable; **cela ne se comprend pas,** it's incomprehensible; there's no accounting for it; **compris!** understood! *F:* **je le comprends,** I don't blame him; (*b*) **comprenez-vous ce qu'il fait?** do you realize, are you aware of, what he is doing? **je comprends que vous soyez fâché,** I can understand your being angry; **maladie que je comprends être très grave,** illness which I understand is very serious; *F:* **je comprends, oui!** yes, sure enough! I should think so (too)! **je comprends bien!** I can well imagine it! (*c*) **cet appartement est mal compris,** this flat is badly planned.

comprenette [kɔ̃prənɛt], *s.f.*, **comprenoir** [kɔ̃prənwa:r], *s.m. Hum: F:* understanding; **avoir la comprenette difficile,** to be slow in the uptake.

compresse [kɔ̃prɛs], *s.f. Med:* compress.

compresser [kɔ̃prɛse], *v.tr.* **1.** to compress. **2.** *F:* to pack; **les prisonniers étaient compressés dans des fourgons,** the prisoners were packed in trucks.

compresseur [kɔ̃prɛsœ:r], *s.m.* **1.** (*a*) *Mec.E:* compressor (of air, gas, fluid, etc.); **c. à double effet,** double-acting compressor; **c. à double, à simple, entrée,** double-, single-, entry compressor; **c. à flux axial,** axial-flow compressor; **c. à flux radial,** radial-flow compressor; **c. à flux mixte,** mixed-flow compressor; **c. à mouvement alternatif, c. à piston,** reciprocating compressor; **c. à plusieurs étages, c. multiétage,** multi-stage compressor; **c. à un, deux, trois, étages,** single-, two-, three-, stage compressor; **c. à seuil réglable,** variable-threshold compressor; **c. centrifuge,** centrifugal compressor, turbo-compressor; **c. commandé, entraîné, par l'échappement,** exhaust-drive compressor; **c. compound,** compound compressor; **c. de cabine,** cabin super-charger; **c. de volume, c. volumétrique,** volume compressor; positive displacement compressor; (*b*) *I.C.E:* supercharger; **c. à plusieurs vitesses,** multi-speed supercharger; **à c.,** supercharged; (*c*) *Civ.E:* (**rouleau**) **c.,** road roller. **2.** *Surg:* constrictor. **3.** *Anat:* compressor (muscle). **4.** *a.m.* compressing; constricting.

compressibilité [kɔ̃prɛsibilite], *s.f.* compressibility (of air, etc.).

compressible [kɔ̃prɛsibl], *a.* (*a*) *Ph:* compressible; (*b*) reducible (expenses, etc.).

compressif, -ive [kɔ̃prɛsif, -i:v], *a.* **1.** compressive (bandage, stress, etc.). **2.** repressive (measures, etc.).

compressimètre [kɔ̃prɛsimɛtr], *s.m. Civ.E:* compressometer.

compression [kɔ̃prɛsjɔ̃], *s.f.* **1.** *Mec:* compression (of gas, fluid, steam, spring, etc.); *I.C.E:* **taux, rapport, de c.,** compression ratio; **temps de c.,** compression stroke; **chambre de c.,** compression chamber; **allumage par c.,** compression ignition; **robinet de c.,** compression cock, faucet; **c. adiabatique,** adiabatic compression; **c. isotherme, isothermique,** isothermal compression; *Aer:* **c. en un étage, c. simple,** single-stage compression; **c. en deux, trois, étages,** two-, three-, stage compression; **c. en plusieurs étages,** multi-stage compression; **pompe de c.,** compression pump; **ressort de c.,** compression spring. **2.** (*strength of materials*) compression, crushing; **effort de c.,** compressive stress; **essai à la c.,** compression, crushing, test; **résistance à la c.,** resistance to compression, to crushing; compressive strength; **soumis à des efforts de c.,** subjected to compression stresses; *Av:* **barre, nervure, de c.** (**d'aile**), compression rib; *Mec:* **pièce travaillant à la c.,** member in compression. **3.** (*a*) *Physiol:* **c. du cerveau par une tumeur,** compression of the brain by a tumour; (*b*) *Ind:* **moulage par c.,** compression moulding; (*c*) squeezing (of sponge, etc.); (*d*) *Fin:* **c. des dépenses budgétaires, compressions budgétaires,** retrenchment; cuts in budgetary expenditures; **c. de personnel,** reduction of staff. **4.** repression, constraint; **mesures de c.,** repressive measures.

comprimable [kɔ̃primabl], *a.* compressible.

comprimant [kɔ̃primɑ̃], *a.* compressing (force, etc.).

comprimé [kɔ̃prime]. **1.** *a.* (*a*) compressed; **air c.**, compressed air; **outil à air c.**, pneumatic tool; *Metall:* **acier c.**, pressed steel; *Mec.E:* **pièce comprimée**, member in compression; strut; (*b*) *Ich: etc:* compressed (body). **2.** *s.m. Pharm:* (compressed) tablet; **acheter des comprimés d'aspirine**, to buy some aspirins.

comprimer [kɔ̃prime], *v.tr.* **1.** to compress (gas, artery, etc.); **c. la taille**, to squeeze the waist in; **certains métaux peuvent se c. par pression**, some metals may compress under pressure; **le coton peut se c. en balles**, cotton can be compressed into bales. **2.** to curb, repress, restrain (one's feelings, etc.); to repress (tears); to hold (nation, etc.) in check; **c. sa colère**, to restrain, *F:* bottle up, one's anger.

compris [kɔ̃pri], *a.* **bien c.**, (thoroughly) understood; **mal c.**, misunderstood; misinterpreted; *s.a.* COMPRENDRE.

compromettant [kɔ̃prɔmɛtɑ̃], *a.* compromising (situation, etc.); incriminating (remark, etc.).

compromettre [kɔ̃prɔmɛtr̥] (*conj. like* METTRE) **1.** *v.tr.* (*a*) to compromise (s.o., s.o.'s reputation, etc.); **être compromis dans un crime**, to be implicated, mixed up, in a crime; **être compromis dans une faillite**, to be involved in a bankruptcy; (*b*) to endanger, jeopardize, imperil (life, safety, etc.); to impair (s.o.'s authority). **2.** *v.i.* to accept arbitration, to compromise.

se compromettre, to compromise oneself; to commit oneself.

compromis [kɔ̃prɔmi], *s.m.* compromise, arrangement; **mettre une affaire en c.**, to submit an affair for arbitration; **passer un c. avec qn**, to come to an arrangement with s.o.; *Com:* **obtenir un c.**, to compound (with creditors); *M.Ins:* **c. d'avarie**, average bond; *Dipl:* **c. d'arbitrage**, compromise.

compromissaire [kɔ̃prɔmisɛːr], *s.m. Jur:* arbitrator, referee.

compromission [kɔ̃prɔmisjɔ̃], *s.f.* **1.** compromising (with one's conscience); surrender (of principle); **c. avec le devoir**, playing fast and loose with one's duty. **2.** *usu. Pej:* compromise.

compromissoire [kɔ̃prɔmiswaːr], *a. Jur:* **clause c.**, arbitration clause (in agreement).

compsognathus [kɔ̃psɔgnatys], *s.m. Paleont:* compsognathus.

comptabiliser [kɔ̃tabilize], *v.tr.* to account for (sth.), to enter (sth.) in the accounts.

comptabilité [kɔ̃tabilite], *s.f.* **1.** book-keeping, accountancy; **c. en partie simple, double**, single-, double-, entry book-keeping; **c. de prix de revient**, cost accounts; **livre de c.**, account book; **service de la c.**, accounts department; **tenir la c. d'une maison**, to keep the books, the accounts, of a firm; **chef de c.**, chief accountant; **commission de c.**, audit committee; **c. publique**, public accountancy; **c. matière**, (i) *Ind:* stock record, stores accounts; (ii) *Mil:* property accounts; *Mil:* **c. deniers**, money accounts; **pièce de c.**, voucher; *Ind:* **c. de temps (du personnel)**, time keeping. **2.** accounts, accountancy, department; *Com:* counting house.

comptable [kɔ̃tabl̥]. **1.** *Com: etc:* (*a*) *a.* book-keeping (work, etc.); **pièce c.**, accountable receipt; voucher; **quittance c.**, formal receipt; (*b*) *s.m.* accountant, book-keeper; **expert c.**, (i) auditor; (ii) = chartered accountant; **c. contrôleur**, auditor. **2.** *a.* (*a*) accountable, responsible; **être c. à qn de qch.**, to be accountable to s.o. for sth.; (*b*) *Com:* **machine c.**, accounting machine.

comptage [kɔ̃taːʒ], *s.m.* **1.** enumeration, numbering; counting, reckoning; **faire un c. rapide**, to make a quick count; **faire le c. des voitures sur une autoroute**, to count the number of cars on a motorway. **2.** *Atom.Ph:* count; *Elcs:* **c. (d'impulsions)**, scaling; **circuit de c.**, scaling circuit; **dispositif de c., appareillage de c.**, scaling unit; **échelle de c.**, scaler. **3.** *El: Tp: etc:* metering, *U.S:* registration; *Tp:* **c. à la durée**, time metering; timing.

comptant [kɔ̃tɑ̃]. **1.** *a.* **argent c.**, ready money, spot cash, *U.S:* call money; **payer cent francs comptant(s)**, to pay a hundred francs cash down; **prendre tout pour argent c.**, to take everything for gospel truth, to take it all in. **2.** *adv.* **payer c.**, to pay (in) cash, in ready money. **3.** *s.m.* **acheter, vendre, qch. (au) c.**, to buy, sell, sth. for ready money, *St.Exch:* for delivery; **payable (au) comptant**, (i) terms: cash; (ii) payable on presentation; **paiement (au) c.**, cash payment; **marché, opération, au c.**, cash transaction; **valeurs au c.**, securities dealt in for cash; **le marché du c.**, the spot market.

compte [kɔ̃ːt], *s.m.* account; (*a*) reckoning, calculation; **faire le c. des dépenses**, to add up; *F:* tot up, expenses; **faire son c. de qch.**, to reckon, count, on sth.; **cela fait mon c.**, that's the very thing I wanted, it's just the thing for me; **je ne sais pas comment ils firent leur c., mais . . .**, I don't know how they managed it, but . . .; **y trouver son c.**, to profit by it, get sth. out of it, turn it to account; **on n'y trouve pas son c.**, it doesn't pay; **être loin de c.**, to be sadly out in one's calculations, in one's reckoning; to be wide of the mark; **où en sont nos comptes?** how do we stand? **le c. y est, n'y est pas**, the account is correct, incorrect; **avez-vous votre c.?** have you the right amount?; **c. rond**, round sum, even money; **au bout du c. qu'est-ce que cela fait?** after all, when all is said and done, what does it matter? **en fin de c. . . ., tout c. fait . . .**, all things considered . . ., after all . . ., taking everything into account . . ., in the long run . . ., eventually; **la femme qu'il épousa en fin de c.**, the woman he eventually married; **il est donc bien coupable à votre c.?** so you think him very much to blame? **à ce c. . . .**, in that case . . ., things being so . . ., at that rate . . .; **tenir c. de qch.**, to take sth. into account, into consideration, to make allowance for sth.; **il y a autre chose dont il faut tenir c.**, there is another consideration; **tenir c. des marchandises retournées**, to allow for goods returned; **je tiendrai c. de votre avis**, I shall bear, keep, your words in mind; **je tiendrai c. de cette promesse**, I shall not overlook this assurance; **ne tenir aucun c. de qn, de qch.**, to ignore s.o., sth.; **ne tenir aucun c. des ordres de qn**, to take no notice of, no heed of, to disregard, set at nought, s.o.'s orders; **tenir le plus grand c. d'un fait**, to attach the greatest importance to a fact; **c. tenu des circonstances atténuantes**, taking into account the extenuating circumstances; **acheter qch. à bon c.**, to buy sth. cheap; *F:* **il a son c., il en a pour son c.**, (i) he's done for, it's all up with him; (ii) he's drunk, he's had as much as he can carry; *F:* **j'ai eu mon c.**, I've had enough; *F:* **son c. est bon**, (i) I'll settle, (ii) I've settled, his hash for him; *Prov:* **les bons comptes font les bons amis**, short reckonings make long friends; (*b*) count; *Box:* **rester sur le plancher pour le c.**, to be counted out; *Golf: etc:* **c. des points**, score, card; (*c*) (*transactions*) **tenir les comptes d'une maison**, to keep the accounts of a firm; **payer un c.**, to pay a bill; **régler son c.**, to settle one's account; *F:* **régler son c. à qn**, to settle s.o.'s hash, to put paid to s.o.'s account; **une nouvelle congestion lui réglerait son c.**, another stroke would finish him; **avoir un (petit) c. à régler avec qn**, to have a bone to pick with s.o.; **régler de vieux comptes**, to pay off old scores; **règlement de c.**, (i) settling of accounts; (ii) *F:* settling of scores; **suivant c. remis**, as per, to, account rendered; **solde de c.**, settlement; **pour solde de tout c.**, in full settlement; **avoir un c. chez qn, être en c. chez qn**, to have an account with s.o.; **c. en banque**, banking account; **c. courant**, current account; **c. spécial**, current account with interest; **c. à terme** = deposit account; **c. courant postal** = Post Office account; **c. de chèques postaux** = Giro account (at Post Office); *Tp:* (*communication*) **sur c. courant**, (call) on credit card system; **c. découvert**, overdrawn account; **relevé de c.**, statement (of account); *Mil:* **c. d'avances**, imprest account; **livre de comptes**, (i) account book; (ii) (tradesman's) pass-book; **c. des profits et (des) pertes**, profit and loss account; **c. d'autre part**, contra account; **(livre de) comptes faits**, ready reckoner; **la Cour des Comptes**, the Audit Office; **donner son c. à qn**, to pay s.o. off (on dismissal); **faire ses comptes**, to make up one's accounts; **créances qui n'entrent pas en ligne de c.**, credits which are not taken into account, which do not appear in the accounts; **considérations qui n'entrent pas en ligne de c.**, extraneous considerations; **cela n'entre pas en ligne de c.**, that has nothing to do with the matter; **versement à c.**, payment on account, in part; **mettre qch. au, sur le, c. de qn**, to enter, put, sth. down to s.o.'s account; **mettre un malheur sur le c. de qn**, to ascribe, attribute, a misfortune to s.o., to blame s.o. for a misfortune; **dire, apprendre, qch. sur le c. de qn**, to say, learn, sth. about s.o.; **il n'y a qu'une opinion sur son c.**, there is only one opinion concerning him; **prendre qch. à son c.**, (i) to buy sth. on one's own account; (ii) to accept responsibility for sth.; **être, se mettre, s'établir, s'installer, à son c.**, to be, to set up, in business on one's own account; **acheter qch. pour le c. de qn**, to buy sth. on s.o.'s account, on s.o.'s behalf; **pour mon c., j'aimerais mieux rester ici**, for my part, as far as I am concerned, I should prefer to stay here; **laisser des marchandises pour c.**, to leave goods on a merchant's hands; **c. à demi**, joint account; **se mettre de c. à demi avec qn**, to go halves, fifty-fifty, with s.o.; **livre édité à c. d'auteur**, book published at author's expense; *F:* **bois un coup sur mon c.**, have one on me; (*d*) **demander des comptes à qn**, to call s.o. to account; **demander c. à qn de qch.**, to call upon s.o. to account for sth., to bring s.o. to book for sth.; **demander c. à qn de sa conduite**, to call s.o. to account for his conduct; **il ne doit de comptes à personne**, he is answerable to nobody; **rendre c. de qch.**, to give an account of sth.; to account for sth.; **rendre c. de sa gestion**, to give an account of one's stewardship; **c. rendu**, report; **faire le c. rendu d'un ouvrage**, to review a book; **comptes rendus**, book reviews; **c. rendu de lecture**, précis writing; **se rendre c. de qch.**, (i) to verify, ascertain, sth.; (ii) to realize, understand, sth.; **soudain il se rendit c. du danger**, he suddenly became aware of the danger; **je me rendis bientôt c. de ses intentions**, I soon saw what he was up to; **se rendre bien c. de qch.**, to be well aware of sth.; **je me rends clairement c. que . . .**, I fully appreciate that . . .; **se rendre c. de l'importance de qch.**, to be aware of, to appreciate, the importance of sth.; *F:* **tu te rends c.!** would you believe it! *F:* **vous m'en rendrez c.!** you shall answer for it! (*e*) **c. à rebours**, count down.

compte-fils [kɔ̃tfil], *s.m.inv. Tex:* linen-prover, thread-counter; weaver's glass.

compte-gibier [kɔ̃tʒibje], *s.m.inv. Ven:* game-scorer.

compte-gouttes [kɔ̃tgut], *s.m.inv.* (*a*) *Pharm: etc:* dropping-tube, (medicine) dropper, pipette; stactometer; **mesurer qch. au c.-g.**, to dole sth. out in driblets; (*b*) *Mec.E:* drip-feed lubricator; (*c*) fountain-pen filler.

compte-minutes [kɔ̃tminyt], *s.m.inv. Dom.Ec:* timer.

compte-pas [kɔ̃tpɑ], *s.m.inv.* **1.** pedometer. **2.** surveying-wheel.

compte-pose [kɔ̃tpoːz], *s.m. Phot:* timer; *pl. compte-poses.*

compter [kɔ̃te]. **1.** *v.tr.* (*a*) to count (up), reckon (up), compute (numbers, etc.); to number; **il comptait son argent**, he was counting (up) his money; **c. jusqu'à dix**, to count up to ten; *F:* **savoir c. jusqu'à cinq**, to know how many beans make five; **comptant à partir d'hier . . .**, reckoning from yesterday . . .; **dix-neuf tous comptés**, nineteen in all, all told; **jusqu'à dix-huit ans comptés**, up to and including eighteen years; *s.a.* RABATTRE 2; **la société compte quelques poètes parmi ses membres**, the society numbers some poets among its members; **être compté au nombre des membres**, to be counted as a member; **marcher à pas comptés**, to walk with measured tread; **il comptait plus de quatre-vingts ans**, he was over eighty; **ses jours sont comptés**, his days are numbered; **il y a de cela vingt ans bien comptés**, a good twenty years have passed since then; **il est obligé de c.**, he has to watch every penny; **donner sans c.**, to give without stint(ing); **dépenser sans c.**, to spend lavishly; **sans c. . . .**, not counting . . ., not including . . ., not to mention . . ., exclusive of . . ., let alone . . .; **nous serons quatre sans c. le chauffeur**, there will be four of us besides, not counting, the driver; **sans c. que . . .**, not to mention that . . ., let alone that . . ., besides the fact that . . .; **mal c.**, to miscount; **ne pas c. qn**, to leave s.o. out of account; **les réussites ne se comptent plus**, the successes have been innumerable; **il faut c. une heure pour nous habiller**, we must allow one hour for dressing; *Prov:* **qui compte sans son hôte compte deux fois**, don't reckon without your host; *prep.phr.* **à c. de . . .**, (reckoning) from . . .; **à c. de demain**, reckoning from to-morrow; *Adm:* **à c. du 1er janvier**, to take effect on, with effect from, January 1st; (*b*) **c. cent francs à qn**, to pay s.o., count s.o. out, a hundred francs; (*c*) *Com:* to charge; **je vous compterai cet article vingt francs**, I will charge you twenty francs for this article; **nous ne comptons pas l'emballage**, we don't charge for packing; (*d*) to count, value, deem; **c. sa vie pour rien**, to hold one's life of no account; **c. qn pour mort**, to count s.o. as dead; (*e*) **c. faire qch.**, to expect to do sth.; to count, reckon, on doing sth.; **je compte le voir**

demain, I expect to see him tomorrow; **que comptez-vous faire?** what do you propose to do, intend doing? **je comptais qu'il serait à m'attendre,** I expected him to be waiting for me. **2.** *v.i.* (*a*) **compter sur qn, sur qch.,** to reckon, count, depend, rely, bank, on s.o., sth.; **je compte sur vous pour m'aider,** I rely on you to help me; **comptez sur moi,** depend upon me; **vous pouvez c. entièrement sur moi,** I won't let you down; **vous pouvez y c.,** you may depend upon it; **il ne peut c. que sur lui-même,** he is entirely dependent on himself; **je compte sur le plaisir de vous revoir,** I am looking forward to seeing you again; *Prov:* **il ne faut pas c. sur les souliers d'un mort pour se mettre en route,** he who waits for dead men's shoes is in danger of going barefoot; (*b*) **c. avec qn, qch.,** to reckon with s.o., sth.; (*c*) **il compte parmi mes meilleurs amis,** he counts among my best friends; **ce tableau compte parmi les trésors du musée,** this painting is numbered among the treasures of the gallery; **c. parmi les meilleurs,** to rank among the best; (*d*) to count, to be of consequence; **ne compter pour rien,** to stand for nothing; **cela ne compte pas,** that goes for nothing; **il ne compte pas,** he doesn't count, doesn't signify, he's of no account; **le mot qui compte,** the operative word.

compte-secondes [kɔ̃tsəgɔ̃:d], *s.m.inv.* stop-watch.

compte-temps [kɔ̃ttɑ̃], *s.m.inv. Av:* running time meter.

compte-tours [kɔ̃ttu:r], *s.m.inv. Mch:* revolution counter; motometer; tachometer.

compteur, -euse [kɔ̃tœ:r, -ø:z]. **1.** (*a*) *s.* (*pers.*) counter; checker; *s.f.* **compteuse,** worker who assembles paper in quires; (*b*) *s.m.* loader (in slate quarry). **2.** *s.m.* (*a*) meter, recorder, register, counter; **c. d'électricité, électrique,** electricity, electric meter; **c. de, à, gaz, à, d', eau,** gas, water, meter; **c. de tours,** revolution counter; *Aut:* **c. de vitesse,** speedometer; **c. de trajet, c. journalier,** trip recorder (of speedometer); **c. kilométrique,** mileage recorder, mileometer, odometer; cyclometer; **c. de stationnement,** parking meter; **c. pour entrées, d'entrées,** turnstile; **c. à paiement préalable, à prépaiement,** slot meter; **c. de temps,** time meter; **c. horaire,** hour meter; **c. de watt-heures,** watt-hour meter; **c. avec remise à zéro,** set back counter; **c. d'air,** air(-flow) meter; **c. à dépassement,** excess meter; **c. auxiliaire,** sub-meter; **c. totalisateur,** integrating meter; (*b*) *Atom.Ph: Elcs:* **c. à feuille,** foil counter; **c. à plaques,** plate counter; **c. d'impulsions,** scaler; (im)pulse counter; **c. de neutrons, de particules alpha,** neutron, alpha, counter; **c. de radiation, de radio-activité,** radiation counter (tube); survey meter; **c. (de) Geiger(-Muller),** Geiger(-Muller) counter; **c. à, de, scintillations,** scintillation counter; (*c*) *Tp:* **c. d'appels,** call meter; **c. d'appels d'abonné,** subscriber's meter; **c. de communications,** message recorder; (*d*) *Nau:* deck chronometer, hack watch, job watch; (*e*) **c. universel,** calculating machine.

compteur-indicateur [kɔ̃tœ:rɛ̃dikatœ:r], *s.m. Aut:* speedometer; **c.-i. de vitesse avec totalisateur journalier,** speedometer with trip-recorder; *pl. compteurs-indicateurs.*

comptine [kɔ̃tin], *s.f.* counting(-out) rhyme.

comptoir [kɔ̃twa:r], *s.m.* **1.** *Com:* counter; **c. de recette,** cashier's desk, cash desk; **c. de cabaret,** bar; **boire au c.,** to drink at the bar; **garçon de c.,** bartender; *A:* **demoiselle de c.,** (i) *Com:* saleswoman; (ii) barmaid. **2.** *Asian etc: Com:* godown, warehouse, factory. **3.** *Fin:* (*a*) bank; **c. d'escompte,** discount bank; (*b*) branch bank, agency.

comptoir-caisse [kɔ̃twa:rkɛs], *s.m.* pay-desk, cash desk; *pl. comptoirs-caisses.*

comptométrice [kɔ̃tɔmetris], *s.f.* comptometer operator.

compulsation [kɔ̃pylsasjɔ̃], *s.f.* examination, checking (of documents).

compulser [kɔ̃pylse], *v.tr.* to examine, check, compare, inspect, go through (documents, books, etc.).

compulseur [kɔ̃pylsœ:r], *s.m. Com: Jur:* examiner (of documents).

compulsif, -ive [kɔ̃pylsif, -i:v], *a.* **1.** *A:* compelling, restraining (force). **2.** *Psy:* compulsive (drinker, etc.).

compulsion [kɔ̃pylsjɔ̃], *s.f.* compulsion.

compulsoire [kɔ̃pylswa:r], *s.m. Jur:* **1.** authorized examination of documents. **2.** order to produce documents.

comput [kɔ̃pyt], *s.m. Ecc:* computation (of calendar).

computateur [kɔ̃pytatœ:r], *s.m. Av:* computer (of distance and route); computing scale.

computation [kɔ̃pytasjɔ̃], *s.f.* computation.

computer [kɔ̃pyte], *v.tr.* to compute.

computiste [kɔ̃pytist], *s.m.* computist.

comtadin, -ine [kɔ̃tadɛ̃, -in], *a. & s. A.Geog:* (native, inhabitant) of the comtat Venaissin.

comtal, -aux [kɔ̃tal, -o], *a.* of, pertaining to, a count, an earl; **couronne comtale,** earl's coronet.

comtat [kɔ̃ta], *s.m. A:* county; *Hist:* **le c. Venaissin,** the (papal state of the) comtat Venaissin (the department of Vaucluse covers approximately the same area).

comte [kɔ̃:t], *s.m.* count; (*in Engl.*) earl; **monsieur le c.,** my lord, your lordship; his lordship.

comté [kɔ̃te], *s.m.* **1.** (*a*) *Hist:* earldom; (*b*) county; (*c*) *Fr.C: Pol:* electoral circumscription. **2.** *Cu:* Franche-Comté cheese.

comtesse [kɔ̃tɛs], *s.f.* countess; **madame la c.,** my lady, your ladyship; her ladyship.

comtisme [kɔ̃tism], *s.m. Phil:* comtism, positivism.

comtiste [kɔ̃tist], *a. & s.m. & f. Phil:* comtist, positivist.

comtois, -oise [kɔ̃twa-wa:z]. **1.** *a. & s.* (native) of Franche-Comté. **2.** *s.f.* **comtoise,** grandfather clock.

con [kɔ̃], *s.m. V:* (*a*) idiot, clot, nit; **va pas faire le c. là-dedans,** don't go arsing about in there; **il est c. comme la lune,** he's a prize nit; (*b*) cunt.

conard [kɔna:r], *s.m. P:* clot, idiot.

conasse [kɔnas], *s.f. V:* (*a*) tart; (*b*) stupid bitch.

conatif, -ive [kɔnatif, -iv], *a. Ling:* conative.

conation [kɔnasjɔ̃], *s.f. Psy:* conation.

concamération [kɔ̃kamerasjɔ̃], *s.f. Arch:* concameration.

concarnois, -oise [kɔ̃karnwa, -wa:z], *a. & s. Geog:* (native, inhabitant) of Concarneau.

concassage [kɔ̃kɑsa:ʒ], *s.m.,* **concassation** [kɔ̃kɑsasjɔ̃], *s.f. Civ.E: Min: etc:* breaking, crushing, pounding (of ore, etc.).

concassé [kɔ̃kɑse], *s.m. Civ.E:* (crushed) ballast material.

concassement [kɔ̃kɑsmɑ̃], *s.m.* pulverization.

concasser [kɔ̃kɑse], *v.tr.* to break, crush (ore); to bray (colours); to grind (pepper, etc.); to pound.

concasseur [kɔ̃kɑsœ:r], *s.m. Ind: etc:* breaker, crusher, crushing-mill; *Paperm:* disintegrator; **c. de coke, de pierres,** coke-breaker, stonebreaker; **c. à plâtre,** gypsum crusher; **rouleau c.,** (stone or ore) crushing-roller.

concasseuse [kɔ̃kɑsø:z], *s.f.* crushing mill.

concaténation [kɔ̃katenasjɔ̃], *s.f. Log:* concatenation, chain (of propositions, syllogisms).

concaténé [kɔ̃katene], *a. Poet:* **strophes concaténées,** concatenated stanzas.

concave [kɔ̃ka:v], *a.* concave.

concavité [kɔ̃kavite], *s.f.* (*a*) concavity; (*b*) concave side (of lens, etc.); (*c*) hollow, cavity; (*d*) *Av:* dishing.

concavo-concave [kɔ̃kavokɔ̃ka:v], *a. Geom: Opt:* concavo-concave, double-concave; *pl. concavo-concaves.*

concavo-convexe [kɔ̃kavokɔ̃vɛks], *a. Geom: Opt:* concavo-convex; *pl. concavo-convexes.*

concéder [kɔ̃sede], *v.tr.* (**je concède, n. concédons; je concéderai**) **1.** to concede, grant, allow (privilege, etc.); **se faire c. des terres,** to obtain a grant of land; **c. l'exécution d'une entreprise à qn,** to place a contract with s.o., to grant s.o. the concession, for an undertaking; **terres non encore concédées,** land awaiting settlement. **2. c. qu'on a tort,** to concede, allow, admit, that one is wrong.

concélébration [kɔ̃selebrasjɔ̃], *s.f. Ecc:* concelebration.

concélébrer [kɔ̃selebre], *v.tr. Ecc:* to concelebrate.

concentrateur [kɔ̃sɑ̃tratœ:r]. *Ch: Min: etc:* **1.** *s.m.* concentrator, concentrating apparatus. **2.** *a.m.* concentrating.

concentration [kɔ̃sɑ̃trasjɔ̃], *s.f.* concentration. **1.** (*a*) *Ph: Ch:* concentration, concentrating (of heat, etc.); **c. des rayons lumineux,** concentration of rays of light (on an object); **c. moléculaire,** molecular concentration; **c. à l'eau, par voie humide,** wet concentration; **c. à sec, par voie sèche,** dry concentration; **pile à c.,** concentration cell; (*b*) *Atom.Ph:* concentration, focusing; **c. de faisceaux électroniques,** electron-beam focusing; **c. ionique,** ion concentration; **c. magnétique,** magnetic focusing; **c. par déphasage,** phase focusing; (*c*) *Mil:* **c. des troupes,** troop concentration; **c. du feu, du tir,** concentration of fire; (*d*) *Pol:* **camp de c.,** concentration camp; (*e*) **les grandes concentrations urbaines,** the large urban concentrations, agglomerations; (*f*) *Pol.Ec:* integration (of enterprises). **2.** concentration (of the mind); **travail qui exige une grande c.,** work which requires great concentration.

concentrationnaire [kɔ̃sɑ̃trasjɔnɛ:r]. **1.** *a.* (*a*) pertaining to, reminiscent of, concentration camps; (*b*) totalitarian; **un système c.,** a totalitarian system. **2.** *s.m. or f.* prisoner in a concentration camp.

concentré [kɔ̃sɑ̃tre], *a.* **1.** (*a*) concentrated; *Ch:* at high concentration; **solution concentrée,** concentrated solution; **lait c.,** condensed milk; *Geog:* **ruissellement c.,** concentrated run-off; (*b*) **violence concentrée,** concentrated violence; **l'odeur concentrée des fleurs,** the concentrated, pungent, scent of the flowers. **2. c. en soi-même,** wrapped up in oneself; **caractère c.,** reserved character; **air c.,** abstracted look. **3.** *s.m.* extract, concentrate; **c. de viande,** meat extract; **c. de tomates,** tomato concentrate; **donner du c. aux vaches,** to feed the cows on concentrates.

concentrer [kɔ̃sɑ̃tre], *v.tr.* **1.** to concentrate (syrup, heat, troops, etc.); to focus (sun's rays, etc.); to centre; **l'attention de tous était concentrée sur . . .,** the general attention centred on . . . **2.** *A: & Lit:* to hold back, repress (one's feelings, etc.); **je n'ai pu c. ma fureur,** I could not contain my fury, my fury knew no bounds.

se concentrer. 1. to concentrate, to centre; **l'activité de Pascal se concentre autour de cette idée,** Pascal's activity centres round this idea; **toutes ses espérances se concentraient sur, dans, cet enfant,** all his hopes centred, were centred, in, (up)on, round, this child; **troupes qui se concentrent,** troops (that are) concentrating, effecting a concentration. **2. se c. (sur),** to concentrate (on); **taisez-vous, je me concentre,** be quiet, I'm trying to concentrate; **se c. en soi-même,** to retire within oneself, to withdraw oneself from the world.

concentrique [kɔ̃sɑ̃trik], *a. Geom: etc:* concentric; *Mec.E:* **mandrin à serrage c.,** self-centring chuck.

concentriquement [kɔ̃sɑ̃trikmɑ̃], *adv.* concentrically.

concept [kɔ̃sɛpt], *s.m.* concept.

conceptacle [kɔ̃sɛptakl̩], *s.m. Bot:* conceptacle.

concepteur [kɔ̃sɛptœ:r], *s.m. Com:* conceiver (of ideas), *F:* ideas man.

conceptibilité [kɔ̃sɛptibilite], *s.f.* conceivability, conceivableness.

conceptible [kɔ̃sɛptibl̩], *a.* conceivable.

conceptif, -ive [kɔ̃sɛptif, -i:v], *a.* conceptive.

conception [kɔ̃sɛpsjɔ̃], *s.f.* **1.** conception, conceiving (i) of offspring; (ii) of idea; *Ecc:* **l'Immaculée C.,** the Immaculate Conception; **c. dirigée,** birth control; **avoir la c. lente,** to be slow to understand (things), *F:* to be slow in the uptake; **avoir la c. vive,** to have a ready grasp (of things). **2.** conception, idea; *F:* **c'est une c.!** that's one way of looking at it! **3.** design.

conceptionnel, -elle [kɔ̃sɛpsjɔnɛl], *a.* conceptional.

conceptisme [kɔ̃sɛptism], *s.m. Spanish Lit:* conceptism.

conceptiste [kɔ̃sɛptist], *s.m. & f. Spanish Lit:* conceptist.

conceptivité [kɔ̃sɛptivite], *s.f. Physiol:* fecundity.

conceptualisme [kɔ̃sɛptɥalism], *s.m. Phil:* conceptualism.

conceptualiste [kɔ̃sɛptɥalist]. **1.** *s.m. Phil:* conceptualist. **2.** *a.* conceptualistic.

conceptuel, -elle [kɔ̃sɛptɥɛl], *a. Phil: Physiol:* conceptual.

concernant [kɔ̃sɛrnɑ̃]. **1.** *pr.p.* concerning, touching, relating to; **les frais me c.,** the expenses for which I am liable, my share of the expenses. **2.** (*with prepositional force*) concerning, about, respecting, with regard to, regarding, dealing with; **votre lettre c. votre frère,** your letter about, regarding, your brother.

concerner [kɔ̃sɛrne], *v.tr.* (*used in third pers. only*) to concern, affect; **pour, en, ce qui c. . . .,** concerning . . ., with respect to, with regard to . . ., regarding, as regards, in regard to . . .; as far as . . . is concerned; **en ce qui me concerne,** as far as I am concerned; **est-ce que cela concerne vos intérêts?** does it affect your interests? are your interests involved? **est-ce que cela vous concerne?** is it any concern of yours? what business is it of yours? **(parlant) pour ce qui me concerne . . .,** (speaking) for myself . . .

concert [kɔ̃sɛ:r], *s.m.* concert. **1.** (*a*) *A:* harmony, agreement; *Hist:* **le c. européen,** the concert of Europe; (*b*) *Jur:* conspiring (to commit an offence); **agir de c. avec qn,** (i) to act in concert, in consort, in conjunction, in consultation, in unison, with s.o., to go hand in hand with s.o.; (ii) to conspire with s.o. **2.** (*a*) *Mus:* concert; **c. spirituel,** concert of sacred music; **c. impromptu,** sing-song; **salle de c.,** concert-hall; *Poet:* **le c. des oiseaux,** the birds' chorus; (*b*) **ce fut un c. d'approbations,** there was a chorus of approval.

concertant, -ante [kɔ̃sɛrtɑ̃, -ɑ̃:t]. **1.** *a. Mus:* concerted (composition); concertante (part). **2.** *s. A:* concert performer.
concerté [kɔ̃sɛrte], *a.* **1.** concerted, united (action). **2.** studied, stiff, composed (manner, etc.).
concerter [kɔ̃sɛrte]. **1.** *v.tr.* (*a*) to concert, arrange (plan, etc.); to plan (scheme); **déclarations concertées entre eux,** declarations prearranged between them; **projet concerté d'avance,** preconcerted plan; **mesures bien concertées,** well-concerted, well-thought-out, measures; (*b*) to compose, settle (one's countenance, etc.). **2.** *v.i.* (*of voices, instruments*) to join (in concert); to harmonize.
se concerter (avec qn), (i) to act in concert (with s.o.); (ii) *Pej:* to connive (with s.o.); **concertez-vous avec lui là-dessus,** discuss the matter with him; **ils se concertèrent,** they put their heads together; **ils se sont concertés pour atteindre leur but,** they worked together to attain their end; **ils se concertèrent sur le moyen d'agir,** they took counsel together as to how to act.
concertina [kɔ̃sɛrtina], *s.f. Mus:* concertina.
concertino [kɔ̃sɛrtino], *s.m. Mus:* concertino.
concertiste [kɔ̃sɛrtist], *s.m. & f.* **1.** concert performer. **2.** soloist (in a concerto).
concerto [kɔ̃sɛrto], *s.m. Mus:* concerto; *pl. concertos.*
concesseur [kɔ̃sɛsœ:r], *s.m. Jur:* grantor.
concessible [kɔ̃sɛsibl̩], *a.* concessible.
concessif, -ive [kɔ̃sɛsif, -i:v], *a.* concessive.
concession [kɔ̃sɛsjɔ̃], *s.f.* concession. **1.** granting (of land, etc.); yielding (of point in dispute, etc.); **faire des concessions,** to make concessions; to meet (s.o.). **2.** grant, allowance; lease; **c. de terrain,** concession, grant, of land; **c. minière,** mineral claim, mining concession; *Adm:* **c. de quinze ans, de trente ans, à perpétuité,** grant (of a grave) for fifteen, thirty, years, in perpetuity.
concessionnaire [kɔ̃sɛsjɔnɛ:r]. **1.** *a.* concessionary (company, etc.). **2.** *s.* grantee (of land); claim-holder; concessionnaire, licence-holder; *Com:* agent.
concetti [kɔ̃tʃetti], *s.m.pl. Lit.Hist:* conceits, concetti.
concevable [kɔ̃səvabl̩, kɔ̃zvabl̩], *a.* conceivable, imaginable, thinkable.
concevabilité [kɔ̃s(ə)vabilite], *s.f.* conceivability.
concevoir [kɔ̃səvwa:r], *v.tr.* (*pr.p.* **concevant;** *p.p.* **conçu;** *pr.ind.* **je conçois, n. concevons, ils conçoivent;** *pr.sub.* **je conçoive, n. concevions;** *p.d.* **je concevais;** *p.h.* **je conçus;** *fu.* **je concevrai**) **1.** to conceive (child); to become pregnant; **hors d'âge de c.,** past child-bearing. **2.** (*a*) to conceive, imagine, form, devise, (idea, plan, etc.); **c. de l'amitié pour qn,** to take a liking to s.o.; **c. des soupçons contre, sur, qn,** to become suspicious of s.o.; **c. des doutes sur qch.,** to form doubts about sth.; **les espoirs que j'avais conçus à votre sujet,** the hopes I had conceived of you; **bâtiment conçu pour lancer des torpilles,** vessel designed to launch torpedoes; (*b*) **je ne conçois pas de vivre en Laponie,** I cannot imagine that I could live in Lapland; (*c*) to conceive, understand; **je ne conçois rien à cela,** I don't understand it at all; **cela se conçoit facilement,** that is easily understood; **conçoit-on!** fancy! (*d*) to word, express (letter, etc.); **dépêche ainsi conçue,** telegram worded as follows, that reads as follows; **l'article est ainsi conçu,** the terms of the article are as follows.
conche [kɔ̃:ʃ], *s.f.* **1.** *A:* conch, marine shell. **2.** *Dial:* (*in S.W. Fr.*) creek, cove.
conchier [kɔ̃ʃje], *v.tr.* to soil (with excrement); **conchié de mouches,** fly-blown.
conchifère [kɔ̃kifɛ:r]. *Moll:* **1.** *a.* conchiferous. **2.** *s.m.pl.* **conchifères,** Conchifera.
conchiforme [kɔ̃kifɔrm], *a.* conchiform, shell-shaped.
conchille [kɔ̃ki:j], *s.m. Bot:* kermes oak.
conchoïdal, -aux [kɔ̃kɔidal, -o], *a. Geom: Min:* conchoid(al).
conchoïde [kɔ̃kɔid]. **1.** *a.* conchoid(al). **2.** *s.f. Geom:* **conchoïde,** conchoid (curve).
conchostracés [kɔ̃kɔstrase], *s.m.pl. Crust:* Conchostraca.
conchotomie [kɔ̃kɔtɔmi], *s.f. Surg:* conchotomy.
conchyliculteur [kɔ̃kilikyltœ:r], *s.m.* shell-fish breeder.
conchyliculture [kɔ̃kilikylty:r], *s.f.* shell-fish breeding.
conchylien, -ienne [kɔ̃kiljɛ̃, -jɛn], *a. Geol:* conchylaceous (ground).
conchylifère [kɔ̃kilifɛ:r], *a.* conchiferous.
conchyliologie [kɔ̃kiljɔlɔʒi], *s.f. Conch:* conchology.
conchyliologique [kɔ̃kiljɔlɔʒik], *a.* conchological.
conchyliologiste [kɔ̃kiljɔlɔʒist], *s.m.* conchologist.
concierge [kɔ̃sjɛrʒ], *s.m. & f.* (house) porter, portress; doorkeeper; caretaker (of flats, etc.), *U.S:* janitor; lodge-keeper (of country estate); keeper (of prison); *F:* **quel(le) c.!** what a talker! *F:* **c'est une vraie c.,** she's a terrible gossip; *F:* **ne fais pas la c.!** don't be so nosy!
conciergerie [kɔ̃sjɛrʒəri], *s.f.* **1.** caretaker's lodge. **2.** duties, post, of caretaker. **3.** *Hist:* **la Conciergerie,** the Conciergerie (prison).
concile [kɔ̃sil], *s.m.* **1.** *Ecc:* council, synod; *Hist:* **le c. de Trente,** the Council of Trent; **les conciles de Latran,** the Lateran Councils. **2.** *pl.* **conciles,** conciliar records and decrees.
conciliable [kɔ̃siljabl̩], *a.* reconcilable (qualities, etc.).
conciliabule [kɔ̃siljabyl], *s.m.* **1.** *Ecc:* conventicle. **2.** (*a*) secret meeting, secret assembly; (*b*) *F:* confabulation.
conciliaire [kɔ̃siljɛ:r], *a.* conciliar.
conciliant [kɔ̃siljɑ̃], *a.* conciliating, conciliatory, conciliative (reply, etc.).
conciliateur, -trice [kɔ̃siljatœ:r, -tris]. **1.** *a.* conciliating. **2.** *s.* conciliator, peacemaker; appeaser.
conciliation [kɔ̃siljasjɔ̃], *s.f.* **1.** (*a*) conciliation, reconciliation; **la c. d'intérêts opposés,** the reconciliation of opposing interests; (*b*) conciliation; reconcilement; *Jur:* **ordonnance de non-conciliation,** (*in divorce suit*) order *pendente lite* regarding wife's domicile and alimony and wardship of children; **bureau de c.,** court of conciliation. **2.** good will; **esprit de c.,** conciliatory spirit.
conciliatoire [kɔ̃siljatwa:r], *a.* conciliatory (measure, etc.).
concilier [kɔ̃silje], *v.tr.* (*p.d. & pr.sub.* **n. conciliions, v. conciliiez**) **1.** to conciliate, reconcile (two parties, etc.); **c. un différend,** to adjust a difference, to bring about an agreement; **c. des textes,** to harmonize, reconcile, texts. **2.** to win, gain (hearts, esteem, etc.); **se c. qn, la faveur de qn,** to gain s.o.'s good will; **se c. les auditeurs,** to win the good feeling of, to win over, the audience.
se concilier, to agree (**avec,** with); **cela ne se concilie pas avec mes idées,** that does not fit in with my ideas.
concis [kɔ̃si], *a.* concise, terse.
concision [kɔ̃sizjɔ̃], *s.f.* concision, conciseness, brevity; terseness; **avec c.,** concisely; tersely.
concitoyen, -enne [kɔ̃sitwajɛ̃, -ɛn], *s.* **1.** fellow-citizen, fellow-townsman, -townswoman. **2.** fellow-countryman, -countrywoman.
concitoyenneté [kɔ̃sitwajɛnte], *s.f.* fellow-citizenship.
conclave [kɔ̃kla:v], *s.m. Ecc:* conclave.
conclaviste [kɔ̃klavist], *s.m. Ecc:* conclavist.
concluant [kɔ̃klyɑ̃], *a.* conclusive, decisive (experiment, etc.); **peu c., non c.,** inconclusive.
conclure [kɔ̃kly:r], *v.tr.* (*pr.p.* **concluant;** *p.p.* **conclu;** *pr.ind.* **je conclus, n. concluons, ils concluent;** *p.d.* **je concluais;** *p.h.* **je conclus;** *fu.* **je conclurai**) to conclude. **1.** (*a*) to end, finish; to bring (speech, etc.) to an end, to a conclusion; (*b*) to arrive at (an understanding); **c. la paix,** to conclude peace, to arrange a peace; **l'affaire fut conclue,** the matter was settled, fixed up; **c. un accord,** to conclude an agreement; *Fin:* **l'emprunt sera conclu pour vingt ans,** the loan shall be for a term of twenty years; **c. un marché,** to drive, strike, clinch, a bargain; **c. un engagement,** to enter into an engagement; **c'est une affaire conclue,** (i) that's settled; (ii) it's a bargain; *F:* done; (*c*) *abs.* to come to a conclusion. **2.** *v.ind.tr.* (*a*) to decide, infer; **qu'en concluez-vous?** what do you infer, conclude, from that? **il en conclut tout de suit que . . .,** he jumped to the conclusion that . . .; **nous avons conclu que . . .,** we have come to the conclusion that . . .; (*b*) **c. à qch.,** to conclude, declare, judge, in favour of sth.; **c. aux mesures de rigueur,** to conclude in favour of rigorous measures; **arguments concluant à l'ajournement,** arguments which concluded in favour of postponement; **c. à une opération immédiate,** to come to the conclusion, to decide, that an immediate operation is necessary; **le jury a conclu au suicide,** the jury returned a verdict of suicide; **son avocat a conclu à ce que la cause soit remise à huitaine,** his counsel moved that the case be adjourned for a week; **c. à faire qch.,** (i) to decide to do sth.; (ii) *occ.* to end by doing sth.
conclusif, -ive [kɔ̃klyzif, -i:v], *a.* conclusive.
conclusion [kɔ̃klyzjɔ̃], *s.f.* conclusion. **1.** close, end (of speech, meeting, etc.); **la c. de l'affaire, ce fut que . . .,** the upshot of the business was that . . .. **2.** concluding, settlement (of treaty, agreement, etc.). **3.** (*a*) inference; **tirer une c. de qch.,** to draw an inference, a conclusion, from sth.; **tirer des conclusions hâtives,** to jump to conclusions; **formuler une c.,** to make an inference, **en c. . . .,** in short . . ., when all is said and done . . .; *F:* **c., il n'y a rien à faire,** in short, there's nothing to be done; (*b*) *Jur:* finding, decision; **les conclusions du jury,** the finding(s) of the jury; **le jury se retire pour formuler ses conclusions,** the jury retire to find their verdict; **conclusions contradictoires,** inconsistent findings; (*c*) *pl. Jur:* pleas, (points at) issue; **accepter les conclusions,** to join issue; **conclusions de l'avocat (en dommages-intérêts),** statement of claim; **plaise au tribunal adopter mes conclusions,** that is my case, my Lord.
concoction [kɔ̃kɔksjɔ̃], *s.f. A:* digestion (of food in stomach).
concolore [kɔ̃kɔlɔ:r], *a.* self-coloured; *Ent:* concolorous.
concombre [kɔ̃kɔ̃:br̩], *s.m.* **1.** *Bot:* cucumber. **2.** *Echin:* **c. de mer,** sea cucumber.
concomitamment [kɔ̃kɔmitamɑ̃], *adv.* concomitantly.
concomitance [kɔ̃kɔmitɑ̃:s], *s.f.* concomitance, co-existence.
concomitant [kɔ̃kɔmitɑ̃], *a.* concomitant, attendant, accompanying (circumstance, symptoms, etc.).
concordance [kɔ̃kɔrdɑ̃:s], *s.f.* **1.** concordance, agreement (of evidence, etc.). **2.** *Gram:* concord, agreement (of adjectives, etc.); sequence (of tenses). **3.** (Bible) concordance.
concordant [kɔ̃kɔrdɑ̃], *a.* concordant, agreeing, harmonious; **témoignages concordants,** concordant, harmonious, depositions; *Geol:* **couches concordantes,** conformable strata.
concordat [kɔ̃kɔrda], *s.m.* **1.** *Ecc.Hist:* concordat, agreement (between pope and sovereign). **2.** *Com:* (bankrupt's) certificate; **c. préventif (à la faillite),** (i) scheme of composition; (ii) composition, legal settlement (between merchant and creditors).
concordataire [kɔ̃kɔrdatɛ:r], *a. & s.* **1.** *Ecc.Hist:* (prelate, church) accepting the Concordat of 1801. **2.** *Com:* certificated (bankrupt).
concorde [kɔ̃kɔrd], *s.f.* concord, harmony; **maintenir la c.,** to keep the peace; **rétablir la c. entre des ennemis,** to establish a reconciliation between, to reconcile, to make peace between, enemies.
concorder [kɔ̃kɔrde], *v.i.* **1.** (*of dates, evidence*) to agree, to tally (**avec,** with). **2.** *Com:* to compound (with creditors).
concourant [kɔ̃kurɑ̃], *a.* concurrent, converging (lines, etc.).
concourir [kɔ̃kuri:r], *v.i.* (*conj. like* COURIR) **1.** (*of lines, etc.*) to converge, to concur; (*of events, etc.*) to concur, to coincide. **2.** to combine, unite; **c. avec qn,** to co-operate with s.o.; **c. à qch.,** to contribute to sth.; **les témoignages concourent à prouver que . . .,** all evidence goes to prove that . . .; **ses ennemis concourent à le ruiner,** his enemies conspire to ruin him. **3.** to compete; **c. (avec qn) pour un prix, pour une place,** to compete (with s.o.) for a prize, for a post. **4.** *Jur:* to rank equally (with other creditors, etc.).
concours [kɔ̃ku:r], *s.m.* **1.** coming together, meeting; (*a*) *A: & Lit:* concourse, gathering (of people); **grand c. de curieux,** great concourse of sightseers; (*b*) concourse, conjunction, (of circumstances); coincidence (of events); **par un c. de circonstances,** by a combination of circumstances; (*c*) *Geom:* **point de c.,** point of convergence, of concurrence. **2.** co-operation, assistance, help; **prêter (son) c. à qn,** to help s.o.; to collaborate with s.o.; to give s.o. a hand; **emprunter le c. de qn,** to get s.o. to help one; **par le c. de . . .,** through the instrumentality, the agency, of . . .; **son c. fut décisif,** his intervention was the deciding factor; *Th: etc:* **avec le c. de . . .,** with the following cast . . .; those taking part were . . .; **avec l'aimable c. de X,** assisted by X; by courtesy of X. **3.** (*a*) competition; competitive examination; *Sp:* field events; **mettre un prix au c.,** to offer a prize for competition; **c. de musique,** band contest; **c. de tir,** shooting competition, contest; *Sp:* **c. de saut en longueur,** long jump event; *Golf:* **c. par coups,** stroke play; *Sch:* **c. général,** competition between all the *lycées* at *baccalauréat* level; **c. d'admission, d'entrée,** entrance examination; **admis sur, par**

voie de, après, c., admitted by competitive examination; *F:* **bête à c.,** examination fiend; **hors c.,** (i) hors concours; (ii) *F:* ace player, world-beater; (*b*) (competitive) show; **c. agricole,** agricultural show; **c. hippique,** horse show; *Aut:* **c. d'élégance,** concours d'élégance. **4.** *Com: Jur:* equality of rank and rights (between creditors).

concréfaction [kɔ̃kreʃaksjɔ̃], *s.f. Metall:* sintering.

concrescible [kɔ̃krɛs(s)ibl̩], *a.* concrescible, coagulable, congealable.

concrescence [kɔ̃krɛsɑ̃:s], *s.f. Bot:* concrescence.

concrescent [kɔ̃krɛsɑ̃], *a. Bot:* concrete, concrescent.

concret, -ète [kɔ̃krɛ, -ɛt], *a.* **1.** concrete, solid (oil, etc.); **suc c.,** dry juice. **2.** *Gram: Log:* concrete (term, etc.); **cas c.,** actual case, concrete example. **3.** *s.m.* (the) concrete (as opposed to the abstract).

concréter [kɔ̃krete], *v.tr.* **(je concrète, n. concrétons; je concréterai)** to solidify, make concrete; to congeal (blood, oil).

se concréter, to concrete, coagulate, set.

concrétion [kɔ̃kresjɔ̃], *s.f.* **1.** (*a*) coagulation; (*b*) caking. **2.** concrete mass, concretion; *Med:* **concrétions biliaires,** biliary concretions; **concrétions calcaires,** chalk stones.

concrétionnaire [kɔ̃kresjɔnɛ:r], *a. Geol:* concretionary (rock, etc.).

concrétionné [kɔ̃kresjɔne], *a. Geol:* **roches sédimentaires concrétionnées,** sedimentary rocks in which concretions have formed.

concrétionnement [kɔ̃kresjɔnmɑ̃], *s.m. Geol:* (the) formation of concretions.

concrétionner [kɔ̃kresjɔne], *v.tr. El.E:* to sinter (lamp filament).

se concrétionner, to form into concretions, to cake together.

concrétisation [kɔ̃kretizasjɔ̃], *s.f.* concretization.

concrétiser [kɔ̃kretize], *v.tr.* to put (idea, question) in concrete form, to concretize.

se concrétiser, nos projets commencent à se c., our plans are beginning to take shape.

concubin, -ine [kɔ̃kybɛ̃, -in]. **1.** *a. & s.m.* concubinary. **2.** *s.f.* **concubine,** (i) concubine; (ii) kept mistress.

concubinage [kɔ̃kybina:ʒ], *s.m.* concubinage; **vivre en c.,** to live together (as man and wife).

concubinaire [kɔ̃kybinɛ:r], *a. & s.m. & f. A:* concubinary.

concubinairement [kɔ̃kybinɛrmɑ̃], *adv. A:* **vivre c.,** to live in concubinage.

concubinat [kɔ̃kybina], *s.m.* concubinage.

concubiner [kɔ̃kybine], *v.i.* to cohabit, to live in sin.

concupiscence [kɔ̃kypisɑ̃:s], *s.f.* concupiscence; lusts of the flesh.

concupiscent [kɔ̃kypisɑ̃], *a.* concupiscent; lustful.

concupiscible [kɔ̃kypisibl̩], *a. Phil: Theol:* concupiscible.

concurremment [kɔ̃kyramɑ̃], *adv.* **1.** concurrently, jointly; **agir c. avec qn,** to act jointly, in conjunction, with s.o. **2.** *Jur:* (*of creditors*) **venir c.,** to rank equally. **3.** competitively, in rivalry, in competition **(avec,** with).

concurrence [kɔ̃kyrɑ̃:s], *s.f.* **1.** (*a*) concurrence, coincidence (of events); (*b*) *Jur:* **créanciers qui viennent en c.,** creditors with equality of rights, who rank equally; (*c*) *Com: etc:* **(jusqu') à c. de . . .,** to the amount of . . ., not exceeding . . ., up to a maximum of . . .; to the extent of . . .. **2.** competition, rivalry; **c. vitale,** struggle for existence; **entrer en c. avec qn,** to enter into competition with s.o.; **capacité de c.,** competitive power; *Com:* **faire c. à qn, à qch.,** to compete with s.o., with sth.; **prix défiant toute c.,** prices defying all competition; **articles sans c.,** unrivalled goods.

concurrencer [kɔ̃kyrɑ̃se], *v.tr.* **(je concurrençai(s); n. concurrençons)** to compete with (s.o., sth.) (in trade, in the open market).

concurrent, -ente [kɔ̃kyrɑ̃, -ɑ̃:t]. **1.** *a.* (*a*) (*of forces, actions, etc.*) co-operative, contributing to the same effect; (*b*) competitive, competing, rival (industries, etc.). **2.** *s.* competitor, competitress (for prize, etc.); candidate (for post, etc.); **il a un c.,** he has a candidate running against him.

concurrentiel, -ielle [kɔ̃kyrɑ̃sjɛl], *a.* rival, competing, competitive (companies, etc.).

concussion [kɔ̃kysjɔ̃], *s.f.* **1.** misappropriation (of public funds). **2.** extortion (by public official); peculation; *A:* concussion.

concussionnaire [kɔ̃kysjɔnɛ:r], *a. & s.* (official) guilty of (i) misappropriation; (ii) extortion; peculator; *A:* concussionary.

condamnable [kɔ̃dɑnabl̩], *a.* condemnable, blamable, blameworthy.

condamnateur, -trice [kɔ̃dɑnatœ:r, -tris]. **1.** *a.* condemning, condemnatory. **2.** *s.* condemner.

condamnation [kɔ̃dɑnasjɔ̃], *s.f.* condemnation. **1.** (*a*) *Jur:* conviction, judgment, sentence; **c. d'un voleur,** conviction of a thief; **c. à vie,** life sentence, sentence for life; **c. à mort,** death sentence, capital sentence; **prononcer c.,** to pronounce, pass, sentence or judgment; **subir sa condamnation,** to undergo one's sentence; **subir c.,** to accept, acquiesce, in the judgment pronounced on one; **passer c.,** to admit that one is in the wrong; **payer, acquitter, les condamnations,** to pay the damages, fines, costs; **purger une c.,** to serve one's sentence; (*b*) putting (of door, window) out of use; *s.a.* POIGNÉE 2. **2.** reproof, blame, censure.

condamnatoire [kɔ̃dɑnatwa:r], *a.* condemnatory.

condamné, -ée [kɔ̃dɑne], *s.* convict; condemned man, woman.

condamner [kɔ̃dɑne], *v.tr.* to condemn. **1.** (*a*) *Jur:* to convict, sentence, pass judgment on (criminal, etc.); **c. qn à mort,** to condemn, sentence, s.o. to death; **il est condamné à mort,** he is under sentence of death; **c. qn à trois mois de prison,** to pass sentence of three months' imprisonment on s.o.; **c. qn à cinq cents francs d'amende,** to fine s.o. five hundred francs; **être condamné à un mois de prison,** *F:* to get thirty days; **condamné à vivre sans espoir,** condemned, doomed, to lead a hopeless existence; **tentative condamnée à l'insuccès,** attempt doomed to failure; **le médecin l'a condamné,** the doctor has given him up; (*b*) **c. une porte, une fenêtre,** (i) to block up, fill in, a door, a window; to board up a window; (ii) to forbid the use of a door, window; to nail, screw up a door; *Nau:* **c. un panneau,** to batten down a hatch; (*c*) **c. sa porte,** to be "not at home" to visitors; (*at university*) to sport one's oak. **2.** to blame, censure, reprove (s.o., s.o.'s conduct, a book, etc.).

condensabilité [kɔ̃dɑ̃sabilite], *s.f.* condensability.

condensable [kɔ̃dɑ̃sabl̩], *a.* condensable.

condensant [kɔ̃dɑ̃sɑ̃], *a.* condensing.

condensateur, -trice [kɔ̃dɑ̃satœ:r, -tris]. **1.** *a. El: etc:* condensing (agent); *s.a.* MICROPHONE 2. **2.** *s.m. El: Opt: etc:* condenser; capacitor; *Opt:* **c. d'Abbe,** Abbe condenser (of a microscope); **c. prismatique de Fresnel,** prismatic condenser; **c. d'antenne,** antenna capacitor; **c. cardioïde,** cardioid condenser; *El:* **c. à plaques, à plateaux,** plate condenser; **c. réglable, variable,** variable condenser; *W.Tel:* **c. d'accord, de syntonisation,** tuning condenser; **condensateurs à blocs combinés,** ganged condensers; *El: etc:* **c. d'appoint, de correction,** trimming capacitor; trimmer-capacitor; **c. d'arrêt,** blocking, stopping, capacitor; **c. de couplage,** coupling capacitor; **c. de découplage, de dérivation,** by-pass capacitor; **c. d'équilibrage,** balancing capacitor; trimmer; **c. de filtrage,** smoothing capacitor; **c. de grille,** grid capacitor; **c. de réaction,** feedback capacitor; **c. double, c. triple,** two-cell, three-cell, capacitor; **c. en série,** series capacitor; **c. polarisé,** polarized capacitor; **c. neutrodyne,** neutralizing condenser.

condensation [kɔ̃dɑ̃sasjɔ̃], *s.f.* condensation, condensing; **machine (à vapeur) à c.,** condensing engine; **sans c.,** non-condensing (engine); **eau de c.,** condensate; *Av:* **traînée de c.,** condensation trail; *Psy:* **c. des idées,** coalescing, blending, condensation, of ideas.

condensé [kɔdɑ̃se]. **1.** *a.* condensed; **lait c.,** condensed milk. **2.** *s.m. Journ:* résumé (of a literary work); digest.

condenser [kɔ̃dɑ̃se], *v.tr.* to condense (gas, lecture, etc.) (en, into); **c. un article,** to cut down an article.

se condenser, to condense.

condenseur [kɔ̃dɑ̃sœ:r], *s.m. Mch: Gasm:* condenser; *Mch:* **c. par surface,** surface condenser; **c. à siphon,** syphon condenser; **c. à injection, c. à, par, mélange,** jet condenser; **c. à récupération,** regenerative condenser; **c. à ruissellement,** evaporative condenser, counter-current condenser; **c. à simple effet,** single action condenser; **c. tubulaire,** condenser by contact; **baromètre de c.,** condenser gauge; (*in refrigerator etc.*) **c. à air,** condenser.

condescendance [kɔ̃dɛsɑ̃dɑ̃:s], *s.f.* **1.** (gracious) condescension. **2.** act of condescension.

condescendant [kɔ̃dɛsɑ̃dɑ̃], *a.* condescending, gracious.

condescendre [kɔ̃dɛsɑ̃:dr̩], *v.i.* to condescend **(à faire qch.,** to do sth.); **c. aux désirs de qn,** to yield to, comply graciously with, s.o.'s wishes.

condiction [kɔ̃diksjɔ̃], *s.f.* (*a*) *Rom.Jur:* condictio(n); (*b*) *Jur:* action brought against a person for specific offences.

condiment [kɔ̃dimɑ̃], *s.m. Cu:* condiment, seasoning.

condisciple [kɔ̃disipl̩], *s.m.* fellow-student, school-fellow.

condit [kɔ̃di], *s.m.* **1.** candied fruit, candied peel. **2.** *Vet:* confection, electuary.

condition [kɔ̃disjɔ̃], *s.f.* condition. **1.** (*a*) state; **examiner la c. d'un bâtiment,** to look into the state of a building; **en c.,** in (good) condition; **cheval en c.,** horse in condition, in good fettle; **équipe en excellente c.,** team in splendid fettle; in top form; **mettre en c.,** to train; *Com:* to condition; **être en c. de faire qch.,** to be in a position, in a fit state, to do sth.; **la c. du pauvre,** the poor man's lot; (*b*) *pl.* conditions, circumstances; **être dans les conditions requises pour agir,** to be entitled to act; **voyager dans les, aux, meilleures conditions,** to travel under the most favourable conditions; **dans ces conditions . . .,** in these circumstances . . .; this being so . . .; (*c*) rank, station, status, position; *A: & Lit:* estate; **la c. d'homme libre,** the state of being a free man; **la c. humaine,** the human condition; **personne de c.,** person of rank; **gens de c.,** people of fashion, of quality; **gens de simple c.,** persons in humble circumstances; **épouser une jeune fille de sa c.,** to marry a girl of one's own station, of one's own class; **améliorer sa c.,** to better oneself; **déchu de sa haute c.,** fallen from his high estate. **2.** condition, stipulation; *pl.* terms; **conditions d'une vente,** clauses governing a sale; **conditions d'un contrat,** terms, articles, of a contract; **c. provisionnelle,** proviso; **faites vos conditions vous-même,** make, name, your own terms; **conditions de faveur,** preferential terms; **c. à remplir, c. nécessaire, c. requise,** requirement, qualification; **conditions d'exploitation, de fonctionnement, d'utilisation,** operating conditions; **faire de meilleures conditions à qn,** to give s.o. better terms; **imposer une c.,** to lay down a stipulation; **poser des conditions à qn,** to impose conditions on s.o.; **imposer de dures conditions à qn,** to drive a hard bargain with s.o.; **offre sans c.,** unconditional offer; *Com:* **sans conditions, sans c. aucune,** unconditionally; *F:* no strings attached; **se rendre sans c.,** to surrender unconditionally; **signer un engagement sous c.,** to sign an agreement conditionally, provisionally; **accepter, mais à c.,** to accept but only conditionally, provisionally; **marchandises à, sous, c.,** goods (i) on sale or return; (ii) on approval; *F:* on appro; **à cette c., à ces conditions, j'accepte,** on this understanding, on these terms, I accept; *Nau:* **conditions d'affrètement,** terms under which a ship is chartered; *Log: Mth:* **c. nécessaire et suffisante,** necessary and sufficient condition; *prep.phr.* **à condition de** + *inf.* **attendre est sage à c. d'attendre quelque chose,** it is wise to wait providing, provided, that one has something to wait for; *conj. phr.* **à condition que** + *ind.* or *sub.*, on condition, on the understanding that, provided that, providing that. **3.** *O:* **être en c., entrer en c. (chez qn),** to be in service, to go into service (with s.o.).

conditionnalisme [kɔ̃disjɔnalism], *s.m. Theol:* conditionalism.

conditionné [kɔ̃ndisjɔne], *a.* **1.** (*a*) (*of work, goods*) in (good, bad) condition; **à air c.,** air-conditioned; **mal c.,** (i) out of condition; (ii) badly done, botched; (*b*) *Com:* packed; **viande conditionnée,** prepackaged meat. **2.** *Log: Med: Psy:* conditioned (proposition, reflex).

conditionnel, -elle [kɔ̃disjɔnɛl]. **1.** *a.* conditional (promise, etc., *Gram:* mood); *Psy:* **stimulus c.,** stimulus provoking a conditioned reflex. **2.** *s.m. Gram:* conditional (mood).

conditionnellement [kɔ̃disjɔnɛlmɑ̃], *adv.* conditionally.

conditionnement [kɔ̃disjɔnmɑ̃], *s.m.* **1.** (*a*) *Mec.E: etc:* conditioning (of air, etc.); *Ind:* conditioning (of silk, etc.), *U.S:* processing; (*b*) *Com:* (i) packaging; (ii) package. **2.** *Psy:* conditioning.

conditionner [kɔ̃disjɔne], *v.tr.* **1.** to condition (wool, silk, air, etc.). **2.** to put (goods) into good condition; to season (wood). **3.** to condition; **tout ce qui conditionne les lois,** everything that conditions laws. **4.** *Com:* to package. **5.** *Psy:* to establish a new mode of behaviour in a living being; to condition (s.o., an animal).

conditionneur, -euse [kɔ̃disjɔnœ:r, -ø:z], *s.* (*a*) *s.m.* **c. d'air,** air-conditioner, *U.S:* conditioner; (*b*) *s.m. & f. Com:* packager, packer.

condoléance [kɔ̃dɔleɑ̃ːs], *s.f.* (*often in pl.*) condolence; **lettre de c.,** letter of condolence; **veuillez agréer mes sincères condoléances,** accept my sincere sympathy; **offrir, présenter, ses condoléances,** to offer one's condolences, one's sympathy.

condom [kɔ̃dɔ̃], *s.m. Hyg:* contraceptive sheath; *P:* French letter.

condominium [kɔ̃dɔminjɔm], *s.m. Pol:* condominium.

condomois, -oise [kɔ̃dɔmwa, -waːz], *a. & s.* **1.** *Geog:* (native, inhabitant) of Condom. **2.** *s.m.* the country around Condom. **3.** *s.m.* the wines and spirits of this region.

condor [kɔ̃dɔːr], *s.m.* **1.** *Orn:* condor; **c. papa,** king vulture. **2.** *Num:* doubloon.

condottiere [kɔ̃dɔtjɛːr], *s.m. Hist:* condottiere; *pl. condottieri.*

conductance [kɔ̃dyktɑ̃ːs], *s.f. El:* conductance, conductivity; **c. de fuite, de perte,** leakage; **c. de transfert,** transconductance; **c. mutuelle,** mutual conductance; **c. thermique,** thermal conductance.

conducteur, -trice [kɔ̃dyktœːr, -tris]. **1.** *s.* (*a*) leader, guide, conductor, conductress (of men, etc.); (*b*) **c. de bestiaux,** cattle-driver; drover; (*c*) driver (of lorry, etc.); *F:* **c. du dimanche,** weekend driver; (*d*) **c. d'une machine,** machine operator, machine minder; **c. de travaux,** clerk of the works, works foreman; **c. de(s) travaux publics,** assistant civil-engineer; (*e*) *Navy:* (*of ship*) **c. de flottille,** flotilla leader; (*f*) *Sw.Fr:* **c. d'orchestre,** conductor (of an orchestra). **2.** *a.* (*a*) *Ph: El:* conducting, transmitting; **mauvais c.,** non-conducting (substance); **tuyau c.,** conduit; *El:* **tige conductrice,** conducting rod; **lacune conductrice,** conduction hole; (*b*) **fil c.,** clew (through labyrinth); (*c*) *Mec.E:* driving; *s.a.* BRIN 4. **3.** *s.m.* (*a*) *El: Ph:* conductor (of heat, electricity, etc.); **mauvais c.,** bad conductor, non-conductor; **c. souple,** flex (wire); (*b*) *El.E:* lead (wire), main; **c. auxiliaire,** branch (wire), tap; **c. blindé,** screened conductor; **c. chargé, c. en charge,** live conductor; **c. d'alimentation,** supply lead, power lead, power conductor; **c. d'arrivée,** electric lead, lead(ing)-in wire, cable; **c. de retour,** return wire; **c. de terre,** earth or ground connection; **c. neutre,** neutral wire or conductor; **c. principal,** main (conductor); **c. résistant,** resistor conductor; **c. unique,** single wire; (*c*) *Min:* leader (vein).

conductibilité [kɔ̃dyktibilite], *s.f. El: Ph:* conductibility, conductivity; **c. spécifique,** (specific) conductance.

conductible [kɔ̃dyktibl], *a. El: Ph:* conductive.

conductimètre [kɔ̃dyktimetr], *s.m.* conductimeter, conductometer.

conductimétrie [kɔ̃dyktimetri], *s.m. El:* conductimetry.

conductimétrique [kɔ̃dyktimetrik], *a. El:* conductometric, conductimetric.

conduction [kɔ̃dyksjɔ̃], *s.f.* **1.** *El:* conduction; **courant de c.,** conduction current; **c. gazeuse,** gaseous conduction; **c. par lacunes,** hole conduction; **décharge de c.,** conductive discharge (of condenser). **2.** *Physiol:* conduction (of excitation through living tissue); **récepteur à c. osseuse,** osophone.

conductivité [kɔ̃dyktivite], *s.f. Ph:* conductivity; **c. spécifique,** conductance; **c. équivalente,** equivalent conductivity; **c. moléculaire,** molecular conductivity; **c. thermique,** heat conductivity, thermal conductivity.

conduire [kɔ̃dɥiːr], *v.tr.* (*pr.p.* **conduisant;** *p.p.* **conduit;** *pr.ind.* **je conduis, il conduit, n. conduisons, ils conduisent;** *p.d.* **je conduisais;** *p.h.* **je conduisis;** *fu.* **je conduirai**) **1.** (*a*) to conduct, escort (party, etc.); to lead (horse, blind man, troops, etc.); to guide (child's first steps, etc.); **c. qn à la gare,** to take, drive, s.o. to the station; **on le conduisit à sa chambre,** he was shown to his room; **c. à bien une affaire,** to bring off a piece of business; *abs.* **chemin qui conduit à la ville,** road that leads to the town; **quel est le chemin qui conduit à la gare?** which is the way to the station? **c. à un résultat,** to lead to a result; **la santé conduit au bonheur,** health is conducive to happiness; (*b*) **c. qn à faire qch.,** to lead, induce, prevail on, s.o. to do sth.; **je fus conduit à conclure que . . .,** I was led to the conclusion that . . . . **2.** (*a*) to drive (horse, carriage, car, etc.); *abs.* **savez-vous c.?** can you drive? **il conduit bien,** he is a good driver; *F:* **c. comme un manche,** to be a rotten driver; *s.a.* PERMIS 2; (*b*) to steer, row, manage (boat); *s.a.* BARQUE 1. **3.** (*a*) convey; **c. de l'eau par des tuyaux,** to convey water by pipes; (*b*) to conduct; **canal qui conduit l'eau au moulin,** canal that carries the water to the mill; **c. un canal jusqu'à la mer,** to carry a canal as far as the sea; **corps qui conduit bien l'électricité,** good conductor of electricity. **4.** to conduct, direct, manage, supervise, attend to (sth.); **c. une maison,** to manage, run, a house; **c. un orchestre,** to conduct an orchestra; **c. une machine,** to operate a machine; **c. un arbre,** to train a tree; **c. toute l'affaire,** *F:* to boss the show; *Games:* **c. le jeu,** to be on top.

se conduire. 1. être d'âge à se c., to be old enough to take care of oneself. **2.** to conduct oneself, to behave; **se mal c.,** to misconduct oneself, to misbehave; **se c. bien, mal, avec qn,** to behave well, badly, towards s.o.; to treat s.o. well, badly, shabbily; **se c. en honnête homme,** to behave as a gentleman; **je n'aime pas sa façon de se c.,** I don't like the way she goes on, carries on; **quelle manière de se c.!** what a way to behave!

conduit [kɔ̃dɥi], *s.m.* (*a*) *Tchn:* conduit, duct, pipe, passage, channel; *Civ.E: Mec.E:* **c. à air, c. d'aérage, c. d'aération,** air-duct, air-pipe, air-passage; **c. de ventilation,** ventilating passage, ventilation-shaft; **c. coudé,** bent pipe, elbow; **c. d'eau (d'un toit),** leader; **c. d'échappement,** exhaust pipe, blast pipe, blast main; **c. de dérivation,** by-pass passage, tube; **c. de fumée,** smoke pipe; **c. souterrain,** underground pipe, underground duct, conduit; *Hyd.E:* **c. de décharge (d'eau),** (i) delivery canal; (ii) waste (water) pipe; drain; *Mch:* **c. d'admission de vapeur,** steam inlet, steam feed pipe; **c. de balayage,** scavenging duct; **c. de vapeur,** steam passage, way; **c. de régulateur de pression,** pressure balance duct; *Nau:* **c. de chaîne, d'ancre,** chain pipe, spill pipe; **c. de dalot,** scupper pipe, shoot; **c. pour cordage(s), pour amarre(s),** fair-lead(er); **c. de soute,** bunker pipe; (*b*) *Physiol:* **c. auditif,** auditory meatus; **c. salivaire,** salivary duct; (*c*) shoot (for coal, ashes, etc.); (*d*) *El:* **c. isolant,** insulating trough; *W.Tel:* **c. d'entrée,** leading-in tube; (*e*) ink-feed (of fountain pen).

conduite [kɔ̃dɥit], *s.f.* **1.** (*a*) conducting, leading, escorting (of s.o.); **faire la c. à qn,** to escort s.o.; **faire un bout de c. à qn,** to set s.o. on his way, to go part of the way with s.o.; *s.a.* GRENOBLE; (*b*) driving (of cart, motor car, etc.); **c. tout terrain, à travers champs,** cross-country driving; navigation (of boat, balloon); *Aut:* drive; **c. à gauche,** left-hand drive; **leçons de c.,** driving lessons; **c. intérieure,** (i) *Aut:* saloon, *U.S:* sedan; (ii) *Av:* enclosed cockpit, closed cabin; (*c*) treatment, conduct (of play, poem); (*d*) *El:* conduction (of current); (*e*) **c. de flammes,** flame baffling. **2.** direction, management, control (of affairs, etc.); command (of army, fleet, etc.); **être sous la c. de qn,** to be (i) under s.o.'s leadership; (ii) under s.o.'s guidance, in s.o.'s care or charge; **sous la c. de la bonne ils font une promenade,** escorted by the nurse they go for a walk; *Sw.Fr:* **orchestre sous la c. de . . .,** orchestra conducted by . . .; **c. des travaux,** superintendence of works; **c. d'une maison,** management of a house; *Mch:* **c. du feu,** stoking, firing (of boilers); **la c. des dispensaires est assurée par . . .,** the work of the dispensaries is carried out by . . .; *Mil:* **c. à tenir en cas d'attaque ennemie,** action to be taken in case of enemy attack; **c. des opérations,** conduct, control, of operations; **c. des troupes,** leading of troops; leadership; **c. du combat,** battle procedure; **c. du feu, du tir,** fire control; **appareil de c. de tir,** predictor. **3.** conduct, behaviour; *O:* **avoir de la c.,** to be steady, well-behaved; *O:* **il n'a pas de c.,** he cannot conduct himself, he is given to loose living; **il faut changer de c.,** you must turn over a new leaf; **sa belle c. dans la bataille,** his gallant bearing in the battle; *s.a.* ACHETER 1; **ligne de c.,** line of conduct; policy; course; **c'est ma seule ligne de c.,** it is the only course open to me; **c. honteuse,** disgraceful conduct; **c. inconvenante,** improper conduct; **c. séditieuse,** riotous conduct; **mauvaise c.,** misbehaviour; **avoir une mauvaise c.,** to misbehave. **4.** (*a*) pipe, conduit, duct; piping, tubing; **c. à air, d'air,** air-duct, -passage, -line; air-hose; **c. d'aérage, d'aération,** breather-line, air-channel; **c. d'amenée, d'alimentation,** delivery-pipe, feed-pipe, supply-pipe; **c. d'aspiration,** suction-pipe; **c. en élévation,** standpipe; **c. de cheminée,** flue; **c. d'eau,** water-pipe, -main(s); **c. de gaz,** gas-pipe, -main(s); **c. de gaz naturel** = **GAZODUC;** **c. d'évacuation des fumées,** waste-heat flue; **c. d'huile,** oil-duct; **c. de produits pétroliers** = OLÉODUC; **c. de refoulement,** delivery-pipe (of pump); **c. de vapeur,** steam-pipe; **c. maîtresse, c. principale,** main; **c. souple,** hose, flexible pipe; **tuyau de c.,** conduit pipe; **tuyau de c. de la vapeur,** steam-feed piping; *Metall:* **c. de vent,** blast-pipe, -main; *Hyd.E: Hyd.El: etc:* **c. forcée,** penstock, (pressure) pipe-line; **c. libre,** (open) channel; **c. montante (d'une tuyauterie d'eau chaude de ménage),** flow-pipe; (*b*) *El: Elcs:* conduit, duct, feeder; **c. multitubulaire,** line of ducts; *Tg:* **c. sous-marine,** submarine cable; *El:* **c. secondaire,** sub-feeder.

conduplicatif, -ive [kɔ̃dyplikatif, -iːv], *a. Bot:* conduplicate.

condurango [kɔ̃dyrɑ̃go], *s.m. Bot:* condurango.

condyle [kɔ̃dil], *s.m. Anat:* condyle.

condylien, -ienne [kɔ̃diljɛ̃, -jɛn], *a. Anat:* condylar.

condyloïde [kɔ̃dilɔid], *a. Anat:* condyloid.

condylome [kɔ̃dilom], *s.m. Med:* condyloma.

cône [koːn], *s.m.* **1.** (*a*) *Geom:* cone; **c. de révolution,** cone of revolution; **c. droit,** right cone; **c. droit (à base) circulaire,** right circular cone; **c. oblique,** oblique cone; **c. parabolique,** curvilinear cone; **sommet d'un c.,** vertex of a cone; *s.a.* TRONC 3, TRONQUÉ; (*b*) *Geol:* cone (of volcano); **c. adventif,** parasitic cone, lateral cone; **c. de cendres, de scories,** cinder cone; **c. de coulée, de lave, c. lavique,** lava cone; **c. d'éboulis, c. d'éboulement,** scree, talus; **c. d'éruption,** cone of eruption; **c. de débris,** (i) tuff-cone (of volcano); (ii) debris cone (of glacier); **c. de déjection, c. d'alluvions,** alluvial cone, alluvial fan; **c. emboîté,** nested cone, ringed cone, crater; **c. mixte,** composite cone; (*c*) *Astr:* **c. d'ombre, de pénombre,** umbra, penumbra (of a planet, etc.); (*d*) *Opt:* **c. de lumière,** cone of light, of rays; **ouverture maximum, minimum, du c. de lumière,** cone of light of maximum, minimum, angular extent; (*e*) *Nau:* **c. de mauvais temps, de tempête,** storm cone; **c. de signalisation,** signal cone. **2.** (*shape*) taper; **tailler qch. en c.,** to taper sth.; **en forme de c.,** cone-shaped, tapering. **3.** *Mil:* (*a*) *Artil:* **c. de dispersion,** cone of dispersion, cone of spread; **c. de forcement,** forcing cone; (*b*) *Exp:* **c. de charge (d'une torpille, d'un missile),** warhead (of torpedo, missile); **c. de charge atomique, nucléaire,** atomic, nuclear, warhead; **c. de charge classique, conventionnel,** conventional warhead; **c. d'exercice,** dummy head, practice head. **4.** (*a*) *Mec.E:* **c. (poulie),** cone(-pulley); **c. à corde,** cone-sheave, grooved cone; **c. à courroie,** belt-cone; **c. à gradins,** step-cone, stepped cone; **c. à deux, trois, quatre, gradins,** two-, three-, four-step cone; **c. conduit,** driven cone; **c. denté,** toothed-cone clutch; **c. d'échappement,** exhaust cone; **c. de commande,** driving cone; **c. d'embrayage,** clutch cone; **c. de réglage,** adjusting cone; **c. d'engrenage,** cone of gears; **c. d'entraînement,** gearing cone; **c. direct,** direct cone; **c. inversé, renversé,** inverted cone; **c. mâle, c. femelle,** male, female, cone; **c. Morse,** Morse taper (of machine-tool); **c. primitif,** pitch-cone; **accouplement à c.,** cone coupling; **commande par cônes(-poulies),** cone(-pulley) drive, driving; **embrayage à cônes,** cone-clutch; **frein à c.,** cone-brake; (*b*) *Metall:* **c. de fermeture,** cone, bell (of blast furnace); (*c*) *A: Phot:* daylight enlarger. **5.** *Av:* **c. avant,** nose cone (of aircraft); **c. d'entrée, de sortie,** entrance cone, exit cone (of wind tunnel); **c. de pénétration de l'hélice,** spinner-cone, propeller-cone, hub-cone; **c. d'appui du moyeu de l'hélice,** propeller-hub securing cone; *Aer:* **c. d'ancrage,** mooring cone. **6.** *El: Elcs:* cone (of cathode-ray tube); *W.Tel:* **c. de haut-parleur,** moving cone; **c. de silence,** cone of silence; **faux c. de silence,** fake cone of silence; *Radar:* **c. mort,** blind cone. **7.** (*a*) *Bot:* **c. de pin, de sapin, de houblon,** pine-, fir-, hop-, cone; (*b*) *Moll:* cone, conus. **8.** *Cer:* **c. de Seger,** Seger cone; **c. pyrométrique,** pyrometric cone.

côné [kone], *a. Conch:* cone-shaped.

cône-ancre [konɑ̃ːkr], *s.m.* (*a*) *Nau:* drag (-anchor); deep-sea anchor; cone-anchor; (*b*) *Aer:* drogue; *pl. cônes-ancres.*

conéine [konein], *s.f.* = CONICINE.

cône-en-cône [koːnɑ̃koːn], *a.inv. Geol:* cone-in-cone (structure, etc.).

conépate [konepat], *s.m. Z:* hog-nosed skunk, conepate.

côner [kone], *v.tr. Mec.E:* to cone, taper.

conessine [konɛsin], *s.f. Ch:* conessine.

confabulation [kɔ̃fabylasjɔ̃], *s.f. A:* confabulation, chat.

confabuler [kɔ̃fabyle], *v.i. A:* to confabulate, chat.

confarréation [kɔ̃fareasjɔ̃], *s.f. Rom.Jur:* confarreation.

confection [kɔ̃fɛksjɔ̃], *s.f.* **1.** (*a*) making, construction (of machine, road, etc.); putting together, making up (of parts of garment, etc.); manufacture (of goods); mixing, compounding (of drugs); compilation (of inventory); drawing-up (of deed); **elle nous offrit des gâteaux de sa c.,** she offered us cakes of her own making; (*b*) (ready-to-wear) clothing industry. **2.** (*a*) confection, ready-to-wear dress, etc.; **acheter une robe de c.,** to buy a ready-made dress; **maison de c.,** shop selling ready-made clothes; **vêtements de c.,** off-the-peg clothes; (*b*) *A.Pharm:* confection.

confectionnement [kɔ̃fɛksjɔnmɑ̃], *s.m.* = CONFECTION 1 (*a*).

confectionner [kɔ̃fɛksjɔne], *v.tr.* **1.** to make (up) (dress); to construct, put together (machine, etc.); to manufacture (clothing); to prepare (dish, etc.); **confectionnés sur demande, à la douzaine,** made up to order, turned out by the dozen; **article confectionné,** ready-made article. **2.** to make up (balance-sheet).

confectionneur, -euse [kɔ̃fɛksjɔnœːr, -øːz], *s.* (*a*) maker (of articles, dishes, etc.); (*b*) *Com:* ready-made clothier, outfitter.

confédéral, -aux [kɔ̃federal, -o], *a.* confederal.

confédérateur, -trice [kɔ̃federatœːr, -tris]. **1.** *a.* confederating. **2.** *s.* confederationist.

confédératif, -ive [kɔ̃federatif, -iːv], *a. A:* confederal, confederative.

confédération [kɔ̃federasjɔ̃], *s.f.* (con)federation, confederacy; *Fr.C. Hist:* **les Pères de la C.,** the Fathers of the Confederation.

confédéré [kɔ̃federe]. **1.** *a.* confederate (nations); associated (merchants); *Ind: Pol:* **syndicat non c.,** non-affiliated union. **2.** *s.* **les Confédérés,** the Confederates (of American Civil War).

confédérer [kɔ̃federe], *v.tr.* (**je confédère, n. confédérons; je confédérerai**) to confederate, unite.

se confédérer, to confederate, unite (**avec,** with).

confer [kɔ̃fɛːr], *Lt. imp.* cf, compare.

conférence [kɔ̃ferɑ̃ːs], *s.f.* **1.** (*a*) *A:* conference, congress, conclave; (*b*) conference, discussion; **c. entre médecins,** conference, consultation, between doctors; **c. contradictoire, c. débat,** (public) debate; **tenir c.,** to hold a conference; **il est en c. avec . . .,** he is conferring with . . .; **c. de presse,** press conference. **2.** lecture; **maître de conférences,** lecturer; **maîtrise de conférences,** lectureship; *s.a.* PROJECTION 1; **salle de conférences,** lecture-room. **3.** comparison (of texts, etc.).

conférencier, -ière [kɔ̃ferɑ̃sje, -jɛːr], *s.* **1.** (*a*) *A:* president; (*b*) member of a conference or congress. **2.** lecturer.

conférer [kɔ̃fere], *v.* (**je confère, n. conférons; je conférerai**) **1.** *v.tr.* (*a*) to compare, collate (texts); *Typ:* **c. des épreuves,** to check proofs; (*b*) to confer, bestow, grant, award (privileges, etc.); **c. le grade de docteur à qn,** to confer a doctor's degree on s.o. **2.** *v.i.* (*a*) to confer (**avec,** with); to converse; **nous avons conféré de votre affaire,** we talked your business over; (*b*) **il a conféré des affaires de l'Orient,** he discoursed, lectured, on Eastern affairs.

confervacées [kɔ̃fɛrvase], *s.f.pl. Algae:* Confervaceae.

conferve [kɔ̃fɛrv], *s.f. Algae:* conferva; *F:* silk-weed, crow-silk; blanket-weed.

confès, -esse[1] [kɔ̃fɛ, -ɛs], *a. A:* (= CONFESSE[2]) **mourir confès, confesse,** to die shriven.

confesse[2], *s.f.* confession (to a priest); used only in **aller, se rendre, être, à c.,** to go to, to be at, confession; **mener à c.,** to take to confession; **venir, revenir de c.,** to return from confession; **retourner à c.,** to go back to confession.

confesser [kɔ̃fɛse], *v.tr.* **1.** to confess, own, avow, acknowledge; to plead guilty to (sth.), to own (up) to (sth.); **c. à qn que** + *ind.*, to confess, own, to s.o. that . . .; *A:* (*with object and complement*) **il se confessa l'auteur du livre,** he confessed to the authorship of the book. **2.** *Ecc:* (*a*) to confess (one's sins); (*b*) to declare one's belief in (God, etc.); to confess (one's faith). **3.** (*of priest*) to confess (penitent); to hear (penitent) in confession; *F:* **je me charge de le c.,** I undertake to get the truth out of him; **c'est le diable à c.,** it is the dickens of a job; *abs.* **ce prêtre ne confesse pas,** this priest doesn't hear confessions.

se confesser, to confess one's sins; **se c. toutes les semaines,** to go to confession every week; **se c. de qch.,** to confess to (having done) sth.

confesseur [kɔ̃fɛsœːr], *s.m. Ecc:* **1.** (father-)confessor; spiritual director. **2.** *Hist:* confessor (of one's religion, faith); **Édouard le C.,** Edward the Confessor.

confession [kɔ̃fɛsjɔ̃], *s.f.* **1.** confession, avowal, admission (of crime, etc.); **faire la c. de qch.,** to confess, own up to, sth. **2.** *Ecc:* (*a*) **c. (auriculaire, privée),** (auricular) confession (of sins); (*b*) **c. de foi,** confession of faith; **la C. d'Augsbourg,** the Confession of Augsburg; the Augustan Confession; (*c*) religious persuasion. **3.** *Ecc:* hearing of confession; **entendre la c. de qn,** to hear s.o.'s confession; *F:* **on lui donnerait le bon Dieu sans c.,** butter wouldn't melt in his, her, mouth.

confessionnal, -aux [kɔ̃fɛsjɔnal, -o], *s.m.* **1.** *Ecc:* confessional (-box). **2.** *Furn:* grandfather-chair.

confessionnel, -elle [kɔ̃fɛsjɔnɛl], *a.* confessional (= pertaining to confessions of faith); denominational (matters, disputes); **école confessionnelle,** denominational school.

confessionniste [kɔ̃fɛsjɔnist], *s.m. Ecc.Hist:* confessionist, Lutheran, adherent of the Confession of Augsburg.

confetti [kɔ̃fɛtti, -feti], *s.m.pl.* confetti.

confiance [kɔ̃fjɑ̃ːs], *s.f.* **1.** confidence, faith, trust, reliance, dependence; **avoir c. en qn, qch., faire c. à qn, qch.,** to put trust in s.o., sth., to rely on s.o., sth., to trust s.o., sth.; **faire c. à qn pour toute action à poursuivre,** to give s.o. discretionary powers to act; **faire c. à l'avenir,** to trust in the future; **inspirer c.,** to inspire confidence; **il n'a pas c. dans les médecins,** he places no reliance on doctors, he doesn't believe in doctors; **faire c. au peuple,** to place confidence in the people, to trust the people; **la c. qui m'a été témoignée,** the confidence placed in me; **acheter qch. de c.,** to buy sth. on trust; **il me faut un homme de c.,** I want a man whom I can trust, whom I can rely on; **être l'homme de c. de qn,** to be s.o.'s confidential agent; **cela m'a donné c.,** this gave me confidence; **avoir c. en, dans, l'avenir,** to have confidence, faith, in the future; **abus de c.,** breach of trust; **abuser de la c. de qn,** to break faith with s.o.; **répondre à la c. de qn,** to deserve s.o.'s confidence; **j'ai sa c.,** I enjoy his confidence, he trusts me; **digne de c.,** trustworthy, reliable; **maison de c.,** trustworthy, reliable, firm; **commis de c.,** confidential clerk; **domestique de c.,** trusty servant; *adv.phr.* **avec c.,** (i) confidently; (ii) trustingly, trustfully; **affirmer qch. avec c.,** to assert sth. boldly; **je vous parle en toute c.,** I know I can trust you (with what I have to say); **de c.,** confidently; **vous pouvez l'acheter de c.,** you may buy it with confidence; *Com.Corr:* **vous remerciant de la c. que vous avez bien voulu nous accorder jusqu'ici,** thanking you for past favours; *Pol:* **vote de c.,** vote of confidence; **poser la question de c.,** to ask for a vote of confidence. **2.** confidence, sense of security; **parler en toute c.,** to speak with perfect confidence; **manquer de c. en soi,** to lack self-assurance.

confiant [kɔ̃fjɑ̃], *a.* **1.** confiding, trusting, trustful (**dans,** in); **Napoléon était c. dans son étoile,** Napoleon had implicit confidence in his star; **c. en l'avenir, en ses amis,** trusting to the future, to his friends. **2.** confident, sanguine (disposition, etc.). **3.** self-confident, assured (manner, etc.).

confidemment [kɔ̃fidamɑ̃], *adv. A:* confidentially, in confidence.

confidence [kɔ̃fidɑ̃ːs], *s.f.* confidence (imparted as a secret); **faire une c. à qn,** to tell a secret to s.o., to trust s.o. with a secret; **il m'a fait ses confidences,** he poured out his soul to me; **faire c. de qch. à qn,** to confide sth. to s.o.; **mettre qn dans la c.,** to let s.o. into the secret; **dire qch. en c.,** to say sth. in confidence, as a secret, confidentially.

confident, -ente [kɔ̃fidɑ̃, -ɑ̃ːt], *s.* confidant, *f.* confidante.

confidentiel, -ielle [kɔ̃fidɑ̃sjɛl], *a.* confidential; **à titre c.,** confidentially, in confidence, privately; **à titre purement, strictement, c.,** in strict confidence.

confidentiellement [kɔ̃fidɑ̃sjɛlmɑ̃], *adv.* confidentially, in confidence.

confier [kɔ̃fje], *v.tr.* (*p.d. & pr.sub.* **n. confiions, v. confiiez**) **1.** to trust, entrust, commit; **c. qch. à qn, à la garde de qn, aux mains de qn,** to entrust s.o. with sth.; to commit, consign, sth. to s.o.'s care, to place sth. in s.o.'s charge, to deliver sth. into s.o.'s charge; **le poste à lui confié,** the position entrusted to him; *Jur:* **c. une affaire à qn,** to put a matter in the hands of s.o.; **c. qn à qn,** to commit s.o. to s.o., to s.o.'s care, to the charge of s.o.; **c. des vers à la mémoire,** to commit lines of poetry to memory. **2.** to confide, impart, disclose; **c. qch. à qn,** to confide sth. to s.o., to tell s.o. sth. in confidence; **confiez-moi ça, confiez-le-moi,** leave it to me.

se confier. 1. se c. à qn, à qch., *occ.* **se c. en, qn, qch.,** to put, repose, one's trust in s.o., to put oneself in s.o.'s hands, to trust to, rely on, sth.; **se c. au hasard,** to trust to luck. **2. se c. à qn,** to confide in s.o., to unbosom oneself to s.o.

configuration [kɔ̃figyrasjɔ̃], *s.f.* **1.** configuration, outline; profile; form, shape; lay, lie (of the land, etc.); *Elcs:* **c. électronique,** electronic configuration. **2.** *Astr:* configuration (of planets).

configurer [kɔ̃figyre], *v.tr.* to configure, fashion, shape.

confiné [kɔ̃fine], *a.* (*a*) confined (atmosphere, etc.); (*b*) **être c. au logis,** to be confined to the house; **poète c. dans l'imitation des anciens,** poet who confines himself to the imitation of the ancients.

confinement [kɔ̃finmɑ̃], *s.m.* **1.** *Jur:* solitary confinement. **2.** congestion, over-crowding (of people in one place).

confiner [kɔ̃fine]. **1.** *v.i.* to abut on, against sth.; (*of country, etc.*) **c. à, avec, un pays,** to border upon, be contiguous to, a country; *occ.* to confine with a country; **courage qui confine à la témérité,** courage verging on, little short of, foolhardiness; **conduite qui confine à la trahison,** conduct that comes near to treachery. **2.** *v.tr.* (*a*) to confine, imprison, restrain (s.o.); **c. qn dans un couvent,** to shut s.o. up, confine s.o., in a convent; **se c. dans la science,** to confine oneself to the pursuit of science; (*b*) to confine, limit, restrict, restrain; **c. ses recherches à la fission nucléaire,** to confine, limit, one's investigations to nuclear fission.

confinité [kɔ̃finite], *s.f.* contiguity, adjacency (of two countries, etc.).

confins [kɔ̃fɛ̃], *s.m.pl.* **1.** confines, borders (of country); **les c. de la science,** the confines of science. **2.** *adv.phr.* **aux c. de,** within the limits of.

confire [kɔ̃fiːr], *v.tr.* (*pr.p.* **confisant;** *p.p.* **confit;** *pr.ind.* **je confis, n. confisons, ils confisent;** *p.d.* **je confisais;** *p.h.* **je confis;** *fu.* **je confirai**) **1.** to preserve (fruit, etc.); to candy (peel, etc.); **c. au sel, au vinaigre,** to pickle; **fruit confit au soleil,** sun-dried fruit. **2.** *Tan:* to dip, soak, steep (skins). **3.** *F:* **se c. en dévotion,** to lose oneself in one's devotions.

confirmand, -ande [kɔ̃firmɑ̃, -ɑ̃ːd], *s. Ecc:* confirmand.

confirmateur, -trice [kɔ̃firmatœːr, -tris], *s.* confirmer, one who confirms (piece of news, etc.).

confirmatif, -ive [kɔ̃firmatif, -iːv], *a.* confirmative (judgment); corroborative (statement).

confirmation [kɔ̃firmasjɔ̃], *s.f.* **1.** confirmation, corroboration (of piece of news, etc.); **en c. de ma lettre,** confirming my letter; **c. d'un jugement,** confirmation of a sentence; **c. d'un traité,** ratification of a treaty. **2.** *Ecc:* (sacrament of) confirmation; **donner la c. à qn,** to confirm s.o.; **recevoir la c.,** to be confirmed.

confirmatoire [kɔ̃firmatwaːr], *a.* confirmatory (declaration, etc.).

confirmé [kɔ̃firme], *a.* **1.** (*a*) *Ecc:* (person who has been) confirmed; (*b*) confirmed, corroborated. **2.** experienced, practised.

confirmer [kɔ̃firme], *v.tr.* **1.** to confirm (news, judgment, etc.) to strengthen (s.o. in resolution, etc.); **c. un traité,** to ratify a treaty; **c. la déposition de qn,** to corroborate, bear out, s.o.'s evidence; **cela confirme mon dire,** that bears out my assertion; **l'exception confirme la règle,** the exception proves the rule; **le bruit ne s'est pas confirmé,** the news proved false; *Av:* **vol confirmé,** confirmed flight. **2.** *Ecc:* to confirm (s.o.).

confiscable [kɔ̃fiskabl̩], *a.* confiscable, liable to be seized, forfeited.

confiscateur, -trice [kɔ̃fiskatœːr, -tris], *s.* confiscator.

confiscation [kɔ̃fiskasjɔ̃], *s.f.* confiscation (of contraband goods, etc.); forfeiture, seizure (of property, etc.); **perdre qch. par c.,** to forfeit sth.

confiserie [kɔ̃fizri], *s.f.* **1.** (*a*) preserving (of fruit, etc.) in sugar; (*b*) confectioner's shop; (*c*) confectionery, sweet(meat)s, preserves. **2.** (*a*) preserving (of sardines, olives, gherkins); (*b*) sardine (olive, gherkin) canning factory.

confiseur, -euse [kɔ̃fizœːr, -øːz], *s.* maker, seller, of preserves and sweetmeats; confectioner.

confisquer [kɔ̃fiske], *v.tr.* to confiscate, seize (goods, property, etc.).

confit [kɔ̃fi]. **1.** *a.* **fruits confits,** crystallized fruit; **c. au sucre,** candied; *F:* **être c. en dévotion, dans l'optimisme,** to be steeped in piety, optimism; **un air c.,** a sanctified, saint-like, air; **être c. de vanité,** to be eaten up with vanity. **2.** *s.m.* (*a*) *Leath:* (i) sour-water, bate; **mettre en c.,** to bate (skins); (ii) maceration tub, vat; (*b*) *Husb:* **c. de son,** bran-mash; (*c*) *Cu:* conserve (of goose, etc.).

confiteor [kɔ̃fiteɔːr], *s.m.inv. Ecc:* confiteor.

confiture [kɔ̃fityːr], *s.f. often pl. Cu:* preserve(s), jam; **c. d'abricot(s),** apricot jam; **c. d'oranges,** (orange) marmalade; **tartine de confiture(s),** slice of bread and jam; *F:* **mettre, réduire, qn en c.,** to pound s.o. to a jelly.

confiturerie [kɔ̃fityrri], *s.f.* **1.** manufacture of jam, of preserves. **2.** jam factory or warehouse.

confiturier, -ière [kɔ̃fityrje, -jɛːr], *s.* **1.** jam-maker, -seller. **2.** *s.m.* jam-pot, -jar, -dish.

conflagration [kɔ̃flagrasjɔ̃], *s.f.* conflagration, blaze.

conflictuel, -elle [kɔ̃fliktɥɛl], *a. Psy:* **situation conflictuelle,** conflict situation.

conflit [kɔ̃fli], *s.m.* (*a*) conflict, struggle; clash(ing) of interests; **le c. des armes,** the clash of arms; **c. armé,** war; **c. d'opinions,** conflict of opinion, disagreement; **les conflits du travail,** trade disputes; **en c.,** conflicting (doctrines, etc.); **être en c.,** (i) to be at variance; *F:* at loggerheads (**avec,** with); (ii) (*of interests, etc.*) to clash (**avec,** with); **entrer en c. avec qn,** to come to loggerheads with s.o.; to come up against s.o.; (*b*) *Jur:* conflict (of authority or scope); clashing, overlapping (of authority); **être en c. positif,** (of both sides) to claim competence; **être en c. négatif,** (of both sides) to disclaim competence; **règles de c.,** rules to determine which court is competent.

confluence [kɔ̃flyɑ̃ːs], *s.f.* **1.** *Med:* running together (of vesicles). **2.** *Geog:* junction.

confluent [kɔ̃flyɑ̃]. **1.** *a. Med: Bot:* confluent; *s.a.* VARIOLE 1. **2.** *s.m.* confluence, meeting, junction (of rivers, veins, etc.).

confluer [kɔ̃flye], *v.i.* to meet, join, unite; **l'Oise conflue avec la Seine,** the Oise flows into the Seine; *abs.* **l'Allier et la Loire confluent près de Nevers,** the confluence of the Loire and the Allier is near Nevers; **à Pâques les touristes confluent à, vers, Paris,** at Easter, tourists flock to Paris.

confondant [kɔ̃fɔ̃dɑ̃], *a.* confounding; damning (evidence, etc.).

confondre [kɔ̃fɔ̃ːdr̥], *v.tr.* to confound. **1.** (*a*) to merge, mingle, intermingle; **rivières qui confondent leurs eaux,** rivers that mingle their waters, that interflow; (*b*) to mistake, confuse; **c. le coupable avec l'innocent,** to mistake the innocent for the guilty; **c. des noms,** to confuse, muddle up, names. **2.** to discomfit, disconcert (one's enemies, etc.); to abash, nonplus, stagger (s.o.); to put (s.o.) to confusion; **l'assassin a été confondu par M. X,** the murderer was shown up by Mr X; **c. la calomnie,** to silence calumny; **c. les projets de qn,** to confound, baffle, s.o.'s plans; to bring s.o.'s plans to naught; **c. l'ennemi,** to put the enemy to confusion, to throw the enemy into disorder; **ça confond l'imagination,** that makes the mind boggle.

se confondre. 1. (*a*) (*of colours, etc.*) to blend (**en,** into); to merge into one another; (*b*) (*of streams, etc.*) to intermingle, interflow; **race où se confondent des éléments divers,** race in which diverse elements are mingled, intermingle; (*c*) (*of interests, etc.*) to be identical. **2. se c. en excuses,** to be profuse in one's apologies; to apologize profusely.

confondu [kɔ̃fɔ̃dy], *a.* **1.** disconcerted, abashed; **je suis tout c. de votre bonté,** I am overwhelmed by your kindness. **2.** dumbfounded (**de,** at); **avoir l'air c.,** to look blank; **regarder qn d'un air c.,** to look blankly at s.o.

conformateur [kɔ̃fɔrmatœːr], *s.m.* **1.** *Tchn:* conformator; *Plastics:* device used to avoid deformation of a moulding during cooling. **2.** *El: Elcs:* **c. d'impulsions,** pulse shaper, pulse shaping network.

conformation [kɔ̃fɔrmasjɔ̃], *s.f.* conformation, structure (of hills, parts of body, etc.); **mauvaise c.,** malconformation; *s.a.* VICE 2.

conforme [kɔ̃fɔrm], *a.* conformable, true, according (**à,** to); consistent, consonant (**à,** with); **c. à l'esprit de justice,** conformable to the spirit of justice; **copie c. à l'original,** copy corresponding to the original; **cette interprétation n'est pas c. à l'esprit du traité,** this interpretation does not correspond with the spirit of the treaty; **ses goûts sont conformes aux miens,** his tastes are consonant, in harmony, with mine; our tastes are identical; **ses actions sont conformes à ses principes,** his acts conform with, are consistent with, in accordance with, in conformity with, his principles; **ces articles ne sont pas conformes aux conditions requises,** such items do not come within the requirements; *Geom:* **figures conformes,** congruent figures; *Adm: etc:* **pour copie c.,** certified true copy; *Com:* **c. à l'échantillon,** up to sample; *Book-k:* **écriture c.,** corresponding entry.

conformé [kɔ̃fɔrme], *a.* **bien c.,** well-formed (child, etc.); **mal c.,** mis-shapen (limb, etc.).

conformément [kɔ̃fɔrmemɑ̃], *adv.* conformably, according (**à,** to); in conformity, in accordance, in compliance (**à,** with); **c. aux stipulations de cet article,** in pursuance of this article; **c. à la loi,** according to (the) law; **c. à vos ordres,** in obedience to, in compliance with, your orders; **c. à l'échantillon joint à votre lettre,** as per sample attached to your letter; *Mil:* **c. au plan,** according to plan.

conformer [kɔ̃fɔrme], *v.tr.* to form, shape; to give form, shape, to (s.o., sth.); **c. qch. à qch.,** to conform sth. to sth.; **c. sa vie à certains principes,** to shape one's life according to certain principles; *Book-k:* **c. les écritures,** to agree the books.

se conformer à qch., to conform, adapt oneself, to sth.; to comply with, fall in with, abide by, sth.; **je me suis conformé à vos ordres,** I have complied with, followed, your instructions; **me conformant à mon mandat,** in conformity, in accordance, with my instructions; *Com:* **se c. au modèle,** to keep to the pattern.

conformisme [kɔ̃fɔrmism], *s.m.* (*a*) conventionalism; conformism, *U.S:* conformity; *Pol: etc:* orthodoxy; (*b*) *Ecc:* conformity.

conformiste [kɔ̃fɔrmist], *s.m. & f.* (*a*) *Ecc:* conformist (of Ch. of Eng.); **église c.,** established church; (*b*) conventionalist, conformist.

conformité [kɔ̃fɔrmite], *s.f.* conformity, conformability, agreement, resemblance, correspondence; *Ecc:* conformity; **c. de qch. avec qch.,** conformity of sth. with sth.; **être en c. de goûts avec qn,** to have similar tastes to s.o.; **en c. de, avec, qch.,** conformably to, in accordance with, sth.; **agir en c. des ordres reçus,** to act in compliance with, conformably to, orders received; **en c. des dispositions de . . .,** in accordance with the provisions of . . .; *Book-k:* **passer une écriture en c.,** to reciprocate an entry; **écriture de c.,** corresponding entry.

confort [kɔ̃fɔːr], *s.m.* comfort(s); **hôtel avec tout le c. moderne,** hotel with every modern comfort; *A:* **niveau du c.,** standard of comfort, of living; **c. intellectuel,** intellectual complaisance; *Aut: A:* **pneus c.,** balloon tyres.

confortable [kɔ̃fɔrtabl̥]. **1.** *a.* (*a*) comfortable, snug, cosy; (*b*) *F:* well-off, comfortably off; **des appointements confortables,** a comfortable salary; **le coureur avait pris une avance c.,** the competitor was well ahead. **2.** *s.m.* (*a*) *O:* comfort, ease; (*b*) (upholstered) easy chair; (*c*) *F: pl.* carpet slippers.

confortablement [kɔ̃fɔrtabləmɑ̃], *adv.* comfortably, in comfort; snugly, cosily.

confortant [kɔ̃fɔrtɑ̃], *a. & s.m. A.Med:* strengthening, corroborant; *s. A:* (*medicine*) corroborant.

conforter [kɔ̃fɔrte], *v.tr.* **1.** *A:* to comfort, console, solace (s.o.). **2.** *Med:* to strengthen, fortify.

confraternel, -elle [kɔ̃fratɛrnɛl], *a.* confraternal, brotherly.

confraternité [kɔ̃fratɛrnite], *s.f.* **1.** confraternity, brotherhood, fellowship. **2.** brotherliness, good fellowship.

confrère [kɔ̃frɛːr], *s.m.* colleague, confrère, fellow-member (of profession, society); brother (-writer, -teacher, -doctor, etc.); man in the same line (of business).

confrérie [kɔ̃freri], *s.f.* (religious) brotherhood or sisterhood; confraternity.

confrontation [kɔ̃frɔ̃tasjɔ̃], *s.f.* **1.** (*a*) *Jur:* confrontation, confronting (of accused person with witness); (*b*) *Jur:* identification, picking out (of prisoner from group of persons); (*c*) *Journ: Sp: F:* encounter; (*d*) *Med:* **c. radio-anatomo-clinique,** clinico-pathological conference. **2.** comparison (**à, avec,** with); collation (of MSS., etc.).

confronter [kɔ̃frɔ̃te], *v.tr.* **1.** *Jur: etc:* to confront; to bring (prisoner) face to face (**avec, à,** with); **confronté à de nouvelles énigmes . . .,** confronted with new enigmas . . .. **2.** to collate (MSS.); to compare (materials, etc.) (**avec, à,** with).

confucianisme [kɔ̃fysjanism], *s.m. Rel.H:* Confucianism.

confucianiste [kɔ̃fysjanist], *s.m.&f.* Confucian(ist).

confus [kɔ̃fy], *a.* **1.** (*a*) confused, mixed, chaotic, jumbled (heap, etc.); indistinct (noise); dim (vision); obscure, ambiguous (style, etc.); ragged (fire); **des voix confuses,** a hubbub of voices; **souvenirs c.,** blurred memories; **mélange confus,** jumble (**de,** of); (*b*) *Jur:* **droits c. en une personne,** rights which merge, are merged, in one person. **2.** confused, embarrassed, abashed, ashamed; **je suis c. de vos bontés,** your kindness makes me ashamed, overwhelms me, overpowers me; **je suis c. de vous déranger,** I'm so sorry to disturb you.

confusément [kɔ̃fyzemɑ̃], *adv.* confusedly, vaguely, indistinctly; **voir qch. c.,** to have a blurred vision of sth.; **objets entassés c.,** objects piled up in confusion; *F:* higgledy-piggledy.

confusion [kɔ̃fyzjɔ̃], *s.f.* confusion. **1.** (*a*) disorder, jumble, medley; **tous ses papiers sont en, dans la, c.,** all his papers are in confusion; in a muddle; **une c. de papiers,** a jumble of papers; **tout était en c.,** *F:* everything was all over the shop; **jeter la c. parmi les troupes,** to cause confusion among the troops, to throw troops into disorder; **ces interruptions mettent la c. dans mon travail,** *F:* these interruptions play the devil with my work; **mettre tout en c.,** to upset everything; *Med:* **c. mentale,** mental aberration, derangement of mind, confusion; (*b*) mistake, error, misunderstanding; **c. de dates, de noms,** confusion of, mistake in, dates, names; **commettre une c.,** to make a mistake. **2.** confusion, embarrassment, shame, abashment; **être rouge de c.,** to blush for shame; **orgueil mêlé de c.,** conscious pride; **il répondit sans aucune c. . . .,** he replied unabashed . . .. **3.** *Jur:* (*a*) extinguishment of a debt through one debtor or creditor succeeding to the estate of the other; (*b*) **avec c. des deux peines,** the two sentences to run concurrently.

confusionnel, -elle [kɔ̃fyzjɔnɛl], *a. Med: Psy:* confusional; **état c.,** confusion.

confusionnisme [kɔ̃fyzjɔnism], *s.m.* **1.** *Psy:* the confused thinking of a child. **2.** *Pol:* policy of deliberately confusing people.

conga [kɔ̃ga], *s.f. Danc:* conga.

conge [kɔ̃ːʒ], *s.m.* **1.** *Rom.Ant:* congius. **2.** *Min:* ore basket.

congé [kɔ̃ʒe], *s.m.* **1.** (*a*) leave, permission (to depart); **prendre c. de qn,** to take leave of s.o.; (*b*) leave (of absence); *Mil:* long leave; **en c.,** on leave; **aller en c.,** to go on leave; **c. de maladie,** sick leave; *Adm: Mil: etc:* **c. de réforme,** discharge for physical (or any other) unfitness for service; **c. pour affaires de famille, pour affaires personnelles,** leave on private affairs, on private business; (*c*) holiday; (*esp. U.S:*) vacation; **être en c.,** to be on holiday; **un après-midi de c.,** an afternoon off; **donner, accorder, (un) c. à qn,** to give s.o. a holiday; *Ind:* **c. payé,** (i) holidays with pay; (ii) *F:* holiday-maker. **2.** (*a*) (notice of) discharge, dismissal; **donner c. à qn,** to discharge s.o., to give s.o. notice; **donner c. un mois d'avance,** to give a month's notice; **demander son c.,** to hand in one's resignation, to give notice; **donner son c. à un prétendant,** to give a suitor his *congé*; (*b*) **donner c. à un locataire, à son propriétaire,** to give a tenant notice to quit, to give one's landlord notice of leaving. **3.** *Mil:* (*a*) period, term, of service; (*b*) discharge (from service); **prendre son c.,** (i) *Mil: Navy:* to take one's discharge; (ii) *Nau:* to be paid off; **mettre qn en c.,** to discharge s.o.; *Nau:* to pay s.o. off; (*of apprentice*) **recevoir son c. d'acquit,** to take up one's indentures. **4.** authorization, permit; *Ecc:* **c. d'élire,** leave to elect (bishop), *congé d'élire*; *Adm: Com:* **c. pour le transport des vins,** release of wine from bond; **c. d'un bâtiment,** clearance of a vessel. **5.** *Tchn:* (*a*) bead, fillet, bend (of pipe); (*b*) *Arch:* congé, apophyge, escape (of column), neck-moulding, necking; (*c*) *Tls:* neck-moulding plane.

congédiable [kɔ̃ʒedjabl̥], *a.* liable to be discharged; due for discharge.

congédiement [kɔ̃ʒedimɑ̃], *s.m.* **1.** dismissal (of worker, etc.). **2.** *Mil: Navy:* discharging (of men); *Nau:* paying off (of crew).

congédier [kɔ̃ʒedje], *v.tr.* (*p.d. & pr.sub.* **n. congédiions, v. congédiiez**) **1.** to dismiss (servant, etc.). **2.** (*a*) to dismiss (caller); (*b*) *Mil: Navy:* to discharge (men); *Nau:* to pay off (crew); **c. une armée,** to disband an army.

congelable [kɔ̃ʒlabl̥], *a.* **1.** congealable, freezable (liquid, etc.). **2.** *F:* coagulable.

congelant [kɔ̃ʒlɑ̃], *a.* congealing, freezing (mixture, etc.).

congélateur [kɔ̃ʒelatœːr], *s.m.* refrigerator, freezing-machine, freezer.

congélation [kɔ̃ʒelasjɔ̃], *s.f.* **1.** (*a*) congelation, congealment; freezing (of water, etc.); solidification (of oil); fixing, setting (of cast-iron, etc.); **point de c. de l'eau,** freezing point of water; **chambre de c.,** freezing chamber; (*b*) (i) cold storage; **viande dans la c.,** meat in cold storage; (ii) quick-freezing, deep-freezing; (*c*) *Bot: Med:* frost-bite; (*d*) coagulation, setting. **2.** (*a*) *Geol:* calcareous tufa; (*b*) *Arch:* stalactited ornament, rock work.

congeler [kɔ̃ʒle], *v.tr.* **(il congèle; il congèlera) 1.** to congeal; to freeze (water, etc.); to deep-freeze (food); **viande congelée,** frozen meat; *s.* **du congelé,** frozen meat, fish, fruit, etc. **2.** to coagulate (blood, etc.). **3.** *Fin:* **crédits congelés,** frozen credits.

se congeler. 1. to congeal; to freeze (up). **2.** *F:* to set, coagulate.

congénère [kɔ̃ʒenɛːr]. **1.** *a. Biol:* congeneric, of the same species; *Anat:* congenerous (muscle); *Ling:* **mots congénères,** cognate words. **2.** *s.m. Biol:* congener; **lui et ses congénères,** he and his like.

congénital, -aux [kɔ̃ʒenital, -o], *a.* congenital; *F:* **résistance congénitale,** built-in resistance.

congénitalement [kɔ̃ʒenitalmɑ̃], *adv.* congenitally.

congère [kɔ̃ʒɛːr], *s.f.* snow-drift; *F:* **c. de sable,** sand drift.

congestible [kɔ̃ʒɛstibl̩], *a. Med:* liable to congestion.

congestif, -ive [kɔ̃ʒɛstif, -iːv], *a.* **1.** *Bot:* congested (organs, etc.). **2.** *Med:* congestive (disposition, etc.).

congestion [kɔ̃ʒɛs(t)jɔ̃], *s.f. Med:* congestion; **c. cérébrale,** congestion of the brain; *F:* stroke; **succomber aux suites d'une c.,** to die of apoplexy; **c. pulmonaire,** congestion of the lungs, pneumonia; **c. vasculaire,** engorgement.

congestionné [kɔ̃ʒɛs(t)jɔne], *a.* **1.** flushed, red (face). **2. rue congestionnée,** crowded, congested, street.

congestionner [kɔ̃ʒɛs(t)jɔne], *v.tr.* **1.** *Med:* to congest; *F:* **bébé a tant crié qu'il s'est congestionné le visage,** baby has cried till he's blue in the face; **2. la foule congestionnait le trottoir,** the crowd was blocking the pavement.

se congestionner, to become congested. **1. son visage se congestionna,** he turned purple, black, in the face. **2. Paris se congestionne de plus en plus,** Paris is becoming more and more congested.

conglobé [kɔ̃glɔbe], *a. Bot:* conglobate.

conglober [kɔ̃glɔbe], *v.tr. & pr.* to conglobate, conglobe; to form into a ball or mass.

conglomérat [kɔ̃glɔmera], *s.m.* **1.** *Geol:* conglomerate, pudding-stone; *Goldmin:* **c. aurifère,** banket. **2.** *Const:* cemented gravel. **3. c. (de personnes, etc.),** cluster, gathering (of people).

conglomération [kɔ̃glɔmerasjɔ̃], *s.f.* conglomeration.

conglomératique [kɔ̃glɔmeratik], *a.* conglomeratic.

conglomérer [kɔ̃glɔmere], *v.tr.* **(je conglomère, n. conglomérons; je conglomérerai)** to conglomerate (particles of matter, etc.).

se conglomérer, to conglomerate, to unite, cluster together; *Anat:* **glandes conglomérées,** conglomerate glands, acinous glands.

conglutinant [kɔ̃glytinɑ̃], *Med: A:* **1.** *a.* conglutinative. **2.** *s.m.* conglutinator.

conglutinatif, -ive [kɔ̃glytinatif, -iːv], *a. & s.m.* = CONGLUTINANT.

conglutination [kɔ̃glytinasjɔ̃], *s.f. Med:* conglutination.

conglutiné [kɔ̃glytine], *a.* conglutinate.

conglutiner [kɔ̃glytine], *v.tr.* to conglutinate, to stick together (edges of wound, etc.).

se conglutiner, to conglutinate, adhere.

Congo [kɔ̃go], *Pr.n.m.* **1.** *Geog:* (river) Congo. **2.** *Geog:* **la république du C.,** the Republic of the Congo; **République démocratique du C.,** Congolese Republic; *Hist:* **C. belge,** Belgian Congo. **2.** *Dy:* **rouge C.,** Congo red; **jaune C.,** Congo yellow.

congolais, -aise [kɔ̃gɔlɛ, -ɛːz], (*a*) *a. & s.* (native, inhabitant) of the Congo; Congolese; (*b*) *s.m. Cu:* coconut cake.

congou [kɔ̃gu], *s.m.* congou (tea).

congratulateur, -trice [kɔ̃gratylatœːr, -tris], *Iron: F:* **1.** *s.* congratulator. **2.** *a.* congratulatory, complimentary.

congratulation [kɔ̃gratylasjɔ̃], *s.f. Iron: F:* congratulation.

congratulatoire [kɔ̃gratylatwaːr], *a. Iron: F:* congratulatory.

congratuler [kɔ̃gratyle], *v.tr. Iron: F:* to congratulate.

congre[1] [kɔ̃ːgr], *s.m.* conger(-eel).

congre[2], *s.m.* fish preserve (in river).

congréage [kɔ̃greaːʒ], *s.m. Nau:* worming (of rope).

congréer [kɔ̃gree], *v.tr. Nau:* to worm (rope); **filin à c.,** worming.

congréganisme [kɔ̃greganism], *s.m. Ecc.Hist:* the Congregation system (under the Fr. Restoration).

congréganiste [kɔ̃greganist], *Ecc:* **1.** *a.* congreganist (school, etc.). **2.** *s.m. & f.* member of the Congregation (under the Fr. Restoration).

congrégation [kɔ̃gregasjɔ̃], *s.f. Ecc:* **1.** (*a*) community, congregation (= group of monasteries); (*b*) the Congregation (under the Fr. Restoration). **2.** committee (of College of Cardinals); congregation. **3.** (*a*) congregation, body of worshippers (of Protestant Church); (*b*) sodality.

congrégationalisme [kɔ̃gregasjɔnalism], *s. Ecc:* Congregationalism.

congrégationaliste [kɔ̃gregasjɔnalist]. **1.** *a.* Congregational (church, etc.). **2.** *s.m. & f.* Congregationalist.

congrès [kɔ̃grɛ], *s.m.* (*a*) congress; **C. des États-Unis,** United States Congress; **membre du C.,** congressman; (*b*) **c. de l'enseignement, etc.,** educational, etc., congress or conference.

congressionnel, -elle [kɔ̃grɛsjɔnɛl], *a. Hist:* congressional.

congressiste [kɔ̃grɛsist], *s.m. & f.* member of a congress; *s.m. U.S:* congressman.

congrier [kɔ̃gri(j)e], *s.m.*, **congrois** [kɔ̃grwa], *s.m.* = CONGRE[2].

congru [kɔ̃gry], *a.* **1.** *O:* sufficient, adequate; **portion congrue,** (i) *Ecc:* adequate emolument (of priest); (ii) *F:* (income providing a) bare living; *F:* **réduire qn à la portion congrue,** to put s.o. on short allowance; *Theol:* **grâce congrue,** congruous grace. **2.** *Mth:* congruent.

congruence [kɔ̃gryɑ̃ːs], *s.f. Mth:* congruence (of numbers, lines).

congruent [kɔ̃gryɑ̃], *a.* congruent (**à,** with).

congruisme [kɔ̃gryism], *s.m. Theol:* congruism.

congruiste [kɔ̃gryist], *a. & s. Theol:* congruist.

congruité [kɔ̃gryite], *s.f.* **1.** *Theol:* congruity (of grace). **2.** adequacy.

congrûment [kɔ̃grymɑ̃], *adv.* **1.** congruously, appropriately, pertinently. **2.** adequately.

conicine [kɔnisin], *s.f. Ch:* coni(c)ine, conine.

conicité [kɔnisite], *s.f.* conicity, conicality, conical shape; taper (of bullet, etc.); **c. de 1 sur 12,** taper of 1 in 12.

conidés [kɔnide], *s.m.pl. Moll:* Conidae.

conidie [kɔnidi], *s.f. Fung: Bot:* conidium.

conifère [kɔnifɛːr], *Bot:* **1.** *a.* coniferous, cone-bearing. **2.** *s.m.pl.* **conifères,** Coniferae, conifers.

coniforme [kɔnifɔrm], *a.* coniform, conical.

coniine [kɔniin], *s.f.*, **conine** [kɔnin], *s.f.* = CONICINE.

coniose [kɔnjoːz], *s.f. Med:* coniosis.

conique [kɔnik, ko-], *a.* **1.** cone-shaped, conical. **2.** *Geom:* conic; **(sections) coniques,** conics, conic sections; *s.a.* PROJECTION 3. **3.** *Mec.E: etc:* coned, taper(ing) (shank, pin, etc.); **soupape c.,** mitre valve; **pignon c.,** bevel pinion; **engrenage c.,** bevel gearing; **pas c.,** taper thread (of screw); **roue c.,** cone wheel; **joint c., raccord c.,** union cone; **fraise c.,** cone countersink.

conirostre [kɔnirɔstr̩], *Orn:* **1.** *a.* conirostral. **2.** *s.m.* coniroster, *pl.* conirostres.

conjectural, -aux [kɔ̃ʒɛktyral, -o], *a.* conjectural.

conjecturalement [kɔ̃ʒɛktyralmɑ̃], *adv.* conjecturally, by guess.

conjecture [kɔ̃ʒɛktyːr], *s.f.* conjecture, surmise, guess; **faire, former, des conjectures sur qch.,** to make, form, conjectures about sth.; **par c.,** as a guess; **être réduit à des conjectures,** to be reduced to conjecture; **se perdre en conjectures,** to be lost in conjecture.

conjecturer [kɔ̃ʒɛktyre], *v.tr.* to conjecture, surmise, guess; **c. qch. de qch.,** to surmise sth. from sth.; *abs.* **c. sur ce qu'on ignore,** to make guesses about what one doesn't know about.

conjoindre [kɔ̃ʒwɛ̃ːdr̩], *v.tr.* (*conj. like* JOINDRE) to unite (two people) together in matrimony; to join in marriage; **conjoints par le mariage,** united in wedlock.

se conjoindre, (*rare*) to get married (**à,** to); to marry.

conjoint, *a.* [kɔ̃ʒwɛ̃]. **1.** conjoined, united, joint; *Fin:* **compte courant c.,** joint current account; *Jur:* **legs c.,** joint legacy; **légataires conjoints,** co-legatees; *Ar:* **règle conjointe,** *s.f.* **conjointe,** chain-rule; *Bot: Geom:* **feuilles, lignes, conjointes,** conjugate leaves, lines; *Mus:* **degré c.,** conjoint, conjunct, degree; *Med:* **maladies conjointes,** co-existing diseases; *s.a.* SOLIDAIRE 1. **2.** *Jur:* married; *s.m.* **les (deux) conjoints,** husband and wife; *F:* **les (futurs) conjoints,** (i) the engaged couple; (ii) the bride and bridegroom.

conjointement [kɔ̃ʒwɛ̃tmɑ̃], *adv.* (con)jointly; **agir c. avec qn,** to act in conjunction with s.o..

conjoncteur [kɔ̃ʒɔ̃ktœːr], *s.m. El:* circuit-closer; cut-in; switch, key, connector; *Tp:* jack.

conjoncteur-disjoncteur [kɔ̃ʒɔ̃ktœrdisʒɔ̃ktœːr], *s.m. El:* make-and-break (key, etc.); cut-out; self-closing circuit-breaker; *pl. conjoncteurs-disjoncteurs.*

conjonctif, -ive [kɔ̃ʒɔ̃ktif, -iːv], *a.* conjunctive; connective (tissue, etc.); *Gram:* **locution conjonctive,** conjunctive phrase; **pronom c.,** relative pronoun.

conjonction [kɔ̃ʒɔ̃ksjɔ̃], *s.f.* **1.** conjunction, union, connection; *O:* **c. par le mariage,** wedlock; *Astr:* **en c.,** in conjunction; conjoined. **2.** *Gram:* conjunction.

conjonctionnel, -elle [kɔ̃ʒɔ̃ksjɔnɛl], *a. Gram:* conjunctional.

conjonctionnellement [kɔ̃ʒɔ̃ksjɔnɛlmɑ̃], *adv. Gram:* conjunctionally, as a conjunction.

conjonctival, -aux [kɔ̃ʒɔ̃ktival, -o], *a. Physiol:* conjunctival.

conjonctive [kɔ̃ʒɔ̃ktiːv], *s.f. Anat:* conjunctiva (of the eye).

conjonctivite [kɔ̃ʒɔ̃ktivit], *s.f. Med:* conjunctivitis; **c. granuleuse,** trachoma; *F:* granular lids.

conjoncture [kɔ̃ʒɔ̃ktyːr], *s.f.* conjuncture, contingency; combination of circumstances; **dans la c. actuelle des choses,** at this (present) juncture, under the present circumstances; **se trouver dans une malheureuse c.,** to find oneself in an unfortunate situation, in a predicament; **dans cette c. . . .,** at this juncture . . .; *Pol: Ec:* **(période de) haute c.,** boom; **c. économique,** overall economic situation.

conjoncturel, -elle [kɔ̃ʒɔ̃ktyrɛl], *a. Pol.Ec:* cyclical.

conjugable [kɔ̃ʒygabl̩], *a. Gram:* conjugable, (verb) that can be conjugated.

conjugaison [kɔ̃ʒygɛzɔ̃], *s.f.* **1.** *Gram: Biol: etc:* conjugation (of verb, of cells, etc.). **2.** pairing (of engines, of guns on turret); mating (of gears); *Artil: etc:* combining (of sights). **3.** *Atom.Ph:* **c. de charge,** charge conjugation.

conjugal, -aux [kɔ̃ʒygal, -o], *a.* conjugal; **amour c., vie conjugale,** married love, life; *Com:* **société conjugale,** partnership between husband and wife; *Jur:* **le domicile c.,** home (of married couple); **les liens conjugaux,** the marriage tie; **remplir son devoir c., ses devoirs conjugaux,** to fulfil one's marital obligations; **droits conjugaux,** conjugal rights.

conjugalement [kɔ̃ʒygalmɑ̃], *adv.* conjugally.

conjugué [kɔ̃ʒyge]. **1.** *a.* (*a*) *Mth: Opt:* conjugate; **diamètres conjugués,** conjugate diameters; **droites conjuguées,** conjugate lines; **foyers conjugués,** conjugate foci; **hyperboles conjuguées,** conjugate hyperbolas; **miroirs conjugués,** conjugate mirrors; **plans, points, conjugués,** conjugate planes, points; *El:* **impédances conjuguées,** conjugate impedances; *Bot:* **feuilles conjuguées,** conjugate leaves; (*b*) combined; **parcours c. métro-autobus,** combined tube and bus journey; (*c*) *Mec.E:* paired, twin, interconnected; **machines conjuguées,** paired engines; *Artil: etc:* **hausses conjuguées,** combined sights; *Aut: etc:* **freinage c.,** coupled, interacting, brakes; **commandes conjuguées,** inter-connected controls; *s.a.* DÉVIATION. **2.** *s.f. Algae:* **conjuguées,** conjugatae.

conjuguer [kɔ̃ʒyge], *v.tr.* **1.** *Gram:* to conjugate. **2.** to pair (engines, guns); *Artil: etc:* to combine (sights). **3. ils conjuguèrent leurs efforts,** they united their efforts.

conjungo [kɔ̃ʒœ̃go], *s.m.* no *pl.* **1.** *F:* marriage; **prononcer le c.,** *F:* to tie the knot. **2.** *Pal:* continuous writing (without spacing or punctuation).

conjurateur, -trice [kɔ̃ʒyratœːr, -tris]. **1.** (*a*) *s.* **c. (de démons),** exorcist; (*b*) *a.* magical. **2.** *s.* conspirator.

conjuration [kɔ̃ʒyrasjɔ̃], *s.f.* **1.** conspiracy, plot. **2.** incantation, exorcism, conjuration. **3.** *pl.* entreaties, supplication.

conjuré, -ée [kɔ̃ʒyre], *s.* conspirator.

conjurer [kɔ̃ʒyre], *v.tr.* **1.** to plot, conspire; (*a*) **c. la ruine de qn,** to plot s.o.'s ruin; (*b*) *v.i.* **c. contre qn,** to conspire against s.o. **2.** (*a*) to exorcise (demon); (*b*) to cope with, avert, ward off (danger, etc.); **c. un désastre, la ruine,** to stave off a disaster, ruin. **3. c. qn de faire qch.,** to entreat, beg, beseech s.o. to do sth.; **je le conjurai de céder,** I entreated, begged, him to yield.

se conjurer, to conspire (together); to league together.

conjureur [kɔ̃ʒyrœːr], *s.m.* conjuror, exorcist.

connaissable [kɔnɛsabl̩], *a.* **1.** *Phil:* cognizable, cognoscible; knowable. **2.** recognizable, easily known (**à,** by).

connaissance [kɔnɛsɑ̃:s], s.f. 1. (a) acquaintance, knowledge; faire c. avec qch., to become acquainted with, obtain knowledge of, sth.; prendre c. de qch., to make oneself acquainted with, to study, examine, to enquire into, sth.; prendre c. d'un dossier, to go through a dossier; j'en prendrai c., I will look into it; avoir c. de qch., to be aware of sth.; il est arrivé à ma c. que . . ., it has come to my knowledge that . . .; porter qch. à la c. de qn, to inform, apprise, advise, s.o. of sth., to make sth. known to s.o., to bring sth. to s.o.'s knowledge; A: cela n'est pas à ma c., this is not within my ken; il n'a jamais, à ma c., été malade, he has never had a day's illness, to my knowledge, so far as I know; en c. de cause, en pleine c. des faits, advisedly, with full knowledge of the facts, on good grounds; O: être en âge de c., to have arrived at years of discretion; (b) Nau: avoir c. de terre, to sight land; (c) Ven: (distinguishing feature of) tracks of quarry; (d) une personne de ma c., someone I know, an acquaintance; faire c. avec qn, faire la c. de qn, to make s.o.'s acquaintance, to become acquainted with s.o., to come to know s.o.; faire faire c. à deux personnes, to make two persons acquainted; to bring two persons together; quand je fis sa c., when I first knew him; faire plus ample c. avec qn, to become better acquainted with s.o.; refaire c., to renew acquaintance; lier c. avec qn, to strike up an acquaintance with s.o.; cultiver la c. de qn, to cultivate s.o.'s acquaintance; des gens de c., people one knows well, friends; une figure de c., a familiar face, the face of an old acquaintance; en pays de c., among familiar faces, among people one knows, on familiar ground; (e) c'est une de mes connaissances, he is an acquaintance of mine; avoir un cercle de connaissances très étendu, to have a wide circle of acquaintances; (f) F: je l'ai rencontré avec sa c., I met him with his girl-friend. 2. (a) knowledge, understanding; c. de soi, self-knowledge; avoir la c. de plusieurs langues, to know several languages; c. approfondie du français, thorough command of French; sa c. du droit, des langues, his knowledge of the law, of languages; une c. vague, superficielle, a nodding acquaintance; Nau: c. des temps, nautical almanac; (b) Jur: cognizance; ces faits ne sont pas dans la c. du tribunal, these facts are not within the cognizance of the court; (c) Phil: cognition; (d) pl. learning, attainments, acquirements; les connaissances de droit que chacun doit posséder, the knowledge of the law that everyone ought to possess; avoir de profondes connaissances en mathématiques, to be deeply versed in mathematics; avoir quelques connaissances en français, to have some knowledge of French; accroître ses connaissances, to add to one's (store of) knowledge; homme sans grandes connaissances, man of no great attainments; exploiter les connaissances de qn, F: to pick, suck, s.o.'s brains. 3. consciousness; perdre c., to lose consciousness, to swoon, faint; reprendre c., to regain consciousness, to recover one's senses, one's wits; F: to come to, to come round; faire reprendre c. à qn, to bring s.o. round, to; sans c., unconscious, in a dead faint; il a conservé sa c. jusqu'au bout, he was conscious to the end.

connaissant [kɔnɛsɑ̃], a. Jur: A: gens à ce connaissants, persons acquainted with the matter, experts.

connaissement [kɔnɛsmɑ̃], s.m. Nau: Com: bill of lading, shipping-bill; Com: c. direct (avec rupture de charge), through bill of lading (with transhipment).

connaisseur, -euse [kɔnɛsœ:r, -ø:z]. 1. s. expert, connoisseur; être bon c. en qch., to be a good judge of, an authority on, sth.; to be a connoisseur of, in, sth. 2. a. regarder qch. d'un œil c., to look at sth. with a critical eye; il prit un air c., he assumed an air of superior knowledge, the air of an expert.

connaître [kɔnɛtr̥], v.tr. (pr.p. connaissant; p.p. connu; pr.ind. je connais, il connaît, n. connaissons; p.d. je connaissais; p.h. je connus; fu. je connaîtrai) to know. 1. to be acquainted with (sth.); c. les chemins, to be familiar with the roads; un endroit de moi seul connu, a place known to me alone; c. un fait, to be aware of, acquainted with, a fact; je connais tous les détails, I am aware of all the circumstances; il ne connaît pas l'amour, he does not know what love is, has no experience of love; il connaît la faim, he knows what hunger is; il ne connaît pas le monde, he is ignorant of the world; (with obj. and complement) cette terre que nous connaissons fertile, this land that we know is, to be, fertile; il connut alors qu'il lui était pardonné, he then knew that he was forgiven; je lui connaissais du talent, I knew he had talent; je ne lui connais pas de défaut, I see no fault in him; on ne lui connaît pas de domicile, he is not known to have any fixed address; la source de lumière la plus intense que l'on connaisse, the brightest light known; faire c. qch., to bring sth. to light, to make sth. known; Equit: cheval qui connaît les éperons, horse that is obedient to the spurs; cette région connaît actuellement une famine, that region is now experiencing a famine; F: je ne te connaissais pas cette robe, I didn't know you had that dress; connaissez-vous la nouvelle? have you heard the news? il est bien connu que . . ., it is well known that . . .; F: il connaît Paris comme le fond de sa poche, he knows every inch of Paris, he knows Paris like the back of his hand, inside out; si tu te tais, ni vu ni connu, if you hold your tongue, no one will be any the wiser; il en connaît bien d'autres, he has plenty more tricks up his sleeve; P: il la connaît (dans les coins), he knows what's what, he's a wily old bird. 2. (a) to be acquainted with (s.o.); c. qn de nom, de vue, to know s.o. by name, by sight; prétendre c. qn, to claim acquaintance with s.o.; c. son monde, to know the people one has to deal with; gagner à être connu, to improve on acquaintance; être connu pour menteur, to be known as a liar; je l'avais connu pauvre, I had known him when he was poor, I had known him as a poor man; ils ne se connaissent plus, they have become estranged; je n'ai pas l'honneur d'être connu de vous, I have not the honour of your acquaintance; B: ton langage te fait connaître, thy speech bewrayeth thee; F: c. qn comme le fond de sa poche, to know s.o. through and through, to read s.o. like a book; connu! I've heard that one before! ça me connaît, you can't teach me anything about that; je ne connais que lui! don't I know him! (b) to make the acquaintance of (s.o.), to come to know (s.o.); ils se sont connus en 1970, they met, they became acquainted in 1970; c'est moi qui les ai fait se c., it was I who made them acquainted; se faire c., (i) to introduce oneself by name; (ii) to come to the front, to become known, to rise to notice; je vous le ferai c., I shall introduce him to you; faire c. qn, (i) to reveal s.o.'s identity; (ii) to bring s.o. into notice; (iii) to show s.o. up; le premier ministre a fait c. la composition de son ministère, the prime minister has announced his cabinet. 3. (a) to be versed in (science, art, language, etc.); c. qch. à fond, to be thoroughly conversant with sth., to have a thorough knowledge of sth.; to have a thorough command of (a language); c. aussi bien l'anglais que le français, to be equally at home in English and French; (b) to distinguish; c. le bien d'avec le mal, to know good from evil. 4. A: to recognize, acknowledge; c. qn pour maître, to acknowledge s.o. as master; je le connais à sa voix, I recognize him by his voice; il est grandi à ne plus le c., he has grown beyond all recognition, out of all knowledge; il ne connaît ni Dieu ni diable, he has no religious beliefs; Prov: à l'œuvre on connaît l'artisan, the workman is known by his work; s.a. BESOIN 2. 5. B: to know, have commerce with (woman); et Adam connut Ève, sa femme, and Adam knew Eve his wife. 6. v.i. Jur: c. de qch., to take cognizance of sth.; c. d'un grief, to deal with a grievance; c. d'un différend, to hear and determine a dispute; F: action dont seul j'ai à c., action that concerns me alone.

se connaître. 1. se c. à, en, qch., to know all about, be a good judge of, sth.; je ne me connais pas, ne m'y connais pas, en chevaux, I am no judge of horse-flesh; F: il s'y connaît, he is an expert; he knows what's what; je ne m'y connais plus, I am all adrift, all at sea. 2. il ne se connaît plus, he has lost control of himself; dans l'ivresse il ne se connaît plus, when under the influence of drink he does not know what he is doing; il ne se connaît plus de joie, he is beside himself with joy; he is walking on air.

conné [kɔne], a. connate (leaf, etc.).

connecter [kɔnɛkte], v.tr. El: Elcs: to connect.

connecteur [kɔnɛktœ:r], s.m. El: connector, connecting condenser, (electric) coupler, transfer switch; c. à fusible, fuse connector; c. annulaire, splicing clamp; Space: c. ombilical, umbilical cord; c. interétages, interstage connector.

connectif, -ive [kɔnɛktif, -i:v]. 1. a. Anat: Ling: connective (tissue, etc.). 2. s.m. Bot: connective (of anther).

connerie [kɔnri], s.f. V: piece of rank stupidity; V: balls; faire une c., to do a darned silly thing; c'est des conneries, it's all cock; V: ne dis pas de(s) conneries, don't talk cock.

connétable [kɔnetabl̥], s.m. Hist: High Constable; (a) first official of the French king's household; (b) commander-in-chief of the French armies (abolished in 1627); (c) title of several dignitaries under Napoleon I.

connétablie [kɔnetabli], s.f. Hist: 1. office of High Constable. 2. military jurisdiction of the High Constable.

connexe [kɔn(n)ɛks], a. Jur: Bot: etc: connected; allied; industries connexes de . . ., industries related to . . ., connected with . . .; assurances sociales et services connexes, social insurance and allied services.

connexion [kɔn(n)ɛksjɔ̃], s.f. 1. connection (of parts, ideas, etc.); en c. avec, in connection with; Mec.E: c. directe, positive drive; machine à c. directe, direct-acting engine; El: appareil en c. avec la terre, apparatus connected with the earth; barrette de c., connecting strap, strip, bar; connector-block; fil de c., connecting wire; relais de c., connecting relay, U.S: cut-through relay; c. à la masse, (i) earth connection, U.S: ground connection; (ii) Aut: etc: frame connection; Rail: triangle de c., tie-rod (of points). 2. Geom: connex. 3. connecting organ or part; El.E: lead; (cell-to-cell) connector, lead, connection; c. à un conducteur, single connector; c. à deux conducteurs, twin connector; c. d'électrode, lead-in wire; c. de mise à la terre, earth connection, U.S: ground connection; c. du couple thermo-électrique, thermo-couple lead; c. interne, internal connection or lead; c. rigide, connector rod; c. volante, jumper-lead; les connexions, the connectors.

connexité [kɔn(n)ɛksite], s.f. Jur: etc: connexity, relatedness (of ideas, etc.); Phil: le principe de c., the principle of relationship.

connil [kɔnil, -ni], s.m. Her: A: cony, rabbit.

connivence [kɔnivɑ̃:s], s.f. connivance, complicity; agir, être, de c. avec qn, to act in complicity, in collusion, with s.o.; gendarmerie de c. avec les contrebandiers, police in connivance, in league, with smugglers.

connivent [kɔnivɑ̃], a. Biol: connivent (petals, wings, etc.).

conniver [kɔnive], v.i. A: Lit: to connive, wink (à, at); c. avec qn, to be in collusion with s.o.

connotateur [kɔnɔtatœ:r], s.m. Ling: Log: significant, connotative element.

connotatif, -ive [kɔnɔtatif, -i:v], a. connotative.

connotation [kɔnɔtasjɔ̃], s.f. Log: connotation.

connoter [kɔn(n)ɔte], v.tr. Log: to connote.

connu [kɔny]. 1. a. (a) well-known, clear; famous; un écrivain c., a well-known writer; c'est une chose bien connue, it's a well-known thing; elle est bien connue, celle-là! everybody knows that one, that joke, that's an old one! (b) le monde c., the known world. 2. s.m. passer, aller, du connu à l'inconnu, to go from the known to the unknown.

conocarpe [kɔnɔkarp], s.m. Bot: conocarpus.

conocéphale [kɔnɔsefal], s.m. Z: conocephalum.

conoïdal, -aux [kɔnɔidal, -o], a. conoidal (calyx, mollusc, etc.).

conoïde [kɔnɔid]. 1. a. conoid (ligament, surface, etc.). 2. s.m. Geom: conoid.

conolophe [kɔnɔlɔf], s.m. Rept: conolophus, land iguana.

conopée [kɔnɔpe], s.m. Ecc: canopy (of tabernacle).

conopidés [kɔnɔpide], s.m.pl. Ent: Conopidae.

conque [kɔ̃:k], s.f. 1. conch, marine shell; la c. de Triton, Triton's conch. 2. concha; (a) Anat: external ear; (b) Arch: A: apse, conch. 3. I.C.E: volute chamber, delivery space.

conquérant [kɔ̃kerɑ̃]. a. conquering (nation, etc.); s. Guillaume le Conquérant, William the Conqueror; F: air c., swaggering air, swagger; il a un air c., he's a regular lady-killer.

conquérir [kɔ̃keri:r], v.tr. (pr.p. conquérant; p.p. conquis; pr.ind. je conquiers, n. conquérons, ils conquièrent; p.d. je conquérais; p.h. je conquis; fu. je conquerrai) (a) to conquer, subdue (country, people); la province qu'il avait conquise sur ses ennemis, the province he had conquered from his enemies; on se demande s'il est conquis à l'ennemi, we are wondering whether he has been won over to the enemy cause; il se conduit comme en pays conquis, he's behaving as if he owned the place; traiter qn en pays conquis, to ride roughshod over s.o.; (b) to gain, win (over), make a conquest of (s.o., sth.); c. l'estime, le cœur, de qn, to win, gain, s.o.'s esteem, heart.

conquêt [kɔ̃kɛ], *s.m. Jur:* acquisition (of goods, wealth, by husband or wife); acquired real estate.

conquête [kɔ̃kɛt], *s.f.* **1.** (act of) conquest; (*a*) **faire la c. d'un pays,** to conquer a country; **pays de c.,** conquered country; *F:* **vivre comme en pays de c.,** to lord it over everyone; (*b*) **faire la c. de qn,** to gain s.o.'s sympathy, esteem, to make a conquest of s.o.; **vous avez fait sa c.,** you have won his or her heart; (*of a woman*) **entreprendre la c. d'un homme,** to set one's cap at a man. **2.** conquered territory; acquisition, possession; **administrer ses conquêtes,** to administer one's conquests.

conquistador [kɔ̃kistadɔːr], *s.m.* (*a*) *Hist:* conquistador; (*b*) *F:* lady-killer; *pl. conquistadors.*

consacrant [kɔ̃sakrɑ̃], *Ecc:* **1.** *a.* consecrating (bishop, etc.). **2.** *s.m.* consecrating priest; consecrator.

consacré [kɔ̃sakre], *a.* **1.** consecrated, sacred (vessel, etc.); hallowed (ground). **2.** sanctioned, established, time-honoured (custom, etc.); **expression consacrée,** accepted, recognized, expression; stock phrase.

consacrer [kɔ̃sakre], *v.tr.* **1.** (*a*) to consecrate (altar, bread and wine, etc.); **c. un évêque, un prêtre,** to consecrate a bishop, ordain a priest; **il fut consacré évêque de Chartres,** he was consecrated Bishop of Chartres; (*b*) to dedicate (one's life to God, etc.); to devote (one's holidays to study, etc.); to assign (sum of money to a purpose, etc.); **c. toute son énergie à une tâche,** to bend, devote, (all) one's energies to a task; **se c. à une entreprise,** to give oneself up to an undertaking; **combien de temps pouvez-vous me c.?** how much time can you spare me? **2.** to sanctify, hallow (memory, place, etc.); **c'est l'habitude qui consacre une erreur,** it is custom that sanctions an error; **c. la gloire de qn,** to establish s.o.'s reputation; **expression consacrée par l'usage,** an expression hallowed by usage.

consanguin [kɔ̃sɑ̃gɛ̃], *a.* **1.** *Jur:* consanguine(an), consanguineous (through the father); **frère c., sœur consanguine,** half-brother, half-sister (on the father's side). **2.** inbred (horse, etc.); **accouplement c., mariages consanguins,** inter-breeding; intermarriage; in-breeding, breeding in. **3.** *Geol:* consanguineous.

consanguinité [kɔ̃sɑ̃gɥinite], *s.f.* **1.** *Jur:* consanguinity (through the father). **2.** in-breeding. **3.** *Geol:* consanguinity.

consciemment [kɔ̃sjamɑ̃], *adv.* consciously, knowingly.

conscience [kɔ̃sjɑ̃ːs], *s.f.* **1.** consciousness; *Phil:* self-consciousness; **perdre c.,** to lose consciousness, (i) to faint; (ii) to fall asleep; **reprendre c.,** to regain consciousness; **avoir c. de qch., d'avoir fait qch.,** to be conscious, aware, of sth., of having done sth.; **lorsque je commençai à avoir c. de mon malheur,** when I awoke to the consciousness of my misfortune; **c. de soi-même,** self-awareness; **prendre c. de soi-même, de ses talents, de ses capacités,** to find oneself; **nation en train de prendre c. d'elle-même,** nation beginning to feel its feet; **agir avec la pleine c. des conséquences,** to act in full consciousness of the consequences; **prise de c.,** sudden awareness; **c'est la première fois que j'en ai pris c.,** it's the first time that it has come home to me; **prendre c. d'être seul,** to realize that one is alone; **prendre c. que . . .,** to become aware that . . .. **2.** (*a*) conscience; **c. chargée, mauvaise c.,** burdened, bad, guilty, conscience; **c. endurcie,** hardened, seared, conscience; **n'avoir pas la c. tranquille,** to have twinges of conscience, a guilty conscience; **c. large,** accommodating conscience; **il a la c. large, élastique,** he is not over-scrupulous; **sans c.,** unscrupulous; unconscionable (rogue, etc.); **scrupule de c.,** conscientious scruple; **cas de c.,** point of conscience; **(se) faire (un cas de) c. de qch.,** to scruple to do sth.; **c'est une affaire de c.,** it is a matter of conscience; *A:* **c'est (une) c. de . . .,** it goes against the conscience to . . .; *A:* **dans le for de ma c.,** in my heart of hearts; *s.a.* ÂME 1; **faire qch. en (toute) sûreté de c.,** to do sth. with a clear conscience; **avoir qch. sur la c.,** to have sth. on one's conscience; **quelque chose lui pèse sur la c.,** something is weighing, lying, on his conscience; **je vous le mets sur la c.,** may your own conscience deal with you; **faire qch. par acquit de c., pour l'acquit de sa c.,** to do sth. for conscience' sake, for form's sake, as a matter of duty; **dire qch. en (bonne) c.,** to say sth. in good faith; **je peux vous assurer, la main sur la c., que . . .,** I can assure you upon my conscience, in all conscience, that . . .; **manque de c.,** unscrupulousness; **j'ai la c. nette, j'ai bonne c.,** I have a clear conscience, my conscience is clear; *s.a.* EXAMEN, OBJECTEUR, OBJECTION; (*b*) conscientiousness; **avoir de la c.,** to be scrupulous, conscientious; **c. professionnelle,** conscientious approach to one's work; **avoir la c. de faire qch.,** to be conscientious enough to do sth.; **faire qch. en, avec, c.,** to do sth. conscientiously; *Typ:* **travail en c.,** time-work; **être en c.,** to be on time-work, on the establishment; **ouvrier en c.,** establishment-hand, job-compositor; (*c*) **liberté de c.,** liberty of conscience; **article sauvegardant la liberté de c.,** conscience clause (in an Act). **3.** (*a*) *P:* stomach; **ça m'est resté sur la c.,** it's lying heavy on my stomach; (*b*) *Tls:* breast-plate, palette, conscience; **drille à c.,** breast-drill.

consciencieusement [kɔ̃sjɑ̃sjøzmɑ̃], *adv.* conscientiously.

consciencieux, -ieuse [kɔ̃sjɑ̃sjø, -jøːz], *a.* conscientious (person, work).

conscient [kɔ̃sjɑ̃], *a.* **1.** conscious (de, of; que, that); *Phil:* self-conscious; **c. de la gravité de . . .,** (fully) aware of the gravity of . . .. **2.** **être c.,** sentient being.

conscriptible [kɔ̃skriptibl̩], *a. & s.m. Mil:* (man) liable for service.

conscription [kɔ̃skripsjɔ̃], *s.f. Mil:* conscription, enrolment for military service, *U.S:* draft; **c. des chevaux,** census of horses; **c. des fortunes,** conscription of wealth; capital levy.

conscriptionnel, -elle [kɔ̃skripsjɔnɛl], *a.* concerning conscription.

conscrit [kɔ̃skri]. **1.** *a. Rom.Ant:* **les pères conscrits,** the conscript fathers. **2.** *s.m.* (*a*) *Mil:* (i) one liable to conscription; (ii) (raw) conscript, recruit; *U.S:* draftee; (*b*) *F:* novice, greenhorn.

consécrateur [kɔ̃sekratœːr], *a. & s.m.* (*a*) *a. Ecc:* = CONSACRANT; (*b*) *s.m.* **ce théâtre a été le c. de nombreux talents,** this theatre has given the stamp of success to many talented artists.

consécration [kɔ̃sekrasjɔ̃], *s.f.* **1.** consecration (of church, bishop, etc.); ordination (of priest). **2.** dedication (of one's life, etc.) (**à**, to). **3.** ratification; establishing (of a reputation); **expression qui a reçu la c. du temps,** expression which has received the sanction of time.

consécutif, -ive [kɔ̃sekytif, -iːv], *a.* **1.** consecutive; **deux jours consécutifs,** two consecutive days, two days running; **pendant trois mois consécutifs,** for three months on end, in succession; *Gram:* **proposition consécutive,** consecutive clause, result clause; *Mus:* **quintes consécutives,** consecutive fifths; *Med: Opt:* **image consécutive,** after-image. **2.** **fatigue consécutive à une longue marche,** fatigue resulting from a long march; **infirmité consécutive à une blessure,** infirmity due to, following upon, consequent upon, a wound.

consécution [kɔ̃sekysjɔ̃], *s.f.* consecution; *A: Astr:* **mois de c.,** lunar month, synodic month.

consécutivement [kɔ̃sekytivmɑ̃], *adv.* consecutively, in succession.

conseil [kɔ̃sɛːj], *s.m.* **1.** (*a*) *A. & Lit:* counsel, purpose, plan; **les conseils de Dieu,** the counsels of God, the decrees of Providence; **ne savoir quel c. prendre,** not to know what decision to make; *Theol:* **les conseils de perfection,** counsels of perfection; **les conseils évangéliques,** evangelical counsels; (*b*) counsel, (piece of) advice; **un bon c.,** a sound piece of advice; **homme de bon c.,** man worth consulting, sensible man; **donner c. à qn,** to advise s.o.; **demander c. à qn, prendre c. de qn,** to consult s.o., seek s.o.'s advice; **suivre le c. de qn,** to take s.o.'s advice; **agir selon le c. de qn,** to act on s.o.'s advice; **je viens sur le c. de . . .,** I have come on the advice of . . .; **il ne prend c. que de sa tête,** he takes no-one's advice; *Prov:* **la nuit porte c.,** seek advice of your pillow; sleep on it; *s.a.* ARBRE 2; **deux conseils valent mieux qu'un,** two heads are better than one; **pouvez-vous me donner quelques conseils?** can you give me some hints? **2.** (*a*) *Jur:* counseller, counsel; **consulter un c.,** to take counsel's opinion; **servir de c. pour une question,** to advise on a question; *A:* **c. judiciaire,** guardian, administrator of estate (of young spendthrift); **pourvu d'un c. judiciaire,** under guardianship; (*b*) **chimiste c.,** consulting chemist; **ingénieur c.,** consulting engineer; **c. fiscal** = chartered accountant. **3.** council, committee, board; **chambre du c.,** council chamber, board-room; *s.a.* CHAMBRE 2; **tenir c.,** to hold (a) council; **le c. des ministres,** the Cabinet; **c. privé, d'État,** Privy Council, Council of State; **c. municipal** = (i) town council; (ii) parish council; **c. général** = county council; *Com:* **c. d'administration,** (i) board of directors; (ii) board-meeting; **c. de surveillance,** board of trustees; *Mil: Navy:* **c. de guerre,** (i) war-council; (ii) court-martial; **passer en c. de guerre,** to be court-martialled; **faire passer qn au c.,** to have s.o. court-martialled; *Navy:* **c. des prises,** prize court; **le c. supérieur de la Guerre,** the Army Council; **le c. supérieur de la Marine,** the Board of Admiralty; *Hist:* **le c. supérieur interallié,** the Supreme War Council; **c. d'enquête,** court of enquiry; **c. de santé,** medical board; *Jur:* **c. de famille,** board of relations (in family matters), family council, board of guardians; **c. de sécurité (de l'O.N.U.),** (U.N.O.) Security Council; **C. de l'Europe,** Council of Europe; *A:* **C. de la République,** Upper House of French Parliament; *s.a.* FABRIQUE 3, ORDRE 4, RÉVISION 2.

conseillable [kɔ̃sɛjabl̩], *a.* advisable, recommendable.

conseiller[1] [kɔ̃sɛje], *v.tr.* to advise, counsel; **c. qn,** to counsel, advise, give advice to, s.o.; **c. qch. à qn,** to recommend sth. to s.o.; **je vous conseille la prudence,** I advise you to be prudent; **je ne vous le conseille pas,** I shouldn't if I were you; **c. à qn de faire qch.,** to advise, recommend, s.o. to do sth.

conseiller[2], **-ère** [kɔ̃sɛje, -jɛːr], *s.* **1.** counsellor, adviser; **c. juridique, technique,** legal, technical, adviser; **c. fiscal** = tax consultant. **2.** **c. municipal,** town councillor; = alderman; **c. général,** = county councillor. **3.** *Jur:* **c. à la cour (d'appel, de cassation),** judge of appeal.

conseilleur, -euse [kɔ̃sɛjœːr, -øːz], *s.* (*a*) adviser; (*b*) *Pej:* person who is always giving (unwanted) advice; *F:* busybody.

consensuel, -elle [kɔ̃sɑ̃sɥɛl], *a. Jur:* consensual (contract); *Physiol:* **réflexe c.,** consensual light reflex.

consensus [kɔ̃sɛ̃syːs], *s.m.* consensus (of opinion, etc.).

consentant [kɔ̃sɑ̃tɑ̃], *a.* (*a*) *Jur:* consenting (party, etc.); **il y est c.,** he consents, agrees; (*b*) **elle est consentante,** she is willing.

consentement [kɔ̃sɑ̃tmɑ̃], *s.m.* **1.** consent, assent; **c. exprès,** formal consent; **c. verbal, par écrit,** verbal assent, written consent; **d'un commun c.,** by common consent, assent; **du c. de tous . . .,** by universal consent . . .; **donner son c. à qch.,** to assent, consent, to sth. **2.** yielding, depression (of beam, etc.).

consenti [kɔ̃sɑ̃ti], *a.* (*a*) sprung, wrung (mast, etc.); (*b*) **discipline librement consentie,** voluntary discipline.

consentir [kɔ̃sɑ̃tiːr], *v.* (*conj. like* SENTIR) **1.** *v.i.* (*a*) to consent, agree; **c. à qch.,** to consent to sth.; **c. à faire qch.,** to consent to do sth.; **je consens (à ce) qu'il vienne,** I consent, agree, to his coming; **assurances sur la vie consenties par l'industrie automobile,** life insurances agreed to by the motor industry; **il a fini par c.,** *F:* he came round in the end; *Prov:* **qui ne dit mot consent,** silence gives consent; (*b*) (*of beam, etc.*) to yield; *Nau:* (*of mast, etc.*) to spring, break. **2.** *v.tr.* (*a*) *Jur:* **c. la vente des effets,** to authorize the sale of effects; *Com:* **c. un prêt,** to grant a loan; **c. une remise, un prix réduit, à qn,** to allow a discount, a reduced price, to s.o.; **c. un sacrifice,** to make a sacrifice; (*b*) to accept, admit (opinion, etc.).

conséquemment [kɔ̃sekamɑ̃], *adv.* **1.** consistently. **2.** consequently, in consequence, accordingly.

conséquence [kɔ̃sekɑ̃ːs], *s.f.* consequence; (*a*) outcome, sequel, result; **subir les conséquences d'une erreur,** to suffer the consequences of a mistake; **il faut en subir les conséquences,** we, you, must take the consequences; **qu'est-ce que cela aura pour c.?** what will be the effect, the result, of it? **tirer à c.,** (i) to be a precedent; (ii) to be of importance; **cela ne tire pas à c.,** it is of no consequence; *adv.phr.* **en c.,** in consequence, consequently, accordingly; **agir en c.,** to take appropriate action; *prep.phr:* **en c. de . . .,** (i) in consequence of . . .; (ii) in pursuance of . . .; (*b*) inference; **tirer une c. de qch.,** to draw an inference from sth.; *Fr.C:* **(jeu des) conséquences,** (game of) consequences; (*c*) *Phil:* consistency; (*d*) importance; **personne sans c.,** person of no importance, consequence; **affaires de la dernière c.,** matters of the highest moment, of the first importance.

conséquent [kɔ̃sekɑ̃]. **1.** *a.* (*a*) consistent, rational (mind, speech, etc.); **conclusion conséquente aux prémisses,** conclusion consistent with the premises; (*b*) *Mus:* **partie conséquente,** *s.m.* **conséquent,** *s.f.* **conséquente d'une fugue,** counter-subject of a fugue; *El:* **points, pôles, conséquents,** consequent points, consecutive poles; (*c*)

following; **septicémie conséquente d'une coupure,** septicaemia following (on) a cut, due to a cut; (*d*) *P:* **homme c., affaire conséquente,** important man, business. **2.** *s.m. Gram: Log: Mth:* consequent; *adv.phr.* **par c.,** consequently, accordingly, therefore.

conséquentiel, -ielle [kɔ̃sekɑ̃sjɛl], *a.* (*rare*) consequent(ial).

conservable [kɔ̃sɛrvabl̩], *a.* (*of butter, etc.*) that will keep.

conservateur, -trice [kɔ̃sɛrvatœːr, -tris]. **1.** *s.* (*a*) conservator, guardian, keeper, warden; **c. de bibliothèque,** librarian; **c. d'un musée,** curator, keeper, of a museum; **c. des hypothèques,** registrar of mortgages; **c. d'un parc national,** warden of a national park; (*b*) *Pol:* conservative; *a.* **parti c.,** conservative party; (*c*) *Ind: O:* canner (of foodstuffs); (*d*) *s.m. Av:* **c. de cap,** course indicator, directional gyro; (*e*) *s.m. Dom.Ec:* freezer. **2.** *a.* preserving, preservative (process, etc.); **lois conservatrices de nos libertés,** laws that guard our liberties.

conservatif, -ive [kɔ̃sɛrvatif, -iːv], *a.* preservative.

conservation [kɔ̃sɛrvasjɔ̃], *s.f.* **1.** (*a*) conserving, conservation; preserving, preservation (of fruit, meat, etc.); *Ph:* **c. de l'énergie,** conservation of energy; (*b*) preservation, care (of buildings, archives, health, etc.); keeping (of archives, etc.); **instinct de conservation,** instinct of self-preservation; *Adm:* **c. des forêts,** (i) conservancy of forests; (ii) preservation of timber; **veiller à la c. des archives,** to keep the archives; (*c*) retaining, keeping (of rights, situation, etc.); *Mil:* **c. d'une position,** holding of a captured position; (*d*) registration (of mortgages); (*e*) curing (of concrete). **2.** (state of) preservation; **meubles d'une belle c.,** well-preserved, well-kept, furniture. **3.** (*thing kept*) *Typ:* standing type; *A.Lith:* work still on the stone.

conservatisme [kɔ̃sɛrvatism], *s.m. Pol: etc:* conservatism.

conservatoire [kɔ̃sɛrvatwaːr]. **1.** *a. Jur:* conservatory (act, etc.); **mesures conservatoires,** measures of conservation. **2.** *s.m.* (*a*) repository, museum; **c. des Arts et Métiers,** museum and college of higher technology for training students in the application of science to industry; (*b*) school, academy (of music, of dramatic art), conservatoire, *U.S:* conservatory.

conserve [kɔ̃sɛrv], *s.f.* **1.** (*a*) preserve, preserved food; **conserves de fruits en bocaux,** bottled fruits; **conserves en pots,** potted meats; **conserves au vinaigre,** pickles; **bœuf de c.,** tinned beef, corned beef, *U.S:* canned beef; *F:* bully beef; **petits pois en c.,** tinned green peas; **se nourrir de conserves,** to live on tinned foods; **mettre en c.,** to tin, can; **mise en c.,** tinning, canning; *s.a.* ALIMENTAIRE 2; *Typ:* **mettre une composition en c.,** to keep type standing; *P:* **que vas-tu faire de cet argent? pas des conserves, bien sûr!** what are you going to do with this money? I'm not going to hang on to it for long! *F:* **musique de c.,** canned music; (*b*) *Pharm:* conserve. **2.** *pl. A:* dark or tinted spectacles, coloured glasses, sunglasses. **3.** *Nau:* convoy, consort; **naviguer de c.,** to sail in company, together (**avec,** with); *F:* **nous y sommes allés de c.,** the whole crowd of us went, we went as a party.

conservé [kɔ̃sɛrve], *a.* **tableaux bien conservés,** pictures in a good state of preservation; *F:* **femme bien conservée,** well-preserved woman.

conserver [kɔ̃sɛrve], *v.tr.* **1.** (*a*) to preserve, conserve (fruit, meat, etc.); **aliments conservés,** tinned or bottled foods; *s.a.* BŒUF 2; (*b*) to preserve, take care of (building, furniture, clothes, etc.); **c. le gibier,** to preserve game; **c. précieusement qch.,** to treasure sth.; (*c*) to cure (concrete). **2.** to keep, retain, maintain (rights, situation, servants, etc.); **c. un usage,** to keep up a custom, **c. toutes ses facultés,** to retain all one's faculties; **c. ses opinions,** to cling to one's opinions; **c. son sang-froid, sa tête,** to remain cool, to keep one's head; **c. l'allure,** to keep up, maintain, the speed or the pace; **conserve ton âme toujours pure,** keep your soul ever pure; *Mil:* **c. une position,** to hold a position; *Nau: etc:* **c. les feux allumés,** to keep (up) steam; *Tp:* **c. la ligne,** to hold the line; *Mil:* **c. la tête droite,** to keep the eyes to the front (as in marching past); **c. les, ses, distances,** to keep one's distance. **3.** *Nau:* to convoy.

se conserver, (*of goods, etc.*) to keep; **articles qui ne se conservent pas,** articles that will not keep, perishable articles.

conserverie [kɔ̃sɛrvəri], *s.f.* **1.** (food-)packing trade; canning industry. **2.** packing-house (for tinned foods, etc.); cannery.

conserveur [kɔ̃sɛrvœːr], *s.m. Ind:* canner.

considérable [kɔ̃siderabl̩], *a.* considerable. **1.** notable, eminent (person, position, etc.); well-to-do (person); (man) of established position. **2.** large, extensive (property, population, etc.); **dépenses considérables,** heavy expenditure; **j'ai fait des dépenses considérables,** I have been, have gone, to considerable expense; **cela m'a rendu un service c.,** it has been of material service to me; **peu c.,** inconsiderable.

considérablement [kɔ̃siderabləmɑ̃], *adv.* considerably, materially.

considérant [kɔ̃siderɑ̃], *s.m. usu. pl. Jur:* preamble (of a law); grounds (of a judgment); (*cf.* CONSIDÉRER 1.)

considération [kɔ̃siderasjɔ̃], *s.f.* consideration. **1.** (*a*) attention, thought; **agir avec, sans, c.,** to act considerately, inconsiderately; **apporter de la c. à ce qu'on fait,** to take thought over, pay attention to, what one is doing; **prendre qch. en c.,** to take sth. into consideration, into account; to consider (offer, etc.); *Pol:* **prise en c., d'un projet de loi,** second reading of a bill; *prep.phr.* **en c. de,** in consideration of, on account of; for the sake of; (*b*) *pl.* **considérations sur l'histoire,** reflexions on history; **échanger des considérations sur qch.,** to exchange views on sth. **2.** reason, motive; **considérations d'honneur, d'intérêts,** considerations, motives, of honour, of interest. **3.** regard, esteem, respect; **avoir une grande c. pour qn,** to have a great regard for s.o.; **n'avoir de c. pour personne,** to have no consideration for anyone, to be most inconsiderate; **jouir d'une grande c.,** to enjoy a high reputation, to be highly respected; **jouissant de la plus haute c. morale,** of the highest moral standing; (*letter formula*) **agréez, Monsieur, l'assurance de ma parfaite, de ma haute, c.,** I am, Sir, yours very truly; *prep.phr.* **par c. pour,** out of consideration, regard, for.

considéré, *a.* [kɔ̃sidere]. **1.** circumspect (behaviour, etc.). **2.** esteemed, respected (person); **c'est un homme c.,** he is greatly esteemed.

considérément [kɔ̃sideremɑ̃], *adv.* considerately, advisedly; circumspectly.

considérer [kɔ̃sidere], *v.tr.* (**je considère, n. considérons; je considérerai**) to consider. **1.** to ponder, weigh (matter); **ce n'est pas à c.,** it is not to be thought of; **il faut c. que . . .,** it must be borne in mind that . . .; **à tout c. . . ., tout bien considéré . . .,** taking all things into consideration . . ., all things considered . . ., after making every allowance . . ., on the whole . . .; **considérant cette réponse . . .,** in view of this answer . . .; *Jur:* **considérant que . . .,** whereas . . .. **2.** to contemplate, gaze on, look at (sth.); **se c. dans le miroir,** to look at oneself in the glass. **3.** to regard, deem; **c. qn avec mépris,** to look down on s.o.; **je considère votre lettre comme frivole,** I regard your letter as flippant; **vous êtes considéré comme responsable,** you are deemed liable, you are held to be liable; **se c. comme responsable,** to consider, hold, oneself responsible; **on le considère beaucoup,** he is highly thought of.

consignataire [kɔ̃siɲatɛːr], *s.m. & f.* **1.** *Jur:* depositary; trustee. **2.** *Com:* consignee; **c. de la coque,** bareboat consignee.

consignateur, -trice [kɔ̃siɲatœːr, -tris], *s. Com:* consignor; shipper.

consignation [kɔ̃siɲasjɔ̃], *s.f.* **1.** consignation, lodging, deposit (of money); *Jur:* **faire une c. à greffe,** to deposit a sum with the registrar; **caisse des dépôts et consignations,** Deposit and Consignment Office. **2.** *Com:* consignment (of goods); **envoyer qch. à qn en c.,** to consign sth. to s.o.; **marchandises en c.,** goods on consignment.

consigne [kɔ̃siɲ], *s.f.* **1.** *Mil: Navy:* (*a*) order(s) instructions (to sentry, etc.); **forcer la c.,** (i) to force a sentry; (ii) *F:* to force one's way in; **il a pour c. de ne laisser passer personne,** his orders are to let nobody pass; *F:* **je ne connais que la c., la c. c'est la c., c.-c.,** I must obey orders; orders are orders; **consignes de la garde,** guard duties; **consignes d'une sentinelle,** sentry's orders; **consignes générales,** general orders; **consignes particulières,** special orders; **c. permanente,** standing order; **c. verbale,** temporary, special, order; **consignes de tir,** fire discipline; **consignes relatives au camouflage, aux convois,** camouflage, convoy, discipline; **appliquer la c.,** (i) to enforce; (ii) to obey, orders; **lever la c.,** to cancel, rescind, an order; **passer les consignes,** to hand over (orders); **prendre les consignes,** to take over (orders); **transmettre les consignes,** to pass on, turn over, orders; **violer la c., manquer à la c.,** to disregard, break, orders; **violation de c.,** breach of orders; (*b*) order-board. **2.** (*a*) *Mil: Navy:* confinement (to barracks, etc.); *A:* **c. à la chambre,** close arrest; (*b*) *Adm:* **marchandises en c. à la douane,** goods stopped, held up, at the customs; (*c*) *Sch:* detention, keeping in, gating. **3.** (*a*) *Mil:* guard-room; (*b*) *Navy:* steerage (where order-board is located); (*c*) *Rail:* cloak-room, left-luggage office; **mettre, déposer, ses bagages à la c.,** to leave one's luggage at the cloak-room; **c. automatique,** left-luggage lockers.

consigner [kɔ̃siɲe], *v.tr.* **1.** (*a*) to deposit (money, etc.); **emballage non consigné,** non-returnable packing; (*b*) *Com:* to consign (goods, etc.) (**à,** to); **c. un navire à qn,** to address a ship to s.o. **2. c. qch. (par écrit),** to register, write down, enter, record, put on record (fact, answer, etc.). **3.** (*a*) to confine (soldier) to barracks; to keep in, detain, gate (pupil); **la troupe est consignée,** the troops are standing by, are confined to quarters; (*b*) **marchandises consignées par la douane,** goods stopped by the customs; (*c*) to refuse admittance to (s.o.); **la gare est consignée aux civils,** the station is closed to civilians; **je lui ai consigné ma porte,** I gave orders that he was not to be admitted; **c. sa porte à qn,** to bar one's door to s.o.; *Mil: etc:* **c. un cabaret,** to put a public house out of bounds; **"Consigné à la troupe,"** "Out of bounds." **4.** *Mil: Adm:* **c. à qn de faire qch.,** to give orders to s.o. to do sth. **5.** *Rail:* **c. ses bagages,** to put one's luggage in the cloakroom.

consistance [kɔ̃sistɑ̃ːs], *s.f.* **1.** (*a*) consistence, consistency (of syrup, cream, etc.); **terrain sans c.,** loose ground; **étoffe sans c.,** flimsy material; **donner de la c. à la peinture,** to give body to paint; (*b*) stability, firmness (of mind, character); **temps qui n'a pas de c.,** unsettled weather; *O:* **atteindre l'âge de c.,** to attain full growth. **2.** credit; **homme sans c.,** man of no consideration, of no standing; **bruit qui prend de la c.,** rumour that is gaining ground; **bruit sans c.,** unfounded rumour. **3.** *Jur:* **héritage en c. d'une maison,** inheritance consisting of a house.

consistant [kɔ̃sistɑ̃], *a.* **1.** firm, solid, stable (substance); **graisse consistante,** (i) set grease; (ii) stiff lubricant; **bruit c.,** well-grounded rumour; **plat c.,** substantial dish; **homme c.,** man who knows his own mind. **2.** *inv. Jur:* **propriété consistant en bois et prés,** estate composed of wood and meadow land.

consister [kɔ̃siste], *v.i.* to consist; **c. en, dans, qch.,** to consist, to be composed, of sth.; **le bonheur consiste à rendre heureux les autres,** happiness consists, lies, in making others happy.

consistoire [kɔ̃sistwaːr], *s.m. Ecc:* **1.** consistory; consistory court. **2.** church session (in Calvinist Church).

consistomètre [kɔ̃sistɔmɛtr̥], *s.m. Tchn:* consistometer; viscosimeter.

consistorial, -iaux [kɔ̃sistɔrjal, -jo]. *Ecc:* **1.** *a.* consistorial. **2.** *s.m.* member of a consistory.

consistorialement [kɔ̃sistɔrjalmɑ̃], *adv. Ecc:* consistorially, in consistory.

consœur [kɔ̃sœːr], *s.f.* fellow-member, sister-member, colleague; **les fiançailles de notre c. X avec notre confrère Y,** the engagement between our colleagues X and Y.

consol [kɔ̃sɔl], *s.m. Av: Nav:* consol.

consolable [kɔ̃sɔlabl̩], *a.* consolable.

consolant [kɔ̃sɔlɑ̃], *a.* consoling, comforting.

consolateur, -trice [kɔ̃sɔlatœːr, -tris]. **1.** *s.* consoler, comforter; **la consolatrice des affligés,** the Virgin Mary. **2.** *a.* consoling, comforting.

consolation [kɔ̃sɔlasjɔ̃], *s.f.* consolation, solace, comfort; **apporter de la c. à qn,** to bring comfort to s.o., to comfort s.o.; **c'est là une piètre c.,** that is cold comfort; **paroles de c.,** words of comfort, comforting words; *P:* **un petit verre de c.,** a little drop of comfort; **lot, prix, de c.,** consolation prize.

consolatoire [kɔ̃sɔlatwaːr], *a.* consolatory.

console [kɔ̃sɔl], *s.f.* **1.** *Arch:* console, corbel, bracket; *Civ.E: Const:* bracket, wall-bracket; **c. d'isolateur,** insulator bracket; **grue à console,** wall-crane; *Tchn:* **c. à équerre,** angle-bracket; *Tp:* **c. d'ancrage,** stay crutch; *Nau:* **c. de bossoir,** cathead support. **2.** *Furn:* console (-table), pier-table. **3.** *Mus:* console (of organ). **4.** *Elcs:* console (of data processor).

console-équerre [kɔ̃sɔlekɛːr], *s.f.* angle-bracket, knee(-bracket); *pl. des consoles-équerres.*

consoler [kɔ̃sɔle], *v.tr.* to console, solace, comfort; **c. qn de qch.,** to console s.o. for sth.

se consoler d'une perte, to get over a loss; **consolez-vous,** *Lit:* be comforted; *F:* cheer up! *F:* **elle s'est vite consolée,** she soon got over it.

consolidable [kɔ̃sɔlidabl̩], *a. Med: etc:* capable of being consolidated.

consolidatif, -ive [kɔ̃sɔlidatif, -iːv], *a.* consolidating, strengthening.

consolidation [kɔ̃sɔlidasjɔ̃], *s.f.* **1.** consolidation, strengthening (of foundation, position, power, etc.); bracing (of construction); **nervure de c.,** stiffening rib; *Min:* **c. d'un ciel,** propping, staying, of a roof. **2.** *Med:* healing, uniting (of wound, fracture). **3.** *Fin:* funding (of floating debt). **4.** *Jur:* merger (of usufruct in ownership). **5.** *Rail:* heavy engine (2-8-0) for mixed purposes.

consolidé [kɔ̃sɔlide], *a. Fin:* **dette consolidée,** funded debt; **dette non consolidée,** floating debt; **les fonds consolidés,** *s.* **les consolidés,** the funded, consolidated, debt; *F:* consols.

consolider [kɔ̃sɔlide], *v.tr.* **1.** to consolidate, strengthen (foundations, position, treaty, etc.); *F:* to settle more firmly; **c. un mur,** to brace a wall; **c. sa fortune,** to put one's fortune on a sound basis. **2.** *Med:* to heal, unite (wound, fracture). **3.** to fund (debt); to consolidate (rates).

se consolider. 1. to grow firm. **2.** *Med:* to heal, unite.

consommable [kɔ̃sɔmabl̩], *a.* consumable.

consommateur, -trice [kɔ̃sɔmatœːr, -tris], *s.* **1.** *Theol:* perfecter, finisher (of work). **2.** (*a*) consumer (of products); (*b*) customer (in restaurant, café).

consommation [kɔ̃sɔmasjɔ̃], *s.f.* **1.** consummation, accomplishment (of work, crime, etc.); **c. du mariage,** consummation of marriage; *B:* **en la c. des temps,** in the fullness of time; **jusqu'à la c. des siècles,** until the end of time. **2.** consumption (of wheat, petrol); use; *Mil: Nau:* expenditure (of stores, equipment, etc.), article; **produit de c. courante,** expendable article, *U.S:* expendable item; *Av:* **c. spécifique, kilométrique,** specific fuel consumption; *Aut:* **c. d'essence aux 100 kilomètres** = miles per gallon; *s.a.* BIEN II 2; **concours de c.,** economy run; *Mch:* **c. à la vitesse, au régime, économique,** cruising consumption; **c. horaire,** consumption per hour; **essais de c.,** consumption test; **taxe de c.,** purchase tax; *Com:* **société de c.,** (i) co-operative supply stores; (ii) consumer society. **3.** drink, snack (in café); **payer les consommations,** to pay for the drinks, to stand the round.

consommé [kɔ̃sɔme]. **1.** *a.* consummate (skill, etc.); **homme c. dans son art,** man who is a master of his art; **musicien c.,** thorough, accomplished, musician; **l'œuvre est traduite avec un talent c.,** the work has been most skilfully translated. **2.** *s.m. Cu:* stock, beef-tea; clear soup, consommé; **faire un c. de viande,** to boil down meat for stock.

consommer [kɔ̃sɔme], *v.tr.* **1.** to consummate accomplish, achieve (work, crime, etc.); **c. un mariage,** to consummate a marriage; **c. un divorce,** to go through with a divorce. **2.** to consume, use up (produce, etc.). **3.** *abs.* (*a*) **voiture qui consomme (beaucoup),** car that is heavy on petrol; (*b*) **c. au bar,** to have a drink in the bar.

se consommer, (*of stock*) to boil down.

consomptible [kɔ̃sɔ̃ptibl̩], *a. Pol.Ec:* consumable.

consomptif, -ive [kɔ̃sɔ̃ptif, -iːv], *a. Med:* wasting; **diabète c.,** diabetes mellitus.

consomption [kɔ̃sɔ̃psjɔ̃], *s.f.* **1.** (*a*) consumption, consuming (of food); (*b*) consuming, destruction (by fire). **2.** *Med:* wasting, decline; *O:* **atteint de c.,** in a decline, suffering from consumption.

consonance [kɔ̃sɔnɑ̃ːs], *s.f. Mus: Ling:* consonance; *Mus:* concordance; **noms aux consonances bizarres,** queer-sounding names; **nom à c. anglaise,** English-sounding name.

consonant [kɔ̃sɔnɑ̃], *a. Mus: Ling:* consonant; *Mus:* concordant.

consonantique [kɔ̃sɔnɑ̃tik], *a. Ling:* consonan(tal).

consonantisme [kɔ̃sɔnɑ̃tism], *s.m. Ling:* consonantism, consonantal system.

consoner [kɔ̃sɔne], *v.i.* = CONSONNER.

consonne [kɔ̃sɔn], *s.f. Ling:* consonant; **c. occlusive sonore, c. moyenne,** media.

consonner [kɔ̃sɔne], *v.i. Mus:* to be consonant, concordant, to harmonize.

consort, -orte [kɔ̃sɔːr, -ɔrt], *s.m. & f.* **1.** *A. & Eng.Hist:* consort; **reine consort(e),** queen consort. **2.** *pl.* (*a*) *Jur:* jointly interested parties; (*b*) *Pej:* associates (in intrigue), fellow-plotters.

consortial, -iaux [kɔ̃sɔrsjal, -jo], *a. Com: Fin:* relating to a consortium or syndicate.

consortium [kɔ̃sɔrsjɔm], *s.m. Com: Fin:* consortium, syndicate; horizontal combine.

consoude [kɔ̃sud], *s.f. Bot:* comfrey, consound; **c. royale,** field larkspur.

conspirateur, -trice [kɔ̃spiratœːr, -tris]. **1.** *s.* conspirator, conspirer; **air de c.,** conspiratorial air. **2.** *a.* conspiring.

conspiration [kɔ̃spirasjɔ̃], *s.f.* conspiracy, plot; **ourdir, tramer, une c. contre qn,** to hatch a plot against s.o.; **c. du silence,** conspiracy of silence; *s.a.* POUDRE 3.

conspirer [kɔ̃spire], *v.i.* **1.** to conspire, plot; **c. contre qn,** to conspire, be in conspiracy, against s.o.; *A: v.tr.* **c. la mort de qn,** to plot s.o.'s death. **2.** to conspire, tend, concur; **tout conspire à grossir l'incident,** everything conspires, tends, to exaggerate the incident.

conspuer [kɔ̃spɥe], *v.tr.* **1.** to decry, run down (s.o., sth.). **2.** (*a*) to boo, hoot (play, speaker); *P:* to give (actor, etc.) the bird; **conspuez X!** down with X! (*b*) *Sp:* to barrack (member of team).

constamment [kɔ̃stamɑ̃], *adv.* **1.** with constancy, steadfastly, perseveringly, unswervingly. **2.** constantly, continually; **cet article est c. demandé,** this article is in constant, steady, demand.

constance¹ [kɔ̃stɑ̃ːs], *s.f.* **1.** constancy, steadfastness; **avec c.,** steadfastly; **c. à faire qch.,** steadfastness in doing sth. **2.** persistence, perseverance, firmness. **3.** constancy, invariability (of temperature, etc.); *El:* **c. d'un élément,** constancy of a cell.

Constance². *Pr.n.* (*a*) *m.* Constantius; (*b*) *f.* Constance; (*c*) *Geog:* **le lac de C.,** the Lake of Constance.

constant, -ante [kɔ̃stɑ̃, -ɑ̃ːt], *a.* **1.** (*a*) constant, steadfast (heart, friendship, etc.); **c. en amour, dans l'adversité,** steadfast in love, in adversity; (*b*) firm, unshaken (perseverance, etc.). **2.** established, patent (fact, etc.); **délit c.,** patent offence; **il reste c. que . . .,** the fact remains that . . .. **3.** (*a*) constant, unchanging, uniform, invariable (temperature, etc.); **vents constants,** constant winds; *Mec.E:* **charge constante,** (i) dead load; (ii) steady load; (*b*) *s.f.* **constante,** *Mth: Ph: etc:* constant; **constante de temps,** time factor or coefficient. **4.** *prep. A. & Jur:* during.

constantan [kɔ̃stɑ̃tɑ̃], *s.m.* German silver, constantan.

Constantin [kɔ̃stɑ̃tɛ̃], *Pr.n.m.* Constantine.

constantinois, -oise [kɔ̃stɑ̃tinwa, -waːz], *a. & s. Geog:* (native, inhabitant) of Constantine.

constat [kɔ̃sta], *s.m.* **1.** *Jur:* certified, official, statement or report (on accident, etc.); **c. d'huissier,** affidavit made by a process-server. **2.** established fact; **les constats scientifiques,** the established facts of science.

constatable [kɔ̃statabl̩], *a.* easily established (fact); verifiable.

constatation [kɔ̃statasjɔ̃], *s.f.* **1.** verification, establishment (of fact, etc.); *Jur:* **le parquet a procédé aux constatations,** the magistrates proceeded to the official investigation; **constatations d'usage,** routine investigations; **c. d'identité,** proof of identity; **faire la c. de qch.,** to (i) note, (ii) acknowledge, sth. as a fact; **l'enquête m'a amené aux constatations suivantes,** the enquiry has enabled me to establish the following facts. **2.** certified statement; **constatations d'une enquête,** findings of an enquiry; *s.a.* DÉCÈS.

constaté [kɔ̃state], *a. Fin:* **valeur constatée,** registered value.

constater [kɔ̃state], *vtr.* **1.** to establish, verify, ascertain, note (fact, etc.); **c. la réalité d'un fait,** to establish a fact; **l'appel nominal constate deux cents présences,** the roll-call establishes that two hundred were present; **je constate un déficit de 2.000 francs,** I find a deficit of 2,000 francs; **c. une erreur,** to discover a mistake; **c. que . . .,** to note that . . .; **vous pouvez c.!** you can see for yourself! **2.** to state, record (sth.); **c. un décès,** to certify a death.

constellation [kɔ̃stɛl(l)asjɔ̃], *s.f.* constellation.

consteller [kɔ̃stɛl(l)e], *v.tr.* to constellate; **ciel constellé d'étoiles,** star-spangled sky; **robe constellée de pierreries,** dress studded, starred, with jewels.

consternant [kɔ̃stɛrnɑ̃], *a.* alarming, dismaying, (news).

consternation [kɔ̃stɛrnasjɔ̃], *s.f.* consternation, dismay.

consterné [kɔ̃stɛrne], *a.* dismayed; **être consterné par une nouvelle,** to be struck with dismay at a piece of news; **contempler, regarder, qch. d'un air consterné,** to gaze aghast at sth., to gaze at sth. in blank dismay.

consterner [kɔ̃stɛrne], *v.tr.* to dismay, stagger; to strike (s.o.) with consternation, with dismay; to appal.

constipant [kɔ̃stipɑ̃], *a. Med:* constipating, binding.

constipation [kɔ̃stipasjɔ̃], *s.f. Med:* constipation, costiveness.

constipé [kɔ̃stipe], *a.* (*a*) constipated, costive; (*b*) *F:* (*of manner, etc.*) embarrassed, strained.

constiper [kɔ̃stipe], *v.tr. Med:* to constipate; to make (s.o.) costive; *abs.* **nourriture qui constipe,** constipating food.

constituant, -ante [kɔ̃stitɥɑ̃, -ɑ̃ːt]. I. *a.* constituent. **1.** forming an integral part of a whole; **partie constituante, élément constituant,** component part, element, constituent part, element; *Atom.Ph:* **particule constituante,** constituent particle. **2.** *Pol:* having authority to frame a constitution; **l'Assemblée nationale constituante,** the Constituent Assembly (of 1789).

II. **constituant,** *s.* **1.** *s.m. Ch: Ph: etc:* constituent (part). **2.** *Pol:* **la Constituante,** the Constituent Assembly (of 1789); **un Constituant,** a member of this Assembly. **3.** (*a*) *Jur:* constituent (who appoints another as his proxy); (*b*) *Jur:* grantor (of annuity or dowry); (*c*) *Pol:* elector; **mes constituants,** my constituency.

constitué [kɔ̃stitɥe], *a.* **1.** constituted, organized (authority, etc.); **les corps constitués,** the official bodies; *Mil:* **fraction constituée,** self-contained unit. **2. argent c. en viager,** money invested, sunk, in an annuity. **3. enfant bien c.,** fine healthy child.

constituer [kɔ̃stitɥe], *v.tr.* to constitute. **1.** (*a*) to form, frame, make (up); **le poisson constituait leur principal aliment,** fish was their main article of diet; **parties qui constituent le tout,** parts that constitute, go to make up, the whole; **qualités qui constituent un grand homme,** qualities that go to make a great man; **cela ne constitue pas un engagement,** that does not constitute a commitment; **c. une menace pour . . .,** to constitute a threat to . . .; **appartement constitué de six pièces,** flat, *U.S:* appartment, consisting of, made up of, six rooms; (*b*) to set up, institute (committee, etc.); to incorporate (an order, a society); **c. un ministère,** to form, establish, a ministry; **ils se constituèrent en commission,** they resolved themselves into a committee; **c. une ville en ville libre,** to establish a city as a free city. **2.** *Jur: etc:* (*a*) to constitute, appoint; **c. qn son héritier,** to constitute, make, s.o. one's heir; **c. qn procureur,** to confer on s.o. power of attorney, to make s.o. one's proxy; **c. qn prisonnier,** to take s.o. into custody; **se c. prisonnier,** to give oneself up (to justice); **se c. partie civile,** to institute a civil action (in criminal case); (*b*) **c. une dot, une rente, à qn,** to settle a dowry, an annuity, on s.o.; (*c*) **c. un avoué,** to brief a lawyer; (*d*) **c. qn en frais, en dépenses,** to put s.o. to expense; (*e*) **c. le jury,** to empanel the jury.

constitutif, -ive [kɔ̃stitytif, -iːv], *a.* **1.** *Jur:* constitutive; (*a*) conferring a right; **titres constitutifs (d'une propriété),** title-deeds; (*b*) **éléments constitutifs d'un délit,** factors that constitute an offence. **2.** constituent; **les éléments constitutifs de l'air, de l'eau, du lait,** the constituent elements of air, water, milk.

constitution [kɔ̃stitysjɔ̃], *s.f.* **1.** constituting, appointing, establishing; **frais de c. (d'une société),** preliminary expenses (in company promoting); **c. d'un comité,** institution of a committee; **c. de dot, de pension,** settling, settlement, of a dowry, of an annuity; *Jur:* **c. d'avoué,** briefing of lawyer. **2.** constitution; (*a*) **avoir une bonne c.,** to have a sound constitution, to be bodily fit; **avoir une forte c., une c. de fer,** to have an iron constitution; (*b*) *Pol:* **c. républicaine, monarchique,** republican, monarchic, constitution. **3.** composition (of air, water, etc.).

constitutionnaliser [kɔ̃stitysjɔnalize], *v.tr. Jur:* to constitutionalize.

constitutionnalité [kɔ̃stitysjɔnalite], *s.f.* constitutionality, constitutional character (of law, etc.).

constitutionnel, -elle [kɔ̃stitysjɔnɛl]. **1.** *a.* constitutional (disease, government, party); temperamental (laziness); **rendre c.,** to constitutionalize; *Fr.Hist:* **les évêques constitutionnels,** the constitutional, conforming, bishops (in 1790). **2.** *s. Pol:* constitutionalist.

constitutionnellement [kɔ̃stitysjɔnɛlmɑ̃], *adv.* constitutionally.

constricteur [kɔ̃striktœːr], *s.m. & a.* **1.** *Physiol:* (muscles) **constricteurs,** constrictors. **2.** *Rept:* **boa c.,** boa constrictor.

constrictif, -ive [kɔ̃striktif, -iːv]. **1.** *a.* constrictive. **2.** *s.f. Ling:* constrictive.

constriction [kɔ̃striksjɔ̃], *s.f.* constriction (of muscle, chest, etc.).

constrictor [kɔ̃striktɔːr], *a. & s.m. Rept:* **boa c.,** boa-constrictor.

constringent [kɔ̃strɛ̃ʒɑ̃], *a. Med:* constringent.

constructeur [kɔ̃stryktœːr], *s.m.* constructor; maker, manufacturer, (structural) engineer; (engine-)builder; designer; **c. de chaudières,** boiler-manufacturer; **c. de navires, de bateaux,** ship-builder, boat-builder; **c. mécanicien,** mechanical engineer; **c. (d')automobile(s),** car manufacturer; **c. de machines,** engine-builder, -maker; **c. de maisons, d'immeubles,** master-builder, house-builder.

constructible [kɔ̃stryktibl̩], *a.* constructible.

constructif, -ive [kɔ̃stryktif, -iːv], *a.* constructive.

construction [kɔ̃stryksjɔ̃], *s.f.* construction. **1.** (*a*) constructing, erecting, erection, building; building operations; **matériaux de c.,** building materials; **c. en fer,** iron-work; **c. de navires,** ship-building; **bâtiment en c.,** ship under, in course of, construction, on the stocks; **de c. anglaise,** English built; **c. de routes,** road-making; **c. mécanique,** (mechanical) engineering; **service des constructions mécaniques,** engineering department; **les constructions navales,** marine engineering; **c. hydraulique,** hydraulic engineering; **acier de c.,** construction steel; **c. de chaudières,** boiler-making; **jeu de c.,** (i) box of bricks; (ii) construction set, constructional toy; *s.a.* BOÎTE 1; (*b*) design(ing) (of machine, etc.); **défaut de c.,** fault in design; **détails de c.,** constructional, structural, details; **c. à bordages croisés, en diagonale,** diagonal build; **c. à clins,** clinker build; **c. à franc-bord,** carvel build; (*c*) **c. d'un roman,** construction of a novel; **c. d'un poème,** composition of a poem; **c. d'une phrase,** construction of a sentence. **2.** (*a*) edifice, structure, building; **c. en briques,** brick building; **c. entièrement métallique,** all-metal structure; **c. mixte,** composite construction; (*b*) *Phil:* construct (of the mind).

construire [kɔ̃strɥiːr], *v.tr.* (*pr.p.* **construisant;** *p.p.* **construit;** *pr.ind.* **je construis, il construit, n. construisons;** *p.d.* **je construisais;** *p.h.* **je construisis;** *fu.* **je construirai**) to construct. **1.** to build, erect; to make, build, lay out (road, etc.); *Fort:* **c. des ouvrages,** to throw up works; **machine construite dans un but spécial,** machine designed for a special purpose; **pendant qu'on construit la maison,** while the house is being built; **Louis XIV fit c., construisit, Versailles,** Louis XIV had Versailles built, built Versailles. **2.** to assemble, put together (machine, etc.); *Gram:* **c. une phrase,** (i) to construct, (ii) to construe, a sentence; *Mth:* **c. une figure,** to draw, construct, a figure; **c. une théorie,** to build up a theory.

consubstantialité [kɔ̃sypstɑ̃sjalite], *s.f. Theol:* consubstantiality (of the Godhead).

consubstantiation [kɔ̃sypstɑ̃sjasjɔ̃], *s.f. Theol:* consubstantiation, real presence.

consubstantiel, -ielle [kɔ̃sypstɑ̃sjɛl], *a. Theol:* consubstantial; of one substance (**à, avec,** with).

consubstantiellement [kɔ̃sypstɑ̃sjɛlmɑ̃], *adv. Theol:* consubstantially.

consuétudinaire [kɔ̃sɥetydinɛːr], *s.m. & f.* habitual sinner.

consul [kɔ̃syl], *s.m.* consul; **le c. de France,** the French consul.

consulaire [kɔ̃sylɛːr], *a.* consular; *F:* **personnage c.,** statesman; *A:* **juge c.** = **juge au tribunal de commerce,** *q.v.* under JUGE; *Adm: Com:* **payer les droits consulaires,** to pay for consulages; **facture c.,** consular invoice.

consulat [kɔ̃syla] *s.m.* consulate; (i) consulship; (ii) consular offices; (iii) consul's residence; **c. général,** Consulate General; **Le c. de France,** the French Consulate; *Fr.Hist:* **Le Consulat,** the Consulate (1799-1804).

consultable [kɔ̃syltabl̩], *a.* consultable.

consultant, -ante [kɔ̃syltɑ̃, -ɑ̃ːt]. **1.** *a.* consulting; **médecin c.,** consulting physician, consultant; *s.a.* AVOCAT[1] 1. **2.** *s.* (*a*) person consulted; *Med:* consultant; (*b*) consulter.

consultatif, -ive [kɔ̃syltatif, -iːv], *a.* consultative, advisory, consulting (committee, board, etc.); advisory (opinion); **avoir une voix consultative,** to be present in an advisory (but non-voting) capacity; **à titre c.,** in an advisory capacity.

consultation [kɔ̃syltasjɔ̃], *s.f.* (*a*) consultation, conference; **entrer en c. avec qn sur qch.,** to consult, confer, with s.o. about sth.; **c. populaire,** popular vote, public expression of opinion; (*b*) (medical) advice, (legal) opinion; **après c. d'avocat,** after taking counsel's opinion; (*c*) *Med:* visit to a doctor; **il m'a fait payer la c.,** he made me pay for consulting him; **cabinet de c.,** consulting room, surgery; **heures de c.,** consulting hours; **consultation externe,** out-patients department; *Jur:* **cabinet de c.,** chambers.

consulte [kɔ̃sylt], *s.f. Hist:* **c. d'État,** State council (in Italy, Switzerland), consulta; **c. sacrée,** judiciary court (at Rome).

consulter [kɔ̃sylte]. **1.** *v.tr.* (*a*) to consult, to take the advice of, the opinion of, to refer to (s.o., sth.); **c. un médecin,** to take medical advice; **c. un avocat,** to take legal opinion; **c. qn sur qch.,** to consult s.o. about sth.; **ils se sont consultés,** they put their heads together; **c. le pays,** to go to the country, to hold (i) a general election, (ii) a referendum; **c. l'assemblée sur une question,** to take the opinion of the meeting on a point; **c. un dictionnaire,** to consult a dictionary; **ouvrage à c.,** work of reference; *abs.* **médecin, avocat, qui consulte,** doctor, barrister, who gives advice; (*b*) **c. ses intérêts,** to consult one's interests; *F:* **c. son oreiller,** *A:* **son chevet, son bonnet de nuit,** to take counsel of one's pillow; "to sleep on it"; **c. ses forces,** to take stock of oneself, of one's strength. **2.** *v.i.* (*a*) *A:* **c. en soi-même,** to deliberate; (*b*) (i) *A:* **c. avec qn,** to take counsel with s.o.; (ii) *Med:* **c. avec un confrère,** to hold a consultation with a colleague, to call in a colleague.

consulteur, -trice [kɔ̃syltœːr, -tris], *a. & s.m. Hist: Ecc:* adviser.

consumable [kɔ̃symabl̩], *a.* consumable (by fire).

consumant [kɔ̃symɑ̃], *a.* consuming (fire, fever, passion).

consume [kɔ̃sym], *s.f.* ullage.

consumer [kɔ̃syme], *v.tr.* to consume. **1.** to wear away; to destroy; **consumé par le feu,** consumed by fire, burnt up; **consumé de rouille,** eaten away, corroded, by rust; **le temps qui consume tout,** all-devouring time; **consumé par le chagrin,** worn away, worn to a shadow, by grief; **consumé par l'ambition,** eaten up with ambition; **fumier bien consumé,** well-rotted, well-decayed, manure. **2.** to use up, waste, spend (fortune, time, energy, etc.); **lampe qui consume beaucoup d'huile,** lamp that burns a great deal of oil.

se consumer, to waste away, pine away; **se c. de douleur,** to pine away with grief; **se c. dans les larmes,** to weep one's eyes out; **se c. en efforts inutiles,** to exhaust oneself, wear oneself out, in useless efforts; **la chandelle s'était consumée entièrement,** the candle had burnt itself out.

consumptible [kɔ̃sɔ̃ptibl̩], *a. Jur:* = CONSUMABLE.

contabescence [kɔ̃tabɛs(s)ɑ̃ːs], *s.f. Bot: Med:* contabescence; atrophy; wasting away; abortion (of pollen).

contabescent [kɔ̃tabɛs(s)ɑ̃], *a.* contabescent (pollen, etc.).

contact [kɔ̃takt], *s.m.* **1.** contact, touch; **être, entrer, en c. avec qn,** to be in contact, come into contact, with s.o., sth.; **mettre deux personnes en c.,** to put two people in(to) touch with one another; **prendre c., se mettre en c., avec qn,** to get in(to) touch with s.o., to contact s.o.; *Mil:* **être en c. avec l'ennemi,** to be in contact, in touch, with the enemy; **établir, opérer, prendre le c. avec l'ennemi,** to establish, gain, contact, touch, with the enemy; **prise de c.,** (i) preliminary conversation; (ii) *Mil:* gaining of contact; **garder, perdre, le c.,** to keep, lose, touch, *Mil:* contact; **rompre le c.,** to break contact; *Mil:* **c. étroit, serré,** close contact; **c. fluide,** fluid, loose, contact; **éléments au c.,** elements in contact; **éléments de c.,** contact elements; **patrouille de c.,** contact patrol; *Geom:* **avoir un c. d'ordre supérieur avec une ligne,** to osculate with a line; *Opt:* **c. par immersion,** immersion contact; **verre de c.,** contact lens; *Phot:* **épreuve, copie, par c.,** contact print; *Geol:* **filon, veine, de c.,** contact lode, vein; **métamorphisme de c.,** contact metamorphism; **minéral, roche, de c.,** contact mineral, rock. **2.** *El:* (*a*) connection, contact; **"contact!"** "switch on!" **c. à la masse,** earth to frame (of car, etc.); **c. de terre,** earth (connection, contact); **c. à la terre,** earth fault; **c. par frottement,** frictional contact; **couteau de c.,** contact knife; **défaut de c.,** contact fault; **électrode de c.,** contact electrode; **fiche de c.,** contact plug; **mauvais c.,** poor contact; **microphone de c.,** contact microphone; **pertes dues au c.,** contact losses; **point de c.,** contact point; *Aut:* **clef de c.,** ignition key; **établir, mettre, le c.,** to make contact; to switch on; *Av:* **demander le c. au pilote,** to ask the pilot for contact; **rompre, couper, le c.,** to break contact; to switch off; *Tp:* **avoir le c.,** to get through; (*b*) switch, contact; **c. fixe, mobile,** fixed, mobile, contact; **c. glissant,** sliding contact; **c. élastique,** spring contact; **c. à cheville, à fiche,** plug(-contact); **c. de relais,** relay contact; **c. redresseur,** contact rectifier; **c. de sûreté,** (electric) alarm; *Tg:* **c. de repos,** back contact, break contact, resting contact; **c. de travail,** make contact; **c. repos-travail,** make-and-break contact.

contacter [kɔ̃takte], *v.tr.* to contact (s.o.).

contacteur [kɔ̃taktœːr], *s.m. El.E:* contactor; contact-maker; *Aut:* **c. au pied,** starter pedal; **c. à temps,** timer; **c. à lame-ressort,** strap-key (contactor), *U.S:* tapping key; **c. multipolaire,** multiple switch.

contacteur-annonceur [kɔ̃taktœːranɔ̃sœːr], *s.m. El:* acknowledging contactor; *pl. contacteurs-annonceurs.*

contadin, -ine [kɔ̃tadɛ̃, -in], *s. A:* peasant, rustic.

contage [kɔ̃taːʒ], *s.m. Med:* virus of contagion; contagium.

contagier [kɔ̃taʒje], *v.tr.* (*p.d. & pr.sub.* **n. contagiions, v. contagiiez**) (*rare*) to communicate a contagious disease to (s.o.); to infect.

contagieux, -ieuse [kɔ̃taʒjø, -jøːz], *a.* **1.** contagious, infectious, communicable; *F:* catching (disease, etc.); *F:* **le bâillement est c.,** yawning is infectious, catching; **rire c.,** infectious laugh. **2.** noxious, pestiferous.

contagifère [kɔ̃taʒifɛːr], *a.* (*rare*) (*of clothing, etc.*) carrying contagion, infected.

contagion [kɔ̃taʒjɔ̃], *s.f.* **1.** *Med: etc:* contagion. **2.** *F:* **la c. du rire, de l'exemple,** the contagiousness of laughter, of example.

contagionner [kɔ̃taʒjɔne], *v.tr. Med:* to infect.

se contagionner, to become infected.

contagiosité [kɔ̃taʒjozite], *s.f. Med:* contagiousness.

container [kɔ̃tɛnɛːr], *s.m. Trans:* container; **avion (de transport) porte-containers,** container-plane, -aircraft; **navire porte-containers,** container-ship; **poste (à quai) pour navire porte-containers,** container-berth; **transports maritimes par containers,** container-shipping; *Rail:* **wagon porte-containers,** container-wagon, *U.S:* container truck.

contaminant [kɔ̃taminɑ̃], *a. & s.m.* contaminant.

contamination [kɔ̃taminasjɔ̃], *s.f.* (*a*) contamination, pollution; (*b*) *Med:* infection.

contaminer [kɔ̃tamine], *v.tr.* (*a*) to contaminate, pollute (water, etc.); (*b*) *Med:* to infect.

conte [kɔ̃ːt], *s.m.* **1.** story, tale; **un c. vrai,** a true story; **livre de contes,** story-book; **c. de fées, c. de ma mère l'Oie,** fairy-tale, nursery tale; **contes de bonne femme,** old wives' tales; **contes rimés,** nursery rhymes; **c. gras,** broad story; *s.a.* BLEU 1. **2.** *F:* story, fib, yarn; **un vrai c.,** an improbable story; **c. fait à plaisir,** idle tale; **c. à dormir debout,** cock-and-bull story; **c'est un grand faiseur de contes,** he can spin a good yarn.

conté [kɔ̃te], *s.m. Cu:* = COMTÉ 2.

contemplateur, -trice [kɔ̃tɑ̃platœːr, -tris], *s.* contemplator.

contemplatif, -ive [kɔ̃tɑ̃platif, -iːv]. **1.** *a.* contemplative; *Ecc:* **ordre c.,** contemplative order. **2.** *s.* meditator, dreamer; *Ecc:* contemplative.

contemplation [kɔ̃tɑ̃plasjɔ̃], *s.f.* contemplation. **1. c. de qch.,** viewing of sth., gazing upon sth. **2.** meditation; **être plongé dans la c.,** to be lost in contemplation, in meditation. **3.** *Ecc:* spiritual communion between God and man.

contemplativement [kɔ̃tɑ̃plativmɑ̃], *adv.* contemplatively.

contempler [kɔ̃tɑ̃ple], *v.tr.* to contemplate. **1.** to behold, view, to gaze at, upon, (nature, picture, etc.). **2.** to meditate, reflect, upon (sth.); *abs.* **passer sa vie à c.,** to spend one's life in meditation.

contemporain, -aine [kɔ̃tɑ̃pɔrɛ̃, -ɛn]. **1.** *a.* (*a*) contemporary; recent, latter-day, (opinions, etc.); (*b*) contemporaneous (**de,** with); of the same date (as). **2.** *s.* contemporary.

contemporanéité [kɔ̃tɑ̃pɔraneite], *s.f.* contemporaneity, contemporaneousness.

contempteur, -trice [kɔ̃tɑ̃ptœːr, -tris]. **1.** *s.* despiser, scorner; **les contempteurs de la vertu,** the contemners of virtue. **2.** *a.* contemptuous, scornful.

contemptible [kɔ̃tɑ̃ptibl̩], *a. A:* despicable, contemptible.

contenable [kɔ̃tnabl̩], *a.* controllable (crowd, passions).

contenance [kɔ̃tnɑ̃:s], *s.f.* **1.** capacity, content (of bottle, etc.); **c. thermique d'un mélange,** heat-content of a mixture; **c. d'un véhicule,** carrying capacity, accommodation, of a vehicle; **c. d'un navire,** burden of a vessel; **c. d'un champ,** content, area, of a field; **d'une c. de dix litres,** capable of holding ten litres. **2.** countenance, bearing; **c. assurée,** assured bearing; **se donner, se faire, une c.,** to keep one's countenance; **faire bonne c.,** (i) to show a bold front, put a good face on it; *F:* to carry it off; (ii) to keep smiling; **perdre c.,** to lose face, not to know which way to look, to be or stand abashed; **faire perdre c. à qn,** to put, stare, s.o. out of countenance; **faire qch. par c., pour se donner une c.,** to do sth. to avoid losing face.

contenant [kɔ̃tnɑ̃]. **1.** *a.* containing. **2.** *s.m.* container.

contendant, -ante [kɔ̃tɑ̃dɑ̃, -ɑ̃:t]. **1.** *a.* contending, competing, rival (parties, etc.). **2.** *s.* contestant, competitor.

conteneur [kɔ̃tnœ:r], *s.m.* container; *Metall:* cylinder containing metal before wire drawing.

contenir [kɔ̃tni:r], *v.tr.* (*conj. like* TENIR) to contain. **1.** to hold, have the capacity for (certain quantity, number); **théâtre qui contient mille places,** theatre that seats a thousand; *Rail:* **compartiment qui contient huit personnes,** compartment for eight people; **livre qui contient beaucoup d'erreurs,** book with many mistakes; **lettre contenant chèque,** letter enclosing cheque; **rapport qui contient le résultat de nos travaux,** report on the result of our work. **2.** to restrain; to keep (crowd, feelings, etc.) in check; to control (passion); **c. ses sentiments,** to repress one's feelings, to keep one's feelings under control; *Mil:* **c. l'ennemi,** to hold, contain, the enemy, to keep the enemy in check.

se contenir, to contain, control, possess, oneself; to hold oneself in; to keep one's temper.

content [kɔ̃tɑ̃]. **1.** *a.* (*a*) content; **être c. de son sort,** to be content, satisfied, with one's lot; **nous vivions contents avec dix mille francs de rente,** we lived contentedly on an income of ten thousand francs; (*b*) satisfied, pleased (de, with); **êtes-vous c. de mon travail?** are you satisfied with my work? **il a l'air c. de lui,** he looks very pleased with himself, there is something smug about him; (*c*) pleased; **je suis très c. de vous voir,** I am very pleased to see you; **votre père ne sera pas c.,** your father will not be pleased, won't like it; **si vous faites cela il ne sera pas c.,** *F:* he won't like your doing that; (*d*) glad; **comme elle était contente!** how glad she was! **je suis fort c. que vous soyez venu,** I am so glad you've come. **2.** *s.m.* sufficiency, *in such phrases as* **manger tout son c.,** to eat one's fill; **s'amuser tout son c.,** to enjoy oneself to one's heart's content; **j'ai mon c. de vos injures,** I've had enough of your insults; *s.a.* PLEURER 2.

contentement [kɔ̃tɑ̃tmɑ̃], *s.m.* (*a*) content(ment), contentedness; *Prov:* **c. passe richesse,** contentment is better than riches; (*b*) satisfaction (de, at, with).

contenter [kɔ̃tɑ̃te], *v.tr.* to content, satisfy (s.o.); to gratify (curiosity, whim, etc.).

se contenter de qch., de faire qch., to be content, satisfied, with sth., with doing sth.; to make shift with sth.; **je me contenterai de faire remarquer que . . .,** I will merely point out that . . .; **plante qui se contente de fumures peu abondantes,** plant that requires only light dressings; **quand il se fut contenté,** when he had satisfied his desire, when he had taken his fill.

contentieusement [kɔ̃tɑ̃sjøzmɑ̃], *adv.* contentiously.

contentieux, -ieuse [kɔ̃tɑ̃sjø, -jø:z]. **1.** *a.* (*a*) contentious (matter); (*b*) *A:* quarrelsome. **2.** *s.m.* *Adm:* contentious business, matters in dispute; law business (of a firm); **bureau, service, du c.,** disputed claims office or department; law bureau; legal department (of bank, administration, etc.); **agent, chef, du c.,** (company's, etc.) solicitor.

contentif, -ive [kɔ̃tɑ̃tif, -i:v], *a.* *Med:* retentive (appliance, bandage).

contention[1] [kɔ̃tɑ̃sjɔ̃], *s.f.* **1.** application, exertion (of faculties); **c. d'esprit,** intentness of mind. **2.** *A:* contention, dispute.

contention[2], *s.f.* *Med:* (*a*) retention (of fracture, etc.) in place; holding; (*b*) restraint (of psychotic patient); (*c*) *Vet:* **moyen de c.,** (any sort of) restraining apparatus.

contenu [kɔ̃tny]. **1.** *a.* restrained (passion, style, etc.); pent-up (anger); reserved (character). **2.** *s.m.* contents (of parcel, volume, etc.); **le c. de sa lettre,** the subject matter, tenor, of his letter.

conter [kɔ̃te], *v.tr.* to tell, relate (story, etc.); **on conte que . . .,** the story is that . . ., people say that . . .; *F:* **allez c. ça ailleurs!** go and tell that to the marines! **en c. (de belles, de bien bonnes,) à qn,** to take s.o. in, pull s.o.'s leg; **vous m'en contez de belles!** that's a tall story! **s'en laisser c.,** to believe everything one is told; **en avoir long à c.,** to have a long tale to tell; *s.a.* FLEURETTE.

contestabilité [kɔ̃tɛstabilite], *s.f.* *Lit:* contestableness.

contestable [kɔ̃tɛstabl̩], *a.* contestable, debatable, questionable.

contestablement [kɔ̃tɛstabləmɑ̃], *adv.* contestably, questionably.

contestant, -ante [kɔ̃tɛstɑ̃, -ɑ̃:t], *a.* & *s.* *Lit:* *Jur:* *Pol:* contending (party).

contestataire [kɔ̃tɛstatɛ:r], *a.* & *s.m.* & *f.* *Pol:* *etc:* contestant.

contestation [kɔ̃tɛstasjɔ̃], *s.f.* contestation, dispute; *Pol:* contestation (on the part of a minority of left-wing students); **sujet de c.,** subject of contestation; *F:* bone of contention; **matières en c.,** matters at issue, in dispute; **matières à c.,** subjects open to discussion; **être en c. avec qn,** to be at variance, at issue, with s.o.; **mettre un droit en c.,** to dispute, question, a right; **c. qui s'élève entre A et B,** difference arising between A and B; **sans c. possible,** beyond all question; **point hors de c.,** point beyond dispute.

conteste [kɔ̃tɛst], *s.f.* (*a*) *A:* = CONTESTATION; (*b*) *adv.phr.* **sans c.,** indisputably, unquestionably, irrefutably, without question, beyond question.

contester [kɔ̃tɛste]. **1.** *v.tr.* to contest, dispute, challenge (point, right, etc.); **ce point est contesté,** this point is at issue, in dispute; **c. à qn le droit de faire qch.,** to challenge s.o.'s right to do sth.; **je lui conteste son droit,** I dispute, question, his right; **c. un dommage,** to put a loss in issue; **c. un juré,** to challenge a juryman. **2.** *v.i.* to dispute, wrangle (avec, with).

conteur, -euse [kɔ̃tœ:r, -ø:z], *s.* **1.** narrator, teller. **2.** storyteller, romancer; **c'est un c. de sornettes, d'histoires,** he talks a lot of nonsense, he likes to tell tall stories, to spin a yarn. **3.** *a.* *A:* **dans sa conteuse vieillesse,** in his anecdotage.

contexte [kɔ̃tɛkst], *s.m.* **1.** (*a*) context; (*b*) **c. historique (d'un événement),** historical background (of an event). **2.** *Jur:* text (of deed, etc.).

contextuel, -elle [kɔ̃tɛkstɥɛl], *a.* contextual.

contexture [kɔ̃tɛksty:r], *s.f.* **1.** (con)texture (of bones, muscles, etc.). **2.** structure, framework (of story, poem); *Pol:* composition; make-up.

contigu, -uë [kɔ̃tigy], *a.* contiguous, adjoining, adjacent, conterminous; **c. à, avec, qch.,** contiguous to, next to, bordering on, sth.; **maison contiguë à la nôtre,** house contiguous to, adjoining, ours; **idées contiguës,** analogous, related, ideas; *Geom:* **angles contigus,** adjacent angles.

contiguïté [kɔ̃tigɥite], *s.f.* contiguity, adjacency; *Surg:* **amputation dans la c.,** amputation in contiguity.

continence [kɔ̃tinɑ̃:s], *s.f.* continence, continency.

continent[1] [kɔ̃tinɑ̃], *a.* **1.** continent, chaste. **2.** *Med:* **fièvre continente,** continued, unintermitting, fever.

continent[2], *s.m.* *Geog:* **1.** continent; **l'ancien, le nouveau, c.,** the old, the new, world. **2.** (*a*) land mass; (*b*) mainland.

continental, -aux [kɔ̃tinɑ̃tal, -o], *a.* **1.** continental. **2.** belonging to the mainland.

continentalisme [kɔ̃tinɑ̃talism], *s.m.* continentalism.

contingence [kɔ̃tɛ̃ʒɑ̃:s], *s.f.* **1.** *Phil:* contingency; *F:* details, incidents. **2.** *Geom:* **angle de c.,** angle of contingence.

contingent [kɔ̃tɛ̃ʒɑ̃]. **1.** *a.* *Phil:* contingent. **2.** *s.m.* (*a*) contingent; *Mil:* **c. annuel,** annual contingent; **le c. annuel d'une classe est de 250.000 hommes,** the annual intake, call-up, totals 250,000 men; **un homme, un militaire, un soldat, du c.,** a conscript, a national service man; *U.S:* a draftee, an inductee; **les contingents britanniques au sein de l'O.T.A.N.,** the British contingents within N.A.T.O.; (*b*) quota (*e.g.* immigration quota); **plein c. d'étudiants,** full quota of students; *Jur:* **réclamer son c.,** to claim one's proportionate share; *Adm:* *etc:* **c. de jours disponibles,** days not appropriated, reserved for contingencies; (*c*) ration, allowance, allocation (of paper, etc.).

contingentement [kɔ̃tɛ̃ʒɑ̃tmɑ̃], *s.m.* *Adm:* "quota" system of distribution; apportioning, fixing, of quotas; **c. des films cinématographiques dans l'industrie britannique,** application of the quota to the British film industry.

contingenter [kɔ̃tɛ̃ʒɑ̃te], *v.tr.* *Adm:* **1.** to establish, apportion, fix, quotas for (imports, etc.). **2.** to distribute, allocate (films, etc.) according to a quota.

continu [kɔ̃tiny]. **1.** *a.* continuous, of long continuance, unbroken; unceasing; sustained (eloquence, etc.); **ligne continue,** continuous, unbroken line; **mouvement c.,** incessant movement; **suite continue de désastres,** unbroken chain of disasters; **fièvre continue,** continued, unintermitting, fever; *El:* **courant c.,** direct current; *s.m.* **alimenter une ligne en c.,** to feed a line with direct current; *s.a.* BAS IV, 1, MÉTIER 2; *Mth:* **fonction continue,** continuous function; **fraction continue,** continued fraction; **politique continue,** settled policy. **2.** *s.m.* *Phil:* *Ph:* continuum; continuous matter or space. **3.** *s.f.* **continue,** *Ling:* continuant.

continuateur, -trice [kɔ̃tinɥatœ:r, -tris], *s.* (*a*) continuer; (*b*) continuator (of s.o. else's literary work).

continuation [kɔ̃tinɥasjɔ̃], *s.f.* **1.** continuation (of history, road, etc.); carrying on (of work, war); extension (of leave, etc.); *F:* **bonne c.!** good luck! **2.** continuance, continuation (of war, etc.); long spell, run (of bad weather, etc.).

continuel, -elle [kɔ̃tinɥɛl], *a.* continual, unceasing, ceaseless; never-ending, unintermitting.

continuellement [kɔ̃tinɥɛlmɑ̃], *adv.* continually; steadily.

continuer [kɔ̃tinɥe], *v.tr.* & *i.* to continue; (*a*) to carry on, go on with, keep on with (studies, efforts, etc.); **c. la tradition de famille,** to carry on the family tradition; **c. sa route,** to continue, pursue, one's journey, to proceed on one's way; (*of ship*) to keep her course; **c. qn dans son emploi,** to keep s.o. on in his, her, employment; **c. à, de, faire qch.,** to continue to do sth., to go on, keep on, continue, doing sth.; **il continua à marcher,** he walked on; **continuez!** go on! go ahead! keep it up! *F:* peg away! *Mil:* *Navy:* carry on! **continuez (votre récit),** *F:* fire away! go on! **continuez à chanter,** sing away, sing on; **continuez à travailler,** work away; **la guerre continue toujours,** the war still goes on; (*b*) to extend; **c. une ligne,** to continue, prolong, a line; **route qui continue jusqu'à la rivière,** road that extends to the river.

continuité [kɔ̃tinɥite], *s.f.* continuity; uninterrupted connection; ceaselessness; *s.a.* SOLUTION 1; *Nau:* *Ins:* *Jur:* **c. du voyage,** continuous voyage; *Surg:* **amputation dans la c.,** amputation in continuity.

continûment [kɔ̃tinymɑ̃], *adv.* continuously, without cessation, without a break.

continuum [kɔ̃tinyɔm], *s.m.* *Mth:* *Ph:* *etc:* continuum; **c. espace-temps,** space-time continuum.

contondant [kɔ̃tɔ̃dɑ̃], *a.* contusive, blunt (instrument).

contorniate [kɔ̃tɔrnjat], *a.* & *s.* *Num:* (*a*) *a.* contorniate, contorniated; (*b*) *s.m.* contorniate.

contorsion [kɔ̃tɔrsjɔ̃], *s.f.* contortion; **faire des contorsions,** (i) to writhe; (ii) to make faces; *El:* **c. du champ magnétique,** distortion of the magnetic field; *F:* **donner une c. à la vérité,** to give the truth a twist.

contorsionner [kɔ̃tɔrsjɔne], *v.tr.* to contort (body, face, etc.).

se contorsionner, to contort one's body, to writhe.

contorsionniste [kɔ̃tɔrsjɔnist], *s.m.* & *f.* contortionist.

contorté [kɔ̃tɔrte], *Bot:* **1.** *a.* contorted, convolute. **2.** *s.f.pl.* **contortées,** Contortae.

contour [kɔ̃tu:r], *s.m.* **1.** outline, contour; **contours gracieux d'une statue,** graceful lines of a statue. **2.** *Surv:* contour(-line). **3.** (*a*) circuit, circumference (of town, forest, etc.); (*b*) = CONTOURNEMENT 2; bend, turn (of road, etc.). **4.** *Mil:* edging (of epaulette).

contournage [kɔ̃turna:ʒ], *s.m.* = CONTOURNEMENT.

contourné [kɔ̃turne], *a.* **1.** shaped; **vase mal c.,** mis-shapen vase. **2.** (*a*) twisted, contorted, crooked (limb, tree, etc.); **style c.,** tortuous style; **coquille contournée,** helical shell; (*b*) *Her:* (i) contournée; (ii) **croissant c.,** moon in decrement, decrescent moon.

contournement [kɔ̃turnəmɑ̃], *s.m.* **1.** shaping, outlining (of figure, etc.). **2.** passing round, working round, skirting (base of mountain, etc.); *Rail:* **ligne de c.,** loop line (avoiding busy centre, etc.); *Aut:* **route de c.,** by-pass (road). **3.** twist, distortion; **contournements d'un sentier,** windings of a path. **4.** *El:* arc-over (of spark); flash-over; **arc de c.,** insulator arc-over; **c. d'isolant,** insulation breakdown.

contourner [kɔ̃turne], *v.tr.* **1.** to shape, to trace the outline of (design, vase, etc.). **2.** to wind round, pass round, work round, circumvent, skirt (hill, wood, etc.); *F:* **c. la loi, une difficulté,** to get round, evade, the law, a difficulty. **3.** to twist, warp, contort, distort, deform; **la peur lui contourne les traits,** fear distorts his features.

contraceptif, -ive [kɔ̃trasɛptif, -iːv], *a. & s.m.* contraceptive.

contraception [kɔ̃trasɛpsjɔ̃], *s.f.* contraception.

contractable [kɔ̃traktabl̩], *a.* contractable.

contractant [kɔ̃traktɑ̃], *Jur:* **1.** *a.* contracting (party); **hautes parties contractantes,** high contracting parties. **2.** *s.m.* contracting party, (i) bargainer; (ii) bargainee.

contracte[kɔ̃trakt], *a.Gram:* contracted (verb, etc.).

contracté [kɔ̃trakte], *a.* (*a*) *Gram:* contracted; **articles contractés,** contracted articles; (*b*) tense (muscles, etc.); **les mâchoires contractées,** with jaws set.

contracter[1] [kɔ̃trakte], *v.tr.* **1.** (*a*) to contract (alliance, marriage, etc.); (*b*) to incur, contract (debt); **c. une obligation envers qn,** to lay oneself under an obligation to s.o.; **les engagements pécuniaires par lui contractés,** the pecuniary obligations into which he has entered; (*c*) **c. une assurance,** to take out an insurance policy. **2. c. une habitude,** to contract, develop, acquire a habit; **c. une maladie,** to contract, catch, a disease.

contracter[2], *v.tr.* to contract, draw together; **le froid contracte les corps,** cold contracts bodies; **traits contractés par la douleur,** features drawn with pain; **visage contracté par le dépit,** face contorted by vexation; *Ling:* **c. "de le" en "du,"** to contract **"de le"** into **"du."**

se contracter, to contract; (*of stuff*) to shrink; **son visage se contracta,** his features contracted.

contractif, -ive [kɔ̃traktif, -iːv], *a.* contractive (force, etc.).

contractile [kɔ̃traktil], *a. Physiol:* contractile, contractible (muscle, etc.).

contractilité [kɔ̃traktilite], *s.f. Physiol:* contractility.

contraction [kɔ̃traksjɔ̃], *s.f.* (*a*) contraction, shrinking, shrinkage (of body, etc.); narrowing (of road, etc.); (*b*) *Ling:* contraction; (*c*) contraction (of muscle); spasm; **c. nerveuse des paupières,** spasm of the eyelids; **c. des traits,** contraction, distortion, of the features.

contractuel, -elle [kɔ̃traktɥɛl]. **1.** *a. Jur:* contractual (obligation, etc.); (liability) *ex contractu*; **action contractuelle,** action for breach of contract; **date contractuelle,** contract date, date of agreement; **vitesse contractuelle,** designed speed (of ship, etc.); **main-d'œuvre contractuelle,** contractual labour; *Jur:* **droits contractuels,** rights granted by contract. **2.** *s.* employee on contract; non-established civil servant; *esp.* traffic warden.

contractuellement [kɔ̃traktɥɛlmɑ̃], *adv.* contractually, by contract.

contracture [kɔ̃traktyːr], *s.f. Arch: Med:* contracture (of pillar, of muscle).

contracturé [kɔ̃traktyre], *a. Med:* contractured (muscle).

contracturer [kɔ̃traktyre], *v.tr. Arch:* to diminish, taper (shaft of column).

contradicteur [kɔ̃tradiktœːr], *s.m.* **1.** contradictor, gainsayer; opposer. **2.** *Jur:* adversary, opposing counsel.

contradiction [kɔ̃tradiksjɔ̃], *s.f.* **1.** contradiction; *Jur:* opposition; **il n'y a pas de c. possible,** there is no gainsaying it, no denying it; **être en c. avec qn, avec les faits,** to be at variance with s.o., with the facts; **témoignage qui défie toute c.,** incontrovertible evidence; **esprit de c.,** contrariness. **2.** contradiction, inconsistency (of human mind, etc.); **c. entre deux récits,** discrepancy between two accounts; **en c. avec qch.,** inconsistent, incompatible, with sth.; **en c. absolue avec . . .,** diametrically opposed to . . .

contradictoire [kɔ̃tradiktwaːr]. **1.** *a.* (*a*) contradictory (à, to); inconsistent (à, with); conflicting (accounts, etc.); **termes contradictoires,** contradiction in terms; **passions contradictoires,** conflicting passions; (*b*) *Jur:* (*of verdict, decree*) after full argument on both sides; **jugement c.,** judgment after trial; **expertise c.,** counter-survey; **examen c.,** cross-examination; **les débats sont contradictoires,** the defence is given a full hearing; (*c*) **conférence c.,** debate; (*d*) *Ch: etc:* **essai c.,** control test; check. **2.** *s.f. Log:* contradictory proposition.

contradictoirement [kɔ̃tradiktwarmɑ̃], *adv.* **1.** contradictorily. **2.** *Jur:* **arrêt rendu c.,** judgment given after full argument on both sides, after free discussion.

contraignable [kɔ̃trɛɲabl̩], *a. Jur:* compellable, coercible; **c. par corps,** attachable, liable to arrest.

contraindre [kɔ̃trɛ̃ːdr̩], *v.tr.* (*pr.p.* **contraignant;** *p.p.* **contraint;** *pr.ind.* **je contrains, n. contraignons, ils contraignent;** *p.d.* **je contraignais;** *p.h.* **je contraignis;** *fu.* **je contraindrai**) to constrain. **1.** to restrain, put restraint on (s.o., one's feelings). **2.** to compel, force; **c. qn à,** *occ.* **de, faire qch.,** to constrain, force, s.o. to do sth.; to coerce s.o. into doing sth.; **je fus contraint d'obéir,** I was obliged to obey; **il vous payera s'il y est contraint,** he will pay you under compulsion, under coercion; **on la contraignit d'entrer au couvent,** they forced her into a convent, she was forced into a convent; **c. l'ennemi à la bataille,** to force an action on the enemy; *Jur:* **c. qn en justice,** to sue s.o., to bring an action against s.o.; **c. qn par saisie de biens,** to distrain upon s.o.; **c. qn par corps,** to imprison s.o. for debt.

se contraindre, (*a*) to keep one's feelings in check; to restrain oneself, to control oneself; (*b*) **se c. à faire qch.,** to force oneself to, to make oneself, do sth.

contraint [kɔ̃trɛ̃], *a.* constrained, cramped (posture, style, etc.); forced, wan (smile); stiff, starched (manner); **elle eut un sourire c.,** she forced a smile; *s.a.* BAS IV. 1.

contrainte [kɔ̃trɛ̃ːt], *s.f.* constraint. **1.** restraint; **tenir son zèle en c.,** to hold one's zeal in restraint, to put a restraint on one's zeal; **parler avec c.,** to speak restrainedly; **parler sans c.,** to speak freely, to speak one's mind; **vacances libres et sans c.,** free and easy holiday. **2.** compulsion, coercion; **faire qch. par c.,** to do sth. under constraint, under coercion, under compulsion; **livre écrit à la hâte et sous la c. des circonstances,** book written hastily and under pressure; **agir sans c.,** to act freely; **la c. de la rime,** the shackles, fetters, trammels, of rhyme; *Jur:* **exercer la c. par saisie de biens,** to distrain (on s.o.); **c. par corps,** imprisonment for debt; **porteur de c.,** writ-server, bailiff; *Jur:* **arrêts et contraintes de princes,** arrests and restraints of princes. **3.** *Tchn:* stress; **c. à la rupture,** strain on breaking point; **c. de cisaillement,** shear(ing) stress; **c. résiduelle,** residual stress; **indicateur de c.,** strain-indicator; **jauge de c.,** strain-gauge; **relâchement des contraintes,** stress-relief. **4.** *Adm:* **contraintes budgétaires,** tight budget.

contraire [kɔ̃trɛːr], *a. & s.m.* **1.** *a.* contrary, opposite (direction, etc.); opposed (opinion, interest, etc.); **en sens c.,** in the opposite direction; **à moins d'avis c., sauf avis c.,** unless I hear to the contrary; **jusqu'à avis c.,** until further notice; **c. à la règle, aux règlements,** against the rules; **c. à la raison,** contrary, opposed, to common sense; **voilà qui est c. à ses habitudes,** that is a departure from his usual habits; **argument c.,** counter-argument; **mouvement c.,** counter-movement. **2.** *a.* (*a*) adverse, opposed; **le sort lui est c.,** fate is against him; **si la fortune nous est c.,** if fate goes against us; **vent c.,** adverse, contrary, foul, wind; **mer c.,** cross sea; (*b*) injurious, bad; **le climat lui est c.,** the climate does not agree with him; **le vin lui est c.,** wine disagrees with him. **3.** *s.m.* opposite; **avoir preuve du c.,** to have proof to the contrary; **c'est le c.,** it's the other way round; **c'est tout le c.,** it's just the opposite, the boot is on the other foot; **je sais le c.,** I know better; *Jur:* **défense au c.,** counter-claim; *adv.phr.* **au c.,** on the contrary; *prep.phr.* **au c. de,** contrary to; **aller au c. de qch.,** to go against sth., to oppose sth.; **aller au c. de qn,** to run counter to, go against, s.o.

contrairement [kɔ̃trɛrmɑ̃], *adv.* contrarily; **faire qch. c. à l'opinion publique,** to do sth. in opposition to public opinion; **c. à son habitude, il sortit . . .,** contrary to his habit, he went out . . .; *Aut:* **dépasser c. au règlement,** to overtake improperly.

contralte [kɔ̃tralt], *s.m.*, **contralto** [kɔ̃tralto], *s.m. Mus:* contralto; **voix de c.,** contralto voice; *pl. contraltes, contralto(s), contralti.*

contrapointiste [kɔ̃trapwɛ̃tist], *s.m. Mus:* contrapuntist.

contrapontique [kɔ̃trapɔ̃tik], *a. Mus:* contrapuntal.

contrapontiste [kɔ̃trapɔ̃tist], *s.m. Mus:* contrapunist.

contraposé [kɔ̃trapoze], *a. Geol:* **côte contraposée,** contraposed shoreline.

contraposition [kɔ̃trapozisjɔ̃], *s.f. Log:* contraposition.

contrapuntique [kɔ̃trapɔ̃tik], *a. Mus:* contrapuntal.

contrapuntiste [kɔ̃trapɔ̃tist], *s.m. Mus:* contrapuntist.

contrariant [kɔ̃trarjɑ̃], *a.* (*a*) provoking, irritating (person, spirit); (*b*) vexatious (measure); trying (circumstance, etc.); **comme c'est c.!** how annoying! what a nuisance!

contrarié, *a.* **1.** (*a*) thwarted; **être c. dans son amour,** to be crossed in love; (*b*) annoyed, vexed, upset (de, at). **2.** *Const:* (*of bricks, etc.*) with broken joints.

contrarier [kɔ̃trarje], *v.tr.* (*p.d. & pr.sub.* **n. contrariions, v. contrariiez**) **1.** to thwart, oppose, cross; to run counter to (s.o.); **c. les desseins de qn,** to interfere with s.o.'s schemes; **c. les désirs de qn,** to thwart s.o.'s wishes; **nous ne fîmes que nous c. tout du long,** from first to last we were at cross purposes; **c. les mouvements de l'ennemi,** to impede the enemy's movements; **navire contrarié par les vents,** wind-bound ship; **ressort qui contrarie l'effet d'une force,** spring acting against a force. **2.** to vex, annoy; *F:* to put (s.o.) out; **cela me contrarie qu'il soit là,** I am vexed, annoyed, at his being there. **3.** to contrast; to put (colours, etc.) in contrast. **4.** *Tchn:* to set (bricks, boiler, plates, etc.) in alternation; **c. les joints,** to break joint. **5.** *abs.* **il aime à c.,** he likes to thwart people.

contrariété [kɔ̃trarjete], *s.f.* **1.** (*a*) contrariety; clash(ing) (of interests, tastes, colours, etc.); **la c. des précédents fait qu'on ne saurait les invoquer,** the contradictory nature of precedents makes it impossible to appeal to them; (*b*) **esprit de c.,** contrariness; perversity. **2.** vexation, annoyance; **quelle c.!** how annoying! **éprouver une vive c.,** to be very much annoyed; **c. passagère,** momentary irritation.

contrarotatif, -ive [kɔ̃trarɔtatif, -iːv], *a. Mec.E: etc:* contrarotating; *Aer: Nau: etc:* **hélice contrarotative,** contrarotating propeller.

contrastant [kɔ̃trastɑ̃], *a.* contrasting (colours, etc.).

contraste [kɔ̃trast], *s.m.* **1.** contrast; set-off; **mettre une chose en c. avec une autre,** to bring one thing into contrast with another, to contrast one thing with another, to set sth. against sth.; **être en c., faire c., avec . . .,** to contrast with . . ., to offer a contrast with . . ., to stand out against . . .; **comme c. à . . .,** by way of contrast to . . .; **par c. avec,** in contrast with. **2.** *Phot: Cin:* contrast; **c. d'éclairement,** light contrast; **c. insensible, c. léger,** slight contrast; **filtre de c.,** contrast filter; **papier c.,** contrast paper, hard, vigorous, paper; **plaque c.,** contrast plate; **négatif sans contrastes,** flat negative. **3.** *Elcs: T.V:* **c. des brillants,** brightness ratio; **c. d'image,** picture contrast; **c. des radiations,** ray contrast; **excès de c.,** clouding.

contrasté [kɔ̃traste], *a. Phot:* contrasty, hard (print).

contraster [kɔ̃traste], *v.* to contrast. **1.** *v.i.* **c. avec qch.,** to contrast, stand in contrast, with sth.; to form a contrast to sth.; **couleurs qui contrastent,** colours that set one another off. **2.** *v.tr.* to put, set, (colours, etc.) in contrast.

contrat [kɔ̃tra], *s.m.* contract, agreement, deed; **action en exécution de c.,** action for specific performance of contract; **rupture de c.,** breach of contract; **passer un c. avec qn,** to enter into, conclude, an agreement with s.o.; **c. translatif de propriété,** conveyance; **c. de société,** deed, articles, of partnership; **c. de mariage,** ante-nuptial contract, marriage settlement; *U.S:* premarital agreement; **c. d'apprentissage,** indenture, articles of apprenticeship; **c. d'assurance,** insurance policy; *Com: Fin:* **c. de vente,** bill of sale; **c. d'arrangement,** deed of arrangement; *Nau:* **c. d'affrètement,** charter-party, contract of affreightment; **résilier le c.,** to cancel the charter; **contrat d'engagement,** ship's articles; **c. de sauvetage,** salvage agreement; **le c. social,** the social compact; *Cards:* **réaliser son c.,** to make one's contract; **c. de manche,** game contract; **c. de location, de louage,** contract of hire; **c. de travail,** service agreement; *U.S:* labor contract; **c. collectif,** collective agreement; **c. de gage,** bailment.

contravention [kɔ̃travɑ̃sjɔ̃], *s.f.* (*a*) contravention, infringement, breach (**au règlement,** of regulations); (*b*) *Jur:* **c. de simple police,** petty offence, minor infraction of the law (as opposed to **délit**); breach of police regulations, police offence; (*c*) *F:* ticket; **dresser une c. à qn,** *F:* to give s.o. a ticket, to book s.o.; to take s.o.'s name and address (with a view to prosecution); often = to summons s.o.; *F:* **se mettre en c.,** to trespass; **être en c. avec,** to contravene.

contraventionnel, -elle [kɔ̃travɑ̃sjɔnɛl], *a. Jur:* **délit c.,** police misdemeanour.

contravis [kɔ̃travi], *s.m. A:* **1.** counter-advice, contrary opinion. **2.** notification to the contrary; countermand; **sauf c.,** unless I hear to the contrary.

contre[1] [kɔ̃:tr̥]. **1.** *prep.* against; (*a*) contrary to; **nager c. le courant,** to swim against the stream; **se battre c. qn,** to fight against, with, s.o.; **se fâcher c. qn,** to get angry with s.o.; **agir c. la loi,** to act against, in defiance, of the law; **c. toute attente,** contrary to all expectation; **c. son habitude,** contrary to his usual practice; **Eton c. Harrow,** Eton *versus* Harrow; **ranger l'opinion publique c. soi,** to antagonize public opinion; **avoir raison c. qn,** to be right in disagreeing with s.o.; *Nau:* **avancer c. le vent,** to steam in the wind's eye; (*b*) from; **s'abriter c. la pluie,** to shelter from the rain; **s'assurer c. l'incendie,** to insure against fire; (*c*) (*in exchange*) for; **échanger une chose c. une autre,** to exchange one thing for another; **livraison c. remboursement,** cash on delivery; (*d*) to; **parier à cinq c. un,** to bet five to one; **résolution adoptée à dix voix c. six,** resolution passed by ten votes to six; (*e*) (close) to, by; **s'appuyer c. le mur,** to lean against the wall; **assis c. la porte,** sitting by, close to, the door; **sa maison est tout contre la mienne,** his house adjoins mine. **2.** *adv.* against; **parler pour et c.,** to speak for and against; **la maison est tout c.,** the house is close by, hard by; **laisser la porte (tout) c.,** to leave the door to; *s.a.* CI-CONTRE, LÀ-CONTRE. **3.** *s.m.* (*a*) **disputer le pour et le c.,** to discuss the pros and cons; **il y a du pour et du c.,** there is something to be said on both sides; *adv.phr:* **par c.,** on the other hand, by way of compensation; *Nau:* (*of two ships*) **courir à c.,** to run in opposite directions, to opposite points; **abattre à c.,** to cast in the wrong way; **chasser à c.,** (*of high clouds*) to blow across the wind; (*b*) *Box: Fenc:* counter; (*c*) *Bill:* kiss; (*d*) *Cards:* double; **c. d'appel,** informative double; **c. de pénalité,** penalty double.

contre[2], *s.m. Tls:* hafted wedge (for splitting timber).

contre-, *pref.* **1.** contra-; **contrebasse,** contrabass. **2.** counter; **contre-accusation,** counter-charge. **3.** anti-; **contrepoison,** antidote. **4.** back-; **contre-courant,** back-current.

contré [kɔ̃tre], *a. Cards:* **non c.,** undoubled.

contre-accélération [kɔ̃trakselerasjɔ̃], *s.f. Mec:* retardation; *Space:* deceleration.

contre-acclamations [kɔ̃traklamasjɔ̃], *s.f.pl.* counter-cheers.

contre-accusation [kɔ̃trakyzasjɔ̃], *s.f.* counter-charge; *pl. contre-accusations.*

contre-à-contre [kɔ̃trakɔ̃:tr̥], *adv. A: Nau:* alongside.

contre-aiguille [kɔ̃tregɥi:j], *s.m. Rail:* stock-rail (at points); *pl. contre-aiguilles.*

contre-alésage [kɔ̃traleza:ʒ], *s.m. Min:* counter-bore; *pl. contre-alésages.*

contre-alizé [kɔ̃tralize], *a. & s. Meteor:* counter-trade; *pl. contre-alizés.*

contre-allée [kɔ̃trale], *s.f.* side-walk, -lane; lateral avenue; *pl. contre-allées.*

contre-allumage [kɔ̃tralyma:ʒ], *s.m. I.C.E:* back-fire; **coup de c.-a.,** kick; *pl. contre-allumages.*

contre-amiral [kɔ̃tramiral], *s.m.* **1.** rear-admiral. **2.** rear-admiral's flagship; *pl. contre-amiraux.*

contre-analyse [kɔ̃tranali:z], *s.f.* check analysis; *pl. contre-analyses.*

contre-appel [kɔ̃trapɛl], *s.m.* **1.** *Fenc:* caveating. **2.** *Mil:* check roll-call, second call. **3.** *Tg:* counter-signal, -call. **4. c.-a. d'air,** back-draught; *pl. contre-appels.*

contre-approches [kɔ̃trapɾɔʃ], *s.f.pl. Fort:* counter-approaches.

contre-appui [kɔtrapɥi], *s.m.* counter-bracing; **corde de c.-a.,** guy(rope); *pl. contre-appuis.*

contre-arbre [kɔ̃trarbr̥], *s.m. Mec.E:* counter-shaft; *pl. contre-arbres.*

contre-arc [kɔ̃trark], *s.m. N.Arch:* sag(ging); **avoir du c.-a.,** to sag; *pl. contre-arc(s).*

contre-assemblée [kɔ̃trasɑ̃ble], *s.f. A: Pol: etc:* opposition meeting; *pl. contre-assemblées.*

contre-assiéger [kɔ̃trasjeʒe], *v.tr.* (*conj. like* ASSIÉGER) *Mil:* to conduct a counter-siege against (an investing force).

contre-assurance [kɔ̃trasyrɑ̃:s], *s.f.* reinsurance; *pl. contre-assurances.*

contre-attaque [kɔ̃tratak], *s.f. Mil:* **1.** counter-attack; counter-stroke. **2.** *pl. Fort:* counter-works; *pl. contre-attaques.*

contre-attaquer [kɔ̃tratake], *v.tr.* to counter-attack.

contre-aube [kɔ̃tro:b], *s.f. Hyd.E:* counter-paddle; *pl. contre-aube(s).*

contrebalancer [kɔ̃trəbalɑ̃se], *v.tr.* (**je contrebalançai(s); n. contrebalançons**) to counter-balance, counterpoise, offset, compensate.

se contrebalancer, to counterbalance; *F:* to cancel out.

contrebalancier [kɔ̃trəbalɑ̃sje], *s.m. Min: etc:* balance-bob (of pump).

contrebande [kɔ̃trəbɑ̃:d], *s.f.* **1.** contraband, smuggling; **articles de c.,** contraband goods; **faire la c.,** to smuggle, to engage in smuggling; **faire entrer des marchandises en c.,** to smuggle in goods; **c. d'armes,** gun-running, *U.S:* **c. des boissons alcooliques,** bootlegging; *A: F:* **homme de c.,** intruder; *F:* gate-crasher. **2.** contraband goods, smuggled goods; **c. de guerre,** war contraband.

contrebandier, -ière [kɔ̃trəbɑ̃dje, -jɛ:r], *s.* smuggler, contrabandist; **c. d'armes,** gun-runner, *U.S:* **c. de boissons alcooliques,** bootlegger; *a.* **vaisseau c.,** smuggling vessel.

contre-barré [kɔ̃trəbare], *a. Her:* counter-faced, counter-fessed; bendy sinister per bend counter-changed.

contrebas (en) [ɑ̃kɔ̃trəbɑ], *adv.phr.* **1.** (lower) down, on a lower level, below; **être en c. de qch.,** to be lower than sth., below the level of sth.; **le café est en c. de la rue,** the café is below street-level. **2.** downwards; **le jardin s'étend en c. vers la rivière,** the garden runs down to the river on the other side (of the house, etc.); **mesure prise en c.,** measurement taken downwards.

contrebasse [kɔ̃trəbɑ:s], *s.f. Mus:* **1.** (*a*) (stringed) double-bass, contrabass; (*b*) (*brass bands*) tuba, bombardon. **2.** double-bass (player), tuba (player).

contrebassier [kɔ̃trəbɑsje], *s.m. O:* = CONTREBASSISTE.

contrebassiste [kɔ̃trəbɑsist], *s.m. Mus:* (*a*) double-bass (player); contrabassist; (*b*) tuba player.

contrebasson [kɔ̃trəbɑsɔ̃], *s.m. Mus:* double-bassoon (instrument or player); contra-bassoon.

contrebatterie [kɔ̃trəbatri], *s.f. Mil:* counter-battery; **tir de c.-b.,** counter-battery fire.

contrebattre [kɔ̃trəbatr̥], *v.tr.* (*conj. like* BATTRE) *Mil:* to counter-batter.

contre-biais [kɔ̃trəbjɛ], *s.m.inv.* diagonal cut against the twist (of cloth), against the grain (of wood); *adv.phr.* **à c.-b.,** against the grain, contrariwise, the wrong way.

contre-bon-sens [kɔ̃trəbɔ̃sɑ̃:s], *s.m.inv. A:* piece of unreason; absurdity.

contre-bord (à) [akɔ̃trəbɔ:r], *adv.phr. Nau:* **courir à c.-b.,** to sail (i) on opposite tacks; (ii) on parallel and opposite courses; **navires à c.-b.,** ships passing; **s'amarrer à c.-b. l'un de l'autre,** to moor head and tail.

contre-boutant [kɔ̃trəbutɑ̃], *s.m.* **1.** *Arch: etc:* buttress; *a.* **murs contre-boutants,** buttressing walls. **2.** *Const: Civ.E:* shore; *pl. contre-boutants.*

contre-bouter [kɔ̃trəbute], *v.tr. Civ.E: etc:* to buttress; to shore up.

contre-bouterolle [kɔ̃trəbutrɔl], *s.f. Tchn:* bucking bar; *pl. contre-bouterolles.*

contre-brasser [kɔ̃trəbrase], *v.tr. Nau:* to counter-brace (yard); **c. devant,** to brace round the head yards.

contre-bride [kɔ̃trəbrid], *s.f. Tchn:* counter-flange; adapter; *pl. contre-brides.*

contre-buter [kɔ̃trəbyte], *v.tr.* = CONTRE-BOUTER.

contre-cacatois [kɔ̃trəkakatwa], *s.m.inv. Nau:* skysail.

contre-cadence [kɔ̃trəkadɑ̃:s], *s.f. Nau:* preventer-plate; *pl. contre-cadences.*

contre-calque [kɔ̃trəkalk], *s.m.* blueprint; *pl. contre-calques.*

contre-calquer [kɔ̃trəkalke], *v.tr.* to take a reversed tracing of, to blueprint (sth.).

contre-carlingue [kɔ̃trəkarlɛ̃:g], *s.f. N.Arch:* sister-keelson; *pl. contre-carlingues.*

contrecarrer [kɔ̃trəkɑre], *v.tr.* (*a*) to cross, thwart, oppose (s.o., plans); **c. un effet,** to counteract an effect; (*b*) *A:* **nous nous contrecarrons,** we are at cross purposes.

contre-caution [kɔ̃trəkosjɔ̃], *s.f. Jur:* additional security; *pl. contre-cautions.*

contre-champ, contrechamp [kɔ̃trəʃɑ̃], *s.m. Cin:* reverse shot; *pl. contre(-)champs.*

contre-chant [kɔ̃trəʃɑ̃], *s.m. Mus:* counter-melody; accompaniment figure; *pl. contre-chants.*

contre-charme [kɔ̃trəʃarm], *s.m.* counter-charm; *pl. contre-charmes.*

contre(-)châssis [kɔ̃trəʃɑsi], *s.m.inv.* **1.** double sash (of window); double window. **2.** *Metall:* top-flask, -box (of mould).

contre-civadière [kɔ̃trəsivadjɛ:r], *s.f. Nau:* sprit-topsail; *pl. contre-civadières.*

contre-clavette [kɔ̃trəklavɛt], *s.f. Mec.E:* gib, fox-wedge, nose-key; **clavette et c.-c.,** gib and cotter; *pl. contre-clavettes.*

contreclef [kɔ̃trəkle], *s.f. Const:* voussoir next to the keystone (of arch); second voussoir.

contre-coalition [kɔ̃trəkɔalisjɔ̃], *s.f.* opposition league; *pl. contre-coalitions.*

contrecœur [kɔ̃trəkœ:r], *s.m.* **1.** *adv.phr.* **à. c.,** unwillingly, reluctantly, grudgingly; **je l'ai fait mais à c.,** I did it but it went against the grain. **2.** (*a*) *Const:* back-plate (of fire-place, of forge); fire back; (*b*) *Rail:* guard-rail, wing-rail (at centre of cross-over).

contrecollage [kɔ̃trəkɔla:ʒ], *s.m. Bookb:* pasting down of the end-papers.

contrecoller [kɔ̃trəkɔle], *v.tr. Bookb:* to glue, to paste down the end-papers; *Tch:* **bois contre-collé,** thick plywood.

contrecoup [kɔ̃trəku], *s.m.* (*a*) rebound (of bullet, etc.); recoil; *Bill:* kiss; *Metalw:* **faire c.,** to receive, support, the blow (in riveting); to hold on; (*b*) jar (of blow, etc.); (*c*) repercussion, backlash (of explosion); kick-back (of motor); *Mec:* backlash; *El:* return shock; by(e)-effect, after-effects, consequence (of action, disaster); **les contrecoups de la guerre,** the repercussions of war; **les prix augmentent par c.,** the prices go up in consequence; (*d*) *Equit:* sudden start, jump (of horse).

contre-courant [kɔ̃trəkurɑ̃], *s.m.* **1.** (*a*) *Hyd:* counter-current; **c.-c. marin,** oceanic counter-current; **nager, naviguer, à c.-c.,** to swim, sail, against the stream; (*of water*) **couler à c.-c.,** to flow backwards; **à c.-c. de,** counter to; (*b*) *El:* back-current, counter-flow; **condensateur à c.-c.,** reflux condenser; (*c*) *Nucl:* counter-current flow; **c.-c. continu,** continuous counter-current flow; (*d*) (*of vehicle*) **rouler à c.-c.,** to drive against the stream (of traffic). **2.** back-draught (of air); *pl. contre-courants.*

contre-courbe [kɔ̃trəkurb], *s.f. Arch:* counter-curve; *pl. contre-courbes.*

contre-course [kɔ̃trəkurs], *s.f. Mch:* reverse-, return-stroke (of piston); *pl. contre-courses.*

contre-coussinet [kɔ̃trəkusinɛ], *s.m. Mec.E:* top-brass (of bearing); *pl. contre-coussinets.*

contre-critique [kɔ̃trəkritik], *s.f.* counter-criticism; *pl. contre-critiques.*

contredanse [kɔ̃trədɑ̃:s], *s.f.* **1.** quadrille (dance, air). **2.** (*in Eng.*) country dance. **3.** *F:* ticket; **flanquer une c. à qn,** *F:* to give s.o. a ticket, to book s.o.

contre-déclaration [kɔ̃trədeklarasjɔ̃], *s.f.* counter-declaration; *pl. contre-déclarations.*

contre-dégagement [kɔ̃trədegaʒmɑ̃], *s.m. Fenc:* counter-disengagement; *pl. contre-dégagements.*

contre-dégager [kɔ̃trədegaʒe], *v.tr. & i.* (*conj. like* DÉGAGER) *Fenc:* to counter-disengage.

contre-dépouille [kɔ̃trədepu:j], *s.f. Metalw:* undercut; **pièce en c.-d.,** undercut piece; *pl. contre-dépouilles.*

contre-digue [kɔ̃trədig], *s.f. Civ.E:* strengthening dike; *pl. contre-digues.*

contredire [kɔ̃trədi:r]. **1.** *v.tr.* (*pr.ind.* **je contredis, n. contredisons, v. contredisez;** *other tenses like* DIRE) to contradict; (*a*) to gainsay; *Jur:* to confute; (*b*) to be inconsistent with, contrary to (sth.), to belie (expectations); **propositions qui se contredisent,** propositions that are inconsistent; **les faits contredisent ces assurances,** the facts are at variance with these assurances; *abs.* **il aime à c.,** he likes contradicting. **2.** *v.i. A:* **c. à qch.,** to oppose, go against, sth.; **nul n'y contredit,** no one has a word to say against it.

se contredire, to contradict oneself; *F:* to give oneself away.

contredisant [kɔ̃trədizɑ̃]. **1.** *a.* argumentative, given to contradicting. **2.** *a. & s. Jur:* opposing (party).

contre-distorsion [kɔ̃trədistɔrsjɔ̃], *s.f. Elcs:* equalization; **intervalle de c.-d.,** frequency range of equalization; **limite de c.-d.,** frequency limit of equalization; *pl. contre-distorsions.*

contredit [kɔ̃trədi], *s.m.* **1.** *A:* contradiction, objection; *Jur:* reply, rejoinder. **2.** *adv.phr.* **sans c.,** indisputably, unquestionably.

contrée [kɔ̃tre], *s.f.* (geographical) region; province (in a wide sense); country (in an indeterminate sense); **les longues nuits d'hiver des contrées du nord,** the long winter nights of northern countries, of the northern regions.

contre-écartelé [kɔ̃trekartəle], *a. Her:* counter-quartered quarter.

contre-échange [kɔ̃treʃɑ̃:ʒ], *s.m.* (mutual) exchange; *pl. contre-échanges.*

contre-écriture [kɔ̃trekrity:r], *s.f. Book-k:* contra-entry; *pl. contre-écritures.*

contre-écrou [kɔ̃trekru], *s.m. Mec.E:* lock-nut, check-nut, jam-nut, keeper; **c.-é. de réglage,** adjustment lock-nut; *pl. contre-écrous.*

contre-effet [kɔ̃trefɛ], *s.m.* contrary effect; *pl. contre-effets.*

contre-électromoteur, -trice [kɔ̃trelɛktrɔmɔtœ:r, -tris], *a. El:* **force contre-électromotrice,** back, counter, electromotive force.

contre-empreinte [kɔ̃trɑ̃prɛ̃:t], *s.f.* fossil imprint; *pl. contre-empreintes.*

contre-enquête [kɔ̃trɑ̃kɛ:t], *s.f. Jur:* counter-enquiry; *pl. contre-enquêtes.*

contre-épaulette [kɔ̃trepolɛt], *s.f. Mil:* epaulette without fringe; (shoulder-)scale (worn on one shoulder with epaulette on the other); *pl. contre-épaulettes.*

contre-épreuve [kɔ̃treprœ:v], *s.f.* **1.** *Engr:* (*a*) counter-proof, reverse(d) proof, reverse transfer; **presse à c.-é.,** (proving and) reversing press; (*b*) second proof. **2.** *Tchn:* check-test, repetition test. **3.** *Adm:* counter-verification (of votes); *pl. contre-épreuves.*

contre-épreuver [kɔ̃treprœve], *v.tr. Engr:* to counter-prove; **presse à c.-é.,** (proving and) reversing press.

contre-espionnage [kɔ̃trɛspjɔna:ʒ], *s.m.* counter-espionage; *s.a.* ESPIONNAGE.

contre-essai [kɔ̃tresɛ, -ɛsɛ], *s.m.* control experiment, check test; *pl. contre-essais.*

contre-étambot [kɔ̃tretɑ̃bo], *s.m. N.Arch:* inner sternpost; *pl. contre-étambots.*

contre-étrave [kɔ̃tretra:v], *s.f. N.Arch:* apron; *pl. contre-étraves.*

contre-expertise [kɔ̃trɛkspɛrti:z], *s.f.* re-survey, counter-valuation; *pl. contre-expertises.*

contre-extension [kɔ̃trɛkstɑ̃sjɔ̃], *s.f. Surg:* counter-extension; *pl. contre-extensions.*

contrefaçon [kɔ̃trəfasɔ̃], *s.f.* **1.** counterfeiting; fraudulently copying or imitating (trade-mark, etc.); infringement (of patent, of copyright); *F:* piracy; **procès en c.,** action for infringement (of copyright, etc.); *s.a.* ASSIGNER 2. **2.** counterfeit, forgery, fraudulent imitation; *F:* pirated edition or copy.

contrefacteur [kɔ̃trəfaktœ:r], *s.m.* (*a*) counterfeiter, forger (of document); (*b*) infringer (of patent, of copyright); *F:* pirate.

contrefaction [kɔ̃trəfaksjɔ̃], *s.f.* counterfeiting (of coins, etc.); forgery (of bank-notes, signature, etc.).

contrefaire [kɔ̃trəfɛ:r], *v.tr.* (*conj. like* FAIRE) **1.** (*a*) to imitate, mimic; *F:* to take off, to ape (s.o., s.o.'s voice, etc.); (*b*) to feign; **c. le mort,** *F:* to sham dead; (*c*) to disguise (one's voice, writing, etc.). **2.** (*a*) to counterfeit (coin, etc.); to forge (signature, currency, etc.); (*b*) *F:* to pirate (book, etc.); **c. un objet breveté,** to infringe a patent. **3.** to distort, deform (shape, features, etc.); **corps contrefait par une maladie,** body deformed by an illness.

contrefait [kɔ̃trəfɛ], *a.* **1.** feigned (zeal, etc.); disguised (writing, etc.). **2.** counterfeit, forged, spurious (money, etc.); **édition contrefaite,** pirated edition. **3.** deformed (person).

contre-fanon [kɔ̃trəfanɔ̃], *s.m. Nau:* buntline; *pl. contre-fanons.*

contre-fenêtre [kɔ̃trəfnɛ:tr̥], *s.f.* inner sash; *pl. contre-fenêtres.*

contre-fer [kɔ̃trəfɛ:r], *s.m. Tls:* top-iron, back-iron, break-iron (of plane); *pl. contre-fers.*

contre-feu [kɔ̃trəfø], *s.m.* **1.** = CONTRECŒUR 2 (*a*). **2.** (*a*) *Metall:* back-draught (of flames in furnace); (*b*) *I.C.E:* backfire. **3.** (any) fire lit as defensive measure; counter-fire; *U.S:* backfire; *pl. contre-feux.*

contre-fiche [kɔ̃trəfiʃ], *s.f. Carp: Const: Mec.E:* brace, strut, stay; angle-brace (of truss, etc.); racking shore (of wall); *Av:* **c.-f. de potence,** upper support arm; *pl. contre-fiches.*

contre-ficher [kɔ̃trəfiʃe], *v.tr. Carp: Const: Mec.E: etc:* to strut, truss.

se contrefiche(r), *P:* **je m'en fiche et m'en contrefiche,** I don't care a hang, give a damn.

contre-fil [kɔ̃trəfil], *s.m.* opposite direction, wrong way (of watercourse, stuff, etc.); **à c.-f. de l'eau,** up-stream; **travailler du bois à c.-f.,** to work wood against the grain; *pl. contre-fils.*

contre-filet [kɔ̃trəfilɛ], *s.m. Cu:* hind brisket; *pl. contre-filets.*

contre-finesse [kɔ̃trəfinɛs], *s.f.* counter-stratagem; *pl. contre-finesses.*

contre-foc [kɔ̃trəfɔk], *s.m. Nau:* inner jib, middle jib; *pl. contre-focs.*

contrefort [kɔ̃trəfɔ:r], *s.m.* **1.** *Arch: Fort: etc:* (close) buttress, abutment; *N.Arch:* **contreforts de l'arcasse,** transom knees; **contreforts (de la cuirasse),** backing; *Rail:* **c. d'un coussinet,** shoulder of a chair. **2.** *Geog:* counterfort, spur, underfeature (of mountain); *pl.* buttresses; foot-hills. **3.** stiffening, counter (of boot).

contre-fossé [kɔ̃trəfose], *s.m. Fort:* advanced fosse; *pl. contre-fossés.*

contre-foulement [kɔ̃trəfulmɑ̃], *s.m. Hyd.E:* backset, surging (in pipe); *pl. contre-foulements.*

contre-fracture [kɔ̃trəfrakty:r], *s.f. Surg:* counter-fracture; *pl. contre-fractures.*

contre-fruit [kɔ̃trəfrɥi], *s.m. Arch:* inner batter (of wall); *pl. contre-fruits.*

contre-fugue [kɔ̃trəfyg], *s.f. Mus:* counter-fugue; *pl. contre-fugues.*

contre-garde [kɔ̃trəgard], *s.f. Fort: etc:* counter-guard; *pl. contre-gardes.*

contre-gouvernement [kɔ̃trəguvɛrnəmɑ̃], *s.m.* shadow government; *pl. contre-gouvernements.*

contre-greffe [kɔ̃trəgrɛf], *s.f. Hort:* double-grafting; *pl. contre-greffes.*

contre-greffer [kɔ̃trəgrɛfe, -efe], *v.tr. Hort:* to double-graft.

contre-griffer [kɔ̃trəgrife], *v.tr. F:* to countersign (document, etc.).

contre-hacher [kɔ̃trəaʃe], *v.tr. Art: Engr:* to cross-hatch.

contre-hachure [kɔ̃trəaʃy:r], *s.f. Art: Engr:* cross-hatch(ing); *pl. contre-hachures.*

contre-haut (en) [ɑ̃kɔ̃trəo]. **1.** *adv.phr.* (*a*) higher up, on a higher level; (*b*) **mesure prise en c.-h.,** measurement taken from the foot upwards. **2.** *prep.phr.* **berge en c.-h. de la rivière,** bank on a higher level than the river.

contre-hermine [kɔ̃trɛrmin], *s.f. Her:* counter-ermine; *pl. contre-hermines.*

contre-heurtoir [kɔ̃trəœrtwa:r], *s.m.* plate (of door-knocker); *pl. contre-heurtoirs.*

contre-hublot [kɔ̃trəyblo], *s.m. Nau:* deadlight; *pl. contre-hublots.*

contre-hus [kɔ̃try], *s.m.inv.* lower half (of stable door).

contre-indication [kɔ̃trɛ̃dikasjɔ̃], *s.f. Med:* contra-indication, counter-indication; *pl. contre-indications.*

contre-indiquer [kɔ̃trɛ̃dike], *v.tr.* (*a*) *Med:* to contra-indicate; **ce traitement est contre-indiqué,** this treatment is inadvisable; (*b*) **il est contre-indiqué de prendre l'avion par temps de brouillard,** it is unwise to fly in foggy weather.

contre-interrogatoire [kɔ̃trɛ̃terɔgatwa:r], *s.m. Jur:* cross-examination; *pl. contre-interrogatoires.*

contre-interroger [kɔ̃trɛ̃terɔʒe], *v.tr.* (*conj. like* INTERROGER) *Jur:* to cross-examine.

contre-jour [kɔ̃trəʒu:r], *s.m.* **1.** unfavourable light (from behind) (for picture, etc.); **tableau pendu à c.-j.,** picture hung against the light; **photo prise à c.-j.,** photograph taken against the light; **assis à c.-j.,** sitting with one's back to the light, in one's own light. **2.** *Art: Cin: Phot:* back-light(ing); *pl. contre-jours.*

contre-lattage [kɔ̃trəlata:ʒ], *s.m. Const:* counter-lathing; *pl. contre-lattages.*

contre-latte [kɔ̃trəlat], *s.f. Const:* counter-lath; *pl. contre-lattes.*

contre-latter [kɔ̃trəlate], *v.tr. Const:* to counter-lath (partition, etc.).

contre-lettre [kɔ̃trəlɛtr̥], *s.f. Jur:* counter-deed, pocket-agreement, defeasance; *pl. contre-lettres.*

contre-ligue [kɔ̃trəlig], *s.f.* opposition league; *pl. contre-ligues.*

contre-maille [kɔ̃trəmɑ:j], *s.f. Fish:* double mesh (of net); *pl. contre-mailles.*

contre-mailler [kɔ̃trəmɑje], *v.tr. Fish:* to double-mesh (net).

contremaître, -tresse [kɔ̃trəmɛ:tr̥, -trɛs]. **1.** *s.* foreman, forewoman; overseer, ganger; *F:* boss, gaffer. **2.** *s.m. Nau: A:* boatswain's mate; *Navy: A:* petty officer.

contremandement [kɔ̃trəmɑ̃dmɑ̃], *s.m. A:* countermand(ing), cancelling (of order).

contremander [kɔ̃trəmɑ̃de], *v.tr. O:* to countermand, cancel, revoke (order, invitation, etc.); **c. une grève,** to call off a strike; **c. ses invités,** to put off one's guests.

contre-manifestant, -ante [kɔ̃trəmanifɛstɑ̃, -ɑ̃:t], *s.* counter-demonstrator; *pl. contre-manifestants, contre-manifestantes.*

contre-manifestation [kɔ̃trəmanifɛstasjɔ̃], *s.f.* counter-demonstration; *pl. contre-manifestations.*

contre-manifester [kɔ̃trəmanifɛste], *v.i. Pol:* to counter-demonstrate.

contre-manœuvre [kɔ̃trəmanœ:vr̥], *s.f.* counter-manœuvre; *pl. contre-manœuvres.*

contre-manœuvrer [kɔ̃trəmanœvre], *v.tr.* to out-manœuvre.

contremarche [kɔ̃trəmarʃ], *s.f.* **1.** (*a*) *Mil:* countermarch; (*b*) *Navy:* alteration of course (16 points) in succession. **2.** *Const:* (*a*) height (of stair); (*b*) riser; **c. palière,** landing-riser.

contremarcher [kɔ̃trəmarʃe], *v.i.* to countermarch.

contre-marée [kɔ̃trəmare], *s.f.* **1.** undertow (of tide); counter-tide. **2.** *adv.phr.* **à c.-m.,** against the tide; *pl. contre-marées.*

contremarque [kɔ̃trəmark], *s.f.* **1.** countermark (on coin, gold plate, etc.). **2.** *Farr:* bishoping (of horse's teeth); countermark. **3.** *Th:* **c. de sortie,** pass-out ticket or check.

contremarquer [kɔ̃trəmarke], *v.tr.* **1.** to countermark (gold, bale of goods, etc.). **2.** *Farr:* to bishop (horse's teeth).

contremarqueur, -euse [kɔ̃trəmarkœ:r, -ø:z], *s. Th:* issuer of pass-out checks.

contre-matrice [kɔ̃trəmatris], *s.f. Mec.E:* reversed die; *pl. contre-matrices.*

contre-mémoire [kɔ̃trəmemwa:r], *s.m. Jur:* counter-statement; *pl. contre-mémoires.*

contre-mesure [kɔ̃trəmzy:r], *s.f.* **1.** counter-measure. **2.** *Mus:* **jouer à c.-m.,** to play against the beat; *pl. contre-mesures.*

contre(-)mine [kɔ̃trəmin], *s.f. Mil:* countermine; *pl. contre(-)mines.*

contre(-)miner [kɔ̃trəmine], *v.tr.* to countermine.

contre-mineur [kɔ̃trəminœ:r], *s.m.* counterminer; *pl. contre-mineurs.*

contre-mont (à) [akɔ̃trəmɔ̃], *adv.phr. A:* (*a*) uphill; (*b*) upstream.

contre-mot [kɔ̃trəmo], *s.m. Mil: A:* password in reply to countersign; *pl. contre-mots.*

contre-mur [kɔ̃trəmy:r], *s.m.* **1.** *Mil: etc:* countermure, outer wall. **2.** *Metall:* lining wall (of furnace); *pl. contre-murs.*

contre-murer [kɔ̃trəmyre], *v.tr. Mil: etc:* to countermure; to protect with an outer wall.

contre-note [kɔ̃trənɔt], *s.f.* (diplomatic) counter-note; *pl. contre-notes.*

contre-offensive [kɔ̃trɔfɑ̃si:v], *s.f. Mil:* counter-offensive; *pl. contre-offensives.*

contre-opération [kɔ̃trɔperasjɔ̃], *s.f. Mil:* countermeasure; counter-move; counter-manœuvre; *pl. contre-opérations.*

contre-opposition [kɔ̃trɔpozisjɔ̃], *s.f. Pol:* minority within an opposition; *pl. contre-oppositions.*

contre-ordre [kɔ̃trɔrdr̥], *s.m.* = CONTRORDRE.

contre-ouverture [kɔ̃truvɛrty:r], *s.f. esp. Surg:* counter-opening; *pl. contre-ouvertures.*

contre-paroi [kɔ̃trəparwa], *s.f. Metall:* casing (of furnace); *pl. contre-parois.*

contrepartie [kɔ̃trəparti], *s.f.* **1.** (*a*) opposite (view) (in debate); **soutenir la c.,** to speak against the motion; (*b*) *Com: Fin:* (i) other party, other side (in transaction); *Pol.Ec:* reciprocal arrangement, quid pro quo; (ii) *St.Exch:* **c. dissimulée, occulte,** market-making; **faire de la c.,** to operate against one's client; **maison de c.,** bucket shop. **2.** (*a*) *Book-k:* contra; **en c.,** per contra; **réclamer des garanties en c. d'une aide efficace,** to claim guarantees as a set-off against effective aid; (*b*) counterpart, duplicate (of document, etc.); (*c*) *Mus:* (i) counterpart; (ii) opposed part (in counterpoint); (*d*) *adv.phr.* **en c.,** on the other hand.

contrepartiste [kɔ̃trəpartist], *s.m. St.Exch:* market-maker; "runner"; **se porter c. de son donneur d'ordres,** to run stock against one's client.

contre-pas [kɔ̃trəpɑ], *s.m.inv. Mil:* **1.** half-pace (taken when changing step). **2.** *adv.phr.* **marcher à c.-p.,** to be out of step (**de,** with).

contre-passation [kɔ̃trəpasɑsjɔ̃], *s.f.,* **contre-passement** [kɔ̃trəpɑsmɑ̃], *s.m.* **1.** *Com: Fin:* return (of bill to drawer). **2.** *Book-k:* (*a*) reversing, contra-ing, transferring (of item, entry); (*b*) cross-entry; *pl. contre-passations, -passements.*

contre-passer [kɔ̃trəpɑse], *v.tr.* **1.** *Com: Fin:* to return, to endorse back (bill to drawer). **2.** *Book-k:* to reverse, contra, transfer (item, entry); (*of two entries*) **se c.-p.,** to cancel each other.

contre-pente [kɔ̃trəpɑ̃:t], *s.f.* reverse gradient; counterslope; *pl. contre-pentes.*

contreperçage [kɔ̃trəpɛrsa:ʒ], *s.m.* counterboring; drilling through a template.

contrepercer [kɔ̃trəpɛrse], *v.tr.* (*conj. like* PERCER) **1.** to counterpierce. **2.** *Mec.E:* to drill (sth.) through a template.

contre-performance [kɔ̃trəpɛrfɔrmɑ̃:s], *s.f. Sp:* shock defeat; *pl. contre-performances.*

contre-peser [kɔ̃trəpəze], *v.tr.* (*conj. like* PESER) *Lit: A:* to counterbalance, counterpoise.

contrepèterie [kɔ̃trəpɛtri], *s.f.* spoonerism.

contre-pétition [kɔ̃trəpetisjɔ̃], *s.f.* counter-petition; *pl. contre-pétitions.*

contre-pétitionnaire [kɔ̃trəpetisjɔnɛːr], *s.* counter-petitioner; *pl. contre-pétitionnaires.*

contre-pétitionner [kɔ̃trəpetisjɔne], *v.i.* to counter-petition.

contrepetterie [kɔ̃trəpɛtri], *s.f.* = CONTREPÈTERIE.

contre-pied [kɔ̃trəpje], *s.m.* **1.** *Ven:* back-scent; **prendre le c.-p.,** (i) (*of dog*) to run heel; to run counter; (ii) to take the opposite course or view (**de,** to); **prendre une observation à c.-p.,** to misconstrue a remark, to take s.o. up the wrong way; **à contre-pied de,** contrary to; **plaider à c.-p. de qch.,** to argue against sth. **2.** *Sp:* **jouer le c.-p., prendre son adversaire à c.-p.,** to wrong-foot one's opponent, to catch one's opponent moving in the wrong direction; **prendre la balle à c.-p.,** to take the ball on the wrong foot; *pl. contre-pieds.*

contreplacage [kɔ̃trəplakaːʒ], *s.m.* plywood construction.

contre-plainte [kɔ̃trəplɛ̃ːt], *s.f. Jur:* counter-charge; *pl. contre-plaintes.*

contre-planche [kɔ̃trəplɑ̃ːʃ], *s.f. Engr:* second plate; *pl. contre-planches.*

contre-plaque [kɔ̃trəplak], *s.f. Mch:* foundation plate, reinforcing plate, anchor-plate; guard-plate; wall-plate (of bracket); back-plate (of furnace); cheek-plate; *pl. contre-plaques.*

contre-plaqué [kɔ̃trəplake], *a. & s.m.* laminated, built up in layers; **(bois) c.,** plywood; **c. à deux épaisseurs,** two-ply (wood); **c. en trois,** three-ply (wood); **meubles en c.,** laminated furniture.

contreplaquer [kɔ̃trəplake], *v.tr.* to laminate (sheets of wood to form plywood).

contre-plongée [kɔ̃trəplɔ̃ʒe], *s.f. Cin:* ground angle shot, low angle shot; *pl. contre-plongées.*

contrepoids [kɔ̃trəpwɑ], *s.m.* **1.** (*a*) *Mec.E: Mch:* balance-weight (of clock, lift, etc.), balancing weight; counterweight, counterpoise; counter-balance; **c. de régulateur de machine à vapeur,** fly-weight, fly-ball of governor; **c. de frein,** brake-weight; **c. du tiroir,** slide-valve balance-weight; **c. oscillant,** balance-weight vibration absorber; **c. tendeur,** balanced tension-block; **soupape (de sûreté) à c.,** weighted safety-valve; **faire c. à qch.,** to (counter)balance sth.; *Elcs: W.Tel:* **c. d'antenne,** counterpoise, capacity earth of radio condenser antenna; *Rail:* **aiguille à c.,** self-acting point, tumbler-point; **c. de levier de manœuvre (d'aiguille),** counter-weight of point-lever; **levier (de manœuvre d'aiguille) à c.,** point-tumbler; (*b*) balancing-pole (of rope-dancer). **2.** *Equit:* seat (of rider).

contre-poil (à) [akɔ̃trəpwal], *adv.phr.* the wrong way (of the nap, of the hair); **caresser un chat à c.-p.,** to stroke a cat the wrong way; *F:* **prendre qn à c.-p.,** to rub s.o. up the wrong way; **prendre une affaire à c.-p.,** to start at the wrong end.

contre-poinçon [kɔ̃trəpwɛ̃sɔ̃], *s.m. Metalw:* **1.** counter-punch. **2.** bolster; *pl. contre-poinçons.*

contre-poinçonner [kɔ̃trəpwɛ̃sɔne], *v.tr. Metalw:* to stamp (metal) in relief.

contrepoint [kɔ̃trəpwɛ̃], *s.m.* **1.** *Mus:* counter-point. **2.** *Lit: etc:* **la musique doit servir de c. aux images,** the music must offset the pictures; **en c.,** as a counterbalance to, to counterbalance, this.

contre-pointe [kɔ̃trəpwɛ̃ːt], *s.f.* **1.** (*a*) false edge (of sword); (*b*) edge play (of fencers). **2.** *Mec.E:* tail-stock, loose head(-stock) (of lathe). **3.** *El:* further terminal (of spark-gap). **4.** *A:* = COURTEPOINTE; *pl. contre-pointes.*

contre-pointer [kɔ̃trəpwɛ̃te], *v.tr.* to quilt; to stitch through and through (skirt, coverlet, etc.).

contrepointiste [kɔ̃trəpwɛ̃tist], *s.m. Mus:* = CONTRAPUNTISTE.

contrepoison [kɔ̃trəpwazɔ̃], *s.m.* antidote (**de,** to).

contre-porte [kɔ̃trəpɔrt], *s.f.* (*a*) *Const:* screen-door, inner door, baffle-door, *U.S:* storm-door; (*b*) *Fort:* second gate; (*c*) fire-door liner; shield (of furnace); *pl. contre-portes.*

contre-poser [kɔ̃trəpoze], *v.tr. Book-k:* to enter (item) on the wrong side of the ledger.

contre-position [kɔ̃trəpozisjɔ̃], *s.f. Book-k:* mis-entry (in ledger); *pl. contre-positions.*

contre-pousser (se) [səkɔ̃trəpuse], *v.pr.* (*of forces*) to thrust one against the other; **les matériaux se contre-poussent,** the thrusts meet.

contre-préparation [kɔ̃trəpreparasjɔ̃], *s.f. Mil:* counter-preparation; *pl. contre-préparations.*

contre-pression [kɔ̃trəprɛsjɔ̃], *s.f.* counterpressure; negative pressure; *Mch:* back-pressure (to piston); *pl. contre-pressions.*

contre-profil [kɔ̃trəprɔfil], *s.m. Arch:* reversed moulding, reversed curve (of cyma); *pl. contre-profils.*

contre-profiler [kɔ̃trəprɔfile], *v.tr. Arch:* to reverse the curve of (moulding).

contre-projet [kɔ̃trəprɔʒɛ], *s.m.* counter-project; *pl. contre-projets.*

contre-promesse [kɔ̃trəprɔmɛs], *s.f. Jur:* counter-bond; *pl. contre-promesses.*

contre-propagande [kɔ̃trəprɔpagɑ̃d], *s.f.* counter-propaganda; *pl. contre-propagandes.*

contre-proposition [kɔ̃trəprɔpozisjɔ̃], *s.f.* counter-proposition, -proposal; alternative proposal; *pl. contre-propositions.*

contre-puits [kɔ̃trəpɥi], *s.m.inv. Mil.E:* defensive mine.

contre-quille [kɔ̃trəkiːj], *s.f. N.Arch:* rising wood, keelson; *pl. contre-quilles.*

contrer [kɔ̃tre]. **1.** *v.tr. Box:* to counter (blow). **2.** *v.i. Cards:* to double. **3.** *v.tr. F:* to thwart.

contre-rail [kɔ̃trərɑːj], *s.m. Rail:* guard-, check-rail (at points); side-, safety-, rail, edge-rail; *pl. contre-rails.*

contre-raison [kɔ̃trərɛzɔ̃], *s.f. A:* counter-reason; *pl. contre-raisons.*

contre-réaction [kɔ̃trəreaksjɔ̃], *s.f. Elcs:* negative reverse, feed back; *pl. contre-réactions.*

Contre-réformation [kɔ̃trərefɔrmasjɔ̃], **Contre-réforme** [kɔ̃trərefɔrm], *s.f.* **1.** *Rel.H:* Counter-Reformation. **2.** *Mil:* **contre-réforme,** revision, reconsideration, of exemptions from military service (1914-17).

contre-ressort [kɔ̃trərəsɔːr], *s.m. Mec.E:* counter-spring; *pl. contre-ressorts.*

contre-révolution [kɔ̃trərevɔlysjɔ̃], *s.f.* counter-revolution; *pl. contre-révolutions.*

contre-révolutionnaire [kɔ̃trərevɔlysjɔnɛːr]. **1.** *a.* counter-revolutionary. **2.** *s.* counter-revolutionist, -revolutionary; *pl. contre-révolutionnaires.*

contre-révolutionner [kɔ̃trərevɔlysjɔne], *v.tr.* (*rare*) to counter-revolutionize.

contre-rezzou [kɔ̃trərɛdzu], *s.m.* (*in North Africa*) (*a*) counter-raiding troops; (*b*) counter-raid; *pl. contre-rezzous.*

contre-riposte [kɔ̃trəripɔst], *s.f. Fenc:* counter (-riposte); *pl. contre-ripostes.*

contre-rivure [kɔ̃trərivyːr], *s.f. Metalw:* (*a*) rivet-washer; (*b*) (riveting-)burr; (*c*) rivet-plate; *pl. contre-rivures.*

contre-ronde [kɔ̃trərɔ̃ːd], *s.f. A: Mil:* check-round (of sentry-posts, etc.); *pl. contre-rondes.*

contre-ruse [kɔ̃trəryːz], *s.f.* counter-stratagem; *pl. contre-ruses.*

contre-sabord [kɔ̃trəsabɔːr], *s.m. N.Arch:* port-lid; *pl. contre-sabords.*

contre-saison (à) [akɔ̃trəsɛzɔ̃], *adv.phr.* out of season.

contre-salut [kɔ̃trəsaly], *s.m. Mil: Nau:* return salute; *pl. contre-saluts.*

contre-sangle [kɔ̃trəsɑ̃gl], *s.f.,* **contre-sanglon** [kɔ̃trəsɑ̃glɔ̃], *s.m. Harn:* girth-leather, girth-strap; *pl. contre-sangles; contre-sanglons.*

contrescarpe [kɔ̃trɛskarp], *s.f. Fort:* counter-scarp.

contre-sceau [kɔ̃trəso], *s.m. A:* **contre-scel** [kɔ̃trəsɛl], *s.m.* counter-seal; *pl. contre-sceaux, -scels.*

contre-sceller [kɔ̃trəsɛle, -ele], *v.tr.* to counter-seal.

contreseing [kɔ̃trəsɛ̃], *s.m.* counter-signature; **avoir le c. de qn,** to be authorized to sign for s.o.

contresens [kɔ̃trəsɑ̃ːs], *s.m.* **1.** misconstruction, misconception (of words, etc.); misinterpretation (of a part, etc.); mistranslation (of passage, etc.); **faire un c.,** to be guilty of a mistranslation, to misunderstand a passage; **prendre le c. des paroles de qn,** to attach a wrong meaning to, to misconstrue, put a wrong construction on, s.o.'s words. **2.** wrong way (of material); **prendre le c. de la marée,** to go against the tide; *F:* **prendre le c. d'une affaire,** to set about a thing the wrong way. **3.** *adv.phr.* **à c.,** in the wrong sense, way, direction; **interpréter une phrase à c.,** to misconstrue, mistranslate, a sentence; **autos qui défilent à c.,** cars passing in opposite directions; *prep.phr.* **à c. de,** in the contrary direction to (sth.).

contre-signal [kɔ̃trəsiɲal], *s.m. Mil: Navy:* counter-signal, repeated signal; *pl. contre-signaux.*

contresignataire [kɔ̃trəsiɲatɛːr], *a. & s.m.* (member of firm, etc.) who countersigns.

contresigner [kɔ̃trəsiɲe], *v.tr.* **1.** to countersign; *F:* to O.K. (order, etc.); **c. un mandat d'amener, de perquisition, etc.,** to back a (magistrate's) warrant.

contre-sortie [kɔ̃trəsɔrti], *s.f. Mil:* counter-sortie; *pl. contre-sorties.*

contre-sujet [kɔ̃trəsyʒɛ], *s.m. Mus:* counter-subject (of fugue); *pl. contre-sujets.*

contre-sûreté [kɔ̃trəsyrte], *s.f. Jur:* counter-surety, -security; *pl. contre-sûretés.*

contre-taille [kɔ̃trətɑːj], *s.f.* **1.** cross-cut; *Engr:* cross-hatch. **2.** *Com:* counter-tally; *pl. contre-tailles.*

contre-tailler [kɔ̃trətɑje], *v.tr.* **1.** (*a*) to cross-cut; (*b*) to cross-hatch (engraving). **2.** *Com:* to counter-tally (amount).

contre-tape [kɔ̃trətap], *s.f. N.Arch:* port-lid; *pl. contre-tapes.*

contretemps [kɔ̃trətɑ̃], *s.m.* **1.** (*a*) mishap, hitch, untoward event; *contretemps;* **quel c.!** how disappointing! (*b*) delay, inconvenience. **2.** note played, step danced (i) against the beat, on the unaccented portion of the beat, (ii) out of time. **3.** *adv.phr.* **à c.,** (*a*) at the wrong moment, unseasonably, inopportunely; (*b*) *Mus:* (i) contra tempo; (ii) out of time; **mesure à c.,** syncopated music; *F:* rag-time.

contre-tenir [kɔ̃trətniːr], *v.tr.* (*conj. like* TENIR) **1.** *Metalw: etc:* to hold up (rivet, etc.). **2.** *Nau:* to pay out (rope) slowly.

contre-tension [kɔ̃trətɑ̃sjɔ̃], *s.f. El:* back-pressure (of battery during charging); *pl. contre-tensions.*

contre-terrasse [kɔ̃trətɛras], *s.f. Arch:* lower terrace; *pl. contre-terrasses.*

contre-terrorisme [kɔ̃trətɛrɔrism], *s.m.* counter-terrorism.

contre-terroriste [kɔ̃trətɛrɔrist], *a. & s.* counter-terrorist; *pl. contre-terroristes.*

contre-tige [kɔ̃trətiːʒ], *s.f. Mec.E:* guide-rod, tail-rod; **c.-t. de piston,** extended piston-rod; *pl. contre-tiges.*

contre-timbre [kɔ̃trətɛ̃bʀ], *s.m.* counterstamp; *pl. contre-timbres.*

contre-tirage [kɔ̃trətiraːʒ], *s.m.* **1.** back-draught (in flue, etc.). **2.** tracing; *pl. contre-tirages.*

contre-tirer [kɔ̃trətire], *v.tr.* **1.** to counter-draw, take a counter-proof of (engraving). **2.** to trace, take a tracing of (plan).

contre-torpilleur [kɔ̃trətɔrpijœːr], *s.m. A: Navy:* (*a*) destroyer; (*b*) light cruiser; *pl. contre-torpilleurs.*

contre-trame [kɔ̃trətram], *s.f. A:* counterplot; *pl. contre-trames.*

contre-tranchée [kɔ̃trətrɑ̃ʃe], *s.f. Mil:* counter-trench; *pl. contre-tranchées.*

contre-transfert [kɔ̃trətrɑ̃sfɛːr], *s.m. Psy:* counter-transference; *pl. contre-transferts.*

contretypage [kɔ̃trətipaːʒ], *s.m.* making of reproductions by electrotyping, stereotyping, etc.; *Cin:* duping (process).

contre(-)type [kɔ̃trətip], *s.m.* **1.** *Phot: etc:* counterpart (of negative, etc.); reproduction, duplicate (made by electrotyping, stereotyping, etc.); *Cin:* **c. positif,** duplicate positive. **2.** *Com:* counter-sample; *pl. contre(-)types.*

contretyper [kɔ̃trətipe], *v.tr.* to make reproductions by electrotyping, stereotyping, etc.; *Cin:* to duplicate.

contre-vair [kɔ̃trəvɛːr], *s.m. Her:* countervair.

contre-valeur [kɔ̃trəvalœːr], *s.f. Fin:* exchange value, value in exchange; *pl. contre-valeurs.*

contrevallation [kɔ̃trəvalasjɔ̃], *s.f. Fort: A:* contravallation.

contre-vapeur [kɔ̃trəvapœːr], *s.f.inv. Mch:* reversed steam, back-pressure, steam cushion.

contrevariance [kɔ̃trəvarjɑ̃ːs], *s.f.* countervariance.

contrevenant, -ante [kɔ̃trəvnɑ̃, -ɑ̃ːt]. **1.** *a.* contravening (party, etc.). **2.** *s.* contravener, infringer (of police regulations); offender, delinquent.

contrevenir [kɔ̃trəvniːr], *v.ind.tr.* (*conj. like* VENIR) to contravene, infringe, transgress; **c. aux règlements,** to contravene, act contrary to, the regulations.

contrevent [kɔ̃trəvɑ̃], *s.m.* **1.** outside shutter (of window). **2.** *Civ.E:* (*a*) wind-brace; (*b*) straining piece (of bridge, etc.). **3.** back-draught (in furnace, etc.).

contreventement [kɔ̃trəvɑ̃tmɑ̃], *s.m. Civ.E:* wind-bracing; **entretoise de c.,** wind-brace.

contreventer [kɔ̃trəvɑ̃te], *v.tr.* to brace, stiffen, (door, bridge, etc.) against wind-pressure; to wind-brace, sway-brace.

contre-vérité [kɔ̃trəverite], *s.f.* **1.** untruth, untrue statement. **2.** ironical statement (intended to convey the contrary); *pl. contre-vérités.*

contre-visite [kɔ̃trəvizit], *s.f.* (*a*) *Adm: Mil: Mec.E: Nau: etc:* check survey; second inspection, check inspection; (*b*) *Med:* check visit; *pl. contre-visites.*

contre-visiter [kɔ̃trəvizite], *v.tr.* to make a second inspection, a check inspection, of (troops, etc.).

contre-voie (à) [akɔ̃trəvwa], *adv.phr. Rail:* **1. circuler à c.-v.,** to travel in the reverse of the usual direction. **2. descendre à c.-v.,** to get out on the wrong side of the train.

contribuable [kɔ̃tribɥabl̩]. **1.** *a.* taxpaying or rate-paying. **2.** *s.m. & f.* taxpayer; **c. à l'impôt foncier** = ratepayer.

contribuant [kɔ̃tribɥɑ̃]. **1.** *a.* contributing (cause, etc.). **2.** *s.m.* contributor (to expenses, etc.).

contribuer [kɔ̃tribɥe], *v.i.* **1.** to contribute, to pay jointly with others; **c. à qch.,** to contribute to sth.; **nous y avons contribué pour une bonne part,** we made a handsome contribution to it; *abs.* **on a fait c. tout le pays,** the whole country has been laid under contribution. **2.** to contribute, conduce; **c. au succès d'une entreprise,** to contribute, tend, be conducive, conduce, to the success of an enterprise; **cela contribue pour beaucoup à la rendre heureuse,** that goes a long way towards making her happy; **il a beaucoup contribué à . . .,** he has played a great part in . . .; he has been instrumental in . . ..

contributaire [kɔ̃tribytɛːr], *a.* contributory (citizen, share).

contributif, -ive [kɔ̃tribytif, -iːv], *a.* contributive, contributory.

contribution [kɔ̃tribysjɔ̃], *s.f.* **1.** (*a*) *Adm:* tax or rate; **contributions indirectes,** indirect taxation; **contributions foncières,** land-tax; **c. mobilière,** rates on income derived from renting flats, houses; **bureau des contributions,** tax office; **lever, percevoir, une c.,** to collect a tax; (*b*) *Mil:* **contributions de guerre,** forced contribution (by inhabitants of occupied territory). **2.** (*a*) contribution, share; **donner qch. comme c.,** to give sth. as one's contribution; **c. à une entreprise,** contribution to, share in, an undertaking; **mettre qch., qn, à c.,** to put sth. into requisition, to make use of s.o., sth.; *Fin:* **mettre à c. les réserves,** to draw upon the reserves; (*b*) contribution (to learning).

contributoire [kɔ̃tribytwaːr], *a.* contributory.

contristant [kɔ̃tristɑ̃], *a. A:* saddening, dismal, doleful (news, etc.).

contrister [kɔ̃triste], *v.tr. A:* to sadden, grieve; to make (s.o.) sad; **se c. facilement,** to be easily depressed.

contrit [kɔ̃tri], *a.* contrite, penitent; **être c. de qch., d'avoir fait qch.,** to be grieved, mortified, at sth., at having done sth.; **d'un air c.,** penitently.

contrition [kɔ̃trisjɔ̃], *s.f.* contrition, penitence.

contrôlable [kɔ̃trolabl̩], *a.* that may be checked, verified, verifiable.

contrôlage [kɔ̃trolaːʒ], *s.m. A:* (*a*) checking (of accounts, etc.); (*b*) hall-marking (of gold, silver).

contro-latéral, -aux [kɔ̃trolateral, -o], *a. Med:* contralateral.

contrôle [kɔ̃troːl], *s.m.* **1.** *Mil: etc:* roll, muster-roll, list, register; **c. nominatif,** nominal roll, list of names; **c. de service,** duty roster; **porter qch. sur les contrôles,** to take sth. on charge; **porter qn sur les contrôles,** to take s.o. on the strength, to put s.o. on the rolls; **rayer qn des contrôles,** (i) **(de l'unité),** to strike, drop, s.o. off the rolls, off strength; (ii) **(de l'armée),** to remove s.o. from the army list. **2.** (*a*) testing, assaying (of gold, silver); (*b*) hall-marking (of gold and silver); **cachet de c.,** hall-mark; **poinçon de c.,** hall-mark stamp; (*c*) assay office. **3.** (*a*) checking, verification (of information, statements, etc.); (*b*) *Adm:* inspection, supervision (of services); registration (of deeds, etc.); *Com:* auditing, checking (of accounts, etc.); **c. de vitesse par radar,** radar speed check; *Av:* **tour de c.,** control tower; **le service du c. des mines,** the Inspection of Mines; **c. postal,** postal censorship; **c. sur un mandat,** supervision of a mandate; *Ind:* **c. de présence,** time-keeping; *Fin:* **c. des changes,** exchange control; *Th: etc:* **c. des billets,** issuing of tickets; **(bureau de) c.,** ticket-office; (*c*) checking point, station; *Sp: Aut:* (i) check, checkpoint; (ii) control (point) (in reliability run, etc.); (*d*) *Sch:* **examen de c.,** second chance exam. **4.** (*a*) authority; **être chargé du c., de qn, de qch.,** to be given control over s.o., sth.; **exercer un c. sévère sur la conduite de qn,** to keep s.o. under strict supervision, to keep a strict eye on s.o.; (*b*) **c. de soi-même,** self-control; (*c*) **c. des naissances** birth control. **5.** *Tchn:* control, monitoring, testing, regulation (of machine, craft, etc.); **appareil de c.,** testing instrument; **boîte de c.,** control-box; **méthodes de c.,** monitoring techniques; **panneau de c.,** test board; **pupitre, table, de c.,** observation desk; *Av: etc:* **feuille de c.,** check-list; *s.a.* TOUR[1] 1; *Av:* **c. aérien,** air control; **c. d'approche,** approach control; **station de c. d'approche,** ground control approach; **c. de la circulation aérienne,** air-traffic control; **c. de l'espace aérien,** airspace control; **c. de la région aérienne,** area control; **c. radar de la région aérienne,** area radar control; **centre de c. de la circulation aérienne,** air-traffic control centre; *Mil.Av:* **centre de c. tactique aérien,** tactical air control centre; **radar de c. de la circulation (aérienne),** traffic-control radar; **zone de c. aérien,** (air-)control zone; *Elcs: Tp:* **c. d'amplitude,** amplitude control; **c. de brillance,** brightness control; **c. de fréquence,** frequency control; **c. de grille,** grid control; **c. de rayonnement,** monitoring of radiation; **c. de voie,** channel monitor(ing); **c. de volume,** volume control; *T.V:* **c. régie,** master monitor(ing); *Space:* **c. d'attitude (d'un satellite),** attitude control (of satellite); **dispositif de c. d'attitude,** attitude control system.

contrôlement [kɔ̃trolmɑ̃], *s.m.* (*rare*) *Adm:* checking, supervision.

contrôler [kɔ̃trole], *v.tr.* **1.** to hall-mark, stamp (gold, silver). **2.** to inspect, supervise (work, etc.); to check, audit (accounts); **c. des billets,** to check tickets; **c. les passeports,** to examine the passports; **c. des renseignements, un fait,** to verify, check (up), information, a fact. **3.** to hold (s.o.) in check; to control. **4.** *W.Tel:* to monitor.

se contrôler, to keep control of oneself, to control oneself.

contrôleur, -euse [kɔ̃trolœːr, -øːz], *s.* **1.** (*a*) comptroller (of Mint); (*b*) controller (of government department); **c. aux liquidations,** controller in bankruptcy; **c. des contributions directes,** assessor, inspector, of taxes; **c. des comptes d'une société,** auditor of a company's accounts; (*c*) inspector, examiner, supervisor (of work, etc.); *Th:* check taker; *Rail:* ticket collector, inspector; *F:* **c. du gaz,** gas-man; (*d*) *Com: Ind:* (i) tallyman; (ii) time-keeper; (*e*) *Av:* **c. de la circulation aérienne,** air traffic controller; *Mil. Av:* **c. de la défense aérienne, air defence controller.** **2.** *s.m.* checking machine, apparatus; tell-tale; tester; **c. d'atelier,** time-recorder; **c. de ronde,** tell-tale clock, watchman's clock; **c. de vitesse,** speed-controller; *I.C.E:* **c. d'allumage,** spark-tester; *Aut: Av: etc:* **c. de pression (des pneus),** pressure gauge; *Av:* **c. de vol,** flight indicator; flight-controller; **c. de pression différentielle,** differential pressure regulator; **c. de route,** heading control; *Av: Space:* **c. d'attitude,** attitude controller (of satellite, aircraft, etc.); *Atom.Ph:* **c. (de l'activité) de l'eau,** water-monitor. **3.** *a.* **appareil c.,** checking, control(ling), apparatus, device.

contrordre [kɔ̃trɔrdr̩], *s.m.* counter-order, countermand; **donner un c.,** to countermand an order; **sauf c., à moins de c.,** unless ordered to the contrary, unless otherwise directed.

controuvé [kɔ̃truve], *a.* false, of pure imagination.

controuver [kɔ̃truve], *v.tr.* (*chiefly used in p.p.*) to invent, fabricate (news, etc.).

controversable [kɔ̃trɔvɛrsabl̩], *a.* controversial, controvertible.

controverse [kɔ̃trɔvɛrs], *s.f.* controversy, disputation, discussion; **hors de c.,** beyond dispute, indisputable; **soutenir une c.,** to carry on a controversy (**contre,** with, against).

controverser [kɔ̃trɔvɛrse], *v.tr.* **1.** to discuss, debate (question, etc.); *abs.* to have, hold, a discussion; **question controversée,** controversial, much debated, question. **2.** to controvert (opinion, etc.).

controversiste [kɔtrɔvɛrsist], *s.m. Rel:* controversialist, disputant.

contumace[1] [kɔ̃tymas], *s.f. Jur:* (*a*) contumacy, non-appearance (in court); **condamné par c.,** sentenced in absentia, sentenced in his absence; **purger sa c.,** to surrender oneself to the law (after being sentenced in one's absence); (*b*) contempt of court.

contumace,[2] **contumax** [kɔ̃tymaks], *Jur:* **1.** *a.* contumacious, defaulting. **2.** *s.m. & f.* contumacious person, defaulter; absconder.

contus [kɔ̃ty], *a.* contused, bruised; **plaie contuse,** bruise.

contusion [kɔ̃tyzjɔ̃], *s.f.* contusion, bruise.

contusionner [kɔ̃tyzjɔne], *v.tr.* to contuse, bruise (limb, etc.).

conurbation [kɔnyrbasjɔ̃], *s.f.* conurbation.

convaincant [kɔ̃vɛ̃kɑ̃], *a.* convincing.

convaincre [kɔ̃vɛ̃ːkr̩], *v.tr.* (*conj. like* VAINCRE) **1.** to convince (de, of, que, that); **c. qn de faire qch.,** to prevail upon, persuade, s.o. to do sth.; **j'en suis convaincu,** I am sure, persuaded, of it; **je ne demande qu'à être convaincu,** I am open to conviction; **se laisser c.,** to let oneself be persuaded, won over; **se c. d'un fait,** to convince oneself of a fact; **peu à peu il se laissa c. que . . .,** it was gradually borne in upon him that . . .. **2.** to convict (de, of); to prove (s.o.) guilty (de, of); **c. qn d'un mensonge,** to bring a lie home to s.o.

convaincu [kɔ̃vɛ̃ky], *a.* **1.** convinced; **parler d'un ton c.,** to speak earnestly, with conviction; **être terriblement c.,** to be terribly in earnest; **démocrate c.,** out-and-out democrat. **2.** convicted; *Jur:* **atteint et c. d'un crime,** guilty of a crime in fact and in law.

convalescence [kɔ̃valɛsɑ̃ːs], *s.f.* convalescence; **entrer, être, en c.,** to become, be, convalescent; **maison de c.,** (i) convalescent home; (ii) nursing home (for rest cure); *Mil: etc:* **congé de c.,** sick leave.

convalescent, -ente [kɔ̃valɛsɑ̃, -ɑ̃ːt], *a. & s.* convalescent; **être c. d'une grave maladie,** to be recovering from a serious illness.

convallaire [kɔ̃valɛːr], *s.f. Bot:* convallaria.

convalo [kɔ̃valo], *Mil: P:* **1.** *s.m.* convalescent. **2.** *s.f.* sick-leave.

convecteur [kɔ̃vɛktœːr], *s.m. Const: etc:* convector.

convection [kɔ̃vɛksjɔ̃], *s.f. Ph:* convection.

convenable [kɔ̃vnabl̩], *a.* **1.** suitable, fit(ting), befitting, becoming, appropriate, proper; **c. à qch.,** suitable for, to, suited to, sth.; **juger c. de faire qch.,** to think it proper, advisable, to think fit, to do sth.; **prendre un prix c.,** to charge a fair price. **2.** decent, respectable; well-behaved (person); seemly, decorous (behaviour); **peu c.,** unseemly, indecorous; **vous n'avez pas l'air c.,** you don't look respectable. **3. un déjeuner c.,** a decent lunch.

convenablement [kɔ̃vnabləmɑ̃], *adv.* **1.** suitably, fitly, befittingly, becomingly, beseemingly, appropriately. **2.** decorously, with propriety; decently. **3. on peut manger très c. à la cantine,** you can eat quite well in the canteen; **il a soutenu sa thèse très c.,** he has presented his thesis very satisfactorily.

convenance [kɔ̃vnɑ̃ːs], *s.f.* **1.** conformity, agreement (of tastes, etc.). **2.** suitability, fitness, convenience, appropriateness, advisableness, advisability; **pour des raisons de c.,** on grounds of expediency; **mariage de c.,** marriage of convenience; **être à la c. de qn,** to meet with s.o.'s requirements, approval; to meet s.o.'s fancy; **trouver qch. à sa c.,** to find sth. suitable; **trouver qn à sa c.,** to like, get on with s.o.; **faire qch. à sa c.,** to do sth. (i) as it suits, pleases, one, (ii) at one's convenience, leisure; **avoir qch. à sa c.,** to have sth. at one's convenience. **3.** propriety, decency, decorum; **manque de c.,** breach of (good) manners; **par c.,** for the sake of decency; **convenances (sociales),** (i) social conventions; etiquette, proprieties, the rules of decorum; (ii) common decency; **respecter les convenances,** to observe convention; **braver les convenances,** to defy convention; **oublier les convenances,** to forget one's manners, to fail in good-breeding.

convenant [kɔ̃vnɑ̃], *a. A:* suitable, fit, proper (procedure, etc.).

convenir [kɔ̃vniːr], *v.i.* (*conj. like* VENIR) **1.** (*conj. with* avoir) (*a*) to suit, fit; **c. à qn, qch.,** to suit, to be suitable to, s.o., sth.; **le livre convient aux débutants,** the book is suitable for beginners; **vêtements qui conviennent à sa position,** clothes that become, befit, are in keeping with, his position; **le fer convient aussi bien que le bois,** iron is as suitable, answers (the purpose) just as well, as wood; **sa figure me convient,** I like his face; **ils se conviennent,** they suit each other, they like each other; **si cela vous convient,** if that is agreeable to you, suits your convenience; **la date qui conviendrait le mieux,** the most suitable date; (*b*) *impers.* **il convient de . . .,** it is fitting, advisable, to . . .; **ce qu'il convient de faire,** (i) the right thing to do; (ii) the proper measures to take; **il convient que vous y alliez,** it is advisable for you to go, it would be better for you to go; you should go, you ought to go; **agir comme il convient,** to act suitably (to the occasion); to act appropriately, rightly; to take appropriate action. **2.** (*conj. with* **avoir,** *and with* **être** *to denote a state of agreement*) (*a*) to agree; to come to an agreement; **c. de qch.,** to agree on, about, (as) to, sth.; **c. du prix avec qn,** to agree, settle, with s.o. as to the price; **ils sont convenus de le faire venir, qu'ils le feraient venir, qu'ils le fassent venir,** they are agreed to send for him; *impers.* **il fut convenu qu'ils le feraient venir,** it was agreed, arranged, that they would send for

him; (*b*) **c. de qch.**, to acknowledge, admit, sth.; **il convient qu'il a eu tort,** he admits, owns, that he was wrong; **il a convenu de son erreur,** he acknowledged his mistake; **j'ai eu tort, j'en conviens,** I was wrong, I admit; (*c*) **c. à qch.**, to agree with, conform to, sth.

convent [kɔ̃vɑ̃], *s.m.* general assembly of Freemasons.

conventicule [kɔ̃vɑ̃tikyl], *s.m.* conventicle.

convention [kɔ̃vɑ̃sjɔ̃], *s.f.* convention. **1.** (*a*) covenant, agreement, compact; **c. par écrit,** agreement in writing; **c. (à l')amiable,** amicable arrangement; **c. relative à une question,** convention on a question; **projet de c.,** draft agreement; **c. collective** = collective bargaining; collective wage agreement; *Pol:* **c. internationale, postale,** international, postal, convention; **la C. de Genève,** the Geneva Convention; (*b*) *usu. pl. Jur:* articles, clauses (of deed, etc.); **sauf c. contraire,** unless there be any (unknown) clause to the contrary; *F:* **ce n'était pas dans nos conventions,** I didn't bargain for that. **2.** standard, rule; **les conventions sociales,** the social conventions; *adj.phr.* **de c.,** conventional; **signes de c.,** conventional signs; **adresse de c.,** accommodation address. **3.** *Pol:* (extraordinary) assembly; *Fr: Hist:* **La C. (nationale),** the (National) Convention (1792-95).

conventionalisme [kɔ̃vɑ̃sjɔnalism], *s.m.* conventionalism.

conventionné [kɔ̃vɑ̃sjɔne], *a.* officially agreed, accepted; **médecin c.,** National Health service doctor.

conventionnel, -elle [kɔ̃vɑ̃sjɔnɛl]. **1.** *a.* (*a*) conventional (value, symbol, etc.); *Mapm: Surv:* **cartouche contenant les signes conventionnels,** reference; **tableau des signes conventionnels,** characteristic sheet, conventional signs sheet; *Mil:* **arme, guerre, conventionnelle,** conventional weapon, warfare; (*b*) conventionary (lease, etc.); **obligations conventionnelles,** treaty obligations; *Jur:* **communauté conventionnelle,** community (between husband and wife) by agreement. **2.** *s.m. Fr.Hist:* member of the National Convention.

conventionnellement [kɔ̃vɑ̃sjɔnɛlmɑ̃], *adv.* **1.** *Jur:* by agreement. **2.** conventionally.

conventualité [kɔ̃vɑ̃tɥalite], *s.f.* monastic life.

conventuel, -elle [kɔ̃vɑ̃tɥɛl]. **1.** *a.* conventual (house, rule, etc.); **bâtiments conventuels,** monastery buildings. **2.** *s.m.* conventual (friar).

conventuellement [kɔ̃vɑ̃tɥɛlmɑ̃], *adv.* conventually.

convenu [kɔ̃vny], *a.* **1.** agreed; stipulated (price (etc.); appointed (time); **l'heure convenue,** the hour agreed upon; **c'est c.!** agreed! it's a bargain! that's settled! *s.m.* **s'en tenir au c.,** to abide by the agreement. **2.** conventional (language, etc.).

convergence [kɔ̃vɛrʒɑ̃:s], *s.f.* convergence, convergency (of lines, etc.); *Mil:* concentration (of fire); *F:* **c. des efforts,** concentration of effort; *Geog: Oc:* **c. antarctique, subtropicale,** Antarctic, sub-tropical, convergence; *Biol:* **c. des espèces,** convergent evolution of the species.

convergent [kɔ̃vɛrʒɑ̃], *a.* convergent, converging (lines, etc.); **tir c.,** converging, concentrated, fire.

converger [kɔ̃vɛrʒe], *v.i.* (**convergeant; ils convergeaient**) (*of roads, lines, etc.*) to converge; *Mil:* **faire c. les feux d'une batterie,** to concentrate the fire of a battery.

convers, -erse [kɔ̃vɛ:r, -ɛrs], *a.* **1.** *Ecc:* lay (brother, sister). **2.** *Log:* **proposition converse,** *s.f.* **converse,** converse (proposition).

conversation [kɔ̃vɛrsasjɔ̃], *s.f.* **1.** (*a*) conversation, talk; *A:* converse; **lier c., entrer en c., engager la c., avec qn,** to enter, get, into conversation with s.o.; to engage s.o. in conversation; *A:* to hold speech with s.o.; **faire la c. à qn,** to chat with s.o., to entertain s.o.; **alimenter la c.,** to keep the conversation going; **faire (tous) les frais de la c.,** to do all the talking; **reprendre le fil de la c.,** to resume the conversation; **mettre la c. sur un sujet,** to start a topic of conversation; to bring the conversation round to a subject; to turn the talk to a subject; **être à la c.,** to be in the conversation; **je n'étais pas à la c.,** I was not attending, my thoughts were wandering; **langage, expressions, de la c.,** colloquial language, expressions; **parler sur le ton de la c.,** to speak in a conversational tone; *s.a.* ACCAPARER; (*b*) **avoir de la c.,** to be versed in the art of conversation; *F:* to have plenty of small talk; **un homme de bonne c.,** a good conversationalist; (*c*) *Tp:* **c. téléphonique,** telephone call; **c. payable à l'arrivée,** reverse charge call, transferred charge call; **c. de service,** service call; *U.S:* official call or message; **c. interurbaine,** (inland) trunk call; **c. non taxée,** free call; **c. taxée,** chargeable call; **position de c.,** speaking position; *U.S:* talking position; **unité de c.,** traffic unit. **2.** *Jur:* **c. criminelle,** criminal conversation, "*crim. con.*", adultery.

converser[1] [kɔ̃vɛrse], *v.i.* to converse, talk (**avec,** with); to discourse; **c. avec soi-même,** to commune with oneself.

converser[2]. **1.** *v.i. Mil:* to change front, change direction; to wheel. **2.** *v.tr.* to swing (bridge) into position.

conversible [kɔ̃vɛrsibl̩], *a.* convertible.

conversion [kɔ̃vɛrsjɔ̃], *s.f.* conversion. **1.** spiritual change; **c. des païens au christianisme,** conversion of the heathen to Christianity. **2.** (*a*) conversion, change (**en,** into); **c. de l'eau en vapeur,** conversion of water into steam; *Fin:* **c. de la rente 5% en $3\frac{1}{2}$%,** conversion of Government 5% stock into $3\frac{1}{2}$ per cents; *Mth:* **c. des équations, des fractions,** conversion of equations, of fractions; *Jur:* **c. de saisie,** sale of attached estate by ordinary auction (after permission has been obtained from the court); (*b*) *St.Exch:* changing over from bear to bull (or *vice versa*). **3.** (*a*) *Log:* conversion (of proposition, etc.); (*b*) *Mil: etc:* wheel(ing), change of front, of direction; **faire une c.,** to wheel; (*c*) *Skiing:* kick turn; (*d*) swinging out (of bridge). **4.** *El:* conversion; **gain de c.,** conversion gain; **pente de c.,** conversion (trans)conductance.

converti, -e [kɔ̃vɛrti]. **1.** *a.* converted (sinner, etc.). **2.** *s.* convert.

convertibilité [kɔ̃vɛrtibilite], *s.f.* convertibility.

convertible [kɔ̃vɛrtibl̩]. **1.** *a.* convertible (**en,** into). **2.** *a. & s.m. Av:* **(avion) c.,** convertiplane, convertaplane. **3.** *s.f. Aut:* convertible.

convertir [kɔ̃vɛrti:r], *v.tr.* to convert. **1.** (*a*) **c. qn au christianisme,** to convert s.o. to Christianity; (*b*) **c. qn à ses opinions,** to bring over, win over, s.o. to one's opinions; to bring s.o. round to one's opinions. **2. c. qch. en qch.,** to convert, change, turn, sth. into sth.; **c. un champ en terrain de golf,** to convert, turn, a field into a golf-course; **c. ses idées en ordres,** to translate one's ideas into orders; *Com: Fin:* **c. des rentes,** to convert stock. **3.** *Log:* to convert, transpose (proposition).

se convertir, (*a*) to become converted (to a faith, etc.); **il s'est converti à ma façon de penser,** he came round to my way of thinking; (*b*) **la neige s'était convertie en boue,** the snow had turned (in)to slush; **son amour se convertit en haine,** his love turned to hate.

convertissable [kɔ̃vɛrtisabl̩], *a.* **1.** convertible. **2.** transformable (**en,** into).

convertissement [kɔ̃vɛrtismɑ̃], *s.m. St.Exch: Fin:* conversion (of securities into money).

convertisseur [kɔ̃vɛrtisœ:r], *s.m.* **1.** *Metall:* converter; **c. à soufflage latéral,** side-blow converter; **c. basique, acide,** basic, acid, converter; **c. Bessemer,** Bessemer converter. **2.** *El: Elcs:* converter; **c. de fréquence,** frequency converter; **c. dynamoteur,** dynamotor; **c. rotatif, c. synchrone,** rotary converter, synchronous converter; **c. statique,** current changer, *U.S:* rectifier; **c. à thyratron,** thyratron inverter; **c. à vapeur de mercure,** mercury-vapour rectifier; **groupe c.,** converter set, *U.S:* motor converter. **3.** *Mec.E:* **c. de couple,** torque rectifier.

convexe [kɔ̃vɛks], *a.* convex; **fond c. d'une chaudière,** dished end of a boiler.

convexion [kɔ̃vɛksjɔ̃], *s.f. Ph:* convection.

convexité [kɔ̃vɛksite], *s.f.* convexity.

convexo-concave [kɔ̃vɛksokɔ̃ka:v], *a.* convexo-concave; *pl. convexo-concaves.*

convexo-convexe [kɔ̃vɛksokɔ̃vɛks], *a.* convexo-convex, double-convex; *pl. convexo-convexes.*

convict [kɔ̃vikt], *s.m.* convict.

conviction [kɔ̃viksjɔ̃], *s.f.* conviction. **1.** firm belief; **avoir la c. que . . .,** to be convinced that . . .; **agir par c.,** to act from conviction; **agir d'après ses convictions,** to act up to one's convictions; **sans grande c.,** without much conviction. **2.** *A:* proof of guilt; *still used in Jur:* **pièce à, de, c.,** object, etc., produced in evidence; exhibit (in criminal case).

convictionnel, -elle [kɔ̃viksjɔnɛl], *a. Jur:* convictive.

convié, -ée [kɔ̃vje], *s.* person invited (to ceremony, to dine, etc.); guest.

convier [kɔ̃vje], *v.tr.* (*p.d. & pr.sub.* **n. conviions, v. conviiez**) **1.** to invite, bid; **c. qn à un mariage, à assister à un mariage,** to invite s.o. to a marriage, to be present at a marriage. **2. c. qn à faire qch.,** to urge s.o. to do sth.

convive [kɔ̃vi:v], *s.m. & f.* (*a*) guest (at table); **le seul c. étranger,** the only stranger at the table; (*b*) table companion; *Navy: etc:* messmate.

convivialité [kɔ̃vivjalite], *s.f.* conviviality.

convocable [kɔ̃vɔkabl̩], *a.* liable to be convoked, to be called.

convocateur, -trice [kɔ̃vɔkatœ:r, -tris]. **1.** *s.* convoker, convocator. **2.** *a.* **circulaire convocatrice,** notice of meeting.

convocation [kɔ̃vɔkasjɔ̃], *s.f.* convocation, summons; calling together, convening (of assembly, etc.); **recevoir une c.,** (i) to receive notice of a meeting; (ii) *Adm:* to be asked to call; to receive a letter fixing an appointment; *Mil:* (*of reservist*) **recevoir sa c.,** to be called up for training.

convoi [kɔ̃vwa], *s.m.* **1.** convoy; **en c.,** in convoy; (*a*) *Mil:* (i) (protecting) escort; (ii) vehicles, etc., under escort; **c. administratif, c. de subsistances,** supply column; **c. automobile,** motor convoy, motor transport column; **c. de munitions,** ammunition supply column; **chef de c.,** convoy commander; (*b*) *Nau:* (i) escorting vessel; (ii) merchant fleet under escort; **dispositif de marche du c.,** diagram of convoy formation; **escorte mer et air du c.,** surface and air escort of convoy. **2. c. (funèbre),** funeral procession, funeral *cortège*; **aller au c., suivre le c., de qn,** to attend s.o.'s funeral. **3.** train, convoy; (*a*) **c. de bêtes de somme,** pack-train; **c. de prisonniers,** gang of convicts; **c. automobile,** motorcade; (*b*) *Rail:* **c. de voyageurs,** passenger train; **c. de bestiaux,** cattle train; **c. direct,** express train; **c. de marchandises,** goods train; *Mil:* **c. d'artillerie,** ammunition supply train; **c. de ravitaillement,** supply train; (*c*) *Nau:* string, train (of barges, etc.).

convoiement [kɔ̃vwamɑ̃], *s.m.* (i) convoying; (ii) conveyance.

convoitable [kɔ̃vwatabl̩], *a.* covetable, desirable.

convoiter [kɔ̃vwate], *v.tr.* to covet, desire; to lust after, *F:* hanker after (s.o., sth.); **c. qch. des yeux,** to cast covetous eyes on sth.

convoiteur, -euse [kɔ̃vwatœ:r, -ø:z]. **1.** *a.* covetous (**de,** of). **2.** *s.* coveter (**de,** of).

convoitise [kɔ̃vwati:z], *s.f.* (*a*) covetousness; **regarder qch., qn, d'un œil, avec un œil, de c.,** to cast covetous glances on sth., to cast lustful eyes on s.o.; (*b*) covetous desire; **faire naître, allumer, des convoitises,** (i) to kindle unholy desires; (ii) to arouse cupidity.

convol [kɔ̃vɔl], *s.m.* re-marriage (of widow).

convoler [kɔ̃vɔle], *v.i.* (*of widow, widower*) to re-marry, to marry again; **c. en troisièmes noces,** to marry for the third time; *F:* **c. en justes noces,** to marry.

convoluta, convolute [kɔ̃vɔlyta, -yt], *s.m. Ann:* convoluta.

convoluté [kɔ̃vɔlyte], *a. Nat.Hist:* convolute(d), whorled.

convolution [kɔ̃vɔlysjɔ̃], *s.f.* convolution; *F:* twist, winding.

convolvulacé [kɔ̃vɔlvylase], **convolvulé** [kɔ̃vɔlvyle], *Bot:* **1.** *a.* convolvulaceous. **2.** *s.f.pl.* **convolvulacées,** Convolvulaceae.

convolvulus [kɔ̃vɔlvylys], *s.m. Bot:* convolvulus; *F:* bindweed.

convoquer [kɔ̃vɔke], *v.tr.* **1.** (*a*) to summon, call together, convoke (assembly); to convene (meeting); *Com:* **c. ses créanciers,** to call one's creditors together; (*b*) *Mil:* to call up (reservists for training, etc.). **2.** *Adm:* to invite (s.o.) to an interview; **êtes-vous convoqué?** have you an appointment?

convoyage [kɔ̃vwaja:ʒ], *s.m.* (i) convoying; (ii) conveyance; **système de c.,** conveyor system; **pilote de c.,** ferry pilot.

convoyer [kɔ̃vwaje], *v.tr.* (**je convoie, n. convoyons, ils convoient; je convoierai**) *Mil: Navy:* to convoy, escort (train, fleet, etc.).

convoyeur, -euse [kɔ̃vwajœ:r, -ø:z]. **1.** (*a*) *s.m. Mil:* officer in charge of convoy; (*b*) *s.m. Nav:* (i) convoying officer; (ii) convoy(-ship), escort (-ship); (*c*) *s.f. Mil:* **convoyeuse,** (woman) officer in charge of ambulance, plane, etc.; (*d*) *s.m.* (i) guard (of train); (ii) mate (of lorry driver). **2.** *s.m. Mec.E: Ind:* conveyor; **c. à bande,** belt-conveyor, endless belt; **c. à crochets,** hook-conveyor; **c. à godets,** bucket-conveyor; **c. à palettes, à raclettes,** pallet-, scraper-, conveyor; trough-conveyor; *U.S:* drag-conveyor; **c. à plateaux,** tray-conveyor; **c. à secousses,** shaker-conveyor, vibrating conveyor; **c. à vis sans fin,** screw-, spiral-, conveyor.

convulser [kɔ̃vylse], *v.tr. Physiol:* to convulse; **visage convulsé par la terreur,** face convusled by, with, terror.

convulsif, -ive [kɔ̃vylsif, -iːv], *a.* convulsive; **pris d'un rire c.,** seized with uncontrollable laughter, convulsed with laughter; *Med:* **toux convulsive,** convulsive, spasmodic, cough.
convulsion [kɔ̃vylsjɔ̃], *s.f.* convulsion; **donner des convulsions à qn,** to throw s.o. into convulsions; *F:* to throw s.o. into a fit; **convulsions cloniques,** clonic spasms; *F:* **convulsions de rage,** convulsions of rage; **c. politique,** political upheaval.
convulsionnaire [kɔ̃vylsjɔnɛːr], *s.m. & f.* (*a*) *Fr. Hist:* **les convulsionnaires de Saint-Médard,** the convulsionaries (whose manifestations took place in Paris, in the cemetery of Saint-Médard); (*b*) fanatic, raving lunatic.
convulsionner [kɔ̃vylsjɔne], *v.tr.* to convulse; **bruit qui convulsionne un pays,** rumour that throws a country into a state of upheaval.
convulsivement [kɔ̃vylsivmɑ̃], *adv.* convulsively.
conyse, conyze [kɔniːz], *s.f. Bot:* fleawort, fleabane, ploughman's-spikenard.
coobligation [koɔbligasjɔ̃], *s.f. Jur:* joint obligation, joint liability.
coobligé, ée [koɔbliʒe], *s. Jur:* co-obligant, co-obligor.
cooccupant, -ante [koɔkypɑ̃, -ɑ̃ːt], *s.* co-occupier.
coolie [kuli], *s.m.* coolie.
coop [koɔp], *s.f. F:* co-operative stores; *F:* co-op.
coopérateur, -trice [koɔperatœːr, koɔ-, -tris]. **1.** *s.* co-operator; fellow-worker. **2.** *a.* **agent c.,** co-operating agent, co-agent.
coopératif, -ive [koɔperatif, koɔ-, -iːv]. **1.** *a.* co-operative (society, etc.). **2.** *s.f. F:* **coopérative,** co-operative stores; *F:* co-op; **coopérative immobilière,** building society; *Mil:* **coopérative militaire** = Navy, Army and Air Force Institute, NAAFI; *U.S:* Post Exchange.
coopération [koɔperasjɔ̃, koɔ-], *s.f.* co-operation.
coopératisme [koɔperatism, koɔ-], *s.m. Pol.Ec:* co-operation, the co-operative system.
coopérativement [koɔperativmɑ̃, koɔ-], *adv.* co-operatively.
coopérer [koɔpere, koɔ-], *v.i.* (**je coopère, n. coopérons; je coopérerai**) to co-operate; to work together; **c. avec qn à un travail, à faire qch.,** to co-operate with s.o. on a piece of work, in doing sth.; **c. au succès de qch.,** to contribute to the success of sth.
cooptation [koɔptasjɔ̃, koɔ-], *s.f.* co-optation, co-option.
coopter [koɔpte, koɔ-], *v.tr.* to co-opt.
coordination [koɔrdinasjɔ̃, koɔ-], *s.f.* co-ordination; *Gram:* **conjonction de c.,** co-ordinating conjunction.
coordinence [koɔrdinɑ̃s, koɔ-], *s.f. Ch:* co-ordination number.
coordonnant [koɔrdɔnɑ̃, koɔ-], *a. Gram:* co-ordinating (conjunction).
coordonnateur, -trice [koɔrdɔnatœːr, koɔ-, -tris], *a.* co-ordinating.
coordonné, -ée [koɔrdɔne, koɔ-]. **1.** *a.* (*a*) co-ordinated (movement, etc.); **travaux coordonnés,** joint work; **ordres coordonnés,** systematic orders; (*b*) *Gram: etc:* co-ordinate (clause, etc.). **2.** *s.f.pl.* **coordonnées;** (*a*) *Geom: Geog: Astr:* co-ordinates, coordinates; *Geom: Astr:* **coordonnées astronomiques,** astronomical co-ordinates; **coordonnées cartésiennes,** Cartesian co-ordinates; **coordonnées cartésiennes de télévision,** television-type Cartesian co-ordinates; **coordonnées célestes,** celestial co-ordinates; **coordonnées équatoriales,** equatorial co-ordinates; **coordonnées horizontales,** horizontal co-ordinates; **coordonnées polaires,** polar co-ordinates; **coordonnées rectangulaires,** rectangular co-ordinates; **coordonnées rectilignes,** rectilinear co-ordinates; **coordonnées sphériques,** spherical co-ordinates; *Geog:* **coordonnées géographiques,** geographic co-ordinates; **coordonnées hectométriques,** grid, hectometric, co-ordinates; **coordonnées littérales,** lettered co-ordinates; **coordonnées topographiques, cartographiques,** map co-ordinates; *Mil: etc:* **les coordonnées d'un point, d'un objectif,** the co-ordinates of a point, of a target; *F:* **établir des coordonnées,** to establish points of contact; *F:* **donnez-moi vos coordonnées,** give me your address and 'phone number; (*b*) *Cost: Com:* coordinates.
coordonner [koɔrdɔne, koɔ-], *v.tr.* to co-ordinate (**à, avec,** to, with), to arrange.
copahu [kɔpay], *s.m. Pharm:* copaiba; **baume de c.,** copaiba balsam.
copahier, copaïer [kɔpaje], *s.m. Bot:* copaiba (-tree).
copain [kɔpɛ̃], *s.m. F:* pal, mate.
copal [kɔpal], *s.m.,* **copale** [kɔpal], *s.f.* copal (-resin); **c. tendre,** gum-elemi; *s.a.* VERNIS 1.
copaline [kɔpalin], *s.f.,* **copalite** [kɔpalit], *s.f. Miner:* copaline, copalite.
copalme [kɔpalm], *s.m. Pharm: Bot:* copalm, sweet gum; liquidambar.
copartage [kɔpartaːʒ], *s.m. Jur:* coparcenary.
copartageant, -ante [kɔpartaʒɑ̃, -ɑ̃ːt], *s.* coparcener, co-heir, co-heiress, joint heir(ess).
copartager [kɔpartaʒe], *v.tr.* (*conj. like* PARTAGER) *Jur:* **c. une succession,** to succeed jointly, to be coparcener(s) in a succession.
coparticipant [kɔpartisipɑ̃], *s.m. Jur:* copartner, partner in joint account.
coparticipation [kɔpartisipasjɔ̃], *s.f. Jur:* copartnership, copartnery; *Com: Ind:* **c. des employés, des travailleurs, dans les bénéfices,** profit-sharing by the employees, by the workmen.
copaternité [kɔpatɛrnite], *s.f.* joint sponsorship.
copayer [kɔpaje], *s.m. Bot:* copaiba(-tree).
copeau, -eaux [kɔpo, ko-], *s.m.* **1.** shaving (of wood); chip, cutting (of wood, metal); swarf; (*if cut with knife*) whittling; **c. de tour,** turnings; **c. d'alésage,** borings; **vin de c.,** (new) wine clarified with chips; *Cu:* **c. (de chocolat),** (chocolate) shavings, shaves. **2. c. de placage,** sheet of veneer.
copeck [kɔpɛk], *s.m. Num:* copeck.
copélates [kɔpelat], *s.m.pl. Z:* Copelata.
Copenhague [kɔpɛnag], *Pr.n.f. Geog:* Copenhagen.
copépodes [kɔpepɔd], *s.m.pl. Crust:* Copepoda.
copermutant, -ante [kɔpɛrmytɑ̃, -ɑ̃t], *s. esp. Ecc:* one who takes part in an exchange of benefices.
copermutation [kɔpɛrmytasjɔ̃], *s.f. esp. Ecc:* exchange (of benefices).
copermuter [kɔpɛrmyte], *v.tr. esp. Ecc:* to exchange (benefices).
Copernic [kɔpɛrnik], *Pr.n.m. Hist:* Copernicus.
copernicien, -ienne [kɔpɛrnisjɛ̃, -jɛn], *a.* Copernican.
cophte [kɔpt, kɔft], *a. & s.m.* = COPTE.
copiage [kɔpjaːʒ], *s.m. Sch:* cribbing, copying.
copie [kɔpi], *s.f.* **1.** copy, transcript; (*a*) **c. figurée,** facsimile; **tirer plusieurs copies d'un manuscrit,** to make several copies of a manuscript; *Adm: Jur:* **"pour c. conforme,"** "certified true copy"; *s.a.* AUTHENTIQUE; (*b*) *Com:* **c. de change,** second of exchange; **prendre c. d'une lettre,** to take a copy of a letter; **livre de c. de lettres,** *s.m.* **c. de lettres,** letter-book; **le c. des factures,** the invoice book; (*c*) *Typwr:* carbon copy; (*d*) *Journ: Typ:* (i) manuscript; (ii) copy; **manquer de c.,** to wait copy; (*e*) *Sch:* (i) fair copy (of exercise, written task); **remettre, rendre, sa c.,** to hand in, give in, one's work; (ii) (candidate's) paper; **bonne c.,** good exercise or paper; **c. nulle,** worthless script. **2.** copy, reproduction (of picture, statue, etc.); imitation (of novel, style, etc.); **se faire la c. de qn,** to model oneself on s.o. **3.** (*a*) *Phot:* print; **c. à la colle, à la gomme,** glue-, gum-, print; **c. à l'albumine bichromatée,** albumen print, helio-process; **c. sur métal,** metal-print; **c. sur papier bromure,** bromide print; **c. sur papier au ferroprussiate,** blueprint, cyanotype; (*b*) *Cin:* print; **c. de montage,** first-answer print; **c. de travail,** studio print; **c. originale,** master print; (*c*) *Rec: etc:* copy, *U.S:* dub.
copier [kɔpje], *v.tr.* (*p.d. & pr.sub.* **n. copiions, v. copiiez**) **1.** to copy, transcribe (manuscript, music, etc.); **c. qch. au propre,** to make a fair, a clean, copy of sth., to copy out sth.; *Com:* **c. une lettre,** to press-copy a letter; **machine à c.,** copying-machine; copying-press. **2.** to copy, reproduce (statue, picture); to imitate (s.o., style, etc.); **c. les gestes de qn,** to copy, mimic, s.o.'s gestures; **c. qch. sur qch.,** to copy sth. from sth.; *Sch:* **c. (un devoir sur un autre élève),** to crib (an exercise from another pupil); **c. sur son voisin,** to copy from one's neighbour; *abs.* **il a copié,** he copied. **3.** *Phot:* **c. sur métal,** to print down on metal plate; **châssis à c.,** printing-down frame.
copieur, -ieuse [kɔpjœːr, -øːz], *a. & s.* (*a*) copier; *Sch:* cribber; (*b*) *s.m.* copying machine, duplicator.
copieusement [kɔpjøzmɑ̃], *adv.* copiously; **boire c.,** to drink deep.
copieux, -ieuse [kɔpjø, -jøːz], *a.* copious; **repas c.,** heavy, hearty, square, meal.
copilote [kɔpilɔt], *s.m. Av:* second pilot, co-pilot.
copine [kɔpin], *s.f. P:* friend; *cf.* COPAIN.
copiste [kɔpist], *s.m. & f.* copier. **1.** copyist, transcriber; **faute de c.,** clerical error. **2.** imitator; *a.* **esprit c.,** imitative spirit.
coplanaire [kɔplanɛːr], *a. Math:* coplanar (forces, etc.).
copocléphile [kɔpɔklefil], *s.m. & f.* key-ring collector.
copocléphilie [kɔpɔklefili], *s.f.* key-ring collecting.
copolymère [kɔpɔlimɛːr], *s.m. Ch: etc:* copolymer.
copolymérisation [kɔpɔlimerizasjɔ̃], *s.f. Ch: etc:* copolymerization.
coporteur [kɔpɔrtœːr], *s.m. Fin:* joint holder (of stock).
coposséder [kɔpɔsede], *v.tr.* (*conj. like* POSSÉDER) *Jur:* to own jointly, to have joint ownership of (sth.).
copossesseur [kɔpɔsɛsœːr], *a. & s.m. Jur:* **1.** joint owner. **2.** cotenant.
copossession [kɔpɔsɛsjɔ̃], *s.f. Jur:* **1.** joint ownership. **2.** cotenancy.
copra(h) [kɔpra], *s.m., A:* **copre** [kɔpr̥], *s.m. Com:* copra; **huile de c.,** coco-nut oil.
copreneur, -euse [kɔprənœːr, -øːz], *s. Jur:* co-lessee, cotenant.
coprésident [kɔprezidɑ̃], *s.m.* copresident.
coprin [kɔprɛ̃], *s.m. Fung:* coprinus.
coproduction [kɔprɔdyksjɔ̃], *s.f.* coproduction.
coprolalie [kɔprɔlali], *s.f. Med: Psy:* coprolalia.
coprolit(h)e [kɔprɔlit], *s.m.* (i) *Geol:* coprolite; (ii) *Med:* coprolith.
coprologie [kɔprɔlɔʒi], *s.f.* **1.** *Biol: Med: Agr:* coprology; scatology. **2.** pornography.
coprophage [kɔprɔfaːʒ], *Ent: etc:* **1.** *a.* coprophagous (insect, etc.). **2.** (*a*) *s.m.pl.* **coprophages,** Coprophagi; (*b*) *s. Med:* coprophagist.
coprophagie [kɔprɔfaʒi], *s.f. Med:* coprophagy, coprophagia.
coprophile [kɔprɔfil], *Ent: etc:* **1.** *a.* coprophilous. **2.** *s.m.* coprophilus.
copropriétaire [kɔprɔprietɛːr], *s. Jur:* co-proprietor; joint owner, part owner, co-owner.
copropriété [kɔprɔpriete], *s.f. Jur:* co-property; joint ownership, co-ownership.
copte [kɔpt], *a. & s.m.* **1.** *s.m.* (*a*) *Ecc.Hist:* Copt; (*b*) *Ling:* Coptic. **2.** *a.* Coptic.
coptée [kɔpte], *s.f. A. & Dial:* toll, stroke (of bell).
copter [kɔpte], *v.tr. A. & Dial:* to toll (bell).
coptique [kɔptik], *a.* Coptic.
coptis [kɔptis], *s.m. Bot:* coptis.
copulateur, -trice [kɔpylatœːr, -tris], *a. Z:* copulatory, copulative (organ, etc.).
copulatif, -ive [kɔpylatif, -iːv], *Gram: Log:* **1.** *a.* copulative (conjunction). **2.** *s.f.* **copulative,** copulative.
copulation [kɔpylasjɔ̃], *s.f.* **1.** *Physiol:* copulation. **2.** *Ch:* coupling.
copule [kɔpyl], *s.f.* **1.** *Gram:* copula. **2.** *Jur: A:* copula, sexual union.
copurchic [kɔpyrʃik], *A: P:* **1.** *a.inv. in f.* ultra-smart (young man, etc.). **2.** *s.m.* out-and-out swell.
copyright [kɔpirajt], *s.m.* copyright.
copyrighter [kɔpirajte], *v.tr.* to copyright.
coq¹ [kɔk], *s.m.* **1.** (*a*) cock, *U.S:* rooster; **c. nain,** bantam; **jeune c.,** cockerel; **chant du c.,** crowing of the cock; **au (premier) chant du c.,** at cock-crow; **combat, concours, de coqs,** cock-fight(ing); **c. de combat,** game cock; *F:* **rouge comme un c.,** red as a turkey-cock; **fier comme un c.,** all cock-a-hoop; **hardi comme un c. sur son fumier,** as bold as a cock on his own dunghill; **vivre comme un c. en pâte,** to live like a fighting cock; **le c. du village, de la paroisse,** the cock of the walk, of the roost; **à nous le c.,** we are on top, we are top-dog; *Box:* **poids c.,** bantam weight; *s.a.* HERBE 4, SAUTER 2; (*b*) cock, male, of various birds; **c. faisan,** cock-pheasant; **c. de la perdrix,** cock-partridge; **c. d'Inde** [kɔkdɛ̃ːd], turkey-cock; **grand c. de bruyère,** capercaillie; **petit c. de bruyère, c. des bouleaux,** black grouse; **c. des marais,** hazel grouse; **c. de montagne,** black grouse; **c. de roche,** cock-of-the-rock. **2.** weather cock, vane. **3.** (*a*) *Laund:* flounce iron; (*b*) *Clockm:* (balance-)cock. **4. c. de mer,** (i) *Crust:* calappa, box-crab; (ii) *Ich:* sea-cock.
coq², *s.m. Nau:* **(maître-)c.,** (ship's) cook; **matelot c.,** cook's mate.
coq-à-l'âne [kɔkalaːn], *s.m.inv.* **1.** desultory discourse; **faire des coq-à-l'âne,** to skip from one subject to another. **2.** *Lit: A:* skit, parody.
coquard, coquart [kɔkaːr], *s.m. F:* **1.** (*a*) old cock; (*b*) *F:* old beau, old fop; (*c*) *F:* ninny, booby. **2.** (hybrid of pheasant and domestic fowl) pero. **3.** *P:* black eye.
coque [kɔk], *s.f.* **1.** (*a*) shell (of egg); **un œuf à la c.,** a (soft-)boiled egg; **faire cuire un œuf à la c.,** to boil an egg; *P:* **dîner à la c.,** rattling good dinner; (*b*) shell, husk (of nut, fruit); *Bot:* coccus; (*c*) *Bot:* **c. du Levant,** Indian berry; (*d*)

Ent: (= COCON) cocoon; **se renfermer dans sa c.**, to retire into one's shell; (*e*) *Ent: Moll:* **c. ovigère**, ootheca, *pl.* oothecæ; (*f*) *Moll:* cockle. **2.** (*a*) *N.Arch:* hull (of boat, dredger, amphibian craft); **c. extérieure**, outer skin; **c. métallique**, metal(lic) hull, all-metal hull; **c. renforcée**, strengthened hull; **c. soudée**, welded hull; **double c.**, double hull; *Com:* **affrètement "coque nue,"** bareboat charter, demise charter; **assurance sur corps et c.**, hull insurance; (*b*) *Av:* hull (of aircraft, *esp.* flying boat); **c. à fond plat**, flat-bottomed hull; **c. à simple, à double, redan**, single-step, double-step, hull; (*c*) *Mil:* body, hull (of tank, etc.); **plaque (de blindage) de c.**, hull plate; **plaque latérale de c.**, hull side plate; **position c. défilée**, hull-down position; (*d*) *Veh: Mch:* body, shell (of car, boiler, etc.). **3.** (*a*) loop (of bow-tie, of ribbon, of hair, etc.); (*b*) kink (in rope).

coquebin, -ine [kɔkbɛ̃, -in], *F:* **1.** *a.* naïve, innocent; *F:* green. **2.** *s.m.* greenhorn.

coquecigrue [kɔksigry], *s.f.* **1.** *Lit:* legendary bird, chimaera; **à la venue des coquecigrues**, never. **2.** *A: pl.* twaddle, balderdash. **3.** *Bot:* smoke-bush, -plant.

coque-fuselage [kɔkfyzlaːʒ], *s.m. Av:* hull (of flying-boat); *pl. coques-fuselages.*

coquelet [kɔklɛ], *s.m.* cockerel.

coqueleux [kɔklø], *s.m. Dial:* breeder of game-cocks; cocker; cockfighter.

coquelicot [kɔkliko], *s.m. Bot:* red poppy, corn poppy, red-weed; *a.inv.* **rouge c.**, poppy red; **robe c.**, scarlet dress.

coquelle [kɔkɛl], *s.f. Dial: Cu:* stew-pan.

coquelourde [kɔklurd], *s.f. Bot:* **1.** pasque-flower, dane-flower, pulsatilla. **2.** rose campion.

coqueluche [kɔklyʃ], *s.f.* **1.** *Cost: A:* hood, cowl; *F:* **être la c. de toutes les femmes, de la ville**, to be the ladies' darling, the darling of the town. **2.** *Orn:* reed-bunting. **3.** *Med:* whooping-cough.

coquelucheux, -euse [kɔklyʃø, -øːz], *a.* suffering from whooping-cough.

coqueluchon [kɔklyʃɔ̃], *s.m.* **1.** *A:* hood, cowl. **2.** *Bot:* monk's-hood, wolf's-bane.

coquemar [kɔkmaːr], *s.m. Cu:* (big-bellied) pot, cauldron; kettle.

coquerelle [kɔkrɛl], *s.f. Bot: F:* (*a*) strawberry-tomato, winter-cherry, bladder-herb; (*b*) *Her:* bunch of three hazel nuts.

coqueret [kɔkrɛ], *s.m. Bot: F:* strawberry-tomato, winter-cherry, bladder-herb; **c. du Pérou**, Cape gooseberry.

coquerico [kɔkriko], *Onomat. & s.m.* cock-a-doodle-doo.

coquerie [kɔkri], *s.f. Nau:* **1.** cook-house (on wharf). **2.** ship's galley, caboose.

coqueriquer [kɔkrike], *v.i.* (*rare*) (*of cock*) to crow.

coqueron [kɔkrɔ̃], *s.m. Nau:* **1.** issue-room, store-room. **2.** peak (of ship); **c. avant**, forepeak; **c. arrière**, after-peak. **3.** *Dial:* stack of hay or wheat.

coquet, -ette [kɔkɛ, -ɛt]. **1.** *a.* (*a*) coquettish (woman, smile, etc.); **elle est coquette**, (i) she likes pretty clothes; (ii) she likes to look attractive; (*b*) smart, stylish, dainty, neat (garment, etc.); **jardinet c.**, trim little garden; **appartement coquet**, attractive flat; *F:* **fortune assez coquette**, tidy fortune. **2.** *s.m. A:* coxcomb, lady-killer. **3.** *s.f.* **coquette**; (*a*) flirt, coquette; (*b*) (botanist's) (i) vasculum; (ii) press.

coqueter [kɔkte], *v.i.* (**je coquette, n. coquetons; je coquetterai**) **1.** (*of a cock*) to mate. **2.** to coquet(te), play the coquette; **c. avec qn**, to flirt; *F:* carry on, with s.o.; **c. avec une idée**, to toy with an idea.

coquetier, -ière [kɔktje, -jɛːr]. **1.** *s.* wholesale egg-merchant; poulterer; egg-man, -woman. **2.** *s.m.* (*a*) egg-cup; (*b*) *Sp: Hum:* cup, *F:* pot; *F:* **gagner le c.**, to hit the jack-pot, to win the prize, to come into big money. **3.** *s.f.* **coquetière**, egg-boiler.

coquettement [kɔkɛtmɑ̃], *adv.* smartly, daintily (dressed, etc.).

coquetterie [kɔkɛtri], *s.f.* **1.** (*a*) coquetry; **dire des coquetteries à qn**, to flirt with s.o.; **faire des coquetteries à qn**, to make advances to s.o., to lead s.o. on; *F:* to carry on with s.o.; **être en c. avec qn**, to be carrying on a flirtation with s.o.; (*b*) coyness, affectation; (*c*) love of finery; (*d*) fastidiousness (in dress); **avoir de la c. pour sa tenue**, to be fastidious, particular, about one's dress; **mettre une certaine c. à vieillir**, to take pains to grow old gracefully. **2.** smartness, stylishness, daintiness (of dress, etc.).

coquillage¹ [kɔkijaːʒ], *s.m.* **1.** shell-fish (excluding crustaceans). **2.** (empty) shell (of shell-fish).

coquillage², *s.m. Metall:* (i) chilling; chill-casting; (ii) **c. (sous pression)**, die-casting; **c. de la fonte**, chilled cast iron, chilled iron.

coquillard [kɔkijaːr], *s.m.* **1.** *Geol:* shelly bed, stratum of shells. **2.** *A:* beggar in the Middle Ages; **les coquillards**, a band of rogues in the time of Villon. **3.** *V:* eye.

coquillart [kɔkijaːr], *s.m.* (*a*) *Geol:* shelly bed, stratum of shells; (*b*) *Const:* shell limestone.

coquille [kɔkiːj], *s.f.* **1.** shell (of snail, oyster, etc.); **escalier en coquille**, spiral staircase; *F:* **ne jamais sortir de sa c.**, never to leave one's home, *F:* one's burrow; **rentrer dans sa c.**, to retire into one's shell. **2.** *Moll:* **c. Saint-Jacques**, (i) scallop; (ii) scallop-shell, comb(-shell), pecten; (iii) *Her:* (e)scallop; *Cu:* **huîtres en c.**, scalloped oysters; **c. de poisson**, fish served up in scallop-shells; *A:* **coquilles de pèlerins**, pilgrims' scallops or cockles; *F:* **portez vos coquilles ailleurs**, take your wares elsewhere (in allusion to consecrated shells offered for sale by returned pilgrims). **3.** (*a*) shell (of egg, nut, etc.); **être à peine sorti de sa c.**, to be only just hatched; (*of boat*) **c'est une vraie c. de noix**, it's a mere cockle-shell; *Paint:* **fini c. d'œuf**, egg-shell finish; *Cer:* **c. d'œuf**, egg-shell china or ware; (*b*) **c. de beurre**, flake, shell, of butter; **coquilles du pain**, blisters on bread; **coquilles d'un anémomètre**, cups of a wind-gauge; **c. de loquet**, thumb of a latch; **c. d'une épée**, hand-guard, shell, basket-hilt, of a sword. **4.** (*a*) *Cu:* (shell-shaped) portable grate (of Dutch oven); (*b*) *Veh:* foot-board, -rest (of carriage-board); (*c*) *Cost:* preformed cup (of swimsuit brassière). **5.** (*a*) casing, housing (of motor, etc.); *Hyd.E:* case (of spiral pump); *Typ:* (copper) shell (of electrotype); *Const:* soffit, underpart (of spiral stair); *Aut:* **c. de radiateur**, radiator shell; *Mec.E:* **c. de coussinet**, bearing shell, bush brasses; *El:* **c. de condenseur**, condenser cover; (*b*) *Metall:* chill, chill-mould; **coulée en c.**, (i) chilling; (ii) (*sous pression*) die-cast; **couler en c.**, (i) to chill; (ii) (*sous pression*) to die-cast; **moulage en c.**, (i) chill-casting, chilled casting; (ii) (*sous pression*) die-casting; **trempage en c.**, chill-hardening; **tremper en c.**, to chill-harden; **fonte (coulée) en c.**, (i) chilled iron, chill-cast iron; (ii) (*sous pression*) die-cast iron; **palier coulé en c.**, (i) chill-cast bearing; (ii) (*sous pression*) die-cast bearing. **6.** *Paperm:* (*a*) **papier c., c. anglaise**, bank paper, bank post; **c. pelure**, foreign note-paper; (*b*) (format) (post) demy, small post (paper). **7.** *Typ:* printer's error, misprint, "literal."

coquillé [kɔkije], *a. Const:* shelly (limestone, etc.).

coquiller [kɔkije]. **1.** *v.tr.* (*a*) to cockle (lace, etc.); (*b*) *Metall:* to chill; to cast (metal) in a chill-mould. **2.** *v.i.* (*a*) (*of silk, etc.*) to cockle up; (*b*) (*of bread*) to blister.

coquillet [kɔkijɛ], *s.m. Const:* shelly limestone.

coquillette [kɔkijɛt], *s.f. Cu:* kind of noodle.

coquilleux, -euse [kɔkijø, -øːz], *a.* **1.** *Geol:* conchitic, shelly. **2.** *F: A:* crusty (disposition, temper).

coquillier, -ière [kɔkije, -jɛːr]. **1.** *a. Geol:* conchitic, shelly. **2.** *s.m.* (*a*) collection of shells; (*b*) shell cabinet.

coquin¹, -ine [kɔkɛ̃, -in]. **1.** *s.* rogue, rascal, wretch; *f. A:* hussy, jade; **c. de la plus belle eau**, villain of the deepest dye; **tour de c.**, knavish trick; **ce c. de Pierre**, that young rascal of a Peter; (*in Provence*) **c. de sort!** hang it! damn it! **petite coquine!** you little mischief! you cheeky little thing! **2.** *a. F:* (*a*) roguish; jaunty (air); (*b*) *A:* **vie coquine**, lazy, idle, life.

coquin², *s.m. Miner:* nodule of phosphate of lime (in greensand).

coquiner [kɔkine], *v.i. A:* to lead the life of a beggar; to mump.

coquinerie [kɔkinri], *s.f.* **1.** knavery, knavishness, roguery; **il est d'une c. fieffée**, he is a thorough-paced scoundrel. **2.** knavish, rascally trick; piece of rascality.

coquinet, -ette [kɔkine, -ɛt], *s. F:* little rogue, little rascal.

coquioule [kɔkjul], *s.f. Bot:* sheep's fescue.

cor [kɔːr], *s.m.* **1.** *Ven:* tine (of antler); **un cerf (de) dix cors**, a five-pronger. **2.** (*a*) *Ven:* **cor (de chasse)**, (hunting-)horn; **donner, sonner, du c.**, to sound, wind, blow, the horn; **chasser la bête à c. et à cri**, to hunt the animal with hound and horn; *F:* **chasser qn à c. et à cri**, to raise a hue and cry after s.o.; **chasse à c. et à cri**, stag-hunting; *F:* **réclamer qch. à c. et à cri**, to clamour for sth.; *Mil:* **manteau en c. de chasse**, rolled greatcoat; (*b*) *Mus:* **c. d'harmonie**, French horn; **c. anglais**, English horn, tenor oboe, cor anglais; (*c*) *Mus:* horn-player. **3.** (*a*) corn (on the toe or foot); (*b*) *Vet:* sitfast.

coraciadidés [kɔrasjadide], *s.m.pl. Orn:* Coraciidae, the rollers.

coraciadiformes [kɔrasjadifɔrm], *s.m.pl. Orn:* Coraciiformes.

coracias [kɔrasjas], *s.m. Orn:* chough.

coracle [kɔrakl], *s.m. Nau:* coracle, currach, curragh.

coraco- [kɔrako-], *pref. Anat:* coraco-.

coraco-claviculaire [kɔrakɔklavikylɛːr], *a. Anat:* coraco-clavicular (ligament); *pl. coraco-claviculaires.*

coracoïde [kɔrakɔid], *a. & s.f. Anat:* coracoid.

corail, -aux [kɔraːj, -o], *s.m.* **1.** coral; **c. simple**, cup coral; **récif de c., de coraux**, coral reef; *F:* **lèvres de c.**, coral lips. **2.** *Bot: F:* **c. des jardins**, pimento. **3.** *Com:* **bois (de) c.**, padouk.

coraillé [kɔraje], *a.* (*of bracelet, etc.*) set with coral.

corailler [kɔraje], *v.i.* to caw.

coraillère [kɔrajɛːr], *s.f.* coral-fishing boat.

corailleur, -euse [kɔrajœːr, -øːz], *s.* **1.** (*a*) coral fisher; (*b*) coral worker. **2.** *s.m.* coral-fishing boat.

corailleux, -euse [kɔrajø, -øːz], *a.* coralline.

corallaire [kɔral(l)ɛːr], *a.* coralloid, coralline.

corallidés [kɔralide], *s.m.pl. Coel:* Coralliidae.

corallien, -ienne [kɔraljɛ̃, -jɛn], *a.* coralline; **récif c.**, coral reef.

corallifère [kɔralifɛːr], *a.* coralliferous.

coralliforme [kɔralifɔrm], *a.* coralliform.

coralligène [kɔraliʒɛn], *a.* coralligenous; *Geol:* **calcaire c.**, coral limestone.

coralligère [kɔraliʒɛːr], *a.* = CORALLIFÈRE.

corallin, -ine¹ [kɔralɛ̃, -in], *a.* red as coral, coral-red.

coralline² [kɔralin], *s.f.* **1.** *Bot:* corallina. **2.** *Miner:* coralline.

Coran (le) [ləkɔrɑ̃], *s.m.* The Koran.

coranique [kɔranik], *a.* Koranic.

coraux [kɔro]. *See* CORAIL.

corbeau, -eaux [kɔrbo], *s.m.* **1.** *Orn:* (*a*) crow; *F:* rook; **c. (proprement dit), grand c.**, raven; **noir comme un c.**, raven-black; **cheveux noir de c.**, raven locks; **c. gris, c. mantelé**, hooded crow; **c. corneille**, carrion crow; **c. freux**, *F:* **corbeau**, rook; (*b*) *F:* **c. blanc**, vulture; **c. des clochers**, jackdaw; **c. cornu**, hornbill; **c. de mer, d'eau**, cormorant; **c. de nuit**, (i) tawny owl; (ii) nightjar, goatsucker. **2.** (*a*) *Arch:* corbel, bracket; (*b*) *Rom.Ant:* boarding-bridge, *corvus*; (*c*) *Nau:* grappling-iron; **nid de c.**, crow's-nest; (*d*) *P:* (i) priest, parson; (ii) funeral mute; (iii) body-snatcher, ghoul; (iv) person of ill-omen; *F:* bird of ill-omen; (v) writer of poison-pen letters; (vi) rapacious person, shark.

corbeautière [kɔrbotjɛːr], *s.f.* rookery.

corbéen, -enne [kɔrbeɛ̃, -ɛn], *a. & s.* (native) of Corbie.

corbeillais, -aise [kɔrbɛjɛ, -ɛːz], *a. & s.* (native) of Corbeil.

corbeille [kɔrbɛːj], *s.f.* **1.** (open) basket (without a bow-handle); **c. à pain, à ouvrage**, bread-basket, work-basket; **c. à papier**, waste-paper basket; **la c. de mariage, de noces**, the wedding presents (given to bride by bridegroom); **c. à linge**, laundry basket; **c. pour correspondance, pour documents à classer**, filing basket; *Typewr:* **c. à caractères**, type-basket; *Fort: A:* **c. (défensive)**, gabion; *s.a.* SOUTIEN-GORGE. **2.** (*a*) *Arch:* corbe(i)l, bell, base (of Corinthian capital); (*b*) *Ent:* corbicula, pollen-basket, -plate (of bee); (*c*) *Hort:* (round) flower-bed; (*d*) **c. de protection**, wire guard (of lamp); *Mch:* **c. de la soupape**, valve cage; *Turb:* **c. de régulateur**, governor frame. **3.** (*a*) stockbroker's central enclosure (in Paris Stock Exchange); (*b*) *Th:* (i) dress-circle; (ii) first three rows of stalls. **4.** *Bot:* **c. d'or**, rock-alyssum, madwort; **c. d'argent**, sweet alison, alyssum.

corbeillée [kɔrbɛje, -eje], *s.f.* basketful.

corbeillois, -oise [kɔrbɛjwa, -waːz], *a. & s. Geog:* = CORBEILLAIS.

corbillard [kɔrbijaːr], *s.m.* hearse; *P:* **monter dans le c.**, to step into one's last bus.

corbillat [kɔrbija], *s.m.* young crow; young raven.

corbillon [kɔrbijɔ̃], *s.m.* **1.** small (open) basket. **2.** (parlour game of) crambo.

corbin [kɔrbɛ̃], *s.m.* crow; raven; **c. crave**, chough; *cf.* BEC-DE-CORBIN.

corbine [kɔrbin], *s.f.* carrion-crow.

corbleu [kɔrblø], *int.* = CORDIEU.

Corcyre [kɔrsiːr], *Pr.n.f. A.Geog:* Corcyra.

cordage [kɔrdaːʒ], *s.m.* 1. (*a*) roping (of bales, etc.); stringing (of racket, etc.); (*b*) measuring (of firewood) by the cord. 2. (*a*) rope; **c. (de fils) d'acier**, (steel-)wire rope; **c. en chanvre**, hemp rope; **commettre un c.**, to lay a rope; **c. commis en câble**, cable-laid rope; *Nau:* **défense en c.**, rope fender; *Harn:* **c. de trait**, trace-rope; **c. en manille**, manilla rope; **c. en nylon**, nylon rope; *Nau:* **c. d'ancre**, anchor-rope; **c. de rechange**, spare rope; (*b*) *pl.* cordage, ropes; *Nau:* gear; **vieux cordages**, junk; **nager entre les cordages (d'une plage)**, to swim between the life-lines; (*c*) *Coll:* strings (of racket, etc.).

cordasson [kɔrdasɔ̃], *s.m. Com:* coarse canvas.

cordat [kɔrda], *s.m.* 1. coarse serge. 2. coarse wrapping-cloth; sacking.

corde [kɔrd], *s.f.* 1. (*a*) rope, cord, line; **mettre qch. en c.**, to twist sth. into a cord; **tabac (mis) en c.**, twist tobacco; **c. en acier**, steel rope; **c. à linge**, clothes-line; **danseur de c.**, tightrope dancer; **c. raide**, tightrope; **marcher, danser, être, faire de l'équilibre, sur la c. raide**, to be (walking) on a tightrope, to be in a precarious situation; **politique de la c. raide**, brinkmanship; **c. lâche**, slack rope; **c. tendue**, taut rope; *Mount:* **c. d'assurance, d'attache**, climbing rope; **escalade à la double c.**, double-roping technique; *Gym:* **c. à nœuds**, knotted climbing rope; **c. lisse**, climbing rope; **c. de traction**, tug-of-war rope; **c. à sauter**, skipping-rope; **sauter à la c.**, to skip; **c. de tambour**, brace of a drum; **mettre des chevaux à la c.**, to picket horses; *F:* **être au bout de sa c.**, to be at the end of one's tether; **(trop) tirer sur la c.**, to go too far; to push one's luck; **dormir à la c.**, to sleep in a doss-house; *Com:* **vendre qch. sous c.**, to sell sth. without breaking bulk; *Mec.E:* *O:* **c. plate**, belt; **c. en cuir**, round leather belt(ing); **c. de manœuvre**, (of hoist, pulley-block, etc.) handrope; *Aer:* guy; **c. (du panneau) de déchirure**, rip(ping)-cord; *Min: etc:* **c. à feu**, slow match, fuse; *Nau:* **c. de halage, de remorqu(ag)e**, tow-rope, tow(ing)-line; *F:* **il tombe, pleut, des cordes**, it's raining cats and dogs; (*b*) string; **c. à boyau**, catgut; **c. à fouet**, whipcord; **cordes à raquette**, racket strings; **c. à piano**, (i) piano wire; (ii) *Av:* flying wire, lift wire; *Mus:* **c. de piano**, piano string; **c. de violon**, violin string; **instrument à cordes**, stringed instrument; (*in orchestra*) **les cordes**, the strings; **c. filée**, covered string; **c. sourde**, muted string; **grosse c.**, lowest string; **double c.**, double stopping; (*in organ pipes*) **c. métallique**, wolf; **sa voix est claire dans les cordes élevées**, his voice is clear in the high notes; *F:* **la grosse c. d'un parti**, the most important person, *F:* the big noise, in a party; **c'est une c. qu'il ne faut pas toucher**, it is a sore subject; *s.a.* ARC[1] 1, SENSIBLE 2; (*c*) halter, hangman's rope; gallows; *F:* **se mettre la corde au cou**, (i) to put a halter round one's own neck; (ii) to get married, *F:* tied up, hooked; **supplice de la c.**, death by hanging; **friser la c.**, to miss the gallows by a hair's breadth; *F:* **il y va de la c.**, it is a hanging matter; **avoir de la c. de pendu dans sa poche**, to have the devil's own luck; **il ne vaut pas la c. pour le pendre**, he is not worth hanging; *Prov:* **il ne faut pas parler de c. dans la maison d'un pendu**, never talk of rope in the house of a man who has been hanged; *s.a.* SAC[1] 1; (*d*) *Fish:* trawl-line; (*e*) *Rac:* **la c.**, the rails; **tenir la c.**, (i) to hug the rails, to be on the inside (lane); (ii) to have the advantage; *Aut:* *F:* **prendre un virage à la c.**, to cut a corner close; *Box:* **les cordes**, the ropes; (*f*) *Tex:* thread; **drap usé jusqu'à la c., qui laisse voir la c.**, threadbare cloth; *P:* **plaisanterie usée jusqu'à la c.**, joke that has worn threadbare; **homme qui montre la c.**, (i) man down at heel; (ii) man who is played out. 2. *Geom:* chord (of segment, of arc); *Civ.E:* span (of arch); chord (of bridge); *Av:* **c. aérodynamique**, aerodynamic chord; **c. (du profil) d'aile**, chord of wing, of an airfoil; length of chord; **c. de référence**, mean aerodynamic chord. 3. *Anat:* (*a*) cord; **cordes vocales**, vocal cords; *F:* **ce n'est pas dans mes cordes**, it's not in my line, it's not my cup of tea; **c'est dans mes cordes**, it suits me, it's right up my street; (*b*) ligament; **c. du jarret**, hamstring; **c. d'Hippocrate**, Achilles tendon. 4. *Meas:* *A:* *Dial:* cord (of cut wood).

cordé[1] [kɔrde], *a.* 1. *Bot:* *Conch:* cordate, heart-shaped. 2. *s.m.pl. Z:* Cordata.

cordé[2]. 1. twisted (hemp, etc.). 2. corded (wood, etc.). 3. (*a*) **céleri cordé**, stringy celery; **vieilles mains cordées de veines**, old hands with corded veins; (*b*) ropy (lava, etc.).

cordeau, -eaux [kɔrdo], *s.m.* 1. (*a*) (tracing-)line, chalk-line, string; **tiré au c.**, perfectly straight, straight as a bowstring; (*b*) **c. de mesure**, measuring-tape. 2. *Min:* *Mil:* *Exp:* fuse, match; **c. Bickford**, Bickford fuse, safety-fuse; **c. détonant**, quickmatch, detonating-fuse; *Min:* cord. 3. rope, cord; *Nau:* tow-rope; **c. de tirage**, tent-rope; *Artil:* **c. tire-feu**, firing lanyard. 4. *Tex:* selvedge (of coarse woollen materials).

cordée [kɔrde], *s.f.* 1. *Com:* **c. de bois**, cord of wood. 2. *Fish:* long-line, eel-fishing line. 3. *Mount:* rope (of roped mountain climbers); roped (climbing) party; **premier de c.**, leader, first on the rope; **en c.**, roped together. 4. strings, stringing (of racquet). 5. *Min:* wind.

cordeler [kɔrdəle], *v.tr.* **(je cordelle, n. cordelons; je cordellerai)** to twist, twine, (hemp, etc.) into rope.

cordelette [kɔrdəlɛt], *s.f.* (*a*) small cord, small string; *Aer:* **c. de déclenchement**, rip-cord; (*b*) **cheveux tressés en cordelettes**, hair braided in small plaits.

cordelier, -ière [kɔrdəlje, -jɛːr]. 1. *s.* Franciscan friar or nun; grey friar or sister; *m.* cordelier; *A:* *F:* **aller sur la mule d'un c.**, to go on Shanks's pony, Shanks's mare; *Hist:* **les Cordeliers**, Revolutionary club (during the French Revolution. 2. *s.f.* **cordelière**, (*a*) girdle ((i) worn by Franciscan friar, (ii) of dressing gown, etc.); cord (of pyjamas); (*b*) *Arch:* cable, moulding, twisted fillet; *Typ:* (ornamental) border (of page); (*c*) *Her:* cordelière, tressure.

cordelle [kɔrdɛl], *s.f. Nau:* tow-line, warp; **haler un bateau à la c.**, to tow a boat.

corder [kɔrde], *v.tr.* 1. to twist (hemp, etc.) into rope; **c. du tabac**, to twist tobacco. 2. (*a*) to cord (trunk, bale, etc.); (*b*) to string (racquet, etc.). 3. *Com:* to measure (wood) by the cord. 4. *v.i. P:* to die; *P:* to snuff out, to snuff it.

se corder, (*of vegetables*) to become stringy.

corderie [kɔrd(ə)ri], *s.f.* 1. (*a*) ropery, rope-walk; (*b*) *Nau:* rope store-room. 2. (*a*) rope manufacture; rope trade; (*b*) rope factory.

cordial, -iaux [kɔrdjal, -jo], *a.* 1. *Pharm:* stimulating (medicine); *s.m.* cordial; stimulant; restorative. 2. cordial, hearty, warm (welcome, etc.); **devenir plus c.**, to warm up.

cordialement [kɔrdjalmɑ̃], *adv.* cordially, heartily; **"c. à vous,"** "sincerely yours."

cordialité [kɔrdjalite], *s.f.* cordiality, heartiness; **nous fûmes accueillis avec la plus grande c.**, the heartiest of welcomes awaited us.

cordier, -ière [kɔrdje, -jɛːr]. 1. *a.* rope(-business, etc.); rope-making (industry, etc.). 2. *s.m.* (*a*) rope-maker; (*b*) dealer in rope and twine; (*c*) *Fish:* long-line fisherman; (*d*) (*of ship*) drifter. 3. *s.m.* tail-piece (of violin).

cordiérite [kɔrdjerit], *s.f. Miner:* cordierite.

cordieu [kɔrdjø], *int. A:* (= **corps de Dieu**) by Jove! by the powers! *A:* odsbodikins! ods bodkins!

cordifolié [kɔrdifɔlje], *a. Bot:* with cordate leaves.

cordiforme [kɔrdifɔrm], *a. Biol:* cordiform, heart-shaped.

cordillère [kɔrdijɛːr], *s.f. Geog:* cordillera; **les Cordillères**, the Cordilleras (of America); **c. bétique**, Betic cordillera; *s.a.* ANDES.

cordite [kɔrdit], *s.f. Exp:* cordite.

cordon [kɔrdɔ̃], *s.m.* 1. (*a*) strand, twist (of cable, rope); **corde à trois cordons**, three-stranded rope; (*b*) cord, string, tape, band; **c. de soie**, silk cord; **c. de coton**, cotton tape; **cordons de bonnet**, bonnet strings; **c. de rideaux**, curtain cord; **c. de sonnette**, bell-rope, -pull; **c. de la porte**, door-pull (controlled by the *concierge*, in French blocks of flats); *O:* **demander le c.**, to ask the *concierge* (at night) to open the door; **tirer le cordon**, to open the door from the "*loge*"; **"cordon, s'il vous plaît!"** "door, please!"; **c. de soulier**, shoe-lace; **faire périr qn par le cordon**, to bowstring s.o.; *s.a.* BOURSE 1, POÊLE[2] 2; (*c*) *Artil:* **c. tire-feu**, firing lanyard; (*d*) ribbon, decoration (of an order, etc.); *cf.* CORDON BLEU; (*e*) (i) *Anat:* funiculus; **cordons nerveux**, funiculi of a nerve; (ii) *Bot:* funicle; (*f*) *Obst:* **c. ombilical**, umbilical cord; *Anat:* **c. médullaire**, spinal cord; (*g*) *El:* *Elcs:* cord, flex; **attache de c.**, cord fastener (or grip); **c. armé**, armoured cord; **c. chauffant, c. résistant**, line-cord resistor; resistance flex; flexible resistance; **c. d'alimentation**, line-cord, power-cord; **c. de secteur**, power-cord; **c. de shunt**, shunt-cord; **c. prolongateur**, extension cord; **c. souple**, flex(ible) cord, wire; **extrémité de c.**, cord tip; *Tp:* *Tg:* **c. à deux fiches**, double-ended cord; **c. à trois fils**, three-conductor cord; **c. de réponse**, answering cord; **ferret de c.**, cord-terminal; **répéteur sur c.**, cord-circuit repeater. 2. (*a*) row, line (of trees, etc.); **c. d'agents de police, de troupes**, cordon of police, of troops; **c. sanitaire**, sanitary cordon; **c. de postes d'observation**, chain of observation stations; **on isola la rue par un c. de police, on établit un c. de police aux entrées de la rue**, the street was cordoned off; (*b*) *Arch:* (i) string-course, cordon (in wall); (ii) coping; *Const:* barge-course; (*c*) *Hort:* (i) **c. de gazon**, turf border; (ii) cordon (tree); (*d*) rim, edge-ring, milled edge (of coin, etc.). 3. *Com:* **petit c.**, lyre isinglass; **gros c.**, leaf isinglass. 4. *Geol:* (*a*) stringer; (*b*) **c. littoral**, offshore bar. 5. *Bot:* *F:* **c. de cardinal**, persicaria. 6. **c. de soudure**, bead.

cordon(-)bleu [kɔrdɔ̃blø], *s.m.* 1. (*a*) (i) blue ribbon, (ii) knight, of the order of the Holy Ghost; (*b*) first-rate cook, cordon bleu. 2. (*a*) *Conch:* apple-shell; (*b*) *Ent:* owl-moth; (*c*) *Orn:* wax-bill; *pl. des cordons(-)bleus.*

cordonnage [kɔrdɔnaːʒ], *s.m. Num:* milling (of coin).

cordonné, *a.* [kɔrdɔne], *Arch:* cordoned.

cordonner [kɔrdɔne], *v.tr.* 1. to twist, twine, cord (silk, hemp, etc.). 2. *Num:* to edge-roll, mark, mill (coins). 3. *Arch:* to ornament (wall, etc.) with a cordon.

cordonnerie [kɔrdɔnri], *s.f.* 1. boot and shoe manufacture or trade; shoe-making. 2. (*a*) shoe-maker's or cobbler's shop; (*b*) shoe-room, -closet (in schools, etc.).

cordonnet [kɔrdɔnɛ], *s.m.* 1. braid, cord, twist. 2. *Num:* = CORDON 2 (*d*).

cordonnier, -ière [kɔrdɔnje, -jɛːr]. 1. *s.* shoe-maker; shoe repairer; *Prov:* **les cordonniers sont les plus mal chaussés**, the shoemaker's wife is always the worst shod; **c., mêlez-vous de votre pantoufle! c., tiens-t'en à la chaussure!** the cobbler should stick to his last. 2. *s.m. F:* (*a*) *Ent:* boat-fly; (*b*) *Ich:* stickleback; (*c*) *Orn:* skua (gull).

cordotomie [kɔrdɔtɔmi], *s.f. Surg:* cordotomy, chordotomy.

cordouan, -ane [kɔrdwɑ̃, -an]. 1. *a.* & *s. Geog:* Cordovan. 2. *s.m. Leath:* *A:* cordwain; Cordovan (leather); Spanish leather.

Cordoue [kɔrdu], *Pr.n.f. Geog:* Cordova; **cuir de Cordoue** = CORDOUAN 2.

cordulie [kɔrdyli], *s.f. Ent:* cordulia.

corduroy [kɔrdyrwa], *s.m. Min: etc:* corduroy.

cordylidés [kɔrdilide], *s.m.pl. Rept:* Cordylidae.

cordyline [kɔrdilin], *s.f. Bot:* cordyline.

Coré [kɔre], *Pr.n.m. B.Hist:* Korah.

corédacteur, -trice [kɔredaktœːr, -tris], *s.* co-editor, joint editor; *f.* joint editress.

corée[1] [kɔre], *s.f. Med:* = CHORÉE.

Corée[2], *Pr.n.f. Geog:* Korea; *Hist:* **la guerre de C.**, the Korean war.

coréen, -enne [kɔreɛ̃, -ɛn], *a.* & *s. Geog:* Korean.

corégence [kɔreʒɑ̃ːs], *s.f.* co-regency, (con)joint regency.

corégent [kɔreʒɑ̃], *s.m.* co-regent, joint regent.

corégnant [kɔreɲɑ̃], *a.* co-regent, co-regnant.

corégones [kɔregɔn], *s.m.pl. Ich:* Coregonidae, Coregonids.

coréidés [kɔreide], *s.m.pl. Ent:* Coreidae.

coreligionnaire [kɔrəliʒjɔnɛːr], *s.* co-religionist.

coréopsis [kɔreɔpsis], *s.m. Bot:* coreopsis.

corèthre [kɔrɛtr], *s.f. Ent:* plume-fly.

corfiote [kɔrfjɔt], *a.* & *s. Geog:* Corfiote.

Corfou [kɔrfu], *Pr.n.f. Geog:* Corfu.

coriace [kɔrjas], *a.* 1. tough, leathery (meat, etc.); *Nat.Hist:* coriaceous. 2. hard, grasping (person).

coriacé [kɔrjase], *a.* coriaceous, leathery.

coriacité [kɔrjasite], *s.f.* toughness, leatheriness.

coriambe [kɔrjɑ̃ːb], *s.m.* = CHORIAMBE.

coriandre [kɔrjɑ̃ːdr], *s.f. Bot:* coriander.

coricide [kɔrisid], *s.m. Pharm:* corn cure.

corindon [kɔrɛ̃dɔ̃], *s.m. Miner:* corundum; **c. jaune**, oriental topaz; **c. artificiel**, aloxite.

Corinne [kɔrin], *Pr.n.f.* 1. *Cl.Lit:* Corinna. 2. *F:* Cora.

Corinthe [kɔrɛ̃ːt], *Pr.n.f. Geog:* Corinth; *Cu:* **raisins de C.**, currants.

corinthien, -ienne [kɔrɛ̃tjɛ̃, -jɛn], *a.* & *s.* corinthian (order, etc.).

Coriolan [kɔrjɔlɑ̃], *Pr.n.m. Rom.Hist:* Coriolanus.

corion [kɔrjɔ̃], *s.m.* = CHORION 1.

corise [kɔriːz], *s.f. Ent:* water-boatman.

corisidés [kɔriside], *s.m.pl. Ent:* Coreidae; Corizidae; Corixidae.

corli, corlis [kɔrli], *s.m. Orn:* = COURLIEU.

cormaillot [kɔrmajo], *s.m. Moll:* sting-winkle.

corme [kɔrm], *s.f. Hort:* service-berry, -apple.

cormé [kɔrme], *s.m.* service-apple cider.

cormier [kɔrmje], *s.m. Hort:* service, sorb(-tree, -wood).

cormière [kɔrmjɛːr], *s.f. N.Arch:* counter-timber of the poop.
cormophytes [kɔrmɔfit], *s.m.pl. Bot:* Cormophyta.
cormoran [kɔrmɔrɑ̃], *s.m. Orn:* cormorant; **grand c.**, cormorant (*phalacrocorax carbo*); **c. pygmée**, pygmy cormorant; **c. moyen**, southern cormorant; **c. huppé, c. largup**, shag.
cornac [kɔrnak], *s.m.* elephant-keeper, carnac, mahout; *F:* **servir de c. à qn**, to act as s.o.'s guide.
cornacées [kɔrnase], *s.f.pl. Bot:* Cornaceae.
cornade [kɔrnad], *s.f.* goring; **donner la c.**, to gore.
cornage [kɔrnaːʒ], *s.m.* **1.** horns (of animal). **2.** *Vet:* wheezing, whistling, roaring, wind-sucking (of horse).
cornaline [kɔrnalin], *s.f. Lap:* cornelian, carnelian.
cornaquer [kɔrnake], *v.tr. F:* to shepherd (tourists).
cornard[1] [kɔrnaːr], *s.m.* **1.** person with horns; *P:* **(mari) c.**, deceived husband, cuckold. **2.** *Ent: F:* stag-beetle. **3.** *Glassm:* hook.
cornard[2], *a. & s.m. Vet:* **(cheval) c.**, roarer, whistler, wheezer, wheezy horse, wheezing horse, wind-sucker.
corne[1] [kɔrn], *s.f.* **1.** (*a*) horn; **bêtes à cornes**, horned beasts; **bêtes à longues cornes, à cornes courtes**, long-, short-horned beasts; **bêtes sans cornes**, hornless beasts; **montrer les cornes**, (i) (*of ram*) to show its horns; (ii) *F:* to show fight; **coup de c.**, (i) thrust; (ii) butt; (iii) malicious attack; **donner un coup de c. à qn**, (*of bull*) to horn s.o., to gore s.o.; (*of ram, goat*) to butt s.o.; **être attaqué, tué, à coups de c. par un taureau**, to be gored (to death) by a bull; (*of husband*) **porter des cornes**, to be deceived by his wife; **faire les cornes à qn**, to jeer, mock, at s.o.; *A:* **mettre des cornes à un enfant**, to put a dunce's cap on a child; **peigne de c.**, horn comb; **c. à chaussure**, shoe-horn; *Pharm: A:* **esprit de c. de cerf**, spirit of hartshorn; *s.a.* TAUREAU 1; (*b*) horn, feeler (of snail); horn, antenna (of stag-beetle); *F:* **rentrer les cornes**, to draw in one's horns; (*c*) *Bot:* cornu, spur, horn; (*d*) *pl. Anat:* cornua. **2.** (*a*) horn(-trumpet); *A: Aut:* **c. (d'appel)**, horn; *Nau:* **c. de brume**, fog-horn; (*b*) *Nau:* gaff (of fore-and-aft sail); **c. de charge**, cargo boom; **le pavillon à la c.**, with the flag at the peak, with colours high; (*c*) tip (of crescent, etc.); **cornes de la lune**, horns, cusps, of the moon; **cornes d'un arc**, tips of a bow; **c. d'une montagne**, peak of a mountain; **chapeau à cornes**, cocked hat; **c. d'un châle**, corner of a shawl; **c. d'une page**, turned down corner, dog's-ear of a page; **faire une c. à une carte de visite**, to turn down the corner of a visiting card; *El.E:* **cornes d'un disjoncteur, d'un commutateur**, horns of a switch; **disjoncteur à cornes**, horn-gap switch; **éclateur, parafoudre, à cornes**, horn (lightning) arrester, horn-gap; *Elcs:* **c. (de tube électronique)**, top-cap, side-contact (of valve); *Fort:* **ouvrage à cornes**, horn-work. **3.** horny matter; **cornes cutanées**, callosities; **c. du sabot (d'un cheval, etc.)**, horn, rind, of the hoof (of a horse, etc.). **4.** (*a*) **c. d'abondance**, (i) cornucopia; horn of abundance, of plenty; (ii) *Ich: F:* tunny; (*b*) *Arch:* **c. de bélier**, horn, volute (of Ionic capital). **5.** *Bot:* **c. de cerf**, buck's horn plantain; **c. du diable**, bird's-foot trefoil; **cornes d'élan**, staghorn fern.
corne[2], *s.f. Bot:* cornel-berry.
corné [kɔrne], *a.* **1.** corneous, horny (substance). **2.** horn-like (leaf, etc.); **silex c.**, hornstone; **lune cornée, argent c.**, horn-silver.
cornéal, -aux [kɔrneal, -o], *a. Anat:* corneal.
corneau, -eaux [kɔrno], *s.m.* **1.** *Nau:* (*a*) soil-pipe; (*b*) *pl.* (crew's) water-closets; *Navy:* the heads. **2.** cross between a mastiff and a hound.
corned beef [kɔrnbif], *s.m.inv.* corned beef.
cornée [kɔrne], *s.f. Anat:* cornea; **c. opaque**, sclerotic, sclera; *Surg:* **greffe de la c.**, corneal grafting.
cornéen, -enne [kɔrneɛ̃, -ɛn], *a. Anat:* corneal.
corneillard [kɔrnɛjaːr], *s.m. Orn:* young crow, young rook; young jackdaw.
corneille [kɔrnɛj], *s.f. Orn:* crow, rook; *F:* jackdaw; **c. noire**, carrion-crow; **c. mantelée, cendrée, grise**, hooded crow; **c. chauve**, rook; **c. d'église, des clochers**, jackdaw; **c. à bec rouge**, chough; **c. à bec jaune**, alpine chough; jackdaw; *s.a.* BAYER 1.
corneillon [kɔrnɛjɔ̃], *s.m.* = CORNEILLARD.
Cornélie [kɔrneli], *Pr.n.f.* Cornelia.
cornéliane [kɔrneljan], *s.f. Miner:* cornelian, carnelian.
cornélien, -ienne [kɔrneljɛ̃, -jɛn], *a. Fr.Lit.Hist:* in the style or spirit of Corneille.
cornement [kɔrnəmɑ̃], *s.m.* **1.** *Med:* buzzing, ringing (in the ears). **2.** *Mus:* ciphering (of organ pipe).
cornemuse [kɔrnəmyːz], *s.f. Mus:* bagpipe(s); **joueur de c.**, piper.
cornemuser [kɔrnəmyze], *v.i.* to play the bagpipes, to pipe.
cornemuseur [kɔrnəmyzœːr], *s.m.* piper.
cornemuseux [kɔrnəmyzø], *s.m. F:* piper.
cornéole [kɔrneɔl], *s.f. Bot: F:* woadwaxen, dyer's greenweed.
corner[1] [kɔrne], *v.tr.* **1.** (*a*) to trumpet, proclaim, blare forth (sth.); **c. une nouvelle**, (i) to proclaim news by sound of horn; (ii) *F:* to trumpet news abroad; *F:* **c. qch. aux oreilles de qn**, (i) to shout, (ii) to din, sth. into s.o.'s ears; (*b*) *abs.* to sound, wind, a horn; *Aut:* to sound the horn, to hoot, honk; **cornez!** sound (your) horn! (*c*) *Mus:* (*of organ pipe*) to cipher; *Vet:* (*of horse*) to roar, wheeze, whistle; (*d*) **les oreilles lui cornent**, his ears are ringing; **on a parlé de vous, les oreilles ont dû vous c.**, we spoke of you, your ears must have been burning; (*e*) *v.i.* **l'automobiliste corne**, the motorist hoots; *F:* **la radio nous cornait dans les oreilles**, the radio was blaring. **2.** (*of goat, ram*) to horn (s.o.); (*of bull*) to gore (s.o.). **3.** to turn down the corner of (page, visiting card, etc.); **page cornée**, dog-eared page.
corner[2] [kɔrnɛːr], *s.m.* **1.** *Fb:* corner. **2.** *Com:* ring.
cornet [kɔrnɛ], *s.m.* **1.** (*a*) small horn, trumpet; *Aut: A:* **c. (avertisseur)**, horn; **c. à bouquin**, (i) herdsman's horn; (ii) fog-horn; (*b*) *Mus:* (i) **c. à pistons**, cornet; *A:* cornopean; (ii) cornet stop (of organ); (iii) cornet(-player), cornetist. **2.** (*a*) **c. acoustique**, ear trumpet; **mettre sa main en c.**, to cup one's hand to one's ear; *A:* **c. de téléphone**, telephone receiver; **c. à dés**, dice box; (*for sweets, tobacco, etc.*) **c. de papier**, cornet; screw, twist, of paper; paper bag; **c. de crème glacée, de glace**, ice-cream cornet, ice-cream cone, ice cone; **c. de pâtisserie**, pastry horn; *Bot:* **c. de l'enveloppe florale**, cornet; *Nau:* **c. d'un mât**, tabernacle, case, of a mast; *Tp: W.Tel:* cornet, mouthpiece (of microphone); **c. d'alimentation (d'antenne)**, feeder horn (of antenna); **c. rayonnant**, horn-radiator; *Elcs:* (electromagnetic) horn; *Mil:* **c. de repérage par le son**, horn collector; *P:* **se coller quelque chose dans le c.**, to put something down one's gullet, to have something to eat; **acheter qch. dans un c.**, to buy a pig in a poke; (*b*) *Archeol:* **c. d'encrier**, ink-horn; (*c*) *Anat:* scroll-bone, turbinate bone. **3.** (*a*) *Bot: F:* wake-robin; (*b*) *Moll: F:* **c. de mer**, paper nautilus. **4.** *Vet:* mark of mouth.
cornette [kɔrnɛt], *s.f.* **1.** (*a*) (woman's) mob-cap; (*b*) (nun's winged) coif, cornet; (*c*) *Leath:* flesher. **2.** (*a*) *Mil: A:* (i) pennant, standard (of cavalry); (ii) *s.m. A:* cornet, ensign (of cavalry); (*b*) *Nau:* burgee; **c. de commandement**, commodore's broad pendant. **3.** *Bot: F:* cow-wheat.
cornettiste [kɔrnɛtist], *s.m. & f. Mus:* cornetist, cornet player.
cornéule [kɔrneyl], *s.f. Ent:* corneal surface (of an ommatidium of a compound eye).
corneur, -euse [kɔrnœːr, -øːz], *s.* **1.** horn blower. **2.** = CORNARD[2].
corniaud [kɔrnjo], *s.m.* **1.** cross between a mastiff and a hound. **2.** *P:* clot.
corniche[1] [kɔrniʃ], *s.f.* **1.** (*a*) *Arch: Furn:* cornice; (*b*) *N.Arch:* counter-rail. **2.** ledge (of rock); overhang, cornice; **c. (de neige)**, (snow) cornice; **(route en) c.**, corniche (road).
corniche[2], *s.f. Bot:* fruit of water caltrop.
corniche[3], *s.f. Sch: P:* army class (preparing for Saint-Cyr).
cornichon [kɔrniʃɔ̃], *s.m.* **1.** *Hort:* gherkin. **2.** *P:* (*a*) greenhorn; *F:* **cornichon!** clot! (*b*) *Sch:* member of Army class (preparing for Saint-Cyr). **3.** *Echin:* **c. de mer**, sea-cucumber, holothurian.
cornicule [kɔrnikyl], *s.f.* (i) *A: Biol: Ent:* cornicle; (ii) *Ent:* **c. (de puceron)**, nectary.
corniculé [kɔrnikyle], *a. Bot:* corniculate (petal).
cornier[1], **-ière** [kɔrnje, -jɛːr]. **1.** *a.* (at the) corner, angle; *Const:* **poteau c.**, *s.m.* **cornier**, corner-, angle-post; **tuile cornière**, corner-tile; valley tile; hip tile; *Aut:* **pied c.**, rear corner (of body). **2.** *s.f.* **cornière**; (*a*) *Const:* valley (joining roofs); (*b*) angle(-iron, -bar); **cornières adossées**, double angle; **c. à boudin**, bulb angle; (*c*) *Typ:* cramp, corner-iron; (*d*) *N.Arch:* **c. gouttière**, stringer bar.
cornier[2], *s.m. Bot: F:* cornel(-tree, -wood).
cornifle [kɔrnifl], *s.f. Bot:* hornwort.
corniforme [kɔrnifɔrm], *a.* corniform.
cornigère [kɔrniʒɛːr], *a.* cornigerous.
cornillas [kɔrnija], *s.m.* = CORNILLON[2].
cornillon[1] [kɔrnijɔ̃], *s.m. Z:* core of the horn.
cornillon[2], *s.m. Orn: F:* (*a*) young crow; (*b*) young jackdaw.
corniolle [kɔrnjɔl], *s.f. Bot: F:* **1.** water-chestnut, (fruit of the) water-caltrop. **2.** fruit of the scorpion-senna.
corniot [kɔrnjo], *s.m.* = CORNIAUD.
cornique [kɔrnik], *a. & s.m. Ling:* Cornish.
corniste [kɔrnist], *s.m. Mus:* horn player.
cornouaillais, -aise [kɔrnwajɛ, -ɛːz], *Geog:* **1.** (*a*) *a.* Cornish; (*b*) *s.* Cornishman, -woman. **2.** (*a*) (native, inhabitant) of the ancient district of Cornouaille (in Brittany); (*b*) a Breton dialect spoken in the South of Finistère.
Cornouaille [kɔrnwɑːj], *Pr.n.f. Geog:* **1.** Cornouaille (in Brittany). **2.** *occ.* Cornwall. **3. île de C.**, Cornwallis Island.
Cornouailles [kɔrnwɑːj], *Pr.n.f. Geog:* Cornwall.
cornouille [kɔrnuːj], *s.f. Bot:* cornel-berry; dog-berry.
cornouiller [kɔrnuje], *s.m.* **1.** *Bot:* cornel(-tree); **c. sanguin**, dogwood-tree. **2.** *Com:* dogwood.
cornu [kɔrny], *a.* **1.** (*a*) horned (beast); (*b*) *Log: A:* **l'argument c.**, the Cornutus; *hence:*—(*c*) *A:* preposterous, absurd (reason, etc.). **2.** *Bot:* cornute (leaf); spurred (wheat). **3 cheval c.**, horse with hips above croup. **4.** *s.m.* (i) bull; (ii) *F:* the Devil.
cornue [kɔrny], *s.f.* **1.** (*a*) *Ch: Gasm:* retort; **charbon de c.**, gas-carbon; **c. à goudron**, tar still; (*b*) *Metall:* steel converter. **2.** *Bot:* water-caltrop.
cornwallite [kɔrnwalit], *s.f. Miner:* cornwallite.
Corogne (la) [lakɔrɔɲ], *Pr.n.f. Geog:* Corunna.
corollacé [kɔrɔl(l)ase], *a. Bot:* corollaceous.
corollaire[1] [kɔrɔl(l)ɛːr]. **1.** *s.m.* (*a*) *Log: Mth:* corollary; (*b*) consequence. **2.** *a.* corollary.
corollaire[2], *Bot:* **1.** *a.* corolline. **2.** *s.m.* corollary tendril.
corollairement [kɔrɔl(l)ɛrmɑ̃], *adv.* **c. à**, as a corollary to.
corolle [kɔrɔl], *s.f. Bot:* corolla.
corollé [kɔrɔl(l)e], *a. Bot:* corollate.
corollifère [kɔrɔl(l)ifɛːr], *a. Bot:* corolliferous.
corolliflore [kɔrɔl(l)iflɔːr], *a. Bot:* corollifloral, corolliflorous.
corolliforme [kɔrɔl(l)ifɔrm], *a.* corolliform, corolla-shaped.
corollin [kɔrɔlɛ̃], *a. Bot:* corolline.
Coromandel [kɔrɔmɑ̃dɛl], *Pr.n.m. Geog:* **la côte de Coromandel**, the Coromandel Coast; *Com:* **bois de Coromandel**, calamander (wood); *Furn:* **laques de C.**, Coromandel lacquer work.
coron[1] [kɔrɔ̃], *s.m. Tex:* fluff, refuse (of wool, etc.).
coron,[2] *s.m.* miners' quarters, mining village (in north of France and Belgium).
coronadite [kɔrɔnadit], *s.f. Miner:* coronadite.
coronaire [kɔrɔnɛːr], *a. Anat:* coronary (veins, etc.); *Vet:* **os c.**, small pastern.
coronal, -aux [kɔrɔnal, -o]. **1.** *a. & s.m. Anat: etc:* coronal. **2.** *a. Astr:* of the solar corona.
coronarien, -ienne [kɔrɔnarjɛ̃, -jɛn], *a.* coronary; **insuffisance coronarienne**, coronary insufficiency.
coronarite [kɔrɔnarit], *s.f. Med:* coronaritis.
coronelle [kɔrɔnɛl], *s.f. Rept:* coronella.
coroniforme [kɔrɔnifɔrm], *a.* crown-shaped, coroniform.
coronille [kɔrɔniːj], *s.f. Bot:* coronilla; *F:* **c. des jardins**, scorpion-senna.
coronographe [kɔrɔnɔgraf], *s.m. Astr:* coronagraph, coronograph.
coronographie [kɔrɔnɔgrafi], *s.f.* (selective) coronary arteriography.
coronoïde [kɔrɔnɔid], *a. Anat:* coronoid; **apophyse c.**, coronoid process.
coronope [kɔrɔnɔp], *s.m. Bot:* wart-cress.
coronule [kɔrɔnyl], *s.f. Crust:* coronule.
corossol [kɔrɔsɔl], *s.m. Bot: F:* custard-apple (tree, fruit); **c. hérissé**, sour-sop; **c. écailleux**, sweet-sop.
corossolier [kɔrɔsɔlje], *s.m. Bot: F:* custard-apple-tree.
corozo [kɔrɔzo, korozo], *s.m.* (*a*) *Bot:* corozo-nut, ivory-nut; (*b*) *Com:* vegetable ivory.
corporal, -aux [kɔrpɔral, -o], *s.m. Ecc:* corporal (-cloth).
corporatif, -ive [kɔrpɔratif, -iːv], *a.* corporate, corporative.
corporation [kɔrpɔrasjɔ̃], *s.f. Jur: Pol:* corporation, corporate body, public body; *Com.Hist:* (trade-)guild.
corporatisme [kɔrpɔratism], *s.m. Pol.Ec: Phil:* corporatism, corporativism.

corporatiste [kɔrpɔratist]. 1. *a.* corporatist. 2. *s.m. & f.* a supporter of corporatism.

corporativement [kɔrpɔrativmɑ̃], *adv.* corporately, as a corporation.

corporéal, -aux [kɔrpɔreal, -o], *a. Surg:* corporeal.

corporéité [kɔrpɔreite], *s.f.* corporeity.

corporel, -elle [kɔrpɔrɛl], *a.* (*a*) corporeal (being, etc.); corporal (punishment, etc.); bodily (infirmity, etc.); tangible (property); (*b*) *Psy:* **schéma c.,** body schema.

corporellement [kɔrpɔrɛlmɑ̃], *adv.* corporeally, corporally, bodily.

corporifier [kɔrpɔrifje], *v.tr.* (*p.d. & pr.sub.* **n. corporifiions, v. corporifiiez**) *A.Ch:* to corporealize (angels, etc.); to materialize; to render (sth.) corporeal.

corps [kɔːr], *s.m.* body. 1. **le c. humain,** the human body; **un c. robuste,** a strong, robust, frame; *F:* **avoir un c. de fer,** to have an iron constitution; **un beau c. de femme,** a fine figure of a woman; **mortifier son c.,** to mortify the flesh; **saisir qn autour du c.,** to catch s.o. round the waist; *Jur:* **saisir qn au c.,** to arrest s.o.; **passer sur le c. de, à, qn,** (i) to run over s.o.; (ii) to ride s.o. down; **tomber à qn sur le c.,** to come down on s.o.; **faire bon marché de son c.,** not to value one's life, one's skin; *F:* **il faut voir ce qu'il a dans le c.,** we must see (i) what he's got in him, what stuff he's made of, (ii) what makes him tick; *F:* **avoir le diable au c.,** (i) to be possessed; (ii) to be full of devilment; (iii) to be tireless; **prendre du c.,** to put on flesh; **prendre c.,** to take, assume, shape; **sans c.,** bodiless, disembodied; **douleur du c.,** bodily pain; **garde du c.,** bodyguard; **les gardes du c.,** the bodyguards, the lifeguards; *F:* **un pauvre c.,** a poor creature; **c'est un drôle de c.,** he's a queer chap; *Jur:* **séparation de c.,** separation from bed and board; *adv.phr.* **saisir qn à bras-le-c.,** to seize s.o. round the waist, to grapple with s.o.; **lutter c. à c.,** to fight hand to hand, to come to grips; **combat c. à c.,** hand-to-hand fight(ing); *Box:* in-fighting; *s.m.* **un c.-à-c.,** a tussle; hand-to-hand fight(ing); *Box:* a clinch; **c.-à-c. jovial,** rough-and-tumble; **répondre de qn c. pour c.,** to be personally responsible, answerable, for s.o.; *s.a.* CONTRAINDRE 2, CONTRAINTE 2, DÉFENDRE 1, PERDU 4, PERTE 1, SAIN. 2. corpse, body; **des c. entassés,** piles of corpses; **la levée du c. aura lieu à onze heures,** the funeral will start from the house at eleven o'clock. 3. (*a*) *Ch: Ph:* body, substance, material; **c. simple,** element; **c. composé,** compound (body); **c. pur,** pure substance; (*b*) *Atom.Ph:* **c. noir,** blackbody; (*c*) *Physiol:* **c. jaune,** yellow body; *corpus luteum, pl. corpora lutea*; **c. strié,** striated body; *corpus striatum, pl. corpora striata*; **c. vitré,** vitreous body; *Med: Ch:* **c. étranger,** foreign body; (*d*) *Astr:* **c. céleste,** celestial, heavenly body. 4. **étoffe qui a du c., qui n'a pas de c.,** strong, flimsy, material; **vin, tabac, qui a du c.,** full-blooded wine, full-flavoured tobacco; **c. de la voix,** range, volume and quality of the voice; **voix qui manque de c.,** thin voice. 5. (*a*) main part (of sth.); body (of coach, hub, impeller, bomb, shell); body, shank (of connecting-rod, bolt, propeller blade, etc.); barrel (of cylinder, turnbuckle, etc.); **c. (de chaudière, de palan,** etc.), shell (of boiler, pulley-block, etc.); **c. cylindrique (de chaudière),** barrel (of boiler); **c. de pompe,** barrel, body, casing, cylinder, of pump; **c. (de dynamo, de palmer),** frame (of generator, micrometer); **c. de lanterne (de projection),** lamp-housing; **faire c. avec qch.,** to be an integral part of sth.; *A:* to corporate with sth.; (*b*) centre (of axle, wheel); **c. de roue à rayons, à voile plein,** spoke-, disc-wheel centre; (*c*) *Dressm:* body, bodice (of dress); (*d*) *Const:* **c. de bâtiment,** main (part of a) building; **caserne en trois corps de bâtiment,** barracks consisting of three main buildings; **le c. d'un édifice,** the main walls, foundations, of a building; **dalle en c. creux,** hollow floor slab; (*e*) *Nau:* **c. d'un bâtiment,** body, hull, of a ship; **perdu c. et biens,** lost with all hands; (*f*) dolphin, moorings; **(bouée de) c. mort,** (anchor-) buoy; **prendre le c. mort,** to make fast, to moor; **filer, larguer, le c. mort,** to cast off (from the buoy); (*g*) (*section*) **les corps d'une canne à pêche,** the joints of a fishing-rod; *Phot:* **c. (d')avant, c. (d')arrière (d'une chambre photographique),** front, back (of camera); *Mus:* **c. de rechange,** (tuning) crook (of horn, etc.); (*h*) *Typ:* **force de c.,** size of type body; **composé en c. douze,** set up in twelve point (body); (*i*) *Jur:* **c. du délit,** *corpus delicti.* 6. (organized body of men) (*a*) **c. constitué,** corporate body, public authority; **le c. diplomatique,** the diplomatic corps; **c. des sapeurs-pompiers,** the fire brigade; **le c. médical,** the medical profession; **le c. politique,** the body politic, the State; **grand c. de l'État,** public body; **un c. d'inspecteurs,** a body of inspectors, of supervisors; **un c. savant,** a learned body; **ils ont donné leur démission en c.,** they resigned in a body; **venir en c.,** to come in a body; *s.a.* BALLET, ESPRIT 5, MÉTIER 1; (*b*) *Mil:* **c. d'armée,** corps; **c. d'armée aérienne,** air corps; **éléments organiques de c. d'armée,** corps units, corps troops; **le c. de bataille,** (i) *Army:* the field forces; (ii) *Navy:* the battle fleet; *O:* **c. de cavalerie,** cavalry corps; **c. de garde,** (i) *A:* guard; (ii) guard-house, -room; **plaisanterie de c. de garde,** barrack-room joke; **c. d'élite,** crack regiment, crack unit; body of picked troops; **c. de troupe,** independent unit, self-contained unit; **c. expéditionnaire,** expeditionary force(s), oversea force(s); **c. franc,** commando. 7. corpus, collection of writing; *Jur:* **c. du Droit Civil,** corpus of civil law; **c. de preuves,** body of evidence.

corpulence [kɔrpylɑ̃ːs], *s.f.* stoutness, corpulence, corpulency, burliness; **de faible c.,** of slight build.

corpulent [kɔrpylɑ̃], *a.* stout, fat, corpulent; portly, burly.

corpus [kɔrpyːs], *s.m. Lit: Jur: Pal:* corpus.

corpusculaire [kɔrpyskylɛːr], *a.* corpuscular.

corpuscule [kɔrpyskyl], *s.m.* corpuscle.

corral [kɔr(r)al], *s.m.* (*in Sp.Amer. and U.S.*) corral; *pl. corrals.*

corrasion [kɔrazjɔ̃], *s.f. Geol:* corrasion.

correct [kɔrɛkt], *a.* correct, proper (language, etc.); accurate (copy, drawing, etc.); (*of pers.*) **très c.,** very "just so"; *Fr.C: F:* **c'est c.!** agreed!

correctement [kɔrɛktəmɑ̃], *adv.* correctly; accurately.

correcteur, -trice [kɔrɛktœːr, -tris]. 1. *s.* corrector; *Sch:* reader (of examination papers); *Typ:* proof-reader. 2. *s.m. Tchn:* corrector, compensator, equalizer; (*a*) *Artil: etc:* corrector-gear (of fuse-setter); **c. de fusée,** fuse-prediction number; **c. de pointage, de visée,** aim-corrector; **c. de site,** site-corrector; (*b*) *Av: Nau: etc:* **c. de latitude,** latitude corrector; **c. de vitesse (de gyrocompas),** speed corrector (of gyro-compass); *Av:* **c. automatique de lacet,** automatic yaw-damper; (*c*) *El: Elcs: Tp:* **c. d'impédance,** impedance corrector or compensator; **c. de ligne,** line equalizer; **c. de phase,** delay equalizer; **c. de tonalité,** tone-corrector device; **c. en dérivation,** parallel equalizer. 3. *a. Av: Nau: etc:* **aimant c.,** compensating magnet; *Av:* **moteur c.,** corrector motor; *Tp:* **réseau c.,** attenuation corrector (or compensator); *Opt:* **verres correcteurs,** corrective lenses.

correctif, -ive [kɔrɛktif, -iːv], *a. & s.m.* 1. corrective (de, of, to); **phrase corrective,** qualifying statement; rider; **un c. à la pauvreté,** a remedy for poverty; **un c. à mes critiques,** a toning down of my criticisms; *Med:* **gymnastique corrective,** remedial, corrective, exercises, gymnastics. 2. *Med:* guard, corrective, **mêler un c. à un narcotique,** to guard a drug.

correction [kɔrɛksjɔ̃], *s.f.* 1. (*a*) correction, correcting (of exercise, of fault, of typographical matter); reading (of proofs); rectification (of scientific observation, etc.); emendation (of text); **c. des mœurs,** reformation of manners; **sauf c. . . .,** subject to correction . . ., under correction . . .; *Th:* **recevoir une pièce à c.,** to accept a play subject to alteration; (*b*) *Artil: Missiles:* **c. aérologique,** meteorological correction, metro-correction; **c.-but,** lead, aim-off, aiming-off; **c.(-but) en direction,** lateral deflection; **c.-but en gisement,** lateral lead; **c. (-but) en hauteur,** vertical deflection; **c.-but en site,** vertical lead; **c. de dérive,** drift-correction; off-course correction; **c. de gisement,** deflection correction; **c. en portée,** range correction; **c. en site,** elevation correction; **c.-vent,** wind correction, aiming-off for wind; (*c*) *Av: Nau: etc:* **aimant de c.,** compensating magnet (of compass); **coefficient de c.,** correcting factor; **c. du compas,** adjustment of the compass, compass error; **c. de dérive,** drift correction, correction, allowance, for leeway; **angle de c. de route,** drift correction; (*d*) *Mec: E: etc:* **c. de température,** correction for temperature; **c. du zéro (d'un appareil de mesure),** index correction (of measuring instrument); **c. hors-tout,** overall correction; *Elcs:* **c. de tonalité,** tone correction (or control); **c. de fréquence,** frequency correction, line equalization; *Ph:* **c. de Bouguer,** Bouguer correction; (*e*) *Opt: etc:* **c. de l'astigmatisme, de la parallaxe, de la réfraction,** correction for astigmatism, for parallax, for refraction; *Surv:* **c. d'alignement,** correction for alignment. 2. reproof, punishment, castigation; **administrer, infliger, une c. à qn,** (i) to rebuke s.o.; (ii) to chastise s.o., to give (child) a thrashing; *A:* **maison de c.,** reformatory, penitentiary. 3. correctness (of dress, speech, etc.); propriety (of speech, conduct); **perdre sa c. de surface,** to drop one's outward correctness, to break out (into abuse, etc.).

correctionnaire [kɔrɛksjɔnɛːr], *s.m. & f.* one who is undergoing or has undergone a *peine correctionnelle, q.v.* under CORRECTIONNEL.

correctionnalisation [kɔrɛksjɔnalizasjɔ̃], *s.f. Jur:* action of sending (case) before a court of summary jurisdiction.

correctionnaliser [kɔrɛksjɔnalize], *v.tr. Jur:* to send (case) before a court of summary jurisdiction.

correctionnel, -elle [kɔrɛksjɔnɛl], *a. Jur:* **délit c.,** minor offence (entailing more than five days' imprisonment); **peine correctionnelle,** penalty of more than five days' (but less than five years') imprisonment; **tribunal de police correctionnelle,** *s.f. F:* **correctionnelle,** court of summary jurisdiction.

correctionnellement [kɔrɛksjɔnɛlmɑ̃], *adv. Jur:* **être condamné c.,** to be sentenced (to imprisonment of more than five days) by a court of summary jurisdiction.

correctivement [kɔrɛktivmɑ̃], *adv.* correctively.

Corrège (le) [ləkɔrɛːʒ], *Pr.n.m. Hist. of Art:* Correggio.

corregidor [kɔr(r)eʒidɔːr], *s.m. Spanish Adm: A:* corregidor.

corrélatif, -ive [kɔr(r)elatif, -iːv], *a. & s.m.* correlative.

corrélation [kɔr(r)elasjɔ̃], *s.f.* correlation; **coefficient de c.,** correlation coefficient.

corrélativement [kɔr(r)elativmɑ̃], *adv.* correlatively.

correler [kɔr(r)ɔle], *v.i.* **(je corrèle, nous correlons; je corrèlerai)** *Statistics:* to correlate.

corrélogramme [kɔr(r)elɔgram], *s.m. Statistics:* correlogram, correlation curve.

correspondance [kɔrɛspɔ̃dɑ̃ːs], *s.f.* 1. (*a*) correspondence, agreement (of tastes, between things, etc.); **c. des grades des armées de terre, de mer et de l'air,** corresponding ranks in the Army, Navy and Air Force; (*b*) *Mth:* correspondence. 2. (*a*) communication (between places); (*b*) *Rail:* connection (between trains); interchange service; *Av:* connecting flight; **manquer,** *F:* **rater, la c.,** to miss the connection; (*of train, boat, etc.*) **faire c. avec, assurer la c. avec . . .,** to connect with . . .; **(voiture de) c.,** railway omnibus; **billet de c.,** transfer ticket (on bus, etc.). 3. (*a*) intercourse, dealings (avec, with); (*b*) correspondence (with s.o. by letter); **être en c., entretenir une c., avec qn,** to correspond, be in correspondence, with s.o.; **notre c.,** the letters that have passed between us; **faire la c.,** to do the correspondence; **école par c.,** correspondence school; **enseignement par c.,** correspondence course; *Journ:* **petite c.,** personal column, agony column; (*c*) mail, post; **ouvrir la c.,** to open the mail.

correspondancier, -ière [kɔrɛspɔ̃dɑ̃sje, -jɛːr], *s.m. Adm: Com: etc:* correspondence clerk, (correspondence) secretary.

correspondant, -ante [kɔrɛspɔ̃dɑ̃, -ɑ̃ːt]. 1 *a.* (*a*) corresponding (à, to, with); corresponding (angle, etc.); associated; (*b*) *Rail:* **train c.,** connection, train running in connection; (*c*) corresponding (member of learned society); (*d*) *Mil.Intelligence:* **"honorable c.",** agent. 2. *s.* (*a*) *Com: Journ:* correspondent; **c. de guerre,** war-correspondent; (*b*) *Sch:* friend acting *in loco parentis* (in respect of pupils in boarding schools); (*c*) pen-friend.

correspondre [kɔrɛspɔ̃ːdr], *v.i.* 1. (*a*) to tally, agree, square (à, with); to correspond (à, to, with); to suit; **articles qui correspondent à nos besoins,** articles that meet our needs, articles adapted to our needs; **la théorie ne correspond pas aux faits,** the theory does not square with the facts; **ornements qui se correspondent,** ornaments that match; (*b*) *A:* to respond (to friendliness, affection, etc.). 2. (*a*) to communicate; **deux pièces qui (se) correspondent,** two rooms which communicate with one another; **deux mers qui correspondent par un détroit,** two seas which are joined by a strait; (*b*) **ce train correspond avec la Flèche d'Or,** this train connects with the Golden Arrow. 3. **c. avec qn,** to correspond (by letter) with s.o.

corrézien, -ienne [kɔrezjɛ̃, -ɛn], *a. & s. Geog:* (native, inhabitant) of the department of Corrèze.

corrida [kɔrida], *s.f.* **1.** corrida, bullfight. **2.** *P:* free-for-all.

corridor [kɔridɔːr], *s.m.* corridor, passage; *Fort:* gallery communication; *Av:* **c. aérien,** (air) corridor; *Hist:* **le c. polonais,** the Polish Corridor.

corrigé [kɔriʒe], *s.m. Sch:* **1.** fair copy (of exercise, after correction). **2.** key; *F:* crib; **manuel d'arithmétique avec corrigé des exercices,** arithmetic with answers.

corriger [kɔriʒe], *v.tr.* **(je corrigeai(s); n. corrigeons) 1.** to correct, mark (exercise, etc.); to read (proofs); to sub-edit (article); to rectify (mistake, etc.); **c. l'acidité d'une substance,** to correct the acidity of a substance; **c. les défauts (d'une machine, etc.),** to repair, cure, make good, the defects (in a machine, etc.); **c. les erreurs d'exécution,** to correct, compensate for, defects in workmanship; **c. qn d'une mauvaise habitude,** to cure, break, s.o. of a bad habit; **c. le dire de qn,** to set s.o. right; *Nau:* **c. les compas,** to adjust the compasses; *Mec.E:* **c. le jeu,** to take up play; *Av: Nau:* **c. la dérive,** to correct for drift, for leeway; *Opt:* **champ corrigé,** flat field. **3.** to correct, (i) to chastise (dog, child, etc.); (ii) to set (s.o.) right.

se corriger d'une habitude, to break oneself of a habit; **il a promis de se corriger,** he has promised to mend his ways, to turn over a new leaf; *s.a.* TARD.

corrigeur [kɔriʒœːr], *s.m. Typ:* corrector.

corrigible [kɔriʒibl̥], *a.* corrigible, rectifiable.

corrigiole [kɔriʒjɔl], *s.f. Bot:* strapwort.

corroborant [kɔr(r)ɔbɔrɑ̃]. **1.** *a. & s.m. Med: A:* corroborant, tonic. **2.** *a.* corroborative (proof).

corroboratif, -ive [kɔr(r)ɔbɔratif, -iːv], *a.* **1.** *A:* = CORROBORANT 1. **2** corroborative, confirmatory (evidence, etc.).

corroboration [kɔr(r)ɔbɔrasjɔ̃], *s.f.* **1.** *Med: A:* strengthening (of delicate constitution, etc.). **2.** corroboration, confirmation (of statement, etc.).

corroborer [kɔr(r)ɔbɔre], *v.tr.* **1.** *Med: A:* to strengthen, fortify. **2.** to corroborate, confirm (statement, etc.); **c. le dire de qn,** to bear s.o. out.

corrodabilité [kɔr(r)ɔdabilite], *s.f. Ch:* corrodibility, corrosibility.

corrodable [kɔr(r)ɔdabl̥], *a.* corrodible, corrosible.

corrodant [kɔr(r)ɔdɑ̃], *a. & s.m. Ch: Med:* corrodent, corrosive.

corrodé [kɔr(r)ɔde], *a.* corroded, eaten away; (*of metal plate*) perished.

corroder [kɔr(r)ɔde], *v.tr.* to corrode, erode, eat away, wear away (metal, stone, etc.).

se corroder, to corrode, become corroded.

corroi [kɔrwa], *s.m.* **1.** currying (of leather). **2.** puddle (of clay and sand). **3.** *Nau:* anti-fouling compound, preserving compound.

corroi(e)rie [kɔrwari], *s.f. Leath:* (*a*) currying; (*b*) curriery.

corrompre [kɔr(r)ɔ̃ːpr̥], *v.tr.* **1.** (*a*) to corrupt (morals, etc.); to deprave, vitiate, spoil (taste, etc.); **c. les juges,** to corrupt, buy (over), bribe, the judges; **essayer de c. un témoin,** to tamper with a witness, to try to suborn a witness; (*b*) **c. la viande,** to taint meat. **2.** *A:* = CORROYER.

se corrompre, (*a*) to become corrupt(ed); (*b*) (*of meat, etc.*) to taint, to become tainted.

corrompu [kɔr(r)ɔ̃py], *a.* (*a*) corrupt, depraved (person, morals); vitiated (taste); **témoin c.,** suborned, bribed, witness; (*b*) tainted, putrid; (*c*) corrupt (text).

corrosif, -ive [kɔr(r)ozif, -iːv], *a. & s.m.* **1.** *a.* corrosive, biting, caustic, etching; *O:* **soucis corrosifs,** gnawing anxiety. **2.** *s.m.* corrodent, corrosive, etching, agent.

corrosion [kɔr(r)ozjɔ̃], *s.f.* (*a*) corrosion, corroding, etching, pitting (of metal, etc.); fretting (of gears); **c. fissurante,** cracking corrosion; *Miner:* **figure de c.,** etching-figure (of crystal); (*b*) *Geol:* corrosion, erosion (of river banks, etc.).

corrosivement [kɔr(r)ozivmɑ̃], *adv.* corrosively.

corrosiveté [kɔr(r)ozivte], *s.f.* corrosiveness.

corroyage [kɔrwajaːʒ], *s.m.* currying (of leather); trimming, rough-planing (of wood); puddling (of clay); welding (of metal); rolling (of iron).

corroyer [kɔrwaje], *v.tr.* **(je corroie, n. corroyons; je corroierai) 1.** to curry (leather); to trim, rough-plane (wood); to puddle, work (clay), to mix (mortar); to weld, to pass, (iron, steel) through the rolling-mill; **acier corroyé,** welded, wrought, steel; shear-steel, rolled steel. **2.** *Hyd.E:* to line (basin, etc.) with puddle.

se corroyer, *Metall:* to weld.

corroyeur, -euse [kɔrwajœːr, -øːz], *s.* **1.** currier, leather dresser. **2.** *Metall:* blacksmith (in ironworks).

corrugateur [kɔr(r)ygatœːr], *a. & s.m. Anat:* corrugator (muscle).

corrugation [kɔr(r)ygasjɔ̃], *s.f.* corrugation; wrinkling (of skin).

corrupteur, -trice [kɔr(r)yptœːr, -tris]. **1.** *s.* corrupter, *f.* corruptress (of youth, etc.); suborner, briber (of witness, etc.); falsifier (of text, etc.). **2.** *a.* corrupt(ing) (influence, etc.); (of presents, etc.) given as a bribe.

corruptibilité [kɔr(r)yptibilite], *s.f.* corruptibility.

corruptible [kɔr(r)yptibl̥], *a.* corruptible; (*of pers.*) bribable, open to bribery.

corruptif, -ive [kɔr(r)yptif, -iːv], *a.* corruptive, corrupting.

corruption [kɔr(r)ypsjɔ̃], *s.f.* corruption. **1. c. de témoins,** suborning, bribing, bribery, of witnesses; *Jur:* **c. de mineurs,** debauchery of youth. **2.** putrefaction, tainting (of food, etc.); fouling (of air, etc.). **3.** (*a*) corruption, corruptness, depravity (of morals, tastes); (*b*) corrupt practices. **4.** corruptness (of a text).

corsage [kɔrsaːʒ], *s.m.* **1.** chest (of horse, stag, etc.); *A:* bust (of woman). **2.** (*a*) bodice, body (of dress); (*b*) blouse, *U.S:* waist.

corsagière [kɔrsaʒjɛːr], *s.f. Dressm:* bodice-hand.

corsaire [kɔrsɛːr], *a. & s.m.* **1.** (*ship*) (commerce-) raider; *A:* corsair, privateer. **2.** (*a*) corsair, privateer(sman); *F: A:* **c'est un vrai c.,** he is a regular shark; *Prov:* **à c., c. et demi,** set a thief to catch a thief; *Cost:* **pantalon c.,** pirate, toreador, pants; (*b*) *Croquet:* **(balle) c.,** rover.

corse[1] [kɔrs], *a. & s. Geog:* Corsican; *Hist:* **le C. à cheveux plats,** Napoleon.

Corse[2] **(la),** *Pr.n.f. Geog:* Corsica.

corsé [kɔrse], *a.* full-bodied (wine, etc.); *A:* thick, stout (cloth, etc.); *A:* strong, vigorous (horse, attack, etc.); **orchestration ample et corsée,** full and highly-coloured scoring; *F:* **repas c.,** substantial meal; **histoire corsée,** broad story; **roman c.,** spicy novel; **pièce à effets corsés,** blood-and-thunder play; **affaire corsée,** business that causes a great stir.

corselet [kɔrsəlɛ], *s.m.* **1.** *Ent: Mil: Cost:* corselet. **2.** *Cost:* bodice.

corser [kɔrse], *v.tr.* to give body, volume, flavour, to (sth.); to enliven (sth.); **c. du vin,** to give body to wine (by adding spirits); **c. l'action d'un drame,** to intensify the action of a drama; *F:* **c. un problème,** to make a problem harder to solve.

se corser, (*of weather, business*) to take a turn for the worse; *F:* **l'affaire se corse,** (i) the plot thickens; (ii) things are getting serious.

corset [kɔrsɛ], *s.m.* **1.** corset; *F:* pair of corsets; **c. orthopédique,** (orthopaedic) corset. **2.** *Nau: A:* **c. de sauvetage,** life-jacket. **3.** *Arb:* fence (round a tree to protect it from animals).

corseter [kɔrsəte], *v.tr.* **(je corsète, n. corsetons; je corsèterai)** to corset; to make corsets for (s.o.); to fit a corset on (s.o.).

corsetier, -ière [kɔrsətje, -jɛːr], *s.* corset-, staymaker.

corsite [kɔrsit], *s.f. Geol:* napoleonite, corsite.

corso [kɔrso], *s.m.* **1.** promenade, corso (*esp.* in Rome). **2.** procession of floral floats; *pl. corsi.*

cortège [kɔrtɛːʒ], *s.m.* **1.** train, retinue, suite, following (of sovereign, etc.); cortège; **ces infirmités forment le c. de la vieillesse,** these infirmities are the concomitants of, follow one in, old age. **2.** procession; (*a*) **aller en c.,** to walk in procession; *F:* to process; **c. funèbre,** burial procession; funeral (cortège); **c. nuptial,** bridal procession; **fermer le c.,** to bring up the rear; (*b*) **c. historique,** pageant. **3.** *Atom.Ph:* **c. électronique,** electron(ic) shell.

cortéger [kɔrteʒe], *v.tr.* **(je cortège, n. cortégeons; je cortégeai(s); je cortégerai)** *A: F:* to accompany, escort, (king, etc.) in a procession.

cortenais, -aise, -ois, -oise [kɔrtenɛ, -ɛːz, -wa, -waːz], *a. & s. Geog:* (native, inhabitant) of Corte [kɔrte].

Cortès [kɔrtɛs], *s.f.pl. Spanish Pol:* Cortes.

cortex [kɔrtɛks], *s.m. Anat: Bot:* cortex.

cortical, -aux [kɔrtikal, -o], *a. Anat: Bot:* cortical.

cortication [kɔrtikasjɔ̃], *s.f. Bot:* cortication.

corticectomie [kɔrtisɛktɔmi], *s.f. Surg:* corticectomy.

corticifère [kɔrtisifɛːr], *a. Bot:* corticiferous, cortex-bearing.

corticiforme [kɔrtisifɔrm], *a. Bot:* corticiform, bark-like.

corticine [kɔrtisin], *s.f. Bot: Ch:* corticin.

corticoïde [kɔrtikɔid], *s.m. Bio-Ch:* corticoid.

corticostéroïde [kɔrtikɔsterɔid], *s.m. Anat: Pharm:* corticosteroid.

corticostérone [kɔrtikɔsterɔn], *s.f. Physiol:* corticosterone.

cortico-surrénale [kɔrtikɔsyrrenal], *s.f. Anat:* cortex of the suprarenal gland.

corticosurrénalome [kɔrtikɔsyrrenaloːm], *s.m. Med:* corticosurrenaloma.

corticothérapie [kɔrtikɔterapi], *s.f. Med:* corticotherapy.

corticotrop(h)ine [kɔrtikɔtrɔfin], *s.f. Bio-Ch: Pharm:* corticotrophin, corticotropin.

cortine [kɔrtin], *s.f.* **1.** *Bot:* cortina. **2.** *Physiol:* cortin.

cortiqueux, -euse [kɔrtikø, -øːz], *a. Bot:* corticous, corticose.

cortisol [kɔrtizɔl], *s.m. Anat: Pharm:* hydrocortisone, cortisol.

cortisone [kɔrtizɔn], *s.f. Med:* cortisone.

corundophyllite [kɔrɔ̃dɔfilit], *s.f. Miner:* corundophilite.

coruscant [kɔryskɑ̃], *a. Lit:* coruscating, glittering; *F:* **dames en toilettes coruscantes,** ladies in dazzling get-up.

coruscation [kɔryskasjɔ̃], *s.f. Meteor:* coruscation.

corvéable [kɔrveabl̥], *a. & s.* **1.** *a. & s.* (*person*) liable to forced or statute labour; *F:* **il est c. à merci,** he's at everyone's beck and call; *s.a.* TAILLABLE. **2.** *a. Mil:* liable to fatigue duty.

corvée [kɔrve], *s.f.* **1.** *A:* forced or statute labour; corvée. **2.** *Mil: etc:* (*a*) fatigue-duty; *Navy:* duty; **c. de bois, de charbon, etc.,** fuel fatigue; **c. d'eau,** water(ing) fatigue; **c. de casernement, de quartier,** barrack fatigue; *U.S:* barracks police, police call; **c. de cuisine(s), d'ordinaire,** cookhouse fatigue; *U.S:* kitchen police; **c. supplémentaire,** extra-fatigue, extra-duty; **homme de c.,** fatigue-man; **service de c.,** fatigue-duty; **tenue de c.,** fatigue-dress; **désigner un homme de c.,** to detail, tell off, a man for a fatigue; **être de c.,** to be on fatigue(-duty); **être puni de c.,** to have extra-duty, extra-fatigue; **mettre de c.,** to put on extra-duty, on extra-fatigue; (*b*) **(détachement de) c.,** fatigue-party; **c. de bois, de charbon, etc.,** fuel party; **c. d'eau,** watering party; **c. de vivres,** ration party. **3.** thankless job; **quelle c.!** what a bind!

corvettard [kɔrvɛtaːr], *s.m. Navy: F:* lieutenant-commander.

corvette [kɔrvɛt], *s.f. Navy:* (*a*) corvette; (*b*) captain of a corvette.

corvidés [kɔrvide], *s.m.pl. Orn:* Corvidae.

corvin [kɔrvɛ̃], *a. Orn:* corvine.

corvusite [kɔrvyzit], *s.f. Miner:* corvusite.

corybante [kɔribɑ̃ːt], *s.m. Gr.Ant:* Corybant.

corybantiasme [kɔribɑ̃tjasm], *s.m. Gr.Ant:* corybantic frenzy; *Med:* corybantiasm.

corybantique [kɔribɑ̃tik], *a.* corybantic.

Coryce [kɔris], *Pr.n.f. A: Geog:* Corycia.

corycien, -ienne [kɔrisjɛ̃, -jɛn], *a. & s. A: Geog:* Corycian.

corycium [kɔrisjɔm], *s.m. Geol:* corycium.

corydale [kɔridal], *s.m.* **1.** *Ent:* corydalus. **2.** *Bot:* corydalis.

corydalidés [kɔridalide], *s.m.pl. Ent:* Corydalidae.

corydal(l)is [kɔridalis], *s.m.* **1.** *Ent:* corydalus. **2.** *Bot:* corydalis.

corylus [kɔrilys], *s.m. Arb:* corylus.

corymbe [kɔrɛ̃ːb], *s.m. Bot:* corymb.

corymbé [kɔrɛ̃be], **corymbeux, -euse** [kɔrɛ̃bø, -øːz], *a. Bot:* corymbose, corymbous.

corymbifère [kɔrɛ̃bifɛːr], **corymbiflore** [kɔrɛ̃biflɔːr], *a. Bot:* corymbiferous.

corymbiforme [kɔrɛ̃bifɔrm], *a. Bot:* corymbiform.

corynébactérie [kɔrinebakteri], *s.f.*, **corynébactérium** [kɔrinebakterjɔm], *s.m.* corynebacterium.

coryphée [kɔrife], *s.m.* **1.** *Gr.Drama:* coryphaeus, leader of the chorus. **2.** (*a*) *Th:* leader of the ballet, principal dancer; (*b*) *s.f.* ballerina in the *corps de ballet*; (*c*) leader, chief (of a party).

coryphène [kɔrifɛn], *s.m. Ich:* coryphene, dorado, dolphin (fish).

coryphodon [kɔrifɔdɔ̃], *s.m. Paleont:* coryphodon.

coryste(s) [kɔrist], *s.m. Crust:* corystes.

coryza [kɔriza], *s.m. Med:* coryza, cold in the head; **c. chronique,** chronic rhinitis.

cos [kɔs], *s.m. F: Mth:* cos.

cosalite [kɔzalit], *s.f. Miner:* cosalite.

cosaque [kɔzak]. **1.** *s.m.* cossack; *Mil:* **avant-poste à la c.,** cossack post; *F: O:* **c'est un c.,** he's a regular cossack, a brute. **2.** *s.f. A:* cossack dance.

cosécante [kɔsekɑ̃ːt], *s.f. Mth:* cosecant.

cosignataire [kosiɲatɛːr], *s.m.* co-signatory.

cosinus [kɔsinyːs], *s.m. Mth:* cosine.

cosinusoïde [kɔsinyzɔid], *s.f. Trig:* cosine curve.

cosismal, -aux [kɔsismal, -o], *a. Meteor:* coseismal.

cosiste [kɔsist], *s.f. Geog:* coseismal line.

Cosme [koːm], *Pr.n.m.* **1.** *Ecc.Hist:* Cosmas. **2.** *Ital.Hist:* Cosimo. **3.** *Gr.Hist:* governor of a Cretan city.

cosmétique [kɔsmetik], *a. & s.m.* cosmetic; **c. pour cils et sourcils,** eye make-up.

cosmétiquer [kɔsmetike], *v.tr.* to put cosmetic(s) on (one's hair); **moustache cosmétiquée,** waxed moustache.

cosmétologie [kɔsmetɔlɔʒi], *s.f.* cosmetology.

cosmétologiste [kɔsmetɔlɔʒist], *s.* cosmetologist; beautician.

cosmia [kɔsmja], **cosmie** [kɔsmi], *s.f. Ent:* cosmia.

cosmique [kɔsmik], *a.* cosmic(al); *Ph:* **rayons cosmiques,** cosmic rays; **rayonnement c.,** cosmic radiation; **voyage c.,** space flight.

cosmiquement [kɔsmikmɑ̃], *adv.* cosmically.

cosmo- [kɔsmɔ], *pref.* cosmo-; **cosmogénie,** cosmogeny.

cosmobiologie [kɔsmɔbiɔlɔʒi], *s.f.* cosmobiology.

cosmodrome [kɔsmɔdrom], *s.m.* launching base (for spacecraft).

cosmogénie [kɔsmɔʒeni], *s.f.* cosmogeny.

cosmogénique [kɔsmɔʒenik], *a.* cosmogenic.

cosmogonie [kɔsmɔgɔni], *s.f.* cosmogony.

cosmogonique [kɔsmɔgɔnik], *a.* cosmogonic(al).

cosmographe [kɔsmɔgraf], *s.m. & f.* cosmographer.

cosmographie [kɔsmɔgrafi], *s.f.* cosmography.

cosmographique [kɔsmɔgrafik], *a.* cosmographic(al).

cosmoline [kɔsmɔlin], *s.f. A:* cosmoline, heavy petroleum grease.

cosmologie [kɔsmɔlɔʒi], *s.f.* cosmology.

cosmologique [kɔsmɔlɔʒik], *a.* cosmological.

cosmologiste [kɔsmɔlɔʒist], **cosmologue** [kɔsmɔlɔg], *s.m.* cosmologist.

cosmonaute [kɔsmɔnoːt], *s.m.f.* cosmonaut.

cosmonautique [kɔsmɔnotik], *s.f.* cosmonautics, *F:* space travel.

cosmonette [kɔsmɔnɛt], *s.f.* spacewoman, cosmonette.

cosmopolite [kɔsmɔpɔlit]. **1.** *a.* cosmopolitan (life, etc.). **2.** *s.m.& f.* cosmopolitan, cosmopolite.

cosmopolitisme [kɔsmɔpɔlitism], *s.m.* cosmopolit(an)ism.

cosmorama [kɔsmɔrama], *s.m.* cosmorama.

cosmos [kɔsmɔs], *s.m.* **1.** cosmos. **2.** *Bot:* cosmos.

cosmotron [kɔsmɔtrɔ̃], *s.m. Atom.Ph:* cosmotron, bevatron, proton-synchroton.

cosphimètre [kɔsfimɛtr̥], *s.m.* power-factor meter.

cossard [kɔsaːr]. **2.** *s.m. Orn:* buzzard. **2.** (*a*) *s.m. P:* lazy fellow, sluggard; (*b*) *a. P:* lazy.

cosse[1] [kɔs], *s.f.* **1.** (*a*) pod, husk, hull (of leguminous plants); (*b*) *Leath:* **parchemin en c.,** unscraped sheepskin. **2.** (*a*) *Nau:* thimble, eyelet (of rope); **c. de l'estrope,** eye of the rope, rope-thimble; (*b*) *El: Elcs:* **cosse (de câble),** eye, lug, tag, terminal, terminal-connector (of cable); **c. à œillet,** spade lug, terminal; **c. à ressort,** clip (terminal); (*c*) *Metalw:* **c. à souder,** soldering-lug, -tag; sweating-lug. **3.** *P:* **avoir la c.,** to feel lazy, slack, half-asleep. **4.** *Geol: Min:* overburden; overlay, top (of slate-quarry).

cosse[2], *s.m.* = COSSUS.

cosser [kɔse], *v.i.* (*of rams*) to butt; *A: F:* **c. contre qch.,** to run one's head against sth.

cossettes [kɔset], *Com:* (*a*) *s.f.pl.* dry chicory roots; (*b*) *s.f.sg. Sug.-R:* **cossette (de betterave),** cossette.

cossidés [kɔside], *s.m.pl. Ent:* Cossidae.

cosson[1] [kɔsɔ̃], *s.m. Ent: F:* **1.** pea-beetle, -weevil. **2.** = COSSUS.

cosson[2], *s.m.* new shoot (on cut vine-stock).

cossu [kɔsy], *a.* **1.** *A:* (*of beans, etc.*) strong in the pod, well-podded. **2.** *F:* (*a*) wealthy, well-to-do, monied (person); rich (dress); (*b*) *A:* rich (story).

cossûment [kɔsymɑ̃], *adv.* (*rare*) *F:* richly, wealthily.

cossus [kɔsyːs], *s.m. Ent:* cossus; **c. gâte-bois,** goat-moth.

costal, -aux [kɔstal, -o], *a. Anat:* costal.

costard [kɔstaːr], *s.m. P: Cost:* man's suit.

costaricain, -aine [kɔstarikɛ̃, -ɛn], **costaricien, -ienne** [kɔstarisjɛ̃, -jɛn], *a. & s. Geog:* Costa Rican.

costaud, *f.* **costaude** [kɔsto, -oːd], *a. & s. F:* strapping, beefy, hefty (individual); solid (building, etc.); tough (material, etc.); (*of drink*) **ça c'est c.!** that's powerful, strong! *Cy:* **les costauds de la course,** the stalwarts of racing.

costectomie [kɔstɛktɔmi], *s.f. Surg:* costectomy.

costiase [kɔstjaːz], *s.f. Ich: Path:* costiasis.

costière [kɔstjɛːr], *s.f.* **1.** *pl. Metall:* tuyere-, twyer-sides, side hearthstones (of blast furnace). **2.** *Th:* cut (in stage flooring).

costo- [kɔstɔ-], *pref. Anat:* costo-.

costo-abdominal [kɔstɔabdɔminal], *a. Anat:* costo-abdominal; *pl. costo-abdominaux.*

costotome [kɔstɔtɔm], *s.m. Surg:* costotome.

costresse [kɔstrɛs], *s.f. Min:* extraction drift.

costule [kɔstyl], *s.f. Z:* costula.

costume [kɔstym], *s.m.* costume, dress; uniform; apparel; **c. national,** national costume; **c. de cour,** court dress; **c. de carnaval,** fancy dress; **c. de golf,** plus-fours; **en grand c.,** in full dress, (of diplomat, *préfet,* etc.) in full uniform; **c. de cérémonie,** formal dress; **en c. ecclésiastique,** in clerical garb; **drôle de c.,** queer rig-out; *Th:* **répéter en c.,** to have a dress rehearsal; *s.a.* BAIN 1.

costumé [kɔstyme], *a.* **bal c.,** fancy-dress ball.

costumer [kɔstyme], *v.tr.* to dress (s.o.) (up); **se c. en Turc,** to dress up as a Turk.

costumier, -ière [kɔstymje, -jɛːr], *s.* **1.** costumier, dealer in (fancy) costumes. **2.** *Th:* wardrobe-keeper.

cosujet [kosyʒɛ], *s.m.* fellow-subject.

cosy [kozi], *s.m. Dom.Ec:* tea-, egg-, cosy.

cosy(-corner) [kozi(-kɔrnɛːr)], *s.m. Furn:* corner divan-bed surrounded by right-angle bookshelves and cupboards; *pl. cosy-corners.*

cotable [kɔtabl̥], *a. St.Exch: Fin:* quotable (security, etc.).

cotangente [kotɑ̃ʒɑ̃ːt], *s.f. Mth:* cotangent.

cotation [kɔtasjɔ̃], *s.f. Fin:* quotation, quoting, *Tch:* **c. fonctionnelle,** method of illustrating the most important dimensions of machine parts on the drawing.

cote [kɔt], *s.f.* **1.** (*a*) quota, share, proportion (of expense, taxes, etc.); **c. mal taillée,** (i) compounding in gross (of account), rough and ready settlement; (ii) *F:* rough and ready compromise; **faire une c. mal taillée,** *F:* to call it square; (*b*) *Adm:* assessment; **c. foncière,** assessment on land; **c. mobilière,** assessment on income; *W.Tel: T.V:* **c. d'écoute,** popularity rating (of programme); (*c*) *Typ:* take (of each compositor). **2.** (*a*) *Mec.E: etc:* (indication of) dimensions; **cotes d'une machine,** dimension figures of a machine; **usiné aux cotes requises,** tooled to the required dimensions; **ligne de c., trait de c.,** dimension line; **cotes d'encombrement,** overall dimensions; **c. d'origine,** standard size; **c. de réalésage,** reaming allowance; **c. nominale, c. normale,** nominal, normal, size; **usiner à la c. de finition,** to finish to size; (*c*) *Surv:* altitude (of a point in figures); elevation (above sea level); height; **c. de niveau, de nivellement,** height, reference, to datum plane, to datum level; **c. de cent pieds au-dessus (du niveau) de la mer,** elevation of a hundred feet above sea level; *Hyd.E:* **c. d'alerte,** critical level, danger point; *Mil.Surv:* **la c. 304,** hill 304; (*d*) reading (on topographical instrument); **cotes lues sur la mire,** rod-readings; **c. de profondeur,** depth-reading; (*e*) *Mil:* **cotes d'une position,** co-ordinates of a position (on grid map). **3.** (*a*) *Com: Jur:* (classification) mark, letter, figure, number (of document, etc.); (library) shelf-mark, press-mark; (*b*) *Nau:* character, classification (of ship); **de première c. (au Lloyd),** A1 (at Lloyd's). **4.** (*a*) *St.Exch: Com:* quotation; **c. des prix,** (i) share-list; (ii) *Com:* list of prices, price-current; **actions inscrites à la c.,** listed shares; **marché hors c.,** curb market; *St.Exch:* **admission à la c.,** admission to quotation; *F:* **c. d'amour,** (i) favouritism; (ii) confidential report (on s.o.); (iii) arbitrary appreciation of a subordinate by a superior; **avoir la c.,** to be in the public eye; in the news; **il n'a plus la c.,** his star has set; **avoir la c. auprès de qn,** to be in s.o.'s good books, to be popular with s.o.; (*b*) *Turf:* **c. d'un cheval,** odds on or against a horse; **quelle c. fait son cheval?** what is the betting on his horse? **forte, faible, c.,** long, short, odds or price; (*c*) *Sch:* marks awarded (for exercise, etc.).

côte [koːt], *s.f.* **1.** rib; (*a*) *Anat:* **vraies côtes,** true, sternal, ribs; **fausses côtes,** false, short, asternal, ribs; **côtes flottantes,** floating ribs; *F:* **se tenir les côtes de rire,** to hold one's sides with laughter; **on lui compterait les côtes,** he is nothing but skin and bone, he is a regular skeleton; **avoir les côtes en long,** to be lazy; **être (sorti) de la c. de Jupiter, de Charlemagne, de Saint Louis,** to be of noble birth; *s.a.* ADAM; *Eng.Hist:* **Côtes de fer,** Ironsides; *Cu:* **c. de bœuf,** rib of beef; **c. d'aloyau,** wing-rib; **côtes (découvertes) de porc,** spare-ribs (of pork); **c. première,** loin-chop; *adv.phr.* **c. à c.,** (i) side by side; (ii) cheek by jowl; **marcher c. à c. avec qn,** to walk alongside of s.o.; (*b*) **côtes d'un navire, d'une colonne, d'un melon, etc.,** ribs of a ship, of a column, of a melon, etc.; **c. d'une feuille,** midrib of a leaf; **étoffe à côtes,** ribbed, corded, material; **tapis en caoutchouc à côtes,** grooved rubber matting. **2.** (*a*) slope (of hill); *Civ.E:* gradient; **vitesse en c.,** speed uphill, on a gradient; *Aut:* **départ en c.,** hill-start; **rendement en c. d'une auto,** hill-climbing efficiency of a motor car; *Sp:* **course de c.,** hill climb; (*b*) hill, rise; **à mi-côte,** halfway up, down, the hill. **3.** coast, shore; **les côtes de (la) France,** the coast of France; *Nau:* **c. au vent,** weather-shore; **c. sous le vent,** lee-shore; **faire c.,** to beach, run aground; **jeter un navire à la c.,** drive a ship ashore, to strand a ship; *F:* **être à la c.,** to be on the rocks, on one's beam ends, hard up; **frère de la c.,** beachcomber; *Geog: A:* **La Côte de l'Or,** the Gold Coast; *s.a.* ARGENT 1, AZUR 1, ÉMERAUDE 1, OPALE 1, VERMEIL 1.

côté [kote], *s.m.* **1.** side (of human body); **être couché sur le c.,** to be lying on one's side; *F:* **être sur le c.,** (i) to be laid up; (ii) to be in a bad way; **il est assis à mes côtés,** he is sitting by my side; **être toujours aux côtés de qn,** to dance attendance on s.o. **2.** (*a*) side (of mountain, road, triangle, sheet of paper, table, etc.); wall (of gun-turret, etc.); **table carrée de deux mètres de c.,** table two metres square; **se parler d'un c. à l'autre de la table,** to talk to each other across the table; **passer de l'autre c. de la rue,** to cross the street; **demeurer de l'autre c. de la rue,** to live across the street, on the other side of the street; **appartement c. midi,** flat with southern aspect; *Ten:* **le choix du service ou du c.,** the choice of service or end, side or service; *Cu:* **haut c. de mouton,** target of mutton; **la tour penche d'un c.,** the tower inclines on one side, leans sideways; *Nau:* **présenter le c. à qch.,** to be broadside on to sth.; **navire qui a un faux c.,** lop-sided ship; **navire sur le c.,** ship on her beam-ends; *s.a.* VENT 1; *Typ:* **c. de première,** outer form; **c. de deux,** inner form; (*b*) **le bon c., le mauvais c., d'une affaire,** the good side, bad side, aspect, of a matter; **le vent vient du bon c.,** the wind is in the right quarter; **prendre les choses par le bon c.,** to look on the bright side of things; **c'est son c. faible,** that is his weak spot; **se marier avec qn du c. gauche,** to cohabit, live, with s.o. without benefit of clergy; **être du c. gauche,** to be illegitimate; **d'un c. à l'autre,** from side to side; **d'un c. . . ., de l'autre c. . . .,** on the one hand . . ., on the other hand . . .; **de mon c. . . .,** for my part . . .; **par certains côtés,** in certain respects, in some ways; **de notre c. nous vous prions de vouloir bien . . .,** for our part we would request you to . . .; **prendre une plaisanterie par le, du, bon c.,** to take a joke in good part; **elle écrit beaucoup de son c.,** she writes a great deal on her own account; **nous venons de visiter la ville, chacun de notre c.,** we have been visiting the town, each on our own (account); (*c*) side, direction, way; **de tous (les) côtés,** on all sides, far and wide; **emprunter, devoir, de l'argent de tous les côtés,** to borrow, to owe, money right and left; **chercher qch. de tous côtés,** to look for sth. high and low, up and down; **les balles arrivaient de tous les côtés,** the bullets came from all quarters; **vous n'êtes jamais venu de nos côtés?** you have never come our way? **courir de c. et d'autre,** to run about in all directions; **se diriger du c. de Paris,** to go towards, in the direction of, Paris; **il habitait du c. de Hampstead,** he lived Hampstead way; **la maison se trouve sur les Champs-Élysées du c. de l'Étoile,** the house is at the Étoile end of the Champs-Élysées; **se ranger d'un c.,** to take sides; **se ranger du c. des plus forts,** to take the side of, to take sides with, to side with, the stronger, the strongest; **les parents du c. du père,** the relations on the father's side; **venez de ce c.,** come (i) this way, (ii) on this side; **de ce c.-ci, -là,** on this side, on that side; **je ne peux pas regarder des deux côtés,** I can't look both ways; **vous ne regardez pas du bon c.,** you are not looking the right way, in the right direction; **ils s'en allèrent chacun de son c.,** they departed each one his own way, they went their several ways; **de quel c.?** in which direction? **de quel c. est l'hôtel?** whereabouts is the hotel? **je sais que vous êtes de leur c.,** I know you are in sympathy with them; (*d*) **(du) c. (de la) vitesse, cette voiture est remarquable,** as regards, in the matter of, speed this car is remarkable. **3.** *adv.phr.* (*a*) **de c.,** on one side, sideways; **porter son chapeau de c.,** to wear one's hat on one side; **faire un saut de c.,** to leap aside, to jump sideways; **pas de c.,** side-step; **vent de c.,** side-wind; **regard de c.,** sidelong glance; **mettre qch. de c.,** to put sth. aside, on one side; **mettre**

de l'argent de c., to put, set, money by; to save money (for the future); **laisser de c. ses vêtements d'hiver,** to discard, cast (off), one's winter clothing; **laisser qn de c.,** to neglect s.o.; **se tenir de c.,** to hold oneself apart; **mettre de c. un travail,** to lay aside a piece of work; *Equit:* **porter un cheval de c.,** to passage a horse; (*b*) **à c.,** to one side, near; **la maison est tout à c.,** the house is quite near, hard by; **les gens d'à c.,** the people next door; **mon voisin d'à c.,** my next door neighbour; **tirer à c.,** to miss the mark; **répondre à c.,** to miss the point (in one's answer); *Com:* **articles à c.,** side-lines; *prep.phr.* **à c. de,** by the side of, next to, beside; **il se tenait à c. de moi,** he stood at, by, my side; he stood beside me; **il se tenait tout à c. de moi,** he stood close beside me, at my elbow; **à c. l'un de l'autre,** side by side; **travailler à c. de qn,** to work side by side with s.o.; **il habite à c. de nous,** he lives next door to us; **c'est à c. de la question,** that is beside the question; **mes maux sont petits à c. des vôtres,** my troubles are small compared with yours; **il n'est rien à c. de vous,** *F:* he can't hold a candle to you.

coteau, -eaux [kɔto, koto], *s.m.* slope, hillside; hillock; *occ.* vineyard; **c. boisé,** wooded hillside.

côtelé [kotle], *a. Tex:* ribbed, corduroy (velvet); corded (material); **bas côtelés,** ribbed stockings.

côtelette [kotlɛt, kɔ-], *s.f.* **1.** *Cu:* (*a*) (mutton) cutlet; **c. à manche,** neck chop; **côtelettes premières,** best end of the neck; (*b*) **c. de filet,** loin-chop; **c. de gigot,** chump chop; (*c*) **c. de veau,** veal cutlet; **c. de porc,** pork chop; *F:* **favoris en c.,** *F:* **côtelettes,** mutton-chop whiskers. **2.** *pl. Th: P: A:* **manger des côtelettes,** to be greeted with applause.

cote-part [kɔtpaːr], *s.f.* = QUOTE-PART.

coter [kɔte], *v.tr.* **1.** to impose a contribution on (s.o.); to assess. **2.** *Mec.E: Surv: etc:* to mark the dimensions on, to dimension (drawing, etc.); to put down references on (maps, etc.); **c. les niveaux d'un chemin de fer,** to mark the levels of a railway; **croquis coté,** dimensioned sketch; *Surv:* **point coté,** (i) reference point, landmark, (ii) spot height (on map, etc.). **3.** (*a*) *Com: Jur:* to classify, number, letter (documents, etc.); (*b*) *Nau:* to class (ship). **4.** (*a*) *Com: St.Exch:* to quote (price, etc.); (*b*) **très coté,** (i) *Turf:* well-backed; (ii) highly thought-of, esteemed. **5.** *Sch:* to mark, award marks for (exercise, etc.).

coterie [kɔtri], *s.f.* (political, literary) set, clique, circle, coterie.

cot(t)eron [kɔtrɔ̃], *s.m. Hist.Cost:* sleeveless peasant blouse.

coteur [kɔtœːr], *s.m. St.Exch:* marking clerk.

cothurne [kɔtyrn], *s.m. Ant:* cothurnus, buskin; *Lit:* **chausser le c.,** (i) to write tragedies; (ii) to act in tragedy; (iii) to affect a tragic manner; *cf.* BRODEQUIN.

cotice [kɔtis], *s.f. Her:* cot(t)ise.

coticé [kɔtise], *a. Her:* cotised.

cotidal, -aux [kɔtidal, -o], *a.* co-tidal.

côtier, -ière [kotje, -jɛːr]. **1.** *a.* (*a*) coast(ing) (pilot, etc.); coastal (defence, population, etc.); coastwise (trade, etc.); inshore (fishery); **navigation côtière,** coasting; (*b*) **chemin c.,** coast road; **fleuve c.,** coastal river, small river flowing into the sea; (*c*) *Oc:* **zone côtière,** coastal zone. **2.** *s.m.* (*a*) coaster, coasting-vessel; (*b*) coasting-pilot; (*c*) trace-horse. **3.** *s.f.* **côtière;** (*a*) range of hills; (*b*) *Hort:* sloping-bed; (*c*) *Brew:* malt-floor; (*d*) *Metall:* = COSTIÈRE 1; (*e*) (one side of) mould (for lead pipes).

cotignac [kɔtiɲak], *s.m.* quince marmalade.

cotignelle [kɔtiɲɛl], *s.f.* quince wine.

cotillon [kɔtijɔ̃], *s.m.* **1.** petticoat; *F:* girl; **homme qui court le c.,** man who runs after women. **2.** *Danc:* (*a*) cotill(i)on; **coiffure de c.,** paper cap, hat; **accessoires de c.,** carnival novelties; (*b*) souvenir (given away at public dance).

cotillonner [kɔtijɔne], *v.i. O:* **1.** *Danc:* to dance the cotillon. **2.** *F:* to run after women.

cotillonneur, -euse [kɔtijɔnœːr, -øːz], *s. O: Danc:* cotillon dancer.

cotinga [kɔtɛ̃ga], *s.m. Orn:* cotinga; *F:* chatterer.

cotingidés [kɔtɛ̃ʒide], *s.m.pl. Orn:* Cotingidae.

cotir [kɔtiːr], *v.tr. Dial:* (*of hail, etc.*) to bruise (fruit).

cotisant, -ante [kɔtizɑ̃, -ɑ̃t], *a.* & *s.* paying member; subscriber (de, to).

cotisation [kɔtizasjɔ̃], *s.f.* **1.** clubbing together (to raise a sum, etc.). **2.** assessment (of tax-payer). **3.** quota, share; contribution (to common fund); subscription (to club, etc.); **c. d'admission,** entrance fee; **assurance à cotisations,** contributory insurance; **percevoir les cotisations,** to collect contributions.

cotiser [kɔtize], *v.tr.* **1.** *Adm:* **c. qn à tant,** to assess s.o. at so much. **2.** *abs. F:* to contribute (**pour,** towards).

se cotiser, to subscribe, to club together (in order to raise sum); to get up a subscription.

cotissure [kɔtisyːr], *s.f. Dial:* bruise (on fruit).

côtoiement [kotwamɑ̃], *s.m.* coming into contact with (society, a situation, etc.).

coton [kɔtɔ̃]. **1.** *s.m.* cotton; *Bot: Ind:* (*a*) **c. en longue soie,** black-seed cotton; **c. en courte soie,** green-seed cotton; **c. en liane, c. brut,** raw cotton, cotton-wool; **fil de c., c. à coudre,** sewing cotton; **c. retors,** cotton thread; **c. à broder,** embroidery cotton, nun's-thread; **c. à repriser,** *O:* pla(i)t, darning cotton; **ruban de c.,** tape; **c. (à) longues fibres,** long-staple cotton; **huile de c.,** cotton-seed oil; (*b*) *P:* trouble, difficulty; *F:* **filer un mauvais c.,** to be in a bad way (in health or business); *P:* **il va y avoir du c.,** there's going to be trouble, we're going to catch it; (*c*) *Bot:* **c. sauvage,** silk-weed, swallow-wort; (*d*) *Exp:* **c. azotique, c. nitré, c. fulminant,** *Nav: F:* **c.** = COTON-POUDRE; (*e*) **c. minéral,** mineral wool, slag-wool. **2.** *s.m.* (*a*) cotton-wool; *F:* **se sentir tout en c.,** to feel flabby; *F:* **j'ai, je me sens, les jambes en c.,** (i) my legs feel like cotton-wool; (ii) I feel (all) weak at the knees (with emotion, etc.); **élever un enfant dans du c.,** to (molly-)coddle a child, to bring up a child in cotton-wool; *Med:* **c. hydrophile,** cotton-wool; (*b*) down (on plants); (*c*) fluff (on cloth, etc.); (*of cloth*) **jeter son c.,** to get fluffy, to shed its fluff; (*d*) **c. de verre,** glass-wool. **3.** *a. F:* difficult; **ça, c'est plutôt c.!** that's rather difficult.

coton-collodion [kɔtɔ̃kɔlɔdjɔ̃], *s.m. Exp:* pyroxyle, pyroxylin(e), collodion cotton; *U.S:* pyro-collodion.

cotonéaster [kɔtɔneastɛːr], *s.m. Bot:* cotoneaster.

cotonnade [kɔtɔnad], *s.f.* (*a*) cotton fabric; (*b*) *pl.* cotton goods.

cotonnage [kɔtɔnaːʒ], *s.m.* (*of raw silk*) shedding of fluff (during reeling).

cotonne [kɔtɔn], *s.f. Tex:* cotton (fabric).

cotonné, [kɔtɔne], *a.* **voile cotonnée,** cottoned, chafed, sail; **menton c.,** downy chin; **poire cotonnée,** sleepy pear; **cheveux cotonnés,** woolly hair.

cotonner [kɔtɔne]. **1.** *v.tr.* (*a*) to cover (sth.) with cotton, with down; (*b*) to wad; to pad (with cotton-wool). **2.** *v.i.* & *pr.* (*a*) to become covered with down; **fruit qui se cotonne,** fruit that (i) becomes covered with down, (ii) becomes woolly, sleepy; (*b*) (*of material*) to become fluffy.

cotonnerie [kɔtɔnri], *s.f.* **1.** cotton-growing. **2.** (*a*) cotton plantation; (*b*) cotton mill.

cotonnette [kɔtɔnɛt], *s.f.* cotton (fabric).

cotonneux, -euse [kɔtɔnø, -øːz], *a.* cottony; downy (leaf, etc.); fleecy (cloud); **fruits c.,** woolly fruit; **poire cotonneuse,** sleepy pear; **style c.,** woolly style; **jambes cotonneuses,** shaky legs.

cotonnier, -ière [kɔtɔnje, -jɛːr]. **1.** *a.* cotton (industry, products, etc.). **2.** *s.* cotton worker, spinner. **3.** *s.m. Bot:* cotton plant. **4.** *s.f. Bot:* **cotonnière,** cottonweed, cudweed.

cotonnine [kɔtɔnin], *s.f.* cotton canvas, cotton sailcloth.

coton-poudre [kɔtɔ̃pudr̥], *s.m. Exp:* gun-cotton, nitrated cotton; *U.S:* nitrocotton, pyrocotton; *pl. cotons-poudre.*

côtoyer [kotwaje], *v.tr.* (**je côtoie, n. côtoyons; je côtoierai**) **1.** to coast along, keep close to, hug (shore, etc.); to skirt (forest, etc.). **2.** to border on (river, etc.); **conceptions qui côtoient la vérité,** conceptions bordering on the truth; **cette année-là je côtoyais la misère,** that year I came close to being destitute; **il avait rarement côtoyé des gens simples,** he had rarely come into contact with simple people.

cotre [kɔtr̥], *s.m. Nau:* cutter.

cotret [kɔtrɛ], *s.m.* **1.** *O:* (*a*) faggot, bundle (of wood); (*b*) stick (of faggot); *F:* **jambes de c.,** spindle-shanks; **sec comme un c.,** as thin as a lath; *A:* **administrer de l'huile de c. à qn,** to give s.o. a good drubbing, a good lathering. **2.** *Text:* wooden pieces supporting the warp beams.

cotriade [kɔtrijad], *s.f. Cu:* (Breton) fish soup.

cottage [kɔtaːʒ], *s.m.* (country) cottage.

cotte[1] [kɔt], *s.f. Cost:* (*a*) *A:* coat, tunic; *Mil. Cost:* **c. d'armes,** (i) tunic (worn over armour), cyclas, cyclatoun, gypoun; (ii) coat of banded mail; **c. de mailles,** coat of mail; **vêtu d'une c. de mailles,** clad in mail; (*b*) *A:* short, skirt, petticoat; (*c*) (workmen's) overalls.

cotte[2], *s.m. Ich:* cottus, *F:* miller's-thumb, bullhead.

cotte-hardie [kɔtardi], *s.f. A.Cost:* cote-hardie; *pl. cottes-hardies.*

cotterézien, -ienne [kɔtrezjɛ̃, -jɛn], *a.* & *s. Geog:* (native, inhabitant) of Villers-Cotterets [vilɛr-kɔtrɛ].

cottérite [kɔterit], *s.f. Miner:* cotterite.

cotte-scorpion [kɔtskɔrpjɔ̃], *s.m. Ich:* hardhead; *pl. cottes-scorpions.*

cottidés [kɔtide], *s.m.pl. Ich:* Cottidae.

Cottiennes [kɔtjɛn], *a.f.pl. A.Geog:* Cottian (Alps).

cotton [kɔtɔ̃], *s.m.* knitting machine (for making several pairs of full-fashioned stockings simultaneously).

cotula [kɔtyla], *s.f.,* **cotule** [kɔtyl], *s.f. Bot:* cotula.

cotutelle [kɔtytɛl], *s.f. Jur:* joint guardianship (of husband with wife).

cotuteur, -trice [kɔtytœːr, -tris], *s. Jur:* joint guardian.

cotyle[1] [kɔtil], *s.f.* **1.** *Gr.Ant:* cotyle. **2.** *Anat:* cotyle, cotyla, acetabulum.

cotyle[2], *s.f. Orn:* cotile, sand-martin.

cotylédon [kɔtiledɔ̃], *s.m.* **1.** *Anat: Bot:* cotyledon; *Bot:* seed-leaf, seed-lobe. **2.** *Bot:* navelwort, pennywort.

cotylédonaire [kɔtiledɔnɛːr], *a. Anat: Bot:* cotyledonary.

cotylédoné [kɔtiledɔne], *a. Bot:* cotyledonous.

cotylifère [kɔtilifɛːr], *a. Bot:* cotyligerous.

cotyloïde [kɔtilɔid], *a. Anat:* cotyloid(al); **cavité c.,** acetabulum.

cotylosauriens [kɔtilɔsɔrjɛ̃], *s.m.pl. Paleont:* Cotylosauria, Cotylosaurians.

cotype [kɔtip], *s.m. Biol:* cotype.

cou [ku], *s.m.* **1.** neck (of animal, bottle, etc.); **la peau du c.,** the scruff of the neck; **rentrer le c. entre, dans, les épaules,** to make oneself small; **couper le c. à qn,** to behead s.o.; **tendre le c.,** (i) to lay one's head on the block; (ii) to offer oneself as a ready victim; (iii) to crane one's neck (in order to see); **serrer le c. de qn, à qn,** (i) to strangle s.o.; (ii) *F:* to wring s.o.'s neck; **se jeter, sauter, au c. de qn,** to throw one's arms round s.o.'s neck; **il me tenait par le c.,** he held me round the neck; *Min:* **travail à c. tordu,** work lying on one's side; *F:* **être dans les dettes jusqu'au c.,** to be up to the eyes in debt; **prendre ses jambes à son c.,** to take to one's heels. **2.** *Hyd.E: etc:* **c. de cygne,** swan-, goose-neck. **3.** *Orn:* **c. rouge,** redbreast; **c. tors,** wry-neck.

couac [kwak]. **1.** *s.m. Mus:* squawk, goose-note; *F:* goose (on clarinet, etc.). **2.** *int.* (*cry of raven, etc.*) arrk!

couagga [kwaga], *s.m. Z:* quagga.

couaille [kwaːj], *s.f.* (*wool*) dag, dagging; britch, breech.

couaquer [kwake], *v.i.* to croak like a raven.

couard [kwaːr]. **1.** *a.* (*a*) *Lit: Dial:* cowardly; **chien c.,** skulking hound; (*b*) *Her:* **lion c.,** lion coward, *coué.* **2.** *s.m.* coward. **3.** *s.m. Cu:* buttock, round (of beef).

couardement [kwardəmɑ̃], *adv. A:* in a cowardly manner, cravenly.

couardise [kwardiːz], *s.f. O:* cowardice, cowardliness, cravenness.

cou-blanc [kublɑ̃], *s.m. Orn: F:* wheatear; *pl. cous-blancs.*

coucal [kukal], *s.m. Orn:* coucal.

couch [kuʃ], *s.m.* recipient for collecting resin (from pine tree).

couchage [kuʃaːʒ], *s.m.* **1.** (*a*) lying in bed; (*b*) bed, night's lodging; (*c*) **(matériel de) c.,** bedding, bedclothes; **sac de c.,** sleeping bag; *Nau:* **postes de c.,** berthing; (*d*) *P:* sexual intercourse. **2.** layering (of plants). **3.** coating (of paper, photographic plate, film, etc.).

couchant [kuʃɑ̃]. **1.** *a.* (*a*) **soleil c.,** setting sun, sunset; (*b*) *Ven:* **chien c.,** setter; **faire le chien c. auprès de qn,** to fawn on, cringe to, s.o. **2.** *s.m.* (*a*) sunset, setting of the sun; **être à son c.,** (i) (*of fame, etc.*) to be on the decline, on the wane; (ii) (*of pers.*) to be nearing the end of one's life; (*b*) **le c.,** the west; **les pays du c.,** the countries in the west; the West.

couche [kuʃ], *s.f.* **1.** (*a*) *Lit:* bed, couch; **c. nuptiale,** marriage (bed); (*b*) *usu. pl.* childbed, confinement, labour; **femme en couche(s),** woman in labour; **couches laborieuses, pénibles,** difficult (child)birth; **suite de couche(s),** period following childbirth; *Med:* **suites de couches,** lochia; **retour de couches,** first menstruation after childbirth; **fausse c.,** miscarriage; **trois enfants d'une même c.,** triplets; **elle est morte en couches,** she died in childbirth; (*c*) **c. (de bébé),** (baby's) napkin; *F:* nappy, *U.S:* diaper. **2.** (*a*) *Geol:* bed, layer, stratum; **c. de houille,** coal bed, seam; **c. pétrolifère,** oil-bearing stratum; **c. aquifère,**

aquifer; *Agr:* **c. arable,** topsoil; *Oc:* **c. diffusante profonde,** deep scattering layer; *Av:* **c. limite,** boundary layer; (*b*) *Arb:* **c. annuelle,** annual ring, zone; **arbre à couches minces, épaisses,** fine-, broad-, ringed tree, fine-, broad-, zoned tree; *Hort:* **c. de fumier,** hot bed, forcing bed; **semer sur c.,** to sow in heat; **champignons de c.,** cultivated mushrooms; (*c*) **couches sociales,** social strata, classes of society; (*d*) coat, coating (of paint, etc.); **c. d'apprêt,** primer; **c. de fond,** undercoat; **c. de teinte,** final coat; **c. de glace (sur un objet),** sheet of ice (on sth.); **c. de neige,** layer of snow; *Phot:* **c. de gélatine,** film of gelatine; (*e*) *Meteor:* **c. de Heaviside,** Heaviside layer; (*f*) *P:* **il en a, il en tient, une c.!** he's absolutely daft! did you ever see such an idiot! *O:* **se donner une belle c.,** to drink oneself blind. **3.** (*a*) *Const:* ground sill, sole timber; **c. isolante, hydrofuge, imperméable,** damp (proof) course; *Civ.E:* **c. de fondation,** base course, bottom layer; **c. de liaison,** binder (course); **c. de roulement,** carpet, surface, layer; (*b*) *Mec.E:* **arbre de c.,** engine shaft, main shaft, power shaft. **4.** *Sm.a:* (*a*) **mettre un fusil à la c. de qn,** to fit a rifle to s.o.; (*b*) **plaque de c.,** butt plate. **5.** *Atom.Ph:* **couche(s) électronique(s),** electron shell (in atom); **c. nucléaire,** nuclear shell; **c. électronique externe,** outer shell; **c. électronique interne,** inner shell, core. **6.** *Anat:* **c. cornée,** stratum corneum; **c. de Malpighi,** Malpighian layer; **c. granuleuse,** stratum granulosum.

couché, [kuʃe], *a.* (*a*) lying (down), recumbent, prone (position); **être c.,** to be in bed, to have gone to bed; **à soleil c.,** at sunset; (*b*) **blés couchés,** lodged wheat; **lettres couchées, écriture couchée,** slanting, sloping, letters, writing; *Her:* **chevron c.,** chevron couched; *Needlew:* **fils couchés,** couched threads; *Geol:* **pli c.,** recumbent fold; (*c*) **papier c.,** art paper; coated paper.

couche-culotte [kuʃkylɔt], *s.f. Cost:* pilch (for infant); *pl. couches-culottes.*

couchée [kuʃe], *s.f.* **1.** (action of) lying down, going to bed. **2.** *A:* (*a*) sleeping-place, night's lodging, bed; (*b*) overnight expenses (in hotel, etc.).

couche-point [kuʃpwɛ̃], *s.m. Bootm:* rand; *pl. couche-points.*

coucher [kuʃe]. **I.** *v.* **1.** *v.tr.* (*a*) to put (child, etc.) to bed; (*b*) **être couché et nourri chez qn,** to get board and lodging, bed and board, at s.o.'s house; **je ne peux pas vous c.,** I can't put you up; (*c*) to lay (s.o., sth., down horizontally); **la pluie a couché les blés,** the rain has beaten down, lodged, flattened, the wheat; **c. le poil d'un chapeau,** to smooth down the nap of a hat; **c. un navire,** to throw a vessel on her beam-ends; **c. un fusil en joue,** to aim a gun; **c. qn en joue,** to take aim at s.o.; **c. un blessé par terre,** to lay down a wounded man; **c. son homme par terre,** *F:* **sur le carreau,** to bring down one's man, to lay one's man out; *Poet:* **c. qn au tombeau,** to lay s.o. in his grave; *Gaming:* **c. cinq francs sur une couleur,** to lay five francs on a colour; **c. gros,** to stake heavily; (*d*) to lay, spread (colour on surface, etc.); to coat (paper); **c. un enduit,** to lay on a coat; (*e*) *Ind:* **c. les feux,** to bank the fires; (*f*) **c. qch. par écrit,** to set, put, sth. down in writing; **c. les faits sur le papier,** to write down the facts; **c. qn sur, dans, son testament,** to mention s.o. in one's will; (*g*) *Hort:* **c. (des branches),** to layer. **2.** *v.i.* (*a*) **c. à l'hôtel, chez un voisin,** to sleep, have a bedroom, at the hotel, at a neighbour's; *F:* **c. avec un homme, avec une femme,** to sleep, to go to bed, with a man, with a woman; (*b*) (*of ship*) to heel over; (*c*) (*to dog*) **va c.!** down! **couché!** sit! *P:* (*to pers.*) **va te c.!** go to blazes, to hell! (*d*) *F:* **avoir un nom à c. dehors,** to have an impossible name.

II. **coucher,** *s.m.* **1.** (*a*) going to bed; **l'heure du c.,** bedtime; (*b*) night's lodging; **le c. et la nourriture,** board and lodging; (*c*) bed(ding). **2.** setting, going down (of sun, star); **au c. du soleil,** at sunset, at sundown.

se coucher, (*a*) to go to bed; **aller se c.,** to go to bed, to retire for the night; *F:* to turn in; **il est l'heure d'aller se c.,** it is bedtime; **je rentre me c.,** I am going home to bed; **nous nous sommes couchés assez tard,** we turned in, we went to bed, rather late; **je ne veux pas vous empêcher de vous c., je ne veux pas vous faire c. tard,** I don't want to keep you up; *F:* **se c. avec, comme, les poules,** to go to bed early; *F:* **va te c.!** be off! get along with you! **envoyer c. les enfants,** to send, *F:* to pack, the children off to bed; *Prov:* **comme on fait son lit on se couche,** as we make our bed, so must we lie; (*b*) to lie down; **se c. de tout son long,** to lie down at full length; *Row:* **se c. sur les avirons,** to throw one's weight on the oars; (*c*) *Nau:* (*of ship*) **se c. sur le flanc,** to heel over; **se c. horizontalement,** to lie on her beam-ends; (*d*) (*of sun, stars*) to set, go down; **nous avons vu le soleil se c.,** we saw the sun set; **le soleil est couché,** the sun is down; (*e*) (*of wheat*) to lodge.

coucherie [kuʃri], *s.f. P:* sexual intercourse.

couche-tard [kuʃtaːr], *s.m. inv. F:* late bedder; **c'est un c.-t.,** he sits up until all hours of the night.

couche-tôt [kuʃto], *s.m. inv. F:* early bedder.

couchette [kuʃɛt], *s.f.* **1.** (child's) cot, bed. **2.** *Nau:* berth, bunk; *Rail:* couchette. **3. c. en bois,** plank bed. **4.** *F: A:* **mignon de c.,** elegant young man, young dandy.

coucheur, -euse [kuʃœːr, -øːz], *s.* **1.** (*a*) bedfellow; *F:* **il a dû être un fameux c., ce vieux-là,** that old man must have taken plenty of women to bed with him in his time; (*b*) *F:* **c'est un mauvais c.,** he's an awkward customer. **2.** *a. & s. Paperm:* **feutre c.,** *s.m.* **coucheur,** couching felt; **presse coucheuse,** *s.f.* **coucheuse,** drying press.

couchis [kuʃi], *s.m.* **1.** *Civ.E:* bed (of earth or sand for roadway). **2.** *Const:* (i) sole-piece; (ii) wall piece (for strut). **3.** *Hort:* layer (attached to parent plant).

couchoir [kuʃwaːr], *s.m. Tchn:* gilder's palette.

couci-couça [kusikusa], **couci-couci** [kusikusi], *adv. F:* so so; moderately; tolerably; **ça va c.-c.,** I'm fair to middling.

coucou [kuku], *s.m.* **1.** (*a*) *Orn:* cuckoo; **c. geai,** great spotted cuckoo; **c. à longue queue (de Tahiti),** long-tailed cuckoo (of Tahiti); **c. terrestre (de Californie),** Californian roadrunner; **(pendule à) c.,** cuckoo clock; (*b*) *int.* (i) cuckoo; (ii) *F:* **c.! (me voilà!)** peep-bo! peek-a-boo! **2.** *Bot:* (*a*) cowslip; (*b*) wild daffodil; (*c*) ragged robbin; (*d*) barren strawberry; (*e*) white clover, Dutch clover; (*in Ireland*) shamrock. **3.** (*a*) *A.Veh:* post-chaise; (*b*) *Rail: F:* shunting engine; (*c*) *Av: P:* old plane, ancient kite; (*d*) *Aut: F:* old crock; (*e*) *P:* watch. **4.** *F:* (*from similarity in sound with* **cocu**) cuckold, deceived husband.

coucoumelle [kukumɛl], *s.f. Fung:* sheathed agaric, grisette.

coude [kud], *s.m.* **1.** (*a*) elbow; **manches au c.,** elbow-length sleeves; **c. à c.,** (i) *adv.phr.* side by side, close together, shoulder to shoulder; (ii) *s. Mil:* elbow touch; **travailler c. à c.,** to work, (i) shoulder to shoulder, (ii) in a spirit of solidarity; **le c. à c. des stations estivales,** the jostling of holiday resorts; **coup de c.,** (i) poke with the elbow; (ii) nudge; **donner un coup de c. à qn,** to nudge, jog, s.o.; **écarter la foule à coups de coudes,** to elbow the crowd aside; **jouer des coudes,** (i) to elbow one's way (through the crowd); (ii) to manœuvre (to gain one's own ends); **se sentir les coudes,** (i) *Mil:* to touch elbows; (ii) to support one another; *F:* **lever, hausser, le c.,** to lift the elbow, to booze; *F:* **lâche-moi le c.!** leave me alone! don't bother me! *F:* **huile de c.,** elbow grease; *F:* **ne pas se moucher du c.,** (i) to be stuck up; (ii) to do oneself well; *P:* **se fourrer le doigt dans l'œil jusqu'au c.,** to be completely wrong, to make a bad blunder; (*b*) *Cost:* elbow (of sleeve); **être troué aux coudes,** to be out at elbows; (*c*) *Z:* elbow (of horse). **2.** (*a*) bend (in road, etc.); **c. brusque,** sharp bend, sharp turning; **la route fait un c.,** the road bends sharply; *Geog:* **c. de capture,** elbow of capture (of river); (*b*) *Mec.E:* bend, elbow (of bar, pipe, etc.); crank (of shaft); **c. complet,** elbow assembly (of piping, etc.); **c. de croisement,** cross-over bend; **c. d'équerre,** right-angled bend; **c. d'essieu,** axle crank; **c. en U,** U-bend, return bend; *Mch: I.C.E:* **arbre à deux coudes,** two-throw crank-shaft; *Rec:* **c. mobile,** tone-arm floater (of record player); *Dist:* **c. de tête d'injection,** goose neck; (*c*) *pl. Cu:* **coudes,** elbow-shaped noodles.

coudé [kude], *a.* bent, kneed, cranked; **levier c.,** bent lever, angle lever, bell crank; **arbre c.,** crankshaft; **essieu c.,** crank axle; **conduit c.,** elbow duct; **raccord c.,** elbow joint.

coudée [kude], *s.f.* **1.** (*a*) *A.Meas:* cubit; (*b*) **dépasser qn de cent coudées,** to be vastly superior to s.o., to stand head and shoulders above s.o. **2.** *pl.* **avoir ses coudées franches,** (i) to have elbow room; (ii) to have free play, full liberty; to have a free hand, to have free scope; **donnez-moi mes coudées franches,** give me free play, don't hamper me.

cou-de-pied [kudpje], *s.m.* instep; *pl. cous-de-pied.*

couder [kude], *v.tr.* to bend (pipe) into an elbow; to crank (shaft).

se couder, to bend; to form a bend, an elbow.

coudoiement [kudwamɑ̃], *s.m.* (*a*) elbowing; (*b*) contact, association.

coudou [kudu], *s.m. Z:* kudu; **petit c.,** lesser kudu.

coudoyer [kudwaje], *v.tr.* (**je coudoie, n. coudoyons; je coudoierai**) **1.** (*a*) *A:* to elbow (s.o.); (*b*) **c. des inconnus dans la foule,** to brush against strangers in the crowd. **2.** (*a*) to be in contact with (s.o.); to rub shoulders with (s.o.); (*b*) **le crime et la faiblesse se coudoient,** crime and weakness are near neighbours.

coudraie [kudrɛ], *s.f.* hazel-grove, -wood.

coudre[1] [kudr̥], *v.tr.* (*pr.p.* **cousant;** *p.p.* **cousu;** *pr.ind.* **je couds, il coud, n. cousons, ils cousent;** *p.d.* **je cousais;** *p.h.* **je cousis;** *fu.* **je coudrai**) **1.** to sew, stitch; **c. un bouton à une robe,** to sew, stitch, a button on a dress; **c. une marque sur une chemise,** to sew a name tab on a shirt; **c. un vêtement à gros points,** to tack up a garment; **machine à c.,** sewing-machine; **c. à la machine,** to machine; **c. une plaie,** to sew up, to suture, a wound; **c. des épithètes à des mots,** to tack epithets on to words; **c. la peau du renard à celle du lion,** to be as wily as a fox and as strong as a lion; *Prov:* **bien taillé, mais il faut c.!** you have laid the foundation, now you must build. **2.** *Nau:* to tack on, rivet on (planking).

coudre[2], *s.m. A:* hazel(-tree).

coudrement [kudrəmɑ̃], *s.m. Tan:* preparation (of skins) for tanning.

coudrer [kudre], *v.tr. Tan:* to prepare (skins) for tanning.

coudreuse [kudrøːz], *s.f. Tan:* vat.

coudrier [kudrie], *s.m.* hazel(-tree).

coudrette [kudrɛt], *s.f.* small hazel-grove.

coué [kue], *a.* **1.** *A:* undocked (dog, etc.). **2.** *Pros:* tailed (rhyme).

couenne [kwan], *s.f.* **1.** (*a*) (thick) skin (of pig, porpoise, etc.); pork rind; *P:* **se gratter la c.,** to scratch oneself; **quelle c.!** what a fool! (*b*) rind (of bacon); crackling (of roast pork). **2.** mole (on face, body). **3.** *Med:* (*a*) **c. inflammatoire,** buffy coat, buff, size (of clotted blood); (*b*) (diphtheric) membrane.

couenneux, -euse [kwanø, -øːz], *a.* **1.** resembling, covered with, a thick skin. **2.** *Med:* (*a*) (*of blood*) buffy; (*b*) *A:* **angine couenneuse,** diphtheria.

couet [kwɛ], *s.m.* (cast-iron) stewpan.

couette[1] [kwɛt], *s.f.* **1.** *Dial:* feather bed. **2.** *Mec.E:* (= COUSSINET) bearing. **3.** *pl. N.Arch:* **couettes courantes,** bilge ways; **couettes mortes,** standing ways, ground ways; **couettes vives,** sliding ways.

couette[2], *s.f.* (hare's, rabbit's) scut; *Dial:* lock (of hair); **elle était coiffée avec des couettes,** she wore her hair in bunches.

couette[3], *s.f. Orn: F:* seagull.

couffa [kufa], *s.m. Nau:* gufa, goofa(h).

couffe [kuf], *s.f.,* **couffin** [kufɛ̃], *s.m. Fish: etc:* frail, basket.

cougna(r)de [kuɲad, kuɲard], *s.f. Cu:* compote of heart cherries.

cougouar [kugwaːr], *s.m.* = COUGUAR.

cougourde [kugurd], *s.f. Dial:* (*Provence*) (*a*) pumpkin; (*b*) (vegetable) marrow.

cougourdette [kugurdɛt], *s.f. Dial:* (*Provence*) small marrow, courgette.

couguar [kugaːr, -gwaːr], *s.m. Z:* cougar, puma, American panther.

couic [kwik], *s.m.* chirp, cheep (of young bird); squeak (of mouse); *P:* **faire c.,** to give one's last gasp, to die; *F:* **n'y voir, n'y comprendre que c.,** to see, understand, nothing at all.

couillard [kujaːr]. **1.** *a. V:* with large testicles; *V:* big-balled. **2.** *s.m. Nau:* bunt gasket.

couille [kuj], *s.f. V:* testicle, *V:* ball; **c'est de la c.,** that's all rot, *V:* balls; **une c. molle,** a milksop, a wet; **avoir des couilles au cul,** to have guts.

couillon [kujɔ̃], *a. & s.m. P:* idiot, fathead, dimwit.

couillonnade [kujɔnad], *s.f. P:* bosh, nonsense; (*a*) **quelle c.!** *V:* balls! (*b*) **dire des couillonnades,** to talk cock.

couillonner [kujɔne], *P:* **1.** *v.tr.* to get the better of (s.o.); **je me suis laissé c.,** I have been had; **du travail couillonné,** ballsed (up) work. **2.** *v.i.* **ce n'est pas le moment de c.,** it's not a time to arse around.

couillonnerie [kujɔnri], *s.f. P:* stupidity.

couinement [kwinmɑ̃], *s.m.* (*a*) squeak; squeal; (*b*) screeching (of brakes); squealing (of tyres); squeaking (of new shoes); cracking (of whip).

couiner [kwine], *v.i.* (*a*) to squeak; to squeal; (*of rabbit, hare*) to scream; (*b*) *F:* to whimper; (*c*) *F: Tg:* to send Morse signals; (*d*) *F:* (*of brakes*) to screech; (*of tyres*) to squeal; (*of new shoes*) to squeak.

couineur [kwinœːr], *s.m.* (*a*) *W.Tel: F:* street loud-speaker; (*b*) *F: Tg:* tapping key for sending signals.

cou-jaune [kuʒoːn], *s.m. Orn:* yellowthroat; *pl. cous-jaunes.*

coulage [kulaːʒ], *s.m.* **1.** (*a*) pouring, running; *Metall: etc:* casting; pouring (of molten metal, glass, soap, etc.); **c. en terre,** loam casting; **c. à noyau,** hollow casting; (*b*) *Mch: I.C.E:* **coulage (d'une bielle, d'un palier, etc.),** burn-out (of connecting-rod, bearing, etc.). **2.** (*a*) leaking, leakage (of liquid); guttering (of candle); *Wine: Dist:* ullage; **maison où il y a beaucoup de c.,** house where there is a great deal of waste; *Ind:* **tenir compte du c.,** to allow for (i) wastage, (ii) petty theft; (*b*) *Metall:* break out (of metal from moulds). **3.** sinking, scuttling (of ship).

coulant [kulɑ̃]. **1.** *a.* running, flowing (liquid); loose (ground); *F:* (*of pers.*) easy-going; **nœud c.,** slip knot, running knot; noose; *Nau:* running bowline; **style c.,** easy, flowing, style; *F:* **homme c. en affaires,** accommodating man; **cheval c., d'allure coulante,** horse of easy gait. **2.** *s.m.* (*a*) sliding ring, sliding runner; **c. pour écharpe, c. de cravate,** scarf-ring; **c. d'une ceinture,** keeper, loop, of a belt; (*b*) *Min:* cage-guide, -slide (of shaft); (*c*) *Opt:* draw-tube, sliding tube (of microscope, etc.); (*d*) *Hort:* runner (of a plant).

coulanter [kulɑ̃te], *v.tr. Min:* to put cage-slides into (mine shafts).

coulard [kulaːr], *a.* (plant) that grows runners.

coule[1] [kul], *s.f. P:* (i) waste (in household), leakage; (ii) petty pilfering; *hence* **mettre qn à la c.,** to teach s.o. the tricks of the trade; **il est à la c.,** he knows what's what, he knows the ropes.

coule[2], *s.f.* (monk's) cowled robe.

coulé [kule]. **1.** *a.* (*a*) cast (metal); **pièce coulée,** casting; **dalle coulée,** concrete flooring; (*b*) sunk(en) (ship, etc.); *F:* **c'est un homme c.,** he's done for, gone under, finished, sunk; (*c*) **fruits coulés,** fruit nipped in the bud; (*d*) **carte coulée,** (conjuror's) substituted card. **2.** *s.m.* (*a*) *Bill:* follow, run-through (stroke); (*b*) *Metall:* cast(ing); (*c*) *Mus:* (i) slide, coulé; (ii) legato; (iii) slur.

coulée [kule], *s.f.* **1.** running, flow(ing) (of liquid); rush (of torrent); **c. de lave,** lava flow; **c. de boue,** lahar, mud avalanche. **2.** *Metall:* (*a*) casting (of molten metal); **c. en barbotine,** slip casting; **c. en moule permanent,** permanent-mould casting; **c. en sable,** sand casting; **c. à la descente, en chute,** top pouring, top casting; **c. à talon,** side pouring; **c. en source,** bottom casting; (*b*) tapping (of molten metal); **trou de c.,** tap(ping) hole, draw hole; **venu de c. avec . . .,** cast in one piece with . . .; (*c*) cast(ing). **3.** (**écriture**) **c.,** running hand. **4.** *N.Arch:* **c. arrière,** run (of ship). **5.** *Ven:* track, run (followed by animal in wood). **6.** *Swim:* plunge (dive).

coulemelle [kulmɛl], *s.f. Fung:* parasol mushroom.

coulement [kulmɑ̃], *s.m. A:* running, flowing (of liquid).

couler [kule], *v.* **1.** *v.tr.* (*a*) to run, draw, pour (liquid); **c. l'eau d'une chaudière,** to run, draw, the water out of a boiler; **c. (à travers un filtre),** to strain, filter; (*b*) *Metall:* to cast, pour, run, teem (molten metal into mould); **c. une gueuse de fer, un lingot,** to cast, teem, a pig, an ingot; **c. une pièce, une statue,** to cast a piece, a statue; **c. plein (une statue, etc.),** to cast (a statue, etc.) solid; **c. en coquille, en matrice, sous pression,** to die-cast; **c. en source,** to cast with gate in bottom of mould; **c. à découvert,** to cast in open sand; **c. à vert,** to cast in green sand; (*c*) to tap, run off (molten metal from furnace); (*d*) *Mch: I.C.E:* **c. (une bielle, un palier, etc.),** to burn out (a connecting-rod, a bearing, etc.); (*e*) *Const: etc:* to grout (masonry); to pour (concrete); **c. du plomb dans un joint,** to run lead into a joint; *Civ.E:* **c. du goudron sur une chaussée,** to run tar on a roadway; (*f*) to sink; **c. bas, à fond, un navire,** to sink a ship; (i) to send a ship to the bottom; (ii) to scuttle a ship; *A:* **c. une question à fond,** to settle a question once and for all; **c. qn (à fond),** to ruin s.o. completely; **ce scandale l'a coulé,** this scandal has done for him; (*g*) to slip, glide; **c. une pièce dans la main de, à, qn,** to slip a coin into s.o.'s hand; **c. un mot (dans la conversation),** to slip in a word; **c. un mot à, dans, l'oreille de qn,** to drop, whisper, a word in s.o.'s ear; **il coula un regard dans ma direction,** he cast a glance in my direction; **c. un faux chèque,** to pass a forged cheque; *Mus:* **c. un passage,** to slur a passage; *Bill:* **c. (la bille),** to play a follow; (*h*) to pass, spend (time smoothly, pleasantly); **il coule ses jours dans la prospérité,** his days glide by in prosperous ease; **c. une vie heureuse,** to lead, spend, a happy life; *F:* **se la c. douce,** to take life easily, to have a good time. **2.** *v.i.* (*a*) (*of liquids, cheese, etc.*) to flow, run; **faire c. l'eau,** to turn the water on; **laisser c. l'eau,** to let things take their course; **la sueur coule sur son front,** sweat is trickling, running, down his forehead; **les larmes coulaient sur ses joues,** tears coursed down her cheeks; **cette question a fait c. beaucoup d'encre,** much ink has been spilt about this question; **sentiment qui coule de source,** feeling that comes from the bottom of one's heart; **ça coule de source,** it's obvious; **sa langue coule de source,** he writes easily, naturally, spontaneously; **son récit coule de source,** he tells a straightforward tale; **l'argent lui coule des doigts,** money runs through his fingers; **les années coulent,** the years slip, glide, by; (*b*) (*of barrel, etc.*) to leak; (*of candle*) to gutter; (*of nose*) to run; (*of molten metal*) to run, break, from the mould; (*of verse*) to flow; (*of dye*) **c. au lavage,** to run; **mon stylo coule,** my fountain-pen is leaking, running, blobbing; (*c*) (*of ship*) **c. à fond, c. bas,** to sink; **le navire coula,** the ship foundered, went down; **c. de, par, l'avant, par l'arrière,** to sink by the bow, stern foremost; **le navire coula à pic,** the ship sank like a stone; (*of pers.*) **c. à pic,** to sink and drown; (*d*) to slide, slip; **l'échelle, le nœud, coula,** the ladder, the knot, slipped; **piston qui ne coule pas,** piston that sticks; **c. sur un fait,** to pass over, touch lightly on, a fact.

se couler. **1.** to glide, slip; **se c. dans un trou,** to creep into a hole; **se c. entre les draps,** to slip into bed; **se c. dans la foule,** to slip, disappear, into the crowd; **se c. auprès de qn, vers qn,** to sidle up to s.o.; **se laisser c. le long d'une corde,** to slide down a rope; **se c. au ras du mur,** to hug the wall. **2.** to ruin, *F:* do for, oneself (*esp.* through some scandal).

coulette [kulɛt], *s.f. Fish:* landing net; spoon net.

couleur[1] [kulœːr], *s.f.* **1.** (*a*) colour; tint; hue; *Petroleum Ind:* cast; *pl.* **insensible aux couleurs,** colour-blind; **couleurs primaires, génératrices,** primary colours; **couleurs binaires, composites,** secondary colours; **c. complémentaire,** complementary colour; **c. claire, foncée,** light, dark, colour; **c. vive,** bright colour; *Ethn:* **gens de c.,** coloured people; **chemise de c.,** coloured shirt; *F:* **couleurs,** coloureds (clothes); **photographie, télévision, en couleurs,** colour photography, television; **carte (postale) en couleurs,** coloured postcard; **la c. d'un journal,** the (political) colour, tone, of a paper; **c. locale,** local colour; **pour faire c. locale,** in order to fit in with the landscape; in order to add local colour; **de quelle c. est-ce?** what colour is it? **l'eau était d'une c. de sang,** the water was the colour of blood; **suivant la c. du temps,** according to the state of things; **je ne connais pas la c. de son argent,** I've never seen the colour of his money; **je ne connais pas la c. de sa voix, de ses paroles,** he's never said a word to me; he never opens his mouth; **tromper qn sous c. d'amitié,** to put up a show of friendship (in order) to deceive s.o.; **sous c. de me rendre service,** under the pretext of helping me, of doing me a service; **de toutes couleurs,** of all colours; *F:* **en avoir vu de toutes les couleurs,** to have had all sorts of experiences; to have been through the mill; to have had a lot of trouble; **on m'en dit de toutes les couleurs sur votre compte,** I've heard you maligned in every way; *F: A:* **conter des couleurs,** to tell lies, to draw the long bow; **prendre c.,** to take colour; *Cu:* (*of joint*) to brown; **l'affaire prend c.,** things are beginning to take shape; **peindre qch. de belles, de riantes, couleurs,** to paint sth. in glowing colours; to put sth. in a favourable light; *Prov:* **des goûts et des couleurs on ne discute pas, il ne faut pas disputer,** everyone to his taste; there's no accounting for taste; *Metall:* **fer de c.,** red-short iron; (*b*) colour, complexion; **elle a des couleurs aujourd'hui,** she has a good colour, red, rosy, cheeks, today; **perdre ses couleurs,** to become pale, to lose one's colour; **reprendre des couleurs, retrouver ses couleurs,** to get back one's colour; **sans c.,** colourless, pale; **être haut en c.,** to have a high colour; **elle a changé de c.,** she changed colour; *Med:* **pâles couleurs,** chlorosis, green sickness; (*c*) *Mil: etc:* colours, flag; **les couleurs nationales,** the national colours, flag; **couleurs à la corne, couleurs hautes,** with colours high; **couleurs déployées, battantes,** with flying colours; **envoyer, hisser, les couleurs,** to hoist the colours, the flag; **amener, rentrer,** *Nav:* **haler bas, les couleurs,** to strike, *Nau:* to haul down, the colours, the flag; (*d*) *Sp: Turf:* colours (of club, stable); **jouer sous les couleurs d'un club,** to play in a club's colours; (*e*) *a.inv.* **c. (de) paille (etc.),** straw (etc.)-coloured; **ruban c. de feu,** flame-coloured ribbon; **bas c. de chair,** flesh-coloured stockings; **tout voir c. de rose,** to see everything through rose-coloured spectacles; (*Note: esp. A: occ. in modern French,* **couleur** *becomes s.m. when the a.inv. is used as a noun, e.g.* **le c. de feu,** flame red). **2.** (*a*) colour, paint; **c. organique,** organic pigment; **c. vitrifiable,** enamel, fusible, colour; **c. à l'eau, à l'aquarelle,** water colour; **c. à l'huile,** oil colour, paint; **boîte de couleurs,** box of paints; **c. pour bois,** wood stain; **impression en couleurs,** colour printing; *Ind:* **mettre qch. en c.,** to colour, stain, sth.; **metteur en c.,** colourer, stainer; *F:* **connaître ses couleurs,** to know what's what; (*b*) *Com:* **marchand de couleurs,** paint-shop proprietor, manager. **3.** *Cards:* suit; **fournir à, donner de, jouer dans, la c.,** to follow suit; (*as opposed to trumps*) **les trois couleurs,** the three plain suits; **annoncer la c.,** (i) to call (spades, etc.); (ii) *F:* to have one's say; to state one's case.

couleur[2], **-euse** [kulœːr, -øːz], *s.* **1.** *Metall:* caster, pourer, foundry hand. **2.** candle maker.

couleuvre [kulœːvr], *s.f.* snake; **c. à collier,** common snake, grass snake; **c. lisse,** European smooth snake; **c. d'Esculape,** Aesculapian snake; **c. léopard,** leopard snake; **c. jarretière,** ribbon snake; *pl.* **les couleuvres venimeuses,** the cobras; **parasseux comme une c.,** bone-lazy; bone-idle; **avaler des couleuvres,** (i) to pocket an insult; (ii) to believe, swallow, anything; **faire avaler des couleuvres à qn,** to lead s.o. up the garden path; **la c. est de taille (à avaler),** it's a hard, bitter, pill to swallow.

couleuvreau, -eaux [kulœvro], *s.m.* young snake.

couleuvrée [kulœvre], *s.f. Bot: F:* **1.** traveller's-joy. **2.** white bryony.

couleuvrin, -ine [kulœvrɛ̃, -in], *a.* colubrine, snake-like.

couleuvrinier [kulœvrinje], *s.m. A.Artil:* culverine(e)r.

coulevrine [kuləvrin], *s.f. A.Artil:* culverin.

couli [kuli], *s.m. A:* coolie.

coulicou [kuliku], *s.m. Orn:* cuckoo; **c. à bec noir, à bec jaune,** black-billed, yellow-billed, cuckoo.

coulin [kulɛ̃], *s.m. Orn: F:* wood pigeon.

coulinage [kulinaːʒ], *s.m. Hort:* singeing (of fruit-trees).

couliner [kuline], *v.tr. Hort:* to singe (fruit-trees, in order to destroy pests).

coulis[1] [kuli], *a.m.* **vent c.** (insidious) draught (through crevice, etc.); *s.m.* **des c. d'air froid,** draughts of cold air.

coulis[2], *s.m.* **1.** (*a*) *Const:* grout(ing); (*b*) (liquid) filling. **2.** *Metall:* molten metal; **c. réfractaire,** grog. **3.** *Cu:* (meat) broth; **c. de tomates,** tomato sauce.

coulis[3], *s.m. A:* coolie.

coulissant [kulisɑ̃], *a.* sliding (spindle, bench, door, contact, etc.).

coulisse [kulis], *s.f.* **1.** (*a*) groove, slot; **fenêtre, siège, porte, à c.,** sliding window, seat, door; **couvercle à c.,** draw-lid; *Tls:* **pied à c.,** slide calipers, slide square; (shoe-maker's) size-stick; *F:* **regard en c.,** sidelong glance; **faire les yeux en c. à qn,** (i) to look at s.o. out of the corner of one's eye; (ii) to make eyes at s.o.; (*b*) slide; **trombone à c.,** slide trombone; *Mch:* (i) **coulisses du tiroir,** slideways of the slide valve; (ii) **la c.,** the link-motion; **c. de changement de marche,** reversing link; *Mec.E:* **coulisses de banc de tour,** slide bars of a lathe-bed; (*c*) *Civ.E: Const:* wooden shoot (for bricks, rubbish, etc.). **2.** *Needlew:* hem (through which to pass tape). **3.** (*a*) *Th:* (scenery) flat; **les coulisses,** the wings, the slips; backstage; **le jargon des coulisses,** theatre slang; **les coulisses de la politique,** behind the scenes in politics; **savoir ce qui se passe dans la c.,** to know what is happening behind the scenes; **être dans la c.,** to be pulling the strings; (*b*) *St.Exch:* **la c.,** the outside market.

coulissé [kulise], *a.* grooved, slotted.

coulisseau, -eaux [kuliso], *s.m.* **1.** (*a*) slide (of piece of machinery); tool-slide, cross-side (of lathe); (*b*) block (sliding in guides); (*c*) runner (of drawer, etc.). **2.** (*a*) chute, shoot (for parcels in stores, etc.); (*b*) race-trough (for unloading, etc.).

coulissement [kulismɑ̃], *s.m. Mec.E:* sliding motion.
coulisser [kulise], *Mec.E: etc:* **1.** *v.i.* to slide. **2.** *v.tr.* (*a*) to provide (sth.) with slides; (*b*) *Needlew:* to run up (seam, etc.).
coulissier, -ière [kulisje, -jɛːr], *St.Exch:* **1.** *a.* relating to outside brokers; **transactions coulissières,** outside transactions. **2.** *s.m.* outside broker.
couloir [kulwaːr], *s.m.* **1.** *A:* strainer. **2.** (*a*) corridor, passage; **train à c.,** corridor train; *Pol:* **couloirs de la Chambre** = lobby of the House; **intrigues de couloir,** wire-pulling; **faire les couloirs,** to lobby; (*b*) *Sp:* (*athletics*) lane; *Ten:* **les couloirs,** the tramlines. **3.** *Ind: etc:* shoot, chute; *Cin:* **c. du film,** film channel, track; *Artil: Sm.a:* **c. d'alimentation,** feed slot, guide; **c. de chargement,** feed trough; **c. d'éjection,** ejection chute. **4.** (*a*) channel, gully (for water); **fleuve encaissé dans de profonds couloirs,** river flowing through deep gorges; (*b*) *Geog:* **c. karstique,** sinkhole, (limestone) sink. **5.** (*a*) *Meteor:* **c. de basse pression,** low pressure corridor; *Av:* **c. aérien,** air corridor; (*b*) *Hist:* **le c. de Dantzig,** the Polish Corridor.
couloire [kulwaːr], *s.f. Cu: etc:* strainer.
coulomb [kulɔ̃], *s.m. El.Meas:* coulomb.
coulommiers [kulɔmje], *s.m.* Coulommiers cheese.
coulon [kulɔ̃], *s.m. Dial: N. of Fr:* pigeon; **c. de mer,** seagull.
coulonneux [kulɔnø], *s.m. Dial: N. of Fr:* pigeon fancier.
coulpe [kulp], *s.f. A:* guilt; **dire sa c.,** to confess one's sins, **battre sa c.,** to beat one's breast (as a sign of penitence).
coulure [kulyːr], *s.f.* **1.** *Metall:* run-out, break-out (from the mould). **2.** *Vit:* washing away of the pollen (by spring rains); abortion, failure, of the crop.
coumaline [kumalin], *s.f. Ch:* coumalin.
coumalique [kumalik], *a. Ch:* coumalic.
coumaranne [kumaran], *s.m. Ch:* coumaran(e).
coumarine [kumarin], *s.f. Ch:* coumarin, cumarin.
coumarinique [kumarinik], *a. Ch:* coumarinic.
coumarique [kumarik], *a. Ch:* coumaric.
coumarone [kumarɔn], *s.f. Ch:* coumarone.
coumarou [kumaru], *s.m. Bot:* coumarou, cumara, cumaru, tonka-bean (tree).
coumarouna [kumaruna], *s.m. Bot:* coumarouna.
Coumassie [kumasi], *Pr.n.f. Geog:* Kumassi.
coumis, coumys [kumis], *s.m.* kumiss.
coup [ku], *s.m.* **1.** knock, blow; (*a*) **frapper trois coups à la porte,** to give three knocks, three raps, on the door; *Th:* **les trois coups,** the three knocks (given just before the curtain rises); **donner de grands coups dans la porte,** to pound, bang, at the door; **se donner un c. contre qch.,** to knock against sth.; **c. du bout du doigt,** poke, dig (with the finger); **c. de coude,** (i) poke with the elbow; (ii) nudge; **c. de tête,** butt; *s.a.* 4 (*a*); **c. de bec,** peck; **la corneille lui donna un c. de bec,** the crow pecked at him, gave him a peck; **c. de bâton,** blow, whack (with a stick); **c. sur les doigts,** rap over the knuckles; **recevoir un mauvais c.,** to get hurt (at the hands of a criminal, in a fight); **c. de couteau, de poignard,** stab (with knife, dagger); **c. de sabre,** (i) slash, cut (with a sword); (ii) sword wound; **coup d'épée,** thrust, lunge; *Fenc:* **c. d'arrêt,** stop hit; **c. droit,** lunge; **porter un c. au bras,** to score a hit on the arm; *s.a.* TEMPS 2; **c. de lance, de baïonnette,** lance-, bayonet-thrust; **c. de hache,** blow, stroke (with an axe); *s.a.* HACHE; **porter un c. à qn,** to aim, deal, strike, a blow at s.o., to strike s.o.; **porter le c. mortel à son adversaire,** to give the death blow to one's opponent; **porter c.,** to hit home; **le reproche porta c.,** the reproach struck home; **le c. a porté,** that was a home-thrust; **cela m'en a donné un c.!** it gave me such a shock! **cela m'a donné un vrai c.,** it gave me quite a turn; **sa mort est un rude c. pour sa famille,** his death is a sad blow to his family; **les coups de la fortune,** the buffets of fortune; **tenir le c.,** (i) to meet the emergency, to withstand the blow, the shock; (ii) to hold out; *F:* to stick it; **en venir aux coups,** to come to blows; **rendre c. pour c.,** to return blow for blow; to hit back, strike back; **il lui porta c. sur c.,** he dealt him blow after blow; **il n'est pas capable de tenir le c.,** he can't take it; *F:* **en mettre un c.,** to put some vim, guts, into it; *F:* **faire les quatre cents coups,** to commit all sorts of excesses; to go the pace; **un c. dur,** a staggering blow, a hard knock; **s'il nous arrive un c. dur,** should the worst happen; **donner, décocher, un c. bas,** to hit below the belt; **faire d'une pierre deux coups,** to kill two birds with one stone; *Jur:* **coups et blessures,** assault and battery; **corps couvert de coups,** body covered with bruises; *Prov:* **le premier c. en vaut deux,** the first blow is half the battle; *prep.phr.* **à coups de,** with blows from (sth.); **abattre qn à coups de masse,** to knock s.o. down with a club, to club s.o.; **abattre un arbre à coups de cognée,** to fell a tree with an axe; *F:* **faire la guerre à coups de canon,** to wage war in earnest; **chasser un chien à coups de pierres,** to drive a dog away with a shower of stones; **faire une traduction à coups de dictionnaire,** to look up every word in the dictionary in translating a passage; *s.a.* CISEAU 2, CORNE[1] 1, ÉPÉE 1, FOUET 2, GRÂCE 3, FRANÇOIS, JARNAC 1, LAPIN, MAIN 1, MARTEAU 1, ONGLE 1, PATTE 1, PIED 1, POING, RAQUETTE 1, TAMPON 6; (*b*) **c. de feu,** shot; *s.a.* FEU[1] II; **c. de fusil,** (i) (gun-, rifle-)shot; (ii) report (of a gun); **c. sec d'un fusil,** crack of a rifle; **tirer un c. de fusil, de canon,** to fire a shot; **c. au but,** direct hit; **c. de blanc,** inner (shot); **c. manqué,** miss; **fusil à un c., à deux coups,** single-, double-barrelled gun; **il fut tué d'un c. de fusil,** he was shot (dead); *Navy:* **rendre un salut c. pour c.,** to return a salute gun for gun; **c. de grisou,** firedamp explosion; *s.a.* DIANE[1], DOUBLE 1, FOUDRE[1] 1, FUSIL 3, MINE[1] 1, RETRAITE 2; (*c*) **c. de vent,** (i) puff, gust, blast, of wind; (ii) sudden gale, squall; *Nau:* strong gale; *Nau:* **petit, fort, c. de vent,** fresh, whole, gale; **entrer dans une pièce en c. de vent,** to burst into a room; **coiffé en c. de vent,** with tousled hair; *F:* **c. de chien, de tabac,** (i) squall; (ii) uprising, trouble; *Nau:* **c. d'eau,** rush of water; **embarquer un c. de mer,** to ship a heavy sea, a green sea; **c. de roulis,** roll; **c. de tangage,** pitch; **c. de froid,** (i) *Meteor:* cold wave, cold snap; (ii) *Med:* chill, cold; **c. de sang,** apoplectic fit; *F:* stroke; *F:* **il a failli crever d'un c. de sang,** he nearly burst a blood vessel; *s.a.* AIR I. 2, CHALEUR 1, LANGUE 1, POMPE[2] 1, SOLEIL 2, VIEUX 1. **2.** stroke (*normal action of sth.*) (*a*) **c. d'aile,** stroke, flap, of the wing; **c. de dents,** bite; **c. de queue,** flick of the tail; **c. de reins,** heave (of the muscles of the back); *P:* **c. de gueule,** shout; **c. de gosier,** (i) shout; (ii) gulp, swallow; **boire son vin d'un c.,** to swallow, gulp down, one's wine at one draught; **boire qch. à petits coups,** to sip sth.; *F:* **un c. de rouge, de blanc,** a glass of red, white, wine; *s.a.* BOIRE I. 1; **c. de baguette,** wave, touch, of the wand; **c. de crayon, de plume,** pencil-stroke, stroke of the pen; **c. d'aviron,** stroke (of the oar); **saluer qn d'un c. de chapeau,** to raise one's hat to s.o.; **c. d'archet,** stroke of the bow; *Tchn:* **c. de lime,** file stroke; **c. de cloche, de timbre,** stroke of the bell; **le premier c. des vêpres a sonné,** the first bell for vespers has rung, has gone; **l'horloge sonna trois coups,** the clock struck three; **sur le c. de midi,** on the stroke of twelve; *Nau:* **six coups,** six bells; **c. de filet,** (i) cast; (ii) haul (of a net), draught (of fishes); **la police les a ramassés d'un seul c. de filet,** the police made a haul of them, collected them up in one haul; **c. de piston,** stroke (of the piston); *s.a.* BROSSE 1, MANQUER II. 1, LUNETTE 1, 1 ŒIL 3; (*b*) *Games:* (i) stroke, hit, drive; *Ten:* **c. droit,** forehand, forearm stroke; **drive de c. droit,** forehand drive; **prendre tout en c. droit,** to run round one's backhand; *Hockey:* **c. de crosse,** hit; **c. franc,** free hit; (ii) *Golf:* shot, stroke; **c. d'approche,** approach shot; **c. roulé,** putt; **concours par coups,** stroke play, medal play; (iii) *Fb:* kick; **c. d'envoi,** kick-off; **c. placé,** place kick; **c. de pied à ras de terre,** drop kick; **c. de tête,** header; (iv) *Bill:* stroke, shot; **faux c. de queue,** miscue; (v) *Cards:* **finir le c.,** to finish the hand; (vi) *Chess: etc:* move; **il fit un beau c.,** he played a fine stroke, shot, or move; *s.a.* DÉ[1] 1; (vii) *Wr:* butt; **c. de tête,** head butt; **c. de bélier,** flying head butt; (viii) *Box:* **c. bas,** below-the-belt blow; *F:* low blow; (*c*) **c. de bonheur,** *F:* **c. de veine, c. de pot,** stroke of luck, piece of good fortune; **c. d'État,** coup d'état; **c. d'audace,** piece of daring, bold stroke; **c. d'éclat,** distinguished action, glorious deed; *s.a.* HASARD 1, THÉÂTRE 3; (*d*) (*sound*) **c. de tonnerre,** clap, peal, of thunder; **c. de sifflet,** (i) blast of a whistle; (ii) whistle; **c. de sirène,** blast of a buzzer, of a siren; **c. de sonnette,** ring, peal, of the bell; **c. de clairon, de trompette,** blast on the bugle, on the trumpet; bugle-call, trumpet-call; **c. de téléphone,** telephone call. **3.** influence, power; instancy, threat; **sous le c. de la peur, de l'effroi,** possessed, smitten, by fear; **agir sous le c. de la peur,** to act through fear, out of fear; **prendre une décision sous le c. de la peur,** to take a decision under the immediate influence of fear; **j'ai répondu sous le c. de la colère,** I answered in a fit of temper; **tomber sous le c. de la loi,** (i) to come within the provisions of; (ii) to fall foul of, the law; **être sous le c. d'une terrible accusation,** to lie under a terrible accusation; **être sous le c. de plaintes au parquet,** to be threatened with the law; **être sous le c. d'un arrêté d'expulsion,** to be under a deportation order; **peuple sous le c. d'une grande épreuve,** people undergoing a great trial. **4.** (*a*) attempt; deed (often evil deed); **essayer un c.,** to have a try; *F:* a go (at it); **c. d'essai,** trial shot, stroke; **on gagne à tous les coups,** you win every time; **marquer le c.,** (i) to mark the occasion; (ii) to put one's foot down; **accuser le c.,** to mark the occasion; *F:* **cela vaut le c.,** it's worth while; it's worth trying; **ça ne vaut pas le c.,** it isn't worth it; **faire son c.,** to achieve one's end; **faire un bon c.,** to make a hit; **c. de tête,** impulsive act; **faire qch. par, sur un, c. de tête,** to act impulsively, without weighing the consequences; *Iron:* **il a fait là un beau c.!** he made a fine mess of it! he's gone and done it! **il médite un mauvais c.,** he's up to mischief; *F:* **un sale c.,** a dirty trick; **ça, c'est un sale c.!** it's a blow! **c'est lui qui a fait le c.!** he's the one who did it! *F:* **il a fait le c.,** he's gone and done it; *P:* **être dans le c.,** (i) to be on to sth.; (ii) to know what's going on; to be with it; (iii) to be in on sth.; *P:* **si on cherche à vous faire le c. . . .,** if people try it on with you . . .; *F:* **un de ces jours il fera un mauvais c.,** one of these days he'll get himself into real trouble; **le c. de la lettre Zinovieff,** the Zinoviev letter stunt; *s.a.* CENT 1, FRAPPER 1, MONTÉ 3, MONTER II. 4, VALOIR 1; (*b*) *F:* **avoir le c. pour faire qch.,** to have the knack of doing sth.; **attraper le c. de main pour faire qch.,** to get the knack, the hang, of doing sth.; (*c*) *adv.phr.* **tout d'un c., d'un seul c.,** at one go, at one fell swoop; **du même c.,** at the same time; **disposer de plusieurs choses du même c.,** to settle several affairs at one (and the same) time; *Phot:* **répandre le révélateur sur la plaque d'un seul c.,** to cover the plate with the developer at one sweep; **faire qch. du premier c.,** to do sth. right away, at the first attempt, shot; **j'ai deviné du premier c.,** I guessed straight off, at the first go; **du c.,** (i) now at last; (ii) this time, in this emergency; **du c. je comprends,** now at last I understand; **du c. je ne sus que répondre,** this fairly stumped me; **elle jeta un cri et du c. laissa tomber le plateau,** she screamed and promptly dropped the tray; **il fut tué sur le c.,** he was killed outright, on the spot; **sur le c., je n'ai pas compris,** at the time, I didn't understand; **pour le c.,** (i) for the moment; (ii) this time; **après c.,** after the event; **arriver après c.,** to come too late; **réflexion après c.,** after-thought; **tout à c.,** suddenly, all at once, all of a sudden; abruptly; **c. sur c.,** in close, in rapid, succession; **boire trois verres c. sur c.,** to drink three glasses one after the other; **encore un c. . . .,** once again . . ., once more . . .; **à tous coups, à tout c.,** (i) constantly; (ii) every time; **à c. sûr,** definitely. **5.** *Civ.E: Const:* (*of wall, etc.*) **prendre c., faire c.,** to get out of plumb; to settle; to sink in. **6.** *Fish:* (baited) pitch; **pêche au c.,** ground-bait fishing.
coupable [kupabl̩]. **1.** *a.* (*a*) guilty (person); **c. de vol,** guilty of theft; **c. envers Dieu,** guilty of an offence against God; **il n'y a pas que lui de c.,** the guilt does not lie with him only, he is not the only guilty party; *Jur:* **s'avouer c.,** to plead guilty; **prononcer, déclarer, qn c.,** to find s.o. guilty, to convict s.o.; *s.a.* PLAIDER; (*b*) **action c.,** culpable act; **plaisirs coupables,** sinful pleasures; **faiblesse c.,** culpable, unpardonable, weakness. **2.** *s.m. & f.* culprit; *Jur:* delinquent; **le grand c., c'est le sport,** sport is the chief offender.
coupablement [kupabləmɑ̃], *adv.* **1.** guiltily. **2.** culpably.
coupage [kupaːʒ], *s.m.* **1.** cutting (of hay, etc.); cutting off (of branch, etc.); cutting down, felling (of tree); **c. à l'arc,** arc cutting. **2.** (*a*) blending, mixing (of wines); (*b*) diluting (of wine, etc., with water). **3.** *Husb:* green meat.
coupailler [kupɑje], *v.tr. F:* to cut away at (sth.) clumsily; to whittle (sth. down).
coupant [kupɑ̃], *a.* **1.** cutting, sharp; **une voix coupante,** a sharp, severe, voice; **outils coupants,** edge tools; **gelée coupante,** nipping frost; *F:* **herbe coupante,** (i) grass you can cut yourself on; (ii) grass that mows well. **2.** *Geom:* secant, cutting (line, surface). **3.** *s.m.* (= TRANCHANT 2) (cutting) edge (of knife, etc.).

coup-de-poing [kudpwɛ̃], *s.m.* **1.** (*a*) pocket pistol or revolver; (*b*) **c.-de-p. américain,** knuckle-duster; (*c*) *Prehist:* chellean pick, hand axe, *coup-de-poing.* **2.** *Mec.E: etc:* **(graisseur à) c.-de-p.,** hand-pump lubricator; *pl. coups-de-poing.*

coupe[1] [kup], *s.f.* cup; (*a*) **c. à champagne,** champagne glass; **c. à fruits,** fruit-stand, -bowl; **c. d'une fontaine,** basin of a fountain; **la c. déborde, est pleine,** my cup runs over, is full; **boire la c. (des plaisirs) jusqu'à la lie,** to drain the cup of pleasure to the dregs; *Prov:* **il y a loin de la c. aux lèvres,** there's many a slip 'twixt the cup and the lip; (*b*) *Com:* ice-cream tub, cup; (*c*) *Sp:* (gold or silver) cup; *Turf:* plate; *Ten:* **la c. Davis,** the Davis cup.

coupe[2], *s.f.* **1.** (*a*) cutting (of hay, coal, stone, etc.); cutting out (of garment); **table de c.,** cutting-out table; **c. de cheveux,** hair-cut; **c. d'une forêt,** cutting (down), chopping down, felling, of the trees of a forest; **mettre un bois en c. réglée,** to make periodical cuttings in a wood; *F:* **mettre qn en c. réglée,** to batten on, exploit, s.o.; **une bande de voleurs qui met en c. réglée tout un quartier,** a gang of thieves working systematically through a district; **c. sombre,** (i) slight thinning (of forest area); (ii) comb(ing) out (of undesirables in factory, etc.); (iii) (through misunderstanding of original meaning) drastic cut (in personnel, in estimates); **c. claire,** thinning (of forest area); *For:* **c. par bandes,** strip felling; **c. secondaire,** after-felling; **c. blanche, à blanc,** clear felling; *For:* **possibilité de c.,** allowable cut; **c. des câbles sous-marins,** cable cutting; (*b*) cut; **c. d'un vêtement,** cut of a garment; **complet de bonne c.,** well-cut suit; *Pros:* **c. d'un vers,** division in a line of verse; *Haird:* **une c. moderne,** a modern hair style; (*c*) *Tls:* cut; **angle de c.,** cutting angle; **c. d'onglet,** mitre cut; **fausse c.,** bevel cut; **assemblage en fausse c.,** bevel joint; *Paperm: etc:* **ligne de c.,** trim-line (of paper-cutting machine); (*d*) *Arch: Draw: etc:* section; **c. en long, c. longitudinale,** longitudinal section; *Nau:* inboard profile; **c. en travers, c. transversale,** cross-section, transverse section; **c. verticale, c. en hauteur,** vertical section, sectional elevation; **en hauteur,** vertical section, sectional elevation; *Nau:* **c. au maître,** midship section; **figurer une machine en c.,** to show a machine in section; **arbre qui a six pieds de c.,** tree that is six feet across; (*e*) outline (of face, etc.); *A: F:* **il a une vilaine, une sale, c.,** I don't like the cut of his jib. **2.** *Cards:* cut, cutting; (*a*) **être sous la c. de qn,** (i) to lead after one's opponent has cut; (ii) *F:* to be under s.o.'s thumb; *F:* **avoir qn sous sa c.,** to have s.o. in one's power; *F:* to have s.o. where one wants him; **avoir une entreprise sous sa c.,** to control an undertaking; **il a deux journaux sous sa c.,** *F:* he has two newspapers in his pocket; **sous la c. des prêtres,** priest-ridden; (*b*) (*card tricks*) **faire sauter la c.,** to make the pass, to slip the cut. **3.** *Min:* **c. d'ouvriers,** gang, shift, of workmen. **4.** *Swimming:* **c. (indienne),** overarm stroke. **5. une c. de drap,** a bolt of cloth.

coupé [kupe]. **1.** *a.* (*a*) cut up, broken up; **pays c.,** much intersected country; **sommeil c.,** broken sleep; **style c.,** jerky style; *Pros:* **vers bien c.,** line with well-marked caesura; *Tchn:* **position "coupé,"** off-position; *El:* **circuit c.,** open, broken, circuit; (*b*) **vin c. d'eau,** wine and water; (*c*) cut off; **armée coupée de ses communications avec, coupée d'avec, la mer,** army cut off from the sea; (*d*) *Ten:* **coup c.,** drive with a cut; **volée coupée-arrêtée,** chop; (*e*) *Her:* (i) party per fesse; (ii) couped, coupé. **2.** *s.m.* (*a*) *Veh:* brougham, coupé; *Aut:* coupé; *Rail:* half-compartment, coupé; (*b*) *Danc:* coupee.

coupe-air [kupɛːr], *s.m.inv. Plumb:* trap (in pipe).

coupe-bordure [kupbɔrdyːr], *s.m. Tls:* edge-trimmer (for lawns); edging-iron, -knife; *pl. coupe-bordure(s).*

coupe-boulons [kupbulɔ̃], *s.m.inv. Tls:* bolt-cutter, -clipper, -cropper.

coupe-bourgeon [kupburʒɔ̃], *s.m. Ent:* common vine-grub; *pl. coupe-bourgeons.*

coupe-bourse [kupburs], *s.m. A:* pickpocket, cutpurse; *pl. coupe-bourses.*

coupe-cercle [kupsɛrkl̩], *s.m. Tls:* washer-cutter; *pl. coupe-cercles.*

coupe-choux [kupʃu], *s.m.inv.* (*a*) *A.Arms:* short (infantry) sabre; (*b*) *Mil: P:* bayonet, *P:* pig-sticker; (*c*) *F:* cut-throat razor; (*d*) *attrib. F:* **frère c.-c.,** lay brother.

coupe-cigare(s) [kupsigaːr], *s.m.* cigar-cutter; *pl. coupe-cigares.*

coupe-circuit [kupsirkɥi], *s.m.inv. El.E:* cut-out, circuit-breaker; **c.-c. à fusible,** fuse; **c.-c. à bain d'huile,** oil breaker-switch, oil fuse cut-out; **c.-c. à l'air libre,** air breaker-switch, open fuse cut-out.

coupe-cors [kupkɔːr], *s.m.inv.* corn-razor, -plane, -cutter.

coupe-coupe [kupkup], *s.m.inv.* = machete, matchet.

coupée [kupe], *s.f. Nau:* gangway (opening or port), gang-port; **échelle de c.,** accommodation ladder.

coupe-épreuves [kupeprœːv], *s.m.inv. Phot:* (*a*) trimming knife; (*b*) print-trimmer, -cutter.

coupe-feu [kupfø]. **1.** *s.m.inv. For:* avenue, cutting (to stop the spread of fire); firebreak. **2.** *a.inv.* **porte c.-f.,** fire-proof door, fire-door; *Nav: Arch:* **cloison c.-f.,** fire-proof bulkhead.

coupe-ficelle [kupfisɛl], *s.m.inv.* twine-cutter.

coupe-fil [kupfil], *s.m.inv. Tls:* wire-cutters; **pince c.-f.,** cutting pliers.

coupe-file [kupfil], *s.m.inv.* (police) pass; **un c.-f. de journaliste,** a press pass.

coupe-filets [kupfilɛ], *s.m.inv. Navy:* net-cutter.

coupe-flamme [kupflam], *s.m.inv.* flame arrester.

coupe-foin [kupfwɛ̃], *s.m.inv. Husb:* hay-knife.

coupe-frites [kupfrit], *s.m.inv. Dom.Ec:* chip cutter.

coupe-froid [kupfrwɑ], *s.m.inv.* weather-strip (for window).

coupe-gaz [kupgɑːz], *s.m.inv.* cut-off (on gas appliance).

coupe-gazon [kupgazɔ̃], *s.m.inv.* lawn mower; = TONDEUSE.

coupe-gorge [kupgɔrʒ], *s.m.inv.* cut-throat place, death-trap, thieves' alley; gambling den; **la vie politique est un affreux c.-g.,** politics are a terribly cut-throat business.

coupe-jambon [kupʒɑ̃bɔ̃], *s.m.inv.* ham-slicer.

coupe-jarret [kupʒarɛ], *s.m.* (hamstringer, *hence*) cut-throat, ruffian, assassin; *pl. coupe-jarrets.*

coupe-julienne [kupʒyljɛn], *s.m.inv. Dom.Ec:* vegetable shredder.

coupe-légumes [kuplegym], *s.m.inv. Dom.Ec:* vegetable cutter.

coupé-lit [kupeli], *s.m. Rail:* sleeping compartment; *pl. coupés-lits.*

coupellation [kupɛl(l)asjɔ̃], *s.f.* cupellation, assaying (of gold, etc.).

coupelle [kupɛl], *s.f.* **1.** (*a*) cupel, test; **passer de l'or à la c.,** to cupel, assay, test, gold; **or de c.,** fine gold; (*b*) *Metalw:* cupel. **2.** *Artil:* (*a*) gas-check cup (of cartridge-case); (*b*) obturator ring (of gun). **3.** *Ind: Atom.Ph:* **coupelle (de colonne à plateaux),** bell-cap (of bubble-tower); **c. à bulle, c. de plateau,** bubble-cap; **plateau à coupelles,** bubble-plate.

coupeller [kupɛl(l)e], *v.tr.* to cupel, assay, test (gold, etc.).

coupement [kupmɑ̃], *s.m.* **1.** cut (with saw), saw-cut. **2.** *Rail:* diamond crossing (of lines).

coupe-mottes [kupmɔt], *s.m.inv. Agr:* clod-crusher, brake harrow.

coupe-net [kupnɛt], *s.m.inv. Tls:* wire-cutter.

coupe-œufs [kupø], *s.m.inv. Cu:* (*a*) egg-scissors, -cutter; (*b*) egg-slicer.

coupe-ongles [kupɔ̃gl̩], *s.m.inv.* nail-clippers.

coupe-paille [kuppɑːj], *s.m.inv. Husb:* chaff-cutter, -chopper.

coupe-pain [kuppɛ̃], *s.m.inv.* bread-cutter, -slicer.

coupe-papier [kuppapje], *s.m.inv.* **1.** paper-knife. **2.** paper cutter.

coupe-pâte [kuppɑːt], *s.m.inv.* **1.** dough-knife. **2.** paste-cutter.

couper [kupe], *v.tr.* to cut. **1.** (*a*) **c. de la viande en morceaux,** to cut up meat; **se c. le doigt, au doigt,** to cut one's finger; **il se couperait en quatre pour son ami,** he'd do anything, he'd cut himself in pieces, for (the sake of) his friend; **c. un arbre,** to cut down, chop down, fell, a tree; *For:* **c. à blanc,** to clean fell, to clear fell; **c. le bras, la tête, à qn,** to cut off s.o.'s arm, head; **c. les bras, c. bras et jambes, à qn,** to leave s.o. helpless, powerless to act; **la nouvelle m'a coupé les jambes,** the news struck me all of a heap; **c. l'herbe sous les pieds de qn,** to cut the ground from under s.o.'s feet; *abs.* **c. dans le vif,** (i) to cut to the quick; (ii) to take extreme measures (to settle sth.); **c. le mal dans sa racine,** to strike at the root of an evil; **c. la poire en deux,** to split the difference; **c. une haie,** to trim, clip, a hedge; **c. les cheveux à qn,** to cut, trim, s.o.'s hair; **brouillard à c. au couteau,** fog you could cut with a knife; **c'est une bêtise à c. au couteau,** it's a piece of crass stupidity; **c. un vêtement,** to cut out a garment; (*b*) *Cards:* (i) to cut (the cards); *abs.* **c'est à vous de c.,** it's your turn to cut; (ii) to trump; (*c*) *Games:* **c. une balle,** (i) *Cr: Ten: Golf:* to cut, slice, a ball; *Hockey:* to give sticks; (*d*) *Husb:* to geld (animal). **2.** (*a*) to cut, cross, intersect; **ligne qui en coupe une autre,** line that intersects, cuts, another; **sentier qui coupe la route,** path that cuts across the road; **pays coupé de canaux,** country intersected by canals; *abs.* **c. à travers champs,** to cut across country; **c. au plus court,** to take a short cut; **par ici, cela coupe court à la ville,** this is a short cut to the town; (*b*) *Aut:* **c. la route à qn,** to cut in; *Nau:* **c. la route d'un navire,** to cut across the bows of a ship; *Sp:* **c. un concurrent, c. la ligne,** to cut in; *Turf:* to bore; *Polo: etc:* **c. un adversaire,** to cross an opponent. **3.** to cut off, interrupt, stop; (*a*) **c. (le) chemin à qn,** to cut s.o. off, to bar s.o.'s way; **c. chemin à un incendie,** to stop a fire from spreading; **être coupé du gros de l'armée,** to be cut off from the main body of the army; **c. la retraite à qn,** to cut off, intercept, s.o.'s retreat; **c. les vivres à l'ennemi,** to cut off the enemy's supplies; *F:* **c. les vivres à qn,** to stop s.o.'s allowance, to starve s.o. out; **c. la fièvre,** to stop, allay, fever; **c. l'appétit à qn,** to spoil s.o.'s appetite, to take s.o.'s appetite away; **c. la parole à qn,** *abs. F:* **c. (court à) qn,** to interrupt s.o., to cut s.o. short; **les sanglots lui coupaient la voix,** his, her, voice was stifled by sobs; **c. la respiration, le souffle, à qn,** (i) to wind s.o.; (ii) to take s.o.'s breath away, to flabbergast s.o.; *P:* **ça te la coupe!** that shakes you! *P:* **c. le sifflet à qn,** (i) to cut s.o.'s throat, to do s.o. in; (ii) to shut s.o. up; *F:* **il m'a coupé mes effets,** he took the wind out of my sails; *Tp:* **c. la communication,** to ring off; **être coupé,** to be cut off; *abs.* **ne coupez pas!** (i) don't cut me off! (ii) hold the line! (*b*) *Tchn:* **c. l'eau,** to turn off, cut off, the water; **c. la vapeur,** to shut down steam, to shut off, cut off, the steam; **c. le gaz à un locataire,** to cut off a tenant's gas; *El:* **c. le courant,** to switch off the current; **c. un circuit,** to break, open, a circuit; *I.C.E:* **c. l'allumage,** to cut off, switch off, the ignition; *I.C.E: F:* **c. les gaz,** to cut off the engine; *Th:* **c. la lumière,** to black out; *Med: Vet:* **c. le lait,** to stop lactation. **4. c. du vin,** (i) to blend; (ii) to water down, dilute, wine. **5.** *v.ind.tr. F:* to avoid, get out of, dodge, doing sth.; **c. à une corvée,** to dodge, shirk, an unpleasant job; **il ne coupera pas au service militaire, il n'y coupera pas des travaux forcés,** he won't dodge, get out of, his military service; he's in for hard labour.

se couper. 1. (*of skin, etc.*) to crack; **tissu qui se coupe,** material which splits (where it is folded, creased). **2.** (*of lines, roads, etc.*) to intersect; to cross. **3.** *F:* to contradict oneself (after having told a lie); to give oneself away; to let the cat out of the bag. **4.** (*of horse*) to interfere.

coupe-racines [kuprasin], *s.m.inv. Agr:* root slicer, turnip chopper, cutter.

couperet [kuprɛ], *s.m.* **1.** (meat) chopper; cleaver. **2.** blade, knife (of the guillotine).

coupe-rondelle [kuprɔ̃dɛl], *s.m. Tls:* washer-cutter; *pl. coupe-rondelle(s).*

couperose [kuproːz], *s.f.* **1.** *Com:* **c. verte,** green vitriol, copperas, ferrous sulphate; **c. bleue,** blue vitriol, copper sulphate. **2.** *Med:* acne rosacea; blotchiness.

couperosé [kuproze], *a. Med:* (*of the skin*) affected with acne rosacea; *F:* with grog blossoms; blotched; **teint c.,** blotchy complexion.

couperoser [kuproze], *v.tr.* to blotch; to make (face) blotchy.

coupe-sève [kupsɛːv], *s.m.inv. Arb:* ringing knife.

coupe-sucre [kupsykr̥], *s.m.inv.* sugar cutter.

coupe-tête [kuptɛt], *s.m.inv. A: F:* executioner, headsman.

coupe-tiffes [kuptif], *s.m.inv. F:* hairdresser.

coupe-tige [kuptiʒ], *s.m.inv. Hort:* secateur(s).

coupe-tirage [kuptiraːʒ], *s.m.inv.* damper (of boiler, etc.).

coupe-tout [kuptu], *s.m.inv. El:* master switch.

coupette [kupɛt], *s.f.* linoleum cutter.

coupe-tube(s) [kuptyb], *s.m.inv.*, **coupe-tuyaux** [kuptɥijo], *s.m.inv. Tls:* tube-cutter, pipe-cutter.

coupeur, -euse [kupœːr, -øːz], *s.* **1.** (*a*) cutter (of clothes, etc.); (*b*) **c. de bourses,** pickpocket; **c. de fils, de cheveux, en quatre,** hair-splitter; *F:* **c. d'oreilles,** braggart, bully. **2.** *s.m. Orn:* **c. d'eau,** scissor-bill, skimmer. **3.** *s.f.* **coupeuse,** (*a*) (paper-, rail-)cutting machine; *Paperm:* **coupeuse à bois,** chipper, chopper; (*b*) *Min:* header; (*c*) *Ent:* **coupeuse (de feuilles),** leaf-cutter (bee).

coupe-vent [kupvɑ̃], *s.m.inv.* **1.** wind-cutter (on railway engine, etc.); **profil en c.-v.,** sharp-cut profile. **2.** *Cost: Fr.C:* windcheater.

coupe-verre [kupvɛːr], *s.m.inv. Tls:* glass-cutter; **c.-v. à molette,** wheel glass-cutter.

couplage [kuplaːʒ], *s.m.* (*a*) *Mec.E:* coupling, connecting (of wheels, etc.); coupling (of railway engines); **c. direct,** direct coupling; **à c. direct,** gearless; (*b*) *El.E: Elcs:* coupling, connection, interlocking; **c. à réaction,** back coupling, regenerative coupling; **c. automatique,** automatic interlocking; **c. capacitif,** capacitive coupling; **c. d'un transformateur,** vector-group of a transformer; **c. en parallèle,** connection in parallel, parallel connection; **c. en série,** connection in series, series connection; **c. entre étages,** **c. cathodique,** interstage coupling; **c. lâche,** loose coupling; **c. par bobine d'arrêt,** choke coupling; **c. par capacité,** capacitance coupling; **c. par induction,** induction, inductive, coupling; **c. par résistance,** resistance, resistor, coupling; **c. par transformation,** transformer coupling; **c. polygonal, c. à phases reliées entre elles,** mesh connection; **c. en carré,** four-phase mesh connection; **c. en triangle,** three-phase mesh connection; **c. réactif,** feed-back coupling, reaction coupling; **c. résistance-capacité,** resistance-capacitance coupling; **coefficient de c.,** coupling coefficient, coupling factor; **résistance de c.,** load-shifting resistor; (*c*) *Space:* docking (of two spacecraft).

couple [kupl]. I. *s.m.* **1.** pair, couple; married couple, man and wife; **c. de pigeons, de perdrix,** pair of pigeons, of partridges; **c. de bœufs,** yoke of oxen; **arrangés par couples,** arranged in pairs; *Danc:* (*quadrille*) **c. no. 1, 2, 3, 4,** top, bottom, side-top, side-bottom, couple. **2.** (*a*) *Mec: Ph:* **couple (de forces),** couple (of forces); **couple (moteur),** (motor) torque; **c. antagoniste,** opposing couple, torque; (*b*) *Mec.E: etc:* **couple (de torsion),** torque; **c. au frein,** locked-rotor torque; **c. de rappel,** restoring torque, force; **c. de serrage,** torque load; **c. maximum constant à vide, c. de décrochage,** pull-out torque; **c. maximum constant en charge, c. d'accrochage,** pull-in torque; **c. de renversement,** torque reaction, torque; **c. résistant,** resisting torque; **c. renvoi d'angle,** bevel gear; *Av:* **c. redresseur,** restoring torque, force; *Av: etc:* **c. d'hélice,** propeller torque; *Av:* **c. de décrochage,** stalling torque; (*c*) *El:* cell, element (of battery); **c. voltaïque,** voltaic couple; **c. thermo-électrique,** thermocouple. **3.** (*a*) *N.Arch:* frame, timber; **c. de levée, droit,** chief frame, timber; **c. de remplissage,** filling frame; **c. renforcé,** deep frame; **c. dévoyé,** cant timbers; (*b*) *Nau:* **avirons à c.** double sculls; **nager à, en, c.,** to double-scull; **canot armé en c.,** double-banked boat; **remorquer un navire à c.,** to tow a ship alongside; **s'amarrer à c. d'un navire,** to moor alongside of a ship. **4.** *Fish:* spreader.

II. **couple,** *s.f.* **1.** *Ven: etc:* leash (for hounds, etc.). **2. une bonne c. de soufflets,** a couple of good blows.

couplé [kuple], *a.* coupled, joined; connected; *Navy:* **pièces couplées en tourelles,** twin turret guns; *Mec.E:* **roues couplées,** coupled wheels; *Phot:* **télémètre c.,** built-in, coupled, range-finder; *Turf:* **pari c.,** double.

couplement [kupləmɑ̃], *s.m.* = COUPLAGE.

couplemètre [kupləmɛtr], *s.m. Mec.E:* torque-meter.

coupler [kuple], *v.tr.* **1.** to couple; to attach (things) together; *El:* to join up, connect (cells). **2.** to leash (hounds). **3.** (*of wolves*) to couple.

couplet [kuplɛ], *s.m.* **1.** hinge. **2.** (*a*) verse (of song); *pl.* song; *F:* **il n'a pas manqué de placer son c. sur la vie chère,** he couldn't resist coming out with his little piece about the high cost of living; (*b*) *Th:* declamatory speech.

coupleter [kuplәte], *v.tr. A:* (**je couplète, n. coupletons; je couplèterai**) to lampoon (s.o.).

coupleteur [kuplәtœːr], **coupletier** [kuplәtje], *s.m.* song writer, lyric writer.

coupleur [kuplœːr], *s.m. El:* make-and-break; **c. de faisceau longitudinal,** longitudinal beam coupler; *Mec.E:* **c. centrifuge,** centrifugal clutch.

coupoir [kupwaːr], *s.m.* cutter, cutting-out tool; *Typ:* lead-cutter.

coupoir-biseautier [kupwaːrbizotje], *s.m. O: Typ:* (hand) mitring and lead-cutting machine.

coupole [kupɔl], *s.f.* (*a*) *Arch:* cupola, dome; **être reçu sous la c.,** to be made a member of the *Académie Française*; **discours prononcé sous la c.,** speech delivered before one of the *Académies* of the *Institut de France*; (*b*) *Fort: Navy:* cupola, (gun-)turret; *Mil.Av:* (gun-)blister; **c. à pivot,** pivot-mounted cupola; **c. tournante,** revolving cupola, revolving (gun-)turret; (*c*) *Av:* **c. de navigation astronomique, c. vitrée du navigateur,** astrodome.

coupon [kupɔ̃], *s.m.* **1.** portion cut off; cutting; (*a*) *Com:* remnant; **c. de robe,** dress length; (*b*) *Mec:* test-bar; *Rail:* short length (of rail). **2.** (*a*) coupon; *Fin:* **c. d'action,** sub-share; **c. de dividende, d'intérêt,** dividend, interest, warrant, coupon; **c. attaché,** cum dividend; with, cum, coupon; **c. détaché,** ex dividend, ex coupon; **c. arriéré,** coupon in arrear; (*b*) *Th:* **c. de loge, de fauteuil d'orchestre,** box, stall, ticket; *Rail:* **c. d'aller, de retour,** outward half, return half (of ticket).

coupon-prime [kupɔ̃prim], *s.m. Com:* gift voucher; *pl. coupons-prime.*

coupon-réponse [kupɔ̃repɔ̃ːs], *s.m. Post:* **c.-r. international,** international reply coupon; *pl. coupons-réponse.*

coupure [kupyːr], *s.f.* **1.** (*a*) cut, gash (on finger, etc.); crack (in skin, etc.); (*b*) cut(ting), drain, irrigation channel. **2.** (*a*) cutting, piece cut out; **c. de journal,** newspaper cutting; *Typ:* **imposition avec c.,** imposition with offcut; (*b*) *Th: etc:* cut, excision (in play, document); **faire des coupures dans le rôle de qn,** to cut s.o.'s part, lines; (*c*) *El:* **c. (de courant),** (power) cut; **pouvoir de c.,** breaking capacity; **essai de c.,** break test; **polarisation de c.,** grid bias, cut-off bias; (*d*) gap, gulf; **la c. entre son passé et son avenir,** the gap, break, between his past and his future; **la c. entre le monde communiste et le monde libre,** the gulf between the communist and the free worlds. **3.** (*a*) *Fin:* (bank-)note (of less than 50 francs); **c. de dix francs,** ten-franc note; **c. d'action,** sub-share; (*b*) map sheet. **4.** (*a*) *Geol: Geog:* fault; rift; (mountain) ravine; **c. transversale,** transverse valley; **c. de méandre,** cut-off; (*b*) *Mil:* obstacle; **s'installer derrière, tenir, une c.,** to take up position behind, to hold, an obstacle; *Civ.E: Mil.E:* **c. en brèche humide, c. en brèche sèche,** wet gap, dry gap. **5.** (*a*) *Mec.E:* gap (in lathe-bed); (*b*) *W.Tel:* **c. d'antenne,** spark micrometer.

couque [kuk], *s.f. Cu:* (*a*) Flemish cake; (*b*) (*in Flanders, Champagne*) gingerbread.

cour [kuːr], *s.f.* **1.** court (of prince, etc.); (*a*) **à la c.,** at court; **dame de la c.,** lady at court, court lady; **gens de c.,** courtiers; **être bien, mal, en c.,** to be in favour, out of favour; **ami de c.,** false, insincere, friend; **abbé de c.,** worldly cleric; **eau bénite de c.,** empty words; *s.a.* PÉTAUD; (*b*) **faire sa c. au roi,** to pay one's court, homage, to the king; **faire sa c. à un personnage influent,** to curry favour with an influential person; **faire la c. à une jeune fille,** to court a girl; **pendant qu'il lui faisait la c.,** during his courtship. **2. c. de justice,** court of justice; **haute c.,** High Court of Justice; **mettre qn hors de c.,** to dismiss s.o.'s case, to nonsuit s.o.; *s.a.* AIDE[1], COMPTE (*c*). **3.** (*a*) court, yard, courtyard; **c. de ferme,** farmyard; **c. d'honneur,** main courtyard; **c. anglaise,** (basement) area; **c. d'école,** school playground; *Mil:* **c. de quartier,** barrack square; *Rail:* **c. de marchandises,** goods yard; *Th:* **côté c.,** "O.P." (side) (opposite prompter); *cf.* JARDIN 1; (*b*) (*in cafés, etc., of the N. of Fr.*) lavatory.

courable [kurabl], *a. Ven:* **cerf c.,** warrantable, runnable, stag.

courage [kuraːʒ], *s.m.* courage; valour; pluck; **perdre c.,** to lose courage, to lose heart; **avoir assez de c. pour refuser,** to be man enough, courageous enough, to refuse; **se sentir le c. de faire qch.,** to feel up to doing sth.; **je ne m'en sens pas le c.,** I don't feel equal to it; *F:* up to it; **prendre c.,** to take courage, to take heart; *F:* **prendre son c. à deux mains,** to take one's courage in both hands; to pluck up courage; **s'armer de c. pour faire qch.,** to brace, steel, oneself to do sth.; to summon up the courage to do sth.; **cela leur donnera du c.,** that will put a bit of fresh life into them; **être plein de c.,** to be full of energy; **(du) c.!** (i) cheer up! buck up! (ii) keep it up! keep going! **avoir le c. de ses opinions,** to have the courage of one's convictions; **vous n'auriez pas le c. de les renvoyer!** you wouldn't have the heart to dismiss them! **travailler avec c.,** to work with a will, with spirit; **déployer tout son c.,** to summon up all one's courage; **le c. me manqua,** my courage failed me; *O:* **leur c. faiblit,** their spirit is flagging; **vous n'avez pas le c. d'une souris!** you haven't the courage, *F:* the guts, of a louse! **combattre avec c.,** to fight bravely, courageously.

courageusement [kuraʒøzmɑ̃], *adv.* (*a*) courageously, bravely; (*of a man*) manfully; (*b*) zealously, with energy.

courageux, -euse [kuraʒø, -øːz], *a.* **1.** courageous, brave. **2.** zealous, energetic; **il n'est pas très c. pour l'étude,** he doesn't show much enthusiasm for his studies; **élève c.,** hard-working pupil.

courailler [kurɑje], *v.i. usu. Pej: F:* to gad about; to gallivant.

courailleur, -euse [kurɑjœːr, -øːz], *usu. Pej:* **1.** *s.* gallivanter, gadabout. **2.** *a.* gallivanting.

couramment [kuramɑ̃], *adv.* **1.** easily, readily; **lire, parler, c. une langue étrangère,** to read, speak, a foreign language fluently. **2.** generally, usually; **outils c. employés,** tools in general use; **ce mot s'emploie c.,** this word is in current use.

courant, -ante [kurɑ̃, -ɑ̃ːt]. **1.** *a.* (*a*) *A:* running; *Her:* courant; **chien c.,** hound; **(écriture) courante,** running, cursive, (hand)writing; *Typ:* **titre c.,** running headline; *A: Mec.E:* **courroie courante,** running belt; *Mill:* **(meule) courante,** running millstone, runner; *Nau:* **manœuvres courantes,** running rigging; (*b*) (*of measurements*) linear, running; **mètre c.,** running metre; **prix par pied c.,** price per foot run; (*c*) flowing, running (water, etc.); **chambre avec eau courante,** bedroom with running water; (*d*) current (account, interest, etc.); **dette courante,** floating debt; **le mois c.,** the present, current, month; **le cinq du (mois) c., le cinq c.,** the fifth inst.; **fin c.,** at the end of this month; **vie courante,** everyday life; **opinion courante,** current opinion; **mot d'usage c.,** word in current, ordinary, general, use; **ce qu'en langage c. on appelle . . .,** what is commonly known as . . .; **c'est de pratique courante,** it is the usual practice; **marchandises de vente courante,** goods that have a ready sale; **monnaie courante,** legal currency; *F:* **ces personnes sont monnaie courante de nos jours,** these people are two a penny nowadays; *F:* **l'homme d'affaires c.,** the average business man; **prix c.,** (i) current price; (ii) price list; **barème c. de rémunération,** ordinary scale of remuneration; **épaisseur courante de tôles,** standard thickness of sheet iron; *Com:* **marque courante,** standard make; **de taille courante,** of standard size; **dépenses courantes,** running expenses. **2.** *s.m.* (*a*) current; running water; **c. d'eau,** (i) current, stream, of water; (ii) tidal current; **c. fluvial,** river current; **c. de dérive,** drift current; *Oc:* **c. de flot, de jusant,** flood, ebb, current; *Hyd.E:* **c. d'arrachement,** rip current; **lutter contre, remonter, le c.,** to stem the tide; **suivre le c.,** to go, to drift along, with the tide; to drift downstream; **aller contre le c.,** to go against the tide; **c. de fond,** undercurrent (in lake, etc.); **c. marin,** marine current; **c. sous-marin,** undercurrent (in sea); undertow; **c. d'air,** (i) draught; (ii) *Meteor:* air current; (iii) *Metall:* blast; **c. inférieur,** undercurrent (in air); **secret c. de mécontentement,** undercurrent of discontent; **c. d'immigration,** steady flow of immigrants; **le c. de l'opinion publique,** the main stream of public opinion; **écrire au c. de la plume,** to let one's pen run on; *Med:* **c. sanguin,** flow; (*b*) *El:* **c. électrique,** electric current; **courants de Foucault,** eddy currents; **condenseur à courants contraires, à courants dans le même sens,** counter-flow, parallel-flow, condenser; **couper le c.,** to cut off the current, to break contact; **fil hors c., fil sans c.,** dead wire; **rail de c.,** live rail; **c. électronique,** electronic current; **c. force,** power (circuit); **c. spatial,** space current; **c. thermo-électrique,** thermo-current; **c. à vide,** no-load current; **c. de charge,** (i) load current; (ii) charging current (of battery); **c. de crête, de pointe,** peak current; **c. de repos,** quiescent current; **c. de retour,** back current; **c. direct,** forward current; **c. d'obscurité,** dark current; **c. inverse,** inverse, reverse, echo, current; **c. perturbateur,** interference current; **c. universel, tous courants,** all-mains; A.C.-D.C. current; **établir, mettre, le c.,** to switch on (the current); **lancer le c.,** to cut in the current; **mettre le c. à la terre,** to earth, *U.S:* ground, a circuit; (*c*) **c. de flammes,** flue (of boiler); **c. de flammes de bas en haut,** upper flue; **c. de flammes de haut en bas,** down flue; **c. de flammes longitudinal,** flash flue; *Tchn: Mec.E: Min:* **c. d'air ascendant,** upcast, updraught; **c. d'air descendant,** downcast, downdraught; *Metall:* **c. d'air chaud,** hot blast; (*d*) course; **dans le c. de l'année,** in the course of the year, some time during the year; **dans le c. de la semaine,** within the next week, some day this week; **c. des affaires,** course of events; **c. du marché,** current market prices; **être au c. de l'affaire,** to know all about, be

conversant with, the matter; *F:* to be in the know, in the picture; **il est au c. de toute l'affaire,** he has the whole business at his finger-tips; **quand vous serez au c. . . .,** when you have got into the swing, into the way (of things); *F:* when you've got the hang of things . . .; **mettre qn au c. des faits, d'une décision,** to acquaint s.o. with the facts, to inform s.o. of a decision; **j'ajouterai, pour vous mettre au c., que . . .,** let me add, for your benefit, that . . .; **se mettre au c. de qch.,** to become, make oneself, acquainted with sth.; **tenir qn au c. (des événements),** to keep s.o. well informed on, well posted on, up to date on, in touch with, current events; **il m'a mis au c.,** he told me all about it; **mes livres de comptes sont au c.,** my account books are up to date, are posted up; **mettre le grand livre au c.,** to write up, post up, the ledger; **se remettre au c.,** to make up arrears (of work); **être au c. de son travail,** to be keeping up with one's work; **professeur qui est très au c. des nouvelles méthodes,** professor who is very conversant with new methods; **touristes au c. des problèmes de l'architecture,** architecturally-minded tourists; **se tenir au c. de l'actualité politique,** to keep abreast of political events; *(e) Nau:* **courant (d'une manœuvre),** running part, hauling part (of rigging); **c. de palan,** tackle-fall. **3.** *s.f.* **courante,** *(a) A:* coranto (dance); *(b) P:* diarrhœa.

courantille [kurɑ̃tiːj], *s.f. Fish:* tunny nét.

courantin, -ine [kurɑ̃tɛ̃, -in], *s. A:* **1.** vagabond, loafer. **2.** *Dial: (W.Fr.)* messenger, errand-boy, -girl.

courant-jet [kurɑ̃ʒɛ], *s.m. Meteor:* jet(-)stream; *pl. courants-jets.*

courantographe [kurɑ̃tɔgraf], *s.m. Oc:* current meter.

couraquet [kurakɛ], *s.m. Orn: F:* sedge warbler.

couratari [kuratari], *s.m. Bot:* couratari.

courbage [kurbaːʒ], *s.m.* curving, bending; warping; deflection.

courbant [kurbɑ̃], *a. & s.m. Com:* **(bois) c.,** compass-timber, crooked, curved, timber.

courbaril [kurbaril], *s.m.* **1.** *Bot:* *(a)* courbaril; locust-tree, varnish-tree; *(b)* locust-wood. **2.** *Com:* gum-animé.

courbarine [kurbarin], *s.f. Com:* gum-animé.

courbaton [kurbatɔ̃], *s.m. N.Arch:* bracket.

courbatu [kurbaty], *a.* **1.** *(of pers.)* tired-out, knocked-up, aching, sore, stiff all over. **2.** *Vet: (of horse)* foundered.

courbature [kurbatyːr], *s.f.* **1.** stiffness, tiredness; **avoir une c., des courbatures,** to be aching all over, stiff all over. **2.** *Vet:* founder.

courbaturer [kurbatyre], *v.tr.* **1.** to tire (s.o.) out, to knock (s.o.) up; **je me sens tout courbaturé,** I'm stiff all over, aching all over. **2.** to founder (horse).

courbe [kurb]. **1.** *a.* curved; **la rue fait une ligne c. autour du château,** the street curves round the castle, skirts the castle; *Mil: Ball:* **tir c.,** high-angle fire, curved fire; *Rail:* **rail c.,** bent rail; curved rail; *Com:* **bois c.,** compass-timber, crooked, curved, timber. **2.** *s.f.* *(a)* curve; graph; *Geom:* **c. à grand, de fort, rayon,** flat, long-radius, curve; **c. de faible rayon,** sharp, short-radius, curve; **c. gauche,** tortuous curve, twisted curve; **c. plane,** plane curve; **c. polaire,** polar curve; *Mth:* **c. en cloche, de probabilité,** probability curve; **c. de lieux géométriques,** loci curve; *Mec:* **c. d'énergie potentielle,** potential energy curve; *Ph:* **c. caractéristique,** characteristic curve; *Opt:* **c. d'intensité lumineuse,** candle-power curve; **c. de visibilité,** visibility curve; **c. du spectre,** spectrum locus; *Nau:* **c. de déplacement,** curve of displacement; **c. des charges,** curve of loads; *El: Elcs:* **c. de charge, de débit,** load curve; **c. de réponse,** response curve, characteristics; **c. de résonance,** resonance curve; *Atom.Ph:* **c. de décroissance,** decay curve; **c. d'effet de dose,** dose-effect curve; *(b) Mapm: Surv:* **c. de niveau, de nivellement,** contour (line); **carte en courbes,** contoured map; **c. bathymétrique,** submarine contour, bathymetric contour; **c. hypsométrique,** hypsometric contour; **c. intercalaire,** intercalary contour line; **c. non levée,** approximate contour; **exécution du tracé des courbes,** contouring; *Agr:* **culture en courbes de niveau,** contour farming; *(c) Geog:* **c. de débit (d'un cours d'eau),** hydrograph; **c. de lit, d'équilibre,** grade; *(d) Rail:* **c. d'évitement,** siding; **c. de raccord(ement),** junction curve; **c. de transition,** transition curve; **c. raide,** sharp curve; *(e) N.Arch:* knee (of ship framing); **c. d'arcasse,** transom-knee; **c. d'étambot,** heel-knee; **c. de barrot,** beam-knee; **c. du pont,** deck-knee; **c. horizontale,** lodging knee; **c. oblique,** dagger-knee, raking knee; **c. verticale,** hanging knee; *(f) Av:* **c. de poursuite,** pursuit curve; **c. balistique,** trajectory (of spacecraft); *(g) Vet:* curb (on horse's leg).

courbé [kurbe], *a.* curved, bent (line, etc.); bowed (figure, etc.); **vieillard c. sous un pesant fardeau,** old man bending under a heavy load; **c. sous le joug,** bent under the yoke; **marcher les épaules courbées, le dos c.,** to walk with a stoop; **c. sur ses livres,** poring over his books; **il était c. en deux de rire,** he was doubled up with laughter.

courbement [kurbəmɑ̃], *s.m.* bending, curving.

courber [kurbe]. **1.** *v.tr.* to bend, curve; **c. en deux,** to bend double; **taille courbée par l'âge,** figure bowed with age; **c. le front, la tête,** (i) to bow one's head; (ii) to submit; **c. l'échine devant qn,** to grovel before s.o., to kowtow to s.o. **2.** *v.i.* to bend; **toit qui courbe,** roof that sags.

se courber, to bow, bend, stoop; **se c. devant qn,** (i) to bow; (ii) to kowtow to s.o.; **se c. jusqu'à terre devant qn,** to bend low before s.o.; **il se courba pour ramasser l'épingle,** he stooped to pick up the pin.

courbet [kurbɛ], *s.m. Tls:* billhook.

courbette [kurbɛt], *s.f.* *(a) Equit:* curvet; **caracoler et faire des courbettes,** to prance and curvet; *(b) F:* **faire des courbettes à qn,** to bow and scrape, to kowtow, to s.o.

courbetter [kurbɛte, -ete], *v.i. Equit:* to curvet.

courbevoisien, -ienne [kurbəvwazjɛ̃, -jɛn], *a. & s. Geog:* (native, inhabitant) of Courbevoie.

courbotte [kurbɔt], *s.f.* rock-staff (of forge-bellows).

courbure [kurbyːr], *s.f.* *(a) Geom: Ph:* curvature (of earth, space, etc.); **c. double,** S curve; dog's leg (in pipe); **rayon de c.,** radius of curvature; *Opt:* **c. de champ,** curvature of field; *(b)* bend, curve (of piece of wood, etc.); *Sm.a:* **c. de la crosse,** bend of the stock; *Sp:* **c. de ski,** arch of ski; **grande c. de ski,** spring of ski; *(c)* camber (of road, aircraft wing, etc.); *Av:* **plan à c. variable,** variable-camber plane; **volet de c.,** camber-flap; *(d)* sweep (of the lines of a ship); *(e)* sagging (of beam, etc.); *(f) Anat:* **c. sigmoïde,** sigmoid flexure.

courcailler [kurkaje], *v.i.* *(of female quail)* to call.

courcaillet [kurkajɛ], *s.m.* *(a)* quail call; *(b)* quail pipe.

courçon [kursɔ̃], *s.m. Mil:* submerged stake.

coureau, -eaux [kuro], *s.m.* **1.** channel, passage (between shoals). **2.** *Dial: Nau:* smack, yawl.

courette [kurɛt], *s.f.* small (court)yard, small court.

coureur, -euse [kurœːr, -øːz], *s.* **1.** *s.m.* *(a)* runner; *Mil:* runner, messenger; *Sp:* runner, racer; **c. de fond,** (i) long-distance runner; (ii) stayer; **c. cycliste,** racing cyclist; **c. automobile** *(pl. coureurs automobile),* racing driver; **c. de vitesse,** sprinter; *a.* **jument coureuse,** racing mare; *(b)* **les coureurs,** (i) *Orn:* Ratitae; (ii) *Ent:* Cursoria; *Orn:* **c. indien,** Indian runner (duck). **2.** *s.m.* *(a)* wanderer, rover; *Com:* (bookseller's) collector, runner; **c. de routes,** tramp; *A:* **c. des bois,** (i) *(in Canada)* trapper; (ii) backwoodsman; *(b)* gadabout; **c. de spectacles,** inveterate playgoer; **c. de tripots,** frequenter of gambling dens; **c. de cabarets,** pub crawler; **c. de filles,** *F:* skirt-chaser; **c. de femmes, de jupons, de cotillons,** womaniser; *F:* wolf, wencher; *(c)* **c. d'aventures,** seeker of adventures, adventurer; **c. de dots,** fortune hunter; *Sp:* **c. de prix,** pot-hunter; *(d) Nau: F:* **c. de bordée,** leave-breaker. **3.** *s.f.* **coureuse,** woman of loose morals.

courge [kurʒ], *s.f.* **1.** *Bot:* gourd; **c. potiron,** red and yellow gourd, *U.S:* winter squash; **c. citrouille,** pumpkin; **c. à la moelle, c. aubergine,** vegetable marrow; **c. éponge,** loofah, vegetable sponge. **2.** *P:* clot.

courgette [kurʒɛt], *s.f. Hort:* (small) marrow, courgette.

courir [kuriːr], *v.* *(pr.p.* **courant;** *p.p.* **couru;** *pr.ind.* **je cours, il court, n. courons, ils courent;** *pr.sub.* **je coure;** *p.h.* **je courus;** *fu.* **je courrai)** *the aux. is* **avoir. 1.** *v.i.* to run *(a)* **c. après qn, qch.,** to run after s.o., sth.; *F:* **on lui court après,** they are running after him; **c. aux armes,** to rush, fly, to arms; **j'ai couru le prévenir,** I ran to warn him; **j'y cours,** I'm going directly; **acteur qui fait c. tout Paris,** actor who draws the whole of Paris; **monter, descendre, la colline en courant,** to run up, down, the hill; **s'enfuir en courant,** to run off; **c. çà et là,** to run about; **arriver en courant, tout courant,** to come running up; **faire qch. en courant,** to do sth. in a hurry; **cours jusqu'au bout de la rue voir s'il est là,** run to the end of the street and see if he's there; **cours acheter des saucisses,** run out and get some sausages; *F:* **il est bien loin s'il court encore,** he left ages ago; **c. à sa fin,** to draw to an end; *F:* **tu peux toujours c.!** you've got another think coming! *P:* **c. (sur l'haricot à qn),** to get on s.o.'s nerves; to pester s.o.; *P:* **tu me cours (sur l'haricot),** you give me the willies; you get on my tits; *F:* **elle est toujours à c.,** she's always gadding about; **il ferait mieux de travailler, au lieu de c.,** he would be better employed working, instead of running after women; **c. comme un Basque,** to run like a hare; *(b)* to race, to run (in a race); **faire c. des chevaux,** to race, run, horses; **faire c.,** to keep a racing stable; *Sp: Aut:* **c. pour une maison,** to race for a firm; *(c) (of ship)* to sail; **c. au large,** to stand out to sea; **c. à terre,** to stand in for the land; **c. sur qch.,** to bear down upon sth.; **c. devant le vent,** to run, scud, before the wind; **c. au plus serré,** to sail close-hauled; **c. de l'avant,** to forge ahead; **c. à sec,** to run under bare poles; *(d)* to be current; **le bruit court que . . .,** rumour has it that . . ., there's a report that . . ., they say that . . .; **faire c. un bruit,** to spread a rumour; *impers.* **il court des bruits sur son compte,** there are rumours going round about him; **il court des potins,** some gossip is flying around; **maladies qui courent pendant l'été,** illnesses that are prevalent in summer; **la mode qui court,** the present, prevailing, fashion; *(e)* **le sang court dans les artères,** the blood flows, circulates, through the arteries; **ruisseau qui court vers l'est,** stream that flows, runs, eastward; **le chemin court au bord du lac,** the road runs, lies, along the lake-side; **par les temps qui courent, par le temps qui court,** nowadays, as things go, are, at present; **le mois qui court,** the current month; *Fin:* **les intérêts qui courent,** the accruing interest; **le bail n'a plus qu'un an à c.,** the lease has only one year to run; *(f) (of knot)* to slip. **2.** *v.tr.* *(a)* to run after (sth.); to pursue, to chase; **c. un cerf,** to hunt, chase, a stag; **c. un lièvre,** to course a hare; *s.a.* LIÈVRE; **c. une place,** to seek, go after, a situation; **c. un risque,** to run a risk; **c. la chance de qch., de faire qch.,** to take one's chance(s) of sth., of doing sth.; *A:* **c. la quintaine,** to tilt at the quintain; *(b)* to overrun; **la région était courue par des bandits,** the district was overrun by bandits; **c. les champs,** to run about the fields. **3.** *with cogn. acc.* *(a)* **c. une course,** to run a race; **la coupe se courra demain,** the cup will be run for, competed for, to-morrow; *(b)* **c. le monde,** (i) to roam the world over; (ii) to gad about; *s.a.* RUE[1] 1; **passer son après-midi à c. les magasins,** to spend one's afternoon shopping; **c. les cafés,** to pub-crawl; **c. les spectacles,** to be an inveterate theatre-goer; *(c)* **c. le grand galop,** to go at full speed; *s.a.* POSTE[1] 1; *(d) Nau:* **c. un bord,** to make a tack; **c. des bords,** to tack, beat.

courlan [kurlɑ̃], *s.m. Orn:* courlan.

courlandais, -aise [kurlɑ̃dɛ, -ɛːz], *a. & s.* (native) of Kurland.

Courlande [kurlɑ̃ːd], *Pr.n.f. Geog:* Courland, Kurland.

courlieu [kurljø], *s.m.*, **courlis** [kurli], *s.m. Orn:* curlew, *Scot: F:* whaup; **c. cendré, grand c.,** curlew *(Numenius arquata)*; **c. esquimau,** eskimo curlew; **c. à bec grêle,** slender-billed curlew; **c. de terre,** stone-curlew; *F:* thick knee; **c. corlieu,** whimbrel.

couroir [kurwaːr], *s.m. Nau:* passage, corridor (between cabins).

couronne [kurɔn], *s.f.* **1.** wreath, crown (of flowers, laurel, etc.); **c. mortuaire,** (funeral) wreath; *O:* **c. de perles,** artificial wreath (very common on graves in Fr.); **c. de martyr,** martyr's crown; **c. académique,** academic reward, prize. **2.** (king's) crown; **prendre la c.,** to assume the crown; **sans c.,** uncrowned; **c. de comte, de duc,** count's coronet, ducal coronet; **la triple c.,** the (pope's) tiara; *s.a.* DISCOURS 3. **3.** *(a) A: Num:* crown; **une demi-c.,** half-a-crown; *(b) Paperm:* crown (size); **double c.,** elephant. **4.** *(a)* ring; *Geom:* annulus; *Bot:* corona; **c. de fil,** coil of wire; **c. d'une dent,** crown of a tooth; **c. de pâturon,** coronet of (horse's) hoof; *A:* **c. de sauvetage,** life-buoy; *Astr:* **c. solaire,** solar corona; *(b)* loaf of bread (in the shape of a ring); *(c) Gothic Arch:* **c. entre arêtes,** cusp between ribs. **5.** *(a) Mec.E:* rim (of pulley, wheel); **c. dentée,** crown gear, crown wheel, ring gear (of differential, etc.); sprocket wheel (of capstan, etc.); calyx; **c. à embrayage,** clutch ring; **c. de démarrage,** starter ring-gear; **c. de serrage,** clamping ring; **c. de billes,** ball ring; **c. à double rangée de billes,** double-row ball race; **c. de galets,** roller ring;

c. inférieure, lower race; **c. supérieure,** upper race; **c. d'ailettes, d'aubes,** blade rim, ring (of turbine); **c. fixe, c. directrice,** guide ring (of turbine); **c. mobile,** runner, wheel (of turbine); **c. fixe de réducteur,** fixed ring gear; **c. d'un piston,** packing ring, junk ring; **c. filetée,** ring nut; (*b*) *Civ.E:* head (of pile), ferrule (of stake); (*c*) *Av:* **c. du disque de l'hélice,** propeller annulus; (*d*) *El.E:* **c. porte-balai,** brush ring, rocker (of dynamo); **effet de c.,** corona; **étincelle due à l'effet de c.,** corona discharge; (*e*) *Min:* **c. à molettes,** core bit. **6.** *Fort:* crown work. **7.** *Mus:* corona, pause.

couronné [kurɔne], *a.* **1.** (*a*) wreathed; **c. de fleurs,** wreathed with flowers; **élève trois fois c.,** scholar who has won three prizes; **roman c.,** prize novel; (*b*) crowned (sovereign); *Her:* crowned. **2.** *Bot:* coronate(d). **3.** *Arb:* dry-topped, stag-headed (tree). **4.** *Vet:* **cheval c.,** broken-kneed horse.

couronnement [kurɔnmɑ̃], *s.m.* **1.** (*a*) crowning, coronation (of king); (*b*) capping (of pier, etc.); crowning, coping (of wall, etc.); *Civ.E:* crest, crown (of a dam); *N.Arch:* (**lisse de**) **c.** (**de la poupe**), taffrail; (*c*) climax; **c. d'une belle vie,** crowning, consummation, of a splendid life. **2.** (*a*) scar (on horse's knee), broken knees; (*b*) withering (of tree) from the top.

couronner [kurɔne], *v.tr.* **1.** (*a*) to crown (with a wreath); **c. un élève,** to award a pupil a (wreath together with a) prize; *F:* **pour c. tout . . .,** to cap, crown, it all . . .; **mes efforts furent couronnés de succès,** my efforts were crowned with success; **c. le dîner d'une tasse de café,** to round off the dinner with a cup of coffee; *Prov:* **la fin couronne l'œuvre,** the end crowns all; (*b*) to crown; **couronné d'épines,** crowned with thorns; (*with object and complement*) **c. qn roi,** to crown s.o. king. **2.** to head, surmount (column, etc.); to cap (pier, etc.); to cope, crown (wall, etc.); *Dent:* **c. une dent,** to crown a tooth; *Mil:* **c. les hauteurs,** to occupy, make good, crown, the high ground. **3. c. un cheval,** to let a horse down on its knees; **se c. le genou,** to graze, skin, one's knee.

se couronner. 1. (*of horse*) to come down on its knees, to break its knees. **2.** (*of tree*) to wither at the top.

couronnure [kurɔnyːr], *s.f.* crown (of antlers).

couroucou [kuruku], *s.m. Orn:* trogon.

cou-rouge [kuruːʒ], *s.m. Orn:* robin, redbreast; *pl. cous-rouges.*

couroupita [kurupita], *s.m. Bot:* couroupita, cannon-ball tree.

courre [kuːr], *v.tr. & i. A:* (= COURIR). **1.** *Ven:* **c. un cerf,** to hunt a stag; **c. un lièvre,** to course a hare; *still used in* **chasse à c.,** hunt(ing); **chasser à c.,** to ride to hounds, to hunt; **laisser c. les chiens,** (i) to lay on the pack; (ii) to slip the hounds. **2. c. un cheval,** to race, gallop, a horse.

courrier [kurje], *s.m.* **1.** courier; **c. de cabinet, diplomatique, d'ambassade** = King's, Queen's, messenger; *A:* **salle des courriers,** guests' servants' hall (at hotel); *Post:* **c. ambulant,** sorter (employed on mail train); **c. convoyeur,** mail-van driver. **2.** (*a*) mail, post, letters; *Mil: etc:* **le c.,** correspondence section (of the secretariat); **c. à deux vitesses,** two-tier postal service; **à quand le prochain départ du c.?** (at) what time does the next post leave? **par retour du c.,** by return of post; **dépouiller son c.,** to open one's correspondence, letters, mail; **faire son c.,** to do one's correspondence, to write one's letters; **c'est l'heure du c.,** it's post time; (*b*) (i) *A:* mail coach; (ii) mail boat; (iii) aircraft (flying a regular transport service); *Mil.Av:* courier, liaison aircraft; *s.a.* LONG-COURRIER, MOYEN-COURRIER. **3.** *Journ:* column; **c. des théâtres,** theatre column; **c. des modes,** fashion page; **c. de Paris,** Paris day by day; **c. des lecteurs,** letters to the editor; **c. du cœur,** women's advice column; *F:* problem page.

courriériste [kurjerist], *s.m. Journ:* columnist.

courroie [kurwa], *s.f.* **1.** strap; **c. à boucle,** strap and buckle; **c. de lance,** sling of a lance; *Harn:* **c. d'arrêt,** breeching strap; *Harn:* **c. d'attelle,** (i) hame strap; (ii) hip strap; *Harn:* **c. porte-traits,** trace bearer; **c. de brêlage,** lashing strap; **c. avant (de ski),** toe strap (of ski); *A: F:* **allonger la c.,** to make things go a long way; **serrer la c. à qn,** to keep s.o. on a short allowance; **lâcher la c. à qn,** to let s.o. have his head; **attacher qch. avec une c.,** to fasten sth. with a strap, to strap sth. (up); *B:* **et je ne suis pas digne de délier la c. de ses souliers,** whose shoe's latchet I am not worthy to unloose; *s.a.* CUIR 2. **2.** *Mec.E:* belt; **c. sans fin,** endless belt; **c. de transmission, de commande,** driving belt; **c. en caoutchouc,** rubber belting; **c. articulée,** chain belt; **c. trapézoïdale,** V-belt; **c. transporteuse,** belt, band, conveyor, conveyor belt; **c. d'entretoise,** transom belt; **agrafe, joint, de c.,** belt clamp; **c. croisée,** cross(ed) belt; **c. semi-croisée,** quarter-turn, -twist, belt.

courroucé [kuruse], *a. esp. Lit:* angry (person, voice, sea); *Lit:* wroth; incensed; **il m'a envoyé une lettre courroucée,** he sent me an angry letter.

courroucer [kuruse], *v.tr. Lit:* (**je courrouçai(s), n. courrouçons**) to anger, incense (s.o.).

se courroucer, (*esp. of sea*) to get angry, to become turbulent.

courroux [kuru], *s.m. Lit:* anger, wrath, ire; **être en c.,** to be angry, wroth; **entrer en c.,** to wax wroth; **mer en c.,** angry, raging, sea.

cours [kuːr], *s.m.* **1.** (*a*) course, flow (of river); course, path (of heavenly bodies); *Min:* run (of lode); **c. d'eau,** river, watercourse, waterway, stream; **c. d'eau intermittent,** seasonal, intermittent, stream; **c. inférieur, supérieur, d'un fleuve,** lower, upper, course of a river; **rivière qui a 200 km de c.,** river 200 km long, in length; **le c. des siècles,** the course of years; **le c. du sang,** the blood stream; **poursuivre le c. de ses idées,** to pursue the train of one's thoughts; **le c. de ses pensées,** the trend of his thoughts; **donner libre c. à ses pensées, à son imagination,** to let one's thoughts run freely, to give free rein, free play, to one's imagination; **donner libre c. à sa douleur,** to give free course, to give vent, to one's grief; **laisser libre c. à la justice,** to let justice take its course; **la justice suivit son c.,** the law had its way; **la maladie suit son c.,** the illness is running its course; **affaires en c.,** outstanding business; **travail en c.,** work in progress, on hand; **négociations en c.,** negotiations now proceeding, in progress; **année en c.,** current, present, year; **bâtiment en c. de construction,** building under construction; **en c. de route,** (i) during the march; on the way; (ii) in transit; **au c. de l'hiver,** during the winter; **dans le c. de la journée de jeudi,** in the course of Thursday; **en c. de production,** in production; **une expérience importante est en c.,** an important experiment is under way; **les discussions sont toujours en c.,** discussions are still going on; **la révision du dictionnaire est en c.,** the revision of the dictionary is in progress; **au c. de la séance,** in the course of the sitting, as the sitting progressed; **au c. de la conversation,** in course of conversation; **tué au c. d'une rixe,** killed during a brawl; (*b*) *Const:* **c. d'assise,** course, layer (of bricks, etc.); (*c*) *Med: A: F:* **c. de ventre,** diarrhoea; (*d*) *Nau:* **long c.,** foreign trade; **voyage au long c.,** ocean voyage, sea voyage; *Nau:* **capitaine au long c.,** master mariner; captain, master, of an ocean-going vessel; **navigation au long c.,** deep-sea, ocean, navigation; **navire au long c.,** ocean-going vessel. **2.** (*a*) circulation, currency (of money); (*of coinage*) **avoir c.** (**légal**), to be legal tender; to be in circulation; **c. forcé,** forced currency; (*b*) **donner c. à un bruit,** to spread a rumour; **tous les romans en c.,** all the current novels. **3.** *St.Exch: etc:* quotation, price; **c. du marché,** market prices, rates; **c. de clôture, derniers c.,** closing price; **c. d'ouverture, premier c.,** opening price; **c. du change,** rate of exchange; **c. étranger,** foreign exchange; **c. des devises,** foreign exchange rate; **c. à terme,** price for the account; **c. au comptant,** price for cash; **c. d'achat,** offer price; **c. de rachat,** buying-in price; **c. en bourse, c. officiel,** (i) official price; (ii) (*in London*) house price; **c. hors bourse, c. hors cote,** unofficial price; **c. du jour,** current daily price; **bulletin des cours,** (official) list of quotations; **c.** (**des changes**) **à terme,** forward (exchange) rates; **c. du comptant,** spot price, rate; **c. commerciaux,** commodity prices; **c. du disponible,** price for prompt delivery; spot price, rate; **c. du livrable,** forward delivery price; **c. du fret,** freight rate; **quel est le c. du sucre?** what is sugar quoted at? what is the quotation for sugar? **c. faits,** bargains marked. **4.** (*a*) course (of lectures, etc.); **professer un c.,** to give a course of lectures (sur, on); **faire un c. d'histoire,** (i) to give a history lesson; (ii) to lecture on history; **faire son c. de droit,** to lecture in law; **c. de vacances,** holiday course; **c. de dessin,** drawing lesson; drawing class; **c. de danse,** dancing class; **il n'assiste jamais aux c.,** he never attends lectures; **finir ses c.,** to finish one's studies; (*b*) handbook; text book. **5.** promenade, walk.

course [kurs], *s.f.* **1.** run, running; **au pas de c.,** at a run; *Mil:* at the double; **rattraper qn à la c.,** to catch up with s.o. running; **prendre sa c.,** to set off (running); to start; **arrêté en pleine c.,** checked in full career; **le cheval avait déjà fourni une longue c.,** the horse had already had a long run; **cheval capable de fournir une longue c.,** stayer; *Gym:* **c. volante,** giant stride. **2.** race, racing; *pl.* (*athletics*) track events; **c. à pied,** foot-race; **c. de chevaux,** horse-race; **les courses,** (i) horse-racing; (ii) the races; **c. plate,** flat race; **c. au clocher,** point-to-point race; **c. de haies, c. d'obstacles,** (i) steeplechase; (ii) hurdle-race; **monter en c.,** to ride in races, to race; **c. de fond,** long-distance race; **c. sur 500 m.,** 500 metres race; **c. de vitesse,** sprint; **champ, terrain, de courses,** racecourse; **c. sur route,** road race; **courses sur route,** road racing; **auto de c.,** racing car; *Aut:* **c. de côte,** hill climb; **courses de bateaux,** (i) boat racing; (ii) boat races; **c. à l'aviron,** pulling race; **c. poursuite,** bumping race; **c. de taureaux,** bullfight; *F:* **être dans la c.,** to be with it; to be in the know. **3.** (*a*) excursion, outing, trip; *Mount:* climb; route; **faire une belle c.** (**à pied, à cheval, en voiture**), to have a pleasant walk, ride, outing; (*b*) journey, run (*esp.* in hired conveyance); **payer** (**le prix de**) **sa c.,** to pay one's fare; *Aut: Com:* **c. d'essai** (**que l'on fait faire à un client**), trial run; **il y a une longue c. d'ici là,** it is a long way from here; (*c*) (business) errand; **faire une c., aller en c.,** to go out on business; **être en c.,** to be out (on business); **faire des courses,** (i) to go out shopping; (ii) to run errands, messages; *F:* **elle ramenait ses courses,** she was bringing back her shopping; **garçon de courses,** errand boy; (*d*) *Nau:* day's run. **4.** *A: Nau:* privateering; **faire la c.,** to privateer; **aller en c.,** (i) to cruise; (ii) to go out commerce destroying; **bâtiment armé en c.,** commerce destroyer, raider; privateer; **guerre de c.,** commerce destroying. **5.** (*a*) path, way, course (of person, ship, planet, etc.); course, flight (of projectile); **arrêter le soleil dans sa c.,** to stop the sun in its course; **la lune poursuit sa c.,** the moon keeps on her way; **je poursuivis ma c.,** I went on my way; **il est arrivé au terme, au bout, de la, sa, c.,** his race is run; *F:* (*of pers.*) **être à bout de c.,** to be worn out, exhausted; *F:* done in; **rien n'arrêtait Napoléon dans sa c.,** nothing could stop Napoleon in his course; (*b*) *Mec.E: etc:* travel (of tool, etc.); stroke (of piston); lift (of valve); throw (of eccentric); **c. arrière, de retour,** back stroke, *U.S:* instroke (of piston); **c. aller,** forward stroke, *U.S:* outstroke (of piston); *Aut:* **c. de l'embrayage,** clutch travel; *Machine Tls:* **c. à vide,** idle stroke, non-cutting stroke; **c. utile,** cutting stroke; **c. du chariot,** (i) travel of lathe carriage; (ii) traverse of crab (of crane); **c. longitudinale, transversale, du chariot,** longitudinal, transverse, movement of carriage; **c. de relevage,** range of luffing (of crane jib); **arriver à fond de c., à bout de c.,** (i) (*of piston*) to reach the dead centre; (ii) (*of switch-points, signal, etc.*) to go fully on, to come completely off.

course-croisière [kurskrwazjɛːr], *s.f. Sp: Nau:* (*yachting*) ocean race; *pl. courses-croisières.*

coursier, -ière [kursje, -jɛːr]. **1.** *s.m.* (*a*) *Lit:* (i) (war-)horse, charger; (ii) steed, courser; (*b*) *Hyd.E:* mill race; (*c*) *Naval Artil:* bow chaser, bow gun. **2.** *s.m. & f.* (*office, etc.*) messenger. **3.** *s.f.* (*a*) small path (across fields); (*b*) *Ecc.Arch:* (narrow) triforium passage; (*c*) *Fort:* chemin de ronde; (*d*) *Metalw:* channel (for molten metal); (*e*) shuttle race (of sewing machine).

coursive [kursiːv], *s.f.* passageway; gallery (connecting rooms); *Nau:* alleyway, gangway.

courson, -onne [kursɔ̃, -ɔn]. **1.** *Arb:* (*a*) *a.* spur-bearing; (*b*) *s.m.* spur bearer. **2.** *s.m. Mil:* submerged stake.

court[1] [kuːr]. **1.** *a.* (*a*) (*in space*) short; **herbe courte,** short grass; **phrases courtes,** short sentences; **avoir les jambes courtes, être c. de jambes,** to be short in the leg, to have short legs; **avoir la vue courte,** (i) to be short-sighted; (ii) to lack forethought, *F:* not to see farther than the end of one's nose; **homme à courtes vues,** man of limited outlook; **avoir l'esprit c.,** to be of limited intelligence; **mes moyens sont trop courts pour cela,** my means will not stretch, run, to that; *Nau:* **vague, mer, courte,** choppy sea, short sea; *Artil:* **coup c.,** short; **le chemin le plus c.,** *abs.* **le plus c.,** the quickest way; **le chemin le plus c. pour y arriver,** the quickest way there; **prendre, couper, au plus c.,** to take a short cut; *F:* **savoir le c. et le long d'une affaire,** to know the long and short of a matter; (*b*) (*in time*) **c. intervalle,** short, brief, interval; **courte vie,** short

life; *F:* **la faire courte et bonne,** to have a short life and a merry one; **de courte durée,** short-lived; **avoir la mémoire courte, avoir courte mémoire, être c. de mémoire,** to have a short memory; to be forgetful; *Fin:* **papiers à courts jours, papiers courts,** short-dated bills; **pour faire c.,** to cut a long story short, to cut it short; (*c*) *Cer:* **pâte courte,** short paste; *Cu:* **sauce courte,** thick sauce. **2.** *adv.* short; **s'arrêter c.,** to stop short, suddenly; **demeurer, rester, c. (dans un discours),** to stop short (in a speech), to break down; *F:* to dry up; **tourner c. à droite,** to turn sharp to the right; **respirer c.,** to be short-winded; **cheveux coupés tout c.,** short-, close-cropped hair; **barbiche c. taillée,** short beard; **couper c. à qn,** to cut s.o. short; **couper c. à une explication,** to cut an explanation short. **3.** (*a*) *adv.phr.* **tout c.,** simply, only, merely; **il s'appelait Jean tout c.,** he was just called John, he had no other name but John; (*b*) *adv.phr.* **de c.; tenir un chien, un cheval, de c.,** to hold a dog on a short leash, a horse on a tight rein, tightly reined; **tenir qn de c.,** to keep a tight hold on s.o.; **il tient son fils de c.,** he doesn't allow his son any freedom; **prendre qn de c.,** (i) to give s.o. short notice; (ii) to catch s.o. unawares; **être pris de c.,** to be caught unprepared; (*c*) *prep.phr.* **à c. (de),** short of; *Ind:* **à c. de main-d'œuvre, de personnel,** short-handed, short-staffed; **à c. de place,** short of space, of room; **à c. (d'argent),** short of money, hard up; **je suis à c. de tabac,** I've run out of tobacco; **il n'est jamais à c. d'arguments,** he's never at a loss for an argument, for an answer; **à c. (de mots),** at a loss for words, for sth. to say.

court² [ku:r], *s.m. Ten:* court; **c. sur gazon,** grass court; **c. dur,** hard court.

courtage [kurta:ʒ], *s.m. Com:* **1.** broking, brokerage; **faire le c.,** to be a broker; **c. en immeubles,** real-estate agency. **2.** brokerage, commission.

courtaud, -aude [kurto, -o:d], *a. & s.* **1.** *A:* dock-tailed, crop-eared (animal); **étriller qn comme un chien c.,** to give s.o. a sound thrashing. **2.** (*a*) dumpy, squat, stocky (person); **notre bonne était une grosse courtaude,** our servant was short and thick-set; (*b*) *A:* **c. (de boutique),** shop assistant, shop-hand, *F:* counter-jumper.

courtauder [kurtode], *v.tr.* to dock the tail, crop the ears, of (an animal).

court-bouillon [kurbujõ], *s.m. Cu:* (*a*) court-bouillon; (*b*) fish cooked in a court-bouillon; *pl. courts-bouillons.*

court-bouillonner [kurbujɔne], *v.tr. Cu:* to cook (fish) in a court-bouillon.

court-circuit [kursirkɥi], *s.m.* (*a*) *El:* short-circuit; **mettre (une résistance, etc.) en court-circuit,** to short-circuit (a resistance, etc.); **dispositif de mise en c.-c.,** short-circuiting device; **c.-c. avec (jaillissement d')étincelles,** flash-over; (*b*) *Elcs:* (*in magnetron*) strapping; *pl. courts-circuits.*

court-circuitage [kursirkɥita:ʒ]. *s.m. El:* short-circuiting.

court-circuiter [kursirkɥite], *v.tr.* (*a*) *El:* to short-circuit (resistance, etc.); **bobine court-circuitée,** burnt-out coil; (*b*) to short-circuit, bypass (s.o.).

court-circuiteur [kursirkɥitœ:r], *s.m. Elcs:* short-circuiter; short-circuiting device; *pl. court-circuiteurs.*

courte-botte [kurtəbɔt], *s.m. A:* short-legged little man, Tom Thumb; *pl. courtes-bottes.*

courtement [kurtəmɑ̃], *adv.* shortly, briefly.

courtepointe [kurtəpwɛ̃:t], *s.f.* quilt; (quilted) bedspread.

courte-queue [kurtəkø]. **1.** *a.* (*of dog, horse*) docked, dock-tailed. **2.** *s.f.* short-stemmed cherry; *pl. courtes-queues.*

courter [kurte]. **1.** *v.tr.* to sell; to offer (goods) for sale. **2.** *v.i.* to buy and sell on commission.

courtes-cornes [kurtəkɔrn], *s.m. & f. Husb:* shorthorn (ox, cow).

courtier, -ière [kurtje, -jɛ:r], *s. Com: Fin:* broker; agent; **c. de commerce, de marchandises,** general broker, commercial broker; **c. d'assurances,** insurance broker; **c. d'assurances maritimes,** marine insurance broker; **c. de change,** bill broker; **c. maritime,** ship broker; **c. libre,** outside, street, broker; **c. marron, clandestin,** unlicensed broker; bucket-shop proprietor; **c. en librairie,** travelling book salesman, *U.S:* book agent; **c. électoral,** election agent; *A:* **courtier, courtière de mariages,** marriage broker; **c. de chair humaine,** white-slave trader, white slaver.

courtil [kurti], *s.m. A:* cottage garden.

courtilière [kurtiljɛ:r], *s.f. Ent:* mole-cricket.

courtille [kurti:j], *s.m. A:* (large) public (pleasure) garden, enclosure (*esp.* on outskirts of Paris).

courtine [kurtin], *s.f.* **1.** *A:* curtain (round a bed). **2.** *Arch:* façade (between two pavilions). **3.** *Mil:* (*a*) curtain (between two bastions); (*b*) line of trenches between two strong points. **4.** *Her:* mantling. **5.** *P:* **les courtines,** (horse) racing, the races; **jouer aux courtines,** to bet (on the horses).

courtisan [kurtizɑ̃], *s.m.* courtier; *a.* **manières courtisanes,** flattering, obsequious, manners.

courtisane [kurtizan], *s.f.* (*a*) *A: & Lit:* courtezan, courtesan; (*b*) *O:* prostitute.

courtisanerie [kurtizanri], *s.f. O:* ways, habits, of courtiers; flattery, obsequiousness; fawning (on the great).

courtiser [kurtize], *v.tr.* (*a*) to court; to pay court to (s.o.); (*b*) to court; to make love to (s.o.); **c. la brune et la blonde,** to make love to all women alike; **c. la dame de pique,** to be an inveterate gambler; (*c*) **c. les grands, les riches,** to ingratiate oneself with, *F:* play up to, lick the boots of, the great, the wealthy.

court-jointé [kurʒwɛ̃te], *a.* (*of horse*) short-pasterned, short in the pastern; *pl. court-jointé(e)s.*

court-noué [kurnwe, -nue], *s.m. Bot:* degeneration disease of the vine.

courtois [kurtwa], *a.* courteous (**envers, avec, pour,** to); courtly; polite, urbane; *Lit.Hist:* **épopée courtoise,** court epic; *A:* **lance courtoise,** lance with coronal tip; **armes courtoises,** blunted weapons, arms of courtesy; **combattre, discuter, à armes courtoises,** to show a courteous attitude towards one's opponent; *F:* to keep to the rules of the game.

courtoisement [kurtwazmɑ̃], *adv.* courteously, politely; urbanely.

courtoisie [kurtwazi], *s.f.* **1.** courtesy, courteousness (**envers,** to, towards); politeness; urbanity; *Dipl:* **c. internationale,** comity of nations. **2.** (act of) courtesy; **échange de courtoisies,** exchange of courtesies.

court-pendu [kurpɑ̃dy], *s.m. Hort:* short-start, -shank (apple); *pl. court-pendus.*

court-vêtue [kurvɛty], *a.f.* short-skirted; *pl. court-vêtues.*

couru, *a.* [kury]. **1.** sought after; **opéra, prédicateur, très c.,** favourite, popular, opera, preacher; **réunion sportive très courue,** well-attended, well-patronized, favourite, sporting event; *F:* **c'est c. (d'avance),** it's a cinch, a cert; **c'était c.,** it was bound to happen. **2.** *Fin:* **intérêt c.,** accrued interest.

courvite [kurvit], *s.m. Orn:* courser; **c. gaulois, isabelle,** cream-coloured courser.

cousage [kuza:ʒ], *s.m.* stitching, sewing (of a book).

cousailler [kuzɑje], *v.i. F:* to stitch away at, patch up, old garments.

couscou [kusku], *s.m. Z:* cuscus.

couscous [kuskus], *s.m. Cu:* couscous.

couscoussier [kuskusje], *s.m. Dom.Ec:* couscous pan.

cousette [kuzɛt], *s.f.* **1.** *F:* dressmaker's assistant, apprentice, hand. **2.** needle-case, (portable) sewing kit.

couseuse [kuzø:z], *s.f.* **1.** (*a*) *A:* sewer, seamstress; (*b*) *Bookb:* stitcher. **2.** stitching machine.

cousin¹, -ine [kuzɛ̃, -in], *s.* cousin; **c. germain,** first cousin, full cousin, cousin german; **cousins au second degré, cousins issus de germains,** second cousins; **c. par alliance,** cousin by marriage; *F:* **cousin à la mode de Bretagne,** distant relation, sort of relation; *F:* **ils sont grands cousins,** they are great friends; **le roi n'est pas son c.,** he thinks no small beer of himself, he's as proud as a peacock.

cousin², *s.m. Ent: F:* gnat, midge; *occ.* daddy-long-legs.

cousinage [kuzina:ʒ], *s.m. F:* **1.** cousinship, cousinhood; relationship. **2. tout le c.,** all the cousins, the whole cousinry, all one's kith and kin; *esp.* all the poor relations.

cousinaille [kuzinɑ:j], *s.f. F:* = COUSINAGE 2.

cousiner [kuzine]. **1.** *v.tr. A:* to call (s.o.) cousin; to call cousins with (s.o.). **2.** *v.i.* (*a*) **c. chez qn,** to sponge on a relative; (*b*) **ils ne cousinent pas ensemble,** they don't get on well together, don't hit it off.

cousinet [kuzinɛ], *s.m. Bot:* pulvinus, cushion.

cousinière [kuzinjɛ:r], *s.f.* (*rare*) mosquito net.

cousoir [kuzwa:r], *s.m.* **1.** *Bookb:* sewing press. **2.** (*glovemaking*) stitching frame.

coussiège [kusjɛ:ʒ], *s.m. Arch:* window seat.

coussin [kusɛ̃], *s.m.* **1.** (*a*) cushion; **siège garni de coussins,** cushioned seat; **c. à air, c. élastique,** air-cushion, -pillow; (*b*) pad(ding) (of horse's collar, etc.); (*c*) *Aut:* squab; (*d*) *Med:* **lit sur c. d'air,** hoverbed; *Veh:* **véhicule sur c. d'air,** air-cushion vehicle, A.C.V.; **appareil à c. d'air,** hovercraft. **2.** *Tchn:* (*a*) (engraver's) sandbag; (*b*) (bookbinder's) gold cushion; (*c*) (lace maker's) pillow. **3.** *Nau:* (*a*) bolster (of hawse-hole, etc.); pillow (of bowsprit); (*b*) chock.

coussiner [kusine], *v.tr.* to cushion; to pad; to line (carriage, etc.) with cushions; to fit (car) with squabs.

coussinet [kusinɛ], *s.m.* **1.** small cushion; pad; *Anat:* **c. plantaire,** pad. **2.** *Mec.E: etc:* (*a*) bearing, bush(ing); **c. à billes,** ball-bearing; **c. à collet,** collar-bearing; **c. à galets, à rouleaux,** roller bearing; **c. antifriction,** antifriction bearing, babbitted bearing; **c. autolubrifiant,** self-oiling bearing; **c. de fusée, de boîte d'essieu,** journal bearing, axle-box bearing; **c. de ligne d'arbre,** line-shaft bearing, plummer-block; **c. de palier,** (i) journal bearing; (ii) bearing brass, bearing shell; **c. à galets,** journal-bearing sleeve; **c. de pied, de tête, de bielle,** small-end, big-end, bearing; **c. de tourillon(s),** trunnion bearing; **c. de vilbrequin,** crankshaft bearing; **c. lisse,** plain bearing; **c. régulé,** white metal bearing; babbitted bearing; **demi-c.,** split bearing; **portée de c.,** bearing surface; **garnir d'un c.,** to bush; (*b*) *Rail:* **c. de rail,** rail chair; **c. de joint,** joint chair; (*c*) *Arch: Civ.E:* coussinet, cushion (of Ionic column, arch pier); (*d*) (engraver's) sandbag; (*e*) (bookbinder's) gold cushion. **3.** *Bot:* pulvinus, cushion. **4.** *Bot: F:* **c. des marais,** bilberry.

coussinette [kusinɛt], *s.f. Bot:* pulvinus, cushion.

cousu [kuzy], *a.* sewn; *Her:* cousu; **c. à la main,** *F:* **c. main,** hand-sewn; *P:* **c'est du c. main,** it's first rate, super; **c. à la machine,** machine-stitched; **avoir, tenir, la bouche cousue,** to keep one's mouth shut; to keep a secret; **bouche cousue!** not a word! **c. de fil blanc,** obvious; blatant; **malices cousues de fil blanc,** open malice; **cheval qui a les flancs cousus,** thin-flanked horse; **avoir les joues cousues,** to be hollow-cheeked; **visage c. de cicatrices,** face lined with scars; **texte c. d'anglicismes,** text full of Anglicisms; *F:* **avoir les yeux cousus de sommeil,** to be heavy with sleep, to be unable to keep one's eyes open; *F:* **être c. d'or,** to be rolling in money.

cousure [kuzy:r], *s.f.* stitching, sewing (of book).

coût [ku], *s.m.* cost; **le c. de la vie,** the cost of living; **le c. d'une imprudence,** the price, the consequences, of a rash action; **menus coûts,** petty expenses, minor expenses.

coutançais, -aise [kutɑ̃sɛ, -ɛ:z], *a. & s. Geog:* (native, inhabitant) of Coutances.

coûtant [kutɑ̃], *a.m. used only in the phr.* **au, à, prix c.,** at cost price.

coute [kut], *s.m.* long-handled billhook (for cutting reeds).

couteau, -eaux [kuto], *s.m.* **1.** knife; (*a*) **c. de table, de cuisine,** table, kitchen, knife; **c. à fromage, à dessert, à poisson,** cheese, dessert, fish, knife; **c. à découper,** carving knife, carver; **c. électrique,** electric carver; **c. à huîtres,** oyster knife; **c. économe,** potato peeler; **c. à scie,** knife with a serrated edge; (bread) saw; **c. de poche,** pocket knife; **c. automatique, c. à cran (d'arrêt),** flick knife (with folding blade), *U.S:* switch-blade (knife); **c. à lame rentrante,** flick knife (with retractable blade); **c. à papier,** paper knife; **c. à palette,** palette knife; **c. à mastiquer,** putty knife; *Surg:* **c. interosseux,** catling; *Equit:* **c. de chaleur,** sweating iron (for rubbing down horse); **c. de chasse,** hunting knife, *U.S:* bowie knife; **roue à couteaux,** rotary cutter; **coup de c.,** stab; **en lame de c.,** knife-edged; **figure en lame de c.,** hatchet face; **être à couteaux tirés (avec qn),** to be at daggers drawn (with s.o.); **le c. sur la gorge,** at the point of the sword; **avoir le c. sur la gorge, être sous le c.,** to be under an immediate threat (of sth.); **mettre le c. sous, sur, la gorge à qn,** (to force s.o. (to do sth.), to frighten s.o. (into doing sth.) (against his will); (*b*) *Bookb:* **c. à rogner,** (i) guillotine; (ii) plough; (*c*) *Carp:* **c. de rabot,** plane iron; (*d*) *Mec.E: etc:* cutter (of gear-cutter, etc.); **c. droit,** spur cutter; (*e*) *Ph:* knife-edge, fulcrum (of balance-beam); knife (of pendulum, etc.); **suspension par c.,** knife-edge suspension; (*f*) *El:* blade (of switch); **interrupteur à c.,** knife switch; **c. de contact,** contact knife. **2.** *Moll:* **(manche de) c.,** solen, razor shell, razor clam.

couteau-poignard [kutopwaɲa:r], *s.m.* hunting knife, *U.S:* bowie knife; *pl. couteaux-poignards.*

couteau-scie [kutosi], *s.m.* knife with serrated edge; bread (etc.) saw; *pl. couteaux-scies.*

coutel [kutɛl], *s.m.* long-handled billhook (for cutting reeds).

coutelas [kutlɑ], *s.m.* **1.** (*a*) *Nau:* cutlass; (*b*) pig-sticker; (*c*) *Dom.Ec:* broad-bladed knife. **2.** *Ich: F:* sword-fish.
coutelet [kutlɛ], *s.m.* (*a*) small knife; (*b*) *A:* (i) toothpick; (ii) nail cleaner; (iii) earpick.
coutelier, -ière [kutəlje, -jɛːr], *s.* **1.** cutler. **2.** *s.f. A:* **coutelière,** knife-box, -case.
coutellerie [kutɛlri], *s.f.* **1.** cutlery (trade or wares). **2.** (*a*) cutlery shop; (*b*) **(fabrique de) c.,** cutlery works.
coûter [kute], *v.i.* **1.** to cost; **cela coûte cinq francs,** it costs five francs; **les cinq mille francs que le tableau m'a coûté,** the five thousand francs that the picture cost me; **c. cher, peu,** to be expensive, inexpensive; **cela vous coûtera cher,** you shall pay dearly for this; **les voyages coûtent,** travelling is expensive; **coûte que coûte,** at any cost, at any price, at all costs, whatever the cost; *F:* **ça coûtera ce que ça coûtera!** to hell with the expense! **l'argent ne lui coûte guère,** money means nothing to him; **cela coûte les yeux de la tête,** it costs the earth; **la bataille coûta la vie à 2000 hommes,** the battle cost 2000 men their lives; **les efforts que ce travail m'a coûtés,** the efforts that this work cost me; *impers.* **il lui en a coûté un bras, la vie,** it cost him an arm, his life; **je voulus l'aider; il m'en coûta,** I tried to help him, to my cost; **ça m'a coûté chaud,** (i) it cost me a pretty penny; (ii) I had to smart for it; *F:* **pour ce que ça vous coûte!** as if it made any difference to you! **2. rien ne lui coûte,** (i) nothing is an effort to him; (ii) he spares no effort, he thinks nothing too much trouble; **rien ne lui coûtera pour le faire,** he will stick at nothing, spare no pains, to do it; **tout lui coûte,** he does nothing with a good grace; **ça ne coûte rien de rêver,** there's no harm in dreaming; **cela me coûte à dire, il m'en coûte de le dire,** it pains me, I regret, to have to say this, I say it reluctantly; **il m'en coûtera de les quitter,** it will be a wrench for me to leave them.
coûteusement [kutøzmɑ̃], *adv.* expensively; at great cost.
coûteux, -euse [kutø, -øːz], *a.* costly; expensive; **peu c.,** inexpensive; **la victoire a été coûteuse,** the victory cost us, them, dear, was won at a great price.
coutil [kuti], *s.m. Tex:* drill, twill; duck; **c. pour matelas,** ticking; **pantalon de c.,** ducks.
coutilier [kutilje], *s.m. A.Mil:* pikeman.
coutille [kutiːj], *s.f. A.Arms:* langue de boeuf; pike.
couton [kutɔ̃], *s.m.* pin-feather (of chicken, etc.).
cou-tors [kutɔːr], *s.m. Orn:* wryneck; *pl. cous-tors.*
coutrasien, -ienne [kutrazjɛ̃, -jɛn], *a. & s. Geog:* (native, inhabitant) of Coutras.
coutre [kutr̥], *s.m.* **1.** (wood-)chopper. **2.** coulter (of plough).
coutrier [kutrije], *s.m. Agr:* subsoil plough.
coutrillon, -onne [kutrijɔ̃, -ɔn], *a. & s. Geog: Dial:* (native, inhabitant) of Coutras.
coutume [kutym], *s.f.* **1.** custom, habit, use, practice; **selon la c. du pays,** according to the custom of the country; **avoir c. de faire qch.,** to be in the habit of doing sth.; to be accustomed to do sth.; **j'irai chez vous comme de c.,** I'll call on you as usual; **je me suis levé plus tard que de c.,** I got up later than usual; **il est de c. de faire qch.,** it is customary, usual, to do sth.; *Prov:* **une fois n'est pas c.,** this is only once in a way; it may never happen again; one swallow does not make a summer; **cela coûtera cher, mais une fois n'est pas c.,** it will cost a lot, but it doesn't matter for once, we're not making a habit of it. **2.** *Jur:* customary law (of a province, etc.); customary.
coutumier, -ière [kutymje, -jɛːr]. **1.** *a.* (*a*) (i) *A:* in the habit of, used to (doing sth.); **il est c. de mentir,** he is an habitual liar; (ii) *usu. Pej:* **il est c. du fait,** it's not the first time he's done that; (*b*) customary; **le travail c.,** the ordinary, usual, routine; **droit c.,** (i) customary law; (ii) unwritten law, common law; **jurisconsulte en droit c.,** common lawyer. **2.** *s.m. Jur:* customary, collection of customs (of a province, etc.).
coutumièrement [kutymjɛrmɑ̃], *adv.* customarily, according to custom.
couturage [kutyraːʒ], *s.m.* machine stitching.
couture [kutyːr], *s.f.* **1.** sewing, needlework; **c. à la main,** hand-stitching; **elle est dans la c.,** (i) she does needlework; (ii) she does dressmaking; **haute c.,** haute couture; **maison de haute c.,** fashion house; *a.* **une veste c.,** a fashionable jacket. **2.** (*a*) seam (in dress, pipe, etc.); rivet seam; **sans c.,** (i) seamless; (ii) *Metalw:* weldless; **c. rabattue,** run and fell seam; flat seam; **c. double, c. anglaise,** French seam; **c. en baguette,** welted seam; **c. piquée,** outside-stitched seam; **battre qn à plate(s) couture(s),** to beat s.o. hollow; **être battu à plate(s) couture(s),** to be utterly, totally, defeated; to be beaten out and out; (*in a race*) to be nowhere; **visage marqué d'une c.,** face marked with a scar; **examiner qn, qch., sur, sous, toutes les coutures,** to examine s.o., sth. from every aspect; **connaître la vie sous toutes ses coutures,** to know the seamy side of life; (*b*) *Nau:* seam; **c. à clin,** lapped seam; *Bot:* **herbe sans c.,** adder's tongue.
couturé [kutyre], *a.* seamed; **visage c.,** scarred face.
couturer [kutyre], *v.tr.* to scar, seam, score; **mur couturé d'humidité,** wall streaked with damp.
couturerie [kutyr(ə)ri], *s.f.* (*a*) dressmaking; (*b*) *A:* (dressmaker's) workroom.
couturier, -ière [kutyrje, -jɛːr], *s.* **1.** (*a*) *s.m. & f.* dressmaker; couturier; (*b*) *s.f.* seamstress, needlewoman; (*c*) *s.f. Th:* rehearsal preceding the final dress rehearsal. **2.** *Anat:* **(muscle) c.,** sartorial muscle, sartorius; *F:* tailor('s) muscle. **3.** *Orn:* **couturier, fauvette couturière,** tailor-bird.
couvade [kuvad], *s.f. Anthr:* couvade, man-childbed.
couvage [kuvaːʒ], *s.m.* incubation, hatching (of eggs).
couvain [kuvɛ̃], *s.m.* **1.** nest of insect eggs. **2.** *Ap:* brood-comb.
couve [kuːv], *s.f.* **1.** *Dial:* (*S.E. France*) broody hen. **2.** *Bot:* cembra pine.
couveau, -eaux [kuvo], *s.m. Husb:* china, glass, plaster, stone egg; nest egg.
couvaison [kuvɛzɔ̃], *s.f.* (*a*) brooding time, sitting time (of bird, fowl); (*b*) incubation, hatching (of eggs).
couvée [kuve], *s.f.* **1.** sitting, clutch, set (of eggs). **2.** brood, hatch(ing) (of chicks).
couvent [kuvɑ̃], *s.m.* (*a*) convent, nunnery; **entrer au c.,** to go into a convent; (*b*) convent school; **elle a été élevée au c.,** she was educated in a convent; (*c*) monastery; (*d*) (religious) community.
couventine [kuvɑ̃tin], *s.f.* (*a*) nun conventual; (*b*) girl at convent school.
couver [kuve]. **1.** *v.tr.* (*a*) (*of hen, etc.*) to sit on (eggs); *abs.* to brood, sit; **poule qui veut c.,** broody hen; **mettre une poule à c.,** to set a hen; (*b*) to incubate, to hatch (out) (eggs); (*c*) **c. le feu,** to brood over the fire; **c. des projets de vengeance,** to brood over, meditate, schemes of vengeance; **c. un complot,** to hatch a plot; **c. une maladie,** to be sickening for an illness; **c. qn, qch., des yeux,** (i) to gaze intently at, to keep one's look fixed on, s.o., sth.; (ii) to look longingly at sth.; (iii) to look fondly at s.o.; **c. du regard sa victime,** to gloat over one's victim. **2.** *v.i.* (*of fire, passion*) to smoulder; **le feu couve sous les cendres,** the fire is smouldering under the embers; **un orage couvait,** a storm was brewing; *F:* **j'ai un rhume qui couve,** I've got a cold brewing, coming (on); **conspiration qui couvait depuis longtemps,** conspiracy that had been hatching for a long time; **il faut laisser c. cela,** we must let it develop.
couvercle [kuvɛrkl̥], *s.m.* (*a*) lid, cover (of box, pot, saucepan, etc.); cap (of jar, etc.); **c. vissé,** screw cap; **flacon à c. vissé,** screw-capped bottle; **c. à glissière(s),** sliding lid; (*b*) *Mec.E: Tchn:* cover (of cylinder, pump, valve, etc.); **c. de fermeture,** cover plate; **c. d'épurateur d'air,** air-filter cap; **c. de trou de visite,** manhole, inspection hole, cover; *I.C.E:* **c. de (carter de) distribution,** timing-case cover; *Mch:* **c. de cylindre,** cylinder head, top cover; *Opt:* **c. d'oculaire,** eyepiece cap, cover; **c. d'objectif,** objective, lens, cap, cover; *El:* **c. de prise de courant,** plug socket cover; *Nau:* **c. de panneau,** dead light.
couvert[1] [kuvɛːr], *a.* covered. **1. allée couverte,** shady walk; **pays c.,** wooded country; **parler à mots couverts,** to speak (i) cryptically, (ii) not too bluntly, with due caution; **laisser entendre qch. à mots couverts,** to hint at sth.; **ciel c., temps c.,** overcast sky, weather; *A:* **ennemi c.,** covert enemy; *A:* **servir qn à plats couverts,** to intrigue against s.o. **2.** wearing one's hat; **rester c.,** to keep one's hat on. **3.** dressed; **c. chaudement, bien c.,** warmly dressed, well wrapped up.
couvert[2], *s.m.* **1.** cover(ing), shelter; **arbre à c. léger,** light-foliaged tree; (*in S. of France*): **les couverts,** street, square, with covered footpaths; **le vivre et le c.,** board and lodging; **être à c.,** (i) to be under cover; (ii) *Com:* to be covered (for a credit); **se mettre à c.,** to take cover; **se mettre à c. de la pluie,** to shelter from the rain; **son honneur est à c.,** his honour is safe; **mettre ses intérêts à c.,** to safeguard one's interests; *St. Exch:* **vendre à c.,** to sell for delivery; **sous le c., de la nuit,** under cover of night; **sous le c. de l'amitié,** under the cover, cloak, pretence, of friendship; **sous le c. d'une visite à rendre,** under the pretext of a call to be made; **sous le c. d'un contrat,** within the terms of a contract; **il a agi sous le c. de ses chefs,** he acted with the authority of his superiors. **2.** *A:* cover, wrapper, envelope (of letter, etc.). **3.** (*a*) fork and spoon; **c. à poisson,** fish knife and fork; **douze couverts d'argent en écrin,** one dozen silver forks and spoons in a case; (*b*) cover, place (at table); **mettre, dresser, le c.,** to lay, set, the table; **ôter le c.,** to clear the table; **mettre trois couverts,** to set the table, to lay, for three; **la table est de vingt couverts,** the table is laid for twenty; **une table à deux couverts, s'il vous plaît,** a table for two, please; **votre c. est à l'autre table aujourd'hui, monsieur,** I have put you at the other table to-day, sir; **vous trouverez toujours votre c. mis,** there will always be a meal for you any time you (would) like to come; (*c*) (*in restaurant*) **(frais de) c.,** cover charge; house charge.
couverte [kuvɛrt], *s.f.* **1.** *Cer:* glaze; **peinture sous c.,** under-glaze painting. **2.** *F: & Dial:* blanket; **passer qn à la c.,** to toss s.o. in a blanket; **passage à la c.,** blanketing. **3.** *Paperm:* deckle.
couverture [kuvɛrtyːr], *s.f.* **1.** covering, cover; **c. de fourgon,** waggon cover; **c. de cheval, d'attente,** horse-cloth, -blanket; **c. de selle,** saddle-cloth, numdah; **c. de voyage,** (travelling) rug; **c. de lit,** coverlet, counterpane, bedspread; **c. piquée,** quilt; **c. de laine,** blanket; **c. chauffante,** electric blanket; *F:* **passer qn à la c.,** to toss s.o. in a blanket; **passage à la c.,** tossing in a blanket, blanketing; **faire la c.,** to turn down the bed; **tirer la c. à soi,** (i) to take all the bedclothes; (ii) to take the lion's share, to look after number one; **c. d'un livre,** cover of a book; **c. en papier,** paper wrapper; **lettre de c.,** covering letter; **sous c. de dévotion, d'amitié,** under the cover, the cloak, of devotion, of friendship; **agent opérant sous (une) c.,** undercover agent; **servir de c. à qn,** to cover up for s.o.; **son métier n'était qu'une c.,** his profession was only a front, a blind; *Mil:* **éléments, troupes, de c.,** covering, protective, elements, troops; **c. et protection sous roc,** cover and rock protection; *Av:* **c. aérienne,** air cover; **c. de chasse,** (i) fighter cover (for land forces); (ii) fighter escort (for bombers, transports, etc.); **c. photographique,** (i) photographic cover; (ii) photographic coverage; **c. radar,** (i) radar cover; (ii) radar coverage; *W.Tel: etc:* **c. d'une antenne,** aerial coverage. **2.** *Const:* roofing; **c. de tuiles,** tiled roof. **3.** *Agr:* topping; **engrais en c.,** surface dressing; top dressing (of fertilizer); **c. d'humus,** surface mulch; *Agr: For:* **c. du sol,** surface; **incendie dans la c. du sol,** surface fire; **plantes de c.,** cover crop. **4.** (*a*) *Com:* cover; **commande sans c.,** order without security, without cover; **exiger une c. de 20% en espèces,** to claim a margin of 20% in cash; (*b*) *St.Exch:* margin, cover; (*c*) *Ins:* covering (of risks). **5.** *Geol: Min:* **terrain(s) de c.,** (over) burden; **c. sédimentaire,** sedimentary mantle. **6.** *pl. Orn:* coverts.
couvet [kuvɛ], *s.m.* brazier.
couveuse [kuvøːz], *s.f.* **1.** sitting hen, brood-hen, brooder, hatcher. **2. c. artificielle,** incubator (for eggs, for infants). **3.** *a. Atom.Ph:* **pile c.,** breeder reactor.
couvi [kuvi], *a.m.* addle(d), rotten (egg).
couvoir [kuvwaːr], *s.m.* (*a*) incubator; (*b*) hatchery.
couvrant [kuvrɑ̃], *a.* covering, giving cover; *Mil:* **hauteur couvrante,** height of cover (in trench); *Phot:* **pouvoir c.,** covering power; *Paint:* **pouvoir c.,** (i) masking power; (ii) coverage, spreading capacity.
couvrante [kuvrɑ̃t], *s.f. P:* blanket.
couvre-amorce [kuvramɔrs], *s.m.* primer-cap; cap chamber (of cartridge); *pl. couvre-amorces.*
couvre-bec [kuvrəbɛk], *s.m.* cap (of clarionet, etc.); *pl. couvre-becs.*
couvre-bouche [kuvrəbuʃ], *s.m. Artil: Sm.a:* muzzle cover, tampion (of gun); *pl. couvre-bouches.*
couvre-chaussure [kuvrəʃosyːr], *s.m.* **1.** galosh, overshoe. **2.** snow-boot; overboot; **c.-c. de protection,** protective overboot; *pl. couvre-chaussures.*
couvre-chaîne [kuvrəʃɛn], *s.m. Cy:* chain-case; *pl. couvre-chaînes.*
couvre-chef [kuvrəʃɛf], *s.m. F: & Hum:* head-dress, headgear; *pl. couvre-chefs.*
couvre-culasse [kuvrəkylas], *s.m.* breech-cover (of gun); *Mil:* back-plate; *pl. couvre-culasses.*

couvre-engrenages [kuvrɑ̃grənaːʒ], *s.m.inv. Mec.E:* gear-box, -case.
couvre-essieu [kuvrɛsjø], *s.m.* axle-tree sleeve, collar; *pl. couvre-essieux.*
couvre-feu [kuvrəfø], *s.m.inv.* **1.** damper-lid (for charcoal fire, etc.). **2.** curfew; **sonner le c.-f.,** to sound the curfew (bell).
couvre-galets [kuvrəgalɛ], *s.m.inv. Mec.E:* roller dust-cap.
couvre-joint [kuvrəʒwɛ̃], *s.m.* **1.** *Carp:* covering, bead, batten. **2.** *Mec.E: etc:* butt-strap, -strip; flat cover-plate; welt (of butt-joint); *pl. couvre-joints.*
couvre-lit [kuvrəli], *s.m.* coverlet, bedspread, counterpane; *pl. couvre-lits.*
couvre-livre [kuvrəliːvr], *s.m. Bookb:* (dust-) jacket; wrapper; *pl. couvre-livres.*
couvre-lumière [kuvrəlymjɛːr], *s.m.inv. Artil:* apron (of canon); *pl. couvre-lumières.*
couvre-manche [kuvrəmɑ̃ːʃ], *s.m. Ten:* grip (for racquet); *pl. couvre-manches.*
couvre-moyeu [kuvrəmwajø], *s.m. Veh:* hub-cap; *pl. couvre-moyeux.*
couvre-nuque [kuvrənyk], *s.m.* **1.** sun-curtain (of cap). **2.** rear-peak (of helmet); *pl. des couvre-nuques.*
couvre-objectif [kuvrɔbʒɛktif], *s.m.* lens cap; objective cap, cover; *pl. couvre-objectifs.*
couvre-objet [kuvrɔbʒɛ], *s.m.* cover-glass, cover-slip (of microscope slide); *pl. couvre-objets.*
couvre-œil [kuvrœːj], *s.m.* (eye-)patch; *pl. couvre-œils.*
couvre-pied(s) [kuvrəpje], *s.m.* coverlet, bedspread; **c. piqué,** (eiderdown) quilt, *NAm:* comforter; *pl. couvre-pieds.*
couvre-plat [kuvrəpla], *s.m.* dish-cover; *pl. couvre-plats.*
couvre-radiateur [kuvrəradjatœːr], *s.m. Aut:* radiator muff; *pl. couvre-radiateurs.*
couvre-selle [kuvrəsɛl], *s.m.* saddle-cover; *pl. couvre-selles.*
couvre-théière [kuvrətejɛːr], *s.m.* tea-cosy; *pl. couvre-théières.*
couvreur [kuvrœːr], *s.m.* roofer; **c. en tuiles,** tiler; **c. en ardoise,** slater; **c. en chaume,** thatcher; *Freemasonry:* **(frère) c.,** tiler.
couvrir [kuvriːr], *v.tr.* (*pr.p.* **couvrant;** *p.p.* **couvert;** *pr.ind.* **je couvre, il couvre, n. couvrons;** *pr.sub.* **je couvre;** *p.d.* **je couvrais;** *p.h.* **je couvris;** *fu.* **je couvrirai) 1.** to cover, to overlay, to screen (de, with); **c. les yeux de qn avec un bandeau,** to cover (up) s.o.'s eyes with a bandage, to blindfold s.o.; **elle se couvrit le visage de ses mains,** she hid, buried, her face in her hands; **être couvert de poussière,** to be covered with dust, all over dust; **tout couvert de boue,** bespattered with mud; **c. qn de honte, de ridicule,** to cover s.o. with shame, with ridicule; **une rougeur lui couvrit le visage,** a flush spread over his face; **c. qn de sa protection,** to shield s.o. with one's protection, to screen s.o.; **c. ses employés,** to cover, take responsibility for, one's staff; **c'est à vous de c.,** it is for you to accept responsibility; **c. la retraite de l'armée,** to cover the army's retreat; **c. un train,** to protect a train (with adequate signals); *Rail:* **c. la ligne,** to block the line; **mur couvert de lierre,** wall overgrown, covered, with ivy; **couvert de neige, par la neige,** covered with snow; **le bruit de la cascade couvre les voix,** the noise of the waterfall drowns the sound of voices; **c. des desseins,** to hide, keep, one's plans, one's intentions, secret; **c. ses fautes,** to make up for one's mistakes; **c. le feu,** to cover up the fire; *Ind: etc:* **c. les feux,** to bank (up) the fires; *Cards:* **c. une carte,** to cover a card; **c. la table,** to lay the table; **c. cinquante kilomètres en une heure,** to cover fifty kilometres in an hour; *Com:* **le prix de vente couvre à peine les frais,** the selling price barely covers the cost; **prière de nous c. par chèque,** kindly remit by cheque; **c. les frais de port,** to refund the postage, the carriage; **c. une enchère,** to make a higher bid; *Journ:* **c. un événement,** to report, cover, an event. **2.** *Const:* **c. une maison,** to roof a house; **maison couverte de, en, tuiles,** house roofed with tiles, house with tiled roof; **maison couverte en ardoise, en chaume,** slated, thatched, house. **3.** (*of male animal*) to cover (female).
se couvrir. 1. (*a*) to put on one's (outdoor) clothes; **couvre-toi bien,** wrap yourself up; (*b*) to put on one's hat. **2.** *Sp: Mil:* to cover, protect, oneself; *Fenc:* to guard one's body; *Mil:* **se c. sur les flancs,** to protect one's flanks. **3.** (*of weather*) to become overcast. **4. les arbres se couvrent de feuilles,** the trees are coming into leaf.
couvrure [kuvryːr], *s.f.* wrappering (of book).
covalence [kovalɑ̃ːs], *s.f. Ch:* covalency.
covariant [kovarjɑ̃], *s.m. Mth:* covariant.
covariation [kovarjasjɔ̃], *s.f.* covariation.
covelline [kɔvɛlin], *s.f.,* **covellite** [kɔvɛlit], *s.f. Miner:* covelline, covellite.
covenant [kɔvnɑ̃], *s.m.* covenant; **le c. de Versailles,** the Versailles covenant.
covenantaire [kɔvnɑ̃tɛːr], *s.m. Hist:* covenanter.
covendeur, -euse [kovɑ̃dœːr, -øːz], *s.* co-vendor, joint-seller.
cover-coat [kɔvœrkot], *s.m.inv. Tex:* covert-coating; *Tail:* **paletot en c.-c.,** covert-coat.
cover-crop [kɔvœrkrɔp], *s.m. Agr:* disc harrow; *pl. cover-crops.*
cover-girl [kɔvœrgœrl], *s.f. F:* cover-girl; *pl. cover-girls.*
covoyageur, -euse [kovwajaʒœːr, -øːz], *s.* travelling companion.
cow(-)boy [kaubɔj], *s.m.* cowboy; *pl. cow(-)boys.*
cow-catcher [kaukatʃɛːr], *s.m. Rail:* cow-catcher; *pl. cow-catchers.*
cowpérite [kauperit], *s.f. Med:* cowperitis.
cow-pox [kaupɔks], *s.m. Vet:* cow-pox.
coxa [kɔksa], *s.f. Z:* coxa; hip segment.
coxal, -aux [kɔksal, -o], *a. Anat:* coxal; **os c.,** hip bone.
coxalgie [kɔksalʒi], *s.f. Med:* coxalgia.
coxalgique [kɔksalʒik], *a. Med:* coxalgic (pain, patient, etc.).
coxarthrie [kɔksartri], *s.f. Med:* senile coxitis.
coxarthrose [kɔksartroːz], *s.f. Med:* coxitis.
coxodynie [kɔksodini], *s.f. Med:* coxodynia.
coxo-fémoral, -aux [kɔksofemɔral, -o], *a. Anat:* coxofemoral.
coxopodite [kɔksopɔdit], *s.m. Crust:* coxopodite.
coxotuberculose [kɔksotybɛrkyloːz], *s.f. Med:* tuberculosis of the hip-joint.
coyau, -aux [kwajo, kɔjo], *s.m. Const:* furrings (of roof).
coyer[1] [kwaje], *s.m.* whetstone sheath.
coyer[2], *s.m. Const:* horizontal timber (supporting corner rafter of hipped roof).
coyote [kɔjɔt], *s.m. Z:* coyote, prairie wolf.
coypou [kɔjpu], *s.m. Z:* coyp(o)u; **fourrure de c.,** nutria.
crabe [krɑb], *s.m.* **1.** *Crust:* crab; **c. laineux,** swimming crab; **c. des cocotiers,** robber, crab, coconut crab; **c. enragé,** green crab, shore crab; **petit c. velu,** hairy porcelain crab; **c. masqué,** masked crab; **c. armé,** masked crab; **c. sillonné,** xantho, furrowed crab; **c. des Moluques,** sea-louse, (East Indian) king-crab; **marcher en c.,** to walk side-ways, crabwise; *Av:* **vol en c.,** drifting; *F:* **le panier de crabes,** the rat race. **2.** *P:* (*a*) *Mil:* corporal; (*b*) **c'est un vieux c.,** he's a pig-headed old fool. **3.** caterpillar tracked vehicle.
crabier [krɑbje], *s.m.* **1.** *Z:* (*a*) water-opossum; (*b*) crab-eating racoon. **2.** *Orn:* boatbill (heron); **c. chevelu,** squacco heron.
crabot [krabo], *s.m. Mec.E: Aut:* direct-drive dog clutch.
crabotage [krabɔtaːʒ], *s.m.* **1.** first shaft (of a slate quarry). **2.** *Aut:* **c. du différentiel,** four wheel drive system.
crabro [krabro], **crabron** [krabrɔ̃], *s.m. Ent:* **1.** sphecid wasp. **2.** *A:* hornet.
crabroniforme [krabrɔnifɔrm], *a. Ent:* vespiform.
crac [krak], *int. & s.m.* **1.** crack, snap; **entendre un c.,** to hear a snap, a cracking noise; *F:* **crac! le voilà parti,** he was off before you could say Jack Robinson. **2.** *Fin:* crash (of stock markets, etc.). **3. Monsieur de C.** = Baron Munchhausen; *cf.* CRAQUE[2].
crachat [kraʃa], *s.m.* **1.** (*a*) spittle, spit; *Med:* sputum; *Med:* **c. sanguinolent,** blood-stained sputum; (*b*) *P:* gob; *F:* **se noyer dans un c.,** to make a mountain out of a molehill; **c. de coucou, de grenouille,** cuckoo-spit; *s.a.* BOUE 2. **2.** *Algae:* **c. de lune,** star jelly, nostoc. **3.** *F:* star, Grand Cross (of an order); *F:* gong. **4.** crackle mark (defect in glass).
craché [kraʃe], *a. F:* **c'est son père tout c.,** he's the dead spit, the spit and image, of his father; **c'est lui tout c.!** that's him and no mistake about it!
crachement [kraʃmɑ̃], *s.m.* **1.** (*a*) (i) spitting; (ii) expectoration; **c. de sang,** spitting of blood; (*b*) *El.E:* sparking, spitting, spluttering (of collector of dynamo, etc.); arcing over (of arc-lamp); *W.Tel:* crackling; (*c*) back-firing (of rifle, etc.). **2.** (*a*) *Mch: Metall:* blowing out (of packing, of metal from mould); (*in welding*) expulsion; *Nau:* spewing, chewing (of oakum in seams); starting of the seams; (*b*) *Mch:* fizzing (of steam).
cracher [kraʃe]. **1.** *v.i.* (*a*) to spit, expectorate; *P.N:* **défense de c.,** no spitting; *F:* **il ne faut pas c. dessus,** it's not to be sneezed at; *Prov:* **quand on crache en l'air votre crachat vous retombe sur le nez,** spit into the wind and you'll get it in the eye; (chickens and) curses come home to roost; *P:* **c. (au bassin(et)),** to cough up, to fork out; *P:* **ça ne se fait pas en crachant dessus,** it's not so easy as it looks; (*b*) (*of pen*) to splutter; **le robinet crache,** the tap splashes; (*c*) *El.E:* (*of collector, etc.*) to spark, spit, splutter; (*of arc-lamp*) to arc over. **2.** *v.tr.* (*a*) (i) to spit (out) (saliva, blood, etc.); (ii) to expectorate; **c. du, le, sang,** (*with adverbial adj.*) **c. rouge,** to spit blood; *A: F:* **c. du latin,** to spout Latin; **c. des injures,** to hurl abuse; *F:* **j'ai dû c. mille francs,** I had to fork out, stump up, cough up, a thousand francs; (*b*) *Mch:* (*of cylinder*) **c. l'étoupe,** to blow out the packing; *Nau:* (*of ship*) **c. ses étoupes,** to spew, chew, oakum; to start at the seams.
cracheur, -euse [kraʃœːr, -øːz], *s.* **1.** spitter, expectorator. **2.** *Ich:* **poisson c.,** archerfish.
crachin [kraʃɛ̃], *s.m.* fine drizzle.
crachiner [kraʃine], *v.i.* to drizzle, to spit (with rain).
crachoir [kraʃwaːr], *s.m.* spitoon, *U.S:* cuspidor; *F:* **tenir le c.,** to monopolize the conversation, to do all the talking; to talk at great length; **tenir le c. à qn,** to talk up, play up, to s.o.
crachotement [kraʃɔtmɑ̃], *s.m.* sputtering, spluttering; *W.Tel:* crackling.
crachoter [kraʃɔte], *v.i.* to keep on spitting; to sputter, to splutter; *W.Tel:* to crackle.
crachoteur, -euse [kraʃɔtœːr, -øːz], **crachoteux, -euse** [kraʃɔtø, -øːz]. **1.** *a.* spitting; spluttering; crackling. **2.** *s.* spitter; splutterer.
crachouiller [kraʃuje], *v.i. F:* to be always spitting; to splutter.
cracidés [kraside], *s.m.pl. Orn:* Cracidae, the curassows.
crack [krak], *s.m. F:* crack horse, player; star pupil.
cracking [krakiŋ], *s.m.* (*a*) cracking (of crude oil); (*b*) cracking plant; **unité de c.,** cracking unit.
Cracovie [krakɔvi], *Pr.n.f. Geog:* Cracow.
cracovien, -ienne [krakɔvjɛ̃, -jɛn], *a. & s. Geog:* Cracovian.
cra(-)cra[1] [krakra], *s.m. Orn: F:* great reed warbler.
cra(-)cra[2], **crado** [krado], *a.inv. P:* filthy.
crafe [kraf], *s.f.* (*in slate quarry*) intrusive vein, layer (of different rock) (which hampers exploitation).
crag [krag], *s.m. Geol:* crag (of the Pliocene series).
craie [krɛ], *s.f.* chalk; **c. de tailleur, de Meudon,** French chalk; **écrit à la c.,** written in chalk; **inscrire qch. à la c.,** to chalk sth. up; **tracer les grandes lignes à la c.,** to chalk out the main lines; *Miner:* **c. de Briançon,** steatite, soapstone.
craillement [krɑjmɑ̃], *s.m.* cawing (of rooks etc.).
crailler [krɑje], *v.i.* (*of rooks, etc.*) to caw.
crain [krɛ̃], *s.m. Min: Dial:* (*N. of France*): fault (in coal seam).
craindre [krɛ̃ːdr], *v.tr.* (*pr.p.* **craignant;** *p.p.* **craint;** *pr.ind.* **je crains, il craint, n. craignons, ils craignent;** *pr.sub.* **je craigne;** *p.d.* **je craignais;** *p.h.* **je craignis;** *fu.* **je craindrai)** (*a*) to fear, dread, to stand in awe of, be afraid of (s.o., sth.); **c. la mort,** to fear, be afraid of, death; **c. Dieu,** to fear God; **homme craignant Dieu,** God-fearing man; **ne craignez rien!** don't be alarmed! **ne craignez rien! je le ferai moi-même,** don't worry! don't be afraid! I'll do it myself; **je crains de le laisser entrer,** I am afraid to let him in, I dread letting him in; **je crains d'oublier,** I am afraid of forgetting; **je crains d'être oublié,** I am afraid of being forgotten; **il n'a pas craint de déclarer . . .,** he did not scruple to declare . . .; **je crains qu'il (ne) soit mort,** I fear, I'm afraid, he is dead; **je craignais qu'il (ne) s'échappât,** I was frightened that he would escape; **je ne crains pas qu'il me suive,** I am not afraid of his following me; **il est à c., il y a lieu de c., que . . . (ne) . . .,** it is to be feared that . . .; **il n'y a pas à c. qu'il revienne,** there is no fear of his coming back; *abs.* **c. pour qn,** to have fears for s.o.'s safety, future, to be anxious about s.o.'s safety; **c. pour sa vie,** to go about in terror of one's life; **faire c. qch. à qn,** to put s.o. in fear of sth.; **on leur fait c. pour leur vie,** they are put in terror of their lives; (*b*) **plante qui craint la gelée,** plant that cannot stand the frost; **animal qui craint l'eau,** animal that shrinks from water; **je crains le froid, le chaud,** I cannot stand the cold, the heat; *Com:* **craint l'humidité, la chaleur,** to be kept dry, cool.

crainte [krɛ̃ːt], *s.f.* fear, dread; **la c. du Seigneur,** the fear of the Lord; **c. mystérieuse,** awe; **avoir une c. respectueuse de qn,** to stand in awe of s.o.; **dans la c. de, de c. de,** *F:* **c. de, tomber,** for fear of falling; **de c. que . . . (ne)** + *sub.*, lest; **parlez plus bas de c. qu'on (ne) vous entende,** speak more quietly, for fear you are overheard; **sans c.,** (i) fearless; (ii) fearlessly; **soyez sans c.,** have no fear; **motiver des craintes,** to give cause for apprehension; **avoir des craintes au sujet de qch.,** to entertain fears, to be under some apprehension, about sth.; **je n'ai aucune c. au sujet de . . .,** I am under no apprehensions about . . .; *Med:* **c. de fracture,** suspected fracture.

craintif, -ive [krɛ̃tif, -iːv], *a.* timid, timorous, fearful, apprehensive.

craintivement [krɛ̃tivmɑ̃], *adv.* timidly, timorously.

craken [krakɛn], *s.m.* kraken.

crambe[1] [krɑ̃ːb], *s.m.*, **crambé** [krɑ̃be], *s.m. Bot:* crambe; **c. maritime,** seakale.

crambe[2], *s.m. Ent:* grass moth.

crambus [krɑ̃bys], *s.m. Ent:* Crambus; *pl.* the grass moths; the sod, grass, web-worms.

cramé [krame], *s.m.* concentrated residue of cooked meat juices.

cramer [krame]. **1.** *v.tr.* to burn slightly; to scorch. **2.** *v.i. P:* **toute la bicoque a cramé,** the whole place went up in flames.

craminage [kraminaːʒ], *s.m. Leath:* softening (of leather).

craminer [kramine], *v.tr. Leath:* to soften (leather).

cramoisi [kramwazi], *a.* crimson; **devenir c.,** to flush crimson, to crimson up; *F:* to get purple in the face; *s.m.* **teindre qch. en c.,** to dye sth. crimson.

crampe[1] [krɑ̃ːp], *s.f.* **1.** (*a*) *Med:* cramp; **c. des écrivains,** writer's cramp; **c. du tennis,** tennis arm, tennis elbow; **être pris, saisi, d'une c.,** to be seized with cramp; **avoir des crampes d'estomac,** (i) to have cramp in the stomach; (ii) to feel (severe) pangs of hunger; (*b*) *F:* (*of pers., thg*) **quelle c.!** what a bore! **2.** *Ich:* torpedo, cramp fish, numb fish, electric ray.

crampe[2], *s.f.* cramp(-iron), staple.

crampillon [krɑ̃pijɔ̃], *s.m.* staple.

crampon [krɑ̃pɔ̃], *s.m.* **1.** *Const: etc:* (*a*) cramp (-iron), staple, dog; clamp, holdfast; spike; **c. de fixation,** cleat; (*b*) hook-nail; **c. fileté,** hook-bolt; (*c*) *Rail:* (dog-)spike. **2.** (*a*) climbing-iron; (*b*) stud (for sole of boot); calk, cog (of horse's shoe); **c. à glace,** (i) frost-nail; (ii) crampon. **3.** *Bot:* crampon, aerial root, adventitious root. **4.** *a. & s.m. F:* **quel c.! qu'il est c.!** what a limpet! what a bore!

cramponnage [krɑ̃pɔnaːʒ], *s.m. Mount:* climbing with crampons.

cramponnant [krɑ̃pɔnɑ̃], *a.* **1.** *Bot:* clutching, holding (tendril), etc.). **2.** *F:* importunate, pestering; **tu es c. avec ta politique!** can't you stop talking politics!

cramponné, *a.* [krɑ̃pɔne], *Her:* **croix cramponnée,** cross cramponnée.

cramponnement [krɑ̃pɔnmɑ̃], *s.m.* clutching, clinging.

cramponner [krɑ̃pɔne], *v.tr.* **1.** (*a*) *Const:* to clamp, cramp, (stones, etc.) together; to fasten (sth.) with a cramp-iron, with a clamp; (*b*) *F:* to buttonhole, pester; to stick like glue to (s.o.). **2.** to rough, cog, calk (horseshoe).

se cramponner à qch., à qn, to hold on to, hang on to, fasten on to, cling (on) to, to keep tight hold of, to clutch, sth., s.o.; **cramponne-toi!** hold on! steady! **cramponné à sa mère,** clinging to his mother; **il s'est cramponné toute sa vie à cette idée,** he clung to this idea all his life.

cramponnet [krɑ̃pɔnɛ], *s.m.* **1.** small cramp-iron. **2.** staple (of lock).

cram(p)ser [kramse], *v.i.* **se cram(p)ser,** *v.pr. P:* to die, to peg out, to kick the bucket.

cran[1] [krɑ̃], *s.m.* **1.** notch; (*a*) catch, tooth (of ratchet, pothook, etc.); cog (of wheel); **c. d'arrêt,** (i) lock notch, stop notch; (ii) catch (of knife); **c. de détente,** expansion notch; **c. de point mort, c. neutre,** dead centre; neutral notch; *Artil: Sm.a:* **c. de l'armé, c. de départ,** full cock notch; **au c. de l'armé,** at full cock; **au c. de repos,** at half cock; **c. de sûreté,** safety catch; **au c. de sûreté,** at safety; *F:* **être à c.,** to be on the point of losing one's temper, to be ready to explode; *F:* **j'avais les nerfs à c.,** my nerves were on edge; (*b*) distance between holes (in strap, on upright for high jump, etc.); **lâcher une courroie d'un cran,** to let a strap out a hole; *F:* **il ne me lâche pas d'un cran,** he won't leave me for a moment, I can't shake him off; **serrer sa ceinture d'un c., se faire un c. de plus à sa ceinture,** to tighten one's belt another hole; *F:* **se serrer d'un c., se mettre un c.,** to tighten one's belt; to draw in one's horns; *F:* **avancer, descendre, d'un c.,** to go up, come down, a peg or two; **son crédit a baissé d'un c.,** his stock has gone down a bit; (*c*) nick; *Sm.a: Artil:* **c. de mire,** sighting notch; **c. de mire de la hausse,** back sight, *U.S:* rear sight, notch; *Typ:* **c. d'une lettre,** nick of a letter; (*d*) *Hairdr:* wave (in hair); (*e*) *F:* **avoir du c.,** to have plenty of pluck, of go, of guts; to be game (for anything); **manquer de c.,** to be spineless, to have no guts. **2.** *Metall:* flaw, fault; *Geol:* **c. de retour,** overthrust fault. **3.** *Mil: P:* **quatre crans,** four days' C.B.

cran[2], *s.m. Nau: A:* **mettre un navire en c.,** to careen a ship.

cran[3], *s.m. Fish:* = cran (of herrings).

cranage[1] [kranaːʒ], *s.m.* hand-finishing of the teeth (of wheel).

cranage[2], *s.m. A:* careening (of ship).

crâne [krɑːn]. **1.** *s.m.* (*a*) cranium, skull; brainpan; **fracture du c.,** fracture of the skull; **défoncer, fendre, le c. à qn,** to brain s.o.; *A: Fb:* **réussir un c.,** to get in a header; (*b*) **avoir le c. étroit,** to be of limited intelligence; *F:* dim-witted; **bourrer le c. à qn,** to stuff s.o. with stories, to (try to) lead s.o. up the garden path. **2.** *a.* (*a*) *O:* swaggering, jaunty (air); **faire le c.,** to swagger; (*b*) *F:* outstanding, first rate; (*c*) **depuis sa maladie il n'est pas bien c.,** since his illness he hasn't been quite up to the mark.

crânement [krɑnmɑ̃], *adv. F:* (*a*) *O:* in a swaggering, jaunty, manner; jauntily; (*b*) **il s'en est acquitté c.,** he did it fearlessly; (*c*) very; **elle est c. belle,** she's staggeringly beautiful.

craner[1] [krane], *v.tr.* to hand-finish the teeth of (wheel).

craner[2], *v.tr. A:* to careen (ship).

crâner [krɑne], *v.i. F:* (*a*) to swagger; to swank; to put on a jaunty air; (*b*) to brazen it out.

crânerie [krɑnri], *s.f. F:* swaggering.

crâneur, -euse [krɑnœːr, -øːz], *s. F:* braggart, swaggerer, swanker; **faire le c.,** to swagger; *a.* **il est un peu c.,** he puts it on a bit.

crangon [krɑ̃gɔ̃], *s.m.* shrimp.

crania [kranja], *s.f. Moll:* crania.

crâniectomie [krɑnjɛktɔmi], *s.f. Surg:* craniectomy.

crânien, -ienne [krɑnjɛ̃, -jɛn], *a. Anat:* cranial; **la boîte crânienne,** the skull, the brain-pan.

crani(o)- [krɑnj(ɔ)], *pref. Anat: Med:* crani(o)-; **craniologique,** craniological.

cranioclasie [krɑnjɔklazi], *s.f. Obst:* cranioclasis.

cranioclaste [krɑnjɔklast], *s.m. Obst:* cranioclast.

craniographe [krɑnjɔgraf], *s.m.* craniograph.

craniologie [krɑnjɔlɔʒi], *s.f.* craniology.

craniologique [krɑnjɔlɔʒik], *a.* craniological.

craniologiste [krɑnjɔlɔʒist], **craniologue** [krɑnjɔlɔg], *s.m. & f.* craniologist.

craniomalacie [krɑnjɔmalasi], *s.f. Med:* craniomalacia.

craniomètre [krɑnjɔmɛtr], *s.m. Anthr:* craniometer.

craniométrie [krɑnjɔmetri], *s.f.* craniometry.

craniométrique [krɑnjɔmetrik], *a.* craniometric.

craniophore [krɑnjɔfɔːr], *s.m. Anthr:* craniophore.

cranioplastie [krɑnjɔplasti], *s.f. Surg:* cranioplasty.

cranioscopie [krɑnjɔskɔpi], *s.f.* cranioscopy.

craniostat [krɑnjɔsta], *s.m. Anthr:* craniophore.

craniotabès [krɑnjɔtabɛs], *s.m. Med:* craniotabes.

craniotome [krɑnjɔtɔm], *s.m. Surg:* craniotome.

craniotomie [krɑnjɔtɔmi], *s.f. Surg:* craniotomy.

crannoge [kranɔːʒ], *s.m. Archeol:* crannog.

cranoir [kranwaːr], *s.m. Tls: Clockm:* notching file.

cranson [krɑ̃sɔ̃], *s.m. Bot:* horse-radish.

cranté [krɑ̃te], *a.* (*a*) notched; serrated; (*b*) *Bootm:* **semelle caoutchouc c.,** treaded rubber sole; (*c*) *Dom.Ec: etc:* **manche c., queue crantée,** finger-grip handle.

cranter [krɑ̃te], *v.tr.* **1.** to notch; *Dressm:* **c. une couture, une emmanchure,** to notch, to pink, a seam, an armhole. **2.** *Hairdr:* to wave, set in waves.

crapaud [krapo], *s.m.* **1.** toad; (*a*) **c. des roseaux** running toad, natterjack; **c. vert,** European variable toad; **c. sonneur,** fire-bellied toad; **c. à griffes,** clawed toad; **c. accoucheur,** midwife-toad, obstetric frog; **c. de Surinam,** Surinam toad, pipa; *F:* **avaler un c.,** (i) to bring oneself to do a particularly unpleasant task; (ii) to pocket an insult; *P:* **c'est un vilain c.,** he's an ugly little squirt; *Miner:* **pierre de c.,** toadstone; (*b*) *F:* child; (*c*) *Ich:* **c. de mer, c. pêcheur,** fishing-frog, angler-fish, sea-devil; (*d*) *Orn:* **c. volant,** nightjar; (*e*) *Lap:* blemish; (*f*) *P:* purse; (*g*) *P:* padlock. **2.** *Nau:* **c. de mouillage, d'amarrage,** mooring clump; sinker (of mine). **3.** *Pyr:* jumping cracker. **4.** *Rail:* sleeper clip. **5.** *Vet:* pododermatitis, grease, greasy heel. **6.** (*a*) tub easy-chair; (*b*) baby grand (piano). **7.** *a.* hideous, ugly; deformed.

crapaudé [krapode], *a.* **arbre c.,** tree with rough, rugged, bark.

crapaudière [krapodjɛːr], *s.f.* **1.** toad-hole. **2.** (*a*) nasty wet, boggy, place; (*b*) **c. d'usuriers,** den of moneylenders.

crapaudine [krapodin], *s.f.* **1.** *Miner:* toadstone. **2.** (*a*) *Bot:* ironwort; (*b*) *Ich:* wolf-fish. **3.** *Cu:* **poulet à la c.,** pullet boned and grilled; spatchcocked chicken. **4.** *Hyd.E:* (*a*) grating, strainer (of inlet pipe of pond); (*b*) discharging valve (of pond); (*c*) waste hole (of bath). **5.** *Mec.E: etc:* (*a*) pivot-bearing, -box, -hole; step-bearing, -box; thrust-bearing (of vertical shaft); **c. annulaire,** collar-slip bearing; (*b*) socket, gudgeon (of door-hinge, rudder, etc.); *Nau:* **c. de bossoir, de chandelier,** davit, stanchion, socket. **6.** *Vet:* crapaudine.

crapette [krapɛt], *s.f. Cards:* crapette, Russian bank.

crapois [krapwa], *s.m. A.Cu:* salted whale meat.

craponne [krapɔn], *s.f. Tls:* (watchmaker's) file.

crapouiller [krapuje], *v.i. Mil: P: A:* to fire trench-mortars.

crapouillot [krapujo], *s.m. Mil: P: A:* **1.** trench-mortar. **2.** trench-mortar shell.

crapoussin [krapusɛ̃], *s.m. P:* dwarf; freak.

crapulados [krapyladoːs], *s.m. P: A:* cheap cigar; *P:* stinkador.

crapule [krapyl], *s.f.* **1.** *A:* debauchery, dissoluteness, profligacy, lewdness. **2.** *Coll. F:* dissolute, profligate, lewd, mob. **3.** (*a*) *A:* dissolute person, debauchee; (*b*) rogue, scoundrel; *a.* dishonest, low-down (pers., action).

crapuler [krapyle], *v.i. A:* to wallow in vice.

crapulerie [krapylri], *s.f.* **1.** debauchery, dissoluteness. **2.** (*a*) piece of profligacy; (*b*) foul trick.

crapuleusement [krapyløzmɑ̃], *adv.* (*a*) *A:* dissolutely, profligately, lewdly; (*b*) dishonestly; in a low-down manner.

crapuleux, -euse [krapylø, -øːz], *a.* (*a*) *A:* debauched, dissolute, lewd; (*b*) *Lit:* **fêtes crapuleuses,** dissolute festivities; (*c*) foul (language); **crime c.,** sordid, loathsome, crime.

crapulos [krapyloːs], *s.m. P: A:* cheap cigar; *P:* stinkador.

craquage [krakaːʒ], *s.m.* cracking (of heavy oil); **c. isomérisant,** isocracking; **c. catalytique, thermique,** catalytic, thermal, cracking; **essence de c.,** cracked petrol, *U.S:* cracked gasoline; **four de c.,** cracking furnace, kiln; **appareil, installation, matériel de c.,** cracker, cracking installation.

craquant [krakɑ̃], *a.* cracking, crackling; **souliers craquants,** squeaky shoes.

craque[1] [krak], *s.f. Geol:* crystalliferous vein; geode, druse.

craque[2], *s.f. P:* (*a*) lie; (*b*) tall story.

craquelage [kraklaːʒ], *s.m.* (*a*) *Cer:* crackling; (*b*) *Paint:* cracking.

craquelé [krakle]. **1.** *a.* crackled; *Cer:* craquelé. **2.** *s.m. Cer:* crackle-ware, -china, -glass; crackle.

craquèlement [krakɛlmɑ̃], *s.m.* crackling.

craqueler [krakle], *v.tr.* **(je craquelle, n. craquelons; je craquellerai)** *Cer:* to crackle, to cover (china, etc.) with small cracks; **front craquelé de rides,** forehead criss-crossed with wrinkles.

se craqueler, to crackle; to become crackled.

craquelin [kraklɛ̃], *s.m.* **1.** *Cu:* (*a*) cracknel (biscuit); (*b*) canary bread. **2.** *Crust:* crackler. **3.** *Nau:* (*a*) crazy ship; (*b*) little shrimp of a man. **4.** wrinkle (in stocking).

craquellement [krakɛlmɑ̃], *s.m.* crackling.

craquelot [kraklo], *s.m.* **1.** bloater, bloated herring. **2.** *Crust:* crackler.

craquelure [kraklyːr], *s.f.* (i) crack; (ii) small cracks (in paint, etc.); *pl. Art:* craquelure.

craquement [krakmɑ̃], *s.m.* (*a*) cracking (sound); crack, snap; (*b*) crackling (of dried leaves, etc.); crunching (of snow); (*c*) creaking (of shoes, etc.).

craquer [krake], *v.i.* **1.** (*a*) to crack; to make a cracking sound; (*b*) (*of dried leaves, etc.*) to crackle; (*of hard snow*) to crunch (under the feet); (*c*) (*of shoes, etc.*) to creak, to squeak; **faire c. ses doigts,** to crack one's finger-joints; **faire c. un mât, un aviron,** to spring a mast, an

oar; **habit qui a craqué dans le dos,** coat that has split, slit, down the back; **faire c. les coutures,** to start the seams; **projet qui craque,** scheme that threatens to come to grief; (*c*) *F:* to crack up; (*d*) *v.tr.* **c. une allumette,** to strike a match; *F:* **c. un héritage,** to spend, go through, a legacy. **2.** *O: P:* to tell lies; to tell a tall story. **3.** *v.tr. Ind:* to crack (mineral oil).

craquerie [krakri], *s.f. O: P:* lie; tall story.

craquètement [krakɛtmɑ̃], *s.m.* **1.** crackling, crackle. **2.** (*a*) chirping (of cricket); (*b*) clattering (of stork).

craqueter [krakte], *v.i.* **(il craquette; il craquettera) 1.** to crackle. **2.** (*a*) (*of cricket*) to chirp; (*b*) (*of stork*) to clatter.

craquettement [krakɛtmɑ̃], *s.m.* **1.** crackling, crackle. **2.** (*a*) chirping (of cricket); (*b*) clattering (of stork).

craqueur, -euse [krakœːr, -øːz], *s. A: P:* fibber, teller of tall stories.

craqûre [krakyːr], *s.f.* split, crack (in armour-plate, etc.); spring (in a mast).

crase [krɑːz], *s.f. Gr.Gram:* crasis.

crash [kraʃ], *s.m. Av: F:* crash landing.

craspédote [kraspedɔt], *a. Coel:* craspedote.

crassane [krasan], *s.f. Hort:* kind of pear.

crasse [kras]. **1.** *a.f.* gross, crass; *used esp. in* **ignorance c.,** crass ignorance. **2.** *s.f.* (*a*) (body) dirt, filth; *Tchn:* sordes; **né dans la c.,** born in squalor, in the gutter; (*b*) *Med:* **c. sénile,** senile keratosis; *Vet:* **c. des porcelets,** keratosis of pigs; (*c*) *Mch:* fur, scale (in boiler); *Metall:* dross, scum, skin, slag, clinker; *Metalw:* hammer-scale, forge-scale; *Fire-arms:* fouling; *Metall:* sullage (in casting-ladle); (*d*) *Nau: F:* black clouds, thick weather; (*e*) avarice, meanness, stinginess; **être d'une c. outrée,** to be mean beyond expression; (*f*) *F:* **faire une c. à qn,** to play s.o. a dirty trick, to do the dirty on s.o.

crassement[1] [krasmɑ̃], *adv.* meanly, stingily; in a low-down manner.

crassement[2], *s.m.* fouling (of barrel of fire-arms).

crasser [krase], *v.tr.* to foul, clog (gun-barrel).

se crasser, (*of fire-arm*) to get, become, foul; to foul.

crasserie [krasri], *s.f. F:* avarice; sordidness.

crasseux, -euse [krasø, -øːz]. **1.** *a.* (*a*) dirty, filthy, soiled (hands, linen, etc.); squalid (dwelling, etc.); **des étudiants c.,** dirty students; *s. F:* **les crasseux,** the great unwashed; (*b*) *F:* mean, stingy. **2.** *s. F:* mean person; skinflint.

crassier [krasje], *s.m.* slag-heap, ash-heap, cinder-bank, tip; dump.

crassicaule [krasikoːl], *a. Bot:* thick-stemmed.

crassilingue [krasilɛ̃ːg], *a. Rept:* crassilingual.

crassulacées [krasylase], *s.f.pl. Bot:* Crassulaceae.

crassule [krasyl], *s.f. Bot:* crassula; *F:* thick-leaf.

cratægus [kratɛgys], *s.m. Bot:* crataegus.

cratæva [kratava], *s.m. Bot:* crataeva; **c. gynandra,** garlic-pear.

-crate [krat], *s.suff. m. & f.* -crat; **aristocrate,** aristocrat; **démocrate,** democrat; **plutocrate,** plutocrat; **bureaucrate,** bureaucrat.

cratère [kratɛːr], *s.m.* crater. **1.** *Gr.Ant:* crater; (wine) bowl. **2.** (*a*) *Geog:* crater (of volcano); **c. adventif,** parasitic, lateral, crater; **c. météorique,** crater formed by a meteorite; **cratères lunaires,** craters of the moon; (*b*) (bomb) crater; shell hole. **3.** *El:* crater (of arc-lamp carbon).

craterelle [kratrɛl], *s.f. Fung:* craterellus.

cratériforme [krateriform], *a.* crateriform, crater-like, bowl-shaped.

cratérope [kraterɔp], *s.m. Orn:* babbler.

craticulage [kratikylaːʒ], *s.m.* drawing of perspective from oblique photograph (correcting the deformation).

craticulaire [kratikylɛːr], *a.* grill-like; in the form of a grid.

craticulation [kratikylasjɔ̃], *s.f.* reduction of a drawing with the aid of squares, grid; graticulation.

craticuler [kratikyle], *v.tr.* to divide (drawing, etc.) into squares, to graticulate.

-cratie [krasi], *s.suff.f.* -cracy; **aristocratie,** aristocracy; **bureaucratie,** bureaucracy.

cratinien [kratinjɛ̃], *a.m. Gr.Pros:* Cratinean (verse).

Cratippe [kratip], *Pr.n.m. Gr.Hist:* Cratippus.

-cratique [kratik], *a.suff.* -cratic; **aristocratique,** aristocratic; **démocratique,** democratic.

cravache [kravaʃ], *s.f.* riding whip, hunting-crop.

cravachée [kravaʃe], *s.f.* (horse-)whipping; **administrer une c. à qn,** to horse-whip s.o., to give s.o. a horse-whipping.

cravacher [kravaʃe], (*a*) *v.tr.* to flog (horse); to horsewhip (person); (*b*) *v.i. F:* to make a desperate effort; to go full speed ahead.

cravan(t) [kravɑ̃], *s.m.* **1.** *Moll:* barnacle. **2.** *Orn:* brent(-goose).

cravate [kravat]. **1.** *s.m. A:* (*a*) Croatian horse; (*b*) *Hist:* Croat, light-mounted mercenary. **2.** *s.f.* (*a*) *Cost:* (i) tie; (ii) scarf; cravat; (woman's) fur tie; **être en c. blanche,** to be in full evening dress, in tails; **c. toute faite,** made-up tie; **c. de sport,** stock; **coulant de c.,** scarf ring; **épingle de c.,** tie-pin; *Mil:* **c. d'un drapeau,** bow and tassels of colour-stave; **c. de commandeur de la Légion d'Honneur,** insignia of a *commandeur de la Légion d'Honneur*; *A: F:* **c. de chanvre, de justice,** hangman's rope; *P:* **s'envoyer, s'en jeter, un derrière la c.,** to knock back a drink; (*b*) *Wr:* hold in chancery; head-lock; (*c*) *Nau:* sling; **mettre l'ancre en c.,** to hang the anchor over the stern; (*d*) *Mec.E: etc:* (metal) collar; ferrule (of sword, etc.); (*e*) *Orn:* ruff, ruffle; **pigeon à c.,** ruff.

cravaté [kravate], *a. Orn:* **pigeon c.,** ruff.

cravate-plastron [kravatplastrɔ̃], *s.f. A.Cost:* four-in-hand tie; *pl. cravates-plastrons.*

cravater [kravate], *v.tr.* **1.** to put a tie on (s.o.); **se c.,** to put on one's tie; **vous êtes mal cravaté,** your tie's crooked; *Mil:* **c. le drapeau,** to tie the bow and tassels on the colour. **2.** *Wr:* to hold (one's opponent) round the neck; to get one's opponent's head in chancery. **3.** *P:* to nab, to collar (a thief, etc.). **4.** *P:* to dupe, hoodwink (s.o.).

cravatier, -ière [kravatje, -jɛːr], *s.* maker, seller, of ties; haberdasher, outfitter.

crave [krɑːv], *s.m. Orn:* **c. à bec rouge,** chough.

crawl [krol], *s.m. Swim:* crawl(-stroke); **c. sur le dos,** back-crawl.

crawler [krole], *v.i. Swim:* to do the crawl, to crawl.

crawleur [krolœːr], *s.m.* crawl-swimmer.

crayer[1] [krɛje], *v.tr.* **(je craye, je craie, n. crayons; je crayerai, je craierai)** to mark (sth.) with chalk; to chalk.

crayer[2] [kraje], *s.m. A.Nau:* crayer, crare.

crayère [krɛjɛːr], *s.f.* chalk pit.

crayeux, -euse [krɛjø, -øːz], *a.* chalky; **collines crayeuses,** chalk hills.

crayon [krɛjɔ̃], *s.m.* **1.** (*a*) pencil; **c. à mine de plomb,** lead pencil; **écrit au c.,** written in pencil; pencilled; **c. de couleur,** coloured pencil, crayon; **marquer une faute au c. bleu,** to blue-pencil a mistake; **c. violet, à encre (indélébile),** indelible pencil; **c. feutre,** felt pen; **c. pastel,** crayon; **c. à bille,** ball-point pencil; **c. Conté,** Conté crayon; **c. litho,** litho, *U.S:* grease, crayon; **c. pour porcelaine,** chinagraph pencil; **dessin au c.,** pencil drawing; **dessin à deux crayons,** sketch in charcoal and (white) chalk; **coup de c.,** pencil stroke; *s.a.* TAILLER 1; (*b*) pencil drawing, sketch; (*c*) *A:* portrait. **2.** stick; *Med:* pencil (of caustic, etc.); *Toil:* **c. à lèvres,** lipstick; **c. pour les sourcils,** eyebrow pencil; *Th:* **c. gras,** stick of greasepaint; *El:* **c. de zinc,** zinc rod; **c. d'une lampe à arc,** carbon(-pencil) of an arc-lamp. **3.** chalk soil, marl.

crayon-lèvres [krɛjɔ̃lɛːvr], *s.m.* lipstick; *pl. crayons-lèvres.*

crayonnage [krɛjɔnaːʒ], *s.m.* **1.** pencilling; pencil marks. **2.** pencil sketch.

crayonner [krɛjɔne], *v.tr.* **1.** to draw (sth.) in pencil, to make a pencil sketch of (sth.). **2.** to pencil; to write, jot, (sth.) down (on paper); to make a pencil note of (sth.). **3.** *A:* to sketch, outline, describe (character, one's feelings, etc.). **4.** to make pencil marks on (sth.).

crayonneur, -euse [krɛjɔnœːr, -øːz], *s.* **1.** (rough) sketcher. **2.** poor artist.

crayonneux, -euse [krɛjɔnø, -øːz], *a.* marly (soil, etc.).

crayonniste [krɛjɔnist], *s.m. & f.* **1.** pencil-seller, -maker. **2.** sketcher, drawer in pencil.

cré [kre], *a.inv.* (*abbr. of* sacré) *P:* **c. nom de nom!** hell!

créance [kreɑ̃ːs], *s.f.* **1.** belief, credence, credit; **hors de c.,** unbelievable; **trouver c.,** to be believed, to find acceptance; **ces récits ne trouvent plus c.,** these stories are no longer credited; **donner, ajouter, c. à qn, à qch.,** to believe s.o., sth.; to give credit to, to credit (rumour, etc.). **2.** trust; **perdre toute c.,** to lose the confidence of the public; **lettre(s) de c.,** (i) credentials (of diplomatic agent); (ii) *Com:* letter of credit (to bank); letter of credence (to correspondent). **3.** debt; *Jur:* claim; **mauvaises créances, créances véreuses,** bad debts; **c. exigible,** debt due; **c. garantie,** secured debt; **c. privilégiée,** preferential, preferred, debt; **nos créances,** moneys owing to us; **créances gelées,** frozen credits. **4.** *Ven:* creance.

créancier, -ière [kreɑ̃sje, -jɛːr], *s.* creditor; holder of debt claim; **créanciers importuns,** duns; **c. hypothécaire,** mortgagee; *a.* **les peuples créanciers d'indemnités de guerre,** the nations to whom war indemnities are owing.

créat [krea], *s.m.* (*a*) *Ich: Dial:* sturgeon; (*b*) *Fish:* sturgeon net.

créateur, -trice [kreatœːr, -tris]. **1.** *a.* creative (power, genius). **2.** *s.* creator; (*a*) **le C.,** the Creator, God; **recevoir son C.,** to take (Holy) Communion; (*b*) maker; establisher (of bank, etc.); *Com:* **c. d'un chèque,** drawer of a cheque; **c. d'un article,** inventor of an article; (*c*) *Th:* creator (of a rôle); *Th:* **la pièce fut rejouée avec plusieurs de ses créateurs,** the play was put on again with several members of the original cast.

créatif, -ive [kreatif, -iːv], *a.* creative.

créatine [kreatin], *s.f. Ch:* creatin(e).

créatinine [kreatinin], *s.f. Ch:* creatinin(e).

créatininémie [kreatininemi], *s.f.* creatininaemia.

création [kreasjɔ̃], *s.f.* **1.** (*a*) creation, creating; **esprit de c.,** creativeness; **la c. du monde,** the creation of the world; (*b*) founding, establishment (of institution, etc.); creation (of peer, of work of art); setting up (of a court, etc.); issuing, drawing (of cheque, bill, etc.); *Com:* **c. d'un nouveau produit,** invention of a new product; *Th:* **c. d'un rôle,** creation of a part; **poste de c. récente,** newly instituted office. **2.** (*a*) **les merveilles de la c.,** the wonders of creation, of the universe; (*b*) **sa robe était une c. de chez Vénus et Cie,** her dress was a creation by Venus & Co.

créationisme [kreasjɔnism], *s.m. Theol:* creationism.

créativité [kreativite], *s.f.* creativity.

créature [kreatyːr], *s.f.* creature. **1.** created being. **2.** *F:* (*a*) person, individual; **c'est une bonne c., une étrange c.,** he's a good creature, an odd creature; (*b*) *Pej:* (*of woman*) **l'insolente c.!** the impudent creature! **3. c. d'un ministre,** creature, tool, of a minister.

crebleu [krəblø], *int. P:* (*abbr. of* **sacrebleu**) confound it! damn it!

crécelle [kresɛl], *s.f.* (hand-)rattle; *F:* **c'est une c.,** she's a regular chatterbox; **voix de c.,** rasping voice, corn-crake voice.

crécerelle [kresrɛl], *s.f. Orn:* **(faucon) c.,** kestrel, windhover.

crèche [krɛʃ], *s.f.* **1.** (*a*) *Husb:* manger, crib; (*b*) (Christ child's) crib; (*c*) plate-rack. **2.** (*a*) (child's) crib; (*b*) day-nursery, crèche; (*c*) *P:* home; digs. **3.** *Hyd.E:* **c. de pourtour,** pile sheathing (of pier, etc.).

crécher [kreʃe], *v.i. P:* to live; **où que tu crèches?** where do you hang out?

Crécy [kresi]. **1.** *Pr.n.m. Geog:* Crécy. **2.** *s.f. Cu:* carrot (*as grown at* Crécy); **(potage à la) c.,** carrot soup.

crédence [kredɑ̃ːs], *s.f.* **1.** (*a*) *A:* credence (table where yeoman for the mouth tasted dishes); (*b*) credence; sideboard, buffet. **2.** *Ecc:* credence (-table). **3.** *A:* buttery.

crédencier [kredɑ̃sje], *s.m. A:* yeoman for the mouth.

crédibilité [kredibilite], *s.f.* credibility, believableness.

crédible [kredibl], *a.* credible; **la dissuasion nucléaire est plus c. que les armements classiques,** a nuclear deterrent is more credible than conventional weapons.

crédieu [kredjø], *int. P: O:* (*shortened form of* **sacré nom de Dieu**), (God) damn it (all)!

crédirentier, -ière [kredirɑ̃tje, -jɛːr], *s. Jur:* recipient of an allowance, of an income, an annuity.

crédit [kredi], *s.m.* **1.** *Lit:* credit, repute, influence; prestige (of country, etc.); **avoir du c. à la cour, auprès de qn,** to have credit, influence, at court, with s.o.; **mettre une opinion en c.,** to accredit an opinion, to get an opinion credited; **mettre une mode en c.,** to bring in a fashion; **nouvelle qui prend c.,** news that is gaining credence; **rumeurs jusqu'ici sans c.,** rumours hitherto uncredited. **2.** *Fin: Com:* credit; **c. bancaire,** bank credit; **banque de c.,** credit bank; **c. en blanc, à découvert,** blank, open, credit; **lettre de c.,** letter of credit; **c. documentaire,** documentary letter of credit; **carte de c.,** credit card; **vendre, acheter, qch. à c.,** to sell, buy, sth. (i) on credit, *F:* on tick, (ii) on hire purchase; **faire c. à qn,** to give s.o. credit, to trust s.o.; **ouvrir un c. chez qn,** to open a credit account, *F:* an account, with s.o.; **ouvrir un c. à qn,** to open a credit account in s.o.'s favour; **établissement, société, de c.,** loan society; credit establishment; bank; **c. municipal,** (municipal) pawn office; le

c. foncier, (government-controlled) building society. **3.** credit(or) side (of ledger, balance sheet); **porter une somme au c. de qn,** to place a sum to s.o.'s credit, to credit s.o. with a sum. **4.** sum voted by Parliament for supply; **voter des crédits,** to vote supplies; **crédits supplémentaires,** (voting of) supplementary estimates.

créditer [kredite], *v.tr.* (*a*) **c. qn du montant d'une somme,** to credit s.o., s.o.'s account, with a sum; to place, carry, put, a sum to s.o.'s credit; **c. un compte,** to credit an account; (*b*) **c. qn de,** to give s.o. credit for; to credit s.o. with.

créditeur, -trice [kreditœːr, -tris]. **1.** *s.* creditor. **2.** *a.* having a credit; **compte c.,** account in credit, credit account; **solde c.,** credit balance; **nation créditrice,** creditor nation.

crednérite [krɛdnerit], *s.f. Miner:* crednerite.

credo [kredo], *s.m.inv.* creed, *esp.* the Apostles' Creed; credo; **c. politique,** political creed.

crédule [kredyl], *a.* credulous; **population c. à tous les bruits,** population ready to believe any rumour; **confiance c.,** blind confidence.

crédulement [kredylmã], *adv.* credulously.

crédulité [kredylite], *s.f.* credulity, credulousness; **avec c.,** credulously.

creep [krip], **creeping** [kripiŋ], *s.m. Geog:* creep; saltation.

créer [kree], *v.tr.* **1.** to create. **2.** (*a*) **c. un courant d'air,** to create a draught; **c. une chaire,** to found, institute, establish, a professorial chair; **c. une armée,** to form an army; **créer qch. de toutes pièces,** to create sth. out of nothing; **fantômes qu'ils se créent eux-mêmes,** phantasms of their own creation; **c. une maison de commerce, un tribunal,** to set up a business, a court; **se c. une clientèle,** to build up a connection; **agence récemment créée,** recently established agency; **c. un effet de commerce,** to draw up, issue, a bill; **c. un chèque,** to write out, make out, a cheque; **c. une obligation, des obligations, à qn,** to put s.o. under an obligation, under obligations; **c. des difficultés à qn,** to create difficulties for s.o., to put difficulties in s.o.'s way; *Th:* **c. un rôle,** to create a part; (*b*) (*with object and complement*) **c. qn chevalier, comte,** to create s.o. a knight, a count. **3.** *Com:* **chemises créées par Dumaine,** shirts styled by Dumaine.

creillois, -oise [krɛjwa, -waːz], *a. & s. Geog:* (native, inhabitant) of Creil.

creittonite [krɛtɔnit], *s.f. Miner:* kreittonite.

crémage [kremaːʒ], *s.m.* **1.** (*action of*) colouring (sth.) cream. **2.** *Physical Ch:* movement in suspension of a disperse(d) phase.

crémaillère [kremajɛːr], *s.f.* **1.** (*a*) pot-hanger, -hook; trammel(-hook); chimney-hook; *F:* **pendre la c.,** to give a house-warming party; **à quand la c.?** when will the house-warming be? **2.** (*a*) *Mec.E: etc:* toothed rack, arc; rack-bar; **c. et pignon,** rack and pinion; **engrenage à c.,** rack-gearing; **fauteuil à c.,** armchair with adjustable back; *Phot:* **c. de mise au point,** focusing rack; (*b*) *Rail:* cog-rail, rack(-rail); **locomotive, chemin de fer, à c.,** rack-engine, -railway; **c. d'avance,** feed rack (of machine tool); **cric à c.,** rack jack; (*c*) *Fort:* crémaillère; **ligne, tracé, à c.,** indented line, trace; (*d*) **fermeture à c.,** zip fastener. **3.** *Veh: Rail:* (arm) sling.

crémaillon [kremajɔ̃], *s.m.* small pot-hook, -hanger.

crémant [kremã], *a. & s.m.* slightly sparkling (wine).

crémaster [kremastɛːr], *s.m. Anat: Ent:* cremaster.

crémation [kremasjɔ̃], *s.f.* cremation.

crématoire [krematwaːr], *a. & s.m.* crematory; (four) crématoire, crematorium.

crématorium [krematɔrjɔm], *s.m.* crematorium; *pl. crematoria.*

crème [krɛm], *s.f.* **1.** (*a*) cream; **c. fouettée,** whipped cream; **fromage à la c.,** cream cheese; **c. (de gruyère, etc.),** processed cheese; **fraises à la c.,** strawberries and cream; **café c.,** white coffee; (*b*) *F:* (*of pers.*) top-notcher; **c'est la c. des hommes,** he's the best of men, one of the best; *O:* (*of literary work*) **ce n'est que de la c. fouettée,** there's nothing solid about it; (*c*) *Cu:* **c. anglaise, c. renversée,** (egg) custard; **c. pâtissière,** confectioner's custard; **c. brûlée,** crème brûlée; **c. caramel,** caramel custard; cream caramel, crème caramel; **c. au café,** coffee cream; **c. glacée,** *Fr.C:* **c. à la glace,** ice cream; **c. d'asperges,** cream of asparagus soup. **2.** (*a*) **c. pour chaussures,** shoe cream, polish; (*b*) *Toil:* **c. de beauté,** face cream; **c. fond de teint,** foundation cream; **c. à raser,** shaving cream; (*c*) *Ch:* **c. de tartre,** cream of tartar; **c. de soufre,** flowers of sulphur; (*d*) *Cu:* **c. de riz,** ground rice, rice flour. **3. c. de menthe,** *crème de menthe,* peppermint liqueur. **4.** *a.inv.* cream(-coloured); **des gants c.,** cream-coloured gloves.

crémer[1] [kreme], *v.tr.* (**je crème, n. crémons; je crémerai**) to cremate.

crémer[2]. **1.** *v.i.* (*of milk, etc.*) to cream. **2.** *v.tr. Dy:* to dye (sth.) cream.

crémerie [krɛmri], *s.f.* **1.** creamery, dairy, milk shop. **2.** *O:* small restaurant (serving light meals); *F:* **changer de c.,** to move on; to go elsewhere; to make a change.

crémeux, -euse [kremø, -øːz]. **1.** *a.* creamy. **2.** *s.f.* **crémeuse,** cream-setting pan.

crémier, -ière [kremje, -jɛːr], *s.* **1.** (*a*) dairyman, dairy-woman, dairy-keeper; (*b*) *O:* keeper of a small restaurant. **2.** *s.f.* **crémière,** cream-jug.

crémier-glacier [kremjeglasje], *s.m.* confectioner who makes ice creams; *pl. crémiers-glaciers.*

Crémone [kremɔn]. **1.** *Pr.n.f. Geog:* Cremona; **un violon de C.,** a Cremona violin. **2.** *s.f.* casement bolt; espagnolette.

crénage [krenaːʒ], *s.m. Typ:* **1.** kerning (of type). **2.** nicking (of shank of type).

créneau, -eaux [kreno], *s.m.* **1.** (*a*) *Fort:* crenel, crenelle, embrasure; *pl.* battlements, crenellation; (*b*) loop-hole; slit (in armoured turret, tank, etc.); **c. de visée,** aiming slit, peep; **c. d'observation,** lookout, observation, slit; (*c*) *Mec.E:* **écrou** *m* **à créneaux,** castle-nut, castellated nut. **2.** breach, gap, hiatus, interval, distance; *Aut:* gap (in line of traffic) where a passing car can slip in; *Aut: Adm:* **garer en c.,** to park between two cars lengthwise along the kerb; *Mil:* **c. d'une colonne,** distance between the units of a column; **les créneaux de la ligne de contact,** gaps, intervals, in the front line. **3.** *Elcs: Radar:* strobe marker.

crénelage [krɛnlaːʒ], *s.m.* **1.** *Fort:* (*a*) crenellation, castellation; (*b*) cutting of, or series of, loopholes (in wall, etc.). **2.** toothing; *Num:* milling (of coin).

crénelé [krɛnle]. **1.** *Fort:* (*a*) crenel(l)ated, castellated, embattled, battlemented (wall, etc.); *Mec.E:* **écrou c.,** castle-nut, castellated nut; (*b*) loop-holed. **2.** *Bot:* crenate(d), crenelled (leaf, etc.). **3.** toothed, notched; *Num:* milled (coin). **4.** *Her:* embattled.

créneler [krɛnle], *v.tr.* (**je crénelle, n. crénelons; je crénellerai**) **1.** *Fort:* (*a*) to crenel(l)ate, embattle, notch (wall, etc.); (*b*) to cut loopholes in, to loophole (wall, etc.). **2.** to notch, tooth (wheel, etc.); *Num:* to mill (coin).

crénelure [krɛnlyːr], *s.f.* crenellation, indentation, series of notches; *Bot:* crenelling (of leaf).

créner [krene], *v.tr.* (**je crène, n. crénons; je crénerai**) *Typ:* **1.** to kern (type). **2.** to nick the shank of (type).

crénom [krenɔ̃], *int. P: O:* (*shortened form of* **sacré nom (de Dieu)**), (God) damn it (all)!

crénon [krenɔ̃], *s.m.* (*slate quarrying*) block of schist.

crénothérapie [krenɔterapi], *s.f. Med:* crenotherapy.

créole [kreɔl], *a. & s. Ethn:* Creole.

créoliser [kreɔlize], *v.tr.* to creolize.

Créon [kreɔ̃], *Pr.n.m. Gr.Lit:* Creon.

créosol [kreɔzɔl], *s.m. Ch:* creosol.

créosotage [kreɔzɔtaːʒ], *s.m.* creosoting.

créosote [kreɔzɔt], *s.f.* creosote.

créosoter [kreɔzɔte], *v.tr.* to creosote.

crêpage [krɛpaːʒ], *s.m.* **1.** crimping, crisping (of hair, of crêpe); *F:* **c. de chignons,** fight, set-to (between women). **2.** *Paperm:* manufacture of crêpe paper.

crêpe [krɛːp]. **1.** *s.f. Cu:* pancake; **faire sauter une crêpe,** to toss a pancake; *F: A:* (*of car*) **faire la c.,** to turn turtle; *F:* **s'aplatir comme une c.,** to fall flat on one's face. **2.** *s.m.* (*a*) *Tex:* crape; crêpe; **c. lisse, c. français,** soft crape, crêpe; **c. de Chine,** crêpe de Chine; **c. ninon,** ninon; **c. satin,** satin crêpe; **chaussettes c. mousse,** crêpe nylon socks; **c. crêpé,** crisped, hard, crape; **c. anglais,** black mourning crape; **porter un c.,** to wear a mourning band (round one's arm, one's hat); **brassard de c.,** band (round arm); **voile de c.,** mourning veil; (*b*) crêpe-rubber; **semelles de c.,** crêpe(-rubber) soles; (*c*) *Paperm:* **papier c.,** crêpe paper, crinkled paper.

crêpé [krepe], *s.m.* (*a*) hair-pad; (*b*) switch of hair.

crêpelé [krɛple], *a.* (*of hair*) crimped, frizzy.

crêpeline [krɛplin], *s.f. Tex:* crêpeline, crêpoline.

crêpelu [krɛply], *a.* (*of hair*) frizzy, fuzzy.

crêpelure [krɛplyːr], *s.f.* frizziness, fuzziness (of hair).

crêper [krepe], *v.tr. F:* to frizz, crimp, (the hair), to back-comb; to crisp, crimp, crape; *F:* **se c. (le chignon),** (of women) to fight, to tear each other's hair, to have a set-to.

crêperie [krɛpri], *s.f.* pancake bar.

crêpeuse [krɛpøːz], *s.f.* machine for the manufacture of crêpe paper.

crépi [krepi]. **1.** *a.* (*a*) **cuir c.,** pebble-leather; (*b*) *Const:* rough-cast, pargeted, pebble-dashed. **2.** *s.m.* rough-rendering; rough coat (of plaster); **c. moucheté,** rough-cast, pebble-dash.

crépide[1] [krepid], *s.m. Bot:* crepis.

crépide[2], *s.f.* **1.** *Ant:* Greek sandal. **2.** *Const:* quay wall.

crepidula [krepidyla], *s.f. Moll:* Crepidula.

crépidule [krepidyl], *s.f. Rom.Ant:* small sandal.

crêpier, -ière [krepje, krɛ-, -jɛːr], *s.* **1.** *s.m. & f.* pancake seller. **2.** *s.m.* pancake griddle.

Crépin [krepɛ̃]. **1.** *Pr.n.m.* Crispin. **2.** *s.m.pl. A:* **crépins,** (leather-)grindery.

crépine [krepin], *s.f.* **1.** fringe (on upholstered furniture); **garni, orné, de c.** fringed. **2.** *Cu:* caul. **3.** strainer, rose (of pump, etc.); *Petroleum Min:* linear; *Min: Nau:* filter (of pump, etc.).

crépiner [krepine], *v.tr.* **1.** to decorate (furniture, etc.) with a fringe. **2.** *Hyd.E:* to put a rose, a strainer, on (pump, etc.).

crépinette [krepinɛt], *s.f. Cu:* flat sausage.

crépir [krepiːr], *v.tr.* **1.** (*a*) to frizz, crimp (horse-hair); (*b*) to grain, pebble (leather). **2.** *Const:* to rough-cast; (*a*) to rough-render (wall); (*b*) to parget; (*c*) to give a pebble-dash finish to (wall); to pebble-dash.

crépis [krepi], *s.m. Bot:* crepis.

crépissage [krepisaːʒ], *s.m.* **1.** (*a*) frizzing, crimping (of horse-hair); (*b*) graining, pebbling (of leather). **2.** *Const:* rough-casting; (*a*) rough-rendering; (*b*) pargeting; (*c*) pebble-dashing.

crépisseuse [krepisøːz], *s.f. Leath:* grainer.

crépissoir [krepiswaːr], *s.m.* hard brush (for rough-casting walls).

crépissure [krepisyːr], *s.f. Const:* rough-cast; (*a*) rough-rendering; (*b*) parget; (*c*) pebble-dash finish.

crépitant [krepitã], *a.* crackling (sound, etc.); *Med: Surg:* crepitant; *W.Tel:* **son c.,** sizzling, crackling.

crépitation [krepitasjɔ̃], *s.f.* **1.** crackling (of sparks, rifle-fire, etc.); sputtering (of melted butter, of arc-lamp). **2.** *Med: Surg:* crepitation.

crépitement [krepitmã], *s.m.* crackling; sputtering.

crépiter [krepite], *v.i.* **1.** (*of fire*) to crackle; (*of rain*) to patter; (*of candle-flame, melted butter, etc.*) to sputter; (*of cricket*) to chirp. **2.** *Med: Surg:* to crepitate.

crépon [krepɔ̃], *s.m.* **1.** *Tex:* crepon. **2.** hair-pad, hair-frame.

crépu [krepy], *a.* **1.** woolly, crisp, frizzy, fuzzy (hair). **2.** crinkled, crisp, (leaf, etc.).

crépure [krepyːr], *s.f.* **1.** frizzing, crimping (of hair). **2.** crimped appearance (of crêpe, etc.).

crépusculaire [krepyskylɛːr]. **1.** *a.* (pertaining to the) twilight; crepuscular; **lumière c.,** twilight, half-light; **cercle c.,** twilight parallel; **beauté c.,** beauty on the wane; **période c.,** dim period, dawn (of history). **2.** *s.m. pl.* **crépusculaires;** *Ent: A:* Crepuscularia; *F:* sphinxes, hawk-moths.

crépuscule [krepyskyl], *s.m.* (*a*) twilight (at dawn, and *esp.* at evening); **c. du soir,** evening twilight; dusk; (*b*) decline.

crèque [krɛk], *s.f. Bot:* sloe.

créquier [krekje], *s.m. Bot:* sloe bush, blackthorn.

cresane [krəzan], *s.f.* = CRASSANE.

crescendo [krɛʃɛdo, -ʃɛ̃], *adv. & s.m.inv.* (*a*) *Mus:* crescendo; (*b*) *adv. F:* **son mal va c.,** he's getting worse and worse.

crésol [krezɔl], *s.m. Ch:* cresol.

crésorcine [krezɔrsin], *s.m. Ch:* cresorcin.

cressiculteur [krɛsikyltœːr], *s.m.* watercress grower.

cressiculture [krɛsikyltyːr], *s.f.* cultivation of watercress.

cresson [krɛsɔ̃], *s.m. Bot:* cress; **c. de fontaine,** watercress; **c. alénois,** garden cress, golden cress; **c. des prés, élégant,** cuckoo-flower, lady's-smock, mayflower; **c. de cheval, de chien,** brooklime; *P:* **il n'a plus de c. sur la fontaine,** he's lost his hair, *F:* his thatch.

cressonnette [krɛsɔnɛt], *s.f. Bot: F:* cardamine.

cressonnière [krɛsɔnjɛːr], *s.f.* **1.** watercress bed, pond. **2.** seller of watercress.

crestmoréite [krɛstmɔreit], *s.f. Miner:* crestmoreite.

crestois, -oise [krɛstwa, -waːz], *a. & s. Geog:* (native, inhabitant) of Crest.

Crésus [krezys], *Pr.n.m. A.Hist:* Croesus; **c'est un vrai C.,** he's as rich as Croesus.
Crésyl [krezil], *s.m. R.t.m: Ch:* cresyl (disinfectant).
crésylage [krezila:ʒ], *s.m.* disinfecting with Cresyl.
crésylate [krezilat], *s.m. Ch:* cresylate.
crésyle [krezil], *s.m. Ch:* cresyl.
crésylène [krezilɛn], *s.m. Ch:* cresylene.
crésyler [krezile], *v.tr.* to disinfect (sth.) with cresyl.
crésylique [krezilik], *a. Ch:* **acide c.,** xylenol, cresylic acid.
crésylite [krezilit], *s.m. Exp:* cresylite.
crêt [krɛ], *s.m.* (*a*) *cret;* **c. monoclinal,** monoclinal escarpment; (*b*) (*in Pr.n.*) = (i) peak; (ii) ridge.
crétacé [kretase], *a. & s.m. Geol:* cretaceous.
Crète [krɛt], *Pr.n.f. Geog:* Crete.
crête [krɛ:t], *s.f.* **1.** comb, crest (of bird); **c. de coq,** cockscomb; *O: F:* **lever la c.,** (i) to hold one's head high; (ii) to bristle up; **il levait la c.,** his hackles were up; **rabaisser la c. à qn,** to snub s.o., to take s.o. down a peg or two; **baisser la c.,** to look crestfallen. **2.** (*a*) crest, ridge (of mountain); **c. anticlinale,** anticlinal ridge; **la c. de Vimy,** Vimy ridge; **ligne de c.,** skyline; **vagues aux crêtes blanches,** white-crested waves; *Mil:* **c. militaire,** firing ridge; (*b*) *Const:* crest, ridge (of roof); crest, top (of parapet, wall); crest, coping, crown (of dam); (*c*) *Anat:* crest (of bone); (*d*) crest (of helmet); *Sm.a:* **c. du chien,** cocking piece, hammer comb. **3.** *El:* peak; **bobine de c.,** peaking coil; **courant de c.,** peak current; **courant anodique, cathodique, de c.,** peak-anode, -cathode, current; **puissance de c. d'impulsion,** peak pulse power; **tension de c.,** peak voltage; **tension inverse de c.,** peak reverse voltage.
crêté [krete], *a. Z: Her:* crested.
crête-de-coq [krɛtdəkɔk], *s.f.* **1.** *Bot:* (*a*) cockscomb; (*b*) yellow rattle. **2.** *Med:* cockscomb; *pl. crêtes-de-coq.*
crételer [kretle], *v.i.* (**elle crételle, elle crétellera**) (*of hen*) to cackle.
crételle [kretɛl], *s.f. Bot:* dog's-tail grass; **c. des prés,** crested dog's-tail.
crêter [krete], *v.tr. Dressm:* (i) to crest; (ii) to tack; (iii) to vandyke.
crétification [kretifikasjɔ̃], *s.f. Med:* cretification.
crétin, -ine [kretɛ̃, -in]. **1.** *s.* (*a*) cretin, (deformed) idiot; (*b*) *F:* hopeless ass, idiot, dead loss; **quel c.!** what a dope! **2.** *a. F:* idiotic; **vous êtes encore plus c. que lui,** you're even more of an idiot than he is.
crétinerie [kretinri], *s.f.* imbecility; stupidity; **j'ai eu la c. de le croire,** I was fool enough to believe it.
crétineux, -euse [kretinø, -ø:z], *a. Med:* cretinous.
crétinisant [kretinizɑ̃], *a. F:* that makes (s.o.) stupid.
crétinisation [kretinizasjɔ̃], *s.f. F:* (action of) becoming or making stupid; **les élèves semblent subir une lente c.,** the pupils seem to grow gradually more and more stupid, dim-witted.
crétiniser [kretinize], *v.tr. F:* to make (s.o.) stupid.
se crétiniser, *F:* to grow stupid, dim-witted; to sink into stupidity.
crétinisme [kretinism], *s.m.* **1.** *Med:* cretinism. **2.** *F:* stupidity, dim-wittedness.
crétinoïde [kretinɔid], *a. Med:* cretinoid.
crétique [kretik], *a. & s.m. A.Pros:* cretic.
crétois, -oise [kretwa, -wa:z], *a. & s. Geog:* Cretan.
cretonne [krətɔn], *s.f. Tex:* cretonne; **c. d'ameublement,** tapestry cretonne.
cretons [krətɔ̃], *s.m.pl. Cu:* greaves, cracklings (from rendered fat); **pain de c.,** *s.m.* **creton,** dog biscuit.
creusage [krøza:ʒ], *s.m.,* **creusement** [krøzmɑ̃], *s.m.* **1.** hollowing (out), grooving (of wood, etc.). **2.** digging (of hole, etc.); sinking (of well, etc.). **3. creusement d'une dépression,** deepening of a depression.
creuser [krøze], *v.tr.* **1.** (*a*) to hollow (out) (cylinder, etc.); to groove (wood, metal, etc.); to plough (a furrow); **c. le sol,** *abs.* **creuser,** to dig, to scoop out the ground; **c. sous sol,** to dig underground; **front creusé de rides,** brow furrowed with wrinkles, deeply lined forehead; **la maladie lui avait creusé les joues,** illness had hollowed his cheeks; **aux joues creusées,** hollow-cheeked, gaunt(-faced); *F:* **travail qui creuse (l'estomac),** work that gives you an appetite, that whets the appetite; **se c. la cervelle,** to rack one's brains; **j'ai beau me c. la tête . . .,** however much I puzzle (my head) over it . . .; (*b*) to wear (sth.) hollow. **2.** (*a*) to excavate; to dig (out) (trench, etc.); to cut (canal); **c. un puits,** to bore, drill, a well; **c. un chemin sous terre,** to burrow one's way underground; **c. sa fosse, son tombeau,** to bring about one's own death, downfall; (*b*) to deepen (well, etc.); (*c*) to examine (a problem, etc.); **c. une question,** to go thoroughly, deeply, into a question.
se creuser, to grow hollow; **un vallon ombrageux se creuse entre les collines,** a shady vale lies deep between the hills; **la mer se creuse,** the sea is rising; **ses joues se creusent,** his cheeks are falling in, are growing gaunt; *F:* **se c. sur un problème,** to puzzle one's head, to rack one's brains, over a problem; **tu ne t'es pas trop creusé!** you didn't exactly kill yourself with the effort! that wasn't much of a strain on the brain!
creuset [krøzɛ], *s.m.* **1.** *Ch: Ind:* crucible, melting-pot; **passer par le c. de l'adversité,** to go through the test of adversity, to be proved by adversity; **le bassin méditerranéen fut le c. de la civilisation occidentale,** the Mediterranean was the melting-pot of western civilisation. **2.** *Metall:* crucible, well, hearth (of blast furnace); **acier (fondu) au c.,** crucible (cast) steel.
creusetier [krøzətje], *s.m.* crucible maker.
creuseur [krøzœ:r], *s.m.* **1.** digger. **2.** thoughtful person, person who goes to the root of things.
creusiste [krøzist], *s.m.* crucible maker.
creusois, -oise [krøzwa, -wa:z], *a. & s. Geog:* (native, inhabitant) of the department of Creuse.
creusotin, -ine [krøzətɛ̃, -in], *a. & s. Geog:* (native, inhabitant) of Le Creusot.
creusure [krøzy:r], *s.f.* small hole, hollow.
creute [krø:t], *s.f. Dial:* disused quarry.
creux, -euse [krø, -ø:z]. **1.** *a.* hollow; **dent creuse,** hollow tooth; **yeux c.,** sunken, deep-set, eyes; **joues creuses,** gaunt, hollow, cheeks; **voix creuse,** deep, bass, voice; **avoir l'estomac c., la dent creuse,** to be ravenous; **aliments c.,** unsubstantial food; **avoir la tête creuse,** to be empty-headed; *P:* **avoir le nez c.,** to be shrewd, far-seeing; **toux creuse,** hollow cough; **chemin c.,** sunken road; **heures creuses,** off-peak hours; **année creuse,** poor, unproductive, year; **saison creuse,** slack season; **assiette creuse,** soup plate; **paroles creuses,** empty words; **idées creuses,** futile, barren, *F:* airy-fairy, ideas; *Aut:* **roue à base creuse,** wheel with well base; *Dressm:* **pli c.,** inverted pleat; *Fin:* **marché c.,** sagging market; *Nau:* **mer creuse,** rough sea. **2.** *adv.* **tousser c.,** to give a hollow cough; **songer c.,** to dream futile dreams, to strive after impossibilities; **tout ce qu'il dit sonne c.,** everything he says sounds false. **3.** *s.m.* (*a*) hollow (of the hand, in the ground, etc.); hole (in the ground); pit (of the stomach, in metal surface, etc.); trough (of wave, curve); belly (of sail); **c. d'un rocher,** cavity of a rock; **le c. des reins,** the small of the back; **c. de l'aisselle,** armpit; *N.Arch:* **c. sur quille,** moulded depth (of ship); **c. de cale,** depth of hold; **c. de membrure,** framing depth; *Mec.E:* **c. d'une roue dentée,** clearance of a toothed wheel; **c. d'une vis,** groove of a screw; *F:* **avoir un c. dans l'estomac,** to be ravenous; (*b*) *F:* **avoir un bon, beau, c.,** to have a fine deep bass voice; (*c*) mould (for plastic cast, etc.); (*d*) **sculpture en c.,** sunk carving; **gravure en c.,** (i) intaglio engraving, incised work; (ii) die sinking; **grand c.,** deep etching; **simili c.,** deepened half-tone.
crevable [krəvabl̩], *a.* puncturable that can be punctured, burst; **pneu non c.,** puncture-proof tyre.
crevaille [krəvɑ:j], *s.f. P:* tuck-in, spread, blow-out.
crevaison [krəvɛzɔ̃], *s.f.* **1.** (*a*) puncture (in tyre), *U.S:* flat; (*b*) bursting (of boiler, tyre, etc.). **2.** *P:* (*a*) death; (*b*) extreme fatigue; **quelle c.!** what a fag! what a slog!
crevant [krəvɑ̃], *a. P:* **1.** boring, tiresome. **2.** funny, side-splitting, killing (story, etc.). **3.** killing, exhausting (work).
crevard, -arde [krəva:r, -ard], *a. & s. P:* (*a*) dying (person); (*b*) hungry, starving (person).
crevasse [krəvas], *s.f.* crack (in skin, etc.); chap (in skin); split, rift (in clouds, etc.); chink, crevice (in wall, etc.); flaw (in metal, etc.); shake (in tree); fissure (in ground); crevasse (in glacier); **muraille fendue de longues crevasses,** wall showing long cracks; **avoir des crevasses aux mains,** to have chapped hands; *Vet:* **crevasses au paturon,** scratches (on the heel); cracked heel.
crevasser [krəvase], *v.tr.* to crack; to make cracks, chinks, in (sth.); to chap (the hands).
se crevasser, to crack; (*of the hands, etc.*) to get chapped, to chap; **arbre crevassé,** shaky tree.
crève [krɛ:v], *s.f. P:* death; *esp. in* **attraper la c.,** (i) to catch one's death of cold; (ii) to die; *P:* to kick the bucket.
crevé [krəve]. **1.** *a.* (*a*) burst; punctured (tyre); *Nau:* **navire c.,** bilged ship; (*b*) *P:* dead; (*c*) *P:* worn out, tired out. **2.** *s.m.* (*a*) *A.Cost:* slash; **manches à crevés,** slashed sleeves; (*b*) *P:* **petit c.,** (i) *A:* fop, dandy; (ii) *P:* little runt.
crève-chien [krɛvʃjɛ̃], *s.m.inv. Bot: F:* (i) black nightshade; (ii) deadly nightshade; (iii) wayfaring-tree.
crève-cœur [krɛvkœ:r], *s.m.inv.* heartbreaking affair, keen disappointment; wrench (at parting, etc.).
crève-de-faim [krɛvdəfɛ̃], **crève-la-faim** [krɛvlafɛ̃], *s.m.inv. F:* down-and-out.
crever [krəve], *v.* (**je crève, n. crevons; je crèverai**) **1.** *v.i.* (*a*) to burst, split; **nuage, abcès, retenue, qui crève,** cloud, abscess, dam, that bursts, breaks; **mon pneu arrière a crevé,** I've a puncture in my back tyre; **c. de jalousie, d'orgueil,** to be bursting with jealousy, with pride; **c. dans sa peau,** to be bursting (i) with overeating, (ii) with conceit, (iii) with spite; **c. de rire,** to split (one's sides) with laughter; (*b*) (*of animals*), *P:* (*of people*) to die; *F:* **c. de faim,** to be famished, starving, to be dying of hunger; *P:* **c. la faim, la c.,** to starve; **c. d'ennui,** to be bored to death; *F:* **je crève de chaleur,** I'm baking, boiling. **2.** *v.tr.* (*a*) to burst (balloon, bag, dam, etc.); to bilge (ship); to stave in (cask, etc.); to puncture (tyre); *abs. F:* **j'ai crevé (en route),** I had a puncture (on the way); **c. un abcès,** (i) *Med:* to burst an abscess; (ii) *F:* to settle an explosive situation; **se c. les yeux à lire,** to ruin one's eyes reading (too much); *F:* **il les creva de bonne chère,** he stuffed, crammed, them with good things to eat; **c. le cœur à qn.,** to break s.o.'s heart; **spectacle qui crève le cœur,** heart-breaking sight; **c. un œil à qn,** to put out s.o.'s eye, to blind s.o. in one eye; **il eut un œil crevé à . . .,** he lost one eye at . . .; **le coup partit et lui creva les yeux,** the gun went off and blinded him; *F:* **ça vous crève les yeux,** it's staring you in the face, it's under your very nose; it stands out, sticks out, a mile; **fait qui crève les yeux,** obvious, glaring, fact; (*b*) **c. un cheval,** to ride or work a horse to death.
se crever. 1. to burst. **2.** *P:* (*a*) *A:* to be greatly amused, to enjoy oneself enormously; (*b*) *A:* stuff oneself (with food); (*c*) **se c. de travail,** to work oneself to death.
crevette [krəvɛt], *s.f.* (*a*) **c. grise,** shrimp; **c. rose, rouge,** prawn; **faire la pêche à la c.,** to shrimp, to go shrimping; **pêcheur de crevettes,** shrimper; (*b*) **c. d'eau douce,** camaron, freshwater crayfish.
crevettier [krəvɛtje], *s.m.* shrimper, shrimp boat.
crevettière [krəvɛtjɛ:r], *s.f.* prawn-, shrimp-net; shove-net.
crevettine [krəvetin], *s.f. Crust:* sand-flea.
cri [kri], *s.m.* (*a*) cry (of persons and animals); (*b*) shout, call; **les cris de Paris,** the street cries of Paris; **cri du cœur,** *cri de cœur;* **c. du sang, de la nature,** the call of the blood; **il fut accueilli aux cris de "vive l'Empereur,"** he was received with shouts of "Long live the Emperor"; **cri de guerre,** (i) war-cry; (ii) *Pol: etc: F:* slogan; **cris de chasse,** hunting cries; **c. d'angoisse,** shriek, scream, of anguish; **pousser des cris,** to utter cries, to shout out; **pousser un c. aigu,** to scream, to give a scream, to shriek out; **pousser un c. d'horreur,** to shriek with horror; **pousser, jeter, les hauts cris,** to make loud protests, to give vent to one's indignation; **ne faire, ne jeter, n'avoir, qu'un c.,** to keep up one continuous shout; **appeler qn à grands cris,** to call loudly to, for, s.o.; *s.a.* COR 2, RÉCLAMER 2; **c. d'appel,** call, halloo; **annoncer qch. à c. public,** to make sth. known by public proclamation; **c. du grillon, d'un oiseau,** chirp of the cricket, of a bird; **c. d'un rat, d'une souris,** squeak of a rat, of a mouse; **c. perçant (d'un animal),** squeal; **c. de l'étain,** crackling of tin, tin-cry; *F:* **le dernier c.,** the latest fashion, style; **des chaussettes dernier c.,** the latest thing, the last word, in socks; **c'est le dernier c.,** it's all the rage; it's the latest thing (out); **c'est tout à fait dernier c.,** it's quite the latest fashion.
criage [kria:ʒ], *s.m. Com:* crying (of wares, etc.).
criaillement [kriajmɑ̃], *s.m.* **1.** crying, shouting, bawling, squalling. **2.** whining, complaining, *F:* grousing. **3.** *usu. pl.* nagging, scolding.

criailler [kriɑje], *v.i.* **1.** (*of pheasant, guinea-fowl*) to cry; (*of goose*) to honk. **2.** to cry out, bawl, shout, squall. **3.** to whine, complain; *F:* grouse; **c. après qn, qch.,** to scold s.o., to nag at s.o., *F:* to go on at s.o., sth.; **plume qui criaille,** scratchy pen.
criaillerie [kriɑjri], *s.f. usu. pl.* **1.** crying, shouting. **2.** whining, complaining. **3.** nagging, scolding.
criailleur, -euse [kriɑjœːr, -øːz], *s. F:* **1.** bawler, shouter. **2.** whiner, complainer; *F:* grouser. **3.** nagger.
criant [kriɑ̃], *a.* crying; calling for notice; *esp. in* **injustice criante,** crying, flagrant, gross, rank, injustice; **couleurs criantes,** (i) gaudy, (ii) clashing, colours.
criard [kriaːr]. **1.** *a.* (*a*) crying, squalling, peevish (child, etc.); **mari c.,** nagging husband; (*b*) **voix criarde,** shrill, high-pitched, screechy, voice; **gonds criards,** creaking, squeaking, hinges; **créanciers criards,** insistent, dunning, creditors; **dettes criardes,** pressing debts; **couleur criarde,** loud, gaudy, colour; **bijoux d'un luxe c.,** flashy jewels; **sa toilette est un peu criarde,** she is rather overdressed. **2.** *s.* (*a*) bawler, squaller; (*b*) grumbler; nagger; **une criarde,** a scold, a shrew.
cribellate [kribɛlat], *a. Arach:* cribellated.
cribellum [kribɛlɔm], *s.m. Arach:* cribellum.
criblage [kriblaːʒ], *s.m.* sifting, riddling (of grain, etc.); screening (of coal, gravel, etc.).
crible [kribl̩], *s.m.* **1.** sieve; riddle; *Min: Civ.E:* screen, jig, jigger; **c. à gravier, à sable,** gravel, sand, screen; **c. mécanique,** screening machine; **c. à tambour, c. rotatif,** drum sieve; rotary screen; **c. oscillant,** oscillating, swinging, screen; **c. classeur,** sizing screen; **c. à grille fixe, mobile,** fixed-sieve, movable-sieve, jig; **c. vibrant,** shaking, vibrating, jigging, screen, sieve; *Min:* **c. laveur,** rocker; **passer qch. au c.,** (i) to pass sth. through a sieve; to sift, sieve, screen, sth. (ii) to go through sth. with a fine toothcomb; **passer les faits au c. de la raison,** to sift out the facts; **il a passé par le c.,** he was closely examined, screened. **2.** *A.Engr:* criblé process. **3.** *Bot:* sieve tube.
criblé [krible], *a.* riddled; **visage c. de petite vérole,** face pitted with smallpox; **être c. de dettes,** to be up to one's eyes in debt.
cribler [krible], *v.tr.* **1.** to sift, riddle, sieve; to pass (sth.) through a sieve; **c. du gravier, du charbon,** to screen gravel, coal. **2.** to pierce (sth.) with holes, to riddle (sth.); *F:* to pepper (with bullets, etc.); **c. qn, qch., de balles,** to riddle s.o., sth., with bullets, with shot; **c. qn de coups,** to beat s.o. black and blue; **c. qn de reproches,** to heap reproaches on s.o.; **c. qn de ridicule,** to cover s.o. with ridicule; **c. qn de questions,** to bombard s.o. with questions.
criblette [kriblɛt], *s.f. Moss:* lattice moss.
cribleur, -euse [kriblœːr, -øːz], *s.* (*a*) sifter, riddler, screener; (*b*) *s.f.* **cribleuse,** sifter, sifting machine.
cribleux, -euse [kriblø, -øːz], *a. Nat.Hist:* sieve-like, cribriform; *Anat:* ethmoid (bone, etc.).
criblure [kriblyːr], *s.f.* siftings (of corn, etc.); screenings (of coal, etc.); riddlings.
cribreux, -euse [kribrø, -øːz], *a.* = CRIBLEUX.
cribriforme [kribrifɔrm], *a. Nat.Hist:* cribriform; *Anat:* ethmoid (bone, etc.).
cribwork [kribwəːk], *s.m. Civ.E:* cribwork.
cric[1] [kri(k)], *s.m.* **1.** (lifting) jack; **c. hydraulique,** hydraulic jack; **c. à vis,** screw-jack; **c. à (pignon et) crémaillère,** rack (-and-pinion) jack; *U.S:* ratchet jack; **c. à double engrenage,** double-rack, double-purchase, jack; **c. à levier,** lever-jack; **c. à main,** hand-jack; **c. à une griffe, à deux griffes,** single-clawed, double-clawed, jack; **griffe, pointe, d'un c.,** claw, spike, of a jack; **c. roulant, c. de garage,** garage jack; *Rail:* **c. relève-rails, c. relève-voie,** rail-jack; (railway-) track jack, track lifter; **c. de tirage,** pulling jack; **soulever (qch.) avec un c., à l'aide d'un c.,** to jack (sth.) up; **mettre une voiture sur c.,** to jack up a car. **2.** *P:* (poor quality) brandy; *P:* rot-gut.
cric[2] [krik]. **1.** *int.* crack! snap! **2.** *s.m.* **on entendit un petit c.,** there was a tearing noise.
cric-crac [krik(k)rak], *int.* crack! snap!
cricétidés [krisetide], *s.m.pl. Z:* Cricetidae, the hamsters.
cricket [kriket], *s.m. Sp:* cricket; **joueur de c.,** cricketer.
cricketeur [kriktœːr], *s.m. Sp:* (*a*) cricketer; (*b*) cricket enthusiast.
crico-aryténoïdien, -ienne [krikoaritenɔidjɛ̃, -jɛn], *a. Anat:* cricoarytenoid.
cricoïde [krikɔid], *a. & s.m. Anat:* cricoid (cartilage).
crico-thyroïdien, -ienne [krikotirɔidjɛ̃, -jɛn], *a. Anat:* cricothyroid.
cri(-)cri [krikri], *s.m.inv.* **1.** chirping (of cricket). **2.** *Ent: F:* cricket.
cric-tenseur [kriktɑ̃sœːr], *s.m.* wire stretcher, wire strainer; *pl. crics-tenseurs.*
crid [krid], *s.m.* kris, Malay dagger.
criée [krie], *s.f.* auction; **vente à la c.,** sale by auction; **chambre des criées,** (public) auction room, sale room.
crier [krie], *v.* (*pr.sub. & p.h.* **n. criions, v. criiez**) **1.** *v.i.* (*a*) to cry; to call out, to shout; to bawl; to squall; **c. de douleur,** to cry out, to scream, shriek, with pain; **il crie avant qu'on l'écorche,** he cries out before he's hurt; **c. comme un pourceau,** to squeal like a pig; **enfant qui crie,** squalling child; **ce sont ceux qui crient le plus fort qui l'emportent,** it is the most vocal who carry the day; **crier après qn,** to carp at s.o.; **ne criez pas (après moi)!** don't shout (at me)! **c. contre qn,** to cry out, rail, against s.o.; **c. contre l'injustice,** to rail against injustice; **c. à l'injustice, à l'oppression,** to complain loudly about injustice, oppression; **couleurs qui crient,** colours that jar; (*b*) (*of mouse, etc.*) to squeak; (*of cricket*) to chirp; (*of birds*) to call; (*c*) (*of door, axle, etc.*) to squeak, creak; (*of bowels*) to rumble; **chaussures qui crient,** squeaky shoes; **les cailloux criaient sous nos pieds,** the stones crunched under our feet. **2.** *v.tr.* (*a*) **c. des légumes,** to cry, hawk, vegetables; **faire c. qch. par la ville,** to have sth. proclaimed, cried, through the town; *F:* **c. qch. sur les toits,** to cry sth. from the house-tops; **la ronde de nuit cria l'heure,** the watch called the hour; (*b*) to put (furniture, etc.) up for auction; (*c*) **c. un ordre,** to shout out an order; **c. des injures à qn,** to shout abuse at s.o.; **c. à qn de faire qch.,** to shout to s.o. to do sth.; **c. son innocence,** to protest one's innocence; **c. famine, misère,** to complain that one is starving, to complain of hardship, distress; **ses vêtements criaient misère,** his clothes betrayed his poverty; **crime qui crie vengeance,** crime that calls aloud for vengeance; **c. au secours,** to shout for help; **c. au voleur,** to shout "Stop thief!"
crierie [kriri], *s.f. usu. pl.* **1.** squalling, crying, wailing. **2.** grumbling; *F:* grousing.
crieur, -euse [kriœːr, -øːz], *s.* **1.** (*a*) shouter; (*b*) grumbler. **2.** crier (at sale). **3.** (*a*) **c. des rues,** street hawker; **c. de journaux,** newspaper seller; *A:* **c. public,** town crier; *A:* **c. de nuit,** night watchman; (*b*) *Th:* call boy.
crime [krim], *s.m.* (*a*) crime, *Jur:* felony; **c. contre nature,** unnatural offence; **c. capital,** capital offence, capital crime; **c. d'État,** treason; **c. de faux,** forgery; **c. d'incendie,** arson; **commettre un c.,** to commit a crime, a felony; (*b*) **c'est un c. que d'avoir démoli cette maison,** it's a crime to have demolished that house; **faire un c. d'une bagatelle,** to make much ado about nothing, to make a mountain out of a molehill; **faire un c. d'une chose innocente,** to treat something harmless as a crime; **ce n'est pas un grand c.!** it's not (really) a crime! it's not really serious!
Crimée [krime], *Pr.n.f. Geog:* Crimea; **la guerre de C.,** the Crimean war.
criméen, -enne [krimeɛ̃, -ɛn], *a. & s.* Crimean.
criminalisable [kriminalizabl̩], *a. Jur:* (case) that may be referred to a criminal court.
criminaliser [kriminalize], *v.tr. Jur:* **c. une cause,** to refer a case to a criminal court (from a civil court).
criminalisme [kriminalism], *s.m.* criminalism.
criminaliste [kriminalist], *s.m.* **1.** criminal jurist. **2.** criminalist.
criminalistique [kriminalistik]. **1.** *a.* criminalistic. **2.** *s.f.* criminalistics.
criminalité [kriminalite], *s.f.* (*a*) criminality, criminal nature (of an act); (*b*) crime, delinquency; **c. juvénile,** juvenile delinquency.
criminatoire [kriminatwaːr], *a.* criminative, criminatory.
criminel, -elle [kriminɛl], *a.* **1.** (*a*) guilty (of crime); **je le crois c.,** I believe he is guilty; (*b*) *s.* criminal, felon. **2.** criminal (law, attempt, etc.); *Jur:* **chambre criminelle,** criminal division, section; **cour criminelle,** penal court; **peine criminelle,** (i) penalty of more than five years' imprisonment (with or without hard labour); (ii) deportation to a penal settlement; (iii) death; *s.m.* **être jugé au c.,** to be tried in a criminal court; **avocat au c.,** criminal lawyer; **poursuivre qn au c.,** to take criminal proceedings against s.o.
criminellement [kriminɛlmɑ̃], *adv.* **1.** criminally (inclined, etc.). **2. poursuivre qn c.,** to prosecute s.o. in a criminal court, to take criminal proceedings against s.o.
criminogène [kriminɔʒɛn], *a.* criminogenic.
criminologie [kriminɔlɔʒi], *s.f.* criminology.
criminologique [kriminɔlɔʒik], *a.* criminological.
criminologiste [kriminɔlɔʒist], **criminologue** [kriminɔlɔg], *s.m. & f.* criminologist.
crin [krɛ̃], *s.m.* **1.** (*a*) horsehair; **matelas de c.,** (horse) hair mattress; **les crins,** the mane and tail; **cheval d'un beau c.,** horse with a fine coat; *F:* **se faire tailler les crins,** to have one's hair cut; *F:* **ils se prenaient aux crins,** they were tearing each other's hair fighting; *O:* **une chevelure à tous crins,** a fine head of hair; **révolutionnaire à tous crins,** thorough, out and out, revolutionary; **hommes de tous crins et de tous poils,** men of every description and background; *F:* **être comme un c.,** to be bad-tempered, cantankerous; (*b*) *Equit:* mounting lock; (*c*) **c. végétal,** vegetable horsehair; (*d*) *Fish:* **c. de Florence, d'Espagne,** silk gut, silkworm gut. **2.** *Ann:* **c. de fontaine, de mer,** hair worm, hair eel. **3.** *Geol:* stringer.
crinal [krinal], *s.m. Rom.Ant:* (ornamental) hair comb.
crincrin [krɛ̃krɛ̃], *s.m. F:* **1.** squeaky violin, fiddle. **2.** *A:* fiddler, scraper.
crinier [krinje], *s.m.* horsehair worker.
crinière [krinjɛːr], *s.f.* **1.** mane (of horse, lion, etc.); **c. en brosse,** hogged mane; **c. d'un casque de dragon,** (horse-)tail of a dragoon's helmet. **2.** *F:* (*of pers.*) abundant crop of (untidy) hair; mane. **3.** *Agr:* strip of land left lying fallow.
criniforme [krinifɔrm], *a.* capilliform, hair-like.
crinkle [kriŋkl̩], *s.m. Hort:* crinkle (of apples, potatoes.
crinoïde [krinɔid]. **1.** *a. Z:* crinoid(al). **2.** *s.m. Echin:* crinoid; *pl.* Crinoidea.
crinol [krinɔl], *s.m.* artificial horsehair (made of rayon acetate).
crinoline [krinɔlin], *s.f.* **1.** *Tex: A: Cost:* crinoline. **2.** *Nau:* (*a*) crinoline (of cable vessel); (*b*) **c. d'échelle,** safety loop.
criocéras [kriɔseras], *s.m. Paleont:* Crioceras.
criocératidés [kriɔseratide], *s.m.pl. Paleont:* Crioceratites.
criocère [kriɔsɛːr], *s.m. Ent:* crioceris; **c. de l'asperge,** asparagus beetle.
cripart [kripar], *s.m. Orn: F:* tree creeper.
crique[1] [krik], *s.f.* creek, cove, bay, bight.
crique[2], *s.f. Metalw:* tear, split (in steel); **c. saisonnière,** season crack.
criquer[1] [krike], *v.i.* (*of steel*) to crack, split (on cooling).
criquer[2] **(se),** *v.pr. P:* to skedaddle, to make tracks, to clear off.
criquet [krikɛ], *s.m.* **1.** *Ent:* locust; **c. pèlerin, voyageur,** migratory locust. **2.** *F:* (*a*) small pony; nag; (*b*) shrimp (of a man). **3.** *F:* poor, thin, wine. **4.** *Toys: F:* clicker.
criqueter [krikte], *v.i.* (**il criquette; il criquettera**) **1.** (*of metal, etc.*) to crackle; to give a scratchy sound. **2.** (*of locust, etc.*) to chirp, chirrup.
criquetis [krikti], *s.m. Engr:* scratching (of the burin on copper).
criqûre [krikyːr], *s.f.* crack, defect, flaw (in steel, in armour-plate); *Metall:* **c. de recuit,** fire crack.
crise [kriːz], *s.f.* **1.** crisis; emergency; **c. politique,** political crisis; *Pol:* **c. de confiance,** national loss of confidence; **c. ministérielle,** interregnum (between resignation of one government and formation of the next); **c. économique,** economic crisis; slump; **la c. du logement,** the housing shortage, crisis; **la c. du papier,** the paper shortage; **la c. du recrutement des professeurs,** the shortage of teachers; **la c. du livre,** the slump in the book trade; **impôt de c.,** emergency tax; **passer par une c.,** to go through a crisis; **subir, traverser, une c.,** to undergo a critical period, a crisis; **mettre fin à, dénouer, résoudre, une c.,** to end a crisis; **la c. est proche,** things are coming to a head. **2.** (*a*) *Med:* crisis (in an illness); (*b*) attack; **c. cardiaque,** heart attack; **c. d'épilepsie,** epileptic fit; **c. de goutte,** attack of gout; **c. aiguë du foie,** sharp liver attack; **c. nerveuse, c. de nerfs,** attack of nerves; fit of hysterics; **avoir une c. de larmes,** to have a fit of crying, to burst into tears; **c. de désespoir,** paroxysm of despair; *F:* **piquer une c.,** (i) to have a fainting fit, to pass out; to have hysterics; (ii) to get in a rage; *F:* **faire piquer une c. (de nerfs) à qn,** to send s.o. up the wall; (*c*) *Vet:* **c. du rouge,** blackhead.
crispant [krispɑ̃], *a. F:* irritating, aggravating, annoying; **enfant c.,** child that gets on one's nerves.

crispateur [krispatœːr], *s.m. Gym:* spring-grip.

crispation [krispasjɔ̃], *s.f.* (*a*) crispation, shrivelling up (of leather, etc.); cockling (of paper); puckering (of the face, etc.); (*b*) **crispations nerveuses des mains,** nervous twitching, clenching, of the hands; **c. de douleur,** wince of pain; **donner des crispations à qn,** to get on s.o.'s nerves.

crispé [krispe], *a.* (*a*) contorted; contracted; **main crispée,** clenched hand; **sa main crispée sur le fusil,** with his hand clutching the gun; (*b*) (*of pers.*) on edge.

crisper [krispe], *v.tr.* to contract; to clench; **elle crispait ses mains dans ses cheveux,** she clutched at her hair; **visage crispé par la souffrance,** face contorted, screwed up, with pain; **bruit qui crispe les nerfs,** noise that sets one's teeth on edge, that jars upon the nerves; *F:* **cela me crispe,** it sets my teeth on edge, it gets on my nerves, makes me wince.

se crisper, to contract; to become wrinkled; **sa figure se crispa,** his face puckered up, he screwed up his face.

crispiflore [krispiflɔːr], *a. Bot:* with curled, crinkled, petals, crispifloral.

crispifolié [krispifɔlje], *a. Bot:* crispifolious.

Crispin [krispɛ̃]. **1.** *Pr.n.m. Lit.Hist:* (*in Italian comedy*) Crispino. **2.** *s.m.* (*a*) *Th: A:* manservant, valet (of comedy); (*b*) *A:* short cloak; (*c*) gauntlet (of glove).

criss [kris], *s.m.* kris, Malay dagger.

crissement [krismɑ̃], *s.m.* grating, grinding (of teeth); squeaking (of chalk on blackboard, etc.); squealing, screeching (of brakes); **le c. du gravier sous les roues,** the crunching of the gravel under the wheels.

crisser [krise], *v.i.* to grate; to make a grating, grinding, rasping, sound; (*of brakes*) to squeal, screech; **c. des dents,** to grind one's teeth; **gravier qui crisse sous les pas,** gravel that crunches under one's feet.

crissure [krisyːr], *s.f.* ridge, wrinkle (in forged steel).

cristal, -aux [kristal, -o], *s.m.* **1.** crystal; **c. droit, gauche,** right-handed, left-handed, crystal; **se dissocier en cristaux,** to crystallize out; **c. de roche,** rock crystal; **c. d'Islande,** Iceland spar. **2.** (*a*) crystal (glass); *pl.* **cristaux,** crystal (glass) ware; **c. taillé,** cut glass; *Ind:* **c. armé,** ferroglass, wire(d) glass; **voix de c.,** crystal-clear voice; (*b*) *Lit: Poet:* **la nappe de c. de la cascade,** the crystal sheet of the waterfall; **le c. d'un rire d'enfant,** the crystalline sound of children's laughter. **3.** *pl. F:* **cristaux (de soude),** *P:* **du cristau(x),** washing soda. **4.** *Psychics:* (i) **boule de c.,** crystal (ball); (ii) **vision dans le cristal,** crystal-gazing.

cristalblanc [kristalblɑ̃], *s.m. Ch:* alban.

cristallerie [kristalri], *s.f.* (*a*) crystal (glass) manufacture; glass cutting; (*b*) (crystal) glassworks; crystal (glass) (ware).

cristallier [kristalje], *s.m.* (*a*) glass cutter and engraver; (*b*) glass (display) cabinet.

cristallière [kristaljɛːr], *s.f.* (*a*) rock-crystal mine; (*b*) rock-crystal cutting machine.

cristallifère [kristalifɛːr], *a.* crystalliferous, crystal-bearing.

cristallin, -ine [kristalɛ̃, -in]. **1.** *a.* (*a*) crystalline (rock, etc.); crystal-clear (water, etc.); (*of sound*) as clear as a bell; (*b*) **systèmes cristallins,** crystal systems; (*c*) **humeur cristalline,** crystalline humour (of the eye). **2.** *s.m. Anat:* crystalline lens (of the eye). **3.** *s.f. Bot:* **crystalline,** ice plant.

cristallinien, -ienne [kristalinjɛ̃, -jɛn], *a. Anat:* crystalline (lens, etc.).

cristallinité [kristalinite], *s.f.* crystallinity.

cristallisabilité [kristalizabilite], *s.f.* crystallizability.

cristallisable [kristalizabl̩], *a.* crystallizable.

cristallisant [kristalizɑ̃], *a.* crystallizing.

cristallisation [kristalizasjɔ̃], *s.f.* crystallization, crystallizing.

cristallisé [kristalize], *a.* (*a*) crystallized; **sucre c.** = granulated sugar; (*b*) frosted (enamel, gelatine).

cristalliser [kristalize], *v.tr. & i.* to crystallize.

se cristalliser, to become crystallized, to crystallize; **ses opinions politiques commencent à se c.,** his views on politics are beginning to crystallize.

cristallisoir [kristalizwaːr], *s.m. Ch:* crystallizer, crystallizing dish, pan.

cristallite [kristalit], *s.f. Geol:* crystallite.

cristallitique [kristalitik], *a.* crystallitic.

cristalloblastique [kristalɔblastik], *a.* crystalloblastic.

cristallogénèse [kristalɔʒenɛːz], *s.f.* crystallogenesis.

cristallogénie [kristalɔʒeni], *s.f.* crystallogeny.

cristallogénique [kristalɔʒenik], *a.* crystallogenic.

cristallographe [kristalɔgraf], *s.m. & f.* crystallographer.

cristallographie [kristalɔgrafi], *s.f.* crystallography.

cristallographique [kristalɔgrafik], *a.* crystallographic(al).

cristalloïdal, -aux [kristalɔidal, -o], *a. Ch:* crystalloidal.

cristalloïde [kristalɔid]. **1.** *a.* crystalloid. **2.** *s.m. Bot: Ph: Ch:* crystalloid.

cristalloluminescence [kristalɔlyminɛsɑ̃ːs], *s.f.* crystalloluminescence.

cristallomancie [kristalɔmɑ̃si], *s.f.* crystallomancy, crystal-gazing.

cristallomancien, -ienne [kristalɔmɑ̃sjɛ̃, -jɛn], *s.* crystal-gazer.

cristallométrie [kristalɔmetri], *s.f.* crystallometry.

cristallométrique [kristalɔmetrik], *a.* crystallometric.

cristallophyllien, -ienne [kristalɔfiljɛ̃, -jɛn], *a. Geol:* crystallophyllian; **roches cristallophylliennes,** foliated crystalline rocks.

cristatelle [kristatɛl], *s.f. Z:* cristatella.

cristau(x) [kristo], *s.m. P:* washing soda.

cristé [kriste], *a. Nat.Hist:* cristate, crested.

cristel [kristɛl], *s.m. Orn: F:* kestrel.

criste-marine [kristəmarin], *s.f. Bot:* (rock-) samphire, sea fennel; *pl. cristes-marines.*

cristi [kristi], *int. P:* (*abbr. of* **sacristi**) Good Lord!

cristobalite [kristɔbalit], *s.f.* cristobalite.

critère [kritɛːr], *s.m.* criterion; test; **soumettre qch. à un c.,** to put sth. to the test; **son seul c. c'est l'avis de son père,** his father's opinion is his only criterion.

critériologie [kriteriɔlɔʒi], *s.f.* criteriology.

critérium [kriterjɔm], *s.m.* **1.** *O:* criterion, test. **2.** *Sp:* (*a*) *Box:* **c. des jeunes,** junior championship (matches); (*b*) *Turf:* **c. des deux ans,** races to select the best two-year-old; (*c*) (eliminating) heat.

crithme [kritm], **crithmum** [kritmɔm], *s.m. Bot:* rock samphire, sea fennel.

criticailleur [kritikajœːr], *s.m.* carping critic; criticaster.

criticalité [kritikalite], *s.f. Atom.Ph:* criticality.

criticisme [kritisism], *s.m.* critical philosophy, Kant(ian)ism.

criticiste [kritisist], *a. & s.m.* critical philosopher; Kantian, Kantist.

critiquable [kritikabl̩], *a.* criticizable, open to criticism.

critiquant [kritikɑ̃], *a.* criticizing, censorious.

critique[1] [kritik], *a. & s.m.* **1.** *a.* (*a*) *Med:* **phase c.,** critical phase (of an illness); *Physiol:* **temps, âge, c.,** critical age, period, *esp.* menopause, *F:* change of life; **jours critiques,** menses, monthly period; (*b*) critical; decisive; crucial; **un moment c. de ma vie,** a critical moment in my life; **être dans une situation c.,** to be in a critical, *F:* ticklish, situation, position; to be in a tight corner; **dans cette situation c.,** in this emergency; *Mil:* **article c.,** critical item; (*c*) *Mth: Ph:* **angle, point, température, c.,** critical angle, point, temperature; *Mec:* **limite c.,** breaking (down) point; *El:* **tension c.,** critical voltage. **2.** *s.m. Atom.Ph:* **c. différé, c. retardé,** delayed critical; **c. instantané,** prompt critical.

critique[2], *a. & s.* **1.** *a.* (*a*) (*passing judgement*) critical; **examen c. d'un ouvrage,** critical examination of a work; **examiner qch. d'un œil c.,** to examine sth. critically, with a critical eye; **remarques littérales et critiques,** textual and critical notes; **édition c.,** critical, annotated, edition; **appareil c.,** critical apparatus; **esprit c.,** critical mind; (*b*) *Pej:* censorious, fault-finding, carping (mind, etc.). **2.** *s.m.* critic; **c. d'art,** art critic; **c. musical,** music critic; **c. théâtral,** theatre critic, drama(tic) critic; **c. acerbe,** harsh critic; **c. en chambre,** armchair critic. **3.** *s.f.* (*a*) (art of) criticism; **c. des textes,** textual criticism; **c. des sources, c. historique,** historical criticism; **c. dramatique,** dramatic criticism; (*b*) critical article, paper; review; **c. acerbe,** caustic, *F:* slashing, review; **faire la c. d'une pièce,** to write a criticism, a critique, of a play; to review a play; (*c*) censure; **être l'objet des critiques du public,** to incur the censure of the public, to be a target for public criticism; **se répandre en critiques sur qch.,** to criticize sth. severely; **diriger des critiques contre qn,** to make s.o. a target for criticism; **la c. est aisée,** it is easy to criticize, to be censorious; **on n'a fait aucune c. sur . . .,** no criticism was passed on . . .; nothing was said against . . .; (*d*) *Coll:* **la c.,** (the body of) critics.

critiquer [kritike], *v.tr.* to criticize; (*a*) to write a criticism, a review, of (sth.); (*b*) to censure; to pass censure on, find fault with (s.o., sth.); **c. qn de faire qch.,** to criticize s.o. for doing sth.

critiqueur, -euse [kritikœːr, -øːz], *s.* critic, criticizer, fault-finder.

Criton [kritɔ̃], *Pr.n.m. Gr.Lit:* Crito.

croassant [krɔasɑ̃], *a.* cawing (crow, rook); croaking (raven, *F:* person).

croassement [krɔasmɑ̃], *s.m.* **1.** caw(ing) (of crow, rook); croak(ing) (of raven, *occ.* of frog; *F:* of person). **2.** (malicious) rumours; **les croassements des envieux,** the carping, criticizing, of the envious.

croasser [krɔase], *v.i.* **1.** (*of crow, rook*) to caw; (*of raven, occ. of frog, F: of person*) to croak. **2.** to spread (malicious) rumours.

croate [krɔat], *Geog:* **1.** *a.* Croatian. **2.** *s.* Croat, Croatian. **3.** *s.m. Ling:* Croatian.

Croatie [krɔasi], *Pr.n.f. Geog:* Croatia.

croc[1] [krɔk], *int.* crunch! scrunch!

croc[2] [kro], *s.m.* **1.** (*a*) hook; **c. à ciseaux,** clasp, clip, hooks; clove, sister, hooks; **c. à échappement,** slip hook; **c. à émerillon,** swivel hook; **c. de boucher, de boucherie, à viande,** (i) butcher's hook, meat hook; (ii) long arm; **c. à levier,** cant hook; **c. de remorquage,** towing hook; *Agr: Hort:* **c. à pommes de terre,** potato hook, Canterbury hoe; **c. à sarcler,** weed lifter; **c. à fumier,** muck rake; *Nau:* **c. à chaînes,** chain hook; **c. de charge, de cargaison,** cargo hook; **c. à échappement,** pelican hook; **c. de vérine,** rope hook; **c. de marinier, de batelier,** boathook; **c. de traversière,** fish-hook; **mettre, pendre, qch. au c.,** to postpone sth., to put sth. off (indefinitely); to give sth. up; **pendre, mettre, son épée au c.,** to hang up one's sword; (*b*) *Mec.E:* pawl, catch. **2.** canine tooth; fang (of dog, wolf); tusk (of walrus); claw (of crab, etc.); *F:* tooth (of pers.); *F:* **avoir mal aux crocs,** to have toothache; **moustache en c.,** curled-up moustache; **montrer ses crocs,** to show one's teeth, one's fangs; *P:* **avoir les crocs,** to be famished, ravenous.

crocéine [krɔsein], *s.f. Ch:* crocein(e).

croc-en-jambe [krɔkɑ̃ʒɑ̃ːb], *s.m.* trip (to bring down opponent); click; *Wr:* leg-trip; **faire, donner, un c.-en-j. à qn,** (i) to trip s.o. up; (ii) to pull a fast one over on s.o.; *pl. crocs-en-jambe* [krɔkɑ̃ʒɑ̃ːb].

croche [krɔʃ]. **1.** *a.* (*a*) *A:* (= CROCHU) hooked, bent; (*b*) *P:* **avoir les mains, les pattes, croches,** to be avaricious, mean, close-fisted. **2.** *s.f.* (*a*) *pl. Metalw:* crook-bit tongs; (*b*) *Mus:* quaver; **double c.,** semiquaver; **triple c.,** demisemiquaver; **quadruple c.,** hemidemisemiquaver.

croche-pied [krɔʃpje], *s.m.,* **croche-patte** [krɔʃpat], *s.m. F:* trip (to bring down an opponent); click; **faire, donner, un c.-p. à qn,** to trip s.o. up; *pl. croche-pieds, croche-pattes.*

crocher [krɔʃe], *v.tr.* **1.** (*a*) to hook (on to) (sth.), to seize (sth.) with a hook; *abs. Nau:* **l'ancre croche,** the anchor grips, bites, holds; *F:* **je l'ai croché amicalement,** I took his arm in a friendly manner; *F:* **les gendarmes l'ont croché,** the police have nabbed him; (*b*) *Nau:* to sling, swing (hammock). **2.** to twist, bend, (sth.) into a hook. **3.** *v.i. Nau:* **c. dans la toile,** to hand in the sail.

crochet [krɔʃɛ], *s.m.* **1.** hook; (*a*) **clou à c.,** hook nail; **c. à vis,** screw hook; **c. à lame-ressort,** flat spring hook; **c. double,** double hook, ram's horn hook; **c. fermé,** closed hook, eye hook; **c. pivotant,** swivel hook; **c. méplat,** flat hook; **c. à bois,** timber hook; **c. d'assemblage,** dog iron; **c. d'attelage,** (i) *Rail:* coupling hook; (ii) *Veh:* trace hook; **c. de brélage,** lashing hook; **c. de remorquage, de remorque,** towing hook; **c. de suspension,** hanger; suspension hook; **c. de traction,** drag hook, draw hook; **c. et porte,** hook and eye (dress fastener); **c. à œillet,** hook and eye (door fastening); **c. à boutons,** button-hook; **c. de chiffonnier,** street cleaner's hooked stick; **c. de portefaix,** porter's crotchet; **c. de bureau,** spike file; *Agr:* **c. (pour pommes de terre, etc.),** Canterbury hoe; *F:* **vivre aux crochets de qn,** to live off, sponge on, s.o.; *Aut:* **c. de fermeture,** bonnet fastener; *Const:* **c. de gouttière,** gutter bracket; *Tp:* **c. commutateur,** switch hook; **c. du récepteur,** receiver hook; *Mil:* **c. bélière,** (sword, rifle) sling hook; (*b*) *Metalw:* hook tool (of slide lathe); *Metall:* rabble(r) (for puddling); **c. de fonderie,** gagger; (*c*) *Tex:* tenterhook; (*d*) *Dent:* clasp; **c. à bras, à**

potence, bar clasp; **c. coulé,** cast, wrought, clasp; (*e*) crochet hook; **dentelle, travaux, au c.,** crochet work; **faire du c.,** to crochet; **faire qch. au c.,** to crochet sth.; (*f*) *A:* kiss-curl. **2.** (*a*) *Mec.E:* **c. d'arrêt,** pawl, catch; **c. de retenue,** latch hook; **c. de sûreté,** safety-hook; *Sm.a:* **c. éjecteur,** ejector hook, ejecting hook; (*b*) **c. de serrurier,** picklock, skeleton key; (*c*) *Nau:* **c. d'épontille,** stanchion hook; **c. de vérine,** rope hook; **c. de voilier,** sail hook. **3.** (*a*) canine tooth (of stag); (*b*) poison fang (of snake); (*c*) *pl.* talons (of eagle). **4.** *pl. Typ:* square brackets. **5.** (*a*) **faire un c.,** (i) to make a detour; (ii) (*of road*) to take a sudden turn; *Nau:* **faire un c. sur la droite,** to swing to starboard; (*b*) *Mil:* sharply thrown back defensive flank. **6.** *Box:* hook; **c. du gauche,** left hook. **7.** *Mus:* hook (of quaver). **8.** *Meteor:* **c. de grain,** squall depression; squall kink. **9.** *Arch:* crocket. **10.** (*a*) **c. (radiophonique),** talent contest (on radio, T.V.); (*b*) *int. F:* (*to bad performer*) **c.!** out!

crochetable [krɔʃtabl], *a.* (lock) that can be picked, pickable (lock).

crochetage [krɔʃtaːʒ], *s.m.* **1.** picking (of a lock). **2.** hoeing (of ground). **3.** *Typ:* taking up or taking down (of end of line) to previous or succeeding line.

crochet-bascule [krɔʃɛbaskyl], *s.m.* steelyard; *pl. crochets-bascules.*

crochetée [krɔʃte], *s.f. A:* porter's load.

crocheter [krɔʃte], *v.tr.* (**je crochète, n. crochetons; je crochèterai**) **1.** to pick (lock); **c. une porte,** to force a door. **2.** (*a*) to hook, to pick up with a hook; (*b*) *F:* to crochet; **ganse crochetée,** crocheted braid; **c. sur métier,** to tambour, to do tambour work. **3.** *Typ:* to hook in (end of line of verse, etc.). **4.** *v.i. Fb:* to swerve.

se crocheter, *P:* to fight, to come to blows.

crocheteur[1] [krɔʃtœːr], *s.m.* picklock; housebreaker.

crocheteur[2], *s.m. A:* porter, carrier; **métier de c.,** vile occupation; thankless job; **langage de c.,** coarse language.

crochetier [krɔʃtje], *s.m.* hook maker.

crocheton [krɔʃtɔ̃], *s.m.* small hook.

crochu [krɔʃy], *a.* **1.** hooked (wire, nose, etc.); beaked (nose); unciform (bone); *F:* **avoir les doigts crochus, les mains crochues,** (i) to be light-fingered; (ii) to be mean, close-fisted; *Gr.Phil:* **atomes crochus,** interlocking atoms; *F:* **avoir des atomes crochus,** to click (with s.o.). **2.** crooked (stick, ideas). **3.** cow-hocked (horse).

crocidolite [krɔsidɔlit], *s.f. Miner:* crocidolite.

crocidure [krɔsidyːr], *s.f. Z:* (*a*) (*genus*) Crocidura, musk shrew; (*b*) **c. aquatique du Tibet,** Szechwan water shrew.

crocine [krɔsin], *s.f. Ch:* crocin.

croco [krɔko], *s.m. F:* crocodile (skin); **un porte-feuille en c.,** a crocodile (-skin) wallet.

crocodilage [krɔkɔdilaːʒ], *s.m. Const:* alligatoring, crocodiling.

crocodile [krɔkɔdil], *s.m.* **1.** (*a*) crocodile; **c. des marais,** mugger; **larmes de c.,** crocodile tears; (*b*) **sac à main en c.,** crocodile (skin) handbag. **2.** *Rail:* alarm contact, automatic stop. **3.** alligator ore-crusher; *Min:* **gueule de c.,** alligator grab.

crocodiler [krɔkɔdile], *v.tr. Rail:* to fit with an automatic stop.

crocodilidés [krɔkɔdilide], *s.m.pl. Rept:* Crocodilidae.

crocodilien [krɔkɔdiljɛ̃], *s.m. Rept:* crocodilian.

crocoïse [krɔkɔiːz], *s.f.,* **crocoïte** [krɔkɔit], *s.f. Miner:* crocoite, crocoisite.

croconique [krɔkɔnik], *a. Ch:* croconic (acid, etc.).

crocus [krɔkys], *s.m. Bot:* crocus.

croire [krwaːr, krwɑːr], *v.* (*pr.p.* **croyant;** *p.p.* **cru;** *pr.ind.* **je crois, il croit, n. croyons, ils croient;** *p.d.* **je croyais;** *p.h.* **je crus;** *fu.* **je croirai**) **1.** *v.tr.* (*a*) **c. qch.,** to believe sth.; **ne pas croire qch.,** to disbelieve sth.; not to believe sth.; **je crois ce que vous dites,** I believe what you say; **vous ne sauriez c. combien je suis content,** you can't think, imagine, how glad I am; **j'aime à c. que** + *ind.,* I hope, trust, that . . .; **il est à c. que** + *ind.,* it is probable that . . .; **cela me fait c. que . . .,** that leads me to think, believe, that . . .; **tout porte à c. que . . .,** there are many indications, there is every indication, that . . .; **je crois que cela suffira,** that ought to do, to be enough; **je ne crois pas que cela suffise,** I don't think that will be enough; **c'est à ne pas c.,** it is beyond all belief; *F:* **je crois bien que . . .,** I think that . . .; **je crois bien qu'il est sorti,** I am afraid he's out; **je (le) crois bien!** I should think so! I dare say! rather! *F:* you bet! **je crois que oui,** I believe, think, so; **je crois que non,** I don't believe, think, so, I think not; **je ne sais qu'en, que, c.,** I don't know what to believe; **n'en croyez rien!** don't believe it! *F:* not a bit of it! **vous croyez?** do you really think so? **à ce que je crois . . .,** in my opinion . . .; *with object and complement;* **c. qn riche,** to believe s.o. to be rich; **on ne me croit pas levé,** they don't think I've got up; **se c. perdu,** to give oneself up for lost; **on se serait cru en octobre,** it felt like October; you would have thought that we were in October; **je vous croyais anglais,** I thought you were English; I took you, had taken you, for an Englishman; **on le croyait anglais,** he was thought to be English; **je ne suis pas celle que vous croyez,** I'm not that kind of girl; **c'était à c. tous les éléments déchaînés,** you would have thought all the elements were let loose; **j'ai cru nécessaire de . . .,** I deemed it necessary to . . .; **j'ai cru bien faire,** I believed, thought, I was doing right; **je crois savoir que . . .,** I have reason to believe that . . .; **l'avare croit ne jamais mourir,** the miser thinks he will never die; **j'ai cru devoir le prévenir,** I thought I ought to warn him; **il crut entendre des pas,** he thought, fancied, he heard footsteps; **il se croit de l'esprit,** he thinks himself a wit; **il se croit tout permis,** he thinks he can do, get away with, anything; *F:* **il se croit,** he thinks a lot of himself, he's (a bit) conceited, he thinks no small beer of himself; **on lui croit des chances,** he is believed to have a chance; **je lui croyais du talent,** I thought he had talent; **je croyais à cet homme plus de droiture,** I thought this man had more integrity; **je n'aurais pas cru cela de lui,** I wouldn't, would never, have thought it, that, of him; *F:* (*intensive*) **crois-tu! croyez-vous! quel temps, crois-tu!** what foul weather! (*b*) **c. qn,** to believe s.o., take s.o.'s word; **me croira qui voudra, mais . . .,** believe me or not, as you like, as you wish, but . . .; *F:* **je te, vous, crois!** (i) I should think so! you bet! rather! (ii) of course! naturally! **en croire qn,** (i) to take s.o.'s word for it; (ii) to take s.o.'s advice; **vous pouvez m'en c.,** take my word for it, depend upon it, you can take it from me; **croyez-m'en,** believe me; take my advice; **s'il faut l'en c., à l'en c., ce n'est pas difficile,** according to him, it is not difficult; **je ne pouvais en c. mes yeux, mes oreilles,** I couldn't believe my eyes, my ears; **il s'en croit un peu,** he fancies himself a bit. **2.** *v.i.* (*a*) to believe (in the existence of sth.); **c. aux fées,** to believe in fairies; **c. à l'innocence de qn,** to believe in s.o.'s innocence; **le médecin crut à une rougeole,** the doctor thought it was measles; **c'est à ne pas y c.,** it's beyond all belief; **veuillez c., je vous prie de c., à l'assurance de mes salutations empressées,** yours truly, yours faithfully; **veuillez c., je vous prie de c., à l'expression de mes sentiments distingués.** yours sincerely; (*b*) to believe (in), trust (in), to have faith in; **c. aux témoignages des sens,** to believe, trust, the evidence of one's senses; **je ne crois pas à ses promesses,** I have no faith in his promises; **c. en qn, qch.,** to trust (in) s.o., sth.; **c. en Dieu,** to believe in God; **c. à la Sainte-Vierge, au Saint-Esprit,** to believe in the Virgin Mary, in the Holy Ghost; *abs.* **il ne croit plus,** he has lost his faith (in God); **c. en soi,** to be self-confident; **c. en son étoile,** to believe in one's lucky star.

croisade [krwazad, krwɑ-], *s.f.* (*a*) *Hist:* crusade; **partir en c.,** to go on a crusade; (*b*) **c. contre l'alcoolisme,** campaign against alcoholism.

croisé [krwaze, krwɑ-]. **1.** *a.* (*a*) crossed; **feu c.,** cross-fire; *Box:* **coup c.,** overarm blow; *Needlew:* **point c.,** herring-bone stitch; *Th: etc:* **éclairage à feux croisés,** cross-lighting; *Games:* **mots croisés,** crossword; *Ten:* **balle croisée,** ball played across the court; *Pros:* **rimes croisées,** alternate rhymes; *Biol:* **fécondation croisée,** cross-fertilization; *Bot:* allogamy. *Husb:* **race croisée,** cross-breed; (*b*) double-breasted (coat, etc.); (*c*) *Med:* crucial, figure-of-eight (bandage); (*d*) *Tex:* twilled (material); (*e*) *Her:* ensigned with a cross. **2.** *s.m.* (*a*) *Hist:* Crusader; (*b*) *Tex:* twill; (*c*) (*animal*) cross-breed.

croisée [krwaze, krwɑ-], *s.f.* **1.** crossing; **c. de deux chemins,** crossroads; **être à la c. de deux chemins,** to stand at the crossroads, at the parting of the ways. **2.** (*a*) casement; (*b*) casement window. **3.** *Arch:* **c. (du transept),** crossing (of church). **4.** *Nau:* **c. d'une ancre,** breadth of an anchor from bill to bill. **5.** *Opt:* cross hairs (of telescope). **6.** *Arch:* **c. d'ogives,** intersecting ribs (of a vault). **7.** cross guard (of sword).

croisement [krwazmɑ̃, krwɑ-], *s.m.* **1.** crossing, meeting; *Aut:* **lors d'un c.,** when two vehicles cross each other; *Rail:* **c. fixe,** scheduled crossing (of trains); *Av:* **altitude de c.,** crossing altitude; **c. d'idées,** interchange of ideas. **2.** (*a*) crossing, intersection (of lines, roads, etc.); **c. de routes, de rues,** crossroads; **c. dangereux,** dangerous crossroads; dangerous corner; **voie de c.,** crossing loop (on railway, road); *Rail:* **c. de voie,** crossing, cross-over; **c. oblique,** diamond crossing; **c. à pointes mobiles,** movable-point crossing; frog; **c. rigide,** rigid frog; **pointe de c.,** point (rail); (*b*) *Mus:* overlapping (of voices in part singing). **3.** (*a*) crossing, interbreeding (of animals); **faire des croisements de races,** to cross breeds; (*b*) cross-breed; cross (**entre . . . et . . .,** between . . . and . . .).

croiser [krwaze, krwɑ-]. **1.** *v.tr.* (*a*) to cross; **chemin de halage qui croise une route,** towpath which crosses a road; **c. le fer avec qn,** to cross swords with s.o.; **c. les jambes,** to cross one's legs; (se) **c. les bras,** (i) to fold one's arms; (ii) to refuse to work; **rester les bras croisés,** (i) to stand with arms folded; (ii) to remain idle; **elle croisa son châle sur sa poitrine,** she folded her shawl over her bosom; **c. qn dans l'escalier,** to meet, pass, s.o. on the stairs; **ils restèrent immobiles, croisant leurs regards,** they stood still, each gazing at the other; **leurs regards se croisèrent,** their eyes met; **nos lettres se sont croisées,** our letters have crossed in the post; *A:* **je regardais la foule qui se croisait,** I was watching the crowd passing to and fro; *A:* **il me croise dans tout ce que je fais,** he crosses me, thwarts me, in everything I do; *Nau:* **c. une vergue,** to cross a yard; (*b*) *A:* to cross (sth.) out; **c. tout un alinéa,** to put one's pen through a whole paragraph; (*c*) *Biol: Husb:* to cross, interbreed (animals, plants); (*d*) *Tex:* to twill (cloth); to weave (rushes, etc.); (*e*) *Mil:* **c. la baïonnette,** to level one's rifle, to charge bayonets; **c. les feux,** to cross-fire. **2.** *v.i.* (*of garment*) to lap, fold over; **habit qui ne croise pas assez,** coat that has not sufficient overlap. **3.** *v.i. Nau:* to cruise, to sail about.

se croiser. **1.** to (inter)cross; to intersect; **se c. avec qn,** to meet and pass s.o.; **ma lettre s'est croisée avec la vôtre,** my letter has crossed yours. **2.** (*a*) *Hist:* to take the cross; (*b*) to league, band, together (contre, against). **3.** *Husb:* **le cheval peut se c. avec l'âne,** the horse can breed with, can be crossed with, the donkey.

croiserie [krwazri, krwɑ-], *s.f.* basket-work, wicker-work, article.

croiseté, croisetté [krwazte, krwazɛte, krwɑ-], *a. Her:* crossleted.

croisette [krwazɛt, krwɑ-], *s.f.* **1.** (*a*) small cross; *Her:* crosslet; (*b*) *Nau:* top-crosstree. **2.** *Bot:* crosswort. **3.** *Miner:* cross-stone.

croiseur [krwazœːr, krwɑ-], *s.m. Navy:* cruiser; **c. à propulsion atomique, nucléaire,** nuclear-powered cruiser; **c. anti-aérien,** anti-aircraft cruiser; **c. auxiliaire,** armed merchantman (cruiser), armed merchant cruiser; **c. cuirassé,** armoured cruiser; **c. de bataille,** battle-cruiser; **c. lance-engins, c. lance-missiles,** guided-missile cruiser; **c. mouilleur de mines,** cruiser minelayer; **c. porte-hélicoptères,** helicopter-carrier cruiser; **c. protégé,** protected cruiser.

croisicais, -aise [krwazikɛ, -ɛːz], *a.* & *s. Geog:* (native, inhabitant) of le Croisic.

croisière [krwazjɛːr, krwɑ-], *s.f.* **1.** *Nau: etc:* (*a*) cruising; **navire en c.,** ship cruising; **vitesse de c.,** cruising speed; (*b*) cruise; **c. océanographique,** ocean-sounding expedition; *Aut: Hist:* **la C. noire,** the first trans-African car expedition; (*c*) cruising fleet; blockage fleet. **2.** *Mil:* ferrule (of bayonet). **3.** *Rail:* crossing (of lines).

croisillon [krwazijɔ̃, krwɑ-], *s.m.* **1.** cross piece, strut; brace; *Arch:* (arm of the) transept; *Nau:* cross-shaped bitt, bollard; *Aut:* **croisillons,** centre bracing, cross braces; **c. d'entrejambe,** (cross) bar (of chair, etc.); **croisillons d'une fenêtre,** window bars; **croisillons d'une roue,** arms, spiders, of a wheel; **bras de c.,** spider arm; *El.E:* **c. inducteur,** field spider; **induit à c.,** spider armature; *Mec.E:* **joint de Cardan à c.,** cross-pin Cardan joint. **2.** *Mch:* cross-head (of slide valve); bracing (of turbine). **3.** *Mec.E:* star, handle, wheel.

croisillonnement [krwazijɔnmɑ̃, krwɑ-], *s.m. Av:* bracing; **c. de recul,** drag trussing.

croisillonner [krwazijɔne, krwɑ-], *v.tr. Av:* to cross-brace (wing).

croissance [krwasɑ̃ːs, krwɑ-], *s.f.* growth; **l'âge de c.,** the growing age; **douleurs de c.,** growing pains; **prendre toute sa c.,** to attain one's full growth; **en pleine c.,** growing rapidly; **finir sa c.,** to stop growing; **arrêté dans sa c.,** stunted (in one's growth); **à c. rapide,** quick-growing.

croissant[1] [krwasɑ̃, krwɑ-], *a.* growing (plant, tendency, etc.); increasing (wealth, anxiety, etc.); rising (prices, flood, colour of cheeks); **avec une force croissante,** with gathering force; **en ordre c.,** in ascending order; *Mth:* **progression croissante,** ascending series.

croissant[2], *s.m.* **1.** (*a*) *O:* waxing (of moon); **la lune est à son c.,** the moon is waxing; (*b*) crescent (of moon); en (**forme de**) **c.,** crescent-shaped; *Hist:* **L'Empire du C.,** the Turkish Empire; **le C. Rouge,** the Red Crescent; *Her:* **c. tourné,** moon in increment, increscent moon; **c. contourné,** moon in decrement; (*c*) *Geom:* lune. **2.** (*crescent-shaped object*) (*a*) *Cu:* croissant; (*b*) **c. à élaguer,** billhook; pruning hook; (*c*) *A:* tread (of tyre); (*d*) *Nau:* (e)uphroe; (*e*) *Nau:* saddle, crutch (of boom); (*f*) *Geog:* **c. de plage,** beach cusp; (*g*) *Av:* **bombardier à aile en c.,** crescent wing bomber; (*h*) s-shaped hook.

croissanté [krwasɑ̃te, krwɑ-], *a. Her:* **croix croissantée,** cross croissanté.

croisure [krwazyːr, krwɑ-], *s.f.* **1.** (*a*) *Pros:* alternating of (i) rhymes, (ii) line of verse; (*b*) **c. de vergues,** squaring of yards. **2.** *Tex:* twill weave. **3.** *Tail:* cross-over (of front of coat). **4.** *Min:* steel lining (of shaft).

croît [krwa], *s.m. Husb:* (*a*) (natural) increase in stock (by breeding); (*b*) increase in weight (of fat stock).

croître [krwaːtr], *v.i.* (*pr.p.* **croissant;** *p.p.* **crû,** *f.* **crue;** *pr.ind.* **je croîs, il croît, n. croissons, ils croissent;** *p.h.* **je crûs;** *fu.* **je croîtrai;** *pr.sub.* **je croisse;** *p.sub.* **je crûsse**) to grow, increase (in size); (*a*) **c. en volume,** to increase in volume; **la rivière a crû,** the river has risen; **le vent croît,** the wind is rising; **la pluie croît,** the rain is becoming heavier; **les jours croissent,** the days are lengthening, getting longer; **c. en sagesse, en beauté,** to grow in wisdom, in beauty; **elle ne fait que c. et embellir,** she gets more beautiful every day; *F:* **cela ne fait que c. et embellir,** (i) it's getting better and better; (ii) *Iron:* it's getting worse and worse; **aller croissant,** to go on increasing, to go, keep, on growing; **c. dans l'estime de qn,** to rise in s.o.'s esteem; (*b*) (*of plants*) to grow; **joncs qui croissent dans l'eau,** rushes which grow in the water; **les pays où croissent la vigne et l'olivier,** lands of the vine and olive; *Prov:* **mauvaise herbe croît toujours,** ill weeds grow apace; (*c*) (*of the moon*) to wax.

croix [krwa, -a], *s.f.* cross. **1.** (*a*) **la Sainte C.,** the Holy Cross; *A:* the Holy Rood; **la vraie C.,** the True Cross; **le mystère de la C.,** the Redemption; **la mise en C.,** the crucifixion; **la descente de C.,** the descent from the Cross; **le chemin de la C.,** (i) the Way of the Cross, Via Dolorosa; (ii) the stations of the Cross; **faire le chemin de la C., un chemin de C.,** to do the stations of the Cross; **le signe de la c.,** the sign of the cross; **faire le signe, un signe, de la c.,** to cross oneself; **porter sa c.,** to bear one's cross; **chacun a sa c.,** everyone has his cross to bear; **aller à la c. avant le temps,** to meet trouble half-way; **mourir pour la c.,** to die for the Cross, for the (Christian) faith; (*b*) **c. processionnelle,** processional cross; *F:* **aller au-devant de qn avec la c. et la bannière,** to receive s.o. with pomp and circumstance, with full honours; **il a fallu la c. et la bannière pour le faire consentir,** it was the devil and all, the very devil, the devil of a job, to get him to consent; **la c. rouge (de Genève),** the Red Cross (sign); **la Croix-Rouge,** the Red Cross (organization); **une ambulance de la Croix-Rouge,** a Red Cross ambulance; **c. de feu, c. sanglante,** fiery cross; *Hist:* **prendre la c.,** to take the cross (for a crusade); **la c. de la Légion d'honneur,** the Cross of the Legion of Honour; **recevoir la c.,** to receive the Legion of Honour; *Mil:* **la c. de guerre,** the Military Cross; *O: P:* **gagner la c. de bois,** to be killed in action; *F:* **c. de bois, c. de fer,** cross my heart. **2.** (*a*) **en forme de c.,** cross-shaped; **église construite en forme de c.,** cruciform church, church built on a cruciform plan; **mettre des bâtons en c.,** to lay sticks crosswise; *Opt:* **fils en c.,** cross-threads, cross-wires, cross-hairs; *Nau:* **mettre les vergues en c.,** to square the yards; **les vergues en c.,** with yards across; **poutre en c.,** cruciform, cross-shaped, girder; **signer en faisant une c.,** to make one's mark, to sign with a cross; **faire, mettre, une c., sur, à, qch.,** to give sth. up for good; to call sth. off; *F:* **elle va venir enfin, il faut faire une c. (à la cheminée),** she's coming at last, put out the flags! mark it with a red letter! (*b*) **c. de Saint-André,** (i) St. Andrew's cross; (ii) *Her:* saltire; (iii) *Civ.E: etc:* diagonal struts, braces, cross-stays, counter-braces; **c. de Saint-Antoine, c. en tau,** St. Anthony's cross, tau(cross); **c. grecque,** Greek cross; **c. latine,** Latin cross; **c. de Lorraine,** cross of Lorraine; **c. de Malte,** (i) Maltese cross; (ii) *Hor: Mec.E:* Maltese cross, Geneva stop; (iii) *Cin:* Maltese cross; **c. gammée,** swastika; *A:* **c. de par Dieu,** criss-cross-row; *A: F:* **il en est à la c. de par Dieu,** he is still learning the ABC of it; (*c*) *A:* head-side, obverse (of coin); **c. ou pile,** heads or tails; **jouer qch. à c. ou pile,** to toss a coin for sth.; (*d*) *Typ:* dagger, obelisk, obelus; (*e*) *Astr:* **la c. du Sud,** the Southern Cross; (*f*) *Bot:* **c.-de-Malte,** land caltrops; **c. de Jérusalem, c.-de-Malte,** Maltese cross, London pride; **c. de Saint-André,** cross-wort; **c. de Saint-Jacques,** jacobean (lily); (*g*) *Miner:* **pierre de c.,** staurolite.

cromaltite [krɔmaltit], *s.f. Miner:* cromaltite.

cromesquis [krɔmɛski], *s.m. Cu:* kromesky.

cromlech [krɔmlɛk], *s.m. Prehist:* cromlech.

cromorne [krɔmɔrn], *s.m. Mus:* **1.** krumm horn, cromorne. **2.** krumm horn, cromorne, stop (of organ).

crône[1] [kroːn], *s.f. Fish:* hole (under bank of stream).

crône[2], *s.m.* (dock)crane.

cronstadt [krɔ̃stat, -ad], *s.m. A:* cronstadt (kind of top hat).

cronstedtite [krɔ̃stetit], *s.f. Miner:* cronstedtite.

crookésite [krukezit], *s.f. Miner:* crookesite.

crooner [krunœːr], *s.m.* crooner.

crop(p)etons (à) [akrɔptɔ̃], *adv.phr.* squatting; on one's haunches.

croquade [krɔkad], *s.f. Art:* (rough) sketch (in pencil or colour).

croquaillon [krɔkajɔ̃], *s.m. F:* poor sketch.

croquant[1] [krɔkɑ̃]. **1.** *a.* crisp, crunchy (biscuit, etc.). **2.** *s.m. Cu:* (*a*) gristle; (*b*) crisp petit four.

croquant[2], *s.m.* **1.** *Fr.Hist:* **les croquants,** name given to peasant revolutionaries during the reigns of Henry IV and Louis XIII. **2.** *Pej:* (*a*) clodhopper; (*b*) insignificant man, nonentity.

croque(-)au(-)sel (à la) [alakrɔkosɛl], *adv.phr. Cu:* raw, and unseasoned except for salt; **manger des radis à la c. au s.,** to eat radishes dipped in salt.

croque-en-bouche [krɔkɑ̃buʃ], *s.m.inv. Cu:* (*a*) crisp cake, pastry; (*b*) sweet made of fruit and (tiny) cream buns covered with caramel.

croque-lardon [krɔklardɔ̃], *s.m. A:* parasite, sponger; *pl. croque-lardon(s).*

croque-madame [krɔkmadam], *s.m.inv. Cu:* toasted ham sandwich sprinkled with grated cheese.

croquembouche [krɔkɑ̃buʃ], *s.m. Cu:* (*a*) crisp, cake, pastry; (*b*) sweet made of fruit and (tiny) cream buns covered with caramel.

croquement [krɔkmɑ̃], *s.m.* crunching.

croque(-)mitaine [krɔkmitɛn], *s.m.* bogey (man); *pl. croque(-)mitaines.*

croque-monsieur [krɔkməsjø], *s.m.inv.Cu:* toasted ham sandwich sprinkled with grated cheese.

croque-mort [krɔkmɔːr], *s.m. F:* (undertaker's) mute; **avoir une figure de c.-m.,** to have a funereal look; *pl. croque-morts.*

croqueneau [krɔkno], *s.m. P:* shoe, beetle-crusher.

croque-noix [krɔknwa], *s.m.inv.,* **croque-noisette** [krɔknwazɛt], *s.m. Z: F:* dormouse; *pl. croque-noisettes.*

croquenot [krɔkno], *s.m. P:* shoe, beetle-crusher.

croque-note [krɔknɔt], *s.m. F:* poor musician, bad, indifferent, performer (on his instrument); *pl. croque-notes.*

croquer[1] [krɔke]. **1.** *v.i.* (*of sugar, etc.*) to scrunch (between the teeth); **soupe qui croque,** gritty soup. **2.** *v.tr.* (*a*) to crunch, munch; **c. une noisette (sous la dent),** to crack a nut (with one's teeth); **c. un poulet en moins de rien,** to gobble up a chicken in no time; **chocolat à c.,** slab chocolate; **c. de l'argent, c. un héritage,** to squander one's money, a legacy; *P:* **c. une poulette,** to have, get, a girl, *P:* a bird; (*b*) to sketch; *F:* **elle est jolie, mignonne, à c.,** she's as pretty as a picture; *F:* she's a sweetie; (*c*) *Mus:* **c. des notes,** to leave out notes; (*d*) (*at croquet*) to tight croquet (the balls); **coup croqué,** tight croquet; (*e*) *F:* **c. le marmot,** to cool one's heels.

croquer[2], *v.tr. Nau:* to hook (sth.); to catch hold of (sth.) on a hook.

croque-sol [krɔksɔl], *s.m. F:* poor, indifferent, musician; *pl. croque-sols.*

croquet[1] [krɔkɛ], *s.m.* (*a*) *Cu:* crisp almond biscuit; (*b*) *F: A:* snappy person.

croquet[2], *s.m. Games:* croquet.

croquet[3], *s.m. Needlew:* scalloped braid.

croquette [krɔkɛt], *s.f.* **1.** (*a*) *Cu:* croquette; rissole; **c. de poisson,** fish croquette, fishcake; (*b*) chocolate drop. **2.** *Bot:* (corn) rattle.

croqueur, -euse [krɔkœːr, -øːz]. **1.** *a.* who, which, eats, devours (sth.). **2.** *s.* (*a*) **le renard est grand c. de poules,** the fox is always on the lookout for a chicken to devour; (*b*) *F:* **c. de femmes,** Don Juan, womanizer; **une croqueuse de diamants,** an expensive mistress, a gold-digger; (*c*) *A:* **c. de rimes,** rhymester.

croquignole [krɔkiɲɔl], *s.f.* **1.** (*a*) flick (on the nose with the finger); (*b*) insult. **2.** *Cu:* crisp biscuit.

croquignolet, -ette [krɔkiɲɔlɛ, -ɛt], *a. F:* sweet, pretty, *U.S:* cute.

croquis [krɔki], *s.m.* sketch; *Geog:* sketch map; **c. à la plume,** pen-and-ink sketch; **c. en couleurs,** coloured sketch; **cahier, album, de c.,** sketch book; **faire un c. de qch.,** to make a (rough) sketch of sth., to sketch sth.; *F:* **tu veux que je te fasse un petit c.?** do I have to spell it out for you? *Arch: etc:* **c. de projet, c. sommaire,** rough sketch; rough plan; **c. coté,** dimensional sketch; *Mil:* **c. d'objectif,** plan of target; **c. des parties vues et cachées,** visibility diagram; **c. de repérage, c. étalonné,** range card.

croquis-calque [krɔkikalk], *s.m.* skeleton tracing (of a frontier, etc.); *pl. croquis-calques.*

croskill [krɔskil], *s.m. Agr:* toothed roller.

croskillage [krɔskilaːʒ], *s.m. Agr:* rolling with a toothed roller.

croskiller [krɔskile], *v.tr. Agr:* to roll (the soil) with a toothed roller.

croskillette [krɔskilɛt], *s.f. Agr:* small toothed roller.

crosne [kroːn], *s.m. Hort:* Japanese, Chinese, artichoke.

cross[1] [krɔs], *s.m.inv. Box:* cross-counter.

cross[2], **cross-country** [krɔskuntri], *s.m. Sp:* cross-country run, race; **c. équestre,** cross-country steeplechase.

crossbar [krɔsbaːr], *s.m.* crossbar automatic telephone control system.

crosse [krɔs], *s.f.* crooked stick, crook. **1.** (*a*) **c. d'évêque,** bishop's crook, crozier; (*b*) crutch. **2.** *Sp:* (*a*) (hockey) stick; (golf) club; (lacrosse) crosse; (cricket) bat; (*at hockey*) **couper, donner, des crosses,** to give sticks; (*b*) (game of) lacrosse; (*c*) *F:* **chercher des crosses à qn,** to pick a quarrel with s.o. **3.** (*a*) crook; **courbé en c.,** crooked [krukt]; *Anat:* **c. de l'aorte,** arch of the aorta; (*b*) *Cu:* knuckle (of leg); (*c*) *Mch:* cross-head, slipper block (of piston); (*d*) *Mil:* butt (of rifle); grip (of pistol); shoulder piece (of quick-firing gun); **béquille de c.,** stock rest; **battant de c.,** butt swivel; *F:* **lever, mettre, la c. en l'air,** (i) to desert; (ii) to mutiny; (iii) to surrender; *P:* **autant pour les crosses!** start again! (*e*) *Artil:* **c. d'affût,** trail (of gun); (*f*) scroll (of violin, etc.); (*g*) *Av:* **c. d'appontage,** arrestor hook (for landing on aircraft carrier); (*h*) *Bot:* crosier (of a fern).

crossé [krɔse], *a. Ecc:* crosiered (bishop, etc.).

crosser [krɔse], *v.tr.* **1.** to hit, strike (ball) (with golf-club, hockey-stick, etc.). **2.** *abs.* (*a*) to play (i) hockey, (ii) lacrosse; (*b*) *P:* (*of hour*) to strike. **3.** *P:* **c. qn,** (i) to beat, go for, s.o.; (ii) to scold, s.o., to tell s.o. off.

se crosser, *P:* to wrangle, scuffle.

crosseron [krɔsrɔ̃], *s.m.* head (of bishop's crook).

crossette [krɔsɛt], *s.f.* **1.** *Arch:* crossette. **2.** *Hort:* slip, cutting (formed of shoot and piece of its parent stem).

crosseur [krɔsœːr], *s.m.* **1.** (hockey, lacrosse) player. **2.** *P:* quarrelsome person. **3.** *P:* = Attorney General.

crossing-over [krɔsiŋovœːr], *s.m.inv. Biol:* crossing-over.

crossite [krɔsit], *s.f. Miner:* crossite.

cross-leg [krɔslɛg], *s.m.inv. Surg:* cross-legged skin graft.

crossman, -men [krɔsman, -mɛn], *s.m. Sp:* cross-country runner.

crossope [krɔsɔp], *s.f. Z:* European water-shrew.

crossoptérygien [krɔsɔpteriʒjɛ̃], *s.m. Ich: Paleont:* crossopterygian; *pl.* **les crossoptérygiens,** the Crossopterygii.

crosswoman, -women [krɔswumən, -wimen], *s.f.* woman cross-country runner.

crotalaire [krɔtalɛːr], *s.f. Bot:* crotalaria; Bengal-hemp, sunn(-hemp).

crotale [krɔtal], *s.m.* **1.** *Gr.Ant:* crotalum, castanet. **2.** *Rept:* crotalus; rattlesnake, *U.S:* rattler.

crotalidés [krɔtalide], *s.m.pl. Rept:* Crotalidae.

croton [krɔtɔ̃], *s.m. Bot:* croton; *Pharm:* **huile de c.,** croton oil.

Crotone [krɔtɔn], *Pr.n.f. Geog:* Crotona.

crotoniate [krɔtɔnjat], *a. & s. A.Geog:* (native, inhabitant) of Crotona.

crotonique [krɔtɔnik], *a. Ch:* **acide c.,** crotonic acid; **aldéhyde c.,** crotonaldehyde.

crotte [krɔt], *s.f.* **1.** (*a*) dung, dropping (of horse, sheep, etc.); *F:* **c'est de la c. de bique,** it doesn't count, it's nothing; (*b*) **une c. de chocolat,** a chocolate; **c. de fromage,** small, round cheese; *F:* **ma petite c.,** my dear, (my) darling; (*c*) *Av: P:* bomb; (*d*) *int. F:* **c.!** damn! **2.** *O:* mud, slush, dirt; **demeurer (les pieds) dans la c.,** to live in squalor.

crotté [krɔte], *a.* dirty; mud-bespattered; **être c. jusqu'aux oreilles, jusqu'à l'échine, comme un barbet,** to be coated with mud from head to foot, bespattered all over with mud; to be muddied all over; *O:* **il fait c. dans les rues,** the streets are filthy, full of mud; *A:* **poète c.,** starveling poet.

crotter [krɔte], (*a*) *v.tr.* to dirty, soil; **tu crottes le parquet avec tes chaussures sales,** you're making the floor filthy with your dirty shoes; (*b*) *v.i. P:* (*of animal*) to make droppings; **chien qui crotte sur le trottoir,** dog that makes a mess on, fouls, the pavement.

se crotter, to get dirty; to get covered with mud.

crotteux, -euse [krɔtø, -øːz], *a.* dirty, muddy.

crottin [krɔtɛ̃], *s.m.* (*a*) (horse)dung; (sheep) droppings; (*b*) small goat's-milk cheese.

crotylique [krɔtilik], *a. Ch:* crotylic.

croulant [krulɑ̃]. **1.** *a.* (*a*) (*of building*) tottering, tumble-down, ramshackle, on the point of collapsing; **empire c.,** tottering empire; (*b*) **beauté croulante,** fading beauty; **c. de sommeil,** dropping with sleep; (*c*) **des êtres croulants,** people bent under the weight of old age. **2.** *s.m. P:* (*teenagers' slang*) back number; (*esp. of one's parents*) **les croulants,** the old folk; the oldsters; **c'est un c.,** he's a square.

croule [krul], *s.f. Ven:* woodcock shooting.

croulement [krulmɑ̃], *s.m.* collapse, falling in, tumbling down (of building, etc.).

crouler[1] [krule]. **1.** *v.tr.* (*a*) *A:* to shake, wag (tail, etc.); (*b*) *Nau:* **c. un vaisseau,** to start a ship on the ways (in launching). **2.** *v.i.* (*of building, etc.*) (*a*) to be sinking, giving way, to be on the point of collapse, to totter; (*b*) to collapse, crumble, tumble down, fall in; to fall with a crash; **faire c. qch.,** to bring down, disrupt, overthrow (wall, etc.); to ruin (project, plan, etc.); *Th:* **faire c. la salle (sous les applaudissements),** to bring down the house; **empire qui croule,** crumbling, tottering, empire.

crouler[2], *v.i.* (*of woodcock*) to call.

croulier, -ière [krulje, -jɛːr]. **1.** *a.* marshy, boggy (land, etc.). **2.** *s.f.* **croulière,** quagmire.

croup [krup], *s.m. Med: Vet:* croup; **faux c.,** false croup, childcrowing.

croupade [krupad], *s.f. Equit:* croupade.

croupal, -aux [krupal, -o], *a. Med:* croupy (cough); croupous (membrane).

croupe [krup], *s.f.* **1.** (*a*) croup, crupper, rump, hindquarters (of horse); **monter en c.,** to ride behind (the rider in the saddle); (of woman) to ride pillion; **prendre qn en c.,** to take s.o. up behind, on the crupper; (*b*) *Anat: F:* behind, backside (*esp.* of woman); *P:* **onduler de la c.,** to sway, wiggle, one's hips (when walking). **2.** (*a*) brow, crest (of hill); (*b*) *Arch:* hip; **toit en c.,** hipped roof.

croupé [krupe], *a.* **bien, mal, c.,** (horse) having a well-, badly-, shaped croup.

croupetons (à) [akruptɔ̃], *adv.phr.* squatting, crouching; **se tenir à c.,** to squat down.

croupeux, -euse [krupø, -øːz]. **1.** *a. Med:* croupous (complaint); croupy (child, cough). **2.** *s.m. & f.* child suffering from croup.

croupi [krupi], *a.* (*of water*) stagnant, foul.

croupiat [krupja], *s.m. Nau:* spring; **amarrer avec un c.,** to make fast with a spring.

croupier [krupje], *s.m.* **1.** croupier (in casino). **2.** *A:* partner (in financial enterprise); *St.Exch:* (broker's) backer.

croupière [krupjɛːr], *s.f.* **1.** *A.Arm:* croupière; *Harn:* crupper; **tailler des croupières à l'ennemi,** to follow hot upon the enemy (close enough to cut the cruppers); to rout the enemy; **tailler des croupières à qn,** to put difficulties, obstacles, in s.o.'s way. **2.** *Nau:* (*a*) spring; (*b*) stern-fast; **mouiller en c.,** to anchor by the stern.

croupion [krupjɔ̃], *s.m.* **1.** (*a*) rump (of bird); *Eng.Hist:* **le Parlement C.,** the Rump (Parliament); (*b*) *F:* parson's nose (of cooked fowl). **2.** (*a*) end of spine, tail-base (of mammals); (*b*) (*of man*) coccyx; *F:* tail; *P:* **se décarcasser le c.,** to go to no end of trouble (to do sth.).

croupir [krupiːr], *v.i.* **1.** (*of pers.*) to lie, be sunk, wallow (in filth, etc.); **c. dans le vice,** to wallow in vice; **c. dans l'oisiveté,** to wallow in idleness. **2.** (*of water, etc.*) to stagnate, grow foul; (*of air*) to grow stale. **3.** to rot (in stagnant water).

croupissant [krupisɑ̃], *a.* stagnating; **eaux croupissantes,** stagnant water; **richesses croupissantes,** money lying idle, stagnant wealth; **vie croupissante,** life of idleness.

croupissement [krupismɑ̃], *s.m.* **1.** wallowing (in vice, etc.). **2.** stagnation, spoiling.

croupon [krupɔ̃], *s.m. Leath:* butt.

crouponnage [krupɔnaːʒ], *s.m. Leath:* cropping.

crouponner [krupɔne], *v.tr. Leath:* to crop.

crouponneur [krupɔnœːr], *s.m. Leath:* cropper.

croustade [krustad], *s.f. Cu:* pie, pasty (with short crust); croustade.

croustance [krustɑ̃ːs], *s.f. P:* food; *P:* grub.

croustillant [krustijɑ̃], *a.* **1.** crisp (biscuit, pie, etc.); crusty (loaf). **2.** *F:* spicy (story); sexy (woman).

croustille [krustij], *s.f.* **1.** small crust; crisp, crunchy, crust (of loaf, etc.). **2.** *Cu:* **croustillants,** game chips; (potato) crisps. **3.** *A.Cost:* woman's head ornament.

croustiller [krustije], *v.i.* **1.** *A:* to munch, nibble, crusts (with one's wine). **2.** (*of food*) to crunch (under the teeth); **pain qui croustille,** crisp, crunchy, bread.

croustilleux, -euse [krustijø, -øːz], *a. F:* (*of story, etc.*) spicy.

croûtage [krutaːʒ], *s.m.* hardening, caking (of surface of soap).

croûte [krut], *s.f.* **1.** (*a*) crust (of bread, pie, etc.); **c. de dessous,** undercrust; **la c. terrestre,** the earth's crust; **faire c.,** to crust, cake; **former une c.,** to cake over; *Cu:* **c. au pot,** soup with crusty bread or toast in it; **c. aux champignons,** mushrooms served on fried bread; **c. de fromage,** cheese rind; *F:* **casser la c., manger une c.,** to have a snack; **viens casser la c. avec moi,** come and have a bite with me; *P:* **à la c.!** let's eat! *F:* **gagner sa c.,** to earn one's daily bread, one's bread and butter; *Prov:* **c. de pâté vaut bien pain,** (only) the best is good enough for me; (*b*) *Geol:* hardpan; **bombe en c. de pain,** volcanic bomb. **2.** (*a*) scab, crust (on wound, etc.); (*b*) skin (of casting); (*c*) *Med: F:* **croûtes de lait,** milk crust; (*d*) **c. de rouille,** layer of rust. **3.** *Leath:* flesh split (of split hide). **4.** (*in sawmill*) **croûtes,** pieces of waste timber (*usu.* including bark). **5.** *F:* (*a*) daub, badly painted picture; **quelle c.!** what a daub! (*b*) **c'est une (vieille) c.,** (i) he's hidebound, he's a stick-in-the-mud, an old fossil; (ii) he's a nitwit.

croûtelette [krutlɛt], *s.f.* small crust.

croûter [krute], *v.i.* **1.** to form a crust; to crust over. **2.** *P:* (*a*) to eat, feed; (*b*) *v.tr.* **tu vas c. ça,** take a bite of that.

croûteux, -euse [krutø, -øːz], *a.* **1.** scabby, covered with scabs. **2. bœuf c.,** beef with a thick layer of fat.

crouth [krut], *s.m. A.Mus:* cr(o)wth, crowd.

croûtier [krutje], *s.m. F:* (*poor artist*) dauber.

croûton [krutɔ̃], *s.m.* **1.** (*a*) piece of crust; (*b*) crusty end, heel (of loaf). **2.** *Cu:* croûton (for soup). **3.** *P:* **(vieux) c.,** (i) (old) fossil, stick-in-the-mud; (ii) (old) nitwit. **4.** *F:* dauber.

crown(-glass) [kraun(glas)], *s.m.* crown-glass; *Opt:* **lentille en c.-g.,** crown-lens (of achromatic lens).

croyable [krwajabl, krwa-], *a.* **1.** (*of pers.*) trustworthy, to be believed. **2.** (*of thg*) believable, credible.

croyance [krwajɑ̃ːs, krwa-], *s.f.* (*a*) belief (**à,** in); **c. en Dieu,** belief in God; **c. aux esprits, au diable,** belief in spirits, in the devil; **donner c. à qn, à qch.,** to believe s.o., sth.; (*b*) belief, conviction; **croyances religieuses,** religious beliefs; **la c. des chrétiens,** the Christian faith; **c. politique,** political opinion.

croyant, -ante [krwajɑ̃, -ɑ̃ːt, krwa-]. **1.** *a.* believing. **2.** *s.* (*a*) believer; (*b*) *pl.* (*Islam*) the Faithful; **le chef, commandeur, des croyants,** the Father, Commander, of the Faithful; **père des croyants,** Abraham.

cru[1] [kry], *a.* **1.** (*a*) raw (meat, silk, material, etc.); crude (ore, art, play, etc.); **vin c.,** wine not yet matured; **cuir c.,** raw hide; **bois c.,** plain unvarnished wood; *Cer:* **pièce crue,** unbaked, unfired, piece; **couleur crue,** crude, garish, colour; **lumière c.,** glare; garish light; **dans le jour c.,** in broad daylight; **parler en termes crus,** to speak (i) in rough, coarse, language, (ii) in plain terms; **réprimande trop crue,** too harsh a reprimand; **anecdote crue,** coarse, broad, anecdote; **dire la chose toute crue,** to say sth. without beating about the bush; **je vous le dis tout c.,** I'm not mincing my words; (*b*) indigestible; **mets c. à l'estomac,** indigestible dish; **eau crue,** hard water. **2.** *adv.phr.* **à c.;** (*a*) next to the skin; **être chaussé à c.,** to wear one's boots without any socks; **monter (un cheval) à c.,** to ride (a horse) bareback(ed); (*b*) *Const:* **maison qui porte à c.,** house built without any foundations; *Veh:* **charge portée à c. sur l'essieu,** unsprung weight on the axle; (*c*) **la lumière tombait à c. sur sa tête,** the light beat straight down on his head. **3.** *s.m.* (*a*) **manger du c.,** to eat raw food; (*b*) *Cer:* unfired clay.

cru[2], *s.m.* **1.** (*rare*) growth (of a plant). **2.** locality in which vines are grown; **les meilleurs crus,** (i) the best vineyards; (ii) the best wines; **vin d'un bon c.,** wine of a good vintage; **vin du c.,** local wine, wine of the country; **sentir le c.,** to smack of the soil, to be redolent of the soil; **bouilleur de c.,** home distiller; **les divers crus politiques,** different political opinions; **une histoire de son (propre) c.,** a story of his own invention.

cruauté [kryote], *s.f.* **1.** cruelty (**envers,** to). **2.** act of cruelty; **exercer des cruautés,** to perpetrate acts of cruelty; **les cruautés du sort,** the cruelty of fate.

cruche [kryʃ], *s.f.* **1.** (*a*) jug, pitcher; **c. à eau,** water jug; *Prov:* **tant va la c. à l'eau (qu'à la fin elle casse),** the pitcher goes so often to the water that in the end it is broken; everything has its day; *F:* **être bête comme une c.,** to be as stupid as they make them; to plumb the depths of stupidity; (*b*) jugful, pitcherful. **2.** *F:* (*a*) idiot, ass, nitwit; (*b*) *a.* **jamais je n'ai vu des enfants si cruches,** I've never seen such stupid children.

cruchée [kryʃe], *s.f.* jugful, pitcherful.

crucherie [kryʃri], *s.f. F:* **1.** foolishness, stupidity. **2.** piece of foolishness, stupid action.

cruchette [kryʃɛt], *s.f.* (*a*) small jug; (*b*) small jugful.

cruchon [kryʃɔ̃], *s.m.* **1.** (*a*) small jug, carafe; **c. de bière,** pot of beer; (*b*) (stoneware) hot-water bottle. **2.** *F:* idiot, ass, nitwit.

crucial, -iaux [krysjal, -jo], *a.* **1.** crucial, cross-shaped (incision, etc.). **2.** (*a*) *Phil:* **expérience cruciale,** crucial experiment; (*b*) **le point c.,** the crucial point.

crucianella [krysjanɛla], *s.f. Bot:* crucianella.

crucifèracées [krysiferase], *s.f.pl. Bot:* Cruciferae.

crucifère [krysifɛːr]. **1.** *a.* cruciferous. **2.** *s.f.pl. Bot:* **crucifères,** Cruciferae, crucifers.

crucifié [krysifje], *a.* crucified; *s.* **le Crucifié,** Christ crucified.

crucifiement, *A:* **crucifîment** [krysifimɑ̃], *s.m.* (*a*) crucifying, crucifixion; **le C.,** the nailing of Christ to the cross; (*b*) *Art:* (painting of the) Crucifixion; (*c*) **c. de la chair,** mortifying of the flesh.

crucifier [krysifje], *v.tr.* (*pr.sub. & p.d.* **n. crucifiions, v. crucifiiez**) to crucify; **c. la chair,** to crucify, mortify, the flesh.

crucifix [krysifi], *s.m.inv.* crucifix; *P:* **mangeur de c.,** sanctimonious hypocrite.

crucifixion [krysifiksjɔ̃], *s.f.* crucifixion.

cruciforme [krysifɔrm], *a.* cruciform, cross-shaped; *Anat:* **ligaments cruciformes,** crucial ligaments; **vis (à tête) c.,** cross-headed screw; **tournevis c.,** cross-headed screwdriver; *R.t.m:* Phillips screwdriver.

cruciverbiste [krysivɛrbist], *s.m. & f.* crossword enthusiast.

crude ammoniac [krydamɔniak], *s.m.* ammonium sulphate (used as a fertilizer).

crudité [krydite], *s.f.* **1.** (*a*) indigestibility (of foods); hardness (of water); (*b*) *Cu:* raw vegetable hors d'œuvres; **manger des crudités,** (i) to eat indigestible things; (ii) to eat raw fruit and vegetables; (*c*) *A:* indigestion. **2.** crudity, crudeness (of colours, etc.); glare (of light). **3.** (*a*) coarseness (of expression, etc.); **parler avec c.,** to speak crudely, coarsely, to call a spade a spade; (*b*) **livre plein de crudités,** book full of crude, coarse, passages.

crue [kry], *s.f.* **1.** *A:* growth (of plant, child, etc.). **2.** (*a*) rising, swelling (of waters, river, etc.); (*b*) flood; **les crues du Nil,** the floods of the Nile; **rivière en c.,** river in spate; (*c*) *Geog:* alluvial deposits (brought by flood waters).

cruel, -elle [kryɛl], *a.* **1.** cruel (**envers, pour, avec,** to); **homme c.,** cruel man; **sort c.,** hard fate; **expérience cruelle,** bitter experience; **perte, déception, cruelle,** grievous loss, bitter disappointment; **cruelle épreuve,** sore trial; **remords cruels,** acute, bitter, remorse; **cruelle maladie,** terrible disease; *F:* **un c. raseur,** a terrible bore. **2.** *s. Lit:* **un cruel, une cruelle,** cruel, heartless, lover.

cruellement [kryɛlmɑ̃], *adv.* cruelly, bitterly, grievously; **c. éprouvé,** sorely tried; *F:* **c. ennuyeux,** terribly annoying; terribly boring.

cruenté [kryɑ̃te], *a.* **plaie cruentée,** raw, bleeding, wound.

cruiser [kruzœr], *s.m.* (luxury cruising) yacht.

crûment [krymɑ̃], *adv.* (*a*) crudely, roughly; **dire qch. c.,** to say sth. bluntly; (*b*) **éclairé c.,** crudely, garishly, lit; lit with an unshaded light.

cruor [kryɔːr], *s.m. Physiol: Med:* cruor, coagulated blood.

crural, -aux [kryral, -o], *a. Anat:* crural.

cruro-pelvimètre [kryropɛlvimɛtr̥], *s.m. Anthr:* cruro-pelvimeter.

Crusoé [krysɔe], *Pr.n.m. Lit:* **Robinson C.,** Robinson Crusoe.

crustacé [krystase]. **1.** *a.* crustaceous (lichen, etc.); crustacean (animal, etc.). **2.** *s.m.pl.* **crustacés,** Crustacea, crustaceans; *F:* shellfish.

crustacéen, -enne [krystaseɛ̃, -ɛn], *a. Z:* crustacean.

crustacéologie [krystaseɔlɔʒi], *s.f.* crustaceology.

crustacéologue [krystaseɔlɔg], *s.m. & f.* crustaceologist.

cruzade [kryzad], *s.f. A.Num:* crusado, cruzado.

cruzeiro [krusejro], *s.m. Num:* cruzeiro.

cryanesthésie [kriɑnɛstezi], *s.f.* cryanaesthesia.

cryesthésie [kriɛstezi], *s.f.* cryaesthesia.

crymothérapie [krimɔterapi], *s.f. Med:* crymotherapy.

cryocautère [kriɔkotɛːr, -kɔ-], *s.m. Med:* carbon dioxide snow pencil.

cryoclastie [kriɔklasti], *s.f.* disintegration (of rocks) caused by ice.

cryoconite [kriɔkɔnit], *s.f. Geol:* cryoconite.

cryodéshydration [kriɔdezidrasjɔ̃], *s.f.* lyophilization, freeze-drying.

cryogène [kriɔʒɛn], *s.m. Ph:* cryogen, freezing mixture.

cryogénie [kriɔʒeni], *s.f. Ph:* cryogenics.

cryogénique [kriɔʒenik], *a. Ph:* cryogenic.

cryohydrate [kriɔidrat], *s.m. Ch:* cryohydrate.

cryolit(h)e [kriɔlit], *s.f. Miner:* cryolite, Greenland spar.

cryomagnétisme [kriɔmaɲetism], *s.m.* cryomagnetism.

cryomètre [kriɔmɛtr̥], *s.m. Ph:* cryometer, low temperature thermometer.

cryométrie [kriɔmetri], *s.f. Ph:* low-temperature thermometry, cryometry.

cryophore [kriɔfɔːr], *s.m. Ph:* cryophorus.

cryoscope [kriɔskɔp], *s.m. Ph:* cryoscope.

cryoscopie [kriɔskɔpi], *s.f. Ph:* cryoscopy.

cryoscopique [kriɔskɔpik], *a.* cryoscopic.

cryostat [kriɔsta], *s.m. Ph:* cryostat.

cryothérapie [kriɔterapi], *s.f. Med:* crymotherapy, cryotherapy.

cryotron [kriɔtrɔ̃], *s.m. Elcs:* cryotron.

cryoturbation [kriɔtyrbasjɔ̃], *s.f. Geol:* cryoturbation.

crypte [kript], *s.f. Ecc: Arch: Anat: Bot:* crypt.

cryptesthésie [kriptɛstezi], *s.f. Psy:* cryptaesthesia.

cryptique [kriptik], *a.* (*a*) *Anat:* cryptal; (*b*) (person) living in a crypt, a catacomb; troglodytic; (*c*) cryptic (message, colouring, etc.).

crypto- [kriptɔ]. **1.** *pref.* crypto-; **cryptocalviniste,** crypto-Calvinist. **2.** *s.m. & f.* **crypto,** *Pol: F:* crypto-communist.

cryptobranche [kriptɔbrɑ̃ʃ], *a. Z: A:* cryptobranchiate.

cryptocalvinisme [kriptɔkalvinism], *s.m.* crypto-Calvinism.

cryptocalviniste [kriptɔkalvinist]. **1.** *s.m. & f.* crypto-Calvinist. **2.** *a.* crypto-Calvinistic.

cryptocéphales [kriptɔsefal], *s.m.pl. Ent:* Cryptocephala.

cryptocérates [kriptɔserat], *s.m.pl. Ent:* Cryptocerata.

crypto-communiste [kriptokɔmynist], *s.m. or f.* crypto-communist.

cryptodères [kriptɔdɛːr], *s.m.pl. Rept:* Cryptodira.

cryptogame [kriptɔgam]. *Bot:* **1.** *a.* cryptogamous, cryptogamic. **2.** *s.f.* cryptogam.

cryptogamie [kriptɔgami], *s.f. Bot:* cryptogamy.

cryptogamique [kriptɔgamik], *a.* cryptogamic.

cryptogamiste [kriptɔgamist], *s.m. & f.* cryptogamist, mycologist.

cryptogénétique [kriptɔʒenetik], **cryptogénique** [kriptɔʒenik], *a. Med:* cryptogenetic (disease), cryptogenic.

cryptogramme [kriptɔgram], *s.m.* cryptogram; cipher (message).

cryptographe [kriptɔgraf], *s.m. & f.* **1.** cryptographer, cryptographist. **2.** *s.m.* ciphering machine, cryptograph.

cryptographie [kriptɔgrafi], *s.f.* cryptography, writing in cipher.

cryptographier [kriptɔgrafje], (*a*) *v.i.* to write in cipher; (*b*) *v.tr.* to cipher, encode (sth.).

cryptographique [kriptɔgrafik], *a.* cryptographic.

cryptolite [kriptɔlit], *s.f. Miner:* cryptolite.

cryptologie [kriptɔlɔʒi], *s.f.* cryptology.

cryptologue [kriptɔlɔg], *s.m. & f.* (*a*) cryptologist; (*b*) cryptographer.

cryptomeria [kriptɔmerja], *s.m. Bot:* cryptomeria.

cryptomnésie [kriptɔmnezi], *s.f.* cryptomnesia.

cryptomonadales [kriptɔmɔnadal], *s.m.pl. Biol:* Cryptomonadales.

crypton [kriptɔ̃], *s.m. Ch:* crypton.

cryptonémiales [kriptɔnemjal], *s.f.pl. Algae:* Cryptonemiales.

cryptonyme [kriptɔnim]. **1.** *a.* cryptonymous. **2.** *s.m.* cryptonym.

cryptophagidés [kriptɔfaʒide], *s.m.pl. Ent:* Cryptophagidae.

cryptophtalmie [kriptɔftalmi], *s.f. Med:* cryptophthalmos.

cryptophyte [kriptɔfit], *s.f. Bot:* cryptophyte.

cryptopine [kriptɔpin], *s.f. Ch:* cryptopine.

cryptoportique [kriptɔpɔrtik], *s.m. Arch:* cryptoporticus.

cryptoprocte [kriptɔprɔkt], *s.m. Z:* **c. féroce,** fossa, foussa.

cryptorchide [kriptɔrkid], *a. & s. Med:* cryptorchid.

cryptorchidie [kriptɔrkidi], *s.f. Med:* cryptorchidism.

cryptorhynque [kriptɔrɛ̃ːk], **cryptorhynchus** [kriptɔrɛ̃kys], *s.m. Ent:* cryptorhynchus.

cryptostegia [kriptɔsteʒja], *s.m. Bot:* cryptostegia, indiarubber vine.

cryptotélégraphe [kriptɔtelegraf], *s.m.* code telegraph.

cryptotélégraphie [kriptɔtelegrafi], *s.f.* code telegraphy.

cryptozyge [kriptɔziːʒ], *a. Anthr:* cryptozygous.

cryptozygie [kriptɔziʒi], *s.f. Anthr:* cryptozygy.

crystal [kristal], *s.m. Fish:* hook (for fresh-water fishing).

csardas [ksardɑːs, -das], *s.f. Danc:* (Hungarian) csardas, czardas.

cténaires [ktenɛːr], *s.m.pl. Coel:* Ctenophora.

cténidie [ktenidi], *s.f. Moll: Ent:* ctenidium.

cténocéphale [ktenosefal], *s.m. Ent:* ctenocephalus.

cténodactylidés [ktenɔdaktilide], *s.m.pl. Z:* Ctenodactylidae.

cténoïde [ktenɔid], *a. Z:* ctenoid, comb-like (scale, etc.).

cténomyidés [ktenɔmjide], *s.m.pl. Z:* Ctenomyidae.

cténophore [ktenɔfɔːr], *s.m.* **1.** *Ent:* crane fly. **2.** *pl. Coel:* **cténophores,** Ctenophora.

Cuba [kyba], *Pr.n.f. Geog:* Cuba.

cubage [kybaːʒ], *s.m.* **1.** cubage, cubature; finding the cubic contents (of pile of wood, etc.); *Const:* **relever le c.,** to take out quantities. **2.** cubic content; volume (of reservoir, etc.); air-space (of room, etc.).

cubain, -aine [kybɛ̃, -ɛn], *a. & s. Geog:* Cuban.

cubanite [kybanit], *s.f. Miner:* cubanite.

cubature [kybatyːr], *s.f. Mth:* cubature (of solids).

cube [kyb]. **1.** *s.m.* (*a*) *Mth:* cube; **c. d'un nombre,** cube of a number; **élever (un nombre) au c.,** to cube (a number); (*b*) *pl. Toys:* building blocks, bricks; (*c*) cubic space (of air, etc.); (*d*) *Sch: F:* (i) third-year student in a class preparing for the *grandes écoles* or in a *grande école*; (ii) pupil staying down for the second time. **2.** *a.* cubic; **mètre c., centimètre c.,** cubic metre, cubic centimetre.

cubèbe [kybɛb], *s.m. Bot: A.Pharm:* cubeb.

cubébin [kybebɛ̃], *s.m.,* **cubébine** [kybebin], *s.f. Ch:* cubebin.

cuber [kybe]. **1.** *v.tr.* (*a*) *Mth:* to cube (number, etc.); (*b*) to cube, gauge; to find the cubical contents of (sth.). **2.** *v.i.* **réservoir qui cube vingt litres,** tank with a cubic capacity of twenty litres; *P:* **ça cube, ça finit par c.,** it's expensive.

cubilot [kybilo], *s.m. Metall:* cupola (furnace), smelting cupola.

cubique [kybik]. **1.** *a.* (*a*) cubic(al); *Arch:* **chapiteau c.,** cubic capital; *Cryst:* **système c.,** cubic system; (*b*) *Mth:* **racine c.,** cube root; (*c*) *Ph:* **dilatation c.,** cubic expansion; (*d*) *F:* (*of mass, occ. of pers.*) heavy, squat, massive. **2.** *s.f.* cubic (curve).

cubisme [kybism], *s.m. Art:* cubism.

cubiste [kybist], *a. & s.m. & f. Art:* cubist.

cubital, -aux [kybital, -o], *a. & s.m. Anat:* cubital (muscle, artery, nerve).

cubitière [kybitjɛːr], *s.f. A.Arm:* cubitière, couter.

cubito-palmaire [kybitopalmɛːr], *a. & s.f. Anat:* cubito-palmar (artery); *pl. cubito-palmaires.*

cubito-radial [kybitoradjal], *a. & s.m. Anat:* cubito-radial (muscle); *pl. cubito-radiaux.*

cubitus [kybitys], *s.m. Anat:* cubitus, ulna.

cubocube [kybɔkyb], *s.m. A.Mth:* ninth power; *A:* cubo-cubo-cube.

cubo-dodécaèdre [kybodɔdekaɛdr̥], *s.m. Cryst:* cubo-dodecahedron; *pl. cubo-dodécaèdres.*

cuboïde [kybɔid], *a. & s.m. Anat: Geom:* cuboid.

cubo-octaèdre [kybooktaɛdr̥], *s.m. Cryst:* cub(o-)octahedron; *pl. cubo-octaèdres.*

cuceron [kysrɔ̃], *s.m. Ent: F:* pea weevil, bean weevil.

cuchia [kuʃia], *s.f. Ich:* cuchia.

cucu [kyky], *a. F:* = CUCUL.

cucubale [kykybal], **cucubalus** [kykybalys], *s.m. Bot:* cucubalus, campion.

cucuje [kykyʒ], **cucujus** [kykyʒys], *s.m. Ent:* cucujid.

cucujidés [kykyʒide], *s.m.pl. Ent:* Cucujidae.

cucul [kyky], *a. F:* stupid, idiotic, dim-witted; **il est c., ce film,** this film's stupid, below anything; **ce qu'il est c.!** what a fool he is!

cuculé [kykyle], *a. Bot:* cucullate.

cuculidés [kykylide], *s.m.pl. Orn:* Cuculidae, the cuckoos.

cuculiformes [kykylifɔrm], *s.m.pl. Orn:* Cuculiformes.

cuculle [kykyl], *s.f. Ecc:* (*a*) (monk's) hood, cowl; (*b*) (Carthusian's) scapular.

cucullifère [kykyl(l)ifɛːr], *a. Nat.Hist:* cucullated.

cuculliforme [kykyl(l)ifɔrm], *a.* cuculliform, cowl-shaped, hood-shaped.

cucurbitacé [kykyrbitase], *a. Bot:* cucurbitaceous; gourd-shaped.

cucurbitacées [kykyrbitase], *s.f.pl. Bot:* Cucurbitaceae, the gourd family.

cucurbitain [kykyrbitɛ̃], *s.m. Ann:* terminal segment (of tapeworm).

cucurbite [kykyrbit], *s.f.* boiler, cucurbit (of distilling apparatus).

cucurbitin [kykyrbitɛ̃]. **1.** *a.* cucurbitine. **2.** *s.m. Ann:* terminal segment (of tapeworm).

cueillage [kœjaːʒ], *s.m.* **1.** (*rare*) picking, gathering (of fruit, etc.). **2.** *Glassm:* gathering (of glass).

cueillaison [kœjɛzɔ̃], *s.f.* **1.** (*a*) *Lit:* gathering, harvesting; (*b*) fruit-picking season. **2.** *Glassm:* gathering (of glass).

cueille [kœj], *s.f.* **1.** picking (of fruit). **2.** *Nau:* (*a*) cloth (of sail); (*b*) coil (of rope).

cueillée [kœje], *s.f. Const:* (floating) screed.

cueille-essaims [kœjɛsɛ̃], *s.m.inv. Ap:* swarm catcher.

cueille-fleurs [kœjflœːr], *s.m.inv.* (*implement*) flower-gatherer.

cueille-fruits [kœjfrɥi], *s.m.inv.* (*implement*) fruit picker.

cueillette [kœjɛt], *s.f.* **1.** (*a*) gathering, picking (of fruit, flowers, etc.); **faire la c. des fraises,** to gather, pick, the strawberries; **c. des airelles,** cranberrying; (*b*) (*fruit, etc.*) picking season; (*c*) **c. des chiffons,** rag-picking. **2.** *Nau:* **navire chargé à, en c.,** ship loaded with a general cargo; **navigation à la c.,** tramping.

cueilleur, -euse [kœjœːr, -øːz], *s.* **1.** picker, gatherer (of fruit, etc.); *O:* **c. de pommes,** badly dressed person. **2.** *Glassm:* gatherer.

cueilli [kœji], *a. Const:* **porte cueillie en plâtre,** door with plain plaster reveal.

cueillie [kœji], *s.f. Const:* (floating) screed.

cueillir [kœjiːr], *v.tr.* (*pr.p.* **cueillant;** *p.p.* **cueilli;** *pr.ind.* **je cueille, il cueille, n. cueillons;** *p.d.* **je cueillais;** *p.h.* **je cueillis;** *fu.* **je cueillerai**) to gather, pick, pluck (flowers, fruit, etc.); **c. un baiser,** to snatch a kiss; **c. des lauriers,** to win laurels; *Glassm:* **c. le verre,** to gather the glass; *Nau:* **c. une corde,** to coil a rope; *F:* **c. qn (au passage),** (i) to nab s.o. (as he goes by); (ii) to buttonhole s.o.; **se faire c.,** to get nabbed, caught; *Rugby:* **c. le ballon,** to gather the ball; *F:* **où as-tu cueilli ça?** where did you fish that out from, dig that up?

cueilloir [kœjwaːr], *s.m.* **1.** (*implement*) fruit picker. **2.** fruit basket.

cuesta [kwɛsta], *s.f. Geol:* cuesta.

cuffa, cuf(f)at [kyfa], *s.m. Min:* skip, tub, kibble, (hoisting-)bucket; **c. à fond mobile,** drop-bottom bucket.

cuic [kɥik], **cui-cui** [kɥikɥi], *int. & s.m.* peep; **on entendait le c. des oiseaux,** you could hear the birds cheeping, chirruping.

cuider [kɥide], *v.tr. A:* to think, believe.

se cuider, *A:* to overestimate one's own importance.

cuiller, cuillère [kɥijɛːr], *s.f.* **1.** (*a*) spoon; **c. à servir,** tablespoon; **c. à dessert, à entremets,** dessert spoon; **c. à soupe,** soup spoon; **c. à café, à moka,** (large, small) coffee spoon; **c. à thé,** teaspoon; **c. à moutarde, à sel,** mustard, salt, spoon; **c. automatique à thé,** tea infuser; **c. à pot,** ladle; **c. à punch,** punch ladle; **œuf à la c.,** boiled egg; *Prov:* **il faut laisser chacun manger avec sa c.,** live and let live; *F:* **il n'y va pas avec le dos de la c.,** (i) he doesn't mince his words; (ii) he's quite ruthless, he goes the whole hog; *F:* **en deux, trois, coups de c. (à pot),** in less than no time, in two shakes (of a lamb's tail); *F:* **être à ramasser à la petite c.,** (i) to be badly hurt, smashed up; (ii) to be completely exhausted, all in; *F:* **avaler sa c.,** to be scared stiff; *Bot:* **herbe aux cuillers,** scurvy grass; *Nau:* **rouler à faire cuiller,** to roll gunwhale under; *Ten: F:* **servir à la c.,** to serve underhand; (*b*) *Fish:* spoon (bait), trolling spoon; **pêcher à la c.,** to troll, to spin (for trout, etc.); (*c*) *Metall:* **c. à couler,** casting ladle; **c. de plombier,** lead ladle; (*d*) *Tls:* spoon drill; **mèche à c.,** spoon bit. **2.** *Civ.E:* scoop, bucket (of dredger); **c. à excavation,** earth grab; *I.C.E:* **c. d'huile (de tête de bielle),** dipper, scoop, splasher (of big end). **3.** *P:* hand, mitt.

cuillerée [kɥij(ə)re], *s.f.* spoonful; **servir une c. de potage à qn,** to serve s.o. a ladleful of soup; (*to child*) **une c. pour maman,** have a nice spoonful for mummy!

cuilleron [kɥijrɔ̃], *s.m.* **1.** bowl (of spoon); **en c.,** spoon-shaped (leaf, etc.). **2.** *Ent:* alula, alulet, winglet (of dipter).

cuir [kɥiːr], *s.m.* **1.** (*a*) skin; *still so used in* **blessure entre c. et chair,** oblique flesh wound; *F:* **jurer entre c. et chair,** to swear under one's breath; *F:* **il a le c. épais,** he's got a hide like a rhinoceros; *P:* **tanner le c. à qn,** to give s.o. a good hiding; *Anat:* **c. chevelu,** scalp; (*b*) hide (of elephant, etc.). **2.** (*a*) leather; **c. vert, cru, brut,** raw hide, green hide; **c. d'œuvre,** undressed leather; **c. de molleterie,** shoe leather; **c. en suif,** waxed leather; **c. jaune,** tan leather; **c. aluné, blanc,** white leather; **c. fort, c. à, pour, semelles,** sole leather; **c. de Russie,** russia, Russia leather, Russia calf; **c. verni,** patent leather; **c. de sellerie,** saddle leather; **c. bouilli,** cuir-bouilli; *F:* **visage de c. bouilli,** leathery face; **chaussures en c.,** leather shoes; **rond de c.,** (i) leather washer; (ii) leather cushion; (iii) *F: Pej:* civil service clerk; pen-pusher; *Mec.E:* **c. d'embrayage,** clutch leather; *F: A:* **faire du c. d'autrui large courroie,** to be generous with other people's money, property; (*b*) **c. à rasoir,** razor strop; (*c*) *F:* leather jacket; *Av:* leather suit. **3.** *Miner:* **c. fossile, de montagne,** fossil flax, mountain flax. **4.** *F:* incorrect "liaison," often an epenthetic [t] or [z], as: **j'étais avec lui** [ʒetɛtavɛk lɥi], **il a fait une erreur** [il a fez yn ɛrœːr], **s'en va en guerre** [sɑ̃vatɑ̃gɛːr]; **faire un c.,** to make an incorrect liaison; *F:* to "drop a brick" (in speaking); **elle parlait sans cuirs,** her way of speaking didn't give her away.

cuirasse [kɥiras], *s.f.* **1.** cuirass, breast-plate; *Z: Ent:* armour; shell (of insect, etc.); **le défaut de la c.,** the join between the breast-plate and the back-plate or the thigh-pieces; the chinks in the armour, the joints of the harness; **trouver le défaut dans la c. de qn,** to find s.o.'s weak, vulnerable, spot; *Nau:* **c. marine, flottante,** cork jacket; *Med:* **cancer en c.,** scirrhous cancer. **2.** armour (of warship, tank); **plaque de c.,** armour-plate; **c. verticale,** side-armour; **c. de ceinture,** belt armour. **3.** sheath (of cable).

cuirassé [kɥirase]. **1.** *a.* (*a*) armour-plated, armoured; *Mil:* **division cuirassée,** armoured division; *Navy:* **bâtiments cuirassés,** armoured ships; (*b*) **électro-aimant c.,** screened (type) electromagnet; **transformateur c.,** shell (type) transformer; (*c*) **être c. contre (les supplications, etc.),** to be proof, be hardened, against (entreaties, etc.). **2.** *s.m.* armoured ship; **c. (de ligne),** battleship; **c. d'escadre,** first-class battleship; **c. de poche,** pocket battleship; *A:* **c. moyen,** monitor.

cuirassement [kɥirasmɑ̃], *s.m.* **1.** armouring (of ship, etc.). **2.** armour, armour-plating.

cuirasser [kɥirase], *v.tr.* **1.** to supply (soldier) with a cuirass; to put a cuirass on (soldier); **se c.,** to put on one's cuirass; **se c. contre qch.,** to steel oneself, one's heart, against sth. **2.** to armour(-plate) (ship); to enclose, protect (machine).

cuirassier [kɥirasje], *s.m. Mil:* cuirassier.

cuire [kɥiːr], *v.* (*pr.p.* **cuisant;** *p.p.* **cuit;** *pr.ind.* **je cuis, il cuit, n. cuisons, ils cuisent;** *p.d.* **je cuisais;** *p.h.* **je cuisis;** *fu.* **je cuirai) 1.** *v.tr.* (*a*) to cook; **c. à l'eau,** to boil; **c. au four,** to bake, to roast; **c. du pain,** to bake bread; **viande cuite à point,** meat done to a turn; **bien cuit,** well done; **trop cuit,** overdone; **pas assez cuit,** underdone (not to s.o.'s taste); **pas trop cuit,** underdone (to s.o.'s taste); *F:* **être dur à c.,** to be stubborn; to be hard-boiled; *F:* **un dur à c.,** a tough nut, a tough customer; (*b*) to boil (sugar); (*c*) to burn, fire, bake, kiln (bricks, pottery, etc.); (*d*) *Ch: Ind:* to calcine; (*e*) *Tex:* to degum (silk). **2.** *v.i.* (*a*) (*of food*) to cook; **c. à petit feu,** to cook slowly; to simmer; **faire c. de la volaille,** to cook poultry; **chocolat à c.,** cooking chocolate; **pomme à c.,** cooking apple, cooker; *F:* **c. dans son jus,** (i) to be terribly hot; (ii) to stew in one's own juice; *F:* **on cuit dans cette salle,** it's boiling (hot) in this room; this room's like an oven; *P:* **va te faire c. un œuf,** to hell with you! (*b*) to burn, smart; **les yeux, les joues, me cuisent,** my eyes are smarting; my cheeks are tingling; *impers.* **il vous en cuira,** you'll be sorry for it; **il lui en a cuit,** he had good reason to repent of it, be sorry for it; *Prov:* **trop gratter cuit, trop parler nuit,** least said soonest mended.

cuiret [kɥirɛ], *s.m.* **1.** skin from which the hair has been removed. **2.** *Hatm:* sweat band.

cuirier [kɥirje], *s.m.* (fisherman's) leather apron.

cuir-lanière [kɥirlanjɛːr], *s.m.* belt strop (for razor); *pl. cuirs-lanières.*

cuirot [kɥiro], *s.m.* haired and dried sheepskin.

cuisant [kɥizɑ̃], *a.* **1.** smarting, burning (pain, etc.); biting (cold); caustic, biting, bitter (remarks); **poivre c.,** hot pepper; **déception cuisante,** bitter disappointment; **désir c.,** burning desire; **la douleur cuisante d'une blessure,** the sting, the smarting, of a wound. **2. légumes cuisants,** easily cooked vegetables.

cuiseur [kɥizœːr], *s.m.* **1.** (*pers.*) (*a*) (brick, lime, porcelain) burner; fireman; (*b*) travelling spirit distiller. **2.** (large) cooking pot; steamer; **c. à pression,** pressure cooker; **c. pour poissons,** fish kettle.

cuisinage [kɥizinaːʒ], *s.m. F:* grilling (of prisoner, suspect).

cuisine [kɥizin], *s.f.* **1.** kitchen; *Mil:* cookhouse; *Nau: Av:* (cook's) galley; **elle fait partie de la c.,** she belongs to the kitchen staff; *Com:* **articles de c.,** hollow ware, cooking utensils; **batterie de c.,** (i) cooking utensils; (ii) *F: Hum:* percussion instruments; (iii) *F: Hum:* (military, etc.) decorations; *F:* gongs; *Mil:* **c. roulante,** field kitchen; **latin de c.,** dog Latin. **2.** (*a*) (art of) cooking, cookery; cuisine; **apprendre la c.,** to learn to cook, to learn cookery; **c. à la vapeur,** steam cooking; **c'est de la bonne c. bourgeoise,** it's good home cooking, good plain cooking; **haute c.,** high class cuisine; **livre de c.,** cookery book, *U.S:* cook book; **faire la c.,** (i) to do the cooking; (ii) *Games:* (*at dominoes*) to shuffle; (iii) *Journ:* to play to the public, the readers; (*b*) *F:* **les petites cuisines du métier,** the little tricks of the trade; **la c. parlementaire,** parliamentary intrigue; **la sale c. des politiciens,** the dirty scheming of politicians; (*c*) *Journ:* subediting. **3.** (cooked) food; *Com:* **c. à emporter,** ready-cooked dishes (for sale); **hôtel où la c. est bonne,** hotel renowned for its good cooking; *P:* **quelle c.!** what a ghastly mix-up!

cuisine-poêle [kɥizinpwɑːl, -wal], *s.f. O:* kitchen range, kitchener; *pl. cuisines-poêles.*

cuisiner [kɥizine]. **1.** *v.i.* to cook; **elle cuisine bien,** she is a good cook. **2.** *v.tr.* to cook (meat, etc.); *F:* to concoct, cook up (a scheme of revenge); *Com:* **plats cuisinés,** ready-cooked dishes; *F:* **c. des comptes,** to cook accounts; **c. une nomination pour qn,** to intrigue, pull the wires, in order to get s.o. an appointment; **c. un prévenu,** to interrogate, *F:* grill, a man in custody.

cuisinier, -ière [kɥizinje, -jɛːr], *s.* **1.** cook; **ma femme est bonne cuisinière,** my wife's a good cook; **trop de cuisinières gâtent la sauce,** too many cooks spoil the broth. **2.** *s.m.* cookery book, *U.S:* cook book. **3.** *s.f.* **cuisinière,** cooker, *U.S:* cookstove; **c. à gaz,** gas stove, cooker; **c. électrique,** electric cooker; **c. à charbon,** (kitchen) range.

cuissage [kɥisaːʒ], *s.m. Hist:* **droit de c.,** jus primae noctis.

cuissard [kɥisaːr], *s.m.* **1.** *A.Arm:* cuisse, cuish, thigh-piece. **2.** *Mch:* (water-)leg (of boiler). **3.** socket, bucket (of artificial leg). **4.** *pl.* overall leggings, seatless trousers (of cyclist, etc.).

cuissardes [kɥisard], *s.f.pl. & a.* **(bottes) c.,** (i) thigh-boots; (ii) waders.

cuisse [kɥis], *s.f.* thigh; **os de la c.,** thigh bone; *Cu:* **c. de poulet,** chicken leg; *F:* drumstick; **cuisses de grenouilles,** frogs' legs; *F:* **se croire sorti de la c. de Jupiter,** to think a lot, no small beer, of oneself; to be stuck-up; *P:* **avoir la c. légère, hospitalière, facile,** to be a woman of easy morals.

cuisseau, -eaux [kɥiso], *s.m. Cu:* leg (of veal).

cuisse-de-nymphe [kɥisdənɛ̃ːf]. **1.** *s.f. Hort:* white rose with pink tints; *pl. cuisses-de-nymphe.* **2.** *a.inv.* **c.-de-n. (émue)** *Lit:* flesh pink.

cuisse-madame [kɥismadam], *s.f. Hort:* cuisse-madame (pear); *pl. cuisses-madame.*

cuissière [kɥisjɛːr], *s.f.* (drummer's) leg-guard.

cuisson [kɥisɔ̃], *s.f.* **1.** (*a*) cooking, baking; **c. à la vapeur,** steam cooking; **c. sur le gril,** grilling; **pain de c.,** home-made bread; *Sug.-R:* **c. du sucre,** sugar boiling; (*b*) burning, firing (of bricks, porcelain, etc.); *Ch: Ind:* calcining, calcination; (*c*) burning in (of photo-engraving). **2.** burning (sensation); smarting (pain). **3.** *Cu:* liquid in which food is cooked; stock.

cuissot [kɥiso], *s.m.* **1.** *A.Arm:* cuisse. **2.** *Cu:* haunch (of venison).

cuistance [kɥistɑ̃ːs], *s.f. Mil: P:* cookery, cooking.

cuistancier [kɥistɑ̃sje], *s.m.,* **cuisteau, -eaux, cuistot** [kɥisto], *s.m. Mil: Nau: etc: P:* cook.

cuistre [kɥistr̥], *s.m.* (*a*) *Sch: A:* usher; (*b*) *O:* (conceited) pedant; (*c*) *O:* ill-bred person.

cuistrerie [kɥistrəri], *s.f. O:* (*a*) pedantry; (*b*) lack of breeding, good manners.

cuit [kɥi]. **1.** *a.* (*a*) cooked; **terre cuite,** terra cotta; *F:* **un socialiste c. et recuit,** a dyed-in-the-wool socialist; *F:* **il a son pain c.,** he's all right for the rest of his life; (*b*) *Tex:* **soie cuite,** degummed silk; (*c*) *Art:* warm (tone); (*d*) *F:* (*of pers.*) ruined; (*of pers., thg*) done for; **je suis c.,** it's all up with me, I'm done for; **ça, c'est c.!** that's had it; (*e*) *F:* **c'est du tout c.,** it's all settled, all buttoned up, it's a cinch. **2.** *s.m.* **vin avec un goût de c.,** wine with a taste of cooked grapes.

cuite [kɥit], *s.f.* **1.** baking, firing, burning (of bricks, etc.); *Sug.-R:* boiling; *Tex:* boiling (of silk). **2.** batch (of things baked at one time). **3.** *F:* **prendre une (bonne) c.,** to get drunk; **il a sa c.,** he's drunk, he's had one over the eight. **4.** whey (from Gruyère cheese); abnormal hole (in curd for Gruyère cheese).

cuiter (se) [səkɥite], *v.pr. P:* to get drunk, tight.

cuit-légumes [kɥilegym], *s.m.inv. Dom.Ec: Husb:* (large) cooking pot (*esp.* for vegetables).

cuit-œufs [kɥitø], *s.m.inv. Dom.Ec:* egg boiler.

cuivrage [kɥivraːʒ], *s.m.* **1.** coppering (of metals, etc.); copper-plating. **2.** *F:* blaring (of brass instruments).

cuivre [kɥiːvr̥], *s.m.* **1.** (*a*) **c. (rouge),** copper; **c. brut,** raw copper; **c. embouti,** pressed copper; **c. en feuilles,** sheet copper; **c. (de) rosette,** rosette (copper); **casserole en c.,** copper saucepan; **fonderie de c.,** copper foundry; **monnaie de c.,** copper coins; **doublé en c.,** (i) copper-plated, copper-sheathed; (ii) copper-bottomed; **eau de c.,** (liquid) metal polish; *Prehist:* **l'âge du c.,** the Copper Age; (*b*) **c. jaune,** brass; **les cuivres,** (i) *Mus:* the brass; (ii) *Nau:* the brasswork, the brightwork; **faire, astiquer, les cuivres,** to do, polish, the brass(es); (*c*) *Miner:* **minerai de c.,** copper ore; **c. manganésé, au manganèse,** manganese copper; **c. sulfuré,** copper glance, chalcocite, chalcosine; **c. vitreux rouge,** cuprite; **c. gris,** grey copper ore, tetrahedrite; **c. pyriteux,** chalcopyrite, copper pyrites; (*d*) copper (colour); **ciel de c.,** copper-coloured sky. **2.** (*a*) *Engr:* copperplate; **gravure sur c.,** copperplate engraving; (*b*) electrotyped plate, block.

cuivré [kɥivre], *a.* **1.** copper-coloured; **peau cuivrée,** copper skin; **teint c.,** bronzed complexion; **ciel c.,** coppery sky; **cheveux aux reflets cuivrés,** auburn hair. **2. voix cuivrée,** resounding, ringing, voice; *Mus:* **sons cuivrés** brassy tones; **les accents cuivrés de la trompette,** the blare of the trumpet.

cuivrer [kɥivre], *v.tr.* **1.** to copper; to coat, sheath, (sth.) with copper. **2.** to make (sth.) copper-coloured; **c. le teint,** to bronze the complexion. **3.** *Mus:* (*of band*) **c. le son,** to play with a brassy tone, to blare.

se cuivrer, to turn the colour of copper, to turn coppery.

cuivrerie [kɥivrəri], *s.f.* **1.** copper foundry. **2.** coppersmith's work; brasswork. **3.** copper goods, copper ware.

cuivreur [kɥivrœːr], *s.m.* (*pers.*) copper plater.

cuivreux, -euse [kɥivrø, -øːz], *a.* **1.** (*a*) coppery; copper (colour, etc.); cupreous (ore, etc.); **sulfure c.,** copper glance, cuprous sulphide; (*b*) *Ch:* cuprous (oxide). **2.** blaring, brassy (sound).

cuivrique [kɥivrik], *a. Ch:* cupric; **liseré c.,** copper line.

cul [ky], *s.m.* (*except in technical meanings this word is not used in polite society*) **1.** (*a*) *P:* backside, bottom, bum, behind, posterior; *V:* arse (of person); *V:* **le trou du c.,** the anus; *V:* shit-hole; *P:* **bas du c., bout de c.,** short and stumpy man; *V:* short-arse; *A:* **cul goudronné,** sailor, tar; **c. terreux,** country bumpkin, yokel, *U.S:* rube; *P:* **renverser qn c. par-dessus tête,** to knock s.o. head over heels, to send s.o. flying; **il en est tombé, il en est resté, sur le c.,** he was knocked all of a heap, he was flabbergasted; **être sur le c.,** to be worn out; **se taper le c. par terre,** to roar with laughter; *A:* **enlever le c. à qn,** to give s.o. a kick in the pants; **baiser, lécher, le c. à qn,** to lick s.o.'s boots; *V:* to lick s.o.'s arse; **ils sont comme c. et chemise,** they are great buddies, inseparable; **montrer le c.,** (i) to be in rags; (ii) to run away; **avoir le feu au c.,** to go like greased lightning; **avoir le c. sur selle,** (i) to be in the saddle; (ii) *F:* to be always sitting down; **être, demeurer, le c. entre deux selles, être, demeurer, entre deux selles le c. à terre,** to fall between two stools; **ça vaut mieux qu'un coup de pied au c.,** it's better than a kick in the pants; **avoir qn dans le c.,** to be fed up with s.o.; *V:* **en avoir plein le c.,** to be fed up; **l'avoir dans le c.,** to have had it; *Mil: P:* **tirer au c.,** to swing the lead; *P:* to shirk; **c'est un tire-au-c.,** he's a shirker; *P:* **quel c.!** *a.* **ce qu'il est c.!** what a ruddy idiot! *P:* **quel c. (il a)!** what disgusting (*i.e.* good) luck (he has)! *P:* **mon c.!** my foot! (*b*) *P:* haunches, rump (of animal); **arrêter un cheval sur c.,** to pull a horse up on its haunches; **tirer un oiseau au c. levé,** to shoot a bird on the rise; (*c*) *A.Cost:* **faux c.,** bustle. **2.** (*a*) bottom (of bag, bottle); base, punt (of bottle); arse (of pulley-block); tail (of cart); **c. de basse-fosse,** deepest dungeon, oubliette; **faire c. sec,** to leave no heel-taps, to drink up; **c. sec!** bottoms up! knock it back! **mettre une charrette à c.,** to tip up a cart; **mettre un tonneau à c.,** to tip up, to up-end, a barrel; *F:* **mettre qn à c.,** to clean s.o. out; **être à c.,** (i) to have one's back to the wall; (ii) to be at the end of one's resources; (*b*) *Nau:* stern (of ship); **trop sur c.,** too much by the stern; **arrière en c. de poule,** counter stern; *P:* **faire la bouche en c. de poule,** to pull a face; to pout; (*c*) *Vet:* **c. de verre,** web cataract (of horse's eye).

culasse [kylas], *s.f.* **1.** (*a*) *Artil: Sm.a:* breech (of gun, rifle); **c. mobile, fermeture de c.,** bolt (of rifle); **tête de c. mobile,** bolt head; **arrêtoir de c. mobile,** bolt stop; **fusil se chargeant par la c.,** breech-loading gun, breech-loader; **bloc de c.,** breech block; **boîte de c.,** breech casing, *U.S:* receiver group; **manchon de c., porte c.,** breech ring; **volet de c.,** breech-clock carrier; **couvre-c., coiffe de c.,** breech cover; *P: A:* **tomber sur la c.,** to fall on one's behind, to land on one's backside; (*b*) *Lap:* culet, collet (of diamond). **2.** *El.E:* yoke (of electro-magnet, relay, transformer, etc.); **c. magnétique,** magnetic yoke; **champ de dispersion de c.,** yoke stray field. **3.** *I.C.E:* cylinder head; **c. amovible, c. rapportée,** detachable cylinder head; **c. à soupapes en tête,** overhead-valve cylinder head; **joint de c.,** cylinder-head gasket. **4.** *Nau:* stockhole (of anchor shank).

culasser [kylase], *v.tr.* to breech (gun, rifle).

cul-blanc [kyblɑ̃], *s.m. Orn:* white-tail, wheatear; **c.-b. gris, cendré,** fallow finch; *pl. culs-blancs.*

cul-brun [kybrœ̃], *s.m. Ent:* brown-tail moth; *pl. culs-bruns.*

culbutage [kylbytaːʒ], *s.m.* **1.** turning a somersault. **2.** *a*) knocking over, upsetting (of sth.); (*b*) tipping (of cart); dumping (of ore, etc.).

culbutant [kylbytɑ̃], *a. & s.m.* **1.** *Orn:* **(pigeon) c.,** tumbler (pigeon). **2.** *P:* trousers.

culbute [kylbyt], *s.f.* (*a*) somersault; **faire la c.,** to turn a somersault; (*b*) tumble; heavy fall; **faire une violente c.,** to come a heavy cropper; (*c*) *F:* **faire la c.,** (i) (*of ministry*) to collapse, to fall; (*in business*) to fail, to become bankrupt; (ii) *Com:* to make a scoop; to make 100% profit; **au bout du fossé la c.!** he's, you're, riding for a fall.

culbutement [kylbytmɑ̃], *s.m.* **1.** turning a somersault. **2.** (*a*) knocking over, upsetting (sth.); tipping (of cart); dumping (of ore, etc.). **3.** (*astronautics*) abnormal rotation; *F:* wobble.

culbuter [kylbyte]. **1.** *v.i.* (*a*) to turn a somersault; (*b*) **c. du haut de l'escalier,** to fall head over heels downstairs; (*c*) *F:* to come to ruin, to fail (in business); (*of ministry*) to fall, to collapse; (*d*) to topple over. **2.** *v.tr.* (*a*) to overthrow, knock down, knock over, upset (s.o., sth.); to knock (s.o.) head over heels; **tout c. dans la chambre,** to turn everything topsy-turvy in the room; **c. un ministère,** to overthrow a ministry; (*b*) *V:* to lay (a woman); (*c*) to tip, tilt (cart, etc.); to dump, shoot (ore, etc.); **c. un tonneau,** to stand a barrel on end; (*d*) to trip (lever, etc.).

culbuterie [kylbytri], *s.f. I.C.E:* set of rocker arms.

culbuteur [kylbytœːr], *s.m.* **1.** *Toys:* tumbler. **2.** *El:* indicator switch; **interrupteur à c.,** tumbler-switch. **3.** *I.C.E:* rocker arm; **c. d'admission,** intake rocker arm; **c. d'échappement,** exhaust rocker arm; **arbre, axe, de c.,** rocker shaft, *U.S:* rockshaft; **boîtier de c.,** rocker box; **moteur à c.,** push-rod-operated overhead-valve engine. **4.** *Mec.E:* (*a*) tripper device; catch, tumbler; (*b*) tipping apparatus, tipper, (for trucks, etc.).

culbutis [kylbyti], *s.m.* **1.** *A:* confused mass, jumbled heap, jumble. **2.** series of somersaults.

cul-de-bouteille [kydbutɛj]. **1.** *a.inv.* bottle-green. **2.** *s.m.pl.* **culs-de-bouteille,** broken bottle-ends (on top of wall); **fenêtre en culs-de-bouteille,** bull's-eye window.

cul-de-chaudron [kydʃodrɔ̃], *s.m. Mil:* bottom of a mine crater; *pl. culs-de-chaudron.*

cul-de-four [kydfuːr], *s.m. Arch:* half dome (of apse); cul-de-four (of niche); *pl. culs-de-four.*

cul-de-jatte [kydʒat], *s.m.* legless cripple; *pl. culs-de-jatte.*

cul-de-lampe [kydlɑ̃ːp], *s.m.* **1.** *Arch:* (*a*) pendant, cul-de-lampe; (*b*) bracket, corbel. **2.** outside plate (of barrel lock). **3.** *Typ:* tail-piece, cul-de-lampe; *pl. culs-de-lampe.*

cul-de-plomb [kydplɔ̃], *s.m. P:* **1. c'est un c.-de-p.,** his bottom never leaves his chair, he just sits around all day, he just sits on his backside all day. **2.** clumsy fellow; *pl. culs-de plomb.*

cul-de-porc [kydpɔːr], *s.m.,* **cul-de-pot** [kydpo], *s.m. Nau:* wall knot, wale-knot; **c.-de-p. simple,** single wall knot; **c.-de-p. double,** double wall knot; *pl. culs-de-porc, culs-de-pot.*

cul-de-poule [kydpul], *s.m.* **1.** knob (of window bolt). **2.** *Nau:* **arrière en c.-de-p.,** rounded stern, counter stern. **3.** *Sm.a:* heel (of rifle-butt). **4.** *Dom.Ec:* (round-bottomed) mixing bowl; *pl. culs-de-poule.*

cul-de-sac [kydsak], *s.m.* **1.** blind alley, cul-de-sac; *Rail:* blind siding; *Nau:* inlet without issue; creek; *Geog:* blind valley; *Rail:* **quai en c.-de-s.,** bay; **votre emploi est un c.-de-s.,** your job is a blind alley, a dead end. **2.** *Anat:* caecum; cul-de-sac (of the vagina); **c.-de-s. de Douglas,** cul-de-sac, pouch, of Douglas; *pl. culs-de-sac.*

cul-doré [kydɔre], *s.m. Ent:* yellow-tail moth; *pl. culs-dorés.*

culdoscopie [kydɔskɔpi], *s.f. Med:* coelioscopy made via the posterior cul-de-sac of the vagina, culdoscopy.

-cule [kyl], *s.suff.* **1.** -cule, -cle; **animalcule,** *m.* animalcule. **2.** *Pej: with connecting vowel* **i; théâtricule,** *m.* small theatre; **principicule,** *m.* princeling.

culebutis [kylbyti], *s.m.* = CULBUTIS.

culée [kyle], *s.f.* **1.** butt (of hide). **2.** *Arch:* pier (of buttress); *Civ.E:* abutment(-pier) (of bridge). **3.** *Nau:* stern-way. **4.** *For:* tree stump (left after felling).

culement [kylmɑ̃], *s.m.* **1.** backing, going backwards (of cart, etc.). **2.** *Nau:* making stern-way, falling astern.

culer [kyle], *v.i.* **1.** (*a*) to go backwards, to back; (*b*) *Nau:* to make, gather, stern-way; to drop astern; **nagez à c.!** backwater! **brasser à c.,** to brace aback; **appareiller en culant,** to go out stern first. **2.** (*of wind*) to veer astern. **3.** *v.tr. Sch: F:* to bump (s.o.).

culeron [kylrɔ̃], *s.m. Harn:* crupper-loop, dock-piece.

culex [kylɛks], *s.m. Ent:* gnat, midge.

culicidés [kyliside], *s.m.pl. Ent:* Culicidae, mosquitoes and gnats.

culiciforme [kylisifɔrm], *a. Ent:* culiciform.

culicivore [kylisivɔːr], *a. Z:* gnat-eating, midge-eating.

culière[1] [kyljɛːr], *s.f. Harn:* crupper.

culière,[2] *s.f. Const:* channel stone, gutter stone.

culinaire [kylinɛːr], *a.* culinary.

culm [kylm], *s.m. Geol:* culm.

culmifère [kylmifɛːr], *a. Bot:* culmiferous, straw-bearing.

culminance [kylminɑ̃ːs], *s.f.* culmination, highest point.

culminant [kylminɑ̃], *a.* (*a*) *Astr:* culminant; (*b*) **point c.,** culminating, highest, point (of range of mountains, of one's fortunes, etc.); zenith (of power, etc.); height, climax, peak (of glory).

culmination [kylminasjɔ̃], *s.f.* (*a*) *Astr:* culmination, transit; **c. inférieure, c. supérieure,** lower, upper, culmination, transit; (*b*) summit, culminating point.

culminer [kylmine], *v.i.* (*of star, etc.*) to culminate, reach its highest point.

culot [kylo], *s.m.* **1.** (*a*) bottom, base (of lamp, etc.); punt, kick (of a bottle); (*b*) *Artil: Sm.a:* base (of cartridge-case, shell, etc.); head (of cartridge); **c. à chanfrein,** boat-tailed base (of bullet, shell, etc.); **c. conique,** tapered base (of shell); *Ball:* **pression de c.,** base pressure; (*c*) *El:* base, cap (of lamp, valve); **c. à baïonnette,** bayonet cap, base; **c. à contact unipolaire, à plot central,** single-contact bulb, single-contact type base; **c. à vis,** screw cap, base; *Elcs:* **c. adaptateur,** valve-adapter; (*d*) *I.C.E:* **c. de bougie,** body of sparking plug; **c. pour bougie,** sparking plug adaptor; (*e*) *F:* **avoir du c.,** to have plenty of cheek, nerve, *U.S:* gall; **eh bien, tu ne manques pas de c.!** well, you're a cool one! **il a un c. monstre,** he's got a hell of a (lot of) cheek; **alors je lui ai dit "oui," au c.,** "yes," I said, cool as you please; **y aller c.,** to bluff. **2.** (*a*) *Metall:* slag, residue (left in crucible); *Ch:* button; (*b*) dottle (in tobacco pipe); (*c*) *Geol:* plug (of volcano). **3.** baffle-plate, -brick (of furnace). **4.** *F:* (*a*) last chick hatched, last animal born (of litter); (*b*) baby of the family; (*c*) *Sch:* **c. (d'une promotion)** = wooden spoon.

culottage [kylɔtaːʒ], *s.m.* (*a*) colouring, seasoning, breaking in (of pipe); (*b*) *Art:* mellowing, darkening (of old pictures).

culotte [kylɔt], *s.f.* **1.** *Cu:* buttock, aitch bone (of beef). **2.** (*a*) **une c.,** *occ.* **des culottes,** (i) a pair of knee-breeches; (ii) a pair of knicker-bockers; (iii) *occ.* a pair of trousers; **c. courte,** (boy's) short trousers, shorts; **c. de cheval,** riding breeches; *O:* **c. de golf,** plus fours; **c. de peau,** (i) *A.Mil.Cost:* buckskins; (ii) *Pej: Mil:* officer of limited outlook, who doesn't see further than the end of his nose, colonel Blimp; *F:* **c'est la femme qui porte la c.,** it's the wife who wears the breeches, trousers, pants; *F:* **user ses fonds de c. sur les bancs de l'école,** to idle away one's time at school; *F:* **trembler,** *P:* **faire, dans sa c.,** to be scared stiff, to have the jitters, to have the wind up; *F:* **jouer ses culottes,** to stake all that one has, to put one's shirt on (a horse); (*b*) (woman's) briefs, panties. **3.** *Hyd.E: etc:* breeches pipe, Y pipe, breeching; *Mch:* **c. de cheminée,** uptake of a flue. **4.** *F:* **prendre une c.,** (i) to lose heavily, to come a cropper (at cards, etc.); (ii) to get drunk, tight.

culotté [kylɔte], **1.** (*a*) (*of pipe*) seasoned, broken in; (*b*) (*of old painting*) mellowed; (*c*) *F:* (*of book, etc.*) well-thumbed; rather the worse for wear. **2.** *F:* full of cheek, nerve; **il est c. comme tout,** he's got a, the, hell of a nerve.

culotter [kylɔte], *v.tr.* **1.** to put breeches, trousers, on (s.o.). **2.** (*a*) to colour, season; *F:* break in (a pipe); (*b*) (*of smoke, etc.*) to darken (paintwork, etc.). **3.** *Sch: F: A:* to swot up (a subject).

se culotter. **1.** to put on one's trousers, breeches. **2.** (*of painting*) to mellow; (*of pipe*) to colour, season. **3.** *P:* to get drunk, tight.

culotteur [kylɔtœːr], *s.m.* **c. de pipes,** great pipe smoker.

culottier, -ière [kylɔtje, -jɛːr], *s.* trousers maker; breeches maker.

culottin [kylɔtɛ̃], *s.m. A: F:* (little) boy wearing his first pair of trousers.

culpabilité [kylpabilite], *s.f.* culpability, culpableness, guiltiness, guilt; *Jur:* **nier sa c.,** to plead not guilty; **déclaration de c.,** verdict of guilty; *Psy:* **complexe de c.,** guilt complex.

cul-rousselet [kyruslɛ], *s.m. Orn: F:* redstart; *pl. culs-rousselets.*

culte [kylt], *s.m.* **1.** worship; **c. privé, public,** private, public, worship; **le c. divin,** divine worship; **le c. des héros,** hero worship; **avoir le c. du passé,** to make a fetish of the past; **avoir un c. pour qn; rendre, vouer, un (véritable) c. à qn,** to worship s.o.; **c. de la personnalité,** personality cult; **avoir le c. du drapeau, de la tradition,** to be devotedly attached to the flag, to tradition. **2.** form of worship, cult, creed; religion; **liberté du c.,** freedom, liberty, of worship; *P.N:* **c. protestant, 10 h.,** protestant service, 10 a.m. **3.** *Adm:* **les Cultes,** ecclesiastical matters, public worship.

cultellaire [kyltɛl(l)ɛːr], *a. Nat.Hist:* knife-shaped, cultrate.

cultellation [kyltɛlasjɔ̃], *s.f. Surv:* cultellation.

cultéranisme [kylteranism], *s.m. Lit:* cultism, gongorism.

cul-terreux [kytɛrø], *s.m. F: Pej:* clodhopper, *U.S:* redneck; *pl. culs-terreux.*
cultisme [kyltism], *s.m. Lit:* cultism, Gongorism.
cultiste [kyltist], *s.m. Lit:* cultist, cultorist, Gongorist.
cultivable [kyltivabl̥], *a.* cultivable; that can be cultivated; arable (land).
cultivar [kyltivaːr], *s.m. Bot:* cultivar, clone.
cultivateur, -trice [kyltivatœːr, -tris], *s.* **1.** agriculturist; farmer; **petits cultivateurs,** small farmers; smallholders; **c. de roses,** rosarian, rose-grower; *a.* **les peuples cultivateurs,** agricultural people, farming communities. **2.** *s.m.* **c. (canadien),** cultivator, light plough; **c. à disques lourd,** cover crop (*machine*).
cultivé [kyltive], *a.* **1.** cultivated (land, etc.); under cultivation. **2.** cultured (mind, etc.); well-read; **les gens cultivés,** cultured, educated, people.
cultiver [kyltive], *v.tr.* **1.** to cultivate, farm, till (the soil, etc.). **2.** to cultivate (plants, one's mind, etc.); to breed (oysters, etc.); **c. des céréales,** to cultivate, raise, grow, cereals; **c. son esprit,** to improve one's mind; **c. un goût, un don,** to develop a taste, a gift. **3. c. ses amis, l'amitié de qn,** to cultivate one's friends, s.o.'s friendship; **c'est une relation à c.,** it is a connection that should be cultivated, kept up; **c. la bienveillance de qn,** to keep s.o. sweet. **4.** to take an interest in (sth.); **c. les sciences,** to take up, study, devote oneself to, science; *F:* **c. la bouteille,** to take to drink.
se cultiver, to broaden one's mind; to deepen one's culture.
cultriforme [kyltrifɔrm], *a. Bot:* cultriform, cultrate.
cultrirostre [kyltrirɔstr̥], *a. Orn:* cultrirostral.
cultuel, -elle [kyltɥɛl]. **1.** *a.* of, pertaining to, worship; **formes cultuelles,** forms of worship; **édifice c.,** place of worship. **2.** *s.f.* **cultuelle,** church society.
cultural, -aux [kyltyral, -o], *a.* pertaining to agriculture, to farming; **procédés culturaux,** farming methods.
culture [kyltyːr], *s.f.* **1.** (*a*) cultivation, tilling (of the soil); **la grande, la petite, c.,** large-scale, small-scale, farming; **c. à sec, c. sèche,** dry farming; **c. sans sol,** hydroponics; **c. en courbes de niveau,** contour farming; **c. mécanique,** mechanized farming; **c. alterne, rotation de c.,** crop rotation, rotation of crops; **c. de rechange,** break crop; **c. de labour,** arable agriculture, culture; (*b*) *pl.* (i) land under cultivation; (ii) crops; **cultures associées,** companion crops; **cultures dérobées,** catch crops; **cultures fruitières,** fruit crops; **c. maraîchère,** market gardening, *U.S:* truck farming. **2.** cultivation, cultivating (of plants, of the mind); culture, rearing, breeding (of bees, fish, oysters, snails, etc.). **3.** *Biol: Bac:* culture (of tissue, bacteria, etc.); **tube à c.,** culture tube; **c. sur plaques,** plate culture; **bouillon de c.,** culture medium. **4.** (*a*) culture; education; **avoir une forte c.,** to be (highly) cultured; **c. générale, classique, technique,** general, classical, technical, education; **c. physique,** physical training, culture; **la c. scientifique de ce chercheur,** the scientific background of this research worker; *Adm:* **maison de c.** = arts centre; (*b*) **la c. gréco-romaine,** Graeco-Roman culture, civilization.
culturel, -elle [kyltyrɛl], *a.* cultural; educational; *Dipl:* **conseiller, attaché, c.,** cultural counsellor, attaché.
culturisme [kyltyrism], *s.m.* body building.
culturiste [kyltyrist], *a. & s.* body builder.
cumacés [kymase], *s.m.pl. Crust:* Cumacea.
cumberlandite [kœbɛrlɑ̃dit], *s.f. Miner:* cumberlandite.
cumbraïte [kœ̃brait], *s.f. Miner:* cumbraite.
cuméen, -enne [kymeɛ̃, -ɛn], *a. & s. A.Geog:* Cumaean.
cumène [kymɛn], *s.m. Ch:* cumene.
cumengéite [kymɛ̃ʒeit], *s.f. Miner:* cumengite.
Cumes [kym], *Pr.n.f. A.Geog:* Cumae.
cumidine [kymidin], *s.f. Ch:* cumidin(e).
cumin [kymɛ̃], *s.m. Bot:* cum(m)in; **c. bâtard,** wild cumin; **c. des prés,** caraway.
cuminique [kyminik], *a. Ch:* cuminic; cumic; **aldéhyde c.,** cumaldehyde.
cuminoïne [kyminɔin], *s.f. Ch:* cuminoin.
cummingtonite [kymiŋtɔnit], *s.f. Miner:* cummingtonite.
cumul [kymyl], *s.m.* (*a*) **c. de fonctions,** plurality of offices, pluralism: *Jur:* **c. des peines,** non-concurrence of sentences; (*b*) *Cmptr:* cumulative total; **c. des frais,** cumulative costs.
cumulard [kymylaːr], *s.m. F: Pej:* pluralist; holder of several (paid) jobs, *U.S: F:* moonlighter.
cumulatif, -ive [kymylatif, -iːv], *a.* cumulative (shares, etc.).
cumulation [kymylasjɔ̃], *s.f.* = CUMUL.
cumulativement [kymylativmɑ̃], *adv.* **1.** pluralistically. **2.** by accumulation, cumulatively. **3.** *Jur:* non-concurrently.
cumulé [kymyle], *a. Fin:* accrued (interest).
cumuler [kymyle], *v.tr.* **1.** *Jur:* to cumulate (proofs, etc.). **2. c. des fonctions,** to hold a plurality of offices; **c. deux traitements,** to draw two (separate) salaries; *abs.* **il cumule,** he has more than one job, *U.S: F:* he's a moonlighter.
cumulo-cirrus [kymylɔsirys], *s.m.inv. Meteor:* cumulo-cirrus.
cumulo-nimbus [kymylɔnɛ̃bys], *s.m.inv. Meteor:* cumulo(-)nimbus.
cumulo-stratus [kymylɔstratys], *s.m.inv. Meteor:* cumulo-stratus.
cumulo-volcan [kymylɔvɔlkɑ̃], *s.m.* cumulo-volcano; *pl. cumulo-volcans.*
cumulus[1] [kymylys], *s.m.inv. Meteor:* cumulus.
Cumulus[2], *Pr.n.m. R.t.m:* electric storage water heater.
cumyle [kymil], *s.m. Ch:* cumyl.
cunéaire [kyneɛːr], *a.* cuneate, wedge-shaped.
Cunégonde [kynegɔ̃ːd], *Pr.n.f.* Cunegonde.
cunéifolié [kyneifɔlje], *a. Bot:* with cuneate, wedge-shaped, leaves.
cunéiforme [kyneifɔrm]. **1.** *a.* (*a*) *Bot:* cuneate; wedge-shaped; arrow-headed; (*b*) *Anat:* cuneiform (bone); (*c*) **écriture c.,** cuneiform writing. **2.** *s.m.* (*a*) *Anat:* cuneiform (bone); (*b*) cuneiform (writing).
cunette [kynɛt], *s.f.* **1.** *Fort:* cunette. **2.** *Civ.E:* drain (of sewer); gutter (of road). **3.** *N.Arch:* waterway.
cuni(culi)culteur [kyni(kyli)kyltœːr], *s.m.* rabbit breeder.
cuni(culi)culture [kyni(kyli)kyltyːr], *s.f.* rabbit-breeding.
cuphæa [kyfea], *s.m. Bot:* cuphea.
cupide [kypid], *a.* covetous, greedy, grasping.
cupidement [kypidmɑ̃], *adv.* covetously, greedily.
cupidité [kypidite], *s.f.* cupidity, covetousness, greed; graspingness.
Cupidon [kypidɔ̃]. **1.** *Pr.n.m. Myth:* Cupid. **2.** *s.m.* (*a*) *Art:* cupid; (*b*) (i) handsome youth; *F:* glamour boy; (ii) ladies' man; (*c*) *Orn:* **c. des prairies,** prairie grouse, chicken, hen.
cuprate [kyprat], *s.m. Ch:* cuprate.
cuprène [kyprɛn], *s.m. Ch:* cuprene.
cupressacées [kyprɛsase], *s.f.pl. Bot:* Cupressaceae.
cupride [kyprid], *s.m. Ch:* cupride.
cuprifère [kyprifɛːr], *a.* cupriferous, copper-bearing.
cuprique [kyprik], *a.* cupric (acid).
cuprite [kyprit], *s.f. Miner:* cuprite, red copper.
cupritungstite [kypritœkstit], *s.f. Miner:* cuprotungstite.
cupro-alliage [kyprɔaljaːʒ], *s.m.* copper alloy.
cupro-aluminium [kyprɔalyminjɔm], *s.m.* aluminium bronze.
cuproammoniacal, -aux [kyprɔamɔnjakal, -o], *a. Ch:* cuproammoniacal; *Paperm:* **liqueur cuproammoniacale,** cuprammonium.
cuproammoniaque [kyprɔamɔnjak], *s.f. Ch:* cuprammonium, cupro-ammonia.
cuprodescloizite [kyprɔdeklwazit], *s.f. Miner:* cuprodescloizite.
cupromanganèse [kyprɔmɑ̃ganɛːz], *s.m.* cupro-manganese.
cupronickel [kyprɔnikɛl], *s.m. Ch:* cupronickel.
cuproscheelite [kyprɔʃelit], *s.f. Miner:* cuproscheelite.
cuprosilicium [kyprɔsilisjɔm], *s.m.* cuprosilicon.
cuproxyde [kyprɔksid], *s.m. Ch:* cuproxide, cupric oxide; *El:* **valve c.,** metal-oxide rectifying valve.
cupulaire [kypylɛːr], *a. Bot:* cupular, cup-shaped.
cupule [kypyl], *s.f.* **1.** (*a*) *Bot:* cupule, cupula; husk (of filbert, chestnut, etc.); cup (of acorn); (*b*) *Ent:* cupule; (*c*) *Ap:* (artificial) queen cell cup. **2.** (*a*) *Mec.E:* cupule cup; (*b*) *W.Tel:* **c. du cristal,** crystal cup; (*c*) *Elcs:* **c. de concentration, de focalisation,** concentrating, focusing, cup.
cupulé [kypyle], *a. Bot:* cupulate.
cupuliféracées [kypyliferase], *s.f. pl. Bot:* Cupuliferae.
cupulifère [kypylifɛːr], *Bot:* **1.** *a.* cupuliferous, cupule-bearing. **2.** *s.f.pl. A:* **cupulifères,** Cupuliferae.
cupuliforme [kypylifɔrm], *a. Bot:* cupuliform, cup-shaped.
curabilité [kyrabilite], *s.f.* curability (of disease).
curable [kyrabl̥], *a.* curable (disease, etc.).
curaçao [kyraso], *s.m.* curaçao (liqueur).
curage[1] [kyraːʒ], *s.m.* **1.** (*a*) picking (of the teeth, etc.); (*b*) clearing, cleaning out (of drain, harbour, etc.); flushing (of drain); (*c*) *Tex:* grassing (of flax). **2.** *pl.* refuse, dirt (from drains, etc.).
curage[2], *s.m. Bot:* water-pepper.
curaillon [kyrajɔ̃], *s.m. F: Pej:* (*a*) **petit c. de village,** petty parish priest; (*b*) young priest.
curare [kyraːr], *s.m.* curare.
curarine [kyrarin], *s.f. Ch: Med:* curarine.
curarisant [kyrarizɑ̃], *a.* curariform; having an effect similar to that of curare.
curarisation [kyrarizasjɔ̃], *s.f. Med:* curarization.
curariser [kyrarize], *v.tr.* to curarize; to administer curare (to animal).
curatelle [kyratɛl], *s.f. Jur:* trusteeship, guardianship.
curateur, -trice [kyratœːr, -tris], *s. Jur:* curator, curatrix; trustee (of vacant succession, etc.); guardian (of emancipated minor); committee (for lunatic); administrator, administratrix (appointed by court); **c. au ventre,** administrator to child unborn.
curatif, -ive [kyratif, -iːv], *a. & s.m.* curative.
curation [kyrasjɔ̃], *s.f. Med:* (course of) treatment; cure.
curculionidés [kyrkyljɔnide], *s.m.pl. Z:* Curculionidae.
curcuma [kyrkyma], *s.m. Bot:* curcuma, turmeric.
curcumine [kyrkymin], *s.f. Ch:* (*a*) curcumin; (*b*) curcumine.
cure [kyːr], *s.f.* **1.** care; *used only in* **n'avoir c. de,** not to care about, not to take any notice of. **2.** *R.C.Ch:* (*a*) cure of souls; office of a parish priest; **obtenir une c.,** to be appointed parish priest, to be appointed to a parish; (*b*) presbytery. **3.** *Med:* (*a*) (course of) treatment, cure; **c. d'air,** open-air cure; **c. de sommeil,** hypnotherapy; **c. thermale,** hydropathy, hydrotherapy; **c. d'amaigrissement,** slimming cure; **faire une c. de lait,** to go on a milk diet; **faire la c. à Vichy,** to take the cure, the waters, at Vichy; (*b*) *A:* (= GUÉRISON) cure, recovery.
curé [kyre], *s.m. R.C.Ch:* (i) parish priest; (ii) *F:* (any) priest; *F:* **les curés,** the clergy; **bonjour, Monsieur le C.,** good morning, Father; **il va se faire c.,** he's going in for the priesthood; *P:* **bouffer du c.,** to be (violently) anti-clerical; *Prov:* **quand il pleut sur le c. il dégoutte sur le vicaire,** you are bound to come in for your share of unpleasantness; *F:* **avoir affaire au c. et aux paroissiens,** to be between the devil and the deep sea.
cure-casserole(s) [kyrkasrɔl], *s.m.* pot scourer; *pl. cure-casseroles.*
cure-dent(s) [kyrdɑ̃], *s.m.* **1.** toothpick; *F:* **venir en c.-d.,** to be invited to coffee (after a dinner at which there have been other guests). **2.** *Mil: A: P:* bayonet; *pl. cure-dents.*
curée [kyre], *s.f.* (*a*) *Ven:* parts of the stag given to the hounds; *A:* quarry; **mettre les chiens en c., faire c.,** to flesh the hounds; **sonner la c.,** *A:* to blow the quarry; *A:* **faire c. de l'honneur de qn,** to tear s.o.'s reputation to pieces; (*b*) *F:* the rush for the spoils; the rat race; **être âpre à la c.,** to be on the make; **se ruer à la c., (des places),** to rush after the jobs (etc.); to join the rat race.
cure-feu [kyrfø], *s.m. Tls: Metall: etc:* poker, pricker; *pl. cure-feu(x).*
curement [kyrmɑ̃], *s.m.* = CURAGE[1] 1.
cure-môle [kyrmoːl], *s.m. Hyd.E:* dredger; *pl. cure-môles.*
cure-ongles [kyrɔ̃gl̥], *s.m.inv. Toil:* nail-cleaner.
cure-oreille [kyrɔrɛj], *s.m.* aural scoop; ear-pick; *pl. cure-oreilles.*
cure-pied [kyrpje], *s.m. Farr:* picker; *pl. cure-pieds.*
cure-pipe [kyrpip], *s.m.* pipe-cleaner; *pl. cure-pipes.*
curer [kyre]. **1.** *v.tr.* (*a*) to pick (one's teeth, etc.); **se c. les ongles,** to clean one's nails; (*b*) to clear, clean out (drain, harbour, etc.); to dredge (river, etc.); (*c*) to scrape (sth.) clean; (*d*) *Petroleum Ind:* **c. un puits,** to bail down; (*e*) *Tex:* to grass (flax); (*f*) *Vit:* **c. une vigne en pied,** to scrape the vine (of surplus wood). **2.** *v.i.* (*of bird of prey*) to seize the prey.
curetage [kyrtaːʒ], *s.m.* = CURETTAGE.
cureter [kyrte], *v.tr. Surg:* to curette.
cureton [kyrtɔ̃], *s.m. F: Pej:* (*a*) parish priest, curé; (*b*) young priest.

curettage [kyrɛta:ʒ], *s.m.* **1.** scraping; *Surg:* curetting, curettage; **c. utérin,** curetting of the womb; **faire le c. de l'utérus,** to curette the womb. **2.** *Town: P:* slum clearance.
curette [kyrɛt], *s.f.* scraper, cleaning tool; *Surg:* curette; *Min:* fluke, spoon (for boreholes).
curetter [kyrɛte], *v.tr. Surg:* to curette.
cureur [kyrœ:r], *s.m.* clearer, cleaner out (of drains, etc.).
Curiaces (les) [lekyrjas], *Pr.n.m.pl. Rom.Ant:* the Curiatii.
curial[1], **-iaux** [kyrjal, -jo], *a. Ecc:* relating to the parish, parochial; **maison curiale,** presbytery.
curial,[2] **curiate** [kyrjat], *a. Rom.Ant:* curial (assembly, etc.).
curie[1] [kyri], *s.f. Rom.Ant: R.C.Ch:* curia.
curie[2], *s.m. Rad.-A: Meas:* curie; **point de C.,** Curie point.
curiethérapie [kyriterapi], *s.f.* radiumtherapy, curietherapy.
curieusement [kyrjøzmɑ̃], *adv.* **1.** (*a*) interestedly, inquiringly; (*b*) curiously, inquisitively; (*c*) curiously, surprisingly. **2.** curiously, (i) *A:* delicately (engraved, worked, etc.); (ii) quaintly, oddly, peculiarly.
curieux, -ieuse [kyrjø, -jø:z], *a.* **1.** *A. & Lit:* (*of pers.*) (*a*) careful (de, of); meticulous; **éviter un soin trop c.,** to avoid being over-meticulous; **être c. de ses livres,** to take care of one's books; (*b*) inquiring (mind); interested (de, in); **c. de fleurs rares, de littérature,** interested in rare flowers, in literature. **2.** (*a*) curious, interested; **c. observateur des affaires contemporaines,** keen observer of contemporary affairs; **je serai c. de voir cela,** I shall be curious, interested, to see it; (*b*) curious, inquisitive; *F:* nosy; **c. des affaires d'autrui,** inquisitive about other people's business; **d'un caractère c.,** of a prying disposition; *s.* **un c., une curieuse,** (i) an interested person; (ii) a sightseer; **un attroupement de c.,** a crowd of interested spectators; **il était venu en c.,** he came as an observer; (iii) *s.m. P:* examining magistrate. **3.** (*of thg*) curious; (*a*) *A:* delicate, careful (workmanship, etc.); (*b*) odd, peculiar; **c'est c.,** that's odd; **chose curieuse à voir,** quaint, curious, odd, sight; **bêtes curieuses,** strange beasts; **ne me dévisage pas comme si j'étais une bête curieuse,** don't look at me as if I were a strange animal; **chose assez curieuse . . .,** curiously enough . . .; (*c*) *s.m.* **il est c. que** (+ *sub.*), it is curious, strange, odd, that . . .; **le c. de l'affaire est que . . .** (+ *ind.*), the odd part of the business, the odd thing about it, is that . . ..
curiosité [kyrjozite], *s.f.* curiosity. **1.** (*a*) interestedness; **c. pour les choses extraordinaires,** eager interest in unusual things; **c. d'esprit,** inquisitiveness of mind; **n'avez-vous jamais eu la c. de savoir qui vivait dans cette maison?** were you never curious enough to find out who lived in this house? (*b*) inquisitiveness; **par c.,** out of curiosity; (*c*) oddness, peculiarity, quaintness; **pour la c. du fait,** as a matter of curiosity. **2.** curio; interesting thing, sight; **collectionner des curiosités,** to collect curios; **magasin de curiosités,** curio shop; **visiter les curiosités de Paris,** to visit the sights of Paris; *F:* (*of pers.*) **lui, c'est une c.!** he's an odd type!
curiste [kyrist], *s.m. & f.* patient taking the cure, the waters (at a spa).
curium [kyrjɔm], *s.m. Ch:* curium.
curling [kœrliŋ], *s.m. Sp:* curling.
curlu [kyrly], *s.m. Orn: F:* curlew.
curriculum vitae [kyrikylɔmvite], *s.m.* curriculum vitae.
curry [kyri], *s.m.* curry.
curseur [kyrsœ:r], *s.m. Tchn:* cursor, slider, slide, runner, traveller (of mathematical or mechanical instrument); *Artil:* tangent scale; *El:* cursor, slider, slide (contact), *U.S:* sliding contact; *El:* **bobine à c.,** slider coil; **pont à c.,** slide bridge; *Sm.a.* **c. de hausse,** back sight slide; *Tls:* **calibre à c.,** sliding gauge; *Typewr:* **c. de marge,** marginal stop.
cursif, -ive [kyrsif, -i:v]. **1.** *a.* (*a*) cursive, running (handwriting); (*b*) cursory. **2.** *s.f.* **cursive;** cursive script, running hand; *Typ:* script (type).
cursivement [kyrsivmɑ̃], *adv.* **1.** cursively; in a running hand. **2.** cursorily.
curtirostre [kyrtirɔstr̥], *a. Orn:* brevirostrate, short-billed.
curule [kyryl], *a. Rom.Ant:* curule (chair, magistrate).
curure [kyry:r], *s.f. usu. pl.* dirt, mud, muck (from pond, drain).
curvatif, -ive [kyrvatif, -i:v], *a. Bot:* (leaf) with a tendency to curl.
curvation [kyrvasjɔ̃], *s.f.* curving; curvature.
curvi- [kyrvi], *pref.* curvi-; **curviforme,** curviform.
curvicaude [kyrviko:d], *a. Z:* curvicaudate, having a curved tail.
curvicaule [kyrviko:l], *a. Bot:* having a curved stem.
curvidenté [kyrvidɑ̃te], *a. Z:* curvidentate.
curvifolié [kyrvifɔlje], *a. Bot:* curvifoliate.
curviforme [kyrvifɔrm], *a.* curviform.
curvigraphe [kyrvigraf], *s.m. Mth:* curve tracer; curvograph.
curviligne [kyrviliɲ], *a.* curvilinear, curvilineal, rounded; **talus c.,** rounded bank.
curvimètre [kyrvimɛtr̥], *s.m. Surv:* curvometer.
curvinervé [kyrvinɛrve], *a. Bot:* curvinervate.
curvirostre [kyrvirɔstr̥], *a. Orn:* curvirostral.
cuscute [kyskyt], *s.f. Bot:* dodder; *F:* devil's-guts.
cuscuté [kyskyte], *a. Bot:* overgrown with dodder.
cuspide [kyspid], *s.f. Anat: Bot:* cusp; *Dent:* **c. secondaire,** supplemental cusp; **l'abrasion des cuspides,** cuspal wear.
cuspidé [kyspide], *a. Bot:* cuspidate.
cuspidifolié [kyspidifɔlje], *a. Bot:* with cuspidate leaves.
cuspidine [kyspidin], *s.f. Miner:* cuspidine.
cusseron [kysrɔ̃], **cusson** [kysɔ̃], *s.m. Ent:* pea weevil, bean weevil.
cussonné [kysɔne], *a.* (*of tree*) worm-eaten.
custode[1] [kystɔd], *s.m. Ecc:* (*in mendicant orders*) monk acting for the provincial.
custode[2], *s.f.* **1.** *Ecc:* (*a*) altar curtain; (*b*) pyx-cloth; (*c*) custodial (for the host, for relics). **2.** *Aut:* rear side panel (of car); **glace de c.,** fixed (*i.e. non-opening*) side window.
custodie [kystɔdi], *s.f. Ecc:* province (of mendicant order).
cutané [kytane], *a.* cutaneous; **maladies cutanées,** skin diseases.
cut-back [kœtbak], *s.m. Civ.E:* cut(-)back.
cuti [kyti], *s.f. Med. F:* cuti-reaction; **c. positive,** positive reaction to a skin test.
cuticole [kytikɔl], *a.* subcutaneous (parasite, etc.).
cuticulaire [kytikylɛ:r], *a.* cuticular, of the skin.
cuticule [kytikyl], *s.f.* cuticle, epidermis.
cuticuleux, -euse [kytikylø, -ø:z], *a.* skin-like, cuticular.
cutine [kytin], *s.f. Ch:* cutin.
cutinisation [kytinizasjɔ̃], *s.f. Bot:* cutinization.
cutiniser (se) [səkytinize], *v.pr. Bot:* to become cutinized, infiltrated with cutin.
cuti-pronostic [kytiprɔnɔstik], *s.m. Med:* prognosis based on cuti-reaction.
cuti-réaction [kytireaksjɔ̃], *s.f. Med:* cuti-reaction.
cutose [kyto:z], *s.f. Ch:* cutin.
cuvage [kyva:ʒ], *s.m.,* **cuvaison** [kyvɛzɔ̃], *s.f.* **1.** fermenting (of wine, beer) in vats. **2.** vat room.
cuve [ky:v], *s.f.* **1.** (*a*) vat, tun (for fermenting wine, etc.); **mettre le raisin en c.,** to vat the grapes; *Brew:* **c. matière,** mash tub, tun; (*of sparkling wine*) **produit en c. close,** produced under pressure, by injection; (*b*) (storage) tank; cistern; **c. à mazout,** oil (storage) tank; **c. à tanner,** tan(ning) pit; **c. à lessive,** (i) copper; (ii) (*in washing machine*) tub, drum; *Ch:* **c. à mercure,** mercury trough; *Phot:* **c. à lavage, à développement,** washing, developing, tank; *Paperm:* **papier à la c.,** hand-made, vat, paper; **ouvrier de c.,** dipper, vatman; *Ind:* **c. à chicanes,** baffle tank; **c. de décantation, de repos,** settling tank; **c. de filtration,** filtration tank; **c. à, sous, vide,** vacuum tank; (*c*) *I.C.E:* **c. (à niveau constant, de carburateur),** float chamber (of carburettor); (*d*) *El.E:* **c. électrolytique,** electrolytic vat, cell; **c. de transformateur,** transformer tank; **c. à câbles,** cable tank (of cable ship); (*e*) *Atom. Ph:* **c. de réacteur,** reactor vessel; **c. pour échantillons (radioactifs),** (radioactive) sample container; **c. sous pression,** pressure vessel; (*f*) *Engr:* **c. de morsure,** etching trough; (*g*) *Furn: A:* bath. **2.** *Metall:* shaft, tunnel (of blast furnace).
cuveau, -eaux [kyvo], *s.m.* small vat, tun, tank.
cuvée [kyve], *s.f.* (*a*) vatful, tunful; **vin de première c.,** wine of the first growth, cuvée; **tête de c. hors ligne,** grand first growth; **mettre des vins en c.,** to blend wines; **encore un conte de la même c.,** another story of the same kind, sort; (*b*) *P:* drinking bout.
cuvelage [kyvla:ʒ], *s.m.* lining, timbering, tubbing (of mine-shaft, etc.); lining (of borehole); casing (of well); *Const:* **fondations en c.,** floating foundations.
cuveler [kyvle], *v.tr.* (**je cuvelle, n. cuvelons; je cuvellerai**) to line, timber, tub (mine-shaft, etc.); to line (borehole); to case, consolidate (well).
cuvellement [kyvelmɑ̃], *s.m.* lining material (for mine-shaft, etc.).
cuver [kyve], **1.** *v.i.* (*of wine, beer*) to ferment, work (in the vats). **2.** *v.tr.* **c. du vin,** to work, ferment, wine; *F:* **c. son vin,** to sleep off the effects of wine, to sleep oneself sober; *F:* to sleep it off; **c. sa colère,** to work off one's rage, to simmer down.
cuverie [kyvri], *s.f. Winem:* fermenting room.
cuvette [kyvɛt], *s.f.* **1.** wash basin, (wash) bowl; *O:* **marbre à c.,** marble top (of washstand, etc.). **2.** dish, cup, bowl; pan (of W.C.); cup, cistern (of barometer); bulb (of thermometer); bowl (of compass); *Phot:* (developing) dish; *Watchm:* cap (of watch); *Const:* hopper head (of drain-pipe); rainwater head; *El:* (accumulator) tray; *Civ.E:* channel (of drainage canal, etc.); *Hort:* shallow basin (round tree, for watering); *Fort:* cunette; *Mec.E:* **c. (d'un roulement) à billes,** ball race; **c. de fixation,** retainer, retaining, cup; **c. d'égouttage,** drip cup, pan (of bearing); sump (of crank case); **c. de ressort,** spring seat; *I.C.E:* **c. de flotteur,** float chamber (of carburettor); *Sm.a:* **c. de tête mobile,** face of bolt head; **c. de fourreau de baïonnette,** bayonet scabbard mouthpiece; **en c.,** dished (cover, etc.); *Tls:* **meule en c.,** cup wheel. **3.** *Geol:* basin, depression; punchbowl; **c. à sel,** salt pan. **4.** *Mus:* pedestal (of harp).
cuvette-rotule [kyvɛtrɔtyl], *s.f. Mec.E:* ball-cup, ball-socket; *pl. cuvettes-rotules.*
cuvier [kyvje], *s.m.* (*a*) *A: Dial:* wash tub; (*b*) *Paperm:* vat; (*c*) *occ.* = CUVERIE.
cyame [sjam], **cyamus** [sjamys], *s.m. Crust:* cyamus, whale louse.
cyamélide [sjamelid], *s.f. Ch:* cyamelid(e).
cyan [sjɑ̃], *s.m. Phot:* cyan.
cyan-. *See* CYANO-.
cyanacétique [sjanasetik], *a. Ch:* cyanacetic, cyano-acetic.
cyanamide [sjanamid], *s.f. Ch:* cyanamide.
cyanate [sjanat], *s.m. Ch:* cyanate.
cyanées [sjane], *s.f.pl. Coel:* Cyanea.
cyanhydrine [sjanidrin], *s.f. Ch:* cyanhydrin, cyano-hydrine.
cyanhydrique [sjanidrik], *a. Ch:* **acide c.,** hydrocyanic acid; *F:* Prussic acid; hydrogen cyanide.
cyanidrose [sjanidro:z], *s.f.* cyanidrosis.
cyanine [sjanin], *s.f. Dy:* cyanin(e).
cyanique [sjanik], *a. Ch:* cyanic (acid).
cyaniser [sjanize], *v.tr. Ch:* to cyanize.
cyanite [sjanit], *s.m. Miner:* cyanite.
cyan(o)- [sjan(ɔ)], *comb.f.m. Ch:* cyan(o)-; **cyanamide,** cyanamide; **cyanhydrine,** cyanhydrin; **cyanofer,** ferrocyanogen; **cyanhydrique,** hydrocyanic.
cyanofer [sjanɔfɛ:r], *s.m. Ch:* ferrocyanogen.
cyanoferrate [sjanɔferat], *s.m. Ch:* ferrocyanide, ferrocyanate.
cyanoferrique [sjanɔferik], *a. Ch: A:* ferrocyanic (acid).
cyanogène [sjanɔʒɛn], *s.m. Ch:* cyanogen.
cyanogénèse [sjanɔʒenɛ:z], *s.f.* cyanogenesis.
cyanogénétique [sjanɔʒenetik], *a.* cyanogenetic.
cyanomètre [sjanɔmɛtr̥], *s.m. Meteor:* cyanometer.
cyanophycées [sjanɔfise], *s.f.pl. Algae:* Cyanophyceae.
cyanose [sjanɔ:z], *s.f.* **1.** *Miner:* cyanose, cyanosite, chalcanthite. **2.** *Med:* cyanosis.
cyanoser [sjanɔze], *v.tr. Med:* to cause, give (s.o.), cyanosis.
cyanotique [sjanɔtik], *a. Med:* cyanotic.
cyanotrichite [sjanɔtrikit], *s.f. Miner:* cyanotrichite.
cyanurage [sjanyra:ʒ], *s.m.* destroying (of pests, etc.) with cyanide, cyaniding.
cyanuration [sjanyrasjɔ̃], *s.f.* **1.** *Ch:* cyanization. **2.** *Goldmin:* cyanide process, cyanidation, cyaniding.
cyanure [sjany:r], *s.m. Ch:* cyanide.
cyanurer [sjanyre], *v.tr.* **1.** to cyanize, convert into cyanide. **2.** to cyanide (gold, etc.). **3.** to destroy (pests, etc.) with cyanide, to cyanide.
cyanurique [sjanyrik], *a. Ch:* cyanuric.
cyathacées [sjatase], **cyathéacées** [sjatease], *s.f.pl. Bot:* Cyatheaceae.
cyathe [sjat], *s.m.* **1.** *Gr.Ant:* cyathus. **2.** *Bot:* cyathus.
cyathophyllidés [sjatɔfilide], *s.m.pl. Paleont:* Cyathophyllidae.
Cybèle [sibɛl], *Pr.n.f. Gr.Myth:* Cybele.
cybernéticien, -ienne [sibɛrnetisjɛ̃, -jɛn], *s.* cyberneticist, cybernetician, cybernetics expert.
cybernétique [sibɛrnetik]. **1.** *s.f.* cybernetics. **2.** *a.* cybernetic.
cycadacées [sikadase], **cycadées** [sikade], *s.f.pl. Bot:* Cycadaceae.
cycadales [sikadal], *s.f.pl. Bot:* Cycadales.

cycadophytes [sikadɔfit], *s.f.pl. Bot: Paleont:* Cycadophyta.

cycas [sikɑːs], *s.m. Bot:* cycas; cycad.

cyclable [siklabl̥], *a.* **piste c.,** cycle track.

cyclade [siklad], *s.m. Moll:* sphaerium.

Cyclades (les) [lesiklad], *Pr.n.f.pl. Geog:* the Cyclades.

cyclage [siklaːʒ], *s.m. Tchn:* cycling.

cyclamen [siklamɛn]. **1.** *s.m. Bot:* cyclamen. **2.** *a.inv.* cyclamen (-coloured).

cyclamine [siklamin], *s.f. Ch:* (*a*) cyclamin; (*b*) cyclamine.

cyclane [siklan], *s.m. Ch:* cyclane.

cyclanthacées [siklɑ̃tase], *s.f.pl. Bot:* Cyclanthaceae.

cyclas [siklas], *s.f. Ant: Cost:* cyclas.

cycle [sikl̥], *s.m.* **1.** cycle (of events, poems, etc.); series (of lectures, etc.); **durée du c.,** cyclic period, operating time; **c. infernal,** vicious spiral; *Astr:* **c. lunaire,** lunar cycle, Metonic cycle; **c. solaire,** solar cycle; *Pol.Ec:* **c. économique,** business, trade, cycle; *Lit:* **le cycle d'Arthur,** the Arthurian cycle; *Geog:* **c. d'érosion,** cycle of erosion; *Ch:* **c. de l'azote, du carbone,** nitrogen, carbon, cycle; *Atom.Ph:* **c. de réaction,** reaction cycle; **c. de régénération, de surgénération,** breeding cycle; **c. du combustible,** fuel cycle; **c. de Bethe, de carbone-azote,** Bethe cycle, carbon-nitrogen cycle; *Elcs:* **compteur de cycles,** cycle-rate counter (of radar); *Magn:* **c. d'aimantation,** hysteresis cycle; *Med:* **c. cardiaque,** cardiac cycle; **c. menstruel,** menstrual cycle; *Sch:* **enseignement du premier c.,** first stage of secondary education; **enseignement du second c.,** second stage in secondary education. **2.** *Veh:* cycle; *F:* **le c.,** cycling; **fabricant de cycles,** cycle manufacturer.

cyclecar [siklɛkaːr], *s.m.* cycle-car.

cyclène [siklɛn], *s.m. Ch:* cyclene.

cycler [sikle], *v.i. A:* to cycle, ride a cycle.

cyclide [siklid], *s.f. Mth:* cyclide.

cyclique [siklik], *a.* cyclic(al); recurrent, recurring; *Ch:* **composés cycliques,** ring compounds.

cyclisation [siklizasjɔ̃], *s.f. Ch:* cyclization.

cyclisme [siklism], *s.m. Sp:* cycling.

cycliste [siklist]. **1.** *s.m. & f.* cyclist. **2.** *a.* cycling (race, etc.).

cyclite [siklit], *s.f. Med:* cyclitis.

cyclo- [siklɔ], *pref.* cyclo-; **cyclocéphale,** cyclocephalous.

cyclobutane [siklɔbytan], *s.m. Ch:* cyclobutane.

cyclocéphale [siklɔsefal], *a. & s.m. Ter:* cyclocephalous (monster).

cyclo-cross [siklokrɔs], *s.m. Sp:* cyclo-cross; *F:* rough stuff.

cyclographe [siklɔgraf], *s.m. Mth:* arcograph, cyclograph.

cycloheptane [siklɔɛptan], *s.m. Ch:* cycloheptane.

cyclohexane [siklɔɛksan], *s.m. Ch:* cyclohexane.

cyclohexanol [siklɔɛksanɔl], *s.m. Ch:* cyclohexanol.

cyclohexanone [siklɔɛksanɔn], *s.f. Ch:* cyclohexanone.

cyclohexène [siklɔɛksɛn], *s.m. Ch:* cyclohexene.

cyclohexyle [siklɔɛksil], *s.m. Ch:* cyclohexyl.

cycloïdal, -aux [siklɔidal, -o], *a. Mth:* cycloidal (curve, pendulum, etc.).

cycloïde [siklɔid], *s.f.* **1.** *Mth:* cycloid; **c. allongée,** prolate cycloid; **c. raccourcie,** curtate cycloid. **2.** *Clockm:* **horloge à c.,** clock with cycloidal pendulum. **3.** *attrib. Ich:* **écailles cycloïdes,** cycloid scales.

cyclomètre [siklɔmɛtr̥], *s.m.* cyclometer, curve measurer.

cyclométrie [siklɔmetri], *s.f.* cyclometry.

cyclomoteur [siklɔmɔtœːr], *s.m.* auto-cycle, moped.

cyclomotoriste [siklɔmɔtɔrist], *s.m. & f.* auto-cycle rider.

cyclonal, -aux [siklɔnal, -o], *a. Meteor:* cyclonic; cyclonal.

cyclone [sikloːn], *s.m.* **1.** *Meteor:* cyclone; **œil de c.,** centre of cyclone. **2.** *Tchn:* **(séparateur à) c.,** cyclone (separator).

cycloner [siklɔne], *v.tr. Min:* to pass through a cyclone separator.

cyclonique [siklɔnik], *a. Meteor:* cyclonic.

cyclonite [siklɔnit], *s.f. Expl:* cyclonite.

cyclope [siklɔp], *s.m.* **1.** (*a*) *Gr.Myth: Crust:* cyclops; (*b*) *F:* one-eyed man; (*c*) **travail de c.,** colossal undertaking. **2.** *Z:* Cyclopes, two-toed anteater.

cyclopéen, -enne [siklɔpeɛ̃, -ɛn], *a.* (*a*) *Archeol:* Cyclopean (wall, etc.); *Civ.E:* **béton c.,** cyclopean concrete; (*b*) gigantic; colossal.

cyclopentadiène [siklɔpɛ̃tadjɛn], *s.m. Ch:* cyclopentadiene.

cyclopentane [siklɔpɛ̃tan], *s.m. Ch:* cyclopentane.

cyclopentanone [siklɔpɛ̃tanɔn], *s.f. Ch:* cyclopentanone.

cyclopentène [siklɔpɛ̃tɛn], *s.m. Ch:* cyclopentene.

cyclophrénie [siklɔfreni], *s.f. Med:* cyclophrenia.

cyclopie [siklɔpi], *s.f. Ter:* cyclopia.

cycloplégie [siklɔpleʒi], *s.f. Med:* cycloplegia.

cyclo-pousse [siklɔpus], *s.m.* trishaw, pedicab, cycle rickshaw.

cyclopropane [siklɔprɔpan], *s.m. Ch:* cyclopropane.

cyclops [siklɔp(s)], *s.m. Crust:* cyclops.

cycloptère [siklɔptɛːr], *s.m. Ich:* cyclopteroid.

cyclorama [siklɔrama], *s.m. Th:* cyclorama.

cyclorhaphes [siklɔraf], *s.m.pl. Ent:* Cyclorrhapha.

cyclostomates [siklɔstɔmat], *s.m.pl. Z: Paleont:* Cyclostomata.

cyclostome [siklɔstɔm], *s.m. Z:* cyclostome; *pl.* **les cyclostomes,** the Cyclostomata; the lampreys.

cyclothyme [siklɔtim], *s.m. & f. Med:* cyclothyme.

cyclothymie [siklɔtimi], *s.f. Med:* cyclothymia.

cyclothymique [siklɔtimik], *a. Med:* cyclothymic.

cyclotornides [siklɔtɔrnid], *s.m.pl. Ent:* Cyclotornidae.

cyclotourisme [siklɔturism], *s.m.* touring on bicycles.

cyclotouriste [siklɔturist], *s.m. & f.* cycling tourist.

cyclotron [siklɔtrɔ̃], *s.m. Atom.Ph:* cyclotron; **faisceau du c.,** cyclotron beam.

cycnoche, cycnoque [siknɔk], *s.m. Bot:* cycnoches; swan-neck, swan-flower; swan orchid.

cycnoïde [siknɔid], *a.* swan-like.

cygne [siɲ], *s.m.* (*a*) swan; **jeune c.,** cygnet; **c. mâle,** cob; **c. femelle,** pen; **c. chanteur, sauvage,** whooper swan; **c. de Bewick, c. nain,** Bewick's swan; **c. muet, tuberculé,** mute swan; **duvet de c.,** swansdown; **chant du c.,** swan song; **faire un c. d'un oison,** to consider (all) one's geese swans; (*b*) *Mec.E:* **cou, col, de c.,** swan neck; **en col de c.,** swan-necked.

cylindrage [silɛ̃draːʒ], *s.m.* **1.** rolling (of roads, gardens, steel, etc.); *P.N:* **c.,** steam roller at work. **2.** *Tex:* calendering, mangling (of cloth); *Mch.Tls:* cylindrical turning; *Metall:* **c. à froid,** cold rolling.

cylindraxe [silɛ̃draks], *s.m. Anat:* axis-cylinder (of nerve).

cylindre [silɛ̃ːdr̥], *s.m.* **1.** *Geom:* cylinder; **c. droit,** right cylinder; **c. de révolution,** cylinder of revolution. **2.** *Tchn:* cylinder, drum; barrel (of pump); (*a*) *Mch: I.C.E:* **c. de piston,** piston cylinder; **alésage du c.,** cylinder bore; **bloc cylindres,** cylinder block; **chemise de c.,** cylinder sleeve; **jeu de c.,** piston clearance; **moteur à quatre cylindres,** four-cylinder engine; *F:* **une quatre cylindres,** a four-cylinder car; *Clockm:* **échappement à c.,** cylinder escapement; *Ind:* **cylindres sécheurs,** (hot) drying cylinders; (*b*) *Typ:* **presse (d'imprimerie) à cylindre(s),** cylinder-press; **c. de blanchet,** blanket-cylinder; **c. d'impression, c. imprimeur,** printing cylinder, drum; **c. de plaque,** plate cylinder; **c. habillé,** packed cylinder; **habillement de c.,** cylinder packing; (*c*) *Mus:* **c. noté,** barrel (of barrel organ); **cylindres (d'un instrument à cuivre),** cylinders, rotary valves (of a brass instrument); *Nau:* **c. (de signalisation),** (signal) drum; **c. de tempête,** storm drum; (*d*) *Rel:* **c. à prières,** prayer mill, prayer wheel; (*e*) *Archeol:* **c.(-sceau),** cylinder seal; (*f*) roller, roll (of rolling mill, mangle, calender, etc.); **c. à tôle,** plate roller; **c. dégrossisseur, ébaucheur,** roughing roller, cylinder; **c. étireur,** drawing roller; **c. compresseur,** (i) *Metalw: etc:* (rotary) squeezer; (ii) road roller; (iii) lawn roller; *Paperm:* **c. porte-lames, c. travailleur,** beater roll; **c. enrouleur,** winding drum; (*g*) *Furn:* **bureau à c.,** roll-top desk. **3.** *Bot:* **c. central,** stele.

cylindrée [silɛ̃dre], *s.f. Mch: I.C.E:* **1.** cubic capacity (of cylinder, engine); piston displacement; **(voiture) de grosse, de petite, c.,** (car) with a large engine, a small engine. **2.** cylinderful; cylinder charge; *I.C.E:* charge (of explosive mixture).

cylindre-enveloppe [silɛ̃drɑ̃vlɔp], *s.m. Ind: etc:* steam-jacket; *pl. cylindres-enveloppes.*

cylindre-équerre [silɛ̃drekɛːr], *s.f.* cylindrical slide; *pl. cylindres-équerres.*

cylindrer [silɛ̃dre], *v.tr.* **1.** to roll (road, lawn, metal, etc.); to roll down (surfacing of road, etc.). **2.** *Tex:* to calender, mangle (cloth).

cylindre-sceau [silɛ̃drəso], *s.m.* cylinder seal; *pl. cylindres-sceaux.*

cylindreur, -euse [silɛ̃drœːr, -øːz], *s.* **1.** *Civ.E: etc:* man in charge of roller, roller-man. **2.** *Tex:* calender-man, mangler.

cylindricité [silɛ̃drisite], *s.f.* cylindricity.

cylindriforme [silɛ̃drifɔrm], *a.* cylindriform, cylindrical.

cylindrique [silɛ̃drik], *a.* cylindrical.

cylindrite [silɛ̃drit], *s.f. Miner:* cylindrite.

cylindro-conique [silɛ̃drɔkɔnik], *a.* cylindro-conical; *Sm.a:* **plomb c.-c.,** slug; **cartouche c.-c.,** cartridge with pointed end; *pl. cylindro-coniques.*

cylindroïde [silɛ̃drɔid], *a.* cylindroid, cylinder-shaped.

cylindro-ogival [silɛ̃drɔɔʒival], *a.* cylindro-ogival; **cartouche c.-ogivale,** cartridge with rounded end; *pl. cylindro-ogivaux.*

cylindrurie [silɛ̃dryri], *s.f. Med:* cylindruria.

cymaise [simɛːz], *s.f. Arch:* cyma, moulding, dado.

cymbalaire [sɛ̃balɛːr], *s.f. Bot:* ivy-leaved toad-flax; mother-of-thousands.

cymbale [sɛ̃bal], *s.f. Mus:* cymbal.

cymbalier [sɛ̃balje], **cymbaliste** [sɛ̃balist], *s.m.* cymbal-player, cymbalist.

cymbalum [sɛ̃balɔm], *s.m. Mus:* cimbalom, cymbalom, cymbalo.

cymbiforme [sɛ̃bifɔrm], *a. Nat.Hist:* cymbiform.

cyme [sim], *s.f. Bot:* cyme.

cymène [simɛn], *s.m. Ch:* cymene.

cymomètre [simɔmɛtr̥], *s.m. W.Tel:* cymometer, wave-meter.

cymophane [simɔfan], *s.f. Miner:* cymophane.

cymoscope [simɔskɔp], *s.m. El:* cymoscope.

cymothoé [simɔtɔe], *s.m. Crust:* sea-louse.

cymrique [simrik], *a.* Cymric.

cynanche [sinɑ̃ːʃ], **cynanchum** [sinɑ̃kɔm], **cynanque** [sinɑ̃ːk], *s.m. Bot:* cynanchum.

cynégétique [sineʒetik]. **1.** *a.* cynegetic. **2.** *s.f.* cynegetics, hunting.

cynipidés [sinipide], *s.m.pl. Ent:* Cynipidae.

cynips [sinips], *s.m. Ent:* cynips; *F:* gall-wasp, -fly.

cynique [sinik]. **1.** *a.* (*a*) cynic(al) (philosophy, etc.); *Med:* **spasme c.,** cynic spasm; (*b*) shameless (morals); brazen (insolence); unblushing (indecency); bare-faced (lie); **il fut assez c. pour . . .,** he had the calm audacity to . . .. **2.** *s.m.* (*a*) cynic; (*b*) shameless, brazen, person.

cyniquement [sinikmɑ̃], *adv.* cynically; shamelessly, brazenly, unblushingly.

cynisme [sinism], *s.m.* **1.** *Phil:* cynicism. **2.** shamelessness, effrontery.

cynocéphale [sinɔsefal]. **1.** *a.* cynocephalous, dog-headed. **2.** *s.m. Z:* cynocephalus; *F:* dog-faced baboon. **3.** *Pr.n.f.pl. A.Geog:* **les Cynocéphales,** (the) Cynoscephalae (mountains).

cynodon [sinɔdɔ̃], *s.m. Bot:* cynodon, Bermuda grass.

cynodontes [sinɔdɔ̃ːt], *s.m.pl. Paleont:* Cynodontia.

cynodrome [sinodroːm], *s.m.* greyhound, *F:* dog, racing-track.

cynoglosse [sinɔglɔs], *s.f.,* **cynoglossum** [sinɔglɔsɔm], *s.m. Bot:* cynoglossum; *F:* hound's-tongue.

cynophile [sinɔfil], *s.m. & f.* dog lover; *a. Mil:* **unité, équipe, peloton, c.,** dog-training, -handling, unit.

cynor(r)hodon [sinɔrɔdɔ̃], *s.m. Bot:* hip, hep; *Pharm:* **sirop de c.,** rose-hip syrup.

Cynoscéphales (les) [lesinɔsefal], *Pr.n.f.pl. A. Geog:* (the) Cynoscephalae (mountains).

cynosure [sinɔzyːr], *s.f.* **1.** *Astr:* cynosure, Little Bear. **2.** *Bot:* Cynosurus; *F:* dog's-tail grass.

cynotechnique [sinɔtɛknik], *a. Mil:* relative to use of dogs.

cyon [sjɔ̃], *s.m. Z:* cuon, Asian wild dog.

cypéracées [siperase], *s.f.pl Bot:* Cyperaceae, the sedge family.

cyphoscoliose [sifɔskɔljoːz], *s.f. Med:* cyphoscoliosis.

cyphose [sifoːz], *s.f. Med:* cyphosis, kyphosis.

cyphotique [sifɔtik], *a. Med:* kyphotic.

cyprès [siprɛ], *s.m. Bot:* cypress (tree); **c. chauve,** bald, black, cypress.

Cyprien [sipriɛ̃], *Pr.n.m.* Cyprian.

cyprière [sipriɛːr], *s.f.* cypress plantation, grove.

cyprin [siprɛ̃], *s.m. Ich:* Cyprinus; (fish of) carp (family); **c. doré,** goldfish; **c. à queue de voile,** veiltail.

cyprinide [siprinid], *Ich:* **1.** *a.* cyprinid (fish). **2.** *s.* cyprinid; member of the family Cyprinidae.

cyprinidé [sipriníde], *s.m. Ich:* cyprinid; *pl.* **les cyprinidés,** the Cyprinidae.

cyprinodontes [siprinɔdɔ̃ːt], **cyprinodontidés** [siprinɔdɔ̃tide], *s.m.pl. Ich:* Cyprinodontidae. Microcyprini.

cypriote [sipriɔt], *a. & s. Geog:* Cypriot.

cypripède [sipripɛd], *s.m. Bot:* Cypripedium; *F:* lady's slipper.

cypripédiées [sipripedje], *s.f.pl. Bot:* Cypripedieae.

Cypris [sipris]. 1. *Pr.n.f. A.Lit:* Cypris, Cyprian Venus. 2. *s.f. Crust:* Cypris; *F:* water-flea.

Cyrard [sira:r], *s.m. F:* = SAINT-CYRIEN.

Cyrénaïque [sirenaik]. 1. *Pr.n.f. A.Geog:* Cyrenaica. 2. *a. & s.* (a) Cyrenian; (b) *Hist. of Phil:* Cyrenaic.

Cyrène [sirɛn], *Pr.n.f. A.Geog:* Cyrene.

cyrénéen, -enne [sireneɛ̃, -ɛn], *a. & s. A.Geog:* Cyrenian.

Cyrille [siril], *Pr.n.m.* Cyril.

cyrillien, -ienne [siriljɛ̃, -jen], **cyrillique** [siril(l)ik], *a.* Cyrillic (alphabet, etc.).

Cyropédie (la) [lasirɔpedi], *s.f. Gr.Lit:* the Cyropaedia.

cyrtomètre [sirtɔmɛtr̩], *s.m.* cyrtometer.

cyst-, cysti-, cysto- [sist, sisti, sistɔ], *pref.* cyst-, cysti-, cysto-; **cysthépatique**, cysthepatic; **cystirrhée**, cystirrhoea.

cystalgie [sistalʒi], *s.f. Med:* cystalgia.

cystectomie [sistɛktɔmi], *s.f. Surg:* cystectomy.

cystéine [sistein], *s.f. Ch:* cysteine.

cysthépatique [sistepɔtik], *a. Med:* cysthepatic.

cysticerque [sistisɛrk], *s.m. Z:* cysticercus; *F:* bladder-worm.

cysticercose [sistisɛrko:z], *s.f. Med:* cysticercosis.

cystidés [sistide], *s.m.pl. Paleont:* Cystoidea.

cystine [sistin], *s.f. Ch:* cystin(e).

cystinurie [sistinyri], *s.f. Med:* cystinuria.

cystique [sistik], *a.* 1. *Anat: Med:* cystic (duct, calculus, etc.). 2. *Z:* cystic, encysted; **ver c.,** cystic worm, bladder-worm.

cystirrhée [sistire], *s.f. Med:* cystirrh(o)ea, cystorrhea.

cystite [sistit], *s.f. Med:* cystitis, inflammation of the bladder.

cystocarpe [sistɔkarp], *s.m. Bot:* cystocarp.

cystocèle [sistɔsɛl], *s.f. Med:* cystocele, hernia of the bladder.

cystodynie [sistɔdini], *s.f. Med:* cystodynia.

cystographie [sistɔgrafi], *s.f. Med:* cystography.

cystoïde [sistɔid]. 1. *a.* cystoid. 2. *s.m.pl. Paleont:* Cystoidea.

cystolithe [sistɔlit], *s.m.* 1. *Bot:* cystolith. 2. *Med:* cystolith, urinary calculus; *F:* stone.

cystoplastie [sistɔplasti], *s.f. Surg:* cystoplasty.

cystoscope [sistɔskɔp], *s.m. Med:* cystoscope.

cystoscopie [sistɔskɔpi], *s.f. Med:* cystoscopy.

cystostomie [sistɔstɔmi], *s.f. Med:* cystostomy.

cystotome [sistɔtɔm], *s.m. Surg:* cystotome.

cystotomie [sistɔtɔmi], *s.f. Surg:* cystotomy.

cytase [sita:z], *s.f. Ch:* cytase.

cyte [sit], *s.m. or f. Biol:* cyte.

Cythère [sitɛ:r], *Pr.n.f. A.Geog:* Cythera.

cytise [siti:z], *s.m. Bot:* 1. cytisus. 2. laburnum; **c. des Alpes,** Alpine laburnum.

cyto- [sitɔ], *pref.* cyto-; **cytothèque**, cytotheca.

cytoblaste [sitɔblast], *s.m. Biol:* cytoblast.

cytochimie [sitɔʃimi], *s.f.* cytochemistry.

cytochrome [sitɔkro:m], *s.m. Biol: Ch:* cytochrome.

cytode [sitɔd], *s.m. Biol:* cytode.

cytodiagnostic [sitɔdjagnɔstik], *s.m. Med:* cytodiagnosis.

cytogénétique [sitɔʒenetik], *a.* cytogenetic.

cytogénie [sitɔʒeni], *s.f. Biol:* cytogenesis.

cytogène [sitɔʒen], *a. Biol:* cytogenous.

cytogénie [sitɔʒeni], *s.f. Biol:* cytogenesis.

cytologie [sitɔlɔʒi], *s.f. Biol:* cytology.

cytologiste [sitɔlɔʒist], *s.m. & f.* cytologist.

cytolyse [sitɔliz], *s.f. Physiol:* cytolysis.

cytopharynx [sitɔfarɛ̃ks], *s.m. Z:* cytopharynx.

cytoplasma [sitɔplasma], **cytoplasme** [sitɔplasm], *s.m. Biol:* cytoplasm.

cytoprocte [sitɔprɔkt], *s.m. Z:* cytoproct.

cytosine [sitɔzin], *s.f. Ch:* cytosine.

cytostome [sitɔstɔm], *s.m. Z:* cytostome.

cytothèque [sitɔtɛk], *s.f. Ent:* cytotheca.

cytotoxine [sitɔtɔksin], *s.f.* cytotoxin(e).

cytotoxique [sitɔtɔksik], *a.* cytotoxic.

cytotropisme [sitɔtrɔpism], *s.m. Biol:* cytotropism.

cytozoaire [sitɔzɔɛ:r], *s.m. Prot:* cytozoon; *pl.* cytozoa.

cyzicénien, -ienne [sizisenjɛ̃, -jen], *a. & s. A.Geog:* Cyzicene.

Cyzique [sizik], *Pr.n. A.Geog:* Cyzicus.

Czar [tsa:r, dza:r], *s.m.,* Czarévitch, Czaréwitch [tsarevitʃ, dzarevitʃ], *s.m.,* Czarine [tsarin, dzarin], *s.f.* = TSAR, TSARÉVITCH, TSARINE.

czardas [tsardaʃ], *s.m. Mus:* (Hungarian) czardas, csardas.

czimbalum [sɛ̃balɔm], *s.m. Mus:* cimbalom, cymbalom, cymbalo.

D

D, d [de], *s.m.* (the letter) D, d; *Tp:* **D comme Désiré**, D for David; *F:* **le système D** (= **débrouille-toi**), resourcefulness, wangling; **employer le système D**, to wangle; *Mec.E:* **tiroir en D**, D-valve.

da, *A:* **dà** [da], *int. F:* (*intensive after* **oui**) **oui-d.**, yes, indeed! yes, of course!

dab(e) [dɑːb], *s.m. P:* (a) *A:* pa, pop, the old man; **mes dabs**, my, the, parents, the old people; (b) the boss.

dabesse [dabɛs], *s.f. P:* (a) ma, mum; (b) the boss; (*said by charwoman*) the lady I oblige, my lady.

daboia [dabɔja], *s.m. Rept:* daboia, daboya, Russell's viper.

d'abord [dabɔːr], *adv.phr.* See ABORD.

dac, d'ac [dak], *int. F:* O.K.

dace [das], *a. & s.m. & f. A.Hist:* Dacian.

dache [daʃ], *s.m. P:* **envoyer qn à d.**, to send s.o. packing; **il est parti à d.**, he's gone off into the blue; **va(-t'en) à d., va le dire à d.**, go to the devil! go to blazes!

dachshund [daksund], *s.m.* dachshund.

Dacie [dasi], *Pr.n.f. A.Geog:* Dacia.

dacique [dasik], *a. A.Hist:* Dacian.

dacite [dasit], *s.f. Miner:* dacite.

dacitique [dasitik], *a. Geol:* dacitic.

dacoït [dakɔit], *s.m. Hist:* dacoit.

dacquois, -oise [dakwa, -waːz], *a. & s. Geog:* (native) of Dax.

Dacron [dakrɔ̃], *s.m. R.t.m: Tex:* Dacron.

dacryadénite [dakriadenit], *s.f. Med:* dacryadenitis.

dacryde [dakrid], **dacrydion** [dakridjɔ̃], *s.f. Bot:* dacrydium.

dacryoadénite [dakriɔadenit], *s.f. Med:* dacryoadenitis.

dacryocystectomie [dakriɔsistɛktɔmi], *s.f. Surg:* dacryocystectomy.

dacryocystite [dakriɔsistit], *s.f. Med:* dacryocystitis.

dacryogène [dakriɔʒɛn], *a. Physiol:* tear-producing.

dacryolithe [dakriɔlit], *s.m. Med:* dacryolith.

dacryon [dakriɔ̃], *s.m. Anat:* dacryon.

dacryops [dakriɔps], *s.m. Med:* dacryops.

dactyle [daktil], *s.m. 1. Pros:* dactyl. **2.** *Bot:* dactylis; **d. pelotonné**, orchard-grass, cock's-foot.

dactylé [daktile], *a. Nat.Hist:* dactylate.

dactyliographie [daktiljɔgrafi], *s.f. Archeol:* dactyliography.

dactyliologie [daktiljɔlɔʒi], *s.f. Archeol:* dactyliology.

dactyliomancie [daktiljɔmɑ̃si], *s.f.* dactyliomancy.

dactylion [daktiljɔ̃], *s.m. 1. Mus:* dactylion. **2.** *Z: Anat:* syndactyly.

dactyliothèque [daktiljɔtɛk], *s.f. Archeol:* dactyliotheca.

dactylique [daktilik], *a. Pros:* dactylic.

dactylite [daktilit], *s.f. Med:* dactylitis.

dactylo [daktilo], (a) *s.f.* (*may be applied to a man*) typist; (b) *s.f.* typing; **il est bon à la d.**, he's good at typing; (c) *s.m. Fr.C:* typewriter.

dactylo-facturière [daktilofaktyrjɛːr], *s.f.* typist invoice-clerk; *pl.* **dactylos-facturières**.

dactylogramme [daktilɔgram], *s.m.* dactylogram, fingerprint.

dactylographe [daktilɔgraf], *A:* **1.** *s.m.* typewriter. **2.** *s.m. & f.* typist.

dactylographie [daktilɔgrafi], *s.f.* **1.** typing, typewriting. **2.** touch method of communication with a blind deaf-mute.

dactylographier [daktilɔgrafje], *v.tr.* (*pr.sub. & p.d.* n. **dactylographiions**, v. **dactylographiiez**) to type(write); **document dactylographié**, typed, typewritten, document.

dactylographique [daktilɔgrafik], *a.* typing (material); **exercices dactylographiques**, typing exercises.

dactyloïde [daktilɔid], *a.* dactyloid.

dactylologie [daktilɔlɔʒi], *s.f.* dactylology.

dactylomégale [daktilɔmegal], *a. Med:* afflicted with dactylomegaly.

dactylomégalie [daktilɔmegali], *s.f. Med:* dactylomegaly.

dactylonomie [daktilɔnɔmi], *s.f.* dactylonomy.

dactylopius [daktilɔpjys], *s.m. Ent:* Dactylopius.

dactylopodite [daktilɔpɔdit], *s.m. Crust:* dactylopodite.

dactyloptère [daktilɔptɛːr], *Ich:* **1.** *a.* dactylopterous. **2.** *s.m.* Dactylopterus, flying gurnard, flying fish; **les dactyloptères**, the Dactylopteridae.

dactyloscopie [daktilɔskɔpi], *s.f.* dactyloscopy.

dactyloscopique [daktilɔskɔpik], *a.* dactyloscopic; **examen d. d'un accusé**, examination of a prisoner's fingerprints.

dactylozoïde [daktilɔzɔid], *a. & s.m. Z:* dactylozooid.

dacus [dakys], *s.m. Ent:* Dacus.

dada [dada], *s.m. F:* **1.** (*in nursery language*) gee-gee; **aller à d.**, (i) to ride a-cock-horse; (ii) to ride a horse. **2.** (a) *A:* hobby(-horse); (b) pet subject; **son dernier d.**, his latest craze; **enfourcher son d.**, to get on to one's pet subject. **3.** *a. Art: Lit:* **le mouvement d.**, the Dada movement, Dadaism.

dadais [dadɛ], *s.m. F:* silly, awkward boy, youth; **allons donc, grand d.!** come on, you silly, awkward lump!

dadaïsme [dadaism], *s.m. Art: Lit:* Dadaism.

dadaïste [dadaist], (a) *s.m.* Dadaïst; (b) *a.* Dadaistic.

dadoxylon [dadɔksilɔ̃], *s.m. Paleont:* dadoxylon.

dagard [dagaːr], *s.m. Ven:* brocket; pricket.

dagorne [dagɔrn], *s.f.* one-horned cow.

dague [dag], *s.f.* **1.** dagger; *Navy:* dirk; *Iron:* **être fin comme une d. de plomb**, to have an elephantine sense of humour, to be heavily jocular. **2.** cat-o'-nine-tails. **3.** *Tls:* scraping-knife (for leather). **4.** *Ven:* (a) dag (of two-year-old deer); (b) tusk (of wild boar).

daguer [dage], *v.tr. Ven:* **1.** to stab (a wild boar, etc.). **2.** (*of stag*) to couple with, cover (a doe).

se daguer, (*of goats*) to butt (each other).

daguerréotype [dagɛreɔtip], *s.m. A.Phot:* daguerreotype.

daguerréotyper [dagɛreɔtipe], *v.tr. A:* to daguerreotype.

daguerréotypie [dagɛreɔtipi], *s.f. A.Phot:* daguerreotypy.

daguet [dagɛ], *s.m. Ven:* brocket; pricket.

daguette [dagɛt], *s.f.* small dagger.

dahabieh [daabje], *s.f. Nau:* (*Nile sailing boat*) dahabeeyah, dahabiah, dahabieh.

dahlia [dalja], *s.m.* **1.** *Bot:* dahlia. **2.** *Ch: Dy:* dahlia.

dahllite [dalit], *s.f. Miner:* dahllite.

dahoméen, -enne [daɔmeɛ̃, -ɛn], *a. & s. Ethn:* Dahoman.

Dahomey [daɔmɛ], *Pr.n.m. Geog:* Dahomey.

daigner [deɲe], *v.tr.* to deign, condescend; **il n'a même pas daigné me répondre**, he didn't even deign to answer (me); **le roi a daigné lui parler**, the king condescended, was pleased, to speak to him.

daikon [daikɔ̃], *s.m. Bot:* daikon.

dail [dajl], *s.m.*, **daille** [daj], *s.f.* (a) scythe stone, whetstone (for scythes); (b) (short-handled) scythe.

d'ailleurs [dajœːr], *adv.phr.* See AILLEURS.

daim [dɛ̃], *s.m.* **1.** *Z:* (fallow-)deer; buck; **chasse au d.**, deer-stalking; **(peau de) d.**, (i) buckskin, doeskin; (ii) suède; **chaussures de d.**, suède shoes. **2.** (a) *A: F:* buck, dandy; (b) *P: O:* simpleton, mug, sucker.

daïmio [daimjo], *s.m.inv. Jap.Hist:* daimio.

daine¹ [dɛn; *Ven:* din], *s.f. Z:* doe (of fallow-deer).

daine² [dɛn], *s.m. Min:* floor, pavement, sole, sill (of mine level).

daintiers [dɛ̃tje], *s.m.pl. Ven:* testicles (of deer).

dais [dɛ], *s.m.* **1.** canopy; **recouvert d'un d.**, canopied; **les feuilles formaient un d. verdoyant**, the leaves formed a green canopy. **2.** *A:* dais, platform.

daisne [dɛn], *s.m. Min:* floor, pavement, sole, sill (of mine level).

dakhma [dakma], *s.m.* (*in India*) dakhma, tower of silence.

dalaï-lama [dalailama], *s.m.* Dalai Lama.

dalbergia [dalbɛrʒja], *s.m.*, **dalbergie** [dalbɛrʒi], *s.f. Bot:* dalbergia.

daleau [dalo], *s.m.* = DALOT.

Dalila [dalila], *Pr.n.f. B.Hist:* Delilah.

dallage [dalaːʒ], *s.m.* **1.** paving (with flags, slabs, etc.); flagging, slabbing. **2.** pavement, flagging; **d. de marbre**, marble pavement, floor; **d. en céramique**, tiled flooring, tiled floor; **d. en verre**, éclairant, pavement lights.

dalle [dal], *s.f.* **1.** (a) *Const:* flag(stone), paving stone, flooring tile; **d. coulée**, concrete flooring; **pièce pavée de dalles**, room floored with stone flags; **d. de verre**, pavement light; **d. flottante**, floating floor; (b) slab (of marble, plate glass, etc.); **d. funéraire, tumulaire**, ledger (stone), (flat) memorial stone; *Mil:* **d. d'éclatement**, detonating slab; *Geol:* **roche en dalles**, foliate rock; (c) *P:* **se rincer, se mouiller, la d.**, to have a drink, to wet one's whistle; **avoir la d. en pente**, to have a permanent thirst. **2.** *Const:* rainwater head, leader head; *Nau:* spout. **3.** *A:* (silver) five-franc piece. **4.** (collotype) plate. **5.** slice, slab (of fish). **6.** scythe stone, whetstone (for scythes). **7.** *P:* **que d.**, nothing; **je n'y comprends, n'y pige, que d.**, I don't get it, I don't understand what it's all about; **je n'ai fichu que d. aujourd'hui**, I've done damn all today.

daller [dale], *v.tr.* to pave (with slabs, flagstones, etc.); to flag, slab (pavement, etc.); to tile (floor); **salle dallée de marbre**, marble-paved hall.

dalleur [dalœːr], *s.m.* paviour, flagsetter, flag layer.

dalmanites [dalmanit], *s.f. Paleont:* Dalmanites.

dalmate [dalmat], *a. & s. Geog:* Dalmatian.

Dalmatie [dalmasi], *Pr.n.f. Geog:* Dalmatia; **chien de D.,** Dalmatian (dog).

dalmatien, -ienne [dalmasjɛ̃, -jɛn], *s.* Dalmatian (dog).

dalmatique [dalmatik], *s.f. Ecc.Cost:* dalmatic.

dalot [dalo], *s.m.* **1.** *Nau:* **d. de pont,** scupper (hole); **d. de pompe,** pump dale; **conduit de d.,** scupper pipe. **2.** *Arch: Civ.E:* channel, water leader, box culvert.

daltonien, -ienne [daltɔnjɛ̃, -jɛn], *a. & s.* daltonian, colour-blind (person).

daltonisme [daltɔnism], *s.m.* daltonism, colour-blindness.

dam [dɑ̃], *s.m.* **1.** (*a*) *A:* injury, prejudice, hurt; **agir au d. de qn,** to act in a manner prejudicial to s.o.; (*b*) **au grand d. de qn,** to s.o.'s detriment. **2.** *Theol:* **peine du d.,** eternal damnation.

damage [damaːʒ], *s.m. Civ.E:* ramming, tamping; tamp work.

daman [damɑ̃], *s.m. Z:* hyrax, dassie, coney; **d. de Syrie,** daman; **d. arboricole africain,** dendrohyrax, African tree hyrax.

Damas [damɑːs]. **1.** *Pr.n.m. Geog:* Damascus; **trouver son chemin de D.,** to see the light. **2.** *s.m.* [damɑ] (*a*) *Tex:* damask (linen, silk, etc.); (*b*) *Sm.a:* Damascus blade; (*c*) *Bot:* (i) damson (plum); (ii) *F:* dame's violet.

damascène [damasɛn], *a. & s. Geog:* Damascene.

damasquette [damaskɛt], *s.f. A.Tex:* damassin.

damasquin [damaskɛ̃], (*a*) *a. & s.* Damascene; (*b*) *a.* **glaive d.,** Damascus blade; (*c*) *s.m. Tex:* damask.

damasquinage [damaskinaːʒ], *s.m. Metalw:* damascening.

damasquiner [damaskine], *v.tr. Metalw:* to inlay, damascene (blade, etc.).

damasquinerie [damaskin(ə)ri], *s.f.* (art of) damascening.

damasquineur [damaskinœːr], *s.m. Metalw:* damascener.

damasquinure [damaskinyːr], *s.f. Metalw:* damascening.

damassé [damɑse], (*a*) *a. & s.m. Tex:* damask, damassé; **nappe damassée,** damask tablecloth; (*b*) *a. Metalw:* **acier d.,** damask steel.

damasser [damɑse], *v.tr. Tex: Metalw:* to damask.

damasserie [damɑsri], *s.f. Tex:* **1.** damask linen manufacture, trade. **2.** damask linen factory. **3.** damask pattern (on linen).

damasseur, -euse [damɑsœːr, -øːz], *s.* damask weaver.

damassin [damɑsɛ̃], *s.m. Tex:* light cotton damask.

damassure [damɑsyːr], *s.f. Tex:* damask design.

dambonite [dɑ̃bɔnit], *s.f. Ch:* dambonitol, dambonite.

dambose [dɑ̃boːz], *s.m. Ch:* dambose.

dame[1] [dam], *s.f.* **1.** (*a*) *A:* (noble) lady; **les dames de France,** the royal princesses of France; *F:* **elle fait la grande d.,** she puts on airs, she's all lah-di-dah; **elle était trop grande d. pour s'abaisser jusqu'à cela,** she was too much the lady to stoop to that; (*b*) lady, woman; *Rail:* **compartiment de dames seules,** ladies only compartment; *P.N:* (*on public convenience*) **dames,** ladies; (*in café, etc.*) **que prendront ces dames?** (i) what will the ladies take? (ii) what will you take, ladies? *Iron:* **et ces dames d'entrer,** and in walked their ladyships; *A:* **mourir pour sa d.,** to die for one's lady; *F: Hum:* **la d. de ses pensées,** the woman of his dreams, the woman on whom his affections are set; *Myth:* **la D. blanche,** the White Lady; *P:* **une d. blanche,** a bottle of white wine; (*c*) **d. nature,** mother nature; (*d*) married woman; **est-ce une d. ou une jeune fille?** is she married? *P:* **votre d.,** your good lady, your missus; *Com: P:* **et pour vous, ma petite d.?** and what can I get you, mum? what's yours, duck? *P:* (*in shop, etc.*) **bonjour monsieur d.,** good morning, sir, good morning madam; *Jur:* **la d. Simon,** Mrs Simon; (*e*) **d. d'honneur,** (i) lady-in-waiting; (ii) matron of honour; **d. de compagnie,** lady's companion; *O:* **dames de charité,** district visitors; *O:* **d. de comptoir,** (woman) cashier; **la d. du vestiaire,** (woman) cloakroom attendant; *Ecc:* **les dames du Sacré-Cœur,** the religious of the Sacred Heart; (*f*) (gentleman's) partner (at dance). **2.** (*a*) **jeu de dames** = (game of) draughts, *U.S:* checkers; **jouer aux dames,** to play draughts; (*b*) (*at draughts*) = king; *Chess: Cards:* queen; (*at backgammon*) piece, man; *Cards:* **d. troisième,** guarded queen; **d. quatrième, cinquième, etc.,** four, five, etc. cards to the queen; *F:* **courtiser, taquiner, la d. de pique,** to be fond of cards, to be an inveterate card player; **aller à d.,** (i) (*at draughts*) to make a king; (ii) *Chess:* to queen (a pawn); (iii) *P:* to fall down. **3.** *Nau:* (*a*) carrick bitt (of windlass); (*b*) **dames (de nage),** (i) rowlocks, thole pins, (ii) outriggers. **4.** *Civ.E: etc:* (paving) beetle; (earth) rammer, punner. **5.** *Bot:* **dame d'onze heures,** star of Bethlehem; *F:* **dame-nue,** naked lady. **6.** *Orn: F:* **d. des marais, d. au long bec,** woodcock. **7.** *Ent:* **belle d.,** painted lady. **8.** *Geol:* rock pinnacle.

dame[2], *int. F:* (*intensive*) **d. oui!** I should say so! you bet! **ça vous étonne?—d. oui!** does it astonish you?—it does indeed! I should think it does! **pourquoi y allez-vous?—(mais) d., il le faut!** why are you going?—well, simply because I must; **vous y allez?—d.!** you're going?—what else can I do?

dame[3], *s.f. Civ.E:* **1.** old-man, dumpling (in excavation work). **2.** dam (across section of canal under construction); *Metall:* dam-stone (of furnace); **(plaque de) d.,** dam-plate. **3.** *Fort:* turret (of batardeau).

dame-blanche [damblɑ̃ːʃ], *s.f. A.Veh:* (white) stage-coach (divided into two compartments); *pl. dames-blanches.*

dame-jeanne [damʒɑːn, -ʒan], *s.f.* demijohn; *pl. dames-jeannes.*

dame-pipi [dampipi], *s.f. P:* (female) lavatory attendant; *pl. dames-pipi.*

damer [dame], *v.tr.* **1.** (*at draughts*) to crown (a piece); *Chess:* to queen; *F:* **d. le pion à qn,** to outwit, outdo, s.o.; to go one better than s.o.; **je lui ai damé le pion,** I spiked his guns for him; I did him down. **2.** *Civ.E: etc:* to ram, tamp (earth, etc.).

dameret [damrɛ], *A:* **1.** *s.m.* fop, dandy. **2.** *a.* **vieillard d.,** foppish, dandified, old man.

dame-ronde [damrɔ̃ːd], *s.f.* pillar (to prevent free passage along coping of wall, etc.); *pl. dames-rondes.*

Damien [damjɛ̃], *Pr.n.m. Ecc.Hist:* Damian.

damier [damje], *s.m.* **1.** (*a*) draught-board (in Fr. with 100 squares); *U.S:* checker-board; (*b*) *Tex: etc:* **en damier,** in check pattern; **étoffe en d.,** check, chequered, material; (*c*) *Arch:* chequer work, checkerwork; (*d*) *Town P:* grid layout, chequer-board layout.

Damiette [damjet], *Pr.n.f. Geog:* Damietta.

dammar [damaːr], *s.m. Com:* dammar (resin).

dammara [damara], *s.m. Bot:* Dammara; agathis; dammar pine; **d. austral,** kauri-pine.

damnable [dɑnabl], *a.* **1.** *Theol:* deserving of damnation. **2.** detestable, damnable, loathsome, abominable (action, etc.); heinous (crime).

damnablement [dɑnabləmɑ̃], *adv.* damnably.

damnation [dɑnasjɔ, da-], *s.f. & int. Theol: etc:* damnation; *int.* **enfer et d.!** hell and damnation!

damné [dɑne], *a. & s.* damned; **les damnés,** the souls in torment, the damned; *F:* **souffrir comme un d.,** to suffer the pains of hell, to go through hell; *F:* **être l'âme damnée de qn,** to be (i) someone's tool, stooge, (ii) someone's evil genius; *F:* **cette damnée affaire,** this confounded, damn(ed), business; *A:* **un d. coquin,** a damned rascal.

damner [dɑne], *v.tr.* to damn; *Lit:* **dieu me damne!** damme! *F:* **faire d. qn,** to drive s.o. crazy, to drive s.o. to exasperation; **cela ferait d. un saint,** it's enough to make a saint swear.

se damner, to incur damnation; **il se serait damné pour elle,** he would have sold his soul for her.

Damoclès [damɔklɛːs], *Pr.n.m. A.Hist:* Damocles; **l'épée de D.,** the sword of Damocles.

damoir [damwaːr], *s.m. Civ.E: etc:* (paving) beetle; (earth) rammer.

damoiseau, -eaux [damwazo], *s.m.,* **damoisel** [damwazɛl], *s.m. A:* **1.** squire, page. **2.** *F:* fop, dandy.

damoiselle [damwazɛl], *s.f. A:* damsel, damozel.

damourite [damurit], *s.f. Miner:* damourite.

damper [dampœːr], *s.m. Mec.E:* damper.

dan [dan], *s.m.* (*judo*) dan.

Danaé [danae], *Pr.n.f. Myth:* Danaë.

Danaïde [danaid], *s.f.* **1.** *Myth:* **les Danaïdes,** the Danaides; **c'est le tonneau des Danaïdes,** (i) it is a fruitless, endless, task; (ii) money runs through his fingers like water through a sieve. **2.** *Ent:* danaid, monarch butterfly; milkweed butterfly; *pl.* Danaidae, the danaids.

danaïte [danait], *s.f. Miner:* danaite.

danalite [danalit], *s.f. Miner:* danalite.

danburite [dɑ̃byrit], *s.f. Miner:* danburite.

dancing [dɑ̃siŋ], *s.m.* dance hall.

dandin [dɑ̃dɛ̃], *s.m. A:* simpleton, ninny, booby.

dandinant [dɑ̃dinɑ̃], *a.* waddling, rolling, swinging (gait, etc.).

dandinement [dɑ̃dinmɑ̃], *s.m.* **1.** dandling (of baby, etc.). **2.** (*a*) rolling gait; swinging (of the body); waddle; (*b*) strutting. **3.** *Aut:* shimmy.

dandiner [dɑ̃dine], *v.tr.* to dandle (baby); *abs.* **d. des hanches,** to sway one's hips.

se dandiner (*a*) to have a rolling gait; **avancer en se dandinant,** to waddle along; **se d. comme un canard,** to waddle like a duck; (*b*) to strut.

dandinette [dɑ̃dinɛt], *s.f. Fish:* dap; **pêcher à la d.,** to dap; **pêche à la d.,** dapping.

dandrelin [dɑ̃drəlɛ̃], *s.m. Vit:* dosser.

dandy[1] [dɑ̃di], *s.m.* dandy; *pl. dandys.*

dandy[2], *s.m. Nau:* dandy.

dandysme [dɑ̃dism], *s.m.* dandyism.

daneau, -eaux [dano], *s.m. Z:* fawn.

Danemark [danmark], *Pr.n.m. Geog:* Denmark.

danger [dɑ̃ʒe], *s.m.* danger; peril; risk, hazard; **d. pour la sécurité nationale,** danger to national security; **dangers maritimes,** shipping hazards; **cela est un d. pour la santé publique,** this constitutes a health hazard; **au plus fort du d.,** in the place of greatest danger; **hors de d.,** out of danger; *Med:* off the danger list; **à l'abri du d.,** out of harm's way; **courir un d.,** to be in danger; to run a risk; **il se rendait compte du d. qu'il courait,** he realized his danger; **s'exposer au d.,** to expose oneself to danger; **s'exposer au d. de . . .,** to run the risk of . . .; **conjurer, détourner, éloigner, écarter, un d.,** to ward off, avert, a danger; **il n'y a pas de d.,** there's no danger, it's quite safe; **il y a du d. à y aller,** it's not safe to go there; **quel d. y a-t-il à l'avertir?** what danger, what harm, is there in warning him? **sans d.,** safe(ly); securely; **notre liberté est en d.,** our liberty is in jeopardy; **mettre en d. la vie, les intérêts, de qn,** to endanger, jeopardize, imperil, s.o.'s life, s.o.'s interests; **mettre sa vie en d.,** to endanger one's person; **en d. de mort,** in danger, peril, of death; in danger of one's life; **être en d. de tomber,** to be in danger of falling; *F:* **pas de d.!** no fear! not likely! **il y a quelque d. que . . . (ne) +** *sub.,* there is some danger lest . . .; **il n'y a pas de d. qu'il vienne,** there is no fear of his coming, that he will come; **se rendre compte du d.,** to see the red light; **suivre qn à travers tous les dangers,** to follow s.o. through thick and thin.

dangereusement [dɑ̃ʒrøzmɑ̃], *adv.* dangerously; **d. malade,** seriously, critically, ill.

dangereux, -euse [dɑ̃ʒrø, -øːz], *a.* dangerous **(pour,** to, for); unsafe; **un d. adversaire,** a dangerous opponent; **des concurrents peu d.,** competitors of little account; **c'est d. pour la circulation,** it is a danger to traffic; **une rivière dangereuse à traverser,** a dangerous river to cross; *Mil:* **zone dangereuse,** danger zone; *Rail:* **point d. (d'un croisement),** fouling point; *Nau:* **côte dangereuse,** foul coast; **passage d.,** dangerous crossing.

danien [danjɛ̃], *a. & s.m. Geol:* Danian.

dannemorite [danmɔrit], *s.f. Miner:* dannemorite.

danois, -oise [danwa, -waːz]. **1.** *a.* Danish; *Hist:* **impôt d.,** Danegeld; *Husb:* **porc d.,** (Danish) Landrace; **chien d.,** *s.m.* **Danois,** great Dane; **(chien) petit d.,** lesser Dane. **2.** *s. Ethn:* Dane. **3.** *s.m. Ling:* Danish.

dans [dɑ̃], *prep.* **1.** (*position, denoting varying degrees of interiority*) in; (*a*) **garder son argent d. un coffre-fort,** to keep one's money in a safe; **d. une boîte,** in(side) a box; **être d. sa chambre,** to be in one's room; **il est quelque part d. la maison,** he is somewhere about the house; **d. la forêt,** in the forest; **d. la rue,** in the street; **flâner d. la ville, d. les ruines,** to stroll about the town, among the ruins; **apercevoir qn d. la foule,** to catch sight of s.o. in the crowd; **regarder un nuage d. le ciel,** to watch a cloud in the sky; **nager d. la mer,** to swim in the sea; **assis d. un fauteuil,** sitting, seated, in an armchair; **couché d. son lit,** lying in his bed; (*b*) **se promener d. Rome,** to go for a stroll in Rome; **il habite d. Paris même,** he lives (right) in(side) Paris (*i.e.* not in the suburbs, *cp.*; **il est à Paris,** he is in Paris); (*c*) **d. la France moderne,** in modern France; **d. le Pakistan Oriental,** in East Pakistan (*cp.* **en France,** in France; **au Pakistan,** in Pakistan); **d. les Pyrénées,** in the Pyrenees; **d. le Var,** in the Var department; **d. le Sussex,** in Sussex; (*d*) **lire qch. d. un livre, d. un journal,** to read sth. in a book, in a newspaper; **apprendre qch. d. un livre,** to learn sth. from a book; **j'ai trouvé cette expression d. Corneille,** I found that expression in Corneille; (*e*) within; **d. un rayon de dix kilomètres,** within a radius of ten kilometres; **d. les limites de l'État,** within the limits of the State; **l'ennemi est d. nos frontières, d. nos murs,** the enemy is within our

frontiers, within our walls; (*f*) *Cu:* **un morceau d. la poitrine,** a cut off the breast. **2.** (*figurative situation, with analogical uses implying state, condition, circumstance, manner, purpose, etc.*) **être d. les affaires,** to be in business; **d. la misère,** in poverty; **être d. la nécessité de . . .,** to be under the necessity of . . .; **être d. le doute, d. une grande inquiétude,** to be in doubt, in great anxiety; **d. la force de l'âge,** in the prime of life; **d. les circonstances,** in, under, the circumstances; **d. mon ignorance,** in my ignorance; **terme employé d. un sens très large,** term used in a very broad sense; **elle disparut d. un doux bruissement de soie,** she disappeared with a soft rustling of silk; **"j'accepte," fit-elle d. un sourire de joie,** "I accept," she said with a happy smile; **dans l'espoir de,** in the hope of; **d. le dessein de,** with the object of. **3.** (*with certain verbs, indicating position from which sth. is taken*) **prendre qch. d. qch.,** to take sth. out of sth.; **boire d. un verre,** to drink out of a glass; **le chien mange d. ma main,** the dog eats out of my hand; **copier qch. d. un livre,** to copy sth. out of, from, a book; **prendre qch. d. un tiroir,** to take sth. out of a drawer; **découper qch. d. un journal,** to cut sth. out of a newspaper; **traits sculptés, taillés, d. la pierre,** features carved out of stone. **4.** (*motion tending to a point within sth.*) (*a*) into, in; **mettre qch. d. une boîte,** to put sth. in(to) a box; **il entra d. la chambre,** he came into, went into, the room; **enfoncer un clou d. le mur,** to drive a nail into the wall; (*b*) (*figuratively*) **sans entrer d. le détail,** without going into detail; **tomber d. l'oubli,** to sink into oblivion; to be forgotten. **5.** (*time*) (*a*) in, during, within; **d. l'après-midi,** in, during, the afternoon; **d. le temps,** in days gone by, long ago; at one time; **d. mon enfance,** in my childhood; **vivre d. le passé,** to live in the past; **payer d. les dix jours,** to pay within ten days; **il mourut d. la semaine,** he died in the course of the week; **nous la trouverons d. les 48 heures,** we'll find her in the next forty-eight hours; (*b*) **je serai prêt à partir d. cinq minutes,** I shall be ready to start in five minutes (*cp.* **on peut aller à Londres en cinq heures,** you can get to London in five hours); **dans cinq ans,** in five years' time, five years hence. **6.** (*approximation*) *F:* **(une somme) d. les dix mille francs,** somewhere about 10,000 francs, something in the neighbourhood of 10,000 francs; **il a d. les quarante ans,** he's about forty, he's fortyish; **ça va faire d. les trois mois qu'on est sans nouvelles,** it is about three months since we had any news.

dansable [dɑ̃sabl], *a.* **une valse qui n'est pas d.,** a waltz you can't dance to.

dansant [dɑ̃sɑ̃], *a.* **1.** dancing; **pas d.,** springy step; **troupe dansante,** dancing troupe. **2. thé d.,** tea dance, thé dansant; **donner une soirée dansante,** to give a dance; **fête dansante,** village dance. **3.** good (tune) to dance to, lively (tune).

danse [dɑ̃:s], *s.f.* dance, dancing; **aimer la d.,** to be fond of dancing; **salle de d.,** dance hall, ballroom; **d. du ventre,** belly dance; **d. de caractère,** character dance, step-dance; **musique de d.,** dance music; **(air de) d.,** dance tune; *Med:* **d. de Saint-Guy,** St Vitus's dance; *F:* **entrer en d.,** (i) to join the dancers, to take one's place in the dance; (ii) to join in; **les canons entrèrent en d.,** the guns began; *s.a.* RENTRER I. 1; **mener la d.,** (i) to lead the dance; (ii) *F:* to run the show; **ouvrir la d.,** (i) to open the dance; (ii) to set the ball rolling; (iii) *F:* to start the fight, the battle; **voilà la d. qui va commencer,** now the fun is beginning, now we are for it; **gare la d.!** there will be the devil to pay; **n'avoir pas le cœur à la d.,** to be in no mood for jollity; **payer la d.,** to pay the piper; *P:* **donner une d. à qn,** to give s.o. a good drubbing, a good dressing down, a thrashing.

danser [dɑ̃se], *v.i.* **1.** (*a*) to dance; *with cogn. acc.* **d. une valse,** to dance a waltz; **faire d. qn,** (i) to dance with s.o.; (ii) *F:* to lead s.o. a dance; *F:* **un disque qui se danse,** a record you can dance to; **le vent faisait d. les ombres,** the wind made the shadows dance; **faire d. les écus,** to make the money fly; **d. sur un volcan,** to dance on the edge of a volcano; **d. devant le buffet,** to have a bare cupboard; *F:* **faire d. l'anse du panier,** to make a bit on the side; **ne savoir sur quel pied d.,** not to know which way to turn, to be all at sea; **avec lui on ne sait jamais sur quel pied d.,** you never know where you are with him; *A: P:* **tu vas la d.,** you'll catch it, you're in for a good thrashing; (*b*) **le bouchon danse sur l'eau,** the cork is bobbing up and down on the water; **des flammes qui dansent,** dancing flames; (*c*) *Typ:* **lettres qui dansent,** letters out of alignment. **2.** *Equit:* (*of horse*) to prance. **3.** *v.tr. Cu:* **d. la pâte à biscuit,** to knead the biscuit dough.

danseur, -euse [dɑ̃sœ:r, -ø:z], *s.* **1.** (*a*) dancer; **d. de ballet,** ballet dancer, *f.* ballerina; (*b*) **d. de corde,** tight-rope dancer; (*c*) *Cy:* **monter une côte en danseuse,** to cycle up a hill standing up on one's pedals. **2.** partner (at dance). **3.** *Orn:* manakin, weaverbird. **4.** *a. Rail:* **traverse danseuse,** yielding sleeper.

dansotter [dɑ̃sɔte], *v.i. F:* to dance a bit (without any real knowledge of the art).

Dante [dɑ̃:t], *Pr.n.m. Ital.Lit:* Dante.

dantesque [dɑ̃tɛsk], *a.* Dantesque, Dantean.

dantonisme [dɑ̃tɔnism], *s.m. Pol.Hist:* the doctrine of Danton.

dantoniste [dɑ̃tɔnist], *a.* & *s. Hist:* Dantonist.

Dantzig [dɑ̃tsig, -dz-], *Pr.n.f. Geog:* Danzig.

dantzicois, -oise [dɑ̃tsikwa, -dz-, -wa:z], *a.* & *s. Geog:* (native, inhabitant) of Danzig; Danziger.

Danube (le) [lədanyb], *Pr.n.m. Geog:* the Danube; **paysan du D.,** (i) plain speaker; (ii) boor.

danubien, -ienne [danybjɛ̃, -jɛn], *a. Geog:* Danubian.

Daours [daur], *s.m.pl. Ethn:* **les D.,** the Daur.

Daphné [dafne]. **1.** *Pr.n.f. Myth:* Daphne. **2.** *s.m. Bot:* daphne.

daphnéphories [dafnefɔri], *s.f.pl. Gr.Hist:* Daphnephoria.

daphnétine [dafnetin], *s.f. Ch:* daphnetin.

daphnia [dafnja], *s.f. Crust:* daphnia.

daphnie [dafni], *s.f. Crust:* daphnid.

daphnine [dafnin], *s.f. Ch:* daphnin.

daphnite [dafnit], *s.f. Miner:* daphnite.

dapifer [dapifɛ:r], *s.m. Hist:* dapifer.

darbysme [darbism], *s.m. Rel.H:* Darbyism.

darbyste [darbist], *s.m.* & *f: Rel:* Darbyite; **les darbystes,** the Plymouth brethren.

Darc, d'Arc [dark]. *See* JEANNE.

darce [dars], *s.f.* harbour, open basin, wet dock, camber, (*esp.* in the Mediterranean).

darcy [darsi], *s.m. Meas:* darcy.

dard [da:r], *s.m.* **1.** (*a*) *A:* dart, javelin; **les dards de la satire,** the stings, barbs, of satire; (*b*) *Fish:* (eel-)spear, harpoon; (*c*) spike; (*d*) *Sm.a:* chape (of scabbard). **2.** (*a*) *Z:* sting (of insect); forked tongue (of serpent); (*b*) tongue, tip (of flame). **3.** *Bot:* pistil. **4.** *Hort:* fruit spur. **5.** *Ich:* dace. **6.** *Arch:* dart.

darder [darde], *v.tr.* **1.** to hurl, shoot forth, dart (pointed object); **le serpent darde sa langue,** the snake shoots out its tongue; **il darda sur moi un regard chargé de haine,** he shot a glance of hatred at me; **le soleil darde ses rayons,** the sun darts its rays; *v.i.* **le soleil dardait,** the sun was beating down. **2.** (*a*) *Fish:* to spear, harpoon (whale); (*b*) **d. qn de sarcasmes,** to hurl sarcasm at s.o.

dardière [dardjɛ:r], *s.f. Ven:* stag trap.

dardille [dardij], *s.f.* **1.** small dart. **2.** stalk of a carnation.

dardillon [dardijɔ̃], *s.m.* **1.** small dart. **2.** barb (of fish-hook).

dare-dare [darda:r], *adv. F:* post-haste, in less than no time.

Darfour [darfu:r], *Pr.n.m. Geog:* Darfur.

dari [dari], *s.m. Agr:* Indian millet, durra.

dariole [darjɔl], *s.f. Cu:* (sort of) almond-flavoured custard tart; dariole.

darne [darn], *s.f. Cu:* slice, steak (of fish).

daron [darɔ̃], *s.m. P: A:* father, old man; **les darons,** parents, the old people.

daronne [darɔn], *s.f. P: A:* mother.

darse [dars], *s.f.* harbour, open basin, wet dock, camber (*esp.* in the Mediterranean).

dartre [dartr̥], *s.f.* **1.** *Med:* (generic term for any slight dry) skin trouble (of a passing nature); scurfy affection; scurf, dartre; herpes; **d. furfuracée,** pityriasis. **2.** *Metall:* scab (of a casting).

dartrer [dartre], *v.i. Metall:* to scab.

dartreux, -euse [dartrø, -ø:z], *a.* **1.** *Med:* herpetic, scabby, dartrous. **2.** *Metall:* scabby.

darwinien, -ienne [darwinjɛ̃, -jɛn], *a.* Darwinian.

darwinisme [darwinism], *s.m.* Darwinism.

darwiniste [darwinist], *s.m.* & *f.* Darwinist.

dash-pot [daʃpɔt], *s.m. Mec.E: El.E:* dashpot.

dasyatidés [daziatide], *s.m.pl. Ich:* Dasyatidae.

dasypodidés [dazipodide], *s.m.pl. Z:* Dasypodidae, the armadillos.

dasyproctidés [dazipr̥ɔktide], *s.m.pl. Z:* Dasyproctidae.

dasyure [dazjy:r], *s.m. Z:* dasyure, dasyurus; Australian native cat.

dasyuridés [daziyride], *s.m.pl. Z:* Dasyuridae.

datable [databl̥], *a.* datable.

datage [data:ʒ], *s.m.* dating; **il oublia de faire le d. du document,** he forgot to write down the date on, to date, the document.

dataire [datɛ:r], *s.m. Ecc:* datary.

data-logger [deitələgɛ:r], *s.m.* data handling system.

datation [datasjɔ̃], *s.f.* dating; **d. d'une couche géologique,** dating of a geological stratum; **d. par radio-carbone, par carbone 14,** dating by radiocarbon, carbon 14; **d. isotopique, par les isotopes,** isotopic dating.

date [dat], *s.f.* date; **d. de naissance, date of birth; mettre, indiquer, la d.,** to date (a document); **la lettre porte la d. du 12 juin,** the letter is dated (the) 12th of June; **sans d.,** undated (letter, etc.); **erreur de d.,** misdating, mistake in the date; **faire une erreur de d.,** to misdate (an event, a document); **prendre d. pour qch.,** to fix a date for sth.; **prendre d. avec qn,** to make an appointment with s.o.; (*of event*) **faire d.,** to mark an epoch; **être le premier en d.,** to come first, to have a prior claim; **amitié de fraîche d.,** recent, newly-formed, friendship; **amitié de vieille, de longue, d.,** friendship of old, of long, standing; long-standing friendship; **je le connais de longue d.,** I have known him for a long time; **en d. du 15 courant,** dated the 15th inst; **en d. de Paris,** dated from Paris; **à trente jours de d.,** thirty days after date; *Fin:* **emprunt à longue, à courte, d.,** long-dated, short-dated, loan; **d. d'échéance,** date of maturity; **d. limite,** deadline; *Jur:* **d. authentique,** certified date; **d. certaine,** legal date (of a private agreement); **d. d'annulation, de résiliation,** cancelling date, date of cancellation; **d. d'entrée en vigueur,** effective date (of regulation, etc.); **à cette d.,** by then, by that time; **les derniers en d. des rois d'avant la Conquête,** the later kings of the pre-Conquest period; **cet événement a mille ans de d.,** this event took place a thousand years ago; **une légende qui n'a pas de d.,** an age-old legend; **robe qui porte sa date,** dress that dates, that is out of fashion; **c'est une d. dans sa vie,** it's a day he will never forget.

dater [date]. **1.** *v.tr.* to date (letter, etc.); **votre lettre datée d'aujourd'hui,** your letter dated today; *Com:* your letter of even date; **lettre datée de Londres,** letter dated from London; **non daté,** undated. **2.** *v.i.* to date (de, from); **à d. de ce jour,** (i) from to-day; (ii) from that day; **à d. du 15,** on and after the 15th; **ces lettres datent de plus d'un siècle,** these letters date more than a hundred years back, are more than a century old; **leur amitié date de loin,** their friendship is of long standing; **ce que je vous raconte là date de loin,** what I am telling you now goes back a long way, a long time; **famille qui date de loin,** family which goes a long way back; *abs.* **événement qui date,** epoch-making, memorable, event; **la pièce commence à d.,** the play is beginning to date; **robe qui date,** dress that dates, old-fashioned, out-of-date, dress; **cela ne date pas d'hier,** this is far from being recent, new; **de quand date votre dernier repas?** when did you last eat?

daterie [datri], *s.f. Ecc:* dataria, datary.

dateur, -euse [datœr, -ø:z]. **1.** *a.* dating; **tampon d., composteur d.,** dating stamp, dater. **2.** *s.m.* date marker, date-stamp, dater.

datif, -ive [datif, -i:v]. **1.** *a.* & *s.m. Gram:* dative (case); **au d.,** in the dative. **2.** *a. Jur:* **tutelle dative,** tutory dative; **tuteur d.,** tutor dative.

dation [dasjɔ̃], *s.f. Jur:* dation; (legal act of) giving, conferring (guardianship, etc.); **d. d'arrhes,** paying of earnest money; **d. en paiement,** dation in payment.

datis(ca)cées [datis(ka)se], *s.f.pl. Bot:* Datiscaceae.

datisme [datism], *s.m. Rh:* fondness for the accumulation of synonyms where one word would suffice.

datisque [datisk], *s.m. Bot:* datisca.

datolite [datɔlit], *s.f. Miner:* datolite.

datte [dat], *s.f.* (*a*) *Bot:* date; **dattes farcies,** marzipan dates; *P:* **des dattes!** nothing doing! (*b*) *Moll:* **d. de mer,** date mussel.

dattier [datje], *s.m. Bot:* date palm, date tree; **suc de d.,** date-palm juice.

datura [datyra], *s.m. Bot:* datura; **d. stramonium,** thorn-apple, *U.S: F:* stinkweed, jimsonweed.

daturine [datyrin], *s.f. Bot:* daturine.

daturique [datyrik], *a. Ch:* daturic.

daube [do:b], *s.f. Cu:* stew; **bœuf en, à la, d.,** stewed, braised, beef; *P:* **c'est de la d.,** it's worth damn all, it's not worth a bean.

daubentoniidés [dobɑ̃tɔniide], *s.m.pl. Z:* Daubentoniidae; the aye-aye family.

dauber[1] [dobe], *v.tr. Cu:* to stew, braise (beef, chicken, etc.).

dauber[2], *v.tr. A: F:* **1.** (*a*) to beat, drub, thump (s.o.); (*b*) to jeer at, insult (s.o.). **2.** *v.i.* **d. sur qn,** to pull s.o. to pieces behind his back.

se dauber, to fight.

daubeur, -euse [dobœːr, -øːz], *s.* **1.** *A:* scoffer, mocker. **2.** *Metalw:* smith's hammerman.

daubière [dobjɛːr], *s.f. Cu:* stewpan, braising-pan.

daubréelite [dobrelit], *s.f. Miner:* daubreelite.

daubréite [dobreit], *s.f. Miner:* daubre(e)ite.

dauciforme [dosifɔrm], *a. Bot:* carrot-shaped.

Daumont [domɔ̃], *Pr.n.m. A: Veh:* **attelage à la, en, D.,** *s.* **une d.,** carriage and four with two postillions.

dauphin [dofɛ̃], *s.m.* **1.** (*a*) *Z: Her:* dolphin; (*b*) *Astr:* **le D.,** Delphinus. **2.** *Constr:* shoe (of drainpipe). **3.** *Nau:* dolphin, mooring-post. **4.** *pl. A.N.Arch:* cheeks (of mast). **5.** (*a*) *Hist:* Dauphin (eldest son of French king); (*b*) *F:* heir apparent (to important position).

dauphine [dofin]. **1.** *s.f. Fr.Hist:* Dauphine, Dauphiness, wife of the Dauphin. **2.** *a.f.* (*a*) **édition d.,** Delphin edition (of the classics, prepared for the son of Louis XIV); (*b*) *Cu:* **pommes dauphines,** dauphine potatoes.

Dauphiné [dofine], *Pr.n.m. Geog:* province of ancient France with capital Grenoble; **en D.,** in Dauphiné.

dauphinelle [dofinɛl], *s.f. Bot:* delphinium, larkspur.

dauphinois, -oise [dofinwa, -waːz], *a.* & *s.* (native) inhabitant of Dauphiné.

daurade [dɔrad], *s.f. Ich:* chrysophrys; sea bream, chad, *F:* gilthead.

davallia [davalja], **davallie** [davali], *s.f. Bot:* Davallia; hare's foot fern.

davantage [davɑ̃taːʒ], *adv.* more; (*a*) **que voulez-vous d.?** what more do you want? **j'en ai, mais il m'en faut d.,** I have some, but I need still more; **je n'en dis pas d.,** I shall say no more; **il n'en sait pas d.,** he doesn't know any more about it; **je le ressens chaque jour d.,** I feel it more and more every day; **je ne donnerai pas d. d'exemples,** I won't give any more examples; **c'est un bon ami, rien d.,** he's just a good friend, nothing more; **il ne faut pas d. pour le finir,** nothing more is needed to finish it; **je ne l'interrogeai pas d.,** I did not question him any further; **vous êtes riche, mais il l'est d.,** you are rich but he is more so; **nous ne resterons pas d.,** we will not stay any longer, we will stay no longer; **il ne semble pas d. que . . .,** nor does it seem that . . .; **s'approcher d.,** to draw near(er); **se reculer d.,** to draw further back; **se baisser d.,** to stoop lower; (*b*) *F:* **d. que** (= **plus que**); **j'en ai d. que lui,** I have more than he (has).

David [david], *Pr.n.m.* David.

davidia [davidja], *s.m. Bot:* Davidia; dove tree.

davidsonite [davidsɔnit], *s.f. Miner:* davidsonite.

davier [davje], *s.m.* **1.** *Tls:* (*a*) *Dent:* forceps; **d. à racine,** alveolar forceps; **d. à crampons, d. porte-crampons,** clamp forceps; (*b*) *Carp:* cramp. **2.** *Nau:* bow sheave, roller chock; davit.

daviésite [daviezit], *s.f. Miner:* daviesite.

davis [davi], *s.m. Coop:* dog.

dawsonite [dɔːsɔnit], *s.f. Miner:* dawsonite.

Dayaks [dajak], *s.m.pl. Ethn:* Dyaks, Dayaks.

de [də], *before vowels and h "mute"* **d'**; **de** *and def. art.* **le, les,** *are contracted into* **du, des.** I. *prep.* **1.** *forming adv. phrases;* (*a*) (*point of departure in space or time*) from; **il vient de Paris, de France, de l'école,** he comes from Paris, from France, from school; **j'ai appris cela de mon père,** I learnt that from my father; **cette signature n'est pas de moi,** that signature is not mine; **l'idée est de vous,** the idea is yours, comes from you; **je l'ai oublié? c'est bien de moi,** did I forget it? It's just like me; **de lui, d'elle, c'est étonnant,** it's surprising, coming from him, her; **du matin au soir,** from morning till night; **croyez-vous que je suis né d'hier?** do you think I was born yesterday? **de vous à moi . . .,** between ourselves . . .; **de vingt à trente personnes,** between twenty and thirty people; **de jour en jour,** from day to day; **de mal en pis,** from bad to worse; **de haut en bas,** from top to bottom; (*b*) (*time vaguely indicated*) **il partit de nuit,** he left by night; **du temps de nos pères,** in the days of our fathers; (*c*) (*agent, means, instrument*) **accompagné de ses amis,** accompanied by his friends; **la statue est de Rodin,** the statue is by Rodin; **elle avait eu un enfant de lui,** she had had a child by him; **j'ai fait cela de ma propre main,** I did it with my own hand; **d'un coup de sabre,** with a stroke of the sword; **je l'ai frappé de mon bâton,** I hit him with my stick; **vivre de fruits,** to live on fruit; **vivre de sa plume,** to live by one's pen; (*d*) (*manner*) **il me regarda d'un air amusé,** he looked at me with an amused expression; **pourquoi agissez-vous de la sorte?** why do you act in such a manner? **répondre d'une voix douce,** to answer in a gentle voice; (*e*) (*cause, origin*) **sauter de joie,** to leap for joy; **je tombe de fatigue,** I am ready to drop with tiredness; **on le loua de sa prudence,** he was praised for his prudence; **il est paresseux de son naturel,** he is lazy by nature; **faire qch. de soi-même,** to do sth. of one's own accord; (*f*) (*measure*) **je suis âgé de seize ans,** I am sixteen years old; **ma montre retarde de dix minutes,** my watch is ten minutes slow; **il est plus grand que moi de la tête,** he is a head taller than I am; **la terrasse a vingt mètres de long, est longue de vingt mètres,** the terrace is twenty metres long; *F:* **placement qui rapporte quinze du cent,** investment yielding fifteen per cent; **un ami qu'il n'avait vu de trente ans,** a friend he had not seen for thirty years; **un chèque de £10,** a cheque for £10; (*g*) (*introducing complement of adj.*) **digne d'éloges,** worthy of praise; **avide de gloire,** eager, *F:* all out, for glory; **altéré de sang,** thirsting for blood. **2.** *forming adj. phrases;* (*a*) (*genitive equivalents*) **le livre de Pierre,** Peter's book; **le toit de la maison,** the roof of the house; **l'arrivée des invités** (*subjective genitive*), the arrival of the guests; **l'oubli du passé** (*objective genitive*), forgetting of the past; **oublieux du passé,** forgetful of the past; **le partage des vivres,** the dividing of the provisions; **le meilleur élève de la classe,** the best pupil in the class; **les rues de Paris,** the streets in Paris, the streets of Paris, the Paris streets; **les petits oiseaux des bois,** the little birds in the woods; **la conférence de Berlin,** the Berlin conference; **la chambre du second,** the room on the second, *U.S:* third, floor; **un hôtel de la rive gauche,** a hotel on the left bank; **nos conversations de Rome,** our conversations in Rome; **scène de rivière hollandaise,** scene on a Dutch river; (*b*) (*material*) **un pont de fer,** an iron bridge; **robe de soie,** silk dress; (*c*) (*distinguishing mark*) **le chien de berger,** the sheep dog (*cp.* **le chien du berger,** the shepherd's dog); **mes visions d'enfant,** my childish visions; **le journal d'hier,** yesterday's paper; **à quatre heures de l'après-midi,** at four o'clock in the afternoon; **la route de Paris,** the Paris road; **le professeur de français,** the French master; (*d*) (*partitive*) **un verre de vin,** a glass of wine; **une livre de café,** a pound of coffee; **beaucoup de paroles,** many words; **pas de fleurs,** no flowers; **je n'ai pas de sœurs,** I haven't any sisters; **être de la noce,** to be one of the wedding party, at the wedding; **il est de la maison,** he is one of the household; **je ne l'ai pas vu de la soirée,** I never saw him the whole evening. **3.** *forming compound prepositions;* **près de la maison,** near the house; **autour du jardin,** round the garden; **hors de Paris,** outside Paris; **à partir de ce jour-là,** from that day onward; (*and many more, shown under their head words*). **4.** *connecting verb, and object:* **nous approchons de Paris,** we are getting near Paris; **j'ai changé d'avis,** I have changed my mind; **jugez de ma surprise,** fancy, judge of, my surprise; **manquer de courage,** to lack courage; **convenir d'une erreur,** to admit an error; **s'acquitter d'une dette,** to discharge a debt; **se servir de qch.,** to use sth. (*these uses will be found under the respective verbs.*)

II. **de,** *serving as a link word.* **1.** *introducing an inf.* (*a*) *the inf. is the logical subject;* **il est honteux de mentir,** it is shameful to lie; **cela le soulageait de s'accuser,** it relieved him to accuse himself; **c'est à vous de jouer,** it is your turn to play; **le mieux était de rire,** it was best to laugh; (*b*) *the inf. is the object;* **je crains d'être en retard,** I am afraid of being late; (*c*) *in comparisons;* **j'aime mieux attendre que de me faire mouiller,** I would rather wait than get wet; **rien de plus facile que de s'en assurer,** there is nothing easier than to make sure; (*d*) *the inf. is complement to an adj.;* **ils sont indignes de vivre,** they are unfit to live; (*e*) *the so-called "historical infinitive" has the force of a finite verb;* **ainsi dit le renard, et flatteurs d'applaudir,** thus spoke the fox and his flatterers applauded. **2.** *introducing an apposition or a predicative complement;* (*a*) **la ville de Paris,** the town of Paris; **la comédie du Misanthrope,** the comedy of the Misanthrope; **il fut traité de lâche,** he was called a coward; **j'ai une heure, trois heures, de libre(s),** I have an hour, three hours, free; **un drôle de garçon,** a funny chap; **ce coquin de Scapin,** that rogue of a Scapin; **quel bijou d'enfant!** what a jewel of a child! **il y eut trois hommes de tués,** three men were killed; **c'est un grand pas de fait,** that is a great step forward; **je n'en ai jamais vu de pareil,** I never saw one like it, I never saw the like; *F:* **si j'étais de vous,** if I were you; *F:* **et d'un(e), et de deux, et de trois,** that's one, that's two, that's three; *F:* **c'est plutôt le vôtre, de fils, qui serait capable de faire cela,** it is rather *your* son, who would be capable of doing this; **j'en ai une, d'idée,** I've got an idea and it's a good one; (*b*) **surprenant de beauté,** surprisingly beautiful; **il était magnifique de santé,** he was bursting with health.

III. **de,** *partitive particle: used also as pl. of* **un, une; n'avez-vous pas de la santé, de la fortune, des amis?** haven't you (got) health, fortune, friends? **épeler sans faire de fautes,** to spell without making any mistakes; **il ne peut parler sans faire des fautes,** he cannot speak without making mistakes; **je n'ai d'ami que vous,** I have no friend but you; **je ne veux pas qu'on lui mette de collier,** I won't have a collar put on him; **je ne pense pas qu'on lui fasse de mal,** I don't think they will hurt him; **de grands artistes se trouvaient là,** there were some great, distinguished, artists there; **avez-vous jamais vu de si méchants enfants?** did you ever see such naughty children? **je bois de l'eau,** I drink water; **ses membres avaient perdu de leur souplesse,** his limbs had lost something of their suppleness; **donnez-nous de vos nouvelles,** let us hear from you; **avez-vous du pain?** have you any, some, bread? **nous avons bu d'un vin exquis,** we drank some superb wine; **donnez-moi de ce vin,** give me some of that wine; **du sang sur le plancher,** blood on the floor; **vous êtes des lâches,** you are cowards; **il y eut des ennemis de tués, des nôtres aussi,** some of the enemy were killed, some of our men also; **je m'adresserai à des amis,** I shall apply to some friends; **il s'adressa à de très anciens amis de la famille,** he applied to some very old friends of the family; **donnez-moi du bon vin,** *A:* **de bon vin;** give me (some) good wine; **manger de tous les plats,** to partake of every dish; (*intensive*) **mettre des heures à faire qch.,** to spend hours over sth.; **il lui fallait rester des vingt minutes à attendre,** he would have to wait as long as twenty minutes; **il gagne jusqu'à des douze francs par heure,** he earns anything up to twelve francs an hour; *occ. as pron.* **toute une troupe d'enfants, des grands et des petits,** a whole band of children, big and small; *F:* **et des comme ça, j'en connais pas mal,** and people like that I know in plenty; **elle a quatre-vingts et des années,** she's eighty odd.

dé[1] [de], *s.m.* **1.** (*a*) *Gaming:* die, *pl.* dice; **dés pipés, chargés,** loaded dice; **cornet à dé(s),** dice box; **jeter les dés,** to throw, cast, the dice; **vous avez le dé, à vous le dé,** (i) it's your throw; (ii) *A:* it's your turn (to speak, etc.); **coup de dé,** cast of the dice; **jouer aux dés,** to play dice; **jouer sa vie sur un coup de dé(s),** to stake one's life on the throw of the dice; *A:* **tenir le dé de, dans, la conversation,** to monopolize the conversation; *A:* **quitter le dé,** to throw in one's hand, to give up; **le dé en est jeté, les dés (en) sont jetés,** the die is cast; (*b*) *Cu:* **couper en dés,** to dice (vegetables, etc.). **2.** *Arch:* dado, die (of pedestal, etc.). **3.** (*a*) *Mec.E:* bearing (bush), brass; split collar (of valve); *Aut: etc:* **dé de cardan,** (trunnion) block; (*b*) bush(ing) (of pulley sheave); (*c*) *Carp: etc:* coak; dowel; **assemblage à dé,** coaking.

dé[2], *s.m.* **1.** (*a*) **dé (à coudre),** thimble; **dé ouvert,** tailor's thimble; (*b*) *F:* **dé (à coudre),** (i) very small glass; (ii) thimbleful. **2.** shoe (of lance, etc.).

dé[3], *s.m.* **1.** (the letter) D. **2.** dee(ring) (on strap, lance, etc.). **3.** *Atom.Ph:* dee (of cyclotron); **distance des dés,** dee gap.

dé-, dés- [dez], *pref. privative.* **1.** dis-; **décharger,** to discharge; **déshériter,** to disinherit; **désobliger,** to disoblige; **déloyal,** disloyal; **désobligeant,** disobliging; **déplaisir,** displeasure; **désordre,** disorder. **2.** de-; **décarburer,** to decarbonize; **désacidifier,** to deacidify; **désoxyder,** to deoxidize. **3.** un-; **débrider,** to unbridle; **décharger,** to unburden; **dévernir,** to unvarnish.

dead-heat [dɛdit], *s.m. Sp:* dead-heat.

déal, -aux [deal, -o], *s.m.* tailor's thimble.

déalbation [dealbasjɔ̃], *s.f.* dealbation (of bones).

déambulation [deɑ̃bylasjɔ̃], *s.f.* (de)ambulation, strolling about; stroll.

déambulatoire [deɑ̃bylatwaːr], *s.m. Ecc.Arch:* ambulatory.

déambuler [deɑ̃byle], *v.i.* to stroll (about), to walk up and down, to saunter.

débâchage [debɑʃa:ʒ], *s.m.* uncovering, untilting (of cart, etc.).

débâcher [debɑʃe], *v.tr.* to uncover, untilt (cart, etc.).

débâclage [debɑkla:ʒ], *s.m. A:* clearing (harbour) (of empty ships).

débâcle [debɑ:kl], *s.f.* **1.** break(ing) up of drift-ice), débâcle. **2.** *(a)* débâcle; collapse, breakdown (of business, of a government, etc.); *Pol:* landslide; *Fin:* crash; **d. générale**, general débâcle; **d. de la santé**, breakdown in health; *Com:* **d. des cotons**, heavy drop in cottons; *(b) F:* attack of diarrhoea (following a period of constipation).

débâclement [debɑklmɑ̃], *s.m.* débâcle, break(ing) up of drift ice.

débâcler [debɑkle]. **1.** *v.i.* (*of ice*) to break up. **2.** *v.tr.* *(a)* to clear (harbour, etc.) (of ice, of empty ships); *(b) A:* to unfasten, unbar (doors, windows, etc.).

débagoulage [debagula:ʒ], *s.m. P:* **1.** vomiting. **2. d. de rhéteur**, rhetorical mouthings, outpourings.

débagouler [debagule], *v.tr. P:* to throw up, to bring up (one's dinner, etc.); **d. un torrent d'injures**, to spew out a torrent of abuse.

débâillonner [debajɔne], *v.tr.* to ungag.

déballage [debala:ʒ], *s.m.* **1.** unpacking. **2. (vente au) d.**, (i) spread of hawker's wares; (ii) clearance sale; (iii) mountain of goods spread out on display. **3.** *P:* (*of woman*) lavish display of one's personal charms; **être volé au d.**, to find the wrapping better than the goods. **4.** *F:* show-down.

déballé [debale], *a. F:* depressed, discouraged, down in the mouth.

déballer [debale], *v.tr.* *(a)* to unpack (goods, etc.); to expose (goods for sale); *F:* **allons, déballe tes connaissances!** come on, do your stuff! *(b) abs. F:* to get it off one's chest.

déballeur [debalœ:r], *s.m.* **1.** unpacker. **2.** hawker, book pedlar.

déballonner (se) [sədebalɔne], *v.pr. P:* **1.** to confess, come clean, open up. **2.** to funk it.

débandade [debɑ̃dad], *s.f.* rout (of army, etc.); helter-skelter flight; stampede (of horses, etc.); **il y eut une d. générale**, there was a general stampede; **à la d.**, in disorder, in confusion, helter-skelter; **mettre tout à la d.**, to turn everything upside down; **marcher à la d.**, to straggle along; **vivre à la d.**, to muddle along.

débander[1] [debɑ̃de], *v.tr.* **1.** to relax (sth. under tension); to unbend (bow); to unbrace (drum); to let down (spring); to uncock (fire-arm). **2. d. une plaie**, to remove a bandage from, to unbandage, a wound; **d. les yeux à qn**, (i) to take the bandage off s.o.'s eyes; (ii) to rob s.o. of his illusions.

se débander[1]. **1.** to relax. **2.** to work loose; to come unbound, undone.

débander[2], *v.tr. A:* to disband (troops, crew).

se débander. *(a)* to disband; (of crowd, etc.) to disperse; *(b) Mil: etc:* to break ranks in disorder, to break into a rout.

débanquage [debɑ̃ka:ʒ], *s.m. Gaming:* breaking of the bank.

débanquer[1] [debɑ̃ke], *v.tr. Gaming:* **d. le banquier**, to break the bank.

débanquer[2]. *Nau:* **1.** *v.tr.* to remove the seats of (boat). **2.** *v.i.* *(a)* to clear, leave, a bank; *(b)* to leave the Banks (after the fishing season); *(c) A: F:* to clear out, to make oneself scarce.

débaptiser [debatize], *v.tr.* to change the name of (person, street, etc.); to rename.

débaraquement [debarakmɑ̃], *s.m.* removal of planking, boarding, etc.

débarbouillage [debarbuja:ʒ], *s.m.* washing (of (face); cleaning (of window, etc.).

débarbouiller [debarbuje]. **1.** to wash (s.o.'s) face; to clean (window, etc.). **2.** *F:* to get (s.o.) out of a scrape. **3.** *P:* **débarbouille-moi ça**, put me in the picture.

se débarbouiller. 1. to wash one's face. **2.** *F:* *(a)* **qu'il se débarbouille**, let him get out of it as best he can, let him shift for himself; *(b)* **le temps se débarbouille**, the weather is clearing up.

débarbouillette [debarbujɛt], *s.f. Fr.C:* (face) flannel.

débarbouilloir, *s.m.*, **débarbouilloire**, *s.f.* [debarbujwa:r] (face) flannel.

débarcadère [debarkadɛ:r], *s.m. Nau:* landing-stage, wharf, unloading dock; *Rail:* platform, unloading bay (in goods yard).

débardage [debarda:ʒ], *s.m.* **1.** *Nau:* unloading, unlading, discharging (of timber). **2.** conveyance (of timber) to the railhead.

débarder[1] [debarde], *v.tr.* **1.** *Nau:* to unload, discharge (timber, etc.); to dismember (timber-raft). **2.** to convey (lumber, quarried stone) to the railhead. **3.** to break up (old ship).

débarder[2], *v.tr. Cu:* to remove bards from (a joint).

débardeur [debardœ:r], *s.m.* **1.** docker, stevedore, longshoreman. **2.** *with f.* **débardeuse** [debardø:z], fancy-dress imitation of longshoreman's costume (popular in the 19th century).

débarouler [debarule], *v.tr.* to tumble down; **il déboula la pente**, he came (i) tumbling, (ii) rushing, down the slope.

débarquage [debarka:ʒ], *s.m.* unloading (of barge, etc.).

débarqué, -ée [debarke], *s.* **1.** one who has just landed, disembarked, stepped off a train; **un nouveau d.**, a country cousin; **c'est une nouvelle débarquée à Paris**, she's fresh from the provinces. **2.** *s.m.* disembarkation, landing, arrival; **au d.**, on arrival; on landing.

débarquement [debarkəmɑ̃], *s.m.* **1.** unloading, discharge, unshipment (of cargo); landing, disembarkation (of passengers); *Rail:* arrival (of passengers); *Nau:* **carte de d.**, landing ticket; *Rail:* **quai de d.**, arrival platform. **2.** *(a) Mil. Trans:* (i) *Rail:* detraining; (ii) *Road Trans:* debussing, *U.S:* detrucking; (iii) *Av:* deplaning; (iv) *Nau:* disembarkation, *U.S:* debarkation; **d. de troupes par avion**, landing of troops by plane; *Rail: Road Trans:* **chantier, point, de d.**, detraining point; debussing point, *U.S:* detrucking point; **zone de d.**, detraining area; debussing area, *U.S:* detrucking area; deplaning area; *(b) Mil: Navy:* (*amphibious operations*) landing; **d. sur plage**, beaching; **d. d'assaut, de vive force**, assault landing; **bâtiment de d.**, assault ship, *U.S:* landing ship; **chaland, péniche, de d.**, landing barge; **transport de chalands de d.**, assault ship, *U.S:* dock landing ship; **transport de personnel et de chalands de d.**, assault ship, *U.S:* landing personnel dock; **troupes de d.**, landing force, party units; *Navy: A:* **compagnie de d.**, landing party. **3.** *Nau:* paying off, discharge (of crew); *Navy:* **certificat, ordre, de d.**, discharge note, ticket.

débarquer [debarke]. I. *v.* **1.** *v.tr.* *(a)* to unship, unload, discharge (cargo); to disembark, land (passengers); to put, set, (passengers, etc.) ashore; to drop (pilot); (*of bus*) to set down (passengers); **d. une embarcation**, to launch a boat (from ship); *(b)* to pay off, discharge (crew); *F:* **d. qn**, to dismiss s.o., to give s.o. the sack; **d. un ministre** (**d'État**), to get rid of a minister; **il faut le d.!** he's got to go! **2.** *v.i.* *(a)* to land, disembark, go ashore (from boat); to deplane, disembark (from aircraft); to alight (from train); *(b) Mil.Trans:* (i) *Rail:* to detrain; (ii) *Road Trans:* to debus, *U.S:* to detruck; (iii) *Av:* to deplane; (iv) *Nau:* to disembark, debark; *(c) Mil: Navy: Av:* (*amphibious or airborne operations*) to land; **d. sur plage**, to beach; **d. en force**, to operate an assault landing; *(d) F:* **d. chez qn**, to drop in on s.o., to land on s.o.; **il débarque**, (i) he's a bit green, he's easily taken in; (ii) he's not with it.

II. **débarquer**, *s.m.* disembarkation, landing, arrival.

débarras [debarɑ], *s.m.* riddance; **bon d.!** good riddance! **ce serait un bon d.**, it would be a good thing to get rid of him, her, it; **(chambre, pièce, de) d.**, lumber room, boxroom; *F:* glory hole.

débarrasser [debarase], *v.tr.* to disencumber; to clear away; to clear (table, etc.); **d. qn de qch.**, to relieve s.o. of sth.; **d. qn de qn**, to rid s.o. of s.o., to take s.o. off s.o.'s hands; **je suis heureux d'en être débarrassé**, I'm glad, thankful, to see the back of him, it; **débarrassez-moi de tout cela**, clear all that out of my way; clear all this out of here; **laissez-moi vous d. de votre chapeau**, let me take your hat; **d. le plancher**, (i) to clear the floor; (ii) *F:* to clear out.

se débarrasser (de qch.), to get rid (of sth.); to extricate, disentangle, oneself (from sth.); to clear (sth.) out of the way; **se d. de ses dettes**, to get clear of one's debts; **se d. de son pardessus**, to take off, get rid of, one's overcoat; **se d. de qn**, to get rid of s.o., to shake s.o. off.

débarrer [debare], *v.tr.* to unbar (door, etc.).

débarricader [debarikade], *v.tr.* to unbarricade.

débat [deba], *s.m.* **1.** (oral) discussion; debate; **soulever un d.**, to provoke a discussion; **mettre une question en d.**, to discuss a question; *pl. Pol:* (parliamentary) debates, proceedings; **diriger les débats**, to conduct the proceedings, to be in the chair; *Jur:* **les débats d'une affaire criminelle**, the (public) trial, hearing, of a criminal case, the proceedings in court; **d. intérieur, d. de conscience**, debating with one's conscience. **2.** *(a)* dispute, quarrel; **trancher un d.**, to settle a dispute; **être en d. sur une question**, to be at issue on a question; **accepter le d.**, to join issue; **à eux le d.**, let them fight it out between themselves.

débatelage [debatla:ʒ], *s.m. Nau:* unlading, discharging.

débateler [debatle], *v.tr.* (**je débatelle, n. débatelons; je débatellerai**) to unlade, discharge (goods, fish).

débâter [debɑte], *v.tr.* to take the pack-saddle off, to unsaddle (horse, mule).

débâtir[1] [debɑti:r], *v.tr.* to demolish, pull down (building).

débâtir,[2] *v.tr.* to unbaste, untack; to take the tacking (threads) out of (garment).

débâtissage [debɑtisa:ʒ], *s.m. Needlew:* (action of) removing the tacking (from a garment).

débattable [debatabl], *a.* debatable.

débattement [debatmɑ̃], *s.m.* **1.** *(a)* struggling; *(b)* floundering (in water, etc.). **2.** *Aut: etc:* (range of) spring movement; clearance, deflection.

débattre [debatr], *v.tr.* (*conj.* like BATTRE) to debate, discuss; **d. une question**, to discuss, argue, a question, to talk a matter over; *abs.* **on se mit d'accord après avoir longtemps débattu**, we came to an agreement after having debated for a long time; **cette question se débat en ce moment**, this question is being debated at the moment; **d. un compte**, to question the items of an account; **prix à d.**, price to be discussed, price by arrangement; **je n'ai pas débattu le prix**, I didn't haggle about the price.

se débattre, *(a)* to struggle; **se d. des mains et des pieds**, to kick and struggle; to thrash about; **se d. contre la misère**, to fight against poverty; *(b)* **se d. dans l'eau**, to flounder, to splash (about) in the water; *(c)* **les gens qui n'ont pas à se d. avec des enfants ne savent pas ce que c'est que la vie**, people who haven't got to cope with children don't know what life is.

débauchage [deboʃa:ʒ], *s.m.* **1.** enticing away (of workman from his work, of soldier from his duty, etc.). **2.** *Ind:* discharging of workmen; turning off, laying off, of hands.

débauche [debo:ʃ], *s.f.* debauchery, dissolute living; **mener une vie de d.**, to live a debauched life, a life of debauchery; *F:* **faire une petite d. (de table)**, to make a pig of oneself; **le décor est une d. de couleurs**, the décor, setting, is a riot of colour; **l'auteur se livre à des débauches d'imagination**, the author's imagination has run riot; *Jur:* **aux fins de d.**, for immoral purposes; **excitation de mineurs à la d.**, incitement of minors to vice; **maison de d.**, disorderly house.

débauché, -ée [deboʃe]. **1.** *a.* debauched, profligate. **2.** *s.* debauchee, libertine, rake; *f.* debauched woman. **3.** *s.f. Nau: etc:* **débauchée**, knock-off time.

débauchement [deboʃmɑ̃], *s.m.* = DÉBAUCHAGE.

débaucher [deboʃe], *v.tr.* **1.** to entice (s.o.) away, to lead (s.o.) astray; to debauch (s.o.); **d. un ouvrier**, to entice a workman away (from his work), to induce him to strike; **d. un soldat**, to induce a soldier to desert. **2.** *Ind:* *(a)* to discharge, turn off (hands); to lay off (hands); *abs.* to reduce one's staff; *(b) v.i. F:* (*of workman*) to knock off (at the end of the day). **3. d. la jeunesse**, to corrupt the young; **d. une jeune fille**, to seduce, ruin, a girl. **4.** *F:* **laissez-là vos livres et débauchez-vous un peu**, put your books away and enjoy yourself.

se débaucher, to become corrupted; to go astray; *F:* to go to the dogs.

débaucheur, -euse [deboʃœ:r, -ø:z], *s.* seducer, debaucher, corrupter.

débavage [debava:ʒ], *s.m. Tex:* removing of floss (from silkworm cocoon).

débaver [debave], *v.tr. Tex:* to remove floss from (silkworm cocoon).

débecquage [debɛka:ʒ], *s.m. Husb:* cauterizing the beaks of chicken (to prevent their pecking each other).

débecqueter, débecter [debɛkte], *v.tr.* (**je débecquette, n. débecquetons, je débecquetterai**) *P:* to disgust, to make (s.o.) sick; **il me débecte**, he makes me spew; **ça me débecte**, I can't stomach that.

débenzolage [debɛ̃zɔla:ʒ], *s.m. Ch:* debenzolization.

débenzoler [debɛ̃zɔle], *v.tr. Ch:* to debenzolize.

débéquiller [debekije], *v.tr. Nau:* to remove prop, shore, leg, from (a ship, etc.).
débet [debɛ], *s.m. Fin:* debit balance.
débiffé [debife], *a. A: F:* out of sorts, run down; drawn, haggard (face).
débiffer [debife], *v.tr. A: F:* to weaken, upset (the stomach, etc.).
se débiffer, *A: F:* to get run down, out of sorts.
débile [debil]. **1.** *a.* weakly (child); weak (stomach); sickly (plant); feeble; **au cerveau d.,** feeble-minded; moronic; **avoir une volonté d.,** to lack decision. **2.** *s.* **un(e) d. mental(e),** a mentally deficient, feeble-minded, person, a mental defective.
débilement [debilmɑ̃], *adv.* weakly, feebly.
débilitant [debilitɑ̃], *a.* debilitant, debilitating, weakening; **remède d.,** *s.m.* **débilitant,** debilitant.
débilitation [debilitasjɔ̃], *s.f. Med:* debilitation.
débilité [debilite], *s.f.* debility, weakness; **d. mentale,** mental deficiency.
débiliter [debilite], *v.tr.* to debilitate, weaken, enfeeble.
débillarder [debijarde], *v.tr.* to saw, cut (wood) diagonally.
débinage [debina:ʒ], *s.m. P:* disparagement, running down.
débine [debin], *s.f. F:* poverty, straitened circumstances; **tomber dans la d.,** to fall on evil times; **être dans la d.,** to be down on one's luck, stony-broke.
débiner [debine], *v.tr. P:* to disparage; to speak slightingly of (s.o.); **d. ses amis,** to run one's friends down; **se d.,** to run each other down.
se débiner. 1. *A:* to fall into straitened circumstances, to come down in the world. **2.** *P:* to make off, to make oneself scarce, to slip away quietly, to hop it.
débineur, -euse [debinœ:r, -ø:z], *s. P:* disparager, detractor.
débirentier [debirɑ̃tje], *s.m.* payer of an allowance.
débit[1] [debi], *s.m.* **1.** *(a)* (retail) sale; **marchandises de bon d.,** marketable, saleable, goods; **article d'un d. assuré,** article certain to sell, of ready sale; **ces marchandises ont peu de d.,** there is little demand for these goods; *(b)* (retail) shop; *esp.* **d. de tabac,** tobacconist's (shop); **obtenir un d. de tabac,** to obtain a licence to open a tobacconist's shop; **d. de vin,** wine shop; **d. (de boissons)** = public house; *F:* pub; **d. clandestin,** shebeen, *U.S:* speak-easy. **2.** cutting up (of logs, meat, etc.); **d. sur maille, sur quartier,** cutting (of timber) on the quarter. **3.** *(a) Hyd: Ph: etc:* discharge, flow (of river, tap, weir, etc.); flow (of air stream, flux, etc.); flow, yield (of spring, oil-well); discharge, delivery, duty (of pump); yield (of mine); feed (of air into furnace, of fluid from injector); **d. d'alimentation,** feed rate; **d. unitaire,** flow rate; **d. total,** mass flow; **d. spécifique,** flow density; **indicateur de d.,** flowmeter; **pompe à grand d.,** heavy-duty pump; **régulateur de d.,** flow regulator; **courbe de d.,** load curve; **d. maximum,** peak load; *(b) Trans:* traffic capacity, output (of road, bridge, railway line); **d. horaire,** hourly capacity, output per hour; **d. du courant de circulation,** rate of traffic flow; *(c) Ind: Mec.E:* output, delivery rate, throughput, throughput rate, (of a machine); *El:* output, power, supplied (by a motor). **4.** delivery, utterance (of orator); **avoir le d. monotone,** to have a monotonous delivery; **avoir le d. facile,** *F:* to have the gift of the gab, a glib tongue; **avoir le d. très lent,** to be slow of speech.
débit[2], *s.m. Com:* debit; debit side; **note de d.,** debit note; **porter, inscrire, une somme au d. de qn,** to debit s.o. with a sum, to enter sth. to s.o.'s debit; **d. de caisse,** cash debit.
débitable [debitabl], *a. (of wood, meat, etc.)* that can be cut up, sawn up.
débitage [debita:ʒ], *s.m.* cutting up, sawing up, conversion (of wood); sawing (of stone).
débitant, -ante [debitɑ̃, -ɑ̃:t], *s.* retail dealer, retailer; *esp.* **d. de boissons,** licensed victualler; **d. de tabac,** often *abs.* **débitant(e),** tobacconist.
débiter[1] [debite], *v.tr.* **1.** to retail; to sell (goods) retail; *abs.* **on débite beaucoup dans cette boutique,** this shop has a large turnover; *F:* **il débite bien sa marchandise,** he has the gift of the gab. **2.** to cut up, saw up, convert, side (timber); to cut up (meat); to saw (stone). **3.** to discharge, yield; **fontaine qui débite mille litres par heure,** spring that yields a thousand litres an hour; **machine qui débite beaucoup d'ouvrage,** machine with a large output; **courant débité par une dynamo,** current delivered by a dynamo. **4.** *(a) Th:* **d. son rôle,** to pronounce, recite, one's part; *abs.* **cet acteur débite mal,** this actor has a bad delivery; **d. trop vite son rôle,** to gabble one's part; *(b) F: usu. Pej:* **d. une longue harangue,** to deliver a long speech; **d. des mensonges,** to utter lies; **d. des histoires,** to spin yarns; **d. des âneries,** to turn out strings of platitudes; **d. une nouvelle,** to spread, retail, a piece of news; **d. tout ce que l'on sait sur un sujet,** to give all the details on a subject; **il ne faut pas croire tout ce qui se débite sur son compte,** do not believe all the things they say about him; *s.a.* SOTTISE 2.
débiter[2], *v.tr. Com:* to debit; **d. une somme à qn, d. qn d'une somme,** to debit s.o. with an amount; **faut-il vous d. le montant?** am I to charge the amount? **d. les frais postaux au client,** to debit the customer with the postage, to charge the postage to the customer; **d. un compte,** to debit an account.
débiteur[1], **-euse** [debitœ:r, -ø:z], *s.* **1.** *usu. Pej:* utterer (of lies, etc.); **d. de calomnies,** scandalmonger; **d. de nouvelles,** newsmonger, spreader of gossip. **2.** assistant (in large stores) who conducts customers to the pay-desk. **3.** *Tchn: (a) Min:* slate-splitter; stone-cutter; *(b)* wood-cutter, sawyer; *(c) s.f.* **débiteuse à lames,** stone-saw. **4.** *Mec.E: etc:* feeding device; *Cin:* top sprocket-wheel (of projector).
débiteur[2], **-trice** [debitœ:r, -tris]. **1.** *(a) s.* debtor; **d. hypothécaire, sur hypothèque,** mortgager, mortgagor, mortgage debtor; *(b) a.* **compte d.** debit account; **solde d.,** debit balance, balance due, balance owing; **solde (de banque) d.,** overdraft. **2.** *s.f.* **débitrice** = DÉBITEUR[1] 2. **3.** *a.* **bobine débitrice,** (i) *Cin:* upper reel, spool; top spool, delivery spool, supply spool; (ii) *Computers:* file reel.
débitmètre [debimɛtr], *s.m.* flowmeter.
débitter [debite], *v.tr. Nau:* to unbitt (cable).
débituminisation [debityminizasjɔ̃], *s.f.* debituminization.
débituminiser [debityminize], *v.tr.* to debituminize.
déblai [deblɛ], *s.m. Civ.E: Rail: etc:* **1.** excavation, cut(ting); clearing; **terrain en d.,** land which has been cleared; **route en d.,** sunk road; **voie en d.,** (railway) cutting; *s.a.* REMBLAI 3. **2.** *(a)* spoil (earth), excavated material, waste; *(b)* debris.
déblaiement [deblɛmɑ̃], *s.m.* **1.** *(a)* excavation, trenching; *(b)* clearing (of ground, of railway-track after accident, etc.). **2.** clearing (away), removal (of excavated material).
déblatération [deblaterasjɔ̃], *s.f.* **1.** abusing, reviling (**contre,** of); railing (**contre,** at, against). **2.** *pl.* abuse.
déblatérer [deblatere], *v.* **(je déblatère, n. déblatérons; je déblatérerai) 1.** *v.tr.* **d. des sottises,** to talk nonsense; *F:* to spout nonsense; **d. des injures,** to fling abuse (**contre,** at); **d. des menaces,** to bluster out threats. **2.** *v.i.* **d. contre qn,** to rail against s.o., to run s.o. down.
déblaver [deblave], *v.tr.* to cut and remove the corn harvest from.
déblayage [deblɛja:ʒ], *s.m.* **1.** *F:* = DÉBLAIEMENT. **2.** *Th: (a)* emphasizing the main speeches of a role by rushing through the others. **3.** *F:* **faire le d. de sa correspondance, de ses affaires,** to clear up one's correspondence, to put one's affairs in order.
déblayement [deblɛmɑ̃], *s.m.* = DÉBLAIEMENT.
déblayer [debleje], *v.tr.* **(je déblaye, je déblaie, n. déblayons) 1.** to clear away, remove (spoil earth, etc.); **d. (à la pelle)** to shovel away. **2.** *(a)* **d. un terrain,** to clear a piece of ground; *F:* **déblayer le terrain,** to clear the ground, the way (for negotiations, etc.); to clear the decks; *Rail:* **d. la voie,** (i) to clear a train out of the way; (ii) to clear the track (*e.g.* after an accident); *s.a.* MACHINE 1; *(b) Th: F:* **d. un rôle,** *abs.* **déblayer,** to emphasize the main speeches in a role by rushing through the others.
déblayeuse [deblejø:z], *s.f. Civ.E:* large bulldozer.
déblocage [deblɔka:ʒ], *s.m.* **1.** = DÉBLOQUEMENT. **2.** freeing; releasing; unjamming (of brake); unclamping (of instrument); **mécanisme de d.,** release gear; unlocking mechanism, device; **levier de d.,** release, unlocking, lever; **poignée de d. de secours,** emergency release, unlocking, handle. **3.** *(a) Rail:* **d. d'une section,** opening, unblocking, of a section. **4.** *Fin:* unfreezing (of capital, prices, wages, etc.). **5.** *Typ:* insertion of the proper sorts in place of the turned letters.
déblocus [deblɔkys], *s.m. Mil:* relief of a town.
débloquement [deblɔkmɑ̃], *s.m. Mil:* raising of a blockade.
débloquer [deblɔke], *v.tr.* **1.** *Mil:* to raise the blockade of (town, port). **2.** to unclamp (instrument), to unjam (brake). **3.** *Rail:* **d. une section,** to open, unblock, a section. **4.** *F:* to free, to release; *Fin:* to unfreeze capital, etc. **5.** *Typ:* to insert the proper sorts in place of the turned letters (set type). **6.** *v.i. P:* to ramble; to talk nonsense; **tu débloques,** you're crackers.
débobinage [debɔbina:ʒ], *s.m.* unreeling; *El:* unwinding, stripping (of coil).
débobiner [debɔbine], *v.tr.* to unreel; *El:* to unwind, strip (coil, etc.).
déboëtter [debwɛte], *v.tr. Fish:* to remove the bait from (a line), to unbait (a line).
déboire [debwa:r], *s.m.* **1.** *A:* (disagreeable) after-taste (of wine, etc.). **2.** (i) disappointment, vexation, blighted hope; (ii) **essuyer bien des déboires,** to suffer many disappointments, many rebuffs.
déboisage [debwaza:ʒ], *s.m. Min:* prop-drawing.
déboisement [debwazmɑ̃], *s.m.* deforestation; clearing of land (of trees); tree-cutting, -felling.
déboiser [debwaze], *v.tr.* **1.** to deforest, untimber (land); to clear (country) of trees. **2.** to untimber (mine-shaft, etc.).
se déboiser, to become, to grow, bare of trees; **montagne qui s'est déboisée,** mountain that has become bare (of trees); **la Sibérie s'est déboisée,** Siberia has lost its forests.
déboiseuse [debwazø:z], *s.f.* clearing plough.
déboîtement [debwatmɑ̃], *s.m.* **1.** dislocation (of limb, etc.), luxation. **2.** *(a) Aut:* filtering (from line of traffic); *(b) Mil:* breaking out of column; *(c) Navy:* hauling out (of the line).
déboîter [debwate], *v.tr.* **1.** to disjoint, disconnect, uncouple (pipe, etc.); **d. une porte,** to take a door off its hinges. **2.** to dislocate (joint), to luxate, to put out of joint; **se d. l'épaule,** to put one's shoulder out; **se d. le genou,** to twist one's knee. **3.** to remove (watch, etc.) from its case; *Bookb:* to uncase (book). **4.** *v.i.* *(a) Aut:* to filter (from line of traffic); *(b) Navy:* **d. de la ligne,** to haul out of the line; *(c) Mil:* **faire d.,** to order a file of soldiers to right-, left-, wheel; to break out of column; **d. vers la droite,** to move off to the right; **d. de la route,** to get off the road; *(d) Skiing:* to move off the track.
se déboîter, *(of shoulder, etc.)* to come out of joint, to be dislocated.
débombage [debɔ̃ba:ʒ], *s.m. Mil:* bomb disposal, clearance.
débomber [debɔ̃be], *v.tr. Mil:* to clear (an area) of bombs.
débonder [debɔ̃de]. **1.** *v.tr.* to unbung (cask); to open the vent of (cask); **d. un réservoir,** to open the sluice gates of a reservoir; *F:* **se d. le cœur, d. son cœur,** *abs.* **débonder,** to pour out one's heart; *P:* **ce purgatif l'a débondé,** this purgative unplugged him, got him going. **2.** *v.i.* *(of liquid)* to burst forth, gush out ,escape; **le lac a débondé,** the lake has burst its dam.
se débonder. 1. *(of cask)* to become unbunged. **2. l'étang s'est débondé cette nuit,** the pond gushed out during the night. **3.** to pour out one's heart; to give vent to one's feelings.
débondonner [debɔ̃dɔne], *v.tr.* to unbung.
débonnaire [debɔnɛ:r], *a.* **1.** *A:* meek, mild, soft. **2.** good-natured, -humoured; easy-going, -tempered; compliant; *A:* debonair; **hautain mais d.,** haughty but condescending; *Iron:* **mari d.,** accommodating husband; *Pej:* **air d.,** indulgent air.
débonnairement [debɔnɛrmɑ̃], *adv.* good-humouredly, good-temperedly, in an easy-going fashion.
débonnaireté [debɔnɛrte], *s.f. Lit:* good humour, good nature, easy temper.
débonneter [debɔnte], *v.i. Hort:* *(of fruit)* to shed dry flowers, remnants of flowers.
déboqueter [debɔkte], *v.tr. Civ.E:* to remove the formwork, the shuttering, the casing (from a concrete pile).
Débora(h) [debɔra], *Pr.n.f.* Deborah.
débord [debɔ:r], *s.m.* **1.** *(a)* (over)flow; *A.Med:* defluxion (of the humours); *(b) Rail:* **voie de d.,** (i) side-track (to works, etc.); (ii) track alongside a road. **2.** edge, rim (of coin); border (of road). **3.** *Dressm:* piped lining.
débordage [debɔrda:ʒ], *s.m.* edging, trimming (of sheet-iron, of a lens, etc.).
débordant [debɔrdɑ̃], *a.* **1.** overflowing, brimming over (**de,** with); *F:* **sa joie était débordante,** he was brimming over, bubbling over, with joy; **gaieté débordante,** boisterous spirits; **enthousiasme d.,** overflowing, utmost, enthusiasm; **d. de santé,** bursting with health, exuberantly healthy; *F:* **train d. de voyageurs,** train bulging with passengers. **2.** *(a)* projecting, protruding; *Av:* **plan d.,** overlapping plane; top plane that projects beyond the lower plane; *(b) Mil:* **attaque débordante,** outflanking attack.

débordé [debɔrde], *a.* **1.** overflowed, overflowing (river, lake, etc.); **eau débordée,** overflow. **2.** être **d. de travail, de requêtes,** to be overwhelmed, *F:* snowed under, with work, with requests; **être d. de visiteurs,** to have a flood of callers; *Com:* **nous sommes débordés,** we are very pressed, very much rushed; **d. par les événements,** unable to keep pace with developments, events. **3.** *A:* licentious, dissipated (man, life). **4.** outflanked (battalion). **5. drap d., couverture débordée,** untucked sheet, blanket; sheet, blanket which has come untucked; *F:* **malade d.,** patient, who has come untucked, whose bed has come untucked.

débordement [debɔrdəmɑ̃], *s.m.* **1.** *(a)* overflow(ing) (of river, etc.); *F:* **d. d'injures,** outburst of abuse; **d. de fureur,** explosion of wrath; **d. d'esprit,** overflowing wit; *El:* **d. d'étincelles,** emission of sparks; **d. d'étincelles entre les bornes,** flash across the terminals; *(b) A.Med:* defluxion (of humours); *(c) usu. pl.,* debauchery, excess, dissipation; dissolute living, licentiousness; **les débordements de sa jeunesse,** the excesses of his youth. **2.** *(a) Mil: Navy:* outflanking (of enemy); **manœuvre de d.,** encircling movement; *Mil:* **d. d'un îlot de résistance,** envelopment of an island of resistance; *(b) Fb:* encircling the defence, sweep-play. **3.** *Nau:* unshipping, unshipment (of oars).

déborder [debɔrde]. **1.** *v.i.* to overflow, brim over, run over; (of milk, etc.) to boil over; **la rivière a débordé,** the river has overflowed (its banks); **la coupe déborde,** the cup is running over; **verre plein à d.,** glass full to overflowing; **verre de bière plein à d.,** glass brim-full of beer; *Prov:* **c'est la goutte d'eau qui fait d. le vase,** it is the last straw that breaks the camel's back; **cette remarque a fait d. le vase,** that remark was the last straw; **mon cœur déborde,** my heart is overflowing; **d. en injures,** to break out into abuse; **livre qui déborde d'esprit,** book brimming over with wit; **faire d. qn,** to push s.o. to the limit; **sa bile a débordé,** he lost his temper; **se laisser d. par le travail, les événements,** to let events, work, get on top of one; **elle déborde de vie, de joie, d'enthousiasme,** she is bubbling over with vitality, joy, enthusiasm; **elle déborde de reconnaissance,** she is brimming over with gratitude; **Londres déborde d'étrangers,** London swarms with foreigners; **le train déborde de voyageurs,** the train bulges with passengers; **d. de son rôle,** to go outside one's province. **2.** *v.tr.* *(a)* to project, jut out, stick out, protrude, extend, beyond (sth.); to overlap (sth.); **d. le cadre de la question,** to go beyond the limits of the question; **pierre qui déborde le mur,** stone projecting, jutting out, from the wall; **les événements nous débordent,** we can't keep pace with events; **doublure qui déborde le gilet,** lining that shows beyond the waistcoat; **dents qui débordent les lèvres,** protruding teeth; *(b) Mil:* to outflank (the enemy); *(c)* to remove (sth.) from a border; **d. un navire,** to rip off a ship's planks; **d. les avirons,** to unship the oars; **d. (les couvertures d')un lit,** to untuck a bed; *Nau:* **d. une embarcation d'un vaisseau,** *abs.* **déborder,** to shove off, bear off, sheer off; **d. les voiles,** to let go; *v.i.* **l'embarcation débordera du quai à deux heures,** the boat will put off from the quay at two o'clock; *(d)* to remove the border from (sth.); **d. une nappe,** to remove, cut off, the border, the edging, from a cloth; **d. une tôle, une table de plomb,** to trim the edges of an iron, a lead plate.

se déborder, *A:* **1.** = DÉBORDER 1. **2. se d. en injures,** to break into abuse.

débordoir [debɔrdwa:r], *s.m. Tchn:* edging tool (of plumber, etc.).

débosquage [debɔska:ʒ], *s.m.* timber haulage.

débosseler [debɔsle], *v.tr.* **(je débosselle, n. débosselons; je débossellerai)** to remove the dents, bumps, from (sth.); *Tchn:* **marteau à d.,** bumping hammer.

débosser [debɔse], *v.tr. Nau:* to take the stopper off (cable).

débotter [debɔte]. I. **1.** *v.tr.* to take off (s.o.'s) (top) boots, to unboot (s.o.). **2. se débotter,** to take off, pull off, one's boots.

II. **débotter,** *s.m.,* **débotté,** *s.m.* [debɔte], *A:* action, moment, of taking off one's (top)boots; *F:* **au débotté,** immediately upon arrival, at once, right away; *A:* **prendre qn au d.,** to take s.o. unawares.

débouchage [debuʃa:ʒ], *s.m.* **1.** clearing, unchoking (of pipe). **2.** uncorking, unstopp(er)ing (of bottles). **3.** *Mil:* setting (of time-fuse).

débouché [debuʃe], *s.m.* **1.** *(a)* outlet, opening, issue (of passage, sap, mountain gorge, etc.); exit (from building, etc.); *Mil:* point of arrival (of column); *Civ.E:* waterway (of bridge); outfall (of sewer); *(b)* inlet (into pond). **2.** opening, opportunity; **quels débouchés y a-t-il pour un jeune homme?** what openings are there for a young man? *Com:* **se créer des débouchés pour un article,** to find openings, a market, for an article; **créer de nouveaux débouchés,** to open up new channels, new avenues, for trade; *Com:* **port qui est le d. des pays de l'Est,** harbour which serves as the outlet of the Eastern countries; **l'Allemagne est un bon d.,** Germany is a good market; **vous pouvez compter sur un bon d., pour cette marchandise,** you may count on a ready sale for these goods. **3.** *(a)* **au d. des bois ils tombèrent sur des braconniers,** on emerging from the woods they ran into poachers; *(b) Mil:* debouching, emerging; jump(ing)-off; **ligne de d.,** start(ing) line, jump(ing)-off line, *U.S:* line of departure.

débouche-becs [debuʃbɛk], *s.m.inv. in pl.* probe, pricker (for acetylene jets, etc.).

débouchement[1] [debuʃmɑ̃], *s.m.* = DÉBOUCHAGE.

débouchement[2], *s.m.* = DÉBOUCHÉ 1, 2.

déboucher[1] [debuʃe], *v.tr.* **1.** to clear, unchoke (pipe, etc.); *I.C.E:* **d. le gicleur,** to clean out the jet; *Med: F:* **d. qn,** to open, clear, s.o.'s bowels. **2.** to uncork, unstopper, open (bottle); *F:* **d. l'intelligence d'un enfant,** to awaken, arouse, a child's intelligence. **3.** to set, punch (time-fuse).

déboucher,[2] *v.i.* **1.** to emerge, issue forth; **l'armée déboucha du défilé dans la plaine,** the army emerged from the pass into the plain; **d. sur l'ennemi,** to come out upon the enemy; **rues qui débouchent sur la place du marché,** roads that open on to, that run into, the market place; **escalier débouchant sur le trottoir,** stairway opening on the pavement; **le Rhône débouche dans la Méditerranée,** the Rhone flows into the Mediterranean; **tandis que nous débouchions au soleil . . .,** as we stepped out into the sunshine . . .; **nous débouchions sur la route quand . . .,** we were coming on to the road when . . .. **2.** *Ven:* = DÉBUCHER 1.

débouchoir [debuʃwa:r], *s.m.* **1.** *Dom.Ec:* rubber plunger. **2.** *Lap:* clearing-iron. **3.** *Mil:* fuse-borer; *Artil:* fuse-setter, (fuse-)punch. **4.** *Agr:* pointed stick for scraping mud off plough-shares.

débouchure [debuʃy:r], *s.f. Mil:* punching (of fuse).

déboucler [debukle], *v.tr.* **1.** *(a)* to unbuckle (belt, etc.); *F:* **d. sa ceinture,** to loosen one's purse-strings; *(b) P:* to release (prisoner). **2.** to take the curl out of, to uncurl (hair).

se déboucler. **1.** *(of belt)* to become unbuckled. **2.** to become uncurled; *(of hair)* to fall out of curl, to uncurl.

débouillage [debuja:ʒ], *s.m.* = DÉBOUILLISSAGE.

débouilli [debuji], *s.m. Dy:* testing dye by boiling; *Tex:* bleaching.

débouillir [debuji:r], *v.i. Dy:* to boil for testing dye; *Tex:* to bleach; *Tex:* **cuve à d.,** kier.

débouillissage [debujisa:ʒ], *s.m.* **1.** *Tex:* boiling off. **2.** *Dy:* testing dye by boiling.

débouler [debule]. I. *v.i.* **1.** to fall head over heels, to roll down; *v.tr.* **d. l'escalier,** to roll downstairs. **2.** *(a) Ven:* *(of game)* to start, bolt (from cover); *(b) F:* to clear out, off; **allons, il faut d.,** come on, we must be off, get going; *(c) Sp:* to make a quick start, to race away, shoot off, (from the starting line).

II. **débouler,** *s.m.,* **déboulé** [debule], *s.m.* *(a)* **tirer un lapin au d.,** to shoot a rabbit, as it bolts from cover; *(b) Sp:* quick start; *(c) Danc:* **déboulés,** déboulés.

déboulonnage [debulɔna:ʒ], *s.m.,* **déboulonnement** [debulɔnmɑ̃], *s.m.* **1.** unriveting; unbolting. **2.** knocking, throwing, over, down; *F:* debunking.

déboulonner [debulɔne], *v.tr.* **1.** to unrivet; to unbolt. **2.** *F:* *(a)* to knock, to throw, over, down; *(b)* to knock (s.o.) off his pedestal; *F:* to debunk (s.o.); *(c)* to fire, to sack (s.o.).

débouquement [debukmɑ̃], *s.m. Nau:* **1.** disemboguing, disemboguement. **2.** passage, strait (between islands, etc.).

débouquer [debuke], *v.i. A:* *(of ship)* to disembogue.

débourbage [deburba:ʒ], *s.m.* **1.** clearing out of the mud (from ditch, etc.). **2.** *Min:* washing, trunking, sluicing (of ore); *Winem:* **cuve de d.,** settling vat. **3.** hauling (of sth.) out of the mire.

débourber [deburbe], *v.tr.* **1.** to cleanse, to clear (of mud); **d. un égout,** to sluice a sewer; **d. une citerne,** to clean out a cistern; **d. une rivière,** to dredge a river; *Min:* **d. du minerai,** to trunk, clean, wash, sluice, ore; *Winem:* **d. le vin,** to rack, draw off, decant, wine; *Pisc:* **d. des carpes,** to put carp into clean water (to make them lose their muddy taste). **2.** to haul (carriage, etc.) out of the mire; *F: A:* **d. qn,** to get s.o. out of a mess.

débourbeur [deburbœ:r], *s.m. Gold Min:* sluice.

débourgeoiser [deburʒwaze], *v.tr.* to rid (s.o.) of middle-class ways or prejudices; **d. un cousin de province,** to smarten, polish up, a country cousin; **famille qui s'est débourgeoisée,** family that has climbed the social ladder.

débourrage [debura:ʒ], *s.m.* **1.** *(a) Leath:* unhairing; scraping off the hair (of skin); *(b) Tex:* stripping, cleaning (of carding-machine). **2.** *(a)* removal of the wad (from fire-arm), of wadding, padding, stuffing (from furniture, etc.); *(b) Min:* untamping.

débourrement [deburmɑ̃], *s.m. Bot:* opening of buds, budding (of trees in spring).

débourre-pipes [deburpip], *s.m.inv.* pipe cleaner.

débourrer [debure], *v.tr.* **1.** *(a) Leath:* to unhair; to scrape the hair off (skins); *(b) Tex:* to strip, clean (carding-machine). **2.** to remove the wad from (fire-arm); to remove the padding, stuffing, from (armchair, etc.); to remove the tobacco from (pipe); to loosen the ballast under (railway sleeper, etc.); *Min:* to untamp (blast-hole); *V:* **d. (sa pipe),** to clear one's bowels. **3. d. un cheval,** to break in a horse; *F:* **d. qn,** to give s.o. easier, more polished, manners; to smarten s.o. up. **4.** *v.i. Bot:* *(of buds)* to open.

se débourrer, *F:* to smarten up.

débourroir [deburwa:r], *s.m. Tls:* padding extractor.

débourrure [debury:r], *s.f. Tex:* waste.

débours [debu:r], *s.m. usu. pl.* **1.** disbursement; out-of-pocket expenses; outgoings; **faire des d.,** to lay out money; **rentrer dans ses d.,** to recover one's outlay. **2.** extra charges on delivery note.

déboursé [deburse], *s.m.* = DÉBOURS.

déboursement [deburs(ə)mɑ̃], *s.m.* paying out, disbursement, disbursing, laying out.

débourser [deburse], *v.tr.* *(a)* to disburse, spend, lay out (money); **sans rien d.,** without spending a penny; *(b) abs.* to part with one's money, to pay up; *F:* to fork out; **je suis toujours à d.,** I am always dipping my hand into my pocket.

déboussoler [debusɔle], *v.tr. P:* to disconcert, to confuse; **un enfant déboussolé,** a bewildered child.

debout [dəbu], *adv.* **1.** *(a)* *(of thg)* upright, on end; *(of pers.)* standing; **mettre, dresser, qch. d.,** to stand sth. up(right), on end; to raise, rear (mast, etc.); *Nau:* **mâts d.,** vertical masts; **remettre les quilles d.,** to set the skittles up again; **tenir qch. d.,** to keep sth. upright; **"tenir debout," "keep upright";** se **tenir d.,** to stand; *(of dog)* to stand on its hind legs; **vingt personnes peuvent s'y tenir d.,** twenty people can stand there, there is standing room for twenty people; **personne debout,** person standing, *U.S:* standee; **le projet ne tient pas d.,** the scheme is preposterous, is half-baked; **argument qui ne tient pas d.,** argument that won't hold water; **phrase qui tient d.,** sentence that makes sense; se **(re)mettre d.,** to stand up, to rise to one's feet, to get on one's feet; **rester d.,** (i) to remain standing; (ii) to keep one's footing, one's feet; **(re)tomber d.,** to fall on one's feet; **il ne restait pas une colonne d.,** not a column was left standing; **passer la nuit d.,** to stay up all night; **malgré ses revers le gouvernement est encore d.,** in spite of set-backs the government is still on its feet; **le vieux chêne, la maison, est encore d.,** the old oak, the house, is still standing, still stands; *F:* **mourir d.,** to die in harness; *Mil:* **debout!** (i) stand up! (ii) (stand to) attention! **debout, les gardes!** up guards! *Sp:* **record encore d.,** unbeaten record; *Const:* **assise d.,** brick-on-end course; *s.a.* BOIS 2, DORMIR 1, MAGISTRATURE 2; *(b) (of pers.)* **être d.,** to be up; **allons, d.!** (i) wake up! (ii) get up! **debout!** stand up; **il n'est pas encore d.,** he is not up, out of bed, yet; *Nau:* **d. au quart, d.!** wakey, wakey! **il va mieux, il est d. maintenant,** he is better, he is up now; *Ven:* **mettre une bête d.,** to start an animal; *(c) Cust:* **passer d.,** to have a permit for transire; *s.a.* PASSE-DEBOUT. **2.** *Nau:* **d. à la mer, à la lame, au vent,** (with) bows on to the sea; head on to the sea, to the wind; **vent d.,** head wind; **avoir vent d., la mer d.,** to have a head wind, the wind in one's teeth; to have a head sea; *F:* **avoir vent d.,**

to go into the teeth of (the) opposition; *F:* **il a une figure de vent d.**, he is like a bear with a sore head; **prendre les lames d.**, to head the waves; **marcher vent d.**, to thrash, thresh, to windward. **3.** *Av:* **décoller, atterrir, vent d.**, to take off, to land, into the wind.
débouté [debute], *s.m. Jur:* nonsuit.
déboutement [debutmɑ̃], *s.m. Jur:* nonsuit.
débouter [debute], *v.tr. Jur:* **1.** to dismiss, reject (suit). **2. d. qn (de sa demande)**, to dismiss s.o.'s claim, to nonsuit s.o.; **vous serez débouté de votre demande**, you have no case.
déboutonnage [debutɔnaːʒ], *s.m.* **1.** unbuttoning (of garment). **2.** *Fenc:* taking the button off (the foil). **3.** *F:* unloading of one's mind. **4.** *Mec.E:* flying (of rivets).
déboutonner [debutɔne], *v.tr.* **1.** to unbutton (garment, child); **son manteau est déboutonné**, his coat is unbuttoned; *F:* **manger à ventre déboutonné**, to gorge; **rire à ventre déboutonné**, to laugh immoderately, to heave with laughter. **2.** to take the button off (foil).
se déboutonner. **1.** (*a*) to unbutton oneself; (*b*) *F:* to unburden one's mind; *F:* to get it off one's chest. **2.** (*of garment*) to come unbuttoned. **3.** *Mec.E:* (*of riveting*) to fly.
débraillé [debrɑje]. **1.** *a.* untidy, all unbuttoned (person); **tenue débraillée**, untidy, hardly decent, appearance; **mœurs débraillées**, loose morals; bohemian habits; **conversation débraillée**, free, coarse, conversation. **2.** *s.m.* slovenliness; carelessness; **d. artistique**, artistic disorder, disarray.
débrailler (se) [sədebrɑje], *v.pr.* to unbutton (one's waistcoat, shirt, blouse, etc.), to undo one's front buttons; *F:* **la conversation se débraille**, the conversation is getting somewhat free, near the knuckle.
débraisage [debrɛzaːʒ], *s.m. Tchn:* removing of embers.
débraisement [debrɛzmɑ̃], *s.m. Tchn:* removing of embers.
débraiser [debrɛze], *v.tr. Tchn:* to remove embers.
débranchement [debrɑ̃ʃmɑ̃], *s.m.* **1.** *El.E: etc:* disconnection, disconnecting; *Computer:* make and break. **2.** *Rail:* splitting-up (of train); **voie de d.**, making-up siding.
débrancher [debrɑ̃ʃe], *v.tr.* **1.** *El.E: etc:* to disconnect. **2.** *Rail:* to split up (a train).
débrayage[1] [debrejaːʒ], *s.m.* **1.** *Aut: Mec.E:* declutching, uncoupling, disconnecting; throwing, putting, out of gear; (clutch) disengagement, throw-out; *Mec.E:* (i) release, releasing; throwing out of action, out of operation, out of feed; (ii) laying-off, throwing-off, shifting (of belt); *Aut:* **à d. automatique**, with automatic clutch; **manchon de d.**, disconnecting clutch; **fourche(tte) de d.**, disconnecting, disengaging, fork; **levier de d.**, clutch arm, throw-out lever; **mécanisme, dispositif, de d.**, (i) *Aut: Mec.E:* disconnecting, disengaging, declutching, mechanism; (ii) *Mec.E:* (*of belt*) (belt-)shifter, striker; *Aut: etc:* **pédale de d.**, clutch pedal. **2.** *F:* going on strike, downing of tools, stoppage.
débrayage[2], *s.m.* removing a coating of tar, pitch.
débrayer[1] [debreje], *v.tr.* (**je débraye, je débraie, n. débrayons; je débrayerai, je débraierai**) **1.** *Mec.E:* to disconnect, disengage (part); to throw, put, (part) out of gear; to put (part) out of action; to ungear (part). **2.** *abs. Aut:* to let the clutch out, to release the clutch. **3.** *F:* (*a*) to go on strike, to down tools, to come out (on strike); (*b*) (*of workman*) to knock off.
débrayer[2], *v.tr.* to remove a coating of tar, pitch.
débrayeur [debrejœːr], *s.m. Mec.E:* **d. de courroie**, (belt-)shifter, striker.
débréler [debrele], *v.tr. Rail: etc:* to unlash (load on truck, etc.).
débridé [debride], *a.* **1.** unbridled (appetite, tongue, etc.). **2.** *Cu:* untrussed (chicken, etc.).
débridement [debridmɑ̃], *s.m.* **1.** unbridling (of horse, etc.). **2.** unslinging (of a load, stone, etc.); **3.** *Surg:* incision, slitting up (of adhesions, etc.); debridement; (wound) excision.
débrider [debride], *v.tr.* **1.** (*a*) to unbridle (horse, etc.); (*hence*) to halt; *abs. F:* **travailler dix heures sans d.**, to work ten hours without stopping, non-stop, at a stretch; **il faut d. après ce travail**, one must (take a) rest after this work; (*b*) *A: F:* **d. ses prières**, to gabble through one's prayers; (*c*) *Cu:* to untruss (a chicken, etc.). **2.** *Tchn:* to unsling (a stone, etc.). **3.** *Surg:* to incise, slit up (adhesion, etc.); to open up (an abscess); **d. une plaie**, to excise a wound; *F:* **d. les yeux à, de, qn**, to open s.o.'s eyes.
se débrider, to become free, independent.

débris [debri], *s.m.pl.* remains, remnants, leftovers; wreckage, debris, fragments; waste, rubbish; **tomber en d.**, to fall to pieces; **d. d'un vase**, broken fragments of a vase; **d. de navires naufragés**, driftwood of wrecked vessels; wreckage; **d. d'une volaille**, remains, scraps, carcass, of a chicken; **d. d'un repas, d'un plat, etc.**, scraps of a meal, of food, etc.; *Prehist:* **d. de cuisine**, kitchen-midden; **d. de drap**, scraps of cloth; **réunir les d. de sa fortune**, to gather together what is left of one's fortune; **d. d'or**, trimmings (from gold leaf); **d. de bois**, shavings, chips; sawdust; *Ind:* **d. métalliques**, scrap-iron, -steel; *occ. in sg.* **un d. de vase antique**, a fragment from an ancient vase; *P:* **un vieux d.**, a decrepit old man.
débrochage [debrɔʃaːʒ], *s.m. Bookb:* stripping, unstitching.
débrocher [debrɔʃe], *v.tr.* **1.** to remove (roast, etc.) from the spit; to unspit (chicken, etc.). **2.** *Bookb:* to strip, unstitch (book); **se d.**, to become unstitched.
débronzer [debrɔ̃ze], *v.tr.* **1.** to remove the bronzing from (sth.). **2.** *abs. F:* to lose one's tan.
débrouillage [debrujaːʒ], *s.m.* **1.** *F:* shifting for oneself, extricating oneself (from difficulties); *F:* wangling. **2.** unravelling.
débrouillard, -arde [debrujaːr, -ard]. **1.** *a. F:* (*a*) resourceful; canny (*esp.* at getting out of difficulties); (*b*) clear-headed. **2.** *s. F:* resourceful young chap or young woman; **c'est un d.**, he's all there, he's got his wits about him, he can fend for himself; he has plenty of gumption; he's a smart lad.
débrouillardise [debrujardiːz], *s.f. F:* smartness; resourcefulness.
débrouille [debruːj], *s.f. F:* wangling, fixing.
débrouillé, -ée [debruje], *a.* **c'est un enfant très d. pour son âge**, he is very bright for (a child of) his age.
débrouillement [debrujmɑ̃], *s.m.* unravelling, disentangling, sorting out.
débrouiller [debruje], *v.tr.* to unravel, disentangle (thread, etc.); to sort out (papers, etc.); **d. une affaire**, to clear up, unravel, straighten out, an affair; to put matters straight; to put things right; **d. les abords d'une question**, to clear the approaches to a question; **je n'ai pas pu d. la signature**, I was not able to make out, to decipher, the signature; **d. un enfant**, to awake a child's intelligence, mind; *F:* **d. qn**, to get s.o. out of a jam.
se débrouiller. **1.** (*of the sky, complexion, etc.*) to clear (up). **2.** to extricate oneself (from difficulties); **qu'il se débrouille!** let him shift for himself! **il s'agit de se d.**, we've got to get out of this; **arriver à se d. à l'étranger**, to manage to get along abroad; **il s'est débrouillé pour l'obtenir**, he wangled to get it; **débrouillez-vous!** that's your look-out! *F:* **se d. sur le voisin**, to pass the baby, to pass the buck; *P:* **débrouille-toi avec les parents de la fille, débrouille-toi tout seul**, that's your baby!
débrouilleur, -euse [debrujœːr, -øːz], *s. F:* unraveller (of difficulties, etc.); decipherer (of manuscripts, etc.).
débroussaillant [debrusajɑ̃], *a. & s.m.* brushwood killer.
débroussaillement [debrusajmɑ̃], *s.m.* clearing (ground) of undergrowth.
débroussailler [debrusaje], *v.tr.* to clear (ground) of undergrowth; *F:* to clear the way (for); to do the spade-work on (project, etc.).
débroussailleur [debrusajœːr], *s.m.* workman who clears undergrowth.
débroussailleuse [debrusajøːz], *s.f. Hort:* treedozer.
débrutir [debrytiːr], *v.tr.* to rough-cut (gem, marble, etc.).
débrutissement [debrytismɑ̃], *s.m.* rough-cutting (of gem, marble, etc.).
débucher [debyʃe]. I. *v.i. Ven:* (*of big game*) to break cover; **faire débucher**, *v.tr.* **débucher, un cerf**, to unharbour, dislodge, start, a stag, to drive, force, a stag from cover; **faire d. le blaireau**, to draw the badger; *v.tr.* **d. l'ennemi de la ville**, to dislodge the enemy from the town.
II. **débucher**, *s.m.*, **débuché** [debyʃe], *s.m. Ven:* (i) breaking cover; (ii) (*on the horn*) "gone away"; **au débuché . . .**, at the start . . . .
débuscable [debyskabl], *a.* that can be dislodged, driven out.
débusquement [debyskəmɑ̃], *s.m.* (*a*) *Mil:* dislodgment (of enemy from under cover); (*b*) ousting (of s.o.) (from a situation).

débusquer [debyske]. **1.** *v.tr.* (*a*) *Mil:* to drive (enemy) out of ambush, from under cover; **l'artillerie eut bientôt fait de les d.**, the artillery soon hunted them out; (*b*) to oust (s.o.) (from a situation); (*c*) *Ven:* = DÉBUCHER. **2.** *v.i.* (*a*) *Mil: etc:* to come out of ambush, from under cover); to come out of hiding; (*b*) *Ven:* = DÉBUCHER.
début [deby], *s.m.* **1.** *Games:* first turn, first play; *Dice:* first throw, first cast; *Cards:* lead. **2.** first appearance, début (of actor, etc.); **faire son début**, to make one's first appearance; **sa fille fait son d., ses débuts, (dans le monde) cet hiver**, his daughter is coming out this winter; **société à ses débuts**, association in its infancy. **3.** beginning, commencement, start, outset, first steps; **dès le d.**, from the outset (de, of), at the very outset; **depuis le d. jusqu'à la fin**, from first to last, from beginning to end; **au d. des hostilités**, at the outbreak, commencement, of hostilities; **au d. de sa carrière**, at the outset of his career, early in his career; **jusqu'au d. du dixième siècle**, until the beginning of the tenth century; **avant le d. de l'hiver**, before winter sets in, begins; **aux appointements de d. de sept mille francs**, at a starting salary of seven thousand francs; **discours de d.**, maiden speech; **formule de d.**, opening phrase; **livre de d.**, first book; **j'en reviens à mon d.**, I come back to what I said at first; **la maladie n'est qu'au d. de son évolution**, the disease is only in the initial stages; **d. de pleurésie**, incipient pleurisy; **les difficultés du d.**, the initial difficulties; **dans les débuts, au d.**, in the beginning, at first, initially, to start with; **au d. de l'année**, early in the year, at the beginning of the year; **j'y étais dès le d.**, I was there from the very start, beginning, from the first; **dès le d. de la pièce**, (i) from the very beginning of the play; (ii) as soon as the play started, began; **il en est à son d.**, he is just starting; *Pej:* **il n'en est plus à ses débuts**, he is no novice; **un d. de sourire aux lèvres**, with the beginnings, a hint, of a smile on his, her, lips.
débutanisation [debytanizasjɔ̃], *s.f. Petroleum Ind:* debutanization.
débutaniser [debytanize], *v.tr. Petroleum Ind:* to debutanize.
débutaniseur [debytanizœːr], *s.m. Petroleum Ind:* debutanizer.
débutant, -ante [debytɑ̃, -ɑ̃ːt], *s.* **1.** beginner, novice; actor, etc., making his first appearance; inexperienced driver, etc.; **d. dans une profession**, entrant into a profession; **classe de débutants**, beginners' class; **ce n'est qu'un d.**, he is only a beginner. **2.** *s.f.* **débutante**, girl who has just come out, débutante; *F:* deb.
débuter[1] [debyte], *v.i.* **1.** *Games:* to play first; *Dice:* to throw first; *Cards:* to lead; *Bill:* to string. **2.** to make one's first appearance (on the stage, etc.); to make one's début; **il débuta avec . . .**, his first book, play, film, etc., was . . .; **faire d. une jeune fille dans le monde**, to bring out a girl; **elle doit d. cet hiver**, she is coming out this winter. **3.** to begin, start, commence; **vous débutez à mille francs par mois**, you start at a thousand francs a month; **il débuta dans la vie comme employé de bureau**, he began life as an office clerk; **il me faut de l'argent pour d.**, I must get money to start with; **vous travaillerez ici pour d.**, you will work here for a start; **la pièce débute par un prologue**, the play begins, opens, starts off, with a prologue; **dans son article il débute sur un accident d'automobile**, he starts off his article with a car accident.
débuter,[2] *v.tr. Sp:* to remove (a ball, etc.), from near a goal.
débuttage [debytaːʒ], *s.m.* laying bare the roots (of tree).
déc(a)- [dek(a)], *pref.* dec(a)-; **décac(h)orde**, decachord; **décastyle**, decastyle.
deçà [dəsa], *adv.* on this side; **d. et delà, deçà delà**, here and there, on this side and that, on all sides; **jambe d., jambe delà**, astraddle; **la flèche tomba en d.**, the arrow fell short; *prep.phr.* **en d. de qch.**, (on) this side of sth.; **ni en d. ni au-delà**, neither this side nor beyond; **être en d. de la vérité**, to be well within the truth.
décabillotter [dekabijɔte], *v.tr. Nau:* to untoggle (rope, etc.).
décabristes [dekabrist], *s.m.pl. Russian Hist:* Decembrists.
décachetable [dekaʃtabl], *a.* that can be unsealed, broken open, (letter, etc.).
décachetage [dekaʃtaːʒ], *s.m.* unsealing, opening (of letter, etc.).
décacheter [dekaʃte], *v.tr.* (*conj. like* CACHETER). to unseal, open, break open (letter, etc.).

décac(h)orde [dekakɔrd], *s.m. Mus:* decachord.

décadactyle [dekadaktil], *a.* decadactylous.

décadaire [dekadɛːr], *a. Fr.Hist: (Revolution):* decadal (month).

décade [dekad], *s.f.* **1.** period of ten days. **2.** period of ten years; *F:* decade. **3.** *Adm:* tobacco ration (for ten days in 1939-45). **4.** decade (series of ten); **les décades de Tite-Live,** the Decades of Livy.

décadenasser [dekadnɑse], *v.tr.* to unpadlock.

décadence [dekadɑ̃ːs], *s.f. (a)* decadence, decline, decay; **la d. de l'Empire romain,** the decline of the Roman Empire; **d. des arts,** decadence of the arts; **être en d.,** to be on the downgrade; **tomber en d.,** to sink into decay, to decline; *(b) Lit: Art:* decadence, decadency; decadent period.

décadent [dekadɑ̃]. **1.** *a.* decadent, declining, in decay. **2.** *s.m. Lit: Art:* decadent.

décadentisme [dekadɑ̃tism], *s.m. Lit: Art:* decadentism.

décadi [dekadi], *s.m. Fr.Hist:* tenth day of the decade (in Fr. Republican calendar).

décadrage [dekadraːʒ], *s.m. (a) Cin: T.V:* misframe; *(b) Computers:* off-registration.

décadré [dekadre], *a. Computers:* off-gauge.

décaèdre [dekaɛːdr̥], *Geom:* **1.** *a.* decahedral. **2.** *s.m.* decahedron.

décaféination [dekafeinasjɔ̃], *s.f.* decaffeinization.

décaféiner [dekafeine], *v.tr.* to decaffeinate, to decaffeinize; **café décaféiné,** decaffeinated, decaffeinized, caffeine-free, coffee.

décagénaire [dekaʒenɛːr], *s.m. & f. Sociology:* adolescent.

décager [dekaʒe], *v.tr.* to uncage.

décagonal, -aux [dekagɔnal, -o], *a. Geom:* decagonal.

décagone [dekagɔn], *s.m. Geom:* decagon.

décagramme [dekagram], *s.m. Meas:* decagram (me) (= ⅓ oz.).

décagyne [dekaʒin], *a. Bot:* decagynian, decagynous.

décaissage [dekɛsaːʒ], *s.m.* **1.** unpacking, uncasing, unboxing (of goods, etc.), taking out of a box, case. **2.** *Hort:* planting out (of plant, shrub).

décaissement [dekɛsmɑ̃], *s.m.* **1.** = DÉCAISSAGE. **2.** *Com: Fin:* withdrawal (of a sum of money, of funds), payment, paying-out (of cash).

décaisser [dekese], *v.tr.* **1.** to unpack, uncase, unbox (goods, etc.), to take out of a box, case. **2.** *Hort:* to plant out (plant, shrub). **3.** *Com: Fin:* to withdraw (a sum of money, funds); to pay out (cash).

décalage [dekalaːʒ], *s.m.* **1.** *(a) Mec.E: etc:* unwedging, unkeying (of pistons, etc.); *(b)* unscotching (of wheel). **2.** (i) staggering; (ii) stagger (of rivets, of aircraft wings); *Av:* **d. latéral (des plans),** overhang (of wing); **d. (des plans) vers l'avant,** forward, front, stagger; positive stagger (of wing); **d. (des plans) vers l'arrière,** backward, rear, stagger; negative stagger (of wing); **angle de d.,** angle of stagger. **3.** *(a)* shifting of the zero (of an instrument); *El.E:* **d. des balais,** brush-shifting, displacement of the brushes; *(b) (time, etc.)* lag; *Adm:* **d. de l'heure,** altering of the time (to summer time); **entre Tokyo et Paris il y a un d. horaire de 8 heures,** local time in Tokyo is 8 hours ahead of (that of) Paris; *(c)* (amount of) shift; *El.E:* (angular) displacement; difference of phase (of current); *Astr:* **d. vers le rouge,** red shift; **d. de phase,** phase shift; **d. en avant,** lead; **d. en arrière,** lag; **d. de fréquence,** frequency slippage. **4.** getting out of step (of operations), time lag (between operations). **5.** *(a)* lack of connection; **il y a d. entre l'Est et l'Ouest,** there is a lack of understanding between East and West; *(b) Pol. Ec:* gap.

décalaminage [dekalaminaːʒ], *s.m.* **1.** *I.C.E:* decarbonizing; *F:* decoking (of cylinders). **2.** *Metall:* descaling.

décalaminant [dekalaminɑ̃], *a. I.C.E:* **carburant additionnel d.,** carbon-preventative fuel; anti-carbon fuel.

décalaminer [dekalamine], *v.tr.* **1.** *I.C.E:* to decarbonize; *F:* decoke (cylinders). **2.** *Metall:* to descale.

décalcifiant [dekalsifjɑ̃], *a. Med:* **régime d.,** decalcifying diet.

décalcification [dekalsifikasjɔ̃], *s.f. Med: Geol:* decalcification (of bones, of rock).

décalcifier [dekalsifje], *v.tr. Med: Geol:* to decalcify.

se décalcifier, *(of bones, rocks, etc.)* to become decalcified.

décalcomanie [dekalkɔmani], *s.f. Cer: etc:* decalcomania; transfer (process or picture).

décaler [dekale], *v.tr.* **1.** *(a) Mec.E: etc:* to unwedge, unkey; **d. le piston de sa tige,** to force the piston off the rod; **d. une table,** to remove the wedge from under a table; *(b)* to unscotch (wheel). **2.** to set off (part of machine, etc.); to stagger (rivets, aircraft wings, etc.); **transmission décalée vers la gauche,** drive-off set to the left. **3.** to shift the zero of (an instrument); *El.E:* to displace, shift (the brushes, etc.); **magnéto décalée,** magneto out of adjustment; *Adm:* **d. l'heure,** to alter the time (to summer-time); **d. tous les trains d'une heure,** to shift all the trains one hour forward or back; *Cin:* **d. les deux impressions d'un film sonore,** to adjust the interval on the film between the picture and the sound impression; *Ph:* **ondes décalées,** waves out of phase; *El.E:* **décalé en phase sur le courant,** differing in phase from the current.

décaleur [dekalœːr], *s.m. El.E:* **d. de phase,** phase shifter, phase converter.

Décaline [dekalin], *s.f. R.t.m:* Decaline.

décalitre [dekalitr̥], *s.m. Meas:* decalitre.

décalobé [dekalɔbe], *a. Bot:* decalobate.

décalogue [dekalɔg], *s.m.* (the) decalogue.

décalotter [dekalɔte], *v.tr.* to remove the cap of, to uncap, to cut off the end (of a lemon), the top (of an egg); *Surg:* to circumcize.

décalquage [dekalkaːʒ], *s.m.* = DÉCALQUE 1.

décalque [dekalk], *s.m.* **1.** *(a)* transferring; *(b)* tracing off; **papier à d.,** (i) transfer paper; (ii) carbon paper or tracing paper. **2.** *(a)* transfer; *(b)* tracing.

décalquer [dekalke], *v.tr.* **1.** to transfer (design, coloured picture). **2.** to trace (off); **papier à d.,** (i) transfer paper; (ii) carbon paper, tracing paper.

décalvant [dekalvɑ̃], *a. Med:* decalvant, hair-destroying.

décalvation [dekalvasjɔ̃], *s.f.* **1.** *Med:* destruction of hair, decalvation. **2.** shaving (of prisoner's head).

Décaméron (le) [lədekamerɔ̃], *s.m. Lit:* the Decameron.

décamètre [dekamɛtr̥], *s.m.* **1.** *Meas:* decametre. **2.** decametre, ten-metre measuring tape.

décamétrique [dekametrik], *a. W.Tel:* **onde d.,** decametric wave.

décampement [dekɑ̃pmɑ̃], *s.m. Mil: A:* striking camp, decampment.

décamper [dekɑ̃pe], *v.i.* **1.** *Mil: A:* to strike camp. **2.** *F:* to decamp, make off, pack up; to make oneself scarce, run away, clear out, abscond, bolt; *P:* to vamoose; **décampe!** run away! *P:* buzz off! beat it! **il a décampé,** the bird has flown.

décan [dekɑ̃], *s.m. Astr:* decan.

décanailler [dekanɑje], *v.tr. F:* to rub the corners off (s.o.).

se décanailler, to acquire some polish; to move up in the world.

décanal, -aux [dekanal, -o], *a.* decanal.

décanat [dekana], *s.m.* deanship.

décandre [dekɑ̃dr̥], *a. Bot:* decandrian, decandrous.

décane [dekan], *s.m. Ch:* decane.

décaniller [dekanije], *v.i. P:* **1.** = DÉCAMPER 2. **2.** to get out of bed; to show a leg.

décanol [dekanɔl], *s.m. Ch:* decanol.

décantage [dekɑ̃taːʒ], *s.m.,* **décantation** [dekɑ̃tasjɔ̃], *s.f.* decantation, decanting; *Petroleum Ind:* elutriation; *Ch:* **ballon de d.,** separatory funnel; *Ind:* **d. (sédimentaire)** settling; **bassin de d.,** settling tank.

décanter [dekɑ̃te], *v.tr. (a)* to decant, pour off; *Ch:* to separate; *Petroleum Ind:* to elutriate; **laisser d.,** to allow to settle; *(b) F:* to clarify; **d. ses idées,** to clarify one's thoughts.

décanteur [dekɑ̃tœːr], *s.m. Tchn:* decanter.

décapage [dekapaːʒ], *s.m.* scouring, cleaning, scraping (of metals); pickling, dipping (of metal articles); **d. de tôles,** scaling of sheet iron; **d. au jet de sable,** sand-blasting; **d. à la grenaille,** shot-blasting; *s.a.* ÉCONOMISEUR 2; **d. électrolytique,** anodic etching; *Engr:* counter-etching, deoxidizing; **solution de d.,** counter-etching solution; *Civ.E:* **d. d'un accotement,** scraping, levelling, of a bank.

décapant [dekapɑ̃], **1.** *s.m.* scouring or pickling solution; **d. pour vernis,** varnish remover; **d. pour peintures,** paint remover. **2.** *a.* **lotion décapante,** scouring solution.

décapelage [dekaplaːʒ], **décapèlement** [dekapɛlmɑ̃], *s.m. Nau:* unrigging, stripping (of mast, yard).

décapeler [dekaple], *v.tr. Nau:* **(je décapelle** [ʒədekapɛl], **n. décapelons** [dekaplɔ̃], **je décapellerai** [dekapɛlre]) **1.** to unrig, strip (mast, yard). **2. d. le double d'une amarre,** to take off, cast off, the bight of a rope.

décapement [decapmɑ̃], *s.m.* = DÉCAPAGE.

décaper[1] [dekape], *v.tr.* to scour, clean, scrape, (metal, etc.); *(with acid)* to pickle, dip (metal objects); **d. au jet de sable,** to sandblast; **d. une tôle,** to scale a sheet of iron; *Civ.E:* **d. un accotement,** to scrape, level, a bank.

décaper[2], *v.i. Nau: A:* to clear, double, a cape.

décapétalé [dekapetale], *a. Bot:* decapetalous.

décapeur [dekapœːr], *s.m.* **1.** *(substance)* cleaner, scourer (of metals). **2.** *(pers.)* pickler, dipper (of metal articles); scourer, scraper.

décapeuse [dekapøːz], *s.f. Civ.E:* scouring machine, drag scraper.

décapitalisation [dekapitalizasjɔ̃], *s.f.* depriving a town of its status as a capital, decapitalization.

décapitation [dekapitasjɔ̃], *s.f.* decapitation, beheading.

décapité [dekapite]. **1.** *a.* decapitated, beheaded; **on retrouva son corps d.,** we found his decapitated, headless, body. **2.** *s.* **un(e) décapité(e,)** one who has been decapitated, beheaded.

décapiter [dekapite], *v.tr.* to decapitate, behead; to cut (s.o.'s) head off; **d. un arbre, un clou,** to cut the head, the top, off a tree, off a nail; *F:* **d. une bouteille,** to open, uncork, a bottle; **sa mort a décapité le parti républicain,** his death has deprived the republican party of its leadership.

décapode [dekapɔd], *Crust:* **1.** *a.* decapod(al), decapodalous. **2.** *s.m.* decapod; **les décapodes,** the Decapoda.

Décapole (la) [dekapɔl], *Pr.n.f. A.Geog:* Decapolis.

décapotable [dekapɔtabl̥], *a. & s.f. Aut:* convertible, drop-head (coupé).

décapoter [dekapɔte], *v.tr. Aut:* to open the hood, top, roof (of a car); *Av:* to remove the cowl(ing) (of an aircraft engine).

décapsul(at)eur [dekapsyl(at)œːr], *s.m.* bottle-opener.

décapsulation [dekapsylasjɔ̃], *s.f. (a)* opening (of bottle); taking-off the crown-cork (of a bottle); *(b) Surg:* decapsulation (of a kidney).

décapsuler [dekapsyle], *v.tr. (a)* to open (a bottle); to take off a crown-cork; *(b) Surg:* to decapsulate.

décapuchonner [dekapyʃɔne], *v.tr.* **1.** *(a)* to remove s.o.'s hood; *(b)* to remove a cover from (typewriter, etc.); *(c)* to unscrew the cap of (a fountain pen, etc.). **2.** to defrock, to unfrock (a priest).

décarbonatation [dekarbɔnatasjɔ̃], *s.f. Ch:* decarbonation.

décarbonaté [dekarbɔnate], *a.* decarbonated.

décarbonater [dekarbɔnate], *v.tr.* to decarbonate.

décarboniser [dekarbɔnize], *v.tr. Metall:* to decarbonize, decarburize (steel, iron, etc.).

décarboxylase [dekarbɔksilaːz], *s.f. Ch:* decarboxylase.

décarboxylation [dekarbɔksilasjɔ̃], *s.f.* decarboxylation.

décarburant [dekarbyrɑ̃]. *Metall: etc:* **1.** *a.* decarbonizing, decarburizing. **2.** *s.m.* decarbonizer, decarburizer.

décarburation [dekarbyrasjɔ̃], *s.f. Metall: etc:* decarburization, decarbonization.

décarburer [dekarbyre], *v.tr. Metall:* to decarbonize, decarburize (steel, iron, etc.).

décarcasser [dekarkase], *v.tr. F:* to bone (a chicken).

se décarcasser, *F:* to slave, drudge; to wear oneself to a shadow; **je me suis décarcassé pour vous procurer ce billet,** I sweated blood to get you this ticket.

décarêmer (se) [sədekareme], *v.pr. F:* to have a good tuck-in to mark the end of Lent.

décarrelage [dekarlaːʒ], *s.m.* taking up, tearing up, the tiles, the flags (from floor, etc.).

décarreler [dekarle], *v.tr.* **(je décarrelle; n. décarrelons; je décarrellerai,** to take up, tear up, the tiles, the flags from (floor, etc.).

décarrer [dekɑre], *v.i. P:* **d. (de belle),** to escape (from prison, etc.); to make oneself scarce.

décartellisation [dekartelizasjɔ̃], *s.f. Pol.Ec:* decartelization.

décartelliser [dekartɛlize], *v.tr. Pol.Ec:* to decartelize.

décartonner [dekartɔne], *v.tr.* to strip cardboard from (sth.).

décarver [dekarve], *v.tr. Nau:* to cross-chock (two timbers).

décasement [dekɑzmɑ̃], *s.m.* moving from a compartment; *Chess: etc:* moving (a piece) from a square.

décaser [dekɑze], *v.tr.* **1.** to move (sth.) from its compartment; *Chess: etc:* to move (piece) from its square. **2.** *A:* to turn out (tenant).

décasquer [dekaske], *v.tr.* to remove s.o.'s helmet.

décastère [dekastɛːr], *s.m. Meas:* decastere (= ten cubic metres).

décastyle [dekastil], *s.m. Arch:* decastyle.

décasyllabe [dekasillab], **décasyllabique** [dekasillabik], *a.* decasyllabic; *s.m.* **poème écrit en décasyllabes,** poem written in decasyllabic verse, in lines of ten syllables.

décathlon [dekatlɔ̃], *s.m.* (*at Olympic games, etc.*) decathlon.

décatholiciser [dekatɔlisize], *v.tr.* to decatholicize (a country).

décati [dekati], *a.* (*of face*) wrinkled; wanting in freshness; **femme décatie,** woman who has lost her looks; **vieillard d.,** worn old man.

décatir [dekatiːr], *v.tr. Tex:* to sponge, steam; to take the gloss, the finish, off (cloth).

se décatir, *F:* to lose one's freshness, one's looks; to show the effects of age.

décatissage [dekatisaːʒ], *s.m. Tex:* sponging, steaming (of cloth); taking off the gloss, the finish.

décatisseur [dekatisœːr], *s.m. Tex:* (cloth) sponger.

Décatron [dekatrɔ̃], *s.m. Elcs: R.t.m:* Dekatron.

decauville [dəkovil], *s.m.* narrow-gauge railway.

décavage [dekavaːʒ], *s.m. P:* ruin, bankruptcy.

décavaillonner [dekavajɔne], *v.tr.* to plough between the rows of vine.

décavaillonneur [dekavajɔnœːr], *s.m.,* **décavaillonneuse** [dekavajɔnøːz], *s.f.* vineyard plough.

décavé, -ée [dekave], *a. & s. F:* ruined, broken; *F:* stony-broke (person); **visage d.,** pinched face; *St.Exch:* lame duck.

décaver [dekave], *v.tr.* (*a*) *Cards: etc:* **d. qn,** to win the whole of s.o.'s money on the table; (*b*) *F:* to ruin (s.o.) at gaming; *F:* to clean (s.o.) out; to break (s.o.).

decazevillien, -ienne [dəkɑzviljɛ̃, -jɛn], *a. & s. Geog:* (native, inhabitant) of Decazeville.

decca [dɛka], *s.m. Av: Nau:* radio-navigation system which gives a continuous plot of position on appropriate chart.

Deccan [dɛkɑ̃], *Pr.n.m. Geog:* Deccan.

Dèce [dɛs], *Pr.n.m. A.Hist:* Decius.

décédé, -ée [desede], *a. & s.* deceased, defunct, departed; **fils de père et mère décédés,** son of parents deceased; **sonner pour un d.,** to toll (for a death); **faire un discours sur la tombe du d.,** to make a speech over the grave of the deceased.

décéder [desede], *v.i.* (*the aux. is* **être**) *used only in official language;* to die, to decease; **il est décédé le premier mars,** he departed this life on the first of March.

déceindre [desɛ̃ːdr̥], *v.tr.* (*conj. like* CEINDRE) *A:* to ungird (sword, etc.).

décelable [des(ə)labl̥], *a.* perceptible, discernible.

décèlement [desɛlmɑ̃], *s.m.* disclosure, revelation, betrayal (of plot, secret).

déceler [desle], *v.tr.* (**je décèle, n. décelons; je décèlerai**) **1.** to disclose, to reveal, to divulge, to detect, to uncover; **d. une intrigue,** to uncover an intrigue; **d. un secret,** to divulge, reveal, *F:* give away, a secret. **2.** (*a*) *A:* to betray, to denounce, s.o.; (*b*) to betray, to disclose, to prove, to show; **son action décèle une âme corrompue,** his action betrays, discloses, a corrupt mind; **un bruit décela sa présence,** a noise disclosed his presence, gave away the fact that he was there. **3.** *Tchn: El.E: etc:* **d. des fuites,** (i) to test for faults; (ii) to detect, to find out, faults.

se déceler. son véritable caractère n'a pas tardé à se d., his true character was not long in showing, revealing, itself.

décélérateur [deseleratœːr], *s.m. Av:* **d. à réaction,** retro-rocket.

décélération [deselerasjɔ̃], *s.f.* deceleration.

décélérer [deselere], *v.tr. & i.* to decelerate.

décéléromètre [deselerɔmɛtr̥], *s.m.* decelerometer.

déceleur, -euse [deslœːr, -øːz], *s.* **1.** divulger. **2.** *A:* betrayer. **3.** *s.m. El.E:* **d. de fuites,** leakage detector or indicator.

décembre [desɑ̃ːbr̥], *s.m.* December; **en d.,** in December; **au mois de d.,** in the month of December; **le premier, le sept, d.,** (on) the first, the seventh, of December, (on) December (the) first, (the) seventh; **une température du mois de d.,** December weather.

décembriste [desɑ̃brist], *s.m. Russian Hist:* Decembrist.

décemment [desamɑ̃], *adv.* decently, with decency; **je ne peux pas d. refuser,** I can't very well refuse.

décemvir [desɛmviːr], *s.m. Rom.Hist:* decemvir.

décemviral, -aux [desɛmviral, -o], *a. Rom.Hist:* decemviral.

décemvirat [desɛmvira], *s.m. Rom.Hist:* decemvirate.

décence [desɑ̃ːs], *s.f.* (*a*) decency; **être vêtu avec d.,** to be decently, modestly, dressed; **garder une certaine d.,** to maintain a certain respectability (of appearance); (*b*) propriety, decency, decorum; **choquer la d.,** to shock the proprieties; **il va de la plus élémentaire d. que** + *sub.,* common decency demands that . . ..

décennal, -aux [desɛn(n)al, -o], *a.* decennial.

décennie [deseni], *s.f.* decade, decennary, decennium.

décent [desɑ̃], *a.* (*a*) decent; modest (attire, etc.); (*b*) proper, seemly, reasonable (behaviour, etc.); **peu d.,** indecent, unseemly.

décentrage [desɑ̃traːʒ], *s.m.* **1.** *Opt: Mec.E: etc:* putting (of lenses, centres, etc.) out of centre, out of true; decentring; **d. en hauteur,** rising front. **2.** *Mec.E: etc:* eccentricity; *Bowls:* bias (of bowl).

décentralisable [desɑ̃tralizabl̥], *a.* that can be decentralized.

décentralisateur, -trice [desɑ̃tralizatœːr, -tris]. **1.** *a.* decentralizing (system, etc.). **2.** *s. Pol:* decentralist, advocate of decentralization, of devolution.

décentralisation [desɑ̃tralizasjɔ̃], *s.f.* decentralization; **d. administrative,** devolution; extension of local government.

décentraliser [desɑ̃tralize], *v.tr.* to decentralize (administration).

décentralisme [desɑ̃tralism], *s.m. Pol:* decentralism.

décentraliste [desɑ̃tralist], *s.m. Pol:* decentralist.

décentration [desɑ̃trasjɔ̃], *s.f.* = DÉCENTREMENT.

décentré [desɑ̃tre], *a.* (*of load, etc.*) out of centre, of true, off-centre; eccentric; **être décentré** (*of wheel, etc.*) to be out of true, to run out of true.

décentrement [desɑ̃trəmɑ̃], *s.m. Opt: Phot:* putting, throwing (lenses, etc.) off centre, off-centring; **appareil à d.,** camera with sliding front.

décentrer [desɑ̃tre], *v.tr. Opt: Mec.E: etc:* to put (lenses, axes, etc.) off centre; to decentre; *Bowls:* to bias (a bowl); (*of wheel, etc.*) **se d.,** to run out of true, to get out of true; *Phot:* **objectif se décentrant en hauteur,** lens on rising front.

déception [desɛpsjɔ̃], *s.f.* **1.** *A:* deception, deceit; **agir sans d.,** to act above-board. **2.** disappointment; set-back; *F:* let-down; **éprouver une cruelle d.,** to meet with a sad disappointment; to be sadly disappointed; **d. sentimentale,** unhappy love-affair.

décercler [desɛrkle], *v.tr.* to unhoop (cask, etc.).

décernement [desɛrnəmɑ̃], *s.m.* awarding (of prize, etc.).

décerner [desɛrne], *v.tr.* **1.** (*a*) *A:* to decree, order; (*b*) *Jur:* **d. un mandat d'arrêt contre qn,** to issue a writ, a warrant, for the arrest of s.o. **2.** to award, assign, bestow; **d. un prix à qn,** to award s.o. a prize, to make an award to s.o.; **d. un honneur à qn,** to confer an honour on s.o.; *s.a.* PALME[1] 2.

décerveler [desɛrvəle], *v.tr.* (*a*) to beat, *F:* bash, out (s.o.'s) brains; (*b*) to deprive (s.o.) of all capacity of reasoning.

décès [desɛ], *s.m. used only in official language;* decease, (natural) death; *Jur:* demise; **notifier un d.,** to notify a death; **acte de d.,** death certificate; **constatation de d.,** proof of death; **fermé pour cause de d.,** closed on account of death; **contrat exécutoire après d.,** post obit bond; **au d. du dernier survivant . . .,** upon the demise of the last survivor . . ..

décesser [desese], *v.tr. F:* **ne pas d. de . . .** = **ne pas cesser de . . .; il ne décesse pas de pleurnicher,** he never stops whimpering; **la pluie n'avait pas décessé,** it hadn't stopped raining.

décevable [des(ə)vabl̥], *a. A:* deceivable, gullible, easily deceived, easily taken in.

décevant [des(ə)vɑ̃], *a.* **1.** deceptive, delusive (appearance, etc.); fallacious; **paroles décevantes,** misleading words. **2.** disappointing; unsatisfactory (result, etc.).

décevoir [desəvwaːr], *v.tr.* (*conj. like* RECEVOIR) **1.** *A:* to deceive, delude. **2.** to disappoint; **d. les espérances de qn,** to disappoint, deceive, s.o.'s hopes; **il fut un peu déçu de ce qu'on ne l'invitait pas,** he was rather disappointed at not being invited; **cela m'a beaucoup déçu,** I was very disappointed with it; it did not come up to my expectations.

déchaînement [deʃɛnmɑ̃], *s.m.* **1.** letting loose, unchaining (of dog, etc.); unfettering (of prisoner). **2.** (*a*) breaking loose; unbridling; **le d. de la tempête,** the bursting, breaking, of the storm; **un d. de l'opinion amena sa chute,** a great wave of public opinion brought about his downfall; (*b*) outburst (of passion); **d. furieux,** outburst of fury, fit of rage; **être dans un perpétuel d. contre qn,** to be perpetually vituperating, inveighing, against s.o.

déchaîner [deʃene], *v.tr.* (*a*) to unchain, to let loose (dog, etc.); to loose the chains of, to unfetter (prisoner); *F:* **il est déchaîné,** nothing will stop him; **les diables sont déchaînés,** hell has broken loose; **c'est le diable déchaîné,** he is a devil let loose; *Lit:* **Prométhée déchaîné,** Prometheus unbound; (*b*) *Bac:* **facteur déchaînant,** bursting factor; (*c*) **d. toutes les passions,** to loose every passion; **d. la guerre,** to unleash, let loose, the dogs of war; **d. l'hilarité,** to set everyone laughing, to raise, to provoke, a storm of laughter; **mer déchaînée,** wild sea.

se déchaîner, (*a*) (*of dog, etc.*) to break loose; (*b*) to break (out); **la tempête se déchaîna,** the storm broke; **enfin sa fureur s'est déchaînée,** at length, his wrath exploded; (*c*) **se d. contre qn,** to break out, fly out, against s.o., to storm at s.o.

déchalasser [deʃalase], *v.tr. Hort:* to remove props from (a vine).

déchalement [deʃalmɑ̃], *s.m.* ebb(ing), fall(ing) (of the tide).

déchaler [deʃale], *v.i.* (*of the tide*) to ebb, fall.

déchant [deʃɑ̃], *s.m. A.Mus:* descant, discant.

déchanter [deʃɑ̃te], *v.i.* to lower one's tone; to come down a peg; to sing a different tune; **ils comptaient sur lui mais il leur fallut d.,** they relied on him but they had to face their disappointment.

déchapage [deʃapaːʒ], *s.m.* peeling (of tyre).

déchapeauter [deʃapote], *v.tr. P:* **d. qn,** to take s.o.'s hat off.

se déchapeauter, *P:* to take off one's hat.

déchapellement [deʃapɛlmɑ̃], *s.m. Dent:* removing of the crown of a tooth.

déchaper [deʃape], *v.tr. Tchn:* to remove the cope from a mould.

se déchaper, (*of tyre*) to peel.

déchaperonner [deʃaprɔne], *v.tr.* **1.** to unhood (hawk). **2.** to remove the coping from (wall).

déchard, -arde [deʃaːr, -ard], *s. P:* hard-up individual.

décharge [deʃarʒ], *s.f.* **1.** (*a*) *O:* unloading (of cart, etc.); unlading, discharging (of boat, cargo); **faire la d. de marchandises,** to unload goods; **navire en d.,** ship being unloaded, ship discharging; (*b*) discharge, volley (of rifle-fire, etc.); **d. de coups de bâton,** volley of blows; (*c*) *El:* discharge, discharging (of accumulator, cell); **batterie en d.,** discharging battery; **d. disruptive,** spark discharge; **d. en retour,** back-kick; **d. lumineuse,** glow discharge; **d. superficielle,** surface leakage; **d. autonome, auto-entretenue,** self-maintained discharge; **d. dans le vide,** discharge in vacuo; **d. en aigrette,** brush-discharge; **d. non-autonome,** non-self-maintained discharge; **d. oscillante,** oscillating, oscillatory, discharge; **d. oscillatoire,** vibrational, vibratory, discharge; (*d*) output (of accumulator). **2.** (*a*) relief, relieving, lightening, easing; *Arch:* **arc de d.,** relieving arch; **d. d'une poutre,** brace, strut, of a beam; *Turf:* **une d. de cinq livres,** an allowance of five pounds; (*b*) **d. d'un impôt,** tax rebate; **donner d. d'une livraison,** to give a receipt for the delivery of a consignment; **payer une somme à la d. de qn,** to pay in a sum to s.o.'s credit; **porter une somme en d.,** to mark a sum as paid; *Com:* **d. de 50 pour cent,** composition 50%; (*c*) *Jur:* **témoin à d.,** witness for the defence; **il convient de dire à sa d.,** it should be said in his defence; **témoignage à votre d.,** evidence that exonerates you; (*d*) *Jur:* release, acquittal (of accused person); (*e*) *Bank:* letter of indemnity. **3.** (*a*) discharge, outlet, eduction; **tuyau de d.,** exhaust pipe; waste pipe, discharge pipe, overflow pipe; **égout de d.,** outfall sewer; **arche de d.,** draining arch (of bridge); *s.a.* CANAL 1; **soupape, robinet, de d.,** delivery-valve, -cock; **d. de fond,** drain, bottom outlet; *Tex:* **cylindre de d.,** delivery roll; (*b*) *Dy:* fading; running (of colour of material). **4.** (*a*) **(lieu de) d. publique,** rubbish tip, dumping ground, dump, rubbish heap; *P.N:* **"d. interdite,"** "tipping prohibited"; **camion à d. automatique,** self-tipping, -dumping, lorry, *U.S:* truck; **d. des résidus, des déchets, dans la mer,** discharge, disposal, of wastes into the sea; *A:* **(chambre de) d.,** lumber-room; *F:* glory-hole; (*b*) outfall (of sewer); (*c*) **bras de d. (d'une rivière),** backwater; (*d*) reservoir, dam. **5.** *Typ:* offset blanket; set-off sheet.

déchargé [deʃarʒe], a. clean-built (horse).

déchargement [deʃarʒəmɑ̃], s.m. unloading (of cart, fire-arm); off-loading (of pack); removal, withdrawal of the charge (from mine, etc.); unloading, unlading (of ship); discharging, unshipment (of cargo); dumping (of rubbish); Atom.Ph: unloading (of reactor); discharge, unloading (of nuclear fuel); expulsion (of moderator); Nau: commencer le d., entrer en d., to break bulk.

décharger [deʃarʒe], v.tr. (je déchargeai(s); n. déchargeons) 1. (a) to unload (cart, horse, etc.); to unload, to unlade, to discharge (boat); to unload, to unship, to discharge (cargo, goods); d. une charretée de gravier, to tip, to dump down, to shoot, a cartload of gravel; abs. j'ai fini de d., I have finished unloading; (b) d. un revolver, (i) to unload, to withdraw the charge from a revolver; (ii) to discharge, let off, fire (off), a revolver (sur, contre, qn, at s.o.); d. une mine, une cartouche, to remove, to withdraw, the charge from a mine, from a cartridge; d. un coup à qn, to deal s.o. a blow; (c) d. sa conscience, to ease one's mind, to clear one's conscience; j'ai déchargé ma conscience en allant le voir, I did my duty by going to see him; d. son cœur, to unburden one's heart, to make a clean breast of it; d. sa bile, sa colère, sur qn, to vent one's spleen, one's ill-humour, one's anger, on s.o.; (d) d. un accumulateur, to discharge an accumulator. 2. (a) to relieve, lighten, ease, (person, horse, ship, etc.) of part of his, its, load; d. une poutre, to take the strain off a beam; F: d. le plancher, to clear out; d. son estomac, se d. l'estomac, (i) to relieve oneself; (ii) to bring up one's food; d. un arbre, (i) to cut back, to remove excess wood (from a tree); (ii) to disbud a tree; (b) d. qn de qch., to discharge, exonerate, release, s.o., to set s.o. free, from (an obligation); je vous déchargerai de cette tâche, I will let you off this task; d. le livre d'un messager, to receipt, sign, a messenger's book; d. qn d'un impôt, to exempt s.o. from (paying) a tax; d. qn d'une dette, to remit a debt; Jur: d. ses cautions, to surrender to one's bail; d. qn d'une accusation, to acquit s.o. of an accusation; failli déchargé, non déchargé, discharged, undischarged, bankrupt; il a été déchargé de l'amende, he has been let off the fine. 3. (a) to discharge, empty; d. un réservoir, to empty a reservoir; d. la boue d'une chaudière, to draw off the sludge from a boiler; d. les feux d'un fourneau, to draw, blow out, a furnace; (b) Dy: étoffe qui décharge (sa couleur), material whose colour runs, fades; Typ: encre qui décharge, ink that sets off, that rubs, comes, off; (c) Typ: to pass waste sheets through (the machine); d. une couleur, to ease, lighten, a colour.

se décharger. 1. (a) (of gun, etc.) to go off; (b) El: (of storage battery) to run down; to discharge; (c) (of anger) to vent itself (sur, on). 2. se d. de qn, de qch., to get rid of s.o., of sth.; to get s.o., sth., off one's hands; se d. d'un fardeau, to put down, lay down, a burden; se d. d'une commission, to carry out a commission; se d. sur qn du soin de qch., to make s.o. responsible for sth., to shift the responsibility of sth. on to s.o. 3. le fleuve se décharge dans la mer, the river flows, empties itself, discharges (itself), into the sea. 4. couleur qui se décharge, colour which runs, fades.

déchargeur [deʃarʒœːr], s.m. 1. dock labourer, docker, stevedore; market porter; d. de charbon, coal heaver. 2. (a) El.E: (spark, lightning) arrester; conductor; (b) Tex: doffer, doffing machine; (c) Ind: Agr: unloader.

décharné [deʃarne], a. 1. fleshless (bones, etc.). 2. emaciated, scraggy (limbs, etc.); lank (body); bare (tree); visage d., pinched, gaunt, face; doigts décharnés, skinny, bony, fingers; style d., bald style.

décharnement [deʃarnəmɑ̃], s.m. fleshlessness, emaciation.

décharner [deʃarne], v.tr. 1. to strip the flesh off (bone). 2. to emaciate (s.o.). 3. d. son style, to strip one's style (of figures of speech, etc.).

se décharner, to lose flesh, to waste away; F: plus il écrit, plus son style se décharne, the more he writes, the barer his style becomes.

déchassé [deʃase], s.m. Danc: chassé to the left.

déchasser [deʃase]. 1. v.tr. to drive out (bolt, pin). 2. v.i. Danc: to chassé to the left.

déchaulage [deʃolaːʒ], s.m. Tan: deliming.

déchauler [deʃole], v.tr. Tan: to delime.

déchaumage [deʃomaːʒ], s.m. Agr: stubble-ploughing.

déchaumer [deʃome], v.tr. Agr: 1. to plough up the stubble of (field). 2. to break (new ground); to break ground.

déchaumeur [deʃomœːr], s.m., **déchaumeuse** [deʃomøːz], s.f. Agr: stubble-plough, grubber, scarifier; d. à disques, one-way disc plough.

déchaussage [deʃosaːʒ], s.m. = DÉCHAUSSEMENT.

déchaussé [deʃose], a. bare-foot(ed); Ecc: discalced (Carmelite); pierre, dent, déchaussée, exposed stone, tooth; d. par la gelée, lifted by frost.

déchaussement [deʃosmɑ̃], s.m. 1. removal of (s.o.'s) shoes, or shoes and stockings. 2. laying bare the roots (of tree); baring of foundations; Dent: recession of the gums; Husb: unearthing; d. par la gelée, frost lifting.

déchausser [deʃose], v.tr. 1. to take off (s.o.'s) shoes, (s.o.'s) shoes and stockings; il n'est pas digne de vous d., he is not fit to tie your shoe-laces, not fit to black your boots. 2. to lay bare the roots of (tree); to bare, expose (tooth, foundations).

se déchausser. 1. to take off one's shoes, etc. 2. ses dents se déchaussent, his teeth are getting loose, his gums are shrinking.

déchausseuse [deʃosøːz], s.f. vineyard plough.

déchaux [deʃo], a.m. Ecc: = DÉCHAUSSÉ.

dèche [dɛʃ], s.f. P: poverty, distress; être dans la d., to be hard up, on the rocks, on one's beam ends, in low water, stony-broke, down on one's luck.

déchéance [deʃeɑ̃ːs], s.f. 1. fall (from grace); downfall (from high estate, from honour, etc.); ils ont contribué à sa d., they helped to bring him down; d. d'un souverain, fall, deposition, dethronement, of a sovereign; l'oisiveté amène la d. individuelle, idleness leads to loss of will-power, to moral decay; nation en d., nation on the decline. 2. forfeiture (of rights, etc.); Jur: Fin: d. d'un administrateur, disqualification of a (company) director; d. de titres, forfeiture of shares; action en d. de brevet, action for forfeiture of patent; d. d'un pouvoir, loss of a right; d. de propriété littéraire, lapse of rights in literary matter; d. de la puissance paternelle, loss of parental authority; d. de la propriété littéraire, lapse of copyright; d. quadriennale, lapse of all claims against the State after four years; d. de nationalité, loss, withdrawal of nationality; Hist: d. nationale, loss of civil rights by reason of indignité nationale; Ins: d. d'une police, expiration, running out, of a policy.

déchénite [deʃenit], s.f. Miner: dechenite.

déchet [deʃɛ], s.m. 1. loss, decrease, diminution (of weight, value, quantity); loss, falling off (of reputation, authority); d. de route, loss (of wine in cask, etc.) in transit. 2. usu. pl. (a) Ind: etc: waste, refuse; déchets de la nutrition, waste products of nutrition; déchets de coton, cotton waste; Typ: d. du papier, (allowance for) waste; spoilage; d. de métal, scrap (metal); déchets de carrière, quarry chips; déchets radioactifs, radioactive waste; Petroleum Ind: déchets de raffinage, (refinery) sludge, bottoms; Min: déchets de criblage, screenings; déchets de cannelle, cinnamon chips; déchets de viande, scraps; déchets d'abattage, offal; destructeur de déchets, refuse destructor; Prehist: déchets ménagers, kitchenmidden; (b) les déchets de nos écoles, our school failures; un d. de la société, an outcast of society; les déchets de la société, the dregs of society, Mil: Sp: etc: d. à l'entraînement, training loss.

décheux, -euse [deʃø, -øːz], a. P: poverty-stricken, hard up; F: stony-broke.

déchevelé [deʃəvle], a. dishevelled, tousled.

décheveler [deʃəvle], v.tr. (je déchevelle [deʃɛvl], n. déchevelons [deʃəvlɔ̃]; je déchevellerai [deʃɛvlre]) to ruffle, tousle (s.o.'s, hair).

se décheveler, to ruffle, to tousle (one's hair).

déchevêtrer [deʃvɛtre], v.tr. A: to unhalter, take the halter off (horse, etc.); Tchn: to break up (a parquet floor).

décheviller [deʃvije], v.tr. to unpin, unpeg.

déchiffonner [deʃifɔne], v.tr. to smoothe out (crumpled material, etc.).

déchiffrable [deʃifrabl̩], a. decipherable (inscription); legible (writing).

déchiffrage [deʃifraːʒ], s.m. Mus: sight-reading.

déchiffrement [deʃifrəmɑ̃], s.m. deciphering, making out (of inscription, etc.); d. d'une dépêche, decoding of a telegram.

déchiffrer [deʃifre], v.tr. to decipher, puzzle out, make out (inscription, etc.); to decode (message); to decipher (cryptogram); to read, interpret (signals); to read or play (music) at sight; to read back (shorthand, etc.); F: d. qn, to make s.o. out; d. une affaire, to clear up, unravel, an affair; machine à d., cipher machine.

déchiffreur, -euse [deʃifrœːr, -øːz], s. decipherer (of inscription); decoder (of message); player or reader (of music) at sight; d. de radar, radar scanner.

déchiquetage [deʃiktaːʒ], s.m. shredding, cutting into pieces; slashing.

déchiqueté [deʃikte], a. 1. (a) jagged (edge, etc.); indented (coast line); papier à bords déchiquetés, deckle-edge paper; (b) Bot: laciniate (leaf). 2. (object) cut to bits. 3. style d., jerky style.

déchiqueter [deʃikte], v.tr. (je déchiquette [deʃikɛt], n. déchiquetons [deʃiktɔ̃]; je déchiquetterai [deʃikɛtre]) 1. to cut, slash, tear, (material, flesh, etc.) into strips, into shreds, into ribbons; to shred (cooked fish, etc.); F: to hack (chicken, etc.); to cut (reputation) to shreds, to pieces. 2. to pink out (leather, pattern).

déchiqueteur [deʃiktœːr], s.m. Paperm: chipper, chopper.

déchiqueture [deʃiktyːr], s.f. slash, long tear, cut (in cloth, etc.); indentation (in coast line); laciniation (in embroidery pattern).

déchirage [deʃiraːʒ], s.m. breaking up (of old ships, of timber raft).

déchirant [deʃirɑ̃], a. 1. heartrending, harrowing, agonizing, distressing, (scene, cry, etc.); excruciating (pain). 2. toux déchirante, racking cough.

déchiré [deʃire], a. (a) torn; (b) F: (of pers.) tattered and torn, in rags; (c) A: femme pas trop déchirée, woman who is still attractive; (d) voix déchirée, choky, strangled, voice.

déchirement [deʃirmɑ̃], s.m. tearing, (of material, etc.); laceration (of flesh); d. d'un muscle, tearing of a muscle; F: d. d'entrailles, griping of the bowels; d. de cœur, heartbreak; cette séparation fut un d. affreux, this separation was a terrible wrench; l'État avait souffert de cruels déchirements, the State had been severely torn apart, ravaged, by faction.

déchirer [deʃire], v.tr. to tear, Lit: to rend (garment, etc.); to lacerate (flesh); to tear up (paper, etc.); to tear open (envelope); d. un morceau d'étoffe, to tear, rip, a piece of cloth; d. qch. en morceaux, to tear sth. to pieces, to bits; d. qch. en deux, to tear sth. asunder; d. une proie à belles dents, to tear a prey to pieces; d. la terre, to plough; l'anarchie déchirera le pays, anarchy will divide the country; pays déchiré par la guerre civile, country torn apart by civil war; Nau: d. une voile, to split a sail; d. un vieux bateau, to break up, rip up, an old boat; le train déchira l'air de son sifflet, the train rent the air with its shrill whistle; sons qui déchirent l'oreille, ear-splitting sounds; cris qui déchiraient le cœur, heartrending cries; déchiré par le remords, par l'angoisse, torn with remorse, with anguish; d. une personne à belles dents, to vilify, slander, a person, to tear s.o.'s character to rags, to pieces; d. une réputation, to ruin a reputation; d. le voile, to unveil, to disclose, the truth; se d. un muscle, to pull a muscle.

se déchirer. 1. (of material, etc.) to tear; papier qui se déchire facilement, paper that tears easily; mon foulard s'est déchiré, my scarf is torn. 2. les femmes se déchirent souvent entre elles, women often tear each other to pieces; mon cœur s'est déchiré en le voyant partir, my heart sank when I saw him leave.

déchireur [deʃirœːr], s.m. 1. one who tears (sth.). A: d. de bateaux, de balles, ship-, bale-breaker. 2. shredder, shredding machine.

déchirure [deʃiryːr], s.f. (a) tear, rent, slit, rip; d. de voile, split in a sail; gap, split, rift (in clouds, etc.); fissure (in ground); crevasse (in glacier); avoir une d. à sa robe, to have a tear in one's dress; (b) lacerated wound, laceration; (c) Med: tear (of perineum, etc.); Sp: etc: il s'est fait une d., he has pulled, torn, a muscle.

déchloruration [deklɔryrasjɔ̃], s.f. Med: dechloridation.

déchloruré [deklɔryre], a Med: salt-free (diet).

déchlorurer [deklɔryre], v.tr. Med: to dechloridize.

déchoir [deʃwaːr], v.i. (p.p. déchu; pr.ind. je déchois, n. déchoyons, ils déchoient; pr. sub. je déchoie, n. déchoyons; p.h. je déchus; p.d. je déchoyais; fu. je déchoirai; the aux. is être or avoir) to fall (from high estate, from honour, etc.); la ville déchoit, the town is decaying, falling into decay; ce quartier, jadis prospère, a déchu, the neighbourhood, once prosperous, has gone down; ses facultés commencent à d., his faculties are beginning to fail; sa popularité déchoit, his popularity is falling off, is on the wane; la maison déchoit de son prestige, the firm is declining, going down (in public estimation);

d. en entrant dans une profession, to lose caste by entering a profession; **d. au degré de . . .,** to sink to the level of . . .; **ce serait d.** (i) it would mean loss of prestige; (ii) it would mean losing one's standing; *Jur:* **d. d'un brevet,** to forfeit a patent; **être déchu de ses droits,** to have forfeited one's rights; **d. de ses espérances,** to see one's hopes fade, vanish.

déchouement [deʃumɑ̃], *s.m.* refloating, floating off (of a boat).

déchouer [deʃwe], *v.tr.* to refloat, to float off (a boat).

déchristianisation [dekristjanizasjɔ̃], *s.f.* dechristianization.

déchristianiser [dekristjanize], *v.tr.* to dechristianize, unchristianize; to turn (s.o.) from Christianity.

se déchristianiser, to turn from, give up, Christianity.

déchu [deʃy]. **1.** *a.* fallen; **ange d.,** fallen angel; **empire d. de son antique splendeur,** empire fallen from its ancient glory; **d. de sa renommée il se retira du monde,** having fallen from great fame he retired from the world; **d. de ses espérances . . .,** seeing his hopes blighted . . .; *Ins:* **police déchue,** expired policy; **membre d.,** lapsed member; **roi d.,** dethroned king; **d. de la nationalité française,** having lost his French nationality. **2.** *s.* **les déchus de la société,** the social outcasts.

déci- [desi], *pref.* deci-.

déciare [desia:r], *s.m. Meas:* deciare.

décibar [desiba:r], *s.m. Meteor:* decibar.

décibel [desibɛl], *s.m. Ph:* decibel; volume-unit (of sound), V.U.

décibelmètre [desibɛlmɛtr], *s.m. Ph:* decibelmeter; V.U.-metre.

décidabilité [desidabilite], *s.f. Phil:* decidability.

décidable [desidabl], *a. Phil:* decidable.

décidé [deside], *a.* **1. chose décidée,** settled matter; **il n'y a rien de d., pour le moment,** nothing is settled, *F:* everything is still in the air at present. **2.** resolute, confident (person); determined (character); **un homme d.,** a resolute, determined, man; **d'un ton d.,** decisively, resolutely. **3. être d. à faire qch.,** to be determined, resolved, to have made up one's mind, to do sth.; to have set one's heart on doing sth.; to be bent on doing sth.; **avoir un goût d. pour les mathématiques,** to have a bent for mathematics. **4. avoir une supériorité décidée sur qn,** to have a decided superiority over s.o.

de-ci, de-là [dəsidəla], *adv.phr. See* CI[1].

décidément [desidemɑ̃], *adv.* **1.** resolutely, firmly. **2.** decidedly, positively, definitely; **il va d. nous quitter,** he is definitely going to leave us; *F:* **d., je n'ai pas de chance aujourd'hui,** there's no doubt about it, it's not my lucky day; *F:* **d., vous êtes fou!** but you must be mad!

décider [deside], *v.tr.* **1.** *(a)* to decide, settle (question, dispute); **d. un point de droit,** to determine, decide, a point of law; **manœuvre qui décida la victoire,** manœuvre which brought about, determined, the victory; **son sort se décide en ce moment,** his fate is now being decided; **voilà qui décide tout!** that settles it! **d. une querelle par un combat,** to settle a quarrel by a fight; **que déciderons-nous si . . .,** what should we decide if . . ., what decision should we make if . . .; **je vous laisse d. pour moi,** I'll let you decide for me; *(b)* **l'assemblée décida la guerre, la paix, la grève,** the assembly decided on war, on peace, on a strike. **2. décider qn à faire qch.,** to persuade, induce, prevail upon, s.o. to do sth.; *abs.* **cela le décida,** that brought him to a decision, that decided him; **je suis bien décidé à ce qu'il m'entende,** I am determined that he should listen to me. **3.** *abs.* *(a)* **il faut que je décide,** I must decide, make up my mind; **vous pouvez d. mieux que personne,** you know best; **d. en faveur de qn,** to decide, *Jur:* to rule, give a ruling, in favour of s.o.; *Jur:* **d. en faveur du demandeur,** to find for the plaintiff; **le sort en a décidé autrement,** fate has decided differently; **tu aimes à d., décide!** you like making decisions, decide! *(b)* **d. de qch.,** to decide sth.; **événement qui décida de sa carrière,** event that determined, decided, his career; **d. de la vie de qn,** to dispose of s.o.'s life; **droit de d. soi-même de son sort,** right of self-determination; *(c)* **il décide de tout, sur tout,** he decides about everything; **d. sur qch.,** to make, to come to, a decision on sth. **4. d. de** + *inf.,* to decide (after deliberation) to (do sth.); **je décidai de partir aussitôt,** I decided, determined, resolved, to start at once; **d. que** + *ind., occ.* + *condit.,* to decide, settle, that . . .; **il a décidé qu'il n'irait pas travailler,** he decided not to go to work; + *sub.* **il avait décidé que la chambre fût peinte en bleu,** he decided that the room should be painted blue; *impers.* **il fut décidé qu'on attendrait sa réponse,** it was decided to await his reply; **je n'ai pas encore décidé ce que je ferai, quelle réponse je ferai, si j'irai,** I have not yet made up my mind what I shall do, what answer I shall give, whether I shall go; **d. à** + *inf.,* **cela m'a décidé à vous écrire,** that decided me to write to you; **je suis décidé à y aller,** I am determined to go.

se décider. 1. to make up one's mind; to come to a decision. **2. se d. à faire qch.,** to make up one's mind (somewhat reluctantly), to decide, to do sth.; **je ne puis pas me d. à le faire,** I cannot bring myself to do it; **allons, décidez-vous,** come on, make up your mind. **3. se d. pour qn, pour qch.,** to decide in favour of s.o., of sth.; to decide on s.o., for sth.

décidu [desidy], *a. Bot:* deciduous (calyx, etc.).

déciduale [desidɥal], *a.f. Obst:* **membrane d.,** decidua.

déciduome [desidɥom], *s.m. Med:* deciduoma.

décigrade [desigrad], *s.m. Trig:* one-tenth of a grade.

décigramme [desigram], *s.m. Meas:* decigram(me).

décile [desil], *s.m. Statistics:* decile.

décilitre [desilitr], *s.m. Meas:* decilitre.

déciller [desije], *v.tr.* = DESSILLER.

décimable [desimabl], *a.* tithable.

décimal, -aux [desimal, -o], *a.* decimal; **fraction décimale,** decimal fraction; **système d.,** decimal system; *Fr.C:* **point d.,** decimal point; **calcul d.,** decimals; **je ne suis pas bon en calcul d.,** I am bad at, can't do, decimals.

décimale [desimal], *s.f.* decimal; **logarithmes à cinq décimales,** five-figure logarithms; **exact jusqu'à la cinquième d.,** correct to five places of decimals; **donner le résultat à deux décimales près,** to give one's answer to two places of decimals.

décimalisation [desimalizasjɔ̃], *s.f.* decimalization (of coinage).

décimaliser [desimalize], *v.tr.* to decimalize (coinage, etc.).

décimateur [desimatœ:r], *s.m. Ecc:* tithe-owner.

décimation [desimasjɔ̃], *s.f.* decimation.

décime[1] [desim], *s.m.* **1.** *(a)* one tenth of a franc; *(b)* ten-centime piece. **2.** ten-per-cent tax.

décime[2], *s.f. Ecc: Jur:* (extraordinary) tithe (levied on the clergy).

décimer [desime], *v.tr.* to decimate; *F:* **la peste décima le peuple,** the plague thinned out, decimated, the people; the plague took its tithe, toll, of the people.

décimètre [desimɛtr], *s.m. Meas:* **1.** decimetre. **2.** decimetre rule(r).

décimétrique [desimetrik], *a. Ph:* **ondes décimétriques,** decimetre waves.

décimilli- [desimili], *pref.* ten thousandth (part of).

décimo [desimo], *adv.* tenthly.

decineper [desinepɛ:r], *s.m. Ph:* decineper.

décinormal, -aux [desinɔrmal, -o], *a. Ch:* (*en parlant d'une solution*), decinormal.

décintrage [desɛ̃tra:ʒ], *s.m.,* **décintrement** [desɛ̃trəmɑ̃], *s.m. Civ.E: Const:* striking of the centre, centring, centre-striking (of arch); **appareil de décintrement,** down-striking apparatus.

décintrer [desɛ̃tre], *v.tr. Civ.E: Const:* to strike, remove, the centre, centring, of (arch, etc.).

décirage [desira:ʒ], *s.m.* removal of wax; *Engr:* removal of the (etching) ground.

décirer [desire], *v.tr.* to unwax (floor, etc.); *Engr:* to remove the (etching) ground.

décisif, -ive [desizif, -i:v], *a.* **1.** decisive (answer, battle, etc.); conclusive (evidence); deciding factor; **c'est un argument d.,** that clinches the argument; **victoire décisive,** decisive victory; **le moment d. approche,** things are drawing to a crisis; **au moment d.,** at the critical, crucial, moment. **2.** *A:* (*of pers.*) prompt to decide; *F:* cock-sure. **3.** positive, authoritative, peremptory (tone).

décision [desizjɔ̃], *s.f.* decision. **1.** *(a)* **prendre, arriver à, une décision,** to arrive at, come to, reach, a decision; to make up one's mind (quant à, au sujet de, about, as to); **la d. que nous allons prendre,** the step that we are about to take; **se battre jusqu'à une d.,** to fight to a finish; **forcer une décision,** to bring matters to a head; **s'en tenir à sa décision,** to abide by one's decision; **décisions d'une assemblée,** conclusions reached at a meeting; *Mil:* **chercher la d. par une manœuvre de débordement,** to seek the issue in an out-flanking movement; **la prise de la cote 304 emporta la d.,** the capture of hill 304 decided the issue, proved decisive; *(b) Jur:* ruling, award; **prononcer, rendre, une d.,** to give a ruling; *(c) Mil:* (regimental) orders; *U.S:* bulletin; **la d. journalière,** the daily orders; *U.S:* the daily bulletin. **2.** *(a)* resolution, determination; **agir avec d.,** to act with decision; **il a de la d.,** he can make decisions; **avec d.,** decisively; **manquer de d.,** to lack decision; **esprit de d.,** decisiveness; *(b)* quickness of resolve.

décisivement [desizivmɑ̃], *adv.* decisively.

décisoire [desizwa:r], *a. Jur:* **serment d.,** decisive oath.

décistère [desistɛ:r], *s.m. Meas:* decistere, one tenth of a stere.

décivilisateur, -trice [desivilizatœ:r, -tris], *a.* decivilizing.

décivilisation [desivilizasjɔ̃], *s.f.* decivilization.

déciviliser [desivilize], *v.tr.* to decivilize.

se déciviliser, to become decivilized.

decizois, -oise [dəsizwa, -wa:z], *a. & s. Geog:* (native, inhabitant) of Decize.

deck-tennis [dektenis], *s.m.* deck-tennis.

déclamateur, -trice [deklamatœ:r, -tris], *s.* **1.** *(a) Rom.Ant:* declaimer, declamator; *(b) A:* reciter, elocutionist. **2.** *(a)* stump orator, ranter; *P:* tub-thumper; *(b)* high-flown, bombastic, writer; phrasemonger. **3.** *a.* = DÉCLAMATOIRE.

déclamation [deklamasjɔ̃], *s.f.* **1.** *(a) (art of)* declamation; elocution, oratory; *(b)* **il a une mauvaise d., une d. outrée,** his delivery is bad, exaggerated. **2.** *(a)* declamation, harangue; *(b)* ranting, spouting; **discours plein de d.,** bombastic, high-falutin', speech.

déclamatoire [deklamatwa:r], *a.* declamatory, inflated, high-flown (style); ranting (speech).

déclamer [deklɑme]. **1.** *v.tr.* to declaim (speech); to recite (poem, etc.). **2.** *v.i.* to rant, spout, harangue; **d. contre qn, qch.,** to inveigh, to rail, against s.o., sth.

déclanche [deklɑ̃:ʃ], *s.f.* = DÉCLENCHE.

déclanchement [deklɑ̃ʃmɑ̃], *s.m.* = DÉCLENCHEMENT.

déclancher [deklɑ̃ʃe], *v.tr.* = DÉCLENCHER.

déclancheur [deklɑ̃ʃœ:r], *s.m.* = DÉCLENCHEUR.

déclarable [deklarabl], *a.* declarable; *Cust:* liable to duty; dutiable.

déclarant, -ante [deklarɑ̃, -ɑ̃:t], *s.* **1.** *Jur: Adm:* informant; *Jur:* avowant. **2.** *Cards:* bidder.

déclaratif, -ive [deklaratif, -i:v], *a. Jur:* declaratory (act, statute, etc.); *Gram:* **verbes déclaratifs,** verbs of saying and thinking.

déclaration [deklarasjɔ̃], *s.f.* declaration; *(a)* proclamation, announcement; **d. de guerre,** declaration of war; **d. de faillite,** declaration of bankruptcy, filing of one's petition; **la d. du jury,** the finding of the jury; **d. de naturalisation,** letters of naturalization; **d. d'intention,** declaration of intent; *(b)* notification (of birth, death, etc.); *(c)* statement; **émettre, faire, une d.,** to make a statement; **d. sous serment,** affidavit; **d. de succession,** statement (by heir) concerning the estate of deceased; **suivant sa propre d.,** according to his own statement; **d. de revenu,** return of income; income-tax return; **fausse d.,** (i) misrepresentation, wilful mis-statement; (ii) false return, declaration; *Adm:* **d. de versement, de quittance,** receipt; *Rail:* **d. d'expédition,** invoice; *R.C.Ch:* **d. de ses péchés,** confession; *(d)* **d. d'amour,** declaration of love; **faire sa d.,** to propose; *A:* to declare oneself; *F:* to pop the question; *(e) Cust:* declaring (of dutiable goods); **d. en douane,** customs declaration, bill of entry; **d. d'entrée, de sortie,** clearance inwards, outwards; **faire la d. (d'un navire) à la sortie,** to clear a ship; **d. d'entrée en entrepôt,** warehousing entry; **d. de transit,** transit entry; **faire une d. en douane de produits manufacturés,** to pass a customs entry of manufactured goods; *(f) Nau:* **d. d'avarie (à la cargaison),** (ship's) protest; *(g) Pol: Hist:* **d. des droits de l'homme et du citoyen** = bill, declaration, of rights; *(h) St.Exch:* **jour de la d. des noms,** ticket day; *(i) Cards:* declaration.

déclaratoire [deklaratwa:r], *a. Jur:* = DÉCLARATIF.

déclaré [deklare], *a.* declared, avowed (enemy, intention, etc.); **ennemi d. du Gouvernement,** open, professed, enemy of the Government.

déclarer [deklare], *v.tr.* **1.** *(a)* to declare, make known (one's intentions, wishes, one's love, etc.); **d. ses complices,** to reveal, disclose, the names of one's accomplices; **il déclara qu'il n'avait rien vu,** he declared, asserted, that he had seen nothing; **il déclara avoir vingt ans,** he gave twenty as his age, he gave his age as twenty;

il déclara qu'il lui faudrait partir le lendemain, he announced that he would have to leave the next day; **il déclara que . . .,** he made the following statement . . .; (*b*) *Cards:* **d. trèfle,** to declare, call, clubs. **2.** to declare, proclaim, announce, make public; (*a*) **d. qn roi,** to declare s.o. king; **le jury l'a déclaré coupable,** the jury found him guilty, brought him in guilty; **déclaré coupable de vol,** convicted of theft; **d. qn en faillite,** to adjudge, adjudicate, s.o. bankrupt; **son mariage a été déclaré nul,** his marriage was annulled; (*b*) **d. un enfant à la mairie,** to register a (new-born) child at the town hall; **d. une naissance, un décès,** to notify a birth, a death; (*c*) **d. la guerre à qn,** to declare war on s.o.; **d. qch. officiellement,** to declare sth. officially; to make an official declaration of sth.; **d. sous serment,** to declare under oath; *F:* **d. la guerre aux anglicismes,** to declare war on anglicisms; (*d*) *Cust:* **avez-vous quelque chose à d.?** have you anything to declare, anything liable to duty? **d. une cargaison,** to manifest a cargo; **d. un vaisseau,** to report a ship; *Fin:* **transferts déclarés,** certified transfers.

se déclarer. 1. (*a*) to declare one's opinions, etc.; to speak one's mind; **se d. pour, contre, qn, qch.,** to declare for, against, s.o., sth.; (*b*) to declare, avow, one's love. **2.** (*with complement*) **se d. jacobite,** to declare oneself a Jacobite; **se d. l'auteur du méfait,** to own up to the deed. **3.** (*a*) (*of fire, disease, storm*) to break out; (*b*) (*of disease*) to declare itself.

déclassé, -ée [deklɑse], *a. & s.* **1.** (one) who has come down in the world, lost his social position; déclassé(e); *Fin:* **valeurs déclassées,** displaced stock. **2.** obsolete (ship, etc.).

déclassement [deklɑsmɑ̃], *s.m.* **1.** transfer (of passengers) from one class to another; change of class; *s.a.* BILLET 3. **2.** coming down in the world, lowering of one's social position. **3.** abandonment, dismantling (of obsolete fortress); striking (of warship, etc.) off the list. **4.** *Navy:* disrating (of seaman). **5.** *Mil: etc:* downgrading (of classified documents).

déclasser [deklɑse], *v.tr.* **1.** (*a*) to transfer (passengers) from one class to another; (*b*) **d. des papiers,** (i) to put papers out of order; (ii) to change the order of papers. **2.** to lower the social position of (s.o.); to bring (s.o.) down in the world. **3.** *Mil: Navy:* to abandon, dismantle (obsolete fortress); to declare (weapon) obsolete; to strike (warship, etc.) off the list; **4.** *Navy:* to disrate (seaman). **5.** *Sp:* to penalize (runner). **6.** *Mil: etc:* to downgrade (a classified document).

déclaveter [deklavte], *v.tr.* (**je déclavette** [deklavɛt], **n. déclavetons** [deklavtɔ̃]; **je déclavetterai** [deklavɛtre]) to unkey (pulley, etc.).

déclenche [deklɑ̃:ʃ], *s.f. Mec.E:* disconnecting gear, release device, trip-gear, trigger mechanism.

déclenche-marge [deklɑ̃ʃmarʒ], *s.m.inv. Typewr:* margin-release.

déclenchement [deklɑ̃ʃmɑ̃], *s.m.* **1** *Mec.E:* (*a*) releasing, throwing out of gear, disengaging (of part); *Rail:* unlocking (of signal); **d. différé, retardé,** delayed-action release, tripping; **dispositif de d.,** release, trip(ping), device; **mécanisme de d.,** disconnecting gear; trip(ping) gear, mechanism; trigger mechanism; *Machine-Tls:* **d. des avances,** feed-tripping; *El: Elcs:* **circuit de d.,** trip circuit; **signal de d.,** trip signal; **d. par bobines en dérivation,** shunt tripping; **d. périodique,** gating; **d. retardé,** delay-action circuit-breaking; **d. périodique, cyclique,** gating; **circuit à d. périodique,** gate; **amplificateur à d. périodique,** gated amplifier; *Phot:* **d. de l'obturateur,** shutter-release; **d. par poire, pneumatique,** bulb-, pneumatic, release; (*b*) trigger action, triggering; **d. au doigt,** trigger release. **2.** starting; setting (of sth.) in motion; *Mil:* launching (of attack); opening (of fire).

déclencher [deklɑ̃ʃe], *v.tr.* **1.** *A:* to unlatch (door); *Rail:* **d. un signal,** to unlock a signal. **2.** (*a*) *Mec.E:* to release, throw out of gear, disconnect, disengage, trip (part); *Phot:* **d. l'obturateur,** to release the shutter; (*b*) *El: Elcs:* to trigger, trip; **d. périodiquement,** to gate. **3.** to set off (mechanism); *F:* to trigger off; to start (apparatus); to set (apparatus) in motion; *Mil:* **d. une attaque,** to launch an attack; **d. le feu,** to open fire; *Fin:* **la nouvelle qui a déclenché la hausse,** the news that started the rise (in prices); *F:* **d. la conversation,** to set everyone talking, to start the ball rolling; **négligence qui a déclenché une série de difficultés,** carelessness that caused, brought about, a series of mishaps; **d. une guerre nucléaire,** to unleash a nuclear war.

déclencheur [deklɑ̃ʃœ:r], *s.m.* (*a*) *Mec.E:* release, trip; **d. de cliquet,** pawl-release; **d. à action différée, retardée,** delayed-action trip; (*b*) *El: Elcs:* **d. à maxima, à minima,** over-, under-current trip; **d. périodique,** gate; (*c*) *Phot:* **d. d'obturateur,** shutter-release; **d. à action différée, retardée,** delayed-action release; **d. automatique,** automatic, self-, timer; **d. à poire, pneumatique,** bulb-, pneumatic, release.

déclic [deklik], *s.m.* **1.** (*a*) pawl, catch, click (of sprocket wheel, etc.); nippers, releasing hooks, trigger (of pile-driver); **levier à d.,** trip-lever; **chronomètre à d.,** stop-watch; *El:* **d. de contact,** contact-release; (*b*) click(ing sound). **2.** *Sm.a:* hair-trigger.

déclimater [deklimate], *v.tr.* to declimatize (s.o., plant, etc.).

déclin [deklɛ̃], *s.m.* decline, close (of day, of life); wane, waning (of moon, volcano); fall (of the year); falling-off (of talent); **le soleil est à, sur, son déclin,** the sun is sinking, setting; **la lune est sur son d.,** the moon is on the wane; **beauté, empire, sur son d.,** beauty, empire, on the wane; **l'Empire romain penchait vers, sur, son d.,** the Roman Empire was on the eve of its decline; **au d. de sa vie,** in his declining years.

déclinable [deklinabl̩], *a. Gram:* declinable.

déclinaison [deklinɛzɔ̃], *s.f.* **1.** (*a*) *Astr:* declination (of star, etc.); **cercle de d.,** declination circle; (*b*) *Magn:* **d. (de l'aiguille) magnétique,** magnetic declination, variation; declination, variation, of the needle; **ligne d'égale d. magnétique,** isogonic line, isogonal; **boussole de d.,** declination compass; **d. de la boussole,** declination, variation, of the compass. **2.** *Gram:* declension; **nom de la première d.,** first-declension noun.

déclinateur [deklinatœ:r], *s.m. Surv:* surveyor's compass.

déclination [declinasjɔ̃], *s.f.* (i) *A:* declination, slope; (ii) decline.

déclinatoire [deklinatwa:r]. **1.** *Jur:* (*a*) *a.* declinatory (plea, etc.); (*b*) *s.m.* plea in bar of trial. **2.** *s.m. Surv:* = DÉCLINATEUR.

décliné [dekline], *a. Bot:* declinate.

décliner [dekline]. I. *v.i.* **1.** to decline, to deviate (from the true line); **boussole qui décline de 3°,** compass that has a deviation, a variation, of 3°. **2.** to decline, to wane; (*of star*) to decline; **le jour, le soleil, décline,** day is drawing to a close, the sun is sinking; **force, fièvre, qui décline, qui va en déclinant,** strength, fever, that is diminishing, abating; **sa beauté décline,** her beauty is falling off, is fading, is on the wane; her looks are failing; **le malade décline à vue d'œil,** the patient is failing, sinking, visibly; **sa vie décline,** his life is ebbing away. **3. l'Empire déclinait déjà,** the Empire was already in decay.

II. **décliner,** *v.tr.* **1.** to decline, refuse (offer, etc.); to decline (responsibility); **d. une juridiction,** to refuse to acknowledge a jurisdiction. **2.** (*a*) *Gram:* to decline (noun, etc.); **ce nom se décline sur la première déclinaison,** this is a first-declension noun; (*b*) **d. ses nom et prénoms,** to state, give, one's name. **3.** *Surv:* to set (plane table) by the compass.

déclinomètre [deklinɔmɛtr̥], *s.m.* declinometer; declination compass.

déclinquer [deklɛ̃ke], *v.tr.* **1.** *N.Arch:* to unclinch; to rip the planking off (clinker-built boat). **2.** *F:* to dismantle, break up (watch, car, etc.).

décliquer [deklike], *v.tr.* to release (pawl); *Civ.E:* **d. le mouton,** to release, trip, the monkey (of pile-driver).

décliquetage [deklikta:ʒ], *s.m. Mec.E:* unclicking, uncogging (of sprocket wheel); undoing (of escapement).

décliqueter [deklikte], *v.tr.* (**je décliquette** [deklikɛt], **n. décliquetons** [deklikt̃ɔ]; **je décliquetterai** [deklikɛtre]) *Mec.E:* to unclick, uncog (sprocket wheel), to undo (escapement).

déclive [dekli:v]. **1.** *a.* declivitous, declivous, sloping, inclined; **terrain d.,** sloping ground; **des pentes moins déclives,** slopes less steep, gentler slopes. **2.** *s.f.* slope; **muraille prolongée en d. vers le fleuve,** wall sloping down to the river.

décliver [deklive], *v.i.* to slope.

déclivité [deklivite], *s.f.* declivity, slope, incline, gradient; **angle de d.,** slope, angle, of gradient; **les déclivités de la montagne,** the slopes of the mountain.

déclochage [deklɔʃa:ʒ], *s.m. Hort:* removing the cloches from, uncovering, (melons, etc.).

déclocher [deklɔʃe], *v.tr. Hort:* to remove the cloches from, to uncover, to decloche (melons, etc.).

décloisonner [deklwazɔne], *v.tr.* to decompartmentalize, to break down the divisions between (administrations, etc.).

décloîtrer [deklwatre, -wɑ-], *v.tr.* to remove (s.o.) from the cloister; to uncloister (s.o.).

se décloîtrer, to leave the cloister, to give up religious life.

déclore [deklɔ:r], *v.tr.* (*conj. like* CLORE) **1.** to throw open, disenclose (park, etc.); to remove the fence from round a garden, a field. **2.** *A:* **lèvres décloses,** parted lips; **fleur déclose,** open flower, flower in bloom.

déclôture [deklotyːr], *s.f.* disenclosing.

déclôturer [deklotyre], *v.tr.* to disenclose, throw open (park, etc.); to remove the fence from round a garden, a field.

déclouer [deklue], *v.tr.* **1.** (*a*) to unnail, undo; to draw the nails from (packing-case, etc.); (*b*) **d. un tableau,** to take down a picture (from its nail). **2.** *P:* to redeem (sth.), to take (sth.) out of pawn.

décoagulation [dekoagylasjɔ̃], *s.f.* liquefaction.

décoaguler [dekoagyle], *v.tr. Ph:* to liquefy, dissolve (curdled substance).

se décoaguler, to liquefy, dissolve.

décochement [dekɔʃmɑ̃], *s.m.* (*rare*) shooting, loosing (of arrow, etc.); **d. d'une épigramme,** firing off of an epigram.

décocher [dekɔʃe], *v.tr.* **1.** to shoot, let off, let fly (bolt from crossbow); *F:* **d. un coup à qn,** to deal s.o. a lightning blow, to hit out at s.o.; **d. un coup de fouet à un chien,** to lash out at a dog; **d. un juron,** to rap out an oath; **d. une épigramme,** to fire off, let off, an epigram; **d. une épigramme contre qn,** to fling an epigram at s.o.; **d. un regard, une œillade, un sourire, à qn,** to shoot, dart, a glance, to flash a glance, a smile, at s.o. **2.** *Metall:* to strip (casting).

décoconnage [dekɔkɔna:ʒ], *s.m. Ser:* gathering, picking, cocoons (from bushes, etc.).

décoconner [dekɔkɔne], *v.tr. Ser:* to gather, pick, cocoons from (bushes, etc.).

décocté [dekɔkte], *s.m. Pharm:* decoction (extract produced by boiling).

décoction [dekɔksjɔ̃], *s.f.* decoction (action of decocting); *P:* **une d. de coups de bâton,** a shower of blows, a good thrashing.

décodage [dekɔda:ʒ], *s.m.* decoding.

décoder [dekɔde], *v.tr.* to decode.

décodeur [dekɔdœr], *s.m.* decoder.

décoffrage [dekɔfra:ʒ], *s.m. Civ.E:* dismantling of the form(work).

décoffrer [dekɔfre], *v.tr. Civ.E:* to strike, dismantle, the form(work).

décognoir [dekɔɲwa:r], *s.m. Typ:* shooting-stick.

décohéreur [dekɔerœ:r], *s.m. W.Tel: A:* decoherer.

décohésion [dekɔezjɔ̃], *s.f.* (magnetic) decoherence; *A:* **d. par percussion,** decoherence by shaking.

décoiffage [dekwafa:ʒ], *s.m. Mil:* uncapping, uncorking (of fuse).

décoiffement [dekwafmɑ̃], *s.m.* **1.** removal of head-dress; uncapping (of fuse); removing the foil cap (from a bottle); uncorking (of bottle). **2.** (*a*) taking down of one's hair; (*b*) disarranging (of s.o.'s hair).

décoiffer [dekwafe], *v.tr.* **1.** to remove (s.o.'s) head-dress, (s.o.'s) hat; to uncap (fuse); to remove the foil cap (from a bottle); to uncork (bottle); **colonnes décoiffées de leurs chapiteaux,** columns bared of their capitals; *Biol:* **d. une préparation,** to remove the cover-glass from a preparation. **2.** (*a*) (i) to take (s.o.'s) hair down; (*b*) to undo, to ruffle (s.o.'s) hair; to disarrange (s.o.'s) hair; **le vent l'a décoiffée,** the wind has blown her hair about, *F:* she is all windswept. **3.** *F: A:* **d. qn d'un dessein,** to get s.o. to drop a project, to get a project out of s.o.'s head.

se décoiffer. 1. to remove one's head-dress; *F:* **se d. d'une idée,** to put an idea out of one's head. **2.** (*a*) to take one's hair down; (*b*) to disarrange one's hair.

décoincement [dekwɛ̃smɑ̃], *s.m.* loosening (of jammed part); unwedging, knocking out of the wedges (of mast, etc.); *Rail:* unkeying, unwedging (of rails).

décoincer [dekwɛ̃se], *v.tr.* (**n. décoinçons; je décoinçai(s)**) to loosen (jammed part); to unwedge, knock out the wedges of (mast, etc.); *Rail:* to unwedge, unkey (rails).

se décoincer, (of part) to work loose, to get unwedged.

décolérer [dekɔlere], *v.i.* (**je décolère, n. décolérons; je décolérerai**) *F:* to calm down, cool down; *used esp. in the neg.* **il ne décolérait pas,** he was in a constant state of anger, he was still furious; *F:* he was still like a bear with a sore head.

décollage [dekɔlaːʒ], *s.m.* **1.** unsticking, ungluing. **2.** *Av:* taking off, rising, leaving the ground; **épreuves de d.,** taking-off trials; **faire un d. prudent,** to effect a careful take-off; **d. assisté (par fusée),** rocket assisted take-off; **d. (à) pleins gaz,** full-throttle take-off; **d. catapulté,** catapult(-assisted) take-off; **d. par vent nul,** take-off without wind; **d. face au vent, vent arrière,** take-off into, with, the wind; **d. vent de travers,** cross-wind take-off; **d. vertical,** vertical take-off, V.T.O.; **avion à d. vertical,** vertical take-off plane; **avion, engin, à d. court,** short-haul craft; **d. à pleine charge,** full-load take-off. **3.** *Pol.Ec:* take-off point (of the development of an economy).

décollation [dekɔlasjɔ̃], *s.f.* (*a*) *A:* decollation, decapitation, beheading; (*b*) *Surg:* decollation, decapitation.

décollé [dekɔle], *a.* (*of ears*) sticking out, standing out, prominent; *Cost:* **encollure décollée,** stand-away neck.

décollement [dekɔlmɑ̃], *s.m.* **1.** (*a*) unsticking, ungluing; (*b*) *Surg:* separation, detachment (of adhesions, etc.). **2.** coming unstuck, unglued; unsticking, loosening (of tyre canvas, etc.); *Phot:* frilling (of plate); *Metalw:* loosening (of rivet head); *Med:* **d. de la rétine,** detachment of the retina; *Paperm:* **décollements (dans les papiers couchés),** cracking; *Av:* **d. des filets d'air,** break-down, separation, of air-flow; *Av: Ph:* **d. des filets fluides,** break-down, separation, of stream-lines.

décoller[1] [dekɔle], *v.tr.* **1.** *A:* to decollate, decapitate, behead. **2.** *Fish:* to cut off (cods') heads.

décoller[2]. **1.** *v.tr.* (*a*) to unstick, unglue (paper, furniture, etc.); (*b*) to loosen, disengage, release (part); *Surg:* to separate, detach (adhesions, etc.); *Bill:* **d. la bille, se d.,** to bring the ball off the cushion. **2.** *v.i.* (*a*) (*of aircraft*) to leave the ground; to lift; (*of pilot*) to take off, to pull the plane off the ground; (*b*) *F:* **il ne décolle pas,** he sticks there, doesn't budge; **deux heures sans d.,** two hours at a stretch; (*c*) *P:* (*of married persons*) to separate; (*d*) *Sp:* (*of cyclist*) to lose touch with his pacer, to drop behind; to give up; (*e*) *Nau:* **d. d'un quart,** to sheer off a point; (*f*) to work one's way up (from a low social or intellectual level); (*g*) *P:* **il a drôlement décollé,** he's got terribly thin.

se décoller, (*a*) to come unstuck, undone; to work loose; (*b*) *P:* (*of pers.*) to become feeble, to be in a bad way; (*c*) *Sp:* (*of runner, cyclist*) to draw ahead.

décolletage [dekɔltaːʒ], *s.m.* **1.** (*a*) cutting out of the neck, lowering of the neck line (of dress); (*b*) baring of the neck, wearing of low-necked dresses, décolleté; **un d. modeste, inconvenant,** a modest, immodest, décolleté; (*c*) neck-line (of dress). **2.** *Agr:* cutting of the tops (of root crop). **3.** *Tchn:* screw-cutting, turning; *Metalw:* cutting-off, free-cutting; undercut, under-cutting.

décolleté [dekɔlte], *s.m.* **1.** *a.* (*a*) **femme décolletée,** woman in low-necked, low-cut, dress, in evening dress, in décolleté; **robe décolletée,** low-necked, low-cut, dress, décolleté dress; **robe décolletée dans le dos,** dress cut low in the back, low-backed dress; backless dress; **cette robe est trop décolletée,** that dress is too revealing, too décolleté, too low-cut; **soulier d.,** court shoe; (*b*) *A. & Lit:* **propos décolletés,** loose, licentious, talk; (*c*) *Metalw:* free-cut, cut from bar, machine-made (bolts, screws, etc.). **2.** *s.m.* (*a*) neck-opening, neck-line (of dress); **d. bateau,** boat neck(-line); **d. carré,** square neck; **d. en pointe,** V neck; **d. profond,** very deep neckline; **d. plongeant,** plunging neckline; **en grand d.,** in a low-cut evening-dress, in full décolleté; **en petit d.,** in semi-evening dress; (*b*) **elle a un beau d.,** she has beautiful, nice, shoulders.

décolleter [dekɔlte], *v.tr.* (**je décollète, je décollette,** are theoretical forms; the pronunciation is always [dekɔlt]) **1.** to cut out the neck of (dress), to lower the neckline of a dress; **d. qn,** to bare s.o.'s neck, to make s.o. wear a low-necked dress; **cette robe la décollette trop,** this dress is too revealing, has too low a neckline. **2.** *Agr:* to cut the tops of (root crops). **3.** *Metalw:* to cut off, cut (screw, etc.); **tour à d.,** cutting-off, free-cutting, screw-cutting, lathe; **machine à d.** = DÉCOLLETEUSE.

se décolleter, to wear a low-necked dress; *A:* **les conversations se décollettent** [dekɔlt] **de plus en plus,** conversations grow more and more free and easy, licentious.

décolleteur, -euse [dekɔltœːr, -øːz]. **1.** *s.m. & f.* screw-cutting machine operator. **2.** *s.f. Metalw:* **décolleteuse,** cutting-off, free-cutting; screw-cutting, machine.

décolleur, -euse [dekɔlœːr, -øːz], *s.m. & f. Fish:* **1.** person who cuts off cods' heads. **2.** *s.m.* knife for cutting off cods' heads.

décolonisation [dekɔlɔnizasjɔ̃], *s.f.* decolonization.

décoloniser [dekɔlɔnize], *v.tr.* to decolonize.

décolorant [dekɔlɔrɑ̃], *Ch:* **1.** *a.* bleaching, decolo(u)rizing, decolorant, discolouring (properties, etc.). **2.** *s.m.* bleaching, discolouring, decolo(u)rizing, agent; decolorant.

décoloration [dekɔlɔrasjɔ̃], *s.f.* (*a*) discolouration, fading; (*b*) *Hairdr:* bleaching, decolo(u)rization; (*c*) colourlessness (of complexion, of style).

décoloré [dekɔlɔre], *a.* **robe d'un bleu d.,** faded blue dress; **visage, teint, d.,** colourless face, complexion; **mener une existence décolorée,** to lead a colourless, drab, existence.

décolorer [dekɔlɔre], *v.tr.* to discolour; to fade; to take the colour out of (sth.), to decolo(u)rize; **se d. les cheveux,** to bleach one's hair; **rideaux décolorés par le soleil,** curtains faded by the sun; **d. son style,** to make one's style colourless.

se décolorer, to lose colour, to fade, to bleach; to discolour; (*of pers.*) to lose one's colour, to grow pale, to become colourless.

décombant [dekɔ̃bɑ̃], *a. Bot:* decumbent.

décomblement [dekɔ̃bləmɑ̃], *s.m. A:* emptying; cleaning out (of hole, etc.).

décombler [dekɔ̃ble], *v.tr. A:* to empty; clean out (hole, etc.).

décombrement [dekɔ̃brəmɑ̃], *s.m. A:* clearing (of piece of ground, etc.).

décombrer [dekɔ̃bre], *v.tr. A:* to remove the rubbish from, to clear (piece of ground, etc.).

décombres [dekɔ̃ːbr̥], *s.m.pl.* (*a*) rubble, debris (of buildings); (*b*) ruins.

décommandement [dekɔmɑ̃dmɑ̃], *s.m.* countermanding, cancelling; calling off.

décommander [dekɔmɑ̃de], *v.tr.* to countermand; **d. une réunion, un dîner,** to cancel a meeting, a dinner; **d. une grève,** to call off a strike; **d. un invité,** to cancel s.o.'s invitation, to put off a guest; *Sp:* **d. un match,** to scratch a match.

se décommander, to excuse oneself (from an appointment, an invitation previously accepted).

décommettre [dekɔmɛtr̥], *v.tr.* (*conj. like* METTRE); to unlay (rope); **bout décommis,** fag-end (of rope).

décompensation [dekɔ̃pɑ̃sasjɔ̃], *s.f.* decompensation.

décompléter [dekɔ̃plete], *v.tr.* (**je décomplète, n. décomplétons; je décompléterai**) (*rare*) to render (collection, etc.) incomplete; to spoil, break up (set).

décomplexer [dekɔ̃plɛkse], *v.tr.* to relieve (s.o.) of his complexes.

décomposable [dekɔ̃pozabl̥], *a. Math: Ch: etc:* decomposable.

décomposant [dekɔ̃pozɑ̃], *a. Ch:* decomposing (agent, etc.).

décomposé [dekɔ̃poze], *a.* **1.** *Bot:* decomposite (leaves, etc.). **2.** (*a*) *Mch: I.C.E:* **huile décomposée,** spent oil; *s.a.* ESPRIT 2; (*b*) **visage d.,** drawn face; face distorted by grief or terror; (*c*) decomposed, decayed, rotten.

décomposer [dekɔ̃poze], *v.tr.* **1.** (*a*) *Ph: Ch: etc:* to decompose, break up, resolve (into); **d. un tout en ses éléments,** to break up a whole into its constituent parts; **d. la lumière,** to disperse, break up, split, light; *Mec:* **d. une vitesse en ses composantes,** to resolve a velocity into its components; **d. des forces,** to resolve forces; *El:* **d. un système polyphasé,** to resolve a polyphase system; (*b*) **d. une propriété,** to break up an estate; (*c*) *Mth:* **d. une fraction,** to split up, break down, a fraction; (*d*) *Com:* **d. un compte,** to analyse, break down, an account; *Gram:* **d. une phrase,** to analyse, construe, a sentence; (*e*) *Gym: Mil: etc:* **d. un mouvement,** to go through a movement by detail, by numbers; **en décomposant,** by numbers; **sans d.,** judging the time. **2.** to decompose, rot (organic matter). **3.** to convulse, distort (features).

se décomposer. **1.** (*a*) (*of organic matter*) to decompose, rot, decay; (*b*) *Ch: etc:* to break down. **2.** (*of face, features*) to become convulsed (with terror, etc.); to undergo a terrible change.

décomposition [dekɔ̃pozisjɔ̃], *s.f.* **1.** (*a*) *Ph: Ch: etc:* decomposition; breaking up, breakdown, into component parts; **d. double,** metathesis; **d. des forces,** resolution of forces; (*b*) *Mth:* **d. en fractions partielles,** splitting up, breakdown, into partial fractions: (*c*) *Com:* **d. des dépenses,** analysis, breakdown, of expenses; (*d*) *Gram:* construe, construing, analysis (of sentence); (*e*) *Gym: Mil: etc:* **d. d'un mouvement,** going through a movement by detail, by numbers. **2.** decomposition, decay, rotting, putrefaction. **3.** distortion, awful change (of features).

décompresseur [dekɔ̃prɛsœːr], *s.m. I.C.E:* (*a*) compression tap, relief cock; (*b*) exhaust(-valve) lifter; (*c*) decompressor.

décompression [dekɔ̃prɛsjɔ̃], *s.f. Mch: etc:* decompression; expansion (after compression), pressure relief; **soupape de d.,** relief valve; **caisson, chambre, de d.,** decompression chamber; **robinet de d.,** (i) *I.C.E:* compression tap; (ii) *Mch:* pet cock.

décomprimer [dekɔ̃prime], *v.tr.* to decompress.

décomptable [dekɔ̃tabl̥], *a.* deductible, deductable, that can be deducted (from an account).

décompte [dekɔ̃ːt], *s.m.* **1.** (*a*) deduction (from sum to be paid); **faire le d.,** to make a deduction (from sum to be paid); *F:* **trouver, éprouver, du d.,** to be disappointed (**à,** in); to be disillusioned (by), to find sth. less advantageous than expected; (*b*) **payer le d.,** to pay the balance due on (an account); *Sp: Games: etc:* **d. des points,** scoring. **2.** *Adm: Com:* detailed account; breakdown.

décompter [dekɔ̃te], *v.tr.* **1.** to deduct (sum from account); *abs.* **ils ont trouvé à d.,** they found things far short of what they expected, they were disappointed; **il leur faudra en d.,** (i) they will have to get over it; (ii) they will have to climb down. **2.** to work out the charges on (bills, etc.); to calculate (interest, etc.). **3.** *v.i.* (*of clock*) to miscount (in striking).

déconcentration [dekɔ̃sɑ̃trasjɔ̃], *s.f. Adm:* devolution.

déconcentrer [dekɔ̃sɑ̃tre], *v.tr.* (*a*) to decentralize; to disperse; (*b*) to distract (s.o.), to make (s.o.) lose concentration.

déconcert [dekɔ̃sɛːr], *s.m. A:* **1.** disaccord. **2.** perturbation, disconcertment; **sans d.,** imperturbably.

déconcertant [dekɔ̃sɛrtɑ̃], *a.* disconcerting.

déconcerté [dekɔ̃sɛrte], *a.* disconcerted, abashed, put out; **il eut l'air assez d.,** he looked rather taken aback, rather put out.

déconcertement [dekɔ̃sɛrtəmɑ̃], *s.m.* disconcertment.

déconcerter [dekɔ̃sɛrte], *v.tr.* **1.** (*a*) *A:* to put (musicians) out of time, out of tune; (*b*) **d. les projets de qn,** to upset, confound, frustrate, s.o.'s plans. **2. d. qn,** to disconcert s.o.; to annoy s.o.; to abash s.o.; to take s.o.'s breath away; **la nouvelle ne laissa pas de le d.,** he was none the less shaken by the news. **3.** *abs.* to be disconcerting.

se déconcerter, to lose one's assurance, to be put out; **sans se d.,** unabashed.

déconfès, -esse [dekɔ̃fɛs], *a. & s. A:* **mourir d.,** to die without confession; *A:* to die unshriven.

déconfire [dekɔ̃fiːr], *v.tr.* (*conj. like* CONFIRE) **1.** *A:* to discomfit; to defeat utterly. **2.** to nonplus; to disconcert; to annoy (s.o.).

déconfit [dekɔ̃fi], *a.* discomfited.

déconfiture [dekɔ̃fityːr], *s.f.* **1.** *A:* discomfiture; defeat, rout (of army). **2.** collapse, failure, downfall, ruin; *Jur:* insolvency; bankruptcy (of non-trader); *St.Exch:* **proclamer la d. d'un agent en défaut,** to hammer a defaulter; **tomber en d.,** to fail to meet one's liabilities; *St.Exch:* to default; *F:* to be hammered.

déconfort [dekɔ̃fɔːr], *s.m. A:* discouragement.

décongélation [dekɔ̃ʒelasjɔ̃], *s.f.* defrosting, defreezing, thawing (of frozen meat, etc.).

décongeler [dekɔ̃ʒle], *v.tr.* (**je décongèle, n. décongelons; je décongèlerai**) to defreeze, defrost, thaw (frozen meat, etc.).

décongestion [dekɔ̃ʒɛstjɔ̃], *s.f. Med:* decongestion, relieving congestion (in the lungs, etc.); *Adm:* clearing (of slum area); relieving congestion (in town).

décongestionner [dekɔ̃ʒɛstjɔne], *v.tr. Med:* to relieve congestion (in the lungs, etc.); *Adm:* to clear (slum area); **cette nouvelle rue va d. le centre de la ville,** this new road will relieve the congestion in the centre of the town.

déconnecter [dekɔnɛkte], *v.tr. El.E:* to disconnect (lead, etc.).

déconner [dekɔne], *v.i. V:* to talk cock.

déconsacrer [dekɔ̃sakre], *v.tr.* to deconsecrate.

déconseiller [dekɔ̃seje], *v.tr.* **d. qch. (à qn), d. à qn de faire qch.,** to advise (s.o.) against sth.; against doing sth., to advise s.o. not to do sth.; **un livre à d. pour les jeunes gens,** a book not to be recommended for young people.

déconsidération [dekɔ̃siderasjɔ̃], *s.f.* disrepute, discredit; **tomber dans la d.,** to fall into disrepute; **jeter la d. sur qn, qch.,** to throw discredit on s.o., sth.

déconsidérer [dekɔ̃sidere], *v.tr.* (**je déconsidère, n. déconsidérons; je déconsidérerai**) to bring (s.o., sth.) into disrepute; to cast discredit, a slur, on (s.o., sth.); *F:* to run (s.o.) down.

se déconsidérer, to bring discredit upon oneself, to fall into discredit; **je ne voudrais pas me d. auprès de lui,** I do not want to belittle myself in his eyes; I do not want to lose his esteem.

déconsigner [dekɔ̃siɲe], *v.tr.* **1.** *Mil:* **d. des troupes,** to cancel the order confining troops to barracks. **2.** *Rail:* **d. ses bagages,** to take one's luggage out of the left-luggage office, *U.S:* baggage, check, room. **3.** *Com:* to return the deposit (on bottles, etc.).

déconsolider [dekɔ̃sɔlide], *v.tr.* to weaken.

déconstipation [dekɔ̃stipasjɔ̃], *s.f. Med:* relief of constipation.

déconstiper [dekɔ̃stipe], *v.tr. Med:* to relieve (s.o.'s) constipation.

décontamination [dekɔ̃taminasjɔ̃], *s.f.* decontamination.

décontaminer [dekɔ̃tamine], *v.tr.* to decontaminate.

décontenance [dekɔ̃tnɑ̃:s], *s.f.* loss of self-assurance, countenance; sheepishness, confusion.

décontenancé [dekɔ̃tnɑ̃se], *a.* confused, abashed, put out; taken aback; **être tout d.,** to look blank.

décontenancement [dekɔ̃tnɑ̃smɑ̃], *s.m.* losing countenance; intimidation, embarrassment.

décontenancer [dekɔ̃tnɑ̃se], *v.tr.* (**je décontenançai(s); n. décontenançons**) to put (s.o.) out of countenance; to embarrass, intimidate, s.o.

se décontenancer, to lose countenance, to lose one's self-assurance, to be embarrassed, intimidated.

décontracté [dekɔ̃trakte], *a.* relaxed.

décontracter [dekɔ̃trakte], *v.tr.* to relax (muscle, mind, etc.).

se décontracter, to relax.

décontraction [dekɔ̃traksjɔ̃], *s.f.* relaxation.

déconvenue [dekɔ̃vny], *s.f.* disappointment, mortification; (mortifying) set-back, failure.

décor [dekɔ:r], *s.m.* **1.** decoration (of house, etc.); **porcelaine d'un d. ancien,** china with antique decoration. **2.** *Th:* setting, arrangement (of stage); décor; set; *pl.* scenery; **d. de trois fermes et plafond,** box-set; **d. simultané,** multiple staging; **pièce à décors,** spectacular play; **peintre de décors,** scene-painter; **changement de décors,** (i) change of scenery; (ii) scene-shifting, scene-change; *F:* **il lui faudrait un changement de d.,** he needs a change (of scenery, of air); *F:* **l'envers du d.,** the other side of the picture; **tout cela n'est que d.,** it's all a façade; *Pol: F:* **d. de théâtre,** window-dressing; *F: Aut:* **rentrer, aller, dans le d.,** to run, smash, into a wall, house, bank, etc., to drive off the road; **d. de verdure,** green landscape; **d. de montagnes,** background of mountains.

décorateur, -trice [dekɔratœ:r, -tris]. **1.** *s.* (*a*) (interior) decorator; (*b*) stage-designer or scene-painter. **2.** *a.* **peintre d.,** interior decorator; **artiste d.,** decorative artist.

décoratif, -ive [dekɔratif, -i:v], *a.* decorative, ornamental; **les arts décoratifs,** the decorative arts; **pièce d'eau décorative,** (i) ornamental lake; (ii) ornamental pool.

décoration [dekɔrasjɔ̃], *s.f.* **1.** decoration, ornamentation, embellishment (of house, etc.). **2.** *A: Th:* scenery. **3.** decoration; badge of honour; medal; ribbon, star (of an order); **porter toutes ses décorations,** to wear all one's orders, all one's medals, all one's decorations; **remise de décorations,** investiture; **procéder à une remise de décorations,** to hold an investiture.

décorativement [dekɔrativmɑ̃], *adv.* decoratively, in a decorative manner.

décorder [dekɔrde], *v.tr.* **1.** to unlay, untwist (rope, hemp). **2.** (*a*) to uncord (box); take the string off (sth.); (*b*) to set (animal) loose.

se décorder, *Mount:* to unrope.

décoré [dekɔre], *a.* wearing an order, a decoration, or its ribbon in one's buttonhole; *s.* **décorés de guerre,** holders of war decorations.

décorer [dekɔre], *v.tr.* **1.** to decorate, ornament, embellish; *F:* to do up (house, etc.); **rues décorées de fleurs,** streets decorated with flowers. **2.** to decorate (s.o.); to confer the Cross of the Legion of Honour, the *Croix de guerre,* etc., on (s.o.); **il a été décoré des palmes académiques,** he was decorated with, he received, the *palmes académiques.* **3. il décore sa brutalité du nom de courage,** he flaunts his brutality under the guise of courage; **taudis décoré du nom d'hôtel,** hovel adorned with the name of hotel.

décoriste [dekɔrist], *s.m.* scene-painter; stage-designer.

décornage [dekɔrna:ʒ], *s.m.* dehorning, dishorning.

décorner [dekɔrne], *v.tr.* **1.** to dehorn, dishorn (cattle, etc.); *F:* **il fait un vent à d. les bœufs,** there's a howling gale, it is blowing great guns. **2. d. une page,** to smoothe out a dog's-ear.

décorticage [dekɔrtika:ʒ], *s.m.,* **décortication** [dekɔrtikasjɔ̃], *s.f.* **1.** decortication; disbarking (of timber); husking (of rice); hulling (of barley, rice, coffee-berries); peeling (of fruit, vegetables); shelling (of nuts, peas). **2. décortication,** *Surg:* decortication.

décortiquer [dekɔrtike], *v.tr.* **1.** to decorticate; to bark, disbark (timber); to husk (rice); to hull (barley, rice, coffee-berries); to peel (fruit, vegetables); to shell (nuts, almonds, peas). **2.** *F:* to scrutinize (news, document).

décortiqueur, -euse [dekɔrtikœ:r, -ø:z], *s.* **1.** *Agr:* (*person, machine*) decorticator. **2.** *Carp:* scraper.

décorum [dekɔrɔm], *s.m. no pl.* decorum, seemliness, propriety; **observer le d.,** to observe the proprieties; **pour observer, garder, le d.,** for decency's sake; **d. royal,** court ceremonial.

décoster [dekɔste], *v.i.* to sail away (from a quay); to leave (a quay).

décote [dekɔt], *s.f. Fin:* allowance, deduction, rebate.

découchage [dekuʃa:ʒ], *s.m.* **1.** sleeping away from home; **frais de d.,** hotel expenses. **2.** staying out all night.

découcher [dekuʃe], *v.i.* **1.** to sleep away from home, out of barracks, etc.; to sleep out. **2.** to stay out all night.

découdre [dekudr], *v.tr.* (*conj. like* COUDRE) (*a*) to unpick, unstitch (needlework, garment); to rip up (seam); **d. un bouton,** to take a button off; (*b*) (*of horned animal*) to rip open, to gore (dog, etc.); (*of boar*) to tusk; *Nau:* **d. le bordage d'un navire,** to rip off, unnail, the planking, sheathing, of a vessel, ship; *F:* **il était toujours prêt à en d.,** he was always ready to cross swords with s.o., to fight; (*c*) *F:* **ne pas oser d. les lèvres,** not to dare to open one's mouth, lips.

se découdre, (*of seam, etc.*) to come unsewn, unstitched; (*of sail*) to rip along the seams; **mon bouton s'est décousu,** my button has come off.

découennage [dekwana:ʒ], *s.m.* removing rind, crackling (of pork).

découenner [dekwane], *v.tr.* to remove rind (from pork, ham, bacon, etc.), to remove crackling (from roast pork).

découlant [dekulɑ̃], *a. B:* **terre découlante de lait et de miel,** land flowing with milk and honey.

découler [dekule], *v.i.* **1.** *A:* to trickle, drip, flow; to run (down); **le sang découle de la plaie,** the blood trickles, flows, from the wound. **2.** to issue, spring, be derived, proceed, follow (from); **cette conclusion découle de sa déposition,** this conclusion follows from his evidence; **la règle découle d'elle-même,** the rule follows at once; **Dieu, de qui découlent toutes les grâces,** God, from whom all blessings flow; **ces avantages découlent de . . .,** these advantages are due to, derived from . . .; **la guerre, et tous les maux qui en découlent,** war and all the evils that it brings in its wake.

découpage [dekupa:ʒ], *s.m.* **1.** cutting up (of paper, cake, etc.); carving (of fowl, etc.). **2.** (*a*) cutting out (of advertisement, article, out of newspaper; of patterns, etc.); cutting, shearing (of sheet-metal); fret-cutting, -sawing (of curved outlines); blanking, punching (out), stamping (of metal with hollow punch or die); punching, pinking (of leather, etc.); **matrices pour d.,** cutting dies; (*child's game*) **faire des découpages,** to do cutouts; (*b*) *Typ:* (i) cutting of the overlays; (ii) overlay; (*c*) *El: Elcs:* chopping (of transponder, wave, etc.). **3.** *Cin:* (i) preparation of shooting-script; (ii) scenario, screen play (shooting-)script. **4.** *Pol:* **d. électoral,** warding, putting into wards.

découpe [dekup], *s.f.* **1.** (*a*) *Cost:* slash; (*b*) *pl.* scallops. **2.** cutting up (of wood, etc.).

découpé [dekupe], *a.* (*a*) cut out; **article d.,** (i) newspaper cutting; (ii) press cutting; **bois d.,** fretwork; *Geog:* **côte découpée,** jagged coastline; (*b*) *Bot:* denticulate; *F:* jagged.

découpe-neige [dekupnɛʒ], *s.m.inv.* snow gauge.

découper [dekupe], *v.tr.* **1.** to cut up (paper, cake, etc.); to carve (fowl, etc.); **couteau à d.,** carving-knife, carver. **2.** to cut out (design, pattern, etc.); to stamp (out), to punch, cut (metals); to punch, pink (leather); to scallop (material); *Tchn:* **d. à l'emporte-pièce,** to punch (out); **d. un article dans un journal,** to cut, clip, an article out of a newspaper; **figure découpée dans du carton,** figure cut out of cardboard; *Leath:* **fer à d.,** pinking iron; **scie à d.,** fret-saw, jig-saw; **la mer a découpé la côte,** the sea has indented the coast; **côte découpée en golfes profonds,** coast cut up into deep bays; **le château découpe ses tourelles sur l'horizon,** the castle turrets stand out on, are outlined against, the horizon.

se découper, to stand out (**sur,** on), show up, project (**sur,** against).

découpeur, -euse [dekupœ:r, -ø:z], *s.* **1.** (*a*) carver; (*b*) **d. en cuir,** (i) leather cutter; (ii) pinker; (*c*) *Cin:* cutter. **2.** *s.f.* **découpeuse;** *Tex: etc:* shearing-, cutting-, pinking-machine. **3.** *s.f. Ent:* **(abeille) découpeuse de feuilles,** leaf-cutter (bee), leaf-cutting bee.

découplage [dekupla:ʒ], *s.m. W.Tel:* decoupling; **condensateur de d.,** decoupling condenser.

découple [dekupl̥], *s.m. Ven:* uncoupling, slipping (of hounds).

découplé [dekuple], *a. usu.* **bien d.,** well-built, muscular; **un jeune homme bien d.,** a strapping young man; **grande jeune fille bien découplée,** tall, well-built girl.

découpler [dekuple]. I. *v.tr.* **1.** to slip, unleash, uncouple (hounds); *F:* **d. les agents après qn,** to send the police after s.o. **2.** to uncouple (horses, railway trucks, etc.); *abs. Mus:* to uncouple, to push in the coupler (of organ); *W.Tel:* to decouple.

II. **découpler,** *s.m.* = DÉCOUPLE.

découpoir [dekupwa:r], *s.m.* **1.** *Metalw: etc:* cutter; (i) shear, (ii) stamp; **d. à l'emporte-pièce,** punch(ing apparatus), cutting-press. **2.** *Needlew:* **d. à figures,** pinking-iron.

découpure [dekupy:r], *s.f.* **1.** (*a*) cutting out; (*b*) punching, stamping (out); (*c*) pinking; (*d*) fretwork. **2.** (*a*) piece cut out (by punch, etc.), punching; stamping; (*b*) (newspaper) cutting, *U.S:* clipping. **3.** (ornamental) cut-out; indentation (in coast, etc.); *Bot:* denticulation (in leaf).

découragé [dekuraʒe], *a.* discouraged, despondent, cast down, broken-spirited; **il a l'air d.,** he looks downhearted, down in the mouth, down in the dumps.

décourageant [dekuraʒɑ̃], *a.* discouraging, dispiriting, disheartening, depressing; **personne décourageante,** *F:* wet blanket; **enfant d.,** hopeless child; **vous êtes d.,** you're hopeless; **il est d'une honnêteté décourageante,** he is incredibly, impossibly, honest.

découragement [dekuraʒmɑ̃], *s.m.* discouragement, dejection; **il n'a jamais connu le d.,** he has never known despair; **renoncer à qch. par d.,** to give up sth. in a fit of despondency; **se laisser aller au d.,** to lose heart; **tomber dans le d.,** to become disheartened.

décourager [dekuraʒe], *v.tr.* (**je décourageai(s); n. décourageons**) **1.** to discourage, dishearten; to damp (s.o.'s) courage; to take the heart out of (s.o.); to put (s.o.) out of heart; **d. qn de qch., de faire qch.,** to discourage, deter, s.o. from sth., from doing sth.; **vous m'avez découragé de travailler,** you have put me off working. **2. d. un projet,** to discourage, *F:* pour cold water on, a scheme.

se décourager, to become discouraged, disheartened, dejected, dispirited; to lose heart, to become despondent; **il ne se décourage jamais,** he never loses heart, he is never daunted; **ne vous découragez pas!** don't lose heart! *F:* keep your pecker up! chin(s) up! cheer up!

décourber [dekurbe], *v.tr.* to straighten (out), unbend (sth.).

découronnement [dekurɔnmɑ̃], *s.m.* (*rare*) **1.** uncrowning (of king). **2.** blowing off of tree tops; pollarding (of tree).

découronner [dekurɔne], *v.tr.* **1.** (*a*) to discrown, uncrown, depose (king, etc.); **saint découronné de son auréole,** saint stripped of his halo; (*b*) *F:* to debunk (hero, etc.). **2.** to pollard (tree); **arbre découronné par le vent,** tree stripped of its branches by the wind; *Mil:* **d. une hauteur,** to clear a height (of the enemy's troops).

décours [deku:r], *s.m.* **1.** waning (of the moon); **lune à son d.,** moon on the wane. **2.** abatement (of fever); waning, decline (of illness).

décousu [dekuzy]. **1.** *a.* (*a*) (*of seam, etc.*) unsewn, unstitched, undone; (*b*) disconnected, disjointed, unconnected, incoherent (words, ideas, etc.); rambling, desultory (remarks); unmethodical

(work); **conversation décousue,** scrappy conversation; **vie décousue,** unsystematic, unmethodical, way of living; **travailler d'une façon décousue,** to work by snatches, by fits and starts, unmethodically; **cheval d.,** loose-limbed horse. **2.** *s.m.* disconnectedness (of operations, ideas, etc.); **d. (du style),** jerkiness (of style).

décousure [dekuzy:r], *s.f.* **1.** seam-rent, place that has come unsewn. **2.** gash, rip (caused by horns or tusks of animal).

découvert [dekuvɛ:r]. **1.** *a.* (*a*) uncovered; **avoir la tête découverte, être d.,** to be uncovered, bare-headed; **à visage d.,** openly, frankly; (*b*) open (country, carriage, car, etc.); *Mil:* **attaque en terrain d.,** attack in the open; *Aut:* **virage d.,** open corner; **coin de ciel d.,** bit of blue sky; (*c*) exposed, unprotected (town, etc.); (*troops*) unsupported; exposed, treeless (country); *Ten:* **région découverte,** part of the court left uncovered (by player); (*d*) *Bank: etc:* **compte d.,** overdrawn account; (*e*) *Jur:* **vendre à deniers découverts,** to sell for hard cash. **2.** *s.m.* (*a*) *Bank: etc:* uncovered balance, unsecured bank loan, overdraft; **accorder à qn un d. de . . .,** to allow s.o. to overdraw to the amount of . . ., an overdraft of . . .; **d. en blanc,** unsecured overdraft; *s.a.* CHASSER 1; (*b*) *Ins:* parts, things, not covered by insurance; (*c*) *Adm:* (budgetary) deficit; *Pol.Ec:* **d. de la balance commerciale,** trade gap; (*d*) open space (in country). **3. à d.,** uncovered, unprotected, open; *Mil:* exposed (to the enemy's fire); **vêtement qui laisse le cou à d.,** garment that leaves the neck bare, uncovered; **engrenages à d.,** exposed gearing; **agir, parler, à d.,** to act, speak, openly; **mettre qch. à d.,** (i) to expose sth. to view; (ii) to uncover, disclose, sth.; (iii) *Banking:* to overdraw (an account); **crédit à d.,** unsecured credit; *St.Exch:* **vente à d.,** time bargain, sale for futures, short sale; **vendre à d.,** *F:* to bear the market.

découverte [dekuvert], *s.f.* **1.** (*a*) uncovering; *Min:* **pratiquer la d.,** to remove the overburden; (*b*) *Fenc: etc:* unguarded position. **2.** discovery (of land, etc.); *Mil:* scouting, reconnoitring; **aller à la d.,** to explore, prospect; *Mil:* to scout, reconnoitre; to go reconnoitring; *Nau:* **bâtiment de d.,** scout vessel, look-out vessel (in convoy); **se lancer à la d. de . . .,** to set out to discover . . .; **voyage de d.,** voyage of discovery; **faire la d. de qch.,** to discover sth.; *Min:* **d. de pétrole,** oil strike. **3.** (*a*) discovery, exposure, detection (of plot, etc.); (*b*) discovery; **une grande d.,** a great discovery. **4.** *Cin:* background, back-drop.

découverture [dekuvɛrty:r], *s.f.* unroofing (of house).

découvrement [dekuvrəmɑ̃], *s.m. Mch:* opening (of steam-port).

découvreur, -euse [dekuvrœ:r, -ø:z], *s.* discoverer.

découvrir [dekuvri:r], *v.tr.* (*conj. like* COUVRIR) **1.** (*a*) to uncover; to remove the cover, the covering, from, off (sth.); **d. un pot,** to take the lid off a pot; **d. une maison,** to take the roof off, to unroof, untile, a house; (*b*) to uncover, expose, lay bare (part of one's body, etc.); to unveil (statue, etc.); to disclose (secret); to uncover (a plot); to disclose, reveal (plan); **se d. la tête,** to remove one's hat, to bare one's head; **d. ses dents,** to show one's teeth; **d. son cœur,** to lay bare, to open, one's heart; *s.a.* PIERRE[2]; *Mil:* **d. son flanc,** to expose one's flank (to the enemy); *Sp:* **d. son but,** to leave one's goal undefended; *Cards:* **d. son jeu,** (i) to expose, lay down, one's hand; (ii) *F:* to show one's hand; *Chess:* **d. une pièce,** to uncover a piece. **2.** to perceive, discern, *Nau:* to sight (land, etc.). **3.** (*a*) to discover, find out (plot, etc.); to detect (error, criminal); to track down (criminal); to bring (crime, etc.) to light; to find, ferret out (the truth); **il ne parvint jamais à en d. la cause,** he never managed to discover the cause of it; **elle ne put d. qui il était,** she could not find out who he was; **c'est mon métier de d. les fraudes,** it is my business to detect, *F:* to nose out, frauds; **d. le siège du mal,** to locate the seat of the disease; **le projecteur découvrit l'avion,** the search-light picked out the plane; **craindre, éviter, d'être découvert,** to fear, to escape, detection; (*b*) to discover (oxygen, etc.); to strike (oil); to be the first to find (sth.); **d. la cause d'une maladie,** to discover the cause of a disease. **4.** *v.i.* (*of reef*) to uncover, become uncovered, to be awash (at low tide).

se découvrir. 1. (*a*) to remove one's head-gear, to bare one's head, to take off one's hat; *O:* to uncover; **découvrez-vous!** hats off! (*b*) to take off some of one's (outer) clothing; **ne vous découvrez pas, vous attraperez froid,** don't take off too much, you'll catch cold; **le malade se découvre,** the patient kicks, throws off the bed-clothes, uncovers himself. **2.** *Box: Fenc:* to break guard; to lower one's guard, to expose oneself. **3.** (*of sky*) to clear up. **4.** to become perceptible; **lentement la scène se découvre,** slowly the scene unfolds; **la tour se découvrit sur la gauche,** the tower became visible, came into sight, on the left. **5.** to come to light; **comment cela s'est-il découvert?** how did it come to light, come out, leak out? **la vérité se découvre toujours,** truth will out; **vous vous découvrez trop,** you reveal your feelings too much, you do not conceal your feelings well enough. **6. se d. soi-même,** to get to know oneself.

décrampiller [dekrɑ̃pije], *v.tr. Tex:* to unravel (silk after dyeing).

décramponner [dekrɑ̃pɔne], *v.tr.* **1.** to unclamp; to unspike (rail, etc.). **2.** *F:* to make (s.o.) let go.

décrassage [dekrasa:ʒ], *s.m.*, **décrassement** [dekrasmɑ̃], *s.m.* cleansing, scouring, scraping; *Mch:* cleaning (of tubes); scaling (of boilers); slicing, pricking (of grate); *O:* **le d. d'un nouveau-riche,** the polishing up of a *nouveau-riche.*

décrassant [dekrasɑ̃], *s.m. Tchn:* scour.

décrasser [dekrase], *v.tr.* to clean, cleanse (skin, etc.), scour, scrape (pan, etc.); *P:* **d. le linge,** to soak clothes before washing; **d. un fourneau,** to clean, clinker, draw, a furnace; to rake out the slag from a furnace; **d. une chaudière,** to scale, fur, a boiler; **d. un canon de fusil,** to remove the fouling from a gun-barrel; *O:* **d. un rustre,** to polish up, rub the rough corners off, a country bumpkin; **d. sa mémoire,** to rub up one's memory.

se décrasser, (*a*) to clean oneself up; (*b*) *F:* (i) to have the corners knocked off one; (ii) to rise in the world.

décrassoir [dekraswa:r], *s.m.* **1.** tooth-comb. **2.** comb-cleaner.

décravater [dekravate], *v.tr.* to remove s.o.'s tie; **il ne veut pas se d.,** he does not want to take off his tie.

décrayonnage [dekrɛjɔna:ʒ], *s.m.* slicing, pricking (of grate).

décréditer [dekredite], *v.tr. Lit:* **d. qn,** to injure s.o.'s credit or reputation; to bring s.o. into discredit, into disrepute.

se décréditer, *Lit:* to lose one's credit, one's reputation, to fall into disrepute, into discredit **(auprès de qn,** in s.o.'s eyes).

décrémage [dekrema:ʒ], *s.m.* skimming (of milk).

décrément [dekremɑ̃], *s.m.* **1.** *Math:* decrement. **2.** *El.E: Elcs:* decay-factor, damping factor, decrement.

décremètre [dekremɛtr̥], *s.m. Mth:* decremeter.

décrépi [dekrepi], *a.* unplastered; peeling; dilapidated.

décrépir [dekrepi:r], *v.tr.* to strip the plaster, the rough-cast, off (wall, etc.).

se décrépir, (*of wall, etc.*) to peel; to fall into disrepair.

décrépissage [dekrepisa:ʒ], *s.m.* (*a*) unplastering, stripping off the plaster; (*b*) peeling; falling into disrepair.

décrépit [dekrepi], *a.* decrepit, senile, worn-out; **cheval d.,** broken-down horse; **vieillard d.,** decrepit old man; *F:* **maison décrépite,** tumble-down, dilapidated, house.

décrépitation [dekrepitasjɔ̃], *s.f. Ch:* decrepitation.

décrépiter [dekrepite], *v.i. Ch:* to decrepitate.

décrépitude [dekrepityd], *s.f.* decrepitude; (*a*) senile decay; (*b*) decay (of a nation); last stage of dilapidation (of a building); **tomber dans la d.,** to become senile.

descrescendo [dekresẽdo, -ʃɛn-], *adv. & s.m. Mus:* decrescendo.

décrescent [dekresɑ̃], *a. Bot:* decrescent.

décret [dekrɛ], *s.m.* **1.** decree, fiat, order, edict, *U.S:* executive order; *Adm:* **d. présidentiel** = Order in Council; **d. général, réglementaire,** enactment; **d. spécial, individuel,** decree (of appointment to a post, etc.); **d. du pape,** papal decree; *F:* **les décrets de la Providence,** the decrees of Providence. **2.** *Jur: A:* writ, warrant (of arrest).

décrétale [dekretal], *s.f. Ecc: Jur:* decretal.

décrétaliste [dekretalist], *s.m.* decret(al)ist; canonist.

décréter [dekrete], *v.tr.* **(je décrète, n. décrétons; je décréterai) 1.** to decree; to issue (decision, etc.) as an order, as an edict; to enact (law); **d. une coutume,** to give force of law to a custom; **il avait été décrété que . . .,** it had been enacted that . . .; *F:* **il décréta qu'il partirait,** he declared, stated, said, firmly that he was going to leave. **2.** *Jur: A:* to issue a writ, warrant, against (s.o.); **il fut décrété de prise de corps,** a writ was issued for his arrest.

décret-loi [dekrɛlwa], *s.m.* = Order in Council; *Jur:* **légiférer par décrets-lois,** to govern by decree(s); *pl. décrets-lois.*

décreusage [dekrøza:ʒ], *s.m. Paperm:* boiling; *Tex:* degumming (of silk); discharging (of cotton, silk, etc.).

décreusement [dekrøzmɑ̃], *s.m. Tex:* = DÉCREUSAGE.

décreuser [dekrøze], *v.tr. Paperm:* to boil (vegetable fibre); *Tex:* to degum (silk); to discharge (cotton, silk, etc.); **non décreusé,** unboiled.

décri [dekri], *s.m. A:* **1.** (*a*) crying down, depreciation by proclamation (of coinage, values); (*b*) fall in value. **2.** disparagement, running down (of s.o., sth.); **tomber dans le d.,** to fall into disrepute, into discredit.

décrier [dekrije], *v.tr.* (*conj. like* CRIER) **1.** to decry, cry down (coinage, value). **2.** to disparage, decry, discredit (s.o., sth.); to run (s.o., sth.) down; **d. la conduite de qn,** to run s.o. down, to vilify s.o.; **un homme décrié,** a man who has fallen in public esteem; **d. sa marchandise, les siens,** to foul one's own nest.

se décrier. 1. to disparage, underrate, oneself. **2.** to lose one's good name, to fall in public esteem.

décrire [dekri:r], *v.tr.* (*conj. like* ÉCRIRE) **1.** to describe, to depict; **cela ne peut pas se d.,** it is beyond description, it beggars description. **2.** (*a*) *Geom: etc:* to describe, trace, draw, (curve, circle); (*b*) **la route décrit une courbe autour du lac,** the road curves, sweeps, round the lake.

décrochable [dekrɔʃabl̥], *a.* that can be unhooked; detachable.

décrochage [dekrɔʃa:ʒ], *s.m.*, **décrochement** [dekrɔʃmɑ̃], *s.m.* **1.** unhooking, taking down (of coat from peg, of telephone receiver, etc.); uncoupling, disconnecting (of railway carriages, etc.); *Rail:* **levier de d.,** (un)coupling lever. **2.** *Ph:* falling out of step, out of tune, (with oscillatory system); *T.V:* jitter. **3.** *Mil:* (*a*) **décrochage,** breaking of contact (with the enemy), disengagement, disengaging (from the enemy); beating a retreat; pulling back; (*b*) **décrochement,** loss of touch (between units). **4.** *Geol:* transverse fault. **5.** *Av:* (*a*) stall; **vitesse de décrochage,** stalling speed; (*b*) breaking formation. **6.** *Arch:* **décrochement,** set-back.

décrocher [dekrɔʃe]. **1.** *v.tr.* to unhook, take down (coat from peg, picture, etc.); to unsling (hammock); to uncouple, disconnect (railway carriages, etc.); *Tp:* to pick up, lift (the receiver); **ne voulant pas être dérangé, il a décroché son téléphone,** not wishing to be disturbed, he has taken off the receiver; *F:* **au bout d'une semaine de cours, il a décroché,** he gave up after one week of lectures; (*of thg*) **je ne peux pas le d.,** I can't get it down; **d. une agrafe,** to undo a clasp; **se d. la mâchoire,** to dislocate one's jaw, to put one's jaw out; **phrase à d. la mâchoire,** tongue-twister; *s.a.* BAILLER 1; **vouloir d. la lune,** to reach for the moon; *P:* **se faire d.,** to get shot; *P:* **d. sa montre,** to redeem one's watch; **d. une décoration,** (i) to receive a decoration; (ii) to wangle a decoration; *F:* **il eut tôt fait de d. ses galons de caporal,** he wasn't long in getting his corporal's stripes; **d. une commande,** to (manage to) get an order; **d. les quatre chiffres,** (*of receipts, etc.*) to touch four figures; **il a décroché une bonne position,** he has tumbled into a nice berth; **d. le grand succès,** to make a big hit; *Sp:* **d. ses concurrents,** to get, draw ahead of other competitors (in race, etc.); *s.a.* TIMBALE 2; (*b*) *Arch:* **ligne décrochée,** (i) stepped line; (ii) split level. **2.** *v.i.* (*a*) *Mil:* to beat a retreat, retire, withdraw, pull back; (*b*) *Av:* to stall; (*c*) *Av:* to break formation; *Sp:* to drop out (from a race).

se décrocher, *Ph:* to fall out of step, out of tune (with oscillatory system); *Mount:* to slip; **le tableau s'est décroché du mur sous l'effet de l'explosion,** the picture fell from the wall with the force of the explosion; *F:* **réussir à se d. d'un engagement,** to manage to slip away from an engagement.

décrochez-moi-ça [dekrɔʃemwasa], *s.m.inv. F:* **1.** cheap second-hand garment; reach-me-down. **2.** cheap second-hand clothes' shop; **s'habiller au décrochez-moi-ça,** to dress in reach-me-downs.

décrochoir [dekrɔʃwa:r], *s.m. Ind:* unhooker.

décroire [dekrwa:r], *v.i.* used only in **je ne crois ni ne décrois,** I neither believe nor disbelieve.

décroisement [dekrwazmɑ̃], *s.m.* uncrossing; *N.Arch:* **d. des abouts,** shifting of butts.

décroiser [dekrwaze], *v.tr.* to uncross (one's legs, threads in weaving, etc.); *Mil:* **d. les échelons,** to form direct from oblique échelons; *Nau:* **d. les garants,** to take out the cross of the falls; *N.Arch:* **d. les abouts,** to shift butts.

décroissance [dekrwasɑ̃:s], *s.f.* **1.** decrease; diminution (of population, etc.); decline (of strength, of empire, etc.); abatement (of fever); **d. de la vitesse,** falling off of the speed; **nos importations sont en d.,** our imports are decreasing. **2.** (*a*) *Mth:* **courbe, facteur, de d.,** die-away curve, factor; (*b*) *Elcs: Atom.Ph:* damping, decay; **courbe, loi, de d.,** decay curve, law; **d. radio-active,** radioactive decay; **d. exponentielle,** exponential decay.

décroissant [dekrwasɑ̃], *a.* (*a*) decreasing; tapering (subsidy); *Mth:* **progression décroissante,** series descending; **en ordre d.,** in descending order; (*b*) *Her:* decrescent (moon).

décroissement [dekrwasmɑ̃], *s.m.* **le d. de la lune,** the waning of the moon; **le d. des jours,** the shortening of days.

décroît [dekrwa], *s.m.* **1.** *Husb:* decrease of live stock. **2.** *Astr:* last quarter (of moon); **la lune est sur son d.,** the moon is in its last quarter.

décroître [dekrwatr̥, -wɑ-], *v.i.* (*pr.p.* **décroissant;** *p.p.* **décru;** *pr.ind.* **il décroît, ils décroissent;** *pr.sub.* **il décroisse;** *p.h.* **décrut;** *fu.* **il décroîtra)** (*a*) to decrease, decline, diminish; **les jours commencent à d.,** the days are beginning to shorten, to draw in; **la rivière décroît,** the river is falling, going down, subsiding; **la lune décroît,** the moon is on the wane; **son qui décroît,** sound that is dying away, becoming fainter; **lumière qui décroît,** light that is getting dimmer; **charge d'électricité qui décroît,** electric charge that is leaking away; **aller (en) décroissant,** to decrease; to grow gradually less; to taper; **l'émotion décroît,** emotion is dying down; **la fièvre décroît,** the fever is abating; **les eaux ont décru, sont décrues,** the water has subsided; (*b*) *Mth: etc:* (*of curve*) to droop, fall.

décrottage [dekrɔta:ʒ], *s.m.* cleaning (of boots, etc.).

décrotter [dekrɔte], *v.tr.* to clean (boots, etc.); to remove the mud from, to brush the dirt off (boots, etc.); to scrape (one's boots); *F:* **d. qn,** to polish up (the manners of) s.o., to knock the corners off s.o.; *s.a.* BROSSE 1.

décrotteur, -euse [dekrɔtœ:r, -ø:z], *s.* **1.** *s.m.* (*a*) shoe-black, boot-black; (*b*) (*in hotel*) boots; (*c*) *Agr:* root-cleaner. **2.** *s.f.* **décrotteuse,** hard brush (for shoes).

décrottoir [dekrɔtwa:r], *s.m.* **1.** shoe-scraper, boot-scraper, door-scraper; **tapis d.,** (woven wire) door-mat; **grille d.,** steel-scraper mat. **2.** mud-scraper (of steam-roller).

décrottoire [dekrɔtwa:r], *s.f.* hard brush (for cleaning shoes).

décroûtage [dekruta:ʒ], *s.m.* removing the matrix from a diamond.

décroûter [dekrute], *v.tr.* **1.** *Metall:* to skin (casting). **2.** to remove the matrix from (a diamond).

décruage [dekrya:ʒ], **décrusage** [dekryza:ʒ], *s.m.* *Tex:* = DÉCREUSAGE.

décrue [dekry], *s.f.* **1.** fall, subsidence (of river, etc.); **la d. a été d'un mètre,** there has been a fall of one metre. **2.** decrease, diminution, fall (in numbers, etc.).

décrûment [dekrymɑ̃], **décrusement** [dekryzmɑ̃], *s.m. Tex:* = DÉCREUSEMENT.

décruser [dekryze], *v.tr. Tex:* = DÉCREUSER.

décryptement [dekriptəmɑ̃], *s.m.* deciphering (of code).

décrypter [dekripte], *v.tr.* to decipher (cryptogram in unknown code).

décrypteur [dekriptœ:r], *s.m.* person who deciphers cryptograms, decoder.

décubitus [dekybitys], *s.m.* **1.** (*dorsal, ventral*) decubitus. **2.** decubitus (ulcer), decubital ulcer; bedsore.

décuirassement [dekɥirasmɑ̃], *s.m. O:* stripping (of battleship).

décuirasser [dekɥirase], *v.tr. O:* to strip (battleship).

décuiter [dekɥite], *v.tr. P:* to sober (s.o.) up.

se décuiter, to sober up, to get over one's drink.

décuivrage [dekɥivra:ʒ], *s.m.* removing the copper-plating (from metals).

décuivrer [dekɥivre], *v.tr.* to remove the copper-plating from (metals).

de cujus [dekyʒys], *s.m. Jur:* deceased person.

déculassement [dekylasmɑ̃], *s.m. Artil:* unbreeching.

déculasser [dekylase], *v.tr.* **1.** *Artil:* to unbreech. **2.** *Aut:* to remove the cylinder head.

déculottée [dekylɔte], *s.f. P:* **1.** heavy defeat. **2.** heavy loss (at gambling); **chaque fois que l'on joue avec eux, on prend une d.,** each time we play them, we take a licking.

déculotter [dekylɔte], *v.tr.* **1.** to take off (s.o.'s) trousers; to take the breeches off (s.o.); *F:* to debag (s.o.). **2.** to scrape out (a pipe). **3.** *P:* **d. sa pensée,** to speak openly, freely.

se déculotter. 1. *F:* (i) to take off, (ii) to let down, one's trousers. **2.** *P:* to speak openly, freely.

décuman, -ane [dekymɑ̃, -an], *a. Rom.Ant:* decuman; **porte décumane,** decuman gate.

décuple [dekypl̥], *a. & s.m.* tenfold, decuple; **trente est (le) d. de trois,** thirty is ten times as much as three; **proportion d.,** ten-to-one ratio.

décuplement [dekypləmɑ̃], *s.m. Mth:* multiplication by ten.

décupler [dekyple], *v.tr. & i. Mth: etc:* to decuple; to increase, multiply, tenfold; **la colère décuplait ses forces,** anger gave him the strength of ten; **fortune qui décuple,** fortune that is increasing rapidly.

décurie [dekyri], *s.f. Rom.Ant:* decury, decuria.

décurion [dekyrjɔ̃], *s.m. Rom.Ant:* decurion.

décurionat [dekyrjɔna], *s.m. Rom.Ant:* decurionate.

décurrence [dekyrɑ̃s], *s.f. Bot:* decurrency.

décurrent [dekyrɑ̃], *a. Bot:* decurrent.

décursif, -ive [dekyrsif, -i:v], *a. Bot:* decursive, decurrent.

décuscutage [dekyskyta:ʒ], *s.m. Agr:* removing of dodder.

décuscuter [dekyskyte], *v.tr. Agr:* to remove dodder.

décuscuteuse [dekyskytø:z], *s.f. Agr: Tls:* instrument for removing dodder.

décussation [dekysasjɔ̃], *s.f. Anat: Bot:* decussation.

décussé [dekyse], *a. Bot:* decussate.

décuvage [dekyva:ʒ], *s.m.*, **décuvaison** [dekyvɛzɔ̃], *s.f.* tunning, racking (of wine).

décuver [dekyve], *v.tr.* to tun, rack (wine).

décyle [desil], *s.m. Ch:* decyl.

décylène [desilɛn], *s.m. Ch:* decylene.

décylique [desilik], *a. Ch:* **alcool d.,** decyl alcohol.

dédaignable [dedɛɲabl̥], *a.* **cette proposition n'est pas d.,** this proposal is not to be despised.

dédaigner [dedɛɲe, -eɲe], *v.tr.* to disdain, scorn, contemn (riches, etc.); to despise, disregard; to slight; **il dédaigne mes offres,** he scorns, turns up his nose at, pooh-poohs, my offers; **cette offre n'est pas à d.,** this offer is not to be disdained, despised; **d. qn,** to look down on s.o., to ignore s.o.; **elle dédaigne les hommes,** she will not look at a man; **il dédaigna de répondre,** he did not deign, did not condescend, to answer.

dédaigneusement [dedɛɲøzmɑ̃], *adv.* disdainfully, contemptuously, scornfully; with disdain, contempt, scorn.

dédaigneux, -euse [dedɛɲø, -ø:z], *a.* disdainful, contemptuous, scornful (de, of); **d. des applaudissements,** disdainful of applause; **être d. de faire qch.,** to scorn to do sth., to be above doing sth.; **faire le d.,** (i) to sniff at sth.; (ii) to affect superiority; (iii) to be fastidious, finicky, difficult to please; **lèvre dédaigneuse,** disdainful expression, superior air.

dédain [dedɛ̃], *s.m.* disdain, scorn (**de,** of); disregard (**de qch.,** of sth., **pour qn,** for s.o.); **avec d.,** disdainfully, scornfully; **en relevant la lèvre avec d.,** with a curl of the lip; **témoigner du d. à qn,** to show contempt for s.o., to despise s.o.; **avoir le d. de qch.,** to have a contempt for sth.; **prendre qn en d.,** to look down on s.o.

Dédale [dedal]. **1.** *Pr.n.m. Gr.Myth:* Daedalus. **2.** *s.m.* labyrinth, maze (of streets, etc.); **les dédales de la loi,** the intricacies of the law.

dédaléen, -éenne [dedaleɛ̃, -eɛn], **dédalien, -ienne,** [dedaljɛ̃, -jɛn], **dédalique** [dedalik], *a.* daedalian; intricate, involved.

dedans [dədɑ̃]. **1.** *adv.* inside; within; in (it, them, etc.); **la bourse est vide, il n'y a rien d.,** the purse is empty, there is nothing in it, inside (it); *F:* **mettre qn d.,** (i) to take s.o. in; to get the better of s.o.; (ii) to put s.o. in clink, jug, to put s.o. inside; *F:* **on m'a mis, fichu, d.,** I've been had; *P:* **donner, entrer, rentrer, d. qch.,** to knock, bash, into sth.; *P:* **il va lui rentrer d.,** he's going to give him what for; *F:* **donner d.,** to fall into the trap, to be had; *F:* **ne pas savoir si l'on est d. ou dehors, n'être ni d. ni dehors,** not to know where one stands, not to know if one is standing on one's head or one's heels; *Nau:* **toutes voiles d.,** with all sail furled; *adv.phr.* **de d.,** from inside, from within; **la porte s'ouvre de d.,** the door opens from (the) inside; **en d.,** (on the) inside, within; **il n'était pas si calme en d.,** he was not so calm inwardly; **mesures en d.,** internal measurements; **tourner les pieds en d.,** to turn one's toes in; **marcher les pieds en d.,** to walk with one's toes turned in; *F:* **personne en d.,** reserved, uncommunicative, person; *prep.phr.* **en d. de,** on the inner side of, within. **2.** *s.m.* (*a*) inside, interior (of house, box, etc.); innermost heart (of person); **d. du pied,** inside of the foot; *Equit:* **la rêne du d.,** the near rein; **agir du d.,** to act from within (a party, etc.); (*b*) *Nau:* belly (of sail); (*c*) (*skating*) inside edge; (*d*) *adv.phr.* **au d.,** (on the) inside, within; **au d. et au dehors,** (i) inside and out; (ii) at home and abroad; *prep.phr.* **au d. de,** inside, within. **3.** *prep. A:* **d. et dehors le royaume,** within and without the realm.

dédicace [dedikas], *s.f.* **1.** *Ecc:* dedication, consecration (of building, etc.). **2.** dedication (of book, etc.); dedicatory inscription (on building).

dédicacer [dedikase], *v.tr.* (**je dédicaçai(s); n. dédicaçons**) to dedicate (book, etc.); to write a dedication in (book, etc.); to autograph (a book); **livre dédicacé,** book bearing a printed or a manuscript dedication from the author.

dedicataire [dedikatɛ:r], *s.m. & f.* dedicatee.

dédicateur, -trice [dedikatœ:r, -tris], *s.* dedicator.

dédication [dedikasjɔ̃], *s.f. Rom.Jur:* dedication (of temple, etc.).

dédicatoire [dedikatwa:r], *a.* dedicatory.

dédier [dedje], *v.tr.* (*p.d. & pr.sub.* **n. dédiions, v. dédiiez**) **1.** *Ecc:* to dedicate, consecrate (building, etc.); **d. un jour au plaisir,** to dedicate a day to, set apart a day for, to keep a day for, pleasure. **2.** to dedicate, inscribe (book, etc.).

dédifférenciation [dediferɑ̃sjasjɔ̃], *s.f. Biol:* dedifferentiation.

dédire [dedi:r], *v.tr.* (*conj. like* **dire,** *except pr.ind.* **v. dédisez**) to deny (a fact); to disown (s.o.); **en d. qn,** to contradict s.o.

se dédire. 1. se d. d'une affirmation, to take back what one has said, to retract a statement; **les témoins se sont dédits,** the witnesses contradicted themselves; **je me dédis de mes paroles d'hier,** I unsay all I said yesterday. **2. se d. d'une promesse, d'un engagement,** to go back on one's word, to break, to back out of, an engagement; *F:* to cry off; **je ne puis pas m'en d.,** I cannot go back on my word; **il n'y a pas, plus, à se d.,** there's no going back; *F:* **Normand,** *P:* **cochon, qui s'en dédit,** I won't go back on it, *P:* cross my heart!

dédit [dedi], *s.m.* **1. d. d'une affirmation,** retraction, withdrawal, of an affirmation. **2. d. d'un engagement,** breaking of a promise; **il a son dit et son d.,** he often goes back on his word. **3.** forfeit, penalty (for breaking contract, etc.); *Nau:* **d. pour défaut de chargement,** dead freight.

dédite [dedit], *s.f.* breaking, throwing up (of contract); renunciation (of promise); going back (on one's word).

dédommagement [dedɔmaʒmɑ̃], *s.m.* **1.** indemnification, indemnifying (**de qn,** of s.o.). **2.** indemnity, compensation, damages; **réclamer un d.,** to claim compensation; **recevoir une somme en d. (de qch.) à titre de d.,** to receive a sum as, in, compensation (for sth.); **ce sera un d.,** that will make amends; *F:* **trouver un d. à ses malheurs,** to find compensation for one's misfortunes.

dédommager [dedɔmaʒe], *v.tr.* (**je dédommageai(s); n. dédommageons**) to indemnify, compensate (s.o.); to make amends to (s.o.); **d. qn de qch.,** to indemnify, recoup, compensate, s.o. for sth.; **d. qn d'une perte, d'un manque,** to make good a loss, a deficiency, to s.o.; **se faire d. par qn,** to recover, recoup, from s.o.; **comment pourrai-je jamais vous d.?** how can I, ever repay you, make it up to you?

se dédommager, to recoup oneself (**de,** fo,); **se d. de ses pertes,** to recoup one's losses.

dédorage [dedɔra:ʒ], *s.m.* ungilding, removing the gilt from (sth.).

dédoré [dedɔre], *a.* **cadre, ornement, d.,** frame, ornament, with the gilt rubbed off; **aristocratie dédorée,** (i) tarnished, (ii) shabby-genteel, aristocracy; **blason d.,** impoverished house, family.

dédorer, [dedɔre], *v.tr.* to ungild, remove the gilt from (sth.).

se dédorer, to lose its gilt.

dédorure [dedɔry:r], *s.f.* ungilding, removing the gilt from (sth.).

dédossement [dedɔsmɑ̃], *s.m.* **1.** *Hort:* splitting up (of herbaceous plant). **2.** *Carp:* edging.

dédosser [dedɔse], *v.tr.* **1.** *Hort:* to split up (herbaceous plant). **2.** *Carp:* to edge.

dédouanage [dedwana:ʒ], *s.m.*, **dédouanement** [dedwanmɑ̃], *s.m. Cust:* clearance (of goods); taking out of bond.

dédouaner [dedwane], *v.tr. Cust:* to clear (goods); to take (goods) out of bond; **d. ses bagages,** to clear one's luggage through the customs; *F:* **d. qn,** to clear s.o.'s name.

dédoublable [dedublabl̩], *a.* divisible into two. **1.** *Ch:* (*of double salts, etc.*) decomposable by double decomposition. **2.** (*train*) that may run in two portions. **3.** *Phot:* **objectif d.,** doublet lens (either component of which may be used alone); convertible lens.

dédoublage [dedubla:ʒ], *s.m.* **1.** diluting (of alcohol). **2.** unlining (of coat); unsheathing (of ship).

dédoublé [deduble], *s.m.* brandy made from diluted alcohol.

dédoublement [dedubləmɑ̃], *s.m.* **1.** undoubling unfolding, opening out, (of folded cloth, etc.). **2.** (*a*) dividing, splitting, into two; **d. de la personnalité,** dual, split, personality; dissociation; *Rail:* **voie de d.,** passing-place, passing-track, shunting loop (on single track); (*b*) *Ch:* double decomposition; (*c*) *Opt:* duplication of image (in binoculars); (*d*) (i) *Rail:* running (of train) in two portions; (ii) *Trans:* duplication (of rail, road, air service); (*e*) *Mil:* **d. constitutif,** subdivision of a unit into two, splitting up of a unit (on mobilisation, etc.).

dédoubler [deduble], *v.tr.* **1.** (*a*) to undouble, unfold, open out (folded cloth, etc.); (*b*) **l'étroitesse du sentier nous força à nous d.,** the narrowness of the path forced us to walk in single file; *Mil:* **d. les rangs,** to form single file; *Nau:* **d. les amarres,** to single the ropes. **2.** (*a*) to divide, cut, split, (sth.) into two; **d. un régiment, une classe,** to divide a regiment, a class, into two; **d. un brin de fil,** to separate the strands of a thread; *Tchn:* **d. une pierre,** to cut, split, a stone lengthwise; (*b*) *Ch: etc:* to divide into two; to decompose (double salts, etc.); **l'impossibilité de d. un corps simple,** the impossibility of splitting up an element; (*c*) to dilute (wine, alcohol); (*d*) *Opt:* (*of binoculars*) to duplicate (the image); (*e*) to run (train) in two parts; to run an extra train. **3.** to remove the lining of, to unline (garment); to unsheathe (ship).

se dédoubler. 1. to unfold. **2.** to divide, split (into two). **3.** (*a*) *Psy:* to suffer from split personality; (*b*) *Psychics:* **avoir le pouvoir de se d.,** to have the power of bilocation.

déductibilité [dedyktibilite], *s.f.* deductibility.

déductible [dedyktibl̩], *a.* deductible.

déductif, -ive [dedyktif, -i:v], *a. Phil:* deductive (reasoning).

déduction [dedyksjɔ̃], *s.f.* **1.** (*a*) deduction, inference, conclusion; **d. erronée,** false conclusion; **ce n'est pas là une d. légitime,** that does not follow; (*b*) *A:* enumeration, recital (of events); *F: A:* **faire une longue d. de ses griefs,** to give a long recital of one's grievances, to dwell at length on one's grievances. **2.** *Com: etc:* deduction, allowance, abatement; **faire d. des sommes payées d'avance,** to deduct, to allow for, sums paid in advance; **sous d. de 10%,** less, minus, 10%; **somme qui entre en d. de . . .,** sum that falls to be deducted from . . .; **sans d.,** terms net cash; **d. personnelle,** personal allowance.

déductivement [dedyktivmɑ̃], *adv. Phil:* deductively, inferentially.

déduire [dedɥi:r], *v.tr.* (*conj. like* CONDUIRE) **1.** (*a*) *A:* to deduce, enumerate, recite (facts, grievances, etc.); (*b*) to deduce, infer (result); **d'où nous déduisons que . . .,** whence we infer that . . .; **d. les conséquences,** to reason out the consequences. **2.** *Com: etc:* to deduct; **d. 5%,** to take off, allow, deduct, 5%; **d. £20 par an pour l'usure,** to write off £20 a year for wear and tear; **l'emballage ne peut être déduit,** packing is not allowed for.

se déduire, to follow, result (**de,** from); **la conclusion se déduit des prémisses,** the conclusion follows from the premises.

déduit [dedɥi], *s.m. A:* (*a*) amusement, diversion; (*b*) love-making, gallantry; (*c*) hunt(ing party); **suivre le d.,** to follow the hunt.

déesse [deɛs], *s.f.* goddess; (*of woman*) **c'est une d.,** she's a goddess, a Venus; she's majestically beautiful; **être digne du lit des déesses,** to be born under a lucky star; **allure de d.,** majestic, regal, bearing.

défâcher (se) [sədefɑʃe], *v.pr. F:* to calm down, cool down; **s'il est fâché, qu'il se défâche,** if he is furious, he will just have to calm down.

défaçonner [defasɔne], *v.tr.* to put (sth.) out of shape; to deform (sth.).

se défaçonner, to get out of shape.

de facto [defakto], *Lt.phr. Jur:* de facto.

défaillance [defajɑ̃:s], *s.f.* **1.** *A:* extinction, decay (of family, race). **2.** (*a*) (moral, physical) lapse, failing, failure; **d. cardiaque,** heart failure; **sans d.,** without flinching; **politique sans d.,** unflinching policy; **moment de d.,** weak, feeble, moment; **d. de mémoire,** lapse of memory; (*b*) *Jur:* default(ing), non-appearance; (*c*) **d. mécanique,** mechanical failure; **le moteur a des défaillances,** the engine breaks down occasionally; *Fin:* **d. du marché,** sagging of the market; **d. du franc,** weakening of the franc; (*d*) fainting fit; **être pris de d.,** to feel faint.

défaillant, -ante [defajɑ̃, -ɑ̃:t]. **1.** *a.* (*a*) *A:* (*of race, family*) dying out, becoming extinct; (*b*) failing, faltering (strength, memory, etc.); waning (light); sinking (heart); **main défaillante,** unsteady, trembling, hand; **ses pas défaillants,** his faltering steps; (*c*) (*of pers.*); **d. de fatigue,** dropping with fatigue; *O:* **d. d'amour,** love-sick; (*d*) (*of pers.*) faint, feeling faint, on the point of fainting. **2.** *Jur: Fin:* (*a*) *a.* defaulting; (*b*) *s.* defaulter, absconder.

défaillir [defaji:r], *v.i. def.* (*pr.p.* **défaillant;** *p.p.* **défailli;** *pr.ind.* **il défaille,** *A:* **il défaut, n. défaillons, ils défaillent;** *p.d.* **je défaillais;** *p.h.* **je défaillis;** *fu:* **je défaillerai, je défaillirai;** *A:* **je défaudrai**) **1.** *A:* to be absent, lacking, wanting. **2.** (*a*) to become feeble, to lose strength; **sa mémoire, sa force, commence à d.,** his memory, his strength, is beginning to fail; **je me sens d. de jour en jour,** I feel weaker every day; **son courage défaille,** his courage is giving way, is faltering; (*b*) to flinch; *A:* **d. à son devoir,** to fail in one's duty; **sans d.,** without flinching; (*c*) to faint; **se sentir prêt à d.,** to feel about to faint; **d. de faim,** to feel faint with hunger; **à cette nouvelle son cœur défaillit,** her heart sank at the news.

défaire [defɛ:r], *v.tr.* (*conj. like* FAIRE) **1.** to demolish; to pull (sth.) to pieces; to tear, pull, (sth.) down; to cancel, annul (treaty); to break off (alliance, marriage); to destroy, ruin (reputation); to remove (creases, pleats); **cette maladie l'a défait,** this illness has pulled him down; **la terreur avait défait son visage,** fear had distorted his features. **2.** (*a*) to undo; to untie (parcel, knot, shoe, etc.); to unwrap (parcel); to strip (a bed); to unpack (trunk); to unpick, unstitch (seam); to undo, unfasten (one's dress, etc.); **d. sa cravate,** (i) to undo, (ii) to take off, one's tie; **d. ses cheveux,** to let one's hair down, to undo one's hair; **le vent a défait sa coiffure,** the wind has ruffled her hair; **d. le couvert,** to clear the table; (*b*) **d. qn de qn, de qch.,** to rid s.o. of s.o., of sth.; **d. qn d'une mauvaise habitude,** to get s.o. out of a bad habit. **3.** to defeat, rout, overthrow (army, etc.); to get the better of (s.o.); **d. qn dans une discussion,** to vanquish, outwit, s.o. in a debate. **4. faire et d. les rois,** to make and unmake kings; **faire et d. qn,** to make and break s.o.

se défaire. 1. (*a*) to undo one's clothes; (*b*) (*of clothes, knot, etc.*) to come undone; (*of hair*) to come down; (*of things joined together*) to come apart. **2.** (*a*) to lose one's health, one's good looks; (*b*) *A:* to commit suicide. **3.** (*a*) **se d. de qn,** to kill, dispatch, s.o.; (*b*) **se d. de qn, de qch.,** to get rid of s.o., of sth.; to rid oneself of s.o., of sth.; **se d. de ses marchandises,** to get rid of, sell off, one's goods; **je ne veux pas m'en d.,** I don't want to part with it; **se d. d'une mauvaise habitude,** to throw off, get out of, break oneself of, a bad habit; **se d. d'un fâcheux,** to shake off a bore; **se d. d'un domestique,** to dismiss a servant; **se d. d'une charge,** to give up a responsibility.

défaisable [defəzabl̩], *a.* that can be undone.

défaiseur, -euse [defəzœ:r, -ø:z], *s.* undoer; destroyer; **le faiseur et d. de rois,** the maker and unmaker of kings.

défait [defɛ], *a.* **1.** (*of knot, screw, etc.*) undone, loose. **2.** (*of army, etc.*) defeated, overthrown. **3.** (*a*) drawn, discomposed (features, face); (*b*) with one's clothes in disorder; dishevelled; disarranged; ruffled (hair).

défaite [defɛt], *s.f.* **1.** *A:* disposal; **marchandises de prompte d.,** saleable goods, goods that command a ready sale, a ready market; **de difficile d.,** hard to get rid of, difficult to dispose of. **2.** *A:* lame excuse; mere pretext; **ce n'est qu'une d.,** it is only a subterfuge, a quibble, it is a mere put-off; **chercher une d.,** to look for an excuse, a pretext. **3.** defeat; **essuyer une d.,** to suffer (a) defeat, to be defeated; **aller au-devant d'une d.,** to court failure; to ride for a fall.

défaitisme [defetism], *s.m.* defeatism; lack of self-confidence.

défaitiste [defɛtist], *a.* & *s.* defeatist; pessimist; **propos défaitistes,** pessimistic, defeatist, talk.

défalcation [defalkasjɔ̃], *s.f. Com: etc:* (*a*) deduction, deducting; abatement (of sum); writing-off (of bad debt); (*b*) sum, weight, etc., deducted; abatement (from income tax).

défalquer [defalke], *v.tr. Com: etc:* to deduct, abate, take off (sum from total); **d. la tare,** to make allowance for the tare; **d. une mauvaise créance,** to write off a bad debt.

défarder [defarde], *v.tr.* to remove the make up from (one s face); **d. la vérité,** to reveal the naked truth.

défatiguer [defatige], *v.tr.* to refresh, rest; **le bain m'a défatigué,** I feel refreshed after my bath.

défaufilage [defofila:ʒ], *s.m. Needlew:* taking out the tacking, basting.

défaufiler [defofile], *v.tr. Needlew:* to take out the tacking, basting.

défausse [defos], *s.f. Cards:* discard.

défausser[1] [defose], *v.tr.* to true, straighten (rod, blade, etc.).

défausser[2] **(se)** [sədefose], *v.pr. Cards:* to discard; **se d. à trèfle,** to discard clubs.

défaut [defo], *s.m.* **1.** (*a*) default, absence, deficiency, insufficiency, (total) lack, want (of s.o., sth.); **d. de courage, d'attention,** lack of courage, want of attention; **d. de paiement,** failure to pay, default in paying; non-payment; *Com:* **intérêts pour d. de paiement,** default interest; **d. de jugement,** lack of judgment; **faire d.,** (i) to be absent, lacking, wanting; (ii) to fail, give out; **trois mouchoirs font d.,** there are three handkerchiefs short, missing; **cette année les pommes font absolument d.,** this year the apple crop is a complete failure; there are no apples this year; **le temps me fait d.,** I haven't enough time; I can't spare the time; **les provisions font d.,** (i) there is a scarcity, a shortage, of provisions; (ii) provisions are running short, are running low; **la mémoire lui fait d.,** (his) memory fails him; **pécher par d.,** to fall short (of what is required); *Bank:* **d. de provision,** no funds, no effects; *prep.phr.* **à d. de,** *A:* **au d. de,** qn, qch., in default of, for lack of, for want of, in the absence of, failing, s.o., sth.; **un travail bien rémunéré, à d. d'être intéressant,** a job which is well paid, if not interesting; *A:* **boire de l'eau au d. de vin,** to drink water in default of wine; **à d. de paiement,** failing payment; (*b*) break in continuity; **les défauts de l'armure,** the joints in the harness the chinks in the armour, the vulnerable points; **trouver le d. dans la cuirasse de qn,** to find s.o.'s weak, vulnerable, spot; **le d. de l'épaule,** the hollow below the shoulder; **frappé au d. des côtes,** struck below the ribs; **glisser au d. du trottoir,** to slip off the kerb; (*c*) *Jur:* default; **d. de comparution,** failure to appear, non-appearance; **faire d.,** to fail to appear, to default, to make default; **jugement par d., d. contre partie,** judgment by default; **juger par d.,** to deliver judgment by default; *St.Exch:* **agent en d.,** defaulter. **2.** (*a*) fault, shortcoming; weakness, weak point (in system, etc.); **chacun a ses défauts,** everyone has his weak points, his failings; **fermer les yeux sur les défauts de qn,** to shut one's eyes to s.o.'s faults; **la curiosité est un d.,** curiosity is a fault, a weakness; **c'est là son moindre d.,** that is the last thing one can accuse him of; **c'est son grand d.,** it is his besetting sin, his great weakness; (*b*) defect, flaw (in metal, diamond, fabric, etc.); **d. de conformation,** malformation, difformity, deformation; **d. d'exécution,** defect, flaw, in the making, fault of workmanship, faulty workmanship; **d. de fabrication,** manufacturing defect; *U.S:* bug; **d. de matière,** defective, faulty, material; **ce poème a ses défauts,** this poem has its faults; **sans d.,** faultless, flawless, without blemish; *El:* **d. d'isolement,** insulation fault, faulty insulation; *Atom.Ph:* **d. de masse,** mass defect, packing loss; **d. de masse relatif, rapport du d. de masse,** packing fraction; *Opt:* **d. de planéité, de surface,** flatness, surface, defect, imperfection; *Paint:* **d. d'enrobage,** patch left unpainted, *U.S:* holiday; **d. d'usinage,** defect in machining; **recherche, localisation, des défauts,** fault locating; **il y a un d. de fonctionnement,** there's sth. wrong with the works; it isn't working properly, *U.S:* something's malfunctioning; (*c*) *Ven:* **mettre les chiens en d.,** to throw the hounds off the scent; **les chiens ont relevé le d.,** the hounds have picked up the scent again; **mettre qn en d.,** to put s.o. on the wrong track; **mettre en d. la vigilance de qn,** to elude the

vigilance of s.o.; (*of hound, person, memory, etc.*) **être en d.,** to be at fault; **sa mémoire est souvent en d.,** his memory often fails him, is often at fault; **trouver, surprendre, prendre, qn en d.,** to catch s.o. out.

défaveur [defavœːr], *s.f.* disfavour, discredit; **tomber en d.,** to fall into disfavour, out of favour, to become unpopular (**auprès de,** with); *Fin:* **actions en d.,** shares at a discount.

défavorable [defavɔrabl̥], *a.* unfavourable (**à,** to); **se montrer d. à un projet,** to be opposed to, to be against, a plan; **les conditions nous sont défavorables,** conditions are against us; *Fin:* **balance d.,** adverse balance.

défavorablement [defavɔrabləmɑ̃], *adv.* unfavourably.

défavorisé [defavɔrise], *a.* at a disadvantage; *Pol. Ec:* underprivileged; **enfants défavorisés,** underprivileged children.

défavoriser [defavɔrize], *v.tr.* to be unfair, unjust, to (s.o.); to treat (s.o.) unfavourably; to handicap (s.o.); **loi qui défavorise qn,** law that bears unjustly upon s.o.

défécation [defekasjɔ̃], *s.f.* **1.** *Pharm: Sug.R: etc:* defecation, clarification. **2.** *Physiol:* defecation.

défectible [defɛktibl̥], *a.* **1.** *A:* imperfect; incomplete. **2.** liable to be found wanting, fallible.

défectif, -ive [defɛktif, -iːv], *a. Gram:* defective (verb, etc.); *Mth:* deficient (hyperbola); *Cryst:* hemihedral.

défection [defɛksjɔ̃], *s.f.* defection from, desertion of, falling away from, an allegiance or cause; **faire d.,** (i) to fall away, to desert, to defect; *F:* to rat; (ii) to be missing, absent; *A.Astr:* **d. de la lune,** eclipse of the moon.

défectionnaire [defɛksjɔnɛːr], *s.* deserter (from party); defector.

défectionner [defɛksjɔne], *v.i.* to desert; *Pol:* to defect.

défectivité [defɛktivite], *s.f. Gram:* defectiveness (of verb, etc.).

défectoscope [defɛktɔskɔp], *s.m.* defectoscope.

défectueux, -euse [defɛktɥø, -øːz], *a.* **1.** defective, incomplete (title-deed, etc.). **2.** defective, faulty, imperfect, unsound (work, text, condition, etc.); unsatisfactory (result, etc.); **articles défectueux,** defective articles, rejects; *Com:* **endos d.,** incorrect endorsement.

défectueusement [defɛktɥøzmɑ̃], *adv.* defectively, imperfectly, faultily, unsoundly.

défectuosité [defɛktɥozite], *s.f.* **1.** defectiveness, faultiness, unsoundness. **2.** defect, flaw, imperfection.

déféminiser [defeminize], *v.tr.* to make (woman) mannish; **une jeune fille qui se déféminise,** a girl who adopts a mannish attitude, appearance.

défendable [defɑ̃dabl̥], *a.* defensible (position, etc.); justifiable (cause); **opinion d.,** opinion that can be defended.

défendeur, -eresse [defɑ̃dœːr, -(ə)rɛs], *s. Jur:* (*a*) defendant; (*b*) (*in equity, admiralty, or divorce cases*) respondent.

défendre [defɑ̃ːdr̥], *v.tr.* **1.** (*a*) to defend, fight for, (cause, military position, prisoner at the bar, etc.); to champion (opinion, cause); to maintain, uphold (opinion, right); to stand up, *F:* stick up, for (one's friends, etc.) (**contre,** against); **il sait d. son opinion,** he can hold his own; **tuer qn à son corps défendant,** to kill s.o. in self-defence; **faire qch. à son corps défendant,** to do sth. reluctantly, grudgingly, under protest; **agir à son corps défendant,** to act under duress, under coercion; **à mon corps défendant!** over my dead body! *F:* **d. sa peau,** to fight for one's life; (*b*) to protect, shield, guard (**contre,** against, from); **d. une forteresse,** to hold a fortress; **batterie qui défend le défilé,** battery that commands the defile; **ces arbres défendent la maison du vent,** these trees shelter, screen, the house from the wind. **2.** to forbid, prohibit; **fruit défendu,** forbidden fruit; **d. qch. à qn,** to forbid s.o. sth.; **d. sa maison, sa porte, à qn,** to forbid s.o. the house; **d. à qn de faire qch.,** to forbid s.o. to do sth.; **je vous défends de le faire,** (i) I forbid you to do it; (ii) *P:* I dare you to do it; **il est défendu de fumer,** smoking prohibited; **il m'est défendu de fumer,** I am forbidden to smoke, I am not allowed to smoke; **sa religion le lui défend,** his religion forbids it, it is forbidden by his religion; **d. que** + *sub.* **il défendit qu'on passât par là,** he forbade anyone to pass, that anyone should pass, he ordered that no one should pass, that way.

se défendre. 1. (*a*) to defend oneself; to stand up, *F:* stick up, for oneself; to hit back; **se d. contre une accusation,** to refute an accusation; **se d. contre le sommeil,** to fight against sleep; **se d. jusqu'à la dernière minute,** to die hard; *F:* **on se défend,** we are getting along; we are holding our own; **ce vieillard se défend,** this old man is still hale and hearty; **il se défend au bridge,** he's quite good at bridge; (*b*) **se d. de qch., d'avoir fait qch.,** to deny sth., to deny having done sth.; **je ne m'en défends pas,** I don't deny it; **se d. d'être difficile,** to protest against being thought hard to please; **se d. de toute arrière-pensée,** to disclaim any ulterior motive; **il se défend de faire des vers,** he will not admit that he writes verse. **2.** (*a*) **se d. de, contre, qch.,** to protect, shield, oneself from, against, sth.; **se d. de ses ennemis,** to protect oneself against one's enemies; **porter un manteau pour se d. du froid,** to wear a coat to protect oneself from the cold; (*b*) *Equit:* (*of horse*) to jib, to refuse. **3. se d. de faire qch.,** to refrain from doing sth., to forbear to do sth.; *esp.* in the negative; **on ne peut se d. de l'aimer,** one can't help liking him; **il ne put se d. de sourire,** he could not refrain from smiling; **dans ce monde là on ne peut pas se d. de boire,** in that crowd you can't get out of drinking, you simply have to drink. **4.** (*the pronoun is the indirect object*) **se d. tout plaisir,** to deny oneself all pleasure; **se d. de faire qch.,** not to allow oneself to do sth.; **elle s'était défendu de penser à lui,** she had made up her mind not to think of him.

défends [defɑ̃], *s.m. For:* **bois en d.,** plantation, area of young woodland, where access is forbidden to grazing animals.

défendu [defɑ̃dy], *a. Her:* (*a*) tusked; (*b*) horned.

défenestration [defənɛstrasjɔ̃], *s.f.* (*a*) *Hist:* **la D. de Prague,** the Defenestration of Prague; (*b*) *F:* (action of) throwing s.o. out of the window.

défenestrer [defənɛstre], *v.tr.* (*a*) *A:* to suppress, block up, the windows; (*b*) *F:* to throw s.o. out of the window.

défens [defɑ̃s], *s.m.* = DÉFENDS.

défense [defɑ̃ːs], *s.f.* **1.** (*a*) defence; **sans d.,** unprotected, defenceless; **combattre pour la d. de son pays,** to fight in defence of one's country; **prendre la d. de qn,** to undertake s.o.'s defence, to champion, take up, s.o.'s cause; **la d. de la langue française,** the defence of the French language; **prendre la d. d'un enfant en faute,** to find excuses for a child who has misbehaved; **d. nationale,** national defence; **d. méthodique, d. conçue et préparée dans le détail,** deliberate defence; **d. sans esprit de recul,** defence at all costs, to the bitter end; obstinate defence; **d. ponctuelle,** pinpoint defence; **d. tous azimuts, d. en point d'appui fermé, d. circulaire, d. périphérique,** all-round, perimeter, defence; **d. opérationnelle du territoire (D.O.T.), d. intérieure (du territoire),** home defence; **guerre de d.,** defensive warfare; **ligne de d.,** line of defence; **d. côtière,** coastal defence; **d. anti-aérienne, d. contre avions, la D.C.A.,** anti-aircraft defence; *F:* ack-ack; **d. passive,** civil defence; air raid precautions, A.R.P.; **poste de d. passive,** warden's post; **la meilleure d., c'est l'attaque,** the best form of defence is attack; *Jur:* **cas de légitime d.,** case of self-defence; **en état de légitime d.,** in self-defence; **se mettre, être en d.,** (i) to stand on one's guard; (ii) to take up a defensive position; **mettre une ville en état de d.,** to put a town in a state of defence, to put a town on a defence footing; **cette place est de d.,** this town is strong; **être hors de d.,** not to be able, to be unable, to defend oneself; **muraille de d.,** protecting wall; *For:* **bois en d.,** wood where the trees are sufficiently grown, so that animals may be allowed to enter; *Psy:* **névroses de d.,** defensive neuroses; **instinct de d.,** defence mechanism; (*b*) *Jur:* defence; **présenter la d.,** to put the case for the defence; **la d. a demandé d'ajourner,** the defence requested an adjournment; **avocat de la d.,** counsel for the defence; **défenses, moyens de la d.,** plea (of the defendant); **d. au contraire,** counter claim; **conclusions de la d., signification des défenses,** statement of defence; (*c*) *Sp:* **la d.,** the defence; **jouer la d.,** to play defence. **2.** (*means of defence*) (*a*) *O:* **les défenses d'une ville,** the defences, defensive works, fortifications, of a town; **d. aérienne,** air defence, aircraft cover; **ouvrage de d.,** (i) fortification; (ii) outwork; *Z:* **défenses d'un éléphant, d'un sanglier, d'un morse,** tusks of an elephant, of a boar, of a walrus; *Bot:* **défenses,** thorns, prickles; *Nau:* **d. (de canot),** fender; **boudin, bourrelet, de d.,** pudding (fender), puddening, rubber; **d. fixe en bois,** skid; **d. de gréement,** scotchman; **d. d'appontement,** rubber of a landing stage; *Nau:* **d. en filin, en cordage,** rope fender; (*b*) *Bookb:* end-paper; (*c*) guard (of newly planted tree); (*d*) *Tchn:* safety-rope (of roofer). **3.** prohibition, interdiction; *P.N:* **défense d'entrer, de fumer, d'afficher,** no admittance; no smoking; no billsticking, *U.S:* post no bills; *P.N:* **d. d'entrer sous peine d'amende,** trespassers will be prosecuted; *P.N:* **d. de passer,** no thoroughfare; **d. de parler!** silence! **faire d. à qn de faire qch.,** to forbid s.o. to do sth.; **on l'expulsa avec d. expresse de jamais revenir,** he was expelled and strictly forbidden ever to return; *Jur:* **défenses à exécution,** order of court of appeal forbidding the enforcement of a judgement; *s.a.* INHIBITION 1.

défenseur [defɑ̃sœːr], *s.m.* **1.** (*a*) protector, defender (of child, town, etc.); *Hist:* **d. de la foi,** Defender of the Faith; (*b*) supporter, upholder, champion, (of an opinion, of a cause). **2.** *Jur:* counsel for the defence.

défensif, -ive [defɑ̃sif, -iːv]. **1.** *a.* defensive; *Mil:* **ouvrage(s) défensif(s),** defences; **armes défensives,** defensive weapons. **2.** *s.f.* **défensive: être, se tenir, sur la d.,** to be, stand, on the defensive; to be on one's guard.

défensivement [defɑ̃sivmɑ̃], *adv.* defensively.

déféquer [defeke], *v.tr.* (**je défèque, n. déféquons; je déféquerai**) **1.** *Ch:* to clarify, clear, purify; *Sug.R:* to defecate. **2.** *abs. Physiol:* to defecate.

déférence [deferɑ̃ːs], *s.f.* deference, respect, regard; **avoir de la d. pour qn, se montrer plein de d. pour qn,** to hold s.o. in respect, to have respect for s.o., to be deferential to s.o., to show regard for s.o.; **avec d.,** deferentially, respectfully; **par d. pour . . .,** in, out of, deference to . . ., out of regard for . . ..

déférent [deferɑ̃], *a.* **1.** deferential (manner, etc.); **être, se montrer d., envers, à l'égard de qn,** to be deferential, respectful, to s.o. **2.** *a. & s.m. Anat:* deferent; **canal d., s. d.,** vas deferens; *A.Astr:* **cercle d., s. d.,** deferent. **3.** *s.m. Num:* mint mark.

déférentiel, -ielle [deferɑ̃sjɛl], *a. Anat:* deferential.

déférentite [deferɑ̃tit], *s.f. Med:* deferentitis.

déférer [defere], *v.* (**je défère, n. déférons; je déférerai**) **I.** *v.tr.* **1.** *Jur:* (*a*) to submit, refer (case to a court); to bring (case before a court); **d. une cause à la cour d'appel,** to remove, transfer, a case to the Court of Appeal; (*b*) to denounce, to inform against (s.o.), to give (s.o.) up; **d. un criminel,** to inform against a criminal; **d. qn en, à la, justice,** to hand over, give up, s.o. to justice; **déféré au juge,** brought before the judge; (*c*) **d. le serment à qn,** to administer, tender, an oath to s.o.; to put s.o. on his oath; to swear (witness); to swear in (jury). **2.** *A:* **d. un honneur, un titre, à qn,** to confer, bestow, an honour, a title, on s.o.

II. **déférer,** *v.i.* **d. à qn,** to defer to s.o.; **d. à la décision de qn,** to defer to s.o.'s decision; **d. aux ordres de qn,** to comply with s.o.'s orders; **d. à une demande,** to accede to a request.

déferlage [defɛrlaːʒ], *s.m. Nau:* unfurling (of sail, flag); breaking (of flag).

déferlant [defɛrlɑ̃], *a. Nau:* (*of wave*) breaking; **vague déferlante,** beachcomber; breaker.

déferlement [defɛrləmɑ̃], *s.m.* breaking (of waves); unfurling (of sail, flag); breaking (of flag, signal); **un d. d'enthousiasme,** a wave of enthusiasm.

déferler [defɛrle]. **1.** *v.tr. Nau:* to unfurl, shake out (sail, flag); to break (flag, signal); to set (sail). **2.** *v.i.* (*of waves*) to break (into foam); to comb; *Mil: F:* (*of wave of attack*) to break up; **la foule déferle dans la rue,** the crowd surges down the street; **les manifestants déferlèrent sur la place,** the demonstrators swarmed into the square.

déferrage [defɛraːʒ], *s.m.* removal of the iron (from sth.); unshoeing (of horse); **d. d'un forçat,** removal of a convict's irons, unfettering of a convict.

déferré [defɛre], *a.* (*of horse, etc.*) unshod.

déferrement [defɛrmɑ̃], *s.m.* = DÉFERRAGE.

déferrer [defɛre], *v.tr.* **1.** (*a*) to remove the iron from (sth.); **d. un chemin de fer,** to take up the rails of a railway; **d. un lacet,** to take the tags off a shoelace; **d. un forçat,** to unfetter a convict; (*b*) to unshoe (horse); *F:* **d. qn (des quatre pieds),** to disconcert s.o., to put s.o. out; **c'est un homme qu'on déferre aisément,** he's easily put out, flummoxed; (*c*) *Nau: A:* **d. un navire,** to slip the anchor. **2.** *abs. A:* to draw one's sword.

se déferrer, (*of horse*) to cast a shoe; *F:* **homme qui ne se déferre pas facilement,** man who is not easily put out, flummoxed.

déferrisation [defɛrizasjɔ̃], *s.f.* deferrization.

déferriser [defɛrize], *v.tr.* to remove the iron from (water, etc.).

déferrure [defɛryːr], *s.f.* **1.** unshoeing (of horse). **2.** (*of horse*) casting of a shoe.

défertiliser [defɛrtilize], *v.tr.* to make (land) unproductive.

défervescence [defɛrvɛs(s)ɑ̃ːs], *s.f. Med:* defervescence.

défet [defɛ], *s.m. Bookb: usu. pl.* imperfections, oddments, waste sheets.

défeuillage [defœjaːʒ, -ø-], *s.m.* stripping the leaves off (trees); stripping (tree) of its leaves; defoliating (of shrub).

défeuillaison [defœjɛzɔ̃, -ø-], *s.f.* defoliation; fall of the leaf.

défeuiller [defœje, -øje], *v.tr.* to strip the leaves off (tree); to strip (tree) of its leaves; to defoliate (shrub); **rose défeuillée,** rose which has shed it's petals.

se défeuiller, (*of tree*) to shed its leaves; (*of flower*) to shed its petals.

défi [defi], *s.m.* (*a*) challenge; **lancer, adresser, jeter, un d. à qn,** to challenge s.o., to send s.o. a challenge; *A:* to challenge s.o. to combat; **relever un d.,** to accept, take up, a challenge; **une flamme de d. s'alluma dans son regard,** his eyes flashed a challenge; (*b*) **regard de d.,** defiant look; **regarder qn d'un air de d.,** to look defiantly at s.o.; **jeter un d. à qn,** to hurl defiance at s.o.; **mettre qn au d. de faire qch.,** to defy, dare, s.o. to do sth.

défiance [defjɑ̃ːs], *s.f.* **1.** mistrust, distrust, suspicion; wariness; **motion de d.,** motion of no confidence; **inspirer de la d. à qn,** to inspire s.o. with distrust; **éveiller la d. de qn, mettre qn en d.,** to arouse s.o.'s suspicions; **éprouver, ressentir, de la d. pour qn,** to feel suspicious of s.o.; **faire qch. sans d.,** to do sth. unsuspectingly; **regarder qn avec d.,** to look distrustfully, suspiciously, at s.o. **2. d. de soi-même,** diffidence, lack of self-confidence.

défiant [defjɑ̃], *a.* mistrustful, distrustful, cautious; wary; timid; **regarder qn d'un air d.,** to look distrustfully at s.o.; **mari d.,** jealous husband.

défibrage [defibraːʒ], *s.m.* (*a*) *Paperm:* grinding (of wood for pulping); (*b*) *Sug.-R:* shredding.

défibrer [defibre], *v.tr.* **1.** *Paperm:* to grind (wood for pulping). **2.** *Sug.-R:* to disintegrate, to remove the fibres of (sugar-cane). **3.** *Tex:* to disintegrate.

défibreur [defibrœːr], *s.m.* **1.** *Paperm:* wood-stuff-grinder; **d. en continu,** caterpillar grinder. **2.** *Sug.-R:* cane-shredder. **3.** *Tex:* disintegrator.

défibrination [defibrinasjɔ̃], *s.f.* defibrination.

défibriner [defibrine], *v.tr.* to defibrinate, defibrinize.

déficeler [defisle], *v.tr.* (**je déficelle, n. déficelons; je déficellerai**) to take the string off, to untie, undo (parcel, etc.).

se déficeler, to come untied, undone.

déficher [defiʃe], *v.tr. Vit:* to remove the props from (vines).

déficience [defisjɑ̃ːs], *s.f.* deficiency; **d. mentale,** mental deficiency; **d. (alimentaire),** malnutrition.

déficient, -ente [defisjɑ̃, -ɑ̃ːt], (*a*) *a.* deficient; **enfant d.,** mentally deficient child; (*b*) *s.* **d. mental, déficiente mentale,** mental defective; mentally deficient, mentally handicapped, person; (*c*) *a. Mth:* deficient (number); **hyperbole déficiente,** deficient hyperbola; (*d*) *a.* **machine déficiente,** defective machine.

déficit [defisit], *s.m.* deficit (in cash, balance-sheet); deficiency (in revenue); shortage (in cash, weight); **être en d.,** to show a deficit; **combler le d.,** to make up, make good, the deficit, the shortage; **d. commercial,** trade gap; trade deficit.

déficitaire [defisitɛːr], *a.* (account) showing a debit balance; (budget, etc.) showing a deficit; **être d.,** to be in the red; **rétablir un budget d.,** to balance an adverse budget; **récoltes déficitaires,** short crops; **année d. en blé,** lean year, bad year for wheat.

défier [defje], *v.tr.* (*p.d.* & *pr.sub.* **n. défiions, v. défiiez**) **1.** (*a*) to challenge; **d. qn au combat, aux échecs,** to challenge s.o. to fight, to a game of chess; **d. qn à courir cent mètres,** to challenge s.o. to run a hundred metres; **d. qn à qui boira le plus,** to challenge s.o. to a drinking match; **je te défie en vers,** I challenge you to a contest in poetry; **d. qn du regard,** to glare defiantly at s.o.; *Com:* **prix défiant toute concurrence,** unbeatable prices; (*b*) to defy, set at defiance (s.o., sth.); **ce monument a défié les siècles,** this monument has withstood the passage of time; **le spectacle défie toute description,** the sight baffles, defies, is beyond, (all) description; **d. qn de faire qch.,** to defy s.o. to do sth.; **je vous défie de deviner qui c'est,** I defy you to, I'll bet you won't, guess who it is; **je te défie de courir plus vite que moi,** I bet you can't run faster than me; (*c*) to brave, to face (danger, death); **d. l'orage,** to brave the storm; **aller d. qn chez lui,** to beard the lion in his den; **d. le bon sens,** to go against common sense. **2.** *Nau:* **d. qch., d. (le navire) de qch.,** to look out for (a danger), to dodge sth.; **d. de la lame,** to dodge a sea; **d. (de) la terre,** to bear off the land; **défiez!** fend off! **défiez l'embardée!** don't let her yaw! **défiez l'aulofée!** don't let her come up! **défiez du vent!** don't let her shake!

se défier de qn, de qch., to mistrust, distrust, s.o., sth.; **il se défie de moi,** he doesn't trust me; **se d. de soi-même,** to have no self-confidence, to be diffident; **je me défie de ses promesses,** I don't believe in his promises; **il faut vous d. des pièces de cinq francs,** you must be on your guard when offered a five-franc piece; **elle ne se défiait pas de ce qui allait arriver,** she did not suspect what was going to happen.

défiger [defiʒe], *v.tr.* (**je défigeai(s); n. défigeons**) (*a*) to liquefy (solidified, oil, etc.); (*b*) *F:* to put some life into (s.o.), to liven (s.o.) up.

se défiger, (*a*) (*of oil, etc.*) to liquefy; (*b*) *F:* (*of pers.*) (i) to thaw, unbend; (ii) to rouse oneself, to liven up.

défigurant [defigyrɑ̃], *a.* disfiguring.

défiguration [defigyrasjɔ̃], *s.f.*, **défigurement** [defigyrmɑ̃], *s.m.*, disfigurement, disfiguration; **d. d'une statue,** defacement of a statue; **d. de la vérité,** distortion of the truth.

défigurer [defigyre], *v.tr.* (*a*) to disfigure (s.o., sth.); to deface (statue, etc.); **défiguré par une maladie de peau,** disfigured by a skin disease; **d. un tableau en le retouchant,** to spoil a picture by touching it up; (*b*) to distort (meaning, the truth); **d. qn,** to misrepresent s.o.; **d. un texte en le traduisant,** to mistranslate a text; to massacre a text in translation.

défilade [defilad], *s.f.* **1. d. de la flotte,** passing of the fleet in line ahead. **2.** procession, succession; **aller à la d.,** to trail along, to trail past.

défilage [defilaːʒ], *s.m.* **1.** drawing (of thread); **2.** *Paperm:* breaking in.

défilateur [defilatœːr], *s.m. Paperm:* breaker.

défilé[1] [defile], *s.m. Paperm:* half-stuff.

défilé[2], *a.* defiladed, concealed, under cover; *Mil:* **cheminement d.,** approach under cover; **batterie défilée,** screened battery; **d. aux vues,** protected, hidden, from view; sight defiladed.

défilé[3], *s.m.* **1.** defile, gorge, (mountain) pass; *Nau:* narrow channel. **2.** (*a*) *Mil: etc:* march past; *Av:* **d. (aérien, d'aviation, d'avions),** fly past; (*b*) **d. de modes,** fashion parade; **d. de voitures,** procession of cars, motorcade; **d. ininterrompu de visiteurs,** endless stream of visitors.

défilement[1] [defilmɑ̃], *s.m. T.V:* **d. des lignes,** movement of lines; line crawl; *Cin: etc:* **vitesse de d.,** tape speed.

défilement[2], *s.m. Mil:* **1.** (*a*) defilading, concealment (of gun, troops, etc.); (*b*) defilade; (*of tank*) **d. à hauteur de coque, de tourelle,** hull-, turret-down, position. **2.** cover.

défiler[1] [defile], *v.tr.* **1.** *Tex:* to ravel, tease out (woven material). **2.** *Paperm:* to break in (rags, etc.).

se défiler[1], (*of stocking, etc.*) to ladder, to run.

défiler[2], *v.tr.* **1.** to unstring, unthread (beads, necklace, etc.); **d. son chapelet,** to have one's say, to speak one's mind. **2.** *Mil:* to defilade (fortress); to put (company, etc.) under cover; to conceal (guns, battery).

se défiler[2]. **1.** (*of beads, etc.*) to come unstrung, unthreaded. **2.** (*a*) *Mil:* **se d. du feu de l'adversaire,** to take cover from the enemy's fire; (*b*) *F:* to make off, clear out; to slip off on the quiet.

défiler[3], *v.i.* (*a*) *Mil:* to defile, to file off; **d. en colonne par deux,** to file off two by two, in twos, to pair off; (*b*) *Mil:* to march past; **d. par compagnies,** to march past by companies; **d. devant le général,** to march past the general; (*c*) to walk in procession; (*d*) **des centaines de voitures défilaient vers la côte,** hundreds of cars were streaming towards the coast; **les avions défilaient dans un ciel bleu,** the aircraft were flying past against a blue sky; **sur toutes les voies ferrées défilaient d'interminables rames de wagons vides,** all along the lines rolled endless streams of empty railway trucks.

défileur, -euse [defilœːr, -øːz]. **1.** *s.m.* (*a*) *Nau:* cod smack, codman; (*b*) *Paperm:* breaker (engine). **2.** *a. Paperm:* **pile défileuse,** *s.f.* **défileuse,** breaker (engine).

défilocher [defilɔʃe], *v.tr.* to shred (rags, etc.).

défini [defini]. **1.** *a.* (*a*) definite, clearly defined; **je suis parti sans raison bien définie,** I left for no particular reason; **j'ai un travail bien d. à faire,** I have a set piece of work to do; (*b*) *Gram:* definite (article, etc.); **passé d.,** past definite, preterite, past historic; (*c*) *Mth: Bot:* definite; *Ch:* **loi des proportions définies,** law of constant, definite, proportions. **2.** *s.m.* (*a*) *Phil:* **le d.,** the object defined; (*b*) *Gram:* definite article.

définir [definiːr], *v.tr.* to define; to give the definition of; **d. un mot,** to define a word, to give, explain, the meaning of a word; **d. un terrain,** to define, establish, the limits of a plot of land; *Theol:* **d. un dogme,** to define a dogma; **conditions à d.,** conditions to be determined; **homme difficile à d.,** man difficult to describe, to portray; *Tchn:* **d. les types de production,** to standardize products.

se définir, (*of coast, etc.*) to become clear, distinct.

définissable [definisabl], *a.* definable, that can be defined.

définiteur [definitœːr], *s.m. Ecc:* definitor.

définitif, -ive [definitif, -iːv], *a.* **1.** (*a*) definitive, final (resolution, judgement, etc.); **édition définitive,** definitive edition; **destination définitive d'un colis,** ultimate destination of a parcel; **être nommé à titre d.,** to be permanently appointed; **rien n'est d. sur la terre,** nothing on this earth is permanent; *Jur:* **jugement d.,** final decree, judgement, decree absolute; *Aut: etc:* **être au stop, à l'arrêt, d.,** to have broken down beyond repair; (*b*) *adv.phr.* **en définitive,** finally, in short, in a word. **2.** *s.m.* what is final, definitive.

définition [definisjɔ̃], *s.f.* (*a*) definition; **donner la d. de qch.,** to give the definition of sth., to define sth.; **par d.,** by that very fact, automatically; (*b*) clue (of cross-word puzzle); (*c*) **d. d'une image,** (i) *Opt:* definition of an image; (ii) *T.V:* picture resolution.

définitivement [definitivmɑ̃], *adv.* definitively, finally, permanently; **il est parti d.,** he has gone away for good.

déflagrant [deflagrɑ̃], *a.* deflagrating; **explosif d.,** low explosive.

déflagrateur [deflagratœːr], *s.m.* deflagrator; *El:* spark-gap; **d. pour mines,** (electric) mine-igniter, (shot-)firer.

déflagration [deflagrasjɔ̃], *s.f.* deflagration, combustion.

déflagrer [deflagre], *v.i.* to deflagrate.

déflation [deflasjɔ̃], *s.f.* **1.** deflation (of balloon, of the currency); dropping (of wind). **2.** *Geog:* wind erosion.

déflationniste [deflasjɔnist], *a.* & *s.m. Pol.Ec:* deflationist; *a.* deflationary (measures, etc.).

défléchir [defleʃiːr], *v.tr.* & *i.* to deflect; *Bot:* **rameau défléchi,** deflected branch.

déflecteur [deflɛktœːr], *s.m. Mch: etc:* deflector, baffle, plate; *Atom.Ph:* divertor; *Aut:* (i) ventilator, ventilating window; (ii) *A:* insect deflector; *Av:* **d. de souffle,** blast screen; **d. Venturi,** Venturi windscreen; *a.* **déflecteur, -trice;** *Elcs:* **plaques déflectrices,** deflecting plates.

déflection [deflɛksjɔ̃], *s.f. Ph:* deflection.

déflegmateur [deflɛgmatœːr], *s.m. Ch:* dephlegmator, fractionating column.

déflegmation [deflɛgmasjɔ̃], *s.f. Ch: Ind:* dephlegmation, concentration (of alcohol, etc.); **colonne de d.,** fractionating column.

déflegmer [deflɛgme], *v.tr. Ch: Ind:* to dephlegmate, rectify, concentrate (alcohol, etc.); **colonne à d.,** fractionating column.

défleuraison [deflœrezɔ̃], *s.f.* falling of blossom, shedding of flowers.

défleurir [deflœriːr]. **1.** *v.i.* & *pr.* (*of tree, etc.*) to lose its blossom; **rosier défleuri,** rose-bush that has shed its flowers. **2.** *v.tr.* to take, nip, the blossom or flowers off (plant); to take the bloom off (fruit); **la gelée a défleuri le pommier,** the frost has stripped the blossom from the apple tree.

déflexion [deflɛksjɔ̃], *s.f. Elcs: Obst: etc:* deflection; *Av:* downwash.

défloculant [deflɔkylɑ̃], *s.m. Ch:* deflocculant.

défloculation [deflɔkylasjɔ̃], *s.f. Ch:* deflocculation.

défloculer [deflɔkyle], *v.i. Ch:* to deflocculate.

défloraison [deflɔrɛzɔ̃], *s.f.* falling of blossom, shedding of flowers.

défloration [deflɔrasjɔ̃], *s.f.* defloration.

défloré [deflɔre], *a.* **1.** *Bot:* deflorate. **2.** (*a*) (*bush, etc.*) stripped of its blooms; (*b*) deflowered (virgin); stale (news).

déflorer [deflɔre], *v.tr.* **1.** to strip (plant) of its blooms. **2.** to deflower, seduce (virgin); **la publicité déflore tout,** publicity takes the bloom off, the freshness out of, everything.

défluent [deflyɑ̃], *s.m. Geog:* distributary.
défluorescent [deflyɔrɛsɑ̃], *a. Petroleum Ind:* deblooming.
défocalisation [defɔkalizasjɔ̃], *s.f.* defocusing.
défoliaison [defɔljɛzɔ̃], *s.f.* defoliating.
défoliant [defɔljɑ̃], *s.m. Agr:* defoliant.
défoliation [defɔljasjɔ̃], *s.f.* defoliation.
défonçage [defɔ̃sa:ʒ], *s.m.*, **défoncement** [defɔ̃smɑ̃], *s.m.* **1.** staving in (of cask, boat); smashing in (of box); breaking down (of fence). **2.** (*a*) **d. d'un chemin par les pluies,** breaking up, cutting up, of a road by the rains; (*b*) *Agr:* deep digging, breaking up (of ground).
défoncé [defɔ̃se], *a.* **1.** bashed in; (*of ship, cask*) stove in; **chapeau d.,** battered hat; **lit d.,** bed with broken springs; **clôture défoncée,** broken-down fence. **2. chemin d., route défoncée,** broken, bumpy, rutted, road; road full of potholes.
défoncer [defɔ̃se], *v.tr.* (**je défonçai(s); n. défonçons**) **1.** to stave in (cask, boat); to smash in (box, etc.); **d. une boîte,** to knock out the bottom of a box; **un camion a défoncé le mur,** a lorry has knocked down the wall; **d. un argument,** to knock the bottom out of an argument; *Mil:* **d. une armée,** to cut up an army; *Nau:* (*of wind*) **d. une voile,** to tear away a sail. **2.** to break up, cut up, make potholes in (road); *Agr:* **d. un terrain,** to break up, to deep-plough, to trench, a piece of ground.
se défoncer, (*of roof, etc.*) to fall in, collapse; (*of ship, road, etc.*) to break up; (*of chair seat*) to give way.
défonceuse [defɔ̃sø:z], *s.f.* (*a*) *Agr:* heavy plough, trenching plough; (*b*) *Civ.E:* ripper.
déforestation [defɔrɛstasjɔ̃], *s.f.* deforestation.
déformable [defɔrmabl̩], *a.* that can be put out of shape, distorted; *Metall:* ductile; **ballon d.,** flexible balloon.
déformage [defɔrma:ʒ], *s.m. Bootm:* (*a*) polishing, finishing; (*b*) de-lasting, last-slipping.
déformant [defɔrmɑ̃], *a.* distorting.
déformateur, -euse [defɔrmatœ:r, -ø:z], *a.* deforming; distorting.
déformation [defɔrmasjɔ̃], *s.f.* **1.** (*a*) deformation; **d. professionnelle,** professional idiosyncrasy; vocational bias; (*b*) *Phot:* distortion (of map projection, of photographic image); (*c*) *Mth:* distortion; (*d*) *Atom.Ph:* **d. du noyau,** nuclear distortion; **d. du col,** saddle-point distortion. **2.** *Mec.E: etc:* (*a*) distortion, strain, set (of materials); buckling, warping; **d. due au, par, cisaillement,** shear(ing) strain; **d. due à la, par, flexion,** bending strain; **d. due à la, par, torsion,** torsion(al) strain; twist; **d. due à la, par, traction,** tensile strain; (*b*) buckled, warped, condition.
déformer [defɔrme], *v.tr.* **1.** to deform; **d. un chapeau,** to put a hat out of shape; **d. une langue,** to distort a language; *Phot:* **image déformée,** distorted image; *Ph:* **onde déformée,** deformed wave; *P.N:* **chaussée déformée,** uneven road surface. **2.** (*a*) *Mec.E: etc:* to warp, buckle, twist, distort; to give a set to (plate, etc.); (*b*) **lecture qui déforme les pensées,** reading which distorts, corrupts, one's ideas.
se déformer. 1. to get out of shape, to become deformed. **2.** to warp, buckle.
défortifier [defɔrtifje], *v.tr.* (*p.d. & pr.sub.* **n. défortifiions, v. défortifiiez**) to dismantle the fortifications, defences, of (town, etc.); *A:* to slight (a town).
défouetter [defwɛte], *v.tr. Bookb:* to untie whipcord from (book).
défouir [defwi:r], *v.tr.* to free (sth. buried), to dig, (sth.) out; **les coques sont défouies par le courant,** cockles are dug out by the tidal flow.
défoulement [defulmɑ̃], *s.m. Psy:* liberation (of complexes, etc.).
défouler [defule], *v.tr. Psy:* to liberate; *F:* to work off (complexes, etc.).
se défouler, to get rid of one's inhibitions, complexes; *F:* to let off steam.
défournage [defurna:ʒ], *s.m.*, **défournement** [defurnəmɑ̃], *s.m.* drawing (of pottery) from the kiln, (of bread) from the oven; discharging (of coke from oven); **aire de défournement,** coking wharf.
défourner [defurne], *v.tr.* to draw (pottery) from the kiln; to draw (bread) from the oven; to discharge (coke from coke-oven).
défourneur [defurnœ:r], *s.m. Gasm:* (*pers.*) oven drawer; *Bak:* peeler, oven man.
défourneuse [defurnø:z], *s.f.* ram (of coke-oven), coke ram.
défourrer [defure], *v.tr.* **1.** to remove the fur from (coat, etc.). **2.** *Agr:* to thresh (corn). **3.** *Nau:* to unserve (cable).
défoxer [defɔkse], *v.tr. Vit:* to remove the foxy taste from (wine).
défrai [defrɛ], *s.m. A:* defraying, payment, of expenses.
défraîchi [defrɛʃi], *a.* **articles défraîchis,** (shop-)soiled goods; **gants un peu défraîchis,** slightly soiled gloves; **fleurs défraîchies,** flowers that have lost their freshness, faded flowers; **beauté défraîchie,** beauty that has lost its bloom; *F:* that is past its best, has seen better days; **ce livre est un peu d.,** *F:* this book is a bit tatty.
défraîchir [defrɛʃi:r], *v.tr.* to take away the newness, freshness, of (sth.); to soil (sth.); **le soleil a défraîchi la couleur du papier,** the sun has faded the paper.
se défraîchir, to lose one's, its, freshness; to fade; **ce tissu se défraîchira très vite,** this fabric will soon lose its crispness, its freshness.
défraiement, défrayement [defrɛmɑ̃], *s.m.* expenses *pl.*
défrancisation [defrɑ̃sizasjɔ̃], *s.f.* degallicising.
défranciser [defrɑ̃size], *v.tr.* to degallicise.
défrapper [defrape], *v.tr. Nau:* to unbend (cable); to unlash (tackle); to cast off (standing part of tackle).
défrayer [defreje], *v.tr.* (**je défraie, je défraye, n. défrayons; je défraierai, je défrayerai**) **1. d. qn,** to defray, pay, meet, settle, s.o.'s expenses; **être défrayé de tout,** to have all expenses paid. **2. d. la conversation,** (i) to be the life of the conversation; (ii) to be the subject of conversation, to provide a topic of conversation; **d. la compagnie,** (i) to keep the company amused; (ii) to be the butt, the laughing-stock, of the company; **d. la chronique,** to be in the news; to hit the headlines; to be the talk of the town; **des aventures à d. un roman policier,** enough adventures to provide material for a thriller.
défretter [defrɛte], *v.tr. Tchn:* to remove metal hoop, band from (pipe, etc.).
défrichable [defriʃabl̩], *a. Agr:* (land) that can be cleared.
défrichage [defriʃa:ʒ], *s.m. Agr:* clearing, grubbing (of land).
défriche [defriʃ], *s.f.*, **défriché** [defriʃe], *s.m.*, *Agr:* clearing, cleared patch (in forest land, etc.).
défrichement [defriʃmɑ̃], *s.m. Agr:* **1.** clearing, grubbing (of land). **2.** cleared land, clearing.
défricher [defriʃe], *v.tr.* (*a*) *Agr:* to clear, grub, reclaim (land for cultivation); to bring (land) into cultivation; to break (new ground); (*b*) **d. un sujet,** to do pioneer work, to break new ground, in a subject.
défricheur, -euse [defriʃœ:r, -ø:z], *s.* **1.** (*a*) settler; reclaimer of land (for cultivation); (*b*) pioneer (in a subject). **2.** *s.f.* **défricheuse,** breaking plough, breaker.
se défringuer [sədefrɛ̃ge], *P:* to undress.
défripement [defripmɑ̃], *s.m.* smoothing out (of crumpled garment), ironing out (of creases in a dress, suit, etc.).
défriper [defripe], *v.tr.* to smoothe out (crumpled garment); **d. une robe en la repassant,** to iron out the creases in a dress.
défrisement [defrizmɑ̃], *s.m.* (*a*) straightening, uncurling (of hair); (*b*) *F:* disappointment.
défriser [defrize], *v.tr.* (*a*) to uncurl, straighten (hair); to put (hair) out of curl; **je suis toute défrisée,** my hair has lost its curl, has gone straight; (*b*) *F:* **ça vous défrise?** are you disappointed, put out?
se défriser, (*a*) (*of hair*) to come out of curl, to uncurl, to lose its curl; (*b*) to uncurl one's hair.
défroisser [defrwase], *v.tr.* to take the creases out of (dress, etc.).
défroncement [defrɔ̃smɑ̃], *s.m.* taking out of gathers (in a dress, etc.).
défroncer [defrɔ̃se], *v.tr.* (**je défronçai(s); n. défronçons**) to undo, take out, the gathers in (skirt, etc.); **il défronça les sourcils,** he stopped frowning.
défroque [defrɔk], *s.f.* **1.** effects (of dead monk). **2.** *usu. pl.* cast-off clothing.
défroqué [defrɔke], *a. & s.m.* unfrocked (priest); ex-priest, ex-monk.
défroquer [defrɔke], *v.tr.* to unfrock, defrock, (priest).
se défroquer, (*of monk*) to give up the frock.
défruiter [defrɥite], *v.tr.* (*a*) to strip (fruit tree); (*b*) to remove the fruity flavour of (olive oil).
défrusquer (se) [sədefryske], *v.pr. F:* to undress.
défubler [defyble], *v.tr.* to unmuffle, unwrap (s.o.).
défunt, -unte [defœ̃, -œ̃:t], *a. & s.* defunct, deceased; **le roi d.,** the late king; **le d.,** the defunct, deceased; **faire un discours sur la tombe du d.,** to make a speech over the grave of the deceased; **prier pour les défunts,** to pray for the dead; **royauté défunte,** extinct monarchy; *F:* **amour d.,** old love.
défunter [defœ̃te], *v.i.* (*aux.* être), *P:* to die, to kick the bucket.
dégagé [degaʒe]. I. *a.* **1.** (*a*) free, untrammelled (movements, etc.); clear (weather); **marcher d'une allure dégagée,** to stride along; to swing along; **horizon d. de brume,** horizon clear of haze; (*b*) cavalier; pert, free and easy (tone, manner); **d'un air d.,** in an off-hand manner, airily, perkily; **propos dégagés,** somewhat free conversation. **2. chambre dégagée,** room with independent exit; **escalier d.,** private staircase; **vue dégagée,** open view, unrestricted view; **route dégagée,** clear road (with no blind corners); *Tp:* **ligne dégagée,** free line.
II. **dégagé,** *s.m.* (*a*) *Danc:* dégagé; (*b*) *Fenc:* disengaging (of blade).
dégagement [degaʒmɑ̃], *s.m.* **1.** redemption (of pledge, mortgage); taking out of pawn; **d. de sa parole,** (i) carrying out of one's promises; (ii) taking back of one's word; **d. de titres,** release of (pledged) securities. **2.** (*a*) disengagement, release (of brake, etc.); *Mec.E:* backing off (a tool); *Fenc:* disengaging (of one's point); disengagement; *Mil:* withdrawal (of troops); relieving, relief (of town); *s.a.* TOUCHE 2; (*b*) loosening, slackening (of bolt, etc.); (*c*) relieving of congestion; clearing (of road, of the lungs, etc.); *Obst:* freeing of the head of the fœtus during childbirth; **d. des cadres de l'armée,** cutting down of the number of officers; **escalier de d.,** (i) private staircase; (ii) emergency stairs; (*d*) private passage (in suite of rooms); **dégagements d'un théâtre, etc.,** exits of a theatre, etc.; (*e*) *Fb:* **les dégagements d'arrière à l'avant,** the clearances from the backs to forwards; **d. en touche,** kicking into touch; (*f*) *Pol: Mil:* disengagement; (*g*) *Mth:* isolation of unknown quantity. **3.** (*a*) escape, release (of steam, gas, etc.); **tuyau de d.,** waste pipe; bypass; (*b*) *Ch:* separation (of gas); **d. de chaleur,** emission, evolution, liberation, of heat. **4.** (*a*) **d. d'un véhicule au-dessus du sol,** clearance of a vehicle above the ground; (*b*) clearance, angle of relief (of lathe-tool, etc.); (*c*) toe room (of wardrobe).
dégager [degaʒe], *v.tr.* (**je dégageai(s); n. dégageons**) **1.** to redeem (pledge, mortgage); to take (sth.) out of pawn; **d. des titres,** to release (pledged) securities; **d. sa montre,** to take one's watch out of pawn; to redeem one's watch; **d. sa parole,** (i) to make good one's promise; (ii) to take back one's word. **2.** (*a*) to disengage, release (s.o., sth.); to unhook (team of artillery horses); **d. le frein,** to release the brake; **d. un organe (d'une machine),** to put a part out of gear, out of action; **d. un navire d'un récif,** to get a ship off a reef; **elle tenta de d. sa main,** she tried to pull away, release, her hand; **d. des prisonniers,** to rescue prisoners; **d. une troupe,** to extricate a body of troops (from critical position); **d. une ville,** to relieve a town; **d. qn d'une promesse,** to release, absolve, s.o. from a promise; **cela me dégage de toute responsabilité,** it relieves me of all responsibility; **d. qn de dessous les débris,** to dig, pull, s.o. out from under the debris, to pull s.o. clear of the wreckage; **d. son esprit de préjugés,** to clear one's mind of prejudices; **d. la vérité de l'erreur,** to separate, sift (out), truth from error; **texte dégagé de toutes ses difficultés,** text cleared of all its difficulties; *Ch:* **d. l'oxygène de l'eau,** to disengage oxygen from water; (*b*) to relieve the congestion in, to clear (ground, road, deck, the breathing passages, etc.); *Rail:* **d. la voie,** to clear the line; *Nav:* **d. les pièces pour le combat,** to clear away for action; *Nau:* **d. le pont,** to clear the deck; **d. les chaînes,** to clear hawse; **d. les cadres (de l'armée),** to cut down the commissioned ranks, to reduce the number of officers; *Med:* **d. la poitrine,** to clear congestion in the lungs; **d. les intestins,** to loosen, clear, the bowels; *Arch:* **d. les vues,** to open vistas; **d. un appartement,** to construct a private passage in a suite of rooms; (*c*) *abs. Mil:* to break contact (with the enemy), to disengage; *Av:* to break out of formation; *F:* **dégagez, s'il vous plaît,** gangway, (please); mind your backs, (please); *Nau:* **dégagez,** stand clear; *P:* **dégage!** buzz off! clear off! (*d*) **habit qui dégage bien la taille,** coat that sets off the figure well; **ce décolleté dégage à peine le cou,** this neckline hardly shows the neck; (*e*) to make clear, to define (one's impressions, etc.); *Mth:* **d. l'inconnue,** to isolate the unknown quantity, *usu.* to pick out the

terms in x; **d. des conclusions d'un récit,** to draw conclusions from an account; **d. le sens intime d'un passage,** to bring out, elucidate, the inner meaning of a passage; *F:* **qu'est-ce que tu en dégages?,** what do you make of it? **d. son style,** to give ease, freedom, to one's style; (*f*) *Mec.E: etc:* to free (a part); to loosen, slacken (bolt); to ease, relieve (pressure); *Mec.E:* to back off (a tool); *I.C.E:* **outil pour d. les soupapes,** valve-freeing tool; (*g*) *Sp: Fencing:* to disengage (the blade); *Box:* to break (away); *Fb:* to kick (ball) over the touch-line; to clear (ball); *Danc:* to dégagé, to perform a dégagé. 3. to emit, give off (vapour, smell); to exhale (odour, etc.); to liberate, emit, give out (heat); **toute sa personne dégage un air d'élégance,** his whole person expresses elegance; **orateur qui dégage l'enthousiasme,** orator who radiates enthusiasm; **fleurs qui dégagent un parfum délicat,** flowers that give off a delicate scent.

se dégager. 1. to free oneself, to get free (de, from); to get clear (de, of); to break loose, break away (de, from); to disengage oneself (de, from); to extricate oneself (de, from); **se d. de ses liens,** to burst one's bonds; **se d. des mains de qn,** to shake s.o. off; **se d. de l'étreinte de qn,** to free oneself, to shake oneself free, from s.o.'s embrace; **d'un effort violent il se dégagea,** he wrenched himself free; **le chien se dégagea de son collier,** the dog slipped its collar; **se d. d'une promesse, d'une affaire,** to break, back out of, a promise; to withdraw from an affair; **se d. de toutes attaches,** to cut oneself free of, break, all ties; **le ciel se dégage,** the sky is clearing; **la rue s'est dégagée rapidement,** the street cleared quickly; **sa toux se dégage,** his cough is easier. 2. (*of gas, vapour, odour, etc.*) to be given off (de, by); to escape, emanate (de, from); to arise, to come off; **il se dégage de l'oxygène,** oxygen is given off; **de la cuisine se dégage une odeur d'ail,** a smell of garlic drifts, floats, from the kitchen; **dans la cuisine se dégage une odeur d'ail,** the kitchen reeks of garlic. 3. to emerge, come out; **la lune se dégage des nuages,** the moon emerges from the clouds; **la silhouette du navire se dégagea du brouillard,** the ship loomed up out of the fog; **enfin la vérité se dégage,** at last the truth is coming out, is emerging; **cette nécessité se dégage de l'étude des faits,** this need becomes apparent from a study of the facts; **rumeur qui se dégage de la foule,** rumours, murmur, rising from the crowd; **l'impression se dégage que les négociations aboutiront,** everything points to a happy issue of the negotiations.

dégainage [degɛnaːʒ], *s.m. Atom.Ph:* decanning.

dégaine [degɛn], *s.f. F:* gait; *usu.* awkward gait; awkward bearing, awkward way of carrying oneself.

dégainement [degɛnmã], *s.m.* unsheathing, drawing (of sword).

dégainer [degɛne, -ene], *v.tr.* 1. to unsheathe, draw (sword); *abs.* to draw; *s.m. A:* **brave jusqu'au d.,** bold in words rather than in deeds. 2. *Atom.Ph:* to decan.

dégalonner [degalɔne], *v.tr.* to strip braid from (coat, etc.).

déganter [degãte], *v.tr.* to unglove (hand).

se déganter, to take off one's gloves.

dégarni [degarni], *a.* empty; depleted; stripped; **armoire dégarnie,** bare cupboard; **mes stocks sont un peu dégarnis,** my stocks are rather low; **arbre d.,** tree bare of leaves; **avoir les tempes dégarnies,** to be bald at the temples; **région dégarnie (d'herbes, de poils, de cheveux),** bald patch.

dégarnir [degarniːr], *v.tr.* to dismantle (room, etc.); to untrim (dress); to strip (bed, etc.); to unrig (ship); to unharness, unsaddle (horse); to thin out (tree); **d. un navire d'hommes,** to unman a ship; *Mil:* **d. une place, une position,** to withdraw the garrison from a fort, troops from a position; *Nau:* **d. le cabestan,** to unrig the capstan; **d. la chaîne (du cabestan),** to take the cable off the capstan; *Rail:* **d. la voie,** to clear away the ballast; *Chess:* **d. une pièce,** to uncover a piece; *Sp:* **d. ses buts,** to leave the goals unguarded, open.

se dégarnir. 1. to lose one's hair, to get bald; (*of tree*) to lose its leaves. 2. to empty, clear; **la salle se dégarnissait peu à peu,** the hall gradually emptied. 3. to run (oneself) short of ready money.

dégarnissage [degarnisaːʒ], *s.m.* 1. *Const:* raking out of the jointing (of wall). 2. *Rail:* clearing away of ballast. 3. stripping off. 4. *Mil:* **d. du front, des arrières,** thinning out of the front line, of the rear.

dégarnissement [degarnismã], *s.m.,* dismantling (of room, etc.); stripping (of bed); unharnessing, unsaddling (of horse); *Mil:* **d. d'une place,** withdrawal of the garrison from a fort; *Nau:* **d. du cabestan,** unrigging of the capstan.

dégasolinage [degazɔlinaːʒ], *s.m. Petroleum Ind:* recovery, extraction, of crude oil (from natural gas); **d. de l'huile,** oil stripping.

dégasoliner [degazɔline], *v.tr. Petroleum Ind:* to extract, recover, crude oil from (natural gas).

dégât [dega], *s.m.* 1. *usu. pl.* damage; **payer les dégâts,** to pay for the damage; **les gelées ont fait des dégâts dans les vignobles,** the frosts have made havoc of, played havoc in, the vineyards; **la guerre avait fait de grands dégâts dans tout le pays,** the war had ravaged, devastated, the whole country. 2. waste (of food, wine, etc.).

dégauchir [degoʃiːr], *v.tr.* to rough-plane, to surface, to try up, shoot (board, etc.); to trim, dress (wall, stone); to straighten, to true up, to take the winding out of (piece of machinery, etc.); *F:* **d. un jeune homme,** to knock the corners off a young man.

dégauchissage [degoʃisaːʒ], *s.m.,* **dégauchissement** [degoʃismã], *s.m.* rough-planing, surfacing, trying up (of board, etc.); trimming (of stone); straightening, truing up.

dégauchisseuse [degoʃisøːz], *s.f.* planing-machine (for surfacing); surfacer, surfacing machine.

dégausser [degose], *v.tr.* to degauss.

dégaussement [degosmã], *s.m.* degaussing.

dégazage [degazaːʒ], *s.m.* removal, extraction, of gas; degasification; degassing; *Atom.Ph:* outgassing, gas entrainment; *I.C.E:* de-aerating.

dégazer [degaze], *v.tr.* (*a*) to degas, degasify; to outgas (a liquid); (*b*) *Atom.Ph:* to getter (gas(es)); (*c*) *I.C.E:* to de-aerate.

dégazeur [degazœːr], *s.m.* (*a*) *Ind: etc:* gas remover, extractor; (*b*) *Elcs: Atom.Ph:* getter; **d. de lampes radio,** radio-tube getter; (*c*) *I.C.E:* de-aerator.

dégazolinage [degazɔlinaːʒ], *s.m.,* **dégazoliner** [degazɔline], *v.tr.* = DÉGASOLINAGE, DÉGASOLINER.

dégazonnage [degazɔnaːʒ], *s.m.,* **dégazonnement** [degazɔnmã], *s.m.,* turf-cutting, paring.

dégazonner [degazɔne], *v.tr. Agr:* to unturf; to cut the turf off, to pare (ground).

dégazonneuse [degazɔnøːz], *s.f.* turf-cutting machine.

dégel [deʒɛl], *s.m.* thaw; **le temps est, se met, au d.,** the thaw is setting in; the frost has broken; **le vent est au d.,** there is a softness in the wind; **d. diplomatique,** thaw (in relations between two countries); *Adm:* **barrière de d.,** barrier closing road to heavy traffic during a thaw.

dégelée [deʒle], *s.f. P:* shower of blows; **une d. de coups de bâton,** a good thrashing; a good hammering.

dégèlement [deʒɛlmã], *s.m.* thawing (of pipes, etc.).

dégeler [deʒle], *v.tr. & i., v.impers.* (**il dégèle**; **il dégèlera**) (*a*) to thaw; **il dégèle,** it is thawing; **d. un tuyau,** to thaw out a pipe; *F:* **je ne peux pas me d.,** I can't get warm; (*b*) *Fin:* to unfreeze (assets, etc.); (*c*) *F:* **d. qn,** to thaw s.o. out; **d. un auditoire,** to warm up an audience.

se dégeler, *F:* (*of pers.*) to thaw; **après le dîner il a commencé à se d.,** after dinner he began to thaw (out).

dégénérant [deʒenerã], *a.* degenerating.

dégénératif, -ive [deʒeneratif, -iːv], *a.* degenerative.

dégénération [deʒenerasjõ], *s.f.* degeneration, degeneracy.

dégénéré, -ée [deʒenere], *a. & s.* degenerate.

dégénérer [deʒenere], *v.i.* (**je dégénère,** n. **dégénérons**; **je dégénérerai**) to degenerate (de, from, en, into); **querelle qui à dégénéré en rixe,** quarrel that degenerated into a brawl; **rhume qui a dégénéré en catarrhe,** cold that developed into catarrh; **il croirait d. en acceptant,** he would think he was lowering himself, losing caste, if he accepted; *abs.* **cet écrivain a bien dégénéré,** this writer has gone down, deteriorated, a lot.

dégénérescence [deʒeneresãːs], *s.f. Med:* degeneration; degenerescence; decay; **d. graisseuse du cœur,** fatty degeneration of the heart; *Bot:* **maladies de d.,** degeneration diseases.

dégénérescent [deʒeneresã], *a. Med:* degenerating, degenerative.

dégermer [deʒɛrme], *v.tr. Brew: Agr:* to degerm.

dégingandage [deʒɛ̃gãdaːʒ], *s.m.,* **dégingandement** [deʒɛ̃gãdmã], *s.m. F:* awkwardness, ungainliness.

dégingandé, -ée [deʒɛ̃gãde], *a. & s. F:* gangling, awkward, ungainly, loosely built (person); **un grand (garçon) d.,** a gawky, loose-limbed, boy; **style d.,** loose, slovenly, style.

dégingander [deʒɛ̃gãde], *v.tr. F:* **d. sa taille, se d.,** to walk, sit, in an awkward, ungainly manner; to flop about.

dégiter [deʒite], *v.tr. Ven:* to dislodge, to unharbour (quarry).

dégivrage [deʒivraːʒ], *s.m. Av: Aut:* de-icing; *Dom.Ec:* de-frosting.

dégivrer [deʒivre], *v.tr. Aut:* to de-ice; *Dom.Ec:* to de-frost.

dégivreur [deʒivrœːr], *s.m. Aut: Av:* de-icer, de-icing device; *Dom.Ec:* de-froster; **d. automatique,** automatic defroster; **revêtement de d.,** de-icer boot, shoe.

déglabration [deglabrasjõ], *s.f.* falling, losing, of hair.

déglaçage [deglasaːʒ], *s.m.,* **déglacement** [deglasmã], *s.m.* 1. thawing, melting, of ice. 2. unglazing (of paper).

déglacer [deglase], *v.tr.* (**je déglaçai(s)**; n. **déglaçons**) 1. to thaw, to melt the ice on (pond, etc.); to remove the ice (from road); to defrost (refrigerating apparatus). 2. to unglaze (paper). 3. *Cu:* to make a sauce by adding liquid (water, wine, etc.) to residue left after cooking (roasting meat, etc.).

déglaciation [deglasjasjõ], *s.f. Geol:* deglaciation; retreating of glaciers.

déglinguer [deglɛ̃ge], *v.tr. F:* to dislocate; to put out of order; to bust up, to smash up.

déglobulisation [deglɔbylizasjõ], *s.f.* diminution of the number of red corpuscles.

dégluer [deglye], *v.tr.* to remove any sticky substance from (sth.); *esp.* **d. un oiseau,** (i) to remove the bird-lime from a bird; (ii) to release a bird.

se dégluer, *F:* (*a*) to extricate oneself (from a difficult position); (*b*) to free oneself from debt.

déglutination [deglytinasjõ], *s.f. Ling:* aphesis.

déglutiné [deglytine], *a. Ling:* aphetic.

déglutir [deglytiːr], *v.tr. Physiol:* to swallow.

déglutition [deglytisjõ], *s.f. Physiol:* deglutition, swallowing.

dégobillade [degɔbijad], *s.f.,* **dégobillage** [degɔbijaːʒ], *s.m. P:* (*a*) spewing, vomiting; (*b*) spew, vomit.

dégobiller [degɔbije], *P:* 1. *v.i.* to be sick, spew, puke, throw up. 2. *v.tr.* to bring up (one's food).

dégobillis [degɔbiji], *s.m. P:* spew, vomit.

dégoisement [degwazmã], *s.m. F:* pouring out (o excuses, of abuse, of gossip).

dégoiser [degwaze], *v.tr. P:* to spout (abuse, etc.); **d. un discours,** to spout a speech; *abs.* **en d.,** to rattle on, to talk away, to spout; **dégoise! speak up!**

dégommage [degɔmaːʒ], *s.m.* 1. (*a*) ungumming (of sth.); *I.C.E:* **robinet de d.,** pet-cock; (*b*) boiling off (of raw silk). 2. *F:* dismissal, firing, sacking.

dégommer [degɔme], *v.tr.* 1. (*a*) to ungum, unstick (sth.); (*b*) to boil off (raw silk); (*c*) to clean off the old oil from (machine). 2. *F:* (*a*) to dismiss (s.o. from office); *F:* to fire, sack (s.o.), to give (s.o.) the sack, his marching-orders, *U.S:* walking-orders; **se faire d.,** to get the sack; (*b*) to push out, oust (s.o.); (*c*) to beat; *F:* to lick (s.o.) (at a game).

dégonder [degõde], *v.tr.* to unhinge, unhang (door).

dégonflage [degõflaːʒ], *s.m.* (*a*) deflating, letting down (of balloon, etc.); (*b*) *P:* collapse, backing out.

dégonflard [degõflaːr], *s.m. P:* funk, *U.S:* yellow-belly.

dégonflé [degõfle]. 1. *a.* flat, soft (tyre); **j'ai un pneu d.,** one of my tyres is down. 2. *s.m. & f. P:* funk, *U.S:* yellowbelly.

dégonflement [degõfləmã], *s.m.* 1. (*a*) deflating, deflation (of balloon, tyre, etc.); (*b*) reducing, bringing down (of swelling). 2. (*a*) collapse (of tyre, etc.); (*b*) subsiding (of swelling). 3. *F:* debunking (of hero, etc.).

dégonfler [degõfle], *v.tr.* 1. to deflate, let the air out of (balloon, etc.); *F:* **se d. de ses soucis,** to pour out one's troubles; **elle dégonfla son cœur,** (i) she had her say out; (ii) she had her cry out. 2. to reduce, bring down (swelling). 3. *F:* to debunk (hero, etc.); to prick the bubble of . . .; **d. une fausse nouvelle,** to show up, expose, a false report.

se dégonfler. 1. (*a*) (*of tyre, balloon, etc.*) to collapse, to go flat; (*b*) (*of swelling*) to go down, to subside. 2. *P:* to get into a funk; to lose one's nerve; to wilt.

dégorgement [degɔrʒ(ə)mɑ̃], *s.m.* **1.** disgorging (of food, bile, etc.); *F:* **d. d'injures,** outpouring of abuse. **2.** freeing, clearing, unstopping (of obstructed passage); cutting of embrasure (through parapet). **3.** (*a*) purifying, scouring (of wool, leather); (*b*) *Winem:* extraction of the sediment-coated cork (of champagne bottle). **4.** outflow, discharging (of sewer, etc.); **d. de la foule,** outflow, pouring out, of the crowd. **5.** (*a*) discharge-pipe; (*b*) mouth (of sewer).

dégorgeoir [degɔrʒwa:r], *s.m.* **1.** outlet, outflow (of pond, etc.); spout (of pump). **2.** *Tls:* (*a*) *Metall:* (moulder's) venting-wire, pricker; (*b*) *Fish:* disgorger, gobstick; (*c*) *Metalw:* (i) fuller, creaser; (ii) round-nosed chipping chisel; (*d*) *Woodw:* mortice boring-bit; (*e*) *Sm.a: etc: A:* priming wire. **3.** *Nau:* **d. de voile,** slab-line.

dégorger [degɔrʒe], *v.* (**je dégorgeai(s); n. dégorgeons**) **1.** *v.tr.* (*a*) to disgorge; **le train dégorge ses voyageurs,** the train disgorges its passengers; **gouttière qui dégorge de l'eau,** gutter which pours out water; **faire d. un oiseau,** to make a bird disgorge (its prey); *F:* **faire d. qn,** to make s.o. disgorge (ill-gotten gains, etc.); (*b*) to free, clear, unstop (passage, pipe, groove, etc.); **machine à d.,** die-slotting machine; (*c*) to purify, scour, cleanse (wool, leather); *Winem:* to remove the sediment from (champagne); *Pisc:* **faire d. un poisson,** to purge a fish (by transferring it to clear water); **d. un poisson,** to remove the hook from a fish's gullet; (*d*) *Metalw:* to fuller (iron). **2.** *v.i. & pr.* (*a*) (*of sewer, pond, etc.*) to flow out, to discharge (**dans,** into); (*b*) (*of pipe, passage*) to become free, clear; (*c*) (*of abscess*) to discharge; (*d*) (*of gutter, stream*) to overflow.

dégot(t)er [degɔte], *v.tr. F:* **1.** to knock over, knock away (cork, opponent's marble) with one's quoit, marble. *Hence* **2.** *F:* (*a*) **d. qn,** to oust, supplant, s.o.; *F:* to knock s.o. off his perch; (*b*) **d. qn, qch.,** to get the better of, beat, lick, s.o., sth., *U.S:* to have the bulge on s.o. **3.** to get, find; **impossible de le d. nulle part,** I can't find him anywhere; **j'ai dégotté ça chez un antiquaire,** I unearthed it in an antique shop. **4.** *v.i. P:* **c'est fou, ce qu'il dégot(t)e!** he's got an air about him all right! **il dégot(t)e mal,** he doesn't look up to much, I don't care for the look of him.

dégoudronnage [degudrɔna:ʒ], *s.m.* removal of tar; extraction of tar (from gas).

dégoudronner [degudrɔne], *v.tr.* to remove the tar from (ship, etc.); to extract the tar from (gas).

dégoudronneur [degudrɔnœ:r], *s.m.* tar extractor.

dégoulinade [degulinad], *s.f. F:* drip (of paint, etc.).

dégoulinage [degulina:ʒ], *s.m. F:* trickling, dripping.

dégoulinant [degulinɑ̃], *a.* **un mur d.,** an oozing, a weeping, wall.

dégouliner [deguline], *v.i. F:* to trickle; **l'eau dégoulinait le long de l'escalier,** the water was trickling, dripping, down the stairs; **une grosse larme lui dégoulinait des cils,** a large tear was oozing off his eyelashes.

dégoupillage [degupija:ʒ], *s.m. Tchn:* removal of the pin.

dégoupiller [degupije], *v.tr.* to take the pin out of (lock-nut, hand-grenade, etc.).

dégourdi [degurdi], *a.* **1.** (*of pers.*) alive, wide-awake, sharp; *s.* **c'est une dégourdie,** she's lively; *F:* **il n'est pas d. pour deux sous,** (i) he's an old stick-in-the-mud; (ii) he's a bit slow in the uptake. **2.** (*of water*) tepid, luke-warm, with the chill off. **3.** *s.m. Cer:* (*a*) biscuit, bisque; (*b*) biscuiting; (*c*) biscuit-oven.

dégourdir [degurdi:r], *v.tr.* **1.** (*a*) to remove stiffness, numbness, from (the limbs); to revive (by warmth, movement, etc.); *F:* **je vais sortir pour me d. les jambes,** I'm going out to stretch my legs a bit; **d. les mains à qn,** to chafe s.o.'s hands; **d. qn,** to sharpen s.o.'s wits; *F:* **d. une recrue,** to lick a recruit into shape; **Paris l'a dégourdi,** Paris has smartened, brightened, polished, him up; *F:* Paris has taught him a thing or two; (*b*) **(faire) d. de l'eau,** to take the chill off water. **2.** *Cer:* **d. la porcelaine,** to give the biscuit baking to porcelain.

se dégourdir. 1. to restore the circulation; to lose one's numb, stiff, feeling. **2.** (*of water*) to grow warm. **3.** (*a*) to grow smarter, more alert; to brighten up; (*b*) *F:* to lose one's innocence.

dégourdissage [degurdisa:ʒ], *s.m. Fuel:* preheating (of fuel oil).

dégourdissement [degurdismɑ̃], *s.m.* **1.** removal of numbness (from limbs). **2.** taking the chill off (liquid).

dégourdisseur [degurdisœ:r], *s.m. Fuel:* preheater, preheating device.

dégoût [degu], *s.m.* **1.** disgust, distaste, loathing; **avoir, éprouver, du d. pour le lait,** to loathe milk; **elle a du d. pour les bananes,** she can't stand bananas. **2.** dislike, repugnance; **avoir du d. pour qch.,** to feel a dislike for sth., an aversion from sth.; **prendre qch. en d.,** to conceive a distaste for sth., to take a dislike to sth.; **il prit sa vie en d.,** he grew sick, weary, of the life he was leading; **cheval qui a du d.,** horse off his feed; *A:* **essuyer des dégoûts,** to meet with discouragement, humiliation.

dégoûtamment [degutamɑ̃], *adv.* disgustingly, in a disgusting manner.

dégoûtant [degutɑ̃], *a.* disgusting, loathsome, sickening, nauseating, nasty (sight, smell, etc.); **homme d. par sa laideur,** repulsively ugly man; **d'une saleté dégoûtante,** filthy; *F:* **c'est d. de travailler aussi mal,** it's sickening, shocking, to work so badly; **c'est un d. personnage,** *s.* **un d.,** he's a dirty old man, a disgusting character.

dégoûtation [degutasjɔ̃], *s.f. P:* disgusting person, thing; **tout ça c'est de la d.,** all that's disgusting.

dégoûté [degute], *a.* **1.** disgusted, wearied, sick at heart; **j'en suis d.,** I can't stomach it any longer, I'm sick of it; **d. de la viande,** off meat. **2.** *F:* fastidious, squeamish; *F:* **vous n'êtes pas d.!** (i) you're not squeamish! (ii) *Iron:* you don't want much! **elle a fait la dégoûtée,** she turned up her nose at it; **ne faites pas trop le d.,** don't be too squeamish.

dégoûter [degute], *v.tr.* to disgust; **d. qn de qch.,** to give s.o. a distaste for sth.; **d. qn de son propre travail,** to put s.o. off his own work; **d. qn de faire qch.,** to give s.o. a dislike for doing sth.; *F:* to put s.o. off doing sth.; **tout cela me dégoûte absolument,** I'm dead sick of it all, it makes me sick.

se dégoûter de qn, de qch., to grow disgusted with, sick of, s.o., sth., to take a dislike to s.o., sth.; **je suis dégoûté de la vie,** I am sick, tired, weary, of life; *s.a.* GOÛTER 3.

dégouttant [degutɑ̃], *a.* dripping; **parapluie d. d'eau,** dripping wet umbrella.

dégouttement [degutmɑ̃], *s.m.* dripping, drip (of rain, etc.).

dégoutter [degute], *v.i.* **1. d. de qch.,** to drip, trickle, to fall drop by drop, from sth.; **la pluie dégoutte de son chapeau,** the rain is dripping from his hat; *s.a.* CURÉ. **2. d. de qch.,** to be dripping with sth.; **les fleurs dégouttent de rosée,** the flowers are dripping with dew; **les toits dégouttent encore,** there is still water dripping from the roofs.

dégoutture [deguty:r], *s.f.* dripping liquid; **les dégouttures des arbres,** the drippings from the trees.

dégradant [degradɑ̃], *a.* degrading, lowering.

dégradateur [degradatœ:r], *s.m. Phot:* vignetter; **d. iris,** iris vignetting mask.

dégradation[1] [degradasjɔ̃], *s.f.* **1.** degradation (from office, etc.); **d. militaire,** (i) dismissal from the army; (ii) reduction to the ranks; **d. civique,** (*1939-45 war*) **d. nationale,** loss of civil rights. **2.** degradation, degraded existence; **tomber dans la d.,** to lose all self-respect. **3.** (*a*) defacement; **d. des monuments historiques,** defacement of historic monuments; (*b*) *O: Geog:* weathering (of rock); (*c*) *usu. pl.* damage; dilapidation, wear (of road, etc.); wear and tear (of furniture, etc.); **ce monument est dans un état de d. pitoyable,** this monument is in a state of dilapidation, in a shocking state of repair; **les dégradations sont à la charge du locataire sortant,** the outgoing tenant is liable for all dilapidations; **d. de la situation politique, économique,** deterioration of the political, economic, situation. **4.** *Ph:* dissipation, gradual loss (of energy).

dégradation[2], *s.f. Paint:* shading off, graduation (of colours, light); *Phot:* vignetting.

dégradé [degrade], *s.m. Paint: Phot:* (gradual) range of colours.

dégrader[1] [degrade], *v.tr.* **1.** (*a*) to degrade (s.o.) (from office, etc.); *Mil:* (i) to dismiss (s.o.) (from the service); (ii) to reduce (s.o.) to the ranks; (*b*) to lower; **vivre en meublé l'aurait dégradée,** to live in furnished apartments would have been a come-down in the world. **2.** to degrade, besot; **l'ivrognerie l'a dégradé,** he's gone to pieces through drinking. **3.** to deface, damage, dilapidate; *O:* (*of atmospheric agents*) to weather; (*of running water*) to scour, wash; *Geol:* to degrade (by erosion, etc.); *Ph:* to degrade (energy); **murs dégradés par le temps,** weather-beaten walls; **remparts dégradés,** ramparts in disrepair, fallen in ruins.

se dégrader. 1. to lower oneself, to lose caste. **2.** to sink into vice, to go to the dogs; to go to pieces. **3.** to dilapidate, to fall into disrepair; **la situation se dégrade,** the situation is worsening. **4.** *Ph:* (*of energy*) to dissipate, leak away.

dégrader[2], *v.tr.* to shade off, to graduate (colours, light); to wash out, lighten (colour); *Phot:* to vignette; **écran dégradé,** graduated light-filter; **écran de ciel dégradé,** gradual sky filter; **teintes dégradées,** shading off tints.

dégrafer [degrafe], *v.tr.* **1.** to unhook, unfasten, undo (dress, etc.); to unclasp (bracelet). **2. d. qn,** to unfasten, undo, s.o.'s dress.

se dégrafer. 1. (*of garment, etc.*) to come unhooked, unfastened, undone; (*of buckle*) to come unclasped. **2.** (*of pers.*) to unhook, undo, one's dress.

dégrafeuse [degrafø:z], *s.f.* staple remover.

dégraissage [degrɛsa:ʒ], *s.m.* **1.** skimming (of soup, etc.). **2.** dry-cleaning (of clothes, etc.); degreasing (of leather); scouring (of wool).

dégraissant [degrɛsɑ̃], *a. & s.m.* **1.** *a.* which removes grease, grease-removing. **2.** *s.m.* grease remover, extractor; *Tex:* scour.

dégraissement [degrɛsmɑ̃], *s.m.* = DÉGRAISSAGE.

dégraisse-peigne [degrɛspɛɲ], *s.m.* comb-cleaner; *pl. dégraisse-peignes.*

dégraisser [degrɛse], *v.tr.* **1.** (*a*) to take the fat from (carcass of animal, etc.); **d. la soupe,** to skim the fat off the soup; **d. la terre,** to impoverish the soil; (*b*) **se d. les cheveux,** to cleanse one's hair of oil; to shampoo one's hair; *Winem:* **d. le vin,** to treat wine for ropiness. **2.** to dry-clean (clothes); to degrease (leather); *Leath:* to kill (a skin before tanning); to scour (wool). **3.** to bevel off, trim (corner, edge). **4.** *A:* to impoverish, drain, bleed (province).

dégraisseur, -euse [degrɛsœ:r, -ø:z], *s.* **1.** dry-cleaner (of clothes, etc.); scourer (of wool). **2.** *s.m.* (*a*) *Ind:* grease remover; (*b*) *Mch:* **d. de vapeur,** oil separator. **3.** *s.f.* **dégraisseuse;** (*a*) *Tex:* scouring machine; (*b*) *Leath:* grease extractor.

dégraissoir [degrɛswa:r], *s.m. Tex:* wringing machine (for scouring wool).

dégramer [degrame], *v.tr. Agr:* to remove the couch-grass from (a newly-ploughed field in order to burn it).

dégras [degrɑ], *s.m. Leath:* degras, dubbin(g).

dégrat [degra], *s.m. Nau:* (*of fishing vessel*) **être en d.,** to set out for the cod fisheries.

dégraveler [degravle], **dégraver** [degrave], *v.tr.* to clear sand, gravel, from (sth.).

dégravoiement [degravwamɑ̃], *s.m.* (*a*) undermining (of foundations, etc.) (by action of running water); (*b*) washing away of gravel.

dégravoyer [degravwaje], *v.tr.* (**il dégravoie; il dégravoyait; il dégravoiera**) (*of running water*) to undermine, lay bare, (foundations, etc.) by erosion; to wash away the gravel from (river bed).

degré [dəgre], *s.m.* **1.** (*a*) step (of stair, ladder); degree (of musical scale); **les degrés de l'autel,** the altar steps; (*b*) *Ph: Mth: etc:* degree (of circle, latitude, heat); **angle de 30 degrés,** angle of 30 degrees; **le thermomètre marque quinze degrés,** the thermometer registers, stands at, fifteen degrees; **dix degrés au-dessous de zéro,** ten degrees below zero; ten degrees of frost; (*c*) **d. alcoolique d'un spiritueux,** alcoholic strength of a spirit. **2.** degree (of relationship, comparison, etc.); **cousins au troisième d.,** cousins three times removed; **d. de parenté ou d'alliance,** degree of consanguinity or affinity; **mariage entre parents ou alliés au d. prohibé,** marriage within the prohibited degrees; **le plus haut d. de perfection,** the highest degree, the acme, of perfection; **heureux au suprême d.,** supremely happy; **il est généreux au plus haut d., au suprême d.,** he is generous to a degree; **le dernier d. de (la) honte,** the lowest depths of shame; *Med:* **brûlure au troisième d.,** third-degree burn; **être tuberculeux au dernier d.,** to be in the last stage of tuberculosis; **passer par tous les d.,** to pass through all the stages; **la demande devra passer par tous les degrés hiérarchiques,** the request will have to pass through the regular channels; **un tel d. d'insolence,** such a pitch of insolence; **par degrés,** by degrees, gradually; *Mth:* **équation du second d.,** quadratic equation, equation of the second degree; **équation du troisième d.,** cubic equation; *Mec:* **d. de liberté,** degree of freedom; *Sch:* **enseignement du second d.,** secondary education; *Sch: A:* **d. de docteur,** doctor's degree.

dégréage [degrea:ʒ], *s.m.*, **dégréement** [degremɑ̃], *s.m. Nau:* unrigging, stripping (of mast, ship, etc.); taking down, dismantling (of crane, etc.).

dégréer [degree], *v.tr. Nau:* **1.** to unrig, strip (mast, ship, etc.); to dismantle, take down (crane). **2. d. une vergue,** to send down a yard; **d. un hamac,** to unsling a hammock.

dégressif, -ive [degresif, -i:v], *a.* degressive, decreasing, graded (tax, etc.); **impôt d.,** degressive taxation; **tarif d.,** decreasing tariff, sliding-scale tariff.

dégression [degresjɔ̃], *s.f.* degression.

dégressivité [degresivite], *s.f. Adm:* (system of) decreasing scale (of taxation).

dégrèvement [degrɛvmɑ̃], *s.m.* **1.** *Adm:* reduction, abatement (of tax); **d. pour charges de famille, pour entretien d'immeubles,** allowance for dependent relatives, for repairs. **2.** relief from taxation, derating (of industry). **3.** disencumbering (of an estate).

dégrever [degrəve], *v.tr.* **(je dégrève, n. dégrevons; je dégrèverai) 1.** to reduce, diminish (tax, duty). **2.** to relieve (s.o.) of a tax; to diminish (s.o.'s) taxes; to derate (industry); to reduce the assessment on (building). **3.** to disencumber (estate); to clear off the mortgage on (an estate).

dégringolade [degrɛ̃gɔlad], *s.f. F:* tumble; **faire une d.,** to come a cropper; **il y eut un bruit de d.,** we heard someone come clattering down; **quelle d. après sa dernière situation!** what a come-down after his last job! **d. du franc, d'un financier,** collapse of the franc, downfall of a financier.

dégringolée [degrɛ̃gɔle], *s.f. F:* clutter (of people, animals, thgs).

dégringoler [degrɛ̃gɔle], *v.tr. & i. F:* **1.** to tumble down; to come a cropper; to come rushing, clattering, down; **il a dégringolé l'escalier,** he came rushing, tearing, down the stairs; **il a dégringolé dans l'escalier,** he fell down the stairs, he came a cropper on the stairs. **2.** to shoot down (bird, etc.); **d. l'administration,** to bring about the fall of the government, to bring the government toppling down; **maison de commerce qui dégringole,** firm that is losing business rapidly, that is going to pieces.

dégripper [degripe], *v.tr. Mec.E:* to release (stuck part).

dégrisement [degrizmɑ̃], *s.m.* *(a)* sobering up; *(b)* disillusionment; cooling down (from passionate love, etc.).

dégriser [degrize], *v.tr.* *(a)* to sober (s.o.) up; *(b)* to disillusion (s.o.); to bring (s.o.) to his senses.

se dégriser *(a)* to sober up, to get sober; *(b)* to come to one's senses.

dégrossage [degrosa:ʒ], *s.m. Metall:* drawing out (of silver and gold).

dégrosser [degrose], *v.tr. Metall:* to draw down (wire).

dégrossi [degrosi], *a.* licked into shape; **recrues mal dégrossies,** raw recruits.

dégrossir [degrosi:r], *v.tr.* to give a rough, preliminary, dressing to (sth.); to trim, to rough down (timber); to rough-hew, scabble (stone); to rough-plane (piece of wood); to bloom (mass of iron); to rough out (design, plan); **outil, meule, à d.,** roughing tool, wheel; **tour à d.,** roughing-down lathe; *Artil:* **d. les réglages,** to make an approximation to the range; *F:* **d. qn,** to polish s.o. up, to knock the corners off s.o., to lick s.o. into shape.

se dégrossir, *F:* *(of pers.)* to lose one's uncouth ways, to acquire polish, to get one's corners knocked off.

dégrossissage [degrosisa:ʒ], *s.m.,* **dégrossissement** [degrosismɑ̃], *s.m.* **1.** rough preliminary operation; roughing; scabbling (of stone); rough-planing, trimming (of piece of wood); roughing out, mapping out (of design); *Metall:* drawing down (of silver, gold); **d. du fer,** blooming; **d. à la meule,** rough grinding; **passe de d.,** roughing pass, cut. **2.** *F:* licking (of s.o.) into shape.

dégrossisseur [degrosisœ:r], *s.m. Metall:* roughing roll, muck-roll; **train, équipage, d.,** roughing mill.

dégrouiller (se) [sədegruje], *v.pr. P:* to get a move on, to buck up.

dégroupement [degrupmɑ̃], *s.m.* dispersal.

dégrouper [degrupe], *v.tr.* to disperse.

déguenillé [degənije], *a.* ragged, tattered; **être tout d.,** to be all in rags, in tatters; *s.* **un petit d.,** a little ragamuffin.

déguerpir [degɛrpi:r]. **1.** *v.tr. Jur: A:* to give up, abandon (property, inheritance, etc.). **2.** *v.i.* *(a)* *(of tenant)* to move out; *F:* to clear out (under compulsion); *(b)* to clear out, decamp; **d. au plus vite,** to bolt; *F:* to skedaddle; **faire d. un locataire,** to evict a tenant; **faire d. un renard,** to rout out a fox; **faire d. l'ennemi,** to drive the enemy out of his positions; *F:* **faire d. qn,** to send s.o. packing.

déguerpissement [degɛrpismɑ̃], *s.m.* **1.** *Jur: A:* giving up, abandonment (of property, inheritance, to creditors or rightful owners). **2.** *F:* decamping, clearing out, skedaddling.

dégueulade [degølad, -œ-], *s.f.* vomit, spew.

dégueulasse [degølas, -œ-], *a. & s.m. & f. P:* disgusting, repulsive (person).

dégueulée [degøle, -œ-], *s.f. P:* *(a)* vomit, spew; *(b)* **d. d'injures,** volley of abuse.

dégueuler [degøle, -œ-], *P:* **1.** *v.i.* to spew, to puke, to cat. **2.** *v.tr.* **d. des injures contre qn,** to pour forth, let fly, a torrent of abuse against s.o.

déguignonner [degiɲɔne], *v.tr. F:* to turn (s.o.'s) luck; to bring better luck to (s.o.).

déguinder [degɛ̃de], *v.tr.* to unrack, unlash (load, etc.).

déguisable [degizabl̩], *a.* easily disguised.

déguisé, -ée [degize]. **1.** *a.* disguised, in disguise; **bal d.,** masked ball; fancy-dress ball; **d. en brigand,** disguised, masquerading, got up, as a brigand; **hostilité à peine déguisée,** hardly veiled hostility. **2.** *s.* masquerader.

déguisement [degizmɑ̃], *s.m.* **1.** *(a)* disguise, get-up, make-up; *(b)* fancy dress. **2.** dissimulation, concealment (of feelings, etc.); **sans d.,** plainly, openly.

déguiser [degize], *v.tr.* **1.** to disguise; **d. un enfant en clown,** to dress up a child as a clown; **d. sa voix, son écriture,** to disguise one's voice, one's writing. **2.** to disguise, conceal (thoughts, feelings, truth, etc.); **parler sans rien d.,** to speak plainly, openly; **d. sa pensée,** to dissemble, to hide one's feelings; **d. son jeu,** to conceal one's intentions, to act in an underhand manner.

se déguiser. 1. *(a)* to disguise oneself, to make up; **se d. en moine,** to get oneself up as a monk; *(b)* to put on fancy dress. **2.** to dissemble, act a part, wear a mask.

dégustateur, -trice [degystatœ:r, -tris], *s.* taster (of wines, tea, etc.).

dégustation [degystasjɔ̃], *s.f.* **1.** *Com:* tasting (of wines, tea, etc.); **cabinet de d.,** tasting-room; **d. gratuite du vin du pays,** free tasting of the local wine; **prendre une d. d'huîtres,** to sample the oysters, to have a (small) dish of oysters. **2. verre à d.,** balloon glass, snifter, *U.S:* inhaler.

déguster [degyste], *v.tr.* **1.** to taste, sample (tea, wine, etc.); **d. son vin,** to sip one's wine. **2.** to eat, drink, with relish; **d. un bon vin,** to savour, appreciate, a good wine; **il dégustait sa liberté comme un plat fin,** he was enjoying, savouring, his freedom like a finely-cooked dish; **d. un conte de Voltaire,** to appreciate one of Voltaire's stories. **3.** *P:* **d. des coups,** to get a good hiding; **qu'est-ce qu'on a dégusté!** didn't we catch it!

déhalage [deala:ʒ], *s.m. Nau:* hauling, shifting, warping (of ship); moving (of ship by her own power); **bouée de d.,** hauling buoy; **treuil de d.,** warping winch.

déhaler [deale], *Nau:* *(a)* *v.tr.* to warp out, haul out, heave off (ship); **d. un navire échoué,** to shift a stranded ship; *(b)* *v.i.* *(of ship)* to move.

se déhaler. 1. *Nau:* to haul off, to claw off. **2.** to extricate oneself (from an affair).

déhâler [deɑle], *v.tr.* to clear, whiten (the complexion); **pommade pour d. le teint,** cream for removing sunburn.

déhanché [deɑ̃ʃe], *a.* *(a)* hip-shot (horse, etc.); *(b)* *(of pers.)* who sways the hips when walking.

déhanchement [deɑ̃ʃmɑ̃], *s.m.* **1.** *Med: Vet:* dislocation of the hip. **2. d. en marchant,** swaying walk.

déhancher [deɑ̃ʃe], *v.tr.* to dislocate (s.o.'s, horse's) hip.

se déhancher, *F:* to sway, wiggle, one's hips when walking.

déharnachement [dearnaʃmɑ̃], *s.m.* *(a)* unsaddling; *(b)* unharnessing (of horse).

déharnacher [dearnaʃe], *v.tr.* *(a)* to unsaddle; *(b)* to unharness.

déhiscence [deis(s)ɑ̃:s], *s.f. Bot:* dehiscence.

déhiscent [deis(s)ɑ̃], *a. Bot:* dehiscent.

déhonté [deɔ̃te], *a. A:* shameless.

dehors [dəɔ:r]. **1.** *adv.* *(a)* out, outside, without; **coucher, dîner, d.,** to sleep, dine, (i) out of doors, in the open, (ii) away from home; **je dîne d. ce soir,** I am dining out this evening; **mettre qn d.,** (i) to put, turn, s.o. out (of doors); (ii) *F:* to give s.o. the sack; **mettez-le d.!** put him out! out with him! **ne pas se pencher d.!** do not lean out of the window! *Nau:* **mettre d. une voile,** to spread, set, a sail; **toutes voiles d.,** with every sail set, with every stitch of canvas; *s.a.* DEDANS 1; *(b)* *Nau:* **le brick est d.,** the brig is in the offing; *(c)* *Sp: Cr:* out; *Box:* **compter qn d.,** to count s.o. out; *(d)* *adv.phr.* **de d.,** from outside; **en d.,** (on the) outside; **tourner les pieds en d.,** to turn one's toes out; **la fenêtre s'ouvre (de dedans) en d.,** the window opens outwards, to the outside; *Mus:* **chaque attaque assez en d.,** each entry well emphasized; *prep.phr.* **en d. de la maison,** outside the house; **en d. de lui, personne ne m'aime,** apart from him, nobody loves me; **en d. de mes pouvoirs,** not within my competence; **en d. du sujet,** outside, beside, the question; **agir en d. de ses associés,** to act without the assent, without the co-operation, of one's partners; **cela s'est fait en d. de moi,** it was done (i) without my knowledge; (ii) without my participation; I had no part in it; **se tenir en d. d'une cause,** to stand aloof from a cause; **événements en d. de notre action,** events beyond our control; **se sentir en d. du mouvement,** to feel out of it; **en d. de cette question . . .,** in addition to this question . . ., apart from this question . . .; **occupation en d. de mon bureau,** occupation outside my office work; **passer par d. la ville,** to skirt the town. **2.** *s.m.* *(a)* outside, exterior (of a house, etc.); **affaires du d.,** foreign, external, affairs; **agir du d.,** to act from outside (a party, etc.); *Equit:* **rêne, jambe, du d.,** off rein, off leg; *adv.phr.* **au d.,** on the outside; **mettre une embarcation au d.,** to get out a boat; **capitaux placés au d.,** capital invested abroad; *prep.phr.* **au d. de ce pays,** outside, beyond, this country; *(b)* *usu. in pl.* (outward) appearance; **maison aux d. imposants,** house with an imposing exterior; **personne aux d. aimables,** prepossessing person; **sous les d. de la religion,** under the cloak of religion; **garder, sauver, les d.,** to keep up, to save, appearances; *(c)* *pl. Fort:* outworks; *(d)* *Skating:* outside edge. **3.** *prep. A:* **dedans et d. le royaume,** within and without the kingdom.

déhouillage [deuja:ʒ], *s.m. Min:* working of coal seam; extraction of coal.

déhouiller [deuje], *v.tr.* to extract (coal); *abs.* to work a coal seam.

déhourdage [deurda:ʒ], *s.m.* **1.** *Const:* removing of deafening, of pugging. **2.** *Min:* **d. d'une cheminée,** loosening, unkeying, of a clogged chute.

déhourder [deurde], *v.tr.* **1.** *Const:* to remove the deafening, the pugging, of (wall, etc.). **2.** *Min:* **d. une cheminée,** to loosen, unkey, a clogged chute.

déhydracétique [deidrasetik], *a. Ch:* dehydr(o)-acetic.

déicide[1] [deisid], *s.m.* deicide, *esp.* the crucifixion of Christ.

déicide[2]. **1.** *s.m. & f.* *(pers.)* deicide. **2.** *a.* deicidal.

déictique [deiktik], *a. Ling:* deictic.

déification [deifikasjɔ̃], *s.f.* deification.

déifier [deifje], *v.tr.* *(p.d. & pr.sub.* **n. déifiions, v. déifiiez) 1.** to deify; **d. l'argent,** to make a god of money. **2.** *A:* **d. qn,** to make s.o. as happy as a god.

déiforme [deifɔrm], *a.* deiform.

déionisation [deiɔnizasjɔ̃], *s.f. El:* deionization.

déisme [deism], *s.m.* deism.

déiste [deist]. **1.** *s.m. & f.* deist. **2.** *a.* deistic(al).

déité [deite], *s.f.* deity.

déjà [deʒa], *adv.* **1.** already; **le soleil se lève d.,** the sun is rising already; **d. le soleil se levait,** even then the sun was rising; **il est d. loin,** by this time he is far away; **d. en 1900,** as far back, as early, as 1900. **2.** before, previously; **je vous ai d. vu,** I have seen you before; **ce devrait être d. fait,** it ought to have been done before now. **3.** yet; **faut-il que vous partiez d.?** need you go yet? **ça fait deux ans d.,** it's two years ago now; *(intensifying)* **vous avez d. trop d'amis,** you have too many friends as it is; **ça n'est d. pas si mal,** it's not too bad at all; **qu'est-ce que vous faites d.?** what did you say your job was?

déjaler [deʒale], *v.tr. Nau:* to unstock; take the stock off (anchor).

Déjanire [deʒani:r], *Pr.n.f. Gr.Myth:* Deianira.

déjantage [deʒɑ̃ta:ʒ], *s.m. Aut:* taking off (of tyre).

déjanter [deʒɑ̃te], *v.tr. Aut:* to remove (tyre) from rim.

déjauger [deʒoʒe], *v.i.* **(il déjaugeait) 1.** *Nau:* *(of ship)* to sew (up), sue (up). **2.** *Av:* **vitesse au d.,** hump speed (of seaplane).

se déjauger, *(of floats of seaplane)* to lift (off the water).

déjection [deʒɛksjɔ̃], *s.f.* **1.** *Med:* dejection, evacuation (of the bowels). **2.** *pl.* dejecta (of body, of volcano); **déjections de lombric,** earth-worm casts.

déjeté [deʒte, deʃte], *a.* (*of body, shape*) crooked, twisted, lopsided; (*of wood*) warped; (*of metal*) buckled; *Geol:* asymmetric (fold); **elle a la taille déjetée,** she has one shoulder higher than the other; **épaules déjetées,** shoulders off the straight.

déjeter [deʒte, deʃte], *v.tr.* (**il déjette; il déjettera**) to make (shape, etc.) lopsided; to warp (wood); to buckle (metal).

se déjeter, to become lopsided; (*of wood*) to warp; (*of metal*) to buckle; (*of wall, etc.*) to bulge.

déjettement [deʒɛtmɑ̃], *s.m.* crookedness, lopsidedness; warping (of wood); buckling (of metal); curvature (of the spine).

déjeuner [deʒœne, -øne]. I. *v.i.* (*a*) to (have) breakfast; **je n'avais pas encore déjeuné,** I had not yet had my breakfast, any breakfast; **d. d'un morceau de pain,** to breakfast off a piece of bread, to break one's fast with a piece of bread; **d. avec du café au lait,** to have white coffee for breakfast; (*b*) to lunch; **nous déjeunons à midi,** we have lunch at mid-day, twelve o'clock; **faire bien déjeuner qn,** to lunch s.o. well, to give s.o. a good lunch; **on me pria de rester à d.,** I was asked to stay to lunch.

II. **déjeuner,** *s.m.* **1.** (*a*) (**petit**) **d.,** breakfast; **d. à la fourchette,** English breakfast; (*b*) luncheon, lunch; **d. sur l'herbe,** picnic lunch; **c'est un d. de soleil,** (i) it's a material that fades rapidly; (ii) it's only a passing phase. **2.** (*a*) breakfast set, service; (*b*) (large) breakfast cup and saucer.

déjeuneur, -euse [deʒœnœːr, -øːz], *s.* (*a*) breakfaster; (*b*) luncher; **il y avait trente déjeuneurs,** there were thirty (i) to breakfast, (ii) to lunch.

déjoindre [deʒwɛ̃ːdr], *v.tr.* (*conj. like* JOINDRE) to sever, disjoint.

déjouer [deʒwe]. **1.** *v.i.* (*a*) (*in chess, draughts, etc.*) to take back a move; (*b*) to be off one's game. **2.** *v.tr.* to thwart, baffle, foil, baulk (s.o.); to frustrate (plot, design); **d. la vigilance de ses créanciers,** to evade the vigilance of, to outwit, one's creditors; **d. les plans de qn,** to spoil s.o.'s game; *Nau:* **d. une manœuvre,** to upset a manœuvre.

déjuc [deʒy], *s.m.* cock crow.

déjucher [deʒyʃe]. **1.** *v.i.* (*of fowls*) to come off the roost; *F:* (*of pers.*) to get out of bed. **2.** *v.tr.* to unroost (fowls); *F:* **d. qn, faire d. qn,** to make s.o. come down from his perch.

déjuger (se) [sədeʒyʒe], *v.pr.* (*conj. like* JUGER) to reverse one's judgment, one's decision, etc.

déjuguer [deʒyge], *v.tr.* to unyoke (oxen, etc.).

de jure [deʒyre], *Lt.adv.phr. Jur:* de jure.

Dekkan [dekɑ̃], *Pr.n.m. Geog:* Deccan.

delà [dəla], beyond. **1.** *prep. A. & Lit:* **d. les monts,** beyond the mountains; *prep.phr.* **par-d. les mers,** beyond the seas; **par-d. l'Atlantique,** on the other side of the Atlantic; **par-d. trois siècles,** three centuries back; **de d. les mers,** from beyond the seas. **2.** *adv.* **deçà et d.,** here and there; on all sides; *adv.phr:* **au-d.,** beyond; **j'ai ce qu'il me faut et au-d.,** I have what I need and to spare; **il m'a satisfait et au-d.,** he has more than satisfied me; **voyageurs à destination d'Orléans et au-d.,** passengers for Orleans and stations beyond; **en d.,** further away; *s.m.* **l'au-d.,** the beyond; the next world; **il entendit une voix qui l'appelait de l'au-delà,** he heard a voice calling from beyond the grave; *prep.phr.* **au-d. de,** beyond, on the other side of; **au-d. des mers,** beyond the seas; **au-d. de la frontière,** over the border; **c'est aller au-d. de mes désirs,** it is more than I asked for; **n'allez pas au-d. de dix francs,** don't go above ten francs; **il est allé au-d. de ses promesses,** he was better than his word.

délabialisation [delabjalizasjɔ̃], *s.f. Ling:* delabialization.

délabré [delɑbre], *a.* dilapidated, out of repair; broken-down (furniture); **vieille maison délabrée,** ramshackle, tumble-down, old house; **santé délabrée,** impaired health; **sa santé est délabrée,** his health has broken down.

délabrement [delɑbrəmɑ̃], *s.m.* dilapidated, broken-down, condition, dilapidation, disrepair, decay (of house, garment, etc.); ruin, wreck (of one's fortune); **le d. de sa santé,** his impaired health.

délabrer [delɑbre], *v.tr.* to dilapidate, wreck, ruin (house, garment, fortune); to impair (health, digestion).

se délabrer, (*of house, etc.*) to fall to pieces, into decay; to go to rack and ruin; (*of health*) to become impaired.

délacer [delase], *v.tr.* (**je délaçai(s); n. délaçons**) to unlace; to loosen (corset); to undo (shoes).

se délacer, to come unlaced, undone.

delafossite [dəlafɔsit], *s.f. Miner:* delafossite.

délai [delɛ], *s.m.* **1.** delay; **agir sans d.,** to act without delay, without loss of time, straight away. **2.** respite, time allowed (for completion of a job, etc.); time lag; **à l'expiration du délai de six mois,** at the end of the six months allowed; **je ne peux pas le faire à aussi court d.,** I cannot do it at so short notice; **dans le plus bref, le plus court, d., dans les meilleurs délais,** in the shortest possible time, as soon as possible; **dans les délais prescrits, réglementaires, voulus,** within the prescribed, required, time; **action à bref d.,** action in the near future; *Com:* **d. de paiement,** term of payment; **d. de livraison,** delivery time; **d. de livraison un mois,** delivery within a month; **livrable dans un d. de trois jours,** can be delivered at three days' notice, within three days; **dans un d. de deux heures,** within two hours; *Jur:* **d. de grâce,** respite of debt; days of grace; **d. de congé, de préavis,** term of notice (to employee, to employer); **d. de protection** (**littéraire**), term, duration of copyright; **obtenir un d.,** to get an extension of time, a respite; **d. de révision,** overhaul period; *Mil:* **d. de route,** travelling time; *Ind:* **d. de fabrication,** processing time; **d. de livraison, d. de suite** (**à donner à un projet pour qu'il puisse être réalisé**), lead time; *Mec.E:* **d. de déclenchement,** releasing time.

délai-congé [delɛkɔ̃ʒe], *s.m. Jur:* term of notice (to employee or employer); *pl. délais-congés.*

délainage [delɛnaːʒ], *s.m.,* fellmongering (of sheepskins), dewooling.

délainer [delɛne], *v.tr.* to remove the wool from, to dewool (sheepskins).

délaissé [delese]. **1.** *a.* forsaken; **femme délaissée,** grass-widow, neglected wife; **maîtresse délaissée,** cast-off mistress; **orphelin délaissé,** friendless orphan; *s.* **pauvres délaissés,** poor forlorn creatures. **2.** *s.m. Ph.Geog:* cut-off meander; ox-bow (lake); cut-off.

délaissement [delɛsmɑ̃], *s.m.* **1.** desertion, abandonment, neglect (of wife, children, etc.); **être dans un grand d.,** to be completely friendless, to have lost touch with everyone. **2.** *Jur:* relinquishment, renunciation (of right, etc.); abandonment (of ship to insurer); **d. par hypothèque,** abandonment of mortgaged property.

délaisser [delese], *v.tr.* **1.** to forsake, desert, abandon (s.o.). **2.** *Jur:* to relinquish, forgo (right, succession, etc.); to abandon (ship to insurer, etc.); **d. des poursuites,** to abandon a prosecution.

délaitage [delɛtaːʒ], *s.m.,* **délaitement** [delɛtmɑ̃], *s.m. Husb:* working, drying (of butter).

délaiter [delɛte], *v.tr. Husb:* to work, dry (butter).

délaiteuse [delɛtøːz], *s.f. Husb:* butter-drying machine.

délardement [delardəmɑ̃], *s.m.* **1.** removal of the fat (of pig). **2.** *Cu:* unlarding (of meat). **3.** (*a*) thinning down, paring (of wood); (*b*) chamfering, bevelling.

délarder [delarde], *v.tr.* **1.** to remove the fat (of pig). **2.** *Cu:* to unlard (meat). **3.** (*a*) to thin down, pare (wood); (*b*) to chamfer, bevel (an edge); (*c*) to splay (opening).

délassant [delɑsɑ̃], *a.* refreshing (bath, rest, etc.); **lectures délassantes,** light reading.

délassement [delɑsmɑ̃], *s.m.* **1.** rest, relaxation; **prendre du d.,** to take a rest, to relax; **la pêche est son seul d.,** fishing is his only relaxation, his only diversion, pastime; **toute cette région est un lieu de d.,** all this region is a holiday ground. **2.** *Mus:* trifle, light piece, entertainment.

délasser [delɑse], *v.tr.* to rest, refresh (the body, etc.); **ce travail me délasse l'esprit,** this work is a relaxation for my mind.

se délasser, to take some rest, some relaxation; **il se délasse à lire,** he finds relaxation in reading.

délateur, -trice [delatœːr, -tris], *s.* **1.** *usu. Pej:* informer, spy. **2.** *s.m. Tchn:* detector (of lock).

délation [delasjɔ̃], *s.f. usu. Pej:* denunciation (of crime, *usu.* in self-interest); informing, denouncement.

délatter [delate], *v.tr.* to take the laths off, remove the laths from (roof, ceiling, etc.).

délavage [delavaːʒ], *s.m.* washing out (of colours, etc.).

délavé [delave], *a.* washed out (colour); colourless, pale (complexion); weak, diluted (wine, beer).

délaver [delave], *v.tr.* (*a*) to make faint in colour; to dilute, to weaken; **d. une aquarelle,** to tone down a water colour; (*b*) **les grandes pluies délavent les terres,** heavy rainfall soaks the earth, the soil.

délayage [delejaːʒ], **délayement** [delemɑ̃], *s.m.* (*a*) thinning (out) (of colour, etc., with liquid); mixing (of flour, etc.) (**dans,** with); (*b*) **toute cette page n'est que du d.,** this page is nothing but padding, is mere verbosity, mere verbiage.

délayé [deleje], *a.* (*a*) thin, watery; **sol d.,** sodden ground; (*b*) prolix, wordy, verbose (style).

délayer [deleje], *v.tr.* (**je délaie, je délaye, n. délayons; je délaierai, je délayerai**) (*a*) to add water to (powdered material, etc.); to thin (paint, etc.) (**dans,** with); to water (liquid); **d. de la farine dans de l'eau, dans du lait,** to mix flour with water, with milk; (*b*) **d. un discours,** to spin out, draw out, a speech; to pad a speech; **d. sa pensée,** to lose oneself in verbosity.

Delco [dɛlko], *s.m. Aut: R.t.m:* distributor (*made by the Dayton Engineering Laboratory Company*).

déléatur [deleatyːr], *s.m.inv. Typ:* delete (mark); dele.

délébile [delebil], *a.* delible; **encre d.,** washable ink.

délectable [delɛktabl], *a.* delectable; delicious, delightful (wine, food, etc.); pleasant (spot).

délectablement [delɛktabləmɑ̃], *adv.* delectably, deliciously, delightfully.

délectation [delɛktasjɔ̃], *s.f.* delectation, delight, enjoyment; **manger avec d.,** to eat with relish.

délecter [delɛkte], *v.tr. A:* to delight (the senses, the heart).

se délecter de qch., à qch., à faire qch., to take delight, great pleasure, in sth., in doing sth.; to revel in sth., in doing sth.; to thoroughly enjoy doing sth.

délégant, -ante [delegɑ̃, -ɑ̃ːt], *s. Jur:* delegant, delegator.

délégataire [delegatɛːr], *s. Jur:* delegatee.

délégateur, -trice [delegatœːr, -tris], *s. Jur:* delegant, delegator.

délégation [delegasjɔ̃], *s.f.* **1.** (*a*) delegation (of authority); **agir en vertu d'une d., par d.,** to act vicariously, on the authority of s.o.; **être chargé par d. d'une inspection,** to act as deputy inspector; **d. judiciaire,** delegation of powers to the *commissaire de police* by the Public Prosecutor's Department; **commissaire aux délégations judiciaires,** *commissaire de police* holding delegated powers; (*b*) delegation, deputing (of representatives); (*c*) *Jur:* assignment, transfer (of debt); *Mil: Navy:* **d. de solde,** assignment, allotment, of pay (to relatives at home, etc.); (*d*) acting-order. **2.** *Coll.* delegation, body of delegates, commission.

délégatoire [delegatwaːr], *a.* delegatory (power, authority).

délégué, -ée [delege], *a. & s.* (*a*) delegate (at meeting, etc.); **d. spécial,** special representative; (*b*) deputy (professor, etc.); **administrateur d.,** managing director; (*c*) *Ind:* **d. syndical,** union representative; **d. d'usine, du personnel, d'atelier,** shop steward.

déléguer [delege], *v.tr.* (**je délègue, n. déléguons; je déléguerai**) **1. d. qn pour faire qch.,** to delegate, depute, s.o. to do sth.. **2. d. ses pouvoirs,** to delegate, hand over, one's powers; *Com:* **d. une créance,** to assign a debt; *Mil: Navy:* **d. sa solde à sa femme, etc.,** to allot one's pay to one's wife, etc.

délenter [delɑ̃te], *v.tr.* to free (hair) of nits.

délentoir [delɑ̃twaːr], *s.m.* nitting-comb, tooth-comb.

délestage [delɛstaːʒ], *s.m.* (*a*) unballasting (of ship, balloon); (*b*) *El:* load-shedding; (*c*) *Adm: Aut:* **itinéraire de d.,** alternative route.

délester [delɛste], *v.tr.* (*a*) to unballast (ship, balloon), to lighten (aircraft); (*b*) **d. qn d'un fardeau,** to relieve s.o. of a burden; **se d. le cœur,** to open one's heart, to unburden oneself; *F:* **d. qn de son argent,** to relieve s.o. of his money, to steal s.o.'s money; (*c*) *El: abs.* to shed the load.

se délester. 1. to throw out ballast; **se d. de la cargaison,** to jettison the cargo; *Pol:* **se d. d'un projet de loi,** to jettison a bill. **2.** *F:* to relieve one's feelings; to get it off one's chest.

délesteur [delɛstœːr], *s.m.* (*a*) ballast-master; (*b*) ballast-heaver.

délétère [deletɛːr], *a.* deleterious; noxious (gas, plant); poisonous (gas); offensive (smell); **doctrine d.,** pernicious doctrine.

délétion [delesjɔ̃], *s.f. Biol:* deletion.

déliage [deljaːʒ], *s.m.* undoing, untying (of parcel, etc.).

déliaison [deljɛzɔ̃], *s.m.* **1.** *Nau:* frapping, racking, seizing. **2.** *Const:* racking.

déliaque [deljak], *a. & s. A.Geog:* Delian; *Geom:* **le problème d.,** the Delian problem.

délibérant [deliberɑ̃], *a.* deliberative (assembly).

délibératif, -ive [deliberatif, -iv], *a.* deliberative (function); **avoir voix délibérative,** to be entitled to speak and vote.

délibération [deliberasjɔ̃], *s.f.* **1.** deliberation, debate, discussion; **d. touchant une affaire,** discussion on a question; **la question est en d.,** the question is under consideration, is being debated; **l'affaire en d.,** the matter in hand; under discussion. **2.** reflection, cogitation; **après mûre d.,** after due deliberation, after careful consideration. **3.** resolution, decision, vote (of an assembly); **prendre une d.,** to carry, pass, a resolution.

délibératoire [deliberatwa:r], *a.* deliberative.

délibéré [delibere]. **1.** *a.* deliberate; (*a*) determined, resolute (tone, manner, step); (*b*) intentional; **agir de propos d.,** (i) to act deliberately, advisedly; (ii) to act of set, deliberate, purpose, of malice prepense, in cold blood. **2.** *s.m. Jur:* consultation, private sitting (of judges); **affaire en d.,** case under private consideration (by the judge(s); **vider un d.,** to make an award.

délibérément [deliberemɑ̃], *adv.* deliberately; (*a*) resolutely; (*b*) intentionally.

délibérer [delibere], *v.* (**je délibère, n. délibérons; je délibérerai**) **1.** *v.i.* (*a*) to deliberate; to take counsel; to consult together; **d. (avec qn) de, sur, qch.,** to deliberate (with s.o.) on sth., to discuss a matter (with s.o.); **le jury se retira pour d.,** the jury retired to consult together, to consider its verdict; **après avoir délibéré pendant deux heures . . .,** after two hours' deliberation . . .; (*b*) to reflect, ponder; **d. (avec soi-même) de, sur, qch.,** to think sth. over; to turn sth. over in one's mind. **2.** *v.tr.* (*a*) to deliberate over (a question); to turn (a question) over in one's mind; **Sophonisbe délibère si elle se tuera pour éviter l'esclavage,** Sophonisba considers whether she shall kill herself to avoid slavery; (*b*) to debate, discuss (a matter); **c'est une affaire délibérée,** the matter is settled, decided. **3.** *v.tr. Equit: A:* **d. un cheval,** to train a horse to stride freely.

délicat [delika], *a.* delicate. **1.** dainty (dish, etc.); **travail d.,** delicate workmanship; **toucher d. sur le piano,** light touch on the piano; **pinceau, ciseau, d.,** (painter's, sculptor's) light, delicate, touch. **2.** fine, refined, discerning, aesthetic (mind, taste, person, etc.); delicate (attentions); tactful (behaviour); **oreille délicate,** delicate, fine, ear; **distinctions délicates,** fine, nice, distinctions; **je vais lui en toucher quelques mots délicats,** I'll drop him a tactful hint. **3.** sensitive, tender (skin, flower, etc.); delicate, frail, weak (health); **d. dès son enfance,** delicate, fragile, from childhood; **il est d'une santé délicate,** he is not robust; **produits délicats,** perishable goods. **4.** difficult, critical; *F:* ticklish (situation, problem, etc.); tricky (job); **manier une situation délicate,** to handle a delicate, an awkward, situation. **5.** scrupulous, particular; **être d. sur le point d'honneur,** to be particular, touchy, on points of honour; **d. sur la nourriture,** fastidious, fussy, about one's food; **ne faites pas le d.,** don't be squeamish; **il est loyal et d. au suprême degré,** he is loyal and punctilious to a degree; **peu d. en affaires,** not over-scrupulous in one's dealings; **conscience délicate,** tender conscience; **caissier peu d.,** dishonest cashier.

délicatement [delikatmɑ̃], *adv.* delicately. **1.** daintily, tastefully; **il toucha d. le vase précieux,** he touched the precious vase gingerly. **2.** tactfully. **3. il a été élevé trop d.,** he has been too much coddled.

délicatesse [delikatɛs], *s.f.* delicacy. **1.** (*a*) fineness, daintiness, softness (of texture, colouring, etc.); **les délicatesses de la table,** table delicacies; *Art:* **manier le pinceau avec d.,** to have a light, delicate, touch (of the brush); (*b*) **délicatesses d'une langue,** niceties of a language. **2.** refinement (of taste); delicacy (of ear); scrupulousness, squeamishness (of conduct, feelings); fastidiousness (of taste); tactfulness (of behaviour); **avec d.,** tactfully; **fausse d.,** false modesty; **manque de d.,** (i) want of tact; (ii) want of good taste; **ils ont leur d., ces gens-là,** these people have their susceptibilities; **d. sur le point d'honneur,** touchiness on points of honour; **d. de conscience,** tenderness of conscience. **3.** fragility, frailness, weakness; delicate state of health. **4.** difficulty, awkwardness (of situation, etc.); **nous sommes en d.,** our relations are slightly strained; **vivre en d. avec qn,** to have a strained relationship with s.o.

délice [delis], *s.m.* delight, extreme pleasure; **c'est un d. de vivre ainsi,** it is delightful to live like this; **cet entremets est un véritable d.,** this sweet is a sheer delight.

délices, *s.f.pl.* delight(s), pleasure(s), delectation, joy(s); **en un lieu de d.,** in pleasant places; **les d. de la campagne,** the delights of the country; **faire les d. de qn,** to be the delight of s.o.; **elle fait toutes mes d.,** she is all the world to me; **faire ses d. de qch.,** to delight, take delight, in sth.; to revel in sth.; **regarder qch. avec d.,** to feast one's eyes on sth.; **jardin des d.,** earthly paradise.

délicieusement [delisjøzmɑ̃], *adv.* deliciously; **s'habiller, chanter, d.,** to dress, sing, delightfully, charmingly.

délicieux, -ieuse [delisjø, -jø:z], *a.* delicious (food), delightful, charming (scenery, person, etc.).

délicoter (se) [sədelikɔte], *v.pr.* (*of horse, etc.*) to slip the halter.

délictuel, -elle [deliktɥɛl], *a.* delinquent; criminal.

délictueux, -euse [deliktɥø, -ty-, -ø:z], *a. Jur:* **1.** punishable; **acte d.,** misdemeanour, offence. **2.** felonious; malicious (intent); **vagabondage d.,** loitering with felonious intent.

délié [delje]. **1.** *a.* slender, fine; **fil d.,** fine thread; **taille déliée,** slim, supple, figure; **doigts déliés,** tapering fingers; **un esprit d.,** (i) a sharp, subtle, mind; (ii) a nimble wit; **avoir la langue déliée,** to have a glib tongue. **2.** *s.m. Typ: etc:* thin stroke; **les pleins et les déliés,** the downstrokes and upstrokes (in writing).

déliement [delimɑ̃], *s.m.* undoing, unbinding, loosening (of sth.).

délien, -ienne [deljɛ̃, -jɛn], *a. & s. Geog: Myth:* Delian, of Delos.

délier [delje], *v.tr.* (*p.d. & pr.sub.* **n. déliions, v. déliiez**) **1.** to untie, undo, unbind; to loose (fetters); to unfetter; unbind (prisoner); to start (seams of ship); **d. les mains à qn,** to untie, unbind, s.o.'s hands; **le vin délie la langue,** wine loosens the tongue; **sans bourse d.,** without spending a penny. **2.** to release; *Theol:* to absolve; **le pouvoir de d.,** the power of absolution; **le pouvoir de lier et de d.,** the power to bind and to loose; **d. qn d'un serment,** to release s.o. from an oath; **se d. de ses engagements,** to free oneself from one's commitments.

se délier. 1. to come undone, unbound; to come loose; (*of seams of ship*) to start; **sa langue se déliait,** (i) his tongue was beginning to wag; (ii) he was beginning to find his tongue. **2.** *Nau:* **le navire se délie,** the ship is, the fastenings are, weakening.

délignification [deliɲifikasjɔ̃], *s.f. Paperm:* delignification.

délimitateur [delimitatœ:r], *s.m.* member of boundary commission; delimiter.

délimitation [delimitasjɔ̃], *s.f.* delimitation; **poteau de d.,** boundary post.

délimiter [delimite], *v.tr.* to delimit, demarcate; to mark the boundaries of, mark off (territory); to define (powers).

délimoner [delimɔne], *v.tr.* to clean, scale (fish by scalding).

délinéament [delineamɑ̃], *s.m.* outline, shape, contour.

délinéation [delineasjɔ̃], *s.f.* delineation, outlining.

délinéer [delinee], *v.tr.* to delineate, outline.

délinquance [delɛ̃kɑ̃:s], *s.f.* delinquency; **d. juvénile,** juvenile delinquency.

délinquant, -ante [delɛ̃kɑ̃, -ɑ̃:t], *a. & s. Jur:* (*a*) delinquent; **l'enfance délinquante,** juvenile delinquents; **enfant d., d. juvénile,** juvenile delinquent; **un d. primaire,** a first offender; (*b*) *s.* trespasser.

déliquescence [delik(ɥ)ɛs(s)ɑ̃:s], *s.f.* deliquescence; **tomber en d.,** to deliquesce.

déliquescent [delik(ɥ)ɛs(s)ɑ̃], *a.* deliquescent.

déliquium [delikɥiɔm], *s.m. Ph:* deliquium.

délirant [delirɑ̃], *a.* delirious, raving, wandering, light-headed; **fièvre délirante,** fever accompanied by delirium; **conceptions délirantes,** ravings; **joie délirante,** delirious, frenzied, joy; **imagination délirante,** disordered, frenzied, imagination.

délire [deli:r], *s.m.* delirium; **avoir le d., être en d.,** to be delirious, to rave; to wander (in one's mind); **le d. du désespoir, de la colère,** the frenzy of despair, of passion; **le d. de la joie, de l'enthousiasme,** the ecstasy, transport, of joy, of enthusiasm.

délirer [delire], *v.i.* to be delirious, light-headed; to wander (in one's mind); to rave; **d. de colère,** to be raving with anger; **d. de joie,** to be in an ecstasy, in transports, of delight.

delirium (tremens) [delirjɔm(tremɛ̃:s)], *s.m. no pl. Med:* delirium tremens; **avoir une crise de d.,** to have an attack, a fit, of delirium tremens; *F:* the d.t.'s.

délissage [delisa:ʒ], *s.m. Paperm:* shredding (of rags).

délisser [delise], *v.tr. Paperm:* to shred (rags).

délit¹ [deli], *s.m. Jur:* misdemeanour, offence; **d. civil,** tort; **d. contre l'ordre public,** breach of the peace; **d. de presse,** violation of the laws governing the Press; **être pris en flagrant d.,** to be caught red-handed, in the act.

délit², *s.m.* **1.** *Const:* false bedding (of schistous stone); **pierre posée en d.,** stone bedded against the grain. **2.** cleavage, rift (in schists); joint.

délitation [delitasjɔ̃], *s.f.* **1.** (*a*) splitting; (*b*) exfoliation (of stone). **2.** *Const:* surbedding (of stones).

déliter [delite], *v.tr.* **1.** to exfoliate, split (stone). **2.** *Const:* to surbed (stones). **3.** to slake (lime).

se déliter, (*of stone*) to exfoliate, split.

délitescence¹ [delitɛs(s)ɑ̃:s], *s.f. Med:* subsiding, sudden disappearance (of tumour, etc.).

délitescence², *s.f. Ch:* efflorescence.

délitescent [delitɛs(s)ɑ̃], *a. Ch:* efflorescent.

délivrance [delivrɑ̃:s], *s.f.* **1.** deliverance, rescue, release; **apporter à qn la d. de ses maux,** to rid s.o. of his troubles. **2.** *Obst:* (*a*) delivery of the afterbirth; (*b*) child-birth, confinement. **3.** delivery, handing over (of property, patent, certificate, etc.); **d. des billets,** issue of tickets; **d. d'une bombe H,** delivery of an H bomb to its place of explosion.

délivre [deli:vr], *s.m. Obst:* afterbirth.

délivrer [delivre], *v.tr.* **1.** to deliver; to rescue (captive, etc.); to release (prisoner); **d. qn de ses ennemis,** to deliver s.o. from, to rid s.o. of, his enemies; **d. qn de ses liens,** to loose s.o. from his bonds; **d. qn de l'inquiétude,** to free s.o. from worry. **2.** *Obst:* (*a*) **d. une femme,** to deliver a woman, (i) of the afterbirth, (ii) of a child; (*b*) *v.i.* to give birth (normally); **la vache a bien délivré,** the cow calved without difficulty. **3.** to deliver, hand over (goods, etc.); to deliver, issue (certificate, ticket, receipt); **on leur délivre une carte spéciale,** they are issued with a special card; **d. un brevet à qn,** to grant a patent to s.o.; *Const:* **d. des ouvrages,** to give a builder work to do. **4.** *Nau:* **d. un bordage,** to take off a plank (temporarily).

se délivrer de qn, de qch., to rid oneself, to get rid, of s.o., of sth.; **se d. de ses liens, d'une obligation,** to free oneself from one's bonds, from an obligation.

délivreur, -euse [delivrœ:r, -ø:z], *s.* **1.** *A:* deliverer, liberator. **2.** distributor, issuer (of provisions, tickets, etc.). **3.** *a. & s.m. Tex:* **(cylindre) d.,** doffing cylinder, delivery roll.

délocalisation [delɔkalizasjɔ̃], *s.f.* delocalization.

délocaliser [delɔkalize], *v.tr.* to delocalize (interests, etc.).

délogement [delɔʒmɑ̃], *s.m.* **1.** removal, moving house. **2.** departure, moving off.

déloger [delɔʒe], *v.* (*conj. like* LOGER) **1.** *v.i. F:* (*a*) to move, move house; **il faudra d. à mi-terme,** we shall have to move, turn out, at the half-quarter; (*b*) to go off, get away; **délogez de là!** clear out! out of it! (*c*) *Mil:* to march off, to decamp; **d. sans tambour ni trompette,** to steal away, to make oneself scarce. **2.** *v.tr.* to oust; to drive (s.o.) out; **d. un locataire,** to eject, turn out, a tenant; **d. l'ennemi,** to dislodge the enemy (from his position); **d. un lièvre,** to start a hare.

delorenzite [dəlɔrɑ̃zit], *s.f. Miner:* delorenzite.

Délos [delɔs, -ɔ:s], *Pr.n.f. Geog:* Delos.

délot [delo], *s.m.* finger-stall (worn by lacemakers, caulkers).

délover [delɔve], *v.tr. Nau:* to uncoil (rope).

déloyal, -aux [delwajal, -o], *a.* disloyal, unfaithful, false (friend, etc.); dishonest, unfair (practice, proceedings); **concurrence déloyale,** unfair competition; *Sp:* **jeu d.,** foul play; **coup d.,** foul; *Box. & F:* blow below the belt.

déloyalement [delwajalmɑ̃], *adv.* disloyally, treacherously, dishonestly, unfairly; *Box:* **frapper d.,** to hit below the belt.

déloyauté [delwajote], *s.f.* **1.** disloyalty, perfidy. **2. commettre une d.,** (i) to commit a disloyal act; to play s.o. false; (ii) to act unfairly.

Delphes [dɛlf], *Pr.n.f.pl. A.Geog:* Delphi.

delphien, -ienne [dɛlfjɛ̃, -jɛn], *a.* Delphian; Delphic (oracle).

delphinaptère [dɛlfinaptɛ:r], *s.m. Z:* Delphinapterus, beluga, white whale.

delphinidés [dɛlfinide], *s.m.pl. Z:* Delphinidae.

delphinine [dɛlfinin], *s.f. Ch:* delphinin.

delphinium [dɛlfinjɔm], *s.m. Bot:* delphinium.

delta [dɛlta], *s.m. Gr.Alph: Geog:* delta; *Geog:* **d. renversé,** shingle spit (at mouth of river); *Av:* **aile en d.,** delta wing.

deltaïque [dɛltaik], *a. Geog:* deltaic (land, etc.).

delthyridium [dɛltiridjɔm], *s.m. Moll:* delthyrium.

deltidial, -aux [dɛltidjal, -o], *a. Moll:* deltidial.

deltidium [deltidjəm], *s.m. Moll:* deltidium.

deltoïde [dɛltɔid]. 1. *a. Anat: Bot:* deltoid(al) (muscle, leaf, etc.). 2. *s.m.* deltoid.

déluge [dely:ʒ], *s.m.* (*a*) deluge, flood; **d. de larmes,** flood of tears; **d. d'injures,** torrent of abuse; **après moi le déluge!** when I'm gone I don't mind what happens! *F:* **cela remonte au d.,** it's as old as Adam, as old as the hills; it goes back to Methuselah; *Lit:* **avocat, ah! passons au d.!** get on with your story! cut it short! (*b*) downpour (of rain).

déluré [delyre], *a.* sharp, knowing, smart, cute, wide-awake; **elle est délurée,** she's not at all shy; *Pej:* **une fille bien délurée,** a cheeky girl.

délurer [delyre], *v.tr.* to sharpen the wits of (s.o.); to smarten (s.o.) up.

se délurer, to lose one's shyness, one's awkwardness.

délustrage [delystra:ʒ], *s.m. Tex:* taking the sheen, the gloss, the lustre, off cloth; sponging, steaming (cloth).

délustrer [delystre], *v.tr.* (*a*) *Tex:* to take the sheen, the gloss, the lustre, off (cloth); to sponge, steam (cloth); (*b*) *F:* to take the shine off (sth.).

se délustrer, (*of material*) to lose its gloss, its lustre; to grow shabby; **sa gloire s'est délustrée,** his reputation, fame, has faded, has dimmed.

délutage [delyta:ʒ], *s.m.* (*a*) *Cer:* unluting; (*b*) opening (of gas retort).

déluter [delyte], *v.tr.* (*a*) *Cer:* to unlute; (*b*) to open (gas retort).

démagnétisant [demaɲetizɑ̃], *a.* demagnetizing.

démagnétisateur [demaɲetizatœ:r]. 1. *a.* (*a*) *Ph:* demagnetizing; (*b*) *Nau:* degaussing; **bâtiment d.,** degaussing vessel. 2. *s.m. Ph:* demagnetizer.

démagnétisation [demaɲetizasjɔ̃], *s.f.* 1. *Ph:* demagnetization. 2. *Nau:* degaussing; **parcours de d.,** degaussing lane. 3. demesmerization (of s.o.).

démagnétiser [demaɲetize], *v.tr.* 1. *Ph:* to demagnetize. 2. *Nau:* to degauss (ship, etc.). 3. to demesmerize (s.o.).

démagogie [demagɔʒi], *s.f.* demagogy.

démagogique [demagɔʒik], *a.* demagogic.

démagogue [demagɔg], *s.m.* demagogue.

démaigrir [demɛgri:r], *v.tr.* to thin (down) (plank, stone).

démaigrissement [demɛgrismɑ̃], *s.m. Carp: etc:* thinning (down) (of plank, stone).

démaillage [démɑja:ʒ], *s.m.* 1. *Nau:* unshackling (of chain). 2. unravelling, undoing (knitting, net, etc.); laddering (of stocking).

démailler [demɑje], *v.tr.* 1. to unshackle (chain). 2. to undo the meshes of (net); **ce bas est démaillé,** this stocking is laddered.

se démailler, (*of stocking*) to ladder.

démailloter [demajɔte], *v.tr.* to unswaddle, unswathe (infant).

demain [dəmɛ̃], *adv. & s.m.* tomorrow; **d. (au) soir,** tomorrow evening; **d. est jour de fête, c'est d. jour de fête,** tomorrow is a holiday; **venez d. matin,** come tomorrow morning; **(de) demain en huit,** tomorrow week; **qu'est-ce que d. nous réserve?** what has the future in store for us? **à d.,** see you tomorrow; good-bye till tomorrow; **vous lirez cela dans le journal de d.,** you will read it in tomorrow's paper; **la mode de d.,** coming, tomorrow's, fashions; *F:* **aujourd'hui pour d.,** at any time; **il bavarderait jusqu'à d.,** he would talk till the cows come home; **ce n'est pas pour d.,** you won't see that in a hurry; **d. il fera jour,** tomorrow is another day.

démanché [demɑ̃ʃe]. 1. *a.* (*a*) (*of knife, tool, etc.*) (i) loose in the handle; (ii) without a handle; (*b*) *F:* rickety (furniture, etc.); loose-jointed, ungainly (person). 2. *s.m.* shift (in playing the violin).

démanchement [demɑ̃ʃmɑ̃], *s.m.* 1. (*a*) removal or loosening of the handle (of broom, tool, etc.); (*b*) dislocation. 2. *Mus:* shift (in playing the violin).

démancher[1] [demɑ̃ʃe]. 1. *v.tr.* (*a*) to remove the handle of, to unhaft (tool, etc.); (*b*) to dislocate, disjoin; **se d. le bras, la mâchoire,** to put one's arm, one's jaw, out (of joint); *F:* **d. un complot,** to upset a plot. 2. *v.i. Mus:* to shift (in playing the violin).

se démancher. 1. (*of tool, etc.*) to lose its handle; to work loose in the handle. 2. *F:* to fall to pieces, to collapse; **il y a quelque chose qui se démanche,** there's a screw loose somewhere. 3. to put one's arm out (of joint); *esp. F:* **se d. pour obtenir qch.,** to move heaven and earth in order to get sth.; *P:* **qu'avez-vous besoin de tant vous d.?** what d'you want to go to all that trouble for?

démancher[2]. 1. *v.tr.* to remove the sleeve of (garment). 2. *v.i. Nau:* (*of ship*) to clear the channel.

demande [dəmɑ̃:d], *s.f.* 1. (*a*) request, petition, application (**de,** for); **d. d'argent, de crédits,** request for money, for funds; **accorder, faire droit à, une d.,** to grant a request; **faire, formuler, une d.,** to make a request; **adresser une d. à qn,** (i) to address a petition, an application, to s.o.; (ii) to make a request to s.o.; **faire la d. de qch.,** to ask for sth.; **d. en mariage,** offer, proposal, of marriage; **sur d.,** on application, on request; **agir sur d.,** to act when requested; **faire qch. sur, à, la d. de qn,** to do sth. at s.o.'s request; **être relevé, remplacé, sur sa d.,** to be relieved (of one's office), superseded, at one's own request; *Com:* **(envoi d')échantillons sur d.,** samples (are sent) on application; **suite à votre d.,** as requested; *Adm:* **d. de remboursement de voyage,** fares claim; *F:* **il faut faire une d.,** you must fill in a form; **à la d., sur d.,** (i) at, on, call; on demand; (ii) as required, to order; *Mil:* **tir à la d.,** fire on call; (*b*) *Com: Fin:* demand; **l'offre et la d.,** supply and demand; **argent payable, remboursable, à la d., sur d.,** call money; *Ind: etc:* **construit, fabriqué, réalisé, à la d.,** custom built; made to the customer's specifications; **pièce de bois allant à la d.,** timber cut exactly to shape; (*c*) *Adm:* indent; **faire une d. de qch.,** to indent for sth.; (*d*) *Jur:* claim, action; (plaintiff's) declaration; **d. en dommages-intérêts,** claim for damages; **d. en divorce,** action for divorce; **d. compensatoire, reconventionnelle,** counter-claim; *Ins:* **d. d'indemnité,** claim; (*e*) *Nau:* **filer à la d.,** to snub (the cable); (*to helmsman*) **à la d.!** handsomely! (*f*) *Cards:* call (at solo whist, etc.). 2. question, enquiry; **demandes et réponses,** questions and answers; *Com: O:* **votre estimée d. du dix ct,** your valued enquiry of the 10th inst.

demandé [dəmɑ̃de], *s.m. Tp:* called party, person.

demander [dəmɑ̃de], *v.tr.* 1. (*a*) to ask (for); **d. une pomme, du pain,** to ask for an apple, for bread; *s.a.* PAIN 1; **on nous demanda nos passeports,** we were asked for our passports; **d. notre catalogue,** write for our catalogue; *F:* **d. un poste,** to apply for a job; **d. qch. à grands cris,** to call out for sth.; **d. la permission,** to ask permission; **d. pardon,** to beg pardon; **d. la paix,** to beg, sue, for peace; **d. des dommages-intérêts,** to claim damages; **d. des hommes de bonne volonté,** to call for volunteers; *F:* **ne d. que plaies et bosses,** to be always asking for trouble; *A:* **ne d. qu'amour et simplesse,** to ask only for peace and quiet; **il n'y a qu'à le d.,** it is to be had for the asking; **on vous demande,** you are wanted, somebody wants to see you; **combien demandez-vous pour une voiture à la journée?** how much do you charge for a car by the day? **combien demandez-vous de l'heure?** how much do you charge an hour? **combien ce fauteuil?—j'en demande cinq cents francs,** how much for this armchair?—I am asking, I want, five hundred francs for it; (*b*) **d. qch. à qn,** to ask s.o. for sth.; **d. une audience, une faveur, à qn,** to request, ask an audience, a favour, of s.o.; **il demande à ce qu'on lui rende justice,** he asks for justice, he asks that justice may be done him; (*c*) **demander à,** *occ.* **de, faire qch.,** to ask (permission) to do sth.; **je demande à parler, à être entendu,** I ask to be allowed to speak, I ask to be heard; **il demande de ne pas vous accompagner,** he asks to be excused from accompanying you; **d. à travailler,** to ask for work; **d. à manger,** to ask for something to eat; **il ne demande qu'à travailler,** he only asks to be allowed to work; **je ne demande qu'à rester ici,** I am all for staying here; (*d*) **d. à qn de faire qch.,** to desire s.o. to do sth., to ask s.o. to do sth.; **puis-je vous d. de me passer le journal?** would you please pass me the paper? **ne serait-ce pas trop vous d. (que de)?** would you very much mind (doing . . .)? I wonder whether you'd mind (doing . . .). 2. to desire, want, need, require; **on demande maçon,** bricklayer wanted; **article très demandé,** article in great demand, in great request; **cela demande le plus grand soin,** it requires the greatest care; **toute la question demande à être ventilée,** the whole question requires to be aired; **la situation demande à être maniée avec tact,** the situation needs, wants, calls for, tactful handling; **le voyage demande trois heures,** the journey takes three hours; **cela ne demandera pas beaucoup de temps,** it won't take long; *s.a.* MIEUX 1. 3. to demand; **d. un discours à qn,** to call on s.o. for a speech; **d. à qn plus qu'il ne peut faire,** to demand, expect, from s.o. more than he can do; **faire ce que demande sa position,** to do what one's position demands, requires, of one; **l'honneur demande que nous refusions,** honour demands that we should refuse; **c'est trop me d.,** it's too much to ask of me; **en d. trop à qn,** (i) to be too exacting with s.o.; (ii) to ask s.o. more than he can answer. 4. to ask, enquire; **d. quelle heure il est, d. l'heure,** to ask the time; **demandez-lui quand il viendra,** ask him when he will come; **d. son chemin à un agent,** to ask, enquire, one's way of a policeman; **d. après qn,** to ask after s.o.; **d. à qn son avis,** to ask s.o.'s opinion; *F:* **je vous demande un peu en quoi cela le regarde,** what the dickens has he to do with it? **en voilà des histoires, je vous demande un peu!** what's all the fuss about, I ask you? **je te le demande!** tell me if you can! **demandez-moi pourquoi,** ask me another! **cela ne se demande pas,** it's obvious.

se demander, to ask oneself, to wonder; **je me demande pourquoi il ne vient pas,** I wonder why he doesn't come; **c'est ce que je me demande,** that's what I should like to know; **on peut se d., si . . .,** it may be asked whether . . .; **on se demande si . . .,** there are speculations as to whether . . .; **je me demande bien pourquoi, ce que, où,** I (really) can't think why, what, where; **c'est à se d. s'il ne l'a pas fait exprès,** one wonders whether he hasn't done it on purpose.

demandeur, -euse [dəmɑ̃dœ:r, -ø:z], *s.* 1. (*a*) petitioner, constant applicant for favours; (*b*) **d. d'un brevet,** applicant for patent; (*c*) *Cards:* declarer. 2. *Jur:* (*f.* **demanderesse**) plaintiff. 3. *Pol.Ec:* demander. 4. *Tp:* **d. (de la communication),** caller.

démangeaison [demɑ̃ʒɛzɔ̃], *s.f.* itching; *F:* **une d. de faire qch.,** a longing, an itching, to do sth.; **j'avais une d. de lui demander si . . .,** I was itching to ask him whether . . .; **d. d'écrire,** the itch to put pen to paper; **avoir des démangeaisons dans les jambes,** to be itching to get going.

démanger [demɑ̃ʒe], *v.i.* **(il démangea(it),** *usu. with dative of person*) to itch; **l'épaule me démange,** my shoulder is itching; **ma main me démange,** my hand tickles; *F:* **la langue lui démangeait,** he was longing, itching, to speak; **la main me démangeait de lui flanquer une gifle,** my fingers were tingling to box his ears; **gratter qn où ça le d.,** to scratch s.o.'s back, to toady to s.o.

démanillage [demanija:ʒ], *s.m. Nau:* unshackling.

démaniller [demanije], *v.tr. Nau:* to unshackle.

démantèlement [demɑ̃tɛlmɑ̃], *s.m.* (*a*) dismantling; (*b*) *Geol:* destruction of a complete stratum by erosion.

démanteler [demɑ̃tle], *v.tr.* **(je démantèle, n. démantelons; je démantèlerai)** (*a*) to dismantle, raze, demolish (fortifications, etc.); **le temps a démantelé ces murs,** these walls have crumbled, fallen into ruin, with the passage of time; (*b*) to break up (an empire, an institution, a spy ring).

démantibuler [demɑ̃tibyle], *v.tr. F:* (*a*) to dislocate (the jaw); to put (the jaw) out (of joint); (*b*) **d. une pendule, une machine,** (i) to interfere with the works; to put a clock out of order, to throw a machine out of gear; (ii) to take a clock, a machine, to pieces; (iii) to break a clock, a machine, to pieces.

se démantibuler, *F:* to come to pieces, to break up.

démantoïde [demɑ̃tɔid], *s.f. Miner:* demantoid.

démaquer [demake], *v.tr. Fish:* to free (fish) caught in the net.

démaquillage [demakija:ʒ], *s.m. Toil:* **crème de d.,** cleansing cream; make-up remover.

démaquillant [demakijɑ̃], *s.m. Toil:* cleansing cream, make-up remover.

démaquiller [demakije], *v.tr.* 1. to remove make-up. 2. *F:* **d. un projet,** to upset a plan.

se démaquiller, to remove one's make-up.

démarcage [demarka:ʒ], *s.m.* 1. removal of the mark from (linen, etc.). 2. plagiarism.

démarcatif, -ive [demarkatif, -i:v], *a.* demarcating (line, etc.).

démarcation [demarkasjɔ̃], *s.f.* demarcation; **ligne de d.,** dividing line; line of demarcation; boundary line; *Hist:* (1940-42) demarcation line; **la d. nette des partis politiques,** the sharp alignment of political parties.

démarchage [demarʃa:ʒ], *s.m.* canvassing.

démarche [demarʃ], *s.f.* 1. gait, step, walk, bearing; **d. majestueuse,** majestic bearing; **la d. mesurée d'un agent,** the measured tread of a policeman; **il avait une d. digne,** he moved with dignity. 2. step; *Dipl:* **d. collective,** joint representations; **démarches suspectes,** suspicious proceedings; **faire une d. auprès de qn,** to approach s.o., to apply to s.o.; **faire les premières**

démarches, to take the first steps; to make the advances; **faire les démarches nécessaires,** to take the necessary steps; **faire des démarches en faveur de la candidature de qn,** to canvass for s.o.; **les visites et démarches des candidats ne sont pas admises,** no canvassing is allowed.

démarcher [demarʃe], *v.tr.* to canvass.

démarcheur, -euse [demarʃœːr, -øːz], *s.* canvasser; door-to-door salesman; *F:* tout.

démargariner [demargarine], *v.tr.* to destearinate, to winterize (a fatty oil).

démariage [demarjaːʒ], *s.m.* **1.** annulment of marriage; divorce. **2.** *Hort:* thinning (out), singling (of plants).

démarier [demarje], *v.tr.* (*p.d. & pr.sub.* **n. démariions, v. démariiez**) **1.** to sever the marriage tie of (man and wife); to unmarry. **2.** *Hort:* to thin (out) (plants).

se démarier, to sever one's marriage tie.

démarquage [demarkaːʒ], *s.m.* **1.** removal of the mark (from linen, plate, etc.). **2.** plagiarism; "lifting". **3.** *Com:* = DÉMARQUE.

démarque [demark], *s.f. Com:* marking down (of goods at sales *usu.* from a fictitious original price).

démarqué [demarke], *a. Fb: Hockey:* unmarked.

démarquement [demarkmɑ̃], *s.m. For:* removal of the reserve mark on a tree (in order to cut it down fraudulently).

démarquer [demarke]. **1.** *v.tr.* (*a*) to remove the identification marks from (linen, plate, etc.); *For:* to remove the reserve mark from (a tree) (in order to cut it down fraudulently); **d. un livre,** (i) to remove the marker from a book; (ii) to plagiarize a book, to dish up its contents in another form; (*b*) *Sp:* to leave one's opponent unmarked; (*c*) *Com:* to mark down (goods, *usu.* from a fictitious original price). **2.** *v.i.* (*of horse*) to lose mark of mouth.

se démarquer, *Sp:* to get unmarked; to elude, break free from, one's opponent.

démarqueur, -euse [demarkœːr, -øːz], *s.* **1.** remover of the marks (from linen, plate, etc.). **2.** plagiarist.

démarrage [demaraːʒ], *s.m.* **1.** unmooring (of boat). **2.** (*a*) start, starting (of train, car, aircraft); **d. doux,** smooth start, get-away; **d. automatique,** automatic starting, self-starting; **moteur (auxiliaire) de d.,** starter motor; **d. à inertie,** inertia starting; **bouton, pédale, de d.,** (self-) starter switch, pedal; *I.C.E:* **d. à froid,** starting from cold; **d. à cartouche,** cartridge, combustion, starting; *Motor Cy:* **d. au pied,** kick starting; *Av:* **groupe de d.,** (ground) starting unit; (*in jet aircraft*) **soupape de d.,** starting valve; **d. avec surchauffe,** hot start; (*b*) *Atom.Ph:* start-up (of nuclear reactor); (*c*) *Sp: Rac:* (i) get-away; (ii) (sudden) spurt; **d. d'une usine,** start(ing) of a factory's production; **le d. de l'industrie atomique,** the sudden spurt made by the atomic industry.

démarrer [demare]. **1.** *v.tr.* (*a*) to unmoor, cast off (ship); to untie, unbend (rope); (*b*) to start (train, motor car, etc.); **d. le moteur,** to start up the engine. **2.** *v.i.* (*a*) to cast off; (*b*) (*of train, car, etc.*) to start (off), move off, get away; (*of driver*) to drive away, to drive off; **faire d.,** to start (car, etc.); **d. doucement,** to start off smoothly; *F:* **ne démarrez pas d'ici,** don't move from here; (*c*) *Sp:* (i) to get off the mark, to get away; **d. vivement,** to be quick off the mark; (ii) to put on a spurt, to spurt, to force the pace (in race); **une entreprise qui a du mal à d.,** a business which has difficulty in getting under way, started.

démarreur [demarœːr], *s.m.* **1.** *Aut: Mch: etc:* starter; **d. automatique,** self-starter; **d. mécanique,** starter motor; **moteur d.,** barring engine, pony engine; **d. à cartouche,** cartridge, combustion, starter; **d. à manivelle,** crank starter; **contact de d.,** starter switch; **noix de d.,** starting dog; jaw; *Motor Cy:* **d. au pied,** kick starter; *Av:* **d. aérodrome, de piste,** field, ground, starter; **d. de bord,** cockpit starter; *El:* **d. à cylindre,** drum-starter. **2.** *Sp:* (*f* **démarreuse**) runner always able to raise a spurt, force the pace.

démascler [demaskle], *v.tr.* to strip the outer cork from (cork-oak).

démasquer [demaske], *v.tr.* to unmask; remove the mask from; **d. un imposteur,** to expose, to show up, an imposter; *Mil:* **d. une position, une batterie,** to unmask a position, a battery; **d. ses batteries,** to show one's hand; *Mch:* **d. une lumière,** to uncover a port; *Nau:* **d. un feu,** to show a light.

se démasquer, (i) to take off one's mask, to unmask; (ii) to show one's true character, to drop the mask.

démasticage, démastiquage [demastikaːʒ], *s.m.* (action of) removing putty from (sth.).

démastiquer [demastike], *v.tr.* to remove putty from (sth.).

démâtage [demɑtaːʒ], *s.m.*, **démâtement** [demɑtmɑ̃], *s.m. Nau:* dismasting, unmasting.

démâter [demɑte]. **1.** *v.tr.* (*a*) to dismast, unmast (ship); to take down the masts of (ship); **d. qn,** to disconcert s.o., to take s.o. aback; not to leave s.o. a leg to stand on; (*b*) **une cheminée était démâtée,** a funnel was down. **2.** *v.i. & pr.* (*of ship*) to lose her masts, to be dismasted.

dématérialisation [dematerjalizasjɔ̃], *s.f.* dematerialization; *Atom.Ph:* annihilation (of matter).

dématérialiser [dematerjalize], *v.tr.* to dematerialize.

dématiacées [dematjase], *s.f.pl. Fung:* Dematiaceae.

dème [dɛm], *s.m. Hist: Biol:* deme.

démêlage [demɛlaːʒ], *s.m.* **1.** disentangling (of string, etc.); combing (out) (of hair); teasing (out) (of wool). **2.** *Brew:* mash(ing).

démêlé [demele], *s.m. usu. pl.* contention, (unpleasant) dealings; **des démêlés survinrent entre eux,** contentions, differences, arose between them; **avoir des démêlés avec la justice,** to be up against the law.

démêler [demele], *v.tr.* **1.** (*a*) to disentangle, unravel (string, silk, etc.); to comb out (hair); to tease (out) (wool); **d. un malentendu,** to clear up a misunderstanding; **d. ses affaires,** to straighten out one's affairs; *F:* **avoir quelque chose à d. avec qn,** to have a bone to pick with s.o.; **qu'avez-vous à d. avec lui?** what quarrel have you with him? **je ne veux rien avoir à d. avec lui,** I wish to have no dealings with him; (*b*) *F:* **d. qn parmi la foule, dans l'ombre,** to make out s.o. in the crowd, in the gloom; **je ne peux pas d. ses raisons,** I can't make out, fathom, his reasons; **d. qch. de, d'avec, qch.,** to distinguish sth. from sth.; **d. la vérité du mensonge, d'avec le mensonge,** to distinguish, sift, truth from falsehood; to sift out the truth. **2.** *Brew:* to mash (the grains of malt).

se démêler. 1. (*a*) (*of string, thread, etc.*) to become disentangled; (*b*) to comb (out) one's hair. **2.** (*a*) to extricate oneself (from difficulty); (*b*) **la vérité se démêle,** the truth is coming out; *A:* **l'île se démêlait parmi les nuages,** the island could just be made out amid the clouds.

démêleur, -euse [demelœːr, -øːz], *s. Tex:* picker.

démêloir [demelwaːr], *s.m.* **1.** large-toothed comb, dressing comb. **2.** *P:* **vous faut-il un d.!** can't you get it out, spit it out?

démêlures [demelyːr], *s.f.pl.* combings.

démembrement [demɑ̃brəmɑ̃], *s.m.* dismembering (of body); dismemberment, disruption (of empire, etc.; breaking up (of ship, of empire).

démembrer [demɑ̃bre], *v.tr.* to dismember; **d. un poulet,** to cut up a chicken; **d. un royaume,** to divide up a kingdom; **d. une famille,** to break up a family.

se démembrer, (*of ship, empire*) to break up.

déménagement [demenaʒmɑ̃], *s.m.* removal, moving house, moving out; **voiture de d.,** furniture van, removal van; *F:* **d. à la cloche (de bois),** moonlight flit(ting).

déménager [demenaʒe], *v.tr. & i.* (**je déménageai(s); n. déménageons**) **d. (ses meubles),** to move (house), to move out; **d. une maison,** to remove the furniture from a house; *F:* **d. à la cloche (de bois),** to shoot the moon; *F:* **il, sa tête, déménage,** his mind is unhinged, he has taken leave of his senses, he's off his head, off his nut; *F:* **allez, déménagez!** scram! shift! get a move on!

déménageur [demenaʒœːr], *s.m.* furniture remover.

démence [demɑ̃ːs], *s.f.* insanity, madness; *Jur:* lunacy, aberration of mind; *Med:* dementia; **d. précoce,** dementia praecox; **être en d.,** to be insane, demented, of unsound mind; **tomber en d.,** to go out of one's mind, off one's head.

démener (se) [sədemne], *v.pr.* (*conj. like* MENER) **1.** to toss about, throw oneself about; to struggle; **se d. comme un possédé,** to fling oneself about like a madman; **se d. comme un beau diable,** to jump about like a cat on hot bricks, *U.S:* on a hot tin roof. **2.** to be active; to take a great deal of trouble about (sth.); **il se démène pour réussir,** he's making great efforts to succeed.

dément, -ente [demɑ̃, -ɑ̃ːt], *a. & s.* crazy, mad (person); *Jur:* lunatic.

démenti [demɑ̃ti], *s.m.* **1.** (flat) denial, contradiction; **donner un d. formel à qn, à une assertion,** to give the lie direct to s.o., to an assertion; **ses actions donnent un d. à ses paroles,** his actions belie his words; **vous vous donnez d'étranges démentis,** you are involving yourself in strange contradictions; **opposer un d. à une déclaration,** to deny, contradict, a statement; **le témoignage reste sans d.,** the testimony remains uncontradicted. **2.** failure (of efforts); disappointment (of expectations); **il en a eu le d.,** he failed ignominiously.

démentiel, -ielle [demɑ̃sjɛl], *a.* utterly mad; **accès d.,** fit of madness; **politique démentielle,** insane policy.

démentir [demɑ̃tiːr], *v.tr.* (*conj. like* MENTIR) **1.** to give the lie to, to contradict (s.o., sth.); **d. formellement une assertion,** to give the lie direct to an assertion; **d. un fait,** to deny a fact; **d. sa signature,** to disown, deny, one's signature. **2.** to belie; **ses actions démentent ses paroles,** his actions belie his words; **il a démenti nos espérances,** he has not come up to our expectations, he has disappointed us; **les événements ont démenti nos craintes,** events proved our fears to be unfounded.

se démentir. 1. to contradict oneself, one's own words; **vous avez promis, ne vous démentez pas,** you have promised, mind you keep your word, do not go back on your word; **c'est un homme qui ne se dément point,** he is a man who is true to himself, whose character is consistent; **politesse qui ne se dément jamais,** unfailing courtesy; **l'assiduité à ce cours ne se dément jamais,** the attendance at this class never falls off, drops off. **2.** *Const:* (*of building, etc.*) to give way, to bulge.

démerder (se) [sədemɛrde], *v.pr. V:* **1.** to (bloody well) get a move on. **2.** to get out of a mess.

démérite [demerit], *s.m.* demerit; **auteur qui a le d. d'être vivant,** author who suffers from the fact that he is still alive; **faire un d. à qn de qch.,** to urge, put forward, sth. against s.o.

démériter [demerite], *v.i.* **1.** to act in a blameworthy, reprehensible, manner; *Theol:* to fall from grace. **2.** (*a*) *A:* **d. de qn,** to break faith with s.o.; (*b*) **d. auprès de qn,** to forfeit s.o.'s esteem; (*c*) **d. de qch.,** to become unworthy of sth.

déméritoire [demeritwaːr], *a.* demeritorious, blameworthy, reprehensible (action).

démersal, -aux [demɛrsal, -o], *a. Ich:* (*a*) (*of fish*) bottom-dwelling; (*b*) (*of eggs*) demersal.

démesure [deməzyːr], *s.f.* disproportion, excessiveness.

démesuré [deməzyre], *a.* **1.** beyond measure, enormous, huge; **cou d.,** neck of inordinate length; **orgueil d.,** pride beyond measure, inordinate pride; **soif démesurée,** excessive, immoderate, thirst; **ambition démesurée,** unbounded ambition. **2. d. à qch.,** disproportionate to sth.

démesurément [deməzyremɑ̃], *adv.* beyond measure, enormously, hugely, inordinately, excessively, immoderately.

Déméter [demetɛːr], *Pr.n.f. Gr.Myth:* Demeter.

déméthanisation [demetanizasjɔ̃], *s.f.* extraction of methane.

déméthaniser [demetanize], *v.tr.* to extract methane from.

déméthyliser [demetilize], *v.tr. Ch:* to demethylate.

démettre[1] [demɛtr], *v.tr.* (*conj. like* METTRE) to dislocate (joint); to put (knee, etc.) out (of joint); *usu. with dative pron.* **il s'était démis l'épaule,** he had put his shoulder out.

démettre[2], *v.tr.* (*conj. like* METTRE) **1. d. qn de ses fonctions,** to deprive s.o. of his office. **2.** *Jur:* **d. qn de son appel,** to dismiss s.o.'s appeal.

se démettre, to resign, to retire; **se d. de ses fonctions,** to resign office, to resign one's appointment.

démeublé [demœble], *a.* unfurnished; stripped of its appurtenances; *F:* **bouche, mâchoire, démeublée,** toothless mouth, jaws.

démeublement [demœbləmɑ̃], *s.m.* **1.** unfurnishing. **2.** unfurnished state (of house, etc.).

démeubler [demœble], *v.tr.* to unfurnish; to remove the furniture from (house, etc.); to strip (house, etc.) of its appurtenances.

demeurant, -ante [dəmœrɑ̃, -ɑ̃ːt]. **1.** *a. & s. Jur:* resident. **2.** *s.m.* (*a*) *A:* remainder; (*b*) *adv.phr.* **au d.,** after all, all the same, howbeit.

demeure [dəmœːr], *s.f.* **1.** (*a*) *A:* tarrying, delay; *still so used in such phrases as* **sans plus longue d.,** without further delay; **il y a péril en la d.,** there is danger in delay; **il n'y a pas péril en la d.,** there's no harm in waiting; (*b*) *adj. & adv.phr.*

en d., in arrears; **je serai toujours en d. envers vous,** I shall always be in your debt; **mettre qn en d. de faire qch.,** to call upon s.o. to do sth., to summon s.o. to perform a contract; **mise en d. (de faire qch.),** formal notice, summons (to do sth.); (*c*) stay; **faire une longue d. dans une ville,** to make a long stay in a town; *adj. & adv.phr.* **à d.,** fixed, permanent(ly); **meuble à d.,** fixture; **machine à d.,** stationary engine; **institutrice à d.,** resident governess; **je suis ici à d.,** I am here permanently, for good; **canalisation électrique à d.,** permanent wiring; *Mec.E:* **goupille à d.,** set pin. **2.** (*place of*) residence, dwelling-place; **établir sa d. à Paris,** to fix, take up, one's residence in Paris; **j'ai fait ici ma d.,** I have settled down here, made my home here; **se diriger vers sa d.,** to bend one's steps homewards; **accompagner qn à sa dernière d.,** to attend s.o.'s funeral, to accompany s.o. to his last resting place.

demeuré, -e [dəmœre], *a.* **un enfant demeuré,** a mentally retarded child; *s.* **les demeurés,** the mentally deficient.

demeurer [dəmœre], *v.i.* **1.** (*conj. with* **être**) (*a*) *A:* to tarry; *B:* **il demeura dans Jérusalem,** He tarried behind in Jerusalem; *F:* **elle demeure des heures à s'habiller,** she takes hours to dress; (*b*) to remain; to stay, stop (in a place); **je demeure convaincu que . . .,** I remain convinced that . . .; **demeurez là!** stay, stop, there! **la police est demeurée sur les lieux,** the police have remained on the spot; **il reprit sa lecture où il en était demeuré,** he resumed his reading where he had left off; **l'affaire n'en demeurera pas là,** the matter will not rest, stop, there; **demeurons-en là,** let us leave it at that; **d. immobile,** to stand stock-still; **ne pouvoir d. en place,** to be unable to keep still; *F:* **d. sur place, y d.,** to be killed on the spot; **elle demeurait assise à nous écouter,** she sat listening to us; **d. en reste, en arrière, avec qn,** to remain under an obligation to s.o.; **son dîner lui était demeuré sur l'estomac,** his dinner was lying heavily on his stomach; **d. sur le cœur,** (i) (*of food*) to lie heavily on the stomach; (ii) (*of grievance*) to rankle (in the mind); **le temps demeurait mauvais,** the weather continued bad; **la tache en est demeurée à son nom,** the slur has stuck to his name; **la victoire nous demeure,** the victory rests with us; **pièce qui demeure au théâtre,** play that remains in the repertoire; *s.a.* COURT[1] 2. **2.** (*conj. with* **avoir**) to live, reside; **d. à Bristol, dans une ville, à la campagne,** to live in, at, Bristol, in a town, in the country; **il demeure numéro 7, rue de Rivoli,** he lives at no. 7, rue de Rivoli; **où demeurez-vous?** where do you live?

demi [dəmi]. **1.** *a.* (*a*) half; **un an et d.,** a year and a half; **deux heures et demie,** (i) two and a half hours, two hours and a half; (ii) half-past two; **un d.-congé,** a half-holiday; **une d.-heure,** half an hour; (*b*) semi-; **d.-cercle,** semicircle; (*c*) demi-; **d.-dieu,** demigod; (*d*) *used adverbially;* **d.-cuit,** half-cooked; **d.-mort,** half-dead. **2.** *s.m.* (*a*) **deux demis,** two halves; **deux plus un d.,** two plus one half; **à fripon, fripon et d., à voleur, voleur et d.,** set a thief to catch a thief; *F:* **un d.** (= DEMI-SETIER), a large glass of beer; (about ½ pint); *s.a.* MOITIÉ 1; (*b*) *Fb:* **les demis,** the half-backs; the halves; *Rugby:* **d. de mêlée,** scrum half; **d. d'ouverture,** fly half, stand-off half; **les demis aile,** the wing halves; **d. centre,** centre half; (*c*) *adv.phr.* **à d.,** (i) half; **elle se releva à d.,** she half got up; **à d. mort,** half-dead; **il ne comprend qu'à d.,** he only half understands; **faire les choses à d.,** to do things by halves; *F:* **il n'y en avait pas à d.,** there were an awful lot of them; *s.a.* COMPTE; (ii) semi-; **à d. fluide,** semi-fluid; half liquid; **à d. transparent,** semi-transparent. **3.** *s.f.* **demie,** half-hour; **la demie de dix heures,** half-past ten; **la demie sonne,** the half-hour is striking; **est-il six heures?—il est la demie,** is it six o'clock?—it's half past.

demi-à-droite [dəmiadrwat], *s.m. Mil:* half-right, right half-wheel; *pl. demis-à-droite.*

demi-à-gauche [dəmiagoːʃ], *s.m. Mil:* half-left, left half-wheel; *pl. demis-à-gauche.*

demi-arbre [dəmiarbr̥], *s.m. Aut:* half-shaft; *pl. demi-arbres.*

demiard [dəmjaːr], *s.m. Fr.C: Meas:* half-pint.

demi-armé [dəmiarme], *s.m.* half-cock.

demi-arrière [dəmiarjɛːr], *s.m. Fb:* half-back; *pl. demi-arrières.*

demi-axe [dəmiaks], *s.m.* semi-axis (of ellipse, etc.); *pl. demi-axes.*

demi-bain [dəmibɛ̃], *s.m.* hip-bath; *pl. demi-bains.*

demi-bande [dəmibɑ̃ːd], *s.f. Nau:* parliament heel; *pl. demi-bandes.*

demi-bas [dəmibɑ], *s.m.inv. Cost:* (calf-length) sock; *Com: pl.* half-hose.

demi-bastion [dəmibastjɔ̃], *s.m. Fort:* half-bastion, demi-bastion; *pl. demi-bastions.*

demi-bâton [dəmibɑtɔ̃], *s.m. Mus:* breve rest, double rest, two-bar baton; *pl. demi-bâtons.*

demi-batterie [dəmibatri], *s.f. Mil:* half-battery; *pl. demi-batteries.*

demi-bau [dəmibo], *s.m. N.Arch:* half-beam; *pl. demi-baux.*

demi-bec [dəmibɛk], *s.m. Ich:* half-beak; *pl. demi-becs.*

demi-blanc, -blanche [dəmiblɑ̃, -blɑ̃ːʃ], *a. Tex:* half-bleached; *pl. demi-blancs, -blanches.*

demi-bosse [dəmibɔs], *s.f. Sculp:* demi-relief, half-relief, mezzo-rilievo; *pl. demi-bosses.*

demi-botte [dəmibɔt], *s.f.* half-boot, calf-length boot; Wellington boot; *pl. demi-bottes.*

demi-boucle [dəmibukl̥], *s.f. Av:* (*aerobatics*) **d.-b. inversée,** bunt; *pl. demi-boucles.*

demi-bouteille [dəmibutɛːj], *s.f.* half-bottle; *pl. demi-bouteilles.*

demi-brigade [dəmibrigad], *s.f.* (*a*) *Hist:* regiment (during the French Revolution); (*b*) *Mil:* group of two or three battalions under a colonel; *pl. demi-brigades.*

demi-brique [dəmibrik], *s.f. Cer:* brick back, grog; *pl. demi-briques.*

demi-cadence [dəmikadɑ̃s], *s.f. Mus:* half-cadence, half-close; *pl. demi-cadences.*

demi-cage [dəmikaːʒ], *s.f. Tchn:* **d.-c. de roulement,** (ball-)bearing retainer; *pl. demi-cages.*

demi-canon [dəmikanɔ̃], *s.m. A.Artil:* demi-cannon; *pl. demi-canons.*

demi-carré [dəmikare], *s.m. Paperm:* demy-folio; *pl. demi-carrés.*

demi-ceint [dəmisɛ̃], *s.m. Arch:* semi-column; *pl. demi-ceints.*

demi-cellule [dəmisɛlyl], *s.f. El:* half cell; *pl. demi-cellules.*

demi-cercle [dəmisɛrkl̥], *s.m.* **1.** *Geom:* semi-circle, half-circle; *Fenc:* half-circle parry; *A:* **pincer, repincer, qn au d.-c,** to catch s.o. off his guard, *F:* on the hop; to get even with s.o.; **en d.-c.,** semicircular. **2.** *Surv:* demi-circle, graphometer. **3.** *Bill:* **d.-c. de départ,** balk; *pl. demi-cercles.*

demi-circulaire [dəmisirkylɛːr], *a.* semicircular; *pl. demi-circulaires.*

demi-clef [dəmikle], *s.f. Nau:* half-hitch; **d.-c. à capeler,** clove-hitch, marline-hitch; **d.-c. renversée,** clove-hitch inverted; *pl. demi-clefs.*

demi-colonne [dəmikɔlɔn], *s.f. Arch:* semi-column; *pl. demi-colonnes.*

demi-coupe [dəmikup], *s.f. Draw:* half-section; *pl. demi-coupes.*

demi-couronne [dəmikurɔn], *s.f. A: Num:* **une d.-c.,** half a crown, a half-crown; **deux demi-couronnes,** two half-crowns.

demi-croupon [dəmikrupɔ̃], *s.m. Leath:* bend; *pl. demi-croupons.*

demi-cylindrique [dəmisilɛ̃drik], *a.* semi-cylindrical; *pl. demi-cylindriques.*

demi-deuil [dəmidœj], *s.m.* half-mourning; **être en d.-d.,** to be in half-mourning; *pl. demi-deuils.*

demi-diamètre [dəmidjamɛtr̥], *s.m.* semi-diameter; *pl. demi-diamètres.*

demi-dieu [dəmidjø], *s.m.* demigod; **se faire un d.-d. de qn,** to make a (little) god, a demigod, of s.o.; *pl. demi-dieux.*

demi-droite [dəmidrwat], *s.f. Geom:* half line, half ray; *pl. demi-droites.*

demi-douzaine [dəmiduzɛn], *s.f.* half-dozen; *pl. demi-douzaines.*

demi-dunette [dəmidynɛt], *s.f. N.Arch:* raised quarter-deck; *pl. demi-dunettes.*

demi-épaisseur [dəmiepɛsœːr], *s.f. Atom.Ph:* half thickness; *pl. demi-épaisseurs.*

démieller [demjɛle], *v.tr.* **1.** to remove the honey from (honeycomb). **2.** *P:* to get (s.o.) out of a mess, a jam.

demi-feuille [dəmifœj], *s.f. Paperm:* folio; *pl. demi-feuilles.*

demi-feuilletage [dəmifœjtaːʒ], *s.m. Cu:* flaky pastry; *pl. demi-feuilletages.*

demi-fin, -fine [dəmifɛ̃, -fin], *a. & s.m.* **1.** twelve-carat (gold); **bracelet (en) d.-f.,** twelve-carat bracelet. **2. écriture en d.-f.,** fine, medium-sized, hand-writing; *pl. demi-fins, -fines.*

demi-finale [dəmifinal], *s.f. Sp:* semi-final; *pl. demi-finales.*

demi-finaliste [dəmifinalist], *s.m. & f. Sp:* semi-finalist; *pl. demi-finalistes.*

demi-fleuron [dəmiflœrɔ̃], *s.m. Bot:* semifloret, ligulate floret; *pl. demi-fleurons.*

demi-flosculeux, -euse [dəmiflɔskylø, -øːz], *a. Bot:* liguliflorous; *pl. demi-flosculeux, -euses.*

demi-fond [dəmifɔ̃], *s.m.inv. Sp:* **(course de) d.-f.,** middle-distance race.

demi-frère [dəmifrɛːr], *s.m.* (*a*) half-brother; (*b*) step-brother; *pl. demi-frères.*

demi-futaie [dəmifytɛ], *s.f.* forest of trees 40-60 years old; *pl. demi-futaies.*

demi-gros [dəmigro], *s.m.inv.* **commerce de d.-g.,** wholesale dealing in small quantities.

demi-guêtre [dəmigɛːtr̥], *s.f.* gaiter, spat; *pl. demi-guêtres.*

demi-heure [dəmiœːr], *s.f.* **une d.-h.,** half an hour; **deux demi-heures,** two half-hours; **prendre une cuillerée de d.-h. en d.-h., toutes les demi-heures,** a spoonful to be taken every half-hour; **l'entr'acte pousse parfois jusqu'à la d.-h.,** the interval sometimes runs to as much as half an hour; *pl. demi-heures.*

demi-jeu (à) [ad(ə)miʒø], *adv.phr. Mus:* with half the power of the instrument.

demi-Jésus [dəmiʒezy], *s.m.inv. Paperm:* imperial folio.

demi-jour [dəmiʒuːr], *s.m.* **1.** *Art: etc:* half-light; half-lighting (of parts of picture, etc.). **2.** (*a*) half-light (of dawn); morning twilight; (*b*) *occ.* twilight, dusk; *pl. demi-jours.*

demi-journée [dəmiʒurne], *s.f.* half a day; **faire des demi-journées, travailler à la d.-j.,** to work half-days, to work half the day; *pl. demi-journées.*

démilitarisation [demilitarizasjɔ̃], *s.f.* demilitarization, demilitarizing.

démilitariser [demilitarize], *v.tr.* to demilitarize.

demi-litre [dəmilitr̥], *s.m.* half-litre; *pl. demi-litres.*

demi-long, -longue [dəmilɔ̃, -lɔ̃ːg], *a.* of medium length; *pl. demi-longs, -longues.*

demi-longueur [dəmilɔ̃gœːr], *s.f.* half-length; *Phon:* half-length sign; *Sp:* half a length; *pl. demi-longueurs.*

demi-louis [dəmilwi], *s.m.inv. A:* (gold) ten-franc piece.

demi-lune [dəmilyn], *s.f.* **1.** half-moon. **2.** *Fort:* (*a*) demilune; (*b*) ravelin. **3.** *Mch:* eccentric catch; *pl. demi-lunes.*

demi-main [dəmimɛ̃], *s.f.* = half quire (of paper); *pl. demi-mains.*

demi-mal [dəmimal], *s.m. F:* small harm; **il n'y a que d.-m.,** the harm is not so great, after all; it might have been worse; *pl. demi-maux.*

demi-membraneux [dəmimɑ̃branø], *a. & s.m. Anat:* **(muscle) d.,** the semimembranosus.

demi-mesure [dəmimzyːr], *s.f.* half-measure; **avec lui il n'y a pas de d.-m.,** there's no half-way with him; *pl. demi-mesures.*

demi-métal [dəmimetal], *s.m. Ch:* semi-metal; *pl. demi-métaux.*

demi-métallique [dəmimetalik], *a. Ch:* semi-metallic; *pl. demi-métalliques.*

demi-mondain, -aine [dəmimɔ̃dɛ̃, -ɛn]. **1.** *a.* belonging to the *demi-monde.* **2.** *s.f.* **demi-mondaine,** demi-mondaine; *pl. demi-mondains, -mondaines.*

demi-monde [dəmimɔ̃ːd], *s.m. demi-monde,* outskirts of society.

demi-mort [dəmimɔːr], *a.* half-dead; **femmes demi-mortes de faim,** women half-dead with hunger; *pl. demi-mort(e)s.*

demi-mot (à) [ad(ə)mimo], *adv.phr.* **entendre (qn) à d.-m.,** to (know how to) take a hint; **il comprit à d.-m.,** (i) he caught on at once (to what I meant); (ii) he took the hint.

déminage [deminaːʒ], *s.m.* mine clearance; bomb disposal.

demi-napoléon [dəminapɔleɔ̃], *s.m. A.Num:* half Napoleon, (gold) ten franc piece; *pl. demi-napoléons.*

déminer [demine], *v.tr.* to clear (a field) of mines; to dispose of bombs.

déminéralisation [demineralizasjɔ̃], *s.f.* **1.** *Med:* demineralization. **2.** *Tchn:* demineralization, deionization.

déminéraliser [demineralize], *v.tr.* **1.** *Med:* to demineralize. **2.** to demineralize, de-ionize (water, etc.).

démineur [deminœːr], *s.m.* bomb disposal expert; **équipe de démineurs,** mine-clearance, bomb disposal, squad, unit.

demi-nœud [dəminø], *s.m.* overhand knot; *pl. demi-nœuds.*

demi-obscurité [dəmiɔpskyrite], *s.f.* half light.

demi-oncial, -aux [dəmiɔ̃sjal, -o], *a.* half uncial.

demi-onde [dəmiɔ̃d], *s.f. Ph:* half-wave; *pl. demi-ondes.*

demi-opale [dəmiɔpal], *s.f. Miner:* semi-opal; *pl. demi-opales.*

demi-opaque [dəmiɔpak], *a.* semi-opaque; *pl. demi-opaques.*

demi-paon [dəmipɑ̃], *s.m. Ent:* hawkmoth; *pl. demi-paons.*

demi-pause [dəmipoːz], *s.f. Mus:* minim rest; *pl. demi-pauses.*

demi-pension [dəmipɑ̃sjɔ̃], *s.f.* half board, demi-pension; *pl. demi-pensions.*

demi-pensionnaire [dəmipɑ̃sjɔnɛːr], *s.m. & f.* half boarder; *Sch:* day boarder; *pl. demi-pensionnaires.*

demi-période [dəmiperjɔd], *s.f. Ph:* half-period (of oscillation); *Ph: Elcs:* half-cycle, semi-period; *Atom.Ph:* **d.-p. radioactive, biologique,** radioactive, biological, half-life; *pl. demi-périodes.*

demi-pièce [dəmipjɛs], *s.f.* **1.** half-piece (of material). **2.** half-cask, half-hogshead (of wine); *pl. demi-pièces.*

demi-pique [dəmipik], *s.f. A.Arms:* spontoon, half pike.

demi-place [dəmiplas], *s.f.* half-fare (when travelling); half-price (at theatre, etc.); **voyager à d.-p.,** to travel at half-fare; *pl. demi-places.*

demi-pointe [dəmipwɛ̃ːt], *s.f. Danc:* **sur (la) d.-p.,** on half toe; **marcher sur la d.-p. des pieds,** to tread on the ball of the foot; *pl. demi-pointes.*

demi-portion [dəmipɔrsjɔ̃], *s.f. F:* pint-sized person; *pl. demi-portions.*

demi-pose [dəmipoːz], *s.f. Phot:* bulb exposure; *pl. demi-poses.*

demi-produit [dəmiprɔdɥi], *s.m. Ind:* semi-manufactured product; *pl. demi-produits.*

demi-quart [dəmikaːr], *s.m.* **1.** *Nau:* half point (of the compass). **2.** *Meas:* (*a*) = 2 ounces; (*b*) *Mil: F:* **un d.-q. de vin,** half a mug of wine; *pl. demi-quarts.*

demi-queue [dəmikø], *s.m.inv. Mus:* boudoir grand (piano).

demi-raisin [dəmirɛzɛ̃], *s.m. Paperm:* royal folio; *pl. demi-raisins.*

demi-relief [dəmirəljɛf], *s.m. Art:* mezzo-relievo; *pl. demi-reliefs.*

demi-reliure [dəmirəljyːr], *s.f. Bookb:* quarter-binding; **d.-r. à petits coins,** half-binding; **d.-r. amateur,** three-quarter binding; *pl. demi-reliures.*

demi-rond [dəmirɔ̃], *s.m. Tls:* (currier's) parer; *pl. demi-ronds.*

demi-ronde [dəmirɔ̃ːd], *s.f. Tls:* half-round file; *pl. demi-rondes.*

demi-saison [dəmisɛzɔ̃], *s.f.* between-season, mid-season; **tissus de d.-s.,** spring suitings; **vêtements de d.-s.,** between-season clothes; *pl. demi-saisons.*

demi-sang [dəmisɑ̃], *s.m.inv.* half-bred horse; half-bred.

demi-savant [dəmisavɑ̃], *s.m.* sciolist; man of superficial knowledge; semi-intellectual; *pl. demi-savants.*

demi-savoir [dəmisavwaːr], *s.m.* sciolism; superficial (intellectual) knowledge.

demi-sec [dəmisɛk], *a. & s.m.* **un (vin) d.-s.,** a medium dry wine; *pl. demi-secs.*

demi-section [dəmisɛksjɔ̃], *s.f. Mil:* two *escouades* (of infantry); *pl. demi-sections.*

demi-sel [dəmisɛl]. **1.** *s.m.* (*a*) slightly salted cream-cheese, *demi-sel*; (*b*) souteneur; (*c*) (petty) criminal; *F:* crook; (*d*) dimwit; *pl. demi-sel(s).* **2.** *a.inv.* **beurre d.-sel,** slightly salted butter.

demi-setier [dəmisətje], *s.m. A.Meas:* quarter of a litre (*esp.* of wine); (half-pint) glass of wine (in taverns, etc.); *pl. demi-setiers.*

demi-sœur [dəmisœːr], *s.f.* (*a*) half-sister; (*b*) stepsister; *pl. demi-sœurs.*

demi-solde [dəmisɔld]. **1.** *s.f. Mil:* half-pay; **en d.-s.,** on half-pay; *pl. demi-soldes.* **2.** *s.m.inv. in pl.* half-pay officer.

demi-sommeil [dəmisɔmɛːj], *s.m.* drowsiness, somnolence; *pl. demi-sommeils.*

demi-soupir [dəmisupiːr], *s.m. Mus:* quaver rest; *pl. demi-soupirs.*

démission [demisjɔ̃], *s.f.* **1.** resignation; **donner sa d.,** to tender, send in, hand in, one's resignation, to resign; (*in Parliament*) to vacate one's seat; *Mil:* to send in one's papers, to resign one's commission. **2.** failure.

démissionnaire [demisjɔnɛːr], *a. & s.* (one) who has resigned (his office, commission, seat in Parliament, etc.); resigner; resigning (officer, etc.); out-going (ministry, etc.); **se déclarer d.,** (i) to announce one's resignation; (ii) to announce that one will not seek re-election.

démissionner [demisjɔne]. **1.** *v.i.* to resign (**de,** from); **d. de la présidence de . . .,** to resign as president of . . .. **2.** *v.tr. F:* **d. qn,** to dismiss; *F:* to sack, s.o.

demi-tarif [dəmitarif], *s.m.* half-fare; **billet à d.-t.,** half-fare ticket; *pl. demi-tarifs.*

demi-tasse [dəmitɑs], *s.f.* **1.** small (coffee-)cup. **2.** half a cup; **une d.-t. de café,** a "small coffee," *U.S:* demi-tasse; *pl. demi-tasses.*

demi-teinte [dəmitɛ̃ːt], *s.f. Art: Phot: etc:* half-tone, half-tint; *pl. demi-teintes.*

demi-tendineux [dəmitɑ̃dinø], *a. & s.m.inv. Anat:* (*musculus*) *semitendinosus.*

demi-terme [dəmitɛrm], *s.m.* **1.** half-quarter; **payer un d.-t. d'avance,** to pay half a quarter's rent in advance; *pl. demi-termes.* **2.** *Med:* **accoucher à d.-t.,** to be delivered when one's time is only half up.

demi-tige [dəmitiʒ], *s.f. Arb:* half standard; *pl. demi-tiges.*

demi-ton [dəmitɔ̃], *s.m. Mus:* semitone; *pl. demi-tons.*

demi-tonneau [dəmitɔno], *s.m. Av:* half-roll; *pl. demi-tonneaux.*

demi-tour [dəmituːr], *s.m.* **1.** (*a*) half-turn; *Mil:* about turn; **faire demi-tour,** (i) to turn back; (ii) to turn (right-)about; to about-turn; **demi-tour, droite! demi-tour à droite! marche!** (right-)about turn! **faire faire d.-t. à son cheval,** to turn one's horse; (*b*) *Nau:* **faire d.-t.,** to turn a half-circle. **2.** spring-bolt (of lock); **fermé au d.-t.,** on the latch. **3.** *Nau:* cross (in the hawse); *pl. demi-tours.*

demi-transparence [dəmitrɑ̃sparɑ̃ːs], *s.f.* semi-transparency; *pl. demi-transparences.*

demi-transparent [dəmitrɑ̃sparɑ̃], *a.* semi-transparent; *pl. demi-transparents.*

démiurge [demjyrʒ], *s.m. A.Phil:* demiurge.

démiurgique [demjyrʒik], *a. A.Phil:* demiurgic.

demi-valétudinaire [dəmivaletydinɛːr], *s.m. & f.* semi-invalid; *pl. demi-valétudinaires.*

demi-varangue [dəmivarɑ̃ːg], *s.f. N.Arch:* half-floor; *pl. demi-varangues.*

demi-varlope [dəmivarlɔp], *s.f. Tls:* jack-plane; *pl. demi-varlopes.*

demi-vérité [dəmiverite], *s.f.* half-truth; *pl. demi-vérités.*

demi-vie [dəmivi], *s.f. Atom.Ph:* half-life; **d.-v. biologique,** biological half-life; **d.-v. radioactive,** radioactive half-life; *pl. demi-vies.*

demi-vierge [dəmivjɛrʒ], *s.f.* demi-vierge; *pl. demi-vierges.*

demi-voix (à) [ad(ə)mivwa], *adv.phr.* **1.** in an undertone, in a subdued tone; under one's breath. **2.** *Mus:* mezza-voce.

demi-volée [dəmivɔle], *s.f. Ten:* half-volley; *pl. demi-volées.*

demi-volte [dəmivɔlt], *s.f. Equit:* demi-volte; *pl. demi-voltes.*

demi-watt [dəmiwat]. **1.** *a.inv. & s.m. El:* half-watt. **2.** *s.f. Tchn:* half-watt lamp; *pl. demi-watts.*

démobilisation [demɔbilizasjɔ̃], *s.f.* demobilization, demobilizing (of troops); discharge (of soldier after active service); **1.500.000 démobilisations,** 1,500,000 service releases.

démobilisé [demɔbilize], *s.m.* recently demobilized man.

démobiliser [demɔbilize], *v.tr.* to demobilize (troops); to discharge (soldier after active service); *abs.* **la France démobilise,** France demobilizes.

démocrate [demɔkrat]. **1.** *a.* democratic (principles, etc.). **2.** *s.* democrat.

démocratie [demɔkrasi], *s.f.* democracy.

démocratique [demɔkratik], *a.* democratic (constitution, etc.).

démocratiquement [demɔkratikmɑ̃], *adv.* democratically.

démocratisation [demɔkratizasjɔ̃], *s.f.* democratization.

démocratiser [demɔkratize], *v.tr.* to democratize. **se démocratiser,** to become democratized; to tend towards democracy.

démocratisme [demɔkratism], *s.m. Pol:* democratism.

Démocrite [demɔkrit], *Pr.n.m. Gr.Phil:* Democritus.

démodé [demɔde], *a.* old fashioned, out of fashion; obsolete, out of date; outdated; **méthodes démodées,** antiquated, obsolete, methods; **les grands chapeaux sont démodés,** large hats have gone out of fashion.

démodécie [demɔdesi], *s.f. Vet:* demodectic mange.

démodécique [demɔdesik], *a. Vet:* demodectic.

démoder [demɔde], *v.tr.* to send (clothes, etc.) out of fashion, *U.S:* to outmode.

se démoder, (*of clothes, etc.*) to go out of fashion, to become old-fashioned, antiquated.

démodex [demɔdɛks], *s.m.inv. in pl. Arach: Med:* demodex; itch-mite.

démodulateur [demɔdylatœːr], *s.m. Elcs:* demodulator.

démodulation [demɔdylasjɔ̃], *s.f. Elcs:* demodulation.

démographe [demɔgraf], *s.m.* demographer.

démographie [demɔgrafi], *s.f.* (*a*) demography; (*b*) population.

démographique [demɔgrafik], *a.* demographic; *Adm: Pol.Ec:* **statistiques démographiques,** vital statistics; **accroissement, poussée, d.,** increase in population; **explosion d.,** population explosion.

demoiselle [dəmwazɛl], *s.f.* **1.** (*a*) spinster, single woman, unmarried woman; **elle est d.,** she is single, unmarried; **je l'avais connue d.,** I had known her when she was single, before she was married, when she was Miss X; **son nom de d.,** her maiden name; (*b*) **d. d'honneur,** (i) maid of honour; (ii) bridesmaid; **d. de compagnie,** lady companion; **d. de magasin,** shop-assistant, shop-girl. **2.** (*a*) young lady; **ces demoiselles sont avec vous?** are these young ladies with you? *s.a.* MADEMOISELLE 2; (*b*) *P:* **comment va votre d.?** how is your daughter? **3.** *F:* (*a*) *Orn:* long-tailed tit; **d. de Numidie,** demoiselle crane, crown crane, Numidian crane; (*b*) *Ent:* dragonfly, damsel-fly, flying-adder, adder-fly; (*c*) *Ich:* (i) hammer-head (shark); (ii) damsel-fish. **4.** (*a*) (paviour's) rammer, paving-beetle, punner; (*b*) glove-stretcher; (*c*) *A:* hot-water bottle; (*d*) *Mus:* tracker (of organ); (*e*) rowlock, thole-pin; (*f*) *Mec.E: F:* **l'arbre fait la d.,** the shaft runs untrue. **5.** *Geol:* erosion column, chimney-rock.

démoli [demɔli], *s.m. F:* cripple, *esp.* crippled acrobat.

démolir [demɔliːr], *v.tr.* (*a*) to demolish, pull down (house, etc.); to batter down (wall, etc.); to break up (ship); *F:* to overthrow (institution, government); *F:* to ruin (health, reputation); **mur à moitié démoli,** tumble-down wall; **table aux pieds démolis,** table with broken legs; (*b*) *F:* **d. qn,** to thrash s.o. soundly; to knock s.o. into a cocked hat; **j'ai démoli son argument,** I knocked the bottom out of his argument, I didn't leave him a leg to stand on.

se démolir, to break up, to go to pieces.

démolissage [demɔlisaːʒ], *s.m.* = DÉMOLITION.

démolissement [demɔlismɑ̃], *s.m. A:* = DÉMOLITION.

démolisseur, -euse [demɔlisœːr, -øːz], *s.* **1.** demolisher, overthrower (of argument, government, etc.). **2.** *Tchn:* (*a*) housebreaker; demolition contractor; (*b*) ship-breaker.

démolition [demɔlisjɔ̃], *s.f.* **1.** demolition; pulling down (of structure); *N.Am:* wrecking; **chantier de d.,** (i) housebreaker's yard; (ii) shipbreaker's yard; **d. de navires,** ship breaking; **poudre de d.,** blasting powder. **2.** *pl.* old, partworn, material (from demolished house, etc.); scrap.

démon [demɔ̃], *s.m.* **1.** *Myth:* daemon, (good, evil) genius; spirit. **2.** demon, devil, fiend; *F:* **c'est un vrai d.,** he is the devil incarnate; **cet enfant est un petit d.,** that child is a little demon, a little imp; **le d. de la jalousie,** the demon of jealousy; **faire le d.,** to kick up a shindy, to raise Cain; **il a de l'esprit comme un d.,** he has the devil's own wit; **d. de midi,** middle age love.

démonétisation [demɔnetizasjɔ̃], *s.f.* **1.** demonetization; calling in, withdrawal from circulation (of coinage, etc.). **2.** *F:* discrediting (of politician, etc.).

démonétiser [demɔnetize], *v.tr.* to demonetize (metal, etc.); to call in, withdraw (coinage, etc.) from circulation; *F:* **d. qn,** to discredit, throw discredit on, s.o.

démoniaque [demɔnjak]. **1.** *a.* demoniac(al); possessed of the, a, devil; **soumettre (qn) à une influence d., rendre d.,** to diabolize. **2.** *s.m. & f.* demoniac; *B:* man possessed of a devil.

démonisme [demɔnism], *s.m.* demonism.

démoniste [demɔnist], *s.m. & a.* demonist.

démonographe [demɔnɔgraf], *s.* = DÉMONOLOGUE.

démonographie [demɔnɔgrafi], *s.f.* = DÉMONOLOGIE.

démonolâtre [demɔnɔlɑːtr], *s. & a.* (one) who worships demons.

démonolâtrie [demɔnɔlɑtri], *s.f.* demonolatry.

démonologie [demɔnɔlɔʒi], *s.f.* demonology.

démonologique [demɔnɔlɔʒik], *a.* demonologic(al).

démonologue [demɔnɔlɔg], *s.* demonologist

démonomanie [demɔnɔmani], *s.f. Med: Psy:* demonomania.

démonstrateur, -trice [demɔ̃stratœːr, -tris], *s.* **1.** *Sch:* demonstrator, professor's assistant; **d. en anatomie,** demonstrator in, of, anatomy. **2.** *Com: Ind:* demonstrator; **ingénieur d.,** exhibit engineer.

démonstratif, -ive [demɔ̃stratif, -i:v], *a.* **1.** (logically) conclusive. **2.** *Gram:* demonstrative (adjective, pronoun). **3.** demonstrative, expansive (person); **peu d.**, undemonstrative, staid; **un Écossais peu d.**, a dour Scotsman.

démonstration [demɔ̃strasjɔ̃], *s.f.* demonstration. **1.** (*a*) proof (of theorem, of a law of nature, etc.); **d. par l'absurde,** proof by *reductio ad absurdum*, demonstration *ab absurdo*; (*b*) conclusive experiment; (*c*) exhibition (of process, etc.); *Box:* **assaut de d.,** sparring match or exhibition; (*d*) *Ind: Com:* demonstration (of an article on show or for sale); **appareil de d.,** demonstration model. **2.** (*a*) *Pol:* demonstration; *Mil:* show of force; **faire une d. (pour dérouter l'ennemi),** to demonstrate, make a demonstration (in order to mislead the enemy); (*b*) *esp. pl.* **faire de grandes démonstrations d'amitié à qn,** to make great demonstrations of friendship to s.o.; to make a great show of friendship to s.o.

démonstrativement [demɔ̃strativmɑ̃], *adv.* demonstratively, conclusively.

démontable [demɔ̃tabl̩], *a.* (*of machine. etc.*) demountable, detachable, removable, dismountable; **construction d.,** building made in sections, portable building; **canot d.,** collapsible boat; *Artil:* **affût d.,** take-down carriage; *Av:* **manche à balai d.,** detachable control-stick.

démontage [demɔ̃ta:ʒ], *s.m.* taking down, taking to pieces, dismantling; disassembling, overhauling (of machine, etc.); teardown (of motor); dismounting, stripping (of gun for cleaning, etc.); unshipping (of rudder, etc.); removal (of tyre); **clé de d.,** disassembly wrench; **ordre de d.,** dismantling sequence.

démonté [demɔ̃te], *a.* **1. escadron de cavalerie d.,** dismounted squadron of cavalry. **2.** stormy, raging, rolling (sea). **3.** (*of pers.*) abashed, flustered; put out (of countenance); upset. **4.** taken to pieces, dismantled.

démonte-pneu [demɔ̃t(ə)pnø], *s.m.* **(levier) d-p.,** tyre-lever; *pl. démonte-pneus.*

démonter [demɔ̃te], *v.tr.* **1.** to unhorse, unseat (rider); **son cheval l'a démonté,** his horse threw him; *F:* **la nouvelle m'a démonté,** I was greatly cut up, upset, put out, by the news, the news unnerved me; **se laisser d.,** to get upset; **il ne se laisse pas d.,** he isn't easily flummoxed, abashed; he's a cool hand. **2.** to take down, take to pieces; dismantle; to disassemble, overhaul (machine, etc.); to dismount, to strip (gun for cleaning); to strike (sheers); to unship, to unhang (rudder, etc.); to unhinge, unhang (door); to remove (pneumatic tyre); to unset, unmount (diamond); to strike (tent). **3.** *Navy: F:* **d. un officier,** to supersede an officer.

se démonter. 1. (*of machine, etc.*) to take to pieces, take down; **échelle qui se démonte,** ladder that takes to pieces; *F:* **la machine commence à se d.,** the whole thing is beginning to go to pieces. **2.** (*a*) (*of mechanism*) to come apart; (*b*) *F:* **il ne se démonte pas pour si peu,** he is not so easily put out (of countenance); he is not so easily disconcerted, upset.

démonte-soupapes [demɔ̃tsupap], *s.m.inv. in pl. Aut:* valve-spring compressor, valve-lifter.

démonteur, -euse [demɔ̃tœ:r, -ø:z], *s.* **1.** dismantler, disassembler. **2.** *s.f.* **démonteuse,** *Tex:* bobbin-setter.

démontrabilité [demɔ̃trabilite], *s.f.* demonstrability.

démontrable [demɔ̃trabl̩], *a.* demonstrable, provable.

démontrer [demɔ̃tre], *v.tr.* **1.** to demonstrate; (*a*) to prove, to establish the truth of (proposition, etc.); **cela se démontre facilement,** that's easily proved; (*b*) to give practical instruction in (sth.). **2.** to give clear indication of (sth.); **action qui démontre la bonté,** act that betokens, evinces, kindliness.

démontreur [demɔ̃trœ:r], *s.m.* demonstrator (of a truth, etc.).

démophile [demɔfil], *s.m.* demophil, friend of the people.

démoralisant [demɔralizɑ̃], *a.* demoralizing.

démoralisateur, -trice [demɔralizatœ:r, -tris]. **1.** *s.* corrupter, demoralizer. **2.** *a.* demoralizing.

démoralisation [demɔralizasjɔ̃], *s.f.* demoralization.

démoraliser [demɔralize], *v.tr.* to demoralize. **1.** to corrupt, deprave. **2.** to undermine, destroy, the discipline of (troops); to dishearten.

se démoraliser, to become demoralized; (*of troops*) to lose their morale.

démordre [demɔrdr̩], *v.i.* (*a*) to let go one's hold (with the teeth); (*b*) *F: usu.* with negative; **ne pas d. de ses opinions,** to stand by, to stick to, one's opinions; **il ne veut pas en d.,** he won't give up his point, he sticks to it; **sans jamais d. d'un de ses principes,** without ever departing from one of his principles.

démorphiner [demɔrfine], *v.tr.* to detoxicate, detoxify, a morphia addict.

démorphinisation [demɔrfinizasjɔ̃], *s.f.* detoxification of a morphia addict.

démosponges [demɔspɔ̃:ʒ], *s.m.pl. Z:* Demospongea, Demospongiae.

Démosthène [demɔstɛn], *Pr.n.m. Gr.Hist:* Demosthenes.

démotique [demɔtik], *a. & s.m.* **1.** *Pal:* demotic (writing). **2.** *Ling:* demotic.

démouchetage [demuʃ(ə)ta:ʒ], *s.m. Fenc:* taking of the button off (foil).

démoucheter [demuʃte], *v.tr.* **(je démouchette, n. démouchetons; je démouchetterai)** *Fenc:* to take the button off (foil).

se démoucheter, (*of foil*) to lose its button.

démoulage [demula:ʒ], *s.m.* (*a*) withdrawing (of pattern) from the mould; (*b*) stripping (of casting); (*c*) lifting (of porcelain, etc.); (*d*) *Cu:* **d. d'un gâteau,** turning out of a cake.

démouler [demule], *v.tr.* (*a*) to withdraw (pattern) from the mould; (*b*) to strip (casting); (*c*) *Cer:* to lift (porcelain); (*d*) *Cu:* to turn out (a cake).

démucilagination [demysilaʒinasjɔ̃], *s.f. Tchn:* removal of mucilages from (crude oil).

démucilaginer [demysilaʒine], *v.tr. Tchn:* to remove mucilages from crude oil.

démuétiser [demɥetize], *v.tr. Ling:* to voice (consonant).

démultiplicateur [demyltiplikatœ:r], *a. & s.m.* **1.** *a.* (*a*) *Mec.E:* gearing-down, reducing; **engrenage d.,** reducing, step-down, gear; **mécanisme d.,** gearing-down mechanism; (*b*) *El.E: Elcs:* **circuit d.,** scaling circuit. **2.** *s.m.* (*a*) *Mec.E:* reducing, step-down, gear; reduction-gear, -unit; **d. de vitesse,** motor reduction-unit; (*b*) *El.E: Elcs:* vernier (arrangement); **cadran à d.,** vernier dial; **condensateur à d.,** vernier control condenser; (*c*) *Atom.Ph:* scaler; **d. de décades,** decade scaler.

démultiplication [demyltiplikasjɔ̃], *s.f.* **1.** *Mec.E:* (i) reduction, gearing down; (ii) gear ratio; **rapport de d.,** reduction ratio, speed reduction percentage; **valeur de d.,** range of gear reduction. **2.** *El.E: Elcs:* scaling; **rapport de d.,** scaling ratio; **d. de (la) fréquence,** skip keying. **3.** *Atom. Ph:* scale, scaling; **d. à décades,** decade scaling.

démultiplier [demyltiplie], *v.tr.* (*p.d. & pr.sub.* **n. démultipliions, v. démultipliiez)** *Mec.E:* to reduce the gear ratio; to gear down; **voiture très démultipliée,** car geared very low.

démuni [demyni], *a.* **1.** unprovided (de, en, with); **titre d. de coupons,** bond minus its coupons; **je ne peux pas rester d. de mes fonds,** I cannot lie out of my money; *F:* **je me trouvais d.,** I was at a loss. **2.** *Com:* **être d. de qch.,** to be out of sth., sold out of sth.

démunir [demyni:r], *v.tr.* **1.** to strip, deprive, (fortress, etc.) of munitions. **2.** to clear (shopkeeper, etc.) out of stock.

se démunir de qch. 1. to allow oneself to run short of sth. **2.** to part with sth.

démurer [demyre], *v.tr.* to remove the masonry from, to open up (door, window, etc.).

démuseler [demyzle], *v.tr.* **(je démuselle, n. démuselons; je démusellerai)** to unmuzzle (dog); *F:* **d. les passions,** to let loose passions.

démutisation [demytizasjɔ̃], *s.f. Psy:* first phase in the teaching of deaf-mutes.

démystification [demistifikasjɔ̃], *s.f. F:* debunking.

démystifier [demistifje], *v.tr.* (*p.d. and pr.sub.* **n. démystifiions, v. démystifiiez)** *F:* to debunk.

démythification [demitifikasjɔ̃], *s.f.* **1.** = DÉMYSTIFICATION. **2.** demythification.

démythifier [demitifje], *v.tr.* (*p.d. and pr.sub.* **n. démythifiions, v. démythifiiez) 1.** = DÉMYSTIFIER. **2.** to divest sth., s.o., of its mythical quality.

dénager [denaʒe], *v.i.* (*conj. like* NAGER) *Nau:* (*to stop way*) to back the oars, to back water; **dénage partout!** back all!

dénaire [denɛ:r], *a. Hist:* denary, decimal (system, etc.).

dénantir [denɑ̃ti:r], *v.tr.* to deprive (creditor, etc.) of pledges, of his securities.

se dénantir, to part with one's securities; *F:* **se d. de tout ce qu'on possède,** to give up all that one possesses.

dénasalisation [denazalizasjɔ̃], *s.f. Ling:* denasalization.

dénasaliser [denazalize], *v.tr. Ling:* to denasalize (a vowel, etc.) to deprive (vowel, etc.) of its nasal sound.

se dénasaliser, (*of vowel, etc.*) to be denasalized, to lose its nasal sound.

dénatalité [denatalite], *s.f.* fall in the birth-rate.

dénationalisation [denasjɔnalizasjɔ̃], *s.f.* denationalization.

dénationaliser [denasjɔnalize], *v.tr.* to denationalize.

se dénationaliser, *A:* to lose one's nationality.

dénatter [denate], *v.tr.* to unplait; to unbraid (one's hair).

dénaturalisation [denatyralizasjɔ̃], *s.f.* denaturalization.

dénaturaliser [denatyralize], *v.tr.* to denaturalize (person).

dénaturant [denatyrɑ̃], *Ch:* **1.** *a.* denaturing. **2.** *s.m.* denaturant, denaturing agent; **d. nucléaire,** nuclear denaturant.

dénaturateur [denatyratœ:r], *s.m.* (*a*) person employed by the (French) Excise to denature alcohol; (*b*) person who sells denatured alcohol under the control of the Excise.

dénaturation [denatyrasjɔ̃], *s.f.* denaturation, changing the nature of (sth.); **d. de l'alcool,** denaturing of alcohol.

dénaturé [denatyre], *a.* **1. alcool d.,** denatured alcohol, methylated spirits. **2.** unnatural; **père d.,** unnatural, hard-hearted, father; **goûts dénaturés,** unnatural, perverted, tastes.

dénaturer [denatyre], *v.tr.* **1.** (*a*) to denature, disnature, to change the nature of (sth.); **d. l'alcool,** to denature, to methylate, alcohol; (*b*) **d. les paroles, les actions, de qn,** to misrepresent, distort, s.o.'s words, s.o.'s actions; **d. la conduite de qn,** to place s.o.'s conduct in a false light; **d. un texte,** to distort the meaning of a text; **d. les faits,** to garble the facts. **2.** to render (s.o., sth.) unnatural; **d. l'âme,** to pervert the soul.

dénazification [denazifikasjɔ̃], *s.f.* denazification.

dénazifier [denazifje], *v.tr.* (*p.d. and pr.sub.* **n. dénazifiions, v. dénazifiiez)** *Pol:* to denazify.

denché [dɑ̃ʃe], *a. Her:* indented.

dendraspis [dɑ̃draspis], *s.m. Z:* Dendraspis.

dendrite [dɑ̃drit, dɛ̃-], *s.f. Geol: Metall:* dendrite.

dendritique [dɑ̃dritik, dɛ̃-], *a. Geol: Metall:* dendritic.

dendr(o)- [dɑ̃dr(ɔ)], *pref.* dendr(o)-.

dendrobates [dɑ̃drɔbat], *s.m. Z:* Dendrobates.

dendrochronologie [dɑ̃drɔkrɔnɔlɔʒi], *s.f.* dendrochronology.

dendrographie [dɑ̃drɔgrafi], *s.f. Arb:* = DENDROLOGIE.

dendrographique [dɑ̃drɔgrafik], *a. Arb:* dendrographic.

dendroïde [dɑ̃drɔid, dɛ̃-], *a. Bot:* dendroid, branching, tree-like.

dendroïque [dɑ̃drɔik], *s.m. Orn:* dendroeca; *F:* yellow-bird.

dendrolague [dɑ̃drɔlag], *s.m. Z:* tree-wallaby; *pl.* (*genus*) Dendrolagus.

dendrologie [dɑ̃drɔlɔʒi, dɛ̃-], *s.f.* dendrology.

dendromètre [dɑ̃drɔmɛtr], *s.m.* dendrometer, dendrograph.

dendrométrie [dɑ̃drɔmetri], *s.f. Arb:* dendrography.

dénébulation [denebylasjɔ̃], *s.f. Av:* fog dispersal.

dénégateur, -trice [denegatœ:r, -tris], *s.* denier.

dénégation [denegasjɔ̃], *s.f.* denial; *Jur:* traverse; **d. de responsabilité,** disclaimer, denial, of responsibility.

dénerver [denɛrve], *v.tr. Cu:* to draw the sinews from (meat).

dengue [dɛ̃:g], *s.f. Med:* dengue(-fever); breakbone fever; *F:* dandy(-fever).

déni [deni], *s.m. Jur:* denial, refusal (of sth. which is due); **d. de justice,** denial of justice.

déniaisé [denjɛze], *a.* **1.** smartened up; who has been taught a thing or two. **2.** who has lost his or her innocence.

déniaisement [denjɛzmɑ̃], *s.m. F:* **1.** education in the ways of the world. **2.** (sexual) initiation; loss of innocence.

déniaiser [denjɛze], *v.tr.* **1.** to educate (s.o.) in the ways of the world. **2.** *F:* to initiate (s.o.) sexually.

se déniaiser. 1. to learn the ways of the world, to learn one's way about. **2.** *F:* to lose one's innocence.

dénichement [deniʃmɑ̃], *s.m.* **1.** robbing (of bird's nest). **2.** finding (of sth. after a search).

dénicher [deniʃe]. **1.** *v.tr.* (*a*) to take (bird, eggs) out of the nest; **aller d. des nids,** to go bird(s')-nesting; (*b*) to find, discover (bird or eggs) in a nest; *F:* **nous avons déniché un bon chauffeur,** we have discovered, unearthed, a good chauffeur; **comment m'avez-vous déniché?** how did you ferret me out, discover my whereabouts? **il**

dénicha tous nos trésors cachés, he unearthed, routed out, all our hidden treasures; **où as-tu bien pu d. ce vieux tacot?** where the devil did you dig up that old crate? (*c*) to dislodge (bird); to rout out (animal); *F:* **d. l'ennemi d'un bois,** to dislodge the enemy from a wood. **2.** *v.i.* (*of birds*) to forsake the nest, to fly away; *O: F:* **d. de la ville,** to quit the town; *F:* **les oiseaux ont déniché, sont dénichés,** the birds have flown; **d. sans tambour ni trompette,** to move off quietly, without attracting attention.

dénicheur, -euse [deniʃœːr, -øːz], *s.* **1.** (bird's)-nester. **2.** *F:* searcher, ferreter out; **d. de curiosités,** curio-hunter; *F:* **d. de talent(s),** talent scout; **d. de merles,** (i) trickster, rogue; (ii) cute fellow; **à d'autres, d. de merles!** *P:* no you don't! I've had some!

dénickelage [denikəlaːʒ], *s.m. Metall:* removal of nickel from a piece of metal.

dénickeler [denikəle], *v.tr. Metall:* to remove the nickel from a piece of metal.

dénicotiniser [denikɔtinize], *v.tr.* to denicotinize, denicotine.

dénicotinisation [denikɔtinizasjɔ̃], *s.f.* denicotinizing.

denier [dənje], *s.m.* **1.** (*a*) *Rom.Ant:* denarius; (*b*) *A:* (Fr.) denier, (*Eng.*) penny; **le d. de la veuve,** the widow's mite; **d. à Dieu,** deposit (on transaction); (*when taking a house*) key-money; tip (to *concierge* from new tenant); **le d. de saint Pierre,** Peter's pence; **payer jusqu'au dernier d.,** to pay to the last farthing; **tirer un bon d. de qch.,** to make a pretty penny out of sth. **2.** *A:* (rate of) interest; **intérêt au d. vingt, au d. quatre,** interest at the rate of one in twenty, one in four, *i.e.* 5%, 25%; *still used in* **prêter à un d. honnête,** to lend at fair interest. **3.** sum of money, funds, **deniers personnels,** one's own money; **je l'ai acheté de mes (propres) deniers,** I paid for it out of my own pocket; **acheter (qch.) à (beaux) deniers comptants,** to buy (sth.) for hard cash; **détournement des deniers de l'État, des deniers publics,** misappropriation of public funds; **allocation en deniers,** money allowance; *R.C.Ch:* **d. du culte,** church-offering (given privately to parish priest). **4.** *Hosiery:* denier; **un bas 30 deniers,** a 30 denier stocking.

dénier [denje], *v.tr.* (*p.d. & pr.sub.* **n. déniions, v. déniiez**) **1.** to deny (crime, etc.); **d. une dette,** to refuse to acknowledge a debt; **d. toute responsabilité,** to disclaim all responsibility. **2.** to refuse (justice, etc.); **d. qch. à qn,** to refuse, deny, s.o. sth.

dénigrant [denigrɑ̃], *a.* disparaging.

dénigrement [denigrəmɑ̃], *s.m.* disparagement, denigration; running down (of s.o., sth.); **par d.,** disparagingly.

dénigrer [denigre], *v.tr.* to disparage, denigrate; to run down, to speak ill of (s.o., sth.); *F:* to crab (s.o.).

dénigreur, -euse [denigrœːr, -øːz], *s.* depreciator, disparager, denigrator; detractor.

Denis [dəni], *Pr.n.m.* Den(n)is, Dionysius; *F:* **Monsieur et Madame D.,** Darby and Joan (of the substantial bourgeois class as sung by Désaugiers).

Denise [dəniːz], *Pr.n.f.* Denise.

dénitrage [denitraːʒ], *s.m. Ind:* the removal of volatile acids from molasses.

dénitrant [denitrɑ̃], *a. Ind:* denitrating; **tour, colonne, dénitrante,** denitrator tower.

dénitration [denitrasjɔ̃], *s.f. Ind:* denitration.

dénitrer [denitre], *v.tr. Ind:* to denitrate.

dénitreur [denitrœːr], *s.m. Ind:* denitrator.

dénitrification [denitrifikasjɔ̃], *s.f.* denitrification.

dénitrifier [denitrifje], *v.tr.* (*p.d. & pr.sub.* **n. dénitrifiions, v. dénitrifiiez**) to denitrify (the soil, etc.).

dénivelé [denivle], *a.* **1.** uneven, unlevel (roadway); **poutre dénivelée,** beam out of true, out of level. **2.** contoured (survey).

dénivelée [denivle], *s.f.* difference, variation, in level (*esp.* between firearm and target).

déniveler [denivle], *v.tr.* (*conj. like* NIVELER) **1.** *Civ.E: etc:* to put (surface, etc.) out of level, to make (surface, etc.) uneven; to diversify (a park, etc.) by changes of level. **2.** *Surv:* to determine differences in level; to contour (survey).

se déniveler, (*of supports, piers, etc.*) to subside, to sink, to settle.

dénivellation [denivelasjɔ̃], *s.f.,* **dénivellement** [denivɛlmɑ̃], *s.m.* **1.** (*a*) difference or variation in level (of supports of girder, etc.); **d. d'une route,** (i) unevenness, (ii) gradients, ups and downs, departures from the level, of a roadway; *Aut:* **d. des roues,** uneven footing of the wheels, disalignment; (*b*) *Hyd.E:* loss of pressure, of head. **2.** subsidence, sinking (of bridge, of engine-bed, etc.); settling (of piers, of supports); *Geol:* drop; change of level. **3.** *Surv:* determination of level; contouring.

dénombrable [denɔ̃brabl], *a.* countable.

dénombrement [denɔ̃brəmɑ̃], *s.m.* enumeration, counting (of persons, things); census (of population); *Log:* **d. imparfait,** undistributed middle; *Med:* **d. des hématies,** blood count.

dénombrer [denɔ̃bre], *v.tr.* to count, enumerate, number (persons, things); to take a census of (population); **trop riche pour pouvoir d. ses troupeaux,** too rich to tell the tale of his flocks.

dénominateur [denɔminatœːr], *s.m. Ar:* denominator; *Ar: and Figurative:* **d. commun,** common denominator.

dénominatif, -ive [denɔminatif, -iːv], *a. & s.m. Ling:* denominative (term, etc.).

dénomination [denɔminasjɔ̃], *s.f.* denomination, name, appellation; type (of equipment, etc.); *Rel:* denomination.

dénommer [denɔme], *v.tr.* to denominate, name, designate, give a name to (s.o., sth.); **certains orateurs non dénommés,** certain unspecified speakers; *Ins:* **personne dénommée,** nominee (for life annuity); *F:* **un dénommé Mathieu,** a man named Matthew.

dénoncer [denɔ̃se], *v.tr.* (**je dénonçai(s); n. dénonçons**) **1.** (*a*) *A:* to declare, proclaim (war, etc.); (*b*) **d. un traité,** to denounce a treaty; **d. un armistice,** to proclaim that an armistice is at an end; (*c*) *Jur:* to give notice of (steps about to be taken, documents to be produced, etc.); (*d*) **son visage dénonce la grossièreté de sa vie,** his face denotes, proclaims, the coarseness of his life. **2.** (*a*) to denounce, expose (s.o.); to inform against (s.o.); *F:* to give (s.o.) away; **se d.,** to give oneself up; **d. ses complices** = to turn King's evidence; (*b*) **d. le vice,** to expose vice; **d. les méfaits de qn à la police,** to make s.o.'s misdeeds known to the police, to lay information against s.o. with the police; to report s.o. to the police.

dénonciateur, -trice [denɔ̃sjatœːr, -tris]. **1.** *s.* (*a*) informer, denouncer; (*b*) person who denounces injustice. **2.** *a.* (*a*) tell-tale (look, blush, etc.); (*b*) **lettre dénonciatrice,** letter laying information.

dénonciation [denɔ̃sjasjɔ̃], *s.f.* **1.** (*a*) declaration, proclamation, official notice; (*b*) notice of termination (of partnership, treaty, etc.); (*c*) *Jur:* notice (of steps about to be taken). **2.** denunciation; information (**de qn,** against s.o.); *Jur:* **d. calomnieuse,** false accusation.

dénotation [denɔtasjɔ̃], *s.f. Log:* denotation.

dénoter [denɔte], *v.tr.* to denote, mark, betoken, show; **indices qui dénotent une maladie,** signs that denote, indicate, a disease; **terme qui dénote le mépris,** expression indicative of contempt; **rien ne semble d. qu'il soit coupable,** nothing seems to show that he is guilty, to point him out as guilty; **visage qui dénote l'énergie,** face that denotes, betokens, expresses, energy.

dénouable [denwabl], *a.* (knot) that may be untied, undone; (difficulty) that may be untangled.

dénouement, dénoûment [denumɑ̃], *s.m.* **1.** *A:* untying, undoing, loosening, untangling (of knot, etc.). **2.** issue, upshot, result, outcome (of event); solution (of difficulty); crisis (of illness); dénouement, ending (of plot, story); *Th:* dénouement; **heureux d.,** happy ending; **le d. de l'aventure,** the end of the adventure.

dénouer [denwe], *v.tr.* **1.** to unknot; to untie, undo, loose (knot, scarf, bootlace, bonds, etc.); **d. ses cheveux,** to undo, let down, unbind, one's hair; **d. une situation, une intrigue,** to clear up, unravel, untangle, a situation, a plot; **d. une action dramatique,** to lead up to the final event of a drama; **d. une question,** to bring a question to a decision. **2.** to make (limbs, etc.) more supple; **d. la langue à qn,** to loosen s.o.'s tongue.

se dénouer. 1. to come undone; **vos cheveux se dénouent,** your hair is falling loose, is coming undone. **2.** (*of story, etc.*) to end, to wind up. **3. sa langue se dénouait,** he was finding his tongue.

dénoueur, -euse [denwœːr, -øːz], *s.* loosener (of knot, etc.); solver, unriddler (of problem, difficulty, etc.).

dénoyage [denwajaːʒ], *s.m. Min:* unwatering (of mine).

dénoyauter [denwajote], *v.tr.* to stone (fruit).

dénoyauteur [denwajotœːr], *s.m.* stoner; fruit-stoning gadget.

dénoyer [denwaje], *v.tr. Min:* to pump out, unwater (mine).

denrée [dɑ̃re], *s.f. usu. pl.* commodity, article, of trade; *esp.* produce, foodstuff; **denrées alimentaires,** provisions, food products, foodstuffs; **denrées coloniales, du pays,** colonial produce, home produce; **denrées périssables,** perishables.

dense [dɑ̃ːs], *a.* **1.** *Ph:* dense; *Mth:* **ensemble d.,** dense set. **2.** dense, crowded; close (formation of troops); thick (atmosphere); (*applied to literary work*) full of matter; **population d.,** dense population; **c'est sur la place que la foule était le plus d.,** the crowd was thickest in the square; **population peu d.,** sparse population.

densification [dɑ̃sifikasjɔ̃], *s.f.* densifying of wood.

densifié [dɑ̃sifje], *a.* densified (wood).

densimètre [dɑ̃simɛtr̥], *s.m. Ph:* densimeter, density-meter, -gauge.

densimétrie [dɑ̃simetri], *s.f. Ph:* densimetry.

densimétrique [dɑ̃simetrik], *a. Ph:* densimetric.

densité [dɑ̃site], *s.f.* **1.** density (of metal, fluid, current, electron beam, etc.); (*a*) *Ph:* **d. moyenne,** mean specific weight, average, mean, density; **flacon à d.,** specific gravity flask, pycnometer; **d. gravimétrique,** gravimetric density; *Ch:* **d. de précipitation,** deposition density; (*b*) *El: Elcs:* **d. d'impulsion,** pulse density; (*c*) *Atom.Ph:* **d. de chocs,** collision density; **d. de ralentissement,** slowing-down density; **d. de rayonnement,** radiation density; **d. du flux de radiation(s),** radiant-flux density; **d. ionique, neutronique,** ion, neutron, density. **2.** denseness, density (of population, etc.); (*a*) **population de faible d.,** sparse population; **région de, à, faible d. de population,** sparsely populated area; (*b*) *Mil:* **d. du feu, du tir,** density of fire; **d. des coups, des points d'impact,** density, grouping, of hits; **d. de l'objectif,** density, compactness, of target.

densitomètre [dɑ̃sitɔmɛtr̥], *s.m. Phot:* densitometer.

dent [dɑ̃], *s.f.* **1.** (*a*) tooth; **dents incisives,** incisors; **d. de sagesse,** wisdom-tooth; **dents de lait,** milk-teeth, first teeth; **dents définitives,** permanent teeth, second teeth; **d. antérieure, d. du devant,** anterior tooth; **d. postérieure, d. du fond, grosse d.,** posterior tooth, back tooth, molar; **d. inférieure, d. du bas, d. d'en bas,** lower, mandibular, tooth; **d. supérieure, d. du haut, d. d'en haut,** upper, maxillary, tooth; **d. de l'œil,** eye-tooth; **dents qui se chevauchent,** crowded, overlapping, teeth; **chevauchement des dents,** tooth-crowding; **d. vitale, vivante,** vital tooth; **d. avitale, morte,** non-vital, dead, tooth; **d. branlante,** loose tooth; **d. sensible,** sensitive tooth; **en forme de dent,** dentoid; **d. artificielle,** artificial, prosthetic, tooth; **fausse d.,** false tooth; **d. à crampon, à pivot,** pin-, pivot-tooth; **d. incluse,** unerupted tooth; *Nat.Hist:* **d. d'éclosion,** egg-tooth; **faire, percer, ses dents,** to cut one's teeth; **l'enfant fait ses dents,** the child is teething; **mal de dents,** toothache; **avoir mal aux dents,** to have toothache; *P:* **il n'a pas, n'aura plus (jamais) mal aux dents,** he is out of all his troubles (*i.e.* he is dead); **se faire arracher une d.,** to have a tooth out; **d. creuse,** hollow tooth; *F:* **il n'y en avait pas pour ma d. creuse,** there was hardly a toothful; **coup de dent(s),** bite; **donner un coup de d. à qn,** (i) (*of dog*) to snap at s.o.; (ii) *F:* (*of pers.*) to have a rap at s.o.; **il ne perdait pas un coup de d.,** he went on eating steadily, he did not miss a mouthful; **n'avoir rien à se mettre sous la d.,** to have nothing to eat; **nous n'avons pas de quoi nous mettre sous la d.,** we haven't a bite of food; **manger à belles dents, manger de toutes ses dents,** to eat away steadily, to eat hungrily; **jouer des dents,** to ply one's teeth; **rire à belles dents,** to laugh heartily; to give a broad grin; **déchirer qn à belles dents,** to tear s.o., s.o.'s reputation, to shreds; **avoir, conserver, garder, une d., contre qn,** to have a grudge against s.o.; **il était tombé sous la d. de X,** he had fallen into the hands of X; **manger du bout des dents,** to eat without appetite, to pick at one's food; **rire du bout des dents,** to force a laugh; **avoir les dents longues,** (i) to be very hungry, famishing; (ii) to be greedy, grasping; **se casser les dents sur qch.,** to run into trouble over sth., to fail; *F:* **avoir la d.,** to be hungry, to be famished; **montrer les dents,** to show one's teeth, to show fight; **armé jusqu'aux dents,** armed to the teeth; **avoir la d. dure,** to be very caustic, critical; **grincer des dents,** to grind one's teeth; **son qui agace les dents,** sound that sets one's teeth on edge; **il n'a pas desserré les dents de la soirée,** he didn't open his mouth the whole evening; **parler entre ses dents,** to mumble; **répondre entre ses dents,** to answer between one's teeth; **couper une corde avec ses dents,** to bite through a rope; to bite a rope through; *F:* **il tient la mort entre les dents,**

he is just holding on (to life); **être sur les dents,** (i) *A:* to be done up, worn out, knocked up; (ii) to be on edge; (iii) to be on the alert; **mettre son personnel sur les dents,** to work one's staff to death; **avoir de la d.,** (i) (*of horse*) to have mark of mouth; (ii) *F:* (*of pers.*) to be still young; *s.a.* LUNE 1, MORS 2, ŒIL 1, POULE 1, SERRER 3; (*b*) **d. d'éléphant,** elephant's tusk. **2.** (*a*) *Tchn: etc:* **d. d'un peigne,** tooth of a comb; **d. d'une lime,** tooth of a file; **d. d'une scie,** tooth, jag, of a saw; **dents contournées, dents pour scier de travers,** cross-cut teeth; **d. double,** champion tooth (of cross-cut saw); **d. droite,** fleam-tooth; **en dents de scie,** tooth-shaped, saw-tooth(ed), serrated; *El:* **tension en dents de scie,** sweep voltage; **d. d'une roue,** tooth, cog, of a wheel; **roue à dents,** cogged wheel; **d. d'arrêt,** ratchet tooth; **d. de repère,** master spline, guide tooth; **fermoir à dents,** toothed, notched, chisel; **dents d'une clé,** bits, steps, wards, of a key; **dents d'une feuille,** serrations of a leaf; **dents d'une broderie,** scallops of a piece of embroidery; **dents d'une fourche, d'une fourchette,** prongs of a pitchfork, of a fork; **d. de herse,** harrow tine; **d. d'une chaîne de montagnes,** jagged peak of a mountain-range; *Clockm: etc:* **d. conique,** club tooth; **pas de la d.,** tooth-pitch (of gear, saw, etc.); (*b*) *El.E:* tooth (of rotor); **d. d'induit,** armature tooth; **induction dans les dents,** tooth-induction.

dentaire [dɑ̃tɛːr]. **1.** *a.* (*a*) *Anat:* dental, dentary (pulp, etc.); **formule d.,** dental formula; (*b*) **l'art d.,** dentistry; **pièce d.,** denture; *F:* plate; **cabinet d.,** dental practice, dental surgery; **école, institut, d.** = dental school; **chirurgie d.,** dental surgery; **installation, matériel, d.,** dental equipment. **2.** *s.f. Bot:* dentaria, coralwort, toothwort.

dental, -aux [dɑ̃tal, -o]. **1.** *a.* dental (nerve, *Ling:* consonant). **2.** *s.f. Ling:* **dentale,** point consonant, dental consonant.

dentale, *Moll:* dentalium, tooth-shell.

dentaria [dɑ̃tarja], *s.m. Bot:* dentaria.

dent-de-chien [dɑ̃d(ə)ʃjɛ̃], *s.f.* **1.** *Bot:* dog's-tooth (violet). **2.** *Tls:* dog's-tooth; *pl. dents-de-chien.*

dent-de-lion [dɑ̃d(ə)ljɔ̃], *s.f. Bot:* dandelion; *pl. dents-de-lion.*

dent-de-loup [dɑ̃dlu], *s.f.* **1.** *Veh:* pin, bolt (of carriage). **2.** gullet-tooth (of saw). **3.** *Aut:* ratchet-tooth, skew-dog, catch (engaging the starting handle). **4.** *Tls:* burnisher; *pl. dents-de-loup.*

dent-de-scie [dɑ̃tsi], *s.f. Arch:* tooth-ornament; *pl. dents-de-scie.*

denté [dɑ̃te], *a.* **1.** cogged, toothed (wheel); **roue dentée,** cog-wheel. **2.** *Bot:* dentate (leaf); **d. en scie,** serrate. **3.** *Ich:* dentex. **4.** *s.f. Ven:* **dentée,** bite (of hound, boar, etc.).

dentelaire [dɑ̃tlɛːr], *s.f. Bot:* plumbago, leadwort.

dentelé [dɑ̃tle], *a.* jagged, notched, indented (edge, etc.); serrated (leaf); scalloped (design, etc.); *Anat:* **muscle d.,** serratus.

denteler [dɑ̃tle], *v.tr.* (**je dentelle, n. dentelons; je dentellerai**) (*a*) to notch, jag, indent; **rivage dentelé de petites baies,** shore cut up, indented, by small bays; (*b*) to pink (out) (leather); **machine à d.,** pinking machine; **ciseaux à d.,** pinking shears.

dentelle [dɑ̃tɛl], *s.f.* **1.** (*a*) lace; **d. à la main,** hand-made lace; **d. à l'aiguille,** needle-point lace, point-lace; **d. aux fuseaux,** pillow-lace, bobbin-lace; **d. à la machine,** machine-made lace; **d. de Bruxelles,** Brussels lace; **d. au tricot,** knitted lace; *P:* **avoir les pieds en d.,** to jib at a job; to be work-shy; *Fb:* **faire de la d.,** to indulge in elegant and dainty teamwork (to detriment of play), to weave pretty patterns and get nowhere; (*b*) wrought ironwork (of balustrade, etc.). **2.** (*a*) *Typ:* (ornamental) border; (*b*) *pl. Bookb:* ornamental gold tooling; inside border, dentelle.

dentellerie [dɑ̃tɛlri], *s.f.* **1.** lace manufacture. **2.** lace factory. **3.** lace(work).

dentellier, -ière [dɑ̃tɛlje, -jɛːr]. **1.** *a.* lace (industry, etc.). **2.** *s.* lace-maker, -worker.

dentelure [dɑ̃tlyːr], *s.f.* denticulation, indentation; serration (of leaf); scalloping (of edge of embroidery, etc.); perforation (at edge of postage-stamp); **dentelures d'une côte,** jagged outline of a coast.

denter [dɑ̃te], *v.tr.* to provide (wheel, etc.) with teeth, with cogs.

denticètes [dɑ̃tisɛːt], **denticétidés** [dɑ̃tisetide], *s.m.pl. Z:* (*a*) Delphinidae, the dolphin genus; (*b*) the porpoises.

denticule [dɑ̃tikyl], *s.m.* (*a*) *Arch:* dentil, denticle; (*b*) *Anat:* denticle.

denticulé [dɑ̃tikyle], *a. Arch:* denticular, denticulated; *Bot:* denticulate, serrulate(d).

dentier [dɑ̃tje], *s.m.* set of false teeth, denture; *F:* plate; **d. complet,** complete, full, denture; **d. partiel,** partial denture; **d. amovible,** removable denture; **d. fixe,** fixed denture; **d. définitif,** permanent denture; **d. provisoire,** temporary denture.

dentiforme [dɑ̃tifɔrm], *a.* dentiform, tooth-like.

dentifrice [dɑ̃tifris]. **1.** *s.m.* dentifrice; tooth-paste, -powder; mouth-wash. **2.** *a.* **pâte d.,** tooth-paste; **eau d.,** mouth-wash.

dentigère [dɑ̃tiʒɛːr], *a. Biol:* dentigerous.

dentine [dɑ̃tin], *s.f. Anat:* dentine.

dentinogénèse [dɑ̃tinoʒenɛːz], *s.f. Anat:* dentinogenesis.

dentinoïde [dɑ̃tinɔid], *a. Anat:* dentinoid.

dentirostre [dɑ̃tirɔstr̥], *s.m. Orn:* sicklebill.

dentiste [dɑ̃tist], *s.m. & f.* dentist; **chirurgien d.,** dental surgeon.

dentisterie [dɑ̃tistəri], *s.f.* dentistry.

dentition [dɑ̃tisjɔ̃], *s.f.* dentition. **1.** *Physiol:* (*a*) cutting of the teeth; teething; (*b*) **d. de lait,** milk-teeth; **d. définitive, permanente,** permanent teeth; **d. caduque, d. temporaire,** deciduous, temporary, dentition. **2.** *Anat:* arrangement of the teeth.

dento-labial, -aux [dɑ̃tolabjal, -o], *a. O: Ling:* labiodental, lip-teeth (consonant).

denture [dɑ̃tyːr], *s.f.* **1.** (*a*) *Anat:* set of (natural) teeth; (*b*) **d. artificielle,** denture. **2.** serrated edge. **3.** *Mec.E:* (*a*) teeth, cogs (as a whole); gearing; **d. à droite, à gauche,** right-hand, left-hand, toothing; **d. à chevrons,** herring-bone teeth, double-helical teeth; **d. en spirale,** spiral teeth; **d. épicycloïdale,** epicyclic teeth; **d. hélicoïdale,** helical teeth; **d. inclinée,** skew teeth; **d. tronquée,** stub teeth; **rapport des dentures,** gear ratio; (*b*) pitch (of cogged wheel).

dénucléarisation [denyklearizasjɔ̃], *s.f.* denuclearization.

dénucléarisé [denyklearize], *a.* atom-free, nuclear free.

dénucléariser [denyklearize], *v.tr.* to denuclearize.

dénudation [denydasjɔ̃], *s.f.* denudation, laying bare, stripping; *Geol:* denudation (of the land, etc.).

dénudé [denyde], *a.* bare, denuded (country); stripped (tree, etc.); bald (head, hill-top); *El:* bare (wire); **région dénudée,** dust-bowl.

dénuder [denyde], *v.tr.* to denude, to bare, to lay bare (bone, the roots of a tooth, etc.); **d. un arbre (de son écorce),** to strip a tree of its bark, to strip the bark off a tree; **d. un câble sous caoutchouc,** to strip a rubber cable; *Tls:* **pinces à d.,** stripping pliers; **d. qn,** to strip s.o. (naked); **dénudé de tous ses biens,** stripped of all his worldly goods.

se dénuder. 1. to grow bare. **2.** to strip (naked).

dénué [denɥe], *a.* (*a*) **être d. d'argent,** to be without money, out of cash; (*b*) **projet d. de sens,** plan devoid of sense; **d. de raison, de sens,** senseless; **d. d'intelligence,** unintelligent; **style d. de toute recherche,** style free from affectation.

dénuement [denymɑ̃], *s.m.* (*a*) destitution, penury, need; **être dans le d.,** to be destitute, to be in want; **dans le d. où j'étais,** in my state of destitution, in my destitute condition; (*b*) **d. d'idées,** dearth, poverty, of ideas; (*c*) bareness (of room, etc.).

dénuer [denɥe], *v.tr.* to divest, strip (s.o.) (de, of); **ces pertes l'ont dénué de tout,** these losses have left him absolutely destitute.

se dénuer, *Lit:* **se d. de ses biens,** to part with all one's possessions, to leave oneself penniless; **se d. pour sa famille,** to strip oneself bare for one's family.

dénûment [denymɑ̃], *s.m. A:* = DÉNUEMENT.

dénutri [denytri], *a. Med:* suffering from denutrition.

dénutrition [denytrisjɔ̃], *s.f. Med:* denutrition, wasting.

Denys [dəni], *Pr.n.m.* Dionysius.

deodar [deɔdaːr], *s.m. Bot:* deodar, deodar cedar, deodara.

déodatien, -ienne [deɔdasjɛ̃, -jɛn], *a. & s. Geog:* (native, inhabitant) of Saint-Dié.

déodorant [deɔdɔrɑ̃], *s.m. Hyg:* = DÉSODORISANT.

déodore [deɔdɔːr], *s.m. Bot:* deodar, deodar cedar, deodara.

déodorisation [deɔdɔrizasjɔ̃], *s.f.* = DÉSODORISATION.

déodoriser [deɔdɔrize], *v.tr.* = DÉSODORISER.

déontologie [deɔ̃tɔlɔʒi], *s.f. Phil:* deontology; **d. médicale,** medical ethics.

déontologique [deɔ̃tɔlɔʒik], *a.* deontologic(al).

dépagnoter (se) [sədepaɲɔte], *v.pr. P:* to get out of bed.

dépaillage [depɑjaːʒ], *s.m.* removing of straw, stripping (chair) of its rush bottom.

dépaillé [depɑje], *a.* stripped of its straw; **siège d.,** seatless (chair).

dépailler [depɑje], *v.tr.* to remove the straw from (sth.), to strip (chair) of its rush bottom.

se dépailler; la chaise se dépaille, the rush bottom, the seat, of the chair is giving way, coming away.

dépaissance [depɛsɑ̃ːs], *s.f. Husb:* **1.** grazing. **2.** grazing-ground, pasture-ground.

dépaisselage [depɛslaːʒ], *s.m. Vit:* removal of vine-props.

dépaisseler [depɛsle], *v.tr. Vit:* to remove the props from (vines).

dépaler [depale], *v.tr. used esp. in the passive; Nau:* **être dépalé,** to drift, sag, to leeward; **se laisser d.,** to (miss stays and) drift on-shore; **être dépalé par le courant,** to be carried out of one's course by the current.

dépannage [depanaːʒ], *s.m.* (*a*) emergency repairs (to engine, etc.), *U.S:* troubleshooting; road repairs (to motor car); breakdown service; **équipe de d.,** breakdown gang; *Mil:* breakdown group, party, light aid detachment; **camion de d.,** breakdown lorry, *U.S:* breakdown truck; **service de. d,** breakdown service, repair service; *Mil:* **détachement, section, de d.,** maintenance crew, section; (*b*) *El.E:* fault location, locating, repairing; **trousse de d.,** test kit; **pont de d.,** fault locating bridge; (*c*) **lit de d.,** emergency, reserve, extra bed; (*d*) *F:* fresh start (in one's career, etc., after getting into a rut).

dépanner [depane], *v.tr.* (*a*) to repair and set going (broken-down engine, car, etc.); *U.S: F:* to troubleshoot; (*b*) to tow (broken-down vehicle); (*c*) *F:* to tide over, to help out, to get (s.o.) out of a hole.

dépanneur [depanœːr], *s.m.* (*a*) break-down mechanic; service man; *U.S: F:* troubleshooter; *Mil:* maintenance man; **d. de T.S.F.,** radio repairman, radio serviceman; (*b*) *Navy:* speedboat used for troubleshooting.

dépanneuse [depanøːz], *s.f. Aut:* break-down lorry, *U.S:* breakdown truck.

dépaquetage [depaktaːʒ], *s.m.* unpacking (of goods).

dépaqueter [depakte], *v.tr.* (*conj. like* PAQUETER) to unpack (goods, etc.).

déparaffinage [deparafinaːʒ], *s.m. Petroleum Ind:* paraffin extraction; dewaxing.

déparaffiner [deparafine], *v.tr. Petroleum Ind:* to dewax.

déparaffineur [deparafinœːr], *s.m. Petroleum Ind:* wax chiller.

dépareillé [depareje], *a.* odd, unmatched, unpaired; *Com:* **articles dépareillés,** oddments, job lot; **rayon des dépareillés,** "separates" department (in a shop); **quelques tomes dépareillés,** a few odd volumes; **quelques restes dépareillés,** a few odds and ends; **collection dépareillée,** odd set, incomplete collection.

dépareiller [depareje], *v.tr.* to spoil, break (set, pair, collection).

déparer [depare], *v.tr.* **1.** to strip (sth.) of ornaments; to divest (s.o.) of jewellery, medals, etc. **2.** to mar, to spoil the beauty of (s.o., sth.); **de graves imperfections déparent son œuvre,** serious defects mar his work; **sa robe la déparait,** her dress gave her a dowdy appearance; *Com:* **d. des fruits, des légumes,** to spoil the display (by picking out the best).

déparier [deparje], *v.tr.* (*p.d. & pr.sub.* **n. déparions, v. dépariiez**) (*a*) to remove one of a pair of, to spoil a pair of (objects); **gant déparié,** odd glove; (*b*) to separate (pair of doves, couple of yoke-oxen).

déparler [deparle], *v.i. F:* **1.** to talk nonsense; to become incoherent or inarticulate (when drunk). **2.** *always in the negative:* **il ne déparle pas,** he never stops talking.

déparquement [deparkəmɑ̃], *s.m.* **1.** unpenning (of cattle); letting (of sheep) out of a fold. **2.** *Ost:* collection (of the oysters) from the culture-beds.

déparquer [deparke], *v.tr.* **1.** to let (sheep) out of a fold, to unfold (sheep); to let (cattle) out of a pen, to unpen (cattle). **2.** *Ost:* to collect (oysters) from the beds.

départ [depaːr], *s.m.* **1.** (*a*) *O:* division, separation, sorting (out); **faire le d. entre qch. et qch.,** to sort out sth. from sth., to discriminate between sth. and sth.; (*b*) *Ch: Metall:* parting, elutriation. **2.** (*a*) departure, starting (of person, vehicle, etc.); sailing (of ship); start (of race, etc.); *Mil:* start, jump off (of an attack); *Trans:* **départs,** departures; **au moment de son d.,** just

as he was starting, setting out; **après mon d.,** after I have, had, gone; after my departure; **au d.,** at the outset; **point de d.,** starting point; **revenir à son point de d.,** to go back to where one started (from), to go back to square one; **produit de d.,** original material (of an experiment); **on lui fit entendre que c'était un beau d.,** he was given to understand that he had made a good start; **excursions au d. de Chamonix,** trips from Chamonix; **exiger le d. d'un employé,** to insist on the dismissal of an employee; *Nau:* **navire sur son d.,** outward bound ship; **liste des départs,** sailing list; *Mil:* **base, position, de d.,** jump-off position, position of departure; **ligne de d.,** jump-off line, starting line, line of departure; **ordre de d.,** (i) order of departure; (ii) marching orders; *Sp:* **d. arrêté,** standing start; **d. lancé, en flèche, foudroyant,** flying start; **faux d.,** false start; **manquer le d.,** to be left at the post; *Golf:* **tertre de d.,** teeing ground; (*at croquet*) **position de d.,** balk; *Bill:* **demi-cercle de d.,** balk; *Post:* **courrier au d.,** outgoing mail; **bureau de d.,** originating office; *Tp:* originating exchange; *Tp:* **communication de d.,** outgoing call; *Civ.E:* **rive de d.,** bank from which a bridge is built (or dismantled); *Com:* **au d. de,** starting from; **valeur de d.,** initial value; **prix d. usine,** price ex works; (*at auction sale*) **prix de d.,** upset price; *Tchn:* **tuyau de d.,** outgoing pipe; outlet pipe; **anneau de d.,** butt ring; *El:* **d. de ligne, de câble,** leading-out cable; **circuit de d.,** outgoing circuit; (*b*) discharge (of firearm); **lueur du, des, départ(s),** muzzle flash, flash of discharge; (*c*) *Ch:* onset (of reaction); (*d*) *Ch:* loss; **perte de poids par d. d'eau,** diminution in weight by loss of water. 3. (*a*) *Rail:* departure platform; (*b*) *Sp:* starting-post; (*c*) **d. d'escalier,** foot of stairs.

départage [departa:ʒ], *s.m. Coop:* the splitting of stave-wood.

départager [departaʒe], *v.tr.* (*conj. like* PARTAGER) to decide between (opinions, etc.); **d. les voix, les votes,** to give the casting vote; **seule une longue pratique pourra d. les deux procédés,** only a long trial will decide which of the processes is the better.

département [departəmɑ̃], *s.m. Adm:* Department; (*a*) Ministry, *U.S:* Department; **le D. des Finances, de la Guerre,** the Ministry of Finance, the War Office; *F:* **cela n'est pas dans mon d.,** that is not in my line, not within my province; (*b*) *Adm:* sub-division (of France) administered by a prefect; department; **chef-lieu de d.,** capital of a department (= Eng. county-town); *F:* **les départements,** the provinces.

départemental, -aux [departəmɑ̃tal, -o]. 1. *a.* departmental; *A:* **chemin de fer d.,** local line; *s.a.* ROUTE 1. 2. *s.f.* **départementale** = "B" road.

départementalement [departəmɑ̃talmɑ̃], *adv.* departmentally, by departments.

départementalisation [departəmɑ̃talizasjɔ̃], *s.f. Adm:* turning (of former colony, etc.) into a department.

départementaliser [departəmɑ̃talize], *v.tr. Adm:* to turn (a former colony, etc.) into a department.

départir [departi:r], *v.tr.* (*conj. like* PARTIR, *occ. like* FINIR) 1. *Ch: Metall: A:* to separate, part (metals). 2. (*a*) *A:* to divide (one's property amongst heirs, etc.); (*b*) to distribute, dispense, deal out (favours, etc.).

se départir, se d. de qch., to part with, give up, depart from, deviate from, sth.; **se d. de ses opinions,** to renounce, desist from, one's opinions; **se d. de ses instructions,** to depart from one's instructions; **se d. de son devoir,** to swerve, deviate, from one's duty; **se d. de ses habitudes usuelles,** to drop, give up, one's usual habits; **se d. d'une prétention,** to relinquish, waive, a claim; **se d. de sa réserve,** to throw off one's reserve.

départoir [departwa:r], *s.m. Tls: Coop:* divider (for splitting stave-wood).

dépassant [depɑsɑ̃], *s.m. Cost:* edging.

dépassé [depɑse], *a.* out of date; obsolete.

dépassement [depɑsmɑ̃], *s.m.* 1. (*a*) excess; going beyond (a mark); overshooting (of one's aim, etc.); surpassing (of oneself); overstepping (one's credit, etc.); **d. du taux normal,** manifold increase; *El:* **tarif à d.,** overload tariff; (*b*) **d. d'honoraires,** overcharging by doctor of a patient who is under the national insurance scheme. 2. (*a*) *Veh: Aut:* overtaking; **effectuer un d.,** to overtake another car; *s.a.* FEU[1] 4; (*b*) *Mil:* (*of units*) passing (over), leap-frogging; **effectuer, opérer, un d.,** to pass (over); **relever des unités de premier échelon par d.,** to relieve forward units by leap-frogging. 3. *Nau:* striking (of topmast); underrunning (of tackle); unreaving (of rope).

dépasser[1] [depɑse], *v.tr.* 1. (*a*) to pass beyond, go beyond (s.o., sth.); to overrun (signal, etc.); **d. l'endroit où il fallait s'arrêter,** to pass the place where one ought to have stopped; **d. le but,** to overshoot the mark; **ces questions dépassent le but de ce discours,** these questions lie outside the scope, purpose, of this address; **d. les bornes,** (i) to overstep the bounds, the mark, to carry things too far, to overdo it; (ii) to be beyond all bounds; **nous avons dépassé le milieu de l'été,** we are past midsummer; **le thermomètre a dépassé 33°,** the thermometer rose above 33°; **il a dépassé la trentaine,** he has turned thirty, is over thirty; *Nau:* **d. un cap,** to pass a headland; **d. le lit du vent,** to be in stays; (*b*) **d. qn (à la course, à la voile, etc.),** to overtake, outdistance, outrun, outstrip, outsail, s.o.; to draw ahead of (s.o., ship, etc.); to overhaul (ship); *Aut:* to pass, to overtake (s.o., another car); **d. tous ses concurrents,** to forge ahead; **élève qui est en train de dépasser ses camarades,** pupil who is outstripping his schoolfellows. 2. **d. qch en hauteur,** to (over-)top sth.; **d. qn de la tête,** to stand a head taller than s.o., to top s.o. by a head; **maison qui dépasse l'alignement,** house that projects beyond the others; **votre jupon dépasse,** your petticoat is showing (below your skirt); **tâche qui dépasse la mesure de mes forces,** burden heavier than I can bear; **la tâche dépasse mes moyens,** the task is beyond my means; **élève qui dépasse ses camarades,** pupil who outshines, excels, his schoolfellows; **il les dépasse tous en mérite,** he transcends them all in merit; **cela dépasse ma compétence,** it lies beyond, outside, my competence; **cela dépasse mon entendement,** it is above my comprehension; *F:* **cela me dépasse,** it is beyond me; it goes over my head; this defeats me; **il y a un clou qui dépasse du mur,** there's a nail sticking out of the wall; **son mouchoir dépasse de sa poche,** his handkerchief is sticking out of his pocket; **je suis dépassé par les événements,** things are getting too much for me. 3. to exceed; **d. son congé,** to overstay one's leave; **d. ses instructions,** to go beyond, to exceed, one's instructions; **d. la limite de vitesse,** to exceed the speed-limit; **d. la vérité,** to overstep the truth, to go beyond the truth; **le succès a dépassé nos espérances,** we have succeeded beyond our hopes; **le prix ne doit pas d. dix francs,** the price must not exceed ten francs; **ne pas d. son revenu,** to live within one's income; **toutes ces voitures dépassent mes moyens,** all these cars are beyond my means; **les recettes dépassent mille livres,** the takings have topped a thousand pounds; **si les cotisations dépassent la somme requise,** if the subscriptions should be in excess of the sum required; **ne pas d. la dose prescrite,** do not exceed the stated dose. 4. *Mil:* (*of units*) to pass over.

se dépasser, to surpass oneself.

dépasser[2], *v.tr.* (*a*) **d. un ruban, un lacet,** to remove a ribbon, a lace (from object in which it has been inserted); (*b*) **d. la bandoulière (de sa harpe, etc.) de dessus son épaule,** to unsling (one's harp, etc.) from one's shoulder; **d. les rênes,** to pass the reins over the horse's head; (*c*) *Nau:* **d. un cordage,** to unreeve a rope; **d. un palan,** to underrun a tackle; **d. les mâts de perroquet,** to strike, send down, the top-gallant masts.

dépassionner [depasjɔne], *v.tr.* 1. to eliminate passion from (debate, discussion). 2. to free (s.o.) from, rid (s.o.) of, his passions.

dépâtisser [depɑtise], *v.tr. Typ:* to sort out (pie).

dépavage [depava:ʒ], *s.m.* unpaving, taking up the pavement.

dépaver [depave], *v.tr.* to unpave, take up the pavement of (yard, street).

dépayolage [depajɔla:ʒ], *s.m. N.Arch:* removal of ceiling.

dépaysé [depeize], *a.* removed from one's usual surroundings; out of one's element; **se sentir d.,** to feel strange, like a fish out of water; not to feel at home, to feel out of place; **il a l'air d.,** he seems lost, at a loss.

dépaysement [depeizmɑ̃], *s.m.* removal (of s.o.) from his usual surroundings, from his element.

dépayser [depeize], *v.tr.* 1. (*a*) to remove (s.o.) from his usual surroundings, from his element; (*b*) to put (s.o.) on the wrong road, to mislead (s.o.). 2. to embarrass, bewilder (s.o.).

se dépayser, to exile oneself; to remove to another country or part of the country.

dépeçage [depəsa:ʒ], **dépècement** [depɛsmɑ̃], *s.m.* 1. (*a*) cutting-up (of a slaughtered or hunted animal); dismembering (of a country), breaking-up (of a ship); **le dépècement du pays fut complété par les barbares,** the barbarians completed the dismemberment of the country; (*b*) *Glove making:* operation consisting of cutting each skin into a number of rectangles. 2. (*of a whale*) **dépeçage,** flensing, flenching; *Nau:* **pont de d.,** cutting-up deck, flensing deck.

dépecer [depəse], *v.tr.* (**je dépèce, n. dépeçons; je dépècerai**) to cut up (stone, carcass, etc.); to dismember, to cut (carcass) into pieces; to carve, cut up (fowl); to flense (whale); to break up (ship, estate); to rip open (a bale of cotton); **le lion dépèce sa proie,** the lion tears its prey.

dépeceur, -euse [depəsœ:r, -ø:z], *s.* cutter-up (of carcass, etc.); **d. (de baleines),** flenser; **d. de gants,** glove-cutter; *A:* **d. de vaisseaux,** ship-breaker.

dépêche [depɛʃ], *s.f.* (*a*) (official) despatch, dispatch, message; (*b*) **d. télégraphique,** telegram; *F:* wire; **envoyer une dépêche à qn,** to telegraph, *F:* to wire, s.o.

dépêcher [depeʃe], *v.tr.* 1. to dispatch; to do (sth.) speedily; **d. une besogne,** to dispatch, rush, polish off, a piece of work; **d. son déjeuner,** to dispatch one's luncheon, to take a hurried luncheon; *F:* **travailler, se battre, à dépêche compagnon,** to do one's work slap-dash, to fight blindly. 2. *A. & Lit:* **d. qn d'un coup d'épée,** to dispatch s.o., put s.o. to death, with the sword. 3. **d. un courrier, un messager,** to dispatch a messenger.

se dépêcher, to hurry; to hasten; *O:* to make haste; to be quick; **dépêchez-vous!** *F:* **dépêche!** hurry up! get a move on! buck up! look alive! **une omelette, et dépêchez-vous!** an omelet, and be quick about it! **se d. de faire qch.,** to be quick to do sth.; **dépêchez-vous de guérir,** hurry up and get well; **se d. de rentrer,** to hurry home.

dépeçoir [depəswa:r], *s.m. Tls:* (*a*) glove stretcher; (*b*) cutter.

dépeigner [depeɲe], *v.tr.* **dépeigner qn,** to ruffle, rumple s.o.; to make s.o.'s hair untidy; **personne dépeignée,** person with tousled hair, unkempt person.

dépeindre [depɛ̃:dr], *v.tr.* (*conj. like* PEINDRE) to depict, picture, describe (s.o., sth.); **je ne saurais vous d. la scène,** words cannot describe the scene; **d. qn tel qu'il est,** to give a true description of s.o.; **il n'est pas si sévère qu'on le dépeint,** he is not so severe as people make him out; **d. les passions,** to paint the passions.

dépelotonner [deplɔtɔne], *v.tr.* unwind (ball of wool, etc.).

se dépelotonner, (*a*) (*of ball of wool, etc.*) to come unwound; (*b*) *F:* (*of cat, etc.*) to uncurl.

dépenaillé [depnɑje], *a.* ragged, tattered, torn; **il était tout d.,** he was all in rags, in tatters, unkempt; **chapeau d., fortune dépenaillée,** dilapidated hat, fortune.

dépenaillement [depnɑjmɑ̃], *s.m.* ragged state, tattered state.

dépendage [depɑ̃da:ʒ], *s.m.* taking down (of hanging object).

dépendamment [depɑ̃damɑ̃], *adv. A:* dependently, in a dependent manner.

dépendance [depɑ̃dɑ̃:s], *s.f.* 1. dependence (of sth. on sth.); **d. de l'effet à cause,** dependence of the effect on the cause. 2. (*a*) dependency (of a country); (*b*) *pl.* outbuildings, offices; **d. d'un hôtel,** annex to a hotel; **les dépendances de la ferme,** the outlying farm buildings; **maison et dépendances,** house and outbuildings, *Jur:* messuage; *s.a.* CIRCONSTANCE 2. 3. dependence, subjection, subordination; **être sous la d. de qn,** to be under s.o.'s domination, control; **tenir qn sous sa d.,** to hold s.o. in subjection; *Gram:* **syntaxe de d.,** syntax of subordinate clauses.

dépendant [depɑ̃dɑ̃], *a.* 1. (*a*) dependent; **fonctions dépendantes l'une de l'autre,** functions dependent on each other, interdependent functions; (*b*) **terres dépendantes de la couronne,** land appertaining to the Crown. 2. dependent, subordinate; **être d. de qn,** to be dependent on s.o.; *F:* to be under s.o.'s thumb; *Gram:* **proposition dépendante,** subordinate clause.

dépendeur, -euse [depɑ̃dœ:r, -ø:z], *s.* one who takes down, unhangs; *F:* **d. d'andouilles,** tall and lanky good-for-nothing.

dépendre[1] [depɑ̃:dr], *v.tr.* to take down (hanging object).

dépendre[2], *v.i.* to depend. 1. **d. de qn, de qch.,** to depend on s.o., on sth.; **sa destinée dépend de vous,** his fate lies in your hands, rests with you; **tout dépend des circonstances,** everything

depends on circumstances; **tout dépend de sa réponse,** everything hangs on, hinges on, turns on, his answer; **nous dépendons tous de la fortune,** we are all at the mercy of fortune; **événements qui ne dépendent pas de nous,** events that are not within our control; **il dépend de vous de** + *inf.*, it lies, rests, with you, it depends on you, it lies within your own discretion, to + *inf.*; **cela dépend,** that depends, we shall see; *F:* **ça dépend s'il est marié,** it depends whether he's married. **2.** (*a*) (*of land, etc.*) to be a dependency (**de,** of); to appertain to, belong to (the Crown); **territoire qui dépend de la France,** territory that belongs to, is a dependency of, France; (*b*) (*of ship*) to hail (from a port); (*c*) (*of wind*) to blow (from a quarter); (*d*) *adv.phr. Nau:* **en dépendant,** crabwise, edging down or away; **doubler une pointe en dépendant,** to clear a point edging down; **arriver sur un bateau en dépendant,** to edge down on a ship; **s'éloigner en dépendant,** to edge away; **accoster en dépendant,** to sheer up, alongside. **3.** to be subordinate, subject (**de,** to); to be under (s.o.'s) domination; to report to (s.o.); **je ne dépends pas de lui,** *F:* I do not take my orders from him; **ne d. que de soi,** to be one's own master; *F:* to stand on one's own feet.

dépens [depɑ̃], *s.m.pl.* **1.** *Jur:* costs; *Com:* cost, expenses; **être condamné aux d.,** to be ordered to pay costs; **payer les d.,** to pay costs. **2.** *prep. phr.* **aux d. de,** at the expense of (s.o., sth.); **vivre aux d. de son voisin,** to live at one's neighbour's expense; **s'amuser aux d. de ses études,** to enjoy oneself at the expense of one's studies; **aux d. de l'honneur,** at the cost of honour, with loss of honour; **devenir sage à ses propres d., à ses frais et d.,** to pay dearly for one's experience; **il apprit à ses d. que . . .,** he learnt to his cost that . . .

dépense [depɑ̃:s], *s.f.* **1.** expenditure, expense, outlay (of money); **dépenses de ménage,** household expenses; **faire la d.,** to be responsible for the expenditure; **carnet de dépenses,** housekeeping book; **dépenses courantes,** current expenditures; **dépenses diverses,** general, sundry, expenses; **dépenses d'acquisition, d'équipement,** procurement costs; **dépenses d'établissement, dépenses en immobilisations,** capital expenditures; **dépenses d'exploitation, de fonctionnement,** operating costs, working expenses; **contrôler les dépenses,** to check expenditure; **faire des dépenses,** to incur expenses; **faire beaucoup de d.,** to go to great expense; **faire qch. au prix de dépenses énormes,** to do sth. at enormous cost; **je ne peux pas faire cette d.,** I cannot go to this expense; **faire la d. d'une voiture,** to go to the expense of buying, hiring, a car; **faire trop de d.,** to spend too much money; **se mettre en d.,** (i) to incur expense; (ii) *F:* to put oneself to a great deal of trouble; **prendre à sa charge toutes les dépenses de la noce,** to defray all the expenses of the wedding; **cela entraîne une forte d.,** it entails a large expenditure; **on ne regardait pas à la d.,** there was no stinting; they did not mind the cost, they spared no expense; **faire de folles dépenses,** to spend money extravagantly; **recettes et dépenses,** receipts and expenditure; **les dépenses excèdent les recettes,** expenditure exceeds income; **dépenses publiques,** government expenditure; **une d. inutile de temps,** a useless expenditure of time. **2.** *Tchn:* **d. d'eau,** outflow, discharge, efflux, of water; **d. de vapeur, d'essence,** steam, petrol, consumption; **d. à vide,** wasted energy. **3.** storeroom, buttery, pantry; dispensary (of hospital); *s.a.* GUICHET 1.

dépenser [depɑ̃se], *v.tr.* **1.** to spend, expend, lay out (money); **il dépense peu en livres,** he spends little on books; **je préfère d. mon argent à des choses utiles qu'en bagatelles,** I prefer to spend my money on useful things rather than on trivialities; **d. son revenu,** to live up to one's income; **d. sans compter,** to spend lavishly, to be free with one's money; *Prov:* **autant dépense chiche que large,** skimping is no saving. **2.** to spend, consume (time, energy, etc.); **d. inutilement son éloquence,** to waste one's eloquence; *F:* **d. sa salive,** to speak.

se dépenser, se d. en vains efforts, to spend oneself, waste one's energy, in useless efforts; **se d. pour qn,** to spare no trouble on s.o.'s behalf; **il s'était dépensé en soins pour elle,** he had been all attention to her; **se d. à l'excès,** to exert oneself overmuch; **vous vous dépensez trop,** you shouldn't do (i) so much, (ii) so much for others.

dépensier, -ière [depɑ̃sje, -jɛ:r]. **1.** *s. A:* storekeeper (of establishment); bursar, manciple. **2.** (*a*) *a.* extravagant, fond of spending, thriftless; (*b*) *s.* spendthrift.

dépentanisation [depɛ̃tanizasjɔ̃], *s.f. Petroleum Ind:* depentanization.

dépentaniser [depɛ̃tanize], *v.tr. Petroleum Ind:* to depentanize.

déperditeur [depɛrditœ:r], *s.m. Av:* **d. de potentiel,** static discharger.

déperdition [depɛrdisjɔ̃], *s.f.* waste, wastage, destruction (of tissue, etc.); loss (of heat, energy); dwindling (of capital); **d. de volonté,** weakening of will; **d. de gaz,** escape of gas; *El:* **d. par dispersion,** leakage.

dépérir [deperi:r], *v.i.* **1.** to waste away, pine, dwindle; (*of health*) to decline; (*of trees, flowers*) to wither, decay; (*of race*) to die out; **maisons qui dépérissent faute d'entretien,** houses falling into decay for want of upkeep; **industrie qui dépérit,** industry that is falling off, declining industry; **condamner une industrie à d.,** to cripple an industry. **2.** *Jur:* (*of debt, proof*) to become more and more doubtful (with the passing of time).

dépérissement [deperismɑ̃], *s.m.* **1.** declining, pining, wasting away; withering, decaying (of tree, etc.); dying out (of race); decay, dilapidation (of building); deterioration (of machinery); decline (of industry); dwindling (of capital); *Hort:* die back; **signes de d.,** signs of decay. **2.** *Jur:* **d. de preuves,** loss of validity of proof (with the passing of time).

dépersonnalisation [depɛrsɔnalizasjɔ̃], *s.f.* depersonalization.

dépersonnaliser [depɛrsɔnalize], *v.tr.* to depersonalize.

se dépersonnaliser, to loose one's personality, one's character.

dépersuader [depɛrsɥade], *v.tr.* **1.** to alter (s.o.'s) conviction. **2. d. qn d'une entreprise,** to dissuade s.o. from an undertaking.

dépêtrer [depetre], *v.tr.* to extricate, free (s.o.) (from entanglement); **d. qn d'une mauvaise affaire,** to get s.o. out of a scrape.

se dépêtrer, to extricate oneself; *F:* **se d. de qn,** to get rid of s.o., to shake s.o. off.

dépeuplement [depœpləmɑ̃], *s.m.* depopulation (of country, etc.); unstocking, drawing (of pond); thinning, clearing (of forest); *For:* depletion.

dépeupler [depœple], *v.tr.* to depopulate (country, etc.); to unstock, draw (pond); to thin, clear (forest); **la pluie avait dépeuplé les rues,** the rain had emptied, cleared, the streets.

se dépeupler, to become depopulated; (*of region*) to lose its population.

déphasage [defɑza:ʒ], *s.m. El.E:* phase displacement; dephasing; difference in phase; **d. en avant,** (phase) lead; **d. en arrière,** lag; phase-shifting, -splitting; **d. capacitatif,** electrostatic displacement; **d. unitaire,** unity phase-shift; **angle de d.,** phase angle, angle of phase difference.

déphasé [defɑze], *a.* **1.** *El.E:* (*of current*) out of phase; **d. en arrière,** lagging (current); **d. en avant,** leading (current); **être d. sur le courant,** to differ from the current. **2.** *F:* disoriented; (i) **je suis un peu d. aujourd'hui,** I'm all haywire today; (ii) **il est complètement d.,** he's got a screw loose; he's off his rocker.

déphaseur [defɑzœ:r], *a. & s.m. El.E:* **1.** *a.* phase-shifting; **système d.,** phase-shifting device; **tube d.,** phase-inverter tube. **2.** *s.m.* phase-shifter, -converter.

déphosphoration [defɔsfɔrasjɔ̃], *s.f. Metall:* dephosphorization; **scories de d.,** basic slag.

déphosphorer [defɔsfɔre], *v.tr. Metall:* to dephosphorize.

dépiauter [depjote, -ote], *v.tr. F:* to skin, flay (rabbit, etc.); **d. un auteur, une pièce,** to pull an author, a play, to pieces.

dépiècement [depjɛsmɑ̃], *s.m.* pulling to pieces, taking to pieces.

dépiécer [depjese], *v.tr.* (**je dépièce, n. dépiéçons; je dépiéçai(s); je dépiécerai**) to pull, cut (chicken, etc.) to pieces; to dismember.

dépigmentation [depigmɑ̃tasjɔ̃], *s.f.* depigmentation (of skin, etc.).

dépigmenter [depigmɑ̃te], *v.tr.* to depigment; to deprive (sth.) of pigment.

dépilage[1] [depila:ʒ], *s.m. Leath:* unhairing, graining, depilation (of skins).

dépilage[2], *s.m. Min:* removal of pit-props.

dépilatif, -ive [depilatif, -i:v], *a.* = DÉPILATOIRE.

dépilation [depilasjɔ̃], *s.f.* (*a*) depilation, removal, of hair; (*b*) loss of hair.

dépilatoire [depilatwa:r], *a. & s.m. Toil:* depilatory; **pâte d.,** superfluous hair remover; depilatory (cream).

dépiler[1] [depile], *v.tr.* (*a*) to depilate; to remove the hair from (face, etc.); (*b*) *Leath:* to unhair, scrape, grain (skin).

dépiler[2], *v.tr.* to remove surplus pit-props from (a mine).

dépingler [depɛ̃gle], *v.tr.* to unpin.

dépiquage [depika:ʒ], *s.m. Husb:* (action of) treading out (corn).

dépiquer[1] [depike], *v.tr.* **1.** *Husb:* to tread out (corn). **2.** *Hort:* to transplant (shoots).

dépiquer[2], *v.tr.* **1.** (*a*) to unquilt; (*b*) to unstitch (garment, etc.). **2.** *P:* to take (sth.) out of pawn.

dépistage [depista:ʒ], *s.m. Med:* tracking down, (early) detection (of disease, virus, etc.); **d. de la tuberculose,** T.B. check-up; *Rockets:* **station de d.,** tracking station.

dépister[1] [depiste], *v.tr.* to track down (game); to run (game, *F:* s.o.) to earth, to detect (a disease); **d. (le gibier),** to smell out (game).

dépister[2], *v.tr.* to put (hounds; *F:* s.o.) off the scent; **d. la police,** to cover up one's tracks; to baffle, outwit, the police; *Fb:* **d. un joueur,** to dodge a player.

dépit [depi], *s.m.* **1.** spite, spleen, resentment, chagrin; **ressentir un d. secret contre qn,** to cherish a secret grudge, a secret resentment, against s.o.; **ne tournez pas votre d. contre moi,** don't vent your spleen on me; **par d.,** out of spite; **pleurer de d.,** to cry with vexation; **répondre avec dépit que . . .,** to answer spitefully that . . .. **2.** *prep.phr.* **en d. de . . .,** in spite of, in defiance of . . .; **en d. du bon sens,** (i) contrary to common sense; (ii) upside down, topsy-turvy; **en d. de l'hostilité,** in the teeth of hostility; **je n'en crois rien en d. de vos affirmations,** I don't believe it for all you (may) say; **en d. de son savoir il ne sait pas enseigner,** for, with, all his learning he can't teach; **en d. de ce que** + *ind.*, in spite of the fact that . . .; *F:* **en d. qu'elle en dise . . ., en d. qu'elle en ait . . .,** for all she may say to the contrary . . ., whatever she may say to the contrary . . .

dépiter [depite], *v.tr.* to vex, chagrin, upset (s.o.), to cause (s.o.) annoyance; **je l'ai dit pour la d.,** I said it to spite her.

se dépiter, to take offence, to be annoyed; **je suis fort dépité,** I am very sore about it; **amant dépité,** disappointed lover.

déplacé [deplase], *a.* **1.** out of its place; displaced (heart, etc.); *F:* **vertèbre déplacée,** slipped disk; **2.** out of place, misplaced, ill-timed; **paroles déplacées et de mauvais goût,** words that are out of place and in bad taste; **observation déplacée,** unwarranted, uncalled-for, remark. **3.** *Pol:* **personnes déplacées,** displaced persons.

déplacement [deplasmɑ̃], *s.m.* **1.** (*a*) displacement, shifting (of boundary marks, of goods, of womb, etc.); removing (of wreck, etc.); **d. d'un fonctionnaire,** transfer of an official; **d. d'une usine,** removal of a works; **d. latéral d'un pont roulant,** traversing of an overhead crane; *Geol:* **d. latéral (d'une faille),** heave (of fault); *Equit:* **d. d'assiette,** unsteadiness of seat; *Pol: etc:* **d. de quatre voix,** turn-over of four votes; *Mch:* **d. du piston,** displacement, travel, of the piston; *Machine-Tls:* **fin de d.,** travel end; *Elcs:* **d. de fréquence,** frequency displacement, shift; *Atom.Ph:* displacement, shift, drift (of electron, isotope, etc.); **d. isotopique,** isotope shift; **coefficient de d.,** displacement factor; *Mil:* **d. du tir,** shifting of fire; *Med:* **d. des vertèbres,** slipped disk; **d. dans les fractures,** fracture-displacement, fracture dislocation; (*b*) altering of the time (of a train, etc.). **2.** (*a*) change of location, of site, of position; *Mil:* change of station (of troops, etc.); (*b*) travelling; moving, movement; journey; **déplacements continuels,** constant moving (from one house to another); *Adm: etc:* **d. de grande amplitude,** big scale movement; **être en d.,** to take a trip, to go on a journey; to go on a (regular) business trip; *Sp:* **jouer en d.,** to play away; **frais de d.,** (i) travelling or removal expenses; (ii) *Bank: etc:* porterage (of documents, etc.); *Nau:* **déplacements,** movements of ships. **3.** (*a*) *N.Arch:* **d. d'un navire,** displacement of a ship; **d. en charge,** displacement loaded, load displacement; **d. lège, d. à vide,** light displacement; **d. hors membrure,** moulded displacement; (*b*) **d. d'air,** air displacement; *Av:* down-wash.

déplacer [deplase], *v.tr.* (**je déplaçai(s); n. déplaçons**) **1.** (*a*) displace, shift (an object); to change the place of (s.o., sth.); **meubles difficiles à d.,** furniture difficult to move; **d. un fonctionnaire,** transfer, move, a civil servant; **d. la question,** to shift one's ground; **d. la cargaison,** to shift the

cargo; **d. qch. à la main,** to move sth. by hand; **d. qch. à force de bras,** to manhandle sth.; *Mil:* **d. le tir,** to shift, switch, (the) fire; to change from one target to another; to shift the aim to a new target; **il nous fallut d. la batterie,** we had to move the battery; (*b*) to alter the time of (train, etc.). **2.** to oust, take the place of (s.o.). **3.** *Nau:* **ce navire déplace dix mille tonneaux,** this ship has a displacement of ten thousand tons.

se déplacer, (*a*) to change one's place, one's residence; *Mil:* to change position, station; (*b*) to move about, to travel; (*c*) to get out of place, to shift; (*c*) *Mil:* to move, to execute a movement; *Mil: etc:* **se d. à découvert,** to move openly, in the open.

déplafonnement [deplafɔnmɑ̃], *s.m. F:* removal of the upper limit (of prices).

déplafonner [deplafɔne], *v.tr.* (*a*) to take down a ceiling; (*b*) to remove the upper limit of.

déplaire [deplɛ:r], *v.ind.tr.* (*conj. like* PLAIRE) (*a*) to displease; **d. à qn,** (i) to displease, offend, s.o.; (ii) to fail to please s.o., to be displeasing to s.o.; **au risque de lui d. . . .,** at the risk of incurring his disapproval . . .; **musique qui lui déplaît,** music that offends his ear, that grates on his ear; **odeur qui déplaît,** offensive, disagreeable, smell; **tu lui déplais,** he dislikes you; **ils se déplaisent,** they dislike each other; **cela me déplaît (de faire qch.),** it is distasteful to me (to do sth.); I object (to doing sth.); **cela ne me déplairait pas,** I shouldn't mind; (*b*) *impers.* **il me déplairait de vous contredire,** I should not like to contradict you; **n'en déplaise à la compagnie,** with all due deference to those present; **n'en déplaise à votre Altesse!** may it please your Highness! **ne vous en déplaise,** if you have no objection, with your permission; *F:* **aujourd'hui il a trois voitures, ne vous en déplaise!** to-day he has three cars, if you please!

se déplaire, to be displeased, dissatisfied; **il se déplaît à Paris,** he does not like Paris; he dislikes living in Paris; **plante qui se déplaît dans ce climat,** plant that does not flourish, thrive, in this climate.

déplaisamment [deplezamɑ̃], *adv.* unpleasantly.

déplaisant [deplezɑ̃], *a.* unpleasing, unpleasant, disagreeable.

déplaisir [deplezi:r], *s.m.* **1.** *A:* grief, distress. **2.** displeasure, dissatisfaction, annoyance, vexation, chagrin; **causer du d. à qn,** to displease, annoy, s.o.; **le d. qu'il éprouve à vous rencontrer,** his annoyance when he meets you.

déplancher [deplɑ̃ʃe], *v.tr.* to remove the planking from (floor, shed, etc.).

déplantage [deplɑ̃ta:ʒ], *s.m.*, **déplantation** [deplɑ̃tasjɔ̃], *s.f.* displantation. **1.** unplanting (of garden, etc.); taking up (of plant). **2.** transplantation, transplanting.

déplanter [deplɑ̃te], *v.tr.* to displant. **1.** to unplant (garden, etc.); to take up (plant). **2.** to transplant. **3.** to uproot (s.o.).

déplantiner [deplɑ̃tine], *v.tr.* to sort out plantain seeds from corn, grass, seeds.

déplantoir [deplɑ̃twa:r], *s.m.* hand fork.

déplasmolyse [deplasmɔli:z], *s.f. Biol:* deplasmolysis.

déplatiner [deplatine], *v.tr. Ind:* to remove a temporary stop (in pipe, etc.).

déplâtrage [deplɑtra:ʒ], *s.m.* **1.** removal of the plaster (from wall, ceiling, etc.). **2.** *Surg:* taking (limb) out of plaster.

déplâtré [deplɑtre], *a.* (*a*) unplastered; (*b*) dilapidated (wall, building); (*c*) *F:* **elle accuse son âge quand elle est déplâtrée,** she looks her age when she isn't made up.

déplâtrer [deplɑtre], *v.tr.* **1.** to remove the plaster from (wall, ceiling, etc.). **2.** *Surg:* to take (limb) out of plaster.

se déplâtrer, (*of ceiling, etc.*) to shed its plaster; to scale.

déplétion [deplesjɔ̃], *s.f. Med:* depletion.

dépliage [deplija:ʒ], *s.m.* (action of) unfolding, spreading out, etc.

dépliant [depliɑ̃, -ijɑ̃], *s.m.* (*a*) folding album; set of folding views; **carte (en) d.,** folding map; (*b*) *Com:* folder, brochure.

dépliement [deplimɑ̃], *s.m.* = DÉPLIAGE.

déplier [deplie, -ije], *v.tr.* (*pr.sub. & p.d.* **n. dépliions, v. dépliiez**) to unfold, open out, spread out (newspaper, handkerchief, etc.); to unpack, open out (tackle, etc.); *Mil:* **d. le bipied du fusil-mitrailleur,** to mount the gun.

se déplier, to unfold, to open out.

déplissage [deplisa:ʒ], *s.m.* unpleating, taking the pleats out (of material, skirt, etc.).

déplisser [deplise], *v.tr.* to unpleat, to take the pleats out of (material, skirt, etc.).

se déplisser, (*of material, skirt, etc.*) to come unpleated, to come out of pleat.

déploiement [deplwamɑ̃], *s.m.* **1.** (*a*) spreading out, unfolding (of newspaper, wings, etc.); unfurling (of flag); (*b*) *Mil: Navy:* deployment (of troops, ships, weapons, equipment, etc.); **plan de d.,** deployment plan (of troops, of ships); deployment pattern (of weapons); **d. en vue du combat,** deployment for action; **d. en tirailleurs,** deployment in extended order, as skirmishers; **d. en éventail,** fan-shaped deployment; **d. tactique, stratégique,** tactical, strategical, deployment. **2.** display (of forces, of courage); display, show (of goods, etc.); **un imposant d. d'outils,** an imposing array of tools.

déplombage [deplɔ̃ba:ʒ], *s.m.* **1.** removal of custom-house seals (from goods). **2.** removal of the stopping (from tooth); unstopping (of tooth).

déplomber [deplɔ̃be], *v.tr.* **1.** to remove the custom-house seals from (package, etc.). **2.** to remove the stopping from (a tooth); to unstop (tooth).

déplorable [deplɔrabl̩], *a.* (*a*) deplorable, lamentable (incident, etc.); (*b*) pitiable (sight).

déplorablement [deplɔrabləmɑ̃], *adv.* deplorably, lamentably.

déploration [deplɔrasjɔ̃], *s.f. Lit: Rel:* lamentation, deploration, lament.

déplorer [deplɔre], *v.tr.* to deplore, lament, regret deeply (sth.); **d. la mort de qn,** to grieve over, to mourn, s.o.'s death; **d. son destin,** to bewail one's lot; **d. d'avoir ou de n'avoir pas fait qch.,** to regret having or not having done sth.

déployer [deplwaje], *v.tr.* (**je déploie, n. déployons; je déploierai**) **1.** to unfold, open out, spread out (newspaper, handkerchief, etc.); to unfurl, display (flag); to spread (sails, wings); to deploy (troops); *Nau:* to set (a sail). **2.** to display, show, make a show of (merchandise, patience, etc.); **je déployai toute ma force,** I put forth all my strength; **d. toute son éloquence en faveur de . . .,** to wax eloquent in support of . . .; **d. sa vengeance contre qn,** to wreak one's vengeance on s.o.; **d. une audace inattendue,** to show unexpected daring. **3.** *Metalw:* **métal déployé,** expanded metal.

se déployer. 1. (*a*) (*of sail, flag*) to unfurl; (*b*) (*of flag*) to fly (on a building, etc.); (*c*) (*of breaker*) to spread (after breaking). **2.** *Mil: Navy:* to deploy; to spread out; to extend; **se d. pour le combat, pour combattre,** to deploy for action; **se d. en tirailleurs,** to deploy in extended order; **se d. en éventail,** to fan out.

déplumé [deplyme], *a.* (*a*) featherless; *F:* **avoir l'air d.,** to look shabby, threadbare; (*b*) bald; **un vieux d.,** an old baldpate.

déplumer [deplyme], *v.tr.* to pluck (chicken, etc.).

se déplumer. 1. (*of bird*) to moult, to lose its feathers. **2.** *F:* (*of pers.*) to become bald, to lose one's hair.

dépocher [depɔʃe], *v.tr. F:* to produce (sth.) from one's pocket; to fork out (money).

dépoétiser [depɔetize], *v.tr.* to depoetize; to deprive (sth.) of its poetic character, to take all the poetry out of (an action, etc.).

dépointage [depwɛ̃ta:ʒ], *s.m.* (*of firearm*) loss of aim; *Artil:* after fire.

dépointé [depwɛ̃te], *a.* (*of firearm*) off the aim, off the target.

dépointer [depwɛ̃te], *v.tr.* (*of firearm*) to disturb the aim of, to put off the target.

se dépointer, (*of firearm*) to get off the target.

dépoisser [depwase], *v.tr.* to clean (sth.) of pitch, of anything sticky.

se dépoisser, *P:* to extricate oneself (from financial difficulties, etc.); to get out of a mess.

dépoitraillé [depwatraje], *a.* with shirt, blouse, coat, etc., (indecently) wide open, all unbuttoned.

dépolarisant [depɔlarizɑ̃], *Ph:* **1.** *a.* depolarizing. **2.** *s.m.* depolarizer.

dépolarisation [depɔlarizasjɔ̃], *s.f. Ph:* depolarization.

dépolariser [depɔlarize], *v.tr. Ph:* to depolarize.

dépoli [depɔli]. **1.** *a.* ground, frosted (glass). **2.** *s.m. Phot:* focusing screen.

dépolir [depɔli:r], *v.tr.* **1.** to take the polish off (sth.); to dull (surface). **2.** to grind, frost (glass).

se dépolir, to become dull; to lose its polish.

dépolissage [depɔlisa:ʒ], *s.m.*, **dépolissement** [depɔlismɑ̃], *s.m.* **1.** taking the polish off (sth.); dulling (of surface). **2.** grinding, frosting (of glass).

dépolitisation [depɔlitizasjɔ̃], *s.f.* taking sth. outside the sphere of politics.

dépolitiser [depɔlitize], *v.tr.* to take (sth.) outside, to remove (sth.) from, the sphere of politics.

dépolluer [depɔlɥe], *v.tr.* to cleanse.

dépolymérisation [depɔlimerizasjɔ̃], *s.f. Ch:* depolymerization.

dépolymériser [depɔlimerize], *v.tr. Ch:* to depolymerize.

dépommoir [depɔmwa:r], *s.m. Vet:* probang (for cattle).

déponent [depɔnɑ̃], *a. & s.m. Gram:* deponent (verb).

dépopulariser [depɔpylarize], *v.tr.* to depopularize (s.o., sth.), to make (s.o., sth.) unpopular.

se dépopulariser, to lose one's popularity, to become unpopular.

dépopulateur, -trice [depɔpylatœ:r, -tris]. **1.** *a.* depopulating. **2.** *s.* depopulator.

dépopulation [depɔpylasjɔ̃], *s.f.* depopulation; fall in population.

déport [depɔ:r], *s.m.* **1.** *Mec.E: etc:* offset, off-centring. **2.** *Elcs:* retransmission (of radar data). **3.** *St.Exch:* (i) (*stock dealings*) backwardation; (ii) (*exchange dealings*) premium.

déportation [depɔrtasjɔ̃], *s.f.* **1.** deportation (of undesirable alien, etc.). **2.** transportation (of convict); deportation (of political prisoners, etc.); **colonie de d.,** penal settlement; **camp de d.,** deportation camp.

déporté,[1] **-ée** [depɔrte], *a. & s.* **1.** deported (person); deportee. **2.** transported (convict); *Adm:* transport.

déporté[2], *a.* **1.** *Mec.E:* off-set; off-centre; **meule à moyeu d.,** depressed-centre grinding-wheel. **2.** *St.Exch:* backwardized (stock).

déportement [depɔrtəmɑ̃], *s.m.* **1.** *pl.* **déportements,** misbehaviour. misconduct, excesses, dissolute life. **2.** *Aut:* skidding.

déporter[1] [depɔrte], *v.tr.* **1.** to deport (undesirable alien). **2.** to transport (convict); to deport (a prisoner of war, political prisoners), to send to a concentration camp.

déporter[2]. **1.** *v.tr.* (*a*) to carry away; **voiture déportée par la violence du vent,** car blown off the road, out of its course, by the violence of the wind; (*b*) *Mec.E: etc:* to off-set (part). **2.** *v.i. Av:* to drift.

se déporter, *Jur: A:* (*a*) **se d. de ses prétentions,** to withdraw one's claims; (*b*) *abs.* = SE RÉCUSER.

déposable [depozabl̩], *a.* (*of securities, etc.*) that may be deposited.

déposant, -ante [depozɑ̃, -ɑ̃:t], *s.* **1.** (*a*) depositor (of money in bank, etc.); (*b*) *Jur:* bailor. **2.** *Jur:* deponent, witness.

dépose[1] [depo:z], *s.f.* removal, taking up (of paving-stones, rails, carpet, etc.); demounting (of engine, etc.); recovery (of telephone line).

dépose[2], *s.f.* landing (by helicopter).

déposer[1] [depoze], *v.tr.* **1.** to remove, take up (paving-stones, etc.); **d. des rails,** to take up rails (from track). **2. d. les rideaux,** to take down the curtains.

déposer[2], *v.tr.* **1.** (*a*) to deposit; to lay, set, (sth.) down; **d. un fardeau, un panier, sur le plancher,** to lay down, deposit, a burden, a basket, on the floor; **ma voiture vous déposera à l'hôtel,** my car will set you down, *F:* will drop you, at the hotel; **déposez-moi où vous m'avez pris,** set me down where you picked me up; **d. son chapeau au vestiaire,** to leave one's hat in the cloak-room; **d. sa carte chez qn,** to leave one's card on s.o.; **d. des ordures,** to shoot rubbish; **d. les armes,** to lay down one's arms, to surrender; **d. son arrogance,** to lay aside one's arrogance; **d. le masque,** to lay aside, put off, the mask; **d. la couronne,** to give up the crown; *F:* **d. son orgueil,** to pocket one's pride; **d. ses hommages aux pieds de qn,** to lay one's homage at s.o.'s feet; *Lit:* **d. un baiser sur le front de qn,** to imprint a kiss on s.o.'s forehead; *Lit:* **d. un secret dans le sein d'un ami,** to confide a secret to a friend; *Mil:* **d. un drapeau (quand un régiment est dissous),** to lay up the colours; (*b*) (*of liquid*) to deposit (sediment); *abs.* **il faut laisser au liquide le temps de d.,** we must allow the liquid some time to settle; **vin qui dépose,** wine that throws down, deposits, a sediment, a crust. **2.** (*a*) to deposit, lodge, (sth.) in a safe place; **d. son argent, des documents, à la banque,** to lodge, deposit, one's money, documents, at the bank; **d. un colis postal au guichet,** to hand in a parcel over the (post-office) counter; **d. un télégramme à la poste,** to hand in a telegram at the post-office; **d. du courrier à la poste, dans une boîte aux lettres,** to post mail; (*b*) *Com:* **d. une demande de brevet,** to file an application for a patent; **modèle déposé,** registered pattern; **d. une marque de fabrique,** to register a trade-mark;

marque déposée, registered trade-mark; **d. des exemplaires d'un livre,** to deposit duty copies of a book (for copyright); (*c*) *Jur:* **d. une plainte contre qn,** to prefer a charge, lodge a complaint, against s.o.; **d. une pétition,** to file a petition; *Com:* **d. son bilan,** to file one's petition (in bankruptcy); (*d*) **d. un projet de loi (sur le bureau de la Chambre),** to table, bring in, a bill; **d. un amendement,** to put down, introduce, present, an amendment; **d. une liste électorale,** to put forward a list of candidates; (*e*) *abs. Jur:* **déposer (en justice),** to give evidence (**contre,** against); to depose; **il déposa** *que* + *ind.*, he deposed that . . .. 3. to depose (monarch, etc.).

se déposer, (*of matter*) to settle, to form a deposit.

dépositaire [depozitɛːr], *s.m. & f.* depositary, trustee; *Jur:* bailee; **d. de valeurs,** holder of securities on trust; *Lit:* **faire de qn le d. d'un secret,** to confide in s.o., to make s.o. the repository of a secret; *Com:* **(seul) d. des produits de qn,** sole agent for s.o.'s products; **d. des enjeux,** stake-holder; **d. de journaux,** newsagent.

déposition [depozisjɔ̃], *s.f.* **1.** *Jur:* deposition, evidence, testimony; statement (made by witness); **d. rigoureuse en témoignage,** affidavit; **recueillir une d.,** to take s.o.'s evidence. **2.** deposing, deposition, deposal, dethronement (of king, etc.). **3.** *Art:* **la D. de croix,** the Deposition from the Cross.

dépositoire [depozitwaːr], *s.m.* mortuary.

déposséder [depɔsede], *v.tr.* **(je dépossède, n. dépossédons; je déposséderai)** (*a*) to dispossess (**de,** of); to oust (**de,** from); **d. qn de sa place,** to deprive s.o. of, oust s.o. from, his seat; (*b*) *Jur:* **d. qn d'une terre,** to disseize s.o. of an estate; *F:* **noblesse dépossédée de toute autorité,** nobility stripped of all authority.

dépossession [depɔsesjɔ̃], *s.f.* (*a*) dispossession; (*b*) *Jur:* eviction, dispossession (from land); disseizin, ouster (of rightful owner).

déposter [depɔste], *v.tr.* to drive (enemy) from his position.

dépôt [depo], *s.m.* **1.** (*a*) depositing; lodgement (of money, etc., in bank, etc.); handing in (of telegram); submission (of report, etc.); registration (of trademark); *Fin:* ear-marking transaction; *Jur:* bailment (of goods); **d. au guichet,** handing in over the counter; **d. du courrier à la poste, dans une boîte aux lettres,** posting of the mail; *Com:* **effectuer, opérer le d. d'une marque (de fabrique),** to register a trade-mark; **d. d'une demande de brevet,** filing an application for a patent; **récépissé de d.,** safe-custody receipt; **société de d.,** joint-stock bank; *Publ:* **d. légal d'un livre,** copyrighting of a book (by depositing duty copies); *Pol:* **d. d'un projet de loi, d'un amendement (sur le bureau de la Chambre),** bringing in, tabling, of a bill, an amendment; laying of a bill, of an amendment, on the table; **d. d'une liste électorale,** putting forward (of) a list of candidates; *Jur:* **d. d'une plainte contre qn,** lodgement of a complaint against s.o.; **d. d'une pétition,** filing (of) a petition; (*b*) deposit; **d. sacré,** sacred trust; **d. de garantie,** earnest money; **d. en banque,** bank deposit; **effectuer un d. de fonds à la banque, dans une banque,** to deposit, lodge, funds at a bank, with a bank; **d. à échéance fixe, argent en d. à terme,** deposit for a fixed period; **compte de dépôts,** deposit account; (*c*) **en d.,** on trust, in trust; **avoir, détenir, qch. en d.,** to hold sth. in trust, on trust; **mettre des documents en d. dans une banque,** to place documents on deposit, in safe custody, to deposit documents, with a bank; **marchandises en d.,** (i) *Cust:* goods in bond; (ii) *Com:* goods on trust, on sale or return; **livrer une marchandise en d. permanent,** to deliver goods on consignment. **2.** depository, repository, store(house), depot; **d. de mendicité,** workhouse; **d. de la Préfecture de Police,** central police station (in Paris); **écroué au d.,** committed to the cells; *F:* put in the lock-up; *Jur:* **mandat de d.,** mittimus, committal, commitment (of prisoner); **délivrer un mandat de d.,** to grant, issue, a mittimus; *Rail:* **d. des machines,** engine shed; **d. des marchandises,** goods depot; **d. de marchandises,** warehouse; **avoir qch. en d.,** to have sth. in stock, **en d. chez . . .,** stocked by . . .; **d. de bois,** timber yard; **d. de charbon,** coal depot, yard; *Nau:* coaling station; **d. d'essence,** petrol storage depot, petrol station; *Petroleum Ind:* **d. de carburants,** tank farm; *Rail: etc:* **d. de(s) bagages,** left-luggage office; *Const:* **d. de matériel,** storage yard. **3.** *Civ.E: etc:* dump, dumping-ground (for waste); **prévoir un emplacement pour le d. des ordures ménagères, des déchets radioactifs,** to provide a site for dumping household refuse, radioactive waste. **4.** (*a*) deposition, settling (of precipitate, mud, etc.); **d. électrolytique,** electro-deposition; (*b*) deposit, sediment; silt (of harbour, etc.); settlings (of liquid); **d. de vin,** crust (in the bottle); **d. d'une chaudière,** scale of boiler; *I.C.E:* **d. de calamine,** carbon deposit. **5.** *Med:* concrement, concretion; deposit; accumulation of matter (in organ); abscess (in lung, etc.); **d. calcaire, d. membraneux,** calcareous, membranous, deposit; *Dent:* **d. de tartre,** calcular deposit. **6.** (*a*) *Mil:* **d. (permanent),** depot; **d. (temporaire),** dump; **d. avancé,** advanced depot, forward dump; **d. d'armée,** army depot; **d. de base,** base depot; **d. de corps de troupe,** regimental depot; **d. central,** general depot; **d. particulier,** branch depot; **d. monovalent,** one-item depot; **d. polyvalent,** multi-item depot; **d. linéaire,** linear dump; **d. en surface,** area dump; **d. d'effectifs,** manning depot; **d. de recomplètement,** replacement depot; **d. du génie,** engineer store, engineer dump; **d. d'explosifs,** explosives store; **d. de l'intendance,** R.A.S.C. (Royal Army Service Corps) depot, *U.S:* quartermaster depot; **d. d'approvisionnements, de vivres,** supply depot, victualling yard; **d. d'habillement,** reclothing point; **d. de carburant(s), d. d'essence,** petrol dump; P.O.L. (Petrol, Oil, Lubricant) depot, dump; **d. (du Service) du Matériel,** R.A.S.C. depot, R.E.M.E. (Royal Electrical and Mechanical Engineers) depot, *U.S:* ordnance depot; **d. de matériel,** equipment depot, dump; **un d. clandestin,** a cache (for arms, etc.); **d. de récupération (du matériel),** salvage depot, dump; **d. de munitions,** ammunition depot, dump; **d. de poudre,** (powder) magazine; **Service des Dépôts,** Supplies and Stores, Ordnance; **d. du Service de Santé,** medical depot; **d. de matériel médical,** depot of medical stores; **d. de convalescents,** convalescent depot; **d. d'éclopés,** walking wounded clearing station; (*b*) *Navy:* **d. des équipages, de la flotte,** naval barracks.

dépotage [depɔtaːʒ], *s.m.*, **dépotement** [depɔtmɑ̃], *s.m.* **1.** decanting (of liquid). **2.** discharge (of a cargo of oil, etc.). **3.** unpotting; planting out, bedding out (of plants).

dépoter [depɔte], *v.tr.* **1.** to decant (liquid). **2.** to unpot (plants); to plant out, bed out (seedlings). **3.** to dump. **4.** to discharge, empty (oil, etc.)

dépotoir [depɔtwaːr], *s.m.* (*a*) (town) night-soil dump; *F:* **ma classe est le d. de l'école,** I've got the dregs of the school in my class; (*b*) refuse dump; (*c*) (refuse) disposal plant.

dépoudrer [depudre], *v.tr.* to take the powder off (face, hair, etc.).

se dépoudrer, to remove the powder from one's face, from one's hair.

dépouille [depuːj], *s.f.* **1.** skin, hide (taken from animal); slough (of reptile); **le serpent jette sa d.,** the serpent casts its slough; **d. mortelle,** mortal remains; *Poet:* **la d. des champs, des jardins,** the crops, the fruits. **2.** (*a*) *usu. pl.* spoils, booty (of war); *F:* **s'enrichir des dépouilles d'autrui,** to get rich at the expense of others; *s.a.* OPIMES; (*b*) effects, clothes (of deceased person). **3.** (*a*) *Mec.E:* backing off, relief, rake, clearance (of drill, of machine-tool); (*b*) *Metall:* draw, draught, draft, taper (of pattern); **offrir de la d.,** to deliver easily.

dépouillé [depuje], *a.* reduced to essentials, spare, severe.

dépouillement [depujmɑ̃], *s.m.* **1.** (*a*) skinning (of eel, rabbit, etc.); stripping (of cable, etc.); *Phot:* **d. de la pellicule de gélatine,** stripping of the emulsion; (*b*) spoliation; deprivation (of s.o.) of his belongings; despoiling, plundering (of country); **d. volontaire de ses biens,** relinquishment, renouncement, of one's property. **2. d. d'un rapport,** examination, analysis, of a report; **d. d'un compte,** abstract of an account; **d. des votes, d'un scrutin,** returning operations, counting of the votes (at a ballot or an election); **d. de la correspondance,** opening of the mail, going through the mail; *Radar:* **d. des données,** data processing. **3.** *Mec.E:* backing off, clearance, relief (of drill, etc.).

dépouiller [depuje], *v.tr.* **1.** (*a*) to skin (eel, rabbit, etc.); **l'hiver dépouille les champs,** winter makes the fields bare, winter strips the fields; (*b*) to cast off, lay aside; **d. ses vêtements,** to throw off one's clothes; to strip; **d. tout ressentiment,** to cast aside all resentment; (*of insect, reptile*) **d. sa première enveloppe,** to cast (off), shed, its skin, its slough; *B. & F:* **d. le vieil homme,** to put off the old man. **2.** to deprive, strip, despoil; **d. qn de ses habits,** to strip, divest, s.o. of his clothes; **arbres dépouillés de leurs feuilles,** trees stripped, denuded, bared, of their leaves; **d. qn de son argent, de ses droits,** to deprive, rob, s.o. of his money, of his rights; *F:* to skin s.o.; **d. un pays,** to plunder, despoil, a country; **il m'a dépouillé d'une grosse somme,** *F:* he has done me out of a large sum; *El.E:* **d. un câble,** to strip a cable; **d. l'extrémité d'un fil,** to bare the end of a wire; *Phot:* **d. un papier au charbon,** to strip off a carbon tissue. **3. d. un inventaire,** to examine, analyse, an inventory; **d. un compte,** to make an abstract of an account; **d. le scrutin,** to count the votes; **d. le courrier,** open, go through the mail; to open mail; **d. les renseignements,** etc., to process information, etc.; *Radar:* **d. des données,** to process data. **4.** (*a*) *Metall:* to taper (pattern); (*b*) *Mec.E:* to back off, relieve, give clearance to (drill, machine-tool, etc.).

se dépouiller. 1. (*of insect, reptile*) to cast (off) its skin, its slough; (*of tree*) to shed its leaves; (*of wine*) to lose colour. **2. se d. de qch.,** to deprive, divest, rid, oneself of sth.; **se d. de ses vêtements,** to strip off one's clothes; *F:* to strip; **se d. de ses biens en faveur de ses enfants,** to divest oneself of one's property in favour of one's children; **se d. de toute haine,** to throw aside, cast aside, all hatred; **il ne se dépouille jamais de sa réserve,** he never casts off his reserve.

dépourvoir [depurvwaːr], *v.tr.* (*conj. like* POURVOIR; *used only in the inf., p.p., and compound tenses*) to deprive (s.o.) (**de,** of).

dépourvu [depurvy], *a.* destitute, bereft, short, devoid (**de,** of); -less; **d. d'intelligence,** wanting in intelligence; destitute of, devoid of, intelligence; **pays d. d'arbres, de pluie,** treeless, rainless, country; **être d. d'argent,** to be without money, short of cash; *adv.phr.* **être pris au d.,** to be caught off one's guard; to be taken or caught napping, unawares.

dépoussiérage [depusjeraːʒ], *s.m. Ind:* freeing from dust; dust removal; de-dusting; **d. électrostatique,** electrostatic dust precipitation; **d. par le vide,** vacuum-cleaning.

dépoussiérer [depusjere], *v.tr. Ind:* to vacuum-clean; to free from dust, to remove the dust; to de-dust; **salle des accumulateurs dépoussiérée,** de-dusted accumulator room; *Typ:* **d. le blanchet,** to lint off blanket.

dépoussiéreur [depusjerœːr], *s.m. Ind:* dust remover; de-duster, duster; **d. électrostatique,** electrostatic dust precipitator; **d. par le vide,** vacuum-cleaner.

dépravant [depravɑ̃], *a.* depraving.

dépravateur, -trice [depravatœːr, -tris]. **1.** *s.* depraver, corrupter. **2.** *a.* **exemple d.,** depraving, vicious, example.

dépravation [depravasjɔ̃], *s.f.* **1.** depravation (of taste, etc.). **2.** (moral) depravity.

dépravé, -ée [deprave]. **1.** *a.* depraved. **2.** *s.* depraved, vicious, profligate, person.

dépraver [deprave], *v.tr.* to deprave.

se dépraver, to become depraved.

déprécatif, -ive [deprekatif, -iːv], *a. Ecc:* deprecative, deprecatory (form of absolution).

déprécation [deprekasjɔ̃], *s.f. Ecc:* **1.** deprecation; prayer for the averting of or deliverance from evil or disaster. **2.** prayer for forgiveness; *A:* deprecation.

déprécatoire [deprekatwaːr], *a.* = DÉPRÉCATIF.

dépréciateur, -trice [depresjatœːr, -tris]. **1.** *s.* depreciator (of currency, etc.); disparager, belittler (of s.o.'s character, etc.). **2.** *a.* depreciatory, depreciative, depreciating, disparaging, belittling.

dépréciatif, -ive [depresjatif, -iːv], *a. Ling:* depreciatory (suffix, etc.).

dépréciation [depresjasjɔ̃], *s.f.* **1.** depreciation; (*a*) fall in value; (*b*) wear and tear. **2.** (*a*) underrating, undervaluing; (*b*) disparagement, belittlement; *F:* running down (of s.o.).

déprécier [depresje], *v.tr.* (*p.d. & pr.sub.* **n. dépréciions, v. dépréciiez**) **1.** to depreciate (coinage, etc.). **2.** (*a*) to underrate, undervalue (goods, merits); (*b*) to disparage, belittle (s.o.); *F:* to run down (s.o., book).

se déprécier. 1. (*a*) (*of values*) to depreciate, to fall; (*b*) (*of goods*) to depreciate, to fall in value. **2.** (*of pers.*) to make oneself cheap.

déprédateur, -trice [depredatœːr, -tris]. **1.** *s.* (*a*) depredator, pillager; (*b*) peculator, embezzler. **2.** *a.* depredatory.

déprédation [depredasjɔ̃], *s.f.* **1.** depredation, pillaging. **2.** peculation; misappropriation, corrupt administration (of funds, etc.).

dépréder [deprede], *v.tr.* (**je déprède, n. déprédons; je déprèderai**) **1.** *A:* to pillage, lay waste. **2.** to peculate; to misappropriate (funds, etc.).

déprendre (se) [sədeprɑ̃:dr], *v.pr.* (*conj. like* PRENDRE) **1.** to detach oneself, to get free; **se d. de soi-même,** to cast off one's own personality. **2.** (*of jelly, etc.*) to melt, to run. **3.** (*of objects stuck together*) to separate, part.

dépressage [deprɛsa:ʒ], *s.m. For:* thinning out, clearing.

dépresser [deprɛse], *v.tr.* **1.** to remove the pressure from (object); *Bookb:* to remove (book) from the press. **2.** *Tex:* to remove the lustre from (cloth). **3.** to thin out (copse, etc.).

dépresseur [deprɛsœ:r], *s.m.* **1.** *Ch:* depressor. **2.** *Med:* **d. de l'appétit,** appetite depressant.

dépressif, -ive [deprɛsif, -i:v], *a.* **1.** bearing down (force). **2.** depressing, depressive (news, etc.).

dépression [deprɛsjɔ̃], *s.f.* depression. **1.** hollow, dip (in floor, ground); flattening (of skull, etc.); *Oc:* trough; *Astr:* **d. de l'horizon,** dip of the horizon; *Artil:* **angle de d.,** angle of depression (of gun). **2.** (*a*) fall (in value); *St.Exch:* depression (of stock); *Pol.Ec:* **d. économique,** economic depression, slump; *Phot:* **d. de la sensibilité,** lowering of sensitiveness; (*b*) *Meteor:* **d. (barométrique),** lowering of barometric pressure; (barometric) depression; low; trough; **d. mobile,** cyclonic depression; **d. mère,** parent depression; **d. secondaire,** secondary depression; (*c*) *Ph: Mec.E:* depression, partial vacuum (in boiler, in tank, in tube, etc.); *s.a.* CENTRE 2. **3.** (moral) depression, dejection; *Med:* **d. nerveuse,** nervous breakdown; **malade en proie à la d.,** depressed patient. **4.** depreciation, disparagement, belittlement.

dépressionnaire [deprɛsjɔnɛ:r], *a.* **1.** *Meteor:* **zone d.,** depression, trough of low pressure, trough of depression. **2.** depressionary, depressional; **déclencher une tendance d. dans l'économie française,** to start a depressionary movement in the French economy.

dépressoir [deprɛswa:r], *s.m. Surg:* depressor.

déprimant [deprimɑ̃], *a. Med:* depressing; lowering (to the system).

déprimé [deprime], *a.* depressed; (*a*) low, flat, flattened (surface, etc.); **front d ,** low forehead; **arc d.,** flat arch; *Bot:* **tige déprimée,** flattened stem; (*b*) **pouls d.,** feeble pulse; **marché d.,** depressed market; **malade d.,** patient in a low state, depressed patient; (*c*) down-hearted, cast down, downcast, down in the mouth, low-spirited, dejected; *F:* hipped; **se sentir d.,** to feel rather low, to be in a despondent mood.

déprimer [deprime], *v.tr.* (*a*) to depress, flatten down, lower (surface, etc.); (*b*) **d. le moral de l'ennemi,** to lower the enemy's morale; **fièvre qui déprime le système,** fever that lowers the system; (*c*) *A:* **d. l'orgueil de qn,** to bring down s.o.'s pride; **d. le mérite,** to belittle merit.

se déprimer, to get depressed, miserable; *F:* to get down in the mouth.

déprimomètre [deprimɔmɛtr], *s.m. Ph:* vacuum gauge.

dépriser [deprize], *v.tr. Lit: A:* to undervalue, underrate.

déprolétarisation [deprɔletarizasjɔ̃], *s.f.* deproletarianization.

déprolétariser [deprɔletarize], *v.tr.* to deproletarianize.

dépromettre [deprɔmɛtr], *v.tr.* (*conj. like* PROMETTRE) *A:* **d. qch.,** to break one's promise about sth.

dépropanisateur [deprɔpanizatœ:r], *s.m. Petroleum Ind:* = DÉPROPANISEUR.

dépropanisation [deprɔpanizasjɔ̃], *s.f. Petroleum Ind:* depropanization.

dépropaniser [deprɔpanize], *v.tr. Petroleum Ind:* to depropanize.

dépropaniseur [deprɔpanizœ:r], *s.m. Petroleum Ind:* depropanizer.

déprovincialiser [deprɔvɛ̃sjalize], *v.tr. F:* to break (s.o.) of his country manners; to smarten (s.o.) up.

se déprovincialiser, to lose one's uncouthness, one's country manners.

dépucelage [depys(ə)la:ʒ], *s.m. F:* defloration.

dépuceler [depys(ə)le], *v.tr. F:* to deflower.

depuis [dəpɥi], *prep.* **1.** (*a*) (*of time*) since; for; **je ne suis pas sorti d. hier,** I have not been out since yesterday; **je n'ai pas mangé d'huîtres d. des années,** I haven't eaten oysters for, in, years; **d. quand êtes-vous ici?** how long have you been here? **je suis ici d. trois jours,** I have been here for three days; **je le connais d. six ans,** I have known him these last six years, for the last six years; **depuis quelques années . . .,** of late years . . .; **il était à l'étranger d. quelques mois,** he had been abroad for some months; **d. combien?** how long since? **d. ce temps-là,** since then, since that time; **je suis là d. le déjeuner,** I have been here ever since lunch; **d. quand répond-on comme cela à sa mère?** since when do children answer their mothers back like that? **d. son enfance il a fait preuve d'une grande intelligence,** from childhood he showed great intelligence; **d. toujours,** right from the start, from the very beginning; **d. Cézanne,** since the time of Cézanne; (*b*) *adv.* since (then), since that time; afterwards, later; **je l'ai vu dimanche, mais pas d.,** I saw him on Sunday, but not since; **je l'ai connu d.,** I made his acquaintance later; (*c*) *conj.phr.* **depuis que** + *ind.*, since . . .; **nous ne l'avons pas vu d. qu'il est marié,** we haven't seen him since he was married; **d. que j'habite Paris,** since the time I came to live in Paris, ever since I lived in Paris; **d. le temps que je me tue à te répéter que . . .,** for years I've told you time and again that . . .. **2.** (*of time, place, etc.*) from; **d. le matin jusqu'au soir,** from morning till night; **d. la ferme jusqu'à la rivière,** from the farm to the river; **il ne m'a pas parlé d. Rouen,** he hasn't spoken to me since (we left) Rouen; **bons vins d. deux francs la bouteille,** good wines from two francs a bottle. **3.** *W.Tel:* broadcast from . . .; **radio-reportage du Grand Prix d. Longchamp,** running commentary on the Grand Prix from Longchamp.

dépulpation [depylpasjɔ̃], *s.f. Dent:* pulpotomy.

dépulpé [depylpe], *a. Physiol: Dent:* (*of tooth*) pulpless.

dépulper [depylpe], *v.tr.* to remove the pulp (from fruit); to pulp (fruit, wood, etc.).

dépulpeur [depylpœ:r], *s.m. Tls: etc:* pulper.

dépurateur, -trice [depyratœ:r, -tris], *a.* purifying.

dépuratif, -ive [depyratif, -i:v], *a. & s.m. Med:* depurative; blood-cleansing, -cleanser.

dépuration [depyrasjɔ̃], *s.f.* depuration; cleansing (of blood); purification (of metal, etc.); clearing (of liquid).

dépuratoire [depyratwa:r], *a. Med:* depurative.

dépurer [depyre], *v.tr.* to depurate, cleanse, clear (the blood); to purify (metal, water).

se dépurer, to (become) clear.

députation [depytasjɔ̃], *s.f.* **1.** (*a*) deputing, delegating (of s.o.); (*b*) deputation, delegation, body of representatives. **2.** *Pol:* (*a*) position as member of Parliament; membership (of Parliament); **se présenter à la d.,** to stand (as candidate) for Parliament, for a seat in Parliament; **candidat à la d.,** parliamentary candidate; (*b*) *Coll.* **la d. d'un département,** the members for a department.

député [depyte], *s.m.* **1.** deputy, delegate. **2.** *Pol:* (*a*) (*in Fr.*) Deputy; **La Chambre des Députés,** the Chamber of Deputies; (*b*) (*in Engl.*) Member of Parliament, M.P.; parliamentary representative.

députer [depyte], *v.tr.* to depute (s.o.), to appoint (s.o.) as deputy, as delegate (à, vers, to).

déqualifier [dekalifje], *v.tr.* (*p.d. & pr.sub.* **n. déqualifiions, v. déqualifiiez**) to deprive (s.o.) of a title.

se déqualifier, to renounce one's title.

déquiller [dekije], *v.tr.* **1.** *abs.* to knock a ninepin out of bounds. **2.** *F:* **d. qn,** (i) to knock s.o. off his pins, to bowl s.o. over; (ii) to cripple s.o.; (iii) to oust s.o. from his job.

der [dɛ:r], *s. F:* (*short for dernier, -ère*) **le, la, der** (**des der**), the last (of all); **la der des der,** the war to end all wars.

déracinable [derasinabl], *a.* that can be uprooted.

déraciné [derasine], *a. & s.* **1.** *a.* uprooted, torn from the ground. **2.** *a. F:* (*of pers.*) torn from one's usual surroundings, uprooted; **se sentir d.,** to feel oneself in a strange land, to feel like a fish out of water, to feel uprooted. **3.** *s.* exile; uprooted person.

déracinement [derasinmɑ̃], *s.m.* **1.** uprooting, deracination (of stump); extirpation (of corn); eradication (of fault). **2.** deracination (of emigrant); tearing, uprooting, from one's surroundings.

déraciner [derasine], *v.tr.* **1.** (*a*) to uproot, grub up, deracinate; to tear (tree, etc.) up by the roots; (*b*) to extirpate (corn, etc.). **2.** to eradicate (fault, abuse). **3.** to deracinate (s.o.); to tear, uproot, (s.o.) from his homeland, from his surroundings.

déracineur, -euse [derasinœ:r, -ø:z], *s.* uprooter.

dérader [derade]. **1.** *v.i. Nau:* (*a*) to leave the roadstead, the anchorage; (*b*) to be driven out of shelter, out to sea. **2.** *v.tr.* to lay up (the fishing-boats) (for the winter).

dérager [deraʒe], *v.i.* (*conj. like* RAGER) *F:* = DÉCOLÉRER.

déraidir [derɛdi:r], *v.tr.* **1.** to unstiffen, take the stiffness out of (limb, material, etc.).

se déraidir. **1.** (*of limb, material, etc.*) to lose its stiffness. **2.** *F:* (*of pers.*) to unbend, to thaw.

déraillement [derɑjmɑ̃], *s.m. Rail:* derailment, leaving the metals; **équerre de d.,** derailer; **aiguille de d.,** derailing switch.

dérailler [derɑje], *v.i.* **1.** (*a*) (*of train, tram*) to run off the metals, off the line; to jump the metals, to become derailed; **faire d. un train,** to derail a train; **le train n'a pas déraillé,** the train kept the rails; (*b*) (*of record-player needle*) to jump, leave, the sound groove; (*c*) **voix, instrument, qui déraille,** voice, musical instrument, which is going off pitch. **2.** *P:* (*of pers.*) (i) to take the wrong path, the wrong turning; (ii) to talk nonsense, rubbish; *P:* to be right off it.

dérailleur [derɑjœ:r], *s.m.* (*a*) *Rail:* shifting track; (*b*) *Cy:* derailleur (gear change).

déraison [derɛzɔ̃], *s.f.* unreasonableness; want of sense, foolishness, unwisdom; unreason, irrationality.

déraisonnable [derɛzɔnabl], *a.* unreasonable, irrational; unwise, senseless, foolish; preposterous; **mettre un temps d. à faire qch.,** to take an unconscionable time to do sth.

déraisonnablement [derɛzɔnabləmɑ̃], *adv.* unreasonably, senselessly; foolishly, unwisely.

déraisonnement [derɛzɔnmɑ̃], *s.m.* raving; nonsensical talk.

déraisonner [derɛzɔne], *v.i.* to talk nonsense; (*in illness*) to rave.

déramer [derame], *v.i.* to backwater.

dérangé [derɑ̃ʒe], *a.* (*of machine*) out of order; (*of mind*) deranged, unbalanced; (*of stomach*) upset; (*of bowels*) loose.

dérangement [derɑ̃ʒmɑ̃], *s.m.* derangement; (*a*) disarrangement (of books, furniture, etc.); (*b*) disturbance, trouble; **causer du d. à qn,** to give s.o. trouble, to disturb s.o.; **aux prix de dérangements personnels considérables,** at great personal inconvenience; *F:* **causer un d. dans notre train(-)train quotidien,** to cause an upset, a disturbance, in our daily routine; (*c*) disturbed or unsettled state; upset; **d. atmosphérique,** atmospheric disturbance; (*d*) *Med:* trouble, upset, derangement; **d. du cerveau, de l'esprit,** mental derangement; **d. de l'intestin,** upset stomach, diarrhoea; (*e*) *Mec.E:* trouble (of engine), derangement (of mechanism); *El.E:* fault (in electric line, etc.); *Tp:* **la ligne est en d.,** the line is out of order, *U.S:* is in trouble; **ligne en d.,** faulty line, *U.S:* line in trouble; **d. d'appel,** signalling fault, *U.S:* signalling trouble; **recherche des dérangements,** fault locating, *U.S:* troubleshooting; **service des dérangements,** fault complaint service.

déranger [derɑ̃ʒe], *v.tr.* (**je dérangeai(s); n. dérangeons**) to derange; (*a*) to disarrange (papers, books, etc.); **ne dérangez pas mes papiers,** don't meddle with my papers, don't touch my papers; (*b*) to disturb, trouble; **pardon, excusez-moi, de vous déranger; pardon si je vous dérange,** excuse my disturbing, my troubling, you; **si cela ne vous dérange pas,** if it is not troubling you, if quite convenient to you, if I am not intruding upon you, if it's no trouble to you; (*c*) to put (sth.) out of order, to upset (s.o.); **machine dérangée,** machine out of order; **d. la raison de qn,** to unsettle s.o.'s reason, to derange s.o.'s mind; **l'orage a dérangé le temps,** the storm has upset, unsettled, the weather; **cela dérange mes plans,** it upsets, interferes with, my plans; **quelque chose lui a dérangé l'estomac,** something has upset his digestion.

se déranger. **1.** (*a*) to move, stir; **ne vous dérangez pas,** please don't move, don't trouble, don't bother (yourself); **se d. pour obliger qn,** to go out of one's way to oblige s.o.; (*b*) *Nau:* to give way (**pour,** to). **2.** to deviate from the path of virtue; *F:* to get into bad ways, to run wild. **3.** (*of machine*) to get out of order; (*of stomach*) to become disordered, to get upset; (*of mind*) to become deranged, unbalanced.

dérangeur, -euse [derɑ̃ʒœ:r, -ø:z], *s.* disturber, interrupter.

dérapage [derapa:ʒ], *s.m.* **1.** *Nau:* (*a*) tripping (of anchor); (*b*) dragging (of anchor). **2.** (*a*) *Aut: etc:* skid(ding); **d. à sec,** dry skid; **d. contrôlé,** controlled skid; (*b*) *Av:* side-slip; *Skiing:* (i) side-slip; (ii) side-slipping.

déraper [derape], *v.tr. & i.* **1.** *A. & Dial:* to tear away, tear out; to tear oneself away. **2.** *Nau:* (*a*) to heave up, trip, weigh, the anchor; **l'ancre est dérapée**, the anchor is atrip, aweigh, apeak; **dérapez!** break ground! (*b*) (*of anchor*) to drag, to pull out; (*of ship*) to drag its anchor. **3.** *Aut: etc:* to skid, to side-slip.

dérasement [derazmɑ̃], *s.m. Const:* levelling (down).

déraser [deraze], *v.tr. Const:* to level down.

dératé [derate], *a.* **1.** spleened; *F:* **courir comme un d.**, to run like a hare. **2.** *F: A:* harum-scarum, scatter-brained.

dérater [derate], *v.tr.* to spleen (dog, etc.).

dérationner [derasjɔne], *v.tr.* to deration.

dératisation [deratizasjɔ̃], *s.f.* extermination of rats; deratization.

dératiser [deratize], *v.tr.* to clear of rats, to derat.

dérayage [dereja:ʒ], *s.m. Cin. T.V:* polishing (out).

dérayer [dereje], (*conj. like* RAYER) **1.** *v.tr.* to cut the boundary-furrow, the last furrow (of ploughed field). **2.** *v.tr.* to unscotch (wheel). **3.** *v.i.* (*of spokes*) to work loose.

dérayure [derɛjy:r], *s.f. Agr:* (*a*) water-furrow; (*b*) boundary-furrow.

derby [dɛrbi], *s.m.* **1.** (*a*) *Turf:* **le d. d'Epsom,** the Derby; (*b*) *Sp: Fb:* local derby. **2.** *Cost:* derby (shoe). **3.** *Veh:* wagonette.

derche [dɛrʃ], *s.m. V:* backside.

déréalisation [derealizasjɔ̃], *s.f. Psy:* the loss of a sense of reality.

derechef [dərəʃɛf], *adv.* a second time, yet again, once more; **la porte s'ouvrit d.**, the door opened again.

déréel, -elle [dereel, -ɛl], *a. Psy:* dereistic.

déréglable [dereglabl], *a.* liable to get out of order.

déréglage [deregla:ʒ], *s.m.* (*a*) *Mec.E: etc:* misadjustment; disarrangement; maladjustment; getting out of order, out of balance; (*b*) *Elcs:* detuning (of radio receiver); (*c*) *Artil: etc:* disadjustment; maladjustment (of aim).

déréglé [deregle], *a.* **1.** (*a*) (*of machine, clock, compass, etc.*) out of order; out of adjustment; (*b*) *Elcs:* (*of radio receiver*) detuned, mistuned; (*c*) *Artil: etc:* (*of aim*) off target; (*of fire*) out of adjustment, maladjusted. **2.** disordered (mind, digestion); irregular (pulse). **3.** lawless, wild, dissolute (life, habits, person); immoderate (appetite, desires).

dérèglement [derɛgləmɑ̃], *s.m.* **1.** disordered state (of house, imagination, etc.); unsettled state (of weather); irregularity (of pulse); **d. de l'esprit**, mental derangement. **2.** dissoluteness, profligacy; **le d. des mœurs de notre époque**, the dissolute morals of the day; **le d. des passions sous la Régence**, the profligacy that was rampant under the Regency; **vivre dans le d.**, to lead a disorderly life.

déréglément [dereglemɑ̃], *adv.* in a disordered manner.

dérégler [deregle], *v.tr.* (**je dérègle, n. déréglons; je déréglerai**) **1.** (*a*) *Mec.E: etc:* to disarrange; to put (mechanism, etc.) out of order; to put out of balance; (*b*) *Elcs:* to detune (radio receiver); (*c*) *Artil: etc:* **d. le pointage**, to lose aim, to get the aim off the target. **2.** to upset, disarrange, disorder (habits, etc.); to unsettle (the stomach, trade, etc.).

se dérégler. 1. (*a*) (*of clock, etc.*) to get out of order; (*b*) *Sp:* to go off one's game; *F:* to go to pieces. **2.** (*of pers.*) to get into evil ways.

dérélict [derelikt], *s.m. Nau:* derelict.

déréliction [dereliksjɔ̃], *s.f. Rel:* dereliction.

dérelier [derəlje], *v.tr.* (*p.d. & pr.sub.* **n. dereliions, v. dereliiez**) to remove the binding from (book).

déréquisition [derekizisjɔ̃], *s.f.* derequisition.

déréquisitionner [derekizisjɔne], *v.tr.* to derequisition.

dérider [deride], *v.tr.* to smoothe, to unwrinkle; to remove the lines, the wrinkles, from (the brow); *F:* to cheer (s.o.) up; to brighten (s.o.) up.

se dérider, to brighten up, to cease to frown; **il ne se déride jamais**, he never unbends, never has a smile on his face.

dérision [derizjɔ̃], *s.f.* derision, mockery; **tourner qn, qch., en d.**, to hold s.o., sth., up to ridicule; **tourner une opinion en d.**, to deride an opinion; **dire qch. par d.**, to say sth. derisively, in mockery, mockingly; **rires de d.**, derisive laughter.

dérisoire [derizwa:r], *a.* ridiculous, laughable (offer, etc.); **vendre qch. à un prix d.**, to sell sth. at an absurdly, ridiculously, low price; **appointements dérisoires**, paltry, beggarly, salary.

dérisoirement [derizwarmɑ̃], *adv.* ridiculously.

dérivable [derivabl], *a.* derivable. **1.** that can be derived (from a source). **2.** that can be diverted.

dérivant [derivɑ̃], *a.* drifting (mine, etc.); **filet d.**, drift-net.

dérivateur [derivatœ:r], *s.m. El.E:* shunting device; shunter; *Elcs:* hybrid ring junction; *F:* rat-race (of radio waves).

dérivatif, -ive [derivatif, -i:v], *a. & s.m.* derivative; derived (word); counter-irritant (agent); relief, distraction (à, de, from); **trouver un d. dans le travail**, to find relief, a wholesome distraction, in work.

dérivation[1] [derivasjɔ̃], *s.f.* **1.** (*a*) diversion, tapping (of water-course); *Mch: etc:* off-take; **fossé de d.**, drain; **canal de d.**, headrace, penstock, leat; **conduite de d.**, by-pass; **amener la vapeur en d.**, to by-pass the steam; (*b*) *Med:* derivation (of blood, etc., from inflamed part); counter-irritation; (*c*) branching off; *El.E:* shunt(ing), branching, tapping (of current); *Tg:* (i) branch-circuit; (ii) leakage; **interrupteur de d.**, branch switch; **branchement en d.**, branching off; **boîte de d.**, dividing box; **bobine en, de, d.**, shunt coil; **moteur, dynamo, monté(e) en d.**, shunt motor, shunt dynamo; **rapport de d.**, shunt ratio; **en d.**, (in) shunt; **monter, mettre, en d.**, to shunt; **excité en d.**, shunt-wound (motor, etc.); **monter un condensateur en d.**, to shunt a condenser; **monté en d.**, shunt connected; **effectuer, faire, une d. à une bobine**, to tap a coil; (*d*) *Rail:* loop(-line). **2.** *Ling:* derivation (of word); **d. régressive, rétrograde**, back-formation.

dérivation[2], *s.f.* **1.** *Nau:* drift. **2.** *Artil: etc:* (*a*) lateral deviation, drift (due to rifling); (*b*) windage.

dérive[1] [deri:v], *s.f.* **1.** (*a*) drift; *Nau:* leeway, drift; **d. littorale**, littoral, (long)shore, drift; **angle de d.**, drift angle; *Av:* **d. en vol**, drift in flight; *Nau:* **aller en d.**, to drift; **avoir de la d.**, to have plenty of sea-room; **à la d., en d.**, adrift, at the mercy of the waves; **partir en d.**, to break adrift; **laisser aller qch. à la d.**, to cut sth. adrift; **jeter qch. à la d.**, to cast sth. adrift; (**quille de**) **d.**, (i) drop-keel, centre-board, centre-plate; (ii) *Aer:* keel (of airship); *Av:* fin; **d. latérale, aile de d.**, lee-board; *s.a.* PLAN[1] 2, SAUMON; (*b*) *Rail:* break-away, running back (of trucks); (*c*) *Geog:* **d. des continents**, continental drift; (*d*) *Atom.Ph:* drift (of nuclear, thermal, power). **2.** *Artil: Missile:* (i) deflection; (ii) allowance for lateral deflection, lateral sight allowance; **écart de d.**, deflection error; **correction de la d. due au vent**, wind deflection; **tambour des dérives**, deflection drum.

dérive[2], *s.f. Rail:* = DÉRIVATION[1] 1 (*d*).

dérivé[1] [derive]. I. *a.* **1.** originated (**de**, from, in, with); sprung (**de**, from); derived, secondary (meaning, etc.); *Mth:* derived (function, curve); *Ch: Ind:* **produit d.**, derived product, by-product. **2.** *El.E:* shunt(ed); **courant d.**, shunt current; **circuit d.**, shunt circuit, branch circuit. **3.** *Mus:* **accord d.**, inversion of a chord; derivative of a chord. **4.** *Civ.E:* diverted (stream, canal, etc.). **5.** *Nau:* adrift, drifting.

II. **dérivé, -ée.** *s.* **1.** *s.m. Ling: etc:* a derivative, an off-shoot; *Ch: Ind:* derivative, derived product, by-product; **les dérivés du pétrole**, the derivatives of, the products derived from, petroleum; the petroleum chemicals; petroleum derivatives; **dérivés nitrés**, nitro-compounds; *Atom.Ph:* **les dérivés fissiles**, fissionable derivatives. **2.** *s.f. Mth:* **dérivée (continue)**, derivative; differential coefficient; **dérivée partielle**, partial derivative; **équation aux dérivées partielles**, (partial) differential equation; *Av:* **dérivée partielle polaire**, rotary derivative.

dérivé[2], *a. Nau:* adrift, drifting.

dériver[1] [derive]. **1.** *v.tr.* (*a*) to divert, tap, the course of (running water); *El.E:* to shunt, branch (current); *Rail:* **d. un train sur une voie de garage**, to shunt, switch, a train on to a siding; (*b*) *Ling: Mth:* to derive (**de**, from); (*c*) *Nau:* to surge (cable). **2.** *v.i.* (*a*) (*of stream*) to be diverted, to flow (**de**, from); (*b*) to spring, arise, be derived (from a source); **mot qui dérive du grec**, word that is derived from Greek; **préjugés qui dérivent de l'ignorance**, prejudices that originate in, spring from, ignorance.

dériver[2]. **1.** *v.tr.* to free (timber-float) from the bank (of river, etc.). **2.** *v.i.* to leave the shore.

dériver[3], *v.tr.* **1.** to unrivet. **2.** to unhead (rivet); to unclinch (nail).

dériver[4], *v.i.* **1.** *Nau:* to drift; **d. à la côte**, to drive ashore; **d. à la voile**, to make leeway; **d. sur son ancre**, to club (down); **d. à vau-l'eau**, to drift down stream. **2.** *Artil:* (*of projectile*) to deviate, to be deflected, to drift.

dériveter [derivte], *v.tr.* (**je dérivette, n dérivetons; je dérivetterai**) to unrivet; to drive out the rivets from (boiler, etc.).

dériveur [derivœ:r], *s.m. Nau:* **1.** (*a*) drop-keel, centre-board; (*b*) lee-board. **2.** storm-spanker. **3.** (i) drifter; (ii) sailing-ship under storm-sails.

dérivomètre [derivɔmɛtr], *s.m. Av:* drift-indicator, -meter, -recorder, -sight.

dermaptères [dɛrmaptɛ:r], *s.m.pl. Ent:* Dermaptera, the earwigs.

dermaptéroïdes [dɛrmapterɔid], *s.m.pl.* Dermapteroidea.

dermatite [dɛrmatit], *s.f. Med:* dermatitis.

dermatobie [dɛrmatɔbi], *s.f. Ent:* dermatobia.

dermatologie [dɛrmatɔlɔʒi], *s.f.* dermatology.

dermatologique [dɛrmatɔlɔʒik], *a.* dermatological.

dermatologiste [dɛrmatɔlɔʒist], *s.m. & f.*, **dermatologue** [dɛrmatɔlɔg], *s.m. & f.* dermatologist.

dermatome [dɛrmatɔm], *s.m. Surg:* dermatome.

dermatomycose [dɛrmatɔmiko:z], *s.f. Med:* dermatomycosis.

dermatophyte [dɛrmatɔfit], *s.m. Med: Fung:* dermatophyte.

dermatose [dɛrmato:z], *s.f. Med:* dermatosis, skin disease.

derme [dɛrm], *s.m. Anat:* derm; cutis, true skin.

dermeste [dɛrmɛst], *s.m. Ent:* dermestes.

dermique [dɛrmik], *a. Anat:* dermic, dermal.

dermite [dɛrmit], *s.f. Med:* dermatitis; *Vet:* poll evil.

dermographie [dɛrmɔgrafi], *s.f. Med:* dermographia.

dermographisme [dɛrmɔgrafism], *s.m. Med:* dermographism.

dermoïde [dɛrmɔid], *a. Med:* dermoid.

dermoptère [dɛrmɔptɛ:r], *s.m. Z:* flying lemur; **les dermoptères**, the Dermoptera.

dermovaccin [dɛrmɔvaksɛ̃], *s.m. Med:* dermovaccine.

dernier, -ière [dɛrnje, -jɛ:r], *a. & s.* **1.** last, latest; (*a*) **au d. moment**, at the last (moment); *F:* at the eleventh hour; *F:* **l'homme de la dernière heure**, the man of the eleventh hour; (**changement**, etc.) **de dernière minute**, last minute (change, etc.); **faire un d. effort**, to make a final effort; **mettre la dernière main à qch.**, to give, put, the finishing, the final touches to sth.; **la raison dernière de qch.**, the final justification for sth.; **j'aurais donné mon d. sou pour l'aider**, I would have given my last farthing to help him; **j'ai payé jusqu'au d. sou**, I paid to the last farthing; **avec quelques dernières recommandations**, with a few parting directions; **les derniers préparatifs**, the final preparations; **je m'en souviendrai jusqu'à mon d. jour, jusqu'à ma dernière heure**, I shall remember it to my dying day; **il veut toujours avoir le d. mot**, he must always have the last word; **il arriva le d.**, he arrived last, was the last to arrive; **ils se soulevèrent jusqu'au d.**, they rose to a man; **dans ces derniers temps**, lately; **au cours des dernières années**, over the past few years; **ces dernières années tout est changé**, of late years everything has altered; **le d. ouvrage de cet auteur**, this author's latest work; **informations de dernière heure, dernières nouvelles**, (i) latest news; (ii) *Journ:* stop-press news; **la dernière mode**, the latest fashion, the latest thing; *St.Exch:* **d. cours**, closing price; (*b*) (*last of series*) **le mois d.**, last month; **les six derniers**, the last six; **étant arrivé à la dernière marche**, having reached (i) the bottom stair, (ii) the top stair; **le d. rang**, the rear rank; **assis au d. rang du parterre**, seated at the very back of the pit; **dans les derniers rangs**, far back; **la dernière moitié de juin**, the latter half of June; **dernier paiement**, final payment; **d. délai pour l'inscription**, last date for registering; **en dernier ressort**, in the last resort; **les dernières années de la vie**, the closing years of life; **les derniers jours du mois de mars**, the last days, the closing days, of March; *Com:* **le plus offrant et le d. enchérisseur**, the highest bidder; **la petite Marthe était notre dernière**, little Martha was our youngest (child); **le d. élève de la classe**, the last, bottom, boy in the form; **il passa chez moi en d.**, he visited me last of all; **en d. il fut obligé de . . .**, in the end he was obliged to . . .; *B:* **les derniers seront les premiers**, the last shall be first; (*c*) **ce d. répondit . . .**, the latter answered . . .. **2.** (*a*) utmost, highest; **de la dernière importance**, of the utmost, greatest, importance; **les derniers confins du monde**, the utmost ends of the earth; **au d. degré**, to the utmost, highest, degree; **il me déplaît au d. point**, I dislike him intensely; **entrer dans les derniers détails**, to enter into the minutest details; **le d. supplice**, the extreme penalty; **il se**

conduisit avec la dernière gaucherie, he behaved with extreme awkwardness; **dans la dernière misère,** in dire want, in dire distress; **c'est du d. vulgaire,** it is the height of vulgarity; **coiffure du d. bien,** highly becoming style of hairdressing; **je suis du d. bien avec lui,** I am on the very best terms with him; **hôtel qui est le d. mot du confort,** hotel that is the last word in comfort; (*b*) lowest, worst; **le d. prix,** the lowest price; **ça, c'est le d. de mes soucis,** that is the least of my worries, I don't care a fig about that; **le d. des hommes,** the vilest, meanest, of men; **le d. des derniers,** the lowest of the low.

dernièrement [dɛrnjɛrmɑ̃], *adv.* lately, latterly, of late, not long ago.

dernier-né [dɛrnjene], *s.m.*, **dernière-née** [dɛrnjɛrne], *s.f.* last-born child; *F:* latest arrival (in a family); *pl. derniers-nés, dernières-nées.*

dérobade [derɔbad], *s.f.* **1.** escape, evasion, avoidance (of s.o., sth.). **2.** shy, swerve, jib (of a horse).

dérobé [derɔbe], *a.* **1.** *Farr:* **pied d.,** worn hoof. **2.** (*a*) *Agr:* **culture, récolte, dérobée,** catch-crop, snatch-crop; (*b*) hidden, concealed, secret (staircase, door, etc.); *Arch:* **porte dérobée,** jib-door; *adv.phr.* **à la dérobée,** stealthily, secretly, on the sly; **boire à la dérobée,** to drink on the quiet; **regarder qn à la dérobée,** to steal a glance at s.o., to watch s.o. furtively; **sortir à la dérobée,** to steal out.

dérobement [derɔbmɑ̃], *s.m. Navy:* turn-away (from the enemy).

dérober [derɔbe], *v.tr.* **1.** (*a*) *A:* to denude, strip (s.o.); (*b*) to skin (broad beans); to blanch (almonds). **2.** (*a*) to steal, to make away with (sth.); **d. qch. à qn,** to filch sth. from s.o.; **on m'a dérobé mon argent,** I have been robbed of my money, they have stolen my money; *Nau: A:* **d. le vent à un vaisseau,** to blanket, wrong, a ship; **d. ses idées à qn,** to appropriate s.o.'s ideas; **d. un secret,** to surprise a secret; **d. un baiser,** to steal a kiss; **d. quelques heures à ses études,** to steal, snatch, a few hours from one's studies; (*b*) **d. qn au danger,** to rescue, save, s.o. from danger. **3.** to hide, conceal, screen; **d. qn, qch., aux vues,** to screen s.o., sth.; **d. une batterie aux coups,** to cover, screen, a battery from fire; **mur qui dérobe la vue,** wall that hides, intercepts, the view; **d. sa marche,** to conceal one's movements (**à l'ennemi,** from the enemy).

se dérober. **1.** (*a*) to escape, steal away, slip away (**à,** from); *F:* to back out; **se d. à l'étreinte, aux mains, de qn,** to get out of s.o.'s clutches; **se d. à ses créanciers,** to avoid one's creditors, to give one's creditors the slip; **se d. aux regards,** to escape observation, to avoid notice; **se d. aux coups,** to dodge the blows; **se d. à la curiosité,** to elude curiosity; **se d. à un devoir,** to evade, shirk, a duty; **de tels événements se dérobent à toute prévision,** it is impossible to foresee such occurrences; (*b*) (*of horse*) to swerve, shy (at a jump); to jib; to refuse. **2.** to give way, to fail (**sous,** under); **le sol se déroba sous nos pas,** the ground gave way under our feet; **ses genoux se dérobèrent sous lui,** his knees gave way beneath him.

dérobeur, -euse [derɔbœːr, -øːz], *a. & s.* **1.** stealer (de, of). **2. cheval d.,** shyer.

dérochage [derɔʃaːʒ], *s.m.* **1.** *Civ.E:* = DÉROCHEMENT. **2.** *Metalw:* scouring, pickling, dipping.

dérochement [derɔʃmɑ̃], *s.m.* removal of rocks (from river-bed, land, etc.).

dérocher[1] [derɔʃe], *v.tr. Metalw:* to scour, pickle, dip.

dérocher[2]. **1.** *v.tr.* to clear (ground, river-bed, etc.) of rocks. **2.** (*a*) *v.tr.* to make (sheep) fall from the rocks, to dislodge (sheep) from the rocks; (*b*) *v.i. & pr.* (*of sheep, etc.*) to fall down a mountain-side, to fall from the rocks.

dérocheuse [derɔʃøːz], *s.f. Civ.E:* rock-breaker.

déroder [derɔde], *v.tr.* to clear, to remove, the tree-stumps and dead wood from (a forest).

dérogation [derɔgasjɔ̃], *s.f.* derogation, impairment (**à une loi,** of a law); **d. à un principe,** waiving of a principle; **faire d. à l'usage,** to make a departure from the custom; **d. à ses instructions,** deviation from one's instructions; **par, en, d. à cette règle,** this rule notwithstanding; **par d. aux dispositions de . . .,** notwithstanding the provisions of . . .; **sauf dérogations prévues au présent traité . . .,** except where otherwise provided for in this treaty . . ..

dérogatoire [derɔgatwaːr], *a. Jur:* derogatory (clause).

dérogeance [derɔʒɑ̃s], *s.f. Hist:* derogation, losing of caste.

dérogeant [derɔʒɑ̃], *a.* derogatory.

déroger [derɔʒe], *v.i.* (**je dérogeai(s); n. dérogeons**) (*a*) **d. à l'usage, à la loi,** to depart from custom, from the law; **d. à une condition,** not to conform to a condition; **d. à un principe,** to waive a principle; (*b*) to derogate; **les termes vulgaires dérogent à la dignité de la tragédie,** vulgarisms derogate from the dignity of tragedy; **d. à son rang, à noblesse,** to lose caste, to derogate; *F:* to make oneself cheap; **je croirais d. en faisant une chose pareille,** I cannot see myself stooping to such a thing; **sans d.,** without derogation (**à,** from).

déroidir [derwɑdiːr], *v.tr.* = DÉRAIDIR.

dérompoir [derɔ̃pwaːr], *s.m. Paperm:* rag-cutting machine; devil.

dérompre [derɔ̃ːpr], *v.tr.* to break up (land, etc.); *Paperm:* to cut (rags).

dérotation [derɔtasjɔ̃], *s.f. Surg:* derotation.

dérougir [deruʒiːr], (*a*) *v.tr.* to take the redness out of sth.; (*b*) *v.i.* to lose one's redness; **elle ne dérougit pas,** she does not stop blushing.

dérouillée [deruje], *s.f. P:* beating-up, shellacking.

dérouillement [derujmɑ̃], *s.m.* removal of rust.

dérouiller [deruje]. **1.** *v.tr.* (*a*) to take, rub, the rust off (sth.); (*b*) *F:* **se d. les jambes,** to stretch one's legs; **se d. la mémoire,** to refresh one's memory; **d. son français,** to brush up one's French; (*c*) *F:* **d. qn,** to rub the corners off s.o.; (*d*) *P:* to give (s.o.) a beating-up. **2.** *v.i. P:* (*a*) to pick up one's first client (of the day); (*b*) to get a beating-up; **j'ai drôlement dérouillé quand il m'a arraché la dent,** I really went through it, I felt it good and proper, when he pulled out my tooth.

se dérouiller, to lose (its) rust; **lire du grec pour se d.,** to brush up one's Greek.

déroulable [derulabl], *a.* that may be unrolled, unwound; that unrolls.

déroulage [derulaːʒ], *s.m.* **1.** = DÉROULEMENT. **2.** *Woodw:* wood-peeling, veneer-peeling.

déroulement [derulmɑ̃], *s.m.* (*a*) unrolling (of blind, map, etc.); unwinding, uncoiling (of cable, etc.); *Geom:* evolution (of curve); *Rec:* **vitesse de d.,** tape speed; (*b*) unfolding, development, progress (of plot, events); **assister au d. de la procession,** to witness the passing of the procession.

dérouler [derule], *v.tr.* (*a*) to unroll (blind, map, etc.); to unwind, unreel, wind off, uncoil (cable); to peel (tree-trunks); to uncoil, let down (one's hair); **le serpent déroula ses anneaux,** the serpent uncoiled itself; **fleuve qui déroule ses eaux,** river that rolls along; (*b*) *Geom:* **d. une courbe,** to describe the evolute of a curve; (*c*) **d. ses plans à qn,** to unfold, make known one's plans, to s.o.

se dérouler. **1.** (*of map, etc.*) to come unrolled, to unroll; (*of cable, etc.*) to come unwound; **ses cheveux se déroulèrent,** her hair came tumbling down; **le serpent se déroula,** the snake uncoiled (itself). **2.** to unfold, to develop; **le paysage se déroule devant nous,** the landscape unfolds, spreads, stretches out, before us; **la procession se déroula dans le plus bel ordre,** the procession passed along in perfect order; **ses pensées se déroulent avec ordre,** his thought unfolds in an orderly manner; **les événements qui se déroulent à Paris,** the events that are being enacted, that are taking place, in Paris; **la manifestation s'est déroulée sans désordre,** the demonstration passed off without disorder.

dérouleur [derulœːr], *s.m. Computers:* **d. (de bande magnétique),** tape handler, tape unit.

dérouleuse [deruløːz], *s.f.* **1.** *El.E:* cable-drum. **2.** *Woodw:* wood-peeling, veneer-peeling machine.

déroutage [derutaːʒ], *s.m.* re-routing.

déroutant [derutɑ̃], *a.* confusing, baffling, misleading.

déroute [derut], *s.f.* (*a*) rout, disorderly retreat; **être en (pleine) d.,** to be in (full) flight; **mettre en d.,** to rout; **l'armée fut mise en d.,** the army was put to flight, was routed; **mettre la d. dans les plans de qn,** to upset, overthrow, s.o.'s plans; (*b*) ruin, downfall (of a family, etc.); **affaire en d.,** concern that is falling to pieces.

déroutement [derutmɑ̃], *s.m.* **1.** *Nau: Com: M.Ins:* deviation (of ship, etc., from normal route without sufficient cause). **2.** *Nau: Av: etc:* diversion (of ship, aircraft, etc. from normal route by movement control authority); **autorité de d.,** diverting authority; *Av:* **aérodrome de d.,** diversion airfield.

dérouter [derute], *v.tr.* **1.** (*a*) to throw, lead, (s.o., sth.) out of the right way; **d. un voyageur,** to lead a traveller astray, out of his course; **d. la police,** to throw the police off the scent; **d. les soupçons,** to throw people off the scent; **ces interruptions me déroutent,** these interruptions put me off; (*b*) to divert, re-route, (ship, aircraft, etc.), to steer (ship, aircraft), take (train), out of its normal course. **2.** to confuse, baffle; **d. les recherches,** to baffle all attempts at discovery; **la question a dérouté le candidat,** the question nonplussed the candidate.

se dérouter. **1.** to go astray. **2.** to lose one's head, become confused; **je suis tout dérouté,** I am all at sea.

derrick [dɛrik, de-], *s.m. Petroleum Ind:* derrick; **d. flottant,** (oil-)drilling platform.

derrière [dɛrjɛːr]. **1.** *prep.* (*a*) behind, at the back of, in the rear of (s.o., sth.); *U.S:* back of (sth.); **il se cacha d. le rideau,** he hid behind the curtain; **avoir des réserves d. soi,** to have reserves at one's back, to have sth. to fall back upon; **laisser qn d. soi,** to leave s.o. behind; (*b*) *Nau:* (i) abaft; (ii) astern of (the ship). **2.** *adv.* (*a*) behind, at the back, in the rear; **laisser qn d.,** to leave s.o. behind; **attaquer qn par d.,** to attack s.o. from behind, from the rear, in the rear; **cheveux coupés ras par d.,** hair cropped close behind, at the back; **cette robe s'attache par d.,** this dress does up at the back; **il dut passer par d.,** he had to go round (to) the back; **wagons de d.,** rear carriages; **porte de d.,** back door; **jardin de d.,** back garden; **pattes de d.,** hind legs; *s.a.* DEVANT 2; (*b*) *Nau:* (i) aft; (ii) astern. **3.** *s.m.* (*a*) back, rear, hinderpart (of building, etc.); tail (of cart); **le d. de la tête,** the back of the head; **ma chambre donne sur le d.,** my room looks out on the back; **une chambre sur le d.,** a back bedroom; **elle a sa chambre au 3ème étage sur le d.,** she lives in the third-floor back; *O:* **les derrières d'une ville,** the back streets of a town; *Mil:* **les derrières d'une armée,** the rear of an army; (*b*) *F:* behind, backside, bottom, buttocks, rump; **tomber sur le d.,** to fall on one's behind, to sit down suddenly; **chien assis sur son d.,** dog sitting on its haunches.

derviche [dɛrviʃ], *s.m.*, **dervis** [dɛrvi], *s.m.* dervish; **d. tourneur,** dancing, whirling, dervish.

dès [dɛ], *prep.* since, from, as early as, as long ago as (a certain time); **d. ce moment elle l'aima,** she loved him from that moment; **d. sa jeunesse . . .,** from childhood . . .; **d. l'abord,** from the outset, from the (very) first; **d. maintenant, d. à présent,** already, henceforth, from now on, onward; **d. avant notre ère,** even before our era; **d. 1840,** as far back as 1840; **d. les premiers jours de juin,** since early June; **d. dix heures,** as early as ten o'clock; **d. le matin,** first thing in the morning, in the day; **d. son arrivée il saura tout,** the minute he arrives, the moment he arrives, he will know everything; **je vous verrai d. mon retour,** I shall see you immediately on my return; **je commencerai d. aujourd'hui,** I will begin this very day, here and now; **d. mon entrée dans la salle,** on my entering the room; **d. la porte il commença à crier,** he had no sooner reached the door than he began to shout; **d. le jour venu,** as soon as it is, was, light; **d. en naissant nous pleurons,** no sooner are we born than we begin to weep; *conj.phr.* **dès que** + *ind.* **d. qu'il sera arrivé,** as soon as he arrives; **d. que la guerre éclata,** the moment the war broke out; **d. que l'on essaie d'être impartial on est accusé d'injustice,** at any attempt at being impartial one is accused of being unjust; *adv.phr.* **dès lors,** (i) from that time onwards, ever since (then); (ii) consequently; therefore; *conj.phr.* **dès lors que** + *ind.*, since, seeing that; **d. lors que vous refusez,** since, seeing that, you refuse.

désabonnement [dezabɔn(ə)mɑ̃], *s.m.* stopping (of subscription).

désabonner [dezabɔne], *v.tr.* **d. qn à un périodique,** to remove s.o.'s name from the list of subscribers to a periodical.

se désabonner, to stop subscribing, being a subscriber, to withdraw, stop, one's subscription (**à,** to); **se d. à un journal,** to give up a paper.

désabusable [dezabyzabl], *a.* capable of being disabused or disillusioned.

désabusé [dezabyze], *a. & s.* disillusioned, embittered (person, etc.).

désabusement [dezabyzmɑ̃], *s.m.* **1.** disabusing, undeceiving. **2.** disillusionment; loss of (one's) illusions.

désabuser [dezabyze], *v.tr.* to disabuse, disillusion, undeceive (s.o.); to open (s.o.'s) eyes; **d. qn de qch.,** to undeceive s.o. with regard to sth.; **esprit désabusé du monde,** disillusioned mind.

se désabuser (de qch.), to lose one's illusions (about sth.), to have one's eyes opened (to the facts regarding sth.).

désacclimater [dezaklimate], *v.tr.* to change (s.o.'s) climate; to remove (s.o., sth.) from his, its, normal climate; to remove (s.o.) from his normal environment.
désaccorage [dezakɔraːʒ], *s.m.* unshoring.
désaccord [dezakɔːr], *s.m.* **1.** (*a*) disagreement, dissension; **être, se trouver, en d. avec qn sur qch.,** to be at variance, at issue, with s.o. about sth.; **ils sont toujours en d.,** they are always at odds, at loggerheads; **sujet de d.,** bone of contention; (*b*) clash (of interests, etc.); **idées en d. avec les miennes,** ideas that clash with mine; **il y a d. entre ses paroles et sa conduite,** his words are inconsistent, not in keeping, with his conduct; **le d. entre la théorie et les faits,** the discrepancy between the theory and the facts. **2.** (*a*) *Mus:* discord, lack of harmony; **en d.,** out of tune; (*b*) *Elecs: TV:* detuning.
désaccordé [dezakɔrde], *a.* out of tune.
désaccorder [dezakɔrde], *v.tr.* **1.** to set (persons) at variance. **2.** *Mus:* to put (instrument) out of tune; to untune.
se désaccorder, to get out of tune.
désaccorer [dezakɔre], *v.tr.* to unshore, to remove the shores from (a ship).
désaccouplement [dezakupləmɑ̃], *s.m.* **1.** unpairing (of doves, etc.). **2.** uncoupling (of horses, trucks, etc.).
désaccoupler [dezakuple], *v.tr.* **1.** to unpair (doves, etc.). **2.** (i) = DÉCOUPLER I; (ii) *El: Mec:* to disconnect.
se désaccoupler, (*of dogs*) to become uncoupled.
désaccoutumance [dezakutymɑ̃ːs], *s.f.* **d. de qch.,** loss of the habit of, of familiarity with, sth.
désaccoutumer [dezakutyme], *v.tr.* **d. qn de qch.,** to disaccustom s.o. to sth.; **je l'ai désaccoutumé du jeu,** I got him out of the habit of gambling, made him leave off gambling; **d. qn de faire qch.,** to break s.o. of the habit of doing sth.
se désaccoutumer de qch., de faire qch. 1. to become unused to sth., to doing sth.; to become unfamiliar with sth. **2.** to get out of the habit of doing sth.; to break oneself of the habit of doing sth.; to leave off doing sth.
désachalandage [dezaʃalɑ̃daːʒ], *s.m. A: Com:* loss, falling off, of custom, of business.
désachalander [dezaʃalɑ̃de], *v.tr. A:* to take away the custom, the business, of (shop, etc.).
se désachalander, *A:* (*of shop*) to lose its business, its custom.
désacidification [dezasidifikasjɔ̃], *s.f.* deacidizing, deacidification.
désacidifier [desasidifje], *v.tr.* (*p.d. and pr.sub.* **n. désacidifions, v. désacidifiiez**) *Ch:* to deacidize.
désaciérer [dezasjere], *v.tr.* (**je désacière, n. désaciérons; je désaciérerai**) (*a*) to unsteel (blade, etc.); (*b*) to remove the steel face from (copperplate, etc.).
désacralisation [desakralizasjɔ̃], *s.f.* desacralization.
désacraliser [desakralize], *v.tr.* to desacralize.
désactivation [dezaktivasjɔ̃], *s.f. Atom.Ph:* decontamination, removal of radio-active elements.
désactiver [dezaktive], *v.tr. Atom.Ph:* to decontaminate, to remove radio-active elements (from).
désadaptation [dezadaptasjɔ̃], *s.f.* loss of adaptability.
désadapté [dezadapte], *a. & s.* (*of pers.*) maladjusted.
désadapter [dezadapte], *v.tr.* to make (s.o., sth.) unsuitable.
se désadapter, *v.pr.* to become alienated from one's environment; to become maladjusted.
désaérer [dezaere], *v.tr.* (*conj. like* AÉRER) to deaerate; **béton désaéré,** vibrated concrete.
désaffectation [dezafɛktasjɔ̃], *s.f.* **1.** putting (of public building, etc.) to another purpose; deconsecration, secularization (of church, etc.). **2.** *Mil:* transfer (of soldier on account of physical unfitness).
désaffecter [dezafɛkte], *v.tr.* **1.** to put (public building, etc.) to another purpose; **église désaffectée,** deconsecrated, secularized, church; **route désaffectée,** abandoned road. **2.** *Mil:* to transfer (soldier) on account of physical unfitness.
désaffection [dezafɛksjɔ̃], *s.f.* disaffection, disaffectedness (envers, to).
désaffectionner [dezafɛksjɔne], *v.tr.* **1.** to alienate (s.o.'s) affections. **2.** to disaffect (followers, etc.).
se désaffectionner (de qn). 1. to lose one's affection (for s.o.), to grow cold (towards s.o.). **2.** to become disaffected (towards s.o.); **troupes désaffectionnées,** disaffected troops.
désaffiliation [dezafiljasjɔ̃], *s.f.* disaffiliation.
désaffilier [dezafilje], *v.tr.* (*conj. like* AFFILIER) to disaffiliate (**de,** from).
désaffleurant [dezaflœrɑ̃], *a.* out of level; **lames de mica désaffleurantes,** proud micas (of electric condenser); **coussinet d.,** offset bearing.
désaffleurement [dezaflœrmɑ̃], *s.m.* unevenness (of floor, etc.).
désaffleurer [dezaflœre, -øre]. **1.** *v.tr.* to push (tiles, etc.) out of level. **2.** *v.i.* to be out of level, to project.
désaffourchage [dezafurʃaːʒ], *s.m. Nau:* unmooring.
désaffourcher [dezafurʃe], *v.tr. & i.* to unmoor.
désaffranchir [dezafrɑ̃ʃiːr], *v.tr.* to disfranchise.
désaffubler [dezafyble], *v.tr.* to unmuffle, unwrap (s.o.); **d. qn de son déguisement,** to strip, relieve, s.o. of his disguise.
désagencement [dezaʒɑ̃smɑ̃], *s.m.* disorganization, disarrangement (of sth.); throwing (of machine) out of gear, out of order.
désagencer [dezaʒɑ̃se], *v.tr.* (**je désagençai(s); n. désagençons**) to disorganize, disarrange (sth.); to throw (machine) out of gear, out of working order.
désagréable [dezagreabl], *a.* disagreeable, unpleasant (**à,** to); **caractère d.,** surly, forbidding, grumpy, nature; **comme vous êtes d. aujourd'hui!** you're very disagreeable to-day! **odeur d.,** offensive, nasty, smell; **son d. à l'oreille,** sound that grates on the ear; **d. à voir,** unpleasant to the sight; unsightly; **d. au goût,** distasteful, unpalatable; **nouvelle d.,** unpleasant, unwelcome, news; **vous pouvez vous figurer ce que ma situation offrait de d.,** you can imagine the unpleasantness of my position.
désagréablement [dezagreabləmɑ̃], *adv.* disagreeably, unpleasantly.
désagréer [dezagree], *v.ind.tr. A:* **d. à qn,** to displease s.o.; **il me désagrée,** I don't like him.
désagrégation [dezagregasjɔ̃], *s.f.* (*a*) disaggregation, disintegration; weathering (of rock); **d. sélective,** differential weathering; (*b*) breaking up (of a family).
désagréger [dezagreʒe], *v.tr.* (**je désagrège, n. désagrégeons; je désagrégeai(s); je désagrégerai**) to disaggregate, disintegrate; to weather (rock).
se désagréger, to break up; (*of rock*) to weather.
désagrément [dezagremɑ̃], *s.m.* source of annoyance, unpleasant occurrence, nuisance; **attirer à qn du d., des désagréments,** to cause s.o. unpleasantness, to lead s.o. into difficulties, to get s.o. into a scrape, into trouble; **quel d.!** how vexing!
désaguerrir [dezageriːr], *v.tr.* to make (soldier, etc.) unwarlike; **troupes désaguerries,** troops out of training, that have become soft.
désaimantation [dezɛmɑ̃tasjɔ̃], *s.f.* demagnetization, demagnetizing.
désaimanter [dezɛmɑ̃te], *v.tr.* to demagnetize.
se désaimanter, to become demagnetized; (*of magnet*) to unbuild.
désaimer [dezeme], *v.tr.* to fall out of love with (s.o.).
désairer [dezɛre], *v.tr.* to capture (a young bird of prey) in its nest.
désajustement [dezaʒystəmɑ̃], *s.m.* disarrangement (of hair, etc.); throwing (of mechanism) out of gear, out of adjustment.
désajuster [dezaʒyste], *v.tr.* (*a*) to disarrange, disorder; **chevelure désajustée,** hair in disorder, dishevelled hair; (*b*) to throw (mechanism) out of adjustment.
se désajuster, to become disarranged; to work loose; to fall out of adjustment.
désaligné [dezaliɲe], *a.* out of alignment, out of line, disaligned.
désalignement [dezaliɲmɑ̃], *s.m.* **1.** falling or throwing out of line; (*of ranks, etc.*) disalignment. **2.** irregular alignment.
désaligner [dezaliɲe], *v.tr.* to throw (soldiers, etc.), put (building, etc.), out of line, to disalign.
se désaligner, to fall out of line.
désalkylation [dezalkilasjɔ̃], *s.f. Ch:* dealkylation.
désalkyler [dezalkile], *v.tr. Ch:* to dealkylate
désallier [dezalje], *v.tr.* (*p.d. & pr.sub.* **n. désalliions, v. désalliiez**) to disunite (nations, etc.).
désaltérant [dezalterɑ̃]. **1.** *a.* thirst-quenching (fruit, etc.). **2.** *s.m.* thirst-quencher.
désaltérer [dezaltere], *v.tr.* (**je désaltère, n. désaltérons; je désaltérerai**) (*a*) to slake, quench, (s.o.'s) thirst; (*b*) to refresh, to water, (plant).
se désaltérer, to slake, quench, one's thirst; to have sth. to drink; *Lit:* **se d. de sang,** to sate, slake, one's thirst for blood.
désamarrer [dezamare], *v.tr.* to unmoor; to untie.
désamidonner [dezamidɔne], *v.tr.* to unstarch.
désamorçage [dezamɔrsaːʒ], *s.m.* **1.** *Exp: etc:* unpriming (of cartridge, fuse, siphon, etc.); defusing (of bomb, shell, etc.). **2.** (*a*) **d. d'une pompe,** draining, dewatering, of a pump; drawing off the water, the petrol, etc., in a pump; (*b*) *Mch:* **d. d'un injecteur,** failing, stopping, of an injector. **3.** (*a*) *El.E:* running down (of dynamo); de-energization, de-energizing (of electromagnet); (*b*) *Elcs:* misfiring (of fluorescent-tube).
désamorcer [dezamɔrse], *v.tr.* (**je désamorçai(s); n. désamorçons**) **1.** *Exp: etc:* to unprime (cartridge, fuse, siphon, etc.); to defuse (bomb, shell, etc.). **2.** (*a*) to drain, dewater (pump); to draw off the water, the petrol, etc., in a pump; (*b*) *Mch:* **d. un injecteur,** to stop an injector. **3.** *El.E:* to run down (dynamo); to de-energize (electro-magnet). **4.** to render (sth.) harmless; to take the sting out of (sth.).
se désamorcer. 1. (*a*) (*of pump, etc.*) to fail, to run dry; (*b*) *Mch:* (*of injector*) to fail, stop. **2.** (*a*) *El.E:* (*of dynamo*) to run down; (*of electromagnet*) to de-energize; (*b*) *Elcs:* (*of fluorescent tube*) to misfire.
désamouracher [dezamuraʃe], *v.tr. Pej:* to disenamour (**de,** of).
se désamouracher, *Pej:* to get over one's infatuation (**de,** for).
désancrer [dezɑ̃kre]. **1.** *v.i. Nau:* to weigh anchor. **2.** *v.tr. O: F:* to tear (s.o.) from his surroundings.
désannexé [dezanɛkse], *a.* disannexed (territory).
désannexer [dezanɛkse], *v.tr.* to disannex (territory).
désannexion [dezanɛksjɔ̃], *s.f.* disannexation, restitution (of territory).
désappareiller [desapareje, -eje], *v.tr.* to unrig, take down (crane, etc.).
désapparier [dezaparje], *v.tr.* (*a*) to remove one of a pair, to spoil a pair (of objects); (*b*) to separate (pair of birds, animals).
désapplication [dezaplikasjɔ̃], *s.f.* lack of application, of diligence.
désappliquer (se) [sədezaplike], *v.pr.* **1.** to become detached. **2.** (*of pers.*) to cease to apply oneself (to work).
désappointement [dezapwɛ̃tmɑ̃], *s.m.* disappointment.
désappointer[1] [dezapwɛ̃te], *v.tr.* to disappoint; *F:* to let (s.o.) down.
désappointer[2], *v.tr.* to break the point of (needle, etc.); to blunt (tool).
désapprendre [dezaprɑ̃ːdr], *v.tr.* (*conj. like* PRENDRE) to forget (what one has learnt); to unlearn; **d. tout son grec,** to forget all one's Greek; **d. à monter à cheval,** to forget how to ride; **faire d. qch. à qn,** to unteach s.o. sth.
désapprobateur, -trice [dezaprɔbatœːr, -tris]. **1.** *s.* disapprover, censurer (**de,** of). **2.** *a.* disapproving, disapprobative, disapprobatory, censorious; **regard d.,** look of disapproval.
désapprobation [dezaprɔbasjɔ̃], *s.f.* disapproval, disapprobation (**de,** of).
désappropriation [dezaprɔprijasjɔ̃], *s.f. Jur:* renunciation of property.
désapproprier [dezaprɔprije], *v.tr.* (*p.d. & pr.sub.* **n. désappropriions, v. désappropriiez**) *Jur:* to disappropriate.
se désapproprier, to renounce one's property.
désapprouver [dezapruve], *v.tr.* to disapprove, disapprove of, object to (s.o., sth.); **il désapprouve que je vienne,** he objects to my coming, he does not think it right that I should come, for me to come.
désapprovisionnement [dezaprɔvizjɔnmɑ̃], *s.m.* deprival, deprivation (of supplies); unstocking (of house); unloading (of rifle, etc., magazine); *Fin:* overdrawing (of bank account).
désapprovisionner [dezaprɔvizjɔne], *v.tr.* to deprive (army, etc.) of supplies; to unstock (house); to remove cartridges from (magazine of rifle); *Fin:* **compte désapprovisionné,** overdrawn account.
désarborer [dezarbɔre], *v.tr.* to strike, haul down (colours, etc.).
désarçonnant [dezarsɔnɑ̃], *a.* dumbfounding, staggering (news, etc.).
désarçonnement [dezarsɔnmɑ̃], *s.m.* **1.** throwing (of rider). **2.** disconcertment, dumbfounding (of s.o.).
désarçonner [dezarsɔne], *v.tr.* **1.** (*of horse*) to unseat (rider); **il fut désarçonné,** he was unhorsed, he was thrown; he lost his seat. **2.** to confound, dumbfound, stagger (s.o.).
désargentage [dezarʒɑ̃taːʒ], *s.m.,* **désargentation** [dezarʒɑ̃tasjɔ̃], *s.f.* **1.** desilvering (of plated object). **2.** desilverization (of ore).

désargenté [dezarʒɑ̃te]. **1.** (*a*) (*of plated spoon, fork, etc.*) worn, rubbed; that has lost its silver; (*b*) desilverized (lead). **2.** *F:* short of cash; out of cash; **revenir d'un voyage entièrement d.,** to come back from a journey stony-broke, without a penny in one's pocket.

désargenter [dezarʒɑ̃te], *v.tr.* **1.** (*a*) to desilver (plated object); (*b*) to desilverize (ore). **2.** *F:* to drain (s.o.) of his cash; **ces dépenses m'ont complètement désargenté,** these expenses have completely cleared me out.

se désargenter, (*of plate*) to wear bare (of silver).

désargenture [dezarʒɑ̃ty:r], *s.f.* desilvering (of plated object).

désarmant [dezarmɑ̃], *a. F:* disarming (smile, frankness, etc.).

désarmé [dezarme]. **1.** (*a*) disarmed; (*b*) (ship) laid up, out of commission. **2.** (*a*) unarmed, defenceless, undefended; (*b*) unloaded (gun).

désarmement [dezarməmɑ̃], *s.m.* **1.** disarming (of s.o.). **2.** disarmament; **la Conférence du d.,** the Disarmament Conference. **3.** *Pol.Ec:* **d. douanier,** lifting of customs barriers. **4.** *Nau:* (*a*) laying up, paying off, putting out of commission (of ship); (*b*) **d. des avirons,** unshipping of the oars.

désarmer [dezarme]. **1.** *v.tr.* (*a*) to disarm; **d. qn de son fusil,** to disarm s.o. of his rifle; **d. la critique, la colère,** to disarm criticism, anger; *F:* **il montrait une franchise qui vous désarmait,** he was disarmingly frank; **les enfants me désarment,** I can never resist children; (*b*) *Mil:* (i) to unload (gun); (ii) to uncock (rifle); (iii) to remove guns from (fort); (*c*) *Nau:* to lay up, pay off, de-store, de-ammunition (ship); to put (ship) out of commission, to decommission (a ship); **d. un canot,** to dismiss a boat's crew; (*d*) **d. les avirons,** to unship the oars. **2.** *v.i.* (*a*) to disarm; to disband one's naval or military forces; (*b*) *Nau:* (*of ship*) to be laid up, paid off, put out of commission; (*c*) to relent; **ne pas d.,** to refuse to be mollified; **haine qui ne désarme pas,** unrelenting hatred.

désaromatisation [dezarɔmatizasjɔ̃], *s.f.* dearomatizing (of petroleum products).

désaromatiser [dezarɔmatize], *v.tr.* to dearomatize (petroleum products).

désarrimage [dezarima:ʒ], *s.m. Nau:* **1.** breaking bulk, breaking the stowage. **2.** shifting (of cargo).

désarrimer [dezarime], *v.tr. Nau:* **1.** to unstow (cargo); **d. la cale,** to break bulk, to break the stowage. **2.** to put (ship) out of trim.

se désarrimer, (*of cargo*) to shift.

désarroi [dezarwa], *s.m.* (*a*) disarray, disorder, confusion; **troupes en d.,** troops in disarray, in confusion; **tout est en d.,** everything is upside down, topsy-turvy, in confusion; **tout mettre en d.,** to turn everything upside down; (*b*) mental, spiritual, distress.

désarticulation [dezartikylasjɔ̃], *s.f.* (*a*) *Surg:* disarticulation, disjointing; amputation through the joint; (*b*) dislocation.

désarticulé [dezartikyle], *a.* dislocated, out of joint.

désarticuler [dezartikyle], *v.tr.* (*a*) *Surg:* to disarticulate, disjoint; (*b*) to dislocate.

désasphaltage [dezasfalta:ʒ], *s.m. Petroleum Ind:* de-asphalting.

désasphalter [dezasfalte], *v.tr. Petroleum Ind:* to de-asphalt.

désassemblage [dezasɑ̃bla:ʒ], **désassemblement** [dezasɑ̃bləmɑ̃], *s.m.* taking to pieces; disengaging, disconnecting (of joints, etc.); disassembly.

désassembler [dezasɑ̃ble], *v.tr.* to take (sth.) to pieces; to take (machine) apart; to disengage, disconnect (joints, etc.).

désassimilation [dezasimilasjɔ̃], *s.f. Biol:* disassimilation.

désassimiler [dezasimile], *v.tr. Biol:* to disassimilate.

désassociation [dezasɔsjasjɔ̃], *s.f.* disassociation, dissociation.

désassocier [dezasɔsje], *v.tr.* (*p.d. & pr.sub.* **n. désassociions, v. désassociiez**) to disassociate, dissociate (**de,** from); to sever the connection (**de,** with).

se désassocier de qn, to sever one's connection, one's partnership, with s.o.

désassombrir [dezasɔ̃bri:r], *v.tr.* (*a*) to lighten, brighten (sth.); (*b*) to cheer (s.o.) up.

se désassombrir, (*a*) (*of weather, etc.*) to become brighter; to brighten up, clear up; (*b*) (*of pers.*) to cheer up, to brighten up.

désassortiment [dezasɔrtimɑ̃], *s.m.* **1.** spoiling, breaking up (of collection). **2.** unstocking (of shop).

désassortir [dezasɔrti:r], *v.tr.* (*conj. like* ASSORTIR) (*a*) to spoil, break up (set, collection, etc.); **service de table désassorti,** dinner service made up of odd pieces; (*b*) *Com:* **je suis désassorti de cet article,** this article is out of stock; I am out of this article.

désassurer [dezasyre], *v.tr.* to cease to insure (property).

désastre [dezastr̥], *s.m.* disaster, calamity; **un d. financier,** a financial disaster, a crash; **une imprudence vous précipiterait au d.,** an imprudence would spell, be a, disaster; **ce serait le d.!** it would be a disaster!

désastreusement [dezastrøzmɑ̃], *adv.* disastrously.

désastreux, -euse [dezastrø, -ø:z], *a.* disastrous, calamitous.

désatomisation [dezatɔmizasjɔ̃], *s.f.* nuclear disarmament.

désatomiser [dezatɔmize], *v.tr.* to de-atomize; to undertake the nuclear disarmament of (a country).

désatteler [dezatle], *v.tr.* (**je désattelle, n. désattelons; je désattellerai**) to unharness; to unyoke (oxen).

désattrister [dezatriste], *v.tr.* to cheer, comfort (s.o.).

se désattrister, to cheer up, to brighten up.

désavantage [dezavɑ̃ta:ʒ], *s.m.* disadvantage, drawback; **c'est un d.,** it is a drawback, a handicap; **se montrer à son d.,** to show oneself to a disadvantage, in an unfavourable light; **cette affaire a tourné à mon d.,** I came off badly in that business; **avoir le d.,** (i) to be handicapped; (ii) to get the worst of it; *Nau:* **d. du vent,** lee-gauge.

désavantager [dezavɑ̃taʒe], *v.tr.* (**je désavantageai(s); n. désavantageons**) to injure, harm (s.o.); to affect (s.o.) unfavourably; to handicap (s.o.); **être désavantagé par suite de qch.,** to be handicapped by sth., to be at a disadvantage owing to sth.

désavantageusement [dezavɑ̃taʒøzmɑ̃], *adv.* disadvantageously, unfavourably.

désavantageux, -euse [dezavɑ̃taʒø, -ø:z], *a.* disadvantageous, unfavourable (position, etc.); **se montrer sous un jour d.,** to show oneself in an unfavourable light, to (a) disadvantage.

désaveu, -eux [dezavø], *s.m.* disavowal, denial; repudiation of the action (of s.o.); disowning (of s.o.); disclaiming (of authorship, etc.); *Jur:* **d. de paternité,** bastardizing of issue.

désaveugler [dezavœgle, -øgle], *v.tr.* to disabuse (s.o.).

désavouable [dezavwabl], *a.* deniable; repudiable; that should be repudiated.

désavouer [dezavwe], *v.tr.* to disavow, deny (promise, etc.); to disclaim (authorship, etc.); to disown (offspring); to retract (opinion); **d. sa promesse,** to repudiate, to go back on, one's promise; **d. un agent,** to disown, refuse to acknowledge, an agent; to repudiate the action of an agent; **faire ce que la morale désavoue,** to do that which morality disapproves.

se désavouer, to go back on one's word; to retract.

désaxage [dezaksa:ʒ], *s.m. Mec.E: etc:* setting over, staggering, throwing off centre.

désaxé [dezakse], *a.* **1.** *Mec.E:* (*a*) excentric (hinge, cam, etc.); off-set, (thrown) off centre; staggered; non axial; out of alignment; (*b*) **roue désaxée,** (i) splayed, dished, wheel; (ii) wheel out of true; (*c*) *I.C.E:* **cylindres désaxés,** offset, désaxé, cylinders. **2.** (*a*) unbalanced (mind); *s.* s.o. of unbalanced mind; (*b*) **sa vie était désaxée,** his life was out of joint.

désaxer [dezakse], *v.tr. Mec.E:* to set over (cylinder, etc.); to offset, stagger; to throw off centre, out of alignment.

désazotation [dezazɔtasjɔ̃], *s.f.* denitrification.

désazoter [dezazɔte], *v.tr.* to denitrify.

descellement [desɛlmɑ̃], *s.m.* **1.** unsealing, breaking the seal (of sth.); forcing (of safe). **2.** loosening (of iron bar from stonework, etc.).

desceller [desɛle, -sele], *v.tr.* **1.** to unseal, to break the seal of (document, etc.); to force (safe). **2.** to loosen (iron post from stonework, etc.); **se d.,** to work loose.

descendance [desɑ̃dɑ̃:s, de-], *s.f.* **1.** descent, lineage; **en d. directe de . . .,** in lineal descent from . . . **2.** descendants.

descendant, -ante [desɑ̃dɑ̃, de-, -ɑ̃:t]. **1.** *a.* (*a*) *Rail:* **train d.,** (i) up train (towards main town); (ii) down train (away from main town); **voie descendante,** (i) up line; (ii) down line; (*b*) **ligne descendante,** (genealogical) line of descent. **2.** *s.* descendant; *pl.* **descendants,** descendants, issue; **ses innombrables descendants,** his vast progeny.

descenderie [desɑ̃dri, de-], *s.f. Min:* descending shaft; winze.

descendeur [desɑ̃dœ:r, de-], *s.m. Cy. Rac:* rider who scores on fast descents; *Skiing:* **un bon d.,** a good downhill slopes skier.

descendre [desɑ̃:dr, de-]. I. *v.i.* (*the aux. is* **être,** *occ.* **avoir**) **1.** (*a*) to descend; to come down, go down; *Med:* (*of womb, etc.*) to prolapse, drop; **d. d'une colline, d'un arbre,** to come down from a hill, from a tree; **descendez de cette échelle,** get down off that ladder; **l'ange est descendu du ciel,** the angel descended from heaven; **d. à la cave,** to go down to the cellar; **les fleuves descendent vers la mer,** the rivers flow down to the sea; **d. bien vite,** to hurry down; **d. avec bruit,** to clatter down; **d. en glissant,** to slide down, to slither down; *Furs:* **peaux descendues,** dropped skins; **la marée descend,** the tide is falling, going down; *F:* **mon dîner ne descend pas,** my dinner won't go down; *Nau:* **le vent descend,** the wind is backing; **le baromètre descend,** the glass is falling; **le thermomètre a descendu de deux degrés,** the thermometer has fallen two degrees; *B:* **l'Esprit de Dieu a descendu sur lui,** the spirit of God has descended on him; **les Goths descendirent sur Rome,** the Goths descended upon Rome; *Jur:* **d. sur les lieux,** to visit the scene (of a crime, etc.); **la police est descendue, a descendu, dans la boîte de nuit,** the police made a descent on, raided, the night-club; *Av:* **d. en piqué,** to dive; **d. en spirale, en vrille, en vol plané,** to spiral, spin, glide, down; **d. à plat,** to pancake down; *Mil:* **d. de garde,** to come off guard, off duty; (*b*) **d. en soi-même,** to examine oneself, one's conscience; (*c*) to come, go, downstairs; **je descends dîner,** I'm going, coming, down to dinner; **d. dans la rue,** to come, go, down into the street; **il n'est pas encore descendu,** he is not down yet; **faites-le d.,** (i) send him down; (ii) call him down; (*d*) to lower oneself, to stoop, condescend; **d. jusqu'à la familiarité,** to stoop to familiarity; **d. jusqu'au mensonge,** to descend, stoop, to lying; **je ne peux pas d. jusqu'à faire cela,** I cannot go so low as to do that; **d. jusqu'aux moindres détails,** to enter into the minutest details. **2.** (*a*) to alight (from vehicle); **d. du train,** get out of, off, the train; **d. de cheval,** to get down from one's horse; to dismount; **c'est ici que je descends,** this is where I get off (the bus, etc.); **tout le monde descend!** all change! **faire d. qn,** (i) to help s.o. out (of a car), off (a train); (ii) to turn s.o. off (a bus); (iii) *Nau:* *Av:* to land s.o.; **d. à terre,** to go ashore, to land; (*b*) **d. à un hôtel,** to put up at a(n) hotel; **à quel hôtel êtes-vous descendu?** at what hotel are you staying, stopping, putting up? **d. chez des parents,** to stop, stay, with relations. **3.** (*a*) to extend downwards; (*of road, street*) to go downhill; **manteau qui descend jusqu'aux pieds,** cloak that reaches to the feet; **le chemin descend, va en descendant, jusqu'à la vallée,** the road slopes, stretches down, sweeps down, falls, sinks, to the valley; **sa barbe descend sur sa poitrine,** his beard falls over his chest; (*b*) **faire d. une histoire jusqu'aux temps modernes,** to bring a history up to modern times. **4.** to be descended (from); **sa famille descend des croisés,** his family is descended from, goes back to, the crusaders; **il descend de familles de paysans,** he is, comes, of peasant stock.

II. **descendre,** *v.tr.* (*aux.* **avoir**) **1. d. les marches, la colline, la rue,** to go down the steps, the hill, the street; **il descendit la rue en courant, au galop,** he ran, galloped, down the street; **d. la rivière,** to row, swim, float, etc. down the river; *Mus:* **d. la gamme,** to run down the scale. **2.** (*a*) to take, bring, (sth.) down; **d. les bagages,** to carry down, bring down, the luggage; **d. un tableau,** to take down a picture; **je ne peux pas le d.,** I can't get it down; (*b*) to lower, let down (man by rope, etc.); *Mus:* **d. une corde d'un demi-ton,** to lower a string a semitone; *Paint:* **d. une peinture d'un ton,** to make the paint lighter; (*c*) to shoot down, bring down, pick off, kill (partridge, man); **d. un avion,** to bring down, shoot down, an aircraft; (*d*) to set down (passenger); **je vous descendrai à votre porte,** I will put you down, drop you, at your door; **il m'a descendu en ville,** he gave me a lift into town, *U.S:* a lift down-town; (*e*) to dismount (gun).

descenseur [desɑ̃sœ:r, de-], *s.m.* chute (for goods, parcels, etc.); (spiral) conveyor.

descensionnel, -elle [desɑ̃sjɔnɛl, de-], *a.* descensional.

descente [desɑ̃:t, de-], *s.f.* descent. **1.** (*a*) coming down, going down (from a height); *Skiing:* run; **d. directe,** schuss; **d. dans un puits de mine,** going down, descending, a mine-shaft; **d. de cheval,** dismounting; **à sa d. de chaire . . .,** as, when, he came down from the pulpit . . .; **la d. d'un ballon,** the descent of a balloon; *Av:* **d. en (vol) piqué,** dive; **d. en (vol) plané,** glide; **d. en spirale,** spiral descent; **d. en vrille,** (tail) spin; **d. à plat,** pancaking; *Mil:* **d. de garde,** coming off guard, off duty; *Mch:* **mouvement de d.,** descending motion; down-stroke (of piston, etc.); (*b*) **d. à un hôtel,** putting up at a hotel; (*c*) raid; **faire une descente dans un pays,** to make a descent, an incursion, into a country; **d. des pirates sur la côte,** pirate raid; *Jur:* **d. sur les lieux,** visit to the scene (of a crime, etc.); **d. de police,** police raid; **faire une d. dans une boîte de nuit,** to raid a night-club; *Fb:* **une d. des avants,** a raid by the forwards; *Fin:* **d. sur une banque,** run on a bank; (*d*) *Med:* (i) dropping, falling, prolapse, prolapsus (of womb, rectum); (ii) **d. (de boyau),** hernia. **2.** letting down, lowering (of man by rope, etc.); *Art:* **La D. de croix,** the Descent from the Cross; **d. d'un tableau,** taking down of a picture. **3.** (*a*) place where s.o., sth., descends; **une d. rapide,** a steep slope; *P.N: Aut:* **d. dangereuse,** dangerous hill; **sentier en forte d.,** steep path; **d. de mine,** descending shaft; *Mil:* **d. de fossé,** descent into the ditch; (*b*) **d. de bain,** bath mat; **d. de lit,** (bedside) rug; (*c*) cellar steps; descending stair; (*d*) *Nau:* companion-way, hatch(way); (*e*) *Const:* down pipe, rainwater pipe; fall pipe; *Mec.E:* down feed; *F:* **avoir une bonne d.,** to be a great eater and drinker; (*f*) *W.Tel: etc:* down lead, lead in (of aerial); **d. de paratonnerre,** down inductor.

déschisteur, -euse [deʃistœ:r, -ø:z], *s. Coalmin:* caster.

déschlammage [deʃlama:ʒ], *s.m. Min:* removal of sludge.

déschlammer [deʃlame], *v.tr. Min:* to remove the sludge from, to sludge.

descloizite [dɛklwazit], *s.f. Miner:* descloizite.

descripteur [dɛskriptœ:r], *s.m.* **1.** describer. **2.** classification category (for documentation).

descriptible [dɛskriptibl], *a.* describable; **à peine d.,** virtually indescribable.

descriptif, -ive [dɛskriptif, -i:v]. **1.** *a.* descriptive. **2.** *s.m. Civ.E:* specification (of work to be carried out).

description [dɛskripsjɔ̃], *s.f.* description, picturing; delineation; **faire la d. de qn, de qch.,** to describe s.o., sth.; **conforme à la d.,** as represented; *Jur:* **d. des meubles,** inventory, specification, of the furniture; **d. de brevet,** patent specification.

Desdémone [dezdemɔn], *Pr.n.f.* Desdemona.

desdits [dedi]. *See* LEDIT.

déséchafauder [dezeʃafode], *v.tr.* to remove the scaffolding from (monument).

déséchouage [dezeʃwa:ʒ], *s.m.*, **déséchouement** [dezeʃumɑ̃], *s.m. Nau:* refloating, floating off (of ship).

déséchouer [dezeʃwe], *v.tr. Nau:* to refloat; to set (ship) afloat, to float off (ship).

se déséchouer, to get afloat, to float off, come off.

déségrégation [desegregasjɔ̃], *s.f. Pol:* desegregation.

désemballage [dezɑ̃bala:ʒ], *s.m.* unpacking (of goods).

désemballer [dezɑ̃bale], *v.tr.* to unpack (goods).

désembarquement [dezɑ̃barkəmɑ̃], *s.m.* disembarking; landing (of s.o.); unshipping (of goods).

désembarquer [dezɑ̃barke], *v.tr.* to disembark; to put (person) ashore; to unship (goods).

désembarrasser [dezɑ̃barase], *v.tr.* to disembarrass.

désembattage [dezɑ̃bata:ʒ], *s.m. Rail:* unshoeing (of wheel).

désembattre [dezɑ̃batr̥], *v.tr.* (*conj. like* BATTRE) *Rail:* to unshoe (wheel).

désembellir [dezɑ̃beli:r], *A: Lit:* **1.** *v.tr.* to disfigure (s.o., sth.); to spoil the beauty of (s.o., sth.). **2.** *v.i.* to lose one's beauty.

désemboîter [dezɑ̃bwate], *v.tr.* to dislocate.

désembourber [dezɑ̃burbe], *v.tr.* to extricate (vehicle, etc.) from the mud, from a morass.

désembourgeoisement [dezɑ̃burʒwazmɑ̃], *s.m.* removal of, loss of, escape from, bourgeois outlook, mentality.

désembourgeoiser [dezɑ̃burʒwaze], *v.tr.* to free (s.o.) from bourgeois habits and ways of thinking; **il s'est désembourgeoisé,** he's lost his bourgeois outlook, mentality.

désembrayage [dezɑ̃brɛja:ʒ], *s.m. A:* = DÉBRAYAGE.

désembrayer [dezɑ̃brɛje], *v.tr. A:* = DÉBRAYER.

désembuage [dezɑ̃bɥa:ʒ], *s.m.* demisting.

désembuer [dezɑ̃bɥe], *v.tr.* to demist.

désemparé [dezɑ̃pare], *a.* (ship) in distress; helpless, crippled, disabled (ship); (aircraft) out of control; **être tout d. dans une discussion,** to be all at sea in a discussion; **ils sont tout désemparés,** they are in great trouble, do not know where to turn, what to do next; **l'étranger se trouve d. quand il veut nous comprendre,** the foreigner is at a loss when he tries to understand us.

désemparer [dezɑ̃pare]. **1.** *v.tr.* (*a*) *Nau:* to disable (ship); (*b*) to break (piece of furniture) in pieces; (*c*) to undo. **2.** *v.i.* (*a*) *A:* **d. d'un lieu,** to quit, abandon, a place; (*b*) **sans d.,** without stopping, without intermission; **garder la pose une demi-heure sans d.,** to pose for half an hour on end; **ils travaillent sans d.,** they work away; **ils tirent, pompent, sans d.,** they fire away, pump away (without a pause).

désempeser [dezɑ̃pəze], *v.tr.* (*conj. like* EMPESER) to take the starch out of (shirt, etc.); to unstarch.

se désempeser, (*of linen*) to become limp, lose its starch.

désempêtrer [dezɑ̃petre, -etre], *v.tr.* = DÉPÊTRER.

désempilage[1] [dezɑ̃pila:ʒ], *s.m.* unstacking (of timber).

désempilage[2], *s.m. Fish:* unmounting (of hook).

désempiler[1] [dezɑ̃pile], *v.tr.* to unstack (timber).

désempiler[2], *v.tr. Fish:* to unmount (hook).

désemplir [dezɑ̃pli:r]. **1.** *v.tr.* to empty partially (bath, bottle, etc.). **2.** *v.i. & pr. usu. in the negative;* **son magasin ne (se) désemplit pas,** his shop is always full (of customers).

désemplumer [dezɑ̃plyme], *v.tr.* to remove the feathers from (hat).

se désemplumer, *F:* to lose one's hair; to go bald.

désempoissonner [dezɑ̃pwasɔne], *v.tr.* to unstock (pond, etc. of fish).

désemprisonner [dezɑ̃prizɔne], *v.tr.* to free (s.o.), set (s.o.) free from prison.

désémulsification [dezemylsifikasjɔ̃], *s.f. Ch:* demulsification, demulsifying.

désémulsionner [dezemylsjɔne], *v.tr. Ch:* to demulsify.

désenamourer (se) [sədezɑ̃namure], *v.pr.* to fall out of love (de, with).

désencadrer [dezɑ̃kadre], *v.tr.* to take (a picture) out of its frame.

désencanailler [dezɑ̃kanɑje], *v.tr. F:* to get (s.o.) out of low, vulgar, ways.

se désencanailler, (*a*) to drop one's low, vulgar, ways; (*b*) to get on, rise, in the world.

désenchaîner [dezɑ̃ʃɛne, -ʃene], *v.tr.* to unchain, unfetter.

désenchanté, -e [dezɑ̃ʃɑ̃te], *a. & s.* disillusioned (person).

désenchantement [dezɑ̃ʃɑ̃tmɑ̃], *s.m.* (*a*) disenchantment; (*b*) disillusion.

désenchanter [dezɑ̃ʃɑ̃te], *v.tr.* (*a*) to disenchant; to free (s.o., sth.) from a spell; (*b*) to disillusion, undeceive (s.o.); **sourire désenchanté,** wistful smile.

se désenchanter, to lose one's illusions.

désenchanteur, -eresse [dezɑ̃ʃɑ̃tœ:r, -(ə)rɛs], *a.* (*a*) disenchanting, spell-breaking; (*b*) disillusioning.

désenchâsser [dezɑ̃ʃɑse], *v.tr.* to remove (gem) from its setting.

désenchevêtrer [dezɑ̃ʃəvɛtre, -etre], *v.tr.* to disentangle.

désenclaver [dezɑ̃klave], *v.tr.* **1.** to disenclose (piece of land). **2.** *Surg:* to free (blocked organ).

désenclouer [dezɑ̃klue], *v.tr.* **1.** to draw a nail from (horse's foot). **2.** *A:* to unspike (gun).

désencombrement [dezɑ̃kɔ̃brəmɑ̃], *s.m.* disencumberment, clearing, freeing (of passage, etc.).

désencombrer [dezɑ̃kɔ̃bre], *v.tr.* to disencumber; to clear, free (passage, etc.).

désencoquiller (se) [sədezɑ̃kɔkije], *v.pr. F:* to come out of one's shell.

désencorder (se) [sədezɑ̃kɔrde], *v.pr. Mount:* to unrope.

désencrasser [dezɑ̃krase], *v.tr.* to clean (sth. greasy); *I.C.E:* to decarbonize (engine).

désencroûtement [dezɑ̃krutmɑ̃], *s.m.* **1.** scaling (of boiler). **2. d. de qn,** broadening of s.o.'s outlook.

désencroûter [dezɑ̃krute], *v.tr.* (*a*) to scale (boiler, etc.); (*b*) to broaden (s.o.'s) outlook; to polish (s.o.) up.

se désencroûter, to get out of the rut.

désendettement [dezɑ̃dɛtmɑ̃], *s.m.* (action of) getting out of debt.

désendetter [dezɑ̃dete, -ete], *v.tr.* to free (s.o.) of debts.

se désendetter, to get out of debt.

désendormir [dezɑ̃dɔrmi:r], *v.tr.* (*conj. like* ENDORMIR) to rouse (s.o.).

désenfiler [dezɑ̃file], *v.tr.* to unthread (needle); to unstring (beads, etc.).

se désenfiler, to come unthreaded; (*of beads*) to come unstrung.

désenflammer [dezɑ̃flame], *v.tr.* (*a*) *Med:* to reduce the inflammation in (wound, etc.); (*b*) to quench (s.o.'s passion); (*c*) to extinguish (fire).

désenflement [dezɑ̃fləmɑ̃], *s.m.* reduction, diminution, of swelling.

désenfler [dezɑ̃fle]. **1.** *v.tr.* (*a*) to reduce the swelling of (ankle, etc.); (*b*) to deflate (balloon, tyre, etc.). **2.** *v.i. & pr.* to become less swollen; **ma joue se désenfle,** the swelling (in my cheek) is going down.

désenflure [dezɑ̃fly:r], *s.f.* reduction, diminution of swelling.

désenfourner [dezɑ̃furne], *v.tr.* to take out of the oven.

désenfumer [dezɑ̃fyme], *v.tr.* to clear (room) of smoke; to renovate (picture).

désengagement [dezɑ̃gaʒmɑ̃], *s.m. Pol: F:* disengagement.

désengager [dezɑ̃gaʒe], *v.tr.* (**je désengageai(s); n. désengageons**) **1.** (*a*) to free (s.o.) from an obligation; (*b*) **d. sa parole,** to obtain release from a promise. **2.** to take (sth.) out of pawn. **3.** *Mec.E:* to throw (pulley, etc.) out of gear; to disengage (pulley).

se désengager, to obtain release, free oneself, from an engagement, appointment, invitation.

désengainer [dezɑ̃gene, -ene], *v.tr.* to uncase, unwrap (mummy, etc.); to unsheath, unwrap (cable).

désengorgement [dezɑ̃gɔrʒəmɑ̃], *s.m.* unchoking, unstopping (of pipe, etc.).

désengorger [dezɑ̃gɔrʒe], *v.tr.* (**je désengorgeai(s); n. désengorgeons**) to unchoke, unstop (pipe, etc.).

désengouer (se) [sədezɑ̃gwe], *v.pr. F:* to get over one's infatuation (**de,** for).

désengrenage [dezɑ̃grəna:ʒ], *s.m.* disengaging (of toothed wheels, etc.); throwing (of machine, etc.) out of gear.

désengrènement [dezɑ̃grɛnmɑ̃], *s.m. Vet:* separation of wall from laminar matrix in horse's hoof resulting from laminitis.

désengrener [dezɑ̃grəne], *v.tr.* (*conj. like* ENGRENER) to disengage, ungear (toothed wheels, etc.); to throw (machine, etc.) out of gear.

se désengrener, to get out of gear.

désenivrer [dezɑ̃nivre]. **1.** *v.tr.* to sober (s.o.). **2.** *v.i.* **il ne désenivre pas,** he is never sober.

se désenivrer, to sober up.

désenlacer [dezɑ̃lase], *v.tr.* (*conj. like* LACER) (*a*) *A:* to unbind; (*b*) **ils se désenlacèrent brusquement,** they suddenly let go their embrace.

désenlaidir [dezɑ̃ledi:r]. **1.** *v.tr.* to make (s.o.) less ugly. **2.** *v.i.* to become better looking, to lose one's plain looks.

désennuyer [dezɑ̃nɥije], *v.tr.* (**je désennuie, n. désennuyons; je désennuierai**) to amuse, divert (s.o.); to help (s.o.) to pass the time.

se désennuyer, to find entertainment, diversion (**à faire qch.,** in doing sth.); **faire une réussite pour se d.,** to play a game of patience in order to while away the time; **se d. de qch.,** to seek diversion from sth.

désenrayement [dezɑ̃rɛjmɑ̃, -rej-], *s.m.* releasing (brake, jammed mechanism, etc.).

désenrayer [dezɑ̃rɛje, -reje], *v.tr.* **1.** to release (brake, jammed part, mechanism). **2.** to unscotch (wheel).

désenrhumer [dezɑ̃ryme], *v.tr.* to cure (s.o.) of a cold; to cure (s.o.'s) cold.

se désenrhumer, to get rid of one's cold.

désenrôlement [dezɑ̃rolmɑ̃], *s.m.* (*a*) removal from the roll; (*b*) *Mil:* discharging; taking (a man) off the strength.

désenrôler [dezɑ̃role], *v.tr.* (*a*) to remove (s.o.) from the roll; (*b*) *Mil:* to take (man) off the strength; to discharge.

désenrouer [dezɑ̃rue], *v.tr.* to cure (s.o.'s) hoarseness.

désensablement [dezɑ̃sabləmɑ̃], *s.m.* (*a*) (action of) getting (ship, car, etc.) off, out of, the sand; fishing (cockles, etc.) out of the sand; excavation (of buried building, etc.) from the sand; (*b*) dredging of sand from (channel, etc.).

désensabler [dezɑ̃sɑble], *v.tr.* (*a*) to get (ship) off the sand; to get (car, etc.) out of the sand; to fish (cockles, etc.) out of the sand; to excavate (building, etc.) from the sand; (*b*) to dredge (channel, etc.) of sand; to free (channel, etc.) from sand.

désenseller [dezɑ̃sɛle, -ele], *v.tr.* (*of horse*) to throw (rider).

désensevelir [dezɑ̃səvliːr], *v.tr.* **1.** to disinter, exhume (corpse), to dig up (sth.). **2.** to unshroud (corpse).

désensevelissement [dezɑ̃səvlismɑ̃], *s.m.* **1.** disinterment, disinterring, exhumation, exhuming (of corpse, etc.). **2.** unshrouding (of corpse).

désensibilisant [desɑ̃sibilizɑ̃], *s.m. Med:* desensitizer.

désensibilisateur, -trice [desɑ̃sibilizatœːr, -tris], *Phot:* **1.** *a.* desensitizing. **2.** *s.m.* desensitizer.

désensibilisation [desɑ̃sibilizasjɔ̃], *s.f.* **1.** *Phot:* desensitizing. **2.** *Med:* desensitization.

désensibiliser [desɑ̃sibilize], *v.tr. Med: Phot:* to desensitize.

désensorceler [dezɑ̃sɔrsəle], *v.tr.* (**je désensorcelle, n. désensorcelons; je désensorcellerai**) **1.** to disenchant (sth.); to free (sth.) from a magic spell. **2.** *F:* (*a*) to free (s.o.) from an infatuation; (*b*) to turn (s.o.'s) luck (at cards, etc.).

désensorcellement [dezɑ̃sɔrsɛlmɑ̃], *s.m.* disenchantment.

désenterrer [dezɑ̃tɛre, -ere], *v.tr.* to disinter, exhume (body); **d. de vieux griefs,** to dig up old grievances.

désenthousiasmer [dezɑ̃tuzjasme], *v.tr.* to damp the enthusiasm of (s.o.).

se désenthousiasmer, to lose one's enthusiasm.

désentoilage [dezɑ̃twalaːʒ], *s.m.* removal of the canvas from (picture), the fabric from (glider-wing, windmill-sail, etc.).

désentoiler [dezɑ̃twale], *v.tr.* to remove the canvas from (picture), the fabric from (glider-wing, windmill-sail, etc.).

désentortiller [dezɑ̃tɔrtije], *v.tr.* to untwist (thread, paper, etc.); to disentangle, unravel (wool, intricate business, etc.).

désentraver [dezɑ̃trave], *v.tr.* **1.** to unhobble, unshackle (horse, etc.). **2.** to clear (affair) of difficulties.

désenvaser [dezɑ̃vɑze], *v.tr.* **1.** to clean out (sewer, harbour). **2.** to extract, to get, (sth.) out of the mud.

désenvelopper [dezɑ̃vlɔpe], *v.tr.* to unwrap (parcel); to unshroud (corpse).

désenvenimer [dezɑ̃vnime], *v.tr.* to cleanse (wound, etc.); to make (conversation, etc.) less venomous.

désépaissir [dezepesiːr], *v.tr.* to thin (hair, etc.).

désépingler [dezepɛ̃gle], *v.tr.* to unpin.

déséquilibre [dezekilibr̥], *s.m.* (*a*) *Ph: Mec: Pol. Ec: etc:* want, lack, of balance, imbalance; **le d. financier des transports aériens,** the financial imbalance of air transport; *Pol.Ec:* **d. de la balance commerciale,** unfavourable, adverse, trade balance; *El.E:* **d. de l'inductance,** inductance imbalance; (*b*) *Med: Psy:* unbalance, imbalance; **d. émotif,** emotional maladjustment.

déséquilibré [dezekilibre], *a.* **1.** (*of thg*) out of balance, unbalanced. **2.** unbalanced (person, mind); *s.* **un(e) déséquilibré(e),** an unbalanced person.

déséquilibrer [dezekilibre], *v.tr.* to unbalance; to throw (sth.) out of balance; to throw (s.o.) off balance; **l'alcool déséquilibre,** alcohol causes lack of balance.

déséquiper [dezekipe], *v.tr.* **1.** to take the equipment off (s.o., sth.); to lay up (ship). **2.** to take down (machine); to unrig (sheers, etc.); *Th:* to dismantle the scenery of (stage).

se déséquiper, to take off, remove, one's equipment.

désert[1] [dezɛːr, dɛ-], *a.* **1.** deserted, forsaken, abandoned (place); **la rue était déserte,** there was nobody on the street; **l'endroit était d.,** there was nobody about. **2.** desert, uninhabited (country, island, etc.); lonely (spot); unfrequented (resort).

désert[2], *s.m.* desert, wilderness; **le d. du Sahara,** the Sahara (Desert); **prêcher dans le d.,** to preach in the wilderness; *F:* to talk to the wind, to deaf ears.

déserter [dezɛrte, dɛ-], *v.tr.* to desert, abandon; **d. la maison paternelle,** to run away from home; **d. son poste,** to abandon, quit, one's post; **d. l'église,** to forsake the church; *Mil:* **d. l'armée,** to desert from the army; *abs.* **soldat qui déserte,** deserter; **d. à l'ennemi,** to go over to the enemy, to defect.

déserteur [dezɛrtœːr, dɛ-], *s.m.* (*a*) deserter; (*b*) defector.

désertion [dezɛrsjɔ̃, dɛ-], *s.f.* **1.** desertion (from the colours, from a party). **2. d. des campagnes,** rural depopulation, the drift from the land.

désertique [dezɛrtik, dɛ-], *a. Geog:* of, pertaining to, the desert; **région d.,** desert region; **l'Afrique d.,** the deserts of Africa.

désescalade [dezɛskalad], *s.f.* de-escalation.

désespéramment [dezɛsperamɑ̃], *adv.* despairingly.

désespérance [dezɛsperɑ̃ːs]. *s.f. Lit:* loss of hope; despair; **mourir de d.,** to be dying of unrequited love.

désespérant [dezɛsperɑ̃], *a.* heart-breaking; **chagrin, enfant, d.,** sorrow, child, that drives one to despair; **temps d.,** hopeless weather; **c'est d.,** (i) it is heart-breaking; (ii) it's a hopeless job.

désespéré, -ée [dezɛspere]. **1.** *a.* desperate; (*a*) hopeless, to be despaired of; **malade d.,** patient whose life is despaired of; **être dans un état d.,** to be in a hopeless, desperate, state, to be far gone (in illness, etc.); to be past recovery; (*b*) prompted by despair; despairing (look, etc.); **lutte déseperée,** desperate struggle, life-and-death struggle; (*c*) driven to despair; *F:* **être d. de qch., d'apprendre qch.,** to be dreadfully sorry, *F:* awfully sorry, about sth.; to be dreadfully sorry to hear sth. **2.** *s.* desperate person; **agir en d.,** to act desperately, like a madman; *F:* **travailler en d.,** to work like mad.

désespérément [dezɛsperemɑ̃], *adv.* **1.** despairingly, hopelessly. **2.** desperately (in love, etc.).

désespérer [dezɛspere], *v.* (**je désespère, n. désespérons; je désespérerai**) **1.** *v.i.* to despair, despond; to lose hope; **il ne faut pas d.,** we must hope for the best; **il ne faut jamais d.,** never say die, we must hope against hope; **d. de qn,** to despair of s.o., to lose all hope in s.o., of s.o.; **d. de qch., de faire qch.,** to despair of sth., of doing sth.; **on désespère de le sauver,** his life is despaired of, he is past hope; **je désespère qu'il réussisse,** I despair of his succeeding; **c'est à d. de jamais réussir,** it seems a hopeless task. **2.** *v.tr.* to reduce, drive, (s.o.) to despair.

se désespérer, to be in despair, to give way to despair; **il se désespère de n'avoir pas réussi, que vous n'ayez pas réussi,** he is in despair that he, you, did not succeed.

désespoir [dezɛspwaːr], *s.m.* **1.** despair; **être au d., dans le d.,** to be in despair; **peuple au d.,** people in despair, despairing people; **enfant qui fait le d. des siens,** child who is the despair of his relations; **se livrer au d.,** to give way to despair; **tomber dans le d.,** to sink into despair; **coup de d.,** act of despair; **accès de d.,** fit of despair, despairing fit; **se tuer par d. d'amour,** to make away with oneself out of disappointed love; **ces formulaires à remplir font mon d.,** these forms to be filled drive me to despair. **2.** desperation; **réduire qn au d.,** to drive s.o. to desperation, to despair; **en d. de cause,** in desperation, when all else fails, as a last resource, as a desperate shift; **y renoncer en d. de cause,** to give up in despair. **3.** *Bot:* **d. des peintres,** London pride.

désessenciement [dezɛsɑ̃simɑ̃], *s.m. Oil Ind:* stripping.

désessencier [dezɛsɑ̃sje], *v.tr.* (*p.d. and pr.sub.* **n. désessenciions; v. désessenciiez**) *Oil Ind:* to strip.

désétablir [dezetabliːr], *v.tr.* to disestablish.

désétablissement [dezetablismɑ̃], *s.m.* disestablishment.

désétamage [dezetamaːʒ], *s.m.* untinning, detinning.

désétamer [dezetame], *v.tr.* to untin, detin.

déséthanisation [dezetanizasjɔ̃], *s.f. Oil Ind:* de-ethanization.

déséthaniser [dezetanize], *v.tr. Oil Ind:* de-ethanize.

déséthaniseur [dezetanizœːr], *s.m. Oil Ind:* de-ethanizer.

désétouper [dezetupe], *v.tr.* to uncaulk (ship).

désexcitation [dezɛksitasjɔ̃], *s.f. El.E:* **courant, tension, puissance, de d.,** drop-out.

désexciter [dezɛksite], *v.tr.* (*a*) to calm (sth., s.o.) down; (*b*) *El.E:* to de-energize.

se désexciter, to calm down.

désexualiser [desɛksɥalize], *v.tr.* to desexualize.

déshabilitation [dezabilitasjɔ̃], *s.f. Jur:* disqualification.

déshabiliter [dezabilite], *v.tr. Jur:* to disqualify.

déshabillage [dezabijaːʒ], *s.m.* (*a*) undressing; *Mus.Hall:* strip-tease; (*b*) *F:* slating (of a play); (*c*) *Tch:* stripping.

déshabillé [dezabije], *s.m.* **1.** négligé; housecoat. **2. être en d.,** to be *en déshabillé*; *F:* **recevoir des amis en d.,** to receive friends informally; **des femmes en déshabillé(s),** women in scanty attire.

déshabiller [dezabije], *v.tr.* **1.** (*a*) to undress (s.o.); *F:* **d. qn,** (i) to lay bare s.o.'s innermost thoughts, s.o.'s soul; (ii) to give s.o. a dressing-down; **d. une pièce,** to slate a play; (*b*) to disrobe; unrobe (judge, etc.). **2** *Nau:* to strip (mast, yard).

se déshabiller. 1. to undress (oneself); to take off one's clothes; to strip. **2.** (*a*) to change into everyday garments; (*b*) to take off one's outdoor clothes; (*of judge, etc.*) to disrobe.

déshabituer [dezabitɥe], *v.tr.* **d. qn de qch.,** to disaccustom s.o. to sth.; **d. qn de faire qch.,** to break s.o. of the habit of doing sth.

se déshabituer. 1. to grow unused (**de,** to). **2.** to break oneself of the habit (**de,** of).

désherbage [dezɛrbaːʒ], *s.m. Agr:* cleaning (of field, etc.); *Hort:* weeding, weed-killing.

désherbant [dezɛrbɑ̃], *s.m.* weed-killer.

désherber [dezɛrbe], *v.tr. Agr:* to clean (field, etc.), to weed (garden).

déshérence [dezerɑ̃ːs], *s.f. Jur:* default of heirs, escheat; **succession en d.,** intestate succession to which there are no next of kin; **tomber en d.,** to escheat.

déshérité [dezerite], *a.* (*a*) disinherited, deprived of one's inheritance; (*b*) underprivileged; **enfant d.,** deprived child; (*c*) plain; **nos sœurs déshéritées,** our plain sisters; (*d*) barren; desolate; bleak; **un pays d.,** a desolate region.

déshéritement [dezeritmɑ̃], *s.m.* disinheritance, disinheriting.

déshériter [dezerite], *v.tr.* to disinherit (s.o.), to deprive (s.o.) of an inheritance; to will one's property away from (s.o.); **je le déshériterai,** I shall strike his name out of my will; *F:* I shall cut him off with a shilling.

désheurer [dezœre]. **1.** *v.tr. Rail:* to change the time of a train so that it runs later than indicated on the timetable. **2.** *v.i. Clockm:* (*of timing device*) to ring at times other than those indicated by the hands.

déshonnête [dezɔnɛːt], *a. A:* improper, immodest, unseemly.

déshonnêtement [dezɔnɛtmɑ̃], *adv. A:* improperly, immodestly.

déshonnêteté [dezɔnɛt(ə)te], *s.f. A:* impropriety, immodesty, unseemliness.

déshonneur [dezɔnœːr], *s.m.* dishonour, disgrace; **faire d. à qn,** to disgrace s.o.; **tenir à d. de manquer à une promesse,** to consider it dishonourable to fail to keep a promise; **il n'y a pas de d. à cela,** there is no disgrace in that.

déshonorable [dezɔnɔrabl̥], *a.* dishonourable, disgraceful, shameful.

déshonorablement [dezɔnɔrabləmɑ̃], *adv.* dishonourably.

déshonorant [dezɔnɔrɑ̃], *a.* dishonouring, discreditable.

déshonorer [dezɔnɔre], *v.tr.* (*a*) to dishonour, disgrace; to bring dishonour, disgrace, upon (s.o.); **d. une jeune fille,** to bring shame upon a girl; **d. le nom de qn,** to tarnish s.o.'s name; (*b*) to maltreat, disfigure, spoil (picture, etc.).

se déshonorer, to disgrace oneself, to lose one's honour.

déshuilage [dezɥilaːʒ], *s.m.* extraction, separation, of oil, grease; de-oiling.

déshuiler [dezɥile], *v.tr.* to extract, separate, remove, oil, grease, from (sth.); to de-oil.

déshuileur [dezɥilœːr], *s.m. Mch:* oil-separator; grease-extractor; de-oiler.

déshumanisation [dezymanizasjɔ̃], *s.f.* dehumanization.

déshumaniser [dezymanize], *v.tr.* to dehumanize.

déshumidificateur [dezymidifikatœːr], *s.m.* dehumidifier.

déshumidification [dezymidifikasjɔ̃], *s.f.* dehumidification.

déshumidifier [dezymidifje], *v.tr.* (*conj. like* HUMIDIFIER) to dehumidify.

déshydrase [dezidraːz], *s.f. Ch:* dehydrogenase.

déshydratant [dezidratɑ̃], *a. & s.m.* desiccant.

déshydratation [dezidratasjɔ̃], *s.f. Ch: Ind: Med:* dehydration; **d. sous vide,** vacuum dehydration.

déshydrater [dezidrate], *v.tr.* (*a*) to dehydrate; **produits (alimentaires) déshydratés,** dehydrated food; (*b*) to desiccate; **noix de coco déshydratée,** desiccated coconut.

se déshydrater, to become dehydrated, desiccated.

déshydrateur [dezidratœːr], *s.m. Ch: Ind:* dehydrator.

déshydrogénation [dezidrɔʒenasjɔ̃], *s.f. Ch:* dehydrogenation.

déshydrogéné [dezidrɔʒene], *a. Ch:* dehydrogenate.

déshydrogéner [dezidrɔʒene], *v.tr.* (**je déshydrogène, n. déshydrogénons; je déshydrogènerai**) *Ch:* to dehydrogenate.

déshypothéquer [dezipɔteke], *v.tr.* (*conj. like* HYPOTHÉQUER) to disencumber (estate).

désidératif, -ive [dezideratif, -iːv], *a. & s.m. Gram:* desiderative (verb).

desideratum [dezideratɔm], *s.m.* desideratum; *pl. desiderata.*

désignatif, -ive [deziɲatif, -iːv], *a.* designative.

désignation [deziɲasjɔ̃], *s.f.* designation. **1.** (*a*) indication, pointing out (of s.o., sth.); (*b*) description (of title-deeds, goods, etc.). **2.** appointment; **d. de qn pour un poste,** appointment, nomination, of s.o., to a post.

désigné [deziɲe], *a.* **évêque d.,** bishop designate.

désigner [deziɲe], *v.tr.* **1.** (*a*) to designate, show, indicate, point out; **d. qch. à l'attention de qn,** to call s.o.'s attention to sth.; **d. qn sous le nom de . . .,** to call s.o., refer to s.o., by the name of . . .; **d. qch. du doigt,** to point sth. out, to point at sth.; **ce succès le désigne pour un grand avenir,** this success marks him out for a great future; (*b*) to describe (title-deeds, etc.). **2.** (*a*) **d. un jour, un lieu de rendez-vous,** to appoint, set, fix, a day, a meeting-place; **je le rejoignis à l'endroit désigné,** I joined him at the appointed place; **il prit le siège qu'on lui avait désigné, à lui désigné,** he took the seat indicated to him; **d. un fondé de pouvoir,** to nominate an agent or a proxy; **d. un expert,** to appoint an expert; **il est tout désigné pour le faire,** he is just the man to do it; he is cut out for it; **une proie toute désignée pour . . .,** a perfect prey for . . .; (*b*) **d. qn à, pour, un poste,** to appoint, draft, nominate, s.o. to a post; *Mil: etc:* **d. qn pour un service,** to detail, tell off, s.o. for a duty; **d. qn pour un commandement,** to post s.o. to a command; **d. qn pour Toulon, pour Brest,** to order s.o. to Toulon, to Brest.

se désigner aux regards, to stand out conspicuously; **se d. au feu de l'ennemi,** to draw the enemy's fire.

désilage [desilaːʒ], *s.m. Husb:* removal of a part, the whole, of the contents of a silo.

désiler [desile], *v.tr. Husb:* to remove from a silo a part, the whole, of its contents.

désileuse [desiløːz], *s.f. Husb:* device for removing contents from a silo.

désiliciage [desilisjaːʒ], *s.m. Ch:* desilication (of industrial waste water).

désillusion [dezil(l)yzjɔ̃], *s.f.* disillusion; **une amère d.,** a rude awakening.

désillusionnant [dezil(l)yzjɔnɑ̃], *a.* disillusioning.

désillusionnement [dezil(l)yzjɔnmɑ̃], *s.m.* disillusionment, disillusioning, undeceiving; cynicism.

désillusionner [dezil(l)yzjɔne], *v.tr.* to disillusion, disillusionize, undeceive; **être désillusionné,** *F:* to be a sadder and wiser man.

désincarnation [dezɛ̃karnasjɔ̃], *s.f.* disincarnation.

désincarné [dezɛ̃karne], *a.* disincarnate.

se désincarner [sədezɛ̃karne], *v.pr. Psychics:* to become disembodied.

désincorporation [dezɛ̃kɔrpɔrasjɔ̃], *s.f.* disembodiment (of company, etc.).

désincorporer [dezɛ̃kɔrpɔre], *v.tr.* to disincorporate, disembody (company, etc.).

désincrustant [dezɛ̃krystɑ̃]. **1.** *a.* scaling (substance); *Toil:* **produit d.,** cleanser, cleansing product (for the skin). **2.** *s.m.* disincrustant; anti-scale (boiler) composition, scale preventive.

désincrustation [dezɛ̃krystasjɔ̃], *s.f.* scaling (of boiler).

désincruster [dezɛ̃kryste], *v.tr.* to scale (boiler).

désincrusteur [dezɛ̃krystœːr], *s.m.* boiler-scaling device or material.

désinculpation [dezɛ̃kylpasjɔ̃], *s.f.* **d. de qn,** withdrawal of the charge against s.o.; clearing of s.o.

désinculper [dezɛ̃kylpe], *v.tr.* to withdraw the charge against (s.o.); to clear (s.o.).

désinence [dezinɑ̃ːs], *s.f.* **1.** *Gram:* termination (of word); flexional ending; desinence. **2.** *Bot:* terminal of certain organs of a plant.

désinentiel, -elle [dezinɑ̃sjɛl], *a. Ling:* desinential.

désinfatuer [dezɛ̃fatɥe], *v.tr.* **d. qn (de qn),** to cure s.o. of his infatuation (for s.o.).

se désinfatuer, to get over one's infatuation (de, for).

désinfectant [dezɛ̃fɛktɑ̃], *a. & s.m.* disinfectant.

désinfecter [dezɛ̃fɛkte], *v.tr.* to disinfect.

désinfecteur [dezɛ̃fɛktœːr]. **1.** *a.m.* disinfecting (apparatus, etc.). **2.** *s.m.* disinfecting apparatus, disinfector.

désinfection [dezɛ̃fɛksjɔ̃], *s.f.* disinfection.

désinsection [dezɛ̃sɛksjɔ̃], *s.f.* (*rare*), **désinsectisation** [dezɛ̃sɛktisasjɔ̃], *s.f.* disinsectization.

désinsectiser [dezɛ̃sɛktize], *v.tr.* to remove insects from (buildings, etc.).

désintégrateur [dezɛ̃tegratœːr], *s.m.* **1.** *Civ.E: etc:* disintegrator, (ore-)crusher. **2.** *Paperm:* machine for reducing cellulose sheets to fragments.

désintégration [dezɛ̃tegrasjɔ̃], *s.f.* disintegration, breaking up; weathering (of rocks); collapse (of structure, organization, etc.); *Atom.Ph:* (nuclear) disintegration, decay; splitting, smashing (of the atom); **d. alpha, d. héliogène,** alpha (-particle) disintegration, decay; **d. bêta, d. négatogène,** beta(-particle) disintegration, decay; **d. positogène, d. avec émission de positons,** positron disintegration, decay.

désintégrer [dezɛ̃tegre], *v.tr.* (**je désintègre, n. désintégrons; je désintégrerai**) to disintegrate; to crush (ore, etc.); to break up (a structure, an organization, etc.); to weather (rocks); *Atom.Ph:* to disintegrate (matter); to split, smash (the atom).

se désintégrer, to disintegrate; (*of structure, organization, etc.*) to break up, collapse, decay; (*of rocks*) to weather; *Atom.Ph:* (*of matter*) to disintegrate; (*of atom*) to smash, split; *F:* **il s'est désintégré,** he's gone all to pieces.

désintéressé [dezɛ̃terese]. **1.** *a.* not involved, not implicated; **être d. dans une affaire,** to have no interest at stake in a business; **d. de toute ambition,** free from all ambition. **2.** *a.* (*a*) disinterested, unprejudiced, unbias(s)ed, candid (opinion, advice, etc.); (*b*) unselfish (motive, etc.). **3.** *s.m.* disinterestedness, disinterested act.

désintéressement [dezɛ̃terɛsmɑ̃], *s.m.* **1.** disinterestedness; (i) impartiality; (ii) unselfishness. **2.** buying out (of partner, etc.); satisfying, paying off (of creditor, etc.).

désintéresser [dezɛ̃terese], *v.tr.* to buy out (partner); to satisfy, pay off (creditor); to reimburse (s.o.).

se désintéresser de qch., de qn, to take (i) no further interest, (ii) no part, in sth.; to dissociate oneself from (an action, s.o.'s fate, etc.); to hold aloof from (a matter); to ignore (s.o., sth.); **il semble se d. de l'affaire,** he seems reluctant to take the matter up; **se d. de toute ambition,** to lay aside all ambition; **se d. de qch.,** to let a thing slide; **se d. de tout,** *F:* to let things slide.

désintérêt [dezɛ̃terɛ], *s.m.* disinterest, indifference.

désinterligner [dezɛ̃tɛrliɲe], *v.tr. Typ:* to unlead (type).

désintoxication [dezɛ̃tɔksikasjɔ̃], *s.f. Med:* detoxication.

désintoxiquer [dezɛ̃tɔksike], *v.tr. Med:* to detoxicate.

désinvagination [dezɛ̃vaʒinasjɔ̃], *s.f. Surg:* disinvagination.

désinvestir [dezɛ̃vestiːr], *v.tr.* to raise the blockade of (town).

se désinvestir d'une fonction, to lay aside, give up, an office.

désinvestiture [dezɛ̃vestityːr], *s.f. Adm:* dismissal (of a magistrate, etc.).

désinviter [dezɛ̃vite], *v.tr.* to cancel an invitation to (s.o.).

désinvolte [dezɛ̃vɔlt], *a.* (*a*) easy, free (gait); (*b*) airy, detached, unembarrassed, unselfconscious (manner); **d. à l'égard de qn,** off-hand with s.o.; (*c*) *F:* cheeky (answer); (*d*) rakish; (*e*) cavalier.

désinvolture [dezɛ̃vɔltyːr], *s.f.* (*a*) unconstraint, unselfconsciousness (in action, manner, conduct, etc.); ease, gracefulness (of movement) (*b*) free and easy manner; off-hand, airy, manner; breeziness; (*c*) lack of deference (towards one's elders, etc.); **avec d.,** in an off-hand manner, airily; cheekily, rakishly; **porter avec d. son chapeau sur l'oreille,** to wear one's hat at a rakish angle.

désionisation [dezjɔnizasjɔ̃], *s.f. Ph:* deionization.

désioniser [dezjɔnize], *v.tr. Ph:* to deionize.

désiphonner [desifɔne], *v.tr. Hyd.E:* to unsiphon (exhaust-pipe).

désir [deziːr], *s.m.* (*a*) desire, wish; **avoir un d. de qch.,** to have a desire for something; **exprimer le d. de faire qch.,** to express a wish, the wish, a desire, to do sth.; **un vif d. de qch.,** a longing for sth.; **d. de plaire,** wish to please; **grand d. de plaire,** anxiety to please; **ardent d. de qch.,** craving, longing, hunger, for sth.; **ardent d. de réussir,** eagerness to succeed; **éprouver le d. de faire qch.,** to feel the desire to do sth.; **accéder à un d.,** to grant a request; **sur, selon, le d. de son père,** at, by, his father's wish; **cela s'est fait à l'encontre de mon d.,** it was done against my wishes; **prendre ses désirs pour des réalités,** to be a wishful thinker, to indulge in wishful thinking; (*b*) **d. sexuel,** sexual desire; **éveiller le d. chez qn,** to arouse (desire in) s.o.

désirable [dezirabl], *a.* desirable, to be desired; **peu d.,** undesirable.

Désiré [dezire], *Pr.n.m.* Desiderius.

désirer [dezire], *v.tr.* **1.** to desire, want; to wish for (sth.); to be desirous of (sth.); **d. ardemment qch.,** to yearn, long, for sth.; to crave for sth.; *F:* to hanker after sth.; to be eager for sth.; **c'est de l'argent qu'il désire,** *F:* money is what he is after; **d. qch. de qn,** to want sth. of, from, s.o.; **je désire le voir,** I want, wish, desire, to see him; I am anxious to see him; **cela me fit d. de le voir,** this made me desirous of seeing him, this made me want to see him; **je désire qu'il vienne,** I want him to come; *F:* **il se fait d.,** he is keeping you, me, us, waiting; **il est à désirer que . . .,** it is to be desired, it is desirable, that . . .; **cela laisse (un peu) à d.,** it is not quite satisfactory, not quite up to the mark; **cela laisse beaucoup à d.,** it leaves much to be desired, there is much room for improvement; **cela ne laisse rien à d.,** it is all that one could wish for, it is quite satisfactory; **je n'avais plus rien à d.,** I had nothing left to wish for; **que désirez-vous?** what would you like? *Com:* **madame désire . . .?** what can I show you, madam? **je peux le faire si je le désire,** it is open to me to do so; **elle désirait vivement accepter cette offre,** *F:* she was all for accepting this offer. **2. d. une femme,** to lust after, for, a woman.

désireux, -euse [dezirø, -øːz], *a.* desirous; **d. de qch.,** desirous of, eager for, sth.; **d. de plaire,** eager to please.

désistement [dezistəmɑ̃], *s.m.* desistance (de, from); (*a*) *Jur:* waiver (of claim); withdrawal (of suit); confession of defence, of plea; *retraxit;* (*b*) withdrawal of one's candidature; standing down; (*c*) recession.

désister (se) [sədeziste], *v.pr.* (*a*) *Jur:* **se d. d'une poursuite,** to desist from, withdraw, an action; **se d. d'une demande,** to waive a claim; (*b*) *abs.* **se désister,** to withdraw (one's candidature) (**en faveur de,** in favour of); to stand down.

desman [dɛsmɑ̃], *s.m. Z:* desman; **d. musqué,** muskrat.

desmidiales [dɛsmidjal], *s.f.pl. Algae:* Desmidiales.

desmine [dɛsmin], *s.f. Miner:* desmine.

desmode [dɛsmɔd], *s.m. Z:* desmodus, American vampire bat.

desmodium [dɛsmɔdjɔm], *s.m. Bot:* Desmodium; *pl. desmodiums.*

desmodontes [dɛsmɔdɔ̃ːt], *s.m.pl. Moll:* Desmodonta.

desmodromique [dɛsmɔdrɔmik], *a. Mec:* positive (drive).

desmognathe [dɛsmɔgnat], *s.m. Z:* desmognathus.

desmographie [dɛsmɔgrafi], *s.f. Anat:* desmography.

desmolase [dɛsmɔlɑːz], *s.f. Biol:* desmolase.

desmologie [dɛsmɔlɔʒi], *s.f. Anat:* desmology.

desmolyse [dɛsmɔliːz], *s.f. Ch:* desmolysis.

desmoncus [dɛsmɔ̃kys], *s.m. Bot:* Desmoncus.

desmotomie [dɛsmɔtɔmi], *s.f. Surg:* desmotomy.

desmotropie [dɛsmɔtrɔpi], *s.f. Ch:* desmotropism, desmotropy.

désobéir [dezɔbeiːr], *v.ind.tr.* to disobey; **d. à qn,** to disobey s.o.; **d. à une règle, à un ordre,** to break a rule, an order; *may be used in the passive;* **mes ordres ont été désobéis,** my orders were disobeyed; **je ne veux pas être désobéi,** I won't be disobeyed.

désobéissance [dezɔbeisɑ̃ːs], *s.f.* **1.** disobedience; **d. à un ordre,** disobedience of an order; **d. à une règle,** disregard for, breaking of, a rule; **d. à qn,** disobedience to s.o. **2.** act of disobedience.

désobéissant [dezɔbeisɑ̃], *a.* disobedient (à, to).

désobligeamment [dezɔbliʒamɑ̃], *adv.* (*a*) disobligingly; (*b*) disagreeably, unkindly.

désobligeance [dezɔbliʒɑ̃ːs], *s.f.* (*a*) disobligingness; (*b*) disagreeableness, unkindness (**envers,** to).

désobligeant, -ante [dezɔbliʒɑ̃, -ɑ̃ːt], *a.* (*a*) disobliging; (*b*) disagreeable, unkind, ungracious, offensive (person, manner, words, etc.) (**envers,** to); **comparaison d.,** invidious comparison.

désobliger [dezɔbliʒe], *v.tr.* (**je désobligeai(s); n. désobligeons**) **1.** to disoblige (s.o.), to be disobliging to (s.o.). **2.** to offend; **j'ai accepté son invitation pour ne pas le d.,** I accepted his invitation so as not to offend him, displease him, in order not to hurt his feelings; **ne riez pas, vous me désobligeriez,** don't laugh, I should take it unkindly, I should resent it.

désobstruant [dezɔpstryɑ̃], **désobstructif, -ive** [dezɔpstryktif, -iːv], a. & s.m. Med: deobstruent, aperient.

désobstruction [dezɔpstryksjɔ̃], s.f. removal of obstructions (from sth.); freedom from obstructions.

désobstruer [dezɔpstrye], v.tr. to remove obstructions from (sth.); to clear, free, (sth.) of obstructions; to clear (pipe, etc.).

désobusage [dezobyza:ʒ], s.m. bomb, shell, clearance; **équipe de d.**, bomb disposal squad.

désobuser [dezobyze], v.tr. to clear (wood, battlefield, etc.) of shells.

désoccupation [dezɔkypasjɔ̃], s.f. Lit: want of occupation, idleness.

désoccupé [dezɔkype], a. Lit: unoccupied, idle.

désodée [desode], a. Med: sodium free (diet, etc.).

désodorisant [dezodorizɑ̃], a. & s.m. Hyg: deodorant; **bâtonnet d.**, deodorant stick.

désodorisation [dezodorizasjɔ̃], s.f. deodorization; sweetening (of air of a room, etc.).

désodoriser [dezodorize], v.tr. to deodorize; to sweeten (the air of a room, the breath, etc.).

désodoriseur [dezodorizœ:r], s.m. Food Ind: deodorizing apparatus.

désœuvré [dezœvre, -øvre], a. unoccupied, idle; **me trouvant d.**, finding myself with nothing to do, F: at a loose end; **il errait le long des quais**, at a loose end, having nothing better to do, he wandered along the riverside; **les riches désœuvrés**, the idle rich; s. **les désœuvrés**, people with nothing to do.

désœuvrement [dezœvrəmɑ̃], s.m. idleness; **par d.**, to kill time, having nothing better to do, for want of occupation, of something to do.

désœuvrer [dezœvre, -øvre], v.tr. to take away (s.o.'s) occupation; to reduce (s.o.) to idleness.

désolant [dezolɑ̃], a. distressing, sad, disheartening (news, etc.); F: **un enfant d.**, a tiresome, provoking, child.

désolation [dezolasjɔ̃], s.f. desolation. 1. (a) devastation, laying waste; (b) desolateness (of region, etc.). 2. grief, sorrow, affliction; **être plongé dans la d.**, to be plunged in grief; **cri de d.**, desolate cry, disconsolate cry.

désolé [dezole], a. 1. (a) desolate, dreary (region, etc.); (b) devastated (country, etc.). 2. very sorry; grieved, disconsolate; sore at heart; **nous sommes désolés d'apprendre . . .**, we regret very much to hear . . .; **avoir l'air d.**, (i) to look heartily sorry; (ii) to have a woe-begone look; **je suis d. de vous déranger**, I hate to trouble you.

désoler [dezole], v.tr. to desolate. 1. to devastate, ravage, lay waste (country, etc.). 2. to afflict, distress, grieve (s.o.); **son échec à l'examen l'avait désolé**, he was very upset, F: cut up, at his failure in the exam.

se désoler, to grieve; **ne vous désolez pas comme cela**, do not grieve so; F: don't be so upset; P: don't take on so.

désolidariser [desolidarize], v.tr. to disunite; to separate (parts); to unmesh, disengage (gears); Pol: **d. un parti**, to break the solidarity of a party, to loosen the ties that keep a party together.

se désolidariser, **se d. de, d'avec, ses collègues**, to break (one's ties) with one's colleagues, to go one's own way; **se d. d'une cause**, to withdraw one's support from a cause.

désoperculateur [dezopɛrkylatœ:r], s.m. Ap: knife for uncapping (honeycomb).

désoperculation [dezopɛrkylasjɔ̃], s.f. Ap: uncapping (of comb).

désoperculer [dezopɛrkyle], v.tr. Ap: to uncap (honeycomb).

désopilant [dezopilɑ̃], a. screamingly funny, highly amusing, mirth-provoking, side-splitting.

désopiler [dezopile], v.tr. Med: A: to open, relieve (spleen, liver); F: **d. la rate à qn**, to provoke s.o.'s mirth.

se désopiler, F: to laugh immoderately, to shake with laughter.

désorber [dezɔrbe], v.tr. to desorb.

désorbité [dezɔrbite], a. A: removed from one's sphere; in unfamiliar surroundings; like a fish out of water.

désordonné [dezɔrdɔne], a. (a) disordered (ranks, etc.); disorganized (life, action); reckless (expenditure); immoderate (appetite); inordinate (pride); Mil: ragged (fire); **maison désordonnée**, (i) untidy house; (ii) ill-managed house; **courir par bonds désordonnés**, to run helter-skelter; (b) (of person) (i) disorganized; (ii) untidy; (iii) disorderly; **ménagère désordonnée**, happy-go-lucky housekeeper; (c) disorderly, dissolute (person, life, etc.).

désordonnément [dezɔrdɔnemɑ̃], adv. in a disorderly, ill-regulated, manner.

désordonner [dezɔrdɔne], v.tr. to throw (sth.) into disorder, into confusion.

se désordonner, to fall into disorder, into confusion.

désordre [dezɔrdr], s.m. 1. (a) disorder, confusion, chaos; **le d. de sa chambre**, the untidiness of his room; **d. artistique**, artistic disarray; **tout est en d.**, everything is in disorder, out of order, in confusion, at sixes and sevens; **cheveux en d.**, tangled, untidy hair; **mettre qch. en d.**, to turn sth. upside down; **mettre le d. partout**, to turn the place into a bear garden; **mettre le d. dans les rangs**, to throw the ranks into disorder, into confusion; (b) Med: **d. nerveux**, nervous disorder; **désordres dus à la dentition**, ailments due to teething. 2. disorderliness, licentiousness, evil-living, disorderly life. 3. pl. disturbances, riots; **de graves désordres ont éclaté**, serious disturbances have broken out.

désorganisateur, -trice [dezɔrganizatœ:r, -tris]. 1. a. disorganizing. 2. s. disorganizer; upsetter (of plans, etc.).

désorganisation [dezɔrganizasjɔ̃], s.f. disorganization.

désorganiser [dezɔrganize], v.tr. to disorganize (society, system, etc.); **d. une armée**, to throw an army into confusion; **d. les plans de qn**, to upset s.o.'s plans.

se désorganiser, to become disorganized, to fall into confusion; F: to go to pieces.

désorientation [dezɔrjɑ̃tasjɔ̃], s.f. 1. confusion, uncertainty, as to one's bearings; loss of bearings. 2. F: confusion, bewilderment.

désorienté [dezɔrjɑ̃te], a. F: puzzled, bewildered, at a loss; lost; **être tout d.**, to have lost one's bearings, to be all at sea, in a maze, at a loss; **je suis tout d.**, I don't know where I am; **être, se trouver, d.**, to lose one's bearings; **le monde est d.**, the times are out of joint.

désorienter [dezɔrjɑ̃te], v.tr. 1. (a) to make (s.o.) lose his bearings, to disorientate (s.o.); (b) to throw (compass, instrument) out of adjustment. 2. F: to disconcert, bewilder; to put (s.o.) out.

se désorienter. 1. to lose one's bearings, to get out of one's reckoning. 2. F: to get confused.

désormais [dezɔrmɛ], adv. henceforward, henceforth, from now on(wards); hereafter, for the future, in future; now; **une belle récolte est d. assurée**, a good harvest is now assured.

désorption [dezɔrpsjɔ̃], s.f. Ch: desorption.

désossé [dezose]. 1. a. (a) boned; (b) F: (i) flabby, boneless (person); (ii) supple (person). 2. s.m. P: acrobat.

désossement [dezosmɑ̃], s.m. boning (of meat, etc.).

désosser [dezose], v.tr. 1. to bone (meat, fish). 2. F: to dissect (sentence, book).

se désosser, to become (i) flabby, (ii) supple.

désoufrage [desufra:ʒ], s.m. desulphur(iz)ation.

désoufrer [desufre], v.tr. to desulphur (wool); to desulphurate, desulphurize (ore, etc.).

désourdir [dezurdi:r], v.tr. to unweave.

désoxy- [dezɔksi-], pref. deoxy-.

désoxydant [dezɔksidɑ̃], Ch: 1. a. deoxidizing. 2. s.m. Metall: etc: deoxidizer.

désoxydation [dezɔksidasjɔ̃], s.f. Ch: Metall: deoxidation, deoxidization.

désoxyder [dezɔkside], v.tr. Ch: Metall: to deoxidate, deoxidize; to reduce (oxide).

se désoxyder, Ch: to lose its oxygen.

désoxygénant [dezɔksiʒenɑ̃], a. deoxygenating (agent).

désoxygénation [dezɔksiʒenasjɔ̃], s.f. deoxygenation.

désoxygéner [dezɔksiʒene], v.tr. (je désoxygène, n. désoxygénons; je désoxygénerai) to deoxygenize.

désoxyribonucléique [dezɔksiribɔnykleik], a. Ch: Biol: **acide d.**, desoxyribonucleic acid.

despatch money [dispatʃmœni], s.m. Nau: Com: despatch money.

despotat [despɔta], s.m. (i) rank of despot; (ii) despotate.

despote [dɛspɔt], s.m. despot, absolute ruler; a. **prince d.**, despotic prince; **homme, femme, d.**, despotic man, woman.

despotique [dɛspɔtik], a. despotic (power, etc.).

despotiquement [dɛspɔtikmɑ̃], adv. despotically.

despotisme [dɛspɔtism], s.m. despotism; **d. éclairé**, enlightened despotism.

desquamatif, -ive [dɛskwamatif, -iːv], a. Med: desquamative.

desquamation [dɛskwamasjɔ̃], s.f. Med: desquamation; F: peeling (of skin); Geol: **d. en écailles**, exfoliation.

desquamer [dɛskwame], v.tr. Med: to make (the skin) desquamate, F: to scale, peel.

se desquamer, to desquamate, to scale off, to peel.

desquels, desquelles [dekɛl]. See LEQUEL.

dessablage [desabla:ʒ], s.m., **dessablement** [desabləmɑ̃], s.m. removing of sand, desanding.

dessabler [desable], v.tr. to remove sand from, to desand, (path, river-bed, etc.); to clean (casting, etc.); s.a. TONNEAU 1.

dessableur [desablœ:r], s.m. Civ.E: desanding pool.

dessaigner [desɛɲe], v.tr. Leath: to clean (skins when they have left the slaughter-house).

dessaisir [desezi:r, -se-], v.tr. 1. to let go, release (captive, etc.). 2. Jur: **d. qn de qch.**, to disseize, disseise, dispossess, deprive, s.o. of sth. 3. Nau: to unlash.

se dessaisir de qch. 1. to relinquish sth.; to part with, give up, sth. 2. **le tribunal s'est dessaisi de l'affaire**, the court decided not to proceed with the case.

dessaisissement [desɛzismɑ̃, -se-], s.m. 1. Jur: disseisin, dispossession. 2. **d. de qch.**, relinquishing, relinquishment, of sth.; parting with sth., giving sth. up.

dessalage [desala:ʒ], s.m., **dessalaison** [desalɛzɔ̃], s.f. 1. removal of salt (from fish, meat, etc.); soaking. 2. F: **dessalage (d'un canot)**, capsizing (of small boat).

dessalé [desale], a. 1. (of meat, fish, etc.) freed of salt. 2. F: awake, sharp (person); up to snuff. 3. s. F: **un d., une dessalée**, man, woman, of the world.

dessalement [desalmɑ̃], s.m. Ind: freshening, desalination, desalinization (of sea water).

dessaler [desale], v.tr. 1. to remove the salt from (meat, fish), to de-salt, freshen (sea water, salt fish, etc.); to put (meat, fish) in soak. 2. F: **d. qn**, to sharpen s.o.'s wits, to put s.o. up to a thing or two.

se dessaler, F: to learn a thing or two.

dessaleur [desalœ:r], s.m. Oil Ind: desalter.

dessalure [desaly:r], s.f. freshening (of sea-water).

dessangler [desɑ̃gle], v.tr. to ungirth, take the girths off (horse); abs. to slacken girths.

se dessangler, F: to unfasten, undo, one's clothes (esp. tight uniform, etc.).

dessaouler [desule] = DESSOULER.

desséchant [deseʃɑ̃]. 1. a. drying, desiccating; **vent d.**, parching wind. 2. s.m. desiccant.

desséché [deseʃe], a. 1. dry (pond, bed of torrent). 2. dry, withered; **branche desséchée**, withered, sapless, branch; **bras d.**, withered, wasted, arm. 3. F: shrivelled, seared (heart).

dessèchement [deseʃmɑ̃], s.m. 1. drying up (of pond); drainage, reclamation (of land). 2. seasoning, drying (of wood); desiccation (of cereals). 3. withering (of plants); emaciation (of the body); withering (of arm, etc.).

dessécher [deseʃe], v.tr. (je dessèche, n. desséchons; je dessécherai) 1. to dry up (ground); to reclaim, drain (land). 2. to season (wood); to desiccate (food stuffs); **d. (la viande) au soleil**, to jerk. 3. (a) (of wind, heat) to wither (plant); to dry (the skin); to parch (the mouth); (b) (of illness, etc.) to emaciate (the body); to wither (limb); **corps desséché par la maladie**, body wasted by disease; (c) (of vice, etc.) to sear (the heart); (d) **d. le cœur de qn**, to harden s.o.'s heart.

se dessécher. 1. to dry up, to become dry; (of pond, etc.) to go dry; (of pers.) to become insensitive. 2. to wither; to waste away.

dessécheur, -euse [deseʃœ:r, -øːz], s. 1. (pers.) (a) Ind: drier; (b) s.m. drainer of marshland. etc.). 2. s.f. Ind: **dessécheuse**, desiccator, drier.

dessein [desɛ̃], s.m. 1. design, plan, scheme, project; **changer de d.**, to change one's plans; **ruiner les desseins de qn**, to upset, thwart, s.o.'s schemes; **marcher sans d.**, to walk about aimlessly. 2. intention, purpose; **avoir le d. de faire qch.**, to have the intention of, to purpose, doing sth.; **former le d. de faire qch.**, to plan to do sth.; **accomplir son d.**, to accomplish, effect, one's purpose; **dans ce dessein. . .**, with this intention . . .; **dans le d. de l'avertir**, with a view to, for the purpose of, warning him; **sans d.**, unintentionally; **avec d.**, designedly; **à d.**, on purpose, purposely, intentionally, advisedly; **à d. de faire qch.**, in order to do sth.; **à d. que + sub.**, to the end that (sth. should be done).

desseller [desele, -se-], v.tr. to unsaddle (horse); abs. to off-saddle.

dessemeler [desəmle], v.tr. (je dessemelle, n. dessemelons; je dessemellerai) to remove the soles from (shoes).

desserrage [desɛra:ʒ], s.m. 1. (a) loosening; (b) easing, slackening, releasing, release; (c) unclamping. 2. looseness, slackness (of part).

desserre [desɛːr], *s.f. F:* untying of one's purse strings; *P:* forking out; **être dur à la d.,** to be close-fisted, stingy.
desserré [desere], *a.* loose, slack (belt, nut, etc.).
desserrement [desɛrmɑ̃], *s.m.* looseness, slackness.
desserrer [desere], *v.tr.* to loosen (screw); to ease, slacken (belt, knot); to unclamp; to unscrew (nut); to unclench (fist, teeth); to release (brake); **d. son étreinte, un blocus,** to relax one's hold, a blockade; **d. son cœur,** to unbosom oneself; *Typ:* **d. la forme,** to unlock the form; *F:* **je n'ai pas desserré les dents, les lèvres,** I did not open my lips, did not utter a word; **d. sa ceinture d'un cran,** to slacken, loosen, one's belt another hole.
se desserrer. 1. to work loose. **2.** (*of grip, etc.*) to relax.
dessert[1] [desɛːr, dɛ-], *s.m.* dessert (*in Fr. consisting of sweets, cheese, fruit, etc.*); **service à d.,** dessert service; **vin de d.,** dessert wine.
dessert[2]. *See* DESSERVIR[1].
desserte[1] [desɛrt, dɛ-], *s.f.* **1.** *Ecc:* duties of an officiating clergyman; care (of parish). **2.** (*a*) **d. d'un port par voies ferrées,** railway service to a port; **chemin de d.,** (i) service road, *U.S:* frontage road; (ii) cart track; **voie de d.,** railway line connecting up with a locality; (*b*) *Trans: etc:* service area.
desserte[2], *s.f.* **1.** *A:* broken meat; remains of food. **2.** (*a*) dumb-waiter, butler's tray; (*b*) sideboard; (*c*) **table d. roulante,** dinner wagon.
dessertir [desɛrtiːr], *v.tr.* to unset (precious stone).
se dessertir, (*of stone*) to come unset.
dessertissage [desɛrtisaːʒ], *s.m.* unsetting (of stone).
desservant [desɛrvɑ̃], *s.m. Ecc:* priest in charge (of chapel of ease).
desservir[1] [desɛrviːr], *v.tr.* (*conj. like* SERVIR) **1.** *Ecc:* to minister to (chapel of ease, etc.). **2.** (*of railways, steamers, etc.*) to serve; **localité desservie par deux lignes,** district served by two lines; **train qui ne dessert pas toutes les gares,** train that does not stop at every station; **ce bateau dessert Cherbourg,** this boat calls at Cherbourg; **car qui dessert quinze petites villes,** bus that connects up fifteen small towns; **chemin qui dessert la fabrique,** road that connects up with the works; **région desservie par une compagnie d'électricité,** district served, supplied, by an electricity company; **région desservie: la région parisienne,** service area: the Paris district; **quai desservi par quatre grues,** wharf equipped with four cranes.
desservir[2], *v.tr.* (*conj. like* SERVIR) **1.** to clear (the table); *abs.* to clear away; to remove the cloth. **2. desservir qn,** to be a bad friend to s.o.; to do s.o. a disservice, an ill-turn; *F:* to play s.o. a dirty trick; **d. qn auprès de qn,** to carry tales to s.o. about s.o.; **les fêtes ont été desservies par le mauvais temps,** the bad weather militated against the festivities, spoilt the festivities; **il s'est desservi lui-même,** he has been his own worst enemy; **cela desservirait mes intérêts,** it would be detrimental to my interests.
dessévage [desevaːʒ], *s.m. For. Ind:* removal of the sap from tree trunks (after felling).
dessévér [desevé], *v.tr. For. Ind:* to remove the sap from tree trunks (after felling).
dessiccant [desikɑ̃, de-], *a. Ind:* desiccant.
dessiccateur [desikatœːr, de-], *s.m. Ind:* desiccator, drier.
dessiccatif, -ive [desikatif, -iːv, de-], *a.* desiccative, drying (process, etc.).
dessiccation [desikasjɔ̃, de-], *s.f. Ind:* desiccation, drying; seasoning (of wood); *Nat.Hist: Z:* dehydration.
dessillement [desij(ə)mɑ̃], *s.m. F:* opening of s.o.'s eyes (to sth.).
dessiller [desije], *v.tr.* **1.** *A:* to unseal (eyes of hawk). **2.** *F:* **d. les yeux à, de, qn,** to open s.o.'s eyes (to facts); to undeceive s.o.; **ses yeux furent dessillés, ses yeux se dessillèrent,** the scales fell from his eyes; his eyes were opened.
dessin [desɛ̃], *s.m.* **1.** (*a*) (art of) drawing, sketching; **d. à main levée,** freehand drawing; (*b*) drawing, sketch; **d. au trait,** outline drawing; **d. ombré,** shaded drawing; **d. linéaire,** linear, lineal, drawing, design; **d. à la plume,** pen-and-ink sketch; *Cin:* **d. animé,** motion-picture cartoon, animated cartoon; **d. humoristique,** cartoon; **d. publicitaire,** publicity drawing; **d. d'après nature,** drawing from life, from nature; **d. en vraie grandeur, en grandeur naturelle,** *F:* **d. grandeur nature,** full-size drawing; **d. d'après la bosse,** drawing from the round; **d. au crayon litho(graphique),** (lithographic) chalk drawing; *Lith:* **d. au trait,** line drawing, line work; **d. au fusain,** charcoal drawing; **d. au lavis, d. lavé,** wash(ed) drawing; *F:* **il vous faut un d.?** do you need a diagram? **2.** design, pattern; **d. d'ornement,** decorative design; **dessins de haute nouveauté,** designs, patterns, in the latest style; **d. bariolé, d. bigarré,** disrupted design, disrupted pattern (for camouflage, etc.); **étoffes à dessins,** patterned fabrics; figured materials. **3.** *Tchn:* (*a*) **(l'art du) d.,** draughtsmanship; **bureau de d.,** drawing office; **planche à d.,** drawing-board; **instruments de d.,** mathematical instruments; (*b*) draught, draft, drawing, plan (of building, machine, etc.); **d. industriel, d. de machine(s),** engineering drawing, machine drawing, mechanical drawing; **d. coté,** drawing showing dimensions, with dimensions marked on it; dimensioned drawing, sketch; **d. en coupe,** section drawing, sectional drawing, cut-away drawing; **d. de projet,** preliminary drawing; **d. d'exécution,** working drawing; **d. de montage,** assembly drawing; **d. d'ensemble,** general assembly drawing; *Mapm: etc:* **d. de lettres,** lettering.
dessinateur, -trice [desinatœːr, -tris], *s.* **1.** (*a*) sketcher, drawer; *F:* **d. de trottoir,** pavement-artist; (*b*) black-and-white artist; (*c*) cartoonist. **2.** designer (of wallpapers, etc.); dress-designer. **3.** *Tchn:* draughtsman, draftsman, -woman; pattern-drawer; **d. détaillant,** detail draughtsman; **d. d'études,** design draughtsman; **d. en architecture,** architectural draughtsman; **d. industriel,** mechanical draughtsman; **d. d'outillage,** tool designer; **d. lithographe,** lithographer draughtsman; **d. topographe,** topographical draughtsman.
dessiner [desine], *v.tr.* **1.** to draw, sketch; **d. qch. d'après nature,** to draw sth. from nature; **d. à l'encre, à la craie,** to draw in ink, in chalk; **d. qch. à l'échelle,** to draw sth. to scale; **d. qch. à grands traits,** to make a rough sketch of sth.; **d. au trait,** to draw, sketch, in outline; *Tchn:* **machine à d.,** draughting machine; **tableau mal dessiné,** picture out of drawing. **2.** to design (wall-paper, material, etc.); **jardins magnifiquement dessinés,** beautifully laid-out gardens. **3.** to show, delineate, outline (sth.); **les montagnes dessinent leur courbe sur le ciel,** the line of the mountains stands out against the sky; **vêtement qui dessine bien la taille,** garment that shows off the figure; **le littoral dessine une série de courbes,** the coast-line forms a series of curves; **visage bien dessiné,** finely chiselled face.
se dessiner, to stand out, take form; to be outlined; **les arbres se dessinent sur le ciel, à l'horizon,** the trees stand out, show up, are outlined, against the sky, on the horizon; **une forme se dessina dans l'obscurité,** a form loomed up in the darkness; **nos projets se dessinent,** our plans are taking shape.
dessolement [desɔlmɑ̃], *s.m. Agr:* change in crop rotation.
dessoler[1] [desɔle], *v.tr. Agr:* **d. une terre,** to change the rotation of crops on a piece of land.
dessoler[2], *v.tr.* to remove the sole (of a horse's hoof).
dessolure [desɔlyːr], *s.f.* removal of the sole (of a horse's hoof).
dessoucher [desuʃe], *v.tr. Agr:* to clear (ground) of tree stumps.
dessoucheur [desuʃœːr], *s.m.* rooter, stumper.
dessouder [desude], *v.tr.* **1.** to unsolder (sth.). **2.** to reopen (brazed or welded seam).
dessoudure [desudyːr], *s.f.* **1.** (*a*) unsoldering; (*b*) reopening (of welded seam). **2.** unsoldered, unbrazed, unwelded, part or seam.
dessoufrer [desufre], *v.tr.* = DÉSULFURER.
dessouler [desule]. **1.** *v.tr.* to sober (s.o.), to make (s.o.) sober. **2.** *v.i. & pr.* to become sober, to sober off; **quand il sera dessoulé,** when he is sober again; **il ne dessoule pas,** he is never sober; **dessoulez-vous!** come on, sober up!
dessous [dəsu]. **1.** *adv.* under(neath), below, beneath; **voilà une table, mettez vous d.,** here is a table, get underneath it; **mettre son adversaire d.,** to get one's opponent under; **marcher bras dessus bras d.,** to walk arm-in-arm; **vêtements de d.,** underclothing; **notre voisin de d.,** our neighbour in the flat below; **gare d.!** look out below! below there! *Nau:* **la barre d.!** down helm! helm alee! *adv.phr.* **en d.,** underneath; **placer qch. face en d.,** to lay sth. face down(wards); **regarder qn en d.,** to look at s.o. furtively, stealthily; **agir en d.,** to act in an underhand way; *Ten:* **servir par en d.,** to serve underhand; **service en d.,** underhand service; *s.a.* SENS 4. **2.** *s.m.* (*a*) lower part, underpart, bottom; **d. d'une table,** underpart of a table; **d. d'une assiette,** bottom of a plate; **d. d'assiette,** table-mat; **d. de carafe,** decanter stand; **d. de bouteille,** (i) bottle-mat; (ii) slider, coaster; **d. d'une étoffe,** wrong side of a material; *F:* **avoir le d.,** to get the worst of it, to be defeated; *F:* **être (tombé) dans le troisième, trente-sixième, d.,** (i) to be completely discredited; (ii) to be down and out; *Cost:* **d. de robe,** (under-)slip; *Metalw:* **d. d'étampe,** bottom swage; **d. de châssis,** drag; bottom part of flask; *abs.* **les d.,** (i) (*women's*) underclothing; *F:* undies; (ii) *Th:* below-stage; (*b*) *F:* **il y avait là un d. que je ne comprenais pas,** there was some mystery about it that I did not understand; **les d. de la politique,** the shady side of politics; *s.a.* CARTE 3, DESSOUS-DE-PLAT, DESSOUS-DE-BRAS, DESSOUS-DE-TABLE. **3.** *prep.* **blessure d. le sein,** wound under the breast; **chercher qch. dessus et d. la table,** to look for sth. on and underneath the table; *prep.phr.* **ses boucles ressortaient de d. son chapeau,** her curls peeped out from under her hat; *s.a.* AU-DESSOUS, CI-DESSOUS, LÀ-DESSOUS, PAR-DESSOUS.
dessous-de-bras [d(ə)sudbra], *s.m.inv.* dress preserver, dress shield.
dessous-de-plat [d(ə)sudpla], *s.m.inv.* dish-stand.
dessous-de-table [d(ə)sudtabl̥], *s.m.inv. F:* golden handshake; **verser un d.-de-t.,** to pay (s.o.) a bribe; (*in property transactions*) to pay a sum over and above the stated price, under the counter.
dessuintage [desɥɛ̃taːʒ], *s.m. Tex:* scouring (of wool).
dessuinter [desɥɛ̃te], *v.tr. Tex:* to scour (wool).
dessuinteuse [desɥɛ̃tøːz], *s.f. Tex:* scouring machine.
dessus [dəsy]. **1.** *adv.* above, over; (up)on (it, them); thereon; **l'un d., l'autre dessous,** one above, the other below; **votre mouchoir est tombé, ne marchez pas d.,** your handkerchief has fallen, don't tread on it; **on a répandu de l'encre d.,** someone has spilt ink over it; **j'ai failli lui tirer d.,** I nearly fired at him, nearly shot him; **la terre et tout ce qu'il y a d.,** the earth and all that is thereon; **mettre la main d.,** to lay hands on it, on them; *F:* **vous avez mis le doigt d.,** you have hit the nail on the head; **un vêtement de d.,** an outer garment, a top garment; *Nau:* **avoir le vent d.,** to be aback; **se mettre vent d., mettre (les voiles d'artimon) vent d.,** to bagpipe; *adv.phr.* **en d.,** at the top, on top, above; **le couteau est tombé le tranchant en d.,** the knife fell with the edge up, with the edge uppermost; **mettre les meilleures pommes (en, au) d.,** to put the best apples on top; *s.a.* SENS 4. **2.** *s.m.* (*a*) top, upper part (of table, etc.); *Mus:* treble part, soprano; **d. de plateau,** tray-cloth; **d. de buffet,** sideboard cover, strip; **d. d'assiette,** doily; **d. de lit,** coverlet, bedspread; **d. de cheminée,** mantelpiece; **d. de porte,** overdoor; *Harn:* **d. du nez,** nose-band; *Metalw:* **d. d'étampe,** top swage; **d. de châssis,** cope; top part of flask; *Th:* **les d.,** rigging-loft, flies; **le d. d'une étoffe,** the right side of a material; **le d. de la main,** the back of the hand; *F:* **le d. du panier,** the pick of the basket; (*b*) **avoir le d.,** to have the upper hand, the whip hand; to have the best of it, the best of the argument; *F:* to be top dog; **prendre le d.,** (i) to rally (from illness); (ii) to overcome one's feelings (of sorrow, etc.); **prendre le d. de qn,** to take the lead, to get the advantage, over s.o.; *Nau:* **avoir le d. du vent,** to have the weather-gauge. **3.** *prep.* **chercher qch. d. et dessous la table,** to look for sth. on and beneath the table; *prep.phr.* **de d.,** from, off; **arracher le bandeau de d. les yeux de qn,** to tear the bandage from somebody's eyes; **tomber de d. sa chaise,** to fall off one's chair; **elle ne leva pas les yeux, de d. son ouvrage,** she did not lift her eyes from, take her eyes off, her work; **enlevez ça de d. mon chapeau!** take that off my hat! *s.a.* AU-DESSUS, CI-DESSUS, LÀ-DESSUS, PAR-DESSUS.
dessus-de-lit [dəsydli], *s.m.inv.* coverlet, bedspread.
dessus-de-plat [dəsydpla], *s.m.inv.* dish cover.
déstalinisation [destalinizasjɔ̃], *s.f. Pol:* destalinization.
déstaliniser [destalinize], *v.tr. Pol:* to destalinize.
destin [dɛstɛ̃], *s.m.* fate, destiny; **d. inéluctable,** ineluctable doom; **se soumettre à son d.,** to submit to one's fate, to one's lot; to accept the inevitable.
destinataire [dɛstinatɛːr], *s.m. & f.* addressee, recipient (of letter, etc.); consignee (of goods); payee (of money order).
destinateur, -trice [dɛstinatœːr, -tris], *s.* sender.

destination [dɛstinasjɔ̃], *s.f.* **1.** destination; **lieu de d.,** place of destination; **arriver à sa d.,** to arrive at one's destination; **lettre arrivée à d.,** letter come to hand; **ce paquet est à votre d.,** this parcel is addressed to you; **trains à d. de Paris,** trains for, (running) to, Paris; **navire à d. de Bordeaux,** ship bound for, making for, Bordeaux; **articles à d. de la province et de l'étranger,** goods for consignment to the provinces and abroad; **lignes aériennes à d. ou en provenance de l'Amérique,** air-lines to and from America. **2.** destination, intended purpose (of building, sum of money, etc.); *Jur:* **immeubles par d.** = landlord's fixtures.

destinée [destine], *s.f.* **1.** (*a*) destiny; **envier la d. de qn,** to envy s.o.'s lot; **abréger sa d.,** to cut short one's life; **unir sa d. à celle de qn,** (i) to throw in one's lot with s.o.; (ii) to marry s.o.; (*b*) *pl.* destinies, fortunes. **2.** = DESTIN.

destiner [destine], *v.tr.* **1.** to destine; to fix the destiny of (s.o.); **destiné à devenir célèbre,** destined to become famous; **être destiné à mourir sur l'échafaud,** to be fated, doomed, to die on the scaffold. **2.** (*a*) **d. qch. à qn,** to intend, mean, sth. for s.o.; **j'avais destiné ce cadeau à un ami,** I had intended this gift for a friend; **c'est à vous qu'il avait destiné le coup,** he meant the blow for you; **la balle vous était destinée,** the bullet was aimed at you; **prix destiné à honorer la mémoire de qn,** prize intended, designed, to commemorate s.o.; **renseignements destinés aux voyageurs,** information for travellers; (*b*) **il avait destiné son fils au barreau,** he had intended his son for the bar, had intended that his son should be called to the bar; (*c*) **d. une somme d'argent à un achat,** to allot, assign, a sum of money to a purchase; **je n'avais pas destiné ce roman à l'écran, à être filmé,** I had not intended this novel for the screen, had not intended this novel to be filmed.

se destiner à qch., to intend to take up sth. (as a profession); **il se destine au barreau, à la médecine,** he intends to go to the bar, to be a doctor; **il se destine aux beaux-arts,** he means to go in for art.

destinézite [destinezit], *s.f. Miner:* destinezite.

destituable [dɛstitɥabl], *a.* dismissible, liable to dismissal.

destitué [dɛstitɥe], *a. A:* without; deprived (**de,** of); lacking (**de,** in); **d. de sens commun,** totally lacking in common sense.

destituer [dɛstitɥe], *v.tr.* to dismiss, discharge (s.o.); to remove (official) from office; **d. un général de son commandement,** to relieve a general of his command; **d. un général,** to strip a general of his rank.

destitution [dɛstitysjɔ̃], *s.f.* dismissal (of official, etc.); removal (of officer).

destrier [dɛstrie], *s.m. A:* charger, war-horse, *A:* destrier.

destroyer [dɛstrwajœːr, -e], *s.m. Nav:* destroyer.

destructeur, -trice [dɛstryktœːr, -tris]. **1.** *a.* destroying (agent, etc.); destructive (child, war, etc.). **2.** *s.* destroyer, destructor. **3.** *s.m.* **d. de déchets,** refuse-destructor.

destructibilité [dɛstryktibilite], *s.f.* destructibility.

destructible [dɛstryktibl], *a.* destructible.

destructif, -ive [dɛstryktif, -iːv], *a.* destructive (**de,** of).

destruction [dɛstryksjɔ̃], *s.f.* **1.** destruction, destroying; disposal; scrapping (of a ship); **d. des ordures ménagères, des déchets atomiques,** disposal of household refuse, of atomic waste; *Mec.E:* **essai (d'endurance) jusqu'à d.,** destruction test, test to destruction; *Mil:* **d. des projectiles non éclatés,** destruction, disposal, of unexploded projectiles, of blind projectiles; *F:* destruction of duds. **2.** *Mil:* (*a*) demolition (by blasting, etc.); **avant de se retirer, l'ennemi procéda à de vastes destructions,** before retreating the enemy carried out widespread demolitions; **d. méthodique,** deliberate demolition; **d. sommaire,** hasty demolition; **dispositif de d.,** demolition set; **détachement chargé, équipe chargée, des destructions,** demolition party, squad; *Atom.Ph:* **charge, mine, atomique de d.,** atomic demolition mine; (*b*) **potentiel (théorique) de d.,** (ideal) kill potential; **taux de d.,** kill rate; **probabilité de d.,** kill probability.

destructivité [dɛstryktivite], *s.f.* destructiveness.

désucrer [desykre], *v.tr.* to desugar(ize).

désuet, -ète [desɥɛ, -ɥɛt], *a.* obsolete (word); **théories désuètes,** antiquated, out-of-date, theories; **doctrine désuète,** *F:* shibboleth.

désuétude [desɥetyd], *s.f.* disuse, desuetude; **tomber en d.,** to fall, pass, into disuse; to become a dead letter; (*of right, etc.*) to lapse; (*of law*) to be no longer enforced, to fall into abeyance; **mot tombé en d.,** obsolete word.

désulfitage [desylfitaːʒ], *s.m.,* **désulfitation** [desylfitasjɔ̃], *s.f. Vit:* removal of the sulfite from (wine or must).

désulfiter [desylfite], *v.tr. Vit:* to remove the sulfite (from wine or must).

désulfurant [desylfyrɑ̃], *a.* desulphurizing.

désulfuration [desylfyrasjɔ̃], *s.f.* desulphurization.

désulfurer [desylfyre], *v.tr.* to desulphurize, desulphurate.

désuni [dezyni], *a.* (*of people*) disunited, at variance; (*of parts, etc.*) disjoined, disconnected; (*of manœuvre*) unco-ordinated; **maison, nation, désunie,** house, nation, divided against itself.

désunifier [dezynifje], *v.tr.* (*conj. like* UNIFIER) to disunite.

désunion [dezynjɔ̃], *s.f.* disunion (of people, etc.); disjunction, disconnection, taking apart (of parts, etc.); **jeter la d. dans une famille,** to bring disunion, dissension, into a family.

désunir [dezyniːr], *v.tr.* to disunite, divide (people, etc.); to disjoin, disconnect (parts, etc.); to take apart (planks); **questions qu'on ne peut pas d.,** questions that cannot be treated apart.

se désunir. 1. to become disunited, estranged. **2.** to lose coherence; (*of parts*) to come apart, to work loose.

desvrois, -oise [dɛvrwa, -waːz], *a. & s. Geog:* (native, inhabitant) of Desvres.

détachable[1] [detaʃabl], *a.* detachable.

détachable[2], *a.* from which stains can be removed.

détachage [detaʃaːʒ], *s.m.* removal of stains (from clothes, etc.).

détachant [detaʃɑ̃]. **1.** *a.* stain-removing. **2.** *s.m.* stain-remover.

détaché [detaʃe], *a.* **1.** (*a*) loose, detached (part); untethered (horse, etc.); (*b*) isolated (farm, etc.); *Mil:* **troupes détachées,** troops on detachment; (*c*) **être d. à un autre service,** to be seconded to another branch; (*d*) **vainqueur d.,** clear winner. **2.** *F:* indifferent, casual, detached, unconcerned (manner, etc.); **sourire d.,** detached smile, smile of unconcern; **d. de ce monde,** unworldly. **3.** *s.m. Mus:* staccato (bowing); **petit d.,** light staccato (with the point of the bow).

détachement [detaʃmɑ̃], *s.m.* **1.** detaching, cutting off (of sth.). **2.** indifference (**de,** to); lack of interest (**de,** in); detachment (**de,** from); **d. des richesses,** indifference to wealth; **d. de ce monde,** otherworldliness, unworldliness. **3.** (*a*) detaching, detachment, attachment (of body of troops, etc.); secondment, seconding (of person); **d. d'un officier à l'état-major,** detachment, attachment, of an officer to headquarters; **il est en d. à l'université de Cambridge,** he has been seconded to the University of Cambridge; (*b*) *Mil:* detachment, party, draft (of troops), *U.S:* detail; **d. de corvée,** fatigue party; **envoyer des troupes en d.,** to draft troops; **d. précurseur,** advance billeting, quartering, party; **d. postcurseur,** rear party; *U.S:* left-behind party; **d. de coup de main,** raiding party; *Nau: Navy:* **d. de visite, d'abordage,** boarding party.

détacher[1] [detaʃe], *v.tr.* to detach; (*a*) to (un)loose, to unfasten, untie, unbind, unlash; **d. un bateau,** to unfasten, unlash, a boat; **d. un wagon,** to uncouple a carriage or truck; **d. un cheval,** to untether a horse; **d. un nœud,** to untie, undo, a knot; **d. un rideau,** to take down, unhook, a curtain; **d. ses cheveux,** to unbind, loose, one's hair; **d. un chien de sa chaîne,** to loose a dog from its chain; *F:* **je ne peux pas en d. mes yeux,** I cannot take my eyes off it; (*b*) to separate, disjoin (**de,** from); **d. un morceau de qch. (de qch.),** to detach, cut off, pull off, break off, bite off, saw off, chisel off, a piece of sth. (from sth.); **d. un coupon d'une action,** to detach a coupon from a bond; **le coupon de ces actions se détache le 1**er **août,** this stock goes ex-coupon on the first of August; **d. un chèque du carnet,** to tear out a cheque from the book; **d. une fleur d'une plante,** to pick, pluck, a flower from a plant; **d. une brique d'un mur,** to remove a brick from a wall; **d. un bout de fil de la bobine,** to break off a piece of thread from the reel; **d. quelques chapitres d'un ouvrage,** to detach, extract, a few chapters from a work; (*c*) **d. qn de ses amis,** to detach, alienate, s.o. from his friends; **d. qn de ses opinions,** to wean s.o. away from his opinions; (*d*) *Mil: etc:* to detach, attach, second; **d. une compagnie d'un bataillon,** to detach a company from a battalion; **d. un officier auprès de qn,** to detach an officer to serve with s.o., to lend an officer to s.o.; **d. un officier à l'état-major de la 6ième division,** to detach an officer to, with, 6 Division headquarters; to attach an officer to 6 Division headquarters; *abs.* **d. une compagnie, un officier,** to detail, draft, a company; to detail, second, an officer; **fonctionnaire détaché à un autre service,** official temporarily attached, seconded, to another department; (*e*) *Art:* **d. une figure dans un tableau,** to make a figure stand out, to bring out a figure, in a picture; *Mus:* **d. les notes,** to detach the notes to play the notes *staccato*; (*f*) *F:* **d. un coup à qn,** to hit out at s.o.; (*of horse*) **d. une ruade, un coup de sabot, à qn,** to let fly a kick at s.o.

se détacher. 1. (*a*) (*of knot, etc.*) to come undone, unfastened, untied, loose; (*of planking, etc.*) to start; (*b*) (*of animal*) to slip its chain, to break loose. **2.** to break off, break loose, become detached; to separate; (*of parts*) to come apart; (*of paint*) to flake away, off; **une branche se détacha de l'arbre et tomba,** a branch broke off from the tree and fell; **un bouton s'est détaché,** a button has come off; **l'écrou se détacha,** the nut worked off, worked loose; **le plombage (de la dent) s'est détaché,** the stopping has come out; **l'écorce se détache,** the bark is peeling off the tree. **3.** (*a*) **se d. sa famille,** to separate, break away, from one's family; to become alienated from one's family; **se d. des plaisirs du monde,** to achieve detachment from worldly pleasures; to turn one's back on the world; **se d. (de qn),** to fall out of love (with s.o.); (*b*) **se d. (des rangs, etc.),** to step forward (from the ranks, etc.); **un petit groupe de coureurs se détacha en avant,** a small group, bunch, pulled ahead (of the field). **4. se d. sur un fond, sur l'horizon,** to stand out against a background, against the horizon; **se d. nettement sur qch.,** to stand out in sharp contrast to sth.

détacher[2], *v.tr.* to remove stains, spots, from (clothing, etc.); **terre à d.,** fuller's earth.

détacheur, -euse [detaʃœːr, -øːz], *s.m.* stain-remover.

détail [detaːj], *s.m.* **1.** (*a*) dividing up, cutting up (of cloth, meat, etc.); (*b*) *Com:* retail; **vendre au d.,** to sell (goods) retail, to retail (goods); **commerce en gros et au d.,** wholesale and retail business; **marchand au d.,** retail dealer, retailer; **prix de d.,** retail price. **2.** detail; small point; (*a*) **le d., les détails, d'un événement,** the details, particulars, of an event; **donner tous les détails,** to enter, go, into all the details, to give full particulars; **raconter qch. en d., entrer dans le d.,** to give a detailed, circumstantial, account of sth., to relate sth. in detail, to go into the details of sth., to go circumstantially into a matter; **donner un fait sans détails,** to state a fact barely; **se perdre dans les détails,** to go too deeply into details; **il connaît l'affaire dans tous ses détails,** *F:* he knows all the ins and outs of the matter, knows the business inside out; **il y a des questions de d. à régler,** there are points of detail to be settled; **le d. d'un compte,** the items of an account; **le d. d'une facture,** the breakdown of an invoice; (*b*) **détails techniques,** technical features; specifications; *Surv:* **levé des détails,** filling in, mapping, the detail; **d. de tracé (de route, etc.),** plotting detail (of road, etc.); *s.a.* REVUE. **3.** *Adm: Mil: etc:* (*a*) internal economy, interior economy; **service de d.,** executive duties, routine (administrative) work; **officier de détail,** quartermaster officer (= supply and pay officer); (*b*) special duty.

détaillant, -ante [detajɑ̃, -ɑ̃ːt], *s.* retailer, retail dealer.

détaillé [detaje], *a.* **1.** detailed, circumstantial (narrative, etc.); **donner un compte-rendu d. des événements,** to give a circumstantial account of the events, to go into every detail of the events. **2.** *Com:* **état d. de compte,** detailed, itemized, statement of account. **3.** *Tchn:* detailed; specific (of plan, diagram, etc.); *Surv:* **tracé d. (de route, etc.),** detailed plotting (of road, etc.); *Mec.E:* **description détaillée,** specification.

détailler [detaje], *v.tr.* **1.** (*a*) to divide up, cut up (piece of stuff, side of beef, etc.); (*b*) *Com:* to retail (goods), to sell (goods) retail; (*c*) *Com: abs.* to sell one's goods separately; **je ne détaille pas,** I sell them only in sets. **2.** (*a*) to detail, enumerate; to relate in detail; to itemize (account); *Th:* **d. les mots, la phrase,** to give full value to each word; (*b*) **d. qn,** to scrutinize s.o., to look s.o. up and down.

détaler [detale]. **1.** *v.tr. Com:* to pack up, put away (unsold goods that have been on show). **2.** *v.i.* (*a*) to decamp, to take oneself off; **la souris détala vers son trou,** the mouse scampered away, scurried off, to its hole; (*b*) *Nau:* to forge ahead.

détalinguer [detalɛ̃ge], *v.tr. Nau:* to unbend (cable); to unshackle (anchor, etc.).

dételler [detale], *v.tr. Hort:* to cut the suckers off (a plant).

détalonnage [detalɔnaːʒ], *s.m.* backing off (of tool).

détalonner [detalɔne], *v.tr.* to back off (tool).

détalonneur [detalɔnœːr], *s.m.* person who backs off tools.

détaper [detape], *v.tr. Navy: Artil:* to remove the tampion from, to unplug (gun).

détapisser [detapise], *v.tr.* (i) to take down the tapestry, (ii) to remove the wallpaper, from (a room).

détartrage [detartraːʒ], *s.m.* **1.** descaling (of boilers); *Dent:* scaling (of teeth). **2.** *I.C.E:* decarbonizing.

détartrant [detartrɑ̃], *s.m.* scaling substance.

détartrer [detartre], *v.tr.* to scale, fur, descale (boiler); *Dent:* to scale (teeth), to remove tartar from (teeth).

détartreur [detartrœːr], *s.m.* **1.** *Mch:* scaling device (for boilers); *a.* **outils détartreurs,** scaling tools. **2.** *Ind:* water-purification appliance or material. **3.** *Dent:* tooth scaler.

détatouage [detatwaːʒ], *s.m.* tattoo-removing.

détatouer [detatwe], *v.tr.* to remove the tattoo marks from (s.o.).

détaxation [detaksasjɔ̃], *s.f.* reduction, remission, of duty, of tax; *Rail:* reduction of carriage.

détaxe [detaks], *s.f.* **1.** remission of tax. **2.** de-controlling.

détaxer [detakse], *v.tr.* to take the duty, the tax, off (sth.); *Rail:* to reduce the carriage of (sth.); **d. (la viande),** to de-control the price of (meat).

détectable [detɛktabl̩], *a.* detectable.

détecter [detɛkte], *v.tr.* to detect.

détecteur, -trice [detɛktœːr, -tris]. I. *a. Tchn:* detecting, sensing; *Elcs:* **diode détectrice,** detector diode; **lampe détectrice,** detector valve; **relais d.,** sensing relay; **organe d.,** sensing device, sensing unit.

II. **détecteur,** *s.m. Tchn:* detector, locator; (*a*) **d. de fumée,** smoke detector, smoke indicator; **d. d'objets, de corps, métalliques,** metal detector, metal locator; *Mil:* **d. de mines,** mine detector; **d. (d'armes, d'engins) par le son,** sound detector; *Min:* **d. de grisou,** gas-detector, -indicator; *Jur:* **d. de mensonges,** lie detector; (*b*) *Mec.E:* **d. d'écarts,** deviation detector; **d. de fuites,** leak detector, leak sensor (in motor, in hydraulic or pressurization system); **d. de température, d. thermique,** thermal detector, thermal unit; **d. de défauts,** flaw detector; *Metall:* **d. de fissures,** crack detector; (*c*) *El.E: Elcs:* detector, sensor; demodulator; **d. à contact,** contact detector; **d. à cristal, d. à quartz,** crystal detector; **d. à lampe,** valve detector; **d. à tube à vide,** vacuum tube detector; **d. électronique,** radio detector, radio locator; **d. linéaire,** linear rectifier; **d. par effet Doppler,** Doppler indicator; **d. quadratique,** quadratic detector, square-law detector; **d. de fuites (de courant),** leak locator; **d. d'ondes,** wave detector; (*d*) *Av:* **d. d'angle d'incidence,** incidence probe; **d. d'erreur,** error sensor; (*e*) *Space:* **d. solaire,** sun-sensor (of satellite, etc.); **d. stellaire, d. d'étoiles,** star-sensor; **d. de Canope,** star Canopus sensor; (*f*) *Atom.Ph:* detector, monitor; **d. de radioactivité,** radioactive monitor; **d. de rayonnement, d. de radiations,** radiation detector, radiation monitor; **d. (de rayonnement, de radiations) à balayage, à courant, gazeux,** gas-flow (radiation) detector; **d. à scintillation(s),** scintillation detector; **d. à séparation élevée,** high-resolution, high-resolving power, detector; **d. d'expériences atomiques, nucléaires,** (i) atomic, nuclear, test detector; (ii) (*of satellite*) atomic, nuclear, test detection sensor; **d. d'explosions atomiques, nucléaires,** (i) atomic, nuclear, explosion detector; (ii) (*of satellite*) atomic, nuclear, explosion detection sensor.

détection [detɛksjɔ̃], *s.f.* detection, location; (*a*) *Elcs:* **appareil de détection,** detection device, detection set; sensor device; **tête de d.,** detection head, probe unit; **portée de d.,** detection range; **d. électromagnétique,** radio-location; **d. radar,** radar detection, radar location; **radar de d.,** search radar; **d. par le son,** sound detection; **d. sonore,** echo ranging; **d. quadratique,** parabolic detection, square-law detection; **d. sous-marine,** submarine detection, underwater detection, subaqueous detection; *W.Tel:* **d. grille,** grid detection, bias detection; **d. plaque,** anode detection; (*b*) *Mil: Navy:* **d. des mines,** mine detection; *Air Defence:* **réseau de d.,** detection net; **d. des avions volant bas,** detection of low-flying aircraft; **système de d. lointaine,** early warning system; (*c*) *Atom.Ph:* detection, monitoring.

détective [detɛktiːv], *s.m.* **1.** (*a*) detective; (*b*) **d. (privé),** private detective; *F:* private eye. **2.** *Phot:* box camera.

détectrice [detɛktris], *s.f. Elcs: etc:* detector; **d. à réaction, à régénération,** regenerative detector.

déteindre [detɛ̃ːdr̩], *v.* (*conj. like* TEINDRE) **1.** *v.tr.* to take the colour out of (sth.). **2.** *v.i. & pr.* (*a*) to fade, to lose colour; **ces étoffes se déteignent vite,** the colour soon comes out of these materials; (*b*) *Dy:* (*of colour*) to bleed; **se d. au lavage,** to run in the wash; **le ruban s'est déteint, a déteint, sur ma robe,** the colour of the ribbon has come off on my dress; **blue-jeans de coton déteint,** blue-jeans of washed-out, faded, cotton; *F:* **homme qui déteint sur tous ceux qui le fréquentent,** man who leaves his mark on, who influences, all who associate with him; *F:* **cela déteint sur eux,** it rubs off on them.

dételage [detlaːʒ], *s.m.* **1.** (*a*) unharnessing; (*b*) unhitching (of horses). **2.** uncoupling (of wag(g)ons).

dételer [detle], *v.tr.* (**je dételle, n. dételons; je détellerai**) **1.** (*a*) to unharness; (*b*) to unhitch, take out (horse(s)); to unhook (team); to unyoke (oxen); (*c*) *abs. F:* (*of elderly pers.*) to put off one's harness, to ease off. **2.** *Rail:* to uncouple (trucks, etc.).

détendeur [detɑ̃dœːr], *s.m.* (pressure-) reducing valve, pressure reducer; **d. de pression,** relief-, escape-valve; **d. de vapeur,** steam-relief valve, steam-reducing valve.

détendre [detɑ̃ːdr], *v.tr.* **1.** to slacken, relax, loosen (sth. that is taut); to unbend (bow); **d. un ressort,** (i) to let down, (ii) to release, a spring; **d. une corde,** to slacken a rope; **d. l'esprit,** (i) to relax, give relaxation to, the mind; (ii) to calm the mind; **d. les nerfs,** to steady the nerves; *F:* **d. le câble,** to ease off (from work); *s.a.* ARC 1. **2.** *A:* (*a*) to unhang, take down (curtains, hanging objects); (*b*) **d. un mur, un lit,** to take down the hangings of a wall, of a bed; (*c*) **d. une tente,** to strike a tent. **3.** *Mch:* **d. la vapeur,** to expand, cut off, the steam.

se détendre. 1. to become slack, to slacken, relax; **mes nerfs se détendent,** my nerves are calming down; **ses traits durs se détendaient graduellement,** his hard features gradually unbent; **se d. pendant une heure,** to relax for an hour; **sa colère se détend,** his anger is cooling down; **son visage se détendit dans un sourire,** his face relaxed into a smile; **le temps se détend,** the weather is becoming milder; **la situation se détend,** the situation is easing, is a little easier. **2.** (*of steam, etc.*) to expand.

détendu [detɑ̃dy], *a.* **1.** slack, slackened; **ressort d.,** weakened spring; *Av:* **aile détendue,** slack wing. **2.** relaxed (conversation, etc.).

détente [detɑ̃ːt], *s.f.* **1.** (*a*) relaxation, loosening, slackening (of sth. that is taut); relaxing (of muscles); *Ling:* off-glide; (*b*) easing (of political situation, etc.); **d. du temps,** mild spell of weather; **la d. après le travail du jour,** relaxation after the day's toil; **d. des esprits,** easing of minds; **une d. s'est produite (entre les deux nations),** the situation has become less strained, easier (between the two nations); there is an improvement in the situation, this has eased the situation; *Com:* **le coton a accusé une d.,** cotton was easier; *Mil:* **permission de d.,** furlough after strenuous service; (*c*) *Sm.a:* pull-off (of trigger); **d. douce, dure,** light, hard, pull-off; **à d. brusque,** with snap action; **arme dure à la d.,** fire-arm hard on the trigger; *F:* **personne dure à la d.,** close-fisted, stingy, person. **2.** (*a*) expansion (of steam, of gases); **machine à d.,** expansion steam-engine; **d. triple,** triple expansion; **marche à la d.,** expansive working; **soupape de d.,** expansion valve; **dispositif de d.,** (i) cut-off; (ii) expansion-gear, link-motion; **d. au dixième,** cut-off at 10% of stroke; *Ph:* **chambre à d. de Wilson,** Wilson's discharge cloud chamber; (*thermodynamics*) **d. de Joule-Thomson,** Joule-Thomson effect; (*b*) *I.C.E:* explosion stroke, power stroke; (*c*) *Mec.E:* **réservoir de d.,** blow-tank. **3.** (*a*) trigger (of pistol, rifle, etc.); **d.-gâchette,** *pl.* **détentes-gâchettes,** trigger and sear in one; **d. à double bossette,** double-pull trigger; **ressort de d.,** trigger-spring, release-spring; **mécanisme de d.,** firing mechanism; **presser, peser, sur la d.,** to pull, press, *F:* squeeze, the trigger; **lâcher la d.,** to let go the trigger; (*g*) *Artil:* firing gear, firing key.

détenteur, -trice [detɑ̃tœːr, -tris], *s.* **1.** (*a*) holder, custodian (of securities, etc.); holder (of challenge cup, etc.); **d. de titres,** stockholder scrip-holder; *Jur:* **tiers d.,** third holder (of mortgaged land, etc.); (*b*) owner (of copyright, etc.). **2.** withholder (of property, etc.).

détention [detɑ̃sjɔ̃], *s.f.* **1.** holding (of securities, etc.); possession (of fire-arms, etc.). **2.** detention, imprisonment, confinement (of s.o.); **d. arbitraire,** illegal imprisonment; **d. préventive,** detention under remand; **d. perpétuelle, à vie,** life imprisonment; **maison de d.,** (i) house of detention; (ii) (preventive) remand home. **3.** withholding (of property, etc.); **d. illégale des biens d'autrui,** unlawful possession of other people's property.

détenir [detniːr], *v.tr.* (*conj. like* TENIR) **1.** to hold, to be in possession of (sth.); **d. des titres en garantie,** to hold stocks as security; **d. un grade,** to hold a rank; **d. le record,** to hold the record; *A:* **d. la vie économique d'une région,** to control the economic life of a region. **2.** (*a*) to detain (s.o.); to keep (s.o.) prisoner, in captivity; (*b*) to withhold, keep back (property, etc.).

détenu, -e [detny], *s.* (*a*) prisoner; **prison des jeunes détenus,** reformatory; (*b*) convict.

détergence [detɛrʒɑ̃ːs], *s.f.* detergency.

détergent [detɛrʒɑ̃]. **1.** *a. & s.m. Med:* detergent. **2.** *s.m. Com:* detergent, cleaning product, household washing powder. **3.** *I.C.E:* **huile détergente,** detergent oil.

déterger [detɛrʒe], *v.tr.* (**détergeant**) *Med:* to deterge, clean, cleanse, wash (wound, etc.).

détérioration [deterjɔrasjɔ̃], *s.f.* **1.** deterioration, deteriorating; **d. de marchandises, de la qualité, des mœurs,** deterioration of goods, in quality, in morals; *Med:* **d. mentale,** mental deterioration. **2.** *pl. Jur:* dilapidations, damage (to property); **payer les détériorations,** to pay for (i) the wear and tear, (ii) the damage.

détériorer [deterjɔre], *v.tr.* to make (sth.) worse; to spoil, mar, damage.

se détériorer, to deteriorate, to become spoilt, to spoil; **caoutchouc qui s'est détérioré,** rubber that has perished; **sa santé se détériore,** his health is becoming worse, is suffering.

déterminabilité [detɛrminabilite], *s.f.* determinability.

déterminable [detɛrminabl̩], *a.* determinable.

déterminant [detɛrminɑ̃]. **1.** *a.* determinant, determinative, determining (factor, cause, etc.); **jouer un rôle d. dans . . .,** to play a decisive, an instrumental, role in . . . . **2.** *s.m. Mth:* determinant.

déterminatif, -ive [detɛrminatif, -iːv], *a. & s.m. Ling: Gram:* determinative (word, etc.); **incidente déterminative,** defining clause.

détermination [detɛrminasjɔ̃], *s.f.* **1.** determination (of species, noun, date, area, etc.); typing (of bacteria); **d. du groupe sanguin,** blood typing. **2.** determination, resolution, fixity of purpose; **agir avec d.,** to act resolutely. **3.** resolve, determination; **prendre une d.,** to make up one's mind; **une d. soudaine de faire qch.,** a sudden determination to do sth.

déterminé [detɛrmine], *a.* **1.** determined, definite, well-defined (area, purpose, etc.); specific, particular (aim); **dans un sens d.,** (i) in a determinate sense; (ii) in a given direction; **à un nombre de tours d.,** at a given number of revolutions; **depuis un temps d.,** since a given date. **2.** (*a*) determined, resolute (person, manner, etc.); firm of purpose; (*b*) **être d. à faire qch.,** to be resolved, determined, to do sth., to be bent on doing sth.; *F:* to be dead set on, to have set one's heart on, doing sth.

déterminément [detɛrminemɑ̃], *adv. Lit:* determinately, resolutely, with determination.

déterminer [detɛrmine], *v.tr.* **1.** to determine (species, value, noun, area, etc.); **d. un lieu de rendez-vous,** to fix, settle, a meeting-place; **d. le budget,** to fix the budget; **d. une méthode de travail,** to decide upon a method of work; **d. les dimensions d'un cylindre,** to find the dimensions of a cylinder; **d. l'emplacement de qch.,** to locate sth. **2.** to cause; to give rise to (sth.); to bring (sth.) to pass; **blessure qui a déterminé sa mort,** wound that brought about his death; **une simple négligence peut d. un incendie,** a simple act of carelessness may cause, lead to, a fire. **3.** (*a*) *v.i. A:* **d. de faire qch.,** to resolve, decide, to do sth.; (*b*) **d. qn à faire qch.,** to induce, move, impel, s.o. to do sth.; **qu'est-ce qui vous a déterminé à partir?** what decided you, prevailed upon you, to depart? what made you go?

se déterminer, to determine, resolve, make up one's mind; **se d. à qch.,** to resolve upon a course; **se d. à faire qch.,** to make up one's mind to do sth.

déterminisme [determinism], *s.m. Phil:* determinism, necessitarianism.
déterministe [determinist]. **1.** *s.m. & f. Phil:* determinist, necessitarian. **2.** *a.* determinist(ic).
déterrage [detɛra:ʒ], *s.m.* **1.** unearthing; *Agr:* (action of) lifting (a plough-share). **2. d. du blaireau,** badger-baiting, -drawing.
déterré, -ée [detɛre], *a. & s.* disinterred (corpse); *F:* **il a l'air d'un d., il a une mine de d.,** he looks as if he had risen from the grave; he looks ghastly.
déterrement [detɛr(ə)mɑ̃], *s.m.* **1.** unearthing; exhuming; disinterment. **2.** = DÉTERRAGE 2.
déterrent [detɛrɑ̃], *s.m. Mil:* deterrent.
déterrer [detɛre, -ere], *v.tr.* **1.** to dig up, unearth (buried treasure, etc.); to exhume, disinter (corpse); *F:* **d. un secret,** to dig out, ferret out, a secret; **d. des manuscrits,** to bring manuscripts to light; **où as-tu donc déterré ce chapeau?** where ever did you unearth that hat? **2. d. le blaireau,** to draw the badger.
déterreur [detɛrœ:r], *s.m.* **1.** exhumer; *F:* body-snatcher. **2.** *F:* discoverer (of old manuscripts, etc.).
détersif, -ive [detɛrsif, -i:v]. **1.** *a. & s.m. Med:* detersive, detergent, abstersive, abstergent. **2.** *s.m. Dom.Ec:* (*a*) detergent, cleaning product; (*b*) cleansing product.
détersion [detɛrsjɔ̃], *s.f. Med:* detersion, abstersion; cleansing (of wound, etc.); *Dom.Ec:* cleaning with a detergent.
détestable [detɛstabl̩], *a.* detestable, hateful (person, place, etc.); very bad, execrable (work, etc.).
détestablement [detɛstabləmɑ̃], *adv.* detestably, hatefully; **chanter d.,** to sing execrably.
détestation [detɛstasjɔ̃], *s.f.* detestation; **d. du péché,** abhorrence of sin; *Lit:* **avoir de la d. pour qn, qch.,** to have an abhorrence of s.o., sth., to hold s.o., sth., in detestation.
détester [detɛste], *v.tr.* to detest, hate; **je déteste être dérangé,** I hate to be disturbed, I hate being disturbed; **se faire d. de tous, par tout le monde,** to get oneself disliked by everyone; **d. faire qch.,** to abominate doing sth.
détirer [detire], *v.tr.* to stretch (linen, leather, etc.); **d. ses bras, ses jambes, se d.,** to stretch one's arms, one's legs, to stretch oneself (in yawning).
détiser [detize], *v.tr.* to rake out (fire).
détisser [detise], *v.tr. Tex:* to unweave.
détitrer [detitre], *v.tr.* **1.** to deprive (s.o.) of a title. **2.** (*a*) **d. un alcool,** to bring an alcohol below proof; (*b*) **d. une monnaie,** to lower the title of a coinage; to debase a coinage.
détonant [detɔnɑ̃]. **1.** *a.* detonating, detonative, explosive (substance); **mélange d.,** explosive mixture; **explosif d.,** high explosive. **2.** *s.m.* explosive.
détonateur [detɔnatœ:r], *s.m.* (*a*) *Exp:* detonator; igniting fuse, fuze; blasting cap; **d. primaire,** primer detonator; **d. secondaire,** booster (detonator); **d. de la charge d'éclatement,** burster detonator; **d. à double effet,** double-action detonator fuse; **d. à percussion,** percussion detonator; **d. de mine à percussion,** contact mine detonator; **d. chimique,** chemical detonator; **d. électrique,** electrical detonator; (*b*) *Rail:* fog-signal.
détonation [detɔnasjɔ̃], *s.f.* (*a*) detonation; **d. par influence,** detonation by influence, by proximity; **d. prématurée,** predetonation (of H-bomb, etc.); (*b*) report (of fire-arm).
détoner [detɔne], *v.i. Exp:* to detonate, explode; **faire d.,** to detonate (dynamite, etc.).
détonneler [detɔnle], *v.tr.* (**je détonnelle, n. détonnelons; je détonnellerai**) to draw (wine, etc.) from the cask.
détonner [detɔne], *v.i.* (*a*) to be, play, sing, out of tune; to flatten, sing flat; (*b*) (*of colours*) to jar, clash; **ses bijoux détonnent dans ce milieu,** her jewels are out of place, out of keeping, in these surroundings.
détordeuse [detɔrdø:z], *s.f. Ind:* machine for untwisting, untwining, unravelling (yarn, etc.).
détordre [detɔrdr̩], *v.tr.* to untwist, untwine, unravel (yarn, etc.); **d. un cordage,** to unlay a rope.
se détordre, (*of yarn, etc.*) to come untwisted, to untwist.
détorquer [detɔrke], *v.tr. A:* to distort the meaning of (text, etc.).
détors, -orse [detɔ:r, -ɔrs], *a.* untwisted (thread, etc.); unlaid (rope).
détorsion [detɔrsjɔ̃], *s.f.* untwisting (of rope, etc.).
détortiller [detɔrtije], *v.tr.* (*a*) to untwist (yarn, hair, etc.); (*b*) to disentangle; (*c*) to unwrap (mummy, etc.).
se détortiller, to come untwisted.
détoucher [detuʃe], *v.i. Nau:* (*of ship*) to get afloat, to float off (after grounding).
détouper [detupe], *v.tr.* = DÉSÉTOUPER.
détour [detu:r], *s.m.* **1.** turning, deviation (from direct way); detour; roundabout way, circuitous way; **faire un d.,** to go a roundabout way, to take a by-way; **faire un d. de vingt milles,** to go twenty miles out of one's way; to make a detour of twenty miles; **faire un long d.,** to go a long way round, to make a wide circuit; *F:* **user de détours pour arriver à un but,** to achieve one's end in a roundabout way; **sans détour(s),** plainly, frankly; **répondre sans détours,** to give a plain, straightforward, answer; **d. qui permet de surmonter la difficulté,** dodge that allows us to overcome the difficulty. **2.** turn, curve, bend (in road, river, etc.); **suivre tous les détours du fleuve,** to follow all the windings of the river; **la route fait un brusque d.,** the road takes a sharp turn; **je connais tous les tours et détours de ces ruines,** I know all the twists and turns, all the ins and outs, of these ruins; **connaître Paris dans ses tours et détours,** to know Paris inside out.
détourage [detura:ʒ], *s.m. Tchn:* routing.
détouré [deture], *a. Phot: Engr: etc:* **portrait, etc., d.,** head, etc., with background blocked out; *F:* a cut-out.
détourer [deture], *v.tr. Tchn:* to rout; *Phot: Engr: etc:* to block out the background of (a profile, etc.).
détourne [deturn], *s.f. F:* **vol à la d.,** shop-lifting.
détourné [deturne], *a.* **1.** indirect, circuitous, roundabout (road or route); **chemin d.,** by-road; **sentier d.,** by-path; **par des voies détournées,** indirectly, in a roundabout way. **2.** *A:* unfrequented, secluded, out-of-the-way (locality, etc.).
détournement [deturnəmɑ̃], *s.m.* **1.** diversion, diverting, turning aside (of water-course, etc.); *Trans: Tp:* **d. du traffic,** diversion, diverting, *U.S:* rerouting, of traffic. **2.** (*a*) misappropriation, fraudulent misuse (of funds); embezzlement; **commettre un important d.,** to embezzle a large sum; **l'auteur du d. a passé en Belgique,** the embezzler has crossed into Belgium; (*b*) *Jur:* **d. de mineur,** abduction of a minor.
détourner [deturne], *v.tr.* **1.** (*a*) to divert (water-course, etc.); to turn (weapon, etc.) aside; *Trans: Tp: etc:* **d. le traffic,** to divert, *U.S:* to reroute, the traffic; **d. l'attention de qn,** to divert, distract, draw off, s.o.'s attention; **d. qn de faire qch.,** to dissuade s.o. from doing sth.; **d. qn de sa route, de son dessein,** to lead s.o. out of his way; to divert, dissuade, s.o. from his design; **je vais essayer de le d. de ce projet,** I shall try to put him off this plan; **d. qn de son devoir,** to seduce, entice, s.o. from his duty; **il essaya de la d. de son mari,** he tried to alienate her from her husband; **cette menace ne le détourna pas,** this threat did not deter him; **d. qn de la bonne voie,** to lead s.o. astray; **d. la conversation,** to turn, change, the conversation; **d. les soupçons,** to avert suspicion; **d. son attention sur qch.,** to be side-tracked by sth.; **d. le sens d'un mot, d. un mot de son sens ordinaire,** to distort, twist, the meaning of a word; (*b*) to turn away, avert (one's head, eyes, etc.); **elle détourna les yeux,** she looked away, in another direction; she averted her eyes; **d. l'oreille, les oreilles,** to refuse to listen; *s.a.* REGARD 1. **2.** (*a*) to untwist, unlay (rope); (*b*) to wind off (rope from drum). **3.** *F:* (= TOURNER) **d. la tête,** to turn one's head, to turn round. **4.** (*a*) to misappropriate, embezzle (funds) (**à,** from); *F:* **il avait détourné dc nombreuses bouteilles de vin,** he had abstracted, made away with, numerous bottles of wine; (*b*) **d. une jeune fille,** to lead a girl astray; *Jur:* **d. un(e) mineur(e),** to abduct a minor.
se détourner, to turn away, turn aside; **se d. de son chemin pour éviter une difficulté,** to step aside from one's path to avoid a difficulty; **se d. d'un projet,** to abandon a scheme.
détourneur, -euse [deturnœ:r, -ø:z], *s.* (*a*) abductor; (*b*) *F:* shoplifter; (*c*) **d. de fonds,** embezzler.
détoxication [detɔksikasjɔ̃], *s.f.* detoxication.
détoxifiant [detɔksifjɑ̃], *s.m.* detoxifier.
détoxification [detɔksifikasjɔ̃], *s.f. Ind:* detoxification.
détoxiquer [detɔksike], *v.tr.* to detoxicate.
détracter [detrakte], *v.tr. A:* to disparage, depreciate, belittle.
détracteur, -trice [detraktœ:r, -tris], *s.* detractor, disparager, vilifier.
détraction [detraksjɔ̃], *s.f. A:* depreciation, belittlement.
détraqué [detrake], *a.* **1.** *Equit:* broken-gaited (horse). **2.** (*of mechanism, digestion, etc.*) out of order; (*of pers.*) deranged; **il a le cerveau d.,** his mind is unhinged; **avoir les nerfs détraqués,** to be a nervous wreck; **sa santé est détraquée,** he is broken in health, his health has broken down; **c'est un détraqué,** he is shattered in mind and body; **le temps est d.,** the weather is unsettled, has broken.
détraquement [detrakmɑ̃], *s.m.* **1.** *Equit:* breaking up, ruining (of horse's gait). **2.** (*a*) putting (of mechanism, etc.) out of order, out of gear; (*b*) breakdown (of mechanism, health, digestion, etc.); *F:* **le d. des facultés intellectuelles,** the ruin of the intellectual faculties.
détraquer [detrake], *v.tr.* **1. d. un cheval,** to ruin a horse's gait. **2.** to put (apparatus) out of order; to throw (mechanism) out of gear; to rack (machinery) to pieces; **son intervention a tout détraqué,** his intervention has upset everything; **cette déception lui a détraqué le cerveau,** this disappointment has unhinged his mind; **se d. l'estomac, les nerfs,** to wreck one's digestion, one's nerves.
se détraquer, (*a*) (*of mechanism, etc.*) to get out of order, out of gear; (*of health*) to break down; (*of digestion*) to get upset; (*b*) *F:* (*of pers.*) to go all to pieces; (*c*) (*of weather*) to break, to become unsettled.
détrempe¹ [detrɑ̃:p], *s.f.* **1.** (*a*) *Art:* distemper (-painting); (*b*) *Paint:* distemper, size-colouring. **2.** *F:* **ouvrage en d.,** (i) poor imitation of another work; (ii) *A:* wishy-washy work; **personne en d.,** insignificant person; *F:* poor stick; **ressemblance en d.,** faint resemblance. **3.** *Cu:* dough.
détrempe², *s.f. Metall:* annealing, softening (of steel).
détremper¹ [detrɑ̃pe], *v.tr.* to dilute, moisten, soak (sth.); **d. des peaux,** to soak, soften, hides; **d. de la chaux,** to slake lime; **champ détrempé,** sodden, soppy, waterlogged, field.
détremper², *v.tr. Metall:* to anneal, soften (steel).
se détremper, (*of steel*) to lose its temper; *F:* **son caractère s'est détrempé,** he has lost his drive, his energy.
détresse [detrɛs], *s.f.* distress. **1.** grief, anguish. **2.** (*a*) (financial) straits, difficulties; **sa famille est dans la plus grande d.,** his family is in dire straits; (*b*) *esp. Nau:* danger; **navire en d.,** ship in distress, in difficulties; **signal de d.,** distress signal; *F:* S O S; (*c*) **le train est en d.,** the train has got stuck, has broken down.
détresser [detrese], *v.tr.* to unbraid, unplait (hair, etc.); to unweave (garland, etc.); to unravel (rope).
détret [detrɛ], *s.m. Dial: Tls:* hand-vice.
détriment [detrimɑ̃], *s.m.* **1.** detriment, injury, loss; *prep.phr.* **au d. de qn, de qch.,** to the detriment, prejudice, of s.o., of sth.; **gaspillages au d. des malheureux,** extravagance at the expense of the poor; **je l'ai appris à mon d.,** I found it out to my cost. **2.** *A: pl.* detritus, debris (of rock, etc.).
détritage [detrita:ʒ], *s.m.* crushing (of olives, etc.).
détriter [detrite], *v.tr.* to crush (olives, etc.).
détrition [detrisjɔ̃], *s.f.* detrition; wearing away (of teeth, fossils, etc.); disintegration (of rock).
détritique [detritik], *a.* detrital (deposit, etc.).
détritoir [detritwa:r], *s.m.* crushing mill (for olives, etc.).
détritophage [detritɔfa:ʒ], *Ent:* **1.** *a.* detritivorous, rubbish-eating (larvae, etc.). **2.** *s.m.* rubbish-eater.
détritus [detrity:s], *s.m.* (*a*) detritus, debris (of rock, etc.); **d. de carrière,** quarry chips; (*b*) rubbish; (*c*) refuse; offal; *Physiol:* roughage (of food).
détroit [detrwɑ], *s.m.* **1.** *Geog:* strait(s), sound; *Hist:* **les Établissements des Détroits,** the Straits Settlements. **2.** *Geog: A:* (narrow mountain) pass; **le d. des Thermopyles,** the pass of Thermopylae. **3.** *Anat:* **détroits du bassin,** straits of the pelvis.
détromper [detrɔ̃pe], *v.tr.* to undeceive, enlighten (s.o.); to correct (s.o.'s) mistake. **détrompez-vous!** don't you believe it!
détrônement [detronmɑ̃], *s.m.* **1.** dethronement. **2.** superseding, discrediting.
détrôner [detrone], *v.tr.* **1.** to dethrone. **2.** to supersede, overthrow (old method, etc.); to discredit.
détrôneur [detronœ:r], *s.m.* dethroner; unmaker (of kings).
détroquage [detrɔka:ʒ], *s.m.* detaching of oysters (from the cultch before fattening).
détroquer [detrɔke], *v.tr.* to detach oysters (from the cultch before fattening).

détroussement [detrusmã], *s.m. A: or Hum:* (highway) robbery; (action of) rifling, picking, s.o.'s pockets.
détrousser [detruse], *v.tr.* **1.** *A:* to untuck, let down (one's apron, sleeves, etc.). **2.** *Hum:* to rob (s.o.) (on the highway); to relieve (s.o.) of his valuables; to rifle, pick, (s.o.'s) pockets.
se détrousser, to let down, untuck, a garment.
détrousseur [detrusœ:r], *s.m. A:* highwayman, footpad.
détruire [detrɥi:r], *v.tr.* (*pr.p.* **détruisant;** *p.p.* **détruit;** *pr.ind.* **je détruis, il détruit, n. détruisons;** *p.d.* **je détruisais;** *p.h.* **je détruisis;** *fu.* **je détruirai)** **1.** (*a*) to demolish, pull down, raze (building, town, etc.); to overthrow (empire, etc.); (*b*) to break up, scrap (ship, etc.); *Av:* **trois appareils ont été détruits,** three machines were written off; (*c*) to dispose of (rubbish). **2.** to destroy, ruin; **la pluie a détruit la moisson,** the rain has ruined the harvest; **d. les espérances de qn,** to destroy, dash, blast, s.o.'s hopes; **son argument est détruit de fond en comble,** he hasn't a leg to stand on.
se détruire. 1. to fall into decay, to rot. **2.** to destroy oneself, to make away with oneself. **3. se d. deux à deux,** (i) *Mth:* (*of factors*) to cancel out; (ii) *Mec:* (*of forces*) to neutralize one another. **4. critiques qui se détruisent mutuellement,** criticisms that cancel out.
détruisant [detrɥizã], *a.* destroying, destructive.
dette [dɛt], *s.f.* debt; (*a*) **dettes de jeu,** gambling debts; **faire des dettes,** to run into debt; **avoir des dettes,** to be in debt; **n'avoir plus de dettes,** to be out of debt; **avoir pour dix mille francs de dettes,** to be ten thousand francs in debt; **être perdu, criblé, accablé, de dettes, avoir des dettes par-dessus la tête,** to be head over ears in debt; **le montant de ma d.,** the amount of my indebtedness, my total debts; **acquitter une d.,** to pay off a debt; *Book-k:* **dettes compte,** book debts; **dettes actives,** book debts ranking as assets; **dettes passives,** liabilities; *Fin:* **la d. publique flottante,** the Floating Debt; **la d. publique perpétuelle en rentes sur l'État,** the National Debt, the Consolidated Debt, Fund; *F:* consols; **Le grand-livre de la d. publique,** the National Debt Register; *s.a.* HONNEUR 1, JEU 4, PRISON 1; (*b*) **avoir une d. de reconnaissance envers qn,** to owe a debt of gratitude, to be under an obligation, to s.o.; **notre d. envers la Grèce,** our indebtedness to Greece; **d. sacrée envers la patrie,** sacred duty towards one's country; **payer sa d. à la nature,** to pay one's debt to nature, to go the way of all flesh, to die; *Prov:* **qui paie ses dettes, s'enrichit** = out of debt, out of danger.
détumescence [detymɛsɑ̃:s], *s.f. Med:* detumescence.
deuil [dœ:j], *s.m.* **1.** (*a*) mourning, sorrow, affliction (for the loss of s.o.); **le pays est plongé dans le d.,** the country is plunged into mourning; **sa mort fut un d. général,** his death was universally mourned; **faire son deuil de qch.,** to give sth. up as lost, as beyond recovery, as gone beyond recall; (*b*) bereavement; **en raison d'un d. récent,** owing to a recent bereavement. **2.** (*a*) mourning (clothes, etc.); **grand d.,** deep mourning; **se mettre en d.,** to go into mourning; **porter le d., être en d., de qn,** to be in mourning for s.o.; **prendre le d. de qn,** to go into mourning for s.o.; **quitter le d.,** to go out of mourning; **d. de veuve,** widow's weeds; **papier (de) d.,** black-edged notepaper, mourning paper; **église tendue de d.,** church hung with mourning; *F:* **il avait toujours les ongles en d.,** his nails were in constant mourning; *F:* **porter le d. de sa blanchisseuse,** to wear dirty linen; (*b*) funeral procession; the mourners; **conduire le d.,** to be chief mourner.
deuillant [dœjɑ̃], *s.m. Sculp:* weeper, mourner (on mediaeval tomb).
deusse [døs], *int. Gym: Mil: etc:* = DEUX; **une, d.! une, d.!** one, two! one, two!
deutéragoniste [døteragɔnist], *s.m. Th:* deuteragonist.
deutéranomalie [døteranɔmali], *s.f. Med:* deuteranomaly.
deutéranope [døteranɔp], *Med:* **1.** *a.* deuteranopic. **2.** *s.m. & f.* deuteranope.
deutéranopie [døteranɔpi], *s.f. Med:* deuteranopia.
deutérium [døterjɔm], *s.m. Ch:* deuterium, heavy hydrogen.
deutérocanonique [døterɔkanɔnik], *a. B.Lit:* **les livres deutérocanoniques,** the Apocrypha.
deutéromycètes [døterɔmisɛt], *s.m.pl. Fung:* Deuteromycetes.
deutéron [døterɔ̃], *s.m. Ch:* deuteron, deuton; duterium nucleus.
Deutéronome [døterɔnɔm], *s.m. B:* Deuteronomy.
deutéropathie [døterɔpati], *s.f. Med:* deuteropathy.
deutéroscopie [døterɔskɔpi], *s.f.* deuteroscopy.
deuton [døtɔ̃], *s.m. Ch:* deuton, deuteron; duterium nucleus.
deutoplasma [døtɔplasma], *s.m.* deutoplasm.
deux [dø; *before a vowel sound in the same word group,* døz], (*a*) *num.a.inv. & s.m.* two; **d. enfants** [døzɑ̃fɑ̃], two children; **d. hommes** [døzɔm], two men; **j'en ai d.** [dø], I have two; **d. et trois** [dø(z)etrwɑ] **font cinq,** two and three are five; **d. ou trois** [døzutrwɑ], two or three; **dans un mois ou d.,** in a month or two, in a month or so; **le d. août** [lədøzu], (on) the second of August; **Charles D.,** Charles the Second; **il est arrivé d. ou troisième,** he arrived second or third; *Cards:* two, deuce; **le d. de cœur,** the two, deuce, of hearts; (*in dicing*) **d. et un,** deuce-ace; **chapitre d.,** chapter two; **le numéro d.,** number two; **"elle" s'écrit: e, deux l, e,** "elle" is spelt: e, double l, e; **c'est clair comme d. et d. font quatre,** it's as plain as a pikestaff; **d. fois,** twice; **d. fois d. font quatre,** twice two is four; **il a d. fois mon âge,** he is twice as old as I am; **notre maison est d. fois plus grande que la vôtre, est d. fois grande comme la vôtre,** our house is twice as big, is as big again, as yours; **il vaut mieux être sage que belle.—Mais on peut être les d. en même temps!** it is better to be good than beautiful.—But one may be both at the same time! **tous (les) d.,** both; **des d. côtés du fleuve,** on either side, on both sides, of the river; **tous les d. jours;** *A:* **de d. jours l'un,** every other day; on alternate days; **j'étais entre les d.,** I stood, sat, between them; **c'est entre les d.,** it's so-so, fair to middling; **casser qch. en d.,** to break sth. in two; **plier une feuille en d.,** to fold a sheet double, in two; to double a sheet; **déchirer qch. en d.,** to tear sth. asunder; **diviser, couper, une ligne, un angle, en d.,** to bisect a line, an angle; **marcher d. par d.,** to walk two and two, in pairs; **marcher par d.,** to march two abreast, *Mil:* in file; **entrer d. par d.,** to come in by twos, in twos, two by two; **piquer des d.,** to clap spurs to one's horse; *F:* **il était entre d. vins,** he'd had one or two; **entre d. âges,** middle-aged; **entre d. soleils,** (i) *A:* between sunrise and sunset, in one day; (ii) between sunset and sunrise; **voiture à d. chevaux,** two-horse carriage; **la vie à d.,** (i) married life, (ii) keeping house, living, together; **combien d'argent avez-vous à vous d.?** how much money have you between you? **à nous d. maintenant!** now we two will have it out! *Ten:* **à d.,** deuce; **à d. de jeux,** five (games) all; *F:* **nous sommes à d. de jeu,** two can play at that game; *Mus:* **à deux,** (i) divisi; (ii) the two instruments to play in unison; *Danc:* **pas de d.,** two-step; *Turf:* **coup de d.,** double; **d. s'amusent, trois s'embêtent,** two's company, three's a crowd, none; *F:* **il fera ça en moins de d.,** he will do it in two ticks; **c'est à d. pas d'ici,** it is close at hand, only a short distance off; **à d. rebords,** double-flanged; **il y en a plus de d. comme moi,** I'm not the only one! **il n'y a pas d. voix là-dessus,** there are no two opinions about it; **un médecin de d. sous,** a twopenny-ha'penny doctor; **nous d., vous d., eux d.,** (i) the two of us, you, them; (ii) us two, you two, those two; (iii) we two, you two, those two; **promettre et tenir sont d.,** *F:* **c'est d., ça fait d.,** promising and keeping one's promise are not the same thing, are different things; *s.a.* MOT 1, SOU, UN 1; (*b*) *s.m. Row:* pair.
deux-ans [døzɑ̃], *s.m.inv. Horse Rac:* **un d.-a,** a two-year old.
deux-huit [døɥit], *s.m.inv. Mus:* two-eight (time).
deuxième [døzjɛm], *num. a. & s.* second; **appartement au d. (étage),** flat on the second, *U.S:* third, floor; *Com:* **d. de change,** second of exchange; *Mth:* **équation du d. degré,** quadratic equation.
deuxièmement [døzjɛmmɑ̃], *adv.* secondly, in the second place.
deux-mâts [dømɑ], *s.m.* two-masted vessel; two-master.
deux-pièces [døpjɛs], *s.m.inv.* **1.** *Cost:* (*a*) two-piece swimsuit; (*b*) two-piece (dress, suit). **2.** two-roomed flat, apartment.
deux-points [døpwɛ̃], *s.m. Typ:* colon.
Deux-Ponts[1] [døpɔ̃], *Pr.n. Geog:* Zweibrücken.
deux-ponts[2], *s.m.inv. Nau:* double-decker (ship); *Av:* double-decker (aircraft).
deux-quatre [døkatr̥], *s.m.inv. Mus:* **1.** two-four (time); duple measure. **2.** piece in two-four time.
Deux-Roses [døro:z], *s.f.pl. Hist:* **la guerre des D.-R.,** the Wars of the Roses.
deux-roues [døru], *s.m.inv.* two-wheeled vehicle.
Deux-Siciles (les) [ledøsisil], *Pr.n.f.pl. Hist:* the Two Sicilies.
deux-temps [døtɑ̃], *s.m.* **1.** *Mus:* = DEUX-QUATRE. **2.** (*a*) two-stroked engined vehicle, light motor cycle; (*b*) **(mélange) d.-t.,** two-stroke mixture.
dévalaison [devalɛzɔ̃], *s.f.* (*of fish*) (action of) going downstream, descending the river.
dévaler [devale]. **1.** *v.i.* to descend, go down; (*of stream*) to rush down; (*of fish*) to go downstream; to descend the river; **la rivière dévale de 600 mètres,** the river tumbles down 600 metres; **lave qui dévale de la montagne,** lava that comes down, flows down, the mountain; **le jardin dévale jusqu'à la rivière,** the garden slopes down, extends down, to the river. **2.** *v.tr.* (*a*) **d. la colline, l'escalier,** to descend, hurry down, the hill, the stairs; **d. la rue à toute vitesse,** to race down the street; (*b*) *A:* **d. du vin à la cave,** to let down wine into the cellar.
dévalisement [devalizmɑ̃], *s.m.* (action of) robbing; burgling.
dévaliser [devalize], *v.tr.* to rob (s.o. of his money, etc.); **d. une maison,** to rifle, burgle, a house.
dévaliseur, -euse [devalizœ:r, -ø:z], *s.* (*rare*) thief, burglar.
dévaloir [devalwa:r], *s.m. Sw.Fr:* rubbish chute, shoot.
dévalorisation [devalɔrizasjɔ̃], *s.f.* **1.** *Fin:* devalorization, devaluation (of currency). **2.** *Com:* fall in value, loss of value. **3.** discrediting (of s.o., a policy).
dévaloriser [devalɔrize], *v.tr.* **1.** *Fin:* to devalue, devaluate (currency); **d. une monnaie de 10%,** to devalue a currency by 10%. **2.** to mark down (goods). **3.** to discredit (s.o., a policy).
se dévaloriser, *Com:* to decrease, fall, in value.
dévaluateur, -trice [devalyatœ:r, -tris], (*a*) *a. Pol.Ec:* **menées dévaluatrices,** devaluation manœuvres; (*b*) *s. Pol.Ec:* advocate of devaluation.
dévaluation [devalyasjɔ̃], *s.f. Fin: Pol.Ec:* devaluation.
dévaluer [devalɥe], *v.tr.* to devalue, devaluate (currency).
devancement [dəvɑ̃smɑ̃], *s.m.* (*a*) preceding, going before; (*b*) out-distancing (of s.o., sth.); (*c*) forestalling (of s.o., sth.); *Mil:* **d. d'appel,** enlistment before call-up.
devancer [dəvɑ̃se], *v.tr.* **(je devançai(s); n. devançons) 1.** to precede; to go or come before (s.o., sth.); **l'avant-garde devance le gros de l'armée,** the advance(d) guard precedes the main body; **les générations qui nous ont devancés,** the generations which came before us. **2.** to leave (the others) behind; to out-distance, overtake, outrival, outstrip; (*in riding*) to outride; (*in walking*) to outwalk; *Sw.Fr: Aut:* to overtake; **je vous ai devancé,** (i) I got here before you; (ii) I anticipated, forestalled, you; **d. son époque,** to be ahead of one's times; **d. ses rivaux,** to outmatch, get the start of, beat, one's rivals; **se laisser d.,** to drop behind. **3. d. les désirs de qn,** to anticipate s.o.'s desires; *Mil:* **d. l'appel,** to enlist before call-up.
devancier, -ière [dəvɑ̃sje, -jɛ:r], *s.* (*a*) precursor; (*b*) predecessor; **nos devanciers,** our forefathers.
devant [dəvɑ̃]. **1.** *prep:* (*a*) before, in front of (s.o., sth.); **regardez d. vous,** look in front of you; **se chauffer d. le feu,** to warm oneself in front of the fire; **assis d. un verre de vin,** sitting over a glass of wine; **je vous rencontrerai d. le cinéma,** I'll meet you outside the cinema; **ne dites rien d. lui,** don't say anything in front of him, in his presence; **marchez tout droit d. vous,** go straight ahead, on; *F:* follow your nose; **fuir d. qn,** to run away from s.o.; **être courageux d. le danger,** to show courage in the face of danger; **d. son insistance je ne savais que décider,** in the face of his insistence, I didn't know what to decide; **égaux d. la loi,** equal in the eyes of the law; **sa position d. ce problème,** his position with regard to this problem; **j'ai de l'argent d. moi,** I've some money saved, some money in hand; **loin d.,** far ahead of; *F:* streets ahead of; **navire d. Calais,** ship off Calais; **d. cet état de choses, d. votre silence,** in view of this state of affairs, of your silence; **la France d. la dévaluation de la livre,** the attitude of France to the devaluation of the pound; *Sp:* **la France mène par 2 à 1, d. la Belgique,** France is leading Belgium 2-1; (*b*) *A:* = AVANT; **mettre l'honneur d. toutes choses,** to put honour first, before everything. **2.** *adv.* (*a*) before, in (the) front; **envoyer qn d.,** to send

s.o. on (in front); **aller d.,** (i) to go in front, to lead the way; (ii) *Nau:* to go forward; **porter qch. sens d. derrière,** to wear sth. back to front; *Nau:* **un navire d.** ship ahead! **veillez d.!** look out afore there! **par bâbord d., par tribord d.,** on the port, starboard, bow; **être vent d.,** to be in stays, to be wind ahead; **être pris d.,** to be taken aback; *adv.phr.* **saisir qch. par d.,** to seize sth. in front; **recevoir une blessure par d.,** to receive a wound in front; *s.a.* PAR-DEVANT; (*b*) *A: Lit:* **il revint plus effaré que d.,** he came back more scared than before; (*c*) *conj.phr. A:* **d. que** = AVANT QUE. **3.** *s.m.* front (part), forepart; **d. d'un habit,** breast of a coat; **d. (de chemise)** (shirt-)front; **d. d'autel,** altar frontal; **d. de cheminée, de feu,** fire-screen; **d. de foyer,** hearth rug; **d. d'un vaisseau,** fore-part of a ship; **d. d'un mât, d'une vergue,** foreside of a mast, of a yard; **chambre sur le d.,** front room; *F:* **bâtir sur le d.,** to get a corporation; **dents de d.,** front teeth; **roue de d.,** fore-wheel, front wheel; **cheval de d.,** leader; **jambes de d. (d'un cheval), pattes de d. (d'un chien),** fore-legs; **prendre les devants,** (i) to go on ahead; (ii) to make the first move; **prendre les devants sur qn,** to get the start of s.o., to forestall s.o.; **gagner les devants,** to forge ahead, to take the lead; *prep. phr.* **terrasse au d. de la maison,** terrace in front of the house; *s.a.* AU-DEVANT, CI-DEVANT.

devanteau, -eaux [dəvɑ̃to], *s.m.*, **devantier** [dəvɑ̃tje], *s.m.*, **devantôt** [dəvɑ̃to], *s.m. Dial:* apron.

devanture [dəvɑ̃tyːr], *s.f.* (*a*) front(age) (of building); front (of boiler, furnace); **local avec une belle d.,** premises with a good frontage; (*b*) **d. de magasin,** shop-front, shop-window; **marchandises à la d.,** goods in the window; **fermer les devantures,** to put up the shutters, to close the shutters.

dévasement [devɑzmɑ̃], *s.m.* dredging, clearing, unsilting (of harbour).

dévaser [devɑze], *v.tr.* to dredge, unsilt; to clear (harbour).

dévastateur, -trice [devastatœːr, -tris]. **1.** *s.* devastator, ravager. **2.** *a.* devastating.

dévastation [devastasjɔ̃], *s.f.* devastation, destruction, havoc.

dévaster [devaste], *v.tr.* to devastate, lay waste, ravage (country, etc.); **pays dévasté,** devastated area; **région dévastée par la guerre,** war-stricken area; **villages dévastés,** wrecked villages; **pays dévasté par la peste,** plague-stricken country.

déveinard [devɛnaːr], *s.m. F:* (*a*) gambler whose luck is out; (*b*) man consistently unlucky.

déveine [devɛn], *s.f. F:* (run of) ill-luck; **avoir la d., être en d., dans la d.,** to be out of luck, down on one's luck; to be up against it; **j'ai la d., je suis en d.,** my luck is out; **il a eu une d. extraordinaire,** he had rank bad luck.

développable [devlɔpabl̩], *a. Geom: etc:* developable.

développante [devlɔpɑ̃ːt], *s.f. Geom:* involute (of curve).

développateur [devlɔpatœːr], *s.m. Phot:* developer.

développé [devlɔpe], *s.m.* **1.** *Sp:* (*weight lifting*) press. **2.** *Danc:* développé.

développée [devlɔpe], *s.f. Geom:* evolute (curve).

développement [devlɔpmɑ̃], *s.m.* **1.** (*a*) spreading out, opening out (of wings); stretching out (of arm); *Fenc:* lunge; (*b*) *Alg:* expansion (of contracted expression); *Geom:* evolution (of curve); **d. en série,** series expansion; **d. en série entière,** power series expansion. **2.** (*a*) spread (of branches of tree, etc.); length (of road, etc.); **piste d'un d. de six kilomètres,** track six kilometres in extent; (*b*) **bicyclette avec un d. de 5 m. 25,** bicycle with a 66 inch gear, geared to 66 inches; (*c*) *N.Arch:* girth (of a vessel); **d. du bordé extérieur,** shell expansion plan. **3.** development, growth (of the body); development (of muscles, flower, faculties, etc., *Phot:* of image); **d. d'un commerce,** growth of a business; **d. d'une mine,** exploitation of a mine; **arbre qui a atteint son d. complet,** full-grown tree; *Pol.Ec:* **pays en voie de d.,** developing countries. **4.** (*a*) *Mus: Lit: Art:* development. (of a theme); (*b*) *Lit:* exposition; *Journ:* article.

développemental, -aux [devlɔpmɑ̃tal, -o], *a.* developmental.

développer [devlɔpe], *v.tr.* **1.** (*a*) to spread out, open out (wings, folded cloth, etc.); to stretch out (arm); to unroll, display (map, banner, etc.); to unwrap, undo, open (parcel, etc.); to unwind (cable, etc.); **d. une affaire compliquée,** to unravel a complicated matter; (*b*) *Alg:* to expand (contracted expression); *Geom:* **d. un cube,** to develop a cube; (*c*) **bicyclette qui développe . . .,** bicycle that has a gear of . . ., that is geared to . . .. **2.** to develop (muscles, faculties, trade, etc.; *Phot:* a negative); to foster (vice, friendship, etc.); to evolve (theory, etc.); **d. ses dons naturels par l'étude,** to improve one's natural gifts by study; **d. un projet,** to work out, amplify, a plan; **d. un sujet,** to develop a subject, to treat a subject at greater length; **il nous a développé son projet,** he explained (the details of) his plan to us; **d. ce qui n'est qu'indiqué,** to expatiate on what is merely hinted at; **d. une mine,** to exploit a mine.

se développer. 1. to spread out, open out, expand, extend; **rouleau qui se développe,** roll (of material) that opens out, unrolls; **la plaine se développe à perte de vue,** the plain extends, stretches out, as far as the eye can see. **2.** (*of organs, flowers, the intelligence, etc.*) to develop; **l'enfant se développe rapidement,** the child is developing, *F:* coming on, rapidly; **son esprit se développe,** his mind is expanding; **pays développé,** advanced country.

développeur, -euse [devlɔpœːr, -øːz], *s.* (*pers.*) developer.

devenir [dəvniːr]. I. *v.pred.* (*conj. like* VENIR; *the aux. is* être) (*a*) to become; **il est devenu mon ami,** he became my friend; **il devint général,** he became a general; **il devint le chef de l'entreprise,** he became the head of the undertaking; **que devenez-vous ces temps-ci?** what are you doing these days? **qu'est-il devenu?** what has become of him? **que deviendra-t-il?** what will become of him; **je ne sais que d.,** I don't know what is to become of me; **que devient votre cousin?** how is your cousin getting on? **que devins-je à cette nouvelle!** what were my feelings at the news! *F:* **il avait l'air de ne savoir que d.,** he looked utterly lost; (*b*) to grow into; **d. jeune homme, d. femme,** to shoot up into a young man, into a woman; **il était devenu homme,** he had grown into a man; *P:* **c'était devenu un beau gars,** he had grown into a fine young fellow; **c'était devenu une belle fille,** she had grown into a fine girl; (*c*) to grow, get, turn; **d. grand,** (i) to grow tall; (ii) to grow up; *F:* **d. à rien,** to shrink to next to nothing; **d. vieux,** to grow, get, old; **d. sur, rose,** to turn sour, pink; **d. blanc de rage,** to go, turn, white with rage; **il devint agriculteur,** he turned farmer; **d. de plus en plus éloquent,** to wax more and more eloquent; **vous allez me faire d. fou,** you will drive me mad; **c'est à d. fou!** it's enough to drive one mad!

II. **devenir,** *s.m.* gradual growth, development; **la langue est dans un perpétuel d.,** language is in a constant state of flux.

déventer [devɑ̃te], *v.tr. Nau:* **1.** to take the wind out of (sail); to shiver, spill (sail). **2.** *Y.Rac:* to blanket (opponent's yacht).

déverbal, -aux [devɛrbal, -o], **déverbatif, -ive** [devɛrbatif, -iːv], *a. & s.m. Gram:* deverbal; deverbative.

déverdir [devɛrdiːr], *v.i.* to lose its green colour.

dévergondage [devɛrgɔ̃daːʒ], *s.m.* **1.** licentiousness, profligacy. **2.** extravagance (of style, imagination).

dévergondé, -ée [devɛrgɔ̃de]. **1.** *a.* (*a*) licentious, profligate, shameless, abandoned; (*b*) extravagant (style, imagination). **2.** *s.* profligate; man, woman, of pleasure.

dévergonder (se) [sədevɛrgɔ̃de], *v.pr.* **1.** to fall into dissolute ways. **2. littérature qui se dévergonde,** literature that is extravagant in style.

déverguer [devɛrge], *v.tr. Nau:* to unbend (sail).

dévernir [devɛrniːr], *v.tr.* to take the varnish, the polish, off (furniture, etc.); **meubles dévernis,** rubbed furniture.

dévernissage [devɛrnisaːʒ], *s.m.* removal of varnish (*esp.* from a painting).

déverrouillage [devɛrujaːʒ], *s.m.* unbolting, unlocking (of door); *Mec.E:* release (of locking device), unlock(ing); *Rail:* unlocking (of switch); *Artil: Sm.a:* unlock(ing), unbolting, bolt release; *Mec.E:* **d. de secours,** emergency release; *Artil:* **d. électrique,** electric unlock.

déverrouiller [devɛruje], *v.tr.* to unbolt, unlock (door); *Mec.E:* to release (locking device); *Rail:* to unlock (switch); *Artil: Sm.a:* to unlock, unbolt; to release the bolt of (a gun).

devers[1] [dəvɛːr], *prep.* (*a*) *A:* towards; **d. Toulon,** towards, in the direction of, Toulon; **d. Pâques,** towards Easter; (*b*) *prep.phr.* **par(-)devers;** (i) **retenir ses papiers par(-)d. soi,** to keep papers in one's possession; (ii) *A:* **par(-)d. les juges,** in the presence of the judges; (iii) **par(-)d. soi,** in one's heart of hearts; **conserver qch. par(-)d. soi,** to keep sth. to oneself.

devers[2], *s.m.* **1.** *N.Arch:* flare (of hull). **2.** *Veh:* set, take (of the axle pin).

dévers [devɛːr]. **1.** *a.* (*a*) *A:* leaning, sloping, out of plumb; (*b*) warped (timber, etc.); out of truth. **2.** *s.m.* (*a*) inclination, cant, slope (of wall, etc.); banking (of road at a bend); tilt (of cart); *Rail:* **d. du rail extérieur,** vertical slant, cant, super-elevation, of the outer rail (at curve); (*b*) warp, twist (in timber, etc.).

déversé [devɛrse], *a.* **1.** sloping, banked. **2.** lopsided; **mur d.,** overhanging wall; *Geol:* **pli d.,** overfold. **3.** warped.

déversement[1] [devɛrs(ə)mɑ̃], *s.m.* (*a*) inclination, sloping, yielding (of wall, etc.); (*b*) warping; warp.

déversement[2], *s.m.* discharge, overflow (of liquid); tipping, tilting (of cart); **lieu de d. (de matériaux, etc.)** dump(ing ground); **plateforme de d.,** tipping-stage; *Town P:* **d. de population,** overspill of population.

déverser[1] [devɛrse]. **1.** *v.tr.* (*a*) to slope, slant (wall, etc.); to bank (road at a bend); to raise the outer rail (of a railway-track); (*b*) to warp (timber). **2.** *v.i. & pr.* (*a*) (*of wall, etc.*) to incline, lean, get out of plumb, jut out; (*b*) (*of wood*) to warp.

déverser[2], *v.tr.* **1.** to divert (channel). **2.** to pour, shed (water); to discharge (overflow of canal, etc.); to tip, dump (material, rubbish, etc.); **le train les déversa sur le quai,** the train deposited them on the platform; **chaque gare déverse sur la ville des milliers de visiteurs,** thousands of visitors pour into the town from each station; **d. le mépris sur qn,** to pour contempt on s.o.

se déverser, (*of river, etc.*) to empty, flow (**dans,** into).

déversoir [devɛrswaːr], *s.m.* **1.** overflow-shoot (of tank, basin, etc.); ash-shoot (of ship); *Hyd.E:* overfall, waste-weir; spillway, wasteway (of dam). **2.** channel (draining water into roadside ditch); outfall (of sewer, etc.). **3.** outlet, safety-valve (for one's energies, etc.). **4.** overspill area; **on fit de la Sibérie un d. pour les grandes villes de l'ouest,** they treated Siberia as an overspill area for the western cities.

dévêtir [devetiːr], *v.tr.* (*conj. like* VÊTIR) (*a*) to undress, strip (s.o.); to divest (s.o.) of his clothing; to unrobe (s.o.); (*b*) to take off (garment); (*c*) *Metall:* to open up (mould).

se dévêtir. 1. (*a*) to undress, strip; to take off one's clothes; (*b*) to leave off some of one's clothing (*e.g.* in warm weather). **2. se d. de son bien,** to divest oneself of, to renounce, one's property.

déviance [devjɑ̃ːs], *s.f. Psy:* deviance, deviancy, deviation (from the norm).

déviant [devjɑ̃], *a. Psy:* deviant.

déviateur, -trice [devjatœːr, -tris], *a.* deviative, deviatory (force, etc.).

déviation [devjasjɔ̃], *s.f.* deflection; deviation (of light, projectile, etc.); deflection (of tool, etc.); deviation, variation (of compass); leaking (of electric current); curvature (of the spine); diversion (of road, traffic); *Min:* deflection (of well); **d. par jet de boue,** jetting; **d. (de qch.) de la verticale,** deviation, deflection (of sth.) from the vertical; **d. verticale,** vertical deflection, deviation; **d. magnétique, d. de la boussole, du compas,** magnetic deflection, deviation, variation; **d. absolue,** absolute deflection, deviation; *Nau:* **d. due à la bande,** heeling error; **d. quadrantale,** quadrantal deviation; *Trans:* **d. de route,** change of route; *Mch:* **d. du régulateur,** throw of the governor; **soupape de d.,** deflecting valve; **d. du zéro d'un appareil,** index error; *Av:* **d. du, de, jet,** jet deflection; *Elcs: El:* **champ de d.,** deflecting field; **coefficient, bobine, de d.,** deflection coefficient, factor; deflecting, deflector coil; **électrode de d.,** deflecting electrode; **plaque de d.,** deflection plate (of radar, etc.); **tension de d.,** deflection voltage; *Med:* **d. conjuguée des yeux,** conjugate deviation of the eyes; **d. du septum,** deviated septum; *A:* **d. des bonnes mœurs,** divergence, deviation, from morality.

déviationnisme [devjasjɔnism], *s.m. Pol:* deviationism.

déviationniste [devjasjɔnist], *a. & s.m. or f. Pol:* deviationist.

dévidage [devidaːʒ], *s.m. Tex: etc:* (*a*) unwinding; (*b*) reeling, winding off, spooling.

dévider [devide], *v.tr. Tex: etc:* (*a*) to unwind; (*b*) to reel, wind off, spool (thread, etc.); *F:* **il me dévida toute l'histoire,** he reeled off the whole story to me.

dévideur, -euse [devidœːr, -øːz], *s. Tex:* (*a*) (*pers.*) reeler, wind(st)er; (*b*) reeling machine, reel, winder, spool.

dévidoir [devidwa:r], *s.m.* (*a*) *Tex:* reeling machine, reel, winder, spool; (*b*) **d. (de machine à coudre),** shuttle winder; (*c*) **d. (à flexible, à manche d'incendie),** hose reel; (*d*) *El.E:* (i) drum (for cable, etc.); (ii) drum barrow.

dévié [devje], *a.* **route déviée,** diversion; **rayon de lumière d.,** refracted ray of light; **avoir la taille un peu déviée,** to have one shoulder slightly higher than the other.

dévier [devje], *v.* (*pr.sub.* & *p.d.* **n. déviions, v. déviiez**) **1.** *v.i.* to deviate, swerve, diverge; *Sp:* (*of ball*) to break; *Mec.E:* to run out of true; **d. de la verticale,** to run out of the vertical; **d. de sa direction,** to deviate, turn aside, from one's direction; **faire d. une balle,** to deflect a bullet; **il ne dévie jamais de ses principes,** he never deviates, never departs, never swerves, from his principles; *Nau: Av:* **d. de sa route,** to deviate from one's course; **ne pas d. de sa route,** to keep one's course; **l'ouragan nous fit d.,** the hurricane drove us out of our course. **2.** *v.tr.* (*a*) to turn (blow, etc.) aside; to deflect (ray, etc.); *Min:* **d. un puits,** to deflect a well; **d. la justice,** to pervert, interfere with, the course of justice; **accident qui lui a dévié la colonne vertébrale,** accident that gave him curvature of the spine; (*b*) *Surg:* to abduct (an organ).

se dévier, (*of the spine, etc.*) to become, grow, crooked, curved; (*of timber*) to warp.

devin, devineresse [dəvɛ̃, dəvinrɛs], *s.* **1.** deviner; soothsayer; *f.* fortune-teller; *F:* **je ne suis pas d.,** I'm not a thought reader; **pas besoin d'être d. pour comprendre,** you don't have to be a wizard to understand. **2.** *F:* **(serpent) d.,** boa constrictor.

devinable [dəvinabl], *a.* guessable.

deviner [dəvine], *v.tr.* **1.** *abs.* to divine, to practise divination; **l'art de d.,** the art of soothsaying. **2.** to guess (riddle, secret, etc.); to predict (the future); to read (s.o.'s character); **je devine ce que vous allez répondre,** I can guess your answer; **d. la pensée de qn,** to read s.o.'s thoughts; **je le devinais dans la pénombre,** I could make him out in the darkness; **on devine la mer toute proche,** one can feel the sea not far off; **je lui devine de l'intelligence,** I should say he has intelligence; *pred.* **on la devine (être) intelligente,** one can tell she is clever; *F:* **cela se devine,** that's obvious; **vous avez deviné,** that's right, you've guessed right, you've got it; **d. bien, mal,** to guess right, wrong.

devineresse. *See* DEVIN.

devinette [dəvinɛt], *s.f.* riddle, conundrum.

devineur, -euse [dəvinœ:r, -ø:z], *s.* guesser (of riddle, etc.).

dévirage[1] [devira:ʒ], *s.m.* (*a*) working back, coming unscrewed (of breech-block, etc.); (*b*) *Nau:* unwinding (of capstan); (*c*) sluing over (of sail, etc.).

dévirage[2], *s.m.* curve (of a timber).

dévirer[1] [devire]. **1.** *v.tr.* (*a*) to turn back (screw); to feather (oar); *Nau:* to veer (the capstan); (*b*) to put about (a sail, etc.). **2.** *v.i.* & *pr.* (*of winch, capstan*) to take charge, to get out of control.

dévirer[2], *v.tr.* to bend, curve (a timber).

dévirginiser [devirʒinize], *v.tr.* to deprive (woman) of her virginity, *U.S:* to devirginate (woman).

déviriliser [devirilize], *v.tr.* to emasculate (s.o.).

devis [dəvi], *s.m.* **1.** *A:* chat, talk. **2.** (*a*) estimate (of work to be done, etc.); scheme; **d. descriptif,** specification; **d. estimatif,** estimate of quantities and costs; **d. d'architecte,** bill of quantities; **faire le d.,** to take out quantities; *N.Arch:* **d. de poids,** weights estimate; (*b*) *Av:* load sheet, weight breakdown.

dévisager [devizaʒe], *v.tr.* (**je dévisageai(s); n. dévisageons**) **1.** *A:* to disfigure, to claw (s.o.'s) face. **2.** to stare at (s.o.); to look (s.o.) full in the face.

devise [dəvi:z], *s.f.* **1.** (*a*) *Her:* device; emblematic figure; (*b*) motto; (*c*) slogan; (*d*) *Nau:* name (of ship). **2.** *Fin:* currency; *used esp. in* **devises étrangères,** foreign currency; **effet en d.,** bill in foreign currency; **d. forte,** hard currency; **d. faible,** soft currency; **d. convertible,** convertible currency.

deviser [dəvize], *v.i.* to chat, gossip; **d. de choses et d'autres,** to chat about one thing and another.

devise-titre [dəviztitr], *s.f.* property currency; *pl. devises-titres.*

dévissage [devisa:ʒ], *s.m.* **1.** (*a*) unscrewing (of bolt, etc.); (*b*) taking the screws out of (lock, etc.). **2.** *Mount: F:* fall.

dévisser [devise]. **1.** *v.tr.* (*a*) to unscrew (bolt nut, etc.); to screw out (breech-block); (*b*) to take the screws out of (lock, etc.); (*c*) *P:* **d. son billard,** to die, peg out. **2.** *v.i. Mount: F:* to fall.

se dévisser, to come unscrewed, to unscrew.

de visu [devizy], *Lt. adv.phr.* as an eye-witness; first-hand.

dévitalisation [devitalizasjɔ̃], *s.f. Dent: etc:* devitalisation.

dévitaliser [devitalize], *v.tr.* to devitalize; *Dent:* **d. une dent,** to devitalize the pulp, *F:* to kill the nerve, of a tooth.

dévitrification [devitrifikasjɔ̃], *s.f.* devitrification.

dévitrifier [devitrifje], *v.tr.* (*p.d.* & *pr.sub.* **n. dévitrifiions, v. dévitrifiiez**) to devitrify (glass).

dévocalisation [devɔkalizasjɔ̃], *s.f.* devocalization.

dévoiement [devwamɑ̃], *s.m.* **1.** (*a*) canting, tilting (of funnel, etc.); (*b*) cant, tilt. **2.** diverting (of pipe, flue). **3.** *N.Arch:* flaring (of timbers). **4.** *A:* **d. de corps,** diarrhoea; looseness of the bowels; **être pris d'un d.,** to have an attack of diarrhoea.

dévoilement [devwalmɑ̃], *s.m.* (*a*) unveiling; (*b*) revealing, disclosure (of name, secret, etc.).

dévoiler [devwale], *v.tr.* **1.** to unveil (face, statue); *Lit: Poet:* to unshroud (statue, light, etc.). **2.** to reveal, disclose (name, secret, etc.); to unmask (conspiracy); to lay bare (fraud). **3.** *Cy: Aut:* **d. une roue,** to straighten a buckled wheel.

se dévoiler. 1. (*of pers.*) to remove one's veil(s); to unveil. **2.** (*of secret, etc.*) to come to light.

dévoîment [devwamɑ̃], *s.m. A:* = DÉVOIEMENT.

devoir [dəvwa:r]. I. *v.tr.* (*pr.p.* **devant;** *p.p.* **dû,** *f.* **due;** *pr.ind.* **je dois, il doit, n. devons, ils doivent;** *pr.sub.* **je doive, n. devions, ils doivent;** *p.d.* **je devais;** *p.h.* **je dus;** *fu.* **je devrai**) **1.** (*duty*) should, ought; (*a*) (*general precept*) **tu dois honorer tes parents,** you should, it is your duty to, honour your parents; **fais ce que dois, advienne que pourra,** do your duty come what may; (*b*) (*command*) **vous devez, devrez, vous trouver à votre poste à trois heures,** you must be at your post at three o'clock; **vous devrez manger plus que vous ne faites,** you will have to eat more than you do; **les commandes doivent être adressées à . . .,** orders should be sent to . . .; (*c*) **je ne savais pas ce que je devais faire,** I did not know what (I ought) to do; **elle ne savait si elle devait rire ou pleurer,** she did not know whether to laugh or cry; **vous ne devriez pas rester plus longtemps,** you ought not to stay any longer; **vous devriez lire Dickens,** you ought to read Dickens; **il aurait dû m'avertir,** he should have warned me; **il crut d. se retirer,** (i) he thought it his duty to retire; (ii) he thought it advisable to retire. **2.** (*compulsion*) must, have to; **tous les hommes doivent mourir,** all men must die; **je dois, devais, me plier à ses caprices,** I have, I had, to yield to his whims; **enfin j'ai dû, je dus, céder,** at last I had to yield, I was obliged to yield. **3.** (*futurity*) am to; (*a*) **je dois partir demain,** I am to start tomorrow; **je devais le rencontrer à Paris,** I was to meet him in Paris; **je devais le rencontrer à Paris, mais . . .,** I was to have met him in Paris, but . . .; **le train doit arriver à midi,** the train is due (to arrive) at twelve o'clock; **dût-il m'en coûter la vie,** were I to die for it; **dussé-je, quand je devrais, tout perdre,** even though I were to lose everything; (*b*) **il ne devait plus les revoir,** he was (destined) never to see them again; **une pluie qui semblait ne devoir jamais finir,** rain that seemed as though it would never end; **que voulez-vous! cela devait être,** well, well! it was meant to be, to happen. **4.** (*opinion expressed*) must; **vous devez avoir faim,** you must be hungry; **il doit avoir mené une vie bien dure,** he must have led a hard life; **il dut, a dû, avait dû, me prendre pour un autre,** he must have taken me for some one else; **il doit être trois heures,** it must be three o'clock; **il ne devait pas être loin de midi,** it must have been getting on for noon; **il ne doit pas avoir plus de 40 ans,** he can't be more than 40; **il doit y avoir beaucoup de gens qui . . .,** there must be many people who . . .; **celui-là? ce doit être le père de la mariée,** that man? he must be the bride's father; **on lui fit une proposition qui devait lui plaire,** they made a proposal that was likely to appeal to him. **5. d. qch. à qn,** to owe s.o. sth.; (*a*) **il me doit mille francs,** he owes me a thousand francs; **tout l'argent qui m'est dû,** all the money owing to me, due to me; **la somme à elle due par son frère,** the sum owed (to) her by her brother; **il doit de tous (les) côtés,** he owes money all round; (*b*) **d. du respect à son père,** to owe respect to one's father; **est-ce à vous que je dois cela?** am I indebted to you for that? **c'est à vous qu'elle doit son bonheur,** she owes her happiness to you; she has you to thank for her happiness; **je lui dois d'être en vie,** I owe my life to him; **c'est à votre ami que je dois ma nomination,** I owe my appointment to your friend; your friend was instrumental in getting me appointed; **je dois à mes amis de leur éviter ce chagrin,** I owe it to my friends to spare them this sorrow; **vous vous devez à vous-même de faire de votre mieux,** you owe it to yourself to do your best; **l'honnête homme se doit de ne jamais mentir,** a gentleman ought never to lie, should never lie; **on lui doit d'attendre son explication,** it is only fair to await his explanation; **la peine due à ces forfaits,** the penalties which these crimes deserve; *A:* **en devoir à qn,** to have a bone to pick with s.o.; **ils ne s'en doivent guère,** there is not much to choose between them.

II. **devoir,** *s.m.* **1.** (*a*) duty; **accomplir son d.,** to do one's duty; **manquer à son d.,** to fail in one's duty; **rentrer dans le d.** (*of mutineers, etc.*) to return to duty; **rappeler, ramener, remettre, qn à son d.,** to recall s.o. to his duty; **faire, remplir, son d. (envers qn, envers la patrie),** to do one's duty (by s.o., by one's country); **se faire un d. de (faire qch.),** to make a point of (doing sth.), to make it one's business to (do sth.); **se mettre en d. de faire qch.,** to prepare to do sth., to set about doing sth.; **il est de mon d. de . . .,** it is my duty, my business, to . . ., I am in duty bound to . . ., it is incumbent on me to . . .; **il est du d. des parents de . . .,** it is the duty of parents to . . .; **je sais ce qui est de mon d.,** I know where my duty lies; **je le fis par d.,** I did it from a sense of duty; (*b*) obligation; **mes devoirs de citoyen, de père,** my duties, obligations, as a citizen, as a father; (*c*) *Sch:* exercise, task; prep; **un d. de latin,** a Latin exercise; **je n'ai pas encore fait mes devoirs,** I haven't done my home-work, prep, yet; (*d*) *Cards:* book (at whist). **2.** *pl.* respects, duty; **rendre ses devoirs à qn,** to pay one's respects to s.o.; **aller présenter ses devoirs à qn,** to pay a formal call on s.o.; **mes devoirs à madame votre mère,** my respects to your mother; **rendre à qn les derniers devoirs,** to pay the last honours to s.o.; to pay a last tribute of respect to s.o. **3.** *Book-k:* debit; **avoir et d.,** debit and credit.

se devoir. 1. to have to devote oneself to s.o., sth.; **je me dois à ma famille,** I must devote myself to my family. **2.** to be compulsory; to be proper; **comme il se doit,** as is proper, right; **ils refusèrent comme faire se devait,** they very properly refused.

dévoiser [devwaze], *v.tr. Ling:* to unvoice (consonant).

dévoltage [devɔlta:ʒ], *s.m.* reduction of voltage; stepping down.

dévolter [devɔlte], *v.tr. El:* to reduce the voltage of, to step down (current).

dévolteur [devɔltœ:r], *s.m. El:* reducing transformer, stepdown transformer; negative booster.

dévolu [devɔly]. **1.** *a. Jur:* (*a*) (*of inheritance, etc.*) devolved; devolving (à, to, upon); transmitted down (to s.o.); **part dévolue à la ligne paternelle,** share that devolves to, upon, the heirs, that falls to the heirs, on the father's side; **succession dévolue à l'État,** escheated succession; (*b*) **droit d. à la Couronne,** right vested in the Crown; (*c*) **d. par péremption,** lapsed; (*d*) **d. à (qn, qch.),** reserved, left, for (s.o., sth.); **être d. à qn de faire qch.,** to fall to s.o.'s lot to do sth. **2.** *s.m.* (*a*) *Ecc:* lapse (of benefice); **bénéfice tombé en d.,** lapsed benefice; (*b*) **jeter son dévolu sur qch.,** (i) to have designs on sth., to set one's heart upon sth.; (ii) to lay claim to sth.; (iii) to choose sth.

dévolutaire [devɔlytɛ:r], *s.m. Ecc:* devolutionary.

dévolutif, -ive [devɔlytif, -i:v], *a. Jur:* devolutionary.

dévolution [devɔlysjɔ̃], *s.f. Jur:* (*a*) devolution, transmission (of property, etc.); **d. d'un héritage à l'État,** escheat; *Hist:* **la guerre de D.,** the War of Devolution; (*b*) *Ecc:* lapsing, devolution (of benefice).

devon [dəvɔ̃], *s.m. Fish:* minnow.

dévonien, -ienne [devɔnjɛ̃, -jɛn], *a.* & *s.m. Geol:* Devonian.

dévonite [devɔnit], *s.f. Miner:* devonite.

dévorant [devɔrɑ̃], *a.* **1.** ravenous; **faim dévorante,** gnawing hunger; **avoir une soif dévorante,** to be parched with thirst, to have a consuming thirst. **2.** consuming (fire, care, climate); wasting (disease); devouring (passion).

dévorateur, -trice [devɔratœːr, -tris]. **1.** *s.* devourer, consumer. **2.** *a.* devouring, consuming.

dévorer [devɔre], *v.tr.* (*a*) to devour (prey); (*of human beings*) to devour, eat greedily, gobble up, wolf (food); *Prov:* **les loups ne se dévorent pas entre eux,** there is honour among thieves; (*b*) **d. un livre,** to devour a book; **d. qn des yeux,** to devour s.o. with one's eyes, to gaze intently on s.o.; **d. une injure,** to swallow, pocket, an insult; **d. sa fortune,** to squander, run through, one's fortune; **les flammes ont dévoré le bâtiment,** the flames destroyed, consumed, the building; **l'orgueil le dévore,** he is eaten up, consumed, with pride; **la soif me dévore,** I am consumed, parched, with thirst; (*c*) **d. la route,** to tear along; to eat up the miles; (*of car, etc.*) to hurtle along; (*d*) **le visage dévoré,** with an anguished face.

dévoreur, -euse [devɔrœːr, -øːz], *s. F:* devourer; **grand d. de livres,** a glutton for books.

dévot, -ote [devo, -ɔt]. **1.** (*a*) *a.* devout, religious, pious; **attitude dévote,** devotional attitude; **livre d.,** (i) religious book; (ii) devotional book; **être d. à un saint,** to be a votary of a saint; *A:* **être d. à la bouteille,** to be addicted to the bottle, to worship the bottle; (*b*) *s.* devout person; *O:* **faux d.,** hypocrite. **2.** *a. & s. Pej:* sanctimonious (person); *s.f.* **dévote,** bigoted churchwoman. **3.** *s.* fanatic, devotee.

dévotement [devɔtmɑ̃], *adv.* devoutly.

dévotieusement [devosjøzmɑ̃], *adv. O:* devotedly.

dévotieux, -euse [devosjø, -øːz], *a. O:* **1.** imbued with formalism (in matters of worship). **2.** who makes a show of devoutness.

dévotisme [devɔtism], *s.m.* pietism.

dévotion [devosjɔ̃, -vɔ-], *s.f.* **1.** devotion, *esp.* devoutness, piety; **d. à la Sainte Vierge,** devotion to the Blessed Virgin; **avoir d. à un saint,** to show special devotion to a saint; **tomber, se jeter, dans la d.,** to take to religion; *R.C.Ch:* **fête de d.,** feast of devotion; **livres de d.,** devotional books; **tableau de d.,** religious picture; **faire ses dévotions,** to make one's devotions, say one's prayers; **fausse d.,** assumed piety. **2.** **avoir une grande d. pour qn, qch.,** to have a great devotion for, to be extremely attached to, s.o., sth.; **être à la dévotion de qn,** to give oneself up to the service of s.o., to be at s.o.'s disposal; **sénat à la d. de l'empereur,** senate devoted to the emperor.

dévoué [devwe], *a.* devoted, staunch, loyal (friend, etc.); **d. à qn, à la cause de qn,** devoted to s.o., to s.o.'s cause; **ils sont dévoués l'un à l'autre,** they are devoted to each other, are all in all to each other; (*letter formulae*) **votre d. serviteur,** your obedient servant; **votre tout d.** = yours sincerely; *Com:* **toujours entièrement d. à vos ordres,** always at your service.

dévouement [devumɑ̃], *s.m.* **1.** (*a*) *A:* self-immolation; (*b*) self- sacrifice, devotion to duty, devoted courage; **le d. d'Assas sauva l'armée,** Assas saved the army by sacrificing his own life; **il périt victime de son d.,** he died the victim of his courage, through his devotion to duty. **2.** devotion, devotedness, affection; **d. à la chose publique, au bien public,** public spirit; **servir qn avec d.,** to serve s.o. devotedly; **son d. pour son ami,** his devotion, attachment, to his friend; (*letter formulae*) **croyez, monsieur, à mon entier d., recevez l'assurance de mon d.,** your obedient servant; yours faithfully.

dévouer [devwe], *v.tr.* **1.** *A:* (*a*) to dedicate, consecrate (s.o., sth.); to give (s.o., sth.) up (to God, to the service of one's country, etc.); (*b*) to consign, deliver (s.o., sth.), to hand (s.o., sth.) over (to damnation, public wrath, etc.). **2.** **d. son temps, son énergie, à une cause,** to devote, sacrifice, one's time, one's energy, to a cause.

se dévouer. **1.** *O:* to devote oneself, dedicate oneself, give oneself up (to God, to one's country, to a cause, etc.); **se d. au secours des pauvres,** to devote oneself to the poor. **2.** **se d. pour qn,** to sacrifice oneself for s.o.; **se d. pour la patrie,** to lay down one's life for one's country; *abs.* **il est toujours prêt à se d.,** he is always ready to sacrifice himself; *F:* **personne ne veut aller chercher le pain? allons, dévoue-toi!** does nobody want to go and fetch the bread? come on, show willing!

dévoûment [devumɑ̃], *s.m. A:* = DÉVOUEMENT.

dévoyé [devwaje], *a.* **1.** (a)stray; *A:* **voyageur d.,** traveller who has lost his way, who has been misled; **esprit d.,** (i) mind at fault; (ii) warped mind; *s.* **un d.,** a bad lot, black sheep. **2.** *Tchn:* (*a*) sloping, canted, oblique (pipe, funnel, etc.); *N.Arch:* **couples dévoyés,** cant timbers; (*b*) out of truth; out of plumb; warped. **3.** *A:* (*of pers.*) suffering from diarrhoea.

dévoyer [devwaje], *v.tr.* (**je dévoie, n. dévoyons; je dévoierai**) **1.** *Lit:* (*a*) to mislead; to lead (s.o.) astray; **d. la jeunesse,** to lead youth astray, to corrupt youth; (*b*) to decoy. **2.** *Tchn:* (*a*) to place (sth.) obliquely, to give a cant to (sth.); to cant; (*b*) to lead (pipe, flue, etc.) round an obstacle; to divert. **3.** *A:* to loosen, relax, (s.o.'s) bowels; to give (s.o.) diarrhoea.

se dévoyer, to go astray; to stray (*esp* from the path of duty, etc.); to go wrong.

Dewar [dewaːr], *Pr.n. Ch:* **vase de D.,** Dewar flask.

déwatté [dewate], *a. El:* wattless; reactive; idle (current); **puissance déwattée,** wattless power, reactive power, reactive volt-amperes; **composante déwattée,** wattless component, reactive component.

deweylite [dewelit], *s.f. Miner:* deweylite.

dextérité [dɛksterite], *s.f.* dexterity, skill, skilfulness; **d. à manier les armes à feu,** skill in handling fire-arms; **conduire ses affaires avec d.,** to manage one's business with tact, cleverness, skill.

dextralité [dɛkstralite], *s.f.* right-handedness.

dextran [dɛkstrɑ̃], *s.m. Ch: Pharm:* dextran.

dextre [dɛkstr̥]. **1.** *a.* (*a*) *Her:* dexter (side of of shield, etc.); (*b*) *A:* skilful (hand, etc.). **2.** *s.f. A: & Lit:* right-hand.

dextrement [dɛkstrəmɑ̃], *adv. A:* dexterously, adroitly, skilfully.

dextrine [dɛkstrin], *s.f. Ch: Ind:* dextrin, British gum.

dextro- [dɛkstrɔ], *pref.* dextro-; **dextroracémate,** dextroracemate; **dextrotartrate,** dextrotartrate.

dextrocardie [dɛkstrɔkardi], *s.f. Anat: Med:* dextrocardia.

dextrochère [dɛkstrɔkɛːr], *s.m. Her:* **d. armé, paré,** right arm in armour, clothed.

dextrogyre [dɛkstrɔʒiːr], *a. Ch:* dextrogyre, dextrorotatory; **composé d.,** dextro-compound.

dextrorse [dɛkstrɔrs], **dextrorsum** [dɛkstrɔrsɔm]. **1.** *a.inv. Bot: etc:* dextrorse. **2.** *adv. occ.* clockwise.

dextrose [dɛkstroːz], *s.m. Ch: O:* dextrose.

dextrovolubile [dɛkstrɔvɔlybil], *a. Bot:* dextrorse.

dey [dɛ], *s.m. Hist:* dey (of Algiers).

dézincage [dezɛ̃kaːʒ], **dézingage** [dezɛ̃gaːʒ], *s.m.* dezincation.

dézinguer [dezɛ̃ge], *v.tr.* to dezinc.

di- [di], *pref.* di-; **dichromatique,** dichromatic; **dibenzyle,** dibenzyl; **dihydrate,** dihydrate; **diphénol,** diphenol.

dia- [dia, dja], *pref.* dia-; **diaphonie,** diaphony; **diacaustique,** diacaustic.

dia [dja], *int.* driver's signal to horse to turn to the left, *U.S:* haw! *s.a.* HUE.

diabase [djabaːz], *s.f. Miner:* diabase.

diabète [djabɛt], *s.m. Med:* diabetes; **d. sucré,** diabetes mellitus, sugar diabetes; **d. insipide,** diabetes insipidus.

diabétique [djabetik], *a. & s.* diabetic.

diabétogène [djabetɔʒɛn], *a.* diabetogenic.

diabétomètre [djabetɔmɛtr̥], *s.m. Med:* diabetometer; saccharometer.

diable [djɑːbl̥], *s.m.* **1.** devil; **le d.,** the devil, Satan; *P:* Old Nick; **en d.,** extremely; **méchant en d.,** very wicked; *F:* **faire le d. (à quatre),** to kick up a row, a shindy; **les diables sont déchaînés,** it's hell let loose; **il faut rendre justice au d.,** give the devil his due; **il ne faut pas faire d'un d. deux,** don't make a bad business worse; **tirer le d. par la queue,** to be hard up; **ce serait le d. si . . .,** it would be surprising if . . .; **du d. si je le sais!** I'm damned, hanged, if I know! **allez au d.!** go to blazes! go to the devil! go to Jericho! **au d. votre associé!** your partner be hanged! bother your partner! **au d. le marmot!** drat the brat! **que le d. l'emporte!** the devil take him! confound him! **(que) le d. m'emporte si j'y comprends quelque chose!** I'll be hanged, blest, if I understand! **cette affaire s'en va au d.,** this business is going to the dogs; **il demeure au d.,** he lives miles away; **aller au d. vauvert,** *often corrupted to* **aller au d. auvert, au d. (au) vert,** to go out into the wilds, to go a long way; **c'est au d. auvert,** it's the hell of a way, miles from anywhere; **c'est le d. pour lui faire entendre raison,** it is the devil (and all), it's damned hard, to make him see reason; **tout le d. et son train,** one damn thing after another; **c'est là le d.!** there's the rub! **c'est le d. à confesser,** it's a devil of a business; **ce n'est pas le d.,** (i) it's not so very difficult; (ii) it's nothing to worry about; **où d. est-il allé?** where the devil has he gone? **qui d. peut venir à cette heure?** who on earth, who the dickens, who in heaven's name, can be coming at this time? **quel d. d'intérêt cela peut-il avoir pour vous?** what possible interest can you have in it? **que d.!** hang it! *int.* **d.!** heavens! oh dear! **bruit de tous les d.,** the devil of a din; **avoir un trac de tous les diables, une frousse du d.,** to be in a devil, a hell, of a funk; to be in a blue funk; **j'ai eu un travail de tous les diables,** I had, the hell, the very dickens, of a job; *adv.phr.* **à la d.,** anyhow; **écrire à la d.,** to have a terrible style; **travail fait à la d.,** perfunctory, scamped, work; *Mil.Hist:* (*name given to chasseurs alpins, 1914-18 war*) **Diables bleus,** French light infantry; **c'est un d. incarné, un d. à quatre,** he's a devil incarnate, a regular devil; **un d. d'homme,** a devil of a man; **pauvre d.!** poor beggar! **un drôle de petit d.,** a funny little chap; **un grand d.,** a big fellow; **un grand d. de cheval,** a huge beast of a horse; **c'est un bon d.,** he is not a bad type; **ce d. de parapluie,** that wretched umbrella; **un d. de temps, un temps du d.,** wretched, lousy, weather; **le d. bat sa femme et marie sa fille,** it's rain and shine together; **un d. de tour,** a rotten trick; **une d. d'affaire,** a devil of a business; **quelle d. de langue que l'anglais!** English is an awful language! *a.* **il est très d.,** he's full of spirit, of fun, of mischief; **elle est très d.,** she's a regular tomboy; **il n'est pas aussi d. qu'il est noir,** he's not so black as he's painted; *s.a.* AVOCAT 2, BEAUTÉ 1, CORPS 1, PEIGNER 1. **2.** (*a*) (two-wheeled) trolley; (railway porter's) barrow, luggage truck; (stone) lorry; (*b*) *Toys:* **d. (à ressort),** Jack-in-the-box; (*c*) *Ich:* **d. de mer,** (i) angler (fish), frog fish; (ii) devil fish, manta ray; (*d*) *Tex:* devil, devilling machine; **conducteur de d.,** deviller; (*e*) *Z:* **d. de Tasmanie,** Tasmanian devil; **d. de Java,** pangolin.

diablement [djɑbləmɑ̃], *adv. F:* devilish (strong, good, funny, etc.); **c'est d. embêtant,** it's an infernal nuisance; **il y a d. longtemps,** it's a hell of a long time ago; **nous en avons d. besoin,** we need it badly; **il faisait d. froid,** it was hellishly cold.

diablerie [djɑbləri], *s.f.* **1.** *A:* devilry, diabolical art, sorcery. **2.** *F:* mischievousness, boisterousness; fun, devilry. **3.** *Lit.Hist:* diablerie, (i) play or scene acted by imps, devils; (ii) Satan and his attendants (in a mystery play, etc.).

diablesse [djɑblɛs], *s.f.* **1.** she-devil. **2.** (*a*) *A:* termagant, virago; (*b*) tomboy. **3.** (*a*) **une grande d. de paysanne,** a great strapping peasant-woman; **une bonne d.,** a good-natured woman; (*b*) **quelle d. de vie menait-il?** what extraordinary sort of a life was he leading?

diablotin [djɑblɔtɛ̃], *s.m.* **1.** (*a*) little devil, imp; (*b*) *F:* mischievous child, imp. **2.** (Christmas) cracker. **3.** *Nau:* mizzen-top staysail. **4.** scud, fleck (of cloud); *pl.* flying rags of cloud; rack. **5.** *Toys:* **d. (à ressort),** Jack-in-the-box. **6.** *Ent:* larva of the empusa.

diabolique [djɑbɔlik], *a.* diabolic(al), fiendish; **possession d.,** demoniacal possession; **frénésie d.,** demoniac(al) frenzy; **elle prend un plaisir d. à l'irriter,** she takes a fiendish delight in aggravating him.

diaboliquement [djɑbɔlikmɑ̃], *adv.* diabolically, fiendishly.

diabolisme [djɑbɔlism], *s.m.* diabolism.

diabolo [djɑbɔlo], *s.m.* **1.** *Games:* diabolo. **2.** *Av: Aut:* dual wheel, twin wheel assembly. **3.** *Fish:* bobbin (of trawl net). **4.** lemonade drink with syrup.

diacaustique [diakostik], *a. Opt:* diacaustic (curve, etc.).

diacétique [diasetik], *a. Ch:* diacetic (acid).

diacéturie [diasetyri], *s.f. Med:* diaceturia.

diachromie [djakrɔmi], *s.f. Phot:* screen-plate colour-photography.

diachronie [djakrɔni], *s.f. Ling:* diachrony.

diachronique [djakrɔnik], *a. Ling:* diachronic, diachronistic, diachronous.

diachylon, diachylum [djaʃilɔ̃, djaʃilɔm], *s.m. Pharm:* diachylon, diachylum; **emplâtre d.,** lead plaster, diachylon plaster.

diacide [diasid], *s.m. Ch:* diacid.

diacinèse [djasinɛːz], *s.f. Biol:* diakinesis.

diaclase [djaklɑːz], *s.f. Surg:* diaclasis, fracture; *Geol:* diaclase.

diacode [djakɔd], *a. & s.m. Pharm:* **(sirop) d.,** diacodion, diacodium, syrup of poppies.

diaconal, -aux [djakɔnal, -o], *a. Ecc:* diaconal.

diaconat [djakɔna], *s.m. Ecc:* diaconate, deaconship.

diaconesse [djakɔnɛs], *s.f.* **1.** deaconess. **2.** deacon's wife.

diacre [djakr̥], *s.m. Ecc:* deacon.

diacritique [djakritik], *a.* **1.** *Ling:* diacritic(al) (sign); **signe d.,** diacritic. **2.** *Med:* characteristic (symptom).

diade [diad], *s.f. Biol:* dyad.

diadelphe [diadɛlf], *a. Bot:* diadelphous, diadelphian.
diadème [djadɛm], *s.m.* (*a*) diadem; (*b*) tiara.
diadochite [djadɔkit], *s.f. Miner:* diadochite.
diadoque [djadɔk], *s.m.* (*a*) *A.Hist:* **les diadoques,** the Diadochi (of Alexander the Great); (*b*) Crown prince (in modern Greece).
diagénèse [djaʒenɛ:z], *s.f. Geol:* diagenesis.
diagnose [djagno:z], *s.f.* **1.** *Med:* (art of) diagnosis. **2.** *Biol:* diagnosis; assignment of species.
diagnostic [djagnɔstik], *s.m. Med:* diagnosis (of disease).
diagnostique [djagnɔstik], *a. Med:* diagnostic (skill, sign, etc.).
diagnostiquer [djagnɔstike], *v.tr. Med:* to diagnose.
diagomètre [djagomɛtr̥], *s.m. El:* diagometer.
diagonal, -aux [djagɔnal, -o]. **1.** *a. Geom: etc:* diagonal; *Rail:* **voie diagonale,** cross-over. **2.** *s.f.* **diagonale;** (*a*) diagonal (line); **en diagonale,** diagonally; *Ten:* **jouer en d.,** to play across the court; (*b*) *Tex:* (i) diagonal cloth; (ii) twill; (*c*) *Civ.E:* cross-brace.
diagonalement [djagɔnalmɑ̃], *adv.* diagonally.
diagonite [djagɔnit], *s.f. Miner:* brewsterite.
diagramme [djagram], *s.m.* diagram; chart; graph; *Ph:* pattern (of diffraction, etc.); **d. d'une fleur,** floral diagram; *Mch:* **d. d'indicateur,** indicator diagram, card; **aire du d.,** work area; **plein du d.,** efficiency of cycle; *Ind:* **d. des opérations successives,** (process and) flow diagram, chart, sheet; *W.Tel: etc:* **d. de rayonnement d'antenne,** antenna pattern; *Med:* **d. de croissance (des os, etc.),** growth pattern (of bones, etc.).
diagraphe [djagraf], *s.m.* diagraph.
diagraphie [djagrafi], *s.f.* **1.** diagraphics. **2.** *Petroleum Min:* well-logging.
dial [dial], *s.m. Ch:* dialdehyde; *pl.* **dials.**
dialcool [dialkɔl], *s.m.* dialcohol.
dialdéhyde [dialdeid], *s.m. Ch:* dialdehyde.
dialectal, -aux [djalɛktal, -o], *a. Ling:* dialectal.
dialecte [djalɛkt], *s.m.* dialect.
dialecticien, -ienne [djalɛktisjɛ̃, -jɛn], *s.* dialectician; *a. Phil:* **matérialiste d.,** dialectical materialist.
dialectique [djalɛktik]. **1.** *a.* dialectic(al) (argument); *Phil:* **matérialisme d.,** dialectical materialism. **2.** *s.f.* dialectics.
dialectiquement [djalɛktikmɑ̃], *adv.* dialectically.
dialectologie [djalɛktɔlɔʒi], *s.f. Ling:* dialectology, study of dialects.
dialectologue [djalɛktɔlɔg], *s.m. & f.* dialectologist.
diallage [djala:ʒ], *s.f. Miner:* diallage.
diallagique [djalaʒik], *a. Miner:* diallagic.
diallèle [djalɛl], *s.m. Log:* diallelon.
dial(l)ogite [djalɔʒit], *s.f. Miner:* dial(l)ogite.
dialogique [djalɔʒik], *a.* dialogic(al) (discussion, etc.).
dialogisme [djalɔʒism], *s.m.* the art of dialogue, of conversation.
dialogue [djalɔg], *s.m.* dialogue; *Pol:* talks; **engager le d.,** to start talks; *F:* **c'est un d. de sourds,** we're, they're, not on the same wavelength.
dialoguer [djalɔge]. **1.** *v.i.* (*a*) to hold a dialogue, to converse; to dialogue; *F:* **d. avec les bouteilles,** to linger over one's cups; (*b*) to write dialogue(s). **2.** *v.tr.* (*a*) *Lit:* to write (literary work) in dialogue form; (*b*) *Ecc:* **messe dialoguée,** dialogue mass.
dialogueur [djalɔgœr], *s.m.* dialogist.
dialoguiste [djalɔgist], *s.m. & f. Cin:* screenwriter.
dialurique [dialyrik], *a. Ch:* dialuric.
dialycarpellé [dialikarpɛle], *a. Bot:* apocarpous.
dialypétale [dialipetal], *Bot:* **1.** *a.* **(corolle) d.,** dialypetalous (corolla). **2.** *s.f.pl.* *A:* **dialypétales,** Dialypetalae.
dialypétalie [dialipetali], *s.f. Bot:* dialypetalous condition.
dialysable [dializabl̥], *a. Ch:* dialysable.
dialysat [dializa], *s.m. Ch:* dialysate.
dialyse [dializ:e], *s.f. Ch: Rh:* dialysis.
dialysépale [dialisepal], *a. Bot:* dialysepalous (calyx).
dialyser [dialize], *v.tr. Ch:* to dialyse.
dialyseur [dializœr], *s.m. Ch:* dialyser, dialysing apparatus.
diamagnétique [djamaɲetik], *a. Ph:* diamagnetic.
diamagnétisme [djamaɲetism], *s.m. Ph:* diamagnetism.
diamant [djamɑ̃], *s.m.* **1.** diamond; **d. de première eau,** diamond of the first water; **d. brut,** rough diamond; **d. à pointes naïves,** point diamond; **d. taillé,** cut diamond; **d. en rose,** rose(-cut) diamond; **d. en table,** table(-cut) diamond; **d. brillant,** brilliant; **d. savoyard,** brown diamond; **d. factice,** (piece of) paste; **les diamants de la couronne,** the Crown jewels; *Tls:* **d. à rabot, de vitrier,** glazier's diamond, diamond point; **d. d'une pince,** heel of a crowbar. **2.** *Nau:* crown (of anchor). **3.** *Typ:* three-point type; diamond.
diamantaire [djamɑ̃tɛ:r]. **1.** *a.* diamond-like, sparkling. **2.** *s.m.* (*a*) diamond cutter; (*b*) diamond merchant.
diamanté [djamɑ̃te], *a.* (*a*) set with diamonds; (*b*) **fleurs diamantées,** frosted (artificial) flowers.
diamanter [djamɑ̃te], *v.tr.* (*a*) to set (piece) with diamonds; (*b*) to make (sth.) shine like a diamond.
diamantifère [djamɑ̃tifɛ:r], *a. Geol: etc:* diamantiferous (region, etc.); diamond-yielding (gravel, etc.); diamond (shares, etc.); **puits, cheminée, d.,** diamond pipe.
diamantin [djamɑ̃tɛ̃], *a.* diamond-like, diamantine, diamantoid.
diamantine [djamɑ̃tin], *s.f.* diamantine.
diamétral, -aux [djametral, -o], *a.* diametrical, diametral (line, etc.); *N.Arch:* **plan d.,** sheer plan.
diamétralement [djametralmɑ̃], *adv.* diametr(ic)-ally; (*of thgs*) **d. opposés,** diametrically opposite; (*of pers.*) **ils sont d. opposés,** they are diametrically opposed, poles apart.
diamètre [djamɛtr̥], *s.m. Geom: etc:* diameter; *Ph: etc:* bore; **la roue a 60 cm. de d.,** the wheel is 60 cm. in diameter, across; **d. intérieur,** internal diameter; **d. extérieur,** external diameter; *Mec.E:* **d. primitif,** pitch diameter (of toothed wheel); *Av: etc:* **d. de l'hélice,** circle of the propeller; *Nau:* **d. de giration, d'évolution,** final diameter; tactical diameter; *Phot:* **d. d'ouverture,** aperture.
diamide [diamid], *s.m. Ch:* diamide.
diamido- [diamido-], *pref. Ch:* diamido-.
diamidophénol [diamidɔfenɔl], *s.m. Ch:* diamidophenol; *Phot:* amidol.
diamine [diamin], *s.f. Ch:* diamine.
diamino- [diamino-], *pref: Ch: etc:* diamino-.
diammonique [diamɔnik], *a. Ch:* diammonium.
diandre [diɑ̃:dr̥], **diandrique** [diɑ̃drik], *a. Bot:* diandrous, two-stamened.
diane[1] [djan], *s.f. Mil: Nau:* reveille; **battre, sonner, la d.,** to sound the reveille.
Diane[2], *Pr.n.f.* **1.** *Myth:* Diana; *s.a.* CHASSERESSE. **2.** *s.f. Ent:* Diana butterfly.
dianite [djanit], *s.f. Miner:* dianite.
dianthera [diɑ̃tera], *s.m. Bot:* dianthera.
diantre [djɑ̃:tr̥], *int. A. & Lit:* (*euphemistic form of* DIABLE) **que d. désirez-vous?** what the deuce do you want? **d. soit des militaires!** a plague on all military men! **d., c'est cher!** hell, it's expensive!
diantrement [djɑ̃trəmɑ̃], *adv. A. & Lit:* devilishly.
diapason [djapazɔ̃], *s.m. Mus:* **1.** diapason, pitch; **d. normal,** (i) French pitch (A = 435 vibrations); (ii) concert pitch (A = 440 vibrations); **faire baisser le d. à qn,** to make s.o. sing small; **se mettre au d. de la compagnie,** to adapt oneself to the company, to fall in with the mood of the company. **2.** tuning fork; **d. de bouche,** pitch-pipe. **3.** compass, range (of the voice).
diapasonner [djapazɔne], *v.tr.* to tune, bring (instrument) to concert pitch.
diapause [djapo:z], *s.f. Ent:* diapause; (state of) suspended animation.
diapédèse [djapedɛ:z], *s.f.* diapedesis.
diaphane [djafan], *a.* (*a*) diaphanous; translucent; (*b*) transparent.
diaphanéité [djafaneite], *s.f.* (*a*) diaphaneity, diaphanousness; (*b*) translucence, translucency.
diaphanoscope [djafanɔskɔp], *s.m. Med:* diaphanoscope.
diaphanoscopie [djafanɔskɔpi], *s.f. Med:* diaphanoscopy.
diaphone [djafɔn], *s.m. Nau:* diaphone.
diaphonie [djafɔni], *s.f.* **1.** *Mus:* diaphony. **2.** *Tp: etc:* cross talk.
diaphonomètre [djafɔnɔmɛtr̥], *s.m. Tp:* cross-talk meter.
diaphorèse [djafɔrɛ:z], *s.f. Med:* diaphoresis, perspiration.
diaphorétique [djafɔretik], *a. & s.m. Med:* diaphoretic, sudorific.
diaphorite [djafɔrit], *s.f. Miner:* diaphorite.
diaphragmatique [djafragmatik], *a. Anat: Med:* diaphragmatic, pertaining to the diaphragm.
diaphragmation [djafragmasjɔ̃], *s.f. Phot:* stopping down (of lens).
diaphragme [djafragm], *s.m.* **1.** *Anat:* diaphragm. **2.** *Tchn:* (*a*) diaphragm, dividing plate (of pipe, electric cell, etc.); *Mch:* sliding stop valve; *N.Arch:* sluice valve (of bulkhead); *Phot:* diaphragm stop (of lens); **d. iris,** iris diaphragm; (*b*) sound-box (of gramophone); **membrane du d.,** diaphragm of the sound-box; (*c*) *Med:* (contraceptive) diaphragm; *F:* cap.
diaphragmer [djafragme], *v.tr.* **1.** to provide (tube, telescope, etc.) with a diaphragm. **2.** *Phot:* to stop down (lens).
diaphyse [djafi:z], *s.f. Anat: Bot:* diaphysis.
diapir [djapir], *a. & s.m. Geol:* diapiric (fold).
diapirique [djapirik], *a. Geol:* diapiric.
diapirisme [djapirism], *s.m. Geol:* diapirism.
diaplégie [djapleʒi], *s.f. Med:* diplegia, bilateral paralysis.
diapo [djapo], *s.f. Phot: F:* slide, transparency.
diapositive [djapɔzitiv], *s.f. Phot:* diapositive, transparency; **d. en couleurs,** colour transparency, colour slide; **d. de projection,** (lantern) slide.
diapré [djapre], *a.* variegated, mottled, speckled; *Her:* diapered (shield); *Tex:* **toile diaprée,** diaper.
diaprer [djapre], *v.tr.* to variegate, mottle, speckle; to diversify (sth.) with many colours; **le printemps diapre les champs de mille couleurs,** spring paints the fields with a thousand colours; **d. ses phrases de mots latins,** to lard one's sentences with Latin words.
diaprure [djapry:r], *s.f.* **1.** variegated, mottled, appearance. **2.** variegated pattern.
diarche [diarʃ], *a. Bot:* diarch.
diarrhée [djare], *s.f. Med:* diarrhoea.
diarrhéique [djareik]. **1.** *a. Med:* diarrhoeic, diarrhoeal. **2.** *s.* diarrhoeic subject.
diarthrodial, -aux [djartrɔdjal, -o], *a. Anat:* diarthrodial.
diarthrose [djartro:z], *s.f. Anat:* diarthrosis.
diaschisis [djaskisis], *s.m. Med:* diaschisis.
diascope [djaskɔp], *s.m.* diascope.
diascopie [djaskɔpi], *s.f.* diascopy.
diascopique [djaskɔpik], *a.* **projections diascopiques,** (lantern-)slide projections.
diascordium [djaskɔrdjɔm], *s.m. Pharm:* diascordium.
diaspis [djaspis], *s.m. Ent:* diaspis.
Diaspora (la) [ladjaspɔra], *s.f. Jew.Rel:* the Diaspora.
diaspore [djaspɔ:r]. **1.** *s.m. Miner:* diaspore. **2.** *s.f. Bot:* diaspore.
diastaltique [djastaltik], *a. Anat:* diastaltic.
diastase [djastɑ:z], *s.f.* **1.** *Surg:* diastasis. **2.** *Ch: Physiol:* diastase; enzyme.
diastasique [djastɑzik], *Ch: Physiol:* diastatic, enzymic.
diastasis [djastɑzis], *s.m. Med:* diastasis.
diastème [djastɛm], *s.f.* **1.** *Anat: Biol:* diastem. **2.** *Z:* diastema.
diastole [djastɔl], *s.f. Physiol:* diastole.
diastolique [djastɔlik], *a. Physiol:* diastolic.
diathermane [djatɛrman], *a. Ph:* diathermic, diathermanous.
diathermanéité [djatɛrmaneite], *s.f.,* **diathermansie** [djatɛrmɑ̃si], *s.f. Ph:* diathermancy, diathermaneity.
diathermie [djatɛrmi], *s.f. Med:* diathermy.
diathermique [djatɛrmik], *a. Ph:* diathermic, diathermanous.
diathèse [djatɛ:z], *s.f. Med:* diathesis, disposition, tendency, predisposition (to disease); **d. sanguine,** sanguine diathesis.
diathésique [djatezik], *Med:* diathetic, constitutional (disease, etc.).
diatomée [djatɔme], *s.f. Algae:* (*a*) diatom; (*b*) *pl.* **diatomées,** Diatoma.
diatomique [djatɔmik], *a. Ch:* diatomic.
diatomite [djatɔmit], *s.f. Miner:* diatomite, diatom earth.
diatonique [djatɔnik], *a. Mus:* diatonic (scale, interval).
diatoniquement [djatɔnikmɑ̃], *adv. Mus:* diatonically.
diatribe [djatrib], *s.f.* (*a*) diatribe; (*b*) abusive tirade.
diaule [diol], *s.f.* **1.** *A.Gr.Mus:* diaulos, double flute. **2.** *Gr.Ant: Sp:* diaulos, double course.
diazo [diazo], *s.m. Ch: F:* diazo compound.
diazoaminé [diazoamine], *s.m. Ch:* diazoamine.
diazoaminobenzène [diazɔaminobɛ̃zɛn], *s.m. Ch:* diazoaminobenzene.
diazoanhydride [diazɔanidrid], *s.m. Ch:* diazoanhydride.
diazobenzène [diazɔbɛ̃zɛn], *s.m. Ch:* diazobenzene.
diazoïmide [diazɔimid], *s.m. Ch:* diazoimide.
diazoïque [diazɔik], *a. & s.m. Ch:* diazo (compound).
diazole [diazol], *s.m. Ch:* diazole.
diazoma [djazoma], *s.m. A.Gr.Arch:* diazoma.

diazométhane [diazɔmetan], *s.m. Ch:* diazomethane.

diazo-réaction [diazɔreaksjɔ̃], *s.f. Ch: Biol:* diazo reaction.

diazoter [diazɔte], *v.tr. Ch:* to diazotize.

dibasique [dibazik], *a. Ch:* dibasic, bibasic.

dibenzopyrrole [dibɛ̃zɔpirɔl], *s.m. Ch:* dibenzopyrrole, carbazole.

dibenzoyle [dibɛ̃zɔil], *a.m. Ch:* dibenzoyl.

dibenzylamine [dibɛ̃zilamin], *s.f. Ch:* dibenzylamine.

dibenzyle [dibɛ̃zil], *s.m. Ch:* bibenzyl, dibenzyl.

dibit [dibi], *s.m.* (*computers*) dibit.

dibranches [dibrɑ̃:ʃ], *s.m.pl. Moll:* Dibranchia(ta).

dibromobenzène [dibrɔmɔbɛ̃zɛn], *s.m. Ch:* dibromobenzene.

dibromohydrine [dibrɔmɔidrin], *s.f. Ch:* dibromohydrin.

dibromosuccinique [dibrɔmɔsyksinik], *a. Ch:* dibromosuccinic (acid).

dibutyrine [dibytirin], *s.f. Ch:* dibutyrin.

dicaéidés [dikeide], *s.m.pl. Orn:* Dicaeidae.

dicaryon [dikarjɔ̃], *s.m. Bot:* dikaryon, dicaryon.

dicaryotique [dikarjɔtik], *a. Bot:* dikaryotic, dicaryotic.

dicastère [dikastɛ:r], **dicastérion** [dikasterjɔ̃], *s.m. Gr.Hist:* dicastery.

dicée [dise], *s.m. Orn:* flower-pecker; **d. à ventre orange,** orange-breasted flower-pecker.

dicéidés [diseide], *s.m.pl. Orn:* Dicaeidae.

dicentre [disɑ̃tr̥], *s.m. Bot:* bleeding heart; lyre flower; dicentra.

dicéphalie [disefali], *s.f. Ter:* dicephalism.

dicérion [diserjɔ̃], *s.m. Ecc:* dicerion, dikerion.

dicétone [disetɔn], *s.f. Ch:* diketone.

dichapétale [dikapetal], *s.m. Bot:* dichapetalum.

dicharyon [dikarjɔ̃], *s.m. Bot:* dikaryon, dicaryon.

dichlamydé [diklamide], *a. Bot:* dichlamydeous, hermaphrodite.

dichloracétique [diklɔrasetik], *a. Ch:* dichloracetic.

dichloracétone [diklɔrasetɔn], *s.f. Ch:* dichloroacetone.

dichloréthane [diklɔretan], *s.f. Ch:* dichloroethane, ethylidene (di)chloride.

dichlorobenzène [diklɔrɔbɛ̃zɛn], *s.m. Ch:* dichlorobenzene.

dichlorohydrine [diklɔrɔidrin], *s.f. Ch:* dichlorohydrin.

dichogame [dikɔgam], *a. Bot:* dichogamous.

dichogamie [dikɔgami], *s.f. Bot:* dichogamy.

dichotome [dikɔtɔm], *a.* **1.** *Astr:* dichotomized (moon). **2.** *Bot:* dichotomous, dichotomal.

dichotomie [dikɔtɔmi], *s.f.* **1.** *Astr: Bot: Log:* dichotomy. **2.** *Med: etc: F:* fee-splitting.

dichotomique [dikɔtɔmik], *a.* dichotomic.

dichotomiquement [dikɔtɔmikmɑ̃], *adv.* dichotomically.

dichroanthe [dikrɔɑ̃t], *a. Bot:* dichromatic.

dichroïque [dikrɔik], *a. Ph:* dichroic (crystal).

dichroïsme [dikrɔism], *s.m. Ph:* dichroism.

dichroïte [dikrɔit], *s.f. Miner:* dichroite.

dichromatique [dikrɔmatik], *a.* dichromatic.

dichroscopique [dikrɔskɔpik], *a.* dichroscopic.

dicible [disibl̥], *a.* (*rare*) sayable, expressible in words.

dickinsonite [dikɛ̃sɔnit], *s.f. Miner:* dickinsonite.

dicksonia [diksɔnja], *s.m. Bot:* dicksonia.

dicksoniacées [diksɔnjase], *s.f.pl. Bot:* Dicksoniaceae.

dicline [diklin], *a. Bot:* diclinous.

dico [diko], *s.m. Sch: F:* dictionary.

dicotyle [dikɔtil], **dicotylé** [dikɔtile], *a. Bot:* dicotyledonous.

dicotylédone [dikɔtiledɔn], *Bot:* **1.** *a.* dicotyledonous. **2.** *s.f.* (*a*) dicotyledon; (*b*) *pl.* (*as a class name*) Dicotyledones.

dicotylédoné [dikɔtiledɔne], *a. Bot:* dicotyledonous.

dicoumarine [dikumarin], *s.f.,* **dicoumarol** [dikumarɔl], *s.m. Med:* dicoumarin.

dicranocère [dikranɔsɛ:r], *s.m. Z: A:* pronghorn.

dicranure [dikrany:r], *s.f. Ent:* **d. vinule,** puss-moth.

dicrote [dikrɔt], *a. Med:* dicrotic.

dicrotisme [dikrɔtism], *s.m. Med:* dicrotism.

dicruridés [dikryride], *s.m.pl. Orn:* Dicruridae.

dictagraphe [diktagraf], *s.m.* dictagraph.

dictame [diktam], *s.m.* **1.** *Bot:* (*a*) dittany (of Crete), Cretan dittany; (*b*) **d. blanc,** white dittany; **d. bâtard,** bastard dittany. **2.** *Lit:* solace, comfort, balm.

dictamen [diktamɛn], *s.m.* dictate (of conscience, etc.).

Dictaphone [diktafɔn], *s.m. R.t.m:* Dictaphone.

dictateur [diktatœ:r], *s.m.* dictator; **ton de d.,** dictatorial tone.

dictatorial, -iaux [diktatɔrjal, -jo], *a.* dictatorial.

dictatorialement [diktatɔrjalmɑ̃], *adv.* dictatorially.

dictature [diktaty:r], *s.f.* dictatorship.

dictée [dikte], *s.f.* dictation; (*a*) (action of) dictating (sth.); **écrire qch. sous la d. de qn,** to write sth. at, from, s.o.'s dictation; (*b*) *Sch:* dictation (exercise).

dicter [dikte], *v.tr.* to dictate; **machine à d.,** dictating machine; **d. une lettre à qn,** to dictate a letter to s.o.; **d. des conditions,** to dictate, lay down, conditions; **mesure dictée par la prudence,** measure dictated by prudence; **votre conscience vous dictera votre devoir,** you must follow the dictates of your conscience; **d. sa volonté à qn,** to impose one's will on s.o.

diction [diksjɔ̃], *s.f.* diction; (*a*) style, choice of words; (*b*) manner of speech, delivery; **professeur de d.,** teacher of elocution.

dictionnaire [diksjɔnɛ:r], *s.m.* dictionary; lexicon; **d. anglais-français,** English-French dictionary; **d. de géographie,** gazetteer; **d. chiffré,** code book; *F:* **c'est un d. ambulant,** he is a walking encyclopaedia; *s.a.* COUP 1.

dicton [diktɔ̃], *s.m.* dictum, (common) saying; maxim; **comme dit le vieux d. . . .,** as the old tag has it.

dictynidés [diktinide], *s.m.pl. Arach:* Dictynidae.

dictyoptères [diktjɔptɛ:r], *s.m.pl. Ent:* Dictyoptera.

dictyosome [diktjɔzo:m], *s.m. Biol:* dictyosome.

dictyota [diktjɔta], *s.f. Algae:* dictyota.

dictyotales [diktjɔtal], *s.f.pl. Algae:* Dictyotales.

dicyanodiamide [disianɔdjamid], *s.m. Ch:* dicyanodiamide.

dicynodontidés [disinɔdɔ̃tide], *s.m.pl. Paleont:* Dicynodontidae.

dicypellion [disipɛljɔ̃], *s.m. Bot:* pink-wood.

didacticien, -ienne [didaktisjɛ̃, -jɛn], *s.* didactician.

didactique [didaktik]. **1.** *a.* didactic. **2.** *s.f.* didactics.

didactiquement [didaktikmɑ̃], *adv.* didactically.

didactyle [didaktil], *Z:* **1.** *a.* didactyl(e), didactylous. **2.** *s.m.pl.* **didactyles,** Didactyla.

didascalie [didaskali], *s.f. Gr.Ant:* didascaly, didascalia.

didelphe [didɛlf], *a. Anat:* didelphic.

didelphes [didɛlf], *s.m.pl.,* **didelphiens** [didɛlfjɛ̃], *s.m.pl. Z:* Didelphia; marsupials, didelphians.

delphidés [didɛlfide], *s.m.pl. Z:* Didelphidae, the opossum family.

didodécaèdre [didɔdekaɛdr̥], *a. Cryst:* didodecahedral.

Didon [didɔ̃], *Pr.n.f. Lt.Lit:* Dido.

diducteur, -trice [didyktœ:r, -tris], *a. Anat:* diductor (muscle, etc.).

diduction [didyksjɔ̃], *s.f. Anat: Z:* diduction.

didoncule [didɔ̃kyl], **didunculus** [didɔ̃kyly:s], *s.m. Orn:* didunculus.

didyme[1] [didim]. **1.** *a. Bot:* didymous. **2.** *s.m. Miner:* didymium.

Didyme[2], *Pr.n.m. B.Hist: etc:* Didymus.

Didyme[3], *Pr.n.f. A.Geog:* Didyma.

didyname [didinam], *a. Bot:* didynamian, didynamous.

didynamie [didinami], *s.f. Bot: O:* didynamia.

didynamique [didinamik], *a. Bot:* didynamian, didynamous.

dièdre [djɛ:dr̥]. **1.** *a. Geom: Av:* dihedral (angle). **2.** *s.m. Geom:* dihedron; *Av:* dihedral. **3.** *s.m. Mount:* open corner, groove.

diélectrique [dielɛktrik], *El:* (*a*) *a.* dielectric; insulating (medium); **rigidité d.,** dielectric strength; **constante d.,** dielectric constant; **hystérésis d.,** dielectric hysteresis; **polarisation d.,** dielectric polarization; (*b*) *s.m.* dielectric, non-conductor (of electricity), insulator.

diencéphale [diɑ̃sefal], *s.m. Anat:* diencephalon.

diencéphalique [diɑ̃sefalik], *a. Anat:* diencephalic.

diène [diɛn], *s.m. Ch:* diene.

dieppois, -oise [djɛpwa, -wa:z], *a. & s.* (native, inhabitant) of Dieppe.

diérèse [djerɛ:z], *s.f.* **1.** (*a*) *Ling:* diaeresis, division of one syllable into two; (*b*) *A:* = TRÉMA. **2.** *Surg:* diaeresis.

diergol [djɛrgɔl], *s.m.* bipropellant.

dièse [djɛ:z], *s.m. Mus:* sharp; **fa d.,** F sharp; **double d.,** double sharp.

diesel [diezɛl], *s.m. I.C.E:* diesel (engine).

diesel-électrique [diezɛlelɛktrik], *a. & s.m.* diesel-electric (locomotive); *pl. diesel-électriques.*

diésélisation [diezelizasjɔ̃], *s.f. Rail:* dieselization.

diéséliser [diezelize], *v.tr. Rail: etc:* to dieselize.

diesel-oil [diezɛlɔjl], *s.m.* diesel oil; *pl. diesel-oils.*

diéser [djeze], *v.tr.* (je dièse, n. diésons; je diéserai) *Mus:* to raise (note) a semitone; to sharpen, *U.S:* sharp (note).

diésis [diezis], *s.m. Typ:* double dagger.

diète[1] [djɛt], *s.f.* diet; **d. lactée,** milk diet; **d. absolue,** starvation diet; **être à la diète,** to be (i) on a low, short, diet; (ii) on starvation diet; **mettre qn à la d.,** to put s.o. on a (low or starvation) diet, to diet s.o.; **se mettre à la d.,** to diet oneself; **les loups supportent longtemps la d.,** wolves can go without food, can starve, for a long time.

diète[2], *s.f. Hist: Pol:* diet.

diététicien, -ienne [djetetisjɛ̃, -jɛn], *s.* dietician.

diététique [djetetik], *Med:* **1.** *a.* dietetic. **2.** *s.f.* dietetics.

diéthanolamine [dietanɔlamin], *s.f. Ch:* diethanolamine.

diéthylénique [dietilenik], *a.* diethylenic, diethylene.

diétrichite [djetrikit], *s.f. Miner:* dietrichite.

dietzéite [djetzeit], *s.f. Miner:* dietzeite.

dieu, -ieux [djø], *s.m.* God. **1. les dieux d'Égypte,** the gods of Egypt; **le d. des combats,** the god of war; **grands dieux!** heavens! ye gods (and little fishes)! **un festin des dieux,** a feast for the gods; **se faire un d. de qn,** to make a (little) god of s.o.; **il fait un d. de son ventre,** he makes a god of his belly. **2.** (*a*) **la voix de Dieu,** the voice of God; **blasphémer le nom de D.,** to take God's name in vain; **un homme de D.,** a holy man; **un homme tout en D.,** a very devout man; **s'il plaît à D.,** please God, God willing, D.V.; **D. merci!** (*on solemn occasions*) thank God! thanks be to God! (*b*) **le bon D.,** God; **le bon D. vous voit, mes enfants,** God sees you, children; **recevoir le bon D.,** to receive the Holy Sacrament; **on lui donnerait le bon D. sans confession,** he looks as innocent as a new-born babe; *Ent:* **bête à bon D.,** ladybird; (*c*) *P:* **un bon D.,** a religious statue, statuette; (*d*) (*F. uses*) **D. merci!** thank heaven! thank goodness! **pour l'amour de D.,** for goodness' sake; **faire qch. comme pour l'amour de D.,** to do sth. grudgingly; **D. sait si j'ai travaillé,** heaven knows I have worked hard enough; **c'est comme ça tous les jours que (le bon) D. fait,** it's like that every blessed day; **c'est la maison du bon D.,** it is a very hospitable house; they are kindness itself; **cela va comme il plaît à D.,** things are allowed to drift, things are going all anyhow; **cela va D. sait comme,** things are going none too well; *P:* **ce n'est pas D. possible,** it ain't ruddy possible. **3.** *int.* (*a*) (*admitted*) **mon D.! grand D.!** dear me! heaven's (above)! **mon D., mon D.!** good heavens! really! **mon D. oui!** why, yes; **mon D. non!** well, no! **mon D. je veux bien!** well, I don't mind! **mon D. je n'en sais rien!** indeed I don't know! (*b*) (*profane*) **bon D.! D. de D.! bon D. de bon D.!** (**sacré**) **nom de D.!** for Christ's sake! God almighty! hell! **quel bon d. d'imbécile!** what a bloody fool!

Dieudonné [djødɔne], *Pr.n.m.* Deodatus.

diffa [difa], *s.f.* (*in Algeria*) diffa.

diffamant [dif(f)amɑ̃], *a.* defamatory, slanderous, libellous.

diffamateur, -trice [dif(f)amatœ:r, -tris], *s.* defamer, slanderer, libeller.

diffamation [dif(f)amasjɔ̃], *s.f.* defamation, slander, libel; *Jur:* **intenter un procès en d. à qn,** to bring an action for libel against s.o.

diffamatoire [dif(f)amatwa:r], *a.* defamatory, slanderous, libellous.

diffamé [dif(f)ame], *a. Her:* defamed, tailless (lion, etc.).

diffamer [dif(f)ame], *v.tr.* to defame, slander, libel; to cast aspersions, a slur, on (s.o.'s) reputation.

différé [difere], *a.* deferred (payment, call, annuity, etc.); *El:* **coupe-circuit à action différée,** time-lag cut-out; *Phot:* **obturateur à action différée,** delayed-action shutter; *W.Tel: T.V:* **émission en d.,** (pre)recorded broadcast; *s.* **le d.,** prerecording, (pre)recorded broadcasting.

différemment [diferamɑ̃], *adv.* differently; **d. de,** in a different way, manner, from.

différence [diferɑ̃:s], *s.f.* difference; **d. de goûts,** differences of taste; **la d. de A à B, entre A et B, de A et de B,** the difference between A and B; **il n'y a pas de d. entre eux,** there's nothing to choose between them; **la d. consiste dans le climat,** the difference lies in the climate; **cela fait une grande d.,** it makes a great difference, a big difference; **cela ne fait pas grande d.,** it doesn't make much difference; **cela ne fait pas de d.,** it makes no odds; **quelle d. avec . . .!**

what a difference from . . .! **faire la d. d'une chose avec une autre, entre une chose et une autre,** to distinguish, discriminate, see the difference, between two things; **d. de nature (de deux obligations, etc.),** different nature (of two obligations, etc.); *Mth:* **d. de deux sinus,** difference between two sines; *Nau:* **navire sans d. de tirant d'eau,** ship without difference in draught of water, on an even keel; *Metall:* **d. de poids entre acier et fer,** weight differential between steel and iron; *prep.phr.* **à la d. de . . .,** unlike . . ., contrary to . . .; **la vie des grandes villes, à la d. de celle de la campagne,** town life as distinct from, as opposed to, country life; *conj.phr.* **à la d. que . . .,** with this difference that . . ., except that . . ..

différenciatif, -ive [diferɑ̃sjatif, -iːv], *a. Ling:* differentiating.

différenciation [diferɑ̃sjasjɔ̃], *s.f.* differentiation.

différenciateur, -trice [diferɑ̃sjatœːr, -tris], *a.* differentiating.

différencier [diferɑ̃sje], *v.tr.* (*p.d. & pr.sub.* **n. différenciions**) to differentiate (**de, d'avec,** from); (*a*) to distinguish, to mark the difference (**entre . . . et . . .,** between . . . and . . .); (*b*) *Mth:* to obtain the differential (coefficient) of (equation, etc.); **expression non différenciée,** undifferentiated expression.

se différencier, to be different (from each other), to differ; to become different.

différend [diferɑ̃], *s.m.* difference, dispute, disagreement (**entre,** between; **relatif à,** as to); **avoir un d. avec qn,** to be at variance with s.o.; **vider, régler, un d.,** to settle a difference, a dispute.

différent [diferɑ̃]. **1.** *a.* different; (*a*) unlike; **mœurs différentes des nôtres,** habits different from ours; (*b*) not the same; **ils habitent des maisons différentes,** they live in different houses; (*c*) various; **différentes personnes l'ont vu,** different people saw him; **différents degrés de petitesse,** various degrees of smallness; **à différentes reprises,** at various times, off and on. **2.** *s.m. Num:* mint-mark.

différentiation [diferɑ̃sjasjɔ̃], *s.f. Mth:* differentiation.

différentiel, -ielle [diferɑ̃sjɛl]. **1.** *a.* differential (calculus, tariff, diagnosis, gear, etc.); discriminating, discriminatory, (duty, tariff); **vis à filets différentiels,** differential screw; *Ac:* **son d.,** differential tone, difference tone; *Psy:* **seuil d.,** differential threshold. **2.** *s.m. Aut: etc:* differential; **d. à roues anglées, d. conique,** bevel (gear) differential. **3.** *s.f. Mth:* **différentielle,** differential.

différentier [diferɑ̃sje], *v.tr.* (*p.d. and pr.sub.* **n. différentiions**) *Mth:* to differentiate.

différer [difere], *v.* (**je diffère, n. différons; je différerai**) **1.** *v.tr.* to defer, postpone (judgment); to put off, hold over (payment); **d. de faire qch.,** to defer, put off, doing sth.; **d. l'échéance d'un effet,** to let a bill lie over. **2.** *v.i.* to differ; (*a*) **il diffère beaucoup de son frère,** he differs greatly from, is very different from, is a great contrast to, his brother; **ils diffèrent entre eux par la taille,** they differ from one another in height; **ils diffèrent de race et d'idiome,** they are different in race and speech; **sa maison ne diffère pas beaucoup de la nôtre,** his house is not so very unlike ours; (*b*) **d. d'opinion,** to differ in opinion; **les historiens diffèrent (entre eux) sur ce point,** historians are at variance, are not in agreement (among themselves), on this point.

difficile [difisil], *a.* **1.** difficult (work, situation, etc.); **travail assez d.,** rather difficult work, work of some difficulty; **raisonnement d. à suivre,** argument that is difficult, hard, to follow; **circonstances difficiles,** trying circumstances; **agir dans les circonstances les plus difficiles,** to act under circumstances of the greatest, utmost, difficulty; **question d.,** hard, difficult, question; **les temps sont difficiles,** times are hard; **le plus d. est fait,** we've done the hardest part; we've turned the corner; **il est d. à, pour, de jeunes élèves d'exprimer leurs idées,** it is hard, difficult, for young pupils to express their ideas; **il m'est d. d'accepter,** it is difficult for me to accept, I can't very well accept; **il m'est d. de ne pas accepter,** I can't very well not accept. **2.** *F:* difficult to get on with, hard to please, particular, choosy; **humeur d.,** difficult, crotchety, temper; **individu d'humeur d.,** crotchety individual; **enfant d.,** difficult, problem, child; **homme d. à contenter,** hard man to satisfy; **il est d. à vivre,** he is difficult to get on with; **les femmes jalouses sont difficiles à manier,** jealous women are difficult to handle; **il est d. sur la nourriture,** he is particular, fastidious, faddy, about his food; **il n'est pas d. quant au choix de ses relations,** he is not particular about his choice of friends; **cheval d.,** stubbornly disobedient horse; *s.* **faire le d.,** to be hard to please; to pick and choose; **ne faites pas le d.,** don't be difficult, fussy, about it.

difficilement [difisilmɑ̃], *adv.* with difficulty; not easily; **faire qch. d.,** to have difficulty in doing sth.; **il apprend d.,** he is slow at learning; **d. prononçable,** hardly pronounceable; **vérités d. transmissibles,** truths which cannot easily be conveyed.

difficulté [difikylte], *s.f.* difficulty; **il est en d.,** he is in trouble; **lever une d.,** to remove a difficulty; **tourner une d.,** to get round, evade, a difficulty; **un moyen de tourner la d.,** a way out of the difficulty; **cela ne présente aucune d.,** there is no difficulty about it, there is nothing difficult about it; **ce n'est pas une d. pour lui,** he makes nothing of it; **faire, élever, des difficultés,** to create obstacles, raise objections, make difficulties; **faire des difficultés pour accepter,** to make difficulties about accepting; **avoir de la d. à faire qch.,** to have difficulty in doing sth., to find it hard, difficult, to do sth.; **si vous saviez les difficultés que j'ai eu à surmonter,** if you only knew the difficulties I had to overcome, the difficulties I was under! **susciter des difficultés à qn,** to put difficulties in s.o.'s way; **aplanir toutes les difficultés,** to remove all difficulties; **cela ne fera pas de d. que je sache,** I'm sure that will be all right; **elle signa le contrat sans plus de d.,** she signed the contract without further ado; **avoir une légère d. avec qn,** to have a slight difference of opinion with s.o.

difficultueux, -euse [difikyltɥø, -øːz], *a.* **1.** *A:* difficult to please, fussy, over-particular, captious; **il est peu d. dans les affaires,** he is not too scrupulous in business. **2.** *F:* **entreprise difficultueuse,** undertaking bristling with difficulties; sticky job.

diffluence [diflyɑ̃s], *s.f.* diffluence.

diffluent [diflyɑ̃], *a.* diffluent (tumour, stream, etc.).

diffluer [diflye], *v.i.* to flow away; (*of pus, etc.*) to run.

difforme [difɔrm], *a.* deformed, mis-shapen (person, limb); **ongles difformes,** shapeless, unshapely, nails; **troncs d'arbres difformes,** gnarled tree trunks.

difformité [difɔrmite], *s.f.* deformity; malformation.

diffracter [difrakte], *v.tr. Opt:* to diffract.

diffractif, -ive [difraktif, -iːv], *a. Opt:* diffractive.

diffraction [difraksjɔ̃], *s.f. Opt:* diffraction; *Atom.Ph:* **d. d'électrons, de neutrons,** electron, neutron, diffraction.

diffractomètre [difraktɔmɛtr̥], *s.m.* diffractometer; **d. à neutrons,** neutron diffraction meter.

diffringent [difrɛ̃ʒɑ̃], *a. Opt:* diffracting, diffractive.

diffus [dify], *a.* diffused (light); diffuse (matter, inflammation, etc.); **éclairs diffus,** sheet lightning; **style d.,** diffuse, prolix, style; **orateur d.,** verbose, wordy, long-winded, orator; *Med:* **phlegmon d.,** diffuse phlegmon.

diffusant [difyzɑ̃]. **1.** *a.* diffusing. **2.** *s.m.* diffuser.

diffusat [difyza], *s.m. Atom.Ph:* diffusate.

diffusé [difyze], diffused; *esp.* **lumière diffusée,** (i) flood-lighting; (ii) indirect lighting.

diffusément [difyzemɑ̃], *adv.* diffusedly; wordily, verbosely; in a long-winded fashion.

diffuser [difyze], *v.tr.* **1.** to diffuse, spread (light, heat, etc.); *Atom.Ph:* to scatter (particles, etc.). **2.** (*a*) *W.Tel:* to broadcast (programme, etc.); (*b*) to spread, propagate, (ideas, news); (*c*) to distribute, circulate (books, newspapers).

se diffuser, to diffuse.

diffuseur [difyzœːr], *s.m.* **1.** *I.C.E:* mixer, spray cone, diffuser; *Hyd.E: El:* diffuser; *Sug.-R:* diffusion battery; *W.Tel:* cone loudspeaker; *Atom.Ph:* scatterer; *I.C.E:* **buse de d.,** (i) choke tube (of carburettor); (ii) diffuser nozzle (of jet aircraft). **2.** (*pers.*) (*a*) spreader, broadcaster (of ideas, news, etc.); (*b*) distributor (of books, newspapers). **3.** *a. Phot:* **écran d.,** diffusion screen.

diffusibilité [difyzibilite], *s.f.* diffusibility.

diffusible [difyzibl̥], *a.* diffusible.

diffusif, -ive [difyzif, -iːv], *a.* diffusive.

diffusiomètre [difysjɔmɛtr̥], *s.m.* diffusiometer.

diffusion [difyzjɔ̃], *s.f.* **1.** diffusion (of light, heat, gases, etc.); *Atom.Ph:* **d. (de particules),** scattering (of particles); **d. ionosphérique, troposphérique,** ionospheric, tropospheric, scatter; **d. cohérente, incohérente, multiple,** coherent, incoherent, multiple, scattering; **d. simple,** single scattering; **d. ambipolaire,** ambipolar diffusion; **d. coulombienne,** Coulomb scattering; **d. des neutrons,** neutron diffusion; **coefficient de d. axial, radial,** axial, radial, diffusion coefficient; *Opt: Phot:* **cercle de d.,** circle of confusion; *Mec.E:* **cone de d.,** venturi; **plateau de d.,** diffuser plate; **pompe de d.,** diffusion pump. **2.** (*a*) spreading, diffusion, propagation, dissemination, circulation, broadcasting (of news, etc.); distribution (of official document); **d. des connaissances,** spread of knowledge; (*b*) spread (of disease, etc.). **3.** verbosity, wordiness, diffuseness (of style, etc.).

digamie [digami], *s.f. Bot:* digamy.

digastrique [digastrik], *a.* digastric (muscle).

digénèse [diʒenɛːz], *s.f. Biol:* digenesis.

digérable [diʒerabl̥], *a.* digestible.

digérer [diʒere], *v.tr.* (**je digère, n. digérons; je digérerai**) **1.** (*a*) to digest, tabulate, classify (laws, etc.); (*b*) to digest, think over, assimilate (what one reads or learns); **plans mal digérés,** ill-digested, ill-matured, raw, schemes. **2.** (*a*) to digest (food); **il digère bien,** his digestion is good; **je ne digère pas le porc,** pork does not agree with me; **aliments qui se digèrent difficilement,** food that does not digest easily; **difficulté à d.,** sluggish digestion; (*b*) *F:* to swallow, stomach, put up with (insult, etc.); **il n'a pas digéré cette remarque,** this remark sticks in his gizzard, still rankles in his mind; **vérités dures à d.,** unpalatable truths. **3.** (*a*) *Med: A:* to mature (tumour); (*b*) *Pharm:* **(faire) d. une poudre,** to digest a powder (in warm liquid); (*c*) *Cu:* **faire d. qch. à feu doux,** to let sth. simmer over a slow fire.

digest [daidʒest, diʒest], *s.m. Journ: F:* digest.

digeste[1] [diʒest], *s.m.* **1.** digest (of laws, etc.). **2.** *Journ: F:* digest.

digeste[2], *a. F:* easily digestible.

digesteur [diʒestœːr], *s.m. Ch: etc:* digester.

digestibilité [diʒestibilite], *s.f.* digestibility.

digestible [diʒestibl̥], *a.* digestible.

digestif, -ive [diʒestif, -iːv]. **1.** *a.* digestive; **le tube d.,** the alimentary canal. **2.** *s.m.* (*a*) *Med:* digestive; aid to digestion; (*b*) brandy; liqueur.

digestion [diʒestjɔ̃], *s.f.* **1.** *Physiol:* digestion; **aliments d'une d. facile,** easily digested food; **faire une promenade de d.,** to walk one's lunch off; *F:* **un affront de dure d.,** an insult difficult to swallow, to stomach; *F:* **lettre de d.,** bread-and-butter letter. **2.** (*a*) *Ch: Hyg: etc:* digestion; (*b*) *Med: A:* maturing (of tumour).

digital, -ale, -aux [diʒital, -o]. **1.** *a.* (*a*) digital (nerve, etc.); **empreinte digitale,** finger-print; (*b*) digital (computer). **2.** *s.m. Fung:* clavaria. **3.** *s.f. Bot:* **digitale,** digitalis; **d. pourprée,** foxglove.

digitaléine [diʒitalein], *s.f. Ch:* digitalein.

digitaline [diʒitalin], *s.f. Ch: Pharm:* digitalin, digitalis.

digitalisation [diʒitalizasjɔ̃], *s.f.* digitalization.

digitaliser [diʒitalize], *v.tr.* to digitalize.

digitaria [diʒitarja], *s.m. Bot:* crabgrass.

digitation [diʒitasjɔ̃], *s.f.* digitation.

digité [diʒite], *a. Bot: Z:* digitate(d).

digitifolié [diʒitifɔlje], *a. Bot:* digitate-leaved.

digitiforme [diʒitifɔrm], *a.* digitiform, fingerlike.

digitigrade [diʒitigrad], *a. & s.m. Z:* digitigrade.

digitinerve [diʒitinɛrv], **digitinervé** [diʒitinɛrve], *a. Bot:* digitinerved, digitinervate.

digitipenné [diʒitipɛne], *a. Bot:* digitipinnate.

digitoxine [diʒitɔksin], *s.f. Pharm:* digitoxin.

digitoxose [diʒitɔksoːz], *s.f. Pharm:* digitoxose.

diglyphe [diglif], *s.m. Arch:* diglyph.

digne [diɲ], *a.* **1.** (*a*) deserving, worthy (**de,** of); **sa conduite est d. de récompense,** his conduct deserves a reward; **elle est d. qu'on fasse davantage pour elle,** she deserves to have more done for her; **caractère d. de respect,** character worthy, deserving, of respect; **d. d'éloges,** praiseworthy; **d. de remarque,** noteworthy; **d. d'envie,** enviable; **d. de pitié,** pitiable; **d. d'une mère,** motherly; **peu d. d'une mère,** unmotherly; **d. de ce nom,** worthy of the name; **il n'est pas d. de vivre,** he is not fit to live; **livre d. d'être lu,** book worth reading; **c'est bien d. de lui,** that's just like him; (*b*) **un d. homme,** a worthy man. **2.** dignified; **air d.,** dignified, stately, air; air of dignity.

dignement [diɲmɑ̃], *adv.* **1.** deservedly, suitably; **récompenser qn d.,** to reward s.o. properly, adequately. **2.** with dignity; **représenter d. qn,** to represent s.o. with dignity.

dignitaire [diɲitɛːr], *s.m.* dignitary (of the Church, etc.).

dignité [diɲite], *s.f.* **1.** dignity; **air, ton, de d.,** dignified air, tone; **la d. d'un sujet,** the seriousness, importance, of a subject; **il ne serait pas de ma d. de . . .,** it would be *infra dig.* for me to . . .; **se retrancher derrière sa d.,** to stand on one's dignity; **elle fit une entrée pleine de d.,** she sailed into the room. **2.** high position, dignity; **d. de chancelier,** dignity of chancellor; **s'élever aux dignités,** to rise to high rank; **d. héréditaire,** hereditary dignity; **la plus haute d. militaire,** the highest military rank.

dignois, -oise [diɲwa, -waːz], *a. & s. Geog:* (native, inhabitant) of Digne.

digoinais, -aise [digwanɛ, -ɛːz], *a. & s. Geog:* (native, inhabitant) of Digoin.

digon [digɔ̃], *s.m.* **1.** *Nau:* flagstaff. **2.** *Fish:* fishgig.

digramme [digram], *s.m.* digraph.

digraphe [digraf], *a. Typ:* digraphic.

digraphie [digrafi], *s.f. Com:* double-entry book-keeping.

digresser [digrɛse], *v.i.* to digress, to wander from the subject.

digressif, -ive [digrɛsif, -iːv], *a.* digressive.

digression [digrɛsjɔ̃], *s.f.* **1.** digression, side issue, departure from the subject; **faire une d., se perdre, se lancer, dans une d.,** to digress, to wander from the point; to fall, go off, into a digression; to lose oneself in a digression. **2.** *Astr:* digression (of planet).

digressivement [digrɛsivmɑ̃], *adv.* digressively.

digue [dig], *s.f. Hyd.E:* (*a*) dyke, dam, causeway, embankment (of waterway, etc.); front, esplanade (of seaside town); (*b*) breakwater, pier (of stone); sea wall; jetty; (*c*) barrier (to passions, etc.); **opposer une d. aux eaux, à la colère,** to stem the waters, a flood of anger.

digue-digue [digdig], *s.f. A: P:* epileptic fit; **tomber en d.-d.,** (i) to have a fit; (ii) to faint.

diguer [dige], *v.tr.* **1.** *Hyd.E:* to dike, to dam (up) (river, etc.). **2.** to spur (horse); to dig one's spurs into (one's horse).

diguette [digɛt], *s.f.* (*in paddy-field*) bund.

digyne [diʒin], *a. Bot:* digynous (flower).

dihexaèdre [diɛgzaɛdr̥]. **1.** *s.m. Geom: Cryst:* dihexahedron, hexagonal pyramid. **2.** *a.* dihexahedral.

dihybride [diibrid], *s.m. Biol:* dihybrid.

dihybridisme [diibridism], *s.m. Biol:* dihybridism.

dihydracridine [diidrakridin], *s.f. Ch:* dihydroacridine.

dihydranthracène [diidrɑ̃trasɛn], *s.m. Ch:* dihydroanthracene.

dihydrate [diidrat], *s.m. Ch:* dihydrate.

dihydrite [diidrit], *s.f. Miner:* dihydrite.

dihydrobenzène [diidrɔbɛ̃zɛn], *s.m. Ch:* dihydrobenzene.

dihydrocarvéol [diidrɔkarveɔl], *s.m. Ch:* dihydrocarveol.

dihydrocarvone [diidrɔkarvɔn], *s.f. Ch:* dihydrocarvone.

dihydroergotamine [diidrɔɛrgɔtamin], *s.f. Ch:* dihydroergotamine.

dihydronaphtalène [diidrɔnaftalɛn], *s.m. Ch:* dihydronaphthalene.

dihydrostreptomycine [diidrɔstrɛptɔmisin], *s.f. Ch:* dihydrostreptomycin.

dihydroxyacétone [diidrɔksiasetɔn], *s.m. Ch:* dihydroxyacetone.

dihydroxyanthracène [diidrɔksiɑ̃trasɛn], *s.m. Ch:* dihydroxyanthracene.

dihydroxybenzoïque [diidrɔksibɛ̃zɔik], *a. Ch:* dihydroxybenzoic (acid).

diiambe [diiɑ̃ːb], *s.m. Pros:* diiamb(us).

diiodobenzène [dijɔdɔbɛ̃zɛn], *s.m. Ch:* diiodobenzene.

diiodoforme [dijɔdɔfɔrm], *s.m.* diiodoform.

dijonnais, -aise [diʒɔnɛ, -ɛːz], *a. & s. Geog:* (native, inhabitant) of Dijon.

dik-dik [dikdik], *s.m. Z:* dik-dik; dig-dig.

dike [dik], *s.m. Geol:* dyke.

diktat [diktat], *s.m. Pej:* dictate, diktat.

dilacération [dilaserasjɔ̃], *s.f.* dilaceration.

dilacérer [dilasere], *v.tr.* (*conj. like* LACÉRER), to break, tear, in pieces, to dilacerate.

dilapidateur, -trice [dilapidatœːr, -tris]. **1.** *a.* (*a*) spendthrift; (*b*) peculating. **2.** *s.* (*a*) spendthrift, squanderer; (*b*) peculator.

dilapidation [dilapidasjɔ̃], *s.f.* **1.** wasting, dilapidation, squandering (of fortune, etc.). **2.** peculation.

dilapider [dilapide], *v.tr.* **1.** to waste, squander (fortune, public funds). **2.** to misappropriate (trust funds, etc.).

dilatabilité [dilatabilite], *s.f. Ph:* dilatability, expansibility.

dilatable [dilatabl̥], *a.* dilatable, expansible.

dilatant [dilatɑ̃]. **1.** *a.* dilating (force, etc.). **2.** *s.m. Surg:* dilator.

dilatateur, -trice [dilatatœːr, -tris]. **1.** *a.* dilating; **muscle d.,** dilator. **2.** *s.m. Surg: Anat:* dilator.

dilatation [dilatasjɔ̃], *s.f.* (*a*) dila(ta)tion, expansion; **d. de la pupille,** dilation of the pupil; **d. des gaz,** expansion of gases; *Const:* **joint à d. libre, joint de d.,** expansion joint; *Civ.E:* **chariot de d.,** expansion slide (of girder, etc.); expansion truck (of steel bridge, etc.); *Metall:* **d. (à la chaleur),** (metal) creep; *Mec.E:* **effort de d.,** expansion stress; **d. de prise,** setting expansion (of cement, etc.); (*b*) distension, dilation (of stomach, etc.).

dilater [dilate], *v.tr.* (*a*) to dilate, expand; *F:* **d. le cœur,** to cheer, gladden, the heart; (*b*) to distend (the stomach).

se dilater, (*a*) to dilate, swell, expand; **la pupille se dilate dans l'obscurité,** the pupil dilates in the dark; **pores dilatés,** enlarged pores; (*b*) (*of the stomach*) to become distended.

dilatoire [dilatwaːr], *a. Jur: etc:* dilatory.

dilatoirement [dilatwarmɑ̃], *adv.* in a dilatory manner.

dilatomètre [dilatɔmɛtr̥], *s.m. Ph:* dilatometer.

dilatométrie [dilatɔmetri], *s.f. Ph:* dilatometry.

dilection [dilɛksjɔ̃], *s.f.* dilection; **d. du prochain,** love of one's neighbour.

dilemmatique [dilɛm(m)atik], *a. Log:* dilemmatic.

dilemme [dilɛm], *s.m. Log:* dilemma; **les termes d'un d.,** the horns of a dilemma; **enfermer qn dans un d.,** to fix s.o. on the horns of a dilemma, to put s.o. in a fix, to drive s.o. into a corner.

dilettante [dilɛt(t)ɑ̃ːt], *s.* dilettante, amateur; **occupations de d.,** dilettantist pursuits; **faire des sciences en d.,** to toy with, play at, dabble in, science; *pl. dilettanti, dilettantes.*

dilettantisme [dilɛt(t)ɑ̃tism], *s.m.* dilettantism, amateurism.

diligemment [diliʒamɑ̃], *adv.* **1.** diligently, industriously. **2.** promptly, quickly.

diligence [diliʒɑ̃ːs], *s.f.* **1.** (*a*) diligence, industry, application; **travailler avec d.,** to work diligently; **montrer beaucoup de d. à faire qch.,** to show great diligence in doing sth.; (*b*) haste, dispatch; **en toute d.,** with all possible dispatch, with all expedition; **faire d.,** to hurry, to make haste; *Com:* **vos commandes seront exécutées avec la plus grande d.,** your orders will be executed promptly. **2.** *Jur:* proceedings; **faire (ses) diligence(s) contre qn,** to take proceedings against s.o.; **à la diligence de qn,** at the suit of s.o. **3.** *A.Veh:* (stage-)coach; *A:* **se rendre en d. à . . .,** to coach, stage, to . . .; *F:* **c'est la diligence embourbée,** we, things, are stuck in a rut; **du temps des diligences,** in the old days.

diligent [diliʒɑ̃], *a.* **1.** diligent, industrious, painstaking; **l'abeille diligente,** the busy bee; **soins diligents,** assiduous care. **2.** speedy, prompt (messenger, etc.).

diligenter [diliʒɑ̃te], *v.tr. A: & Jur:* to press on, urge on (s.o., sth.); to hasten (work).

se diligenter, *A:* to make haste; to exert oneself.

dilobé [dilɔbe], *a.* bilobed, bilobate.

dilogie [dilɔʒi], *s.f.* **1.** *Rh:* dilogy. **2.** *Lit:* play with a double plot.

diluant [dilyɑ̃]. **1.** *a.* diluent. **2.** *s.m.* diluter, diluent, thinner.

dilué [dilɥe], *a.* diluted; **solution diluée,** dilute(d) solution; **acide acétique d.,** dilute, weak, acetic acid; *Mil:* **formation diluée,** deployed, loose, formation.

diluer [dilɥe], *v.tr.* **1.** to dilute (de, with); to water down (drink, etc.); to thin down (paint); *Fin:* **d. le capital,** to water the stock. **2.** to space out, extend (troops, etc.).

se diluer, to become diluted.

dilutif [dilytif], *s.m. Paint:* thinning agent, thinner.

dilution [dilysjɔ̃], *s.f.* **1.** dilution; thinning down; watering down (of liquid); *Ph:* **d. isotopique, moléculaire,** isotopic, molar, dilution; *Mec.E:* **dispositif de d. d'huile,** oil dilution system; *Fin:* **d. de capital,** watering of stock. **2.** bypass (of jet engine); **taux de d.,** bypass ratio; **réacteur à taux de d. élevé,** high bypass engine.

diluvial, -iaux [dilyvjal, -jo], **diluvien, -ienne** [dilyvjɛ̃, -jɛn], *a.* **1.** diluvian (fossils, etc.); diluvial (deposit, clay, etc.). **2. pluie diluvienne,** deluge of rain, torrential rain, downpour.

diluvium [dilyvjɔm], *s.m. Geol: O:* diluvium, river drift.

dîmable [dimabl̥], *a.* tithable.

dimanche [dimɑ̃ːʃ], *s.m.* **1.** Sunday; **d. des Rameaux, de Pâques, de la Pentecôte,** Palm Sunday, Easter Sunday, Whit Sunday; **d. gras,** Quinquagesima Sunday; **observer le d.,** to keep the sabbath; **venez me voir d.,** come and see me on Sunday; **il vient le d., il vient les dimanches,** he comes on Sundays; **il vient tous les dimanches,** he comes every Sunday; **habits du d.,** one's Sunday best; **s'habiller en d.,** to put on one's Sunday best; **ma robe des dimanches,** my best, party, dress; **un air de d.,** a festive appearance; *F:* **c'est d. aujourd'hui,** today's a holiday; *F:* **chauffeur du d.,** weekend driver; **peintre du d.,** amateur, spare-time, painter; *s.a.* RIRE. **2.** *Paint:* bare patch, *U.S:* holiday.

dîme [dim], *s.f.* **1.** tithe; **faire payer la d. à qn,** to tithe s.o.; **lever la d. sur qch.,** to tithe sth.; **payer la d. sur qch.,** to tithe sth.; **prélever la d. sur qch.,** to exact a proportion, a percentage, of sth. as dues; **grange de la d.,** tithe barn. **2.** (*with ref. to U.S.*) dime, ten cents.

dimension [dimɑ̃sjɔ̃], *s.f.* dimension, size; **bouteille de grandes dimensions,** large-sized bottle; **de dimensions ordinaires,** of ordinary size; **géométrie à deux, à trois, dimensions,** two-, three-dimensional geometry; **prendre les dimensions de qch.,** to take the measurements of sth.; *F:* **prendre les dimensions de qn,** to size up s.o.; **prendre ses dimensions,** to size up work, the facts; *Mec.E:* **mettre (un trou, etc.) à dimensions,** to size (a hole, etc.); **taillé à la d.,** cut to size; *Mth: Ph:* **équation de dimensions,** dimensional equation.

dimensionné [dimɑ̃sjɔne], *a.* dimensioned; **largement d.,** of ample dimensions.

dimensionnel, -elle [dimɑ̃sjɔnɛl], *a.* dimensional.

dîmer [dime], *v.tr. & i.* to levy tithe on (corn, etc.); *abs.* to levy tithes; **d. sur les récoltes,** to levy tithes on crops, to tithe crops.

dimère [dimɛːr]. **1.** *a.* (*a*) *Bot: Ent:* dimerous; (*b*) *Ch:* dimeric. **2.** *s.m. Ch:* dimer.

diméthylacétique [dimetilasetik], *a. Ch:* dimethylacetic (acid).

diméthylamine [dimetilamin], *s.f. Ch:* dimethylamine.

diméthylaniline [dimetilanilin], *s.f. Ch:* dimethylaniline.

diméthylarsine [dimetilarsin], *s.f. Ch:* dimethylarsine.

diméthylbenzène [dimetilbɛ̃zɛn], *s.m. Ch:* dimethylbenzene, xylene.

dimètre [dimɛtr̥], *a. & s.m. Pros:* (vers) **d.,** dimeter.

dîmier [dimje], *s.m. A:* tithe-proctor, -collector.

diminué [diminɥe]. **1.** *Mus:* diminished (interval). **2.** *Knitting: etc:* **rang d.,** row in which the number of stitches is decreased; **bas entièrement d.,** fully-fashioned stocking. **3. colonne diminuée,** tapering column. **4. un vieillard d.,** an old man whose powers are waning; **c'est un homme diminué,** he is failing, he is not what he used to be; *s.m.* **un diminué,** a man whose powers are failing him; **un diminué physique,** a physically handicapped person.

diminuendo [diminɥɛ̃do], *adv. & s.m. Mus:* diminuendo.

diminuer [diminɥe]. **1.** *v.tr.* to lessen; to diminish; reduce; to shorten; *Knitting:* to decrease (number of stitches); **d. les prix,** to reduce, bring down, prices; **d. les dépenses,** to curtail, cut down, reduce, expenses; **d. l'autorité de qn,** to lessen, detract from, s.o.'s authority; **cela vous diminuerait aux yeux du public,** it would lower you in the eyes of the public; **d. les chagrins de qn,** to lighten s.o.'s grief; **d. l'ardeur de qn,** to damp s.o.'s ardour; **d. le son,** to reduce the volume of sound; *Arch:* **d. une colonne,** to diminish, taper, a column. **2.** *v.i.* to diminish, decrease, lessen, grow less; (*of fever, etc.*) to abate; (*of profits*) to fall off, decline; (*of prices*) to fall; (*of cold*) to relax; **les recettes diminuent,** the takings are falling off, dropping off; **d. de vitesse,** to slow down, to reduce speed; **les jours diminuent,** the days are drawing in, are shortening, are growing shorter; **la crue diminue,** the flood is subsiding, abating; **malade qui diminue à vue d'œil,** invalid who is visibly wasting away; **il sentait ses forces d.,** he felt his strength ebb; **cet accident l'a beaucoup diminué,** this accident has greatly handicapped him; **sa gloire diminue,** his fame is waning; **la colonne diminue vers le haut,** the column tapers upwards; *Nau:* **d. de toile,** to shorten sail; (*of water*) **d. de profondeur, de fond,** to shoal.

se diminuer, (*a*) to grow less; (*b*) to lower oneself.

diminutif, -ive [diminytif, -iːv], *a. & s.m.* diminutive; **appeler qn par, de, son d.,** to call s.o. by his pet name, by his nickname; **temple qui est un d. du Parthénon,** temple that is a miniature Parthenon.

diminution [diminysjɔ̃], *s.f.* diminution, lessening; reduction, decrease, lowering (of price, etc.); abatement (of flood, fever, etc.); curtailing, cutting down (of expenses); slackening (of speed); tapering (of column); **d. générale de richesse,** general falling off in wealth; **d. des espèces,** depreciation of money value; **d. d'impôts,** (i) lowering of taxation; (ii) drop in yield of taxation; **d. de prix, sur le prix,** reduction in price; **faire une d. à une robe,** (i) to shorten, (ii) to take in, a dress; **faire une d. sur un compte,** to allow a rebate on an account; **subir une d. rapide, to diminish rapidly;** *N.Arch:* **bordages de d.,** diminishing planks.
dimissoire [dimiswaːr], *s.m. Ecc:* dimissory letter, letters di(s)missory.
dimissoriales [dimisɔrjal], *a.f.pl. Ecc:* **lettres d.,** dimissory letter, letters di(s)missory.
dimorphe [dimɔrf], *a. Biol: Cryst:* dimorphic, dimorphous.
dimorphisme [dimɔrfism], *s.m., occ.* **dimorphie** [dimɔrfi], *s.f. Biol: Cryst:* dimorphism.
dinanais, -aise [dinanɛ, -ɛːz], *a. & s. Geog:* (native, inhabitant) of Dinan.
dinanderie [dinɑ̃dri], *s.f.* copper, brass, kitchen utensils; brass ware, copper ware; coppersmith's work; braziery.
dinandier [dinɑ̃dje], *s.m.* coppersmith; brazier.
dinandois, -oise [dinɑ̃dwa, -waːz], *a. & s.* (native, inhabitant) of Dinan.
dinantais, -aise [dinɑ̃tɛ, -ɛːz], *a. & s. Geog:* (native, inhabitant) of Dinant.
dinantien, -ienne [dinɑ̃sjɛ̃, -jɛn], *a. & s.m. Geol:* Dinantian.
dinaphtyle [dinaftil], *s.m. Ch:* dinaphthyl.
dinar [dinaːr], *s.m. Num:* dinar.
dinarique [dinarik], *a. Geog:* **Alpes dinariques,** Dinaric Alps.
dinassaut [dinaso], *s.f. Mil:* (= *Division navale d'assaut*), naval assault force.
dînatoire [dinatwaːr], *a. Dial:* **déjeuner d.,** substantial lunch, midday dinner.
dinde [dɛ̃ːd], *s.f.* **1.** turkey-hen; *Cu:* turkey. **2.** *F:* stupid woman; **petite d.!** you little goose! **quelles dindes que mes élèves cette année!** I have a lot of stupid, clottish, pupils this year; **prendre le thé avec un tas de vieilles dindes,** to take tea with a lot of old hens.
dindet [dɛ̃dɛ], *s.m. Nau:* ketch.
dindon [dɛ̃dɔ̃], *s.m.* **1.** turkey-cock. **2.** *F:* fool, idiot, clot; **être le d. de la farce,** to be fooled, duped; to have to pay the piper.
dindonneau, -eaux [dɛ̃dɔno], *s.m.* young turkey, turkey-poult.
dindonner [dɛ̃dɔne], *v.tr.* to dupe, fool (s.o.), to take (s.o.) in; **mari dindonné,** deceived husband.
dindonnier, -ière [dɛ̃dɔnje, -jɛːr], *s.* turkey-keeper.
dîné [dine], *s.m.A:* dinner.
dîner [dine]. I. *v.i.* to dine, to have dinner; **il est en train de d.,** he is having, eating, his dinner; **d. en ville,** to dine out; **il dîne souvent en ville,** he is a great diner-out; **à quelle heure dînez-vous?** what time do you have dinner? **d. de légumes,** *F:* **avec des légumes,** to dine off, on, vegetables; **nous venions de commencer de d.,** we had just begun dinner; **donner à d.,** to give a dinner (party); **d. à la fortune du pot,** to take pot luck; **d. sur le pouce,** to snatch a hasty dinner; **d. avec les chevaux de bois,** to go without one's dinner; *Prov:* **qui dort dîne,** (i) he who sleeps forgets his hunger; (ii) no work no dinner.
II. **dîner,** *s.m.* dinner; *Fr.C: Belg:* lunch; *Fr.C:* **salle à d.,** dining room; **d. prié, d'invitation,** (formal) dinner party; **nous avons ce soir un grand d.,** we have a big dinner party this evening; **qu'est-ce que nous avons à d.?** what have we got for dinner? **faire son d. de,** *F:* **avec, qch.,** to dine off, on, sth.; **l'heure du d.,** dinner time; **d. de têtes,** a dinner at which each guest represents a historical figure by means of masks or use of make-up, wig, etc., though wearing normal dress; *Prov:* **qui garde son d., il a mieux à souper,** we must put something by for a rainy day.
dînette [dinɛt], *s.f. F:* **1.** (*a*) dolls' dinner party; **faire la d.,** to give a dolls' dinner party; (*b*) doll's tea-set. **2.** light meal between intimate friends.
dîneur, -euse [dinœːr, -øːz], *s.* diner; **un beau d.,** a great eater, a good trencherman.
dineutron [dinøtrɔ̃], *s.m. Ph:* di-neutron.
dinghy [dingi], *s.m. Nau:* dinghy; *pl. dinghies.*
dingo [dɛ̃go], *s.m. Z:* dingo (of Australia).
dingo(t) [dɛ̃go], **dingue** [dɛ̃ːg], *a. & s.m. & f. P:* (*a*) *a.* cracked, daft, off his nut, bats, loony; (*b*) *s.* idiot, loony, clot.
dinguer [dɛ̃ge], *v.i. P: used only in* **envoyer d. qch.,** (i) to chuck sth. up; (ii) to fling sth. away; **envoyer d. qn,** (i) to send s.o. to the devil, to send s.o. packing; (ii) to send s.o. spinning (**contre,** against).
dinitrobenzène [dinitrobɛ̃zɛn], *s.m. Ch:* dinitrobenzene.
dinitrocrésol [dinitrokresɔl], *s.m. Ch:* dinitrocresol.
dinitrométhane [dinitrometan], *s.m.* dinitromethane.
dinitronaphtalène [dinitronaftalɛn], *s.m.* dinitronaphthalene.
dinitrophénol [dinitrofenɔl], *s.m. Ch:* dinitrophenol.
dinotrotoluène [dinitrotɔlɥɛn], *s.m. Ch:* dinitrotoluene.
dinocéras [dinɔseras], *s.m. Paleont:* dinoceras.
dinornis [dinɔrnis], *s.m. Paleont:* dinornis.
dinosaure [dinɔsɔːr], *s.m. Paleont:* dinosaur.
dinosauriens [dinɔsɔrjɛ̃], *s.m.pl. Paleont:* Dinosauria, dinosaurians, dinosaurs.
dinotherium [dinɔtɛrjɔm], *s.m. Paleont:* dinotherium.
diocésain, -aine [djɔsezɛ̃, -ɛn], *a. & s. Ecc:* diocesan.
diocèse [djɔsɛːz], *s.m. Ecc:* diocese.
diochotomique [diɔkɔtɔmik], *a.* diochotomizing.
Dioclétien [djɔklesjɛ̃], *Pr.n.m. Hist:* Diocletian.
dioctaèdre [diɔktaɛdr̥], *s.m.* dioctahedral crystal.
diode [djɔd], *a. & s.f. W.Tel:* diode; two-electrode tube; **d. détectrice,** detector diode; **d. en montage croisé,** cross-connected diode; **d. à pointe,** cat whisker diode; **détection par d.,** diode detection.
diodon [djɔdɔ̃], *s.m. Ich:* diodon, porcupine-fish, sea porcupine, globe fish.
Diodore [djɔdɔːr], *Pr.n.m. Hist:* Diodorus.
Diogène [djɔʒɛn]. **1.** *Pr.n.m. Gr.Hist:* Diogenes. **2.** *s.m. Crust:* Diogenes crab.
dioïque [djɔik], *a. Bot:* dioecious.
diois, -oise [diwa, -waːz], *a. & s. Geog:* (native, inhabitant) of Die.
Diomède [djɔmɛd], *Pr.n.m. Gr.Lit:* Diomedes.
diomédéidés [djɔmedeide], *s.m.pl. Orn:* Diomedeidae.
dionée [djɔne], *s.f. Bot:* dionaea; *F:* catch-fly, Venus's fly-trap.
dionysiaque [djɔnizjak]. **1.** *a. Gr.Ant:* dionysiac, dionysian. **2.** *s.f.pl.* **dionysiaques,** dionysia, dionysiac festivals.
dionysien, -ienne [djɔnizjɛ̃, -jɛn], *a. & s. Geog:* (native, inhabitant) of Saint-Denis.
dionysies [djɔnizi], *s.f.pl. Gr.Ant:* Dionysia.
Dionysos [djɔnizɔs], *Pr.n.m. Gr.Myth:* Dionysus.
Diophante [djɔfɑ̃ːt], *Pr.n.m. Hist. of Mth:* Diophantus.
diophantine [djɔfɑ̃tin], *a. Mth:* diophantine (analysis, equation).
diopside [djɔpsid], *s.m. Miner:* diopside.
dioptase [djɔptaːz], *s.f. Miner:* dioptase.
dioptides [diɔptid], *s.m.pl. Ent:* Dioptidae.
dioptre [djɔptr̥], *s.m.* **1.** *Astr: Surv:* diopter, dioptra, theodolite. **2.** *Opt:* dioptre.
dioptrie [djɔptri], *s.f. Opt:* (*unit of refractive power*) dioptre.
dioptrique [djɔptrik]. **1.** *a.* dioptric, refractive. **2.** *s.f.* (study of) refraction, dioptrics.
diorama [djɔrama], *s.m.* diorama.
dioramique [djɔramik], *a.* dioramic (effect, etc.).
diorite [djɔrit], *s.f. Geol:* diorite.
dioscoréacées [djɔskɔrease], *s.f.pl. Bot:* Dioscoreaceae.
Dioscures (les) [ledjɔskyːr], *s.m.pl. Gr.Myth:* the Dioscuri.
diosphénol [djɔsfenɔl], *s.m. Ch:* diosphenol.
dioxane [diɔksan], *s.m. Ch:* dioxane.
dioxime [diɔksim], *s.m. Ch:* dioxime.
dioxyde [diɔksiːd], *s.m. Ch:* dioxide; **d. de carbone,** carbon dioxide.
dioxytartrique [diɔksitartrik], *a. Ch:* dioxytartaric.
dipalmitine [dipalmitin], *s.f. Ch:* dipalmitin.
diparachlorobenzyle [diparaklɔrɔbɛ̃zil], *s.m. Ch:* diparachlorobenzyl.
dipétale [dipetal], *a. Bot:* dipetalous.
diphasé [difaze], *a. El.E:* two-phase, quarter-phase (system, armature, etc.); diphasic.
diphénique [difenik], *a. Ch:* diphenic.
diphénylacétylène [difenilasetilɛn], *s.f. Ch:* diphenylacetylene.
diphénylamine [difenilamin], *s.f. Ch:* diphenylamine.
diphényle [difenil], *s.m. Ch:* biphenyl, diphenyl.
diphénylméthane [difenilmetan], *s.m. Ch:* diphenylmethane.
diphényline [difenilin], *s.f. Ch:* diphenyline.
diphtérie [difteri], *s.f.* **1.** *Med:* diphtheria. **2.** *Vet:* **d. aviaire, des volailles,** fowlpox.
diphtérique [difterik], *a. Med:* diphther(it)ic.
diphtéroïde [difterɔid], *a. Med:* diphtheroid.
diphtongaison [diftɔ̃gɛzɔ̃], *s.f. Ling:* diphthongization.
diphtongal, -aux [diftɔ̃gal, -o], *a. Ling:* diphthongal.
diphtongue [diftɔ̃ːg], *s.f. Ling:* diphthong; **d. ascendante, croissante,** ascending, rising, diphthong; **d. descendante, décroissante,** descending, falling, diphthong.
diphtonguer [diftɔ̃ge], *v.tr.Ling:* to diphthong(ize).
diplacousie [diplakuzi], *s.f. Med:* diplacusis.
diplégie [dipleʒi], *s.f. Med:* diplegia, bilateral paralysis.
diplex [diplɛks], *a.inv. & s.m. Tg:* diplex (transmission, etc.).
diplexeur [diplɛksœːr], *s.m. Elcs:* diplexer.
dipl(o)- [diplɔ], *pref.* diplo-.
diplocéphale [diplɔsefal], *Ter:* **1.** *a.* diplocephalous. **2.** *s.m.* diplocephalus.
diplocéphalie [diplɔsefali], *s.f.* diplocephaly.
diplocoque [diplɔkɔk], *s.m. Bac:* diplococcus.
diplodocus [diplɔdɔkyːs], *s.m. Paleont:* diplodocus.
diploèdre [diplɔɛdr̥], *s.m. Cryst:* diplohedron.
diploédrique [diplɔedrik], *a.* diplohedral.
diplogénèse [diplɔʒenɛːz], *s.f. Biol:* diplogenesis.
diploglosse [diplɔglɔs], *s.m. Rept:* diploglossus.
diploïde [diplɔid], *a. Biol:* diploid.
diplomate [diplɔmat], *s.m.* **1.** diplomat(ist); *a.* **un air d.,** a diplomatic appearance; **une femme d.,** (i) a woman diplomat; (ii) a diplomatic woman. **2.** *Cu:* = trifle.
diplomatie [diplɔmasi], *s.f.* **1.** diplomacy; **d. par allocation de crédits,** dollar diplomacy; **user de d.,** to be diplomatic. **2. entrer dans la d.,** to enter the diplomatic service.
diplomatique[1] [diplɔmatik], *Pal:* **1.** *a.* diplomatic, textual (copy, document, etc.). **2.** *s.f.* diplomatic(s), science of deciphering ancient documents, etc.
diplomatique[2], *a.* diplomatic (service, body, etc.); **valise d.,** diplomatic bag, *U.S:* (diplomatic) pouch; **réponse d.,** diplomatic answer; **avoir un air d.,** to have an air of discretion; **avoir une maladie d.,** to have a diplomatic illness.
diplomatiquement [diplɔmatikmɑ̃], *adv.* (*a*) diplomatically; (*b*) tactfully, discreetly.
diplomatiser [diplɔmatize], *v.i.* to use diplomacy, to finesse.
diplomatiste [diplɔmatist], *s.m.* specialist in diplomatics.
diplôme [diploːm], *s.m.* **1.** *A:* diploma, charter, official document. **2.** diploma (of teacher, doctor, etc.); **pourvu de tous ses diplômes,** fully qualified; **(cérémonie de la) remise des diplômes aux étudiants** = graduation ceremony; *Sch:* **d. d'études supérieures** = (*approx*) M.A., M.Sc.; **il a ses diplômes,** he has his degree, he is a graduate.
diplômé, -ée [diplome], *a. & s.* graduate; **architecte d.,** fully qualified architect; **instituteur d.,** qualified teacher.
diplômer [diplome], *v.tr.* to grant a diploma to (s.o.).
diplophase [diplɔfaːz], *s.f. Biol:* diplophase.
diplopie [diplɔpi], *s.f. Med:* diplopia, double vision.
diplopodes [diplɔpɔd], *s.m.pl. Ent:* Diplopoda, the millipedes.
diploures [dipluːr], *s.m.pl. Ent:* Diplura, Entotrophi.
diploptère [diplɔptɛːr], *Ent:* **1.** *a.* diplopterous. **2.** *s.m.pl.* **diploptères,** Diploptera.
diplosome [diplɔzoːm], *s.m. Biol:* diplosome.
diplozoon [diplɔzɔɔ̃], *s.m. Z:* diplozoon.
dipneumone [dipnømɔn], *a. Z:* dipneumonous.
dipneustes [dipnøst], *s.m.pl. Paleont:* Dipneusti.
dipode [dipɔd], *a. Nat.Hist:* dipodous, having two feet.
dipodidés [dipɔdide], *s.m.pl. Z:* Dipodidae.
dipolaire [dipɔlɛːr], *a. El:* dipolar; **moment d.,** dipole moment.
dipôle [dipoːl], *s.m. El:* dipole; (*radar*) **antenne d.,** doublet.
diprotodon [diprɔtɔdɔ̃], *s.m. Paleont:* diprotodon.
diprotodontes [diprɔtɔdɔ̃ːt], *s.m.pl. Z:* Diprotodontia.
diproton [diprɔtɔ̃], *s.m. Atom.Ph:* di-proton.
dipsacacées [dipsakase], **dipsacées** [dipsase], *s.f.pl. Bot:* Dipsacaceae.
dipsadinés [dipsadine], *s.m.pl. Rept:* Dipsadinae.
dipsomane [dipsɔman], **dipsomaniaque** [dipsɔmanjak], *a. & s.* dipsomaniac.
dipsomanie [dipsɔmani], *s.f.* dipsomania.
diptère[1] [diptɛːr], *Ent:* **1.** *a.* dipterous, two-winged. **2.** *s.m.* dipter(an); **les diptères,** the Diptera.

diptère[2], *a. & s.m.*, **diptérique** [dipterik], *a. Arch:* dipteral (temple).

diptérocarpacées [dipterɔkarpase], *s.f.pl. Bot:* Dipterocarpaceae.

diptyque [diptik], *s.m.* diptych.

dipyre [dipiːr], *s.m. Miner:* dipyre.

dipyréné [dipirene], *a. Bot:* dipyrenous.

dire [diːr]. I. *v.tr.* (*pr.p.* **disant**; *p.p.* **dit**; *pr.ind.* **je dis, tu dis, il dit, n. disons, vous dites, ils disent**; *imp.* **dis, disons, dites**; *p.d.* **je disais**; *p.h.* **je dis**; *fu.* **je dirai**) **1.** to say, tell; (*a*) **d. qch. à qn,** to tell s.o. sth., to say sth. to s.o.; **j'avais oublié de vous d. que . . .,** I had forgotten to mention that . . .; **vous ne m'en avez jamais rien dit,** you never mentioned it; **envoyer d. à qn que . . .,** to send word to s.o. that . . .; **ce disant . . .,** with these words . . .; **d. du mal de qn,** to speak ill of s.o.; **qu'en dira-t-on?** what will people say? *s.a.* QU'EN-DIRA-T-ON; **il doit en avoir à d.,** he must have a lot to say; **je n'ai rien à d. contre lui,** I have nothing to say against him, have no objection to him; **il n'y a rien à d. à sa conduite,** no fault can be found with his behaviour; **d. un secret,** to tell a secret; **d. ce qu'on pense,** to speak one's mind; **un ami, disons mieux, un frère,** a friend, or rather, a brother; **un ami, que dis-je! un frère,** a friend, no, a brother! **quand je vous le disais! je vous l'avais bien dit!** didn't I say so? didn't I tell you so? **je le disais bien que . . .,** didn't I say that . . .; **c'est justement ce que j'allais d.!** that's just what I was about to say! you've taken the very word(s) out of my mouth! **laissez-moi d. un mot,** let me get a word in; **vous (me) dites cela si gentiment . . .,** you put it so nicely . . .; **d. bonjour à qn,** to say good-day, good morning, good afternoon, to s.o.; to wish s.o. good-day, good morning, good afternoon; **d. bonsoir à qn,** to say goodnight to s.o.; to wish s.o. goodnight; **comme dit l'autre, comme on dit,** as the saying goes, as the phrase goes; **comment est-ce que cela se dit, comment dites-vous cela, en français?** how do you say that in French? what is the French for that? **cela ne se dit pas,** that isn't said, that expression isn't used; **qui vous dit qu'il viendra?** how do you know he will come? **puisque je vous le dis,** you can take it from *me*; **qu'est-ce qui me dit que vous payerez?** how do I know whether you will pay? **c'est moi qui vous le dis!** I can tell you! *F:* **à qui le dites-vous?** don't I know it? you're telling me! *F:* **vous l'avez dit!** you've said it! *F:* **que tu dis!** that's what *you* say! *F:* **il faut le d. vite!** tell it to the marines! *F:* **on se l'est dit,** they passed it round; **dites-le avec des fleurs,** say it with flowers; (*at auction sale*) **qui dit mieux?** any advance? **je vais vous d., commencez par . . .,** I'll tell you what: begin by . . .; **dites toujours!** go on! say it! *F:* fire away! **venez déjeuner un de ces jours, disons dimanche,** come and have lunch one of these days, say (on) Sunday; **d. que oui,** to say yes; **je vous dis que non,** I tell you, no; **d. d'un, puis d'un autre,** to say first one thing, then another; to contradict oneself; **comment vous d. merci!** how can I thank you! **je ne sais comment d.,** I don't know how to put it; **je me disais que tout était fini,** I thought all was over; **que dites-vous de ce tableau?** what do you think of this picture? **que dites-vous de cela?** what do you say to that? **à vrai d. . . .,** to tell the truth . . .; **pour ne pas d. . . .,** not to say . . .; **pour tout d. . . .,** in a word . . .; **c'est tout d.,** I need say no more; **tout est dit,** that is an end of, to, the matter; **tout n'est pas dit,** we haven't heard the last of it; **pour ainsi d.,** so to speak, as it were; *F:* **comme qui dirait . . .,** as you might say . . .; **vous êtes comme qui dirait de la famille,** you are so to speak one of the family; **à ce qu'il dit,** according to him; **j'ai dit ce que j'avais à d.,** I (have) had my say, I (have) said my say; **vous l'avez dit,** quite so, exactly; **ainsi dit, ainsi fait; sitôt dit, sitôt fait,** no sooner said than done; **cela va sans dire,** that goes without saying, that stands to reason; **tenez-vous cela pour dit,** don't let me have to tell you that again; **j'ai dit,** I have spoken; **alors c'est dit,** well then, that's settled, decided; **en moins de temps qu'il n'en faut pour le d.,** in less time than it takes to tell; **on dit que . . .,** the story goes that . . .; **on dit que c'est lui le coupable,** he is said to be the culprit; **on dirait que . . .,** one would think that . . .; **on dirait qu'il va pleuvoir,** it looks like rain; **on dirait un fou,** he acts like a madman, you would think he was mad; **on aurait dit que . . .,** it seemed as though . . .; **on dirait (d')une aquarelle,** it might be taken for, it looks like, a water-colour; **on se dirait en Suisse,** you might think you were in Switzerland; **il n'y a pas à d.,** there is no denying it, there is no doubt about it; **c'est de la déveine, il n'y a pas à d.!** it is bad luck and no mistake! **il n'y a pas à d., il fait chaud!** it is warm, and no mistake! **au-delà de tout ce qui peut se d.,** more than words can say, can express; **dites donc, dis donc,** (i) tell me now . . .; (ii) look here, I say (that's enough)! **et d. qu'il n'a que vingt ans!** and to think that he's only twenty! **c'est beaucoup d.,** that's going rather far; **ce n'est pas peu d.,** that's saying a lot; **on dirait qu'il pleut,** it looks as if it is raining; **on dirait du Mozart,** it sounds like Mozart; **on dirait du gin,** it tastes like gin; *Cards:* **à vous de d.,** it's your call; *s.a.* PARLER I 1, ENVOYER 1; (*b*) *pred.* **on le dit mort,** he is reported (to be) dead, they say he's dead; **ils se disaient (de) nos amis,** they made out that they were, professed to be, friends of ours; **un navire est dit gîter lorsqu'il penche sur le côté,** a ship is said to list when it leans over to one side. **2.** (*a*) **d. à qn de faire qch.,** to tell, order, bid, s.o., to do sth.; **on nous a dit de partir,** we have been told to leave; **dites-lui d'entrer,** ask him to come in; **faites ce qu'on vous dit,** do as you are told; (*b*) **d. que** + *sub.* **dites qu'on le fasse entrer,** ask them to show him in; **dites qu'on porte cette lettre à la poste,** have this letter taken to the post; **il avait dit qu'on le réveillât à six heures,** he had asked to be woken up at six o'clock. **3. d. des vers,** to recite poetry; **d. son chapelet,** to tell one's beads; **d. la messe,** to say mass. **4.** (*a*) to show, express, betoken, bespeak; **horloge qui dit l'heure,** clock that tells the time; **ses vêtements disaient sa pauvreté,** his clothes revealed his poverty; **sa mine disait beaucoup,** his looks spoke volumes; **cela en dit long sur son courage,** it speaks volumes for his courage; **ce nom ne me dit rien,** the name conveys, means, nothing to me; **visage qui ne dit rien,** face that expresses nothing; **cela ne me disait rien de bon,** I didn't like the look of it; (*b*) to suit (s.o.), appeal to (s.o.); **cette musique ne me dit rien,** this music does not appeal to me, I don't care for, take to, this music; **son offre ne me dit rien,** I don't fancy his offer; **cela ne me dirait rien d'être médecin,** I shouldn't like to be a doctor; **si cela te dit,** if you feel like it; **qu'est-ce que dit le temps?** what's the weather like? **plus je regarde ce tableau plus il me dit,** that picture grows on me; **qui dit danger dit crainte,** danger spells fear; *s.a.* CŒUR. **5.** (*a*) **vouloir d.,** to mean; **je veux d. . . .,** that is to say . . .; **que voulez-vous d. par là?** what do you mean by that? **je ne veux pas d. que ce soient là des chiffres précis,** these figures are not meant to be accurate; **que veut d. ce mot?** what does this word mean? **cela veut d. qu'il ne reviendra pas,** it means that he won't come back; (*b*) **qu'est-ce à d.?** what does this mean? **est-ce à d. que . . .?** do you mean to imply that . . .? **ce n'est pas à d. que** + *sub.*, it does not mean, follow, that . . .; (*c*) **faire d. qch. à qn,** to send word of sth. to s.o.; **je lui ai fait d. de venir,** I sent to ask him to come; **je lui ai fait d. que . . .,** I sent him word, notified him, that . . .; **il ne se le fit pas d. deux fois,** he didn't wait to be told twice; **Madame fait d. qu'elle est prête,** Mrs X asks me to say that she is ready; (*d*) **faire d. qch. à qn,** to make s.o. say, tell, sth.; *F:* **je ne vous le fais pas d.,** I'm not telling you anything you don't know, you know that very well already; (*e*) **faire d. qch. par qn,** to send word of sth. through s.o.; (*f*) *with inf.* **vous m'avez dit adorer la musique,** you told me you adored music.

II. **dire,** *s.m.* statement, assertion; *Jur:* allegation; **on ne peut pas se fier à leurs dires,** one cannot trust their statements; **cela confirme mon d.,** that bears out my assertion; **je reviens à mon d.,** I reaffirm what I said before; **selon d. d'expert,** according to expert opinion; **selon son d. . . ., d'après son d. . . .,** according to him . . ., by his own account . . .; **à d. d'experts,** at a valuation; **au d. de chacun, il était présent,** everyone agrees that he was present; **au d. de tout le monde . . .,** by, from, all accounts . . ., everybody agrees that . . ., by common consent . . .; **à votre d. . . .,** by, according to, what you say . . .; **aux dires de . . .,** according to the statement of . . ..

direct [dirɛkt], *a.* (*a*) direct, straight; **ligne directe,** straight line; **descendre de qn en ligne directe,** to be a direct descendant of s.o.; **impôts directs,** direct taxes; **une personne directe,** a straight-forward person; **démenti d.,** flat denial; **deux opinions en contradiction directe,** two opinions at complete variance with, flatly opposed to, one another; *Gram:* **complément d.,** direct object; *Phot:* **papier à noircissement d.,** printing, out paper, P.O.P.; *Rail:* **train d.,** through train, express train; **voiture directe,** through carriage; **prendre un billet d. pour Paris,** to take a ticket straight through to Paris; *Mth:* **sens d.,** positive direction; (*b*) *s.m. W.Tel:* **émission en d.,** live broadcast; **antenne montée en d.,** direct-coupled aerial; (*c*) *s.m. Box:* **d. du droit,** straight right.

directement [dirɛktəmɑ̃], *adv.* directly, direct, straight; **maison d. en face de la nôtre,** house directly, exactly, immediately, opposite ours; **il est venu d. vers nous,** he came straight to us, made a bee-line for us; **se diriger d. au nord,** to go due north; **répondre d. à la question,** to give a direct, straight, answer to the question; **témoignages d. contradictoires,** pieces of evidence diametrically opposed to one another; **expédier des marchandises d. à qn,** to dispatch, send, goods direct to s.o.; *Rail:* **le train va d. à B.,** the train runs through to B.

directeur, -trice [dirɛktœːr, -tris]. **1.** *s.* director; manager, manageress; head (of industrial concern, etc.); headmaster, headmistress (of school); principal (of school); governor, warden (of prison); conductor (of orchestra); editor (of paper); leader (of undertaking); *Com: Ind:* **d. gérant,** managing director; **(président) d. général,** general manager; **d. commercial,** sales manager; **d. de succursale,** branch manager; **d. régional,** district manager; *Adm:* **d. général (d'un ministère),** permanent under-secretary; **d. général des postes, télégraphes, et téléphones** = Postmaster General; *Ecc:* **d. de conscience,** director, confessor; *Mil:* **d. de l'arrière,** general in charge of operations in the rear of the front line; *Mil: Navy:* **d. de tir,** fire-control officer. **2.** *a.* directing, managing, controlling (force, etc.); guiding (principle); **comité d.,** board of directors; **idée directrice d'un ouvrage,** leading idea of a work; *Hyd.E:* **ouvrages directeurs,** training works; **digue directrice,** training wall; *Aut: Cy:* **roue directrice,** front wheel; *Mch:* **bielle directrice,** driving rod; *Artil:* **pièce directrice,** directing gun; *Mil:* **plan d.,** battle map; *Mth:* **cercle d. (d'une ellipse),** director circle; *Geol:* **ligne directrice (d'un pli),** fold axis; *T.V:* **élément d.,** director (of aerial). **3.** *s.f.* **directrice,** (*a*) *Geom: Artil:* directrix; (*b*) *Turb:* guide vane.

directif, -ive [dirɛktif, -iːv]. **1.** *a.* directing, guiding (rule, etc.); *Mth:* **algèbre directive,** directional calculus. **2.** *s.f.pl.* **directives,** rules of conduct; *Mil:* general directions, directives, broad lines (laid down for a battle); *Pol:* guide lines; **directives politiques d'un parti,** main lines, general lines, of a party's policy.

direction [dirɛksjɔ̃], *s.f.* **1.** (*a*) guidance, direction: conduct (of undertaking, war); management, control (of business, house, etc.); directorate (of railways, etc.); editorship (of newspaper); headmastership (of school); leadership (of a party); **c'est à vous de prendre la d.,** it is for you to take the lead, to assume the direction of affairs; *Mus:* **orchestre (placé) sous la d. de X,** orchestra conducted by X; *Navy:* **d. du tir,** gunnery control; (*b*) (i) board of directors; board; directorate; (ii) administrative staff; management; **secrétaire de d.,** executive secretary; *Mil:* directorate (of infantry, artillery, etc.); (iii) *Jur: A:* **d. de créanciers,** meeting of creditors (in a case of bankruptcy, etc.); (*c*) (i) offices (of the board); manager's office; (ii) head office (of firm, etc.); **d. régionale,** district headquarters. **2.** (*a*) direction, driving, guiding (of engine, etc.); *Aut:* steering; **mécanisme de d.,** steering gear; **d. assistée,** power-assisted steering, *U.S:* power steering; (*b*) steering (of boat); **d. par levier à main,** tiller steering. **3.** direction, course; *Nau:* bearing; *Geol:* bearing, course (of vein); *Av: Nau:* **indicateur (gyroscopique) de d.,** direction indicator, directional gyro; *Nau:* **d. d'où vient le vent,** quarter from which the wind is blowing; **changer de d.,** to change one's direction; to alter one's course, one's route; **quelle d. ont-ils prise?** which way did they go? *P.N:* **d. de la gare,** to the station; **ce train va en d. de, dans la d. de, d., Paris,** this train goes to Paris, this is a Paris train, a train for Paris; **la d. de la marée,** the set of the tide; **le courant de l'opinion prend cette direction,** opinion is setting that way; **il imprima à la maison une d. douce mais ferme,** he brought a gentle but firm hand to bear upon the firm; **donner une mauvaise d. aux études de qn,** to misdirect s.o.'s studies. **4.** *pl.* directions, instructions; **donner d'utiles directions,** to supply useful directions.

directionnel, -elle [dirɛksjɔnɛl], *a.* directional; *W.Tel: Elcs:* **antenne directionnelle,** directional aerial, antenna; **relais d.,** directional relay; **couplage d., détecteur d. de mesures,** directional coupler; *Av: Nav:* **gyroscope d.,** directional gyro.

directivité [dirɛktivite], *s.f. El: etc:* directivity.

directoire [dirɛktwa:r], *s.m.* **1.** *Ecc:* directory. **2.** *Fr.Hist:* **le D.,** the Directoire (1795-9); **style D.,** Directoire style.

directorat [dirɛktɔra], *s.m.* (*rare*) (*a*) directorate; directorship; (*b*) managership.

directorial[1], **-aux** [dirɛktɔrjal, -o], *a. Fr.Hist:* directorial (constitution, government).

directorial[2], **-aux,** *a.* pertaining to the management (of business, theatre, etc.); directorial, managerial.

directrice [dirɛktris]. *See* DIRECTEUR.

diremption [dirɑ̃psjɔ̃], *s.f. Jur:* dissolution (of a marriage).

dirigé [diriʒe], *a.* **1.** controlled, managed, planned; **efforts mal dirigés,** misguided, misdirected, efforts; **économie dirigée,** planned economy; *Fin:* **monnaie dirigée,** managed, controlled, currency; *Sch:* **jeux dirigés,** organized games. **2.** *W.Tel: Elcs:* directional; *W.Tel:* **antenne dirigée,** directional aerial (fixed for one station); **émission aux ondes dirigées,** beam transmission; **liaison radio, hertzienne, dirigée,** directional radio, directional transmission.

dirigeabilité [diriʒabilite], *s.f. Aer:* dirigibility, navigability (of airship).

dirigeable [diriʒabḷ]. **1.** *a.* dirigible; *W.Tel:* **antenne d.,** directional aerial. **2.** *s.m. Aer:* dirigible (balloon); airship; **d. rigide, souple,** rigid, non-rigid, airship; *A: Mil: Navy:* **d. de reconnaissance, d'observation,** *F:* blimp.

dirigeant, -ante [diriʒɑ̃, -ɑ:t]. **1.** *a.* directing, guiding (power, principle, etc.); **les hommes d'État dirigeants de l'Europe,** the leading statesmen of Europe; **classes dirigeantes,** ruling classes. **2.** *s.* leader; **les dirigeants,** the rulers, those at the head of affairs, the leaders; **la dirigeante d'un mouvement féminin,** the leader of a women's movement.

diriger [diriʒe], *v.tr.* (**je dirigeai(s); n. dirigeons**) **1.** to direct, control, manage; to run (business, school, theatre, farm, etc.); to conduct (orchestra); to edit (newspaper); to superintend, conduct (proceedings, election, etc.); **mal d. une entreprise,** to misdirect, mismanage, an undertaking; **d. la production,** to control production; *Artil:* **d. le feu, le tir,** to control the fire. **2.** (*a*) to direct, guide, lead (sth., s.o.); to drive (horse, car); to steer, navigate (ship, airship); to sail (ship); **d. un colis sur Paris,** to send a parcel off to Paris; **je suis en retard parce qu'on m'a mal dirigé,** I am late because I was misdirected, sent the wrong way; (*b*) **d. ses pas vers . . .,** to go, move, towards . . .; **d. ses pas vers la maison,** to make for home, to be going home; **d. un cheval vers un obstacle,** to put a horse at an obstacle; **d. son attention sur qch.,** to turn one's attention to sth.; **d. des accusations, des sarcasmes, contre qn,** to level, aim, accusations, sarcasms, at s.o.; **d. un blessé sur un hôpital,** to send an injured man to a hospital; (*c*) to aim (rifle) (**sur,** at); to train (gun) (**sur,** on); to level, point (telescope) (**sur,** at); to bring (telescope) to bear (**sur,** on).

se diriger. 1. (*a*) **se d. vers un endroit,** to turn towards a place; to make one's way towards a place; to make for, head for, a place; **l'embarcation se dirigea vers le rivage,** the boat pulled for the shore; **le navire se dirigea vers le port,** the vessel steered, headed, for the harbour; (*b*) **se d. vers qn,** to go up to s.o. **2.** (*of river, lode of ore, etc.*) **se d. du nord au sud,** to run north and south; to follow a course from north to south.

dirigisme [diriʒism], *s.m.* dirigisme; (*a*) *Pol.Ec:* planning; **d. économique,** planned economy, economic planning; (*b*) controlled finance.

dirigiste [diriʒist], *s.m. & f. Pol.Ec:* advocate, exponent, of dirigisme, of planned economy.

dirimant [dirimɑ̃], *a. Jur:* diriment, nullifying; **cause dirimante de mariage,** diriment impediment to marriage.

dirimer [dirime], *v.tr. Jur:* to nullify, invalidate (contract, etc.).

dis- [dis], *pref.* (*privative*) **1.** *v.pref.* (*a*) dis-; **discontinuer,** discontinue; **disqualifier,** disqualify; **disparaître,** disappear; (*b*) **disculper,** exculpate. **2.** *s.pref.* (*a*) dis-; **discrédit,** discredit; **discontinuité,** discontinuity; **dissymétrie,** dissymmetry; (*b*) **disconvenance,** unsuitableness. **3.** *a.pref.* dis-; **discourtois,** discourteous; **dissemblable,** dissimilar.

disable [dizabḷ], *a.* speakable, expressible, sayable (idea, etc.).

disaccharide [disakarid], *s.f. Ch:* disaccharide.

disant [dizɑ̃], *s.m.* **le moins d.,** the lowest bidder.

discal [diskal], *a. Med:* **hernie discale,** slipped disc; **se faire une hernie discale,** to slip a disc.

discale, -aux [diskal, -o], *s.f. Com:* loss of weight in transit, (of bulk goods).

discaler [diskale], *v.i.* (*of bulk goods*) to lose weight in transit.

discarthrose [diskartro:z], *s.f. Med:* spinal arthritis.

discernable [disɛrnabḷ], *a.* discernible, visible.

discernement [disɛrnəmɑ̃], *s.m.* **1.** perception, distinguishing (by sight); discrimination (**de . . . et de . . .,** between . . . and . . .); **faire le d. de deux choses,** to distinguish, discriminate, between two things. **2.** discernment, judgment; **agir avec d.,** to act with discrimination; **âge de d.,** age of understanding; *Jur:* **l'enfant a agi sans d.,** the child acted without cognizance.

discerner [disɛrne], *v.tr.* to discern, distinguish (sth.); **on discernait une maison dans le lointain,** we could (just) see, make out, a house in the distance; **but facile à d.,** object easy to detect; **d. qch. de qch.,** to distinguish sth. from sth., to discriminate between sth. and sth.; **d. le bien du mal,** to tell right from wrong.

disciflore [disiflɔ:r], *a. Bot:* discifloral, disciflorous.

disciple [disipḷ], *s.m.f.* disciple, follower.

disciplinable [disiplinabḷ], *a.* disciplinable.

disciplinaire [disiplinɛ:r]. **1.** *a.* disciplinary (punishment, etc.). **2.** *s.m.* (*a*) disciplinarian; (*b*) (*Fr. Army*) soldier in a disciplinary company.

disciplinairement [disiplinɛrmɑ̃], *adv.* disciplinarily; as a matter of discipline.

discipline [disiplin], *s.f.* **1.** (*a*) *A:* chastisement; (*b*) scourge, discipline (for chastisement, *esp.* for self-flagellation); **se donner la d.,** to scourge oneself. **2.** discipline; (*a*) **d. à la prussienne,** iron discipline; **garder la d.,** to maintain discipline, order; **ployer qn à une d. sévère,** to bend s.o. to a strict discipline; **maintenir une d. rigoureuse,** to keep strict discipline; **il ne sait pas maintenir la d.,** he cannot keep discipline, he is no disciplinarian; (*Fr. army*) **compagnies de d.,** punishment companies; **salle de discipline,** guard-room; (*b*) branch of instruction; **élevé dans la forte d. du latin et du grec,** educated in the stern discipline of Latin and Greek; **les différentes disciplines sportives,** the various forms of sport.

discipliné [disipline], *a,* disciplined, amenable to discipline; well-schooled.

disciplinement [disiplinmɑ̃], *s.m.* disciplining, reducing to discipline.

discipliner [disipline], *v.tr.* **1.** *A:* to chastise (monk, etc.). **2.** to discipline (school); to bring (troops, students, etc.) under control, under discipline; **d. sa voix, son geste,** to school one's voice, one's gestures; **se d. à une habitude,** to train oneself in a habit; **d. son travail,** to work methodically.

discission [disisjɔ̃], *s.f. Surg:* discission.

discite [diskit], *s.f. Med:* discitis.

discoblastula [diskɔblastyla], *s.f. Biol:* discoblastula.

discobole [diskɔbɔl], *s.m.* **1.** (*a*) *Gr.Ant:* discobolus; (*b*) *Sp:* discus thrower. **2.** *Ich:* discobolus.

discodactyle [diskɔdaktil], *a. Z:* discodactyl(ous).

discogastrula [diskɔgastryla], *s.f. Biol:* discogastrula.

discoglosse [diskɔglɔs], *s.m. Amph:* discoglossid (toad); *F:* painted toad.

discoglossidés [diskɔglɔside], *s.m.pl. Amph:* Discoglossidae.

discographie [diskɔgrafi], *s.f.* discography.

discoïde [diskɔid], **discoïdal, -aux** [diskɔidal, -o], *a.* discoid(al); disc-shaped.

discolore [diskɔlɔ:r], *a. Bot:* **1.** bicoloured. **2.** of different colours.

discolichens [diskɔlikɛn], *s.m.pl. Moss:* discolichens.

discoméduses [diskɔmedy:z], *s.f.pl. Coel: O:* Discomedusae; Discomedusans.

discomycètes [diskɔmisɛt], *s.m.pl. Fung:* Discomycetes.

discontinu [diskɔ̃tiny], *a.* discontinuous; *Ind:* **production discontinue,** batch production; *Atom. Ph:* **réacteur à charges discontinues,** batch reactor; *Mth:* **fonction discontinue,** discontinuous function; *s.m. Phil:* **les concepts du continu et du d.,** the concepts of continuity and of discontinuity.

discontinuation [diskɔ̃tinɥasjɔ̃], *s.f.* (*rare*) discontinuance, cessation.

discontinuer [diskɔ̃tinɥe], *A: & Lit: rarely used now except in the phrase* **sans d. 1.** *v.tr.* to discontinue, break off, stop (sth.); **il veut d. le latin,** he wishes to drop Latin; **d. de faire qch.,** to leave off, to stop, doing sth. **2.** *v.i.* to discontinue, stop, cease, leave off; **fièvre qui ne discontinue pas,** continuous fever; **parler pendant des heures sans d.,** to talk for hours on end, without a break.

discontinuité [diskɔ̃tinɥite], *s.f.* discontinuity; **travailler sans d.,** to work without stopping, without interruption; *Mth:* **point de d.,** (point of) discontinuity (of a function).

disconvenance [diskɔ̃vnɑ̃:s], *s.f. Lit:* **1.** unsuitableness, unfitness (of climate, occupation, etc.). **2.** disparity, dissimilarity (between persons, objects); **d. de mots,** incongruity of terms, mixed metaphor; **d. de construction,** faulty construction (of sentence); **d. d'âge,** disproportion in age (**entre . . . et . . .,** between . . . and . . .).

disconvenant [diskɔ̃vnɑ̃], *a. Lit:* incongruous; disproportionate.

disconvenir [diskɔ̃vni:r], *v.i.* (*conj. like* VENIR; *the aux. is* **avoir**) **1. d. à qn, à qch.,** to be unsuited to, unsuitable for, s.o., sth.; **cette vie lui disconvient,** this life does not suit him; **ses opinions disconviennent aux miennes,** his opinions clash with mine. **2. d. de qch.,** not to agree with sth.; **on ne peut pas en disconvenir,** there is no denying it; **je n'en disconviens pas,** I admit it, I don't deny it; **d. que** + *sub.*, to deny that . . ..

discophile [diskɔfil], *s.m. & f.* discophile; record, disc, enthusiast.

discophilie [diskɔfili], *s.f.* record, disc, collecting.

discord [diskɔ:r]. **1.** *a.m. A: Mus:* (*of instrument*) out of tune; **esprit d.,** inconsequent mind. **2.** *s.m. A: & Lit:* discord; dispute.

discordance [diskɔrdɑ̃:s], *s.f.* discordance, dissonance (of sounds); clashing (of colours); difference (of opinions); disagreement (of evidence, etc.); *Geol:* unconformability (of strata); **couches en d.,** unconformable strata; **d. des parties d'un édifice,** lack of harmony between the parts of a building.

discordant [diskɔrdɑ̃], *a.* discordant, dissonant, inharmonious (sound); grating, jarring (noise); clashing (colours); conflicting, discrepant (evidence, opinions, etc.); **piano d.,** piano out of tune; *Geol:* **couches discordantes,** uncomformable strata.

discorde [diskɔrd], *s.f.* discord, dissension, strife; **mettre la d. entre deux personnes,** to set two people at variance; to make bad blood between two people; **semer la d.,** to make trouble; **pomme de d.,** apple of discord, bone of contention.

discorder [diskɔrde], *v.i.* (*rare in modern Fr.*) **1.** *Mus:* to be discordant, out of tune. **2.** (*of pers.*) not to be in agreement; (*of colours*) to clash.

discothèque [diskɔtɛk], *s.f.* (*a*) record library; (*b*) record cabinet; (*c*) discothèque.

discoureur, -euse [diskurœ:r, -ø:z], *Pej:* **1.** *s.* (great) talker; speechifier; **c'est un grand d.,** he likes the sound of his own voice. **2.** *a.* talkative (person); given to holding forth.

discourir [diskuri:r], *v.i.* (*conj. like* COURIR) *usu. Pej:* to discourse, to air one's opinions (**sur,** on); **perdre son temps à d.,** to waste one's time talking, speechifying; **d. longuement sur les avantages de . . .,** to expatiate, enlarge, on the advantages of . . ..

discours [disku:r], *s.m.* **1.** *A:* talk, conversation; **ce sont des d. en l'air,** it's all talk, all idle talk. **2.** discourse, dissertation, treatise; **d. sur la matière,** treatise on matter. **3.** speech, oration; **prononcer, faire, un d.,** to make, deliver, a speech; **d. d'ouverture,** opening address; **tenir un d. à qn,** to address s.o. at length; **le d. de la couronne, du trône,** the King's, Queen's, speech from the Throne; *F:* **reprendre le fil de son d.,** to get back to one's subject, to take up the thread of one's speech again. **4.** diction, language; *Gram:* **parties du d.,** parts of speech; **d. indirect,** indirect, reported, speech.

discourtois [diskurtwa], *a.* discourteous, uncivil, rude.

discourtoisement [diskurtwazmɑ̃], *adv.* discourteously; rudely.

discourtoisie [diskurtwazi], *s.f. A:* discourtesy, incivility.

discrédit [diskredi], *s.m.* discredit, loss of credit; disrepute; **entreprise tombée dans le d.,** undertaking fallen into discredit, into disrepute; **jeter du d. sur . . .,** to reflect, throw, discredit upon . . .; **faire tomber qch. dans le d.,** to bring sth. into disrepute.

discréditer [diskredite], *v.tr.* (*a*) to discredit (bill, etc.); (*b*) **d. qn, les œuvres de qn,** to disparage, run down, s.o., s.o.'s works; **d. une affirmation,** to discredit a statement; (*c*) **d. l'autorité de qn,** to bring s.o.'s authority into disrepute; **bévues qui discréditent la maison,** blunders which give the firm a bad name.

se discréditer, to become discredited; (**auprès de qn,** in s.o.'s eyes).

discret, -ète [diskrɛ, -ɛt], *a.* **1.** (*a*) discreet, cautious, circumspect (behaviour, conversation, etc.); **mon agent est très d., vous pouvez vous confier à lui,** my agent is very discreet, you may confide in him; **être trop d.,** to be too reticent; **d. comme la tombe,** silent as the tomb; *Post: Com:* **sous pli d.,** under plain cover; (*b*) quiet, unobtrusive (taste in dress, etc.); sober, quiet (dress); inconspicuous (smoke-trail, etc.); modest (request, etc.); **lieu d.,** quiet, unpretentious, spot; **causerie discrète,** subdued, hushed, conversation. **2.** *Mth:* discrete, discontinuous (quantity). **3.** *Med:* discrete (smallpox).

discrètement [diskrɛtmɑ̃], *adv.* **1.** discreetly, judiciously, with discretion. **2.** quietly, unobtrusively, modestly; **mouchoir d. parfumé,** handkerchief with just a touch of scent.

discrétion [diskresjɔ̃], *s.f.* discretion. **1.** prudence, circumspection, judgment; **user de qch. avec d.,** to use sth. in moderation; **mettre de la d. dans l'exercice de son droit,** to use discretion in the exercise of one's rights; **avoir de la d.,** to be discreet; **âge de d.,** age, years, of discretion; **je me fie à votre d.,** I leave it to you, to your discretion; **recommander la plus grande d. à qn,** to enjoin the strictest secrecy on s.o. **2. être à la d. de qn,** to be (i) at s.o.'s disposal, (ii) at s.o.'s mercy; **fruits à la d. de tous promeneurs,** fruit free to all (comers); *adv.phr.* **à d.,** (i) at one's own discretion; (ii) unconditionally; **se rendre à d.,** to surrender unconditionally; **manger à d.,** to eat as much as one pleases; (*on menu*) **pain à d.,** unlimited bread, bread *ad lib.*

discrétionnaire [diskresjɔnɛːr], *a.* discretionary (powers, etc.).

discrétionnairement [diskresjɔnɛrmɑ̃], *adv.* discretionarily.

discriminant [diskriminɑ̃], *a. & s.m. Mth:* discriminant.

discriminateur [diskriminatœːr]. **1.** *a.m.* discriminating; *Elcs:* **filtre d.,** discrimination filter. **2.** *s.m. El: etc:* discriminator; **d. d'amplitude,** pulse amplitude discriminator.

discrimination [diskriminasjɔ̃], *s.f.* discrimination; differentiation; **d. raciale,** racial discrimination; *Elcs:* **courbe de d.,** discriminator curve; **seuil de d.,** discriminator threshold value.

discriminatoire [diskriminatwaːr], *a.* discriminatory.

discriminer [diskrimine], *v.tr. Lit:* to discriminate, to distinguish.

disculpation [diskylpasjɔ̃], *s.f.* (*rare*) exculpation, exoneration.

disculper [diskylpe], *v.tr.* **1.** to exculpate, exonerate (de, from); **d. qn d'un crime,** to clear s.o. of a crime. **2.** *A:* to justify (sth.).

se disculper, to exculpate oneself (de, from); to clear oneself (de, of).

discursif, -ive [diskyrsif, -iːv], *a.* discursive.

discursivement [diskyrsivmɑ̃], *adv.* discursively, in a discursive manner.

discussion [diskysjɔ̃], *s.f.* **1.** discussion, debate; **un sujet de d.,** a subject for discussion; **la question en d.,** the question under discussion, in debate, under debate, at issue; **mettre un sujet en d.,** (i) to debate a subject; (ii) to ventilate, air, a subject; **la question est revenue en d.,** (i) the question is being, has been, debated anew; (ii) the question has cropped up again, is once more to the fore; **aborder la d. d'une question,** to take up a matter; **l'emporter dans une d.,** to get the better of an argument; **sans d. possible,** indisputably; **le fait ne souffre pas de d.,** the fact is beyond dispute, beyond controversy; **courage au-dessus de toute d.,** courage beyond question; **il s'exécuta sans d.,** he complied without arguing (the point), without argument; **entrer en d. avec qn,** to enter into an argument with s.o. **2.** *Jur:* **d. de biens,** enquiry into the assets of a debtor (with a view to recovery of debt); **bénéfice de d.,** benefit of discussion.

discutable [diskytabl̩], *a.* debatable, questionable, arguable (point, etc.); **question d.,** doubtful matter, open question; **son droit n'est pas d.,** his rights are beyond question.

discutailler [diskytɑje], *v.i.* to argue the toss, to argy-bargy; to quibble.

discuté [diskyte], *a.* disputed (question); much discussed (book, subject).

discuter [diskyte]. **1.** *v.tr.* (*a*) to discuss, debate; **discutons la chose,** let us talk the matter over, let us talk it over; **d. un cas,** to go into the merits of a case; **d. le prix,** to argue about the price; *F:* **d. le coup,** to talk about things in general, to have a natter; (*b*) to question, dispute; **d. un droit,** to call a right into question; to controvert a right; **il n'y a pas à d.,** there is no question, there are no two ways, about it. **2.** *Jur:* **d. un débiteur,** (i) to enquire into, to establish, the assets of a debtor; to discuss a debtor; (ii) to sell up a debtor. **3.** *v.i.* **d. avec qn sur qch.,** to argue with s.o. about sth.; **d. (de) politique,** to discuss politics; **d. sur des pointes d'aiguille,** to split hairs; **d. dans le vide,** to argue without having anything to support one's views; **ne discutez pas,** no arguing.

discuteur, -euse [diskytœːr, -øːz], *s.* arguer.

disert [dizɛːr], *a.* eloquent, fluent (orator).

disertement [dizɛrtəmɑ̃], *adv.* eloquently, fluently.

disette [dizɛt], *s.f.* scarcity, dearth, want (*esp.* of food); **d. d'eau,** drought; **d. d'un article,** shortage, short supply, of an article; **la guerre amène la d.,** war brings famine (in its train); **vivre dans la d.,** to live in want, in poverty.

disetteux, -euse [dizɛtø, -øːz], *a. A:* necessitous, needy.

diseur, -euse [dizœːr, -øːz], *s.* (*a*) monologuist; diseur, diseuse; reciter; **d. de chansonnettes,** humorist (at concert); entertainer; (*b*) teller, sayer, utterer (of sth.); **d., diseuse, de bonne aventure,** fortune-teller; **d. de nouvelles,** newsmonger; **beau d.,** fine talker; *Prov:* **les grands diseurs ne sont pas les grands faiseurs,** great talkers are little doers.

disgrâce [dizgrɑːs, dis-], *s.f.* **1.** disfavour, disgrace; **encourir la d. de qn,** to incur s.o.'s displeasure; **tomber dans la d. (de qn),** to fall out of favour (with s.o.); *F:* to get into s.o.'s bad books; **attirer une d. à qn,** to bring s.o. into disgrace. **2.** (*a*) *A:* misfortune; (*b*) *Lit:* plainness (of looks); lack of charm; uncomeliness.

disgracié [dizgrasje, dis-], *a.* (*a*) out of favour; *s.* **les disgraciés de la fortune,** the unlucky, the unfortunate; (*b*) (i) ill-favoured, plain-featured; (ii) deformed.

disgracier [dizgrasje, dis-], *v.tr.* (*p.d. & pr.sub.* **n. disgraciions, v. disgraciiez**) to deprive (s.o.) of one's favour; to dismiss (s.o.) from favour; to disgrace; *esp. A:* (*of sovereign*) to dismiss (s.o.) from court, to banish (s.o.) to his estates.

se disgracier, to fall into disfavour, into disgrace (**auprès de,** with).

disgracieusement [dizgrasjøzmɑ̃, dis-], *adv.* **1.** uncouthly, awkwardly. **2.** ungraciously.

disgracieux, -ieuse [dizgrasjø, dis-, -jøːz], *a.* **1.** uncouth, unlovely, awkward, ungraceful (person). **2.** ungracious (answer). **3.** ugly (face, etc.); unsightly (spot, etc.).

dishley [diʃle], *s.m. Husb:* (*sheep*) Leicester.

disilane [disilan], *s.m. Ch:* disilane.

disjoindre [dizʒwɛːdr, dis-], *v.tr.* (*conj. like* JOINDRE) to disjoin, sever, disjoint, separate (the parts of a whole).

se disjoindre, to come apart, to separate; to come asunder; to break up; **le bordage du bateau commençait à se d.,** the ship's planks had begun to start.

disjoint [dizʒwɛ̃, dis-], *a.* (*a*) disjoined, disjointed (parts, etc.); (*b*) *Mus:* disjunct (motion).

disjoncter [dizʒɔ̃kte, dis-], *v.i. El:* to trip.

disjoncteur [dizʒɔ̃ktœːr, dis-], *s.m. El:* (*a*) circuit-breaker, cut-out, switch; underload release; **bouton d.,** disconnecting key; (*b*) switch-board.

disjonctif, -ive [dizʒɔ̃ktif, dis-, -iːv], *a. Log: Gram:* disjunctive (proposition, conjunction, etc.).

disjonction [dizʒɔ̃ksjɔ̃, dis-], *s.f.* **1.** disjunction, sundering, separation (of parts of whole); *Jur:* severance (of causes, of parts of a resolution). **2.** *El:* switching, trip-out. **3.** *Med:* **d. crânio-faciale,** pyramidal fracture.

dislocation [dislɔkasjɔ̃], *s.f.* dislocation (of limb, business); taking to pieces, taking down (of machine, etc.); dismemberment (of empire, etc.); dislodgement (of stones in a wall); *Geol:* fault; *Cryst:* dislocation; *Mil: etc:* dispersal, breaking up, separation, split up (of troops, etc.); *Nau:* split up (of convoy); **point de d.,** (i) *Mil:* break(ing)-up point, separation point; (ii) *Mil.Av:* dispersal point; (iii) *Nau:* split up position (of convoy, etc.).

disloqué [dislɔke]. **1.** *a.* (*of limb*) dislocated; out of joint; (*of machine*) out of order; (*of empire, etc.*) dismembered, broken up; (*of stones*) dislodged; **pièce disloquée,** play that does not hang together; *Geol:* **gîte d.,** faulted deposit. **2.** *s.m.* contortionist.

disloquement [dislɔkmɑ̃], *s.m.* (state of) dislocation.

disloquer [dislɔke], *v.tr.* to dislocate; to put (limb) out of joint; to put (machine) out of order; to break up, distribute (troops in garrisons); to dismember (state); to upset (system, etc.); to dislodge (stones in a wall); *Geol:* to fault (the strata).

se disloquer, to break up, to fall to pieces; **tout se disloque,** everything is going to pieces.

disluite [dislɥit], *s.f.,* **dislyite** [disliit], *s.f. Miner:* disluite.

dismutation [dismytasjɔ̃], *s.f. Ch:* dismutation.

disodique [disɔdik], *a. Ch:* disodic, disodium; **phosphate d.,** disodium phosphate.

disomie [disɔmi], *s.f. Biol:* disomic condition.

dispache [dispaʃ], *s.f. M.Ins:* average adjustment.

dispacheur [dispaʃœːr], *s.m. M.Ins:* average-stater, average adjuster.

dispair [dispɛːr], *a. A:* **yeux dispairs,** eyes that do not match, that are not a pair.

disparaissant [disparɛsɑ̃], *a.* disappearing, vanishing (target).

disparaître [disparɛːtr̥], *v.i.* (*conj. like* PARAÎTRE) to disappear. **1.** to vanish, to pass out of sight, knowledge; **d. aux yeux de qn,** to vanish before s.o.'s eyes; to vanish into thin air; **la côte disparut aux regards, disparut de l'horizon,** the coast faded out of sight, faded from the horizon; **je le vis d. sous les flots,** I saw the waters close over him; I saw him go down; **il est entré dans le bois et a disparu,** he ran into the wood and disappeared, vanished, from sight; **il est disparu depuis longtemps,** he disappeared long ago; *F:* **disparais(sez)!** get lost! buzz off! **ces vieux amis ont, sont, maintenant disparu(s),** these old friends have now passed away; **amis disparus,** vanished friends; **faire d. qn, qch.,** (i) to make away with s.o., sth.; to rub out, wash out, remove (stain, etc.); to smooth out (crease); (ii) to put s.o., sth., out of sight; to clear away (sth.); **on a fait d. le musée,** the museum has been done away with; **cette mode disparaît,** this fashion is going out; **sa timidité disparaît peu à peu,** his shyness is wearing off. **2.** to be hidden; **la muraille disparaît sous le lierre,** the wall is hidden under the ivy; **ses traits disparaissaient dans la graisse,** his features were buried in fat.

disparate [disparat]. **1.** *a.* (*a*) disparate, dissimilar, incommensurable; (*b*) ill-matched, ill-assorted, motley; jarring; **meubles disparates,** heterogeneous furniture; **couleurs disparates,** clashing colours; **bas disparates,** stockings that are not a pair, odd stockings. **2.** *s.f.* (*a*) disparity, lack of conformity; (*b*) incongruity; clash (of colours).

disparation [disparasjɔ̃], *s.f. Opt:* **d. rétinienne,** disparation.

disparité [disparite], *s.f.* disparity (of age, etc.).

disparition [disparisjɔ̃], *s.f.* **1.** disappearing, vanishing. **2.** disappearance; **remarquer la d. de qch.,** to miss sth.; **depuis sa d. . . .,** since he disappeared . . .; **depuis sa d. sa femme est inconsolable,** his wife has been inconsolable since his death.

disparu, -ue [dispary]. **1.** *a.* (*a*) *Mil: etc:* missing; **être porté d.,** to be reported missing; *Nau:* **d. en mer,** lost at sea; (*b*) extinct (race, etc.); **dans un monde d. où on circulait librement,** in a world (which has) now disappeared, which no longer exists, where one could move around freely. **2.** *s.* (*a*) **le d. laisse une veuve et deux enfants,** the deceased leaves a widow and two children; **le(s) cher(s) disparu(s),** the dear departed; (*b*) *Mil:* **les disparus,** the missing.

dispatcher [dispatʃœːr], *s.m. Rail:* controller, *U.S:* dispatcher.

dispatching [dispatʃiŋ], *s.m. Rail: Petroleum Ind:* control system, *U.S:* dispatching system.

dispendieusement [dispɑ̃djøzmɑ̃], expensively; extravagantly.

dispendieux, -ieuse [dispɑ̃djø, -jøːz], *a.* expensive, costly (process, etc.); **goûts d.,** expensive tastes.

dispensable [dispɑ̃sabl̩], *a.* dispensable (oath, offence, etc.); subject to dispensation.

dispensaire [dispɑ̃sɛːr], *s.m. Med:* **1.** *A:* pharmacopoeia, dispensatory. **2.** = out-patients' department (of hospital); (*ante-natal, child welfare*) clinic; welfare centre; (*in Africa, etc.*) dispensary; **d. antivénérien,** V.D. clinic.

dispensataire [dispɑ̃satɛːr], *s.m. & f.* (one of the) recipient(s) (of a sum of money).

dispensateur, -trice [dispɑ̃satœːr, -tris], *s.* dispenser, distributor (of charity, justice, etc.).

dispensation [dispɑ̃sasjɔ̃], *s.f. A:* dispensation; (*a*) distribution, meting out (of charity, favours, etc.); (*b*) administration.

dispense [dispɑ̃:s], *s.f.* **1.** (*a*) exemption; **d. du service militaire,** exemption from military service; **d. d'âge,** waiving of age limit; (*b*) *Ecc:* dispensation; **d. de jeûne,** dispensation from fasting. **2.** certificate of exemption; **d. de bans** = marriage licence.

dispensé, -ée [dispɑ̃se], *s. Mil: etc:* person exempt (from service, etc.).

dispenser [dispɑ̃se], *v.tr.* **1. d. qn de qch., de faire qch.,** to dispense, exempt, excuse, s.o. from sth., from doing sth.; to absolve s.o. from (an obligation); **d. qn d'une tâche,** to relieve s.o. of, to excuse s.o. from, to let s.o. off, a task; **dispensez-moi de ce voyage,** spare me this journey; **d. qn du service militaire,** to exempt s.o. from military service; **d. qn de travailler,** to relieve s.o. from (the necessity of) working; *Ecc:* **d. qn du jeûne,** to give s.o. dispensation from fasting; **dispensé de timbrage, d'affranchissement,** (i) (*of letters*) Official Paid; (ii) (*of documents*) free from stamp duty; **je vous dispense de ces observations,** you can keep your remarks to yourself. **2.** (*a*) to dispense, mete out, distribute (charity, favours, etc.); to administer (the sacraments); (*b*) *Pharm: A:* to dispense, make up (medicine).

se dispenser de qch., to excuse oneself from sth., to get out of sth.; to dispense with sth.; **se d. de faire qch.,** to get out of, excuse oneself from, doing sth.; **vous pouvez vous d. de m'accompagner,** there is no need for you to go with me; **on peut s'en d.,** it can be dispensed with.

dispersal [dispɛrsal], *s.m. Av: F:* dispersal area.

dispersant [dispɛrsɑ̃], *a. & s.m.* **1.** *a.* dispersing. **2.** *Ch: Ind:* dispersant.

dispersé [dispɛrse], *a. Mil:* **ordre d.,** extended order.

dispersement [dispɛrsəmɑ̃], *s.m.* dispersal, dispersing, dispersion, scattering.

disperser [dispɛrse], *v.tr.* **1.** to disperse, scatter; to spread (far and wide); **d. une foule,** to disperse, break up, a crowd; **d. ses efforts,** to dissipate ones' efforts; *Artil:* **d. le tir,** to split up the fire; **d. un obstacle,** to blow away, destroy, an obstacle; *Mil:* **d. une armée,** to rout an army. **2.** *Opt:* (i) to disperse, split up, decompose (light); (ii) to scatter (light).

se disperser, to disperse, scatter; (*of clouds, crowd, etc.*) to break up, to melt away.

disperseur [dispɛrsœ:r], *s.m. Agr:* centrifugal spreader.

dispersibilité [dispɛrsibilite], *s.f.* dispersibility, degree of solubility (of dried milk).

dispersif, -ive [dispɛrsif, -i:v], *a. Opt: etc:* dispersive (power, etc.).

dispersion [dispɛrsjɔ̃], *s.f.* **1.** dispersion, dispersal (of people); breaking up (of crowd); scattering abroad (of coins, etc.); rout (of army); spread, scattering (of shot); blowing away (of obstacle); *Mil:* **zone de d.,** dispersal area; *Mil.Av:* **aire de d.,** dispersal area. **2.** (*a*) scattering (of light); dissipation, leakage, straying (of magnetic force, etc.); **champ de d.,** stray-field (of magnet); (*b*) *Opt:* dispersion, decomposition (of light).

dispersivité [dispɛrsivite], *s.f. Aut:* dispersiveness, dispersive quality (of lubricant).

dispersoïde [dispɛrsɔid], *s.m. Ch:* dispersoid.

disponibilité [dispɔnibilite], *s.f.* **1.** availability (of seats, lodgings, capital, etc.); **avoir la d. de qch.,** to have the disposal of sth.; *Mil:* **la d.,** the reserve; **mettre qn en d.,** to release s.o.; **mise en d.,** release; **être en disponibilité,** to be unattached, on half-pay; *Navy:* **bâtiment en d. armée,** ship with reduced crew. **2.** *pl.* (*a*) available time, means; **s'occuper de qch. selon ses disponibilités,** to attend to sth. when at leisure, when free to do so; (*b*) *Fin:* available funds, liquid assets.

disponible [dispɔnibl], **1.** *a.* available; at (s.o.'s) disposal; disposable; **trois places disponibles,** three vacant, unoccupied, seats (in bus, etc.); **livres disponibles,** books in print; **avoir peu de monde d.,** to be short-handed; **nous avons peu d'argent d.,** we have little money in hand, at our disposal; *Com:* **marché du d.,** spot market; *Fin:* **capital d.,** spare capital; **actif d., valeurs disponibles,** *s.m.* **le disponible,** available assets, liquid assets; *Jur:* **biens disponibles, portion d. (par testament),** disposable portion of property; *Mil:* **officier d.,** unattached officer, half-pay officer. **2.** *s.m. Mil:* member of the reserve.

dispore [dispɔ:r], *s.m. Bot:* Disporum.

dispos [dispo], *a.m.* (*a*) fit, well, fresh, in good form, in good spirits, in good fettle; **frais et d.,** hale and hearty; in top form; (*b*) **esprit d.,** fresh, alert, mind.

disposant, -ante [dispozɑ̃, -ɑ̃:t], *s. Jur:* settlor (of annuity, etc.).

disposé [dispoze], *a.* **1.** disposed; **être bien, mal, d.,** to be in a good, bad, humour, mood; **être bien d. pour, envers, qn,** to be well disposed towards s.o.; **être mal d. envers qn,** to be ill-disposed towards s.o.; **être, se sentir, d. à faire qch.,** to feel disposed, prepared, inclined, in the mood, to do sth.; **je suis tout d. à pardonner,** I am fully prepared to forgive; **êtes-vous d. à m'accompagner?** would you like to come with me? **2.** *A:* **être d. au rhumatisme,** to have a predisposition, to be predisposed, to rheumatism.

disposer [dispoze]. **1.** *v.tr.* (*a*) to dispose, set out, arrange (objects in order, in position); to lay out (garden); to set (fuse, etc.); *Mil:* **d. des troupes en ordre dilué, en éventail,** to arrange troops in extended order, in fan order; *Prov:* **l'homme propose et Dieu dispose,** man proposes but God disposes; (*b*) **d. qn à qch., à faire qch.,** to dispose, incline, s.o. to sth., to do sth.; **d. qn à la mort,** to prepare s.o. for death; **rien ne dispose mieux le corps à supporter la fatigue que,** nothing enables the body so well to stand fatigue as. **2.** *v.ind.tr.* (*a*) **d. de qn, de qch.,** to dispose of s.o.; of sth.; to have s.o., sth., at one's disposal; **droit des peuples de d. d'eux-mêmes,** right of peoples to self-determination; **d. d'un criminel,** to deal with a criminal; **d. de sa vie,** to order one's own life; **disposez de moi,** I am at your service; **d. de la presse,** to command the press; **essayer de tous les moyens dont on dispose,** to try every available means; **toutes les heures dont je puis d.,** every hour I can spare; **les renseignements dont je dispose,** the information in my possession; **les moyens dont je dispose,** the means at my disposal, at my command; **d. de capitaux importants,** to have a large capital at one's command, in hand; to command a large capital; **vous pouvez d. de mon dictionnaire,** you may use my dictionary; (*at the end of an interview*) **vous pouvez d.,** you may go; (*b*) **d. de ses biens en faveur de qn,** to make over one's property to s.o.; (*c*) **d. sur qn pour une somme,** to draw on s.o. for a sum of money. **3.** to prescribe, enjoin; **la loi ne dispose que pour l'avenir,** the law applies only to the future; **règlement qui dispose que . . .,** regulation which enjoins that . .; **la loi dispose que . . .,** the law provides that . ..

se disposer à qch., à faire qch., to get ready for sth., to get ready to do sth.; **se d. au sommeil, à dormir,** to prepare to go to sleep; to compose oneself to sleep; **se d. à partir,** to get ready to start.

dispositif [dispozitif], *s.m.* **1.** *Jur:* purview, enacting terms (of statute, etc.). **2.** *Mil:* disposition (of troops in battle, in billets, etc.); *Navy:* **d. d'éclairage,** scouting order; **d. de mines,** system of mines. **3.** *Tchn:* apparatus, device, contrivance, appliance; **d. pour économiser la vapeur,** steam-saving appliance; **d. de commande, de manœuvre,** driving-gear, controlling gear, mechanism; **d. de sûreté,** (safety) locking device; *Av:* **d. d'injection au démarrage,** primer; *W.Tel: etc:* **d. antiparasites,** parasitic suppressor; (*computers*) **d. d'entraînement,** drive; **d. d'entrée manuelle,** manual word generator, manual input unit.

disposition [dispozisjɔ̃], *s.f.* disposition. **1.** arrangement, ordering (of house, troops, of work, etc.); laying out, lay-out (of garden, etc.); **d. du terrain,** lie of the land; *Typ:* **d. typographique,** layout (of advertisement, etc.). **2.** (*a*) state (of mind, body); frame of mind; **être dans la d. de partir,** to be intending to leave, to be prepared to leave; **être en bonne d. pour faire qch.,** to be disposed, inclined, in the humour, to do sth.; **être en mauvaise d.,** not to feel up to the mark; not to be in the mood (to do sth.); **avoir des dispositions favorables pour qn,** to be favourably disposed towards s.o.; (*b*) *A:* predisposition; **avoir une d. au rhumatisme,** to be predisposed to rheumatism; **avoir une d. à s'enrhumer,** to have a tendency to catch cold, to be liable to catch cold; (*c*) *pl.* natural aptitude, aptness (for sth.); **dispositions naturelles pour la musique,** natural bent for music; **avoir des dispositions pour la peinture,** to have an aptitude, a taste, a turn, for painting; to be cut out for an artist; **enfant qui a des dispositions,** (naturally) gifted child. **3.** *pl.* (*a*) arrangements; **prendre des dispositions pour faire qch.,** to prepare, arrange, for doing sth.; **prendre des dispositions pour que qch. se fasse,** to arrange, make the necessary arrangements, for sth. to be done; **nous avons pris des dispositions dans ce sens,** we have made provision to this effect; **j'avais pris toutes mes dispositions,** I had made all my arrangements; **prendre toutes dispositions utiles,** to make the necessary arrangements, to take the necessary steps; **quand on a pris de bonnes dispositions, la bataille, la partie, est à moitié gagnée,** to be well prepared is half the battle; *Mil:* **dispositions de combat!** prepare for action! (*b*) provisions, conditions, dispositions (of will, law, treaty, etc.); clauses (of law); **les dispositions contenues dans l'article 34,** the provisions of article 34; **arrêter des dispositions générales,** to lay down general rules. **4.** (*a*) disposal; **avoir la libre d. de son bien,** to be free to dispose of one's property; *Jur:* **d. entre vifs,** donation *inter vivos*; **je n'ai pas la d. de moi-même,** I am not my own master; **libre d. de soi-même,** self-determination; *Adm:* **mise en d. (d'un fonctionnaire),** loan, temporary transfer (of civil servant) to another department; **fonds à ma d.,** funds at my disposal, at my command, under my control; **le peu qu'il y a est à votre d.,** you are welcome to what little there is; **mettre qch. à la d. de qn,** to place sth. at s.o.'s disposal; **il mit sa maison à ma d.,** he gave me the run of his house; **je suis à votre (entière) d.,** I am (entirely) at your service; **avoir les journaux à sa d.,** to command the press; (*b*) *Com:* **d. sur qn,** (i) drawing on s.o.; (ii) advice of date on which client will be drawn upon.

disproportion [disprɔpɔrsjɔ̃], *s.f.* disproportion, lack of proportion (**entre,** between).

disproportionné [disprɔpɔrsjɔne], *a.* disproportionate, (**à, avec,** to); out of proportion (**à, avec,** with).

disproportionnel, -elle [disprɔpɔrsjɔnɛl], *a.* disproportional, unequal (quantities, etc.).

disproportionnellement [disprɔpɔrsjɔnɛlmɑ̃], *adv.* disproportionally.

disproportionnément [disprɔpɔrsjɔnemɑ̃], *adv.* disproportionally, disproportionately, out of (all) proportion (**à,** to, with).

disputable [dispytabl], *a.* disputable, debatable (point, question).

disputailler [dispytɑje], *v.i. F:* to wrangle, bicker, squabble (**sur,** about).

disputaillerie [dispytɑjri], *s.f. F:* squabble, petty argument; bickering.

disputailleur, -euse [dispytɑjœ:r, -ø:z], *F:* **1.** *a.* given to arguing; fond of wrangling, bickering, squabbling; cantankerous. **2.** *s.* wrangler, bickerer, squabbler.

disputant [dispytɑ̃], *s.m. Sch: A:* disputant.

disputation [dispytasjɔ̃], *s.f. Sch: A:* disputation.

dispute [dispyt], *s.f.* **1.** *A:* (*a*) debate, controversy, dispute; **sujet en d.,** subject under discussion; (*b*) contest, competition; **mettre qch. à la d.,** to offer sth. for competition. **2.** altercation, quarrel; **chercher d. à qn,** to pick a quarrel with s.o.; **c'est un sujet de d. entre eux,** it is a bone of contention between them; **ils ont eu une d.,** they had words; they had a dispute; they quarrelled.

disputer [dispyte], *v.tr. & i.* **1.** *A:* **disputer qch., de qch., sur qch.,** to dispute, debate, about sth.; to discuss sth. **2. disputer qch., de qch.,** to dispute, contest, sth.; **d. le terrain,** to dispute every inch of ground; **d. qch. à qn,** to contend with s.o. for sth.; **trophée chaudement disputé,** hard-won trophy; **le disputer en beauté avec qn,** to vie with s.o. in beauty; **en beauté elle le disputait à toutes ses rivales,** in beauty she held her own with all her rivals; **deux chiens qui se disputent un os,** two dogs fighting over a bone; **des passions contradictoires se disputent son âme,** his soul is torn between conflicting passions; **d. un match,** to play a match; **le match de boxe s'est disputé hier,** the boxing match took place yesterday; **d. une course sur mille mètres,** to run a thousand metre race; *Nau: A:* **d. le vent (à un autre navire),** to contend for the weather-gauge. **3.** *v.i.* to quarrel, wrangle, argue (**avec,** with); **d. de savoir si . . .,** to argue as to whether . . . **4.** *F:* **d. qn,** to tick s.o. off.

se disputer, to quarrel, wrangle, argue (**pour,** over, about; **avec,** with); to have words; **ils se disputent entre eux,** they quarrel, squabble, among themselves; **ils se disputent à qui aura le plus gros morceau,** they are quarrelling as to which of them should have the biggest share, they are arguing about who is to, shall, get the biggest share.

disputeur, -euse [dispytœ:r, -ø:z], *A: & Lit:* **1.** *a.* contentious, quarrelsome. **2.** *s.* wrangler, disputer, arguer.

disquaire [diskɛ:r], *s.m.* (gramophone) record dealer.

disqualificatif, -ive [diskalifikatif, -iːv], *a. Sp:* disqualifying) blow, etc.).
disqualification [diskalifikasjɔ̃], *s.f. Sp:* disqualification.
disqualifier [diskalifje], *v.tr.* (*pr.sub. & p.d.* **n. disqualifiions, v. disqualifiiez**) (*a*) *Sp:* to disqualify; (*b*) to discredit (s.o.).
disque [disk], *s.m.* **1.** *Sp:* discus. **2.** disc, *occ.* disk; (*a*) disc (of moon, etc.); (*b*) *Tchn:* disc, plate; **d. de perceuse,** drill plate; **d. en buffle,** buff wheel; **d. d'embrayage,** clutch plate, disc; **frein à d.,** disc brake; **d. d'excentrique,** eccentric sheave; *El:* **d. d'épreuve,** test plate; **enroulement en d.,** disc winding; *Tp:* **d. d'appel,** calling dial; (*c*) *Rail:* (disc) signal, target disc; **d. à distance,** distance signal; **d. de fermeture,** block signal; **siffler au d.,** to whistle for the road; (*d*) *Rec:* record, disc; **d. original,** original recording; **d. père,** master matrix; **d. mère,** mother matrix; **d. magnétique,** magnetic disc; **d. microsillon, (de) longue durée,** microgroove, long-playing, record; *F:* L.P.; **d. souple,** acetate; *F:* **changer de d.,** (i) to change one's tune; (ii) to change the subject; (*computers*) **d. codeur,** code wheel; **d. magnétique,** magnetic disk; (*e*) *Nau:* **d. de franc bord,** free board disc; (*f*) *Anat:* **d. intervertébral,** (intervertebral) disc; (*g*) *Adm: Aut:* **d. de stationnement,** parking disc; *P.N:* **zone bleue, d. obligatoire** = parking meter zone.
disque-lotion [disk(ə)losjɔ̃], *s.m. Toil:* cleansing pad; *pl. disques-lotion.*
disquisition [diskizisjɔ̃], *s.f.* disquisition.
disrupteur [disryptœːr], *s.m. El.E:* (spark) interrupter; break.
disruptif, -ive [disryptif, -iːv], *a.* disruptive (force, electric discharge, etc.).
dissatisfaction [disatisfaksjɔ̃], *s.f.* dissatisfaction.
dissatisfaire [disatisfɛːr], *v.tr.* (*conj. like* FAIRE) to dissatisfy.
dissécable [disekabl̩], *a.* dissectable.
dissecteur [disɛktœːr], *s.m.* dissector; (*computers*) **d. optique,** image dissector.
dissection [disɛksjɔ̃], *s.f.* dissection (of body, plant, accounts, literary work, etc.).
dissector [disɛktɔːr], *s.m. T.V:* image dissector tube.
dissemblable [dis(s)ɑ̃blabl̩], *a.* dissimilar, different, unlike; **d. à, de, qch.,** unlike sth., dissimilar to sth., different from sth.
dissemblablement [dis(s)ɑ̃blabləmɑ̃], *adv.* dissimilarly; in a different way.
dissemblance [dis(s)ɑ̃blɑ̃ːs], *s.f.* dissimilarity (entre, between); unlikeness.
dissemblant [dis(s)ɑ̃blɑ̃], *a.* dissimilar, different, unlike.
disséminateur, -trice [dis(s)eminatœːr, -tris], *s.* disseminator.
dissémination [dis(s)eminasjɔ̃], *s.f.* **1.** sowing, scattering (of seeds, etc.); spreading (of germs). **2.** dissemination, spreading (of ideas, etc.).
disséminement [dis(s)eminmɑ̃], *s.m.* (state of) dissemination.
disséminer [dis(s)emine], *v.tr.* **1.** to sow, scatter (seeds, etc.); to spread (germs). **2.** to disseminate (ideas, etc.).
se disséminer, to spread.
dissension [dis(s)ɑ̃sjɔ̃], *s.f.* dissension, discord, disagreement; **dissensions domestiques,** family feuds; family quarrels; **fomenter les dissensions,** to stir up strife.
dissentiment [dis(s)ɑ̃timɑ̃], *s.m.* disagreement, dissent, difference of opinion.
dissépiment [disepimɑ̃], *s.m. Z:* dissepiment (of coral formation).
disséquant [dis(s)ekɑ̃], *a.* dissecting; **anévrisme d.,** dissecting aneurism.
disséquer [dis(s)eke], *v.tr.* (**je dissèque, n. disséquons; je disséquerai**) to dissect (corpse, plant, accounts, literary work, etc.).
disséqueur, -euse [dis(s)ekœːr, -øːz], *s.* dissector.
dissertateur, -trice [disɛrtatœːr, -tris], *s.* dissertator, dissertationist; *Pej:* **grand d.,** great talker, great speechifier.
dissertation [disɛrtasjɔ̃], *s.f.* (*a*) dissertation, essay, discourse, treatise (**sur,** (up)on); (*b*) *Sch:* **d. française,** French essay; **d. latine,** (original) composition in Latin; Latin essay.
disserter [disɛrte], *v.i.* (*a*) **d. sur un sujet,** to discourse, expatiate, on a subject; to develop a subject; (*b*) to talk at length; *F:* to hold forth; **il aime à d.,** he's (rather) long-winded; he likes to hold forth, to hear himself talk.
disserteur, -euse [disɛrtœːr, -øːz], *s.* dissertator, dissertationist.
dissidence [dis(s)idɑ̃ːs], *s.f. Ecc: etc:* dissidence, schism, dissent; **tribu en d.,** dissident, disaffected, tribe.
dissident, -ente [dis(s)idɑ̃, -ɑ̃ːt]. **1.** *a.* dissident, dissentient, dissenting (sect, party, etc.); disaffected (tribe, etc.). **2.** *s.* (*a*) dissentient; (*b*) *Ecc:* dissenter, nonconformist.
dissimilaire [dis(s)imilɛːr], *a.* dissimilar, unlike.
dissimilarité [dis(s)imilarite], *s.f.* dissimilarity, unlikeness.
dissimilation [dis(s)imilasjɔ̃], *s.f. Ling:* dissimilation.
dissimiler [dis(s)imile], *v.tr. Ling:* to dissimilate.
dissimilitude [dis(s)imilityd], *s.f.* **1.** dissimilitude, dissimilarity. **2.** *Rh:* dissimile.
dissimulateur, -trice [dis(s)imylatœːr, -tris], *s.* dissimulator, dissembler, deceiver.
dissimulation [dis(s)imylasjɔ̃], *s.f.* **1.** dissimulation, dissembling, deceit, double-dealing; **user de d.,** to dissemble. **2.** concealment, covering up (of the truth, etc.); *Jur:* **d. d'actif,** (fraudulent) concealment of assets.
dissimulé [dis(s)imyle], *a.* **1.** hidden; secret. **2.** dissimulating, dissembling, secretive, double-dealing (man, character). **3.** latent, bound (electricity).
dissimuler [dis(s)imyle], *v.tr.* **1.** to dissemble, dissimulate, hide, conceal (feelings, etc.); to conceal (trench, etc.); to cover up (fault); *abs.* to dissemble; **d. un fait,** to keep back, hold back, a fact; **d. qch. à qn,** to hide sth., keep sth. back, from s.o.; **se d. la vérité,** to shut one's eyes to the truth; **je ne me dissimule pas que . . .,** I fully appreciate, realize, that . . .; **je ne peux pas me d. que . . .,** I cannot overlook the fact that . . ., I cannot conceal from myself that . . .; **il n'y a pas à se d. que . . .,** there is no blinking the fact that . . .; **robe qui dissimule les défauts de la silhouette,** dress that hides, covers (up), the defects of the figure; **ils dissimulèrent qu'ils eussent** (*occ.* **qu'ils avaient**) **eu part à l'affaire,** they concealed the fact that they had played a part in the business; **je ne dissimule pas qu'il en est ainsi, qu'il n'en soit ainsi,** I do not conceal the fact that it is so; **je ne me dissimule pas que mon cas est grave, ne soit grave,** I do not close my eyes to the fact that my case is a serious one. **2.** *A:* to ignore, take no notice of (insult, etc.).
se dissimuler, to hide; **se d. derrière les rideaux,** to hide, skulk, behind the curtains; **il parvint à se d. dans la foule,** he managed to lose himself in the crowd; **parmi tant de qualités se dissimule un défaut,** among so many qualities lurks a weakness.
dissipateur, -trice [disipatœːr, -tris]. **1.** *s.* spendthrift, squanderer, waster. **2.** *a.* **administration dissipatrice,** wasteful administration; **fils d.,** prodigal son.
dissipation [disipasjɔ̃], *s.f.* **1.** (*a*) dissipation, dispersion (of clouds, etc.); (*b*) dissipation, wasting (of money, energy, time, etc.); squandering (of fortune); making away (with stores, etc.); *Mil:* **d. d'effets,** making away with effects. **2.** (*a*) dissipation, dissolute living; (*b*) frivolous conduct (in school, etc.); fooling; inattention.
dissipé [disipe], *a.* (*a*) dissipated, dissolute; gay (woman); **mener une vie dissipée,** to lead a gay life; (*b*) *Sch:* inattentive, talkative (pupil).
dissiper [disipe], *v.tr.* **1.** (*a*) to dissipate, disperse, scatter, dispel (clouds, etc.); to clear up (misunderstanding); **d. une armée,** to rout, break up, an army; **d. les craintes de qn,** to dispel s.o.'s fears; **d. les soupçons,** to dispel suspicions, to allay suspicion; **d. une illusion,** to dispel an illusion; **d. la haine,** to put an end to hatred; **les anciennes rancunes ne sont pas entièrement dissipées,** the old rancours are not all gone; (*b*) to dissipate, waste (fortune, time, energy, etc.); to make away with (stores, etc.); **d. tout son argent,** to fritter away, squander, all one's money. **2.** (*a*) *A:* to divert; to occupy the spare time of (s.o.); **ces petits travaux me dissipent,** these little jobs come as a relaxation; **d. l'ennui du voyage,** to relieve, while away, the tedium of the journey; (*b*) **d. un élève,** to distract the attention of a pupil.
se dissiper. 1. (*of visions, suspicions, etc.*) to vanish, disappear; **le brouillard se dissipe,** the fog is lifting, is clearing (away), is dissipating; **l'orage s'est dissipé,** the storm is over, has blown over; **les nuages se dissipent,** the clouds are breaking; **sa fatigue s'était dissipée,** his fatigue had worn off; **ses doutes se sont dissipés,** his doubts faded. **2.** (*a*) *A:* to enjoy oneself, seek relaxation; (*b*) to fall into dissipated ways, to begin to run wild; to lead a dissipated life; (*c*) to be frivolous, inattentive (in school, etc.).
dissociabilité [dis(s)ɔsjabilite], *s.f.* dissociability.
dissociable [dis(s)ɔsjabl̩], *a.* dissociable.
dissociation [dis(s)ɔsjasjɔ̃], *s.f.* (*a*) *Ch:* dissociation, decomposition; **d. électrolytique,** electrolytic dissociation; (*b*) *Psy:* dissociation; (*c*) *Med:* **d. auriculo-ventriculaire,** Stokes Adams' syndrome; heart block.
dissocier [dis(s)ɔsje], *v.tr.* (*p.d. and pr.sub.* **n. dissociions, v. dissociiez**) **1.** *Ch:* to dissociate (compound). **2.** to disunite, separate, dissociate (ideas, etc.).
dissolu [dis(s)ɔly], *a.* dissolute, loose, corrupt, profligate (person, life).
dissolubilité [dis(s)ɔlybilite], *s.f.* dissolubility.
dissoluble [dis(s)ɔlybl̩], *a.* **1.** *A:* soluble. **2.** *Jur:* dissolvable, dissoluble (contract, etc.); *Pol:* **assemblée d.,** assembly which can be dissolved.
dissolutif, -ive [dis(s)ɔlytif, -iːv], *a. Ch: Pharm:* (dis)solvent.
dissolution [dis(s)ɔlysjɔ̃], *s.f.* **1.** disintegration, dissolution, decomposition (of body, etc.). **2.** (*a*) *Ch:* dissolving (of substance in liquid, etc.); (*b*) solution; **d. de caoutchouc,** rubber solution. **3.** dissolution (of parliament, marriage, partnership, etc.); breaking up (of meeting); winding up (of company); *Mil:* disbandment (of unit). **4.** dissoluteness, licentiousness, profligacy; **vivre dans la d.,** to lead a dissolute life.
dissolvant [dis(s)ɔlvɑ̃], *a. & s.m.* (*a*) (dis)solvent; **d. (pour ongles),** nail varnish remover; (*b*) **livre d., doctrine dissolvante,** corrupt book, doctrine.
dissonance [dis(s)ɔnɑ̃ːs], *s.f.* **1.** *Mus: etc:* dissonance. **2.** *Mus:* discord; **résoudre une d.,** to resolve a discord.
dissonant [dis(s)ɔnɑ̃], *a.* **1.** dissonant, discordant. **2.** (word, etc.) offensive to the ear, that grates on the ear; out of place.
dissoudre [dis(s)udr̩], *v.tr.* (*pr.p.* **dissolvant;** *p.p.* **dissous,** *f.* **dissoute;** *pr.ind.* **je dissous, il dissout, n. dissolvons;** *pr.sub.* **je dissolve;** *p.d.* **je dissolvais;** *p.h. & p.sub. are lacking, the past historic of* **faire dissoudre** *is available in sense 1; fu.* **je dissoudrai**) to dissolve. **1.** to melt (substance) in a liquid. **2.** (*a*) to disintegrate, decompose (body, etc.); *Med:* **d. une tumeur,** to disperse a tumour; (*b*) to dissolve (parliament); to dissolve, break (partnership); to annul (marriage); *Mil:* to disband (unit).
se dissoudre, to dissolve. **1.** (*a*) (*of sugar, etc.*) **se d. dans l'eau,** to dissolve, melt, in water; **faire d. une substance,** to dissolve, melt, a substance; (*b*) **colère qui se dissout en larmes,** anger that dissolves into tears. **2.** (*of assembly*) to break up.
dissous [dis(s)u], *a.* dissolved, in solution; *Ch:* **corps d.,** solute.
dissuader [dis(s)ɥade], *v.tr.* **d. qn de qch., de faire qch.,** to dissuade s.o. from sth., from doing sth.; to argue s.o. out of doing sth.; **d. qn de partir,** to persuade s.o. not to go away; **je l'ai dissuadé de se battre,** I persuaded him not to fight.
dissuasif, -ive [disɥazif, -iːv], *a.* dissuasive.
dissuasion [dis(s)ɥazjɔ̃], *s.f.* dissuasion (**de,** from); *Mil: Pol:* **arme de d.,** deterrent.
dissyllabe [disil(l)ab]. **1.** *a.* di(s)syllabic. **2.** *s.m.* di(s)syllable.
dissyllabique [disil(l)abik], *a.* di(s)syllabic.
dissymétrie [dis(s)imetri], *s.f.* asymmetry, dissymmetry.
dissymétrique [dis(s)imetrik], *a.* asymmetric(al), dissymmetrical, unsymmetrical; *Med:* **névrite d.,** unilateral neuritis; *Ch:* **atome d.,** asymmetric atom.
distal, -aux [distal, -o], *a. Nat.Hist:* distal, terminal.
distance [distɑ̃ːs], *s.f.* distance; **d. d'un lieu à un autre, entre deux lieux,** distance from one place to another, between two places; **on ne voyait rien à cette d.,** one could see nothing from that distance; **suivre qn à d., à peu de d.,** to follow s.o. at a distance, at a short distance; **la ville est à deux lieues de d.,** the town is five miles away; **à quelle d. sommes-nous de la ville?** how far are we from the town? **maison à un kilomètre de d., à peu de d.,** house that is a kilometre off, a kilometre away; not far off, not far away; **à courte d.,** within easy reach (**de,** of); **c'est à une grande d.,** it is a long way off (**de,** from); **ils sont à une d. d'un kilomètre l'un de l'autre,** they are a kilometre apart; **d. de dix ans entre deux événements,** ten years' interval between two events; **de d. en d. se trouvent des cabines téléphoniques,** at intervals there are telephone boxes; **tenir qn à d.,** to keep s.o. at a distance, at arm's length; **conserver, garder, ses distances, se tenir à d.,** to keep at a distance, to keep aloof, to hold off; **tenir ses distances,** (i) (*of subordinate*) to know one's place; (ii) (*of employer, etc.*) to keep oneself aloof; **prendre ses distances,** (i) *Mil: Gym:* to dress; (ii) to stand aloof; *Sp:*

tenir la d., to go the distance, to stay, last, the course; *Mec.E:* commande à d., remote control; *Opt:* d. focale, focal length; (objectif) de courte d. focale, short focus (lens); *Artil: etc:* appréciation des distances, distance judging; à petite d., à faible d., at short range; bâtiment à d. de lancement d'une torpille, ship within torpedo range; *I.C.E: etc:* d. explosive, spark-gap; *Nau:* d. parcourue, day's run; *Aut:* d. d'arrêt, de freinage, braking distance.

distancé [distɑ̃se], *a. Rac:* (*of horse*) disqualified.

distancement [distɑ̃smɑ̃], *s.m. Rac:* disqualifying, disqualification (of winner).

distancer [distɑ̃se], *v.tr.* (je distançai(s); n. distançons) *Rac: etc:* 1. to outdistance, outrun, outstrip; to outpace; *Nau:* to outsail; se laisser d., to drop away, to fall behind; se laisser d. par les autres élèves, to fall, lag, behind the other pupils. 2. to disqualify (winner).

distanciation [distɑ̃sjasjɔ̃], *s.f. Th:* alienation effect.

distant [distɑ̃], *a.* 1. distant; nos deux maisons sont distantes d'un kilomètre l'une de l'autre, our two houses are a kilometre apart. 2. il est très d., he is very stand-offish, always very aloof.

distendre [distɑ̃:dr̥], *v.tr.* 1. to distend (stomach, bladder, etc.); to over-inflate (balloon). 2. to overstretch, strain (muscle, etc.); to stretch (a rope, etc.) to breaking point.

se distendre. 1. to become distended; to swell (out). 2. to relax, to slacken; il sentait se d. les derniers liens qui retenaient son âme à ce monde, he felt the last links which bound him to this world giving way.

distension [distɑ̃sjɔ̃], *s.f. Med:* 1. distension (of stomach, etc.). 2. overstretching, straining (of muscle, etc.).

disthène [distɛn], *s.m. Miner:* disthene, cyanite.

distillable [distilabl̥], *a.* distillable.

distillat [distila], *s.m. Ch: Ind:* distillate.

distillateur [distilatœ:r], *s.m.* 1. distiller; owner of a distillery. 2. *Nau:* (*a*) distilling condenser, fresh-water condenser; (*b*) (navire) d., distilling ship.

distillation [distilasjɔ̃], *s.f.* distillation; distilling; d. sèche, dry distillation; d. fractionnée, fractional distillation; d. discontinue, batch distillation.

distillatoire [distilatwa:r], *a.* 1. *Ind:* distillatory, distilling, (apparatus, etc.). 2. *Bot:* plante d., pitcher-plant, nepenthes.

distiller [distile]. 1. *v.tr.* (*a*) to distil, exude, secrete (drops of moisture, etc.); d. sa rage, etc., to exude anger, etc.; (*b*) *Ind:* to distil (spirits, etc.); to condense; eau distillée, distilled water. (*c*) (*of bee*) to elaborate (honey); *Lit:* to distil (a philosophy, etc.); to refine (one's thoughts). 2. *v.i.* to distil, exude (de, from).

distillerie [distilri], *s.f.* 1. distillery. 2. distilling (trade).

distinct [distɛ̃(:kt)], *a.* 1. distinct, separate (de, from); presse à imprimer des feuilles distinctes, press for printing separate sheets. 2. distinct, clear (outline, voice, etc.); audible (voice); unblurred (outline, print).

distinctement [distɛ̃ktəmɑ̃], *adv.* distinctly, clearly; audibly.

distinctif, -ive [distɛ̃ktif, -i:v], *a.* distinctive, characteristic, distinguishing (sign, feature, etc.); trait d., characteristic, peculiarity; le signe d. de la civilisation, the hallmark of civilization.

distinction [distɛ̃ksjɔ̃], *s.f.* distinction. 1. d. de qch. d'avec qch., point of difference between sth. and sth.; faire une d. entre deux choses, to make a distinction, to discriminate, differentiate, distinguish, between two things; faire la d. des personnes, to distinguish between people; sans d., indiscriminately; sans d. de rang, without distinction of rank; d. des classes, class distinction; sans d. de race ou de couleur, irrespective of race or colour. 2. (*a*) distinction, honour; distinctions académiques, academic honours; (*b*) decoration (*e.g.* medal, star). 3. (*a*) distinction, eminence; un personnage de haute d., a highly distinguished person; (*b*) avoir de la d. dans les manières, to have a distinguished bearing.

distinctivement [distɛ̃ktivmɑ̃], *adv.* distinctively.

distinguable [distɛ̃gabl̥], *a.* distinguishable.

distingué [distɛ̃ge], *a.* distinguished. 1. eminent, noted (writer, politician, etc.). 2. (*a*) refined (taste, bearing, etc.); avoir un air d., to look gentlemanly, lady-like, distinguished; les manières distinguées de l'ancien temps, old-world manners; (*b*) smart (costume, etc.). 3. (*letter formula*) croyez à ma considération distinguée, yours truly. 4. *s.m. F:* large glass of beer (one litre).

distinguer [distɛ̃ge], *v.tr.* to distinguish. 1. to mark, characterize; œuvres distinguées par le bon goût, works characterized by good taste; sa mise soignée le distinguait de la foule, his impeccable appearance singled him out, made him stand out, from the crowd. 2. (*a*) to honour; to single (s.o.) out for distinction; (*b*) *A:* to pay particular attention to (s.o.), to honour (s.o.) with particular attention. 3. d. entre deux choses, to distinguish between two things; d. qch. de qch., d'avec qch., to distinguish, tell, sth. from sth.; la raison distingue l'homme des autres animaux, reason distinguishes, differentiates, man from other animals; on peut à peine le d. d'avec son frère, you can hardly tell him from his brother; il faut apprendre à d. entre les gens, you must learn to discriminate between people. 4. to discern, perceive; je ne peux pas d. ses traits, I cannot make out his features; je l'ai distingué parmi la foule, I singled him out amongst the crowd; il faisait trop noir pour bien d., it was too dark to see clearly; d. le point de chute d'un obus, to mark the fall of a shell.

se distinguer. 1. to distinguish oneself (par ses talents, by one's talents). 2. se d. des autres, to be distinguishable, marked off, from others (par, by); il se distingue de son frère par son grand nez, one can tell him from his brother by his big nose; il se distingue de son frère par son goût pour la musique, he differs from his brother in that he has a taste for music; his love of music distinguishes him from his brother. 3. to be noticeable, conspicuous; le besoin de se d., the desire to be different, to stand out; parmi tant de toiles se distingue un petit chef-d'œuvre, among so many canvases a small masterpiece stands out; l'arbre se distingue contre le ciel, the tree stands out against the sky; rien ne se distinguait qu'un petit sifflement, all that could be heard was a slight hissing sound.

distinguo [distɛ̃go], *s.m. F:* distinction; faire le d., to make a subtle distinction.

distique[1] [distik], *s.m. Pros:* 1. (*Gr. or Lt. verse*) distich. 2. (*Fr. verse*) couplet.

distique[2], *a. Bot:* distichous.

distomatose [distɔmato:z], *s.f. Vet:* rot (in sheep).

distome [distɔm], *s.m. Z: Vet:* distome, distomian.

distomiens [distɔmjɛ̃], *s.m.pl. Z:* Distomians.

distordre [distɔrdr̥], *v.tr.* 1. to distort. 2. to twist (one's ankle, etc.).

distors [distɔ:r], *a.* twisted; distorted; deformed.

distorsiomètre [distɔrsjɔmɛtr̥], *s.m. Ac:* distortion meter.

distorsion [distɔrsjɔ̃], *s.f.* distortion (of limb, of optical image, of wireless reproduction, etc.); *Opt:* d. en barillet, barrel-shaped distortion (by a lens); d. en croissant, en coussinet, pincushion distortion; pillow distortion; *Ac:* d. non uniforme, d. amplitude-fréquence, attenuation distortion.

distraction [distraksjɔ̃], *s.f.* 1. *A:* & *Jur:* (*a*) division, severance (of part from a whole, etc.); (*b*) appropriation; faire une d. dans une intention spéciale, to set aside a sum, make an appropriation, for a special purpose; (*c*) misappropriation (of funds, supplies, etc.). 2. absentmindedness, absence of mind, inadvertence, abstraction; une d., a fit of absentmindedness; il est sujet à des distractions, he is subject to fits of absentmindedness; his mind wanders at times; par d., inadvertently, absentmindedly. 3. diversion, amusement, distraction; relier des livres comme d., to bind books as a hobby.

distractivité [distraktivite], *s.f.* inability to concentrate (on anything).

distraire [distrɛ:r], *v.tr.* (*conj. like* TRAIRE) 1. (*a*) to divert, separate (part from whole, etc.); d. tant sur ses économies, to set aside, apart, so much out of one's savings; (*b*) to abstract, misappropriate (funds, supplies, etc.). 2. to distract, divert (s.o.'s attention, etc.); d. l'attention de qn, to take s.o.'s attention, mind, off sth.; ce spectacle avait distrait sa pensée, the sight had turned his thoughts in another direction; d. qn de son chagrin, to take s.o.'s mind off his sorrow; d. qn de ses travaux, to take s.o. from his work. 3. to divert, entertain, amuse.

se distraire, to amuse oneself; se d. à faire de la peinture, to amuse oneself with painting, to paint as a hobby; le besoin de se d., the need for amusement, for relaxation; afin de se d. de son chagrin, in order to take his mind off his sorrows.

distrait [distrɛ], *a.* (*a*) absentminded; (*b*) inattentive, listless; air d., abstracted, vacant, look; accorder une attention distraite à qn, to pay s.o. divided attention; il laissait errer ses mains distraites sur l'ivoire du clavier, his fingers wandered idly over the keys; vous êtes d., you're wool-gathering; you're not paying attention; d'une oreille distraite, abstractedly; inattentively; with only half an ear.

distraitement [distrɛtmɑ̃], *adv.* absentmindedly, absently, abstractedly, listlessly; errer d., to wander idly.

distrayant [distrɛjɑ̃], *a.* diverting, entertaining (book, spectacle); les romans policiers sont d'une lecture distrayante, detective stories make good light reading.

distribuable [distribɥabl̥], distributable.

distribuer [distribɥe], *v.tr.* 1. to distribute, deal out, give out (orders, prizes, etc.); to issue, serve out, portion out, share out (provisions, etc.); (*of postman*) to deliver (letters); *Typ:* to distribute (type); d. des coups à droite et à gauche, to deal (out) blows right and left; d. des prospectus, distribute, to give out, handbills; d. les fleurs, les animaux, en plusieurs classes, to classify flowers, animals; d. les cartes, to deal out the cards; *Th:* d. les rôles, to assign, cast, the parts (in a play); to cast a play. 2. d. un appartement, to arrange (the furniture, etc., in) a flat.

distributaire [distribytɛ:r], *s.m.* & *f.* recipient (in distribution); *Jur:* distributee.

distributeur, -trice [distribytœ:r, -tris]. 1. (*a*) *s.* distributor, dispenser (of alms, prizes, favours, etc.); (*b*) *s.m. Cin:* film distributor. 2. *s.m. Tchn:* distributor; d. (d'essence), petrol pump; d. automatique, automatic vending machine, slot machine; d. automatique de timbres-poste, stamp machine; d. de lames de rasoir, razor blade dispenser; d. de billets, ticket machine; *I.C.E:* d. de courant, distributor; d. à étincelles sautantes, gap type distributor; pièce mobile du d., distributor arm; rotor; (*computers*) d. d'impulsions d'horloge, d. de rythmes, time-pulse distributor; *Mch:* d. de vapeur, steam distributor, regulator; steam valve; d. compte-gouttes, drip-feed (of oil); d. d'ordonnancement, sequence valve; d. alimentaire, perforated feed pipe; *Typ:* d. d'encre, ink fountain and vibrator; *Tex:* d. au fil, guide finger, thread guide; *Agr:* d. d'engrais, fertilizer spreader.

distributif, -ive [distribytif, -i:v], *a.* 1. *Log: Gram:* distributive (term, pronoun, etc.). 2. justice distributive, distributive justice.

distribution [distribysjɔ̃], *s.f.* distribution; allotment (of duties, cabins, etc.); issue (of rations); delivery (of letters, goods); arrangement (of furniture, etc.); *Typ:* distribution (of type); *Com:* handling; *Com:* circuit de d., distribution channel; d. des plantes, classification of plants; *Sch:* d. de prix, prize-giving, speech-day; *Th:* d. des rôles d'une pièce, (i) casting; (ii) cast, of a play; *Th: Cin: W.Tel:* d. (par ordre d'entrée en scène, en ondes), characters (in order of appearance, of speaking); d. d'eau (de la ville), water supply, water service; *El.E:* tableau de d., switchboard; tension de d., supply pressure, service voltage; *Mch:* mécanisme de d. (de la vapeur), (steam) valve-gear; *I.C.E:* (engrenages de) d., valve gear, timing gear; d. à cames, cam gear; arbre de d., camshaft, timing shaft.

distributivement [distribytivmɑ̃], *adv.* distributively.

district [distrik(t)], *s.m.* district, region; *Adm:* d. urbain, urban district; d. aurifère, houiller, gold-field, coalfield; cela n'est pas de mon d., that's not within my province, my scope.

distyle [distil]. 1. *a.* (*a*) *Arch:* distyle (columniation); (*b*) *Bot:* distylous. 2. *s.m. Arch:* distyle.

disubstitué [disybstitɥe], *a. Ch:* disubstituted.

disulfonique [disylfɔnik], *a. Ch:* disulphonic.

disulfure [disylfy:r], *s.m. Ch:* disulphide.

dit [di]. 1. *a.* (*a*) settled, fixed; prendre qch. pour d., to take sth. for granted; à l'heure dite, at the appointed time, at the hour indicated; (*b*) (so-)called; Pierre d. le Cruel, Peter, called the Cruel; la zone dite tempérée, the so-called temperate zone. 2. *s.m. A:* (*a*) given word; il a son d. et son dédit, he often goes back on his word; his word is not to be relied on; (*b*) *Jur:* statement; (*c*) maxim, saying; (*d*) *Lit:* familiar story (usually in verse); le d. des trois larrons, the story of the three thieves.

dithéisme [diteism], *s.m. Rel:* ditheism.

dithéiste [diteist], *Rel:* 1. *a.* ditheistic. 2. *s.m.* & *f.* ditheist.

dithiobenzoïque [ditjɔbɛ̃zɔik], *a. Ch:* dithiobenzoic.

dithionique [ditjɔnik], *a. Ch:* dithionic.

dithyrambe [ditirɑ̃:b], *s.m.* (*a*) *Lit:* dithyramb; (*b*) extravagant eulogy; *F:* rhapsody.
dithyrambique [ditirɑ̃bik], *a.* (*a*) *Lit:* dithyrambic; (*b*) extravagant (eulogy, etc.).
ditolyle [ditɔlil], *s.m. Ch:* ditolyl.
dito [dito], *adv.* ditto, do.
diton [ditɔ̃], *s.m. Mus: A:* ditone.
dittographie [ditɔgrafi], *s.f.* dittography.
dittologie [ditɔlɔʒi], *s.f.* dittology.
diurèse [djyrɛ:z], *s.f. Med:* diuresis.
diurétique [djyretik], *a.* & *s.m. Med:* diuretic.
diurnal, -aux [djyrnal, -o]. 1. *a. A:* diurnal, daily. 2. *s.m. Ecc:* (*R.C.Ch.*): diurnal.
diurne [djyrn], *a.* 1. diurnal (motion of planet, etc.). 2. **insectes diurnes**, diurnal insects; **oiseau d.**, day bird.
diva [diva], *s.f. O:* diva, prima donna.
divagant [divagɑ̃], *a.* wandering, straying; (*of speech, etc.*) rambling, incoherent.
divagateur, -trice [divagatœ:r, -tris]. (*rare*) 1. *a.* wandering (imagination); rambling (speech, etc.). 2. *s.* wanderer, rambler.
divagation [divagasjɔ̃], *s.f.* 1. (*a*) *A:* divagation, wandering; *Jur:* straying (of cattle, etc.); (*b*) shifting (of river) from its course. 2. digression (in a speech, etc.); **divagations d'un fou**, maunderings, ravings, incoherent utterings, of a madman.
divaguer [divage], *v.i.* 1. (*a*) *A:* to divagate, wander; *Jur:* (*of cattle, etc.*) to stray; (*b*) (*of river*) to shift its course. 2. (*a*) to digress, to wander away from the point, to make irrelevant remarks; to be wide of the mark; (*b*) **malade qui divague**, person whose mind is wandering, who rambles in his speech; *F:* **vous divaguez!** you're raving!
divalent [divalɑ̃], *a.* & *s.m. Ch:* divalent, bivalent; **radical d.**, dyad.
divan [divɑ̃], *s.m.* 1. *Hist:* divan, (i) oriental council; (ii) council-room. 2. *Furn:* divan; couch.
divan-coffre [divɑ̃kɔfr], *s.m. Furn:* (box-)ottoman; *pl. divans-coffres.*
divarication [divarikasjɔ̃], *s.f.* divarication.
divariqué [divarike], *a. Biol: Bot:* divaricate.
divariquer [divarike]. 1. *v.tr. Surg:* to open up (wound). 2. *v.i. Biol: Bot: etc:* to divaricate, diverge.
dive [di:v], *a.f. A:* divine; *A: or F:* **la d. bouteille**, wine, the bottle; **être adorateur de la d. bouteille**, to be over-fond of one's wine.
divergence [divɛrʒɑ̃:s], *s.f.* divergence, divarication (of lines, paths, opinions, rays, etc.); spread (of bullets, etc.); differences (of opinion); *Alg:* **d. d'une série**, divergence of a series; *Bot:* **angle de d.**, angle of divergence; *Aut:* **d. des roues avant**, toe-out; *Atom.Ph:* (*of nuclear reactor*) **entrer en d.**, to start a (fission) chain reaction.
divergent [divɛrʒɑ̃]. 1. *a.* divergent (lines, paths, opinions, lens); negative (optical system); *Ch: Atom.Ph:* chain (reaction); *Alg:* **série divergente**, divergent series; *Bot:* **rameaux divergents**, diverging branches. 2. *s.m.* diffuser nozzle (of jet aircraft).
diverger [divɛrʒe], *v.i.* (**il divergea(it); n. divergeons**) (*a*) (*of lines, paths, rays, etc.*) to diverge (de, from); to spread out in opposite directions, to divaricate; (*b*) **nos opinions divergent sur certains points**, our opinions differ on certain points; (*c*) (*of nuclear reactor*) to start a (fission) chain reaction.
divers [divɛ:r], *a.* 1. *A:* changing, changeful, varying (nature, etc.); **un monde toujours d.**, an ever-changing world; a world never the same, of endless variety. 2. (*a*) *pl.* diverse, different, varied; **ces diverses opinions, ces opinions diverses**, these varied, diverse, opinions; **des opinions très diverses**, very varied opinions; (**frais**) **d.**, sundry expenses, sundries; **articles d.**, sundry articles, sundries; *Nau:* **marchandises diverses**, *s.m.* **des divers**, general cargo; **remarques diverses**, miscellaneous remarks; (*b*) *Journ:* **avis d.**, miscellaneous column; **faits d.**, news items; **un fait d.**, incident; **en présence de ces d. faits**, faced with these diverse, varied, facts; (*c*) *indef. adj., always preceding the sb.* various, sundry; **en diverses occasions**, on various occasions; **diverses personnes l'ont vu**, various people saw him.
diversement [divɛrsəmɑ̃], *adv.* diversely; (*a*) differently; (*b*) in various ways, variously.
diversicolore [divɛrsikɔlɔ:r], *a. Bot:* diversicoloured, variegated.
diversifiable [divɛrsifjabl], *a.* diversifiable, that can be diversified.
diversification [divɛrsifikasjɔ̃], *s.f.* diversification.
diversifier [divɛrsifje], *v.tr.* (*pr.sub.* & *p.d.* **n. diversifiions, v. diversifiiez**) to diversify, vary (conversation, pursuits, etc.); to variegate (colours).
se diversifier, (*of matter, interests, etc.*) to change; (*a*) to vary; (*b*) to become different.
diversiflore [divɛrsiflɔ:r], *a. Bot:* diversiflorous.
diversiforme [divɛrsifɔrm], *a. Nat.Hist:* diversiform.
diversion [divɛrsjɔ̃], *s.f.* 1. *Mil:* diversion. 2. diversion, change, distraction; **faire d.**, to create a diversion; **faire d. à la tristesse de qn**, to take s.o.'s mind off his sorrow, to cheer s.o. up. 3. *Med:* drawing off (of inflammation, etc., from one point to another).
diversité [divɛrsite], *s.f.* diversity; (*a*) variety; (*b*) difference; **d. d'opinions**, variety of opinions; **d. d'opinion**, conflict of opinion; (*c*) *Elcs:* **monté en d.**, diversity coupled; **radar d.**, diversity radar.
diverticule [divɛrtikyl], *s.m. Anat:* diverticulum; *Med:* **d. du côlon**, diverticulosis.
diverticulite [divɛrtikylit], *s.f. Med:* diverticulitis.
diverticulose [divɛrtikylo:z], *s.f. Med:* diverticulosis.
divertir [divɛrti:r], *v.tr.* to divert. 1. *A:* (*a*) to turn aside, ward off (blow, etc.); to turn (s.o.) away (from project, etc.); (*b*) **d. une somme**, to misappropriate a sum of money; (*c*) to divert (attention, etc.); **d. la tristesse de qn**, to take s.o.'s mind off his sorrow. 2. to divert, entertain, amuse; **ce spectacle nous divertit beaucoup**, the sight afforded us a great deal of amusement, of fun.
se divertir, to enjoy oneself; **se d. aux dépens de qn**, *A:* **se d. de qn**, to make fun of s.o., to poke fun at s.o.; **vous avez l'air de vous d.**, you seem to be enjoying yourself; **elle se divertissait à faire des réussites**, her hobby was playing patience.
divertissant [divɛrtisɑ̃], *a.* diverting, amusing, entertaining.
divertissement [divɛrtismɑ̃], *s.m.* 1. **d. de fonds**, misappropriation of funds. 2. (*a*) diversion; entertainment, amusement, recreation, relaxation; **faire qch. par d.**, to do sth. by way of recreation, as a hobby, for pleasure; (*b*) *Th: A:* divertis(s)ement, entr'acte; (*c*) *Mus:* divertimento.
divette [divɛt], *s.f.* (*music-hall or light opera*) star.
dividende [dividɑ̃:d], *s.m. Mth: Fin:* dividend; **toucher un d.**, to draw a dividend; **dividendes d'actions**, dividends on shares; **distribuer des dividendes**, to distribute the dividends, *U.S: F:* to cut a melon; **avec d., sans d.**, cum div(idend), ex div(idend); **acompte de d., sur d., d. provisoire**, interim dividend; **solde de d.**, final dividend.
dividuel, -elle [dividɥɛl], *a. Log:* dividual.
divin [divɛ̃], *a.* divine (majesty, worship, etc.); holy (word, etc.); sacred (blood, etc.); **le d. Enfant** [divinɑ̃fɑ̃], the Holy Child; **le d. Achille**, heaven-born Achilles; **le d. Ulysse**, godlike Ulysses; **poésie divine**, exquisite, sublime, divine, poetry; **charme d.**, divine charm; *s.m.* **le d.**, the divine.
divinateur, -trice [divinatœ:r, -tris]. 1. *s. A:* diviner, soothsayer. 2. *a.* foreseeing, prophetic.
divination [divinasjɔ̃], *s.f.* 1. divination, soothsaying. 2. instinctive foresight.
divinatoire [divinatwa:r], *a.* divinatory; **baguette d.**, divining rod, dowsing rod.
divinement [divinmɑ̃], *adv.* divinely.
divinisation [divinizasjɔ̃], *s.f.* divinization, deification.
diviniser [divinize], *v.tr.* to divinize; to deify.
divinité [divinite], *s.f.* divinity. 1. divine nature; godhead (of Christ, etc.). 2. deity; god, goddess; (*of woman*) **une d.**, a goddess, a Venus.
divinyle [divinil], *s.m. Ch:* divinyl.
divis [divi], *Jur:* (*a*) *a.* (*used only as opposite of* **indivis**) divided (property, ownership); *adv. phr.* **par d. et indivis**, jointly and severally; (*b*) *s.m.* divided ownership (of property); severalty.
diviser [divize], *v.tr.* to divide. 1. **d. une ville par, en, arrondissements** = to divide (up) a town into wards; **d. son argent entre ses amis**, to divide one's money between, among, one's friends; **d. le travail**, to portion out the work; **d. un acte en scènes**, to split up an act into scenes; *Mth:* **d. un nombre par un autre**, to divide one number by another; **d. un angle en deux parties égales**, to bisect an angle; **machine à d.**, graduator; dividing, graduating, machine. 2. (*a*) to part, separate; **les Pyrénées divisent la France d'avec l'Espagne**, the Pyrenees divide, separate, France from Spain; **divisés d'opinion**, divided, separated, in opinion; (*b*) to set (people, etc.) at variance; **maison divisée contre elle-même**, house divided against itself; **provinces divisées de sentiments et d'intérêts**, provinces divided in feelings and in interests; *Hist: Pol:* **d. pour régner**, divide and rule.
se diviser. 1. to divide, to break up (en, into). 2. **l'examen se divise en trois parties**, the examination is divided into three parts; **vingt-cinq se divise par cinq**, twenty-five is divisible by five.
diviseur [divizœ:r], *s.m.* & *a.inv.* 1. *Mth:* divisor; **plus grand commun d.**, highest common factor, H.C.F.; **d. premier**, prime factor; **la fraction diviseur**, the divisor fraction. 2. divider; *El:* **d. de courant**, current divider; *Hyg:* **système d.** (**de vidange**), tight-cesspool system.
diviseuse [divizø:z], *s.f. Tchn:* graduator; dividing, graduating, machine.
divisibilité [divizibilite], *s.f.* divisibility.
divisible [divizibl], *a.* divisible.
division [divizjɔ̃], *s.f.* division. 1. partition (en, into); dividing (of whole into parts); *Mth:* division; **d. à un chiffre** = simple division; **d. du travail**, division of labour; **d. par arrondissements**, division into wards. 2. part, portion, section (of whole); (administrative) department, branch; *Sch:* division; set; *Mil: Navy:* division; *Mil:* **d. blindée, aéroportée**, armoured division; airborne division. 3. discord, dissension, disagreement; **mettre la d. dans une famille**, to bring division, discord, into a family; to set a family at variance. 4. (*a*) *Typ:* hyphen; (*b*) *Mus:* double bar.
divisionnaire [divizjɔnɛ:r], *a.* 1. (*a*) *Mil: etc:* divisional; **tranche d.**, divisional slice; *Adm:* **commissaire d.** = superintendent (of police); (*b*) *s.m. Mil:* major general. 2. *Com:* **monnaie d.**, subsidiary coins.
divisionnisme [divizjɔnism], *s.m. Art:* divisionism.
divisme [divism], *s.m. Cin:* stardom; the star system.
divisoire [divizwa:r], *a.* 1. dividing (line, etc.). 2. *Jur:* divisory (action, etc.).
divitisme [divitism], *s.m. A:* extreme wealth, divitism.
divorce [divɔrs], *s.m.* 1. divorce; **intenter une action en d.** (**contre qn**), to take divorce proceedings (against s.o.); **demander le d.**, to sue for a divorce, to file a petition for divorce; *B:* **lettre de d.**, bill of divorcement; *A:* **faire d. avec les plaisirs**, to renounce, take leave of, pleasures. 2. **le d. de la langue écrite avec la langue parlée**, the gulf between the written and the spoken language.
divorcé, -ée [divɔrse]. 1. *a.* divorced; **ils sont divorcés**, they have been divorced. 2. *s.* divorced man, woman, divorcee.
divorcer [divɔrse], *v.i.* (**je divorçai(s); n. divorçons**) (*a*) **d.** (**d'**)**avec qn, se d. de qn**, to divorce s.o.; *abs.* **il veut d.**, he wants to be divorced, to obtain a divorce; (*b*) (*rare in modern Fr.*) **d. avec qch.**, to renounce; to break with, to abandon sth.; to give sth. up.
divortialité [divɔrsjalite], *s.f.* **taux de d.**, divorce rate.
divulgateur, -trice [divylgatœ:r, -tris]. 1. *a.* revealing, tell-tale. 2. *s.* discloser, betrayer (of secrets); informer.
divulgation [divylgasjɔ̃], *s.f.* divulgation, divulgement, divulgence, disclosure (de, of); **d. d'un secret**, disclosure of a secret.
divulguer [divylge], *v.tr.* to divulge, reveal, disclose, to make public, to let out (secret, etc.); **d. la présence de qn**, to make s.o.'s presence known.
se divulguer, (*of news, secret, etc.*) to leak out; to become known.
divulseur [divylsœ:r], *s.m. Surg:* divulsor.
divulsion [divylsjɔ̃], *s.f. Med:* divulsion.
dix, *num.a.inv.* & *s.m.inv.* ten. 1. *card. a.* (*at the end of the word-group* [dis]; *before sb. or adj. beginning with a vowel sound* [diz]; *before sb. or adj. beginning with a consonant* [di]) **d. hommes** [dizɔm], ten men; **d. petits enfants** [dipətizɑ̃fɑ̃], ten little children; **il est d. heures** [dizœ:r], it is ten o'clock; **j'en ai d.** [dis], I have ten. 2. *s.m.inv. usu.* [dis] (*a*) **d. et demi** [disedmi], ten and a half; (*b*) (*ordinal uses, etc.*) **le d. mai** [lədimɛ], the tenth of May; **le d. août** [lədisu], the tenth of August; **Charles D.**, Charles the Tenth; **le numéro d.**, number ten; **le d. de cœur**, the ten of hearts; *F:* **je vous le donne en d.**, you'll never guess; *F:* **ça vaut d.**, (i) it's first rate; (ii) (*of story, etc.*) that's a good one!
dix-cors [dikɔ:r], *s.m.inv. Ven:* (*stag*) ten-pointer; **grand d.-c.**, royal.
dixénite [diksenit], *s.f. Miner:* dixenite.

dix-huit [dizɥi(t)], *num.a.inv. & s.m.inv.* **1.** eighteen; (*for rules of pronunciation see* HUIT.) **2.** [dizɥi] **le dix-huit mai,** the eighteenth of May.
dix-huitième [dizɥitjɛm]. **1.** *num.a. & s.m. & f.* eighteenth. **2.** *s.m.* eighteenth (part).
dix-huitièmement [dizɥitjɛmmɑ̃], *adv.* eighteenthly; in the eighteenth place.
dixième [dizjɛm]. **1.** *num.a. & s.m. & f.* tenth. **2.** *s.m.* tenth (part).
dixièmement [dizjɛmmɑ̃], *adv.* tenthly, in the tenth place.
dix-neuf [diznœf], *num.a.inv. & s.m.inv.* **1.** nineteen; (*for rules of pronunciation see* NEUF.) **2.** (*always* [diznœf]) **le dix-neuf mai,** the nineteenth of May.
dix-neuvième [diznœvjɛm]. **1.** *num.a. & s.m. & f.* nineteenth. **2.** *s.m.* nineteenth (part).
dix-neuvièmement [diznœvjɛmmɑ̃], *adv.* nineteenthly, in the nineteenth place.
dix-sept [disset], *num.a.inv. & s.m.inv.* **1.** seventeen; (*for rules of pronunciation see* SEPT.) **2.** (*always* [disset]) **le dix-sept mai,** the seventeenth of May.
dix-septième [dis(s)ɛtjɛm]. **1.** *num.a. & s.m. & f.* seventeenth. **2.** *s.m.* seventeenth (part).
dix-septièmement [dis(s)ɛtjɛmmɑ̃], *adv.* seventeenthly, in the seventeenth place.
dizain [dizɛ̃], *s.m.* **1.** packet of ten packs of cards. **2.** *Pros:* ten-line stanza. **3.** *A:* decade (of rosary).
dizaine [dizɛn], *s.f.* (*a*) *Arith:* ten; **colonne des dizaines,** the tens column; **compter par dizaines,** to count in tens; (*b*) about ten; **une d. de personnes,** ten or a dozen people, ten people or so, about ten people; **il y a une d. d'années,** some ten years ago; **revenir dans la d.,** to return within ten days; (*c*) **d. (de chapelet),** decade (of rosary).
dizygote [dizigɔt], **dizygotique** [dizigɔtik], *a. Biol:* dizygotic.
djaïn [dʒain], *a. & s.m. Hindu Rel:* Jain.
djaïnisme [dʒainism], *s.m. Hindu Rel:* Jainism.
Djakarta [dʒakarta], *Pr.n. Geog:* Djakarta.
djebel [dʒebɛl], *s.m.* (*in N. Africa*) jebel, mountain; **le d. Haoûran,** Jebel Hauran.
djellaba [dʒɛlaba], *s.f. Cost:* jellaba.
Djerba [dʒɛrba], *Pr.n. Geog:* Djerba.
Djibouti [dʒibuti], *Pr.n.m. Geog:* Djib(o)uti.
djihad [dʒiad], *s.m.* Jihad; holy war.
djinn [dʒin], *s.m. Arab.Myth:* djinni, djin(n); *pl.* **les djinns,** the djin(n), the djinns.
do [do], *s.m. Mus:* **1.** (= UT) (*the note*) C. **2.** (*in the fixed do system*) doh.
doberman [dɔbɛrman], *s.m. Breed:* doberman (pinscher).
Dobroudja [dɔbrudʒa], *Pr.n.f. Geog:* (the) Dobrudja, Dobruja.
dochmiaque [dɔkmjak], *a. & s.m.*, **dochmius** [dɔkmjyːs], *s.m. Gr.Pros:* (*a*) *a.* dochmiac; (*b*) *s.m.* dochmius.
docile [dɔsil], *a.* (*a*) docile, apt, teachable (pupil, etc.); (*b*) submissive, manageable, gentle, amenable, biddable (child); tractable (animal, etc.); **d. à des conseils,** amenable to advice; **cheval d. au feu,** horse steady under fire; **moteur d.,** flexible engine.
docilement [dɔsilmɑ̃], *adv.* submissively, quietly, obediently, with docility.
docilité [dɔsilite], *s.f.* docility; (*a*) readiness to learn; (*b*) tractability, submissiveness, amenableness; steadiness (of horse, etc.).
docimasie [dɔsimazi], *s.f. Gr.Ant: Med:* docimasy.
dock [dɔk], *s.m.* **1.** *Nau:* (*a*) dock; **d. de carénage,** dry dock; **d. flottant,** floating dock; **mettre un navire au d.,** to dock a ship; **mise, entrée, au d.,** docking; (*b*) **d. de sauvetage,** salvage-vessel (for submarines); (*c*) dock(s), dockyard; **droits de d.,** dock dues. **2.** *Com:* (dock) warehouse; bonded warehouse.
docker [dɔkɛːr], *s.m.* docker; stevedore.
docte [dɔkt], (*a*) *a. Lit: or* (*when it precedes noun*) *Iron:* learned; (*b*) *s.m.pl.* **les doctes,** scholars.
doctement [dɔktəmɑ̃], *adv. Lit: or Iron:* in a learned manner, learnedly.
docteur [dɔktœːr], *s.m.* doctor. **1.** (*a*) *A:* scholar, learned man; **il était grand d. en matière de grec,** he was a first class Greek scholar; (*b*) **les docteurs de l'Église,** the Doctors of the Church. **2.** *Sch:* **d. en droit,** Doctor of Laws, LL.D.; **d. ès lettres,** Doctor of Literature, D.Litt; **d. en théologie,** Doctor of Divinity, D.D.; **Mlle X est docteur ès sciences,** Miss X is a doctor of science. **3. d. (en médecine),** doctor (of medicine); **leur fille est d.,** their daughter is a doctor; **il n'aime pas les femmes docteurs,** he doesn't like women doctors; **entrez, d.,** come in, Doctor; **le d. Petit,** Dr Petit.
doctissime [dɔktisim], *a. usu. Iron:* very learned.
doctoral, -aux [dɔktɔral, -o], *a.* **1.** doctoral. **2.** pompous, heavy (manner); grandiloquent (tone).
doctoralement [dɔktɔralmɑ̃], *adv.* pompously, grandiloquently; ex cathedra.
doctorat [dɔktɔra], *s.m. Sch:* degree of doctor; doctorate; **passer son d.,** to take one's doctorate; **d. d'État** (*the highest grade of doctorate in Fr.*) = D.Sc., D.Litt., etc.; **d. d'université** = Ph.D.
doctoresse [dɔktɔrɛs], *s.f.* (*a*) *O: or F:* woman doctor; (*b*) *F:* bluestocking.
doctrinaire [dɔktrinɛːr]. **1.** *a.* (*a*) doctrinary (school of thought); (*b*) **pédant d.,** pedantic theorist, doctrinaire pedant. **2.** *s.m.* (*a*) doctrinarian; (*b*) *Fr.Hist:* doctrinaire.
doctrinairement [dɔktrinɛrmɑ̃], *adv.* in a doctrinaire manner, doctrinarily.
doctrinal, -aux [dɔktrinal, -o], *a.* doctrinal.
doctrinalement [dɔktrinalmɑ̃], *adv.* doctrinally.
doctrinarisme [dɔktrinarism], *s.m.* doctrinairism, doctrinarianism.
doctrine [dɔktrin], *s.f.* doctrine, tenet; **il est d. que . . .,** it is a matter of doctrine that . . .; **d. chrétienne,** Christian doctrine; **d. politique,** political doctrine, beliefs; **changer de d. tous les jours,** to change one's opinion, beliefs, every day.
document [dɔkymɑ̃], *s.m.* (*a*) document; **d. de travail,** working document; (*b*) *pl. Hist: etc:* documents, records.
documentaire [dɔkymɑ̃tɛːr], *a. & s.m.* **1.** *a.* documentary (proof, etc.); *Com:* **traite d.,** draft with documents attached; *Cin:* **film d.,** documentary. **2.** *s.m. Cin:* documentary.
documentaliste [dɔkymɑ̃talist], *s.m. or f.* (*a*) *Adm:* filing clerk; keeper of records; (*b*) research assistant.
documentariste [dɔkymɑ̃tarist], *s.m. & f.* director of documentary films; documentarist.
documentation [dɔkymɑ̃tasjɔ̃], *s.f.* **1.** documentation. **2.** *Coll.* documents; information; literature.
documenter [dɔkymɑ̃te], *v.tr.* to document (matter); to support (statement, etc.) by documentary evidence; **roman très documenté,** novel that shows a great deal of research, very well documented novel; **d. qn sur une question,** to brief s.o. on a question; **il est bien documenté,** he is well-informed, well documented, on the subject.
se documenter, to gather documentary evidence; **se d. pour un ouvrage,** to gather material for a book.
dodéc(a)- [dɔdek(a)], *pref.* dodec(a)-; **dodécafide,** dodecafid; **dodécapétale,** dodecapetalous; **dodécarchie,** dodecarchy.
dodécaèdre [dɔdekaɛdr], *s.m. Geom: Cryst:* dodecahedron.
dodécaédrique [dɔdekaedrik], *a.* dodecahedral.
dodécagonal, -aux [dɔdekagɔnal], *a. Geom:* dedecagonal, twelve-sided.
dodécagone [dɔdekagɔn], *s.m. Geom:* dodecagon.
dodécane [dɔdekan], *s.m. Ch:* dodecane.
Dodécanèse (le) [lədɔdekanɛːz], *Pr.n.m. Geog:* the Dodecanese.
dodécaphonie [dɔdekafɔni], *a.f. Mus:* dodecaphony.
dodécaphonique [dɔdekafɔnik], *a. Mus:* twelve-tone, dodecaphonic.
dodécaphonisme [dɔdekafɔnism], *s.m. Mus:* twelve-tone system, dodecaphony.
dodécaphoniste [dɔdekafɔnist], *Mus:* **1.** *a.* twelve-tone, dodecaphonic. **2.** *s.m. & f.* dodecaphonist.
dodécastyle [dɔdekastil], *a. Arch:* dodecastyle.
dodécasyllabe [dɔdekasilab], *s.m.* dodecasyllable.
dodécathéon [dɔdekateɔ̃], *s.m. Bot:* dodecatheon.
dodécatomorie [dɔdekatɔmɔri], *s.f. Astr:* dodecatemory.
dodécuple [dɔdekypl], *a.* dodecuple.
dodelinement [dɔdlinmɑ̃], *s.m.* **1.** wagging, (tremulous) shaking (of head); nodding (with age). **2.** dandling (of child, etc.).
dodeliner [dɔdline]. **1.** *v.i.* (*of old person*) **d. de la tête,** to wag one's head, to nod. **2.** *v.tr.* to dandle (child, etc.); to rock (child) in one's arms.
dodinage [dɔdinaːʒ], *s.m.* rocking (of sifting-machine, etc.).
dodiner [dɔdine]. **1.** *v.tr. A:* (*a*) = DODELINER 2; (*b*) to coddle (child, etc.); (*c*) to rock (sifting-machine, etc.). **2.** *v.i. A:* (*of pendulum*) to wag.
se dodiner, *A:* (*a*) to rock; (*b*) to coddle oneself, to lie abed.
dodinette [dɔdinɛt], *s.f.* **1.** *A:* = DODO[1]. **2.** *Mus:* lullaby.
dodo[1] [dodo], *s.m.* (*in nursery language*) (*a*) sleep, bye-bye; **faire d.,** to go to sleep; to sleep; (*b*) bed; **aller à d., au d.,** to go to bed, to bye-bye; **dans mon petit d.,** in my little bed.
dodo[2], *s.m. Orn:* dodo.
Dodone [dɔdɔn], *Pr.n. A.Geog:* Dodona.
dodu [dɔdy], *a. F:* plump.
doéglique [doeglik], *a. Ch:* doeglic (acid).
dogaresse [dɔgarɛs], *s.f. Hist:* doge's wife, dogaressa.
dogat [dɔga], *s.m. Hist:* dog(e)ate, dogeship.
dog-cart [dɔgkart], *s.m. Veh:* dog-cart; *pl. dog-carts.*
doge [dɔʒ], *s.m. Hist:* doge.
dogger [dɔgɛːr], *s.m. Geol:* dogger.
dogmatique [dɔgmatik]. **1.** *a.* dogmatic. **2.** *s.f.* dogmatics.
dogmatiquement [dɔgmatikmɑ̃], *adv.* dogmatically.
dogmatisation [dɔgmatizasjɔ̃], *s.f.* dogmatization.
dogmatiser [dɔgmatize], *v.i.* to dogmatize; *F:* to lay down the law.
dogmatiseur, -euse [dɔgmatizœːr, -øːz]. **1.** *a.* given to dogmatizing; dogmatic. **2.** *s.* dogmatizer.
dogmatisme [dɔgmatism], *s.m.* dogmatism.
dogmatiste [dɔgmatist], *s.m.* dogmatist.
dogme [dɔgm], *s.m.* dogma, tenet.
dogre [dɔgr], *s.m. Fish:* dogger(boat).
dogue [dɔg], *s.m.* **1.** large watch-dog with drooping ears and pendulous lips; **d. anglais,** mastiff; **d. du Tibet,** Tibetan mastiff; **petit d.,** pug; *F:* **être d'une humeur de d.,** to be like a bear with a sore head. **2.** *Nau: A:* **d. d'amure,** chesstree.
doguer (se) [sədɔge], *v.pr.* (*of rams*) to butt one another.
doguin, -ine [dɔgɛ̃, -in]. **1.** *s. Breed:* (*a*) mastiff puppy; (*b*) pug. **2.** *s.m. Mec.E:* (lathe) dog, driver, carrier.
doigt [dwa], *s.m.* **1.** finger; *Anat: Z:* digit; (*a*) **les dix doigts,** the ten fingers; **troisième d., grand d.,** second finger, middle finger; **le petit d.,** the little finger; *F:* (*to child*) **mon petit d. me l'a dit,** a little bird told me so; *F:* **faire qch. avec le petit d.,** *P:* **les doigts dans le nez,** to do sth. with one's eyes shut, standing on one's head; **ne pas lever, remuer, le petit d.,** not to lift a finger; **compter sur ses doigts,** to count on one's fingers; **mes cousins se comptent sur les doigts de la main,** I can count my cousins on the fingers of one hand; **porter une bague au d.,** to wear a ring on one's finger; **promener ses doigts sur qch.,** to finger, feel, sth.; to run one's fingers over, along sth.; **donner, taper, sur les doigts à qn,** to rap s.o. over the knuckles; *F:* **se faire taper sur les doigts,** to take the rap; **savoir qch. sur le bout du d.,** to have sth. at one's finger tips; **il a de l'esprit jusqu'au bout des doigts,** he has a great fund of wit; **anglais jusqu'au bout des doigts,** every inch an Englishman, English to his finger tips; *F:* **avoir mal au bout du d.,** to have a pain in one's little finger, a trifling ailment; **toucher la mort du d.,** to be within an ace of death; **c'est un sujet qu'il ne faut toucher que du bout du d.,** it is a subject which had better be left alone; **il ne sait rien faire de ses dix doigts,** he has never done a hand's turn of work yet; **menacer qn du d.,** to shake, wag, one's finger at s.o.; **le d. de Dieu, du destin,** the finger of God, of Fate; **il lui fit signe du d. (de venir),** he beckoned to him (to come); **montrer qn, qch., du d.,** to point at s.o., sth.; **montrer qn du d., au d.,** to point the finger of scorn at s.o.; **mettre le d. sur la source du mal,** to lay, put, one's finger on the cause of the trouble; **vous avez mis le d. dessus,** you have hit the nail on the head; *P:* **se mettre, se fourrer, le d. dans l'œil,** to be entirely mistaken; *F:* **cela se voit au d. et à l'œil,** it's obvious, as plain as can be; (*of clock*) **aller au d. et à l'œil,** to keep very bad time; *s.a.* MENER 1, OBÉIR; **se mordre les doigts,** to bite one's nails with impatience; **se mordre les doigts d'avoir menti,** to repent of having told a lie; **s'en mordre les doigts,** to repent (of) it, to rue it; **fourrer le d. partout,** to interfere with everything; **il fourre le d. partout,** he's so interfering; **ils sont ensemble comme les doigts de la main,** they are hand in glove; (*b*) finger's breadth; **la robe est trop courte d'un d.,** the dress is too short by a finger's breath, is a trifle too short; **un d. de cognac,** a nip, spot, of brandy; *Knitting:* **il m'en reste quelques doigts à faire,** (i) I've still several inches to do; (ii) I've still a few fingers to knit (of gloves); **faire un d. de cour à qn,** to have a little flirtation with s.o.; **être à deux doigts de la mort, de la ruine,** to be within an ace of death, at death's door; to be

on the brink, on the verge, of ruin; (*c*) **d. de pied,** toe. **2.** (*finger-shaped object*) **doigts d'un gant,** fingers of a glove; **d. de chocolat,** stick of chocolate, *Mec.E: etc:* **d. de came,** swell of a cam; **d. d'encliquetage,** iron finger, pawl, click (of ratchet-wheel, etc.); **d. d'entraînement,** driving-plate pin, driver, catch pin (of lathe); *El:* **d. de contact,** contact finger.

doigté, doigter [dwate], *s.m.* **1.** *Mus:* fingering (of piece of music); **exercices de d.,** five-finger exercises; **d. fourchu,** cross-fingering (on wind-instrument); **passage qui demande un d. léger,** passage requiring a light touch. **2. commande au d.,** finger-touch control. **3.** adroitness (in appreciating circumstances and acting accordingly); **diplomate plein de d.,** diplomatist full of tact, of judgment; **manquer de d.,** to be tactless, to be apt to bungle; **tâche qui exige du d.,** tricky job.

doigter [dwate], *v.tr.* to finger (piece of music); to mark (music) with the proper fingering.

doigtier [dwatje], *s.m.* **1.** finger-stall. **2.** *Bot:* common foxglove.

doit [dwa], *s.m. Com:* debit, liability; **d. d'un compte,** debit (side), debtor-side, of an account; **d. et avoir,** debit and credit, debtor and creditor.

dol [dɔl], *s.m. Jur:* fraud, *dolus malus,* wilful misrepresentation.

dolage [dɔlaːʒ], *s.m.* planing, paring (of staves, etc.); skiving (of skins); sleeking, slicking (of casting-mould).

dolce [dɔltʃe], *adv. Mus:* dolce, softly.

dolcissimo [dɔltʃisimo], *adv. Mus:* dolcissimo, very softly.

doldrums [dɔldrœmz], *s.m.pl. Meteor:* doldrums.

doléances [dɔleɑ̃ːs], *s.f.pl.* complaints, whining; **conter ses d.,** to tell one's tale of woe, to air one's grievances; **écouter les d. de qn,** to listen to s.o.'s grievances.

dolemment [dɔlamɑ̃], *adv. A:* dolefully.

dolence [dɔlɑ̃s], *s.f. A: & Lit:* dolefulness, plaintiveness.

dolent [dɔlɑ̃], *a.* **1.** whining, doleful, plaintive, complaining (voice, person, etc.). **2.** *A: & Lit:* (*a*) painful, swollen (arm, etc.); **cœur d.,** aching heart; (*b*) out of sorts; **se sentir d.,** not to feel up to the mark.

doler [dɔle], *v.tr.* to adze, pare, shave (wood); to skive, pare, whiten (skins); to sleek, slick (casting-mould).

dolérite [dɔlerit], *s.f. Miner:* dolerite.

dolérophane [dɔlerɔfan], *s.f. Miner:* dolerophanite.

doleur [dɔlœːr], *s.m. Leath:* (*pers.*) skiver.

doleuse [dɔløːz], *s.f. Leath:* (*machine*) skiver.

dolic [dɔlik], *s.m. Bot:* dolichos; **d. asperge,** asparagus bean.

dolichocéphale [dɔlikɔsefal]. **1.** *a.* dolichocephalic, dolichocephalous, long-headed. **2.** *s.m. & f.* dolichocephal.

dolichocéphalie [dɔlikɔsefali], *s.f.* dolichocephalism, dolichocephaly.

dolichocôlon [dɔlikɔkolɔ̃], *s.m. Med:* dolichocolon.

dolichocrâne [dɔlikɔkrɑːn], *a. Anthr:* dolichocranial.

dolichocrânie [dɔlikɔkrɑni], *s.f. Anthr:* dolichocrany.

doliidés [dɔliide], *s.m.pl. Moll:* Doliidae.

doliman [dɔlimɑ̃], *s.m. Cost:* (Turkish) dolman.

doline [dɔlin], *s.f. Geol:* doline, sinkhole.

dolique [dɔlik], *s.m. Bot:* dolichos; **d. asperge,** asparagus bean.

dollar [dɔlaːr], *s.m. Num:* dollar.

dolman [dɔlmɑ̃], *s.m. A.Mil.Cost:* (*a*) dolman; (*b*) short-skirted jacket (of hussars, etc.).

dolmen [dɔlmɛn], *s.m. Prehist:* dolmen; **d. à galerie,** passage grave.

doloir [dɔlwaːr], *s.m. Leath:* skiver, parer, whitening knife.

doloire [dɔlwaːr], *s.f.* (carpenter's) broad axe; (cooper's) adze; (mason's) larry; *A:* **d. de guerre,** battle-axe; *Bot:* **feuille en d.,** dolabriform leaf.

dolois, -oise [dɔlwa, -waːz], *a. & s. Geog:* (native, inhabitant) of Dol.

dôlois, -oise [dolwa, -waːz], *a. & s. Geog:* (native, inhabitant) of Dôle.

dolomie [dɔlɔmi], *s.f.,* **dolomite** [dɔlɔmit], *s.f. Miner:* dolomite (marble); magnesian limestone; *Geog:* **les Dolomites,** the Dolomites.

dolomitique [dɔlɔmitik], *a. Geol:* dolomitic.

dolomitisation [dɔlɔmitizasjɔ̃], *s.f. Geol:* dolomitization.

dolosif, -ive [dɔlɔzif, -iːv], *a. Jur:* fraudulent, dolose, dolous.

dom [dɔ̃], *s.m. Ecc: etc:* (*title*) Dom.

domaine [dɔmɛn], *s.m.* **1.** domain; (real) estate, property; *Jur:* demesne; **domaines de la Couronne,** Crown lands; **d. public, de l'État,** public property (property of the State, or of a municipality, when used for public purposes); **le d. forestier,** the national forests; **il possède un grand d. minier,** he owns a large mining area; **à vendre château avec d.,** country house and estate for sale; *Jur:* **dans le d. public,** in common use and not coverable by patent; **ouvrage tombé dans le d. public,** work the copyright of which has lapsed, run out; work out of copyright; **invention tombée dans le d. public,** invention the patent of which has expired. **2. d. d'une science,** field, scope, of a science; **cela rentre dans le d. de l'histoire littéraire,** it falls within the domain, within the category, of literary history; **dans le d. matériel de l'existence,** in the material field of life; **ce n'est pas de mon d.,** that is not within my province, not within my sphere; **d. où je puis être utile,** field of action in which I may prove useful; **le d. du possible, des choses possibles,** the realm(s) of possibility.

domanial, -aux [dɔmanjal, -o], *a.* (*a*) domanial (property, rights, etc.); (*b*) (*of estates, etc.*) national, belonging to the State; **forêts domaniales,** State forests, (*in monarchy*) Crown forests.

domanialiser [dɔmanjalize], *v.tr.* to bring (forest, etc.) under State ownership.

dombaslois, -oise [dɔ̃balwa, -waːz], *a. & s.* (native, inhabitant) of Dombasle-sur-Meurthe.

dombiste [dɔ̃bist], *a. & s.m. or f.* (native, inhabitant) of the Dombes (region).

dôme [doːm], *s.m.* **1.** (*in Italy*) cathedral. **2.** (*a*) *Arch:* dome, cupola; (*b*) *Lit:* vault, canopy (of heaven, trees, etc.); (*c*) *Geog:* dome. **3.** (*a*) *Mch:* **d. de prise de vapeur,** steam dome; (*b*) roof, dome (of reverberatory furnace, etc.); (*c*) *N.Arch:* companion; (*d*) **d. du palais,** roof of the mouth; (*e*) *Furn:* **dômes du silence,** domes of silence.

domestication [dɔmɛstikasjɔ̃], *s.f.* (*a*) domestication; (*b*) **la d. de l'énergie atomique,** the harnessing of atomic energy.

domesticité [dɔmɛstisite], *s.f.* **1.** (*a*) menial condition; (state of) dependence; **elle a huit ans de d.,** she has been eight years in (domestic) service; (*b*) domesticated state, domesticity (of animal). **2.** *F:* servile action. **3.** *Coll.* staff of servants; household; **une nombreuse d.,** a large staff of servants.

domestique [dɔmɛstik]. **1.** *a.* (*a*) domestic (animal, life, etc.); **affaires domestiques,** family affairs; **éducation d.,** home training; **économie d.,** domestic economy, housekeeping; **guerre d.,** domestic, intestine, war; (*b*) domestic, menial (service). **2.** *s.m. & f.* (*a*) domestic servant; manservant, maid; (*in formal speech*) domestic; (*b*) *Cy: Rac:* rider who acts as "squire" for his leader. **3.** *s.m. A:* (*a*) *Coll.* staff of servants; (*b*) household, home.

domestiquement [dɔmɛstikmɑ̃], *adv.* **1.** in the capacity of a servant; menially. **2.** *A:* domestically.

domestiquer [dɔmɛstike], *v.tr.* (*a*) to domesticate (animal); (*b*) to bring (s.o.) to a state of subjection; (*c*) to harness (atomic energy, etc.).

se domestiquer, to become domesticated.

domeykite [dɔmɛkit], *s.f. Miner:* domeykite.

domfrontais, -aise [dɔ̃frɔ̃tɛ, -ɛːz], *a. & s. Geog:* (native, inhabitant) of Domfront.

domicile [dɔmisil], *s.m.* residence, dwelling(-place); *Jur:* domicile; **établir son d. à Londres,** to take up one's residence in London; **sans d. fixe,** of no fixed abode; **d. personnel, réel,** place of residence; *Jur:* **élire d. dans un endroit,** to elect domicile at a place; **d. élu,** address for service; *s.a.* RÉINTÉGRATION 3, RÉINTÉGRER 3; *adv.phr.* **à d.,** at one's private house; *Com:* **de d. à d.,** from door to door; **prise, remise, de colis à d.,** collection, delivery, of parcels; **notre épicier livre à d.,** our grocer has a delivery service; **franco à d.,** carriage paid; **payable à d.,** payable at address of payee; **la télévision vous apporte le monde à d.,** television brings the world into your (own) home; *Sp:* **match à d.,** home game; *Adm: A:* **secours à d.,** out-door relief; **institutrice à d.,** visiting governess.

domiciliaire [dɔmisiljɛːr], *a.* domiciliary (visit, etc.).

domiciliataire [dɔmisiljatɛːr], *s.m. Com:* paying agent (of bill of exchange).

domiciliation [dɔmisiljasjɔ̃], *s.f. Com:* domiciliation (of bill of exchange).

domicilié [dɔmisilje], *a.* resident, domiciled (à, at).

domicilier [dɔmisilje], *v.tr.* (*pr.sub. & p.d.* **n. domiciliions, v. domiciliiez**) *Com:* to domicile (bill at banker's, etc.).

se domicilier, to take up one's residence (à, at).

dominance [dɔminɑ̃ːs], *s.f.* **1.** dominance, dominion. **2.** predominance, preponderance (of colour, opinion, etc.); prevalence (of disease, etc.).

dominant, -ante [dɔminɑ̃, -ɑ̃ːt], *a.* **1.** dominating, dominant, ruling (power, passion, etc.). **2.** predominating, prevailing (colour, wind, opinion, etc.); **trait d.,** outstanding feature; **idée dominante,** outstanding, main, idea (of work, etc.); *Biol:* **caractère d.,** dominant. **3.** (*a*) *a. & s.f.* **dominante;** *Mus:* dominant (note); sol (of Movable Do system); (*b*) *s.f. F:* chief characteristic.

dominateur, -trice [dɔminatœːr, -tris]. **1.** *s.* dominator, ruler. **2.** *a.* (*a*) dominating, dominant, ruling (people, influence, etc.); (*b*) domineering, overbearing (person, tone, etc.).

dominatif, -ive [dɔminatif, -iːv], *a.* dominative.

domination [dɔminasjɔ̃], *s.f.* **1.** domination, rule; sovereignty, dominion; **établir sa d. sur un pays,** to establish one's rule, assume dominion, over a country. **2.** *pl. Theol:* dominions, dominations (of angels).

dominer [dɔmine]. **1.** *v.i.* to rule; **d. sur qn,** (i) to rule, have dominion, over s.o.; (ii) to domineer over s.o.; **couleur qui domine,** predominating colour; **l'opinion domine que . . .,** the opinion prevails that . . .; **il aime à d. sur tous,** he likes to domineer, *F:* to lord it, over everyone; **il domine partout,** (i) he makes his authority felt everywhere; (ii) *F:* he throws his weight about, runs the show, everywhere. **2.** *v.tr.* to dominate; (*a*) to rule; **l'ambition le domine,** he is dominated by ambition; **d. ses scrupules,** to master, control, overcome, one's scruples; **sa voix dominait toutes les autres,** his voice overpowered, rose above, was heard above, all others; *Sp:* **d. la partie,** to have the best of the game; to outplay the other side; (*b*) to tower over, above (sth.); to overlook; **fort qui domine la ville,** fort that commands, overlooks, the town; **cette hauteur domine la ville,** this hill dominates, overlooks, the town, rises above the town; **le château domine la vallée,** the castle looks down upon the valley.

se dominer, to have command of oneself, to keep oneself under control; to control one's feelings; to keep down one's anger, one's impatience, etc.

dominicain, -aine [dɔminikɛ̃, -ɛn], *a. & s.* **1.** *Ecc:* dominican (friar, nun); *s.m.* black friar. **2.** *Geog:* (native, inhabitant) of (i) Santo Domingo, (ii) Dominica; **la République Dominicaine,** the Dominican Republic, Santo Domingo.

dominical, -aux [dɔminikal, -o]. **1.** *a.* dominical (letter, etc.); **l'oraison dominicale,** the Lord's prayer; **réunion dominicale en plein air,** open-air Sunday meeting; **le repos d.,** Sunday rest. **2.** *s.f. O:* **dominicale,** Sunday sermon.

dominion [dɔminjɔ̃, -njɔn], *s.m. Pol:* Dominion.

Dominique[1] [dɔminik], *Pr.n.m. & f.* Dominic.

Dominique[2] (la), *Pr.n.f. Geog:* Dominica.

dominique[3], *s.m. Nau: F:* ship's kitty.

domino [dɔmino], *s.m.* **1.** *Cost: Games:* domino; **jouer aux dominos,** to play (at) dominoes; **d. en pêchant, à la pêche, à la pioche,** draw game of dominoes; **d. en boudant,** passing game; **faire d.,** to call "domino," to be (first) out. **2.** *pl. P:* (*a*) teeth; **jouer des dominos,** to munch away, to tuck in; (*b*) **boîte à dominos,** coffin. **3.** *El:* **d. bipolaire,** two-way connecting block.

dominoterie [dɔminɔtri], *s.f.* (i) manufacture of, (ii) trade in, coloured paper (for children's games, etc.).

dominotier, -ière [dɔminɔtje, -jɛːr]. **1.** *s.* (*a*) *A:* worker in factory making coloured paper; (*b*) worker in domino factory. **2.** *s.m. Bot:* wild plum tree.

dômite [domit], *s.f. Geol:* domite.

Domitien [dɔmisjɛ̃], *Pr.n.m. Hist:* Domitian.

dommage [dɔmaːʒ], *s.m.* **1.** (*a*) damage, injury; **causer du d. à qn,** to do s.o. harm, an injury; (*b*) **quel d.!** what a pity! what a shame! **c'est d., il est d., qu'elle ne soit pas venue,** it is a pity that she did not come; **c'est bien d. que . . .,** it is a thousand pities that . . .. **2.** *usu. pl.* (*a*) damage (to property, etc.); **réparer les dommages,** to repair, make good, the damage; to make up the losses; **troupeau trouvé en dommage,** herd found causing damage; *Jur:* herd damage feasant; (*b*) *Jur:* **dommages et intérêts, dommages-intérêts,** damages; **poursuivre qn en dommages-intérêts,** to sue s.o. for damages; to bring an action for damages against s.o.;

déclaration de dommages et intérêts, statement of claim; **se faire accorder des dommages-intérêts,** to recover damages; **dommages de guerre,** war damage (compensation).

dommageable [dɔmaʒabl], *a.* detrimental, injurious; *Jur:* tortious, prejudicial; **acte d.,** tort.

domptable [dɔ̃tabl], *a.* capable of being tamed, subdued; tamable.

domptage [dɔ̃taːʒ], *s.m.* taming (of animals); breaking in (of horses); overcoming (of one's passions).

dompter [dɔ̃te, *P:* dɔ̃pte], *v.tr.* to tame (animal); to break in (horse); to subdue, overcome, master (one's passions); to reduce (s.o.) to obedience; **d. l'orgueil de qn,** to break s.o.'s pride.

dompteur, -euse [dɔ̃tœːr, -øːz; *P:* dɔ̃ptœːr], *s.* tamer (of wild beasts); subduer, vanquisher (of people, etc.); **d. de chevaux,** horse-breaker.

dompte-venin [dɔ̃tvənɛ̃], *s.m.inv. Bot:* white swallow-wort, tame-poison.

don[1] [dɔ̃], *s.m.* **1. d. de qch. à qn,** giving of sth. to s.o., bestowal of sth. on s.o. **2.** (*a*) gift, present; *Jur:* donation; **recevoir qch. en d.,** to receive sth. as a gift; **faire d. à qn de qch.,** to make a present, *Jur:* a donation, of sth. to s.o.; *Lit:* **faire d. de son cœur, de sa main, à qn,** to give one's heart, one's hand, to s.o.; **les dons de la civilisation,** the blessings of civilization; (*b*) gift, natural quality, talent; **le d. des langues,** the gift of languages, a talent for languages; **avoir le d. de faire qch.,** to have a talent, a genius; for doing sth.; **il a le d. de l'à-propos,** he has a (happy) knack of saying, doing, the right thing; **ça n'a pas eu le d. de lui convenir,** it didn't happen to please him, suit him.

don[2], *s.m.* (*Spanish title*) Don; *s.a.* QUICHOTTE.

doña [dɔɲa], *s.f.* (*Spanish title*) Doña.

donace [dɔnas], *s.f. Moll:* donax.

donacidés [dɔnaside], *s.m.pl. Moll:* Donacidae.

Donat [dɔna], *Pr.n.m. Ecc.Hist:* Donatus.

donataire [dɔnatɛːr], *s.m. & f. Jur:* donee; *Scot:* donatary.

donateur, -trice [dɔnatœːr, -tris], *s.* giver; *Jur:* donor, *f.* donatrix.

donation [dɔnasjɔ̃], *s.f.* donation, gift; *Jur:* **d. entre vifs,** donation *inter vivos*; **acte de d. entre vifs,** deed of gift; **faire d. entière de son bien à qn,** to make over the whole of one's estate to s.o.

donatisme [dɔnatism], *s.m. Ecc.Hist:* donatism.

donatiste [dɔnatist], *s.m. Ecc.Hist:* donatist.

donax [dɔnaks], *s.m. Moll:* donax.

donc [dɔ̃ːk]. **1.** *conj.* therefore, accordingly, then, hence, consequently, so; **je pense, donc je suis,** I think, therefore I am. **2.** *adv.* [dɔ̃, *but in oratory often* dɔ̃ːk] (*a*) (*emphatic*) **vous voilà d. de retour,** so you are back again; **que voulez-vous d.?** what ever do you want? **qui d. vous a dit cela?** who ever told you that? **on me l'a dit—qui d.?** I was told so,—by whom? **mais taisez-vous d.!** do be quiet! *F:* do shut up! **allons d.!** (i) nonsense! not a bit of it! (ii) come on! look sharp! **pensez d.!** just think! **lisez d. ça!** just read that! **si on y allait?—où ça?—à la pêche donc!** supposing we went?—where?—fishing, of course! **tu as d. oublié?** did you forget? **dites d.!** (i) tell me now . . .; (ii) look here! I say! (*b*) (*after interruption or digression*) **donc** [dɔ̃ːk], **pour en revenir à notre sujet . . .,** well, to come back to our subject . . .

dondaine [dɔ̃dɛn], *s.f.* **1.** *A:* bagpipes. **2.** (*used in imitation of the drone in refrains of old songs*), fol-de-rol. **3.** *A.Mil:* (*a*) bolt, quarrel (of cross-bow); (*b*) engine of war.

dondon [dɔ̃dɔ̃], *s.f. F:* **grosse d.,** big lump of a girl, of a woman.

donjon [dɔ̃ʒɔ̃], *s.m.* **1.** keep, donjon (of castle). **2.** turret mast (of warship).

don Juan [dɔ̃ʒɥɑ̃], *s.m.* Don Juan, seducer.

donjuanesque [dɔ̃ʒɥanɛsk], *a.* donjuanesque.

donjuaniser [dɔ̃ʒɥanize], *v.i. F:* to act the Don Juan.

donjuanisme [dɔ̃ʒɥanism], *s.m.* donjuanism.

donnant [dɔnɑ̃], *a.* generous, open-handed; **peu d.,** mean, close-fisted; *adv.phr.* **d. d.,** (i) give and take, tit for tat; nothing for nothing; (ii) cash down.

donne [dɔn], *s.f. Cards:* deal; **à vous la d.!** your deal! **fausse d., mauvaise d.,** misdeal; **faire la d.,** to deal.

donné [dɔne]. **1.** *a. & p.p.* (*a*) given; **propriété donnée en dot,** property given as a dowry; **fête donnée au profit d'une bonne œuvre,** fête in aid of charity; **édition donnée par . . .,** edition issued by . . .; *F:* **c'est d.,** it's dirt cheap; it's a gift; *Prov:* **à cheval d. on ne regarde pas la bride,** one shouldn't look a gift horse in the mouth; (*b*) **nombres donnés dans l'énoncé (d'un problème),** numbers given in the data; **à un point d., à une distance donnée,** at a given, certain, point, distance. **2.** (*a*) **dans un temps d.,** within a given time, period; *prep.phr.* **étant donné;** (*in modern Fr.* **donné** *is usu. inv. when preceding the noun it qualifies*) **étant d. deux triangles,** given two triangles; **étant d. deux points, deux points étant donnés,** given any two points; **étant d. l'heure tardive,** in view, in consideration, of the lateness of the hour; (*b*) *conj.phr.* **étant donné que,** since, as; **étant d. qu'il est mineur,** since, as, he is not of age. **3.** *s.m.* (*a*) *Psy:* datum; (*b*) *Ecc.Hist:* oblate; lay brother.

donnée [dɔne], *s.f.* **1.** datum, given information (of problem, etc.); fundamental idea, subject, scheme (of novel, play, etc.). **2.** *pl.* data, particulars; admitted facts; facts as given, as granted; *Elcs:* (*computers*) **élaboration, exploitation, traitement, des données,** data generation, handling, processing; **données alphanumériques,** alphanumeric data; **données analogiques,** analog data; **données de base,** master data; **données variables,** transaction data.

donner [dɔne], *v.tr.* to give. **1.** (*a*) **d. un cadeau à qn,** to give a present to s.o., to give s.o. a present; **je vous le donne volontiers,** I gladly make you a present of it, present you with it; **d. un bal, un dîner,** to give a ball, a dinner-party; *abs.* **d. aux pauvres,** to give to the poor; *Prov:* **qui donne tôt donne deux fois,** he gives twice who gives quickly; **d. un coup de brosse à son chapeau,** to give one's hat a brush; **d. un coup de rame,** to pull a stroke; **d. des caresses à qn,** to caress s.o.; *F:* **je suis trop jeune pour qu'on me donne du "mademoiselle,"** I am too young to be called "mademoiselle," to be addressed as "mademoiselle"; **d. le bonjour à qn,** to wish s.o. a good day; **d. une maladie à qn,** to give, communicate, a disease to s.o.; **d. une entrevue à qn,** to grant, give, s.o. an interview; **d. des conseils,** to give advice; **d. à boire à qn,** to give s.o. something to drink; *F:* **d. aux poules, à un cheval,** to feed the hens, a horse; **je lui ai donné à entendre que . . .,** I gave him to understand that . . .; **cela me donne à croire que . . .,** it leads me to believe that . . .; **je vous donne deux mille francs de votre mobilier,** I will give you two thousand francs for your furniture; **je vous en donne dix francs,** I will give you ten francs for it; **je vous le donne en mille,** you can have as many guesses as you like; I bet you'll never guess it; **d. qch. (pour rien),** to give sth. away (for nothing); **j'ai donné la plupart de mes livres à un ami,** I gave away most of my books to a friend; *P:* **on vous en donnera!** you're very hard to please! **d. un cheval pour, contre, un âne,** to give a horse in exchange for a donkey; **je donnerais beaucoup pour savoir si . . .,** I would give a lot to know whether . . .; **s'en d. (à cœur joie),** to enjoy oneself (to the full), to have a good time; **il n'est pas donné à tout le monde d'être un Milton,** not everybody can be a Milton; **d. au monde,** to give to the world; to make public; (*of engine, train*) **d. de la vitesse,** to get up speed; *Tp:* **d. à qn la communication avec qn,** to get, put, s.o. through to s.o.; *F:* **donnez-moi M. X,** give me, put me through to, Mr X; *Med:* **d. du sang,** to donate, give, blood; (*b*) to give up (sth.); **d. sa vie pour qn,** to sacrifice one's life for s.o.; (*c*) (i) to give, hand (over) (sth. to s.o.); **d. à qn qch. à garder,** to entrust s.o. with sth., to give s.o. sth. to keep; **d. à qn sa fille en mariage,** to give one's daughter to s.o. in marriage; (ii) **d. la main à qn,** to shake hands with s.o.; **elle lui donna sa main,** she gave him her hand (in marriage); **je veux bien que tu sortes avec ton père, mais il faudra lui d. la main,** of course you may go out with your father, but you must give him your hand, let him hold your hand; (*d*) **d. les cartes,** to deal (the cards); **à qui de d.?** whose deal is it? **mal d.,** to misdeal. **2.** (*a*) to provide, furnish; (*of crops*) to yield; **arbre qui donne des fruits,** tree that yields, bears, fruit; **pays qui a donné maints grands hommes,** country that has produced many great men; **d. une domestique à un ami,** to provide a friend with a servant; **d. des preuves à qn,** to furnish s.o. with proofs; **son travail ne lui donne pas de quoi vivre,** his work does not bring him in enough to live on; **je lui donne la nourriture,** I provide him with food; **cela donne à penser,** this gives, provides, food for thought; **le plaisir que donne la musique,** the pleasure one gets from music; **d. de l'inquiétude à qn,** to cause s.o. worry; **cela donne l'idée que . . .,** it conveys the idea that . . .; **d. un bon exemple,** to set a good example; **d. un problème,** to set a problem; **d. une pièce de théâtre,** to produce, perform, a play; **qu'est-ce qu'on donne au cinéma aujourd'hui?** what's on at the cinema today? **auteur qui a donné trente volumes,** writer who (has) produced thirty volumes; *F:* **ça n'a pas donné ce que j'espérais,** it didn't work out, turn out, as I hoped; **je me demande ce que cela va d.,** I wonder what will come out of it, what the result, outcome, of it will be; *abs.* **si les blés donnent cette année,** if there is a good yield of wheat this year; (*b*) **d. faim, soif, sommeil, chaud, à qn,** to make s.o. hungry, thirsty sleepy, hot; (*c*) *P:* to inform on (s.o.). **3.** to ascribe, attribute (sth. to s.o.); **on lui donne une grande fortune,** they say he has a large fortune; **l'histoire lui donne pour maître Leucippe,** history tell us he was a pupil of Leucippus; **je lui donne vingt ans,** I take, reckon, him to be twenty, I put him down as twenty; **on ne lui donnerait pas son âge,** he does not look his age; **d. tort, d. raison, à qn,** to disagree, agree, with s.o. **4.** (*a*) **fenêtre qui donne (jour) sur la cour,** window looks on to the yard; **pièces qui donnent sur le vestibule,** rooms which open on to the hall; **cette porte donne (accès) sur le jardin,** this door leads out into the garden; **ma fenêtre donne sur le parc,** my window looks out over the park; **leur appartement donne sur la mer,** their flat faces the sea, looks on to the sea-front; **le soleil donne sur la porte,** the sun shines on, beats down upon, the door; **pièce où le soleil ne donne pas,** room that gets no sun; **le soleil me donnait dans les yeux,** the sun was in my eyes; *Nau:* **vent qui donne sur la hanche,** wind blowing on the quarter; (*b*) **d. de la tête contre qch.,** to knock, strike, bump, run, one's head against sth.; **ne pas savoir où d. de la tête,** not to know which way to turn; **le navire donna sur les rochers,** the ship ran on to, struck, the rocks; *Nau:* **d. dans un port,** to sail into a port; *Nau:* **d. dans une passe,** to run in for a passage; *Nau:* **d. sur la barre,** to run her into the surf; **d. dans le piège,** to fall into the trap; *F:* **d. dedans,** to let oneself be deceived, to walk right into the trap; **d. dans le luxe,** to have a taste for expensive things, for show; **d. dans le romanesque,** to be romantically inclined; **il me donne sur les nerfs,** he gets, jars, on my nerves; *F:* **d. dans l'œil de, à, qn,** to strike s.o.'s fancy; *Mil:* **faire d. un bataillon,** to send a battalion into action; **la cavalerie n'a pas donné,** the cavalry did not engage; *I.C.E:* **moteur qui donne mal,** engine running, firing, badly; (*c*) **le toit donne,** the roof sags, is giving way; **le cordage a beaucoup donné,** the rope has given a good deal.

se donner. 1. (*a*) **se d. à une cause,** to devote oneself to a cause; **se d. tout entier (à qch.),** to make an all-out effort, to put one's back into sth.; **se d. des airs,** to put on airs, to give oneself airs; **se d. au jeu,** to throw oneself into the game; **se d. en spectacle,** to make an exhibition of oneself; (*b*) (*of woman*) to give oneself ((i) to a husband, (ii) to a lover). **2.** (*a*) **cela se donne,** it can be had for the asking; (*b*) *Hamlet* **se donne ce soir,** they are playing *Hamlet* tonight. **3. se d. des vacances,** to give oneself a holiday; **se d. du tourment,** to worry oneself; **se d. un but à atteindre,** to set oneself a goal; **se d. du mal,** to work hard. **4. elle se donne trente ans,** she professes to be thirty; she says she's thirty; **il se donne pour mon ami,** he professes, pretends, to be my friend; **il se donne pour riche,** he pretends to be wealthy; he lets people think he is wealthy; **se d. pour un honnête homme,** to claim to be an honest man.

donneur, -euse [dɔnœːr, -øːz], *s.* (*a*) giver, donor; **il n'est pas d.,** he doesn't like parting with his money; *Med:* **d. de sang,** blood donor; **d. universel,** universal donor; *Com:* **d. d'ordre,** principal; **d. de caution,** guarantor; *Fin:* **d. d'aval,** guarantor, backer, of bill; **d. d'avis, de conseils,** busybody, *U.S: F:* wise guy; (*b*) *Cards:* dealer; (*c*) *Fin:* seller; *St.Exch:* **d. d'ordres,** client (of a broker); (*d*) *Ch:* donor; (*e*) *P:* (police) informer, nark.

donques [dɔ̃ːk], *conj. & adv. A:* = DONC.

donquichottesque [dɔ̃kiʃɔtesk], *a.* quixotic.

donquichottisme [dɔ̃kiʃɔtism], *s.m.* quixotism, quixotry.

dont [dɔ̃]. **1.** *rel.adv. A:* (= **d'où**) whence; **hauteur d. on découvre la ville lointaine,** hilltop (from) whence one can descry the distant town. **2.** *rel.pron.* (= **de qui, duquel, desquels, etc.**) (*a*) from, by, with, whom, or which; **les aïeux d. je suis descendu,** the ancestors from whom I am

descended; **la chaîne d. il était attaché,** the chain by which he was fastened; **l'amitié d. vous m'honorez,** the friendship with which you honour me; **la femme d. il est amoureux,** the woman he is in love with; **la façon d. il me regardait,** the way (in which) he looked at me; (*b*) (*of, about, concerning*) whom, which; **homme d. on dit beaucoup de bien,** man of whom, about whom, much good is spoken; **le livre d. j'ai besoin,** the book (which, that) I want, need; **le travail approfondi dont témoignent ses œuvres,** the detailed work, which is revealed in his writing; **voici ce d. il s'agit,** this is what it's all about; **dites-moi ce d. il s'agit,** tell me what it's all about; **il a reçu plusieurs visites, d. celle du préfet,** he has had a number of callers, one of whom was the prefect; *Com:* **paiements d. détail ci-dessous,** payments as per details below; **la personne d. mention ci-dessus,** the above-mentioned person; (*c*) whose, of whom, of which; **la dame d. je connais le fils,** the lady whose son I know; **la dame d. le fils vous connaît,** the lady whose son knows you; **la chambre d. la porte est fermée,** the room of which the door, the door of which, is closed; (*d*) *St.Exch:* **(dont** *precedes the option rate*), **livrer des actions à une semaine d. 1 pour cent,** to give 1 per cent put of a stock for a week.

donzelle [dɔ̃zɛl], *s.f.* **1.** (*a*) *F:* (i) fast girl; woman of loose morals; (ii) difficult, capricious, woman; (*b*) *Dial:* (*in Provence*) bridesmaid. **2.** *Ich:* ophidium. **3.** *Dom.Ec: A:* pot hook.

dop [dɔp], *s.m. Diamond Ind:* dop.

dopage [dɔpa:ʒ], *s.m. Elcs: Rac:* doping.

dopant [dɔpɑ̃], *s.m.* dope.

dopa-réaction [dɔpareaksjɔ̃], *s.f. Med:* dopa reaction.

dope [dɔp], *s.m.* (*petrol, etc.*) additive.

doper [dɔpe], *v.tr.* (*a*) *Rac: etc:* to dope; **d. un cheval de course,** to dope a racehorse; **se d.,** to take stimulants, to dope oneself; (*b*) *Elcs:* to dope; *Atom.Ph:* to add to the power of (an H-bomb, etc.); **bombes-H dopées,** power-amplified H-bombs.

doping [dɔpiŋ], *s.m.* **1.** administering of a drug; doping. **2.** dope.

dorade [dɔrad], *s.f.* **1.** *Ich:* (*a*) chrysophrys; (*b*) dorado, dolphin; (*c*) **d. (méditerranéenne),** gilt-head bream; **d. de la Chine,** goldfish. **2.** *Astr:* **la D.,** the Swordfish, Xiphias, Dorado.

doradille [dɔradi:j], *s.f. Bot:* doradilla; **d. nid d'oiseau,** bird's nest scale fern; **d. des murailles,** wall rue.

dorage [dɔra:ʒ], *s.m.* **1.** gilding. **2.** *Cu:* (*a*) glazing (of cake); (*b*) browning (of meat, fish).

doré [dɔre], *a.* **1.** gilded, gilt; **d. au trempé,** gold-washed; *Bookb:* **d. sur tranches,** gilt-edged; **cigarette à bout d.,** gold-tipped cigarette; **moisson dorée,** golden harvest; **jeunesse dorée,** gilded youth; **langue dorée,** smooth, glib, tongue, silver tongue; **cheveux blond d.,** golden hair. **2.** *Cu:* (*a*) glazed (cake); (*b*) browned (meat, etc.). **3.** *s.m. Ich: F:* (*a*) **(Jean) D.,** (John) Dory; (*b*) *Fr.C:* wall-eyed pike, yellow pike.

dorée [dɔre], *s.f. Ich: F:* (John) Dory.

dorénavant [dɔrenavɑ̃], *adv.* henceforth, henceforward, from this time forth, hereafter.

dorer [dɔre], *v.tr.* **1.** to gild; **d. par électrolyse,** to electrogild; **le soleil dorait les cimes,** the sun shed a golden light upon, cast a glow upon, gilded, the hilltops; *F:* **d. la pilule,** to sugar the pill. **2.** *Bookb:* **d. à froid,** to stamp (cover) in blind. **3.** *Cu:* (*a*) to glaze (cake); (*b*) to brown (meat, fish, etc.).

se dorer, to turn a golden colour.

doreur, -euse [dɔrœ:r, -ø:z], *s.* gilder.

Doride [dɔrid], *Pr.n.f. A.Geog:* Doris.

dorididés [dɔridide], *s.m.pl. Moll:* Dorididae.

dorien, -ienne [dɔrjɛ̃, -jɛn], *a.* & *s. Gr.Civ:* Dorian (people); Doric (dialect).

dorine [dɔrin], *s.f. Bot:* opposite-leaved golden saxifrage.

dorique [dɔrik], *a. Arch:* Doric; **l'ordre d.,** *s.* **le dorique,** the Doric (order).

doris[1] [dɔris], *s.f. Moll:* Doris, argo, sea-lemon.

doris[2], *s.m. Nau:* dory.

dorlotement [dɔrlɔtmɑ̃], *s.m.* fondling; coddling (of child, etc.).

dorloter [dɔlɔte], *v.tr.* to fondle; to coddle; to make much of, make a fuss of (child, etc.); to pamper (s.o.).

se dorloter, to coddle oneself, to take great care of oneself.

dorlotine [dɔrlɔtin], *s.f.* lounge chair.

dormance [dɔrmɑ̃:s], *s.f. Bot:* **(période de) d.,** (period of) dormancy.

dormant [dɔrmɑ̃]. **1.** *a.* (*a*) sleeping; *s.m.* **Les Sept Dormants,** the Seven Sleepers (of Ephesus); (*b*) inactive, dormant (account); (*of capital*) unproductive, unemployed, lying idle; (*of water*) stagnant; *Bot:* **œil d.,** dormant bud; (*c*) *Her:* dormant; (*d*) fixed, immovable (post, etc.); **vitrage d.,** light that cannot be opened, fixed fanlight; **pêne d.,** dead lock; *Nau:* **manœuvres dormantes,** standing rigging. **2.** *s.m.* (*a*) **d. d'une fenêtre, d'une porte,** window frame, door frame; window casing, door casing; *Nau:* **d. d'un hublot, d'un sabord,** main frame of a porthole; (*b*) *Nau:* standing end (of tackle); (*c*) *A:* (table) centre-piece.

dormasser [dɔrmase], *v.i. F:* to doze; to snooze.

dormeur, -euse [dɔrmœ:r, -ø:z], *s.* **1.** (*a*) sleeper; *a.* **poupée dormeuse,** sleeping doll; (*b*) *F:* sleepyhead, sluggard. **2.** *s.f.* **dormeuse;** (*a*) lounge chair; (*b*) stud ear-ring. **3.** *s.m. Crust: F:* edible crab.

dormichonner [dɔrmiʃɔne], *v.i. A: F:* to snooze.

dormille [dɔrmi:j], *s.f. Ich:* loach.

dormir [dɔrmi:r], *v.i.* (*pr.p.* **dormant;** *p.p.* **dormi;** *pr.ind.* **je dors, il dort, n. dormons, ils dorment;** *pr.sub.* **je dorme;** *p.d.* **je dormais;** *p.h.* **je dormis;** *fu.* **je dormirai) 1.** to sleep, to be asleep; **il dort,** he has gone to sleep; **d. profondément,** (i) to be fast asleep; (ii) to sleep soundly; **d. d'un profond sommeil,** to be sound asleep; **d. du sommeil du juste,** to sleep the sleep of the just; **j'ai bien dormi,** I've slept well, I've had a good night; **d. tout d'un somme,** to sleep without waking; **il faut le laisser finir de d.,** we must let him have his sleep out; **je n'ai pas dormi de la nuit,** I have not slept a wink all night; **il n'en dort pas,** he can't (get to) sleep for thinking of it; **le bruit l'empêche de d.,** the noise keeps him awake; **d. trop longtemps,** to oversleep; **faire passer une indisposition en dormant,** to sleep off an indisposition; *s.a.* DÎNER I; *with cogn. acc.* (i) *F:* **d. un bon somme,** to have a good sleep; (ii) *Lit:* **dormez votre sommeil . . .,** sleep your sleep . . .; **d. à poings fermés, comme un sabot, comme une souche, comme un loir,** to sleep soundly, like a log; to be fast asleep, in a heavy slumber; **ne d. que d'un œil, ne d. que sur une oreille, d. les yeux ouverts, d. en lièvre, en gendarme,** to sleep with one eye open; **vous pouvez d. sur les, vos, deux oreilles,** you need have no cause for uneasiness, you can trust me (him, etc.); *F:* **il dort sur ses deux oreilles,** he just sits on his behind; **avoir envie de d.,** to be, feel, sleepy, drowsy; **il dormait debout,** he was falling asleep on his feet, he couldn't keep his eyes open; **une histoire, un conte, à d. debout,** a tall story; a cock-and-bull story; a cock-eyed story; *Bot:* **fleur qui dort pendant la nuit,** flower that closes up during the night; *Nau:* **le compas dort,** the compass does not travel, does not traverse; **le manomètre dort,** the manometer isn't working. **2.** to remain inactive, to be dormant; **les passions qui dorment dans son cœur,** the passions dormant in his heart; **laisser d. une affaire,** to sit on a business deal; **ses fonds dorment,** his capital is lying idle; **eau qui dort,** stagnant, still, water; *Prov:* **il n'est pire eau que l'eau qui dort,** still waters run deep.

dormitif, -ive [dɔrmitif, -i:v]. **1.** *a.* dormitive, soporific. **2.** *Med: s.m.* sleeping-draught.

dormition [dɔrmisjɔ̃], *s.f. esp. Ecc:* dormition.

doroir [dɔrwa:r], *s.m.* pastry brush.

doronic [dɔrɔnik], **doronicum** [dɔrɔnikɔm], *s.m. Bot:* doronicum, leopard's bane.

Dorothée [dɔrɔte], *Pr.n.f.* **1.** Dorothy, Dorothea. **2.** *s.f. Ent:* (type of) dragonfly.

dorsal, -aux [dɔrsal, -o], *a.* dorsal; *Anat:* **épine dorsale,** dorsal fin (of fish); *Av:* **parachute d.,** back-type parachute.

dorsalgie [dɔrsalʒi], *s.f.* backache, dorsalgia.

dorsalisation [dɔrsalizasjɔ̃], *s.f. Med:* hypertrophy of the seventh vertebra.

dorsibranche [dɔrsibrɑ̃:ʃ], *Ann:* **1.** *a.* dorsibranchiate, notobranchiate. **2.** *s.m.* dorsibranchiate.

dorsifère [dɔrsifɛ:r], *a. Bot:* dorsiferous.

dorsifixe [dɔrsifiks], *a. Bot:* dorsifixed.

dorsigère [dɔrsiʒɛ:r], *a. Bot:* = DORSIFÈRE.

dorsiventral, -aux [dɔrsivɑ̃tral, -o], *a. Biol:* dorsiventral.

dorso-costal [dɔrsokɔstal], *a. Anat:* dorsocostal; *pl. dorso-costaux, -ales.*

dorso-lombaire [dɔrsolɔ̃bɛ:r], *a. Anat:* dorsolumbar; *pl. dorso-lombaires.*

dorso-ventral [dɔrsovɑ̃tral], *a. Bot:* dorsiventral; **fleur à symétrie dorso-ventrale,** a dorsiventrally symmetrical flower; *pl. dorso-ventraux, -ales.*

dortoir [dɔrtwa:r], *s.m.* dormitory; (*in monastery*) dorter; *Nau:* sleeping cabin; *Ind: etc:* men's sleeping quarters; **ville dortoir,** dormitory town.

dorure [dɔry:r], *s.f.* **1.** (*a*) gilding; **d. à la feuille,** leaf gilding; *Metalw:* **d. galvanique, à la pile,** electrogilding; **d. au froid,** cold gilding; (*b*) *Bookb:* **d. à froid,** blind tooling, stamping; **d. à chaud,** gold tooling; (*c*) *Cu:* (i) glazing (with yolk of egg); (ii) browning (of meat, etc.). **2.** gilt, gilding; **uniforme couvert de dorures,** gold-braided uniform.

doryanthe [dɔriɑ̃t], *s.f. Bot:* Doryanthes; spear lily.

dorylinés [dɔriline], *s.m.pl. Ent:* Dorylinae.

doryphore [dɔrifɔ:r], *s.m.* (*a*) *Ent:* Colorado beetle; (*b*) *F:* German soldier (1939-1945 war), Jerry.

dos [do], *s.m.* back. **1. être étendu sur le d.,** to be (lying) on one's back; **avoir le d. rond,** to be round-shouldered; **il s'est retiré le d. rond,** he went away dejectedly; **voir qn de d.,** to have a back view of s.o.; **je ne l'ai vu que de d.,** I only saw his back; **le sac au d.,** his rucksack on his back; **robe qui s'agrafe dans le d.,** dress that fastens at the back; **tourner le d. à qn,** to turn one's back on s.o.; to stand, sit, with one's back to s.o.; **excusez-moi si je vous tourne le d.,** please excuse my back; **il se moque de vous quand vous avez le d. tourné,** he laughs at you, makes fun of you, behind your back; **tourner le d., montrer le d., à l'ennemi,** to turn tail; **les brigands nous tombèrent sur le d.,** the robbers fell on us, leapt on us; **il va nous tomber sur le d. d'un moment à l'autre,** he will come bursting in on us at any moment; **il me tombe toujours sur le d.,** he's always jumping down my throat, cracking down on me; **faire le gros d.,** (*of cat*) to arch its back; (*of horse*) to buck; (*of pers.*) (i) to put on important airs; (ii) to bristle up; **monter à d.,** to ride barebacked; **monter à d. sur qn,** to ride pick-a-back on s.o.; **voyager à d. de cheval,** to travel on horseback; **aller à d. d'âne, à d. de chameau,** to ride on a donkey, a camel; *s.a.* DOS(-)D'ÂNE; *Swim:* **le 100 mètres d.,** the 100 metres backstroke; **se mettre tout le monde à d.,** to set everybody against oneself; **d. à d.,** back to back; *Jur: F:* **renvoyer les deux parties d. à d.,** to dismiss both parties non-suited; **je n'ai rien à me mettre sur le d.,** I haven't a rag to my back, I haven't anything fit to wear, to put on; **elle porte ses cheveux dans le d.,** she wears her hair down her back; *F:* **avoir qn sur le d.,** to be saddled with s.o.; *F:* **elle est toujours dans mon d.,** she's always nagging at me, always interfering, always on my back; *P:* **l'avoir dans le d.,** to meet with disappointment, to come a cropper; **faire pénitence sur le d. d'autrui,** to make s.o. else take the blame (for one's misdeeds, shortcomings); **il a bon d.,** (i) he's always ready to take on a job; he doesn't mind responsibilities; (ii) he always gets the blame; **le gouvernement a bon d.,** the government has a broad back; *F:* **j'en ai plein le d.,** I'm sick of it, fed up with it; *F:* **je le porte sur mon d.,** *P:* **il me scie le d.,** I've had enough of him; he bores me stiff, bores me to tears; **battre qn d. et ventre,** to hit out blindly at s.o. **2.** back (of chair, blade, page); bridge (of the nose); spine (of a book); **scie à d.,** backed saw; **brosse à d. d'ivoire,** ivory-backed brush; **signer au d. d'un chèque,** to endorse a cheque; **voir au d.!** see the other side! turn over! **3.** *P:* **d. (vert),** pimp, ponce.

dos(-)d'âne [dodɑ:n], *s.m.inv.* dos d'âne; **en d.(-)d'â.,** ridged razor-backed; **colline en d. d'â.,** hog's back (ridge); **toit en d. d'â.,** ridge roof, gable roof; **pont en d. d'â.,** humpbacked bridge; **route en d. d'â.,** high-crowned road; *Furn:* **secrétaire d. d'â.,** = bureau.

dosable [dozabl], *a. Ch: etc:* determinable, measurable (ingredient, etc.).

dos-à-dos [do(z)ado], *s.m. Furn:* double back-to-back settee.

dosage [doza:ʒ], *s.m.* **1.** *Ch: etc:* quantity determination, proportioning, titration (of ingredients); quantitative analysis (of compound); gauging (of cement, etc.); *I.C.E:* control (of mixture); *Ch:* **d. témoin,** blank determination. **2.** dosage (of medicine). **3.** *Winem:* sweetening, dosing (of champagne).

dose [do:z], *s.f.* **1.** *Ch: etc:* proportion, amount (of constituent in compound); *Atom.Ph:* dose. **2.** dose (of medicine); **par petites doses,** in small quantities; **avoir de l'esprit plus que sa d.,** to have more than one's share of wit; **une légère d. d'ironie,** a tinge, a suspicion, of irony; **une forte**

d. de mépris, a large admixture of scorn; *P:* **en avoir, en tenir, une d.,** to be a complete idiot, a proper Charlie; *P:* **avoir sa d.,** (i) to have been badly beaten up; (ii) to be dead.

doser [doze], *v.tr.* **1.** *Ch: etc:* (i) to determine the quantity of; (ii) to proportion, titrate (constituent in compound); to gauge (cement, etc.). **2.** to divide (medicine) into doses. **3.** *Winem:* to liqueur, sweeten, dose (champagne).

doseur [dozœːr], *s.m.* **1.** *Ch: etc:* dosimeter. **2.** *Winem: (of pers.)* liqueurer, sweetener (of champagne). **3.** *Mch: Ind:* feed regulator.

dosimètre [dozimɛtr̥], *s.m. Atom.Ph:* dosimeter, dose meter, dosage meter; **d. à condensateur,** capacitor dosimeter; **d. photographique,** photographic dosimeter; **d. photographique personnel,** film badge.

dosimétrie [dozimetri], *s.f.* dosimetry.

dosimétrique [dozimetrik], *a.* dosimetric.

dosologie [dozɔlɔʒi], *s.f. Med:* posology, dosology.

dossard [dosaːr], *s.m. Sp:* number (fastened on the back of a player or competitor).

dosse [doːs], *s.f.* flitch, slab (of timber).

dosseret [dosrɛ], *s.m.* **1.** *Arch:* pier (of arch, wall, chimney); **d. de porte,** door-jamb. **2.** *Tls:* back, backing (of saw); **scie à d.,** backed saw. **3.** *Furn:* headboard (of a bed).

dosseuse-niveleuse [dosøːzniv(ə)løːz], *s.m. Agr: (machine)* leveller; *pl. dosseuses-niveleuses.*

dossier [dosje], *s.m.* **1.** back (of seat, etc.); backboard (of boat); **d. de malade,** bed-rest; **chaise à d. droit,** straight-backed chair; *Aut:* **d. inclinable,** adjustable back. **2.** *(a)* dossier; **d. d'une affaire,** documents, file, relating to a case; **verser une pièce au d.,** to file a document; *(b)* record, dossier, (of official, prisoner, etc.); *Jur:* **d. d'une procédure,** brief; **établir le d. d'une affaire,** to brief a case; *Mil:* **d. de régiment,** (private's) regimental conduct sheet; **avoir un d. lourdement chargé,** to have a very bad record; *Med:* **d. médical,** case history; *(c) Fin:* holding, investment; *Bank:* portfolio; **mise sous d.,** earmarking transaction; **mettre sous d. des titres (pour le compte d'une autre banque),** to ear-mark securities.

dossière [dosjɛːr], *s.f.* **1.** *Harn:* back-, ridge-strap (supporting the shafts); back-band. **2.** backplate (of cuirass). **3.** backing (of saw); **scie à d.,** backed saw.

dossier-lit [dosjeli], *s.m.* back rest; *pl. dossiers-lits.*

dossier-machine [dosjemaʃin], *s.m. Ind:* instruction book (for assembly, use and maintenance of a machine); *pl. dossiers-machines.*

dot [dɔt], *s.f.* **1.** dowry, marriage portion; marriage settlement in favour of daughter; *Prov:* **fille jolie porte sur son front sa d.,** her face is her fortune; *F:* **coureur de dots,** fortune hunter; *F:* **épouser une d.,** to marry a woman for her money. **2.** portion brought by nun on entering a convent.

dotal, -aux [dɔtal, -o], *a.* dotal (property, etc.); **apport d.,** dowry; *Jur:* **régime d.,** (marriage) settlement in trust.

dotation [dɔtasjɔ̃], *s.f.* **1.** endowment (of hospital, church, etc.); foundation; settlement (made to pers.). **2.** equipment; *Rail:* **d. en locomotives,** locomotive stock.

doter [dɔte], *v.tr.* *(a)* to dower (bride); **être doté de toutes les vertus,** to be endowed with every virtue; *(b)* to make a parliamentary grant to (general, etc.); *(c)* to endow (hospital, institution, etc.); **les mentions honorables sont dotées d'une récompense en nature,** the highly commended receive a reward in kind; *(d)* **d. une usine d'un matériel neuf,** to equip a works with new plant.

douaire [dwɛːr], *s.m.* **1.** (widow's) dower. **2.** jointure, marriage settlement, in favour of wife; **assigner un d. à (qn),** to dower (widow); (ii) to jointure (wife).

douairière [dwɛrjɛːr], *a. & s.f.* dowager; **duchesse d.,** dowager duchess.

douaisien, -ienne [dwezjɛ̃, -jɛn], *a. & s. Geog:* (native, inhabitant) of Douai.

douane [dwan], *s.f. Adm:* customs; **la visite de la d. à Dieppe,** the customs examination at Dieppe; **passer (par) la d.,** to pass, get, through the customs; *Aut:* **carnet (de passage en d.),** (International Customs) carnet; **procéder aux formalités de la d.,** to effect customs clearance; **déclaration en, de, d.,** customs declaration; bill of entry; *Nau:* **déclaration en d. à la sortie,** clearance; **passer des marchandises en d.,** to clear goods; **marchandises (non) passées en d.,** bonded goods; **(bureau de) d.,** customs house; **l'administration des douanes,** the Customs House; **(droits de) d.,** customs duties; customs dues; **soumis aux droits de d.,** dutiable; **franc de d.,** duty paid; *Nau:* **expédier un navire en d.,** to clear a ship at the customs; **cotre de la d.,** revenue cutter; **magasin sous d.,** duty-free shop.

douaner [dwane], *v.tr.* to put the customs seal on (bales, etc.); **marchandises douanées,** duty-paid goods.

douanier, -ière [dwanje, -jɛːr]. **1.** *a.* (pertaining to the) customs; **tarif d.,** customs tariff; **union douanière,** customs union; **poste d.,** (frontier) customs post; **visite douanière,** customs examination, customs formalities; **barrières douanières,** tariff walls; **sentier d.,** coastguard path. **2.** *s.m.* customs officer; *Nau:* tide-waiter, tidesman.

douar [dwaːr], *s.m.* *(a)* (Arab) douar; *(b)* **un d. de bohémiens,** a gipsy camping ground.

douarneniste [dwarnənist], *a. & s.,* **douarnenézien, -ienne** [dwarnenezjɛ̃, -jɛn], *a. & s. Geog:* (native, inhabitant) of Douarnenez.

doublage [dublaːʒ], *s.m.* **1.** *(a)* doubling, folding in half (of sheet of paper, etc.); *(b) Tex:* drawing, doubling (of thread); *(c) Cin:* dubbing. **2.** (process of) lining (coat); plating (metal); sheathing (ship); tabling (sail). **3.** copper bottom (of ship). **4.** *Aut:* passing, overtaking.

doublant, -ante [dublɑ̃, -ɑ̃t], *s. Th:* understudy; *Cin:* double, stand-in.

doublard [dublaːr], *s.m. Mil: P:* N.C.O. wearing a double stripe, *i.e.* **sergent-major** (in infantry) or **maréchal des logis-chef** (in mounted arms).

double [dubl̥]. **1.** *a.* *(a)* double, twofold (measure, quantity, etc.); **maisons doubles,** semi-detached houses; **mot, expression, à d. entente,** word, phrase, with a double meaning; double entendre; **mot à d. sens,** ambiguous word; **mener une vie d.,** to lead a double life; **homme à d. face,** double-faced man; **agent d.,** double agent; **jouer d. jeu avec qn,** to play fast and loose with s.o.; **vêtement à d. face,** reversible garment; **un d. avantage,** a twofold advantage; **coup d.,** right-and-left (in shooting); **faire coup d.,** to kill two birds with one shot; **mot qui fait d. emploi (avec un autre),** redundant word; **discours qui a fait d. emploi avec un autre,** speech that overlapped another; *Book-k:* **article qui fait d. emploi,** item entered twice; duplicated item; **sa canne à pêche a une longueur d. de la mienne,** his fishing-rod is twice the length of mine; **fermer une porte à d. tour,** to double-lock a door; **pompe à d. effet,** double-acting pump, double-action pump; *Book-k:* **comptabilité en partie d.,** book-keeping by double entry; **quittance d.,** receipt in duplicate; *Fin:* **d. option, doubles primes,** double option, put and call; *I.C.E:* **d. allumage,** dual ignition; *Mec.E:* **tour à d. outil,** duplex lathe; **d. joint,** ball-and-socket joint; *Golf:* **partie d.,** foursome; *Cin:* **programme d.,** double-feature programme; **d. whisky,** double, large, whisky; *(b) Const:* **mur d.,** cavity wall; *(c)* **bière d.,** double ale; **encre d.,** ink of superior quality; *A:* **un d. coquin,** an arrant rascal. **2.** *adv.* **voir d.,** to see double; **boire d.,** to drink twice as much. **3.** *s.m.* *(a)* double; **je l'ai vendu pour le d. de ce qu'il m'a coûté,** I sold it for double what it cost me, for twice as much as it cost me; **j'ai le d. de votre âge,** I am twice your age; **plus lent du d.,** twice as slow; **plier qch. en d.,** to fold sth. in half; **plier une feuille en trois doubles,** to fold a sheet in three; **plier une couverture en quatre doubles,** to fold a blanket in four; *Nau:* **mettre une manœuvre en d.,** to double a rope; **amarre passée en d.,** slip-rope; **se mettre en d.,** (i) to bend oneself double; (ii) to make every effort, to bend over backwards (to do sth.); *F:* **mettre les morceaux en d., mettre les bouchées doubles,** (i) to eat quickly, to gobble one's food; (ii) to work double time; **bontés rendues au d.,** kindnesses returned twofold; *Ten:* **d. messieurs, dames, mixte,** men's, ladies', mixed doubles; *(b)* duplicate, counterpart; *Typwr:* carbon copy; **d. d'un acte,** duplicate of a deed; **d. d'une peinture,** replica of a picture; **facture en double,** invoice in duplicate; **pour votre trousseau il vous faudra avoir tout en d.,** for your trousseau you must have two of everything; *(c)* bight (of rope). **4.** *s.f. Nau:* double ration (of wine, on special occasion).

doublé [duble]. **1.** *a.* *(a)* doubled; **fièvre doublée,** intermittent fever; *(b)* lined; *(c)* **bijouterie doublée d'or, d'argent,** gold-, silver-cased jewellery; **montre en or d.,** gold-filled watch; *(d)* **avirons doublés,** double-banked oars; *(e) Cin:* dubbed. **2.** *s.m.* *(a)* gold-, silver-cased jewellery; rolled gold; **d. d'argent,** silver-plated ware; *(b) Bill:* stroke off the cushion; **jouer au d.,** to play off the cushion; *(c) Ven:* doublet (shot); right-and-left; *(d) Sp: F:* **réussir un d.,** to bring off a double.

double-as [dublɑːs], *s.m. (at dominoes, etc.)* double ace, double one; *pl. doubles-as.*

doubleau, -eaux [dublo], *s.m. Const:* (ceiling-) beam; *Arch:* transverse rib.

double-bang [dubləbɑ̃ːg], *s.m. Av:* double bang; *pl. doubles-bangs.*

double-bécassine [dubləbekasin], *s.f. Orn: F:* great snipe; *pl. doubles-bécassines.*

double-blanc [dubləblɑ̃], *s.m. (at dominoes)* double blank; *pl. doubles-blancs.*

double-cinq [dubləsɛ̃k], *s.m. (at dominoes)* double five; *pl. doubles-cinq.*

double-commande [dubləkɔmɑ̃d], *s.f. Av: Aut:* dual control system; *pl. doubles-commandes.*

double-corde [dubləkɔrd], *s.f. Mus:* double-stopping (on violin, etc.); **faire des doubles-cordes,** to double-stop.

double-crème [dubləkrɛm], *s.m.* (type of) cream cheese; *pl. double(s)-crème(s).*

double-dé [dublədе], *s.m. (at dominoes)* double; *pl. doubles-dés.*

double-décimètre [dublədesimɛtr̥], *s.m.* graduated rule two decimetres long = ruler, foot-rule.

double-deux [dublədø], *s.m. (at dominoes, etc.)* double two; *pl. doubles-deux.*

double-face [dubləfas]. **1.** *s.f. Tex:* double-faced cloth. **2.** *a.* **brosse d.-f.,** two-sided brush; *pl. doubles-faces.*

doublement[1] [dubləmɑ̃], *adv.* doubly.

doublement[2], *s.m.* **1.** doubling (of number, etc.); folding in two, doubling (of piece of paper, etc.); duplication (of air service). **2.** *Opt:* duplication (of image).

double-fond [dubləfɔ̃], *s.m. N.Arch:* double bottom; *pl. doubles-fonds.*

double-hunier [dubləynje], *s.m. Nau:* double topsail; *pl. doubles-huniers.*

double-mètre [dubləmɛtr̥], *s.m. P: (man)* six-footer, lamp-post; *pl. doubles-mètres.*

double-pesée [dubləpəze], *s.f.* (method of) double-weighing; *pl. doubles-pesées.*

double-quatre [dubləkatr̥], *s.m. (at dominoes, etc.)* double-four; *pl. doubles-quatre.*

doubler [duble]. **1.** *v.tr.* *(a)* to double (the amount, size, etc.); *(b)* **d. une feuille de papier,** to fold a sheet of paper in half, in two, to double a sheet of paper; *Mil:* **d. les files,** to double the files; *Mus:* **d. les parties,** to double the parts; **d. les avirons,** to double-bank the oars; *Shooting:* **d. une balle,** to cover exactly a preceding bullet; *Nau:* **d. un cap,** to double, make, weather, a cape; *F:* **d. le cap,** to give a creditor a wide berth; *F:* **avoir doublé le cap de la cinquantaine,** to have passed the fifty mark; **d. le cap du terme,** to weather quarter-day; *Sch:* **d. une classe,** to stay down; *Th:* **d. un rôle, un acteur,** to understudy a part, an actor; *Cin:* to stand in for (s.o.); **d. le pas,** to quicken one's pace; **d. sur les avirons,** to pull hard, pull away; **d. un navire,** to overhaul, come up with, a ship; **d. le courant,** to stem the tide; **d. une voiture, un concurrent,** to overtake, pass, a car, a competitor (in a race); *Aut:* **d. en troisième position,** to overtake three abreast; *P.N:* **défense de d.,** no overtaking, *U.S:* no passing; *Ven: (of stag, etc.)* **d. ses voies,** to double back; *Bill:* **d. la bande,** to play off the cushion; *(c) Tex:* to draw, double (the thread); *(d)* to line (coat, etc.); **caisse doublée de zinc,** zinc-lined case; **robe doublée mi-corps,** half-lined dress; *Nau:* **d. une voile,** to table a sail; **fourchettes doublées d'argent,** silver-plated forks; *Nau:* **d. un navire,** to sheath a ship; **navire doublé en cuivre,** copper-bottomed ship; **haine qui se double de mépris,** hatred coupled with contempt; **savant doublé d'un artiste,** scholar who is also an artist; *(e) Cin:* to dub (a film); *(f) F:* to double cross (s.o.). **2.** *v.i. (of population, etc.)* to double, to increase twofold.

double-scull [dubləskœl], *s.m. Row:* double sculler; *pl. doubles-sculls.*

double-six [dubləsis], *s.m. (at dominoes, etc.)* double six; *pl. doubles six.*

doublet [dublɛ], *s.m. Lap: Dice: Ling: etc:* doublet; *Opt: Phot:* doublet (lens).

double-triple [dublətripl̥], *s.m.inv. Mus:* three-two time.

double-trois [dublətrwa], *s.m. (at dominoes, etc.)* double three; *pl. doubles-trois.*

double-un [dublœ̃], *s.m. (at dominoes)* double one; *pl. doubles-uns.*

doubleur, -euse [dublœːr, -øːz], *s. Tex:* **1.** doubler (of wool, silk, etc.). **2.** *s.m.* lapping machine. **3.** *s.f.* **doubleuse,** doubling frame.

double-zéro [dubləzero], *s.m.* (*a*) (*at dominoes, etc.*) double blank; (*b*) *F:* **c'est un d.-z.,** he's a dead loss; *pl. doubles-zéros.*

doublier [dublije], *s.m.* **1.** *Husb:* double sheep rack. **2.** *A:* (*a*) large tablecloth (put double on table); (*b*) large (communal) table napkin; (*c*) large vase; (*d*) large dish. **3.** *a.m. A.Arm:* **haubert d.,** hauberk of double mail; **heaume d.,** tilting helm, heaume.

doublière [dublijɛːr], *s.f. Husb:* ewe, nanny-goat, carrying twins.

doublon[1], **-onne** [dublɔ̃, -ɔn]. **1.** *s.m. Typ:* double. **2.** *s.m. Metall:* doubled bloom. **3.** *s. Husb: Dial:* two-year-old.

doublon[2], *s.m. Num:* doubloon.

doublure [dublyːr], *s.f.* **1.** lining (of garment, etc.); sheathing (of hull, etc.). **2.** *Metall:* flaw, defect, scaling. **3.** *Th:* understudy; *Cin:* double, stand-in; **d. (casse-cou),** stunt man. **4.** *A: Aut:* (overtaking and) passing.

douc [duk], *s.m. Z:* douc.

douçâtre [dusɑːtr], *a. A:* = DOUCEÂTRE.

douce-amère [dusamɛːr], *s.f. Bot:* woody nightshade, bitter-sweet; *pl. douces-amères.*

douceâtre [dusɑːtr], *a.* sweetish; sickly (taste).

doucement [dusmɑ̃], *adv.* (*a*) gently, without noise; (to speak, sing) softly; (to speak) gently; (to smile) sweetly; (to tread) lightly, delicately; (to sleep) calmly, peacefully; (to live) quietly, tranquilly; (to run, work) smoothly; (*b*) gently, cautiously, without haste; **cheval qui va d.,** horse that jogs slowly along; **allez-y d.!** gently does it! easy does it! **parlez d.!** speak slowly! **les affaires vont d.,** business is so-so, none too brisk; **ramer d.,** to row slack; *Nau:* **amener d.,** to lower handsomely; **en avant d.!** slow ahead! easy ahead! **à gauche d.!** starboard a little! *Prov:* **qui va d. va loin,** slow and steady wins the race; *F:* **allez-y d. sur, avec, pour, l'électricité,** go easy on the electricity; *P:* **ça m'a fait d. rigoler,** I had a good laugh over it.

doucereusement [dusrøzmɑ̃], *adv.* **1.** insipidly. **2.** in a mealy-mouthed, soft-spoken, manner.

doucereux, -euse [dusrø, -øːz], *a.* **1.** sweetish, insipid, sickly, mawkish (taste, etc.). **2.** mealy-mouthed, soft-spoken, smooth-tongued (person); smooth, sugary, plausible (voice, tone).

doucet, -ette [dusɛ, -ɛt]. **1.** *a. & s.* meek, mild, demure (person). **2.** *s.m.* (*a*) *Ich:* dragonet, yellow gurnard; (*b*) *Bot:* sweet variety of grape, of apple. **3.** *s.f.* **doucette;** (*a*) *Bot:* corn salad, lamb's lettuce; **campanule doucette,** Venus's looking-glass; (*b*) treacle, molasses.

doucettement [dusɛtmɑ̃], *adv. F:* gently; quietly; cautiously.

douceur [dusœːr], *s.f.* **1.** (*a*) sweetness (of honey, perfume, etc.); (*b*) *pl.* sweets, sweet things; **aimer les douceurs,** to have a sweet tooth. **2.** softness (of sound, material, etc.); smoothness (of trot, of running of engine, etc.); meekness (of disposition); **un rasage en d.,** a smooth shave. **3.** (*a*) pleasantness; (*b*) pleasant thing; **c'est une d. de se savoir aimé,** it is pleasant to know that one is loved; **les douceurs de la vie,** the comforts, sweet things of life; **les douceurs mêlées d'amertume de la vie quotidienne,** the bitter-sweets of everyday life; **dire des douceurs à une femme,** to say sweet nothings to a woman; **accorder de petites douceurs à qn,** to grant little favours to s.o.; **se permettre la d. d'un verre de madère,** to allow oneself the indulgence of a glass of Madeira; to indulge in a glass of Madeira. **4.** gentleness, tenderness (of conduct, character, etc.); sweetness (of smile); mellowness (of colour, wine); mildness (of climate); **traiter qn avec d.,** to treat s.o. gently, with kindness; **mesures de d.,** lenient measures; *adv.phr.* **en d.,** cautiously, carefully, tactfully; *Nau:* handsomely; *Space:* **atterrissage en d.,** soft landing; **allez-y en d.!** gently does it! easy does it! **faire son chemin en d.,** to travel, proceed, by easy stages; **prendre les choses en d.,** to take things calmly, easy; **il veut collectiviser l'agriculture par la d.,** he wants to collectivize agriculture by persuasion; *Prov:* **plus fait d. que violence,** gentleness achieves more than violence.

douche [duʃ], *s.f.* **1.** (*a*) shower(-bath); **d. écossaise,** (i) hot and cold shower; (ii) succession of good and bad news, experiences, etc.; (*b*) *F:* **administrer une d. à qn,** to douse s.o.; **jeter une d. froide sur l'enthousiasme de qn,** to throw cold water on s.o.'s enthusiasm. **2.** *Med:* douche.

doucher [duʃe], *v.tr.* **1.** (*a*) to give (s.o.) a shower; (*b*) *F:* to douse (s.o.); (*c*) *F:* to cool off; **son manque de succès a douché son enthousiasme pour le golf,** his lack of success has cooled off his enthusiasm for golf. **2.** *Med:* to douche.

se doucher, to take a shower; *F:* **se faire d.,** to get a soaking (from the rain).

doucheur, -euse [duʃœːr, -øːz], *s.* (shower-)bath attendant.

douci [dusi], *s.m. Glassm:* grinding down, fine grinding (of plate-glass, etc.).

doucin [dusɛ̃], *s.m. Arb:* wild apple tree (for graft stock).

doucine [dusin], *s.f.* **1.** *Arch:* cyma recta, doucine. **2.** *Tls:* ogee plane, moulding plane, reeding plane.

doucir [dusiːr], *v.tr.* **1.** *Glassm:* to grind down (plate-glass, etc.). **2.** to set (tool) on the oilstone.

doucissage [dusisaːʒ], *s.m.* **1.** *Glassm:* grinding down, fine grinding (of plate-glass, etc.). **2.** setting (of tool).

doucisseur [dusisœːr], *s.m. Glassm:* (rough-) polisher.

doudou [dudu], *s.f. F:* West Indian woman.

doué [dwe], *a.* gifted; **élève bien d.,** pupil of great ability; **il est d. pour les mathématiques,** he has a natural gift, a bent, for mathematics; **il n'est guère d. pour les langues,** he has no gift for languages; he's no linguist.

douelle [dwɛl], *s.f.* **1.** *Coop:* stave. **2.** *Arch:* soffit (of vault, etc.); **d. extérieure,** extrados; **d. intérieure,** intrados.

douer [dwe], *v.tr.* to endow (s.o.) (with qualities, advantages); **la nature l'a bien doué,** he has great natural gifts; **il est doué d'une persévérance rare,** he has, is blessed with, unusual powers of perseverance.

douglasite [duglazit], *s.f. Miner:* douglasite.

douil [duːj], *s.m. Vit:* (*in S.W.Fr.*) vat (of 7-8 hectolitres).

douillard, -arde [dujaːr, -ard], *a. & s. F:* **1.** soft (person). **2.** (person) rolling (in money). **3.** well-thatched (person).

douille [duːj], *s.f.* **1.** tubular casing; (*a*) socket (of tool, bayonet, etc.); **d. de prise de courant,** contact socket, lamp socket (of electric light bulb); **d. à (pas de) vis,** screw lamp holder; **d. voleuse,** screw socket adapter; **d. à clef,** lamp holder with switch; **d. à baïonnette,** bayonet holder, socket; (*b*) case (of cartridge, etc.); *Aut:* **d. d'embrayage,** clutch casing; (*c*) *Mec.E:* bush(ing) (of bearing); (*d*) *Mec.E:* sleeve, boss (of wheel, etc.); *Veh:* **d. de roulement,** nave box; **accouplement à d.,** sleeve coupling; **d. de serrage,** couplet; **joint à d.,** faucet joint; (*e*) nipple (of bicycle spoke, etc.); (*f*) *Cu:* piping nozzle; **poche à d.,** piping bag. **2.** *P:* money, cash. **3.** *pl. P:* hair.

douiller [duje], *v.tr. & i. P:* to pay; to stump up, to fork out; **ça douille!** that's pricey!

douillet, -ette [dujɛ, -ɛt]. **1.** *a.* (*a*) soft, downy (cushion, bed, etc.); **pièce calme et douillette,** quiet and cosy room; (*b*) (*of pers.*) soft, fond of comfort; frightened of getting hurt; self-indulgent; **un d.,** a molly-coddle; (*of child*) a cry-baby. **2.** *s.f.* **douillette,** *Cost:* (*a*) quilted wrap; overcoat (*esp.* of priest); (*b*) quilted housecoat.

douillettement [dujɛtmɑ̃], *adv.* softly, delicately; cosily; **être couché d.,** to lie on a soft, downy, bed, to lie snug in bed; **élever un enfant d.,** to coddle a child.

douilletter [dujete], *v.tr.* to coddle; to pamper.

douillon [dujɔ̃], *s.m. Cu:* (*in Normandy*) apple dumpling; pear dumpling.

Doukhobors [dukɔbɔːr], *s.m.pl. Rel.H:* Doukhobors.

doulcemer [dus(ə)mɛːr], *s.m. A.Mus:* dulcimer.

douleur [dulœːr], *s.f.* suffering. **1.** pain, ache; **sentir une d. aiguë,** to feel a sharp pain, a twinge; **pousser un cri, des cris, de d.,** to cry out with pain; **couché sur un lit de d.,** lying on a sick-bed, on a bed of sickness; **se sentir des douleurs par tout le corps,** to ache all over; **les douleurs de l'enfantement,** the pains, pangs, of childbirth; **sans d.,** painless (operation, etc.). **2.** sorrow, grief; **s'abandonner à sa d.,** to give way to one's grief; **mourir de d.,** to die of grief; **il eut la d. de la perdre dès leur première année de mariage,** he had the sorrow of losing her in the first year of their marriage; **partager la d. de qn,** to share s.o.'s sorrow, to feel with s.o.

doullennais, -aise [dulanɛ, -ɛːz], *a. & s. Geog:* (native, inhabitant) of Doullens [dulɑ̃].

douloir (se) [sədulwaːr], *v.pr. A:* **1.** to suffer. **2.** to grieve, moan, lament.

douloureusement [dulurøzmɑ̃], *adv.* **1.** painfully. **2.** sorrowfully.

douloureux, -euse [dulurø, -øːz], *a.* painful. **1.** aching (wound, etc.); **il a toujours le pied d.,** his foot is still sore, tender; **d. au toucher,** tender, sore, to the touch; *s.a.* TIC. **2.** sad, distressing, grievous (loss, event, etc.); pained, sorrowful (look); **des cris d.,** heart-rending, mournful, cries. **3.** *s.f. F:* **la douloureuse,** the (hotel) bill, the reckoning.

doum [dum], *s.m. Bot:* doum, doom(-palm).

douma [duma], *s.f. Hist:* Duma, Russian parliament.

doura [dura], *s.m. Agr:* Indian millet, durra.

dourdannais, -aise [durdanɛ, -ɛːz], *a. & s. Geog:* (native, inhabitant) of Dourdan.

dourine [durin], *s.f. Vet:* dourine.

douro [duro], *s.m. Num:* duro.

douroucouli [durukuli], *s.m. Z:* douroucouli, durukuli, night-ape, owl-monkey.

doute [dut], *s.m.* doubt, uncertainty, misgiving; **être en d., dans le d.,** to be in doubt, in a state of uncertainty; **avoir des doutes sur qn, qch., au sujet de qn, à l'endroit de qn,** to have misgivings, suspicions, about s.o., sth.; to entertain doubts about s.o.; **être dans le d. au sujet de qch.,** to be doubtful about sth.; **laisser qch. en d.,** to leave sth. in doubt; **laisser qn en d.,** to leave s.o. in doubt; **théorie frappée de d. par un fait nouveau,** theory undermined by a new fact; **mettre, révoquer, qch. en d.,** to question sth.; to cast doubts on sth.; **mettre en d. la parole de qn,** to challenge s.o.'s word; **mettre en d. que** + *sub.* . . ., to question whether . . .; **regarder qn d'un air de d.,** to look dubiously at s.o.; **c'est hors de d., il n'y a pas de d.,** it is beyond doubt, beyond (all) question; **fait hors de d.,** unquestionable fact; **il est hors de d. que** + *ind.*, it is beyond doubt that . . .; **le d. n'est pas permis,** there is no room for doubt; **le d. n'est plus permis,** there is no longer any room for doubt; **cela ne fait plus aucun d.,** there is no longer any doubt about it; **nul d. qu'il (ne) soit mort,** there is no doubt that he is dead; **sans d.,** (i) *A:* doubtless(ly), without doubt, undoubtedly, unquestionably; (ii) no doubt, probably, I dare say; **sans aucun d.,** without (any) doubt; **vous ne me reconnaissez pas, sans d.,** I don't suppose you recognize me; *F:* **sans d. qu'il oubliera,** I dare say, I expect, he will forget; **sans d. viendra-t-il; sans d. qu'il viendra,** I expect he will come, no doubt he will come.

douter [dute], *v.i.* (*and tr. with noun clause as object*) to doubt; **d. du zèle de qn,** to doubt, to question, to have doubts about, s.o.'s enthusiasm; **d. de qn,** to be doubtful about s.o., to mistrust s.o.; **il était à n'en point d. courageux,** his courage was beyond all question; **c'est lui à n'en pas d.,** it is he beyond doubt; **je sais à n'en pas d. que . . .,** I know for certain that . . .; **je doute si j'ai dit cela,** *occ.* **je doute avoir dit cela,** I doubt whether I said that; **je ne doute pas de le voir bientôt,** I have no doubt I shall see him before long; **je doute d'avoir jamais la force de le faire,** I doubt if I shall ever have the strength to do it; **je doute qu'il soit assez fort,** I doubt, have my doubts, whether he is strong enough; **je ne doute pas qu'il (ne) vous vienne en aide,** I am confident that he will help you; **il doute de lui,** he has no self-confidence; **il ne doute de rien,** he is full of self-confidence.

se douter de qch., to suspect, surmise, conjecture, sth.; **je m'en doutais (bien),** I guessed, thought, as much; **il se doute de quelque chose,** he suspects something; *F:* he smells a rat; **vous les ferez (se) d. de quelque chose,** you will make them suspect something; **je me doutais qu'il était là,** I felt sure he was there; **il ne se doute de rien,** he suspects nothing, he has no inkling of the matter; **je ne me doutais pas qu'il fût là,** I had no suspicion, no idea, that he was there; **j'avais, sans m'en d., fait son jeu,** without suspecting it, all unawares, I had played into his hand.

douteur, -euse [dutœːr, -øːz]. **1.** *s.* doubter. **2.** *occ. a.* doubting; **siècle d.,** age of doubt.

douteusement [dutøzmɑ̃], *adv.* doubtfully.

douteux, -euse [dutø, -øːz], *a.* **1.** doubtful, uncertain, questionable; dubious (honour, company); **personne d'une probité douteuse,** person of questionable honesty; shady character; **linge d.,** linen of doubtful cleanliness; **créance douteuse,** bad debt; **clarté douteuse,** dubious, uncertain, light; **une affaire à issue douteuse,** a matter of doubtful issue; *F:* a toss-up; *F:* **ça, c'est une plaisanterie douteuse!** that's a bit near the knuckle! that joke's a bit off! **il est d. que** + *sub.*, it is doubtful whether . . .; **il n'est pas d. que . . . (ne)** + *sub.*, *more usu.* **que** + *ind.*, there is no doubt that . . .. **2.** (*a*) *A:* suspicious, filled with suspicion, anxious; (*b*) **je suis d. sur ce que je dois faire,** I am in doubt (as to) what to do.

douvain [duvɛ̃], *s.m. Coop:* wood, *esp.* oak, used for staving.

douve [du:v], *s.f.* **1.** (*a*) *Agr:* trench, ditch; (*b*) *usu. pl.* moat (of castle); (*c*) *Turf:* water jump, open ditch; the brook. **2.** *Coop:* stave. **3.** *Bot:* **grande d.,** spearwort; **petite d.,** lesser spearwort. **4.** (*a*) *Vet:* fluke(worm); (*b*) **d. du foie,** liver fluke.

douvé [duve], *a. Vet:* fluked.

douvelle [duvɛl], *s.f. Coop:* small stave.

Douvres [du:vr̥], *Pr.n.f. Geog:* Dover.

doux, douce [du, dus], *a.* (*a*) sweet (to the taste, smell, hearing, sight); smooth, soft (to the touch); **plat d.,** sweet dish; **amandes douces,** sweet almonds; **vin d.,** new, unfermented, wine; *s.m.* **préférer le sec au d.,** to prefer dry (wine) to sweet; *F:* **il a avalé cela d. comme lait,** he swallowed it without a murmur; **eau douce,** (i) fresh water; (ii) soft water; *F:* **marin d'eau douce,** landlubber; **poisson d'eau douce,** freshwater fish; **parfum d.,** sweet scent; **douces voix d'enfants,** children's sweet voices; **le vert d. des premières feuilles,** the tender green of the early leaves; **peau douce,** smooth, soft, skin; **à la douce!** cherry ripe! (*b*) pleasant, agreeable (air, tone, recollection, etc.); **douce nouvelle,** pleasant news; **garder un d. souvenir de qn,** to keep a pleasant memory of s.o.; **mener une vie douce,** to lead a calm, tranquil, life; *P:* **se la couler douce;** to have an easy time, take life easily; **j'ai eu la vie douce,** my life has been a pleasant one; **il était d. à ses parents qu'on le louât,** his parents loved to hear him praised; **d. sourire,** sweet, pleasant, smile; **tenir de d. propos,** to say sweet nothings; **faire les yeux d. à qn,** to make sheep's eyes at s.o.; *s.f.* **ma douce,** my fiancée; my girl friend; *Iron:* **douce perspective!** a nice prospect! (*c*) gentle (movement, slope, voice); soft, subdued (light, colour, sound); mellow (light); mild (climate, winter); **cheval d.,** quiet horse; **voiture douce,** smooth-running car; **allure douce,** easy, smooth, gait; **pente douce,** gentle, easy, slope; **temps d.,** mild, open, weather; **chaleur douce,** gentle, moderate, heat; **lumière douce,** soft light; *Cu:* **faire cuire à feu d.,** cook at a low heat, on a low gas; in a low oven; *Phot:* **papier donnant d., pour effets d.,** soft paper; **fer d.,** soft iron; **acier d.,** mild steel; **lime douce,** smooth file; **plume douce,** pen that writes smoothly, smooth pen; **tabac d.,** mild tobacco; *Cu:* **plat trop d.,** insipid, flavourless, dish; **son d.,** soft, gentle, sound; **consonnes douces,** soft consonants; (*d*) gentle (remonstrance, mockery); meek (nature); mild (rule, punishment); **regard d.,** gentle, mild, look; **prix d.,** moderate price; **d. comme un agneau,** as gentle as a lamb; *s.m. F:* **c'est un d.,** he's a gentle creature; (*e*) *F:* **c'est de la folie douce!** it's sheer madness! (*f*) *adv. F:* **filer d.,** to obey, give in; to sing small; *adv.phr. F:* **en douce,** discreetly, quietly, on the Q.T.; **il a filé en douce,** he slipped off quietly.

douzain [duzɛ̃], *s.m.* **1.** *Pros:* (*a*) twelve-line stanza; (*b*) twelve-line poem. **2.** packet of twelve packs of cards.

douzaine [duzɛn], *s.f.* dozen; **une d. d'œufs,** a dozen eggs; **trois douzaines d'œufs,** three dozen eggs; **une d. de personnes,** about a dozen, ten or a dozen, people; **une d. de mouchoirs fait, font, défaut,** a dozen handkerchiefs are missing; **une demi-douzaine,** half a dozen; **à la douzaine,** by the dozen; *F:* **une personne à la d.,** a very ordinary, everyday kind of, person; **il ne s'en trouve pas à la douzaine,** they are not to be picked up every day; **on les a par douzaines,** they are to be had by the dozen, by the score; **treize à la d.,** baker's dozen.

douze [du:z], *num.a.inv. & s.m.inv.* **1.** twelve; **nous sommes d.,** there are twelve of us; **le d. mai,** the twelfth of May; **Louis D.,** Louis the Twelfth; *B.Hist:* **les D.,** the Twelve (apostles); *Rail: etc:* **d. heures,** twelve o'clock (noon). **2.** *Typ:* pica, 12-point. **3.** *Aut: O:* **une d. chevaux,** a twelve horse-power car.

douze-huit [duzɥit], *s.m.inv. in pl. Mus:* **1.** twelve-eight time. **2.** piece in twelve-eight time.

douzième [duzjɛm]. **1.** *num.a. & s.* twelfth. **2.** *s.m.* twelfth (part); *Pol:* **d. provisoire,** monthly supply vote (when the budget is not passed in time).

douzièmement [duzjɛmmɑ̃], *adv.* twelfthly, in the twelfth place.

downingie [daunɛ̃ʒi], *s.f. Bot:* downingia.

doxologie [dɔksɔlɔʒi], *s.f.* doxology.

doxologique [dɔksɔlɔʒik], *a.* doxological.

doxométrie [dɔksɔmetri], *s.f.* the study of public opinion by means of sample surveys, Gallup polls.

doyen, -enne [dwajɛ̃, -ɛn], *s.* **1.** (*a*) *Ecc: Sch:* dean (of chapter, of faculty); (*b*) doyen (of diplomatic corps, etc.). **2.** senior; **être le d., la doyenne, de qn,** to be s.o.'s senior; **d. d'âge,** oldest member (of a club, etc.); **le d. des officiers,** the senior officer.

doyennat [dwajɛna], *s.m. Sch:* deanship (of a faculty).

doyenné [dwajɛne], *s.m.* **1.** deanery; (*a*) office or dignity of dean; (*b*) dean's residence. **2.** *Hort:* doyenné (pear).

doyenneté [dwajɛnte], *s.f.* seniority.

dracéna [drasena], *s.m. Bot:* dracaena, dragon-tree.

dracénois, -oise [drasenwa, -wa:z], *a. & s. Geog:* (native, inhabitant) of Draguignan.

drachme [drakm, dragm], *s.f.* **1.** *Num:* drachma. **2.** *Meas:* dram, drachm.

dracocéphale [drakɔsefal], *s.m. Bot:* (*a*) dragon-head, dragon's head; (*b*) **d. de Virginie,** false dragon's head, physostegia.

dracocephalum [drakɔsefalɔm], *s.m. Bot:* dracocephalum, dragon's head.

Dracon [drakɔ̃], *Pr.n.m. Gr.Hist:* Draco, Dracon.

draconien, -ienne [drakɔnjɛ̃, -jɛn], *a.* Draconian; **réglements draconiens,** harsh, unduly severe, Draconian, regulations; **régime d.,** very strict diet.

draconitique [drakɔnitik], *a. Astr:* dracontic, draconitic.

dracontiase [drakɔ̃tja:z], *s.m. Med:* dracontiasis.

dracontique [drakɔ̃tik], *a. Astr:* dracontic, draconitic.

dracunculose [drakɔ̃kylo:z], *s.f. Med:* dracontiasis.

drag [drag], *s.m.* **1.** *Ven:* drag(hunt). **2.** *Veh:* drag.

dragage [draga:ʒ], *s.m.* **1.** dredging (of river, harbour, etc.); **d. d'entretien,** maintenance dredging. **2.** (*a*) **d. des mines,** mine-sweeping; (*b*) dragging (of river for body, etc.).

dragée [draʒe], *s.f.* **1.** (*a*) sugar(ed) almond, dragée; **tenir la d. haute à un chien,** to make a dog jump for a sweetmeat; **tenir la d. haute à qn,** (i) to keep s.o. waiting; (ii) to make s.o. dance to one's tune, to make s.o. pay through the nose (for a concession); (*b*) *Pharm:* sugar-coated pill; **d. purgative,** laxative pill; **la d. est amère,** it's a bitter pill (to swallow); **avaler la d.,** to swallow the pill. **2.** (*a*) *Ven:* small shot; (*b*) *Mil: P:* bullet. **3.** (*a*) *Husb:* maslin, meslin; (*b*) *Agr:* **d. de cheval,** buckwheat.

dragéification [draʒeifikasjɔ̃], *s.f.* sugarizing (of almonds); coating (of pills).

dragéifier [draʒeifje], *v.tr. Pharm:* **d. une pilule,** to coat a pill; **comprimé dragéifié,** sugar-coated tablet; *Cu:* **d. des amandes,** to sugar almonds.

drageoir [draʒwa:r], *s.m.* **1.** (*a*) (crystal) sweetmeat dish; (*b*) box for holding sweetmeats; *A:* comfit box. **2.** bezel (holding watch-glass, etc.).

drageon [draʒɔ̃], *s.m. Arb: Hort:* sucker; **enlever les drageons d'une plante,** to sucker a plant; (*of plant*) **pousser des drageons,** to sucker.

drageonnage [draʒɔna:ʒ], **drageonnement** [draʒɔnmɑ̃], *s.m. Arb: Hort:* throwing out of suckers; suckering.

drageonner [draʒɔne], *v.i.* (*of plant or tree*) to throw out suckers, to sucker.

dragline [draglin], *s.m. Civ.E:* dragline (excavator).

dragoman [dragɔmɑ̃], *s.m.* dragoman.

dragon [dragɔ̃], *s.m.* **1.** (*a*) *Myth:* dragon; (*b*) *F:* (i) duenna; (ii) shrew, termagant, virago; **d. de vertu, de vigilance,** dragon of virtue, of watchfulness; (*c*) *Rept:* flying lizard; **d. volant oriental,** oriental flying lizard; (*d*) *Ich:* **d. des mers,** flying fish; **d. de mer,** (i) butterfly cod, butterfly fish; (ii) weever, sting fish; (*e*) *Orn:* dragoon (pigeon); (*f*) *Her:* (i) dragon; (ii) wyvern. **2.** *Mil:* (*a*) *A:* cavalry standard; *hence* (*b*) dragoon. **3.** *Nau:* offshore squall. **4.** *Nau:* flying jib. **5.** *Astr:* **le D.,** Draco, the Dragon.

dragonnades [dragɔnad], *s.f. Fr.Hist:* dragonnades (1685); dragooning (of the Huguenots).

dragonne[1] [dragɔn], *s.f.* **1.** (*a*) sword-knot; (*b*) tassel (of umbrella). **2.** tag (connecting parts of harness).

dragonne[2], *a.f.* dragoon-like; *A:* **mission d.,** dragonnade; *adv.phr.* **à la dragonne,** cavalierly, in a cavalier manner.

dragonné [dragɔne], *a. Her:* dragonné, dragony.

dragonneau, -eaux [dragɔno], *s.m.* **1.** *Ann: Med:* guinea-worm. **2.** coloured speck (in diamond).

dragonner [dragɔne], *v.tr.* (*a*) *Hist:* to dragoon (the people); (*b*) to persecute, hector (s.o.).

dragonnet [dragɔnɛ], *s.m. Ich:* dragonet.

dragonnier [dragɔnje], *s.m. Bot:* dracena, dragon tree.

draguage [draga:ʒ], *s.m.* = DRAGAGE.

drague[1] [drag], *s.f.* **1.** (*a*) *Hyd.E:* dredger; **d. suceuse,** pump dredger; **d. à godets,** bucket dredger; **d. à benne piocheuse, à benne preneuse,** grab bucket; **d. à cuiller,** power shovel; (*b*) drag, grappling-hook; (*c*) *Fish:* dredge, dragnet; **ramasser des huîtres à la d.,** to dredge for oysters; **pêcheur à la d.,** dredger. **2.** *Nau:* drogue, sea anchor.

drague[2], *s.f. Brew:* draff.

draguelles [dragɛl], *s.f.pl. Cost:* (fisherman's) waders.

draguer [drage], *v.tr.* **1.** to dredge (river, harbour, etc.). **2.** (*a*) to drag (pond, etc.); *Nau:* **d. une ancre, des mines,** to drag, sweep, for an anchor, for mines; **d. un chenal,** to sweep a channel; (*b*) to dredge for (oysters, etc.). **3.** *P:* to chase (girls).

draguette [dragɛt], *s.f.* small dragnet (for oysters).

dragueur [dragœ:r]. **1.** *s.m.* (*a*) *Hyd.E:* dredgerman; (*b*) fisherman using a dragnet; dragman. **2.** *a. & s.m.* (*a*) **(bateau) d.,** dredger; (*b*) **d. de mines,** minesweeper. **3.** *s.m. P:* girl-chaser, skirt-chaser.

dragueuse [dragø:z], *s.f. Hyd.E:* dredger.

draguignanais, -aise [dragiɲanɛ, -ɛ:z], *a. & s. Geog:* (native, inhabitant) of Draguignan.

draille [drɑ:j], *s.f.* **1.** *Nau:* stay (of certain sails). **2.** *Husb:* track followed by sheep during transhumance.

drain [drɛ̃], *s.m.* **1.** (*a*) drain(pipe), (small) culvert; (*b*) *Min:* watercourse; (*c*) *Surg:* drainage tube, drain. **2.** *A:* draining; *Nau:* **pompe de d.,** bilge-pump.

drainable [drɛnabl̥], *a.* drainable.

drainage [drɛna:ʒ], *s.m.* **1.** drainage, draining (of field, wound, etc.); **tuyau de d.,** drainpipe; *Med: Surg:* **d. à vide,** suction drainage; *Surg:* **d. au point déclive,** dependent drainage; *Min:* **galerie de d.,** lodgment level. **2.** drain (of money, capital).

draine [drɛn], *s.f. Orn:* missel thrush, storm cock.

drainer [drɛne], *v.tr.* (*a*) to drain (soil, abscess); (*b*) to tap (capital, talent, etc.); to draw, attract (trade, workers, etc.); (*c*) **d. une foule,** to channel a crowd.

drainette [drɛnɛt], *s.f. Fish:* small dragnet.

draineur [drɛnœ:r], *s.m.* drainer.

draisienne [drɛzjɛn], *s.f.* **1.** *A:* draisene, hobby-horse. **2.** *Rail:* gauge (used for checking the distance between the rails).

draisine [drɛzin], *s.f. Rail:* line inspection car.

drake [drak], **drakkar** [draka:r], *s.m. Nau: Hist:* Viking ship, long ship, drake.

dramatique [dramatik]. **1.** *a.* dramatic (art, representation); **l'art d.,** the drama; **chanteur, cantatrice, d.,** operatic singer; **auteur d.,** playwright, dramatist; **situation d.,** dramatic, striking, situation; **je ne considère pas son départ comme d.,** I don't think his leaving is a tragedy. **2.** *s.m.* **réussir dans le d.,** to succeed in drama; **scène dans laquelle il y a du d.,** scene in which there is much that is dramatic, sensational.

dramatiquement [dramatikmɑ̃], *adv.* dramatically.

dramatisation [dramatizasjɔ̃], *s.f.* **1.** dramatizing. **2.** dramatization, adaptation for the stage, stage adaptation (of novel, etc.). **3.** *Psy:* dramatization.

dramatiser [dramatize], *v.tr.* **1.** to dramatize; to give a dramatic, sensational, turn to (incident, etc.). **2.** to dramatize, to adapt (novel, etc.) for the stage.

dramatiseur, -euse [dramatizœ:r, -ø:z], *s.* dramatizer, sensationalist.

dramaturge [dramatyrʒ], *s.m.* dramatist, playwright.

dramaturgie [dramatyrʒi], *s.f.* **1.** dramaturgy, drama, the dramatic art. **2.** dramatic effect(s).

drame [dram], *s.m.* **1.** *Lit:* (*a*) drama (as a literary genre); (*b*) (i) *A:* (any) play; (ii) play (of a serious nature); **d. romantique,** play of the Romantic school; **d. lyrique,** opera. **2.** (*a*) catastrophic event; drama, tragedy; **un d. s'est déroulé à Versailles hier,** yesterday Versailles was the scene of (i) a tragedy, (ii) a crime; **la scène a tourné au d.,** the scene took a tragic turn; (*b*) **il ne faut pas en faire un d.,** there's no need to dramatize it; **maman va en faire un d.,** mother's going to make a scene about it.

drap [dra], *s.m.* **1.** cloth; **négociant en draps,** cloth-merchant, woollen-merchant; **le commerce des draps,** the trade in woollens; **d. fin,** broadcloth; **gros d.,** coarse cloth; **d. mortuaire,** pall; **d. d'or,** gold brocade; *Hist:* **Le Camp du d. d'or,**

the Field of the Cloth of Gold; *F:* **tailler en plein d.,** (i) to use sth. lavishly, to be wasteful; (ii) to be free to do as one pleases; **ils sont tous taillés dans le même d.,** they are all tarred with the same brush; **il n'y a que cela de d.,** you must cut your coat according to your cloth; *Prov:* **on ne peut pas avoir le d. et l'argent,** you can't eat your cake and have it. **2. d. (de lit),** sheet; **mettre des draps blancs sur un lit,** to put clean sheets on a bed; *F:* **être dans de beaux, mauvais, vilains, draps,** (i) to be in a fine mess, in a pickle, in a sorry plight, in a predicament; (ii) to be in a bad way, critically ill; **nous voilà dans de beaux draps!** this is a nice mess! *Med:* **d. mouillé,** pack-sheet, packing-sheet; cold pack; **d. d'hôpital,** waterproof sheeting; **d. de plage,** beach towel.

drapage [drapaːʒ], *s.m.* **1.** draping (of material). **2.** finish used to give an impression of down on artificial flowers.

drapant [drapɑ̃], *a. Tex:* **tisserand d.,** cloth weaver.

drapé [drape]. **1.** *a.* (*a*) covered with a sheet, a cloth; **aux roulements des tambours drapés,** to the sound of muffled drums; (*b*) *Tex:* solid (material); (material) with plenty of body; **bas drapés,** woollen stockings made to imitate cloth; (*c*) **robe drapée sur les épaules,** dress pleated on the shoulders. **2.** *s.m.* drape (of a garment).

drapeau, -eaux [drapo], *s.m.* **1.** (*a*) flag; (regimental) colour; **d. parlementaire,** flag of truce; **d. blanc,** white flag; **arborer, hisser, un d.,** to hoist a flag; *Mil:* **présentation du d.** = trooping the colour; **garde du d.,** colour party; (*b*) **être sous les drapeaux,** to serve in the (armed) forces; **être appelé sous les drapeaux,** to be called up (for military service); **se ranger sous les drapeaux de qn,** to embrace, take up, s.o.'s cause; to join s.o.'s party; **c'est lui le d. des contestataires,** it's he who stands out as the symbol of the contestants; **porter le d. de . . .,** to be the first to uphold (an opinion, etc.); to be a pioneer in (a cause); *F:* **mettre son d. dans sa poche,** to conceal one's opinions, convictions; *P:* **planter un d.,** to leave without paying the bill, to bilk; (*c*) *Av:* **mettre une hélice en d.,** to feather a propeller; (*d*) *Rail:* **train d.,** crack express; (*e*) *Sp:* **abaisser le d. à l'arrivée du premier concurrent,** to flag in the winner. **2.** *A:* (*a*) piece of cloth; swaddling clothes; garment; (*street cry*) **vieux linges, vieux drapeaux!** any old rags! (*b*) *pl. Paperm:* rags.

drapeler [draple], *v.tr. Paperm:* to break in (rags).

drapelet [draplɛ], *s.m.* little flag.

drapement [drapmɑ̃], *s.m.* draping (of material).

draper [drape], *v.tr.* **1.** (*a*) to cover (sth.) with cloth; **boutons drapés,** cloth-covered buttons; (*b*) to drape, cover, hang (doorway, carriage, etc.) with black (as a sign of mourning). **2.** to drape (article of furniture, etc.; cloth into folds). **3.** *A: F:* to mock at, jeer at (s.o.). **4.** *v.i. A:* to wear mourning.

se draper. **1.** (*of curtains, etc.*) to drape. **2.** (*a*) to wrap oneself up, drape oneself (**dans, de,** in); (*b*) **se d. dans sa dignité,** to stand on one's dignity; **se d. dans sa vertu,** to pride oneself on one's virtue; to parade one's virtue.

draperie [drapri], *s.f.* **1.** *A:* cloth; garment made of cloth. **2.** (*a*) cloth manufacture; (*b*) cloth factory; (*c*) drapery (trade). **3.** *Paint: Sculp:* drapery. **4.** (*a*) curtains; hangings; (*b*) *Mil: etc:* bunting.

drap-housse [draus], *s.m.* fitted sheet; *pl. draps-housses.*

drapier, -ière [drapje, -jɛːr], *s.* **1.** (*a*) draper, clothier; cloth merchant; (*b*) cloth manufacturer; (*c*) *a.* **marchand d.,** cloth merchant. **2.** (*a*) *s.m. Orn: F:* kingfisher; (*b*) *s.f. Com:* **drapière,** baling pin, blanket pin.

drastique [drastik], *a. & s.m.* drastic (remedy, purgative).

drave[1] [drav], *s.f.* **d. printanière,** whitlow grass.

drave[2], *s.f. Fr.C:* drive (of logs).

draver [drave], *v.tr. Fr.C:* to float, to drive (logs).

draveur [dravœːr], *s.m. Fr.C:* driver, raftsman, rafter, wood floater.

dravidien, -ienne [dravidjɛ̃, -jɛn], *a. & s. Ethn:* Dravidian.

dravite [dravit], *s.f. Miner:* dravite.

drawback [drobak], *s.m. Cust:* drawback; **certificat de d.,** debenture.

drayage [drɛjaːʒ], *s.m. Leath:* fleshing, scraping.

drayer [drɛje], *v.tr. Leath:* to flesh, scrape (skin).

drayeuse [drɛjøːz], *s.f. Leath:* fleshing machine.

drayoire [drɛjwaːr], *s.f. Leath:* fleshing-iron.

drayure [drɛjyːr], *s.f. Leath:* fleshings.

dreadnought [drɛdnɔt], *s.m. Navy: A:* dreadnought.

drèche, drêche [drɛʃ], *s.f.* **1.** *Brew:* draff. **2.** (*in Newfoundland*) crude cod-liver oil.

drège[1] [drɛːʒ], *s.f. Tex:* rippling comb, ripple, hackle (for hemp).

drège,[2] *s.f. Fish:* dragnet.

dréger [dreʒe], *v.tr.* (**je drège, n. drégeons; je drégeai(s); je drégerai**) *Tex:* to ripple (flax, etc.).

drégeur [dreʒœːr], *s.m. Fish:* trawler.

dreige [drɛːʒ], *s.f. Fish:* dragnet.

dreikanter [drekɑ̃tɛːr], *s.m. Geol:* dreikanter.

dreki [drɛki], *s.m. Nau:* Viking ship, long ship, drake.

drelin [drəlɛ̃], *Onomat. & s.m.* ting-a-ling; tinkle.

drenne [drɛn], *s.f. Orn:* missel thrush.

drepanaspis [drepanaspis], *s.m. Paleont:* drepanaspis.

drépanididés [drepanidide], *s.m.pl. Orn:* Drepanididae.

drépanocytose [drepanɔsitoːz], *s.f. Path:* drepanocytosis.

Dresde [drɛzd], *Pr.n.f. Geog:* Dresden.

dressage [drɛsaːʒ], *s.m.* **1.** erection, raising (of monument, etc.); setting (of trap); laying (of ambush, table); pitching (of tent). **2.** preparation, drawing up (of plan, etc.); drafting (of report); drawing (of map); *Cu:* presentation (of a dish for the table). **3.** adjustment, arranging (of sth.); trimming, dressing (of piece of wood, of hedge, etc.); dressing, squaring (of stone); straightening (of rod, bar); truing up (of machine, gun-barrel, etc.). **4.** (*a*) training (of animal); **d. (savant) d'un chien, etc.,** training of a dog, etc., to do tricks; *Equit:* **d. (élémentaire),** breaking in (of horse); **d. (supérieur),** dressage; (*b*) *F:* (severe) disciplining (of child); bringing (of child) to heel.

dressant [drɛsɑ̃], *s.m. Min:* edge seam; edge coal.

dresse [drɛs], *s.f. Ind:* dressing (of gloves).

dressé [drese], *a.* **1.** disciplined; trained; **cheval bien d.,** well-trained horse; **cheval non d.,** unbroken horse; **chien d. à la propreté,** house-trained, *U.S:* housebroken, dog; **chien d. à rapporter,** dog trained to retrieve. **2.** *Bot:* erect (stem, etc.).

dressement [drɛsmɑ̃], *s.m.* **1.** drawing up, making out (of list, account, etc.). **2.** (*a*) straightening out (of wire, etc.); (*b*) *Rail:* **d. d'un talus, d'une voie,** rectification of an embankment, of a track.

dresser [drese], *v.tr.* **1.** to erect, set up, raise (mast, monument, etc.); to rear (pole, ladder); to put up (ladder); to set (trap); to set, lay (ambush); to pitch (tent); *O:* **d. la table, le couvert,** to lay the table; *Cu:* **d. un plat,** to serve a dish, to present a dish (for the table); **d. la tête,** (i) to hold up, lift, one's head; (ii) to look up; **d. les oreilles,** to prick up, cock, one's ears; *Nau:* **d. les vergues,** to square the yards; **dressez la barre!** right the helm! **2.** to prepare, draw up (plan, report, contract, bill, etc.); to make out (cheque, invoice, etc.); to make out, draw up (list); **d. la carte d'un district,** to prepare, draw, the map of a district; **d. plainte contre qn,** to lodge a complaint against s.o. **3.** to adjust, arrange (sth.); to trim, dress, shoot, true up (piece of wood); to dress (up), square (block of stone); to trim (hedge, boat); to straighten out (piece of wire); to true up, line up (machine); **machine à d.,** facing, planing, machine; *Metalw:* **presse à d.,** straightening press; *Carp:* **planche à d.,** shooting board; *Mec.E:* **d. une machine,** to align, line up, an engine; *Mil:* **d. un camp, une batterie,** to lay out, trace, mark out, a camp; to establish a battery. **4.** (*a*) to train (animal); to break in (horse); (*b*) *A: or Pej:* to train, drill (a recruit); *F:* to discipline (s.o.) (severely); to bring (s.o.) to heel; **ça le dressera!** that'll bring him to heel! that'll show him where he gets off!

se dresser, (*a*) to stand up, rise; to hold oneself erect, straight; **se d. contre qch.,** to rise up (in protest) against sth.; **se d. en face d'un abus,** to make a stand against an abuse; **syndicats dressés contre les élus du suffrage universel,** unions at war with, up in arms against, the duly elected representatives of the people; **se d. de toute sa taille,** to draw oneself up to one's full height; **se d. sur la pointe des pieds,** to rise on tip-toe; **c'était à faire d. les cheveux (sur la tête),** it was enough to make one's hair stand on end; **aventures à faire d. les cheveux sur la tête,** hair-raising experiences; **au centre se dresse une statue,** in the centre stands a statue; **les obstacles qui se dressent sur notre chemin,** the obstacles that stand, lie, in our way; (*b*) to sit up, straighten up (in one's chair); to become all attention; (*c*) (*of horse*) to rear.

dresse-tube(s) [drɛstyb], *s.m. Tchn:* tube straightener.

dresseur, -euse [drɛsœːr, -øːz], *s.* **1.** erector; adjuster, trimmer; **d. de chapeaux,** hat blocker; **dresseuse de gants,** glove dresser. **2.** trainer (of animals); **d. de chevaux,** horse-breaker, rough-rider.

dressoir [drɛswaːr], *s.m.* **1.** *Furn:* (*a*) dresser; (*b*) sideboard. **2.** metal plaque (for polishing diamonds).

dreyfusard, -arde [drɛfyzaːr, -ard], **dreyfusiste** [drɛfyzist], *s.m. & f. Hist:* partisan of Dreyfus, Dreyfusite.

dribble [dribḷ], *s.m. Fb: etc:* dribble.

dribbler [drible], *v.tr. Fb: etc:* to dribble.

dribbleur [driblœːr], *s.m. Fb: etc:* dribbler.

dribbling [driblin], *s.m. Fb: etc:* dribbling.

drift [drift], *s.m.* **1.** *Geol:* (*glacial*) drift. **2.** *Elcs:* drift transistor.

drifter [driftɛːr], *s.m. Fish:* herring drifter.

drill[1] [drij], *s.m. Z:* drill; West-African baboon.

drill[2], *s.m. Agr:* (seed-planting) drill.

drille[1] [drij], *s.m. F:* **1.** *A:* vagrant soldier. **2. un bon, joyeux, d.,** a good sort; a cheery type.

drille[2], *s.f. Tls:* hand drill, drill brace, borer; **d. à rochet, à levier,** ratchet drill; **d. à arçon,** bow drill.

driller [drije], *v.tr.* to drill, bore.

drilles [driːj], *s.f.pl. Paperm:* rags.

drimys [drimis], *s.m. Bot:* drimys.

dringue [drɛ̃ːg], *s.f. A:* **1.** *F:* five-franc piece. **2.** *P:* **avoir la d.,** to have diarrhoea.

dringuer [drɛ̃ge], *v.i. A: P:* **1.** to have diarrhoea. **2.** to be in a funk.

drink [drink], *s.m. F:* drink.

drisse [dris], *s.f.* (*a*) *Nau:* halyard, yard-rope; **drisses de basses vergues,** jeers; **d. des signaux,** signal halyard; **pavillon à mi-d.,** flag at the dip; **conduit de d.,** fairlead(er); (*b*) lashing (of scaffolding).

drive [draːjv], *s.m. Ten: Golf:* drive.

drive-in [draiːjvin], *s.m.inv. U.S:* drive-in (cinema).

driver[1] [drivœːr], *s.m.* **1.** *Rac:* (*in trotting races*) driver. **2.** *Golf:* (*club*) driver. **3.** *Elcs:* driver.

driver[2] [drive], *v. Sp:* **1.** *v.i. & tr. Ten: Golf:* to drive (ball). **2.** *v.tr.* (*in trotting races*) to drive (horse).

drogman [drɔgmɑ̃], *s.m.* dragoman.

drogue [drɔg], *s.f.* **1.** (*a*) *A:* pharmaceutical ingredient; dyeing material; (*b*) (i) *A:* drug; nostrum; quack remedy; (ii) *Pej:* **toutes les drogues que lui ordonne son médecin lui font plus de mal que de bien,** all those drugs, that stuff, his doctor prescribes do him more harm than good; (iii) sth. unpleasant to swallow; **cette boisson est une vraie d.,** this drink tastes like medicine; (*c*) narcotic, drug; **la politique c'est comme une d. dangereuse,** politics are a dangerous intoxicant, act on one like a dangerous drug. **2.** *A: F:* (*a*) worthless article, trash; (*b*) disagreeable person.

drogué, -ée [drɔge], *s.* drug addict.

droguer [drɔge]. **1.** *v.tr.* (*a*) to physic (person); to dope, *P:* nobble (racehorse, etc.); **se d.,** (i) to be always taking medicine; (ii) to take drugs; **il se drogue,** he's a drug addict; (*b*) to adulterate, doctor (wine, etc.). **2.** *v.i. F: A:* to wait, to cool one's heels; **faire d. qn,** to keep s.o. waiting; **d. pendant des heures,** to be kept waiting for hours.

droguerie [drɔgri], *s.f.* **1.** *A:* drugs, medicines. **2.** (*a*) = hardware store (selling paint, cleaning materials, toilet preparations, etc.); *O:* drysalter; (*b*) trade in paint, cleaning materials, toilet preparations, etc.

droguet [drɔgɛ], *s.m. Tex:* drugget.

droguiste [drɔgist], *s.m.* **1.** = ironmonger (dealing in paints, household cleaning materials, etc.); *O:* drysalter; **épicier d.,** grocer and general storekeeper. **2.** wholesale distributor of pharmaceutical and chemical products.

droit[1], **droite** [drwa, drwat], *a.* **1.** (*a*) straight, upright; plumb (wall, etc.); **se tenir d.,** to hold oneself erect, to stand up straight; **col d.,** stand-up collar; **d. comme un piquet,** as straight, stiff, as a post; **d. comme un i, comme un cierge, comme un jonc, comme une quille,** as straight as a poker, as a ramrod; **se tenir d. comme un i,** to stand bolt upright; **angle d.,** *s.m.* **droit,** right angle; **au d. de . . .,** at right angles with . . .; *Geom.Draw:* **section droite,** cross-section; (*b*) **gilet d.,** single-breasted waistcoat. **2.** (*a*) direct, straight (road, etc.); **d. comme une flèche,** straight as an arrow; **coup d.,** (i) *Fenc:* straight thrust; (ii) *Ten:* forehand drive; **porter un coup d. à nos libertés,** to aim, strike, a direct blow at our liberties; *Nau:* **mettre la barre droite,** to right the helm; **d. la barre!** helm amidships! (*b*) **ligne droite,** *s.f.* **droite,** straight line; **droites**

parallèles, parallel straight lines; *Rac:* **la ligne droite,** the straight; **en ligne droite,** in a straight line, as the crow flies; **descendre en ligne droite de qn,** to be descended in a direct line from s.o.; **s'avancer en ligne droite vers qch.,** to make a bee-line for sth.; (*c*) *adv.* (in a) straight (line), directly; **marcher d.,** to walk straight; **allez tout d.,** keep straight on; **aller d. vers qch.,** to make a bee-line for sth.; **aller d. au fait,** to go straight, directly, to the point; **je rentre tout d. à la maison,** I am going straight home; *Nau:* **d. devant, d. debout,** right ahead; **abordage d. debout,** head-on collision; **faire route d. vers le sud,** to sail dead south. **3.** (*a*) straightforward, upright, honest (person, conduct); (*b*) **pièce droite,** coin of standard weight and fineness, standard coin. **4.** (*a*) right (hand, side, etc.); **être le bras d. de qn,** to be s.o.'s right-hand man; *Opt:* **cristal d.,** right-handed crystal; **côté d. d'un cheval,** off side of a horse; (*b*) *s.f.* **droite,** right hand, right(-hand) side; (i) (*in Great Britain, etc.*) off side; (ii) (*in U.S., Fr. etc.*) near side (of car); *Av:* **hélice à pas à droite,** right-hand air screw; **tourner à droite,** to turn to the right; **tenir la droite,** to keep to the right; **cheval de droite,** off horse; **le coin à droite de la feuille,** the right-hand corner of the sheet; **j'entends dire à droite et à gauche, de droite et de gauche, que . . .,** I hear from all quarters that . . .; *Nau:* **changer de route sur la droite,** to alter course to starboard; **à droite (la barre)!** starboard! (*A:* port!) (*c*) *s.f. Pol:* **la Droite, les Droites,** the right (wing); (*in Eng.*) the conservatives; **candidat de droite,** right-wing candidate.

droit², *s.m.* **1.** right; (*a*) privilege; **d. divin,** divine right; **d. de grâce, de vie et de mort,** power of pardon, of life and death; **droits civils,** civil rights; **d. de passage,** right of way; *Min:* way-leave; **d. de cité,** freedom of a city; **d. de saisie,** right to attachment; **d. électoral,** elective franchise; **priver qn de ses droits civils, du d. électoral,** to disfranchise s.o.; **d. de vote,** right to vote; **d. de visite,** right of search; **d. d'aînesse,** birthright; **d. d'impression réservé,** copyright; **tous droits réservés,** all rights reserved; (*b*) justification; fair claim; **faire valoir son (bon) d.,** to vindicate one's rights; **faire valoir, renoncer à, ses droits,** to establish, to waive, one's rights; *Prov:* **bon d. a besoin d'aide,** the best cause is none the worse for support; **où il n'y a rien le roi perd ses droits,** you can't get blood out of a stone; **droits acquis,** vested interests; **d. de regard,** right of inspection; **avoir d. à qch.,** to have a right to sth., to be entitled to sth.; **il a d. à mes excuses,** I owe him an apology; *Iron:* **après cela nous eûmes d. aux inévitables recommandations,** after that we were treated to the inevitable good advice; **donner d. à qn,** to give a decision in favour of s.o.; **donner à qn d. à qch., de faire qch.,** to entitle s.o. to sth., to do sth.; **avoir le d., être en d., de faire qch.,** to have a right to do sth.; to have just cause for doing sth.; to be justified in doing sth.; to be entitled to do sth.; **vous n'avez pas le d. de le faire,** you have no business to do so; **agir de (plein) d.,** to act by right, with good reason; **vous pouvez agir de plein d.,** you can proceed without further consideration or enquiry; **s'adresser à qui de d.,** to apply to the proper quarter, to an authorized person; **être dans son d.,** to be within one's rights; **à bon d.,** (i) with good reason; (ii) legitimately; **de d. et de fait,** *de facto* and *de jure*; **de quel d. entrez-vous ici?** by what right do you come in here? **de quel d. m'ordonnez-vous de me taire?** what right have you to tell me to be silent? **faire d. à une demande, à une réclamation,** to comply with, accede to, a request; to admit, allow, a claim; to satisfy a claim; **faire d. à une plainte,** to remove a cause of complaint; *Jur:* **ayant d.,** rightful claimant; interested party; beneficiary. **2.** charge, fee, due, toll; **d. d'entrée (à un club, etc.),** entrance fee; **droits d'auteur,** royalties; **d. de garde,** charge (by bank) for safe custody; **d. de passage (sur une propriété privée),** toll traverse; **droits de port,** harbour dues; **d. de quai, de bassin,** wharfage, quayage; *Cust:* **d. de douane,** duty; **d. d'entrée, de transit,** import, transit, duty; **marchandises assujetties aux droits, exemptes de droits,** dutiable goods, duty-free goods; *Adm:* **d. de timbre,** stamp duty; **d. d'inscription,** registration fee; *Post:* **d. de recommandation,** registration fee; *Jur:* **d. de mutation,** (i) **(entre vifs)** transfer duty, conveyance duty; (ii) **(par décès)** succession duty; **droits de succession,** duties on estate (of deceased person). **3.** law; **d. romain,** Roman law; **d. écrit,** statute law; **d. national,** municipal law; **d. coutumier, commun,** common law; **d. des gens,** law of nations; **d. pénal, criminel,** criminal law; **d. des obligations** = law of contract; **d. commercial,** commercial law; **d. maritime,** maritime law; **d. aérien,** air law; **par voies de d.,** by legal process; **responsable en d.,** legally responsible; **légitime en d.,** legally justifiable; **consacrer une mesure en d.,** to give a measure the force of law; **faire son d.,** to study, read, law; to read for the bar; **étudiant en d.,** law student; **livre de d.,** law book.

droitement [drwatmɑ̃], *adv.* uprightly, righteously, honestly, justly.

droiterie [drwatri], *s.f.* right-handedness.

droit-fil [drwafil], *s.m. Tail:* stiff buckram lining (for pockets, revers, etc.); *pl. droits-fils.*

droitier, -ière [drwatje, -jɛːr], *a. & s.* **1.** right-handed person. **2.** *Pol:* member of the Right; conservative.

droitiste [drwatist], *a. & s.m. & f. Pol:* rightist; right-wing (politician, etc.).

droiture [drwatyːr], *s.f.* **1.** uprightness, straightforwardness, rectitude, honesty; **d'une d. absolue,** *F:* straight as a die. **2.** *adv.phr. A:* **en droiture,** straight; **on le renvoya en d. chez ses parents,** he was sent straight home to his people. **3.** direct delivery (of petroleum products) to the consumer from the refinery.

drolatique [drolatik], *a.* (*a*) comic, humorous, droll; (*b*) spicy, ribald (tale, song).

drolatiquement [drolatikmɑ̃], *adv.* drolly, comically.

drôle¹ [droːl]. **1.** (*a*) *s.m. A:* rascal, knave, scamp; (*b*) *s.m. & f.* curious, queer, person. **2.** *s.m. Dial:* (*S. of Fr.*) youth; young man.

drôle², *a.* (*a*) funny, amusing; **chanson d.,** funny, humorous, song; **la situation actuelle n'est pas très d.,** the present situation is scarcely amusing; **qu'il est d. avec ce petit chapeau!** isn't he funny with that little hat! doesn't he make you laugh with that little hat! (*b*) funny, curious, queer; **je l'ai trouvé d., il doit avoir quelque souci caché,** I found him rather odd, he must be worrying about something; **il est d. qu'il l'ait oublié,** it's strange that he should have forgotten it; *F:* **se sentir tout d.,** to feel queer, not at all up to the mark; *F:* **vous êtes d.! qu'auriez-vous fait à ma place?** don't be funny! what would you have done in my place? (*c*) **drôle de . . .** (i) **une d. d'odeur,** a queer smell; **une d. d'aventure,** a strange, funny, adventure; **quelle d. d'idée!** what a funny idea! **ce sont des drôles de gens,** they're funny, odd, people; *F:* **un d. de type, de numéro,** a queer fish; an odd type; *F:* **la d. de guerre,** the phoney war (1939-40); (ii) *F:* (*intensive*) **il faut une d. de patience,** it needs a heck of a lot of patience; **il a une d. de carrure,** he's terrifically broad-shouldered; (*d*) *adv. P:* **ça m'a fait tout d. de te voir là,** I felt awfully funny, queer, seeing you there.

drôlement [drolmɑ̃], *adv.* **1.** funnily, queerly, oddly. **2.** *F:* excessively; awfully; **il a d. décollé,** he hasn't half changed; **elle est d. bien,** she's gorgeous; **il fait d. froid,** it's awfully, terribly, cold; **nous nous sommes d. amusés,** we had a fabulous time; **il fume d.,** he's in a heck of a temper; **les prix ont d. augmenté,** prices have gone up the hell of a lot.

drôlerie [drolri], *s.f.* (*a*) joking; jesting; fun; (*b*) joke; funny remark; **débiter des drôleries,** to crack jokes.

drôlesse [drolɛs], *s.f.* **1.** *A:* jade, strumpet, hussy. **2. c'est une petite d.,** she's a mischievous little imp.

drôlet, -ette [drolɛ, -ɛt], **drôlichon, -onne** [droliʃɔ̃, -ɔn], *a. F:* quaint, odd, funny (child, etc.).

dromadaire [drɔmadɛːr], *s.m. Z:* dromedary.

dromas [drɔmas], *s.m. Orn:* dromas.

drome¹ [drɔm], *s.f.* **1.** *Nau:* (*a*) spars, etc., lashed together; float, raft; (*b*) spare masts and yards, spare gear; **la d. du pont,** the booms; **mettre les embarcations en d.,** to take the boats in; (*c*) **d. d'un port,** collection or assemblage of small boats in a harbour. **2.** main beam (of forge hammer).

drome², *s.m. Orn:* dromas; **d. ardéole,** crab plover.

dromia [drɔmja], *s.m.,* **dromie** [drɔmi], *s.f. Crust:* dromia.

dromomanie [drɔmɔmani], *s.f. Med:* dromomania.

dromon [drɔmɔ̃], *s.m. A.Nau:* dromon(d).

dromotrope [drɔmɔtrɔp], *a. Physiol:* dromotropic.

drone [drɔn], *s.m. Mil.Av:* drone.

drongo [drɔ̃go], *s.m. Orn:* drongo.

dronte [drɔ̃t], *s.m. Orn:* dodo.

drop¹ [drɔp], *s.m.* (*crane*) drop.

drop², *s.m. Rugby Fb:* drop goal.

droper [drɔpe], *v.i. P:* to run (off), to skedaddle, to beat it.

drop-goal [drɔpgoːl], *s.m. Rugby Fb:* drop goal.

droppage [drɔpaːʒ], *s.m. Av:* parachuting; drop; **zone de d.,** dropping zone.

droschki [drɔʃki], *s.m.* droshky.

drosera [drɔzera], **drosère** [drɔzɛːr], *s.f. Bot:* drosera; sundew; **d. à feuilles rondes,** moor-grass.

droséracées [drɔserase], *s.f.pl. Bot:* Droseraceae.

drosophile [drɔzɔfil], *s.f. Ent:* drosophila, vinegar fly, fruit fly.

drosophilidés [drɔsɔfilide], *s.m.pl. Ent:* Drosophilidae.

drosophyllum [drɔsɔfilɔm], *s.m. Bot:* drosophyllum.

drosse [drɔs], *s.f. Nau:* **1. drosses de gouvernail,** (i) wheel-ropes, tiller-ropes; (ii) rudder chains. **2. d. de vergue,** truss.

drosser [drɔse], *v.tr. Nau:* (*of wind, current*) to drive, drift, carry (ship); **être drossé à la côte,** to be driven ashore.

drouais, -aise [druɛ, -ɛːz], *a. & s. Geog:* (native, inhabitant) of Dreux.

droussage [drusaːʒ], *s.m. Tex:* scribbling, scrabbling (wool).

drousser [druse], *v.tr. Tex:* to scribble, scrabble (wool).

drousseur [drusœːr], *s.m. Tex:* scribbler.

dru [dry]. **1.** *a.* (*a*) thick, strong, close-set (corn, hair, etc.); dense, thick-set (undergrowth); **pluie fine et drue,** fine, close rain; (*b*) (i) (*of birds*) fully-fledged; (ii) *A:* (*of pers.*) full-grown, vigorous, sturdy, lusty, brisk. **2.** *adv.* **tomber d.,** to fall thick and fast; **pousser d.** (*of grass, etc.*) to grow thickly; **semer d.,** to sow thickly; **frapper d.,** to shower blows (on s.o.); **jaser, caqueter, d.,** to talk nineteen to the dozen; **dans la cale on mourait d.,** in the hold they died like flies.

druide, druidesse [drɥid, drɥidɛs], *s.* druid, druidess.

druidique [drɥidik], *a.* druidic(al).

druidisme [drɥidism], *s.m.* druidism.

drumlin [drœmlin], *s.m. Geog:* drumlin.

drupacé [drypase], *a. Bot:* drupaceous.

drupe [dryp], *s.m. or f. Bot:* drupe.

drupéole [drypeɔl], *s.m. Bot:* drupel, drupelet.

druse [dryːz], *s.f. Geol:* druse, geode.

Druses, Druzes [dryːz], *s.m.pl. Ethn: Geog:* the Druses.

drusillaire [dryzijɛːr], *a. Geol:* drusy.

dryade¹ [dri(j)ad], *s.f.* dryad, wood nymph.

dryade², *s.f.,* **dryas** [drijas], *s.m. Bot:* dryas, mountain avens.

dry farming [drajfarmiŋ], *s.m. Agr:* dry farming.

dryobalanops [driɔbalanɔps], *s.m. Bot:* dryobalanops.

dryopithèque [driɔpitɛk], **dryopithecus** [driɔpitekys], *s.m. Paleont:* dryopithecus.

dryopteris [driɔpteris], *s.m. Bot:* dryopteris.

dû, due [dy]. **1.** *a.* due; (*a*) owing; **en port dû,** carriage forward; (*b*) proper; **en temps dû,** in due course; **contrat rédigé en bonne et due forme,** contract drawn up in due form, formal contract. **2.** *s.m.* (*a*) due; **réclamer son dû,** to claim one's due; **donner à chacun son dû,** to give everyone his due; **à chacun son dû,** give the devil his due; **payer son dû,** to pay (amount owed); (*b*) acquittal (of trust, etc.); **pour le dû de ma conscience,** for the acquittal of my conscience.

dual [dɥal], *a. Mth:* dual.

dualine [dɥalin], *s.f. Exp:* dualin.

dualisme [dɥalism], *s.m.* dualism.

dualiste [dɥalist]. **1.** *a.* dualistic. **2.** *s.* dualist.

dualistique [dɥalistik], *a. Ch:* dualistic.

dualité [dɥalite], *s.f.* duality.

dubitatif, -ive [dybitatif, -iːv], *a.* dubitative; **geste d.,** gesture expressive of doubt.

dubitation [dybitasjɔ̃], *s.f. Rh:* dubitation.

dubitativement [dybitativmɑ̃], *adv.* dubitatively, in a manner expressing doubt, in a doubtful tone, with a gesture of doubt.

duc [dyk], *s.m.* **1.** duke; **Monsieur le d.,** my Lord Duke, his Grace; (*2nd pers.*) your Grace. **2.** *Orn:* horned owl; **grand d.,** eagle-owl; **moyen d.,** eared owl; **petit d.,** scops (owl).

ducal, -aux [dykal, -o], *a.* ducal; **la couronne ducale,** the ducal coronet.

ducasse [dykas], *s.f.* (*in Northern France*) patronal feast.

ducat [dyka], *s.m. A.Num:* ducat; **d. d'argent,** ducatoon.

ducaton [dykatɔ̃], *s.m. A.Num:* ducatoon.

duc-d'albe [dykdalb], *s.m.* mooring post.

duce[1] [dys], *s.m.* system of secret signs (used by card-sharpers, illusionists, etc.); *P:* **balancer le d.,** to give the sign.

duce[2] [dutʃe], *s.m. Hist:* **le d.,** the Duce.

duché [dyʃe], *s.m.* duchy, dukedom.

duchesse [dyʃɛs], *s.f.* **1.** duchess; **Madame la d.,** her Grace; (*2nd pers.*) your Grace; *F:* **elle fait la d.,** she puts it on. **2. poire d.,** duchess pear. **3.** *Tex:* **(satin) d.,** duchesse satin; **(guipure) d.,** duchesse lace. **4.** *Cu:* **petite d.,** (type of) petit four. **5.** *Furn:* duchesse.

ducroire [dykrwɑːr], *s.m. Com:* **1.** *del credere* (commission), guarantee commission. **2.** *del credere* agent.

ductile [dyktil], *a.* (*a*) ductile, tensile, malleable; (*b*) **caractère d.,** tractable, pliable, nature.

ductilité [dyktilite], *s.f.* (*a*) ductility, malleability; (*b*) pliableness, docility (of character).

dudgeon [dydʒɔ̃], *s.m. Tls:* tube expander.

dudgeonnage [dydʒɔnaːʒ], *s.m.* expansion (of tubes).

dudgeonner [dydʒɔne], *v.tr.* to expand (tube); to secure (tubes) by flanging over; to bead (tube ends).

dudit [dydi]. *See* LEDIT.

duègne [dɥɛɲ], *s.f. A:* chaperon.

duel[1] [dɥɛl], *s.m.* duel, encounter; **d. à l'épée, au pistolet,** duel with swords, with pistols; **d. à mort,** duel to the death; **provoquer, appeler, qn en d.,** to call s.o. out; **d. oratoire,** battle of words.

duel[2], *s.m. Gram:* dual (number).

duel[3], *s.m. Sch:* diplôme universitaire d'études littéraires.

duellisme [dɥɛlism], *s.m. A:* mania for fighting duels.

duelliste [dɥɛlist], *s.m.* duellist.

duettiste [dɥɛtist], *s.m. & f. Mus:* duettist.

duffel-coat, duffle-coat [dœfœlkot], *s.m. Cost:* duffel coat, duffle coat; *pl. duffel-coats, duffle-coats.*

dufrénite [dyfrenit], *s.f. Miner:* dufrenite.

dufrénoysite [dyfrenwazit], *s.f. Miner:* dufrenoysite.

Dugazon [dygazɔ̃], *Pr.n.f. Th: A:* **jouer les (jeunes) D., les (mères) D.,** to take the young coquettish parts in light opera.

dugong [dygɔ̃], *s.m. Z:* dugong, sea-cow.

duire [dɥiːr], *v.ind.tr.* **(il duit, ils duisent; il duisait; il duira)** *A:* to suit, please; *still used in the Prov:* **ce qui nuit à l'un duit à l'autre,** one man's meat is another man's poison.

duit [dɥi], *s.m.* (*a*) small dam (across tidal river to act as a barrier to fish); (*b*) *Hyd.E:* cross-dyke (in stream).

duite [dɥit], *s.f. Tex:* (*a*) shoot, shot, pick (of weft); weft thread; **d. d'envers,** undershot pick; **d. d'endroit,** overshot pick.

duiter [dɥite], *v.tr. Tex:* to pick (the shuttle).

dulçaquicole [dylsakwikɔl], *a. Biol:* freshwater (flora, fauna).

dulcifiant [dylsifjɑ̃], *a.* sweetening, dulcifying (ingredient, etc.).

dulcification [dylsifikasjɔ̃], *s.f.* **1.** sweetening, dulcification. **2.** *Metall:* (blast) roasting (of lead ore).

dulcifier [dylsifje], *v.tr.* (*pr.sub. & p.d.* **n. dulcifiions, v. dulcifiiez**) **1.** to sweeten, dulcify. **2.** *Metall:* to (blast) roast (lead ore).

dulcine [dylsin], *s.f. Ch:* dulcin.

Dulcinée [dylsine], (*a*) *Pr.n.f. Spanish Lit:* Dulcinea; (*b*) *Hum: Iron:* **il soupire auprès de sa d.,** he spends his time sighing after the lady of his dreams.

dulcite [dylsit], *s.f.*, **dulcitol** [dylsitɔl], *s.m. Ch:* dulcite, dulcitol.

dulie [dyli], *s.f. Theol:* dulia; worship of the saints.

dum-dum [dumdum], *s.f.* dum-dum bullet; *pl. dums-dums.*

dumdum(is)er [dumdum(iz)e], *v.tr.* to nick (bullet).

dûment [dymɑ̃], *adv.* duly, in due form, properly; **d. expédié, reçu,** duly dispatched, received.

dumicole [dymikɔl], *a. Nat.Hist:* bush-dwelling.

dumontite [dymɔ̃tit], *s.f. Miner:* dumontite.

dumortiérite [dymɔrtjerit], *s.f. Miner:* dumortierite.

dumper [dœmpœːr], *s.m. Civ.E: Veh:* dumper.

dumping [dœmpiŋ], *s.m. Com:* dumping.

dumping-syndrome [dœmpiŋsɛ̃drɔm], *s.m. Med:* dumping syndrome; *pl. dumping-syndromes.*

dun [dœn], *s.f. Fish:* dun (fly).

dundasite [dœ̃dazit], *s.f. Miner:* dundasite.

dundee [dœndi, dœ̃-], *s.m. Nau:* ketch.

dune [dyn], *s.f.* dune; sandhill; **d. fixe,** static, fixed, dune; **d. vive, active,** active dune.

dunette [dynɛt], *s.f. Nau:* poop (deck); **échelle de d.,** quarter ladder.

Dunkerque [dœ̃kɛrk], *Pr.n.f. Geog:* Dunkirk.

dunkerquois, -oise [dœ̃kɛrkwa, -waːz], *a. & s.* (native, inhabitant) of Dunkirk.

duo [dɥo], *s.m.* **1.** *Mus:* duet. **2.** *Metall:* two-high rolling mill.

duodécennal, -aux [dɥɔdesɛnal, -o], *a.* duodecennial (period, etc.).

duodécimal, -aux [dɥɔdesimal, -o], *a.* duodecimal.

duodécimo [dɥɔdesimo], *adv.* twelfthly, in the twelfth place.

duodénal, -aux [dɥɔdenal, -o], *a. Anat:* duodenal; *Med:* **ulcère d.,** duodenal ulcer.

duodénectomie [dɥɔdenɛktɔmi], *s.f. Surg:* duodenectomy.

duodénite [dɥɔdenit], *s.f. Med:* duodenitis.

duodéno-jéjunostomie [dɥɔdenɔʒeʒynɔstɔmi], *s.f. Surg:* duodeno-jejunostomy.

duodéno-pancréatectomie [dɥɔdenɔpɑ̃kreatektɔmi], *s.f. Surg:* duodeno-pancreatectomy.

duodénostomie [dɥɔdenɔstɔmi], *s.f. Surg:* duodenostomy.

duodénotomie [dɥɔdenɔtɔmi], *s.f. Surg:* duodenotomy.

duodénum [dɥɔdenɔm], *s.m. Anat:* duodenum; **ulcère du d.,** duodenal ulcer.

duodi [dɥɔdi], *s.m. Hist:* (*Republican calendar*) second day of a decade.

duodiode [dɥɔdiɔd], *s.f. Elcs:* duodiode.

duolet [dɥɔlɛ], *s.m. Mus:* duole.

duopole [dɥɔpɔl], *s.m. Pol.Ec:* duopoly.

dupe [dyp]. **1.** *s.f.* dupe; *F:* mug, sucker; **prendre qn pour d.,** to fool s.o., to take s.o. in; **je ne suis pas d. de vos mensonges,** I'm not taken in by your lies; **c'est un marché de dupes,** I've, he's, etc., been had, taken in, swindled. **2.** *a.* naïve, easily deceived, easily taken in; **on serait meilleur sans la crainte d'être d.,** one would be better if one were not afraid of being taken in, of being swindled.

duper [dype], *v.tr.* to dupe, to fool (s.o.); to victimize (s.o.); to swindle (s.o.); to take (s.o.) in; **se laisser d.,** to allow oneself to be imposed upon; to be taken in.

duperie [dypri] *s.f.* **1.** (*a*) dupery, deception, trickery, (*b*) gullibility, credulity. **2.** take-in; case of victimization.

dupeur, -euse [dypœːr, -øːz], *s.* (*a*) trickster, cheat, swindler; (*b*) hoaxer.

duplex [dyplɛks], *a.inv. & s.m.* (*a*) duplex (telegraphy, pump, etc.); (*b*) *W.Tel:* diplex; (*c*) *s.m.* **(appartement en) d.,** maison(n)ette, *U.S:* duplex apartment.

duplexage [dyplɛksaːʒ], *s.m.* (*a*) *Tg:* duplexing; (*b*) *W.Tel:* diplexing.

duplexer [dyplɛkse], *v.tr.* (*a*) *Tg:* to duplex, to use duplex technique; (*b*) *W.Tel:* to diplex.

duplexeur [dyplɛksœːr], *s.m. Tg:* duplexer.

duplicata [dyplikata], *s.m.inv.* duplicate (copy); **d. de reçu, reçu en d.,** receipt in duplicate, duplicate receipt; **tirer une lettre de change par d.,** to draw a bill of exchange in duplicate.

duplicate [dyplikat], *a. & s.m. Cards:* duplicate (bridge).

duplicateur [dyplikatœːr], *s.m.* **1.** duplicator (of circulars, etc.), duplicating machine; copier. **2.** *El:* doubler.

duplicatif, -ive [dyplikatif, -iːv], *a.* duplicative.

duplication [dyplikasjɔ̃], *s.f.* (*a*) duplication; (*b*) *Biol:* **d. chromosomique,** doubling of chromosomes; (*c*) (i) *Tg:* duplexing; (ii) *W.Tel:* diplexing.

duplicature [dyplikatyːr], *s.f.* **1.** *Anat:* duplicature. **2.** *Bot:* chorisis.

duplice [dyplis], *s.f. Pol:* dual alliance.

duplicidentés [dyplisidɑ̃te], *s.m.pl. Z:* Duplicidentata.

duplicité [dyplisite], *s.f.* duplicity, double dealing.

duplique [dyplik], *s.f. A.Jur:* (*defendant's*) rejoinder.

dupliquer [dyplike], *v.tr.* (*a*) *Tg:* to duplex, to use duplex technique; (*b*) *W.Tel:* to diplex.

dur [dyːr], *a.* **1.** hard (substance); tough (meat, wood); **d. comme le diamant,** hard as a diamond, as adamant; **œufs durs,** hard-boiled eggs; **être d. à cuire,** (i) (*of food*) to take a lot of cooking; (ii) *F:* (*of pers.*) to be a tough nut; **eau dure,** hard water; **fer d.,** chilled iron; **rayons durs,** hard X rays. **2.** hard, difficult (work, etc.); **faire le plus d. du travail à qn,** to break the back of the work for s.o.; **escalier d.,** steep staircase; **dure nécessité,** dire necessity; **c'est d. à croire,** it is difficult to believe; **article d. à la vente,** article difficult to sell; **il fait d. à vivre ici,** life is hard here; **rendre la vie dure à qn,** to make s.o.'s life a burden; **avoir la vie dure,** (i) to be hard to kill; (ii) to have a hard time of it; **vous aurez la vie dure pour commencer,** you will have to rough it at the start; **cette superstition aura la vie dure,** this superstition will be hard to kill; *F:* **enfant d.,** difficult, problem, child. **3.** (*a*) insensitive, unimpressionable; **tempérament d. à la fatigue,** constitution hardened, inured, to fatigue; **avoir l'oreille dure, être d. d'oreille,** to be hard of hearing; **avoir la tête dure,** to be (i) thick-headed, dull-witted, (ii) pig-headed; **avoir le sommeil d.,** to be a heavy sleeper; **bateau d. à la mer,** boat stiff in a seaway; *F:* **être d. à la détente,** to be mean; to find it difficult to pay up, to put one's hand in one's pocket; (*b*) hard, harsh, cruel, callous; **traits durs,** hard features; **voix dure,** harsh voice; **avoir le cœur d.,** to be hard-hearted, callous; **être d. envers, pour, avec, à, qn,** to be hard, rough, on s.o.; to be unkind to s.o.; **mer dure,** rough sea; **hiver d.,** hard, rigorous, severe, winter; **style d.,** harsh style; **vin d.,** harsh wine; *Av:* **atterrissage d.,** rough landing; (*c*) stiff; **commande dure,** stiff control lever. **4.** (*a*) *adv.* **travailler d.,** to work hard; **dormir d.,** to be a heavy sleeper; **le soleil tape d.,** the sun is beating down hard; **cogner d.,** to hit (out) hard; **être couché d.,** to lie on a hard bed; **il croit d. comme (le) fer que . . .,** he firmly believes that . . .; (*b*) *adv.phr.* **à la dure; il a été élevé à la dure,** he's had a hard upbringing. **5.** *s.m.* (*a*) **le d. est le contraire du moelleux,** hard is the opposite of soft; *Const:* **en d.,** in concrete; in stone; (*b*) (*pers.*) **un d.,** (i) *F:* a tough type, a tough guy; (ii) *P:* a bad type, a rotter; *s.m. & f. F:* **un d., une dure, à cuire,** a tough nut, a hard nut to crack; (*c*) *A: P:* train; **brûler le d.,** to travel without a ticket, to bilk the fare; (*d*) *P:* **un verre de d.,** a glass of brandy, of spirits. **6.** *s.f.* (*a*) **coucher sur la dure,** to sleep on the bare boards, on the bare ground; (*b*) *F:* **en dire de dures à qn,** to reproach s.o. severely, to tell s.o. where he gets off; (*c*) *F:* **il en a vu de dures,** he's had a hard, bad, tough, time of it; **en faire voir de dures à qn,** to give s.o. a hard, tough, time of it; to make it hot for s.o.

durabilité [dyrabilite], *s.f.* durability, durableness.

durable [dyrabl̩], *a.* durable, lasting, stable (building, etc.); lasting (friendship, peace); settled (peace).

durablement [dyrabləmɑ̃], *adv.* durably.

durain [dyrɛ̃], *s.m. Miner:* durain.

Duralumin [dyralymɛ̃], *s.m. R.t.m: Metall:* Duraluminium, Duralumin.

duramen [dyramɛn], *s.m. Bot:* duramen.

durant [dyrɑ̃], *prep.* (*may follow a sb. sounded as one syllable*) (*a*) during; **il travailla d. toute sa vie, sa vie d.,** he worked during his whole life, he worked for the whole of his life; **parler des heures d.,** to talk for hours on end, for hours at a time; **d. quelques instants personne ne dit mot,** for a few moments no one uttered a word; (*b*) *conj.phr. A:* **d. que,** while, whilst.

duratif, -ive [dyratif, -iːv], *a. Gram:* durative.

dur-bec [dyrbɛk], *s.m. Orn:* grosbeak; **d.-b. des sapins,** pine grosbeak; *pl. durs-becs.*

durcir [dyrsiːr]. **1.** *v.tr.* (*a*) to harden, to make hard; **d. un œuf,** to hard-boil an egg; (*b*) *Metall:* to chill (casting, etc.); **durci à la surface,** case-hardened, face-hardened; (*c*) *Phot:* to harden (an emulsion). **2.** *v.i. & pr.* (*a*) to harden; to become, grow, hard, tough; **neige durcie,** hard snow; (*b*) (*of clay, etc.*) to become indurated; (*of cement, etc.*) (i) to set; (ii) to harden; **sol durci par le soleil,** earth baked by the sun.

durcissement [dyrsismɑ̃], *s.m.* **1.** hardening; setting (of cement, etc.); chilling (of casting); induration (of clay); toughening, hardening (of skin); *Metall:* **d. par l'âge, d. structural,** age-hardening; **d. à l'air,** air hardening (of cement). **2.** stiffening (of enemy resistance); hardening (of attitude).

durcisseur, -euse [dyrsisœːr, -øːz]. **1.** *a.* hardening (process, etc.). **2.** *s.m. Tchn:* solidifying agent.

durdénite [dyrdenit], *s.f. Miner:* durdenite.

durée [dyre], *s.f.* **1.** lasting quality, wear (of material, building, etc.); **d. d'une ampoule électrique,** life of an electric bulb; **tissu, mode, qui n'est pas de d.,** material, fashion, that will not last long; **le peu de d. d'une mode,** the short life, the ephemeral nature, of a fashion; *Mec.E:* **essai de d.,** endurance test. **2.** (*a*) duration (of

reign, war, etc.); **bonheur de courte d.,** short-lived happiness; (b) **d. d'un bail, du droit d'auteur,** duration, term, of a lease, of a copyright; **pendant la d. de sa peine,** while he was undergoing his sentence; **quelle est la d. de votre congé?** how long does your leave last? how long is your leave? Rec: **disque à d. prolongée,** extended play record, F: **É.P.;** Cin: **d. de projection,** running, projection, time.

durement [dyrmɑ̃], adv. 1. hard, vigorously; **frapper d.,** to hit hard. 2. with difficulty; **repos d. gagné,** hardly earned, hard-earned, rest; **vivre d.,** to live a hard life. 3. (to speak, treat s.o.) harshly, severely, unkindly; **d. éprouvé,** severely tried.

dure-mère [dyrmɛːr], s.f. Anat: dura mater; pl. **dures-mères.**

durène [dyrɛn], s.m. Ch: durene.

durer [dyre], v.i. 1. (of thgs) to last; to continue; (a) **voilà trois ans que cela dure,** it has been going on for three years; **votre congé dure combien de temps?** how long is your leave? **cette minute nous a duré une heure,** that minute seemed like an hour to us; abs. **l'hiver a duré cette année,** it has been a long winter this year; **le temps lui dure,** time hangs heavy on his hands; **ça va d. longtemps, cette plaisanterie?** how long is this going on for? haven't we had about enough of this? (b) **la pierre dure plus que le bois,** stone lasts longer than wood, timber; **fleur qui ne dure qu'un jour,** flower that lasts only one day; **la jeunesse ne dure pas longtemps,** youth is short-lived; youth will not last for ever; F: **ça durera ce que ça durera, mais . . .,** it won't, may not, last long, but . . .; **ce costume a duré deux ans,** this suit has lasted two years; **tissu qui durera,** material which will wear well; abs. **leur amitié a duré,** theirs was a lasting, enduring, friendship. 2. (of pers.) (a) (i) A: to live; (ii) F: to remain alive; Pej: **est-ce qu'il dure toujours?** is he still alive? (b) F: (usu. neg.) to hold out; **nous n'y pouvons plus d.,** we can't hold out, bear it, stick it, any longer; **il ne peut pas d. en place,** he can't stay put; he's like a cat on hot bricks.

duret, -ette [dyrɛ, -ɛt], a. F: rather hard, hardish (substance); rather tough (meat, etc.).

dureté [dyrte], s.f. 1. hardness (of substance, of water); toughness (of meat). 2. difficulty, hardness (of task, etc.); **la d. des temps,** the austerity, hardships, of the times; **d. d'oreille,** hardness of hearing. 3. (a) harshness, callousness, unkindness; **d. d'un père pour ses fils,** severity, harsh attitude, of a father towards his sons; **d. des traits, de la voix,** hardness of features, harshness of voice; **d. de cœur,** hardness of heart, hard-heartedness; callousness; **duretés de caractère,** asperities of disposition; **d. du froid,** severity of the cold; **parler avec d.,** to speak harshly; (b) A: **dire des duretés à qn,** to say unkind, harsh, things to s.o.

durillon [dyrijɔ̃], s.m. 1. callosity (on hand, etc.); corn (on sole of foot). 2. Tchn: hard grain (in marble, etc.); knot (in wood).

durio [dyrjo], s.m. Bot: (fruit or tree) durian, durion.

durion [dyrjɔ̃], s.m. Bot: durian, durion (tree).

durione [dyrjɔn], s.f. Bot: durian, durion (fruit).

durite [dyrit], s.f. Aut: Av: etc: R.t.m: flexible connection piping; hose connection.

duromètre [dyrɔmɛtr], s.m. Tchn: durometer.

duroquinone [dyrɔkinɔn], s.f. Ch: duroquinone.

dusse [dys], s.m. system of secret signs (used by card-sharpers, illusionists, etc.).

duumvir [dyɔmviːr], s.m. Rom.Hist: duumvir; pl. **les duumvirs,** the duumvirs, duumviri.

duumviral, -aux [dyɔmviral, -o], a. Rom.Hist: duumviral.

duumvirat [dyɔmvira], s.m. Rom.Hist: duumvirate.

duvet [dyvɛ], s.m. 1. (a) down (on chin, young bird, peach, etc.); **d. de l'eider, du cygne,** eider down, swan's down; **d. de chardon,** thistledown; F: **coucher sur le d.,** to live in the lap of luxury; (b) underfur (of animal); (c) (i) down mattress; (ii) F: sleeping bag. 2. Tex: nap, fluff (of cloth).

duveté [dyvte], a. downy.

duveter (se) [sədyvte], v.pr. to become downy, fluffy.

duveteux, -euse [dyvtø, -øːz], a. downy, fluffy.

Duvetine [dyvtin], s.f. Tex: R.t.m: Duvetyn.

dyade [djad], s.f. Phil: Poet: dyad, diad.

dyadique [djadik], a. dyadic.

dyarchie [djarʃi], s.f. dyarchy, diarchy.

dyarchique [djarʃik], a. dyarchic, diarchic.

dyarque [djark], s.m. dyarch, diarch.

dyke [dik], s.m. Geol: dyke; **d. de phonolite,** phonolitic dyke.

dynamètre [dinamɛtr], s.m. Opt: dynameter.

dynamique [dinamik]. 1. a. dynamic(al); Aer: **pression d.,** ram pressure; F: **c'est un type d.,** he's lively, dynamic, go-ahead; **il est très d.,** he's got plenty of drive. 2. s.f. (a) dynamics; (b) **la d. des groupes,** group dynamism.

dynamiquement [dinamikmɑ̃], adv. dynamically.

dynamisation [dinamizasjɔ̃], s.f. dynamization.

dynamiser (se) [sədinamize], v.pr. (of force, feeling, etc.), to become dynamic, concentrated.

dynamisme [dinamism], s.m. (a) dynamism; (b) vitality; drive.

dynamiste [dinamist], s.m. dynamist.

dynamitage [dinamitaːʒ], s.m. dynamiting.

dynamite [dinamit], s.f. dynamite; **d. gomme,** explosive gelatine, gum dynamite.

dynamiter [dinamite], v.tr. Exp: to dynamite, to blow up (building, etc.).

dynamiterie [dinamitri], s.f. dynamite factory.

dynamiteur, -euse [dinamitœːr, -øːz], s.m. (a) A: worker in a dynamite factory; (b) dynamiter.

dynamitier [dinamitje], s.m. manufacturer of dynamite.

dynamitière [dinamitjɛːr], s.f. dynamite magazine.

dynamo- [dinamɔ], comb.fm. dynamo; **dynamographe,** dynamo-graph; **dynamogénie,** dynamogeny.

dynamo [dinamo], s.f. El.E: dynamo; **d. excitatrice,** exciter; **d.-quantité,** low-tension dynamo; **d.-tension,** high-tension dynamo.

dynamo-démarreur [dinamɔdemarœːr], s.f. Aut: dynamotor; pl. **dynamos-démarreurs.**

dynamo-électrique [dinamɔelɛktrik], a. dynamoelectric(al); pl. **dynamo-électriques.**

dynamogène [dinamɔʒɛn], **dynamogénique** [dinamɔʒenik], a. dynamogenic, dynamogenous, stimulating.

dynamogénie [dinamɔʒeni], s.f. Physiol: dynamogenesis.

dynamographe [dinamɔgraf], s.m. dynamograph.

dynamométamorphisme [dinamɔmetamɔrfism], s.m. Geol: dynamometamorphism.

dynamomètre [dinamɔmɛtr], s.m. Mec: dynamometer; **d. à écrasement,** crusher gauge.

dynamométrie [dinamɔmetri], s.f. Mec: dynamometry.

dynamométrique [dinamɔmetrik], a. dynamometric(al); **clef d.,** torque wrench.

dynamophore [dinamɔfɔːr], a. Physiol: energy-producing (food, etc.).

dynamoteur [dinamɔtœːr], s.m. Aut: dynamotor.

dynastart [dinastaːr], s.f. Aut: dynamotor.

dynaste [dinast], s.m. 1. dynast. 2. Ent: dynastes.

dynastides [dinastid], s.m. Ent: Dynastes; Dynastid.

dynastie [dinasti], s.f. dynasty.

dynastique [dinastik], a. dynastic.

dynatron [dinatrɔ̃], s.m. El: dynatron.

dyne [din], s.f. Ph.Meas: dyne.

dynode [dinɔd], s.f. Elcs: dynode.

dypnone [dipnɔn], s.f. Ch: dypnone.

dys- [dis], pref. dys-; **dysgénésie,** dysgenesis; **dysopie, dysopsia; dystrophie,** dystrophy; **dyschromatope,** dyschromatoptic.

dysanalyte [disanalit], s.f. Miner: dysanalyte.

dysarthrie [disartri], s.f. Med: dysarthria.

dyschromatopsie [diskrɔmatɔpsi], s.f. Med: dyschromatopsia.

dyschromie [diskrɔmi], s.f. Med: dyschromia.

dyscinésie [disinezi], s.f. Med: dyskinesia.

dyscrase [diskraːz], s.f., **dyscrasite** [diskrazit], s.f. Miner: discrasite.

dyscrasie [diskrazi], s.f. Med: dyscrasia.

dyscrasique [diskrazik], a. Med: dyscrasic, dyscratic.

dysendocrinie [disɑ̃dɔkrini], s.f. Med: endocrinopathy.

dysendocrinien, -ienne [disɑ̃dɔkrinjɛ̃, -jɛn], a. Med: endocrinopathic.

dysenterie [disɑ̃tri], s.f. Med: dysentery.

dysentériforme [disɑ̃terifɔrm], a. Med: dysenteriform.

dysentérique [disɑ̃terik], a. Med: dysenteric.

dysesthésie [disɛstezi], s.f. Med: dys(a)esthesia.

dysfonctionnement [disfɔ̃ksjɔnmɑ̃], s.m. Med: dysfunction.

dysgénète [disʒenɛt], s.m. & f. Biol: disgenetic.

dysgraphie [disgrafi], s.f. Med: dysgraphia.

dysharmonique [disarmɔnik], a. Biol: **symbiose d.,** antagonistic symbiosis.

dyshidrose, dyshydrose, dysidrose [disidroːz], s.f. Med: dyshidrosis, dysidrosis.

dyskératose [diskeratoːz], s.f. Med: dyskeratosis.

dyskinésie [diskinezi], s.f. Med: dyskinesia.

dyslalie [dislali], s.f. Med: dyslalia.

dyslexie [dislɛksi], s.f. Med: dyslexia.

dyslexique [dislɛksik], a. & s. Med: dyslectic.

dyslogie [dislɔʒi], s.f. Med: dyslogia.

dysluite [dislɥit], **dyslyite** [disliit], s.f. Miner: dysluite.

dysménorrhée [dismenɔre], s.f. Med: dysmenorrhoea.

dysménorrhéique [dismenɔreik], a. dysmenorrhoeal.

dysmnésie [dismnezi], s.f. Med: dysmnesia.

dysmorphophobie [dismɔrfɔfɔbi], s.f. Med: dysmorphophobia.

dysorexie [disɔrɛksi], s.f. Med: dysorexia, loss of appetite.

dyspepsie [dispɛpsi], s.f. Med: dyspepsia.

dyspepsique [dispɛpsik], **dyspeptique** [dispɛptik], a. & s. Med: dyspeptic; **aliment néfaste aux dyspeptiques,** food that is bad for dyspeptics.

dysphagie [disfaʒi], s.f. Med: dysphagia.

dysphonie [disfɔni], s.f. Med: dysphonia.

dysphorie [disfɔri], s.f. dysphoria.

dysphrénie [disfreni], s.f. Med: dysphrenia.

dysplasie [displazi], s.f. Med: dysplasia.

dyspnée [dispne], s.f. Med: dyspnoea.

dyspnéique [dispneik], a. Med: dyspnoeal, dyspnoeic.

dysprosium [disprɔzjɔm], s.m. Ch: dysprosium.

dyssymétrie [dis(s)imetri], s.f. asymmetry.

dyssymétrique [dis(s)imetrik], a. asymmetrical, unsymmetrical.

dysthyroïdie [distirɔidi], s.f. Med: dysthyroidism.

dystocie [distɔsi], s.f. Obst: dystocia, dystokia.

dystrophie [distrɔfi], s.f. Med: dystrophy.

dystrophique [distrɔfik], a. Med: dystrophic.

dysurie [disyri], s.f. Med: dysuria, dysury.

dysurique [disyrik], a. Med: dysuric.

dytique [ditik], Ent: 1. a. dytiscid. 2. s.m. dytiscus, water-beetle, diving-beetle; F: diver; water-tiger.

dytiscidés [ditiside], s.m.pl. Ent: Dytiscidae.

dzéta [dzeta], s.m. Gr.Alph: zeta.

Dzoungarie [dzungari], Pr.n.f. Geog: A: Zungaria, Dzungaria.

E

E, e [œ], *s.m.* (the letter) E, e; e ouvert, fermé, open e, closed e; *Tp:* E comme Eugène, E for Edward.

É, é [e], *s.m.* (*in spelling words*) e acute (accent); *Tp:* É comme Émile, E for Edward.

é- [e], *pref.* e-; **édenté**, edentate; **éjecter**, to eject.

Éaque [eak], *Pr.n.m. Myth:* Aeacus.

eau, eaux [o], *s.f.* water. **1.** (*a*) **e. de source**, spring water; **e. dure**, hard water; **e. douce**, (i) fresh water; (ii) soft water; *F:* **marin d'e. douce**, landlubber; *Ecc:* **e. bénite**, holy water; **se ressembler comme deux gouttes d'e.**, to be as alike as two peas (in a pod); **être comme l'e. et le feu**, to be as different as chalk from cheese; **clair comme l'e. de roche**, crystal clear; **laver le plancher à grande e.**, to swill down the floor; **débourber un égout à grande e.**, to flush out a drain; **e. de vaisselle, e. grasse**, dishwater, washing-up water; **e. de savon**, soapsuds; **meuler un outil à l'e.**, to wet-grind a tool; **faire venir l'e. à son moulin**, to turn things to one's own advantage; to feather one's own nest; (*b*) **e. potable**, drinking water; **e. non potable**, water unfit for drinking; **boire un verre d'e. fraîche**, to drink a glass of cold water; **se noyer dans un verre d'e.**, to make a mountain out of a molehill; *F:* **il ne vaut pas l'e. qu'il boit**, he isn't worth his salt; *F:* **croyez ça et buvez de l'e.!** don't you believe it! **vin coupé d'e.**, wine and water; *F:* **mettre de l'e. dans son vin**, (i) to reduce one's expenses; (ii) to draw in one's horns; (iii) to tone it down a bit; (*of spirits*) **sans e.**, neat; **whisky à l'e.**, whisky and water; **boire son whisky à l'eau, sans e.**, to drink one's whisky with water; to drink one's whisky neat; **e. de Seltz**, soda water; **e. gazeuse**, aerated, mineral, water; (*c*) **eaux thermales**, thermal springs, hot springs; **e. minérale**, (natural) mineral water; **ville d'eau(x)**, spa; **prendre les eaux**, to take, drink, the waters; **aller aux eaux**, to go to a spa (to take the waters); (*d*) *Ind: Mch: etc:* **e. d'alimentation**, feed water; **e. de refroidissement**, cooling water; **chambre à e.**, water space (of boiler); (*of locomotive, ship*) **faire de l'e.**, to water, take in water. **2.** (*a*) **e. de pluie**, rainwater; **il tombe de l'e.**, it's raining; **le temps est à l'e.**, it's wet, rainy, weather; (*b*) **cours d'e.**, waterway; stream; river; **cours d'e. navigable**, navigable waterway; **chute d'e.**, waterfall; **jet d'e.**, fountain; **dimanche grandes eaux à Versailles**, the fountains will play at Versailles on Sunday; **pièce d'e.**, (ornamental) lake; pool; **e. dormante, stagnante**, stagnant water; **e. superficielle, eaux de surface, e. folle**, surface water; **au bord de l'e.**, at the water's edge; **sur l'e.**, afloat; **revenir sur l'e.**, to get on one's feet again; to surface; **voler à fleur d'e.**, to skim the water; *Ven:* (*of stag*) **battre l'e.**, to take soil; *Adm:* **service des Eaux et Forêts = Forestry Commission**; **depuis lors il a passé (bien) de l'e. sous le(s) pont(s)**, much has happened since then; a lot of water has flowed, passed, under the bridge since then; **tomber à l'e.**, (i) to fall into the water; (ii) (*of plan*) to fall through; to peter out; **porter de l'e. à la rivière, à la mer**, to bring, carry, coals to Newcastle; **ne pas trouver l'e. à la rivière**, not to know one's way about; not to see what is under one's nose; **l'e. va à la rivière**, money attracts money; *F:* **rester le bec dans l'e.**, to be stuck for a reply; to be tongue-tied; (*c*)

Nau: **l'e.**, the sea; **e. de mer, e. salée**, sea water, salt water; **c'est une goutte d'e. dans la mer**, it's only a drop in the bucket, in the ocean; **mortes eaux**, neap tides; **vives eaux**, spring tides; (*of ship*) **échouer aux vives eaux**, to get neaped; **hautes, basses, eaux**, high, low, water; *F:* **les eaux sont basses**, I'm, he's in low water, hard up; (*in tidal river*) **grandes eaux**, high water; *F:* **ce fut les grandes eaux**, she burst into a flood of tears, she turned on the waterworks; **nager entre deux eaux**, (i) to swim under water; (ii) to sit on the fence; to run with the hare and hunt with the hounds; (*of ship*) **faire e.**, to leak, to spring a leak; **faire e. de toutes parts**, to leak at every seam; **notre barque faisait e. de toutes parts**, our fortunes were in a bad way; **chaussures qui prennent l'e.**, shoes that let in the water, that let in the wet; **être dans les eaux d'un navire**, to be in the wake of a ship, astern of a ship; **mettre un navire à l'e.**, to launch a ship; to set a ship afloat; **mettre un canot à l'e.**, (i) to put out, lower, a boat; (ii) to launch a boat; **mise à l'e.**, launching (of a ship); **e. à courir**, sea room; **manquer d'e. à courir**, to have no sea room; (*in yacht race, etc*) **demander de l'e.**, to ask for sea room; **les eaux d'un port**, the confines of a port; **eaux territoriales**, territorial waters; (*d*) **la compagnie des eaux = the Water Board**; **service des eaux**, water supply; **e. de la ville, main(s) water**; **château d'e.**, water tower; **conduite d'e.**, water main; **arrêter l'e.**, to turn off the water; (*in house, etc*) **e. courante**, running water; **il n'y a pas d'e. courante**, there is no water laid on; **chambre avec e. courante**, room with running water, with a washbasin; *s.a.* PRISE. **3.** (*a*) **juice** (of a melon, etc.); **pêche qui a trop d'e.**, watery peach; **diamant de la première e.**, diamond of the first water; *F:* **imbécile de la première, la plus belle, e.**, out-and-out fool; **ampoules pleines d'e.**, blisters full of fluid, of water; **cela lui fait venir l'e. à la bouche**, it makes his mouth water; **être tout en e.**, to be dripping with perspiration; **suer sang et e.**, to sweat blood (doing sth.); (*b*) urine, water; **faire de l'e.**, to pass water; *Vet:* **eaux rousses**, red water; (*d*) *Obst:* **la perte des eaux**, the breaking of the waters; (*e*) *Ch: Ind: etc:* **e. de Cologne**, eau de Cologne; **e. de rose**, rose water; **socialisme à l'e. de rose**, pale pink socialism, milk-and-water socialism; **e. ammoniacale**, gas liquor; **e. céleste**, eau céleste, solution of cupric ammonium sulphate; **e. oxygénée**, hydrogen peroxide; **e. régale**, aqua regia; **e. de baryte**, baryta water, barium hydroxide; **e. de cristallisation**, water of crystallization; **e. de constitution**, water of constitution; **e. mère**, mother liquor; **e. de Javel**, Javel water; bleach and disinfectant; *Atom.Ph:* **e. lourde**, heavy water; *Paperm:* **e. collée, e. blanche**, white water; *A.Pharm:* **e. blanche**, sugar of lead, lead acetate.

eaubénitier [obenitje], *s.m.* holy-water basin (made of silver).

eau-de-vie [odvi], *s.f.* (*a*) brandy; (*b*) spirits; **e.-de-v. de Dantzig**, Danzig(er) Goldwasser; *pl.* **eaux-de-vie**.

eau-forte [ofɔrt], *s.f.* **1.** *Ch:* aqua fortis, nitric acid; **enlever le métal à l'e.-f.**, to etch away the metal. **2.** *Engr:* (gravure à l')**e.-f.**, etching, etched engraving; **e.-f. pure**, first state of the etched plate; *pl.* **eaux-fortes**.

eaux-vannes [ovan], *s.f.pl. Agr:* liquid manure, sewage (water).

ébahi [ebai], *a.* amazed, stupefied, flabbergasted, staggered, astounded, dumbfounded, tonguetied; **un regard é.**, a look of blank astonishment; **rester tout é.**, to stand gaping; **être é. d'apprendre que . .**, to be amazed to learn that . . .

ébahir [ebaiːr], *v.tr.* to amaze, astound, flabbergast; to take (s.o.'s) breath away.

s'ébahir, to gape, to stare; to stand amazed, to be dumbfounded; **s'é. de qch.**, to wonder, be astounded, amazed, at sth.

ébahissement [ebaismã], *s.m.* amazement, astonishment, wonder.

ébarbage [ebarbaːʒ], *s.m.*, **ébarbement** [ebarbəmã], *s.m.* trimming (of sth.); removing of the rough edges (from sth.); dressing, edging off, scraping (of engraved plate); fettling (of casting); trimming (of vegetables); trimming down (of edges of book); clipping, trimming (of hedge, etc.); burring (of metal); **é. des bavures**, trimming of flash.

ébarber [ebarbe], *v.tr.* to trim; to remove rough edges from (sth.); to dress, to edge off, to scrape (engraved plate); to fettle (casting); to trim (vegetables, edges of a book); to clip, trim (hedge, etc.); **papier à bords non ébarbés**, deckle-edged paper; *Bookb:* **é. les tranches**, to trim down the edges; *Metalw:* **presse à é.**, burr-removing press, edge-finishing press.

ébarbeur, -euse [ebarbœːr, -øːz], *s. Cer: Metall: etc:* (*pers.*) trimmer, fettler, chipper.

ébarbeuse [ebarbøːz], *s.f. Metall: etc:* trimming machine; *a.* **fraise é.**, burring reamer.

ébarboir [ebarbwaːr], *s.m. Tls:* scraper, chipping chisel, burr-cutter.

ébarbure [ebarbyːr], *s.f.* (*a*) burr, paring, shaving (of metal, etc.); (*b*) *pl.* outer leaves (of salad, etc.); trimmings (from paper).

ébardoir [ebardwaːr], *s.m. Tls:* triangular scraper, parer, shavehook.

ébats [eba], *s.m.pl.* disport; revels; playing about; **les é. des cygnes dans les eaux**, swans frolicking (about) in the water; **prendre ses é.**, to play (about), to disport oneself.

ébattement [ebatmã], *s.m.* **1.** *A:* disport; revelling. **2.** swinging, swaying, rocking (of vehicle).

ébattre (s') [sebatr], *v.pr.* (*conj. like* BATTRE) to gambol; to frolic, play (about); to disport oneself; **agneaux qui s'ébattent**, lambs frisking about, gambolling; **les oiseaux s'ébattent dans la volière**, the birds are hopping about the cage.

ébaubi [ebobi], *a. F:* amazed, flabbergasted.

ébaubir [ebobiːr], *v.tr. F:* to amaze, flabbergast.

s'ébaubir, *F:* to be flabbergasted, dumbfounded, *F:* struck all of a heap.

ébaubissement [ebobismã], *s.m. F:* stupefaction, amazement.

ébauchage [eboʃaːʒ], *s.m.* roughing out (of sth.) giving a first shape to sth.); sketching out, blocking out (of picture); outlining (of novel, etc.); *Mec.E:* roughing (out, down); roughing out work; **passe d'é.**, roughing (out) cut, pass.

ébauche [eboʃ], *s.f.* (*a*) rough shape; preliminary shape, adumbration (of sth.); rough sketch (of picture); skeleton, outline, rough draft (of novel, etc.); *Mec.E:* blank, rough model; *U.S:* roughcast; **coupe, passe, d'é.**, roughing (out) cut, pass; **é. d'un sourire**, suspicion, ghost, of a smile; (*b*) *Biol:* anlage (of organ, etc.).

ébauché [eboʃe], *s.m. Ind:* blank.

ébaucher [eboʃe], *v.tr.* to rough (sth.) out, give a first shape to (sth.); to sketch out, outline (picture, plan); to outline, make a skeleton of (novel, etc.); to rough-hew, boast, block out, rough in (statue, etc.); *Mec.E: Ind:* to rough-form, to rough-machine; to rough-forge, cog (metal); **fer ébauché,** muck-iron; **pièce ébauchée,** rough-formed, rough-machined, piece; **é. un sourire,** to give a faint, wan, smile.

ébaucheur [eboʃœːr], *a. & s.m.* **1.** *a.* roughing (-down); **alésoir é.,** roughing reamer; *Metall:* **train é.,** roughing(-down) roll; billeting roll. **2.** *s.m.* (*a*) (*pers.*) rougher; rougher-out, rough-shaper (of article); (*b*) *Metall:* roughing (-down) roll.

ébauchoir [eboʃwaːr], *s.m. Tls:* (*sculptor's, mason's*) boaster; roughing-chisel; (*carpenter's*) paring chisel; (mortise) boring bit.

ébauchon [eboʃɔ̃], *s.m.* (*pipe-making*) briar-block, ébauchon.

ébaudir [ebodiːr], *v.tr. A:* to amuse, enliven.

s'ébaudir, *A:* to frolic; make merry (**de,** over); to be in high glee; **s'é. de qn,** to make merry at s.o.'s expense.

ébaudissement [ebodismɑ̃], *s.m. A:* jollity, glee, frolicking.

ébavurage [ebavyraːʒ], *s.m. Metalw:* fettling.

ébavurer [ebavyre], *v.tr. Metalw:* to fettle.

ebbe, èbe [ɛb], *s.m.* (*a*) *Dial:* ebb (of tide); (*b*) **portes d'èbe,** tide gates (of lock).

ébénacées [ebenase], *s.f.pl. Bot:* Ebenaceae.

ébénales [ebenal], *s.f.pl. Bot:* Ebenales.

ébène [ebɛn], *s.f.* ebony; **collection d'ébènes,** collection of ebony curios; **é. fossile,** jet; **cheveux d'é., d'un noir d'é.,** jet-black hair; *F: Pej:* **(bois d')é.,** negro slaves.

ébéner [ebene], *v.tr.* **(j'ébène, n. ébénons; j'ébénerai)** to ebonize.

ébénier [ebenje], *s.m.* **1.** ebony tree. **2. faux é.,** laburnum.

ébéniste [ebenist], *s.m.* cabinet maker.

ébénisterie [ebenist(ə)ri], *s.f.* **1.** cabinet-making. **2.** cabinet work. **3.** cabinet (for radio set, etc.).

éberġement [ebɛrʒ(ə)mɑ̃], *s.m. Civ.E:* grading of banks (of waterway, when dredging).

éberlué [ebɛrlɥe], *a. F:* flabbergasted.

éberluer [ebɛrlɥe], *v.tr. F: O:* **1. é. qn,** to hoodwink s.o., to throw dust in s.o.'s eyes. **2.** to astound; to strike (s.o.) all of a heap; to flabbergast (s.o.).

Eberth [ebɛrt], *Pr.n. Med:* **bacille d'E.,** Eberth's bacillus; typhoid bacillus.

éberthite [ebɛrtit], *s.f. Med:* septicæmia caused by Eberth's bacillus.

ébionites [ebjɔnit], *s.m.pl. Rel.H:* Ebionites.

ébisèlement [ebizɛlmɑ̃], *s.m.* chamfering, bevelling.

ébiseler [ebizle], *v.tr.* **(j'ébiselle, n. ébiselons; j'ébisellerai)** to chamfer, bevel.

éblouir [ebluiːr], *v.tr.* to dazzle; **beauté qui éblouit,** dazzling beauty; **se laisser é. par des promesses flatteuses,** to be dazzled by flattering promises; **ses succès l'ont ébloui,** success has gone to his head; **il a été ébloui par les phares d'une voiture,** he was dazzled, blinded, by the headlights of a car.

s'éblouir (de qch.), to be dazzled (by sth.).

éblouissant [ebluisɑ̃], *a.* dazzling; **soleil é.,** dazzling, blinding, sunshine; **beauté éblouissante,** radiant beauty; **éloquence éblouissante,** dazzling, brilliant, eloquence.

éblouissement [ebluismɑ̃], *s.m.* **1.** (*a*) dazzling, dazzle, glare; (*b*) **l'é. produit par la neige,** snow blindness; **l'é. causé par les phares d'une voiture est une source de danger,** being blinded, dazzled, by the headlights of a car is a source of danger; (*c*) dizziness, vertigo; **avoir des éblouissements,** to have fits of dizziness. **2.** amazement; (intense) admiration.

ébonite [ebɔnit], *s.f.* ebonite; vulcanite.

ébognage [ebɔrɲaːʒ], *s.m. Arb:* nipping off of buds (on fruit trees); disbudding.

éborgnement [ebɔrɲəmɑ̃], *s.m.* (*a*) blinding (of s.o.) in one eye; (*b*) being blind in one eye, blindness of one eye.

éborgner [ebɔrɲe], *v.tr.* **1.** (*a*) **é. qn,** to blind s.o. in one eye, to put s.o.'s eye out; **j'ai failli m'é.,** I nearly put my eye out; (*b*) *F:* to give (s.o.) a punch in the eye; (*c*) **é. une maison,** to build sth. in front of a house (blocking the light). **2.** *Arb:* to nip the buds off, to disbud (fruit-tree).

ébotter [ebɔte], *v.tr.* **1.** to cut the head off (nail, pin). **2.** *Arb:* to cut back (branches); to pollard (tree).

ébouage [ebuaːʒ], *s.m.* scavenging, sweeping (of streets); *Mch:* **robinet d'é.,** mud-cock.

ébouer [ebue], *v.tr.* to sweep (streets); to clean out (boiler).

éboueur, -euse [ebuœːr, -øːz]. **1.** *s.m.* (*pers.*) street sweeper. **2.** *s.f.* **éboueuse,** (*machine*) street sweeper.

ébouillantage [ebujɑ̃taːʒ], *s.m.* scalding; stifling (of silkworms with steam).

ébouillanter [ebujɑ̃te], *v.tr.* **1.** to scald (person, one's foot, etc.). **2.** to scald (cooking vessel). **3.** to dip (sth.) in boiling water.

ébouillir [ebujiːr], *v.i.* (*conj. like* BOUILLIR) *A:* to boil away, boil down.

éboulée [ebule], *s.f.* mass of scree, of debris, of rubble, of fallen earth.

éboulement [ebulmɑ̃], *s.m.* **1.** falling in, crumbling (of earth, mine, etc.); caving in, collapsing (of wall); *Fort:* éboulement. **2.** rock-fall, fall of rock; **é. de terre,** landslide, landslip.

ébouler [ebule]. **1.** *v.tr.* to bring down, loosen (gravel, earth, etc.); *Mil:* to blow in (wall); to wreck (trench). **2.** *v.i. A:* to fall in, crumble, collapse.

s'ébouler, to fall down, fall in, crumble, collapse, cave in; (*of cliff*) to slip.

ébouleux, -euse [ebulø, -øːz], *a.* loose, crumbling, crumbly (ground, etc.).

éboulis [ebuli], *s.m.* **1.** mass of fallen earth; debris. **2.** *Geog:* scree; **é. de lessivage,** leaching residue.

ébouqueter [ebukte], *v.tr. Hort:* to remove leaf buds from (fruit trees), to disbud.

ébouquetage [ebuktaːʒ], *s.m. Hort:* (*a*) disbudding, pinching off, nipping off (of buds); (*b*) topping.

ébourgeonnage [eburʒɔnaːʒ], *s.m.*, **ébourgeonnement** [eburʒɔnmɑ̃], *s.m. Arb: Vit:* disbudding, nipping off of the buds.

ébourgeonner [eburʒɔne], *v.tr. Arb: Vit:* to disbud, to nip the buds off (fruit tree, etc.); to trim.

ébourgeonneur [eburʒɔnœːr], *s.m. Orn: F:* bud-eater; (i) bullfinch; (ii) hawfinch; (iii) brambling.

ébourgeonnoir [eburʒɔnwaːr], *s.m. Arb:* disbudder.

ébouriffant [eburifɑ̃], *a. F:* amazing, astounding, startling (success, etc.); **histoire ébouriffante,** preposterous story.

ébouriffé [eburife], *a.* **1.** dishevelled, ruffled, rumpled, tousled (hair); **Pierre l'É.,** Shock-headed Peter. **2.** amazed; startled; ruffled (**de, par,** by); **elle a l'air tout ébouriffé(e),** she is all in a fluster.

ébouriffer [eburife], *v.tr.* **1.** to dishevel, ruffle, rumple, tousle (s.o.'s hair). **2.** *F:* to amaze (s.o.); to take (s.o.'s) breath away; to take (s.o.) aback; to ruffle (s.o.).

ébourrage [eburaːʒ], *s.m. Leath:* unhairing (of skins).

ébourrer [ebure], *v.tr. Leath:* to unhair (skins).

ébousiner [ebuzine], *v.tr.* to clean off the soft surface of (quarry stone).

ébouter [ebute], *v.tr.* to cut off, saw off, the end of (beam, etc.).

ébracté [ebrakte], *a. Bot:* ebracteate.

ébraiser [ebreze], *v.tr.* to rake out the embers from (baker's oven).

ébranchage [ebrɑ̃ʃaːʒ], *s.m.*, **ébranchement** [ebrɑ̃ʃmɑ̃], *s.m. Arb:* stripping, lopping; cutting away of the branches.

ébranché [ebrɑ̃ʃe], *a.* branchless, lopped (tree).

ébrancher [ebrɑ̃ʃe], *v.tr.* to cut away, lop off, break off, the branches from (tree); to prune, trim.

ébrancheur [ebrɑ̃ʃœːr], *s.m. Arb:* pruner.

ébranchoir [ebrɑ̃ʃwaːr], *s.m. Arb:* lopping bill, (long-hafted) billhook.

ébranlable [ebrɑ̃labl], *a. A:* **1.** easily shaken or moved. **2.** (*a*) easily daunted, easily intimidated; (*b*) accessible to pity.

ébranlage [ebrɑ̃laːʒ], *s.m. Metall:* rapping (of pattern).

ébranlé [ebrɑ̃le], *a.* shaken; **vitres ébranlées par une explosion,** windows shaken by an explosion; **ce mur est é. mais tient encore debout,** this wall threatens to collapse but is still standing; **confiance ébranlée,** shaken confidence; **santé ébranlée,** impaired health; **nerfs ébranlés,** jangled nerves; **profondément é. par les événements,** deeply shaken, moved, distressed, by events.

ébranlement [ebrɑ̃l(ə)mɑ̃], *s.m.* **1.** shaking, shock, concussion; **é. des vitres,** rattling of the windows; **é. du crédit d'un pays,** blow to the credit of a country. **2.** perturbation, agitation; **nouvelle qui causa un é. universel,** news that caused a general commotion; **la mort de son père fut pour elle un terrible é.,** her father's death was a serious shock to her; **é. de la raison,** unhinging of the mind.

ébranler [ebrɑ̃le], *v.tr.* **1.** (*a*) to shake; to loosen (tooth, etc.); *Metall:* to rap (pattern); **é. la foi, l'opinion, de qn,** to shake, unsettle, s.o.'s faith, s.o.'s opinion; **il était fort ébranlé par ce qu'il apprenait,** he was staggered, much disturbed, by what he heard; (*b*) **se laisser é.,** to allow oneself to be moved (to pity). **2.** (*a*) to set in motion; **é. une cloche,** to set a bell ringing; **é. l'air,** to disturb the air; (*b*) **é. son cheval au galop,** to spur one's horse to a gallop.

s'ébranler. 1. to shake, totter; **fermeté qui ne s'ébranle jamais,** unflinching, unwavering, fortitude; **tout le pays parut s'é.,** the whole country seemed to be disturbed. **2.** to get under way, to move off; to start; **la colonne s'ébranla,** the column marched off, got on the move. **3. les cloches s'ébranlent,** the bells start ringing.

ébrasement [ebrɑzmɑ̃], *s.m. Arch:* (*a*) splaying; (*b*) splay (of window opening, etc.).

ébraser [ebrɑze], *v.tr. Arch:* to splay (embrasure, etc.) outwards; **arc ébrasé,** splayed arch.

ébrasure [ebrazyːr], *s.f.* = ÉBRASEMENT.

Èbre (l') [lɛbr], *Pr.n.m.* the (river) Ebro.

ébrèchement [ebrɛʃmɑ̃], *s.m.* nicking, damaging, making jagged (of blade).

ébrécher [ebreʃe], *v.tr.* **(j'ébrèche, n. ébréchons; j'ébrécherai)** (*a*) to notch; to make a notch, a gap, in (sth.); **é. une assiette,** to chip a plate; **s'é. une dent,** to break one of one's teeth; **é. un couteau,** to nick the blade of a knife; **couteau ébréché,** jagged knife; **souliers ébréchés,** shoes in holes; (*b*) *F:* to damage, impair (reputation); to make a hole in, play ducks and drakes with (one's fortune); **capital fortement ébréché,** greatly reduced capital; (*c*) *Geol:* **cratère ébréché,** breached cone.

ébréchure [ebreʃyːr], *s.f.* **1.** nick, notch, jagged place (on blade). **2.** jaggedness (of blade).

ébrener [ebrəne], *v.tr.* **(j'ébrène, n. ébrenons; j'ébrènerai)** *A:* to wipe (baby) clean.

ébreuiller [ebrœje], *v.tr.* to gut (cod-fish).

ébriété [ebriete], *s.f.* intoxication; (state of) drunkenness; *Jur:* **en état d'é.,** intoxicated; in a state of intoxication; under the influence of drink.

ébrieux, -euse [ebriø, -øːz], *a. Path:* ebrious.

ébroïcien, -ienne [ebrɔisjɛ̃, -jɛn], *a. & s. Geog:* (native, inhabitant) of Évreux.

ébrouage [ebruaːʒ], *s.m.* branning (of wool, before dyeing).

ébrouement [ebrumɑ̃], *s.m.* (*a*) snorting, snort (of horse, etc.); (*b*) flap(ping), clap(ping) (of wings).

ébrouer[1] [ebrue], *v.tr.* to bran (wool, before dyeing).

ébrouer[2] **(s'),** *v.pr.* **1.** (*of horse, etc.*) to snort. **2.** to splash about; (*of bird*) **s'é. dans la poussière,** to take a dust-bath. **3.** to shake oneself.

ébrouissage [ebruisaːʒ], *s.m.* branning (of wool, before dyeing).

ébroussailleuse [ebrusajøːz], *s.f.* undergrowth remover.

ébrousser [ebruse], *v.tr.* (*rare*) *Arb:* **1.** to strip the leaves off (tree). **2.** to disbud.

ébruitement [ebrɥitmɑ̃], *s.m.* spreading (abroad) (of news); disclosure (of secret).

ébruiter [ebrɥite], *v.tr.* to make known; to spread, bruit (news); to divulge, disclose (secret).

s'ébruiter, (of piece of news, etc.) to become known, to spread; **je ne veux pas que cela s'ébruite,** I don't want it to get round.

ébrun [ebrœ̃], *s.m. Agr:* ergotized grain.

ébrutage [ebrytaːʒ], *s.m.* rough cutting (of diamond).

ébulliomètre [ebyljɔmɛtr], *s.m. Ph:* ebulliometer.

ébulliométrie [ebyljɔmetri], *s.f. Ph:* ebulliometry.

ébulliométrique [ebyljɔmetrik], *a. Ph:* ebulliometric.

ébullioscope [ebyljɔskɔp], *s.m. Ph:* ebullioscope, ebulliometer.

ébullioscopie [ebyljɔskɔpi], *s.f. Ph:* ebullioscopy, ebulliometry.

ébullioscopique [ebyljɔskɔpik], *a. Ph:* ebullioscopic.

ébullition [ebylisjɔ̃], *s.f.* **1.** (*a*) ebullition, boiling; **point d'é.,** boiling point; **entrer en é.,** to come to the boil; *F:* **être en é.,** to be boiling, seething, with rage; (*b*) *Ch:* effervescence; (*c*) sudden outburst (of feeling); ferment; turmoil; agitation; **mon cerveau est en é.,** my head is in a whirl; **toute la ville est en é.,** the whole town is in a state of agitation. **2.** *Vet:* skin eruption, rash.

éburnation [ebyrnasjɔ̃], *s.f. Med:* eburnation.

éburné [ebyrne], **éburnéen, -enne** [ebyrneɛ̃, -ɛn], *a.* eburnean, eburneous, ivory-like; *Med:* eburnated; *Anat:* **substance éburnée,** dentine.

Éburons [ebyrɔ̃], *s.m.pl. Hist:* Eburones.

écabochage [ekabɔʃaːʒ], *s.m.* stripping (of tobacco leaves).

écabocher [ekabɔʃe], *v.tr.* to strip (tobacco leaves).

écabochoir [ekabɔʃwaːr], *s.m.* (*implement*) stripper (for tobacco leaves).

écaché [ekaʃe], *a. A:* flattened, flat (nose).

écachement [ekaʃmɑ̃], *s.m.* **1.** *A:* (*a*) crushing, squashing (of fruit, nuts, snail, etc.); (*b*) flattening (of wire, etc.). **2.** smooth-grinding (of tool).

écacher [ekaʃe], *v.tr.* **1.** (*a*) *A:* to crush, squash (nut, strawberry, snail, etc.); (*b*) *Metall:* to flatten, laminate. **2.** to smooth-grind (tool).

écade [ekad], *s.f. Biol:* ecad.

écaillage [ekajaːʒ], *s.m.* **1.** scaling (of fish, etc.); opening, shelling (of oysters, mussels). **2.** flaking off, peeling off (of paint); scaling off, chipping (of enamel, glaze). **3.** *Geol: Ind:* spalling, spawling, chipping (of rocks by the weather; of stone by a mason).

écaille [ekaːj], *s.f.* **1.** (*a*) scale (of fish, etc.); *A.Arm:* **armure à écailles,** scale-armour; (*b*) *Bot: Med:* scale; (*c*) flake; **tableau qui tombe par écailles,** picture that is peeling off, flaking off, coming off in flakes; **la peinture se détache par écailles,** the paint is flaking; **é. de marbre,** chip of marble; **é. de bois,** splinter, sliver; *Metall:* **écailles de fer,** forge scales; **les écailles lui tombèrent des yeux,** the scales fell from his eyes. **2.** (*a*) *A:* shell (of mollusc, etc.); (*b*) **é. de tortue,** tortoise shell; **lunettes à monture d'é.,** tortoiseshell-rimmed spectacles; *Arch:* **moulure en écailles,** scalloped moulding. **3.** *Ent:* arctia; **é. martre,** tiger moth. **4.** *pl.* **écailles,** compressed cattle cake.

écaillé [ekaje], *a. A:* scaled (fish).

écaillement [ekajmɑ̃], *s.m.* scaling; peeling (off), flaking (off).

écailler[1] [ekaje], *v.tr.* **1.** (*a*) to scale (fish); to open (oyster); (*b*) to scale (boiler). **2.** *Arch:* to scallop (moulding).

s'écailler, to scale off, peel off; to flake (off); to come off in flakes.

écailler[2], **-ère** [ekaje, -ɛːr], *s.* **1.** oyster seller; oyster opener, sheller. **2.** *s.f.* **écaillère,** oyster knife.

écaillette [ekajɛt], *s.f.* small scale, flake, splinter.

écailleur, -euse[1] [ekajœːr, -øːz], *s.* scaler (of fish); opener (of oysters).

écailleux, -euse[2] [ekajø, -øːz], *a.* scaly, squamous (animal, bulb, etc.); scutate (animal); splintery (mineral, wood); flaky (paint, etc.); fissile (slate, etc.).

écaillon [ekajɔ̃], *s.m.* tush (of horse).

écaillure [ekajyːr], *s.f.* **1.** *Coll.* scales (of fish). **2.** flake (of paint, etc.).

écalage [ekalaːʒ], *s.m.* shelling, husking; shucking.

écale [ekal], *s.f.* **1.** shell, pod (of peas, etc.); hull, husk (of walnut); shuck (of chestnut). **2.** road metal.

écaler [ekale], *v.tr.* **1.** to shell (peas, beans); to hull, husk (walnuts); to shuck (chestnuts). **2.** **terre écalée,** arable land (which does not form part of a farm).

s'écaler. **1.** (*of peas, etc.*) to fall out (of the pod); (*of walnuts*) to burst the husk. **2.** (*of wood*) to flake.

écalure [ekalyːr], *s.f.* hard skin, husk (of certain fruits, grains).

écalyptré [ekaliptre], *a. Bot:* not calyptrate.

écang [ekɑ̃], *s.m.*, **écangue** [ekɑ̃ːg], *s.f. Tex:* scutching blade, scutcher.

écangage [ekɑ̃gaːʒ], *s.m. Tex:* scutching, swingling, beating (of flax, hemp).

écanguer [ekɑ̃ge], *v.tr. Tex:* to scutch, swingle, beat (flax, hemp).

écardides [ekardid], **écardines** [ekardin], *s.m.pl. Biol:* Ecardines, Inarticulata.

écarlate [ekarlat], *s.f. & a.* scarlet; **elle devint é.,** she blushed, went, scarlet; **endosser l'é.,** to don the scarlet (of a cardinal).

écarlatin, -ine [ekarlatɛ̃, -in], *A:* **1.** *a.* scarlet. **2.** *s.m. Tex:* scarlet woollen stuff.

écarquillement [ekarkijmɑ̃], *s.m.* (*a*) opening wide (of the eyes); (*b*) *A:* straddling (of the legs).

écarquiller [ekarkije], *v.tr.* (*a*) **é. les yeux,** to open the eyes wide; to stare; **regarder qch. les yeux écarquillés de surprise, en écarquillant les yeux,** to look at sth. in open-eyed surprise; to gaze open-eyed at sth.; (*b*) *A:* to straddle, spread out (the legs).

écart[1] [ekaːr], *s.m.* **1.** motion, distance, apart; divergence; (*a*) *A:* **é. de cent francs entre deux comptes,** discrepancy of a hundred francs between two accounts; **é. entre deux essais,** divergence between two tests; **é. entre deux lectures (d'un appareil scientifique),** variation between two readings; **é. du plomb,** spreading, scattering, of small shot; *Av:* **grand é. de vitesse,** wide range of speeds; *Mch:* **é. du régulateur,** throw of the governor; *Ph: Ch: Mec:* **é. admissible,** tolerance; **é. absolu,** absolute deviation; **é. moyen,** mean deviation; **réduire l'é. entre . . .,** to reduce the margin, gap, between . . .; *Pol.Ec:* **l'é. entre les taux d'intérêt des deux pays,** the margin between the rate of interest (ruling) in the two countries; **é. entre les prix agricoles et les prix industriels,** disparity between agricultural and industrial price levels; **é. entre le prix de vente et le prix de revient,** margin between the cost price and the retail price; (*b*) separation, spreading out; straddling (of the legs); *Mus:* wide stretch (on piano); **faire le grand é.,** to do the splits; (*c*) *Vet:* **é. d'épaule,** shoulder strain (of horse, ox); (*of horse, etc.*) **se donner un é.,** to strain its shoulder. **2.** deviation; (*a*) deflection (of compass needle); *Geol:* **é. de la verticale,** hade; (*b*) *Artil: etc:* **é. en portée,** error in range; **é. en hauteur,** vertical error; **angle d'é. initial,** jump; (*c*) swerve, step(ping) aside; **faire un é.,** to step aside; (*of horse*) to shy; **le cheval fit un é.,** the horse shied; (*d*) **é. de l'imagination,** flight, freak, of the imagination, flight of fancy; **écarts de conduite,** delinquencies, wrong-doings; departures from accepted standards of conduct; **écarts de jeunesse,** errors of youth; **écarts de régime,** overeating; *Hum:* dietary indiscretions; (*e*) digression (in speech, etc.); (*f*) (*statistics*) **é. type, é. quadratique moyen,** standard, root-mean-square, deviation. **3.** remote spot; **la commune et ses écarts,** the parish and its dependencies. **4.** *adv.phr.* **à. l'é.,** aside, on one side, apart; **se tenir à l'é.,** to keep out of the way, in the background; **se tenir à l'é. des affaires publiques,** to hold aloof from, to keep out of, public life; **tenir qn à l'é.,** to keep s.o. in the background, out of the public view; **sa timidité le met à l'é. de la société,** his shyness keeps him out of society; **habiter à l'é.,** to live in a retired, lonely, spot; *A:* **mettre de l'argent à l'é.,** to put money by; **mettre à l'é. tout sentiment personnel,** to set aside, banish, any personal feeling; **prendre qn à l'é.,** to take s.o. aside; *F:* **mettre qn à l'é.,** to put s.o. in prison.

écart[2], *s.m. Cards:* **1.** discarding, throwing away. **2.** discarded cards, discard.

écart[3], *s.m. Her:* quarter (of shield).

écart[4], *s.m. Carp: Mec.E:* scarf, scarph; amount of lap (in joint); **assemblage à é.,** scarfing, scarf-joint; **é. simple,** plain scarf; **é. double,** hook-and-butt (joint); bird's mouth scarf; **é. à mi-bois,** box scarf; **é. à croc,** hook scarf; **é. à sifflet,** skew scarf, splayed joint.

écarté[1] [ekarte], *a.* **1.** isolated, lonely, unfrequented, secluded, remote (house, spot, etc.); **rue écartée,** back street, by-street; **chemin, sentier, é.,** by-lane, by-path; *Cr:* **balle écartée,** wide (ball). **2.** (far) apart; **se tenir les jambes écartées,** to stand astraddle, with one's feet (far) apart.

écarté[2], *s.m. Cards:* (game of) écarté.

écarte-lames [ekart(ə)lam], *s.m.inv. Aut:* leaf-spring opener.

écartelé [ekartəle], *a. Her:* quartered, quarterly; **é. en sautoir,** party per saltire.

écartèlement [ekartɛlmɑ̃], *s.m.* (*a*) quartering (of criminal); (*b*) *Her:* quartering (of shield); (*c*) *Wr:* splits; (*d*) **é. entre le bien et le mal,** struggle between good and evil.

écarteler [ekartəle], *v.tr.* (**j'écartèle, n. écartelons; j'écartèlerai**) (*a*) to quarter (criminal); (*b*) *Her:* to quarter (shield); (*c*) **être écartelé entre deux désirs contraires,** to be torn between two conflicting desires.

écartelure [ekartəlyːr], *s.f. Her:* quartering, quarter.

écartement [ekartəmɑ̃], *s.m.* **1.** (*a*) separation, spreading out, spacing; **pièce d'écartement,** spacer, distance piece; *Mch:* **angle d'é. (des boules du régulateur),** angle of deflection (of governor balls); (*b*) setting aside (of objects). **2.** space, distance apart, gap, clearance (between bars, etc.); **poteaux qui ont un é. de dix pieds,** stakes (spaced) ten feet apart; **é. de deux murs,** space between two walls; *El.E:* **é. des balais,** pitch of the brushes; *Rail:* **é. de voie,** gauge (of track); *Tex:* **é. des rouleaux (d'un banc à étirer),** reach (of a drawing-frame); *Veh:* **é. des essieux,** wheelbase; **é. des roues,** track, width between the wheels; *N.Arch:* **é. des membrures,** frame spacing; *I.C.E:* **régler l'é. des pointes, des électrodes d'une bougie,** to set a sparking-plug, to set the spark gap of a plug.

écarter[1] [ekarte], *v.tr.* **1.** to separate, part (two or more objects, the fingers, branches, etc.); to draw aside (curtains); to open (one's arms); to spread (one's legs); to square (one's elbows); **la tempête avait écarté les navires,** the storm had scattered, separated, the ships; **fusil qui écarte (le plomb),** gun that spreads the shot. **2.** (*a*) to move, thrust, (s.o., sth.) aside; **é. les cheveux de son front,** to push back, brush back, the hair from one's forehead; **é. un enfant du bord de l'eau,** to pull, keep, a child away from the water's edge; **é. violemment qch.,** to dash sth. aside, away; **é. qch. d'une poussée,** to push, shove, sth. aside; **é. les obstacles de son chemin,** to brush aside the obstacles in one's path; **é. un coup, un danger,** to ward off, avert, a blow, a danger; to turn (a blow) aside; **é. qn d'un geste,** to wave s.o. aside; **é. une proposition, une objection,** to brush aside, wave aside, set aside, rule out, dismiss, a proposal, an objection; **il écarta cette pensée,** he put the thought from him; **é. une réclamation, une candidature,** to turn down a claim, a candidature; **é. toute prévention,** to set aside, to dismiss, all prejudice; (*b*) **essayez d'é. les gens pendant que je lui parlerai,** try to keep people away while I talk to him. **3.** to divert (suspicion, etc.); **é. qn de la bonne voie,** to lead s.o. astray. **4.** *v.i.* to side-step (an attack); to dodge.

s'écarter. **1.** to move aside; **s'é. pour laisser passer qn,** to draw aside, step aside, stand aside, to allow s.o. to pass; to make way for s.o.; **écartez-vous de la grille,** stand away from, stand clear of, the gates; **s'é. brusquement,** to spring aside (de, from); *Nau:* **s'é. de la terre,** to bear off from the land. **2.** to move apart, diverge; (*of shot*) to spread; **routes qui s'écartent,** roads that diverge. **3.** to deviate, stray (de, from); **s'é. du chemin battu,** to go off the beaten track; **maison écartée du chemin,** house standing back from the road; **s'é. de l'original, du sujet,** to depart from the original (in copying); to depart, deviate, wander, from the subject; **ne vous écartez pas de la question,** speak to the point; **s'é. de son devoir,** to swerve, deviate, from one's duty; **s'é. des règles,** to depart from the rules.

écarter[2], *v.tr. Cards:* to discard.

écarteur [ekartœːr], *s.m.* **1.** *Mec.E: Tchn:* spacer; *Dent:* separator; *Surg:* retractor. **2.** dodger, baiter (of the cow in the cow-baiting displays of the Landes region).

écarver [ekarve], *v.tr.* to scarf (two timbers).

écaudé [ekode], *a. Z:* ecaudate, tailless.

ecballium [ɛkbaljɔm], *s.m. Bot:* ecballium, squirting cucumber.

Ecbatane [ɛkbatan], *Pr.n.f. A.Geog:* Ecbatana.

ecce homo [ɛkeɔmo, ɛkseɔmo], *s.m. Art:* ecce homo.

eccéité [ekseite], *s.f. Phil:* haecceity, thisness.

ecchondrome [ek(k)ɔ̃drɔm], *s.m.*, **ecchondrose** [ek(k)ɔ̃droːz], *s.f. Path:* ecchondrosis, ecchondroma.

ecchymose [ek(k)imoːz], *s.f.* bruise; *Med:* ecchymosis.

ecchymosé [ek(k)imoze], *a.* bruised; *Med:* ecchymosed (tissue, etc.).

ecchymotique [ek(k)imɔtik], *a. Med:* ecchymotic.

ecclésia [eklezja], *s.f. Gr.Ant:* ecclesia.

ecclésial, -aux [eklezjal, -o], *a.* belonging to, connected with, the church; **biens ecclésiaux,** church property.

Ecclésiaste (l') [leklezjast], *s.m. B:* **1.** (the book of) Ecclesiastes. **2.** The Preacher.

ecclésiastique [eklezjastik]. **1.** *a.* ecclesiastical; **chapeau, costume, e.,** clerical hat, dress. **2.** *s.m.* (*a*) ecclesiastic, clergyman; (*b*) *B.Lit:* **l'E.,** Ecclesiasticus.

ecclésiastiquement [eklezjastikmɑ̃], *adv.* ecclesiastically.

ecclésiologie [eklezjɔlɔʒi], *s.f.* ecclesiology.

eccyclème [eksiklɛm], *s.m. A.Gr.Th:* eccyclema.

ecdémite [ekdemit], *s.f. Miner:* ecdemite.

ecdysis [ekdisis], *s.f. Z:* ecdysis.

écéper [esepe], *v.tr.* (**j'écèpe, n. écépons; j'écéperai**) **écepper** [esɛpe], *v.tr. Vit:* to uproot (vine stocks).

écervelé, -ée [esɛrvəle]. **1.** *a.* thoughtless; flighty; harebrained, scatterbrained. **2.** *s.* harum-scarum, scatterbrain.

ecgonine [ekgɔnin], *s.f. Ch:* ecgonin(e).

échafaud [eʃafo], *s.m.* **1.** scaffolding, staging, stand, platform (for workmen, spectators, etc.); *Civ.E:* **é. volant,** hanging stage, travelling cradle. **2.** scaffold; **monter sur l'é., à l'é.,** to go to the scaffold, to mount the scaffold; **crime qui mérite l'é.,** crime that deserves the gallows.

échafaudage [eʃafoda:ʒ], *s.m. Const:* **1.** (*a*) erection of scaffolding; (*b*) building up (of new social order, etc.). **2.** scaffolding; *Civ.E:* **é. volant,** hanging stage, travelling cradle; **tout l'é. d'arguments,** the whole structure, fabric, of argument.

échafauder [eʃafode]. **1.** *v.i.* to erect (a) scaffolding. **2.** *v.tr.* to pile up (objects one on top of another); to build up, construct (system, argument, plan); to compile (book); **é. une hypothèse,** to work out a hypothesis.

échalas [eʃala], *s.m.* **1.** *Agr:* (*a*) cane, prop, stake (to support plant); (*b*) vine prop; (*c*) hope pole. **2.** *F:* (*a*) long, thin leg, *pl.* spindle shanks; (*b*) tall, thin person; bean-pole.

échalassage [eʃalasa:ʒ], *s.m.*, **échalassement** [eʃalasmɑ̃], *s.m. Agr:* propping, staking (of vine, etc.).

échalasser [eʃalase], *v.tr.* to prop, stake (vine, etc.).

échal(l)ier [eʃalje], *s.m.*, **échalis** [eʃali], *s.m.* **1.** (wooden) fence, barrier (closing gap). **2.** stile.

échalote [eʃalɔt], *s.f. Bot:* shallot; **é. d'Espagne,** rocambole.

échamp [eʃɑ̃], *s.m.* space between two rows of vines.

échampelée [eʃɑ̃ple], *a.f.* **vigne é.,** vine the buds of which have not formed before the hot season.

échampir [eʃɑ̃pi:r], *v.tr. Paint:* to pick out, set off (design on panelling, etc.).

échamplure [eʃɑ̃ply:r], *s.f.* retarding of the formation of vine buds due to excessive cold.

échancrer [eʃɑ̃kre], *v.tr.* to make a circular, a V-shaped, cut in (neck of dress, etc.); to indent, notch, gap (plank, etc.); to channel (table of machine-tool); **mouchoir échancré,** scalloped handkerchief; **la mer échancre le littoral,** the sea eats into the coastline; **littoral échancré,** indented coastline; **robe trop échancrée,** dress cut too low (at the neck); *Mec.E:* **bâti échancré,** (i) swept-out, (ii) in-cut, frame.

échancrure [eʃɑ̃kry:r], *s.f.* (*a*) cut-out part, opening (in garment); notch, cut, nick (in piece of wood, etc.); indentation (in coastline, etc.); groove, channel; *Nau:* roach (in sail); *Sm.a:* aiming aperture; *Surv:* re-entrant; (*b*) *Anat:* notch; **é. sciatique,** sciatic notch.

échandole [eʃɑ̃dɔl], *s.f. Const:* (roofing) shingle.

échange [eʃɑ̃:ʒ], *s.m.* (*a*) exchange (of prisoners, ideas, greetings, vows, etc.); **faire un é. de qch. pour, contre, qch.,** to exchange sth. for sth.; **ils avaient fait un é. de chapeaux,** they had changed hats; **é. de vues,** exchange of views; symposium; **recevoir qch. en é. de qch.,** to receive sth. in exchange, in return, for sth.; *F:* **si nous faisions un é.?** shall we swap? *Mec.E:* **roue d'é.,** bevel wheel, *esp.* mitre wheel; *Aut: etc:* **é. standard,** (replacement by) reconditioned spare (part); (*b*) *Com: Pol.Ec:* exchange; barter; **valeur d'é.,** exchange value; **taux de l'é.,** rate of exchange; *s.a.* LIBRE-ÉCHANGE; (*c*) *Bot:* **échanges gazeux,** gaseous interchange; (*d*) *Ph: etc:* exchange, transfer; **é. chimique,** chemical exchange; **é. thermique,** heat transfer; **réaction d'é.,** exchange reaction.

échangeabilité [eʃɑ̃ʒabilite], *s.f.* exchangeability.

échangeable [eʃɑ̃ʒabl], *a.* exchangeable.

échanger [eʃɑ̃ʒe], *v.tr.* (**j'échangeai(s); n. échangeons**) to exchange (information, etc.); to interchange; *Com:* to exchange; to barter; **é. des salutations, des idées, avec qn,** to exchange greetings, ideas, with s.o.; **é. ses impressions,** *F:* to compare notes; **é. qch. pour, contre, qch.,** to exchange, barter, *F:* swap, sth. for sth.; **il y eut quelques coups d'échangés,** there was an exchange of blows; **nous avions échangé quelques lettres,** there had been some correspondence between us; **nous échangeons des timbres,** we exchange (postage) stamps.

échangeur, -euse [eʃɑ̃ʒœ:r, -ø:z]. **1.** *s. Fin: Com: A:* exchanger; barterer. **2.** *s.m. Ch: Ph:* exchanger; **é. de chaleur, thermique, de température,** heat exchanger. **3.** *s.m. Civ.E:* (*on motorway*) clover leaf (intersection).

échangiste [eʃɑ̃ʒist], *s.m. Fin: etc:* exchanger; *s.a.* LIBRE-ÉCHANGISTE.

échanson [eʃɑ̃sɔ̃], *s.m. Hist:* cup-bearer.

échantignole [eʃɑ̃tiɲɔl], *s.f. Const:* cleat (of roof purlin, etc.); bracket.

échantillon [eʃɑ̃tijɔ̃], *s.m.* **1.** *Tchn:* (*a*) *Carp: E: etc:* templet; (*b*) *Com: A:* **é. de taille,** creditor's half of tally; (*c*) *Const:* **brique, tuile, etc., d'é.,** brick, tile, etc., of regulation pattern, of standard dimensions; **bois d'é.,** dimension timber; standard wood; **ardoise d'é.,** sized slate; (*d*) *N.Arch:* scantling; **é. sur le droit,** siding; (*e*) *Metall:* modelling board, loam-board. **2.** (*a*) sample (of wine, etc.); sample, pattern (of cloth, silk, etc.); specimen (of one's work, etc.); **prendre des échantillons de . . .,** to sample . . .; **prise, prélèvement, d'échantillons,** sampling; **boîte é. de . . .,** sample box of . . .; **livre d'échantillons,** pattern book; **conforme, pareil, à l'é.,** up to sample; **é. choisi,** picked sample; **é. type,** representative sample; **é. représentatif,** true, fair, sample, *Post:* **échantillons sans valeur,** sample post, samples of no (commercial) value; *Min:* **é. carotté,** core sample; *Petroleum Ind:* **é. de dosage,** oil thief; **un é. de son éloquence,** a sample, a taste, of his eloquence; *F:* **juger de la pièce par l'é.,** to judge the whole by the part; (*b*) *Pol.Ec:* population sample (for Gallup poll, etc.). **3.** *Const:* bare (of a slate).

échantillonnage [eʃɑ̃tijɔna:ʒ], *s.m.* **1.** (*a*) *Com:* making up of samples (of wine, etc.), of patterns (of cloth, etc.); (*b*) range (of goods, etc.); (*c*) *Min:* sampling; **é. du minerai,** quartering; **é. latéral des formations,** side-wall coring; **é. répété,** resampling. **2.** (*a*) verifying, checking, by the samples; (*b*) *A:* gauging by the templet. **3.** *N.Arch:* scantling. **4.** choice, selection (of people, etc., for Gallup poll, etc.).

échantillonner [eʃɑ̃tijɔne], *v.tr.* **1.** (*a*) *Com:* to prepare patterns, samples, of (sth.); **é. des vins,** to make up wine into samples; **é. du drap,** to cut up cloth into patterns; (*b*) *Min:* to take a core sample of. **2.** (*a*) to verify, check, (articles) by the samples; (*b*) *A:* to gauge (article) by the templet; (*c*) to sample (wine, etc.). **3.** to make (articles) according to sample. **4.** *Leath:* **é. des peaux,** to trim skins (to make them more regular in shape). **5.** to sample the population (for Gallup poll, etc.).

échantillonneur, -euse [eʃɑ̃tijɔnœ:r, -ø:z], (*a*) *s.* (*pers.*) sampler; person collecting statistics (for Gallup poll, etc.); (*b*) *s.m.* (*device*) sampler.

échanvrer [eʃɑ̃vre], *v.tr. Tex:* to hatchel, hackle (hemp).

échanvroir [eʃɑ̃vrwa:r], *s.m. Tex:* hemp comb, hackle.

échappade [eʃapad], *s.f.* **1.** *A:* (*a*) escape; (*b*) indiscreet word; sally of wit; *adv.phr.* **en é.,** secretly, stealthily. **2.** *Engr:* slip (of the burin).

échappatoire [eʃapatwa:r]. **1.** *s.f.* subterfuge, way out, means of evasion, loophole (of escape from obligation, etc.); **chercher des échappatoires,** (i) to hedge; (ii) to try to find excuses (in order not to do sth.). **2.** *s.f. Motor Rac:* escape way. **3.** *a.* **clause é.,** escape clause.

échappé, -ée[1] [eʃape]. **1.** *a.* escaped, runaway, fugitive; **cheval é.,** runaway horse. **2.** *s. A:* escaped person, runaway, escapee; *F:* **é. de Charenton,** crack-brained fellow; loony. **3.** *s.m. Danc:* échappé.

échappée[2], *s.f.* **1.** (*a*) escape (of cattle into field, etc.); *adv.phr.* **à l'é.,** secretly, stealthily; (*b*) (i) *Sp:* sudden spurt (in race); (ii) break-away; get-away; (*c*) escapade. **2.** space, interval; **é. de vue,** vista (sur, over); glimpse (of), peep (at); **une courte é. de clair de lune fit apparaître une voile,** the moon appeared for a moment and we saw a sail; **par une é. des arbres,** through an opening in the trees; **é. de ciel,** patch of sky; **é. de soleil,** sunburst; **é. de beau temps,** spell of fine weather; **faire qch. par échappées,** to do sth. by fits and starts, by snatches. **3.** (*a*) turning space (for vehicles); (*b*) head-room, head-way (in passage, etc.); (*c*) passage (between houses, etc.). **4.** *N.Arch:* run (of ship's bottom).

échappement [eʃapmɑ̃], *s.m.* **1.** escape, leakage (of gas, water). **2.** *Mch:* (i) exhaust, release (of steam); eduction; (ii) exhaust stroke; **tuyau d'é.,** (i) waste-steam pipe; (ii) *I.C.E:* exhaust (pipe); **machine à é. libre,** non-condensing engine; *Mch:* **soupape d'é.,** exhaust valve; *I.C.E:* **pot d'é.,** silencer; *N.Am:* muffler; **(soupape d')é. libre,** cut-out (to silencer); **collecteur d'é.,** exhaust manifold; **chaleur d'é.,** exhaust heat; **gaz d'é.,** exhaust fumes; **clapet d'é.,** exhaust cut-out; **orifice d'é.,** exhaust port; **tuyère d'é.,** exhaust duct; (*in jet engine*) **aubages fixes guides d'é.,** exhaust stator blades. **3.** (*a*) *Clockm:* escapement; **montre à é.,** lever watch; **é. à repos,** dead-beat escapement; (*b*) hopper (of piano). **4.** = ÉCHAPPÉE 3.

échapper [eʃape], *v.i.* (*the aux. is* **être** *or* **avoir**) to escape. **1.** (*a*) **é. à qn, à qch.,** to escape s.o., sth.; **é. à la prison,** to escape imprisonment; **é. à la poursuite,** to elude, baffle, pursuit; **é. à la potence,** to cheat the gallows; **é. à ses gardiens,** to escape from one's warders; **le prisonnier nous a échappé,** the prisoner got away (from us), showed a clean pair of heels; **il n'y a pas moyen d'y é.,** there is no escaping it, no escape from it; **ce fait a, est, échappé à mon attention, ce fait m'a échappé,** this fact escaped my attention, I had overlooked this fact; **il n'a échappé à personne que . . .,** it will not have escaped the notice of anyone that . . .; **pas un mot ne lui a échappé,** he did not miss a single word; **ce propos m'a échappé,** I failed to hear this remark, I lost that remark; **il est vrai que ce propos m'est échappé,** it is true that I let this remark slip out; **la vérité lui échappe parfois,** he sometimes blurts out the truth; **son nom m'échappe,** I can't remember his name; **le mot propre m'échappe,** I can't think of the right word; **é. aux vues de l'ennemi,** to be out of sight of the enemy; **sa gestion échappe à tout contrôle,** there is no possible check on his administration; **é. à toute définition,** to defy definition; **la patience échappe à la longue,** patience gives out in the end; (*b*) (*the aux. is* **avoir**) to dodge (sth.); **é. à un coup,** to dodge a blow; **on n'échappe pas aux conséquences de ses fautes,** your sins will find you out; *F:* **vous l'avez échappé belle,** you've had a narrow escape, a narrow squeak, a close shave; **é. comme par miracle,** to have a miraculous escape; (*c*) **laisser échapper qn, qch.,** to let s.o., sth., escape; to set s.o. free; **laisser é. l'air d'un ballon,** to let out the air from a balloon; **laisser é. la vapeur,** to let off steam; to blow off; **laisser é. sa colère, un soupir,** to give vent to one's anger, to let out a sigh; **laisser é. une larme,** to let fall a tear; **laisser é. un secret,** to let out a secret, to let the cat out of the bag; **laisser é. la vérité,** to blurt out the truth; **laisser é. sa plume,** to let one's pen slip from one's fingers; **laisser é. l'occasion, le moment favorable,** to let the opportunity slip; to miss the opportunity; **laisser é. une faute,** to overlook, pass over, a mistake; (*d*) *A: impers.* **il lui échappa de la tutoyer,** he forgot himself and called her "**tu.**" **2. é. de qch.,** to escape from, out of, sth.; **é. de prison,** to escape, make one's escape, from prison; **la plume m'est échappée des mains,** the pen slipped from my fingers; **il, cela, m'est échappé des doigts,** he, it, slipped through my fingers; **é. d'une maladie, d'un naufrage,** to survive an illness, a shipwreck; **é. d'une tempête,** to weather a storm; **é. du carnage,** to escape the general slaughter.

s'échapper, to escape; to break free, loose. **1. s'é. de prison,** to break prison; **échappez-vous!** run! *F:* scram! beat it! **faire é. qn,** to help s.o. to escape; *F:* **il faut que je m'échappe,** I must be off, I must hurry away. **2. le gaz qui (s')échappe des conduites,** the gas escaping, leaking, from the mains; **voir (s')é. son dernier espoir,** to see one's last hope vanish(ing); **un cri s'échappa de ses lèvres,** a cry burst from his lips; **une larme s'échappa de ses yeux,** a tear stole down her cheek, a tear escaped her. **3.** to break out; *Mch:* (*of steam*) to blow off; **sa douleur s'échappe en reproches,** his grief finds expression in reproaches; **l'âne s'échappa en une ruade,** the donkey let fly with this heels. **4.** *A:* **s'é. jusqu'à faire qch.,** to forget oneself so far as to do sth.

écharbot [eʃarbo], *s.m. Bot:* water-caltrops.

écharde[1] [eʃard], *s.f.* prickle, splinter, thorn, that has lodged under the skin, nail.

écharde[2], *s.f. Ich: F:* stickleback.

échardonnage [eʃardɔna:ʒ], *s.m.* **1.** *Agr:* clearing (ground) of thistles. **2.** *Tex:* (wool) picking.

échardonner [eʃardɔne], *v.tr.* **1.** *Agr:* to clear (ground) of thistles. **2.** *Tex:* to pick (wool).

échardonnet [eʃardɔnɛ], *s.m.*, **échardonnette** [eʃardɔnɛt], *s.f. Agr:* thistle hook, weed hook.

échardonneur, -euse [eʃardɔnœ:r, -ø:z], *s. Tex:* **1.** *A:* (*pers.*) burr picker. **2.** *s.f.* **échardonneuse,** burr-picking machine.

échardonnoir [eʃardɔnwa:r], *s.m. Agr:* thistle hook, weed hook.

écharnage [eʃarna:ʒ], **écharnement** [eʃarn(ə)mɑ̃], *s.m. Leath:* fleshing, scraping (of hides).

écharner [eʃarne], *v.tr. Leath:* to flesh, scrape, whiten (hides).

écharneur [eʃarnœ:r], *s.m. Leath:* (*pers.*) flesher.

écharneuse [eʃarnø:z], *s.f. Leath:* fleshing machine, whitening machine.

écharnoir [eʃarnwa:r], *s.m. Leath:* fleshing knife.

écharnure [eʃarny:r], *s.f. Leath:* **1.** dressing, fleshing (of hide). **2.** *pl.* hide-parings, scrapings.

écharpage [eʃarpa:ʒ], *s.m. Tex: A:* scribbling, carding (of wool).

écharpe [eʃarp], *s.f.* **1.** (*a*) shoulder sash, (municipal) sash worn round the waist; **porter une é. en bandoulière,** to wear a sash over the shoulder; *A:* **é. de chevalier,** knight's colours; *A:* **changer d'é.,** to change one's allegiance; *Poet:* **é. d'Iris,** rainbow; (*b*) *Cost:* (lady's) scarf; **é. de soie,** silk

scarf; **é. de fourrure,** fur stole; (*c*) *Surg:* arm sling; **porter le bras en é.,** to carry one's arm in a sling; (*d*) *adv.phr.* **en é.,** slantwise, aslant; *Mil:* **tirer en é.,** to fire obliquely; **tir d'é.,** oblique fire; **prendre d'é.,** to take obliquely; to attack from an oblique angle; **prendre en é.,** to sideswipe; **les deux trains se sont pris en é.,** the trains collided at the points; *Tchn:* **moise en é.,** diagonal brace, tie. **2.** *Tchn:* (*a*) **é. d'une grue,** jib of a crane; (*b*) body of pulley block; *pl.* sheaves and cordage; (*c*) (hoisting) sling.

écharpement[1] [eʃarp(ə)mɑ̃], *s.m.* = ÉCHARPAGE.

écharpement[2], *s.m. Mil:* diagonal march.

écharper[1] [eʃarpe], *v.tr.* **1.** *Tex: A:* to scribble, scrabble, card (wool). **2.** (*a*) to slash, gash, hack; **s'é. la joue en se rasant,** to gash one's cheek while shaving; (*b*) to hack (up) (fowl); to cut (troops) to pieces; to cut up (troops, etc.); **le chirurgien l'a écharpé,** he was hacked up by the surgeon; **vous allez vous faire é.!** they'll tear you to pieces!

écharper[2]. **1.** *v.tr.* (*a*) to decorate (s.o.) with a sash (as sign of office); (*b*) to pass a sling round (heavy object). **2.** *v.i. Mil:* to march diagonally.

écharpiller [eʃarpije], *v.tr.* **1.** *Tex: A:* to scribble, card (wool). **2.** *F:* to hack to pieces.

échars [eʃaːr], *Num: A:* (*a*) *a.* under weight, light; (*b*) *s.m.* **un louis qui a un dixième d'é.,** a louis that is ten per cent under weight.

écharser [eʃarse], *A:* **écharseter** [eʃarste], *v.tr. Num:* to mint underweight, to debase (coinage).

écharseté [eʃarste], *s.f. Num:* debasement (of coinage).

échasse [eʃɑs], *s.f.* **1.** stilt; **marcher, être monté, sur des échasses,** (i) to be on stilts; (ii) to be stilted, pompous; to ride the high horse; (iii) *F:* to be long in the leg. **2. é. d'échafaud,** scaffolding-pole. **3.** *Orn:* stilt; **é. blanche,** black-winged stilt.

échassier [eʃasje], *s.m.* **1.** *Orn:* wader, stilt-bird, grallatory bird; **échassiers,** Grallatores. **2.** *F:* lanky-legs, spindle-shanks.

échau, -aux [eʃo], *s.m.* channel, runnel, drain (in field).

échauboulé [eʃobule], *a. A:* pimply (face, etc.).

échauboulure [eʃobulyːr], *s.f. A:* (*a*) pimple, pustule; (*b*) *Vet:* (bovine) urticaria.

échaudage[1] [eʃodaːʒ], *s.m.* **1.** scalding. **2.** *Agr:* shrivelling (of cereals by sun).

échaudage[2], *s.m.* **1.** whitewashing, lime-washing. **2.** whitewash, lime-wash.

échaudé [eʃode]. **1.** *a.* (*a*) scalded; *s.a.* CHAT 1; (*b*) *Agr:* **blé é.,** wheat shrivelled by the sun. **2.** *s.m.* (*a*) *Cu: A:* canary-bread; (*b*) *A:* (i) triangular flower-bed; (ii) triangular block of houses; (iii) intersection of three roads, *Dial:* three-went-way; (iv) folding-stool.

échaudement [eʃod(ə)mɑ̃], *s.m. Agr:* shrivelling (of wheat by the sun).

échauder[1] [eʃode], *v.tr.* to scald; *Tex:* to scour (wool); **s'é. le pied,** to scald one's foot; **é. une marmite,** to scald a saucepan; *F:* **se faire é. dans une affaire,** to burn one's fingers over sth.; **je me suis fait é.,** I've been fleeced; I've been had.

échauder[2], *v.tr.* to whitewash, lime-wash.

échaudi(s) [eʃodi], *s.m. Nau:* lashing triangle, span shackle.

échaudoir [eʃodwaːr], *s.m.* **1.** (*in slaughterhouse*) (*a*) scalding room; (*b*) scalding tub. **2.** *Tex:* (*a*) scouring room; (*b*) scouring vat (for wool).

échaudure [eʃodyːr], *s.f.* scald.

échauffant [eʃofɑ̃], *a.* **1.** (*a*) heating (food, etc.); (*b*) causing constipation; binding (food). **2.** exciting (discussion, etc.).

échauffe [eʃoːf], *s.f. Tan:* (*a*) sweat, sweating; (*b*) sweating room.

échauffé [eʃofe]. **1.** *a.* (*a*) overheated (room, blood, etc.); hot (bearings); (*b*) fermented, heated (corn, hay, etc.). **2.** *s.m.* close smell (caused by fermentation, by excessive heat).

échauffement [eʃofmɑ̃], *s.m.* **1.** (*a*) heating (of soil, *Mec:* of bearings, etc.); overheating (of engine, etc.); (*b*) chafing (of rope); (*c*) *Petroleum Ind:* **essai d'é. sulfurique,** acid heat test; (*d*) (over) excitement; **dans l'é. de sa jeunesse,** in the heat of (his) youth; **les échauffements de la colère,** the heat of anger. **2.** (*a*) *Med: F: A:* (i) overheating (of the body); (ii) inflammation; (iii) constipation; (iv) (mild) blennorrhagia; (*b*) *Vet:* **é. de la fourchette,** thrush (in horses). **3.** (= *fermentation*) heating (of cereals, hay, wood, etc.).

échauffer [eʃofe], *v.tr.* **1.** (*a*) *A:* to warm; to warm up; **les oiseaux échauffent leurs petits sous leurs ailes,** birds keep their young warm under their wings; (*b*) to overheat (room, blood, body, etc.); **frottement qui échauffe les roues,** friction that overheats the wheels; **é. l'imagination de qn,** to fire, excite, s.o.'s imagination; **é. la bile, la tête, les oreilles, de qn,** to anger s.o.; to provoke s.o.; to rub s.o. up the wrong way; (*c*) *F: A:* to give (s.o.) constipation, to constipate (s.o.); (*d*) *Ven:* **é. la voie,** to follow hot on the scent. **2.** to cause fermentation in, to heat (cereals, hay, etc.).

s'échauffer. **1.** (*a*) to become, get, overheated; **je me suis échauffé à marcher,** I got hot, warm, walking; **ne vous échauffez pas,** (i) don't over-heat yourself; (ii) don't get excited; **la dispute s'échauffait,** feeling began to run high, words were running high; (*b*) *F:* to get all hot and bothered; (*c*) to warm (up); **il ne s'échauffe pas facilement,** he does not warm up easily; **le conférencier s'échauffait par degrés,** the lecturer was warming to his subject; *Sp:* **le joueur s'échauffait avant la partie,** the player warmed up before the game; **la partie s'échauffait,** the game was warming up. **2.** (*a*) (*of engine*) to run hot; (*of bearings*) to heat; (*b*) (*of rope*) to chafe.

échauffourée [eʃofure], *s.f.* (*a*) *A:* rash, abortive, enterprise; (*b*) *Mil:* affray, brush, scrap; (*c*) scuffle; clash (between mobs); (*d*) *Chess:* rash (and disastrous) move.

échauffure [eʃofyːr], *s.f.* **1.** *A: Med:* heat rash. **2.** *For:* stain (in felled timber). **3.** *Agr:* slight fermentation (of cereals, etc.).

échauguette [eʃogɛt], *s.f. Fort:* watch tower (on wall); échauguette, bartizan.

échaume [eʃoːm], *s.m. Nau:* thole pin.

échaumer [eʃome], *v.tr. Agr:* to clear stubble from (field).

èche [ɛʃ], *s.f. Fish:* bait.

échéable [eʃeabl̩], *a. Fin:* falling due, payable, matured.

échéance [eʃeɑ̃ːs], *s.f.* **1.** date (of payment, of maturity); term, falling due (of bill), date-line; **venir à é.,** to fall due; **payable à l'é.,** payable at maturity; **à longue, courte, é.,** long-, short-, range; **billet à longue é., à courte é.,** long-dated, short-dated, bill; *Fin:* **prêter à longue é.,** to lend long; **emprunter à courte é.,** to borrow short; **résultats à longue é.,** results long of fruition, deferred results; **une politique à longue é.,** a long-term policy; **à brève é.,** shortly; **faire face à une é.,** to meet a bill; **demander une prolongation d'é.,** to ask for an extension of time; **l'intérêt n'a pas été payé à l'é.,** the interest is overdue; **é. à vue,** bill at sight; **à trois mois d'é.,** at three months' date; **é. moyenne,** average due date; **carnet d'é.,** bill book. **2.** expiration (of tenancy, etc.). **3. é. fatale,** death.

échéancier [eʃeɑ̃sje], *s.m. Fin:* bills-receivable book or bills-payable book; *F:* bill book.

échéant [eʃeɑ̃]. **1.** *a. Fin:* falling due. **2.** *adv.phr.* **le cas é.,** should the occasion arise; if necessary; in case of need.

échec [eʃɛk], *s.m.* **1.** (*a*) (*at chess*) check; **é. et mat,** checkmate; **faire (le roi) é. et mat en trois coups,** to checkmate the king in three moves; to mate in three; **é. à la découverte,** discovered check; **en é.,** (i) in check; (ii) (*of army, etc.*) stopped, unable to advance; **tenir l'ennemi en é.,** to keep the enemy at bay, to hold the enemy in check; **tenir un projet en é.,** to thwart, frustrate, a project; (*b*) check, failure, defeat; setback; **essuyer, subir, un é.,** to meet with a check, with a repulse; **vous courez à un é., vous allez au-devant d'un é.,** you are courting failure, disaster; **faire é. à (qch.),** to put a check on, to check (activities, etc.); **faire é., donner (un) é., à qn,** to checkmate s.o., to frustrate s.o.'s plans. **2.** *pl.* (*a*) chess; **faire une partie d'échecs** [eʃɛk], to play a game of chess; (*b*) chessmen.

échelette [eʃlɛt], *s.f.* **1.** (*a*) *A: & Dial:* small ladder (fastened to pack-saddle of mule, etc. for carrying load); (*b*) rack, rail (of cart). **2.** *Orn:* wall creeper.

échelier [eʃəlje], *s.m.* peg ladder.

échelle [eʃɛl], *s.f.* **1.** (*a*) ladder; **é. d'incendie, é. de sauvetage,** fire escape; **é. brisée,** folding steps; **é. de corde,** rope ladder; **é. à coulisse,** extension ladder; **é. à crochet,** (fireman's) hook ladder; *Mil: A:* **é. de siège,** scaling ladder; *Nau:* **é. de commandement, d'honneur,** companion ladder; **é. de commandement, de coupée,** accommodation ladder, side ladder; **é. de coupée, de côté,** gangway ladder; **é. de dunette,** quarter ladder; **é. de passerelle,** bridge ladder; **é. de poupe,** stern ladder; **é. de revers,** Jacob's ladder; **é. de débarquement,** landing steps (of jetty); **faire la courte é. à qn,** to give s.o. (i) a leg up, (ii) a helping hand; **monter à l'é.,** (i) to go up a ladder; (ii) *F:* to flare up, to lose one's temper; (iii) *F:* to be taken in, had; *F:* **ce n'est pas vrai, vous voulez me faire monter à l'é.,** it's not true; you're trying to have me on; **après cela, lui, il faut, il n'y a plus qu'à tirer l'é.,** (i) after that, after what he has done, there's no point in trying any further; it's impossible to do better than that, him; (ii) *Pej:* that's, he's, the limit; *Iron:* **si vous ne savez même pas ça il n'y a plus qu'à tirer l'é.,** if you don't even know that we'd better give up, it's no use going on any further; (*b*) **é. à poissons,** fish ladder; salmon leap; (*c*) *Gym:* **é. suédoise,** rib stall; (*d*) **é. de Jacob,** (i) *B.Hist:* Jacob's ladder; (ii) *Bot:* Jacob's ladder, Greek valerian; (*e*) run, ladder (in stocking). **2.** (*a*) **l'é. sociale,** the social scale; **être au haut, au sommet, de l'é.,** to be at the top of the tree, the ladder; (*b*) *Mus:* **é. diatonique, chromatique, harmonique,** diatonic, chromatic, harmonic, scale; (*c*) **é. des couleurs,** scale of colours; **é. des valeurs,** scale of values; *Pol.Ec:* **é. des salaires, des traitements, des prix,** scale of wages, salaries, prices; **é. mobile,** (i) sliding scale (of prices, etc.); (ii) escalator clause; (*d*) *Mec.E:* **é. de vitesse,** range of speed. **3.** (*a*) scale (of map, plan, etc.); **é. numérique,** representative fraction, R.F.; **carte à petite, à grande, é.,** small-scale, large-scale, map; **à é. réduite,** on a reduced scale; **dessiné à l'é. d'un centimètre pour un mètre,** drawn on, to, a scale of one centimetre to a metre; **é. linéaire,** linear scale; **é. des hauteurs,** vertical scale; (*b*) scale (of thermometer, barometer, etc.); *Phot:* **é. de mise au point,** focusing scale; *Nau:* **é. de tirant d'eau,** water marks, draft marks; *U.S:* immersion scale; *Meteor:* **é. de visibilité,** visibility scale; **é. de Beaufort,** Beaufort scale (of winds); *Oc:* **é. de marée,** tide gauge; *Rail: etc:* **é. de jauge,** tonnage scale; (*c*) **travailler, faire les choses, sur une grande é.,** to work, do things, on a large scale; **ce projet est irréalisable à une si petite é.,** this project is unworkable, cannot be carried out, on such a small scale; **ce problème se pose à l'é. nationale,** this problem must be considered on a nation-wide basis; this problem exists on a national scale. **4.** *A:* (*esp. in the Middle East*) port; **faire é.,** to put into port; *Hist:* **les échelles du Levant,** the (commercial) ports of the Levant.

échelle-observatoire [eʃɛlɔpsɛrvatwaːr], *s.f. Mil:* observation ladder, field observatory; *pl.* *échelles-observatoires.*

échellier [eʃɛlje], *s.m. Bank: St.Exch:* dealer in arbitrage transactions.

échelon [eʃlɔ̃], *s.m.* **1.** (*a*) rung, round (of ladder); (*b*) grade, echelon; level; **le premier é. de ma fortune,** the first step, stage, in my fortune; **monter par échelons,** to rise by degrees, by successive stages; **les échelons de l'administration,** the grades of the civil service; **à l'é. ministériel,** at ministerial level; **à l'é. national,** on a national, countrywide, basis; *Mus:* **é. de la gamme,** degree of the scale. **2.** *Mil:* (*a*) echelon (formation); **é. de combat,** fighting echelon; **unité de premier é.,** leading unit, forward unit; **unité de deuxième é.,** support unit; **en deuxième é.,** in support; **é. de sûreté, é. de surveillance,** security, surveillance, echelon; *Mil.Av:* **en é. vers le haut, vers le bas,** stepped-up, stepped-down, formation; (*b*) column of supply; *Artil:* **é. de combat,** first-line ammunition transport, battery wagon line; (*c*) **échelon (de la hiérarchie),** grade, level; **é. de commandement,** command echelon; command level; headquarters; **à l'é. division, à l'é. corps d'armée,** at division, at corps, level; **les échelons supérieurs,** upper levels, higher grades; (*d*) **évacuation par échelons,** phased withdrawal. **3.** *adv.phr.* **en é.;** (*a*) *Mil:* in echelon, in stepped formation; *Mil: Av:* **vol en é.,** stepped-up formation; (*b*) *Mec.E:* stepped (gearing, etc.).

échelonnage [eʃlɔnaːʒ], *s.m.* staggering (of holidays).

échelonnement [eʃlɔnmɑ̃], *s.m.* **1.** *Mil:* (i) echelonment, echeloning; disposition (of troops) in echelon; staggering; (ii) spacing out, echelonment (of depots, installations, etc.); **é. en profondeur,** echelonment in depth. **2.** (*a*) spreading out (of payments); (*b*) staggering (of holidays). **3.** *El.E:* staggering (of brushes).

échelonner [eʃlɔne], *v.tr.* **1.** *Mil:* to dispose (troops, supply depots) in echelon; to dispose (troops) in depth; to echelon. **2.** (*a*) to space out (objects); to place (objects) at intervals; (*b*) to spread out (payments, over a certain time); to stagger (holidays, etc.); **congés échelonnés,** staggered holidays; **versements échelonnés sur dix ans,** instalments spread over ten years; *Med:* **doses échelonnées,** graded doses; (*c*) to step (gears, etc.); (*d*) *El.E:* to stagger (brushes).

échenal, -aux [eʃnal, -o], **échenau, -aux** [eʃno], **écheneau, -eaux** [eʃno], **échenet** [eʃnɛ], *s.m.* **1.** *Const:* wooden gutter. **2.** *Metall:* gate-channel (of mould).

échenillage [eʃnija:ʒ], *s.m.* **1.** *Agr:* removal of caterpillars (fruit trees trees, etc.). **2.** *F:* clearing up, removing, of undesirable elements.

écheniller [eʃnije], *v.tr.* (*a*) *Agr:* to clear (fruit-trees, etc.) of caterpillars; (*b*) (i) to clean up; (ii) to polish (style, etc.); (iii) to remove undesirable elements from (society, etc.).

échenilleur [eʃnijœ:r], *s.m. Orn:* cuckoo shrike.

échenilloir [eʃnijwa:r], *s.m. Tls:* tree pruner (for removing caterpillar-infested branches, etc.); branch lopper, averruncator, pole pruner.

écheveau, -eaux [eʃ(ə)vo], *s.m.* (*a*) hank, skein (of yarn, etc.); (*b*) **é. de rues,** maze of streets; **embrouiller l'é.,** to obscure the issue; **démêler l'é. d'une intrigue,** to unravel the intricacies of a plot.

échevelé [eʃəvle], *a.* (*a*) dishevelled (hair, person); (person) with dishevelled hair, with tousled hair; (*b*) wild, disorderly (dance, etc.); breathless (style); (*c*) *Lit:* windswept (trees).

écheveler [eʃəv(ə)le], *v.tr.* (**j'échevelle, n. échevelons; j'échevellerai**) (*a*) to dishevel, disarrange, rumple (the hair); (*b*) **un grand vent échevelait les nuages,** a strong wind whipped up the clouds.

échevellement [eʃ(ə)vɛlmɑ̃], *s.m.* **1.** (*a*) dishevelling, untidying; (*b*) dishevelled state (of the hair). **2.** baldness.

écheveria [eʃvəria], *s.m. Bot:* echeveria.

échevetage [eʃ(ə)vəta:ʒ], **échevettage** [eʃ(ə)vɛta:ʒ], *s.m. Tex:* skeining.

échevette [eʃvɛt], *s.f. Tex:* rap, lea (*in Fr.,* 100 metres).

échevin [eʃvɛ̃], *s.m.* **1.** *A:* municipal magistrate. **2.** (*in Belgium*) = alderman.

échevinage [eʃvina:ʒ], *s.m. A:* function, period of office, of an *échevin*; territory administered by an *échevin*; body of *échevins.*

échicoter [eʃikɔte], *v.tr.* to remove the stumps of (branches, trees).

échidné [ekidne], *s.m. Z:* echidna; spiny porcupine, spiny anteater.

échidnisme [ekidnism], *s.m.* snake poisoning.

échif, -ive [eʃif, -i:v], *a. Ven: A:* voracious, ravenous (hound, etc.).

échiffe [eʃif], *s.m.*, **échiffre** [eʃifr], *s.m.* **1.** *Const:* string wall (of staircase). **2.** *A.Fort:* (wooden) watch tower (on city walls).

échignole [eʃiɲɔl], *s.f. Tex:* bobbin (for reeling silk).

échimyidés [ekimjide], *s.m.pl. Z:* Echimyidae.

échimys [ekimis], *s.m. Z:* echimys, spiny rat.

échinant [eʃinɑ̃], *a. P:* exhausting, back-breaking (work).

échine[1] [eʃin], *s.f.* **1.** spine, backbone; (*of animals*) chine; *F:* **crotté jusqu'à l'é.,** all over mud; *F:* **frotter l'é. à qn,** to thrash s.o., to beat s.o. up; to give s.o. a good hiding; **courber, plier, l'é.,** to yield, to give in; *F:* **courber l'é. devant qn,** to kowtow to s.o., to toady to s.o.; to lick s.o.'s boots; **avoir l'é. souple, flexible,** (i) to give way to others; to be a yes-man; (ii) to be obsequious, *F:* a boot-licker. **2.** *Cu:* loin (of pork).

échine[2], *s.f. Arch:* echinus, ovolo, quarter-round (of capital).

échinée [eʃine], *s.f. Cu:* chine, griskin (of pork).

échinement [eʃinmɑ̃], *s.m. A: F:* **1.** fagging, drudging. **2.** back-breaking work; fag.

échiner [eʃine], *v.tr. A:* **é. qn;** (*a*) to break s.o.'s back; (*b*) *F:* to beat s.o. within an inch of his life; (*c*) *F:* to tire s.o. out; (*d*) *F:* to slash, cut, to pieces (army, s.o.'s work, etc.).

s'échiner, *F:* to knock oneself up; to wear oneself out; to work oneself to death; **s'é. à (faire) qch.,** to slave at sth., to break one's back over sth., doing sth.

échineur [eʃinœ:r], *s.m. F:* slashing critic.

échinide [ekinid], *s.m.* (*a*) echinid, sea urchin; (*b*) *pl.* **échinides,** Echinidea, Echinoidea.

échinocactus [ekinɔkaktys], *s.m. Bot:* echinocactus, hedgehog cactus.

échinocaris [ekinɔkaris], *s.m. Paleont:* echinocaris.

échinocarpe [ekinɔkarp], *a. Bot:* echinocarpous.

échinocéréus [ekinɔsereys], *s.m. Bot:* echinocereus.

échinococcose [ekinɔkɔko:z], *s.f. Med:* echinococcosis.

échinocoque [ekinɔkɔk], *s.m. Ann: Med:* echinococcus.

échinocystis [ekinɔsistis], *s.m. Bot:* echinocystis.

échinoderme [ekinɔdɛrm]. **1.** *a.* echinodermatous. **2.** *s.m.* echinoderm; *pl.* **échinodermes,** Echinodermata.

échinoïde [ekinɔid], (*a*) *a. & s.m.* echinoid; (*b*) *s.m.pl.* **échinoïdes,** Echinoidea.

échinon [ekinɔ̃], *s.m.* (metal, wooden) cheese mould.

échinope [ekinɔp], *s.m.*, **échinops** [ekinɔps], *s.m. Bot:* echinops, globe-thistle.

échinorynque [ekinorɛ̃k], **échinorhynchus** [ekinorɛ̃kys], *s.m. Ann:* echinorhynchus.

échinulé [ekinyle], *a. Nat.Hist:* echinulate, prickly.

échinus [ekinys], *s.m. Echin:* echinus.

échiqueté [eʃikte], *a.* chequered, in squares; painted chequerwise; *Her:* checky.

échiquier [eʃikje], *s.m.* **1.** (*a*) chess-board; *adv.phr.* **en é.,** chequerwise, in chequer pattern, chequered; *Her:* **écu en é.,** field checky; *Navy:* **ligne en é.,** (ships) in bow and quarter line; (*b*) *Town P:* chequer-board layout, grid layout. **2.** *Fish:* square fishing-net. **3.** (*in Eng.*) **Chancelier de l'É.,** Chancellor of the Exchequer; **billets de l'É.,** Exchequer bills.

échis [ekis], *s.m. Rept:* echis.

échitès [ekitɛs], *s.m. Bot:* Echites.

échiures [ekjy:r], **échiuriens** [ekjyrjɛ̃], *s.m.pl. Ann:* Echiuroidea.

écho [eko], *s.m.* **1.** echo; (*a*) **faire é.,** to echo; **faire é. à un cri,** to echo back a shout; **se faire l'é. des opinions de qn,** to echo, repeat, s.o.'s opinions; **galerie à é.,** whispering-gallery; (*b*) *Elcs:* **é. fixe,** permanent echo; **échos multiples,** flutter echo; **effet d'é.,** echo effect; **éliminateur, suppresseur, d'é.,** echo suppressor; (*c*) *Elcs:* **échos parasites,** clutter; **échos parasites fixes,** permanent clutter; **échos (parasites) de sol,** ground clutter; **échos parasites en mer,** sea clutter; (*d*) *T.V:* ghost(ing); (*e*) *Nau: Av:* echo; *Radar:* **é., top d'é.,** blip, pip; *Av: Radar:* radar echo; **é. de sol,** ground return. **2.** *Journ:* **échos,** news items; social gossip.

échogramme [ekogram], *s.m.* echogram.

échographe [ekograf], *s.m.* echograph.

échoir [eʃwa:r], *v.i.* (*pr.p.* **échéant;** *p.p.* **échu;** *pr.ind.* **il échoit, il échet, ils échoient, ils échéent;** *p.d.* **il échoyait, il échéait;** *p.h.* **il échut;** *fu.* **il écherra; il échoira;** *the aux is usu.* **être**) **1.** to fall (to s.o.'s lot); **é. en partage à qn,** to fall to s.o.'s share; **la Lombardie lui échut en partage,** Lombardy was allotted to him; **la Lombardie lui échut au sort,** Lombardy fell to him by lot; **le devoir m'échut de lui apprendre la nouvelle,** it fell to me to break the news to him; **la tâche la plus ingrate qui puisse é. à qn,** the most thankless task that can fall to s.o., that can devolve upon s.o.; **le sort échu à . . .,** the fate met with by . . .; **le trône est échu à un neveu,** the throne fell to a nephew. **2.** (*a*) *Fin:* (*of bill, etc.*) to fall due, to mature; **billets échus,** bills (over)due; **intérêts échus,** outstanding interest; **intérêts à é.,** accruing interest; **capitaux dont la date de paiement est échue,** matured capital; (*b*) (*of tenancy*) to expire.

écholalie [ekolali], *s.f. Med:* echolalia.

écholocalisation [ekolɔkalizasjɔ̃], *s.f. Z: Tchn:* echolocation.

écholocation [ekolɔkasjɔ̃], *s.f. Z:* echolocation.

échomètre [ekomɛtr], *s.m. Elcs:* echometer, echo test set.

échométrie [ekometri], *s.f. Ph:* echometry, echo ranging.

échoppage [eʃɔpa:ʒ], *s.m. Engr: etc:* working with a graver, with a burin; graving.

échoppe[1] [eʃɔp], *s.f.* (*a*) booth, covered stall, street stall; (*b*) **é. de cordonnier,** cobbler's small (work)shop.

échoppe[2], *s.f. Tls: Engr: etc:* graver, scoop(er), burin.

échopper [eʃɔpe], *v.tr. Engr: Typ: etc:* to grave, gouge, scoop; to rout (out); *Wood Engr:* to cut away; **machine à é.,** routing machine.

échoppeuse [eʃɔpø:z], *s.f. Typ: etc:* routing machine.

échopraxie [ekopraksi], *s.f. Med:* echopraxia, echopraxis.

écho-sondeur [ekosɔ̃dœ:r], *s.m. Nau:* echo sounder, sonic depth-finder; *pl. écho-sondeurs.*

échotier [ekɔtje], *s.m. Journ:* paragraphist; gossip writer.

échouage [eʃwa:ʒ], *s.m. Nau:* **1.** (*a*) stranding, running aground, grounding; (*b*) beaching (of vessel); **bassin d'é.,** tidal dock; **cale d'é.,** dry dock. **2.** beaching strand, graving beach.

échouement [eʃumɑ̃], *s.m.* **1.** *Nau:* (*a*) stranding, running aground; (*b*) beaching (of vessel). **2.** (*rare*) failure, miscarriage (of plan).

échouer [eʃwe]. **1.** *v.i.* (*a*) *Nau:* to run aground, to be stranded, to ground; **échoué à sec,** high and dry; **navire échoué sur un banc de sable,** ship aground on a sand bank; *F:* **il a échoué sur un banc de jardin public,** he ended up on a park bench; (*b*) to fail, miscarry, come to grief, prove abortive; **son plan a échoué,** his plan did not work, broke down; **l'affaire échoua,** the business fell through; **é. à un examen,** to fail an examination; *F:* to be ploughed, plucked, in an exam.; **il a échoué dans sa tentative contre le record du monde,** he failed in his attempt to break the world record; **faire é. un projet,** to bring about the failure of a plan, to wreck a plan. **2.** *v.tr. Nau:* to beach; to run (ship) aground.

s'échouer, to run aground, to be driven ashore.

écidie [esidi], *s.f. Fung:* aecidium, *pl.* aecidia.

écimage [esima:ʒ], *s.m.* topping, pollarding (of trees).

écimer [esime], *v.tr.* to top, pollard (tree); to tassel (maize).

éciton [esitɔ̃], *s.m. Ent:* eciton.

éclaboussement [eklabusmɑ̃], *s.m.* splashing, (be)spattering.

éclabousser [eklabuse], *v.tr.* to splash, (be)spatter (with mud, etc.); **page éclaboussée d'encre,** page spattered with ink; **é. le monde, ses voisins (de son luxe),** to parade one's wealth; **scandale qui a éclaboussé toute la famille,** scandal that damaged, sullied, the reputation of the whole family.

éclaboussure [eklabusy:r], *s.f.* splash, spatter (of mud, dirty water, etc.); splash (of colour); splinter (of metal); (*b*) blemish, blot, smirch (on reputation); *F:* **recevoir des éclaboussures,** to get a bit of the backwash.

éclair [eklɛ:r], *s.m.* **1.** flash of lightning; **éclairs,** lightning; **éclairs de chaleur,** heat lightning, summer lightning; **é. diffus, en nappe,** (flash of) sheet lightning; **é. en boule,** globe lightning; **é. fulminant, en sillon,** (flash of) ribbon lightning; **é. arborescent, ramifié,** (flash of) forked lightning; **é. sinueux,** (flash of) chain lightning; **é. en chapelet,** (flash of) beaded lightning; **il fait des éclairs,** it's lightening; **rapide comme l'é.,** quick as lightning, as thought; *F:* **visite é.,** lightning visit; **guerre é.,** blitzkrieg; **attaque é.,** lightning raid; **l'auto passa comme un é.,** the car flashed by. **2.** (*a*) flash (of a gun, etc.); **point d'é.,** flash point; (*b*) *Metall:* fulguration, brightening (of gold or silver under assay); **bijoux qui lancent des éclairs,** flashing, glittering, jewels; **ses yeux lançaient des éclairs de colère,** his eyes flashed with anger; **la pensée traversa mon esprit comme un é.,** the thought flashed through my mind; **é. de génie,** flash of genius; (*c*) *Phot:* **é. libre,** open flash; **é. au magnésium,** magnesium flash. **3.** *Cu:* éclair.

éclairage [eklɛra:ʒ], *s.m.* **1.** (*a*) lighting; illumination; **é. électrique,** electric lighting; **é. direct, indirect,** direct, indirect, lighting; **é. de côté, é. à feux croisés,** cross lighting; **é. de secours,** emergency lighting; **é. des rues,** street lighting; *Adm:* **é. public réduit,** half-night lights; **é. public intense,** all-night lights; *Aut:* **é. intérieur automatique,** courtesy-light; **heure d'é.,** lighting-up time (for vehicles); *Aut:* **inculpé d'avoir circulé avec absence totale d'é.,** charged with driving without lights.; **é. de la scène, é. scénique,** stage lighting; *Phot: etc:* **é. d'ambiance,** uniform lighting; flat lighting; (*b*) light; **mauvais é.,** bad light; sous cet é., seen in this light. **2.** *Mil: Navy:* scouting; *Navy:* **rideau d'é.,** scouting screen.

éclairagisme [eklɛraʒism], *s.m.* illuminating engineering.

éclairagiste [eklɛraʒist], *s.m.* (electric) lighting engineer.

éclairant [eklɛrɑ̃]. **1.** *a.* lighting, illuminant, giving light; **pouvoir é.,** illuminating power; **dallage é.,** pavement light. **2.** *s.m.* illuminant.

éclaircie [eklɛrsi], *s.f.* **1.** break, opening, rift (in cloudy sky, smoke, fog, etc.); fair period (of weather); **temps pluvieux avec éclaircies,** rain with bright intervals. **2.** clearing (in forest, through hedge); glade. **3.** *Hort:* thinning out (of fruit, lettuces, etc.).

éclaircir [eklɛrsi:r], *v.tr.* **1.** to clear (up); **vent qui éclaircit le brouillard,** wind that disperses the fog; **s'é. la voix,** to clear one's throat. **2.** (*a*) to lighten; to make (sth.) clear; **é. les vitres,** to clean the windows; **é. le teint,** to clear the complexion; (*b*) **é. un mystère, un malentendu,** to solve, explain, throw light on, clear up, a mystery, a misunderstanding; **é. une situation,** to clarify a situation; **é. un doute,** to clear up a doubt; **é. une idée,** to elucidate an idea; (*c*) **é. qn sur qch.,** to enlighten s.o. on sth.; **é. qn d'un doute,** to remove a doubt from s.o.'s mind. **3.** to thin (forest, sauce); to thin out (seedlings, etc.); to clear (path); **cheveux éclaircis par les soucis,** hair grown thin with worry. **4.** to clarify (liquid).

s'éclaircir. 1. (*a*) (*of the weather*) to clear (up), to become bright(er); **sa figure s'éclaircit,** his face brightened up, lit up; **son teint s'éclaircit,** his complexion is getting clearer; (*b*) **je veux m'é. sur ce point,** I want to get clear on this point; (*c*) **la vérité s'éclaircit,** the truth is coming out. **2.** (*of hair, plants, etc.*) to become thin, to thin; **enfin les arbres s'éclaircirent,** at length the trees thinned out, became fewer and farther between.

éclaircissage [eklɛrsisa:ʒ], *s.m.* **1.** polishing (of glass, etc.); furbishing, burnishing (of metal, etc.). **2.** thinning out (of trees, plants, hair (by the hairdresser)).

éclaircissement [eklɛrsismɑ̃], *s.m.* **1.** (*a*) enlightenment; explanation, elucidation; (*b*) explanatory statement; **é. d'un mystère,** solving, clearing up, of a mystery; **demander des éclaircissements sur qch.,** to ask for explanations about sth.; (*c*) *A:* (piece of) information. **2.** clearing (in forest, etc.). **3.** *Hort:* thinning out.

éclaircisseur [eklɛrsisœ:r], *s.m.*, **éclaircisseuse** [eklɛrsisø:z], *s.f. Agr:* thinning hoe.

éclaire [eklɛ:r], *s.f.* **1.** *Bot:* celandine; **petite é.,** lesser celandine, pilewort. **2.** *Nau:* hatchway (in deck of fishing vessel).

éclairé [eklɛre, -ere], *a.* enlightened, well-informed, educated (person, mind, etc.).

éclairement [eklɛrmɑ̃], *s.m.* **1.** illumination, lighting. **2.** *Opt: etc:* degree of illumination.

éclairer [eklɛre, -ere]. **1.** *v.tr.* (*a*) to light, illuminate, give light to (s.o., sth.); **venez nous é.,** come and show us a light; **je suis nourri, logé, et éclairé,** I get my board, lodging, and lighting; **salle éclairée par quatre fenêtres,** hall lighted by four windows; **maison qui est éclairée, qui s'éclaire, au gaz, à l'électricité,** house lit by gas, by electricity; **la pièce s'éclaire sur le jardin,** the room looks out on the garden; **é. un point obscur,** to shed, throw, light on an obscure point; **é. la lanterne de qn,** to straighten s.o. out; (*b*) *abs.* (*of lamp, etc.*) to give a good light; **cette lampe n'éclaire pas,** this lamp gives a poor light; **les yeux du chat éclairent dans l'obscurité,** a cat's eyes shine, gleam, in the dark; (*c*) *Mil:* **é. le terrain, la marche,** to reconnoitre (the ground); to scout; (*d*) *A: F:* to watch, keep an eye on (s.o.); **é. un suspect,** to watch, shadow, a suspicious character; (*e*) to enlighten, instruct, inform; *Cards: etc:* **é. (le tapis),** to put down one's stake; **é. le jeu,** to convey information to (one's partner); **é. qn sur un sujet, sur les causes de qch.,** to enlighten s.o. on a subject, about the causes of sth.; (*f*) *P:* **é. la dépense;** *abs.* **éclairer,** to pay (up), to foot the bill. **2.** *v.impers. A: & Dial:* **il éclaire,** it's lightening.

s'éclairer. 1. to light up, brighten up; **sa figure s'éclaira d'un sourire,** his face lit up with a smile. **2.** to clear up, become clear. **3.** (*of the mind*) to become enlightened, informed.

éclaireur, -euse [eklɛrœ:r, -ø:z], *s.* **1.** (*a*) *s.m. Mil:* scout; **envoyer qn en é.,** to send s.o. to reconnoitre; (*b*) *s.m. Navy:* scouting vessel, scout, look-out ship; (*c*) *s.m. attrib. Av:* **avion é.,** reconnaissance aircraft; (*d*) *s.m. & f.* (non-Catholic) (boy) scout; (girl) guide; **chef é.,** scoutmaster. **2.** (*a*) *s.m. Aut: A:* **é. de tablier,** dashboard light; (*b*) *a.* **appareil é.,** lighting apparatus.

éclamé [eklame], *a.* (*of bird*) broken-winged, broken-legged.

éclampsie [eklɑ̃psi], *s.f. Med:* eclampsia; *F:* convulsions.

éclamptique [eklɑ̃ptik], *a. & s.f. Obst:* eclamptic.

éclanche [eklɑ̃:ʃ], *s.f. Cu:* shoulder of mutton.

éclancher [eklɑ̃ʃe], *v.tr. Tex:* to remove the creases from, to smooth out (material).

éclat [ekla], *s.m.* **1.** (*a*) splinter, chip (of wood, stone, etc.); flake (of mica); splinter (of bone, glass); **é. d'obus,** shell splinter; **voler en éclats,** to fly, burst, into pieces, to be shattered to pieces; **briser qch. en éclats,** to smash sth. to pieces, to smithereens; **éclats de verre,** (i) broken glass; (ii) flying glass (actually in the air); (*b*) shake (in wood); (*c*) *Hort:* fragment (of root, for propagation). **2.** (*a*) burst (of noise, explosive, thunder, laughter, etc.); **é. de colère,** outburst of anger; **on entendait de grands éclats de voix,** one could hear (i) voices raised in anger, (ii) snatches of loud conversation; **partir d'un grand é. de rire,** to burst into a peal of laughter, to burst out laughing; **rire aux éclats,** to laugh heartily; to roar, scream, with laughter; (*b*) **cette nouvelle fera de l'é.,** this news will create a commotion, a scandal; **éviter, craindre, les éclats,** to avoid, to be afraid of, rows, scandals; *adv.phr.* **sans é.,** quietly; without any fuss, any scandal. **3.** (*a*) flash (of light, of gun); *Nau:* **feu, phare, à éclats,** flashing light; (*b*) glare (of the sun, etc.); glitter, lustre (of diamond, etc.); brilliancy, vividness (of colours, etc.); *Min:* **é. gras,** soapy lustre; *Astr:* **variation d'é.,** light change (of a star); **l'é. de ses yeux,** the sparkle in his, her, eyes; **é. du teint,** freshness of complexion; **dans tout l'é. de sa beauté,** in the full bloom, radiance, of her beauty; **l'é. de la jeunesse,** the bloom, freshness, of youth; **le soleil brille dans tout son é.,** the sun is shining brightly, with full brilliance; **quand le soleil brille de son plus vif é.,** when the sun is (shining) at its brightest, at its most brilliant; *adj.phr.* **sans é.,** dull, lustreless; lack-lustre (eyes); **l'é. soyeux de ses cheveux,** the glossiness of her hair; (*c*) brilliancy (of style, musical execution, etc.); glamour (of glory, etc.); **l'é. de son nom,** the (outstanding) fame of his name; **action d'é.,** action of outstanding brilliance; brilliant feat of arms; **aimer l'é.,** to be fond of show, display, ostentation; **prêter de l'é. à,** to lend glamour to; **faux é.,** (i) false glamour; (ii) tawdriness; false brilliance; *adv.phr.* **sans é.,** quietly, without any show, unostentatiously.

éclatable [eklatabl], *a.* liable to splinter; splintery.

éclatage [eklata:ʒ], *s.m. Hort:* division, partition (of roots).

éclatant [eklatɑ̃], *a.* **1.** bursting; **être é. de santé,** to be bursting with health. **2.** loud, ringing (sound, laughter, etc.); piercing (shriek, etc.); **bruit é.,** crash; **le son é. de la fanfare,** the blare of the brass band. **3.** glaring; dazzling, brilliant, (light, colour, success); bright (light, colour); sparkling, glittering, flashing (jewels, etc.); **services éclatants,** outstanding services; **action éclatante,** brilliant, illustrious, deed; **victoire éclatante,** signal, brilliant, victory; **mensonge é.,** blazing, blatant, lie; **vert é.,** vivid green.

éclatée [eklate], *s.f. Tchn:* exploded view.

éclatement [eklatmɑ̃], *s.m.* bursting, explosion (of boiler, shell, gun); bursting, blow-out (of tyre); rupture (of vein); shattering, flying (of glass); *Mil:* fanning out, breaking out (of column, formation, etc.); dispersal, *U.S:* dispersion (of convoy, etc.); **port d'é.,** dispersal port (for oil tankers); *Av:* (*aerobatics*) **é. d'une formation,** bomb burst; *El:* **pont d'é.,** spark gap; **fréquence d'é.,** spark frequency; *Artil:* **é. en surface,** surface burst; **é. fusant,** air burst; **gerbe d'é.,** sheaf of splinters, of fragments; *Pol:* **é. d'une fédération,** break-up, split-up, of a federation.

éclater [eklate]. **1.** *v.tr.* (*a*) to split, splinter (branch, mast); to burst (tyre); (*b*) *Hort:* to divide, partition (roots of plant, for propagation); (*c*) to disperse (cargo of crude oil). **2.** *v.i.* (*of boiler, shell, gun*) to burst, explode; (*of mine*) to blow up; (*of tyre*) to burst; (*of glass*) to fly (into pieces); (*of mast*) to split, splinter; **faire é. qch.,** to burst, explode, shatter, split, sth.; **faire é. un pétard,** to detonate a fog signal; **la nouvelle éclata comme une bombe,** the news came like a bombshell; **la guerre, la révolution, l'incendie, sa colère, éclata,** war, the revolution, fire, his anger, broke out; **quand la guerre éclata . . .,** at the outbreak of the war . . .; **l'orage éclata,** the storm broke; **le tonnerre éclata,** there was a clap of thunder; *Th: etc:* **la salle éclata en applaudissements,** the house burst into applause; **à son arrivée la fanfare éclata,** on his arrival the band struck up; **é. en larmes,** to burst into tears, to burst out crying; **laisser é. sa colère,** to give vent to one's anger; **é. de rire,** to burst out laughing, to laugh outright; *F:* **ça continuera jusqu'au moment où vous en aurez plein le dos et alors ça éclatera,** you'll go on until you can't stand it any longer and then there will be a flare up. **3.** *v.i.* (*a*) (*of jewels*) to blaze, sparkle, glitter, flash; (*b*) **l'indignation éclatait dans ses yeux,** his eyes were ablaze, flashed, with indignation; **l'admiration éclate dans ses yeux,** his eyes are full of admiration; there comes into his eyes a sparkle of admiration; **sa bonté éclate dans tout ce qu'il fait,** his goodness shines out in everything he does; **la partialité de l'auteur éclate à chaque page du livre,** the author's bias is glaringly apparent on every page of the book.

éclateur [eklatœ:r], *s.m. El: W.Tel:* (i) spark gap; (ii) spark arrester; **é. pour étincelle étouffée,** quenched spark gap.

éclectique [eklɛktik], *a. & s.* eclectic.

éclectiquement [eklɛktikmɑ̃], *adv.* eclectically.

éclectisme [eklɛktism], *s.m.* eclecticism.

écli [ekli], *s.m. Nau:* chip, splinter (of wood); **vergue qui a des éclis,** yard that is chipping off.

éclimètre [eklimɛtr], *s.m.* **1.** *Surv:* eclimeter. **2.** clinometer.

éclipsable [eklipsabl], *a.* retractable; collapsible.

éclipse [eklips], *s.f.* (*a*) eclipse; **é. de soleil, de lune,** eclipse of the sun, of the moon; **é. totale de la raison,** total loss of reason; **revenir après une é. d'un an,** to return after a year's disappearance; **sa renommée s'affirme après avoir subi une é.,** his fame is becoming established after suffering an eclipse; (*b*) disappearing (target, etc.); *Fort: etc:* **tourelle à é.,** disappearing turret; *Nau:* **feu à é.,** occulting, intermittent, light.

éclipser [eklipse], *v.tr.* (*a*) to eclipse; to surpass, outshine, overshadow; to throw (s.o.) into the shade, to put (s.o.) in the shade; (*b*) to obscure (beam of light).

s'éclipser, to become eclipsed; to disappear; *Nau:* (*of light*) to occult; *F:* **au moment du danger il s'éclipsa,** at the moment of danger he vanished, made off, slipped away, made himself scarce.

écliptique [ekliptik], *a. & s.f. Astr:* ecliptic.

éclissage [eklisa:ʒ], *s.m. Civ.E: etc:* (*a*) fishing; fish-plating; *Rail:* **é. électrique,** bonding (of live rail); (*b*) splice; **plaque d'é.,** butt strap, gusset plate.

éclisse [eklis], *s.f.* **1.** (*a*) (wooden) wedge; (*b*) butt-strap. **2.** split wood. **3.** cheese tray. **4.** *Surg:* splint. **5.** *Rail:* (*a*) fish-plate, shim; **é. cornière,** angle fish-plate; (*b*) bond (of live rail); **joint à é. électrique,** bonded joint (of rail). **6. éclisses d'un violon,** ribs of a violin.

éclisser [eklise], *v.tr.* **1.** *Surg:* to put (limb) in splints, to splint. **2.** *Rail:* to fish (rails); to join (rails) by fish-plates.

éclogite [eklɔʒit], *s.f. Miner:* eclogite.

éclopé [eklɔpe], *a.* footsore, lame, limping; unable to walk, crippled; badly hurt; **cheval é.,** lame horse.

écloper [eklɔpe], *v.tr.* (*usu. passive*) (*a*) to make (s.o.) lame, footsore; (*b*) *Turf: F:* to nobble (horse); (*c*) to hurt (s.o.) badly; to cripple (s.o.).

éclore [eklɔ:r], *v.i. def.* (*p.p.* **éclos;** *pr.ind.* **il éclôt, ils éclosent;** *p.d.* **il éclosait, ils éclosaient;** no *p.h.*; *fu.* **il éclora, ils écloront;** *the aux. is usu.* **être,** *occ.* **avoir) 1.** (*of eggs, chicks*) to hatch (out), to be hatched; **faire é. des poussins,** to hatch chickens. **2.** (*a*) (*of flowers*) to open, to blossom (out), to bloom, blow; (*of buds*) to burst; **pavots frais éclos, roses fraîches écloses,** fresh-blown poppies, roses; (*b*) to open out, develop, come to light; **génie près d'é.,** budding genius; **le jour est près d'é.,** dawn is at hand; **faire é. un projet,** to realize a plan.

éclosabilité [eklozabilite], *s.f.* hatchability (of eggs).

éclosion [eklozjɔ̃], *s.f.* **1.** hatching (of eggs, chicks). **2.** (*a*) opening, blossoming, blooming (of flowers); (*b*) blossoming forth (of genius, etc.); birth (of passion, etc.); **nous assistons à l'é. d'un monde nouveau,** we are witnessing the birth of a new world.

éclosoir [eklozwa:r], *s.m. Husb:* hatchery.

éclusage [eklyza:ʒ], *s.m.* passing (of boat) through a lock; *Hyd.E:* locking, lockage.

écluse [ekly:z], *s.f.* **1.** (*a*) (canal) lock; **droit d'é.,** lockage; **porte d'é.,** flood gate, lock gate, sluice (gate); **é. à sas, é. double,** lift lock, twin lock; **sas, chambre, d'é.,** lock chamber; *Hyd.E:* **é. à pas,** pound lock; **é. simple,** flash lock; **é. à air,** air lock (of caisson); **é. de moulin,** mill dam; **lâcher une é.,** to open a sluice gate; (*b*) sluice (gate), flood gate, lock gate; **é. de dégagement,** waste gate; *Hyd.E:* **é. de fuite,** tail lock, tail race; (*c*) tide gate (of dock). **2.** *Geog:* **L'É.,** Sluys.

éclusée [eklyze], *s.f.* lockful (of water); feed; lockage water; sluicing water.

éclusement [eklyzmɑ̃], *s.m.* **1.** passing of boat through a lock; locking. **2.** *Civ.E:* passing of compressed air into a caisson.

écluser [eklyze], *v.tr.* to lock. **1.** to equip (canal) with locks. **2.** to pass (barge) through a lock. **3.** *P:* **é. un verre, un godet,** to knock a drink back, to lift one's elbow.

éclusette [eklyzɛt], *s.f. Civ.E:* materials lock (of pneumatic caisson).

éclusier, -ière [eklyzje, -jɛ:r]. **1.** *a.* relating to locks; **porte éclusière,** lock gate. **2.** *s.* lock keeper.

ecmnésie [ɛkmnezi], *s.f. Med:* ecmnesia.

écobuage [ekɔbɥa:ʒ], *s.m. Agr:* burn-beating, *A:* denshering.

écobue [ekɔby], *s.f.* weeding tool; turfing tool, plough.

écobuer [ekɔbɥe], *v.tr. Agr:* to burn-beat, *A:* densher; to sweal, swale.

écœurant [ekœrɑ̃], *a.* (*a*) nauseating, sickening; **gâteau é.**, sickly sweet cake; (*b*) disgusting, loathsome, revolting, nauseating; **flatterie écœurante**, sickening flattery; (*c*) thankless, demoralizing (work, etc.).

écœurement [ekœrmɑ̃], *s.m.* (*a*) nausea; (*b*) disgust; loathing; repugnance; **on est pris d'é. devant pareil spectacle**, such a sight is nauseating, sickening, disgusting, makes one feel sick; (*c*) **é. causé par des échecs répétés**, demoralization, discouragement, caused by repeated failure.

écœurer [ekœre, -øre], *v.tr.* (*a*) to sicken, nauseate; *abs.* **les gâteaux trop riches écœurent**, cakes that are too rich make one feel sick; (*b*) to disgust, revolt, nauseate; **j'étais écœuré par toutes les bêtises que j'avais vues**, I was disgusted by all the stupidity I had seen; all the stupidity I had seen nauseated me, made me sick; (*c*) to discourage, dishearten, demoralize; **écœuré, il donna sa démission**, he resigned in disgust.

écoffret, écofrai [ekɔfrɛ], *s.m.*, **écofroi** [ekɔfrwa], *s.m. Leath:* cutting board.

écoinçon, écoinson [ekwɛ̃sɔ̃], *s.m.* **1.** *Const:* corner piece; corner stone (of wall); *Join:* sconcheon, scuncheon (of window frame, etc.); *Arch:* spandrel. **2.** (*a*) corner cupboard; (*b*) corner chair.

écoine [ekwan], *s.f. Tls:* adjusting file, rasp.

écoiner [ekwane], *v.tr.* to file, to rasp.

écoinette [ekwanet], *s.f.* small file, rasp.

écolage [ekɔla:ʒ], *s.m.* (*a*) schooling; (*b*) *A: & Sw.Fr:* school fees.

école [ekɔl], *s.f.* **1.** (*a*) school; **é. maternelle**, nursery school, kindergarten; **é. primaire**, *A:* **é. communale**, primary, *A:* elementary, school; *A:* **é. primaire supérieure** = central school; **é. d'État**, state, *U.S:* public, school; **é. libre** = independent school; **é. confessionnelle**, denominational school; **maison d'é.**, school house; **directeur, maître, d'é.**, (primary school) headmaster; (primary) schoolmaster; **tenir é.**, to keep, run, a school; **faire l'é. à des enfants**, to teach children; **vous êtes à bonne é.**, (i) you've got a good teacher; (ii) you're in good hands; **sentir l'é.**, to be pedantic; **aller à l'é.**, to go to school; **faire l'é. buissonnière**, to play truant; **pendant l'é.**, during school(time); **la rentrée des écoles**, the beginning of term, of the school year; (*b*) (= *pupils*) **toute l'é. le savait**, the whole school knew it; (*c*) **les grandes écoles**, colleges of university level specializing in professional training (*they include* **l'É. Polytechnique, l'É. Normale Supérieure, l'É. des Mines, l'É. des Arts et Métiers, l'É. des Ponts et Chaussées**, *and many others*); *Mil:* **É. (supérieure) de Guerre** = Staff College; **é. régimentaire**, regimental school; **é. normale**, college of education; **é. ménagère**, domestic training college; **é. d'été**, summer school; (*in Paris*) **le quartier des Écoles**, the Latin quarter; (*d*) *Mil: etc:* school, drill, training; **é. du soldat**, recruit drill; **é. de compagnie**, company drill; **é. de bataillon**, battalion training; **é. de tir**, rifle drill; *Artil:* **écoles à feu**, target practice; *Nau:* **é. de nœuds**, knotting and splicing; *Av:* **appareil d'é.**, training aircraft; (*e*) school, training; **é. d'équitation**, riding school; **haute é.**, haute école; **cheval qui a de l'é., qui fournit bien à l'é.**, trained horse; (*f*) (i) (*at backgammon*) failure to mark one's score; (ii) *F:* blunder, (piece of) stupidity; *F:* **faire une é.**, to put one's foot into it. **2.** (*a*) school (of thought, art, literature, etc.); **l'é. de Platon**, the Platonic school; **l'é. italienne**, the Italian school (of painting); **faire é.**, (i) to found, be leader of, a school; (ii) to set a fashion; **pourvu qu'il ne fasse pas é.**, I hope he won't get a following, won't start a fashion; **idée qui fait é.**, idea that is gaining ground, becoming popular; (*b*) *Phil.Hist:* **l'É.**, the Schools, the Schoolmen (of the Middle Ages).

écolier, -ière [ekɔlje, -jɛ:r]. **1.** *s.* (*a*) (primary) schoolboy, schoolgirl; **un de mes anciens écoliers**, one of my old pupils, one of my old boys; **bévue d'é.**, (i) schoolboy howler; (ii) stupid, childish, mistake; **se conduire en é.**, to behave like a schoolboy; **le chemin des écoliers**, the longest way round; (*b*) novice, beginner. **2.** *a.* **goûts écoliers**, schoolboy tastes; **papier é.**, exercise paper.

écolleter [ekɔlte], *v.tr.* (**j'écollette, n. écolletons; j'écolletterai**) to hammer out, beat out (metal).

écologie [ekɔlɔʒi], *s.f. Biol:* ecology.

écologique [ekɔlɔʒik], *a. Biol:* ecological.

éconduire [ekɔ̃dɥi:r], *v.tr.* (*conj. like* CONDUIRE) to get rid of (s.o.) (politely); to show (an importunate person) to the door; **é. un soupirant**, to give a suitor the mitten; **être éconduit**, to meet with a refusal; (*of suitor*) to be rejected; *F:* to be given the brush off.

économat [ekɔnɔma], *s.m.* (*a*) stewardship (of estate); treasurership (of institution); bursarship (of college); (*b*) steward's, treasurer's, bursar's, office; (*c*) stationery department (of any large office); (*d*) staff stores.

économe [ekɔnɔm]. **1.** *s.m. & f.* treasurer, bursar (of college, institution, etc.); steward, housekeeper (of castle, large mansion, etc.); agent (of estate); stationery clerk (of any large office); *B:* **l'é. infidèle**, the unjust steward. **2.** *a.* economical, thrifty, sparing (person, etc.); **être é. de paroles**, to be sparing of words, not to have much to say for oneself.

économétricien, -ienne [ekɔnɔmetrisjɛ̃, -jɛn], *s.* econometrician.

économétrie [ekɔnɔmetri], *s.f.* econometrics.

économie [ekɔnɔmi], *s.f.* **1.** (*a*) economy; management; **é. politique**, political economy; **é. dirigée**, planned economy; *Com:* **société d'é. mixte**, private company with government participation; semi-public company; (*b*) **l'é. de la France, the**, French economy, the French economic system. **2.** economy, saving, thrift; **vivre avec é.**, to live economically, frugally; **faire une é. de temps**, to save time; **é. de main-d'œuvre**, labour-saving; **par é.**, for economy's sake; **vous faites ainsi une é. de vingt pour cent**, in this way you save twenty per cent. **3.** *pl.* savings; **faire des économies**, to save money, to save (up); **faire appel à, prendre sur, ses économies**, to draw upon one's savings; *F:* **économies de bouts de chandelles**, cheese-paring economy; *Prov:* **il n'y a pas de petites économies; les petites économies font les bonnes maisons**, take care of the pence and the pounds will take care of themselves; a penny saved is a penny earned, is a penny gained.

économique [ekɔnɔmik], *a.* **1.** economic (problem, doctrine, etc.); **sciences économiques**, economics. **2.** (*a*) economical, inexpensive, cheap (method, apparatus, etc.); **poêle é.**, fuel-saving stove; (*b*) **vitesse é.**, economical speed (of a ship, etc.). **3.** *s.f.* (*rare*) economics.

économiquement [ekɔnɔmikmɑ̃], *adv.* economically; sparingly, frugally, inexpensively; **les é. faibles**, the underprivileged.

économiser [ekɔnɔmize], *v.tr.* to economize, save (money, time); to husband (resources, strength, etc.); **é. ses paroles**, to be sparing of one's words; *abs.* **il faut é.**, we must economize, practise economy; **é. sur qch.**, to save, economize, on sth.; **é. pour l'avenir**, to put by for the future, to save up; **il faut s'é.**, one must conserve one's strength.

économiseur, -euse [ekɔnɔmizœ:r, -ø:z], *s.* **1.** economizer, saver. **2.** *s.m. Mch: etc:* economizer, economizing device; *esp.* exhaust-gas engine; **é. de combustible**, fuel economizer, fuel saver; *Ind:* **é. de décapage**, pickling inhibitor.

économisme [ekɔnɔmism], *s.m.* economism.

économiste [ekɔnɔmist], *s.m.* (political) economist.

écopage [ekɔpa:ʒ], *s.m. P:* (*a*) blow, wound; (*b*) reprimand, slating.

écope [ekɔp], *s.f.* ladle; *Nau:* (bailing) scoop, bailer, piggin; *Dom.Ec:* **é. (pour écrémer le lait)**, skimmer.

écoper [ekɔpe]. **1.** *v.tr.* (*a*) to bail (out); **é. l'eau d'une embarcation**, to bail out a boat; (*b*) *P:* to drink. **2.** *v.i. F:* (*a*) to be hit, wounded; to get a beating; to get the worst of it; to cop it, to get it in the neck; **é. de cinq ans de travaux forcés**, to cop five years' hard labour; (*b*) to get the blame, to catch it.

écoperche [ekɔpɛrʃ], *s.f. Const:* **1.** upright pole, standard (of scaffolding). **2.** derrick.

écopeur [ekɔpœr], *s.m. P:* victim; **c'est toujours lui l'é.**, he's always the one to take the rap, get it in the neck.

écor [ekɔ:r], *s.m.* customs check (on parcels, goods).

écorage [ekɔra:ʒ], *s.m.* **1.** *Fish:* keeping the tally (of fish landed). **2.** *Cust:* checking (of parcels, goods).

écorçage [ekɔrsa:ʒ], *s.m.* barking, stripping (of trees); peeling (of oranges, etc.); husking (of rice).

écorce [ekɔrs], *s.f.* (*a*) *Bot:* cortex, skin; (*b*) bark (of tree); rind, peel (of orange, etc.); husk (of rice); **l'e. terrestre**, the earth's crust; *Tan:* **magasin d'écorces**, barkery, tan-house; *Tan:* **é. de chêne**, oak bark; **cuir tanné à l'é. de chêne**, oak-bark tanned leather; **é. du Pérou**, Peruvian bark.

écorcement [ekɔrs(ə)mɑ̃], *s.m.* = ÉCORÇAGE.

écorcer [ekɔrse], *v.tr.* (**j'écorçai(s); n. écorçons**) to bark (tree); to strip the bark off (tree); to peel (orange, etc.); to husk (rice).

écorceur, -euse [ekɔrsœ:r, -ø:z], *s.* **1.** *s.m. For: Ind:* (*pers.*) barker. **2.** *s.f.* (*machine*) barker.

écorchant [ekɔrʃɑ̃], *a.* (*of sound*) unpleasant; inharmonious; strident, harsh.

écorché [ekɔrʃe]. **1.** *a.* (*a*) flayed, skinned (animal); (*b*) grazed, galled (skin). **2.** *s.m.* (*a*) *Art:* anatomical model, écorché; (*b*) *Tchn:* sectional view.

écorche-cul (à) [aekɔrʃ(ə)ky], *adv.phr. P:* **descendre une pente à é.-c.**, to slither down a slope; **faire qch. à é.-c.**, to do sth. reluctantly; **il n'est venu qu'à é.-c.**, we had to drag him here; *Equit:* **monter à é.-c.**, to ride bareback.

écorchement [ekɔrʃ(ə)mɑ̃], *s.m.* **1.** flaying, skinning. **2.** abrasion, grazing (of the skin); barking (of shin, knuckles).

écorcher [ekɔrʃe], *v.tr.* **1.** to flay (large animal); to skin (eel); **écorché vif**, flayed alive; *F:* **é. une langue, un morceau**, to murder a language, a piece of music; **marchand qui écorche ses clients**, shopkeeper who fleeces his customers; **é. l'anguille par la queue**, to set to work the wrong way; to begin at the wrong end; *F:* **crier comme si on vous écorchait**, to make a song and dance about nothing; *P:* **é. le renard**, to spew, throw up. **2.** (*a*) to abrade, gall, graze, rub off (the skin); **cheval écorché sous la selle**, saddle-galled horse; **col qui écorche la peau**, collar that chafes the skin; **s'é. le coude, le tibia**, to graze, bark, one's elbow, one's shin; (*b*) to scrape, scratch (wall, furniture); to rasp (throat, ear); **son qui écorche l'oreille**, sound that grates on the ear; **boisson qui écorche le gosier**, drink that burns, stings, the throat.

écorcherie [ekɔrʃəri], *s.f.* (*a*) knacker's yard; (*b*) *F: A:* extortionate inn.

écorcheur, -euse [ekɔrʃœ:r, -ø:z]. **1.** *s.* (*a*) flayer; *Mil:* skinner; (*b*) *F:* fleecer, extortioner. **2.** *s.m. Orn:* butcher bird. **3.** *s.f.* **écorcheuse**, road scraper.

écorchure [ekɔrʃy:r], *s.f.* (*a*) *Med:* abrasion, excoriation (of the skin); gall; *Vet:* **é. sous la selle**, saddle gall; (*b*) scratch, graze.

écore [ekɔ:r], *s.f. Fish:* (*in Channel ports*) tally sheet.

écorer [ekɔre], *v.tr.* (*in Channel ports*) to keep tally of (fish landed); *abs.* to keep the tally sheets.

écoreur [ekɔrœ:r], *s.m.* tally keeper.

écornage [ekɔrna:ʒ], *s.m.* dehorning (of cattle).

écorner [ekɔrne], *v.tr.* **1.** to dehorn, to break the horns of (animal); *F:* **vent à é. les bœufs**, howling gale; **il faisait un vent à é. les bœufs**, there was a howling gale; *Nau:* it was blowing great guns. **2.** (*a*) to break, chip, the corner(s) off (sth.); **é. un livre**, (i) to dog('s)-ear a book; (ii) to break the corner of a (bound) book; **é. son capital**, to make a hole in one's capital; **é. la pension de qn**, to curtail, cut down, s.o.'s allowance; **la route a écorné sa propriété**, the road has taken a corner off his land; (*b*) *Carp: etc:* to chamfer, trim (piece of wood, block of stone, etc.); **scie à é.**, edge saw.

écorniflage [ekɔrnifla:ʒ], *s.m. O: F:* cadging, scrounging; sponging.

écornifler [ekɔrnifle], *v.tr. F:* to cadge, scrounge (meal, money, etc.); to sponge.

écornifleur, -euse [ekɔrniflœ:r, -ø:z], *s. F:* sponger, cadger; scrounger.

écornure [ekɔrny:r], *s.f.* **1.** chip, fragment chipped off. **2.** chipped corner (of stone, etc.).

écossais, -aise [ekɔsɛ, -ɛ:z]. **1.** *a.* (*of thg*) Scotch; (*of pers.*) Scottish, Scots; **étoffe écossaise**, tartan, plaid; **la Garde écossaise**, the Scots Guards; **hospitalité écossaise**, disinterested and generous hospitality; *s.a.* DOUCHE. **2.** *s.* Scot; Scotsman, Scotswoman; *Mil:* **les É.**, (i) the Scots Guards; (ii) the London Scottish. **3.** *s.m.* (*a*) tartan, plaid; check material; (*b*) *Ling:* Scotch, Scots (dialect). **4.** *s.f. Danc:* écossaise.

Écosse [ekɔs], *Pr.n.f. Geog:* Scotland; **la Haute É.**, the Highlands; *Tex:* **fil d'É.**, lisle thread.

écosser [ekɔse], *v.tr.* to shell, hull, (un)husk (peas, etc.).

écossette [ekɔsɛt], *s.f. Agr:* bunch of beet.

écosseur, -euse [ekɔsœ:r -ø:z], *s.* (*a*) (*pers.*) sheller (of peas, etc.); (*b*) *s.f.* **écosseuse**, shelling machine.

écosystème [ekɔsistɛm], *s.m. Biol:* ecosystem.

écot[1] [eko], *s.m.* **1.** (*a*) share, quota; **payer chacun son é.**, to pay one's own share; *F:* to go Dutch; (*b*) *A:* score, reckoning (of meal). **2.** *A:* company, party (eating together); *A: F:* **parlez à votre é.**, mind your own business.

écot², *s.m.* **1.** lopped tree, branch. **2.** lop wood, faggot wood, loppings.

écôtage [ekota:ʒ], *s.m.* stripping (of tobacco leaves).

écoté [ekɔte], *a.* lopped (tree or branch).

écôter [ekote], *v.tr.* to stem (tobacco leaves, etc.); **tabac écôté**, stripped leaves.

écôteur, -euse [ekotœ:r, -ø:z], *s.* stripper (of tobacco leaves).

écouailles [ekwɑ:j], *s.f.pl. Tex:* breeching; coarse wool.

écouane [ekwan], *s.f. Tls:* adjusting file, rasp.

écouche [ekuʃ], *s.f. Tex:* scutcher, scutching blade.

écoucher [ekuʃe], *v.tr. Tex:* to scutch, beat (flax, etc.).

écouenne [ekwɛn], *s.f. Tls:* adjusting file, rasp.

écouer [ekwe], *v.tr.* to dock (horse, dog).

écoufle [ekufl̩], *s.m. Orn:* kite.

écoulage [ekula:ʒ], *s.m.* **1.** *Leath:* draining (of skins). **2.** floating (of timber).

écoulé [ekule], *a. Com:* of last month, ultimo; *F:* ult.; **payable fin é.**, due at the end of last month.

écoulement [ekulmɑ̃], *s.m.* **1.** (*a*) outflow, flow, flowing, discharge (of liquid, gas, steam, etc.); *Hyd.E:* flow, run-off; *Geog:* **coefficient d'é.**, coefficient of flow (of a river); **é. glaciaire**, glacier flow; **é. laminaire**, laminar flow; **é. souterrain**, underground run-off; **é. de l'eau**, drainage; **fossé d'é.**, drain; **tube d'é.**, outlet tube; **trou d'é.**, plughole (of a sink); **tuyau d'é.**, drain (of oil sump, etc.); **é. dosé**, metered flow; **é. par gravité, é. en charge**, gravity flow; **vitesse d'é.**, rate of flow; *Av:* **é. (des filets) d'air**, air flow; **é. d'électricité**, flow of electricity; *Petroleum Ind:* **é. complexe**, pattern flow; (*b*) *Med:* **é. purulent, é. séreux**, purulent, serous, discharge; **é. catarrhal**, catarrhal discharge; **é. de l'urètre**, gleet; (*c*) waste pipe (of bath, etc.); (*d*) dispersal (of a crowd); *Trans:* **é. de la circulation**, (i) flow of traffic; (ii) handling of traffic (by traffic controller); **voie d'é.** channel, route (of traffic, etc.); *Mil: etc:* **é. d'une colonne**, passage of a column; **durée d'é. d'une colonne**, time length of a column. **2.** *Com:* sale, disposal, rapid turnover (of goods); **marchandises d'é. facile**, goods easily disposed of, that have a ready sale, that are in good demand.

écouler [ekule]. **1. s'écouler**, *v.pr.* (*a*) (*of liquid, etc.*) to flow out, run out; **la foule s'écoule rapidement**, the crowd (i) flows out, pours out, (ii) disperses, rapidly; **son argent s'écoule peu à peu**, his money is gradually melting away; **notre stock s'écoule rapidement**, our stock is selling fast, is running low; **faire é. l'eau**, to run off, drain off, the water; **faire é. la foule**, to get the crowd (i) to leave the building, (ii) to move on; (*b*) (*of time*) to pass, elapse, slip away; **à mesure que les années s'écoulent**, as the years roll by, slip by, fly by, wear on; **laisser (s')é. la moitié de l'année**, to allow half the year to elapse; **quand cette semaine d'angoisse se fut écoulée**, when this week of anxiety had passed; **après tant d'années écoulées**, after the passing, the lapse, of so many years. **2. écouler**, *v.tr.* (*a*) *Leath:* to drain (the skins); (*b*) *Com:* to sell (off), dispose of, get rid of (goods, etc.); **le charlatan écoulait rapidement sa marchandise**, the quack was doing a roaring trade; **é. de faux billets**, to utter forged notes, to put forged notes into circulation; (*c*) *For:* **é. le flot**, to bring the loose logs (thrown into the river) into port (for rafting).

écoumène [ekumɛn], *s.m. Geog:* ecumene.

écoupe [ekup], *s.f. Nau:* scoop, bailer.

écourgeon [ekurʒɔ̃], *s.m. Agr:* winter barley.

écourter [ekurte], *v.tr.* (*a*) to shorten; to curtail, to cut short; **é. sa barbe**, to trim one's beard short; **é. sa visite**, to cut short, curtail, one's visit; **é. un discours**, to cut a speech short; **pour é. ses heures de captivité**, in order to make the time seem shorter while he was in captivity; (*b*) **é. un chien**, (i) to crop (the ears of); (ii) to dock (the tail of), a dog; **é. un cheval**, to dock a horse.

écoutant, -ante [ekutɑ̃, -ɑ̃:t], *A:* **1.** *a.* listening (person, etc.); **avocat é.**, briefless barrister. **2.** *s.* hearer, listener.

écoute¹ [ekut], *s.f.* **1.** (*a*) *A:* sentinel, watch(man); (*b*) *Ecc:* **sœur é.**, nun accompanying other nun or boarder receiving a visit. **2.** *Mil:* **poste d'é.**, listening post; **service des écoutes**, listening branch; **être, se tenir, aux écoutes**, (i) to eavesdrop; (ii) to keep one's ears open; (iii) to be on the watch. **3.** *Tp: W.Tel:* listening-in; **é. de contrôle**, monitoring; **(service des) écoutes radio-téléphoniques, écoutes radio**, news monitoring; **station, centre, d'é.**, monitoring station; **table d'é.**, (i) listening table (used by police for tapping phone conversation); (ii) monitor desk, observation desk (for checking or testing phone system); **se mettre, se porter, à l'é., prendre l'é.**, to listen in; **être, rester, à l'é.**, to be listening in; **é. en haut parleur**, loudspeaker reception; *Tp:* **ne quittez pas l'é.! restez à l'é.!** hold the line! hold on a minute! one moment please! don't ring off! *W.Tel: T.V:* **l'heure de la plus vaste é.**, peak listening in, viewing, period; **cabine d'é.**, (i) *Cin:* monitor room; (ii) (*in record shop*) listening booth. **4.** *pl. Ven:* ears (of wild boar).

écoute², *s.f. Nau:* sheet (of sail); **fausse é.**, lazy guy; **nœud d'é.**, sheet bend; **point d'é.**, clew; **avoir le vent entre deux écoutes**, to have the wind dead aft.

écouté [ekute], *a. Equit:* **mouvements écoutés**, precise, measured, movements; **pas é.**, regular, uniform, step.

écouter [ekute], *v.tr.* **1.** (*a*) to listen to (s.o., sth.); **vous n'écoutez pas**, you're not listening; **n'é. que d'une oreille**, to listen with half an ear; **é. de toutes ses oreilles**, to listen with both ears; to be all ears; **savoir é.**, to be a good listener; **refuser d'é. qn**, to turn a deaf ear to s.o.; **é. qn jusqu'au bout**, to hear s.o. out; **é. chanter les oiseaux**, to listen to the birds singing; **é. à la porte, aux portes**, to eavesdrop; **écoutez!** look here! I say! I'll tell you what! *P:* **je t'écoute!** sez you! (*b*) *W.Tel:* to listen in; *Tp:* to overhear (at listening table). **2.** to pay attention to (s.o., sth.); **é. les avis de qn**, to take s.o.'s advice; **si on m'écoutait . . .**, if I were listened to . . ., if only people listened to me . . .; **n'écoutant que son courage**, prompted by his courage alone; **n'écoutant que son amour**, with no thought for anything but his love; **é. sa conscience**, to follow the dictates of one's conscience, to listen to one's consience; *Equit:* **é. son cheval**, to give one's horse its head.

s'écouter. 1. to pay too much attention to one's own ideas, feelings; **il s'écoute parler**, he likes the sound of his own voice; **si je m'écoutais je n'irais pas à ce rendez-vous**, if I followed my own advice I wouldn't keep this rendezvous. **2.** to pay too much attention to one's own health; **il s'écoute**, he coddles himself.

écoute-s'il-pleut [ekutsilplø], *s.m.inv. F:* **1.** water mill (fed by stream liable to run dry). **2.** timorous, gutless, man.

écouteur, -euse [ekutœ:r, -ø:z], *s.* **1.** (*a*) listener; **é. aux portes**, eavesdropper; (*b*) *W.Tel:* listener-in. **2.** *s.m.* (telephone) receiver; *W.Tel: etc:* earphone, head-phone.

écouteux, -euse [ekutø, -ø:z], *a.* skittish (horse).

écoutille [ekuti:j], *s.f. Nau:* hatchway; **é. vitrée**, skylight.

écoutillon [ekutijɔ̃], *s.m. Nau:* scuttle; booby-hatch.

écouvette [ekuvɛt], *s.f. Tex: Tail:* (type of) brush, broom.

écouvillon [ekuvijɔ̃], *s.m.* (*a*) (long-handled baker's) oven mop; (*b*) *Mil:* (gun) sponge; (rifle) cleaning brush; (*c*) *Med:* swab; (*d*) flue brush, tube brush.

écouvillonnage [ekuvijɔna:ʒ], *s.m.* mopping out (of oven); swabbing out (of gun; *Med:* of uterus, etc.); cleaning, brushing out (of tube, flue, etc.); *Artil:* **é. à l'eau**, sponging out (of gun); **é. à l'air**, scavenging (of gun).

écouvillonner [ekuvijɔne], *v.tr.* to mop out, clean out (oven); to brush out (rifle, tube, etc.); to sponge out, swab, scavenge (gun); *Med:* to swab.

écrabouillage [ekrabuja:ʒ], **écrabouillement** [ekrabujmɑ̃], *s.m. F:* crushing, squashing.

écrabouiller [ekrabuje], *v.tr. F:* to crush; to reduce (s.o., sth.) to pulp; to squash.

écran [ekrɑ̃], *s.m.* **1.** screen; (*a*) **é. de fumée**, smoke screen; **é. de protection, é. protecteur**, shield; **é. (de protection) contre les radiations**, radiation shield; **é. ignifuge, é. à pied**, fire screen; **é. cache-lueur(s)**, flash screen, glow screen; *Nau:* **é. de fanal, é. de feu de côté**, sidelight screen; **é. de sortie d'eau**, splash board; *Cin:* **é. de sûreté**, cut-off (of projector); **faire é.**, to prevent light, wind, rain, from penetrating; (*b*) *Rail:* **é. paraneige**, snow shield; snow shed; (*c*) *Phot: Opt:* **é. coloré, é. compensateur, é. filtre**, (colour) screen, (light, correction) filter; **é. de ciel**, sky filter; **é. orthochromatique**, orthochromatic screen; **é. sélectif**, separation filter; **coefficient d'un écran coloré**, multiplying factor; **é. à baïonnette**, bayonet screen, filter; **é. à friction**, slip-on, push-on, screen, filter; **é. à vis, é. vissant**, screw-in screen, filter; (*d*) *El.E:* **é. antiarc**, flash barrier; **é. électrostatique**, electrostatic shield; Faraday screen, shield; **é. inductif**, induction sheath; (*e*) **procédé à l'é. de soie**, silk screen (printing) process. **2.** (*a*) *Cin: Phot:* **é. (de projection)**, screen; **é. panoramique**, panoramic screen; *Coll.* **l'é.**, the cinema; **la technique de l'é.**, film technique; **é. de télévision**, television screen; *F:* **le petit é.**, television; *F:* the small screen; *P:* the telly; **mettre, porter, un roman à l'é.**, (i) to film, (ii) to televise, a novel; (*b*) *Elcs:* screen (of cathode-ray tube); **effet d'é.**, screening effect, screening factor; **é. (de) radar**, radar scope, radar screen; **é. lumineux**, display screen; **é. luminescent**, luminescent screen; **é. panoramique**, plan-position indicator, P.P.I.; **é. absorbant**, dark-trace screen; (*X rays*) **é. fluorescent, é. radioscopique**, fluorescent screen. **3.** (*a*) *Mch:* baffle-plate (of boiler); (*b*) **é. acoustique**, (i) baffle (-board) (of loudspeaker); (ii) gobo (of microphone, etc.).

écrancher [ekrɑ̃ʃe], *v.tr. Tex:* = ÉCLANCHER.

écrasable [ekrɑzabl̩], *a.* crushable.

écrasage [ekrɑza:ʒ], *s.m.* crushing (of ores, oil-seeds, etc.).

écrasant [ekrɑzɑ̃], *a.* crushing (weight, contempt, defeat, etc.); **preuves écrasantes**, overwhelming proof; **majorité écrasante**, staggering, overwhelming, majority.

écrasé [ekrɑze], *a.* **1.** crushed, squashed; **é. de soleil**, sun-drenched. **2.** flattened; *Arch:* too low, too flat. **3.** *Journ: F:* **rubrique des chiens écrasés**, odd news items (especially accidents).

écrasement [ekrɑzmɑ̃], *s.m.* **1.** (*a*) crushing, squashing (of fruit, etc.); oppression (of the people); defeat (of army); collapse, breakdown (of building, etc.); prostration, state of collapse (of person); *Mec.E:* **essai d'é.**, crushing test; **résistance à l'é.**, crushing strength; *Typ:* **é. (des caractères)**, batter; (*b*) *Ling:* contraction, reduction; (*c*) *Surg:* ecrasement. **2. é. d'une chaudière**, implosion of a boiler.

écrase-merdes [ekrɑzmɛrd], *s.m.pl. P:* clod-hoppers, beetle-crushers.

écraser [ekrɑze], *v.tr.* **1.** to crush, bruise (fruit, limb, etc.); to flatten out (tin can, etc.); to squash (fruit, black-beetle); *Typ:* to batter (type); **machine à é.**, crushing-mill; **se faire é.**, to get run over; **il a été écrasé par une auto**, he was run over by a car; **il fut écrasé sous les pieds des chevaux**, he was trampled to death by the horses' hooves; *Aut: F:* **é. l'accélérateur**, *P:* **le champignon**, to step on the gas; **é. un peuple d'impôts**, to overburden a people with taxes; to crush a people under taxation; **être écrasé de travail**, to be overwhelmed, *F:* snowed under, with work; *F:* **ce n'est pas l'intelligence qui l'écrase**, he's not overburdened with brains; **pièces en main il écrasa ses adversaires**, documents in hand he crushed, *F:* squashed, his opponents; **le plus faible est toujours écrasé**, the weakest goes to the wall; **tour dont la hauteur écrase le corps de bâtiment**, tower whose height dwarfs the main building; **un silence de mort écrase toute la nature**, a deathlike silence weighs upon the whole of nature; *Fin: F:* **é. le marché**, to glut, bang, the market; *Ten:* **é. la balle**, to kill, smash, the ball; **coup écrasé**, smash; *P:* **en é.**, to sleep soundly, to be sound asleep. **2.** *v.i. P:* **il ferait mieux d'é.**, it would be better not to insist; **écrase!** shut up!

s'écraser. 1. (*a*) to collapse, break down, crumple up; (*of waves*) to break; (*of aircraft*) **s'é. sur le sol**, to crash (to earth); **il tomba du toit et vint s'é. sur la chaussée**, he fell from the roof and crashed down on the roadway; (*b*) **la neige s'écrase sous nos pieds**, the snow crunches under our feet. **2. on s'écrasait aux portes**, there was a dreadful crush, squash, at the doors.

écraseur, -euse [ekrɑzœ:r, -ø:z]. **1.** *s.* (*a*) crusher; (*b*) *Aut: F:* road hog; bad driver. **2.** *s.m.* (*a*) *Civ.E:* steam roller; (*b*) *Surg:* écraseur. **3.** *a.* crushing.

écrasis [ekrɑzi], *s.m.* mass, heap, of crushed material.

écrasite [ekrazit], *s.f. Exp: A:* ecrasite.

écrasure [ekrɑzy:r], *s.f.* **1.** crushed spot (on velvet, etc.). **2.** *pl.* broken pieces, fragments, debris (of sth. that has been crushed).

écrémage [ekrema:ʒ], *s.m.* **1.** *Dom.Ec:* creaming: (i) separating; (ii) skimming (of milk). **2.** *Glassm:* skimming, scumming (of molten glass); *Metall:* drossing.

écrémaison [ekremɛzɔ̃], *s.f. Glassm:* skimming scumming (of molten glass).

écrémer [ekreme], *v.tr.* (**j'écrème, n. écrémons; j'écrémerai**) **1.** (*a*) *Dom.Ec:* to cream: (i) to separate; (ii) to skim (milk); (*b*) to take the best part, the cream, of (sth.); **lait écrémé,** skimmed milk. **2.** *Glassm:* to skim, scum (molten glass); *Metall:* to dross.

écrémeur [ekremœːr], *s.m. Petroleum Ind:* oil separator.

écrémeuse [ekremøːz], *s.f.* **1.** *Dom.Ec:* (cream) separator; creamer. **2.** *Glassm: Metall:* skimmer.

écrémillon [ekremijɔ̃], *s.m. Dial:* (*W.Fr.*) skimmed milk.

écrémoir, *s.m.,* **écrémoire** [ekremwaːr], *s.f.* skimmer.

écrémure [ekremyːr], *s.m. Glassm:* skimmings.

écrêtage [ekrɛtaːʒ], *s.m. El:* chopping, clipping.

écrêtement [ekrɛtmɑ̃], *s.m.* removal of (cocks') combs; knocking off of the tops (of flowers, corn, etc.); cutting down (of parapet, etc., by gun-fire); lowering the crest (of hill).

écrêter [ekrɛte], *v.tr.* (*a*) to remove the comb of (cock); (*b*) to notch (top of wall); (*c*) to knock off the tops of (flowers, corn, etc.); (*d*) to cut down (parapet, etc., by gunfire); (*e*) to lower the crest of (hill); **é. une côte,** to cut down a slope; (*f*) *El:* to chop, to clip.

écrevisse [ekrəvis], *s.f.* **1.** (*a*) (fresh-water) crayfish, *U.S:* crawfish; (*b*) *Dial:* **é. de mer,** lobster; *F:* **rouge comme une é.,** as red as a boiled lobster; *F:* **marcher en é., comme les écrevisses,** (i) to walk backwards; (ii) to walk at a snail's pace. **2.** *Astr:* Cancer, the Crab. **3.** *Metalw:* lever-grip tongs. **4. armure à é.,** écrevisse, splint armour.

écrier[1] [ekrije], *v.tr. & i.* to clean (wire) (by rubbing it with a rag containing grit).

écrier[2] **(s')**, *v.pr.* (*p.d. & pr.sub.* **n.n. écriions, v.v. écriiez**) (*a*) to cry (out), to shout (out); **s'é. de douleur,** to cry out with pain; (*b*) to exclaim; to burst out, break out.

écrille [ekriːj], *s.f. Pisc:* grating (of fishpond).

écrin [ekrɛ̃], *s.m.* (*a*) (jewel)case; (*b*) *A:* casket.

écrire [ekriːr], (*p.pr.* **écrivant;** *p.p.* **écrit;** *pr.ind.* **j'écris, il écrit, n. écrivons, ils écrivent;** *pr.sub.* **j'écrive;** *p.d.* **j'écrivais;** *p.h.* **j'écrivis;** *fu.* **j'écrirai**) to write; (*a*) **é. qch. à l'encre, avec de l'encre,** to write sth. in ink; **il écrit bien,** (i) he is a good writer (of fiction, etc.); (ii) he writes a good hand; **é. sous la dictée de qn,** to write from s.o.'s dictation; **machine à é.,** typewriter; **é. une lettre à la machine,** to type a letter; **écrit à la machine,** typewritten, typed; **é. à qn,** to write to s.o.; **é. une lettre à qn,** to write s.o. a letter; **é. un mot à la hâte,** to scribble a note; **é. un mot à qn,** to drop s.o. a line; **é. en Amérique, au Japon,** to write to America, to Japan; **il m'a écrit la mort de son père,** he has written to tell me of his father's death; **je lui ai écrit de venir,** I have written asking him to come; **lettre écrite par . . .,** letter written by, in the handwriting of . . .; (*b*) to write (sth.) down; **é. l'adresse de qn,** to write down, jot down, s.o.'s address; **ce mot s'écrit avec,** *A:* **par, un g,** this word is written, spelt, with a g; *F:* **il est écrit que je ne peux pas y aller,** I am fated not to get there; *Com:* **é. la comptabilité,** to write up the books; (*c*) to write, compose (book, song, etc.); **é. dans les journaux,** to write for the papers; *abs.* **il écrit,** he's a writer, he writes.

s'écrire, to write, sign, one's name (**de telle façon,** in such and such a way).

écrit [ekri]. **1.** *a.* (*a*) written (word, law, etc.); (*b*) **style trop é.,** over-elaborate style. **2.** *s.m.* (*a*) writing; **consigner, coucher, qch. par é.,** to set down sth. in writing, in black and white; **convention en, par, é.,** agreement in writing, written agreement; **exposer un cas par é.,** to submit a written statement of a case; **exprimer un désir par é.,** to record a wish in writing; (*b*) written document, written work; **faire, signer, un é.,** to draw up, to sign, a document; **il tira un é. de sa poche,** he took from his pocket a paper with something written on it; **les écrits de Bossuet,** the writings, works, of Bossuet; (*c*) *Sch:* **passer, échouer, à l'é.,** to pass, fail in, the written examination; **corriger l'é.,** to mark (examination) papers.

écriteau, -eaux [ekrito], *s.m.* placard; announcement (posted up); **j'ai vu un é. annonçant "à vendre" devant la maison,** I saw a notice "for sale" in front of the house; **un é. portant "passage interdit,"** a sign saying "no thoroughfare."

écritoire [ekritwaːr], *s.f.* **1.** *A:* writing-desk. **2.** inkstand. **3.** writing-room, scriptorium (of monastery).

écriture [ekrityːr], *s.f.* **1.** (hand)writing; **avoir une belle é., une é. lisible,** to write a good hand, a legible hand; **é. affreuse,** abominable hand, awful scrawl; **é. anglaise,** Italian hand, running hand; **é. gothique,** Gothic script; **é. à la machine,** typewriting, typing; *s.a.* BÂTARD 1. **2.** (*a*) *pl.* (legal, commercial) papers, documents, records; **écritures d'une banque,** accounts, books, of a bank; **tenir les écritures,** to keep the accounts; **commis, employé, -ée, aux écritures,** book-keeper, invoicing clerk, entering clerk; (*b*) *Book-k:* entry, item; **écritures en partie double,** double entry; (*c*) **l'É. sainte, les saintes Écritures,** Holy Scripture, the Scriptures, Holy Writ. **3.** writing (as a literary art); **l'é. artiste des Goncourt,** the artistry of the Goncourt brothers.

écrivailler [ekrivɑje], *v.i. F:* (*a*) to be a hack-(writer); (*b*) to dabble in literary work, to scribble.

écrivaillerie [ekrivɑjri], *s.f. F:* mania for writing, scribbling.

écrivailleur, -euse [ekrivɑjœːr, -øːz], *s.,* **écrivaillon** [ekrivɑjɔ̃], *s.m. F:* hack-writer, scribbler.

écrivain [ekrivɛ̃], *s.m.* **1.** (*a*) *A:* scrivener, scribe; **é. public,** (public) letter-writer; (*b*) *Nau:* writer. **2.** author, writer; **femme é.,** *occ.* **une é.,** woman writer; authoress; **é. besogneux,** writer of pot-boilers. **3.** *Ent: F:* common vine grub.

écrivasser [ekrivase], *v.i. F:* (*a*) to be a hack (writer); (*b*) to scribble.

écrivasserie [ekrivasri], *s.f. F:* mania for writing, scribbling.

écrivassier, -ière [ekrivasje, -jɛːr], *s. & occ. a. F:* hack (writer); scribbler.

écriveur, -euse [ekrivœːr, -øːz], *s.* inveterate writer; **grand é. de lettres,** great letter-writer.

écrou[1] [ekru], *s.m. Jur:* (*a*) entry (on prison calendar) of receipt of prisoner into custody; (*b*) committal to gaol; **levée d'é.,** (i) order of release; (ii) release, discharge, from prison.

écrou[2], *s.m. Mch: etc:* (screw)nut, female screw; **é. ailé, à ailettes, à oreilles, à papillon,** thumb nut, screw; wing nut, screw; butterfly nut; **é. d'arrêt, contre-é.,** check nut; **é. d'assemblage, é.-raccord,** union nut, coupling nut; **é. de blocage,** lock nut; **é. borgne,** acorn nut, cap nut, blind nut; **é. brut,** nut blank; **é. carré,** square nut; **é. à chape,** cap nut; **é. à collet,** collar nut; **é. crénelé, à créneaux, à encoches,** castellated nut, castle nut; **é. cylindrique,** round nut, ring nut; **é. de fixation, de réglage,** adjusting nut; **é. hexagonal, (à) six pans,** hexagonal nut; **é. indesserrable,** self-locking nut; **é. moleté, à molette,** milled, knurled nut; **é. noyé, encastré,** flush nut, internal wrenching nut; **é. prisonnier,** anchor nut, plate nut; **é. presse-étoupe,** gland nut; *Artil:* **é. de culasse,** breech bushing.

écrouelles [ekruɛl], *s.f.pl.* **1.** *Med: A:* scrofula, king's evil. **2.** *Bot: F:* **herbe aux écrouelles,** (i) burweed; (ii) figwort.

écrouelleux, -euse [ekruɛlø, -øːz], *a. A:* scrofulous.

écrouer [ekrue], *v.tr.* (*a*) to enter (prisoner's name) on the prison calendar; (*b*) to imprison; to commit, consign, (s.o.) to prison; **écroué au dépôt,** consigned to the cells.

écroui [ekrui], *a. Metalw:* (*a*) hammer-hardened, cold-beaten, cold-hammered; (*b*) cold-drawn; (*c*) cold-rolled.

écrouir [ekruiːr], *v.tr. Metalw:* (*a*) to hammer-harden, to cold hammer; (*b*) to cold draw; (*c*) to cold roll.

écrouissage [ekruisaːʒ], *s.m.,* **écrouissement** [ekruismɑ̃], *s.m. Metalw:* (*a*) hammer-hardening, cold-hammering; work-hardening; (*b*) cold-drawing; (*c*) cold-rolling.

écroulé [ekrule], *a.* **1.** destroyed; in ruins; **mur (à moitié) é.,** tumble-down wall. **2.** (*of pers.*) (*a*) exhausted, in a state of collapse; (*b*) *F:* **être é.,** to be doubled up with laughter.

écroulement [ekrulmɑ̃], *s.m.* collapse, tumbling down, falling in, giving way (of building, etc.); fall (of earth, rock); **é. de toutes mes espérances,** ruin, downfall, of all my hopes; **é. d'une fortune,** crumbling, collapse, of a fortune; **é. d'un système,** breakdown of a system; **é. de la santé,** breakdown in health.

écrouler (s') [sekrule], *v.pr.* (*a*) (*of building, roof, bridge, etc.*) to collapse, fall in, give way, fall to pieces, tumble down; **la terre s'écroule,** the ground is crumbling away; **l'énorme masse s'écroula,** the vast mass (i) toppled over; (ii) crumpled up; **le plafond s'écroula sur nous, tous nos plans s'écroulèrent,** the ceiling, our plans, fell about our ears; **empire près de s'é.,** empire on the verge of ruin, of breaking up; (*b*) *F:* **s'é. sur une chaise,** to drop, flop, on to a chair; *Sp:* **il s'est écroulé dans la ligne d'arrivée,** he collapsed at the tape.

écroûtage [ekrutaːʒ], **écroûtement** [ekrutmɑ̃], *s.m.* (*a*) removing the crust (from bread, etc.); (*b*) *Agr:* scarifying (of land).

écroûter [ekrute], *v.tr.* (*a*) to remove the crust from (bread, etc.); (*b*) *Agr:* to scarify (land).

écroûteuse [ekrutøːz], *s.f. Agr:* scarifier.

écru [ekry], *a. Tex:* (*of material*) unbleached, écru, natural-coloured; **soie écrue,** raw silk; **toile écrue,** holland.

écrues [ekry], *s.f.pl.* scrub of recent growth.

ectase [ɛktaːz], *s.f. Gram:* ectasis.

ectasie [ɛktazi], *s.f. Med:* ectasis.

ecthyma [ɛktima], *s.m. Med: Vet:* ecthyma.

ecto- [ɛkto], *pref.* ecto-.

ectoblaste [ɛktɔblast], *s.m. Biol:* ectoblast.

ectocardie [ɛktɔkardi], *s.f. Med:* ectocardia.

ectocarpales [ɛktɔkarpal], *s.f.pl. Algae:* Ectocarpales.

ectocyste [ɛktɔsist], *s.m. Biol:* ectocyst.

ectoderme [ɛktɔdɛrm], *s.m. Biol:* ectoderm.

ectodermique [ɛktɔdɛrmik], *a. Biol:* ectodermal, ectodermic.

ectogenèse [ɛktɔʒənɛːz], *s.f.* ectogenesis.

ectohormone [ɛktɔɔrmɔn], *s.f. Ap:* queen substance.

ectolécithe [ɛktɔlesit], *a. Biol:* ectolecithal.

ectomorphe [ɛktɔmɔrf]. **1.** *a.* ectomorphic. **2.** *s.m. or f.* ectomorph.

ectomorphisme [ɛktɔmɔrfism], *s.m.* ectomorphy.

ectoparasite [ɛktɔparazit], *Z:* **1.** *a.* ectoparasitic. **2.** *s.m.* ectoparasite.

ectopie [ɛktɔpi], *s.f.* displacement (of organ); ectopia; **e. inguinale des testicules, e. testiculaire,** undescended testes.

ectopiste [ɛktɔpist], *s.m. Orn:* **e. migrateur,** passenger pigeon.

ectoplasme [ɛktɔplasm], *s.m. Biol: Psychics:* ectoplasm.

ectoplasmique [ɛktɔplasmik], *a.* ectoplasm(at)ic.

ectoproctes [ɛktɔprɔkt], *s.m.pl. Z:* Ectoprocta.

ectosome [ɛktɔzɔm], *s.m. Biol:* ectosome.

ectotrophe [ɛktɔtrɔf]. **1.** *a. Nat.Hist:* ectotrophic. **2.** *s.m.pl. Ent:* Ectotrophi, Ectognatha.

ectozoaire [ɛktɔzɔɛːr], *Z:* **1.** *s.m.* ectozoon, ectozoan. **2.** *a.* ectozoan, ectozoic.

ectrodactyle [ɛktrɔdaktyl], *a.* ectrodactylous.

ectrodactylie [ɛktrɔdaktili], *s.f.* ectrodactylia, ectrodactyly, ectrodactylism.

ectromèle [ɛktrɔmɛl], *a. & s.m. or f. Ter:* ectromelian.

ectromélie [ɛktrɔmeli], *s.f. Ter:* ectromelia.

ectropion [ɛktrɔpjɔ̃], *s.m. Med:* ectropion, ectropium; eversion (of eyelid).

ectypal, -aux [ɛktipal, -o], *a. Phil:* ectypal.

ectype [ɛktip], *s.f.* ectype.

écu [eky], *s.m.* **1.** (*a*) *Arm:* shield; (*b*) *Her:* escutcheon, coat of arms. **2.** *Num: A:* (*a*) crown (= three francs); **é. de cinq francs,** five-franc piece; (*b*) *F:* **avoir des écus,** to have plenty of money, pots of money; **c'est le père aux écus,** he's rolling (in money); **je n'ai pas un é. vaillant,** I haven't a penny to bless my name with; **faire valser les écus,** to make the money fly. **3.** *Bot: F:* **herbe aux écus,** moneywort, creeping jenny. **4.** *Ent:* scutum. **5.** *Paperm: approx.* = large post.

écuadorien, -ienne [ekwadɔrjɛ̃, -jɛn], *a. & s. Geog:* Ecuadorian.

écuage [ekɥaːʒ], *s.m. Hist:* **1.** feudal service of squire. **2.** scutage.

écuanteur [ekɥɑ̃tœːr], *s.f. Veh:* dish(ing) (of wheels).

écubier [ekybje], *s.m. Nau:* **é. (de mouillage),** hawse hole, hawse pipe; **é. d'amarrage, de pavois,** mooring pipe, ring; bulwark chock; **é. arrière, d'embossage,** stern pipe, cat hole; **é. de corps mort,** stern mooring pipe; **é. de Panama,** Panama lead, Panama chock, bull ring; **é. de pont,** chain pipe, deck pipe; **é. de remorque,** towing chock; **tampon d'é.,** hawse plug, block.

écueil [ekœːj], *s.m.* reef, shelf; (*of ship*) **donner sur les écueils,** to strike the rocks; **la vie est pleine d'écueils,** life is full of dangers; **se heurter à un é.,** to strike, come across, a snag; **ce manque d'harmonie fut l'é. de l'entreprise,** this lack of harmony was the rock on which the undertaking came to grief.

écuelle [ekɥɛl], *s.f.* **1.** (*a*) bowl, basin; porringer; **manger une é. de soupe,** to eat a bowl(ful) of soup; **manger à la même é.,** (i) to live on intimate terms together; (ii) to have the same interests; (*b*) *P:* plate; (*c*) *Nau:* saucer, bed-plate (of capstan); (*d*) *Min:* pan. **2.** *Bot: F:* **é. d'eau,** marsh pennywort, water-cup.

écuellée [ekɥele], *s.f.* bowlful.
écuellier [ekɥelje], *s.m. A.Furn:* = dresser.
écuer [ekɥe], *v.tr.* to dish (wheel).
écuiage [ekɥija:ʒ], *s.m. Hist:* **1.** feudal service of a squire. **2.** scutage.
écuisser [ekɥise], *v.tr.* to split the trunk of (a tree, in felling it).
éculé [ekyle], *a.* (*a*) down-at-heel; (*b*) well-worn (device, etc.); *F:* **les trucs les plus éculés réussissent toujours,** the corniest tricks, tricks that have been used time and time again, always succeed.
éculer [ekyle], *v.tr.* **é. ses souliers,** to wear one's shoes down at heel.
écumage [ekyma:ʒ], *s.m.* scumming, skimming (of soup, jam, molten metal, etc.); priming (of water in a boiler); *Ind:* **produits d'é.,** skimmings.
écumant [ekymɑ̃], *a.* foaming, frothing (sea, beer, etc.); **é. de rage,** foaming with rage.
écume [ekym], *s.f.* **1.** (*a*) froth (on liquid); foam (on waves, etc.); **cheval couvert d'é.,** foam-covered horse; *Ent:* **é. printanière,** cuckoo-spit; (*b*) scum (on soup, jam, etc.); **é. de la société,** scum, dregs, of society; (*c*) *Metall:* dross, scum. **2. é. de mer,** meerschaum; **pipe en é. de mer, pipe d'é.,** meerschaum (pipe); **é. de manganèse,** bog manganese; **é. de fer,** oligist (iron).
écuménicité [ekymenisite], *s.f.* (o)ecumenicity.
écuménique [ekymenik], *a.* (o)ecumenical.
écuméniquement [ekymenikmɑ̃], *adv.* (o)ecumenically.
écumer [ekyme]. **1.** *v.tr.* (*a*) to scum, skim (soup, molten metal, etc.); **é. le pot, la marmite,** (i) to skim the pot; (ii) to cadge, sponge; (*b*) **é. les mers,** to scour the seas; to buccaneer; **les antiquaires ont écumé la région,** the antique dealers have laid their hands on everything they could find in the region, have cleaned out the region; (*c*) (*of bird of prey*) **é. sa proie,** to skim over its prey. **2.** *v.i.* (*a*) (*of wine, beer, the sea, etc.*) to foam, froth; **cheval qui écume,** foaming horse; (*of pers.*) **é. (de rage),** to foam (at the mouth) with rage; (*b*) to scum, froth; (*c*) *Mch:* (*of boiler*) to prime.
écumeresse [ekym(ə)rɛs], *s.f. Ind:* (large) skimmer.
écumeur, -euse[1] [ekymœ:r, -ø:z], *s.* (*a*) one who scums (soup, molten metal, etc.); **é. de mer,** sea-rover, pirate; **é. littéraire,** plagiarist; *A:* **é. de marmites, de tables,** sponger, parasite, hanger-on; (*b*) *Adm:* (*in Paris*) official in charge of recovering bodies of animals from the Seine.
écumeux, -euse[2] [ekymø, -ø:z], *a.* foamy, frothy (waves, liquor, etc.), scummy (liquid).
écumoire [ekymwa:r], *s.f. Cu: Tchn:* skimmer; *Cu:* skimming ladle; *F:* **en é., comme une é.,** riddled with bullets; **visage en é.,** face seamed with scars.
écurage [ekyra:ʒ], *s.m. A:* cleaning, cleansing, scouring (of pots, pans, etc.); cleaning out (of well); unsilting (of harbour).
écurement [ekyrmɑ̃], *s.m. Agr:* drainage furrow.
écurer [ekyre], *v.tr.* (*a*) *A:* & *Dial:* to clean, cleanse, scour (pots, pans, etc.); to pick (one's teeth); to clean out (well); to unsilt (harbour); (*b*) *Tex:* to clean (teasels).
écurette [ekyrɛt], *s.f. Tex:* (*instrument*) teasel cleaner.
écureuil [ekyrœ:j], *s.m.* **1.** *Z:* (*a*) squirrel; **é. du Canada, de Virginie,** grey squirrel; *N.Am:* **é. d'Amérique,** chickaree; **é. gris,** Gambian tree squirrel; **é. roux,** red squirrel; **vif, agile, comme un é.,** as quick as a squirrel; **cage d'é.,** squirrel-cage; (*b*) **é. de terre, é. rayé indien,** striped Indian squirrel, ground squirrel; *F:* chipmunk; **é. fossoyeur africain,** African ground squirrel; (*c*) **é. volant,** flying squirrel, flying phalanger, polatouche; **é. volant asiatique,** Russian flying squirrel; (*d*) **é. jappant,** prairie dog. **2.** *Ent:* red-humped apple worm. **3.** *A:* treadmill. **4.** *El.E:* **induit à cage d'é.,** squirrel-cage rotor.
écureur, -euse [ekyrœ:r, -ø:z], *s.* (*pers.*) (*a*) *A:* cleaner, cleanser, scourer; (*b*) *Tex:* teasel cleaner.
écurie [ekyri], *s.f.* (*a*) stable; **mettre les chevaux à, dans, l'é.,** to stable the horses; **é. de courses,** racing stable, racing stud; *F:* **sentir l'é.,** to be eager to get back home; (*b*) *Box:* **é. d'entraînement,** boxing school; (*c*) *Nau:* horseboat, -ship; (*d*) *Aut:* stable.
écusson [ekysɔ̃], *s.m.* **1.** *Her:* escutcheon, shield, coat of arms. **2.** keyhole scutcheon, sheave; key-plate. **3.** *Husb:* (milk) escutcheon (of cow). **4.** *Mil:* (*a*) collar-patch, tab, badge (with number, etc.); (*b*) centre portion of epaulet. **5.** *Hort:* (shield)bud (for grafting); **greffe en é.,** budding, shield grafting. **6.** *Ent:* scutellum.
écussonnable [ekysɔnabl̩], *a. Hort:* buddable; suitable for grafting.
écussonnage [ekysɔna:ʒ], *s.m. Hort:* shield grafting, budding.
écussonné [ekysɔne], *a.* **1.** *Ent:* scutellate. **2.** *Ich:* scutate.
écussonner [ekysɔne], *v.tr.* **1.** to put one's coat of arms, on (carriage, etc.). **2.** *Hort:* to bud (a tree), to graft a shield-bud on (fruit tree). **3.** to put a badge on (uniform, etc.).
écussonneur [ekysɔnœ:r], *s.m. Hort:* grafter.
écussonnoir [ekysɔnwa:r], *s.m.* budding knife.
écuyer, -ère [ekɥije, -ɛ:r], *s.* **1.** *s.m. A:* (*a*) squire, esquire; armiger; armour-bearer; **é. tranchant,** esquire trenchant; (*b*) equerry; *Hist:* **grand é.,** Master of the Horse. **2.** (*a*) *s.m.* & *f.* rider; horseman, horsewoman; **être bon é., bonne écuyère,** to ride well, to be a good rider; **é. de cirque,** circus rider; equestrian, *f.* equestrienne; **bottes à l'écuyère,** riding boots; (*of woman*) **monter à l'écuyère,** to ride astride; (*b*) *s.m.* riding-master. **3.** *s.m.* (*a*) prop, stay (of tree); (*b*) hand-rail (on the wall side of staircase).
eczéma [ɛgzema], *s.m. Med:* eczema; **e. humide, suintant,** weeping eczema.
eczémateux, -euse [ɛgzematø, -ø:z], *a. Med:* eczematous.
eczématide [ɛgzematid], *s.f. Med:* seborrheic eczema.
eczématiforme [ɛgzematifɔrm], *a.* eczematoid.
eczématisation [ɛgzematizasjɔ̃], *s.f.* eczematization.
eczématiser (s') [sɛgzematize], *v.pr.* to become eczematous; to develop into eczema.
édaphique [edafik], *a. Biol:* edaphic, relating to the soil.
édaphologie [edafɔlɔʒi], *s.f. Biol:* edaphology.
édaphon [edafɔ̃], *s.m. Biol:* edaphon.
eddique [edik], *a. Lit:* Eddaic, Eddic.
edelweiss [edɛlvais, -vɛs], *s.m. Bot:* edelweiss.
Éden (l') [ledɛn], *s.m. B:* (the Garden of) Eden.
édénien, -ienne [edenjɛ̃, -jɛn], **édénique** [edenik], *a.* paradisiac, like the Garden of Eden.
édénite [edenit], *s.f. Miner:* edenite.
édentation [edɑ̃tasjɔ̃], *s.f.* loss of teeth; extraction of teeth.
édenté [edɑ̃te], *a.* **1.** toothless (person, etc.). **2.** *Z:* edentate; *s.m.pl.* **édentés,** Edentata.
édentement [edɑ̃tmɑ̃], *s.m.* toothlessness.
édenter [edɑ̃te], *v.tr.* **é. qn,** to deprive s.o. of (his) teeth, to break s.o.'s teeth; **la vieillesse l'a édenté,** old age has made him lose his teeth; **é. un peigne,** to break the teeth of a comb.
s'édenter, to lose one's teeth.
Édesse [edɛs], *Pr.n.f. A.Geog:* Edessa.
édestine [edɛstin], *s.f. Bio-Ch:* edestin.
édictal, -aux [ediktal, -o], *a.* edictal (proclamation, etc.).
édicter [edikte], *v.tr.* to enact, decree (penalties, etc.).
édicule [edikyl], *s.m.* **1.** *A:* aedicule, miniature temple; private chapel. **2.** (*a*) kiosk, shelter; (*b*) *F:* public convenience.
édifiant [edifjɑ̃], *a.* edifying (sermon, example, etc.).
édificateur, -trice [edifikatœ:r, -tris]. **1.** *a. Bot:* colonizing (plant). **2.** *s.m.* **édificateur,** builder, constructor (*esp.* of public buildings).
édification [edifikasjɔ̃], *s.f.* **1.** (*a*) erection, construction, building (of monument, etc.); (*b*) **é. d'un empire,** building up of an empire; **é. d'une œuvre littéraire,** creation of a literary work. **2.** (*a*) edification; (*b*) information; **pour votre é., sachez que . . .,** for your information . . ., I think you should know that . . .
édifice [edifis], *s.m.* (*a*) building, edifice, structure, erection; **édifices publics,** public buildings; (*b*) **tout l'é. social,** the whole fabric, structure, of society; (*c*) *Ap:* comb; (*d*) **é. de cheveux,** elaborate hairstyle; **l'é. d'une chevelure,** styling of a head of hair.
édifier [edifje], *v.tr.* (*p.d.* & *pr.sub.* **n. édifiions, v. édifiiez**) **1.** (*a*) to erect, build, construct (public building, etc.); (*b*) to construct, create; **é. un système,** to build up a system; **il a fallu une vie à Mansion pour é. son dictionnaire,** the creation, realization, of his dictionary took Mansion a whole lifetime. **2.** (*a*) to edify; **sermon qui édifie,** edifying sermon; (*b*) to edify, inform; **je vais vous é. là-dessus,** let me explain it to you; **cet incident m'a édifié sur les intentions de mon ami,** this incident clearly revealed my friend's intentions; *Iron:* **nous voilà édifiés!** well, now we know!
édile [edil], *s.m.* (*a*) *Rom.Ant:* aedile; (*b*) *Adm: Journ:* municipal official; magistrate; town councillor.
édilitaire [edilitɛ:r], *a.* (*a*) *Rom.Ant:* aedilitian; (*b*) municipal, civic.
édilité [edilite], *s.f.* (*a*) *Rom.Ant:* aedileship; (*b*) (*rare*) municipal administration; body of magistrates, of public men.
Édimbourg [edɛ̃bu:r], *Pr.n. Geog:* Edinburgh.
édimbourgeois, -oise [edɛ̃burʒwa, -wa:z], *a.* & *s. Geog:* (native, inhabitant) of Edinburgh.
édingtonite [ediŋtɔnit], *s.f. Miner:* edingtonite.
édit [edi], *s.m.* edict; **l'É. de Nantes,** the Edict of Nantes.
éditant [editɑ̃], *a. A:* **libraire é.,** publisher.
éditer [edite], *v.tr.* **1.** to edit (text with notes, etc.). **2.** to publish (book, etc.).
éditeur, -trice [editœ:r, -tris], *s.* **1.** editor (of text). **2.** publisher; *Jur:* **é. responsable,** person responsible at law (for the contents of book).
Édith(e) [edit], *Pr.n.f.* Edith.
édition [edisjɔ̃], *s.f.* **1.** edition, issue, impression (of work); **é. originale, é. princeps,** first, original, edition; **é. ne varietur,** definitive edition; **é. scolaire,** school edition; **é. populaire,** cheap reprint; **ce livre a connu de nombreuses éditions,** this book has run into numerous editions; **il (en) est à sa quatrième é.,** it is in its fourth edition. **2.** (*a*) publishing; **maison d'é.,** publishing house, firm: (*b*) publishing (trade); **travailler dans l'é.,** to be in publishing; to work in a publishing company.
éditorial, -iaux [editɔrjal, -jo], *Journ:* **1.** *a.* editorial; leading (article). **2.** *s.m.* leading article, leader; editorial.
éditorialiste [editɔrjalist], *s.m.* & *f.* (*a*) *Journ:* leader-writer; (*b*) *W.Tel:* programme editor.
Edmond [ɛdmɔ̃], *Pr.n.m.* Edmund.
Édomite [edɔmit], *s.m. or f. B.Hist:* Edomite.
Édoniens [edɔnjɛ̃], *s.m.pl. Hist:* Edoni, Edones.
édossage [edosa:ʒ], *s.m. Agr:* removal of surface soil.
édosser [edose], *v.tr. Agr:* to remove the surface soil from (an area, to clear it of roots).
Édouard [edwa:r], *Pr.n.m.* Edward.
édouardien, -ienne [edwardjɛ̃, -jɛn], *a.* Edwardian.
édredon [edrədɔ̃], *s.m.* (*a*) *A:* eider down; (*b*) **é. (piqué, américain),** eiderdown.
édrioastérides [edrijɔasterid], *s.m.pl. Paleont:* Edrioasteroidea.
édriophtalme [edrijɔftalm], *Crust:* **1.** *a.* edriophthalmous, edriophthalmic, edriophthalmatous. **2.** *s.m.* edriophthalmoan; *pl.* **édriophtalmes,** Edriophthalma(ta).
éducabilité [edykabilite], *s.f.* educability.
éducable [edykabl̩], *a.* educable; (animal) that can be trained.
éducateur, -trice [edykatœ:r, -tris]. **1.** *s.* (*a*) educator, instructor; **la douleur est la plus grande éducatrice des hommes,** suffering is the greatest teacher of mankind; man learns most through suffering; (*b*) educationalist; (*c*) **é. (d'enfants retardés),** teacher of mentally retarded, educationally sub-normal, children. **2.** *a.* **méthodes éducatrices,** educative methods; **ouvrages éducateurs,** educational works; **le rôle é. des parents,** the educational rôle of parents.
éducatif, -ive [edykatif, -i:v], *a.* educative, instructive; informative (book); **filmé.,** educational film.
éducation [edykasjɔ̃], *s.f.* **1.** (*a*) education; **faire l'é. de qn,** to educate s.o.; **il a reçu une forte é.,** he is well educated; **é. professionnelle,** vocational training; **é. physique,** physical training; **é. de l'oreille,** ear training; **maison d'é.,** educational establishment; **maison d'é. surveillée** = approved school; (*b*) training (of animals); (*c*) upbringing, breeding; **personne sans é.,** ill-bred person; **il manque d'é.,** he has no manners. **2.** *A:* rearing, breeding (of silkworms, sheep, etc.); keeping (of bees); growing (of plants).
éducationnel, -elle [edykasjɔnɛl], *a.* educational.
éduction [edyksjɔ̃], *s.f.* eduction.
édulcorant [edylkɔrɑ̃]. **1.** *a.* sweetening. **2.** *s.m.* sweetening substance, sweetener; *Ch:* edulcorator.
édulcoration [edylkɔrasjɔ̃], *s.f.* sweetening; *Ch:* edulcoration.
édulcorer [edylkɔre], *v.tr. Pharm:* **1.** to sweeten (medicine, etc.). **2.** to edulcorate (powdered substance, etc.). **3.** to weaken; to water down; **é. une triste nouvelle,** to break a piece of bad news gently; **compte-rendu édulcoré,** watered-down account, report.
édule [edyl], *a. Bot:* edible, esculent.
éduquer [edyke], *v.tr.* **1.** to bring up, educate (child); **personne mal éduquée,** ill-bred person. **2.** to train (animal).
éfaufiler [efofile], *v.tr.* to unravel, ravel out (material).
efendi [efɛ̃di], *s.m.* (*Turkish title*) effendi.

effaçable [efasabl], *a.* effaceable, erasable.
effaçage [efasa:ʒ], *s.m.* deleting; (*a*) rubbing out, erasing; (*b*) crossing out.
efface [efas], *s.f. Fr.C:* eraser, india rubber.
effacé [efase], *a.* **1.** unobtrusive (manner); **vie effacée**, retired life; **manières effacées**, retiring ways, manners; **rôle e.**, unobtrusive part; small part; **menton e.**, receding chin. **2.** *Fenc: etc:* **position effacée**, sideways position of body (offering least resistance to attack); *Rail:* **signal e.**, open signal, road clear.
effacement [efasmɑ̃], *s.m.* **1.** obliteration (of word, mark, etc.); effacement, wearing away (of carvings, etc.); blotting out, fading (of memories). **2. e. du corps**, sideways position of body (in fencing, etc.); **e. des épaules**, throwing back, set-back, of the shoulders. **3.** retirement, unobtrusiveness (of manners, character, life, etc.); self-effacement.
effacer [efase], *v.tr.* (**j'effaçai(s); n. effaçons**) **1.** (*a*) to efface, obliterate, delete; **e. un mot avec une gomme**, to rub out a word; **e. un mot à la plume**, to cross out a word; **e. une tache**, to wash out, wipe out, a stain; **e. des imperfections**, to smooth out imperfections; **sculptures effacées par le temps**, carvings weathered, worn away, in the course of time; **e. qch. de sa mémoire**, to blot sth. out of one's memory; **sa beauté effaçait toutes les autres femmes**, her beauty threw, put, all (the) other women into the shade; (*b*) *P:* to kill. **2.** *Fenc: etc:* **e. le corps**, to turn (the body) sideways; **e. les épaules**, to throw back, set back, the shoulders.
s'effacer. **1.** to become obliterated; to wear away; to fade (away) (**de**, from); **cela s'effacera à l'eau**, it will wash off; **impression, souvenir, qui s'efface vite**, impression, memory, that soon fades, that soon dies away, grows dim. **2.** to stand aside; **s'e. pour laisser passer qn**, to draw aside, stand on one side, in order to let s.o. pass; **depuis quelque temps il s'était effacé**, for some time he had kept in the background, had taken a back seat. **3.** (*in fencing, etc.*) (*a*) to stand sideways; to show less front; (*b*) to move aside.
effaceur, -euse [efasœ:r, -ø:z], *s.* (*a*) obliterator; (*b*) *s.m. Sch:* board rubber.
effaçure [efasy:r], *s.f.* obliteration, deletion; (*a*) erasure, word(s) rubbed out; (*b*) word(s) crossed out.
effaner [efane], *v.tr. Agr:* to strip (plant) of superfluous leaves.
effanure [efany:r], *s.f. Agr:* superfluous leaves, etc., stripped from plants.
effarade [efarad], *s.f. A:* panic; agitation.
effarant [efarɑ̃], *a.* bewildering, startling, frightening.
effaré [efare]. **1.** frightened, scared, startled, dismayed; bewildered; flurried, in a fluster, in a flurry; flustered. **2.** *Her:* **lion e.**, lion salient.
effarement [efarmɑ̃], *s.m.* fright, alarm, dismay; bewilderment.
effarer [efare], *v.tr.* to frighten, scare, startle, dismay; to bewilder.
s'effarer, to be frightened, scared, startled (**de**, at, by); to take fright (**de**, at); to be bewildered (**de**, by).
effarouchable [efaruʃabl], *a.* easily scared.
effarouchant [efaruʃɑ̃], *a.* frightening; startling.
effarouchement [efaruʃmɑ̃], *s.m.* startling, frightening (away) (of animal, etc.).
effaroucher [efaruʃe], *v.tr.* to startle, scare away, frighten away (animal); **e. la modestie de qn**, to shock s.o.'s modesty.
s'effaroucher, to be startled, frightened away (**de**, at, by); to be scared; to take fright (**de**, at); **s'e. d'une remarque**, to blush at a remark.
effarvatte [efarvat], *s.f. Orn:* (**rousserolle**) **e.**, reed warbler.
effe [ɛf], *s.f.* (the letter) f.
effecteur, -trice [efɛktœ:r, -tris], *Z:* **1.** *a.* effector; reactive. **2.** *s.m.* effector.
effectif, -ive [efɛktif, -i:v]. **1.** *a.* (*a*) effective, efficacious (treatment, etc.); *A:* **un homme e.**, a man of his word; **rendre (un traité, etc.) e.**, to implement (a treaty, etc.); *Mec:* **pression effective**, active pressure; (*b*) effective, actual; *Fin:* **circulation effective**, active circulation; **valeur effective**, real value; **avoir tant de francs effectifs**, to have so many francs in cash; **il est e. que . . .**, it is true that . . . **2.** *s.m.* (*a*) *Mil:* strength, establishment, manpower; *Navy:* complement; **e. budgétaire**, budgetary strength, *U.S:* authorized strength; **e. théorique**, basic strength; **e. réalisé**, available strength; **e. réel**, effective strength; (**à**) **e. complet**, (at) full strength, (on) full establishment; (*of ship*) **avoir son e. au complet**, to have her full complement; **à e. réduit**, under, below, strength; **crise d'effectifs**, shortage of manpower; (**à**) **e. de guerre**, (at) war strength, (on) war establishment; (**à**) **e. (du temps) de paix**, (on) peacetime establishment, (at) peacetime strength; **état des effectifs**, strength return; **tableau d'effectifs**, establishment chart, manning table, *U.S:* table of organization; **figurer sur les effectifs**, to be on the strength; *Sch:* **réduire l'e. des classes à 25**, to reduce the size of classes to 25; **grille d'effectifs**, personnel grid, members grid (for listing members of an association); (*b*) membership (of party, club); (*c*) *Ind:* stock (of material, etc.).
effectivement [efɛktivmɑ̃], *adv.* **1.** effectively, efficaciously. **2.** Actually, in reality, really; in actual fact. **3.** (*as an answer*) that is so; I agree; of course.
effectuer [efɛktɥe], *v.tr.* to effect, carry out, carry into effect, accomplish; to execute (scheme, operation, etc.); to effect, make (payment); to accomplish (journey, voyage); **e. une réconciliation**, to bring about a reconciliation; **e. une retraite**, to make good a retreat; **e. une expérience**, to carry out an experiment; *Mth:* **e. un calcul**, to make a calculation; **e. la parenthèse**, to work out, multiply out, the brackets.
efféminant [efeminɑ̃], *a.* weakening, enervating (pleasures, etc.).
efféminatìon [efeminasjɔ̃], *s.f.* (*a*) effemination; (*b*) effeminacy.
efféminé [efemine], *a.* effeminate, unmanly, womanish; self-indulgent; **caractère e.**, effeminacy.
efféminement [efeminmɑ̃], *s.m.* effeminacy.
efféminer [efemine], *v.tr.* to effeminatize, to make effeminate; **e. un petit garçon**, to make a mollycoddle of a little boy; **le luxe effémine une nation**, luxury weakens a nation.
s'efféminer, to become effeminate.
effendi [efɛ̃di], *s.m.* (*Turkish title*) effendi.
efférent [eferɑ̃], *a.* efferent (nerve, artery, etc.).
effervescence [efɛrvɛs(s)ɑ̃:s], *s.f.* **1.** effervescence; (*of liquid*) **être en e., faire e.**, to effervesce. **2. e. populaire**, popular excitement; agitation; restlessness, restiveness, of the people; **ville en e.**, town seething with excitement, anger, etc.
effervescent [efɛrvɛs(s)ɑ̃], *a.* **1.** effervescent (drink, etc.). **2.** excitable, easily excited (disposition, crowd, etc.); agitated (crowd).
effet [efɛ], *s.m.* **1.** effect, result; **point d'e. sans cause**, no effect without a cause; **tout cela aura pour e. de le fâcher**, the result, consequence, of all that will be to annoy him; **faire de l'e.**, to be effective; **avoir de l'e. sur le résultat**, to affect the result; **mon avertissement produisit l'e. voulu**, my warning had the desired effect; **avoir, faire, son e.**, to take effect; **à cet e.**, for this purpose; with this object, end, in view; **bouton prévu à cet e.**, button provided for the purpose; **à l'e. de**, for the purpose of, in order to; **mes conseils n'eurent aucun e.**, my advice had no effect, was disregarded; **sans e.**, ineffective, ineffectual; **rester sans e.**, to have no effect. **2.** action, performance, operation, working; (*a*) **mettre un projet à l'e., en e.**, to put a plan into action; to carry out a plan; (*of law, etc.*) **prendre e.**, to become operative; **il me faut des effets et non pas des paroles**, I must have deeds not words; **nul et sans e.**, null and void; **considérer une lettre comme sans e.**, to consider a letter as cancelled; (*b*) *Ins:* commencement (of policy); (*c*) *Games:* (i) *Cr: Ten:* spin, break; **balle qui a de l'e.**, ball that breaks, **donner de l'e. à une balle**, to put a spin on a ball; (ii) *Bill:* **e. de côté**, side (screw); **e. à revenir**, screw back; **faire de l'e. (de côté)**, to put side on the ball; **faire de l'e. à revenir**, to put bottom on the ball; **faire des effets de bande**, to play off the cushion; *s.a.* RÉTROGRADE; (iii) *Bill: A:* **e. d'une queue**, tip of a cue; (*d*) *Mec.E:* **e. utile**, efficiency, net result; **e. réactif**, backlash; **à simple e., à double e.**, single-action, single-acting; double-action, double-acting; *Ball:* **e. meurtrier**, killing power (of shell); (*e*) *Elcs:* **e. Edison**, Edison effect; **e. photo-émissif**, photo-emissive effect; **e. photovoltaïque**, photovoltaic effect; *El:* **e. électrophonique**, electrophonic effect; **e. de scintillation**, flicker effect; *Av:* **e. dynamique**, ram effect; *Ph:* **e. corona, de couronne**, corona discharge; **e. Joule**, Joule effect; **e. pelliculaire, de peau**, Kelvin effect; skin effect; *Nau* **e. de coup de ballast**, slamming, pounding; **e. de déliaison transversale**, racking; **e. de souffle**, (i) *Nau:* parting; (ii) *Exp:* blast effect; (*f*) *adv.phr.* **en e.**, as a matter of fact; indeed; *F:* sure enough; **c'est en e. un honnête homme**, he is indeed an honest man; **oui, je m'en souviens, en e.**, yes, I do remember it; **vous oubliez vos paquets!—en e.!** you are forgetting your parcels!—so I am! **il menaça de partir, et il partit en e.**, he threatened to go and go he did. **3.** (*a*) impression; **quel e. a-t-elle produit sur lui?** what impression did she make on him? **voilà l'e. que cela m'a produit**, that is how it impressed me, how it struck me; **elle me fait l'e. d'un moineau**, she puts me in mind of, reminds me of, a sparrow; **la jupe me fait l'e. d'être trop courte**, the skirt seems, looks, too short to me; *F:* **ça m'a fait un e. de la voir si pâle**, it gave me quite a turn to see her so pale; *F:* **si c'est tout l'e. que ça te fait!** if that's the way you feel about it! **faire de l'e.**, to make a show, attract attention; **cela fait bon e.**, it looks well; **cela fait bon e. dans un discours**, it sounds well in a speech; **faire des effets d'érudition**, to make a parade of learning; **manquer son e.**, to fail to attract attention; (*of joke, etc.*) to miss fire, to fall flat; **phrases à e.**, words used for effect; claptrap; **homme à e.**, affected man; **mobilier à e.**, showy furniture; **feuilleton à gros effets**, blood-and-thunder serial story; *F:* sensational serial; cliffhanger; (*b*) *Art:* **e. de lune**, moonlight effect or study; *Cin: etc:* **effets sonores**, sound effects. **4.** *Com:* **e. de commerce**, negotiable instrument; bill; **effets à payer**, bills payable; **e. à vue**, draft at sight; **e. sur place**, local bill; *Fin:* **effets publics**, government stock, securities; public bonds; **effets au porteur**, bearer stock; **effets nominatifs**, registered stock. **5.** *pl.* possessions, belongings, effects; **effets mobiliers**, personal effects; goods and chattels; **effets d'un soldat, d'un matelot**, a soldier's kit, a sailor's slops; **faites vos effets**, pack up your clothes, your things.
effeuillage [efœja:ʒ], *s.m.* **1.** thinning out of leaves; stripping (of fruit-trees, etc.). **2.** *F:* striptease.
effeuillaison [efœjɛzɔ̃], *s.f.* fall of the leaves.
effeuillé [efœje], *a.* leafless (tree).
effeuillement [efœjmɑ̃], *s.m.* **1.** fall of the leaves. **2.** leaflessness, bareness (of trees, wood, etc.).
effeuiller [efœje], *v.tr.* to thin out the leaves of (fruit-tree); to pluck off the petals of (flower); **le temps effeuille nos espérances**, time destroys our hopes one by one; *s.a.* MARGUERITE.
s'effeuiller, (*of tree*) to lose, shed, its leaves; (*of flower*) to shed its petals.
effeuilleur, -euse [efœjœ:r, -ø:z], *s.* **1.** *Hort:* stripper. **2.** *s.f.* strip-teaser, stripper.
effeuillure [efœjy:r], *s.f.* (mass of) fallen leaves.
efficace [efikas]. **1.** *a.* (*a*) efficacious, effectual, effective, adequate (action, remedy, etc.); efficient (person); **orateur e.**, capable speaker; *Mil: etc:* **tir e.**, effective fire; **action peu e.**, ineffectual action; **votre aide e.**, your able assistance; **travaux efficaces**, work efficiently done; **prêter à qn un appui e.**, to give s.o. effectual support; (*b*) *Mth:* **valeur e. d'une quantité variable**, effective value of a variable quantity; *El.E:* **watt e.**, true watt. **2.** *s.f. Theol:* efficacity (of grace, etc.).
efficacement [efikasmɑ̃], *adv.* efficaciously, effectively; effectually; efficiently.
efficacité [efikasite], *s.f.* efficacy, effectiveness (of remedy, prayer, etc.); efficiency (of work, device, etc.); *Opt:* **e. lumineuse**, luminous efficiency; *Atom.Ph:* **e. biologique relative** (**E.B.R.**), relative biological effectiveness (**R.B.E.**) (of radiation); *Mil:* **e. anti-personnel**, casualty-producing potential (of weapon); **zone d'e.**, damage area (of missile).
efficience [efisjɑ̃:s], *s.f. Pol.Ec: & F:* (*of pers.*) efficiency.
efficient [efisjɑ̃], *a.* **1.** *Phil:* **cause efficiente**, efficient cause. **2.** *F:* (*of pers.*) efficient.
effigie [efiʒi], *s.f.* effigy; **brûler, pendre, qn en e.**, to burn, hang, s.o. in effigy; **monnaie frappée à l'e. de . . .**, coinage bearing the effigy of . . . the head of . . ..
effilage [efila:ʒ], *s.m.* **1.** fraying, ravelling out (of material). **2.** *Com:* drawing (of poultry, without removing the gizzard).
effilé [efile], *a.* **1.** *Tex:* frayed, fringed (material); *s.m.* fringe, fringed trimming. **2.** slender, slim slight (figure); tapering (fingers); tapered, sharp, pointed (tool); *Aut: etc:* streamlined; **cheval e.**, fine-shouldered horse.
effilement [efilmɑ̃], *s.m.* tapering.
effiler [efile], *v.tr.* **1.** *Tex:* to fray, unravel, ravel, out. **2.** to taper; to cut, make, (sth.) into a point; *N.Arch:* to fair; *Hairdr:* **e. les cheveux**, to taper hair. **3.** *Ven:* **e. les chiens**, to tire, wear out, the dogs. **4.** *Cu:* to slice, to cut in fine strips.
s'effiler. **1.** (*of material*) to fray (out). **2.** to taper, to become thin, sharp, pointed; to thin out.

effileur, -euse [efilœːr, -øːz], *s.* = EFFILOCHEUR, -EUSE.

effilochage [efilɔʃaːʒ], *s.m.* (*a*) teasing out; (*b*) fraying; (*c*) *Paperm:* (rag-)cutting; (*d*) *Tex:* breaking, tearing (of wool, cotton waste); **drap de laine d'e.,** shoddy.

effiloche [efilɔʃ], *s.f.* fringe (of threads left loose).

effiloché [efilɔʃe], *s.m. Tex:* shoddy.

effilochement [efilɔʃmɑ̃], *s.m.* (*a*) ravelling; fraying; *Tex:* teasing; (*b*) ravelled, frayed, condition.

effilocher [efilɔʃe], *v.tr.* (*a*) to ravel out, tease out; (*b*) to fray (material); (*c*) *Paperm:* to cut, tear, break (the rags); (*d*) *Tex:* to break, tear (wool, cotton waste).

s'effilocher, (*of material*) to fray.

effilocheur, -euse [efilɔʃœːr, -øːz], *s. Tex:* breaker (of waste material); (*pers. or machine*) (shoddy) tearer; (*machine*) devil.

effilochure [efilɔʃyːr], *s.f.* ravelled, teased, material; frayed material.

effiloque [efilɔk], *s.f.* = EFFILOCHE.

effilure [efilyːr], *s.f.* ravelled, frayed, material.

efflanqué [eflɑ̃ke], *a.* (*a*) lean, lean-flanked, raw-boned (animal); (*b*) skinny, gaunt, lanky (person); (*c*) *O:* **style e.,** thin, inadequate, style.

efflanquer [eflɑ̃ke], *v.tr.* to make thin; **la fatigue efflanque les chevaux,** fatigue makes horses become lean, raw-boned.

s'efflanquer, to become thin; to become elongated; **les collines s'efflanquent et prennent un faux air de montagnes,** the hills become tapered and look almost like mountains.

effleurage [eflœraːʒ], *s.m.* (*a*) *Leath:* shaving, buffing (of hide); (*b*) *Med:* light massage.

effleurement [eflœrmɑ̃], *s.m.* **1.** (*a*) (light, gentle) touch; gentle stroking; (*b*) skimming (of the water). **2.** graze.

effleurer [eflœre], *v.tr.* **1.** to touch, stroke, lightly; to skim (the surface of the water); to graze, brush (solid surface); **la balle n'a fait qu'effleurer la peau,** the bullet only grazed the skin; **sa main effleura les cordes (de la harpe),** his hand ran lightly over the strings; **e. un sujet,** to touch (lightly) on a topic. **2.** *Agr:* to plough (land) lightly. **3.** (*a*) *Leath:* to shave, buff (hides); (*b*) *Med:* to massage lightly.

effleurir [eflœriːr], *v.i. & pr. Ch: Min:* to effloresce.

effleurissement [eflœrismɑ̃], *s.m.* efflorescence.

effloraison [eflɔrɛzɔ̃], *s.f. Bot:* flowering.

efflorescence [ef(f)lɔrɛs(s)ɑ̃ːs], *s.f.* **1.** *Bot:* flowering, efflorescence. **2.** *Ch: Min:* efflorescence; bloom (of sulphur on rubber); **former une e.,** to effloresce. **3.** *Med:* rash, eruption (of measles, etc.).

efflorescent [ef(f)lɔrɛs(s)ɑ̃], *a. Bot: Ch:* efflorescent.

effluence [eflyɑ̃s], *s.f.* effluence.

effluent [eflyɑ̃]. **1.** *a.* effluent. **2.** *s.m.* effluent (from sewage tank); **e. radio-actif,** radioactive waste.

effluve [eflyːv], *s.m.* **1.** effluvium, emanation; exhalation; **les premiers effluves du printemps,** the first breath of spring; **les effluves parfumés des roses,** the fragrance of roses (in the air). **2.** *El:* brush discharge, silent discharge, glow discharge.

effluver [eflyve], *v.i.* to exhale.

effondré [efɔ̃dre], *a.* **1.** (*a*) ploughed up; (*b*) boggy (land); (*c*) *Med:* **pied e.,** drop foot. **2.** **e. dans la douleur,** prostrate with grief; **être e.,** to be distraught.

effondrement [efɔ̃drəmɑ̃], *s.m.* **1.** *Agr:* subsoiling, trenching. **2.** breaking down, caving in; subsidence; collapse (of bridge, etc.); falling in (of roof); *St.Exch:* **e. des cours,** slump in prices; **l'e. du mark,** the collapse of the mark; **e. d'un projet,** falling through of a plan; **l'e. du ministère,** the downfall, collapse, of the ministry; **il est dans un état d'e. complet,** he is in a state of absolute prostration. **3.** *Geol: etc:* subsidence; **cratère d'e.,** sinkhole, shakehole; **fossé d'e.,** rift valley.

effondrer [efɔ̃dre], *v.tr.* **1.** (*a*) *Agr:* to subsoil, trench (the ground); (*b*) (*of shells, etc.*) to plough up, cut up (the ground). **2.** to break (sth.) in, down; to break open (door, cupboard); to stave in (barrel); **la chute du toit effondra les planchers,** the fall of the roof caused the floors to give way, broke down the floors. **3.** *A:* to draw (fowl); to gut (fish).

s'effondrer, to fall in, cave in, break down, collapse; (*of credit, prices*) to slump; *F:* (*of pers.*) to be ruined; (*of government*) to collapse; **le toit s'effondra,** the roof fell in, collapsed; *F:* **s'e. dans un fauteuil,** to sink, subside, *F:* flop, into an armchair; **le projet s'est effondré,** the scheme has fallen through, has come to nothing.

effondrilles [efɔ̃driːj], *s.f.pl. A:* deposit (left after boiling liquid).

efforcer (s') [sefɔrse], *v.pr.* (**je m'efforçai(s); n.n. efforçons**) **s'e. de,** *occ.* **à, faire qch.,** to endeavour, strive, do one's utmost, make every effort, make every endeavour, to do sth.; **je m'efforcerai de vous contenter,** I shall endeavour, do my best, to satisfy you; **s'e. vers un but,** to strive after, for, an end; **il s'efforça de sourire,** he did his best, he forced himself, to smile; *abs.* **efforcez-vous,** make an effort.

effort [efɔːr], *s.m.* **1.** effort, exertion; **faire e. pour,** to strive to; **faire un e. pour faire qch.,** to make an effort, to exert oneself, to do sth.; **faire un e. sur soi-même,** to exercise self-control, to try to control oneself; **faire tous ses efforts pour . . .,** to use every effort, strain every nerve, do one's utmost, to . . .; **ce sera mon e. constant de . . .,** it will be my constant endeavour to . . .; **il a fourni un e. immense,** he was indefatigable, he has been a tower of strength; **e. soutenu,** sustained effort; **l'e. soutenu d'un match prolongé,** the strain of a long-drawn-out match; **consacrer tous ses efforts à une tâche,** to bend, devote, all one's energies to a task; **e. financier qu'un état consacre à ses armements,** national outlay on armaments; **sans e.,** easily, without effort; **faire des efforts de mémoire,** to rack, cudgel, one's brains; **après bien des efforts,** after much exertion, much hard work; *F:* **suivre la loi du moindre e.,** to take the line of least resistance; **les efforts du vent,** the force of the wind. **2.** (*a*) *Mec.E: etc:* strain, stress; **e. de tension,** tensile stress, pull; **e. de torsion,** torque; **e. de rupture,** breaking strain; **e. de traction,** pull; **e. de cisaillement,** shearing stress; **e. à la traction,** tensile stress; **e. axial,** thrust load; **indicateur d'e.,** strain-meter; (*b*) *Med: Vet:* strain, (w)rick (in the back, etc.); **se donner, attraper, un e.,** to (w)rick one's back; **cheval qui a un e.,** foundered horse; (*c*) *Med: F:* rupture.

effracteur [efraktœːr], *s.m. A:* burglar.

effraction [efraksjɔ̃], *s.f. Jur:* breach of close, of domicile; *F:* house-breaking; **vol de nuit avec e.,** burglary; **s'introduire par e. dans une maison,** to break into a house; **ouvrir une porte, un couvercle, avec e.,** to break open a door, a lid; **à l'épreuve de l'e.,** burglar-proof.

effraie [efrɛ], *s.f. Orn: F:* barn owl, screech owl, white owl.

effrangement [efrɑ̃ʒmɑ̃], *s.m.* (*a*) fraying; fringing; (*b*) frayed edge; fringe.

effranger [efrɑ̃ʒe], *v.tr.* (**j'effrangeai(s); n. effrangeons**) to fray (out) (edges of material, etc.).

s'effranger, to fray (out), to become frayed.

effrayable [efrɛjabl̩], *a.* easily frightened; timid, shy.

effrayant [efrɛjɑ̃], *a.* (*a*) terrifying, appalling; gruesome, ghastly (sight); (*b*) **cet e. génie,** this terrific genius; (*c*) *F:* tremendous, terrific, appalling, ghastly; **chaleur effrayante,** terrific, appalling, heat; **appétit e.,** tremendous, terrific, appetite.

effrayer [efreje], *v.tr.* (**j'effraie, j'effraye, n. effrayons; j'effraierai, j'effrayerai**) (*a*) to frighten, scare, startle (s.o.); **e. qn par des cris,** to frighten s.o. by shouting; **effrayé, il courut se cacher,** in alarm, full of terror, he ran and hid; (*b*) **l'énormité de la besogne nous effraie,** the magnitude of the task appals us.

s'effrayer, to be, get, frightened, scared; to take fright; **s'e. de qn, de qch.,** to be frightened of, at, s.o., sth.; **s'e. pour rien,** to be alarmed, take alarm, about nothing.

effréné [efrene], *a.* unbridled, unrestrained (passion, curiosity, etc.); **efforts effrénés,** frantic efforts.

effrénement [efrenmɑ̃], *s.m.* lack of all restraint; frenzy.

effrénément [efrenemɑ̃], *adv.* unrestrainedly; frantically.

effritement[1] [efritmɑ̃], *s.m. Agr:* exhaustion (of the soil).

effritement[2], *s.m.* crumbling (into dust), disintegration (of plaster work, etc.); weathering (of rock); *St.Exch:* **e. des cours,** crumbling of prices.

effriter[1] [efrite], *v.tr. Agr:* to exhaust (the soil).

s'effriter[1], (*of land*) to become exhausted.

effriter[2], *v.tr.* to render (sth.) friable; to cause (sth.) to crumble; to disintegrate.

s'effriter[2], (*of plaster work, etc.*) to crumble; (*of rock*) to weather; **bois qui s'effrite en poudre,** wood that crumbles into dust; *St.Exch:* (*of prices*) to crumble.

effroi [efrwa, -ɑ], *s.m.* fright, terror, fear, dread; **inspirer de l'e. à qn,** to fill s.o. with terror; **ils sèment l'e. sur leur passage,** they spread terror in their path; **cri d'e.,** startled cry; **silence qui inspire un e. religieux,** awe-inspiring silence; *Med:* **névrose d'e.,** fear neurosis.

effronté [efrɔ̃te], *a.* shameless, bold, impudent, saucy, barefaced, brazen, brash; **petit e.!** you cheeky little imp, devil! **mensonge e.,** barefaced lie; **e. comme un page, comme un moineau,** as cheeky as a sparrow.

effrontément [efrɔ̃temɑ̃], *adv.* shamelessly, barefacedly, brazenly, impudently; **répondre e.,** to answer as bold as brass; **mentir e.,** to be a barefaced, shameless, liar.

effronterie [efrɔ̃tri], *s.f.* effrontery, insolence, impudence, barefacedness; *F:* cheek; **il faut payer d'e.,** we must brazen it out; **rien n'égale l'e. du moineau,** there's nothing as cheeky as a sparrow.

effroyable [efrwajabl̩], *a.* (*a*) frightful, fearful, dreadful, appalling; **visage e.,** hideous face; (*b*) *F:* tremendous, terrific; **embouteillage e.,** terrific, terrible, (traffic) jam; **dégoût e.,** appalling disgust; **dépense e.,** tremendous expense.

effroyablement [efrwajabləmɑ̃], *adv.* *F:* tremendously, terribly; **je m'ennuyais e.,** I was bored to death.

effruiter [efrɥite], *v.tr.* **1.** to strip fruit from (tree, orchard). **2.** *Agr:* to exhaust (the soil).

effulguration [ɛf(f)ylgyrasjɔ̃], *s.f.* **1.** effulgence. **2.** flash (of light).

effumer [efyme], *v.tr. Art:* to tone down (colour, background).

effusif, -ive [efyzif, -iːv], *a. Geol:* effusive (rock).

effusion [efyzjɔ̃], *s.f.* **1.** effusion, outpouring, overflowing; **e. de sang,** (i) haemorrhage; (ii) bloodshed, spilling of blood; **effusions de tendresse,** demonstrations of love. **2.** effusiveness; **avec e.,** effusively, gushingly. **3.** *Theol:* **l'e. de la grâce divine,** the bestowal of divine grace. **4.** *Ch:* effusion.

éfourceau [efurso], *s.m.* (large) two-wheeled wood-cart.

égagropile [egagrɔpil], *s.m. Vet:* hair-ball.

égaiement [egɛmɑ̃], *s.m.* enlivenment; amusement; **au grand é. de la compagnie,** to the great amusement of the company.

égailler [egaje], *v.tr.* to flush (and scatter) (birds); to scatter, disperse (ships, etc.).

s'égailler, (*of birds, etc.*) to disperse, scatter.

égal, -aux [egal, -o], *a.* **1.** (*a*) equal (**à,** to); **poids é.,** equipoise; **objets placés à écartement é.,** equidistant objects; **contribuer pour une part égale à la dépense,** to contribute equally to the expense; to contribute equal shares to the expense; **rien n'est é. à cette splendeur,** nothing can equal this splendour; **toutes choses égales (d'ailleurs),** other things being equal; **à travail é., salaire é.,** equal pay for equal work; **combattre à armes égales,** to fight on equal terms; **les deux parties sont à peu près en nombre é.,** the two parties are pretty well balanced; *s.* **s'associer avec ses égaux,** to associate with one's equals; **traiter qn d'é. à é.,** to treat s.o. as an equal; **il est votre é.,** he is equal to you; *prep.phr.* **à l'é. de,** as much as, equally with; **haïr qn à l'é. de la peste,** to hate s.o. like poison; **il me chérit à l'é. d'un fils,** he loves me like a son; (*b*) level, even, regular (line, wall, road, etc.); steady (pace, pulse); **souffle é.,** even, regular, breathing; **température égale,** even, equable, temperature; **homme d'humeur égale,** man of equable temperament, even-tempered man; **il est é. à lui-même,** he is always true to himself; **il apprit la nouvelle d'une âme égale,** he received the news with equanimity. **2.** all the same; **cela m'est (bien) é.,** it is all the same, all one, to me; I don't care either way; *F:* **ça lui est bien é.,** he doesn't care a rap, doesn't mind a bit; **tout lui est é.,** all things are alike to him; **si cela vous est é.,** if you don't mind; **cela vous est-il é. de venir?** do you mind coming? *F:* **c'est é., il nous doit des excuses,** all the same, he ought to apologize.

égalable [egalabl̩], *a.* that can be equalled (**à,** to, with).

également[1] [egalmɑ̃], *adv.* **1.** equally, alike; **é. bon,** equally good, no less good; **servir tout le monde é.,** to serve everyone alike. **2.** also, likewise; **j'en veux é.,** I also want some; I want some, too, I want some as well.

également[2], *s.m. A.Jur:* equalization payment (to co-heir).

égaler [egale], *v.tr.* **1.** to equalize; to make (s.o., sth.) equal (**à,** to); **é. deux personnes,** to put two people on the same footing; **il s'égale au roi,**

he considers himself on a level with the king; **é. un auteur à un autre,** to rank one author as the equal of another. **2.** to equal, be equal to (s.o., sth.); **deux et deux égalent quatre,** two and two equal, make, four; **aucun ne pouvait l'é.,** no one could equal him, could hold a candle to him; **rien ne peut é. cette élégance,** nothing can compare with this elegance.

égalir [egali:r], *v.tr. Tchn:* to level; to equalize.

égalisage [egaliza:ʒ], *s.m. Expl:* sifting, sieving (of powder).

égalisateur, -trice [egalizatœ:r, -tris], *a.* (*a*) egalitarian (system); (*b*) *Sp:* **but é.,** equalizing goal, equalizer.

égalisation [egalizasjɔ̃], *s.f.* **1.** equalization, equalizing (à, to); *Mth:* **é. à zéro,** equating to zero; *Fb:* **but d'é.,** equalizer. **2.** levelling, smoothing (of ground, etc.).

égaliser [egalize], *v.tr.* **1.** to equalize, adjust (pressure, values, conditions, etc.); to screen (coal); to size (small shot, etc.); *Sp:* to draw (game); **é. les cheveux de qn,** to trim s.o.'s hair; *Mth:* **é. une expression à zéro,** to equate an expression to zero; *Fb:* **é. (la marque),** to equalize. **2.** to level, smoothe (piece of ground, etc.); to make (ground) even.

s'égaliser, to become (i) equalized, (ii) level, even.

égaliseur [egalizœ:r], *s.m.* **1.** (*device*) equalizer, regulator; *El:* **é. de potentiel,** voltage regulator. **2.** (*pers.*) (*in piano industry*) (master) tuner.

égalisoir [egalizwa:r], *s.m. Expl:* (powder) sieve.

égalitaire [egalitɛ:r], *Pol:* **1.** *a.* levelling (spirit, policy). **2.** *s.m.* equalitarian; egalitarian; leveller.

égalitarisme [egalitarism], *s.m.* egalitarianism.

égalité [egalite], *s.f.* **1.** (*a*) equality; **être sur un pied d'é. avec qn,** to be on an equal footing, on equal terms, with s.o.; *Games: Sp:* **é. de points,** tie; **à é.,** (i) (*of teams*) level; (ii) (*of result*) drawn, tied; *Golf:* all square; *Ten:* deuce; **é. à rien,** love all; *Rac:* **course à é.,** dead heat; tie; **arriver à é.,** to run a dead heat; *Turf:* **parier à é. sur un cheval,** to lay evens, even odds, on a horse; *prep.phr.* **à é. de . . .,** where there is equality of . . .; (*b*) *Typ:* (sign of) equality. **2.** evenness, regularity, smoothness (of surface, of breathing, etc.); **é. d'humeur, de caractère,** evenness of temper; **é. d'âme,** equanimity; *Mus:* **é. de jeu,** evenness, smoothness, of execution.

égard [ega:r], *s.m.* consideration, respect; (*a*) **avoir é. à qch.,** to take sth. into consideration, into account; to make allowance(s), to allow, for sth.; **eu é. à . . .,** in consideration of . . ., due allowance being made for . . ., having regard to . . .; **sans é. à,** regardless of, irrespective of; **phrase traduite sans é. au contexte,** sentence translated without regard to the context; **à tous (les) égards,** in all respects, in every respect, to all intents and purposes; **à certains égards . . .,** in some respects . . .; **n'ayez aucune crainte à cet é.,** have no fear in this connection, on that score, about that; *prep.phr.* **à l'é. de,** with reference to, with regard to, with respect to; **la terre est petite à l'é. du soleil,** compared with the sun the earth is small; **qu'avez-vous à dire à son é.?** what have you to say about him? **être injuste à l'é. de qn,** to be unjust to(wards) s.o.; **à l'é. de votre demande . . .,** with reference to your request . . .; (*b*) **témoigner des égards pour qn,** to show consideration for s.o.; **devoir des égards à qn,** to owe s.o. respect; **faire qch. par é. pour qn,** to do sth. (i) out of regard, out of respect, out of consideration, for s.o., (ii) for s.o.'s sake; **être sans é. pour qn,** to have no consideration for s.o.; **être plein d'égards pour qn,** to be full of attentions to s.o.; **être plein d'égards pour les autres,** to be thoughtful of others; **manquer d'égards envers qn,** to slight s.o.; to behave inconsiderately to s.o.; **manque d'égards envers qn,** lack of consideration for s.o.; slight.

égaré [egare], *a.* **1.** stray, lost (sheep, traveller, etc.); **balles égarées,** stray bullets; **pas égarés,** wandering, straying, steps; **village é.,** remote, out-of-the-way, village. **2.** distraught, distracted, (face, etc.); **regarder qn avec des yeux égarés,** to look at s.o. with wild eyes.

égarement [egarmɑ̃], *s.m.* **1.** (*a*) miscarriage (of letter, etc.); (*b*) mislaying (of object); (*c*) bewilderment; **é. d'esprit,** mental aberration. **2.** deviation (from virtue, etc.); wildness (of conduct); **il est revenu de ses égarements,** he has seen the error of his ways. **3.** frenzy (of grief, anger, etc.); wildness (of expression); **dans un moment d'é.,** in a wild moment, in a moment of mental aberration.

égarer [egare], *v.tr.* **1.** (*a*) to lead (s.o.) astray, out of his way; to mislead, misguide (s.o.); **é. ses pas dans les montagnes,** to lose one's way in the mountains; **é. ses regards dans le ciel,** to let one's eyes wander over the sky; **les mauvais exemples l'ont égaré,** he has been led astray by bad examples; (*b*) to mislay, lose (sth.). **2.** to bewilder, derange (s.o.); **égaré par tant de malheurs,** distraught by so many misfortunes. **3.** *Equit:* **é. la bouche d'un cheval,** to spoil a horse's mouth.

s'égarer. **1.** to lose one's way, to go astray; **colis qui s'est égaré,** parcel that has got lost, gone astray; **s'é. loin du droit chemin,** to wander from the straight path. **2. son esprit s'égare,** his mind is wandering.

égauler [egole], *v.tr.* (*a*) *Arb:* to prune (young shoots); (*b*) to cut down (brushwood).

égayant [egejɑ̃], *a.* cheerful, cheery, lively (conversation, music, etc.).

égayement[1] [egemɑ̃], *s.m.* enlivenment, amusement; **au grand é. de la compagnie,** to the great amusement of the company.

égayement[2], *s.m.* drainage channel (on irrigated land).

égayer [egeje], *v.tr.* (**j'égaie, j'égaye, n. égayons; j'égaierai, j'égayerai**) **1.** to cheer up (patient); to amuse (the guests); to enliven (the company, the conversation); to brighten (up) (room, dress, s.o.'s life); **é. le chagrin de qn,** to divert s.o. from his grief; **é. son deuil,** to relieve the severity of one's mourning; **un feu clair égayait la pièce,** a cheerful fire brightened up the room. **2.** *Hort:* to prune, lop (tree).

s'égayer, (*a*) to amuse oneself; (*b*) **s'é. aux dépens de qn,** to make fun of s.o.

Égée [eʒe]. **1.** *Pr.n.m. Gr.Myth:* Aegeus. **2.** *a. Geog:* **la mer É.,** the Aegean (Sea).

égéen, -éenne [eʒeɛ̃, -eɛn], *a.* Aegean (civilization, etc.).

égérane [eʒeran], *s.f. Miner:* egeran.

Égérie [eʒeri]. **1.** (*a*) *Pr.n.f. Myth:* Egeria; (*b*) *s.f. Lit:* Egeria. **2.** *s.f. Ent:* clearwing.

égermage [eʒɛrma:ʒ], *s.m. Brew:* degerming (of barley).

égermer [eʒɛrme], *v.tr. Brew:* to degerm(inate) (barley).

égide [eʒid], *s.f.* (*a*) *Gr.Myth:* aegis, shield; (*b*) protection, defence; **sous l'é. de . . .,** under the care of . . .; *Lit:* under the aegis of . . .; *Hist:* **mandat sous l'é. de la Société des Nations,** mandate under the League of Nations; **prendre qn sous son é.,** to take s.o. under one's wing.

Égine [eʒin], *Pr.n.f. Geog:* Aegina; *Art:* **les marbres d'É.,** the Aeginetan Marbles.

éginète [eʒinɛt], *a. & s. Geog:* Aeginetan.

éginétique [eʒinetik], *a.* Aeginetic.

Égisthe [eʒist], *Pr.n.m. Gr.Lit:* Aegisthus.

églantier [eglɑ̃tje], *s.m. Bot:* wild rose, dog-rose (bush); **é. odorant,** sweet-briar.

églantine [eglɑ̃tin], *s.f. Bot:* wild rose, dog-rose (flower); **é. odorante,** sweet-briar, eglantine.

églefin [egləfɛ̃], *s.m. Ich:* haddock.

eglestonite [eglɛstɔnit], *s.f. Miner:* eglestonite.

église [egli:z], *s.f.* church. **1. l'É. militante,** the Church militant; **l'É. catholique (romaine),** *abs.* **l'É.,** the (Roman) Catholic Church; **l'É. anglicane,** the Church of England; **l'É. d'État,** the established Church; **l'É. et l'État,** Church and State; **en face de l'É., devant l'É.,** in the eyes of the Church; **terres d'É.,** church lands; **entrer dans l'É.,** to go into the church, to take holy orders; *A:* **être d'É.,** to be in (holy) orders; **se faire d'É.,** to go into the Church; **petite É.,** (i) *Hist:* the non-adherers to the Concordat of 1801; (ii) small coterie. **2. une é.,** a church (building); **l'é. Saint-Pierre,** St. Peter's (church); **é. gothique,** gothic church; **aller à l'é.,** to go to church; **gens d'é.,** the clergy. **3.** *A: F:* chimney jack; rotating cowl.

églogue [eglɔg], *s.f. Lit:* eclogue.

égoblage [egɔbla:ʒ], *s.m.* **1.** rough squaring (of timber). **2.** lopping (of branches of a tree which has been felled).

égobler [egɔble], *v.tr.* **1.** to rough square (timber). **2.** to lop (the branches of a tree which has been felled).

égocentrique [egɔsɑ̃trik], *a.* self-centred, egocentric.

égocentrisme [egɔsɑ̃trism], *s.m.* egocentricity, egocentrism, self-centredness.

égocère [egɔsɛ:r], *s.m. Z:* egocerus; **é. noir,** sable antelope.

égohine, égoïne [egɔin], *s.f.* (small) hand saw.

égoïser [egɔize], *v.i. A:* to egotize.

égoïsme [egɔism], *s.m.* (*a*) *A:* egotism; (*b*) egoism; **être sans é.,** to be altruistic, unselfish.

égoïste [egɔist]. **1.** *s.m. & f.* (*a*) *A:* egotist; (*b*) egoist. **2.** *a.* (*a*) *A:* egotistic(al); (*b*) egoistic, self-centred.

égoïstement [egɔistəmɑ̃], *adv.* (*a*) *A:* egotistically; (*b*) egoistically.

égophonie [egɔfɔni], *s.f. Med:* egophony.

égophonique [egɔfɔnik], *a. Med:* egophonic.

égopode [egɔpɔd], *s.m. Bot:* aegopodium; goutweed, bishop('s)-weed.

égorgement [egɔrʒəmɑ̃], *s.m.* **1.** sticking, cutting the throat (of pig, etc.). **2.** butchery, massacre, slaughter.

égorgeoir [egɔrʒwa:r], *s.m.* **1.** *A:* (*a*) cut-throat den; (*b*) shambles. **2.** *Nau:* spilling line.

égorger [egɔrʒe], *v.tr.* (**j'égorgeai(s); n. égorgeons**) **1.** (*a*) to cut the throat of (pig, sheep, etc.); to stick (pig); (*b*) **é. qn,** to slit s.o.'s throat. **2.** (*a*) to butcher, massacre, slaughter (persons); (*b*) *F:* **é. ses clients,** to fleece one's customers.

égorgeur, -euse [egɔrʒœ:r, -ø:z], *s.* **1.** (pig-, sheep-) sticker. **2.** murderer, butcher, slaughterer; *A:* **les égorgeurs du peuple,** those who batten on the people.

égosiller (s') [segozije], *v.pr.* (*a*) to bawl; to shout (oneself hoarse); to shout like mad; **mais je m'égosille à vous le dire!** I've told you so till I'm blue in the face; (*b*) **oiseau qui s'égosille à chanter,** bird singing a full-throated song, *F:* singing its head off.

égotique [egɔtik], *a.* egotistic.

égotisme [egɔtism], *s.m.* egotism.

égotiste [egɔtist]. **1.** *s.m. & f.* egotist. **2.** *a.* egotistic(al).

égout [egu], *s.m.* **1.** (*a*) draining, drainage (of liquid); **l'é. des eaux des toits,** the drip(ping) of water from the roofs; (*b*) slope (of roof). **2.** (*a*) *Hyd.E:* (i) sewer; (ii) drain; **eaux d'é.,** sewage, sullage; sewerage; **tuyau d'é.,** drain pipe, sullage pipe; **é. collecteur,** main sewer; **tout à l'é.,** main drainage (system); **jeter à l'é.,** (i) to flush away; (ii) to pour down the sink, the drain; **plaque d'é.,** manhole cover; (*b*) *Const:* (i) eaves; (ii) gutter (of roof); **toit à deux égouts,** ridge roof.

égoutier [egutje]. **1.** *s.m.* sewerman; **bottes d'é.,** sewerman's waders. **2.** *a.m.* **miasme é.,** sewer gases.

égouttage [eguta:ʒ], *s.m.* drainage; draining (of cheese, ground, etc.); *Paperm: etc:* **caisse d'é.,** draining tank.

égouttement [egutmɑ̃], *s.m.* **1.** dripping (of water, blood, etc.). **2.** drainage, draining.

égoutter [egute], *v.tr. & i.* to drain (cheese, lettuce, plot of land, etc.); **mettre la vaisselle à é.,** to put the dishes to drain (in rack); **faire é. des légumes,** to strain vegetables; **faire é. l'eau,** to drain off the water; *Husb:* **é. une vache,** to strip a cow.

s'égoutter, to drain, drip.

égoutteur [egutœ:r], *a. Paperm:* **rouleau é.,** dandy-roll, -roller.

égouttoir [egutwa:r], *s.m.* **1.** (*a*) draining board; (*b*) drainer, draining rack (for bottles, etc.); plate rack; dish rack. **2.** (**panier**) **é.,** basket (of deep fryer).

égoutture [eguty:r], *s.f.* (*in either sg. or pl.*) drops, drippings (from roof, tap, bottle, etc.); **boire les égouttures,** to drink the few drops remaining (in bottle); *Ind:* **bac d'égouttures,** drip tray.

égraffigner [egrafiɲe], *v.tr. A: F:* to scratch.

égrainement [egrɛnmɑ̃], *s.m.*; **égrainer** [egrɛne], *v.tr.*; **égraineuse** [egrɛnø:z], *s.f.* = ÉGRÈNEMENT, ÉGRENER, ÉGRENEUSE.

égrappage [egrapa:ʒ], *s.m.* picking off (of grapes, currants, from bunch); removal of the stalks, stalking (of grapes).

égrapper [egrape], *v.tr.* to pick off (grapes, etc.); to remove the stalks from (grapes); to stalk (grapes).

égrappeur, -euse [egrapœ:r, -ø:z], *s.* (*grape, etc.*) picker.

égrappoir [egrapwa:r], *s.m. Winem:* fruit-crushing and stalk-removing machine.

égratigner [egratiɲe], *v.tr.* to scratch. **1.** *Agr:* **é. le sol,** to scratch, rake over, the soil; *Art:* **manière égratignée,** graffito style. **2.** to ruffle (s.o.), to rub (s.o.) up the wrong way.

égratigneur, -euse [egratiɲœr, -ø:z]. **1.** *s.* scratcher; *Art:* graffito artist. **2.** *a.* scratching.

égratignure [egratiɲy:r], *s.f.* **1.** scratch; **je n'ai pas reçu une é.,** I escaped unscathed, without a scratch. **2.** gibe; dig (at s.o.); **ne pouvoir souffrir la moindre é.,** to be touchy, easily offended.

égrefin [egrəfɛ̃], *s.m. Ich:* **haddock.**

égrenage [egrəna:ʒ], *s.m.* shelling (of corn, peas); picking off (of grapes, etc.); ginning (of cotton); rippling, bolling (of flax).
égrène [egrɛn], *s.f.* iron corner (for chest, box).
égrènement [egrɛnmɑ̃], *s.m.* **1. é. d'un chapelet,** telling of beads. **2. é. de lumières,** string of lights.
égrener [egrəne], *v.tr.* **(j'égrène, n. égrenons; j'égrènerai)** (*a*) to shell (maize, fodder crops, peas, etc.); to pick off (grapes, etc., from the bunch); to gin (cotton); to ripple, boll (flax); *Tex:* **machine à é.,** cotton gin; (*b*) **é. son chapelet,** to tell one's beads; **é. un chapelet d'injures,** to give vent to a volley of abuse; **les marronniers égrènent leurs feuilles à l'automne,** the chestnut trees shed their leaves one by one in the autumn; **é. des sujets de conversation,** to try one subject of conversation after another; *F:* **porte qui égrène les visiteurs un à un,** door that lets the visitors through one by one; *F:* **elle égrenait une valse de Chopin,** she tripped nimbly through a Chopin waltz.
s'égrener. 1. (*of corn, grapes, etc.*) to fall, drop, from the ear, from the bunch; to seed; **des lumières s'égrènent le long du quai,** a string of lights stretches along the quay; **la famille s'est égrenée,** the members of the family have dispersed. **2.** (*of steel*) to crack, fly.
égreneuse [egrənø:z], *s.f.* machine for shelling maize, etc.; sheller; **é. à maïs,** *U.S:* corn sheller; **é. de coton,** cotton gin; boiler; **é. de lin,** ripple.
égrillard [egrija:r], *a.* ribald; **histoires égrillardes,** risqué, spicy, stories.
égrillardise [egrijardi:z], *s.f.* ribald remark; risqué remark.
égrilloir [egrijwa:r], *s.m. Fish: Hyd.E:* weir.
égrisage [egriza:ʒ], *s.m.* grinding (of marble, glass, diamonds, etc.).
égrisé [egrize], *s.m.,* **égrisée** [egrize], *s.f.* bort, diamond powder.
égriser [egrize], *v.tr.* to grind (marble, glass, diamonds, etc.); **poudre à é.,** abradant.
égrotant [egrɔtɑ̃], *a.* sickly.
égrugeage [egryʒa:ʒ], *s.m.* **1.** bruising (of grain); pounding (of salt, sugar, etc.); mealing (of gunpowder). **2.** (removal of seeds or bark) seeding (of grapes, etc.); pilling, rippling (of flax).
égrugeoir [egryʒwa:r], *s.m.* **1.** (*a*) *Dom.Ec: etc:* mortar; **é. de table,** salt mill; (*b*) *Exp:* rubber, mealer. **2.** *Tex:* pill comb, flax comb, ripple.
égruger [egryʒe], *v.tr.* **(j'égrugeai(s); n. égrugeons) 1.** to bruise (grain); to pound (salt, sugar, etc.); to meal (gunpowder). **2.** to seed (grapes, etc.); to pill, ripple (flax).
égueulé [egœle], *a.* (gun) worn at the muzzle; breached (crater, etc.).
égueulement [egœlmɑ̃], *s.m. Artil:* running, spewing (of metal, at muzzle of bronze gun).
égueuler [egœle], *v.tr.* to break the mouth of (vessel), the neck of (bottle), the lip of (jug).
s'égueuler. 1. (*of gun*) to wear, run, spew, at the muzzle. **2.** *P:* **s'é. à crier,** to shout oneself hoarse.
Égypte [eʒipt], *Pr.n.f. Geog:* Egypt.
égyptiac [eʒipsjak], *s.m. Vet:* Egyptian ointment.
égyptien, -ienne [eʒipsjɛ̃, -jɛn]. **1.** *a.* & *s.* Egyptian. **2.** *s. A:* gipsy. **3.** *s.f. Typ:* clarendon.
égyptologie [eʒiptɔlɔʒi], *s.f.* Egyptology.
égyptologique [eʒiptɔlɔʒik], *a.* Egyptological.
égyptologue [eʒiptɔlɔg], *s.m.* & *f.* Egyptologist.
eh [e], *int.* hey! **eh bien!** well! now then! **eh bien?** well? **eh! que voulez-vous que je fasse?** why, what can I do? **eh! que c'est beau!** isn't it fine! **eh! là-bas, c'est à vous que je parle!** hullo there, it's you I'm speaking to!
éhanché [eɑ̃ʃe], *a.* hipshot (horse).
ehlite [elit], *s.f. Miner:* ehlite.
éhonté [eɔ̃te], *a.* shameless, barefaced, unblushing.
éhontément [eɔ̃temɑ̃], *adv.* shamelessly.
éhoupage [eupa:ʒ], *s.m.* topping, pollarding (of tree).
éhouper [eupe], *v.tr.* to top, pollard (tree).
ehrétie [ereti], *s.f. Bot:* ehretia.
eichornia [eikɔrnja], *s.m. Bot:* eichhornia.
eicosane [eikɔzan], *s.m. Ch:* eicosane.
eider [ɛdɛ:r], *s.m. Orn:* **e. (à duvet),** eider duck; **e. à tête grise,** king eider; **e. de Fischer,** spectacled, Fischer's, eider; **e. de Steller,** Steller's eider.
eidétique [ɛjdetik], *a. Psy: etc:* eidetic.
Éidophore [eidɔfɔ:r], *s.m. T.V: R.t.m:* Eidophor system.
Eiffel [ɛfɛl], *Pr.n.* **la tour E.,** the Eiffel tower.
Einhorn [ɛjnɔrn], *Pr.n. Med:* **sonde d'E.,** Einhorn's tube.
einsténien, -ienne [ɛjnstenjɛ̃, -jɛn], **einsteinien, -ienne** [ɛjnstejnjɛ̃, -jɛn], *a.* Einsteinian.
einsteinium [ɛjnstɛjnjɔm], *s.m. Ch:* einsteinium.
Eire [ɛ:r], *Pr.n.f. Geog:* Eire.
eisenkiesel [ɛjsɛnkjɛzɛl], *s.m. Miner:* eisenkiesel.
éjaculateur, -trice [eʒakylatœ:r, -tris], *a.* ejaculatory.
éjaculation [eʒakylasjɔ̃], *s.f.* **1.** *Physiol:* ejaculation, emission (of seed, fluid, etc.). **2.** short and earnest prayer; appeal to God.
éjaculatoire [eʒakylatwa:r], *a.* ejaculatory (organ, prayer, etc.).
éjaculer [eʒakyle], *v.tr.* **1.** *abs. Physiol:* to ejaculate. **2.** to ejaculate, put up (short and earnest prayer).
éjarrage [eʒara:ʒ], *s.m.* plucking (of furs).
éjarré [eʒare], *a.* (*of fur*) plucked; without overhair.
éjarrer [eʒare], *v.tr.* to pluck (furs).
éjarreur, -euse [eʒarœ:r, -ø:z], *s.* plucker (of furs).
éject [eʒɛ], *s.m. Phil:* eject.
éjecta [eʒɛkta], *s.m.pl. Geol:* ejecta (of a volcano).
éjectable [eʒɛktabl̩], *a. Av:* **siège é.,** ejector seat.
éjecter [eʒɛkte], *v.tr.* (*a*) to eject (steam, water, etc.); (*b*) *P:* to sack, to fire.
éjecteur [eʒɛktœ:r], *s.m.* **1.** *Mch: Sm.a: etc:* ejector (of stream, water, cartridge, etc.); **é. d'un réservoir,** outlet works of a reservoir; *Nau:* **é. d'escarbilles,** ash-ejector. **2.** *a. Av:* **siège é.,** ejector seat.
éjection [eʒɛksjɔ̃], *s.f.* **1.** ejection (of steam, water, cartridge, etc.; *Av:* of pilot); *Geol:* **éjections volcaniques,** ejecta, ejectamenta. **2.** *Physiol:* evacuation (of urine, faeces).
éjet [eʒɛ], *s.m. Phil:* eject.
éjointage [eʒwɛ̃ta:ʒ], *s.m.* clipping of the wings (of duck, etc.).
éjointer [eʒwɛ̃te], *v.tr.* to clip the wings of (duck, falcon, etc.).
éjouir(s') [seʒwi:r], *v.pr. A:* = SE RÉJOUIR.
ékebergite [ekbɛrʒit], *s.f. Miner:* ekebergite.
élaborant [elabɔrɑ̃], **élaborateur, -trice** [elabɔratœ:r, -tris], *a.* elaborative (organ, etc.).
élaboration [elabɔrasjɔ̃], *s.f.* elaboration (of work, of idea, etc.); assimilation (of food); formulation (of plan); drawing up (of constitution, etc.); production; manufacture (of product); **mesures en cours d'é.,** measures in course of preparation, of elaboration; **l'é. du système militaire de l'Otan,** the Nato military build-up.
élaboré [elabɔre], *a. Bot:* **sève élaborée,** elaborated sap; *Lit:* **style é.,** studied style.
élaborer [elabɔre], *v.tr.* to transform (raw material, etc.); **l'estomac élabore les aliments,** the stomach renders food assimilable; **é. un plan,** to elaborate, work out, think out, prepare, formulate, draw up, a plan.
elæis [eleis], *s.m. Bot:* elaeis, oil palm.
élæodendron [eleɔdɛ̃drɔ̃], *s.m. Bot:* eloeodendron.
élagage [elaga:ʒ], *s.m.* **1.** *Arb:* pruning (of tree); lopping (of branches); *F:* weeding out (of candidates for a post); **é. d'une pièce, d'un livre,** cutting (down), pruning, of a play, of a book. **2.** *pl.* prunings; loppings.
élaguer [elage], *v.tr. Arb:* to prune (tree); to lop (off, away) (branches); to curtail, cut (down) (play, book, etc.); **é. des détails,** to cut out details.
élagueur [elagœ:r], *s.m. Arb:* **1.** (*pers.*) pruner. **2.** (*a*) pruning hook; (*b*) pruning shears.
élaïdine [elaidin], *s.f. Ch:* elaidin.
élaïdique [elaidik], *a. Ch:* elaidic.
élaïomètre [elaiɔmɛtr̩], *s.m.* elaeometer.
élaiter [elɛte], *v.tr.* to work, dry (butter).
élamite [elamit], *B.Hist:* **1.** *a.* & *s.m.* & *f.* Elamite. **2.** *s.m. Ling:* Elamitic.
élan[1] [elɑ̃], *s.m.* **1.** (*a*) spring, bound, dash, dart; **il fit un é. pour se sauver,** he made a dash to escape; **avancer par élans,** to advance by rushes; **d'un seul é.,** at one bound; **prendre son é.,** to take off; **saut sans é., avec é.,** standing jump, running jump; (*b*) **l'é. merveilleux de nos troupes,** the wonderful elan, dash, of our troops; **travailler avec é.,** to work whole-heartedly, enthusiastically; to work with a will; (*c*) impetus; **emporté par mon propre é.,** carried away by my own momentum, by my own impetus; **é. vital,** life force; (*d*) *Arch: Lit:* **l'immense vaisseau de la nef monte d'un é. puissant vers la voûte,** the immense nave surges up to the vaulting. **2.** burst, outburst (of feeling, temper, etc.); glow (of enthusiasm); impulse; **geste d'é.,** impulsive gesture; **mouvement de premier é.,** first impulse; **cette vie avait tué en lui tous les élans,** this life had killed all his enthusiasm; **é. de l'imagination,** flight of fancy; **avoir des élans d'énergie,** to have sudden fits of energy.
élan[2], *s.m. Z:* (*a*) Scandinavian elk, Eurasiatic moose; (*b*) **é. du Canada,** American moose; (*c*) **chien d'é.,** elkhound.
élancé [elɑ̃se], *a.* tall and slim; slender; gracefully shaped (figure, person, etc.); **cheval é.,** lank, lean, horse; *Nau:* **avant é.,** lean, raking, bows.
élancement [elɑ̃smɑ̃], *s.m.* **1.** (*a*) *A:* springing forward, bounding forward, darting forward; (*b*) *Nau:* rake (of stem or stern). **2.** transport (of feeling); **élancements vers Dieu,** yearning towards God. **3.** shooting pain, stabbing pain, twinge.
élancer [elɑ̃se], *v.* **(j'élançai(s); n. élançons) 1.** *v.tr. A:* to hurl (sth.) forth, to launch (spear, etc.); **é. des soupirs vers le ciel,** to sigh to heaven. **2.** *v.tr.* & *i.* (*of part of the body*) to throb, shoot (with pain); **mon doigt m'élance,** my finger is throbbing; **son cor, sa dent, lui élance,** his corn, his tooth, is shooting; **ce souvenir lui élança la conscience,** at this recollection he felt a twinge of conscience.
s'élancer. 1. s'é. en avant, to spring, bound, dash, shoot, forward; **s'é. sur son cheval,** to spring, leap, on to one's horse; **s'é. sur qn,** to rush at s.o.; to make a rush at s.o.; to make a spring at s.o.; *F:* to go for s.o.; **le chat s'élança sur moi,** the cat flew at me; **il s'élança avant de voir l'eau,** he made his bound before he was aware of the water; **s'é. vers un abri,** to make a dash, a bolt, for shelter; **il s'élança derrière le rideau,** he whipped behind the curtain; **s'é. à toute vitesse,** to dash off at top speed; **s'é. à l'assaut,** to throw oneself into the fray. **2.** (*of child, plant, etc.*) to shoot up; **sa taille s'élance,** he, she, is growing taller, is shooting up; *Arch: Lit:* **le vaisseau de la nef s'élance vers la voûte,** the nave soars up to the vaulting.
éland [elɑ̃], *s.m. Z:* **é. du Cap,** eland.
élane [elan], *s.m.,* **élanion** [elanjɔ̃], *s.m. Orn:* swallow hawk; **é. blac, blanc,** black-winged kite.
élaphé [elafe], *s.f. Rept:* Elaphe.
élaphode [elafɔd], **élaphodus** [elafɔdys], *s.m. Z:* elaphodus.
élaphomycès [elafɔmisɛs], *s.m. Fung:* Elaphomyces.
élaphre [elafr̩], *s.m. Ent:* elaphrus.
élapidés [elapide], *s.m.pl. Rept:* Elapidae, the cobras.
élaps [elaps], *s.m. Rept:* elaps.
élargir [elarʒi:r], *v.tr.* **1.** (*a*) to widen (road, etc.); to let out (dress, etc.); to stretch (shoes, etc.); *Tex:* to tenter (cloth); **acteur qui a élargi son jeu,** actor who has broadened his style; **il a élargi son jeu,** his acting has taken on breadth; *Mus:* **é. le temps,** to broaden, slacken, the tempo; **é. des règles,** to make rules less stringent; (*b*) to enlarge, extend, add to (one's estate, ideas, knowledge); to expand (tube); to enlarge (hole, wound); *Nau:* to ream (deck-seam, etc.); *Petroleum Min:* to underream (a borehole); **é. son influence,** to extend one's influence. **2.** to set (prisoner) free, at large; to release (prisoner). **3.** *v.i. F:* **il a élargi,** he has broadened out.
s'élargir, (*a*) to widen out, broaden out; **sa face s'élargit,** his face broadened out into a smile; (*b*) (*of shoes, etc.*) to stretch; (*c*) (*of estate, ideas, circle of friends, etc.*) to grow, extend; (*of tube, etc.*) to expand.
élargissage [elarʒisa:ʒ], *s.m. Tex:* tentering.
élargissement [elarʒismɑ̃], *s.m.* **1.** (*a*) widening, broadening (of road, etc.); letting out (of dress, etc.); stretching (of shoes); *Petroleum Min:* reaming, underreaming (of a borehole); (*b*) enlargement, enlarging (of estate, one's ideas, acquaintances); (*c*) *Med:* dilatation (of heart, etc.). **2.** release, liberation, discharge (of prisoner); **prendre des mesures d'é. à l'égard de qn,** to order s.o.'s release.
élargisseur [elarʒisœ:r], *s.m.* **1.** *Tex:* tentering machine, tenter. **2.** *Petroleum Min:* underreamer.
élargissure [elarʒisy:r], *s.f.* piece let in; *Dressm:* gusset, gore.
élarvement [elarv(ə)mɑ̃], *s.m. Agr:* removal of the larvae of insects (from plants, etc.).
élasmobranches [elasmɔbrɑ̃:ʃ], *s.m.pl. Ich:* Elasmobranchii.
élasmose [elasmo:z], *s.f. Miner:* **1.** elasmosine, nagyagite. **2.** altaite.
elasmotherium [ɛlasmɔterjɔm], *s.m. Paleont:* elasmotherium.
élasticimètre [elastisimɛtr̩], *s.m.* extensometer.
élasticimétrie [elasticimetri], *s.f.* elastometry.
élasticité [elastisite], *s.f.* **1.** (*a*) elasticity (of body, gas, etc.); **é. acoustique,** (acoustic) compliance; **é. de fonctionnement,** flexibility (of machine, etc.); (*b*) springiness, spring (of step, etc.). **2.** (*a*) adaptability; **elle luttait contre ses maux avec une é. surprenante,** she struggled

against her misfortunes with surprising elasticity; *Pej:* **l'é. de conscience d'un homme politique,** a politician's flexibility, lack, of conscience; (*b*) **é. d'une loi,** elasticity of interpretation of a law; (*c*) *Pol.Ec:* **l'é. de l'offre et de la demande,** the elasticity of supply and demand.

élastine [elastin], *s.f. Bio-Ch:* elastin.

élastique [elastik]. **1.** *a.* (*a*) (*which has elasticity*) elastic; **l'acier est le plus é. des métaux,** steel is the metal with the greatest coefficient of elasticity; *Mec:* **limite é. (à la traction, etc.),** (tensile, etc.) strength; (*b*) elastic, rubber; **gomme é.,** indiarubber; **balle é.,** rubber ball; **bretelles élastiques,** elastic braces, *U.S:* suspenders; **bandage é.,** elastic bandage; *Anat:* **tissu é.,** elastic tissue; (*c*) resilient; springy; buoyant; **sommier é.,** spring mattress; **pas é.,** springy, buoyant step; **accouplement é.,** flexible coupling, *Mth:* **courbe é.,** elastic curve; (*d*) **mot é.,** word which can be interpreted in many different ways; *Pej:* **conscience é.,** elastic, lax, conscience; (*e*) *Mil:* **défense é.,** defence in depth. **2.** *s.m.* (*a*) (india) rubber; (*b*) *Dressm: etc:* elastic; **bretelles en é.,** elastic braces, *U.S:* suspenders; **bottines à élastiques,** elastic-sided boots; (*c*) elastic, rubber, band; (*d*) *P:* **lâcher son argent avec un é.,** to pay reluctantly. **3.** *s.f. Mth:* elastic curve.

élastomère [elastɔmɛːr], *Ch: Ind:* **1.** *s.m.* elastomer. **2.** *a.* elastomeric.

élater, élatère¹ [elatɛːr], *s.m. Ent:* elater; *F:* skip jack, click beetle.

élatère² [elatɛːr], *s.f. Bot:* elater (of liverwort, etc.).

élatérides [elaterid], **élatéridés** [elateride], *s.m.pl. Ent:* Elateridae; *F:* click beetles.

élatérion [elaterjɔ̃], *s.m.* **1.** *Bot:* squirting cucumber. **2.** *Pharm:* elaterium.

élatérite [elaterit], *s.f. Miner:* elaterite, elastic bitumen.

élatéromètre [elaterɔmɛtr̥], *s.m. Tchn:* elatrometer.

élatinacées [elatinase], *s.f.pl. Bot:* Elatinaceae.

élatine [elatin], *s.f. Bot:* elatine; waterwort.

élavage [elavaːʒ], *s.m. Paperm:* washing (out) of rags.

élavé [elave], *a. Ven:* (*esp. of coat of hound*) washed out.

élaver [elave], *v.tr. Paperm:* to wash (out) (rags).

Elbe¹ [ɛlb], *Pr.n.f. Geog:* **l'île d'E.,** the island of Elba.

Elbe², *Pr.n.m. Geog:* (the river) Elbe.

elbeuf [ɛlbœf], *s.m. Tex:* tweed (made at Elbeuf).

elbeuvien, -ienne [ɛlbœvjɛ̃, -jɛn], *a. & s. Geog:* (native, inhabitant) of Elbeuf.

elbois, -oise [ɛlbwa, -waːz], *a. & s. Geog:* (native, inhabitant) of Elba.

Elbourz [ɛlburz], *Pr.n.m. Geog:* **l'E.,** the Elburz mountains.

elbovien, -ienne [ɛlbɔvjɛ̃, -jɛn], *a. & s.* (native, inhabitant) of Elbeuf.

elcésaïte [ɛlsezait], *s.m. Rel.H:* Elkesaite.

Eldorado [ɛldɔrado], *Pr.n.m.* El Dorado.

éléagnacées [eleaɲase], *s.f.pl. Bot:* Elaeagnaceae.

Éléates [eleat], *s.m.pl.* (school of) Eleatic philosophers.

éléatique [eleatik], *a. Phil:* Eleatic (school, etc.).

électeur, -trice [elɛktœːr, -tris], *s.* **1.** *German Hist:* elector, *f.* electress. **2.** *Pol:* elector, voter; **les électeurs,** the electorate; **mes électeurs,** my constituents.

électif, -ive [elɛktif, -iːv], *a.* elective; *Psy:* **affinités électives,** selective affinities; *Ch:* **affinité élective,** elective affinity.

élection [elɛksjɔ̃], *s.f.* **1.** *Pol:* election, polling; **élections législatives,** parliamentary election; **é. partielle,** by-election; **jour des élections,** polling day; **procéder à une é.,** to hold an election; **annuler l'é. de qn,** to unseat s.o. **2.** (*a*) election, choice, preference; *Jur:* **faire é. de domicile,** to elect domicile; **mon pays d'é.,** my favourite country, the country of my choice; (*b*) *Theol:* election; **un vase d'é.,** a chosen vessel.

électivement [elɛktivmɑ̃], *adv.* electively, by choice.

électivité [elɛktivite], *s.f.* electivity, electiveness.

électoral, -aux [elɛktɔral, -o], *a.* electoral; **circonscription électorale,** constituency; **collège é.,** electoral college; **comité é.,** election committee; **agent é.,** election agent; **courtier é.,** canvasser; **manœuvres électorales,** vote-catching manœuvres; **propagande électorale,** electoral propaganda, electioneering; **liste électorale,** register (of voters); **droit é.,** franchise; **trucage é.,** gerrymandering; **consulter le corps é.,** to go to the country.

électoralement [elɛktɔralmɑ̃], *adv.* electorally.

électoralisme [elɛktɔralism], *s.m.* vote-catching manœuvres.

électorat [elɛktɔra], *s.m.* **1.** *Hist:* (*a*) electorate; (*b*) rank of Elector. **2.** *Pol: Coll.* electorate **consulter l'é.,** to go to the country; **l'importance de l'é. féminin,** the importance of the feminine vote. **3.** franchise.

Électre [elɛktr̥], *Pr.n.f. Gr.Lit:* Electra; *Psy:* **complexe d'É.,** Electra complex.

électricien, -ienne [elɛktrisjɛ̃, -jɛn], *a. & s.* electrician; (ingénieur) **é.,** electrical engineer.

électricité [elɛktrisite], *s.f.* electricity; **é. positive, vitrée,** positive, vitreous, electricity; **é. négative, résineuse,** negative, resinous, electricity; **é. atmosphérique, dynamique, statique,** atmospheric, dynamic, static, electricity; **é. de friction,** frictional electricity; **é. résiduelle,** electric residuum; **éclairé à l'é.,** lit by electricity; **allumer, donner, l'é.,** to switch on the light; **éteindre, couper, l'é.,** to switch off the light; **remettre l'é.,** to switch on again; **l'é. est coupée,** the electricity's off; there's a power cut; **il y a de l'é. dans l'air,** the atmosphere's electric.

électrification [elɛktrifikasjɔ̃], *s.f.* electrification (of railway, etc.).

électrifier [elɛktrifje], *v.tr.* (*p.d. & pr.sub.* **n. électrifiions, v. électrifiiez**) (*a*) to electrify (railway, etc.); (*b*) **é. un village,** to bring electric light to a village.

électrique [elɛktrik], *a.* **1.** (*of, charged with, worked by, capable of developing, electricity*) electric; **courant, lumière, é.,** electric current, light; **centrale é.,** (electric) power station; **cuisinière é.,** electric cooker; **train é.,** electric train; **commotion é.,** electric shock; **l'atmosphère de la réunion était é.,** the atmosphere of the meeting was electric. **2.** (*relating to electricity*) electrical; **l'industrie de l'équipement é.,** electrical engineering.

électriquement [elɛktrikmɑ̃], *adv.* electrically.

électrisable [elɛktrizabl̥], *a.* electrifiable (substance, audience).

électrisant [elɛktrizɑ̃], *a.* (*of atmosphere*) charged with electricity; (*of eloquence, etc.*) electrifying.

électrisation [elɛktrizasjɔ̃], *s.f.* electrification (of substance, audience); **à é. positive,** positively charged, charged with positive electricity.

électriser [elɛktrize], *v.tr.* to electrify (substance, audience, etc.); to thrill (audience); **fil de fer électrisé,** live wire; **être électrisé par un discours,** to be electrified, thrilled, inspired, by a speech.

électro- [elɛktrɔ], *pref.* electro-; **électrocapillarité,** electrocapillarity.

électro-acoumètre [elɛktrɔakumɛtr̥], *s.m. Med:* (electric) audiometer; *pl. électro-acoumètres.*

électro-acousticien [elɛktrɔakustisjɛ̃], *s.m.* electro-acoustics engineer; *pl. électro-acousticiens.*

électro-acoustique [elɛktrɔakustik]. **1.** *a.* electro-acoustic(al). **2.** *s.f.* electro-acoustics; *pl. électro-acoustiques.*

électro-affinité [elɛktrɔafinite], *s.f.* electro-affinity, electric attraction; *pl. électro-affinités.*

électro-aimant [elɛktrɔɛmɑ̃], *s.m.* (electro-)magnet; *Ind:* **é.-a. de levage,** electric lifting magnet; **é.-a. cuirassé,** iron-clad electro-magnet, electro-magnet screened type, *U.S:* shield electromagnet; *pl. électro-aimants.*

électro-analyse [elɛktrɔanaliːz], *s.f.* electro-analysis; *pl. électro-analyses.*

électro-artériogramme [elɛktrɔarterjɔgram], *s.m. Med:* plethysmogram; *pl. électro-artériogrammes.*

électro-artériographe [elɛktrɔarterjɔgraf], *s.m. Med:* plethysmograph; *pl. électro-artériographes.*

électro-artériographie [elɛktrɔarterjɔgrafi], *s.f. Med:* plethysmography.

électrobéton [elɛktrɔbetɔ̃], *s.m.* electro-cement.

électrobiologie [elɛktrɔbjɔlɔʒi], *s.f.* electrobiology.

électrobiologique [elɛktrɔbjɔlɔʒik], *a.* electrobiological.

électrobiologiste [elɛktrɔbjɔlɔʒist], *s.m. & f.* electrobiologist.

électrocapillaire [elɛktrɔkapilɛːr], *a.* electrocapillary.

électrocapillarité [elɛktrɔkapilarite], *s.f.* electrocapillarity.

électrocardiogramme [elɛktrɔkardjɔgram], *s.m.* electrocardiogram.

électrocardiographe [elɛktrɔkardjɔgraf], *s.m.* electrocardiograph.

électrocardiographie [elɛktrɔkardjɔgrafi], *s.f.* electrocardiography.

électrocardioscope [elɛktrɔkardjɔskɔp], *s.m.* electrocardioscope.

électrocaustique [elɛktrɔkostik], *s.f.* electrocauterization.

électrocautère [elɛktrɔkotɛːr], *s.m. Surg:* electrocautery.

électrochimie [elɛktrɔʃimi], *s.f.* electrochemistry.

électrochimique [elɛktrɔʃimik], *a.* electrochemical; *Ind:* **extraction é.,** electro-extraction.

électrochirurgie [elɛktrɔʃiryrʒi], *s.f.* electrosurgery.

électrochoc [elɛktrɔʃɔk], *s.m. Med:* **traitement par électrochocs,** electric shock treatment, therapy.

électrocinétique [elɛktrɔsinetik], *a.* electrokinetic.

électrocoagulation [elɛktrɔkoagylasjɔ̃], *s.f. Med:* electrocoagulation, diathermic coagulation.

électrocoma [elɛktrɔkɔma], *s.m. Med:* electrocoma.

électrocopie [elɛktrɔkɔpi], *s.f.* xerography.

électrocorticogramme [elɛktrɔkɔrtikɔgram], *s.m. Med:* electrocorticogram, electroencephalogram.

électrocortine [elɛktrɔkɔrtin], *s.f. Physiol:* electrocortin, aldosterone.

électroculture [elɛktrɔkyltyːr], *s.f.* electroculture.

électrocuter [elɛktrɔkyte], *v.tr.* to electrocute.

électrocuteur [elɛktrɔkytœːr], *s.m. U.S:* electrocutioner.

électrocution [elɛktrɔkysjɔ̃], *s.f.* electrocution.

électrode [elɛktrɔd], *s.f.* electrode; **é. positive,** anode, positive pole; **é. négative,** cathode, negative pole; **é. nue,** bare electrode; **é. enrobée,** coated electrode; **é. enduite,** thin-coated electrode; **é. douce,** easy-flowing electrode; **é. dure,** hard-metal electrode; **é. boudinée,** extruded electrode; **é. en anse,** loop-electrode; **é. collectrice,** collector electrode; **é. d'entrée, de sortie,** input, output, electrode.

électrodéposition [elɛktrɔdepɔzisjɔ̃], *s.f.* electrodeposition.

électrodiagnostic [elɛktrɔdjagnɔstik], *s.m.* electrodiagnosis.

électrodialyse [elɛktrɔdjaliːz], *s.f.* electrodialysis.

électrodissolution [elɛktrɔdisɔlysjɔ̃], *s.f.* electrodissolution.

électrodomestique [elɛktrɔdɔmɛstik], *a. A:* = ÉLECTROMÉNAGER.

électrodynamique [elɛktrɔdinamik]. **1.** *a.* electrodynamic(al). **2.** *s.f.* electrodynamics.

électrodynamomètre [elɛktrɔdinamɔmɛtr̥], *s.m.* electrodynamometer.

électroencéphalogramme [elɛktrɔɑ̃sefalɔgram], *s.m.* electroencephalogram.

électroencéphalographe [elɛktrɔɑ̃sefalɔgraf], *s.m.* electroencephalograph.

électroencéphalographie [elɛktrɔɑ̃sefalɔgrafi], *s.f.* electroencephalography.

électro-endosmose [elɛktrɔɑ̃dɔsmoːz], *s.f.* electro-endosmosis.

électrofiltre [elɛktrɔfiltr̥], *s.m. Ind:* precipitator (for controlling pollution of air, etc.).

électroformage [elɛktrɔfɔrmaːʒ], *s.m. Tchn:* electroforming.

électrogalvanique [elɛktrɔgalvanik], *a.* electrogalvanic.

électrogène [elɛktrɔʒɛn], *a. El.E:* generating (plant, etc.); **groupe é.,** generating set.

électrogenèse [elɛktrɔʒenɛːz], *s.f.* electrogenesis.

électrogénérateur [elɛktrɔʒeneratœːr], *s.m. El:* generator.

électrographe [elɛktrɔgraf], *s.m. Tg:* electrograph.

électrographie [elɛktrɔgrafi], *s.f. Tg:* electrography.

électrologie [elɛktrɔlɔʒi], *s.f.* electrology.

électroluminescence [elɛktrɔlyminɛs(s)ɑ̃ːs], *s.f.* electroluminescence.

électroluminescent [elɛktrɔlyminɛs(s)ɑ̃], *a.* electroluminescent.

électrolysable [elɛktrɔlizabl̥], *a.* electrolysable.

électrolysation [elɛktrɔlizasjɔ̃], *s.f.* electrolysing, electrolysation.

électrolyse [elɛktrɔliːz], *s.f.* electrolysis; **é. du zinc,** electrolytic zinc process.

électrolyser [elɛktrɔlize], *v.tr.* to electrolyse.

électrolyseur [elɛktrɔlizœːr], *s.m.* electrolyser.

électrolyte [elɛktrɔlit], *s.m. El:* electrolyte; battery solution; **é. impropre,** foul electrolyte.

électrolytique [elɛktrɔlitik], *a.* electrolytic; **analyse é.,** electroanalysis; **désintégration é.,** electrolytic dissociation; **cuivre é.,** electrolytic copper; **cuve é.,** electrolytic cell, vat; **décapage é.,** electrolytic pickling; **redresseur é.,** electrolytic rectifier.

électrolytiquement [elɛktrɔlitikmɑ̃], *adv.* electrolytically.

électromagnétique [elɛktrɔmaɲetik], *a.* electromagnetic; **champ é.,** electromagnetic field; **dispersion é.,** electromagnetic leakage; **induction é.,** electromagnetic induction; **onde é.,** electromagnetic wave.

électromagnétisme [elɛktrɔmaɲetism], *s.m.* electromagnetism.
électromécanicien [elɛktrɔmekanisjɛ̃], *s.m.* electrical engineer.
électromécanique [elɛktrɔmekanik]. **1.** *a.* electromechanical. **2.** *s.f.* electromechanics.
électromécanisme [elɛktrɔmekanism], *s.m.* electromechanism.
électroménager [elɛktrɔmenaʒe], *a. & s.m.* **(appareils) électroménagers,** electric household appliances, *U.S:* household electricals.
électromère [elɛktrɔmɛːr], *s.m. Ch:* electromer.
électromérie [elɛktrɔmeri], *s.f. Ch:* electromerism.
électrométallurgie [elɛktrɔmetalyrʒi], *s.f.* electrometallurgy.
électrométallurgique [elɛktrɔmetalyrʒik], *a.* electrometallurgic.
électrométallurgiste [elɛktrɔmetalyrʒist], *s.m.* electrometallurgist.
électromètre [elɛktrɔmɛtr], *s.m.* electrometer; **é. à lame vibrante,** vibrating-reed electrometer.
électrométrie [elɛktrɔmetri], *s.f.* electrometry.
électrométrique [elɛktrɔmetrik], *a.* electrometric.
électromobile [elɛktrɔmɔbil], *a.* electrically driven, operated (vehicle).
électromoteur, -trice [elɛktrɔmɔtœːr, -tris]. **1.** *a.* electromotive. **2.** *s.m.* electromotor.
électromusculaire [elɛctrɔmyskylɛːr], *a.* electromuscular.
électromyogramme [elɛktrɔmiɔgram], *s.m. Med:* electromyogram.
électromyographe [elɛktrɔmiɔgraf], *s.m. Med:* electromyograph.
électromyographie [elɛktrɔmiɔgrafi], *s.f. Med:* electromyography.
électron [elɛktrɔ̃], *s.m. Ph:* electron; **paire d'électrons,** electron pair; **é. atomique,** atomic electron, atom-bound electron, orbital electron; **é. nucléaire,** nuclear electron; **é. extra-nucléaire,** extranuclear electron; **é. célibataire,** lone electron; **é. libre,** free electron; **é. captif,** trapped electron; **é. lié,** orbital electron, bound electron; **é. planétaire, é. satellite,** planetary, orbital, electron; **é. interne,** inner(-shell) electron; **é. périphérique,** outer(-shell) electron; **é. primaire, secondaire,** primary, secondary, electron; **é. tournant,** spinning electron; **é. thermique,** thermo-electron, thermion; **é. négatif,** negatron; **é. positif,** positron; **canon à électrons,** electron gun.
électronarcose [elɛktrɔnarkoːz], *s.f. Med:* electronarcosis, electroshock therapy.
électronation [elɛctrɔnasjɔ̃], *s.f.* electron capture; electron attachment.
électronégatif, -ive [elɛktrɔnegatif, -iːv], *a.* electronegative.
électronégativité [elɛktrɔnegativite], *s.f.* electronegativity.
électronicien, -ienne [elɛtrɔnisjɛ̃, -jɛn], *s.* electronics specialist.
électronique [elɛktrɔnik]. **1.** *a.* electronic, electron; **caméra é.,** electron camera; **choc é.,** electron impact; **commande é.,** electronic control; **enregistreur é.,** electronic recorder; **faisceau é.,** electron beam; **flux é.,** electron flow, stream; **gaz é.,** electron gas; **lentille é.,** electron lens; **microscope, télescope, é.,** electron microscope, telescope; **miroir é.,** electron mirror; **mire é.,** electron(ic) pattern; **trajectoire é.,** electron path; **tube é.,** electron tube; **valence é.,** electrovalence, electrovalency; **valve é.,** thermionic valve, electron valve; **calculateur, calculatrice é.,** electronic computer, electronic brain; **ensemble é.,** computer; **petit ensemble é.,** small-scale computer; **grand, gros, ensemble é.,** large-scale computer; **ensemble é. moyen, de moyenne puissance,** medium-scale computer. **2.** *s.f.* electronics; **é. moléculaire,** molecular electronics; **é. aéronautique,** avionics; **é. quantique,** quantum physics of electronics.
électroniquement [elɛktrɔnikmɑ̃], *adv.* electronically.
électron-trou [elɛktrɔ̃tru], *s.m. Elcs:* electron-positron pair; *pl. électrons-trous.*
électronucléaire [elɛktrɔnykleɛːr], *a.* **centrale é.,** nuclear power station.
électron-volt [elɛktrɔ̃vɔlt], *s.m.* electron-volt; *pl. électrons-volts.*
électro-optique [elɛktrɔɔptik]. **1.** *a.* electro-optic(al). **2.** *s.f.* electro-optics.
électro-osmose [elɛktrɔɔsmoːz], *s.f.* electro-osmosis, electrosmosis.
électro-osmotique [elɛktrɔɔsmɔtik], *a.* electro-osmotic.
électropathologie [elɛktrɔpatɔlɔʒi], *s.f. Med:* electropathology.
électrophone [elɛktrɔfɔn], *s.m.* record(-)player.
électrophonique [elɛktrɔfɔnik], *a.* electrophonic (effect).
électrophore [elɛktrɔfɔːr], *s.m.* electrophorus.
électrophorèse [elɛktrɔfɔrɛːz], *s.f.* electrophoresis.
électrophorétique [elɛktrɔfɔretik], *a.* electrophoretic.
électrophotomètre [elɛktrɔfɔtɔmɛtr], *s.m.* electrophotometer.
électrophysiologie [elɛktrɔfizjɔlɔʒi], *s.f.* electrophysiology.
électrophysiologique [elɛktrɔfizjɔlɔʒik], *a.* electrophysiological.
électrophysiologiste [elɛktrɔfizjɔlɔʒist], *s.m. Med:* electrophysiologist.
électroplaxe [elɛktrɔplaks], *s.f. Nat.Hist:* electroplax.
électropneumatique [elɛktrɔpnømatik], *a.* electropneumatic.
électropompe [elɛktrɔpɔ̃ːp], *s.f.* electric, motor-driven, pump.
électroponcture [elɛktrɔpɔ̃ktyːr], *s.f. Med:* electropuncture.
électropositif, -ive [elɛktrɔpɔzitif, -iːv], *a.* electropositive.
électropositivité [elɛktrɔpɔzitivite], *s.f.* electropositivity.
électropuncture [elɛktrɔpœ̃ktyːr], *s.f. Med:* electropuncture.
électropyrexie [elɛktrɔpirɛksi], *s.f. Med:* electropyrexia.
électroradiologie [elɛktrɔradjɔlɔʒi], *s.f.* electroradiology.
électroradiologiste [elɛktrɔradjɔlɔʒist], *s.m. & f.* electroradiologist.
électroraffinage [elɛktrɔrafinaːʒ], *s.m. Ind:* electrorefining.
électrorétinogramme [elɛktrɔretinɔgram], *s.m.* electroretinogram.
électroscope [elɛktrɔskɔp], *s.m.* electroscope; **é. à feuilles d'or,** gold-leaf electroscope.
électrosidérurgie [elɛktrɔsideryrʒi], *s.f.* electrosiderurgy.
électrosmose [elɛktrɔsmoːz], *s.f.* electro-osmosis, electrosmosis.
électrosoudure [elɛktrɔsudyːr], *s.f.* electric welding.
électrostatique [elɛktrɔstatik]. **1.** *a.* electrostatic(al). **2.** *s.f.* electrostatics.
électrosténolyse [elɛktrɔstenɔliːz], *s.f.* electrostenolysis.
électrostriction [elɛktrɔstriksjɔ̃], *s.f.* electrostriction; *(computers)* **effet d'é.,** electrostrictive effect.
électrosynthèse [elɛktrɔsɛ̃tɛːz], *s. Ch:* electrosynthesis.
électrotaxis [elɛktrɔtaksis], *s.f. Biol:* electrotaxis.
électrotechnicien, -ienne [elɛktrɔtɛknisjɛ̃, -jɛn], *s.* electrotechnologist, specialist in electrotechnology.
électrotechnique [elɛktrɔtɛknik]. **1.** *a.* electrotechnic(al). **2.** *s.f.* *(a)* electrotechnology; *(b)* electrical engineering.
électrothérapeute [elɛktrɔterapøt], *s.m. & f. Med:* electrotherapeutist.
électrothérapeutique [elɛktrɔterapøtik], *a.* electrotherapeutic(al).
électrothérapie [elɛktrɔterapi], *s.f. Med:* electrotherapy, electrotherapeutics.
électrothermie [elɛktrɔtɛrmi], *s.f.* electrothermics.
électrothermique [elɛktrɔtɛrmik], *a.* thermoelectric(al), electrothermic.
électrotonique [elɛktrɔtɔnik], *a.* electrotonic.
électrotonus [elɛktrɔtɔnys], *s.m. Physiol:* electrotonus.
électrotrain [elɛktrɔtrɛ̃], *s.m. Rail:* electric multiple unit.
électrotrieuse [elɛktrɔtriøːz], *s.f.* magnetic separator; electromagnetic separator.
électrotropisme [elɛktrɔtrɔpism], *s.m.* electrotropism.
électrotype [elɛktrɔtip], *s.m. Typ:* electrotype; *F:* electro.
électrotyper [elɛktrɔtipe], *v.tr.* to electrotype.
électrotypeur [elɛktrɔtipœːr], *s.m.* electrotyper.
électrotypie [elɛktrɔtipi], *s.f. Typ:* electrotyping.
électrovalence [elɛktrɔvalɑ̃ːs], *s.f.* electrovalence, electrovalency.
électro-valve [elɛktrɔvalv], *s.f.* electro-valve; *pl. électro-valves.*
électrovanne [elɛktrɔvan], *s.f.* electromagnetic sluice gate.
électrum [elɛktrɔm], *s.m. Cl.Ant: Miner:* electrum.
électuaire [elɛktɥɛːr], *s.m. Pharm:* electuary.
élédone [eledɔn], *s.f.* the Mediterranean octopus.
Élée [ele], *Pr.n.f. A.Geog:* Elea.
éléen, -enne [eleɛ̃, -ɛn], *a. & s. A.Geog:* Elean; (i) of Elea; (ii) of Elis.
élégamment [elegamɑ̃], *adv.* elegantly; **bijoux é. ciselés,** delicately chased jewellery; **elle s'habille é.,** she dresses well, fashionably; she is always elegantly dressed; **écrire é.,** to write in an elegant style; **il s'en est tiré é.,** he got out of it very neatly.
élégance [elegɑ̃ːs], *s.f.* elegance; *(a)* **l'é. a toujours l'air facile,** true elegance has always an unstudied, unforced, appearance; **é. de la taille,** grace of figure; **l'é. du chat siamois,** the elegance, grace, of a Siamese cat; **l'é. du mobilier,** the elegant, graceful, style of the furniture; **les œuvres de ce peintre ont plus d'é. que de vigueur,** this painter's works are characterized by elegance, by charm, rather than force; **femme qui a de l'é.,** (i) elegant, graceful, (ii) well-dressed, woman; **s'habiller avec é.,** to dress smartly, in a fashionable style; *(b)* **écrire avec é.,** to write in a distinguished, polished, style; **il s'exprime dans un français correct mais sans é.,** his French is correct but lacks style; *(c)* **é. d'une démonstration, d'une solution,** neatness of a demonstration, a solution; **savoir perdre avec é.,** to be a good loser; **charité qui a l'é. de se cacher,** (commendably) discreet charity; **il est arrivé à ses fins mais ses procédés manquent d'é.,** he got what he wanted, but in a somewhat crude fashion; *(d)* *pl.* **les élégances de la vie,** the refinements of life.
élégant [elegɑ̃]. **1.** *a.* elegant; *(a)* **taille élégante,** elegant, graceful, figure; **mains élégantes,** shapely hands; **architecture élégante,** graceful architecture; **femme élégante,** (i) graceful, elegant, (ii) well-dressed, woman; **robe élégante,** smart, fashionable, dress; **assistance élégante,** fashionable, distinguished, audience; **restaurant é.,** fashionable restaurant; *(b)* **style é.,** elegant, polished, style; **parler d'une manière élégante,** to speak in a distinguished, polished, manner; *(c)* **démonstration élégante,** neat, elegant, demonstration; **plusieurs solutions correctes, dont l'une est plus élégante que les autres,** several correct solutions, one of which is neater than the others; **mensonge é.,** diplomatic lie; **ses procédés sont peu élégants,** his way of going about things is (i) ill-mannered, (ii) undiplomatic, crude, (iii) in dubious taste. **2.** *s.* *(a)* *s.m. A:* **un é.,** a man of fashion; a dandy; *(b)* *s.f.* **une élégante,** a well-dressed, fashionably dressed, woman; **elle veut faire l'élégante,** she wants to appear fashionable, elegant; she tries to look as though she belonged to the smart set.
élégiaque [eleʒjak], *a.* elegiac; **poète é.,** elegist.
élégie [eleʒi], *s.f.* *(a)* elegy; *(b)* *F:* **il nous fatigue avec ses perpétuelles élégies,** he wearies us with his eternal complaints, his perpetual moaning.
élégir [eleʒiːr], *v.tr. Tchn:* to reduce the volume of (sth.); to plane down, file down, fine down (material).
éléis [eleis], *s.m. Bot:* elaeis, oil palm.
élément [elemɑ̃], *s.m.* element. **1.** *(a)* *Ch:* element (simple substance); **le carbone est un é.,** carbon is an element; *(b)* **les quatre éléments,** the (four) elements; **l'eau est l'é. du poisson,** water is the element of the fish; **être, nager, dans son é.,** to be in one's element; *Meteor:* **lutter contre les éléments déchaînés,** to struggle against the (raging) elements; *(c)* *Ph: Atom.Ph:* element; **é. radioactif,** radioactive element; **é. ascendant, é. mère, é. original,** parent element; **é. descendant, é. engendré, é. de filiation,** daughter element; **é. de la même famille,** related element; **é. séparateur, é. de séparation,** separative element; **é. transuranien,** transuranic element; **é. (de) combustible,** fuel element (of atomic reactor); **é. du réseau,** lattice element (of atomic reactor). **2.** *(a)* component, constituent (of sth.); ingredient (of medicine); standardized part (of sectional structure, etc.); **les éléments du bonheur,** the factors which make for happiness; **les éléments conservateurs de notre ville,** the conservative elements in our town; **savourer l'é. comique de la situation,** to enjoy the comic side of the situation; **l'é. décisif,** the deciding, the decisive, factor; **é. d'instabilité,** disturbing factor; **le confort est un é. essentiel de la vie moderne,** comfort is an essential element in modern life; *Jur:* **éléments constitutifs d'un délit,** factors that constitute an offence; *Nau:* **éléments du journal,** entries in the log; *Civ.E: Mec.E:* **é. constitutif,** component, constituent, element, part; **é. de contrôle, de régulation, de réglage,** control unit, element, member; **é. de sécurité,** safety unit, element, member; **é. générateur,** generating unit; **é. chauffant,** heating unit, element; **é. de construction,** construction unit; sub-assembly; **construction par éléments standards,** modular construction; **é. de pont**

mobile, member of portable bridge; éléments auxiliaires d'un système articulé, auxiliary rods, members, of a framework; *N.Arch:* é. d'un panneau de cale, pontoon of a steel hatch cover; *Tchn:* é. filtrant, filter element; *T.V:* é. d'image, image, picture, element; *Furn:* mobilier formé d'éléments, unit furniture; éléments normalisés, standardized units; (*b*) *El:* cell (of battery, accumulator); é. thermo-électrique, thermocouple; é. chargé, active cell; é. témoin, control cell; batterie de cinq éléments, five-cell battery; (*c*) *Elcs:* é. de calculateur, de calculatrice, électronique, computer unit; é. de guide d'ondes, wave-guide section; é. porte, gating unit; é. binaire, binary cell; é. de circuit, circuit modula; é. de mémoire, storage cell; (*d*) *Mil:* element, unit, force; éléments avancés, advanced, leading, elements, forces; é. de couverture, covering, screening, element, force; é. de soutien, supporting element, force; é. de sûreté, security, protection, element, force; é. blindé, é. motorisé, armoured, motorized, force, unit; se heurter à de forts éléments d'infanterie, to meet, run into, strong infantry elements, forces; éléments non endivisionnés, non-divisional elements; éléments organiques d'armée, de corps d'armée, army, corps, troops, units; (*e*) *Geom:* element (of line, surface, solid, etc.); *Surv:* é. d'un cheminement, leg of traverse (between stations); (*f*) individual; member (of a group); les éléments indésirables de la population, the undesirable elements of the population, the undesirables. 3. *pl.* (*a*) elements, rudiments, first principles (of science, theory, etc.); apprendre les éléments de l'arithmétique, to learn the elements, the rudiments, of arithmetic; il faut apprendre les éléments du français avant de partir pour Paris, you should learn some basic French before setting out for Paris; bien connaître ses éléments, to be thoroughly grounded, to have a good grounding; éléments de mathématiques, general mathematics; (*b*) éléments (d'information, d'un problème, etc.), data; *Artil: Ball:* éléments de tir, firing data; *Artil:* éléments extrapolés, prediction data; *Elcs:* traitement des éléments d'information, data processing; *Mapm:* éléments numériques du quadrillage, grid data.

élémentaire [elemɑ̃tɛːr], *a.* 1. elemental (body, part, etc.); *Ch:* analyse é., elementary analysis; *Atom.Ph:* particules élémentaires, elementary particles. 2. elementary (knowledge, algebra, etc.); *Sch:* classes élémentaires, junior forms; classe de mathématiques élémentaires = VIth form mathematical division. 3. (*a*) rudimentary (dwelling, etc.); (*b*) *F:* c'est é., that's the least you can do.

élémental, -aux [elemɑ̃tal, -o], *a. Psychics:* elemental.

élémi [elemi], *s.m. Pharm:* gum elemi.

élémicine [elemisin], *s.f. Ch:* elemicin.

éléocarpacées [eleɔkarpase], *s.f.pl. Bot:* Elaeocarpaceae.

éléolite [eleɔlit], *s.f. Miner:* elaeolite.

Eléonore [eleɔnɔːr], *Pr.n.f.* Eleanor(a), Elinor; *Hist:* É. de Guyenne, d'Aquitaine, Eleanor of Aquitaine.

éléonorite [eleɔnɔrit], *s.f. Miner:* eleonorite.

éléphant [elefɑ̃], *s.m. Z:* 1. (*a*) elephant; é. mâle, femelle, bull, cow, elephant; il agit avec la grâce, la légèreté, d'un é., he treads as delicately as an elephant; *F:* il manquerait un é. dans un tunnel, he couldn't hit a barn door (at three paces); *F:* elle a une peau d'é., she's thick-skinned, she's got a hide like a rhinoceros; *F:* être comme un é. dans un magasin de porcelaine, to be like a bull in a china shop; *F:* faire d'une mouche un é., to make a mountain out of a mole-hill; *F:* il a une mémoire d'é., he never forgets an injury, an insult; *Cost:* pantalon (à) pattes d'é., bell-bottomed trousers, bell-bottoms; (*b*) *F:* heavy, clumsy, person; *Nau:* landlubber. 2. é. de mer, é. marin, sea elephant, elephant seal.

éléphante [elefɑ̃ːt], *s.f.* (*rare*) cow elephant.

éléphanteau, -eaux [elefɑ̃to], *s.m.* elephant calf.

éléphantesque [elefɑ̃tɛsk], *a. F:* elephantine, gigantic, enormous.

éléphantiasique [elefɑ̃tjazik], *a. Med:* elephantiasic.

éléphantiasis [elefɑ̃tjazis], *s.f. Med:* elephantiasis; é. des Arabes, Barbados leg.

éléphantidés [elefɑ̃tide], *s.m.pl. Z:* Elephantidae.

éléphantin [elefɑ̃tɛ̃], *a.* 1. elephantine (epoch, nature, etc.). 2. made of ivory.

éléphantopodie [elefɑ̃tɔpɔdi], *s.f. Med:* elephant leg.

éléphantopus [elefɑ̃tɔpys], *s.m. Bot:* elephantopus; elephant's foot.

élettaria [elɛtarja], *s.m. Bot:* elettaria.

éleusine [elœzin], *s.f. Bot:* eleusine; yard-grass.

éleusinien, -ienne [eløzinjɛ̃, -jɛn], *a. & s. Gr.Ant:* Eleusinian.

éleusinies [eløzini], *s.f.pl. Gr.Ant:* Eleusinia, Eleusinian mysteries.

éleuthérodactyle [eløterɔdaktil], *s.m. Amph:* eleutherodactylus.

éleuthéropétale [eløterɔpetal], *a. Bot:* eleutheropetalous.

éleuthérozoaires [eløterɔzɔɛːr], *s.m.pl. Echin:* Eleutherozoa.

élevable [ɛlvabl, e-], *a.* (*of animal*) that can be reared.

élevage [ɛlvaːʒ, e-], *s.m. Husb:* 1. breeding, rearing (of stock); animal husbandry; stock farming; grazing (of sheep, etc.); raising (of plants); prairie d'é., ranch; é. des moutons, (i) sheep-breeding, -farming; (ii) wool-growing; faire l'é. des moutons, to breed sheep; é. des animaux à fourrure, fur farming; poulet d'é., battery-reared chicken. 2. (stock-)farm; ranch; (*in Austr.*) (sheep-)station; élevages chevalins et mulassiers, mule and horse studs.

élévateur, -trice [elevatœːr, -tris]. 1. (*a*) *a. & s.m. Anat:* elevator (muscle); (*b*) *a.* machine élévatrice d'eau, water elevator, water engine, pumping engine; chariot é. (à fourche), (fork) lift truck. 2. *s.m.* (*a*) elevator, lift, hoist; é. à bascule, tip; *Hyd.E:* é. de bateaux, canal lift; *Sm.a:* é. de chargeur, cartridge carrier, (spring) feed mechanism; planchette de l'é., (magazine) platform (depressor); (*b*) (grain) elevator; é. à augets, à godets, bucket elevator; é. pneumatique, é. aspirateur, pneumatic, sucking, elevator; (*c*) *Av:* é. à fourche, fork lift truck.

élévation [elevasjɔ̃], *s.f.* 1. (*a*) elevation, lifting, raising (of s.o., sth.); é. de l'hostie, *abs.* l'é., elevation of the Host, the elevation; é. de qn au trône, raising of s.o. to the throne; é. de l'eau, pumping (up) of water; é. des prix, raising, putting up, of prices; é. de la voix, raising of the voice; é. morale, moral uplift; (*b*) erection, setting up (of temple, statue, etc.); (*c*) *Mth:* é. à une puissance, raising to a power, exponentiation. 2. (*a*) rise; é. de température, rise in temperature; é. des prix, soaring of prices; (*b*) é. du pouls, quickening of the pulse. 3. (*a*) *O:* loftiness, height, altitude; atteindre une é. de deux cents mètres, to reach a height of two hundred metres; é. du plafond, loftiness, height, of the ceiling; l'é. des prix, the high prices; é. de style, grandeur, nobility, of style; é. d'esprit, d'âme, high-mindedness; (*b*) altitude (of star, etc.); (*c*) *Artil:* angle d'é., angle of elevation (of gun). 4. *Arch: Geom:* elevation, vertical section; *N.Arch:* sheer draught; é. du devant, du derrière, front-, back-view. 5. high ground, height, eminence; une é. bornait la vue, rising ground, a rise in the ground, limited the view.

élévatoire [elevatwaːr]. 1. *a.* elevatory, lifting, hoisting (apparatus, etc.). 2. *s.m. Surg:* elevator.

élévator [elevatɔːr], *s.m. Agr:* grain elevator.

élève[1] [elɛːv], *s.m. & f.* 1. pupil; student; apprentice; trainee; *Mil: etc:* é. officier, cadet; é. officier d'aviation = R.A.F. cadet; é. officier de marine, (i) naval cadet; (ii) cadet of the merchant service; *Av:* é. pilote, pilot trainee, student pilot. 2. *s.f.* (*a*) *Husb:* young rearing animal; (*b*) *Hort:* seedling.

élève[2], *s.f. Husb: etc: A:* raising, breeding, rearing (of stock); raising (of plants).

élevé [elve], *a.* 1. (*a*) high (mountain, position, price, temperature); noble, lofty (style, mind); exalted (position, rank); aux principes élevés, high-principled; sentiment très é. du devoir, very exalted conception of duty; l'officier le plus é. en grade, the senior officer; plafond peu é., low ceiling; (*b*) pouls é., quick pulse. 2. bien é., well brought up, well-mannered, well-bred; mal é., badly brought up, ill-mannered, ill-bred; *F:* c'est très mal é. de dire ça, one shouldn't say that; *s.* il s'est conduit comme un mal é., he behaved like a boor.

élever [elve], *v.tr.* (j'élève, n. élevons; j'élèverai) 1. (*a*) to elevate, raise (s.o., sth.); é. un fardeau, to raise, lift up, hoist, a burden; é. un mur de deux mètres, to raise a wall by two metres, to make a wall two metres higher; é. la température, to raise the temperature; é. la voix, to raise, lift up, one's voice; *Mus:* é. le ton d'un morceau, to transpose a piece to a higher key; é. les prix, to raise prices; é. qn à un rang supérieur, to promote, advance, s.o.; é. l'âme de qn, to elevate s.o.'s mind; é. qn aux nues, to laud s.o. to the skies; *Nau:* é. une côte, un phare, to raise a coast, a lighthouse; (*b*) *Mth:* é. un nombre au carré, au cube, to square, to cube, a number. 2. (*a*) to erect, set up (temple, machine, statue, etc.); é. un parapet, to throw up a parapet; (*b*) é. une objection, de nouvelles difficultés, to raise an objection, fresh difficulties; (*c*) é. une fortune, to found a fortune (sur, on); é. une doctrine, to establish a doctrine (sur, on). 3. to bring up, rear (child); to rear (stock); to breed (cattle, horses, rabbits); to keep (bees, poultry); to grow (plants); é. du vin, to cultivate vines; é. un bébé au sein, au biberon, to breast-feed, bottle-feed, a baby; comment a-t-elle été élevée? how was she brought up? what sort of upbringing has she had? élevé à la campagne, country bred.

s'élever. 1. (*a*) to rise (up); le ballon s'élevait dans les airs, the balloon was rising into the air; l'avion s'est élevé difficilement, the aircraft took off with difficulty; le brouillard s'élève, the fog is lifting; (*b*) to stand; le château s'élève sur la colline, the castle stands on the hill; (*c*) to arise; des protestations s'élevèrent, protests were raised; s'il s'élève des difficultés, if difficulties arise; un cri s'éleva, a shout was heard; le vent s'élève, the wind is rising; (*d*) s'é. contre une accusation, to protest against an accusation; s'é. contre un abus, to make a stand against an abuse; to denounce an abuse; (*e*) *Nau:* (i) to beat off the wind; s'é. au vent vers la terre, to beat up; s'é. au vent d'une côte, to claw off a coast; s'é. dans le vent, to gain the wind, to draw ahead against the wind; (ii) s'é. à la lame, to top the sea, to rise with the sea. 2. (*a*) to raise oneself; s'é. sur les pointes des pieds, to stand on tiptoe; s'é. à force de travail, to work one's way up; (*b*) s'é. au-dessus de ses préjugés, to overcome one's prejudices. 3. (*a*) chaque mois les prix s'élèvent quelque peu, prices are going up a little every month; la température s'élève à mesure que l'on s'approche des tropiques, the temperature rises as one approaches the tropics; (*b*) le compte s'élève à mille francs, the bill comes to, amounts to, a thousand francs.

éleveur, -euse [elvœːr, -øːz], *Husb:* 1. *s.* stock breeder; grazier; horse breeder; é. de chiens, dog breeder. 2. *s.f.* éleveuse, battery, brooder (for chickens); incubator, foster-mother.

élevon [elvɔ̃], *s.m. Aer:* elevator aileron, elevon.

élevure [elvyːr], *s.f.* pimple, pustule; weal (of urticaria, etc.).

elfe [ɛlf], *s.m.* elf.

elginisme [ɛlʒinism], *s.m.* removal from site of architectural or artistic treasures (to put in museum or private collection).

Éliacin [eljasɛ̃], **Éliakim** [eljakim], *Pr.n.m.* Eliakim.

éliasite [eljazit], *s.f. Miner:* eliasite.

élicite [elisit], *a. Phil:* acte é., elicit act.

Élide [elid], *Pr.n.f. Geog:* Elis.

élider [elide], *v.tr. Ling:* to elide (vowel).

Élie [eli], *Pr.n.m.* Elijah, Elias.

Élien [eljɛ̃], *Pr.n.m. Gr.Lit:* Aelianus.

élier [elje], *v.tr.* (*p.d. & pr.sub.* n. éliions, v. éliiez) to draw off (wine).

Éliézer [eljezɛːr], *Pr.n.m. B.Hist:* Eliezer.

éligibilité [eliʒibilite], *s.f.* eligibility; titres d'é., qualifications for membership (à, of).

éligible [eliʒibl], *a.* eligible.

élimage [elimaːʒ], *s.m.* threadbareness.

élimé [elime], *a.* (*of material*) worn, threadbare; shiny (through wear); chemise élimée aux poignets, shirt rubbed at the cuffs.

élimer [elime], *v.tr.* to wear off the nap of (material).

s'élimer, (*of clothes, etc.*) to wear threadbare.

éliminable [eliminabl], *a.* eliminable; that can be eliminated.

éliminateur, -trice [eliminatœːr, -tris]. 1. *a.* eliminating, eliminative (process, etc.); *W.Tel:* circuit é. de bruit de fond, squelch circuit. 2. *s.m.* eliminator; suppressor.

élimination [eliminasjɔ̃], *s.f.* elimination; en procédant par é., by a process of elimination; principe d'é., knock-out principle; concours sur le principe d'é., knock-out competition; *Ind: etc:* é. des déchets, waste disposal; é. des parasites, des échos parasites, suppression of noise, interference; *Cmptr:* deletion.

éliminatoire [eliminatwaːr]. 1. *a.* eliminatory (method, examination, etc.). 2. *a. & s.f. Sp:* (épreuves) éliminatoires, preliminary, eliminating, heats.

éliminer [elimine], *v.tr.* to eliminate, remove, expel; to get rid of (s.o., sth.); *Cmptr:* to reject (erroneous card); **é. par décalage, par filtrage, par masquage,** to shift out, filter out, mask out; **il faut é. cette hypothèse,** this theory must be ruled out; **é. un nom d'une liste,** to strike a name off a list; **é. les incapables,** to weed out the inefficient; *Sp:* **être éliminé,** to be knocked out (in a tournament); *Alg:* **é. une inconnue,** to eliminate an unknown quantity; (*of quantities*) **s'é.,** to cancel out.

élinde [elɛ̃:d], *s.f. Civ.E:* dredging ladder.

élingage [elɛ̃ga:ʒ], *s.m. Civ.E:* slinging.

élingue [elɛ̃:g], *s.f. Civ.E: etc:* sling (of crane); **é. à griffes, à pattes,** can hook; **é. de portage,** carrying sling; **é. de retenue,** snubbing line; **é. en filet, filet d'é.,** cargo net, loading net; *Mil.Av:* **é. de levage des bombes,** bomb hoist sling.

élingué [elɛ̃ge], *a.* without tongue; *Ent:* without proboscis.

élinguée [elɛ̃ge], *s.f. Civ.E: etc:* load (of a sling); **une é. de deux tonnes,** a two-ton load.

élinguer [elɛ̃ge], *v.tr.* to sling; to raise (heavy object) by a sling.

élingueur [elɛ̃gœ:r], *s.m.* (*pers.*) (crane) slinger.

élinvar [elɛ̃va:r], *s.m. Metall:* elinvar.

élire [eli:r], *v.tr.* (*conj. like* LIRE). **1.** to elect, choose (s.o.); **il fut élu à l'Académie,** he was elected to the Academy; **é. un député,** to return, elect, a member of parliament; **il sera certainement élu,** he is sure to get in; *pred.* **é. qn président,** (i) to elect s.o. president; (ii) to vote s.o. into the chair. **2. é. domicile (dans un endroit),** to take up one's residence, to make one's home, to settle down (in a place); *Jur:* to elect domicile.

Élisabeth [elizabɛt], *Pr.n.f.* Elizabeth.

élisabéthain, -aine [elizabetɛ̃, -ɛn], *a. & s.* Elizabethan.

Élise [eli:z], *Pr.n.f.* Eliza.

Élisée [elize], *Pr.n.m. B.Hist:* Elisha, Eliseus.

élision [elizjɔ̃], *s.f. Ling:* elision, eliding.

élite [elit], *s.f.* élite; flower, pick (of the army, etc.); **les élites,** the élite; **personnel d'é.,** picked personnel; **régiment d'é.,** crack regiment; **tireur d'é.,** crack shot; **l'é. de la ville assistait à la représentation,** the élite of the town attended the performance; *Typewr:* **caractères é.,** élite type; *Breed:* **livre d'é.,** stud book.

élixir [eliksi:r], *s.m.* elixir; **l'é. de longue vie,** the elixir of life.

ellagique [elaʒik], *a. Ch:* ellagic.

ellagotannique [elagɔtanik], *a. Ch:* ellagitannic; **acide e.,** ellagitannin.

elle, elles [ɛl], *pers.pron.f.* **1.** (*unstressed, clinging to the verb or its adjuncts*) (*of pers.*) she, they; (*of thg*) it, they; **e. chante, elles dansent,** she sings, they dance; **e. m'a vu,** she saw me; **e. est plus belle qu'elle ne l'était,** she is prettier than she used to be; **quant à la goélette, e. a sombré,** as for the schooner, she foundered; **c'est à vous, cette broche? qu'e. est jolie!** is that your brooch? how pretty it is! **2.** (*stressed*) (*a*) (*subject*) she, it, they; **e. et lui le savent** (both) she and he know it; **e. seule le sait,** she alone knows it; **c'est e., ce sont elles,** it is she, it is they; **je suis plus grand qu'e.,** I am taller than she is; **je fais comme e.,** I do as she does; **e.-même l'a vu,** she saw it herself; (*b*) (*object*) her, it, them; **je suis content d'elle(s),** I am pleased with her, with them; **chez e.,** at her house; **son fils habite chez e.,** her son lives with her; **il pense à e.,** he is thinking of her; **e. ne pense qu'à e.,** she thinks only of herself; **chacune d'elles travaille pour e.-même,** each of them works for herself; **ces gants sont à e., à elles,** these gloves belong to her, to them, are hers, theirs; **la rivière entraîne tout avec e.,** the river carries everything along with it; **il aimait sa patrie et mourut pour e.,** he loved his country and died for it.

ellébore [ɛl(l)ebɔ:r], *s.m. Bot:* hellebore; **e. noir,** Christmas rose; **e. fétide,** bear's foot, helleboraster, stinking hellebore; setterwort; **e. vert,** boar's foot.

elléborisé [ɛl(l)ebɔrize], *a. Pharm:* helleborized (medicine, etc.).

elle-même, elles-mêmes [ɛlmɛ:m], *pers.pron.f. See* ELLE *and* MÊME 1 (*c*).

ellipse [elips], *s.f.* **1.** *Gram:* ellipsis. **2.** *Mth:* ellipse; **e. de Cassini,** Cassinian ellipse; **compas d'e.,** elliptic(al) compass. **3.** *Cin:* jump cut.

ellipsographe [elipsɔgraf], *s.m. Geom:* ellipsograph, trammel.

ellipsoïdal, -aux [elipsɔidal, -o], *a. Geom:* ellipsoidal.

ellipsoïde [elipsɔid], *Geom:* **1.** *a.* ellipsoidal. **2.** *s.m.* ellipsoid.

ellipsoïdique [elipsɔidik], *a.* ellipsoid.

ellipticité [eliptisite], *s.f. Geom:* ellipticity.

elliptique [eliptik], *a. Gram: Geom:* elliptic(al).

elliptiquement [eliptikmɑ̃], *adv.* elliptically.

Elme [ɛlm], *Pr.n.m.* Elmo; *Nau:* **feu Saint-E.,** St. Elmo's fire.

elnois, -oise [ɛlnwa, -wa:z], *a. & s. Geog:* (native, inhabitant) of Elne.

élocution [elɔkysjɔ̃], *s.f.* elocution.

élodée [elɔde], *s.f. Bot:* elodea.

éloge [elɔ:ʒ], *s.m.* **1.** eulogy, panegyric, encomium. **2.** (deserved) praise; **faire l'é. de qn,** to speak in praise of s.o., to eulogize s.o., to speak highly of s.o.; **faire son propre é.,** *F:* to blow one's own trumpet; **adresser des éloges à qn,** to praise, eulogize, s.o.; **action qui vaut des éloges, action digne d'éloges,** praiseworthy, commendable, action; **son é. n'est plus à faire,** it would be superfluous to praise him, it; there is no need to add to his praises; **sa conduite est toute à son é.,** one can have nothing but praise for his conduct, behaviour; **c'est le plus bel é. à lui faire,** that is the highest praise one can offer him; *A:* **être reçu à un examen avec éloges,** to pass an examination brilliantly, *cum laude*.

élogieusement [elɔʒjøzmɑ̃], *adv.* eulogistically.

élogieux, -ieuse [elɔʒjø, -jø:z], *a.* eulogistic, laudatory (speech, poem, etc.); appreciatory (judgment); **parler en termes é. de qn,** to speak (very) highly, flatteringly, of s.o.; to speak in high terms of s.o.; to make flattering remarks about s.o.

Élohim, Éloïm [elɔim], *Pr.n.m.* Elohim.

Élohiste, Éloïste [elɔist], *s.m. B.Lit:* Elohist.

Éloi [elwa], *Pr.n.m.* Eligius, Éloi.

éloigné [elwaɲe], *a.* far (away), distant, remote (place, time); **la ville est éloignée de cinq kilomètres,** the town is five kilometres away; **être é. de sa famille,** to be far away from one's family; **habiter un quartier é.,** to live in an outlying district; **maison très éloignée de la gare,** house a long way from the station; **pays é.,** distant country; **le plus é.,** farthest (off); **remettre un voyage à une date plus éloignée,** to put off a journey to a later date; **récit é. de la vérité,** account far from the truth; **son sentiment n'était pas très é. de l'amour,** his feeling was not far removed from love; **tenir qch. é. du feu,** to keep sth. away from the fire; **parent é.,** distant relation; **avenir peu é.,** near future; **rien n'est plus é. de ma pensée,** nothing is further from my thoughts; **mon occupation me tient é. de la ville,** my occupation keeps me away from town; **un tel sentiment est bien é. de sa nature,** such a feeling is quite foreign to his nature; **se tenir é. de qch.,** to hold (oneself) aloof from sth.; **je suis fort é. de consentir,** I am anything but inclined to consent; **être é. de son compte,** to be far out in one's calculations.

éloignement [elwaɲmɑ̃], *s.m.* **1.** removal, removing, putting away (of s.o., sth.); postponement (of departure, etc.); deferment (of payment, etc.). **2.** (*a*) absence; **pendant mon é.,** while I am, was, away; (*b*) distance, remoteness (in place, time); **é. de deux villes,** distance between two towns; **voir qch. dans l'é.,** to see sth. in the distance; **voir qch. en é.,** to have a distant view, prospect, of sth.; **vivre dans l'é. du monde,** to live apart, aloof, from the world; **é. de ses devoirs,** neglect of one's duties; **é. de Dieu,** estrangement from God; (*c*) *A:* aversion; **avoir de l'é. pour qn, pour qch.,** to have an antipathy to s.o., an aversion to sth.; (*d*) distance (of manner); **traiter qn avec un é. marqué,** to treat s.o. with marked coolness, in a markedly distant manner.

éloigner [elwaɲe], *v.tr.* (*a*) to (re)move, move away (s.o., sth.) to a distance, further off; to get (s.o., sth.) out of the way; **é. qch. de qch.,** to move sth. away from sth.; **ils sont éloignés d'un kilomètre,** they are one kilometre apart; **é. les mouches du visage de qn,** to drive away, keep away, the flies from s.o.'s face; **les verres concaves éloignent les objets,** concave mirrors make objects look far off; **é. toute crainte,** to banish all fears; **é. une pensée,** to dismiss, put away, a thought; **é. les soupçons,** to avert suspicion; **é. qn de faire qch.,** to put s.o. off doing sth.; **trop de plaisir éloigne des devoirs de la vie,** too much dissipation distracts you from the duties of life; (*b*) to postpone, put off (departure, etc.); to defer (payment); (*c*) **é. qn de qn,** to alienate, estrange, s.o. from s.o.; **é. les gens par ses manières brusques,** to estrange people, *F:* to put people off, by one's gruff manners.

s'éloigner. 1. to move off, retire, withdraw; *Nau:* to stand away, bear off (de, from); **s'é. sans dire un mot,** to go away without saying a word; **s'é. en toute hâte,** to hurry away; **s'é. peu à peu de qn,** to edge away from s.o.; **ne vous éloignez pas!** don't go away! **s'é. de son devoir,** to swerve, deviate, from one's duty; **s'é. du sujet,** to wander from the subject; *Mus:* **en s'éloignant,** growing fainter. **2.** (*a*) **voudriez-vous vous é. un peu?** would you please stand further away, further back? **il ne faut pas vous é.,** you must keep in sight, within hail; you must keep in touch with us; (*b*) **s'é. de tout le monde,** to keep aloof from everybody; (*c*) **votre opinion ne s'éloigne pas beaucoup de la mienne,** your opinion does not differ much from mine.

élongation [elɔ̃gasjɔ̃], *s.f.* elongation; *Astr:* digression, elongation; *Med:* elongation; pulled muscle; *Mec.E:* **é. de rupture,** elongation at rupture.

élongement [elɔ̃ʒmɑ̃], *s.m. Nau:* **1.** laying out, running out (cable, anchor, etc.). **2.** passing, coming alongside (ship, etc.).

élonger [elɔ̃ʒe], *v.tr.* (**j'élongeai(s); n. élongeons**) *Nau:* **1.** to lay out, run out (cable, anchor, etc.); *Fish: Nau:* **é. les lignes,** to shoot the lines. **2.** to pass, to come alongside (ship, etc.); **é. la côte,** to skirt the coast.

élongis [elɔ̃ʒi], *s.m. Nau:* longitudinal piece; **é. d'écoutille,** carline, carling; **é. de chouque,** trestle-tree; **é. de tambour,** spring-beam.

élopidés [elɔpide], *s.m.pl. Ich:* Elopidae.

élops [elɔps], *s.m. Ich:* elops.

éloquemment [elɔkamɑ̃], *adv.* eloquently.

éloquence [elɔkɑ̃:s], *s.f.* (*a*) eloquence; (*b*) **é. de la chaire,** pulpit oratory; **é. de barreau,** forensic oratory; **é. de la tribune,** parliamentary oratory.

éloquent [elɔkɑ̃], *a.* eloquent; **un silence é.,** an eloquent silence; **ces chiffres sont éloquents,** these figures speak volumes; **geste é.,** expressive gesture.

elpasolite [ɛlpazɔlit], *s.f. Miner:* elpasolite.

elpidite [ɛlpidit], *s.f. Miner:* elpidite.

Elseneur [ɛlsənœ:r], *Pr.n. Geog: Lit:* Elsinore.

elsholtzia [ɛlʃɔltzja], *s.m. Bot:* elscholtzia.

élu, -e [ely]. **1.** *a.* chosen; elected; successful (candidate); **président é.,** president elect; *B.Hist:* **le peuple é.,** the chosen people. **2.** *s.* (*a*) one chosen (by God, etc.); *Ecc:* **les élus,** the elect; *Pol:* **les élus du peuple,** the people's representatives; **l'élu(e) de son cœur, l'heureux(-euse) élu(e),** fiancé, -ée; the lucky man; the girl of his choice.

éluant [elyɑ̃], *s.m. Ch:* eluent, eluant.

éluat [elya], *s.m. Ch:* eluate.

élucidation [elysidasjɔ̃], *s.f.* elucidation, clearing up.

élucider [elyside], *v.tr.* to elucidate, clear up, clarify (question, mystery, etc.).

s'élucider, to become clearer.

élucubrateur, -trice [elykybratœ:r, -tris], *s. Pej:* lucubrator.

élucubration [elykybrasjɔ̃], *s.f. Pej:* lucubration.

élucubrer [elykybre], *v.tr. Pej:* to lucubrate (literary work).

éluder [elyde], *v.tr.* to elude, evade (law, difficulty, etc.); **é. la question,** to evade, *F:* dodge, the question; **é. la vigilance de qn,** to elude, outwit, s.o.'s vigilance.

éludeur, -euse [elydœ:r, -ø:z]. **1.** *a.* shifty; evasive. **2.** *s.* evader.

éluer [elye], *v.tr. Ch:* to elute.

élusate [elyzat], *a. & s. Geog:* (native, inhabitant) of Eauze.

élusif, -ive [elyzif, -i:v], *a.* elusive.

élution [elysjɔ̃], *s.f. Ch:* elution.

éluvial, -aux [elyvjal, -o], *a. Geol:* eluvial.

éluviation [elyvjasjɔ̃], *s.f. Geol:* eluviation.

éluvion [elyvjɔ̃], *s.f.*, **éluvium** [elyvjɔm], *s.m. Geol:* eluvium.

éluvionnaire [elyvjɔnɛ:r], *a. Geol:* eluvial.

elvan [ɛlvɑ̃], *s.m. Geol:* elvan.

Elvire [ɛlvi:r], *Pr.n.f.* Elvira.

élyme [elim], **elymus** [elimys], *s.m. Bot:* elymus, lyme grass.

Élysée [elize]. **1.** *Pr.n.m.* (*a*) *Myth:* **L'É.,** Elysium; (*b*) **(le palais de) l'É.,** the official residence of the President of the French Republic. **2.** *a.* **Les Champs Élysées,** (i) *Myth:* the Elysian Fields; (ii) the Champs Élysées (avenue in Paris).

élyséen, -enne [elizeɛ̃, -ɛn], *a. A. & Poet:* Elysian (peace, delights).

élysie [elizi], **elysia** [elizja], *s.f. Moll:* elysia.

élysiidés [elizjide], *s.m.pl. Moll:* Elysiidae.

élytral, -aux [elitral, -o], *a. Ent:* elytral.

élytre [elitr], *s.m. Ent:* elytron, wing sheath, wing case; shard.

élytrocèle [elitrɔsɛl], *s.f. Med:* elytrocele.

elzévir [ɛlzevi:r], *s.m. Typ:* elzevir (edition, type).

elzévirien, -ienne [ɛlzevirjɛ̃, -jɛn], *a.* elzevir(ian) (edition, type).

em- [ɑ̃], *pref.* **1.** em-; **embarquer,** to embark. **2.** im-; **emprisonner,** to imprison. **3.** be-; **embarbouiller,** to besmear.

émaciation [emasjasjɔ̃], *s.f.* emaciation.

émacié [emasje], *a.* emaciated, wasted (figure, face, etc.).

émaciement [emasimɑ̃], *s.m.* emaciation.

émacier [emasje], *v.tr.* (*rare*) to emaciate.

s'émacier, to become emaciated, to waste away.

émail, émaux [emaːj, emo], *s.m.* **1.** (*a*) *Art: etc:* enamel; **é. champlevé,** champlevé enamel; **é. cloisonné,** cloisonné enamel; **émaux de niellure,** niello enamels; **é. de cobalt,** smalt; **é. vitrifié,** glazed enamel; *Lit:* **l'é. des prés,** the variegated colours of the meadows; (*b*) *Her:* (i) tincture; (ii) colour (as distinct from metal); (*c*) enamel (of the teeth). **2.** (*pl.* **émails**) (*a*) enamelling material, enamel; (*b*) *Cer: Phot:* glaze; (*c*) *Aut: etc:* **é. cellulosique, à la cellulose,** cellulose enamel.

émaillage [emajaːʒ], *s.m.* **1.** enamelling (of precious metals, etc.). **2.** *Cer: Phot:* glazing; *Cer:* **demi-émaillage,** salt glaze.

émailler [emaje], *v.tr.* **1.** *Art: etc:* to enamel (precious metal, etc.); **émaillé au four,** stove-enamelled. **2.** *Cer: Phot:* to glaze (porcelain, print, etc.). **3.** (*of flowers, etc.*) to dot, fleck, speckle, spangle (the fields, etc.); **style émaillé de métaphores,** style sprinkled with metaphors.

émaillerie [emajri], *s.f.* **1.** (*art of*) enamelling. **2.** enamel works.

émailleur, -euse[1] [emajœːr, -øːz], *s.* enameller, enamellist.

émailleux, -euse[2] [emajø, -øːz], *a.* enamelled.

émaillure [emajyːr], *s.f.* **1.** (*a*) enamelling; enamel work; (*b*) enamelled portion (of vase, etc.). **2.** spot, patch; speckle (of colour in nature, etc.).

émanateur [emanatœːr], *s.m.* vaporizer, atomizer.

émanation [emanasjɔ̃], *s.f. Theol: Ph: Psychics: etc:* emanation; **é. fétide,** foul smell; **é. d'un mets,** (appetizing) smell of a dish; **é. du radium,** radium emanation, radon; **émanations volcaniques,** gaseous volcanic eruption; **é. de la beauté idéale,** manifestation of ideal beauty; **é. du pouvoir,** emanation of power.

émancipateur, -trice [emɑ̃sipatœːr, -tris]. **1.** *a.* emancipatory. **2.** *s.* emancipator.

émancipation [emɑ̃sipasjɔ̃], *s.f.* emancipation; manumission (of slave); *Eng.Hist:* **é. des catholiques,** catholic emancipation.

émancipé [emɑ̃sipe], *a. F:* uninhibited; unconventional.

émanciper [emɑ̃sipe], *v.tr.* to emancipate (people, minor, slave, etc.); to manumit (slave).

s'émanciper. 1. to free oneself (from control); to gain one's freedom (**de,** from); **esprit émancipé de toute influence,** mind freed from all influence. **2.** *F:* (*of young pers.*) to get out of hand, to run wild.

émaner [emane], *v.i.* (*a*) (*of gas, light, etc.*) to emanate, to issue, proceed (**de,** from); (*b*) **ordres émanant de qn,** orders emanating from, sent out by, s.o.; **cette recommandation émane de . . .,** this recommendation was made by . . .; **pétition émanant de . . .,** petition from . . .; **lettres émanées du Saint-Siège,** letters emanating from the Holy See; (*c*) **obligations qui émanent d'une clause,** obligations that result, arise, that are derived, from a clause.

émaniste [emanist], *s.m. & f. Phil:* emanationist, emanatist.

émanomètre [emanɔmɛtr], *s.m.* emanometer.

émanométrie [emanɔmetri], *s.f.* emanometry.

émanon [emanɔ̃], *s.m. Ch:* emanon.

émargement [emarʒəmɑ̃], *s.m.* **1.** *Bookb: etc:* cutting down of the margins, trimming. **2.** (*a*) marginal note; (*b*) receipting, initialling, (of account, etc.) in the margin; **feuille, état, d'é.,** pay sheet.

émarger [emarʒe], *v.tr.* (j'émargeai(s); **n. émargeons**) **1.** *Bookb: etc:* to cut down, trim, crop, the margins of (sheets, etc.). **2.** (*a*) **é. un livre,** to make marginal notes in a book; (*b*) *Adm: etc:* **é. un compte,** to receipt, initial, an account (in the margin); *hence* (*c*) *abs.* (*of official, etc.*) to draw one's salary; **é. au budget,** to be on the payroll; **journalistes qui émargent aux fonds secrets,** journalists subsidized out of the secret funds.

émarginé [emarʒine], *a. Bot:* emarginate (leaf, etc.).

émarginule [emarʒinyl], *s.f. Moll:* emarginula.

émasculateur [emaskylatœːr], *s.m. Vet:* emasculator.

émasculation [emaskylasjɔ̃], *s.f.* emasculation; (*a*) castration; gelding; (*b*) weakening; bowdlerizing, bowdlerization (of literary work).

émasculer [emaskyle], *v.tr.* to emasculate; (*a*) to castrate, to geld; (*b*) to weaken; to render (nation, etc.) effeminate; to bowdlerize (literary work).

embabouiner [ɑ̃babwine]. **1.** *v.tr. F:* to coax, cajole, get round (s.o.). **2.** *v.i. Nau:* (*of ship*) to get into difficulties.

embâcle [ɑ̃bɑːkl], *s.m.* (*in river, etc.*) (*a*) obstruction, blockage; (*b*) ice dam, ice jam.

embâcler [ɑ̃bakle], *v.tr.* to obstruct, to block (river, etc., *esp.* with ice).

emballage [ɑ̃balaːʒ], *s.m.* **1.** (*a*) packing, wrapping (of parcels, goods, etc.); **papier d'e.,** packing paper; **toile d'e.,** pack cloth, canvas wrapper; **fil d'e.,** pack thread; (*b*) packing cases, wrappings, crates, etc.; **e. gras,** pitch paper; **emballages vides,** (returned) empties; **e. perdu, e. non retournable,** non-returnable packing. **2.** *Rac:* burst (of speed), spurt; **faire un e.,** to put on a spurt. **3.** *P:* dressing down, telling off.

emballé [ɑ̃bale], *a. F:* enthusiastic, carried away.

emballement [ɑ̃balmɑ̃], *s.m.* **1.** (*of machine, engine*) racing; **sûreté contre l'e.,** runaway governor. **2.** excitement; burst of enthusiasm, of energy, etc.; *St.Exch:* boom.

emballer [ɑ̃bale], *v.tr.* **1.** (*a*) to pack (goods, etc.); to wrap up, do up (article in paper, etc.); (*b*) *F:* **e. qn dans un train,** to bundle s.o. into a train; **je l'ai emballé pour Turin,** I packed him off to Turin; *P:* **e. qn,** (i) to arrest s.o., to run s.o. in; (ii) to put s.o. in prison. **2.** (*a*) *I.C.E:* **e. le moteur,** to race the engine; (*b*) *abs. Sp:* to (put on a) spurt. **3.** *F:* to fire s.o. with enthusiasm, to excite s.o.; **ça ne m'emballe pas,** I'm not exactly carried away by that, I can't get up much enthusiasm over that; **il ne m'emballe pas,** I'm not terribly impressed by him, I don't think much of him. **4.** *P:* to give (s.o.) a (good) dressing down; to tell (s.o.) where he gets off.

s'emballer, (*a*) (*of horse*) to bolt, to run away; **cheval emballé,** runaway horse; **cheval porté à s'e.,** bolter; (*b*) (*of engine*) to race; (*c*) *F:* to be carried away (by excitement, anger, enthusiasm); **ne vous emballez pas!** keep your head! don't blow off steam like that! calm down! draw it mild! **il s'emballe pour un rien,** he gets all worked up over nothing; **être emballé par qn, qch.,** to be gone on s.o., madly in love with s.o.; to be swept off one's feet by s.o.; to be (mad) keen on sth.

emballeur [ɑ̃balœːr], *s.m.* **1.** (*a*) packer; (*b*) packing agent. **2.** horse liable to run away, bolter.

emballonuridés [ɑ̃balɔnyride], *s.m.pl. Z:* Emballonuridae.

emballoter [ɑ̃balɔte], *v.tr.* to pack (goods) in bales; to bale (goods).

embarbouiller [ɑ̃barbuje], *v.tr.* **1.** to dirty (one's face, hands, etc.). **2.** to muddle (s.o.), to put (s.o.) out.

s'embarbouiller, to get muddled, to get into a muddle.

embarcadère [ɑ̃barkadɛːr], *s.m.* **1.** *Nau:* landing stage; wharf, quay; loading dock; **e. en bout,** end-loading dock. **2.** *A: Rail:* (departure) platform.

embarcation [ɑ̃barkasjɔ̃], *s.f.* boat; small craft; **e. à l'aviron, à avirons,** rowing boat; **e. à moteur,** motor boat, motor launch; **e. de sauvetage,** lifeboat; ship's boat; **e. pliable,** folding boat; **e. à vapeur,** steam launch; *Mil:* **e. d'assaut,** assault boat; **e. de reconnaissance,** reconnaissance boat, craft.

embardage [ɑ̃bardaːʒ], *s.m.* (*a*) *Nau:* yawing, lurching; (*b*) *Aut: etc:* swerving (of car, etc.).

embardée [ɑ̃barde], *s.f.* (*a*) *Nau:* yaw, lurch; **e. à tribord,** lurch to starboard; *A:* **e. hors du sujet,** digression from the subject, from the point; (*b*) *Aut: etc:* swerve; **faire une e.,** (i) (*of boat*) to yaw; (ii) (*of car*) to swerve (across the road); (iii) *F:* (*of pers.*) to lurch across the road.

embarder [ɑ̃barde], *v.i.* (*a*) (*of ship*) (i) to yaw, lurch; (ii) to sheer; (*b*) (*of car, etc.*) to swerve; (*c*) *A:* (*of pers.*) to digress (from the subject).

embargo [ɑ̃bargo], *s.m. Nau: etc:* embargo; **mettre l'e. sur un navire,** to lay an embargo on a ship; to embargo a ship; **mettre l'e. sur un journal,** to suspend a newspaper; **lever l'e.,** to take off, raise, the embargo.

embarillage [ɑ̃barijaːʒ], *s.m.* barrelling (of goods).

embariller [ɑ̃barije], *v.tr.* to barrel (goods).

embarquant, -ante [ɑ̃barkɑ̃, -ɑ̃ːt], *s.* (*a*) member of a ship's crew; (*b*) ship's passenger.

embarqué [ɑ̃barke], *a. Nau:* (officer, etc.) serving afloat; (*of equipment*) (i) ship-borne; (ii) air-borne, satellite-borne, space-borne, etc.; **l'aviation embarquée,** (i) carrier(-based) air forces; (ii) carrier-borne, sea-based, aircraft.

embarquement [ɑ̃barkəmɑ̃], *s.m.* **1.** *Nau:* (*a*) embarkation, embarcation, embarking, *U.S:* embarkment, going on board (of passengers); shipment, shipping (of goods); hoisting in (of boat, etc.); **e. clandestin,** stowing away; **officier d'e.,** embarkation officer; **port d'e.,** port of embarkation; *Com:* **blé canadien, e. novembre, coté à tant la tonne,** Canadian wheat quoted, for November shipment, at so much per ton; *Mil:* **e. type combat,** combat unit loading; **e. type convoi,** convoy unit loading; (*b*) entering (of seaman, passenger) in the ship's register; (*c*) **homme qui a deux ans d'e.,** seaman with two years' service. **2.** (*a*) *Rail:* getting, putting (goods), into (a train), boarding (a train); *Mil: etc:* entraining, entrainment; **quai d'e.,** departure platform (for passengers), loading platform (for goods); **e. à quai,** entraining from platform; **e. en pleine voie,** entraining direct from the tracks; *Mil:* **exercise d'e.,** entraining practice; (*b*) getting, putting, into (a bus, a car, etc.; boarding (a bus); *Mil: etc:* embussing, *U.S:* entrucking (troops, equipment); *Mil: etc:* **lieu, point, d'e.,** embussing, *U.S:* entrucking, site. **3.** *Av:* emplaning, embarking (of passengers, goods); boarding (of aircraft).

embarquer [ɑ̃barke]. **1.** *v.tr.* (*a*) to embark (passengers); to ship (goods), to take (goods) aboard; **e. les canots,** to hoist in the boats; **e. son eau,** to take in (a supply of) water; **e. de l'eau, e. un coup de mer,** *abs.* **embarquer,** to ship a sea; **e. qn dans un procès,** to involve s.o. in a lawsuit; **e. très mal une affaire,** to make a bad start to a piece of business; *F:* **ce n'est pas sans inquiétude que j'embarque tous ces enfants,** I'm a bit worried, taking all these children with me; *P:* **e. une fille,** to pick up a girl; (*b*) *Nau:* to enter (a seaman) on the ship's books; (*c*) *Rail:* to put (goods) into a train; (*of train*) to take on (passengers); *Mil. etc:* to entrain (troops, equipment); (*d*) *Av:* to emplane (passengers); (*e*) to put (goods) into a bus, lorry, etc.; (*of bus*) to pick up (passengers); *Mil: etc:* to embus, *U.S:* entruck (troops, equipment); *F:* **e. qn dans sa voiture,** to give s.o. a lift in one's car; (*f*) *P:* **e. qn,** to arrest s.o., to run s.o. in. **2.** *v.i. & pr.* to embark; (**s'**)**e. sur un navire,** to go aboard, on board (a ship); **s'e. pour Tahiti,** to embark for Tahiti; **la mer s'embarque à chaque instant,** we're shipping water all the time; *Av:* **tendances à s'e.,** yaw characteristics; **s'e. dans un train, un autobus, une voiture,** to get into a train, a bus, a car; *Mil:* to entrain, embus, *U.S:* to entruck; **s'e. dans une discussion,** to embark upon, launch into, a discussion; **s'e. dans une nouvelle guerre,** to embark on a fresh war.

embarras [ɑ̃bara], *s.m.* **1.** (*a*) *A:* obstruction, obstacle, encumbrance; **e. de voitures,** traffic block, hold-up; **e. d'objets,** confused mass of objects; **e. de la langue,** impediment of speech; (*b*) *Med:* **e. gastrique,** bilious attack. **2.** (*a*) difficulty, trouble; **des e. d'argent,** money troubles, financial difficulties; **se trouver dans l'e.,** to be in difficulties (*esp.* financial); **tirer qn d'e.,** to help s.o. out of a difficulty; **je vous donne beaucoup d'e.,** I'm afraid I'm giving you a lot of trouble; **ajouter aux e. de qn,** to add to s.o.'s difficulties; (*b*) *F:* **faire des e., de l'e.,** (i) to be fussy; to make a fuss; (ii) to show off; **ne faites pas tant d'e!** don't make so many bones, such a song and dance, about it! **sans plus d'e.,** without any more ado. **3.** embarrassment; (*a*) perplexity, hesitation; **n'avoir que l'e. du choix,** to have far too much to choose from; **je suis dans l'e.,** I'm in a difficulty, a quandary; I don't know what to do; (*b*) confusion discomposure; **ne pouvoir dissimuler son e.,** to be unable to hide one's embarrassment.

embarrassant [ɑ̃barasɑ̃], *a.* **1.** cumbersome, awkward (parcel, etc.). **2.** (*a*) perplexing, puzzling (question); **question embarrassante,** poser; (*b*) embarrassing, awkward (question, situation, etc.); **se trouver dans une situation embarrassante,** to be in an embarrassing situation.

embarrassé [ɑ̃barase], *a.* **1.** hampered (movements); involved (style); *A:* obstructed (path, etc.); **avoir les mains embarrassées,** to have one's hands full (of parcels, etc.); *A:* **circulation embarrassée,** congested traffic; *Jur:* **biens embarrassés,** encumbered estate; **être dans une situation (financière) embarrassée,** to be in

(financial) difficulties; **il a la parole embarrassée,** he has an impediment in his speech; **explications embarrassées,** involved, confused, explanations; **avoir l'estomac e.,** to feel bilious; *Nau:* **cordages embarrassés,** foul ropes. **2.** embarrassed; (*a*) perplexed, nonplussed, puzzled; **il est bien e. que faire,** he can't decide, he's at a loss to know, what to do; **il n'est jamais e.,** he's never at a loss; **être e. pour trouver un mot,** to be at a loss for a word; **j'étais assez e. pour répondre,** I found it difficult to answer; **je serais bien e. de vous l'expliquer,** it's too difficult for me to explain it to you; (*b*) bashful, sheepish, diffident; **sourire e.,** embarrassed, diffident, smile; **avoir un air e.,** to look embarrassed; **il est e. de ses mains,** he doesn't know where to put his hands; (*c*) **il est bien e. pour peu de chose,** he's very easily put out; he makes mountains out of molehills.

embarrasser [ɑ̃barase], *v.tr.* **1.** to encumber, hamper; **un paquet volumineux l'embarrassait,** he was struggling with a large parcel; **est-ce que ma valise vous embarrasse?** is my case in your way? **son manteau l'embarrasse,** he doesn't know what to do with his coat; *A:* **e. la circulation,** to hold up the traffic; *Med:* **aliments qui embarrassent l'estomac,** indigestible food; *Nau:* **cordages qui s'embarrassent,** ropes that foul each other. **2.** to embarrass; (*a*) to trouble, inconvenience; **sa demande m'embarrasse,** I find his request embarrassing; **sa présence m'embarrasse,** I wish he'd go; I wish I could get rid of him; **il ne se laisse pas e. par des scrupules,** he isn't troubled by scruples; (*b*) to confuse (question); (*c*) to perplex, non-plus, puzzle (s.o.); **choix qui embarrasse,** difficult choice; (*d*) to embarrass (s.o.); to make (s.o.) feel awkward.

s'embarrasser. 1. s'e. de qch., to burden, encumber, hamper, oneself with sth. **2.** (*a*) to trouble oneself, be concerned (about sth.); **il ne s'embarrasse point de cela,** that doesn't bother, trouble, him in the least; he'd never bother his head about that; (*b*) to feel embarrassed, awkward; **ne t'embarrasse pas pour me le dire,** you needn't be shy about, you needn't mind, telling me; **il s'embarrasse de tout,** he makes mountains out of molehills; *F:* he makes a song and dance about everything.

embarrer[1] [ɑ̃bare], *v.tr.* to place a lever, a hand-spike, under (heavy object, in readiness for lifting it).

embarrer[2] **(s'),** *v.pr.* (*of horse*) to get a leg over the pole.

embarriquer [ɑ̃barike], *v.tr.* to barrel (goods); to put (wine, etc.) into casks; to fill a butt with (water).

embase [ɑ̃bɑːz], *s.f.* base (of post, of electric switch, etc.); shoulder (of trunnion, chisel, knife, etc.); bolster (of knife); flange, collar (of shaft, etc.); bed plate, base plate, seating (of machine); **écrou à embase,** collar nut; *I.C.E:* **e. pour l'attache du volant,** flywheel flange (on crankshaft); *Mch:* **e. de la cheminée,** stack base (of locomotive); **e. de raccord,** *Civ.E: Mec.E:* pipe-union; *El.E:* coupling connector.

embasement [ɑ̃bɑzmɑ̃], *s.m. Arch: Const:* base, footing (of wall); ground table.

embastillement [ɑ̃bastijmɑ̃], *s.m. A:* **1.** imprisonment; *esp.* (before 1789) imprisonment in the Bastille. **2.** fortification (of town, etc.).

embastiller [ɑ̃bastije], *v.tr. A:* **1.** to imprison (s.o.), *esp.* in the Bastille. **2.** to fortify (town, etc.).

embastionné [ɑ̃bastjɔne], *a.* bastioned.

embastionnement [ɑ̃bastjɔnmɑ̃], *s.m.* fortifying with bastions.

embastionner [ɑ̃bastjɔne], *v.tr.* to fortify (with bastions).

embatage [ɑ̃bataːʒ], *s.m.* = EMBATTAGE.

embâtage [ɑ̃bɑtaːʒ], *s.m.* saddling (of pack animal).

embatailler [ɑ̃bataje], *v.tr. A:* to draw up (troops) in order of battle.

embataillonner [ɑ̃batajɔne], *v.tr.* to form (men) into battalions.

embâter [ɑ̃bɑte], *v.tr.* to saddle (pack animal).

embâtonné [ɑ̃bɑtɔne], *a. Arch:* cabled (column).

embâtonner [ɑ̃bɑtɔne], *v.tr. Arch:* to cable (column).

embatre [ɑ̃batr], *v.tr.* = EMBATTRE.

embattage [ɑ̃bataːʒ], *s.m.* shoeing, tyring (of wheel), shrinking on (of metal tyre).

embatteur [ɑ̃batœːr], *s.m.* wheel tyrer.

embattre [ɑ̃batr], *v.tr.* (*conj. like* BATTRE) to shoe, tyre, to put a (metal) tyre on (wheel).

embauchage [ɑ̃boʃaːʒ], *s.m.* **1.** (*a*) engaging, taking on (of workmen); hiring (of farm hands); **ouvriers qui attendent l'e.,** workmen waiting to be taken on; (*b*) *A:* recruiting. **2.** *A:* (*a*) crimping (of soldiers, sailors, etc.); enticing, procuring (of women or girls); (*b*) enticing (of soldiers) to go over to the enemy, (of workmen) to enter another workshop.

embauche[1] [ɑ̃boːʃ], *s.f.* **1.** = EMBAUCHAGE 1; **service d'e.,** (industrial) employment agency. **2.** *F:* job; **chercher de l'e.,** to look for a job.

embauche[2], *s.m. Agr:* rich pasture land.

embauchée [ɑ̃boʃe], *s.f.* (*rare*) *Navy:* return to work (in arsenals).

embauchement [ɑ̃boʃmɑ̃], *s.m.* = EMBAUCHAGE.

embaucher [ɑ̃boʃe], *v.tr.* **1.** (*a*) to engage, take on, sign on (workmen); to hire (farm hands); **on n'embauche pas,** no hands wanted; (*b*) *A:* to recruit (soldiers). **2.** *A:* (*a*) to crimp (soldiers, sailors); to entice, procure (women or girls); (*b*) to entice (soldiers) to go over to the enemy; to entice (workmen) away from their work; to win over (electors).

embaucheur, -euse [ɑ̃boʃœːr, -øːz], *s.* **1.** labour contractor; recruiter of labour. **2.** *A:* crimp.

embauchoir [ɑ̃boʃwaːr], *s.m.* boot tree, shoe tree; **e. à forcer,** shoe stretcher.

embaumement [ɑ̃bommɑ̃], *s.m.* embalming (of corpse).

embaumer [ɑ̃bome], *v.tr.* **1.** to embalm (corpse). **2.** to embalm, perfume, scent; **jardin embaumé du parfum des fleurs,** garden fragrant with the perfume of flowers; **air embaumé,** balmy air; *abs.* **ces fleurs embaument,** these flowers have a lovely fragrance; **le chocolat embaume,** there is a delicious smell of chocolate; *with cogn. acc. F:* **l'escalier embaumait l'encaustique,** the staircase smelt of wax polish; **l'église embaume l'encens,** the church is heavy with incense.

embaumeur [ɑ̃bomœːr], *s.m.* embalmer (of corpses).

embecquer [ɑ̃beke], *v.tr.* **1.** (*a*) to feed (bird); (*b*) to cram (fowl). **2.** to bait (fishing-hook).

embecquetage [ɑ̃bektaːʒ], *s.m. Nau:* = EMBOUQUEMENT.

embecqueter [ɑ̃bekte], *v.i.* (**il embecquète; il embecquètera**) *Nau:* = EMBOUQUER.

embéguiner [ɑ̃begine], *v.tr. A:* **1.** to muffle up, wrap up, s.o.'s head; **s'e. d'un capuchon,** to cover one's head with a hood. **2. e. qn d'une idée,** to infatuate s.o. with an idea; **s'e. de qn,** to become infatuated with s.o.

embelle [ɑ̃bɛl], *s.f. Nau: A:* waist (of ship).

embelli, -ie [ɑ̃beli]. **1.** *a.* embellished, beautified. **2.** *s.f.* **embellie;** *Nau:* clearing (in the sky, in the weather); lull (in wind, etc.); smooth (in sea); **courte embellie,** bright interval; short spell of good weather.

embellir [ɑ̃beliːr]. **1.** *v.tr.* to embellish; to beautify (sth.); to improve the looks of (s.o.); **ce chapeau vous embellit,** you look much prettier in that hat; **e. une histoire,** to improve upon, embellish, a story. **2.** *v.i.* to grow more beautiful, (*of man*) more handsome; to improve in looks; **elle a beaucoup embelli, est beaucoup embellie,** she has become much more attractive, beautiful.

s'embellir, (*usu. of thg, occ. of pers.*) to improve; **le jardin s'embellit,** the garden is looking better, is beginning to look attractive.

embellissant [ɑ̃bɛlisɑ̃], *a.* embellishing, beautifying.

embellissement [ɑ̃bɛlismɑ̃], *s.m.* **1.** (*action of*) embellishing, improving, beautifying (of town, house, etc.). **2.** improvement (in looks). **3.** embellishing touch; ornament, adornment; **nous avons fait quelques embellissements à la maison,** we have been making some improvements to the house; **apporter des embellissements à une histoire,** to improve upon a story; to add a few fancy touches to a story.

embellisseur, -euse [ɑ̃bɛlisœːr, -øːz], *s.* person with a mania for embellishing, improving, things; **ville enlaidie par les embellisseurs,** town ruined by the improvers.

emberlificoter [ɑ̃bɛrlifikɔte], *v.tr. F:* **1.** to entangle (s.o.), to tangle (s.o.) up (in barbed wire, in an argument, etc.); to involve (s.o.) in difficulties. **2.** to get round (s.o.); to trick (s.o.); to lead (s.o.) up the garden path; to take (s.o.) in.

s'emberlificoter, *F:* to get entangled, tangled up (in sth.).

emberlificoteur, -euse [ɑ̃bɛrlifikɔtœːr, -øːz], *s. F:* duper; person who leads s.o. up the garden path.

emberloquer(s') [sɑ̃bɛrlɔke], **emberlucoquer (s')** [sɑ̃bɛrlykɔke], *v.pr. O: F:* **s'e. de qch.,** to go crazy about, to go daft over, sth.; **il s'est emberlucoqué de cette idée,** this idea has turned his brain.

embesogné [ɑ̃bəzɔɲe], *a. A:* busy, hard at work.

embêtant [ɑ̃bɛtɑ̃], *F:* (*a*) *a.* annoying; **qu'il est e., celui-là,** what a pest! **c'est bien e., cette histoire,** it's a very annoying, troublesome, worrying, business; (*b*) *s.m.* **l'e. c'est que la valise ne ferme pas à clef,** the annoying thing, the nuisance, is that the case doesn't lock.

embêtement [ɑ̃bɛtmɑ̃], *s.m. F:* annoyance; unpleasantness; worry; **j'ai assez d'embêtements dans ma propre vie,** I've enough trouble, worry, in my own life; **le bruit, la cohue, tous les embêtements de la grande ville,** the noise, the crowds, all the unpleasantness of a large town.

embêter [ɑ̃bete], *v.tr. F:* (*a*) to annoy; **ne l'embête pas!** leave him alone! **il m'embête,** I've no time for him; **ça m'embête de . . .,** (i) I can't be bothered to . . .; (ii) I wish I didn't have to . . .; **ça m'embête d'arriver en retard,** I hate being late; (*b*) **à la campagne on s'embête à cent sous de l'heure,** one gets bored stiff in the country; **il ne s'embête pas,** he's not having a bad time; you don't have to be sorry for him.

embeurrer [ɑ̃bœre], *v.tr.* to butter (bread; *Cu:* inside of pan).

embidonnage [ɑ̃bidɔnaːʒ], *s.m.* filling (of cans, drums).

embidonner [ɑ̃bidɔne], *v.tr.* to fill (cans, drums).

embidonneur, -euse [ɑ̃bidɔnœːr, -øːz]. **1.** *s.m. & f.* (*pers.*) filler (of cans, drums). **2.** *s.f.* (*machine*) automatic can, drum, filler.

embie [ɑ̃bi], *s.m. Ent:* embia.

embiellage [ɑ̃bjɛlaːʒ], *s.m. Mec.E: I.C.E:* connecting rod assembly, assembling; **faire un e.,** to assemble the connecting rods.

embieller [ɑ̃bjɛle], *v.tr. Mec.E: I.C.E: F:* to assemble the connecting rods.

embiidés [ɑ̃biide], *s.m.pl. Ent:* Embiidae.

embioptères [ɑ̃bjɔptɛːr], *s.m.pl. Ent:* Embioptera.

emblavage [ɑ̃blavaːʒ], *s.m.* wheat, cereals.

emblave [ɑ̃blaːv], *s.f. Agr:* land sown with wheat, cereals.

emblavement [ɑ̃blavmɑ̃], *s.m.* = EMBLAVAGE.

emblaver [ɑ̃blave], *v.tr. Agr:* to sow, crop, (field) with wheat, cereals.

emblavure [ɑ̃blavyːr], *s.f. Agr:* land sown with (i) wheat; (ii) any other crop.

emblée (d') [dɑ̃ble], *adv.phr.* directly, at the first attempt, right away, straight off; **accepter d'e. une proposition,** to accept a proposal straight away; **la ville fut prise d'e.,** the town was taken at the first onset, at one fell swoop; **emporter une affaire d'e.,** to be successful at the first attempt, at the first shot, at the first go.

emblématique [ɑ̃blematik], *a.* emblematic(al).

emblématiquement [ɑ̃blematikmɑ̃], *adv.* emblematically.

emblème [ɑ̃blɛm], *s.m.* **1.** (*a*) emblem, device; *Her:* cognizance; (*b*) badge, crest (on uniform, etc.); crest (on boat). **2.** symbol, sign; **les emblèmes de la force,** the attributes of power.

embobeliner [ɑ̃bɔbline], *v.tr.* **1.** *A:* to wrap (s.o., oneself) up (in garments). **2.** *F:* to hoodwink (s.o.); to get round (s.o.); **se laisser e.,** to be taken in.

embobiner [ɑ̃bɔbine], *v.tr.* **1.** *F:* to deceive (s.o.), to take (s.o.) in; **ne vous laissez pas e.,** don't let yourself be hoodwinked, taken in. **2.** (*rare*) to wind (cotton, etc.) on a reel, bobbin.

emboire [ɑ̃bwaːr], *v.tr.* (*conj. like* BOIRE) *Sculp:* to smear, coat, (plaster mould) with grease, with wax.

s'emboire, (*of paint*) to soak in; to become flat, dull.

emboîtage [ɑ̃bwataːʒ], *s.m.* **1.** (*a*) packing (of articles) into boxes; (*b*) box, casing. **2.** *Bookb:* (*a*) French binding (on mull, without bands); (*b*) cover, case, casing; paper, cloth, boards (of book). **3.** *Th: F:* hooting, hissing.

emboîtement [ɑ̃bwatmɑ̃], *s.m.* **1.** (*a*) encasing; nesting (of boxes, boats); (*b*) fitting, jointing (of pipes, etc.); interlocking (of timbers, etc.); (*c*) *A: Biol:* incasement. **2.** fitment; joint; housing, boxing (of tenon, etc.); socket (of pipe); **assemblage à e.,** spigot joint; *Anat: etc:* **e. réciproque,** ball-and-socket joint.

emboîter [ɑ̃bwate], *v.tr.* **1.** (*a*) to encase; **e. des caisses, des embarcations,** to nest boxes, boats; **tubes emboîtés,** nested tubes; *El:* **fusible emboîté,** enclosed fuse; (*b*) *Bookb:* to case (book) on mull. **2.** (*a*) to pack (sardines, etc.) in boxes; *Mil: P:* **e. qn,** to run s.o. in; (*b*) to fit (things) together, to joint, interlock, dovetail; to house, box (tenon, etc.); **e. des tuyaux,** to joint, socket, pipes; **e. un essieu dans le moyeu,** to fit an axle into the nave; (*c*) *Mil:* **e. le pas,** to fall into step (**à, sur,** with); to lock (in marching); **e. le pas à qn,** (i) to follow in s.o.'s footsteps, on s.o.'s heels; (ii) to follow suit, to join in. **3.** *Th: P:* to hoot; to hiss.

s'emboîter, (*of part*) to fit (**dans,** in).
emboîture [ɑ̃bwaty:r], *s.f.* **1.** fit, interlock (of two things); **e. des os,** juncture of the bones. **2.** (*a*) socket; *Plumb:* **joint à e.,** spigot joint, faucet joint; *Veh:* **e. du moyeu,** nave hole; (*b*) **serrer des planches entre deux emboîtures,** to clamp boards between two cross pieces.
embole [ɑ̃bɔl], *s.m. Med:* embolus.
embolectomie [ɑ̃bɔlɛktɔmi], *s.f. Surg:* embolectomy.
embolie [ɑ̃bɔli], *s.f. Med:* **1.** (*a*) embolism; **e. gazeuse,** air embolism; (*b*) clot of blood (in artery, etc.); **e. cérébrale,** clot on the brain. **2.** emboly.
embolique [ɑ̃bɔlik], *a. Med:* embolic.
embolisation [ɑ̃bɔlizasjɔ̃], *s.f. Med:* embolism.
embolisme [ɑ̃bɔlism], *s.m. Chr:* embolism, intercalation.
embolismique [ɑ̃bɔlismik], *a. Chr:* embolismic (month, etc.).
embolite [ɑ̃bɔlit], *s.f. Miner:* embolite.
embolus [ɑ̃bɔlys], *s.m. Med:* embolus.
embonpoint [ɑ̃bɔ̃pwɛ̃], *s.m.* stoutness, plumpness; fullness of figure; **avoir de l'e.,** to be stout, fat; **prendre de l'e.,** to put on flesh, to get fat; **perdre son e.,** to lose weight, to become thinner, slimmer.
emboquer [ɑ̃bɔke], *v.tr.* to cram (fowl).
embordurer [ɑ̃bɔrdyre], *v.tr.* (*rare*) to mount (print).
embossage [ɑ̃bɔsa:ʒ], *s.m. Nau:* mooring broadside on, with a spring.
embosser [ɑ̃bɔse], *v.tr. Nau:* to moor (ship) broadside on, to moor with a spring.
s'embosser sur les coffres, to secure fore and aft.
embossure [ɑ̃bɔsy:r], *s.f. Nau:* (= CROUPIAT) spring (for mooring).
embotteler [ɑ̃bɔtle], *v.tr.* (**j'embottelle, n. embottelons; j'embottellerai**) to truss (hay, etc.).
embouage [ɑ̃bwa:ʒ], *s.m. Min:* mudding off.
embouche [ɑ̃buʃ], *s.m.* (*a*) rich pasture land; (*b*) fattening of livestock (in pastures).
embouché [ɑ̃buʃe], *a.* **1. cheval bien e.,** well-mouthed horse. **2.** *F:* **mal e.,** (i) foul-mouthed (person); coarse of speech; (ii) in a foul mood.
emboucher [ɑ̃buʃe], *v.tr.* **1.** to put (wind instrument) to one's mouth; to blow (wind instrument); *often Iron:* **e. la trompette,** to announce (sth.) with a flourish; to trumpet the news. **2. e. un cheval,** to put the bit in a horse's mouth. **3.** *F:* **e. qn,** to prompt s.o., to tell s.o. what to say. **4.** to fatten (livestock). **5.** *Nau:* **e. une rivière, etc.,** to enter the mouth of a river, etc.
s'emboucher. 1. *Nau:* to enter a narrow opening. **2.** (*of river, etc.*) to flow, empty itself (**dans,** into).
emboucheur [ɑ̃buʃœ:r], *s.m. Husb:* (*pers.*) fattener (of livestock).
embouchoir [ɑ̃buʃwa:r], *s.m.* **1.** upper band (of rifle); **e. à quillon,** upper band with bayonet stud. **2.** *Mus:* mouthpiece (of wind instrument). **3.** shoe tree, boot tree.
embouchure [ɑ̃buʃy:r], *s.f.* **1.** (*a*) mouthpiece (of blowpipe, wind instrument, horse's bit, etc.); **cheval délicat d'e.,** horse with a delicate mouth; (*b*) *Mus:* embouchure, lipping (= lip position, attack of the note, etc., on wind instrument). **2.** (*a*) opening, mouth (of sack, vessel, etc.); (*b*) mouth (of river, pit-shaft, volcano, etc.); entry, outfall (of valley); **les embouchures du Gange,** the mouth of the Ganges.
emboudiner [ɑ̃budine], *v.tr. Nau:* to lay a pudd(en)ing round (ring, etc.).
emboudinure [ɑ̃budiny:r], *s.f. Nau:* pudd(en)ing.
embouer [ɑ̃bwe], *v.tr.* **1.** to coat, smear, (wall, etc.) with mud or clay; *Min:* to mud off. **2.** *A:* to bespatter with mud; **e. la réputation de qn,** to besmirch s.o.'s reputation; *Prov:* **qui se loue s'emboue,** self-praise is no recommendation.
embouquement [ɑ̃bukmɑ̃], *s.m. Nau:* **1.** entering the mouth of (river, etc.). **2.** entry (of waterway).
embouquer [ɑ̃buke], *v.tr. & i. Nau:* to enter the mouth of (waterway); **e. la passe, dans la passe,** to enter the channel.
embourbement [ɑ̃burbəmɑ̃], *s.m.* sinking, sticking, in the mud, in the mire.
embourber [ɑ̃burbe], *v.tr.* (*a*) to bog down (vehicle), to get (vehicle) stuck in the mud; (*b*) to place (s.o.) in a difficult, sticky, situation.
s'embourber, to stick in the mud; **s'e. dans un marécage,** to get bogged (down); **s'e. dans une explication,** to flounder, get tied up, in an explanation.
embourgeoisement [ɑ̃burʒwazmɑ̃], *s.m.* attainment of middle-class respectability.
embourgeoiser [ɑ̃burʒwaze], *v.tr.* (*a*) *Lit:* to bring (one's style) down to the level of the middle classes; to make (one's style) banal, commonplace; (*b*) *A:* (*of workman, etc.*) **e. sa fille,** to marry one's daughter into the middle classes.
s'embourgeoiser, (*a*) (*of workman, etc.*) to rise in the social scale; (*of the aristocracy*) (i) to come down in the social scale; (ii) to marry into the middle classes; (*b*) **il s'embourgeoise en prenant de l'âge,** he's becoming (very) respectable in his old age; **les Russes s'embourgeoisent,** the Russians are becoming bourgeois.
embourrage [ɑ̃bura:ʒ], **embourrement** [ɑ̃burmɑ̃], *s.m.* stuffing, padding, upholstering (of chair, etc.).
embourrer [ɑ̃bure], *v.tr.* to stuff, pad, upholster (chair, etc.).
embourrure [ɑ̃bury:r], *s.f.* ticking; coarse cloth (for undercover of chair, etc.).
embourser [ɑ̃burse], *v.tr.* (*a*) to pocket (money); (*b*) (*rare*) to put (money) aside, in reserve.
embout [ɑ̃bu], *s.m.* **1.** ferrule, tip (of umbrella, stick, etc.); nipple, terminal (of cable, tube, etc.); nozzle (of hose, pipe); connector (of tie-rod, wire, etc.); chape (of scabbard); **e. protecteur,** cap, protecting end, sealing end; **e. fileté,** threaded end, union nut; **e. orientable,** adjustable nipple, adjustable end; **e. de flexible,** flexible shaft adapter; **e. d'accrochage,** grabbing-tip (of gyroscope). **2.** mouthpiece (of speaking, breathing, tube). **3. e. d'une seringue,** syringe adapter.
embouteillage [ɑ̃butɛja:ʒ], *s.m.* **1.** *A:* bottling (of wine, beer, etc.). **2.** bottling up (of harbour mouth, fleet). **3.** traffic jam, congestion (of traffic); **je ne veux pas attendre l'heure de l'e. du métro,** I don't want to wait for the rush hour on the tube; *W.Tel:* **e. de l'éther,** overcrowding of the ether.
embouteiller [ɑ̃buteje], *v.tr.* **1.** *A:* to bottle (wine, beer, etc.). **2.** to bottle up, block up (harbour mouth, fleet, entrance to station); **circulation embouteillée,** congested traffic; **route embouteillée,** road blocked with cars; **les lignes téléphoniques étaient embouteillées,** the telephone lines were blocked; all the (telephone) lines were engaged.
embouteilleur [ɑ̃butɛjœr], *s.m.* bottler (of wines, etc.).
embouter [ɑ̃bute], *v.tr.* to put a metal tip on (sth.); to tip, to ferrule (umbrella, etc.).
embouti [ɑ̃buti], *s.m. Metalw:* pressing.
emboutir [ɑ̃buti:r], *v.tr.* **1.** *Metalw:* (*a*) to stamp, press, swage (metal); **e. la tôle à froid,** to cold press; **pièce emboutie,** pressing; **tôle emboutie,** dished plate; **châssis en tôle emboutie,** pressed steel frame; (*b*) to emboss. **2.** (*a*) to sheathe (cornice, etc.) with metal; (*b*) to tip, cap, (rod, etc.) with a metal ferrule. **3.** to dent (sth.) badly; to bash (sth.) in; **un camion a embouti l'arrière de ma voiture,** a lorry bashed in the back of my car; **j'ai failli e. un arbre, m'e. sur un arbre,** I nearly crashed into a tree; **la voiture s'emboutit contre un mur,** the car crashed into, hit, a wall.
emboutissage [ɑ̃butisa:ʒ], *s.m. Metalw:* (*a*) (drop-) stamping, pressing, swaging (of metals); **e. profond,** deep drawing; **e. d'un fond,** dishing; **matrices pour e.,** stamping dies; (*b*) embossing; (*c*) *F:* (*of cars*) collision.
emboutisseur [ɑ̃butisœ:r], *s.m. Metalw:* stamper, plate bender.
emboutisseuse [ɑ̃butisø:z], *s.f.,* **emboutissoir** [ɑ̃butiswa:r], *s.m. Metalw:* **1.** plate-bending machine, shaping machine, shaper. **2.** stamping press, stamper.
embranchement [ɑ̃brɑ̃ʃmɑ̃], *s.m.* **1.** branching (off) (of tree, road, railway line, pipe, etc.); division, dividing (of mountain range). **2.** (road, rail, pipe) junction; fork (in road); **tuyau d'e.,** branch pipe. **3.** (*a*) side road; branch (of motorway, etc.); (*b*) *Rail:* (i) branch line; (ii) siding; **e. particulier, industriel,** private siding, siding leading to works; (*c*) spur, secondary chain (of mountain range); (*d*) branch (of a science); *Nat.Hist:* sub-kingdom, phylum.
embrancher [ɑ̃brɑ̃ʃe], *v.tr.* to connect up, join up (secondary road, railway line, pipe, etc., with main artery).
s'embrancher, (*of road, etc.*) (i) to form a junction; (ii) to branch off (**sur,** from); to connect up (**sur,** with).
embraquer [ɑ̃brake], *v.tr. Nau:* to haul, rouse, (rope) taut; **e. (un cordage),** to tighten (a rope); **e. le mou,** to haul in the slack, to shorten in.
embrasé [ɑ̃braze] *a.* (*a*) blazing (ship, etc.); glowing (coals, etc.); (*b*) **atmosphère embrasée,** sultry atmosphere; **journée embrasée,** sweltering day; **ciel e.,** fiery sky; *Lit:* **cœur e. d'amour,** heart aflame with passion.
embrasement [ɑ̃brazmɑ̃], *s.m.* (*a*) *A:* burning, conflagration (of town, ship, etc.); (*b*) **e. politique,** political upheaval, conflagration; (*c*) *A:* illumination (of public building, etc., on festive occasion); *Lit:* **l'e. du couchant,** the fiery glow of the sunset.
embraser [ɑ̃braze], *v.tr.* (*a*) *A:* to set fire to (sth.); to set (sth.) ablaze, aflame; **e. du charbon,** to bring coal to a glow; (*b*) **route que le soleil embrase,** road scorched by the sun; **le soleil embrase les pics,** the sun sets the peaks aglow; **ciel qu'embrasait le soleil couchant,** sky aglow with the setting sun; (*c*) **le zèle qui l'embrase,** the zeal that inflames, fires, him; **e. l'imagination,** to fire the imagination; **e. l'Europe,** to set Europe ablaze; (*d*) *A:* to illuminate (public building, etc., on festive occasion).
s'embraser, to catch fire; **toute l'Europe s'embrasa,** all Europe blazed up; **s'e. d'amour pour qn,** to conceive a violent passion for s.o.
embrassade [ɑ̃brasad], *s.f.* embrace; hug.
embrassant [ɑ̃brasɑ̃], *a. Bot:* amplexicaul.
embrasse [ɑ̃bras], *s.f.* **1.** *A:* embracing, embrace. **2.** (*a*) curtain loop; (*b*) *A:* arm-rest (of carriage).
embrassé [ɑ̃brase], *a. Pros:* **rimes embrassées,** introverted, enclosing, rhymes.
embrassement [ɑ̃brasmɑ̃], *s.m. Lit:* embrace.
embrasser [ɑ̃brase], *v.tr.* to embrace. **1.** (*a*) to put one's arms round (s.o., sth.); to clasp (s.o.) (in one's arms); to hug (s.o., sth.); **e. la croix,** to embrace, clasp, the cross; **e. qn jusqu'à l'étouffer,** to hug s.o. to death; **l'équateur embrasse la terre,** the equator encircles the earth; **le lierre embrasse le chêne,** the ivy twines (itself) round the oak; *Equit:* **bien e. son cheval,** to have a firm grip of one's horse (with the knees); (*b*) to kiss; **ils s'embrassèrent,** they kissed; (*letter formula*) **je vous embrasse de tout mon cœur,** with much love; *A:* **n'embrasse pas qui veut,** kissing goes by favour; (*c*) to adopt, take up (career, etc.); to take up (cause); to embrace (doctrine); **e. le parti de qn,** to side with s.o.; **e. une occasion,** to seize an opportunity. **2.** to contain, include, take in; **empire qui embrasse dix nations,** empire that includes, comprises, ten nations; **le regard ne peut pas e. tout le paysage,** the eye cannot take in the whole landscape; **l'explication n'embrasse pas tous les faits,** the explanation does not cover all the facts; **sujet qui embrasse tout le siècle,** subject that spans the whole century.
embrasseur, -euse [ɑ̃brasœ:r, -ø:z], *s.* inveterate (i) hugger, (ii) kisser.
embrassure [ɑ̃brasy:r], *s.f.* **1.** (*a*) *Const:* (i) binding hoop; (ii) ferrule; (*b*) *Veh:* (spring-) shackle. **2.** *Arch:* quatrefoil.
embrasure [ɑ̃brazy:r], *s.f.* **1.** (*a*) embrasure, window recess; (*b*) flanning, inward chamfer (of window jamb, etc.); (*c*) *Fort:* embrasure, crenel; (*d*) *Nau:* gun port. **2.** tuyère arch (of furnace).
embrayage [ɑ̃brɛja:ʒ], *s.m. Aut: Mec.E: etc:* **1.** connecting, coupling; engaging (of the clutch); throwing into gear (of engine parts). **2.** clutch, coupling, connecting gear; **e. automatique,** automatic clutch; **e. centrifuge,** centrifugal clutch; **e. à cône,** cone clutch, coupling; **e. à courroies,** band clutch; **e. à crabots,** dog clutch, coupling; **e. à disque (unique),** (single)-disc clutch, coupling; **e. à disques multiples,** multi(ple)-disc clutch, coupling; **e. à friction,** friction clutch, coupling; **e. à griffes, à dents,** claw coupling; **e. à manchon,** box, sleeve, coupling; **e. à plateau (unique),** (single)-plate clutch, coupling; **e. à plateaux multiples,** multi(ple)-plate clutch, coupling; **e. à ruban,** band clutch, coupling; strap clutch, coupling; **e. à spirale,** coil coupling; **e. flexible,** flexible coupling; **e. mobile,** loose coupling; **e. hydraulique,** fluid coupling, hydraulic coupling; **commande d'e.,** clutch control; **disque, plateau d'e.,** clutch disc, plate; **fourche d'e.,** clutch fork; **garniture d'e.,** clutch facing, lining; **guide d'e.,** clutch guide; **pédale d'e.,** clutch pedal; **ressort d'e.,** clutch spring; **timonerie d'e.,** clutch linkage; **tige d'e.,** striker rod (of gear).
embrayer [ɑ̃breje], *v.tr.* (**j'embraie, j'embraye, n. embrayons; j'embraierai, j'embrayerai**) *Mec.E:* to connect, couple; engage; to throw (parts) into gear; *abs. Aut:* to let in the clutch; *abs. F:* to start work.

s'embrayer, to come into gear.

embrayeur [ɑ̃brɛjœːr], *s.m. Mec.E: etc:* (*a*) clutch lever, fork; (*b*) belt shifter.

embrelage [ɑ̃brəlaːʒ], *s.m. Dial:* lashing down (of cart-load, etc.).

embreler [ɑ̃brəle], *v.tr.* (**j'embrèle, n. embrelons; j'embrèlerai**) *Dial:* to lash down (cart-load, etc.).

embrener [ɑ̃brəne], *v.tr.* (**j'embrène, n. embrenons; j'embrènerai**) *P: A:* to soil, make a mess in (one's pants); **enfant qui s'embrène,** child who makes a mess in his pants.

embrèvement [ɑ̃brɛvmɑ̃], *s.m. Carp:* **1.** joggle (joint). **2.** groove-and-tongue joint.

embrever [ɑ̃brəve], *vt.r.* (**j'embrève, n. embrevons; j'embrèverai**) *Carp:* **1.** to joggle (two joints). **2.** to join (boards) by groove and tongue; to match (boards).

embrigadement [ɑ̃brigadmɑ̃], *s.m.* **1.** *Mil:* brigading (of troops, etc.). **2.** enrolling (of a body of men).

embrigader [ɑ̃brigade], *v.tr.* **1.** *Mil:* to brigade (troops, etc.); **partisans bien embrigadés,** well-organized body of adherents. **2. e. des hommes (pour balayer la neige, etc.),** to enrol a body of men (to sweep away the snow, etc.); **il m'a embrigadé dans son club,** he made me join his club.

embringuer [ɑ̃brɛ̃ge], *v.tr. F:* to involve; **se laisser e. dans qch.,** to get involved in sth.

embrocation [ɑ̃brɔkasjɔ̃], *s.f. Med:* (*a*) application of embrocation; (*b*) embrocation.

embrochage [ɑ̃brɔʃaːʒ], *s.m.* **1.** *Tg:* series mounting; **ligne à e.,** circuit with intermediate receiving stations. **2.** *Surg:* pinning (of fracture).

embrochement [ɑ̃brɔʃmɑ̃], *s.m.* **1.** *Cu:* spitting, putting on the spit (of piece of meat, etc.); *F:* running (s.o.) through (with bayonet, etc.). **2.** *Tg:* (action of) series mounting.

embrocher [ɑ̃brɔʃe], *v.tr.* **1.** *Cu:* to spit, to put (piece of meat) on the spit; *F:* **e. qn d'un coup de baïonnette,** to run s.o. through with a bayonet. **2.** *Tg:* to wire (station) on a circuit. **3.** *Surg:* to pin (fracture).

embroncher [ɑ̃brɔ̃ʃe], *v.tr.* to lay (tiles, slates, etc.) with an overlap.

embrouillage [ɑ̃brujaːʒ], *s.m. F:* confusion, embarrassment.

embrouillamini [ɑ̃brujamini], *s.m. F:* confusion, disorder.

embrouillarder (s') [sɑ̃brujarde], *v.pr.* (*of weather*) to become misty, foggy; *F:* (*of pers.*) to get fuddled (with drink).

embrouille [ɑ̃bruːj], *s.f. P:* complete disorder, hopeless mess, muddle.

embrouillé [ɑ̃bruje], *a.* **1.** tangled, (skein, etc.); complicated, involved (style, business). **2.** dull, threatening (weather).

embrouillement [ɑ̃brujmɑ̃], *s.m.* **1.** entanglement, ravelling (of thread, etc.). **2.** confusion (of ideas, etc.); jumbled state (of things); intricacy (of question).

embrouiller [ɑ̃bruje], *v.tr.* **1.** to ravel, tangle (thread, etc.). **2.** to tangle up, muddle; to mix up (papers); to confuse, muddle (s.o.); **e. une affaire,** to get a piece of business into a muddle; **e. la question,** to confuse, cloud, the issue.

s'embrouiller. 1. (*of thread, etc.*) to get tangled, into a tangle. **2.** (*a*) (*of pers.*) to get muddled, confused, to lose the thread of one's ideas; to lose count; (*b*) **le ciel s'embrouille,** the sky is clouding over; (*c*) **l'affaire s'embrouille,** the business is getting intricate; **ses affaires s'embrouillent,** his business is getting into a muddle.

embrouilleur, -euse [ɑ̃brujœːr, -øːz], *s.* muddler.

embroussaillé [ɑ̃brusaje], *a.* **1.** covered with bushes, with brushwood; **cheveux embroussaillés,** tousled hair. **2.** complicated, involved (business).

embroussaillement [ɑ̃brusajmɑ̃], *s.m. Coll.* brushwood.

embroussailler [ɑ̃brusaje], *v.tr.* to cover with brushwood, with bushes; **ses cheveux lui embroussaillaient le front,** his, her, hair fell in a tangle on his, her, forehead.

embruiné [ɑ̃brɥine], *a.* **1.** *Agr:* (*of crops, etc.*) blighted with cold drizzle. **2. horizon e.,** horizon lost in the drizzle, the mist.

embrumé [ɑ̃bryme], *a.* misty (weather); hazy (horizon); visage e., downcast face.

embrumer [ɑ̃bryme], *v.tr.* to cover (landscape, etc.) with mist, haze, fog; **craintes qui embrument l'avenir,** fears that darken the future.

s'embrumer, to become misty, hazy, foggy; **le ciel s'embruma,** the sky is clouding over; **son visage s'embruma,** his face clouded.

embrun [ɑ̃brœ̃], *s.m. Nau:* **1.** *usu. pl.* spray, spindrift. **2.** (*rare*) fog.

embrunir [ɑ̃bryniːr], *v.tr.* (*a*) to darken, to turn brown; **des nuages qui embrunissaient le paysage,** clouds that darkened the landscape; (*b*) to sadden (s.o.).

s'embrunir, to darken; *F:* **son visage s'était embruni,** his face had clouded over, had taken on a gloomy expression.

embryocardie [ɑ̃briɔkardi], *s.f. Med:* embryocardia.

embryogénèse [ɑ̃briɔʒenɛːz], *s.f. Biol:* embryogenesis.

embryogénie [ɑ̃briɔʒeni], *s.f. Biol:* embryogeny.

embryogénique [ɑ̃briɔʒenik], *a. Biol:* embryogen(et)ic.

embryographie [ɑ̃briɔgrafi], *s.f.* embryography.

embryoïde [ɑ̃briɔid], *a.* embryoid.

embryologie [ɑ̃briɔlɔʒi], *s.f. Biol:* embryology.

embryologique [ɑ̃briɔlɔʒik], *a. Biol:* embryologic(al).

embryologiste [ɑ̃briɔlɔʒist], *s.m. & f.,* **embryologue** [ɑ̃riɔblɔg], *s.m. & f.* embryologist.

embryome [ɑ̃brioːm], *s.m Med:* embryoma.

embryon [ɑ̃briɔ̃], *s.m.* (*a*) *Biol:* embryo; (*b*) **œuvre encore en e.,** work still in embryo.

embryonnaire [ɑ̃briɔnɛːr], *a. Biol:* (*a*) embryonic (period, chick, etc.); **projets embryonnaires,** plans still in embryo; (*b*) embryonary (sac, state); embryo (sac, etc.).

embryopathie [ɑ̃briɔpati], *s.f. Med:* embryopathy.

embryotège [ɑ̃briɔtɛːʒ], *s.m. Bot:* embryotega.

embryotome [ɑ̃briɔtɔm], *s.m. Obst:* (*instrument*) embryotome.

embryotomie [ɑ̃briɔtɔmi], *s.f. Obst:* embryotomy.

embryotrophe [ɑ̃briɔtrɔf], *s.m.* embryotrophy.

embryotrophique [ɑ̃briɔtrɔfik], *a.* embryotrophic.

embu [ɑ̃by]. **1.** *a.* flat, dull (paint, painting). **2.** *s.m.* flatness, dullness, streakiness (of paint, painting).

embûche [ɑ̃byʃ], *s.f.* **1.** *A:* ambush, ambuscade. **2.** (*a*) *usu. pl.* plot (against s.o.); trap; **tendre, dresser, des embûches à qn,** to set a trap for s.o.; to plot against s.o.; **tomber dans l'e.,** to fall into the trap; (*b*) obstacle, difficulty; **sujet plein d'embûches,** tricky subject.

embûcher [ɑ̃byʃe], *v.tr.* **1.** *A:* to ambush (s.o.). **2.** *For:* to start cutting the timber of (forest). **3.** *Ven:* to drive (stag) back to cover(t), to lodge (stag).

s'embûcher, *Ven:* (*of stag*) to enter cover(t), to turn back to cover(t); to lodge.

embuer [ɑ̃bɥe], *v.tr.* (*of steam, etc.*) to dim, cloud (glass, etc.); **yeux embués de larmes,** eyes dimmed with tears.

embuscade [ɑ̃byskad], *s.f.* ambush, ambuscade; **dresser, tendre, une e. à qn,** to lay an ambush for s.o.; **attirer qn dans une e.,** to ambush, waylay, s.o.; **tomber dans une e.,** to be ambushed, to fall into an ambush; **se tenir en e.,** to be, lie, in ambush; to lie in wait.

embuscage [ɑ̃byskaːʒ], *s.m.* placing (of snipers, etc.) under cover, (of troops) in ambush.

embusqué [ɑ̃byske], *s.m.* **1.** *Mil:* (*a*) soldier whose duties exempt him from drill, parade, etc.; *hence* (*b*) *F:* (i) slacker, dodger; (ii) shirker (from enlistment or active service); **nid d'embusqués,** funk hole; (*c*) **cheveux à l'e.,** hair brushed back. **2.** *Rugby Fb:* **les embusqués,** the back row of forwards.

embusquer [ɑ̃byske], *v.tr.* **1.** to place (troops, etc.) in ambush, under cover. **2.** to find (s.o.) a safe job (in wartime).

s'embusquer, (*a*) to lie in ambush, to ambush; (*b*) to take cover; (*c*) (*in war*) to shirk active service.

embusqueur [ɑ̃byskœːr], *s.m. Mil: F:* protector, abettor, of shirkers, dodgers.

embut [ɑ̃by], *s.m. Geog: Dial:* (*Provence*) aven.

éméché [emeʃe], *a. F:* slightly the worse for drink; a bit tipsy, merry, lit up.

émécher [emeʃe], *v.tr.* (**j'émèche, n. éméchons; j'émécherai**) **1.** to divide (hair, etc.) into locks, into strands. **2.** *F:* to make (s.o.) merry.

s'émécher, *F:* to get slightly the worse for drink; to get tight.

émendation [emɑ̃dasjɔ̃], *s.f. A:* emendation, editing (of text).

émender [emɑ̃de], *v.tr. Jur:* to amend (decree, sentence, etc.).

-ement [əmɑ̃], *s.suff.m.* (*a*) (*expressing action*) -ment, -ing; **abaissement,** abatement, lowering; **commencement,** commencement, beginning; **verdissement,** turning green; (*b*) (*expressing result of action*) **agrandissements,** extensions; **établissement,** establishment.

émeraude [ɛmroːd, e-]. **1.** *s.f.* emerald; **é. du Brésil,** Brazilian emerald, green tourmaline. **2.** *a.inv. & s.f.* emerald green; *Geog:* **côte d'É.,** the north coast of Brittany, from Saint-Malo to Roscoff; *Poet: Journ:* **l'île d'É.,** the Emerald Isle, Ireland. **3.** *s.m. Orn:* (*a*) (i) great emerald, (ii) lesser emerald, bird of paradise; (*b*) humming bird.

émergement [emɛrʒmɑ̃], *s.m. Geol:* emergence (of land from sea).

émergence [emɛrʒɑ̃ːs], *s.f.* **1.** emergence (of spring, submerged body; *Opt:* of ray of light; *Biol: Phil:* of quality, character). **2.** *Bot:* (*outgrowth*) emergence; *Anat:* point of emergence (of nerve).

émergent [emɛrʒɑ̃], *a.* emergent. **1.** *Chr:* **année émergente,** emergent year. **2.** *Opt:* **rayons émergents,** emergent rays. **3.** *Pol:* **nations emergentes,** emergent nations.

émerger [emɛrʒe], *v.i.* (**j'émergeai(s); n. émergeons**) **1.** to emerge (from the sea, etc.). **2.** to come into view; **l'un après l'autre les objets émergeaient de l'ombre,** one after the other shapes emerged from the shadows; **les violettes émergent au milieu de l'herbe,** the violets peep from the grass; **la vérité finissait par é.,** the truth finally emerged, came to light.

émeri [ɛmri, e-], *s.m.* emery; **poudre d'é.,** emery powder; **toile, papier, (d')é.,** emery cloth, paper; **bouchon à l'é.,** (ground glass) stopper; **bouché à l'é.,** (i) (*of flask*) stoppered; (ii) *F:* (*of pers.*) narrow-minded; *Toil:* **lime é.,** emery board.

émerillon [ɛmrijɔ̃, e-], *s.m.* **1.** *Orn:* **(faucon) é.,** merlin. **2.** *Tchn:* swivel (hook); *Nau:* **é. d'affourche,** mooring swivel; **croc à é.,** swivel hook; **poulie à é.,** swivel block. **3.** *A.Artil:* merlin.

émerillonnage [ɛmrijɔnaːʒ, e-], *s.m. Tex:* twisting.

émerillonné [ɛmrijɔné, e-], *a. A: & Lit:* bright; gay; (*of pers., expression*) roguish, mischievous.

émerillonner [ɛmrijɔne, e-], *v.tr.* **1.** *A:* to cheer, brighten, (s.o.) up. **2.** *Tex:* to twist (thread).

émeriser [ɛmrize, e-], *v.tr.* **1.** to coat (paper, cloth, etc.) with emery; **papier émerisé,** emery cloth. **2.** *Metalw:* to paper (metal).

émérite [emerit], *a.* **1.** (*a*) *Rom.Mil.Hist:* **soldat é.,** emeritus; (*b*) *A:* **professeur é.,** emeritus professor. **2.** practised, experienced (player, etc.); **chirurgien é.,** eminent surgeon.

émérophonie [emerɔfɔni], *s.f. Med:* hemeraphonia.

émersion [emɛrsjɔ̃], *s.f.* **1.** emergence (of submerged rock, body, etc.); **île d'é.,** emerged island. **2.** *Astr:* emersion (of moon, etc.).

émerveillement [emɛrvɛjmɑ̃], *s.m.* amazement, wonder; **c'était un é.,** it was amazing, wonderful; **il parle avec é. de Versailles,** he speaks of Versailles in terms of breathless admiration.

émerveiller [emɛrvɛje], *v.tr.* to amaze; to fill (s.o.) with wonder, with admiration; **Versailles l'émerveilla,** he was enchanted by Versailles.

s'émerveiller, to be struck with amazement, with admiration; to be enchanted (**de,** with); *F:* **il n'y a pas là de quoi s'é.,** that's nothing to write home about.

émèse [emɛːz], *s.f. Ent:* emesa.

émétine [emetin], *s.f. Ch:* emetin(e).

émétique [emetik]. **1.** *a.* emetic. **2.** *s.m.* (*a*) emetic; (*b*) tartar emetic; **é. de bore,** soluble cream of tartar.

émétisant [emetizɑ̃], *a.* which tends to make one vomit; **la toux émétisante est caractéristique de la coqueluche,** a cough accompanied by vomiting is characteristic of whooping cough.

émétiser [emetize], *v.tr.* **1.** to add an emetic to (drink, etc.). **2.** to administer an emetic to (patient, etc.).

émetteur, -trice [emetœːr, -tris]. **1.** *s.m.* (*a*) *Fin: etc:* issuer (of bank-notes, shares, etc.); (*b*) *Elcs: W.Tel: etc:* transmitter; **é. radio,** radio transmitter; **é. radio-téléphonique,** radio-telephone (R/T) transmitter; **é. de fac-similés,** facsimile transmitter; **é. brouilleur,** jamming station, jamming transmitter; **é. automatique,** automatic transmitter, auto-transmitter; **é. (à) ondes courtes,** short-wave transmitter; **é. à modulation de fréquence,** frequency-modulation (F/M) transmitter; **é. dirigé, é. de radio-alignement,** (directional) beam transmitter; **é (télégraphique) à bande perforée,** tape transmitter; **é. de radiodiffusion,** broadcast(ing) transmitter; **é. régional,** regional transmitter; **é. relais,** repeater station, re-transmitter; **é. de station-relais,** relay transmitter; *T.V:* **é. de télécinéma,** film transmitter; **é. image,** image, picture, transmitter, vision transmitter; **é. son,** aural transmitter; (*radar, etc.*) **é. d'impulsions,** pinger; *Av:* **é. de radioguidage,** glide-path transmitter; **é. de bord,** (i) *Av:* onboard transmitter; (ii) *Nau:* ship's transmitter; (*c*) *Atom.Ph:*

emitter, radiator; **é. (de particules) alpha,** alpha (-particle) emitter, radiator; **é. (de particules) bêta,** beta (-particle) emitter, radiator; **é. primaire,** primary emitter, radiator; **é. pur,** pure emitter. **2.** *a.* issuing (banker, etc.); *W.Tel: etc:* **poste é., station émettrice,** (i) transmitting station; (ii) broadcasting station.

émetteur-récepteur [emetœrreseptœːr], *s.m. W. Tel:* transmitter-receiver, transceiver; **é.-r. (portatif),** portable transceiver; *F:* walkie-talkie; **é.-r. toutes ondes,** multi-frequency radio set; *pl.* **émetteurs-récepteurs.**

émetteur-relais [emetœrrəlɛ], *s.m. W.Tel: T.V:* relay transmitter; *pl.* **émetteurs-relais.**

émettre [emetr], *v.tr.* (*conj. like* METTRE) **1.** (*a*) to emit (sound, heat, ray of light, etc.); to utter (sound); to give off (fumes); to give out (heat); **é. des particules alpha, bêta,** to emit alpha, beta, particles; (*b*) **é. une opinion,** to express an opinion; **é. une objection,** to raise, put forward, an objection; (*c*) *abs. W.Tel: Tg:* to transmit; *W.Tel:* to broadcast. **2.** to issue (bank notes, cheque, etc.); to issue; float (loan); **é. de la fausse monnaie,** to put counterfeit coins into circulation, to utter counterfeit coins.

émeu[1] [emø], *s.m. Orn:* emu; *pl.* **émeus.**

émeu[2], *s.m.* droppings (of falcon, goshawk).

émeulage [emølaːʒ], *s.m.* buffing.

émeuler [emøle], *v.tr.* to buff (metal); **huile à é.,** buffing oil.

émeut [emø], *s.m.* droppings (of falcon, goshawk).

émeute [emøːt], *s.f.* riot, outbreak, disturbance; **exciter une é.,** to stir up a riot; **faire é.,** to riot; **chef d'é.,** riot leader; ringleader.

émeuter [emøte], *v.tr.* to stir up (the people); to rouse (the people) to revolt.

émeutier, -ière [emøtje, -jɛːr], *s.* (*a*) rioter; **bande d'émeutiers,** (rioting) mob; (*b*) riot leader.

émier [emje], *v.tr. Dial:* to crumble.

émiettement [emjɛtmã], *s.m.* **1.** crumbling; **é. du pouvoir,** dispersal of power; **é. d'une fortune,** frittering away of a fortune. **2.** crumbs.

émietter [emjete], *v.tr.* to crumble; **é. du pain pour les oiseaux,** to crumble (up) bread for the birds; **roche émiettée par l'érosion,** rock crumbled (away) by erosion; **é. un domaine,** to fragment, split up, an estate; **é. sa fortune,** to fritter away one's fortune; **é. ses activités,** to disperse one's activities.

s'émietter, to crumble (away); **l'empire s'émietta en une multitude de petits royaumes,** the empire disintegrated, split, into a number of petty, small, kingdoms; **le groupe s'émietta,** the group dispersed.

émigrant, -ante [emigrã, -ãːt]. **1.** *a.* emigrating (population, etc.); migratory (birds). **2.** *s.* emigrant; **navire d'émigrants,** emigrant ship.

émigration [emigrasjɔ̃], *s.f.* **1.** migration (of birds, fishes). **2.** emigration (of people); **é. des savants,** brain drain.

émigré, -ée [emigre], *s.* émigré, (political) exile.

émigrer [emigre], *v.i.* **1.** (*of pers.*) to emigrate. **2.** (*of birds, fish*) to migrate.

Émile [emil], *Pr.n.m. Rel.H:* Aemilius.

Émilie [emili], *Pr.n.f.* **1.** Emily, Amelia. **2.** *Geog:* Emilia.

Émilien[1] [emiljɛ̃], *Pr.n.m.* Aemilian.

émilien[2], **-ienne,** *a. & s. Geog:* (native, inhabitant) of Emilia.

émincé [emɛ̃se], *s.m.* (*a*) thin slice (of meat, onion); (*b*) thinly sliced meat served in sauce.

émincer [emɛ̃se], *v.tr.* (j'éminçai(s); n. éminçons) to slice (meat, etc.) finely; to shred (vegetables).

éminemment [eminamã], *adv.* eminently; highly; to, in, a high degree; **il est é. généreux,** he is outstandingly generous, generous to a degree; *Phil:* **l'effet est contenu é. dans la cause,** the effect is eminently implied in the cause.

éminence [eminãːs], *s.f.* eminence. **1.** (*a*) rising ground, rise, hill, height; (*b*) **é. osseuse,** bony protuberance; **é. du pouce,** ball of the thumb; **éminences vermiformes du cervelet,** vermiform processes of the cerebellum; (*c*) *A:* (moral, intellectual) superiority, distinction; **par é., en é.,** eminently. **2.** *Ecc:* **son É. le Cardinal,** his Eminence the Cardinal; **veuillez bien, É., me permettre de . . .,** votre É. voudra bien me permettre de . . ., will your Eminence kindly allow me to . . .; **l'É. grise,** the power behind the throne.

éminent[1] [eminã], *a.* (*a*) *A:* high (ground, etc.); (*b*) eminent, distinguished; **chirurgien é.,** eminent surgeon; **service é.,** valuable service; **vertu éminente,** outstanding virtue; **il est d'un savoir é.,** he is distinguished by his scholarship; he is an eminent scholar.

éminentissime [eminãtisim], most eminent (cardinal, etc.).

émir [emiːr], *s.m.* emir.

émirat [emira], *s.m.* emirate.

émissaire[1] [emisɛːr], (*a*) *s.m.* emissary, messenger; (*b*) *a.* **bouc é.,** scapegoat.

émissaire[2]. **1.** *a. & s.m.* (**veine**) **é.,** emissary vein. **2.** *s.m.* (*a*) *Geog:* (stream issuing from lake) effluent; (*b*) *Hyd.E:* drainage channel, outlet channel (for lake, etc.); *Rom.Ant:* emissary, emissarium; **é. d'évacuation,** outfall sewer.

émissif, -ive [emisif, -iːv], *a. Ph:* emissive (power, etc.).

émission [emisjɔ̃], *s.f.* **1.** (*a*) emission (of sound, light, fluid, etc.); utterance (of sound); radiation (of heat); sending out (of signals); **tuyau d'é.,** discharge pipe; (*b*) *W.Tel:* (i) transmission; sending out; (ii) broadcasting; (iii) broadcast, transmission; programme; **é. aux ondes dirigées,** beam transmission; **é. en différé,** recorded broadcast; **é. en direct,** live broadcast; **é. simultanée,** simultaneous broadcast; **é. dirigée,** directional transmission; **puissance d'é.,** transmitter power; (*c*) *Elcs:* emission; **é. électronique,** electron emission; **é. (électronique) primaire,** secondaire, primary, secondary, emission; **é. thermo-ionique,** thermionic emission; **é. quantique,** quantum emission; **é. dirigée,** beam emission; **puissance d'é.,** radiating power; (*d*) *Atom.Ph:* emission; **é. de particules,** particle emission; **é. de particules alpha, bêta,** alpha, beta, particle emission; **é. de positrons, é. positogène,** positron emission; **é. en cascade,** cascade emission; **é. gamma en cascade,** gamma cascade, cascade gamma-rays. **2.** (*a*) *Fin: etc:* issue, issuing (of bank-notes, tickets, etc.); issue, floating (of loan); **prix d'é.,** issue price; **banque d'é.,** issuing bank; (*b*) *Jur:* uttering (of counterfeit coin, document).

émissionnaire [emisjɔnɛːr]. **1.** *a.* issuing (bank). **2.** *s.m.* issuer (of bank-notes).

émission-réception [emisjɔ̃resepsjɔ̃], *s.f. W.Tel:* send-receive; *pl.* **émissions-réceptions.**

émissole [emisɔl], *s.f. Ich: F:* (smooth) dogfish, smooth hound.

émittance [emitãːs], *s.m.* **é. énergétique,** luminous flux density.

emmagasinage [ãmagazinaːʒ], *s.m.,* **emmagasinement** [ãmagazinmã], *s.m.* **1.** *Com:* storage, warehousing (of goods); (*b*) storage (charges), warehouse charges. **2.** *Ph: etc:* storing up, storage, accumulation (of electricity, etc.). **3.** *Agr:* accumulation (of water in the soil).

emmagasinateur, -trice [ãmagazinatœːr, -tris], *a. Ph: etc:* accumulating, storing (vessel, etc.).

emmagasiner [ãmagazine], *v.tr.* **1.** *Com:* to store, warehouse (goods); to house (aircraft, etc.); **dates emmagasinées dans la mémoire,** dates stored away in the memory. **2.** *Ph: etc:* to store up, to accumulate (energy, etc.). **3.** *Sm.a:* to fill the magazine with (cartridges).

emmagasineur [ãmagazinœːr], *s.m. Com:* warehouseman.

emmaigrir [ãmegriːr]. **1.** *v.tr. A:* to make (s.o.) thin. **2.** *v.i. & pr. A:* to grow thin, to lose weight.

emmailler [ãmaje], *v.tr.* to catch (fish) in the meshes of a net; **les poissons se sont emmaillés,** the fish got caught in the meshes of the net.

emmaillotement [ãmajɔtmã], *s.m.* (*a*) *A:* swaddling (of infant); (*b*) binding (up) (of limb, etc.).

emmailloter [ãmajɔte], *v.tr.* (*a*) *A:* to swaddle (infant); (*b*) to bind (up) (limb, etc.); **l'homme moderne emmailloté d'innombrables règlements,** modern man entangled, bound up, in countless regulations.

emmanchage [ãmãʃaːʒ], *s.m.,* **emmanchement** [ãmãʃmã], *s.m.* **1.** (*a*) fitting a handle (to tool, etc.); hafting, helving (of tool, etc.); (*b*) jointing, fitting together (of pipes, etc.); coupling, mounting. **2.** sleeve-joint, expansion joint.

emmanché, -ée [ãmãʃe], *s.* clumsy, ham-fisted, person; awkward person, blunderer.

emmancher[1] [ãmãʃe], *v.tr.* **1.** to fix a handle to, to haft, to helve (tool, etc.). **2.** to joint (pipes, etc.); to fit (pipes, etc.) together; to fix (pulley on shaft, etc.); **é. qch. à chaud,** to shrink sth. on; **e. une affaire,** to start, set about, a piece of business; **affaire mal emmanchée,** business muddled at the start.

s'emmancher, to fit (i) into a handle, (ii) together.

emmancher[2], *v.i. Nau:* to enter a channel.

emmanchure [ãmãʃyːr], *s.f.* (*a*) armhole (of coat, etc.); (*b*) *Tls:* eye (of hammer, etc.).

emmanteler [ãmãtle], *v.tr.* (j'emmantèle; n. emmantelons; j'emmantèlerai) to mantle. **1.** *A:* to cover (s.o.) with a mantle. **2.** to surround (place) with fortifications.

Emmanuel [emanɥɛl], *Pr.n.m.* Emmanuel.

emmarchement [ãmarʃmã], *s.m. Const:* tread (of stair); **longueur d'e.,** width of stair.

emmassement [ãmasmã], *s.m. Mil:* **1.** massing, concentrating (of troops). **2.** massed body of troops.

emmasser [ãmase], *v.tr. Mil:* to mass, concentrate (troops).

Emmaüs [em(m)ays], *Pr.n.m. A.Geog:* Emmaus.

emmêlage [ãmɛlaːʒ], *s.m.,* **emmêlement** [ãmɛlmã], *s.m.* **1.** (*a*) tangling (of threads, hair, etc.); (*b*) mixing up, muddling (of facts). **2.** (*a*) tangle (of threads, etc.); (*b*) mix-up, muddle.

emmêler [ãmele], *v.tr.* (*a*) to (en)tangle (thread, hair, etc.); (*b*) to mix up (facts); to muddle (story); **e. ses affaires,** to get one's business into a muddle; **il emmêle tout,** he's an awful muddler.

s'emmêler, to become (i) tangled, (ii) mixed up; to get into a tangle, into a muddle.

emménagement [ãmenaʒmã], *s.m.* **1.** (*a*) moving in(to) (a house); (*b*) installation (of furniture, etc.). **2.** *pl. Aer: Nau:* accommodation, appointments.

emménager [ãmenaʒe], *v.* (j'emménageai(s); n. emménageons) **1.** *v.tr.* (*a*) to move (s.o.) into a new house; to install (s.o., the furniture, etc.); (*b*) *Nau:* **e. un navire,** to fit up the accommodation in a ship. **2.** *v.i.* to move in; **e. dans une maison,** to move into a house.

emménagogue [ɛm(m)enagɔg, ãmen-], *s.m. Med:* emmenagogue.

emmener [ãmne], *v.tr.* (j'emmène, n. emmenons; j'emmènerai) (*a*) to lead, take, (s.o.) away, out; **il fut emmené en prison,** he was taken off, marched off, to prison; **e. les chevaux,** to lead away the horses; **je vous emmène avec moi,** I'm taking you with me; **je l'ai emmené passer l'hiver en Italie,** I took him off to spend the winter in Italy; **le train a brûlé Rugby et j'ai été emmené jusqu'à Crewe,** the train didn't stop at Rugby and I was taken on to Crewe; **le nouvel épicier a emmené toute ma clientèle,** the new grocer has taken away all my customers; *P:* **je t'emmène à la campagne!** go to hell, to blazes! *P:* **être emmené en belle,** to be taken for a ride; *pred.* **il fut emmené prisonnier,** he was taken away in custody; (*b*) *Mil: Sp:* to command; to lead; **chef qui sait e. ses troupes,** leader who knows how to command his troops; **les avants étaient bien emmenés par le capitaine,** the captain led the forwards well.

emmenotter [ãm(ə)nɔte], *v.tr.* to handcuff (prisoner, etc.).

emmensite [ɛmãsit], *s.f. Exp:* emmensite.

emment(h)al [emɛtal], *s.m.* Emment(h)al(er) (cheese).

emmerdant [ãmɛrdã], *a. P:* (bloody) annoying; **c'est e.,** it's a bloody nuisance; **tu es e.,** you're a pain in the neck.

emmerdement [ãmɛrdəmã], *s.m. P:* bloody nuisance; **quel e.!** what a bloody mess! **j'ai des emmerdements,** I've got problems.

emmerder [ãmɛrde], *v.tr. P:* **1.** *A:* to soil, dirty (one's pants, etc.). **2.** (*a*) to plague (s.o.); **tu m'emmerdes,** you bloody well get on my nerves; (*b*) **je l'emmerde,** he can go and get stuffed, knotted; **les voisins? je les emmerde!** the neighbours? they can go to hell!

s'emmerder, *P:* to be bored (stiff).

emmerdeur, -euse [ãmɛrdœːr, -øːz], *s. P:* bloody nuisance; **c'est un e.,** he's a bloody nuisance, the bloody limit.

emmétrope [ãmetrɔp]. **1.** *a.* emmetropic (eye). **2.** *s.* emmetrope.

emmétropie [ãmetrɔpi], *s.f.* emmetropia.

emmeulage [ãmølaːʒ], *s.m. Agr:* stacking (of cereals, etc.).

emmeuler [ãmøle], *v.tr. Agr:* to stack (cereals, etc.).

emmi [ãmi], *prep: A: Lit:* amid, in the midst of.

emmiellé [ãmjele], *a.* honeyed (words, etc.).

emmieller [ãmjele], *v.tr. A:* (*a*) to sweeten (sth.) with honey; (*b*) **e. un refus,** to soften (down) a refusal. **2.** *P: Hum:* (eupheumism for EMMERDER) to pester, plague (s.o.); *Iron:* **tu m'emmielles!** you sweet little so-and-so!

emmitonner [ãmitone], *v.tr. F:* **1.** to wrap (s.o.) up warmly (in shawl, etc.). **2.** to get round (s.o.).

emmitoufler [ãmitufle], *v.tr.* to muffle (s.o.) up (dans, de, in).

s'emmitoufler, to muffle up; **emmitouflée de fourrures, dans ses fourrures,** muffled up in furs, smothered in furs.

emmortaiser [ɑ̃mɔrteze], *v.tr. Carp:* to join (timbers) by tenon and mortise; to insert (end of timber) into a mortise.
emmotter [ɑ̃mɔte], *v.tr.* to cover roots of plant with soil for transport; to ball up.
emmouflage [ɑ̃muflaːʒ], **emmouflement** [ɑ̃mufləmɑ̃], *s.m. Cer:* placing (of pottery) in muffle furnace.
emmoufler [ɑ̃mufle], *v.tr.* to place (pottery) in muffle furnace.
emmouscailler [ɑ̃muskaje], *v.tr. P:* to annoy, plague (s.o.).
emmoustaché [ɑ̃mustaʃe], *a. A:* moustached, mustachioed.
emmurement [ɑ̃myrmɑ̃], *s.m.* walling in, immuring.
emmurer [ɑ̃myre], *v.tr.* to wall in, immure (victim, prisoner); to wall (in) (estate); **nous restions emmurés dans notre silence,** we remained locked in silence.
emmuseler [ɑ̃myzle], *v.tr.* **(j'emmuselle, n. emmuselons; j'emmusellerai)** *A:* **1.** to muzzle (dog). **2.** to gag (s.o.).
émodine [emɔdin], *s.f. Ch:* emodin.
émoi [emwa], *s.m.* emotion, agitation, excitement, anxiety; *(of bird, etc.)* **être (tout) en é.,** to be all of, in, a flutter; to be flurried; **sa visite causa un grand é.,** his visit caused a great commotion; **elle avait le cœur en é.,** her heart was in a flutter; **être en grand é. d'être renvoyé,** to stand in great fear of dismissal; **foule en é.,** excited crowd; **toute la ville était en é.,** the whole town was agog with excitement, was in a commotion; **je vins m'asseoir à côté d'elle non sans é.,** it was not without some emotion, trepidation, that I sat down beside her.
émollient [emɔljɑ̃], *a. & s.m. Pharm:* emollient; counter-irritant.
émolument [emɔlymɑ̃], *s.m.* **1.** *A:* *(a)* fee; *(b)* perquisite, benefit, advantage (derived from office, etc.). **2.** *pl.* remuneration, salary, pay, emoluments.
émolumentaire [emɔlymɑ̃tɛːr], *a.* emolumentary, remunerative (office, etc.).
émonction [emɔ̃ksjɔ̃], *s.f. Physiol:* excretion.
émonctoire [emɔ̃ktwaːr], *s.m. Physiol:* emunctory.
émondage [emɔ̃daːʒ], **émondement** [emɔ̃dmɑ̃], *s.m.* **1.** *Arb: etc:* pruning, trimming. **2.** cleaning (of grain, etc.); blanching (of almonds).
émonde [emɔ̃ːd], *s.f.* *(a)* **(arbre d')é.,** pollarded tree; *(b) pl.* prunings (of trees).
émonder [emɔ̃de], *v.tr.* **1.** *Arb:* to prune, trim; **é. un livre,** to cut down, prune, a book. **2.** to clean (grain, etc.); to blanch (almonds).
émondeur, -euse [emɔ̃dœːr, -øːz], *s. Arb:* pruner.
émondoir [emɔ̃dwaːr], *s.m. Arb:* pruning hook, knife; trimming axe.
émorfilage [emɔrfilaːʒ], *s.m.* removing of the wire edge (of tool), of the rough edge (of leather, etc.).
émorfiler [emɔrfile], *v.tr.* to remove the wire edge from (tool), the rough edge from (leather, etc.).
émotif, -ive [emɔtif, -iːv], *(a) a.* emotive; **peu é.,** irresponsive; *(b) s.* emotive person.
émotion [emosjɔ̃], *s.f.* **1.** emotion; **vive é.,** excitement; thrill; **ressentir une vive é. à la vue de qch.,** (i) to be greatly moved, (ii) to be thrilled, at the sight of sth.; **parler avec é.,** to speak feelingly; **(voyage, etc.) fertile en émotions,** thrilling (journey, etc.); *F:* **j'ai eu une é.,** I've had a shock. **2.** *A:* stir; **é. publique,** public disturbance; **calmer l'é. de la foule,** to calm the agitation of the crowd. **3.** *Med: A:* **é. du pouls,** quickening of the pulse.
émotionnable [emosjɔnabl], *a. F:* *(of pers.)* emotional, easily affected; excitable.
émotionnant [emosjɔnɑ̃], *a. F:* exciting, thrilling; moving (tale, etc.).
émotionnel, -elle [emosjɔnɛl], *F: a.* emotional.
émotionner [emosjɔne], *v.tr. F:* to agitate, thrill, affect, move, touch (s.o.); **le spectacle nous a profondément émotionnés,** we were overcome with emotion, deeply moved, we were thrilled, at the sight.
s'émotionner, *F:* to get excited, *U.S:* to emote.
émotivité [emɔtivite], *s.f.* susceptibility to emotion; emotivity, emotiveness.
émottage [emɔtaːʒ], **émottement** [emɔtmɑ̃], *s.m. Agr: etc:* breaking up of the clods (of field), of the lumps (of sugar).
émotter [emɔte], *v.tr. Agr: etc:* to break up, crush, the clods of (field), the lumps of (sugar, etc.).
émotteur, -euse [emɔtœːr, -øːz]. **1.** *s.* clod-crusher (farm-hand). **2.** *s.m. & f.* clod-crusher (roller).
émotteur-cribleur [emɔtœrkriblœːr], *s.m. Agr:* grain sifter; *pl. émotteurs-cribleurs.*
émottoir [emɔtwaːr], *s.m.* clod beetle.
émou [emu], *s.m. Orn:* emu; *pl. émous.*
émoucher [emuʃe], *v.tr.* *(a)* to drive, switch, whisk, away the flies from (animal, etc.); *(b) A: F:* **é. qn,** to beat, drub, s.o.
s'émoucher, *(of cow, horse, etc.)* to whisk away the flies.
émouchet [emuʃɛ], *s.m. Orn: F:* small hawk, *esp.* kestrel.
émouchetage [emuʃtaːʒ], *s.m.* **1.** breaking off of the point (of tools). **2.** *Tex:* hackling (of flax).
émoucheter [emuʃte], *v.tr.* **(j'émouchette, n. émouchetons; j'émouchetterai) 1.** *Fenc:* to take the button off (foil). **2.** to break off the point of (tool). **3.** *Tex:* to hackle (flax).
émoucheteur [emuʃtœːr], *s.m. Tex:* hackler.
émouchette [emuʃɛt], *s.f.* fly net (for horses).
émouchoir [emuʃwaːr], *s.m.* **1.** fly whisk. **2.** = ÉMOUCHETTE.
émouchure [emuʃyːr], *s.f. usu. pl. Tex:* combings.
émoudre [emudr], *v.tr. (conj. like* MOUDRE) *A:* to grind, sharpen, whet (tool, etc.).
émoulage [emulaːʒ], *s.m. A:* grinding, sharpening, whetting (of tools, etc.).
émouleur [emulœːr], *s.m. A:* (tool-)grinder, knife-grinder.
émoulu [emuly], *a.* **1.** *A:* sharpened, newly ground (tool, weapon); **se battre à armes émoulues,** to fight with sharp swords. **2.** *F:* **jeune homme frais é. du collège, de l'université,** young man fresh from school, down from the university.
émoussage [emusaːʒ], *s.m. Hort:* removal of moss (from trees, lawn, etc.).
émoussé [emuse], *a.* **1.** *(a)* blunt (edge, point, tool, angle); *(b)* blunted, dulled (senses, grief, etc.). **2.** *Geog:* *(a) s.m.* **indice d'é.,** degree of spheroidal weathering (of rock particle); *(b)* **grain é. luisant,** rock particle rounded by river erosion; **grain é. mat,** rock particle rounded by wind erosion.
émoussement [emusmɑ̃], *s.m.* *(a)* blunting (of blade, tool); *(b)* dulling (of the senses, etc.).
émousser[1] [emuse], *v.tr.* *(a)* to blunt (edge, point, tool, angle); to take the edge off (tool); *(b)* to dull, deaden, blunt (the senses, etc.); to take the edge off (appetite, pleasure); **é. la colère de qn,** to take the edge off s.o.'s anger; to mollify s.o.
s'émousser, *(a) (of tool, etc.)* to lose its edge, its point, its keenness; *(of razor)* to get dull; *(b) (of senses, passions)* to become blunted, dull, less keen; to cease to react; *(of stimulus, etc.)* to lose force.
émousser[2], *v.tr. Hort:* to remove the moss from (tree, lawn, etc.).
émoussoir [emuswaːr], *s.m.* moss knife; wire brush (for removing moss).
émoustillant [emustijɑ̃], *a.* *(a)* exhilarating, enlivening, cheering; **vin é.,** exhilarating, heady, wine; *(b)* that excites the passions; **beauté émoustillante,** rousing, exhilarating, beauty.
émoustiller [emustije], *v.tr.* *(a)* to exhilarate; to animate (s.o.); to put (s.o.) in a good humour; to cheer (s.o.) up; **é. ses invités par quelque histoire drôle,** to animate, liven up, rouse, one's guests with a funny story; *abs.* **le champagne émoustille,** champagne is exhilarating; *(b)* to excite, arouse, (s.o.'s) passions, senses.
émouvant [emuvɑ̃], *a.* moving; *(a)* touching (scene, etc.); *(b)* stirring, thrilling (incident).
émouvoir [emuvwaːr], *v.tr. (p.p.* **ému**; *otherwise conj. like* MOUVOIR) to move. **1.** *A:* to set (sth.) in motion; **é. le pouls,** to make the pulse irregular; **é. la bile à qn,** to move s.o. to anger, to rile s.o. **2.** *(a)* to excite, stir up, rouse (mob, etc.); to stir (audience); **é. les passions,** to stir, rouse, the passions; **é. la compassion de qn,** to stir s.o. to pity; *(b)* to affect, touch; **é. le cœur de qn,** to touch s.o.'s heart; **é. qn (jusqu')aux larmes,** to move s.o. to tears; **il est impossible de l'é.,** he is not to be moved; **ne vous laissez pas é.,** don't let yourself be upset; **il est facile à é.,** he is emotional, easily moved.
s'émouvoir. 1. to get excited, to be roused; **le pays s'émeut,** the country is in a state of excitement. **2.** to be touched, affected, moved; **s'é. à la vue de qch.,** to be affected at the sight of sth.; **il s'émeut d'un rien,** the least thing upsets him, puts him out; **il ne s'émeut de rien,** nothing disturbs him, puts him out; **sans s'é.,** calmly.
empaffer (s') [sɑ̃pafe], *v.pr. P:* to get drunk.
empaillage [ɑ̃pajaːʒ], *s.m.* **1.** packing (of goods, etc.) in straw; *Hort:* matting up (of plants); covering (of plants) with a straw litter. **2.** bottoming (of chairs) with straw. **3.** stuffing (of dead animals); taxidermy.
empaillé, -ée [ɑ̃paje]. **1.** *a.* *(a)* stuffed (with straw); *(b)* **oiseau e.,** stuffed bird; *F:* **avoir l'air e.,** to look like a stuffed owl. **2.** *a. & s.* lazy (person); lazybones; stupid (person); idiot, fool.
empaillement [ɑ̃pajmɑ̃], *s.m.* **1.** packing (of goods, etc.) in straw; *Hort:* covering (of plants) with straw. **2.** bottoming (of chairs) with straw. **3.** stuffing (of dead animals); taxidermy. **4.** *Agr:* *(a) Coll.* straw (from cereal crop); *(b)* **e. d'une ferme,** provision of straw (for litter) for a farm; *(c)* composting (of litter).
empailler [ɑ̃paje], *v.tr.* **1.** to pack (goods, etc.) in straw; to mat up (plants, pump, in winter); to cover up (plants) with a straw litter. **2.** to bottom (chair seat) with straw. **3.** to stuff (dead animal).
empailleur, -euse [ɑ̃pajœːr, -øːz], *s.* **1.** chair-bottomer. **2.** taxidermist.
empalement [ɑ̃palmɑ̃], *s.m.* impalement (of criminal, etc.).
empaler [ɑ̃pale], *v.tr.* to impale (criminal, etc.).
s'empaler, to impale oneself; **il s'est empalé sur une fourche en tombant,** he fell and impaled himself on, *F:* stuck himself with, a (garden) fork.
empalmage [ɑ̃palmaːʒ], *s.m.* palming (of coin, card, etc.).
empalmer [ɑ̃palme], *v.tr.* to palm (coin, card, etc.).
empamprer [ɑ̃pɑ̃pre], *v.tr.* to decorate (sth., s.o.) with vine leaves.
empan [ɑ̃pɑ̃], *s.m.* **1.** *Meas:* (22 cm) span (9 inches). **2.** *Psy:* span (of perception).
empanacher [ɑ̃panaʃe], *v.tr.* *(a)* to plume; to decorate (horse's head, helmet, etc.) with plumes; *(b)* **style empanaché,** pompous, flowery, style.
empannage [ɑ̃panaːʒ], *s.m. Nau:* gybe, gybing.
empanner [ɑ̃pane], *v.tr. Nau:* to bring (vessel) by the lee; *abs.* to gybe, to be brought by the lee.
empannon [ɑ̃panɔ̃], *s.m.* **1.** *Const:* jack rafter (of roof). **2.** *Veh:* shaft bar.
empansement [ɑ̃pɑ̃smɑ̃], *s.m. Vet:* blast.
empanser [ɑ̃pɑ̃se], *v.tr. Vet:* *(of food)* to blow (animal).
empantalonné [ɑ̃pɑ̃talɔne], *a.* trousered, in trousers.
empantouflé [ɑ̃pɑ̃tufle], *a. (of pers.)* slippered, in slippers.
empapilloter [ɑ̃papijɔte], *v.tr. O:* to put (hair) in curl-papers.
empaquetage [ɑ̃paktaːʒ], *s.m.* **1.** packing (of goods, etc.); doing up (of goods) into parcels. **2.** packing (material).
empaqueter [ɑ̃pakte], *v.tr.* **(j'empaquette, n. empaquetons; j'empaquetterai)** *(a)* to pack (sth.) up, to make (sth.) into a parcel; **e. un article (dans du papier),** to wrap up, do up, an article (in paper); **e. des gens dans une voiture,** to pack people into a car; *(b)* **e. un bras,** to bandage up an arm.
s'empaqueter, *F:* to wrap oneself up; *(of group of people)* to pack themselves (into a bus, etc.).
empaqueteur, -euse [ɑ̃paktœːr, -øːz], *s. Ind: etc: (pers.)* packer.
emparadiser [ɑ̃paradize], *v.tr. Lit:* to imparadise.
emparer (s') [sɑ̃pare], *v.pr.* *(a)* **s'e. de qch.,** take hold of, lay hands on, seize (upon), secure, possess oneself of, take possession of, to get hold of, sth.; **il s'empara de mon parapluie,** he seized hold of my umbrella; **s'e. de la conversation,** to monopolize the conversation; *(b)* **une grande frayeur s'empara d'elle,** she was seized with great fear; **leur émotion s'était emparée de moi,** their emotion had seized hold of me.
emparquer [ɑ̃parke], *v.tr.* to fold (sheep).
empatage [ɑ̃pataːʒ], *s.m.* = EMPATTEMENT.
empâtage [ɑ̃pɑtaːʒ], *s.m.* **1.** pasting (of covers of book, etc.). **2.** *Soapm:* saponification (of fat, oil). **3.** *(a) Brew:* mashing; *(b) Sugar R:* mixing (of sugar with syrup to remove impurities).
empâté [ɑ̃pɑte], *a.* clogged, choked; **langue, bouche, empâtée,** coated, sticky, tongue, mouth; **voix empâtée,** thick voice; **visage e.,** (i) gross, fleshy, bloated, face; (ii) pudding face; **cheval e.,** coarse, thickset, horse; *Mus:* **jeu e.,** over-slurred execution.
empateliner [ɑ̃patline], *v.tr. A:* to get round (s.o.).
empâtement [ɑ̃pɑtmɑ̃], *s.m.* **1.** pasting (of covers of book, of accumulator plate, etc.). **2.** *(a)* **e. des mains,** stickiness of the hands; **e. de la voix,** thickness, huskiness, of the voice; **e. (des chairs),** (i) putting on of flesh; (ii) fleshiness; *(b) Typ:* over-inking. **3.** *Husb:* fattening, cramming (of fowls). **4.** *Art:* impasting, impasto.

empâter [ɑ̃pɑte], *v.tr.* **1.** to paste (covers of book, accumulator plate, etc.). **2.** (*a*) **e. une lime,** to clog, choke up, a file; **s'e. les mains,** to make one's hands sticky; **boissons qui empâtent la bouche,** drinks that coat the palate; (*b*) *Typ:* to over-ink (type, etc.); (*c*) *Soapm:* **e. le corps gras,** to kill the goods. **3.** *Husb:* to fatten up, cram (fowls). **4.** *Art:* to impaste.

s'empâter, *F:* to put on flesh; **sa taille commence à s'e.,** she is losing her figure.

empâteur, -euse [ɑ̃pɑtœːr, -øːz], *s. Husb:* (poultry) fattener.

empathie [ɑ̃pati], *s.f.* empathy.

empathique [ɑ̃patik], *a.* empathic.

empattement [ɑ̃patmɑ̃], *s.m.* **1.** (*a*) joining, tenoning (of timbers); rooting-in (of turbine-blades); (*b*) **e. de torons,** joining of strands (for splicing). **2.** (*a*) foundation (of erection); footing (of wall, of spoke); racking (of wall); *Arb:* root swelling; flare (of tree); base-plate (of crane); basement (of bridge abutment); (*b*) wheelbase (of car, engine); width (of aircraft); (*c*) *Bot:* node, articulation (of stem); (*d*) *Typ:* serif (at foot of letter).

empatter [ɑ̃pate], *v.tr.* **1.** (*a*) to foot, tenon, joint (timbers); **e. les raies d'une roue,** to let in the spokes of a wheel; **e. les aubes d'une roue,** to root in the blades of a (water) wheel; (*b*) **e. des torons,** to join, lay in, strands (for splice). **2.** to support (crane, etc.); to fix (erection, etc.) on a foundation; **e. un mur,** to give footing to a wall.

empatture [ɑ̃patyːr], *s.f. Carp:* scarf joint.

empaume [ɑ̃pom], *s.f.* palm piece (of glove).

empaumer [ɑ̃pome], *v.tr.* (*a*) to catch (ball, etc.) in the palm of the hand; to strike (ball, etc.) with the palm of the hand, with a racquet, etc.; *A:* **e. la balle,** to seize the opportunity; (*b*) *Ven:* (*of hounds*) **e. la voie,** to get on the scent; (*c*) *A:* **e. une affaire,** to have a matter well in hand, to get a thorough grip of a matter; **e. qn,** to establish one's influence over s.o.; (*d*) *F:* **se laisser, se faire, e.,** to be tricked, taken in; to be swindled; (*e*) to palm (card, coin, etc.).

empaumure [ɑ̃pomyːr], *s.f.* **1.** palm piece (of glove). **2.** *Ven:* palm (of deer's antlers).

empêché [ɑ̃pɛʃe, -pɛ-], *a.* **1.** puzzled, at a loss; embarrassed; **on serait bien e. s'il fallait . . .,** one would be very much at a loss if one had to . . .. **2.** (*of rope, etc.*) fouled. **3.** *F:* être e. de sa personne, to be awkward, not to know what to do with oneself. **4.** unable to attend; unavoidably absent; busy; **faire l'e.,** to look busy.

empêchement [ɑ̃pɛʃmɑ̃], *s.m.* (*a*) obstacle, hindrance, impediment (**à,** to); prevention; **avoir un e.,** to be unable to attend; **je n'ai pas pu venir car j'ai eu un e.,** I couldn't come as something turned up (at the last minute); **excusez-moi de mon retard, j'ai eu un e.,** I'm sorry I'm late, I got held up; **mettre e. à qch.,** to put an obstacle in the way of sth.; **trouver un e. à qch.,** to find an objection to sth.; **être un e. à qch.,** to be a bar to sth.; **sans e.,** without (let or) hindrance; **sauf e.,** if nothing happens to prevent it, all being well, d.v.; **en cas d'e.,** in case of prevention; (*b*) **e. de la langue,** impediment of speech.

empêcher [ɑ̃pɛʃe, -pɛ-], *v.tr.* **1.** to prevent, hinder, impede, preclude; (*a*) **e. un mariage,** to prevent, put a stop to, a marriage; **cette muraille empêche la vue,** this wall obstructs the view; **ce vent empêchera la pluie,** this wind will keep the rain off; **e. la hausse,** to keep prices down; **je ne peux pas l'e.,** I cannot prevent it; *Prov:* **il faut souffrir ce que l'on ne peut e.,** what can't be cured must be endured; (*b*) **e. qn de faire qch.,** to prevent s.o. from doing sth.; **qu'est-ce qui vous a empêché de venir?** what prevented, kept, you from coming? what prevented your coming? **e. qn de partir,** to detain s.o.; to prevent s.o. from leaving; **le bruit l'empêche de dormir,** the noise prevents him from sleeping, keeps him awake; **son âge l'empêche de concourir,** his age debars him from competing; **je ne peux pas l'en e.,** I cannot prevent him; **que rien ne vous en empêche!** do it by all means! (*c*) **la pluie empêche que nous (ne) sortions,** the rain prevents us from going out; **je n'empêche pas que vous (ne) vous amusiez,** I am not preventing you from enjoying yourselves; (*d*) *impers.* **il n'empêche que cela nous a coûté cher,** all the same, and yet, nevertheless, for all that, it has cost us dear; **cela n'empêche qu'elle soit belle,** it doesn't prevent her from being beautiful, it doesn't mean she's not beautiful; *F:* **n'empêche,** (i) all the same; (ii) so what? **2.** *A:* (*of garment, etc.*) **e. qn,** to impede, hamper, s.o.'s movements.

s'empêcher (*usu. neg.*) to refrain (**de,** from); **je ne pouvais m'e. de rire,** I couldn't help laughing, I had to laugh; **on ne peut s'e. de penser qu'il a raison,** one can't help thinking he's right.

empêcheur, -euse [ɑ̃pɛʃœːr, -øːz], *s. F:* hinderer; **e. de danser en rond,** spoil-sport, wet blanket; **c'est un e. de tourner rond,** he's the nigger in the woodpile.

Empédocle [ɑ̃pedɔkl], *Pr.n.m. Gr.Hist:* Empedocles.

empédocléen, -éenne [ɑ̃pedɔkleɛ̃, -eɛn], *a.* Empedoclean.

empeignage [ɑ̃pɛɲaːʒ], *s.m.* maximum width (of material which can be woven on a given loom).

empeigne [ɑ̃pɛɲ], *s.f.* (*a*) vamp, upper (of shoe); (*b*) *P:* **gueule d'e.,** (i) ugly face, mug; (ii) disagreeable person, sourpuss.

empeigner [ɑ̃pɛɲe], *v.tr. Tex:* to warp (loom).

empellement [ɑ̃pɛlmɑ̃], *s.m.* sluice (used to retain water in a pond).

empeloter [ɑ̃p(ə)lɔte], *v.tr.*, **empelotonner** [ɑ̃p(ə)lɔtɔne], *v.tr.* to wind (wool, string, etc.) into a ball; to ball (wool, etc.).

s'empeloter, (*of bird of prey*) to pellet (its food).

empelotonnage [ɑ̃p(ə)lɔtɔnaːʒ], *s.m.* balling (of knitting wool, etc.).

empênage [ɑ̃pɛnaːʒ], *s.m.* **1.** works of a lock. **2.** (box-)staple (of lock).

empêner [ɑ̃pɛne], *v.tr.* to adjust the works of (a lock).

empennage [ɑ̃pɛnaːʒ], *s.m.* (*a*) feathering, feathers (of arrow); (*in archery*) fletching; fins, vanes (of bomb); fins (of torpedo, etc.); (*b*) *Av:* tail unit; stabilizers, rudders (of aircraft); **embase d'e.,** tail cone; **raccord(ement) d'e.,** tail fillet; **saumon d'e.,** stabilizer tip; **surface d'e.,** tail area.

empenne [ɑ̃pɛn], *s.f.* feather (of arrow).

empenné [ɑ̃pɛne], *a.* feathered (arrow, etc.); finned, vaned (bomb, etc.).

empennelage [ɑ̃pɛnlaːʒ], *s.m. Nau:* backing (of anchor).

empenneler [ɑ̃pɛnle], *v.tr.* (**j'empennelle, n. empennelons; j'empennellerai**) *Nau:* to back (anchor).

empennelle [ɑ̃pɛnɛl], *s.f. Nau:* back anchor.

empennement [ɑ̃pɛnmɑ̃], *s.m.* = EMPENNELAGE.

empenner [ɑ̃pɛne], *v.tr.* (*a*) to feather, fletch, (arrow); to fit the fins or vanes on (bomb, etc.); (*b*) to fit the tail unit on to (aircraft).

empennon [ɑ̃pɛnɔ̃], *s.m.* = EMPENNE.

empenoir [ɑ̃pənwaːr], *s.m. Tls:* mortise-lock chisel, lock-mortise chisel.

empercher [ɑ̃pɛrʃe], *v.tr.* **1.** *Agr:* to set up poles for (hops, etc.). **2.** *Ven:* to stake (deer for disembowelling).

empereur [ɑ̃prœːr], *s.m.* **1.** (*a*) emperor; (*b*) *abs.* (Holy Roman) emperor; (*c*) **l'E.,** Napoleon I. **2.** (*a*) *Ent:* silver-washed fritillary; (*b*) *Ich:* (i) swordfish; (ii) emperor fish; (*c*) *Moll:* top-shell; (*d*) *Orn:* wren; (*e*) *Rept:* emperor (boa).

emperler [ɑ̃pɛrle], *v.tr.* (*a*) to ornament (clothes, etc.) with pearls; (*b*) to bead (dress, bag, etc.); **fleurs emperlées par la rosée,** flowers pearled by the dew; **front emperlé de sueur,** forehead beaded with perspiration; **trop e. son style,** to overdecorate one's style.

emperruqué [ɑ̃peryke], *a. A:* bewigged; periwigged.

empesage [ɑ̃pəzaːʒ], *s.m.* (*a*) starching (of linen, etc.); (*b*) starchiness, stiffness (of manner).

empesé [ɑ̃pəze], *a.* (*a*) starched (collar, etc.); (*b*) stiff, starchy, unbending (manner, etc.); stiff, affected (style); **il a l'air e.,** he looks (very) stiff, stand-offish.

empeser [ɑ̃pəze], *v.tr.* (**j'empèse, n. empesons; j'empèserai**) **1.** to starch (linen, etc.). **2.** *Nau:* to wet (sail).

empeseuse [ɑ̃pəzøːz], *s.f. Tex: etc:* starching machine.

empesté [ɑ̃pɛste], *a.* foul, pestilential.

empester [ɑ̃pɛste], *v.tr.* **1.** (*rare*) to infect with the plague, pestilence. **2.** to infect (place, etc.) with bad smells; to make (sth.) stink; **air empesté par le tabac,** air reeking of tobacco; **il nous empestait de son haleine,** his breath was dreadful; **e. le monde de mauvaises doctrines,** to corrupt the world with unsound doctrines. **3.** *abs.* to stink; **e. l'alcool,** to reek of alcohol.

empétracées [ɑ̃petrase], *s.f.pl. Bot:* Empetraceae.

empêtre [ɑ̃pɛːtr̥], *s.m. Bot:* empetrum; **e. à fruits noirs,** crowberry.

empêtré [ɑ̃pɛtre], *a.* awkward, embarrassed.

empêtrement [ɑ̃pɛtrəmɑ̃], *s.m.* entanglement.

empêtrer [ɑ̃pɛtre], *v.tr.* **1.** to hobble (animal). **2.** to entangle; **s'e. les pieds dans les broussailles,** to catch one's feet, get one's feet entangled, in the undergrowth; **elle était empêtrée dans, par, son grand manteau,** she was hampered by her long coat; **e. qn dans une querelle,** to involve s.o. in a quarrel; **e. qn par des questions indiscrètes,** to embarrass s.o. with indiscreet questions; *s.a.* POULE 1.

s'empêtrer, (*a*) to become entangled; **s'e. de colis,** to hamper oneself with luggage; **empêtré dans le varech,** floundering among the seaweed; (*b*) **s'e. dans une mauvaise affaire,** to get involved, entangled, mixed up, in a bad business; **s'e. dans une explication,** to get all tangled up in an explanation.

empeuré [ɑ̃pœre], *a. A:* frightened, scared.

emphase [ɑ̃fɑːz], *s.f.* **1.** (*a*) *Pej:* bombast, turgidity, grandiloquence, pomposity; **écrire avec e.,** to write in a bombastic, high-flown, turgid, style; (*b*) exaggeration; **dévouement sans e.,** simple devotion. **2.** *Ling:* (*a*) emphasis; **prononcer un mot avec e.,** to lay stress on a word; (*b*) metaphorical expression.

emphatique [ɑ̃fatik], *a.* **1.** bombastic, pompous, grandiloquent, turgid (style, speech, etc.). **2.** *Ling:* emphatic (form, word, etc.).

emphatiquement [ɑ̃fatikmɑ̃], *adv.* grandiloquently; in a bombastic manner, style; bombastically.

emphysémateux, -euse [ɑ̃fizematø, -øːz], *a. Med:* emphysematous.

emphysème [ɑ̃fizɛm], *s.m. Med:* emphysema.

emphytéose [ɑ̃fiteoːz], *s.f. Jur:* long lease (18 to 99 years); hereditary lease.

emphytéote [ɑ̃fiteɔt], *s.m. & f. Jur:* holder of a long lease; hereditary lessee.

emphytéotique [ɑ̃fiteɔtik], *a. Jur:* **bail e.,** long lease (18 to 99 years); building lease; **redevance e.,** ground rent.

emphytie [ɑ̃fiti], *s.f. Hort:* enphytotic (disease) (of plants).

empididés [ɑ̃pidide], *s.m.pl. Ent:* Empididae.

empiècement [ɑ̃pjɛsmɑ̃], *s.m.* yoke (of dress, etc.).

empiéger [ɑ̃pjeʒe], *v.tr.* (*conj. like* PIÉGER); (*a*) to trap, snare (bird, etc.); (*b*) to deceive, trick (s.o.).

empierrement [ɑ̃pjɛrmɑ̃], *s.m. Civ.E:* **1.** (*a*) metalling, macadamization (of road); *Rail:* ballasting (of track); (*b*) paving; (*c*) *Agr:* filling (of trench, ditch) with stones (for drainage purposes). **2.** macadam, (road) metal; *Rail:* ballast; **e. de base,** bottoming (of road).

empierrer [ɑ̃pjere, -ere], *v.tr. Civ.E:* (*a*) to metal, macadamize (road); *Rail:* to ballast (track); (*b*) to pave; (*c*) *Agr:* to fill (ditch) with stones (for drainage purposes).

empiétement [ɑ̃pjetmɑ̃], *s.m.* (*a*) encroachment, trespass (**sur,** on); infringement (**sur,** of); *Jur:* **e. des autorités,** abuse of administrative authority; (*b*) **e. de la mer sur les terres,** encroachment of the sea on the land.

empiéter [ɑ̃pjete], *v.* (**j'empiète, n. empiétons; j'empiéterai**) **1.** *v.i.* (*a*) **e. sur le terrain, l'autorité, les loisirs, de qn,** to encroach (up)on s.o.'s land, authority, leisure; **e. sur les droits de qn,** to infringe s.o.'s rights; **la mer empiète sur les côtes,** the sea is encroaching on the land; (*b*) *of tile, etc.*) **e. sur . . .,** to overlap . . .. **2.** *v.tr.* *A:* (*a*) **e. un arpent sur le champ d'un voisin,** to filch an acre from a neighbour's field; (*b*) **e. le pouvoir suprême,** to usurp the supreme power. **3.** *v.tr. Arch: A:* **e. une statue,** to provide a statue with a pedestal. **4.** *v.tr.* (*of goshawk*) to seize (prey) in its talons.

empiffrer [ɑ̃pifre], *v.tr. P:* to cram, stuff (s.o. with food); **e. un enfant de bonbons,** to stuff a child with sweets, *U.S:* candies.

s'empiffrer, *P:* to gorge, guzzle; to have a good tuck-in; **s'e. de gâteaux,** to gorge oneself on cakes.

empilable [ɑ̃pilabl̥], *a.* stackable.

empilage[1] [ɑ̃pilaːʒ], *s.m.* **1.** stacking, piling up. **2.** *Gasm:* **empilages réfractaires,** fire-brick chequer-work (of regenerator).

empilage[2], *s.m. Fish:* mounting (of hook).

empile [ɑ̃pil], *s.f. Fish:* leader, snell, casting line, cast.

empilement [ɑ̃pilmɑ̃], *s.m.* (*a*) stacking, piling (up) (of wood, coal, etc.); (*b*) **un e. invraisemblable de caisses,** an incredible pile, stack, of packing cases; (*c*) *Geol:* piling up (of strata in recumbent overfolds, etc.).

empiler[1] [ɑ̃pile], *v.tr.* **1.** (*a*) to stack, to pile (up) (wood, coal, books, etc.); (*b*) **e. des voyageurs dans un compartiment,** to cram passengers into a compartment; (*c*) **e. des écus,** to amass, pile up, money. **2.** *P:* to cheat, rob (s.o.); **se faire e.,** to get rooked.

s'empiler, to pile up; **les livres s'empilent sur la table,** the books are piling up on the table; **les gens s'empilaient dans les voitures du métro,** people were crowding, piling, into the tube train.

empiler², *v.tr. Fish:* to mount (hook).

empileur, -euse [ɑ̃pilœːr, -øːz], *s.* **1.** stacker, piler (of wood, etc.). **2.** *P:* cheat, swindler, fraud.

empiper [ɑ̃pipe], *v.tr.* to barrel (herrings).

empirance [ɑ̃pirɑ̃s], *s.f.* debasement (of coinage).

empire [ɑ̃piːr], *s.m.* **1.** (*a*) sovereign authority, imperial rule; dominion; sway; **e. des mers,** command of the sea; **sous l'e. d'un tyran,** under the rule, sway, of a tyrant; (*b*) influence, control; **exercer un e. sur qn,** to have an influence, power, over s.o.; **il a perdu son e. sur l'opinion,** he has lost his hold on people's opinion; **e. sur soi-même,** self-command, self-control, self-mastery; **avoir de l'e. sur soi-même,** to be self-restrained, self-possessed, to be master, mistress, of oneself; **perdre l'e. sur soi-même,** to lose one's self-control, to lose control of oneself; **sous l'e. de la nécessité,** under the pressure of necessity; **cœur sous l'e. de l'ambition,** heart dominated by ambition; **agir sous l'e. de la colère,** to be actuated by anger; **l'e. de la mode,** the dominating influence of fashion; **il était sous l'e. de la boisson quand il a commis le crime,** he was under the influence of drink when he committed the murder. **2.** empire; (*a*) reign (of emperor); **Dioclétien abdiqua l'e.,** Diocletian abdicated as emperor; (*b*) (*territory forming an empire*) **l'E. romain, byzantin,** the Roman, Byzantine, Empire; *Rom.Hist:* **le bas E.,** the Lower, Later Empire; *Hist: A:* **l'E. du Milieu, le Céleste E.,** the Celestial Empire (China); *Hist:* **le Saint-E. romain (germanique),** the Holy Roman Empire; **l'E. britannique,** the British empire; **constructeur d'empires,** empire builder; (*c*) *Fr.Hist:* **le premier E.,** *abs.* **l'E.,** the First Empire; **le second E.,** the Second Empire; *a.inv.* **style, meubles, e.,** Empire style, furniture; (*d*) empire (of industrialist, etc.); (*d*) *Lit:* **l'e. des morts,** the realm of the dead; **l'e. de Neptune,** Neptune's empire.

empirement [ɑ̃pirmɑ̃], *s.m.* worsening, deterioration.

empirer [ɑ̃pire], *v.* to worsen. **1.** *v.tr.* to make (sth.) worse, to aggravate (an ill, etc.); **pour e. les choses,** to make matters worse. **2.** *v.i.* to become, grow, worse; **l'état du malade a empiré,** the patient has taken a turn for the worse; **la position a empiré depuis,** the position has since worsened; **les affaires empirent de jour en jour,** business gets worse and worse, is going from bad to worse.

empiriocriticisme [ɑ̃pirjɔkritisism], *s.m. Phil:* empiriocriticism.

empirique [ɑ̃pirik]. **1.** *a.* empiric(al), rule-of-thumb (method, etc.). **2.** *s.m.* empiric, empiricist.

empiriquement [ɑ̃pirikmɑ̃], *adv.* empirically; by rule of thumb.

empirisme [ɑ̃pirism], *s.m.* empiricism; **e. médical,** quackery.

empiriste [ɑ̃pirist], *s.m.* empiricist.

emplacement [ɑ̃plasmɑ̃], *s.m.* **1.** (*a*) site (of, for, building, etc.); (*b*) location (of works, etc.); (*c*) place, spot. **2.** (*a*) *Mil:* emplacement (of gun), gun pit; station (of troops in peace); (dis-) position (of troops, etc., on battlefield); (*b*) berth (of ship); **e. de chargement,** loading berth.

emplage [ɑ̃plaːʒ], *s.m. Constr:* rubble, infilling, filling-in material (for wall).

emplanter [ɑ̃plɑ̃te], *v.tr.* to plant (piece of ground).

emplanture [ɑ̃plɑ̃tyːr], *s.f.* (*a*) step (of mast); **mettre un mât dans son e.,** to step a mast; (*b*) *Av:* root, socket (of wing); (*c*) footing (of turbine blade).

emplastique [ɑ̃plastik], *a.* emplastic.

emplâtre [ɑ̃plɑːtr], *s.m.* **1.** (*a*) *Pharm:* (i) plaster; (ii) sticking plaster; **e. contre, pour, les cors,** corn plaster; *F:* **mettre un e. à sa fortune,** to patch up one's fortune; *F:* **c'est mettre un e. sur une jambe de bois,** it's no earthly use; (*b*) *F:* spineless person; **c'est un e.,** he's got no backbone. **2.** *Aut: Cy:* gaiter (for repair of tyre), outer-cover patch. **3.** *P:* **appliquer un e. sur la figure de qn,** to give s.o. a slap in the face. **4.** *F:* food that lies heavy on the stomach.

emplâtrer [ɑ̃plɑtre], *v.tr.* (*a*) to apply a plaster to (sth.); (*b*) *P:* **e. qn de paquets,** to load s.o. up with parcels.

emplectite [ɑ̃plektit], *s.f. Miner:* emplectite.

emplette [ɑ̃plɛt], *s.f.* **1.** purchase (of goods), shopping; **aller faire ses emplettes,** to go shopping; **faire e. d'un chapeau,** to purchase a hat; **être de bonne e.,** to be worth buying, to be a bargain; **j'ai fait une mauvaise e.,** I've made a bad bargain. **2.** purchase (= *thing purchased*); **mettre ses emplettes dans un panier,** to put one's purchases, one's shopping, into a basket.

empli [ɑ̃pli], *s.m. Soapm:* filling of the moulds.

emplir [ɑ̃pliːr]. **1.** *v.tr.* to fill (up); **la foule emplissait les rues,** the crowd filled the streets; **nouvelle qui m'emplit de joie,** news that fills me with delight. **2.** *v.i. Nau:* (*of ship*) to have a leak.

s'emplir, to fill up, to become full; *Nau:* (*of boat*) to be, become, swamped, waterlogged.

emplissage [ɑ̃plisaːʒ], *s.m.* (= REMPLISSAGE) filling.

emplisseur, -euse [ɑ̃plisœːr, -øːz], *s.* **1.** *s.m. or f.* (*pers.*) filler (of barrels, cans, etc.). **2.** *s.f.* (*machine*) automatic chain filler (of petroleum barrels, etc.).

emploi [ɑ̃plwa], *s.m.* **1.** use, employment (of sth.); **mode d'e.,** manner of using (sth.); directions for use; **je n'en ai pas (le) besoin mais j'en ai l'e.,** I don't need it but I can certainly use it; **il nous expliqua l'e. de sa journée,** he told us how he had spent the day; **e. du temps,** (i) daily routine; (ii) time-table (of work), allotment of time; **l'e. de l'acier dans la construction moderne,** the use of steel in modern building; **l'e. des troupes en temps d'émeute,** the calling out of the armed forces in times of disturbance; **faire e. de la force,** to resort to force; **e. d'un mot,** usage of a word; **mot qui fait double e.,** word that is a useless repetition; *Book-k:* **double e.,** duplication (of entry); (*of book entry, etc.*) **faire double e. avec . . .,** to duplicate with . . .; **faux e.,** wrong entry; **faire un e. de qch.,** to put sth. to a use; **faire un bon e. de qch.,** to make good use of sth., to put sth. to good use; **immeuble sans e.,** building standing empty; *Fin:* **reliquat sans e.,** unexpended balance. **2.** employment, occupation, post, job; **être sans e.,** to be out of work, out of a job, to be unemployed; **quel est son e.?** what is his occupation? what does he do (for a living)? **perdre son e.,** to lose one's job; *Pol.Ec:* **plein e.,** full employment; **e. à temps complet, à plein temps,** full-time employment; **e. à temps partiel,** part-time employment; **il n'est pas dans son e.,** he's a square peg in a round hole; **les emplois militaires et civils,** the military and civil services; **e. public,** public office; **remplir un e.,** to hold a position, an office; *Journ:* **demandes d'e.,** situations wanted; **offres d'e.,** situations vacant; *Th:* **e. d'un acteur,** special line of an actor; **tenir l'e. de père noble,** to play heavy fathers, the heavy father; **tenir plusieurs emplois dans une troupe,** to act several kinds of parts in a company.

emplombé [ɑ̃plɔ̃be], *a.* lead-coated.

employable [ɑ̃plwajabl], *a.* employable; utilizable (material, etc.).

employé, -ée [ɑ̃plwaje], *s.* employee; **e., employée, de magasin,** shop assistant; *U.S:* clerk; **e. à la vente,** salesman; **e. de banque,** bank clerk; **e. (de bureau),** office worker; **e. au classement,** filing clerk; **e. de l'expédition,** shipping clerk; **employés et ouvriers,** black-coated and manual workers; **e. d'administration,** government employee, civil servant; **e. des chemins de fer,** railway employee; **l'e. du gaz,** the gas man (who reads the meters).

employer [ɑ̃plwaje], *v.tr.* **(j'emploie, n. employons; j'emploierai) 1.** (*a*) to employ, use (sth.); **e. toutes sortes de moyens,** to use every possible means; **je ne peux pas e. ces articles,** I can't make use of these things; **e. son argent à l'achat de livres,** to use one's money to buy books; **e. toute son industrie à faire qch.,** to devote all one energies to doing sth.; **e. tout son temps à s'amuser,** to spend all one's time (in) enjoying oneself; **bien e. son temps,** to make good use of, the most of, one's time; **mal e. son temps,** to misuse one's time; **ne savoir à quoi e. son temps,** to be hard up for something to do; **mot qui s'emploie au figuré,** word that is used in the figurative sense; **vêtement qui emploie trois mètres d'étoffe,** garment that requires three metres of material; **machine à écrire qui emploie de grands formats,** typewriter that takes large sizes; (*b*) *Book-k:* **e. une somme en recette, en dépense,** to put, enter, an amount in the receipts, in the expenditure. **2.** (*a*) to employ (workmen, etc.); **je l'emploie à jardiner,** I employ him to do the garden; **je l'ai employé à cela,** I used him on that; I gave him that to do; *pred.* **e. qn comme secrétaire,** to employ s.o. as secretary; (*b*) **e. qn,** to make use of s.o.'s services.

s'employer, to occupy oneself; **il s'emploie à jardiner,** he spends his time gardening; **s'e. à une tâche urgente,** to get busy on an urgent job; **s'e. à fond pour,** to do everything within one's power to; **s'e. pour qn,** to exert oneself, interest oneself on s.o.'s behalf; **il ne s'emploie pas,** he doesn't exert himself.

employeur, -euse [ɑ̃plwajœːr, -øːz], *s.* (*a*) employer (of labour); (*b*) **e. et mandataire,** principal and agent.

emplumé [ɑ̃plyme], *a.* (*a*) feathered; **bête emplumée,** bird; (*b*) *Orn:* feather-legged.

emplumement [ɑ̃plymmɑ̃], *s.m. Orn:* feathering.

emplumer [ɑ̃plyme], *v.tr.* **1.** (*a*) to feather (an arrow); to decorate, trim (sth.) with feathers; (*b*) to tar and feather (s.o.). **2.** *A:* to quill (harpsichord).

s'emplumer. 1. (*of bird*) to grow feathers. **2.** to adorn oneself with feathers. **3.** *F:* to feather one's nest.

emplure [ɑ̃plyːr], *s.f.* gold-beater's skin.

empoche [ɑ̃pɔʃ], *s.f. Com:* cash advance (given to salesman, etc. in order that he can give change).

empocher [ɑ̃pɔʃe], *v.tr.* (*a*) to pocket (money, etc.); (*b*) **e. une insulte,** to pocket an insult; **e. quelques bonnes vérités,** to listen to a few home truths; **e. un coup,** to be hit, to receive a blow.

empodium [ɑ̃pɔdjɔm], *s.m. Ent:* empodium.

empoignade [ɑ̃pwaɲad], *s.f. F:* quarrel, row, *F:* shindy, set-to.

empoignant [ɑ̃pwaɲɑ̃], *a.* thrilling, stirring, poignant (episode, etc.).

empoigne [ɑ̃pwaɲ], *s.f.* (*a*) (*rare*) seizure, grabbing (of s.o., sth.); (*b*) *F:* **acheter qch. à la foire d'e.,** to get sth. on the crook; **la vie n'est qu'une foire d'e.,** life's just a rat race.

empoignement [ɑ̃pwaɲmɑ̃], *s.m.* arrest, capture.

empoigner [ɑ̃pwaɲe], *v.tr.* **1.** (*a*) to grasp, seize, grip, grab, to lay hold of (s.o., sth.); **elle lui empoigna le bras, elle l'empoigna par le bras,** she seized him by the arm; **e. l'occasion,** to seize the opportunity; (*b*) to insult (s.o.); (*c*) **ils se sont empoignés,** they quarrelled, came to blows. **2.** *F:* to catch, arrest, *F:* collar (criminal, etc.). **3.** to thrill, grip, to take hold of (reader, spectator); **pièce qui empoigne les spectateurs,** play that grips the audience.

empointer¹ [ɑ̃pwɛ̃te], *v.tr.* to point (tool, needle, etc.).

empointer², *v.tr.* to tack (down), to give a few stitches to (roll of cloth, etc.).

empointure [ɑ̃pwɛ̃tyːr], *s.f. Nau:* earing, peak (of sail).

empois [ɑ̃pwa], *s.m.* (*a*) starch(paste); (*b*) *Tex:* dressing; **donner de l'e. à un tissu,** to stiffen a material.

empoise [ɑ̃pwaːz], *s.f. Mch:* plummer block; chock (of rolling mill, etc.).

empoisonnant [ɑ̃pwazɔnɑ̃], *a. F:* poisonous; annoying, irritating; **odeur empoisonnante,** stench, putrid smell; **pièce empoisonnante,** putrid, rotten, play.

empoisonné [ɑ̃pwazɔne], *a.* **1.** poisoned; **mourir e.,** to die of poison; **vie empoisonnée de remords,** life embittered with remorse. **2.** (*a*) poisoned (food, arrow, etc.); *P:* **herbe empoisonnée,** deadly nightshade; (*b*) poisonous (doctrine, etc.). **3.** *F:* (*of pers.*) fed up.

empoisonnement [ɑ̃pwazɔnmɑ̃], *s.m.* (*a*) poisoning; **e. par, à, l'arsenic,** poisoning by arsenic; **e. de l'esprit,** poisoning of the mind; **e. des masses,** corruption of the masses; (*b*) *Atom.Ph:* progressive reduction in efficiency (of nuclear fuel in reactor); (*c*) *F:* stench, stink; (*d*) *F:* **cette affaire ne me donne que des empoisonnements,** I've had nothing but trouble from that business; **quel e. que cette femme!** what a pest that woman is!

empoisonner [ɑ̃pwazɔne], *v.tr.* **1.** to poison (s.o.) *abs.* **la belladone empoisonne,** belladonna is poisonous; *F:* **e. la vie de qn,** to embitter, poison, s.o.'s life; **e. la jeunesse,** to corrupt youth. **2.** (*a*) to poison (food, etc.); **odeur qui empoisonne l'air,** smell that infects the air; (*b*) *abs. F:* to stink; *with cogn. acc.* **ça empoisonne le tabac ici,** this room is reeking of tobacco; **ce fromage empoisonne,** this cheese stinks to high heaven. **3.** *F:* to bore (s.o.) to death; to plague, pester (s.o.).

s'empoisonner. 1. to poison oneself, to take poison. **2.** *F:* to get bored.

empoisonneur, -euse [ɑ̃pwazɔnœːr, -øːz]. **1.** *s.* poisoner; *F:* **cet hôtelier c'est un e.!** this hotel keeper wants to poison his customers! **2.** *s. F:* bore. **3.** *a.* poisonous (doctrine, etc.).

empoisser [ɑ̃pwase], *v.tr.* (*a*) (*rare*) to coat with pitch; (*b*) **e. son visage avec de la confiture,** to smear one's face with jam; (*c*) **il s'assit à une table empoissée,** he sat down at a (filthy) greasy table.

empoissonnage [ɑ̃pwasɔnaːʒ], *s.m.*, **empoissonnement** [ɑ̃pwasɔnmɑ̃], *s.m.* stocking (of pond, river).

empoissonner [ɑ̃pwasɔne], *v.tr.* to stock (pond, etc.) with fish.

empoitraillé [ɑ̃pwatraje], *a.* broad-chested (horse, etc.).

empommer (s') [sɑ̃pɔme], *v.pr.* (*of cattle*) to choke (on an apple).

emporétique [ɑ̃pɔretik], *a.* **papier e.**, filter paper.

emporium [ɑ̃pɔrjɔm, ɛmp-], *s.m. Rom.Ant:* emporium; *pl. emporia.*

emport [ɑ̃pɔːr], *s.m. Jur:* **e. d'objets volés**, asportation.

emporté, -ée [ɑ̃pɔrte], *a. & s.* **1.** irascible, quick-tempered, hot-headed (person); *s.* hot-head; **caractère e.**, passionate nature. **2.** runaway (horse, etc.). **3.** *a.* woody (tree).

emportement [ɑ̃pɔrtəmɑ̃], *s.m.* **1.** (*a*) transport (of anger, *occ.* of joy, love, etc.); **dans l'e. de la discussion**, in the heat of debate; (*b*) anger; **se laisser aller à son e.**, to give way to one's anger; **répondre avec e.**, to make a heated reply, to reply angrily. **2.** racing (of propeller, etc.).

emporte-pièce [ɑ̃pɔrtəpjɛs], *s.m.inv. Tls:* punch; *Leath:* pinking iron; *Dom.Ec:* pastry cutter; **découper qch. à l'e.-p. (dans la tôle)**, to stamp sth. out (of sheet-iron); **c'est un e.-p.**, he is very cutting, sarcastic; **style (à l') e.-p.**, sharp, clear, style; style with punch in it; **mots à l'e.-p.**, biting, cutting, words; words that tell; *adv.phr.* **à l'e.-p.**, neatly, trenchantly.

emporter [ɑ̃pɔrte], *v.tr.* **1.** to carry, take (s.o., sth.) away; **e. un blessé sur un brancard**, to carry off, bear away, a wounded man on a stretcher; **emportez tout cela**, take all that away; **ils ont emporté de quoi manger**, they have taken food with them; **vin à e.**, wine for off-consumption; **faire e. ses meubles**, to have one's furniture removed; **il emporta son secret dans la tombe**, he carried his secret to the grave; *F:* **il ne l'emportera pas en paradis**, I'll get my own back sooner or later; *F:* **(que) le diable l'emporte!** the devil take him! he can go to hell! **2.** (*a*) to carry, tear, sweep, (s.o., sth.) away; **l'inondation a emporté le pont**, the flood swept away the bridge; **emporté par les vagues**, washed away by the waves; **un obus lui emporta le bras**, a shell carried away his arm; **le choléra l'emporta**, cholera carried him off; **le vent emporta son chapeau**, the wind blew off his hat; **la haine emporte toute réserve**, hatred breaks down all reserve; **autant en emporte le vent**, it's all idle talk; *F:* **cette moutarde vous emporte la bouche**, this mustard takes the roof off your mouth; (*b*) **e. un fort**, to carry, take, a fort (by assault); **e. la victoire, la journée**, to carry off the victory, to carry the day; (*c*) **e. un morceau de qch.**, to cut a piece of sth. clean off; **outil qui emporte les pièces**, tool that stamps out, punches out, the parts; *A:* **emporter la pièce, le morceau**, to be very trenchant; *F:* **e. le morceau**, to succeed, to get one's own way; (*d*) **cet argument emporta du coup la balance**, this argument at once turned the scale. **3.** (*a*) to carry (s.o., sth.) along; **le torrent emporta le bateau**, the torrent carried the boat along; **son cheval l'emporta à travers champs**, his horse carried him across country; **se laisser e. par, à, la colère**, to give way to, let oneself be carried away by, anger; (*b*) **ce point essentiel emporte tout le reste**, everything hangs on this essential point; (*c*) **tout devoir emporte un droit**, every duty implies a right. **4. l'e. sur qn, qch.**, to get the better of s.o., sth.; to best s.o.; **l'e. sur ses ennemis**, to triumph over one's enemies; **l'e. dans une discussion**, to have the best of an argument; **l'e. sur qn en éloquence**, to surpass s.o. in eloquence; **la société l'emporte en valeur sur l'individu**, society is worth more than the individual; **considérations qui l'emportent sur toutes les autres**, considerations which override all others; **l'e. en nombre sur . . .**, to outnumber . . .; **le bon l'emportait sur le mauvais**, good outweighed bad; **qui à votre avis l'emportera?** who do you think will carry the day? will have the best of it?

s'emporter. 1. to allow oneself to be carried away (by passion, etc.); to lose one's temper, to fly into a passion, into a rage; **s'e. contre qn**, to lose one's temper with s.o.; **s'e. contre le vice**, to declaim against vice; *F:* **s'e. comme une soupe au lait**, to fire up, blaze up, in a moment; to flare up, to go off the deep end. **2.** (*of horse*) to bolt. **3.** *Arb:* (*of tree*) to run to wood.

emposieu, -ieux [ɑ̃pozjø], *s.m. Geol:* (*in the Jura*) aven; swallow-hole.

empotage [ɑ̃pɔtaːʒ], *s.m.* potting (of plants, jam, etc.).

empoté [ɑ̃pɔte], *a. & s.* (*a*) **plante empotée**, potted plant; (*b*) *F:* awkward, clumsy (person); slow-coach.

empotement [ɑ̃pɔtmɑ̃], *s.m.* (*a*) potting (of plants, etc.); (*b*) *Jur:* verification of cubic capacity of wine etc. barrel (by filling from standard measures).

empoter [ɑ̃pɔte], *v.tr.* to pot (plants, jam, etc.); *Min:* to set (pit prop) in its socket.

empouilles [ɑ̃puːj], *s.f.pl. A.Jur:* standing crops.

empouper [ɑ̃pupe], *v.tr. Nau:* **le vent empoupe le navire**, the wind is aft, astern.

empourpré [ɑ̃purpre], *a.* crimson.

empourprer [ɑ̃purpre], *v.tr.* **1.** to tinge (sth.) with crimson. **2.** to give a purple tinge to (grapes, etc.).

s'empourprer, (*a*) to flush; **ses joues s'empourprèrent**, his cheeks flushed scarlet, burned red; **son visage s'empourpra**, he flushed, he turned purple; (*b*) (*of sky, etc.*) to turn crimson; **l'horizon s'empourpre**, the horizon glows with a crimson light.

empoussiéré [ɑ̃pusjere], *a.* covered with dust; dusty.

empoussiérer [ɑ̃pusjere], *v.tr.* (*conj. like* ACCÉLÉRER) to cover with dust.

empoutrerie [ɑ̃putrəri], *s.f.* girderage.

empreindre [ɑ̃prɛ̃ːdr], *v.tr.* (*pr.p.* **empreignant**; *p.p.* **empreint**; *pr.ind.* **j'empreins, il empreint, n. empreignons, ils empreignent**; *p.d.* **j'empreignais**; *p.h.* **j'empreignis**; *fu.* **j'empreindrai**) to impress, imprint, stamp; **e. un sceau dans de la cire**, to impress a seal on wax; **souvenirs qui s'empreignent sur l'esprit**, memories that have made a lasting impression on the mind.

empreint [ɑ̃prɛ̃], *a.* stamped, impressed; **pas empreints sur le sable**, footprints on the sand; **visage e. de mélancolie**, face marked, stamped, with sadness; **visage e. d'énergie**, face characterized by energy; **visage e. de terreur**, face full of terror; **la fatigue empreinte sur son visage**, the marks of fatigue on his face.

empreinte [ɑ̃prɛ̃ːt], *s.f.* **1.** (*a*) impress(ion), (im)print, stamp; **e. en plâtre**, plaster cast; **e. à la cire**, wax impression; **e. des roues**, trace, track, of the wheels; **e. du pied, de pas**, footprint; **e. de doigt**, fingermark; **e. de pouce**, thumb print; *Adm:* **e. digitale**, fingerprint; **e. du génie**, stamp, mark, of genius; **prendre l'e. de qch.**, to take an impression of sth.; **marquer qch. d'une e.**, to stamp sth.; **roue à e.**, toothed marking-wheel; (*b*) *Typ:* mould (from standing type); **prendre l'e. d'une page**, to mould a page; (*c*) *Dent:* impression; **e. pour prothèse (dentaire)**, denture impression; (*d*) *pl. Ven:* track (of game). **2.** *Paint:* priming.

empressé, -ée [ɑ̃prɛse], *a. & s.* eager, zealous; **peu e.**, backward, slow **(à faire qch.**, in doing sth.); **des soins empressés**, assiduous attentions; *Corr:* **agréez mes salutations empressées**, (I am) yours faithfully; *s.* **faire l'e. auprès de qn**, (i) to dance attendance on s.o., to fuss around s.o.; (ii) to show, pay, marked attention to s.o.; **ne faites pas l'e.**, don't fuss, don't be so officious; **écarter les empressés**, to keep busybodies at a distance.

empressement [ɑ̃prɛsmɑ̃], *s.m.* (*a*) eagerness, readiness, willingness, alacrity; **e. de qn à faire qch.**, eagerness, readiness, of s.o. to do sth.; **faire qch. avec e.**, to do sth. readily, with alacrity, *F:* like a shot; **écouter qn avec e.**, to listen eagerly to s.o.; **mettre beaucoup d'e. à faire qch.**, to show great keenness in doing sth.; **marquer un grand e. à faire qch.**, to be eager to do sth.; **montrer peu d'e. à faire qch.**, (i) to show reluctance to do sth.; to hold back; (ii) to do sth. half-heartedly; (*b*) bustling zeal; **témoigner de l'e. auprès de qn**, to pay marked attention(s) to s.o.

empresser (s') [sɑ̃prɛse], *v.pr.* **1.** to hurry; **s'e. de faire qch.**, to make haste to do sth.; **il s'empressa de répondre à ma lettre**, he lost no time in answering my letter; **il s'empressa de rentrer à la maison**, he hurried home. **2. s'e. à faire qch.**, to show eagerness, zeal, in doing sth.; to be sedulous in doing sth.; **s'e. auprès de qn**, (i) to dance attendance on s.o.; (ii) to pay marked attention(s) to s.o.; **la foule s'empresse autour de l'orateur**, the crowd presses round the speaker; **les médecins s'empressent auprès des blessés**, the doctors are busy with the wounded.

emprésurer [ɑ̃prezyre], *v.tr.* to add rennet to (milk).

emprise [ɑ̃priːz], *s.f.* **1.** *A:* (*a*) emprise, enterprise; (*b*) *Her:* device. **2.** (*a*) expropriation or acquisition (of land for public purposes); (*b*) land or ground acquired (for public purposes); **e. du chemin de fer, de la voie ferrée**, railway, *U.S:* railroad, territory. **3.** (*a*) ascendancy (over person or mind); hold **(sur**, on); **tenter des emprises sur les consciences**, to attempt to work on the public conscience; **phénomène qui échappe à l'e. humaine**, phenomenon that eludes the human grasp; (*b*) **sous l'e. de (qn, qch.)**, under the influence of (s.o., sth.).

emprisonnement [ɑ̃prizɔnmɑ̃], *s.m.* imprisonment; **e. à vie**, life imprisonment; **e. cellulaire**, solitary confinement.

emprisonner [ɑ̃prizɔne], *v.tr.* to imprison (s.o.); to put (s.o.) in prison; **e. qn dans sa chambre**, shut s.o. up in his room; **il s'emprisonne dans sa chambre**, he shuts himself up in, refuses to leave, his room; **e. un gaz dans qch.**, to confine a gas in sth.; **chaleur emprisonnée dans qch.**, heat bottled up in sth.; **les rives qui emprisonnent le fleuve**, the banks that hold back the river (in its bed); **son cou emprisonné dans un faux-col raide**, his neck imprisoned in a stiff collar; *abs.* **le parti que l'on sert emprisonne**, the (political) party for which one works holds one prisoner, holds one in its grasp.

emprisonneur, -euse [ɑ̃prizɔnœːr, -øːz], *s.* imprisoner, incarcerator.

emprosthotonie [ɑ̃prɔztɔtɔni], *s.f.*, **emprosthotonos** [ɑ̃prɔztɔtɔnɔs], *s.m. Med:* emprosthotonos.

emprunt [ɑ̃prœ̃], *s.m.* **1.** borrowing; **faire un e. à qn**, to borrow (money) from s.o.; **offrir qch. à qn à titre d'e.**, to offer sth. to s.o. as a loan, on loan; **vivre d'emprunts**, to live by borrowing; **objets d'e.**, borrowed articles; **ce mot est un e. au latin**, this word is a borrowing from Latin; **nom d'e.**, assumed name; **science d'e.**, superficial, sham, learning; **gaieté d'e.**, affected cheerfulness; **route d'e.**, alternative road, by-pass; **e. à une œuvre littéraire**, excerpt, quotation, from a literary work; *Civ.E:* **e. de terre**, borrow pit. **2.** loan; **e. d'État**, government loan; **e. remboursable sur demande**, call money; **contracter un e.**, to raise a loan; **procéder à un nouvel e.**, to make a new issue of capital, a new loan issue.

emprunté [ɑ̃prœ̃te], *a.* **1.** (*a*) assumed, false (name, etc.); sham (learning); (*b*) derived (meaning); borrowed (idea, etc.). **2.** self-conscious, stiff, awkward (manner, appearance, etc.).

emprunter [ɑ̃prœ̃te], *v.tr.* to borrow; **e. de l'argent à qn**, *abs.* **e. à qn**, to borrow (money) from s.o.; **e. une idée de, à, qn**, to borrow, *F:* crib, an idea from s.o.; **mot emprunté, au, du, latin**, word taken, borrowed, from Latin; **la lune emprunte sa lumière du soleil**, the moon derives its light from the sun; **e. de l'argent sur une terre**, to borrow money on the security of an estate, to raise a loan on an estate; **e. à intérêt**, to borrow at interest; *St.Exch:* **e. des actions**, to take the rate; **e. un nom**, to assume a name; **le cortège emprunta la rue de Rivoli**, the procession followed the Rue de Rivoli; (*of train*) **e. une voie**, to make use of a track; *Prov:* **ne choisit pas qui emprunte**, beggars can't be choosers.

emprunteur, -euse [ɑ̃prœ̃tœːr, -øːz]. **1.** *s.* borrower; *Jur:* bailee. **2.** *a.* (*a*) given to borrowing; (*b*) borrowing (state, corporation).

empuantir [ɑ̃pɥɑ̃tiːr], *v.tr.* to infect (the air); to make (sth.) stink.

s'empuantir, to become foul, malodorous, offensive.

empuantissement [ɑ̃pɥɑ̃tismɑ̃], *s.m.* (*a*) (act of) becoming foul, beginning to stink; (*b*) (act of) contaminating (sth.), making (sth.) stink.

empusa [ɑ̃pyza], **empuse** [ɑ̃pyːz], *s.f.* **1.** *Fung:* empusa; **e. de la mouche**, fly fungus. **2.** *Ent:* empusa.

empyème [ɑ̃piɛm], *s.m. Med:* **1.** empyema, pyothorax. **2.** operation for empyema.

empyréal, -aux [ɑ̃pireal, -o], *a.* empyreal, empyrean.

empyrée [ɑ̃pire], *a. & s.m.* empyrean.

empyreumatique [ɑ̃pirømatik], *a.* empyreumatic(al).

empyreume [ɑ̃pirøm], *s.m.* empyreuma.

ému[1] [emy], *a.* affected (by emotion), moved; **voix émue**, voice touched with emotion; **parler d'une voix émue**, to speak with emotion; **parler d'une voix fortement émue**, to speak with deep emotion; **nous étions tous très émus**, we were all (i) deeply moved, deeply affected, (ii) greatly excited; **conserver un souvenir é. de qn**, to have a tender recollection of s.o.; **trop é. pour répondre**, too much affected to answer; **contempler qn d'un air é.**, to look at s.o. with emotion; **vous paraissez tout é.**, you look agitated, upset; **se sentir un peu é.**, to feel a bit nervous.

ému², *s.m. Orn:* = ÉMEU.

émulateur, -trice [emylatœːr, -tris], *s.* **1.** *A:* (*a*) rival, competitor; (*b*) **é. de la gloire de qn,** emulator of s.o.'s fame. **2.** *Elcs:* control unit (which enables a computer to process data designed for another computer).

émulation [emylasjɔ̃], *s.f.* emulation, rivalry, competition; **exciter l'é. de qn,** to put s.o. on his mettle.

émule [emyl], *s.m. & f.* emulator, rival, competitor; **il a été votre é. en courage,** he has been your equal in courage.

émulseur [emylsœːr], *s.m.* (*device*) emulsifier.

émulsibilité [emylsibilite], *s.f.* emulsibility, emulsifiability.

émulsif, -ive [emylsif, -iːv], *a.* emulsive.

émulsifiable [emylsifjabl̩], *a.* emulsifiable.

émulsifiant [emylsifjɑ̃], *a.* **1.** *a.* emulsifying (agent). **2.** *s.m.* emulsifier.

émulsificateur [emylsifikatœːr], *s.m.* emulsifier.

émulsification [emylsifikasjɔ̃], *s.f.* = ÉMULSIONNEMENT.

émulsifier [emylsifje], *v.tr.* to emulsify.

émulsifieur [emylsifjœːr], *s.m.* emulsifier.

émulsine [emylsin], *s.f. Ch:* emulsin.

émulsion [emylsjɔ̃], *s.f.* emulsion.

émulsionnable [emylsjɔnabl̩], *a.* emulsible.

émulsionnant [emylsjɔnɑ̃], (*a*) *a.* emulsifying (agent); (*b*) *s.m.* emulsifier.

émulsionnement [emylsjɔnmɑ̃], *s.m.* emulsification.

émulsionner [emylsjɔne], *v.tr.* to emulsify, emulsionize.

émulsionneur [emylsjɔnœːr], *s.m.* (*device*) emulsifier.

émulsoïde [emylsɔid], *s.m. Ch:* emulsoid.

émyde [emid], *s.f. Rept:* emys; freshwater, marsh, tortoise; emyd.

émydidés [emidide], *s.m.pl. Rept:* Emydidae.

en¹ [ɑ̃], *prep.* **1.** (*place*) (*a*) *introducing a sb. not particularized;* in, (in)to; **être, aller, en ville,** to be in town, to go (in)to town; **en province,** in the country, in the provinces; **être en prison,** to be in prison; **mettre qn en prison,** to put s.o. in prison; **venir en chemin de fer, en auto,** to come by train, by car; **en avion,** by air, by plane; **amener qn à la gare en voiture,** to drive s.o. to the station; **être en bateau, en autobus,** to be in a boat, a bus; **en tête, en queue,** at the head, in the rear; **la suite en quatrième page,** continued on page four; **être en montagne,** to be in the mountains; **il est parti en mer,** he's gone to sea; **il est en mer,** he's at sea; **professeur en Sorbonne,** professor at the Sorbonne; (*with f. names of countries*) **être, aller, en France, en Amérique,** to be in, to go to, France, America; *s.a. under* ARRIÈRE 1, AVANT I. 5, BAS III, 1, DEDANS 1, DEHORS 1, DESSOUS 1, HAUT III. 3, *etc.*; (*b*) *with pers. pron.* **il y a quelque chose en lui que j'admire,** there is something I admire about him; **un homme en qui, en lequel, j'ai confiance,** a man whom I trust; **avoir en soi toutes les qualités d'un bon professeur,** to possess all the qualifications of a good teacher; **ils savent créer le bonheur en eux,** they know how to create happiness within themselves; (*c*) *with def. art., poss. adj., etc.*; **en l'honneur de qn,** in honour of s.o.; **en votre honneur,** in your honour; **regarder en l'air,** to look up at the sky; **s'épuiser en d'inutiles efforts,** to exhaust oneself in useless efforts; **décédé en son domicile,** who passed away in his home; **le mariage aura lieu en l'église Saint-Jean,** the marriage will be celebrated at St. John's (church). **2.** (*time*) in; (*a*) **en été, en automne, en hiver,** in (the) summer, autumn, winter; **né en 1905,** born in 1905; **ne parlez pas tous en même temps,** don't all speak at the same time, at once; **d'aujourd'hui en huit,** to-day week; (*b*) **on peut aller à Londres en cinq jours,** one can go to London in five days; it takes five days to go to London; (*c*) *with def. art., poss. adj., etc.*; **en l'an 1800,** in (the year) 1800; **en ce temps-là,** in those days, at that time; **en nos temps,** in our time; **en l'absence du chef,** in the absence of the chief; **en son absence,** in his absence. **3.** (*a*) (*state*) in; **être en deuil, en loques,** to be in mourning, in rags; **arbres en fleur,** trees in blossom; **être en guerre,** to be at war; **en réparation,** under repair; **en congé,** on leave; **en faction,** on guard; **en tournée,** on tour; **en vacances,** on holiday; **une femme en tablier,** a woman in an apron, with an apron on; **une femme en cheveux,** a woman without a hat; **peindre qch. en bleu,** to paint sth. blue; (*b*) (*material*) **montre en or,** gold watch; **escalier en bois,** wooden staircase; (*c*) (*manner*) **escalier en spirale,** spiral staircase; **chemin en pente,** inclined road; **faire cent à l'heure en palier,** to do 100 kilom. an hour on the level; **docteur en médecine,** doctor of medicine; **peintre en bâtiment,** house painter; **fort, faible, en mathématiques,** good, bad, at mathematics; (*d*) (*change, division*) into; **il fut changé en serpent,** he was changed into a serpent; **traduire une lettre en français,** to translate a letter into French; **briser qch. en morceaux,** to break sth. into bits; **partager qch. en trois portions,** to divide sth. into three; **casser qch. en deux,** to break sth. in two; (*e*) **de . . . en . . .,** from . . . to . . .; **de mal en pis,** from bad to worse; **de fleur en fleur,** from flower to flower; **d'année en année,** from year to year, year by year; **attendre qn de jour en jour,** to wait for s.o. day after day; (*f*) **acheter en vrac,** to buy in bulk; **vendre en paquets, en feuilles,** to sell in packets, in sheets. **4.** *introducing a pred. complement*; as, like, in the manner of; **envoyer qch. en cadeau,** to send sth. as a present; **on lui donna une petite terre en compensation,** he was given a small estate by way of compensation; **il m'a traité en gentilhomme,** he treated me (i) like the gentleman he is, (ii) as was due to a gentleman; **il mourut en brave,** he died like the brave man that he was; **agir en soldat, en honnête homme,** to act like a soldier, like an honest man; **prendre la chose en philosophe,** to take the thing philosophically. **5.** *with gerund*; **il répondit en riant,** he answered laughingly, with a laugh; **menacer qn en plaisantant,** to threaten s.o. by way of a joke; **travailler en chantant,** to sing at one's work; **on apprend en vieillissant,** we learn as we grow older; **se consoler en pensant que . . .,** to console oneself with the thought that . . .; **en faisant cela vous l'offenserez,** by doing that you will offend him; **en arrivant à Paris . . .,** on arriving in Paris . . .; **en vous écrivant hier j'avais oublié de vous dire que . . .,** when writing to you yesterday, I forgot to mention that . . .; **buvez un bock en attendant,** drink a glass of beer while waiting; **tout en chantant je l'observais,** I watched him as I sang; **tout en tricotant elle nous racontait des histoires,** as she knitted she told us stories; **il marchait en lisant son journal,** he walked along reading his paper; **il s'est enrhumé en marchant sous la pluie,** he caught a cold (through) walking in the rain; **elle entra, sortit, en dansant,** she danced into, out of, the room; **il monta l'escalier en soufflant,** he puffed his way upstairs; **en n'en prenant pas davantage,** by not taking any more; **en n'en soufflant mot,** not breathing a word of it; **il sortit en riant,** he went out laughing; **j'ai été fort étonné en voyant cela,** I was very surprised to see that; **vous réussirez en travaillant,** you'll succeed by working, if you work.

en², *unstressed adv. and pron.* I. *adv.* **1.** from there, thence; **vous avez été à Londres?—oui, j'en arrive,** you've been to London?—Yes, I've just come from there. **2.** on that account; **si vous étiez riche, en seriez-vous plus heureux?** if you were rich, would you be happier on that account, any the happier? **s'en trouver mieux,** to feel better for it; **c'est à n'en pas croire ses yeux,** one cannot believe one's eyes.

II. **en,** *pron.inv.* **1.** (*a*) *standing for a sb. governed by* **de**; of (from, by, with, about) him, her, it, them; **vous avez appris la nouvelle?—oui, nous en parlions,** you have heard the news?—yes, we were speaking of it, about it; **j'aime mieux n'en pas parler, ne pas en parler,** I would rather not speak about it; **qu'en pensez-vous?** what do you think about it? **les rues en sont pleines,** the streets are full of it, of them; **il reçut une blessure et en mourut,** he received a wound and died of it; **je ne m'en tairai point,** I refuse to keep quiet about it; **il l'aime et il en est aimé,** he loves her and is loved by her; **il rencontra une jeune fille et en devint amoureux,** he met a girl and fell in love with her; (*b*) *with expressions of quantity,* **combien avez-vous de chevaux?—j'en ai un, trois, plusieurs,** how many horses have you got?—I have one, three, several; **il en est mort un,** one of them is dead; **il y en a un que je vais vendre,** there is one that I am going to sell; **je vais en vendre la moitié, le tiers,** I am going to sell half of them, a third of them; (*c*) *replacing the possessive, when the possessor is inanimate,* **nous avons visité l'église, et en avons admiré les vitraux,** we visited the church and admired its stained glass; **j'ai la valise mais je n'en ai pas la clef,** I have the suitcase but I haven't the key of it; **et grande en fut la ruine,** and great was the fall thereof; (*d*) *neut. standing for a clause,* **vous remplacer, il n'en est pas capable,** he is not fit to take your place; **il ne l'a pas fait, mais il en est capable,** he did not do it but he is capable of it. **2.** *standing for a partitive sb.,* some, any; **j'en ai,** I have some; **je n'en ai pas,** I have none; **en avez-vous?** have you any? **si vous n'avez pas de livres on vous en prêtera,** if you have no books we will lend you some; **parmi ces livres il y en a d'excellents,** among these books are some excellent ones; **des amis, j'en ai beaucoup,** friends I've (got) plenty. **3.** (*indeterminate uses*) **je n'en ai pas encore fini avec lui,** I have not done with him yet; **vous en savez plus long que moi,** you know more (about it) than I do; **si le cœur vous en dit,** if you feel so inclined; **on s'en est donné,** we had a great time; **il en est ainsi,** that's the way it is; **voulez-vous en être?** will you join us? (*many other similar uses will be found under the relevant verbs, e.g.* AVOIR, ÊTRE; ALLER, ARRIVER, VENIR; CROIRE, FAIRE, FALLOIR, POUVOIR, VOULOIR). **4.** *in stressed position after imperative*; **prenez-en,** take some; **prenez-en dix,** take ten; **va-t'en,** go away; **juges-en par toi-même,** judge of it for yourself.

en- [ɑ̃], before *b, m, p,* **em-** [ɑ̃], *pref.* **1.** en-, em-; **embarquer,** to embark; **encadrer,** to enframe; **enlacer,** to enlace; **enrichir,** to enrich. **2.** in-, -im-; **encourir,** to incur; **enfreindre,** to infringe; **emprisonner,** to imprison. **3.** be-; **embarbouiller,** to besmear; **engourdir,** to benumb.

énallage [enalaːʒ], *s.f. Gram:* enallage.

enamouré [ɑ̃namure], **énamouré** [enamure], *a.* **être e. de qn,** to be in love with s.o.; **être e. du théâtre,** to be stage-struck.

enamourer (s') [sɑ̃namure], **énamourer (s')** [senamure], *v.tr.* to fall in love (de, with).

énanthème [enɑ̃tɛm], *s.m. Med:* enanthem(a); *pl.* enanthems, enanthemata.

énantiomorphe [enɑ̃tjɔmɔrf], *a.* enantiomorphous.

énantiomorphisme [enɑ̃tjɔmɔrfism], *s.m. Ch:* enantiomorphism.

énantiose [enɑ̃tjoːz], *s.f. Phil:* enantiosis.

énantiotrope [enɑ̃tjɔtrɔp], *a. Ch:* enantiotropic.

enarbrer [ɑ̃narbre], *v.tr.* to fix (wheel) on an axle, on a shank.

énargite [enarʒit], *s.f. Miner:* enargite.

énarme [enarm], *s.f. A.Arm:* enarme.

énarque [enark], *s.m. Pej:* higher civil servant who graduated at the *École Nationale d'Administration.*

énarration [enarasjɔ̃], *s.f. A:* detailed account.

énarrer [enare], *v.tr. A:* to give a detailed account of (sth.).

enarrher [ɑ̃nare], *v.tr.* to give earnest money to (landlord, etc.).

en-arrière [ɑ̃narjɛːr], *s.m.inv.* (*Skating*) backward glide.

énarthrodial, -aux [enartrɔdjal, -o], *a. Anat:* enarthrodial.

énarthrose [enartroːz], *s.f. Anat:* enarthrosis, ball-and-socket joint.

énaser (s') [senaze], *v.pr.* to hit one's nose hard (against sth.).

en-avant [ɑ̃navɑ̃], *s.m.inv.* **1.** *Fb:* forward pass; *Rugby Fb:* knock-on. **2.** (*skating*) forward glide.

en-but [ɑ̃by], *s.m.inv. Rugby Fb:* in-goal.

encabanage [ɑ̃kabanaːʒ], *s.m.* preparing (of (wicker) trays for silkworms).

encabaner [ɑ̃kabane], *v.tr.* to prepare ((wicker) trays for silkworms).

s'encabaner, *Fr.C:* to shut oneself up; to see nobody; *F:* to hole up, dig in.

encablure [ɑ̃kablyːr], *s.f. Nau: A:* cable('s length) (= one-tenth of a nautical mile, = 185 m. approx.).

encadastrer [ɑ̃kadastre], *v.tr.* to enter (estates) on the public register.

encadenasser [ɑ̃kadnase], *v.tr.* to padlock (sth.) to put (sth.) under lock and key.

encadré [ɑ̃kadre], *s.m. Typ: Journ:* box.

encadrement [ɑ̃kadrəmɑ̃], *s.m.* **1.** (*a*) framing; (*b*) *Mil:* officering (of unit); *Ind: Adm:* **personnel d'c.,** managerial staff; (*c*) *Artil:* bracketing (of target); straddle. **2.** (*a*) framework; frame (of picture, etc.); **e. de porte, de fenêtre,** door-, window-frame, -architrave; **dans l'e. de la porte,** in the doorway; **e. de gazon,** border of turf; *Typ:* **e. en filets,** ruled border (of page); rule box; (*b*) *Nau:* hatch coaming; (*c*) setting (of story, etc.).

encadrer [ɑ̃kadre], *v.tr.* **1.** (*a*) to frame (picture, etc.); **cheveux noirs encadrant un visage pâle,** black hair framing, encircling, a pale face; **e. un journal de noir,** to put a black border round a paper; **jardin encadré de haies,** garden enclosed by hedges; **plates-bandes qui encadrent le jardin,** flower beds that border the garden;

anecdote mal encadrée (dans un chapitre), anecdote in a wrong setting; (*b*) **le prévenu est encadré par deux gendarmes,** the accused (man) is flanked by two policemen. **2.** *Mil:* (*a*) **e. un bataillon,** to officer a battalion; (*b*) **e. des recrues,** (i) to enrol recruits; (ii) to stiffen raw troops with a draft of trained men. **3.** *Artil:* to straddle, bracket (objective). **4.** *Equit:* to get (horse) well under one. **5.** *P:* **je ne peux pas l'e.,** I can't stand him, I hate the sight of him. **6.** *F:* **il a encadré un arbre,** he wrapped his car round a tree.

encadreur [ãkadrœːr], *s.m.* picture framer; picture-frame maker.

encagement [ãkaʒmã], *s.m.* (*a*) caging (of bird, etc.); *Artil:* **tir d'e.,** barrage fire to cut off a point; box-barrage; (*b*) *F:* imprisoning.

encager [ãkaʒe], *v.tr.* (**j'encageai(s); n. encageons**) (*a*) to cage (bird, etc.); **tenir qn encagé,** to keep s.o. caged up, imprisoned; (*b*) *Min:* to cage (truck, etc.).

encageur [ãkaʒœːr], *s.m. Min:* (*a*) cager, cage man; (*b*) (*machine*) cager.

encagoulé [ãkagule], *a.* hooded.

encaissable [ãkɛsabl̩], *a. Fin:* (en)cashable, collectable (bill).

encaissage [ãkɛsaːʒ], *s.m.* **1.** *Hort:* planting (of shrubs, etc.) in tubs; tubbing. **2.** boxing, casing, packing (of goods).

encaissant [ãkɛsã], *a.* (*a*) *Geol:* enveloping (strata); (*b*) beetling, overhanging (rocks, etc.).

encaisse [ãkɛs], *s.f.* **1.** *Com: Fin:* cash (in hand); **e. d'un magasin,** till money; **e. de 1000 francs,** cash balance of 1000 francs; **e. or et argent d'un pays,** gold and silver holding of a country; **e. métallique,** gold and silver coin and bullion; *Bank:* **pas d'e.,** no funds. **2.** *Box: F:* (*blows received*) **homme dur à l'e.,** man who stands punishment.

encaissé [ãkɛse], *a.* boxed in; deeply embanked (river); sunken (road); **vallée encaissée,** deep, narrow, valley; **méandre e.,** incised, enclosed, meander; **tournant e.,** blind corner (of road).

encaissement [ãkɛsmã], *s.m.* **1.** (*a*) incasing; encasing; casing, packing, boxing (of goods); **e. d'arbres,** planting of trees in tubs; tubbing; (*b*) *Fin:* encashment, receipt, collection (of money or bills); (*c*) paying in (of cheque); **donner un chèque à l'e.,** to pay in a cheque. **2.** (*a*) embanking (of river); trenching (of ground for bed of new road); (*b*) embankment (of river); **e. d'une route,** ballast bed of a road; (*c*) *N.Arch:* casing.

encaisser [ãkɛse], *v.tr.* **1.** (*a*) to encase, incase (sth.); **e. des marchandises,** to pack goods into cases or crates; to box, case, goods; **e. des arbres,** to plant trees in tubs; to tub, box, trees; (*b*) to encash, receive, collect (money, bill); *F:* **e. un coup,** (*of boxer*) to take a blow; (*of ship*) to be hit; **apprendre à e. (les coups),** to learn to take a blow, to learn to stand punishment; **il a encaissé,** he was severely punished; **il sait e.,** he can take it; **e. des chocs,** to be jolted; **e. les obus sans sourciller, sans broncher,** to stick it under shell fire, to take a shelling without flinching, without turning a hair; **elle encaisse sans broncher,** she grins and bears it; **j'ai encaissé,** I put up with it; **e. une observation,** to take a remark in good part; **je n'encaisse pas son air professoral,** I can't stand his professorial attitude; **je ne peux pas l'e.,** I can't stand him at any price; I can't stomach him; (*c*) **e. un effet,** to cash a bill. **2.** *Civ.E:* to embark (river); to trench the ground for (new road); to ballast (road).

s'encaisser, (*of river*) to flow into a gorge; (*of road, etc.*) to run through a cutting.

encaisseur [ãkɛsœːr], *s.m.* **1.** *Fin: Com:* (*a*) collector, receiver (of bill, cheque, etc.); payee; (bank) cashier; (*b*) bank messenger; (*c*) collector (of gas company, etc.); (*d*) *a.* collecting (banker, etc.). **2.** *F:* boxer who can stand punishment, who can take it.

encalifourchonné [ãkalifurʃɔne], *a. A:* astraddle.

encalminé [ãkalmine], *a. Nau:* becalmed, in the doldrums.

encan [ãkã], *s.m.* (public) auction; **vendre qch. à l'e.,** to sell sth. by, at, auction; **mettre qch. à l'e.,** to put sth. up for auction; **justice à l'e.,** venal justice.

encanaillement [ãkanɑjmã], *s.m.* mixing with the rabble, keeping low company.

encanailler [ãkanɑje], *v.tr.* (*a*) to degrade (s.o., the mind, etc.); to drag (s.o.) down; (*b*) to fill (one's house) with low company.

s'encanailler, to frequent low company; to get into low habits; **la société s'encanaille,** society is going to the dogs.

encanaquer(s') [sãkanake], *v.pr. F:* to go native.

encapé [ãkape], *a. Nau:* embayed.

encapeler [ãkaple], *v.tr.* (**j'encapelle, n. encapelons; j'encapellerai**) *Nau:* to make fast (rope).

encaper [ãkape], *Nau:* **1.** *v.tr.* to embay (ship). **2.** *v.i.* to get embayed.

encapuchonner [ãkapyʃɔne], *v.tr.* to put a hood, a cowl, on (s.o.); to hood, cover (funnel, piece of machinery, etc.).

s'encapuchonner. 1. (*a*) to put on a hood, a cowl; to wrap up one's head; (*b*) to enter a monastery. **2.** (*of horse*) to curve, arch, the neck.

encaquement [ãkakmã], *s.m.* barrelling (of herrings).

encaquer [ãkake], *v.tr.* to barrel (herrings, etc.); *F:* to pack (passengers, etc.) in like sardines.

encarpe [ãkarp], *s.m. Arch:* encarpus.

encart [ãkaːr], *s.m.* (*a*) *Bookb:* inset (of 4 or 8 pages); insert; (*b*) *Typ:* inset of a small photograph, map, etc., on a larger one.

encartage [ãkartaːʒ], *s.m.* **1.** (*a*) *Bookb:* insetting; (*b*) carding (of pins, etc.). **2.** (*a*) *Bookb:* inset (leaf, advertisement); inlay; insert; (*b*) card (holding pins, etc.).

encartée [ãkarte], *s.f.* registered prostitute.

encarter [ãkarte], *v.tr.* **1.** (*a*) *Bookb:* to inset (pages, leaflets, etc.); to inlay (plates); (*b*) to insert (leaflet, prospectus, in book); **supplément littéraire encarté dans chaque numéro,** literary supplement folded in with each number. **2.** to card (pins, etc.). **3.** *Adm:* to register (prostitute); (*cf.* CARTE 3 (*c*).)

encarteuse [ãkartøːz], *s.f.* machine for carding pins, buttons, etc.

encarteuse-piqueuse [ãkartøːzpikøːz], *s.f. Bookb:* wire-stitcher; *pl. encarteuses-piqueuses.*

encartonner [ãkartɔne], *v.tr.* **1.** *Typ:* to put (printed sheets) between boards (for pressing and glazing). **2.** *Com:* **e. un article,** to box an article.

encartoucher [ãkartuʃe], *v.tr.* to put (explosive) in a cartridge.

encartoucheur [ãkartuʃœːr], *s.m.* (*a*) cartridge manufacturer; (*b*) (*pers.*) cartridge filler.

en(-)cas [ãkɑ], *s.m.inv.* **1.** article kept for emergencies; emergency supply; emergency stock, snack, etc.; *Med:* **en-c. de première nécessité,** first-aid outfit; **avoir une somme en réserve comme en-c.,** to have a sum put by to fall back upon; to have a sum in reserve as a stand-by. **2.** dumpy umbrella.

encasernement [ãkazɛrnmã], *s.m.* quartering (of troops) in barracks; confining to barracks.

encaserner [ãkazɛrne], *v.tr. Mil:* to quarter (troops) in barracks.

encastage [ãkastaːʒ], *s.m. Cer:* encastage.

encastelé [ãkastəle], *a. Vet:* hoof-bound.

encasteler (s') [sãkastəle], *v.pr. Vet:* (*of horse*) to become hoof-bound.

encastelure [ãkastəlyːr], *s.f. Vet:* navicular disease.

encaster [ãkaste], *v.tr. Cer:* to place (pottery for firing) in saggers.

encastré [ãkastre], *a.* imbedded; inserted, sunk; built-in (furniture, etc.); **poutre encastrée,** encastré beam, beam with fixed ends; built-in, tailed-in, beam; **rivet à tête encastrée,** countersunk rivet; **clavette encastrée,** sunk key; **serrure encastrée,** mortise lock.

encastrement [ãkastrəmã], *s.m. Civ.E:* **1.** embedding, fixing, housing (of sth.) (into recess, groove, notch, etc.); impaction; **e. des aubes de la turbine,** footing of turbine buckets. **2.** (*a*) bed, recess, hollow, housing; *Av:* tail-in; **assemblage à e.,** rabbeting; *Artil:* **e. des tourillons,** trunnion bed; (*b*) frame, casing.

encastrer [ãkastre], *v.tr.* to embed, to set in, tail in: to fix, house, impact (beam, stone, etc.); to recess (rivet-head, etc.).

s'encastrer, to be imbedded (**dans,** in); to fit, tail (in, into).

encaustiquage [ãkɔstikaːʒ, -ko-], *s.m.* beeswaxing, wax-polishing (of floor, furniture, etc.); *Phot:* waxing (of print).

encaustique [ãkɔstik, -ko-]. **1.** *a.* & *s.f. Art:* encaustic (painting). **2.** *s.f.* (bees-)wax polish; furniture polish; floor polish.

encaustiquer [ãkɔstike, -ko-], *v.tr.* to beeswax (floor, etc.); to polish (furniture); *Phot:* to wax (print).

encavement [ãkavmã], *s.m.* cellaring (of wine).

encaver [ãkave], *v.tr.* to cellar (wine, etc.).

encaveur [ãkavœːr], *s.m. Com:* cellarman.

-ence [ãːs], *s.suff.f.* -ence, -ency; **adhérence,** adherence; **intermittence,** intermittence; **exigence,** exigency; **cohérence,** coherence, coherency.

enceindre [ãsɛ̃ːdr], *v.tr.* (*conj. like* CEINDRE) to gird, enclose, surround, encompass; **e. une ville de murailles,** to enclose a town with walls.

enceinte[1] [ãsɛ̃ːt], *s.f.* **1.** (*a*) surrounding wall; fence; *Fort:* enceinte; **e. de montagnes,** ring of mountains; (*b*) **parc qui a dix kilomètres d'e.,** park ten kilometres in circumference. **2.** enclosure, enclosed space; chamber, envelope; precinct; **dans l'e. des fortifications,** within the precincts of the fortifications; (*b*) *Box: Turf:* ring; (*c*) **e. acoustique,** loudspeaker enclosure; (*d*) *Atom.Ph:* casing, tank, vessel (of reactor); **e. sous pression,** pressure shell; **e. étanche aux gas,** gas-tight housing.

enceinte[2], *a.f.* with child; pregnant; *B:* great with child; **femme e.,** expectant mother; **elle était e. de lui,** she was pregnant by him, *F:* in the family way; **elle est e. de cinq mois,** she is five months pregnant.

Encelade [ãsəlad], *Pr.n.m. Myth:* Enceladus.

encellulement [ãselylmã], *s.m.* confinement in the cells.

encelluler [ãselyle], *v.tr.* to put (prisoner) in the cells.

encens [ãsã], *s.m.* incense; **e. mâle,** frankincense; **brûler de l'e. devant qn, donner de l'e. à qn,** (i) *Ecc:* to burn incense before, to cense, s.o.; (ii) to shower fulsome praise or flattery on s.o.

encensement [ãsãsmã], *s.m. Ecc:* censing (of the altar, the people, etc.).

encenser [ãsãse], *v.tr. Ecc: etc:* **1.** to cense (altar, etc.); **e. les idoles,** to burn incense to, before, idols; **e. qn,** to shower fulsome praise or flattery on s.o. **2.** *abs. Equit:* (*of horse*) to toss the head up and down.

encenseur, -euse [ãsãsœːr, -øːz], *s.* (*a*) *Ecc:* thurifer, censer-bearer; (*b*) flatterer, sycophant.

encensier [ãsãsje], *s.m. Bot:* rosemary.

encensoir [ãsãswaːr], *s.m.* (*a*) *Ecc:* censer; **donner trois coups d'e. au prêtre,** to cense the priest three times; (*b*) **coup d'e.,** (piece of) fulsome flattery; **casser le nez à qn à coups d'e.,** to overwhelm s.o. with fulsome flattery, praise; **donner de, prendre, manier, l'e.,** to shower flattery.

encépagement [ãsepaʒmã], *s.m.* (a vineyard's) stock of vines.

encéphalalgie [ãsefalalʒi], *s.f. Med:* encephalalgia.

encéphale [ãsefal], *s.m. Anat:* encephalon, brain.

encéphalique [ãsefalik], *a. Anat:* encephalic.

encéphalite [ãsefalit], *s.f. Med:* encephalitis; **e. léthargique,** encephalitis lethargica; *F:* sleepy sickness.

encéphalitique [ãsefalitik], *a.* encephalitic.

encéphalocèle [ãsefalɔsɛl], *s.f. Med:* encephalocele.

encéphalogramme [ãsefalɔgram], *s.m.* (electro)-encephalogram.

encéphalographie [ãsefalɔgrafi], *s.f.* (electro)-encephalography.

encéphaloïde [ãsefalɔid], *a. Med:* encephaloid (tumour, etc.).

encéphalolithe [ãsefalɔlit], *s.m. Med:* encephalolith.

encéphalomalacie [ãsefalɔmalasi], *s.f. Med:* encephalomalacia, softening of the brain.

encéphalomyélite [ãsefalɔmielit], *s.f. Med:* encephalomyelitis.

encéphalopathie [ãsefalɔpati], *s.f. Med:* encephalopathy.

encéphalopathique [ãsefalɔpatik], *a. Med:* encephalopathic.

encerclement [ãsɛrkləmã], *s.m.* encircling.

encercler [ãsɛrkle], *v.tr.* to encircle; to shut in.

enchaîné [ãʃene], *s.m.* **1.** chained book (in library, etc.). **2.** *Cin:* (lap) dissolve, mix.

enchaînement [ãʃɛnmã], *s.m.* **1.** chaining (up) (of animals, prisoners, etc.). **2.** (*a*) chain, series, concatenation, train (of ideas, events, etc.); (*b*) **e. logique,** logical sequence; (*c*) *Cin:* mix, (lap) dissolve.

enchaîner [ãʃene], *v.tr.* **1.** to chain up, enchain (s.o., dog, etc.); **e. qn à un poteau,** to chain s.o. to a stake; **e. un prisonnier,** to put a prisoner in chains, in irons; to fetter a prisoner; **e. les passions,** to curb the passions; **e. les cœurs par sa bonté,** to captivate hearts by one's kindness; **e. l'attention,** to rivet the attention; **e. qn à sa promesse,** to keep, bind, s.o. to his promise; **la peur enchaînait ses pas,** fear paralysed his steps. **2.** (*a*) to link (up), connect (machinery, etc.); **e. des preuves,** to connect up (pieces of) evidence; **e. des idées,** to link up ideas; **e. la conversation,**

to carry on the conversation (where it was broken off); *abs.* **il avait déjà enchaîné sur le whisky,** he had already moved on to whisky; **il enchaîna sur ses propres nouvelles,** he went on to give his own news; (*b*) *Th: abs.* (i) to gag; (ii) to take up quickly; (iii) to continue; (*c*) *Cin:* to fade in; **fondu enchaîné,** mix, (lap) dissolve; (*d*) *abs. Mus:* to play one tune after another without stopping; (*e*) *abs.* (*computers*) to catenate, concatenate.

s'enchaîner, to be connected, to be linked together; *F:* to hang together; **on voit comme les choses s'enchaînent,** one can see how things hang together, are linked with one another, are interdependent.

enchaînure [ɑ̃ʃɛnyːr], *s.f.* **1.** chainwork. **2.** chain, series, sequence.

enchanté [ɑ̃ʃɑ̃te], *a.* **1.** (*a*) enchanted, under a spell, bewitched; **le pays e.,** wonderland; *Th:* **la Flûte enchantée,** the Magic Flute; (*b*) **lieu e.,** charming, delightful, spot. **2. être e. de qch.,** to be delighted, charmed, at, with, sth.; **je suis e. de vous voir,** I am delighted to see you; (*when introduced to s.o.*) **enchanté(e)!** = how do you do?

enchantement [ɑ̃ʃɑ̃tmɑ̃], *s.m.* **1.** enchantment, magic; (magic) spell; **comme par e.,** as if by magic. **2.** charm; **l'e. des grandes villes,** the glamour of large towns. **3.** delight; **être dans l'e.,** to be delighted; to be in the seventh heaven (of delight).

enchanter [ɑ̃ʃɑ̃te], *v.tr.* **1.** to enchant, bewitch (s.o., sth.); to lay (s.o., sth.) under a spell. **2.** to charm, delight, enrapture (s.o.); **artiste qui enchante l'auditoire,** performer who enraptures the audience, who holds the audience spellbound; **cette idée ne l'enchante pas,** he is not greatly taken with the idea; the idea doesn't appeal to him.

enchanterie [ɑ̃ʃɑ̃tri], *s.f.* (*a*) *Coll.* magic formulae, spells; (*b*) enchantment.

enchanteur, -eresse [ɑ̃ʃɑ̃tœːr, -rɛs]. **1.** *s.* (*a*) enchanter, *f.* enchantress; (*b*) **c'est un e.,** he's a charmer. **2.** *a.* bewitching, captivating (smile); entrancing (beauty, dream); enchanting, delightful, charming (speech, view, etc.).

enchaper [ɑ̃ʃape], *v.tr.* to enclose (case, cask) in an outer case or cask.

enchaperonnement [ɑ̃ʃaprɔnmɑ̃], *s.m.* hooding (of falcon).

enchaperonner [ɑ̃ʃaprɔne], *v.tr.* to hood (falcon, etc.).

enchapure [ɑ̃ʃapyːr], *s.f.* buckle loop; dee ring (of belt, etc.).

encharbonner [ɑ̃ʃarbɔne], *v.tr.* to blacken, dirty (garments, etc.) with coal.

encharger [ɑ̃ʃarʒe], *v.tr.* (*conj. like* CHARGER) *A:* to charge, commission, warn (**qn de faire qch.,** s.o. to do sth.).

encharner [ɑ̃ʃarne], *v.tr.* to hinge; to fit (box, etc.) with hinges.

enchâssement [ɑ̃ʃɑsmɑ̃], *s.m.* **1.** enshrining (of relic, etc.). **2.** setting, mounting (of jewel, etc.).

enchâsser [ɑ̃ʃɑse], *v.tr.* to enchase. **1.** to enshrine (relic, etc.). **2.** (*a*) to set, mount (jewel, etc.); **dans la boucle s'enchâsse un rubis,** a ruby is set in the buckle; **brillants enchâssés dans du platine,** diamonds set, mounted, enchased, in platinum; (*b*) to mount, frame, (sth.) in a chassis, casing; to house (axle, etc.).

enchâssure [ɑ̃ʃɑsyːr], *s.f.* **1.** manner in which sth. is mounted, set. **2.** (*a*) setting, mount (of jewel, etc.); (*b*) housing (for axle, etc.).

enchatonné [ɑ̃ʃatɔne], *a.* (*a*) *Med:* (*of stone in bladder*) encased, encapsulated, in the mucous membrane; (*b*) *Obst:* (*of placenta*) retained by the uterus.

enchatonnement [ɑ̃ʃatɔnmɑ̃], *s.m.* **1.** (process of mounting (a jewel). **2.** *Obst:* enclavement (of placenta).

enchatonner [ɑ̃ʃatɔne], *v.tr.* to set, mount (jewel, etc.).

enchaussenage [ɑ̃ʃosnaːʒ], *s.m.* liming (of hides in fellmongering).

enchaussener [ɑ̃ʃosne], *v.tr.* (**j'enchaussène, n. enchaussenons; j'enchaussènerai**) to lime (hides).

enchausser [ɑ̃ʃose], *v.tr.* **1.** *Hort:* to earth up (foot of tree, vegetables, etc.). **2.** to spoke (wheel).

enchaussumer [ɑ̃ʃosyme], *v.tr.* to lime (hides).

enchaux [ɑ̃ʃo], *s.m. Leath:* limewash.

enchemisage [ɑ̃ʃmizaːʒ], *s.m. Bookb:* putting of a dust-cover (**de,** on).

enchemiser [ɑ̃ʃmize], *v.tr. Bookb:* to put a dust-cover on (book).

enchère [ɑ̃ʃɛːr], *s.f.* bid(ding); **après plusieurs enchères,** after several bids; **l'e. a monté jusqu'à deux cents francs,** the bidding rose to two hundred francs; **vente à l'e., aux enchères,** sale by auction; **mettre e.,** to make a bid (**sur,** for); **faire une e. de cent francs,** to bid another hundred francs; **mettre qch. à l'e., aux enchères,** to put sth. up to, for, auction; **le mobilier fut mis aux enchères,** the furniture was put up for auction, came under the hammer; **folle e.,** irresponsible bid (that cannot be made good); *F:* **payer la folle e.,** to pay for one's folly, for one's rashness; **e. au rabais,** Dutch auction; *Cards:* **bridge aux enchères,** auction bridge.

enchérir [ɑ̃ʃeriːr]. **1.** *v.tr.* to raise, put up, the price of (goods, etc.); **sans rien e.,** without exaggeration. **2.** *v.i.* (*a*) to rise, go up, in price; to grow dearer; **le pain a enchéri, est enchéri,** bread has gone up; (*b*) to make a higher bid; **e. de dix francs,** to bid another ten francs; **e. sur qn,** (i) to outbid s.o.; (ii) to go one better than s.o.; **e. sur les idées de qn,** to improve on s.o.'s ideas; **e. sur la bonté de qn,** to outdo, surpass, s.o. in kindness.

enchérissement [ɑ̃ʃerismɑ̃], *s.m.* rise, increase (in price); **e. des vivres, du pain,** rise in the cost of living, in the price of bread; **l'e. des loyers,** the rise in rents.

enchérisseur, -euse [ɑ̃ʃerisœːr, -øːz], *s.* **1.** bidder; **au dernier e., au plus offrant e.,** to the highest bidder; **fol e.,** irresponsible bidder. **2. e. sur . . .,** improver upon (offer, etc.).

enchevalement [ɑ̃ʃ(ə)valmɑ̃], *s.m.* underpinning, shoring up.

enchevaler [ɑ̃ʃ(ə)vale], *v.tr.* to underpin, to shore up (wall, building, etc.).

enchevaucher [ɑ̃ʃ(ə)voʃe], *v.tr.* to fix, lay (tiles, planks, etc.) with an overlap.

enchevauchure [ɑ̃ʃ(ə)voʃyːr], *s.f.* (*a*) overlapping (of tiles, planks, etc.); (*b*) overlap.

enchevêtré [ɑ̃ʃ(ə)vetre], *a.* tangled (skein, etc.); confused, involved (style); intergrown (foliage, etc.); **détails enchevêtrés,** intricate details.

enchevêtrement [ɑ̃ʃ(ə)vetrəmɑ̃], *s.m.* **1.** tangling up. **2.** tangle, jumble, network; **e. de ficelle,** tangle of string; **e. de fils de fer,** criss-cross of wires; **e. de toits,** huddle of roofs; **e. de mots,** jumble of words; **e. de voitures,** traffic jam.

enchevêtrer [ɑ̃ʃ(ə)vetre], *v.tr.* **1.** to halter (horse). **2.** *Const:* to join (joists) by a trimmer. **3.** to mix up, confuse, tangle up; **e. du fil de fer,** to entangle wire.

s'enchevêtrer, to get mixed up, confused, entangled; (*of horse*) to get tangled up (in noose, rope, etc.); **papiers qui s'enchevêtrent dans un désordre sans nom,** papers jumbled together in unspeakable confusion; **tous ces projets s'enchevêtrent dans son esprit,** all these plans form a tangle, are tangled up, in his mind.

enchevêtrure [ɑ̃ʃ(ə)vetryːr], *s.f.* **1.** *Vet:* halter-cast; excoriation of the pastern. **2.** *Const:* trimming work (for chimney shaft).

enchevillement [ɑ̃ʃ(ə)vijmɑ̃], *s.m. Surg:* pinning (of fracture with grafted bone).

encheviller [ɑ̃ʃ(ə)vije], *v.tr.* (*a*) to peg; to fix (sth.) by means of pegs, of pins; (*b*) *Surg:* to pin (fracture with grafted bone).

enchifrènement [ɑ̃ʃifrɛnmɑ̃], *s.m.* blocking of the nose (by a cold in the head).

enchifrener [ɑ̃ʃifrəne], *v.tr.* (**j'enchifrène, n. enchifrenons; j'enchifrènerai**) *Med:* (*of cold*) to block the nose.

s'enchifrener, to get one's nose blocked, stopped up (by a cold).

enchondrome [ɑ̃kɔ̃droːm], *s.m. Med:* enchondroma.

enchytrée [ɑ̃kitre], *s.m.,* **enchytraeus** [ɑ̃kitreys], *s.m. Ann:* enchytraeus.

enchytréidés [ɑ̃kitreide], *s.m.pl. Ann:* Enchytraeidae.

encirement [ɑ̃sirmɑ̃], *s.m.* waxing (of floor, etc.).

encirer [ɑ̃sire], *v.tr.* to wax (floor, etc.).

encise [ɑ̃siːz], *s.f. A.Jur:* murder of pregnant woman.

enclasser [ɑ̃klɑse], *v.tr. A:* to enrol, rate (sailors).

enclave [ɑ̃klaːv], *s.f.* (*a*) *Geog: Hist:* enclave; (*b*) **l'escalier fait e. dans la pièce,** the staircase leads directly from, into, the room; (*c*) *Hyd.E:* recess (for sluice gates); gate chamber; (*d*) *Geol:* inclusion; xenolith; (*e*) *Bot:* enclave.

enclavement [ɑ̃klavmɑ̃], *s.m.* **1.** wedging in (of sth.); dovetailing. **2.** enclavement (of territory). **3.** *Obst:* enclavement.

enclaver [ɑ̃klave], *v.tr.* **1.** to wedge in, dovetail, house, fit in (timbers, etc.); **le prestidigitateur a enclavé ses deux anneaux,** the conjuror linked his two rings (together). **2.** to enclave (territory); **jardin enclavé entre deux rues,** garden hemmed in, wedged in, enclosed, between two streets; **domaine qui enclave deux petites terres,** estate which enclaves, encloses, two small properties (belonging to a different owner).

enclavure [ɑ̃klavyːr], *s.f.* = ENCLAVEMENT.

enclenche [ɑ̃klɑ̃ːʃ], *s.f. Mec.E:* gab.

enclenchement [ɑ̃klɑ̃ʃmɑ̃], *s.m.* (*a*) *Mec.E:* throwing into gear; interlocking (of parts); **appareil d'e.,** interlocking gear, engaging gear; **e. électrique,** electrical interlock; (*b*) *Rail:* interlocking (of points); (*c*) *Ind:* **e. entre deux opérations,** interdependence of two processes of manufacture.

enclencher [ɑ̃klɑ̃ʃe], *v.tr. Mec.E:* to lock, engage; to throw (parts) into gear; *Ind:* **opération enclenchée,** dependent process.

s'enclencher, to engage; to come into gear (**avec,** with).

enclencheur, -euse [ɑ̃klɑ̃ʃœːr, -øːz], *a. Ind:* controlling (operation, etc.).

enclin [ɑ̃klɛ̃], *a.* inclined, disposed; **j'étais e. à le croire,** I was inclined, disposed, to believe it; **e. à l'ivrognerie,** inclined to drunkenness, addicted to drink; **nature encline au mal,** nature prone to evil; **il n'est pas e. à la louange,** he is not given to praise; **e. à faire qch.,** disposed to do sth.; **e. aux accidents,** prone to accidents, accident prone.

enclinomène [ɑ̃klinɔmɛn], *s.m. Ling:* enclitic or proclitic.

encliquetage [ɑ̃kliktaːʒ], *s.m. Mec.E:* (pawl-and-)ratchet mechanism; *Aut:* (starting handle) dogs; **e. d'une horloge,** click-and-ratchet work of a clock; **doigt d'e.,** pawl.

encliqueter [ɑ̃klikte], *v.tr.* (**j'encliquette, n. encliquetons; j'encliquetterai**) *Mec.E:* to cog, ratch (wheel, etc.); **roue encliquetée,** ratchet wheel, cog wheel.

enclise [ɑ̃kliːz], *s.f. Ling:* enclisis.

enclitique [ɑ̃klitik], *a.* & *s.m. or f. Gram:* enclitic.

encloisonné [ɑ̃klwazɔne], *a.* **serrure encloisonnée,** mortise lock.

encloîtrer [ɑ̃klwatre], *v.tr.* to cloister (s.o.); to shut (s.o.) up in a convent, monastery; **je voudrais m'e. dans quelque abbaye jusqu'à la fin de ma vie,** I would like to take refuge, shut myself up, in some abbey for the rest of my life.

enclore [ɑ̃kloːr], *v.tr.* (*conj. like* CLORE) to enclose; to close in, fence in, wall in (piece of ground, etc.); **e. les faubourgs dans la ville,** to bring the suburbs, outlying districts, within the boundaries of the town; **il lui fallait e. sa vie dans les bornes les plus strictes,** he had to restrict his way of living drastically.

enclos [ɑ̃klo], *s.m.* **1.** enclosure, close; paddock; walled farmyard. **2.** ring fence, palisading; (enclosing) wall. **3.** *Pol.Ec:* (*in U.S.S.R.*) area of land which the members of a kolkhoz may cultivate for their private use.

enclôture [ɑ̃klotyːr], *s.f. Hist: Agr.Adm:* enclosure system.

enclouage [ɑ̃kluaːʒ], *s.m.* **1.** *A.Artil:* spiking (of gun). **2.** *Surg:* pinning (of bone); **e. médullaire,** intramedullary nailing.

enclouer [ɑ̃klue], *v.tr.* **1.** *Farr:* to prick (horse) (in shoeing). **2.** (*a*) *A.Artil:* to spike (gun); (*b*) to nail down; (*c*) to block (a lock). **3.** *Surg:* to pin (bone).

s'enclouer, (*of horse*) to prick itself.

encloueur [ɑ̃kluœːr], *s.m. A.Artil:* spiker (of guns).

enclouure [ɑ̃kluyːr], *s.f. Farr:* prick (given in shoeing); *A:* **j'ai découvert l'e.,** I have discovered where the hitch is, where the shoe pinches.

enclume [ɑ̃klym], *s.f.* **1.** *Metalw: etc:* anvil; **table d'e.,** anvil face; **billot d'e.,** anvil block; **e. à limes,** file-cutting block; *Bootm:* **e. de cordonnier,** shoemender's block; **e. universelle,** hobbing foot; **être entre l'e. et le marteau,** to be between the devil and the deep (blue) sea, to be in a dilemma; **remettre un ouvrage sur l'e.,** to start a piece of work again; **dur comme une e.,** as hard as iron. **2.** *Anat:* incus, anvil (of inner ear).

enclumeau, -eaux [ɑ̃klymo], *s.m.,* **enclumette** [ɑ̃klymɛt], *s.f.,* **enclumot** [ɑ̃klymo], *s.m.* **1.** bench anvil, hand anvil; stake (anvil). **2.** *Tg:* **e. de repos,** back contact (of Morse sender).

encochage [ɑ̃kɔʃaːʒ], *s.m.* (*a*) *El: Coll.* slotted armature; (*b*) *Bookb:* cutting of notches (for thumb index).

encoche [ɑ̃kɔʃ], *s.f.* (*a*) notch, nick (in tally-stick, rack, quadrant, etc.); nock (of arrow); (*b*) slot; *Mch:* gab (of eccentric-rod); *El.E:* **armature à encoches,** slotted armature; (*c*) tommy hole (in screw head); (*d*) *Bookb:* **avec encoches,** with thumb index.

encochement [ɑ̃kɔʃmɑ̃], *s.m.* (*a*) notching, nicking; (*b*) slotting.

encocher [ɑ̃kɔʃe], *v.tr.* **1.** (*a*) to notch, nick (stick, etc.); (*b*) to slot; (*c*) to make a tommy hole in (screw head). **2.** (*a*) to nock (arrow on bow-string); (*b*) **e. une cheville,** to insert a peg; to drive a peg, pin, home.

encochure [ɑ̃kɔʃyːr], *s.f. Nau:* notch, groove (at end of yard arm).

encodage [ɑ̃kɔdaːʒ], *s.m.* encoding; *Elcs:* encoding.

encoder [ɑ̃kɔde], *v.tr.* to encode; *Elcs:* (*of computer*) to encode.

encodeur [ɑ̃kɔdœːr], *s.m. Elcs:* encoder (of computer).

encoffrer [ɑ̃kɔfre], *v.tr.* (*a*) to enclose (sth.) in a coffer; to lock (sth.) up; to hoard (money); (*b*) *F:* to misappropriate (money), to take (s.o. else's money) for one's own use; (*c*) *F:* to lock (s.o.) up, to put (s.o.) in the lock-up.

encoignure [ɑ̃kwaɲyːr], *s.f.* **1.** corner, angle (of room. yard, street); **prendre boutique à une e.,** to take a corner shop; **chaîne d'e.,** corner stones (of brickwork). **2.** corner cupboard.

encoléré [ɑ̃kɔlere], *a.* angry.

encolérer [ɑ̃kɔlere], *v.tr.* (**j'encolère, n. encolérons; j'encolérerai**) to anger (s.o.), to make (s.o.) angry.

encollage [ɑ̃kɔlaːʒ], *s.m.* **1.** (*a*) gluing (of wood, etc.); (*b*) gumming, pasting (of paper, etc.); (*c*) sizing; (*d*) *Metalw:* shutting up (of weld). **2.** (*a*) glue; (*b*) gum; (*c*) size.

encoller [ɑ̃kɔle], *v.tr.* (*a*) to glue (wood, etc.); (*b*) to gum, paste (paper, etc.); **e. une carte,** to mount a map; (*c*) to size (paper, etc.); (*d*) *Metalw:* to shut up (weld).

encolleter [ɑ̃kɔlte], *v.tr.* (*conj. like* COLLETER) to snare (rabbits, etc.).

encolleur, -euse [ɑ̃kɔlœːr, -øːz], *s. Tex:* **1.** *s.m. & f.* sizer. **2.** *s.f.* **encolleuse,** sizing machine.

encolpion [ɑ̃kɔlpjɔ̃], **encolpium** [ɑ̃kɔlpjɔm], *s.m. Ecc: A:* encolpion, encolpium.

encolure [ɑ̃kɔlyːr], *s.f.* **1.** (*a*) neck and withers (of horse); neck (of camel, ostrich); **cheval à e. de cygne, à e. penchante,** cock-throttled, lop necked horse; **cheval à e. de cerf, à e. renversée,** ewe-necked horse; **pli de l'e.,** bend of the neck; *Turf:* **gagner d'une, par une, e.,** to win by a neck; (*b*) *F:* **homme de forte e.,** thickset, stocky, man; **je le reconnais à son e.,** I know him by his build. **2.** (*a*) neck opening, neckline (of dress, etc.); **e. carrée,** square neck; **robe à e. dégagée,** low-necked dress; (*b*) (i) (shirt) collar; (ii) size in collars. **3.** *Nau:* crown (of anchor). **4.** *Nau:* **e. d'une varangue,** curve of the throat of a floor; **ligne d'e.,** cutting-down line.

encombrant [ɑ̃kɔ̃brɑ̃], *a.* (*a*) encumbering, cumbrous, cumbersome; clumsy (furniture, etc.); **peu e.,** compact; **colis encombrants,** bulky packages; (*b*) *F:* **c'est un personnage e.,** he's a nuisance, he's always in the way; **passé e.,** murky past.

encombre [ɑ̃kɔ̃ːbr̥], *s.m. A:* cumbrance; *used now only in the adv.phr.* **sans e.,** without (iet or) hindrance; **nous sommes arrivés à Douvres sans e.,** we arrived at Dover without mishap, without difficulty.

encombrement [ɑ̃kɔ̃brəmɑ̃], *s.m.* **1.** (*a*) litter (of articles); congestion (of traffic, etc.), traffic jam, block (of vehicles), traffic block; glut (of goods); **e. de l'espace aérien,** overcrowding of the air space; (*b*) overcrowding (of individuals); (*c*) **e. dentaire,** tooth crowding; overlapping teeth; (*d*) *Med:* obstruction. **2.** (*a*) cumbersomeness, bulkiness (of article); **de faible e.,** compact; *Nau:* **tonneau d'e.,** measured ton; (*b*) floor, ground, space (required); room occupied (by engine, etc.); cubic capacity (of refrigerator, etc.); **coefficient d'e.,** space factor; **e. d'une auto,** width of track of a car; **e. hors tout,** overall dimensions; (*c*) clearance (required by swinging member of bridge, machine, etc.); **e. vertical,** headroom.

encombrer [ɑ̃kɔ̃bre], *v.tr.* to encumber; to saddle (s.o.) with (sth.); **e. les rues,** to congest, overcrowd, the streets; **maison encombrée de vieux meubles,** house cluttered up with old furniture; **table encombrée de papiers,** table encumbered, littered, with papers; **sentier encombré de ronces,** path overgrown, with brambles; **ici le sol était encombré de cadavres,** here the bodies lay thick upon the ground; **e. le marché,** to glut, to overstock, the market; **e. un magasin de stocks,** to overstock a shop; **n'encombrez pas le passavant,** stand clear of the gangway.

s'encombrer, to burden oneself, saddle oneself, load oneself up (de, with).

encontre (à l') [alɑ̃kɔ̃ːtr̥], *adv.phr.* in opposition, to the contrary; **je n'ai rien à dire à l'e.,** I have nothing to say against it; I have no objection; *prep.phr.* **à l'e. de,** against, in opposition to; **aller à l'e. du danger plutôt que de l'attendre,** to go out to meet danger rather than wait for it; **aller à l'e. de la loi,** to run counter to the law, to set the law at defiance; **aller à l'e. de la nature,** to go against nature; **il marche toujours à l'e. de mes projets,** he always opposes, runs counter to, my plans; he always crosses me; **à l'e. des idées reçues,** contrary to accepted ideas; *Nau:* **deux navires à l'e. l'un de l'autre,** two ships end-on to each other.

encoprésie [ɑ̃kɔprezi], *s.f. Med:* incontinence (of faeces).

encor [ɑ̃kɔːr], *adv. Poet:* = ENCORE.

encorbellement [ɑ̃kɔrbɛlmɑ̃], *s.m.* (*a*) *Arch:* corbelling (out) (of wall, etc.); overhang (of upper storey); cantilever; **poutre en e.,** overhung girder, cantilever girder; **fenêtre en e.,** oriel window; *Civ.E:* **trottoir en e.,** overhanging footway, cantilever footway (of bridge); **route en e.,** overhanging road; (*b*) *Metall:* **e. de la tympe,** tymp arch; (*c*) *N.Arch:* sponson.

encorbeller [ɑ̃kɔrbɛle], *v.tr. Const:* to corbel; to cantilever.

encordage [ɑ̃kɔrdaːʒ], *s.m.* **1.** cording, tying up (of parcels, etc.). **2.** *Tex:* heddles (of loom).

encordement [ɑ̃kɔrd(ə)mɑ̃], *s.m. Mount:* roping (up).

encorder [ɑ̃kɔrde], *v.tr.* **1.** *Tex:* to mount the heddles. **2.** *Mount:* to rope (climbers) together.

s'encorder, *Mount:* to rope, to put on the rope.

encore [ɑ̃kɔːr], *adv.* **1.** (*a*) still; **est-ce qu'ils jouent e.?** are they still playing? **je suis e. à chercher une explication,** I am still looking for an explanation; **j'en suis e. à lui trouver un défaut,** I have never found a fault in him yet; **j'ai e. cinq minutes,** I've five minutes in hand; I've five minutes to spare; (*b*) yet; **plus gai que je ne l'avais e. jamais vu,** more cheerful than I had ever seen him before; **je ne suis e. qu'étudiant,** I am only a student yet, so far; **pas e.,** not yet; **il n'a pas e. dix ans,** he is not yet ten; **elle n'est pas e. arrivée,** she has not arrived yet; **un homme que je n'avais e. jamais vu,** a man I had never seen before; (*c*) more, again; **e. un mot,** (just) one word more; **en voulez-vous e.?** do you want, would you like, some more? **e. du mouton, s'il vous plaît!** some more mutton, please! **e. une tasse de café,** another, one more, cup of coffee; **outre l'argent, on lui donna e. un cheval,** besides the money they gave him a horse as well; **quoi e.?** what else? **que vous faut-il e.?** what else do you want? **pendant trois mois e., pendant e. trois mois,** for another three months, three months longer; **e. quelques mois et je serai libre,** a few more months and I shall be free; **pour quelque temps e.,** for some time yet; **réduire e. le prix,** to reduce the price still further; **e. une fois,** once more, once again; **e. et toujours,** over and over again; **nous l'avons vu e.,** we saw him again; **nous l'avons e. vu hier,** we saw him again yesterday; **e. autant,** as much again; **ce serait e. pis,** that would be still worse; **une tâche e. plus difficile,** a still more difficult task; **il est e. plus bête que je ne croyais,** he is even stupider than I took him to be; *F:* **tu es e. gentil, toi!** you're a fine chap too! a nice chap you are! **e. vous!** (what) you again? (*d*) **comment s'appelle t-il encore?** what's his name again? **quel âge a-t-il encore?** what did you say his age was? **2.** moreover, furthermore, in addition; **nous conspirons, et contre toi e.,** we are plotting, and, what is more, against you; **non seulement . . ., mais e. . . .,** not only . . ., but also . . . **3.** (*restrictive*) (*a*) **hier e. je lui ai parlé,** I spoke to him as lately as yesterday, no longer ago than yesterday; I spoke to him only yesterday; **e. si on pouvait lui parler,** if even one could speak to him; **e. s'il était reconnaissant!** if only he was at least grateful; (*b*) (*with inversion of subj. and vb.*) **je n'ai qu'un ciseau, e. est-il émoussé,** I have only one chisel and even that is blunt; **le mot est français; encore n'est-il pas usuel,** the word is French, all the same it is not in common use; **e. vous aurait-il fallu me prévenir,** for all that you should have let me know; (*c*) **il vous en donnera dix francs et e.!** he will give you ten francs for it, if that! **vous l'aurez demain, et e.!** you'll get it tomorrow, if then! (*d*) *conj.phr.* **e. (bien) que** + *sub.*, (although; **e. qu'il ne me soit rien,** although he is nothing to me; **liens forts e. qu'invisibles,** bonds that are strong, although, even though, invisible; **temps agréable e. qu'un peu froid,** pleasant weather if rather cold. **4. il s'est montré très discret—mais e.!** he was very reticent—but what *did* he say?

encornail [ɑ̃kɔrnaːj], *s.m. Nau:* half-sheave.

encorné [ɑ̃kɔrne], *a.* **1.** horned (animal); *F:* **mari e.,** cuckold. **2.** *Vet:* **javart e.,** swelling under the coronet.

encorner [ɑ̃kɔrne], *v.tr.* **1.** to furnish (sth.) with horn(s); **e. un arc,** to tip a bow with horn; *F:* **e. un mari,** to cuckold a husband. **2.** (*of bull, etc.*) to gore, toss (s.o.).

encornet [ɑ̃kɔrnɛ], *s.m. Moll: F:* squid; calamary.

encornure [ɑ̃kɔrnyːr], *s.f. Z:* set, placement, of horns.

encotillonné [ɑ̃kɔtijɔne], *a.* under a woman's thumb, under petticoat government.

encouardir [ɑ̃kwardiːr], *v.tr.* to make a coward of (s.o.).

encourageant [ɑ̃kuraʒɑ̃], *a.* encouraging, cheering; **nouvelles encourageantes,** cheerful news; **la perspective est plus encourageante,** the prospect looks, the outlook is, more hopeful; **les perspectives sont peu encourageantes,** the outlook is bleak.

encouragement [ɑ̃kuraʒmɑ̃], *s.m.* encouragement; **e. à la vertu,** incentive to virtue; **société d'e. au bien,** association for the promotion of good citizenship; **recevoir peu d'e. à faire qch.,** to receive little encouragement, little inducement, to do sth.; **un geste d'e.,** an inviting gesture; *Sch:* **prix d'e.** = progress prize.

encourager [ɑ̃kuraʒe], *v.tr.* (**j'encourageai(s); n. encourageons**) **1.** to encourage, hearten (s.o.); **e. ses soldats,** to put heart into one's soldiers; **e. qn à faire qch.,** to encourage s.o. to do sth.; **e. qn au bien,** to encourage s.o. in well-doing; **il était timide, mais elle l'encourageait,** he was shy but she drew him out; **il m'a encouragé à rester,** he induced me to stay. **2. e. les arts, la propagande,** to encourage, foster, the arts, propaganda; to promote the arts; **e. une croyance,** to foster a belief; **e. le crime,** to put a premium on crime; to abet crime; **e. un projet,** to promote, countenance, a scheme; to give countenance to a scheme.

encourir[1] [ɑ̃kuriːr], *v.tr.* (*conj. like* COURIR) to incur (reproaches, etc.); to bring (punishment, reproaches, etc.) upon oneself; **e. des frais,** to incur expenses; **e. un risque,** to take a chance.

encourir[2] **(s')**, *v.pr.* (*conj. like* COURIR) *A: Lit:* to run, hasten (to a place); **le pauvre homme s'encourut chez son voisin, s'encourut trouver son voisin,** the poor man hastened round to his neighbour.

en(-)cours [ɑ̃kuːr], *s.m.* **1.** *Bank:* total of the bills (remitted by the customer to the bank) outstanding at any one time; **l'e. de la dette,** the outstanding debt. **2.** *Ind:* **e. de fabrication,** material undergoing processing; **e. de route,** material, stock, awaiting transfer (to another department).

encouturé [ɑ̃kutyre], *a. N.Arch:* clinker-built.

encrage [ɑ̃kraːʒ], *s.m. Typ:* inking (up); **excès d'e.,** over-inking.

encrassage [ɑ̃krasaːʒ], *s.m.* dirtying; choking up; clogging up; sooting up; fouling.

encrassé [ɑ̃krase], *a.* dirty; choked, clogged, with dirt; foul (gun, etc.); sooted up (sparking plug, cylinder head, etc.); gummed up (piston).

encrassement [ɑ̃krasmɑ̃], *s.m.* dirtying (of clothes, etc.); fouling (of fire-arms, etc.); fouling, sooting (up), oiling up (of sparking plug); clogging, choking (of machine, etc.); gumming up (of piston); *I.C.E:* **e. charbonneux,** (deposit of) carbon.

encrasser [ɑ̃krase], *v.tr.* to dirty, grease (one's clothes, etc.); to foul (gun, etc.); to oil up; to soot up (sparking plug, etc.); to clog, choke (machine, etc.).

s'encrasser, to get dirty, greasy; to get foul; to foul; to soot up, oil up, gum up.

encre [ɑ̃ːkr̥], *s.f.* ink; **e. communicative, à copier,** copying ink; **e. indélébile,** indelible, waterproof, ink; **e. de Chine,** Indian ink; **e. à marquer,** marking ink; **e. d'impression,** printing ink; **e. d'écrivain litho,** lithographic writing ink; **e. stylographique, à stylo,** fountain pen ink; **e. à tampon,** endorsing ink, stamp pad ink; **e. sympathique,** invisible ink; **écrit à l'e.,** written in ink; **mettre une épure à l'e., repasser un dessin à l'e.,** to ink in a drawing; **mise à l'e.,** inking in; **refusant l'e.,** ink resisting; **retenant l'e.,** ink retentive; **dessinateur à l'e.,** black and white artist; **doigts couverts d'e., visage barbouillé d'e.,** inky fingers, face; *F:* **c'est la bouteille à l'e.,** there's no making head or tail of it, the whole thing is in a hopeless muddle; **noir comme de**

l'e., inky black, murky; **écrire de sa meilleure e.,** to pay attention to one's style; **écrire de bonne e.,** to write without mincing one's words, to put it bluntly; **nuit d'e.,** pitch-black night; **se faire un sang d'e.,** to worry oneself sick; *Bot:* **maladie de l'e.,** ink disease; black canker.

encrèchement [ɑ̃krɛʃmɑ̃], *s.m. Hyd.E:* sheet piling.

encrêper [ɑ̃krɛpe], *v.tr.* to trim, cover, (sth.) with crape.

encrer [ɑ̃kre], *v.tr. Typ: etc:* to ink; **pierre, table, à e.,** inking slab; **pierre à e. cylindrique,** ink cylinder.

encreur [ɑ̃krœːr]. **1.** *s.m.* (*a*) *Typ:* ink(ing) roller; (*b*) *El: Ph: etc:* inker (of a recording apparatus). **2.** *a.* inking; *Typewr:* **ruban e.,** inking ribbon; *Typ:* **rouleau e.,** inker.

encrier [ɑ̃krije], *s.m.* **1.** ink pot, inkstand; **e. pour table percée,** (school) inkwell. **2.** *Typ: etc:* (*a*) ink trough; **rouleau d'e.,** duct roller, fountain roller; **vis d'e.,** feed screw; (*b*) distributing table.

encrine [ɑ̃krin], *s.f. Echin: Paleont:* encrinus; crinoid.

encrinite [ɑ̃krinit], *s.f. Geol:* encrinite.

encrivore [ɑ̃krivɔːr]. **1.** *s.m.* ink(stain) remover. **2.** *a.* ink(stain) removing.

encroisage [ɑ̃krwazaːʒ], *s.m.*, **encroisement** [ɑ̃krwazmɑ̃], *s.m. Tex:* shedding.

encroiser [ɑ̃krwaze], *v.tr. Tex:* to shed.

encroix [ɑ̃krwa], *s.m. Tex:* shed (in weaving); **bâtons d'e.,** healds.

encrotter [ɑ̃krɔte], *v.tr.* to muddy, to cover with mud; **rues encrottées,** muddy streets.

encrouage [ɑ̃kruaːʒ], *s.m.* entanglement (of fallen tree in the branches of another).

encroué [ɑ̃krue], *a.* (*of fallen tree*) entangled, caught (in the branches of other trees).

encroûtant [ɑ̃krutɑ̃], *a.* (*a*) encrusting; (*b*) *F:* soul-destroying (occupation, etc.).

encroûté [ɑ̃krute], *a.* (*a*) encrusted, crusted over; (*b*) **e. de préjugés,** steeped in prejudice, hidebound; **e. dans sa paresse,** sunk in (the slough of) laziness; **e. dans un système,** wedded to, hidebound by, a system; *s.m.* **vieux, vieil, e.,** old fogey, old stick-in-the-mud; (*c*) **élève e.,** stupid ignorant, pupil.

encroûtement [ɑ̃krutmɑ̃], *s.m.* **1.** (*a*) encrusting, crusting over (of sth.); (*b*) sinking into the rut. **2.** crust; *Geol:* (salt) crust; scale (in boiler); fur (in kettle); *Med:* **e. calcique,** chalky deposit.

encroûter [ɑ̃krute], *v.tr.* **1.** to encrust (sth.); to cover (sth.) with a crust; to cake (sth.) with mud, etc.; **e. un mur,** to rough-cast a wall. **2. rien ne nous encroûte comme la paresse,** nothing makes us as ignorant, as stupid, as laziness.

s'encroûter. 1. to become encrusted, crusted over, caked over (**de,** with). **2.** to sink into a rut; to become hidebound; **s'e. dans une technique démodée,** to become wedded to an out-of-date technique.

enculasser [ɑ̃kylase], *v.tr.* to breech (gun, rifle).

enculé [ɑ̃kyle], *s.m.* **1.** *V:* catamite. **2.** *V:* old mucker; idiot.

encuvage [ɑ̃kyvaːʒ], **encuvement** [ɑ̃kyvmɑ̃], *s.m.* (act of) vatting (skins, grapes, etc.).

encuver [ɑ̃kyve], *v.tr.* to vat; to put (skins, grapes, etc.) into a vat, into a tub.

encyclique [ɑ̃siklik], *a. & s.f. Ecc:* encyclical (letter).

encyclographie [ɑ̃siklɔgrafi], *s.f.* encyclop(a)edia (arranged by subjects).

encyclopédie [ɑ̃siklɔpedi], *s.f.* encyclop(a)edia; **une e. vivante,** a walking encyclopaedia.

encyclopédique [ɑ̃siklɔpedik], *a.* encyclop(a)edic.

encyclopédisme [ɑ̃siklɔpedism], *s.m.* encyclop(a)edism.

encyclopédiste [ɑ̃siklɔpedist], *s.m.* encyclop(a)edist.

encyrtidés [ɑ̃sirtide], *s.m.pl. Ent:* Encyrtidae.

endamœbidés [ɑ̃damebide], *s.m.pl. Z:* Endamoebidae.

endartère [ɑ̃dartɛːr], *s.f. Anat:* endarterium.

endartérite [ɑ̃darterit], *s.f. Med:* endarteritis.

endaubage [ɑ̃dobaːʒ], *s.m. Cu:* **1.** (*a*) stewing (of meat); (*b*) stewed meat, stew. **2.** canned, tinned, beef.

endauber [ɑ̃dobe], *v.tr. Cu:* **1.** to stew (meat, etc.). **2.** to tin, can (beef).

endéans [ɑ̃deɑ̃], *prep. A: & Belgian:* within (a certain time).

endécagone [ɛ̃dekagɔn], *Geom:* (*a*) *a.* hendecagonal; (*b*) *s.m.* hendecagon.

endécher [ɑ̃deʃe], *v.tr.* (**j'endèche, n. endéchons; j'endécherai**) *P:* to make (s.o.) short of funds, broke; to bring (s.o.) into low water.

endémicité [ɑ̃demisite], *s.f.* endemicity.

endémie [ɑ̃demi], *s.f.* endemic disease; endemic.

endémique [ɑ̃demik], *a.* endemic.

endémiquement [ɑ̃demikmɑ̃], *adv.* endemically.

endémisme [ɑ̃demism], *s.m.* endemism.

endente [ɑ̃dɑ̃ːt], *s.f. Carp:* notch, scarf, joint.

endenté [ɑ̃dɑ̃te], *a.* **1.** (*a*) (*rare*) having teeth; **les mâchoires fortes et vigoureusement endentées,** with well-marked jaws and strong rows of teeth; (*b*) **gens bien endentés,** people (blessed) with hearty appetites. **2.** (*a*) cogged, toothed (wheel); (*b*) scarf, joggle (joint); (*c*) indented (line, etc.); *Navy:* (**en ordre**) **e.,** in indented order; formed in two bow and quarter lines. **3.** *Dipl: etc:* **charte endentée,** indenture.

endentement [ɑ̃dɑ̃tmɑ̃], *s.m.* **1.** (*a*) cogging, toothing (of wheel); (*b*) meshing (of wheels). **2.** indent(ation), dovetail(ing). **3.** *Carp:* = ENDENTE.

endenter [ɑ̃dɑ̃te], *v.tr.* **1.** (*a*) to furnish (s.o., sth.) with teeth; (*b*) to tooth, cog, ratch (wheel, etc.); (*c*) to mesh (wheels). **2.** to indent (line, etc.). **3.** *Carp:* to join (timbers) by a notch, scarf, joint, to scarf (timbers).

endenture [ɑ̃dɑ̃tyːr], *s.f. Dipl: etc:* indenture.

endetté [ɑ̃dɛte], *a.* in debt.

endettement [ɑ̃dɛtmɑ̃], *s.m.* running into debt.

endetter [ɑ̃dɛte], *v.tr.* to involve (s.o.) in debt; to get (s.o.) into debt.

s'endetter, to get, run, into debt; to run up bills.

endeuiller [ɑ̃dœje], *v.tr.* to put, plunge, (s.o., sth.) into mourning; **maison endeuillée,** house of mourning; **des cyprès endeuillent le premier plan du tableau,** cypresses strike a note of gloom in the foreground; **la journée fut endeuillée par cet événement,** this event cast a gloom over the day.

s'endeuiller, to go into mourning; **la campagne s'endeuille de brouillards,** the countryside is becoming enshrouded in fog.

endêvé [ɑ̃dɛve], *a. O: F:* provoked; angry; furious.

endêver [ɑ̃dɛve], *v.i. O: F:* to be furious, angry; **faire e. qn,** to torment s.o., to drive s.o. wild, mad.

endhyménine [ɑ̃dimenin], *s.f. Bot:* intine, endosporium.

endiablé [ɑ̃djable], *a.* (*a*) *A:* possessed (of the devil); (*b*) reckless, devil-may-care (courage, etc.); (*c*) wild, frenzied (music, etc.); (*d*) devilish (wind, etc.).

endiabler [ɑ̃djable], *A:* **1.** *v.tr.* to make diabolic. **2.** *v.i.* to be furious, to fret and fume; **faire e. qn,** to torment, *F:* to aggravate, to rag, s.o.

endiamanté [ɑ̃djamɑ̃te], *a.* (*a*) studded with diamonds; **mains endiamantées,** hands laden with diamonds; (*b*) sparkling.

endigage [ɑ̃digaːʒ], **endiguement** [ɑ̃digmɑ̃], *s.m.* **1.** (*a*) damming (up); (*b*) embanking (of river, etc.); (*c*) *Mil:* **politique d'endiguement,** policy of containment. **2.** (*a*) dam; (*b*) sea wall; (*c*) embankment, bank, dyke, dike.

endiguer [ɑ̃dige], *v.tr.* **1.** to dam up (river, etc.); **e. la marche des événements,** to stay the course of events. **2.** to (em)bank (river, etc.); to dike (land). **3.** to impound (water).

endimanché [ɑ̃dimɑ̃ʃe], *a.* in Sunday attire, in one's Sunday best; **elle a l'air e.,** she looks all got up for the occasion; **le jour de la fête, la place et la mairie étaient endimanchées,** on the day of the fête, the square and the town hall were all decorated.

endimanchement [ɑ̃dimɑ̃ʃmɑ̃], *s.m.* dressing up in one's Sunday best.

endimancher [ɑ̃dimɑ̃ʃe], *v.tr.* to dress (s.o.) in his (her) Sunday best.

s'endimancher, to put on one's Sunday best.

endive [ɑ̃diːv], *s.f. Bot:* **1.** endive. **2.** witloof, broad-leaved chicory.

endivisionnement [ɑ̃divizjɔnmɑ̃], *s.m. Mil:* formation (of troops) into a division.

endivisionner [ɑ̃divizjɔne], *v.tr. Mil:* to form (troops) into a division.

endlichite [ɑ̃dlikit], *s.f. Miner:* endlichite.

endo- [ɑ̃dɔ], *pref.* endo-; **endométrite,** endometritis.

endobiotique [ɑ̃dɔbjɔtik], *a.* endobiotic.

endoblaste [ɑ̃dɔblast], *s.m. Biol:* endoblast.

endocarde [ɑ̃dɔkard], *s.m. Anat:* endocardium.

endocardiaque [ɑ̃dɔkardjak], *a. Med:* endocardial (murmur, etc.).

endocardite [ɑ̃dɔkardit], *s.f. Med:* endocarditis.

endocarditique [ɑ̃dɔkarditik], *a. Med:* endocarditic.

endocarpe [ɑ̃dɔkarp], *s.m. Bot:* endocarp.

endocarpé [ɑ̃dɔkarpe], *a.* (*of fruit*) having an endocarp, endocarpous.

endoceras [ɑ̃dɔseras], *s.m. Paleont:* endoceras.

endochrome [ɑ̃dɔkroːm], *s.m. Biol:* endochrome.

endocrâne [ɑ̃dɔkrɑːn], *s.m. Anat:* endocrane, endocranium.

endocrânien, -ienne [ɑ̃dɔkranjɛ̃, -jɛn], *a. Anat:* endocranial.

endocrine [ɑ̃dɔkrin], *a.f. Anat:* endocrine, ductless (gland).

endocrinien, -ienne [ɑ̃dɔkrinjɛ̃, -jɛn], *a. Biol: Anat:* endocrine, endocrinal (glands, etc.); *Med:* **à dépendance endocrinienne,** hormone dependent.

endocrinologie [ɑ̃dɔkrinɔlɔʒi], *s.f. Physiol:* endocrinology.

endoctrinable [ɑ̃dɔktrinabl̩], *a.* that may be indoctrinated.

endoctrinement [ɑ̃dɔktrinmɑ̃], *s.m.* indoctrination.

endoctriner [ɑ̃dɔktrine], *v.tr.* **1.** (*a*) to indoctrinate; (*b*) *A:* to instruct (messenger, etc.). **2.** to win over (adherents).

endoctrineur, -euse [ɑ̃dɔktrinœːr, -øːz], *s.* indoctrinator.

endocyste [ɑ̃dɔsist], *s.m. Biol:* endocyst.

endoderme [ɑ̃dɔdɛrm], *s.m. Biol: Bot:* endoderm.

endoénergétique [ɑ̃dɔenɛrʒetik], *a. Ph:* endothermic; endoergic.

endogame [ɑ̃dɔgam], *a. Anthr:* endogamous.

endogamie [ɑ̃dɔgami], *s.f. Anthr:* endogamy; inbreeding.

endogé [ɑ̃dɔʒe], *a. Biol:* **faune endogée,** fauna living in the soil, soil-dwelling fauna.

endogène [ɑ̃dɔʒɛn], *a. Bot: Physiol:* endogenous; *Geol:* endogenetic, endogenic.

endogénèse [ɑ̃dɔʒenɛːz], *s.f. Biol:* endogeny.

endolori [ɑ̃dɔlɔri], *a.* painful, sore; tender (nose, etc.); **avoir le cœur e.,** to suffer heartache.

endolorir [ɑ̃dɔlɔriːr], *v.tr.* to make (limb, etc.) ache; **j'en avais les bras endoloris,** it made my arms ache.

s'endolorir, to become painful.

endolorissement [ɑ̃dɔlɔrismɑ̃], *s.m.* ache, pain (in limb, etc.); tenderness.

endolymphatique [ɑ̃dɔlɛ̃fatik], *a. Anat:* endolymphatic.

endolymphe [ɑ̃dɔlɛ̃ːf], *s.f. Physiol:* endolymph.

endomètre [ɑ̃dɔmɛtr̥], *s.m. Physiol:* endometrium.

endométriome [ɑ̃dɔmetriɔm], *s.m. Path:* endometrioma.

endométriose [ɑ̃dɔmetrioːz], *s.m. Path:* endometriosis.

endométrite [ɑ̃dɔmetrit], *s.f. Path:* endometritis.

endomitose [ɑ̃dɔmitoːz], *s.f. Biol:* endomitosis.

endomixie [ɑ̃dɔmiksi], *s.f. Biol:* endomixis.

endommagement [ɑ̃dɔmaʒmɑ̃], *s.m.* damage, injury (de, to).

endommager [ɑ̃dɔmaʒe], *v.tr.* (**j'endommageai(s); n. endommageons**) to damage, injure; to do damage to (sth.); *Typ:* to batter (type).

endomorphe [ɑ̃dɔmɔrf], *Geol:* **1.** *a.* endomorphic, endomorphous. **2.** *s.m.* endomorph.

endomorphisme [ɑ̃dɔmɔrfism], *s.m. Geol:* endomorphism.

endomycétales [ɑ̃dɔmisetal], **endomycétacées** [ɑ̃dɔmisetase], *s.f.pl. Fung:* Endomycetales, Endomycetaceae.

endonéphrite [ɑ̃dɔnefrit], *s.f. Med:* endonephritis.

endoparasite [ɑ̃dɔparazit], *s.m. Nat.Hist:* endoparasite.

endophasie [ɑ̃dɔfazi], *s.f.* implicit, internal, language; endophasia.

endophragme [ɑ̃dɔfragm], *s.m. Ent: Crust: etc:* endophragm, endophragmal skeleton.

endophyte [ɑ̃dɔfit], *a. & s.m. Biol: Bot:* endophyte.

endoplasme [ɑ̃dɔplasm], *s.m. Biol:* endoplasm.

endoplèvre [ɑ̃dɔplɛːvr̥], *s.f. Bot:* endopleura; tegmen.

endopodite [ɑ̃dɔpɔdit], *s.m. Crust:* endopodite.

endoptérygotes [ɑ̃dɔpterigɔt], *s.m.pl. Ent:* Endopterygota.

endoradiothérapie [ɑ̃dɔradjɔterapi], *s.f. Med:* endoradiotherapy.

endoréique [ɑ̃dɔreik], *a. Geol:* endor(h)eic.

endoréisme [ɑ̃dɔreism], *s.m. Geol:* endor(h)eism.

endormant [ɑ̃dɔrmɑ̃], *a.* **1.** soporific; **potion endormante,** sleeping draught. **2.** *F:* boring, wearisome; humdrum (task).

endormeur, -euse [ɑ̃dɔrmœːr, -øːz], *s.* **1.** one who (i) lulls (s.o.) to sleep, (ii) drugs (s.o.). **2.** *F:* (*a*) cajoler, humbug; (*b*) bore.

endormi, -ie [ɑ̃dɔrmi], *a.* **1.** (*a*) asleep, **sleeping;** *s.* sleeper; **faire l'e.,** to pretend to be asleep; (*b*) sleepy, drowsy; *F:* **être e.,** to have no life in one, to be a slowcoach; *s.* **c'est un e., une endormie,** he, she, is a sleepy-head; (*c*) dormant (passion, etc.). **2.** (*of limb, etc.*) numb; **j'ai la jambe endormie,** my leg has gone to sleep.

endormir [ɑ̃dɔrmiːr], *v.tr.* (*conj. like* DORMIR) **1.** (*a*) to make (s.o.) sleep; to put, send, lull, (s.o.) to sleep; **e. un enfant en chantant,** to sing a child to sleep; (*b*) *F:* to bore (s.o.); (*c*) *Med:* to anaesthetize; to chloroform; *F:* **on l'a endormi,** they drugged him; (*d*) *P:* to kill, murder (s.o.); *Box:* to knock out (opponent). **2.** to benumb, deaden (limb, etc.); to deaden (pain). **3.** *F:* to cajole, humbug, befool (s.o.); to throw dust in the eyes of (s.o.); to hoodwink; **e. les soupçons,** to allay suspicion; **e. qn avec de belles promesses,** to put s.o. off with fine promises.

s'endormir, to fall asleep; to go to sleep; to drop off to sleep; **s'e. profondément, d'un profond sommeil,** to fall into a sound, a deep, sleep; *F:* **s'e. sur une affaire,** to go to sleep over a piece of business, to let it drag on; *s.a.* RÔTI.

endormissement [ɑ̃dɔrmismɑ̃], *s.m. Med:* passing into unconsciousness (of patient under anaesthetic); induction of sleep.

endos [ɑ̃do], *s.m.* endorsement (on bill, cheque); **e. en blanc,** blank endorsement.

endoscope [ɑ̃dɔskɔp], *s.m. Med:* endoscope.

endoscopie [ɑ̃dɔskɔpi], *s.f. Med:* endoscopy.

endoscopique [ɑ̃dɔskɔpik], *a. Med:* endoscopic.

endosmomètre [ɑ̃dɔsmɔmɛtr], *s.m. Ph:* endosmometer.

endosmose [ɑ̃dɔsmoːz], *s.f. Med: Ph:* endosmosis, endosmose.

endosmotique [ɑ̃dɔsmɔtik], *a. Ph:* endosmotic.

endosome [ɑ̃dɔzoːm], *s.m. Biol:* endosome.

endosperme [ɑ̃dɔspɛrm], *s.m. Bot:* endosperm.

endospermé [ɑ̃dɔspɛrme], *a. Bot:* endospermic.

endospore [ɑ̃dɔspoːr], *s.m. Bot:* endospore.

endosquelette [ɑ̃dɔskəlɛt], *s.m. Ent:* endoskeleton.

endossable [ɑ̃dosabl], *a.* endorsable (cheque).

endossage [ɑ̃dosaːʒ], *s.m. Bookb:* = ENDOSSURE.

endossataire [ɑ̃dosatɛːr], *s.m. & f. Com:* endorsee.

endosse [ɑ̃doːs], *s.f. F:* responsibility, trouble; **jeter sur qn l'e. d'une affaire,** to let s.o. else shoulder a piece of business, to shift the responsibility on to s.o.; (*in pl.*) *P:* back; **en avoir plein les endosses,** to have had enough of sth.

endossement [ɑ̃dosmɑ̃], *s.m.* **1.** (*a*) putting on, slipping on (of one's garments, etc.); (*b*) *F:* shouldering (of responsibility). **2.** *Com:* (*a*) endorsing; (*b*) = ENDOS. **3.** *Bookb:* = ENDOSSURE.

endosser [ɑ̃dose], *v.tr.* **1.** to put on (clothes, livery, cuirass, etc.); **e. son armure,** to buckle on one's armour; **e. l'uniforme, la soutane, l'écarlate,** to go into the army, the Church, the legal profession; *F:* **e. une responsabilité,** to assume, shoulder, a responsibility; **e. un enfant,** to adopt, take on, a child. **2. e. un mur en tôle,** to back a wall with sheet iron. **3.** *Com:* to endorse (cheque, bill, etc.); to back (bill). **4.** *Bookb:* to back (book).

endosseur, -euse [ɑ̃dosœːr, -øːz], *s. Com:* endorser (of bill, etc.).

endossure [ɑ̃dosyːr], *s.f. Bookb:* backing, rounding (of back).

endostome [ɑ̃dɔstoːm], *s.f. Bot: Anat:* endostome.

endostyle [ɑ̃dɔstil], *s.m. Z:* endostyle.

endothélial, -aux [ɑ̃dɔteljal, -o], *a. Physiol:* endothelial.

endothéliome [ɑ̃dɔteljɔm], *s.m. Med:* endothelioma.

endothélium [ɑ̃dɔteljɔm], *s.m. Physiol:* endothelium.

endothèque [ɑ̃dɔtɛk], *s.f. Fung:* ascus (of truffle, etc.).

endothérapique [ɑ̃dɔterapik], *a.* pest-destroying; acaricidal.

endothermique [ɑ̃dɔtɛrmik], *a. Ch:* endothermic.

endotoxine [ɑ̃dɔtɔksin], *s.f. Bac:* endotoxin.

endouzainer [ɑ̃duzɛne], *v.tr.* to put up (articles) in dozens.

endroit [ɑ̃drwa, -a], *s.m.* **1.** place, locality, spot; **le plus bel e. de la ville,** the finest spot in the town; **par endroits,** here and there, in places; **l'e. où il fut blessé,** the place where he was wounded; **il est venu à l'e. où je pêchais,** he came to where I was fishing; **l'e. le plus touchant du livre,** the most touching part, passage, in the book; **à cet e. de la conversation,** at this point of the conversation; **rire au bon e.,** to laugh in the right place; **j'ai perdu l'e.,** I have lost the, my, place (in the book); *F:* **le petit e.,** the w.c.; *s.a.* SENSIBLE 2. **2.** side, aspect; **vous ne connaissez l'affaire que par son plus bel e.,** you know only the best side of the matter; **prendre qn par son e. faible;** *F:* to get on the soft side of s.o.; *prep. phr.* **à l'e. de qn, de qch.,** regarding, with regard to, s.o., sth.; **quelles sont ses intentions à votre e.?** what are his intentions regarding you? **avoir des soupçons à l'e. de qn,** to entertain suspicions about s.o.; **il n'éprouve que de la haine à leur e.,** he feels nothing but hatred towards them. **3.** right side (of material); **à l'e.,** right side, way, out, round, up; **une de vos chaussettes n'est pas à l'e.,** one of your socks is wrong side out; **étoffe sans e. ni envers,** reversible material; *Tex:* **duite d'e.,** overshot pick. **4.** sunny side (of valley).

endromididés [ɑ̃drɔmidide], *s.m.pl. Ent:* Endromididae.

enduction [ɑ̃dyksjɔ̃], *s.f.* coating.

enduire [ɑ̃dɥiːr], *v.* (*pr.p.* **enduisant;** *p.p.* **enduit;** *pr.ind.* **j'enduis, il enduit, n. enduisons;** *p.d.* **j'enduisais;** *p.h.* **j'enduisis;** *fu.* **j'enduirai**) **1.** *v.tr.* to smear, besmear, cover, coat, plaster; to pay (ship); to dope (aeroplane wings); **e. des pierres de goudron,** to coat stones with tar; **e. un mur de chaux,** to plaster a wall; **le mur fut enduit de peinture,** the wall was coated with paint; **e. un mur de ciment,** to render a wall with cement; **e. un carneau de ciment,** to lute, line, a flue with cement; **e. la peau de vaseline,** to smear the skin with vaseline, to smear vaseline over the skin; *F:* **enduit de boue,** plastered with mud, overlaid with mud. **2.** *v.i. Ven:* (*of a bird of prey*) to digest well.

enduisage [ɑ̃dɥizaːʒ], *s.m.* (action of) coating; doping (of aeroplane wings); *Phot:* backing (of plate); *Civ.E:* **e. de surface,** surface dressing.

enduisant [ɑ̃dɥizɑ̃], *a.* adherent (matter, etc.).

enduiseur [ɑ̃dɥizœːr], *s.m. Const:* (*pers.*) finisher.

enduiseuse [ɑ̃dɥizøːz], *s.f. Paperm:* coating machine.

enduit [ɑ̃dɥi], *s.m.* **1.** (*a*) coat, coating (of tar, paint, etc.); **e. protecteur,** protective coating; *Av:* dope; *Civ.E:* **e. d'usure,** surface dressing; **e. bitumineux,** bituminous grout; **e. calorifuge,** non-conducting composition; (*b*) *Const:* plastering, coat of plaster, set; **appliquer un e. sur un mur,** to set a wall; **e. de ciment,** cement rendering; **e. de pan de bois,** lath and plaster; *Metalw:* **e. de noir,** blackwash. **2.** (water)proofing (of cloth, etc.). **3.** *Cer:* glaze, glazing. **4.** *Phot:* **e. antihalo,** backing; **plaque à e. antihalo,** backed plate; **plaque sans e. antihalo,** unbacked plate.

endurable [ɑ̃dyrabl], *a.* endurable.

endurance [ɑ̃dyrɑ̃ːs], *s.f.* endurance. **1.** long-suffering, patience. **2.** resistance to wear and tear; *Aut: etc:* **épreuve, course, d'e.,** reliability trial; reliability run. **3.** stamina; staying-power.

endurant [ɑ̃dyrɑ̃], *a.* enduring, patient, long-suffering; **peu e.,** quick-tempered, testy.

endurci [ɑ̃dyrsi], *a.* **1.** hardened; *Tchn:* indurated. **2. cœur e.,** (i) hard, callous, heart; (ii) obdurate heart; **pécheur e.,** hardened sinner; **célibataire e.,** confirmed bachelor; **haine endurcie,** inveterate hatred.

endurcir [ɑ̃dyrsiːr], *v.tr.* **1.** to harden, indurate; **e. le cœur de qn,** to harden s.o.'s heart. **2. e. qn à qch., à faire qch.,** to inure s.o. to sth., to doing sth.; **être endurci à la fatigue,** to be inured, hardened, to fatigue; **l'habitude endurcit,** habit is a hardener.

s'endurcir. 1. to harden, indurate; to become hard; *F:* to become callous; **s'e. aux malheurs d'autrui,** to become callous to the misfortunes of others. **2.** to become hardened, fit, tough.

endurcissement [ɑ̃dyrsismɑ̃], *s.m.* **1.** (*a*) hardening, induration (of substance); (*b*) **e. à la fatigue,** inuring (of s.o.) to fatigue; toughening (up). **2.** (*a*) hardness (of heart); callousness; (*b*) obduracy.

endurer [ɑ̃dyre], *v.tr.* **1.** to endure, bear (hardship, ill-treatment, etc.); **je ne peux e. ses manières grossières,** I can't stand, put up with, his rude manners; *Lit:* I cannot brook his rude manners; **e. des railleries,** to put up with chaff. **2.** *Row:* (*a*) to pull easy; (*b*) to hold.

endymion [ɑ̃dimjɔ̃], *s.m. Bot:* bluebell.

Énée [ene], *Pr.n.m. Lt.Lit:* Aeneas.

Énéide (l') [leneid], *Pr.n.f. Lt.Lit:* the Aeneid.

énéma [enema], *s.m. Med:* enema.

énéolithique [eneolitik], *a. & s.m. Prehist:* aeneolithic (age).

énergamètre [enɛrgamɛtr], *s.m.* machine for measuring the work done by human muscles.

énergamétrie [enɛrgametri], *s.f.* method, study, of the techniques of measuring the work done by human muscles.

énergétique [enɛrʒetik]. **1.** *a.* energizing (medicine, food, etc.); **ressources énergétiques,** (sources of) power; *Ph:* concerning energy; *Ind:* **dépense é.,** expenditure of energy; *Ind: Mec.E: Physiol:* **rendement é.,** energy efficiency. **2.** *s.f.* energetics.

énergétisme [enɛrʒetism], *s.m. Phil:* energetics.

énergie [enɛrʒi], *s.f.* energy. **1.** (*a*) force, vigour; **é. à faire qch.,** energy in doing sth.; **consacrer, apporter, appliquer, toute son é. à une tâche,** to devote, bend, direct, all one's energies to a task; to throw all one's energy into a task; to put one's heart and soul into a task; *F:* to put one's best foot forward; **faire appel à toute son é.,** to summon up all one's energy; **déployer de l'é.,** to put forth, display, energy; **avec é.,** energetically; **sans é.,** listless(ly); (*b*) efficacy (of remedy). **2.** (*a*) *Mec* **é. cinétique,** kinetic energy; **é. potentielle, é. interne,** potential energy; **é. atomique,** atomic energy, nuclear power; **é. emmagasinée,** stored energy; **déplacement d'é.,** energy shift; **é. acoustique,** sound energy; **é. au zéro absolu,** zero point energy; **é. nulle,** zero energy; **é. radiante, é. rayonnante, é. de rayonnement,** radiant energy, radiant flux; *Atom.Ph:* **é. de liaison,** binding energy; **é. de répulsion,** repulsive energy; **é. de désintégration,** disintegration energy; *Ball:* **é. à la bouche,** muzzle energy; **é. au choc,** striking energy; (*b*) *Ind:* (fuel and) power; **fourniture d'é.,** supply of power; **é. consommée,** power consumption; **installation d'é.,** power equipment.

énergique [enɛrʒik], *a.* energetic; (*a*) **être é.,** to be full of grit, to have plenty of go; **travailleur é.,** strenuous worker; (*b*) strong, drastic (measures); forcible (language); emphatic (gesture); **remède é.,** (i) powerful medicine; (ii) drastic remedy, kill or cure remedy.

énergiquement [enɛrʒikmɑ̃], *adv.* energetically; strenuously; forcibly; **s'y mettre é.,** to put one's back into it; **il affirmait é. que . . .,** he strongly maintained that . . .

énergol [enɛrgɔl], *s.m. Rockets:* propellant.

énergumène [enɛrgymɛn], *s.m. & f.* **1.** *Theol:* demoniac, energumen; *F:* **crier comme un é.,** to scream like one possessed. **2.** *F:* (*a*) frenzied fanatic or agitator; (*b*) ranter, tub-thumper. **3.** *F:* freak; outlandish character.

énervant [enɛrvɑ̃], *a.* **1.** enervating (climate, etc.). **2.** *F:* aggravating, irritating (person, habit, etc.); **bruits énervants,** nerve-racking noises.

énervation [enɛrvasjɔ̃], *s.f.* **1.** (*a*) (moral or physical) enervation; (*b*) nervous prostration. **2.** (*a*) hamstringing; (*b*) slaughter by severance of the spinal cord; pithing (of ox); (*c*) *Surg:* denervation.

énervé [enɛrve], *a.* **1.** *O:* nerveless, flabby; *F:* wishy-washy (style). **2.** (*a*) fidgety, nervy, unstrung; **petits rires énervés,** hysterical giggles; **il était tout é.,** his nerves were (all) on edge; (*b*) out of patience. **3.** hamstrung. **4.** *Bot:* (*of leaves, etc.*) without veins, nerves; enervate.

énervement [enɛrvəmɑ̃], *s.m.* state of jangled nerves; nervous irritation; restiveness; **être dans un état d'é. perpétuel,** to be in a constant state of nerves.

énerver [enɛrve], *v.tr.* **1.** (*a*) *O:* to enervate, weaken (body, will, etc.); **é. son style,** to emasculate one's style, *U.S: F:* to take the pep out of one's style; (*b*) to cripple (s.o., animal) by severing the sinews; to hamstring; (*c*) *Surg:* to denervate. **2. é. qn,** to get on s.o.'s nerves, to set s.o.'s nerves on edge, to fray s.o.'s nerves, to irritate s.o.; to try s.o.'s temper; **le moindre bruit l'énerve,** the least sound irritates him; gets on his nerves; **cela m'énerve,** it gives me the fidgets.

s'énerver. 1. *O:* to become languid, flabby (through idleness, etc.); to lose one's stamina. **2.** (*a*) to become irritable, fidgety, nervy; to get excited; **il s'énervait de ces questions,** he chafed, was impatient, under these questions; (*b*) (*of horse, etc.*) to become restive, to get out of hand.

enfaîteau, -eaux [ɑ̃fɛto], *s.m. Const:* hip-tile, ridge-tile.

enfaîtement [ɑ̃fɛtmɑ̃], *s.m. Const:* ridge-tiling, ridging.

enfaîter [ɑ̃fɛte], *v.tr. Const:* to ridge (roof); to finish off (roof) with ridge-tiles, galvanized iron, etc.

enfance [ɑ̃fɑ̃ːs], *s.f.* **1.** (*a*) childhood; **première, petite, e.,** infancy, babyhood; *Med:* **deuxième, seconde, e.,** later childhood; **dès sa plus tendre e.,** from his earliest childhood; **il fut adroit de ses mains dès son e.,** he was clever with his fingers from a child; *F:* **l'e. de la civilisation,** the dawn, beginning, of civilization; *F:* **c'est l'e. de l'art,** it's (mere) child's-play; **industrie encore dans son e.,** industry still in its infancy, in its early stage, still undeveloped; (*b*) boyhood; girlhood. **2.** childishness; **retomber en e.,** to sink into one's second childhood, into one's dotage. **3.** children (collectively).

enfançon [ɑ̃fɑ̃sɔ̃], *s.m. F: A:* little child, babe.
enfant [ɑ̃fɑ̃], *s.m. & f.* **1.** (*a*) child; boy or girl; *F:* youngster; *Jur:* infant; **un(e) e. en bas âge, du premier âge,** an infant, a baby; **e. problème, difficile,** problem, difficult, child; **e. non désiré,** unwanted child; **il n'y a plus d'enfants,** children are all grown up nowadays; **arrivez, mes enfants!** come along, boys (girls)! come along, children! **c'est une belle e.,** she is a beautiful child; **e., trouvé,** (i) foundling; (ii) *A: Nau:* stowaway; *Mil:* **e. de troupe,** soldier's son or orphan (educated at a Preparatory Military School); *F:* **ce n'est qu'un jeu d'e.,** it is (mere) child's play; **babil d'e.,** childish prattle; **se conduire en e., faire l'e.,** to behave childishly; **contes pour les enfants,** nursery tales; **la vérité sort de la bouche des enfants,** "out of the mouth of babes and sucklings"; *s.a.* CHAMBRE 1, CHŒUR 2, TERRIBLE, VOITURE 2; *V:* **e. de putain, de salaud,** son-of-a-bitch; *a.* childlike; babyish; **un sourire e.,** a childlike smile; **ne soyez pas si e.,** don't be so childish; (*b*) *F:* lad, fellow, man; *esp. pl.* (*officer to his men*) **allons-y, mes enfants!** come on, lads! *Mil:* **enfants perdus,** forlorn hope; *a.* **bon e.,** good-natured; **il est trop bon e. pour . . .,** he is too decent a chap to . . .. **2.** (*a*) offspring; **il a trois enfants, deux filles et un fils,** he has three children, two daughters and a son; **c'est l'e. de son père;** *F:* he is his father's child, a chip of the old block; **mourir sans enfants,** to die childless, *Jur:* without issue; **être en travail d'e., en mal d'e.,** to be in labour; **e. de l'amour,** love-child; **le bonheur est e. de la vertu,** happiness is the child of virtue; (*b*) descendant; **les enfants de David,** the descendants of David; **les enfants d'Israël,** the children of Israel; (*c*) **un e. de Paris,** a native of Paris; (*d*) *Hist:* **les Enfants de France,** the Princes and Princesses of the blood; (*e*) *F:* **c'est son e.,** it's his baby, his brainchild, his invention.
enfantelet [ɑ̃fɑ̃t(ə)lɛ], *s.m. Dial: F:* little child, babe.
enfantement [ɑ̃fɑ̃tmɑ̃], *s.m.* **1.** childbirth, confinement; *A:* travail. **2.** giving birth (**d'une œuvre,** to a work).
enfanter [ɑ̃fɑ̃te], *v.tr.* to bear, to bring forth, to give birth to (child); **trois fils enfantés par elle,** three sons born to her; **la discorde enfante le crime,** discord begets crime; **ce fut lui qui enfanta ce grand projet,** he was the father of that great scheme.
enfantillage [ɑ̃fɑ̃tija:ʒ], *s.m.* **1.** childishness; **pas d'e.!** no nonsense! **2.** childish act or saying; *pl. F:* baby tricks.
enfantin [ɑ̃fɑ̃tɛ̃], *a.* **1.** infantile; **classe enfantine,** *s.f.* **enfantine,** infant class. **2.** childish (voice, game, etc.); **littérature enfantine,** children's literature, juvenile literature; **babil e.,** baby talk. **3.** c'est e., *F:* it's just too easy; **travail e.,** child's-play.
enfariner [ɑ̃farine], *v.tr.* **1.** to flour (sth.); to cover (sth.) with flour; *F:* **elle s'est bien enfarinée,** she smothered her face in powder; **piéton qu'enfarine la poussière,** pedestrian smothered in dust; *F:* **aborder qn la langue enfarinée,** to address s.o., (i) in a bumptious manner, (ii) in a mealy-mouthed manner; **j'arrive le bec enfariné pour les féliciter le jour de l'anniversaire de leur mariage . . . et j'apprends qu'ils sont en train de divorcer!** I came bouncing up bubbling with congratulations on their wedding anniversary, only to hear they were getting a divorce; *F:* **e. qn d'un système philosophique,** to win s.o. completely over to a philosophical system. **2.** *A:* **être enfariné d'une science,** to have a smattering, a sprinkling, of a science.
s'enfariner. **1.** to get covered with flour. **2.** *F:* **s'e. de grec,** to acquire a smattering of Greek.
enfer [ɑ̃fɛ:r], *s.m.* **1.** hell; **les enfers,** the underworld, the nether regions; Hades; *Lit:* **l'E. de Dante,** Dante's Inferno; **aller en e.,** to go to hell; *F:* **il a fait de ma vie un e.,** he has made my life a hell upon earth; **aller un train d'e.,** to go at top speed, (i) to ride hell for leather; (ii) (of car, etc.) to scorch along; **bruit d'e.,** hellish noise; **feu d'e.,** roaring fire; **tison d'e.,** limb of Satan; *Mil.Hist:* **l'e. de Stalingrad,** the inferno of Stalingrad; *s.a.* JEU 4, PAVER. **2.** *Tchn: F:* stoke-hole. **3.** library department containing books not available to the public.
enferge [ɑ̃fɛrʒ], *s.f.* hobble.
enfermé [ɑ̃fɛrme], *s.m. used in* **sentir l'e.,** (*of room*) to smell stuffy.
enfermer [ɑ̃fɛrme], *v.tr.* **1.** to shut (s.o., sth.) up; **e. qn dans une cellule,** to confine s.o. in, to, a cell; **e. qch., qn, à clef,** to lock sth., s.o., up; **e. ses papiers,** to lock up one's papers; **e. qn dans une prison,** to clap s.o. into prison; **tenir qn enfermé,** to keep s.o. in confinement, under lock and key; **j'ai été enfermé dans une pièce toute la journée,** I have been cooped up in a room all day; **il enferma les chèvres,** he penned the goats; *F:* **il est bon à e.,** he ought to be shut up (in an asylum); he is stark mad; **e. son chagrin,** to keep one's sorrow to oneself. **2.** to shut, hem, (sth.) in; to enclose, surround; *Sp:* to hem in, to box (an opponent); **montagnes qui enferment la vallée,** mountains that hem in the valley. **3.** *A:* (= RENFERMER) to contain; **passage qui enferme beaucoup de vérités,** passage that contains many truths.
s'enfermer. **1.** (*a*) to lock oneself in, to shut oneself up; **s'e. dans ses études,** to bury oneself in one's studies; **enfermé dans ses pensées,** wrapped up in his thoughts; **s'e. dans son opiniâtreté,** to maintain an attitude of obstinacy; *F:* to dig one's toes in; (*b*) to live shut up, *F:* cooped up; **vivre trop enfermé,** to live too much indoors; **il s'enferma une heure avec le colonel,** he was closeted with the colonel for an hour. **2.** **jardin qui s'enferme de hauts murs,** garden surrounded by high walls.
enferrer [ɑ̃fɛre], *v.tr.* to pierce (s.o.); to run (s.o.) through (with a sword, etc.).
s'enferrer. **1.** (*a*) to spit oneself (on opponent's sword); (*b*) (*of fish*) to swallow the hook. **2.** to give oneself away, to be hoist with one's own petard; *F:* to dish oneself; **aider qn à s'e.,** to lead s.o. on.
enfeu [ɑ̃fø], *s.m. Arch:* recess (tomb).
enfeuiller [ɑ̃fœje], *v.tr.* to cover (sth.) with leaves.
s'enfeuiller, (*of tree, etc.*) to break into leaf.
enficeler [ɑ̃fisle], *v.tr.* (**j'enficelle, n. enficelons; j'enficellerai**) (*rare*) to tie (sth.) round with string.
enfichable [ɑ̃fiʃabl], *a.* plug-in.
enficher [ɑ̃fiʃe], *v.tr. Tp: etc:* to plug in.
enfieller [ɑ̃fjɛle], *v.tr.* **1.** to make (food, etc.) bitter. **2.** to embitter, sour (s.o.'s life, etc.).
enfiévré [ɑ̃fjevre], *a.* fevered (brow, etc.); feverish (activity).
enfièvrement [ɑ̃fjɛvrəmɑ̃], *s.m.* fever(ishness).
enfiévrer [ɑ̃fjevre], *v.tr.* (**j'enfièvre, n. enfiévrons; j'enfiévrerai**) **1.** to give (s.o.) fever; to make (s.o.) feverish. **2.** to fire, animate (s.o.); **enfiévré de joie,** in a fever of joy.
s'enfiévrer. **1.** to grow feverish. **2.** to get excited.
enfilade [ɑ̃filad], *s.f.* **1.** succession, series (of doors, etc.); suite (of rooms, etc.); **chambres en e.,** suite of rooms; **maisons en e.,** row of houses; **e. d'injures, de gens,** string of insults, of people. **2.** *Mil:* enfilade; **tir d'e.,** raking, enfilading, fire; **prendre une tranchée en e.,** to enfilade, rake, a trench.
enfilage [ɑ̃fila:ʒ], *s.m.* = ENFILEMENT.
enfile-aiguilles [ɑ̃filegɥij], *s.m.inv.* needle-threader.
enfilement [ɑ̃filmɑ̃], *s.m.* threading (of needle); stringing (of beads, etc.); filing (of papers on spike-file).
enfiler [ɑ̃file], *v.tr.* **1.** to thread (needle); to file (papers on spike-file); **e. des perles,** (i) to string beads; (ii) *F:* to trifle away one's time; *F:* **e. d'interminables raisonnements,** to go through an endless string of arguments; **e. qn,** (i) to run s.o. through (with a sword, etc.); (ii) *F:* to dupe, swindle, s.o. **2. e. une rue,** to take, go along, a street; **e. les tranchées,** to thread one's way along the trenches; *Nau:* **e. un détroit,** to thread a strait; **e. la rue d'un coup d'œil,** to look down, up, along, the street; *A:* **e. la venelle,** to cut and run. **3. e. ses vêtements,** to slip on, tumble into, one's clothes; **e. son pantalon, ses bas,** to pull on, draw on, one's trousers, one's stockings; **blouse à e.,** slip-on blouse. **4.** *F:* (*a*) **s'e. un bon dîner,** to treat oneself to a good dinner, to get outside a good dinner; **s'e. un pot,** to knock back a drink; (*b*) **s'e. un travail,** to have to plod through a piece of work; **on s'est enfilé tout le chemin à pied,** we had to walk all the way. **5.** *Mil:* to enfilade, rake (trench, etc.). **6.** *Nau:* to run down (ship).
enfileur, -euse [ɑ̃filœ:r, -ø:z], *s.* **1.** threader (of needle); stringer (of pearls). **2.** *F:* swindler, cheat.
enfin [ɑ̃fɛ̃]. **1.** *adv.* (*a*) finally, lastly, after all, in the long run, ultimately; **e. et surtout,** last but not least; (*b*) in fact, in a word, in short; **il est mal élevé et vindicatif, e. un mauvais enfant,** he's rude and spiteful, in short, in a word, a thoroughly bad child; (*c*) at last, at length; **e. vous voilà! vous voilà e.!** here you are at last! **2.** *int.* (*a*) at last! that's that! (*b*) come now! **mais e., s'il acceptait!** but still, if he did accept! (*c*) **e.! ce qui est fait est fait,** well, well! what is done is done; **e., vous pouvez essayer,** anyhow, after all, you can try.
enflammé [ɑ̃flɑme], *a.* **1.** burning, blazing (wood, etc.); fiery (sun, sunset). **2.** blazing, glowing (cheeks). **3.** burning (passion); **e. de colère,** burning, blazing, with anger, in a blaze of anger, ablaze with anger. **4.** *Her:* inflamed.
enflammement [ɑ̃flɑm(ə)mɑ̃], *s.m.* **1.** blazing (of fire, etc.). **2.** *F:* exciting, stirring up (of passions).
enflammer [ɑ̃flɑme], *v.tr.* to inflame. **1.** to ignite; to set (sth.) on fire, in a blaze, ablaze; **e. une allumette,** to strike a match. **2.** to inflame (wound). **3.** to excite, animate, stir up (s.o.); **e. le courage de qn,** to fire s.o.'s courage.
s'enflammer. **1.** to catch fire, to ignite, to burst into flame, to blaze up, to flare up. **2.** (*of wound, etc.*) to become inflamed. **3.** *F:* **s'e. de colère,** to fire up, flare up.
enflé [ɑ̃fle], *a.* swollen (river, limb, etc.); blown out (balloon); *Med:* tumid; **style e.,** turgid, high-flown, bombastic, style; **e. d'orgueil,** puffed up with pride; *s.m. P:* **espèce d'e.!** you idiot!
enflécher [ɑ̃fleʃe], *v.tr.* (**j'enflèche, n. enfléchons; j'enflécherai**) *Nau:* to rattle down (*i.e.* put the ratlines on the shrouds).
enfléchure [ɑ̃fleʃy:r], *s.f. Nau:* ratline.
enflement [ɑ̃fləmɑ̃], *s.m.* (*a*) swelling (of river, limb, etc.); (*b*) *occ.* inflation (of balloon, etc.).
enfler [ɑ̃fle]. **1.** *v.tr.* (*a*) to swell; to cause (sth.) to swell; **e. les joues,** to puff out, blow out, one's cheeks; (*of wind*) **e. les voiles,** to fill the sails; **les pluies ont enflé la rivière,** the rain has swollen the river; **le succès l'enfle,** success has gone to his head; **e. le nombre, la dépense,** to swell the number, the expenditure; (*b*) *occ.* to inflate (balloon, etc.); (*c*) **e. son style,** to inflate one's style. **2.** *v.i. & pr.* (*a*) to swell; **son bras (s')enfle,** his arm is swelling; **la rivière (s')enfle,** the river is rising; **la voile s'enfle,** the sail fills; **mon cœur s'enfle quand j'y pense,** my heart swells when I think of it; (*b*) to grow puffy.
enfleurage [ɑ̃flœra:ʒ], *s.m.* enfleurage (of fats and oils).
enfleurer [ɑ̃flœre], *v.tr. Ind:* to saturate (oils or fat) with the perfume of flowers.
enflure [ɑ̃fly:r], *s.f.* (*a*) swelling (of cheek, limb, etc.); *F:* **e. du style,** inflation, turgidity, of style; (*b*) puffiness.
enfoiré [ɑ̃fware], *s.m. V:* **espèce d'e.!** you silly bugger!
enfoncé [ɑ̃fɔ̃se], *a.* **1.** smashed (in), broken (in); stove in; **côtes enfoncées,** fractured ribs, broken ribs. **2.** (*a*) sunken, deep (cavity, ravine, etc.); **yeux enfoncés,** deep-set, sunken, eyes; **e. dans l'étude,** deep in study; (*b*) low-lying (ground, village, etc.). **3.** *P:* cheated, done, had.
enfoncement [ɑ̃fɔ̃smɑ̃], *s.m.* **1.** (*a*) driving (in) (of pile, nail, etc.); breaking open (of door, etc.); (*b*) sinking (of one's feet in the mud, etc.); (*c*) staving in (of metal, wall, etc.). **2.** (*a*) hollow, depression (in the ground); (*b*) *Nau:* bay, bight; (*c*) *Arch:* alcove, recess; (*d*) *Art:* background; (*e*) *Surg:* **e. du crâne, du bassin (à la suite d'une fracture),** depression in skull or pelvis caused by fracture.
enfoncer [ɑ̃fɔ̃se], *v.* (**j'enfonçai(s); n. enfonçons**) **1.** *v.tr.* (*a*) to drive (in) (pile, nail); **e. à fond,** to push well home; **e. un clou dans le mur,** to drive a nail into the wall; *Tp: etc:* **enfoncez le bouton,** press the button; *s.a.* MARTEAU 1; **e. la main dans sa poche,** to thrust one's hand into one's pocket; *F:* to dive into one's pocket; **e. son chapeau sur sa tête,** to cram one's hat on one's head; **il m'enfonça son coude dans le flanc,** he dug his elbow into my ribs; **s'e. une épine dans le pied,** to run a thorn into one's foot; **e. la clef dans la serrure,** to insert the key in the lock; *Artil:* **e. la charge,** to insert the charge; *F:* **je ne peux pas lui e. cela dans la tête, le crâne,** I can't get, drive, that into his head; (*b*) to break open, beat in, burst in (door, etc.); to stave in (cask); **e. qch. à coups redoublés,** to batter sth. in; **e. un carreau,** to break a window-pane; *F:* **e. une porte ouverte,** (i) to use a steam hammer to crack a nut; (ii) to flog a dead horse; *Mil:* **e. une ligne de défense,** to break through a line of defence; **e. tous les obstacles,** to break through all obstacles; **e. l'ennemi,** to break in upon the enemy, to break up the ranks of the enemy; to rout the enemy; (*c*) *F:* to get the better of (s.o.); to best (s.o.); to worst (s.o.); *F:* to down (s.o.), to bowl (s.o.) over. **2.** *v.i.* to sink (into mud, sea); **le navire enfonçait,** the ship was settling; **nous y**

avons enfoncé jusqu'aux genoux, we sank into it up to our knees. **3.** *v.tr.* to put the bottom into (cask, etc.); to bottom (cask).

s'enfoncer, to penetrate, plunge, go deep (into sth.); **le navire s'enfonça sous les eaux,** the ship sank to the bottom; **le navire s'enfonçait peu à peu,** the ship was settling down; **enfoncé de l'arrière,** down by the stern; **enfoncé par l'avant,** down by the head; **le plancher s'enfonçait,** the floor was subsiding, was giving way; **s'e. dans un bois,** to plunge into a wood; **les montagnes s'enfoncent au nord,** the mountains thrust northwards; **le golfe s'enfonce vers la ville,** the gulf runs inland towards the town; **ici la terre s'enfonce profondément,** here the ground forms a deep hollow; **le mur s'enfonce en cet endroit,** the wall forms a recess at this point; **les racines s'enfoncent profondément dans le sol,** the roots strike deep into the soil; **la balle s'enfonça dans le mur,** the bullet bedded itself in the wall; **s'e. dans l'eau,** to sink into the water; **s'e. dans l'ombre,** to disappear in, be swallowed up by, the darkness; **s'e. dans une rue,** *F:* to dive into a street; **s'e. dans une rêverie,** to sink into a brown study; **s'e. dans l'étude de qch.,** to bury oneself in the study of sth.; **plus on perd au jeu, plus on s'enfonce,** the more one loses at play, the deeper one sinks; **s'e. dans le crime,** to sink deep(er) in crime; **ceux qui sont en train de s'e.,** men who are going downhill.

enfonceur, -euse [ɑ̃fɔ̃sœːr, -øːz], *s.* one who breaks in, through (sth.); **e. de porte(s) ouverte(s),** one who finds difficulties where none exist.

enfonçure [ɑ̃fɔ̃syːr], *s.f.* **1.** cavity (in rock); depression, hollow (in ground); recess (in cavern, etc.). **2.** bottom (of cask).

enforcir [ɑ̃fɔrsiːr]. **1.** *v.tr. A:* to reinforce, consolidate, strengthen (a construction, etc.); to strengthen (s.o.); *F:* to set (s.o.) up. **2.** *v.i. & pr.* (*of pers.*) to gain strength; to grow, become, stronger; to thrive; (*of wine*) to acquire body; *F:* **comme votre petit a enforci!** how your youngster has grown!

enformer [ɑ̃fɔrme], *v.tr.* **1.** to fashion; to give shape to (sth.). **2.** to block (hat).

enfouir [ɑ̃fwiːr], *v.tr.* to hide (sth.) in the ground; to bury (dead animal, money); **avoir des talents enfouis,** to have hidden talents; **e. sa douleur,** to conceal one's grief; **e. (par un labour),** to plough in; **e. (du fumier) avec le râteau,** to rake in (manure).

s'enfouir, *F:* to retire, to hide oneself; **s'e. dans la campagne,** to bury oneself in the country.

enfouissement [ɑ̃fwismɑ̃], *s.m.* hiding (of sth.) in the ground; burying (of dead animal, etc.).

enfouisseur [ɑ̃fwisœːr], *s.m.* **1.** (*rare*) burier. **2.** *Ent:* sexton-beetle.

enfourchement [ɑ̃furʃəmɑ̃], *s.m.* **1.** *Mec.E:* fork link. **2.** *Carp:* (*a*) open mortise-joint, slot-mortise; (*b*) slit-and-tongue joint. **3.** *Arch:* meeting-angle of groin arch. **4.** *Wr:* crutch hold.

enfourcher [ɑ̃furʃe], *v.tr.* **1.** to thrust a (pitch)fork into (sth.). **2.** (*a*) to bestride, get astride, mount (horse, bicycle, etc.); (*b*) *F:* to ride (idea, opinion) to death; *s.a.* DADA. **3.** *Box:* **e. la tête de son adversaire,** to get one's opponent's head in chancery.

enfourchure [ɑ̃furʃyːr], *s.f.* fork, crotch (of tree); fork (of legs, antler, etc.).

enfournage [ɑ̃furnaːʒ], *s.m.,* **enfournée** [ɑ̃furne], *s.f.,* **enfournement** [ɑ̃furnəmɑ̃], *s.m.* **1.** charging (of furnace, kiln, oven); *Atom.Ph:* **enfournement,** loading (of reactor). **2.** placing (of bread, etc.) in the oven.

enfourner [ɑ̃furne], *v.tr.* (*a*) to put (bread, etc.) in an oven, (pottery, bricks) in a kiln; *F:* (*a*) **e. une affaire,** to start sth., to set a matter going; (*b*) **e. qch.,** to gobble sth. up.

s'enfourner, *F:* to get involved, mixed up (in an affair); to get into a fix; *F:* **la foule s'est enfournée dans l'église,** the crowd poured into the church; *F:* **s'e. dans une impasse,** to get into a blind alley.

enfourneur [ɑ̃furnœːr], *s.m.* (*a*) *Baking:* oven-man; peeler; (*b*) kiln-man; charger.

enfourneuse [ɑ̃furnøːz], *s.f. Ind:* charging-machine, coal-car.

enfranger [ɑ̃frɑ̃ʒe], *v.tr.* to trim (dress, etc.) with a fringe.

enfreindre [ɑ̃frɛ̃ːdr], *v.tr.* (*pr.p.* **enfreignant;** *p.p.* **enfreint;** *pr.ind.* **j'enfreins, il enfreint, n. enfreignons, ils enfreignent;** *p.d.* **j'enfreignais;** *p.h.* **j'enfreignis;** *fu.* **j'enfreindrai**) to infringe, transgress, break (the law); to fail to comply with (the law); **e. les dispositions d'un traité, etc.,** to violate a treaty, etc.

enfroquer [ɑ̃frɔke], *v.tr. A: & Iron:* to make a monk of (s.o.).

s'enfroquer, *A: & Iron:* to become a monk.

enfuir (s') [sɑ̃fɥiːr], *v.pr.* (*conj. like* FUIR) **1.** (*a*) to flee, fly; to run away; to slip away; **s'e. de prison,** to escape from prison; *F:* **à mesure que les jours s'enfuyaient,** as the days flew by; **les côtes s'enfuient,** the coast recedes; **terrain qui s'enfuit sous les pas,** ground that gives way under the feet; (*b*) (*of embezzler, etc.*) to abscond; **s'e. du domicile conjugal, de la maison paternelle, avec un(e) amant(e),** to elope. **2.** (*of liquid*) (i) to leak out, run out; to run; (ii) to boil over.

enfumage [ɑ̃fymaːʒ], *s.m.* (*a*) filling (of room, etc.) with smoke; (*b*) blackening (of sth.) with smoke; (*c*) smoking out (of bees, animals).

enfumé [ɑ̃fyme], *a.* **1.** smoky (room, etc.). **2.** smoke-blackened (walls, etc.).

enfumer [ɑ̃fyme], *v.tr.* **1.** (*a*) to fill (room, etc.) with smoke, to smoke out (room); (*b*) to blacken (sth.) with smoke; (*c*) to smoke out (bees, animal from it's lair, etc.). **2.** *F:* to stupefy, fuddle (s.o.) (with wine, etc.).

enfumoir [ɑ̃fymwaːr], *s.m. Ap:* smoking-apparatus, smoker.

enfûtage [ɑ̃fytaːʒ], *s.m.* barrelling (of wine, cider, etc.).

enfutailler [ɑ̃fytɑje], **enfûter** [ɑ̃fyte], *v.tr.* to barrel, cask (wine, cider, etc.).

engagé [ɑ̃gaʒe]. **1.** *a.* (*a*) *Arch:* engaged; **colonne engagée,** engaged, imbedded, column; (*b*) *Nau:* (*of ship*) (i) gunwale under; on her beam-ends; (ii) waterlogged; (*c*) *Nau:* (*of propeller*) foul; (*d*) committed (literature, etc.); **non e.,** uncommitted. **2.** *s.m. Mil:* **e. (volontaire),** (i) volunteer; (ii) man who has enlisted in advance of the statutory age; *Turf:* **la liste des engagés,** the list of entries.

engageable [ɑ̃gaʒabl], *a. Lit:* that may be (i) pawned, pledged, mortgaged, (ii) invested.

engageant [ɑ̃gaʒɑ̃], *a.* engaging, prepossessing, winning, attractive (manners, etc.); inviting (meal, etc.).

engagement [ɑ̃gaʒmɑ̃], *s.m.* **1.** (*a*) pawning, pledging (of jewels, etc.); mortgaging (of estate); (*b*) tying up, locking up (of capital); *Adm:* **e. de dépenses,** commitment of funds; (*c*) receipt (for object pledged). **2.** (*a*) engagement, promise, agreement; contract; liability; commitment; **tenir ses engagements, faire honneur, faire face, à ses engagements,** to keep, observe, carry out, one's engagements; to meet one's obligations, one's liabilities; **prendre l'e. de faire qch.,** to undertake to do sth., to pledge one's word to do sth.; **contracter, prendre, un e.,** to enter into a contract, into an engagement; **mes engagements ne me permettent pas . . .,** my commitments do not allow me to . . .; **sans e.,** without obligation; *Com:* **il a toujours rempli ses engagements,** he has always fulfilled his engagements; *Jur:* **e. signé par la caution,** bail-bond; (*b*) engagement, appointment (of employee); *Com:* indenture; *Mil:* voluntary enlistment; **se trouver sans e.,** to be disengaged, *F:* out of a job; *Th: F:* to be resting; (*c*) *Sp:* (i) entering; (ii) entry (for sporting event); (iii) fixture. **3.** *Fenc:* engage, engagement, engaging; *Hockey:* **e. du jeu,** bully; *Mil: Navy:* engagement, action; *F:* scrap (with the enemy). **4.** (*a*) (*of artist*) booking; (*b*) *Pol: etc:* commitment; alignment. **5.** *Obst:* engagement (of the baby's head).

engager [ɑ̃gaʒe], *v.tr.* (**j'engageai(s); n. engageons**) **1.** (*a*) to pledge, pawn (jewellery, etc.); to mortgage (property); **e. sa parole,** to pledge, plight, one's word; **e. sa foi,** to plight oneself, one's troth; **cette promesse les engage,** this promise is binding on them; **cette lettre ne vous engage pas,** this letter does not bind you, does not commit you; **réponses qui n'engagent à rien,** non-committal answers; **e. qn à dîner,** *F:* to book s.o. for dinner; **tous les frais engagés seront remboursés,** all expenses incurred will be reimbursed; *s.a.* HONNEUR 1, RESPONSABILITÉ; (*b*) **e. un cheval,** to enter a horse (for a race). **2.** (*a*) to engage (servant, etc.); to take on (hands), to sign on (ship's company); **main-d'œuvre engagée à long terme,** indentured labour; (*b*) to enlist (recruit). **3.** (*a*) to catch, foul, entangle (rope, etc.); to jam (part of machine. etc.); **e. une ancre,** to foul an anchor; **e. un aviron,** to catch a crab; **e. un vaisseau,** to run a ship aground; **manœuvre engagée à la poulie,** rope choked in the block; *F:* **e. qn dans une querelle,** to involve s.o. in, draw s.o. into, a quarrel; (*b*) *Fin:* **e. son capital,** to lock up, tie up, one's capital; **ma fortune personnelle est engagée dans l'affaire,** my private means are invested in the business; (*c*) to engage (machinery), to put (machinery) into gear; (*d*) **e. un tube dans une ouverture,** to fit, drive, a pipe into an opening; **e. la clef dans la serrure,** to fit, insert, the key in the lock. **4.** to begin, start; to set (sth.) going; to open (conversation, fight, etc.); **e. la conversation avec qn,** to engage in conversation with s.o.; **e. le combat,** to join battle; to engage; *Navy:* **bord non engagé,** disengaged side (of ship in battle); **e. des négociations,** to enter into, start upon, negotiations; *Jur:* **e. des poursuites,** to institute proceedings, to take legal action (**contre,** against); *Hockey:* **e. le jeu,** to bully off; *Fenc:* **e. (l'épée),** to engage; *Mil:* **e. des troupes,** to bring troops into action, to engage troops. **5. e. qn à faire qch.,** to invite, urge, advise, s.o. to do sth. **6.** *v.i.* (*a*) (*of machinery*) to come into gear; (*b*) *Nau:* (*of ship*) to roll gunwale under.

s'engager. 1. s'e. à, *A:* **de, faire qch.,** to undertake, promise, covenant, agree, bind oneself, pledge one's word, commit oneself, to do sth.; **s'e. d'honneur à faire qch.,** to pledge one's honour that one will do sth.; **s'e. par traité à faire qch.,** to contract to do sth.; **je ne savais pas à quoi je m'engageais,** I did not know what I was letting myself in for; **je ne m'engagerai à rien,** I'll be quite non-committal; **sans s'e. à rien,** without pinning oneself down (to anything); **je suis trop engagé pour reculer,** I have gone too far, am too deeply committed, to draw back. **2.** (*a*) to take service (**chez qn,** with s.o.); (*b*) *Mil:* to enlist; to join up; **s'e. aux dragons,** to enlist in the dragoons; (*c*) *Sp:* **s'e. pour une course,** to enter for a race. **3.** (*a*) (*of rope, propeller*) to foul; to become fouled; (*of machine*) to jam; (*of aeroplane*) to get out of control; *Nau:* **s'e. dans un autre navire,** to run foul of another ship; (*b*) **un tube s'engage dans l'ouverture,** a pipe fits into the opening. **4.** (*a*) **s'e. dans qch.,** to enter, plunge into, sth.; **l'armée s'engagea dans le défilé,** the army entered the pass; **s'e. dans une rue,** to turn into a street; (*b*) (*of battle, conversation, etc.*) to begin.

engainant [ɑ̃genɑ̃], *a. Bot:* sheathing (leaf).

engainer [ɑ̃gɛne], *v.tr.* (*a*) to sheathe (dagger, etc.); *Sculp:* **statue engainée,** gaine; (*b*) (*of leaf, etc.*) to ensheathe (the stalk).

engallage [ɑ̃galaːʒ], *s.m. Tex:* weighting (of silk).

engaller [ɑ̃gale], *v.tr. Tex:* to weight (silk).

engamer [ɑ̃game], *v.i.* (*of fish*) to swallow the hook.

enganter [ɑ̃gɑ̃te], *v.tr.* **1.** *A: F:* to infatuate (s.o.). **2.** *Nau:* to have the heels of, come up with, fore-reach (another ship).

s'enganter, *A: F:* **s'e. de qn,** to become infatuated with s.o.

engaver [ɑ̃gave], *v.tr.* (*of bird*) to feed (nestling).

s'engaver, *A: F:* to gorge.

engazonnement [ɑ̃gɑzɔnmɑ̃], *s.m.* **1.** turfing (of ground). **2.** sowing (of ground) with grass-seed.

engazonner [ɑ̃gɑzɔne], *v.tr.* **1.** to turf (over) (piece of ground). **2.** to sow (ground) with grass-seed.

engeance [ɑ̃ʒɑ̃ːs], *s.f.* **1.** *A:* species, breed, strain (of poultry, etc.). **2.** *F:* **e. de scélérats,** brood of scoundrels; **sale e.!** lousy bunch! **quelle e.!** what a lot, set.

engeancer [ɑ̃ʒɑ̃se], *v.tr.* (**j'engeançai(s); n. engeançons**) *A: F:* **e. qn de qn,** to saddle, burden, s.o. with s.o.

engeigner [ɑ̃ʒɛɲe], *v.tr. A:* to deceive s.o., to get the better of s.o.

s'engeigner, *A:* to get caught in one's own toils.

engelure [ɑ̃ʒlyːr], *s.f.* chilblain.

engendrement [ɑ̃ʒɑ̃drəmɑ̃], *s.m.* **1.** begetting (of children); procreation. **2.** *F:* production; generation (of heat, etc.); breeding (of disease, etc.). **3.** *Civ.E:* **coefficient d'e.,** ratio of traffic flow before and after the building of a new road, bridge, etc.

engendrer [ɑ̃ʒɑ̃dre], *v.tr.* **1.** (*a*) to beget (child); (*b*) (*of stallion, etc.*) to sire. **2.** to engender (strife, etc.); to generate, develop (heat, etc.); to breed (disease); **courant engendré par une pile,** current produced by a cell; **volume engendré par une courbe,** volume generated by a curve; *Prov:* **la familiarité engendre le mépris,** familiarity breeds contempt; **c'est le désir qui a engendré cette pensée,** the wish was father to the thought; *F:* **il n'engendre pas la mélancolie,** he's good company.

engerbage [ɑ̃ʒɛrbaːʒ], *s.m.* **1.** *Husb:* binding (of sheaves). **2.** piling, heaping, (of things) together.

engerber [ɑ̃ʒɛrbe], *v.tr.* **1.** *Husb:* to sheaf (corn); to bind (corn) in sheaves. **2.** to pile (up), heap (up), stack (barrels, sacks, etc.).

engin [ɑ̃ʒɛ̃], *s.m.* **1.** engine, machine; device, contrivance; *Civ.E:* **e. de transport,** haulage unit; *Petroleum Ind:* **e. de forage,** movable derrick platform; **engins de pêche,** fishing tackle; **e. à lever les fardeaux,** gin, hoist; **e. de sauvetage,** rescue appliance; life-saving apparatus; **e. mécanique,** mechanical appliance; *Nau: Av: etc:* **e. de manutention,** cargo-handling gear. **2. engins de guerre,** engines, appliances, of war; **e. amphibie,** amphibian, amphibious, craft or vehicle; **e. téléguidé,** guided missile; **e. autoguidé, e. à tête chercheuse,** homing missile; **e. atmosphérique,** air-breathing missile, cruise-type missile, flying missile, non-ballistic missile; **e. balistique,** ballistic missile; **e. antifusée,** anti-ballistic missile; **e. balistique à portée moyenne, à portée intermédiaire,** medium-range, intermediate-range, ballistic missile; **e. balistique intercontinental,** intercontinental ballistic missile; **e. air-air,** air-to-air missile; **e. air-sol,** *Navy:* **e. air-surface,** air-to-surface missile; **e. sol-air,** *Navy:* **e. surface-air,** surface-to-air missile; **e. sol-sol,** *Navy:* **e. surface-surface,** surface-to-surface missile; *Navy:* **e. mer-sol,** underwater-to-surface missile; **e. à moteur interne,** hot missile; **e. guidé par un faisceau,** beam rider. **3.** *A:* snare, gin.

englaciation [ɑ̃glasjasjɔ̃], *s.f. Geog:* glaciation (of a region).

englanté [ɑ̃glɑ̃te], *a. Her:* acorned.

englober [ɑ̃glɔbe], *v.tr.* to include, embody; to take (sth.) in; **propriété qui englobe plusieurs villages,** estate that takes in, includes, several villages; **e. les innocents parmi les coupables,** to include the innocent with the guilty; **il les englobait tous dans son mépris,** he included them all in his contempt; **ces états furent englobés dans l'Empire,** these states were, became, merged in the Empire.

engloutir [ɑ̃gluti:r], *v.tr.* **1.** to swallow; to gulp (sth.) down; to wolf down, bolt (one's food). **2.** to engulf (sth.), to swallow (sth.) up; **vaisseau englouti par les flots,** vessel swamped, swallowed up, by the waves; *F:* **le jeu a englouti toute sa fortune,** gambling has swallowed up all his fortune; **e. une fortune dans une entreprise,** to sink a fortune in an undertaking.

s'engloutir, (*of ship*) to be engulfed; to sink (like a stone).

engloutissement [ɑ̃glutismɑ̃], *s.m.* **1.** swallowing, gulping down, bolting (of food, etc.). **2.** engulfment (of ship, by sea, etc.); swallowing up (of fortune, etc.).

engluage [ɑ̃glya:ʒ], *s.m.,* **engluement** [ɑ̃glymɑ̃], *s.m.* **1.** (*a*) liming (of twigs, of birds); (*b*) *Arb:* banding; painting (with wax, etc.). **2.** (*a*) bird-lime; (*b*) *Arb:* grafting-wax.

engluer [ɑ̃glye], *v.tr.* (*a*) to lime (twigs, etc.); to smear (twigs, etc.) with bird-lime; (*b*) to lime (bird); to catch (bird) with bird-lime; (*c*) *F:* to ensnare (s.o.); **se laisser e.,** to allow oneself to be caught in the toils; (*d*) **coque engluée de boue,** hull slimed all over with mud.

s'engluer, *v.pr.* **1.** (*of bird*) to get caught (on limed twig). **2.** to get caught in the toils.

engobage [ɑ̃gɔba:ʒ], *s.m. Cer:* slip painting.

engobe [ɑ̃gɔb], *s.m. Cer:* slip.

engober [ɑ̃gɔbe], *v.tr. Cer:* to decorate, coat, (pottery) with slip.

engommage [ɑ̃gɔma:ʒ], *s.m.* **1.** gumming. **2.** *Cer:* glazing.

engommer [ɑ̃gɔme], *v.tr.* **1.** to gum, dress (tissue, etc.); *Bookb:* to gum. **2.** *Cer:* to glaze.

engoncé [ɑ̃gɔ̃se], *a.* **1.** stiff; bundled up in one's clothes; **avoir l'air e.,** to look awkward and stiff. **2. taille engoncée,** (i) hunched-up shoulders; (ii) stiffness (in one's clothes). **3. e. dans la respectabilité,** bound up in one's own respectability, starchily respectable.

engoncer [ɑ̃gɔ̃se], *v.tr.* **(il engonça(it))** (*of clothes*) to sit awkwardly on (s.o.).

engoncement [ɑ̃gɔ̃smɑ̃], *s.m.* stiffness (in one's clothes).

engorgé [ɑ̃gɔrʒe], *a.* choked up (pipe, etc.); foul (pump); congested (railway-station, etc.); swollen (glands); fouled up (boiler); sluggish, congested (liver).

engorgement [ɑ̃gɔrʒəmɑ̃], *s.m.* **1.** choking, stopping (up), obstructing, blocking, clogging (of passage, pipe, etc.); fouling (of pump, etc.); *Metall:* scaffolding, engorgement (of blast-furnace); *Pol.Ec:* **l'e. (des marchés),** glutting (of the markets). **2.** obstruction, stoppage; *Med:* engorgement, congestion; **e. des seins, mammaire,** swelling of the breasts.

engorger [ɑ̃gɔrʒe], *v.tr.* **(j'engorgeai(s); n. engorgeons)** to choke (up), stop (up), to obstruct, block, clog (passage, pipe, etc.); *Pol.Ec:* to glut.

s'engorger, to become choked (up), blocked (up), clogged; (*of pump*) to foul; *Metall:* (*of blast-furnace*) to scaffold, to become engorged; *Med:* to become engorged, congested.

engoué [ɑ̃gwe, -ue], *a.* **1.** *Lit:* choked. **2.** infatuated **(de,** with).

engouement [ɑ̃gumɑ̃], *s.m.* **1.** *Med:* obstruction, choking up (of hernia). **2.** infatuation, craze; **l'e. pour le tennis,** the tennis craze.

engouer [ɑ̃gwe, ɑ̃gue], *v.tr. Lit:* to obstruct, choke up (the breathing passages, etc.).

s'engouer. 1. *Med:* (*of hernia*) to become obstructed. **2. s'e. de qn, de qch.,** to become infatuated with, to go crazy over, s.o., sth.

engouffrement [ɑ̃gufrəmɑ̃], *s.m.* engulfment, engulfing, swallowing up (of vessel by the sea, etc.); **l'e. du vent,** the rushing in of the wind.

engouffrer [ɑ̃gufre], *v.tr.* to engulf; **e. une fortune,** to swallow up a fortune; **e. sa nourriture,** to devour, gulp down, wolf, one's food.

s'engouffrer, to be engulfed, swallowed up, lost to sight; **la foule s'engouffra dans l'édifice,** the crowd surged into the building; **il s'engouffra dans le hall de la gare,** he disappeared into the station; **le vent s'engouffre sous les arches du pont,** the wind blows violently, rushes, under the arches of the bridge; **le vent s'engouffra par la porte,** the wind swept in.

engoujure [ɑ̃guʒy:r], *s.f. Nau:* score (of block); dead sheave, dumb sheave (of mast).

engouler [ɑ̃gule], *v.tr.* (*a*) *A: F:* to gulp (sth.) down; to gobble (sth.) up; (*b*) *Her:* **sautoir engoulé,** saltire engouled, engoulé.

engoulevent [ɑ̃gulvɑ̃], *s.m. Orn:* **e. (d'Europe),** nightjar, goat-sucker, fern-owl; **e. d'Égypte,** Egyptian nightjar; **e. à collier roux,** red-necked nightjar; **e. porte-étendard,** pennant-wing nightjar; **e. d'Amérique,** American night-hawk; **e. de Virginie,** whippoorwill.

engoûment [ɑ̃gumɑ̃], *s.m.* = ENGOUEMENT.

engourdi [ɑ̃gurdi], *a.* **1.** (*a*) numb(ed); **j'ai le pied e.,** my foot has gone to sleep; (*b*) **état e. d'un animal,** torpid state of an animal. **2. esprit e.,** dull, sluggish, mind; numskull. **3.** *Nau:* **filin e.,** stiff rope; **le navire est e.,** the ship is hanging.

engourdir [ɑ̃gurdi:r], *v.tr.* **1.** to (be)numb (limb, etc.). **2. e. l'esprit,** to dull the mind.

s'engourdir. 1. (*of limb, etc.*) to grow numb; *F:* (*of foot, limb*) to go to sleep. **2.** (*of the mind*) to become dull, sluggish, torpid. **3.** (*of hibernating animal*) to become torpid.

engourdissement [ɑ̃gurdismɑ̃], *s.m.* **1.** numbness (of limb, etc.). **2.** dullness, sluggishness, torpor (of mind, etc.); **e. du marché,** sluggishness of the market. **3.** torpor (of hibernating animal).

engrain [ɑ̃grɛ̃], *s.m. Agr:* einkorn.

engrais [ɑ̃grɛ], *s.m.* **1.** *Husb:* fattening pasture or food; **mettre des bœufs à l'e.,** to put oxen to fatten. **2.** *Agr:* manure; **e. artificiels, chimiques,** fertilizers, chemical manure; **e. flamand,** liquid manure; **e. de poisson,** fish manure; **e. d'os,** bone meal; **e. vert,** manure crop.

engraissage [ɑ̃grɛsa:ʒ], *s.m.* = ENGRAISSEMENT 1.

engraissant [ɑ̃grɛsɑ̃], *a.* fattening (food).

engraissement [ɑ̃grɛsmɑ̃], *s.m.* **1.** fattening (of animals); cramming (of fowls). **2.** (*of pers.*) putting on of flesh. **3.** *Geol:* **e. de plage,** beach accretion.

engraisser [ɑ̃grɛse]. **1.** *v.tr.* (*a*) to fatten (animals); to cram (fowls); (*of s.o. drowned in the sea*) *F:* **e. les poissons,** to feed the fishes; (*b*) to make (s.o.) fat; **la bonne chère l'a engraissé,** good living has made him fat; *A: F:* **temps qui engraisse le cimetière,** weather that makes a fat churchyard; (*c*) to manure, fertilize (land); (*d*) *A:* to make (sth.) greasy; **s'e. les doigts,** to grease one's fingers. **2.** *v.i.* to grow stout; to put on flesh; to run to fat; (*of cattle, etc.*) to thrive; **elle va beaucoup mieux, elle a engraissé,** she is much better: she has filled out, put on weight.

s'engraisser, to fatten oneself up; **mes chevaux s'engraissent à ne rien faire,** my horses are eating their heads off; **s'e. de la misère d'autrui,** to batten, thrive, on other people's misfortunes.

engraisseur [ɑ̃grɛsœ:r], *s.m.* fattener; crammer (of fowls, etc.).

engramme [ɑ̃gram], *s.m. Psy:* engram.

engrangement [ɑ̃grɑ̃ʒmɑ̃], *s.m.* garnering, getting in (of corn, etc.).

engranger [ɑ̃grɑ̃ʒe], *v.tr.* **(j'engrangeai(s); n. engrangeons)** to garner, get in (the corn).

engravement [ɑ̃gravmɑ̃], *s.m.* **1.** grounding, stranding (of boat). **2.** covering (of ground) with sand. **3.** silting up (of harbour).

engraver[1] [ɑ̃grave], *v.tr. A:* to engrave.

engraver[2]. **1.** *v.tr.* (*a*) *Nau:* to strand (ship); to run (boat) into the sand; (*b*) (*of flooded river, etc.*) to cover (ground) with sand, with gravel; (*c*) *Const:* (i) to make a notch in a sheet of roofing lead; (ii) to fix a piece of lead by one extremity. **2.** *v.i. & pr.* (*a*) (*of boat*) to ground; to run on to the sand, to settle into the sand; to bed in the sand; (*b*) (*of harbour*) to silt up.

engravure [ɑ̃gravy:r], *s.f. Const:* sheet of roofing-lead.

engrêlé [ɑ̃grɛle], *a. Her:* engrailed.

engrêler [ɑ̃grɛle], *v.tr.* to purl; to put an edging on (lace).

engrêlure [ɑ̃grɛly:r], *s.f.* **1.** *Her:* engrailed border. **2.** purl, edging (on lace); picot-edge.

engrenage [ɑ̃grəna:ʒ], *s.m.* **1.** *Mec.E:* (*a*) gearing, engaging, throwing into gear, coming into gear, meshing; **e. intermédiaire (de machine-outil),** backgear(ing); (*b*) (toothed) gearing; gear; gear-wheels; **e. à crémaillère,** rack-and-pinion gear; **e. à onglet, à 45°,** mitre-gear; **e. à biseau, e. conique,** bevel gear; **e. hélicoïdal,** helical gear, screw-gear; **e. à vis sans fin,** worm gear(ing); **e. à chevrons,** herringbone gear, double-helical gear; **e. cylindrique, droit,** spur gear; **e. (à dents) intérieur(es),** annular, internal, gear; **e. à développante,** involute gear; **e. à denture croisée,** step-tooth gear; **e. multiplicateur, démultiplicateur,** step-up, step-down, gear; **e. sélectif,** pick-off gear, selective transmission; *Aut:* **e. de direction,** steering gear; **système, jeu, d'engrenages,** train, set, of gear-wheels; gearing; **machine à tailler les roues d'e.,** gear-cutting machine; **engrenages d'une montre,** watch-train; **turbine à engrenage(s),** geared turbine; (*c*) **e. de circonstances,** mesh, complication, of circumstances; **être pris dans l'e.,** to become more and more involved, to get caught up in the machine. **2.** *Nau:* stowage (of casks) in the hold.

engrenant [ɑ̃grənɑ̃], *a.* toothed, meshing, gearing (wheel).

engrènement [ɑ̃grɛnmɑ̃], *s.m.* **1.** (*a*) feeding (of mill-hopper or threshing-machine) with corn; (*b*) feeding (of animals) on corn. **2.** *Mec.E:* coming into gear, meshing, engaging; **ligne d'e. (d'une roue dentée),** pitch-line.

engrener [ɑ̃grəne], *v.tr.* **(j'engrène, n. engrenons; j'engrènerai) 1.** (*a*) to feed corn (into threshing machine); (*b*) to feed (animals) on corn. **2.** (*a*) *Mec.E:* to gear, put into gear, connect, engage, mesh (toothed wheels); to put (wheels) into gear, *U.S:* to intermesh; *F:* **e. une affaire,** to set a thing going; to start a deal, an undertaking; (*b*) *v.i. & pr.* **roues qui (s')engrènent,** wheels that gear, engage, into one another; wheels that mesh with one another, that cog. **3.** *Nau:* to stow (casks) in the hold.

engreneur [ɑ̃grənœ:r], *s.m.* (*pers.*) feeder (of threshing-machine).

engreneuse [ɑ̃grənø:z], *s.f.* mechanical feeder (of threshing-machine).

engrenure [ɑ̃grəny:r], *s.f.* **1.** *Mec.E:* (*a*) engaging, catching (of toothed wheels); interlocking; (*b*) gear ratio. **2.** *Anat:* serrated suture, serra (of skull).

engrisailler [ɑ̃grizɑje], *v.tr.* to grey (over) (the whites of an etching, etc.).

engrois [ɑ̃grwa], *s.m.* wedge (in the eye of a hammer).

engrosser [ɑ̃grose], *v.tr. P:* to make (woman) pregnant; *F:* to get (girl) into trouble; to put (woman) in the family way; *P:* to knock (a girl) up.

engrosseur [ɑ̃grosœ:r], *s.m. P:* man who makes women pregnant, *P:* knocks girls up.

engrossir [ɑ̃grosi:r], *A:* **1.** *v.i.* to become pregnant. **2.** *v.tr.* = ENGROSSER.

engrumeler [ɑ̃grymle], *v.tr.* **(il engrumelle; il engrumellera)** (*rare*) to clot, curdle (soap, etc.).

s'engrumeler, (*of soap, etc.*) to clot, curdle.

enguenillé [ɑ̃gənije], *a. F:* clothed in rags, tattered.

engueulade [ɑ̃gœlad], *s.f.,* **engueulement** [ɑ̃gœlmɑ̃], *s.m. P:* scolding, slanging; blowing up; **recevoir une e.,** to be hauled over the coals; *P:* to be told off good and proper; *P:* **envoyer à qn une lettre d'e.,** to send s.o. a rocket.

engueuler [ɑ̃gœle], *v.tr. P:* to abuse, slang (s.o.); to blow (s.o.) up; to go for (s.o.); **si tu rentres tard tu vas te faire e.,** if you come in late, you'll get a rocket, there'll be ructions.

s'engueuler, *P:* **s'e. avec qn,** to have a row with s.o.

enguichure [ɑ̃giʃy:r], *s.f. Hist: Arm:* guige.

enguignonné [ɑ̃giɲɔne], *a. F:* out of luck; suffering from a run of bad luck.

enguirlander [ãgirlãde], *v.tr.* **1.** (*a*) to (en)garland (sth.); **statue enguirlandée de fleurs**, statue garlanded, wreathed, with flowers; **une vigne enguirlande le balcon**, a vine entwines the balcony; (*b*) *O: F:* **e. qn**, to get round s.o. **2.** *F:* = ENGUEULER.

enhaché [ãaʃe], *a. Arch: Surv:* encroaching (portion of building, territory).

enhachement [ãaʃmã], *s.m. Arch: Surv:* encroaching portion (of building, territory).

enhardir [ãardiːr], *v.tr.* to embolden; to put courage into (s.o.); **e. qn à faire qch.**, to encourage s.o. to do sth.

s'enhardir, to pluck up courage, to throw off one's shyness; **s'e. à faire qch.**, to venture, make bold, to do sth.; **s'e. jusqu'à faire qch.**, to make so bold as to do sth.; **ils ne s'enhardissent pas à parler**, they are shy of speaking; **enhardi au crime**, grown bold in crime.

enhardissement [ãardismã], *s.m.* **1.** emboldening. **2.** boldness; **e. au crime**, boldness in crime.

enharmonie [ãnarmoni], *s.f. Mus:* enharmonic change.

enharmonique [ãnarmonik], *a.* enharmonic (modulation, etc.).

enharnachement [ãarnaʃmã], *s.m.* **1.** harnessing. **2.** harness.

enharnacher [ãarnaʃe], *v.tr.* **1.** to harness (horse). **2.** (*a*) *A:* to put s.o.'s armour (on him); (*b*) *O: F:* to get (s.o.) up, deck (s.o.) out, like a guy.

enherbé [ãnerbe], *a.* grass-covered, -grown.

enherbement [ãnerb(ə)mã], *s.m. Agr:* (act of) putting (land) under grass.

enherber [ãnerbe], *v.tr. Agr:* to put (land) under grass.

enhuché [ãyʃe], *a. Naut:* (*of vessel*) moon-sheered; high out of water.

enhydre[1] [ãniːdr], *a.* enhydrous.

enhydre[2], *s.m.* **1.** *Z:* enhydra. **2.** *Miner:* enhydros.

éniellage [enjɛlaːʒ], *s.m. Agr:* weeding out of corn-cockles.

énieller [enjele], *v.tr. Agr:* to rid (crop) of corn-cockles.

énième [enjɛm], *a. & s.m. F:* n^{th}; **je te le dis pour la é. fois**, I'm telling you for the nth, umpteenth, time.

énigmatique [enigmatik], *a.* enigmatic(al).

énigmatiquement [enigmatikmã], *adv.* enigmatically.

énigme [enigm], *s.f.* enigma, riddle; **proposer une é. (à qn)**, to ask (s.o.) a riddle, to put, propound, a riddle (to s.o.); **trouver le mot d'une é.**, to find the answer, the clue, to a riddle; to guess, solve, a riddle; **parler par énigmes**, to speak in riddles; **ce garçon est une é. pour moi**, I can't make the boy out.

enivrant [ãnivrã], *a.* intoxicating, heady.

enivrement [ãnivrəmã], *s.m.* **1.** intoxication, inebriation. **2.** *F:* ectasy (of joy); elation; delirious enthusiasm.

enivrer [ãnivre], *v.tr.* to intoxicate. **1.** (*a*) to inebriate; to make (s.o.) drunk; **la bière l'avait enivré**, the beer had gone to his head; (*b*) to ply (s.o.) with liquor. **2.** *F:* to impassion, elate, exalt.

s'enivrer. 1. to become intoxicated, inebriated (de, with); to get drunk; *F:* to get fuddled. **2.** *F:* **s'e. de mots, de projets**, to get drunk on words, to revel in schemes; **s'e. de colère**, to get into a blind rage.

enjabler [ãʒable], *v.tr. Coop:* to bottom or head (cask).

enjablure [ãʒablyːr], *s.f. Coop:* bottoming.

enjaler [ãʒale], *v.tr. Nau:* to stock (anchor).

enjambé [ãʒãbe], *a.* **haut e.**, long-legged; **court e.**, short-legged.

enjambée [ãʒãbe], *s.f.* stride; **marcher à grandes enjambées**, to stride along, to stalk along; *F:* **d'une e.**, in one go.

enjambement [ãʒãbmã], *s.m.* **1.** *Pros:* enjambment, overflow; run-on-line. **2.** *Civ.E:* fly-over, *U.S:* overpass. **3.** *Biol:* crossing-over.

enjamber [ãʒãbe]. **1.** *v.tr.* (*a*) to bestride (horse); (*b*) to step over, stride over (obstacle); **e. une barrière**, to straddle a gate; **trois ponts enjambent le fleuve**, three bridges span the river. **2.** *v.i.* (*a*) to stride; to step out; to walk with long strides; (*b*) **e. sur qch.**, (i) to jut, project, over sth.; (ii) to encroach on sth.; (*c*) *Pros:* to run the line on; (*of line*) to run on.

enjarreté [ãʒarte], *a.* (*of horse*) hobbled.

enjaveler [ãʒavle], *v.tr.* **(j'enjavelle, n. enjavelons; j'enjavellerai)** *Agr:* to gather (the swath) into handfuls, into sheaves.

enjeu, -eux [ãʒø], *s.m. Gaming:* stake; **mettre son e.**, to put down one's stake; **retirer son e.**, (i) to withdraw one's stake, (ii) *F:* to back out (of an undertaking), to cry off; **lutte dont une vie est l'e.**, struggle in which a life is at stake.

enjoindre [ãʒwɛ̃ːdr], *v.tr.* (*conj. like* JOINDRE) to enjoin, prescribe; **e. (strictement) à qn de faire qch.**, to enjoin, to call upon, to charge, s.o. to do sth.; to give s.o. strict injunctions to do sth.; to enjoin a course of action on s.o.

enjôlement [ãʒolmã], *s.m.* **1.** cajoling, wheedling, inveigling. **2.** cajolery, blandishment, inveiglement.

enjôler [ãʒole], *v.tr.* to coax, inveigle, wheedle; to get round (s.o.); to humbug (s.o.); to talk (s.o.) over.

enjôleur, -euse [ãʒolœːr, -øːz], **1.** *s.* coaxer, cajoler, wheedler. **2.** *a.* coaxing, cajoling, wheedling.

enjolivant [ãʒolivã], *a.* beautifying, embellishing, adorning.

enjolivement [ãʒolivmã], *s.m.* **1.** beautifying, embellishment, adornment (of s.o., sth.); *F:* **l'e. d'un récit**, the embroidering of a tale. **2.** ornamental piece; scroll; **enjolivements**, embellishments.

enjoliver [ãʒolive], *v.tr.* to beautify, embellish, set off (s.o., sth.); **elle sait tout e. autour d'elle**, she knows how to make things attractive; *F:* **e. un récit**, to embroider a tale.

enjoliveur, -euse [ãʒolivœːr, -øːz], *s.* **1.** beautifier, embellisher. **2.** *s.m. Aut:* hub cap; wheel-disk.

enjolivure [ãʒolivyːr], *s.f.* small embellishment.

enjoué [ãʒwe], *a.* playful, vivacious, lively, bright, sprightly; **ton e.**, playful tone of voice; **caractère e.**, sprightly nature.

enjouement, enjoûment [ãʒumã], *s.m.* sprightliness; playfulness.

enjouer [ãʒwe], *v.tr. Lit:* to give a pleasant or sprightly tone to (conversation).

enjuguer [ãʒyge], *v.tr.* to yoke (oxen).

enjuiver [ãʒɥive], *v.tr.* to Judaize; to submit (sth., s.o.) to Jewish influence.

enjuponnée [ãʒypone], *a.f.* in petticoats; in her petticoat.

enjuponner [ãʒypɔne], *v.tr.* to put (s.o.) into petticoats; **s'enjuponner (d'une femme)**, to become attached (to a woman).

enkysté [ãkiste], *a.* encysted.

enkystement [ãkistəmã], *s.m. Med:* encystation, encystment.

enkyster (s') [sãkiste], *v.pr. Med:* (*of tumour, etc.*) to become encysted.

enlaçage [ãlasaːʒ], *s.m.*, **enlacement** [ãlasmã], *s.m.* **1.** intertwining, interlacing. **2.** enlacing, entwining; *Box:* **un e. de jambe**, a trip; *Tex:* **e. de cartons**, card-lacing (for Jacquard loom).

enlacer [ãlase], *v.tr.* **(j'enlaçai(s); n. enlaçons) 1.** to intertwine, interlace (ribbons, branches, etc.). **2.** (*a*) to entwine, enlace; to tie up (papers); **le lierre enlace l'arbre**, the ivy twines round, entwines, the tree; (*b*) to clasp, enfold, (s.o.) in one's arms, to hug (s.o.); *A:* to encircle, hem in (enemy); **amants enlacés**, lovers folded, clasped, in each other's arms; (*c*) *Carp:* **e. un tenon et une mortaise**, to dowel a tenon and mortise. **3.** to net, snare (animal).

s'enlacer. 1. (*of plants, etc.*); (*a*) to intertwine; (*b*) (*of creeper*) **s'e. autour de . . .**, to twine round . . . **2.** (*of wrestlers*) to hug. **3.** *A:* (*of animal*) to fall into a snare.

enlaçure [ãlasyːr], *s.f. Carp:* **1.** dowelled tenon-and-mortise joint. **2.** dowel-hole.

enlaidir [ãlɛdiːr]. **1.** *v.tr.* to uglify; to make (s.o.) ugly; to disfigure (s.o.). **2.** *v.i.* to grow ugly, plain; **elle a enlaidi**, (i) she has lost her good looks; (ii) she looks plainer than ever.

enlaidissement [ãlɛdismã], *s.m.* **1.** (*a*) uglification; (*b*) disfigurement. **2.** growing ugly; loss of good looks.

enlassure [ãlasyːr], *s.f.* = ENLAÇURE.

enlevable [ãlvabl], *a.* removable; (of machine part, etc.) detachable.

enlevage [ãlvaːʒ], *s.m.* **1.** *Row:* spurt; *F:* dust-up. **2.** *Min:* lifting-point (of the rope on the pit-head pulleys). **3.** *Tex:* bleaching, decolo(u)rizing.

enlevant [ãlvã], *a.* rousing (speech); swinging (tune, march, etc.).

enlevé [ãlve], *a.* (*of portrait*) boldly drawn; *Mus:* **morceau e.**, piece played *con brio*.

enlevée [ãlve], *s.f.* cart-load, waggon-load (of hay, etc.).

enlèvement [ãlɛvmã], *s.m.* **1.** removal, removing; carrying off, away; clearing away; *Nau:* unshipment (of mast); **e. des taches**, removal, wiping out, of stains; **e. de marchandises**, snapping up of goods (by customers); **e. de bagages à domicile**, collecting of luggage; *Geol:* **e. de la couverture**, denudation. **2.** kidnapping, carrying off; *Lit:* ravishment; **l'e. des Sabines**, the rape of the Sabine women; **mariage par e.**, elopement; *Jur:* **e. de mineur**, abduction; **e. d'enfant**, baby-snatching. **3.** *Mil:* storming, carrying (of position); *Nau:* taking (of ship) by boarding. **4.** (*a*) raising, lifting up (of weights, etc.); sending up (of balloon); (*b*) translation (to Heaven).

enlever [ãlve], *v.tr.* **(j'enlève, n. enlevons; j'enlèverai) 1.** (*a*) to remove; to take off (clothes); to carry away, take away; to carry off; *Nau:* to unship (mast); to lift (goods); **e. l'écorce, la peau**, to peel off, strip off, the bark; to peel off, tear off, the skin; *F:* **moutarde qui enlève la bouche**, mustard that takes the roof off your mouth; **e. un tapis, un rideau**, to take up a carpet, to take down a curtain; **e. des rails**, to take up rails; *Av: etc:* **e. les cales**, to remove, pull away, the chocks; **e. les meubles pour qu'on puisse danser**, to clear away the furniture, to clear the room, for dancing; **e. le couvert**, to clear away (after a meal); to clear the table; **e. une tache**, to remove, rub out, wash out, take out, a stain; **être enlevé par la mer, par le vent**, to be carried away, washed away, by the sea, blown away by the wind; **matelot enlevé par une lame**, sailor washed overboard; **la mort l'enleva à vingt ans**, death carried him off at twenty; **e. des marchandises**, to snap up, clear, goods; **les billets s'enlèvent comme des petits pains**, the tickets are being snapped up like hot cakes; *Fin:* **e. une émission d'actions**, to snap up an issue of shares; (*b*) **e. qch. à qn**, to deprive s.o. of sth.; to take sth. from s.o.; to snatch sth. (away) from s.o.; **la machine lui enleva un doigt**, the machine took off one of his fingers; **on m'a enlevé mon pardessus**, someone has made off with my overcoat; **il m'a enlevé mes cors**, he removed my corns; **la poésie l'enleva au barreau**, poetry made him desert the Bar; **la mort nous enlève à bien des misères**, death spares us many troubles. **2.** to carry off, steal (s.o., sth.); to kidnap (s.o.); **les voleurs ont tout enlevé**, the thieves went off with everything, made a clean sweep; **e. une jeune fille**, to abduct a girl; **e. une jeune fille pour l'épouser**, to make a runaway match with a girl; **se faire e. par qn**, to elope with s.o. **3.** *Mil:* to carry, storm (position); **e. un petit poste, une sentinelle (par surprise)**, to rush a picket, a sentry; *Nau:* to take (ship) by boarding. **4.** to raise; (*a*) to bear upwards; **il fut enlevé au ciel**, he was translated (in)to heaven; (*b*) **e. le couvercle**, to lift the lid; **e. des fardeaux à l'aide d'une grue**, to lift weights by means of a crane; **le vent enlève la poussière**, the wind raises the dust; **e. un ballon**, to send up a balloon; *P:* **e. le ballon à qn**, to kick s.o.'s behind; *F:* **e. qn**, to reprimand s.o.; to tick, tell, s.o. off; **e. son cheval**, (i) to lift one's horse (to a hurdle, etc.); (ii) to set one's horse off at full speed; **e. des troupes**, to spur on, urge on, cheer on, troops; *F:* **la foule fut enlevée par ces paroles**, the crowd was carried away, transported, by these words; **e. un morceau (de musique)**, to play a piece of music brilliantly, with brio; **e. un article de journal**, to dash off an article; **mouvement bien enlevé**, movement smartly carried out; **c'est à vous d'e. l'affaire**, it is up to you to pull it off; **il a enlevé l'affaire**, he got the order, the contract.

s'enlever. 1. (*a*) (*of paint, etc.*) to come off; (*of bark, etc.*) to strip (off); **la peau s'enlève**, the skin is peeling (off); **cela s'enlèvera par l'usure**, it will wear off; (*b*) *Com:* **marchandises qui s'enlèvent**, goods that sell quickly, that are snapped up. **2.** (*a*) (*of balloon, etc.*) to rise; (*b*) *A:* (*of milk*) to boil over, up; *F:* (*of pers.*) **s'e. (comme une soupe au lait)**, to fly into a passion, to flare up.

enlève-taches [ãlɛvtaʃ], *s.m.inv.* stain-remover.

enleveur [ãlvœːr], *s.m.* abductor, kidnapper.

enliasser [ãljase], *v.tr.* to tie (papers, etc.) into bundles; to file (papers).

enlier [ãlje], *v.tr.* (*pr.sub. & p.d.* **n. enliions, v. enliiez**) *Const:* to bond (bricks, stones).

enlignement [ãliɲmã], *s.m.* **1.** ranging; setting (of objects) in a line. **2.** alignment.

enligner [ãliɲe], *v.tr.* to range; to set (objects) in line.

enlisement, *A:* **enlizement** [ãlizmã], *s.m.* sinking (into quicksand, into a bog); **e. d'un avion à l'atterrissage**, sinking in of a plane on landing.

enliser, *A:* **enlizer** [ãlize], *v.tr.* (*of quicksand, bog*) to suck in, swallow up, engulf.

s'enliser, to sink, be sucked down (into quicksand, bog); (*of car, etc.*) to get bogged; (*of plane*) to sink into the ground (on landing); **les charrettes s'enlisèrent dans les marais**, the carts got caught in the swamps.

enluminer [ɑ̃lymine], *v.tr.* **1.** (*a*) to illuminate (MS); (*b*) to colour (print, map). **2.** *F:* **visage enluminé par la boisson,** face flushed with drink; **nez enluminé,** fiery red nose.

s'enluminer, *F:* **1.** to paint one's face. **2.** (*of face*) to blush or flush.

enlumineur, -euse [ɑ̃lyminœːr, -øːz], *s.* illuminator; *A:* limner (of MSS., etc.).

enluminure [ɑ̃lyminyːr], *s.f.* **1.** (*a*) illumination, illuminating (of MSS.); colouring (of prints, maps, etc.); (*b*) *F:* high colour; **e. du nez,** redness of the nose. **2.** illuminated design, illumination.

enne [ɛn], *s.f.* (the letter) n.

ennéade [ɛn(n)ead], *s.f.* ennead.

ennéagonal, -aux [ɛn(n)eagɔnal, -o], *a. Geom:* enneagonal, nine-angled (figure).

ennéagone [ɛn(n)eagɔn], *Geom:* **1.** *a.* = ENNÉAGONAL. **2.** *s.m.* enneagon, nonagon.

ennéagyne [ɛn(n)eaʒin], *a. Bot:* enneagynous.

ennéandre [ɛn(n)eɑ̃ːdr], *a. Bot:* enneandrous.

ennéasyllabe [ɛn(n)easil(l)ab], *a. Pros:* enneasyllabic.

enneigé [ɑ̃neʒe], *a.* snow-clad, -covered (mountain, etc.).

enneigement [ɑ̃nɛʒmɑ̃], *s.m.* snowing up; snow conditions; the state of being snow-covered; **bulletin d'e.,** snow report.

enneiger [ɑ̃neʒe], *v.t.* to cover with snow.

ennemi, -ie [ɛnmi]. **1.** *s.* enemy; *Lit:* foe; **ennemi No. 1,** enemy No. 1; **ennemis à mort,** bitter enemies; **se faire un e. de qn,** to make an enemy of s.o.; **passer à l'e.,** to go over to the enemy; **être tué à l'e.,** to be killed in action; *Prov:* **le mieux est l'e. du bien,** let well alone. **2.** *a.* (*a*) **l'armée ennemie,** the hostile army; *Lit:* the foe; **le camp e.,** the enemy's camp; **flotte ennemie,** enemy('s) fleet; *F:* **couleurs ennemies,** clashing colours; (*b*) **être e. avec qn,** to be on bad terms with s.o.; **il est e. des persécutions,** he is dead against persecution, he is set against persecution; **être e. du bruit,** to hate noise.

ennoblir [ɑ̃nɔbliːr], *v.tr.* to ennoble (action); to elevate, uplift (mind, etc.).

ennoblissement [ɑ̃nɔblismɑ̃], *s.m.* ennoblement (of action); elevation, uplifting (of mind, etc.).

ennoyage [ɑ̃nwajaːz], *s.m. Geog:* submergence.

ennoyé [ɑ̃nwaje], *a. Geog: Geol:* **vallée ennoyée,** drowned valley.

ennoyer [ɑ̃nwaje], *v.tr. Geog:* to submerge.

ennuager [ɑ̃nɥaʒe], *v.tr.* to becloud.

ennui [ɑ̃nɥi], *s.m.* **1.** worry, annoyance, anxiety; **avoir des ennuis,** to be worried; **pour le moment je n'ai pas d'ennuis,** I have no problems at the moment; **petits ennuis,** petty annoyances; **attirer, créer, susciter, des ennuis à qn,** to make trouble for s.o.; to make things uncomfortable for s.o.; to get s.o. into difficulties, into trouble, into hot water; **se créer des ennuis,** to get oneself into difficulties; **vous vous préparez des ennuis,** you are asking for trouble; **aller au-devant des ennuis,** to meet trouble half-way; **l'e. d'une pareille situation,** the awkwardness of such a situation; **quel e.!** what a nuisance! *Com.Corr:* **nous regrettons d'avoir pu vous causer un e. quelconque,** we are sorry for any inconvenience we may have caused you; *Prov:* **un ennui ne vient jamais seul,** troubles never come singly. **2.** boredom, tedium, ennui; **chasser l'e. de qn,** to cheer s.o. up; **ils me font mourir d'e.,** they bore me to death; **je mourais d'e.,** I was bored to tears, to death; **lire un livre avec e.,** to find a book boring to read; **dissiper, tromper, l'e. du voyage,** to relieve, while away, the tedium of the journey.

ennuyant [ɑ̃nɥijɑ̃], *a. O:* = ENNUYEUX 1.

ennuyé [ɑ̃nɥije], *a.* **1.** annoyed. **2.** bored. **3.** worried.

ennuyer [ɑ̃nɥije], *v.tr.* (**j'ennuie, n. ennuyons; j'ennuierai**) **1.** (*a*) to annoy, worry, vex; **cela m'ennuie de vous demander ce service,** I don't like to ask this service of you; **cela vous ennuierait-il d'attendre?** would you mind waiting? **cela m'ennuierait fort d'être en retard,** I should hate to be late; (*b*) to importune, to pester. **2.** to bore (s.o.); **l'affaire commence à m'e.,** I'm beginning to get tired of, bored with, the business; **il m'ennuie à mourir,** I get dreadfully tired of him; he bores me stiff; *abs.* **l'éloquence continue ennuie,** sustained eloquence palls.

s'ennuyer. 1. to be bored; **je m'ennuie à ne rien faire, d'être désœuvré,** (i) I'm bored, *F:* fed up, with doing nothing; (ii) I get bored if I have nothing to do; **on s'ennuie à mourir ici,** this is a deadly dull place; **je m'ennuie (comme une carpe, un rat mort)!** I'm bored stiff! **j'espère que vous ne vous ennuyez pas à m'écouter,** I hope you are not bored listening to me; **on ne s'ennuie pas à l'écouter,** we never tire of listening to him. **2.** *Dial:* **s'e. de qn, après qn,** to miss s.o., to long for s.o.'s return.

ennuyeusement [ɑ̃nɥijøzmɑ̃], *adv.* **1.** boringly, tediously. **2.** annoyingly.

ennuyeux, -euse [ɑ̃nɥijø, -øːz]. **1.** *a.* (*a*) boring, tedious, tiresome, dull; **mortellement e.,** deadly-dull; *F:* **e. comme la pluie,** as dull as ditch-water; (*b*) importunate; (*c*) annoying, irritating; **comme c'est e.!** what a nuisance! how very annoying! **2.** *s.* tiresome person; bore.

énol [enɔl], *s.m. Ch:* enol.

énolique [enɔlik], *a. Ch:* enolic.

énolase [enɔlaːz], *s.f. Ch:* enolase.

énolisation [enɔlizasjɔ̃], *s.f. Ch:* enolization.

énoncé [enɔ̃se], *s.m.* statement, declaration, expression (of facts, thought, etc.); **é. d'un problème,** terms of a problem; **é. d'un acte,** text, wording, of an act; **simple é. des faits,** mere statement of the facts; **l'é. du prix nous fit sauter,** the price mentioned made us jump.

énoncer [enɔ̃se], *v.tr.* **1.** (**j'énonçai(s); n. énonçons**) to state, to set forth (opinion, fact, etc.); **la quittance doit é. l'origine des deniers,** the receipt must state the source of payment; **convention énoncée dans le contrat,** condition set forth in the agreement; **é. une vérité,** to state a truth; **é. des opinions reçues,** to voice accepted opinions. **2.** to articulate (word, syllable); **phrases qui s'énoncent avec facilité,** sentences that can be spoken with ease.

s'énoncer, to express oneself (clearly, etc.); **un vague concept ne peut s'é. clairement,** a vague concept cannot be expressed clearly, put into simple words.

énonciateur, -trice [enɔ̃sjatœːr, -tris]. **1.** *s.* enunciator. **2.** *a.* **termes énonciateurs d'un principe,** terms expressing a principle.

énonciatif, -ive [enɔ̃sjatif, -iːv], *a.* enunciative (proposition); declaratory (act, etc.).

énonciation [enɔ̃sjasjɔ̃], *s.f.* **1.** stating, declaring, asserting, expressing (of thought, fact, etc.). **2.** enunciation (of syllables, etc.); articulation.

énophtalmie [enɔftalmi], *s.f. Med:* enophthalmus.

enorgueillir [ɑ̃nɔrgœjiːr], *v.tr.* to make (s.o.) proud.

s'enorgueillir, to become proud, elated; to be proud (of); **s'e. de qch., d'avoir fait qch.,** to pride oneself on sth., on having done sth.; to glory in sth.; **s'e. à raconter ses exploits,** to boast of one's exploits; **il s'enorgueillit de ce que . . .,** it is his boast that . . .

énorme [enɔrm], *a. & s.m.* enormous, huge, inordinate; *F:* tremendous; **une bête é.,** a huge beast; **quantité é.,** enormous, immense, quantity; **cela fait une différence é.,** it makes a huge difference; **crime é.,** shocking, outrageous, crime; **perte é.,** grievous, tremendous, loss; **ça m'a fait un bien é.,** it did me an enormous amount of good; **majorité é.,** overwhelming majority; **mensonge é.,** thumping lie; *F:* whopper; **c'est é.,** it's a bit much, a bit thick; **il ne se plaît que dans l'é.,** he likes everything (to be) on a large scale.

énormément [enɔrmemɑ̃], *adv.* **1.** enormously, hugely; *F:* tremendously; **je le regrette é.,** I'm extremely, *F:* awfully, sorry. **2.** a great deal (**de,** of); a great many; *F:* lots of; **il y a é. de gens qui pensent que . . .,** there are any number of people who believe that . . .; **cela m'a fait é. de bien,** it has done me an enormous amount of good; **je me suis amusé é.,** I enjoyed myself hugely; I had a great time.

énormité [enɔrmite], *s.f.* **1.** (*a*) enormity, outrageousness (of demand, sin, etc.); heinousness (of crime, sin); (*b*) enormousness, vastness, hugeness (of ocean, construction, etc.). **2.** *F:* **commettre une é.,** to make a gross blunder; *F:* to put one's foot in it badly; *F:* to drop a brick, a clanger; **dire des énormités,** to say shocking things.

énostose [enɔstoːz], *s.f. Med:* enostosis.

énouage [enwaːʒ], *s.m. Tex:* burling (of cloth).

énouer [enwe], *v.tr. Tex:* to burl (cloth).

énoyautage [enwajotaːʒ, -ɔ-], *s.m.* stoning (of fruit).

énoyauter [enwajote, -ɔ-], *v.tr.* to stone (fruit).

énoyauteur [enwajotœːr, -ɔ-], *s.m.* fruit-stoning machine.

enquérir (s') [sɑ̃keriːr], *v.pr.* (*conj. like* ACQUÉRIR) to inquire, make inquiries (**de,** after); **s'e. du prix,** to ask the price; **il s'est enquis de vous,** he inquired, asked, after you; **il s'enquérait si tu venais,** he inquired whether you were coming; **s'e. auprès de qn,** to seek information from s.o.

enquête [ɑ̃kɛt], *s.f.* inquiry, investigation, (*a*) **après e.,** on inquiry; **e. sommaire,** brief investigation; survey; **e. par sondage,** sample survey; **e. scientifique,** scientific investigation; piece of research; **faire, ouvrir, procéder à, une e. sur qch.,** to hold, institute, set up, conduct, an inquiry, to make investigations, regarding sth.; to inquire into sth.; *Jur:* **e. judiciaire après mort d'homme** = (coroner's) inquest; **conseil, commission, d'e.,** court of inquiry; *Parl:* select committee; *s.a.* SE LIVRER 2, ORDONNER 2; (*b*) *Jur:* hearing of witnesses (before trial).

enquêter [ɑ̃kɛte], *v.i.* to hold an inquiry, to make investigations; **e. sur une affaire,** to inquire into an affair.

s'enquêter, *A:* = S'ENQUÉRIR.

enquêteur, -euse [ɑ̃kɛtœːr, -øːz]. **1.** *a. Jur:* **commissaire e.,** investigating commissioner. **2.** *s.* investigator, inquisitor; *Adm:* poor-law officer; *Journ:* **enquêteuse,** female interviewer, reporter.

enquiquinant [ɑ̃kikinɑ̃]. **1.** *a. F:* infuriating; irritating; **vous êtes e.,** you're a pain in the neck. **2.** *s.* pest.

enquiquinement [ɑ̃kikinmɑ̃], *s.m. F:* real nuisance, bore; (act of) pestering; **comme toujours les enquiquinements sont pour moi,** I'm getting the worst of it as usual.

enquiquiner [ɑ̃kikine], *v.tr. F:* to aggravate, bore, pester, annoy, plague (s.o.); *F:* **je suis bien enquiquiné,** I've got problems.

enquiquineur, -euse [ɑ̃kikinœːr, -øːz], *a. & s. F:* (*a*) *a.* infuriating; (*b*) *s.* pain in the neck, real nuisance.

enraciné [ɑ̃rasine], *a.* deep-rooted (plant, prejudice, etc.); deep-seated.

enracinement [ɑ̃rasinmɑ̃], *s.m.* **1.** (*a*) digging in (of sapling); burying (of foundations); (*b*) rooting, taking root (of tree, etc.); **arbre à e. profond,** deep-rooted tree. **2. e. d'une opinion,** deep-rootedness of an opinion.

enraciner [ɑ̃rasine], *v.tr.* (*a*) to dig in, root (tree, etc.); to dig in (foundations); (*b*) *F:* to establish, implant (principles, etc.).

s'enraciner, (*a*) (*of tree, etc.*) to take root; (*b*) *F:* (*of feelings, emotions, etc.*) to become established, deeply rooted; **ces vices s'enracinent profondément dans l'âme,** these vices become deeply rooted in the soul; **une mauvaise habitude s'enracine peu à peu,** a bad habit gains on one.

enragé, -ée [ɑ̃raʒe]. **1.** *a.* (*a*) mad (dog, etc.); (*of dog*) **devenir e.,** to go mad; *F:* **vie enragée,** wild, rackety, life; *s.a.* VACHE 1; (*b*) *F:* **socialiste e.,** rabid, out-and-out, socialist; **amazone enragée,** enthusiastic horsewoman; **pêcheur e.,** fishing enthusiast, keen angler; **joueur e.,** inveterate gambler, gambling fiend. **2.** *s.* **un e. de golf,** a golf enthusiast, a keen golfer; *Pol:* **les enragés,** the extremists.

enrageant [ɑ̃raʒɑ̃], *a.* maddening; *F:* aggravating; **c'est e.!** it is enough to drive you wild! it's maddening!

enragement [ɑ̃raʒmɑ̃], *s.m.* (fretting and) fuming.

enrager [ɑ̃raʒe], *v.* (**j'enrageai(s); n. enrageons**) **1.** *v.tr.* (*a*) to enrage, madden (s.o.); (*b*) to excite (the passions of) (s.o.), to drive (s.o.) wild (with desire, etc.). **2.** *v.i.* (*a*) to be out of all patience, to (fret and) fume; *O:* **e. des dents,** to be mad with toothache; **j'enrage, ça me fait enrager, rien que d'y penser,** it makes me wild only to think of it; **faire e. qn,** to make s.o. wild; to get a rise out of s.o.; (*b*) *O:* **e. de faire qch.,** (i) to be itching to do sth.; to be all agog to do sth.; (ii) to be extremely fond of doing sth.; **elle enrage de danser,** *F:* she is mad on dancing.

enrayage[1] [ɑ̃rɛjaːʒ], *s.m. Agr:* drawing, laying out (of furrows).

enrayage[2], *s.m.*, **enraiement, enrayement** [ɑ̃rɛ(j)mɑ̃], *s.m.* **1.** (*a*) locking, braking, putting on the skid (of wheel); arresting, checking (of disease); **patin, sabot, d'enrayement,** drag, shoe; skid-pan; (*b*) jamming, stopping (of mechanism). **2.** spoking, fitting of spokes to (wheel).

enrayer[1] [ɑ̃rɛje], *v.tr.* (**j'enraye, j'enraie, n. enrayons; j'enrayerai, j'enraierai**) *Agr:* **1. e. un champ,** to plough the first furrow of a field. **2. e. les sillons,** to draw, lay out, the furrows.

enrayer[2], *v.tr.* **1.** (*a*) to lock, skid (wheel); to put (i) the brake, (ii) the drag, on (wheel); *Mil:* to stop, check, slow up (attack); **e. une maladie,** to arrest, check, a disease; to bring a disease under control; **e. une épidémie,** to stem an epidemic; **e. une crise,** to check a crisis; *F:* to stop the rot; **e. un procès, une grève,** to stop a case, a strike; *F:* **il est temps d'e.,** it is time to call a halt, to go slow; **e. la hausse des prix,** to check rising prices; (*b*) **e. une machine,** to jam, stop (machinery); **mitrailleuse enrayée,** jammed machine-gun; *F:* **les affaires sont enrayées,** business is at a standstill. **2.** to spoke (wheel), to furnish (wheel) with spokes.

s'enrayer. **1.** (*of wheel*) to jam. **2.** (*of epidemic*) to abate.

enrayure[1] [ɑ̃rɛjyːr], *s.f. Agr:* first furrows ploughed in a field.

enrayure[2], *s.f. Veh:* **1.** drag, shoe, skid, trig. **2.** spokes (of wheel).

enrayure[3], *s.f. Const:* **1.** framing (of carcass of roof). **2.** (any system of) beams radiating from a centre.

enrégimentation [ɑ̃reʒimɑ̃tasjɔ̃], *s.f.* **1.** forming (of men, troops) into regiments. **2.** regimentation.

enrégimentement [ɑ̃reʒimɑ̃tmɑ̃], *s.m.* (act of) forming into regiments.

enrégimenter [ɑ̃reʒimɑ̃te], *v.tr.* **1.** to form (men, troops) into regiments. **2.** *F:* (*a*) to enrol (body of helpers, etc.); (*b*) to regiment, to discipline (people).

enregistrable [ɑ̃r(ə)ʒistrabl̩], *a.* recordable.

enregistrement [ɑ̃r(ə)ʒistrəmɑ̃], *s.m.* **1.** (*a*) registration, registry, record(ing); **e. d'une commande,** booking, entering (up), of an order; **bureau d'e.,** (i) registry office; (ii) *Rail:* booking-office (for luggage); **e. d'une compagnie,** incorporation of a company; (*b*) **e. d'une exécution** (sound) recording of a performance; **e. électrique,** electric recording; **e. sur bande,** tape-recording; **e. direct,** direct recording; *Cin: T.V:* **e. sur disques,** sound-on-disk recording; **e. à densité constante,** variable-width recording (on film); **e. à densité variable,** variable-density recording; **e. du son, e. sonore,** sound recording; **camion d'e. (du son),** sound van; **e. (intégral) d'une émission radiophonique,** electrical transcription; **cabine d'e. sonore,** (portable) monitor room; **passer un e.,** to play a (gramophone or tape) recording. **2.** *Adm:* (*a*) registry (office); register office; **droit d'e.,** stamp duty (on property); (*b*) Wills and Probate Department.

enregistrer [ɑ̃r(ə)ʒistre], *v.tr.* to register, record. **1.** (*a*) **e. les faits de l'histoire,** to record the facts of history; **e. une naissance, un acte,** to register a birth, a deed; **e. une commande,** to book, enter up, an order; **l'amélioration enregistrée se maintient,** the improvement noted is being maintained; **société enregistrée,** incorporated company; *Rail:* **e. des bagages pour Paris,** to book, register, luggage for Paris; (*b*) *F:* to memorize. **2.** to record (for gramophone reproduction); **e. sur bande,** to tape, to record on tape; *abs.* **artiste qui enregistre pour les disques Maxim,** artiste who records for Maxims; **musique enregistrée,** recorded music (on tape, record), *U.S: F:* canned music; *Cin:* (*of actor*) **e. la joie, le dédain,** to register joy, disdain; *Computers:* **programme enregistré,** stored programme. **3.** *Fb:* **e. un but,** to score a goal; **aucun but n'a été enregistré,** neither side scored, there was no score.

enregistreur, -euse [ɑ̃r(ə)ʒistrœːr, -øːz]. **1.** *a.* (self-)recording, registering (apparatus, device); **bande enregistreuse,** recording chart; **stylet e.,** recording pen; *s.a.* CAISSE 3. **2.** *s.m.* (*a*) registrar; (*b*) (automatic) recording instrument; recorder; **e. du son, e. sonore,** sound recorder; **e. sur disques,** sound-on-disc recorder; **e. magnétique sur ruban, sur bande, à bande magnétique,** tape-recorder; **e. à bande,** (strip-) chart recorder; *Mec.E: El.E: etc:* **e. à tambour,** drum recorder; *Av:* **e. de trajectoire de vol,** flight path recorder; *Aut: O:* **e. de distance,** distance recorder; *Ind:* **e. de temps,** time clock, time recorder; **e. de débit,** flow recorder; (*computers*) **e. (automatique),** logger; **e. magnétique,** magnetic recorder.

enrênement [ɑ̃rɛnmɑ̃], *s.m.* **1.** reining in (of horses). **2.** arrangement of the reins.

enrêner [ɑ̃rene], *v.tr.* to rein (horse) in.

enrésinement [ɑ̃rezinmɑ̃], *s.m. For:* introduction of resin-producing tree into a wood.

enrhumer [ɑ̃ryme], *v.tr.* to give (s.o.) a cold.

s'enrhumer, to catch (a) cold; to take cold; **être très enrhumé,** to have a bad cold; **être enrhumé du cerveau, de la poitrine,** to have a cold in the head, on the chest.

enrichi, -ie [ɑ̃riʃi], *a. & s.* **1.** *s.* nouveau riche, newly rich, parvenu, upstart. **2.** *a. Ch: Atom.Ph:* enriched (uranium, nuclear fuel, etc.); **e. à l'isotope,** isotope enriched. **3.** *a.* (*of jewels, costume, etc.*) embellished (**de,** with).

enrichir [ɑ̃riʃiːr], *v.tr.* **1.** to enrich; to make (s.o.) wealthy. **2.** *Ch: Atom.Ph:* to enrich (uranium, nuclear fuel, etc.). **3.** **e. une toilette de bijoux,** to set off one's dress with jewels; **e. une langue,** to enrich, add to, a language.

s'enrichir. **1.** to enrich oneself; to grow rich, to make money; *F:* to make one's pile; **s'e. aux dépens d'autrui,** to grow wealthy at the expense of others, to batten on others; **une affaire du genre "enrichissez-vous vite,"** a deal of the "get-rich-quick" type. **2.** to grow richer; **notre théâtre s'enrichit en idées,** our drama is growing richer in ideas; **la langue s'enrichit tous les jours,** the language is becoming richer every day.

enrichissant [ɑ̃riʃisɑ̃], *a.* enriching, rewarding; **j'ai trouvé ce livre très e.,** *F:* I got a lot out of this book.

enrichissement [ɑ̃riʃismɑ̃], *s.m.* **1.** enriching, enrichment; **e. d'un palais,** embellishment of a palace. **2.** *Atom.Ph:* enrichment (of uranium, nuclear fuel, etc.); **e. isotopique,** isotopic enrichment.

enrobage [ɑ̃rɔbaːʒ], *s.m.* coating, covering (of sth.) with, wrapping (of sth.) in, a protecting envelope or layer; **e. de sucre, de chocolat,** sugar, chocolate, coating (for sweet, pill, etc.).

enrobement [ɑ̃rɔbmɑ̃], *s.m.* = ENROBAGE.

enrober [ɑ̃rɔbe], *v.tr.* to coat, cover, (sth.) with, wrap (sth.) in, a protecting envelope; to enrobe, cover (sweets, etc.); **e. des pierres de goudron,** to coat stones with tar; **enrobé de ciment,** embedded in cement; **diamant enrobé dans sa gangue,** diamond encased in its gangue; **e. des viandes,** to coat (cooked) meats with gelatine, fat, etc.; **e. une réprimande d'un sourire,** to sugar the pill with a smile.

enrobeuse [ɑ̃rɔbøːz], *s.f. Mch: R.t.m.* enrober (of sweets, etc.).

enrochement [ɑ̃rɔʃmɑ̃], *s.m. Civ.E: Hyd.E:* **1.** enrockment, riprap, stone packing, stone bedding (of dam, jetty, pier); **barrage en enrochement(s),** rock-fill dam; **barrage en e. en vrac,** dumped rock-fill dam. **2.** rough stone breakwater.

enrocher [ɑ̃rɔʃe], *v.tr. Civ.E: Hyd.E:* to riprap, stone-pack (foundations of bridge, etc.); to make an enrockment for (dam, quay, etc.).

enrôlé [ɑ̃role], *s.m.* person enrolled, on the rolls; **les enrôlés volontaires,** the volunteers.

enrôlement [ɑ̃rolmɑ̃], *s.m.* (*a*) enrolment; (*b*) *Mil:* enlistment; **e. d'office,** (i) *A:* impressment; (ii) *F:* press-ganging; (*c*) *Jur:* enrolment (on the cause-list).

enrôler [ɑ̃role], *v.tr.* (*a*) to enrol, recruit (labour); (*b*) to enlist; **e. (qn) d'office,** (i) *A:* to impress (s.o.); (ii) *F:* to press-gang (s.o.); (*c*) *Jur:* to enrol (on the cause-list).

s'enrôler, (*a*) to enrol (oneself); (*b*) to enlist.

enrôleur [ɑ̃rolœːr], *s.m.* recruiting sergeant; recruiter (of labour, etc.).

enroturer (s') [sɑ̃rɔtyre], *v.pr. A:* (*of nobility*) to become middle-class, common; to marry into the middle class.

enroué [ɑ̃rwe], *a.* hoarse, husky (person, voice).

enrouement [ɑ̃rumɑ̃], *s.m.* hoarseness, huskiness.

enrouer [ɑ̃rwe], *v.tr.* to make (s.o.) hoarse, husky.

s'enrouer, to get hoarse; **s'e. à force de crier,** to shout oneself hoarse.

enrouillé [ɑ̃ruje], *a. O:* rusty (knowledge, etc.).

enrouiller [ɑ̃ruje], *v.tr.* **1.** *O:* to cover (iron) with rust. **2.** *F:* **l'oisiveté enrouille l'esprit,** idleness makes one's, your, mind rusty.

s'enrouiller, *O:* to get covered with rust.

enroulage [ɑ̃rulaːʒ], *s.m.*, **enroulement** [ɑ̃rulmɑ̃], *s.m.* **1.** (*a*) rolling up; winding; **e. en couronne,** coiling (up); (*b*) *El:* **enroulement,** coil; **e. d'une bobine,** winding of a coil; **à deux enroulements,** double-wound; **e. imbriqué,** lap-winding; **e. d'induit,** armature winding; **e. inducteur,** field winding; **e. fermé,** re-entrant winding; *Mec.E: Min:* **tambour, poulie, d'e.,** winding-drum; *Tex:* **e. de la toile,** taking up of the cloth; (*c*) wrapping up (**dans,** in). **2.** *Arch:* volute, scroll, *enroulement.*

enrouler [ɑ̃rule], *v.tr.* (*a*) to roll up (map, etc.); to wind (cable, etc.); **e. (qch.) en couronne,** to coil (cable, etc.); *Tex:* **e. la toile,** to take up the cloth (in weaving); (*b*) to wrap up (**dans,** in); **s'e. dans une couverture,** to wrap oneself (up) in a blanket.

s'enrouler, to wind, coil; to be wound, rolled (**autour de,** round).

enrouleur, -euse [ɑ̃rulœːr, -øːz], *s.m. & a. Tchn:* roller; **cylindre e.,** winding-drum.

enroutiné [ɑ̃rutine], *a.* bound by routine, by red-tape.

enrubanner [ɑ̃rybane], *v.tr.* to decorate, trim, (sth.) with ribbon(s); **enrubanné de la tête aux pieds,** beribboned from top to toe.

enrue [ɑ̃ry], *s.f.* large furrow.

ens [ɛ̃ːs], *s.m. Phil:* ens.

ensablé [ɑ̃sable], *a.* silted up; choked (with sand); *F:* stuck (in the sand).

ensablement [ɑ̃sabləmɑ̃], *s.m.* **1.** running aground, stranding (of ship). **2.** blinding (of roads); *Rail:* boxing, ballasting (of the sleepers). **3.** (*a*) silting up (of harbour); (*b*) choking up (of pipes). **4.** sand-bank; harbour bar.

ensabler [ɑ̃sable], *v.tr.* **1.** to strand; to run (ship) aground. **2.** (*a*) (*of flooded river, etc.*) to cover (land) with sand; **e. un port,** to silt up, sand up, a harbour; **ancre ensablée,** anchor buried in sand; (*b*) *Tchn:* to blind (road); *Rail:* **e. les traverses,** to box, ballast, the sleepers.

s'ensabler. **1.** (*of ship, fish*) to settle in the sand. **2.** (*of harbour, river*) to silt up; (*of pipes*) to get choked up. **3.** *F:* (*of pers.*) to get stuck.

ensaboter [ɑ̃sabɔte], *v.tr.* **1.** *A:* to put (child, etc.) in clogs, in sabots. **2.** to skid (wheel); to put the drag or shoe on (wheel).

ensachage [ɑ̃saʃaːʒ], *s.m.*, **ensachement** [ɑ̃saʃmɑ̃], *s.m.* putting (of corn, ore, etc.) into sacks; bagging, sacking.

ensacher [ɑ̃saʃe], *v.tr.* to put (corn, etc.) into sacks; to sack (corn, etc.); to bag (fruit, plants, etc.); **e. du minerai,** to bag ore.

ensacheur [ɑ̃saʃœːr], *s.m.* bagger.

ensacheuse [ɑ̃saʃøːz], *s.f. Tchn:* machine for bagging, bag-filling machine.

ensaisinement [ɑ̃sɛzin(ə)mɑ̃], *s.m. Jur: A:* enfeoffment; seisin, vesture.

ensaisiner [ɑ̃sɛzine], *v.tr. Jur: A:* to enfeoff; to put (s.o.) in possession; to give seisin, to vest.

ensanglanter [ɑ̃sɑ̃glɑ̃te], *v.tr.* to cover, stain, (sth.) with blood; **mains ensanglantées,** blood-stained, bloody, hands; **pays ensanglanté par la guerre,** country steeped in blood by war.

ensauvager [ɑ̃sovaʒe], *v.tr.* **(j'ensauvageai(s); n. ensauvageons) 1.** to make (animal, s.o.) shy, wild, timorous. **2.** (*a*) to make a savage of (s.o.); (*b*) to make (s.o.) shy, averse to company.

s'ensauvager, to become savage, wild; (*of pers.*) to become shy, averse to company.

ensauver (s'), *v.pr. Dial: F:* to run away.

enseignable [ɑ̃sɛɲabl̩], *a.* teachable, that can be taught.

enseignant [ɑ̃sɛɲɑ̃], (*a*) *a.* teaching; **corps e.,** teaching profession; (*b*) *s.m.* teacher.

enseigne [ɑ̃sɛɲ]. **1.** *s.f.* (*a*) sign, index, token, mark (of character, quality, etc.); *adv.phr.* **à bonnes enseignes,** (i) deservedly; (ii) on sure grounds, on good authority; **à telle e. que . . .,** the proof being that . . ., so much so that . . .; (*b*) sign(-board), shop sign; style, firm (name); **e. en forme d'entablement,** fascia; **e. lumineuse,** electric sign; **e. au néon,** neon sign; **loger à l'e. du Lion d'or,** to put up at the (sign of the) Golden Lion; *F:* **nous sommes tous logés à la même e.,** we are all in the same boat; *Prov:* **à bon vin point d'e.,** good wine needs no bush; (*c*) *Mil:* ensign, colour(s), flag; (cavalry) standard; **"enseignes déployées,"** "with flying colours," "with flags flying," (*d*) *s.m. or f. Nau: Navy: A:* (= PAVILLON 3) ensign, flag; *still used in* **grand e.,** ensign (flown at stern). **2.** *s.m.* (*a*) *Mil: A:* standard-bearer, ensign; (*b*) *Navy:* **enseigne (de vaisseau) (i) de première classe,** sub-lieutenant, *U.S:* lieutenant (junior grade); (ii) **de deuxième classe,** lieutenant (junior grade), *U.S:* ensign.

enseignement [ɑ̃sɛɲmɑ̃], *s.m.* **1.** (*a*) teaching; tuition; **entrer dans l'e.,** to go in for teaching; to adopt the profession of teacher; **e. par correspondance,** postal tuition, correspondence course; **il est dans l'e.,** he is a teacher; he teaches; **méthode d'e.,** teaching method; (*b*) **enseignements de la Guerre,** teachings, lessons, of the War; **tirer un e. de qch.,** to draw a lesson from sth. **2.** education, instruction; **e. privé,** private tuition; **e. professionnel,** professional training; **e. public,** state education; **e. libre,** non-state education; **e. supérieur,** higher education; **film d'e.,** instructional film; *s.a.* COLLÈGE 2, SECONDAIRE 1.

enseigner [ɑ̃sɛɲe], *v.tr.* **1.** to show; to point out; **e. à qn son devoir,** to point out his duty to s.o.; *A:* **enseignez-moi le chemin de la ville,** show me the way to the town. **2.** to teach; (*a*) **e. les enfants,** to teach, give lessons to, children; (*b*) **e. la grammaire à qn,** to teach s.o. grammar; **e. à qn à faire qch.,** to teach s.o. to do sth.; **e. l'anglais,** to teach English.

ensellé [ɑ̃sɛle], *a.* saddle-backed, sway-backed (horse).

ensellement [ɑ̃sɛlmɑ̃], *s.m.* saddle, col (in mountains).

ensellure [ɑ̃sɛlyːr], *s.f.* curve of the back.

ensemble [ɑ̃sɑ̃ːbl̩]. **1.** *adv.* together; (*a*) in company, one with another; **ils se marièrent e.,** they married (each other); **vivre e.,** to live together; **être bien e.,** to be good friends, on good terms; **être mal e.,** to have fallen out; **ils vont mal e.,**

they don't get on; *F:* they don't hit it off; **choses qui vont e.**, things that belong, go, together; **choses qui vont bien e.**, things that harmonize, match; *Equit:* **mettre bien e. son cheval**, to collect one's horse, to keep one's horse collected; **le tout e.**, (i) the general effect; (ii) the whole lot; (iii) *Art:* the "altogether"; *Art:* **figure qui n'est pas e.**, figure that is out of proportion; *adv.phr.* **agir d'e.**, to act in concert, as a body; (b) at the same time; **vendre tous ses meubles e.**, to sell all one's furniture at once. **2.** *s.m.* (a) whole, entirety; **l'e. du travail est bon**, the work on the whole, as a whole, is good; **l'e. d'un tableau**, the general effect of a picture; **vue d'e.**, comprehensive view, overall picture; general view or survey; **enquête d'e.**, general inquiry; **étude d'e.**, comprehensive study; conspectus; **idée d'e.**, broad, general, idea (of a subject); *Ind: etc:* **rendement d'e.**, (i) aggregate output; (ii) all-round efficiency; **dans l'e...**, on the whole .., taken all round .., in the aggregate .., by and large ...; **la situation dans son e.**, the situation as a whole; **pris dans leur e., étaient intègres**, the judges, taken as a body, were honest; *Art:* **poser pour l'e.**, to pose for the nude, for the "altogether"; (b) cohesion, unity; **mouvement d'e.**, combined movement; **e. vocal**, vocal ensemble; **musique d'e.**, concerted music; **un assez bel e.**, a fairly harmonious whole; **e. d'un orchestre**, unity of execution of an orchestra; **e. d'un morceau de musique**, (i) general unity, (ii) general effect, of a piece of music; **l'exécution manque d'e.**, the execution is ragged; **attaque qui manque d'e.**, attack that lacks cohesion; **avec e.**, all together, harmoniously, as one; **e. de couleurs**, harmonious group of colours; *(of horse)* **avoir de l'e.**, to be well built, to have good proportions; (c) unit; *Furn:* suite; *Tchn:* set (of tools, instruments, etc.); assembly, unit (of parts); **e. partiel**, sub-assembly; **e. principal**, major assembly; **e. de réglage automatique**, automatic control unit; **e. de sécurité**, safety assembly; **e. filtrant**, strainer assembly; **e. des pignons**, gear cluster; **e. de bâtiments**, block of buildings; **grand e.**, new residential area consisting of large blocks of flats, hostels; = new town; (d) *Cost:* **e. de voyage**, (lady's) travelling suit; **e. (de) trois pièces**, three-piece suit; (e) *Mth:* **théorie des ensembles**, theory of sets; (f) *Adm: Ind: etc:* **e. des indices**, index set.

ensemblier [ãsãblie], *s.m.* **1.** decorative artist. **2.** interior decorator.

ensembliste [ãsãblist], *a.* *Mth:* = CARTÉSIEN, -IENNE.

ensemencement [ãs(ə)mãsmã], *s.m.* **1.** *Agr:* sowing. **2.** *Med:* seeding (of vaccine lymph); **lymphe d'e.**, seed lymph.

ensemencer [ãsmãse], *v.tr.* (j'ensemençai(s); n. ensemençons) **1.** *Agr:* to sow (field); **e. une terre en blé**, to sow land with wheat, to put land under wheat. **2.** *Biol: Med:* to culture, to seed.

enserrement [ãsɛrmã], *s.m.* **1.** enclosing, encompassing (of town, etc.); hemming in (of army, etc.). **2.** squeezing, crushing.

enserrer¹ [ãsɛre], *v.tr.* **1.** (a) to enclose, encompass (sth.); to hem in (army, etc.); **mur qui enserre la ville**, wall that encircles the town; **armée enserrée dans un étroit espace, entre de hautes montagnes**, army hemmed into a narrow space, hemmed in by, between, high mountains; **lac enserré de montagnes**, lake surrounded by mountains; (b) *(of brake-band, etc.)* to grip round (drum); (c) to squeeze, crush; **le boa enserre sa victime**, the boa crushes its victim (in its coils); **l'ours enserre sa proie**, the bear hugs its prey. **2.** *A:* to lock up, put away, hide away (money, etc.).

enserrer², *v.tr.* *Hort:* to put (plant, etc.) in a hothouse, under glass.

ensevelir [ãsəvliːr], *v.tr.* **1.** to bury, entomb (corpse); **la mer ensevelit ses victimes**, the sea swallowed up its victims; **e. un secret dans son cœur**, to hide away a secret in one's heart. **2.** to wrap (corpse) in a shroud; to shroud (corpse).

s'ensevelir, **s'e. dans ses livres**, to bury oneself in one's books; **enseveli dans la méditation**, lost, sunk, wrapped, in deep thought; **s'e. sous les couvertures**, to bury oneself under the bedclothes.

ensevelissement [ãsəvlismã], *s.m.* **1.** burial, entombment. **2.** shrouding (of corpse).

ensevelisseur, -euse [ãsəvlisœːr, -øːz], *a. & s.m.* **1.** *Ent:* burying (beetle); sexton-beetle. **2.** *s.m. or f.* layer-out (who prepares body for burial).

ensifères [ãsifɛːr], *s.m.pl.* *Ent:* longhorned grasshoppers, longhorns.

ensifolié [ãsifɔlje], *a.* *Bot:* ensiform-leaved, sword-leaved.

ensiforme [ãsiform], *a.* ensiform, sword-shaped.

ensilage [ãsilaːʒ], *s.m.* *Husb:* ensilage (of crops).

ensil(ot)er [ãsil(ɔt)e], *v.tr.* to ensile, ensilage, silo (crop).

ensileuse [ãsiløːz], *s.f.* *Husb:* (ensilage) blower, silo filler.

ensimage [ãsimaːʒ], *s.m.* *Tex:* oiling, greasing (of wool); **huile d'e.**, textile oil.

ensimer [ãsime], *v.tr.* *Tex:* to oil, grease (wool).

en-soi [ãswa], *s.m.inv.* *(Existentialist)* *Phil:* en-soi.

ensoleillé [ãsɔleje], *a.* sunny, sunlit (countryside, etc.); **sourire e.**, sunny smile.

ensoleillement [ãsɔlej(ə)mã], *s.m.* sunning, insolation; **durée, période, d'e.**, period of sunshine.

ensoleiller [ãsɔleje], *v.tr.* (a) to give sunlight to (sth.); to shine upon (sth.); to insolate, to sun; (b) to brighten, light up (s.o.'s life, etc.); **elle ensoleille tout autour d'elle**, she sheds sunshine all round her.

s'ensoleiller, to light up (with the sun); to break into sunshine, to brighten; *Lit:* **son visage s'ensoleilla**, her face lit up.

ensommeillé [ãsɔmeje], *a.* sleepy, drowsy.

ensommeillement [ãsɔmej(ə)mã], *s.m.* drowsiness.

ensorcelant [ãsɔrsəlã], *a.* (be)witching (words; *F:* manners, etc.).

ensorcelé [ãsɔrsəle], *a.* bewitched; under a spell; spellbound.

ensorceler [ãsɔrsəle], *v.tr.* (j'ensorcelle, n. ensorcelons; j'ensorcellerai) (a) to bewitch; to cast a spell, put a spell, (up)on (s.o., sth.); (b) *F:* to captivate (s.o.); to turn (s.o.'s) head.

ensorceleur, -euse [ãsɔrsəlœːr, -øːz]. **1.** *s.* (a) sorcerer, f. sorceress; (b) *F:* charmer. **2.** *a.* = ENSORCELANT.

ensorcellement [ãsɔrsəlmã], *s.m.* **1.** sorcery, witchcraft, bewitchment. **2.** charm, spell.

ensoufrer [ãsufre], *v.tr.* to sulphurate (wool, etc.); **e. des allumettes**, to impregnate matches with sulphur.

ensouple [ãsupl], *s.f.* *Tex:* beam, roller (of loom); **e. dérouleuse**, yarn-beam, yarn-roll, warp-beam; **e. enrouleuse**, fore-beam, cloth-beam.

ensoutaner [ãsutane], *v.tr.* *F:* *Pej:* to send (s.o.) into the church.

enstatite [ãstatit], *s.f.* *Miner:* enstatite.

enstérage [ãstera:ʒ], *s.m.* stacking of wood in steres.

enstérer [ãstere], *v.tr.* to stack wood in steres.

ensuairer [ãsɥere], *v.tr.* to lay out (corpse).

ensuaireuse [ãsɥerøːz], *s.f.* *A:* layer-out (of corpse).

ensuble [ãsybl], *s.f.* = ENSOUPLE.

ensucrer [ãsykre], *v.tr.* to sweeten, to sugar (food).

ensuifer [ãsɥife], *v.tr.* to smear (sth.) with tallow; to tallow.

ensuite [ãsɥit], *adv.* after(wards), then; **travaillons d'abord, nous nous reposerons e.**, let us work first and rest afterwards; **et e. il m'a dit ..**, and then he said to me ..; **e. nous sommes allés chez A**, next, after that, we went to A's; **et e.?** what then? *F:* **e. de quoi ..**, after which ..; **e. de cela ..**, after that ..; **il lui dit e. que ..**, he went on to tell him that ...; **il passa e. au récit de ..**, he went on to tell us of ..; **les pompiers marchaient en tête, e. venait la musique**, the firemen led the procession, next came the band.

ensuivre (s') [sãsɥivr], *v.pr.* *(conj. like* SUIVRE; *used only in the third pers.)* to follow, ensue, result; **les maux qui se sont ensuivis de ce malentendu**, the evils that resulted from this misunderstanding; **les inconvénients qui s'ensuivent**, the attendant disadvantages; *impers.* **il s'ensuit que nous sommes ruinés**, it follows, the consequence is, that we are ruined; **il ne s'ensuit pas que la bague soit perdue**, it does not necessarily follow that the ring is lost; *F:* **et tout ce qui s'ensuit**, and what not, the lot, and the whole boiling. NOTE; **en** *and* **suivre** *are often separated in the compound tenses; see* SUIVRE 2 (b).

entablement [ãtãbləmã], *s.m.* **1.** entablature (of building, power-hammer, etc.); **enseigne en forme d'e.**, fascia. **2.** *Const:* coping, tablet (of wall, quay, etc.).

entabler [ãtãble], *v.tr.* *Const: etc:* to set in (beam, stone).

entacher [ãtaʃe], *v.tr.* **1.** to sully, taint, blemish, besmirch; to cast a slur on (s.o.'s honour, memory, etc.); **réputation entachée**, sullied reputation; **religion entachée de superstition**, religion tainted with superstition; **entaché d'erreur**, erroneous; **rien n'entache mon respect pour vous**, my respect for you remains undim-inished. **2.** *Jur:* to vitiate; **acte entaché d'un vice radical**, act vitiated by a fundamental flaw; **entaché de dol**, tainted with fraud; **transaction entachée de fraude**, fraudulent transaction; **entaché de nullité**, voidable.

entaillage [ãtaja:ʒ], *s.m.* **1.** (a) notching, nicking (of piece of wood, etc.); (b) grooving, slotting. **2.** fitting (of lock, etc.) into a recess.

entaille [ãta:j], *s.f.* (a) notch, jag, nick, cut (in piece of wood, etc.); groove; slot; tommy-hole (in circular nut); **à entailles**, slotted; **assemblage à entailles**, notched joint; (b) gash, cut, slash (in the body); **il s'est fait une e. au menton**, he has gashed his chin; (c) gap (of lathe-bed); (d) **une e. dans la confiance publique**, a blow to public confidence.

entailler [ãtaje], *v.tr.* **1.** (a) to notch, nick (piece of wood, etc.); to groove, slot; (b) to gash, cut, slash; **s'e. le doigt**, to cut one's finger; **e. un arbre à coups de hache**, to hack (away) at a tree. **2.** to fit (lock, etc.) into a recess; *s.a.* SERRURE.

entaillure [ãtajyːr], *s.f.* *A:* = ENTAILLE.

entame [ãtam], *s.f.* **1.** first cut, outside slice (of loaf, joint, etc.). **2.** *Cards:* opening (of a suit).

entamement [ãtam(ə)mã], *s.m.* *O:* **1.** cutting into (loaf, joint, etc.); broaching (of cask); breaking into (capital). **2.** beginning, commencing, starting (of conversation, quarrel, etc.).

entamer [ãtame], *v.tr.* **1.** to cut into, make the first cut in (loaf, joint, etc.); to broach (cask); to open (bottle, pot of jam); to penetrate (defence, armour-plate); to gap (edge); **e. la peau**, to break the skin; **une brèche entame la montagne**, there is a breach, a gash, in the mountain; **doutes qui entament la foi, doubts that undermine one's faith, that shake one's faith; **e. son capital**, to break into one's capital; **e. la réputation de qn**, to cast a slur on s.o.'s reputation; **e. le crédit de qn**, to deal s.o.'s credit a blow; **e. une troupe**, to throw a body of troops into disorder. **2.** to begin, commence, start (conversation, quarrel, etc.); **e. des relations avec qn**, to enter into relations with s.o.; **e. une affaire**, to initiate a deal; *Mil:* **e. les opérations**, to commence operations; **e. des poursuites contre qn**, to initiate, institute, proceedings against s.o.; **e. un sujet**, (i) to broach a subject; (ii) to break the ice; **e. un travail**, to start a piece of work; **e. des négociations**, to open negotiations; *Cards:* **e. trèfle**, to open clubs; *Equit:* **e. un cheval**, to begin breaking in a horse.

entamure [ãtamyːr], *s.f.* = ENTAME 1.

entartrage [ãtartra:ʒ], **entartrement** [ãtartrəmã], *s.m.* furring, incrustation, scaling (of boiler, etc.).

entartrate [ãtartrat], *s.m.* fur, scale, deposit (in boiler, etc.).

entartrer [ãtartre], *v.tr.* *(of water, etc.)* to incrust, fur, scale (boiler, etc.); to foul up (boiler tubes).

s'entartrer, to fur; to become furred, fouled up; to scale, to become scaled.

entasis [ãtazis], *s.f.* *Arch:* bulging, swelling, of the shaft of a column.

entassé [ãtase], *a.* *A:* squat; **être e.**, to have one's head sunk between one's shoulders; to sit hunched up.

entassement [ãtasmã], *s.m.* accumulation. **1.** (a) piling (up), heaping (up) (of stones, coal, etc.); stacking (of cases, etc.); crowding (up), packing together, overcrowding (of passengers, cattle, etc.); congestion. **2.** pile (of goods, etc.); clutter (of furniture).

entasser [ãtase], *v.tr.* (a) to accumulate; to pile (up), heap (up), bank (up) (stones, coal, etc.); **e. des caisses**, to stack (up) cases; *F:* **e. des écus**, to amass money; (b) to pack, crowd, cram, (passengers, cattle, etc.) together; **passagers entassés sur l'arrière-pont**, passengers huddled together on the after-deck.

s'entasser. **1.** *(of thgs)* to accumulate; to pile up; *(of mist)* to bank. **2.** *(of persons)* to crowd, huddle, together.

entasseur, -euse [ãtasœːr, -øːz], *s.* *F:* miser, hoarder.

ente [ãːt], *s.f.* **1.** *Hort:* (a) scion, graft; grafted shoot; (b) stock. **2.** (a) handle (of paint-brush, etc.); (b) branch (of pair of pliers). **3.** *Ven:* straw decay.

enté [ãte], *a.* *Her:* **e. en pointe**, enté en point.

entéléchie [ãteleʃi], *s.f.* *Phil:* entelechy.

entelle [ãtɛl], *s.m.* *Z:* langur, lungoor, hanuman, leaf monkey.

entendement [ãtãdmã], *s.m.* understanding; **discours qui dépasse l'e. de l'auditoire**, speech above the heads of the audience; **homme d'e.**, man of sense, of intelligence, of good judgment;

entendeur [ɑ̃tɑ̃dœːr], *s.m. A:* one who understands; *used only in the phrases* **à bon e., demi-mot suffit, à bon e. salut!** (i) a word to the wise (is enough); (ii) if the cap fits, wear it.

entendre [ɑ̃tɑ̃ːdr̥], *v.tr.* **1.** to intend, mean; **e. faire qch.,** to intend, mean, to do sth.; **je n'entends pas méconnaître ses droits,** I do not mean to ignore his rights; **je n'entends aucunement méconnaître ses droits,** I have no intention of ignoring his rights; **qu'entendez-vous par là?** what do you mean by that? **il n'y entend pas malice,** (i) he means no harm; (ii) he does not mean what he says; (iii) he takes what you say at its face value; **faites comme vous l'entendrez,** do as you think best, do as you please; **quelle suite entendez-vous donner à cette affaire?** what do you propose to do in the matter? **je n'entends pas être traité de la sorte,** I won't stand being treated in such a way; **e. que** + *sub.*; **j'entends que vous veniez,** I expect you to come, you must come; **j'entends qu'on m'obéisse,** I mean, intend, to be obeyed; **je n'entends pas qu'on le vende,** I won't have it sold. **2.** (*a*) to hear; **j'entendis un cri,** I heard a cry; **e. un enfant qui pleure,** to hear a child crying; **on l'entend à peine,** it is scarcely audible, it is almost inaudible; **faire e. des cris,** to utter cries; **un gémissement se fit e.,** a groan was heard; **je pouvais à peine me faire e.,** I could hardly make myself heard; **je l'entendis rire,** I heard him laugh; **on l'entendit rire,** he was heard to laugh; **je l'entendais rire,** I could hear him laughing; **j'entends parler dans la chambre voisine,** I hear people talking, I hear voices, in the next room; **e. parler de qn, de qch.,** to hear of, about, s.o., sth.; **c'est la première fois que j'en entends parler,** this is the first I have heard of it; **j'ai entendu parler de cela,** I have heard (tell) of the matter; **il ne veut pas en e. parler,** he won't hear of it; **on fut longtemps sans e. parler d'eux,** they were not heard of for a long time; **je ne veux plus e. parler de lui,** I don't want to hear him mentioned again; **e. dire que** + *ind.*, to hear it said that . . .; *P:* to hear tell that . . .; **on entend dire que . . .,** it is rumoured that . . .; **je me rappelle avoir entendu dire que . . .,** I remember hearing (tell) that . . .; **je l'ai souvent entendu dire,** I have often heard it said; **je le sais par ce qu'on entend dire,** I know it by hearsay; **on entend dire du vilain sur son compte,** there are unpleasant rumours abroad about him; **cela fait l'effet du déjà entendu,** it strikes one as familiar; **e. dire qch. à qn,** (i) to hear sth. said or told to s.o.; (ii) to hear s.o. say sth.; **je lui ai entendu dire qu'il viendrait,** I heard him say he would come; **je le leur ai entendu dire,** (i) I heard it said to them; (ii) I heard them say it; *abs.* **il entend mal,** *O:* **dur,** he doesn't hear well, he is hard of hearing; **on ne s'entend pas, plus, ici,** one can't hear oneself speak, *F:* think, here; the place is a bear-garden; **bruit à ne pas s'e.,** deafening noise; **ce fut à ne plus s'e.,** the din became deafening; (*b*) to hear, to listen to, *B: Lit:* to hearken to; **on le congédia sans l'e.,** he was dismissed without a hearing; **veuillez m'e.,** give me a hearing; **l'affaire sera entendue demain,** the case comes up for hearing to-morrow; the case comes on to-morrow; **e. la messe,** to attend mass; **à vous e. . . .,** judging from what you say . . ., according to you . . .; **refuser d'e. une requête,** to turn a deaf ear to a request; **e. raison,** to listen to reason; **faire e. raison à qn,** to bring s.o. to reason; **il n'a rien voulu e.,** he would not listen; (*c*) *v.ind.tr. O:* **ils ne veulent pas e. à cet arrangement,** they will not listen to, agree to, hear of, this arrangement; *s.a.* OREILLE 2. **3.** (*a*) to understand; **il ne l'entend pas ainsi,** he doesn't see it that way, he doesn't agree; **e. une langue,** to understand a language; **donner à e. à qn que . . ., faire e. à qn que . . .,** (i) to lead s.o. to believe; (ii) to give s.o. to understand, that . . .; **voulez-vous donner à e. que . . .?** do you mean to insinuate that . . .? **laisser e. qch.,** to throw out hints about sth., to insinuate, imply, sth.; **il n'entend pas la plaisanterie,** he can't take a joke; **les prix s'entendent avec un rabais de 5%,** prices are subject to a 5% discount; **cela s'entend,** *F:* **s'entend,** that is an understood thing; of course; that goes without saying; **je m'entends,** I know very well what I mean; **c'est entendu,** agreed, all right; very well; **il doit être bien entendu que . . .,** it should be clearly understood that . . .; **étant entendu que . . .,** given that, it being understood that; **comme de bien entendu,** as might be expected; **c'est une affaire entendue,** it's all settled; **bien entendu!** of course! certainly! **entendu!** very well! all right! agreed! *F:* right oh! O.K.! *conj.phr.* **bien entendu que . . .,** it is, be it, understood that . . .; of course . . .; this is on the understanding that . . .; (*b*) to know (all about sth.); to be skilled in (sth.); **e. son métier,** to know, to be good at, one's job; **je n'entends rien à l'algèbre,** I don't know the first thing about algebra; **je n'y entends rien,** I don't know the first thing about it.

s'entendre. 1. to understand one another, to agree; **on ne se dispute sur cette matière que faute de s'e.,** people argue on this matter only through misunderstanding; **nous nous entendons du mieux qui soit,** we are on the best possible terms; **ils s'entendent bien,** they get on (well); **ils ne s'entendent pas, ils n'arrivent pas à s'e.,** they don't get on well (together); *F:* they don't hit it off, they don't pull together; **nous ne sommes pas faits pour nous e.,** we are not suited to each other; **s'e. directement avec qn,** to come to a direct understanding with s.o.; **s'e. pour commettre un crime,** to conspire to commit a crime; **ils s'entendent comme larrons en foire, comme les deux doigts de la main,** they are as thick as thieves; **ils s'entendent pour me nuire,** they are ganging up against me; **s'e. avec l'ennemi,** to collaborate (with the enemy); **s'e. avec qn pour se rencontrer quelque part,** to agree with s.o. to meet somewhere. **2.** to be skilled (à, in); **s'e. aux affaires,** to be a good business man; **s'e. aux chevaux,** to understand horses; **s'e. en musique,** to understand, know about, music; **il s'y entend parfaitement,** he is very good at this sort of thing; **s'e. à faire qch.,** to know, understand, how to do sth.; **s'e. mal à mentir,** to be bad, a bad hand, at telling lies.

entendu [ɑ̃tɑ̃dy], *a.* **1.** (*a*) business-like, sensible (person); **être e. aux affaires,** to be well up, well versed, in business matters, to have good business capacity; (*b*) knowing, shrewd (look, etc.); **prendre un (petit) air e.,** to put on a knowing look; to look wise; **il sourit d'un air e.,** he smiled knowingly; **faire l'e.,** (i) to pretend to know all about it; (ii) to pose as an expert, to set up for an expert; (iii) to put on a knowing look. **2. maison bien entendue,** well-arranged house; **zèle mal e.,** mistaken zeal; **intérêt bien e.,** enlightened self-interest.

enténébré [ɑ̃tenebre], *a.* dark, gloomy; **tableaux tristes et enténébrés,** dismal, gloomy pictures.

enténébrer [ɑ̃tenebre], *v.tr.* (**il enténèbre; il enténébrera**) to envelop, plunge, (scene, etc.) in darkness, in gloom.

s'enténébrer, *Lit:* to grow dark, gloomy; **la plaine s'enténébrait,** night was falling over the plain.

entente [ɑ̃tɑ̃ːt], *s.f.* **1.** (*a*) understanding (de, of); skill (de, in); **peintre qui a l'e. du coloris,** artist who understands all about colour; **avoir l'e. des affaires,** to have a good head for business; (*b*) meaning; (*so used in the phr.*) **mot à double e.,** word with a double meaning; double entendre. **2.** agreement, understanding (**entre,** between); **esprit d'e.,** spirit of mutual understanding; **bonne e.,** good feeling; **e. cordiale,** Entente cordiale, friendly understanding; **terrain d'e.,** common ground; **après e. avec les autorités,** after consultation with the authorities; **on arriva bientôt à une e.,** an agreement was soon reached; *Jur:* **e. délictueuse,** conspiracy; *Com: Fin:* **e. industrielle,** combine; **légiférer contre les ententes industrielles,** to legislate against trusts, (restrictive) trade combines, associations.

enter [ɑ̃te], *v.tr.* **1.** to graft, engraft (tree, etc.); **e. qch. sur qch.,** to graft sth. on to sth.; *O:* **e. des bas,** to foot stockings. **2.** *Carp:* to scarf, graft (timbers); to assemble (timbers) by mortises; **canne entée,** jointed cane; **e. les aubes d'une roue,** to root in the blades of a (water-) wheel.

entéralgie [ɑ̃teralʒi], *s.f. Med:* enteralgia.

entérinement [ɑ̃terinmɑ̃], *s.m. Jur:* ratification, confirmation.

entériner [ɑ̃terine], *v.tr. Jur:* to ratify, confirm; *F:* to rubber-stamp.

entérique [ɑ̃terik], *a. Med:* enteric, intestinal (trouble, etc.).

entérite [ɑ̃terit], *s.f. Med:* enteritis.

entéro- [ɑ̃terɔ], *pref.* entero-.

entérocèle [ɑ̃terɔsɛl], *s.f. Med:* enterocele.

entérocolite [ɑ̃terɔkɔlit], *s.f. Med:* enterocolitis.

entérocoque [ɑ̃terɔkɔk], *s.m. Med:* enterococcus; *pl.* enterococci.

entéro-hépatite [ɑ̃terɔepatit], *s.f. Vet:* blackhead.

entérokinase [ɑ̃terɔkinaːz], *s.f. Biol:* enterokinase.

entérolithe [ɑ̃terɔlit], *s.m. Med:* enterolith.

entéromorphe [ɑ̃terɔmɔrf], *s.f. Algae:* enteromorpha.

entéromphale [ɑ̃terɔ̃fal], *s.f. Surg:* umbilical hernia.

entéroptose [ɑ̃terɔptoːz], *s.f. Med:* enteroptosis, visceroptosis.

entéro-rénal, -aux [ɑ̃terɔrenal, -o], *a. Med:* enterorenal.

entérorragie [ɑ̃terɔraʒi], *s.f. Med:* enterorrhagia.

entérovaccin [ɑ̃terɔvaksɛ̃], *s.m.* enterovaccine.

enterrage [ɑ̃tɛraːʒ], *s.m.* planting; *Metall:* bedding.

enterré [ɑ̃tɛre], *a.* sunken, deep (trench, road, etc.); *s.a.* BATTERIE 4.

enterrement [ɑ̃tɛrmɑ̃], *s.m.* (*a*) burial, interment; (*b*) funeral, obsequies; **messe d'e.,** burial service; **e. civil,** funeral without religious ceremony, civil funeral; **e. militaire,** military funeral; **assister à l'e.,** to attend the funeral; *F:* **avoir, faire, une figure d'e.,** to have a funereal, woe-begone, look, to have a face as long as a funeral; *F:* **ne fais pas cette tête d'e.,** don't look so mournful! **avancer à pas d'e.,** to proceed at a funeral pace; *F:* **c'est un e. de première classe,** the thing has been shelved for good.

enterrer [ɑ̃tɛre], *v.tr.* **1.** to put (sth.) in the earth; **e. des oignons,** to plant bulbs; **canalisation faiblement enterrée,** main just underground; *Metall:* **e. le modèle dans le sable,** to bed in the mould. **2.** to bury, inter (corpse); **être enterré vivant,** to be buried alive; *F:* **il nous enterrera tous,** he will outlive us all; **e. sa vie de garçon,** to give a farewell bachelor('s) party; **e. de l'argent dans une entreprise,** to sink money in an undertaking; **e. un projet,** to bury a plan in oblivion; **elle désire e. toute cette affaire,** she wants the whole thing buried and forgotten; *s.a.* MORT[1].

s'enterrer. 1. *F:* **s'e. au fond de la campagne,** to bury oneself in the depths of the country. **2.** *Mil:* to dig oneself in.

enterreur [ɑ̃tɛrœːr], *s. O:* burier (of corpse).

entêtant [ɑ̃tɛtɑ̃], *a.* that gives one a headache; oppressive, stifling (atmosphere, etc.); heady (wine); persistant (smell, scent).

en-tête [ɑ̃tɛt], *s.m.* **1.** heading (of letter, document); **en-tête de facture,** bill-head; **papier à en-tête,** headed note-paper. **2.** *Typ:* headline (of page, column, etc.); *U.S:* caption; *pl. en-têtes.*

entêté, -ée [ɑ̃tɛte], *a. & s.* obstinate, headstrong, stubborn, wilful; perverse; *F:* pigheaded, mulish (person).

entêtement [ɑ̃tɛtmɑ̃], *s.m.* **1.** obstinacy, stubbornness; *F:* pig-headedness, mulishness; **e. à faire qch.,** persistency in doing sth. **2.** headache. **3.** heading (of pins).

entêter [ɑ̃tɛte], *v.tr.* **1.** (*of odours, etc.*) to give (s.o.) a headache; to make (s.o.) giddy; to intoxicate; *F:* **ces louanges l'entêtaient,** this praise went to his head, turned his head. **2.** *A:* = ENTICHER. **3.** to head (pins).

s'entêter. 1. to be obstinate, stubborn; **s'e. dans une opinion,** to persist in an opinion; **s'e. à faire qch.,** to persist in doing sth.; **il s'entête à ne pas vouloir manger,** he stubbornly refuses to eat. **2.** *A:* = S'ENTICHER.

enthalpie [ɑ̃talpi], *s.f. Ph:* enthalpy.

enthousiasme [ɑ̃tuzjasm] *s.m.* enthusiasm, rapture; **parler avec e.,** to speak with warmth, feeling; **faire qch. sans e.,** to do sth. half-heartedly, in a half-hearted way; **accepter d'e.,** to accept enthusiastically.

enthousiasmer [ɑ̃tuzjasme], *v.tr.* to fire (s.o.) with, rouse (s.o.) to, enthusiasm; to enrapture.

s'enthousiasmer, to become enthusiastic; **s'e. pour, de, sur, qn, qch.,** to be enthusiastic, go into raptures, over s.o., sth.; to become keen on s.o., sth.; *F:* to enthuse over sth.; **il s'enthousiasme facilement,** he is easily moved to enthusiasm, easily fired.

enthousiaste [ɑ̃tuzjast]. **1.** *s.m. & f.* enthusiast. **2.** *a.* enthusiastic.

enthymème [ɑ̃timɛm], *s.m. Log:* enthymeme.

entibois [ɑ̃tibwɑ], *s.m. Tls:* (wooden) vice-clamp, -jaw.

entiché [ɑ̃tiʃe], *a.* **1.** *A:* spotted, touched (fruit). **2.** infatuated (**de qn,** with s.o.); *P:* nuts (on s.o.); crazy (about s.o., sth.); **e. de sport,** keen on sport, **e. d'une opinion,** wedded to, taken with, an opinion.

entichement [ɑ̃tiʃmɑ̃], *s.m.* infatuation, enthusiasm (**de, pour,** for); keenness (**pour,** on).

enticher [ɑ̃tiʃe], *v.tr.* **1.** *A:* to spot, touch, spoil (fruit). **2. e. qn de qn, de qch.,** to make s.o. keen on s.o., on sth.; to infatuate s.o. with s.o., sth.

s'enticher de qn, de qch., to become infatuated with, to take a fancy to, s.o., sth.; **elle s'est entichée du théâtre,** she is dying to go on the stage; **il s'est entiché de cette théorie,** he has this theory on the brain; he is wedded to this theory.

entier, -ière [ɑ̃tje, -jɛːr], *a.* **1.** entire, whole; **pain e.,** whole loaf; **lait e.,** full-cream milk; **la France entière,** the whole of France; **manger une oie tout(e) entière,** to eat a whole goose; **l'œuvre est tout entière à recommencer,** the whole work must be done again; **pendant des heures entières,** for (whole) hours together; for hours on end; **des sanglots la secouaient tout entière,** sobs shook her whole frame; **pas une vitre ne reste entière,** not a window remains intact, whole; **conserver sa réputation entière,** to keep one's reputation intact; **la question reste entière,** the question remains untouched; **les choses ne sont plus entières,** things are not unchanged, not as they were; **ne laisser rien d'e.,** to leave nothing as it was; *Mth:* **nombre e.,** *s.m.* **entier,** integer, whole number; *Breeding:* **cheval e.,** *s.m.* **entier,** entire horse, stallion; *Rail: etc:* **payer place entière,** to pay full fare. **2.** complete, full (authority, independence, etc.); **l'entière direction de qch.,** the entire, sole, management of sth.; **elle est tout(e) entière à ce qu'elle fait,** she is completely absorbed in what she is doing; she is engrossed in, intent on, what she is doing; **tout e. à sa vengeance,** intent on revenge; **être tout e. pour une ligne de conduite,** to be all in favour of a course of action. **3.** *F:* **homme e.,** (i) bluff, plain-spoken, man; (ii) unyielding, headstrong, man. **4.** *s.m.* entirety; **raconter une histoire dans son e.,** to relate a story in its entirety; *adv.phr.* **en e.,** wholly, entirely, fully, in full; **nom en e.,** name in full; **lire un volume en e.,** to read a volume right through; to read the whole of a volume; **il mangea le poulet en e.,** he ate the whole chicken.

entièrement [ɑ̃tjɛrmɑ̃], *adv.* entirely, wholly, quite, fully, completely; **il n'est pas e. mauvais,** he is not all bad; **vous avez e. raison,** you are absolutely right; **doublé e. en peau,** leather-lined throughout; *Fin:* **capital e. versé,** fully paid (-up) capital.

entifler [ɑ̃tifle], *v.* **1.** *v.i. P:* to barge in. **2.** *v.tr. P:* to marry; to live with, shack up with.

s'entifler, *P:* **s'e. de sec,** to get married, spliced, hitched.

entité [ɑ̃tite], *s.f. Phil:* entity.

entoilage [ɑ̃twalaːʒ], *s.m.* **1.** (*a*) mounting, pasting, (of maps, etc.) on linen, on canvas; (*b*) covering with canvas; (*c*) *Tail:* stiffening (of collar, of revers, etc.) with canvas. **2.** (*a*) canvas mount; (*b*) *Av: A:* (i) fairing, canvas cover; (ii) fabric.

entoiler [ɑ̃twale], *v.tr.* **1.** to mount, paste (map, etc.) on linen or canvas; **carte entoilée,** map mounted on linen, on cloth. **2.** *Av: etc: A:* to cover (wing, etc.) with canvas, with fabric.

entoir [ɑ̃twaːr], *s.m. Hort:* grafting-knife.

entôlage [ɑ̃tolaːʒ], *s.m. P:* (*esp. of prostitute*) (inveigling and) robbing.

entôler [ɑ̃tole], *v.tr. P:* (*a*) (*esp. of prostitute*) to (inveigle and) rob; (*b*) **e. un chaland,** to fleece a customer; **se faire e. au bridge,** to get fleeced at bridge.

entôleur, -euse [ɑ̃tolœːr, -øːz], *s. P:* inveigler, thief, sharper.

entolome [ɑ̃tɔlɔm], *s.m. Fung:* entoloma.

entomique [ɑ̃tɔmik], *a.* entomic.

entomogame [ɑ̃tɔmɔgam], *a. Bot:* entomophilous.

entomogamie [ɑ̃tɔmɔgami], *s.f. Bot:* entomophily, pollination by insects.

entomologie [ɑ̃tɔmɔlɔʒi], *s.f.* entomology.

entomologique [ɑ̃tɔmɔlɔʒik], *a.* entomological.

entomologiste [ɑ̃tɔmɔlɔʒist], *s.m.* entomologist.

entomophage [ɑ̃tɔmɔfaːʒ], *a. Bot:* entomophagous.

entomophile [ɑ̃tɔmɔfil], *a. Bot:* entomophilous.

entomophilie [ɑ̃tɔmɔfili], *s.f. Bot:* entomophily.

entomostracés [ɑ̃tɔmɔstrase], *s.m.pl. A: Moll:* Entomostraca.

entonnage [ɑ̃tɔnaːʒ], *s.m.,* **entonnement** [ɑ̃tɔnmɑ̃], *s.m.,* **entonnaison** [ɑ̃tɔnɛzɔ̃], *s.f.* barrelling, casking (of wine, etc.).

entonner[1] [ɑ̃tɔne], *v.tr.* **1.** (*a*) to barrel, cask (wine, etc.); *F:* **s'e. du vin dans le gosier,** to swig wine; (*b*) *F: O:* **e. qch. à qn,** to din sth. into s.o. **2.** to fill (sausages).

s'entonner, *A:* (*of the wind*) to rush in, up, down (as into a funnel); **le vent s'entonnait dans la cheminée, dans la vallée,** the wind was blowing violently down (or up) the chimney, the valley.

entonner[2], *v.tr. Mus:* **1.** to intone (psalm, etc.); to sing the opening phrase of (a chant); **e. les louanges de qn,** to sing s.o.'s praises. **2.** to start (a song); to strike up, break into (a song).

entonnoir [ɑ̃tɔnwaːr], *s.m.* **1.** (*a*) funnel; **e. à grille,** straining funnel; **en (forme d')e.,** funnel-shaped; (*of aperture*) bell-mouthed; (*b*) *Ind:* (charging) boot; (*c*) **e. à saucisses,** sausage-filler; (*d*) *P:* gullet, throat. **2.** (*a*) *Mil:* shell-hole, crater; (*b*) hollow (among hills); *Scot:* corrie; *Geol:* sink-hole.

entophyte [ɑ̃tɔfit], *s.m. Bot:* entophyte.

entorse [ɑ̃tɔrs], *s.f.* sprain, wrench, twist, strain (*esp.* of the ankle); **se donner une e.,** to sprain, twist, wrench, one's ankle; *F:* **faire une e. au code, à la loi,** to do violence to the law; to go beyond, to stretch, the law; **donner une e. à la vérité,** to twist, wrench, the truth; **faire une e. au sens d'un passage,** to strain, distort, the meaning of a passage.

entortillage [ɑ̃tɔrtijaːʒ], *s.m.,* **entortillement** [ɑ̃tɔrtijmɑ̃], *s.m.* **1.** (*a*) winding, twisting, wrapping up (**dans,** in); (*b*) twisting, twining, winding, coiling (of snake, convolvulus, etc.). **2** (*a*) entanglement; (*b*) *F:* obscurity, intricacy (of style); circumlocution.

entortiller [ɑ̃tɔrtije], *v.tr.* (*a*) **e. qch. dans qch., autour de qch.,** to wind, twist, twine, wrap, sth. in sth., round sth.; (*b*) *F:* to wheedle; to get round (s.o.); to inveigle; **elle sait l'e.,** she can twist him round her little finger; (*c*) *F:* **e. ses idées,** to state one's ideas in an involved, obscure, fashion; **style entortillé,** involved style.

s'entortiller, to twist, twine, coil (**autour de,** round); **s'e. dans qch.,** to get entangled in sth.

entortilleur, -euse [ɑ̃tɔrtijœːr, -øːz], *s.* cajoler, wheedler.

entotrophe [ɑ̃tɔtrɔf], *a. & s. Ent:* **1.** *a.* entotrophic. **2.** *s.m.pl.* **entotrophes,** entotrophi.

entour [ɑ̃tuːr], *s.m.* **1.** *A:* (*used only in the pl.*) (*a*) environs, surroundings (of town, etc.); (*b*) persons among whom one lives, one's associates. **2.** *adv.phr.* **à l'entour,** around, round about; **les villages à l'e.,** the surrounding villages; *prep. phr.* **à l'entour de,** round; **les montagnes à l'e. de la ville,** the mountains round about the town; *cf.* ALENTOUR 1.

entourage [ɑ̃turaːʒ], *s.m.* **1.** (*a*) surroundings (of place); setting, framework (of sth.); **avec un e. de . . .,** surrounded by . . .; **miniature avec un e. de perles,** miniature set in pearls; (*b*) fencing, casing (of machinery, etc.). **2.** set, circle (of friends, etc.); environment; entourage, associates; attendants; **une personne de son e.,** one of his familiars; **le roi et tout son e.,** the king and all his suite.

entourant [ɑ̃turɑ̃], *a.* surrounding, encompassing; *Bot:* **feuilles entourantes,** sheathing leaves.

entourer [ɑ̃ture], *v.tr.* to surround, encompass (**de,** with); to fence in (field, etc.); to encircle (army); **les murailles qui entourent la ville,** the walls that surround the town; **un large ruban entourait sa taille,** she had a wide ribbon round her waist; **s'e. d'amis,** to surround oneself with friends; **monsieur le maire, entouré du clergé et des officiers de la garnison . . .,** the Mayor, supported by the clergy and the officers of the garrison . . .; **les gens qui nous entourent,** those around us; **il était très entouré,** (i) many people came up to him, he was the centre of attraction; (ii) he had a wide circle of friends; **une affaire entourée de mystère,** an affair wrapped (up) in mystery; **e. qn de soins,** to lavish attentions on s.o.; **il a été bien entouré durant sa maladie,** during his illness he was well looked after by the people around him; **e. de respect,** to show great respect to; **entouré de dangers, de difficultés, d'ennemis,** beset with dangers, with difficulties, with foes; **s'e. de toutes sortes de précautions,** to take all sorts of precautions; **savoir s'e.,** to know how to choose one's counsellors.

entourlouper [ɑ̃turlupe], *v.tr. F:* **e. qn,** to play a dirty trick on s.o.; to cheat, swindle s.o.

entourloupette [ɑ̃turlupɛt], *s.f. F:* nasty, dirty, trick.

entournure [ɑ̃turnyːr], *s.f.* armhole (of coat, frock, etc.); *F:* **être gêné dans les, aux, entournures,** to be awkward, stiff, ill-at-ease (in society); *F:* **être gêné aux entournures,** to be in financial straits.

en-tout-cas [ɑ̃tukɑ], *s.m.inv. in pl. O:* umbrella-sunshade.

entozoaire [ɑ̃tɔzɔɛːr], *s.m. Z:* entozoon; *pl.* entozoa.

entr'abattre (s') [sɑ̃trabatr̥], *v.pr.* (*conj. like* BATTRE) to shoot one another down, to lay one another low.

entr'aborder (s') [sɑ̃trabɔrde], *v.pr.* **1.** to hail one another. **2.** *Nau:* to collide head-on.

entr'accorder (s'), entraccorder (s') [sɑ̃trakɔrde], *v.pr.* to agree together.

entr'accrocher (s') [sɑ̃trakrɔʃe], *v.pr.* to hook together.

entr'accuser (s'), entraccuser (s') [sɑ̃trakyze], *v.pr.* to accuse one another.

entracte [ɑ̃trakt], *s.m. Th:* **1.** interval, intermission; **à l'e.,** during the interval, between the acts. **2.** entracte, interlude; **e. de musique,** musical interlude.

entr'admirer (s'), entradmirer (s') [sɑ̃tradmire], *v.pr.* to admire one another.

entraide [ɑ̃trɛd], *s.f. no pl.* mutual aid.

entraider (s') [sɑ̃trede], *v.pr.* to help one another.

entrailles [ɑ̃trɑːj], *s.f.pl.* **1.** (*a*) entrails, intestines, viscera, bowels; *F:* guts; **avoir des douleurs d'e.,** to have intestinal pains, *F:* pains in one's inside; **entendre crier ses e.,** to feel the pangs of hunger; **les e. de la terre,** the bowels of the earth; *O:* **les e. de la question,** the heart of the question; (*b*) *Ecc: Poet:* **le fruit de vos e. est béni,** blessed be the fruit of thy womb; **s'armer contre ses propres e.,** to take up arms against one's own flesh and blood. **2.** bowels of mercy, heart, compassion, affection; **ému, remué, jusqu'au fond de ses e.,** stirred to the depths of his soul; **avoir pour qn des e. de mère,** to have a motherly affection for s.o.; **être sans e.,** to be heartless, ruthless, unfeeling.

entr'aimer (s') [sɑ̃treme], *v.pr.* to love one another.

entrain [ɑ̃trɛ̃], *s.m.* liveliness, briskness; high spirits; spirit; *F:* go; **être plein d'e.,** to be full of life, of go; to be in high feather; *P:* to be full of beans; **musique pleine d'e.,** lively music; **y mettre de l'e.,** to go briskly at it; *F:* to make things hum; **manger avec e.,** to eat with gusto; **travailler avec e.,** to work with spirit; **jouer avec e.,** to play with zest; **attaque menée avec e.,** attack carried out with dash, smartly carried out; **pour donner plus d'e. à la conversation,** in order to liven up the conversation; **la conversation manque d'e.,** the conversation drags, is rather slow; **faire qch. sans e.,** to do sth. half-heartedly, in a half-hearted manner; **retrouver son e.,** to cheer up, brighten up, again.

entraînable [ɑ̃trɛnabl̥], *a.* easily led, easily influenced.

entraînant [ɑ̃trɛnɑ̃], *a.* inspiriting, stirring (speech, tune, etc.); heart-stirring (speech); lively (music); catchy (music).

entraînement [ɑ̃trɛnmɑ̃], *s.m.* **1.** (*a*) dragging (or being dragged) along; carrying away; **e. de l'opinion publique,** (i) force, (ii) carrying, of public opinion; (*b*) (i) feed (of machine-tool); (ii) drive (of machine); **e. régulier,** smooth drive; **e. par courroie,** belt transmission, belt drive; **à e. par courroie,** belt-driven; **e. par tambour,** drum drive; **clavette, doigt, goupille, d'e.,** drive, driving pin; driving dog; **e. mécanique,** mechanical drive, power drive; **à e. mécanique,** power-driven; **e. progressif,** gradual application of power; **tige d'e.,** driving-plate pin, driver (of lathe); **bout d'e.,** driven end; (*c*) enthusiasm. **2.** leading (or being led) astray; allurement; **préserver qn de mauvais entraînements,** to keep s.o. from being led astray; **e. d'une mélodie,** lure, witchery, of a tune. **3.** *Sp:* training (of race-horses, of athletes); coaching (of team); **être à l'e.,** to be in training; **manquer d'e.,** to lack practice; **partie d'e.,** practice match; **vol d'e.,** practice flight.

entraîner [ɑ̃trɛne], *v.tr.* **1.** (*a*) to drag, draw, carry, along; to carry away; to wash away or down; to sweep along or away (gravel, earth, etc.); *Mch:* (*of steam*) **e. de l'eau,** to prime; **e. qn quelque part,** to drag s.o. off somewhere; **e. vivement qn,** to whisk s.o. off, along; **e. qn en prison,** to drag s.o. off to prison; **entraîné par le courant,** borne along, swept along, by the current; **entraîné au fond de la mer,** sucked down to the bottom of the sea; **être entraîné dans un cataclysme,** to be involved in a cataclysm; **il a été entraîné dans le désastre,** he was engulfed in the disaster; **il vous entraînera dans sa perte,** he will drag you down with him; (*b*) *Mec.E:* to transmit motion to, to drive (part of machine, etc.); **roue entraînée,** follower wheel. **2.** to seduce, inveigle (s.o.); **e. qn à faire qch.,** to lead s.o. to do sth., to inveigle s.o. into doing sth.; **e. qn dans l'erreur,** to lead s.o. into error; **être entraîné dans un piège,** to be lured into a trap; **entraîné par la jalousie, par l'éloquence de l'orateur,** carried away by jealousy, by the speaker's eloquence; **se laisser e.,** to allow oneself to be led into temptation, led away, led astray; **se laisser e. à faire qch.,** to be drawn into doing sth.; **ne vous laissez pas e. dans la politique,** do not let

yourself be drawn, inveigled, into politics. 3. to produce (sth.) as a consequence, to bring (sth.) about; to entail, involve; **cela entraînera un retard,** it will involve, lead to, delay; **cela entraîne de la dépense,** that entails, runs one into, expense; **e. des conséquences,** to be followed, attended, by, to entail, consequences; **e. la ruine de qn,** to bring about s.o.'s ruin, to involve s.o. in ruin; **décision qui peut e. des inconvénients,** decision that may land one in difficulties, give rise to difficulties; **par l'élévation du prix que cette opération, etc., entraîne,** owing to the inevitable increase in price; **e. une condamnation au pénal,** to give rise to, to attract, a sentence under criminal law. 4. (*a*) *Sp:* to train (racehorse, athlete); to coach (team); **entraîné à tous les sports,** trained in every kind of game; **entraîné à fond,** in the pink (of condition); in thorough training; (*b*) *Sp:* to pace (a cyclist); (*c*) **il est entraîné aux affaires difficiles,** he is schooled in difficult business.

entraîneur [ɑ̃trɛnœːr], *s.m.* 1. *Sp:* (*a*) trainer (of horses, etc.); coach (of team); (*b*) **e. (de coureur),** pace-maker, pacer. 2. (*a*) *Mec.E:* driving device; (*b*) *Tex: etc:* **rouleaux entraîneurs,** feed rolls. 3. *Atom.Ph:* carrier; **e. de rétention,** hold-back carrier; **sans e.,** carrier-free.

entraîneuse [ɑ̃trɛnøːz], *s.f. Danc:* dance hostess.

entraison [ɑ̃trɛzɔ̃], *s.f.* spawning time (of salmon, etc.).

entrait [ɑ̃trɛ], *s.m. Const:* (*a*) tie-beam, stringer, binder (of wooden roof); **faux entrait,** collar (-beam, -tie); (*b*) tie-rod (of iron roof).

entrancer [ɑ̃trɑ̃se], *v.tr.* **(j'entrançai(s); n. entrançons)** *A:* to send, put, (s.o.) into a trance.

s'entrancer, *A:* to go or fall into a trance.

entrant, ante [ɑ̃trɑ̃, -ɑ̃ːt]. 1. *a.* (*a*) incoming, ingoing; **fonctionnaires entrants,** newly-appointed officials; **les élèves entrants,** the new boys; (*b*) *A:* **manières entrantes,** insinuating ways; ingratiating manner. 2. *s.* incomer, ingoer; (*at cards*) player cutting in; **entrants et sortants,** comers and goers.

entr'apercevoir [ɑ̃trapɛrsəvwaːr], *v.tr.* (*conj. like* APERCEVOIR) to catch a fleeting glimpse of (sth.).

entr'appeler (s') [sɑ̃traple], *v.pr.* (*conj. like* APPELER) to call one another.

entr'attaquer (s') [sɑ̃tratake], *v.pr.* to attack one another.

entravant [ɑ̃travɑ̃], *a.* hampering, impeding.

entrave [ɑ̃traːv], *s.f.* 1. (*a*) shackle, fetter; (*b*) hobble; (*for cow*) spancel; **mettre des entraves à un cheval,** to hobble a horse. 2. **e. à qch.,** hindrance, impediment, obstacle, to sth.; clog upon sth.; **les entraves de l'étiquette,** the trammels of etiquette; **agir sans entraves,** to act without hindrance; **cela constituerait une e. à nos travaux,** it would hamper our work; *Jur:* **e. à la liberté du travail,** interference with the right to work.

entravé [ɑ̃trave], *a.* impeded, hampered; *A: Cost:* **jupe entravée,** hobble-skirt; *Ling:* **voyelle entravée,** blocked vowel.

entraver[1] [ɑ̃trave], *v.tr.* 1. to shackle, fetter; to clog (animal); to spancel (cow); **e. un cheval,** to hobble a horse. 2. to hinder, hamper, clog, trammel, impede; to interfere with (natural function, etc.); **e. la circulation,** to hold up, block, the traffic; **e. la marche des services,** to clog the wheels of the administration; **entravé par les préjugés,** trammelled by prejudices.

entraver[2], *v.tr. P:* to understand; **je n'y entrave que dalle,** I haven't the first notion about it.

entr'avertir (s') [sɑ̃travɛrtiːr], *v.pr.* to warn one another.

entraxe [ɑ̃traks], *s.m.* = ENTRE-AXE.

entre [ɑ̃ːtr]. I. *prep.* 1. (*a*) between; *A. & Lit:* betwixt; **e. deux haies,** between two hedges; **distance de cinq milles e. deux villes,** distance of five miles between two towns; **e. deux et trois (heures),** between two and three; **femme e. deux âges,** middle-aged woman; **regarder qn e. les yeux,** to look s.o. full in the face; **passer e. les mailles,** to slip through the net; (*b*) **e. les deux,** betwixt and between, neither one thing nor the other; **le gris est e. le blanc et le noir,** grey is something between white and black; **être e. la vie et la mort,** to be betwixt life and death. 2. (*a*) among(st); **nous sommes e. amis,** we are among friends; **nous dinerons e. nous,** there won't be anyone else at dinner; **e. quat'z'yeux,** in private; **il fut laissé e. les morts,** he was left among the dead; *B:* **vous êtes bénie e. toutes les femmes,** blessed art thou among women; **il est doué e. tous,** he outshines all others; **elle était belle e. toutes,** she was beautiful beyond all others; **un homme dangereux e. tous,** a most dangerous man; *F:* **c'est un malin e. tous,** he's as sharp as they make 'em; **j'aime, e. toutes, les peintures de cet artiste,** I particularly like this artist's paintings; **un jour e. mille,** a day in a thousand; **un exemple e. mille,** one example among thousands; **ce problème est délicat e. tous,** the question is one of extreme delicacy; there is no more delicate question; **ce jour e. tous,** this day of all days; **e. autres,** among others, among other things; **e. autres choses il a dit que . . ., il a dit, e. autres, que . . .,** among other things he said that . . .; **moi e. autres . . .,** I, for one . . .; (*b*) **tomber e. les mains de l'ennemi,** to fall into the enemy's hands; **il tomba e. les mains des voleurs,** he fell among thieves; **tenir qch. e. les mains,** to hold sth. in one's hands; **mon sort est e. vos mains,** my fate is in your hands; (*c*) *prep.phr.* **d'e.** (from) among; *used instead of "de" with pers. pron.*; **l'un d'e. eux,** one of their number; **deux d'e. eux,** two of them; **beaucoup, peu, plusieurs, d'e. nous,** many, few, several, of us; **ceux d'e. nous qui . . .,** those of us who . . . 3. in relation to (one another); **ils s'accordent e. eux,** they agree among themselves; **elles vivaient e. elles,** they lived in close companionship; **ils se marient e. eux,** they intermarry; **e. eux trois ils eurent bientôt terminé,** between the three of them they had soon done; **les masses sont e. elles dans un rapport constant,** the masses are in a fixed proportion to each other, one to the other; **soit dit e. nous,** (be it said) between ourselves; *F:* between you and me and the gate-post; **soit dit e. experts,** as one expert to another.

II. **entre-** *used as pref.* 1. (*sense of reciprocity*) **s'entretuer,** to kill one another; **s'entr'embrasser,** to kiss one another. 2. (*a*) (*sense of crossing*) **entrecouper,** to intersect; **entrelacer,** to interlace; **entrelacs,** interlacing; (*b*) (*sense of connecting*) **s'entre-communiquer,** to inter-communicate; (*c*) (*sense "between"*) **s'entremettre,** to interpose; **entremise,** intervention; **entre-rail,** space between the rails. 3. (*sense "half," "partially"*) **entre-bâiller,** to half-open; **entre-bâillement,** half opening.

entre-axe [ɑ̃traks], *s.m.inv. Veh: Rail:* **e.-a. des essieux,** distance between the axles.

entrebâillement [ɑ̃trəbɑjmɑ̃], *s.m.*, **entrebâillure** [ɑ̃trəbɑjyːr], *s.f.* 1. narrow opening, chink (of door, etc.); slit, small gap (between curtains, etc.); **je l'ai vu par l'e. de la porte,** I saw him through the half-open door. 2. *Const:* casement-stay.

entrebâiller [ɑ̃trəbɑje], *v.tr.* to set (door) ajar; to half-open (door, curtain, etc.); **les rideaux s'entrebâillaient, étaient entrebâillés,** there was a gap between the curtains; **la porte était entrebâillée,** the door was ajar.

entrebâilleur [ɑ̃trəbɑjœːr], *s.m. Furn:* door stop; door chain; (*of window*) casement stay.

entre-bande [ɑ̃trəbɑ̃ːd], *s.f. Tex:* coloured end-list, end-selvedge (of piece of cloth); *pl. entre-bandes.*

entre-battre (s'), entrebattre (s') [sɑ̃trəbatr], *v.pr.* (*conj. like* BATTRE) *A:* to fight one another.

entrechat [ɑ̃trəʃa], *s.m. Danc:* (*a*) entrechat; (*b*) *pl. F:* crosscapers; **battre des entrechats,** to cut capers.

entre-chercher (s') [sɑ̃trəʃɛrʃe], *v.pr.* to look for one another, to seek each other out.

entrechoquement [ɑ̃trəʃɔkmɑ̃], *s.m.* collision, shock, clash (between two things, etc.).

entrechoquer (s') [sɑ̃trəʃɔke], *v.pr.* (*a*) to collide, clash, to fall foul of one another; *F:* **gens qui s'entrechoquent à tout propos,** people who disagree, clash, on every occasion; (*b*) *v.pr.* (*of bottles, etc.*) to knock against one another; (*of glasses*) to chink.

entre-clore [ɑ̃trəklɔːr], *v.tr.* (*conj. like* CLORE) (*rare*) to half-close (door, etc.).

entre-clos [ɑ̃trəklo], *a.* half-shut, half-closed (eyes, etc.); half-drawn (curtains); (door) ajar.

entr'éclos [ɑ̃treklo], *a.* half-opened (bud, etc.).

s'entre-cogner [sɑ̃trəkɔɲe], *v.pr. F:* to fight.

entrecolonne [ɑ̃trəkɔlɔn], *s.f.*, **entrecolonnement** [ɑ̃trəkɔlɔnmɑ̃], *s.m.* intercolumniation.

entre-combattre (s') [sɑ̃trəkɔ̃batr], *v.pr.* (*conj. like* BATTRE) to fight one another.

entre-communiquer (s') [sɑ̃trəkɔmynike], *v.pr.* to inter-communicate.

entrecôte [ɑ̃trəkoːt], *s.f. Cu:* steak cut from the ribs (of beef); *F:* rib of beef; **e. minute,** thin grilled steak.

entrecoupé [ɑ̃trəkupe], *a.* interrupted, broken (speech, sleep, etc.); **voix entrecoupée (de sanglots),** voice broken with sobs; broken voice; **d'une voix entrecoupée,** with a catch in one's voice; **(parler) à mots entrecoupés,** (to speak) brokenly.

entrecouper [ɑ̃trəkupe], *v.tr.* 1. to intersect; **prairie entrecoupée de fossés,** meadow intersected with ditches. 2. to interrupt, check; **des soupirs entrecoupaient son discours,** sighs interrupted his speech.

s'entrecouper, to intersect.

entrecoupeuse [ɑ̃trəkupøːz], *s.f. Combmaking:* **e. double,** twinning-machine, -saw.

entr'écrire (s') [sɑ̃trekriːr], *v.pr.* (*conj. like* ÉCRIRE) to write to one another.

entrecroisé [ɑ̃trəkrwaze], *a.* intersected, interwoven; *Tex:* interlock.

entrecroisement [ɑ̃trəkrwazmɑ̃], *s.m.* 1. intersection; criss-cross (of lines, etc.); interlacing (of threads, etc.); *Med:* interdigitation; 2. *Breed:* intercrossing.

entrecroiser [ɑ̃trəkrwaze], *v.tr.* to intersect, cross (lines, etc.); to interlace (threads, etc.); *Med:* to interdigitate; **doigts entrecroisés,** interlocked fingers.

s'entrecroiser, to intersect, intercross, interlace, interlock; to cross one another; to criss-cross.

entrecuisse, entre-cuisse, [ɑ̃trəkɥis], *s.m.* crotch, crutch.

entre-déchirer (s') [sɑ̃trədeʃire], *v.pr.* to tear one another to pieces.

entre-détruire (s') [sɑ̃trədetrɥiːr], *v.pr.* (*conj. like* DÉTRUIRE) to destroy one another.

entre-deux [ɑ̃trədø], *s.m.inv.* 1. space between; interspace, interval; **e.-d. des lames,** trough of the sea; *F:* **la vérité est dans l'e.-d.,** the truth is between the two; **prendre un e.-d.,** to take a middle course; *adv.* **fait-il chaud?—e.-d.,** is it hot?—middling; betwixt and between. 2. (*a*) *Min:* parting (between galleries, etc.); (*b*) *Const:* partition; (*c*) *Dressm: Needlew:* insertion; **e.-d. de dentelle,** lace insertion; (*d*) panel (between pillars, etc.); (*e*) *Cu:* **e.-d. de morue,** middle-cut of cod.

entre-deux-guerres [ɑ̃trədøgɛːr], *s.m. or f.inv.* the inter-war years (1918-1939).

entre-dévorer (s') [sɑ̃trədevɔre], *v.pr.* to devour one another.

entre-donner (s') [sɑ̃trədɔne], *v.pr.* to give one another (sth.).

entrée [ɑ̃tre], *s.f.* 1. (*a*) entry, entering, entrance (of s.o. into room, etc., of an army into town); **e. en scène d'un acteur,** actor's entrance, appearance (on the stage); **à son e. nous nous levâmes,** when he appeared we rose to our feet; **la clef donne e. au jardin,** the key admits to the garden; **faire son e.,** to make one's entrance; **sa fille fera son e. dans le monde cet hiver,** his daughter is coming out this winter; **son e. dans cette carrière,** his first steps in this career; **l'e. des États-Unis dans la politique mondiale,** the entry of the United States into world politics; *Sch:* **e. en vacances,** break(ing) up; *Av: Nau:* **bord d'entrée,** leading edge (of propeller); *W.Tel:* **(fil d')e. de poste,** lead-in; (*b*) *pl.* (i) *Com:* receipts; (ii) *Nau:* arrivals (of ships). 2. (*a*) admission, admittance (to club, college, etc.); **obtenir l'e. d'une société,** to gain admission to a society; **avoir son e., ses entrées, à un théâtre, dans un lieu,** to have one's entrée to a theatre, to have the run of a place; **avoir ses entrées libres dans une maison,** to be free of a house; **avoir ses entrées libres chez qn,** to have free access to s.o.; **donner à qn ses entrées libres,** to make s.o. free of the house; **"e. interdite,"** "no admittance"; **payer ses entrées,** (i) to pay one's admission fee, one's entrance fee; (ii) to pay one's footing; *Com: P.N:* **(magasin à) e. libre,** walk round shop; **"e. libre"** (i) = "no obligation to buy"; (ii) admission free; (*b*) *Com:* import(ation); *Cust:* entry; **droit d'e.,** import duty; **e. en douane,** clearance inward, entry inward. 3. (*a*) way in, entrance (to railway station, building, etc.); (entrance-)hall; lobby; **le phare à l'e. du port,** the lighthouse at the harbour entrance; **e. d'une rivière, d'une caverne, d'un sac,** mouth of a river, of a cave, of a sack; **courant d'e.,** inflowing current; **e. d'une manche,** opening of a sleeve; **e. d'un bas,** leg-hole of a stocking; **e. de tête,** head-size (of hat); **e. de serrure,** (i) keyhole; (ii) escutcheon (over keyhole); **c'est l'e. aux récriminations,** it affords an opportunity, a loop-hole, for recriminations; **à l'e. de l'hiver,** at the beginning of winter; **d'e. (de jeu),** from the very beginning, from the word go, from the outset; *Nau:* **l'e. ouest de la Manche,** the chops of the Channel; (*b*) *Mch:* admission, inlet (of cylinder, etc.); **(orifice d') e.,** inlet; **orifice d'e. (de compresseur),** inlet volute (of compressor); **raccord d'e.,** inlet fitting; **e. d'air,** *Mec.E:* air inlet, air hole; *I.C.E:* air intake; *Av:* **e. d'air fuseau,** nacelle intake ring; *Civ.E:* **cône d'e.,**

tapered inlet pipe (of pipeline); (*c*) *Computers: Elcs:* input. **4.** *Cu:* entrée.

entrefaite [ɑ̃trəfɛt], *s.f. used only in the phr.* **dans l'entrefaite, sur ces entrefaites . . .,** *A:* **sur l'entrefaite . . .,** meanwhile, in the midst of all this . . ., while this was going on . . ., during that time . . ., at this juncture . . ..

entre(-)fenêtre [ɑ̃trəf(ə)nɛtr̥], *s.f. Arch:* pier; *pl. entre-fenêtres.*

entrefer [ɑ̃trəfɛːr], *s.m.* clearance (between metallic surfaces); *esp. El:* air-gap (of dynamo, etc.).

entrefermer [ɑ̃trəfɛrme], *v.tr.* to half close; **entrefermé,** half-closed.

entrefilet [ɑ̃trəfilɛ], *s.m. Journ:* (*a*) paragraph (in newspaper); *F:* par; (*b*) *F:* short.

entre-fin [ɑ̃trəfɛ̃], *a.* medium quality (goods); *pl. entre-fin(e)s.*

entre-frapper (s') [sɑ̃trəfrape], *v.pr.* to strike one another.

entregent [ɑ̃trəʒɑ̃], *s.m.* tact (in handling people); discretion; worldly wisdom.

entr'égorger (s') [sɑ̃tregɔrʒe], *v.pr.* (*conj. like* ÉGORGER) to cut one another's throats.

entre-haïr (s') [sɑ̃trəaiːr], *v.pr.* (*conj. like* HAÏR) to hate one another.

entre-heurter (s') [sɑ̃trəœrte], *v.pr.* = ENTRE-CHOQUER (S').

entreillissé [ɑ̃trejise], *a.* trellised (gate, etc.).

entrejambe [ɑ̃trəʒɑ̃ːb], *s.m. Tail:* (*a*) crutch; (*b*) **(longueur d')e.,** length (of trousers) from fork to heel.

entre-joindre (s') [sɑ̃trəʒwɛ̃ːdr̥], *v.pr.* (*conj. like* JOINDRE) to join together.

entrelacé [ɑ̃trəlase], *a.* interlaced, interwoven; **ils entrèrent les mains entrelacées,** they entered hand in hand.

entrelacement [ɑ̃trəlasmɑ̃], *s.m.* interlacing (of ribbon, etc.); interweaving (of threads, etc.); intertwining, network (of branches, etc.); *Tchn:* wicker-, basket-, wattle-work; *T.V:* interlacing, interlaced scanning.

entrelacer [ɑ̃trəlase], *v.tr.* (*conj. like* LACER) to interlace (ribbon, twigs, etc.); to interweave (threads, etc.); to intertwine (branches, etc.); to interknit; *Typ:* to ligature (letters).

s'entrelacer, to intertwine.

entrelacs [ɑ̃trəlɑ], *s.m.* interlacing, intertwining; interlaced design, tracery; knot-work, strap-work (in embroidery, architecture, etc.); **e. de ronces,** tangle of briars.

entrelardé [ɑ̃trəlarde], *a.* (*of pork, etc.*) streaky; streaked with fat.

entrelardement [ɑ̃trəlardəmɑ̃], *s.m.* (*a*) *Cu:* larding; (*b*) interlarding.

enterlarder [ɑ̃trəlarde], *v.tr. Cu:* to lard (meat); **e. un discours de citations,** to interlard a speech with quotations.

entre-ligne [ɑ̃trəliɲ], *s.m.* **1.** space between lines (of writing, print, etc.). **2.** interlineation, writing inserted between the lines; *pl. entre-lignes.*

entre-louer (s') [sɑ̃trəlwe], *v.pr.* to praise one another; to sing one another's praises.

entre-luire [ɑ̃trəlɥiːr], *v.i.* (*conj. like* LUIRE) to glimmer, glint.

entre-manger (s'), entremanger (s') [sɑ̃trəmɑ̃ʒe], *v.pr.* to eat one another.

entremêlement [ɑ̃trəmɛlmɑ̃], *s.m.* **1.** (inter)-mingling. **2.** (inter)mixture, jumble, medley; **e. de larmes et de rires,** tears intermingled with laughter; **dans un e. de larmes et de rires,** half laughing, half crying.

entremêler [ɑ̃trəmele], *v.tr.* **e. qch. (de, parmi, qch.),** to (inter)mix, (inter)mingle, sth. (with sth.); **e. des couleurs,** to mix, blend, colours; *F:* **e. un discours de citations bibliques,** to interlard a speech with quotations from the Bible; **ordres entremêlés de jurons,** orders interspersed with oaths.

s'entremêler. 1. to (inter)mix, (inter)mingle. **2.** *A:* **s'e. dans une affaire,** to meddle with, mix oneself up in, an affair; to interfere.

entremets [ɑ̃trəmɛ], *s.m. Cu:* (*a*) side-dish, second course; (*b*) **e. sucré,** sweet (as dinner course); **e. salé,** savoury.

entremetteur, -euse [ɑ̃trəmɛtœːr, -øːz], *s.* **1.** *A:* intermediary, mediator; *F:* go-between; *Com:* middleman. **2.** *Pej:* procurer, procuress; *m.* pimp; *f.* bawd.

entremettre (s') [sɑ̃trəmɛtr̥], *v.pr.* (*conj. like* METTRE) to interpose, intervene; **s'e. pour qn,** to intercede for s.o.; **s'e. dans une querelle,** to intervene in a quarrel; **s'e. dans une affaire,** to act as go-between, as intermediary, in an affair.

entremise [ɑ̃trəmiːz], *s.f.* **1.** (*a*) intervention, interposition; (*b*) mediation; **agir par l'e. de qn,** to act through (the agency of) s.o.; **je vous l'envoie par l'e. d'un ami,** I send it you by the hand of a friend. **2.** *N.Arch:* (*below beams*) carling, carline; **courbe d'e.,** carling knee; **e. de bossoir,** davit span.

entre-nerf(s) [ɑ̃trənɛːr], *s.m.inv. Bookb:* panel (of back).

entre-nœud [ɑ̃trənø], *s.m. Bot:* (*a*) internode; (*b*) pipe (of straw); *pl. entre-nœuds.*

entre-nuire (s') [sɑ̃trənɥiːr], *v.pr.* (*conj. like* NUIRE) to injure one another; to do one another harm.

entrepas [ɑ̃trəpɑ], *s.m.* amble, ambling gait (of horse).

entrepénétrer (s') [sɑ̃trəpenetre], *v.pr.* to penetrate one another; to interpenetrate.

entre-percer (s') [sɑ̃trəpɛrse], *v.pr.* to pierce one another; to run one another through.

entrepont [ɑ̃trəpɔ̃], *s.m. Nau:* between-decks; 'tween-decks; **passager d'e.,** steerage passenger.

entreposage [ɑ̃trəpozaːʒ], *s.m.* warehousing, storing; *Cust:* bonding; *Petroleum Ind:* stacking (of a rig).

entreposer [ɑ̃trəpoze], *v.tr.* to warehouse, store; *Cust:* to bond; to put (goods) in bond; **marchandises entreposées,** bonded goods.

entreposeur [ɑ̃trəpozœːr], *s.m.* (*a*) warehouse keeper, warehouseman; *Cust:* officer in charge of a bonded store; (*b*) official in charge of warehousing and sale of state monopoly goods (in France).

entrepositaire [ɑ̃trəpozitɛːr], *s.m. Cust:* **1.** bonder. **2.** warehouseman.

entrepôt [ɑ̃trəpo], *s.m.* **1.** warehouse, store, repository; **e. maritime,** wharf; *Cust:* **e. réel, e. de la douane,** bonded warehouse; bondstore; **e. fictif,** unbonded warehouse; **e. frigorifique,** cold store; **marchandises en e.,** bonded goods, goods in bond; **mettre des marchandises en e.,** to bond goods; **mise en e.,** (i) wharfage; (ii) *Cust:* placing of (goods) in bond; *Com:* **à prendre en e.,** ex-warehouse. **2.** *Mil:* **e. de munitions,** ammunition depot; **e. de réparation,** repair depot.

entreprenable [ɑ̃trəprənabl̥], *a.* attemptable, feasible, practicable.

entreprenant [ɑ̃trəprənɑ̃], *a.* enterprising, venturesome, go-ahead; **montrer un esprit e.,** to show enterprise, initiative; **il est e.,** he has plenty of initiative; *esp.* **un jeune homme e., une jeune femme entreprenante,** a forward young man, young lady.

entreprendre [ɑ̃trəprɑ̃ːdr̥], *v.tr.* (*conj. like* PRENDRE) **1.** to undertake; to take (sth.) in hand; to set one's hand to, address oneself to (task); **e. un commerce,** to open shop, business; **e. une étude,** to enter upon a study; **e. de faire qch.,** to undertake to do sth.; **e. de réaliser un programme,** to undertake a programme; *F:* **e. qn au billard,** to take s.o. on at billiards; **e. qn sur un sujet,** to start a discussion with s.o. on a subject; to take s.o. to task, to tackle s.o. over a matter. **2.** to contract for (piece of work). **3.** *v.i. A:* **e. sur les droits de qn,** to encroach upon s.o.'s rights; **e. sur la liberté,** to make an attempt against liberty.

entrepreneur, -euse [ɑ̃trəprənœːr, -øːz], *s.* contractor; **e. du gouvernement,** contractor to the Government; **e. (en bâtiments)** building contractor; **e. en maçonnerie,** master mason; **e. de déménagements,** furniture remover; **e. de transports,** carrier, forwarding agent; **e. de chargement et de déchargement,** stevedore; **e. de pompes funèbres,** undertaker, *U.S:* mortician.

entreprise [ɑ̃trəpriːz], *s.f.* **1.** (*a*) undertaking, venture; **e. hardie,** bold enterprise; **une folle e.,** (i) a mad venture; (ii) *F:* a wild goose chase; **entreprises (galantes),** advances (towards a member of the opposite sex); (*b*) firm; **e. commerciale,** business undertaking, business concern; **e. rémunératrice,** paying concern; **e. douteuse,** doubtful venture; **e. publique,** public corporation; **e. privée,** private enterprise; **la libre e.,** free enterprise; **e. à risques partagés,** joint venture; **e. artisanale,** (i) small-scale enterprise; (ii) cottage industry; **c'est une grosse e.,** it's a big firm; *F:* **e. de gangsters,** racket; (*c*) **e. de transports, de roulage,** carrying company, forwarding agency. **2. e. de travaux publics,** contract for public works; **travail à l'e.,** work by, on, contract; *Ind:* **recours à l'e.,** contracting; **mettre qch. à l'e.,** to put sth. out to contract; **avoir l'e. de construire une route,** to hold a contract for building a road. **3.** *A:* **e. sur les droits de qn,** encroachment on s.o.'s rights; **e. contre la liberté,** attempt upon liberty.

entre-quereller (s') [sɑ̃trəkərɛle, -ele], *v.pr.* to quarrel (with one another); to bicker.

entrer [ɑ̃tre], *v.i.* (*the aux. is être*) **1.** to enter; to go in(to), to come in(to); to step in(to); (*a*) **e. dans une salle,** to enter, go into, come into, walk into, a room; **e. dans, à, l'épicerie,** to go into the grocer's; **entrez!** come in! **"Entrez sans frapper,"** "please walk in"; **"Entrez, messieurs dames!"** "Walk up!" **"Défense d'e.,"** "no admittance," "private"; **faire e. qn (dans une pièce),** (i) to show s.o. in(to a room); (ii) to call s.o. in; **on les fit e. au salon,** they were shown into the drawing-room; **faites(-le) e.,** show him in; **laisser e. qn, qch.,** to let s.o., sth., in; to admit s.o.; **on ne voulut pas le laisser e.,** he was refused admittance; **e. en passant,** to drop in, look in (on s.o.); **je n'ai fait qu'e. et sortir,** I only just dropped in, *F:* popped in, for a moment; **les employés entraient et sortaient,** the employees came in and out; **j'entrerai un instant en revenant du bureau,** I shall look in on my way back from the office; **empêcher qn d'entrer,** to keep s.o. out; to close the door against s.o.; **l'épine lui est entrée dans le doigt,** the thorn went into, pierced, his finger; **équipement qui entre dans un sac,** outfit that goes into, fits into, a bag; **pièce qui entre dans une autre,** piece that fits into another; **la clef n'entre pas dans la serrure,** the key does not fit the lock; **le vent entre par la fenêtre,** the wind blows in at the window; **faire entrer qch. dans qch.,** to insert sth. in sth., to drive sth. into sth.; **chapeau qui entre bien (dans la tête),** hat which fits well on to the head, that comes well down on the head; **il n'entrait plus dans son pantalon,** he couldn't get into his trousers any longer; **une pareille idée ne lui est jamais entrée dans la tête,** such an idea never occurred to him, never entered his head; *Th:* **Hamlet entre (en scène),** enter Hamlet; *Aut: F:* **e. dans un arbre, dans une voiture,** to run, crash, into a tree, into a car; (*b*) (*of horseman*) to ride in; (*of vehicle*) to drive in; (*of ship*) to sail in; (*c*) **e. en courant,** to run in; **e. en dansant,** to dance in, to skip in; **e. précipitamment,** to dash in; **e. furtivement,** to steal in; **parvenir à e.,** to (manage to) get in; (*d*) **e. dans l'armée, une société,** to join, enter, the army, a company; **il est entré au Ministère de l'Air,** he has been taken into the Air Ministry; **e. dans une carrière,** to take up a career; **e. dans les ordres,** to take, go into, (holy) orders; **e. dans la finance,** to go in for finance; **e. en condition,** to go into (domestic) service; **e. en fonction,** to enter upon one's duties; *Mil:* **e. en campagne,** to take the field; **e. en ménage,** to set up house(keeping); **e. à l'Académie,** to be admitted to the Academy; **e. au collège,** to go to school (for the first time); **e. en vacances,** to break up (for holidays); **e. dans sa soixantième année,** to enter one's sixtieth year; (*e*) **e. dans de longues explications,** to go into long explanations; **e. en correspondance avec qn,** to enter into correspondence with s.o.; (*f*) **e. en colère,** to get angry; **e. en ébullition,** to begin to boil, to come to the boil; **e. en fusion,** to (begin to) melt. **2.** to enter into, be a part of, take part in (sth.); **e. dans un complot,** to take part in a plot; **je n'entrerai pas dans l'affaire,** I will have nothing to do with the matter; **vous n'entrez pour rien dans l'affaire,** you are in no way concerned with the business; *F:* you don't come into it; **e. dans les idées de qn,** to agree with s.o.; **e. dans les sentiments de qn,** to share s.o.'s feelings; **e. dans le jeu,** to enter into the spirit of the game; **e. dans une catégorie,** to fall into a category; **dans tout ceci l'imagination entre pour beaucoup,** in all this imagination plays a large part; **il n'entre pas dans nos intentions de . . .,** it is not our intention to . . .; **pilules où il entre de l'arsenic,** pills that contain arsenic, with arsenic as an ingredient. **3.** *v.tr.* (*the aux. is* avoir) to bring, let, put (sth.) in; **e. des marchandises en fraude,** to smuggle in goods.

entre-rail [ɑ̃trərɑːj], *s.m. Rail:* space between the rails; gauge of track; (*in Engl.*) four-foot way; *pl. entre-rails.*

entre-rang [ɑ̃trərɑ̃], *s.m.* space between the rows, between the ranks; *pl. entre-rangs.*

entre-regarder (s') [sɑ̃trər(ə)garde], *v.pr.* to look at one another.

entre-répondre (s') [sɑ̃trərepɔ̃ːdr], *v.pr.* to answer, reply to, one another.

entresol [ɑ̃trəsɔl], *s.m. Arch:* entresol, mezzanine (floor).

entre-sourcils [ɑ̃trəsursi], *s.m.inv.* space between the eyebrows.

entre-soutenir (s') [sɑ̃trəsut(ə)niːr], *v.pr.* to support each other.

entre-suivre (s') [sɑ̃trəsɥiːvr], *v.pr.* (*conj. like* SUIVRE) to follow one another.
entretaille [ɑ̃trətɑːj], *s.f.* light stroke (in engraving).
entre-tailler (s'), entretailler (s') [sɑ̃trətɑje], *v.pr.* (*of horse*) to interfere, to cut, to brush.
entretaillure [ɑ̃trətɑjyːr], *s.f.* **1.** *Vet:* interference, brushing. **2.** tapestry interwoven with gold and silver threads.
entre-temps, entretemps [ɑ̃trətɑ̃]. **1.** *s.m.inv.* interval; **dans l'e.-t.,** meanwhile, in the meantime. **2.** *adv.* meanwhile, in the meantime, between whiles.
entreteneur, -euse [ɑ̃trətnœːr, -øːz], *s.* **1.** maintainer, preserver. **2.** *s.m.* keeper (of a mistress).
entretenir [ɑ̃trətniːr], *v.tr.* (*conj. like* TENIR) **1.** to maintain; to keep (sth.) up; **e. qch. en bon état,** to keep sth. in repair; **route mal entretenue,** road in bad repair; **la voiture a été bien entretenue,** the car has been well looked after; **j'entretiens la voiture moi-même,** I look after the car myself; **e. son français,** to keep up one's French; **e. une correspondance avec qn,** to keep up a correspondence with s.o.; **e. une vaste correspondance,** to carry on a wide correspondence; **e. l'espoir de qn,** to keep s.o.'s hopes alive; **e. la conversation,** to keep the conversation alive; **e. les craintes de qn,** to keep s.o. in a state of fear; **e. la paix,** to keep the peace; **e. une agitation,** to foster an agitation; **e. les rues,** to maintain, keep, the streets in good condition; **s'e. la main,** to keep one's hand in; **e. le feu,** to keep up, tend, the fire; to keep the fire going; *El:* **e. un accu,** to maintain a battery. **2.** (*a*) to maintain, support, keep (a family, a mistress, a fleet, etc.); **de quoi e. la vie,** enough to sustain life; **e. qn de vêtements,** to keep s.o. in clothes; *F:* **e. qn d'espérances,** to feed s.o. on hopes; **il ne gagne pas de quoi s'e.,** he does not earn enough to live on, to keep himself; (*b*) **e. des soupçons,** to entertain, harbour, suspicions. **3. e. qn (de qch.),** to converse with, talk to, s.o. (about sth.); **pendant ce temps j'ai entretenu les invités,** meanwhile I made conversation with the guests.
s'entretenir. 1. *A:* (*of things*) to hold together. **2. s'e. avec qn (de qch.),** to converse, have a talk, with s.o. (about sth.), to discuss sth. with s.o. **3.** *Sp:* to keep fit.
entretenu [ɑ̃trətny], *a.* **1. femme entretenue,** kept woman. **2.** *W.Tel:* **oscillations entretenues,** sustained oscillations; **ondes entretenues,** undamped, continuous, waves.
entretien [ɑ̃trətjɛ̃], *s.m.* **1.** (*a*) upkeep, maintenance (of roads, buildings, etc.); maintenance (of accumulator); keeping (of machines, etc.) in repair, in good order; care (of supplies, etc.); **personnel d'e.,** maintenance staff; *Ind: Com:* **e. et réparations,** servicing; **e. (d'une auto, d'un poste de radio), par les fournisseurs,** servicing (of a car, radio); **manuel d'e.,** instruction book (of a car, etc.); **les accus exigent un e. journalier,** batteries require daily attention; **produit d'e. (pour cuirs, etc.),** dressing; **produits d'e.,** (household) cleaning materials; *s.a.* DRAGAGE 1; (*b*) *W.Tel:* **limite d'e.,** threshold of oscillation (of valve). **2.** support, maintenance (of family, army, etc.); **frais d'e.,** cost of maintenance; **ce qu'il gagne ne suffit pas à son e.,** he does not earn his keep; **elle dépense trop pour son e.,** she spends too much on dress. **3.** (*a*) conversation, interview; **j'ai eu un e. avec lui,** I had a talk with him; (*b*) subject, topic (of conversation); *A:* **faire l'e. du public,** to be the talk of the town; (*c*) *pl.* **entretiens,** talks, negotiations; **avoir des entretiens avec le Prince des ténèbres,** to hold converse, have dealings, with the Prince of darkness, the Devil.
entretisser, entre-tisser [ɑ̃trətise], *v.tr.* to weave together, to interweave.
entretoile [ɑ̃trətwal], *s.f.* (lace) insertion.
entretoise [ɑ̃trətwaːz], *s.f.* **1.** (*a*) *Const: etc:* brace, strut, cross-bar, cross-piece, distance-piece, tie, stay, cross-bearer; cross-brace; spacer; *Rail:* **e. de rail,** rail tie-bar; **e. butée,** stop spacer; (*b*) *A:* transom (of gun-carriage, in aeroplane). **2.** *Equit:* lower bar (of bit).
entretoisement [ɑ̃trətwazmɑ̃], *s.m. Const:* **1.** bracing, counter-bracing, staying, strutting; **boulon d'e.,** stay-bolt. **2.** = ENTRETOISE 1.
entretoiser [ɑ̃trətwaze], *v.tr. Const: etc:* to (cross-)brace, stay, strut, tie.
entre-toucher (s') [sɑ̃trətuʃe], *v.pr.* to touch (one another).
entre-travée [ɑ̃trətrave], *s.f. Coll. Const:* small beams resting on the main beams; *pl. entre-travées.*
entre-tuer (s') [sɑ̃trətɥe], *v.pr.* to kill, slaughter, one another.
entrevision [ɑ̃trəvizjɔ̃], *s.f.* glimpse.
entre-voie [ɑ̃trəvwa], *s.f. Rail:* space between tracks; (*in Engl.*) six-foot way; **quai d'e.-v.,** island platform; *pl. entre-voies.*
entrevoir [ɑ̃trəvwaːr], *v.tr.* (*conj. like* VOIR) to catch sight, catch a glimpse, of (s.o., sth.); **je n'ai fait que l'e.,** I caught only a glimpse of him; **j'entrevis des arbres dans le brouillard,** I caught a dim sight of trees through the fog; *F:* **il entrevoyait la vérité,** he had an inkling of the truth; **laisser e. qch. à qn,** to drop a hint of sth. to s.o.; **j'entrevois des difficultés,** I foresee difficulties; **il laissa de bonne heure e. son talent,** he early gave an earnest of his talent, he gave early indications of his talent; **il avait entrevu la mort,** he had glimpsed death; **e. de faire qch.,** (i) to envisage the possibility of doing sth.; (ii) to be thinking of doing sth.
entrevous [ɑ̃trəvu], *s.m. Const:* case-bay; space between girders.
entrevoûter [ɑ̃trəvute], *v.tr. Const:* to fill up (the case-bay) with plaster.
entrevue [ɑ̃trəvy], *s.f.* interview.
entr'hivernage [ɑ̃trivernaːʒ], *s.m. Agr:* winter-ploughing.
entr'hiverner [ɑ̃triverne], *v.tr. Agr:* to winter-plough.
entripaillé [ɑ̃tripɑje], *a. F:* fat.
entr'obliger (s') [sɑ̃trɔbliʒe], *v.pr.* to oblige one another.
entropie [ɑ̃trɔpi], *s.f. Ph: etc:* entropy.
entropion [ɑ̃trɔpjɔ̃], *s.m. Surg:* entropion, introversion of eyelid.
entroque [ɑ̃trɔk], *s.m. Paleont:* (en)trochite; (*of rock*) **à entroques,** entrochal.
entr'ouïr [ɑ̃truiːr], *v.tr.* (*conj. like* OUÏR) to half-hear; to catch the sound of (s.o.'s voice, etc.).
entrouvert, entr'ouvert [ɑ̃truvɛːr], *a.* **1.** half-open (window, flower, etc.); **laissez la porte entrouverte,** leave the door ajar; **lèvres entrouvertes,** parted lips. **2.** gaping, yawning (chasm, etc.).
entrouvrir, entr'ouvrir [ɑ̃truvriːr], *v.tr.* (*conj. like* OUVRIR) to half open (door, the eyes, etc.); **e. la porte,** to set the door ajar; **e. les rideaux,** to draw the curtains slightly aside.
s'entrouvrir, s'entr'ouvrir. 1. to half open. **2.** (*of chasm, etc.*) to open up, gape, yawn.
entubage [ɑ̃tybaːʒ], *s.m. P:* swindling.
entuber [ɑ̃tybe], *v.tr. P:* to swindle.
enturbanné [ɑ̃tyrbane], *a.* turbaned (head, etc.).
enture [ɑ̃tyːr], *s.f.* **1.** *Hort:* incision, cut (for grafting). **2.** (*a*) peg, pin (of a peg ladder); (*b*) *Carp:* scarf-joint; **e. à goujon,** pin-joint.
énucléation [enykleasjɔ̃], *s.f.* **1.** *Surg:* enucleation (of tumour, etc.). **2.** stoning (of fruit).
énucléer [enyklee], *v.tr.* **1.** *Surg:* to enucleate (tumour, eye, etc.). **2.** to stone (fruit).
énucloir [enyklwaːr], *s.m.* fruit-stoner.
énumérable [enymerabl], *a.* that may be enumerated.
énumérateur, -trice [enymeratœːr, -tris], *s.* enumerator.
énumératif, -ive [enymeratif, -iːv], *a.* enumerative.
énumération [enymerasjɔ̃], *s.f.* enumeration; recital (of facts); telling (of votes).
énumérer [enymere], *v.tr.* (**j'énumère, n. énumérons; j'énumérerai**) to enumerate; to count up; *Pol:* to tell; **é. les faits,** to detail, recite, facts; **é. les voix,** to tell the votes.
énurèse [enyrɛːz], **énurésie** [enyrezi], **énurésis** [enyrezis], *s.f. Med:* enuresis.
énurétique [enyretik], *a. & s. Med:* enuretic.
envahir [ɑ̃vaiːr], *v.tr.* **1.** to invade, to overrun (country, etc.); **la foule envahit la salle,** the crowd invaded, broke into, the hall; **jardin envahi par les mauvaises herbes,** garden overrun, overgrown, with weeds; **envahi par l'eau,** flooded; **une défaillance l'envahit,** a feeling of faintness came over him; **le rouge lui envahit le visage,** the blood rushed to his face; **quand la crainte nous envahit,** when fear assails us; **la politique envahit tout,** politics obtrude themselves everywhere. **2. e. le terrain de son voisin,** to encroach upon one's neighbour's land.
envahissable [ɑ̃vaisabl], *a. N.Arch:* **longueur e.,** floodable length.
envahissant [ɑ̃vaisɑ̃], *a.* invading (forces, etc.); encroaching (flames, etc.); **plante, mauvaise herbe, envahissante,** overgrown plant, weed; *F:* **il est e.,** he is intrusive.
envahissement [ɑ̃vaismɑ̃], *s.m.* invasion, overrunning (of country, etc.); encroachment (of the tide, etc.); inrush (of water, etc.).
envahisseur [ɑ̃vaisœːr]. **1.** *s.m.* invader. **2.** *a.* (*a*) invading; (*b*) encroaching.
envasement [ɑ̃vɑzmɑ̃], *s.m.* silting; choking (up) (of harbour, etc.) with mud; siltation.
envaser [ɑ̃vɑze], *v.tr.* **1.** to silt; to choke (up) (canal, etc.) with mud. **2.** to run (boat) on the mud.
s'envaser. 1. (*of harbour, etc.*) to silt up. **2.** (*of ship*) to stick, rest, settle down, in the mud.
enveilloter [ɑ̃vɛjɔte], *v.tr.* to put (hay) in cocks.
enveloppant, -ante [ɑ̃vlɔpɑ̃, -ɑ̃ːt]. **1.** *a.* enveloping, enclosing; *Mil:* **mouvement e.,** enveloping movement; *F:* **charme e.,** captivating charm; *Aut:* **pare-choc(s) e.,** wrap-round bumper. **2.** *s.f.* **enveloppante;** *Mth:* envelope.
enveloppe [ɑ̃vlɔp], *s.f.* **1.** (*a*) envelope, cover(ing) (of letter); wrapper, wrapping (of parcel); **mettre une lettre sous e.,** to put a letter in an envelope; **envoyer qch. sous e.,** to send sth. under cover; **e. gommée,** adhesive envelope; **e. à panneau transparent, à fenêtre cristal rapportée,** window envelope; **e. vitrifiée,** window envelope; **e. à panneau découpé, à fenêtre découpée,** aperture envelope; **e. premier jour,** first-day cover; **e.-réponse,** reply-paid envelope; *F:* **passer une e. à qn.,** to give s.o. a (large) tip; to grease s.o.'s palm; **recevoir une e.,** to receive a bribe; (*b*) **e. de voyage,** hold-all. **2.** exterior, external appearance. **3.** *Anat:* investing membrane, tunic (of organ); *Artil: Sm.a:* coating (of projectile); envelope (of bullet); *Mch:* sheathing, casing, jacket, lagging (of boiler, cylinder, etc.); **e. calorifuge,** insulating lagging; *Nau:* skin (of steel ship); *Aut: etc:* outer cover (of tyre), casing (of tyre); *Aer:* gas-bag; **e. de chanvre (d'un cordage),** serving (of a rope); *El.E:* **e. d'un câble,** sheathing of a cable; **e. d'induit,** armature casing; *I.C.E: etc:* **condensateur à e. étanche,** enclosed condenser; *Phys:* **e. de l'atome,** shell; *Atom.Ph:* envelope, shell (of reactor); **e. de sécurité,** containment. **4.** *Mth:* envelope (of a system of curves). **5.** *Geol:* **e. pierreuse externe, interne,** outer, inner, mantle.
enveloppement [ɑ̃vlɔpmɑ̃], *s.m.* **1.** envelopment, wrapping (up); (*a*) *Med:* packing (of a patient), pack; **e. froid,** pack sheet, cold pack; **e. glacé,** ice-pack; (*b*) *Mil: etc:* **manœuvre d'e.,** enveloping movement, encircling movement. **2.** *Biol:* (*a*) embryonic condition; (*b*) sheath (of seed, etc.).
envelopper [ɑ̃vlɔpe], *v.tr.* **1.** to envelop; (*a*) to wrap (s.o., sth.) up; **e. qn dans un manteau,** to wrap s.o. up in a cloak; **enveloppé d'un ample manteau,** wrapped in an ample cloak; **e. un paquet,** to wrap up, do up, a parcel; *Med:* **e. qn (dans un drap mouillé),** to pack a patient; **enveloppé de bandages,** swathed in bandages; **e. qn d'un regard, de ses regards,** to run one's eyes over s.o.; **crime enveloppé de mystère,** crime shrouded, hidden, in mystery; **discours enveloppé de réticences,** speech that gives little away; **paysage enveloppé de brume,** landscape shrouded in mist; (*b*) to cover, case (tube, etc.); *Mch:* **e. une chaudière,** to jacket, lag, a boiler; (*c*) to surround, encircle, close in upon, hem in (enemy, etc.); **la nuit nous enveloppa,** darkness closed in upon us. **2.** to involve, include; **e. qn dans un désastre,** to involve s.o. in a disaster. **3.** *Equit:* to grip (horse) with the knees.
envenimation [ɑ̃vnimasjɔ̃], *s.f. Vet:* poisoning due to (i) snake bite, (ii) bee sting.
envenimement [ɑ̃vnimmɑ̃], *s.m.* **1.** envenoming, poisoning (of finger, etc.). **2.** irritation, aggravation (of wound, of quarrel).
envenimer [ɑ̃vnime], *v.tr.* **1.** to envenom, poison (wound, etc.); **e. une querelle,** to fan, inflame, a quarrel. **2.** to irritate, aggravate (wound); *F:* **e. le mal,** to make matters worse.
s'envenimer, (*of wound*) to fester, suppurate; **la discussion s'envenime,** the discussion is growing acrimonious.
enverger [ɑ̃vɛrʒe], *v.tr. Tex:* to form a shed for (the shuttle).
envergeure [ɑ̃vɛrʒyːr], *s.f. Tex:* shed (of loom).
enverguer [ɑ̃vɛrge], *v.tr. Nau:* to bend (sail).
envergure [ɑ̃vɛrgyːr], *s.f.* **1.** *Nau:* (*a*) head, spread of sail (on yard-arm); **bâtiment qui a beaucoup d'e.,** ship that spreads much cloth; (*b*) **envergures, rabans d'e.,** robands, rope-bands; **ralingue d'e.,** head bolt-rope. **2.** spread, breadth, span (of bird's wings, of aircraft, etc.); wing-spread, wing-span (of bird, aircraft); full span (of the arms); **en e.,** spanwise, *F:* **de grande e.,** far-reaching, wide-spreading; **travaux, attaque, de grande e.,** works, attack, on

a large scale; **une offensive d'e.**, a large-scale offensive; **criminel de grande e.**, criminal on a large scale; **d'une certaine e.**, on a fairly large scale; **esprit de grande e.**, wide-ranging mind; **esprit de peu d'e.**, circumscribed, narrow, intellect; **un homme d'e.**, a man of great ability.

enverjure [ɑ̃vɛrʒyːr], *s.f. Tex:* shedding.

envers[1] [ɑ̃vɛːr], *s.m.* 1. wrong side, reverse, back (of material, etc.); *Tex:* **duite d'e., chaîne de l'e.**, undershot pick, backing warp; **étoffe sans e. (ni endroit)**, reversible material; *F:* **l'e. de la vie**, the seamy side of life; **l'e. de la médaille**, the reverse of the medal; **l'e. vaut l'endroit**, it's six of one and half a dozen of the other; *adv.phr:* **à l'envers**, (i) on the wrong side, inside out; (ii) wrong way up; (iii) wrong side foremost; **le monde à l'e.**, topsy-turvydom; **avoir la raison à l'e.**, to be utterly confused; **j'ai la tête à l'e.**, my brain is in a whirl; **tout est à l'e.**, things are all wrong. 2. cold northern slope (of valley).

envers[2], *prep:* toward(s) (= as regards, in relation to); **bien intentionné e. nous**, well-intentioned towards us; well-disposed to us, towards us; **être juste e. tous**, to be just to(wards) all; **agir loyalement e. qn**, to deal honestly, fairly, with s.o.; **son devoir e. sa patrie**, his duty to his country; **il fit son devoir e. la patrie**, he did his duty by his country; **soutenir une opinion e. et contre tous**, to maintain an opinion against all comers, against the whole world.

envi [ɑ̃vi], *s.m. used only in the adv.phr.* **à l'e.**, emulously, *and the prep.phr.* **à l'e. de**, in emulation of; **ils étudient à l'e. les uns des autres, l'un de l'autre**, they try to outdo each other in their work; **ils prêchaient à l'e. (l'un de l'autre)**, it was a preaching match between them.

enviable [ɑ̃vjabl̩], *a.* enviable.

envidage [ɑ̃vidaːʒ], *s.m. Tex:* winding, spooling.

envider [ɑ̃vide], *v.tr. Tex:* to wind, spool (yarn, etc.).

envie [ɑ̃vi], *s.f.* 1. desire, longing, inclination; **avoir (l')e. de qch.**, to want, to have a fancy for, sth.; **avoir (l')e. de faire qch.**, to wish, feel inclined, have a mind, to do sth.; **j'ai grande e. de lui écrire**, I have a great mind to write to him; **cela me donne l'e. de demander . . .**, that makes me inclined to ask . . .; **j'avais e. de pleurer**, I felt like crying, I felt a lump in my throat; **avoir bien e., presque e., de faire qch.**, to have a good mind, to have half a mind, to do sth.; **il a e. que je fasse cela**, he wants me to do that; **je n'éprouve aucune e. de le revoir**, I feel no desire to see him again; **si vous en éprouvez l'e.**, if you are so minded; **jeter sur qch. des regards d'e.**, to cast longing, covetous, looks on sth.; to look enviously at sth.; **avec e.**, longingly; **l'enfant regardait avec e. l'étalage du boulanger**, the child looked wistfully at the baker's window; **e. de femme enceinte**, craving; *P: abs.* **avoir e.**, to want to pee; **ça l'a pris comme une e. de pisser**, it got him suddenly. 2. envy; **être dévoré d'e.**, to be eaten up with envy; *F:* to be green with envy; **regards d'e.**, envious looks; **faire e. à qn**, to make s.o. envious; **ce livre me fait e.**, I long to have this book; **sa collection ferait e. à un spécialiste**, his collection might be envied by a specialist; **ma collection lui fait e.**, my collection makes him envious; *Prov:* **mieux vaut faire e. que pitié**, it is better to be envied than pitied; **porter e. à qn**, to envy s.o.; **s'attirer l'e. de qn**, to attract s.o.'s envy. 3. (*a*) agnail, hangnail; (*b*) birthmark.

envieillir [ɑ̃vjɛjiːr]. 1. *v.tr. A:* to make (s.o.) look old. 2. *v.i. & pr.* to grow old(er); *A:* **pécheur, ivrogne, envieilli**, hardened sinner, inveterate drunkard.

envier [ɑ̃vje], *v.tr.* (*p.d. & pr.sub.* **n. enviions, v. enviiez**) to envy. 1. to covet; *F:* to hanker after (sth.); to wish for (sth.). 2. to be envious of (s.o., sth.); **e. qch. à qn**, (i) to envy s.o. sth.; (ii) to begrudge s.o. sth.; **lui enviez-vous cet honneur?** do you begrudge him this honour? **je l'envie d'aller à Paris**, I envy his going to Paris.

envieusement [ɑ̃vjøzmɑ̃], *adv.* enviously.

envieux, -ieuse [ɑ̃vjø, -jøːz], *a.* envious (**de**, of); *s.* **faire des envieux**, to excite envy.

environ [ɑ̃virɔ̃]. 1. *adv.* about; **il a e. quarante ans**, he is forty or so, or thereabouts; he is about forty; **quelque chose d'e. dix francs**, something approaching ten francs. 2. *s.m.pl.* **environs**, (*a*) surroundings, vicinity, outskirts, neighbourhood, environs (of a place); **habiter aux, dans les, environs de Paris**, to live in the vicinity, in the outskirts, of Paris; to live near Paris; **aux environs de Noël**, at the approach of, round about, Christmas; *occ. sg.* **dans quelque environ de Paris**, in some outskirt of Paris; (*b*) **notre cap est aux environs du nord**, we are steering roughly north. 3. *prep. A:* **e. le mois d'avril**, (round) about April.

environnant [ɑ̃virɔnɑ̃], *a.* surrounding (country, etc.).

environnement [ɑ̃virɔnmɑ̃], *s.m.* surroundings; environment; **science de l'e.**, environmental science.

environner [ɑ̃virɔne], *v.tr.* to surround, environ, encompass (s.o., place, etc.); **environné de dangers**, beset with dangers.

envisagement [ɑ̃vizaʒmɑ̃], *s.m.* facing, envisagement (of s.o., sth.); looking (s.o.) in the face; consideration, contemplation (of facts, dangers, etc.).

envisager [ɑ̃vizaʒe], *v.tr.* (**j'envisageai(s); n. envisageons**) to face, envisage; (*a*) to look (s.o.) in the face; **e. la mort sans effroi**, to look upon death without fear; (*b*) to consider, contemplate (possibility, etc.); **e. l'avenir**, to look to the future; **le cas que nous envisageons**, the case under consideration; **on n'avait pas envisagé ce fait**, this event had not been anticipated, was unexpected; **les mesures dont on envisage la nécessité**, the measures considered to be necessary; **cas non envisagé**, unforeseen case; **e. différemment les événements**, to take a different view of events; **je n'envisage pas la chose ainsi**, I do not look on, do not view, the thing in that light; **comment envisagez-vous la question?** what are your views on the matter? *F:* **il n'envisageait pas de partir pour Paris**, (i) he wasn't thinking of going off to Paris; (ii) he was not expecting to go off to Paris.

envoi [ɑ̃vwa], *s.m.* 1. (*a*) sending, dispatch, expedition, forwarding, consignment; *Post:* delivery (of goods); **e. par mer**, shipment; **e. groupé**, batched dispatch; **faire un e. tous les mois**, to send, dispatch, goods every month; *Com:* **lettre d'e.**, letter of advice, covering letter; *Jur: Com:* **e. forcé**, forced sale by post; (*b*) **e. de renforts**, dispatch of reinforcements; (*c*) **e. de fonds**, remittance (of funds); **faire un e. de fonds à qn**, to remit funds to s.o.; (*d*) *Jur:* **e. en possession**, (i) livery of seisin; (ii) writ of possession; (*e*) *Fb:* **coup d'envoi**, (i) kick-off, (ii) free kick; *Rugby:* place kick. 2. consignment, parcel; shipment; **un e. de coton, de fruits**, a consignment of cotton, of fruit; **e. groupé**, batched consignment; **"e. de l'auteur,"** "presentation copy," "with the compliments of the author." 3. *Poetry:* envoi, envoy.

envoiler (s') [sɑ̃vwale], *v.pr. Metalw:* (*of steel*) to bend, warp (in tempering).

envoilure [ɑ̃vwalyːr], *s.f. Metalw:* bending, warping (of steel in tempering).

envoisiner [ɑ̃vwazine], *v.tr. A:* to surround (s.o.) with neighbours; **nous sommes bien envoisinés**, we have agreeable neighbours.

envol [ɑ̃vɔl], *s.m.* 1. (*a*) (*of birds*) taking flight, taking wing; (*b*) (*of aircraft*) taking off, flying off; **piste d'e.**, tarmac, airstrip, runway; *Navy: Av:* **pont d'e.**, flight-deck; **pont d'e. à piste oblique**, angled flight-deck. 2. (*a*) flight; (*b*) take-off, start; **prendre son e.**, (*of young person*) to start one's own life; (*c*) **dans un e. de jupes, elles s'enfuirent**, they ran away with a flurry, swirl, of skirts.

envolée [ɑ̃vɔle], *s.f.* (*a*) flight (of birds, aircraft); (*b*) *F:* **e. d'éloquence**, flight of oratory; **lyrisme de haute e.**, high-soaring lyricism.

envolement [ɑ̃vɔlmɑ̃], *s.m.* taking flight.

envoler (s') [sɑ̃vɔle], *v.pr.* (*a*) (*of bird*) to fly away, to fly off; to take flight, to take wing; *Ven:* to flush; **faire e. des oiseaux**, to put birds to flight, to scatter, flush, put up, birds; **laisser e. un oiseau**, to set a bird free; **l'oiseau s'est envolé**, the bird has flown; (*b*) (*of aircraft*) to take off, fly off; (*c*) (*of hat, etc.*) to blow off; **voilà tous mes papiers qui s'envolent!** there blow all my papers! **cheveux envolés**, tousled hair; **le temps s'envole**, time is flying; **les années envolées**, the years that have fled, flown.

envoûtant [ɑ̃vutɑ̃], *a.* captivating.

envoûté, -ée [ɑ̃vute], *s.* victim of sympathetic magic.

envoûtement [ɑ̃vutmɑ̃], *s.m.* (*a*) sympathetic magic, imitative magic; hoodoo; invultuation; (*b*) charm, magic appeal; **l'e. de Paris**, the charm of Paris.

envoûter [ɑ̃vute], *v.tr.* to practise sympathetic magic on (s.o.) (by means of a wax effigy); to hoodoo; to subjugate, to cast a spell over s.o.; **comme envoûté**, as if spellbound; **envoûté par la beauté de qn**, infatuated by s.o.'s beauty; under the spell of s.o.'s beauty.

envoûteur, -euse [ɑ̃vutœːr, -øːz], *s.* 1. worker of spells; caster of spells. 2. fascinating person; charmer, *U.S:* spellbinder.

envoyable [ɑ̃vwajabl̩], *a.* sendable, dispatchable.

envoyé, -ée [ɑ̃vwaje], *s.* messenger, representative; *esp.* (*government*) envoy; **e. extraordinaire et ministre plénipotentiaire**, Envoy Extraordinary and Minister Plenipotentiary; *Journ:* **de notre e. spécial**, from our special correspondent; **un e. du ciel**, a messenger from heaven.

envoyer [ɑ̃vwaje], *v.tr.* (**j'envoie, n. envoyons**; *fu.* **j'enverrai**) 1. to send, to ship; (*a*) **e. qn à Paris**, to send s.o. to Paris; **e. une lettre à qn**, to send s.o. a letter; **e. de l'argent**, to remit money; **e. une dépêche**, to dispatch a telegram; **envoyez-moi un petit mot**, drop me a line; **la somme à lui envoyée**, the sum sent to him; **e. sa démission**, to send in, tender, one's resignation; **e. un baiser à qn**, to blow s.o. a kiss; **e. des pierres dans un étang**, to throw stones into a pond; **e. un soufflet à qn**, to fetch s.o. a box on the ears; **e. chercher qn**, to send for s.o.; **il faut e. le chercher, l'e. chercher**, we must send for him; **envoyez-le chercher**, send for him; **je l'enverrai la chercher**, I shall send him for her; **j'ai envoyé (qn) prendre de ses nouvelles**, I sent (s.o.) to ask after him; **e. dire que . . .**, to send word that . . .; *F:* **je ne le lui ai pas envoyé dire**, I told him straight, to his face; *F:* **e. promener qn**, to send s.o. to the right-about, about his business; *P:* **ça c'est envoyé!** that's got him! that's the stuff to give him! (*b*) *pred.* **e. qn ambassadeur à Londres**, to send s.o. as ambassador to London. 2. *Nau:* **e. vent devant**, to go about; **envoyez!** about ship! 'bout ship! 3. *Nau:* to hoist (colours, etc.); **envoyez la vergue en haut!** send the yard up! **envoyez-moi un bout!** heave me a line!

s'envoyer, *P:* to stand oneself (a treat, etc.); **s'e. un verre de vin (derrière la cravate)**, to knock back a glass of wine; **s'e. une fille**, to get a woman, to stand oneself a tart, a bird; **s'e. une corvée**, to take on an irksome task.

envoyeur, -euse [ɑ̃vwajœːr, -øːz], *s.* sender, forwarder (of goods, letter, etc.); remitter (of money).

enwagonner [ɑ̃vagɔne], *v.tr.* to put (goods) into waggons, carts.

enzootie [ɑ̃zɔɔti, -si], *s.f. Vet:* enzootic disease.

enzootique [ɑ̃zɔɔtik], *a. Vet:* enzootic.

enzymatique [ɑ̃zimatik], *a. Bio-Ch:* enzymatic.

enzyme [ɑ̃zim], *s.f. Bio-Ch:* enzym(e).

enzymologie [ɑ̃zimɔlɔʒi], *s.f. Bio-Ch:* enzymology.

eoanthropus [eɔɑ̃trɔpys], *s.m. Paleont:* eoanthropus.

éocène [eɔsɛn], *a. & s.m. Geol:* eocene (period).

eohippus [eɔipys], *s. Paleont:* eohippus.

Éole [eɔl], *Pr.n.m. Gr.Myth:* Aeolus.

éolide [eɔlid], **éolis** [eɔli(s)], *s.f. Moll:* aeolis; **é. mauve**, plumed aeolis.

Éolie [eɔli], *Pr.n.f. A.Geog:* Aeolis; Aeolia.

éolien, -ienne [eɔljɛ̃, -jɛn], *a. & s.* 1. *Gr.Hist:* Aeolian. 2. **harpe éolienne**, Aeolian harp; **érosion éolienne**, wind erosion; **moteur é.**, wind-engine. 3. *s.f.* **éolienne**, wind-mill (for pumping); wind-engine, air-motor.

éolipile, éolipyle [eɔlipil], *s.m.* 1. *Ph:* aeolipile, -pyle. 2. *A:* wind-valve, ventilator (of chimney). 3. *A:* soldering lamp, blowlamp.

éolique [eɔlik], *a.* = ÉOLIEN.

éolithe [eɔlit], *s.m. Archeol:* eolith, celt.

éolithique [eɔlitik], *a.* eolithic.

éon [eɔ̃], *s.m.* aeon, eon.

éonisme [eɔnism], *s.m. Psy:* eonism.

éosine [eɔzin], *s.f. Ch:* eosin.

éosinophile [eɔzinɔfil], *Physiol:* 1. *s.m.* eosinophil(e). 2. *a.* eosinophilic, eosinophil(e).

éosinophilie [eɔzinɔfili], *s.f. Med:* eosinophilia.

éosphorite [eɔsfɔrit], *s.f. Miner:* eosphorite.

épacridacées [epakridase], *s.f. pl. Bot:* Epacridaceae.

épacte [epakt], *s.f. Chr:* epact.

épagneul, -eule [epaɲœl], *s.* spaniel.

épaillage [epɑjaːʒ], *s.m.* 1. picking (of wool). 2. cleaning (of molten gold).

épailler [epɑje], *v.tr.* 1. to pick (wool). 2. to clean (molten gold).

épair [epɛːr], *s.m. Paperm:* **é. nuageux, irrégulier**, wild look-through.

épais, -aisse [epɛ, -pɛːs]. 1. thick; **mur é.**, thick wall; **mur é. de deux pieds**, wall two foot thick; **cheveux é.**, thick, bushy, hair; **feuillage é.**, dense foliage; **couvert de forêts épaisses**, thickly, densely, wooded; **haie épaisse**, close-set hedge; **fourré é.**, close thicket; **brouillard é.**, heavy, dense, thick, fog; **encre épaisse**, thick, muddy, ink; **avoir la taille épaisse**, to be thickset;

livre é., thick, bulky, book; *F:* **avoir l'esprit é.**, to be dense, dull-witted; **avoir la langue épaisse**, (i) to be thick of speech; (ii) to have a furred tongue; **peu é.**, thin. **2.** *adv.* thick(ly); **semer é.**, to sow thick. **3.** *s.m.* **avoir deux pieds d'é.**, to be two foot thick; **couper dans l'é.**, to cut into the thickest part.

épaisseur [epɛsœ:r], *s.f.* **1.** (*a*) thickness (of wall, etc.); depth (of layer); **le mur a deux pieds d'é.**, the wall is two foot thick; **é. d'un livre**, bulk of a book; **é. d'un cheveu**, hair's breadth; (**courroie**, etc.) **en trois épaisseurs**, three-ply (belt, etc.); *Mec.E:* **feuilles d'é.**, feelers; **mettre (une planche**, etc.) **à d'é.**, to thickness (a board, etc.); **le peu d'é. de . . .**, the thinness of . . .; (*b*) *Atom.Ph:* **é. équivalente**, equivalent; **é. équivalente d'arrêt**, stopping-equivalent; **é. équivalente de plomb**, lead-equivalent. **2.** density, thickness (of foliage, fog, etc.); *F:* **é. d'intelligence**, denseness, dullness, of mind.

épaissir [epesi:r]. **1.** *v.tr.* to thicken ((i) wall, board, etc.; (ii) sauce, etc.); (*of smoke, etc.*) to make (the air) dense; to inspissate (a liquid). **2.** *v.i. & pr.* to thicken, become thick; (*of pers.*) to grow stout; **les ténèbres s'épaississent**, the darkness deepens; **la neige s'épaississait**, the snow was getting deeper; **son esprit s'épaissit**, he is growing dense.

épaississant [epesisã]. **1.** *a.* thickening (matter, etc.). **2.** *s.m. Phot:* thickener (in developer, etc.).

épaississement [epesismã], *s.m.* thickening (of fog, etc.); dulling (of the mind); inspissation (of liquid).

épaississeur [epesisœ:r], *s.m. Ind:* thickener, thickening apparatus.

épamprage [epãpra:ʒ], *s.m.*, **épamprement** [epãprəmã], *s.m. Vit:* thinning out of the leaves.

épamprer [epãpre], *v.tr. Vit:* to thin out the leaves of (vine).

épanalepse [epanalɛps], *s.f. Lit:* epanalepsis.

épanchement [epãʃmã], *s.m.* **1.** (*a*) pouring out, discharge, overflow (of liquid); *Med:* (i) extravasation, (ii) effusion (of blood, etc.); *Geol:* **roche d'é.**, effusive rock; *s.a.* BILE 2; (*b*) outpouring (of thoughts, feelings); effusion (of feeling); **en veine d'é.**, in an expansive mood. **2.** *pl.* effusiveness; outpourings of the heart.

épancher [epãʃe], *v.tr.* to pour out (liquid); to shed (blood); *F:* **é. sa bile**, to vent one's spleen; *s.a.* BILE 2; **é. sa colère sur qn**, to vent one's anger on s.o.; **é. ses chagrins dans le sein de qn**, to unbosom one's sorrows to s.o.; **é. son cœur**, to pour out, to unload, one's heart, to unbosom oneself; **é. son amertume**, to pour out one's bitterness.

s'épancher (*a*) (*of liquid*) to pour out, overflow; *Med:* (*of blood, etc.*) to extravasate; *F:* **l'auditoire s'épancha dans les rues**, the audience poured out into the streets; (*b*) to unbosom oneself.

épanchoir [epãʃwa:r], *s.m. Hyd.E:* outlet, wastepipe; **é. à siphon**, regulation siphon (of canal).

épandage [epãda:ʒ], *s.m. Hyd:* distribution (of water, etc.); spreading, scattering (of manure, etc.); **champ, zone, d'é.**, dissipating area; **champs d'é.**, sewage farm; *U.S:* landfill.

épandeur, -euse [epãdœ:r, -ø:z], *s. Agr:* muck spreader; *Civ.E:* asphalt, gravel, spreader.

épandre [epã:dr], *v.tr.* to distribute (water, etc.); to spread, scatter (manure, etc.); to shed (light, etc.).

s'épandre, (*of water, fire, etc.*) to spread.

épannelage [epan(ə)la:ʒ], *s.m.* rough hewing (of a block of stone).

épanneler [epan(ə)le], *v.tr.* to rough hew (a block of stone).

épanner [epane], *v.tr.* to flatten one side of (a block of millstone).

épanoui [epanwi], *a.* in full bloom; **rose épanouie**, full-blown rose; **visage é.**, joyful, beaming, face; **sourire é.**, broad grin; beaming smile; **rire é.**, whole-hearted laugh.

épanouir [epanwi:r], *v.tr.* to cause (flower, etc.) to open out; **navire qui épanouit ses voiles**, ship that spreads its sails; **le bonheur épanouit le visage**, happiness lights up, brightens up, one's face; **un large sourire lui épanouit le visage**, his face broadened into a grin.

s'épanouir. 1. (*of flower*) to open out, blossom out, bloom, blow; **au-dessus du portail s'épanouit une splendide rosace**, above the west door is the glorious expanse of a rose-window. **2.** (*of face*) to beam, to light up; **son visage s'épanouissait en un large sourire**, she was all smiles; she beamed at us.

épanouissement [epanwismã], *s.m.* **1.** (*a*) opening out, blooming, blowing (of flowers); (*b*) beaming, brightening up (of the countenance). **2.** (full) bloom (of flower, of beauty).

éparcet [eparsɛ], *s.m.*, **éparcette** [eparsɛt], *s.f. Agr: F:* sainfoin.

éparchie [eparʃi], *s.f. Ecc.Hist:* eparchy.

épargnant [eparɲã]. **1.** *a.* saving, sparing, thrifty, parsimonious. **2.** *s.* saver.

épargne [eparɲ], *s.f.* **1.** saving, economy, thrift; **vivre d'é.**, to live thriftily; **é. mesquine**, stinginess; **caisse d'é.**, savings-bank; **caisse nationale d'é.**, post-office savings-bank; *Pol.Ec:* **dépôts d'é.**, savings; **bon d'é.**, national savings certificate; **l'é. privée**, private investors; *s.a.* TAILLE 2. **2.** **vivre de ses épargnes**, to live on one's savings.

épargner [eparɲe], *v.tr. & abs.* **1.** to save (up), economize, put by (money, provisions, etc.); **é. le beurre**, to be sparing with the butter; **é. ses forces**, to husband one's strength; *Prov:* **qui épargne gagne**, waste not, want not; **un sou épargné est un sou gagné**, a penny saved is a penny earned. **2.** to save, spare (energy, time); **je lui épargne autant de fatigue que possible**, I spare him as much fatigue as I can; **é. à qn la peine de faire qch.**, to save s.o. the trouble of doing sth; **il n'épargne rien**, **il ne s'épargne pas**, **pour l'obtenir**, he spares no pains to get it; *Iron:* **épargnez-nous les cris et les pleurs!** spare us the histrionics! **3.** to spare, have mercy on (prisoner, etc.).

éparpillement [eparpijmã], *s.m.* **1.** scattering. **2.** scattered condition.

éparpiller [eparpije], *v.tr.* to disperse, scatter; to spread, strew, (sth.) about; **é. son argent**, to fritter away one's money.

s'éparpiller, (*of crowd, etc.*) to scatter, to disperse; **les chaumières s'éparpillent dans la vallée**, the cottages lie scattered in the valley; *F:* (*of pers.*) **il s'éparpille sans cesse**, he flutters about endlessly.

éparque [epark], *s.m. Ecc.Hist:* eparch.

épars [epa:r], *a.* scattered (troops, villages, etc.); **cheveux é.**, dishevelled hair; **village aux maisons éparses**, straggling village; *Meteor:* **averses éparses**, local showers.

épar(t) [epa:r], *s.m.* **1.** cross-bar (of door, gate, etc.). **2.** transom, shaft-bar (of vehicle). **3.** *A: Nau:* spar.

éparvin [eparvɛ̃], *s.m. Vet:* spavin; **é. sec**, stringhalt, springhalt; **é. calleux**, bone spavin.

épatamment [epatamã], *adv. F:* stunningly, splendidly.

épatant [epatã], *a. F:* wonderful; stunning; fine, capital, splendid; gorgeous (entertainment); **c'est un type é.**, he's a wonderful chap; **un dîner é.**, a slap-up, first-class, rattling good, dinner; **course épatante**, damn good run; **c'est é.**, it's first class! **ce n'est pas bien é.**, it's nothing to write home about.

épate [epat], *s.f. F:* swank, swagger; **faire de l'é.**, (i) to show off, swank, bounce, cut a dash; (ii) to bluff; (iii) to create a sensation, to make a splash; **politique d'é.**, showy policy; *F:* window-dressing.

épaté [epate], *a.* **1.** *O:* crippled (animal, lacking a paw); (glass) that has lost its foot. **2.** (*a*) splay-footed (table, etc.); flat (nose); **au nez é.**, flat-nosed; (*b*) *Nau:* (*of the shrouds*) having spread, outrig. **3.** *F:* dumbfounded, flabbergasted, struck all of a heap.

épatement [epatmã], *s.m.* **1.** flatness (of nose, etc.); *Nau:* outrig, spread (of the shrouds). **2.** *F:* stupefaction, astonishment.

épater [epate], *v.tr.* **1.** *O:* to cripple the foot of (animal); **é. un verre**, to break off the foot of a wineglass. **2.** (*a*) *A:* to send (s.o.) flying, full length; (*b*) *F:* to astound, flabbergast, amaze; to bowl (s.o.) over; **pour é. le bourgeois**, to startle conventional people; **pour é. la galerie**, to swank, to impress the onlookers; **rien ne l'épate**, **il ne se laisse pas é.**, he isn't easily flummoxed, bowled over; **ce qui m'épate, c'est que . . .**, what I can't understand, what beats me, *P:* knocks me, is that . . . . **3.** to flatten out the base of (sth.).

s'épater, to get rattled; **il ne s'épate de rien**, nothing surprises him.

épateur [epatœ:r], *s.m. F:* **1.** swank(er), bouncer. **2.** bluffer.

épaufrer [epofre], *v.tr.* **1.** to knock a flake off (stone) by a clumsy blow of the hammer. **2.** to spall (stone).

s'épaufrer, (*a*) (*of stone*) to flake, to spall; (*b*) (*of concrete*) to crumble (under pressure, etc.).

épaufrure [epofry:r], *s.f. Stonew:* spall.

épaulard [epola:r], *s.m. Z:* grampus, orc; killer whale.

épaule [epo:l], *s.f.* **1.** shoulder; **é. contre é.**, shoulder to shoulder; **large d'épaules**, broad-shouldered; **hausser les épaules**, to shrug one's shoulders; **avoir la tête enfoncée dans les épaules**, to be short-necked, bull-necked; **é. de mouton**, (i) *Cu:* shoulder of mutton; (ii) *Nau:* leg of mutton sail; **coup d'é.**, (i) shove, (ii) effort, (iii) leg-up; *F:* **prêter l'é.**, **donner un coup d'é. à qn**, to lend s.o. one's help; to give s.o. a leg-up; **faire qch. par-dessus l'é.**, to do sth. anyhow; **regarder qn par-dessus l'é.**, to look down one's nost at s.o.; **charger un fardeau sur son épaule**, to shoulder a burden; *Mil:* **arme sur l'é.!** slope arms! **l'arme sur l'é.**, with rifle at the slope; **marcher des épaules**, to walk with a swing of the shoulders; *Equit:* **trotter des épaules**, to trot heavily, stiffly; **courber les épaules devant qn**, to cringe before s.o.; **rouler les épaules**, to swagger; *Tail:* **ligne des épaules**, line of shoulders. **2.** *N.Arch:* (*a*) loof, luff (of bows); (*b*) sny (of planking); spiling.

épaulé [epole]. **1.** *a.* (*of animal*) shoulder-shot, *A:* shoulder-shotten. **2.** *a.* (*of tenon*) shouldered. **3.** *s.m.* (*weight lifting*) **é. jeté**, clean and jerk.

épaulée [epole], *s.f.* (*a*) push with the shoulder; **faire un travail par épaulées**, to have several goes at a job; (*b*) *Const:* quoin; **mur par épaulées**, wall built by steps and quoins; (*c*) *Cu:* target (of mutton).

épaulement [epolmã], *s.m.* **1.** *Const:* revetment wall; *Fort:* epaul(e)ment, breastwork, gun-bank. **2.** *Nau:* bows (of ship). **3.** shoulder (of hill). **4.** shoulder(ing) (of tenon, axle); bolster (of penknife, etc.); shoulder (of tyre).

épauler [epole], *v.tr.* **1.** to put out, splay, the shoulder of (animal). **2.** (*a*) to bring (gun) to the shoulder; to fit (the gun) into the shoulder; *abs:* to level one's gun, to take aim; (*b*) **é. un bataillon**, to protect a battalion by an epaulement; *Civ.E:* **é. un accotement, une route**, to back a driftway, a road; (*c*) *F:* **é. qn**, to give s.o. a leg-up, to back s.o. up; (*d*) *Carp:* to shoulder (beam); (*e*) *N.Arch:* to give a bluff-bow to (ship).

s'épauler, to shelter behind an epaul(e)ment.

épaulette [epolɛt], *s.f.* **1.** *Cost:* (*a*) shoulder-strap; (*b*) *Mil:* epaulet(te); **gagner l'é.**, to obtain a commission. **2.** *Nau:* bolster, shoulder, hound (of mast).

épaulière [epoljɛ:r], *s.f.* **1.** *O: Cost:* brace, shoulder-strap. **2.** *A.Arm:* shoulder-piece, epauliere (of armour). **3.** *Mil:* (butt) hook (of firearm).

épave [epa:v]. **1.** *a. Jur: O:* stray, unclaimed, ownerless (animal). **2.** *s.f.* (*a*) unclaimed object; (*b*) (i) waif, stray; (ii) down-and-out; (*c*) *Nau:* **é. maritime**, wreck, derelict; **épaves d'un naufrage**, wreckage; **épaves flottantes**, flotsam; **épaves rejetées**, jetsam; *Nau:* **inventeur d'épaves**, finder of wreckage; *F:* **é. humaine**, human wreck.

épeautre [epo:tr], *s.m. or f. Agr:* spelt; German wheat; **petit é.**, einkorn.

épée [epe], *s.f.* **1.** straight sword, rapier; *Navy:* admiral's sword; **é. de combat**, duelling sword; **é. à deux mains**, espadon, two-handed sword; **porter l'é.**, to wear, carry, a sword; **faire de l'é.**, to fence with the sword; **se battre à l'é.**, to fight with one's sword; **tirer, mettre, l'é. hors du fourreau**, to draw (one's) sword; **remettre l'é. au fourreau**, (i) to put up, sheathe, one's sword; (ii) to stop fighting; **rendre son é.**, to give up one's sword; **passer une garnison au fil de l'é.**, to put a garrison to the sword; **poursuivre, presser, qn l'é. dans les reins**, (i) to be in hot pursuit of s.o., to press hard upon s.o.; (ii) to prod s.o. on (to do sth.); **il ne faut pas lui mettre l'é. dans les reins**, don't press him too hard; *Fenc:* **aller à l'é.**, to uncover oneself (*e.g.* when parrying); *Mil:* **briser son é.**, to quit the service; *A:* **préférer l'é. à la robe**, to prefer a military to a legal career; **homme d'é.**, soldier; **coup d'é.**, sword-thrust; *F:* **coup d'é. dans l'eau**, wasted effort; **c'est un coup d'é. dans l'eau**, the attempt has come to nothing; **donner des coups d'é. dans l'eau**, to beat the air; **c'est la meilleure é. du régiment**, he is the best swordsman in the regiment; **il rendit son é. au vainqueur**, he surrendered his sword to the victor; *s.a.* CHEVET 1, NOBLESSE 1. **2.** (*a*) *Ropem:* batten; (*b*) *Tex:* **é. de chasse**, picking stick, lathe sword (of loom); *Leathw:* pricker. **3.** *Ich: F:* **é. de mer**, sword-fish, xiphias.

épée-baïonnette [epebajɔnɛt], *s.f.* sword-bayonet; *pl.* **épées-baïonnettes**.

épeiche [epɛʃ], *s.f. Orn:* (pic) **épeiche,** great spotted woodpecker.

épeichette [epɛʃɛt], *s.f. Orn:* (pic) **épeichette,** lesser spotted woodpecker.

épeire [epɛːr], *s.f. Arach:* epeirid; **é. diadème,** garden spider.

épeirogénèse [epeirɔʒenɛːz], *s.f. Geol:* epeirogenesis.

épeirogénique [epeirɔʒenik], *a. Geol:* epeirogenic.

épéiste [epeist], *s.m. Fenc:* fencer who favours the épée (rather than the foil); swordsman.

épeler [eple], *v.tr.* (**j'épelle, n. épelons; j'épellerai**). **1.** to spell (word); **mot mal épelé,** misspelt word. **2.** to spell out (message).

épellation [epelasjɔ̃], *s.f.* spelling.

épendyme [epɑ̃dim], *s.m. Anat:* ependyma.

épendymite [epɑ̃dimit], *s.f. Med:* ependymitis.

épenthèse [epɑ̃tɛːz], *s.f. Ling:* epenthesis.

épenthétique [epɑ̃tetik], *a. Ling:* epenthetic.

épépinage [epepinaːʒ], *s.m.* stoning (of raisins); coring (of apples); seeding (of melons).

épépiner [epepine], *v.tr.* to take out the seeds or pips of (cucumber, melon, etc.); to stone (raisins); to core (apples).

éperdu [epɛrdy], *a.* distracted, bewildered; **résistance éperdue,** desperate resistance; **é. de douleur,** mad with pain or with grief; **é. de joie,** wild with delight.

éperdument [epɛrdymɑ̃], *adv.* distractedly, madly, desperately; **aimer qn é.,** to love s.o. to distraction, to be infatuated with s.o.; **é. amoureux,** head over heels in love; *F:* **je m'en fiche é.,** I couldn't care less, I don't give a damn.

éperlan [epɛrlɑ̃], *s.m. Ich:* smelt, sparling.

éperon [eprɔ̃], *s.m.* **1.** *Equit:* spur; **donner de l'é. à son cheval, piquer de l'é.,** to spur, clap spurs to, one's horse; **cheval sensible à l'é.,** horse that is spur-wise; **chausser, déchausser, ses éperons,** to put on, take off, one's spurs; *s.a.* CHAUSSER 1; *A. & F:* **gagner ses éperons,** to win one's spurs; *Hist:* **la Journée des Éperons,** the Battle of the Spurs (at Guinegatte, 1513). **2.** (*a*) *Bot: Geog: Z:* spur (of columbine, mountain range, cock's leg); (*b*) *A: F:* crow's-foot, wrinkle (near the eye). **3.** (*a*) steel spur (of game-cock); (*b*) *N.Arch:* (i) ram, *F:* beak (of warship); (ii) cutwater, knee. **4.** (*a*) counterfort, buttress (of wall); breakwater, starling, fender (of bridge); (*b*) groyne.

éperonné, [eprɔne], *a.* **1.** spurred (horseman). **2.** *Bot:* calcarate (corolla, etc.). **3.** *A:* (*of the eyes*) crow-footed.

éperonner [eprɔne], *v.tr.* **1.** (*a*) *Equit:* to spur, put spurs to (horse); to rowel; *F:* **é. qn,** to spur, urge, s.o. on; (*b*) *Nau:* to ram (enemy ship). **2.** to spur, put spurs on (boot, game-cock).

éperonnier [eprɔnje], *s.m.* spurrier.

éperonnière [eprɔnjɛːr], *s.f. Bot:* (*a*) larkspur; (*b*) columbine; (*c*) toadflax.

épervier [epɛrvje], *s.m.* **1.** *Orn:* **é. (d'Europe),** sparrow-hawk; **é. à pieds courts,** Levant sparrow-hawk. **2.** *Fish:* cast-net. **3.** *Games:* **jeu de l'é.,** kind of base in which the prisoners form a chain.

épervière [epɛrvjɛːr], *s.f. Bot:* hawkweed (*hieracium*); *a. Orn:* **chouette épervière,** hawk-owl.

épervin [epɛrvɛ̃], *s.m.* = ÉPARVIN.

épeuré [epœre], *a. Lit:* frightened, scared.

épeurer [epœre], *v.tr. Lit:* to frighten, to scare.

épexégèse [epeksεʒɛːz], *s.f.* epexegesis.

épexégétique [epeksεʒetik], *a.* epexegetical.

éph-; *s.a.* ÉPI.

épha [efa], **éphi** [efi], *s.m. Jew.Meas: B:* ephah.

éphèbe [efɛb], *s.m.* (*a*) *Gr.Ant:* ephebe; (*b*) *F:* handsome young man.

ephébogénèse [efebɔʒenɛːz], *s.f. Biol:* = ANDROGENÈSE.

éphectique [efɛktik], *a. & s. Phil:* ephectic.

ephédra [efedra], **éphèdre** [efɛːdr̥], *s.f. Bot:* ephedra, shrubby horsetail.

éphédrine [efedrin], *s.f. Pharm:* ephedrin(e).

éphélide [efelid], *s.f.* freckle; ephelis.

éphémère [efemɛːr]. **1.** *a.* ephemeral; short-lived, transitory, passing, fleeting (happiness, etc.). **2.** *s.m. Ent:* ephemera, ephemeron, day-, may-fly. **3.** *s.f. Bot:* spiderwort, tradescantia.

éphémèrement [efemɛrmɑ̃], *adv. F:* transitorily, fleetingly.

éphéméride [efemerid], *s.f.* **1.** *Astr:* ephemeris; *F:* **calendrier é.,** tear-off calendar, block-calendar. **2.** *pl.* ephemerides; astronomical tables; **éphémérides nautiques,** nautical almanac.

éphéméridés [efemeride], *s.m.pl. Ent:* Ephemeridae, may-flies, day-flies.

éphéméroptères [efemerɔptɛːr], *s.m.pl. Ent:* Ephemeroptera.

Éphèse [efɛːz], *Pr.n.f. A.Geog:* Ephesus.

éphésiaques [efezjak], **éphésies** [efezi], *s.f.pl. Gr.Ant:* feasts held annually (by the Ephesians) in honour of Artemis.

éphésien, -ienne [efezjɛ̃, -jɛn], *a. & s.* Ephesian.

ephestia [efɛstja], *s.f. Ent:* ephestia.

éphialte [efjalt], *s.m. A: Med:* incubus, nightmare.

éphialtes [efjaltɛs], *s.m. Ent:* Ephialtes.

Éphialtès [efjaltɛs], *Pr.n.m. Gr.Hist:* Ephialtes.

éphippe [efip], *s.m. Ich:* spadefish, angel-fish.

éphippie [efipi], *s.f. Z:* ephippium.

éphippigère [efipiʒɛːr], *s.f. Ent:* ephippiger provincialis; wingless grass-hopper of Provence.

éphod [efɔd], *s.m. Jew.Ant:* ephod.

éphorat [efɔra], *s.m. Gr.Ant:* ephoralty.

éphore [efɔːr], *s.m. Gr.Ant:* ephor.

éphydride [efidriːd], *Ent:* **1.** *a.* ephydrid. **2.** *s.m.* ephydrid (insect).

éphydrogame [efidrɔgam], *a. Bot:* ephidrogamous.

éphydrogamie [efidrɔgami], *s.f. Bot:* ephydrogamy.

épi [epi], *s.m.* **1.** (*a*) ear, head (of grain); spike (of flower); **blés en é.,** corn in the ear; (*of corn*) **monter en é.,** to ear; *F:* **é. de cheveux,** feather, cow-lick; *Astr:* **é. de la Vierge,** Spica (of Virgo); (*b*) *Nau:* **é. du vent,** wind's eye. **2.** cluster (of diamonds); *Const:* (cluster of) spikes (on wall); *Arch:* finial; *Rail:* **é. de voies,** nest of short tracks (leading from main line); set of sorting-tracks; *Aut:* **stationnement en épi,** angle parking. **3.** (*a*) *Const:* **assise en é.,** course of diagonal bricks; **appareil en é.,** herring-bone work; (*b*) *Surg:* spica (bandage); (*c*) parting (of horse's mane). **4.** (i) wharf, jetty; **é. de bordage,** camp-shot, campshedding, campsheeting; (ii) **é. à dent,** groyne. **5.** *Artil:* **é. courbe,** emplacement racer (of heavy artillery on rails). **6.** *Bot:* **é. d'eau,** pond-weed, water-spike. **7.** *Oc:* visible part of barrier reef.

ép(i)- [epi], **éph-** [ef], *pref.* ep(i)-, eph-; *Gr.Ant:* **éponymie,** eponymy; *Ch:* **épichlorhydrine,** epichlorhydrin; *Anat:* **éphippion,** ephippium.

épiage [epjaːʒ], *s.m.,* **épiaison** [epjɛzɔ̃], *s.f.,* **épiation** [epjasjɔ̃], *s.f.* earing, heading (of grain).

épiblaste [epiblast], *s.m. Biol:* epiblast.

épiblastique [epiblastik], *a. Biol:* epiblastic.

épibolie [epibɔli], *s.f. Biol:* epiboly.

épicalice [epikalis], *s.m. Bot:* epicalix.

épicanthus [epikɑ̃tyːs], *s.m. Anat:* **epicanthic fold,** epicanthus.

épicarde [epikard], *s.m. Anat:* epicardium.

épicarpe [epikarp], *s.m. Bot:* epicarp.

épicaute [epikot], *s.f. Ent:* epicauta.

épice [epis], *s.f.* **1.** spice; **é. blanche,** ginger; **quatre épices,** allspice; **pain d'é.,** gingerbread. **2.** *pl. A:* douceur (to a judge).

épicé [epise], *a.* highly spiced; hot (seasoning); *F:* **conte é.,** spicy tale; **prix é.,** stiff price.

épicéa [episea], *s.m. Bot:* picea, spruce(-fir).

épicédion [episedjɔ̃], *s.m.* epicedium, funeral **ode.**

épicène [episɛn], *a. Gram:* epicene; (noun) of common gender.

épicentre [episɑ̃tr̥], *s.m.* epicentrum, epicentre (of earthquake).

épicer [epise], *v.tr.* (**j'épiçai(s); n. épiçons**). **1.** to spice (cake, drink, etc.); *F:* to make (a tale, a song) spicy. **2.** *F:* = SALER 1 (*b*).

épicerie [episri], *s.f.* **1.** *A:* spices. **2.** groceries; **être dans l'é.,** to be in the grocery business. **3.** grocer's shop; *U.S:* grocery.

épicerie-droguerie [episridrɔg(ə)ri], *s.f.* general store(s), general shop; *pl. épiceries-drogueries.*

épicier, -ière [episje, -jɛːr], *s.* (*a*) grocer; *F: A:* (*of book, etc.*); **bon pour l'é.,** fit only for making paper bags, for the waste-paper basket; (*b*) *F:* unintellectual person; philistine; (*c*) artist, author, etc. with a strictly mercenary outlook.

épichlorhydrine [epiklɔridrin], *s.f. Ch:* epichlorhydrin.

épiclèse [epiklɛːz], *s.f. Ecc:* epiclesis, epiklesis.

épicome [epikom], *s.m. Ter:* epicomus.

épicondyle [epikɔ̃dil], *s.m. Anat:* epicondyle.

épicondylien, -ienne [epikɔ̃diljɛ̃, -jɛn], *a. Anat:* epicondylic, epicondylian.

épicontinental [epikɔ̃tinɑ̃tal], *a. Oc:* epicontinental.

épicrâne [epikrɑːn], *Anat:* **1.** *s.m.* epicranium, scalp. **2.** *a.* = ÉPICRANIEN.

épicrânien, -ienne [epikrɑnjɛ̃, -jɛn], *a. Anat: Ent:* epicranial (muscle, suture, etc.).

épicrise [epikriːz], *s.f. Med:* epicrisis.

Épictète [epiktɛt], *Pr.n.m. Gr.Phil:* Epictetus.

Épicure [epikyːr], *Pr.n.m. Gr.Phil:* Epicurus.

épicuréisme [epikyreism], *s.m.* = ÉPICURISME.

épicurien, -ienne [epikyrjɛ̃, -jɛn]. **1.** *a. & s. Gr.Phil:* Epicurean. **2.** *s. F:* epicure, sybarite.

épicurisme [epikyrism], *s.m.* **1.** *Gr.Phil:* epicureanism. **2.** epicurism.

épicycle [episikl̥], *s.m. A.Astr: Geom:* epicycle.

épicycloïdal, -aux [episiklɔidal, -o], *a.* epicycloidal (curve, gear); *Mec.E:* **train é.,** epicyclic train.

épicycloïde [episiklɔid], *s.f. Geom:* epicycloid.

Épidaure [epidɔːr], *Pr.n. A.Geog:* Epidaurus.

épidémicité [epidemisite], *s.f.* epidemicity.

épidémie [epidemi], *s.f.* epidemic; outbreak (of contagious disease).

épidémiologie [epidemjɔlɔʒi], *s.f.* epidemiology.

épidémiologique [epidemjɔlɔʒik], *a.* epidemiologic(al).

épidémique [epidemik], *a.* epidemic(al).

épidendrum [epidɛ̃drɔm], *s.m. Bot:* epidendron, epidendrum.

épiderme [epidɛrm], *s.m.* epiderm(is), cuticle; *F:* **avoir l'é. sensible, délicat,** to be thin-skinned, touchy; **chatouiller l'é. à qn,** to scratch s.o.'s back, to fawn on s.o.

épidermique [epidɛrmik], *a.* epidermal, epidermic (tissue, etc.); *Med:* **test é.,** patch-test; *s.a.* GREFFE 2.

épidermoïde [epidɛrmɔid], *a.* epidermoid(al).

épidermomycose [epidɛrmomikoːz], *s.f. Med:* epidermomycosis.

épidiascope [epidjaskɔp], *s.m. Opt:* epidiascope.

épidiascopique [epidjaskɔpik], *a.* epidiascopic.

épididyme [epididim], *s.m. Biol: Anat:* epididymis.

épididymite [epididimit], *s.f.* **1.** *Med:* epididymitis. **2.** *Miner:* epididymite.

épidote [epidɔt], *s.m. Miner:* epidote.

épidural, -aux [epidyral, -o], *a.* epidural; *Vet:* **anesthésie épidurale,** epidural, caudal, anaesthesia.

épié [epje], *a.* spicate (flower, etc.); **queue épiée,** feathery tail (of animal); **chien é.,** dog with a feather on its forehead.

épier¹ [epje], *v.tr.* (*p.d. & pr.sub.* **n. épiions, v. épiiez**). **1.** to watch (s.o.); to spy upon (s.o.); **é. un secret,** to be on the watch for a secret; **é. les démarches, les actes, de qn,** to keep watch on s.o.'s movements, doings. **2.** to be on the look-out, on the watch, for (s.o., occasion, etc.).

épier², *v.i.* (*of grain*) to ear, to head.

épierrage [epjɛraːʒ], *s.m.* **épierrement** [epjɛrmɑ̃], *s.m. Agr:* clearing (of field, etc.) of stones.

épierrer [epjɛre], *v.tr. Agr:* to clear (field, etc.) of stones.

épierreur [epjɛrœːr], *s.m.,* **épierreuse** [epjɛrøːz], *s.f. Husb:* cleanser (of stones from grain, from roots, prior to cutting up); stone-removing machine.

épieu, -ieux [epjø], *s.m.* **1.** *Ven:* boar-spear; *A:* hunting-spear. **2.** *Mil: A:* pike.

épieur, -euse [epjœːr, -øːz], *s.* spier (de, on).

épigamique [epigamik], *a. Biol:* epigamous.

épigastre [epigastr̥], *s.m. Anat:* epigastrium, pit of the stomach; *Box:* **coup d'é.,** blow on, to, the mark.

épigastrique [epigastrik], *a. Anat:* epigastric.

épigé [epiʒe], *a. Bot:* epigeal, epigeous (cotyledon).

épigée [epiʒe], *s.f. Bot:* **épigée rampante,** *U.S:* (trailing) arbutus; mayflower.

épigène [epiʒɛn], *a. Bot: Geol:* epigene.

épigénèse [epiʒenɛːz], *s.f. Biol:* epigenesis.

épigénie [epiʒeni], *s.f. Geol:* supercomposition; pseudomorphism.

épigénique [epiʒenik], *a. Geol:* epigen(et)ic; **rivière, vallée, é.,** superimposed, epigenetic, river, valley.

épiglotte [epiglɔt], *s.f. Anat:* epiglottis.

épiglottique [epiglɔtik], *a. Anat:* epiglottic.

épignathe [epignat], *a. & s.Ter:* (*a*) *a.* epignathous; (*b*) *s.* epignathus.

épigone¹ [epigɔn], *s.m. Bot:* epigone.

épigone². **1.** *Gr.Myth:* **les Épigones,** *s.m.pl.* the Epigoni. **2.** *s.m.* (*a*) one who belongs to the second generation; (*b*) follower, imitator.

épigrammatique [epigramatik], *a.* epigrammatic.

épigrammatiquement [epigramatikmɑ̃], *adv.* epigrammatically.

épigrammatiste [epigramatist], *a. & s.* epigrammatist.

épigramme [epigram], *s.f.* epigram.

épigraphe [epigraf], *s.f.* epigraph; quotation, motto (on title-page of book, or under chapter heading).

épigraphie [epigrafi], *s.f.* epigraphy.

épigraphique [epigrafik], *a.* epigraphic.

épigraphiste [epigrafist], *s.m. & f.* epigraphist.

épigyne [epiʒin], *a. Bot:* epigynous (corolla, stamens, etc.).

épigynie [epiʒini], *s.f. Bot:* epigyny.

épilage [epilaːʒ], *s.m.* depilation; *Leath:* graining; *Toil:* removal of superfluous hair.

épilation [epilasjɔ̃], *s.f.* depilation; removal of superfluous hairs; plucking (of eyebrows).
épilatoire [epilatwa:r], *a. & s.m.* depilatory.
épilé [epile], *a.* **sourcils épilés,** plucked eyebrows.
épilepsie [epilɛpsi], *s.f.* epilepsy.
épileptiforme [epilɛptifɔrm], *a.* epileptiform.
épileptique [epilɛptik], *a. & s.m. & f.* epileptic.
épileptoïde [epilɛptɔid], *a. & s.m. & f. Path:* epileptoid.
épiler [epile], *v.tr.* to depilate; to remove (s.o.'s) superfluous hairs; to pluck (one's eyebrows); **il s'épile pour cacher son âge,** he pulls out his grey hairs to hide his age.
épileur, -euse [epilœ:r, -ø:z], *s.* depilator.
épilimnion [epilimnjɔ̃], *s.m.* epilimnion.
épillet [epijɛ], *s.m. Bot:* spikelet, spicule.
épilobe [epilɔb], *s.m.*, **épilobium** [epilɔbjɔm], *s.m. Bot:* epilobium, willow-herb; **é. à épi(s),** rosebay willow-herb.
épilogue [epilɔg], *s.m.* epilogue.
épiloguer [epilɔge]. **1.** *v.tr.* to pass censure on, to find fault with (s.o.'s actions, etc.). **2.** *v.i.* **é. sur qch., qn,** to carp, cavil, at, about, sth., s.o.; **ce n'est pas la peine d'é.,** no need to comment; no comment is needed.
épilogueur, -euse [epilɔgœ:r, -ø:z], *s.* caviller, fault-finder.
épiloir [epilwa:r], *s.m.* tweezers (for pulling out hairs).
épimaque [epimak], *s.m. Orn:* **é. de Meyer,** long-tailed bird of paradise.
épimède [epimɛd], *s.f. Bot:* barrenwort; **épimède des Alpes,** Alpine barrenwort.
Épiménide de Cnosse [epimeniddəknɔs], *Pr.n.m. A.Hist:* Epimenides of Cnossos.
épimère [epimɛ:r]. **1.** *a. & s.m. Ch:* epimer. **2.** *s.m. Biol:* epimere.
épimérisation [epimerizasjɔ̃], *s.f. Ch:* epimerisation.
épimorphe [epimɔrf], *a. Z:* epimorphic.
épimorphose [epimɔrfo:z], *s.f. Biol:* epimorphosis.
épinaie [epinɛ], *s.f.* brake, thicket (of thorny growth).
Épinal [epinal], *Pr.n.m. Geog:* Epinal; *s.a.* IMAGE 2.
épinard [epina:r], *s.m.* (*a*) *Bot:* spinach; **é. sauvage,** blite, good-King-Henry; **é. fraise,** strawberry-spinach, -blite; **é. de Virginie,** red weed; (*b*) *pl. Cu:* **épinards au naturel, en branches,** braised spinach; *Art: F:* **plat d'épinards,** (*of picture*) plate of spinach; **vert é.,** spinach green; *Mil:* **épaulettes à graines d'épinards,** bullion-fringe epaulets; *s.a.* BEURRE 1.
épinarde [epinard], *s.f. Ich:F:* stickleback.
épinçage [epɛ̃sa:ʒ], *s.m.* **1.** *Tex:* burling (of cloth). **2.** *Arb:* disbudding (of trees); pinching off, nipping off (of buds). **3.** *Civ.E:* cutting, shaping (of paving stones).
épincer [epɛ̃se], *v.tr.* **(j'épinçai(s); n. épinçons), épinceler** [epɛ̃sle], *v.tr.* **(j'épincèle; n. épincelons). 1.** *Tex:* to burl (cloth). **2.** *Arb:* to disbud (tree); to pinch off, nip off (bud). **3.** *Civ.E:* to cut, shape (paving stones).
épincetage [epɛ̃sta:ʒ], *s.m.* = ÉPINÇAGE 1, 3.
épinceter [epɛ̃ste], *v.tr.* **1.** *Tex:* to burl (cloth). **2.** *Arb:* to disbud (tree); to pinch off, nip off (bud). **3.** *Civ.E:* to cut, shape (paving stones).
épincette [epɛ̃sɛt], *s.f. Tex:* burling-iron, -tweezers.
épinçoir [epɛ̃swa:r], *s.m. Civ.E:* paviour's hammer.
épine [epin], *s.f.* **1.** thorn-bush; **é. blanche,** hawthorn; **é. noire,** blackthorn, sloe-bush, sloe-tree; **é. de rat,** knee-holly, butcher's broom; **é. fleurie,** scorpion-broom, scorpion-thorn; *F:* **c'est un fagot d'épines,** he is a crusty, cross-grained, fellow. **2.** thorn, prickle; **la vie est hérissée d'épines,** life bristles with difficulties; **être, marcher, sur des épines,** to be on thorns, on pins and needles; **une é. au pied,** a thorn in the flesh; **tirer à qn une é. du pied,** (i) to get s.o. out of a mess; (ii) to relieve s.o.'s mind; **vous m'avez tiré là une rude é. du pied,** that's a great relief! *Prov:* **(il n'est) point de rose sans épines,** every rose has its thorn. **3.** *Anat:* **é. dorsale,** spine, backbone; **é. de l'omoplate,** spine of the shoulder-blade.
épinéphèle [epinefɛl], *s.m. Ich:* epinephelus; *F:* grouper.
épiner [epine], *v.tr. Arb:* to protect (tree) with thorn branches.
épineuriens [epinœrjɛ̃], *s.m.pl. Z:* Chordata.
épinette [epinɛt], *s.f.* **1.** *Bot:* spruce; **é. noire,** black spruce; **é. rouge,** tamarack. **2.** *Fish:* thorn-hook. **3.** *Husb:* (hen-, chicken-)coop. **4.** *Mus: A:* spinet, virginal.
épineux, -euse [epinø, -ø:z]. **1.** (*a*) thorny, prickly, spiky (bush, stem, etc.); *F:* **affaire épineuse,** thorny, ticklish, knotty, matter; **être dans une situation épineuse,** to be on a bed of thorns, in a ticklish situation; *A:* **é. de caractère,** *F:* prickly; *s.a.* BÂTON[1] 1; (*b*) *Anat:* spiny; **apophyse épineuse,** spinous process of the vertebral column. **2.** *s.m.* thorn-bush.
épine-vinette [epinvinɛt], *s.f. Bot:* berberis, barberry, berberry; *F:* piperidge; *pl. épines-vinettes.*
épinglage [epɛ̃gla:ʒ], *s.m.* **1.** pinning; fixing (of sth.) with a pin. **2.** *Metall:* piercing (of mould, core). **3.** *Civ.E:* underpinning.
épingle [epɛ̃:gl], *s.f.* **1.** pin; **é. de cravate,** tie-pin, breast-pin; **é. à chapeau,** hat-pin; **é. anglaise, de sûreté, de nourrice, é. double,** safety-pin; **é. à cheveux,** hair-pin; *Aut:* **virage en é. à cheveux,** hair-pin bend; *A:* **é. à onduler, à friser,** waving-, curling-pin; **é. à linge,** clothes-peg; **tête d'é.,** pin-head; **attacher qch. avec des épingles,** to pin sth. (up, down); *F:* **tiré à quatre épingles,** dapper, trim, spick and span; **elle était tirée à quatre épingles,** she looked as if she had stepped out of a bandbox; **tirer son é. du jeu,** to get out of a venture without loss, to get well out of it; **coups d'é.,** pin-pricks, petty annoyances; **chercher une é. dans une botte, dans une meule, de foin,** to look for a needle in a haystack, *A:* in a bottle of hay; **monter qch. en é.,** to make much of sth., to give an exaggerated importance to sth.; to seize upon (weak point). **2.** *pl. A:* (*a*) pin-money; (*b*) present, douceur.
épinglé [epɛ̃gle], *a. & s.m. Tex:* terry, uncut (fabric, velvet).
épingler [epɛ̃gle], *v.tr.* **1.** to pin; to fasten (sth.) with a pin; **é. une carte au mur, sur le mur,** to pin a card to, on, the wall; **é. ses cheveux,** to pin up one's hair; *Ent:* **planche à é.,** setting-board. **2.** (*a*) to prick, clean, (sth.) out (with a pin); (*b*) *Metall:* to pierce (mould, core). **3.** *F:* (i) to arrest, to pinch, to nab (s.o.); (ii) to catch s.o. out; **il s'est fait é.,** he got pinched.
épinglerie [epɛ̃gləri], *s.f.* (*a*) pin factory; (*b*) the pin trade.
épinglette [epɛ̃glɛt], *s.f.* (*a*) *O: Exp:* pricker, priming-needle; (*b*) *Min:* boring-tool; (*c*) *Mil:* badge awarded to marksmen.
épinglier, -ère [epɛ̃gli(j)e, -ɛ:r], *s.* **1.** (*a*) manufacturer of pins; (*b*) seller of pins. **2.** *s.m.* pin-tray; pin-box.
épinier [epinje], *s.m. Ven:* thicket.
épinière [epinjɛ:r], *a.f.* **moelle é.,** spinal cord; **maladie de la moelle é.,** spinal complaint.
épinoche[1] [epinɔʃ], *s.f.*, **épinochette** [epinɔʃɛt], *s.f. Ich:* stickleback; prickle-back; **épinoche de mer,** fifteen-spined stickleback.
épinoche[2], *s.f. Com: A:* best quality coffee.
épipélagique [epipelaʒik], *a. Oc:* epipelagic.
Épiphane [epifan], *Pr.n.m.* **1.** *A.Hist:* Epiphanes. **2.** *Rel.H:* Epiphanius.
Épiphanie [epifani], *s.f.* Epiphany, Twelfth Night.
épipharynx [epifarɛ̃:ks], *s.m. Ent:* epipharynx.
épiphénomène [epifenɔmɛn], *s.m. Psy:* epiphenomenon.
épiphénoménisme [epifenɔmenism], *s.m. Phil: Psy:* epiphenomenalism.
épiphénoméniste [epifenɔmenist], *a. & s.m. & f. Phil: Psy:* epiphenomenalist.
épiphléode [epifleɔd], *a. Bot:* epiphloedal, epiphloedic.
épiphora [epifɔra], *s.m. Path:* epiphora.
épiphragme [epifragm], *s.m. Moll:* epiphragm.
épiphylle [epifil], *Bot:* **1.** *a.* epiphyllous (organ). **2.** *s.f.* epiphyllum.
épiphysaire [epifizɛ:r], *a. Anat:* epiphyseal, epiphysial, epiphysary.
épiphyse [epifi:z], *s.f. Anat:* epiphysis.
épiphyte [epifit], *Bot:* **1.** *a.* epiphytal, epiphytic. **2.** *s.m.* epiphyte.
épiphytie [epifiti], *s.f. Bot:* epiphytic disease.
épiphytique [epifitik], *a. Bot:* epiphytic (disease, etc.).
épiploïque [epiplɔik], *a. Anat:* epiploic, omental (vein, etc.).
épiploon [epiplɔɔ̃], *s.m. Anat:* epiploon, omentum.
épipode [epipɔd], *s.m. Bot:* epipodium.
épipodium [epipɔdjɔm], *s.m. Z:* epipodium (of mollusc).
épipyropides [epipirɔpid], *s.m.pl. Ent:* Epipyropidae.
épique [epik], *a.* epic; **poème é.,** epic poem; epic, epos; *F: Iron:* **ce fut une discussion é.!** it was an epic discussion!
Épire [epi:r], *Pr.n.f. A.Geog:* Epirus.
épir(r)hize [epiri:z], *a. Bot:* epir(r)hizous.
épirogénèse [epirɔʒenɛ:z], *s.f. Geol:* epirogenesis.
épirogénique [epirɔʒenik], *a. Geol:* = ÉPÉIROGÉNIQUE.
épirote [epirɔt], *A.Geog:* **1.** *s.m. & f.* Epirot(e). **2.** *a.* Epirotic.
épiscia [episja], *s.m. Bot:* episcia.
épisclérite [episklerit], *s.f. Path:* episcleritis.
épiscopal, -aux [episkɔpal, -o]. **1.** *a. Ecc:* episcopal; **église épiscopale,** Anglican Church; *Scot: U.S:* Episcopal church; **cité épiscopale,** cathedral city. **2.** *s.* Anglican; *Scot: U.S:* Episcopalian.
épiscopalien, -ienne [episkɔpaljɛ̃, -jɛn], *a. & s. Ecc:* (*in Scot. and U.S.*) Episcopalian.
épiscopalisme [episkɔpalism], *s.m.* episcopacy, government by bishops.
épiscopat [episkɔpa], *s.m. Ecc:* **1.** episcopate, office of bishop. **2.** episcopacy, episcopate, (the) bishops.
épiscope [episkɔp], *s.m. Mil: Opt:* episcope.
épiscopique [episkɔpik], *a. Opt:* **projection é., projecteur é.,** projection, projector, of opaque objects.
épisépale [episepal], *a. Bot:* episepalous.
épisiotomie [epizjɔtɔmi], *s.f. Obst:* episiotomy.
épisode [epizɔd], *s.m.* episode; instalment; **film à épisodes,** serial film.
épisodique [epizɔdik], *a.* episodic(al); temporary, transitory; **il n'a qu'un rôle é.,** he only plays an incidental part.
épisodiquement [epizɔdikmɑ̃], *adv.* episodically.
épisome [epizo:m], *s.m. Biol:* episome.
épispastique [epispastik], *a. & s.m. Med:* epispastic.
épisperme [epispɛrm], *s.m. Bot:* episperm.
épisporange [epispɔrɑ̃:ʒ], *s.m. Bot:* epispore.
épissage [episa:ʒ], *s.m.* splicing (of rope).
épisser [epise], *v.tr.* to splice (rope, wire cable).
épissière [episjɛ:r], *s.f.* horse-net, (horse's) fly-net.
épissoir [episwa:r], *s.m.*, **épissoire** [episwa:r], *s.f. Nau:* marline-spike, splicing fid.
épissure [episy:r], *s.f.* splice (in rope); **é. à œillet,** eye-splice, ring-splice.
épistaminé [epistamine], *a. Bot:* gynandrous.
épistase [epista:z], *s.f. Med:* epistasis (of urine).
épistasie [epistazi], *s.f. Biol:* epistasis.
épistaxis [epistaksis], *s.f. Med:* epistaxis.
épistémologie [epistemɔlɔʒi], *s.f. Phil:* epistemology.
épistémologique [epistemɔlɔʒik], *a. Phil:* epistemological.
épisterne [epistɛrn], **épisternum** [epistɛrnɔm], *s.m. Ent:* episternum.
épistolaire [epistɔlɛ:r], *a.* epistolary.
épistole [epistɔl], *s.f. F:* letter.
épistolier, -ière [epistɔlje, -jɛ:r], *s. Lit: F:* letter-writer.
épistolographe [epistɔlɔgraf], *s.m. & f. Gr.Hist:* epistolographer.
épistolographie [epistɔlɔgrafi], *s.f.* epistolography.
épistome [epistɔm], *s.m. Ent:* clypeus; *Nat.Hist:* epistome.
épistrophe [epistrɔf], *s.f. Rh:* epistrophe.
épistyle [epistil], *s.m. Arch:* epistyle, architrave.
épitaphe [epitaf], *s.f.* epitaph.
épitase [epita:z], *s.f. Gr.Drama:* epitasis.
épitaxial, -iaux [epitaksjal, -jo], *a. Cryst:* epitaxial, epitaxic.
épitaxie [epitaksi], *s.f. Cryst:* epitaxy.
épite [epit], *s.f. Nau: etc:* spile, dowel-wedge, treenail-wedge.
épithalame [epitalam], *s.m.* epithalamium.
épithélial, -iaux [epiteljal, -jo], *a. Anat:* epithelial.
épithélioma [epiteljɔma], *s.m. Med:* epithelioma; *Vet:* **é. contagieux des volailles,** fowlpox.
épithélium [epiteljɔm], *s.m. Anat:* epithelium.
épithème [epitɛm], *s.m.* **1.** *O: Pharm:* epithem. **2.** *Bot:* epithem(e).
épithermal, -aux [epitɛrmal, -o], *a. Geol:* epithermal.
épithermique [epitɛrmik], *a. Atom.Ph:* epithermal.
épithète [epitɛt], (*a*) *s.f.* epithet; *Gram:* attributive adjective; (*b*) *a.* **adjectif é.,** epithet adjective.
épithétique [epitetik], *a.* epithetic(al).
épitoge [epitɔ:ʒ], *s.f.* (*a*) *Rom.Ant:* cloak (worn over the toga); (*b*) *Sch:* = CHAPERON 1(*b*).
épitoir [epitwa:r], *s.m. Carp:* spile awl.
épitomé [epitɔme], *s.m.* epitome, abridgment (of book, etc.).
épitoque [epitɔk], *a. Biol:* epitocous, epitokous.
épitoquie [epitɔki], *s.f. Biol:* epitoke.
épître [epi:tr], *s.f.* (*a*) epistle; *Ecc:* **côté de l'é.,** south side, epistle-side (of altar); (*b*) *F:* letter, esp. long letter.
épitrope [epitrɔp], *s.f. Rh:* epitrope.
épizoaire [epizɔɛ:r], *s.m. Z:* epizoon.
épizoanthus [epizɔɑ̃tys], *s.m. Bot:* epizoanthus.
épizoïque [epizɔik], *a. Nat.Hist:* epizoic.

épizone [epizo:n], *s.f. Geol:* epizone.
épizootie [epizɔɔti, -si], *s.f.* epizootic disease, epizooty.
épizootique [epizɔɔtik], *a.* epizootic.
éploiement [eplwamɑ̃], *s.m. Her:* spread(ing) (of the eagle).
éploré [eplɔre], *a. & s.* tearful, weeping (person); **mine éplorée,** face bathed in tears; **être tout éplorée,** to be all tears.
éployé [eplwaje], *a. Her:* displayed; **aigle éployée,** spread eagle.
éployer [eplwaje], *v.tr.* (*rare*) = DÉPLOYER.
épluchage [eplyʃa:ʒ], *s.m.,* **épluchement** [eplyʃmɑ̃], *s.m.* **1.** (*a*) cleaning (of feathers, fur, etc.); picking (of salad, wool, etc.); shelling (of shrimps, etc.); (*b*) peeling, paring (of fruit, potatoes, etc.); (*c*) *Agr:* weeding (of field); thinning out (of fruit-tree). **2.** *F:* hypercritical examination, overhauling (of system, etc.); canvassing (of reputation).
éplucher [eplyʃe], *v.tr.* **1.** (*a*) to clean, pick (sth.); **oiseau qui épluche ses plumes,** bird cleaning, preening, its feathers; **é. une salade,** to pick, clean, a salad; *Tex:* **é. la laine,** to pick, pluck, the wool; (*b*) to peel (fruit, potatoes, etc.); to top and tail (gooseberries); (*c*) *Agr:* to weed (field); to thin out (fruit-tree). **2.** *F:* (*a*) to examine, criticize, (work) closely, in detail; **é. une question,** to sift a question; (*b*) to examine, review, (work) hypercritically; **é. une réputation,** to canvass a reputation; **é. les défauts de qn,** to go over s.o.'s faults.
épluchette [eplyʃɛt], *s.f. Fr.C:* **é. de blé d'Inde,** corn-husking party.
éplucheur, -euse [eplyʃœ:r, -ø:z], *s.* **1.** (*a*) cleaner; **é. de noix,** walnut picker; **é. de laine,** wool picker; *s.a.* POUBELLE; (*b*) **é. de pommes de terre,** potato peeler (person); (*c*) *Agr:* weeder; (*d*) **(couteau) é.,** potato-peeler. **2.** *F:* hypercritical person, fault-finder.
éplucheur-batteur [eplyʃœ:rbatœ:r], *s.m. Tex:* = **ouvreuse,** *q.v.* under OUVREUR 2; *pl. éplucheurs-batteurs.*
épluchoir [eplyʃwa:r], *s.m.* paring-knife.
épluchure [eplyʃy:r], *s.f. usu. pl.* **épluchures,** peeling(s), paring(s) (of potatoes, etc.); offal (of meat); refuse.
épochè [epɔkɛ], *s.f. Phil:* epoche.
épode [epɔd], *s.f. Pros:* epode.
époilant [epwalɑ̃], *a. A: P:* surprising, astounding, wonderful (news).
épointage [epwɛ̃ta:ʒ], *s.m.* breaking the point (of needle, pencil, etc.).
épointé [epwɛ̃te], *a.* **1.** blunt(-pointed) (needle, pencil, etc.). **2.** *Vet:* (*of horse*) hipshot; **chien é.,** dog with a broken thigh.
épointement [epwɛ̃tmɑ̃], *s.m.* bluntness (of pointed instrument).
épointer [epwɛ̃te], *v.tr.* **1.** to break or blunt the point of (needle, pencil, etc.); (*of woman*) **se faire é. les cheveux,** to have one's hair trimmed. **2.** *Bookb:* **é. les nerfs,** to cut the bands into points.
s'épointer, (*of pencil, etc.*) to lose its point.
épointeuse [epwɛ̃tø:z], *s.f. Agr:* scourer.
éponge[1] [epɔ̃:ʒ], *s.f.* **1.** (*a*) *Spong:* sponge; (*b*) *Com:* sponge; *Dom.Ec:* **é. métallique,** (pot-)scourer; **laver qch. avec une é.,** to sponge sth.; **effacer une tache à l'é., d'un coup d'é.,** to sponge out a stain; **passons l'é. là-dessus,** let us say no more about it, let bygones be bygones; **une politique du coup d'é.,** a policy of the clean slate; *Box:* **jeter l'é.,** to throw in the sponge; (*c*) *Tex:* **tissu é.,** (Turkish) towelling; **serviette é.,** Turkish towel; (*d*) **é. végétale,** vegetable sponge, loofah. **2.** *Bot:* bedeguar, rose-gall. **3.** *Metall:* **é. métallique,** metallic sponge; **é. de fer,** spongy iron; *s.a.* PLATINE[2].
éponge[2], *s.f.* **1.** *Farr:* calkin (of horseshoe). *Hence* **2.** *Vet:* abscess (in horse's elbow).
épongeage [epɔ̃ʒa:ʒ], *s.m.* **1.** sponging (of face, etc.); mopping. **2.** *Fin:* absorbing, siphoning off.
éponger [epɔ̃ʒe], *v.tr.* (**j'épongeai(s); n. épongeons**). **1.** to sponge up, mop up (liquid). **2.** to sponge, mop (surface); **s'é. le front, les yeux, avec un mouchoir,** to mop one's brow, dab one's eyes, with a handkerchief; **é. les jambes d'un cheval,** to sponge down a horse's legs. **3.** to remove (sth.) with a sponge; **é. les taches d'une robe,** to sponge the stains off a dress. **4.** *Fin:* to absorb, mop up, drain off, siphon off. **5.** *F:* **é. un retard,** to make up for lost time.
éponte [epɔ̃:t], *s.f. Min:* wall (of lode).
épontillage [epɔ̃tija:ʒ], *s.m. Nau:* shoring, propping.
épontille [epɔ̃ti:j], *s.f. Nau:* **1.** pillar, stanchion. **2.** shore, prop; **é. de chouque,** cap-shore.
épontillé [epɔ̃tije], *a. Navy: F:* **officier très é.,** officer with influence behind him at headquarters, with strong backing at headquarters, who stands well at headquarters.
épontiller [epɔ̃tije], *v.tr. Nau:* to prop, shore (up); to undershore (the deck, booms, etc.).
éponyme [epɔnim]. **1.** *a.* eponymous (hero, etc.). **2.** *s.m.* eponym.
éponymique [epɔnimik], *a.* eponymic.
épopée [epɔpe], *s.f.* (*a*) epos; (*b*) epic, epic poem, epopee.
époque [epɔk], *s.f.* **1.** epoch, era, age; **l'é. glaciaire,** the ice-age; **l'é. des Antonins,** the age of the Antonines; **la belle é.,** the Edwardian era; **meubles d'é.,** (genuine) antique, period, furniture; **faire é.,** to mark an epoch, an era; **découverte qui fait é.,** epoch-making discovery; **sa visite fit é. dans la ville,** his visit was a red-letter day in the town. **2.** time, period, date; **à l'é. de sa naissance,** at the time of his birth; **c'était justement l'é. des vacances,** it happened to be holiday time; **les meilleurs médecins de l'é.,** the best doctors of the day; **dans une é. prospère,** in prosperous times; **il y a un an à pareille é.,** this time last year; *Fin:* **é. d'un compte courant,** period of a current account. **3.** *pl. O:* (woman's) periods, menses.
époucé [epuse], *a. Orn:* without a hind toe.
époufé [epufe], *a. A: F:* breathless, out of breath, puffed.
épouffer (s') [sepufe], *v.pr. A:* **1.** *F:* to lose one's breath, to get puffed; **s'é. de rire,** to burst with laughter; to guffaw. **2.** *P:* to make oneself scarce.
épouillage [epuja:ʒ], *s.m.* cleansing (sth.) of vermin; delousing.
épouiller [epuje], *v.tr.* to cleanse (s.o., sth.) of vermin; to delouse.
époumonage [epumɔna:ʒ], *s.m. F:* shouting that leaves you breathless, hoarse; **maître d'école éreinté après des heures d'é.,** schoolmaster exhausted after hours of stentorian teaching.
époumoner [epumɔne], *v.tr.* to try the lungs of (s.o.); **époumonés par la montée raide,** puffed, breathless, after their stiff climb.
s'époumoner, to shout oneself out of breath; **s'é. à crier,** to shout oneself hoarse.
épousailles [epuzɑ:j], *s.f.pl. A: & Dial:* espousals, nuptials, wedding.
épouse, *see* ÉPOUX.
épousé, -ée [epuze], *s. Dial: or A:* bridegroom, *f.* bride.
épouser [epuze], *v.tr.* **1.** to marry, wed, *A:* espouse (s.o.); to enter into wedlock with (s.o.); **é. une grosse dot,** to marry money; **é. de nouveau (qn dont on est divorcé),** to remarry; **il épouse une jeune fille qui n'est pas de son monde,** he is marrying beneath him; **il a épousé une jeune fille qui appartenait à une famille riche,** he married into a rich family; **il lui demanda de l'épouser,** he proposed to her. **2.** to espouse, take up, adopt (cause, doctrine, etc.); **é. la querelle de qn,** to take up s.o.'s quarrel; *F:* to take up the cudgels on s.o.'s behalf; **elle a épousé les partis pris de son père,** she is wedded to her father's prejudices; *F:* **il faut é. son temps,** one must move with the times. **3. é. la forme de qch.,** to take the exact shape of sth.; to correspond in shape to sth.; to fit sth.; to assume the shape of sth.
épouseur [epuzœ:r], *s.m. A: & Iron:* suitor, wooer; **ici, peu d'épouseurs,** here there are few (i) marrying men, (ii) eligible men.
époussetage [epusta:ʒ], *s.m.* dusting (of furniture, etc.); beating (of carpet, etc.); rubbing down (of horse).
épousseter [epuste], *v.tr.* (**j'époussette** [epusɛt]; **j'époussetterai;** or *F:* **j'époussete** [epust]; **j'épousseterai**) to dust (furniture, etc.); to beat (the dust from) (carpet, clothes, etc.); to rub down (horse); *F:* **é. qn,** to dust s.o.'s jacket for him, to give s.o. a dusting; to beat s.o.
épousseteur, -euse [epustœ:r, -ø:z], *s.* one who dusts; **é. de tapis,** carpet-beater.
époussetoir [epustwa:r], *s.m.* jeweller's dusting brush.
époussette [epusɛt], *s.f.* (*a*) feather-duster; (dusting) whisk; banister brush; (*b*) rag, cloth (for rubbing down horse); stable-rubber.
époussoir [epuswa:r], *s.m. Sw.Fr:* small brush (for dust-pan).
époustouflant [epustuflɑ̃], *a. F:* amazing, astounding, startling.
époustoufler [epustufle], *v.tr. F:* to astound, to flabbergast.
époutí [eputi], *s.m.Tex:* burl (in woollen materials).
époutiage [eputja:ʒ], **époutissage** [eputisa:ʒ], *s.m. Tex:* burling, cleaning, picking (of cloth).
époutier [eputje], *v.tr.,* **époutisser** [eputise], *v.tr. Tex:* to burl, clean, pick (cloth).
épouvantable [epuvɑ̃tabl̩], *a.* dreadful, horrible, terrible, frightful; shocking; appalling.
épouvantablement [epuvɑ̃tabləmɑ̃], *adv.* dreadfully, horribly, terribly, frightfully; shockingly; appallingly.
épouvantail [epuvɑ̃ta:j], *s.m.* **1.** scarecrow. **2.** *F:* (*a*) bugbear, bogy, bugaboo; (*b*) **quel é.!** isn't she a fright!
épouvante [epuvɑ̃:t], *s.f.* terror, fright; **jeter, porter, l'é. dans un pays,** to spread terror in a country; **être saisi d'é.,** to be terror-struck, -stricken, frightened to death, in a deadly fright, half-dead with fright; **partout régnait l'é.,** terror reigned everywhere; **film d'é.,** horror film.
épouvanté [epuvɑ̃te], *a.* terror-stricken.
épouvantement [epuvɑ̃t(ə)mɑ̃], *s.m. Lit:* deadly terror.
épouvanter [epuvɑ̃te], *v.tr.* to terrify, scare (s.o.); to frighten (s.o.) out of his wits; to frighten (s.o.) to death; to appal.
s'épouvanter, to take fright, to become panic-stricken.
époux, -ouse [epu, -u:z], *s.* (*a*) *Adm: Jur:* spouse; consort; husband; *f.* wife; **les é.,** the married couple, the husband and wife; **les jeunes é.,** (i) the young couple; (ii) the newly-weds; **les futurs é.,** the engaged couple; **les é. Dupont,** the man Dupont and his wife; *Theol:* **l'épouse de Jésus-Christ,** the bride of Christ; (*b*) *F:* **vous et votre é.,** you and your good man; **vous et votre épouse,** you and your good lady.
époxyde [epɔksid], *Ch:* **1.** *s.m.* epoxy. **2.** *a.* epoxy; **résine é.,** epoxy resin.
épreindre [eprɛ̃:dr̩], *v.tr.* (*pr.p.* **épreignant;** *p.p.* **épreint;** *pr.ind.* **j'épreins, il épreint, n. épreignons, ils épreignent;** *p.d.* **j'épreignais;** *p.h.* **j'épreignis;** *fu:* **j'épreindrai**); *A:* **1.** to squeeze (lemon, etc.). **2.** to squeeze out, press out (juice of lemon, etc.).
épreintes [eprɛ̃:t], *s.f.pl.* **1.** colic, gripes. **2.** *Ven:* spraints.
éprendre (s') [seprɑ̃:dr̩], *v.pr.* (*conj. like* PRENDRE). to become attached (de, to); to become enamoured (de, of); **s'é. de qn,** to fall in love with s.o.; to lose one's heart to s.o.; **s'é. de qch.,** to take a fancy to sth.; **il s'éprend facilement,** he is quick to lose his heart.
épreuve [eprœ:v], *s.f.* **1.** (*a*) proof, test, trial; assay; **é. d'un pont,** test(ing) of a bridge; **é. des chaudières,** boiler test; **é. à l'eau, à la vapeur,** test by water, by steam; **é. d'endurance,** endurance test; **é. d'outrance,** resistance test; (*of guns*) proof to bursting; *Statistics:* **é. d'hypothèse, de signification,** significance test; **subir une é.,** to undergo a test, to be put through a test; **subir victorieusement l'é.,** to stand the test; **soutenir, supporter, l'é.,** to pass, stand, the test; **il ne supporta pas l'é.,** he was tried and found wanting; **faire l'é. de qch., mettre qch. à l'é.,** to try, test, prove, sth., to put sth. to the test; **voilà qui mettra votre adresse, votre patience, à l'é.,** that will tax your skill, your patience; **sa patience fut mise à rude é.,** his patience was sorely tried; **rester fidèle à qn à travers toutes les épreuves,** to stick to s.o. through thick and thin; **amitié à l'é.,** sure, staunch, friendship; **acheter qch. à l'é.,** to buy sth. on trial, on approval; **à l'é. de qch.,** proof against sth.; **à l'é. du feu, de l'eau,** fire-proof, waterproof; **à l'é. de la tentation,** proof against temptation; **(papier) à l'é. de la graisse,** grease-proof (paper); **à l'é. des balles,** bullet-proof; **à l'é. des mites,** moth-proof; *s.a.* BOMBE 1; **mécanisme à toute é.,** fool-proof mechanism; **bonté à toute é.,** never-failing kindness; (*b*) *Sch:* (examination) test, paper; **épreuves écrites,** written papers; **l'examen comprendra des épreuves pratiques, écrites, et orales,** the examination will consist of practical, written and oral tests; (*c*) *Sp:* event (at athletic meeting); **é. éliminatoire,** (eliminating, preliminary) heat; **épreuves sur terrain,** field events; **épreuves sur piste,** track events; **é. nulle,** dead heat; (*d*) *A:* ordeal; **l'e. du feu,** ordeal by fire. **2.** trial, affliction, ordeal; **passer par de rudes épreuves,** to go through painful experiences, to be sorely tried; *F:* to go through the mill. **3.** (*a*) proof; *Typ:* **é. a la brosse,** brush-proof; **é. en premier,** (i) foul proof; (ii) galley-proof; **é. de révision, deuxième é.,** revise; **é. en bon à tirer,** press proof, press revise; **lire un livre sur épreuves,** to read a book in proof form; *Engr:* **é. avant la lettre,** proof before letters, proof engraving; **é. avec la lettre,** letter-proof; (*b*) *Phot:* print; **é. non collée,** unmounted print.

épris [epri], *a.* **1. é. de qn, de qch.,** in love, *F:* smitten, with s.o., with sth.; enamoured of s.o., of sth.; **ils ne sont pas fort é. l'un de l'autre,** they aren't enamoured of each other. **2. é. d'une folle ambition,** smitten with a mad ambition; **é. de colère,** overcome by anger.

éprouvant [epruvɑ̃], *a.* distressing; tiring.

éprouvé [epruve], *a.* **1.** tested, tried; experienced; **remède é.,** well-tried remedy. **2. troupes très éprouvées,** severely, sorely, tried troops, troops that have suffered severely; **famille, région, éprouvée,** stricken family, hard-hit district.

éprouver [epruve], *v.tr.* **1.** to test, try (s.o., sth.); to put (s.o., sth.) to the test; **é. une arme à feu,** to test a fire-arm; **é. la patience de qn,** to try s.o.'s patience; **il a été cruellement éprouvé,** he has been sorely tried, has met with sad trials. **2.** to feel, experience (sensation, pain, etc.); **é. une perte,** to sustain, suffer, meet with, experience, a loss; **é. des difficultés,** to meet with difficulties, to encounter difficulties; **é. des difficultés à faire qch.,** to have difficulty, to experience difficulty, in doing sth.; **é. des craintes,** to entertain fears; **l'émotion que cette nouvelle nous fit é.,** the emotion which this news aroused within us; **quels sentiments avez-vous éprouvés?** how did you feel?

éprouvette [epruvɛt], *s.f.* **1.** *Ch: Ph: etc:* test-tube, -glass. **2.** *Exp:* eprouvette. **3.** *Metall:* (*a*) test-piece, -bar; (*b*) flux-assay spoon. **4.** *Surg:* probe.

epsilon [ɛpsilɔn], *s.m. Gr.Alph:* epsilon.

epsomite [ɛpsɔmit], *s.f.* epsomite, Epsom salts.

épucer [epyse], *v.tr.* **(j'épuçai(s); n. épuçons);** to clean (dog, etc.) of fleas.

épuisable [epɥizabl̩], *a.* exhaustible.

épuisant [epɥizɑ̃], *a.* exhausting; *F:* fagging (work).

épuise [epɥiːz], *s.f. Hyd.E: Min:* water-elevator, draining-engine, water-engine.

épuisé [epɥize], *a.* exhausted. **1. mine épuisée,** worked-out mine; **filon é.,** dead lode; **édition épuisée,** edition out of print; **acide é.,** spent acid; **énergie épuisée,** spent energy; (*in restaurant*) **plat qui est é.,** dish that is off; **mon mandat se trouve é.,** my mandate has expired; **lettre de crédit épuisée,** invalid letter of credit; *El:* **pile épuisée,** dead cell; *Atom.Ph:* **uranium é.,** depleted, impoverished uranium. **2.** tired out, worn out; spent (with fatigue); *F:* fagged, dead-beat.

épuisement [epɥizmɑ̃], *s.m.* **1.** exhausting, using up (of provisions, etc.); emptying, draining (of cask, cistern); depletion (of resources); *Atom. Ph:* depletion, impoverishment (of uranium, catalyst, etc.); **é. d'une mine,** (i) exhausting, working-out; (ii) drainage, pumping-out, of a mine; **moteur d'é.,** pumping equipment; *Com:* **jusqu'à é. des stocks,** as long as supplies last; *Alg:* **méthode d'é.,** method of exhaustion. **2.** exhaustion, loss of strength; *Med:* depletion; **é. cérébral,** brain-fag; **il a travaillé jusqu'à é.,** he worked until he was exhausted.

épuiser [epɥize], *v.tr.* to exhaust. **1.** to use up, consume (provisions, ammunition, etc.); to drain, empty (well, tank, cask); to dry up (secretions, etc.); **é. une mine,** (i) to work out, exhaust, (ii) to drain, pump out, fork, a mine; *Com:* **é. un article,** to sell out an article; *F:* **é. un sujet,** to exhaust a subject; **é. tous les chagrins,** to drain the cup of sorrow to the dregs; **écrivain qui a épuisé sa veine,** writer who has written himself out. **2.** to wear, tire, (s.o.) out; **é. la patience de qn,** to wear out, exhaust, s.o.'s patience.

s'épuiser, to become exhausted. **1.** (*of spring, etc.*) to dry up, to run dry; (*of stock, money, provisions, etc.*) (i) to run out, give out; (ii) to run low; (*of mineral deposit*) to peter out. **2.** to wear oneself out (**à force de travail, en efforts inutiles,** with work, with useless efforts); **s'é. à faire qch.,** to wear oneself out with doing sth.; **mais je m'épuise à vous le dire,** I've told you so till I'm blue in the face.

épuisette [epɥizɛt], *s.f.* **1.** *Nau:* scoop, bailer. **2.** *Fish:* landing-net, spoon-net, dip-net.

épuise-volante [epɥizvɔlɑ̃ːt], *s.f. Hyd.E:* wind (mill) pump; *pl. épuises-volantes.*

épulide [epylid], **épulie** [epyli], *s.f. Dent:* epulis; *pl.* epulides.

épulon [epylɔ̃], *s.m. Rom.Ant:* epulo; *pl.* epulones.

épulpeur [epylpœːr], *s.m. Agric:* pulp extractor.

épurage [epyraːʒ], *s.m.* purifying, refining, cleansing.

épurant [epyrɑ̃], *a. Ind:* purifying (substance, etc.).

épurateur [epyratœːr], *s.m.* **1.** purifying apparatus; purifier (of liquids, etc.); *Gasm: etc:* scrubber, scrubbing plant; **é. de gaz,** gas-cleaning plant; **é. d'eau,** water-softening plant; *I.C.E:* **é. d'air,** air filter, air scrubber, air cleaner; *Mch:* **é. de vapeur,** steam separator; *Agr:* **é. centrifuge,** (centrifugal) clarifier. **2.** (*pers.*) *Pol:* purger.

épuratif, -ive [epyratif, -iːv], *a.* purifying, (process, apparatus, etc.).

épuration [epyrasjɔ̃], *s.f.* purification, purifying, cleansing; purging (of morals); filtering, scrubbing (of gas); refining (of oil, metals); *Pol:* purge; **é. d'un personnel,** weeding out of a staff; **é. d'un texte,** expurgation of a text; *Gasm: etc:* **colonne d'é.,** separator, scrubber; *Petroleum Ind:* **agent d'é.,** scavenger; *Med:* **épreuve d'é.,** (renal) clearance.

épuratoire [epyratwaːr], *a.* = ÉPURATIF.

épure [epyːr], *s.f.* **1.** diagram; working drawing. **2.** finished design, plan (of building, engine, etc.). **3.** blueprint (of a project).

épurement [epyrmɑ̃], *s.m.* **1.** (act of) purifying (style, etc.); (act of) expurgating (a text); expurgation (of text). **2.** purity (of style).

épurer [epyre], *v.tr.* to purify, filter (gas, water, etc.); to refine (oil, metals); to scrub, clean (gas); **é. les mœurs,** to purify, refine, purge, morals; **é. une administration,** to weed out, purge, a branch of the service; **é. un auteur,** to expurgate an author; *Nau:* **é. l'eau,** to sweeten the water.

épurge [epyrʒ], *s.f. Bot:* euphorbia, spurge; **grande é.,** castor-oil plant.

épyornis [epjɔrnis], *s.m. Paleont:* aepyornis; *pl.* aepyornes.

équanime [ekwanim], *a.* even-tempered, equanimous.

équanimité [ekwanimite], *s.f.* evenness of temper, equanimity.

équarrir [ekariːr], *v.tr.* **1.** to square (timber, stone, etc.); **bois équarri,** scantling(s). **2.** to broach, ream (hole). **3.** to quarter, cut up the carcass of (horse, mule, etc.). **4.** *F:* to rub the corners off (boor, etc.).

équarrissage [ekarisaːʒ], *s.m.,* **équarrissement** [ekarismɑ̃], *s.m.* **1.** (*a*) squaring (of timber, stone, etc.); **bois d'é.,** scantling(s); **é. marchand,** timber for the trade; (*b*) *Meas:* scantling; **avoir un é. de deux pouces sur quatre pouces,** to have a scantling of two inches by four inches. **2.** quartering, cutting up (of animal carcasses); **chantier d'é.,** knacker's yard.

équarrisseur [ekarisœːr], *s.m.* **1.** squarer (of timber, etc.); **é. de pierres,** squareman, stone-cutter. **2.** knacker.

équarrissoir [ekariswaːr], *s.m.* **1.** *Tls:* broach, reamer. **2.** (*a*) knacker's knife; (*b*) knacker's yard.

équateur [ekwatœːr], *s.m.* **1.** equator; equinoctial line; **sous l'é.,** at the equator; *Astr:* **é. céleste,** celestial equator; *Geog:* **é. magnétique,** magnetic equator. **2.** *Pr.n.m. Geog:* **(la République de l') Équateur,** Ecuador.

équation [ekwasjɔ̃], *s.f.* equation. **1.** *Mth:* **é. du premier, du deuxième, degré,** simple equation, quadratic equation; **é. à deux inconnues,** equation with two unknown quantities; **résoudre une é.,** to resolve an equation; **mettre un problème en é.,** to find the equation of a problem; *s.a.* SIMULTANÉ. **2.** *Ch:* equation. **3.** (*a*) *Astr:* **é. du temps,** equation of time; (*b*) *Psy:* **é. personnelle,** personal equation.

équatorial, -iaux [ekwatɔrjal, -jo]. **1.** *a.* equatorial; *Nau:* **calmes équatoriaux,** equatorial doldrums; *Biol:* **plaque équatoriale,** equatorial plate. **2.** *s.m. Astr:* equatorial (telescope).

équatorialement [ekwatɔrjalmɑ̃], *adv.* equatorially, in an equatorial position.

équatorien, -ienne [ekwatɔrjɛ̃, -jɛn], *a. & s. Geog:* Ecuadorian.

équerrage [ekɛraːʒ], *s.m. Carp:* **1.** (*a*) squaring; (*b*) bevelling (of timber). **2.** square or bevel angle; **é. en gras,** obtuse angle (of timber); standing bevelling.

équerre [ekɛːr], *s.f.* **1.** *Tls:* square; **é. à dessin,** set-square; **é. à T,** T-square; **é. à coulisse,** (sliding) caliper gauge; **fausse é.,** bevel square; **fausse é. à rapporteur,** bevel protractor; **é. à centrer,** centre-square; **é. à onglet,** mitre square; *Surv:* **é. d'arpenteur,** cross-staff (head); optical square. **2.** *Const:* **(angle d')é.,** right angle; **en é. d'é.,** at right angles; **hors d'é.,** out of square, out of perpendicular; **couper qch. à fausse é.,** to cut sth. askew, out of square, on the bevel; **mettre qch. d'é.,** to square sth.; **mettre bien d'é.,** to true (of a wheel, etc.); *Plumb:* **coude en é.,** quarter bend; **coude d'é.,** right-angled bend. **3.** *Civ.E: etc:* right-angle bracket; angle iron, iron knee, corner plate; *Const:* corner brace.

équerrer [ekere], *v.tr. Carp:* (*a*) to square; (*b*) to bevel (timber, etc.) according to the template.

équestre [ekɛstr̥], *a.* equestrian (statue, order, etc.).

équeutage [ekøtaːʒ], *s.m.* **1.** stalking, tailing (of fruit). **2.** *Petroleum Ind:* tailing out.

équeuter [ekøte], *v.tr.* **1.** to stalk, tail (fruit). **2.** *Petroleum Ind:* **é. les tiges de pompage,** to tail out rods.

équi- [ekɥi], *pref.* equi-; **équicrural,** equicrural; **équivalve,** equivalved.

équiangle [ekɥiɑ̃ːgl̩], *a. Geom:* equiangular.

équidés [ekɥide], *s.m.pl.* **1.** *Z:* Equidae. **2.** *Com:* hides (horse, pony, zebra, etc.).

équidifférent [ekɥidiferɑ̃], *a. Mth:* equidifferent.

équidistance [ekɥidistɑ̃ːs], *s.f.* **1.** *Geom:* equidistance. **2.** *Surv:* **é. (des courbes),** (contour) interval, vertical interval (of contours); **é. des teintes hypsométriques,** layer step.

équidistant [ekɥidistɑ̃], *a. Geom:* equidistant; **lignes équidistantes,** parallel lines.

équienne [ekɥiɛn], *a For:* **peuplement é.,** plantation containing trees all of the same age.

équilatéral, -aux [ekɥilateral, -o], *a. Geom:* equilateral.

équilatère [ekɥilatɛːr], *a. Mth:* equilater; **hyperbole é.,** equilateral hyperbola.

équilénine [ekɥilenin], *s.f. Vet: Biol:* equilenin.

équilibrage [ekilibraːʒ], *s.m.* **1.** (*a*) counterbalancing, counterpoising; *Mch:* balancing (of slide valve, etc.); **masse d'é.,** counterpoise; (*b*) *El.E: Elcs:* balancing (of circuit); correction (of phases); **câble d'é.,** equalizer lead; **fil d'é.,** equalizing conductor; **é. d'impédance,** impedance match(ing). **2.** trim (of aircraft, etc.).

équilibrant [ekilibrɑ̃], *a.* equilibrating, balancing (system, etc.).

équilibrateur, -trice [ekilibratœːr, -tris], *a.* equilibratory, equilibrating, balancing (action, etc.).

équilibration [ekilibrasjɔ̃], *s.f.* **1.** equilibration, counterbalancing, counterpoising. **2.** balancing (of the body, of the budget).

équilibre [ekilibr̥], *s.m.* equilibrium, balance, (equi)poise; stability (of aeroplane); poise (of mind); (*of pers.*) **avoir un bon é.,** to be well balanced; **mettre qch. en é.,** to balance sth.; **mise en é.,** balancing; **se tenir, être, en é.,** to keep one's balance, to be in equilibrium; **tenir qch. en é. sur son nez,** to balance sth. on one's nose; **perdre l'é.,** (i) to lose one's balance; (ii) to lose one's (mental) equilibrium; **faire perdre l'é. à qn,** to throw s.o. off his balance; **déranger, rompre, l'é. de qch.,** to disturb the balance of sth., to upset (the equilibrium of) sth.; **faire de l'é.,** to do balancing tricks; *Adm:* **parvenir à, rétablir, l'é. budgétaire,** to balance the budget; *Pol:* **é. européen,** balance of power in Europe; **les états qui se font é.,** the balancing powers; **point d'é.,** null position; *Phil: etc:* **l'é. de la nature,** the balance of nature; *El.E:* **fil d'é.,** equalizing conductor; *Ph:* **é. thermique,** calorific balance; *Atom.Ph:* **é. radioactif,** radioactive equilibrium; *s.a.* STABLE 1, INSTABLE.

équilibré [ekilibre], *a.* in equilibrium; balanced; **esprit bien é.,** well-balanced mind, sane mind; **mal é.,** ill-balanced, unbalanced; cranky (mind, boat); crank (boat); *Med:* (*of diabetic*) **malade é.,** controlled patient; **forces non équilibrées,** unbalanced forces; *Mil: etc:* **stocks équilibrés,** balanced stocks.

équilibrer [ekilibre], *v.tr.* to balance, (counter)-poise, equilibrate; **é. un panier sur la tête,** to balance a basket on one's head; **é. qch. par un contrepoids,** to counterbalance sth.; **é. le budget,** to balance the budget; *Oil Ind: Nau: etc:* **é. les réservoirs,** to trim the tanks; *Aut:* **é. les roues,** to balance the wheels.

s'équilibrer, (*of weights, etc.*) to balance; to come into equilibrium.

équilibreur, -euse [ekilibrœːr, -øːz]. **1.** *a.* equilibratory, equilibrating, balancing (action, etc.). **2.** *s.m. Av:* stabilizer; horizontal stabilizing rudder or fin.

équilibriste [ekilibrist], *s.m. & f.* equilibrist; rope-walker; acrobat.

équille [ekiːj], *s.f. Ich:* lesser sand eel.

équimoléculaire [ekɥimɔlekylɛːr], *a. Ch:* equimolecular.

équimultiple [ekɥimyltipl̩], *a. & s.m. Mth:* equimultiple.

équin [ekɛ̃], *a.* equine; **pied é.,** club foot (*talipes equinus*); **variole équine,** horse-pox.

équinisme [ekinism], *s.m. Med:* clubfoot.

équinoxe [ekinɔks], *s.m.* equinox; **é. de printemps,** spring, vernal, equinox; **vent d'é.,** equinoctial gale; **grandes marées d'é.,** equinoctial tides.

équinoxial, -iaux [ekinɔksjal, -jo], *a.* equinoctial. *Hist: A:* **France équinoxiale,** French Guiana.

équinter [ekɛ̃te], *v.tr.* to point the end of (leather strap, etc.).

équipage [ekipa:ʒ], *s.m.* **1.** *Nau:* crew, ship's company; hands; *Av:* aircrew; *Aer:* crew (of airship); **faire son é.,** to man the ship; **maître d'é.,** boatswain; *Aut:* **l'é. d'un camion,** the crew of a lorry; *Mil:* **é. de char,** tank crew. **2.** *Mil:* train, equipment; **é. de siège,** siege train (of guns); siege equipment (of engineers); *A:* **train des équipages,** baggage train, waggon train, = Army Service Corps (of British army); **é. de pont,** bridging train, bridging equipment. **3.** equipage; (*a*) retinue, suite, train; *F:* **arriver, partir, en grand é.,** to arrive, depart, in state; (*b*) *A:* carriage and horses; turn-out; **avoir é.,** to keep a carriage. **4.** *Ven:* pack of hounds; hunt; **maître d'é.,** master of the hounds. **5.** apparel, attire; *F:* get-up, rig-out; *F:* **être en piteux é.,** to be in a sorry plight. **6.** (*general sense of* "*requisites*") **é. d'engrenage(s),** gear-train (of lathe, etc.); **é. d'outils,** set of tools; **é. d'atelier,** workshop equipment, apparatus; **é. de pompe,** pump-gear; **é. de construction,** builder's paraphernalia; **é. radiologique,** X-ray outfit. **7. é. mobile,** (i) *El.E:* moving contact; (ii) *Av: Nau:* gimbal.

équipartition [ekɥipartisjɔ̃], *s.f.* division into equal parts.

équipe [ekip], *s.f.* **1.** *Nau:* train of boats. **2.** (*a*) gang (of workmen); *Rail:* **é. de conduite, de locomotive,** engine crew; **é. de nuit,** night shift; **travailler par équipes,** to work in shifts; **travail par équipes,** shiftwork; **travail d'é.,** team work; **homme d'é.,** gangman, navvy; **chef d'é.,** foreman (of a gang); ganger; charge hand, charge man; **é. volante,** (police) flying squad; **é. de secours,** rescue squad; *Ind:* **é. d'entretien,** maintenance crew; **é. de service,** duty squad; *Oil Ind:* **é. de forage,** drilling crew, rig crew; **é. de montage,** erection gang; (*b*) *Mil:* (i) squad; (ii) team; working party; *Artil:* **é. de pièce,** gun crew. **3.** *Sp:* (*a*) team; side; **é. de football,** football team, eleven; **é. de cricket,** cricket eleven; *s.a.* ESPRIT 5; (*b*) crew (of rowing boat).

équipé [ekipe], *a.* fitted up; ready for use; **troupes mal équipées,** badly equipped troops.

équipée [ekipe], *s.f. F:* escapade, lark; **il a fait là une belle é.!** a nice mess he's made of it!

équipement [ekipmɑ̃], *s.m. Nau: Mil: Av:* equipment. **1.** (*a*) fitting out; **é. en hommes,** manning; (*b*) rigging, fitting up (of sheers, etc.); (*c*) **é. électrique,** electrical fittings; **industrie de l'é. électrique,** electrical engineering industry; **é. mécanique,** mechanical equipment, mechanical plant, mechanical engineering; **é. électronique de bord,** (i) *Av:* avionics; (ii) *Nau:* ship electronics, marine electronics; **é. radio,** radio equipment; **é. de bord,** (i) *Av:* (on-)board equipment, airborne equipment; (ii) *Nau:* ship outfit, ship equipment; ship fittings; **é. aéronautique,** aircraft equipment; **é. astronautique,** astronautic equipment, spacecraft equipment; *s.a.* BIEN II, 2. **2.** outfit (of ship, soldier, etc.); gear, appurtenances; **grand é.,** accoutrement, equipment; **petit é.,** kit; **é. de cheval,** horse appointments, horse furniture.

équiper [ekipe], *v.tr.* to equip (s.o., sth.) (**de,** with); to fit (s.o.) out (**de,** in, with); **é. un navire,** (i) to equip, fit out, (ii) to man, a vessel; **é. des troupes,** to equip troops; **é. une chèvre,** to rig, fit up, sheers; *F:* **é. qn,** to rig s.o. out; **comme vous voilà équipé!** what a guy you look! what a rig-out! *Th: etc:* **é. le décor,** to rig (up).

équipier, -ière [ekipje, -jɛ:r], *s.* **1.** *s.m. A:* one of a gang (of workmen). **2.** *s.m. & f.* member of a team; team-mate; **les équipiers,** (i) the players, the team; (ii) the crew (of rowing-boat); **un é.,** a crew (on a sailing dinghy); **être é.,** to crew (a sailing dinghy).

équiplanation [ekɥiplanasjɔ̃], *s.f. Geol:* antiplanation.

équipol(l)é [ekipɔle], *a. Her:* checky (in nine pieces).

équipollence [ekipɔlɑ̃:s], *s.f. A:* equipollence.

équipollent [ekipɔlɑ̃], *a. A:* equipollent (**à,** with).

équipoller [ekipɔl(l)e], *v.i. A:* **é. à qch.,** to equal sth., to be equipollent with, equivalent to, sth.

équipondérance [ekɥipɔ̃derɑ̃:s], *s.f.* equiponderance.

équipotence [ekɥipɔtɑ̃:s], *s.f. Mth:* equipotence.

équipotent [ekɥipɔtɑ̃], *a. Mth:* equipotent.

équipotentiel, -ielle [ekɥipɔtɑ̃sjɛl], *a. Ph: etc:* equipotential.

équiprobable [ekɥiprɔbabl], *a.* equiprobable.

équirépartition [ekɥirepartisjɔ̃], *s.f. Statistics:* equidistribution.

équiscalaire [ekɥiskalɛ:r], *a.* **ligne é.,** line of scalar quantity.

équisétales [ekɥisetal], *s.f.pl. Palaeobotany:* Equisetales.

equisetum [ekɥisetɔm], *s.m. Bot:* equisetum; *F:* horse-tail.

équitable [ekitabl], *a.* equitable, fair, just, reasonable, upright (dealing, judgment, etc.); **homme é.,** impartial, fair-minded, even-handed, man; **remporter une victoire é.,** to win a deserved victory, to deserve one's victory.

équitablement [ekitabləmɑ̃], *adv.* equitably, fairly, justly, uprightly; **juger é.,** to judge impartially.

équitant [ekitɑ̃, -kɥi-], *a. Bot:* equitant.

équitation [ekitasjɔ̃], *s.f.* equitation, horsemanship; **son docteur lui a ordonné de faire de l'é.,** his doctor has ordered him to take up riding; **école d'é.,** riding-school.

équité [ekite], *s.f.* equity, equitableness, fairness, impartiality, even-handed dealing; *Jur:* adherence to equity (in defiance of statute); *Eng. Jur:* **loi d'équité,** equity.

équivalemment [ekivalamɑ̃], *adv.* (*rare*) equivalently.

équivalence [ekivalɑ̃:s], *s.f.* equivalence (**à,** to).

équivalent [ekivalɑ̃], *a. & s.m.* equivalent (**à,** to); tantamount (**à,** to); *Ind:* **é. thermique,** thermal value; **é. fuel,** fuel oil equivalent; *Surv:* **projection équivalente,** equal area projection.

équivalent-gramme [ekivalɑ̃gram], *s.m. Ch:* gram(me) equivalent; *pl. équivalents-grammes.*

équivaloir [ekivalwa:r], *v.i.* (*conj. like* VALOIR) **é. à qch.,** to be equivalent, equal in value, to sth.; *F:* **cela équivaut à l'appeler lâche,** that is tantamount to, as good as, calling him a coward; **cela équivaut à un refus,** that is in effect a refusal, that amounts to a refusal.

équivoque [ekivɔk]. **1.** *a.* (*a*) equivocal, ambiguous (words, etc.); of double meaning; **allusion peu é.,** pointed allusion, **compliment é.,** back-handed compliment; (*b*) questionable, doubtful, dubious (conduct, reputation, etc.). **2.** *s.f.* (*a*) ambiguity (of expression); **sans é.,** unequivocal(ly); **user d'é.,** to quibble; (*b*) ambiguous expression; (*c*) misunderstanding; **il y a é.,** there is a misunderstanding; **pour dissiper toute é.,** in order to remove any uncertainty, any doubt (**sur,** as to).

équivoquer [ekivɔke], *v.i. A:* to equivocate; to quibble.

s'équivoquer, *A:* to use the wrong word, to make a slip.

érable [erabl], *s.m. Bot:* maple(-tree, -wood); **é. dur,** rock-maple; *Bot:* **é. du Canada,** silver maple; **é. champêtre,** field maple; **é. à sucre,** sugar-maple; **é. plane,** Norway maple; *Join:* **é. madré, é. à broussin,** bird's-eye maple; **sucre d'é.,** maple sugar.

érablière [erablijɛ:r], *s.f.* maple grove.

éradication [eradikasjɔ̃], *s.f.* (*esp. Med:*) eradication; rooting out.

éraflement [erɑfləmɑ̃], *s.m.* **1.** grazing, scoring, scratching. **2.** scratched, scored, condition (of bore of gun, etc.).

érafler [erɑfle], *v.tr.* (*a*) to scratch, graze, to scuff (leather); *Golf:* to scrape, sclaff (ball, the ground); **s'é. les tibias,** to bark one's shins; (s')é., to rub one's skin off; (*b*) to score (inside of gun, etc.).

éraflure [erɑfly:r], *s.f.* (*a*) slight scratch, abrasion; (*b*) score (in bore of gun, etc.).

éraillé [erɑje], *a.* **1.** frayed (collar, etc.); scratched (surface). **2. yeux éraillés,** bloodshot or red-rimmed eyes. **3.** raucous, harsh, hoarse (voice); **notes éraillées d'un violon,** scratchy notes of a fiddle.

éraillement [erɑjmɑ̃], *s.m.* **1.** (*a*) unravelling, fraying (of material, etc.); fretting (of rope); (*b*) grazing, chafing (of surface). **2.** *Med:* **é. de la paupière,** ectropion. **3.** raucousness, harshness, hoarseness (of the voice).

érailler [erɑje], *v.tr.* **1.** to unravel, fray out (material, etc.); to fret (rope). **2.** to graze, chafe, scratch (the skin, etc.). **3.** to roughen (the voice).

s'érailler. 1. to unravel, come unravelled; to fray; (*of rope*) to fret. **2.** (*of skin, voice*) to grow rough.

éraillure [erɑjy:r], *s.f.* **1.** frayed part (of garment, etc.). **2.** = ÉRAFLURE.

éranthe [erɑ̃:t], *s.f. Bot:* eranthis.

Érasme [erasm], *Pr.n.m.* Erasmus.

érasmien, -ienne [erɑ̃smjɛ̃, -jɛn], *a. & s. Theol:* Erasmian.

Éraste [erast], *Pr.n.m.* Erastus.

érastianisme [erastjanism], *s.m. Theol:* Erastianism.

érastien, -ienne [erastjɛ̃, -jɛn], *a. & s. Theol:* Erastian.

Érato [erato], *Pr.n.f. Gr.Myth:* Erato.

Eratosthène [eratɔstɛn], *Pr.n.m.* Eratosthenes.

erbium [ɛrbjɔm], *s.m. Ch:* erbium.

erbue [ɛrby], *s.f. Metall:* clay flux.

ère [ɛ:r], *s.f.* (*a*) era, epoch; **l'è. chrétienne,** the Christian era; **en l'an 1550 de notre è.,** in 1550 A.D.; **le cinquième siècle avant notre è.,** the fifth century B.C.; (*b*) era, age, period; **l'è. des croisades,** the period, time, of the crusades; **avec l'invention de la machine à vapeur s'ouvrit une è. nouvelle,** the invention of the steam engine marked the beginning of a new era; **l'è. de la liberté,** the age of liberty; **une è. de prospérité,** a period of prosperity; (*c*) *Geol:* **è. primaire, secondaire, tertiaire, quaternaire,** primary, secondary, tertiary, quaternary, era.

Érèbe [erɛb], *Pr.n.m. Gr.Myth: Ent:* Erebus.

érébia [erebja], *s.m. Ent:* erebia.

Érechthée [erɛkte], *Pr.n.m. Gr.Myth:* Erechtheus.

Érechthéion [erɛktejɔ̃], *s.m. Gr.Arch:* Erechtheion.

érecteur, -trice [erɛktœ:r, -tris], *a. & s.m.* **1.** *Anat:* erector (muscle, etc.). **2.** *s.m. Civ.E:* erector.

érectile [erɛktil], *a.* erectile (tissue, etc.).

érectilité [erɛktilite], *s.f.* erectility.

érection [erɛksjɔ̃], *s.f.* **1.** erection, setting up, raising (of statue, temple, mast, etc.). **2.** (*a*) establishment, institution, foundation, setting up (of an office, etc.); (*b*) **é. d'une baronnie en duché,** raising of a barony into a dukedom. **3.** *Physiol:* erection (of tissue, etc.).

éreintage [erɛ̃ta:ʒ], *s.m.* = ÉREINTEMENT 2.

éreintant [erɛ̃tɑ̃], *a. F:* back-breaking, exhausting, killing, tiring, fagging (work, etc.); **c'est é.!** it does take it out of you!

éreinté [erɛ̃te], *a. F:* exhausted, fagged; dog-tired, dead-tired, tired to death, dead-beat; *F:* all in, whacked.

éreintement [erɛ̃tmɑ̃], *s.m. F:* **1.** exhaustion, great fatigue. **2.** (*of literary criticism*) slating, cutting-up; savage attack; *F:* **é. avec des fleurs,** damning with faint praise.

éreinter [erɛ̃te], *v.tr.* **1.** (*a*) to break the back of (horse, etc.); (*b*) *F: A:* to thrash (s.o.). **2.** *F:* (*a*) to exhaust; to tire (s.o.) out; to knock (s.o.) up; **ça m'éreinte!** it takes it out of me! (*b*) to ruin (s.o.); (*c*) to beat (s.o.) in argument; *F:* to wipe the floor with (s.o.). **3.** (*a*) *F:* to smash up, ruin (car, etc.); (*b*) to criticize (author, s.o.'s character, etc.) unmercifully; to vilify (s.o.); to slate, slash, cut to pieces, run down (literary work, etc.); to pull (performance) to pieces.

s'éreinter, *F:* (*a*) to exhaust oneself; to tire oneself out; (*b*) to drudge, toil (**à,** at).

éreinteur [erɛ̃tœ:r], *s.m. F:* slashing critic; **c'est un é.,** he never has a good word for anybody.

érémitisme [eremitism], *s.m.* hermit's way of life, eremitism.

érémitique [eremitik], *a.* eremitic(al); **vie é.,** hermit's life, life of a recluse.

eremurus [eremyry:s], *s.m. Bot:* eremurus; *pl. eremuri.*

érepsine [erɛpsin], *s.f. Bio-Ch:* erepsin.

érésipèle [erezipɛl], *s.m. F:* = ÉRYSIPÈLE.

éréthisme [eretism], *s.m.* **1.** *Med:* erethism. **2.** *Lit:* violence of feeling, etc., taken to extremes; nervous excitement.

éréthizontidés [eretizɔ̃tide], *s.m.pl. Z:* Erethizontidae.

éreuth(r)ophobie [erøt(r)ɔfɔbi], **éreutophobie** [erøtɔfɔbi], *s.f. Psy:* ereutrophobia, erythrophobia.

erg[1] [ɛrg], *s.m. Ph.Meas:* erg.

erg[2], *s.m. Geog:* erg (of the Sahara).

ergastoplasme [ɛrgastɔplasm], *s.m. Biol:* ergastoplasm.

ergastule [ɛrgastyl], *s.m. Rom.Ant:* ergastulum.

ergatogyne [ɛrgatɔʒin], *a. Ent:* ergatogyne.

ergatoïde [ɛrgatɔid], *a. Ent:* ergatoid.

ergmètre [ɛrgmɛtr], *s.m. El:* ergmeter.

ergo [ɛrgo], *Lt.conj.* ergo, therefore.

ergocratie [ɛrgɔkrasi], *s.f.* ergatocracy.

ergo-glu [ɛrgogly], *A:* **1.** *adv.phr. F:* that is ridiculous, that proves nothing at all. **2.** *s.m.inv. in pl.* ridiculous argument.

ergographe [ɛrgɔgraf], *s.m. Physiol:* ergograph.

ergomètre [ɛrgɔmɛtr], *s.m. Physiol:* ergometer.

ergonomie [ɛrgɔnɔmi], *s.f.* ergonomics, biotechnology.

ergostérol [ɛrgɔsterɔl], *s.m. Ch:* ergosterol.

ergot [ɛrgo], *s.m.* **1.** (*a*) spur (of cock, etc.); *F:* **monter, se dresser, sur ses ergots,** to get on one's high horse; **quand il monte sur ses ergots . . .,** when his hackles are up . . .; (*b*) dew-claw (in certain mammals). **2.** (*a*) *Hort:* stub (on fruit-tree, etc.); (*b*) *Agr:* **e. (des graminées),** ergot; *Pharm:* **e. (de seigle),** ergot. **3.** *Mec.E: etc:* (*a*) catch, snug, lug, stop (on gearing, etc.); detent; **e. d'arrêt, e. de butée,** stop pin; **e. de centrage,**

locating pin, locating peg, locating dowel; **e. conique,** taper spigot; **e. d'entraînement,** drive pin; (*Computers*) feed pin; (*b*) feather, spline (on shaft); (*c*) pin (of electric bulb).

ergotage [ɛrgɔtaːʒ], *s.m. F:* quibbling, cavilling.

ergotamine [ɛrgɔtamin], *s.f. Pharm:* ergotamine.

ergoté [ɛrgɔte], *a.* **1.** (*of bird, etc.*) spurred; (*of cattle, dog, etc.*) dew-clawed. **2.** *Agr:* ergotted (corn); **seigle e.,** spurred rye.

ergoter [ɛrgɔte], *v.i. F:* to quibble, cavil (**sur,** about); to split hairs; to raise captious objections.

ergoterie [ɛrgɔtri], *s.f. F:* = ERGOTAGE.

ergoteur, -euse [ɛrgɔtœːr, -øːz], *F:* **1.** *a.* cavilling, quibbling, pettifogging. **2.** *s.* caviller, quibbler, pettifogger.

ergothérapie [ɛrgɔterapi], *s.f. Med:* ergotherapy.

ergotine [ɛrgɔtin], *s.f. Pharm:* ergotin(e).

ergotisme[1] [ɛrgɔtism], *s.m. F:* cavilling, quibbling, hair-splitting.

ergotisme[2], *s.m. Med:* ergotism, ergotic poisoning.

ergotiste [ɛrgɔtist], *s.m. & f.* = ERGOTEUR.

érianthe [erjɑ̃ːt], *Bot:* **1.** *a.* erianthous, woolly-flowered. **2.** *s.m.* erianthus.

éricacé [erikase], *a. Bot:* ericaceous.

éricacées [erikase], *s.f.pl. Bot:* Ericaceae.

éricales [erikal], *s.f.pl. Bot:* Ericales.

éricicole [erisikɔl], *a. Bot:* ericeticolous.

éricoïde [erikɔid], *a. Bot:* heath-like, heather-like, ericoïd, (plants).

Érié [erje], *Pr.n.m. Geog:* **le Lac É.,** Lake Erie.

Érigène [eriʒɛn], *Pr.n.m.* Erigena.

ériger [eriʒe], *v.tr.* **(j'érigeai(s); n. érigeons) 1.** to erect, set up, raise (statue, temple, mast, etc.). **2.** to establish, institute, found, set up (office, etc.); **é. un tribunal,** to set up a tribunal. **3.** to elevate, exalt; **é. une église en cathédrale,** to raise a church to (the dignity of) a cathedral; **é. la corruption en système,** to systematize bribery; **l'ironie érigée en art,** irony brought to a fine art; **é. qch. en principe,** to lay sth. down as a principle; **é. une règle en principe,** to give a rule the force of a general principle.

s'ériger, s'é. en critique, to set up as a critic; to pose as a critic.

érigéron [eriʒerɔ̃], *s.m. Bot:* erigeron, flea-bane; **é. du Canada,** horse-weed.

érigne [eriɲ], *s.f.,* **érine** [erin], *s.f.* (surgeon's) tenaculum.

érinacéidés [erinaseide], *s.m.pl. Z:* Erinaceidae.

érinite [erinit], *s.f. Miner:* erinite.

Érinnyes [erinni], *s.f.pl. Gr.Myth:* Erin(n)yes, Furies.

ériocaulacées [erjokɔlase], *s.f.pl. Bot:* Eriocaulaceae.

ériocaule [erjɔkoːl], **ériocaulon** [erjɔkolɔ̃], *s.m. Bot:* eriocaulon.

ériocraniides [erjɔkraniid], *s.m.pl. Ent:* Eriocraniidae.

Ériphyle [erifil], *Pr.n.f. Gr.Myth:* Eriphyle.

érismature [erismatyːr], *s.m. Orn:* erismatura; **é. roux,** ruddy-duck, *U.S:* fool-duck; **é. à tête blanche,** white-headed duck.

éristale [eristal], *s.m. Ent:* eristalis.

éristique [eristik], *a. & s.m. & f.* eristic.

ermenonvillois, -oise [ɛrmənɔ̃vilwa, -waːz], *a. & s. Geog:* (native, inhabitant, of Ermenonville.

erminette [ɛrminɛt], *s.f. Tls:* adze.

ermitage [ɛrmitaːʒ], *s.m.* hermitage.

ermite [ɛrmit], *s.m.* hermit, eremite; **vivre en e.,** to live the life of a recluse.

ernacéen, -enne [ɛrnaseɛ̃, -ɛn], *a. & s.* (native) of Ernée.

Ernest [ɛrnɛst], *Pr.n.m.* Ernest.

Ernestine [ɛrnɛstin], *Pr.n.f.* Ernestine.

éroder [erɔde], *v.tr.* to erode, abrade, denude; to eat away, wear away; to corrode (metals, etc.); *Bot:* **feuille érodée,** gnawed leaf.

érodium [erɔdjɔm], *s.m. Bot:* erodium.

érogène [erɔʒɛn], *a.* erogenic, erogenous.

érogénéité [erɔʒeneite], *s.f.* erogeneity.

Érôs, Éros [erɔs]. **1.** *Pr.n.m. Gr.Myth:* Eros. **2.** *s.m. Psy:* eros.

érosif, -ive [erozif, -iːv], *a.* erosive.

érosion [erozjɔ̃], *s.f.* erosion; wearing away; wear; (*a*) *Dent:* **é. dentaire,** (dental) erosion; (*b*) *Geol: Geog:* erosion, denudation, degradation; **é. différentielle,** differential erosion; **é. latérale,** lateral erosion; **é. (linéaire),** erosion; **é. marine,** marine erosion; **é. glaciaire,** glacial erosion; **é. éolienne,** wind, (a)eolian, erosion; **cycle d'é.,** cycle of erosion.

Érostrate [erɔstrat], *Pr.n.m. Gr.Hist:* Erostratus.

érotématique [erɔtematik], *a.* erotetic, interrogatory.

érotique [erɔtik], *a.* erotic; amatory (poem).

érotiquement [erɔtikmɑ̃], *adv.* erotically.

érotisme [erɔtism], *s.m.* eroticism, erotism.

érotogène [erɔtɔʒɛn], *a.* erotogenic.

érotomane [erɔtɔman], *s.m. & f.,* **érotomaniaque** [erɔtɔmanjak], *s.m. & f.* erotomaniac.

érotomanie [erɔtɔmani], *s.f.* erotomania; (*in women*) nymphomania.

érotyle [erɔtil], *s.m. Ent:* erotylus.

érotylidés [erɔtilide], *s.m.pl. Ent:* Erotylidae.

erpétologie [ɛrpetɔlɔʒi], *s.f.* herpetology.

erpétologique [ɛrpetɔlɔʒik], *a.* herpetologic(al); **faune e.,** herpetofauna.

erpétologiste [ɛrpetɔlɔʒist], *s.m.* herpetologist.

errance [ɛrɑ̃ːs], *s.f.* (state of) wandering, odyssey; **sa vie ne fut qu'une longue e.,** his life was one long odyssey.

errant [ɛr(r)ɑ̃], *a.* **1.** rambling, roaming, roving, wandering (traveller, life, etc.); **chevalier e.,** knight-errant; **chevalerie errante,** knight-errantry; **le Juif e.,** the Wandering Jew; **chien e.,** stray dog; **pensées errantes,** vagrant, wandering, thoughts; *A.Astr:* **étoiles errantes,** errant stars, planets. **2.** erring, misguided (person, action); *s.* **les errants,** those who have gone astray, who have strayed from the fold; the lost sheep.

errata [ɛr(r)ata], *s.m.inv. Typ:* errata slip.

erratique [ɛr(r)atik], *a. Astr: Geol: Med: etc:* erratic (block, pulse, etc.); *Geol:* **bloc e.,** erratic.

erratum [ɛr(r)atɔm], *s.m. Typ:* erratum (misprint or mis-statement); *pl. errata.*

erre[1] [ɛːr], *s.f.* (the letter) r.

erre[2], *s.f.* **1.** *Nau:* (head)way (of ship); **e. pour gouverner,** steerage-way; **prendre de l'e.,** to gather, fetch, headway; **avoir de l'e.,** to have headway, to have way on; **briser, casser, étaler, l'e.,** to check the way; **perdre de l'e., son e.,** to lose way; **couper l'e. à un navire,** to bring a ship to; **donnez de l'e.!** give way! give way ahead! **mouiller avec de l'e.,** to make a running moor. **2.** *pl. Ven:* track, spoor, slot (of stag, etc.); **suivre les erres de qn,** to walk in s.o.'s footsteps. **3.** *A:* **aller grand-e., belle e.,** to move quickly.

errements [ɛrmɑ̃], *s.m.pl.* **1.** *A:* procedure, methods, ways; **suivre les e. de qn,** to follow in s.o.'s track. **2.** erring ways; mistaken ideas; **retomber dans, revenir à, ses anciens e.,** to fall back into the bad old ways.

errer [ɛr(r)e, ere], *v.i.* **1.** to ramble, roam, rove, wander, stroll (about); **e. dans les bois, par les rues,** to wander in the woods, about the streets; **e. à l'abandon,** to wander aimlessly, forlornly; **barques errant sur les flots,** boats drifting on the waves; **laisser e. ses pensées,** to let one's thoughts stray, run on; **un sourire errait sur ses lèvres,** a smile was hovering on his lips; *s.a.* PEINE 1. **2.** *A:* to err; to be mistaken, misguided.

erreur [ɛrœːr], *s.f.* error. **1.** mistake, blunder, slip; **e. de plume,** clerical error, slip of the pen; **e. de date, de calcul,** mistake in the date, in reckoning; **e. de jugement,** error of, in, judgment; **e. judiciaire,** miscarriage of justice; **e. sur le genre,** mistake in gender; **e. typographique,** misprint; **e. de signaux,** error in signalling; *Tchn:* **e. de calibration, d'étalonnage,** calibration error; *Surv:* **e. angulaire, de cheminement,** angular, traverse, error; *Artil:* **e. de pointage, de visée,** error of aim; **e. systématique de visée,** aim bias; **faire, commettre, une e.,** to make a mistake, a slip, a blunder; **par e.,** by mistake; **sauf e.,** if I am not mistaken; *Com:* **sauf e. ou omission,** errors and omissions excepted; **il y a e.,** there's some mistake; **faire e.,** to be mistaken; *F:* **c'est un malin, pas d'e.,** he's a smart one and no mistake; *P:* **y a pas d'e.!** that's so! you're right! **2.** false belief, mistaken opinion; delusion; fallacy; **être dans l'e.,** to labour under a misapprehension, under a delusion; to be mistaken; to be at fault; **une e. courante,** a current fallacy; **induire qn en e.,** to mislead, delude, s.o.; **tirer qn d'e.,** to undeceive s.o., to show s.o. how he was wrong; **tomber dans l'e.,** to fall, run, into error. **3.** folly, imprudence; **les erreurs de la jeunesse,** the errors of youth; **revenir de ses erreurs,** to turn over a new leaf.

erroné [ɛrɔne], *a.* erroneous, wrong, mistaken (statement, belief, etc.); **interprétation erronée de la loi,** misreading of the law.

erronément [ɛrɔnemɑ̃], *adv.* erroneously.

ers [ɛr(s)], *s.m. Bot:* vetch.

ersatz [ɛrzats], *s.m.inv.* substitute (*esp. for articles of food*); **e. de café,** ersatz coffee; **la guerre n'est point une aventure véritable, elle n'est qu'un e. d'aventure,** war is not a real adventure, only a substitute.

erse[1] [ɛrs]. **1.** *a. & s.m. Ling:* Gaelic (of the Highlands). **2.** *a.* **mœurs erses,** Highland customs.

erse[2], *s.f. Nau:* **1.** strop; **e. en bitord,** selvagee; **grosse e.,** garland. **2.** grummet, grommet.

erseau, -eaux [ɛrso], *s.m. Nau:* grummet, grommet.

érubescence [erybɛs(s)ɑ̃ːs], *s.f.* erubescence blushing.

érubescent [erybɛs(s)ɑ̃], *a.* erubescent; *Bot:* rubescent; **fruits érubescents,** fruit that is turning red; **jeune fille érubescente,** blushing girl; *Med:* **tumeur érubescente,** erubescent tumour.

érubescite [erybɛs(s)it], *s.f. Miner:* erubescite, bornite.

éruca [eryka], *s.f. Bot:* eruca, rocket.

éruciforme [erysifɔrm], *a. Ent:* eruciform.

érucique [erysik], *a. Ch:* erucic (acid).

éructation [eryktasjɔ̃], *s.f.* eructation, belching; belch.

éructer [erykte]. **1.** *v.i. Med:* to eruct, to belch. **2.** *v.tr.* **é. des injures,** to belch forth abuse.

érudit [erydi]. **1.** *a.* erudite, scholarly, learned (person, work). **2.** *s.m.* scholar; **les érudits,** the erudite; **c'est un é. en histoire,** he is widely read in history; he's an historian of great scholarship.

érudition [erydisjɔ̃], *s.f.* (*a*) erudition, learning, scholarship; **discourir avec é. de qch.,** to talk learnedly on sth.; (*b*) *A:* scholarly observation.

érugineux, -euse [eryʒinø, -øːz], *a.* (*of bile, sputum, etc.*) resembling copper-rust, aeruginous.

éruptif, -ive [eryptif, -iːv], *a. Med: Geol:* eruptive (disease, rock, etc.); **nappe éruptive,** lava flow.

éruption [erypsjɔ̃], *s.f.* **1.** eruption (of volcano, of water, blood, etc.); **faire é.,** to erupt; *Min:* **é. d'une sonde,** blow-out of an oil well. **2. é. des bourgeons,** bursting forth of the buds; **é. des dents,** cutting of the teeth. **3.** *Med:* eruption, breaking out, rash (on the skin); **l'é. paraît au bout de trois jours,** the rash appears at the end of three days.

érycinides [erisinid], *s.m.pl. Ent:* Erycinidae, Riodinidae, the metal marks.

Érymanthe [erimɑ̃ːt], *Pr.n.m. A.Geog:* Erymanthus.

érynge [erɛ̃ːʒ], **eryngium** [erɛ̃ʒjɔm], *s.m. Bot:* Eryngium; eryngo.

éryon [erjɔ̃], *s.m. Paleont:* eryon.

érysimon [erizimɔ̃], *s.m. Bot:* erysimum.

érysipélateux, -euse [erizipelatø, -øːz], *a. Med:* erysipelatous.

érysipèle [erizipɛl], *s.m. Med:* erysipelas.

érysiphacées [erizifase], *s.f.pl. Fung:* Erysiphaceae.

érysiphe [erizif], *s.m. Fung:* erysiphe.

érythémateux, -euse [eritematø, -øːz], *a. Med:* erythematous.

érythème [eritɛm], *s.m. Med:* erythema.

érythrasma [eritrasma], *s.m. Med:* erythrasma.

érythrée[1] [eritre], *s.f. Bot:* erythraea; lesser, common, centaury.

Érythrée[2]. **1.** *a. A.Geog:* **la mer Érythrée,** the Erythrean Sea (Persian Gulf or Indian Ocean). **2.** *Pr.n.f. Geog:* **l'É.,** Eritrea.

érythréen, -enne [eritreɛ̃, -ɛn], *a. & s. Geog:* Eritrean.

érythrémie [eritremi], *s.f. Med:* erythraemia.

érythrène [eritrɛn], *s.m. Ch:* erythrene.

érythrin [eritrɛ̃], *s.m. Ich:* erythrinus.

érythrine [eritrin], *s.f.* **1.** *Miner:* erythrite, red cobalt. **2.** *Ch:* erythrin. **3.** *Bot:* erythrina.

érythrisme [eritrism], *s.m. Anthr:* erythrism.

érythrite [eritrit], *s.f.,* **érythritol** [eritritɔl], *s.m. Ch:* erythrite, erythritol.

érythroblaste [eritrɔblast], *s.m. Physiol:* erythroblast.

érythroblastose [eritrɔblastoːz], *s.f. Med:* erythroblastosis.

érythrocarpe [eritrɔkarp], *a. Bot:* erythrocarpous.

érythrocyte [eritrɔsit], *s.m. Physiol:* erythrocyte.

érythrocytose [eritrɔsitoːz], *s.f. Med:* erythrocytosis.

érythrodermie [eritrɔdɛrmi], *s.f. Med:* erythrodermia.

érythrol [eritrɔl], *s.m. Ch:* erythrol.

érythrolyse [eritrɔliːz], *s.f. Physiol:* erythrolysis.

érythromycine [eritrɔmisin], *s.f. Pharm:* erythromycin.

érythrone [eritrɔn], *s.m. Bot:* erythronium, dog's tooth (violet).

érythrophagocytose [eritrɔfagɔsitoːz], *s.f. Physiol:* erythrophagocytosis.

érythrophile [eritrɔfil], *a. Biol:* erythrophilous.

érythrophobie [eritrɔfɔbi], *s.f. Psy: Med:* erythrophobia.

érythropoïèse [eritrɔpɔiɛːz], *s.f. Physiol:* erythropoïesis.

érythropsie [eritrɔpsi], *s.f. Med:* erythropia, erythropsia.
érythropsine [eritrɔpsin], *s.f. Biol:* erythropsin.
érythrose[1] [eritro:z], *s.f.* **é. pudique**, pronounced tendency to blush; **é. des pommettes**, flushing of the cheeks (as in tuberculosis).
érythrose[2], *s.m. Ch:* erythrose.
érythrosidérite [eritrɔsiderit], *s.f. Miner:* erythrosiderite.
érythrosine [eritrɔzin], *s.f. Ch:* erythrosin(e).
érythrozincite [eritrɔzɛ̃sit], *s.f. Miner:* erythrozincite.
érythrulose [eritrylo:z], *s.m. Ch:* erythrulose.
éryx [eriks], *s.m. Rept:* eryx.
Erzeroum [ɛrzerum], *Pr.n. Geog:* Erzerum, Erzurum.
ès [ɛs], *contracted article* = **en les**; *still used in names of degrees and names of places;* **docteur ès lettres** = D.Lit(t); **licencié ès lettres, ès sciences** = bachelor of arts (B.A.), bachelor of science (B.Sc.); *A:* **maître ès arts**, master of arts; *Jur:* **agir ès qualités**, to act within the scope of one's attributions.
Ésaü [ezay], *Pr.n.m. B.Lit:* Esau.
esbigner (s') [sɛzbiɲe], *v.pr. P:* to make off, to skedaddle, to decamp.
esbrouf(f)ant [ɛzbrufɑ̃], *a. F:* amazing, unheard of; **c'est e.!** that beats me! that staggers me! **toilette esbroufante**, loud (and unconventional) dress.
esbrouf(f)e [ɛzbruf], *s.f. F:* showing off, bounce; *Box:* hustling tactics; **faire de l'e.**, (i) to show off, to bounce, to put on side; (ii) to hector, to ruffle; **vol à l'e.**, pocket-picking by hustling one's victim; hustling; snatch-and-grab robbery.
esbrouf(f)er [ɛzbrufe], *v.tr. F:* to impress (s.o.), to take (s.o.) in, to bluff (s.o.), with one's grand airs, one's bluster.
esbrouf(f)eur, -euse [ɛzbrufœ:r, -ø:z], *F:* **1.** *a.* (*a*) swanky; swanking; (*b*) hectoring, ruffling. **2.** *s.* (*a*) swank; bouncer, hustler; (*b*) snatch-and-grab thief.
esca [ɛska], *s.f. Bot:* esca, apoplexy (of vine).
escabeau, -eaux [ɛskabo], *s.m.* **1.** (wooden) stool. **2.** step-ladder, pair of steps; *Av: etc:* **e. plateforme d'accès**, work stand.
escabeau-chaise [ɛskaboʃɛ:z], *s.m.* chair with folding steps attached; *pl. escabeaux-chaises.*
escabécher [ɛskabeʃe], *v.tr.* (*conj. like* ACCÉLÉRER) *Cu:* to marinate (sardines, mackerel, etc.) in olive oil (for serving as hors-d'œuvre).
escabelle [ɛskabɛl], *s.f.* three-legged (i) chair, (ii) stool.
escabelon [ɛskablɔ̃], *s.m.* plinth (of silver cup, bust, etc.).
escache [ɛskaʃ], *s.f. Harn:* oval bit.
escadre [ɛskadr̥], *s.f.* (*a*) *Navy:* fleet; squadron; **l'e. de la Méditerranée**, the Mediterranean fleet; **e. de bâtiments de ligne**, battleship squadron; **chef d'e.**, commodore; squadron commander; (*b*) *Av:* **e. aérienne**, wing, station, *U.S:* (air) combat wing.
escadrille [ɛskadri:j], *s.f.* **1.** *Navy:* flotilla, fleet of small vessels. **2.** *Av:* flight (of aircraft).
escadron [ɛskadrɔ̃], *s.m.* (*a*) *Mil:* squadron; **e. de chars**, armoured squadron, *U.S:* tank company; **e. de commandement et des services**, headquarters, *U.S:* service, squadron; **chef d'escadron(s)**, major; (*b*) *Av:* **e. de chasse, de bombardement**, fighter, bomber, squadron; (*c*) (large) band, group; **un e. de jolies filles**, a bevy of beautiful girls; **un e. de malentendus**, a host of misunderstandings.
escadronner [ɛskadrɔne], *v.i.* (*of aircraft A: of cavalry unit*) to perform evolutions.
escalade [ɛskalad], *s.f.* **1.** (*a*) scaling, climbing (of wall, cliff); *Mount:* **e. artificielle**, artificial climbing; (*b*) climb; *Mil:* escalade; (*c*) *Mil:* escalation; (*d*) *Pol.Ec:* **e. des taux d'intérêt**, escalation of rates of interest. **2.** *Jur:* house-breaking.
escalader [ɛskalade], *v.tr.* to scale, climb (wall, etc.); *Mil:* to escalade (fortress, etc.).
escaladeur [ɛskaladœ:r], *s.m.* escalader.
escalator [ɛskalatɔ:r], *s.m.* escalator.
escale [ɛskal], *s.f. Nau: Av:* **1.** port, place, of call; *Av:* intermediate landing, stopover; **e. tête de ligne**, airline terminal; **e. aérienne**, air staging post; **arriver à l'e.**, to arrive at the port of call, at the landing place; **escales prévues**, scheduled stops; *Nau:* **faculté d'e.**, authority (given to the captain of a cargo ship) to stop at any port; *Nau:* **frusques d'e.**, harbour togs, long togs. **2. faire e.**, (i) *Nau:* to put into port; (ii) *Av:* to touch down; **nous avons fait e. à Bordeaux**, (i) *Nau:* we put in, called, at Bordeaux; (ii) *Av:* we touched down, stopped, at Bordeaux; *Av:* **vol sans e.**, non-stop flight; **une e. de quatre heures**, a four hour stop; **visiter une ville pendant l'e.**, to visit a town (i) *Nau:* while the ship is in port, (ii) *Av:* during an intermediate stop, a stopover.
escaler [ɛskale], *v.i. Nau: Av:* to put into port; to touch down, call (**à**, at).
escalier [ɛskalje], *s.m.* staircase; (flight of) stairs; **e. de service**, service staircase, back stairs; **e. entre murs**, box stair; **e. tournant, circulaire, hélicoïdal, en vis, en colimaçon, en escargot, en spirale**, spiral staircase; **e. hors d'œuvre**, external staircase; turret staircase; **e. roulant, mécanique**, *Fr.C:* **e. mobile**, escalator, moving staircase; **e. dérobé**, (i) hidden, concealed, secret, staircase; (ii) devious method; *Nau:* **e. de commande**, accommodation ladder; **e. central**, main companion; *Geol:* **failles en e.**, step faults; **rencontrer qn dans l'escalier**, to meet s.o. on the stairs; **tomber du haut de l'e.**, to fall downstairs; **esprit de l'e.**, after wit, *U.S:* latter wit; **j'ai l'esprit de l'e.**, I always think of a retort when it's too late; *F:* **faire des escaliers dans les cheveux de qn**, to cut s.o.'s hair in a jagged line.
escaliéteur [ɛskaljetœ:r], *s.m.* carpenter specializing in the manufacture of staircases.
escalope [ɛskalɔp], *s.f.* (*a*) *Cu:* escalope; scallop, fillet (of veal, etc.); (salmon) steak; (*b*) *Golf:* **faire sauter une e.**, to take a divot.
escaloper [ɛskalɔpe], *v.tr.* to cut (raw meat) into thin slices.
escalpe [ɛskalp], *s.f.* scalping.
escamotable [ɛskamɔtabl̥], *a.* (*of arm-rest, etc.*) concealable, disappearing; retractable (handle, etc., *Av:* undercarriage); **lit e.**, fold-away bed.
escamotage [ɛskamɔta:ʒ], *s.m.* (*a*) legerdemain, conjuring, sleight of hand; skipping, scamping (of a job); **e. d'une carte**, vanishing of a card; (*b*) **manivelle d'e.**, disappearing handle; *Phot:* **e. d'une plaque**, changing of a plate (in a changing box); *Cin:* **phase d'e.**, cut-off period; (*c*) *Av:* retraction (of undercarriage); (*d*) stealing, filching.
escamote [ɛskamɔt], *s.f.* conjuror's ball.
escamoter [ɛskamɔte], *v.tr.* (*a*) (*of conjuror, etc.*) to vanish (card, etc.); **e. une tâche**, to skip, scamp, a task; **e. la vraie question**, to burke the question, to dodge the question, the issue; **e. son dépit**, to conceal one's annoyance; **e. certains mots**, to glide over certain words; to pronounce certain words inaudibly; (*b*) *Phot: A:* **e. une plaque**, to change a plate (in the changing box); (*c*) *Av:* **e. le train d'atterrissage**, to retract the undercarriage; (*d*) to steal, filch (s.o.'s property); **e. un emploi à qn**, to do s.o. out of a job; **e. un consentement**, to obtain s.o.'s consent by a trick; **on m'a escamoté ma montre**, my watch has been pinched.
escamoteur, -euse [ɛskamɔtœ:r, -ø:z], *s.* (*a*) conjuror; (*b*) person who dodges the issue; (*c*) sneak thief.
escamper [ɛskɑ̃pe], *v.i. F:* to make off, clear out.
escampette [ɛskɑ̃pɛt], *s.f. F: used only in* **prendre la poudre d'e.**, to make off, do a bolt, a bunk, *U.S:* to take a (runout) powder.
escap [ɛskap], *s.m.*, **escape**[1] [ɛskap], *s.f. Ven:* (*training of hawk, etc.*) **faire, donner, e. à (l'oiseau)**, to show (hawk, etc.) its prey.
escapade [ɛskapad], *s.f.* **1.** (*a*) *A:* escape, escaping; (*b*) escapade; **e. d'écolier**, schoolboy's escapade. **2.** *Equit:* caper (of horse).
escape[2], *s.f.* **1.** *Arch:* scape, spring, apophyge (of column). **2.** lower section (of barrel).
escaper [ɛskape], *v.tr. Ven:* **e. le gibier**, to release the game (for the hawk, etc.).
escarbeille [ɛskarbɛ:j], *s.f.* (*ivory trade*) scrivello.
escarbillage [ɛskarbija:ʒ], *s.m.* sifting (of cinders).
escarbille [ɛskarbi:j], *s.f. esp. Nau: Rail:* (*a*) (half-burnt) cinder; (*b*) *pl.* clinkers, ashes; (*c*) *pl.* sparks.
escarbiller [ɛskarbije], *v.tr.* to sift (cinders).
escarbilleur [ɛskarbijœ:r], *s.m.* **1.** cinder sifter. **2.** *Nau: etc:* ash ejector; ash hoist.
escarbit [ɛskarbi], *s.m.* (*caulker's*) oil box, grease box.
escarbot [ɛskarbo], *s.m. Ent:* **1. e. doré**, rose-chafer; **e. de la farine**, meal beetle. **2.** *F:* (*a*) cockchafer; (*b*) dung beetle.
escarboucle [ɛskarbukl̥], *s.f.* (*a*) *A: Lap:* carbuncle; (*b*) **yeux d'e.**, flashing eyes; (*c*) *Her:* escarbuncle.
escarcelle [ɛskarsɛl], *s.f.* (*a*) *A:* (money) pouch, wallet; (*b*) *F:* purse; worldly wealth; **il cherchait un divertissement à portée de son e.**, he was looking for some amusement he could afford.
escargot [ɛskargo], *s.m.* snail; **e. comestible**, edible snail; **parc à escargots**, snailery; **(escalier en) e.**, winding stair(s), spiral staircase; **allure d'e.**, snail's pace; **aller, avancer, comme un e.**, to go along at a snail's pace.
escargotière [ɛskargɔtjɛ:r], *s.f.* **1.** snailery. **2.** dish for serving snails.
escarmouche [ɛskarmuʃ], *s.f.* skirmish, brush (with the enemy); **escarmouches parlementaires**, parliamentary skirmishes.
escarmoucher [ɛskarmuʃe], *v.i.* to skirmish.
escarmoucheur [ɛskarmuʃœ:r], *s.m.* skirmisher.
escarole [ɛskarɔl], *s.f. Bot:* endive.
escarotique [ɛskarɔtik], *a. Med:* escharotic.
escarpe[1] [ɛskarp], *s.f. Fort:* (e)scarp; *Const:* scarp (of wall).
escarpe[2], *s.m. A: F:* cut-throat.
escarpé [ɛskarpe], *a.* (*a*) steep-sloped; steeply sloping; precipitous; abrupt (slope); sheer (cliff); (*b*) **les chemins escarpés de la science**, the hard road to science; (*c*) (*of pers.*) **caractère e.**, difficult character.
escarpement [ɛskarpəmɑ̃], *s.m.* **1.** steepness; acclivity, abruptness (of slope). **2.** (*a*) *Fort:* escarpment; (*b*) *Geog: etc:* escarpment, scarp slope; steep slope; **e. de faille**, (i) fault scarp; (ii) fault-line scarp.
escarper [ɛskarpe], *v.tr.* (*rare*) to (e)scarp; to cut back (rock face).
escarpin [ɛskarpɛ̃], *s.m.* (*a*) (dancing) shoe; pump; (*b*) court shoe; casual (shoe); (*c*) *F:* **e. de Limoges**, sabot; (*d*) *P:* **jouer de l'e.**, to make off, clear out (quickly), to show a clean pair of heels.
escarpolette [ɛskarpɔlɛt], *s.f.* **1.** (child's) swing. **2.** *Th: F:* **faire de l'e.**, to gag; to guy (one's part). **3.** (*house painter's*) platform, stage.
escarre[1] [ɛska:r], *s.f. Her:* L-shaped border of quarter.
escarre[2], *s.f. Med:* (*a*) scab, eschar, slough; (*b*) bed sore.
escarrification [ɛskarifikasjɔ̃], *s.f. Med:* formation of a scab.
escarrifier [ɛskarifje], *v.tr. Med:* to form a scab
Escaut (l') [lɛsko], *Pr.n.m. Geog:* the (river) Scheldt.
eschara [ɛskara], **eschare**[1] [ɛska:r], *s.m. Z:* eschara; escharine.
eschare[2], *s.f. Med:* (*a*) scab, eschar, slough; (*b*) bed sore.
escharification [ɛskarifikasjɔ̃], *s.f. Med:* formation of a scab.
escharifier [ɛskarifje], *v.tr.* to form a scab on.
escharine [ɛskarin], *s.f. Z:* escharine.
escharotique [ɛskarɔtik], *a. Med:* escharotic.
eschatocole [ɛskatɔkɔl], *s.f. Dipl:* eschatocol.
eschatologie [ɛskatɔlɔʒi], *s.f.* eschatology.
eschatologique [ɛskatɔlɔʒik], *a.* eschatological.
esche [ɛʃ], *s.f. Fish:* bait.
escher [ɛʃe], *v.tr. Fish:* to bait (hook).
Eschine [ɛsʃin, eʃin], *Pr.n.m. Gr.Hist:* Aeschines.
Eschyle [ɛsʃil, eʃil], *Pr.n.m. Gr.Lit:* Aeschylus.
escient [ɛsjɑ̃], *s.m.* knowledge, cognizance; *used in* **à bon e.**, well knowing, deliberately, wittingly; *Jur:* scienter; **prouver qu'un acte a été commis à bon e.**, to prove a scienter; *also* **à mon, ton, son, escient**, to my, your, his, (certain) knowledge; **il ne faut prophétiser qu'à bon e.**, don't prophesy unless you know; *F:* **dépenser son argent à bon e.**, to spend one's money judiciously.
escionnement [ɛsjɔnmɑ̃], *s.m. Hort:* disbudding.
escionner [ɛsjɔne], *v.tr. Hort:* to disbud (tree, etc.).
esclaffement [ɛsklafmɑ̃], *s.m.* **e. (de rire)**, burst, roar, of laughter.
esclaffer (s') [sɛsklafe], *v.pr.* **s'e. (de rire)**, to burst out laughing; to roar, shake, shriek, yell, with laughter.
esclandre [ɛsklɑ̃:dr̥], *s.m.* (*a*) *A:* (i) misadventure; (ii) attack; brawl; (*b*) scandal; scene; row; **faire, causer, un e., faire de l'e.**, to cause a scandal; to make a scene.
esclavage [ɛsklava:ʒ], *s.m.* **1.** slavery; **réduire qn en e.**, to enslave s.o., to reduce s.o. to slavery; **l'e. du bureau**, the drudgery of the office; **vivre dans l'e. des passions**, to be the slave of one's passions; **ce travail est un véritable e.**, this work is sheer slavery. **2.** *Cost:* (*a*) necklace (reminiscent of slave collar); (*b*) *pl. A:* ribbons (ornamenting women's shoes).
esclavagisme [ɛsklavaʒism], *s.m.* **1.** (*a*) pro-slavery; (*b*) the slave system. **2.** *Ent:* dulosis.
esclavagiste [ɛsklavaʒist], **1.** *s.m. Hist:* advocate of negro slavery; *a.* **les états esclavagistes**, the slave states (of the U.S.A.). **2.** *a. Ent:* dulotic.
esclave [ɛsklɑ:v], *s.m. & f.* slave; **marchand d'esclaves**, slave trader; **il fut vendu comme e.**, he was sold as a slave, was sold into slavery; **elle est l'e. de sa famille**, she is the family drudge; **obéir en e.**, to obey slavishly; **être e. à son travail**, to be a slave to one's work; **être (l')e.**

de la mode, to be a slave to, the slave of, fashion; **il est e. de sa parole,** his word is his bond, he never goes back on his word; *Geog: A:* **la Côte des Esclaves,** the Slave Coast; **le Grand Lac de l'E., des Esclaves,** the Great Slave Lake; **le Petit Lac des Esclaves,** the lesser Slave Lake.

esclavon, -onne [ɛsklavɔ̃, -ɔn], *a. & s. A: Geog:* Slavonian.

escobar [ɛskɔbaːr], *s.m. A: Pej:* equivocator (*from the Spanish casuist Escobar*).

escobarder [ɛskɔbarde], *v.i. A: Pej:* to equivocate, quibble.

escobarderie [ɛskɔbardəri], *s.f. A: Pej:* equivocation, quibbling; hypocrisy.

escof(f)ier [ɛskɔfje], *v.tr.* (*p.d. & pr.sub.* **n. escofiions, v. escofiiez**) *P:* to kill, murder, bump off.

escogriffe [ɛskɔgrif], *s.m.* **1.** *A:* cadger, sponger. **2.** gawky, lanky, man; *esp.* **un grand e.,** a great lout of a fellow.

escomptable [ɛskɔ̃tabl], *a.* **1.** *Fin:* discountable (securities, etc.). **2.** that can be reckoned upon.

escompte [ɛskɔ̃ːt], *s.m.* **1.** *Com:* discount, rebate; **e. de caisse,** cash discount; **accorder un e. sur les prix,** to allow a discount off the prices; **e. au comptant,** discount for cash; **maison d'e.,** cut-price stores; **à e.,** at a discount. **2.** *Fin:* **e. (de banque),** discount; **e. officiel, taux d'e.,** bank rate (of discount), discount rate; **prendre à l'e. un effet de commerce,** to discount a bill of exchange; **e. en dedans,** true discount; **e. en dehors,** bank discount; **banque d'e.,** discount bank. **3.** *St. Exch:* call for delivery (of securities) before settlement.

escompter [ɛskɔ̃te], *v.tr.* **1.** *Fin:* to discount (bill). **2. e. les variations du marché,** to anticipate, allow for, the variations in prices; **e. un succès,** to take success for granted, to reckon on, anticipate, success; to bank on success. **3.** *Fin:* to call for delivery (of securities), before settlement.

escompteur [ɛskɔ̃tœːr], *s.m. Fin:* discounter, discount-broker; *a.* **banquier e.,** discounting banker.

escope [ɛskɔp], *s.f. Nau:* bailing scoop, bailer.

escopette [ɛskɔpɛt], *s.f. A.Arms:* blunderbuss.

escorte [ɛskɔrt], *s.f. Mil: etc:* escort; *Navy:* convoy; **sous l'e. de . . .,** under the escort of . . .; *Navy:* convoyed by . . .; **sans e.,** unescorted; **navire d'e.,** convoy; **faire e., servir d'e., à qn,** to escort s.o.; **conduire un prisonnier sous e.,** to escort a prisoner.

escorter [ɛskɔrte], *v.tr.* to escort; *Navy:* to convoy, escort; **e. qn jusqu'à la porte,** to show s.o. out.

escorteur [ɛskɔrtœːr], *s.m. Navy:* escort (vessel), frigate; **e. rapide,** fast frigate, *U.S:* destroyer escort; **e. d'escadre,** squadron escort, fleet escort ship; **e. de haute mer,** ocean escort; **e. côtier,** coastal escort.

escouade [ɛskwad], *s.f.* **1.** (*a*) squad, gang (of workmen, etc.); (*b*) group (of people). **2.** *Mil: A:* section (of infantry).

escoupe [ɛskup], *s.f.* (*a*) *Nau:* bailing scoop, bailer; (*b*) *Tchn:* scoop (used in lime kilns).

escourgeon [ɛskurʒɔ̃], *s.m. Agr:* winter barley.

escoussage [ɛskusaːʒ], *s.m. Cer:* crawling (of the glaze).

escrime [ɛskrim], *s.f.* fencing; swordsmanship; **faire de l'e.,** (i) to fence; (ii) to go in for fencing; **leçons d'e.,** fencing lessons; **e. à l'épée,** fencing with the épée, sword; **e. à la baïonnette,** bayonet exercise, drill; **e. au sabre,** backsword play; *Gym:* **e. au bâton,** backsword, singlestick (play); **moniteur d'e.,** fencing master.

escrimer [ɛskrime], *v.i.* (*a*) *A:* to fence; (*b*) *F:* **e. avec un bâton,** to spar, make sword-play, with a stick; (*c*) *occ.* to struggle, make every effort.

s'escrimer, to fight, struggle; to spar; **s'e. de sa canne,** to make play with, to flourish, one's stick; **s'e. des dents, des mâchoires,** to eat heartily; **s'e. des pieds et des mains,** to fight tooth and nail; **s'e. contre qn,** to have a tussle with s.o.; **s'e. sur le piano,** to bang, strum, on the piano; **s'e. à un travail,** to work hard, peg away, at sth.; **s'e. à faire qch.,** to try hard to do sth.; to work like mad at sth.

escrimeur, -euse [ɛskrimœːr, -øːz], *s.* fencer; fencing enthusiast.

escroc [ɛskro], *s.m.* swindler, sharper, crook.

escroquer [ɛskrɔke], *v.tr.* **1. e. qch. à qn,** to cheat, rob, s.o. of sth., to trick s.o. out of sth. **2. e. qn,** to swindle, defraud, s.o.

escroquerie [ɛskrɔkri], *s.f.* **1.** (obtaining of sth. by) false pretences; swindling. **2.** swindle, fraud; **e. au chantage,** blackmail racket.

escudo [ɛskydo], *s.m. Num:* escudo.

Esculape [ɛskylap]. **1.** *Pr.n.m. Myth:* Aesculapius. **2.** *s.m. A: & Hum:* physician. **3.** *Rept:* Aesculapian snake.

esculent [ɛskylɑ̃], *a. O:* esculent, eatable, edible.

esculétine [ɛskyletin], *s.f. Bio-Ch:* esculetin.

esculine [ɛskylin], *s.f. Ch:* aesculin, esculin.

ésérine [ezerin], *s.f. Pharm:* eserin.

esgourde [ɛsgurd], *s.f. P:* ear; **écarquillez vos esgourdes!** pin back your lugholes!

esgourder [ɛsgurde], *v.tr. P:* to listen to.

esker [ɛskɛːr], *s.m. Geol:* esker.

eskimo, -os [ɛskimo], *a. & s. Geog:* Eskimo.

eskimotage [ɛskimɔtaːʒ], *s.m. Sp:* (*canoeing*) roll, rolling.

esmillage [ɛsmijaːʒ], *s.m. Const: Min:* spalling, scabbling.

esmiller [ɛsmije], *v.tr. Const: Min:* to spall, scabble.

ésociculture [ezɔsikyltyːr], *s.f.* pike breeding.

ésocidés [ezɔside], *s.m.pl. Ich:* Esocidae, the pikes.

Ésope [ezɔp], *Pr.n.m. Gr.Lit:* Aesop.

ésophorie [ezɔfɔri], *s.f. Med:* esophoria.

ésopique [ezɔpik], *a. Lit:* Aesopic, Aesopian.

ésotérique [ezɔterik], *a.* esoteric.

ésotérisme [ezɔterism], *s.m.* esoterism.

ésouchement [esuʃmɑ̃], *s.m.* stubbing up, grubbing up (of tree stumps).

ésoucher [esuʃe], *v.tr.* to stub up, grub up (tree stumps).

espace [ɛspas]. I. *s.m.* space. **1.** (*a*) (*defined area*) **laisser de l'e.,** to leave space, room; **il n'y a pas assez d'e.,** there's not enough room; **e. vital,** lebensraum; *Av:* **e. aérien,** airspace; *Town P:* **espaces verts,** open spaces; *Anat:* **e. intercostal,** intercostal space; **e. mort,** (i) *Mil:* dead ground; (ii) *Mch:* clearance (of piston head); *Mch:* **pertes de l'e. mort,** clearance losses; (*b*) (*distance between objects*) **entre les deux grilles se trouvait un e. de dix mètres,** there was a distance, space, of ten metres between the gates; **e. entre les piles d'un pont,** span between the piles of a bridge; (*c*) (*interval of time*) **pendant le même e. de temps,** in the same space of time; **en l'e. d'une semaine,** within a week; **dans l'e. d'un an,** a year from now; (*d*) *Mus:* space. **2.** (*a*) void; infinity; **regarder dans l'e.,** to stare into space; **e. cosmique,** cosmic space, outer space; **les mondes morts perdus dans l'e.,** the dead worlds lost in space; **la conquête de l'e.,** the conquest of space; **voyageur de l'e.,** space traveller, spaceman; **vol, voyage, dans l'e.,** space flight, space travel; **voler, voyager, dans l'e.,** to fly, travel, in space; (*b*) *Elcs: Ph:* **e. d'accélération,** acceleration space; **e. de captation,** catcher space; **e. de modulation,** buncher space (of klystron); **e. intermédiaire,** buffer space; **e. sombre anodique, cathodique,** anode, cathode, dark space; (*c*) *Mth:* **e. à trois, à quatre, dimensions,** three-dimensional, four-dimensional, space; **géométrie de, dans, l'e.,** solid geometry; (*d*) *Psy:* **e. d'attributs,** *U.S:* property space.

II. **espace,** *s.f. Typ:* space; **e. fine,** hair space; **e. moyenne, forte,** middle, thick, space.

espacé [ɛspase], *a.* far between, far apart; **îles espacées,** islands far apart; **troupes largement espacées,** troops at wide intervals; **lignes espacées de dix centimètres,** lines ten centimetres apart.

espacement [ɛspasmɑ̃], *s.m.* spacing (of columns, trees, etc.); pitch (of rivets); *Typ:* spacing, leading (of lines); spacing out (of letters); *Typewr:* spacing, escapement; **barre d'e.,** space-bar, spacer.

espacer [ɛspase], *v.tr.* (**j'espaçai(s); n. espaçons**) **1.** to space; to leave a space between (objects); *Typ:* **e. les lignes,** to lead, space, white out, the lines; **e. les lettres,** to space out, set out, the type. **2.** (*of time*) **il faut e. nos rencontres,** we must meet at longer intervals, make our meetings less frequent.

s'espacer. 1. to get, become, farther apart, spaced out; (*of competitors in a race*) to tail away, off, out; **les maisons s'espaçaient,** the houses became fewer and farther between. **2. ses visites s'espacent,** his visits are becoming less frequent.

espace-temps [ɛspastɑ̃], *s.m.inv. Mth: Ph:* space-time.

espadage [ɛspadaːʒ], *s.m. Tex:* scutching (of hemp).

espade [ɛspad], *s.f. Tex:* (*instrument*) scutch, scutcher (for hemp).

espader [ɛspade], *v.tr. Tex:* to scutch (hemp).

espadon [ɛspadɔ̃], *s.m.* **1.** *A.Arms:* espadon, two-handed sword. **2.** *Ich:* swordfish, xiphias.

espadrille [ɛspadriːj], *s.f.* alpargata, espadrille.

Espagne [ɛspaɲ], *Pr.n.f. Geog:* Spain.

espagnol, -ole [ɛspaɲɔl]. **1.** *a.* Spanish. **2.** *s.* Spaniard. **3.** *s.m. Ling:* Spanish.

espagnolette [ɛspaɲɔlɛt], *s.f.* espagnolette, hasp (of French window, etc.).

espagnolisme [ɛspaɲɔlism], *s.m.* **1.** *Ling:* hispanicism, Spanish turn of phrase. **2.** narrow Spanish patriotism.

espagnoliser [ɛspaɲɔlize], *v.tr.* **1.** *Ling:* to hispanicize. **2.** to hispaniolize.

espalier[1] [ɛspalje], *s.m.* **1.** *Hort:* (*a*) **(arbre en) e.,** espalier (grown on wall); **contre-e.,** espalier (grown on trellis, wires, but not against wall); (*b*) wall (on which espaliers are grown). **2.** *Gym:* rib stall.

espalier[2], *s.m. A.Nau:* stroke (of galley).

espalme [ɛspalm], *s.m. A.Nau:* **1.** coat of tallow and tar (for ship's bottom). **2.** coat of tallow (for racing boat's bottom).

espalmer [ɛspalme], *v.tr. A:* to clean, tallow, pay (ship's bottom).

espar [ɛspaːr], *s.m.* **1.** *Nau:* spar; **e. de tente,** awning spar. **2.** *Artil:* lever (for handling gun). **3.** *Fish:* pole (used for lifting certain types of net).

esparcet [ɛsparsɛ], *s.m.*, **esparcette** [ɛsparsɛt], *s.f. Bot:* sainfoin.

esparcier [ɛsparsje], *s.m. Hyd.E:* small sluice gate (for irrigation ditch).

espargoute [ɛspargut], *s.f. Bot:* spergula, spurrey.

espèce [ɛspɛs], *s.f.* **1.** (*a*) kind, sort; **distinguer deux choses dans l'e.,** to distinguish two things in kind; **gens de toute e.,** people of all kinds, of every description; (*b*) **une e. de,** a kind of; **sous les espèces de,** with the appearance of, in the form of, in the guise of, as a; **il portait une e. d'uniforme brun,** he wore a kind of brown uniform; **j'avais une e. d'impression que . . .,** I had a sort of impression that . . .; *Pej: F:* **cette e. d'idiot,** *P:* (*incorrect grammar*) **cet e. d'idiot,** that silly fool! *P:* **e. d'idiot!** you fool! you idiot! (*c*) *Pharm:* compound preparation; (*d*) *Jur: etc:* case in question, (this) particular case; **question d'e.,** question of fact in each case; **dans chaque cas d'e.,** in each specific case; **loi applicable en l'e.,** law applicable to the case in point; *F:* **mais je suis un cas d'e.,** but I'm a special case; (*e*) *pl. Fin:* (i) *A:* **espèces (monnayées),** specie, cash, coin; (ii) **payer en espèces,** to pay in cash; **espèces sonnantes,** hard cash. **2.** *Nat.Hist:* species (of plants, animals); **l'e. humaine,** mankind; **l'origine des espèces,** the origin of species. **3.** *Theol:* (eucharistic) species; **communion sous les deux espèces,** communion in both kinds.

espérable [ɛsperabl], *a.* that may be hoped for.

espérance [ɛsperɑ̃ːs], *s.f.* hope; **fonder son e. sur qn, qch.,** to found one's hopes on s.o., sth.; **être plein d'e. dans qch., être dans l'e. de qch.,** to be in hopes of sth.; **je nourris la ferme e. de le revoir,** I live in the certain hope of seeing him again; **mettre ses espérances en qch.,** to pin one's faith on sth., to trust in sth.; **garçon de grande e.,** promising boy; **elle donne de belles espérances,** she shows great promise; **victoire en e.,** hoped-for victory; **président en e.,** potential president; person hoping to become president; would-be president; **l'affaire n'a pas répondu à nos espérances,** the business did not come up to our expectations; **avoir des espérances,** (i) to have expectations (of a fortune); (ii) (*of woman*) to be expecting; **régler sa dépense sur ses espérances,** to live up to one's expectations; **e. de vie,** expectation of life.

espérantiste [ɛsperɑ̃tist], *Ling:* **1.** *s.m. & f.* Esperantist. **2.** *a.* Esperanto (society, etc.).

espéranto [ɛsperɑ̃to], *s.m. Ling:* Esperanto.

espère [ɛspɛːr], *s.f. Ven: Dial:* (*S. of Fr.*) **à l'e.,** in wait, on the watch.

espérer [ɛspere], *v.tr.* (**j'espère, n. espérons; j'espérerai**) **1.** to hope; **e. qch.,** to hope for sth.; **espérons des jours meilleurs,** let us hope for better days; **j'espère vous revoir,** I hope to see you again; **j'espérais bien que . . .,** I was hoping that . . .; **j'espère que tout ira bien,** I hope, trust, that all will go well; **j'espère qu'il ne va pas manquer son train,** I hope he doesn't miss his train; **j'espère qu'il viendra,** I hope he will come; **j'espère qu'il n'hésiterait pas à venir dans ce cas-là,** I hope in that case he wouldn't hesitate to come; **je n'espère pas qu'il vienne,** I have no hope of his coming; I don't expect him to come; **espérez-vous qu'il vienne, qu'il viendra?** do you expect him to come? **un jour viendra, je l'espère, où . . .,** a day will come, I hope, when . . .; **e. en qn, en qch.,** to hope, trust, in s.o., sth.; **e. en Dieu,** to trust in God; **e. contre toute espérance, e. quand même,** to hope against

hope; **la réponse espérée,** the expected answer; *A: & Lit:* **e. de faire qch.,** to hope to do sth.; **il aurait pu e. de vous convaincre,** he might have had hopes of convincing you; he might have thought he would convince you. **2.** *(a)* to expect (s.o., sth.); **je ne vous espérais plus,** I had given you up; **j'avais si longtemps e. ce jour,** I had waited so long for that day; *(b) A: & Dial:* **espérez-moi quelques instants,** wait a moment for me.

esperluète [ɛspɛrlɥɛt], *s.f. A:* ampersand.

espiègle [ɛspjɛgl], *a. & s.* mischievous (child, reply, etc.); **regard e.,** arch look; **petit(e) e.,** little mischief, little monkey.

espièglerie [ɛspjɛgləri], *s.f.* **1.** mischievousness; **par pure e.,** out of pure mischief. **2.** prank, monkey trick; **faire des espiègleries à qn,** to play pranks on s.o.

espingole [ɛspɛ̃gɔl], *s.f. A.Arms:* blunderbuss.

espion, -ionne [ɛspjɔ̃, -jɔn], *s.* **1.** *(a)* spy; **e. de la police,** police spy; *(b)* secret agent; **e. double,** double agent. **2.** *s.m.* *(a)* concealed microphone (in room, etc.); detectaphone; bug; *(b)* window-mirror, busybody.

espionnage [ɛspjɔnaːʒ], *s.m.* espionage, spying; **e. et contre-e.** = the secret service.

espionner [ɛspjɔne], *v.tr.* to spy on (s.o., s.o.'s movements, etc.); **il est toujours à e.,** he is always spying.

espionnite [ɛspjɔnit], *s.f. F:* spy mania.

esplanade [ɛsplanad], *s.f.* esplanade; promenade, parade.

espoir [ɛspwaːr], *s.m.* **1.** hope; **avoir l'e. de faire qch.,** to have hopes of doing sth.; **dans l'e. de vous revoir,** in the hope of seeing you again; **perdre (l')e.,** to lose hope; **les pauvres sans e. pour l'avenir,** the poor who have nothing to hope for; **avoir bon e.,** to be full of hope; **ayons bon e.,** let us hope for the best; **j'ai bon e. que tout ira bien,** I am confident that, am living in hope(s) that, all will be well; **mettre (tout) son e. en qch., en qn,** to pin one's faith on sth., on s.o.; to set one's hopes on sth., on s.o.; to trust in sth., in s.o.; **mettre son e. en Dieu,** to trust in God; **nourrir l'e. de faire qch.,** to set one's hopes on doing sth.; **exprimer le ferme e. que . . .,** to express the confident hope that . . .; **on conservait un vague e. que . . .,** there was a vague, lingering, hope that . . .; **exalter l'e. de qn,** to raise s.o.'s hope(s); **tromper l'e. de qn,** to disappoint s.o.'s expectations. **2. il est l'e. de son pays,** he is the hope of his country; **l'e. du tennis français,** the hope of French tennis; **il portera les espoirs olympiques américains,** he will be carrying the hopes of America in the Olympic games.

espoleur [ɛspɔlœːr], **espouleur** [ɛspulœːr], *s.m. Tex: (pers.)* bobbin, spool, winder.

espolin [ɛspɔlɛ̃], **espoulin** [ɛspulɛ̃], *s.m. Tex:* bobbin, spool.

esponton [ɛspɔ̃tɔ̃], *s.m. A:* *(a)* spontoon; *(b) Nau:* boarding pike.

espringale [ɛsprɛ̃gal], *s.f. A.Mil:* springal(d).

esprit [ɛspri], *s.m.* **1.** spirit; *(a)* **le Saint-E., l'E. saint,** the Holy Ghost, the Holy Spirit; **rendre l'e.,** to give up the ghost; **l'e. malin,** the Evil One; *(b)* ghost, phantom; **croire aux esprits,** to believe, in ghosts, in spirits; **il revient des esprits dans cette maison,** this house is haunted; *(c) (of Puck, Ariel, etc.)* sprite; **e. follet,** elfish spirit, hobgoblin. **2.** *(a)* vital spirit; **esprits animaux,** animal spirits; **recueillir ses esprits,** to pull oneself together; *A:* **perdre ses esprits,** to lose consciousness; **reprendre ses esprits,** to regain consciousness; to come to, come round; *(b) Ch: etc:* (volatile) spirit; **e. brut,** raw spirits; **e. de vin,** spirit(s) of wine, alcohol; *A:* **e. de bois,** methyl alcohol, wood alcohol; *A:* **e. de vitriol,** sulphuric acid; *A:* **e. de sel,** spirit(s) of salt, hydrochloric acid; **e. de sel décomposé,** killed spirit. **3.** *Gr.Gram:* **e. rude,** rough breathing; **e. doux,** smooth breathing. **4.** *(a)* mind; **e. dédoublé, schizophrène,** split mind; **d'e. lent,** slow-witted; **d'e. vif,** quick-witted; **vue de l'e.,** (fantastic) notion; **avoir l'e. tranquille,** to be easy in one's mind; **avoir l'e. de travers,** to have an awkward temper; **elle avait l'e. ailleurs,** her thoughts were elsewhere; **les esprits sérieux,** serious-minded people; *Prov:* **les grands esprits se rencontrent,** great minds think alike; **perdre l'e.,** to go mad, out of one's mind; **où aviez-vous l'e.?** what were you thinking of? you must have been out of your mind; **avez-vous perdu l'e.?** are you out of your wits? **il a perdu l'e.,** his mind is unhinged, deranged; **présence d'e.,** presence of mind; **conserver toute sa présence d'e.,** to keep all one's wits about one; **homme à l'e. calme,** cool-headed man; **il m'est venu à l'e. que . . .,** it occurred to me, struck me, that . . .; **une pareille idée ne me serait jamais venue à l'e.,** such an idea would never have entered my head; **cela m'est sorti de l'e.,** it slipped my memory; **avoir l'e. des affaires,** to have a genius, a turn, for business; **avoir l'e. de se taire,** to have the sense to be silent; **un e. fort,** a free-thinker; *(b)* wit; **il fait de l'e.,** he is trying to be funny; **mots d'e., traits d'e.,** witticisms; **c'est un homme d'e.,** (i) he has a nice wit; (ii) he has a sense of humour; *s.a.* BEAU I. 2, ESCALIER; **observation pleine d'e.,** witty remark. **5.** *(a)* spirit, feeling, dominant influence; **e. public,** public feeling; **e. de corps,** esprit de corps; team spirit; **e. d'équipe,** team spirit; **e. de famille,** clannishness; **avoir bon e.,** to be well-meaning; to be good-natured; **personnes de bon e.,** well-disposed people; **avoir mauvais e.,** to be evil-minded, ill-disposed; to be cantankerous; *Sch:* **cette classe a mauvais e.,** this is a difficult form; **les esprits sont très montés,** feeling is running very high; *(b)* spirit, (inner) meaning, sense (of a command, contract, etc.); **entrer dans l'e. de qch.,** to enter into the spirit of sth.; **il faut s'attacher à l'e. de la loi plutôt qu'à la lettre,** one should go by the spirit of the law rather than by the letter. **6. un e. dangereux,** a dangerous man; **un grand e.,** a noble-minded man.

esprot [ɛspro], *s.m. Ich:* sprat.

esquicher [ɛskiʃe], *v.i. & pr.* **1.** *O: Cards:* to play a low card; *F:* to duck. **2.** *F: O:* to avoid committing oneself, to lie low. **3.** *Dial: (S. of Fr.) P:* to crush.

esquif [ɛskif], *s.m. Lit:* small boat, skiff; wherry.

Esquilin [ɛskilɛ̃], *a. Geog:* **le mont E.,** the Esquiline (Hill); **porte Esquiline,** Esquiline Gate.

esquille [ɛskiːj], *s.f.* splinter (*esp.* of bone).

esquilleux, -euse [ɛskijø, -øːz], *a. Surg:* comminuted (fracture, etc.); splintered (bone); *Geol:* splintery (fracture).

esquimau, -aude, -aux [ɛskimo, -oːd, -o], *s. & a. (occ. inv. in f.)* **1.** *(a)* Eskimo, Esquimau, *U.S: F:* Husky; **Esquimaude, femme e.,** Eskimo woman; **la civilisation esquimaude, esquimau,** Eskimo civilization; *(b)* **chien e.,** husky, Eskimo dog; *s.m. Ling:* Eskimo. **2.** *s.m. F: Com.* choc ice. **3.** *s.m. Cost:* (child's) woolly suit.

esquimau-aléoute [ɛskimoaleut], *s.m. Ling:* Aleutian Eskimo (language).

esquimautage [ɛskimotaːʒ], *s.m. Sp: (canoeing)* rolling, roll.

esquimo, -os [ɛskimo], *a. & s.* = ESQUIMAU 1.

esquinancie [ɛskinɑ̃si], *s.f. A.Med:* quinsy; cynanche; *Bot: F:* **herbe à l'esquinancie,** squinancy-wort.

esquine [ɛskin], *s.f.* loins (of horse); **cheval faible, fort, d'e.,** horse weak, strong, in the back.

esquintant [ɛskɛ̃tɑ̃], *a. F:* exhausting, killing, back-breaking (work, etc.).

esquinté [ɛskɛ̃te], *a. F:* **1.** exhausted, dead-beat, dog-tired, all in. **2.** *(of health, etc.)* ruined.

esquinter [ɛskɛ̃te], *v.tr. F:* **1.** to exhaust; to knock (s.o.) up; to tire, wear, (s.o.) out. **2.** *(a)* to smash (sth.); to kill; to do (s.o.) in; **e. sa santé,** to ruin one's health; *(b)* to spoil, damage; **je ne veux pas e. la voiture,** I don't want to ruin the car.

s'esquinter, *F:* **1.** to tire, wear, oneself out (**à faire qch.,** doing sth.). **2.** to get spoilt, damaged; **votre voiture s'esquinte en plein air,** your car is being ruined by standing in the open.

esquisse [ɛskis], *s.f.* (rough) sketch; draft, outline (of portrait, landscape, novel, etc.); **e. d'un bâtiment,** rough plan of a building; **e. au crayon, à la plume,** pencil sketch, pen-and-ink sketch.

esquisser [ɛskise], *v.tr.* to sketch, outline (portrait, design, essay, etc.); **e. un geste de protestation,** to make a vague gesture of protestation; **e. un sourire,** to give the ghost of a smile.

esquive [ɛskiːv], *s.f.* dodging; *Fenc:* slip away, aside; evasion; **faire une e.,** to dodge; **e. de la tête,** duck(ing); *Mil: Av: etc:* **manœuvre d'e.,** evasive action.

esquivement [ɛskivmɑ̃], *s.m.* avoiding, dodging (of blow, creditor, etc.).

esquiver [ɛskive], *v.tr.* *(a)* to avoid, dodge, evade (blow, s.o.'s attentions, etc.); **e. ses créanciers,** to evade, elude, one's creditors; *(b) abs. Fenc:* to slip aside, to dodge; *Box:* **e. de la tête,** to duck.

s'esquiver. **1.** to slip away, off; to steal off; to make oneself scarce; to take French leave. **2.** *Navy:* to avoid action.

essai [esɛ], *s.m.* **1.** *(a)* trial, test(ing); **e. d'un pont, d'une machine,** testing of a bridge, of a machine; **essai en (plateforme d')usine,** shop trial, bench test; **e. de bon fonctionnement,** running test; working test; **e. probatoire,** feasibility test; **e. d'homologation,** type approval test, prototype test; **e. sur le terrain,** field test; **e. à pleine puissance,** full power run; **e. de vitesse,** speed trial; **chambre d'e.,** test chamber; **laboratoire d'e.,** test laboratory, testing plant; **banc d'e.,** testing bench; **terrain d'e.,** testing ground; **vitesse aux essais,** trial speed, speed on trials; **en (cours d') e.,** undergoing trials; **faire l'e. de qch.,** to test sth., to try sth. out; **nous en ferons l'e.,** we'll give it a trial; **mettre qn, qch., à l'e.,** to put s.o., sth., to the test; **engager qn à l'e.,** to engage s.o. on trial, on probation; **prendre qch. à l'e.,** to take sth. on trial, on approval; **conditions d'e.,** test requirements, test limits; **à titre d'e.,** experimentally; as an experiment; as a trial measure; **vente à l'e.,** sale on approval; *Com:* **commande d'e.,** trial order; *Ind:* **essais sur modèles,** model experiments; *Hort: etc:* **jardin, station, d'e.,** experimental garden, station; *Nau:* **e. (de vitesse) sur base,** trial over the measured mile; **e. à la mer,** sea trial, trial trip; **croisière d'essais,** shake-down cruise; *N.Arch:* **essais au bassin (des carènes),** tank trials; *Av:* **vol d'e.,** trial flight; **e. au sol,** ground run; **e. en dépression,** vacuum test; **e. mécanique,** physical test; **pilote d'e.,** test pilot; *Aut:* **essais sur route, e. routier,** road test; *Artil:* **essais de tir,** gun trials; *Ch: Metall:* **e. de coloration,** flame test (in analysis); *Metall:* **e. de fluage,** creep test; *El:* **e. de masse,** earth test; **e. à vide,** off-circuit test; **borne, tension, d'e.,** testing terminal voltage; *Th: Cin:* **théâtre, cinéma, d'e.,** experimental, avant-garde, theatre, cinema; *Mus:* **séance d'e. (d'un musicien),** audition; *s.a.* BALLON 1; *(b) Metall:* assay(ing) (of ore); **e. au chalumeau,** blowpipe analysis; **fourneau d'e.,** assay furnace. **2.** *(a)* attempt(ing), try; **les essais des grands génies,** the first attempts of great geniuses; **coup d'e.,** first attempt, trial shot; *(b) Lit:* (i) essay; (ii) monograph; *(c) Rugby Fb:* try; **marquer un e.,** to score a try; **transformer un e. (en but),** to convert a try. **3.** *Com:* sample (of wine, etc.).

essaim [esɛ̃], *s.m.* *(a)* swarm (of bees, etc.); *(of hive)* **jeter un e.,** to send out, throw off, a swarm; *(b)* **un e. d'étudiants,** a crowd, swarm, of students; **un e. de jeunes filles,** a bevy of girls.

essaimage [esɛmaːʒ], *s.m. Ap:* **1.** swarming, hiving off. **2.** swarming time.

essaimer [eseme, -eme], *v.* **1.** *v.i. Ap:* to swarm, to hive off. **2.** *v.i.* to emigrate. **3.** *v.tr.* to spread (news, etc.).

essandole [esɑ̃dɔl], *s.f. Const:* (roofing) shingle.

essange [esɑ̃ːʒ], *s.f.,* **essangeage** [esɑ̃ʒaːʒ], *s.m.* soaking (of soiled linen before boiling).

essanger [esɑ̃ʒe], *v.tr.* **(j'essangeai(s); n. essangeons)** to soak (soiled linen before boiling).

essanvage [esɑ̃vaːʒ], *s.m. Agr:* destruction of wild mustard, charlock.

essanveuse [esɑ̃vøːz], *s.f.* machine used to destroy wild mustard, etc.

essarder [esarde], *v.tr. Nau:* to swab (deck).

essart [esaːr], *s.m.* **1.** *Agr:* freshly cleared ground; *Jur:* assart. **2.** rock pool uncovered at low tide.

essartage [esartaːʒ], *s.m.,* **essartement** [esartəmɑ̃], *s.m. Agr:* grubbing; clearing of the ground; *Jur:* assart; *For:* **essartement de protection,** safety belt (against fire); firebreak.

essarter [esarte], *v.tr. Husb:* to grub up (trees, roots); to clear (ground); *Jur:* to assart (land); **machine à e.,** grubber.

essarteur [esartœːr], *s.m.* person who cleans land for cultivation.

essartis [esarti], *s.m.* land cleared for cultivation.

essaugue [esoːg], *s.f. Fish:* purse seine.

essaule [ɛsol], **essaune** [ɛson], *s.f. Const:* shingle board.

essaver [esave], *v.tr. Agr:* **1.** to bail out (water from ditch). **2.** to bail (ditch) dry.

essayage [esejaːʒ], *s.m.* **1.** testing, trying (of machine, etc.). **2.** trying on, fitting (of clothes); **salon d'e.,** fitting-room, trying-on room; **cabine d'e.,** trying-on cubicle; **e. à demeure,** final fitting. **3.** *Metall:* assaying (of ore).

essayer [eseje], *v.tr.* **(j'essaie, j'essaye; n. essayons; j'essaierai, j'essayerai)** **1.** *(a)* to test, try (machine, horse, etc.); to try (new remedy, etc.); to taste (wines); *(b)* to try on (garment, etc.); *(c) Metall:* to assay (ore); *(d)* **e. de qch.,** to try, taste, (wine, dish, etc.); **essayons-en,** let us try it, let us see what it tastes like; *(e) v.ind.tr. A:* **quand il refusa, elle essaya d'un sourire,** when

he refused, she tried giving a smile. **2. e. de faire qch.,** to try, attempt, endeavour, to do sth.; to have a try, a shot, a go, at doing sth.; **on n'essayera pas de . . .,** no attempt will be made to . . .; **essayez de l'attraper,** try and catch him; **laissez-moi e.,** let me have a try; **j'eus beau e. . . .,** in spite of all my attempts, of all my endeavours . . ..

s'essayer à, dans, qch., à faire qch., to try one's hand, one's skill, at sth., at doing sth.

essayeur, -euse [esejœːr, -øːz], *s.* **1.** *Ind:* assayer (of metals); analyst, tester; *Adm:* assay master. **2.** *Tail: etc:* fitter; trier-on.

essayiste [esejist], *s.m. & f. Lit:* essayist.

esse [ɛs], *s.f.* **1.** (the letter) s. **2.** *Tchn:* (*a*) S-shaped hook, pin or link; S-hook, snake-fastener; (*b*) *Veh:* linchpin; (*c*) bend (in road). **3.** wire gauge. **4.** sound hole, *f*-hole (of violin).

esseimer [esime], *v.tr. Ven:* to make (hawk, etc.) thin (for quicker flight).

esséminer [esemine], *v.tr. A:* to scatter (seeds, etc.).

essemiller [esmije], *v.tr. Const:* to spall, scabble.

essence [esɑ̃ːs], *s.f.* **1.** *Phil: Theol:* essential being; essence. **2.** (*a*) (essential) oil (of lemons, cloves, etc.); attar (of roses); **e. de térébenthine,** oil of turpentine; (*b*) motor spirit, petrol, *U.S:* gasoline; **e. (ordinaire),** regular grade petrol; **e. super,** premium grade petrol; **e. (pour) avion,** aviation spirit, aircraft fuel; **e. adoucie, e. désulfurisée,** sweet petrol; **e. antidétonnante,** anti-knock petrol; **e. très volatile, e. non stabilisée,** wild petrol; **e. de premier jet,** straight run petrol; **faire de l'e.,** to fill up (with petrol); **poste d'e.,** petrol-pump; filling-station; (*c*) (concentrated) essence, extract (of beef, etc.). **3.** (*a*) nature, spirit, natural quality; **l'e. de l'affaire,** the pith, gist, essence, of the matter; **par e.,** by nature, essentially; (*b*) *For:* species, variety (of tree); **essences résineuses,** resinous trees, conifers.

Essénien [ɛs(s)enjɛ̃], *s.m. B.Lit:* Essene.

essénisme [ɛs(s)enism], *s.m. B.Lit:* Essenism.

essente [esɑ̃ːt], *s.f. Const:* (roofing) shingle.

essenter [esɑ̃te], *v.tr. Const:* to shingle (roof).

essentialité [esɑ̃sjalite], *s.f.* essentiality.

essentiel, -ielle [esɑ̃sjɛl]. **1.** *a.* (*a*) essential (truth, character, oil, etc.); **maladie essentielle,** idiopathic disease; **atteint dans les organes essentiels,** hit in the vital organs; **c'en est une partie essentielle,** that is an essential part of it; (*b*) *A:* **un ami e.,** a friend on whom one can count. **2.** *s.m.* **l'e.,** the great thing, the main point; **l'e. était de ne pas le perdre de vue,** the main thing, the essential, was not to lose sight of him; **il possède l'e. de cette matière,** he has the root of the matter in him.

essentiellement [esɑ̃sjɛlmɑ̃], *adv.* (*a*) essentially, fundamentally; (*b*) primarily.

esser [ese], *v.tr. Metalw:* to gauge (wire).

esseret [ɛsrɛ], *s.m. Tls: Carp:* long borer.

esserter [esɛrte], *v.tr. For:* to lop, prune, trim (trees).

essette [ɛsɛt], *s.f. Tls:* (cooper's) adze.

esseulé [esœle], *a.* solitary, lonely (person).

esseulement [esœlmɑ̃], *s.m.* isolation, solitude.

esseuler (s') [sesœle], *v.pr.* to keep oneself apart; to lead a solitary life.

essévé [eseve], *a.* (*a*) *A: & Dial:* **lait e.,** skim(med) milk; (*b*) *Carp: etc:* **bois e.,** bled timber.

Essi [esi], *s.m. F:* = **S.I. (Syndicat d'Initiative),** tourist information centre.

essieu, -ieux [esjø, ɛ-], *s.m.* axle(-tree) (of wheel); pin (of pulley block); **e. moteur,** driving-axle; **e. porteur,** carrying axle; **e. fixe,** dead, fixed, axle; **e. tournant,** live axle; **e. flottant,** floating axle; **e. libre,** free axle; **e. coudé,** crank axle, bent axle; **e. surbaissé,** drop axle; **e. chappé,** forked axle; **e. avant,** front axle; **fusée d'e.,** axle journal; **courbure d'e.,** axle drop; **flasque d'e.,** axle flange; **carter d'e.,** axle housing; *Rail:* **e. bissel,** poney-truck axle (of locomotive).

essimer [esime], *v.tr. Ven:* to make (hawk, etc.) thin (for quicker flight).

essimplage [esɛ̃plaːʒ], *s.m. Hort:* culling (of flower seedlings).

essimpler [esɛ̃ple], *v.tr. Hort:* to cull (flower seedlings).

essonite [esɔnit], *s.f. Miner:* essonite.

essor [esɔːr], *s.m.* flight, soaring, launch (of bird); **donner l'e. à un oiseau,** to let a bird fly away, to release a bird; **donner libre e. à son génie,** to give full play, full scope, to one's genius; **prendre son e.,** (i) (*of bird*) to take wing, to soar; (ii) to spring into life, into vigorous action; **e. d'une industrie,** rise of an industry; **industrie qui a pris un grand e., industrie en plein e.,** industry that has made great strides, industry making rapid strides; **prendre un e. prodigieux,** to advance, progress, by leaps and bounds; **période d'e.,** boom.

essorage [esɔraːʒ], *s.m.* (*a*) drying (of herbs, etc.); wringing (of linen); **e. (par centrifugation),** (spin) drying (of clothes in a washing machine); (*b*) *Phot:* wiping, blotting off (of negative).

essorant [esɔrɑ̃], *a. Her:* soarant.

essorer¹ [esɔre], *v.tr.* to dry (herbs, etc.); to wring (linen) dry, to spin dry (clothes); *Phot:* to wipe, blot off (negative); **e. un pinceau,** to squeeze out the excess of colour in a brush; **e. un terrain,** to drain a piece of ground.

essorer² (s') [sesɔre], *v.pr.* (*of bird*) to soar, take flight.

essoreuse [esɔrøːz], *s.f.* **1. e. (centrifuge),** (i) *Ind:* drying machine, centrifugal drier; (ii) *Dom.Ec:* spin drier; **e. à tambour horizontal (à mouvement alterné),** tumbler drier. **2. e. (à rouleaux),** wringer; mangle.

essorillement [esɔrijmɑ̃], *s.m.* cropping (of dog's ears).

essoriller [esɔrije], *v.tr.* (*a*) to crop the ears of (dog, horse); (*b*) *F:* to give (s.o.) a close crop.

essouchage [esuʃaːʒ], *s.m.,* **essouchement** [esuʃmɑ̃], *s.m.* stubbing up, grubbing up (of tree stumps).

essoucher [esuʃe], *v.tr.* to stub up, grub up, the stumps of trees from (land); to stump.

essoucheur [esuʃœːr], *s.m.* stump pulling machine, stump puller.

essoufflé [esufle], *a.* out of breath, short of breath, winded; *F:* puffed; **voix essoufflée,** breathless voice; **respiration essoufflée,** shortness of breath, breathlessness; **essoufflé d'avoir couru,** breathless with running.

essoufflement [esufləmɑ̃], *s.m.* shortness of breath, breathlessness, panting; *F:* puffing.

essouffler [esufle], *v.tr.* to blow, wind (horse, man); **la montée l'avait essoufflé,** he was out of breath after the climb.

s'essouffler, to get out of breath, to get winded, *F:* puffed; **s'e. à traîner qch.,** to get out of breath dragging sth.; **s'e. à force de parler,** to talk oneself out of breath.

essuie-glace [esɥiglas], *s.m. Aut:* windscreen, *U.S:* windshield, wiper; **e.-g. à retour automatique,** self-parking windscreen wiper; *pl. essuie-glaces.*

essuie-main(s) [esɥimɛ̃], *s.m.inv.* (hand)towel; **e.-m. à rouleau,** roller-towel; **e.-m. automatique,** automatic roller-towel; **e.-m. pour la cuisine,** kitchen towel.

essuie-meubles [esɥimœbl], *s.m.inv.* duster.

essuie-pieds [esɥipje], *s.m.inv.* doormat; **e.-p. métallique,** wire mat.

essuie-plume(s) [esɥiplym], *s.m.inv.* penwiper.

essuie-rasoir [esɥirazwaːr], *s.m.* razor-wipe; *pl. essuie-rasoir(s).*

essuie-verres [esɥivɛːr], *s.m.inv.* glass cloth; tea towel.

essuyage [esɥijaːʒ], *s.m.* wiping (of dishes, etc.); wiping up, mopping up (of water, etc.).

essuyer [esɥije], *v.tr.* **(j'essuie, n. essuyons; j'essuierai) 1.** to wipe, dry, (dishes, etc.); to wipe (sth.) clean; to wipe up, mop up (water, etc.); **e. la vaisselle,** to wipe up; **s'e. les mains,** to wipe, dry, one's hands; **e. la sueur de son front,** to mop one's brow; **e. les larmes de, à, qn,** to wipe away s.o.'s tears; to console s.o.; **e. furtivement une larme,** to brush away a tear; **le vent essuie les routes,** the wind is drying (up) the roads; *F:* **e. les plâtres,** (i) to be the first occupant of a newly-built house; (ii) to get a job going. **2.** to suffer, endure, be subjected to (defeat, insults, etc.); **e. un refus,** to meet with a refusal; **e. une perte,** to suffer a loss; **e. le feu de l'ennemi,** to come under the fire of the enemy, under enemy fire; **e. un coup de feu,** to be shot at; *Nau:* **e. un coup de vent,** (i) to meet with a gale, to encounter a gale; (ii) to weather (out) a gale; **e. l'orage,** to bear the brunt of the storm.

essuyeur, -euse [esɥijœːr, -øːz]. **1.** *s.* wiper (of dishes, etc.). **2.** *s.m. Tex. (printing):* ductor, doctor.

est [ɛst]. **1.** *s.m. no pl.* east; **résider dans l'e.,** to live in the east (of a country); **un vent (d')e.,** an easterly wind; **le vent d'e.,** the east wind; **à l'e. de Suez,** (to the) east of Suez; eastward of Suez; **vers l'e.,** eastward, towards the east; **borné à l'e. par . . .,** bounded on the east by . . .; *Nau:* **faire de l'e.,** to get easterly; **chemin est,** easting; **e. quart nord-e.,** east by north; **e. quart sud-e.,** east by south. **2.** *a.inv.* **côté e.,** eastern, east, side; **les régions e. de la France,** the eastern parts of France.

estacade [ɛstakad], *s.f.* **1.** line of stakes, piles, barricade of piles; (*a*) *Fort:* stockade; (*b*) *Nau:* (i) breakwater; (ii) pier (on piles); pier (at seaside resort); (*c*) *Rail: etc:* elevated runway; coal tip. **2. e. flottante,** (harbour) boom.

estafette [ɛstafɛt], *s.f.* (*a*) *A:* estafette, courier; *Mil:* mounted orderly; (*b*) *Mil:* liaison officer; dispatch rider; (*c*) *Rail:* **locomotive e.,** pilot-engine.

estafier [ɛstafje], *s.m. A:* **1.** (armed) attendant. **2.** (*a*) bully; (*b*) pimp.

estafilade [ɛstafilad], *s.f.* (*a*) gash in the face (from razor, sword, etc.); (*b*) slash (in clothing).

Est-africain allemand, anglais [ɛstafrikɛ̃almɑ̃, -ɑ̃glɛ], *Pr.n.m. Hist:* German, British, East Africa.

estagnon [ɛstaɲɔ̃], *s.m.* drum, container (made of copper or tin for export of oils, etc.); oil-can.

estain [ɛstɛ̃], *s.m. A: N.Arch:* fashion piece.

est-allemand, -ande [ɛstalmɑ̃, -ɑ̃ːd], *a. & s. Geog:* East German.

estame [ɛstam], *s.f. Tex:* worsted.

estaminet [ɛstaminɛ], *s.m.* **1.** (*in N. of Fr.*): (small) public house; *F:* pub. **2.** bar (in hotel, public house); coffee room.

estampage [ɛstɑ̃paːʒ], *s.m.* **1.** (*a*) stamping, embossing (of silver, leather, etc.); impressing (of pattern on clay, etc.); *Arch:* squeeze; (*b*) *A:* branding (of criminals); (*c*) *Phot:* **e. des épreuves,** plate marking. **2.** *Metalw:* (*a*) stamping, punching; (*b*) drop forging. **3.** *F:* (*a*) swindling, fleecing; (*b*) swindle.

estampe [ɛstɑ̃ːp], *s.f.* **1.** *Tls:* punch. **2.** print, engraving; **e. sur bois,** woodcut; **e. sur acier,** steel engraving; **cabinet des estampes,** print-room (of a library).

estamper [ɛstɑ̃pe], *v.tr.* **1.** (*a*) to stamp, emboss (silver, coin, leather, etc.); to impress (pattern on clay, etc.); (*b*) *A:* to brand (criminal). **2.** to stamp (sheet metal, etc.); to punch; *Metalw:* **pièce estampée,** punched piece; **3.** *F:* to swindle; to fleece (s.o.); to rush (s.o.); **se faire e.,** to be done, to be skinned.

estampeur, -euse [ɛstɑ̃pœːr, -øːz], *s.* **1.** stamper, embosser. **2.** *F:* swindler. **3.** *s.f.* **estampeuse,** stamping machine, stamper.

estampillage [ɛstɑ̃pijaːʒ], *s.m.* stamping, marking, sealing (of goods, inventions, etc.).

estampille [ɛstɑ̃piːj], *s.f.* (official) stamp; identification mark; brand; *Com:* trademark.

estampiller [ɛstɑ̃pije], *v.tr.* to stamp (weights, document, etc.); to mark (goods); to brand; to hall-mark (gold, silver).

estampilleuse [ɛstɑ̃pijøːz], *s.f. Leath: etc:* stamping machine.

estampoir [ɛstɑ̃pwaːr], *s.m. Tchn:* = ESTAMPE.

estampure [ɛstɑ̃pyːr], *s.f.* mouth, splay (of hole in metal plate); nail hole (of horseshoe).

Est-Anglie [ɛstɑ̃gli], *Pr.n.f. Geog:* East Anglia.

estant [ɛstɑ̃], *a. For:* (tree) set aside from felling.

estarie [ɛstari], *s.f. Nau:* **(jours d')e.,** lay days.

estau, -aux [ɛsto], *s.m. Min:* arch (in mine).

est-ce que [ɛskə]. *See* CE¹ 1 (i).

este [ɛst]. **1.** *a. & s. Geog:* Estonian. **2.** *s.m. Ling:* Estonian.

Estelle [ɛstɛl], *Pr.n.f.* Estelle, Stella.

ester¹ [ɛste], *v.i. A:* to stand; *still used in Jur:* **e. en justice,** to go to law, to sue in a civil action; **e. en jugement,** to appear in court, to plead.

ester² [ɛstɛːr], *s.m. Ch:* ester.

estérification [ɛsterifikasjɔ̃], *s.f. Ch:* esterification.

estérifier [ɛsterifje], *v.tr. Ch:* to esterify.

esteuble [ɛstœbl], **esteule** [ɛstœl], *s.f. Agr:* stubble.

Esther [ɛstɛːr], *Pr.n.f.* Esther, Hester.

estheria [ɛsterja], **esthérie** [ɛsteri], *s.f. Crust:* estherian; (*genus*) Estheria.

esthésie [ɛstezi], *s.f.* (a)esthesia.

esthésiogène [ɛstezjɔʒɛn], *a.* (a)esthesiogenic.

esthésiologie [ɛstezjɔlɔʒi], *s.f.* (a)esthesiology.

esthésiomètre [ɛstezjɔmɛtr], *s.m.* (a)esthesiometer.

esthète [ɛstɛt], *s.m. & f.* aesthete.

esthéticien, -ienne [ɛstetisjɛ̃, -jɛn], *s.* **1.** aesthetician. **2.** beauty specialist, beautician.

esthéticisme [ɛstetisism], *s.m.* aestheticism.

esthétique [ɛstetik]. **1.** *a.* aesthetic; **chirurgie e.,** plastic surgery (for aesthetic purposes). **2.** *s.f.* aesthetics.

esthétiquement [ɛstetikmɑ̃], *adv.* aesthetically.

esthétisme [ɛstetism], *s.m.* aestheticism.

esthiomène [ɛstjɔmɛn], *s.m. Med:* esthiomene.

Esthonie [ɛstɔni], *Pr.n.f. A.Geog:* Estonia.

estimable [ɛstimabl], *a.* **1.** estimable. **2.** fairly good, respectable (work, etc.); of reasonable competence.

estimateur, -trice [ɛstimatœːr, -tris], *s.* **1.** estimator; *Com:* appraiser, valuer. **2.** appreciator, esteemer (of merit, etc.).

estimatif, -ive [ɛstimatif, -iːv], *a.* **1.** estimative (faculty, etc.). **2.** estimated (cost, etc.); **devis e.,** estimate.

estimation [ɛstimasjɔ̃], *s.f.* **1.** (*a*) estimation (of the value, price, of sth.); valuing, appraising (of goods, etc.); assessment (of damage); (*b*) estimate, valuation. **2.** *Nau:* (= ESTIME 1) reckoning.

estimatoire [ɛstimatwaːr], *a.* estimatory.

estime [ɛstim], *s.f.* **1.** guesswork; *Nau:* reckoning; **calculateur d'e.,** dead-reckoning computer; **être en avant de son e.,** to be ahead of one's reckoning; *adv.phr.* **à l'e.,** by guesswork; *Nau:* by dead reckoning; **navigation à l'e.,** dead-reckoning (navigation). **2.** (*a*) estimation, opinion; (*b*) esteem, regard; **témoigner de l'e. pour qn,** to show regard for s.o.; **professer une grande e. pour qn,** to profess great esteem, a high regard, for s.o.; **tenir qn en grande, en médiocre, e.,** to think highly, little, of s.o.; **tenir qn, qch., en haute e.,** to have a high regard for s.o., sth.; **être tenu en grande e.,** to be held in high esteem; **être perdu d'e.,** to have lost all respect; **baisser dans l'e. de qn,** to fall in s.o.'s good opinion; **il a monté dans mon e.,** he has risen in my estimation; *s.a.* SUCCÈS 2.

estimé [ɛstime], *a.* **1.** esteemed. **2.** *Nau:* **longitude estimée,** estimated longitude, longitude (calculated) by dead reckoning.

estimée [ɛstime], *s.f. Com:* **votre e.,** your esteemed letter, your favour.

estimer [ɛstime], *v.tr.* **1.** (*a*) to estimate; to value, appraise (goods); to assess (damage); **e. la gloire à sa valeur,** to rate glory at its true value; **des soldats estimés à 200 ont été tués,** an estimated 200 soldiers were killed, it is estimated that 200 soldiers were killed; (*b*) to calculate (distance, etc.); *Nau:* to reckon. **2.** (*a*) to consider; to be of (the) opinion (that); *pred:* **on l'estime sage,** he is considered wise; **s'e. heureux,** to think oneself lucky, to account oneself lucky; **j'estime être aussi renseigné que vous,** I consider I know as much as you; **j'estime qu'il est de mon devoir de . . .,** I consider it my duty to . . .; (*b*) to esteem (s.o.); to have a high opinion of (s.o., sth.); to rate (s.o., sth.) highly; to prize, value (sth.).

estivage[1] [ɛstivaːʒ], *s.m.* **1.** summering (of cattle) in mountain pastures. **2.** spending of the summer (at a resort).

estivage[2], *s.m. Nau:* estivage, steeving (of cargo).

estival, -aux [ɛstival, -o]. **1.** *a.* (a)estival (plant, illness, etc.); **résidence estivale,** summer residence; **station estivale,** summer resort. **2.** *s.m.pl.* **estivaux,** yearling trout used for restocking waters.

estivant, -ante [ɛstivɑ̃, -ɑ̃ːt], *s.* summer visitor; (summer) holiday-maker; summer resident.

estivation [ɛstivasjɔ̃], *s.f.* (a)estivation. **1.** *Z:* (summer) dormancy, torpor (of snakes, etc.). **2.** *Bot:* prefloration.

estive[1] [ɛstiːv], *s.f.* **1.** (*in Pyrenees*) mountain pasture. **2.** (*in edible oil mill*) storage room.

estive[2], *s.f. Nau:* (*a*) stowage; (*b*) compression of cargo into small space; steeving, estivage.

estiver[1] [ɛstive]. **1.** *v.tr.* to move (cattle, etc.) to summer pastures. **2.** *v.i.* (*a*) (*of cattle*) to spend the summer in mountain pastures; (*b*) (*of pers.*) to spend the summer at a resort.

estiver[2], *v.tr. Nau:* to pack, press, (cargo) into small compass; to steeve (cargo).

estiveur [ɛstivœːr], *s.m.* = ESTIVANT.

est-nord-est [ɛstnɔrɛst], *s.m. Nau:* east-north-east.

estoc [ɛstɔk], *s.m.* **1.** stock, trunk (of tree); **couper un arbre à blanc e.,** to cut a tree off at the roots; **être de bon e.,** to be of good stock, of good lineage. **2.** (*a*) *A.Arms:* tuck (short sword); rapier, thrusting weapon; (*b*) *Fenc:* **coup d'e.,** (rapier) thrust; **frapper d'e. et de taille,** (i) to cut and thrust; (ii) to thrash around wildly; **parler d'e. et de taille,** to talk wildly. **3.** rock (uncovered at low tide).

estocade [ɛstɔkad], *s.f.* **1.** (*a*) stab wound; (*b*) *Fenc:* thrust; (*c*) (*in bullfighting*) estocada. **2.** *A.Arms:* tuck (short sword); rapier. **3.** sudden and violent attack.

estomac [ɛstɔma], *s.m.* **1.** (*a*) stomach; **creux de l'e.,** pit of the stomach; **le mal d'e.,** stomach ache; **avoir mal à l'e.,** to have stomach ache; **avoir un bon, un mauvais, e.,** to have good, bad, digestion; **avoir un e. d'autruche,** to have a cast-iron digestion; **avoir petit e.,** to have a small appetite; **avoir l'e. dans les talons,** to be ravenously hungry, to feel faint with hunger; **aliment qui reste sur l'e.,** food that is difficult to digest, indigestible food; **cet échec lui est resté sur l'e.,** he couldn't stand, stomach, this setback; **avoir de l'e.,** (i) to have plenty of pluck; (ii) to have plenty of cheek; (iii) to stand heavy losses without wincing, to be always game; (iv) to be strong financially, to have strong reserves; (*of firm*) to be solid; *F:* **le faire à l'e.,** to bluff, to put it over on s.o.; (*b*) (i) *A:* bosom; (ii) *V:* **estomacs,** bubs; (*c*) *A.Cost:* **pièce d'e.,** stomacher. **2.** (*a*) web, body (of anvil); (*b*) breast plate (of drill, etc.).

estomaquer [ɛstɔmake], *v.tr. F:* **e. qn,** to take s.o.'s breath away; to stagger, astound, flabbergast, s.o.

estompage [ɛstɔ̃paːʒ], *s.m.* shading (off).

estompe [ɛstɔ̃ːp], *s.f. Art:* (*a*) stump; (*b*) **(dessin à l')e.,** stump drawing.

estompé [ɛstɔ̃pe], *a.* soft, indistinct, blurred (outline); **souvenirs estompés,** blurred, dim, memories.

estompement [ɛstɔ̃pmɑ̃], *s.m.* shading (off).

estomper [ɛstɔ̃pe], *v.tr. Art:* to stump; to soften off, shade off, (drawing) with a stump; **la brume estompe les lointains,** the haze makes the distant landscape indistinct, blurs the landscape; **e. des détails trop crus,** to tone down crude details.

s'estomper, to grow blurred, indistinct; to loom up vaguely.

Estonie [ɛstɔni], *Pr.n.f. Geog:* Estonia.

estonien, -ienne [ɛstɔnjɛ̃, -jɛn]. **1.** *a. & s. Geog:* Estonian. **2.** *s.m. Ling:* Estonian.

estoquer [ɛstɔke], *v.tr.* to lunge, thrust, at (bull, etc.).

estoublage [ɛstublaːʒ], *s.m. coll. Agr:* freshly cut straw.

estouffade [ɛstufad], *s.f. Cu:* (dish of) braised meat.

estouffée [ɛstufe], *s.f. Min:* dam (for fire).

estourbir [ɛsturbiːr], *v.tr. P:* to kill (s.o.); to do (s.o.) in.

estrade[1] [ɛstrad], *s.f. A:* road; *still used in* **battre l'e.,** (i) *Mil:* (of cavalry) to scout, raid, reconnoitre; (ii) *F:* to roam about; (iii) to be on the tramp; (iv) (*of highwayman*) to be on the look-out for travellers; **batteur d'e.,** (i) *Mil:* scout; (ii) tramp, vagabond; (iii) footpad, highwayman.

estrade[2], *s.f.* dais; rostrum; platform, stage.

estradiot [ɛstradjo], *s.m. A.Mil:* stradiot.

estragale [ɛstragal], *s.f. Tls:* turning chisel.

estragol(e) [ɛstragɔl], *s.m. Ch:* estragol(e).

estragon [ɛstragɔ̃], *s.m. Bot: Cu:* tarragon.

estran(d) [ɛstrɑ̃], *s.m.* strand, foreshore.

estrapade [ɛstrapad], *s.f.* **1.** *A:* (*a*) strappado (punishment); (*b*) *Nau:* dipping from the yard-arm. **2.** *Equit:* buck jump (of horse). **3.** *Gym:* skinning the cat; **faire l'e.,** to skin the cat. **4.** *Clockm:* mainspring winder.

estrapader [ɛstrapade], *v.tr. A:* (*a*) to punish (s.o.) with the strappado; (*b*) to dip (sailor) from the yard-arm.

estrapasser [ɛstrapase], *v.tr. Equit:* to tire (horse) with prolonged violent exercise.

Estrémadure [ɛstremadyːr], *Pr.n.f. Geog:* Estremadura.

estrope [ɛstrɔp], *s.f. Nau:* strop, strap, grommet (of pulley block, toggle pin, etc.); **poulie à e.,** stropped block.

estroper [ɛstrɔpe], *v.tr. Nau:* to strop (rigging, block, etc.).

estropié, -ée [ɛstrɔpje]. **1.** *a.* crippled, disabled, maimed; **être e. du pied,** to have a crippled foot; **être e. de la jambe, du bras,** to have a lame, game, leg, a game arm. **2.** *s.* **les estropiés,** the maimed.

estropiement [ɛstrɔpimɑ̃], *s.m.* (*a*) crippling, laming, maiming; (*b*) murdering (of piece of music, etc.); misquoting (of author); spelling or pronouncing (word) incorrectly.

estropier [ɛstrɔpje], *v.tr.* (*p.d. & pr.sub.* **n. estropiions, v. estropiiez**) (*a*) to cripple, lame, disable, maim; (*b*) **e. une valse, le français,** to murder a waltz, French; **e. un mot,** to mispronounce a word; **e. une citation,** to misquote a writer; **mots dont on estropie l'orthographe,** words which are mis-spelt, spelt wrongly.

estrouif [ɛstrwif], *s.m. Nau:* thole(pin).

est-sud-est [ɛstsydɛst], *s.m. Nau:* east-south-east.

estuaire [ɛstɥɛːr], *s.m.* estuary.

estudiantin, -ine [ɛstydjɑ̃tɛ̃, -in], *a.* **la vie estudiantine,** student life.

esturgeon [ɛstyrʒɔ̃], *s.m. Ich:* sturgeon.

et [e]. **1.** *conj.* and; **Pierre et Jean,** Peter and John; **il va et vient,** he comes and goes; **j'ai écrit et écrit,** I have written and written; **c'est un homme de grande énergie, et qui arrivera,** he is a man of great energy, who will succeed; **et son frère et sa sœur,** both his brother and his sister; **j'aime le café; et vous?** I like coffee; do you? **je n'aime pas le thé; et vous?** I don't like tea; do you? *F:* **et les dix francs que je vous ai prêtés?** and (what about) the ten francs I lent you? (NOTE: *there is no liaison with* **et**; **Pierre et André** [pjɛːreɑ̃dre]; **j'ai écrit et écrit** [ʒeekrieekri]). **2.** *s.m.* (*a*) *Typ:* **et commercial,** ampersand; (*b*) *Elcs:* (*Boolean operator*) and.

êta [ɛta], *s.m. Gr.Alph:* eta.

établage [etablaːʒ], *s.m.* stalling (of cattle); stabling (of horses).

étable [etabl], *s.f.* cowshed, cattle shed, byre; **é. à pourceaux,** pigsty.

établer [etable], *v.tr. A: & Dial:* to stall (cattle); to stable (horses).

établi[1] [etabli], *s.m.* (work)bench.

établi[2] *a.* established; **réputation (bien) établie,** well-established reputation; **fait é.,** established fact; **l'ordre é.,** the established order; **usages établis,** established, accepted, customs; **sa fille est établie,** his daughter is married, settled in life; *Nau:* **brise établie,** settled wind; **temps é.,** steady weather; settled weather.

établir [etabliːr]. I. *v.tr.* **1.** (*a*) to establish (form of government, business house, peace, fact, relations (with s.o.)); to set up (statue, agency); to put up (building, etc.); to construct (dam, railway); to settle, fix (one's place of residence); to install, fix up (machinery, etc.); to set (a sail); to erect (beacon, etc.); **é. un camp,** to pitch a camp; *Mil:* **é. des emplacements de mitrailleuses,** to site machine-gun emplacements; **é. une facture,** to make out an invoice; **é. un prix,** to quote, fix, a price; **é. son crédit,** to establish, secure, one's credit; **é. un record,** to set up a record; **balcon établi autour de la maison,** balcony set round the house; **route solidement établie,** well-laid road; (*b*) **é. l'innocence de qn,** to establish, prove, s.o.'s innocence; **é. une accusation,** to establish, substantiate, a charge; to make out a case. **2.** (*a*) to work out (plan, proposition, etc.); to draw up (plan); **considérer qch. comme chose établie,** to take sth. for granted; **reliure établie par . . .,** binding designed by . . .; *Com:* **é. un compte, un bilan, un budget,** to draw up, make up, an account, a balance sheet; to draw up a budget; **é. une balance,** to strike a balance; **établi d'après les statistiques,** compiled from statistics; (*b*) **é. des bois, des pierres,** to mark timber for sawing, stone for cutting. **3.** to institute, create (tax, tribunal, etc.); to prescribe, lay down (rule); to lay down (principle); to found (colony, factory, etc.). **4.** to set (s.o.) up in business.

II. **établir,** *v.i. Nau:* (*of sail*) to set, fit (well, badly).

s'établir. **1.** to establish oneself, to take up one's residence (in a place). **2.** **s'é. épicier,** to set up as a grocer; **il est établi à son compte,** he is in business on his own account. **3.** (*of custom, etc.*) to become established; *Nau:* (*of wind*) to settle (in a quarter).

établissement [etablismɑ̃], *s.m.* establishment. **1.** (*a*) setting up, putting up, fixing, installing (of machinery, etc.); setting (of a sail); establishing, building up (of reputation, fortune, etc.); (*b*) establishment, proving (of innocence, guilt). **2.** (*a*) working out (of design, etc.); drawing up, making up (of accounts, schedule, etc.); striking (of balance); (*b*) marking (of timber) for sawing, (of stone) for cutting. **3.** instituting, creating, forming (of government, etc.); laying down (of rules); founding (of colony, industry). **4.** (*a*) establishment, settlement, settling (of one's children, etc.); (*b*) establishment, setting up (of a business); *Com:* **frais d'é., coût de premier é.,** promotion money; initial outlay, investment, expenditure; *Ind:* **capital d'é.,** invested capital. **5.** (*a*) institution; **é. de charité,** charitable institution; **é. de crédit,** bank; (*b*) *Hist:* (colonial) trading centre; **é. colonial,** colonial settlement; (*c*) (i) factory; business; **les établissements Renault,** the Renault works; **les établissements Martin,** Martin & Co.; **é. principal,** main branch (of a business); **fermer son é.,** to close (down) one's business; (ii) **é. d'utilité publique,** public utility service; **é. scolaire,** school, educational establishment; (*d*) (business, etc.) premises; **é. public,** public establishment; **les cafés, restaurants et autres établissements publics,** public houses, restaurants and other public establishments. **6.** *Jur:* domicile; place where a person has his principal interests. **7.** *Astr:* establishment (of a port).

étage [eta:ʒ], *s.m.* **1.** storey, *U.S:* story, floor (of building); level (of mine); **maison à un é., sans é.,** single-storeyed house, bungalow; **à deux étages, avec é.,** two-storeyed; **au troisième é.,** on the third floor, three flights up, *U.S:* on the fourth story; *F:* **à l'é.,** upstairs; (*in hotel*) **service d'é.,** room service; *For:* **futaie à double é.,** two-storeyed forest. **2.** (*a*) tier, range, step; **gâteau à quatre étages,** four-tiered cake; *Dressm:* **jupe à deux étages,** two-tiered skirt; *Fort:* **casemate à étages,** tiered casemate; **le jardin descendait d'é. en é. jusqu'à la rivière,** the garden stretched down to the river in a series of terraces; *F:* **menton à deux étages,** double chin; (*b*) (i) *A: & Lit:* degree, rank; **étages de la société,** strata, levels, of society; (ii) inferior, low, third-rate; **gens de bas é.,** people from the lower strata, the dregs of society; (*c*) *Geol:* stage, layer, formation; **l'é. argovien,** the Argovian (division); (*d*) *Mch: etc:* stage; **compression par étages,** compression by stages; **pompe à quatre étages,** four-stage pump; **fusée à trois étages,** three-stage rocket; **turbine à étages,** stage turbine; *W.Tel: etc:* **é. amplificateur,** amplifier stage; **é. basse, haute, fréquence,** audio-, radio-, frequency stage; (*e*) *Mec.E:* step (of cone pulley).

étagement [etaʒmɑ̃], *s.m.* **1.** arrangement in tiers; **é. des vignes sur les côtes,** terracing of vines on the hillsides. **2.** *Mch:* staging (of turbine).

étager [etaʒe], *v.tr.* **(j'étageai(s); n. étageons) 1.** to range (seats, etc.) in tiers; **jardin étagé,** terraced garden; **plateau étagé en terrasses,** plateau rising in steps, forming a succession of terraces; **poulie étagée,** cone-pulley; **é. des rivets,** to stagger rivets. **2.** to perform (operation) by stages; **compression étagée,** compression by stages; **réduction soigneusement étagée des armes nucléaires,** carefully staged reduction of nuclear weapons.

s'étager, to rise in tiers, one above another.

étagère [etaʒɛ:r], *s.f.* (*a*) whatnot; (*b*) rack; (set of) shelves; (*c*) shelf; **é. de cheminée,** overmantel.

étai[1] [etɛ], *s.m. Nau:* **1.** stay; **é. de tangage, faux é.,** preventer stay; **voile d'é.,** staysail; **tenir un espar en é.,** to stay a spar. **2. étais de bigues,** guys of sheers. **3.** bar, stud (of chain link).

étai[2], *s.m. Const:* stay, prop, shore, strut; **é. de mine,** pit prop; **é. de la société,** mainstay of society.

étaiement [etɛmɑ̃], *s.m.* (= ÉTAYAGE) staying, shoring, propping (up); buttressing.

étain[1] [etɛ̃], *s.m.* **1.** (*a*) tin; *Miner:* **é. de roche,** lode tin; **é. en saumons, en blocs,** block tin; **é. pyriteux,** stannite; **é. oxydé,** cassiterite, tin-stone; **é. de bois,** wood tin, toad's eye tin; **é. battu, é. en feuilles,** tinfoil, thin sheet tin; (*b*) **feuille d'é.,** tinfoil, silver paper. **2.** pewter; **vaisselle d'é.,** pewter (plate).

étain[2], *s.m. N.Arch:* fashion piece.

étainier [etɛnje], *s.m. Ind:* (*a*) tin founder; (*b*) manufacturer of (i) pewter ware, (ii) (fancy) tin ware.

étairion [etɛrjɔ̃], *s.m. Bot:* etaerio, aggregate fruit.

étal, -aux, *occ.* **-als** [etal, -o], *s.m.* (*a*) (i) butcher's stall, meat stall; (ii) (small) butcher's shop; (*b*) (market) stall.

étalage [etala:ʒ], *s.m.* **1.** *Com:* (*a*) display, show (of goods, etc.); **é. de bouquiniste,** secondhand bookstall; **droits d'é. (en place de marché, etc.),** stallage; (*b*) window-dressing; **faire l'é.,** (i) to set out one's wares; (ii) to dress the window(s); **mettre qch. à l'é.,** to display sth., to put sth. in the window; **article qui a fait l'é.,** shop-soiled article; *s.a.* VOL[2] 1, VOLEUR[2] 1; (*c*) showing off; **faire é. de ses bijoux, de son savoir,** to show off, make a show of, to display, parade, one's jewels, one's knowledge; **faire é. de ses opinions,** to air one's opinions; **é. d'érudition,** show, parade, of learning. **2.** *pl. Metall:* bosh (of blast-furnace). **3.** *Tex:* roving (of flax).

étalager [etalaʒe], *v.tr.* **(j'étalageai(s); n. étalageons)** to expose, display, (goods) for sale (in shop window, on the counters).

étalagiste [etalaʒist], *s.m. & f. Com:* (*a*) stall keeper, stall holder; pitcher; (*b*) window-dresser.

étale [etal], *Nau:* **1.** *a.* slack (sea, tide); steady (breeze); (ship) without headway. **2.** *s.m.* (*a*) slack (of rope); (*b*) **é. du flot,** slack water (at flood or at ebb of the tide).

étalé [etale] *a. Arb:* **arbre à cime étalée,** large-crowned tree.

étalement [etalmɑ̃], *s.m.* **1.** (*a*) displaying, showing, exposure (of goods, etc.); (*b*) spreading out (of objects to dry, etc.); (*c*) *Cards:* laying down (of one's hand); (*d*) staggering (of holidays). **2.** *F:* flaunting, showing off.

étaler [etale], *v.tr.* **1.** *Nau:* (*a*) to stem (the current); to weather out, ride out (gale); **é. la voie d'eau avec les pompes,** to keep the water under with the pumps; (*b*) **é. l'erre,** to check the way; **étalez!** hold on! **2.** (*a*) *Com:* **é. sa marchandise,** to display one's goods, to expose one's goods for sale; (*b*) to spread out, lay out (linen to dry, etc.); **é. de la graisse sur qch.,** to smear sth. with grease; **é. des papiers sur la table,** to spread out papers on the table, to strew the table with papers; (*c*) *Cards:* to lay down (one's cards); (*d*) to flaunt, display, show off (one's wealth, charms, etc.); to air (one's knowledge); (*e*) to stagger (holidays, payments).

s'étaler. 1. (*a*) to stretch oneself out; to sprawl (in an armchair, etc.); *F:* **s'é. sur un sujet,** to hold forth, to spread oneself, on a topic; **il s'étala par terre,** (i) he lay down full length on the ground; (ii) *F:* he went sprawling on the ground, he came a cropper; (*b*) **le village s'étale dans la vallée,** the village is spread out in the valley. **2.** *F:* to show off.

étaleuse [etalø:z], *s.f. Tex:* spreader.

étalier [etalje], *a. & s.m.* **(garçon) é.,** butcher's assistant.

étalinguer [etalɛ̃ge], *v.tr. Nau:* to bend (cable) to the anchor; to clinch, shackle (cable).

étalingure [etalɛ̃gy:r], *s.f. Nau:* clinch (of cable to anchor); **é. du puits,** inner clinch, bitter end; **maillon d'é.,** (fore)ganger.

étalon[1] [etalɔ̃], *s.m.* stallion, stud horse; **é. rouleur,** travelling sire; **é. d'essai,** teaser.

étalon[2], *s.m.* **1.** standard (of weights, measures, make, value, etc.); **é. du mètre,** standard metre; *Fin:* **l'é. d'or, l'é. or,** the gold standard; **pays à é. d'argent,** silver-standard country; *Mus:* **é. d'un tuyau d'orgue,** scale, size of bore, proportions, of an organ-pipe; *Ph:* **condensateur é.,** calibration condenser; **électromètre é.,** calibrating electrometer; *Nau:* **compas é.,** standard compass; **il n'y a pas d'é. des mœurs,** there is no absolute standard of morality. **2.** *Arch: Carp:* layout of the plan (of timber work, etc.).

étalonnage [etalɔna:ʒ], **étalonnement** [etalɔnmɑ̃], *s.m.* **1.** standardization (of weights, etc.); calibration (of tubes, etc.); testing, gauging (of instruments); rating (of light); *Phot:* grading (of negatives); *W.Tel:* logging (of stations); **tableau d'é.,** table of dial readings. **2.** stamping, marking (of standardized weights, etc.).

étalonné [etalɔne], *a. Psy:* **test é.,** standard, standardized, test.

étalonner[1] [etalɔne], *v.tr.* (*of stallion*) to serve.

étalonner[2], *v.tr.* **1.** to standardize (weights, etc.); to calibrate (tubes, etc.); to test, gauge, adjust (instruments); to rate (light); *Psy:* to standardize (test); *Phot:* to grade (negatives); *W.Tel:* **é. les stations,** to log the stations. **2.** to stamp, mark (standardized weights, etc.).

étalonnerie [etalɔnri], *s.f. Breed:* stud stable.

étalonnier [etalɔnje], *s.m. Breed:* stud farmer.

étamage [etama:ʒ], *s.m.* **1.** *Metalw:* tinning (of copper, etc.); tinning, tin-plating (of sheet iron). **2.** (*a*) **é. au zinc,** galvanizing, zinc(k)ing; (*b*) silvering (of glass).

étambot [etɑ̃bo], *s.m. Nau:* stern post; **é. arrière,** rudder-post; **é. avant,** propeller-post; **faux é.,** inner, false, stern post; **courbe d'é.,** heel knee; **de l'étrave à l'é.,** from stem to stern.

étambrai [etɑ̃brɛ], *s.m. Nau:* **1.** mast hole (in deck). **2.** partners (of capstan, bowsprit, etc.).

étamer [etame], *v.tr. Metalw:* **1.** to tin (copper, etc.); to tinplate (iron). **2.** (*a*) *A:* to galvanize, zinc, whiten (metals); (*b*) to silver (mirror).

étamerie [etamri], *s.f.* **1.** tinsmithing. **2.** tinsmith's shop, works.

étameur [etamœ:r], *s.m.* **1.** (*a*) tinner, tinsmith; (*b*) **é. ambulant,** tinker. **2.** silverer (of mirrors).

étamine[1] [etamin], *s.f.* **1.** (*a*) coarse muslin, bolting cloth, tammy-cloth; butter muslin, cheese cloth; **é. de crin,** haircloth; (*b*) **é. à pavillon,** bunting. **2.** sieve, strainer; **passer qch. à, par, l'é.,** (i) to sift, bolt, sth.; (ii) *F:* to sift, examine closely (evidence, etc.).

étamine[2], *s.f. Bot:* stamen.

étampage [etɑ̃pa:ʒ], *s.m.* **1.** *Metalw: etc:* stamping, punching. **2.** *Metalw:* (*a*) swaging; (*b*) drop forging.

étampe [etɑ̃:p], *s.f.* **1.** stamp, die. **2.** *Tls:* (*a*) punch; (*b*) swage; **é. supérieure,** swage hammer.

étamper [etɑ̃pe], *v.tr.* **1.** *Metalw: etc:* to stamp (sheet metal, etc.); to punch (horseshoe, etc.); **é. à chaud, à froid,** to hot stamp, cold stamp. **2.** *Metalw:* (*a*) to swage; (*b*) to drop forge; **pièce étampée,** drop forging.

étamperche [etɑ̃pɛrʃ], *s.f. Const:* **1.** upright pole, standard (of scaffolding). **2.** derrick.

étampeur, -euse [etɑ̃pœ:r, -ø:z] **1.** *s.m.* stamper. **2.** *s.f.* **étampeuse,** stamping machine; stamp.

étampois, -oise [etɑ̃pwa, -wa:z], *a. & s.* (native, inhabitant) of Étampes.

étampure [etɑ̃py:r], *s.f.* mouth, splay (of hole in metal plate); nail hole (of horseshoe).

étamure [etamy:r], *s.f. Metalw:* **1.** coating of tin. **2.** tinning metal.

étance [etɑ̃:s], *s.f.* **1.** *N.Arch:* pillar, stanchion. **2.** *Nau:* **é. volante,** ricker.

étanchage [etɑ̃ʃa:ʒ], *s.m.* sealing against leaks.

étanche [etɑ̃:ʃ], *a.* tight, impervious; moisture-proof (cable); **é. à l'eau, à l'air, au gaz,** watertight, airtight, gastight; *Mch:* **chaudière é.,** steamtight boiler; *N.Arch:* **cloison é.,** watertight bulkhead; *Av:* **cabine é.,** pressure cabin; **partie non-é. du fuselage,** non-pressurized section of the fuselage; **é. à l'humidité, à la poussière,** damp proof, dust proof; **é. aux projections horizontales,** splash proof; **é. aux chutes d'eau verticales,** drop proof; *Geol:* **couche é.,** impervious stratum; **rendre qch. é.,** to make sth. watertight, airtight, etc.; to seal sth. (hermetically); *s.f.* **entretenir une toiture é.,** to keep a roof watertight; **système de défense é.,** watertight, foolproof, system of defence.

étanchéité [etɑ̃ʃeite], *s.f.* tightness; **é. à l'eau, à l'air, à la vapeur,** water-, air-, steam-tightness; **é. à l'humidité,** imperviousness to damp; **joint d'é.,** sealing gasket, ring; *Hyd.E:* **écran d'é.,** impervious layer (in dyke wall); **vérifier l'é.,** to check for leaks.

étanchéifier [etɑ̃ʃeifje], *v.tr.* (*p.d. & pr.sub.* **n. étanchéifiions, v. étanchéifiiez)** to make (sth.) water- (air-, gas-)tight.

étanchement [etɑ̃ʃmɑ̃], *s.m.* **1.** (*a*) checking the flow (of liquid); sta(u)nching (of blood); (*b*) **é. de la soif,** quenching, slaking, of thirst; (*c*) clearing of water, drying up. **2.** making (sth.) watertight, airtight.

étancher [etɑ̃ʃe], *v.tr.* **1.** (*a*) to check the flow of (liquid, etc.); to sta(u)nch (blood); **é. les larmes de qn,** to check, dry, s.o.'s tears; **é. une voie d'eau,** to stop a leak; (*b*) **é. sa soif,** to quench, slake, one's thirst; (*c*) to clear (ship, land) of water; to dry up (land). **2.** to make (sth.) watertight, airtight, to seal (sth.).

étançon [etɑ̃sɔ̃], *s.m.* (*a*) *N.Arch:* pillar, stanchion; (*b*) prop, stay, shore; *Min:* pit prop.

étançonnement [etɑ̃sɔnmɑ̃], *s.m.* staying, propping, shoring (up) (of wall, deck, etc.); underpinning (of building).

étançonner [etɑ̃sɔne], *v.tr.* to stay, to prop (up), to shore (up) (wall, deck, etc.); to underpin (building); **chaîne étançonnée,** stud link chain.

étang [etɑ̃], *s.m.* **1.** pond, pool. **2. é. salé,** salt pan.

étape [etap], *s.f.* **1.** *A:* mart, emporium; **(ville d')é.,** trading centre. **2.** (*a*) halting place (after a day's journey; *Mil:* march); **faire é.,** to stop; **nous avons fait é. à Bordeaux,** we stopped overnight at Bordeaux; **ville d'é.,** (good) overnight stop (on a route); **brûler une é.,** to pass a halting place without stopping, to press on; *Rail: etc:* to pass, fail to stop at, a scheduled stop; **brûler les étapes,** to make exceptional progress; to get ahead of schedule; *Sp:* **parc d'é.,** concentration point (of cars in a road race); *Cy: Aut:* **arriver à l'é.,** to complete the stage, the lap; to arrive at the concentration point; *Mil:* **zone des étapes,** area behind the lines; back area; staging area; (*b*) a day's run, march, flight; **à, par, petites étapes,** by easy stages; **nous avons fait Paris Madrid en trois étapes,** we did the journey from Paris to Madrid in three stages; **nous avons fait hier une é. de 500 kilomètres,** we covered, did, 500 kilometres yesterday; *Cy: Aut:* **course par étapes,** stage race; **é. de montagne,** mountain stage; (*c*) **les étapes de la civilisation,** the stages of civilization; **une des étapes qui conduisent à . . .,** one of the stages, steps, leading to . . .; **la première é. vers la conquête de l'espace,** the first step towards the conquest of space; **d'é. en é.,** progressively, stage by stage.

étarque [etark], *a. Nau:* (*of sail, etc.*) hoisted home, taut, trim.

étarquer [etarke], *v.tr. Nau:* to hoist home, hoist taut (sail).

état [eta], *s.m.* **1.** state, condition; (*a*) **é. de choses,** state of things; circumstances; **dans l'é. (actuel) des choses,** in the present state of things, as things stand at present; **l'é. actuel du pays,** the present state of the country; **é. d'une question,** progress achieved in respect of a matter; **en l'é. . . .,** this being the case . . .; **vêtements à l'é. de guenilles,** clothes reduced to rags;

passions à l'é. de souvenirs, passions reduced to memories; é. d'entretien, condition (of stores, etc.); en (bon) é., in good condition, in good order; undamaged; (house) in good repair; navire en bon é. (de navigabilité), seaworthy ship; en mauvais é., hors d'é., out of repair, out of order, in bad condition; (house) in a poor state of repair; flotte en é. d'agir, battleworthy fleet; hors d'é. de rendre aucun service, totally unfit for use; freins en mauvais é., defective brakes; mettre ses affaires en é., to put one's affairs in order; remettre qch. en é., to put sth. to rights; to overhaul, recondition, sth.; to reassemble (engine, etc.); laisser les choses en l'é., to leave things as they stand; bois en é., standing timber; *Jur:* affaire en état, suit ready for hearing; (*b*) state, mode of being; é. d'ivresse, state of intoxication; en é. d'ivresse, in a state of intoxication; en é. de siège, in a state of siege; é. d'esprit, state, frame, of mind; é. de santé, state of health; (*of boxer, etc.*) être en bon é., to be in good shape; en piteux é., in poor condition, shape; ne plus être en é. de travailler, to be past one's work; peuple à l'é. sauvage, people in the savage state; é. de guerre, (i) state of war; (ii) war footing; é. d'urgence, state of emergency; être en é. de faire qch., to be (i) fit, in a fit state, (ii) able, ready, in a position, to do sth.; mettre qn en é. de faire qch., to enable s.o. to do sth.; hors d'é. de faire qch., unable, not in a position, to do sth.; ennemi hors d'é. de nuire, enemy reduced to impotence; *F:* être dans tous ses états, to be in a great state, in a stew; il va se mettre dans un tel é. que . . ., he will work himself into such a state that . . .; *F: Iron:* être dans un bel é., to be in a nice mess; (*c*) é. absolu d'un chronomètre, chronometer error. 2. (*a*) statement, report, list, return; é. des dépenses, é. de compte, statement of expenses, statement of account; é. des dettes actives et passives, account of liabilities and assets; é. de paiements, schedule of payments; *Jur:* é. de frais, bill of costs; é. mensuel, monthly return; é. "néant," "nil" return; é. des lieux, inventory of fixtures (as between landlord and tenant); *Ind: etc:* é. périodique, periodical, progress, report; *Av:* é. de chargement, load distribution manifest; é. de service, (i) record of service; (ii) *Mil: etc:* daily duty sheet; é. des malades, sick list; é. nominatif, list of names, (nominal) roll; rayer qn des états, to strike s.o. off the rolls; (*b*) faire é. de qch., (i) to take sth. into account, to note a fact; (ii) to depend, count, on sth.; fait dont on ne peut faire é. contre l'accusé, fact that cannot be brought up, admitted as evidence, against the defendant; en tout é. de cause . . ., whatever the circumstances, in any case . . .; faire grand é. de qn, to think highly of s.o.; (*c*) *Adm:* é. civil, (i) civil status; (ii) registry office; actes de l'é. civil, certificates of births, marriages, deaths; informer l'é. civil d'un décès, to register a death; les archives de l'é. civil, the Registrar General's office; officier de l'é. civil, mayor, etc., acting as registrar. 3. profession, trade; *Journ:* avocation; il est militaire, épicier, de son é., he is a soldier by profession, a grocer by trade. 4. *Pol:* (*a*) estate (of the realm); le tiers é., the third estate, the commonalty; *Hist:* les États généraux, the States General; (*b*) state, body politic, (form of) government; é. monarchique, monarchic form of government; coup d'é., coup (d'état); homme d'é., statesman; banque d'é., State bank; affaires d'É., affairs of State; Secrétaire d'É., Secretary of State; prisonnier d'é., prisoner of state, state prisoner; pour des raisons d'É., for reasons of State; é. providence, welfare state; être à la charge de l'É. = to be on national assistance; (*c*) nation, state; servir l'é., to serve the nation, the state; tous les états étaient représentés, every state, country, was represented.

étatifier [etatifje], *v.tr.* (*p.d. & pr.sub.* n. étatifiions, v. étatifiiez) *A:* to put (industries, etc.) under State control, to nationalize (industries, etc.).

étatique [etatik], *a.* (of the) State; l'appareil é., the State machine.

étatisation [etatizasjɔ̃], *s.f.* nationalization.

étatisé [etatize], *a.* State-controlled; nationalized.

étatiser [etatize], *v.tr. Pol:* to establish State control over; to nationalize.

étatisme [etatism], *s.m.* etatism, statism; State management, control; State socialism.

étatiste [etatist], *s.m. Pol:* partisan of State control.

état-major [etamaʒɔːr], *s.m.* 1. *Mil: Navy: Av:* (*a*) (general) staff; officier d'é.-m., staff officer; chef d'é.-m., chief of staff; chef d'é.-m. général, chief of general staff; sous-chef d'é.-m., deputy chief of staff; petit é.-m. d'un régiment, noncommissioned officers of regimental headquarters; carte d'é.-m. = ordnance survey map; voyage d'é.-m., staff ride; (*b*) headquarters. 2. directing staff, management (of factory, etc.); *pl. états-majors.*

états-unien, -ienne [etazynjɛ̃, -jɛn], *a. & s.* (citizen, inhabitant) of the United States; American.

États-Unis (les) [lezetazyni], *Pr.n.m.pl.* the United States (of America); *F:* the States.

étau, -aux [eto], *s.m. Tls:* 1. (*a*) vice, *U.S:* vise; é. à main, hand vice; é. à chaud, blacksmith's vice; é. d'établi, bench vice; é. d'ébéniste, joiner's cramp; *Tel: etc:* é. tendeur, draw vice; *Metalw:* é. à tuyaux, tube vice; (*b*) *Leath:* stitching horse; (*c*) être pris, serré, comme dans un é., to be caught in a vice; l'é. des restrictions, the stranglehold of restrictions; avoir le pied dans un é., to be wearing shoes that pinch. 2. é. mortaiseur, slotting machine.

étau-limeur [etolimœːr], *s.m. Metalw:* shaping machine, shaper; *pl. étaux-limeurs.*

étaupinage [etopinaːʒ], *s.m.* destruction of molehills.

étaupiner [etopine], *v.tr. Agr:* to clear (ground) of molehills.

étaupineuse [etopinøːz], *s.f.*, **étaupinoir** [etopinwaːr], *s.m.* instrument for the destruction of molehills.

étau-pionnier [etopjɔnje], *s.m.* portable work bench; *pl. étaux-pionniers.*

étaut [eto], *s.m. Ven:* (*of hounds*) aboyer d'é., to bay at the kill.

étavillon [etavijɔ̃], *s.m.* piece of fine leather (prepared for making glove).

étayage [etejaːʒ], *s.m.* 1. staying, shoring, propping (up); buttressing. 2. *Civ.E:* false works (of bridge).

étayer [eteje], *v.tr.* (j'étaie, j'étaye, n. étayons; j'étaierai, j'étayerai) (*a*) to stay, prop (up), shore (up), support; to buttress, to underpin; (*b*) to support, back up (statement, etc.); é. une thèse, to buttress up an argument; pour é. ses allégations, in support of, to support, his allegations; é. une théorie de son autorité, to bolster up a theory with one's authority.

s'étayer, s'é. contre un choc, etc., to steady oneself against a shock, etc.; s'é. sur un ami influent, to lean upon an influential friend.

et cætera, et cetera [ɛtsetera], *Lt.phr. & s.m.inv.* et cetera; des et c. de notaire engendrent des procès, lawyers' et ceteras lead to lawsuits.

été [ete], *s.m.* summer; en é., in summer; se mettre en robe d'é., to put on a summer dress; hiver comme é., j'habite à la campagne, I live in the country both summer and winter; un jour d'é., a summer('s) day; heure d'é., summer time; passer l'é. à . . ., to spend the summer at . . .; é. de la Saint-Martin, St Martin's summer, Indian summer; être dans l'é. de sa vie, to be in the prime of life.

éteigneur, -euse [etɛɲœːr, -øːz], *s.* extinguisher (of lights, fires).

éteignoir [etɛɲwaːr], *s.m.* 1. (*a*) (candle) extinguisher; en é., conical; *P:* (nez en) é., large nose, beak; (*b*) la crainte de déplaire est l'é. de l'imagination, the fear of displeasing stifles imagination; *P: Fr.C:* c'est un vrai é. de concupiscence, she's as ugly as sin; (*c*) *F:* (*pers.*) wet blanket.

étein [etɛ̃], *s.m. A.N.Arch:* fashion-piece.

éteindre [etɛ̃ːdr], *v.tr.* (*conj. like* TEINDRE) 1. to extinguish, put out (fire, light); to turn off (the gas); to switch off (electric light, radio, etc.); laisser é. le feu, to let the fire go out; é. une bougie d'un souffle, to blow out a candle; é. les feux d'un fourneau, to draw the fires of a furnace; *Th:* é. la rampe, to black out; *abs.* éteignez, turn out, switch off, the light; *Nau:* faire route tous feux éteints, to proceed without lights. 2. to extinguish (race, family); to annul, pay off (a debt); to abolish (a right); to put an end to (a quarrel); é. la soif, to slake, quench, thirst; é. l'espoir, l'ambition, to extinguish hope, to kill ambition; *Mil:* é. le feu de l'ennemi, to silence the enemy's guns. 3. (*a*) to slake, slack, kill (lime); (*b*) *Metalw:* to quench (red-hot iron, etc.). 4. to fade, soften (colours); to stifle, smother, deaden (sound); to appease, allay (passions); to dim (light, flashing, eyes, etc.); tapis qui éteint tout bruit de pas, carpet that muffles, deadens, any sound of footsteps; parole qui éteignit tous les sourires, word that wiped the smile off every face; *Mus:* é. le son, to let the sound die away.

s'éteindre. 1. (*a*) (*of fire, light*) to go out, to die out, (*of fire*) to burn out; (*b*) (*of colour, etc.*) to fade, grow dim; (*of sound*) to die down, to die away; to subside; (*of passion*) to die down; s'é. peu à peu, to die away; le jour s'éteint, daylight is failing, is fading; son sourire s'éteignit, his smile faded (away); l'espoir s'éteignit de ses yeux, hope faded from his eyes. 2. (*a*) (*of race, family*) to become extinct, to die out; (*b*) vieillard qui s'éteint, old man who is nearing his end; sa fortune s'éteindra avec lui, his fortune dies with him; il s'éteignit entre mes bras, he passed away in my arms; (*c*) *Jur:* laisser s'é. une servitude, to allow an easement to be extinguished.

éteint, -einte [etɛ̃, -ɛ̃ːt]. 1. *a.* (*a*) extinguished; le feu est é., the fire is out; (*b*) extinct (race, family, volcano); (*c*) dull, dim, faint (colour, sound); yeux éteints, dull, *Lit:* lack-lustre, eyes; voix éteinte, faint, toneless, far-away, voice; (*d*) chaux éteinte, slaked lime. 2. *s.f. A:* éteinte, extinction; *still used in* adjudication à l'éteinte de chandelle, auction by inch of candle.

ételle[1] [etɛl], *s.f.* tidal wave.

ételle[2], *s.f.* (fairly large) chip (of wood).

ételon [etlɔ̃], *s.m. Arch: Carp:* layout of the plan (of timberwork, etc.).

étemperche [etɑ̃pɛrʃ], *s.f. Const:* 1. upright pole, standard (of scaffolding). 2. derrick.

étendage [etɑ̃daːʒ], *s.m.* 1. (*a*) hanging out (of washing, etc.); spreading (of butter, etc.); (*b*) stretching (of skin, etc.). 2. (*a*) clothes lines; (*b*) drying yard; (*c*) *Tex:* drying room (for dyed cloth, yarn).

étendard [etɑ̃daːr], *s.m.* 1. (*a*) *Mil:* standard (of mounted arms); colour(s); (*b*) lever l'é. de la révolte, to raise the flag of rebellion. 2. *Bot:* vexillum, standard, banner (of Papilionaceae).

étendelle [etɑ̃dɛl], *s.f.* 1. (*in edible oil mill*) press cloth, hair. 2. canvas bag (holding seeds).

étendoir [etɑ̃dwaːr], *s.m.* (*a*) clothes lines; (*b*) drying yard, room; *Paperm:* treble.

étendre [etɑ̃ːdr], *v.tr.* to spread, extend. 1. to spread, stretch, (s.o., sth.) out to full length; é. une nappe, to spread, lay, a cloth; é. de la paille, to spread straw; é. du beurre sur du pain, to spread butter on bread; é. une couche de peinture (sur qch.), to give (sth.) a coat of paint; é. la lessive, to hang out the washing; é. le bras, to stretch out, reach out, one's arm; (*of bird*) é. ses ailes, to spread its wings; (*of tree*) é. ses branches, to spread its branches; é. un malade sur un lit, to lay a sick man (at full length) on a bed; é. qn (par terre) d'un coup de poing, to knock s.o. down; to stretch s.o. on the ground; *F:* to lay s.o. out; il l'étendit mort, he laid him dead at his feet; une balle l'étendit mort, a bullet killed him on the spot; nous l'avons trouvé étendu mort, we found him lying dead; *F:* se faire é. à un examen, to fail an exam. 2. (*a*) to stretch (sth.) out (to more than original size); é. une peau, to stretch a skin; é. l'or, (i) to beat out, hammer out, gold; (ii) to wire-draw gold; *Cu:* é. la pâte, to roll out the dough, the pastry; é. ses connaissances, to extend, enlarge, improve, one's knowledge; é. les termes d'une loi, to widen, broaden, the terms of a law; é. sa propriété, to enlarge one's estates; é. un récit, to lengthen out, fill out, a story; (*b*) to dilute (wine, milk, etc.) (de, with); é. d'eau une boisson, to water (down) a drink.

s'étendre. 1. (*a*) to stretch oneself out, to lie down (at) full length; étendu par terre tout de son long, stretched out at full length on the ground; (*b*) s'é. sur un sujet, to dwell, enlarge, expatiate, (up)on a subject; je ne m'étendrai pas là-dessus, I won't labour the point. 2. (*a*) to extend, stretch; la ligne s'étend depuis . . . jusqu'à . . ., the line stretches, runs, from . . . to . . .; les villes s'étendent toujours à, vers, l'ouest, towns always spread, extend, to the west; aussi loin que la vue, le regard, peut s'é., as far as the eye can reach; (*b*) to spread; *Dy:* (*of colour*) to bleed; empêcher l'incendie de s'é., to prevent the fire from spreading; encre qui ne s'étend pas, ink that will not run; (*of dye*) s'é. au lavage, to run in the wash; (*c*) to expand; nation qui s'étend de tous côtés, nation that is expanding on all sides; ses terres s'étendent de plus en plus, his estate is growing larger and larger.

étendu, -ue [etɑ̃dy]. 1. *a.* (*a*) extensive (knowledge, memory); far-reaching (influence); wide (plain, knowledge); (*b*) outspread (wings); outstretched (hands); (*c*) diluted (de, with). 2. *s.f.* étendue; (*a*) extent, size, dimensions, area; scale (of calamity, etc.); stretch (of water, etc.); tract (of land, etc.); reach (of the mind); sweep (of

country); **vaste é. de mer**, vast stretch, expanse, of sea; **é. d'une voix**, compass, range, of a voice; **é. du savoir de qn**, extent, scope, of s.o.'s knowledge; **l'é. d'un discours**, the length of a speech; **l'é. de la vie**, the duration of life; **sur toute l'é. d'une poutre**, over the whole length of a beam; *Fenc:* **avoir beaucoup d'é.**, to have a long reach; (*b*) *Phil:* extension (of matter, of a body).

Étéocle [eteɔkl̩], *Pr.n.m. Gr.Lit:* Eteocles.

étéocrétois, -oise [eteɔkretwa, -waːz], *a. & s.* **1.** *A.Hist:* Eteocretan. **2.** *s.m. Ling:* Eteocretan.

éter [ete], *v.i. A:* to be standing; *For:* **bois en étant**, standing timber.

éternel, -elle [etɛrnɛl], *a.* (*a*) eternal; **le père é.**, the Father Eternal; *s.m.* **L'É.**, God, the Lord; the Eternal; **l'É. des armées**, the Lord of hosts; (*b*) everlasting, perpetual, unending, ceaseless, endless (life, joy, etc.); *s.m.* **du temps à l'é.**, from time to eternity; **sommeil é.**, eternal sleep, death; *Ecc:* **feu é.**, everlasting fire; **la Ville éternelle**, the Eternal City (Rome); **l'é. féminin**, the eternal feminine; **soucis éternels**, incessant, never-ending, worries; (*c*) **un é. causeur**, an inveterate chatterer; **mon père et son éternelle cigarette**, father and his everlasting cigarettes; **l'éternelle serviette pleine de papiers**, the inevitable brief-case full of papers; **c'est un é. mécontent**, he's a perpetual grumbler; *s.a.* NEIGE.

éternellement [etɛrnɛlmɑ̃], *adv.* (*a*) eternally, for ever, for evermore; (*b*) everlastingly, perpetually, endlessly; *Pej:* **un homme qui gronde é.**, a man who's always grumbling, who never stops grumbling.

éternisation [etɛrnizasjɔ̃], (*a*) perpetuation (of a memory, etc.); (*b*) dragging on, spinning out (of lawsuit, etc.).

éterniser [etɛrnize], *v.tr.* to eternize, eternalize, perpetuate; (*a*) **é. la mémoire de qn**, to immortalize s.o.'s memory; **si nous pouvions é. cette heure**, if only we could make this hour last for ever; (*b*) **é. une discussion**, to drag on a discussion (interminably); **é. sa visite**, to outstay one's welcome.

s'éterniser, to last for ever; to become interminable; **le procès s'éternise**, the case drags on, goes on and on; **c'est ainsi que les abus s'éternisent**, thus are abuses perpetuated; *F:* **s'é. chez qn**, to outstay, overstay, one's welcome; *F:* **elle s'éternisait devant son miroir**, she spent endless hours in front of her mirror.

Éternit [eternit], *s.m. R.t.m:* asbestos board, sheet.

éternité [etɛrnite], *s.f.* eternity; **de toute é.**, from time immemorial; **cela va durer une é.**, it will go on for ever; **il y a une é. que je ne vous ai vu**, it's ages since I saw you, I haven't seen you for ages; **ça va me prendre une é.**, it will take me a month of Sundays.

éternuement [etɛrnymɑ̃], *s.m.* **1.** sneezing. **2.** sneeze.

éternuer [etɛrnɥe], *v.i.* to sneeze; **réprimer une envie d'é.**, to stifle a sneeze; *Bot: F:* **herbe à é.**, sneezewort; *P:* **é. dans le son, dans le sac**, to be guillotined.

éternueur, -euse [etɛrnɥœːr, -øːz], *s.* sneezer.

éternûment [etɛrnymɑ̃], *s.m. A:* **1.** sneezing. **2.** sneeze.

étésien [etezjɛ̃], *a. & s.m.* etesian (wind).

étêtage [etɛtaːʒ], *s.m.*, **étêtement** [etɛtmɑ̃], *s.m.* (*a*) pollarding, topping (of trees); (*b*) (*oil refining*) topping.

étêté [etɛte], *a. Her:* beheaded; headless.

étêter [etɛte, -ete], *v.tr.* (*a*) to remove the head from (fish, pin, nail, etc.); *Fish Ind:* **machine à é.**, heading machine; (*b*) to pollard, top (tree); to head down (tree); (*c*) (*oil refining*) to top.

étêteur [etɛtœːr], *s.m. Fish:* (*a*) (*pers.*) header (of cod); (*b*) header, heading knife.

éteuf [etœf], *s.m.* **1.** leather ball (filled with bran); ball (in old game of tennis); *A:* **prendre l'é. à la volée**, to grasp the occasion; **renvoyer l'é.**, to give tit for tat. **2.** button (of foil).

éteule [etœl], *s.f.*, **éteulière** [etœljɛːr], *s.f. Agr:* stubble.

éthal [etal], *s.m. Ch:* ethal.

éthanal [etanal], *s.m. Ch:* ethanal.

éthane [etan], *s.m. Ch:* ethane.

éthanethiol [etanetjɔl], *s.m. Ch:* ethanethiol.

éthanoïque [etanɔik], *s.m. Ch:* ethanoic acid.

éthanol [etanɔl], *s.m. Ch:* ethanol.

éthanolamine [etanɔlamin], *s.f. Ch:* ethanolamine.

éthanolyse [etanɔliːz], *s.f. Ch:* ethanolysis.

éthène [etɛn], *s.m. Ch:* ethene, ethylene.

éther [etɛːr], *s.m. Poet:* ether, the heavens; *Ph: Ch: Med:* ether; *Ch:* **é. composé**, ethereal salt; *Com:* **é. sulfurique, ordinaire**, sulphuric ether, ethyl oxide; **é. de cellulose**, cellulose ether; *Ph:* **ondes de l'é.**, waves in the ether.

éthéré [etere], *a.* **1.** ethereal, airy (regions). **2.** *Ch:* ethereal (salt).

éthérie [eteri], *s.f. Moll:* etheria.

éthérification [eterifikasjɔ̃], *s.f.* etherification.

éthérifier [eterifje], *v.tr. Ch:* to etherify.

éthériidés [eteriide], *s.m.pl. Moll:* Etheriidae.

éthérisation [eterizasjɔ̃], *s.f. Med:* etherization.

éthériser [eterize], *v.tr. Med:* to etherize (patient).

éthériseur [eterizœːr], *s.m. Med:* (*apparatus*) etherizer.

éthérisme [eterism], *s.m. Med:* etherism.

éthéromane [eterɔman], *s.m. & f.* ether addict.

éthéromanie [eterɔmani], *s.f.* addiction to ether; etheromania.

éthionamide [etjɔnamid], *s.f. Med:* thyroid extract.

éthionique [etjɔnik], *a. Ch:* ethionic (acid).

éthiopianisme [etjɔpjanism], *s.m. Hist:* movement for the eviction of the white races from Africa.

Éthiopie [etjɔpi], *Pr.n.f. Geog:* Ethiopia; Abyssinia.

éthiopien, -ienne [etjɔpjɛ̃, -jɛn], *a. & s.* **1.** Ethiopian; Abyssinian. **2.** *s.m. Ling:* (*a*) Ethiopian; (*b*) Ethiopic.

éthiopique [etjɔpik], *a.* Ethiopic (language, church, etc.).

éthiops [etjɔps], *s.m. A.Ch:* ethiops; **é. martial**, ethiops martial.

éthique [etik]. **1.** *a.* (*a*) ethical (problem, etc.); (*b*) *Gram:* **datif é.**, ethic dative. **2.** *s.f.* ethics; moral philosophy.

ethmoïdal, -aux [ɛtmɔidal, -o], *a. Anat:* ethmoidal.

ethmoïde [ɛtmɔid], *a. & s.m. Anat:* ethmoid (bone).

ethmoïdite [ɛtmɔidit], *s.f. Med:* ethmoiditis.

ethnarchie [ɛtnarʃi], *s.f.* ethnarchy.

ethnarque [ɛtnark], *s.m.* ethnarch.

ethnie [ɛtni], *s.f.* ethnos, ethnic group.

ethnique [ɛtnik]. **1.** *a. Rel.H:* ethnic(al), gentile. **2.** *a.* ethnological, ethnical. **3.** *s.m.* ethnicon.

ethnocentrique [ɛtnɔsɑ̃trik], *a.* ethnocentric.

ethnocentrisme [ɛtnɔsɑ̃trism], *s.m.* ethnocentrism.

ethnogénie [ɛtnɔʒeni], *s.f.* ethnogeny.

ethnographe [ɛtnɔgraf], *s.m. & f.* ethnographer.

ethnographie [ɛtnɔgrafi], *s.f.* ethnography.

ethnographique [ɛtnɔgrafik], *a.* ethnographic(al).

ethnologie [ɛtnɔlɔʒi], *s.f.* ethnology.

ethnologique [ɛtnɔlɔʒik], *a.* ethnological.

ethnologiquement [ɛtnɔlɔʒikmɑ̃], *adv.* ethnologically; from the ethnological point of view.

ethnologue [ɛtnɔlɔg], *s.m. & f.* ethnologist.

éthogène [etɔʒɛn], *s.m. Ch:* aethogen.

éthographie [etɔgrafi], *s.f.* ethography.

étholide [etɔlid], *s.m. Ch:* etholide.

éthologie [etɔlɔʒi], *s.f.* ethology.

éthologique [etɔlɔʒik], *a.* ethological.

éthologue [etɔlɔg], *s.m. & f.*, **éthologiste** [etɔlɔʒist], *s.m. & f.* ethologist.

éthos [etɔs], *s.m.* ethos; **l'é. et le pathos**, ethos and pathos.

éthoxyle [etɔksil], *s.m. Ch:* ethoxyl.

éthrioscope [etriɔskɔp], *s.m. Meteor:* aethrioscope.

éthuse [etyːz], *s.f. Bot:* aethusa; fool's parsley.

éthylamine [etilamin], *s.f. Ch:* ethylamine.

éthylate [etilat], *s.m. Ch:* ethylate; **é. de vanadium**, vanadium ethylate.

éthylation [etilasjɔ̃], *s.f. Ch:* ethylation.

éthylcellulose [etilsɛlyloːz], *s.f. Ch:* ethylcellulose.

éthyle [etil], *s.m. Ch:* ethyl.

éthylé [etile], *a. Ch:* ethylated.

éthylène [etilɛn], *s.m. Ch:* ethylene; ethene; **oxyde d'é.**, ethylene oxide; **é. glycol**, ethylene glycol; **é. diamine**, ethylene diamin(e).

éthylénier [etilenje], *s.m.* ethylene tanker.

éthylénique [etilenik], *a. Ch:* ethylenic; **carbures éthyléniques**, ethylene hydrocarbons.

éthyler [etile], *v.tr. Ch:* to ethylate.

éthylidène [etilidɛn], *s.m. Ch:* ethylidene.

éthyline [etilin], *s.f. Ch:* ethylin.

éthylique [etilik]. **1.** *a. Ch:* ethyl(ic); **alcool é.**, ethyl alcohol. **2.** *s.m. & f.* (*a*) alcoholic; (*b*) ethyl alcohol drinker.

éthylisme [etilism], *s.m.* (*a*) alcoholism; (*b*) ethylism.

éthylmercaptan [etilmɛrkaptɑ̃], *s.m. Ch:* ethyl mercaptan.

éthylmorphine [etilmɔrfin], *s.f. Ch:* ethylmorphine.

éthylsulfurique [etilsylfyrik], *a. Ch:* ethylsulphuric.

éthyluréthane [etilyretan], *s.m. Ch:* ethylurethane.

étiage [etjaːʒ], *s.m.* lowest water level, low water (of river); **le débit d'é. de la Seine**, the rate of flow of the Seine when at its lowest; **échelle d'é.**, floodometer.

Étienne [etjɛn], *Pr.n.m.* Stephen.

étier [etje], *s.m.* (*a*) (*in Brittany*) (small) estuary; (*b*) (i) small canal (joining port to river or sea); (ii) canal, channel (conducting sea-water to salt-pans).

étincelage [etɛ̃slaːʒ], *s.m.* (*a*) **soudure par é.**, flash welding; (*b*) *Med:* electrotherapy (used (i) for destruction of tissues; (ii) as a sedative).

étincelant [etɛ̃slɑ̃], *a.* sparkling, glittering, glistening, flashing (jewels, eyes, etc.); **esprit é.**, sparkling wit.

étinceler [etɛ̃sle], *v.i.* (**il étincelle; il étincelait; il étincellera**) **1.** to throw out sparks. **2.** (*of diamonds, stars, sea, etc.*) to sparkle, glitter, gleam; (*of wit*) to sparkle; **ses yeux étincelaient de joie, de colère**, his eyes sparkled with joy, flashed with anger; **la fureur étincelle dans ses yeux**, his eyes are flashing, glittering, with rage.

étinceleur [etɛ̃slœːr], *s.m. Oil Ind:* sparker.

étincelle [etɛ̃sɛl], *s.f.* spark; (*a*) **lancer des étincelles**, to throw out sparks, to sparkle, flash; *El:* **é. disruptive**, spark discharge; **é. éclatante**, jump spark; **é. de frottement, par came**, wipe spark; **é. bien nourrie**, fat spark; **é. de rupture (de courant)**, break spark, flashover; **retard d'é.**, spark lag; **interruption sans étincelles**, sparkless breaking; *I.C.E:* **allumage par é.**, spark ignition; **distributeur à étincelles sautantes**, jump-spark distributor; (*b*) **é. de génie**, spark, flash, of genius; **faire des étincelles**, (i) to sparkle with wit; (ii) to be very successful.

étincellement [etɛ̃sɛlmɑ̃] *s.m.* sparkling, glittering, scintillation (of gem, etc.); twinkling (of stars).

étiolement [etjɔlmɑ̃], *s.m.* (*a*) *Bot: Med:* chlorosis, etiolation; (*b*) drooping, wilting (of flowers); **é. de l'esprit, de l'intelligence**, atrophy of the mind; weakening of the intellect.

étioler [etjɔle], *v.tr.* **1.** to etiolate, blanch (celery, etc.). **2.** to make (s.o.) sickly, weakly, pale; to enfeeble (s.o.); to make (s.o.) insignificant.

s'étioler, (*a*) to etiolate, blanch; (*b*) (*of tree, plant*) to starve; (*of flowers, etc.*) to grow sickly; to droop, wilt; **intelligence qui s'étiole**, mind that is becoming atrophied.

étiologie [etjɔlɔʒi], *s.f.* aetiology, etiology.

étiologique [etjɔlɔʒik], *a.* aetiological, etiological.

étiologue [etjɔlɔg], *s.m.* aetiologist, etiologist.

étique [etik], *a.* **1.** *A:* consumptive; in a decline. **2.** emaciated, wasted; *F:* skinny; **cheval, poulet, é.**, horse, chicken, all skin and bone.

étiquetage [etiktaːʒ], *s.m.* labelling (of luggage, plants, etc.); docketing (of manuscripts, etc.); ticketing (of goods, etc.).

étiqueter [etikte], *v.tr.* (**j'étiquète, n. étiquetons; j'étiquèterai**) (*a*) to label (luggage); to docket (manuscripts); to ticket (goods); (*b*) to label (politician); to classify, arrange (ideas).

étiqueteur, -euse [etiktœːr, -øːz], *s.* (*a*) (*pers.*) labeller, ticketer; (*b*) *s.f.* **étiqueteuse**, labelling machine (for bottles).

étiquette [etikɛt], *s.f.* **1.** (*a*) label, docket, ticket; **é. à bagages, de direction**, luggage label; **é. à œillets**, tie-on label; tag; **é. gommée**, gummed label, stick-on label; **é. de vitrine**, show card; **apposer une é. à un paquet**, to label, stick a label on, a parcel; (*b*) (political) label. **2.** etiquette, formality, ceremony; **l'é. de la cour**, Court ceremonial; **il n'est pas d'é. de . . .**, it is not etiquette to . . .; **il est contraire à l'é. de . . .**, it is bad form to . . .. **3.** *P:* ear, lughole.

étirable [etirabl̩], *a.* (*of metals*) ductile, drawable; (*of rubber, etc.*) elastic.

étirage [etiraːʒ], *s.m.* **1.** stretching; **é. des métaux**, drawing (out) of metals; **é. à chaud, à froid**, hot, cold, drawing; **é. du fil**, wire drawing; **é. des peaux**, racking of skins; *Tex:* **banc d'é.**, drawing frame. **2.** *Tex:* draught (of frame).

étire [etiːr], *s.f. Leath:* slicker, stretching iron.

étiré [etire], *s.m. Metalw:* drawn bar; drawn tube.

étirer [etire], *v.tr.* **1.** (*a*) to stretch; to draw out (sth.); **é. les métaux**, to draw (out) metals; **é. à froid**, to cold-draw; **é. le fil**, to draw wire; **finement étiré**, fine-drawn; **banc à é.**, draw-bench; *Geol:* **pli étiré**, drag fold; (*b*) **les élastiques sont étirés**, the elastic has worn out. **2.** *Leath:* to slick (skin); *Tan:* to perch, to set (skins); **machine à é.**, setting machine.

s'étirer. **1.** to stretch oneself, one's limbs; **le chat s'étire**, the cat is stretching himself, having a good stretch. **2.** (*of column on the march, of the field in a race, etc.*) to stretch out, to straggle, to become strung out.

étireur, -euse [etirœːr, -øːz]. 1. *a.* drawing (cylinder). 2. *s.* (*a*) drawer (of metals); draw-bench worker; (*b*) wire drawer; (*c*) racker (of skins). 3. *s.f.* étireuse; *Metalw:* (*a*) draw bench; (*b*) wire-drawing bench.

étisie [etizi], *s.f. A.Med:* wasting, decline.

étoc [etɔk], *s.m.* 1. *Arb:* stock, trunk (of tree). 2. rock (exposed at low tide).

étoffe [etɔf], *s.f.* 1. (*a*) *Tchn:* material (used in manufacture of sth.); *A:* *often* = metal; *s.a.* BASSE-ÉTOFFE, CLAIRE-ÉTOFFE; **é. suffisante pour faire un roman,** enough material to make a novel; **roman qui manque d'é.,** thin, flimsy, novel; **on n'a pas épargné, n'a pas plaint, l'é.,** it's good measure; they haven't spared the material; (*b*) **avoir de l'é.,** to have plenty of grit; **manquer d'é.,** to be weak; *F:* not to have what it takes; **il a de l'é.,** there is something in him, there is good stuff in him; **il y a en lui l'é. d'un écrivain,** he has the makings of a writer in him; **son frère est d'une autre é.,** his brother is made of different stuff. 2. *Tex:* material, fabric; **é. pour costumes,** dress material; **é. légère,** light material, tissue; **riches étoffes de soie,** heavy silk fabrics. 3. *pl.* **étoffes;** *Publ:* gross profit (on an impression).

étoffé [etɔfe], *a.* 1. ample, full (garment); stuffed (cushion); upholstered (armchair, etc.); rich, full (voice); well-appointed (house); **homme bien é.,** (i) stout, thickset, man; (ii) well-to-do man; **discours é.,** speech full of substance; **voix bien étoffée,** powerful voice. 2. (*pillar, etc.*) thickened (for greater strength).

étoffer [etɔfe], *v.tr.* 1. (*a*) to use ample material in making (sth.); **é. un roman,** to pack incident into a novel; (*in novel*) **é. un personnage,** to build up, develop, a character; **é. un discours,** etc., to fill out a speech, etc.; (*b*) to stuff (cushion, etc.); to upholster (armchair, etc.); (*c*) **é. la voix,** to give fullness to the voice. 2. to stiffen (gum, etc.); to whip (cream); *Cu:* to stuff (chicken, etc.).

s'étoffer, (*of horse, of pers.*) to fill out.

étoile [etwal], *s.f.* star. 1. (*a*) **é. filante,** shooting star; **l'é. polaire,** the pole star; **ciel (par)semé d'étoiles,** starlit sky, starry sky; **à la clarté des étoiles,** in the starlight; **l'é. du matin,** the morning star; **coucher, dormir, à la belle é.,** to sleep out of doors, in the open, under the stars; **un ciel sans étoiles,** a starless sky; **être né sous une bonne, une mauvaise, é.,** to be born under a lucky, an unlucky, star; **je bénis mon é. de ce que** + *ind.*, I thank my stars that . . .; **son é. pâlit,** his fame is declining, his star is on the wane; *F:* **voir les étoiles en plein midi,** to see stars; (*b*) *Mil:* **é. éclairante,** Very light. 2. (*a*) star (of a decoration); *Pol: Hist:* **é. jaune,** Star of David; (*b*) radial crack (in timber, glass, etc.); star; (*c*) blaze (on horse); (*d*) asterisk, star; *Com:* **cognac trois étoiles,** three star brandy; **hôtel à trois étoiles,** three star hotel; (*e*) *W.Tel:* quad; *El:* **montage, couplage, en é.,** star, Y, connection (of phase system); *A: I.C.E:* **moteur en é.,** radial engine; (*f*) roundabout, circus, *rond-point* (from which many broad streets radiate); *Rail:* system of tracks radiating from a junction; (*g*) *Rail:* spring washer; (*h*) *Lap:* star facet; (*i*) *Echin:* **é. de mer,** starfish; **é. de mer à bras multiples rouges,** sun star(fish); **é. palmée,** duck's foot starfish. 3. (film, operatic) star; ballerina (of international status); **avoir un rôle d'é. dans une pièce,** to star in a play.

étoilé [etwale], *a.* 1. starry, starlit (sky); studded with stars; *Hist:* **la Chambre étoilée,** the Star Chamber; **la Bannière étoilée,** the Star-spangled Banner, the Stars and Stripes (of the U.S.A.). 2. star-shaped, stellate(d) (flower, crack, etc.); **vitre, bouteille, étoilée,** starred window pane, bottle; *Mil:* **fort é.,** star fort; *El:* **tension étoilée,** star voltage; *Bot:* **anis é.,** star anise.

étoilement [etwalmɑ̃], *s.m.* 1. *Lit:* **l'é. du ciel se faisait peu à peu,** the sky gradually became filled with stars. 2. star-shaped crack; star.

étoiler [etwale], *v.tr.* 1. to stud, spangle, (sth.) with stars; **la croix militaire étoilait ses haillons,** the military cross gleamed among his rags. 2. to make a star-shaped crack in, to star (glass, etc.).

s'étoiler. 1. (*of the sky*) to light up, become filled, with stars. 2. (*of window pane, etc.*) to star.

étole [etɔl], *s.f. Ecc: Cost:* stole.

Étolie [etɔli], *Pr.n.f. Geog:* Aetolia.

étolien, -ienne [etɔljɛ̃, -jɛn], *a. & s. Geog:* Aetolian.

étonnamment [etɔnamɑ̃], *adv.* astonishingly, surprisingly, amazingly; wonderfully.

étonnant [etɔnɑ̃], *a.* 1. *A:* stunning, staggering (news, blow); dumbfounding (news). 2. astonishing, surprising; wonderful; amazing; **chose étonnante, il savait sa leçon,** for a wonder he knew his lesson; **ce qu'il y a d'é., c'est que . . .,** the wonder is that . . .; **rien d'é. à cela,** that's no wonder; **il accepta, et rien d'é.,** he accepted, as well he might; **c'est é. qu'il ait réussi,** it is a wonder that he managed it; **ce n'est pas é. qu'il soit malade,** no wonder, it's not to be wondered at, that he is ill; **ce n'est guère é.,** small wonder; *F:* **vous êtes é.!** you're the limit! *s.* **l'é. est qu'il soit venu,** the surprising thing is that he came.

étonné, -ée [etɔne], *a.* 1. *A:* stunned, staggered, dumbfounded. 2. astonished, surprised; taken by surprise; **ouvrir de grands yeux étonnés,** to stare round-eyed; *s.* **jouer, faire, l'é.,** to pretend to be surprised.

étonnement [etɔnmɑ̃], *s.m.* 1. (*a*) astonishment, surprise; wonder; amazement; **frappé, saisi, d'é.,** struck with surprise; **plongé dans l'é.,** lost in astonishment; **j'ai appris, à mon é., que . . .,** I have heard, to my astonishment, that . . .; **faire l'é. de tout le monde,** to be the talk of the town; **revenir de son é.,** to recover from one's amazement; (*b*) *Phil:* (faculty of) wonder. 2. *A:* (i) commotion; (ii) terror; (iii) excessive admiration. 3. crack, fissure (in building); flaw (in diamond).

étonner [etɔne], *v.tr.* 1. *A:* (*a*) to stun; (*b*) to shake, loosen (structure) (by blow or shock); to crack, shiver (flint, etc.); to crack, fissure (arch, etc.). 2. to astonish, amaze, surprise; **cela m'étonne que** + *sub.*, I am astonished that . . .; **cela ne m'étonnerait pas,** I shouldn't wonder (at it); **vous m'étonnez,** (i) you astonish me; (ii) I am surprised at you; **ce qui m'étonne, c'est que . . .,** what surprises me is that . . .; *abs.* **cela étonne de sa part,** that's astonishing, coming from him.

s'étonner. 1. *A:* to become loose, to crack, fissure; (*of arch*) to sink. 2. to be astonished, surprised, to wonder (**de,** at); **je m'étonne de vous voir,** I am surprised to see you, at seeing you; **je m'étonne que** + *sub.*, I wonder that . . .; **je m'étonne qu'il ne voie pas le danger,** it amazes me that he does not see the danger; **comment s'é. qu'il ait refusé?** can you wonder that he refused? **je ne m'étonne plus de rien,** nothing surprises me any more.

étoquiau, -aux [etɔkjo], *s.m. Aut:* stop pin, steady pin (of laminated spring).

étouffade [etufad], *s.f. Cu:* braising.

étouffage [etufaːʒ], *s.m.* 1. stifling (of silkworms, bees, etc.). 2. *P:* stealing, filching.

étouffant [etufɑ̃], *a.* stifling, suffocating, stuffy (atmosphere, etc.); oppressive, sultry (weather); **bureau é. de chaleur,** sweltering office; **gaz é.,** choke damp; **malaise é.,** paralysing malaise uneasiness.

étouffé [etufe], *s.m. Mus:* muted section, phrase.

étouffée [etufe], *s.f. Cu:* 1. **cuire qch. à l'étouffée,** to braise (meat). 2. (dish of) braised meat.

étouffement [etufmɑ̃], *s.m.* 1. suffocation, stifling (of s.o.); smothering (of fire); hushing-up (of rumour). 2. choking sensation; **avoir des étouffements,** to have fits of oppression, of breathlessness.

étouffer [etufe]. 1. *v.tr.* (*a*) to suffocate, choke, smother (s.o.); **plantes qui s'étouffent,** plants that choke one another; *For:* **sous-bois étouffé,** suppressed undergrowth; **on s'étouffait pour entrer,** people crushed in; **à son cri l'émotion faillit m'é.,** his cry brought my heart into my mouth; *F:* **ce n'est pas l'intelligence qui l'étouffe,** he's not overburdened with brains; (*b*) to stifle (cry, passion, industry, conspiracy); to smother (fire); to stamp out (epidemic); to quell, suppress (revolt); to damp (sound, initiative); to mute (musical instrument); *El:* to quench (spark); **é. une affaire,** to hush up a matter; **é. ses sentiments,** to bottle up one's feelings; **é un sanglot,** to choke down a sob; **é. son pas,** to walk, step, lightly; to muffle one's footsteps; **le tapis étouffe tout bruit de pas,** the carpet deadens the sound of footsteps; *El:* **étincelle étouffée,** quenched spark; (*c*) *Nau:* to spill (sail); (*d*) *P:* to steal, pinch (sth.); (*e*) *Cu:* to stew, to braise. 2. *v.i. & pr.* (*a*) to suffocate, choke; **é. de rage, de rire,** to choke with rage, with laughter; (*b*) **on étouffe ici,** it's stifling here.

étouffeur, -euse [etufœːr, -øːz], *s.* (*a*) (*pers.*) stifler; (*b*) *s.m.* **é. de vibrations (pour les tuyauteries rigides),** vibration damper.

étouffoir [etufwaːr], *s.m.* 1. charcoal extinguisher. 2. sound damper; *Mus:* damper (of piano). 3. stuffy room. 4. airtight (bulk) container. 5. *Aer:* choke.

étoupage [etupaːʒ], *s.m. Ind:* **é. de chanvre,** hemp packing.

étoupe [etup], *s.f.* 1. (*a*) **é. blanche,** tow; (*b*) **é. noire,** oakum, junk; (*c*) **é. de coton,** cotton waste; **mettre le feu aux étoupes,** to start trouble. 2. *Mec.E:* packing, stuffing (of piston rod, etc.); **boîte à é.,** stuffing box.

étouper [etupe], *v.tr.* 1. to put tow in (one's ears, etc.); to stop up (crevices, etc.) with tow, oakum; to caulk (boat); to chinse, chintze. 2. *Mec.E:* to stuff, pack (gland, etc.).

étoupeux, -euse [etupø, -øːz], *a.* (*a*) stuffed with tow; **toile étoupeuse,** coarse cloth (resembling tow); towy material.

étoupier, -ière [etupje, -jɛːr], *s.* oakum picker.

étoupille [etupiːj], *s.f.* 1. *Artil:* (*a*) *A:* quick-match; (*b*) firing-tube; **enlever l'é.,** to extract the tube. 2. *Min:* fuse.

étoupiller [etupije], *v.tr. Min:* to fuse (blasting charge, etc.).

étoupillon [etupijɔ̃], *s.m. Artil: A:* vent-plug.

étourderie [eturdəri], *s.f.* 1. thoughtlessness, inadvertence; absentmindedness; **par é.,** through inadvertence, inadvertently; in an unthinking moment. 2. thoughtless action, oversight, blunder; **devoir rempli d'étourderies,** exercise full of careless mistakes; **commettre une é.,** to make a careless blunder.

étourdi, -ie [eturdi]. 1. *a.* thoughtless, scatter-brained, hare-brained, flighty, irresponsible (person); giddy (girl); foolish (answer, etc.); **é. comme un hanneton,** harum-scarum. 2. *s.* scatter-brain, harum-scarum. 3. *adv.phr.* **à l'étourdie,** thoughtlessly, heedlessly, in haste; **lâcher un secret à l'étourdie,** to blurt out a secret.

étourdiment [eturdimɑ̃], *adv.* thoughtlessly; **répondre é.,** to answer foolishly, without thinking.

étourdir [eturdiːr], *v.tr.* 1. to stun, daze; to make (s.o.) dizzy; to make (s.o.'s) head swim; **bruit qui étourdit les oreilles,** deafening noise; **cet enfant nous étourdit,** that child is making an awful din! is deafening us! 2. (*a*) to (be)numb, ease, deaden (pain); to allay, assuage (grief); to appease, take the edge off (hunger); (*b*) *Cu:* **é. l'eau,** to take the chill off water; **é. de la viande,** to cook meat slightly, to parboil meat.

s'étourdir, (*a*) to try to forget; **s'é. dans la boisson,** to drown one's sorrows; (*b*) **s'é. de chimères,** to lose oneself in daydreams.

étourdissant [eturdisɑ̃], *a.* 1. deafening, ear-splitting (noise). 2. staggering, stunning, astounding (news, etc.); *O:* **toilette étourdissante,** shattering, stunning, get-up.

étourdissement [eturdismɑ̃], *s.m.* 1. giddiness, vertigo, dizziness; **avoir un é.,** to feel giddy, to have a fit of giddiness; **j'ai eu un é.,** my head began to swim; **cela me donne des étourdissements,** it makes my head swim; **après mon premier é. . . .,** when I had recovered from the shock . . . 2. numbing, deadening (of pain, grief); dazing (of the mind).

étourneau, -eaux [eturno], *s.m.* 1. (*a*) *Orn:* **e. (sansonnet),** starling; **é. unicolore,** spotless starling; (*b*) *F:* scatter-brain; **répondre comme un é.,** to answer in a scatter-brained manner. 2. *a. & s.m.* flea-bitten (horse).

étouteau, -eaux [etuto], *s.m.* pin, catch (on watch wheel, etc.); **é. d'une baïonnette,** locking pin of a bayonet.

étrange [etrɑ̃ːʒ], *a.* 1. *A:* (*a*) foreign; far-off; **nations étranges,** foreign nations; (*b*) fearsome, distressing; **peine é.,** terrible grief. 2. (*a*) strange, peculiar, odd, queer, weird; **usage é.,** quaint, odd, custom; **chose é., il est revenu,** strange to say, he came back; **le plus é. c'est que . . .,** strangest of all . . .; (*b*) *Atom.Ph:* **particules étranges,** strange particles.

étrangement [etrɑ̃ʒmɑ̃], *adv.* strangely, queerly, oddly, peculiarly; **se tromper é.,** to be sadly mistaken; **cela ressemble é. à la rougeole,** it looks suspiciously like measles; **é. vieilli,** surprisingly aged.

étranger, -ère [etrɑ̃ʒe, -ɛːr], *a. & s.* 1. (*a*) *a.* foreign; **Ministre des affaires étrangères** = Secretary of State for Foreign Affairs; *F:* Foreign Secretary; (*b*) *s.* foreigner, alien; (*c*) *s.m.* foreign parts; **vivre, voyager, à l'é.,** to live, travel, abroad; **voyages à l'é.,** foreign travel; **navire à destination de l'é.,** ship bound for foreign parts; **correspondancier pour l'é.,** foreign correspondence clerk. 2. (*a*) *a.* strange, unknown; **sa voix m'est étrangère,** I don't know, don't recognize, his voice; (*b*) *s.* stranger, outsider; **nous ne vous traitons pas comme un é.,** we don't treat you as a stranger. 3. extraneous, foreign; not belonging

(to sth.), unconnected (**à,** with); **cela est é. à la question,** that is beside the point, irrelevant (to the subject); **je suis é. à l'affaire,** I have nothing to do with it; **être é. au complot,** to have no part in the plot; **la haine lui est étrangère,** hatred is unknown to him; **il est é. à la musique,** he has no knowledge of music; **il est é. à nos usages,** he is a stranger to, ignorant of, our customs.

étrangeté [etrɑ̃ʒte], *s.f.* (*a*) strangeness, quaintness, oddness, peculiarity (of conduct, style, dress, etc.); (*b*) *Atom.Ph:* strangeness.

étranglé [etrɑ̃gle], *a.* constricted, narrow (passage, etc.); over-tight (dress); choked, choking, choky (voice); strangulated (hernia); *Aut:* **châssis é.,** cambered, inswept, chassis.

étranglement [etrɑ̃gləmɑ̃], *s.m.* **1.** (*a*) strangling, strangulation, garrotting (of s.o.); (*b*) constriction, narrowing (of sth.); jamming (of cable); *Mch:* throttling; **soupape d'é.,** throttle valve; *Med:* **é. d'une hernie, é. herniaire,** strangulated hernia, strangulation of a hernia. **2.** (*a*) choke (of gun barrel); *Mec:* **é. calibré,** calibrated choke; (*b*) narrow channel, narrows (of strait, river); bottleneck (of thoroughfare); neck (in pipe).

étrangler [etrɑ̃gle], *v.tr.* **1.** (*a*) to strangle, throttle (s.o.); **é. un condamné,** to garrotte a prisoner; **sa cravate l'étrangle,** his tie is choking him; **é. un complot au berceau,** to nip a plot in the bud; **j'ai un mot qui m'étrangle,** I've got a frog in my throat; (*b*) *v.i.* **é. de soif,** to be parched with thirst. **2.** to constrict; compress (sth.); to strangulate (blood vessel); *Mch:* to throttle (steam, etc.); *Nau:* to nip, jam (stay); *I.C.E:* **é. le moteur,** to throttle down the engine; **é. une manche,** to make a sleeve too narrow; *A:* **taille étranglée par le corset,** tight-laced, constricted, figure; **les chantiers du métro achevaient d'é. les rues,** the works for the underground were practically blocking the streets.

s'étrangler. 1. to strangle oneself. **2.** to choke oneself; **il s'est étranglé à force de crier,** he grew quite hoarse with shouting; **s'é. de colère,** to choke with rage; **s'é. de rire,** to suffocate with laughter; **sa voix s'étrangla,** she could hardly speak. **3.** to swallow sth. the wrong way; **s'é. avec une arête de poisson,** to choke on a fish-bone. **4. la vallée s'étrangle,** the valley narrows.

étrangleur, -euse [etrɑ̃glœːr, -øːz]. **1.** *s.* (*a*) strangler, garrotter; thug; (*b*) *A: P:* scrounger. **2.** *s.m.* (*a*) *Mch:* throttle(-valve); (*b*) *I.C.E:* strangler, choke, air-shutter. **3.** *s.m. pl. Bot:* **les étrangleurs,** the stranglers.

étrangloir [etrɑ̃glwaːr], *s.m.* **1.** *Nau:* throat brail (of sail); **é. de câble, de chaîne,** compressor. **2.** *Pyr:* choking frame.

étranglure [etrɑ̃glyːr], *s.f.* crease (in cloth).

étranguillon [etrɑ̃gijɔ̃], *s.m.* **1.** *Vet:* strangles. **2.** *Hort:* **poire d'é.,** choke pear.

étrave [etraːv], *s.f. Nau:* stem, stem-post (of ship); **de l'é. à l'étambot,** from stem to stern; **lame d'é.,** bow wave; **é. à guibre,** cutwater stem.

être [ɛːtr]. **I.** *v.i. & pred.* (*pr.p.* **étant**; *p.p.* **été**; *pr.ind.* **je suis, tu es, il est, n. sommes, v. êtes, ils sont**; *pr.sub.* **je sois, tu sois, il soit, n. soyons, v. soyez, ils soient**; *imp.* **sois, soyons, soyez**; *p.d.* **j'étais**; *p.h.* **je fus, tu fus, il fut, n. fûmes, v. fûtes, ils furent**; *p.sub.* **je fusse**; *fu.* **je serai**) **1.** to be, to exist; **je pense, donc je suis,** I think, therefore I am; **l'ancien projet n'est plus,** the old plan is dead, is a thing of the past; **cesser d'être,** to cease to be; **elle n'est plus,** she is no more, she is gone; **cela étant,** that being the case, such being the case; **cela n'est pas,** that is not so; **la plus belle voiture qui soit,** the finest car going, the finest car out, the best car in the world; **eh bien, soit!** (i) well, so be it! agreed! (ii) well, it can't be helped! **ainsi soit-il,** so be it; *Ecc:* amen; **on ne peut pas ê. et avoir été,** you can't have your cake and eat it. **2.** (*as copula*) (*a*) **c'est le chef de gare,** he's the station master; **il est, c'est un, chef de gare,** he's a station master; **êtes-vous père?** are you a father? **si j'étais roi,** if I were king; **soit *a* la base d'un triangle,** let *a* be the base of a triangle; **soit un triangle ABC,** given a triangle ABC; *P:* **en être,** to be a queer, to be like that, to be one of them; **vous n'allez pas me dire que Marc en est,** don't tell me Mark is like that; (*b*) **l'homme est mortel,** man is mortal; **le retour fut difficile,** the return proved difficult; **nous étions deux, trois, plusieurs,** there were two, three, several, of us; (*c*) **elle est très mal, beaucoup mieux,** she is very ill, much better; **ê. bien, mal, avec qn,** to be on good, bad, terms with s.o.; **comment êtes-vous avec le patron?** how do you stand with the boss? **quel jour (du mois) sommes-nous?** what's the date (today?); **nous sommes le dix,** it's the tenth (today); (*d*) **ê. dans son lit,** to be in bed; **le village est au-dessous du château,** the village lies below the castle; **ses livres étaient sur la table,** his books were lying on the table; **la vérité est entre ces extrêmes,** the truth lies between these extremes; **il est à Paris,** he is in Paris; **quand il fut pour sortir,** just as he was about to leave; **mon frère était près de l'arbre,** my brother was standing near the tree; (*e*) **ê. au travail,** to be at work; **ê. à l'agonie,** to be dying; **ê. aux appointements,** to receive a salary; **vous n'êtes pas à ce que je dis,** you are not paying attention to what I say, your mind is wandering; **il est tout à son travail,** he is entirely engrossed in his work; *s.a.* Y[2] 1; (*f*) **ce tableau est de Gauguin,** this picture is by Gauguin; **il est d'un bon caractère,** he is good-tempered; **il est de Londres,** he is from London; **il était du conseil municipal,** he belonged to, was a member of, the municipal council; **il n'est pas des nôtres,** he isn't a member of our party, he isn't with us; he isn't one of us; **voulez-vous ê. des nôtres?** will you join our party, make one of us? **il est de mes amis,** he's a friend of mine, one of my friends; **ê. de service,** to be on duty; (*g*) **il est à travailler, à jouer,** he is at work, at play; **on est tout le temps à se demander: est-ce vrai?** we wonder the whole time whether it is true; **son ami est dans le salon à l'attendre,** her friend is waiting for her in the drawing-room; **il fut trois ans à l'écrire,** he took three years to write it; **ils sont toujours à se quereller,** they are always quarrelling; **la maison est à louer,** the house is to be let; (*h*) (*with* **ce** *as neuter subject*) (i) **voilà ce que c'est que de ne pas regarder,** that's what comes of not looking; **je sais ce qui est arrivé,** I know what happened; **est-ce vrai?** can it be true? is it true? **serait-ce vrai?** can it be true? could it (possibly) be true? **ne fût-ce que, ne serait-ce que,** if only; (ii) **vous venez, n'est-ce pas?** you're coming, aren't you? **vous ne venez pas, n'est-ce pas?** you're not coming, are you? **n'est-ce pas qu'il a de la chance?** isn't he lucky? (iii) (*with ellipsis of* **ce**) **je le ferais (si ce) n'était que . . .,** I should do it were it not that . . ., only that . . ., but that . . .; **n'était mon rhumatisme . . .,** were it not for my rheumatism, but for my rheumatism . . .; **n'eût été la pluie . . .,** had it not been for the rain . . ., but for the rain . . .; (*i*) *impers. uses,* (i) **il est midi,** it is twelve o'clock; **il est temps de partir,** it is time to go; **il est vrai que . . .,** it is true that . . .; **il est de mon devoir de** + *inf.*, it is my duty to + *inf.*; **il est bon de** + *inf.*, it is good to + *inf.*; **il n'est que de le voir pour se convaincre que . . .,** you have only to see him to be convinced that . . .; **il n'est que de faire preuve d'énergie,** we, you, need only show energy; **comme si de rien n'était,** as if nothing had happened; *abs.* **trois à quinze francs, soit 45 fr.,** three at fifteen francs, that is 45 fr.; **trois tours de piste, soit deux kilomètres,** three times round the track, (let us) say two kilometres; **soit dit sans offense,** be it said without offence; you won't take offence at my saying so; you don't mind my saying so; (ii) **il est un Dieu,** there is a God! **il est des hommes à qui tout sourit,** there are men on whom fortune always smiles; **il était une fois une fée,** once upon a time there was a fairy; **un héros, s'il en fut (jamais),** a hero, if ever there was one; **joueur s'il en fut (jamais),** a gambler with a vengeance, an inveterate gambler; (*j*) (*with indeterminate* **en**) (i) **où en sommes-nous?** how far have we got? **nous en sommes à la page 10,** we are at, have reached, page 10; **où en étais-je?** where was I? **l'affaire en est là,** so the matter rests; that's the stage things have reached; **il en est à mendier son pain,** he is reduced to begging; **vous n'en êtes pas encore là!** you haven't come to that yet! **il n'en est pas à son coup d'essai,** this is not his first attempt; **nous allons faire l'inventaire pour voir où nous en sommes,** we are going to take stock, in order to see how we stand; **je ne sais plus où j'en suis,** I'm in a fog, all astray; **personne n'en est plus à hausser les sourcils lorsque . . .,** nobody is going to bat an eyelid now when . . .; **nous n'en sommes pas à le renvoyer,** we haven't reached the point of sacking him yet; (ii) **j'en suis pour mon argent,** I've spent my money to no purpose; **j'en suis pour mille francs,** I am the poorer by a thousand francs; **j'en suis pour ma course; il était sorti,** I did the journey for nothing; he was out; **s'il y en a trop, on en sera pour en laisser,** if there is too much, we must just leave some; (iii) **j'en suis pour ce que j'ai dit,** I stick to what I said; **il en est pour les changements,** he believes in change, he's all for change; (iv) **j'en suis!** I'm game! I'm on! I'm with you! count me in! (v) **c'en est trop!** this is past bearing! beyond words! *F:* the end! the limit! (vi) (*impers.*) **il en est de l'homme comme de la nature,** it's the same with man as with nature; **puisqu'il en est ainsi,** since that is how things are; **j'aurais préféré qu'il en fût autrement,** I could have wished it otherwise; **il n'en est rien!** it's not so! nothing of the kind! **par bonheur il n'en fut rien,** fortunately nothing of the kind happened; (vii) **il en est qui disent que . . .,** there are some (people) who say . . .; (*k*) (*with indeterminate* **y**) **il y est pour quelque chose,** he's got something to do with it; **ça y est!** (i) it's done! that's it! (ii) all right! (iii) well, I was sure it would happen! *F:* **vous y êtes?** are you with me? have you got it? **3.** (*a*) **ê. à qn,** to belong to s.o.; **à qui sont ces livres?—ils sont à nous,** whose books are these?—they are ours, they belong to us; **ma vie est-elle à moi?** is my life my own? **je suis à vous dans un moment,** I shall be at your service in a moment; **la victoire est aux forts,** the battle is to the strong; (*b*) **c'est à vous de jouer,** it's your turn to play; **c'est à vous de veiller sur l'enfant,** it's your job to look after the child; **c'est à nous de mener l'affaire à bien,** it rests with us to see the business through; **ce fut à ses fils d'achever le travail,** it was left for his sons to complete the work. **4.** (*aux. use*) (*a*) (*with intr. vbs. denoting change of place or state, etc.*) **il est arrivé,** he has arrived; **il est arrivé hier,** he arrived yesterday; **elle est née en 1950,** she was born in 1950; **attendez qu'il soit arrivé,** wait until he arrives; **il était parti la veille,** he had left the day before; **quand il fut reparti,** when he had gone away again; **on refusa de croire que je fusse venu à pied,** they (simply) wouldn't believe that I had walked; (*b*) (*with pronominal verbs*) **nous nous sommes trompés,** we (have) made a mistake; **elle s'est fait mal,** she (has) hurt herself. **5.** (*as aux. of the passive voice*) **il fut puni par son père,** he was punished by his father; **il est aimé de tout le monde,** he is beloved by everyone; **j'entends être obéi,** I mean to be obeyed. **6.** (*a*) = ALLER (*in compound tenses and in p.h.*); **j'avais été à Paris,** I had been to Paris; **j'ai été voir Jones,** I've been, I went, to see Jones; **il fut se promener dans le parc,** he went for a walk in the park; **on a été jusqu'à prétendre que . . .,** people have gone so far as to claim that . . .; (*b*) = S'EN ALLER (*in p.h. only*) **il s'en fut ouvrir la porte,** he went off to open the door; **il s'en fut sans plus rien dire,** he departed, made off, without another word.

II. **être,** *s.m.* **1.** being, existence; **ceux qui vous ont donné l'ê.,** those to whom you owe your being. **2.** being, nature; **tout mon ê. se révolte à l'idée que . . .,** my whole being revolts at the idea that . . .; **métaphysique conforme à l'ê. véritable des choses,** metaphysics in conformity with the true nature, essence, of things. **3.** being, individual; **L'Ê. suprême,** the Supreme Being; **un ê. humain,** a human being; *Pej:* **c'est un ê. insupportable,** he's unbearable; **pauvres petits êtres!** poor little creatures! poor little things!

étrécir [etresiːr], *v.tr. A:* to narrow (street, etc.); **é. une robe,** (i) to take in, (ii) to shrink, a dress; *Equit:* **é. un cheval,** to cause a horse to narrow.

s'étrécir, *A:* **1.** to become narrower, to narrow; **le chemin va en s'étrécissant,** the road becomes narrower as one goes on; **la prunelle s'étrécit au grand jour,** the pupil contracts in the daylight. **2.** (*of material*) to shrink. **3.** *Equit:* (*of horse*) to narrow.

étrécissement [etresismɑ̃], *s.m. A:* narrowing (of road, of the mind, etc.); contraction (of the pupil of the eye, etc.); **é. d'une robe,** (i) taking in, (ii) shrinking, of a dress.

étrécissure [etresisyːr], *s.f. A:* shrinkage (of material, etc.).

étreignant [etrɛɲɑ̃], *a.* (*a*) clinging (liana); (*b*) moving (experience).

étreignoir [etrɛɲwaːr], *s.m. Carp:* screw clamp, flooring cramp.

étreindelle [etrɛ̃dɛl], *s.f.* (*in edible oil mill*) press cloth, "hair."

étreindre [etrɛ̃ːdr], *v.tr.* (*pr.p.* **étreignant**; *p.p.* **étreint**; *pr.ind.* **j'étreins, il étreint, n. étreignons, ils étreignent**; *p.d.* **j'étreignais**; *p.h.* **j'étreignis**; *fu.* **j'étreindrai**) **1.** to embrace, hug; to clasp (s.o.) in one's arms; **elle lui sauta au cou et l'étreignit,** she flung her arms round his neck; **é. qch. dans la main,** to grasp, grip, sth. (with one's hand); to clutch (pistol, etc.); **é. la main de qn,** to wring s.o.'s hand; **l'émotion m'étreint,** I am in the grip of emotion; **spectacle qui vous étreint le cœur,**

moving sight; *Prov:* **qui trop embrasse mal étreint,** grasp all, lose all. **2.** to fetter, impede (thought, etc.). **3.** *A:* **é. les liens de l'amitié,** to tighten the bonds of friendship.

étreinte [etrɛ̃:t], *s.f.* **1.** (*a*) embrace, hug; (*b*) grasp, grip; **forte é. de mains,** hearty handshake; **échapper à l'é. de qn,** to escape (from) s.o.'s grasp; (*c*) *Wr:* lock. **2.** (exertion of) pressure; **sous l'é. de l'émotion,** under the pressure of emotion. **3.** (*in vegetable oil mill*) canvas bag (holding seed). **4.** *Civ.E:* **triple é.,** triaxial compression.

étrenne [etrɛn], *s.f.* **1.** *usu. pl.* New-Year's gift; **les étrennes du facteur** = the postman's Christmas box; **livre d'étrennes,** giftbook. **2.** (*a*) *A:* (shopkeeper's) first sale of the day; (*b*) **avoir l'é. de qch.,** to have the first use of sth.; *F:* **n'en avoir pas l'é.,** to get sth. secondhand; to get s.o.'s cast-offs.

étrenner [etrene]. **1.** *v.tr.* (*a*) *A:* to give a New-Year's gift to (s.o.); (*b*) *A:* to be the first to buy from (shopkeeper). **2.** *v.i.* (*a*) *A:* to receive money from the first customer of the day; (*b*) *F:* **tu vas étrenner!** you're going to get it! you're going to catch it! **3.** *v.tr.* to use (sth.) for the first time; to christen (object); **é. une robe,** to wear a dress for the first time.

étrèpe [etrɛp], *s.f. Agr:* mattock.

êtres [ɛ:tr], *s.m.pl.* arrangement, ins and outs, of a house; **connaître les ê.,** to know one's way about a house.

étrésillon [etrezijɔ̃], *s.m.* **1.** *Const: Min:* prop, shore, strut, brace. **2.** *Nau:* rigging batten; Spanish windlass.

étrésillonnement [etrezijɔnmɑ̃], *s.m. Const:* propping; shoring (across); strutting, bracing (of wall, trench, etc.).

étrésillonner [etrezijɔne], *v.tr.* to prop; to shore (across); to strut, brace (wall, excavation, etc.).

étrier [etrije], *s.m.* **1.** (*a*) *Harn:* stirrup; *Equit:* **pied de l'é.,** stirrup, left, foot; **à franc é.,** at full gallop; **être fort, ferme, sur ses étriers,** (i) to have a good seat; (ii) to be ready to uphold one's opinions; (iii) to be resolute in carrying out one's plans; **perdre, vider, les étriers,** (i) to lose one's stirrups; (ii) to be thrown, unhorsed; (iii) to lose one's advantage; (iv) to become disconcerted, upset; **avoir le pied à l'é.,** (i) to be about to mount (one's horse); (ii) to be on the point of leaving; (iii) to hold oneself ready; (iv) to be well on the way to success; **tenir l'é. à qn,** (i) to hold s.o.'s horse (for him to mount); (ii) to give s.o. a helping hand; **vin, coup, de l'é.,** stirrup cup; *F:* **le coup de l'é.,** one for the road; **remettre le pied de qn dans l'é.,** to help s.o. to his feet; (*b*) *Mount:* (climbing) stirrup(s); (*c*) *pl. Nau:* stirrups (of the foot ropes); (*d*) *Surg:* (i) stirrup, leg rest (for examination, operation); (ii) caliper (splint) (for fractured leg). **2.** *Anat:* stirrup bone (of ear); stapes. **3.** *Tchn:* stirrup piece, strap, band, brace (for beams, etc.); clip, clevis, yoke; **é. de pression, de serrage,** binding clip; **é. de soupape,** valve clamp; **é. d'attache,** attaching lug (of brake, etc.); **é. pour tuyau,** pipe hanger; *Const:* **é. d'échafaudage,** cradle iron, cradle stirrup; *Rail:* **é. d'attelage,** shackle (of railway coupling); *Tp:* **é. du récepteur,** receiver rest, cradle; *El:* **é. de raccordement,** bridge connector.

étrière [etrijɛ:r], *s.f. Harn:* stirrup strap.

étrieu [etrijø], *s.m. Const:* transverse stay.

étrillage [etrija:ʒ], *s.m.* **1.** curry(comb)ing (of horse). **2.** *F:* (*a*) *A:* thrashing, trouncing, drubbing; (*b*) overcharging, fleecing.

étrille [etrij], *s.f.* **1.** currycomb. **2.** *Crust:* velvet swimming crab.

étriller [etrije], *v.tr.* **1.** to curry(comb) horse. **2.** *F:* (*a*) *A:* to thrash, trounce, drub (s.o.); (*b*) **é. qn aux échecs,** to wipe the floor with s.o. at chess; (*c*) to treat (s.o.) roughly; to make violent criticism of (s.o.), to tear (s.o.) to pieces; (*d*) to overcharge, fleece (s.o.); **nous nous sommes fait é. à cet hôtel,** we were well and truly stung at that hotel.

étripage [etripa:ʒ], *s.m.* gutting (of fish); drawing (of chicken, etc.); *F:* (*of people*) tearing each other's guts out.

étripé [etripe], *a.* frayed, fagged (rope).

étripe-cheval (à) [aetripʃəval], *adv.phr. A:* **courir à é.-c.,** to ride hell-for-leather.

étriper [etripe], *v.tr.* to gut (fish); to draw (chicken, etc.); to disembowel (horse, etc.).

s'étriper, (*of rope*) to become frayed, fagged; to fray; *F:* (*of people*) to tear each other's guts out.

étriqué [etrike], *a.* (*a*) skimpy, tight (garment); **garçon é.,** boy who is growing out of his clothes; **cour étriquée,** narrow, cramped, courtyard; **position étriquée, geste é.,** cramped position, gesture; (*b*) narrow, limited, (outlook); **mener une vie étriquée,** to lead a cramped, restricted, life; (*c*) *Ven:* **chien é.,** thin lanky hound.

étriquement [etrikmɑ̃], *s.m.* cramping; crampedness.

étriquer [etrike], *v.tr.* **1.** *Carp:* to thin (plank, etc.). **2.** (*a*) to skimp (garment); to make (coat, etc.) too tight; **cette coupe de veste vous étrique,** the cut of that jacket gives you a skimped appearance; (*b*) **é. un discours,** to skimp a speech.

étriquet [etrikɛ], *s.m. Fish:* fishing net (with rectangular frame).

étristé [etriste], *a. Ven:* (*of hound*) strong-hocked.

étrive [etri:v], *s.f. Nau:* **1.** throat-seizing. **2.** bend, nip (in rope).

étriver [etrive], *Nau:* **1.** *v.tr.* to cross, seize, jam, nip (rope); **la ralingue est étrivée par l'étai,** **étrive l'étai,** the foot rope nips round the stay; **é. les deux haubans ensemble,** to heave the two shrouds together. **2.** *v.i.* (*of rope*) to become jammed, nipped.

étrivière [etrivjɛ:r], *s.f.* stirrup leather; *A:* **donner les étrivières à qn,** to thrash, strap, s.o.; to give s.o. a belting, a leathering.

étroit [etrwɑ], *a.* **1.** narrow (space, ribbon, etc.); confined (space); **souliers étroits du bout,** shoes narrow at the toe(s); pointed shoes; **chemin de fer à voie étroite,** narrow-gauge railway; **la voie étroite,** the strait and narrow way; **esprit é.,** narrow mind; **personne aux idées étroites,** narrow-minded person; *Com:* **marché é.,** limited market. **2.** tight, close (knot, bond, etc.); tight(-fitting) (coat, etc.); **pantalon é. du bas,** tapered trousers; **alliance étroite,** close, intimate, alliance; **parenté, proximité, étroite,** close relationship, proximity; **règlements étroits,** strict, hidebound, rules; **étroite obligation,** strict obligation; **dans le sens le plus é. du mot,** in the strictest sense of the word. **3.** *adv.phr.* **être à l'é.,** (i) to be pinched, cramped, for room; to be cribbed, cabined, and confined; (ii) to be badly off, in straitened circumstances; **se sentir à l'é.,** to feel cramped for room, confined for room; to feel boxed up; **vivre à l'é.,** to practise strict economy; to live in a very small way. **4.** *s.m. Geog:* gorge.

étroite [etrwat], *s.f. Tls:* broach, reamer.

étroitement [etrwatmɑ̃], *adv.* **1.** narrowly; **être logé é.,** to live in cramped quarters; **être chaussé é.,** to have tight shoes. **2.** tightly, closely (bound, knotted, etc.); **être é. renfermé,** to be closely, strictly, confined; **ils sont é. liés d'amitié,** they are bosom friends; **surveiller qn é.,** to keep a close, strict, watch over s.o.

étroitesse [etrwatɛs], *s.f.* **1.** narrowness (of path, shoulders, etc.); **é. d'esprit,** narrow-mindedness. **2.** tightness, closeness (of bond, knot, etc.); **l'é. de notre budget,** our slender means, our limited budget.

étron [etrɔ̃], *s.m. P:* turd, shit.

étronçonner [etrɔ̃sɔne], *v.tr. Arb:* to head down, to cut the head off, to pollard (tree).

étrope [etrɔp], *s.f. Nau:* strop, strap, grommet (of pulley block, toggle pin, etc.); **poulie à é.,** stropped block.

étroper [etrɔpe], *v.tr. Nau:* to strop (rigging, block).

Étrurie [etryri], *Pr.n.f. A.Geog:* Etruria.

étruscologie [etryskɔlɔʒi], *s.f.* Etruscology.

étruscologue [etryskɔlɔg], *s.m. & f.* Etruscologist.

étrusque [etrysk], *a. & s.* Etruscan, Etrurian.

étude [etyd], *s.f.* study. **1.** (*a*) studying; **l'é. des langues, de l'histoire,** the study of languages, of history; **é. sans maître,** self instruction; **il n'avait pas fait d'études de droit,** he had not studied law; **faire ses études à . . .,** to be educated at . . .; **il a fait ses études à Oxford,** he was at Oxford; **il a fait ses études à Harvard,** *U.S:* he graduated at Harvard; **faire des études de français,** to study French; **études sur le terrain,** field study; **programme d'études,** curriculum; syllabus; **il avait subvenu aux frais d'études de son neveu,** he had paid for his nephew's education; *Sch:* **l'é. du soir,** (evening) preparation; *F:* prep; **(salle d') é.,** preparation, *F:* prep, room; **fait en é.,** done in prep; **faire de bonnes études,** to have a successful school career; **é. du piano,** piano practice; **é. d'une pièce de théâtre,** rehearsing of a play; **mettre une pièce à l'é.,** to rehearse a play; (*b*) (*application of mind*) **faire son é. de qch., mettre son é. à qch., à faire qch.,** to take great pains about sth.; to make a special study of sth.; **cela sent l'é.,** it smells of midnight oil; (*c*) research (work); investigation; survey; **bureau d'études,** (i) research department; (ii) drawing office (of factory, etc.); **atelier, services, d'études,** design department, research and development department; **é. préliminaire,** preliminary, pilot, study; **é. des méthodes,** method analysis; **faire les études d'un chemin de fer,** to survey a railway; **é. d'un canal,** scheme, project, for a canal; **moteur, voiture, d'é.,** test engine, car; *Av:* **é. de route,** route analysis; **é. sur le terrain,** field study; *Mil:* **é. du terrain,** terrain study; **ingénieur d'études,** design engineer; **comité d'é.,** committee of enquiry; **procéder à l'é. d'une question, mettre une question à l'é.,** to study, go into, survey, examine, a question; **le projet est à l'é.,** the plan is being worked out; **cet avion est encore à l'é.,** this aircraft is still (i) on the drawing board, (ii) at the experimental stage; **é. de la situation,** survey of the situation. **2.** *Mus:* étude, study; **é. pour violon,** violin study; *Art:* **é. de tête,** study of a head; **é. de nu,** study from the nude; **é. de bétail,** cattle piece. **3.** (*a*) office (of solicitor); chambers (of barrister); (*b*) (lawyer's) practice; **vendre son é.,** to sell one's practice.

étudiant, -iante [etydjɑ̃, -jɑ̃:t]. **1.** *s.* student; undergraduate; **é. en médecine, en droit, en lettres,** medical, law, arts, student; **é. libre,** external student; **é. de première année,** freshman; *F:* fresher. **2.** *attrib.a.* **organisation étudiante,** student organization.

étudié [etydje], *a.* studied (calm); studied, elaborate, deliberate (effect); set (speech); **manières étudiées,** artificial, affected, manners; **prix très étudiés,** cheapest possible, keenest, prices; **meuble aux lignes étudiées,** well-designed piece of furniture; **é. en vue de . . .,** designed for . . .

étudier [etydje], *v.tr.* (*p.d. & pr.sub.* **n. étudiions, v. étudiiez**) (*a*) to study (language, music, person's character, etc.); *Sch:* to prepare (lessons, etc.); to read (law, medicine); **é. une matière en vue d'un examen,** to read up a subject for an examination; **é. (son piano),** to practise (on the piano); (*b*) to study (one's effect, appearance); to practise (fencing); to rehearse (play); (*c*) to investigate, consider, examine, carefully; go into, enquire into, look into (question, plan, theory); to make a study of (a case); to design (sth.); **rapport bien étudié,** carefully written report; **machine étudiée dans un but spécial,** machine designed for a special purpose.

s'étudier à faire qch., to take pains to do sth., to endeavour to do sth., to make a point of doing sth.; **on s'était étudié à mettre tout le monde à l'aise,** a great effort had been made to make everybody comfortable; **il s'étudiait à m'éviter,** he studiously avoided me; **il s'étudie à plaire,** he makes every effort to please; *F:* **elle s'étudie trop,** (i) she is too affected; (ii) she fusses about herself too much.

étudiole [etydjɔl], *s.f. Furn:* nest of drawers.

étui [etɥi], *s.m.* case, box, cover; **é. de voile,** sail cover; **é. de cartouche,** cartridge case; **é. à lunettes,** spectacle case; **é. à cigares,** cigar case; **é. à cartes,** card case; **é. de revolver,** holster; **é. de, à, chapeau,** hat-box; *A:* **é. de mathématiques,** case of drawing instruments; **(livre en) é.,** (book in a) slip case; **é. à brosse à dents,** toothbrush holder; **é. (de capsules pharmaceutiques),** carrier.

étui-musette [etɥimyzɛt], *s.m.* haversack; *pl. étuis-musettes.*

étuvage [etyva:ʒ], *s.m.,* drying (of sugar, etc.); seasoning, steaming (of wood); stoving, baking (of contaminated clothing); sweating (of leather); *Metall:* stoving, baking (of mould, etc.); *Med:* fomenting.

étuve [ety:v], *s.f.* **1.** (*a*) *A:* bath-house; (*b*) sweating-room (of baths); **é. sèche,** hot-air bath or cabinet; **é. humide,** vapour bath. **2.** *Ch: Ind: etc:* (*a*) drying oven; **séché à l'é.,** oven-dried; (*b*) drying cupboard; **é. à linge,** hot (linen) press; **é. à vide,** vacuum drier; *Metall:* **é. à noyaux,** core oven; *Bac:* **é. à incubation, à cultures,** incubator; *F:* **quelle é.!** what an oven!

étuvée [etyve], *s.f. Cu:* **à l'é.,** braised.

étuvement [etyvmɑ̃], *s.m.* = ÉTUVAGE.

étuver [etyve], *v.tr.* **1.** *Ind: etc:* to dry; to heat; to steam; to stove, bake (contaminated clothing); to sweat (leather); *Metall:* to stove, bake (mould). **2.** *Cu:* to braise (meat, etc.); to jug (hare, etc.); to steam (potatoes, etc.). **3.** *Med:* to foment.

étuveur, -euse [etyvœ:r, -ø:z], *s.* **1.** *A:* bath-house attendant. **2.** *s.m.* steamer (for cattle food). **3.** *s.f. Coop:* steam generator (for moistening timber of barrels).

étymologie [etimɔlɔʒi], *s.f.* etymology; **é. populaire,** popular, folk, etymology.

étymologique [etimɔlɔʒik], *a.* etymological.

étymologiquement [etimɔlɔʒikmɑ̃], *adv.* etymologically.

étymologiste [etimɔlɔʒist], *s.m. & f.* etymologist.

étymon [etimɔ̃], *s.m. Ling:* etymon.

eu- [ø], *pref.* eu-; *Ent:* **eucéphale,** eucephalous; *Miner:* **euchroïte,** euchroite.

eubactériées [øbakterje], *s.f.pl. Bac:* Eubacteria.

Eubée [øbe], *Pr.n.f. Geog:* Euboea.

eubéen, -enne [øbeɛ̃, -ɛn], *a. & s. Geog:* Euboean.

euboïque [øbɔik], *a. Geog:* Euboic (Sea).

eucaïrite [økairit], *s.f. Miner:* eucairite, eukairite.

eucalyptol [økaliptɔl], *s.m. Ch:* eucalyptol.

eucalyptus [økaliptyːs], *s.m. Bot:* eucalyptus; gum(tree); **e. bleu,** blue gum tree; **e. résineux,** iron bark tree, red gum; **e. poivré,** peppermint tree; *Pharm:* **essence d'e.,** eucalyptus oil.

eucarides [økarid], *s.m.pl. Crust:* Eucarida.

eucéphale [øsefal], *a. Ent:* eucephalous.

eucharis [økaris], *s.m.* **1.** *Bot:* eucharis. **2.** *Ent:* eucharid.

eucharistie (l') [løkaristi], *s.f. Ecc:* the eucharist.

eucharistique [økaristik], *a.* eucharistic(al).

euchologe [økɔlɔːʒ], *s.m. Ecc:* euchology, euchologion.

euchre [øːkr̥], *s.m. Cards:* euchre.

euchroïte [økrɔit], *s.f. Miner:* euchroite.

euchromatine [økrɔmatin], *s.f.* euchromatin.

euchromides [økrɔmid], *s.m.pl. Ent:* Euchromiidae, Syntomidae.

euchromosome [økrɔmɔzoːm], *s.m.* euchromosome.

euclase [øklaːz], *s.f. Miner:* euclase.

eucléides [økleid], *s.m.pl. Ent:* Eucleidae, the Euclid (family of) moths.

Euclide [øklid], *Pr.n.m.* Euclid.

euclidien, -ienne [øklidjɛ̃, -jɛn], *a.* Euclidean.

eucnémididés [øknemidide], *s.m.pl. Ent:* Eucnemidae.

eucolite [økɔlit], *s.f. Miner:* eucolite, eukolite, eukolyte.

eucologe [økɔlɔːʒ], *s.m. Ecc:* euchology, euchologion, prayerbook.

eucrasite [økrazit], *s.f. Miner:* eucrasite.

eucryptite [økriptit], *s.f. Miner:* eucryptite.

eudémis [ødemis], *s.m. Ent:* eudemis moth; **e. de la vigne,** vine moth.

Eudémon [ødemɔ̃], *Pr.n. Astrol:* Eudaemon.

eudémonique [ødemɔnik], *a. Astrol:* eudaemonistic.

eudémonisme [ødemɔnism], *s.m. Phil:* eudemonism.

eudémoniste [ødemɔnist], *a. & s.m. & f. Phil:* eudemonist.

Eudes [øːd], *Pr.n.m. Hist:* Odo.

eudialyte [ødjalit], *s.f. Miner:* eudialyte.

eudidymite [ødidimit], *s.f. Miner:* eudidymite.

eudiomètre [ødjɔmɛtr̥], *s.m. Ph:* eudiometer.

eudiométrie [ødjɔmetri], *s.f. Ph:* eudiometry.

eudiométrique [ødjɔmetrik], *a. Ph:* eudiometric(al).

eudiste [ødist], *s.m. R.C.Ch:* Eudist.

eudois, -oise [ødwa, -waːz], *a. & s. Geog:* (native, inhabitant) of Eu.

eufraise [øfrɛːz], *s.f. Bot:* euphrasia; eyebright.

eugénate [øʒenat], *s.m. Ch: Dent:* eugenolate, eugenate.

Eugène [øʒɛn], *Pr.n.m.* Eugene, Eugenius; *Hist:* **le Prince E.,** Prince Eugene.

eugénésie [øʒenezi], *s.f. Biol:* eugenesia.

eugénésique [øʒenezik], *a. Biol:* eugenic.

Eugénie [øʒeni], *Pr.n.f.* Eugenia.

eugénique [øʒenik], *s.f.,* **eugénisme** [øʒenism] *s.m.* eugenics, eugenetics.

eugéniste [øʒenist], *s.* eugenist.

eugénol [øʒenɔl], *s.m. Ch:* eugenol.

euglène [øglɛn], *s.f. Prot:* euglena.

eugléniḋés [øglenide], *s.m.pl. Prot:* Euglenidae.

euglobine [øglɔbin], **euglobuline** [øglɔbylin], *s.f. Bio-Ch:* euglobulin.

eugubine [øgybin], *a. Ant:* **tables eugubines,** Eugubine tables.

euh [ø], *int.* (*expressing surprise, incredulity*) hm! **e.! vous êtes sûr?** uh! are you sure? (*expressing uncertainty, embarrassment*) er . . ., **cela vous plaît?—e.!** you like it?—'m.

euhédral, -aux [øedral, -o], *a.* euhedral.

eukaïrite [økairit], *s.f. Miner:* eucairite, eukairite.

Eulalie [ølali], *Pr.n.f.* Eulalia.

eulimidés [ølimide], *s.m.pl. Moll:* Eulimidae.

eulogie [ølɔʒi], *s.f. Ecc:* eulogia.

eulytène [ølitɛn], *s.f. Miner:* eulytine, eulytite.

Eumée [øme], *Pr.n.m. Gr.Lit:* Eumaeus.

eumène [ømɛn], *s.m. Ent:* eumenid, potter wasp.

Euménides (les) [lezømenid], *s.f.pl. Gr.Myth:* the Eumenides.

euménidés [ømenide], *s.m.pl. Ent:* Eumenidae.

eunecte [ønɛkt], *s.m. Rept:* eunectes; anaconda.

eunice [ønis], *s.f. Ann:* Eunice; eunicid, eunician.

eunicidés [øniside], *s.m.pl. Ann:* Eunicidae.

eunuchisme [ønykism], *s.m.* eunuchism.

eunuchoïde [ønykɔid], *a.* eunuchoid.

eunuque [ønyk], *s.m.* eunuch.

euosmite [øɔzmit], *s.f. Miner:* euosmite.

eupaléodictyoptères [øpaleɔdiktjɔptɛːr], *s.m.pl. Ent: Paleont:* Eupaleodictyoptera.

eupatoire [øpatwaːr], *s.f. Bot:* eupatorium; **e. (à feuilles de chanvre),** hemp agrimony; **e. pourprée,** kidney root.

eupepsie [øpɛpsi], *s.f. Med:* eupepsia.

eupeptique [øpɛptik], *a. Med:* eupeptic.

euphausiacés [øfozjase], *s.m.pl. Crust:* Euphausiacea.

Euphémie [øfemi], *Pr.n.f.* Euphemia.

euphémique [øfemik], *a.* euphemistic.

euphémiquement [øfemikmɑ̃], *adv.* euphemistically.

euphémisme [øfemism], *s.m.* euphemism.

euphonie [øfɔni], *s.f.* euphony.

euphonique [øfɔnik], *a.* euphonic, euphonious.

euphoniquement [øfɔnikmɑ̃], *adv.* euphonically, euphoniously.

euphorbe [øfɔrb], *s.f.* **1.** *Bot:* euphorbia, spurge; **e. arborescente,** tree euphorbia, arborescent euphorbia; **e. des vignes,** wild purslane; **e. réveille-matin,** wart-wort, devil's milk. **2.** *Pharm:* euphorbium.

euphorbiacées [øfɔrbjase], *s.f.pl. Bot:* Euphorbiaceae.

euphorie [øfɔri], *s.f.* euphoria, well-being.

euphorique [øfɔrik]. **1.** *a.* euphoric. **2.** *s.m.* euphoriant; euphoric.

euphorisant [øfɔrizɑ̃], *s.m. Med:* mood elevator.

euphraise [øfrɛːz], *s.f.,* **euphrasie** [øfrazi], *s.f. Bot:* euphrasia; euphrasy, eyebright.

Euphrate [øfrat], *Pr.n.m. Geol:* the (river) Euphrates.

Euphrosyne [øfrɔzin], *Pr.n.f. Gr.Myth:* Euphrosyne.

euphuisme [øfyism], *s.m. Lit.Hist:* euphuism.

euphuiste [øfyist], *s.m. & f.* euphuist.

euplecte [øplɛkt], *s.m. Orn:* bishop bird.

euplectelle [øplɛktɛl], *s.f. Spong:* euplectella; Venus's flower basket.

euplère [øplɛːr], *s.m. Z:* falanouc, falanaka.

euplocome [øplɔkɔm], *s.m. Orn:* euplocomus.

euploïde [øplɔid], *s.m. Biol:* euploid.

eupnée [øpne], *s.f. Med:* eupnea, eupnoea.

eupnéique [øpneik], *a. Med:* eupneic, eupnoeic.

euquinine [økinin], *s.f. Pharm:* euquinine.

eurafricain, -aine [ørafrikɛ̃, -ɛn], *a.* Eurafrican.

Eurafrique [ørafrik], *s.f. Geog:* the Eurafrican area, region.

Eurasie [ørazi], *Pr.n.f. Geog:* Eurasia.

eurasien, -ienne [ørazjɛ̃, -jɛn], *a. & s. Ethn:* Eurasian.

Euratom [øratɔm], *Pr.n.f.* Euratom.

Euripe (l') [lørip], *Pr.n.m.* **Canal de l'E.,** Strait of Euripus, Evripos.

Euripide [øripid], *Pr.n.m. Gr.Lit:* Euripides.

euripidien, -ienne [øripidjɛ̃, -jɛn], *a. Gr.Lit:* Euripidean.

euristique [øristik], *a. & s.f. Phil:* heuristic, euristic.

eurite [ørit], *s.f. Miner:* eurite.

Europe [ørɔp], *Pr.n.f.* **1.** *Gr.Myth:* Europa. **2.** *Geog:* l'E., Europe; **la Pointe d'E.,** Europa Point.

européanisation [ørɔpeanizasjɔ̃], *s.f.* Europeanization.

européaniser [ørɔpeanize], *v.tr.* to Europeanize.

européanisme [ørɔpeanism], *s.m.* Europeanism.

européen, -enne [ørɔpeɛ̃, -ɛn], *a. & s.* European.

européennement [ørɔpeɛnmɑ̃], *adv.* in a European manner, fashion.

européisation [ørɔpeizasjɔ̃], *s.f.* Europeanization.

européiser [ørɔpeize], *v.tr.* to Europeanize.

europium [ørɔpjɔm], *s.m. Ch:* europium.

Eurovision [ørɔvizjɔ̃], *Pr.n.f.* Eurovision.

Euryale [ørjal], *Pr.n.m. Lt.Lit:* Euryalus.

euryales [ørjal], *s.m.pl. Echin:* Euryalida, sea spiders.

eurybathe [øribat], *a. Biol:* eurybathic.

Eurybiade [øribjad], *Pr.n.m. Gr.Hist:* Eurybiades.

eurycéphale [ørisefal], *a. Anthr:* eurycephalic, eurycephalous.

eurycéphalie [ørisefali], *s.f. Anthr:* eurycephaly.

Euryclée [ørikle], *Pr.n.f. Gr.Lit:* Eurycleia.

Eurydice [øridis], *Pr.n.f. Gr.Myth:* Eurydice.

eurygnathe [ørignat], *a. Anthr:* eurygnathous.

euryhalin [ørialɛ̃], *a. Biol:* euryhaline.

euryhalinité [ørialinite], *s.f. Biol:* euryhaline habits, conditions, state.

eurylaime [ørilɛm], *s.m. Orn:* eurylaimus, broadbill.

eurylaimidés [ørilɛmide], *s.m.pl. Orn:* Eurylaimidae.

euryphage [ørifaːʒ], *a. Ent:* euryphagous.

eurypharynx [ørifarɛ̃ːks], *s.m. Ich:* eurypharynx, pelican fish.

euryprosope [øriprɔzɔp], *a. Anthr:* euryprosopic.

euryprosopie [øriprɔzɔpi], *s.f. Anthr:* euryprosopia.

euryptérides, euryptéridés [øripterid, -teride], *s.m.pl. Paleont:* Eurypterida, Eurypteroidea, Gigantostraca, the giant sea scorpions.

Eurysthée [øriste], *Pr.n.m. Gr.Myth:* Eurystheus.

eurytherme [øritɛrm], *a. Biol:* eurythermal, eurythermic, eurythermous.

eurythermie [øritɛrmi], *s.f. Biol:* eurythermal habits, conditions, state.

eurythmie [øritmi], *s.f.* eurhythmy; **e. d'un passage,** happy rhythm, swing, of a passage.

eurythmique [øritmik], *a.* eurhythmic.

eurytomidés [øritɔmide], *s.m.pl. Ent:* Eurytomidae.

euscarien, -ienne, euskarien, -ienne [øskarjɛ̃, -jɛn], *a. & s. Geog:* Euskarian, Basque.

Eusèbe [øzɛːb], *Pr.n.m. Rel.H:* Eusebius.

eusébien, -ienne [øzebjɛ̃, -jɛn], *a. & s. Rel.H:* Eusebian.

Eustache [østaʃ]. **1.** *Pr.n.m.* Eustace, Eustachius; *Anat:* **trompe d'E.,** Eustachian tube. **2.** *s.m. F: O:* clasp-knife, pig-sticker.

eustatique [østatik], *a. Geol:* eustatic.

eustatisme [østatism], *s.m. Geol:* eustacsy, eustatism.

eustyle [østil], *s.m. Arch:* eustyle.

eusynchite [øzɛ̃kit], *s.f. Miner:* eusynchite.

eutectique [øtɛktik], *a. Ch: Ph:* eutectic.

eutectoïde [øtɛktɔid], *s.m. Metall:* eutectoid (alloy).

Euterpe [øtɛrp]. **1.** *Pr.n.f. Gr.Myth:* Euterpe. **2.** *s.f. Bot:* euterpe, assai palm.

eutexie [øtɛksi], *s.f. Ch: Ph:* eutexia.

euthanasie [øtanazi], *s.f.* euthanasia.

euthanasique [øtanazik], *a.* euthanasic.

euthériens [øterjɛ̃], *s.m.pl. Z:* Eutheria, Monodelphia, Placentalia.

eutocie [øtɔsi], *s.f. Obst:* eutocia.

Eutrope [øtrɔp], *Pr.n.m.* Eutropius.

eutrophe [øtrɔf], *a.* eutrophic (lake).

eutrophie [øtrɔfi], *s.f. Physiol:* eutrophy.

eutrophique [øtrɔfik], *a. Physiol:* eutrophic.

eutychéen, -éenne [øtikeɛ̃, -eɛn], *a. Rel.H:* Eutychian.

Eutychès [øtikɛːs], *Pr.n.m. Rel.H:* Eutyches.

eutychianisme [øtikjanism], *s.m. Rel.H:* Eutychianism.

eutychien, -ienne [øtikjɛ̃, -jɛn], *a. & s. Rel.H:* Eutychian.

eux [ø]. *See* LUI².

eux-mêmes [ømɛm]. *See* LUI² and MÊME 1 (*c*).

euxénite [øksenit], *s.f. Miner:* euxenite.

évacuable [evakɥabl̥], *a. Mil:* (*of wounded man*) fit to be moved.

évacuant [evakɥɑ̃], **évacuatif, -ive** [evakɥatif, -iːv], *a. & s.m. Med:* evacuant.

évacuateur, -trice [evakɥatœːr, -tris]. **1.** *a.* **conduit é.,** evacuation channel. **2.** *s.m. Hyd.E:* **é. (de crues),** crest gate, spillway gate.

évacuation [evakɥasjɔ̃], *s.f.* **1.** evacuation, voiding, discharge (of matter from the body, etc.); draining off, emptying, drainage (of water); eduction (of steam); *I.C.E:* exhaust stroke; **tuyau d'é.,** (i) outlet pipe; waste pipe; (ii) exhaust pipe, eduction pipe; *Civ.E:* **canal d'é.,** drainage canal. **2.** (*a*) removal, clearing out (of goods, people, etc.); ejection, eviction (of tenants); **é. de la population du quartier inondé,** evacuation of the population from the flooded district; **é. d'un théâtre par la sortie de secours,** emptying, clearing, of a theatre by the emergency exit; (*b*) *Mil:* evacuation, withdrawal (of troops, wounded men, etc.); **hôpital d'é.,** clearing hospital, station; **centre d'é.,** casualty clearing station; (*c*) vacating (of apartment, etc.); evacuation (of fortress, town). **3.** *Med:* evacuated matter, evacuation.

évacué, -ée [evakɥe], *s.* evacuee.

évacuer [evakɥe], *v.tr.* **1.** to evacuate, discharge, void (matter from the body, etc.); to exhaust (steam); to drain (off) (water); **é. l'eau d'une chaudière,** to empty, blow out, a boiler; *Paperm: Mch: etc:* **é. (une chaudière, un lessiveur, etc.),** to blow (off). **2.** (*a*) **é. des locataires,** to eject, evict, tenants; (*b*) *Mil: etc:* to evacuate, withdraw (troops, wounded, etc.); **é. la population d'une ville bombardée,** to evacuate the population from a bombed town. **3.** to vacate (apartment, etc.); to evacuate (fortress, town); **faire é. une salle,** to have a hall cleared, to clear a

hall; **on avait évacué toutes les maisons menacées de l'inondation,** all the houses threatened by the flood had been evacuated; *Nau:* **é. le bâtiment,** to abandon ship.

s'évacuer, (*of river, etc.*) to empty, discharge (**dans,** into).

évadé, -ée [evade], *a. & s.* escaped (prisoner).

évader (s') [sevade], *v.pr.* to escape (by stealth); to run away; (*of tiger, etc.*) to break loose; **s'é. de prison,** to escape from prison, to break gaol; **il a trouvé moyen de s'é. pour le Venezuela,** he managed to escape to Venezuela.

évagination [evaʒinasjɔ̃], *s.f. Physiol:* evagination.

évaginulé [evaʒinyle], *a. Bot:* evaginate.

évaltonné [evaltɔne], *a. A:* forward, saucy.

évaluable [evalɥabl̩], *a.* appraisable, assessable (goods, property).

évaluateur, -trice [evalɥatœːr, -tris], *s.* valuer, appraiser.

évaluation [evalɥasjɔ̃], *s.f.* valuation, appraisement (of property, etc.); assessment (of damages); estimate (of weight, etc.); *Typ:* cast(ing) off (of MS); **é. en gros,** rough estimate; **é. des coûts,** cost analysis.

évaluer [evalɥe], *v.tr.* to value, appraise (property, etc.); to assess (damages); to estimate, reckon (weight, number); **on évalue sa fortune à deux millions de francs,** his fortune is estimated at two million francs.

Évandre [evɑ̃ːdr̩], *Pr.n.m. Gr. & Rom.Myth:* Evander.

évanescence [evanɛs(s)ɑ̃ːs], *s.f.* evanescence.

évanescent [evanɛs(s)ɑ̃], *a.* evanescent.

évangéliaire [evɑ̃ʒeljɛːr], *s.m. Ecc:* evangelistary, gospel-book.

évangélique [evɑ̃ʒelik], *a.* **1.** *Ecc:* evangelic; according to the Gospel. **2.** *Rel.H:* evangelical, protestant (church, etc.).

évangéliquement [evɑ̃ʒelikmɑ̃], *adv.* evangelically.

évangélisateur [evɑ̃ʒelizatœːr], *s.m.* gospel preacher (*esp.* to the heathen); evangelizer, evangelist.

évangélisation [evɑ̃ʒelizasjɔ̃], *s.f.* evangelization, evangelizing.

évangéliser [evɑ̃ʒelize], *v.tr.* to evangelize; to preach the Gospel to (the heathen, etc.).

évangélisme [evɑ̃ʒelism], *s.m.* evangelicalism.

évangéliste [evɑ̃ʒelist], *s.m.* (*a*) evangelist; (*b*) **se faire l'é. d'une doctrine nouvelle,** to be the propagator of, to preach, a new doctrine.

évangile [evɑ̃ʒil], *s.m.* **1.** (*a*) **l'É.,** the Gospel; **l'É. selon saint Jean,** the Gospel according to St. John; (*b*) **ce livre est devenu son é.,** he has taken this book as his bible; *F:* **prendre qch. pour, croire qch. comme, parole d'É.,** to take sth. for gospel (truth). **2.** *Ecc:* **l'é.,** the gospel (for the day); **côté de l'é.,** north side, gospel side (of altar).

évanie [evani], *s.f. Ent:* ensign fly.

évaniidés [evaniide], *s.m.pl. Ent:* Evaniidae.

évanouir (s') [sevanwiːr], *v.pr.* **1.** to vanish, disappear; *Lit:* to evanesce; *W.Tel:* to fade; **fantôme qui s'évanouit,** ghost that vanishes, fades from sight; **le mendiant s'évanouit dans la nuit,** the beggar faded, melted, into the night; **s'é. dans la nature,** to vanish into thin air; **le bruit de ses pas s'évanouit,** the sound of his footsteps died away; **espérances évanouies,** vanished hopes; *Mth:* **faire é. *y*,** to eliminate *y*; **faire é. les dénominateurs d'une équation,** to clear an equation of fractions. **2.** to faint; **tomber évanoui,** to fall down in a faint; **on l'a trouvé évanoui,** he was found unconscious, in a dead faint.

évanouissement [evanwismɑ̃], *s.m.* **1.** vanishing, disappearance (of ghost, hopes, etc.); dying away (of sound); *W.Tel:* fading; *Mth:* elimination, cancelling out. **2.** faint(ing fit).

évansite [evɑ̃zit], *s.f. Miner:* evansite.

évaporable [evapɔrabl̩], *a.* evaporable.

évaporateur [evapɔratœːr], *s.m. Ch: Ind:* evaporator; **é. à vide,** vacuum evaporator.

évaporatif, -ive [evapɔratif, -iːv], *a.* evaporative.

évaporation [evapɔrasjɔ̃], *s.f.* **1.** evaporation; **réduire par é.,** to evaporate down; *Ch:* **é. discontinue,** batch evaporation. **2.** *F: A:* frivolousness, flightiness.

évaporativité [evapɔrativite], *s.f.* evaporativity.

évaporatoire [evapɔratwaːr], *a.* evaporating (process, apparatus).

évaporé, -ée [evapɔre], *a. F:* feather-brained, irresponsible, flighty (person, conduct); **une blonde évaporée,** a dumb blonde; *s.* **c'est une petite évaporée,** she's a featherbrain.

évaporer [evapɔre], *v.tr.* **1.** *A:* to evaporate (liquid); **é. sa bile,** to (give) vent (to) one's spleen. **2.** *P:* to steal (skilfully); **on m'a évaporé ma montre,** my watch has been pinched.

s'évaporer, (*a*) (*of liquids, perfumes, etc.*) to evaporate; **faire é. un liquide,** to evaporate, dry off, a liquid; **bière qui a un goût évaporé,** beer that tastes flat; *A:* **leur enthousiasme s'évaporait en phrases,** their enthusiasm never got beyond talk; (*b*) *F:* **plus personne; on aurait dit que les assistants s'étaient évaporés,** there was nobody left; it seemed as though the onlookers had vanished into thin air; **ce livre ne s'est tout de même pas évaporé!** all the same the book can't have vanished, disappeared! (*c*) *F: A:* to become frivolous.

évaporimètre [evapɔrimɛtr̩], **évaporomètre** [evapɔrɔmɛtr̩], *s.m.* evaporimeter, evaporometer, atmometer.

évaporométrie [evapɔrɔmetri], *s.f.* atmometry.

évapotranspiration [evapɔtrɑ̃spirasjɔ̃], *s.f.* evapotranspiration.

évasé [evɑze], *a.* bell-mouthed, wide-mouthed, funnel-shaped (vessel, pipe, etc.); flared (skirt, etc.); splayed (window opening, etc.).

évasement [evɑzmɑ̃], *s.m.* **1.** widening out, splaying; *Artil:* enlargement (of bore, etc.). **2.** bell mouth (of vessel, pipe, etc.); flare (of skirt, etc.); splay (of window opening, etc.).

évaser [evɑze], *v.tr.* to widen (out) the opening of (vessel); to bell-mouth (vessel); to open out (pipe, etc.); to flare (skirt); to splay (window opening, etc.); to cove (fireplace).

s'évaser, to widen out at the mouth; *Dressm:* to flare (out); **chenal qui s'évase,** broadening channel; **à cet endroit les murs escarpés de la montagne s'évasaient,** at that point the sheer mountain walls began to open out.

évasif, -ive [evazif, -iːv], *a.* evasive.

évasion [evazjɔ̃], *s.f.* **1.** escape, flight (from prison, etc.); **tentative d'é.,** attempted escape; **un désir d'é. hors de son milieu,** a longing to escape from one's surroundings; **é. des capitaux,** exodus of capital; **é. fiscale,** tax avoidance. **2.** *A:* evasion, shift, quibble. **3.** escapism; **littérature d'é.,** escapist literature.

évasivement [evazivmɑ̃], *adv.* evasively.

évasure [evɑzyːr], *s.f.* bell-mouthed, funnel-shaped, opening; splay.

Ève [ɛːv], *Pr.n.f.* Eva; *B.Lit:* Eve; *F:* **une fille d'Ève,** a daughter of Eve, a frivolous woman; a coquette; *F:* **dans le costume d'È.,** in one's birthday suit; *F:* **je ne le connais ni d'È. ni d'Adam,** I don't know him from Adam.

évêché [eveʃe], *s.m.* **1.** bishopric, diocese, see; **Orléans est un é.,** Orleans is a cathedral city. **2.** bishop's palace.

évection [evɛksjɔ̃], *s.f. Astr:* evection.

éveil [evɛːj], *s.m.* **1.** (*a*) awakening; **l'é. des sens,** the awakening of the senses; (*b*) wide-awake state, state of alertness; **être en é.,** to be wide awake; to be on the alert; **tenir qn en é.,** to keep s.o. on the alert. **2.** warning (**contre,** against); **donner l'é.,** to raise the alarm; **donner l'é. à qn,** to warn s.o.; to give s.o. a hint; to put s.o. on his guard; to excite s.o.'s suspicions.

éveillé [eveje], *a.* **1.** awake, waking; **rêve, sommeil, é.,** waking dream, sleep; **tenir qn é.,** to keep s.o. awake; **rester é.,** to keep awake; **é. ou endormi,** waking or sleeping; **je le trouvai tout é.,** I found him wide awake. **2.** wide-awake, alert, lively, perky (person, etc.); **garçon (à l'esprit) é.,** bright, sharp, quick-witted, boy; **cerveau é.,** active brain. **3.** *Mus:* sprightly, lively, quick.

éveillée [eveje], *s.f. A: F:* **quelle é.!** what an awakening!

éveiller [eveje], *v.tr.* **1.** to awake(n), wake (s.o.) up; to (a)rouse (s.o.) (from sleep); **é. la curiosité, les soupçons, de qn,** to arouse, awaken, s.o.'s curiosity, suspicions; **é. l'envie,** to arouse envy; **le vin lui avait éveillé l'esprit,** the wine had sharpened his wits. **2. é. le poil d'une fourrure,** to raise, brush up, the hair of a fur.

s'éveiller. 1. to awake(n), to wake (up), to come out of one's sleep; **il s'éveilla en sursaut,** he woke with a start. **2.** (*of the senses, of a passion*) to awaken; to be aroused.

éveilleur, -euse [evejœːr, -øːz], *s.* (*a*) awakener (of intelligence, etc.); (*b*) caller, knocker-up.

événement [evɛnmɑ̃], *s.m.* event. **1.** (*a*) *A:* issue, consequence, outcome, result; *still so used in* **dans l'é., en l'é.,** as things turned out; (*b*) *Th:* climax; (*c*) *Ph:* event. **2.** occurrence, incident; **roman plein d'événements,** novel full of incident; **faire é.,** to cause a stir; **suivre le cours des événements,** to follow the course of events; **semaine pleine d'événements, fertile en événements,** eventful week; **en cas d'é.,** in case of emergency; **à tout é.,** in order to provide against emergencies, as a measure of precaution; *F:* **attendre un heureux é.,** to be expecting a happy event.

événementiel, -ielle [evɛnmɑ̃sjɛl], *a.* **histoire événementielle,** factual history.

évent [evɑ̃], *s.m.* **1.** *A:* fresh air, open air, airing; *occ. still used in* **mettre qch. à l'é.,** to air sth.; **c'est une tête à l'é.,** she's feather-brained. **2.** mustiness (of food); flatness (of beverages, due to exposure); **sentir l'évent,** to smell stale, musty; **vin qui a un goût d'é.,** flat wine. **3.** (*a*) *Z:* blowhole, spiracle, spout (of whale); (*b*) *Tchn:* vent, vent-hole, air-hole; *Metall:* riser, air gate; *I.C.E:* breather(pipe) (of crank-case); *Mil:* flash hole (of fuse); **tuyau d'é.,** blow-off pipe (of cesspool); (*c*) flaw (in gun barrel).

éventage [evɑ̃taːʒ], *s.m.* airing; exposure to the air.

éventail [evɑ̃taːj], *s.m.* **1.** (*a*) fan; **jouer de l'é.,** to play with a fan; **en é.,** fan-shaped; *Arch:* **voûte en é.,** fan vaulting; *Geol:* **pli en é.,** fan folding; *Navy:* **disposer la flotte en é.,** to arrange the fleet in fan order; **tailler un arbre en é.,** to cut a tree fan-shape; **(fenêtre en) é.,** fanlight; (*b*) punkah. **2.** spreader (of watering hose). **3.** *Pol.Ec: etc:* range; **l'é. des salaires,** the salary range. **4. é. de mer,** fan coral.

éventaillerie [evɑ̃tajri], *s.f.* fan-making industry, trade.

éventailliste [evɑ̃tajist], *s.m. & f.* **1.** fan maker. **2.** fan painter.

éventaire [evɑ̃tɛːr], *s.m.* (*a*) (hawker's) flat basket, tray; (*b*) (street) stall.

éventé [evɑ̃te], *a.* (*a*) exposed to the wind; (*b*) stale, musty (food, etc.); flat (beer, etc.); (*c*) **complot é.,** plot that has been discovered.

éventement [evɑ̃tmɑ̃], *s.m.* **1.** airing, ventilation. **2.** (*of food, drink*) spoiling, going stale, flat.

éventer [evɑ̃te], *v.tr.* **1.** (*a*) to air; to expose (bedding, skins, grain, etc.) to the air; **é. une carrière,** to open up a quarry; **é. une houillère,** to ventilate a coal pit; *Nau:* **é. la quille,** to heave keel out; (*b*) to damage, spoil (scent, wine, etc.) by exposure to the air; (*c*) *Mil:* **é. une mine, la mèche,** to lay bare a mine, the match; **é. la mèche,** to uncover the plot; **le secret est éventé,** the secret is out. **2.** *Nau:* **é. une voile,** to fill a sail. **3.** to fan; **s'é. avec son mouchoir,** to fan oneself with one's handkerchief. **4.** *Const:* to hold (a stone) from the wall (while hoisting); to steady (a stone). **5.** (*a*) *Ven:* (*of hounds*) to scent, get the scent of (game); (*b*) *F:* to get wind of (sth.); to discover (secret); (*c*) *v.i.* (*of horse*) to raise the nose too much.

s'éventer, (*a*) (*of food, etc.*) to spoil (from exposure to the air); (*of beverages*) to go flat, stale; (*b*) **le secret est, s'est, éventé,** the secret has leaked out.

éventoir [evɑ̃twaːr], *s.m.* **1.** *A.Dom.Ec:* fire fan (for fanning up charcoal). **2.** *Min:* air shaft.

éventration [evɑ̃trasjɔ̃], *s.f. Surg:* eventration.

éventrer [evɑ̃tre], *v.tr.* to disembowel, eviscerate; to gut (fish), draw (game, poultry); to rip, tear open (parcel, envelope); to break, smash, open (cask, box, etc.); to burst open (door); to blow up (barricade); to slit open (sack); to rip (tyre); **une bombe avait éventré le bâtiment,** a bomb had torn the building apart.

éventreur [evɑ̃trœːr], *s.m.* disemboweller; *Hist:* **Jack l'É.,** Jack the Ripper.

éventualité [evɑ̃tɥalite], *s.f.* possibility, contingency, eventuality; **envisager l'é. d'une guerre,** to envisage the possibility of war; **parer à toute é.,** to provide for all contingencies, for all emergencies; **considérer l'é. d'un événement,** to examine the possibility of an event.

éventuel, -elle [evɑ̃tɥɛl]. **1.** *a.* (*a*) possible, contingent, liable to happen; **à titre é.,** as a possible event; **s'assurer contre des accidents éventuels,** to insure against possible accidents; **sortie éventuelle,** emergency exit; *Fin:* **passif é.,** contingent liabilities; **un client é.,** a potential, prospective, customer; **les modifications éventuelles devront être faites plus tard,** the modifications, if any, will have to be made later; (*b*) eventual; **compter sur une part des profits éventuels d'une affaire,** to reckon on a share in the eventual profits of an undertaking. **2.** *s.m.* (*a*) eventuality, contingency, possible event; **l'é. est exprimé dans le système verbal par le conditionnel,** the conditional is used to express possibility; (*b*) fluctuating emoluments, perquisites (of official, etc.).

éventuellement [evɑ̃tɥɛlmɑ̃], *adv.* possibly; if necessary; if required; should the occasion arise; **il n'y a pas de pays où l'on se sente é. plus**

seul, there is no country where one may feel more alone, where one may feel so isolated on occasions; **j'aurais é. besoin de votre concours,** I may need your help (later).

évêque [evɛk], *s.m.* bishop; **monseigneur l'é.,** my Lord Bishop; **Monseigneur X, é. de . . .,** Monsignor X, Bishop of . . .; Bishop X of . . .; **é. suffragant,** suffragan bishop; *Lap:* **pierre d'é.** amethyst; *Prov:* **un chien regarde bien un é.,** a cat may look at a king; **bonnet d'é.,** (i) bishop's mitre; (ii) *F:* parson's nose (of fowl); *attrib.* **violet é.,** episcopal purple.

éverrer [evɛre], *v.tr.* to worm (dog, its tongue).

éversé [evɛrse], *a. Anthr: Nat.Hist:* everted.

éversion [evɛrsjɔ̃], *s.f.* **1.** *A:* eversion, overthrow. **2.** *Med:* (*a*) eversion; (*b*) **l'é. des lèvres est très marquée chez certaines races noires,** certain black races have markedly everted lips.

évertuer (s') [sevɛrtɥe], *v.pr.* to do one's utmost, to exert oneself; **s'é. l'esprit,** to rack one's brains; **s'é. à, pour, faire qch.,** to do one's utmost, to make every effort, to do sth.; **mais je m'évertue à vous le dire!** I've been telling you so till I'm blue in the face!

éveux [evø], *a. Agr:* spewy (soil).

Évhémère [evemɛːr], *Pr.n.m.* Euhemerus.

évhémérisme [evemerism], *s.m. Phil:* euhemerism.

évhémériste [evemerist]. **1.** *a.* euhemeristic. **2.** *s.m. & f.* euhemerist.

éviction [eviksjɔ̃], *s.f. Jur:* eviction, dispossession, ejectment (of tenant), ouster (of official); *Sch:* **é. scolaire,** exclusion from school (of child suffering from contagious disease).

évidage [evidaːʒ], *s.m.* (*a*) hollowing out, scooping out (of stone, flute, etc.); scraping out (of cavity of bone); (*b*) grooving, channelling, fluting (of sword blade, needle, etc.); routing out (of groove); (*c*) cutting away, sloping out (of neck of dress, wooden framework, etc.); (*d*) gutting (of fish); (*e*) pinking (of leather, etc.).

évidé [evide], *a.* **1.** hollow; **rasoir é.,** hollow-ground razor; **excentrique é.,** chambered eccentric; **visage é.,** gaunt face. **2.** grooved; *Mec.E:* **bielle évidée,** U-section connecting rod. **3.** cut away. **4.** *N.Arch:* **navire à l'arrière é.,** ship with a clean run.

évidement [evidmɑ̃], *s.m.* **1.** = ÉVIDAGE. **2.** space hollowed out, hollow, groove, slot, recess, cavity; **embouchure (de tuyau) à é. annulaire,** recessed pipe end. **3.** *N.Arch:* stern run (of ship's lines).

évidemment [evidamɑ̃], *adv.* **1.** evidently, obviously, clearly; **il est é. nécessaire de . . .,** it is clearly, obviously, necessary to . . . **2.** certainly, of course; **é. il se trompe,** of course he is mistaken; **vous acceptez?—é.!** you accept?—naturally! of course!

évidence [evidɑ̃ːs], *s.f.* (*a*) obviousness, manifestness, clearness, evidence (of fact); **se rendre à l'é.,** to yield to the facts, to acknowledge oneself in the wrong; **nier, aller contre, l'é., se refuser à l'é.,** to fly in the face of facts; **comment nier l'é. même?** how can we deny obvious, patent, facts? **on ignore les causes de l'accident, mais elles sont d'é. liées à la mauvaise visibilité,** the causes of the accident are not known but are obviously connected with the poor visibility; **c'est une é.,** it's an obvious fact; *adv.phr.* **à l'é., de toute é.,** clearly, certainly, evidently, obviously; **démontrer à é. que . . .,** to show clearly, without any possible doubt, that . . .; **il est de toute é. que . . .,** it is obvious, it stands to reason that . . .; **il est de toute é. qu'elle l'aime,** anyone can see with half an eye that she is in love with him; (*b*) conspicuousness; **être en é.,** to be in a conspicuous, prominent, position; to be in evidence; **mettre des marchandises en é.,** to display, show off, goods; **mettre en é. les défauts de qn,** to reveal, show up, s.o.'s faults; **se mettre en é.,** (i) to put oneself forward; (ii) to come to the fore; **appuyé bien en é. contre un arbre,** conspicuously propped up against a tree.

évident [evidɑ̃], *a.* evident, obvious, manifest, unmistakable, clear, plain; **erreur évidente,** palpable error, glaring mistake; **c'est é.,** that's evident, that stands to reason; **il est é. que . . .,** it stands to reason that . . ., it is plain that . . .; **je tiens pour é. que,** I take it for granted that . . . .

évider [evide], *v.tr.* **1.** to hollow out, scoop out (slab of stone, flute, etc.); **é. un os,** to scrape the cavity of a bone. **2.** to groove, channel, flute (sword blade, needle, etc.). **3.** to cut away, slope out (neck of dress, etc.). **4.** to gut (fish). **5.** to pink (leather, cloth).

s'évider, to form a cavity; **au-dessous des créneaux s'évident des lucarnes carrées,** square lights are recessed below the battlements.

évidoir [evidwaːr], *s.m. Tls:* groover; scooper; gouge.

évidure [evidyːr], *s.f.* **1.** hollow, cavity. **2.** groove.

évier [evje], *s.m.* **1.** (kitchen) sink. **2.** gutter-stone.

évier-vidoir [evjevidwaːr], *s.m. Dom.Ec:* sink with waste-disposal unit; *pl. éviers-vidoirs.*

évincement [evɛ̃smɑ̃], *s.m.* ousting, supplanting (of rival, etc.).

évincer [evɛ̃se], *v.tr.* (**j'évinçai(s); n. évinçons**) **1.** *Jur:* to evict, dispossess, eject; *F:* turn out (tenant). **2.** to oust, supplant (s.o.); **il voudrait m'é. auprès de mon amie,** he is trying to cut me out with my girl. **3.** to discriminate against (s.o.).

évirer [evire], *v.tr.* to castrate (man).

éviscération [eviserasjɔ̃], *s.f.* evisceration.

éviscérer [evisere], *v.tr.* (**j'éviscère, n. éviscérons; j'éviscérerai**) to eviscerate, disembowel.

évitable [evitabḷ], *a.* avoidable, preventable.

évitage [evitaːʒ], *s.m.*, **évitée** [evite], *s.f. Nau:* **1.** swinging (of ship); **bassin d'é.,** turning basin. **2.** (*a*) room to swing, sea room; **nous n'avons pas notre é.,** we have a foul berth; (*b*) width of channel.

évitement [evitmɑ̃], *s.m.* **1.** shunning, avoiding, avoidance, (of s.o., sth.); *Mil: etc:* **faire une manœuvre d'é.,** to take evasive action; *Biol:* **réaction d'é.,** avoiding reaction. **2.** (*a*) *Rail:* shunting (of train); **voie, gare, d'é.,** siding; **ligne d'é.,** loop line; (*b*) **route d'é.,** by-pass; (*c*) *Elcs:* **radar d'é.,** terrain-following radar. **3.** passing place (in trench, etc.); *Rail:* passing track, loop.

éviter [evite]. **1.** *v.tr.* (*a*) to avoid, shun; to give (s.o., sth.) a wide berth; to keep out of (s.o.'s) way; to keep clear of (s.o.); to fight shy of (s.o.); **c'est un homme à é.,** he is a man to avoid; **é. un danger,** to evade a danger; **é. un coup,** to avoid, evade, dodge, a blow; **é. de la tête,** to duck; **é. une discussion,** to avoid a discussion; **é. de faire qch.,** to avoid doing sth.; **je n'ai pas pu éviter de payer une tournée,** I couldn't help, couldn't avoid, standing a round; **évitez qu'on ne vous voie,** avoid being seen; **é. la question,** to side-step the question; to dodge the issue; (*b*) (= ÉPARGNER) **é. une peine à qn,** to spare s.o. trouble; **la police a évité à l'assassin d'être lynché,** the police prevented the murderer from being lynched; **ce dictionnaire n'a pas été fait pour vous é. de réfléchir,** this dictionary has not been compiled to save you the trouble of thinking; **quelles peines ne s'éviterait-on pas en y réfléchissant davantage!** what a lot of trouble would be saved if one thought about things more! **2.** *v.i. Nau:* (*of ship*) **é. sur l'ancre,** to swing at anchor; **être évité le cap sur la terre,** to ride head to the land; **évité au vent, au courant,** wind-rode, weather-rode.

évocable [evɔkabḷ], *a.* evocable (spirit, memory, etc.); *Jur:* **cause é.,** case that may be summoned, evoked, to a higher court.

évocateur, -trice [evɔkatœːr, -tris]. **1.** *a.* evocative, suggestive (**de,** of); **lieu é. d'anciens souvenirs,** spot that recalls, conjures up, old memories. **2.** *s.* evocator, evoker; *Psy:* signal organ (of animal).

évocation [evɔkasjɔ̃], *s.f.* **1.** (*a*) (i) evocation, calling forth, conjuring up, raising (of spirits, etc.); (ii) **il semblait que ce fût une é. qui vous parlait,** it seemed as if it were a ghost speaking (to you); (*b*) conjuring up, calling up (of the past); **il sourit à l'é. du souvenir,** he smiled as the memory of it came back to him. **2.** *Jur:* evocation (of cause).

évocatoire [evɔkatwaːr], *a.* evocatory; *Jur:* **cause é.,** case summoned to a higher court.

évo(h)é [evɔe], *int. Gr.Ant:* evoe.

évolage [evɔlaːʒ], *s.m. Agr:* exploitation of land on the water-meadow system.

évolagiste [evɔlaʒist], *s.m. & f. Agr:* farmer who exploits land on the water-meadow system.

évolué [evɔlɥe], *a.* (highly) developed, advanced; **race moins évoluée,** backward race; **un homme é.,** (i) a cultured man; (ii) a broad-minded man.

évoluer [evɔlɥe], *v.i.* **1.** (*a*) *Mil: Nau: Av:* (*of vessel, troops, etc.*) to perform evolutions, to manœuvre; (*b*) *Navy:* (*of ships*) to alter course, to turn; (*c*) **la vie réelle n'évolue pas sur le plan politique,** real life does not move on the political plane; (*d*) (i) to move around; (ii) to move (in society). **2.** *Mch:* (*of wheel, etc.*) to revolve, go round. **3.** to evolve, develop; *Biol: etc:* to advance; **camaraderie qui évolue vers l'amour,** friendship that evolves, develops, into love; **la chirurgie a beaucoup évolué depuis 1950,** surgery has made great progress since 1950; **la maladie évolue,** the illness is following its normal course; **il a beaucoup évolué,** he has become much more (i) civilized; (ii) broad-minded; **ses opinions ont évolué,** he has acquired a broader outlook.

évolutif, -ive [evɔlytif, -iːv], *a.* (*a*) *Biol:* evolutionary; (*b*) evolutive; (*c*) *Med:* **maladie évolutive,** disease that follows certain specific stages of development.

évolution [evɔlysjɔ̃], *s.f.* **1.** (*a*) *Mil: Nau:* evolution, manœuvre (of ship, troops, etc.); **évolutions tactiques,** tactical exercises; (*b*) *Navy:* (*of ships*) alteration of course; turn. **2.** (*a*) *Biol: etc:* evolution; development; (*b*) evolvement (of plan, etc.); **é. ultérieure (d'une question),** subsequent development (of a question); (*c*) course (of disease); history (of phenomenon, disease); **é. de la désintégration de la matière en fonction du temps,** time-history of the disintegration of matter.

évolutionnaire [evɔlysjɔnɛːr], *a.* (*a*) *Mil: Nau:* evolutionary (operation); (*b*) *Biol:* evolutionary (doctrine).

évolutionner [evɔlysjɔne], *v.i. Mil: Nau:* to perform evolutions; to manœuvre.

évolutionnisme [evɔlysjɔnism], *s.m. Biol: etc:* evolutionism.

évolutionniste [evɔlysjɔnist], *Biol: etc:* **1.** *a.* evolutionist(ic). **2.** *s.m. & f.* evolutionist.

évoquer [evɔke], *v.tr.* **1.** (*a*) to evoke, call forth, summon, conjure up, raise (spirit); (*b*) to recall, call to mind, call up, conjure up, evoke (memory); to be reminiscent of (sth.); **é. un bruit,** to allude to a rumour; **é. la maison paternelle,** to call to mind the old home; **contes évoquant des enfants,** tales of children. **2.** *Jur:* to evoke (cause).

évrillage [evrijaːʒ], *s.m.* removal of tendrils (from vine).

évulsif, -ive [evylsif, -iːv], *a.* evulsive.

évulsion [evylsjɔ̃], *s.f. A:* evulsion; extraction (of tooth, etc.).

evzone [ɛvzoːn], *s.m. Gr.Mil:* evzone.

ex- [ɛks], *pref.* **1.** ex-; **ex-ambassadeur,** ex-ambassador; **ex-femme,** ex-wife; *F:* **mon ex,** my ex; **ex-hôtesse,** ex-hostess. **2.** late; **ex-président de . . .,** late president of . . ., one time president of . . ..

ex abrupto [ɛksabrypto], *Lt.adv.phr.* impromptu, spontaneously, off the cuff.

exacerbation [ɛgzasɛrbasjɔ̃], *s.f.* exacerbation.

exacerber [ɛgzasɛrbe], *v.tr.* to exacerbate, aggravate (pain, irritation, etc.); **la douleur s'exacerbe,** the pain is growing worse, is becoming more intense.

exact [ɛgza(kt)], *a.* exact; (*a*) accurate, true, right, correct, precise (calculation, etc.); **les sciences exactes,** the exact sciences; **l'heure exacte,** the right, correct, time; **e. à un millimètre près,** correct to a millimetre; **mes chiffres se trouvent exacts,** my figures, calculations, have come right; **historien e.,** accurate historian; **récit e.,** accurate, true, correct, account; **c'est e.,** it is quite true, it is a fact; **au cas où il serait e. que . . .,** should it prove correct that . . .; (*b*) strict, rigorous (diet, etc.); close (copy); (*c*) punctual; **être e. dans ses payements, au bureau,** to be punctual in one's payments, at the office; **e. à payer son loyer,** punctual in paying his rent.

exactement [ɛgzaktəmɑ̃], *adv.* exactly; (*a*) accurately, correctly; **reproduire e. un texte,** to reproduce a text accurately; **viser e.,** to take accurate aim; (*b*) just, precisely; **il avait e. l'air d'un spectre,** he looked just, for all the world, like a ghost; **e. comme si . . .,** exactly, for all the world, as if . . .; **un effet e. contraire,** a directly opposite effect; (*c*) punctually; **payer e. ses dettes,** to pay one's debts punctually.

exacteur [ɛgzaktœːr], *s.m. A:* **1.** exacter, exactor (of his due). **2.** (*a*) extorter (**de,** of); (*b*) extortioner, extortionist.

exaction [ɛgzaksjɔ̃], *s.f.* **1.** exaction (of tax, etc.). **2.** extortion.

exactitude [ɛgzaktityd], *s.f.* (*a*) exactness, exactitude, correctness, accuracy (of statement, calculation, etc.); closeness (of copy); **d'une e. rigoureuse,** accurate to a hair's breadth; (*b*) punctuality; **e. à s'acquitter de ses fonctions,** exactness, punctuality, in carrying out one's duties; **avec e.,** exactly, punctually.

ex æquo [ɛgzeko], *Lt.adj.phr.* of equal merit; **en cas d'ex a. . . .,** in the case of equality of points . . .; **classés ex a.,** bracketed equal (in competition); **premier prix ex a.,** first prize divided; **être troisième ex a.,** to tie for third place.

exagérateur, -trice [ɛgzaʒeratœːr, -tris], *s.* exaggerator; magnifier (of events, etc.).

exagératif, -ive [egzaʒeratif, -i:v], *a.* exaggerative.

exagération [egzaʒerasjɔ̃], *s.f.* exaggeration; overstatement; **dans son récit il faut faire la part de l'e.,** we must take his account with a grain of salt; **e. de la sensibilité,** hypersensitivity.

exagéré [egzaʒere], *a.* **1.** exaggerated; **prix e.,** unduly high price; **pression exagérée,** undue, excessive, pressure; **confiance exagérée (en),** overconfidence (in). **2.** (*of pers.*) given to exaggeration, to making too much of everything. **3.** *s.m.* **ce siècle de l'e.,** this age of exaggeration, when everything is exaggerated.

exagérément [egzaʒeremɑ̃], *adv.* exaggeratedly; **être e. sévère,** to be unduly strict, over strict; **sans vous faire attendre e.,** without keeping you waiting unduly, too, long.

exagérer [egzaʒere], *v.tr.* **(j'exagère, n. exagérons; j'exagérerai)** to exaggerate, magnify (facts, dangers, etc.); to overstate (truth, etc.); to overestimate, overrate (s.o.'s qualities); *abs.* to overdo it; **s'e. la portée de qch.,** to make too much of sth.; **n'exagérez pas!** *F:* come off it! don't pile it on! **vous exagérez!** you're exaggerating! you're going too far! **n'exagérons rien!** let's not, don't, exaggerate!

exalbuminé [egzalbymine], *a. Bot:* exalbuminous.

exaltable [egzaltabl̩], *a.* excitable (person, etc.).

exaltant [egzaltɑ̃], *a.* exciting, stirring (speech, etc.).

exaltation [egzaltasjɔ̃], *s.f.* **1.** (*a*) exaltation (of the Cross, of a pope, of the name of God; *Astrol: A:* of a planet); **fête de l'E. de la Sainte Croix,** Holy Cross Day; (*b*) exalting, glorifying, extolling (of virtue, etc.). **2.** (*a*) exaltation, rapturous emotion, excited state, excitement; (*b*) *Med:* over-excitement.

exalté, -ée [egzalte]. **1.** (*a*) excited, impassioned (speech, etc.); (*b*) hot-headed; quixotic (person); (*c*) uplifted (state of mind, etc.). **2.** *s.* excitable, hotheaded, person; hothead; fanatic.

exalter [egzalte], *v.tr.* **1.** to exalt, praise, glorify, magnify, extol. **2.** to excite, inflame (courage, imagination, etc.); **les nouvelles exaltaient beaucoup la population,** the people were greatly stirred, excited, by the news. **3.** to exalt, dignify, ennoble; **il exalta sa propre existence,** he exalted, ennobled, his own life. **4.** (*a*) *Med:* **certaines influences exaltent la virulence du microbe,** certain influences (greatly) increase the virulence of the microbe; (*b*) *Lit:* **la tiédeur de la pièce exaltait le parfum des fleurs,** the warmth of the room intensified the scent of the flowers.

s'exalter, to grow excited, enthusiastic; to enthuse; **s'e. sur les mérites de qn,** to extol the merits of s.o.; to enthuse over s.o.; **l'imagination s'exalte,** the imagination is fired.

examen [egzamɛ̃], *s.m.* examination; (*a*) investigation; **e. d'une machine,** overhauling of a machine; **après un e. attentif de l'horizon,** after a careful scrutiny, survey, of the horizon; *Med:* **examens de contrôle à distance, à long terme,** follow up; **e. de la vue,** sight testing; **e. des comptes,** inspection, scrutiny, of accounts; **cette assertion ne supporte pas l'e.,** this assertion will not bear examination; **sa réputation ne supporte pas l'e.,** his character will not bear investigation; **la question est à l'e.,** the matter is under examination, under consideration; **la question est encore à l'e.,** the question is still under discussion; **soumettre qch. à un e. minutieux,** to subject sth. to minute inspection, to a careful overhaul; to go carefully over sth.; *Com:* **livre à l'e.,** (i) specimen copy; (ii) book on approval; **e. de conscience,** self-examination; **faire son e. de conscience,** to examine one's conscience (before confession); *Theol: etc:* **libre e.,** liberty of thought; free enquiry; (*b*) *Sch:* **passer, subir, un e.,** to go in, sit, for an examination, *F:* an exam; **être reçu, refusé, à un e.,** to pass, fail in, an examination; **e. d'entrée,** entrance examination; **e. de sortie,** passing-out, final, examination; **e. de passage,** end-of-year examination; **e. d'état,** state examination; **e. d'entrée en 6ème** = eleven plus examination; **jury d'e.,** the examining body, the examiners; *Aut:* **e. du permis de conduire,** driving test.

examinable [egzaminabl̩], *a.* examinable; that can be examined.

examinateur, -trice [egzaminatœ:r, -tris]. **1.** *s.* (*a*) investigator, inspector; (*b*) examiner. **2.** *a.* examining (professor, etc.).

examiner [egzamine], *v.tr.* to examine; (*a*) to investigate, inspect, scrutinize; **e. une machine,** to overhaul a machine; **e. un malade,** to examine a patient; **se faire e. par un médecin,** to have oneself examined, *F:* vetted, by a doctor; **je voudrais l'e. de plus près,** I should like to get a closer look at it; **e. qch. attentivement,** to have a good look at sth.; **e. attentivement l'horizon,** to scan, survey, the horizon; **e. une question,** to look into, go into, consider, a matter; **e. les comptes,** to go through, inspect, scrutinize, the accounts; **e. à nouveau une question,** to reconsider a question; (*b*) *Sch:* **e. qn en algèbre,** to examine s.o. in algebra.

s'examiner, to examine one's conscience.

exanthémateux, -euse [egzɑ̃tematø, -ø:z], **exanthématique** [egzɑ̃tematik], *a Med:* exanthematous.

exanthème [egzɑ̃tɛm], *s.m. Med:* exanthema, rash; **e. sérique,** serum rash.

exarchat [egzarka], *s.m.,* **exarchie** [egzarʃi], *s.f. Hist: Ecc:* exarchate.

exarque [egzark], *s.m. Hist: Ecc:* exarch.

exarthrose [egzartro:z], *s.f. Med:* dislocation.

exaspérant [egzasperɑ̃], *a.* exasperating, irritating, galling, aggravating; **il est e.!** he's exasperating!

exaspération [egzasperasjɔ̃], *s.f.* **1.** *A:* aggravation, exacerbation (of disease, pain, etc.). **2.** exasperation, irritation, aggravation; **il bouillonne d'e.,** he's seething with exasperation, irritation.

exaspéré [egzaspere], *a.* exasperated; **j'étais e.,** I was fuming (**de, at**).

exaspérer [egzaspere], *v.tr.* **(j'exaspère, n. exaspérons; j'exaspérerai) 1.** to aggravate, exacerbate (disease, pain). **2.** to exasperate, irritate; to incense (s.o.), to aggravate (s.o.); to provoke (s.o.) beyond measure.

s'exaspérer. 1. (*of pain, etc.*) to become exacerbated. **2.** (*of pers.*) to lose all patience; to become exasperated (**de,** at).

exaucement [egzosmɑ̃], *s.m.* **1.** granting of the prayer (of s.o.). **2.** granting, fulfilment (of wish).

exaucer [egzose], *v.tr.* **(j'exauçai(s); n. exauçons)** (*of the Deity*) **1. e. qn,** to grant, give ear to, answer, the prayer of s.o. **2.** to fulfil (wish, desire); **exauce ma prière!** hear my prayer!

excavateur, -trice [ɛkskavatœ:r, -tris], *s. Civ.E:* (*a*) digging machine, digger, (steam)navvy, excavator; (*b*) **excavatrice pour fossés,** ditcher; (*c*) *Dent:* dentist's drill.

excavation [ɛkskavasjɔ̃], s.f. **1.** excavation, excavating, digging (out) (of channel, etc.). **2.** (*a*) excavation, hollow, pit; (*b*) hole (in road, etc.); (*c*) *Anat:* **e. pelvienne,** pelvic cavity.

excaver [ɛkskave], *v.tr.* to excavate, to dig out.

excédant [eksedɑ̃], *a.* **1.** surplus (sum, etc.); excess(ive) (luggage, etc.). **2.** importunate, tiresome, exasperating (visitor); overpowering (smell).

excédent [eksedɑ̃], *s.m.* excess, surplus, overplus; **somme en e.,** sum in excess; **vous garderez l'e.,** you will keep what is over; **e. de productions d'un pays,** surplus produce of a country; **e. de poids,** overweight; *Com:* **e. de dépenses,** deficit; **e. dans l'encaisse,** over in the cash; **excédents et déficits,** overs and shorts; *Rail:* **e. de bagages,** excess luggage; *abs.* **payer 50 francs d'e.,** to pay 50 francs excess (charge); *Mch:* **e. de puissance,** margin of power; **e. des exportations sur les importations,** excess of exports over imports.

excédentaire [eksedɑ̃tɛ:r], *a.* which is in excess, excess, surplus; **la balance commerciale est e.,** the trade balance shows a surplus, a credit; **écouler la production e. sur les marchés extérieurs,** to get rid of, dump, surplus production on foreign markets.

excéder [eksede], *v.tr.* **(j'excède, n. excédons; j'excéderai) 1.** to exceed, go beyond (a certain limit); **le résultat a excédé mes espérances,** the result has surpassed my hopes; **e. le montant de son compte (en banque),** to overdraw one's account; **e. ses pouvoirs,** to exceed one's powers. **2.** (*a*) *O:* to tire (s.o.) out, to wear (s.o.) out; **e. un cheval,** to overwork a horse; **excédé de fatigue,** worn out; fagged out; (*b*) to overtax (s.o.'s) patience; **j'étais excédé,** I had lost all patience, I was exasperated; **sa présence m'excède,** his presence irritates me; *F:* I can't stand having him around.

excellemment [ekselamɑ̃], *adv.* **1.** excellently, extremely well. **2.** eminently, superlatively.

excellence [ekselɑ̃:s], *s.f.* **1.** excellence, pre-eminence; *Sch:* **prix d'e.,** first prize (in form); prize for a general all-round standard; *adv.phr.* **par e.,** (i) par excellence, pre-eminently, in the highest sense of the word; (ii) especially, particularly, supremely, above all. **2.** (*title of honour*) **votre E.,** your Excellency; **c'est moi, E., qui . . .,** it is I, your Excellency, who . . .; **puis-je demander à votre E. de . . .,** may I ask your Excellency to . . .; *Pol: F:* **nos Excellences,** the ministers.

excellent [ekselɑ̃], *a.* excellent, first-rate; **nous sommes en excellente santé,** we are in the best of health; **une idée excellente,** a splendid idea; **nous avons passé une excellente soirée,** we had a most enjoyable evening; **il était d'excellente humeur,** he was in the best of moods, in high spirits; **un e. homme,** a very kind man; **e. en latin,** well up in Latin; **il était e. dans le rôle de Hamlet,** he was a success as Hamlet; *F:* **je vous trouve e., vous!** you're pretty good, you are!

excellentissime [ekselɑ̃tisim], *a. often Hum:* most excellent, superb, superlative; **un vin e.,** a superb, superlative, wine.

exceller [eksele], *v.i.* to excel; **e. en latin, dans les mathématiques, au billard,** to excel in, be brilliant at, Latin, mathematics, billiards; **e. à faire qch.,** to excel in doing sth.

excentrage [eksɑ̃tra:ʒ], *s.m. Tchn:* off-cent(e)ring.

excentration [eksɑ̃trasjɔ̃], *s.f.,* **excentrement** [eksɑ̃trəmɑ̃], *s.m. Mec.E:* setting over, offsetting; throwing off centre.

excentré [eksɑ̃tre], *a.* eccentric (shaft, spindle, etc.), offset; **roue excentrée,** wheel out of true.

excentrer [eksɑ̃tre], *v.tr. Mec.E:* to throw off centre; to offset, to set over; to bring (sth.) out of centre.

excentricité [eksɑ̃trisite], *s.f.* **1.** (*a*) eccentricity (of orbit, etc.); *Mec.E:* throw (of eccentric); (*b*) remoteness (of suburb, etc.) from the centre. **2.** eccentricity, peculiarity, oddity (of manners).

excentrique [eksɑ̃trik]. **1.** *a.* (*a*) eccentric (orbit, pulley, etc.); (*b*) remote, outlying (suburb, etc.); (*c*) eccentric, odd, oddish, whimsical (person). **2.** *s.* odd, queer, eccentric, person; **c'est un(e) e.,** he's, she's, an eccentric; he, she, is a little peculiar. **3.** *s.m. Mec.E:* (*a*) eccentric (gear); **tige d'e.,** eccentric rod; **plateau, disque, d'e.,** sheave; (*b*) cam; **e. en cœur,** heart cam; (*c*) eccentric chuck (of lathe).

excentriquement [eksɑ̃trikmɑ̃], *adv.* eccentrically. **1.** out of centre. **2.** oddly, peculiarly.

excepté [eksepte]. **1.** *prep.* except(ing), but, save, besides, with the exception of; **tout le monde était arrivé, e. la mariée,** everyone had arrived except the bride; **personne e. lui,** none but he, nobody except him; **rien e. une maladie grave,** nothing barring a severe illness; **il n'a rien e. ses gages,** he has nothing beyond his wages; *conj. phr.* **e. que** + *ind.*, except that . . ., but that . . .; **nous avons eu beau temps, e. qu'il a un peu plu vers midi,** we had fine weather, except for a little rain about mid-day. **2.** *a.* excepted; **tous les habitants, les femmes exceptées,** all the inhabitants, except the women, apart from the women.

excepter [ɛksɛpte], *v.tr.* to except, exclude (s.o., sth.) (**de,** from); **inviter tous, sans en e. personne,** to invite everyone, without leaving anyone out; **e. qn d'une amnistie,** to except s.o. from a general pardon; **si l'on excepte une seule rue,** with the exception of one (single) street.

exceptif, -ive [ɛksɛptif, -i:v], *a. Log:* **proposition exceptive,** exceptive proposition.

exception [ɛksɛpsjɔ̃], *s.f.* **1.** exception; **une e. à qch.,** an exception to sth.; **faire une e. à une règle,** to make an exception to a rule; **faire e. à une règle,** to be an exception to a rule; **l'e. confirme la règle,** the exception proves the rule; **sans e.,** (i) without exception; (ii) without fail; **tous sans e. refusèrent,** they one and all declined; **sauf e.,** with certain exceptions; **à cette e. que . . .,** with this exception that . . .; **à quelques exceptions près,** with a few exceptions; *adv.phr.* **à titre d'e.,** by way of an exception; *prep.phr.* **à l'e. de . . ., e. faite de . . .,** except . . ., save . . ., with the exception of . . .; **tous, à l'e. du docteur,** all, except the doctor; all, barring the doctor. **2.** (*a*) *Jur:* exception, incidental plea (of defence); **e. péremptoire,** demurrer, plea in bar; **première e.,** (defendant's) plea; **opposer une e.,** to demur, to raise an objection in law; (*b*) **la question a été ainsi résolue sans soulever la moindre e.,** the question was solved in this manner without anyone taking exception to the decision, without any protest being raised, without a single dissentient voice. **3. mesures d'e.,** emergency regulations; **gouvernement d'e.,** emergency government (after a coup); *Jur:* **juridiction d'e.,** jurisdiction of an exceptional court; **tribunal d'e.,** emergency court.

exceptionnel, -elle [ɛksɛpsjɔnɛl], *a.* (*a*) (*which constitutes an exception*) **congé e.,** special leave; **une faveur exceptionnelle,** an exceptional favour; (*b*) exceptional, uncommon; out of the ordinary; **des circonstances exceptionnelles,** exceptional

circumstances; **talent e.,** exceptional, outstanding talent; **un homme e.,** an exceptional, remarkable, man; *Com:* **taille exceptionnelle,** outsize (in garments); **prix exceptionnels,** bargain prices; (*c*) *Log:* exceptive.

exceptionnellement [ɛksɛpsjɔnɛlmɑ̃], *adv.* exceptionally; by way of, as an, exception; **un homme e. beau,** an exceptionally, remarkably, handsome man; **des éléments qui rendent e. complexe la crise,** factors which make the crisis exceptionally, particularly, extraordinarily, complex.

excès [ɛksɛ, ɛk-], *s.m.* (*a*) excess; **e. de qch. sur qch.,** excess, preponderance, of sth. over sth.; **e. des dépenses sur les recettes, de l'offre sur la demande,** excess of expenditure over revenue, of supply over demand; **e. d'un nombre sur un autre,** amount by which one number exceeds another; **pécher par e. de zèle,** to be over-zealous; *Mec.E:* **clapet d'e. de pression,** relief valve; *Phot:* **e. de pose, d'éclairage,** over-exposure, overlighting; *St.Exch:* **e. de vendeurs,** sellers over; **manger, dépenser, avec e.,** to eat, spend, too much; **manger sans e.,** to eat moderately, reasonably; (*b*) *adv.phr:* **(jusqu') à l'e.,** to excess, excessively, in the extreme, unduly, too much; **manger à l'e.,** to eat to excess, to overeat, to eat too much; **se dépenser à l'e.,** to overexert oneself; **scrupuleux à l'e.,** scrupulous to a fault, over-scrupulous; **consciencieux à l'e.,** over-conscientious; **être modeste à l'e.,** to carry modesty too far; (*c*) *usu. pl.* **commettre des e.,** to be intemperate, to commit excesses (of cruelty, violence, etc.); **se porter à des e.,** to commit violence; **e. (de table),** overeating, eating and drinking too much; *Hum:* dietary indiscretions; **e. de conduite,** loose living; (*d*) *Jur:* **e. de pouvoir,** action ultra vires; **révoqué pour e. de pouvoir,** dismissed for exceeding his powers; *Aut:* **e. de vitesse,** exceeding the speed limit; *F:* speeding.

excessif, -ive [ɛksɛsif, -iːv], *a.*(*a*) excessive, extreme (heat, severity, etc.); undue (optimism, etc.); exorbitant (price); immoderate (eating, drinking); inordinate (pride); **prêter une importance excessive à qch.,** to attach exaggerated importance to sth.; **un travail e. l'a rendu malade,** he has become ill through overwork, overworking has made him ill; **il est vraiment e. que ce sujet soit traité en deux pages seulement,** it's really scandalous, absurd, that this subject should be dealt with in only two pages; (*b*) *s.* **l'e. est son domaine naturel,** the excessive, the extravagant, is his natural province; (*c*) (*of pers.*) **les méridionaux sont souvent excessifs,** southerners are often exuberant, tend to go to extremes; **sa nature excessive n'envisage aucun juste milieu,** his exuberant temperament ignores the possibility of a happy medium; (*d*) **cette fille avait des traits d'une excessive douceur,** she looked an exceptionally gentle girl.

excessivement [ɛksɛsivmɑ̃], *adv.* (*a*) excessively, extremely, exceedingly; immoderately; inordinately; **e. cher,** inordinately expensive; **manger e.,** to eat too much; (*b*) very, extremely; **elle est devenue e. curieuse,** she has become extremely inquisitive.

excessiveté [ɛksesivte], *s.f.* excessiveness.

exciper [ɛksipe], *v.i. Jur:* to put in, offer, a plea; **e. de sa bonne foi,** to allege, plead, one's good faith.

excipient [ɛksipjɑ̃], *s.m. Pharm:* excipient, vehicle (for other ingredients).

excise [ɛksiːz], *s.f. Eng.Adm:* **1.** excise; **sujet aux droits d'e.,** excisable. **2.** excise office.

exciser [ɛksize], *v.tr. Surg:* to excise, cut out, dissect out (tumour, etc.).

excision [ɛksizjɔ̃], *s.f. Surg:* excision, cutting out, dissecting out; **pratiquer l'e. de . . .,** to excise (tumour, etc.).

excitabilité [ɛksitabilite], *s.f.* excitability.

excitable [ɛksitabl̩], *a.* excitable.

excitant [ɛksitɑ̃], *a.* **1.** exciting, stimulating (news, etc.). **2.** *Med:* (*a*) stimulating (food); excitant, stimulating (drug); (*b*) *s.m.* excitant, stimulant; *F:* pep pill.

excitateur, -trice [ɛksitatœːr, -tris]. **1.** (*a*) *a.* exciting (cause, etc.); provocative (**de,** of); (*b*) *s.* exciter, instigator (**de,** of). **2.** (*a*) *s.m. El:* discharger, (static) exciter; (*b*) *s.f.* **excitatrice;** *El.E:* exciter, exciting dynamo.

excitatif, -ive [ɛksitatif, -iːv], *a.* (*a*) *A:* exciting, stimulating (drug); (*b*) **moyens excitatifs,** stimuli.

excitation [ɛksitasjɔ̃], *s.f.* **1.** excitation (of the senses, etc.); **e. à la révolte,** instigation, incitement, to rebellion. **2.** (state of) excitement (of a nerve, etc.). **3.** *El:* excitation; **batterie d'e.,** exciting battery; **e. par choc,** shock excitation; **e. en dérivation, e. shunt,** shunt excitation; **groupe d'e.,** exciter set. **4.** *Atom.Ph:* excitation.

excité [ɛksite]. **1.** *a.* (*a*) *F:* excited, heated, het up; (*b*) *P:* randy; (*c*) *Atom.Ph:* **état e.,** excited state; **atome e.,** excited atom. **2.** *s.* **une bande d'excités,** an over-enthusiastic crowd; **quel e.!** what a fanatic!

excitement [ɛksitmɑ̃], *s.m. Physiol:* renewal of energy, excitation (of organs).

exciter [ɛksite], *v.tr.* to excite; (*a*) to provoke, arouse, awaken, stir up (envy, curiosity, etc.); to call forth (admiration); **e. l'indignation de qn,** to move s.o. to indignation; **e. la pitié de qn,** to excite s.o.'s pity; to move s.o. to pity; (*b*) to animate, inflame; **e. un chien,** to irritate, tease, excite, a dog; **e. les combattants,** to urge on the combatants; **e. qn à la révolte, à se révolter,** to incite, urge, egg on, s.o. to revolt; **e. qn contre qn,** to set s.o. against s.o.; (*c*) to stimulate (thirst, etc.); **e. un nerf,** to apply a stimulus to, to excite, a nerve; (*d*) to cause, bring about (war, etc.); **e. une tempête,** to raise a storm; (*e*) *El:* to pick (up), to energize (a relay).

s'exciter. 1. to get excited, worked up. **2.** to respond to a stimulus.

exciteur, -euse [ɛksitœːr, -øːz], *s. F:* exciter, excitor.

excito-moteur, -trice [ɛksitomɔtœːr, -tris], *a. Physiol:* excitomotor (nerves).

excito-secrétoire [ɛksitosekretwaːr], *a. Physiol:* excitosecretory (nerves).

excitron [ɛksitrɔ̃], *s.m. Elcs:* excitron.

exclamatif, -ive [ɛksklamatif, -iːv], *a.* exclamative, exclamatory (phrase, etc.); *Gram:* **point e.,** exclamation mark, *U.S:* exclamation point.

exclamation [ɛksklamasjɔ̃], *s.f.* exclamation; *Gram:* **point d'e.,** exclamation mark, *U.S:* exclamation point.

exclamativement [ɛksklamativmɑ̃], *adv.* exclamatively, exclamatorily.

exclamer (s') [sɛksklame], *v.pr.* (*a*) to exclaim; to utter exclamations; **pas possible! s'exclama-t-il,** impossible! he exclaimed; (*b*) to protest loudly; **il n'y a pas tant à s'e.,** there is nothing to make a fuss about.

exclu, -ue [ɛkskly], (*a*) *a.* excluded, refused, rejected; **candidat e.,** unsuccessful candidate; (*b*) *s.* person excluded, debarred; *s.m. Mil:* **e. de l'armée,** man excluded from the army on account of criminal antecedents; (*c*) **vous apprendrez le texte jusqu'au vers 19 exclu,** you will learn the text (by heart) up to but not including line 19.

exclure [ɛksklyːr], *v.tr.* (*pr.p.* **excluant;** *p.p.* **exclu;** *pr.ind.* **j'exclus, n. excluons;** *p.d.* **j'excluais;** *p.h.* **j'exclus;** *fu.* **j'exclurai**) (*a*) to exclude, shut out, leave out (s.o., sth.); to preclude; **e. qn de qch.,** to exclude s.o. from sth.; to deny s.o. admittance to sth.; **e. qn des champs de courses,** to warn s.o. off the turf; *Sch:* **e. temporairement,** to rusticate, suspend (student); *A:* **e. qn de faire qch.,** to debar s.o. from doing sth.; (*b*) **deux qualités qui s'excluent,** two qualities that are incompatible, that are mutually exclusive; **il n'est pas exclu que . . .,** it is not out of the question that . . ., there is nothing to prevent . . .; **e. la possibilité (de),** to rule out the possibility (of).

exclusif, -ive [ɛksklyzif, -iːv], *a.* **1.** exclusive, sole (right, etc.); **agent e.,** sole agent; *Com:* **article e.,** exclusive article, speciality. **2.** self-opinionated. **3.** *s.m. A.Com:* monopoly of trade (with overseas territories). **4.** *s.f.* **exclusive,** veto.

exclusion [ɛksklyzjɔ̃], *s.f.* **1.** exclusion, excluding, debarring (of s.o., sth., from sth.); *Fin:* **e. par voie d'achat,** buying out (of shareholders); *prep.phr.* **à l'e. de . . .,** excluding . . ., exclusive of . . ., to the exclusion of . . .. **2.** *Mch:* **e. de la vapeur,** cutting off of steam; cut-off. **3.** *Atom.Ph:* **principe d'e.,** exclusion principle.

exclusivement [ɛksklyzivmɑ̃], *adv.* (*a*) exclusively, solely; **il lisait e. des ouvrages philosophiques,** he read nothing but philosophical books; he read philosophical books to the exclusion of everything else; (*b*) **depuis lundi jusqu'à vendredi e.,** from Monday to Friday exclusive; **lisez depuis le chapitre premier jusqu'au vingtième e.,** read from chapter one up to but not including chapter twenty.

exclusivisme [ɛksklyzivism], *s.m.* exclusivism.

exclusiviste [ɛksklyzivist], *s.* exclusivist.

exclusivité [ɛksklyzivite], *s.f.* **1.** (*a*) *A:* exclusiveness; (*b*) *Ind:* **e. syndicale,** closed-shop policy. **2.** sole, exclusive, rights (**de,** in); monopoly; **film en e.,** exclusive film; *Journ:* **article en e.,** exclusive.

excogitation [ɛkskɔʒitasjɔ̃], *s.f.* excogitation, thinking out (of problem, etc.).

excommunication [ɛkskɔmynikasjɔ̃], *s.f.* excommunication.

excommunicatoire [ɛkskɔmynikatwaːr], *a.* excommunicatory.

excommunié, -ée [ɛkskɔmynje], *a. & s.* excommunicate (person); under sentence of excommunication, excommunicated (person).

excommunier [ɛkskɔmynje], *v.tr.* (*p.d. & pr.sub.* **n. excommuniions, v. excommuniiez**) to excommunicate.

excoriation [ɛkskɔrjasjɔ̃], *s.f.* excoriation, abrasion (of the skin).

excorier [ɛkskɔrje], *v.tr.* to excoriate; to peel off (the skin).

s'excorier, (*of the skin*) to peel (off).

excoriose [ɛkskɔrjoːz], *s.f. Vit:* black rot.

ex-coupon [ɛkskupɔ̃], *adv.phr. Fin:* ex coupon, ex dividend.

excrément [ɛkskremɑ̃], *s.m. Physiol:* excrement; *Pej:* **e. de la terre!** scum (of the earth)!

excrémentation [ɛkskremɑ̃tasjɔ̃], *s.f. Physiol:* evacuation.

excrémenteux, -euse [ɛkskremɑ̃tø, -øːz], **excrémen(ti)tiel, -ielle** [ɛkskremɑ̃(ti)sjɛl], *a.* excremental.

excrescence [ɛkskrɛs(s)ɑ̃ːs], *s.f. A:* excrescence.

excréta [ɛkskreta], *s.m.pl. Physiol:* excreta.

excréter [ɛkskrete], *v.tr.* **(j'excrète, n. excrétons; j'excréterai)** *Physiol:* to excrete.

excréteur, -trice [ɛkskretœːr, -tris], *a. Physiol:* excretive; excretory (duct, etc.); **organe e.,** excretory (organ).

excrétion [ɛkskresjɔ̃], *s.f. Physiol:* excretion; (*a*) excreting; (*b*) excreted matter, excreta.

excrétoire [ɛkskretwaːr], *a. Physiol:* excretory; excretionary; **troubles excrétoires,** difficulties in excretion.

excroissance [ɛkskrwasɑ̃ːs], *s.f.* excrescence; outgrowth; (surface) growth.

excurrent [ɛkskyrɑ̃], *a. Bot:* excurrent.

excursion [ɛkskyrsjɔ̃], *s.f.* **1.** excursion; tour; trip; jaunt; outing; ramble; **excursions accompagnées,** conducted tours; **e. à pied,** walking tour; hike; **aimer faire des excursions à pied,** to like (i) walking tours; (ii) hiking, long walks; **e. en montagne,** trip into the mountains; **e. botanique, scientifique,** botanical, scientific, expedition, outing; **faire une e. en Belgique,** to go on a trip, on a tour, to Belgium; **dimanche dernier nous avons fait une e. à la campagne,** last Sunday we went for a trip, an outing, into the country; *Rail:* **billet d'e.,** excursion ticket. **2.** *Mil: A:* raid, excursion; inroad (**dans,** on). **3.** digression, excursion (in speech, etc.); **e. dans la théorie,** excursion into theory; **faire une e. hors du sujet traité,** to digress, to wander from the subject. **4.** *Mec.E:* stroke, travel (of piston, etc.). **5.** *Elcs:* **e. de fréquence,** frequency deviation.

excursionner [ɛkskyrsjɔne], *v.i. F:* to make an excursion.

excursionnisme [ɛkskyrsjɔnism], *s.m.* love of, fondness, taste for, excursions, outings, trips.

excursionniste [ɛkskyrsjɔnist], *s.* excursionist, tourist, tripper; **e. à pied,** hiker.

excursus [ɛkskyrsyːs], *s.m.* excursus.

excurvé [ɛkskyrve], *a.* excurved, curved outwards.

excusabilité [ɛkskyzabilite], *s.f.* excusableness, excusability.

excusable [ɛkskyzabl̩], *a.* excusable, pardonable (error, etc.); (*person*) for whom there is some excuse; **nous sommes excusables de penser que . . .,** we may be forgiven for thinking that . . ..

excusablement [ɛkskyzabləmɑ̃], *adv.* excusably.

excuse [ɛkskyːz], *s.f.* **1.** (*a*) excuse; **il n'y a rien à dire à son e.,** there is nothing to be said in excuse for him; **mauvaise, faible, e.,** poor, lame, excuse; **trouver une e. à qch.,** to find an excuse for sth.; **donner pour e. que . . .,** to excuse oneself on the ground that . . .; **quand je veux m'esquiver, je prends mon travail comme e.,** when I want to slip away I make my work the excuse; (*b*) *A:* **faire e., les excuses, demander e.,** to excuse oneself, to ask (s.o.'s) pardon; *P:* **faites e.!** pardon me! **2.** *pl.* apology; **faire, présenter, ses excuses à qn,** to make one's apologies, to apologize, to s.o.; **se confondre en excuses d'arriver si tard,** to be very apologetic for arriving so late; **veuillez agréer nos excuses,** please accept our apology; **mes excuses pour ne pas l'avoir discerné,** excuse my not having noticed it; **il écrivit une lettre d'excuses,** he wrote to say he was sorry.

excuser [ɛkskyze], _v.tr._ **1.** to make excuses, to apologize, for (s.o.); **e. qn auprès de qn,** to apologize for s.o. to s.o. **2.** (_a_) to excuse, pardon (s.o.); **e. qch. à qn,** to excuse s.o. sth.; **e. qn de faire qch.,** to excuse s.o. (i) for doing sth.; (ii) from doing sth.; **excusez-moi d'arriver si tard,** excuse my coming so late; **vous êtes tout excusé,** that's quite all right; _Jur:_ **e. un juré,** to excuse a juryman (from attendance); (_b_) **l'ignorance de la loi n'excuse personne,** ignorance of the law excuses no man, is no excuse.

s'excuser, to excuse oneself, to apologize; **s'e. auprès de qn,** (i) to make one's apologies to s.o.; (ii) to send excuses for not coming; **s'e. de faire qch.,** (i) to apologize for doing sth.; (ii) to apologize for not doing sth.; (iii) to excuse oneself from doing sth.; **s'e. sur qch.,** (i) to make sth one's excuse; (ii) to apologize for sth.; **s'e. sur sa jeunesse,** to plead the inexperience of youth; **s'e. sur qn,** to shift the blame on to s.o. else; **s'e. de, sur, sa tenue,** to apologize for one's attire; **se faire e.,** to decline, to cry off; **ils commencèrent tous à s'e.,** they all began to make excuse; **il s'en excusa vivement,** he was quite apologetic about it; he was full of apologies; _Prov:_ **qui s'excuse s'accuse,** excuses always proceed from a guilty conscience.

ex-dividende [ɛksdividɑ̃:d], _adv.phr._ _Fin:_ ex dividend.

exeat [egzeat], _s.m._ (_a_) _Ecc: Sch:_ exeat; (_b_) **donner son e. à qn,** to dismiss s.o.; _F:_ to sack, fire, s.o.

exécrable [egzekrabl̩], _a._ execrable; abominable, loathsome (crime, etc.); deplorable, extremely bad (taste, verse, etc.).

exécrablement [egzekrabləmɑ̃], _adv._ execrably, abominably.

exécration [egzekrasjɔ̃], _s.f._ **1.** _A:_ execration, malediction, curse. **2.** execration, detestation (of crime, etc.); **avoir qn en e.,** to loathe s.o. **3.** deconsecration (of church, etc.).

exécratoire [egzekratwa:r], _a._ execratory (speech, etc.).

exécrer [egzekre], _v.tr._ (j'**exècre,** n. **exécrons;** j'**exécrerai**) (_a_) to execrate, loathe, detest; **e. l'hypocrisie,** to detest hypocrisy; **il exècre ce genre de vie,** he detests this kind of life; this kind of life repels, is repellent to, him; **ils s'exècrent mutuellement,** they detest each other; _F:_ they can't stand, bear, the sight of each other; **e. l'odeur de l'essence,** to detest the smell of petrol; to find the smell of petrol abominable, disgusting; **j'exècre le style de cet auteur,** I can't stand this author's style.

exécutable [egzekytabl̩], _a._ practicable, feasible, achievable.

exécutant, -ante [egzekytɑ̃, -ɑ̃:t], _s._ _Mus:_ performer (in band, etc.); executant.

exécuter [egzekyte], _v.tr._ **1.** to execute; to carry out, achieve (work); to follow out, carry out, act upon (orders, etc.); to perform, fulfil (promise); to carry out, give effect to (decree); to enforce (the law); to perform, play (piece of music); to perform (dance); **e. tout le programme,** to go through the whole programme; **l'ordre n'a pas été complètement exécuté,** the order was not fully carried out, implemented; _A:_ **e. sa parole,** to keep one's promise; _Artil:_ **une bouche à feu,** to serve a gun. **2.** (_a_) to execute; to put (criminal, etc.) to death; _F:_ **un jeune critique l'exécuta en deux articles,** a young critic disposed of him, _F:_ settled his hash, in a couple of articles; (_b_) _Jur:_ to distrain upon (debtor); (_c_) _St.Exch:_ to hammer (defaulter); **e. un client,** (i) to buy in, (ii) to sell out, against a client; (_d_) _Sp:_ to suspend (player) indefinitely; to warn (jockey) off the turf; (_e_) _Mil: A:_ **e. militairement une ville,** to punish a town.

s'exécuter. 1. to submit to doing, bring oneself to do, sth. unpleasant; **il faudra bien vous e.,** you'll have to bring yourself to do it; **s'e. de bonne grâce,** to submit gracefully. **2.** to pay up.

exécuteur, -trice [egzekytœ:r, -tris], _s._ **1.** (_a_) _A:_ executor, executer, performer (of undertaking); (_b_) _Jur:_ **exécuteur, -trice,** testamentaire, executor, -trix. **2.** executioner.

exécutif, -ive [egzekytif, -i:v], _a._ executive; **le pouvoir e.,** the executive power, **les agents exécutifs,** _s.m._ **l'exécutif,** the executive; _s.m._ **un e. de cinq membres,** an executive of five.

exécution [egzekysjɔ̃], _s.f._ **1.** execution, performance, carrying out (of plan, orders, agreement); fulfilment (of promise); enforcement (of the law, of a judgment); **e. d'un opéra,** production, performance, of an opera; **droit d'e.,** (i) right of performance; (ii) performing rights, author's fee; **e. d'un morceau de musique,** performance of a piece of music; _Artil:_ **e. de la**

---

bouche à feu, service of the piece; **mettre une idée, une menace, à e.,** to carry out an idea, a threat; **mettre un projet à e.,** to put a plan into execution; **gêner la mise à e. d'un projet,** to interfere with the carrying out of a project; **en e. de cette décision . . .,** in execution of this decision . . .; **plan d'e.,** plan of execution; **travaux en voie d'e.,** work in progress; **ces projets entreront bientôt en voie d'e.,** these plans will soon be put into execution, will soon be carried out, _U.S:_ will soon eventuate; **homme d'e.,** man of deeds; _Nau:_ **signal d'e.,** executive signal. **2.** (_a_) **e. capitale,** carrying out the death sentence; execution; **ordre d'e.,** death warrant; _Mil:_ **peloton d'e.,** firing party; _F:_ **e. d'un écrivain par un critique,** tearing to pieces of an author by a critic; (_b_) _Jur:_ distraint, distress; (_c_) _St.Exch:_ hammering (of defaulter); (_d_) _Sp:_ indefinite suspension (of player); warning (of jockey) off the turf.

exécutoire [egzekytwa:r]. _Jur:_ **1.** _a._ (_a_) (_of decree, contract, etc._) enforceable; to be carried into effect, put in force; **obligation e.,** operative obligation; **jugement e.,** final judgement; **les décisions de la Commission sont exécutoires,** the Commission has executive powers; (_b_) executory (formula, etc.). **2.** _s.m._ writ of execution; **e. de dépens,** order to pay costs; **délivrer un e. pour le montant des dépens,** to issue execution for the amount of the costs.

exécutoirement [egzekytwarmɑ̃], _adv._ enforceably; effectively.

exèdre [egzɛdr̩], _s.f._ _Arch:_ ex(h)edra.

exégèse [egzeʒe:z], _s.f._ exegesis.

exégète [egzeʒɛt], _s.m._ exegete, exegetist.

exégétique [egzeʒetik], _a._ exegetic(al); **théologie e.,** exegetics.

exemplaire¹ [egzɑ̃plɛ:r], _a._ exemplary.

exemplaire², _s.m._ 1. _A:_ exemplar, pattern, model (of virtue, behaviour, etc.). **2.** (_a_) sample, specimen (of work); (_b_) copy (of book, engraving, etc.); **e. de presse,** press copy; _Adm:_ **e. d'archives,** file copy; (_c_) _Lit:_ **les hommes de cette sorte, on en trouve des centaines d'exemplaires,** there are hundreds of men of this kind; **chaque concurrent doit présenter son ouvrage en cinq exemplaires,** each competitor must submit five copies of his work; **en double e.,** in duplicate.

exemplairement [egzɑ̃plɛrmɑ̃], _adv._ exemplarily, in an exemplary fashion.

exemplarité [egzɑ̃plarite], _s.f._ _Lit:_ exemplariness, exemplarity.

exemple [egzɑ̃:pl], _s.m._ example. **1. donner l'e.,** to set an, the, example; **suivre l'e. de qn,** to follow s.o.'s example; **prendre e. sur qn,** to take a leaf out of s.o.'s book; **citer qn en e.,** to hold s.o. up as an example; **citer qch. à titre d'e.,** to cite sth. as an example, as an illustration; **supposons à titre d'e. que . . .,** let us suppose for argument's sake, for example, that . . .; **prêcher d'e.,** to practise what one preaches; **joindre l'e. à la parole,** to suit the action to the word; **s'abstenir de vin pour l'e.,** to abstain from wine in order to show an example; **être un e. de vertu,** to be a model of virtue; **donner un e. d'une règle,** to exemplify a rule; _prep.phr._ **à l'e. de (qn),** following the example of (s.o.). **2.** lesson, warning, caution; **faire un e. de qn,** to make an example of s.o.; **servir d'e. à qn,** to be a lesson, a warning, to s.o.; **infliger une punition pour l'e.,** to inflict a punishment as a caution, as a warning, to others. **3.** instance, precedent; **il n'y en a point d'e.,** there is no precedent for it; **sans e.,** unexampled, without parallel; **par e.,** for instance, for example; **venez déjeuner un de ces jours, par e. dimanche,** come and have lunch one of these days, say on Sunday; **par e.,** (i) _int. phr._ well! who'd have thought it! _P:_ I should think not! (ii) (_intensive_) **cela vous serait utile, mais c'est cher, par e.,** it would be useful to you, but you must admit that it's very expensive; **voilà ce que je ne ferai jamais, par e.,** that's one thing I shall never do; _F:_ **il aime plaisanter avec ses subordonnés, mais, par e., il ne faut rien dire qui lui déplaise,** he likes joking with his subordinates, but mark you, you mustn't say anything he doesn't like.

exemplification [egzɑ̃plifikasjɔ̃], _s.f._ exemplification.

exemplifier [egzɑ̃plifje], _v.tr._ to exemplify.

exempt¹, -empte [egzɑ̃, -ɑ̃:t]. **1.** _a._ exempt (from service, tax, etc.); free (from anxiety, disease, etc.); **bois e. de nœuds,** wood free from knots; **esprit e. d'illusions,** mind free of illusions; **e. de soucis,** carefree; **combustion exempte de fumée,** smokeless combustion; _Cust:_ **e. de droits,** free

---

of duty, duty-free; _Com:_ **e. de frais,** no extra charge; _Mil: Navy:_ **e. de service,** excused (from fatigue, etc.); on the excused list. **2.** _s._ _Sp:_ player who has a bye.

exempt², _s.m._ _A:_ 1. exempt (military officer). **2.** officer of the watch.

exempté [egzɑ̃te], _a. & s.m._ exempted, exempt.

exempter [egzɑ̃te], _v.tr._ **e. qn (de qch.),** to exempt, free, excuse, s.o. (from sth.); **être exempté d'une corvée,** to be excused a fatigue; **e. qn de faire qch.,** to exempt s.o. from doing sth.; **e. qn du service militaire,** to exempt s.o. from military service.

s'exempter de faire qch., to excuse oneself from, get out of, doing sth.

exemption [egzɑ̃psjɔ̃], _s.f._ **1.** exemption (de, from); immunity (from service, tax, etc.); freedom (from anxiety, etc.); _Cust:_ **lettre d'e.,** bill of sufferance; **liste d'exemptions,** free list. **2.** _Sch:_ _A:_ good mark voucher (with which punishments may be redeemed).

exencéphale [egzɑ̃sefal], _Ter:_ (_a_) _a._ exencephalous, exencephalic; (_b_) _s.m._ exencephalus.

exencéphalie [egzɑ̃sefali], _s.f._ _Ter:_ exencephalia.

exentération [egzɑ̃terasjɔ̃], _s.f._ _Surg:_ exenteration.

exequatur [egzekwaty:r], _s.m.inv._ **1.** _Jur:_ proceedings to enforce a foreign judgment or an arbitrator's award. **2.** (consul's) exequatur.

exerçant [egzɛrsɑ̃], _a._ practising (doctor, etc.).

exercé [egzɛrse], _a._ experienced, practised, exercised (à, in); **un œil e.,** a practised, trained, eye; **oreille exercée à saisir tous les sons,** ear tuned to every sound.

exercer [egzɛrse], _v.tr._ (j'**exerçai(s),** n. **exerçons**) to exercise. **1.** (_a_) **e. un cheval, son corps,** to exercise a horse, one's body; **e. son oreille,** to train one's ear; **e. qn à qch., à faire qch.,** to train s.o. for sth., to do sth.; **e. la patience de qn,** to try s.o.'s patience; **e. toutes ses facultés,** to exercise all one's faculties; (_b_) _Mil:_ to drill, train (soldiers). **2.** (_a_) to exert, make use of (force, etc.); **e. le pouvoir,** to wield power; **e. des cruautés sur qn,** to practise cruelties on s.o.; **e. son influence sur qn,** to exert, exercise, one's influence, bring one's influence to bear, on s.o.; **e. une pression sur qch.,** to exert a pressure on sth.; _Jur:_ **e. des poursuites contre qn,** to bring an action against s.o.; **e. ses droits,** to exercise one's rights; **e. un mandat,** to carry out a mandate; (_b_) (_of medicine, etc._) **e. une action sur . . .,** to have an action upon . . ., to act upon . . . **3.** (_a_) to practise, follow, pursue, carry on (profession, business); **e. un métier,** to follow a trade; _abs._ **médecin qui n'exerce plus,** doctor who has given up (his) practice, doctor no longer in practice; (_b_) _abs._ _Adm:_ to visit, inspect, licensed premises.

s'exercer. 1. to drill; to do exercises. **2.** to practise; **s'e. à qch., à faire qch.,** to practise sth., practise doing sth.; **il s'est exercé à l'examen de ces questions,** he is experienced in examining such questions; **les critiques trouvent à s'e.,** critics find much to criticize. **3.** **la pression qui s'exerce sur . . .,** the pressure exerted on . . . **4.** **ces lois s'exercent dans tous les domaines de la Nature,** these laws hold good in every realm of Nature.

exercice [egzɛrsis], _s.m._ exercise. **1.** (_a_) **prendre de l'e.,** to take exercise; **e. physique,** physical exercise; (_b_) _Mil: etc:_ drill(ing), training; **être à l'e.,** to be on parade; **faire l'e.,** to drill; **faire faire l'e. à qn,** to drill s.o.; **exercices de tir,** musketry instruction; **e. de tir réel,** combat practice firing, field firing practice; (_c_) **exercices scolaires,** school exercises; **jouer des exercices au piano,** to practise (exercises) on the piano. **2.** (_a_) (putting into) practice; use (of power, privilege, etc.); carrying out (of mandate, etc.); **entrer en e.,** to enter upon one's duties; **e. d'une profession,** practice of a profession; _e._ **illégal,** illegal practice of a profession; **dans l'e. de ses fonctions,** in the exercise, discharge, of one's duties; **avocat en e.,** practising barrister; **le président en e.,** the president in office; (_b_) **l'e. du culte,** public worship. **3.** visit of inspection (of exciseman). **4.** _Fin: Com:_ (_a_) (i) financial year, year's trading; (ii) budgetary year, fiscal period; **e. social,** company's financial year; **l'e. de ce mois,** this month's trading; (_b_) balance sheet; (_c_) **e. 1970 attaché,** cum dividend 1970.

exerciseur [egzɛrsizœ:r], _s.m._ _Gym:_ exerciser (apparatus).

exercitant, -ante [egzɛrsitɑ̃, -ɑ̃:t], _s._ _Ecc:_ exercitant.

exérèse [egzere:z], _s.f._ _Surg:_ exeresis; cutting away (of foreign or diseased matter).

exergue [egzɛrg], *s.m.* (*a*) *Num:* exergue; **portant en e. . . .**, bearing inscribed below . . .; (*b*) introductory quotation; epigraph; **mettre qch. en e.**, to put sth. forward.
exert [egzɛr], *a. Bot:* exsert(ed).
exertile [egsɛrtil], *a. Biol:* exertile.
exeunt [egzeœ̃t], *Lt.v.i. Th:* (*stage direction*) exeunt.
exfoliatif, -ive [ɛksfɔljatif, -iːv], *a.* exfoliative.
exfoliation [ɛksfɔljasjɔ̃], *s.f.* exfoliation.
exfolier [ɛksfɔlje], *v.tr.* (*p.d. & pr.sub.* **n. exfoliions, v. exfoliiez**) to exfoliate, scale (bone, tree, rod, etc.).
s'exfolier, to exfoliate, scale off.
exhalaison [egzalɛzɔ̃], *s.f.* exhalation, effluvium; *pl.* fumes, effluvia.
exhalation [egzalasjɔ̃], *s.f.* exhalation, exhaling.
exhaler [egzale], *v.tr.* to exhale, emit, give out (smell, vapour, etc.); **e. un soupir**, to breathe a sigh; **e. son dernier soupir**, to breathe one's last, to die; **e. sa rage**, to give vent to, to vent, one's wrath; **ce lieu exhale la tristesse, le crime**, this place breathes an air of sadness, reeks of crime.
s'exhaler, (*of gas, smell, vapour, etc.*) to exhale, to pass off into the air; **une faible odeur s'exhale des genêts**, a faint scent is rising from the broom; **s'e. en menaces**, to give vent to threats.
exhaure [egzoːr], *s.f. Min:* pumping (out), unwatering.
exhaussement [egzosmɑ̃], *s.m.* **1.** raising, increasing the height (of house, heel of shoe, etc.); *Arch:* stilting (of arch). **2.** *Geol:* rise in level (of river bed, through deposition); *Hyd.E:* **remous d'e.**, rise in level (of water above dam). **3. e. du terrain**, rise in the ground; mound, elevation.
exhausser [egzose], *v.tr.* (*a*) to raise, to increase the height of (house, wall, etc.); *Arch:* to stilt (arch); **e. une maison d'un étage**, to add a storey to a house; (*b*) to ennoble; to dignify; **dignité qui est capable d'e. l'humanité**, dignity which can raise humanity to a higher level.
s'exhausser, (*of ground, etc.*) to rise.
exhausteur [egzostœːr], *s.m. Aut:* **1.** suction-pipe (of vacuum-feed tank). **2.** vacuum-feed tank.
exhaustif, -ive [egzostif, -iːv], *a.* (*a*) *occ.* exhausting; (*b*) exhaustive.
exhaustion [egzostjɔ̃], *s.f.* exhaust(ion) (of liquid, gas, etc.); *Nau:* **pompe d'e.**, brine pump; *Mth:* **méthode d'e.**, method of exhaustions.
exhaustivement [egzostivmɑ̃], *adv.* exhaustively.
exhérédation [egzeredasjɔ̃], *s.f. Jur:* exheredation, disinheritance, disherison.
exhérédé [egzerede], *a.* disinherited.
exhéréder [egzerede], *v.tr.* (**j'exhérède, n. exhérédons; j'exhéréderai**) *Jur:* to exheredate, disinherit.
exhiber [egzibe], *v.tr.* **1.** *Jur:* to exhibit, produce (documents, etc.). **2.** (*a*) to present, show, produce (ticket, passport, etc.); (*b*) to exhibit, show (animals, etc.); *usu. Pej:* **e. sa science, ses diamants**, to show off, display, one's knowledge, one's diamonds.
s'exhiber, *Pej:* (*a*) to show off; (*b*) to make an exhibition of oneself.
exhibiteur, -trice [egzibitœːr, -tris], *s.* exhibitor.
exhibition [egzibisjɔ̃], *s.f.* **1.** *Jur:* exhibition, production (of documents, etc.). **2.** (*a*) producing, presenting, showing (of passport, etc.); (*b*) show (of cattle, etc.); exhibition (of pictures, etc.); *Pej:* **faire l'e. de ses bijoux**, to show off, display, one's jewels; (*c*) *Sp:* exhibition; exhibition match.
exhibitionnisme [egzibisjɔnism], *s.m.* (*a*) *Psy:* exhibitionism; indecent exposure; (*b*) exhibitionism; **son e. me dégoûte**, the way he flaunts his emotions disgusts me.
exhibitionniste [egzibisjɔnist]. **1.** *a.* exhibitionistic. **2.** *s.* (*a*) *Psy:* exhibitionist; (*b*) exhibitionist, person who flaunts his emotions, etc.
exhilarant [egzilarɑ̃], *a. & s. A:* exhilarant; **gaz e.**, laughing gas.
exhortatif, -ive [egzɔrtatif, -iːv], *a.* hortative, hortatory.
exhortation [egzɔrtasjɔ̃], *s.f.* exhortation, admonishment; **e. à qch., à faire qch.**, exhortation to sth., to do sth.
exhorter [egzɔrte], *v.tr.* to exhort, urge; **e. qn à faire qch.**, to exhort, urge, s.o. to do sth.
exhumation [egzymasjɔ̃], *s.f.* (*a*) exhumation, disinterment; (*b*) unearthing (of old documents, etc.); (*c*) excavation, digging up (of buried city, etc.); (*d*) *Geol:* exhumation.
exhumé [egzyme], *a.* (*a*) exhumed, disinterred; (*b*) excavated, dug up; (*c*) *Geol:* **relief e.**, exhumed relief.
exhumer [egzyme], *v.tr.* (*a*) to exhume, disinter (body); (*b*) to unearth, bring to light (old documents, etc.); **documents exhumés des archives**, documents brought to light from, dug out of, the archives; **e. de vieilles rancunes**, to dig up old grudges; (*c*) to dig up, excavate; **e. un bâtiment ancien, un vase ancien**, to excavate an ancient building, to dig up an antique, ancient, vase.
exigeant [egziʒɑ̃], *a.* exacting; demanding; hard to please; **être trop e.**, to be over-particular, to expect too much; **malade e.**, demanding patient, invalid; **métier e.**, demanding, exacting, job; **plante exigeante**, plant difficult to rear.
exigence [egziʒɑ̃ːs], *s.f.* **1.** exactingness; **personne d'une e. insupportable**, unreasonable person. **2.** (*a*) unreasonable, arbitrary, demand; **se soumettre aux exigences de qn**, to submit to s.o.'s whims, to humour s.o.; *Com:* **satisfaire aux exigences de ses clients**, to satisfy the demands, the whims, of one's customers; (*b*) exigence, exigency, demand(s), requirement(s); **l'e., les exigences, de l'étiquette**, the demands of etiquette; **selon l'e. du cas**, as may be required; **la marchandise répond à toutes les exigences**, the goods are up to standard in every way; **satisfaire les exigences**, to meet requirements.
exiger [egziʒe], *v.tr.* (**j'exigeai(s); n. exigeons**) **1.** to exact, demand, require (**de**, from); to insist on (sth.); **j'exige de conserver ma liberté**, I insist on keeping my freedom; **e. un impôt**, to exact a tax; **e. l'obéissance de qn**, to demand, insist on, obedience from s.o.; **qu'exigez-vous de moi?** what do you demand of me? what do you require, want me to do? **j'exige de voir le chef de gare**, I insist on seeing the stationmaster; **j'exige qu'il me fasse des excuses**, I insist on his apologizing; **e. qu'une chose soit faite**, to insist on sth. being done; **trop e. des forces de qn**, to overtax s.o.'s strength. **2.** to require, necessitate, call for (care, etc.); **prendre les mesures qu'exigent les circonstances**, to take the requisite, necessary, measures, the necessary steps.
exigibilité [egziʒibilite], *s.f.* **1.** liability to be demanded. **2.** *pl. Com:* current liabilities.
exigible [egziʒibl], *a.* exigible (**de**, from); claimable; (payment) due.
exigu, -uë [egzigy], *a.* exiguous, tiny (dwelling, etc.); scanty (resources); slender (income); diminutive (stature); small (territory, etc.); **ressources exiguës**, slender means.
exiguïté [egzigɥite], *s.f.* exiguity, smallness (of dwelling, etc.); scantiness (of resources); slenderness (of income); diminutiveness (of stature); **il se plaignait de l'e. de son logement**, he complained of his cramped quarters; **l'e. de nos ressources ne nous permet pas de . . .**, our slender means do not allow us to . . .
exil [egzil], *s.m.* exile, banishment; **envoyer qn en e.**, to send s.o. into exile, to banish s.o.; **partir, s'en aller, en e.**, to go into exile; **frapper qn d'un e. temporaire**, to sentence s.o. to temporary exile; **revenir de son e.**, to return from exile.
exilarchat [egzilarka], *s.m. Jewish Hist:* exilarchate.
exilarque [egzilark], *s.m. Jewish Hist:* exilarch.
exilé, -ée [egzile], *s.* (*pers.*) exile.
exiler [egzile], *v.tr.* to exile, banish.
s'exiler, to go into exile; **s'e. du monde**, to withdraw from the world.
exilien, -ienne [egziljɛ̃, -jɛn], **exilique** [egzilik], *a. Jewish Hist:* exilic.
exine [egziːn], *s.f. Bot:* ex(t)ine, exosporium (of a pollen grain).
exinscrit [egzɛ̃skri], *a. Geom:* escribed (circle).
existant [egzistɑ̃]. **1.** *a.* (*a*) existing, living, existent; **lois existantes**, existing laws, laws in force; **majorer les tarifs existants**, to increase existing tariffs; (*b*) extant (species, document, etc.); **le plus ancien document e.**, the earliest extant document; (*c*) (supplies, etc.) on hand. **2.** *s.m.* (*a*) *Com:* **l'e. (en caisse)**, the cash in hand; **l'e. (en magasin)**, the stock in hand; (*b*) *Phil:* living being.
existence [egzistɑ̃ːs], *s.f.* **1.** (*a*) existence, (state of) being; (*b*) life; **mener une e. agréable**, to lead a pleasant existence, a pleasant life; **moyens d'e.**, means of existence; **on ne donne guère à ce gouvernement plus de trois mois d'e.**, people don't give this government more than three months; (*c*) living being; **le mariage qui unit deux existences**, marriage which unites two human beings, two lives. **2.** *Com:* **e. (en magasin)**, stock (in hand).
existentialisme [egzistɑ̃sjalism], *s.m. Phil:* existentialism.
existentialiste [egzistɑ̃sjalist], *a. & s.m. & f. Phil:* existentialist.
existentiel, -elle [egzistɑ̃sjɛl], *a.* existential.
exister [egziste], *v.i.* (*a*) to exist, be; to live; **la plus belle voiture qui existe**, the finest car going, the finest car on the market; **ce modèle existe en plusieurs tailles**, this model comes in several sizes; **le plus grand génie qui ait jamais existé**, the greatest genius that ever lived; **races qui n'existent plus**, races that are extinct, that have died out; **pays où existe un état d'hostilités**, country where hostilities are in progress; **la maison existe depuis 50 ans, existe toujours**, the firm has been in existence for 50 years, is still in existence; **circulaires d'une société qui n'existe pas**, circulars from a bogus company; **rien n'existe pour lui que l'art**, nothing but art exists for him, matters to him; *F:* **ça n'existe pas!** that's stupid! (*b*) to be extant; **il existe encore quelques manuscrits**, there are still a few manuscripts extant.
exit [egzit], *Lt.v.i. Th:* (*stage direction*) **e. Macbeth**, exit Macbeth.
ex-libris [ɛkslibriːs], *s.m.* book plate, ex libris; **collectionneur d'e.-l.**, ex-librist.
exo- [egzɔ], *pref.* exo-.
exoascacées [egzɔaskase], *s.f.pl. Fung:* Exoascaceae.
exoascus [egzɔaskys], *s.m. Fung:* exoascus.
exobaside [egzɔbazid], **exobasidium** [egzɔbazidjɔm], *s.m. Fung:* exobasidium.
exobasidiacées [egzɔbazidjase], *s.f.pl. Fung:* Exobasidiaceae.
exobiologie [egzɔbiɔlɔʒi], *s.f.* extra-terrestrial biology, exobiology.
exocardiaque [egzɔkardjak], *a. Med:* exocardiac.
exocet [egzɔsɛ], *s.m. Ich:* exocoetus; flying fish.
exocranien, -ienne [egzɔkrɑnjɛ̃, -jɛn], *a. Anat:* exocranial.
exocrine [egzɔkrin], *a. Physiol:* exocrine (gland).
exode[1] [egzɔd], *s.m. Gr.Lit:* exodium, exode (of tragedy).
exode[2], *s.m.* (*a*) *B.Hist:* **l'E.**, the Exodus (of the Jews from Egypt); (*b*) exodus; emigration; **l'e. des Irlandais au XIXe siècle**, the (mass) emigration of the Irish during the XIXth century; *Fr.Hist:* **l'e. (de 1940)**, the exodus (of 1940); *Com:* **e. des capitaux**, flight of capital; **e. rural**, rural depopulation; **le premier août est le signal pour l'e. des vacances**, the first of August is the signal for everyone to leave for his summer holidays.
exoderme [egzɔdɛrm], *s.m. Physiol:* exoderm.
exodontie [egzɔdɔ̃ti], *s.f. Dent:* exodontia.
exoénergétique [egzɔenɛrʒetik], *a. Ch:* energy-liberating (reaction).
exogame [egzɔgam], *a. Anthr:* exogamous (tribe).
exogamie [egzɔgami], *s.f. Anthr:* exogamy.
exogène [egzɔʒɛn], *a. Bot: Geol: Med:* exogenous; *Med:* enthetic; **plante e.**, exogen.
exognathie [egzɔgnati], *s.f.*, **exognathisme** [egzɔgnatism], *s.m. Anat:* exognathia, exognathism.
exogonium [egzɔgɔnjɔm], *s.m. Bot:* exogonium.
exogyne [egzɔʒin], *a. Bot:* exogynous.
exogyre [egzɔʒiːr], *s.m. & f. Paleont:* exogyra.
exomorphe [egzɔmɔrf], *a. Geol:* exomorphic.
exomorphisme [egzɔmɔrfism], *s.m. Geol:* exomorphism.
exomphale [egzɔ̃fal], *s.f. Med:* exomphalos, umbilical hernia.
exondation [egzɔ̃dasjɔ̃], *s.f.*, **exondement** [egzɔ̃dmɑ̃], *s.m. Geol: Geog:* emergence.
exonder(s') [segzɔ̃de], *v.pr. Geol: Geog:* (*of land*) to emerge.
exonération [egzɔnerasjɔ̃], *s.f.* exoneration, relieving; remission (of fees, taxes, etc.); **e. des charges de guerre**, immunity from war indemnities.
exonérer [egzɔnere], *v.tr.* (**j'exonère, n. exonérons; j'exonérerai**) (*a*) to exonerate (**de**, from); to free, relieve (s.o. from duty, etc.); **être exonéré de l'impôt sur le revenu**, to be exempted from income tax; (*b*) **e. des marchandises**, to exempt goods from import duty; *Sch:* **e. un candidat**, to remit a candidate's examination fees.
exophorie [egzɔfɔri], *s.f. Med:* exophoria.
exophtalmie [egzɔftalmi], *s.f. Med:* exophthalmus, exophthalmos; exophthalmia.
exophtalmique [egzɔftalmik], *a. Med:* exophthalmic (goitre).
exoplasme [egzɔplasm], *s.m.* ectoplasm.
exopodite [egzɔpɔdit], *s.m. Crust:* exopodite.
exoptérygote [egzɔpterigɔt], *Ent:* **1.** *a.* exopterygotic. **2.** *s.m.pl.* **exoptérygotes**, Exopterygota.
exorable [egzɔrabl], *a.* exorable; accessible to pity.
exorbitamment [egzɔrbitamɑ̃], *adv.* exorbitantly.

exorbitance [egzɔrbitɑ̃:s], *s.f.* exorbitance, extravagance (of demand, etc.).

exorbitant [egzɔrbitɑ̃], *a.* exorbitant, extravagant, unconscionable (demand, etc.); **prix e.,** exorbitant, prohibitive, price; *Jur:* **e. de,** outside the scope, the competence, of.

exorbité [egzɔrbite], *a.* **ils regardaient, les yeux exorbités,** they were looking on, with their eyes popping out of their heads.

exorbiter (s') [segzɔrbite], *v.pr.* (*of eyes*) to stare; *F:* to pop out of one's head.

exorcisation [egzɔrsizasjɔ̃], *s.f.* exorcizing.

exorciser [egzɔrsize], *v.tr.* to exorcize (demon, one possessed, haunted place); to cast out (devil); to lay (ghost).

exorciseur, -euse [egzɔrsizœ:r, -ø:z], *s.* exorcizer, exorcist.

exorcisme [egzɔrsism], *s.m.* **1.** exorcizing. **2.** exorcism.

exorciste [egzɔrsist], *s.* (*a*) exorcist, exorcizer; (*b*) *Rel.H:* exorcist.

exorde [egzɔrd], *s.m.* (*a*) *Rh:* exordium; (*b*) **la fin de cette affaire fut digne de l'e.,** the matter ended in the same way that it had begun.

exoréique [egzɔreik], *a. Geol:* exoreic.

exoréisme [egzɔreism], *s.m. Geol:* exoreism.

exor(r)hize [egzɔri:z], *a. Bot:* exor(r)hizal; **plante e.,** exor(r)hiza.

exosmose [egzɔsmo:z], *s.f. Ph:* exosmose, exosmosis.

exosmotique [egzɔsmɔtik], *a. Ph:* exosmotic.

exosphère [egzɔsfɛ:r], *s.f.* exosphere.

exospore [egzɔspɔ:r], *s.m. Bot:* exospore.

exosporé [egzɔspɔre], *a. Bot:* exosporous.

exosquelette [egzɔskəlɛt], *s.m.* exoskeleton.

exostome [egzɔstom], *s.m. Bot:* exostome.

exostosant [egzɔstozɑ̃], *a. Med:* that causes exostosis.

exostose [egzɔsto:z], *s.f. Med: Bot:* exostosis.

exotérique [egzɔterik], *a.* exoteric.

exotérisme [egzɔterism], *s.m.* exotericism.

exothèque [egzɔtɛk], *s.f. Bot:* exothecium.

exothermique [egzɔtɛrmik], *a. Ch:* exothermic (reaction, etc.).

exotique [egzɔtik], (*a*) *a.* exotic; (*b*) *s.m.* **le goût de l'e.,** taste for, love of, the exotic.

exotiquement [egzɔtikmɑ̃], *adv.* exotically.

exotisme [egzɔtism], *s.m.* exot(ic)ism.

exotoxine [egzɔtɔksin], *s.f. Bac:* exotoxin.

exotype [egzɔtip], *s.m. Biol:* exotype.

expansé [ɛkspɑ̃se], *a.* expanded; **polystyrène e.,** expanded polystyrene.

expanseur [ɛkspɑ̃sœ:r], *s.m.* **1.** *Tls:* tube expander. **2.** *W.Tel: etc:* expandor.

expansibilité [ɛkspɑ̃sibilite], *s.f.* **1.** *Ph:* expansibility (of gas, etc.). **2.** expansiveness (of disposition).

expansible [ɛkspɑ̃sibl], *a. Ph:* expansible (gas, etc.).

expansif, -ive [ɛkspɑ̃sif, -i:v], *a.* **1.** expansive (force, gas, etc.); *Med:* **lésion intracranienne expansive,** space-occupying tumour; *Civ.E:* **ciment e.,** expanding cement. **2.** (*of pers.*) expansive, exuberant, effusive; **se montrer trop e.,** to wear one's heart on one's sleeve; **devenir e.,** to become talkative.

expansion [ɛkspɑ̃sjɔ̃], *s.f.* **1.** expansion; (*a*) expansion (of gases, etc.); **moteur à triple e.,** triple-expansion engine; **frein à e.,** internal expanding brake; *Tchn:* **e. de prise,** setting expansion (of cement, etc.); *Hyd.E:* **vase d'e.,** surge tank; *Anat:* **l'œil doit être regardé comme une e. du nerf optique,** the eye may be regarded as an expansion of the optic nerve; *Astr:* **l'e. de l'univers,** the expansion of the universe; **l'univers en e.,** the expanding universe; (*b*) **e. coloniale,** colonial expansion; **taux d'e. économique,** economic growth rate; **équilibre d'e.,** equilibrium in an expanding economy; **e. démographique,** (net) increase in population; **e. des idées nouvelles,** propagation, spreading, of new ideas. **2.** expansiveness; **accueillir qn avec e.,** to greet s.o. effusively; **le tout se termina par des expansions et des poignées de main,** it all ended with everyone being effusive and shaking hands.

expansionner (s') [sɛkspɑ̃sjɔne], *v.pr. A: F:* (*of pers.*) to expand, to become expansive; to open out, to talk without reserve.

expansionnisme [ɛkspɑ̃sjɔnism], *s.m.* (*a*) *Pol:* colonialism; (*b*) *Pol.Ec:* expansionism.

expansionniste [ɛkspɑ̃sjɔnist]. **1.** *a.* expansionist. **2.** *s.m. & f.* (*a*) partisan of colonial expansion; (*b*) *Pol.Ec:* expansionist.

expansivité [ɛkspɑ̃sivite], *s.f.* expansiveness.

expatriation [ɛkspatriasjɔ̃], *s.f.* expatriation.

expatrié, -ée [ɛkspatrie], *s.* expatriate; exile; emigrant.

expatrier [ɛkspatrie], *v.tr.* (*p.d. & pr.sub.* **n. expatriions, v. expatriiez**) to expatriate, banish; to send (s.o.) out of the country; *Fin:* **e. des capitaux,** to expatriate capital, to invest money abroad.

s'expatrier, to leave one's (own) country; to settle abroad.

expectance [ɛkspɛktɑ̃:s], *s.f.* expectancy.

expectant [ɛkspɛktɑ̃], *a.* (*rare*) expectant (attitude, medicine, etc.); **politique expectante,** wait-and-see policy.

expectateur, -trice [ɛkspɛktatœ:r, -tris], *a. & s.* expectant.

expectatif, -ive [ɛkspɛktatif, -i:v]. **1.** *a. A:* expectative; *Ecc:* **grâce expectative,** expectative grace; **fortune expectative,** anticipated fortune; *F:* expectations. **2.** *s.f.* **expectative;** expectation, expectancy (of inheritance, etc.); **vivre dans l'expectative,** to live in expectation; **nous sommes dans l'expectative,** we are waiting; **rester dans l'expectative,** to wait and see; **avoir qch. en expectative,** to expect sth.; to have hopes of sth.; **sortir de son expectative,** to depart from one's expectant attitude; **triste expectative,** gloomy prospect.

expectation [ɛkspɛktasjɔ̃], *s.f.* (*a*) *A:* expectation, anticipation; (*b*) *Med:* **méthode d'e.,** expectant treatment.

expectorant [ɛkspɛktɔrɑ̃], *a. & s.m. Med:* expectorant.

expectoration [ɛkspɛktɔrasjɔ̃], *s.f.* expectoration. **1.** expectorating. **2.** sputum.

expectorer [ɛkspɛktɔre], *v.tr.* (*a*) to expectorate, to spit; **e. des mucosités,** to hawk up phlegm; (*b*) *F:* to spit out (abuse, etc.).

expédié, -iée [ɛkspedje]. **1.** *a. Surv:* rough, approximate (survey). **2.** *s.f.* **expédiée,** running hand(writing).

expédience [ɛkspedjɑ̃:s], *s.f.* expediency, expedience.

expédient [ɛkspedjɑ̃]. **1.** *a.* expedient, advisable, proper, fit; **vous ferez ce que vous jugez e.,** you will do what you think advisable, fit; **il est e. de prendre les devants,** it is advisable to take the initiative; *Lit:* **il est e. que** + *sub.*, it is expedient, advisable, that + *condit.* **2.** *s.m.* (*a*) expedient, (make)shift, resource; device; **chercher un e.,** to find a way, a means, **homme d'expédients,** resourceful man; **essayer de mille expédients,** to try every possible device; (*b*) *Pej:* device, shift; **vivre d'expédients,** to live by one's wits; **avoir recours à des expédients,** to resort to dubious methods.

expédier [ɛkspedje], *v.tr.* (*p.d. & pr.sub.* **n. expédiions, v. expédiiez**) to dispatch, despatch. **1.** (*a*) to get rid of, dispose of (s.o.); to get (s.o.) out of the way; (*b*) *F: & A:* (i) to ruin, do for (s.o.); (ii) to kill; to do (s.o.) in. **2.** (*a*) to expedite, hurry up with, go quickly through (task, business); **e. la besogne,** to finish off, polish off, one's work; **il eut bientôt expédié sa messe,** he made short work of his mass; **e. son déjeuner,** to hurry through, polish off, bolt, one's lunch; **le dîner fut vite expédié,** dinner was soon disposed of; (*b*) *Cust:* **e. des marchandises en douane,** to clear goods; (*c*) **e. les affaires de qn,** to manage s.o.'s affairs. **3.** *Jur:* to draw up (contract, deed). **4.** to forward, send off (letter, parcel, goods); **e. ses marchandises,** to get one's goods off; **expédiez ceci par le premier courrier,** get this off by the first post; **e. des marchandises par navire,** to ship goods; **e. (qch.) par la poste,** to post, mail (sth.); *F:* **expédiez-le-moi!** send him along (to me)!

expéditeur, -trice [ɛkspeditœ:r, -tris], *s.* **1.** sender (of telegram, letter, etc.); originator (of message); (*on letter, etc.*) **expéditeur, -trice** (*abbr.* **exp.**), from, sender. **2.** (*a*) shipper, consigner, consignor (of goods); (*b*) forwarding agent; (*c*) dispatcher.

expéditif, -ive [ɛkspeditif, -i:v], *a.* (*a*) expeditious, prompt; (*b*) hasty.

expédition [ɛkspedisjɔ̃], *s.f.* **1.** (*a*) expedition, dispatch, disposal (of business, etc.); **je vais rester pour assurer l'e. des affaires courantes,** I shall stay behind to carry on the ordinary business; *A:* **homme d'e.,** energetic man; (*b*) *Cust:* **e. en douane,** (customs) clearance; (*c*) *Wines:* **liqueur d'e.,** sweetener (added to champagne in course of manufacture). **2.** (i) copying; (ii) copy (of deed, contract, etc.); **première e.,** first authentic copy; **en double e.,** in duplicate; **en triple e.,** in triplicate. **3.** (*a*) dispatch(ing), forwarding, sending (of parcels, etc.); **e. par mer,** shipping, shipment; **bulletin d'e.,** waybill; **maison d'e.,** forwarding house; **expédition franco à partir de 1000 francs,** orders of 1000 francs and over delivered free; (*b*) consignment; (*c*) (i) (military, scientific, etc.) expedition; (military) campaign; (police) raid; **e. au pôle sud,** expedition to the South Pole; (ii) *F:* tour, trip; **elle est rentrée fatiguée de son e. en ville,** she came back tired out from her little trip to town; (*of journey involving complicated preparations*) **c'est une véritable e.,** it's a real expedition.

expéditionnaire [ɛkspedisjɔnɛ:r]. **1.** *s.m.* (*a*) sender; (*b*) forwarding agent. **2.** *a. & s.m.* **(commis) e.,** (i) copying clerk; (ii) shipping clerk. **3.** *a. Mil: Navy:* **corps e.,** expeditionary force.

expéditivement [ɛkspeditivmɑ̃], *adv.* expeditiously, speedily, quickly.

expérience [ɛksperjɑ̃:s], *s.f.* **1.** experience; **avoir l'e. de qch.,** to have experience of, in, sth., to be experienced in sth.; **il en a l'e.,** he is an old hand at it; **un homme d'e.,** a man of experience; **il a l'e. du monde,** he is a man of the world; **faire l'e. de qch.,** to experience sth.; **connaître qch. par e.,** to know sth. from experience; **sans e.,** inexperienced (de, in); **l'e. démontre que . . .,** experience shows that . . .; **l'e. rend prudent,** one learns prudence by experience. **2.** experiment, test; **terrain d'e.,** testing ground; **e. de chimie,** chemical experiment; **e. en blanc,** blank determination; **faire une e.,** to carry out an experiment; **faire qch. à titre d'e.,** to do, try, sth. as an experiment; **faire une e. sur qn, sur qch.,** to experiment on s.o., on sth.; **faire l'e. d'un poison,** to test a poison; *Artil:* **expériences de tir,** gun trials.

expérimental, -aux [ɛksperimɑ̃tal, -o], *a.* experimental; **les sciences expérimentales,** the applied sciences; **station expérimentale,** experimental station; **réacteur e.,** development reactor.

expérimentalement [ɛksperimɑ̃talmɑ̃], *adv.* experimentally, by (way of) experiment.

expérimentalisme [ɛksperimɑ̃talism], *s.m.* experimentalism.

expérimentaliste [ɛksperimɑ̃talist], *s.m. & f.* experimentalist.

expérimentateur, -trice [ɛksperimɑ̃tatœ:r, -tris]. **1.** *s.* (*a*) (scientific) research worker; (*b*) experimenter; **la France est à la merci des expérimentateurs,** France is at the mercy of experimenters. **2.** *a.* experimentative (mind, etc.).

expérimentation [ɛksperimɑ̃tasjɔ̃], *s.f.* experimentation, experimenting.

expérimenté [ɛksperimɑ̃te], *a.* (*a*) experienced, efficient; skilled (workman); (*b*) experimented, studied, investigated.

expérimenter [ɛksperimɑ̃te], *v.tr.* (*a*) to test, try (remedy, model, etc.); **on ne peut pas juger de cela sans l'avoir expérimenté,** it is impossible to judge this without having tried, tested, it; **e. un vaccin sur un cobaye,** to try out a vaccine on a guinea-pig; (*b*) *abs.* to experiment(alize), to make experiments; (*c*) **on devient plus indulgent à mesure qu'on expérimente la vie,** one becomes more indulgent as one gains greater experience of life.

expert [ɛkspɛ:r]. **1.** *a.* expert, skilled (**en, dans,** in); able; **la main-d'œuvre la plus experte,** the most highly skilled labour; **mains expertes,** experienced hands; **un œil e.,** the eye of an expert; **il est e. dans la matière,** he is an expert in this field. **2.** *s.m.* expert; connoisseur; *Com:* valuer, appraiser; *Nau:* surveyor; **à dire d'experts,** according to the experts.

expert-comptable [ɛkspɛrkɔ̃tabl], *s.m.* = chartered accountant; *pl. experts-comptables.*

expert-conseil [ɛkspɛrkɔ̃sɛ:j], *s.m. Ind: etc:* consultant; *pl. experts-conseils.*

expertement [ɛkspɛrtəmɑ̃], *adv.* expertly, skilfully; ably.

expertise [ɛkspɛrti:z], *s.f.* **1.** *Com:* expert appraisement, valuation; *Nau:* survey (of ship for damage); **e. d'avarie,** damage survey; **faire l'e. des dégâts, d'un travail, de l'état d'un navire,** to appraise the damage; to value work done; to survey a ship; **faire une e.,** to make a valuation, a survey; **e. judiciaire,** *U.S:* court-ordered appraisal. **2.** expert's report, expert opinion; **l'e. a établi que ce tableau est une copie,** according to expert opinion this picture is a copy.

expertiser [ɛkspɛrtize], *v.tr.* **1.** *Com:* to appraise, value, estimate; *Nau:* to survey (ship for damage); **faire e. qch.,** to have sth. surveyed; to obtain an expert opinion on sth. **2.** *abs.* to give an expert opinion.

expiable [ɛkspjabl], *a.* expiable.

expiateur, -trice [ɛkspjatœ:r, -tris], *a. A:* expiatory.

expiation [ɛkspjasjɔ̃], *s.f.* expiation; *Theol:* atonement; **en e. de**, in expiation of; in atonement for; **fête de l'e.**, Day of Atonement.

expiatoire [ɛkspjatwaːr], *a.* expiatory; *Ecc:* **offrande e.**, atonement money.

expier [ɛkspje], *v.tr.* (*p.d. & pr.sub.* **n. expiions, v. expiiez**) to expiate, atone for, pay the penalty of (sin, etc.); **il expia durement sa faute**, he paid heavily, up to the hilt, for his mistake; **faire e. qch. à qn**, to make s.o. pay the penalty for sth.

expilation [ɛkspilasjɔ̃], *s.f. A.Jur:* **e. d'hérédité**, depredation of decedent's estate.

expirant [ɛkspirɑ̃], *a.* expiring, dying; **flamme expirante**, dying flame; **voix expirante**, barely audible voice.

expirateur [ɛkspiratœːr], *a.m.* expiratory (muscle).

expiration [ɛkspirasjɔ̃], *s.f.* expiration. **1.** breathing out (of air); *Mch:* discharge (of steam). **2.** expiry, termination, end (of lease, term of office, etc.); **venir à e.**, to expire; *Jur:* **e. d'un terme**, effluxion of time; **l'e. des délais**, time limit.

expiré [ɛkspire], *a.* at an end; **mon congé est e.**, my leave is up; **notre bail est e.**, our lease is at an end, has run out.

expirer [ɛkspire], *v.* to expire. **1.** *v.tr.* to breathe out (air, etc.). **2.** *v.i.* (*a*) to die; **il a expiré à sept heures dans mes bras**, he died at seven o'clock in my arms; **être sur le point d'e.**, to be at one's last gasp; **sa voix expira dans le lointain**, his voice died away in the distance; (*b*) to come to an end; **notre bail a expiré hier**, our lease expired, ran out, yesterday; **ce passeport expire le . . .**, the validity of this passport expires on . . . .

explant [ɛksplɑ̃], *s.m. Biol:* explant.

explétif, -ive [ɛkspletif, -iːv], *a. & s.m.* expletive.

explétivement [ɛkspletivmɑ̃], *adv.* expletively.

explicabilité [ɛksplikabilite], *s.f.* explicableness.

explicable [ɛksplikabḷ], *a.* explicable, explainable, that can be explained.

explicateur, -trice [ɛksplikatœːr, -tris]. **1.** *s.* explainer, exponent; (*in museums, etc.*) guide. **2.** *a.* explanatory.

explicatif, -ive [ɛksplikatif, -iːv], *a.* explanatory; *Gram:* **incidente explicative**, circumstantial clause, incidental clause; *Lit:* **notice explicative**, prefatory note; *Com:* **note, notice, explicative**, instructions, directions, for use.

explication [ɛksplikasjɔ̃], *s.f.* explanation; **donner l'e. de qch.**, to account for, to explain, sth.; *Sch:* **e. d'un auteur grec**, construing of a Greek author; *Sch:* **e. de textes, e. littéraire**, literary appreciation, commentary; **demander une e. à qn**, to call s.o. to account; **il reste encore beaucoup de faits qui demandent une e.**, there is still much to be accounted for; **fournir des explications**, to enter into explanations; *F:* **e. armée**, showdown; *F:* **avoir une e. avec qn**, to have it out with s.o.

explicitation [ɛksplisitasjɔ̃], *s.f.* clarification.

explicite [ɛksplisit], *a.* explicit, clear, plain.

explicitement [ɛksplisitmɑ̃], *adv.* explicitly, clearly, plainly.

expliciter [ɛksplisite], *v.tr.* (*a*) to put into words; (*b*) to make (clause of contract, etc.) clear; to clarify, explain (text).

s'expliciter, to be explicit.

expliquer [ɛksplike], *v.tr.* **1.** to explain, make clear, unfold, declare, give details of (one's ideas, plans, etc.). **2.** (*a*) to explain, expound, elucidate (doctrine, difficult subject, etc.); *Sch:* **e. Homère**, to construe Homer; (*b*) to explain, account for (action, etc.); **fait facile à e.**, fact easily accounted for; **je ne m'explique pas sa présence ici**, I don't understand why he is here; I cannot account for his presence here; **je ne m'explique pas pourquoi . . .**, I can't understand why . . ..

s'expliquer, to explain oneself, one's conduct; **je m'explique**, this is what I mean; **forcer qn à s'e.**, to bring s.o. to book; *F:* **s'e. avec qn**, to have it out with s.o.; **nous allons nous e.**, we'll have it out together.

expliqueur, -euse [ɛksplikœːr, -øːz], *s.* explainer, interpreter (of dreams, etc.).

exploit [ɛksplwa], *s.m.* **1.** exploit, feat (of arms, etc.); achievement; prowess; **exploits héroïques**, heroic deeds; *Iron:* **un bel e. que vous avez fait là!** well, that's a fine thing to have done! **2.** *Jur:* writ, process, summons, notice; **signifier un e. à qn.** to serve a writ on s.o.; **dresser un e.**, to draw up a writ.

exploitabilité [ɛksplwatabilite], *s.f.* workableness, payability (of mine, etc.); *For:* **âge d'e. (d'une forêt)**, age of maturity (of a forest).

exploitable [ɛksplwatabḷ], *a.* **1.** workable (quarry, etc.); developable (site, etc.); gettable (coal); paying, payable (ore, etc.). **2.** exploitable (person). **3.** *Jur:* distrainable (goods).

exploitant [ɛksplwatɑ̃]. **1.** *a.* (*a*) *Ind:* operating (staff, etc.); (*b*) *Jur:* writ-serving (officer, etc.); **huissier e.**, process server. **2.** *s.m.* (*a*) owner or operator (of mine, etc.); grower (of forest); cultivator (of land); **e. agricole**, farmer, *U.S:* dirt farmer; **les petits exploitants**, small farmers; smallholders; (*b*) *Cin:* exhibitor.

exploitation [ɛksplwatasjɔ̃], *s.f.* **1.** (*a*) exploitation, exploiting; working (of mine, etc.); running (of railway, newspaper, etc.); *Rail:* working (of line); operating, operation (of machine, etc.); utilization (of invention, patent, etc.); **en e.**, in operation; *Rail: Tp:* **service de l'e.**, traffic department; **e. en régie**, state management; **l'e. des ressources naturelles**, the tapping of natural resources; **société d'e.**, development company; **matériel d'e.**, working plant; **frais d'e.**, working costs, running expenses; **e. agricole**, farming, *U.S:* dirt farming; **e. du sel**, salt mining; *Min:* **e. à ciel ouvert, e. souterraine**, opencast, underground, mining; **e. en profondeur**, deep mining, working; **e. des alluvions par canaux**, ground sluicing; *Tchn:* **e. d'un document**, analysis of a document; **e. de l'information, des données**, data handling; *Mil:* **e. du renseignement**, utilization of information, of intelligence; (*b*) exploitation, taking (unfair) advantage of, making capital out of (s.o.'s ignorance, etc.); **l'e. des touristes**, the exploitation of tourists; **e. patronale**, sweating (of labour); (*c*) swindling. **2.** (*a*) workings; mine; works; **e. industrielle**, industrial undertaking, concern; (*b*) farm (estate); holding; **grande, petite, e.**, large, small, farm; **chemin d'e.**, farm road, track.

exploité, -ée [ɛksplwate], *s.* exploited person, victim of exploitation; **les exploités**, the exploited.

exploiter [ɛksplwate]. **1.** *v.tr.* to exploit; (*a*) to work (mine, patent, etc.); to operate (railway, etc.); to get, win (coal); to farm (land); to run (a farm); **champs mal exploités**, badly cultivated fields; *F:* **e. son talent**, to make the most of one's talent; **e. un succès**, to make capital out of, to exploit, a success; (*b*) to exploit; to take (unfair) advantage of (s.o.); to trade upon (s.o.'s ignorance, etc.); to make capital out of (a scandal, etc.); **e. les ouvriers**, to sweat labour; **e. les connaissances, l'intelligence, de qn**, to pick s.o.'s brains; (*c*) to swindle. **2.** *v.i. Jur:* to serve a writ.

exploiteur, -euse [ɛksplwatœːr, -øːz], *s.* exploiter; (*a*) speculator, jobber; (*b*) sweater, employer of sweated labour; (*c*) swindler.

explorable [ɛksplɔrabḷ], *a.* explorable.

explorateur, -trice [ɛksplɔratœːr, -tris]. **1.** *s.* explorer. **2.** *a.* exploring; *Cin: T.V:* scanning (cell, etc.); *El.E:* **bobine exploratrice**, exploring, search, flip, coil. **3.** *s.m. Surg:* exploring needle, trocar.

exploratif, -ive [ɛksplɔratif, -iːv], *a.* explorative, exploratory.

exploration [ɛksplɔrasjɔ̃], *s.f.* **1.** exploration; **voyage d'e.**, voyage of discovery. **2.** *Mil:* reconnaissance. **3.** (*a*) *Min: etc:* fieldwork; prospecting; **e. à flanc de coteau**, drift mining; (*b*) *Surv:* **levé d'e.**, exploratory survey. **4.** (*a*) *T.V: Elcs:* scanning; **ligne d'e.**, scanning strip; **e. par lignes verticales**, vertical dissection; (*b*) *El.E:* **bobine d'e.**, exploring, search, flip, coil. **5.** *Med:* examination; exploration.

explorer [ɛksplɔre], *v.tr.* **1.** (*a*) to explore (country); (*b*) *Med:* to explore, probe (wound); (*c*) **e. les poches de qn**, to go through s.o.'s pockets; (*d*) *Cin: T.V:* to scan (sound track, image). **2.** *Mil:* to reconnoitre. **3.** *Min: etc:* to prospect.

exploser [ɛksploze], *v.i.* (*a*) (*of boiler*) to explode, to blow up; (*of shell*) to explode; *I.C.E:* (*of mixture*) to fire, burn; **faire e.**, *tr.* **e. une mine**, to explode, fire, touch off, a mine; (*b*) *F: abs.* (*of pers.*) to explode, blow up; (*of temper*) to burst out, explode; **e. en injures**, to burst out into abuse.

exploseur [ɛksplozœːr], *s.m.* blasting machine, exploder, firer; **e. électro-statique**, frictional blasting-machine.

explosibilité [ɛksplozibilite], *s.f.* explosiveness; explosibility.

explosible [ɛksplozibḷ], *a.* explosive (bullet, etc.); explosible, detonable.

explosif, -ive [ɛksplozif, -iːv]. **1.** *a.* (*a*) explosive, detonating; *El:* **distance explosive**, sparking gap, spark gap; (*b*) **situation explosive**, explosive situation; **avoir un tempérament e.**, to have an explosive, a violent, temper. **2.** *s.m.* explosive; **e. à grande puissance, e. détonant, e. brisant**, high explosive; **e. déflagrant**, low explosive; **e. de relais**, booster explosive; **e. de remplissage**, filler explosive (of bomb, etc.); **e. propulsif**, propellant explosive; **e. atomique, nucléaire**, atomic, nuclear, explosive; **travail aux explosifs**, blasting. **3.** *s.f.* **explosive**; *Ling:* explodent, explosive, plosive, stop.

explosion [ɛksplozjɔ̃], *s.f.* explosion, bursting; **e. atomique, nucléaire**, atomic, nuclear, explosion; **e. aérienne**, air burst; **e. en surface**, surface burst; **faire e.**, to explode, blow up; (*of boiler*) to burst; **moteur à e.**, internal combustion engine; **chambre d'e.**, combustion chamber; **e. prématurée**, premature explosion; *I.C.E:* (i) pre-ignition; (ii) back-fire; **e. de fureur, de rires**, (out)burst of fury, of laughter; **e. démographique**, population explosion.

explosivité [ɛksplozivite], *s.f.* explodability, liability to explode.

expoliation [ɛkspɔljasjɔ̃], *s.f. Hort:* removal of dead wood.

expolier [ɛkspɔlje], *v.tr.* (*p.d. & pr.sub.* **n. expoliions, v. expoliiez**) *Hort:* to remove the dead parts of (trees, etc.).

exponction [ɛkspɔ̃ksjɔ̃], **exponctuation** [ɛkspɔ̃ktɥasjɔ̃], *s.f. Pal:* expunction.

exponctuer [ɛkspɔ̃ktɥe], *v.tr. Pal:* to put an expunction sign (under a letter).

exponentiation [ɛkspɔnɑ̃sjasjɔ̃], *s.f. Mth:* exponentiation.

exponentiel, -ielle [ɛkspɔnɑ̃sjɛl], *Mth:* **1.** *a.* exponential. **2.** *s.f.* **exponentielle**, exponential.

exportable [ɛkspɔrtabḷ], *a. Com:* exportable.

exportateur, -trice [ɛkspɔrtatœːr, -tris]. **1.** *s.* exporter. **2.** *a.* exporting.

exportation [ɛkspɔrtasjɔ̃], *s.f.* export, *U.S:* exportation; **articles d'e.**, exports; **faire l'e.**, to export; **les exportations**, (i) the export trade, the shipping trade; (ii) exports; **commerce d'e.**, export trade; **une e. florissante**, a flourishing export trade; **exportations invisibles**, invisible exports; **la France augmente ses exportations vers la Grande-Bretagne**, France is increasing her exports to Great Britain; **prime d'e.**, export subsidy.

exporter [ɛkspɔrte], *v.tr.* to export.

exporteur [ɛkspɔrtœːr], *s.m.* = EXPORTATEUR.

exposant, -ante [ɛkspozɑ̃, -ɑ̃ːt]. **1.** *a.* (*a*) *Jur:* petitioning; (*b*) exhibiting. **2.** *s.* (*a*) *Jur:* petitioner, deponent; (*b*) exhibitor (of work of art, etc.). **3.** *s.m.* (*a*) *Mth:* exponent; (power) index; (*b*) *Typ:* superior figure; (*c*) *Ch:* superior, inferior, figure; (*d*) *Nau:* **e. de charge**, boot topping.

exposé [ɛkspoze]. **1.** *a.* (*a*) in an exposed position; in danger, in peril; *Mil:* (*of flank, etc.*) in the air; **objet e.**, exhibit; (*b*) liable, apt (**à**, to); **objets exposés à être renversés**, objects liable to be knocked over, in danger of being knocked over; (*c*) open (**à**, to); **e. à tous les vents**, open to every wind. **2.** *s.m.* statement, account, report, exposition (of facts, affairs, etc.); **e. public**, public statement; **e. verbal (de mission)**, briefing; **e. d'un brevet**, preamble of a royal warrant; **e. de procédure à adopter**, sketch of procedure to be adopted; **donner un e. d'un projet**, to sketch out a plan; **faire un e.**, to read a paper; **faire un e. complet de la situation**, to give a full account of the situation; **à l'e. de ce projet son visage s'assombrit**, when this plan was put before him his face darkened.

exposemètre [ɛkspozmɛtr̥], *s.m. Phot:* exposure meter.

exposer [ɛkspoze], *v.tr.* **1.** (*a*) to exhibit, show, display (goods, works of art, etc.); **le tableau est exposé rue de la Paix**, the picture is on view in the Rue de la Paix; **on a exposé trois de ses tableaux**, three pictures by him have been hung; *abs.* **je n'expose pas cette année**, I'm not exhibiting this year; **e. des marchandises en vente, à la devanture**, to display goods for sale, to show goods in the window; *Ecc:* **e. le saint sacrement**, to expose the Blessed Sacrament; (*b*) to set forth, set out, state, unfold, make known (plans, reasons, etc.); **e. une réclamation**, to state a claim; **e. des griefs personnels**, to air personal grievances; **e. clairement la situation**, to put the case clearly; **je leur ai exposé ma situation**, I explained to them how I was placed; **e. son avis, un projet, à qn**, to lay one's opinion, a plan, before s.o.; **il m'avait exposé ses projets**, he had told me of his plans. **2.** (*a*) to expose; to lay (s.o., sth.) open (to sth.); **e. qn au froid**, to expose s.o. to the cold; **e. qch. à la pluie**, to expose sth. to the rain, to leave sth. (standing) in the rain; **après avoir été exposé au soleil . . .**, after exposure to the sun . . ., after standing in the

sun. . .; *Phot:* **e. un film,** to expose a film; **maison exposée au nord,** house with a north aspect, facing north; **e. sa vie,** to endanger one's life; **e. qn à la tentation,** to expose s.o. to temptation; **s'e. à des critiques,** to lay oneself open to criticism; **il s'expose à des poursuites,** he is rendering himself liable to proceedings; **il s'expose à devenir ridicule,** he is in danger of becoming, liable to become, ridiculous; (*b*) **le corps fut exposé pendant deux jours,** the body lay in state for two days; (*c*) **e. un nouveau-né,** (i) to expose a new-born infant; (ii) to abandon a new-born infant (in a public place). **3.** (*a*) to expose, lay bare (roots, etc.); (*b*) *A: & Lit:* to expose (hypocrite).

exposeur [ɛkspozœːr], *s.m.* expositor, expounder, exponent.

expositeur [ɛkspozitœːr], *s.m.* (*a*) exposer (of new-born child); (*b*) *Jur: A:* **e. de fausse monnaie,** utterer of false coinage.

expositif, -ive [ɛkspɔzitif, -iːv], **expositoire** [ɛkspɔzitwaːr], *a.* expositive, expository.

exposition [ɛkspozisjɔ̃], *s.f.* **1.** (*a*) exhibition, show (of goods, works of art, etc.); exposition (of Sacrament, etc.); lying in state (of body); **e. internationale,** international exhibition; **e. de fleurs,** flower show; **salle d'e.,** (i) exhibition room; (ii) show room; (*b*) exposure (to a danger, to cold); *Atom.Ph:* **e. brève,** acute exposure; **débit d'e.,** exposure rate; (*c*) *Jur:* exposure, abandoning (of new-born child); (*d*) exposition, statement, setting forth (of facts, reasons, etc.); **e. d'une œuvre littéraire,** introduction to a literary work; (*e*) *Mus: Lit:* exposition. **2.** aspect, exposure (of house); lighting (of picture); **e. au sud,** southern aspect, southerly exposure. **3.** *Phot:* exposure.

exprès¹, -esse [ɛksprɛ, ɛksprɛs, -ɛs]. **1.** *a.* express, distinct, explicit, clear (order, intention, warning, etc.); **les dispositions expresses d'une loi,** the actual provisions of an act; **défense expresse de fumer,** smoking strictly prohibited; **je lui ai dit en termes e. que . . .,** I told him expressly that . . .. **2.** [ɛksprɛs] (*a*) *a. & s.m. A:* express (messenger); (*b*) *a.inv. & s.m.* **(lettre, paquet) e.,** express letter, parcel; **par e.,** by special delivery.

exprès² [ɛksprɛ]. **1.** *adv.* designedly, on purpose, purposely, intentionally, deliberately; **outil façonné e.,** specially designed tool; **elle est venue tout e. pour me voir,** she came on purpose, specially, to see me; **je viens e. de Paris pour le faire,** I have made a special journey from Paris to do it; **je ne l'ai pas fait e.,** I didn't mean (to do) it, I didn't do it on purpose; **il fait e. de vous contredire,** he is deliberately contradicting you; he makes a point of contradicting you; **c'est fait e.,** it's (quite) intentional; I meant (to do) it. **2.** *s.m.* **un fait e.,** an annoying coincidence (which seems deliberate); **on dirait un fait e., le seul livre dont j'ai besoin n'est pas en librairie,** you'd think they'd done it on purpose; there's no copy of the one book I want in the bookshop; **dimanche, ce fut comme un fait e., je m'éveillai plus tôt qu'à l'ordinaire,** of course it would happen that on Sunday I woke up earlier than usual.

express [ɛksprɛs], *a. & s.m.* **1.** *Rail:* express (train). **2.** *a. F:* **café e.,** espresso coffee.

expressément [ɛksprɛsemɑ̃], *adv.* **1.** expressly, distinctly, explicitly. **2.** expressly, purposely; **ne faites pas cela e. pour moi,** don't do it especially for me, just for me.

expressif, -ive [ɛksprɛsif, -iːv], *a.* expressive (language, glance, face); soulful (glance); full of expression; *Mus:* **clavier e.,** swell organ; **pédale expressive,** swell pedal; **boîte expressive,** swell box.

expression [ɛksprɛsjɔ̃], *s.f.* expression. **1.** squeezing, pressing (of water from sponge, of lemon juice, etc.). **2.** utterance, voicing (of opinion, etc.); show, manifestation (of feelings); **prêter à ses sentiments une e. éloquente,** to give eloquent expression to one's feelings; **d'e. française,** French-speaking; **au delà de toute e.,** inexpressible, beyond expression; **visage d'une e. triste,** face with a sad expression; **sans e.,** expressionless, unexpressive; **regard sans e.,** blank look, vacant look; *Mus:* **jouer avec e.,** to play with expression; **signe d'e.,** expression mark; **boîte d'e.,** swell box (of organ). **3.** term, phrase; **selon l'e. de . . .,** in the words of . . ., in the phrase of . . .; **e. familière,** colloquial expression. **4.** *Mth:* **e. algébrique,** algebraic expression; **réduire une équation à sa plus simple e.,** to reduce an equation to its simplest form, expression; **réduire qch. à sa plus simple e.,** to reduce sth. to its bare essentials, to its simplest form.

expressionnisme [ɛksprɛsjɔnism], *s.m.* expressionism.

expressionniste [ɛksprɛsjɔnist], *a. & s.m. & f.* expressionist.

expressivement [ɛksprɛsivmɑ̃], *adv.* expressively; with expression.

expressivité [ɛksprɛsivite], *s.f.* **1.** *Biol:* expressivity. **2.** expressiveness, expressivity.

expresso [ɛksprɛso], *a. & s.m.* **1.** **(café) e.,** espresso coffee. **2.** *s.* espresso (machine).

exprimable [ɛksprimabl̩], *a.* expressible.

exprimer [ɛksprime], *v.tr.* to express. **1.** **e. le jus d'un citron,** to squeeze (out), press, the juice from a lemon; **e. une peau de chamois,** to squeeze out, wring out a chamois leather; **huile de ricin exprimée à froid,** cold-drawn castor oil. **2.** (*a*) to voice, put into words, to convey (one's feelings, thoughts, etc.); **e. l'opinion générale,** to give voice to the general opinion; **un discours où il exprimait son admiration de . . .,** a speech expressive of his admiration for . . .; **mots superflus qui n'expriment rien,** superfluous words that convey nothing; **e. l'espoir que . . .,** to express the hope that . . .; (*b*) (*of looks, gestures,* etc.) to show, manifest (pain, pleasure, etc.); **ses regards exprimaient sa surprise,** his expression revealed his surprise; **attitude qui exprime le dédain,** disdainful attitude; (*c*) *Mapm:* **e. graphiquement,** to depict.

s'exprimer, to express oneself; **je me suis mal exprimé,** I expressed myself badly; I didn't mean it that way; **si l'on peut s'e. ainsi,** if one may put it so, if one may say so; **pour m'e. autrement . . .,** to put it otherwise, another way . . .; **bonheur qui ne saurait s'e.,** inexpressible happiness.

expromission [ɛksprɔmisjɔ̃], *s.f.* expromission.

expropriateur, -trice [ɛksprɔpriatœːr, -tris], *s.* expropriator.

expropriation [ɛksprɔpriasjɔ̃], *s.f. Jur:* compulsory purchase of private property; expropriation; compulsory surrender (of real estate).

exproprié, -ée [ɛksprɔprie], *a. & s.* expropriated (person, property).

exproprier [ɛksprɔprie], *v.tr.* (*p.d. & pr.sub.* **n. expropriions, v. expropriiez**) to expropriate ((i) proprietor, (ii) property); **e. un immeuble pour cause d'utilité publique,** to expropriate, take over, a building for public purposes.

expuition [ɛkspɥisjɔ̃], *s.f. Med:* expuition, spitting.

expulsé, -ée [ɛkspylse], *a. & s.* expelled; ejected, evicted (tenant); *s.* expellee.

expulser [ɛkspylse], *v.tr.* to expel, eject (s.o.); to turn (s.o.) out; to deport (alien); *Sch:* to send down (student); to expel (pupil); **e. un locataire,** to evict a tenant; *Sp:* **e. qn du terrain,** to send s.o. off (the field); *Mch:* **e. l'air,** to blow out the air; **e. la garniture,** to blow out the packing.

expulseur [ɛkspylsœːr], *a.m.* expelling (*the f. form* **expultrice** *is rare*).

expulsif, -ive [ɛkspylsif, -iːv], *a.* expulsive (force, etc.).

expulsion [ɛkspylsjɔ̃], *s.f.* expulsion. **1.** deportation; **arrêté d'e.,** deportation order. **2.** *Jur:* ejection, eviction (of tenant). **3.** *Med:* evacuation.

expurgade [ɛkspyrgad], *s.f. For:* thinning (of trees in a plantation).

expurgation [ɛkspyrgasjɔ̃], *s.f.* **1.** expurgation, bowdlerizing (of book). **2.** *For:* thinning (of young trees in a plantation).

expurgatoire [ɛkspyrgatwaːr], *a.* expurgatory (index, etc.).

expurger [ɛkspyrʒe], *v.tr.* **(j'expurgeai(s); n. expurgeons)** to expurgate; to bowdlerize (book).

exquis [ɛkski], *a.* **1.** exquisite, delicious (food, taste, etc.); **d'une politesse exquise,** exquisitely polite. **2.** *Med:* **douleur exquise,** sharp, localized pain.

exquisement [ɛkskizmɑ̃], **exquisément** [ɛkskizemɑ̃], *adv.* exquisitely.

exquisité [ɛkskizite], *s.f.* (*rare*) exquisiteness.

exsangue [ɛksɑ̃ːg, egz-], *a.* (*a*) exsanguine; anaemic, bloodless; (*b*) cadaverous.

exsanguination [ɛksɑ̃ginasjɔ̃], *s.f. Surg:* exsanguination.

exsanguino-transfusion [ɛksɑ̃ginotrɑ̃sfyzjɔ̃], *s.f. Surg:* exsanguinotransfusion; exchange transfusion.

exsert [ɛksɛːr], *a. Biol:* exsert, exserted.

exsertile [ɛksɛrtil], *a. Biol:* exsertile.

exsiccateur [ɛksikatœːr], *s.m. Ch:* exsiccator.

exsiccation [ɛksikasjɔ̃], *s.f.* exsiccation.

exstrophie [ɛkstrɔfi], *s.f. Med:* exstrophy, extrophy.

exsuccion [ɛksyksjɔ̃], *s.f.* exsuction.

exsudant [ɛksydɑ̃], *a. & s.m. Med:* sudorific.

exsudat [ɛksyda], *s.m. Med:* exudate.

exsudatif, -ive [ɛksydatif, -iːv], *a. Med:* exudative.

exsudation [ɛksydasjɔ̃], *s.f. Physiol:* exudation, sweating.

exsuder [ɛksyde], *v.tr. & i.* to exude.

exsurgence [ɛksyrʒɑ̃ːs], *s.f. Geog:* resurgence (of underground stream).

extant [ɛkstɑ̃], *a. Jur: A:* existing, in being.

extase [ɛkstɑːz], *s.f.* ecstasy. **1.** *Psy: Med:* ecstasy, trance; *Theol:* ecstasy, rapture. **2.** rapture (of admiration, etc.); **être en e. devant qch.,** to be in ecstasies over sth., to be enraptured, entranced, by sth.

extasier (s') [sɛkstɑzje], *v.pr.* (*p.d. & pr.sub.* **n. n. extasiions, v.v. extasiiez**) to be in, go into, ecstasies (**devant,** before); **s'e. sur qch.,** to go into ecstasies, into raptures, over sth.; to be enraptured, entranced, by sth.

extatique [ɛkstatik], *a.* **1.** *Psy: Med:* ecstatic; **état e.,** ecstatic state, (state of) trance. **2.** ecstatic, rapturous, enraptured.

extemporané [ɛkstɑ̃pɔrane], *a.* **1.** unpremeditated (crime, etc.). **2.** *Pharm:* extemporaneous (medicine).

extendeur [ɛkstɑ̃dœːr], *s.m. Paint: etc:* extender.

extenseur [ɛkstɑ̃sœːr]. **1.** *a. & s.m. Anat:* extensor (muscle). **2.** *s.m.* (*a*) *Gym:* chest expander; (*b*) *Av:* (rubber) shock absorber; (*c*) **e. de pantalon,** trouser stretcher.

extensibilité [ɛkstɑ̃sibilite], *s.f.* extensibility.

extensible [ɛkstɑ̃sibl̩], *a.* **1.** extensible; stretchable; extending (table, etc.); expanding (bracelet, etc.). **2.** *Metall: etc:* tensile.

extensif, -ive [ɛkstɑ̃sif, -iːv], *a.* **1.** tensile (force, etc.). **2.** extensive; *Log:* denotative (word); **culture extensive,** extensive agriculture; *Ling:* **sens e.,** extended meaning (of word).

extensile [ɛkstɑ̃sil], *a. Z: etc:* extensile.

extensilingue [ɛkstɑ̃silɛ̃ːg], *a. Z:* with an extensile tongue.

extension [ɛkstɑ̃sjɔ̃], *s.f.* **1.** extension; (*a*) stretching, tension (of limb, muscle, etc.); *Mec:* **travail à l'e.,** tensile stress; (*b*) straining (of muscle, etc.); (*c*) spreading, enlargement, augmentation (of territory, industry, etc.); **e. d'une maladie,** spread of a disease; **e. d'un conflit,** spread, spreading, of a conflict; **donner de l'e. à qch.,** to extend, enlarge, sth.; **être en e., prendre de l'e.,** to spread, grow, increase; **son commerce a pris une e. considérable,** there has been a notable extension of his business, his business has increased considerably; (*d*) *Atom. Ph:* **e. en phase,** phase space. **2.** extent; *Log:* range, denotation (of term); extensive quantity (of proposition); *Gram:* extended meaning (of word); **par e.,** in a wider sense.

extensomètre [ɛkstɑ̃somɛːtr], *s.m. Mec.E:* extensometer.

extente [ɛkstɑ̃ːt], *s.f.* valuation, assessment.

exténuant [ɛkstenɥɑ̃], *a.* exhausting (work, etc.).

exténuation [ɛkstenɥasjɔ̃], *s.f.* **1.** extenuation, softening (of terms, etc.). **2.** (*a*) emaciation, attenuation (of body); (*b*) exhaustion (of body or mind).

exténuer [ɛkstenɥe], *v.tr.* **1.** to extenuate, soften (judgment, etc.). **2.** (*a*) *A:* to emaciate, waste (the body); (*b*) to exhaust; **être exténué (de fatigue),** to be tired out, worn out, fagged out, dog tired, dead tired, *F:* dead beat, all in.

s'exténuer, to work oneself to death; **je m'exténue à vous dire que . . .,** I'm *trying* to tell you that . . .

extérieur [ɛksterjœːr]. **1.** *a.* (*a*) exterior, outer, external; **port e.,** outer harbour; *Mth:* **angle e. d'un triangle,** exterior angle of a triangle; *Nau:* **cabine extérieure,** *Navy:* **chambre extérieure,** outboard cabin; **le côté e. de . . .,** the outer side of . . .; **le monde e.,** the outside world; **jardin e. à ma propriété,** garden that lies outside my grounds; (*b*) foreign (trade, policy, etc.); **dette extérieure,** foreign, overseas, debt. **2.** *s.m.* (*a*) exterior, outside (of building, etc.); **les bruits qui pénètrent de l'e.,** the noises that come in from without, from outside; **à l'e.,** (i) (on the) outside, out of doors; (ii) abroad; **à l'e. et à l'intérieur,** outside and in; **à l'intérieur et à l'e.,** inside and out; *Sp:* **match à l'e.,** away match; *prep.phr:* **à l'e. de la gare,** outside the station; (*b*) **de l'e.,** from abroad; **nos rapports avec l'e.,** our relations with (i) other people, (ii) other firms, (iii) foreign countries; (*c*) (outward) appearance, looks; **juger par l'e.,** to judge by externals, by external appearances; **avoir un e. imposant,** to have an imposing appearance, to look imposing; (*d*) *Cin:* (i) exterior (shot); (ii) location (shot); **il tourne en e.,** he's on location.

extérieurement [ɛksterjœrmɑ̃], *adv.* **1.** externally, on the outside, outwardly. **2.** on the surface, in appearance; **être très bien e.,** to have a prepossessing appearance.

extérioration [ɛksterjɔrasjɔ̃], *s.f. Physiol:* exterioration (of sensation).

extériorisation [ɛksterjɔrizasjɔ̃], *s.f. Phil: Psychics:* exteriorization, externalization.

extérioriser [ɛksterjɔrize], *v.tr.* (*a*) *Phil: Psychics:* to exteriorize, to externalize; (*b*) to manifest outwardly; **e. ses sentiments,** to show one's feelings.

s'extérioriser, to reveal oneself outwardly, to show one's feelings; **sa colère ne s'extériorise pas,** he never shows that he is angry.

extériorité [ɛksterjɔrite], *s.f.* exteriority, externality.

exterminant [ɛkstɛrminɑ̃], *a.* exterminating, destroying.

exterminateur, -trice [ɛkstɛrminatœːr, -tris]. **1.** *s.* exterminator, destroyer. **2.** *a.* exterminating, destroying (angel, etc.).

extermination [ɛkstɛrminasjɔ̃], *s.f.* extermination, destruction (of race, army, etc.); **guerre d'e.,** war of extermination; **camp d'e.,** extermination camp.

exterminer [ɛkstɛrmine], *v.tr.* (*a*) to exterminate, destroy; *F:* to wipe out (race, army, etc.); **ils furent exterminés de la surface de la terre,** they were exterminated from the face of the earth; (*b*) *F:* to kill, exterminate (s.o.).

s'exterminer, *F:* to work oneself to death (**à faire qch.,** doing sth.); **mais je m'extermine à vous le dire!** I've told you so till I'm blue in the face!

externat [ɛkstɛrna], *s.m.* **1.** (*a*) day-school system; (*b*) day school; (*c*) the day pupils (as a body). **2.** (*a*) non-resident medical studentship (at hospital); (*b*) the non-resident medical students (as a body). **3.** out-patients' department (of hospital).

externe [ɛkstɛrn]. **1.** *a.* (*a*) external, outside, outer; **côté e.,** outside; **angle e.,** exterior angle; *Pharm:* **pour l'usage e.,** for external use (only), not to be taken; (*b*) **élève e.,** day pupil; **malade e.,** out-patient (at hospital). **2.** *s.* (*a*) day pupil; (*b*) **e. (des hôpitaux),** non-resident medical student acting as assistant (at hospital).

extérocepteur [ɛksterɔsɛptœːr], *a. & s.m. Physiol:* exteroceptor.

extéroceptif, -ive [ɛksterɔsɛptif, -iːv], *a. Physiol:* exteroceptive.

exterritorial, -aux [ɛksteritɔrjal, -o], *a.* ex(tra)-territorial.

exterritorialité [ɛksteritɔrjalite], *s.f. Jur:* ex(tra)-territoriality (of ambassador, etc.).

extincteur, -trice [ɛkstɛ̃ktœːr, -tris]. **1.** *a.* extinguishing (material, etc.). **2.** *s.m.* **e. d'incendie,** fire extinguisher, sprinkler; **e. à mousse (carbonique),** (chemical) foam extinguisher, sprayer.

extinctif, -ive [ɛkstɛ̃ktif, -iːv], *a.* extinctive.

extinction [ɛkstɛ̃ksjɔ̃], *s.f.* extinction. **1.** (*a*) extinguishing, putting out (of fire, candle, etc.); *Mil:* **e. des feux,** lights out; *U.S:* taps; **e. des lumières,** blackout; *Ind:* **wagon d'e.,** coke car; *Com:* **adjudication, vente, à l'e. des feux,** auction by inch of candle; *Tchn:* **e. du fer rouge,** quenching of red-hot iron; **e. de la chaux,** slaking, slacking, extinction, of lime; *Opt:* **deux nicols à l'e.,** two crossed nicols giving total extinction; (*b*) abolition, suppression (of institution, etc.); paying off, wiping out (of debt, etc.); termination (of contract). **2.** (*a*) dying out, extinction (of race, species, etc.); (*b*) **e. de voix, de vue,** loss of voice, of sight; **attraper une e. de voix,** to lose one's voice.

extinguible [ɛkstɛ̃gibl̩], *a.* (*a*) extinguishable; (*b*) (*rare*) quenchable (thirst).

extirpable [ɛkstirpabl̩], *a.* eradicable.

extirpage [ɛkstirpaːʒ], *s.m. Agr:* scarifying, grubbing (of land).

extirpateur [ɛkstirpatœːr], *s.m.* **1.** (*a*) extirpator, remover (of corns, etc.); (*b*) uprooter (of tree, evil, etc.). **2.** *Agr:* weeding machine, weeder; extirpator, grubber, scarifier; cultivator.

extirpation [ɛkstirpasjɔ̃], *s.f.* eradication; extirpation; uprooting; removal (of corns, etc.).

extirper [ɛkstirpe], *v.tr.* to extirpate, eradicate, root out (plant, growth, evil, etc.); to remove (a corn).

extorquer [ɛkstɔrke], *v.tr.* to extort; **e. de l'argent, une promesse, à qn,** to extort money, wring a promise, from s.o.

extorqueur, -euse [ɛkstɔrkœːr, -øːz], *s.* extortioner.

extorsion [ɛkstɔrsjɔ̃], *s.f.* **1.** extortion, exaction (from the people, etc.). **2.** extortion (of bribe, promise, etc.); blackmail.

extorsionnaire [ɛkstɔrsjɔnɛːr], *a.* guilty of extortion.

extourner [ɛksturne], *v.tr. Fin:* to reverse (a debit, etc.).

extra [ɛkstra]. **1.** *s.m. usu. inv.* (*a*) extra; **un (plat, domestique, d')e.,** an extra (dish, servant); **du vin e.,** extra-special wine; **payer les extra(s),** to pay for the extras; **faire un peu d'e.,** to do things a little more elaborately than usual; to give oneself a little treat; (*b*) temporary job; **faire des extra chez qn,** to give s.o. some extra help. **2.** *a.inv.* extra-special (wine, etc.); first-class, first-rate; *s.m. F:* **c'est de l'e.,** it's extra-special. **3.** *pref.* (*a*) extra(-fine, strong, etc.); **e.-bon,** extra good; (*b*) (= *additional*) extra(-current, etc.); (*c*) (= *outside*) extra(-territorial, etc.).

extra-atmosphérique [ɛkstraatmɔsferik], *a.* extra-atmospheric.

extra-axillaire [ɛkstraaksil(l)ɛːr], *a. Bot:* extra-axillary.

extra-blanc, -blanche [ɛkstrablɑ̃, -blɑ̃ːʃ], *a.* (*petroleum refining*) **huile extra-blanche,** water-white oil.

extra-buccal, -aux [ɛkstrabykal, -o], *a. Physiol:* extra-oral.

extrabudgétaire [ɛkstrabydʒetɛːr], *a. Fin:* (*of expenses, etc.*) extra-budgetary, outside the budget.

extra(-)cardiaque [ɛkstrakardjak], *a. Med:* extracardial.

extra(-)cellulaire [ɛkstrasɛlylɛːr], *a. Biol:* extra-cellular.

extra-champ [ɛkstraʃɑ̃], *s.m. Sp:* (*baseball*) outfield; *pl. extra-champs.*

extra-conjugal, -aux [ɛkstrakɔ̃ʒygal, -o], *a.* extra-conjugal, extra-marital.

extra(-)courant [ɛkstrakurɑ̃], *s.m. El:* extra-current, self-induction current; **e.-c. de rupture,** break impulse.

extra(-)crânien, -ienne [ɛkstrakrɑnjɛ̃, -jɛn], *a. Anat:* extracranial.

extracteur [ɛkstraktœːr], *s.m.* **1.** drawer, extractor (of teeth, etc.). **2.** (*a*) *Sm.a: Ap:* extractor; (*b*) **e. de gaz,** gas exhauster; **e. de dévasement,** suction dredger; (*c*) **e. centrifuge,** centrifugal drier.

extractible [ɛkstraktibl̩], *a.* extractable.

extractif, -ive [ɛkstraktif, -iːv], *a.* extractive.

extraction [ɛkstraksjɔ̃], *s.f.* extraction. **1.** extracting; (*a*) *Med:* avulsion; *Dent:* extraction, pulling out (of teeth); *Surg:* removal (of appendix, etc.); *Min:* mining, extraction (of coal, ore); quarrying (of stone); (*b*) hoisting, drawing up; *Min:* **machine d'e.,** winding machine, winding gear, hoisting engine; **cage d'e.,** hoisting cage; **machiniste, mécanicien, d'e.,** winder; (*c*) *Mth:* extraction (of root); (*d*) *Mch:* **robinet d'e.,** blow-down cock; **tuyau d'e.,** blow-off pipe; **turbine d'e.,** extraction turbine; (*e*) **e. électrochimique,** electro-extraction; **e. électrolytique,** electro-winning; **e. par absorption, par solvant,** absorption, solvent, extraction; (*f*) *Tchn:* **e. de cartes,** card pulling; (*g*) (*petroleum refining*) stripping. **2.** descent, lineage, origin, parentage; **être de haute, de basse, e.,** to belong to the upper classes, to the nobility; to the lower classes.

extradé, -ée [ɛkstrade], *a. & s.* extradited (person).

extrader [ɛkstrade], *v.tr. Jur:* to extradite.

extradition [ɛkstradisjɔ̃], *s.f. Jur:* extradition.

extrados [ɛkstrado], *s.m.* (*a*) *Arch:* extrados, back (of arch); (*b*) *Av:* upper surface (of wing); **panneau d'e.,** upper skin panel.

extradossé [ɛkstradose], *a. Arch:* extradosed (arch).

extradosser [ɛkstradose], *v.tr. Arch:* to build (arch) with an extrados.

extra(-)dur [ɛkstradyːr], *a.* **acier e.,** hardened steel.

extra-européen, -enne [ɛkstraørɔpeɛ̃, -ɛn], *a.* extra-European, not belonging to Europe, outside Europe.

extra(-)fin [ɛkstrafɛ̃], *a.* superfine; of a special brand, vintage, etc.

extrafoliacé [ɛkstrafɔljase], **extrafolié** [ɛkstrafɔlje], *a. Bot:* extrafoliaceous.

extra(-)fort [ɛkstrafɔːr], (*a*) *a.* extra-strong; (*b*) *s.m. Dressm:* selvedge tape; bias binding.

extragalactique [ɛkstragalaktik], *a.* extragalactic.

extra-hospitalier, -ière [ɛkstraɔspitalje, -jɛːr], *a.* **services extra-hospitaliers,** out-patients department.

extra-humain [ɛkstraymɛ̃], *a.* extrahuman.

extraire [ɛkstrɛːr], *v.tr.* (*conj. like* TRAIRE) (*a*) to extract, draw out, take out, pull out; to extract, pull out (tooth); to extract, mine (coal, ore); to quarry (stone); (*of computer*) to read (out); **e. un passage d'un livre,** to copy out a passage, make an extract, from a book; *Hort:* **e. des plants,** to lift seedlings; *Mth:* **e. une racine,** to extract a root; (*b*) **s'e. d'une position difficile,** to get out, wriggle out, of an awkward position; **s'é. de sa voiture,** to wriggle out of one's car; **e. qn de sa prison,** to rescue s.o. from prison.

extrait [ɛkstrɛ], *s.m.* **1.** *Ch: Pharm: etc:* extract; **e. de viande,** meat extract, meat essence; *Bio-Ch:* **e. sec,** dry matter; **e. sec du lait,** milk solids. **2.** extract, excerpt, quotation (from book); abstract (of deed, account); **extraits d'actes de l'état civil,** (birth, marriage, etc.) certificates; **e. de naissance,** birth certificate; **e. de compte,** statement of account; *Nau:* **e. du journal de bord,** abstract of log.

extra(-)judiciaire [ɛkstraʒydisjɛːr], *a. Jur:* extra-judicial; (done) out of court; **serment e.,** voluntary oath.

extra(-)judiciairement [ɛkstraʒydisjɛrmɑ̃], *adv. Jur:* extrajudicially, out of court.

extra(-)légal, -aux [ɛkstralegal, -o], *a.* extra(-)legal, not sanctioned by law.

extra(-)lucide [ɛkstralysid], *a.* clairvoyant.

extralucidité [ɛkstralysidite], *s.f.* clairvoyance.

extra-muros [ɛkstramyroːs]. **1.** *adv.* outside the town. **2.** *a.inv.* **quartier e.-m.,** extramural, suburban, district.

extranéité [ɛkstraneite], *s.f. Jur:* foreign origin, alien status.

extranucléaire [ɛkstranykleɛːr], *a.* extranuclear.

extraordinaire [ɛkstr(a)ɔrdinɛːr]. **1.** *a.* (*a*) extraordinary (meeting, etc.); special (messenger, etc.); **ambassadeur e.,** ambassador extraordinary; **frais, dépenses, extraordinaires,** (i) extras; (ii) non-recurring expenditure; **impôt e.,** emergency tax; *Th:* **représentation e.,** benefit performance; *A:* **vingt personnes d'e.,** twenty extra people; (*b*) extraordinary, unusual, astonishing, fantastic; **costume e.,** extraordinary clothes; **je trouve e. qu'il ne nous ait pas prévenus,** I find it extraordinary, astonishing, that he hasn't let us know; **cela n'a rien d'e.,** that's nothing out of the ordinary; (*c*) extraordinary, remarkable, outstanding; **beauté e.,** remarkable, outstanding, beauty; **succès e.,** outstanding success; **homme e.,** extraordinary man; (*d*) *F:* extraordinarily good; **ce plat est e.,** this dish is superb, first-rate; **ce film n'est vraiment pas e.,** this film's nothing to write home about; (*e*) *Opt:* **rayons extraordinaires,** extraordinary rays. **2.** *s.m.* (*a*) **goût de l'e.,** a taste for the extraordinary; **l'e., ce qu'il y a d'e., c'est que . . .,** the extraordinary thing is that . . .; *A:* **c'est pour lui un e. que de boire du vin,** it is a departure from his usual custom for him to drink wine; (*b*) *A:* (i) emergency fund, extraordinaries; (ii) extraordinary mail, courrier; (iii) *Ecc:* extra-diocesan authority. **3.** *adv.phr.* **par e.,** exceptionally; for a wonder; **par e. nous allons à la mer dimanche,** strange to say we're going to the sea on Sunday; **par e. il fait beau,** for a wonder it's fine; **par e. il est arrivé à l'heure,** for once in his life he arrived on time; **par e. je l'ai rencontré hier,** strangely enough I met him yesterday.

extraordinairement [ɛkstr(a)ɔrdinɛrmɑ̃], *adv.* (*in all senses of extraordinary*) extraordinarily.

extra-organique [ɛkstraɔrganik], *a.* extra-organic.

extra-parlementaire [ɛkstraparləmɑ̃tɛːr], *a.* extra-parliamentary.

extra(-)périosté [ɛkstraperjɔste], *a. Anat:* extra-periosteal.

extrapolation [ɛkstrapɔlasjɔ̃], *s.f.* (*a*) *Mth:* extrapolation; (*b*) *Artil:* prediction; **e. du but,** target prediction.

extrapoler [ɛkstrapɔle], *v.tr.* (*a*) *Mth:* to extrapolate; (*b*) *Artil:* to predict; **éléments extrapolés,** prediction, predicted, data.

extra-professionnel, -elle [ɛkstraprɔfɛsjɔnɛl], *a.* extraprofessional.

extra-réglementaire [ɛkstrareglәmɑ̃tɛːr], *a.* not prescribed by regulations, extra-regular.

extra-rétinien, -ienne [ɛkstraretinjɛ̃, -jɛn], *a.* extra-retinal.

extra-scolaire [ɛkstraskɔlɛːr], *a.* out-of-school; **activités extra-scolaires,** out-of-school activities.

extra-sensible [ɛkstrasɑ̃sibl̩], *a.* extrasensible, that cannot be perceived by the ordinary senses.

extra(-)sensoriel, -ielle [ɛkstrasɑ̃sɔrjɛl], *a. Psy:* extrasensory; **la perception e.(-)sensorielle,** extrasensory perception.

extra(-)statutaire [ɛkstrastatytɛːr], *a.* extra-statutory.

extrasystole [ɛkstrasistɔl], *s.f. Med:* extrasystole.

extratensif, -ive [ɛkstratɑ̃sif, -iːv], *Psy:* **1.** *a.* extratensive, extraverted. **2.** *s.* extravert.

extratension [ɛkstratɑ̃sjɔ̃], *s.f. Psy:* extraversion, extratension.

extra-terrestre [εkstratεrεstɾ], a. extra-terrestrial.

extraterritorialité [εkstratεritɔrjalite], s.f. extra-territoriality.

extra-utérin [εkstrayterɛ̃], a. Obst: extra-uterine.

extravagamment [εkstravagamɑ̃], adv. extravagantly. 1. wastefully. 2. exaggeratedly, unreasonably; (to pay) exorbitantly.

extravagance [εkstravagɑ̃:s], s.f. extravagance. 1. (a) wastefulness; (b) absurdity, folly (of action, request, etc.); exorbitance (of price); immoderateness (of desires). 2. faire, dire, des extravagances, to do, say, absurd, foolish, things; F: il a dit un tas d'extravagances, he talked a lot of wild nonsense.

extravagant [εkstravagɑ̃], a. extravagant. 1. wasteful. 2. absurd, foolish (person, action, etc.); exorbitant (price, demand); immoderate (desire); histoires extravagantes, foolish things. 3. s.m. eccentric, crank.

extravaguer [εkstravage], v.i. 1. (a) to be delirious, to rave; (b) F: to talk nonsense; F: to talk through one's hat. 2. to act wildly, unreasonably.

extravas(at)ion [εkstravɑz(as)jɔ̃], s.f. extravasation (of blood, etc.).

extravaser (s') [sεkstravaze], v.pr. (of blood, sap, etc.) to extravasate.

extravéhiculaire [εkstraveikylε:r], a. extravehicular.

extraversif, -ive [εkstravεrsif, -i:v], Psy: 1. a. extraversive, extraverted. 2. s. extravert.

extraversion [εkstravεrsjɔ̃], s.f. (a) Psy: extraversion; (b) Med: extroversion.

extraverti, -ie [εkstravεrti], a. & s. Psy: extravert.

extravertir [εkstravεrti:r], v.tr. to extravert; to extrovert.

extrémal, -aux [εkstremal, -o], a. extreme (state).

extrême [εkstrεm]. 1. a. extreme; (a) farthest, utmost (point, limit, etc.); Pol: l'e. gauche, the extreme left; Carp: montant e., end post; des montagnes dans l'e. lointain, mountains in the extreme distance; (b) intense, excessive (cold, pleasure, etc.); il est dans une e. misère, he is in extreme poverty, in dire distress, in utter want; (c) drastic, severe (measure, remedy); être e. dans ses opinions, to be extreme in one's views, to hold extreme opinions. 2. s.m. extreme

limit; les extrêmes, the extremes; scrupuleux à l'e., scrupulous in the extreme, to a degree; pousser les choses à l'e., to carry matters to extremes; A: être réduit à l'e., to be reduced to the last extremity; Prov: les extrêmes se touchent, extremes meet; too far east is west.

extrêmement [εkstrεmmɑ̃], adv. 1. extremely, exceedingly; highly (pleased). 2. A: avoir e. d'esprit, to be extremely witty.

extrême-onction [εkstrεmɔ̃ksjɔ̃], s.f. Ecc: extreme unction.

Extrême-Orient (l') [lεkstrεmɔrjɑ̃], s.m. Geog: the Far East.

extrême-oriental [εkstrεmɔrjɑ̃tal], a. Far-Eastern; pl. extrême-orientaux.

extrémiser [εkstremize], v.tr. F: Ecc: to administer extreme unction to, to anoint (s.o.).

extrémisme [εkstremism], s.m. extremism (in politics, etc.).

extrémiste [εkstremist], s.m. & f. extremist.

extrémité [εkstremite], s.f. 1. (a) extremity, end (of rope, etc.); tip (of finger, wing, etc.); point (of needle, billiard cue, etc.); termination (of cable, line); terminal (of radio link); Mth: head (of vector); aux extrémités de la ligne, at the ends of the line; extrémité supérieure, inférieure, d'un lac, head, foot, of a lake; les extrémités de la terre, the uttermost ends of the earth; F: j'ai les extrémités gelées, my hands and feet are frozen; (b) extremity, extreme, last degree (of misery, etc.); pousser qch. à l'e., to carry sth. to extremes; en venir à des extrémités, to resort to violence; l'e. d'un besoin, the urgency of a need; dans cette e., in this extremity; en être réduit à la dernière e., to have one's back to the wall; (c) last moment; attendre à l'e. pour . . ., to wait till the last moment before . . .; être à l'e., à toute e., to be dying, to be at death's door, at the point of death, in the last extremity. 2. pl. pousser qn à des extrémités, to drive s.o. to take extreme measures; to drive s.o. to extremes; se porter aux dernières extrémités sur, contre, qn, to go to all lengths against s.o.

extrémum [εkstremɔm], s.m. Mth: extremum (pl. extrema); pl. extrémums.

extrinsèque [εkstrɛ̃sεk], a. extrinsic; Num: valeur e., face value.

extrinsèquement [εkstrɛ̃sεkmɑ̃], adv. extrinsically.

extrorse [εkstrɔrs], a. Bot: extrorse.

extrospection [εkstrɔspεksjɔ̃], s.f. Psy: extrospection.

extroversion [εkstrɔvεrsjɔ̃], s.f. Med: extroversion.

extroverti, -ie [εkstrɔvεrti], s. Psy: extrovert, extravert.

extrovertir [εkstrɔvεrti:r], v.tr. to extravert; to extrovert.

extrudage [εkstryda:ʒ], s.m. Tch: Metalw: extrusion.

extrusif, -ive [εkstryzif, -i:v], a. Geol: extrusive (rock).

extrusion [εkstryzjɔ̃], s.f. Tchn: Metall: extrusion.

exubérance [εgzyberɑ̃:s], s.f. exuberance, superabundance, luxuriance (of vegetation, ideas, etc.).

exubérant [εgzyberɑ̃], a. exuberant, superabundant, luxuriant (growth, ideas, etc.); overflowing (spirits); e. de santé, bursting with health.

exubérer [εgzybere], v.i. (j'exubère, n. exubérons; j'exubérerai) to be exuberant, full of life.

exulcération [εgzylserasjɔ̃], s.f. Med: ulceration.

exulcérer [εgzylsere], v.tr. (il exulcère; il exulcéra) Med: to ulcerate.

exultant [εgzyltɑ̃], a. exultant, exulting.

exultation [εgzyltasjɔ̃], s.f. exultation.

exulter [εgzylte], v.i. to exult, rejoice.

exultet [εgzyltet], s.m. Ecc: exultet.

exustion [εgzystjɔ̃], s.f. Surg: cauterization, cauterizing, burning (of wound, etc.).

exutoire [εgzytwa:r], s.m. 1. A: Med: exutory. 2. outlet, means of escape; il cherchait un e. à sa colère, he was looking for an outlet for his anger.

exuviable [εgzyvjabl], a. exuviable (skin).

exuvial, -aux [εgzyvjal, -o], a. exuvial (skin).

exuviation [εgzyviasjɔ̃], s.f. Nat.Hist: exuviation, skin-casting (in insects and reptiles); (of snakes) sloughing.

exuvie [εgzyvi], s.f. Nat.Hist: exuvia, shed cuticle (after ecdysis); slough (of snake).

exvoluté [εksvɔlyte], a. Bot: evolute.

ex-voto [εksvɔto], s.m.inv. ex-voto (offering); votive offering.

eyra [eira], s.m. Z: eyra.

Ézéchias [ezekjɑ:s], Pr.n.m. B.Hist: Hezekiah.

Ézéchiel [ezekjεl], Pr.n.m. B.Hist: Ezekiel.

F

F, f [εf], *s.m. & f.* (the letter) F, f; *Tp:* F comme François, F for Frederick; *I.C.E:* cylindre à culasse F, F-head cylinder.

fa [fa], *s.m.inv. in pl. Mus:* 1. (the note) F; clef de **fa**, bass clef, F clef; morceau en **fa**, piece in F. 2. fa (in the Fixed Do system).

fabagelle [fabaʒɛl], *s.f.*, **fabago** [fabago], *s.m. Bot:* bean-caper.

fabien, -ienne [fabjɛ̃, -jɛn], *a.* Fabian.

fabisme [fabism], *s.m. Med:* favism.

fable [faːbl], *s.f.* 1. (*a*) fable; les fables de La Fontaine, La Fontaine's fables; **comme le renard de la f.**, like the fox in the fable; (*b*) story, tale; *F:* **faire courir mille fables à propos de qn**, to spread all sorts of stories, falsehoods, about s.o.; **être la f. de toute la ville**, to be the laughing stock, the talk, of the town. 2. **célèbre dans la f.**, famous in story, in fable. 3. *Psy:* test des **fables**, fables test.

fableau, -eaux [fablo], *s.m.*, **fabliau, -aux** [fabljo], *s.m. A:* short tale in verse; (*in medieval Fr.Lit.*) fabliau.

fablier [fablje], *s.m.* 1. *A:* fabulist. 2. book of fables.

fabrecoulier [fabr(ə)kulje], *s.m. Bot: S. of Fr:* = MICOCOULIER.

fabricant, -ante [fabrikɑ̃, -ɑ̃ːt]. 1. *s.* (*a*) maker, manufacturer; **f. de chapeaux**, hat maker, manufacturer; (*b*) *A:* mill owner. 2. *a.* manufacturing (hatter, etc.).

fabricateur, -trice [fabrikatœːr, -tris], *s. almost always Pej:* fabricator (of lies, etc.); **f. de fausse monnaie**, coiner; **f. d'un document**, forger of a document.

fabrication [fabrikasjɔ̃], *s.f.* 1. (*a*) manufacture, making (of sth.); baking (of bread); brewing (of beer); boiling (of soap, glue); cutting (of files); **n'employer que la meilleure f.**, to employ only the best workmanship; **numéro de f.**, serial number; **programme de(s) fabrication(s)**, production plan, schedule; **article de f. française**, article of French make, French-made article; **unité de f.**, factory unit; (*b*) *Coll.* manufactured goods; **notre f.**, our products. 2. forging (of document); coining (of counterfeit money); **c'est de la f.**, it's pure fabrication, there's not a word of truth in it.

fabricien [fabrisjɛ̃], *s.m. Ecc:* = churchwarden.

fabrique [fabrik], *s.f.* 1. (*a*) making, manufacture; **prix de f.**, cost price, manufacturer's price; **marque de f.**, trade mark, brand; **secret de f.**, trade secret; (*b*) make; **article de mauvaise f.**, article of bad make. 2. factory, works; (cloth, paper, oil)mill; **monter une f.**, to set up, establish, a factory, a works; **valeur en f.**, cost price. 3. *Jur: Ecc:* fabric (of a church); *A:* (conseil de) f. = (parochial) church council; vestry.

fabriquer [fabrike], *v.tr.* 1. (*a*) *Ind:* to manufacture (cloth, bicycles, etc.); (*b*) to make (sth.); **qu'est-ce que tu fabriques?** (i) what's that you're making? (ii) what are you doing? what on earth are you up to? 2. (*a*) to fabricate; **f. des calomnies sur qn**, to make up, invent, calumnies about s.o.; **f. une accusation**, to trump up a charge; **f. un document**, to forge, fabricate, a document; (*b*) to coin, mint (phrase, new word); (*c*) *P:* **qu'avez-vous fabriqué avec mon tabac?** what *have* you done with my tobacco?

fabulateur, -trice [fabylatœːr, -tris], *a. Psy:* **l'enfant est f.**, children are great fabricators.

fabulation [fabylasjɔ̃], *s.f. Lit:* 1. working out, fabulation (of a novel, etc.). 2. texture (of a novel, etc.). 3. *Med: Psy:* fabrication, confabulation.

fabuler [fabyle], *v.i. Med: Psy:* to confabulate.

fabuleusement [fabyløzmɑ̃], *adv.* fabulously, prodigiously (wealthy, etc.).

fabuleux, -euse [fabylø, -øːz], *a.* 1. fabulous (exploits); **les temps f.**, legendary times. 2. incredible; prodigious; **cela vaut une somme fabuleuse**, it is worth a fabulous sum, a mint of money.

fabuliste [fabylist], *s.m.* fabulist.

fac [fak], *s.f. F:* = FACULTÉ 2.

façade [fasad], *s.f.* façade, front(age); *Nau:* **f. du château**, bridge front; **maison à large f.**, wide-fronted house; **local avec façades, en f., sur deux rues**, premises with frontages on two streets; **hôtel en f. sur la place**, hotel facing the square; **patriotisme de f.**, show of patriotism; **ce n'est qu'une f.**, it's all a façade; *F:* **refaire sa f.**, to make up (one's face).

face [fas], *s.f.* face. 1. (*a*) **une f. rubiconde**, a rubicund face; **f. de réprouvé**, sinister face, countenance; **jeter la vérité à la f. de qn**, to cast the truth in s.o.'s face; **sauver la f.**, to save (one's) face; **perdre la f.**, to lose face; (*b*) *Ecc:* **La Sainte F.**, the Holy Face; (*c*) **la f. des eaux, de la terre**, the face of the waters, of the earth; **les affaires ont changé de f.**, the complexion of things has altered. 2. (*a*) face (of sth.); flat (of sword blade); side (of a gramophone record); **f. avant**, front; **f. arrière**, back; *Nau:* **f. arrière du château**, bridge end, after end, of bridge house; *Av:* **f. arrière**, *Nau:* **f. antérieure, (de la pale d'hélice)**, back of propeller blade; **polyèdre à douze faces**, twelve-sided polyhedron; *Opt:* **f. concave, convexe, d'une lentille**, concave, convex, side of a lens; *Tex:* **tissu à double f.**, reversible fabric; **considérer qch. sous toutes ses faces**, to consider sth. from all sides, from all aspects; (*b*) obverse (of medal); head side (of coin); **pile ou f.**, heads or tails; (*c*) *Th:* **f. de la scène**, front of stage, downstage; (*d*) *Mount:* face, wall; (*e*) *Anat:* facet, facies; **f. antéro-postérieure**, antero-posterior facet. 3. (*a*) **faire f. à qn, à qch.**, to face s.o., sth.; **sa maison fait f. à l'église**, his house stands opposite to, faces, fronts, the church; **faire f. à ses échéances, à ses dépenses**, to meet one's liabilities, one's expenses; **faire f. à tous les besoins**, to meet all needs; **faire f. à des difficultés**, to cope with difficulties; **faire f. au malheur**, to bear up against misfortune; *abs:* **faire f.**, to face up to things; (*b*) **portrait de f.**, full-face portrait; **vue de f.**, front view; **regarder un monument de f.**, to look at the front of a monument; **se présenter de f.**, to face (the observer, etc.); *Th:* **loge de f.**, box facing the stage; **la maison (d')en f.**, the house opposite; **les gens d'en f.**, the people from over the way; **regarder qn (bien) en f.**, to look s.o. full, straight, in the face; **regarder les choses en f.**, to face facts; **je lui ai dit en f.**, I said it to his face; **f. à f.**, face to face (avec, with); **mettre deux témoins f. à f.**, to confront two witnesses. 4. *prep.phr.* **f. à**, facing; **position f. à la gare**, position facing the station; *Rail:* **place f. à l'arrière**, seat with back to the engine; **place f. à la direction de marche**, seat facing the engine; *Mil:* **f. à l'ennemi**, face, front to the enemy; **f. aux résultats . . .,**

with regard to the results . . .; **en f. de**, opposite; **il était juste en f. de moi**, he stood right opposite me, he was right in front of me; **les maisons en f. de l'école, F: en f. l'école**, the houses opposite the school; **le problème en f. duquel je me trouve**, the problem with which I am confronted; **mettre qn en f. de qch.**, to confront s.o. with sth.; **en f. l'un de l'autre, l'un en f. de l'autre**, opposite each other, facing each other; **en f. de Dieu et des hommes**, before God and man; **à la f. des autels**, in full view of the altars.

face-à-main [fasamɛ̃], *s.m.* lorgnette; *pl. faces-à-main*.

facétie [fasesi], *s.f.* facetious remark; joke, jest; **dire des facéties**, to crack jokes; **recueil de facéties**, collection of witticisms; **faire des facéties à qn**, to play pranks on s.o.; **connu par f. sous le nom de . . .**, known humorously as . . . .

facétieusement [fasesjøzmɑ̃], *adv.* facetiously.

facétieux, -ieuse [fasesjø, -jøːz], *a.* facetious (person, remark).

facettage [fasɛtaʒ], *s.m.* faceting.

facette [fasɛt], *s.f.* 1. facet (of diamond, of insect's eye); **(taillé) à facettes**, (cut) in facets; **homme à facettes**, man of many parts. 2. flat(ted) surface. 3. *Dent:* facet, facing; **f. pour bridge**, bridge facing; **f. à crampons**, pin facing.

facetter [fasete], *v.tr.* to facet (diamond, etc.).

fâché [faʃe], *a.* 1. sorry; **être f. de qch., pour qn**, to be sorry about sth., for s.o.; **il est f. de l'avoir fait**, he's sorry he did it; **je suis f. qu'il ait été puni**, I'm sorry he was punished. 2. angry, annoyed; **être f. contre, après qn**, to be annoyed, vexed, with s.o.; **il est f. de votre conduite**, he's annoyed, vexed, at your conduct. 3. **être f. avec qn**, to have fallen out with s.o.; **ils sont fâchés**, they have fallen out, they have had a quarrel.

fâcher [faʃe], *v.tr.* 1. to grieve. 2. to anger, annoy; to make (s.o.) angry; **fâcher qn, F:** to put, set, get, s.o.'s back up; **soit dit sans vous f.**, with all due deference; *impers:* **il me fâche de . . .**, it pains, grieves, me to . . .

se fâcher. 1. to get angry, annoyed; to lose one's temper; *F:* to cut up rough; **ne pas se f.**, to keep one's temper; **se f. pour rien**, to get angry over nothing; to take offence at nothing; **se f. contre, après, qn**, to get annoyed with s.o.; **répondre sans se f.**, to reply calmly, coolly; *F:* **se f. tout rouge**, to lose one's temper, to get properly angry, to flare up, blaze up; *F:* **se f. de (la nourriture)**, (i) to be annoyed about (the food); (ii) to complain about (the food). 2. **se f. avec qn**, to quarrel with s.o.

fâcherie [faʃri], *s.f.* bad feeling; quarrel, tiff; **il y a entre eux de la f.**, they are on bad terms, they have had a tiff; **des fâcheries quotidiennes**, daily tiffs.

fâcheusement [faʃøzmɑ̃], *adv.* tiresomely, annoyingly; awkwardly.

fâcheux, -euse [faʃø, -øːz]. 1. *a.* troublesome, tiresome, trying, annoying, unfortunate, untoward (event); **posture fâcheuse**, awkward, trying, position; **nouvelle fâcheuse**, sad, disturbing, distressing, news; **personne fâcheuse**, troublesome, tiresome, person; **il est f. que + *sub.***, it is unfortunate, a pity, that . . .; *s.m.* **le f. de l'affaire, c'est que . . .**, the annoying, trying, part of the business is that . . . 2. *s.m. A:* (society) bore; nuisance (of a man); intrusive fellow.

Fachoda [faʃɔda], Pr.n. Geog: Fashoda.

facial, -iaux [fasjal, -jo], a. 1. Anat: etc: facial (muscle, etc.); massage f., facial massage, face massage; névralgie faciale, facial neuralgia. 2. valeur faciale, face value.

facies, faciès [fasjɛːs], s.m. 1. Bot: Med: Z: facies, aspect, appearance (of plant, person, etc.); Med: f. hippocratique, grippé, facies hippocratica. 2. cast of features. 3. Geol: facies.

facile [fasil], a. 1. easy; (a) chose f. à faire, thing easy to do, easily done; c'est f. à dire, it is more easily said than done; il lui est f. de le faire, it is easy for him to do it; ce n'est pas f., it's not easy, it takes a lot of doing; d'une mise en place f., easily installed; on leur donne des besognes faciles, they are given light tasks, light work; (b) (i) homme f., easy-going man; homme f. à vivre, f. en affaires, man easy to live with, easy to get on with, easy, pleasant, to deal with; homme f. à émouvoir, man easily moved; manières faciles, easy manners; mari f., complaisant husband; femme f., woman of easy virtue; (ii) pliable, weak, easily influenced. 2. facile, ready, quick; génie f., facile genius; avoir le style, la parole, f., to have a fluent style, tongue; écrivain, plume, f., ready writer, pen; je n'ai pas la parole f., words do not come easily to me; elle n'a pas les larmes faciles, she is not easily moved to tears.

facilement [fasilmɑ̃], adv. easily, readily; le fer se rouille f., iron rusts easily; de Versailles on va f. à Paris, Versailles is within easy reach of Paris.

facilitation [fasilitasjɔ̃], s.f. Physiol: Med: facilitation.

facilité [fasilite], s.f. 1. (a) easiness (of task, etc.); ease (with which a thing is done); avec f., easily, with ease; céder à la f., to take the easy way out; (b) avoir la f. de faire qch., to enjoy facilities for doing sth.; facilités d'accès à l'éducation, opportunities for education; Com: facilités de paiement, accommodation, facilities, for payment; easy terms, deferred payments; Bank: consentir des facilités de caisse, to grant overdraft facilities; (c) Mus: easier alternative (for difficult passage); (d) Av: etc: f. d'entretien, serviceability; Mec.E: etc: f. d'accès, accessibility. 2. aptitude, talent, facility; f. pour qch., aptitude, talent, for sth.; f. à faire qch., gift, aptitude, for doing sth.; f. de parole, fluency, readiness, of speech; il parle avec une f. étonnante, he speaks with wonderful fluency. 3. (a) pliancy, complaisance; f. en affaires, etc., accommodativeness; (b) easy virtue (of woman).

faciliter [fasilite], v.tr. to facilitate; to make (sth.) easier, easy; cette invention facilite beaucoup le jardinage, this invention takes much of the hard work out of gardening; f. qch. à qn, to make sth. easier for s.o.; f. le progrès, to promote progress.

façon [fasɔ̃], s.f. 1. (a) (i) making, fashioning; (ii) style; f. d'un habit, (i) making(up), (ii) cut, of a coat; tailleur, ébéniste, à f., bespoke tailor, jobbing cabinet maker; cordonnier à f., shoemaker (who makes shoes to measure); on prend, travaille, à f., customers' own materials made up; la f. n'est pas irréprochable, the workmanship is not beyond criticism; plat de sa f., dish of her own making; poème de sa f., poem of his own composition; robe qui a bonne f., well-cut dress; maison qui a bonne f., handsome house; Agr: donner une f. à la terre, to give the soil a dressing; (b) Nau: façons d'un navire, lines, form, of a ship; A: sweep; façons d'arrière, run (of ship); ligne des façons, rising line; façons d'avant, entrance; façons des œuvres vives, underwater lines; (c) ciseau f. américaine, American pattern chisel; cuir f. porc, imitation pigskin; gants f. cousu main, imitation hand-sewn gloves; (d) Ind: matière et f., material and labour. 2. (a) manner, mode, way (of acting, speaking, etc.); prendre des façons de vivre, to fall into habits of living; vivre à la f. des sauvages, to live like savages; avoir une f. à soi de faire qch., to have one's own way of doing sth.; il est religieux, à sa f., he is religious, after his own manner; je le ferai à ma f., I shall do it (in) my own way; nous n'avons pas la même f., les mêmes façons, de voir, we have different points of view; f. de parler, manner of speaking, form of speech; je lui dis, f. de rire, que . . ., I said to him, by way of a joke, that . . .; c'est une f. de poète, he is a poet of sorts; ses façons étaient agréables, his manners were pleasing; elle a de petites façons engageantes, she has engaging ways; parler d'une f. absurde, to talk in an absurd manner, absurdly; vous ne tenez pas votre plume de la même f. que moi, you don't hold your pen as I do; ils agissent tous de la même f., they all act alike; de quelque f. qu'il s'y prenne . . ., whatever way he sets about it . . .; avec lui il faut s'y prendre de telle et telle f., with him you have got to set about it in such and such a way; regardez de quelle f. il tient son archet, look how he holds his bow; de la bonne f., properly, in good style, nicely; arranger qn de (la) belle, de bonne, f., to give s.o. a good dressing-down; (b) homme sans f., rough-and-ready man; elle n'a ni mine ni f., she has neither good looks nor manners; qu'est-ce que c'est que ces façons? what sort of behaviour is this? en voilà des façons! what a way to behave! il entra sans façon(s), he entered unceremoniously; traiter qn sans façon(s), to treat s.o. in an offhand manner; sans plus de façons, without any more ado; faire des façons, to stand on ceremony, to make a fuss; cela ne mérite pas qu'on y apporte tant de façons, it is not worth so much ceremony; il y faut plus de f., it requires more care; (c) de cette f., thus, in this way; venez avec nous, de cette f. cela ne vous coûtera rien, come with us, (in) that way it won't cost you anything; ne me parlez pas de cette f., don't speak to me like that; comment pouvez-vous mentir de cette f.? how can you tell such lies? voilà de quelle f. il m'a traité, that is the way he treated me; de f. ou d'autre, d'une f. ou d'une autre, (i) (in) one way or another, some way or other; (ii) by some means or other, by hook or by crook; de toutes les façons possibles et imaginables, in every possible way; de toute(s) façon(s) j'irai, anyhow, in any case, I shall go; je ne suis d'aucune f., en aucune f., disposé à céder, I am in no way, by no means, disposed to yield; en aucune f.! not at all! by no means! en quelque f., in a way, in a sense. 3. conj.phr. (a) de f. à, so as to; agir de f. à brouiller tout le monde, to act so as to set everyone by the ears; parlez de f. à vous faire comprendre, speak so that you can be understood; (b) de (telle) f. que, (i) + ind. il pleuvait de telle f. que je fus obligé de rentrer, it was raining so hard that I had to go home; il pleuvait, de f. que je fus obligé de rentrer, it was raining, (and) so I had to go home; (ii) + sub. parlez de f. qu'on vous comprenne, speak so as to be understood; réglez toujours votre vie de telle f. que vous n'ayez pas à en rougir, always so regulate your life that you need not be ashamed of it.

faconde [fakɔ̃ːd], s.f. (often Pej:) fluency of speech, facundity, flow of words; avoir de la f., to have a ready flow of language, F: the gift of the gab; f. impressionnante, impressive gift of speech.

façonnage [fasɔnaːʒ], s.m., **façonnement** [fasɔnmɑ̃], s.m. shaping, working (of iron, wood, etc.); turning (of wood, etc., on lathe); fashioning (of clay, etc.); making (of dress, etc.); dressing (of soil); finishing off (of trade article); decorating (of furniture, etc.); figuring (of cloth, etc.).

façonné [fasɔne], a. & s.m. Tex: figured (fabric, material).

façonner [fasɔne], v.tr. to work, shape (wood, metal, etc.); to turn (sth. on lathe); to fashion (clay, etc.); f. une robe, to make (up) a dress; tissu façonné, figured material; Agr: f. la terre, to dress, work, the soil; f. un enfant, to mould, form, a child's character; les voyages, le commerce du monde, façonnent un jeune homme, travelling, moving in society, improve a young man, F: lick a young man into shape; se f. à la discipline, to accustom oneself to discipline.

façonneur, -euse [fasɔnœːr, -øːz], s. maker, shaper, fashioner.

façonnier, -ière [fasɔnje, -jɛːr], a. & s. 1. (rare) ouvrier f., jobbing tailor, home-worker. 2. fussy, over-ceremonious (person).

fac(-)similaire [faksimilɛːr], a. (copy, etc.) in facsimile; facsimile (copy).

fac-similé [faksimile], s.m. facsimile, exact copy (of signature, writing); pl. fac-similés.

fac-similer [faksimile], v.tr. to reproduce (sth.) in facsimile; to facsimile.

factage [faktaːʒ], s.m. (a) carriage (and delivery); transport (of goods); entreprise de f., parcels-delivery company; payer le f., to pay the carriage; (b) porterage; (c) delivery (of letters).

facteur, -trice [faktœːr, -tris], s. 1. (musical) instrument maker; f. d'orgues, organ-builder. 2. (a) carrier, transport agent; (b) carman (delivering parcels); (c) A: (railway) porter; (d) Adm: postman, postwoman; le facteur est passé, the post has come; f. des télégraphes, f.-télégraphiste, telegraph messenger, telegraph boy. 3. Com: (a) agent, middleman, factor, broker; (b) auctioneer (at the Halles). 4. s.m. (a) factor; Mth: décomposer en facteurs, to factor(ize), to resolve into factors; f. premier, prime factor; f. aléatoire, random factor; le f. humain, the human factor; f. d'évolution, factor of evolution; la religion est un f. important dans la vie d'une nation, religion is an important factor in a nation's life, in the life of a nation; El: f. de puissance, power factor; Mec.E: f. de sûreté, de sécurité, safety factor, coefficient of safety; Pol.Ec: revenu national au coût des facteurs, national income at factor cost; revenu de f., factor income; prix de f., factor price; f. d'utilisation, duty factor, cycle; Atom.Ph: f. antitrappe, resonance escape probability; (b) Biol: factor, gene; s.a. RHÉSUS 2.

facteur-clé [faktœrkle], s.m. key factor; pl. facteurs-clés.

factice [faktis]. 1. a. factitious; artificial, imitation (rocks, gems, etc.); edition f., miscellany; devanture remplie de boîtes factices, shop window full of dummy boxes; Th: (gigot, etc.) f., property (leg of mutton, etc.). 2. s.m. (a) dummy; factices de caoutchouc, rubber imitations, dummies; (b) Rubber Ind: vulcanized oil additive.

facticement [faktismɑ̃], adv. artificially, factitiously.

facticité [faktisite], s.f. Phil: etc: facticity.

factieux, -ieuse [faksjø, -jøːz]. 1. a. factious, seditious, discontented (spirit, etc.). 2. s. factious person, seditionmonger, factionist.

faction [faksjɔ̃], s.f. 1. sentry duty, guard; faire f., être de f., être en f., monter la f., to stand sentry, to be on sentry(-go), to be on guard; mettre (qn) en f., to post (a sentry); relever (qn) de f., to relieve (a sentry); aller, entrer, en f., to go on sentry; sortir de f., to come off sentry-go; mettre les grévistes en f., to place strikers on picket duty. 2. (a) faction; factious party; la Constituante était divisée en factions, the Constituent Assembly was broken up into factions; (b) esprit de f., faction, factiousness.

factionnaire [faksjɔnɛːr], s.m. (a) sentry; poser, relever, un f., to post, relieve, a sentry; (b) man on picket duty; picket.

factitif, -ive [faktitif, -iːv], a. Gram: causative, factitive (verb, etc.).

factorerie [faktɔrəri], s.f. Com: foreign (trading) post, depot.

factoriel, -ielle [faktɔrjel]. 1. a. Mth: etc: factorial; Statistics: Psy: analyse factorielle, factor analysis. 2. s.f. Mth: factorielle, factorial.

factorisation [faktɔrizasjɔ̃], s.f. Mth: factorization, factorizing.

factoriser [faktɔrize], v.tr. Mth: to factorize.

factotum [faktɔtɔm], s.m. 1. factotum; (a) steward (of house property); (b) handyman. 2. Iron: F: nosy parker.

factuel, -elle [faktɥel], a. Phil: factual.

factum [faktɔm], s.m. (a) Jur: statement of the facts (of a case); memorial, factum; (b) (i) controversial pamphlet; (ii) scurrilous pamphlet; pl. factums.

facturation [faktyrasjɔ̃], s.f. Book-k: invoicing; (service de) f., invoice department; travaux de f., invoice work.

facture[1] [faktyːr], s.f. 1. (a) treatment (of music, work of art); Mus: morceau de f., show piece; vers d'une f. heureuse, well-made verses; (b) Com: get-up, make, workmanship (of an article); style (of motor car, etc.); pardessus f. soignée, carefully tailored overcoat. 2. (a) manufacturing (of musical instruments); (b) calibre, scale (of organ pipes).

facture[2], s.f. Com: invoice, bill (of sale); faire, dresser, établir, une f., to make out an invoice; f. simulée, pro forma, pro forma invoice; prix de f., invoice price; f. détaillée, itemized invoice; selon, suivant, f., as per invoice.

facturer [faktyre], v.tr. Com: to invoice; to charge for (sth.) on the invoice.

facturier, -ière [faktyrje, -jɛːr], s. Com: 1. s.m. sales book. 2. s.m. & f. invoice clerk. 3. s.f. facturière, invoicing machine.

facule [fakyl], s.f. Astr: facula.

facultatif, -ive [fakyltatif, -iːv], a. optional, facultative; sujet (d'examen) f., optional subject (in examination); extra subject; P.N: arrêt f., request stop; Jur: législation facultative, permissive legislation.

facultativement [fakyltativmɑ̃], adv. optionally, at discretion.

faculté [fakylte], s.f. 1. (a) option, right, faculty; avoir (la) f. de faire qch., to have (i) the option of doing sth., (ii) power to do sth.; louer un immeuble avec f. d'achat, to rent a building with the option of purchase; St.Exch: f. du double,

call of more; (*b*) faculty, ability, power; **facultés de l'esprit,** intellectual faculties, mental powers; **f. de parler, de sentir,** faculty of speech, of feeling; **jouir de toutes ses facultés,** to be in possession of all one's faculties; **il ne jouissait pas de la plénitude de ses facultés (mentales),** he was not in full possession of his faculties; **homme doué de grandes facultés,** man of great talent, of great abilities; man of parts; **l'aimant a la f. d'attirer le fer,** the magnet has the property of attracting iron; (*c*) *pl.* resources, means. **2.** *Sch:* **la f. des lettres, des sciences, de droit,** the Faculty of Arts, of Science, of Law; **professeur de f.,** (university) professor; **quand j'étais à la f.,** *F:* **à la fac,** when I was at university; **la Faculté,** (i) the Faculty (of Medicine); (ii) *F:* the medical profession.

fada [fada], (*S. Dial.*) (*a*) *s.m. F:* fool; simpleton; clot; (*b*) *a.* foolish, crazy.

fadaise [fadɛːz], *s.f.* (*a*) piece of nonsense, silly remark; (*b*) *pl.* twaddle, nonsense, rot, bosh; stuff and nonsense; **débiter des fadaises,** to talk twaddle; *F:* **fadaises que tout cela!** fiddlesticks! rot!

fadasse [fadas], *a.* insipid, sickly, cloying (taste, etc.); pale, washed out (colour, hair); sloppy (novel, etc.).

fade [fad], *a.* **1.** insipid, flavourless, tasteless (dish, etc.); mawkish (compliments); **odeur f.,** stale odour; **teint f.,** washed-out colour; **avoir le cœur f.,** to feel squeamish; **conversation f.,** dull, insipid, conversation; **plaisanterie f.,** pointless, tame, joke. **2.** *s.m. P:* **avoir son f.,** (i) to have one's full share (of sth.); (ii) to be drunk, tight.

fadé [fade], *a. P:* **1. être f. de qch.,** to be in possession of sth. **2. être f.,** (i) to be in a bad way (through illness, wounds, etc.); (ii) to be drunk, tight; **il est f. de son genre,** he's a prize specimen of his kind.

fadement [fadmɑ̃], *adv.* insipidly.

fader[1] [fade], *v.tr. P:* **1.** to beat, kill. **2.** to punish (s.o.) severely. **3.** to share out (the booty among the thieves); **avec ça je ne serai pas fadé,** I haven't been given my fair share (of the booty); I've been done.

fader[2] [fedœːr], *s.m. Cin: W.Tp:* fader.

fadet [fadɛ], *s.m. Dial:* elf, goblin.

fadette [fadɛt], *s.f. Dial:* fairy.

fadeur [fadœːr], *s.f.* (*a*) insipidity; mawkishness; sickliness (of taste, smell, etc.); (*b*) *pl.* **dire des fadeurs à qn,** to pay insipid compliments to s.o.; (*c*) pointlessness, tameness (of joke).

fading [fediŋ], *s.m. W.Tel:* fading (effect).

faffe [faf], **fafiot** [fafjo], *s.m. P:* **1.** bank note; *P:* flimsy; *U.S: F:* greenback. **2.** (*a*) *A:* **f. à roulotter,** cigarette-paper; (*b*) *pl.* **fafiots,** identity papers.

fagacées [fagase], *s.f.pl. Bot:* Fagaceae.

fagne [faɲ], *s.f. Dial:* upland moss hag (in the Ardennes).

fagopyrisme [fagɔpirism], *s.m. Vet:* fagopyrism, fagopyrismus.

fagot [fago], *s.m.* **1.** faggot, bundle of firewood; *Fort:* **f. de sape,** fascine; **il y a fagots et fagots,** all men, things, are not alike; **sentir le f.,** to savour of heresy; **bouteille de vin de derrière les fagots,** bottle of wine from the hidden store, kept for special occasions; *Rac:* **cheval de derrière les fagots,** rank outsider; *s.a.* BOURRÉE[1], ÉPINE 1. **2.** *A:* bundle (of clothes, etc.); *F:* **elle s'habille comme un f.,** she dresses like a scarecrow; she's like an old sack tied in the middle. **3.** *F: A:* **conter, débiter, des fagots,** to tell silly pointless, stories. **4.** *P:* ticket-of-leave man.

fagotage [fagɔtaːʒ], *s.m.,* **fagotement** [fagɔtmɑ̃], *s.m.* **1.** (*a*) putting, tying, (of sticks) in bundles; faggoting; (*b*) *Metalw: etc:* faggoting; (*c*) *F:* botching (of work). **2.** (*a*) firewood, faggot-wood; (*b*) *F:* botched piece of work; botch. **3.** *F:* ridiculous manner of dressing, ridiculous get-up, dowdy get-up.

fagoté [fagɔte], *a. F:* badly dressed; **mal fagotée,** dowdy; **elle est terriblement fagotée,** she's an awful frump, an awful scarecrow.

fagoter [fagɔte], *v.tr.* **1.** to tie up (wood, etc.) in bundles; to faggot (firewood). **2.** to bungle, botch (work). **3.** *F:* to dress (s.o.) like a scarecrow; **comme les femmes se fagotaient de mon temps!** what dreadful clothes women wore in my day!

fagoteur, -euse [fagɔtœːr, -øːz], *s.* **1.** faggot maker, tier. **2.** jobber, botcher; **f. de romans,** hack novelist.

fagotier [fagɔtje], *s.m.* (fine) woodcutter; firewood seller.

fagotin [fagɔtɛ̃], *s.m.* **1.** bundle of firewood, of kindling. **2.** *A:* (*a*) organ-grinder's monkey; (*b*) clown, buffoon.

faguette [fagɛt], *s.f. Fort:* small fascine.

fahlbande [falbɑ̃ːd], *s.f. Miner:* fahlband.

faiblage [fɛblaːʒ], *s.m.* **1.** weak part, spot (of manufactured article). **2.** (*a*) *A:* diminution of the value or weight (of coins); (*b*) *Mint:* tolerance, allowance (of weight or fineness).

faiblard [fɛblaːr], *a. F:* weak(ish); feeblish; **son vin est f.,** his wine is a bit thin.

faible [fɛbl̩]. **1.** (*a*) *a.* feeble, weak; **l'âge f.,** the tender age; infancy; **le sexe f.,** the weaker sex; **f. d'esprit,** weak-, feeble-minded; mentally deficient; **f. de corps,** weak in body; **l'esprit est prompt, mais la chair est f.,** the spirit is willing, but the flesh is weak; **cheval f. des reins,** horse weak in the back; **point f. d'un projet,** weak point, flaw, in a scheme; **points faibles d'un argument,** weaknesses in an argument; **points faibles chez qn,** shortcomings in s.o.; **son point f.,** his weak (-est) spot; **c'est là son côté f.,** that is his weak side; *Nau:* **vaisseau f. de côté,** cranky, crank-sided, vessel; (*b*) *s.m. & f.* **f. d'esprit,** feeble-minded person; **protéger les faibles,** to protect the weak; **les économiquement faibles,** the underprivileged; (*c*) *a.* **brise f.,** light breeze; **voix f.,** (i) weak voice; (ii) faint voice; **son f.,** faint sound; **f. odeur,** faint smell; **café f.,** weak, thin, coffee; **douleur f.,** slight pain; **f. espérance,** slender, faint, hope; **les chances du malade étaient faibles,** the patient's chances of survival were poor; *Com:* **f. demande,** slack demand; **prix f.,** (i) low price; (ii) discount price; **pièce f.,** light coin; **f. vitesse,** low speed, slow speed; **lampe à f. consommation,** low-consumption lamp; **minerai à f. teneur (d'or, etc.),** low-grade ore; **f. quantité,** small quantity; **f. récolte,** light crop; **f. dose,** small dose; **faibles ressources,** small resources, scanty means; **f. différence,** slight difference; **f. majorité,** bare majority; *Mus:* **temps f.,** unaccented beat; *Nau:* **f. tirant,** shallow draught; **navire de f. tonnage,** ship of small tonnage; *Phot:* **cliché f.,** thin negative; (*d*) *a.* **cette élève est f. en chimie,** this pupil is weak in chemistry. **2.** *s.m.* weakness, failing, foible; **la boisson est son f.,** drink is a failing of his; **le f. de qn, de qch.,** the weak side, weak spot, weak point, in s.o., sth.; **avoir un f. pour qn, qch.,** to have a weakness, a partiality, for s.o., sth., to be partial to s.o., sth., to have a liking for s.o., sth.; **elle semble avoir un f. pour vous,** she seems to like you, she seems to have a soft spot for you; **c'est là son f.,** that's his weak point.

faiblement [fɛbləmɑ̃], *adv.* (*a*) feebly, weakly; (*b*) **entendre qch. f.,** to hear sth. faintly.

faiblesse [fɛblɛs], *s.f.* **1.** (*a*) feebleness, weakness; debility; **f. de la voix, du pouls,** feebleness of the voice, of the pulse; **je tombais de f.,** I was ready to drop with exhaustion; *F:* I was dead-beat; (*b*) faintness; **(accès de) f.,** fainting fit; **tomber en f.,** to fall down in a faint; to faint; **il lui a pris une f.,** (i) she fainted; (ii) she nearly fainted; (*c*) **la f. humaine,** human weakness, frailty; **f. d'une mère pour ses enfants,** a mother's indulgence, partiality, for her children; (*d*) smallness (of sum, number); slightness (of difference); (*e*) *Sch:* **ma f., c'est l'histoire romaine,** my weakest subject is Roman history. **2.** (*a*) **f. chez qn,** failing in s.o.; **je l'aime avec toutes ses faiblesses,** I love him in spite of all his failings; (*b*) slip (in conduct).

faiblir [fɛbliːr], *v.i.* to weaken; to grow weak(er), to lose strength; *I.C.E:* (*of engine*) to lose power; **elle faiblissait de jour en jour,** she was growing weaker every day; **plancher qui commence à f.,** floor that is beginning to give way; **ma vue faiblit,** my sight is failing; **son courage faiblit,** his courage, resolution, is failing, is flagging; **le vent faiblit,** the wind is abating, is dropping.

faiblissant [fɛblisɑ̃], *a.* weakening, growing feeble; failing (sight); failing, waning, dwindling (light); flagging, drooping (spirit, courage).

faiblisseur [fɛblisœːr], *a. & s.m. Phot:* = AFFAIBLISSEUR.

faïence [fajɑ̃ːs], *s.f.* faience, crockery, earthenware, stoneware; **f. fine,** china; **vase de f.,** china bowl.

faïencé [fajɑ̃se], *a.* **1.** like pottery, in imitation of pottery. **2.** crackled (oil-painting).

faïencerie [fajɑ̃sri], *s.f.* **1.** crockery, earthenware. **2.** (*a*) china shop; (*b*) pottery(works); (*c*) pottery (trade).

faïencier, -ière [fajɑ̃sje, -jɛːr]. **1.** *a.* earthenware, pottery (industry, etc.). **2.** *s.* crockery, earthenware, maker, dealer.

faignant, -ante [fɛɲɑ̃, -ɑ̃ːt], *a. & s. P:* = FAINÉANT.

faillant [fajɑ̃], *a.* (*rare*) failing, about to end; **à jour f.,** at close of day.

faille[1] [faːj], *s.f. Tex:* coarse-grained silk material; faille.

faille[2], *s.f. Geol: Min:* (i) fault; (ii) break (in lode); **ressaut de f.,** fault scarp; **f. à charnière,** pivotal fault; **f. à gradins,** step fault; **f. en gradins, en escalier,** distributive fault; **f. inverse,** reverse(d) fault; **f. d'effondrement, d'affaissement,** downthrow fault; **f. de chevauchement,** upthrow fault, thrust fault; **f. serrée,** collapsed fault; **f. rajeunie,** rejuvenated fault; **f. horizontale de décrochement,** strike lip fault; **f. à rejet horizontale,** lateral shearing fault.

faillé [faje], *a. Geol:* faulted.

failli, -ie [faji]. **1.** *a.* (*a*) *Vet:* **tendon f.,** close tendon (in horse); (*b*) *A: P:* **un f. chien d'usurier,** a scoundrelly moneylender. **2.** *s.* (adjudicated) bankrupt.

faillibilité [fajibilite], *s.f.* fallibility.

faillible [fajibl̩], *a.* fallible; **tout le monde est f.,** anybody may make a mistake; accidents will happen.

faillir [fajiːr], *v.i.* (*pr.p.* **faillant;** *p.p.* **failli;** *A: pr.ind.* **je faux, tu faux, il faut, n. faillons;** *p.h.* **je faillis;** *fu.* **je faillirai,** *A:* **je faudrai;** *the parts in commonest use are the past historic, the future and the compound tenses*) **1.** (*a*) to fail; **je faillirais à mon devoir si . . .,** I should be failing in, should fall short of, my duty if . . .; **f. à une promesse,** to fail to keep a promise; **le cœur, la mémoire, me faut,** my heart, memory, fails me; **édifice qui a failli par la base,** building that has given way at the base; **le jour commence à f.,** daylight is beginning to fail; **sans f.,** without fail; *s.a.* AMOUR 1, AUNE[2]; (*b*) *Com:* to go bankrupt; (*c*) *A:* **jeune fille qui a failli,** girl who has lost her virtue. **2. faillir +** *inf.* (*only in past hist. and compound tenses*); **j'ai failli manquer le train,** I all but missed the train; I nearly missed the train; **il faillit être écrasé,** he narrowly missed being run over; **j'ai bien failli me noyer,** I was only just saved from drowning, I was very nearly drowned, I had a narrow escape from drowning.

faillite [fajit], *s.f.* (*a*) *Com:* failure, bankruptcy, insolvency; **être en f., en état de f.,** to be bankrupt, insolvent; **tomber en f., faire f.,** to go bankrupt, to fail; *F:* to go to smash, to break, to go to the wall; **se mettre en f.,** to file a petition in bankruptcy; *F:* to file one's petition; **déclarer, mettre, qn en f., prononcer la f. de qn,** to adjudicate, adjudge, s.o. bankrupt; **faire une f. d'un million,** to fail for a million; *s.a.* JUGEMENT 1; (*b*) failure; **f. d'une politique,** failure of a policy.

faim [fɛ̃], *s.f.* hunger; **réduire une ville par la f.,** to starve a town into surrender; **avoir f., sentir la f.,** to be, feel, hungry; *F:* **avoir une f. de loup, une f. canine,** to be ravenously hungry, *F:* as hungry as a hunter; **j'ai une f. de loup,** I could eat a horse, *U.S:* I'm as hungry as a bear; *F:* **j'ai une de ces faims!** I'm simply ravenous! **manger à sa f.,** to eat one's fill, to eat to repletion; **mourir de f.,** (i) to die of starvation; (ii) *F:* to starve, to be starving; (iii) *F:* to be famished, ravenous; **travailler pour ne pas mourir de f.,** to work to keep body and soul together; *Prov:* **la f. chasse le loup du bois,** necessity knows no law; **avoir f. de gloire,** to hunger, thirst, for glory; **il avait f. de la revoir,** he was longing to see her again; **rester sur sa f.,** (i) to remain hungry; (ii) *F:* to be left in the air; **laisser qn sur sa f.,** to leave s.o. with a sense of frustration; *s.a.* CALMER, DONNER 2.

faim-valle [fɛ̃val], *s.f. A: No pl. Med:* morbid hunger, bulimy, bulimia, boulimia; *Vet:* hungry evil.

faîne [fɛːn], *s.f.* **1.** *Bot:* beechnut. **2.** *pl.* beechmast.

fainéant, -ante [fɛneɑ̃, -ɑ̃ːt]. **1.** *a.* idle, lazy, slothful, do-nothing; *Hist:* **les Rois fainéants,** the *Rois fainéants* (the later Merovingian Kings). **2.** *s.* idler, sluggard, lazybones, slacker; loafer.

fainéanter [fɛneɑ̃te], *v.i.* to idle; to loaf (about).

fainéantise [fɛneɑ̃tiːz], *s.f.* idleness, laziness, sloth; **passer des heures de f.,** to idle the time away.

fainée [fɛne], *s.f.* **1.** beechmast. **2.** beechmast gathering.

faire [fɛːr], *v.tr.* (*pr.p.* **faisant** [fəzɑ̃]; *p.p.* **fait** [fɛ]; *pr.ind.* **je fais, tu fais, il fait, n. faisons** [f(ə)zɔ̃], **v. faites** [fɛt], **ils font;** *pr.sub.* **je fasse;** *imp.* **fais, faisons, faites;** *p.h.* **je fis;** *fu.* **je ferai**) **I.** to make. **1.** to bring into existence; **Dieu a fait l'homme à son image,** God made, created, man in his own

image; *F:* **ils ne veulent pas f. d'enfants,** they don't want to have any children; **f. un enfant à une femme,** to make a woman pregnant; **se f. les dents,** to cut one's teeth; **Paris ne s'est pas fait dans un jour** = Rome was not built in a day; **f. une rente à qn,** to make s.o. an allowance, to allow s.o. an income; **les vieilles gens sont ainsi faits,** old people are like that; **il n'est pas fait pour être soldat,** he is not cut out for a soldier; **il n'est pas fait pour cela,** he is not the man, not fitted, not cut out, for that. **2.** (*a*) **f. un gâteau, du cidre,** to make a cake, cider; **statue faite en, de, marbre,** statue cut, made, out of marble; **vêtements tout faits,** ready-made clothes; **expressions toutes faites,** ready-made phrases, set phrases; *Fb:* **rater un but tout fait,** to miss an easy goal, *F:* a sitter; **jambe bien faite,** shapely leg; **homme bien fait,** handsome man; **comment est-il fait?** (i) what does he look like? (ii) what sort of man is he? *F:* **comme vous voilà fait!** (i) what a sight you are! (ii) what a mess you're in! **la vie est faite de ce que nous y mettons,** life is what you make it; **il n'y aurait pas de blé pour f. du pain,** there would be no corn to make bread; **pain fait avec du seigle,** rye bread; **f. un poème,** to write a poem; **f. un tableau,** to paint a picture; **f. un livre,** to write a book; **f. un chèque,** to write a cheque; **f. un chèque de £10,** to make out a cheque for £10; (*b*) **f. la guerre,** to wage war; **f. une attaque,** to make, deliver, an attack; **f. un miracle,** to work a miracle; **il faut f. l'Europe,** we must unite Europe; **ferme où on fait de la betterave,** farm that grows beetroot; **f. les foins,** to make hay; (*c*) *Com:* **nous ne faisons que la fleur coupée, le gros,** we are only cut-flower, wholesale, dealers; *s.a.* AFFAIRE 2, SE FAIRE 3; (*d*) *F:* **f. de l'œil à qn,** to wink at s.o.; *F:* **je lui ai fait du pied pendant la représentation de Carmen,** I played footsie, footy-footy, with her during Carmen; *F:* **f. du genou sous la table,** to play kneesies under the table; *s.a.* TOUCHÉ. **3.** (*a*) **f. sa fortune,** to make one's fortune; **f. des pertes,** to meet with, sustain, losses; **il se fait 10.000 francs par mois,** he makes 10,000 francs a month; **se f. des amis,** to make friends; (*b*) **faire des provisions,** to lay in provisions; **f. de l'eau, du charbon,** to take in water, coal; *Aut:* **f. le plein,** to fill up; (*c*) *P:* **on m'a fait ma montre,** someone has pinched my watch; **on vous a fait,** you've been done, had; *P:* **tu es fait, mon vieux!** you've had it, chum! *s.a.* RAT 1.

II. **faire,** to do. **1.** (*a*) **faites envers les autres comme vous voudriez qu'ils fissent envers vous,** do as you would be done by; **qu'est-ce que vous faites?** (i) what are you doing? (ii) what are you up to? **il n'a rien fait,** he did nothing; **qu'est-ce qu'il y a à f.?** (i) what is there to do? (ii) what is there (that) wants doing, (that) needs to be done? **il n'y a rien à f. ici,** there is nothing to do here; **il n'y a rien à f.,** there is nothing to be done, there's no help for it; **cela n'a rien à f. avec la situation actuelle,** that has no relation to the present situation; **que f.?** what is, was, to be done? what can, could, he, we, I, do? **je ne sais que f.,** I don't know what to do; **je l'observais, le regardais, f.,** I watched him at it, doing it; **nous l'avons fait à deux,** there were two of us at it, we did it between us; **est-ce que je peux ouvrir la fenêtre?—faites donc!** may I open the window!—do! by all means! **faites vite!** look sharp! **il n'a rien à f. ici,** he has no business here; **avoir fort à f.,** to have a great deal to do, to have one's work cut out, to be kept hard at work, to have one's hands full; **j'ai eu fort à f. pour l'obtenir,** I had a hard job to get it; **nous avons fort à f. pour joindre les deux bouts,** we are hard put to it to make both ends meet; **vous allez avoir de quoi f.,** you have your work cut out; **on n'aurait jamais fait si on voulait tout dire,** one would never have done if one said everything; **je suis heureux de n'avoir plus rien à f. avec eux,** I am glad to get out of further dealings with them; **homme à tout f.,** handy-man, Man Friday; **bonne à tout f.,** maid of all work, general servant, maid; **ces choses-là ne se font pas,** those things are not done; **c'est une chose qui ne se fait pas,** it is not good form, it is bad form; **cela vous fera beaucoup de bien,** it will do you such a lot of good; **grand bien vous fasse!** much good may it do you! **c'est bien fait!** it serves you right! **étant donné un triangle, comment faites-vous pour y inscrire une circonférence?** given a triangle, how do you proceed to inscribe a circle in it? **pour ce que j'en fais,** for my purpose; for all the use, the good, it is to me; (*b*) to say; **"vous partez demain!" fit-il,** "you leave to-morrow!" he said, he ejaculated; **il fit un petit "oh" de surprise,** he gave a little "oh" of surprise; **f. ses prières,** to say one's prayers; **la déclaration à lui faite,** the statement made to him; **les vaches font "meuh,"** cows go "moo". **2.** (to perform, practise) (*a*) **f. son devoir,** to do one's duty; **f. la ronde,** to go one's rounds; *F:* **f. ses besoins,** *abs.* **faire,** to relieve oneself, to go to the loo, *U.S:* the John; *Com:* **f. les cuirs, les laines,** to deal in leather, in wool; **quel article faites-vous?** what is your line? **voilà qui est fait,** that's done, settled; **c'est toujours ça de fait,** that's a good job done; **toute réflexion faite . . .,** all things considered . . .; (*b*) **f. de la bicyclette, du sport, de l'auto, de la politique,** to go in for cycling, for sport, for motoring, for politics; **j'ai fait de l'anglais à l'école,** I did English at school; **il fait sa médecine,** he is doing medicine, studying medicine; **il fait son droit,** he is reading law; **f. du journalisme,** to practise journalism; **f. un peu de droit,** to dabble in law; **il fait beaucoup de musique,** he does a lot of music; **f. une maladie,** to have an illness; **f. de la coqueluche, de la fièvre,** to develop whooping-cough, fever; **f. de l'hypertension,** to have high blood pressure; **f. dix ans de prison,** to serve a sentence of ten years, to do ten years (in prison); **f. son apprentissage,** to serve one's apprenticeship; *F:* **f. le continent,** to do the Continent; **f. les magasins,** to go round the shops; *s.a.* HÔPITAL 1. **3.** (to proceed, go); **f. quelques pas dans le sentier,** to go, take a few steps along the path; **f. une promenade,** to go for a walk; *F:* **f. du cent à l'heure,** = to go, do, a hundred kilometres an hour; **f. dix kilomètres à pied, à cheval,** to walk, ride, ten kilometres; **mon pardessus fera encore l'hiver,** my overcoat will last the winter out, will do for this winter. **4.** to cause; **ces mots firent une profonde sensation,** these words caused a deep sensation. **5.** (*a*) to amount to; **combien cela fait-il?** how much does that come to? **deux fois deux font quatre,** twice two is four; **ce qui ferait dix habitants au mille carré,** which would give ten inhabitants to the square mile; **ça fait trois jours qu'il est parti,** it's three days since he left; **ce poulet fait trois kilos,** this chicken weighs three kilos; (*b*) **"cheval" fait "chevaux" au pluriel,** *cheval* becomes *chevaux* in the plural. **6.** to charge; *F:* **combien ça fait la livre de chocolat?** how much do you charge for a pound of chocolate? **il me fait ce buffet mille francs,** he wants a thousand francs for this sideboard; his price for this sideboard is a thousand francs. **7.** to be, constitute; **f. l'admiration de tous,** to be the admiration of all; **cela fera mon affaire,** (i) that will suit me; (ii) that's just what I'm looking for; **l'argent fait tout,** money is everything; **il fera un bon négociant,** he has the makings of a good business man; **quel taquin vous faites!** what a tease you are! *Prov:* **l'habit ne fait pas le moine,** it is not the cowl that makes the monk. **8.** to matter; **qu'est-ce que ça fait?** what does it matter? who cares? **cela vous ferait-il rien de fermer la porte?** would you mind closing the door? **qu'est-ce que cela vous fait?** what is that to you? **qu'est-ce que cela me fait?** what do I care? **pour ce que ça me fait!** for all I care! **si cela ne vous fait rien,** if you don't mind; **rien ne lui fait,** nothing affects him; **l'argent fait sur lui plus que tout,** money counts with him more than anything; **cela ne fait rien,** that makes no difference, never mind, it doesn't matter. **9.** **faire** *replacing a head verb in the second term of a comparison;* **Charles XII voulait braver les saisons comme il faisait ses ennemis,** Charles XII wanted to defy the seasons as he did his enemies; **pourquoi agir comme vous le faites?** why do you act as you do? **il usait de cet argent comme il eût fait du sien,** he made free with this money as he would have done with his own; **il s'en est acquitté beaucoup mieux que je n'aurais pu le f.,** he acquitted himself much better than I could have done.

III. **faire.** **1.** to form; **ce professeur fait de bons élèves,** this master produces, turns out, good pupils; **se f. une opinion sur qch.,** to frame, form, an opinion on sth.; *F:* **f. ses souliers,** to stretch one's shoes by use; **f. des chaussures à son pied,** to break in a pair of shoes; **démarche faite pour m'étonner,** step calculated to astonish me. **2.** to arrange; **f. la chambre,** to clean, to do, the room; **f. sa malle, sa valise,** to pack one's trunk, one's suitcase; **f. ses ongles,** to (polish and) trim one's nails, to do one's nails; **f. ses chaussures,** to clean one's shoes; **f. les cartes,** (i) to shuffle, (ii) to deal, the cards; **à qui de f.?** whose deal is it? *Th:* **f. la salle,** to pack the house with supporters; *Tp:* **f. le 51848,** to dial 51848; *s.a.* PAQUETAGE 2. **3.** (*pred. uses*) (*a*) **f. qn qch., f. qch. de qn,** to make s.o. sth.; **f. qch. (de) qch.,** to make sth. sth.; **Dieu a fait tous les hommes égaux,** God made all men equal; **elle s'est faite belle,** she has smartened herself up; **l'empereur l'a fait général,** the emperor made him a general; **qu'allez-vous f. de votre fils?** what are you going to make of your son? **qu'avez-vous fait de mon parapluie?** what have you done with my umbrella? **f. d'un théâtre un cinéma,** to turn a theatre into a cinema; **n'avoir que f. de qch.,** to have no occasion, no need, for sth.; not to want sth.; to have no use for sth.; **si vous n'avez que f. de ce livre, prêtez-le-moi,** if you can spare this book, do lend it to me; *s.a.* FAIRE VI 3; *F:* **cela fait riche,** it gives an appearance of wealth; *F:* **ça fait riche,** it looks posh, stylish; **vases qui font bien sur la cheminée,** vases that look well, nice, on the mantelpiece, that make a fine, lovely, effect on the mantelpiece; **il ne fait pas quarante ans,** he doesn't look forty; **elle fait très femme pour dix-huit ans,** she is very much a woman, very grown-up, for an eighteen-year-old; **il ne fait pas père de famille,** he doesn't look like, you'd never think he was, a father; **cette robe fait très jeune,** that dress makes her, you, look very young; **la rue de Rivoli fait un peu clinquant,** the Rue de Rivoli looks a bit flashy and cheap; **rien ne fait moins traité que cet ouvrage,** nothing is less like a treatise than this work; *s.a.* SORT[2] 1; (*b*) *O:* **on le faisait mort,** he was alleged, given out, to be dead; **il se fait plus pauvre qu'il ne l'est,** he makes himself out to be poorer than he is. **4.** (*to act a part*) **il fait Hamlet,** he acts Hamlet; **f. le malade,** to sham illness; **f. le pauvre,** to pretend to be poor; **il fait le mort,** he is shamming dead; **il faisait le libre-penseur,** he affected the free-thinker; **elle ne va pas faire la reine ici,** she isn't going to queen it here! *A:* **f. le gros monsieur,** to act big; **f. l'imbécile,** to play the fool.

IV. **faire.** **1. en f.;** (*a*) **il n'en fait qu'à sa tête,** he follows his own inclination; **ce que j'en fais c'est pour vous,** I am only doing it for your sake; **n'en faites rien,** do no such thing, don't do anything of the kind, don't do it; **dans le genre ingénu elle en faisait tout de même un peu trop,** she was rather overdoing the innocent act; (*b*) **c'en est fait,** the worst has happened; **c'(en) est fait de lui,** it's all up, all over, with him; his fate is sealed; he's done for; (*c*) *P:* **(ne) t'en fais pas** (*i.e.* **de la bile**), don't worry. **2. y faire; rien n'y fit,** nothing availed, it was all of no use; **qu'y faire?** how can it be helped? what remedy is there for it? **que voulez-vous que j'y fasse?** how can I help it? **3.** *F:* **la faire; on ne la lui fait pas,** you can't get a rise out of him; **on ne me la fait pas!** nothing doing! I'm not to be had! you can't bamboozle me! **je la lui ai fait à l'ancien combattant,** I worked the ex-service man on him; **la f. à la vertu,** to pretend to be virtuous; *s.a.* BON 11.

V. **faire,** *impers.* **1. quel temps fait-il?** what is the weather like? *F:* what's the weather doing? **il fait beau (temps),** the weather is fine, it is fine (weather); **il fait du soleil,** it is sunny, the sun is shining; **il fait de la neige,** the weather is snowy, it is snowing; **par le froid qu'il fait,** in this cold weather. **2. il fait mauvais voyager par ces routes en hiver,** it is hard travelling on these roads in winter. **3.** *Dial: F:* **il fait soif, faim, après un travail pareil,** one feels, gets, thirsty, hungry, after work like that; **il fait faim,** I am, we are, getting hungry.

VI. **faire,** *syntactical constructions.* **1. ne f. que** + *inf.* **il ne fait que lire toute la journée,** he does nothing but read all day; **je n'ai fait que le toucher,** I only touched it; **le chien ne fait qu'aboyer,** the dog keeps on barking, does nothing but bark; **le voyage ne fait que commencer,** the journey is only just beginning; **il ne fait qu'entrer et sortir,** (i) *F:* he keeps popping in; (ii) *F:* he's only here for a moment. **2. ne f. que de** + *inf.* **je ne fais que d'arriver,** I have only just arrived. **3. n'avoir que f. de** + *inf.* **vous n'aviez que f. de parler,** you had no business to speak; *s.a.* FAIRE III 3. **4.** (*a*) **f. que** + *ind.* **c'est ce qui fait que je suis venu si vite,** that is why, this is how it happens that, I came so quickly; **cela fait que nous restons toujours ici,** the result is, thus it comes about, that we always remain here; (*b*) **f. que** + *sub.* **pouvais-je f. que cela n'arrivât pas?** could I have prevented it? **fasse le ciel qu'il vienne à temps!** heaven grant, send, that he (may) come in time! **faites qu'il se trouve là demain,** arrange, see to it, that he is there tomorrow.

VII. **faire** + *inf.* = *causative verb. In the comp. tenses the past participle of* **faire** *is invariable.* **1.** (*the noun or pron. object is the subject of the inf.*) (*a*) **le soleil fait fondre la neige,** the sun causes the snow to melt, melts the snow; **f. sécher le linge,** to dry the linen; **je le fis chanter,** I made him sing; **on le fit chanter,** he was made to sing; **je ne peux pas la f. chanter,** I cannot get her, induce her, to sing; **cela me fait rougir,** it makes me blush; **faites venir le médecin,** send for, call in, the doctor; **il nous a fait venir,** he sent for us; **faites-le entrer,** show him in; **la fumée l'a fait tousser,** the smoke made her cough; **cela me fit réfléchir,** that set me thinking; **f. manger le chien,** to get the dog to eat; to feed the dog; **ne me faites pas attendre,** don't keep me waiting; **je l'ai fait monter, descendre, entrer, pour prendre une tasse de thé,** I had him up, down, in, for a cup of tea; **je l'ai fait sortir pour dîner,** I made him come out to dinner; **il veut me f. croire que . . .,** he is trying to persuade me that . . ., he would have me believe that . . .; (*b*) **faire** + *v.pr.* (i) (*reflexive pron. omitted*) **faire asseoir qn,** to make s.o. sit down; **f. coucher un enfant,** to put a child to bed; **f. taire une batterie,** to silence a battery; **je vous en ferai repentir,** you'll be sorry for that; (ii) (*reflexive pron. retained*) **nous l'avons fait se cacher dans une armoire,** we made him hide in a cupboard; **c'est moi qui les ai fait se connaître,** it was I who introduced them to each other; **je le fis s'arrêter,** I made him stop; **cette réponse fit se demander à Marie si elle n'était pas en train de rêver,** this answer made Mary wonder whether she was not dreaming. **2.** (*the noun or pron. is the object of the inf.*) (*a*) **f. bâtir une maison,** to have, to get, a house built; **f. f. deux exemplaires,** to have two copies made; **faites-le réparer,** get it mended; **je les ai fait tous relier,** I have had them all bound; **je le fis arrêter,** I had him arrested; **f. accepter qch.,** to secure acceptance of sth.; to get sth. accepted; (*b*) **se f.** + *inf.*; **se f. photographier,** to have, *F:* get, oneself photographed, to have one's photograph taken; **se f. connaître,** (i) to make oneself known, to reveal one's identity; (ii) to become known; **un bruit se fit entendre,** a noise was heard; **il peut à peine se f. comprendre,** he can hardly make himself understood; **ne vous faites pas tant prier,** don't take so much asking; **il ne se le fit pas dire deux fois,** he did not need to be told twice; **je me suis fait couper les cheveux,** I have had my hair cut; **il se faisait lire le journal par sa femme,** he got his wife to read the paper to him; **il s'est fait punir,** he's got himself punished; **il se faisait respecter de tous,** he commanded everyone's respect. **3. f. qch. à, par, qn,** to cause, get, s.o. to do sth.; to get, have, sth. done by s.o.; **il fit lâcher prise à son adversaire,** he made his opponent let go; **faites-lui lire cette lettre,** get him to read, make him read, this letter; **je la lui ai fait lire,** (i) I got him to read it, I made him read it; (ii) I had it read to him; **vous ne leur ferez jamais f. cela,** you will never bring them, get them, induce them, to do that; **qui est-ce qui vous a fait f. cela?** who put you up to this?; **je lui ai fait observer que . . .,** I called his attention to the fact that . . .; **faites-lui comprendre que . . .,** give him to understand that . . .; **on ne peut pas f. comprendre à tout le monde que . . .,** one cannot bring everybody to understand that . . .; **on m'a fait croire que . . .,** I was led to believe that . . .; **je lui fais f. un pardessus par votre tailleur,** I am having an overcoat made for him by your tailor; **je le ferai examiner par un médecin,** I shall have him examined by a doctor; **f. porter la lettre par la domestique,** to ask the maid to take the letter; **f. raccommoder la boîte par le menuisier,** to get the joiner to mend the box; to get, have, the box mended by the joiner.

VIII. **faire,** *s.m.* **1.** doing, making (of sth.); **il y a loin du f. au dire,** saying is one thing, doing is another. **2.** *Art: Lit:* technique; handling; **tableau d'un f. libre et élégant,** picture of free and elegant execution.

se faire. 1. to become; (*a*) to develop, mature; **jeune fille qui se fait,** girl who is developing, whose character is developing; **ce fromage se fera,** this cheese will ripen; **son style se fait,** his style is forming; (*b*) to become; **se f. vieux,** to become, grow, get, old; **il se sont faits plus aimables,** they have become more amiable; **les murmures se faisaient plus forts,** the murmurs became louder; **se f. soldat,** to become, *F:* go for, a soldier; **se f. catholique,** to turn Roman Catholic; **se f. agriculteur,** to turn farmer, to go in for farming; **la nuit se fait,** it is getting, growing, dark; night is falling; (*c*) to adapt oneself; **se f. à qch.,** to get used, accustomed, to sth.; **nous nous faisons à tout,** we get, become, used to anything; **se f. à la fatigue,** to become inured to fatigue; **fait à la misère,** inured to hardship; **vous vous ferez bientôt à nos habitudes,** you will soon drop into our ways; **vous vous y ferez,** you will get into the way of it; **souliers qui se feront,** shoes that will wear to the shape of the feet; *Mec.E:* **permettre aux engrenages de se f.,** to run in the gears; (*d*) *Nau:* **le courant se fait,** the current makes; **la mer, le vent, se fait,** the sea, the wind, is getting up. **2.** *impers.* (*a*) **il se fait tard,** it is growing late; (*b*) **il se fit un long silence,** a long silence followed, ensued; **comment cela se fait-il?** how does that happen? how does it come about? *esp. U.S:* how come? **comment se fait-il que vous soyez en retard?** how is it that you are late? **3. il est venu voir ce qui se faisait,** he came to see what was happening, doing; **ces dames savent tout ce qui se fait les unes chez les autres,** these ladies know all each other's business; **le miracle s'est fait tout seul,** the miracle came about by itself; **le mariage ne se fera pas,** the marriage will not take place, *F:* will not come off; *F:* the marriage is off.

faire-part [fɛrpaːr], *s.m.inv.* announcement (of birth, death, marriage, etc.); **f.-p. de naissance, de décès,** printed letter announcing s.o.'s birth, death; **f.-p. de mariage,** invitation card to a wedding, wedding card; (*of a funeral*) **le présent avis tiendra lieu de f.-p.,** friends will accept this, the only intimation.

faire-valoir [fɛrvalwaːr], *s.m. inv.* **1.** development; **exploitation en f.-v. direct,** owner farm. **2.** *Th: etc:* foil (to another actor, clown, etc.).

fair-play [fɛrplɛ], *s.m.inv. F:* fair play; **il est f.-p.,** he plays fair.

faisabilité [fəzabilite], *s.f.* feasibility.

faisable [fəzabl̩], *a.* practicable, feasible; achievable; that can be made, done.

faisan [fɛzɑ̃, fə-], *s.m.* **1.** (**coq**) **f.,** (cock) pheasant; **f. doré,** golden pheasant; **f. de chasse,** pheasant (*phasianus colchicus*); **f. de chasse de Chine,** Chinese ring-necked pheasant; **f. bruyant,** grouse. **2.** *P:* crook.

faisances [fɛzɑ̃ːs, fə-], *s.f.pl.* dues in kind paid by tenant farmer over and above his rent.

faisandage [fɛzɑ̃daːʒ, fə-], *s.m. Cu:* hanging (of meat, *esp.* game); allowing (of meat *esp.* game) to get high.

faisandé [fɛzɑ̃de, fə-], *a.* (*a*) high, gamy (meat); (*b*) *F:* spicy (story); (*c*) *F:* decadent (literature, aristocracy, etc.).

faisandeau, -eaux [fɛzɑ̃do, fə-], *s.m.* young pheasant, pheasant poult.

faisander [fɛzɑ̃de, fə-], *v.tr.* **1.** *Cu:* to hang (meat, *esp.* game). **2.** *P:* to cheat.

se faisander, to get high.

faisanderie [fɛzɑ̃dri, fə-], *s.f.* pheasantry, pheasant preserve.

faisandier, -ière [fɛzɑ̃dje, -jɛːr; fə-]. **1.** *a.* pheasant (tribe, etc.). **2.** *s.* pheasant breeder.

faisane [fɛzan, fə-], *s.f.* (**poule**) **f.,** hen pheasant.

faisceau, -eaux [fɛso], *s.m.* (*a*) bundle (of sticks, etc.); *Anat:* fasciculus, bundle, bunch (of fibres); *Rom.Ant:* **f. de verges,** fasces (of lictor); **f. d'ampoules électriques,** cluster of electric bulbs; **f. de fils,** wiring harness; *Arch:* **colonne en f.,** clustered column; *El:* **f. aimanté,** compound magnet, bunch of magnets; *Geol:* **f. de failles,** group of faults; *Mch:* **f. tubulaire,** nest of boiler-tubes, tube stack, tube bank; *Mec.E:* **f. de ressorts,** nest of springs, cluster spring; *Metall:* **fer en f.,** faggot-iron; *Mil:* **f. d'armes,** pile (of arms); **former les faisceaux,** to pile arms; **rompre les faisceaux,** to unpile arms; **aux faisceaux!** fall in! (*b*) *Opt:* beam; **f. lumineux, de lumière,** pencil of rays; **f. parallèle,** parallel beam; **f. d'un phare,** beam of a lighthouse, of a headlight; **se trouver en plein dans le f. des projecteurs,** to find oneself full in the beam of the searchlights; *Aut:* **f. de croisement européen,** Continental dipping beam unit; (*c*) *Rail:* **f. de voies,** group of sidings, gridiron; (*d*) *Artil: Ball:* **f. (de trajectoires, de tir),** sheaf (of trajectories, of fire); (*e*) *Elcs:* **f. hertzien,** wireless beam, micro-wave link; *T.V:* **f. cathodique explorateur,** scanning electron beam; **f. électronique,** electron beam; **f. radar,** radar beam; **f. cathodique,** cathode ray; **f. sonore,** sound beam; **commutation de f.,** beam switching; **tension de f.,** beam voltage; **ouverture de f.,** beam width; **vacillement, balancement, du f.,** beam jitter; *Ball:* **guidage par f.,** beam rider (guidance); *Av:* **f. de radiophare de balisage,** localiser beam.

faiseur, -euse [fəzœːr, -øːz], *s.* **1.** (*now frequently Pej:*) maker, doer; **f. de dentelles,** lace-maker; **f. de miracles,** miracle worker; **f. d'affaires,** financier "on the make," company promoter; **f. de tours,** mountebank; **f. de projets,** schemer; **bon f., bonne faiseuse,** first-rate workman, workwoman; **chapeau du bon f.,** hat from a good hatter; **f. de mariages,** matchmaker; **f. d'horoscopes,** caster of horoscopes; **f. de systèmes,** spinner of theories; **f. d'embarras,** *F:* fuss-pot. **2.** *F:* bluffer, humbug.

faisselle [fɛsɛl], *s.f.* cheese drainer, cheese basket.

fait[1] [fɛ], *a.* fully developed; **cheval f.,** fully developed and trained horse; **homme f.,** (i) (full-)grown man; (ii) man of ripe experience; **fromage f.,** ripe cheese; **temps f.,** settled weather; **mer faite,** grown sea; **vent f.,** steady wind.

fait[2] [fɛ *and sometimes* fɛt], *s.m.* **1.** act, deed, feat, achievement; **faits et dits,** sayings and doings; **f. d'armes,** feat of arms; **revenir sur ses anciens faits d'armes,** to fight one's battles over again; **cela est du f. d'un tel,** this is so-and-so's doing; *Lit:* **ce n'est pas le f. d'un chevalier de,** it does not become a knight to; **c'est le f. d'un homme mal élevé,** it is the act of an ill-bred man; **prendre qn sur le f.,** to catch s.o. in the act, redhanded; **se porter à des voies de f.,** to resort to force, to violence; **parler n'était pas son f.,** he was no talker; talking was not his line; **la vanité n'est pas son f.,** there is no vanity about him; **dire son f. à qn,** to talk straight to s.o., to pitch into s.o., to give s.o. a piece of one's mind; **elle lui a dit son f.,** she told him what she thought of him; **de son f.,** of its, one's own accord; **ce n'est pas de son f.,** it is not like him, her; *s.a.* CHARGE 5, GESTE[2] 2. **2.** (*a*) fact; **f. accompli, situation, état, de f.,** accomplished fact, definite situation; **mettre qn devant le f. accompli,** to present s.o. with a fait accompli; **possession de f.,** actual possession; **le f. de travailler,** the fact of working; **les faits d'une cause,** the facts of a case; **prendre f. et cause pour qn,** to take up the cudgels for s.o., to side wholeheartedly with s.o.; to stand up for s.o.; *F:* to stick up for s.o.; **ceci est un f.,** this is a (matter of) fact; **roi de nom plutôt que de f.,** king in name rather than in fact; **il est de f. que** + *ind.*, it is a fact that . . .; **aller droit au f.,** to go straight to the point; **en venir au f.** (*A:* **et au prendre**), **arriver au f.,** to come to the point; *F:* to get down to brass tacks; **quand on en vint, quand c'est venu, au f. et au prendre . . .,** when it came to the point . . .; **être au f. de la question,** to be acquainted with the facts of the matter, to know how things stand; **être entièrement au f. des derniers événements,** to be well posted up in recent events; **mettre qn au f.,** to give s.o. full information, to make s.o. acquainted with the facts, to acquaint s.o. with the situation; **mettre qn au f. d'un secret,** to let s.o. into a secret; **vous voilà maintenant au f.,** now you know all about it; **se mettre au f. des événements,** to make oneself acquainted with events; **mettre, poser, qch. en f.,** to lay sth. down as a fact; *adv.phr.* (i) **au f., que venez-vous faire ici?** in fact, what have you come here for? (ii) **en f., par le f., dans le f., de f.,** as a matter of fact, in point of fact, in actual fact; in reality, actually; **de f. je ne la trouve pas si sotte,** as a matter of fact I don't think she's such a fool; **de f. cela est un refus,** that is in effect a refusal, that is tantamount to a refusal; to all intents and purposes that is a refusal; (iii) **de ce f.,** thereby, on that account, because of this; **du f. que,** owing to the fact that; **par le f. de . . .,** owing to, because of . . .; **du, par le, seul f. de, que, . . .,** by the mere fact of, that, . . .; merely, simply, only, by . . .; *prep.phr.* **en f. de,** as regards; **en fait d'argent il est des plus insouciants,** in money matters he is most careless; **qu'est-ce que vous avez en f. de rôti?** what have you in the way of a joint? *s.a.* TOUT IV, 1; (*b*) occurrence, happening; **lors de ces faits . . .,** at the time of these occurrences . . .; **ces faits sont assez rares,** these occurrences are few; this seldom happens, seldom occurs; **ces faits ont été observés plus d'une fois,** these things have been noted, this has been known to happen, more than once; **un f. nouveau se produisit,** there was a new development. **3.** *Jur:* **le f. du prince,** restraint of princes.

faîtage [fɛtaːʒ], *s.m. Const:* **1.** ridge-board, -pole; crest (of roof); roof-tree. **2.** ridge tiling, ridge sheathing. **3.** roof timbers or girders. **4.** *Rail: Veh:* sheet supporter (of uncovered truck, etc.).

fait-divers [fedivɛːr], *s.m. Journ:* paragraph, news item; *pl. faits-divers.*

fait-diversier [fedivɛrsje], *s.m. A: Journ:* (news) par writer; *pl. fait-diversiers.*

faîte [fɛ(ː)t], *s.m.* **1.** (*a*) *Const:* ridge (of roof); **poutre de f.,** ridge-pole; (*b*) *Geog:* crest; **ligne de f.,** watershed, crest line; (*c*) *Min:* roof (of a level). **2.** top, summit (of house, tree, etc.); *F:* **le f. de la gloire,** the pinnacle, topmost height, of glory; the acme of glory; **il est plus agréable de monter que de se trouver sur le f.,** it's pleasanter to climb than to be at the top.

faîteau, -eaux [fɛto], *s.m. Const:* **1.** finial. **2.** ornamental ridge-tile.

faîtière [fetjɛːr], *a.f. & s.f. Const:* **(tuile) f.,** ridge tile, arris tile, crest tile; **(lucarne) f.,** skylight; **(panne) f.,** ridge pole, ridge purlin.

faitout [fɛtu], *s.m.*, **fait-tout** [fɛtu], *s.m.inv. Dom. Ec:* stewpan, braising pan.

faix [fɛ], *s.m.* **1.** (*a*) weight, burden, load; **le f. des années,** the weight of years; **le f. des impôts,** the burden of taxation; (*b*) *Obst:* the fœtus (in the womb). **2.** *Nau:* head bolt rope; **raban de f.,** roband; **ralingue de f. d'une tente,** ridge rope of an awning.

fakir [fakiːr], *s.m.* fakir.

fakirisme [fakirism], *s.m.* the art and activities of a fakir.

falaise [falɛːz], *s.f.* cliff; **f. littorale,** sea cliff; **f. de glace,** ice barrier; ice cliff; **f. morte,** abandoned, ancient, cliff; **f. d'éboulement, fausse f.,** undercliff, secondary cliff.

falaisien, -ienne [falɛzjɛ̃, -jɛn], *a. & s. Geog:* (native, inhabitant) of Falaise.

falarique [falarik], *s.f. A.Mil:* phalarica.

Falaschas [falaʃa], *s.m.pl. Ethn:* Falashas.

falbalas [falbala], *s.m.pl. Cost:* (*usu. Pej:*) furbelows, flounces, falbala; **jupe à f.,** flounced skirt.

falbalasser [falbalase], *v.tr.* (*rare*) to trim (dress, etc.) with furbelows.

falciforme [falsifɔrm], *a. Anat: Bot:* falciform, falcate, sickle-shaped.

falconelle [falkɔnɛl], *s.f. Orn:* falconet.

falconidés [falkɔnide], *s.m.pl. Orn:* Falconidae.

falconiformes [falkɔnifɔrm], *s.m.pl. Orn:* Falconiformes.

falculaire [falkylɛːr], *a.* sickle-shaped.

Falériés [faleri], *Pr.n. A.Geog:* Falerii.

falerne [falɛrn], *s.m.* Falernian (wine).

falisque [falisk], *A.Geog:* (*a*) *a.* Faliscan; (*b*) *s.pl.* the Falisci.

fallacieusement [falasjøzmɑ̃], *adv.* fallaciously.

fallacieux, -ieuse [falasjø, -jøːz], *a.* fallacious, deceptive, misleading; **arguments f.,** special pleading.

falle [fal], *s.f. Fr.C:* crop (of bird); chest (of animal).

falloir [falwaːr], *v. impers. def.* (no *pr.p.*; *p.p.* **fallu**; *pr.ind.* **il faut**; *pr.sub.* **il faille**; *p.d.* **il fallait**; *p.h.* **il fallut**; *p.sub.* **il fallût**; *fu.* **il faudra**; *condit.* **il faudrait**) **1.** to be wanting, lacking, necessary, requisite; **il lui faut un nouveau pardessus,** he needs a new overcoat; **avez-vous tout ce qu'il (vous) faut?** have you got all you want, need? **il faut beaucoup d'eau à cette plante,** the plant requires a great deal of water; **faut-il de tout cela?** is all that necessary? **c'est juste ce qu'il (me) faut,** that's the very thing (I want); **que vous faut-il?** what do you require? **ce ne sont pas là les outils qu'il me faut,** those are not the right tools; **voilà ce qu'il vous faut,** here is the very thing you want, the very thing for you; **voilà l'homme qu'il faut,** he's the very man (for the job); *F:* **il faut ce qu'il faut!** hang the expense! **nous en avons plus qu'il ne nous en faut,** we have more than we need; **il lui faut du temps pour se décider,** it takes him some time to make up his mind; **il m'a fallu trois jours pour le faire,** it took me three days to do it; **combien vous faut-il pour me conduire à X?** (i) how much do you want; (ii) how long will it take you, to drive me to X? **il faudrait des volumes, des heures, pour raconter . . .,** it would take volumes, hours, to relate . . .; **il a fallu les horreurs de la guerre pour nous ouvrir les yeux,** it needed the horrors of war to open our eyes; **c'est plus qu'il n'en faut,** that's more than enough; **je ferai tout ce qu'il faudra,** I shall do everything necessary; **il a tout ce qu'il faut pour réussir,** he has everything he needs to be a success; *F:* he's got what it takes to succeed; **s'en f.,** to be lacking, wanting; **il s'en faut de beaucoup,** it falls far short of it; **il s'en faut de deux francs,** it is two francs short; **il s'en faut d'un mètre qu'il m'ait donné la mesure,** he has given me three feet short measure; **s'en faut-il de beaucoup?** is there much lacking? is it far short? **je ne suis pas satisfait, il s'en faut de beaucoup, tant s'en faut,** I am not satisfied, far from it, not by any means, not by a long way; *F:* not by a long chalk; **il s'en faut de beaucoup qu'il soit heureux,** he is far from happy; **bien s'en faut qu'il soit artiste,** he is far from being an artist; **il s'en faut de beaucoup qu'il soit à même de jouer vos accompagnements,** he's nothing like good enough to play your accompaniments; **il s'en est fallu de peu qu'il ne mourût,** it was touch and go whether he died; **il s'en faut de beaucoup que l'autobus (ne) soit plein,** the bus is far from being full; **il s'en faut qu'il (ne) soit aussi bon,** he, it, is not nearly as good, so good (as); **il s'en est fallu de peu qu'il n'ait été écrasé,** he was very nearly run over, he came near to, he was within an ace of, being run over; **peu s'en faut,** very nearly; **c'est la même chose ou peu s'en faut,** it is the same or nearly so, or near it, or not far from it; **cinq livres ou peu s'en faut,** the best part of £5; **il s'en est fallu de peu,** it was a near thing; **peu s'en faut, il s'en faut de peu, qu'il ne soit tombé,** he nearly fell, almost fell, had a narrow escape from falling; **peu s'en fallut qu'il ne pleurât,** he almost cried; he all but cried; **peu s'en fallut qu'il ne se tuât,** he was within an ace of being killed; **il s'en est fallu de rien qu'il (ne) fût écrasé,** he was within an ace of being run over; **il s'en faut de peu qu'il accepte,** he is more than half inclined to accept; *adj.phr. & adv.phr.* **comme il faut,** proper(ly); **se conduire comme il faut,** to behave in a proper, gentlemanly, manner; *Iron:* to behave in a genteel manner; **un jeune homme très comme il faut,** a very gentlemanly young man; **elle est très comme il faut,** (i) she is very well-bred; (ii) she is very prim and proper; (iii) *Iron:* she is very genteel; **ce sont des gens très comme il faut,** they move in the right circles; **votre toilette est tout à fait comme il faut,** your dress is just right, perfect. **2.** (*a*) **f.** + *inf.*, **f. que** + *sub.*, to be necessary; **il faut partir,** I, we, you, etc., must start; **il faut dire qu'il s'est bien comporté,** I am bound to say he behaved well; **il nous faut le voir, il faut que nous le voyions,** we must see him; (*with pron. vbs. in the inf. the dat. of the first and second persons is not expressed*); **il faut nous dépêcher,** we must hurry; *but* **il lui faut se dépêcher,** he must hurry); **il faudra marcher plus vite,** we shall have to walk faster; **il m'a fallu y renoncer,** I had to give it up; **il fallait porter plainte,** you should, ought to, have made a complaint; **il fallait voir ça!** you ought to have seen it! **il fallait le dire!** why didn't you say so? **il fallait que mon visage lui plût, car . . .,** it must have been that he liked my face, for . . .; **il n'aurait pas fallu attendre,** you ought not to have waited; **il faut qu'il ait été fâché pour avoir dit cela,** he must have been angry to have said that; *F:* **faut-il qu'il soit bête!** well, he *is* a fool! **il n'y a pas de train, il (nous) faudra faire le trajet à pied,** there is no train, so we shall have to walk; **il faut vous méfier,** you must be on your guard; *F:* **c'est ce qu'il faudra voir!** we must see about that! we shall have to see about that! **il faudra que je lui en parle,** I shall have to speak to him about it, I must speak to him about it; **faut-il le faire ou non? faut-il que je le fasse ou non?** am I to do it or not? **la police a arrêté l'homme qu'il ne fallait pas,** the police have arrested the wrong man; **il ne faut pas être un génie pour faire cela,** it does not need a genius to do that; **il faudrait être peintre pour . . .,** one would have to be a painter to . . .; **il faut voir ca!** that's worth seeing! *P:* **faut voir!** you should see it! **c'est simple, mais il fallait y penser,** its simple once you've thought of it; **il faut l'entendre,** you should hear him; **il a fallu qu'elle apprenne cet accident!** she *had* to hear of *that* accident! **il faut les féliciter tous les deux,** they are both to be congratulated; **au-delà des champs se trouvait un bois par lequel il lui fallait passer, qu'il lui fallait traverser,** beyond the fields was a wood which he had to cross; **flanque-lui une taloche.—faut-il vraiment?** box his ears.—am I to really? shall I really? **il ne faudrait pas que je les rencontre,** it would never do for me to meet them, to bump into them; **il ne faut pas que cela continue ainsi,** things mustn't go on, continue, like that; **il ne faut pas y aller,** (i) you must not go there; (ii) you are not supposed to go there; **il ne fallait pas y aller,** you, he, she, they, should not have gone there; **il faut toujours qu'il parle quand on ne lui demande rien,** he *will* (always) talk out of turn; (*b*) (*with* **le** = *noun-clause*); **il viendra s'il le faut,** he will come if need be, if necessary, if needs must, if required; **vous dites que vous ne viendrez pas? vous verrez qu'il le faudra bien,** you say you won't come? you will see that you will have to, that you will be obliged, compelled to; **le** *is occ. omitted*; **vous êtes revenu à pied?—il a bien fallu,** you walked back?—there was nothing else for it.

falot¹ [falo], *s.m.* **1.** (hand) lantern; (stable) lamp; *A: Mil:* **f. de ronde,** guard-house lantern. **2.** *P:* court martial.

falot², -ote [falo, -ɔt], *a.* **1.** (*a*) *O:* quaint, curious, queer, droll, odd (person, idea); (*b*) colourless (person). **2.** wan (light); colourless (style).

falourde [falurd], *s.f.* large faggot (of firewood).

falque [falk], *s.f. Nau:* wash strake (of boat).

falqué [falke], *a. Nat.Hist: etc:* falcate.

falquet [falkɛ], *s.m. Orn:* hobby.

falsifiable [falsifjabl̩], *a.* falsifiable; forgeable (document, etc.).

falsificateur, -trice [falsifikatœːr, -tris], *s.* falsifier; forger (of documents); adulterator (of food, etc.).

falsification [falsifikasjɔ̃], *s.f.* falsification; forgery, faking (of documents, etc.); adulteration (of food, etc.); **f. de registres,** tampering with registers.

falsifier [falsifje], *v.tr.* (*p.d. & pr.sub.* **n. falsifiions, v. falsifiiez**) to falsify (text, etc.); to tamper with (register, etc.); to forge, fake (document, etc.); **f. les comptes,** to falsify, *F:* doctor, cook, fake, the accounts; **f. du lait,** to adulterate milk; **monnaie falsifiée,** spurious coins.

faluche [falyʃ], *s.f.* **1.** *Dial:* a kind of bread. **2.** student's beret.

falun [falœ̃], *s.m. Geol:* faluns; *Agr:* shell marl.

faluner [falyne], *v.tr. Agr:* to manure (ground) with shell marl.

falunière [falynjɛːr], *s.f.* shell-marl pit.

falzar [falzaːr], *s.m. P:* (pair of) trousers; *Mil: F:* slacks.

Famagouste [famagust], *Pr.n. Geog:* Famagusta.

famatinite [famatinit], *s.f. Miner:* famatinite.

famé [fame], *a.* **bien, mal, f.,** of good, evil, repute; **mal f.,** ill-famed.

famélique [famelik]. **1.** *a.* famished-looking; half-starved; **chaton f.,** starveling kitten. **2.** *s.* poor starving creature, starveling.

famennien [famɛnjɛ̃], *a. & s.m. Geol:* Famennian (strata, etc.).

fameusement [famøzmɑ̃], *adv.* famously; *F:* **on s'est f. amusé,** we had a whale of a time.

fameux, -euse [famø, -øːz], *a.* **1.** famous; **f. dans l'histoire,** famous, celebrated, renowned, in history; **rocher f. par cent naufrages,** rock notorious for (many) wrecks. **2.** *F:* **fameuse idée,** splendid idea; **vous êtes un f. menteur!** you are a heck of a liar! **c'est une fameuse canaille,** he's an out-and-out scoundrel; **un f. dîner,** a first-rate, slap-up, dinner; **vous commettez une fameuse erreur,** you are making a (mighty) big mistake; **ce n'est pas f.,** it isn't up to much.

familial, -iaux [familjal, -jo]. **1.** *a.* family (life, ties, etc.); **salle familiale,** living-room; *Adm:* **allocation familiale,** family allowance; *Med:* **maladie familiale,** hereditary disease; *Psy:* **test des attitudes familiales,** family attitudes test; *Com:* **en pot f.,** in a family-size jar; *Adm:* **placement f. des enfants,** placing of children in foster-homes. **2.** *Aut:* *s.f.* **familiale,** seven-seater saloon; estate car, station wagon.

familiariser [familjarize], *v.tr.* to familiarize; **f. qn à, avec, qch.,** to make s.o. used to, accustomed to, familiar with, sth.

se familiariser. 1. to familiarize oneself, make oneself familiar (**avec,** with); **se f. avec une langue,** to master a language. **2.** to grow familiar; to make over-free.

familiarité [familjarite], *s.f.* familiarity; (*a*) **être d'une grande f. avec qn,** to be on terms of great familiarity, intimacy, with s.o.; **être admis dans la f. des grands,** to be intimate with the great; *F:* to hob-nob with the great; *Prov:* **la f. engendre le mépris,** familiarity breeds contempt; (*b*) **prendre trop de familiarités avec qn,** to be too familiar, to take liberties, with s.o.; **familiarités de style,** familiarities of style.

familier, -ière [familje, -jɛːr], *a.* **1.** domestic, of the family, familiar; **dieux familiers,** household gods; **esprit f.,** familiar spirit. **2.** familiar; (*a*) **être f. avec qn,** to be on familiar terms, to be intimate, with s.o.; **prendre des airs trop familiers,** to be over-familiar; **expression familière,** colloquial expression; colloquialism; **animal f.,** pet (animal); *s.* **un des familiers de la maison,** a regular frequenter of the house; an intimate friend of the family; (*b*) **visage qui lui est f.,** face which is familiar, well-known, to him; **cette question lui est familière,** he is familiar with, he

is at home in, with, this subject; **cet auteur nous les a rendus familiers,** this author has made us familiar with them; **le mensonge lui est f.,** he is a habitual liar; **il refit encore une fois le voyage f.,** he made once again the familiar journey; **être f. avec les problèmes d'après-guerre,** to be conversant with post-war problems.

familièrement [familjɛrmɑ̃], *adv.* familiarly; **vivre f. avec qn,** to live on familiar terms with s.o.

familistère [familistɛːr], *s.m.* **1.** *Hist. of Pol.Ec:* phalanstery. **2.** workers' co-operative association (mainly in North and East of France).

famille [famiːj], *s.f.* **1.** (*a*) family; household; **la f. Martin,** the Martin family; **elle a une f. de six enfants,** she has a family of six; **a-t-il de la f.?** has he any family? **il faut que je vous présente à ma f.,** I must introduce you to (i) my people (= parents), (ii) my family (= wife and children); **j'ai de la f. à Bourges,** I have relatives at Bourges; **affaire de f.,** family matter; **charges de famille,** dependants; **allocation, indemnité, pour charges de f.,** family allowance; **chef de f.,** (i) head of the family; (ii) householder, head of the household; **soutien de f.,** breadwinner; **fils de f.,** young man of good social position; **garçon de bonne f.,** young man with a good background; **il y a entre eux un air de f.,** there is a family likeness between them; **rentrer dans sa f.,** to go home (after absence, from school, etc.); **en f.,** as a family party; **dîner en f.,** to dine at home (informally) with one's family; **avec eux je me sens en f.,** I feel quite at home with them; **cela tient, vient, de f.,** it runs in the family, in the blood; **la f. des Bourbons,** the family, race, house, of the Bourbons; **entrer dans une f. de négociants,** to marry into a family of merchants; **chez lui cela tient de f.,** in his case it is bred in the bone; **pension, maison, de f.,** (small) boarding house; (*b*) *Jur:* next of kin; **prévenir la f.,** to inform the next of kin. **2. f. de mots, de plantes,** family of words, of plants; *Mth:* **f. de courbes,** family of curves; *Atom.Ph:* **f. radioactive,** radioactive series, family; decay chain; **f. de l'uranium,** uranium series; *Ch:* **f. collatérale,** collateral family, series, chain.

famine [famin], *s.f.* famine, starvation; **prendre, réduire, une ville par la f.,** to starve out a town; **crier f.,** to complain that one is starving; to complain (of hard times); **crier f. sur un tas de blé,** to cry hunger in the midst of plenty; **salaire de f.,** starvation wages.

fan [fan], *s.m. F:* (*of pers.*) (*football, etc.*) fan.

fana [fana], *a. & s.m. & f. P:* enthusiast(ic), *s.* fan; **il est f., c'est un f.,** he's got it on the brain.

fanage[1] [fanaːʒ], *s.m.* tedding, tossing (of hay).

fanage[2], *s.m.* (*a*) (dried or green) leaves (for litter, etc.); litter; (*b*) haulm (of potatoes, etc.).

fanaison [fanɛzɔ̃], *s.f. Hort:* drooping, withering (of flowers, leaves, etc.).

fanal, -aux [fanal, -o], *s.m.* (*a*) lantern, lamp, light; **f. sourd,** dark lantern; **f. morse,** morse blinker light; **f. à, de, signaux,** signal(ling) lamp, lantern, light; **tourelle de f.,** lighthouse; **lumière sans f.,** naked light; *Rail: etc:* **f. de tête,** headlight (of locomotive); (*b*) beacon light; (*c*) *Nau:* (ship's) navigation light, side light; **f. de bord,** ship's lantern; **f. d'embarcation,** boat lamp; **f. portatif,** portable light.

fanariote [fanarjɔt], *s.m. & f.* Phanariot, Fanariot.

fanatique [fanatik]. **1.** *a.* fanatic(al); bigoted; **zèle f.,** fanatical zeal; **être f. de qn, de qch.,** to be a zealous, an enthusiastic, admirer or supporter of s.o., of sth.; **c'est un pêcheur fanatique,** he's an enthusiastic, a keen, fisherman; he's mad on fishing. **2.** *s.* fanatic, zealot, enthusiast; **les fanatiques du football,** football fans; **les fanatiques du bridge,** bridge fiends.

fanatiquement [fanatikmɑ̃], *adv.* fanatically.

fanatiser [fanatize], *v.tr.* to fanaticize; to make a fanatic of (s.o.).

fanatisme [fanatism], *s.m.* fanaticism, zealotry.

fanchon [fɑ̃ʃɔ̃]. **1.** *Pr.n.f.* Fanny (a heroine of folk-song, a good sort and not over-shy). **2.** *s.f.* head scarf.

fandango [fɑ̃dɑ̃go], *s.m. Danc:* fandango.

fane [fan], *s.f.* **1.** (*a*) haulm (of potatoes, etc.); (*b*) **fanes de navets,** turnip tops. **2.** grass drying for hay. **3.** *Bot:* involucre (of buttercup, etc.).

faner [fane], *v.tr.* **1.** to ted, toss (hay). **2.** to make (flowers, colours, etc.) fade; **étoffe fanée par le soleil,** material faded by the sun; **seins fanés,** shrunken breasts; **beauté fanée,** faded beauty, beauty that has lost its freshness.

se faner, (*of flowers, etc.*) to droop, wither, wilt, fade; (*of colours, etc.*) to fade.

faneur, -euse [fanœːr, -øːz], *s.* **1.** *Agr:* (*pers.*) tedder. **2.** *s.f.* **faneuse,** tedding machine, tedder.

fanfan [fɑ̃fɑ̃], *s.m. & f. F:* (*from* **enfant**) small child; *Hist:* **F. la Tulipe,** traditional name for the jolly, amorous, and bibulous soldier of the eighteenth century.

fanfare [fɑ̃faːr], *s.f.* **1.** (*a*) flourish (of trumpets or bugles); **sonner une f.,** to sound a flourish; (*b*) *Ven:* fanfare (on hunting horns); **sonner la f.,** to sound a fanfare. **2.** brass band; *P:* **c'est un sale coup pour la f.,** it's a hell of a blow; **chef de f.,** (i) bandmaster; (ii) *Mil:* (*chasseurs à pied*) bugle major. **3.** *Bookb:* **reliure à la f.,** fanfare binding.

fanfariste [fɑ̃farist], *s.m.* (*rare*) (brass)bandsman.

fanfaron, -onne [fɑ̃farɔ̃, -ɔn]. **1.** *a.* boasting, bragging, swaggering. **2.** *s.* braggart, boaster, swaggerer, swashbuckler; **f. de vices,** flaunter of vices; **faire le f.,** to brag, to bluster.

fanfaronnade [fɑ̃farɔnad], *s.f.* **1.** brag, boasting, swagger, bluster; *F:* bounce. **2.** piece of brag, of boasting, of braggadocio.

fanfaronner [fɑ̃farɔne], *v.i.* to brag, boast, swagger, bluster.

fanfaronnerie [fɑ̃farɔnri], *s.f.* boastfulness, brag, blustering.

fanfreluche [fɑ̃frəlyʃ], *s.f.* **1.** trifle, bauble, trinket. **2.** *pl. Cost:* fallals; frills and furbelows.

fange [fɑ̃ːʒ], *s.f.* mud, mire, filth, muck; **couvrir qn de f.,** to hurl abuse, insults, to throw mud, at s.o.; **la f. du vice,** the slough of vice; **vivre dans la f.,** to live a life of degradation, to live in vice; **il est sorti de la f.,** he rose from the gutter; **bercé dans la f.,** brought up in the gutter, gutter-bred.

fangeux, -euse [fɑ̃ʒø, -øːz], *a.* **1.** miry, muddy. **2.** (*a*) covered with filth; (*b*) filthy (mind, etc.).

fanion [fanjɔ̃], *s.m.* (*a*) *Mil:* (distinguishing) flag; **f. de bataillon, de compagnie,** battalion, company, flag; **f. du général,** general's flag; **f. de commandement,** headquarters flag; **f. d'ambulance,** Red Cross flag; **f. de sécurité, f. signalant un danger,** danger flag; **jalonner une ligne avec des fanions,** to mark out a line with flags; (*b*) **f. de lance,** lance pennon.

fanion-signal [fanjɔ̃siɲal], *s.m. Mil:* signalling flag; *pl. fanions-signaux.*

fanon [fanɔ̃], *s.m.* **1.** (*a*) *A:* pennon (of banner, lance); (*b*) *Nau:* hanging fold, goose-wing (of brailed sail); (*c*) *Ecc:* (i) maniple, fanon; (ii) pendant, lappet, vitta (of mitre). **2.** *Z:* (*a*) dewlap (of ox); (*b*) lappet, wattle (of bird); (*c*) fetlock (of horse). **3.** whalebone, baleen.

fantaisie [fɑ̃tezi], *s.f.* **1.** (*a*) imagination, fancy; **de f.,** imaginary; **portrait de f.,** fanciful portrait; **f. piquante (d'un chapeau),** jauntiness (of a hat); (*b*) *Mus:* (i) fantasia; (ii) **f. sur "Faust,"** selections from "Faust." **2.** (*a*) fancy, desire, whim; **j'ai la f. de me baigner,** I feel like a bathe; **il lui prit la f. d'aller à Brighton,** he had a sudden idea to go to Brighton; **chacun s'amusait à sa f.,** everyone amused himself as the fancy took him, as he pleased; **faire qch. par f.,** to do sth. out of sheer caprice; **se passer la f. de qch.,** to indulge, gratify, one's fancy for sth., to treat oneself to sth.; **articles, prix, (de) f.,** fancy goods, prices; **pain (de) f.,** fancy-bread (*sold by the loaf, not by weight*); **gilet (de) f.,** fancy waistcoat; **bijoux (de) f.,** costume jewellery; (*b*) freakish notion or movement; freak, vagary; **j'en ai assez de ses fantaisies,** I'm tired of his whims.

fantaisiste [fɑ̃tezist]. **1.** *a.* fantastic, whimsical, freakish (artist, writer, work of art). **2.** *s.m. & f.* (*a*) fantasist; (*b*) entertainer; cabaret artiste.

fantasia [fɑ̃tazja], *s.m. Mil: Equit:* fantasia.

fantasmagorie [fɑ̃tasmagɔri], *s.f.* (*a*) phantasmagoria; (*b*) weird spectacle, sight.

fantasmagorique [fɑ̃tasmagɔrik], *a.* (*a*) phantasmagoric(al); (*b*) weird, fantastic.

fantasme [fɑ̃tasm], *s.m.* phantasm, hallucination; *Psy:* fantasy.

fantasque [fɑ̃task], *a.* odd, whimsical (person, idea); temperamental (person).

fantassin [fɑ̃tasɛ̃], *s.m.* foot-soldier, infantryman; **les fantassins,** the infantry, *P:* the P.B.I. (the poor bloody infantry); **quatre cents fantassins,** four hundred infantry, four hundred foot.

fantastique [fɑ̃tastik], *a.* **1.** fantastic, fanciful, imaginary; **lueur f.,** weird, eerie, light. **2. luxe f.** incredible, extravagant, luxury; **histoire f.,** story beyond belief, fantastic yarn. **3.** *s.m.* **le f.,** the uncanny, the fantastic.

fantastiquement [fɑ̃tastikmɑ̃], *adv.* fantastically.

fanti, -ie [fɑ̃ti], *a. & s. Ethn:* Fantee.

fantoche [fɑ̃tɔʃ], *s.m.* **1.** marionette, puppet; **ses personnages sont de purs fantoches,** his characters are mere puppets; *a.* **gouvernement f.,** puppet government. **2.** outrageous fellow; **f. politique,** political jumping jack.

fantomal, -als, -aux [fɑ̃tomal, -o], **fantomatique** [fɑ̃tomatik, fɑ̃tɔ-], *a.* spectral, ghostly, ghost-like, phantasmal.

fantôme [fɑ̃toːm], *s.m.* phantom, ghost, spectre, apparition, spirit; **vaisseau f.,** phantom ship; *Mus: etc:* **le Vaisseau Fantôme,** the Flying Dutchman; **ce n'est plus qu'un f.,** he is a walking skeleton; **c'est un f. de roi,** he is a pale reflection of a king; **fantômes de l'esprit,** mental illusions, phantasms of the mind; **se faire des fantômes,** to create imaginary difficulties; *Pol:* **gouvernement f.,** shadow government; **cabinet f.,** shadow cabinet; *Surg:* **membre f.,** phantom limb; *Tp:* **circuit f.,** phantom circuit; *Elcs:* **image f.,** echo-image.

fanton [fɑ̃tɔ̃], *s.m. Const:* **1.** (*a*) dowel wood, peg wood; (*b*) strip iron. **2.** (*a*) treenail, dowel, pin, peg, plug; (*b*) iron (tie).

fanu [fany], *a.* haulmy, having long haulms or stalks.

fanum [fanɔm], *s.m. Rom.Arch:* fane, temple.

fanure [fanyːr], *s.f.* faded look.

faon [fɑ̃], *s.m.* fawn; roe calf; **f. femelle,** hind calf.

faonner [fane], *v.i.* (*of deer*) to fawn.

faquin [fakɛ̃], *s.m.* low fellow; cad.

faquir [fakiːr], *s.m.* = FAKIR.

farad [farad], *s.m. Meas. El:* farad.

faradique [faradik], *a. El:* faradic (current, etc.).

faradisation [faradizasjɔ̃], *s.f. Med:* faradization, faradism.

faradmètre [faradmɛtr̥], *s.m. El:* faradmeter, faradimeter, faradometer.

faramineux, -euse [faraminø, -øːz], *a. F:* amazing, phenomenal, colossal; **un rhume f.,** an awful cold.

farandole [farɑ̃dɔl], *s.f.* **1.** farandole (popular dance of Provence). **2.** *F:* merry-go-round.

farandoler [farɑ̃dɔle], *v.i.* to dance a farandole.

faraud [faro]. *A:* **1.** *a. F:* vain, affected (counter-jumper, etc.); (youth) toffed up. **2.** *s.m. F:* bumpkin dressed up to kill, to cut a dash; **faire le f.,** to put on side.

farauder [farode], *v.i. A:* to cut a dash; to swank; to tog up, to toff oneself up.

farce [fars], *s.f.* **1.** *Cu:* stuffing; forcemeat. **2.** (*a*) *Th:* farce; **grosse f.,** knock-about farce; **cela tourne à la f.,** this is becoming highly farcical; (*b*) practical joke; prank; **faire des farces à qn,** to play jokes, tricks, pranks, on s.o.; *Com:* **farces et attrapes,** novelties; tricks and jokes; (*c*) **faire des farces,** to run wild; **il a fait ses farces,** he has sown his wild oats; (*d*) *F:* **dire des farces à qn,** to joke with s.o. **3.** *a. A:* funny, comical; **des petits frisons tout à fait farces,** little curls that were really too funny, too quaint; **est-ce assez f.!** what a game!

farceur, -euse [farsœːr, -øːz], *a. & s.* **1.** *s.* practical joker. **2.** *s.* wag, joker, humorist; humbug; **c'est un f. qui vous aura dit cela,** somebody's been pulling your leg. **3.** *s.* dissipated, wild, young man or woman; **se ruiner pour une farceuse,** to ruin oneself over an adventuress. **4.** *a.* given to practical joking; facetious.

farcin [farsɛ̃], *s.m. Vet:* farcy.

farcineux, -euse [farsinø, -øːz], *a. Vet:* farcied (horse); **bouton f.,** farcy bud.

farcir [farsiːr], *v.tr. Cu:* to stuff (poultry, etc., with forcemeat); *F:* **se f. de sucreries,** to stuff, cram, oneself with sweet things; **f. un enfant de latin,** to cram a child with Latin.

se farcir, *P:* **se f. qch.,** (i) to treat oneself to sth.; (ii) to put up with sth.; **se f. qn,** to put up with s.o.

farcot [farko], *s.m. Nau:* steering engine.

fard[1] [faːr], *s.m.* paint, rouge, make-up (for the face); **f. à paupières,** eye shadow; **se mettre du f. aux joues,** to rouge one's cheeks; **sans f.,** without pretence, without disguise, plainly; **la vérité sans f.,** the naked unvarnished, truth; **parler sans f.,** to speak plainly, candidly; *F:* **piquer un f.,** to blush.

fard[2], *s.m. Nau:* sails and yards (of a mast); **f. de grand mât,** mainsails.

fardage[1] [fardaːʒ], *s.m.* (*a*) making up; rougeing; (*b*) *F:* hiding of inferior wares or produce under attractive samples; camouflage (of goods); overfacing (of a basket of apples, etc.).

fardage[2], *s.m. Nau:* **1.** top-hamper (rigging). **2.** dunnage.

farde[1] [fard], *s.f. Com:* bale (of Mocha coffee, of cinnamon, etc.).

farde[2], *s.f. Belg:* file, folder.

fardeau, -eaux [fardo], *s.m.* **1.** burden, load; **le f. des ans,** the weight of years; **c'est un f. qu'il traînera jusqu'à sa mort,** it will be a millstone round his neck till the end of his days; *Jur:* **f. de la preuve,** burden of proof. **2.** *Brew:* mash.

fardeler [fardəle], *v.tr.* (**je fardelle; je fardellerai**) to do up (linen, etc.) into a bundle; to bundle up.

fardeleuse [fard(ə)løːz], *s.f. Tchn:* bundling machine.

farder[1] [farde], *v.tr.* (*a*) to paint; to make (s.o.) up; **visage fardé**, made up face; **f. la vérité**, to gloss, camouflage, disguise, the truth; to put a gloss on the truth; **f. les faits**, to gloss (over) the facts; **f. ses sentiments**, to disguise one's feelings; (*b*) *F:* to hide (inferior wares) under attractive samples; to camouflage (goods); to put the big apples at the top of (the basket), to overface (a basket of apples, etc.).

se farder, to make up, to rouge; to paint one's face.

farder[2], *v.i.* **1.** (*a*) to weigh heavy (**sur**, upon); (*b*) (*of wall, etc.*) to settle (down); to sink. **2.** *Nau:* (*of sails*) to fit, set.

fardier [fardje], *s.m.* trolley, dray, truck, lorry (for carrying building-stones, etc.); *Veh:* log transporter; *For:* bar wheels (for moving logs).

farfadet [farfadɛ], *s.m.* (hob)goblin, brownie; sprite, elf.

farfelu [farfely]. **1.** *s.m. F:* (*a*) whipper-snapper; jerk; (*b*) crazy, irrational, person. **2.** *a. F:* crazy; weird.

farfouillement [farfujmɑ̃], *s.m. F:* rummaging; groping.

farfouiller [farfuje], *v.tr. & i. F:* to rummage (in, among); to grope (among); to explore; **f. (dans) un tiroir**, to rummage about in a drawer.

farfouilleur, -euse [farfujœːr, -øːz], *F:* **1.** *a.* rummaging, searching. **2.** *s.* rummager, searcher.

farfouillis [farfuji], *s.m. F:* rummaging.

fargue [farg], *s.f.* **1.** bow plate, spirketting plate, *U.S:* apron plate. **2.** *pl.* **fargues**, (*a*) wash strakes (of boat); **f. volantes**, washboards; (*b*) *Nau: A:* **f. de sabords**, washboards (of portholes).

farguer[1] [farge], *v.tr.* to fit (boat) with washboards.

farguer[2], *v.i. P: Nau:* (*a*) **f. mal**, to look like a dog's dinner; (*b*) **navire qui fargue bien**, trim ship.

faribole [faribɔl], *s.f.* idle tale; stuff and nonsense; *F:* **fariboles**, moonshine.

faridon [faridɔ̃], *s.f. F:* **faire la f.**, to go on the binge, on a bender; **être de la f.**, to be (stony) broke.

faridondaine [faridɔ̃dɛn], *s.f.*, **faridondon** [faridɔ̃dɔ̃], *s.f.* (*as burden to a song*) **la faridondaine, la faridondon** = tol-de-rol, fol-de-rol-de-rido.

farigoule [farigul], *s.f.* (*in S. of Fr.*) thyme.

farigoulette [farigulɛt], *s.f.* (*in S. of Fr.*) area where wild thyme grows.

farinacé [farinase], *a.* farinaceous, flour-like.

farinage [farinaːʒ], *s.m.* **1.** *Paint:* chalking. **2.** *Mill:* miller's fee.

farine [farin], *s.f.* **1.** flour, meal; **fleur de f.**, pure wheaten flour, whites; **folle f.**, flour dust, mill dust; **f. d'avoine**, oatmeal; **f. de maïs**, cornflour, *U.S:* cornstarch, Indian meal; **f. de lin**, linseed meal; **f. de pois**, pease meal; **f. de riz**, ground rice; **f. de poisson**, fish meal; **f. lactée**, malted milk; *Cu:* **saupoudrer la pâte de f.**, to flour the paste; **mains couvertes de f.**, floury hands; *F:* **ce sont gens de (la) même f.**, they are birds of a feather; they are all of the same kidney, all tarred with the same brush; *Prov:* **d'un sac à charbon ne peut sortir blanche f.**, you can't touch pitch without being defiled; *Ent:* **ver de f.**, meal worm (larva of meal beetle); *F:* **rouler qn dans la f.**, to make a fool of s.o. **2.** *Geol:* **f. fossile**, infusorial earth. **3.** *Mec.E:* **f. de forage**, bore dust.

fariné [farine], *a.* floury, covered with flour; *F:* colourless, pale.

fariner [farine]. **1.** *v.tr. Cu:* to dust, dredge, (sth.) with flour. **2.** *v.i.* to become flour-like, to get mealy.

farinet [farinɛ], *s.m.* **1.** *Fung:* (*a*) clitopilus prunulus; (*b*) hydnum repandum. **2.** *Games:* die marked on one face.

farineux, -euse [farinø, -øːz], *a.* **1.** farinaceous; **aliments f.**, farinaceous foods; **pomme de terre farineuse**, floury, mealy, potato. **2.** covered with flour.

farinier, -ière [farinje, -jɛːr], *s.* **1.** (*a*) *s.m. A:* flour merchant; (*b*) *s.f. A:* **farinière**, flour merchant's wife. **2.** *s.f.* **farinière**, flour bin. **3.** *s.m. F: Fung:* = FARINET.

farlouse [farluːz], *s.f. Orn:* meadow pipit.

farnésol [farnezɔl], *s.m. Toil: Ch:* farnesol.

farniente [farnjɛnte, farnjɑ̃ːt], *s.m. no pl.* (pleasant, luxurious) idleness.

faro [faro], *s.m.* Brussels beer.

faroba [farɔba], *s.m. Bot:* (*a*) locust tree, varnish tree; (*b*) locust wood.

farouch(e)[1] [faruʃ], *s.m. Agr:* (*S. of Fr.*) crimson clover, French clover.

farouche[2], *a.* **1.** fierce, wild, savage (animal, people); **tyran f.**, grim, cruel, tyrant; **femme d'une vertu f.**, aggressively virtuous woman, dragon of virtue. **2.** (*a*) shy, timid, coy (child, etc.); **peu f.**, not shy; (*b*) unsociable.

farouchement [faruʃmɑ̃], *adv.* fiercely, savagely.

farrago [farago], *s.m.* **1.** *Agr:* mixed corn (for feeding). **2.** farrago, (confused) medley.

fart [faːr(t)], *s.m.* wax (for skis).

fartage [fartaːʒ], *s.m.* waxing (of skis).

farter [farte], *v.tr.* to wax (skis).

fasce [fas], *s.f.* **1.** *Arch:* fascia (of column). **2.** *Her:* fess(e).

fascé [fas(s)e], *Her:* fessey.

fascia [fas(s)ja], *s.m. Anat:* fascia, aponeurosis.

fascial, -iaux [fas(s)jal, -jo], *a. Anat:* fascial, aponeurotic.

fasciation [fas(s)jasjɔ̃], *Bot:* fasciation.

fasciculaire [fasikylɛːr], *a.* **1.** *Bot: Z:* (*of hairs, etc.*) fascicular, fasciculate, growing in bunches, in clusters. **2.** *Z:* scopiform.

fascicule [fasikyl], *s.m.* **1.** (*a*) *Pharm:* bunch, bundle (of herbs); (*b*) *Bot: Z:* fascic(u)le, bunch, cluster (of hairs). **2.** instalment, part, section (of publication); **vente par fascicules**, instalment selling; **publier un livre par fascicules**, to publish a book in parts. **3.** *Mil:* **f. de mobilisation**, mobilization instructions (attached to reservist's small book).

fasciculé [fasikyle], *a. Nat.Hist:* fasciculate, growing in bunches, clusters; *Bot:* **racine fasciculée**, fibrous root.

fascié [fas(s)je], *a.* **1.** *Z:* fasciated, banded, striped. **2.** *Bot:* fasciate(d) (stem).

fascinage [fasinaːʒ], *s.m. Civ.E: Fort:* **1.** protection (of river bank, earthworks, etc.) with fascines. **2.** fascine work.

fascinant [fas(s)inɑ̃], **fascinateur, -trice** [fas(s)inatœːr, -tris], *a.* fascinating; *Com:* **prix fascinants**, attractive prices.

fascination [fas(s)inasjɔ̃], *s.f.* fascination; charm.

fascine [fasin], *s.f.* fascine, faggot (of brushwood).

fasciner[1] [fas(s)ine], *v.tr.* (*a*) to fascinate; (*b*) to hypnotize; **se laisser f. par des promesses**, to allow oneself to be drawn on by promises.

fasciner[2], *v.tr. Civ.E: Fort:* to fascine (river bank, earthworks, etc.); *U.S:* to corduroy (road); **route fascinée**, *U.S:* corduroy road.

fascineur [fasinœːr], *s.m. Civ.E:* fascine worker.

fasciola [fasjola], *s.f.inv. Ann:* fasciola.

fasciolaria [fasjolarja], *s.f. Moll:* Fasciolaria.

fasciolariidés [fasjolariide], *s.m.pl. Moll:* Fasciolariidae.

fasciole [fasjɔl], *s.f. Echin:* fasciole.

fascisant, -ante [fasizɑ̃, -ɑ̃ːt, faʃ-], *a. & s. Pol:* pro-Fascist.

fascisme [fasism, faʃ-], *s.m. Pol:* Fascism.

fasciste [fasist, faʃ-], *s.m. Pol:* Fascist.

faséier, faseiller, faseyer [fazeje], *v.i. Nau:* (*of sails*) to shiver, shake.

faséole [fazeɔl], *s.f.* horse bean.

fasiement [fazimɑ̃], *s.m. Nau:* shivering, shaking (of sail).

fasier [fazje], *v.i. Nau:* (*of sails*) to shiver, shake.

fassaïte [fasait], *s.f. Miner:* fassaite.

fassi, -ie [fasi], *a. & s.* (native, inhabitant) of Fez.

faste[1] [fast], *s.m. no pl.* (*a*) ostentation, display; pomp; **mariage sans f.**, quiet wedding; (*b*) *A:* pride.

faste[2], *a.* (*a*) *Rom.Ant:* lawful (day); (*b*) **jour(s) faste(s)**, lucky day(s).

fastes [fast], *s.m.pl.* (*a*) *Rom.Ant:* fasti; (*b*) *A. & Lit:* annals, archives, records (of great deeds, history, etc.).

fastidieusement [fastidjøzmɑ̃], *adv.* tediously; in a dull, wearying, manner; prosily.

fastidieux, -ieuse [fastidjø, -jøːz], *a.* dull, tedious, wearying, wearisome, irksome, tiresome; fulsome (compliments); (food) that palls; **besognes fastidieuses**, drudgery; **orateur f.**, tedious speaker; **discours f.**, dull, boring, speech.

fastigié [fastiʒje], *a. Bot:* fastigiate (tree, etc.).

fastigium [fastiʒjɔm], *s.m. Arch:* fastigium, pediment.

fastueusement [fastɥøzmɑ̃], *adv.* ostentatiously; sumptuously.

fastueux, -euse [fastɥø, -øːz], *a.* ostentatious; showy; sumptuous.

fat [fa(t)]. **1.** *a.* (*the f. form* **fate** *is rare*) (*a*) conceited; self-satisfied; (*b*) *A:* stupid. **2.** *s.m.* (*a*) conceited, self-satisfied, person; (*b*) *A:* miserable wretch.

fatal, -als [fatal], *a.* **1.** fatal; **heure fatale, moment, jour, terme, f.**, fatal hour, hour of death; **coup f.**, deadly, mortal, blow; *Med:* **cancer f., pneumonie fatale**, terminal cancer, pneumonia; **f. à qn**, fatal, disastrous, to s.o.; *Lit:* **les déesses fatales**, the Fates, the Parcae; **femme fatale**, femme fatale. **2.** fated, inevitable, sure to happen; **aboutissement f. d'une action**, inevitable result of an action; **c'est f.**, it is bound to come, bound to happen; **le retardataire f.**, the inevitable latecomer. **3.** *Com:* **terme f.**, last day of grace.

fatalement [fatalmɑ̃], *adv.* fatally; inevitably.

fataliser [fatalize], *v.tr.* **1.** to render (sth.) inevitable. **2.** to put a fatalistic mark upon (doctrine, etc.).

fatalisme [fatalism], *s.m.* fatalism; **avec f.**, fatalistically.

fataliste [fatalist]. **1.** *s.* fatalist. **2.** *a.* fatalistic.

fatalité [fatalite], *s.f.* **1.** fate, fatality; **poursuivi par la f.**, pursued by fate; **c'est la f.!** it's (just) bad luck! **c'est comme une f.!** it is, was, bound to happen! **les fatalités de la guerre**, the hazards of war. **2.** misfortune. **3.** (*casualty*) death.

fatidique [fatidik], *a.* fatidical (number, etc.); fated (hour, encounter); prophetic (utterance, etc.); fateful (word).

fatigabilité [fatigabilite], *s.f.* liability, tendency, to fatigue; fatigability, fatigableness.

fatigable [fatigabl̩], *a.* fatigable, subject to fatigue, easily tired.

fatigant [fatigɑ̃], *a.* **1.** tiring, fatiguing. **2.** tiresome, wearisome; tedious; **un collègue f.**, a (i) tiresome, (ii) boring, colleague; **c'est f. de ne jamais trouver ce qu'on cherche**, it's annoying never to find what one is looking for.

fatigue [fatig], *s.f.* **1.** (*a*) fatigue; tiredness, weariness; **tomber, être mort, de f.**, to be tired out, dead beat; **supporter bien la f.**, to stand up to fatigue, to being tired; **f. nerveuse**, nervous fatigue, exhaustion; **f. cérébrale**, mental fatigue; **f. oculaire**, eyestrain; **la f. de la marche, du cheval**, the fatigue, tiredness, caused by walking, by riding; **se remettre des fatigues du voyage**, to recover from (the strain of) the journey; **la f. des affaires**, the strain of business; **les fatigues de la guerre**, the hardships of war; **tempérament dur à la f.**, tough constitution; (*b*) **souliers de f.**, walking shoes, strong shoes; **habits de f.**, working clothes; **cheval de f.**, cart horse. **2.** straining (of ship); stress, fatigue (of metal); heavy duty (of transmission gear, etc.); *Mec.E:* **pièces de f.**, parts subject to strains; **f. des métaux**, metal fatigue; **défaillance due à la f., rupture par f.**, fatigue failure; **f. acoustique**, acoustic fatigue. **3.** wear and tear (of machines, clothes, etc.); **présenter des traces de f.**, to show signs of wear. **4.** *A:* worry, trouble, anxiety; **ô la grande f. que d'avoir une femme!** what a trial it is to have a wife!

fatigué [fatige], *a.* **1.** (*a*) tired, fatigued; jaded; weary; **il a le cœur f.**, he has a strained heart; **vous êtes f., il faut prendre un congé**, you are run down and need a holiday; **être f. de qch., de faire qch.**, to be tired of sth., of doing sth.; **f. par le voyage**, travel-worn; **f. de rester debout**, tired of standing; **f. d'être resté debout**, tired with standing; **avoir la tête fatiguée**, to suffer from overwork; (*b*) **cheval f.**, worn out, groggy, old horse; (*c*) (*in S. of Fr.*) (i) ill; (ii) *F:* loony. **2.** worn, shabby (clothes, etc.); **livre f.**, well-worn, well-thumbed, book; **câble f.**, worn cable.

fatiguer [fatige]. **1.** *v.tr.* (*a*) to fatigue, tire; to make (s.o.) tired, weary; **ce travail me fatigue**, this work tires me; **f. l'ennemi**, to harass the enemy; **se f. les yeux (à faire qch.)**, to strain one's eyes (doing sth.); *F:* **il ne se fatigue pas les méninges**, he doesn't exactly overwork; *F:* **il me fatigue!** he bores me! **f. le ciel de ses prières**, to weary, importune, heaven with one's prayers; (*b*) to overwork (animal, etc.); to impose a strain on (machine); to overstrain, overdrive (machine, etc.); to strain (ship); **f. un terrain**, to exhaust, impoverish, a piece of ground; **f. un livre**, to give a book hard use, to thumb a book; (*c*) *Nau:* **la mer fatigue le navire**, the ship is labouring; (*d*) **f. la salade**, to mix the salad. **2.** *v.i.* (*a*) to tire oneself; to labour; (*b*) (*of ship, engine*) to labour; **poutre qui fatigue**, beam that bears a heavy strain; *Nau:* (*of ship*) **f. au mouillage**, to ride hard; **ne pas f.**, to ride easy.

se fatiguer, to tire; to get tired; (*of voice, etc.*) to get strained; **se f. de qch.**, to tire, get tired, of sth.; **se f. à faire qch.**, to tire oneself out doing sth.; **se f. à force de danser, de courir, de parler**, to dance, run, talk, oneself tired.

Fatima [fatima], *Pr.n.f.* Fatima.

fatras [fatrɑ], *s.m.* (*a*) jumble, medley, confused mass, hotchpotch (of ideas, events, papers, etc.); (*b*) lumber, rubbish; **esprit encombré d'un f. de connaissances mal assimilées,** mind cluttered up with a mass of half-digested knowledge.

fatrasser [fatrase], *v.i. A: F:* to waste time over trifles, over trash; to potter.

fatrasserie [fatrasri], *s.f. A: F:* **1.** pottering. **2.** collection, jumble, of rubbish.

fatrassier, -ière [fatrasje, -jɛːr], *s. A: F:* **1.** potterer. **2.** hoarder of rubbish.

fatuité [fatɥite], *s.f.* **1.** self-conceit, self-satisfaction, self-complacency. **2.** piece of self-conceit.

fauber(t) [fobɛːr], *s.m. Nau:* (deck-)swab, mop.

fauberder [fobɛrde], **fauberter** [fobɛrte], *v.tr. Nau:* to swab, mop (the decks, etc.).

faubourg [fobuːr], *s.m.* suburb; outlying district (of town); **f. industriel,** industrial suburb; **f. résidentiel,** residential district; **parler avec l'accent des faubourgs,** to speak with a common accent.

faubourien, -ienne [foburjɛ̃, -jɛn]. **1.** *a.* suburban; **accent f.,** common accent. **2.** *s.* suburbanite; inhabitant of a suburb (*esp.* a working-class suburb of Paris).

faucard [fokaːr], *s.m.* long-handled scythe (for clearing ponds, rivers, etc., of weeds).

faucardage [fokardaːʒ], **faucardement** [fokardmɑ̃], *s.m.* clearing of weeds (from fish pond).

faucarder [fokarde], *v.tr.* (*a*) to clear (pond, etc.) of weeds; (*b*) to clear out (weeds).

faucardeur [fokardœːr], *s.m.* boat equipped with mechanical scythe (for clearing weeds from pond).

faucardeuse [fokardøːz], *s.f.* mechanical scythe (for cutting pond weed).

fauchable [foʃabl̩], *a. Agr:* ready for mowing; mowable.

fauchage [foʃaːʒ], *s.m.* **1.** mowing, cutting, reaping (of corn, etc.). **2.** (*a*) mowing down (of troops); (*b*) *Artil: Sm.a:* traversing; (*of machine gun*) **angle de f.,** angle of traverse.

fauchailles [foʃaːj], *s.f.pl.* reaping season; mowing season.

fauchaison [foʃɛzɔ̃], *s.f.* (*a*) (action of) mowing, reaping; (*b*) mowing time, reaping time.

fauchard [foʃaːr], *s.m.* **1.** *A.Arms:* fauchard. **2.** *For: Hort:* double-edged slasher; slash hook.

fauche [foʃ], *s.f.* **1.** *A:* mowing time, reaping time. **2.** *Agr:* swath. **3. prairie de f.,** hay meadow. **4.** *P:* (*a*) petty theft; (*b*) loot.

fauché [foʃe], *a.* **1.** *Agr:* mown, cut, reaped. **2.** *F:* **f. (comme les blés),** (stony) broke, cleaned out, broke to the wide.

fauchée [foʃe], *s.f.* **1.** *Agr:* amount (of corn, etc.) cut (i) in a day, (ii) without resharpening the scythe; day's cutting or mowing. **2.** swath.

faucher [foʃe], *v.tr.* **1.** (*a*) to mow, cut, reap (grass, corn, etc.); **f. une prairie,** to mow a meadow; *F:* **f. l'herbe sons les pieds de qn,** to cut the ground from under s.o.'s feet; **il est revenu de la guerre le pied fauché,** he came back from the war minus a foot; **la voiture a fauché le poteau télégraphique,** the car brought down the telegraph pole; *Fb:* **f. son homme,** to bring down one's man; (*b*) *F:* to swipe; **ils ont fauché mon tabac,** they've pinched, swiped, my tobacco; (*c*) *P:* to guillotine (s.o.). **2.** (*a*) to mow down (troops); (*b*) to sweep (ground) (with machine gun). **3.** *abs.* (*a*) (*of horse, pers.*) to swing one leg out sideways when walking; (*of horse*) to dish, paddle; (*b*) *Bill:* to swing the cue.

fauchet [foʃɛ], *s.m.* **1.** hay rake. **2.** billhook.

fauchette [foʃɛt], *s.f.* billhook.

faucheur, -euse [foʃœːr, -øːz], *s.* **1.** mower, reaper. **2.** *s.m. Arach:* harvester, harvest spider, daddy-long-legs. **3.** *s.f.* (*a*) **faucheuse,** (mechanical) reaper, mower; (*b*) **la (grande) Faucheuse,** the Reaper, Death.

faucheux [foʃø], *s.m. Arach:* harvester, harvest spider, daddy-long-legs; *F:* **avoir des jambes de f.,** to have long, spindly legs.

fauchon [foʃɔ̃], *s.m.* **1.** *A.Arms:* falchion. **2.** (*a*) (type of) short-handled scythe; (*b*) scythe equipped with a rake.

faucille [fosiːj], *s.f.* **1.** sickle, reaping hook. **2.** sickle feather (of cock, etc.).

fauciller [fosije], *v.tr.* to reap, mow, (corn) with a sickle.

faucillon [fosijɔ̃], *s.m.* small sickle.

faucon [fokɔ̃], *s.m.* **1.** *Orn:* falcon; hawk; **f. mâle,** tercel, tiercel; **f. pèlerin,** peregrine falcon; **f. d'Éléonore,** Eleonora's falcon; **f. gerfaut,** gerfalcon; **f. lanier,** lanner falcon, lanner; **f. kobez, f. à pattes rouges,** red-footed falcon; **f. sacre,** saker (falcon); **f. des moineaux,** American sparrowhawk; **f. crécerellette,** lesser kestrel; **f. gris,** sooty falcon; **chasser au f.,** to hawk; **chasse au f.,** hawking. **2.** *A.Artil:* falcon. **3.** *U.S.Pol:* hawk.

fauconneau, -eaux [fokɔno], *s.m.* **1.** young falcon. **2.** *A.Artil:* falconet.

fauconner [fokɔne], *v.i. Equit:* to mount a horse on the off side.

fauconnerie [fokɔnri], *s.f. Ven:* **1.** hawk house, falcon house. **2.** falconry; hawking.

fauconnet [fokɔnɛ], *s.m. Orn:* falconet.

fauconnier [fokɔnje], *s.m.* falconer; **monter à cheval en f.,** to mount a horse on the off side.

fauconnière [fokɔnjɛːr], *s.f.* **1.** hawking pouch. **2.** saddle-bag.

faucre [foːkr̥], *s.m. A.Arms:* rest (for couched lance); faucre; fewter.

faudage [fodaːʒ], *s.m.* **1.** folding (of piece of cloth) in half lengthwise. **2.** crease(mark) (in folded cloth).

fauder [fode], *v.tr.* **1.** to fold (piece of cloth) in half lengthwise. **2.** to mark the centre line of (a strip of cloth).

faudeur [fodœːr], *s.m. Tex:* folder.

faufil(e) [fofil], **faufilage** [fofilaːʒ], *s.m.* (*a*) tacking thread, basting thread; (*b*) tacking, basting; tacking on (of braid, etc.).

faufiler [fofile]. **1.** *v.tr.* (*a*) to tack, baste (seam, etc.); to tack on, baste on (braid, etc.); (*b*) *occ.* to insert, introduce, (s.o., sth.) stealthily, adroitly; to slip (s.o., sth.) in. **2.** *v.i. A:* **f. avec l'aristocratie,** to associate with the aristocracy.

se faufiler, se f. dans la faveur de qn, to insinuate oneself into s.o.'s favour; **il s'était faufilé avec les invités,** he had slipped in among the guests; **se f. dans un endroit, hors d'un endroit,** (i) to slip, edge, into, out of, a place; (ii) to sneak in, out; **se f. entre les voitures,** to thread, twist, one's way through the traffic; to nip in and out of the traffic; **se f. le long du mur,** to creep along the wall; (*rare*) **se f. passage,** to make a way for oneself.

faufilure [fofilyːr], *s.f. Dom.Ec:* tacked seam; tacking, basting.

faujasite [foʒazit], *s.f. Miner:* faujasite.

faulde [fod], *s.f.* charcoal kiln (in the forest).

faultrage [fotraːʒ], *s.m. A.Jur:* **droit de f.,** dues on meadow lands (paid by vassal).

faune¹ [foːn], *s.m. Myth:* faun.

faune², *s.f.* fauna, animal life (of region, etc.); **f. avienne,** avifauna; **f. erpétologique,** herpetofauna; *F:* **la f. des cafés de Montparnasse,** the regular crowd of the cafés of Montparnasse.

faunesque [fonɛsk], *a.* faun-like.

faunique [fonik], **faunistique** [fonistik], *a. Z:* faunal, faunistic, relating to fauna.

faurrade [forad], *s.f. Fish:* barrier of nets (to catch fish as the tide goes out).

faussage [fosaːʒ], *s.m.* warping, buckling.

faussaire [fosɛːr], *s.m. & f.* forger (of documents, etc.); perverter, falsifier (of the truth, etc.).

faussement [fosmɑ̃], *adv.* falsely, erroneously, untruly; **accuser qn f.,** to accuse s.o. wrongfully.

fausse-morue [fosmɔry], *s.f. Ich: F:* false cod, grouper; *pl. fausses-morues.*

fausser [fose]. **1.** *v.tr.* (*a*) to make false; to falsify, to pervert (the truth, etc.); to vitiate (the results of a test); **f. les faits,** to alter the facts, to present the facts in a wrong light; **f. le sens d'un texte,** to distort the meaning of a text; *Cards:* **f. la coupe,** to make a false cut; **f. les idées de qn,** to warp s.o.'s ideas; **esprit faussé,** warped mind; **f. les comptes,** to falsify, *F:* cook, the books; **f. parole à qn,** to break one's word to s.o.; **f. compagnie à qn,** to give s.o. the slip; (*b*) to force, bend, buckle, warp, strain; to put (rod, etc.) out of truth, out of true; **essieu faussé,** sprung axle; **cuirasse faussée,** dented, buckled, breastplate; **roue faussée,** wheel out of true, warped wheel; **f. une clef, une serrure,** to wrench a key, to tamper with a lock; (*of screw, bolt*) **f. un filetage,** to cross thread; *Ph:* **onde faussée,** deformed wave; (*c*) to put (instrument) out of tune; to strain (voice). **2.** *v.i. Mus:* to sing, play, out of tune.

se fausser, (*a*) (*of instrument, etc.*) to get out of true, out of order; (*b*) (*of axle, rail, etc.*) to bend, buckle; (*c*) (*of voice*) (i) to get out of tune; (ii) to crack.

fausse-route [fosrut], *s.f. Med:* false passage (of bougie, probe); *pl. fausse-routes.*

fausset¹ [fosɛ], *s.m. Mus:* **1.** falsetto; **chanter en f.,** to sing falsetto. **2.** falsettist.

fausset², *s.m.*, **fosset** [fosɛ], *s.m.* **1.** spigot, spile, vent plug, vent peg (of barrel); *U.S:* faucet; **trou de f.,** vent hole. **2.** fine pen nib.

fausseté [foste], *s.f.* **1.** falseness, falsity (of judgment, statement, etc.); **démontrer la f. d'un dire,** to disprove, refute, a statement. **2.** falsehood, untruth; **dire des faussetés,** to tell falsehoods. **3.** duplicity; **f. de cœur, de conduite,** treachery; double dealing.

faussures [fosyːr], *s.f.pl.* barrel (of a bell).

faute [foːt], *s.f.* **1.** lack, need, want; **faire f.,** to be lacking; **la main-d'œuvre nous fait f.,** we are short of labour; **vous lui faites f.,** he misses you; **ne se faire f. de rien,** to deny oneself nothing; **nous ne nous faisons jamais f. de lui écrire,** we never fail to write to him, we never miss writing to him; **je ne m'en ferai pas f.,** I shall not fail to do it; **sans f.,** without fail; **écrivez-lui sans f.,** mind you write to him; *A:* **avoir f. de qch.,** to lack, have need of, sth.; *prep.phr.* **f. de,** for want of, for lack of; **f. de réponse satisfaisante . . .,** failing a satisfactory reply . . .; **f. d'argent,** for want of money; **f. d'ordres précis,** in the absence of, in default of, definite instructions; *Jur:* **(à) f. de,** in default of; **f. de quoi . . .,** failing which . . .; as otherwise . . ., or else . . .; **f. de mieux,** for want of, for lack of, something better; **f. d'essayer,** for want of trying; **f. par le gouvernement d'avoir rempli les conditions . . .,** owing to the government's having failed to carry out the conditions . . .; *Com:* **retourner une traite f. de paiement,** to return a bill unpaid; **poursuivre qn pour f. de paiement,** to sue s.o. for non-payment. **2.** (*a*) fault, mistake; **être en f.,** to be at fault; **trouver, prendre, qn en f.,** to catch s.o. in the act; **il n'y a pas (de) f. de ma part, ce n'est pas (de) ma f.,** it is not my fault, I am not to blame; **à qui la f.?** whose fault is it? who is to blame? **il en rejette toute la f. sur elle,** he puts all the blame on her; **la f. en est à moi,** it is my fault, I am to blame; **c'est un peu de ma f.,** I am partly to blame; **ce n'est pas sa f., c'est son malheur,** it is not his fault but his misfortune; **f. d'orthographe,** spelling mistake; **f. de jugement,** error of judgment; **commettre une f. grave,** to make a serious mistake; **f. d'impression,** misprint; **f. de français, d'anglais,** mistake in French, in English; (*b*) misbehaving, misbehaviour; misconduct, lapse (from righteousness); transgression, delinquency, offence; **f. grave,** serious offence; **f. légère,** minor, trifling, offence; peccadillo; **elle n'est jamais allée jusqu'à la f.,** she never went the whole way; *Jur:* **il y eut f.,** intimacy took place; (*c*) *Fb: etc:* foul; **commettre une f. contre qn,** to foul s.o.; (*d*) *Ten:* fault; **f. de pied,** foot fault.

fauter [fote], *v.i. F:* (*a*) (*of woman*) to go wrong, to allow oneself to be seduced; (*b*) **f. par un endroit,** to be defective in sth.

fauteuil [fotœːj], *s.m.* **1.** armchair, easy chair; **f. à oreillettes,** wing chair; **f. à bascule, à balançoire,** rocking chair; **f. pliant,** folding chair, deck-chair; **f. saharien,** Roorkee chair; **f. dentaire, de dentiste,** dentist's chair; **f. roulant, à roulettes,** (i) bath chair, wheel chair; (ii) self-propelling chair; **f. club,** club chair; *Th:* **f. d'orchestre,** seat in the stalls, orchestra stall; **f. de premier balcon,** dress-circle seat; *F:* **arriver dans un f.,** to win in a canter; to win hands down. **2.** (*a*) chair (of meeting); **occuper le f.,** to be chairman (of meeting), to be in the chair; *s.a.* PRÉSIDENTIEL; (*b*) **les quarante fauteuils de l'Académie française,** the forty seats of the French Academy.

fauteuil-lit [fotœjli], *s.m.* chair-bed; *pl. fauteuils-lits.*

fauteur, -trice [fotœːr, -tris], *s.* (*a*) *A:* supporter; protector; (*b*) *Pej:* (*the f. form* **fautrice** *is rare*) abettor; **f. d'une émeute,** instigator of a rising; **f. de troubles,** agitator, trouble maker; **f. de guerre,** warmonger; **f. d'un crime,** aider and abettor of a crime; **être f. d'um crime,** to connive at a crime.

fautif, -ive [fotif, -iːv], *a.* **1.** faulty, incorrect; **calcul f.,** miscalculation, faulty reckoning; **mémoire fautive,** defective memory. **2.** sinning, offending, in fault; (child) who has been naughty.

fautivement [fotivmɑ̃], *adv.* faultily, incorrectly.

fautrage [fotraːʒ], *s.m. A.Jur:* **droit de f.,** dues on meadow lands (paid by vassal).

fautre [foːtr̥], *s.m. A.Arms:* faucre; fewter; rest for couched lance.

fauve [foːv]. **1.** *a.* (*a*) fawn-coloured; buff; fulvous; tawny (hair, etc.); (*of deer*) fallow; **Orpington f.,** buff Orpington; **ciel f.,** lurid sky; (*b*) **odeur f.,** musky smell. **2.** *s.m.* (*a*) fawn (colour); (*b*) **le f., les (bêtes) fauves,** deer; (*c*) **les (grands) fauves,** big game; **la chasse aux grands fauves,** big game

hunting; (*d*) **f. de Bourgogne,** large fawn-coloured rabbit with white spots; (*e*) *Art:* **les Fauves,** the Fauves, Fauvists, the wild men.

fauveau [fovo], *s.m.* fawn-coloured ox.

fauverie [fovri], *s.f.* lion house.

fauvette [fovɛt], *s.f. Orn:* warbler; **f. américaine,** prothonotary warbler; **f. babillarde,** lesser whitethroat; **f. couturière,** tailor bird; **f. épervière,** barred warbler; **f. à gorge noire,** black-throated warbler; **f. grisette,** whitethroat; **f. d'hiver,** hedge sparrow, dunnock; **f. à lunettes,** spectacled warbler; **f. mélanocéphale,** Sardinian warbler; **f. naine,** desert warbler; **f. orphée,** orphean warbler; **f. parula,** parula warbler; **f. passerine, subalpine,** subalpine warbler; **f. pitchou,** Dartford warbler; **f. des roseaux,** reed warbler; **f. de Rüppell,** Rüppell's warbler; **f. sarde,** Marmora's warbler; **f. à tête noire,** blackcap; **elle chante comme une f.,** she sings like a lark.

fauvisme [fovism], *s.m. Art:* Fauvism.

faux[1], **fausse** [fo, foːs]. I. *a.* false. **1.** untrue; **c'est complètement f.,** it is absolutely untrue; **fausse nouvelle,** false report; **f. soupçon,** false, unfounded, suspicion; **f. témoin,** false witness; **f. témoignage,** false evidence, perjury; **porter un f. témoignage,** to bear false witness, to perjure oneself, to commit perjury. **2.** not genuine; (*a*) **fausse cordialité,** bogus cordiality; **il y a un f. air de famille entre eux,** there is a sort of family likeness between them; **c'est une fausse maigre,** she is not so thin as she looks; **fausse monnaie,** false, spurious, counterfeit, base, coin(age); **crime de fausse monnaie,** coinage offence; **fausse clef,** skeleton key; **fausse adresse,** wrong, false, address; **f. fond,** false bottom; **fausse cartouche,** dummy cartridge; **fausses dents,** false teeth; **f. cheveux,** false hair; **devanture toute en fausses boîtes,** shop-window dressed with dummy boxes; **f. bijoux, bijouterie fausse,** imitation jewellery; **fausse fenêtre,** blind, blank, dead, window; *Nau:* **fausse galerie,** badge; *Obst:* **fausse couche,** miscarriage; **acte f.,** forged deed; **f. chèque,** forged cheque; **fausse déclaration,** misrepresentation; **f. bilan,** fraudulent balance sheet; **f. nom,** false name, assumed name; *Anat:* **fausses côtes,** false ribs, floating ribs, short ribs; *Bot:* **f. persil,** false parsley, fool's parsley; **fausse rhubarbe,** false rhubarb; *Mil:* **fausse attaque,** feint, false, dummy, attack; **fausse sortie,** feint sortie; *Th:* sham exit; *Mth: A:* **fausse position,** trial and error (in computation); *Nau:* **fausse amure,** preventer tack; **f. point,** clew rope; *Typ:* **f. titre,** half title, bastard title; **fausse page,** left-hand page; *Aut:* **f. moyeu,** dummy hub; **f. carter,** dummy crank-case; (*b*) treacherous; **homme f.,** untrustworthy man; **f. comme un jeton,** false to the core; **c'est un f. jeton,** he's a hypocrite, a double dealer; **f. bonhomme,** shifty, sly, character. **3.** wrong, mistaken; **fausse date,** wrong date; **raisonnement f.,** unsound reasoning, argument; **être dans un f. jour,** to be in the wrong light; **présenter la conduite de qn sous un f. jour,** to misrepresent s.o.'s conduct; **fausse position,** cramped position; **se trouver dans une fausse position,** to be in a false position, to find oneself awkwardly placed; **situation fausse,** equivocal situation; **balance fausse,** inaccurate balance; **f. poids,** unjust weight; **faire un f. pas,** (i) to take a false step; (ii) to blunder, to make a faux pas; **son seul et unique f. pas,** his one and only indiscretion; **faire fausse route,** to take the wrong road, to go astray, to mistake the way; *F:* to be on the wrong tack; to go the wrong way about sth.; **se faire une fausse opinion de qch.,** to form a wrong, erroneous, mistaken, opinion of sth.; **une fausse appréciation de la distance,** a miscalculation of the distance; **théories reconnues pour fausses,** exploded theories; *Bill:* **faire fausse queue,** to miscue; *Cr:* **fausse balle,** no ball; *Turf: etc:* **f. départ,** false start; *Engr:* **fausse épreuve,** faulty proof; *Ling:* **f. sens,** wrong shade of meaning (in translation); *Mus:* **fausse note,** wrong note; *Pros:* **vers f.,** faulty, defective, verse; *Tp:* **f. numéro,** wrong number; *s.a.* BOND 2.

II. **faux,** *adv.* falsely, wrongly, erroneously; **chanter f.,** to sing out of tune; **rire qui sonne f.,** hollow laughter; **voir f.,** to take a false view of things.

III. **faux,** *s.m.* **1.** (*a*) **le f.,** the false, the untrue; **distinguer le vrai du f.,** to distinguish truth from falsehood; **plaider le f. pour savoir le vrai,** to angle for the truth with a lie; to try to draw s.o. out; *Jur:* **s'inscrire en f. contre qch.,** to indict sth. as false, to plead the falsity of sth., to deny sth., to dispute the validity of sth.; (*b*) **bijouterie en f.,** imitation jewellery; **porter du f.,** to wear imitation, costume, jewellery; (*c*) *adv.phrs.* **à f.,** wrongly; **poser le pied à f.,** to miss one's footing; **accuser qn à f.,** to accuse s.o. wrongly; **interpréter qch. à f.,** to put a false interpretation on sth.; (*of hound*) **aboyer à f.,** to bay at fault; **frapper à faux,** to miss one's mark; **argument qui porte à f.,** argument that (i) rests on erroneous premises, (ii) is irrelevant, beside the mark, beside the point; **mur qui porte à f.,** wall out of plumb, that has an overhang; (*of wheel*) **tourner à f.,** to run untrue, out of true. **2.** *Jur:* forgery; **inscription de f.,** procedure in proof that a document has been forged; plea of forgery; **arguer une pièce de f.,** to put in a plea of forgery.

faux[2], *s.f.* **1.** *Agr:* scythe. **2.** *Anat:* falx, sickle-shaped fold (of brain, etc.).

faux-acacia [fozakasja], *s.m. Bot:* false acacia; *pl. faux-acacias.*

faux-bau [fobo], *s.m. Nau:* carling knee; *pl. faux-baux.*

faux-bord [fobɔːr], *s.m. Nau:* lopside; *pl. faux-bords.*

faux-bourdon [foburdɔ̃], *s.m.* **1.** *Mus:* faux-bourdon. **2.** *Ent:* drone; *pl. faux-bourdons.*

faux-bras [fobra], *s.m.inv. Nau:* preventer brace; **f.-b. de ceinture,** guess rope, guest rope.

faux-col [fokɔl], *s.m.* (*a*) detachable collar; (*b*) *F:* head (on glass of beer); *pl. faux-cols.*

faux-éperlan [foeperlɑ̃], *s.m. Ich:* atherine; *pl. faux éperlans.*

faux-filet [fofilɛ], *s.m. Cu:* sirloin; *pl. faux-filets.*

faux-fuyant [fofɥijɑ̃], *s.m.* **1.** *A:* by-way, by-path. **2.** subterfuge, shift, quirk, evasion, dodge; **chercher des faux-fuyants,** to try to find excuses (in order not to do sth.); to hedge; *pl. faux-fuyants.*

faux-monnayage [fomɔnɛjaːʒ], *s.m.* counterfeiting of currency.

faux-monnayeur [fomɔnɛjœːr], *s.m.* coiner, counterfeiter; *pl. faux-monnayeurs.*

faux-poivrier [fopwavrije], *s. Bot:* schinus, pepper-tree; *pl. faux-poivriers.*

faux-pont [fopɔ̃], *s.m. Nau:* orlop deck; **soute à bagages dans le f.-p.,** baggage room between decks; *pl. faux-ponts.*

faux-quartier [fokartje], *s.m. Vet:* false quarter (of hoof); *pl. faux-quartiers.*

faux-semblant [fosɑ̃blɑ̃], *s.m.* false pretence; pretext, ruse; make-believe; *pl. faux-semblants.*

faux-tampon [fotɑ̃pɔ̃], *s.m. Rail:* buffer box; *pl. faux-tampons.*

favelle [favɛl], *s.f. Algae:* favella.

favellidie [favɛlidi], *s.f. Algae:* favellidium.

favéole [faveɔl], *s.f. Nat.Hist:* small cellule, alveola; faveolus.

favéolé [faveɔle], *a. Nat.Hist:* faveolate.

faverole [favrɔl], *s.f.* field bean, horse bean.

faverolles [favrɔl], *s.m. Husb:* Faverolle (fowl).

faveur [favœːr], *s.f.* favour. **1.** (*a*) **gagner, obtenir, la f. de qn,** to obtain s.o.'s favour, s.o.'s interest; **demander une f. à qn,** to ask a favour of s.o.; **recevoir des marques de f. de qn,** to receive marks of favour from s.o.; **être en f. auprès de qn,** to be in favour with s.o.; **être en grande f. à la cour,** to be in high favour at court; **monter en f. auprès de qn,** to rise, grow, in favour with s.o.; **rentrer en f.,** to be restored to favour; **le gouvernement a perdu la f. du public,** the government has fallen out of favour with the people; **trouver f. auprès de qn,** to find favour with s.o.; **devenir en f., prendre f.,** to come into vogue, into favour; **mettre une mode en f.,** to bring a fashion into favour; *Com:* **prix de f.,** preferential, special, price; **taux de f.,** specially favourable rate; *F:* **faire subir à qn le traitement de f.,** to give s.o. the (full) works, V.I.P. treatment; **jours de f.,** days of grace; *Th: etc:* **billet de f.,** complimentary ticket, free ticket; order; **pas de billets de f.,** the free list is suspended; *prep.phr.* **à la f. de . . .,** by the help of . . ., by means of . . .; **à la f. de la nuit,** under cover of darkness, night; **en f. de . . .,** in favour of . . .; **plaider en f. de qn,** to plead on s.o.'s behalf, in s.o.'s favour; **on lui fit grâce en f. de sa jeunesse,** he was let off in consideration of his youth; **quête en f. de,** collection in aid of; (*b*) **faire une f. à qn,** to do s.o. a favour, a kindness; **combler qn de faveurs,** to load s.o. with favours; (*of woman*) **accorder ses faveurs (à qn),** to encourage (a suitor); **elle lui accorda les dernières faveurs,** she gave herself to him. **2. f. de soie,** silk favour, ribbon.

faveux, -euse [favø, -øːz], **favique** [favik], *a. Med:* favose; **teigne faveuse,** favus; crusted, honeycomb, ringworm.

favisme [favism], *s.m. Med:* favism.

favorable [favɔrabl], *a.* **1.** *A:* pleasing, agreeable. **2.** (*of pers., opinion*) favourable (**à, pour,** to); **mon impression lui fut f.,** he impressed me favourably; **se rendre les dieux favorables,** to propitiate the gods. **3.** favourable (wind, occasion, etc.); propitious (circumstances, wind); auspicious (occasion); fair (wind); **incident f. à mes intérêts,** incident likely to favour, advance, my interests; **le moment était f. pour lui parler,** it was a good moment to speak to him, it was just the moment to speak to him; **peu f.,** unfavourable, unpropitious (**à, pour,** to).

favorablement [favɔrabləmɑ̃], *adv.* favourably, auspiciously; **recevoir f. qn, qch.,** to give s.o., sth., a kind, friendly, favourable, reception; **ma requête a été accueillie f.,** my request was favourably received.

favori, -ite [favɔri, -it]. **1.** *a.* favourite (person, object, racehorse, etc.). **2.** *s.* favourite. **3.** *s.m.pl.* (side)whiskers.

favorisé, -ée [favɔrize]. **1.** *a.* favoured. **2.** *s.* **les moins favorisés,** the underprivileged.

favoriser [favɔrize], *v.tr.* (*a*) to favour; to be partial to (s.o., sth.); **f. une entreprise,** to be in favour of an enterprise; **l'examinateur a favorisé le candidat,** the examiner showed favouritism towards the candidate; **f. les arts,** to patronize, encourage, promote, the arts; **des hommes, favorisés par le talent,** men who have the advantage of being gifted; **nation la plus favorisée** most favoured nation; (*b*) (*of thg*) to be favourable to (s.o.); to help, encourage (sth.); **f. l'essor de la production,** to encourage production; **f. la croissance,** to promote growth; **les événements l'ont favorisé,** events were in his favour; **f. un dessein,** to further an object; **ce beau temps favorise l'optimisme,** this fine weather makes for optimism; **la faiblesse du gouvernement favorisa l'insurrection,** the weakness of the government helped, contributed to the success of, the rebellion; (*c*) *Lit:* **la nature l'a favorisé de ses dons,** nature has favoured him with her gifts; **f. qn d'un regard,** to favour s.o. with a glance.

favoritisme [favɔritism], *s.m.* favouritism.

favosite [favɔzit], *s.f. Paleont:* favosite.

favositidés [favɔzitide], *s.m.pl. Paleont:* Favositidae.

favus [favyːs], *s.m. Med:* favus.

fayalite [fajalit], *s.f. Miner:* fayalite.

fayard [fajaːr], *s.m. Dial:* beech (tree).

fayolisme [fajɔlism], *s.m. Pol.Ec:* doctrine of hierarchism (in industry, etc.).

fayot [fajo], *s.m. P:* **1.** haricot bean, kidney bean; **doubler le cap f.,** to be reduced to a diet of beans. **2.** (*a*) (i) *Mil:* re-engaged man, old sweat; (ii) re-engaged sailor; **faire f.,** to re-enlist; (*b*) eager beaver.

fayotage [fajɔtaːʒ], *s.m. P:* excessive zeal (in one's work); **ça, c'est du f.!** how's that for an eager beaver!

fayoter [fajɔte], *v.i. Mil: P:* to show excessive zeal; **tu es toujours à f., salaud!** you're always sweating to curry favour, you bastard!

féage [feaːʒ], *s.m. Jur: A:* feoffment.

féal[1], **-aux** [feal, -o]. **1.** *a. A:* faithful, trusty (vassal, friend, etc.); **à nos féaux sujets,** to our trusty lieges. **2.** *s.m. Lit: or Hum:* devoted servitor.

féal[2], *s.m.* ferro-aluminium (containing 25% aluminium).

feather-weight [fɛðərweit], *s.m. Box: Turf:* featherweight.

féauté [feote], *s.f. A:* faithfulness, fidelity; *A:* fealty; **faire au roi serment de f.,** to swear fealty to the king.

fébricitant [febrisitɑ̃], *a.* feverish (patient).

fébriciter [febrisite], *v.i.* (*rare*) to be feverish.

fébricule [febrikyl], *s.f. Med:* febricula.

fébrifuge [febrifyːʒ], *a. & s.m. Med:* febrifuge, antifebrile.

fébrigène [febriʒɛn], *a. Med:* febrific, febricant.

fébrile [febril], *a.* (*a*) *Med:* febrile (pulse, etc.); (*b*) feverish (restlessness, preparations).

fébrilement [febrilmɑ̃], *adv.* feverishly.

fébrilité [febrilite], *s.f.* (*a*) *Med:* febricity, febrility, feverishness; (*b*) feverishness, frantic nature (of preparations, etc.).

fébronianisme [febrɔnjanism], *s.m. Ecc:* Febronianism.

fébronien, -ienne [febrɔnjɛ̃, -jɛn], *a. & s. Ecc:* Febronian.

fécal, -aux [fekal, -o], *a. Ch: Physiol:* faecal; *Physiol:* **matières fécales,** faeces.

fécaloïde [fekalɔid], *a.* fecaloid, dung-like.

fécalome [fekalɔm], *s.m. Med:* f(a)ecaloma.

fécalurie [fekalyri], *s.f. Med:* f(a)ecaluria.

fécampois, -oise [fekɑ̃pwa, -waːz], *a. & s.* (native, inhabitant) of Fécamp.

fécer [fese], *v.i. Ch:* to form a sediment, a deposit.

fèces [fɛs], *s.f.pl.* 1. *Ch:* faeces, sediment. 2. *Physiol:* faeces; *Med:* stool.

fécial, -aux [fesjal, -o], *a. & s.m. Rom.Ant:* fetial.

fécond [fekɔ̃], *a.* prolific, fruitful, fertile, fecund; productive (en, of); **terre féconde**, fertile earth, rich soil; **race, femme, féconde**, fruitful, prolific, race, woman; **imagination féconde**, fertile imagination; **esprit f. en inventions**, mind fertile, rich, in inventions; **chaleur féconde**, life-giving heat; **pluies fécondes**, bountiful rain; **source féconde**, abundant spring (of water).

fécondabilité [fekɔ̃dabilite], *s.f. Pol.Ec:* **taux de f.**, fertility rate.

fécondable [fekɔ̃dabl̩], *a.* fertilizable.

fécondant [fekɔ̃dɑ̃], *a.* 1. *Biol:* fecundating, fertilizing; impregnating. 2. life-giving (sun, river, etc.).

fécondateur, -trice [fekɔ̃datœːr, -tris], *a. & s.* (*a*) *a.* fertilizing; (*b*) *s.* fertilizer, fertilizing agent.

fécondation [fekɔ̃dasjɔ̃], *s.f. Biol:* fecundation, fertilization; impregnation; **f. artificielle**, artificial insemination; *Bot:* **f. croisée**, cross fertilization; **f. directe**, self-fertilization.

féconder [fekɔ̃de], *v.tr.* to fecundate. 1. *Biol:* to impregnate. 2. (*of sun, river, etc.*) to make (land) fertile; to bring fertility to (land, etc.).

fécondité [fekɔ̃dite], *s.f.* fecundity. 1. fruitfulness; fecundity (of woman); *Pol.Ec:* **taux de f.**, reproduction rate. 2. fertility (of land, etc.). 3. **f. d'invention**, inventiveness; **f. d'esprit**, fertility of mind; **quelle f. en paroles!** what a flow of words!

fécule [fekyl], *s.f.* f(a)ecula, starch; **f. de pommes de terre**, potato starch, flour.

féculence [fekylɑ̃ːs], *s.f. Ch:* 1. thickness, turbidity, feculence (of solution). 2. starchiness (of solution).

féculent [fekylɑ̃], 1. *a. Ch:* (*a*) thick, turbid, feculent; (*b*) starchy, containing starch. 2. *s.m.* starchy substance, starchy food.

féculer [fekyle], *v.tr.* 1. to reduce (potatoes) to a starch. 2. to add potato flour to (food).

féculerie [fekylri], *s.f.* fecula works, potato-starch works.

féculeux, -euse [fekylø, -øːz], *a.* starchy.

féculier, -ière [fekylje, -jɛːr]. 1. *a.* **pomme de terre féculière**, starch potato. 2. *s.m.* manufacturer of potato starch.

fédéral, -aux [federal, -o]. 1. *a.* federal. 2. *s.m.pl. U.S:Hist:* **les Fédéraux**, the Federals.

fédéraliser [federalize], *v.tr.* to federalize.

fédéralisme [federalism], *s.m.* federalism.

fédéraliste [federalist], *a. & s.* federalist.

fédératif, -ive [federatif, -iːv], *a.* federative (constitution, etc.).

fédération [federasjɔ̃], *s.f.* federation (of states, societies, etc.); **f. syndicale ouvrière**, trade(s) union; **f. de syndicats (ouvriers)**, amalgamated unions.

fédéré [federe]. 1. *a. Pol:* federate (states, etc.). 2. *s.m. Fr.Hist:* federate (of 1790, of 1815, of 1871).

fédérer [federe], *v.tr.* (**je fédère, n. fédérons; je fédérerai**) to federate, federalize (a number of states, etc.).

se fédérer, to federate.

fédie [fedi], *s.f. Bot:* fedia, African valerian.

fée [fe]. 1. *s.f.* fairy; **conte de fées**, fairytale; **pays des fées**, fairyland; **doigts de f.**, nimble fingers; **vieille f.**, old hag; *Geol:* **cheminée des fées**, demoiselle, capped earth pillar. 2. *a.* fairy, magic, enchanted; **clef f.**, magic key.

feed-back [fidbak], *s.m.inv. Elcs:* feedback.

feeder [fidœːr, -ɛːr], *s.m.* (*a*) *El:* feeder (cable); *W.Tel:* feeder; **f. reliant deux stations**, *El:* feeder tie; *Typ:* trunk feeder; (*b*) (gas) pipeline; (*c*) *Nau:* feeder.

féer [fee], *v.tr.* to endow with supernatural, fairy, power.

féerie [fe(e)ri], *s.f.* 1. enchantment, fairyhood. 2. (*a*) fairyland; (*b*) riot of colour, glimpse of fairyland. 3. *Th:* (*a*) fairy play; (*b*) spectacular play (of the pantomime type).

féerique [fe(e)rik], *a.* 1. fairy, magic (castle, etc.). 2. fairy-like, enchanting (sight, etc.); **paysage d'une beauté f.**, entrancing landscape. 3. *Th:* **pièce f.**, fairy play; spectacular play.

féeriquement [fe(e)rikmɑ̃], *adv.* entrancingly; marvellously; fairily.

feignant [fɛɲɑ̃], **feignasse** [fɛɲas], *a. & s. P:* idle, bone lazy.

feignasser [fɛɲase], *v.i. P:* to idle; to loaf.

feindre [fɛ̃ːdr], *v.* (*pr.p.* **feignant**; *p.p.* **feint**; *pr.ind.* **je feins, il feint, n. feignons, ils feignent**; *pr.sub.* **je feigne**; *p.d.* **je feignais**; *p.h.* **je feignis**; *fu.* **je feindrai**) 1. *v.tr.* (*a*) to feign, simulate, act, pretend, sham (fit, illness, etc.); **f. la mort**, to sham, counterfeit, death; to pretend to be dead; **f. de faire qch.**, to pretend to do sth., to make a pretence of doing sth.; (*occ. without* **de**) **il feignait ne rien voir**, he pretended not to see; **tout cela est feint**, all that is pretence, is make-believe, *F:* is put on; *abs.* **inutile de f.**, it's no use pretending; (*b*) *A:* (i) to imagine, invent (tale, etc.); (ii) **il nous feignit qu'on l'avait volé**, he gave it out to us, tried to make us believe, that he had been robbed; (iii) **ne pas f. de faire qch.**, not to hesitate, not to scruple, to do sth. 2. *v.i. Equit:* to go (slightly) short; to put it on.

feint [fɛ̃], *a.* (*a*) *A:* fictitious, imaginary (reason, etc.); (*b*) feigned, assumed, sham (benevolence, etc.); (*c*) **porte feinte**, blind door, dummy door; **joint feint**, imitation joint.

feinte [fɛ̃ːt], *s.f.* 1. (*a*) feint, sham, pretence; *A:* **agir avec f.**, to pretend; *A:* **parler sans f.**, to speak openly, without pretence; **sa maladie n'était qu'une f.**, his illness was only a blind; **ce n'est qu'une f.**, it's mere acting, only pretence; **c'était une f. pour le surprendre**, it was a dodge to catch him out; (*b*) *Box: Fenc:* feint; **faire une f. du gauche**, to feint, make a feint, with the left; *Fb:* (*Rugby*) **faire une f. de passe**, to give, sell, the dummy. 2. (*of horse*) sham lameness. 3. *Typ:* faint impression; friar.

feinter [fɛ̃te]. 1. *v.i. Box:* **f. du gauche**, to feint, make a feint, with the left. 2. *v.tr. F:* to deceive; *P:* **t'es feinté!** you've been had!

feinteur [fɛ̃tœːr], *s.m. Fb:* feinter.

feintise [fɛ̃tiːz], *s.f. A:* deceit, deceiving, pretence.

fêlant [fɛlɑ̃], *a. A: P:* **histoire fêlante**, side-splitting story, killingly funny story.

félatier [felatje], *s.m.* worker in glass industry (who works with a blowpipe).

feld-maréchal [fɛldmareʃal], *s.m.* field-marshal; *pl. feld-maréchaux.*

feldspath [fɛl(d)spat], *s.m. Miner:* fel(d)spar; **f. nacré**, argentine, moonstone; **f. vert**, Amazon stone, amazonite; **f. calcosodique**, lime soda feldspar.

feldspathides [fɛl(d)spatid], *s.m.pl. Miner:* (the) feldspathoids.

feldspathiforme [fɛl(d)spatifɔrm], *a.* resembling feldspar.

feldspathique [fɛl(d)spatik], *a. Miner:* fel(d)spathic, fel(d)spathose.

feldspathisation [fɛl(d)spatizasjɔ̃], *s.f. Miner:* feldspathization.

feldspathoïdes [fɛl(d)spatɔid], *s.m.pl. Miner:* (the) feldspathoids.

fêle [fɛl], *s.f. Glassm:* blowpipe.

fêlé [fɛle], *a.* cracked (glass, voice, etc.); **inventeur à l'esprit f.**, crack-brained inventor; **il a le cerveau f., le timbre f., la tête fêlée**, he's a bit cracked; *s.m.* (*of bell, etc.*) **sonner le fêlé**, to sound cracked.

fêler [fɛle], *v.tr.* to crack (glass, china, etc.).

se fêler, (*of glass, etc.*) to crack.

félibre, -bresse [felibr, -brɛs], *s. Lit:* (*a*) writer in the Provençal language; (*b*) member of the *félibrige.*

félibrée [felibre], *s.f. Lit:* meeting of the *félibrige.*

félibréen, -enne [felibreɛ̃, -ɛn], *a. Lit:* relating to the *félibrige.*

félibrige [felibriːʒ], *s.m. Lit:* society of poets and prose writers formed in 1854 with the object of preserving the Provençal language.

Félicie [felisi]. 1. *Pr.n.f.* Felicia. 2. *s.f. Bot:* felicia.

félicitation [felisitasjɔ̃], *s.f.* congratulation; **adresser des félicitations à qn**, to congratulate s.o.; **je vous en fais mes félicitations; félicitations!** congratulations! **il a reçu de nombreuses félicitations**, many people congratulated him; he was widely congratulated.

félicité[1] [felisite], *s.f.* felicity, bliss(fulness), happiness, joy; **une félicité m'envahit**, I was overcome with joy; a wave of happiness swept over me.

Félicité[2], *Pr.n.f.* Felicity.

féliciter [felisite], *v.tr.* **f. qn de qch., d'avoir fait qch.**, to congratulate, compliment, s.o. on sth., on having done sth.; **f. qn sur ses progrès**, to congratulate s.o. on his progress; *Iron:* **je vous en félicite!** I wish you the joy of it! much good may it do you! so what!

se féliciter, se f. de qch., to be pleased with sth., to express satisfaction at sth.; *abs. F:* to pat oneself on the back; **j'ai tout lieu de me f. de l'issue**, I have every reason to be satisfied with the result; **félicitons-nous de ce que nous avons la vie sauve**, let us be thankful we came out alive; **à la longue nous n'eûmes qu'à nous en f.**, it turned out to be a blessing in disguise; **je n'ai eu qu'à me f. de mes conseillers**, I have been singularly fortunate in my advisers.

félidés [felide], *s.m.pl. Z:* Felidae; the cat family; **un félidé**, a felid.

félin, -ine [felɛ̃, -in], *a.* feline; (*a*) *Z:* cat (family, etc.); **exposition féline**, cat show; *s.* **les grands félins**, the great felines; *F:* the big cats; (*b*) cat-like; **grâce féline**, feline, kittenish, grace.

félinité [felinite], *s.f.* felinity.

félir [feliːr], *v.i.* (*of cat*) to spit.

Félix [feliks], *Pr.n.m.* Felix.

fellag(h)a [fɛlaga], *s.m.* fellagha.

fellah [fɛl(l)a], *s.m.* fellah, Egyptian peasant; **les fellahs**, the fellaheen.

Fellatas [fɛllata], *s.m.pl. Ethn:* Fellatahs, F(o)ulahs.

felle [fɛl], *s.f. Glassm:* blowpipe.

féloïdes [felɔid], *s.m.pl. Z:* Feloidea.

félon, -onne [felɔ̃, -ɔn], *A:* 1. *a.* disloyal, false, traitorous, felon. 2. *s.m.* felon, caitiff.

félonie [felɔni], *s.f. A:* disloyalty, traitorousness; *Feud:* felony.

Feloup(e)s [fɛlup], *s.m.pl. Ethn:* Feloops, Felup.

felouque [fəluk], *s.f. Nau:* felucca.

felsite [fɛlsit], *s.f. Miner:* felsite.

felsobanyite [fɛlsɔbanjit], *s.f. Miner:* felsobanyite.

fêlure [fɛlyːr], *s.f.* crack (in china, etc.); split (in wood, etc.), flaw (in diamond); *Surg:* infraction; **f. du crâne**, fracture of the skull; *Lit:* **une f. dans le cristal de notre amitié**, a rift in the lute; **elle remarqua dans sa voix une f. de dépit**, she observed a break in his voice indicating his resentment; **il a une f.**, he's a bit cracked, a bit touched.

femelle [fəmɛl], *s.f. & a.* 1. (*a*) female (animal, sex, etc.); she-(animal); **portée de trois petits chiens, un mâle et deux femelles**, litter of three pups, one dog and two bitches; **une girafe f.**, a cow-giraffe; **un éléphant f.**, a cow-elephant; **un serin f.**, a hen-canary; (*b*) *F: Pej:* **ce n'est qu'une f.**, after all, she's only a woman; **l'espèce f.**, women, the female species. 2. *a.* (*a*) *Tchn:* female (screw, etc.); *El.E:* **prise f.**, socket connector; (*b*) *Bot:* female, pistillate (flower).

femelot [fəmlo], *s.m. N.Arch:* gudgeon (of rudder).

féminilité [feminilite], *s.f.* 1. womanliness. 2. effeminacy.

féminin, -ine [feminɛ̃, -in]. 1. *a.* feminine (gender, grace, rhyme, etc.); **le sexe f.**, the female sex; *Lit:* the fair sex; **voix féminine**, (i) woman's voice; (ii) womanish voice. 2. *s.m. Gram:* feminine (gender); **ce mot est du f.**, this word is feminine; **adjectif au f.**, adjective in the feminine; **substantif qui prend un -e au f.**, noun that takes an -e in the feminine.

féminisation [feminizasjɔ̃], *s.f.* feminization.

féminiser [feminize], *v.tr.* 1. to feminize; to make feminine, womanish; to give a feminine cast, tone, appearance, to (s.o., sth.). 2. **f. un mot**, to make a word feminine.

féminisme [feminism], *s.m.* feminism.

féministe [feminist], *a. & s.* feminist.

féminité [feminite], *s.f.* femineity, femininity.

femme [fam], *s.f.* 1. (*a*) woman; *Coll.* women; **les femmes**, womankind, womenfolk; *Hum: F:* **ses femmes**, his womenfolk, the women of his family; **l'instinct de la f.**, a woman's instinct; **l'émancipation de la f.**, the emancipation of women; **vertus de f.**, womanly virtues; **voix de f.**, woman's voice, female voice; **cherchez la f.**, cherchez la femme, there's a woman behind this; **réunion entre femmes**, (i) women's meeting; (ii) *F:* hen party; **elle est très f.**, she's very feminine; **elle est plus f. que sa sœur**, she's more of a woman than her sister; **passer f.**, to grow into a woman, to reach womanhood; **devenir f.**, (i) to become, grow into, a woman; (ii) to lose one's virginity; **une f. d'intérieur**, a domesticated woman; **une maîtresse f.**, an authoritative woman; **f. auteur, f. de lettres**, woman author, authoress; **f. médecin**, woman doctor; **elle n'est pas f. à se laisser conter**, she's not the sort of woman who believes everything she is told; **elle est f. à se venger**, she's a revengeful sort of woman; (*b*) *Jur:* **la f. Martin**, (the woman, the accused) Martin; **f. en puissance de mari**, feme covert, married woman; **f. célibataire**, feme sole; spinster. 2. wife; **une jeune f.**, a young married woman; **faire sa f. de qn**, to marry s.o., **chercher f.**, to look for a wife; **prendre f.**, to get married; **avoir f.**, to have a wife, to be married; *s.a.* DIABLE 1. 3. **f. de chambre**, (i) housemaid; (ii)

lady's maid; (iii) chambermaid; *Nau:* stewardess; **f. de charge,** housekeeper; **f. de journée, f. de ménage,** charwoman, daily help; *F:* daily; *A:* **sa f. est une bonne f. de ménage,** his wife is a good housekeeper. **4.** *(a)* **une bonne f.,** a simple, good-natured (old) woman; **sa bonne f. de mère,** his old mother; *(b)* **une vieille bonne f.,** a little old woman; **contes, remèdes, de bonne f.,** old wives' tales, remedies. **5.** *Cards: P:* queen.

femme-agent [famaʒɑ̃], *s.f.* policewoman; *pl. femmes-agents.*

femmelette [famlɛt], *s.f. F:* *(a)* little woman; weak, delicate, woman; silly woman; *(b)* *(of a man)* weakling; **ce n'est pas un homme, c'est une f.,** he's nothing but an old woman.

femme-serpent [famsɛrpɑ̃], *s.f.* (female) contortionist; *pl. femmes-serpents.*

femme-soldat [famsɔlda], *s.f.* servicewoman; *pl. femmes-soldats.*

fémoral, -aux [femɔral, -o], *a. Anat:* femoral (artery, etc.).

femto [fɛmto], *pref. Mth:* femto.

fémur [femyːr], *s.m. Anat:* femur, thigh bone.

fenaison [fənɛzɔ̃], *s.f.* **1.** haymaking, hay harvest; **une fois la f. faite,** once the hay is cut. **2.** haymaking time.

fenasse [fənas], *s.f.* **1.** *Bot: F:* tall meadow oat, false oat grass. **2.** fragments of hay (scattered on the floor of the hayloft).

fenassier [fənasje], *s.m.* stable hand (in charge of fodder).

fenchène [fɛ̃ʃɛn], *s.m. Ch:* fenchene.

fenchol [fɛ̃ʃɔl], *s.m. Ch:* fenchyl alcohol.

fenchone [fɛ̃ʃɔn], *s.f. Ch:* fenchone.

fenchyle [fɛ̃ʃil], *s.m. Ch:* fenchyl.

fenchylique [fɛ̃ʃilik], *a. Ch:* **alcool f.,** fenchyl alcohol.

fendage [fɑ̃daːʒ], *s.m.* **1.** splitting, cleaving, slitting (of wood, etc.). **2.** slotting (of screw head).

fendant [fɑ̃dɑ̃]. **1.** *s.m. A:* *(a)* (sword)cut; *(b)* brawler, braggart, bully; **faire le fendant,** to play the bully. **2.** *a.* bullying, hectoring. **3.** *s.m. Vit:* fendant (grape or wine).

fendante [fɑ̃dɑ̃ːt], *s.f. Tls:* slot(ting) file.

fendard [fɑ̃daːr], *s.m. P:* trousers; slacks.

fenderie [fɑ̃dri], *s.f.* **1.** splitting, slitting, cutting, (of metal, wood) into rods. **2.** *(a)* splitting mill, slitting mill; *(b)* splitting machine, splitting rollers; *(c)* cutting shop.

fendeur, -euse [fɑ̃dœːr, -øːz], *s.* *(a)* splitter, slitter (of slates, leather, etc.); cleaver (of diamonds, etc.); *(b)* woodcutter.

fendille [fɑ̃diːj], (surface) crack; fissure (in paint, china, etc.); small crack (in wood); flaw (in metal).

fendillé [fɑ̃dije], *a.* fissured; cracked; crackled.

fendillement [fɑ̃dijmɑ̃], *s.m.* fissuration; cracking (of paint, wood, etc.); crackling (of glaze); crazing; break (in the surface, the skin, etc.).

fendiller [fɑ̃dije], *v.tr.* to fissure; to crack (wood, etc.); to crackle, craze (glaze).

se fendiller, *(of wood, paint, etc.)* to crack; *(of china, glaze)* to crackle, to craze; *(of concrete)* to craze.

fendoir [fɑ̃dwaːr], *s.m.* chopper, cleaver; splitting axe.

fendre [fɑ̃ːdr], *v.tr.* **1.** *(a)* to cleave (lengthwise); to split, slit, rive (wood, slate, etc.); to rip up (plank, sheet, etc.); *(b)* to part, fissure; **la sécheresse a fendu la terre,** the drought has cracked, fissured, the ground; *Lit:* **le navire fendait les eaux, l'onde,** the boat cut, ploughed, (through) the waters; *(of swimmer)* **f. la lame,** to breast the waves; **f. l'air,** to cleave the air; *(of sound)* to rend the air; **f. la foule,** to force, elbow, break, one's way through the crowd; to squeeze through the crowd; **il gèle à pierre f.,** it is freezing hard; **c'était à f. l'âme,** it was heartbreaking, heartrending; it was enough to break your heart; **pleurer à f. l'âme,** to cry pitifully; **le cœur me fend de voir . . .,** it breaks my heart to see . . .; **cris à f. le cœur,** heartrending cries; **ne me fendez pas la tête,** (i) don't make such a din; (ii) say no more; **bruit à f. la tête, à vous f. les oreilles,** ear-splitting noise; *P:* **se f. la pipe,** to split one's sides laughing; *Mil: P:* **f. l'oreille à qn,** to put s.o. on the retired list. **2.** to slot (screw head).

se fendre. 1. *(of wood, etc.)* to split, crack; **la terre, la muraille, commence à se f.,** the earth, the wall, is beginning to crack, to gape. **2.** *Fenc:* to lunge; **se f. à fond,** to make a full lunge. **3.** *P:* **se fendre (de vingt francs),** to fork out, stump up (twenty francs); **il s'est fendu!** he did the thing handsomely; **il ne s'est pas fendu,** it didn't cost him a penny.

fendu [fɑ̃dy], *a.* split, cloven; **goupille, bague, fendue,** split pin, split ring; **marteau à panne fendue,** claw hammer; **pied f.,** cloven hoof; **jupe fendue,** slashed skirt; **avoir la bouche fendue jusqu'aux oreilles,** to have a mouth that stretches from ear to ear; **yeux bien fendus,** large, wide-open eyes; *F:* **être bien f.,** to be long-legged.

fendue [fɑ̃dy], *s.f. Min:* (*Central & S. Fr.*) mine entry, adit, stulm.

fêne [fɛn], *s.f.* beechnut.

fenestella [fənɛstɛla], *s.f. Arch:* fenestella.

fénestella [fenɛstɛla], *s.f. Paleont:* fenestella.

fénestellidés [fenɛstɛlide], *s.m.pl. Paleont:* Fenestellidae.

fenestrage [fənɛstraːʒ], *s.m.* windows; fenestration (of building).

fenestration [fənɛstrasjɔ̃], *s.f. Arch: Med:* fenestration.

fenestré [fənɛstre], *a.* *(a)* *Anat: Bot:* fenestrate; *Geol:* **structure fenestrée,** lattice structure; *(b)* **des découpures plus frêles et plus fenestrées qu'une dentelle,** a cut-out pattern more delicate and with more open-work than lace.

fenestrelle [fənɛstrɛl], *s.f. Arch:* small window.

fenestrer [fənɛstre], *v.tr. Arch:* to fenestrate.

fenestron [fənɛstrɔ̃], *s.m.* (*S. of Fr.*) small window.

fenêtrage [fənɛtraːʒ], *s.m.* windows; fenestration (of building).

fenêtre [fənɛːtr], *s.f.* **1.** window; **f. à coulisse, à guillotine,** sash window; **f. croisée, à battants,** French window, casement window; **f. en saillie,** bay window, bow window; **f. en lézarde,** gap window; **f. à glissière,** sliding window; **f. à bascule, à charnière, oscillante,** balance window; *Fr.C:* **f. anglaise,** sash window; *Ecc.Arch:* **fenêtres hautes,** clerestory; **fausse f.,** (i) blind, blank, false, window; (ii) *N.Arch:* deadlight; **regarder par la f.,** to look out of the window; **façade sans f.,** windowless façade; *F:* **il faut passer par là ou par la f.,** it is absolutely inevitable; there is no choice, no alternative, nothing else for it; **mettre la tête à la f.,** (i) to thrust one's head out of the window; (ii) *P:* to be guillotined; *P:* **boucher une f. à qn,** to give s.o. a punch in the eye; *P:* *(of prostitute)* **faire la f.,** to make signs to men, to solicit, from the window; *s.a.* JETER. **2.** blank, space (in document). **3.** *Anat:* fenestra, window (of the tympanum). **4.** cut-away portion; opening; aperture; window (in envelope) *Mch:* port (in cylinder); **f. de lecture,** reading window (of instrument); (*Computers*) **carte à f.,** aperture card; *Sm.a:* **f. d'éjection,** ejection slot; *(radar)* **f. de poursuite,** follower gate; **f. de visée d'un blockhaus,** sighting port of a conning tower; *Cin:* **f. de projection,** film gate (of projector); **f. d'observation (de la cabine de projection),** observation port; *Geol:* **f. (dans une nappe de charriage)** inlier.

fenêtré [fənetre], *a.* **1.** windowed. **2.** *Anat: Bot:* fenestrate. **3.** *Surg:* fenestrated (bandage).

fenêtrer [fənetre], *v.tr.* *(a)* to put windows in (house); *(b)* *Med:* to fenestrate (bandage, etc.).

fénian [fenjɑ̃], *s.m. Pol.Hist:* Fenian.

fénianisme [fenjanism], *s.m. Pol.Hist:* Fenianism.

fenier [fənje], *s.m. Dial:* (*in Central Fr.*) (large) haystack.

fenil [fəni(l)], *s.m.* hayloft.

fennec [fɛnnɛk], *s.m. Z:* fennec.

fenouil [fənuːj], *s.m. Bot:* fennel; **f. officinal,** sweet fennel; **f. marin, f. de mer,** sea fennel, samphire; **f. de porc,** hog's, sow's, fennel; sulphur wort, milkweed; **f. bâtard,** dill; **f. sauvage,** hemlock; **f. des Alpes,** spignel, baldmoney.

fenouillet [fənujɛ], *s.m. Bot:* fennel apple.

fenouillette [fənujɛt], *s.f.* **1.** *Bot:* fennel apple. **2.** fennel water.

fente [fɑ̃ːt], *s.f.* **1.** *(a)* crack, crevice, split, slit, fissure, chink (in door, wall, etc.); *Anat:* fissure (of sphenoid bone, etc.); **tube étiré sans f.,** solid-drawn tube; *Geol:* **f. de retrait,** shrinkage crack; *Com:* **bois de f.,** cloven timber; laths; *(b)* slot, cut (in piece of wood, head of screw, etc.); *Av:* **aile à fentes,** slotted wing; *(c)* *Opt: etc:* slit (for admission of light); lookout slit (in gun shield, etc.); **f. d'observation,** observation slit; **f. de visée,** aiming slit; **f. annulaire,** annulus; **faire une f. dans une étoffe,** to cut a slit in a piece of cloth; **f. de poche,** pocket hole. **2.** *(a)* *Fenc: etc:* lunge; *(b)* *Sp:* length of leg (of athlete).

fenton [fɑ̃tɔ̃], *s.m.* **1.** *(a)* dowel wood, peg wood; *(b)* strip iron. **2.** *(a)* treenail, dowel, peg, pin, plug; *(b)* (iron) tie.

fenugrec [fənygrɛk], *s.m. Bot:* fenugreek.

féodal, -aux [feɔdal, -o], **1.** *a.* feudal. **2.** *s.m.* feudal lord; *F:* big landowner.

féodalement [feɔdalmɑ̃], *adv.* feudally.

féodalisation [feɔdalizasjɔ̃], *s.f.* feudalization.

féodaliser [feɔdalize], *v.tr.* to feudalize.

féodalisme [feɔdalism], *s.m.* feudalism.

féodalité [feɔdalite], *s.f.* feudality; the feudal system.

fer¹ [fɛːr], *s.m.* iron. **1.** *(a)* **minerai de f.,** iron ore; **f. des lacs, des marais,** bog iron ore; **f. cru, brut,** raw, crude, iron; **f. fondu,** ingot iron; **f. coulé, de fonte,** cast iron; **f. en saumon, en gueuse,** pig (iron); **f. puddlé,** forge pig (iron); **f. de masse,** scrap iron; **f. doux,** soft iron; **f. affiné,** malleable iron; **f. aigre,** brittle, short, iron; **f. forgé, soudé, battu,** wrought iron; **f. œuvré,** hand-wrought iron; **f. en tôles, en feuilles,** iron sheet, sheet iron; **f. laminé, cylindré,** rolled iron; **f. en barres,** bar, strip, iron; **f. plat, f. feuillard,** hoop iron; *Com:* **f. plat,** flat bar iron; **f. en plaques,** boiler plate; **f. carré,** square iron bar; **f. galvanisé, zingué,** galvanized iron; **fer à, en, T,** T iron; **f. à, en, U,** U iron; **f. à cornière,** angle iron; **fil de f.,** wire; *(b)* **l'âge de f.,** the iron age; **corps, discipline, de f.,** iron constitution, discipline; **digérer du f.,** to have a cast-iron stomach; **dur comme (le) f.,** as hard as iron; **croire dur comme f. (que),** to have a cast-iron, unshakeable, belief (that); **avoir une volonté, une tête, de f.,** to have an iron will, a will of iron; **ne tenir ni à f. ni à clou,** to be in a rickety, ramshackle, state; to be in a state of collapse; **battre le f. quand il est chaud,** to strike while the iron is hot. **2.** *(a)* **f. (d'une canne),** ferrule (of a stick); **f. de lance,** lance head, spear head; *Bot:* **en f. de lance,** lanceolate; **f. de toupie,** peg of a top; **f. de hache,** axe head; **f. de flèche,** arrow head; **f. de gaffe,** boathook; **f. d'un lacet,** tag of a lace; **f. de botte,** heel plate (of boot); **f. de rabot,** plane iron; cutting iron, blade, of a plane; *(b)* shoe, band, cap (of pile, wooden beam, etc.); *(c)* *Bookb:* (i) tool; (ii) brass; **petit f.,** bookbinder's punch; *(d)* sword; **croiser, engager, le f. avec qn,** to cross swords with s.o.; **battre le f.,** to fence; *Fenc:* **tirer dans le f.,** to thrust on the side on which one's opponent is covered; **porter le feu et le f. dans un pays,** to put a country to fire and sword; *(e)* *(of surgeon)* **avoir recours au f.,** to resort to the knife; **employer le f. et le feu,** (i) to use knife and cautery; (ii) to employ drastic means. **3.** *Tls: etc:* **f. à souder,** soldering iron, soldering bit; **f. à marquer,** branding iron; **marquer au f. rouge,** to brand; *Dom.Ec:* **f. à repasser,** (laundry) iron; **f. électrique,** electric iron; **f. (électrique) à vapeur,** steam iron; **f. à tuyauter,** goffering iron; **donner un coup de f. à qch.,** to press, iron, sth.; **mettre les fers au feu,** to set to work; **f. à friser,** curling tongs; *Cu:* **f. à gauffres,** waffle iron; *Golf:* **grand f.,** driving iron; **f. moyen,** mid iron; **coup de f.,** iron shot. **4.** *pl.* irons, chains, fetters, shackles; **mettre qn aux fers,** to clap s.o. in irons; **être aux fers,** to be in irons, in chains; **il avait des fers aux mains et aux pieds,** his hands and feet were fettered; **briser les fers à qn,** to set s.o. free; **rompre ses fers,** to set oneself free; *(b)* *Obst:* forceps. **5. fer à, de, cheval,** horseshoe; *Fort:* **f. à cheval,** horseshoe; *Arch:* **arc en f. à cheval,** horseshoe arch; *Med:* **rein en f. à cheval,** horseshoe kidney; **table en f. à cheval,** horseshoe table; **f. à glace, à crampons,** frost shoe; **mettre un f. à un cheval,** to shoe a horse; *(of horse)* **perdre un f.,** to cast a shoe; **tomber les quatre fers en l'air,** (i) *(of horse)* to fall on its back; (ii) *F:* *(of pers.)* to go sprawling; **il y a quelque f. qui cloche,** there's something wrong, there's a screw loose somewhere; **il ne vaut pas les quatre fers d'un chien,** he's a good-for-nothing.

fer², *s.m.* **f. en meubles,** stuffing, padding (for furniture).

féra [fera], *s.f. Ich:* dace.

fer-à-cheval [fɛraʃ(ə)val], *s.m.* **1.** *Z:* horseshoe bat. **2.** *Bot:* horseshoe vetch; *pl. fers-à-cheval.*

feralia [feralja], **féralies** [ferali], *s.f.pl. Rom.Ant:* Feralia.

ferbérite [fɛrberit], *s.f. Miner:* ferberite.

fer-blanc [fɛrblɑ̃], *s.m.* tinplate; **boîte en f.-b.,** tin, can; **articles en f.-b.,** tinware; *pl. fers-blancs.*

ferblanterie [fɛrblɑ̃tri], *s.f.* **1.** *(a)* tinplate (i) industry, (ii) trade; *(b)* ironmonger's shop. **2.** *(a)* tinware; ironmongery; *(b)* *F: Pej:* medals, *F:* gongs.

ferblantier [fɛrblɑ̃tje], *s.m.* *(a)* tinman, tinsmith, whitesmith; *(b)* ironmonger; *(c)* *Nau: P: A:* naval officer (attached to an administrative unit).

fer-chaud [fɛrʃo], *s.m. A: Med:* heartburn.

fer-de-lance [fɛrdəlɑ̃ːs], *s.m. F:* **1.** *Rept:* fer-de-lance, rat-tailed serpent. **2.** *Z:* (S. American) leaf-nosed bat; *pl. fers-de-lance.*

fer-de-moulin [fɛrdəmulɛ̃], *s.m. Her:* fer-de-moline; *pl. fers-de-moulin.*

Ferdinand [fɛrdinɑ̃], Pr.n.m. Ferdinand.

féret [ferɛ], s.m. Tchn: = FERRET.

ferghanite [fɛrganit], s.f. Miner: ferganite.

fergusonite [fɛrgysɔnit], s.f. Miner: fergusonite.

férial, -aux [ferjal, -o], a. Ecc: ferial (office, etc.).

férie [feri], s.f. 1. Rom.Ant: feria, day of rest, holiday. 2. Ecc: feria, weekday.

férié [ferje], a. jour f., public holiday; Adm: = bank holiday; Ecc: holy day, day of obligation; Jur: dies non.

férier [ferje], v.tr. f. un jour, to appoint, keep, a day as a holiday.

férin [ferɛ̃], a. Med: toux férine, spasmodic cough.

férir [feri:r], v.tr. A: to strike; used only in sans coup f., (i) Lit: without striking a blow; without firing a shot; (ii) without encountering any obstacle; without meeting any resistance.

se férir, (used in inf. and compound tenses) se f. de qn, to fall (madly) in love with s.o.; elle s'est férue d'un cousin, she has fallen in love with a cousin; il s'était féru de libre échange, he had become a rabid free-trader; elle s'était férue du théâtre, she had become stagestruck.

ferlage [fɛrla:ʒ], s.m. furling (of sails).

ferler [fɛrle], v.tr. to furl (sail).

ferlet [fɛrlɛ], s.m. Paperm: etc: peel.

fermage [fɛrma:ʒ], s.m. 1. (tenant) farming. 2. rent (of farm); état des fermages, rent roll.

fermail [fɛrma:j], s.m. (ornamental) clasp; fastening (of garment, bible, etc.); pl. fermaux.

fermaillet [fɛrmajɛ], s.m. small ornamental clasp.

fermant [fɛrmɑ̃]. 1. a. closing; (a) provided with a lock; (b) O: arriver à portes fermantes, to arrive as the gates are closing; à jour fermant, à nuit fermante, at dusk, at close of day. 2. s.m. hinged cover (of painting, mirror).

ferme¹ [fɛrm]. 1. a. (a) firm, steady; hard, solid; poutre f., firm, rigid, beam; gelée f., firm jelly; à la chair f., firm-fleshed; terre f., (i) firm, solid, land; (ii) mainland; terra firma; je n'aime pas les avions; je préfère la terre f., I don't like aircraft; I prefer travelling by land, on terra firma; sur un terrain f., on solid ground; d'un pas f., with a firm tread; d'un ton f., in a decided tone; il répondit d'une voix f., he replied in a firm, steady, voice; être f. à cheval, sur ses étriers, to have a steady seat; tenir les rênes d'une main f., to hold the reins firmly; maintenir ses prix fermes, to keep one's prices steady; le marché reste très f., the market continues very strong; avoir le f. propos, la f. volonté, la f. intention, de faire qch., to have the firm intention of doing sth.; volonté très f., unfaltering will; soyez f., be firm; être f. dans ses desseins, to be firm, steadfast, in one's intentions; toujours f. dans son dessein d'attaquer, persistent in his intention to attack; très f. à maintenir son autorité, very firm in the upholding of his authority; Mil: de pied f., at the halt; attendre qn de pied f., to wait resolutely for s.o.; combattre de pied f., to make a stout resistance; (of horse) sauter de f. à f., to prance without moving forward; (b) vente f., offre f., firm, definite, sale, offer. 2. (a) adv. firmly; clou qui tient f., nail that holds fast, firmly; tenir f., to stand fast, to hold one's own; frapper f., to hit hard; j'y travaille f., I am hard at it, hard at work; nier qch. fort et f., to deny sth. stoutly; croire fort et f. aux esprits, to be a firm believer in spirits; petite ville où on s'ennuie f., small town that bores one to tears; manger f., (i) to eat steadily through the courses; (ii) to be a hearty eater; nous avons discuté f. pendant deux heures, we argued solidly for two hours; condamné à cinq ans de prison f., condemned to five years' imprisonment with no possibility of remission; Com: vendre f., to make a firm sale; acheter qch. f., to buy sth. firm; (b) int: ferme! (i) steady! (ii) pull! (on rope, etc.). 3. s.m. (a) Min: vein adjacent to a gallery; galerie au f., en f., gallery opened in a hitherto unexploited area; (b) Ven: (i) (of wild boar) tenir le f., to stand, be, at bay; (ii) f. roulant, mort; (c) St.Exch: firm stock.

ferme², s.f. 1. (a) farming lease; prendre une terre à f., to take a lease of, to rent, a piece of land; donner à f., to farm out; (b) farm; farmhouse; farmstead; petite f., smallholding; valet de f., farmhand; fille de f., maid (on a farm); dairymaid; il travaille dans une f., he is working on a farm; f. école, agricultural college; college farm, demonstration farm; exploitation d'une f., farming. 2. Adm: A: farming (of taxes); donner un impôt à f., to farm out a tax. 3. (a) truss (of roof, bridge, etc.); f. simple, king-post truss; (b) trussed girder; f. en arc, arch girder; (c) Mch: f. du ciel du foyer, crown bar of the fire box. 4. Th: rigid flat, set piece.

fermé [fɛrme], a. 1. closed (door, window); bureaux fermés au public, offices closed to the public; port f., close harbour; rade fermée, landlocked roadstead; bout f., dead end (of pipe, etc.); voiture fermée, closed conveyance; dormir à poings fermés, to sleep soundly, like a log; je pouvais y aller les yeux fermés, I could go there blindfold, with my eyes shut; O: à la nuit fermée, when night had fallen; avoir la main fermée, to be mean, avaricious; frapper à main fermée, to hit hard; être f. à qch., to have no taste for, no appreciation of, sth.; f. au sentiment du beau, blind to beauty, inaccessible to any feeling of beauty; il a l'esprit f. aux mathématiques, mathematics are a closed book to him; Ling: voyelle fermée, syllabe fermée, closed vowel, syllable; Tchn: position "fermé," off position. 2. visage f., irresponsive, inscrutable, impassive, countenance. 3. monde, cercle, très f., very exclusive society, club.

ferme-circuit [fɛrmsirkɥi], s.m.inv. El.E: circuit-closer.

ferme-imposte [fɛrmɛ̃pɔst], s.m.inv. mechanical window-opener.

fermement [fɛrməmɑ̃], adv. firmly, steadily, unswervingly; je crois f. que . . ., I firmly believe that . . .; soutenir f. une opinion, to maintain an opinion resolutely, stoutly.

ferment [fɛrmɑ̃], s.m. ferment (of wine, of ill-feeling, etc.); leaven (of bread, etc.); Ecc.Hist: fermentum.

fermentable [fɛrmɑ̃tabl], a. fermentable.

fermentatif, -ive [fɛrmɑ̃tatif, -i:v], a. fermentative, producing fermentation.

fermentation [fɛrmɑ̃tasjɔ̃], s.f. 1. fermentation; F: working (of wine, etc.); rising (of dough, etc.); Med: zymosis; f. gastro-intestinale, flatulence. 2. agitation; unrest; ferment.

fermenter [fɛrmɑ̃te], v.i. 1. (of wine, etc.) to ferment, F: work; (of dough, etc.) to rise. 2. les esprits fermentaient, men's minds were seething with excitement, were in a ferment.

fermentescibilité [fɛrmɑ̃tɛsibilite], s.f. fermentability.

fermentescible [fɛrmɑ̃tɛsibl], a. fermentable, fermentescible.

fermenteur [fɛrmɑ̃tœ:r], s.m. fermentor.

ferme-porte [fɛrm(ə)pɔrt], s.m.inv. door spring, U.S: door closer, door check.

fermer [fɛrme]. 1. v.tr. (a) to close, shut; Nau: to batten down; f. hermétiquement, to seal hermetically; f. la porte, la fenêtre, to close the door, the window; f. le store, to pull down the blind; f. la porte au nez de qn, to shut, slam, the door in s.o.'s face; f. violemment la porte, to slam, bang, the door; f. sa porte à qn, to close one's door against s.o.; to deny one's door to s.o.; f. la porte à clef, au verrou, to lock, to bolt, the door; f. la porte à double tour, to double-lock the door; f. les rideaux, to draw, close, the curtains; f. une maison, to shut up a house; f. boutique, to shut up shop; on ferme! closing time! le théâtre fermera ses portes pour un mois, the theatre will close for a month; f. un éventail, to furl a fan; f. un trou, to stop up, block up, a hole; f. une lettre, to close, seal up, a letter; f. une liste, to close a list; f. un débat, to close a debate; f. la serrure, to turn the key in the lock; f. un robinet, to turn off a tap; f. l'eau, to turn off, shut off, the water; f. le gaz, (i) to turn out the gas; (ii) to turn off the gas (at the meter); (iii) Aut: to throttle down (the engine); f. l'électricité, la lumière, to switch off the light; f. la radio, to turn, switch, off the radio; f. un jardin par un mur, au moyen d'un mur, to wall in a garden; cette victoire ferma la mer Égée à notre flotte, this victory closed the Aegean to our fleet; f. l'oreille à un cancan, to close one's ears to a piece of gossip; f. les yeux à la lumière, to shut one's eyes to the truth; Const: f. un cours d'assises, to lay the last stone of a course; f. une voûte, to put the keystone in place; El: f. un circuit, to close a circuit, to switch on (light, current); Nau: f. la voilure, to brace in the sails; Rail: f. la voie, to block the line; Knitting: f. cinq mailles, to cast off five stitches; f. la bouche à qn, to reduce s.o. to silence; P: ferme ta gueule! ferme-la! la ferme! shut up! dry up! shut your trap! (b) f. la marche, to bring up the rear, to close up the rear; le cortège était fermé par les pompiers, the fire brigade closed the procession; (c) Nau: f. deux amers, to come into line with two landmarks; f. un promontoire par un autre, to close one headland with another; (d) Games: (at dominoes) f. le jeu, to block the game. 2. v.i. to close; porte qui ferme bien, door that shuts well; le parc ferme à quatre heures, the park closes at four o'clock; hôtel qui ferme pour l'hiver, hotel that closes down for the winter.

se fermer, to close, shut; la porte se ferma immédiatement, the door shut, closed, at once; la plaie se ferme, n'est pas encore fermée, the wound is healing, has not healed yet; ses yeux se fermèrent, his eyes closed; à cette demande son visage se ferma, at this request his face froze.

fermeté [fɛrməte], s.f. firmness (of jelly, of purpose); steadfastness, steadiness (of purpose); strength (of mind); rigidity (of principles); manquer de f., to be lacking in firmness, to have no backbone; agir avec f., to act firmly, resolutely.

fermette [fɛrmɛt], s.f. 1. Constr: (a) false gable truss; dormer-window truss; (b) sluice-gate truss; barrage à fermettes, needle dam. 2. (a) small farm; (b) (country) weekend cottage.

fermeture [fɛrməty:r], s.f. 1. (a) closing, shutting (of gates, door, etc.); closure; f. des ateliers, (i) knocking off (from work); (ii) closing down of the workshops; (iii) lock-out; f. des bureaux au public, closing of the offices to the public; heure de f., closing time (of shop); knocking-off time (of works); f. de la pêche, de la chasse, close of the fishing season, of the shooting season; Com: f. d'un compte, closing of an account; El: f. du circuit, closing, making, of the circuit; Tg: Tp: fil de f., jumper; Mch: f. de l'admission, cut-off (of steam); (b) fastening; f. à clef, locking; appareil de f., locking apparatus; à f. automatique, self-locking; Hyd.E: etc: f. à eau, f. hydraulique, water seal; (c) f. d'esprit, narrow-mindedness. 2. (a) closing apparatus; f. à grille extensible, sliding lattice; gate; f. à vis, screw stopper; f. à glissière, à crémaillère, R.t.m: f. éclair, zip fastener; (b) shutter (of shop); f. à rouleau, revolving shutter; (c) Sm.a: locking, closing, U.S: fermeture; f. de culasse, (i) breech closure, U.S: fermeture; (ii) breech-closing mechanism.

fermi [fɛrmi]. 1. Pr.n. Atom.Ph: âge de F., Fermi age; constante de F., Fermi constant. 2. s.m. Atom.Ph: Meas: fermi.

fermier, -ière [fɛrmje, -jɛ:r], s. 1. (a) tenant (of farm); tenant farmer; (b) farmer; une fermière, (i) a farmer's wife; (ii) a (woman) farmer. 2. (a) Hist: farmer of taxes, tax farmer; f. général, farmer general; (b) f. d'entreprise, contractor. 3. attrib. (a) société fermière, trust (of a newspaper); compagnie fermière, company to which state property is farmed out; (b) beurre f., farm butter; poulet f., farm chicken, free-range chicken; (c) Tex: satin fermière, printed sateen.

fermion [fɛrmjɔ̃], s.m. Atom.Ph: fermion.

fermium [fɛrmjɔm], s.m. Ch: fermium.

fermoir¹ [fɛrmwa:r], s.m. 1. clasp, hasp, snap, catch, fastener (of book, handbag, etc.); bouton f., clinch button; bouton f. à pression, snap fastener; f. de sûreté, safety catch. 2. Sm.a: cut-off (of box-magazine).

fermoir², s.m. Tls: firmer (chisel), double-bevelled chisel; f. (à) nez rond, f. néron, skew carving chisel.

fermorite [fɛrmɔrit], s.f. Miner: fermorite.

féroce [ferɔs], a. ferocious, savage, wild, fierce; bêtes féroces, wild beasts; vengeance f., ferocious, savage, revenge; une faim f., un appétit f., a ravenous appetite; un regard f., a ferocious look.

férocement [ferɔsmɑ̃], adv. ferociously, savagely, fiercely.

férocité [ferɔsite], s.f. ferocity, ferociousness; savageness, savagery, fierceness.

Féroé [ferɔe], Pr.n. Geog: les iles F., the Faroe Islands.

féroïen, -ienne [ferɔjɛ̃, -jɛn], a. & s.m. Ling: Faroeish.

Féronie [ferɔni], Pr.n.f. Myth: Feronia.

ferrade [fɛrad], s.f. (In S. of Fr.) bull branding.

ferrage [fɛra:ʒ], s.m. covering, fitting, (sth.) with iron; providing (sth.) with iron fittings; shoeing (of wheel, of horse); tagging (of lace); shackling (of convict); putting (of man) in irons; Farr: f. à froid, cold shoeing; f. à glace, rough shoeing, calking; Fish: f. (d'un poisson), striking (of a fish).

ferraillage [fɛrɑja:ʒ], s.m. Const: reinforcement.

ferraille [fɛrɑ:j], s.f. (a) old iron, scrap iron; tas de f., scrap heap; bon pour la f., bon à mettre à la f., good enough for the scrap heap; mettre, envoyer, qch. à la f., to put sth. on, send sth. to, the scrap heap; ma voiture n'était plus qu'un tas de f., my car was reduced to scrap metal, was a complete write-off; bruit de f., clanking noise, rattle; faire un bruit de f., to rattle, clank; marchand de f., scrap merchant; (b) F: je vous

donne toute ma f., I'll give you all my small change.

ferraillement [fɛrɑjmɑ̃], *s.m.* **1.** hammer-and-tongs fighting. **2.** rattling, clanking, noise.

ferrailler [fɛrɑje], *v.i.* **1.** *Pej:* (*a*) to clash swords; to fight; to go at it hammer and tongs; (*b*) to fence clumsily, badly; (*c*) to squabble, wrangle. **2.** to clank, rattle. **3.** *Const:* to reinforce (concrete).

ferrailleur [fɛrɑjœːr], *s.m.* **1.** *Pej:* (*a*) swashbuckler; (*b*) poor fencer; (*c*) squabbler, wrangler. **2.** scrap merchant. **3.** *Const:* worker who prepares reinforcement for concrete.

ferrant [fɛrɑ̃], *a.* **maréchal f.,** shoeing smith, farrier.

ferrarais, -aise [fɛrarɛ, -ɛːz], *a.* & *s.* *Geog:* Ferrarese.

Ferrare [fɛraːr], *Pr.n.f.* *Geog:* Ferrara.

ferrate [fɛr(r)at], *s.m.* *Ch:* ferrate.

ferratier [fɛratje], *s.m.* **1.** scrap merchant. **2.** shoeing smith's hammer.

ferre [fɛːr], *s.f.* *Glassm:* bottle pincers.

ferré [fɛre], *a.* **1.** (*a*) fitted, mounted, with iron; iron-shod (stick, lever, etc.); **poulie ferrée,** iron-bound pulley; **souliers ferrés,** hob-nailed shoes; **voie ferrée,** (i) (railway) track, permanent way (of railway); (ii) railway (line); **réseau f.,** railway system; **cheval f. à glace,** rough-shod, roughed, frost-nailed, sharped, horse; *F:* **être f. (à glace) sur un sujet,** to be perfectly at home with, to know all about, a subject; to be well up in, a subject; to know a subject inside out; (*b*) **route ferrée,** metalled, macadamized, road. **2.** *Med:* *A:* **eau ferrée,** water to which iron nails, etc., have conveyed a certain proportion of rust.

ferrement [fɛrmɑ̃], *s.m.* **1.** (*a*) shoeing (of horse); (*b*) *A:* riveting (of convict's chains). **2.** *pl.* (*a*) (iron) girders (of building); (*b*) **les ferrements d'un coffre,** the ironwork of a chest.

ferréol [fɛreɔl], *s.m.* *Bot:* ironwood.

ferrer [fɛre], *v.tr.* **1.** (*a*) to fit, mount, (sth.) with iron; **f. une porte,** to fit locks and hinges to a door; **f. un bâton,** to put a ferrule on a stick; **f. un lacet,** to tag a lace; **f. une roue,** to tyre, shoe, a wheel; **f. un cheval,** to shoe a horse; **f. à froid,** to cold-shoe; **f. à glace,** to rough-shoe, to calk; *F:* **f. la mule,** (i) to make illicit profits (when buying for others); *F:* to make a bit on the side; (ii) to take a bribe (for obtaining an interview for s.o.); (*b*) *Husb:* **f. un porc,** to ring a pig. **2.** to metal (road). **3.** (*a*) *Fish:* **f. un poisson,** to strike a fish; (*b*) *F:* **f. qn,** to hook s.o.

ferrerie [fɛr(ə)ri], *s.f.* **1.** iron trade. **2.** ironwork.

ferret [fɛrɛ], *s.m.* **1.** tag, tab, a(i)glet (of lace, of aiguillette); *Tp:* **f. de cordon,** cord terminal. **2.** *Glassm:* *A:* ferret. **3.** *Miner:* (*a*) hard kernel, core (in stone); (*b*) **f. (d'Espagne),** red iron ore, haematite.

ferretier [fɛrtje], *s.m.* shoeing-smith's hammer.

ferreur [fɛrœːr], *s.m.* fitter, mounter, (of sth.) with iron; **f. de porte,** lock fitter; **f. de lacets,** tagger; **f. de chevaux, de bœufs,** shoeing-smith.

ferreux, -euse [fɛr(r)ø, -øːz], *a.* *Ch:* *Miner:* ferrous (metal); ferriferous, iron(-bearing) (ore); **alliages ferreux,** iron-alloys, ferro-alloys.

ferri- [fɛr(r)i], *pref.* *Ch:* ferr-; **ferricyanogène,** ferricyanogen.

ferrico- [fɛr(r)iko], *Ch:* (*in double salts*) ferric; **sel ferrico-ammonique,** ferric ammonium salt.

ferricyanhydrique [fɛr(r)isjanidrik], *a.* *Ch:* ferri-(hydro)cyanic (acid).

ferricyanogène [fɛr(r)isjanɔʒɛn], *s.m.* *Ch:* ferricyanogen.

ferricyanure [fɛr(r)isjanyːr], *s.m.* *Ch:* ferricyanide.

ferrière [fɛrjɛːr], *s.f.* (blacksmith's, locksmith's) tool bag.

ferrifère [fɛr(r)ifɛːr], *a.* *Ch:* *Miner:* ferriferous; containing, yielding, iron; iron-bearing, iron-producing.

ferrimagnétique [fɛr(r)imaɲetik], *a.* ferrimagnetic.

ferrimagnétisme [fɛr(r)imaɲetism], *s.m.* ferrimagnetism.

ferriprive [fɛr(r)ipriːv], *a.* *Med:* **anémie f.,** hypoferric, iron-deficiency, anaemia.

ferrique [fɛr(r)ik], *a.* *Ch:* ferric (salt, etc.).

ferrite [fɛr(r)it], *s.m.* *Metall:* ferrite; *Elcs:* **mémoire à f.,** ferrite core memory, storage.

ferritine [fɛr(r)itin], *s.f.* *Physiol:* ferritin(e).

ferro- [fɛr(r)ɔ], *pref.* *Ch:* *Miner:* ferro-; **ferrocyanure,** ferrocyanide.

ferro [fɛr(r)o], *s.m.* **1.** *Print:* *Phot:* blueprint. **2.** (any) ferro-alloy.

ferro-alliage [fɛr(r)oaljaːʒ], *s.m.* *Metall:* ferro-alloy; *pl. ferro-alliages.*

ferro-aluminium [fɛr(r)oalyminjɔm], *s.m.* ferro-aluminium.

ferrobore [fɛr(r)ɔbɔːr], *s.m.* *Metall:* ferroboron.

ferrocalcite [fɛr(r)ɔkalsit], *s.f.* *Miner:* ferrocalcite.

ferrocérium [fɛr(r)ɔserjɔm], *s.m.* ferrocerium.

ferrochrome [fɛr(r)ɔkroːm], *s.m.* *Metall:* ferrochrome, -chromium; chrome iron.

ferrocyanhydrique [fɛr(r)ɔsjanidrik], *a.* ferrocyanic.

ferrocyanogène [fɛr(r)ɔsjanɔʒɛn], *s.m.* ferrocyanogen.

ferrocyanure [fɛr(r)ɔsjanyːr], *s.m.* *Ch:* ferrocyanide.

ferro-électrique [fɛr(r)ɔelɛktrik], *a.* ferro-electric.

ferroferrite [fɛr(r)ɔfɛr(r)it], *s.f.* *Min:* ferrosoferric oxide.

ferrogallique [fɛr(r)ɔgalik], *a.* *Phot:* ferro-gallic (paper).

ferromagnétique [fɛr(r)ɔmaɲetik], ferromagnetic.

ferromagnétisme [fɛr(r)ɔmaɲetism], *s.m.* *El:* ferromagnetism.

ferromanganèse [fɛr(r)ɔmɑ̃ganɛːz], *s.m.* ferromanganese.

ferromolybdène [fɛr(r)ɔmɔlibdɛn], *s.m.* ferromolybdenum.

ferronickel [fɛr(r)ɔnikɛl], *s.m.* ferronickel.

ferronnerie [fɛrɔnri], *s.f.* **1.** iron works, iron foundry. **2.** ironmongery, hardware. **3.** **f. (d'art),** art metalwork; **f. au marteau,** wrought-iron work.

ferronnier, -ière [fɛrɔnje, -jɛːr], *s.* **1.** ironworker; blacksmith; locksmith; **f. (d'art),** wrought-iron worker, art metalworker. **2.** ironmonger. **3.** *s.f.* **ferronnière;** (*a*) wife of an ironworker; (*b*) chain with single jewel worn round the forehead, ferronière (from Leonardo da Vinci's portrait of *La belle Ferronnière*).

ferroprussiate [fɛr(r)ɔprysjat], *s.m.* *Ch:* ferroprussiate; **papier f.,** blueprint paper.

ferrosilicium [fɛr(r)ɔsilisjɔm], *s.m.* ferrosilicon.

ferrosoferrique [fɛr(r)ɔzɔfɛr(r)ik], *a.* ferrosoferric.

ferrotitane [fɛr(r)ɔtitan], *s.m.* ferrotitanium.

ferrotungstène [fɛr(r)ɔtœkstɛn], ferrotungsten.

ferrotype [fɛr(r)ɔtip], *s.m.* *Phot:* ferrotyping.

ferrotypie [fɛr(r)ɔtipi], *s.f.* *Phot:* ferrotype.

ferrotypique [fɛr(r)ɔtipik], *a.* *Phot:* ferrotype (plate, etc.).

ferrovanadium [fɛr(r)ɔvanadjɔm], *s.m.* ferrovanadium.

ferroviaire [fɛrɔvjɛːr], *a.* pertaining to a railway; *U.S:* to a railroad; **les grandes lignes ferroviaires,** the main railway lines; **liaisons ferroviaires,** rail communications; **grave accident f.,** serious railway accident; **trafic f.,** rail(way) traffic.

ferrugineux, -euse [fɛr(r)yʒinø, -øːz], *a.* *Ch:* *etc:* ferruginous; **argile ferrugineuse,** iron clay; **eau, source, ferrugineuse,** chalybeate, ferruginous, water, spring.

ferrure [fɛryːr], *s.f.* **1.** piece of ironwork, iron fitting; iron mounting; **ferrures de porte,** door fittings; **ferrures de carrosserie,** mountings of the coachwork; **f. (de sabot),** clout; **ferrures en cuivre,** brass fittings, mounts; *El.E:* **f. d'isolateur,** insulator pin; *Mec.E:* **f. d'assemblage,** fish-plate; *Nau:* **f. de gouvernail,** brace, iron, of rudder; **f. du bout de vergue,** goose-neck of the yard. **2.** (*a*) shoeing (of horse, mule, etc.); **f. à chaud, à froid,** hot, cold, shoeing; (*b*) *Coll.* the shoes (of horse, etc.).

ferry(-boat) [fɛri(bot)], *s.m.* train, car, ferry; *pl. ferry-boats.*

ferté [fɛrte], *s.f.* *A:* (*still found in place names, as* La Ferté-Milon, *etc.*), stronghold, fort.

fertier [fɛrtje], *s.m.* shoeing smith's hammer.

fertile [fɛrtil], *a.* (*a*) fertile, fruitful; rich (land, imagination, etc.); fat (land); **f. en blé,** fertile in wheat; **terre peu f.,** poor land; **f. en excuses,** prolific in excuses; **semaine f. en événements,** eventful week; (*b*) *Atom.Ph:* fertile (material).

fertilement [fɛrtilmɑ̃], *adv.* fertilely, fruitfully.

fertilisable [fɛrtilizabl], *a.* fertilizable.

fertilisant [fɛrtilizɑ̃]. **1.** *a.* fertilizing. **2.** *s.m.* fertilizer.

fertilisation [fɛrtilizasjɔ̃], *s.f.* fertilization, fertilizing.

fertiliser [fɛrtilize], *v.tr.* to fertilize; to make (sth.) fertile, fruitful.

se fertiliser, (*of land, etc.*) to become fertile.

fertiliseur [fɛrtilizœːr], *s.m.* fertilizer.

fertilisines [fɛrtilizin], *s.f.pl.* *Biol:* fertilisins, fertilizins.

fertilité [fɛrtilite], *s.f.* fertility; fruitfulness, richness (of soil, imagination, etc.); fatness (of soil).

fertois, -oise [fɛrtwa, -waːz], *a.* & *s.* (native, inhabitant) of La Ferté.

féru [fery], *a.* **1.** **f. (d'amour),** (madly) in love; **être f. d'une idée,** to be set on an idea. **2.** *A:* **f. contre qn,** angry, vexed, with s.o. **3.** **cheval f. au tendon,** horse cut on the tendon.

férule [feryl], *s.f.* **1.** *Bot:* ferula, giant fennel; **f. persique,** asafoetida. **2.** *Sch:* cane, ruler; *A:* ferule; **donner de la f. à qn,** to cane s.o.; **être sous la f. de qn,** to be ruled by s.o. with a rod of iron; to be completely under s.o.'s thumb.

férulique [ferylik], *a.* ferulic (acid).

fervanite [fɛrvanit], *s.f.* *Miner:* fervanite.

fervemment [fɛrvamɑ̃], *adv.* fervently.

fervent, -ente [fɛrvɑ̃, -ɑ̃ːt]. **1.** *a.* fervent, ardent (devotion, prayer, etc.); ardent (enthusiasm); enthusiastic (approval, etc.). **2.** *s.* enthusiast; **c'est un f. de Mozart,** he's a Mozart enthusiast; **c'est une fervente du bridge,** she's a bridge fiend, she's mad about bridge; **les fervents du football,** football fans.

ferveur [fɛrvœːr], *s.f.* (*a*) fervour, devotion; **avec f.,** fervently, earnestly; (*b*) **travailler avec f.,** to work with enthusiasm, enthusiastically; **aimer avec f.,** to love with devotion, devotedly, ardently; **avec une ferveur religieuse,** with religious ardour.

fescennin, -ine [fɛsɛnɛ̃, -in], *a.* *Lit:* fescennine (verse).

fesle [fɛl], *s.f.* *Glassm:* blowpipe.

fesse [fɛs], *s.f.* **1.** *Anat:* buttock; *F:* **donner sur les fesses d'un enfant,** to give a child a spanking; *F:* **botter les fesses de qn, donner à qn un coup de pied aux fesses,** to give s.o. a kick in the pants; *P:* **poser ses fesses,** to sit down (on one's backside); *P:* **serrer les fesses,** (i) to be on one's guard; to play a close game; (ii) to sit tight; (iii) to have cold feet, to have the wind up; **il est parti en serrant les fesses,** he went off with his tail between his legs; *P:* **avoir chaud aux fesses,** to have a nasty fright; *P:* **n'y aller que d'une f.,** to go about it half-heartedly; *P:* **occupe-toi de tes fesses,** mind your own bloody business! **2.** *Nau:* **fesses d'un navire,** buttocks, tuck, of a ship.

fessecul [fɛsky], *s.m.* *Bot:* *F:* fat hen, sea purslane.

fessée [fese], *s.f.* spanking, smacking; **donner une f., la f., à un enfant,** to spank a child, to give a child a spanking.

fesse-mathieu [fɛsmatjø], *s.m.* (*a*) *A:* usurer; (*b*) miser, skinflint, screw; *pl. fesse-mathieux.*

fesser [fese], *v.tr.* **1.** (*a*) to spank (s.o.), to smack (s.o.'s) bottom; (*b*) **se faire f.,** to expose oneself to humiliation. **2.** *A:* to do (sth.) hurriedly.

fesseur, -euse [fesœːr, -øːz], *s.* spanker, flogger.

fessier, -ière [fesje, -jɛːr]. **1.** *a.* (*a*) *Anat:* gluteal (muscle, artery, etc.); **la région fessière,** the buttocks; (*b*) *F:* **la poche fessière de son short,** the back pocket of his shorts. **2.** *s.m.* (*a*) *Anat:* **le grand f.,** gluteus maximus; (*b*) *F:* bottom, backside, behind.

fessu [fesy], *a.* broad-bottomed (man).

festin [fɛstɛ̃], *s.m.* feast, banquet; **quel f.!** what a feast! what a spread! **f. de noces,** wedding feast; **salle de f.,** banqueting hall; **faire (un) f.,** to feast, banquet; **nous n'avions que du pain pour tout f.,** we had nothing to regale ourselves with but bread.

festination [fɛstinasjɔ̃], *s.f.* *Med:* festination.

festiner [fɛstine], *A:* **1.** *v.i.* to feast. **2.** *v.tr.* to feast (s.o.).

festival, -als [fɛstival]. **1.** *a.* *Ecc:* *A:* **lettre festivale,** festal letter. **2.** *s.m.* (*a*) (musical) festival; **f. du film,** film festival; (*b*) *F:* *Sp:* **l'avant-centre nous a donné un véritable f.,** the centre-forward gave a spectacular performance.

festivalier, -ière [fɛstivalje, -jɛːr]. **1.** *a.* festival. **2.** *s.* festival-goer.

festivité [fɛstivite], *s.f. usu. pl.* festivity, rejoicing.

festoiement [fɛstwamɑ̃], *s.m.* feasting, banqueting, carousing.

feston [fɛstɔ̃], *s.m.* **1.** festoon (of flowers, etc.); *Arch:* festoon; *F:* **ivrogne qui fait des festons en marchant,** drunkard who staggers, zigzags, along. **2.** *Needlew:* scallop; **point de f.,** buttonhole stitch. **3.** *Anat:* **f. gingival,** festoon of the gum.

festonné [fɛstɔne], *a.* **1.** festooned. **2.** *Needlew:* scalloped (handkerchief, etc.); **brides festonnées,** buttonholed bars.

festonner [fɛstɔne], *v.tr.* **1.** to festoon. **2.** to scallop (hem, etc.).

festoyer [fɛstwaje], *v.* (**je festoie, n. festoyons; je festoierai**) **1.** *v.tr.* *A:* to regale, entertain, feast (s.o.). **2.** *v.i.* to feast, carouse.

festoyeur, -euse [fɛstwajœːr, -øːz], reveller.

fêtard, -arde [fɛtaːr, -ard]. *F:* **1.** *a.* rollicking, gay (life, etc.). **2.** *s.* (*the f. form* **fêtarde** *is rare*), reveller, roisterer.

fetch [fɛtʃ], *s.m.* *Oc:* fetch (of waves).

fête [fɛːt], *s.f.* **1.** feast, festival; *Ecc:* **dimanches et fêtes,** Sundays and feast days; **f. nationale,** national festival, national commemoration day; **la f. de la Toussaint, des Morts,** All Saints' Day, All Souls' Day; **les fêtes de Pâques,** the Easter

holiday; **f. légale** = bank holiday; **f. des mères,** mother's day, mothering Sunday; **f. des pères,** father's day; **f. de charité** = sale of work, (charity) bazaar; *Sch:* **f. sportive,** sports day, school sports; **c'est ma f. demain,** it's my saint's day, name day, tomorrow; **souhaiter la f., une bonne f., à qn** = to wish s.o. many happy returns; *P:* **ça va être ta f.!** you'd better look out! **ce n'est pas tous les jours f.,** life isn't always funny; **c'est triste comme un lendemain de f.,** it's like the morning after the night before. **2.** fête, entertainment; **donner une f.,** to give an entertainment; **donner une (petite) f.,** to give a party; **f. d'aviation, f. aéronautique,** air display, show, pageant; **f. foraine,** fun fair; **f. du village, du pays,** village fête, fair (of a particular village); **f. de village, f. villageoise, f. champêtre,** (any) village fête, fair. **3.** festivity, gaiety, merrymaking, rejoicings; **air de f.,** festive appearance; **le village était en f.,** the village was on holiday; **c'est f. demain,** tomorrow's a holiday; **faire la f.,** to lead a rollicking life; to carouse; to have one's fling; **faire f. à qn,** to welcome s.o. with open arms; **être de la f.,** to be one of the party; *A:* **se faire de f.,** to invite oneself; to obtrude oneself; **se faire une f. de qch., de faire qch.,** to look forward to sth., to doing sth.; **il ne s'était jamais vu à pareille f.,** he had never had such a good time; *F:* **il n'était pas à la f.,** he was having a bad time.

Fête-Dieu [fɛtdjø], *s.f. Ecc:* Corpus Christi; *pl. Fêtes-Dieu.*

fêter [fete], *v.tr.* **1.** (*a*) to keep (day, etc.) as a holiday, as a festival; **f. la naissance de qn,** to celebrate s.o.'s birthday; **f. Noël à l'ancienne mode,** to keep Christmas in the old style; (*b*) **f. un saint,** to keep a saint's day; **c'est un saint qu'on ne fête plus,** he has lost all credit, all authority. **2. f. qn,** (i) to fête s.o.; (ii) to entertain s.o.; to receive s.o. with open arms; **dîner pour f. le nouveau membre,** dinner to welcome the new member.

fêteur, -euse [fetœːr, -øːz], *s.* **1.** holidaymaker. **2.** reveller.

fétial, -aux [fesjal, -o], *a. Rom.Ant:* fetial.

fétiche [fetiʃ], *s.m.* (*a*) fetish; (*b*) mascot; (*c*) object of hero-worship.

féticheur [fetiʃœːr], *s.m.* (*in Africa*) juju priest; medicine man.

fétichisme [fetiʃism], *s.m.* fetishism.

fétichiste [fetiʃist]. **1.** *s.* fetishist. **2.** *a.* fetishistic.

fétide [fetid], *a.* fetid, rank, stinking, offensive, foul (smell, etc.).

fétidité [fetidite], *s.f.* fetidness, foulness (of smell, etc.).

fétu [fety], *s.m.* straw; **être emporté comme un f.,** to be blown along like a straw in the wind; **je m'en soucie comme d'un f.,** I don't care a straw, a rap, about it; **cela ne vaut pas un f.,** it isn't worth a brass farthing, a straw; *A:* **rompre le f. avec qn,** to break with s.o.

fétuque [fetyk], *s.f. Bot:* fescue; **f. ovine,** sheep's fescue.

feu[1], feux [fø], *s.m.* fire. **1.** (*a*) **le f. et l'eau,** fire and water; **craindre qch. comme le f.,** to stand in fear, be in terror, of sth.; **jouer avec le f.,** to play with fire; **soleil de f.,** fiery sun; **faire f. des quatre pieds,** (i) (*of horse*) to make the sparks fly; (ii) (*of pers.*) to be irrepressible; to have plenty of drive; **il n'a pas le f. sacré,** he lacks vital enthusiasm, driving force; *Prov:* **on fait f. de tout bois,** every little helps; **il fait f. de tout bois,** he makes the most of his opportunities; everything is grist to his mill; he can turn anything to account; *F:* **avoir le f. au derrière,** *P:* **au cul,** to be always in a hurry; *F:* to have ants in one's pants; **mettre (le) f. à qch.,** to set fire to sth., to set sth. on fire; *Lit:* **mettre une ville à f. et à sang,** to put a town to fire and sword; **mettre le f. aux poudres,** (i) to fire the powder magazine; to blow up the ship; (ii) to bring a scandal to light; **enlever de la peinture au f.,** to burn off the paint; **ustensiles qui vont au f.,** fireproof utensils; **f. de cheminée,** chimney on fire; **f. de brousse,** bush fire; **la cheminée est en f.,** the chimney is on fire; **mettre l'Europe en f.,** to set Europe ablaze, aflame, alight; **avoir le visage en f.,** to have a flushed face, burning cheeks; **j'avais la bouche en f.,** my mouth was burning; **f. du rasoir,** smarting sensation caused by shaving; *O:* **vin qui a du f.,** fiery wine; *A:* **f. céleste, f. Saint-Antoine,** erysipelas, St. Anthony's fire; **prendre f.,** to catch fire; **il prend f. pour la moindre chose,** he flies into a rage, flares up, on the slightest provocation; **le f. prend,** the fire is catching; **si le f. prenait,** if a fire broke out; **le f. a pris à sa robe,** her dress caught fire; **crier au f.,** to shout "Fire!"; **faire la part du f.,** (i) to clear the ground (to prevent the fire spreading); (ii) to cut one's losses; *F:* **il n'y a pas le f. à la maison,** don't be impatient; there's no particular hurry; **couleur de f.,** *a.inv.* **rouge f.,** flame-coloured; **chien noir et f.,** black and tan dog; **jeter (tout) son f.,** to flare up (and then cool down); **il a jeté tout son f. dans son premier roman,** he wrote himself out in his first novel; **jeter f. et flamme (contre qn),** to rage (at s.o.); **est-ce que vous avez du f.?** have you a light, a match; *s.a.* ENFER 1, FOLLET; (*b*) ardour, enthusiasm; passion; **tout f. tout flamme,** heart and soul; **dans le premier f. de sa colère,** in the heat of his anger; **dans le f. de la discussion,** in the heat of the debate; (*c*) *A:* love, passion; **vous savez de quels feux je brûle pour elle,** you know how ardently, how passionately, I love her; *Lit:* **Vénus et ses feux redoutables,** Venus and the baleful passions that she kindles. **2.** (*a*) **préparer le f.,** to lay the fire; **faire du f.,** to light a fire; **arranger le f.,** to make up the fire; **garniture de f.,** fire irons; **f. dans la cheminée, f. nu,** open fire; **faire du f. de qch.,** to make a fire of sth., to burn sth.; **jeter qch. au f.,** to throw sth. on to, in, the fire; **f. de camp,** camp fire; **f. de joie,** bonfire; beacon; **f. d'artifice,** (i) fireworks; (ii) *Mil: etc:* signals and flares; **leur amitié ne fera pas long f.,** their friendship won't last long; *s.a.* COIN 1, PAILLE 1; (*b*) *Mch:* **mettre une chaudière en f.,** to fire up a boiler; **pousser les feux,** to make all steam; **laisser tomber les feux,** to let the fires down; **mettre les feux au fond, couvrir, coucher, les feux,** to bank up the fires; **mettre bas les feux,** to draw the fires; **rester sous les feux,** (i) to keep up steam; (ii) to bank up the fires; *Metall:* **fourneau hors f.,** furnace out of blast; *Mch: Nau:* **mettre les feux,** to light up; (*c*) **condamner qn au f.,** to condemn s.o. to be burnt at the stake; **je me mettrais, jetterais, dans le f. pour lui,** I would go through fire and water for him, I would do anything for him; **j'en mettrais la main au f.,** I would swear to it; **épreuve du f.,** ordeal by fire; **brûler qn à petit f.,** to torture s.o. (on the grill); **brûler à petit f.,** to be on tenterhooks; **mourir à petit f.,** to die by inches; **faire mourir qn à petit f.,** (i) to kill s.o. by inches; (ii) to keep s.o. on tenterhooks; (*d*) *Cu:* **cuisinière à quatre feux,** four-burner cooker, stove; **faire cuire à f. doux, à petit f.,** to cook gently, over a slow gas, heat; in a slow oven; **faire cuire à grand f., à f. vif,** to cook over a brisk heat, a quick fire, in a quick, hot oven; **poêle à f. continu,** slow-combustion stove; (*e*) (i) *A:* **hameau de 50 feux,** hamlet of 50 homes; (ii) **n'avoir ni f. ni lieu,** to be homeless, to have neither hearth nor home. **3.** gunfire, rifle fire; **armes à f.,** firearms; **bouche à f.,** piece of ordnance, of artillery; **faire f. sur qn,** to shoot at s.o.; **commencer, déclencher, ouvrir, le f.,** to open fire; **ouvrir le f. sur une patrouille ennemie,** to engage an enemy patrol; **faire f. sur qn,** to fire at s.o.; **feu! fire! halte au f.!** suspend firing! **cesser le f.,** to cease fire; **sous le f.,** under fire; (*of pistol, fuse, plan, etc.*) **faire long f.,** (i) to hang fire; (ii) to misfire; **faire faux f.,** to misfire; **aller au f.,** to go into action, under fire; **croiser les feux,** to cross fire; **il n'a jamais vu le f.,** he has never heard a gun fired, never smelt gunpowder; **f. roulant,** running fire, drumfire; **maintenir un f. roulant contre l'ennemi,** to blaze away at the enemy, to keep up a running fire against the enemy; **un f. roulant de questions,** a running fire of questions; **un f. roulant de paradoxes,** a whole series, string, of paradoxes; **être entre deux feux,** to be between two fires; *Navy:* **f. de chasse,** ahead fire; **f. de retraite,** astern fire; **f. de travers, de bordée,** broadside fire; *s.a.* NOURRI, 2, PUISSANCE 1. **4.** (*a*) *Nau:* (i) light (of lighthouse, beacon, etc.); **feux de côte,** coasting lights; **feux (d'entrée) de port,** harbour lights; **f. de marée,** tidal light; **f. de musoir,** pier-head light; **droits de feux,** light dues; **f. à éclats,** flashing light; **f. à occultations, à éclipses,** occulting light; **f. isophase,** intermittent light; **f. à secteur,** sectored light; **f. clignotant,** blinker light; **f. tournant,** revolving light; **f. fixe,** fixed light; **f. flottant,** floating light; floating beacon; **f. non gardé,** unattended, unwatched, light; (ii) **feux de route, de navigation, de position,** navigation lights, running lights, position lights; **feux de mouillage,** anchor lights, riding lights; **feux de côté,** sidelights; **f. de babord,** port light, red light; **f. de tribord,** starboard light, green light; **f. de poupe,** stern light; **f. de tête de mât,** masthead light, steaming light; **f. additionnel, f. de pointe,** range light; **f. de mât arrière,** (after) range light; **f. de hune,** top light; **feux de pêche,** working lights; **f. de remorque,** towing light; **f. d'impossibilité de manœuvre(r),** not-under-command light; (*b*) *Av:* (i) **feux d'aérodrome, d'aéroport,** airfield, airport, lights; **feux de balisage,** boundary lights; **feux de piste,** course lights, runway lights; **f. d'atterrissage,** landing light, contact light; **f. d'obstacle,** obstruction light; **f. signalisateur,** landing flare; (ii) **feux de bord, feux de navigation,** navigation lights, running lights, position lights; **f. de position,** wing-tip light; **f. latéral,** side-light; **f. d'identification,** identification light, recognition light; (*c*) *Veh:* (i) **feux de circulation, de signalisation routière,** *F:* **f. rouge,** traffic lights; **f. rouge, orange, vert,** red, amber, green, light; **f. clignotant,** winking warning light (at crossroads); *F:* **tournez à droite au premier f. rouge,** turn right at the first traffic lights; *F:* **donner le f. vert à qn,** to give s.o. the green light, the go-ahead; (ii) *Aut: etc:* **f. rouge,** rear light (of car); **feux de route,** headlights; **feux de croisement,** dipped headlights; **feux de position, de stationnement,** sidelights, parking lights; **feux de gabarit,** rear corner marker lamps; *Aut: Rail:* **feux d'encombrement,** gauge lights; **f. d'avant d'une locomotive,** headlight of a locomotive; **f. d'arrière d'un train,** tail light, rear light, of a train; (*d*) **feux d'un diamant,** dispersion of a diamond; **yeux pleins de f.,** flashing eyes; **n'y voir que du f.,** (i) to be dazzled; (ii) to be completely taken in; (iii) to be unable to make (either) head or tail of sth. **5. coup de feu:** (*a*) (i) browning (of joint, etc.); (ii) burning (of bread, joint, etc.); (iii) *A:* rush hour; **être dans son coup de f.,** to be at one's busiest; (iv) *O:* **donner un coup de f. à du linge,** to air linen (in front of the fire); (*b*) gun shot, pistol shot; **nous avons reçu des coups de f.,** we were fired on; (*c*) *Min:* fire-damp explosion; (*d*) *Mch:* local overheating.

feu[2], *a.* late (= deceased). **1.** (*between article and sb., and variable*) **le feu roi, la feue reine,** the late king, the late queen; **fils de feue Berthe Dupont,** son of Berthe Dupont, deceased; *occ. pl.* **mes feus parents,** my late parents. **2.** (*preceding the article or poss. adj. and inv.*); **feu la reine,** the late queen; **feu mon père,** my late father; **feu les princesses,** the late princesses.

feudataire [fødatɛːr], *s.m. Hist:* feudatory; vassal (state, etc.).

feudiste [fødist], *s.m. Jur:* feudalist, feudist, expert in feudal law.

feuil [fœːj], *s.m. Ch: Ph:* (surface) film.

feuillage [fœjaːʒ], *s.m.* foliage, leaves; *Arch: etc:* leaf-work.

feuillagé [fœjaʒe], *a.* (*of plant*) in leaf.

feuillaison [fœjɛzɔ̃], *s.f.* **1.** *Bot:* (*a*) foliation; (*b*) vernation. **2.** spring(time).

feuillant, -ante, -antine [fœjɑ̃, -ɑ̃ːt, -ɑ̃tin], *s.* **1.** (*a*) *Ecc:* Feuillant, *f.* Feuillantine; strict Bernardine; (*b*) *Fr.Hist:* Feuillant. **2.** *s.f. Cu:* **feuillantine,** puff pastry.

feuillard [fœjaːr], *s.m.* **1.** *Husb:* leaf-fodder. **2.** *Coop: etc:* (*a*) hoop-wood; (*b*) (fer) **feuillard,** hoop-iron, strip-iron, strap-iron; (metallic) ribbon; **train à feuillards,** strip mill.

feuille [fœːj], *s.f.* **1.** (*a*) leaf (of plant); **f. morte,** dead leaf; *Av:* **descente en f. morte,** dead leaf dive; **les arbres mettent, prennent, leurs feuilles, se couvrent de feuilles,** the trees are coming into leaf; **trembler comme une f.,** to tremble like a leaf; **f. de chou,** (i) cabbage leaf; (ii) *F:* (*newspaper*) rag; *Art:* **f. de vigne,** fig leaf; *Arch:* **remplage en quatre feuilles,** quatrefoil tracery; *F:* **voir la f. à l'envers,** to make love in the open air; (*b*) *Poet: etc:* petal; **f. de rose,** rose leaf, rose petal. **2.** (*a*) **f. de métal,** sheet of metal; **fer en feuilles,** sheet iron; **mince f. de plomb,** lead foil; **f. d'or,** gold leaf, foil; **f. d'étain,** tinfoil; *A:* **f. d'une scie, d'un ressort,** blade of a saw, leaf of a spring; (*b*) **f. de bois,** thin board; **f. d'un contrevent,** leaf of a shutter; (*c*) **f. anglaise,** sheet rubber; (*d*) **f. de boucher,** chopper. **3.** (*a*) sheet (of paper); **f. volante, f. mobile,** loose sheet, fly sheet; leaflet; **feuilles d'un livre,** leaves of a book; *Bookb:* **f. de garde,** fly leaf, end paper (of book); **f. (quotidienne),** (daily) paper; *Publ:* **bonnes feuilles (de publicité),** advance proofs; **lire sous la f.,** to read between the lines; (*b*) *Mapm:* **f. au millionième, au deux millionième,** one in a million sheet, one two million sheet; **f. adjacente,** adjoining, adjacent, sheet; **ligne de raccordement d'une f.,** sheet line; **tableau d'assemblage des feuilles,** index to adjoining sheets; (*c*) **f. de paie, des salaires, des appointements,** payroll, pay sheet; salary list; *Mil:* **f. de soldes,** payroll;

f. de présence, time sheet; attendance list; *M.Ins:* **f. de temps,** time sheet; **f. d'imposition,** form of return (for income tax, etc.); *Bank:* **f. de versement,** paying-in slip; **f. de recensement,** census paper; *Med:* **f. de température,** temperature chart; *Jur:* **f. d'audience,** cause list; *Mil: etc:* **f. d'appel,** muster roll; **f. de punitions,** crime sheet; **f. de service,** (duty) roster; **f. de déplacement,** travel order; **f. de route,** (i) *Com:* waybill; (ii) *Mil: etc:* travel warrant. **4.** *P:* ear, *P:* lug; **être dur de la f.,** to be hard of hearing.

feuillé [fœje]. **1.** *a.* leafy, in full leaf; *Her:* leafed; *Arch:* **colonne feuillée,** foliated, foliaged, pillar. **2.** *s.m.* foliage (in painting, etc.).

feuille-de-sauge [fœːjdəsoːʒ], *s.f.* **1.** *Surg:* bistoury. **2.** *Tls:* cross(ing) file; *pl. feuilles-de-sauge.*

feuillée [fœje], *s.f.* **1.** (*a*) foliage (in painting, etc.); *Lit:* **sous la f.,** under the leafy boughs; (*b*) arbour. **2.** (*a*) **faire la f.,** to gather leaves (for fodder, etc.); (*b*) *Mil: etc:* **les feuillées,** the latrines (in camp).

feuille-morte [fœjmɔrt], *a. & s.m.inv.* **1.** dead-leaf colour(ed); filemot; oak-leaf brown; **manteau f.-m.,** russet coat. **2.** *Ent: F:* dead leaf butterfly.

feuiller [fœje]. **1.** *v.i. & pr.* (*of trees, etc.*) to break into leaf. **2.** *v.tr.* (*a*) *Paint:* **f. les arbres,** to paint the leaves of the trees (in picture); (*b*) *Carp:* to rabbet, groove (a board). **3.** *s.m.* foliage (in painting).

feuilleret [fœjrɛ], *s.m. Tls:* fillister, rabbet plane, grooving plane.

feuillet [fœjɛ], *s.m.* **1.** (*a*) leaf (of book); *Bookb:* **f. de garde,** fly leaf (of unbound book); end paper (of bound book); (*b*) *Adm:* form (for a return); return sheet; **f. à souche,** form with counterfoil. **2.** thin sheet, plate (of wood, metal, etc.). **3. f. de tourneur,** turning saw. **4.** omasum, psalterium (third stomach of ruminant); *Dial:* manyplies. **5.** *Biol:* **f. vasculaire,** parablast. **6.** *El:* **f. magnétique,** magnetic layer. **7.** (*usu. pl.*) *Geol:* **feuillets (de schistes),** folia.

feuilletage [fœjtaːʒ], *s.m. Cu:* (*a*) rolling (of dough for flaky pastry); (*b*) flaky pastry.

feuilleté [fœjte]. **1.** *a.* foliated, laminated, lamellar (rocks, etc.); *El:* laminated (core); *Cu:* **pâte feuilletée,** flaky pastry. **2.** *s.m.* flaky pastry.

feuilleter [fœjte], *v.tr.* **(je feuillette, n. feuilletons; je feuilletterai) 1.** to divide (metal, wood, etc.) into sheets, leaves; *Cu:* to roll and fold (pastry). **2. f. un livre,** to turn over the pages of a book; to glance, skim, flip, through a book; to dip into a book; **livre bien feuilleté,** well-thumbed book.

se feuilleter, (*of mineral, etc.*) to split up, to flake, to cleave.

feuilletis [fœjti], *s.m.* **1.** cleavage line (of slate). **2.** girdle (of diamond); **serrer le f.,** to tighten up the setting (of diamond).

feuilleton [fœjtɔ̃], *s.m.* **1.** (*a*) *Journ:* (literary, scientific) article; feature; (*b*) *Journ: W.Tel: T.V:* (i) instalment (of serial); **publier un roman en feuilletons,** to serialize a novel; to publish a novel in instalments; in serial form; (ii) serial story. **2.** *Paperm:* poor quality thick paper, cardboard.

feuilletoniste [fœjtɔnist], *s.m. & f.* *feuilleton* writer; feature writer; serial writer.

feuillette[1] [fœjɛt], *s.f.* small leaf, leaflet.

feuillette[2], *s.f. A.Meas:* (*approx.* =) quarter cask; half hogshead.

feuillettement [fœjɛtmɑ̃], *s.m.* turning, flipping, over the pages (of book); scanning.

feuillir [fœjiːr], *v.i.* to leaf, to break into leaf.

feuillu [fœjy]. **1.** *a.* leafy; broad-leaved, deciduous (forest); **forêt d'arbres feuillus,** hardwood forest. **2.** *s.m.* foliage.

feuillure [fœjyːr], *s.f.* **1.** *Carp:* groove, rabbet, rebate; fillister (of window, door, etc.); **faire une f., tailler en f.,** to rabbet. **2.** (*a*) *Artil:* head space; (*b*) *Sm.a:* bolt head rim.

feulement [følmɑ̃], *s.m.* (*of tiger*) snarl, (*of cat*) growl, growling.

feuler [føle], *v.i.* (*of tiger*) to snarl, (*of cat*) to growl.

feurre [fœːr], *s.m.* straw.

feutier [føtje], *s.m.* **1.** *A:* fireman, furnace-attendant (of a large establishment). **2.** *Ecc:* lighter of candles; official who attends to the lighting of tapers (at Lourdes, etc.).

feutrable [føtrabl̩], *a.* that can be felted.

feutrage [føtraːʒ], *s.m.* **1.** felting, felt making. **2.** (*a*) felting; covering, coating, packing, (of boiler, etc.) with felt; (*b*) stuffing, padding (of saddle, etc.). **3.** cover(ing), packing, of felt; felt(ing).

feutrant [føtrɑ̃], *a.* felting (property of wool, etc.).

feutre [føːtr̩], *s.m.* **1.** felt; **f. poilu,** hair felt; **f. bitumé,** roofing felt; tarred felt; **f. goudronné,** caulking felt; **papier f.,** carpet felt; **chaussons de f.,** felt slippers; **tableau de f.,** flannelgraph. **2.** **(chapeau de) f.,** felt hat. **3.** *Harn: etc:* (*a*) stuffing, padding (of saddle, etc.); (*b*) guard flap (under buckle). **4.** *Nat.Hist:* tomentum.

feutré [føtre], *a.* padded; covered, lined, with felt; **porte feutrée,** baize door; **à pas feutrés,** with noiseless tread; with velvet tread; **s'éloigner à pas feutrés,** to steal away, slip quietly away; **marcher à pas feutrés,** to pad (about, along); **des rues feutrées de neige,** streets blanketed with snow; **cette démagogie feutrée,** this hypocritical, sneaking, demagogy.

feutrement [føtrəmɑ̃], *s.m.* (*a*) (process of) felting (wool, etc.); (*b*) trimming with felt.

feutrer [føtre], *v.tr.* **1.** to felt; to make (hair, wool, etc.) into felt. **2.** (*a*) to felt, pack; to cover (boiler, etc.) with felt; (*b*) to stuff, pad (saddle, etc.). **3.** *v.i.* to become matted, to felt.

se feutrer, (*of material, etc.*) to become matted; to felt.

feutreuse [føtrøːz], *s.f. Tchn:* felting machine.

feutrier, -ière [føtri(j)e, -jɛːr]. **1.** *a.* (*a*) suitable for felting; (*b*) **ouvrier f.,** felt worker. **2.** *s.m.* felt manufacturer.

feutrine [føtrin], *s.f. Tex:* baize.

fève [fɛːv], *s.f.* **1.** *Bot:* (*a*) **f. (des marais),** broad bean; **f. de Calabar,** Calabar bean; **f. de Lima,** Lima bean; *Fr.C:* **f. verte,** string bean; **petite f. (jaune),** wax bean; **gâteau de la f.,** Twelfth-night cake; **roi de la f.,** bean king (of Twelfth-night); **donner un pois pour avoir une f.,** to throw out a sprat to catch a mackerel; **rendre à qn f. pour pois,** to give s.o. tit for tat; (*b*) **f. de cacao,** cocoa nib. **2.** *Ent: F:* chrysalis. **3.** *Vet:* lampas.

féverole [fɛvrɔl], *s.f.* field bean, horse bean.

févier [fevje], *s.m. Bot: F:* honey-locust (tree).

fèvre [fɛːvr̩], *s.m.* **1.** *A:* metal worker. **2.** boiler-man (at saltworks).

février [fevri(j)e], *s.m.* February; **en f., au mois de f.,** in (the month of) February; **le premier, le sept, f.,** (on) the first, the seventh, of February; (on) February (the) first, (the) seventh; *Fr.Hist:* **les journées de F.,** the revolution of 1848.

fez [fɛːz], *s.m. Cost:* fez.

Fezzan [fɛzɑ̃], *Geog:* **1.** *Pr.n.m.* Fezzan. **2.** *a. & s.* (*f.* **Fezzane**) (native, inhabitant) (i) of the Fezzan; (ii) *A:* of Fez.

fi [fi], *int.* (*a*) *O:* fie! for shame! **fi de la célébrité!** to hell with fame! (*b*) **faire fi de qch.,** to despise, turn up one's nose at, sth.; **faire fi des conseils de qn,** to despise, scorn, s.o.'s advice; **faire fi des conséquences,** not to care what the consequences will be.

fiabilité [fjabilite], *s.f. Tchn:* reliability; **essai de f.,** reliability test; **absence, manque, de f.,** unreliability; **le degré de f. d'un avion,** the degree of reliability of an aircraft.

fiable [fjabl̩], *a. Tchn:* reliable; dependable.

fiacre [fjakr̩], *s.m. A.Veh:* hackney carriage, four-wheeler, cab; **cocher de f.,** cab driver, cab-man; *F:* cabby; **stationnement de fiacres,** cab rank, stand.

fiacrée [fjakre], *s.f. A:* cabful, cab-load.

fiançailles [f(i)jɑ̃sɑːj], *s.f.pl.* engagement (**avec,** to); **anneau, bague, de fiançailles,** engagement ring.

fiancé, -ée [f(i)jɑ̃se]. **1.** *s.* fiancé, fiancée. **2.** *s.m. Ent: F:* owlet moth.

fiancer [f(i)jɑ̃se], *v.tr.* **(je fiançai(s); n. fiançons)** to promise (one's daughter, son) in marriage.

se fiancer, to become engaged (**à, avec,** to).

fiasco [fjasko], *s.m.inv.* fiasco; **leurs projets ont fait f.,** their plans have come to nothing, to grief, have fizzled out; **cette pièce est un f.,** this play is a (complete) flop.

fiasque [fjask], *s.f.* Italian wine flask.

fiat [fjat]. **1.** *s.m.inv. Psy: Jur:* fiat. **2.** *int.* agreed!

fibrage [fibraːʒ], *s.m. Tchn:* drawing out of glass fibre.

fibran(n)e [fibran], *s.f. Tex:* staple fibre; spun rayon.

fibration [fibrasjɔ̃], *s.f. Physiol:* disposition of the fibres, fibration.

fibre [fibr̩], *s.f.* (*a*) *Bot: Anat: Tchn:* fibre; **f. végétale,** vegetable fibre; **coton à fibres longues,** long-staple cotton; **f. du bois,** grain of the wood; **f. de bois (pour emballage),** wood fibre (for packing); **f. textile,** textile fibre; **f. synthétique,** synthetic, man-made, fibre; **f. de carbone, de quartz,** carbon, quartz, fibre; **f. de verre,** fibre-glass (*R.t.m.*), glass fibre, fibrous glass, spun glass, glass wool; **malle en f.,** fibre trunk; **rondelle en f.,** fibre washer; *Anat:* **f. musculaire,** muscle fibre; **f. nerveuse,** nerve fibre; (*b*) *Mec:* **f. neutre,** neutral axis; (*c*) *Lit:* **les fibres du cœur,** the heart-strings; **avoir la f. sensible,** to be susceptible, impressionable; *O:* **avoir la f. de la musique,** to have a soul for music, to respond to music; *F:* **avoir la f. paternelle,** to be a born father.

fibre-cellule [fibrəsɛlyl], *s.f. Anat:* fibre cell; *pl. fibres-cellules.*

fibrer (se) [səfibre], *v.pr.* (*of glass*) to be drawn into fibres.

fibreux, -euse [fibrø, -øːz], *a.* fibrous, stringy, thready; *Anat:* **tissu f.,** fibrous tissue; *Med:* **tumeur fibreuse,** fibrous tumor; *Metall: Miner:* **cassure fibreuse,** fibrous fracture.

fibrillaire [fibril(l)ɛːr], *a.* fibrillar(y).

fibrillation [fibril(l)asjɔ̃], *s.f.* fibrillation.

fibrille [fibril], *s.f. Physiol: Bot:* fibril(la).

fibrilleux, -euse [fibril(l)ø, -øːz], *a.* fibrillous, fibrillose.

fibrine [fibrin], *s.f. Ch:* fibrin.

fibrinémie [fibrinemi], *s.f. Physiol:* fibrinemia.

fibrineux, -euse [fibrinø, -øːz], *a.* fibrinous.

fibrin-ferment [fibrɛ̃fɛrmɑ̃], *s.m. Ch: Physiol:* fibrin ferment, thrombin; *pl. fibrins-ferments.*

fibrino- [fibrino], *comb.fm.* fibrino-; **fibrino-plastique,** fibrino-plastic.

fibrinogène [fibrinɔʒɛn], *s.m. Ch:* fibrinogen.

fibrinolytique [fibrinɔlitik], *a. & s.m.* fibrinolytic.

fibrinurie [fibrinyri], *s.f.* fibrinuria.

fibro- [fibro], *comb.fm.* fibro-; **fibroséreux,** fibro-serous.

fibroblaste [fibrɔblast], *s.m.* fibroblast.

fibrocartilage [fibrɔkartilaːʒ], *s.m. Anat:* fibro-cartilage.

fibrocartilagineux, -euse [fibrɔkartilaʒinø, -øːz], *a. Anat:* fibrocartilaginous.

fibrochondrome [fibrɔkɔ̃drɔm], *s.m. Med:* fibro-chondroma.

Fibrociment [fibrɔsimɑ̃], *s.m. Civ.E: etc: R.t.m:* Fibrocement, asbestos cement.

fibrocyte [fibrɔsit], *s.m. Biol:* fibrocyte.

fibroferrite [fibrɔfɛrit], *s.f. Miner:* fibroferrite.

fibroïde [fibrɔid], *a. & s.m. Med:* fibroid (tumour, etc.).

fibroïne [fibrɔin], *s.f. Ch:* fibroin.

fibrokystique [fibrɔkistik], *a. Med:* fibrocystic.

fibrolite [fibrɔlit], *s.f. Miner:* fibrolite.

fibromateux, -euse [fibrɔmatø, -øːz], *a.* fibro-matous.

fibromatose [fibrɔmatoːz], *s.f. Med:* fibroma-tosis.

fibrome [fibroːm], *s.m. Med:* fibroma, fibrous tumour.

fibromyome [fibromiɔm], *s.m. Med:* fibromyoma.

fibrose [fibroːz], *s.f. Med:* fibrosis; **f. pulmonaire,** pulmonary fibrosis; **f. cardiaque,** myocardial fibrosis.

fibroséreux, -euse [fibrɔserø, -øːz], *a. Med:* fibroserous.

fibrosite [fibrɔzit], *s.f. Med:* fibrositis.

fibro(-)vasculaire [fibrɔvaskylɛːr], *a.* fibro-vascular.

fibule [fibyl], *s.f. Rom.Ant:* fibula, buckle.

fic [fik], *s.m.* (*a*) *Vet:* wart (of horse); fig; (*b*) *Bot: F:* **herbe de f.,** figwort, pilewort, lesser celandine.

ficaire [fikɛːr], *s.f. Bot:* lesser celandine, pilewort.

ficelage [fislaːʒ], *s.m.* tying up (of parcels, etc.).

ficelard [fislaːr], *s.m. F:* an old hand who knows the ropes, all the tricks of the trade.

ficelé [fisle], *a.* (*a*) (*of parcel, etc.*) tied up; (*b*) *F: Pej:* dressed up, got up; **homme mal f.,** man whose clothes do not sit properly, untidily dressed man; **elle est f. comme quatre sous,** she really is a sight; **f. comme une andouille,** wearing clothes that are too tight.

ficeler [fisle], *v.tr.* **(je ficelle, n. ficelons; je ficellerai) 1.** to tie up, do up, (parcel, etc.) with string. **2.** *F:* to dress; **qui donc vous a ficelé ainsi?** whoever got you up like that? **elle met deux heures à se f.,** it takes her two hours to get dressed (and made up).

ficeleur, -euse [fislœːr, -øːz], *s.* (parcel) packer.

ficel(l)ier [fisəlje], *a. & s.m. F:* **1.** (actor) who knows all the stage tricks. **2.** (person) who lives by his wits, who lives from hand to mouth.

ficelle [fisɛl], *s.f.* (*a*) (i) string, twine; (ii) pack-thread; **f. à fouet,** whipcord; *Agr:* **f. à lier, f. lieuse,** binder twine; *Mil:* **f. de nettoyage,** pull-through; *F: Box: Rac: etc:* **les ficelles,** the ropes; **bonhomme en f.,** pin man; (*b*) **ficelles d'une marionnette,** strings of a marionnette; **c'est lui qui tient les ficelles,** he's the one who pulls the strings; **ficelles du théâtre,** stage tricks; **connaître toutes les ficelles,** to be up to all the tricks of the trade, to know all the ropes; *F:* **une vieille f.,** an old hand; **on voit bien la f.,** it's easy to see how that's done; (*c*) *a. & s.f. O:* sharp,

wily, cunning (person); *s.* trickster; **être f.,** to be cunning; **avocat f.,** tricky, wily, lawyer; (*c*) *Mil: F:* = (officer's) pip; **il vient d'avoir sa troisième f.,** he's just been made a captain, just got his third pip; (*e*) *Bak:* long, very thin loaf of bread.

ficellerie [fisɛlri], *s.f.* (*a*) string, twine, factory; (*b*) warehouse where string is stored.

fichage [fiʃaːʒ], *s.m. Const:* pointing (of wall, etc.).

fichaise [fiʃɛːz], *s.f. F:* rubbish, trash; **quelle f.!** what rot! **tout ça, c'est des fichaises!** that's all rot!

fichant [fiʃɑ̃], *a.* **1.** *Mil:* plunging (fire). **2.** *P:* annoying, exasperating; **que c'est f.!** what a bloody nuisance!

fiche[1] [fiʃ], *s.f.* **1.** (*a*) peg, pin (of iron, wood, etc.); (*b*) stake; **f. d'un pieu,** hold of a pile; *Surv:* **f. d'arpenteur,** surveyor's arrow, chain pin; **f. plombée,** drop arrow; (*c*) *Const:* **f. de maçon,** pointing trowel; pointing tool; (*d*) hinge; **f. à bouton,** hinge with knob pin; **f. à nœud,** loose-pin hinge; **f. à vase,** loose-butt hinge; (*e*) *Nau:* **fiches de roulis,** fiddles (for the tables). **2.** (*a*) *El:* plug; **f. banane,** banana plug, pin; **f. de contact,** contact plug; **f. de raccordement,** coupler plug, connecting plug; **f. de terre,** earth plate; **interrupteur à f.,** plug switch; **mettre la f. dans la prise de contact,** to plug in the connection; (*b*) *Tp:* **f. d'appel,** calling plug; **f. d'écoute,** answering plug; **f. d'essai,** test plug; **f. femelle,** jack; **f. de jack,** jack plug. **3.** (*a*) (i) docket, slip (of paper); (ii) memorandum slip, card, chart, list, sheet; voucher; *Com: etc:* **f. de pesage,** weight slip; *Sch:* **f. scolaire,** school record card; *Ind: etc:* **f. de contrôle,** checking form, docket; check list, check sheet; **f. technique,** data sheet; *Adm:* **f. de voyageur** (i) (hotel) registration form; (ii) passport control card; *Med:* **f. médicale,** medical record, case record, medical history sheet; **f. d'examen (médical),** examination record chart; **f. d'observation,** record card; *Dent:* **f. dentaire,** dental chart; (*b*) card, ticket (of membership of club, etc.); (*c*) (index) card; **boîte à fiches,** card-index box, filing box; **jeu de fiches,** card index; **mettre (des informations) sur fiches,** to card(-index); **mise sur fiches,** card-indexing; **fiches matière, fiches sujet,** subject entries; **f. d'affectation,** locator card; **f. d'identité,** identification card; **f. d'immatriculation,** register card; **f. de renseignements,** data card, information card; **f. signalétique,** record card; (*d*) tie-on label, luggage label, luggage tag; (*e*) slide, slider (of microscope). **4.** *Cards: etc:* (bone, ivory) counter, marker; fish.

fiche[2], *see* FICHER 4 *&* SE FICHER.

fiché [fiʃe], *a. Her:* fitchy.

ficher [fiʃe], *v.tr.* **1.** to drive in, fix, plant (stake, nail, etc. into sth.); **f. un clou dans le mur,** to drive a nail into the wall; *F:* **f. les yeux sur qch.,** to fix one's eyes on sth.; to stare at sth.; *F:* **se f. une idée dans la tête,** to get an idea firmly fixed in one's mind. **2.** *Const:* **f. un mur,** to point a wall. **3.** *F:* to card(-index). **4.** *F:* (*the infin. is often* **fiche** *and the p.p.* **fichu**) (*a*) (= METTRE) **f. son chapeau par terre,** to chuck one's hat on the floor; **ça fiche tout par terre,** that ruins everything; **fiche(r) qn à la porte,** to throw, chuck, s.o. out; **f. qn dehors, en l'air,** to give s.o. the sack, to fire s.o.; **fiche(r) qn dedans,** (i) to cheat s.o., to take s.o. in; (ii) to put s.o. in jug, in nick; **on m'a fichu dedans,** I've been had, done; (*b*) (= FAIRE) **il n'a rien fichu, il n'a pas fichu un coup, une secousse, de toute la journée,** he hasn't done a stroke all day; **ça ne fiche rien,** (i) it doesn't matter a scrap; (ii) I don't care a rap; **qu'est-ce ça fiche?** what does it matter? who the hell cares? (*c*) (= DONNER) **f. une gifle, un coup, à qn,** to slap s.o. (in the face), to hit s.o.; **fiche-moi la paix!** (i) leave me alone! (ii) shut up! (*d*) **fiche(r) le camp,** to escape, to get away, to do a bunk; **fiche-moi le camp d'ici!** out you go, get! scram! *P:* **va te faire fiche!** get to hell out of here! **je t'en fiche!** nothing of the sort! not likely! *Iron:* **on t'en fichera!** well, if you want some more you can have it!

se ficher. *F:* (*infin. often* **se fiche;** *p.p.* **fichu**) **1. se f. par terre,** (i) to fling oneself on the ground; (ii) to fall; **il s'est fichu par terre,** he went sprawling. **2.** (*a*) **se fiche(r) de qn, de qch.,** to make fun of s.o., sth.; to pull s.o.'s leg; to make a fool of s.o.; **vous vous fichez de moi,** what do you take me for? **ça, c'est se fiche(r) du monde!** well, of all the nerve! (*b*) **je m'en fiche pas mal!** I don't care a hang! I couldn't care less! **je me fiche bien de ce qu'on pense de moi!** I don't give a damn what they think about me! **ce que je m'en fiche!** as if I cared! **3. se f. dedans,** (i) to make a bad break; to put one's foot in it; (ii) to make a mistake.

ficheron [fiʃrɔ̃], *s.m.* eye bolt.

fichet [fiʃɛ], *s.m.* peg (used for backgammon).

ficheur [fiʃœːr], *s.m. Const:* pointer (of walls).

fichier [fiʃje], *s.m.* (*a*) card-index cabinet, box; filing cabinet; (*b*) card index; (*c*) file (of computer); **f. sur cartes,** card file; **f. sur bande,** tape file; **f. sur disque(s),** disc file; **f. mouvement(s),** transaction file; **f. permanent,** master file.

fichiste [fiʃist], *s.m. & f.* (*a*) filing clerk; (*b*) card indexer.

fichoir [fiʃwaːr], *s.m.* (*rare*) clothes peg.

fichtre [fiʃtr], *int. F:* (*a*) (*expressing surprise, admiration*) good heavens! well . . .! (*b*) (*expressing pain, annoyance*) blast! hell! (*c*) (*intensive*) **f. oui!** rather! of course! I should say so! **f. non!** I should think not! not likely! **je n'en sais f. rien!** I'm damned if I know!

fichtrement [fiʃtrəmɑ̃], *adv. F:* extremely, awfully; confoundedly; **il a f. raison,** he's dead right; **c'est f. bien,** it's damn good; **c'est f. loin!** it's a hell of a way (off).

fichu[1] [fiʃy], *a. F:* **1.** rotten, awful; **quel f. pays!** what a god-forsaken country; **quel f. temps!** what filthy weather! **une fichue position,** a beastly, awkward, rotten, position; **je maudis la fichue idée que j'ai eue de venir ici,** I can't help cursing the terrible idea I had to come here. **2. il est f.,** he's done for; it's all up with him; **tout est f.** it's all up; the game's up; **c'est de l'argent f.,** it's (so much) money down the drain; **ma robe est fichue,** my dress is ruined, done for. **3. être bien f.,** (i) to be well-dressed; (ii) to be good-looking; **être f. comme quatre sous, comme l'as de pique,** to be dressed like a guy; **être mal f.,** (i) to be off colour, out of sorts; (ii) to be badly dressed; (iii) to be ugly, misshapen; **elle n'est pas trop mal fichue,** (i) she's quite well turned-out; (ii) she's not bad-looking. **4. f. de,** capable of; **il est f. d'arriver en retard,** it's quite on the cards that he'll be late; **elle n'est pas fichue de gagner sa vie,** she's not capable of earning her own living; **il est f. de nous faire entrer dans un arbre, en conduisant comme ça!** he's quite likely to crash into a tree, I shouldn't be surprised if he crashed into a tree with us, driving like that!

fichu[2] [fiʃy], *s.m.* small shawl; fichu.

fichûment [fiʃymɑ̃], *adv. F:* extremely, awfully; confoundedly.

ficoïde [fikɔid]. **1.** *a.* ficoid. **2.** *s.f. Bot:* fig marigold; **f. comestible,** Hottentot's fig; **f. cristalline, glaciaire,** ice plant.

fictif, -ive [fiktif, -iːv], *a.* **1.** (*a*) fictitious, imaginary (person, etc.); (*b*) *s.m.* **le réel et le f.,** the real and the imaginary; truth and fiction. **2.** (*a*) false, fictitious; **combat f.,** sham fight; **promesses fictives,** fictitious promises; *Fin:* **dividende f.,** sham dividend; *Com:* **compte f.,** impersonal account; **prix f.,** nominal price; **facture fictive,** pro forma invoice; (*computers*) **circuit de charge f.,** artificial load; *Astr:* **soleil f.,** fictitious sun; *s.a.* ENTREPÔT; (*b*) *Fin:* **valeur fictive (de la monnaie fiduciaire),** face (as opposed to intrinsic) value (of notes, coinage). **3.** *Jur:* feigned (issue, action, pleading).

fiction [fiksjɔ̃], *s.f.* (*a*) *A:* fiction, lie; (*b*) *Lit: etc:* fiction; **la vérité est supérieure à toutes les fictions,** truth is better than fiction; **œuvre de f.,** work of fiction; (*c*) fiction, convention; *Jur:* **f. légale, f. de droit,** fiction of law, legal fiction; **l'or et l'argent sont une richesse de f.,** gold and silver have only a conventional value.

fictivement [fiktivmɑ̃], *adv.* fictitiously.

ficus [fikyːs], *s.m.* **1.** *Bot:* ficus, fig tree. **2.** *Moll:* ficus.

fidéicommis [fideikɔmi], *s.m. Jur:* trust; **acte de f.,** trust deed.

fidéicommissaire [fideikɔmisɛːr], *s.m. Jur:* beneficiary (of a trust); *Rom. Jur:* fideicommissioner; **héritier f.,** feoffee in trust, feoffee of trust.

fidéicommisser [fideikɔmise], *v.i.* to make, leave, a trust.

fidéisme [fideism], *s.m. Phil:* fideism.

fidéiste [fideist]. (*a*) *a.* fideistic; (*b*) *s.m. & f.* fideist.

fidéjusseur [fideʒysœːr], *s.m. Jur:* surety; fidejussor.

fidéjussion [fideʒysjɔ̃], *s.f. Jur:* security, fidejussion.

fidéjussoire [fideʒyswaːr], *a. Jur:* fidejussory, fidejussionary.

fidèle [fidɛl]. **1.** *a.* (*a*) faithful, loyal, true, staunch, constant; **serviteur f.,** faithful servant; **compagnon f.,** loyal, devoted, companion; **f. au roi,** loyal to the king; **f. aux commandements de Dieu,** faithful to God's commandments; **rester f. à une promesse,** to stand by, keep, a promise; **rester f. à soi-même,** to remain true to oneself; **être f. à ses habitudes,** to be conservative in one's habits; to be a creature of habit; **il est resté f. au chapeau melon,** he still clings to his bowler (hat); **être f. à un fournisseur,** to be a regular customer (at a shop); (*b*) faithful, accurate; exact; **traduction f.,** accurate translation; **mémoire f.,** reliable memory; **souvenir f.,** accurate, exact, recollection; **témoin f.,** accurate witness. **2.** *s.m. & f.* (*a*) **les fidèles du gouvernement,** the (loyal) supporters of the government; (*b*) *Com:* regular customer; (*c*) *Ecc:* **les fidèles,** (i) the faithful; (ii) the congregation; **les fidèles trépassés,** the faithful departed.

fidèlement [fidɛlmɑ̃], *adv.* (*a*) faithfully, loyally; **servir qn f.,** to serve s.o. faithfully, loyally; **il continuait à venir f. nous voir,** he continued to come and see us regularly; (*b*) faithfully, accurately; **traduire f. un texte,** to translate a text accurately, to make a faithful translation of a text.

fidélité [fidelite], *s.f.* (*a*) fidelity; faithfulness; integrity, trustworthiness (of an employee); **serment de f.,** oath of allegiance; **f. conjugale,** conjugal fidelity; **la f. du chien,** the faithfulness of the dog; **f. à une promesse,** faithfulness to a promise; **f. à une habitude,** faithfulness, clinging, to a habit; (*b*) accuracy, closeness (of translation); accuracy (in reporting s.o.'s words); fidelity (in sound reproduction); reliability (of memory); *W.Tel: Elcs:* **haute f.,** high fidelity, hi-fi; **à haute f.,** high-fidelity.

fidibus [fidibyːs], *s.m. A: F:* fidibus; spill; pipe-lighter.

Fidji [fidʒi], *Pr.n. Geog:* **les îles F.,** the Fiji Islands.

fidjien, -ienne [fidʒjɛ̃, -jɛn], *a. & s. Geog:* Fijian.

fiduciaire [fidysjɛːr]. **1.** *a.* fiduciary (loan, etc.); (*legacy, etc.*) held in trust; **circulation f., monnaie f.,** fiduciary currency, paper money, token money, credit circulation; **certificat f.,** trustee's certificate. **2.** *s.m.* fiduciary, trustee.

fiduciairement [fidysjɛrmɑ̃], *adv.* fiduciarily; **in trust.**

fiducie [fidysi], *s.f. Jur:* trust.

fiduciel, -ielle [fidysjɛl], *a. Astr: Surv: etc:* fiducial (line, etc.); *Clockm:* **pendule fiducielle,** master clock.

fief [fjɛf], *s.m.* (*a*) *Jur: A:* fief, feoff, fee; *Scot:* feu; **don en f.,** feoffment; **investir qn d'un fief,** to enfeoff s.o.; (*b*) *F:* **f. électoral,** constituency.

fieffataire [fjɛfatɛːr], *s.m. & f. Jur: A:* feoffee.

fieffé [fjefe], *a.* **1.** *Jur: A:* (*a*) (*of pers.*) enfeoffed; (*b*) (*of land*) given in fief. **2.** *F: Pej:* arrant (liar, etc.); rank (impostor); **ivrogne f.,** hopeless drunkard; **f. coquin, coquin f.,** unmitigated, thorough-paced, scoundrel; villain of the deepest dye.

fieffer [fjefe], *v.tr. A:* **1. f. une terre,** to feoff out an estate. **2. f. qn,** to enfeoff s.o., to grant s.o. a fief, a fee.

fiel [fjɛl], *s.m.* **1.** (*a*) gall (of animal); *A:* bile (of person); **f. de bœuf,** ox-gall; (*b*) **épancher son f.,** to vent one's spleen (**sur,** on); **satire pleine de f.,** satire full of bitterness, of venom; **n'avoir point de f.,** to be without malice; **le f. de la vie,** the gall and bitterness of life. **2.** (*a*) *Glassm:* **f. de verre,** glass-gall; (*b*) *Bot:* **f. de terre,** earth-gall, lesser centaury.

fielleux, -euse [fjelø, -øːz], *a.* (*a*) gall-like, bitter; (*b*) rancorous, bitter (remark, etc.).

fiente [fjɑ̃ːt], *s.f.* dung; droppings (of birds).

fienter [fjɑ̃te]. **1.** *v.i.* (*of animals*) to dung; (*of birds*) to mute. **2.** *v.tr. A:* to manure, fertilize (land).

fienteux, -euse [fjɑ̃tø, -øːz], *a.* covered, soiled, with droppings, with dung.

fier[1], **-ère** [fjɛːr], *a.* **1.** *A:* ferocious, cruel. **2.** (legitimately) proud; **au cœur f.,** proud-hearted; **être trop f. pour mendier,** to be too proud to beg; **ne soyez pas trop f. pour accepter,** do not be too proud to accept, do not be above accepting; **courage f.,** lofty courage; **beauté fière,** proud beauty, stately grace; **être f. de qch.,** to be proud of sth.; **il est très f. des succès de son fils,** he takes great pride in his son's achievements; **il est f. d'avoir réussi,** he is proud of having succeeded. **3.** (*a*) proud, haughty, stuck-up; **air f.,** lordly air; **faire le f.,** to swank; **je n'étais pas f.,** I felt rather small, I cut rather a poor figure; **il n'y a pas là de quoi être f.,** that's nothing to boast of; **f. comme Artaban,** as proud as Lucifer; **entrer, sortir, se pavaner, f. comme Artaban,** to strut in, out, about; (*b*) **être f. de sa**

belle voix, de sa belle jambe, to be vain of one's fine voice, of one's shapely leg. **4.** *F: O:* rare, fine, famous; **un f. dîner,** a slap-up, first-rate, dinner; **tu m'as fait une fière peur,** a fine, rare, fright you gave me; **c'est un f. imbécile,** he's a first-class idiot; *Iron:* **tu m'as rendu là un f. service!** a fine service you've done me! **5.** *Art: Lit:* bold. **6.** *Equit:* (*of horse*) lively; graceful.

fier² [fje], *v.tr.* (*p.d. & pr.sub.* **n. fiions, v. fiiez**) *A:* (= CONFIER); **f. son honneur à un ami,** to entrust one's honour to a friend.

se fier, to trust; **se f. à qn,** *occ.* **en qn,** to rely on s.o., to trust s.o.; **ne vous fiez pas à eux,** do not trust them, they are not to be trusted; **je me fie entièrement à vous,** I have complete trust in you, I trust you completely; **on ne sait plus à qui se f.,** one no longer knows whom one can trust; **je me fie à votre discrétion,** I rely on your discretion; **vous pouvez vous f. à ce que je vous dis,** you may depend upon it that what I say is true; **fiez-vous à moi,** leave it to me; you can trust me (to do it); **ne pas se f. à ses yeux, à ses oreilles,** not to believe one's eyes, one's ears; **je me fie à lui pour . . .,** I depend, am depending on him to . . .; **fiez-vous-y,** you can be sure of it; you can count on it; **ne vous y fiez pas,** (i) don't trust it; beware of it; (ii) don't reckon on it; **catalogue auquel on peut se f.,** reliable catalogue.

fier-à-bras [fjɛrabra], *s.m. A:* bully, swaggerer, braggadocio; *pl. fier(s)-à-bras.*

fièrement [fjɛrmɑ̃], *adv.* **1.** proudly. **2.** (*a*) haughtily; (*b*) vainly. **3.** *F: O: Iron:* famously, properly; **être f. bête,** to be a proper fool; **il a été f. attrapé!** he was properly caught! **4.** *Art: Lit:* boldly.

fiérot [fjero], *a. & s. F:* snobbish, stuck-up, snooty; *P:* toffee-nosed (person).

fierté [fjɛrte], *s.f.* **1.** pride, self-respect. **2.** (*a*) pride, haughtiness; (*b*) vanity. **3.** *Art:* boldness (of touch).

Fiesque [fjɛsk], *Pr.n.m. Hist:* Fiesco; *pl.* **les Fiesques,** the Fieschi.

fieu, -eux [fjø], *s.m. Dial:* (= FILS) son, sonny; **c'est un bon f.,** he's a good chap, a good fellow.

fièvre [fjɛːvr̥], *s.f.* **1.** (*a*) fever; **accès de f.,** bout of fever; **forte f.,** high fever; **f. lente,** slight fever; **avoir une f. de cheval,** to have a raging fever; **la f. tombe,** the fever is abating; **la f. battait ses tempes,** his temples were throbbing (with fever); **avoir de la f.,** to be feverish, to have a (high) temperature; *F:* **il a quarante de f.,** he has a temperature of 40°C (104°F); *Med:* **f. des foins,** hay fever; **f. intermittente, paludéenne,** intermittent fever; malaria; *A:* **avoir, prendre, les fièvres,** to have, catch, malaria; **f. jaune,** yellow fever; **f. récurrente, à rechutes,** trench fever; **f. fluviale du Japon,** scrub typhus; **f. de trois jours,** sand-fly fever; *A:* **f. muqueuse,** paratyphoid; *A:* **f. quarte,** quartan ague; *Vet:* **f. aphteuse,** foot and mouth disease; **f. charbonneuse,** anthrax; *Lit:* **tomber de la f. en chaud mal,** to fall from the frying pan into the fire; (*b*) *Bot:* **arbre à f.,** fever tree. **2.** (*a*) excitement, restlessness; **il parlait sans f.,** he was speaking calmly; **dans la f. de la mêlée, de la campagne électorale,** in the heat of the battle, of the electoral campaign; **travailler avec f.,** to work feverishly; (*b*) **la f. des conquêtes,** the passion, desire, for conquest; **la f. d'écrire,** the urge to write; **f. de la lecture,** passion for reading; (*c*) **il en a la f. rien que d'y penser,** it makes him feverish, frantic, even to think of it; **l'attente des résultats lui donne la f.,** he gets frantic, completely worked up, waiting for the results.

fiévreusement [fjevrøzmɑ̃], *adv.* feverishly; **travailler f.,** to work frantically.

fiévreux, -euse [fjevrø, -øːz]. **1.** *a.* (*a*) feverish (pulse, etc.); **se sentir f.,** to feel feverish; **climat f.,** climate that induces fever; **marécage f.,** fever swamp; (*b*) feverish (activity, excitement, etc.); (*of pers.*) excited; frantic; *F:* worked up. **2.** *s.* (*a*) fever patient; **salle des f.,** fever ward (in hospital); (*b*) **c'est un f.,** he's an excitable, nervy, sort of person.

fifi [fifi], *s.m. F:* (*child's word*) little boy; **le f. à sa maman,** mummy's little boy.

fifille [fifiːj], *s.f. F:* (*child's word*) little girl; **la f. à son papa,** daddy's little girl, little girly-wirly.

fiflot [fiflo], *s.m. A: P:* (infantry) soldier.

fifre [fifr̥], *s.m.* **1.** (*a*) fife; (*b*) *F:* **un grand f.,** a tall, lanky fellow. **2.** fifer, fife (player).

fifrelin [fifrəlɛ̃], *s.m. F:* trifle; *used only in the phr.* **cela ne vaut pas un f.,** it isn't worth a brass farthing.

fifrer [fifre], *v.tr.* **f. un air,** to play a tune on the fife; to fife, pipe, a tune; *abs.* to play the fife, to fife, to pipe.

figaro [figaro], *s.m. F:* barber.

figeacois, -oise [fiʒakwa, -waːz], *a. & s.* (native, inhabitant) of Figeac.

figeage [fiʒaːʒ], *s.m. Rail:* weekly halt of goods trains.

figement [fiʒmɑ̃], *s.m.* coagulation, congealing, solidifying (of oil, blood, etc.); clotting (of blood, cream).

figer [fiʒe], *v.tr.* (**figeant, il figeait**) (*a*) (*of blood, oil*) to coagulate, congeal, solidify, fix; **corps figés par la mort,** corpses stark and stiff in death; **cris qui vous figent le sang,** blood-curdling cries; **figé sur place,** rooted to the spot; spellbound; **un regard figé,** a fixed look; (*b*) *Pol.Ec:* to freeze; **les ouvriers spécialisés des industries lourdes ont été figés,** skilled operatives in the heavy industries have been frozen.

se figer, to stand still, to freeze; (*of oil, blood*) to solidify, coagulate, congeal; (*of blood*) to clot; (*of the features*) to set; **son sang se figea (dans ses veines),** his blood ran cold; **sourire figé,** set smile.

fignolage [fiɲɔlaːʒ], *s.m. F:* (*a*) finicking, fiddle-faddling; (*b*) touching up.

fignoler [fiɲɔle]. *F:* **1.** *v.i.* to make a thorough job of sth.; to do things in a finicky way, to finick, to fiddle-faddle; to niggle. **2.** *v.tr.* (*a*) to fiddle, finick, over (job); to prepare (dish) with meticulous care; (*b*) to touch (sth.) up.

se fignoler, to titivate oneself.

fignoleur, -euse [fiɲɔlœːr, -øːz]. *F:* **1.** *a.* finicking, finical, niggling. **2.** *s.* fiddle-faddler, finicky person; niggler.

figue [fig], *s.f.* **1.** fig; **figues noires,** purple figs; **figues blanches,** green figs; **f. d'été, première f.,** fig that takes two seasons to ripen; *F:* **mi-f., mi-raisin,** *A:* **moitié f., moitié raisin,** half one thing and half another; wavering; **un petit sourire mi-f., mi-raisin,** a wry, forced, smile; **ton mi-f., mi-raisin,** tone (of voice), half in jest half in earnest; **ce n'est ni f. ni raisin,** it's neither one thing nor the other; **c'est mi-f., mi-raisin,** it's like the curate's egg; *F:* **faire la f. à qn,** to make a gesture of contempt at s.o., to fig s.o. **2.** (*a*) *Bot:* **f. banane,** plantain; **f. de Barbarie,** prickly pear; (*b*) *Moll:* **f. de mer,** edible sea squirt.

figue-caque [fig(ə)kak], *s.f. Bot:* persimmon; *pl. figues-caques.*

figuerie [figri], *s.f.* fig garden, fig orchard.

figuier [figje], *s.m. Bot:* **1.** fig tree. **2. f. de Barbarie,** prickly pear; **f. d'Égypte,** Egyptian sycamore, oriental sycamore, sycamore fig; **f. d'Adam,** plantain tree, Adam's fig. **3.** *Orn:* **f. à tête cendrée,** magnolia warbler; **f. bleu à gorge noire,** black-throated blue warbler.

figulin, -ine [figylɛ̃, -in]. **1.** *a.* (*a*) figuline, earthenware (vessel, etc.); (*b*) figuline, fictile (clay, etc.). **2.** *s.f.* **figuline;** *Cer:* figuline.

figurable [figyrabl̥], *a.* figurable, representable.

figurant, -ante [figyrɑ̃, -ɑ̃ːt]. **1.** *a. A:* figurative. **2.** *s.* (*a*) *A:* ballet dancer; (*b*) *Th: Cin:* walker-on, crowd artist, supernumerary; *F:* super; **les figurants,** the crowd; **rôle de f.,** walk-on part, bit part; *F:* thinking part; (*c*) figure-head, person whose rôle is purely decorative; **nation réduite au rôle de f. dans une conférence internationale,** nation reduced to observer status in an international conference; **il n'est qu'un f. dans toute cette histoire,** he is taking no active part in this business, he is no more than an onlooker in all this business.

figuratif, -ive [figyratif, -iːv], *a.* (*a*) *A:* symbolic; (*b*) figurative; emblematic; **art f.,** representational art.

figuration [figyrasjɔ̃], *s.f.* **1.** (*a*) figuration, representation; **f. d'un son par un symbole,** notation of a sound by a symbol; (*b*) (*radar*) display; **les données sont introduites dans des figurations de grandes dimensions,** data are fed into large-size displays. **2.** *Coll. Th:* supers, extras; crowd artists; **faire de la f.,** to be, work as, an extra.

figurativement [figyrativmɑ̃], *adv.* figuratively.

figure [figyːr], *s.f.* **1.** (*a*) figure, form, shape; **f. d'un homme,** figure, form, of a man; **portrait de demi-figure,** half-length portrait; **f. de bronze,** bronze figure; **figures de cire,** waxworks; **figures géométriques,** geometrical figures, diagrams; **f. de mots, de rhétorique,** figure of speech; **f. de proue,** figurehead (of ship); **les figures d'une danse,** the figures of a dance; **une des grandes figures de l'histoire,** one of the great figures, of the great characters, in history; (*b*) *Tchn:* figure, pattern; *Cryst:* **f. de corrosion,** corrosion figure; *Opt:* **f. d'interférence,** interference figure; **f. de diffraction,** diffraction pattern. **2.** (*a*) face, countenance; **avoir une jolie f.,** to have a pretty face; **jeter (qch.) à la f. de qn,** (i) to throw (sth.) in s.o.'s face; (ii) to cast (an insult) in s.o.'s teeth; **faire longue f.,** to pull a long face; **sa f. s'allongea,** his countenance fell; *Th:* **faire sa f.,** to make up; *Cards:* **les figures,** the court cards; *F:* **casser la f. à qn,** to beat s.o. up, to push s.o.'s face in; *F:* **se casser la f.,** to come a cropper; (*b*) appearance; **faire f. de,** to give the impression of; **faire f. avec peu de fortune,** to cut a figure, to keep up an appearance, on small means; **faire (très) bonne f. en selle,** to show up to (great) advantage in the saddle; **faire pauvre, sotte, piètre, pâle, f.,** to cut a sorry figure; **faire grande f.,** to play an important rôle.

figuré [figyre], *a.* (*a*) **monument f.,** monument decorated with figures; (*b*) **sens f.,** figurative meaning; *adv.phr.* **au f.,** in the figurative sense; figuratively; (*c*) figured (material); (*d*) **danse figurée,** figure dance; (*e*) *Mus:* **contrepoint f.,** *s.m.* **figuré,** figured, florid, counterpoint; (*f*) *Mil:* **ennemi f.,** marked, indicated, enemy (in manœuvres or musketry training); **plan f.,** *s.m.* **figuré,** representative plan, representation of ground (by a sketch).

figurément [figyremɑ̃], *adv.* figuratively, in a figurative sense.

figurer [figyre]. **1.** *v.tr.* (*a*) *A:* = FAÇONNER; (*b*) to represent; **on figure la Justice avec un bandeau sur les yeux,** Justice is represented, shown, blindfolded; **f. des persiennes sur un mur,** to paint shutters on a wall; **f. un personnage sur la scène,** to act, take the part of, a character; **la partie du salon qui figure la scène,** the part of the drawing-room got up as a stage. **2.** *v.i.* to appear, figure; **il ne figure pas dans l'histoire,** he does not figure in history; **son nom ne figure pas dans l'histoire,** his name does not appear in history; **je ne veux pas que mon nom figure dans l'affaire,** I don't want my name to appear in the matter; **ces articles figurent dans le catalogue,** these articles are listed in the catalogue; *Th:* **f. sur la scène,** to walk on; **Falstaff figure dans "Les Joyeuses Commères de Windsor,"** Falstaff comes into "The Merry Wives of Windsor."

se figurer qch., to imagine sth., to fancy sth.; **se f. les choses autrement qu'elles ne sont,** to fancy things different from what they are; **figurez-vous la situation,** picture the situation to yourself; **figurez-vous que vous êtes, que vous soyez, soldat,** imagine, picture, yourself as a soldier; **ne vous figurez pas que je sois satisfait,** do not imagine that I am satisfied; **je me figure bien que cela puisse arriver,** I can imagine it happening; **il se figure tout savoir,** he fancies he knows everything; **je l'aime, figure-toi,** believe it or not, I am in love with her (him).

figurine [figyrin], *s.f.* figurine, statuette.

figurisme [figyrism], *s.m. Theol:* figurism.

figuriste [figyrist], *s.m. & f.* **1.** *Theol:* figurist. **2.** maker of plaster figures.

fil [fil], *s.m.* **1.** (*a*) thread; yarn; **f. de coton, de nylon,** cotton, nylon, yarn; **f. cardé, peigné,** carded, combed, yarn; **f. de lin,** linen yarn, thread; **des draps pur f.,** (pure) linen sheets; **f. de fouet,** whipcord; **f. de jute,** jute yarn; **f. de caret,** rope yarn; **f. d'emballage,** pack(ing) thread; *Sp:* **f. (de laine),** tape; **bas de f.,** lisle stockings; **gants de f.,** cotton, fabric, gloves; **laine trois, quatre, fils,** three-ply, four-ply, wool; (*b*) **f. à coudre,** sewing cotton, thread; **f. à boutons, gros f.,** button thread; **bobine de f.,** reel of cotton, thread; **finesse cousue de f. blanc,** obvious trick, trick which would deceive nobody; **de f. en aiguille,** little by little; gradually; **brouiller les fils,** to muddle things up, to get muddled; **démêler les fils d'une intrigue,** to unravel the threads of a plot; **donner du f. à retordre à qn,** to create difficulties for s.o.; to give s.o. a headache, sth. to think about; **avoir du f. à retordre,** to have one's work cut out; to have more than one bargained for; **avoir un f. sur la langue,** to have a slight stammer; **mince comme un f.,** as thin as a rake; *F:* **à un f. près,** by a narrow margin; **le f. d'Ariane,** Ariadne's clew; **trouver le f. d'Ariane, le f. conducteur,** to find the clue (to the mystery); (*c*) **les fils d'un câble, d'une corde,** strands of a cable, a rope; **fils de marionnette,** puppet strings; *Fish:* **donner du f. au poisson,** to give the fish some line; **sa vie ne tenait qu'à un f.,** his life hung by a thread; **c'est lui qui tient les fils,** he's the one who can pull the strings; *F:* **avoir un f. à la patte,** (i) not to be a free agent; to be tied down; (ii) to be encumbered (with a mistress); *F:* **se mettre un f. à la patte,** to get married, *F:* tied up; (*d*) **f. d'araignée,** spider's thread; **fils de la Vierge,** gossamer; *Opt:* **f. du réticule, f. d'araignée,** cross wire, cross hair; spider line; **f. vertical, f. collimateur (du réticule),** vertical

cross wire, cross hair; **f. horizontal, f. axial (du réticule),** horizontal cross wire, cross hair; **f. de stadia,** stadia wire, hair; (*e*) *pl.* strings (of French beans, etc.); **ces haricots ont des fils,** these beans are stringy. **2.** (*a*) **f. métallique, f. de fer,** wire; **f. de fer barbelé, galvanisé,** barbed wire; galvanized wire; **clôture en f. de fer,** wire fencing; *F:* **avoir des jambes comme des fils de fer,** to have legs like matchsticks; **f. d'acier, de cuivre, de laiton, d'or,** steel, copper, brass, gold, wire; **f. demi-jonc, f. demi-rond,** half-round wire; **f. tréfilé, étiré,** drawn wire; *Geol:* **fils étirés,** Pele's hair; **f. torsadé,** twin wire; **f. blindé,** shielded wire; **f. d'archal,** brass wire, binding wire; **f. aérien, tendeur,** span wire; **f. plombé,** lead seal wire; **f. d'arrêt,** retaining wire; **f. d'attache, de ligature,** tie wire, binding wire; **f. de hauban,** bracing, staying, wire; guy wire; **f. à suspendre,** picture cord, wire; **f. à trébucher,** trip wire; *Metall:* **f. pour soudure oxygène,** welding wire; *Surg:* **f. de contention, de ligature,** retaining wire, thread; ligature wire, thread; *Dent:* **f. d'arc,** arch wire; **f. à couper le beurre,** cheese, butter, wire; *F:* **il n'a pas inventé le f. à couper le beurre,** he'll never set the Thames on fire; (*b*) *El:* **f. électrique,** electric wire; **f. souple,** flexible wire, flex; **f. d'arrivée (de courant),** (electric) lead; **f. d'amenée, d'aller,** feed wire; **f. de retour,** return wire; **f. de dérivation,** shunt wire; **f. de branchement d'abonné,** service lead; **les fils de ligne,** the mains; **f. de masse, de terre,** earth (wire), *U.S:* ground wire; **f. de raccord de circuit, f. volant,** jumper (wire); **f. conducteur,** conductor, conducting wire; **f. sous tension, f. électrisé,** live wire; **f. nu, dénudé,** bare, naked, wire; **f. fusible,** fuse wire; *Elcs:* **enregistreur sur f.,** wire recorder; (*c*) *Tp:* **f. d'appel,** calling wire; **donner un coup de f. à qn,** to give s.o. a ring, to ring s.o. up, *U.S:* to call s.o.; **être au bout du f.,** to be on the phone, on the line; **je viens d'avoir X au bout du f.,** I've just had X on the line, I've just been through to X; **télégraphie, téléphonie, sans f.,** wireless telegraphy, telephony; *F: O:* **un sans-f.,** a wireless message. **3.** (*a*) grain (of wood, etc.); **contre le f., à contre-f.,** against, across, the grain; **de droit f.,** with the grain; **couper qch. de droit f.,** to cut sth. (i) with, along, the grain, (ii) along the warp, the woof; **tissu droit f.,** cross fabric, interwoven fabric; (*b*) vein (in marble, stone). **4.** (*a*) (i) *A:* current, stream (of river); (ii) **au f. de l'eau,** with the current, downstream; **se laisser aller au f. de l'eau,** to let oneself drift (with the current); **au f. des jours et des ans,** day after day, year after year; **au f. de la plume,** as the pen runs; (*b*) **le f. des événements,** the chain of events; **perdre le f. de la conversation, de ses idées,** to lose the thread of the conversation, of one's ideas; **reprendre le f. de son discours,** to pick up the threads of one's speech. **5.** (*a*) edge (of knife, sword, etc.); **repasser le f.,** to sharpen; **donner le f. à un rasoir,** to put an edge on a razor; *Lit:* **passer des prisonniers au f. de l'épée,** to put prisoners to the sword; **langue qui a le f.,** cutting, sarcastic, tongue; (*b*) *F:* **avoir le f.,** to be wide awake, to be all there.

filable [filabl̩], *a.* spinnable, suitable for spinning, that can be spun.

fil-à-fil [filafil], *s.m.inv. Tex:* end-and-end weave.

filage [filaːʒ], *s.m.* **1.** (*a*) spinning (of cotton, etc.); **f. du tabac,** making of twist; (*b*) yarn. **2. f. d'un tonneau,** lowering of a cask (into a cellar, etc.). **3.** palming (of card). **4.** *Nau:* **f. de l'huile,** pouring of oil (on the water). **5.** *Metalw:* drawing (of metal); extrusion; **f. inverse,** backward extrusion; **f. direct,** forward extrusion. **6.** *Typ:* progressive destruction of printing image of offset plate. **7.** *Bot:* cudweed.

filaire[1] [filɛːr], *s.f. Ann:* filaria; *esp. Med:* guinea-worm.

filaire[2], *a. Mil:* **les moyens filaires,** telegraphic (as opposed to radio) means of transmission.

filament [filamɑ̃], *s.m.* filament, fibre (of plant, etc.); thread (of silk, etc.); *El:* **lampe à filaments métalliques,** metal filament lamp; **f. étiré,** drawn filament; **f. à ruban,** flat filament; **f. chauffant,** heating filament, element; *W.Tel:* **valve à f. obscur,** dull-emitter valve.

filamenteux, -euse [filamɑ̃tø, -øːz], *a.* filamentous; fibrous; *F:* stringy (meat, etc.).

filandière [filɑ̃djɛːr], *s.f. A:* spinner; *Lit:* **les (sœurs) filandières,** the Fates.

filandre [filɑ̃ːdr̥], *s.f.* **1.** fibre; *pl.* stringy parts, strings (of meat, vegetables, etc.). **2.** *pl.* gossamer. **3.** white specks (in glass).

filandreux, -euse [filɑ̃drø, -øːz], *a.* (*a*) (*of meat, vegetables, etc.*) tough, stringy; **explication filandreuse,** long-drawn, involved, confused, explanation; (*b*) (*of wood, marble*) streaked.

filant [filɑ̃], *a.* **1.** ropy (liquid). **2. étoile filante,** shooting star, falling star.

filanzane [filɑ̃zan] (*in Madagascar*) **1.** *s.f.* palanquin, carrying-chair. **2.** *s.m.* palanquin bearer.

filao [filao], *s.m. Bot:* filao.

filarioïdés [filarjɔide], *s.m.pl. Ann:* Filarioidea.

filariose [filarjoːz], *s.f. Med:* filariasis, filariosis.

filasse [filas], *s.f.* **1.** tow, harl, textile fibre, bast; *F:* **cheveux de f.,** tow-like hair, hair of a washed-out colour; **aux cheveux blond f.,** tow-headed. **2.** oakum; **faire de la f.,** to pick oakum. **3.** *Miner: F:* **f. de montagne,** asbestos.

filassier, -ière [filasje, -jɛːr], *s.* tow maker, worker, seller.

filateur, -trice [filatœːr, -tris], *s.* **1.** spinner; owner of a spinning-mill. **2.** (private detective's) spy; shadower; tail; informer.

filatière [filatjɛːr], *s.f. Hist:* decorative scroll.

filature [filatyːr], *s.f.* **1.** spinning. **2.** (*a*) spinning-mill, -factory; **f. de coton,** cotton mill; (*b*) rope-walk. **3.** shadowing (by detective, etc.); **prendre qn en f.,** to shadow s.o.

fildefériste [fildəferist], *s.m. or f.* tightrope walker.

file [fil], *s.f.* file (of soldiers, etc.); **f. creuse,** blank file; **chef de f.,** (i) front-rank man, file leader; (ii) leader (of a party, etc.); (iii) (parliamentary) whip; (iv) leading exponent (of an art, etc.); **aller à la f.,** to go in file, one behind another; **en, à la, f. indienne,** in Indian file; *Nau: etc:* in single file; **deux heures à la f.,** two hours on end; **voter à la f.,** to vote in uninterrupted sequence; **fumeur de cigarettes à la f.,** chain-smoker; **sortir, entrer, traverser, etc., à la f.,** to file out, in, across, etc.; **f. d'attente,** queue; **f. de véhicules,** line of vehicles; **prendre la, sa, f.,** to join one's car on to the end of the line, to line up, to queue up; **stationner en double f.,** to double park; *Navy:* **en ligne de f.,** (single) line ahead; **prendre la ligne de f.,** to form single line ahead; *Mil:* **par f. à droite! à gauche!** right, left, wheel!

fil(-en-trois, -en-quatre, -en-six) [fil(ɑ̃trwa, ɑ̃katr̥, -ɑ̃sis)], *s.m. F:* strong spirits; *F:* rot-gut; **avaler un verre de f.,** to take a dram.

filé [file], *s.m.* **1.** thread; **f. de coton,** yarn; **f. d'or,** gold thread. **2.** *Cu:* **cuire du sirop au f.,** to boil sugar to the pearl. **3.** *Surv:* running (of contour). **4.** *a. Nau:* flowing; **les écoutes filées,** with flowing sail, sheet. **5.** twist tobacco, chewing tobacco (in plug or string shape).

filée [file], *s.f.* row of tiles (in area of tiling).

filer [file]. **I.** *v.tr.* **1.** (*a*) to spin (cotton, flax, glass, etc.); **machine à f. le coton,** spinning jenny; **l'araignée file sa toile,** the spider spins its web; **f. du tabac,** to make twist (tobacco); *F:* **f. un mauvais coton,** to be in a bad way; *s.a.* BERTHE 1; (*b*) to (wire)draw (metal). **2.** (*a*) *Nau:* to pay out, run out (cable); to ease off (sheet); to slip (moorings); to heave (the lead); **filez de la chaîne!** ease off the cable! **f. le corps mort,** to cast off from the buoy; **f. sa chaîne par le bout,** to slip the anchor; **f. de l'huile,** to release oil; **f. le loch,** to stream the log; **f. en grand,** to let go by the run; **f. à la demande,** to slack away; **f. le câble,** to pay out the cable; *F:* **f. son nœud,** to slip one's painter, one's cable; (i) to make off, to make oneself scarce; (ii) to die; *Fish:* **f. la ligne (à un poisson),** to pay out line; (*b*) **f. une barrique,** to lower a cask (into a cellar); (*c*) to prolong, spin out, draw out (sound, story, etc.); to pour out (oil) in a trickle; *Mus:* **f. un son, la voix,** to hold a note. **3.** (*of detective, etc.*) to shadow, *U.S:* tail (s.o.); (*of murderer*) **f. une victime,** to trail a victim. **4.** *Cards:* (*a*) **f. la carte,** (i) to palm, (ii) to palm off, a card; (*b*) **f. les cartes,** to discard a sequence; (*c*) **f. ses cartes,** to run through one's cards. **5.** *Surv:* **f. une courbe de niveau,** to run a contour. **6.** *F:* to give; to procure. **7.** *P:* **f. une danse, une dérouillée, une raclée, une rouste, une avoine (à qn),** to beat s.o. up, to lay into s.o.

II. filer, *v.i.* **1.** (*a*) to flow smoothly; (*of oil, etc.*) to run; (*of wine, etc.*) to rope (when poured out); (*b*) **la lampe file,** the lamp is smoking; (*c*) *F:* **f. doux,** to sing small, to obey without a word; (*d*) *F:* **j'ai une maille qui file,** I've (got) a ladder, *U.S:* run, in my stocking. **2.** (*a*) to slip by, move past; to whisk away; **le temps file,** time flies; **les jours filent et rien ne se fait,** the days go by and nothing is done; **le câble file,** the cable runs out; **laisser f. un câble,** to pay out a cable; **voiture, train, qui file à toute vitesse,** car, train, that goes, rushes along, at full speed; **les voitures filaient sur la route,** cars were speeding along the road; *Nau:* **f. à grande vitesse, à vingt nœuds,** to proceed at a high speed, at twenty knots; **combien filons-nous?—douze nœuds,** how fast are we steaming?—twelve knots; *F:* **f. comme une flèche,** to shoot off; **il a filé,** he made a bolt for it, he made tracks; **je filai à la cuisine,** I hurried to the kitchen; **f. (en vitesse),** to cut and run; *P:* to bunk, to do a bunk; **allez, filez!** take yourself off! clear out! cut along! buzz off! skedaddle! **filez devant,** go on ahead; **f. sur un endroit,** to make for a place; **il fila sur l'Amérique avec l'argent,** he bolted, made off, skipped (off), to America with the money; **f. à l'anglaise,** to take French leave, to slip away; **f. en douceur,** to slip away; **il fila rejoindre ses amis,** he ran off to join his friends; (*of bookie*) **f. avec les enjeux,** to welsh; (*b*) **le sentier file entre les haies,** the path threads its way between the hedges; (*c*) *Ven:* (*of game*) to go off in a straight line.

filerie [filri], *s.f.* **1.** (*a*) hemp spinning; (*b*) hemp-spinning mill. **2.** *Metalw:* (*a*) wire drawing; (*b*) drawplate. **3.** *El:* network (of admittances).

filet[1] [filɛ], *s.m.* **1.** small, fine, thread; (*a*) *F:* **f. de voix,** thin, weak, voice; **f. de lumière,** thin streak of light; **f. d'air,** thin stream, filament, of air; **filets d'air,** airflow; *Av:* **redresseur des filets d'air,** airflow straightener; *Min:* **f. de minerai,** thread of ore; **f. d'eau,** thin trickle, thin jet, runnel, of water; **ajoutez-y un f. de citron,** add a dash of lemon; (*b*) *Mec.E:* **f. (d'une vis),** thread (of screw); worm, fillet, of a screw; **f. à droite,** right-handed thread; **f. à gauche, f. renversé,** left-handed thread; (*c*) *Anat:* frenum; **f. de la langue,** bridle, string, of the tongue; *F:* **avoir le f.,** to be tongue-tied; **elle n'a pas le f.,** she has a glib tongue; **elle a le f. bien coupé,** she has the gift of the gab; (*d*) fillet (of column); purfling (of violin); *Bookb: Arch:* fillet; **filets dorés,** gold lines (on binding, etc.); **f. d'encadrement,** border line (of picture, etc.); *Her:* fillet; (*e*) *Typ:* (brass) rule; **f. maigre, gras,** thin, thick, rule; **f. anglais,** French rule, swell rule; **f. à composer,** setting-rule; (*f*) *Bot:* filament (of stamen); *Hort:* runner (of strawberry plant, etc.). **2.** *Cu:* fillet (of fish); **f. de bœuf,** fillet, undercut, tenderloin, of beef; *Belg:* **f. américain,** steak tartare. **3.** *Harn:* (*a*) snaffle bridle, watering bridle; (*b*) snaffle (bit).

filet[2], *s.m.* net(ting); (*in a circus*) safety-net; *Com:* mesh-bag; *F:* snare, ambush; **f. de chargement,** loading net; **f. de pêche,** fishing net; **f. maillant,** gill net, tangle net; **f. traînant,** drag-net; **coup de f.,** (i) cast; (ii) haul (of a net), draught (of fishes); haul (of criminals, suspects); **f. à mines,** mine net; **jeter, tendre, un f.,** to cast, to spread, a net; **pose des filets,** netting (of wood, etc.); **faire du f.,** to net; **pêche au f.,** net-fishing; **prendre du poisson au f.,** to net fish; **f. à papillons,** butterfly net; **être pris au f.,** to be caught in the net; **faire tomber dans un f.,** to ensnare; **bourse en f.,** net purse; **f. à provisions,** net bag, string bag; **f. pour cheveux,** hair net; *Rail:* **f. à bagages,** luggage rack; *Navy:* **f. de protection,** torpedo net; **f. de débarquement,** scramble net; *Ten:* **jeu au f.,** net play; **mettre la balle dans le f.,** to net the ball; **balle de f.,** let ball; *Aut: etc: A:* **f. chapelière,** hat-net; *Tex:* **dentelle de f.,** filet lace.

filetage[1] [filtaːʒ], *s.m.* **1.** (wire-)drawing (of metal); drawing (of wire). **2.** (*a*) threading (of screw), screw cutting; thread cutting; **f. par vis mère,** threading with lead screw; **calibre pour f.,** thread gauge; (*b*) thread, pitch (of screw). **3.** *Cu:* filleting (of fish).

filetage[2], *s.m.* poaching (with nets), netting.

fileter[1] [filte], *v.tr.* **(je filète, n. filetons; je filèterai) 1.** to (wire-)draw (metal, etc.); to draw (wire). **2.** to cut a thread, worm, screw, on (bolt, etc.); to worm, thread, screw (bolt, etc.); **tige filetée,** threaded rod; **tige filetée sur toute sa longueur,** full thread(ed) rod; **bouchon fileté,** screw plug; **tour à f.,** screw-cutting lathe, threading lathe; **machine à f.,** screw(-cutting), screwing, machine; thread-cutting machine; threading machine, thread cutter, threader; **machine à f. à la fraise,** screw-milling, thread-milling, machine; **machine à f. à la meule,** screw-grinding, thread-grinding, machine. **3.** *Cu:* to fillet (fish).

fileter[2], *v.tr.* to poach (with nets).

fileteur [filtœːr], *s.m.* screw cutter.

filetier [filtje], *s.m.* **1.** (spinning-)mill hand. **2.** net maker. **3.** poacher (who nets the game).

fileur, -euse [filœːr, -øːz], *s.* **1.** *Tex:* (*a*) spinner; (*b*) (silk)thrower, throwster; (*c*) *s.f.* **fileuse,** reeling girl. **2.** gold, silver, wire drawer. **3.** *F:* (private detective's) spy; informer; shadower, *U.S:* tail. **4.** *F:* runaway, quitter. **5.** *s.f.* **fileuse,** ropemaking machine.

filial, -aux [filjal, -o]. **1.** *a.* filial; **peu f.,** unfilial; undaughterly. **2.** *s.f.* **filiale,** (*a*) *Com:* sub-company, subsidiary company; affiliated firm, *U.S:* affiliate; (*b*) provincial branch, offshoot (of association); (*c*) *Ecc:* daughter house.

filialement [filjalmɑ̃], *adv.* filially.

filiation [filjasjɔ̃], *s.f.* **1.** (*a*) consanguinity in direct line, (af)filiation; **en f. directe,** in direct line; (*b*) descendants. **2.** dependence, relationship; **f. des idées,** filiation of ideas. **3.** *Ecc:* **une abbaye de la f. de Cluny,** a daughter house of Cluny. **4.** *Atom.Ph:* **f. radioactive,** radioactive relationship; **produit de f.,** daughter product.

filibranches [filibrɑ̃:ʃ], *s.m.pl. Moll:* Filibranchia (-ta).

filicales [filikal], *s.f.pl. Bot:* Filicales, Filices.

filicine [filisin], *s.f. Pharm:* filicin.

filicinées [filisine], *s.f.pl. Bot:* Filicinae.

filicique [filisik], *a. Ch:* filicic (acid).

filière [filjɛ:r], *s.f.* **1.** (*a*) (stock and) die; **f. simple, f. à truelle,** die plate, screw plate; **f. double,** screw stock and dies; **f. (de métier à tisser la soie artificielle),** nozzle; (*b*) **f. (à étirer),** draw(ing) plate; **travailler un métal à la f.,** to draw a metal; *F:* **il a passé, par, suivi, la f.,** he has worked his way up (to a good position), come through the mill; **il faut que cette demande passe par la f. administrative,** this request must go through the usual official channels; (*c*) gauge (for surgical bougies, etc.); (*d*) *Cu:* pierced plate for moulding vermicelli, etc.; (*e*) (*computers*) **f. (de magasin d'alimentation),** (card) throat. **2.** (*a*) ridge rope (of tent); *Nau:* (man-)rope; **f. d'envergure,** jack-stay; **f. en guirlande,** grab line; (*b*) purlin (of roof); (*c*) ledger (of scaffolding). **3.** *Nat.Hist:* spinneret (of spider, silkworm, etc.). **4.** (*a*) *Com:* transfer note; (*b*) *St.Exch:* trace; **établir la f.,** to draw up the succession of previous holders (of shares). **5.** *Atom.Ph:* line. **6.** *Min:* vein, lode (of metal). **7.** *Ven:* leash (of hawk). **8.** *Fr.C:* filing cabinet.

filifère [filifɛ:r], *s.m. Dom.Ec:* needle threader.

filiforme [filifɔrm], *a.* filiform, thread-like (antenna, etc.); *Anat:* **papille f.,** filiform papilla; *Med:* **pouls f.,** thready pulse; *Av:* **fuselage f.,** pencil-shaped fuselage; *F:* **homme f.,** lanky man.

filigranage [filigrana:ʒ], *s.m. Paperm:* (i) watermarking; (ii) embossing; **laminoir pour faux f.,** embossing calender.

filigrane [filigran], *s.m.* **1.** filigree (work); **boucles d'oreilles en f.,** filigree earrings. **2.** watermark (of banknotes, etc.); waterline; **papier à f.,** watermarked paper; **f. ombré,** embossment. **3.** binding (of sword-grip). **4.** *adv.phr.* **en f.,** implicitly.

filigraner [filigrane], *v.tr.* **1.** to ornament (sth.) with filigree work, to filigree; **verre filigrané,** lace-glass. **2.** *Paperm:* (i) to watermark; (ii) to emboss.

filigraneur, -euse [filigranœ:r, -ø:z], **filigraniste** [filigranist], *s.* filigree worker.

filin [filɛ̃], *s.m.* rope; **f. noir, goudronné,** tarred rope; **franc f., f. blanc,** white rope, untarred rope; **f. mixte,** fibre clad rope; **f. d'acier,** steel rope; **f. en trois, en quatre,** three-, four-stranded rope; **vieux f.,** junk.

filipendula [filipɑ̃dyla], **filipendule** [filipɑ̃dyl], *s.f. Bot:* filipendula; *F:* dropwort.

fillasse [fijas], *s.f. Pej:* coarse, fat, blowsy girl; prostitute.

fillatière [fijatjɛ:r], *s.f. Hist:* decorative scroll.

fille [fij], *s.f.* **1.** daughter; *Hist:* **F. de France,** (legitimate) daughter of the King of France; *F: Lit:* **jouer (à) la f. de l'air,** to disappear, decamp; to make oneself scarce. **2.** (*a*) girl; **petite f.,** little girl; child; **c'est encore une petite f.,** she is a mere child still; **jeune f.,** girl, young woman; *Lit:* maiden, maid; *A:* damsel; *Scot:* lass; **nom de jeune f.,** maiden name; **manières de jeune f.,** maidenly manners or airs; girlish ways; **grande f.,** full-grown girl; **école de filles,** girls' school; **vieille f.,** old maid, spinster; **rester f.,** to remain single, unmarried, *F:* to remain an old maid; **habitudes de vieille f.,** old-maidish habits; *F:* **c'est une bonne f., une brave f.,** she's a good sort, a decent sort (of girl); *Jur:* **la f. Martin,** (the accused) Martin; (*b*) **f. d'honneur,** maid of honour (attached to queen); (*c*) **f. publique,** *F:* **fille,** prostitute; *A:* **f. soumise,** registered prostitute; *F:* **elle a des manières de f.,** she's a bit of a tart; **courir les filles,** to be always after women. **3.** *Ecc:* **les filles de Port-Royal,** the sisters, nuns, of Port-Royal. **4. f. de service,** maidservant, servant-girl; housemaid; **f. de cuisine,** kitchen-maid; **f. de vaisselle,** washer-up; **f. de basse-cour,** poultry maid; *O:* **f. de boutique,** shop girl; **f. de salle (d'un hôtel, etc.),** waitress; **f. de salle (dans un hôpital),** ward maid; **f. de comptoir,** barmaid. **5.** *P:* bottle of wine.

fille-mère [fijmɛ:r], *s.f.* unmarried, *U.S:* unwed, mother; *pl. filles-mères.*

filler[1] [filœ:r], *s.m. Num:* filler.

filler[2], *s.m. Civ. E:* filler.

fillerisation [filərizasjɔ̃], *s.f. Civ.E:* addition of filler (to road tar).

filleriser [filərize], *v.tr. Civ.E:* to add filler to (bitumen); **bitume fillerisé,** filled bitumen.

fillette [fijɛt], *s.f.* **1.** little girl; *Scot:* little lass; lassie. **2.** *F:* half-bottle (of wine).

filleul, -eule [fijœl], *s.* godchild; godson, goddaughter; **f. de guerre,** adopted godson, protégé (during the war).

fillowite [filəwit], *s.f. Miner:* fillowite.

film [film], *s.m.* **1.** film; (*a*) *Phot:* **f. rigide,** cut film, flat film, stiff film; **f. en bobine,** roll film; **f. radiographique,** X-ray film; (*b*) *Cin:* film, *U.S:* motion picture, *F:* movie, picture; **tourner un f.,** (i) to make, produce, a film; (ii) to act a film part; **f. muet,** silent film; **f. parlant, parlé,** talking picture; *F:* talkie; **f. sonore, sonorisé,** synchronized sound film; **f. de reportage, d'actualité,** topical film, news film; **f. à épisodes,** serial film; **f. annonce,** trailer; *U.S:* preview, prevue; **grand f., f. principal,** (main) feature film, *F:* big picture; **f. supplémentaire,** supporting film; **film(s) vierge(s),** (film-)stock; **f. comique,** comic film, comedy film; **f. en couleurs, technicolore,** colour film, film in technicolour; **f. fixe (d'enseignement),** filmstrip; **f. télévisé,** television film, telefilm. **2.** (*a*) **f. (d'huile),** film (of oil); (*b*) *Dent:* **f. dentaire,** dental plaque.

filmage [filma:ʒ], *s.m. Cin:* filming, shooting.

filmer [filme], *v.tr.* **1.** to cover (sth.) with a film. **2.** *Cin:* to film, shoot (scene); **f. un roman,** to put a novel on the screen; to film a novel.

filmique [filmik], *a.* cinematic, filmic.

filmogène [filmɔʒɛn], *a. Paint:* film building, film forming.

filmographie [filmɔgrafi], *s.f. Cin:* catalogue of films (made by a producer, an actor).

filmologie [filmɔlɔʒi], *s.f.* the study of the cinema (from the philosophical and sociological angle).

filmothèque [filmɔtɛk], *s.f.* film library.

film-pack [filmpak], *s.m. Phot:* film-pack; *pl. film-packs.*

filoche [filɔʃ], *s.f. Tex:* net, netting, *esp.* silk netting; butterfly net; *Fish:* gauze net, landing net.

filocher [filɔʃe], *v.i.* **1.** (*a*) to make net, netting; (*b*) to net (butterflies, etc.). **2** *P:* **f. devant une corvée,** to shirk a fatigue. **3.** *F:* to speed; *P:* to belt along.

filo-guidage [filɔgida:ʒ], *s.m.* wire guidance; *pl. filo-guidages.*

filoguidé [filɔgide], *a. Elcs: Ball:* wire-guided (missile, etc.).

filon [filɔ̃], *s.m.* (*a*) *Min:* vein, seam, lode, lead (of metal, etc.); reef (of gold); *Geol: Min:* **f. guide,** leader (vein); **f. en selle,** saddle reef; **f. à géodes,** hollowlode; **f. à pendage fort, vertical,** gash vein, rake vein; (*b*) *P:* cushy job; **il tient le f., il a déniché, trouvé, le (bon) f.,** he has struck it rich, he has struck oil.

filon-couche [filɔ̃ku:ʃ], *s.m. Geol:* sill; bed-vein; *pl. filons-couches.*

filonien, -ienne [filɔnjɛ̃, -jɛn], *s. Geol:* **cuirasse filonienne,** slickenside(s); **roche filonienne,** veinstone.

filoselle [filɔzɛl], *s.f.* filoselle, floss-silk, ferret.

filou [filu], *s.m.* (*a*) pickpocket, thief; *F:* rogue, swindler; (*b*) cheat, sharper (at cards); (*c*) (*of child*) little rascal.

filoutage [filuta:ʒ], *s.m.* (*a*) pocket-picking, stealing; (*b*) *F:* swindling, cheating.

filouter [filute], *v.tr.* **1. f. qch. à qn,** to rob s.o. of sth. **2. f. qn,** to swindle, cheat, s.o.; **il m'a filouté de mille francs,** he robbed me of, swindled me out of, a thousand francs.

filouterie [filutri], *s.f.* **1.** stealing; swindling, cheating. **2.** swindle, fraud.

fils [fis], *s.m.* **1.** son; *B:* **le F. unique du Père,** the only begotten of the Father; **ses deux f.,** her two boys; *F:* **f. à papa,** (i) young man with an influential father; (ii) (young) playboy; **les f. de France,** the male (legitimate) children of the kings of France; *P:* **le f. de mon père,** my father's son (i.e., the speaker); **il n'est f. de bonne mère qui n'eût agi ainsi,** there is no decent man but would have acted thus; **c'est bien le f. de son père,** he's a chip of the old block; **être le f. de ses œuvres,** to be a self-made man; *B:* **f. de Bélial,** son of Belial; **M. Duval f.,** Mr Duval junior; **le f. Duval,** young Duval; *s.a.* PÈRE 1. **2.** *F:* boy, lad, fellow; **viens, mon f.,** come, my lad; **qu'est-ce que tu veux, f.?** what do you want, old chap, sonny? **c'est un bon f.,** he's a decent chap, a good fellow.

filterie [filt(ə)ri], *s.f. Tex:* thread-making factory.

filtrable [filtrabl], *a.* filterable, filtrable (virus).

filtrage [filtra:ʒ], *s.m.* (*a*) filtering, straining (of liquid); percolation; (*b*) *El: Elcs:* filtering, smoothing (of current, voltage); filtering, suppression (of sound); **chargement par f.,** trickle charging; **bobine, self, de f.,** filter choke, smoothing coil; **condensateur de f.,** filter capacitor, smoothing capacitor; (*c*) combing out (of suspects by police).

filtrant [filtrɑ̃], *a.* **1.** filterable, filtrable; **virus f.,** filterable virus, filter passer. **2. bout f.,** filter tip (of a cigarette); *Opt:* **verre f.,** filter lens; **cartouche filtrante, élément f. (de filtre à air),** filter cartridge; **dispositif f.,** filtration unit; *Civ.E:* **galerie filtrante,** filtration channel.

filtrat [filtra], *s.m. Ch: etc:* filtrate.

filtration [filtrasjɔ̃], *s.f.* filtration, percolation; seeping, seepage; *Ch: Ind:* **f. à la terre,** clay filtration; **f. à froid,** cold pressing (of oils).

filtre[1] [filtr], *s.m.* filter, strainer; percolator; **f. double,** twin filter; *a.* **bout f.,** filter tip (of cigarette); *Com:* (*of cigarette*) **avec ou sans f., monsieur?** tipped or plain, sir? *Cu:* **f. à café,** coffee filter; percolator; **(café) f.,** coffee made in an individual filter, drip coffee; **f. à charbon,** carbon filter; **f. à aspiration,** suction filter; **f. rotatif,** rotary, rotating, filter; **papier f.,** filter paper; **f. à sable, à vide,** sand, vacuum, filter; **f. à air,** air filter, strainer, scrubber; **f. pour les eaux d'égout,** sewage filter; *Sugar-R:* **f. à noir,** bone-black filter; *Av:* **f. métallique,** wire-gauze filter; *Opt: Phot:* **f. optique,** optical filter; **f. de couleur, f. coloré,** colour filter, colour screen, light filter; **f. bleuté,** white light filter; **f. de contraste,** contrast filter; **f. compensateur, f. correcteur,** compensating filter, correction filter; **f. neutre,** neutral filter; **f. de mise au point,** dummy filter; *El: Elcs:* **f. électrique, f. de courant, f. de tension,** electric filter, smoothing filter; **f. de fréquence,** frequency filter; **f. à, d', impédances,** choke filter; **f. correcteur,** correcting filter; **f. d'impulsions,** impulse corrector; **f. discriminateur,** discrimination filter; **f. duplexeur,** duplexer filter; **f. redresseur,** rectifier filter; **f. de bande,** band filter, wave filter; **f. éliminateur de bande,** band-stop filter, band-elimination filter; **f. passe-bande,** band-pass filter; **f. passe-bas,** low-pass filter; **f. passe-haut,** high-pass filter; **f. passe-(par)tout,** all-pass filter; **f. piézo-électrique,** crystal filter; *W.Tel: T.V:* **f. de tonalité,** tone filter; **f. anti-parasites,** interference filter, suppressor; **rendement, sélectivité, d'un f.,** filter discrimination, selectivity of filter.

filtre[2], *s.m.* philtre.

filtrée [filtre], *s.f.* trickle (of water, etc.); **f. de lumière,** gleam, streak, of light.

filtre-presse [filtrəprɛs], *s.m. Ind:* filter press; *pl. filtres-presses.*

filtrer [filtre]. **1.** *v.tr.* (*a*) to filter, strain, leach; **eau filtrée,** filtered water; **f. qch. dans le vide,** to filter sth. by suction; (*b*) *El: Elcs:* to filter, smooth; **courant filtré, non filtré,** smoothed, unsmoothed, current; *W.Tel:* **f. un poste émetteur,** to by-pass a station; (*c*) *F:* to screen (visitors). **2.** *v.i. & pr.* to filter, percolate, leach; **l'eau (se) filtre à travers le terrain,** the water filters, seeps, through the earth; **la lumière filtrait à travers, par, les branches,** the light filtered, glimmered, stole, through the branches; **laisser f. une nouvelle,** to let a piece of news leak out, to leak news; **des renseignements filtraient,** information was seeping out.

filtre-tambour [filtrətɑ̃bu:r], *s.m.* rotatory, rotating, filter; *pl. filtres-tambours.*

filtreur [filtrœ:r], *s.m.* filter man, filterer, strainer.

fimbrié [fɛ̃bri(j)e], *a. Bot: Z:* fimbriate, fringed.

fimbrille [fɛ̃bri:j], *s.f. Bot:* **à fimbrilles,** fimbrillate, fimbrillose.

fimbristylis [fɛ̃bristilis], *s.m.*, **fimbristyle** [fɛ̃bristil], *s.f. Bot:* fimbristylis.

fin[1] [fɛ̃], *s.f.* **1.** end, close, termination; **la f. du monde,** the end of the world; **f. d'une lettre,** end, conclusion, of a letter; **la f. du jour,** the close of day; **f. du mois,** end of the month; *Com:* **f. de mois,** monthly statement; **f. de semaine,** weekend; **en f. de soirée, semaine,** towards the end of the evening, the week; **il est venu vers la f. de l'après-midi,** he came late in the afternoon; **cadeaux de f. d'année,** Christmas and New Year gifts; **c'était à la f. de l'été,** it was late summer; **l'année touche, tire, à sa f.,** the year is drawing to an end, is nearly over; **en f. d'année il y a déficit,** at the end of the year there is a deficit; **cela se passait (en) f. 1968,** this happened at the end of 1968; *Com:* **payable f. courant, f. prochain,** payable at the end of the current month, of next month; **jusqu'à la f. des temps, des**

siècles, till the end of time, until doomsday; *adj.phr.* (*applied to art, etc. of the late 19th century*): **f. de siècle,** (i) (*at the time*) ultra modern; (ii) (*now*) decadent; fin de siècle; **le vocabulaire est à la f. du livre,** the vocabulary is at the back of the book; **vis, courroie, sans f.,** endless screw, belt; *Mec:* **f. de filetage,** thread runout; **des activités sans f.,** never-ending activities; **le troisième avant la f.,** the third from the end; **le cinquième en commençant par la f.,** the last but four; the fifth starting from the end; **faire une belle, bonne, f.,** to make a good end; to die fortified with the rites of the Church; **f. prématurée,** untimely death; **il est sur sa f.,** he hasn't much longer to live; **la maison est sur ses fins,** the firm is on its last legs; **mettre f. à qch.,** to put an end, a stop, to sth., to bring sth. to an end; **mettre une entreprise à f.,** to bring an undertaking to an end, to complete an undertaking; (*of pers.*) **faire une f.,** to settle down; **prendre f., avoir une f.,** to come to an end; **prendre f. brusquement,** to come to an abrupt end; **il y a longtemps que cela a pris f.,** that's over long ago, that's all over and done with; **mener une affaire à bonne f.,** to bring a matter to a successful issue, conclusion; **mener une tâche à bonne f.,** to deal successfully with a job; *Bank:* **sauf bonne f.,** under reserve; **attendons la f.,** we must wait and see (what) the end (will be); **toute cette générosité aura pour f. que vous n'aurez plus un sou à vous,** all this generosity will end in your having no money of your own, no money left; **c'est la f.,** (i) this is the end; (ii) this is the last of it, of him, etc.; **c'est le commencement de la f.,** this is the beginning of the end; **à la f. il répondit,** in the end, finally, he answered; *F:* **tu es stupide à la f.!** you really are the end, an idiot! **à la f., c'est trop!** that's really a bit much! **à la f. du compte, en f. de compte,** in the end; in the last resort; to cut a long story short; *F:* **à la f. des fins,** when all's said and done. **2.** end, aim, purpose, object; (*a*) *Prov:* **la f. justifie les moyens,** the end justifies the means; **qui veut la f. veut les moyens,** if you want the end you must not stick at the means; **en venir, arriver, à ses fins,** to achieve one's aim, object, purpose; to attain one's object; to get what one wants; **à cette f. il faut . . .,** in order to attain, achieve, this, one must . . .; **à quelle f.?** for what purpose? with what end in view? why? **à deux fins,** dual-purpose, serving a double purpose; *A:* **robinet à quatre fins,** four-way cock; **à toutes fins,** for all purposes; all-purpose; **à toutes fins utiles,** (i) for whatever purpose it may serve; (ii) to whom it may concern; **aux fins de faire qch.,** with a view to doing sth.; **à bonne f.,** for a laudable purpose; **à seule f. de,** for the sole purpose of; **aller à ses fins,** to pursue one's point; **former un comité aux fins d'enquête,** to set up, establish, a committee for the purpose of investigation, to set up an investigation committee; **il discutait avec lui à la seule f. de l'exaspérer,** he argued with him simply for the sake of annoying him; *Med:* **aux fins d'autopsie,** for a post-mortem examination; *Jur:* **aux fins de débauche,** for immoral purposes; (*b*) *Jur:* **renvoyer qn des fins de sa plainte,** to nonsuit s.o.; **renvoyé des fins de la plainte,** discharged, acquitted; **f. de non-recevoir,** demurrer, plea in bar, estoppel, refusal; **rendre une f. de non-recevoir,** to dismiss a case.

fin[2], **fine** [fɛ̃,fin]. **1** *a.* (*a*) *A:* extreme, farthermost; (*b*) **dans le f. fond du hangar,** right at the back of the shed; **au f. fond de la Sibérie,** in farthest Siberia; **la science en son f. fond est ontologique,** science is fundamentally ontological; *s.a.* MOT 1. **2.** *a.* (*a*) fine; first-class; **vins fins,** choice wines; **or f., argent f.,** pure, fine, gold, silver; **linge f.,** fine linen; *Fish:* **eau fine,** clear water; *s.a.* HERBE 1; (*b*) fine, subtle, shrewd, discriminating; **f. connaisseur de vins,** fine judge of wine; **fine ironie,** subtle irony; **avoir l'oreille fine,** to have a delicate, quick, fine, acute, ear; to be quick of hearing; **esprit f.,** fine, delicate, wit; **f. comme l'ambre,** sharp as a needle; *Iron: F:* **non, mais j'aurai l'air f.!** I really will look a fool, won't I? **il est trop f. pour vous,** he's one too many for you; you're no match for him; **bien f. qui le prendra,** it would take a smart man to catch him; **plus f. que lui n'est pas bête,** *he's* no fool; *F:* **c'est une fine mouche,** he's a sharp customer; she knows what she's after; *Fish:* **fine main,** experienced, skilful, cunning, fisherman; *s.a.* NEZ 1; (*c*) fine, small (rain, grains, etc.); fine (needle); **charbon f.,** small coal, fines, peas; **traits fins,** delicate features; **taille fine,** slender figure, waist; **attaches fines,** neat ankles, wrists; **écriture fine,** small handwriting; *Bill:* **prendre la bille trop fine,** to make too fine a stroke; *N.Arch:* **carène fine,** sharp bottom; **navire à formes fines,** sharp-built boat. **3.** *s.m.* (*a*) **savoir le fort et le f. d'une affaire,** to know the ins and outs of sth.; **le f. de l'affaire,** the crux of the matter; **jouer au (plus) f.,** to have a battle of wits; **f. contre f.,** diamond cut diamond; **le f. du f.,** the ultimate, the ne plus ultra; (*b*) **écrire en f.,** to write a small hand; (*c*) fineness (of gold, silver); *Ind:* **f. de minerai,** mineral pulp; (*d*) *Tex:* fine linen. **4.** *s.f.* (*a*) **une fine,** a liqueur brandy; **une fine à l'eau** = brandy and soda; (*b*) *pl.* **fines,** small coal, fines, peas. **5.** *adv.* (*a*) **tout était f. prêt,** everything was absolutely ready; (*b*) finely; **café moulu f.,** finely ground coffee; **des crayons taillés f.,** sharp-pointed pencils; *Bill:* **prendre la bille trop f.,** to make too fine a stroke.

finage[1] [finaːʒ], *s.m.* (re)fining (of metals).

finage[2], *s.m.* (*a*) *A:* administrative area (of parish or *commune*); (*b*) (*in Burgundy and Franche-Comté*) cultivated land (of a village).

final, -als [final], *a.* final. **1.** (*a*) last (letter, syllable, etc.); *Sp:* **les (épreuves) finales,** the finals; *Cin:* **titre f.,** end-frame; *Com:* **compte f.,** account for the financial year; (*b*) ultimate; **succès f. d'un livre,** ultimate success of a book; *Theol:* **impénitence finale,** final impenitency; **sa prodigalité et sa ruine finale,** his prodigality and his eventual ruin. **2.** (*a*) *Phil:* **cause finale,** final cause; *Phil:* **preuve par les causes finales,** argument from design, teleological argument; (*b*) *Gram:* **proposition finale,** final clause.

final(e)[1] [final], *s.m. Mus:* finale.

finale[2], *s.f.* **1.** end syllable (of word). **2.** *Mus:* (*a*) keynote, tonic; (*b*) (*in plain-song*) final. **3.** *Sp:* final; **f. de coupe,** cup final; **quart de f.,** quarter final; **être en huitième de f.,** to be in the last eight.

finalement [finalmɑ̃], *adv.* finally, at last, in the end; ultimately.

finalisme [finalism], *s.m. Phil:* finalism.

finaliste [finalist], *s.m. & f.* **1.** *Sp:* finalist. **2.** *Phil:* finalist.

finalité [finalite], *s.f. Phil:* finality; *Biol:* adaptation.

finance [finɑ̃ːs], *s.f.* **1.** *A:* ready money; **être court de f.,** to be short of cash; *still so used in* **faire qch. moyennant f.,** to do sth. for a consideration. **2.** finance; **homme de f.,** financier, capitalist, banker; **entrer dans la f.,** to become a banker, a financier; **monde de la f.,** financial world; **la haute f.,** (i) high finance; (ii) the financiers, the bankers. **3.** *pl.* finances, resources; **être mal dans ses finances,** to be hard up; **ministre des Finances,** minister of Finance, = Chancellor of the Exchequer; **le Ministère des Finances** = the Treasury, the Exchequer; *Pol:* **loi de finances,** appropriation bill. **4.** *Fr.Hist:* the financiers, the farmers (of taxes).

financement [finɑ̃smɑ̃], *s.m.* (*a*) financing; (*b*) *Sw.Fr:* fee.

financer [finɑ̃se], *v.* (**je finançai(s); n. finançons**) **1.** *v.i.* to pay out (ready) money. **2.** *v.tr.* to finance (undertaking, etc.); to put up the money for (sth.), to back (s.o.).

financier, -ière [finɑ̃sje, -jɛːr]. **1.** *a.* financial (system, etc.); **l'aristocratie financière,** the aristocracy of finance; **considérations financières,** financial considerations; **solide au point de vue f.,** financially sound; **embarras financiers,** financial, pecuniary, difficulties; **le marché f.,** (i) the money market; (ii) the stock market. **2.** *s.m.* (*a*) financier; (*b*) *Fr.Hist:* financier, farmer (of taxes). **3.** *s.f. Cu:* **financière,** financière.

financièrement [finɑ̃sjɛrmɑ̃], *adv.* financially.

finasser [finase], *v.i. F:* to finesse; to resort to subterfuge, trickery; **f. avec qn,** to play hanky-panky with s.o.

finasserie [finasri], *s.f.* **1.** trickery, artifice, cunning, foxiness. **2.** (*a*) piece of cunning; (*b*) *pl.* subterfuges; *F:* hanky-panky; **les finasseries du métier,** the tricks of the trade.

finasseur, -euse [finasœːr, -øːz], **finassier, -ière** [finasje, -jɛːr]. **1.** *a.* artful, wily, cunning, tricky. **2.** *s.* petty trickster, artful rogue; **c'est une finassière,** she knows how to get her own way.

finaud, -aude [fino, -oːd]. **1.** *a.* wily, cunning (peasant, etc.). **2.** *s.* crafty type; wangler; **petite finaude,** little wretch; **c'est un f.,** he's a sly character, he knows how to look after number one; **c'est une finaude,** she knows how to get her own way, to get what she wants.

finauderie [finodri], *s.f.* trickiness; trickery; cunning trick, dodge, wangle.

fincelle [fɛ̃sɛl], *s.f. Fish:* head line (of net).

fine [fin], *s.f.* **une f.,** a liqueur brandy.

finement [finmɑ̃], *adv.* **1.** finely, delicately, well (executed, designed, etc.). **2.** smartly, subtly; shrewdly; with finesse. **3.** slenderly; **taille f. découpée,** slender, slim, waist; slender figure.

finerie [finri], *s.f. Metall:* finery, refining furnace.

fines [fin], *s.f.pl.* small coal; fines, peas.

finesse [finɛs], *s.f.* **1.** fineness, good quality (of material, etc.); delicacy (of execution, of design); finish (of piece of work); **f. d'un vin,** lingering fragrance of a wine. **2.** (*a*) fineness, subtlety, shrewdness; **f. d'ouïe,** quickness, keenness, acuteness, of hearing; **f. de goût,** nicety of taste; **f. d'esprit,** (i) shrewdness of mind; (ii) smartness of wit; **f. psychologique,** insight into character; **discours plein de f.,** speech full of finesse; **parodie pleine de f.,** clever, subtle, parody; **finesses d'un métier,** fine points of a craft; (*b*) cunning, guile; **elle use de la f. de son sexe,** she takes full advantage of being a woman; **chercher f. (à qch.),** to look for snags; (*c*) piece of cunning; **il craignait quelque f. de ma part,** he feared some trick on my part. **3.** (*a*) fineness (of particles of dust, etc.); slenderness, slimness (of waist, etc.); (*b*) sharpness (of build of ship, of optical image, of wireless tuning); keenness (of cutting edge); (*c*) *Ph: Mec:* aerodynamic efficiency; (*d*) fineness (of wool).

finet, -ette [finɛ, -ɛt]. **1.** *a. A: F:* artful, wily, cute (person, etc.). **2.** *s.f.* **finette;** *Tex:* flannelette (with fluffy under-side).

fini [fini]. **I.** *a.* **1.** finished, ended, over; **des pots de crème finis aux trois quarts,** pots of cream three parts, quarters, empty; **l'orage est f.,** the storm is over; **c'est f.; tout est f.; c'est f., tout ça,** that's all over, all done with; *F:* **il est f., c'est un homme f.,** he's done for, down and out; **finies ces sottises!** enough of that nonsense! **mes copies sont finies de corriger,** I have finished correcting my batch of exercises; **c'est f. de rire,** we've done with laughter; **n i ni, (c'est) fini!** (i) that's an end to that! (ii) it's all over between us; *Turf:* **cheval f.,** overridden horse. **2.** *Pej:* accomplished, finished; **un idiot f.,** a complete idiot. **3.** finite, limited; *Mth:* **grandeur finie,** finite magnitude; **nombre f.,** finite number.

II. **fini,** *s.m.* **1.** finish (of work of art, manufactured article). **2.** *Phil:* finitude; **le f. et l'infini,** the finite and the infinite.

finial [finjal], *s.m.* (*pl. uncertain*) *Arch:* finial.

finir [finiːr]. **1.** *v.tr.* to finish, end; **f. une tâche,** to complete, finish, a task; **avez-vous fini votre travail?** have you finished, *F:* are you through with your work? **f. sa vie, sa carrière,** to end one's life, one's career; **laissez-le f. son somme,** let him have his sleep out; *Lit:* **finissez mes craintes,** put an end to my fears; **f. un tableau, une sculpture,** to finish off a picture, a sculpture; **ce sera fini demain,** it will be over, done (with), tomorrow; **il a fini son temps (de service militaire, d'apprentissage, etc.),** his time is up; **son temps est fini,** his term (of imprisonment, etc.) is up, over. **2.** *v.i.* to end, come to an end, finish; **voir f. qch.,** to see sth. out, through; **c'est fini entre nous,** it's all over between us; *F:* I am through with you; **c'est fini et bien fini,** it is over and done with; **il finira mal,** he will come to a bad end; **je ne sais comment cela finira,** I don't know how it will turn out; **tout est bien qui finit bien,** all's well that ends well; **en f. avec qn, qch.,** to be, have, done with s.o., sth.; **en f. avec une question,** to bring a matter to an issue, to settle a question once and for all, to set a question at rest; **c'en était fini de la guerre,** the war was at an end; **il faut en f.,** we must make an end (of it); **je voudrais en f.,** I want to get it over; **cela n'en finit pas,** there is no end to it; **il n'en finira donc pas!** will he never finish, stop! **pour en f.,** to cut the matter short; **histoires à n'en plus f.,** (i) never-ending, long-winded, interminable, endless, stories; (ii) innumerable stories, stories without end; **f. de faire qch.,** to finish, leave off, doing sth.; **finissez de pleurer,** stop crying; **quand j'aurai fini,** when I have finished; *F:* **finissez donc!** do be quiet! do leave off! stop it! chuck it! **il n'a jamais fini de poser des questions saugrenues,** he never stops asking silly questions; **sa blessure n'en finissait pas de guérir,** his wound wouldn't heal; **cette route n'en finit pas,** this road seems to go on for ever; **f. en pointe,** to end, terminate, in a point; **ce mot finit par une voyelle,** this word ends, terminates, in a vowel; **f. par faire qch.,** to end in, by, doing sth.; **il a fini par se décider,** he finally made up his mind, made up his mind in the end, at last; **quand nous finîmes par découvrir la vérité,** when eventually, ultimately, we found out the truth; **la justice finit par triompher,** justice triumphs

finally, in the end, in the long run; **je finirai bien par l'attraper,** I shall catch him yet! **ce projet finit par se réaliser,** the plan was carried out in the end; **cela finit toujours par se savoir,** it always gets to be known (in the end), it always comes out eventually.

finish [finiʃ], *s.m.* **1.** *Sp:* (*a*) finish; *Box: A:* **match au f.,** fight to the finish; (*b*) final burst; **il a un bon f.,** he has a fast finish. **2.** *adv. P:* no go!

finissage [finisaːʒ], *s.m. Ind:* finishing (off).

finissant [finisɑ̃], *a.* ending, finishing; **le jour f.,** dusk, twilight, gloaming; **société finissante,** decaying society.

finisseur, -euse [finisœːr, -øːz]. **1.** *a. Ind:* finishing (roll, mill, etc.). **2.** *s. Ind:* finisher; *Sp:* finisher; **c'est un bon f.,** he is a fast finisher. **3.** *s.f.* **finisseuse,** (*a*) *Civ.E:* finishing machine (for road surfacing); (*b*) *Tex:* finisher card.

finissure [finisyːr], *s.f. Bookb:* casing in.

finistérien, -ienne [finisterjɛ̃, -jɛn], *a. & s. Geog:* (native, inhabitant) of the department of Finistère.

finition [finisjɔ̃], *s.f.* **1.** *A:* end; **il faut en voir la f.,** we must see the back of it. **2.** finish; finishing; *Ind:* **atelier de f.,** finishing shop; *Hyd.E:* **grille de f.,** protective grill; *Mch: Tls:* **passe de f.,** finishing cut; **les finitions demandent autant de temps que la construction,** the finishing takes, the finishing touches take, as long as the construction.

finitude [finityd], *s.f. Phil:* finitude.

fin-keel [finkil], *s.m. Nau:* fin keel.

finlandais, -aise [fɛ̃lɑ̃dɛ, -ɛːz]. *Geog:* **1.** *a.* of Finland; Finnish. **2.** *s.* Finlander, Finn. **3.** *s.m. Ling:* Finnish.

Finlande [fɛ̃lɑ̃ːd], *Pr.n.f. Geog:* Finland.

finnemanite [fin(ə)manit], *s.f. Miner:* finnemanite.

finnois, -oise [finwa, -waːz]. **1.** *a.* Finnish. **2.** *s.* Finn; *s.m. Ling:* Finnish.

finno-ougrien, -enne [finougri(j)ɛ̃, -ɛn], *a. Ling:* Finno-ugric, -ugrian.

finot, -otte [fino, -ɔt]. **1.** *a. & s. O:* = FINAUD. **2.** *s.m.* fine semolina.

finsenthérapie [fɛ̃sɛ̃terapi], *s.f. Med:* Finsen (light) treatment.

finte [fɛ̃t], *s.f. Ich: F:* shad.

fiole [fjɔl], *s.f.* **1.** (*a*) phial, flask; small bottle; *B:* cruse; *Ch: Ph:* **f. jaugée,** volumetric flask; **f. à vide,** filter flask; (*b*) *P:* head, mug; **se payer la f. de qn,** to make a fool of s.o. **2. f. d'arpentage,** (surveyor's) spirit level.

fion [fjɔ̃], *s.m. F:* **1.** finish (of an article); **donner le coup de f. à qch.,** to give the finishing touch(es) to sth. **2.** *O:* knack; **avoir le f. pour faire qch.,** to have the knack of doing sth.

Fionie [fjɔni], *Pr.n. Geog:* Fyn, Fünen.

fionien, -ienne [fjɔnjɛ̃, -jɛn], *a. & s. Geog:* (native, inhabitant) of Fünen.

fionner [fjɔne], *v.i. P:* to strut, show off.

fiord [fjɔːr], *s.m. Geog:* fjord.

fiorite [fjɔrit], *s.f. Miner:* fiorite.

fioriture [fjɔrityːr], *s.f.* (*a*) *Mus:* fioritura, ornament; (*b*) flourish (to handwriting, etc.); **fioritures de style,** ornaments, embellishments, of style; **sans fioritures,** without fancy work.

fioriturer [fjɔrityre], *v.tr.* (*a*) *Mus:* to add fioriture to, to flourish, to ornament; (*b*) to put flourishes to (handwriting); *F:* to ornament, embellish (one's style, etc.).

firmament [firmamɑ̃], *s.m.* firmament, sky, vault of heaven.

firme [firm], *s.f.* **1.** (business) firm. **2.** *Jur:* style of firm; *Publ:* imprint; **sous la f. de . . .,** under the style of . . .

Firmin [firmɛ̃]. **1.** *Pr.n.m.* Firmin. **2.** *s.m. F:* valet.

firmisternes [firmistɛrn], *s.m.pl. Amph:* Firmisternia.

firmware [fœrmwɛːr], *s.m. Elcs:* firmware.

fisc [fisk], *s.m.* (*a*) the Treasury, the Exchequer; (*b*) the Inland Revenue; **les agents du f., le f.,** the collectors of taxes, of customs and excise; the revenue officials or authorities; *F:* **les gens du f.,** income-tax people.

fiscal,[1] -aux [fiskal, -o], *a.* fiscal; **droits fiscaux,** State dues; taxes; customs and excise dues; **dans un but f.,** for purposes of revenue; **ressources fiscales de l'État,** financial resources of the State; **l'administration fiscale,** the taxation authorities; **charges fiscales, prélèvement f.,** taxation; **timbre f.,** (Inland) Revenue stamp; **fraude fiscale,** tax evasion; *Aut:* **puissance fiscale,** Treasury rating (of car).

fiscal[2], -aux, *s.m. Orn: F:* fiscal (shrike).

fiscalement [fiskalmɑ̃], *adv.* fiscally.

fiscalin [fiskalɛ̃], *s.m. Hist:* (*a*) (i) fief; (ii) feoffee, of the king; (*b*) tax collector.

fiscaliser [fiskalize], *v.tr.* to tax.

fiscalité [fiskalite], *s.f.* **1.** financial system (of a country); **f. excessive,** excessive taxation. **2.** fiscality; financial red tape.

fischérite [fiʃerit], *s.f. Miner:* fischerite.

fissa [fisa], *adv. P:* quick, sharp.

fissi- [fissi], *pref.* fissi-; **fissilingue,** fissilingual; **fissipare,** fissiparous.

fissible [fisibl̩], *a. Ph:* fissionable, fissile.

fissidactyle [fissidaktil], *a. Z:* fissidactyl.

fissile [fisil], *a.* (*a*) fissile; cleavable, tending to split; **roche f.,** fissile rock; (*b*) *Atom.Ph:* fissionable, fissile.

fissilingue [fisilɛ̃g], *a. Rept:* fissilingual.

fissilité [fisilite], *s.f.* cleavability; fissility.

fission [fisjɔ̃], *s.f. Atom.Ph:* fission; **f. atomique, f. de l'atome,** atomic fission, nuclear fission; fission, splitting, of the atom; **f. du noyau (atomique),** fission, splitting, of the (atomic) nucleus; **f. nucléaire,** nuclear fission; **f. de l'uranium,** uranium fission, splitting; **f. en chaîne,** chain fission; **f. provoquée, f. induite,** induced fission; **f. spontanée,** spontaneous fission; **f. rapide, f. par neutrons rapides,** fast (-neutron) fission; **f. par neutrons lents, f. par neutrons thermiques, f. thermique,** slow-neutron fission, thermal fission; **f. par capture,** fission capture; **produit de f.,** fission product.

fissionner [fisjɔne], *v.tr. Atom.Ph:* to split (the atom).

fissipare [fisipaːr]. **1.** *a. Biol:* fissiparous. **2.** *s.m.pl.* Fissipara.

fissiparité [fisiparite], *s.f.* **1.** *Biol:* fissiparism, fissiparous reproduction, schizogenesis, fission. **2.** *Astr:* fissiparity (of nebulae, etc.).

fissipède [fisipɛd], *Z:* (*a*) *a.* fissiped; fissipedal, fissipedate; (*b*) *s.m.pl.* **fissipèdes,** Fissipeda; the fissipeds.

fissirostre [fisirɔstr̩], *Orn:* (*a*) *a.* fissirostral; (*b*) *s.m.pl.* **fissirostres,** Fissirostres.

fissuraire [fisyrɛːr], *a. Med:* fissural.

fissuration [fisyrasjɔ̃], *s.f.* cracking, fissuring; *Geol: Med:* fissuration; *Civ.E:* **f. en étoile,** starring.

fissure [fisyːr], *s.f.* (*a*) fissure, cleft, crack (in rock, etc.); **terrain crevassé de nombreuses fissures,** ground showing numerous cracks; (*b*) *Anat: Med:* fissure; **f. de l'anus,** anal fissure; **f. de Sylvius,** fissure of Sylvius, lateral fissure; *P:* **avoir une f.,** to be a bit cracked.

fissurelle [fisyrɛl], *s.f. Moll:* fissurella.

fissurellidés [fisyrɛlide], *s.m.pl. Moll:* Fissurellidae.

fissurer [fisyre], *v.tr.* to fissure, split, crack.

se fissurer, to fissure, crack.

fiston [fistɔ̃], *s.m. F:* son, youngster; **allons (mon) f.!** now then, young fellow, my lad! **viens ici, (mon) f.,** come here, sonny.

fistot [fisto], *s.m. F:* first-year naval cadet.

fistulaire [fistylɛːr], (*a*) *a. Anat: Geol:* fistular, fistulous, tube-like; (*b*) *s.f. Ich:* fistularia.

fistule [fistyl], *s.f.* **1.** *Med:* fistula; sinus; (*b*) *Vet:* **f. du garrot,** fistulous withers. **2.** dent (in woodwork).

fistuleux, -euse [fistylø, -øːz], *a.* (*a*) *Med:* fistulous; **trajet f.,** sinus tract; (*b*) *Bot:* fistulose.

fistuline [fistylin], *s.f. Fung:* fistulina, beefsteak fungus.

fistulisation [fistylizasjɔ̃], *s.f. Med:* fistulization.

fit [fit], *s.m. Cards:* (*bridge*) fit.

fitis [fitis], *s.m. Orn:* willow-warbler.

five-o'clock [faivɔklɔk; *F:* fiv-], *s.m. A:* afternoon tea.

five-o'clocker [faivɔklɔke; fiv-], *v.i. A: Hum:* to have tea; **on five-o'clockera à quatre heures,** tea at four.

fixable [fiksabl̩], *a.* fixable.

fixage [fiksaːʒ], *s.m.* fixing; (*a*) fastening (of rail, etc.); (*b*) fixing (of drawing, etc.); *Phot:* **bain de f.,** fixing bath; **bain de f. aluné,** hardening-fixing bath.

fixateur, -trice [fiksatœːr, -tris]. **1.** *a.* fixing, fixative. **2.** *s.m.* (*a*) fixer, fastener (for eyelets, etc.); (*b*) *Ind: Tex:* fixer (of dyes, etc.); *Phot:* fixing solution, fixing bath; **f. aluné,** hardening-fixing bath; (*c*) *Biol:* fixative; (*d*) *Hairdr:* dressing.

fixatif [fiksatif], *s.m.* (*a*) fixative (for drawings, etc.); (*b*) *Hairdr:* dressing.

fixation [fiksasjɔ̃], *s.f.* **1.** fixing (of date, indemnity, shelf, etc.); setting (of date); **f. des impôts,** assessment of taxes; **f. des indemnités,** determination of compensation; **f. des prix,** price fixing; **f. du lieu d'un rendez-vous,** deciding on, fixing on, a meeting-place. **2.** *Ch: Ind:* fixation (of nitrogen, etc.). **3.** (*a*) *Mec.E:* attachment, anchor (ing), fixing; mounting (of engine); **f. à baïonnette,** bayonet attachment; **f. par bride, par collier,** clamping; **accessoires, organes, pièces, de f.,** attaching, attachment, parts; **dispositif, point, de f.,** attachment; *Aut: Av:* **dispositif de f. pour ceinture de sécurité,** attachment for safety belt; **boulon de f.,** clamp bolt, hold(ing)-down bolt, holding bolt; **attache de f.,** hold-down clip; **collerette, flasque, de f.,** attaching, attachment, flange; **collier de f.,** bracket clip; support clip (of pipe, etc.); **douille de f.,** attachment bushing; **griffe de f.,** clamp; **manchon de f.,** adapter; **patte de f.,** anchor(ing) clip; attaching, fixing, lug; **plaque de f.,** clamping plate; **trou de f.,** anchor hole; **vis de f.,** fixing screw, set-screw; (*b*) (ski) binding, fittings, harness; **fixations de sécurité,** release bindings; **f. à tendeur,** cable harness; (*c*) *Med:* anchorage (of floating kidney); fixation (of splint); (*d*) *For:* **f. des dunes,** fixation of drifting sands; (*e*) *Psy:* fixation.

fixe [fiks], *a.* **1.** fixed, firm; **étoile f.,** fixed star; **support f.,** fixed base; **idée f.,** fixed idea; **yeux fixes,** set eyes; **regard f.,** intent gaze; **grue f.,** stationary, fixed, crane; **poulie f.,** fast pulley; **essieu f.,** dead axle; *Nau:* **soutes fixes,** permanent bunkers; *Ch:* **corps f.,** fixed body; *Mil:* **f.!** eyes front! **moteur f.,** stationary engine; *El.E:* **enroulement (de champ) f.,** stationary winding. **2.** fixed, regular, settled; **prix f.,** set price; **à prix f.,** at fixed prices; **traitement f.,** *s.m.* **f.,** fixed salary; **résidence f.,** permanent abode; **capital f.,** permanent capital; **agent f.,** local agent; **prendre ses repas à heure f.,** to eat at fixed, set, hours; **beau (temps) f.,** set fair (weather); **il m'écrivait à jour f.,** he had a regular day for writing to me; *P.N:* **arrêt f.,** all buses stop here. **3.** *s.m. Nau:* lower topsail.

fixé [fikse], *a.* fixed. **1. se réunir à des époques fixées,** to meet at fixed, stated, times; **somme fixée,** given, named, sum. **2.** (*a*) **un Français f. aux États-Unis,** a Frenchman resident in, who has settled in, the United States; (*b*) **être f. sur qch.,** to entertain no further doubts about sth.; **maintenant je suis f.,** now I know what I wanted to know; now I know what to think; that settles it; **ne pas être f.,** to have no fixed plans; **le regard f. sur le mur,** his gaze riveted on the wall; (*c*) *F:* **elle est fixée,** she has secured a husband; (*d*) *Psy:* suffering from a fixation. **3.** *Tchn:* attached, fixed, anchored; **f. à demeure,** built-in; integral (**sur,** with).

fixe-assiettes [fiksasjɛt], *s.m.inv.* hanger (for plaque, etc.).

fixe-au-toit [fiksotwa], *s.m.inv. Aut:* elastic or spring clamp for roof rack.

fixe-bouchon [fiksbuʃɔ̃], *s.m.* cork-wire, wiring (of wine bottle); *pl. fixe-bouchons.*

fixe-chaussettes [fiks(ə)ʃosɛt], *s.m.inv.* sock suspender(s); *U.S:* garter(s).

fixe-cravate [fiks(ə)kravat], *s.m.* tieclip; tie pin; *pl. fixe-cravates.*

fixe-majuscules [fiks(ə)maʒyskyl], *s.m.inv. Typwr:* shift-lock (key).

fixement [fiksəmɑ̃], *adv.* fixedly; **regarder f. qch.,** to stare at sth.; to look hard, intently, at sth.

fixe-moustaches [fiks(ə)mustaʃ], *s.m.inv.* moustache-trainer.

fixe-pompe [fiks(ə)pɔ̃ːp], *s.m. Cy:* pump clip; *pl. fixe-pompes.*

fixer [fikse], *v.tr.* **1.** (*a*) to fix; to make (sth.) firm, rigid, fast; **f. un tableau au mur,** to hang, fix, a painting on the wall; **f. un volet,** to fasten a shutter; **les vis qui fixent la serrure,** the screws that hold the lock; **f. qch. dans sa mémoire,** to fix sth. in one's memory; **f. une bougie sur une bouteille,** to stick a candle into a bottle; **f. une lunette sur une étoile,** to bring a telescope to bear on a star; **f. l'attention de qn,** to engage, hold, arrest, s.o.'s attention; **f. tous les regards,** to attract everybody's attention; **f. ses affections sur qn,** to fix, set, one's affections on s.o.; **f. les yeux sur qch.,** to fix one's eyes on sth.; to gaze, stare, at sth.; to look hard, intently, at sth.; *Golf:* **f. la balle,** to keep one's eye on the ball; **f. qn,** to look steadily at s.o.; to hold s.o. with one's eye; to stare at s.o.; *Mil:* **f. l'ennemi,** to fix, hold, the enemy; (*b*) *Ch: Phot:* to fix. **2.** (*a*) to fix, determine; to set (time); **f. la valeur de qch.,** to fix the value of sth.; **f. des règles, un règlement,** to determine rules, regulations; **le jour reste à f.,** the day remains to be settled, fixed, decided upon; **f. un jour,** to appoint, name, a day; **f. l'heure et le lieu,** to appoint the time and the place; **f. une séance à trois heures,** to fix a meeting for three o'clock; **f. des conditions,** to lay down conditions; **il suffira de quelques exemples pour f. les idées à cet égard,** a few instances will help us to clarify our views on the subject; **fixez tel prix que vous voudrez,**

name any price you like; *St.Exch:* **f. un cours,** to make a price; *Jur:* **f. les dommages et intérêts,** to assess the damages; (*b*) **f. qn sur ses intentions,** to give s.o. definite information as to one's intentions; (*c*) *F:* **elle a fixé sa fille,** she has settled, married off, got a husband for, her daughter.

se fixer. **1.** (*a*) **se f. dans un pays,** to settle in a country; **elle n'avait point envie de se f.,** she had no desire to settle down; (*b*) **se f. à une opinion, à une résolution,** to become wedded to an opinion, to a resolve; (*c*) **elle s'est fixée sur cette robe,** she finally chose that dress; (*d*) *F:* to get married.

fixe-tapis [fiks(ə)tapi], *s.m.inv.* carpet tack.

fixisme [fiksism], *s.m.* **1.** *Biol:* creationism. **2.** *Ap:* rearing in a frameless hive.

fixiste [fiksist], *s.m. & f.* **1.** *Biol:* creationist. **2.** *Ap:* beekeeper who uses frameless hives.

fixité [fiksite], *s.f.* fixity; **donner plus de f. à une poutre,** to make a beam steadier; **f. du regard de qn,** steadiness of s.o.'s gaze.

fjeld [fjɛld], *s.m. Geog: Geol:* fjeld.

fjord [fjɔːr], *s.m. Geog:* fjord.

fla [fla], *s.m.* flam (on drum).

flabellé [flabɛl(l)e], *a. Biol:* flabellate.

flabelliforme [flabɛl(l)ifɔrm], *a.* flabelliform.

flabellum [flabɛl(l)ɔm], *s.m. Ecc: Coel:* flabellum.

flac [flak], *s.m. & int.* slap; bang (of blow); crack (of whip); plop (into water); **faire f.,** to plop.

flaccidité [flaksidite], *s.f.* flaccidity, flabbiness, limpness; looseness (of the skin).

flache[1] [flaʃ], *s.f.* **1.** (*a*) *Carp:* wane, flaw, (of plank); (*b*) crack (in stone); (*c*) *For:* blaze (on tree to be felled). **2.** (*a*) (pot-)hole, hollow, depression (in pavement, road); (*b*) **f. (d'eau),** pool, puddle (in roadway, etc.); (*c*) *Rail:* depression (in track); dip (in rails due to slight displacement).

flache[2], *a. Carp:* waney.

flacher [flaʃe], *v.tr. For:* to blaze (tree).

flacherie [flaʃri], *s.f. Ser:* flacherie, flachery; flaccidity (of silkworms).

flacheux, -euse [flaʃø, -øːz], *a.* waney (plank); dull-edged (timber).

flacon [flakɔ̃], *s.m.* bottle, (stoppered) flagon; flask, case-bottle; **f. d'odeur,** smelling-bottle; **f. à parfum,** scent bottle; **f. à liqueur,** liqueur decanter; **qu'importe le f., pourvu qu'on ait l'ivresse,** don't judge anything by appearances, don't judge a book by its cover; *Ch:* **f. à tare,** weighing-bottle; **f. laveur,** washing bottle; **f. doseur,** dropping bottle.

flaconnage [flakɔnaːʒ], *s.m.* bottle manufacture; bottles (collectively), set of bottles.

flaconnerie [flakɔnri], *s.f.* bottle manufacture; *Com:* bottles.

flaconnet [flakɔnɛ], *s.m.* (very) small bottle.

flaconnier [flakɔnje], *s.m.* **1.** (ornamental) bottle-maker. **2.** (scent or toilet) bottle-holder, bottle-case.

flacourtia [flakurtja], *s.m. Bot:* flacourtia.

flacourtiacées [flakurtjase], *s.f.pl. Bot:* Flacourtiacae.

fla-fla [flafla], *s.m. F:* (drumming, *hence*) ostentation, show; *Cost:* ornaments, trimmings; *Paint: etc:* flashy effect, showy style; **faire du f.-f.,** to make a show, a display; to advertise (oneself, one's works).

flagada [flagada], *a.inv. F:* washed out, done up; **pantalon f.,** baggy, crumpled, trousers.

flagellaire [flaʒɛl(l)ɛːr]. **1.** *a. Biol:* flagellate, flagellar, flagelliform, whip-like. **2.** *s.f. Bot:* flagellaria.

flagellant [flaʒɛl(l)ɑ̃], *s.m. Rel.H:* Flagellant.

flagellates [flaʒɛl(l)at], *s.m.pl. Prot:* Flagellata.

flagellateur, -trice [flaʒɛl(l)atœːr, -tris], *s.* scourger, flogger, flagellator.

flagellation [flaʒɛl(l)asjɔ̃], *s.f.* flagellation, scourging, whipping, flogging.

flagelle [flaʒɛl], *s.m. Biol:* flagellum.

flagellé [flaʒɛl(l)e], *a. & s.m. Biol:* flagellate.

flageller [flaʒɛl(l)e], *v.tr.* to scourge, flog, whip, lash.

flagellifère [flaʒɛl(l)ifɛːr], *a. Bot:* flagelliferous.

flagelliforme [flaʒɛl(l)ifɔrm], *a. Biol:* flagelliform, whip-shaped, whip-like.

flagellum [flaʒɛl(l)ɔm], *s.m.* (*a*) *Myth:* flail (of Osiris); (*b*) *Biol:* flagellum.

flageolement [flaʒɔlmɑ̃], *s.m.* shaking, trembling.

flageoler [flaʒɔle], *v.i.* (*of horse's, man's, legs*) to shake, tremble, give way; **les jambes lui flageolent,** he is trembling at the knees.

flageolet[1] [flaʒɔlɛ], *s.m.* (*a*) *Mus:* flageolet; **sons de f.,** flageolet tones, harmonics; (*b*) *F:* **flageolets,** matchstick legs.

flageolet[2], *s.m. Cu:* flageolet, (small) kidney bean.

flagorner [flagɔrne], *v.tr.* to flatter; to fawn upon (s.o.); to toady to (s.o.); to lick (s.o.'s) boots.

flagornerie [flagɔrnəri], *s.f.* flattery, boot-licking.

flagorneur, -euse [flagɔrnœːr, -øːz], *s.* boot-licker, flatterer, toady.

flagrance [flagrɑ̃ːs], *s.f.* (*rare*) *Jur:* flagrancy.

flagrant [flagrɑ̃], *a.* flagrant, glaring (injustice, etc.); **en contradiction flagrante,** in open, glaring, contradiction; **pris en f. délit,** caught in the act, red-handed, in flagrante delicto; *F:* **c'est f.!** it's obvious!

flair [flɛːr], *s.m.* (*a*) (*of dogs*) scent, (sense of) smell; nose; **chien qui a du f.,** dog with a good nose; (*b*) *F:* (*of pers.*) flair; **avoir du f.,** to have a gift for nosing, finding, things out; to be shrewd, far-sighted; **avoir du f. pour qch.,** to have a flair, a nose, for sth.

flairer [flɛre], *v.tr.* **1.** (*a*) (*of dog*) to scent, smell (out), nose out (game, etc.); *F:* **f. le danger,** to scent, smell, suspect, danger; (*b*) to smell, sniff (at) sth. **2.** *P:* (= FLEURER) **f. le musc,** to smell of, like, musk.

flaireur, -euse [flɛrœːr, -øːz], *s.* smeller, scenter; *F:* **f. de cuisine,** sponger, *U.S:* free-loader.

flaiteau-aux [fleto], *s.m. Ich: F:* flounder.

flajolotite [flaʒɔlɔtit], *s.f. Miner:* flajolotite.

flamand, -ande [flamɑ̃, -ɑ̃ːd]. **1.** *a.* Flemish; **d'expression flamande,** Flemish-speaking. **2.** *s.* Fleming. **3.** *s.m. Ling:* Flemish.

flamant [flamɑ̃], *s.m. Orn:* **f. (rose),** flamingo.

flambage [flɑ̃baːʒ], *s.m.* **1.** (*a*) singeing (of hair, cloth, etc.); (*b*) charring (of end of stake, etc.); (*c*) *Metall:* skin-drying (of moulds); (*d*) *Nau:* breaming; (*e*) *Agr:* burning off (of field, etc.). **2.** buckling, lateral flexion, yielding, collapse (of metal plate, etc.); buckle; **charge au f.,** buckling, crippling, load; **résistance au f.,** buckling strength; **f. plastique, secondaire,** plastic, minor, buckling.

flambant [flɑ̃bɑ̃]. **1.** *a.* blazing, flaming (log, sun); *Her:* flamant, flaming; *F:* **il était tout f. dans son uniforme neuf,** he was a brilliant, gorgeous, figure in his new uniform; **habit (tout) f. neuf, robe (toute) f. neuve,** brand-new coat, frock. **2.** *s.f. A: P:* **une flambante,** a match, a light. **3.** *Min:* **houille flambante,** *s.m.* **flambant,** bituminous, soft, coal; **f. gras,** caking, cannel, coal; **f. sec,** non-caking coal.

flambard, -arde [flɑ̃baːr, -ard]. **1.** *a. P:* flashily dressed (person); gaudily furnished (room); *s.* **faire le f.,** to swank. **2.** *s.m.* (*a*) blazing (piece of) coal; (*b*) *Nau:* (*on the Channel coast*) two-masted fishing smack; (*c*) bad oarsman; (*d*) *Cu:* lard; (*e*) *Arms:* kris.

flambart [flɑ̃baːr], *s.m.* **1.** swaggerer. **2.** blazing (piece of) coal. **3.** *Nau:* two-masted fishing smack. **4.** *F:* St. Elmo's fire. **5.** *Arms:* kris.

flambe [flɑ̃ːb], *s.m.* **1.** *Bot: F:* **f. d'eau,** water-flag. **2.** *Dial:* blazing fire. **3.** *Arms:* kris. **4.** *A.Mil:* pennant.

flambé [flɑ̃be]. **1.** *a.* (*a*) *Cu:* flambé, flambéed; (*b*) buckled (metal). **2.** *s.m. Ent:* scarce swallow-tail.

flambeau, -eaux [flɑ̃bo], *s.m.* **1.** (*a*) torch; *A:* link; **à la lueur des flambeaux, aux flambeaux,** by torchlight; *Poet:* **le f. du jour,** the sun; **le f. de l'hymen,** the marriage torch; *Lit:* **le f. (de l'amour),** the flames of love; *Gr.Ant:* **la course des flambeaux,** the torch-race; **retraite aux flambeaux,** torchlight tattoo; (*b*) candle; **f. de cire,** wax candle. **2.** candlestick; sconce; candelabra; **f. électrique,** electric table-standard.

flambée [flɑ̃be], *s.f.* blaze (of shavings, etc.); blazing fire; **une belle f.,** a fine blaze; *F:* **son enthousiasme n'a été qu'une f.,** his enthusiasm was only a flash in the pan; **une f. d'optimisme,** a surge of optimism; **ne faire qu'une f.,** to be over, gone, in a flash.

flambement [flɑ̃bmɑ̃], *s.m.* **1.** buckling, lateral, flexion, yielding, collapse (of metal plate, etc.); **flambements secondaires,** minor buckling; **résistance au f.,** resistance to lateral pressure. **2.** flaming, blazing; *El:* **f. de l'arc,** flaming of the arc.

flamber [flɑ̃be]. **1.** *v.i.* (*a*) to flame, blaze; to be ablaze; (*of fire*) **se mettre à f.,** to burst into flame, into a blaze; to go up in flames; **faire f. le feu,** to make the fire burn up, to stir the fire into a blaze; *F:* **faire f. la maison,** to set the house ablaze; **f. comme une allumette,** to burn like matchwood; (*b*) (*of metal bar, etc.*) to buckle, yield; **faire f. une tige,** to buckle a rod; (*c*) *F:* (i) to gamble; (ii) to play cards. **2.** *v.tr.* to singe (hair, fowl, cloth, etc.); to char (end of stake, etc.); *Metall:* to skin-dry (mould); *Nau:* to bream (ship); *Surg:* **f. une aiguille,** to sterilize a needle (in flame); *Cu:* **f. une volaille,** to singe a bird; *A: Artil:* **f. un canon,** to fire an unshotted charge; *F:* **c'est de l'argent flambé,** it is so much money lost, squandered, gone to blazes; **il est flambé,** he is done for; it's all up with him; his number is up, his goose is cooked.

flamberge [flɑ̃bɛrʒ], *s.f.* **1.** (*a*) *A.Arms:* flamberg, flamberge; (*b*) *A:* sword, blade; **mettre f. au vent,** to draw (one's sword); *F:* to enter the fray. **2.** artificial candle.

flambeur [flɑ̃bœːr]. **1.** (*a*) small flame-thrower (used for the destruction of locusts in the South of France and North Africa); (*b*) *a.m. Tex:* **tuyau f.,** burner (for singeing cloth). **2.** *s.m. F:* (i) gambler; (ii) card player.

flamboiement [flɑ̃bwamɑ̃], *s.m.* flaming; blazing, blaze; flaring (up) (of fire, etc.); *El:* **f. de l'arc,** flaming of the arc.

flamboyant [flɑ̃bwajɑ̃], *a.* **1.** flaming, blazing (fire); flaring (light); blazing (eyes); *Her:* flamant, flaming. **2.** (*a*) *Arch:* flamboyant; (*b*) *F:* flamboyant (speech); gaudy, dazzling (get-up); **cravate d'un rouge f.,** flaming red tie; *Journ:* **des titres flamboyants,** banner headlines. **3.** *s.m. Bot:* coral tree; flamboyant(e).

flamboyer [flɑ̃bwaje], *v.i.* (**il flamboie**) (*of fire*) to blaze; **se mettre à f.,** to flame up, flare up, blaze up; *F:* **ses yeux flamboyaient de colère,** his eyes blazed, glowed, flashed, with anger; **un sabre qui flamboie,** a flashing sword.

flambure [flɑ̃byːr], *s.f. Dy:* uneven colouring.

flamenco [flamɛ̃ko], *s.f. Span.Danc:* flamenco.

flamiche [flamiʃ], *s.f. Cu:* leek pie.

flamine [flamin], *s.m. Rom.Ant:* flamen.

flamingant, -ante [flamɛ̃gɑ̃, -ɑ̃ːt]. **1.** *a.* Flemish-speaking (town, person). **2.** *s.* Flemish nationalist.

flamingantisme [flamɛ̃gɑ̃tism], *s.m. Pol:* policy of the Flemish-speaking party in Belgium; pro-Flemish agitation.

flaminique [flaminik], *s.f. Rom.Ant:* wife of flamen, flaminica.

flamique [flamik], *s.f. Cu:* leek pie.

flammage [flamaːʒ], *s.m. Tex:* uneven colour (of cloth).

flamme[1] [flɑːm, -a-], *s.f.* **1.** (*a*) flame; *El:* candle lamp; **maison toute en flammes,** house all in flames, house on fire, in a blaze, ablaze; **par le fer et la f.,** with fire and sword; **mettre le pays en flammes,** to set the country ablaze, *Lit:* aflame; **ses yeux lançaient des flammes de colère,** his eyes blazed with anger; **jeter feu et f.,** to fly into a rage; **être tout feu tout f.,** to take up (sth.) enthusiastically; *Mch:* **chaudière à f. directe, à retour de f.,** direct-, return-flame boiler; **courant de flamme,** flue; **retour de f.,** back-flash (from gun); *I.C.E:* **retour de f. (au carburateur),** spitting back, popping back (in the carburettor), backfire, backfiring; **donner des retours de f.,** to backfire; **avoir des retours de f.** (*in gas stove*), to light, flash, back; **pointe de f.,** flash-point (of petrol); *Theol:* **les flammes éternelles,** the eternal fire; *Tex: etc:* **passer le drap, etc., à la f.,** to singe the cloth, etc.; **passage à la f.,** singeing; (*b*) *Poet:* passion, love; **avouer sa f.,** to declare one's passion. **2.** *Mil: Nau: etc:* pennant, pendant, pennon, streamer; **f. de lance,** lance pennon; *Nau:* **f. couplée,** waft; *Navy:* **f. de guerre,** action pendant; **f. de fin de campagne,** paying-off pendant. **3. f. (d'oblitération postale),** slogan (accompanying postmark).

flamme[2], *s.m. Vet:* fleam.

flammé [flame], *a. & s.m. Cer:* flambé.

flammèche [flamɛʃ], *s.f.* spark, flake (of fire).

flammerole [flamrɔl], *s.f.* **1.** will-o'-the-wisp. **2.** small pennant, pennon.

flammette [flamɛt], *s.f.* **1.** small flame. **2.** small pennant, small pennon. **3.** *Bot:* (*a*) lesser spear-wort; (*b*) clematis.

flan [flɑ̃], *s.m.* **1.** *Cu:* (i) baked custard; (ii) custard tart; *P:* **du f.,** nothing doing! I'm not having any! *P:* **rester, être, comme deux ronds de f.,** to be flabbergasted. **2.** *Num: etc:* blank, planchet, flan; *Mec.E:* **f. usiné,** finished blank; **f. de fraise,** milling-cutter blank. **3.** *Typ:* mould (from standing type); (newspaper) flong. **4.** *P:* **à la f.** (*perhaps corruption of* FRANQUETTE, *q.v.*), (i) *adj.phr.* happy-go-lucky; (ii) *adv.phr.* in a happy-go-lucky fashion; **travail fait à la f.,** botched work, work done anyhow; **c'est un type tout à la f.,** he's a plain easy-going chap; **j'ai dit ça au f.,** I said that at a venture, for the sake of talking, of saying something.

flanc [flɑ̃], *s.m.* flank, side (of person, animal, ship, army, etc.); *Artil:* edge, side (of groove in rifling); *Her:* flank; *Leath:* belly (of hide); *Geol:*

flank, leg, side (of fold); *Aut:* wall (of tyre); **pneu à flanc(s) blanc(s),** white wall tyre; **f. de coteau,** hillside; **route à f. de coteau,** road following the hillside; **se coucher sur le f.,** (i) to lie down on one's side; (ii) (*of ship*) to heel over; *F:* **être sur le f.,** (i) to be laid up (in bed); (ii) to be quite done up; **mettre un cheval, qn, sur le f.,** to knock up a horse, s.o.; **l'enfant qu'elle a porté dans ses flancs,** the child she carried in her womb; **se battre les flancs,** (i) (*of tiger, etc.*) to lash its tail; (ii) *F:* to waste energy and achieve nothing, to make desperate efforts, to cudgel one's brains; (*of horse, etc.*) **battre du f.,** to heave, pant; *Mil:* **par le f. droit!** by the right! **prendre une armée en f.,** to take an army in the flank; **attaquer de f.,** to attack on the flank; **battre de f.,** to enfilade; **le navire se présentait de f.,** the ship was broadside on (to us); *Fenc. & F:* **prêter le f. à un adversaire,** to give an adversary an opening; **prêter le f. à la critique,** to lay oneself open to criticism; *N.Arch:* **blindage de f., cuirasse des flancs,** side-armour; *Mil: P:* **tirer au f.,** to malinger, to swing the lead, to shirk, to dodge the column; **tireur au f.,** skrimshanker, shirker, lead-swinger, malingerer.

flanc-garde [flɑ̃gard], *s.f. Mil:* flanker; flanking detachment, flank-guard; *pl. flancs-gardes.*

flanchage [flɑ̃ʃaːʒ], *s.m. F:* flinching, wavering, shrinking; ratting.

flanchard, -arde [flɑ̃ʃaːr, -ard], *a. & s.P:* (person) who gives in, knuckles under; shirker; funk; quitter.

flanche[1] [flɑ̃ːʃ], *s.f. P:* **1.** (showman's) patter; speech; newspaper article. **2.** thing, job, business; **une sale f.,** a rotten job.

flanche[2], *s.m. Leath:* finishing.

flanché [flɑ̃ʃe], *a. Her:* flanched.

flancher[1] [flɑ̃ʃe], *v.i. F:* **1.** (*a*) to flinch; to waver; to give in, to knuckle under; (*b*) to rat; to quit. **2.** (*a*) (*of car, etc.*) to break down; (*b*) **j'ai flanché en histoire,** I came a cropper, I came down, I was ploughed, in history; (*c*) *Rac:* (*of horse*) to compound.

flancher[2], *v.tr. Leath:* to finish.

flanchet [flɑ̃ʃɛ], *s.m. Cu:* flank (of beef).

flanchis [flɑ̃ʃi], *s.m. Her:* saltire couped.

flanconade [flɑ̃kɔnad], *s.f. Fenc:* flancon(n)ade, twist and thrust.

Flandre[1] [flɑ̃ːdr], *Pr.n.f.* **1.** *Geog:* **la Flandre,** *A:* **les Flandres,** Flanders. **2.** *Husb:* **(lapin) géant des Flandres,** Flemish giant.

flandre[2], *s.f. Min:* lengthwise timber (under the roof).

flandrien [flɑ̃drjɛ̃], *a. & s.m. Geol:* Flandrian.

flandrin [flɑ̃drɛ̃], *s.m.* **1.** *A:* Fleming. **2.** *F:* **un grand f.,** a tall, lanky, fellow; a great lout of a fellow; **quel grand f.!** what a lamp-post he is!

flâne [flɑːn], *s.f. F:* loafing, strolling; stroll, saunter, loaf.

flanelle [flanɛl], *s.f.* **1.** *Tex:* flannel; **f. (de) coton,** flannelette; **porter un costume de, en, f.,** to wear a flannel suit; *F:* to wear flannels; **porter un gilet de f.,** *F:* **une f.,** to wear a flannel (under)-vest; *Cost: Sp:* **pantalon de f. blanc, blanche,** whites, flannels; **pantalon de f. gris(e),** grey flannels; *F:* **s'envelopper de f.,** to wrap oneself in cotton wool. **2.** *P:* bad customer (who spends very little, *esp.* in disorderly house); **faire f.,** (i) to look in without meaning business; (ii) to loaf.

flanellette [flanɛlɛt], *s.f. Tex:* flannelette.

flâner [flɑne], *v.i.* to stroll, to loaf about; *F:* to mooch about; to dawdle, to saunter; *F:* to hang about (in public places); **f. dans les rues pendant une heure,** to idle about the streets for an hour; **perdre son temps à f.,** to idle away one's time.

flânerie [flɑnri], *s.f.* **1.** dawdling; *F:* mooching; sauntering, lounging about; loaf, mooch. **2. dans mes flâneries le long du boulevard,** in my strolls along the boulevard. **3.** *Ind:* **f. systématique,** go-slow.

flâneur, -euse [flɑnœːr, -øːz], *s.* **1.** (*a*) idler, dawdler, saunterer; (*b*) loafer, drifter. **2.** *s.f.* **flâneuse,** lounge chair.

flanier, -ière [flanje, -jɛːr], *a. Mill:* **meule flanière,** slightly concave runner.

flânier, -ière [flɑnje, -jɛːr], *s.* (*rare*) idler, stroller.

flânocher [flɑnɔʃe], *v.i. F:* to hang or loiter about; to loaf.

flânocheur, -euse [flɑnɔʃœːr, -øːz], *s. F:* idler, stroller, loiterer, dawdler; loafer.

flanquant [flɑ̃kɑ̃], *a.* flanking (battery, fire, etc.).

flanqué [flɑ̃ke], *a. Her:* flanched.

flanquement [flɑ̃kmɑ̃], *s.m.* **1.** flanking (of fortress, regiment, etc.). **2.** *Fort:* flanker.

flanquer[1] [flɑ̃ke], *v.tr.* to flank. **1. arcade flanquée de deux pavillons,** arcade flanked by two pavilions; **chaises qui flanquent le fauteuil du président,** chairs on either side of the presidential chair; **avancer flanqué de deux agents,** to step forward between two policemen; **se f. de qn,** to have someone at one's side. **2.** *Mil:* (*a*) **f. une colonne, etc.,** to protect the flanks of, to flank, a column, etc.; (*b*) **f. l'ennemi,** to take the enemy in flank; (*c*) *Fort:* **deux ouvrages qui se flanquent,** two works flanking, protecting, each other.

flanquer[2], *v.tr. F:* to throw, pitch, chuck; **f. la soupe sur la table,** to plonk, slam, the soup down on the table; **f. une gifle, un coup de pied, à qn,** to fetch s.o. a blow, to land s.o. a kick; **f. son chapeau sur l'oreille,** to cram one's hat over one's ear; **f. qn à la porte,** (i) to turn s.o. out of doors; to bundle s.o. out of the house; (ii) to throw, *F:* boot, s.o. out; (iii) to fire, sack, s.o.; *P:* **f. la trouille à qn,** to give s.o. the jitters; *F:* **se f. par terre,** to fall; to come a cropper; *P:* **se f. un gnon,** to bang into sth., to bruise oneself.

flanqueur [flɑ̃kœːr], *s.m. Mil: A:* flanker.

flanquis [flɑ̃ki], *s.m. Her:* saltire couped.

flapi [flapi], *a. F:* (*of pers.*) fagged out, jaded, washed out; the worse for wear; seedy.

flaque [flak], *s.f.* puddle, pool, plash; **terrain plein de flaques,** plashy, sloppy, ground.

flaquée [flake], *s.f.* splash (of water); glassful (of water, etc.) thrown (at s.o.).

flaquer [flake], *v.* **1.** *v.tr.* to fling, splash (liquid on ground, at s.o., at sth.). **2.** *v.i. Soapm:* (*of soap*) to subside (in the boiler). **3.** *v.tr. Fish:* **f. la morue,** to split, to open, a cod.

flare up [flɛrœp], *s.m. Nau:* flare-up (light).

flash, *pl.* **flashes** [flaʃ], *s.m.* **1.** *Phot:* flash-light; *a. inv.* **des lampes flash,** flash-lights. **2.** *Cin:* short scene. **3.** *Journ:* (news)flash. **4.** *Petroleum Ind:* flash. **5.** *El:* flashover.

flash-back [flaʃbak], *s.m. Cin: etc:* flashback.

flask [flask], *s.m.* flask.

flasque[1] [flask], *a.* flaccid (flesh); flabby (hand, style); limp (cloth, style); floppy (hat); **se sentir f.,** to feel limp.

flasque[2], *s.f.* **1.** *A:* powder-horn. **2.** *Com:* flask (of mercury, etc.).

flasque[3], *s.m.* **1.** cheek (of gun carriage); cheek web (of crank); shear, side, cheek (of lathe); *pl.* boards (of bellows); side plates (of roller-chain link); *Nau:* cheeks (of mast); **f. palier,** end bearing-plate. **2.** support (of dynamo, etc.). **3.** *pl. Nau:* whelps (of capstan); *Av: etc:* flange. **4.** *Aut:* wheel-disc; **f. de frein,** brake flange. **5.** *Nau:* **f. d'ancre,** anchor-fluke chock, bolster, buffalo.

flasquement [flask(ə)mɑ̃], *adv.* flabbily, limply.

flat [fla], *a.m. Ser:* flaccid; (silkworm) attacked by *flacherie.*

flatoir [flatwaːr], *s.m.* **1.** forging hammer (for coin blanks). **2.** engraver's hammer.

flâtrer (se) [səflɑtre], *v.pr. Ven:* (*of hare, wolf, etc.*) to squat; **flâtré,** squatting.

flâtrure [flɑtryːr], *s.f. Ven:* squat (of hare).

flatté [flate], *a.* **portrait f.,** flattering portrait.

flatter [flate], *v.tr.* **1.** to stroke, caress; **se f. le menton de la main,** to stroke one's chin; **f. un cheval,** to make much of, to pat, to gentle, a horse; *Mus:* **f. la corde,** to caress the string, to play with expression. **2.** to delight, please, charm, gratify; **spectacle qui flatte les yeux,** sight that is pleasant to the eye; **vers qui flatte l'oreille,** verse that falls pleasingly on the ear; **f. les caprices de qn,** to humour, gratify, indulge, s.o.'s fancies; **la fortune nous flatte,** fortune favours us; **au fond il était très flatté,** in his heart of hearts he was very much gratified; **f. bassement un goût,** to pander to a taste. **3.** to delude; **f. un malade sur son état,** to deceive an invalid as to his condition; **f. qn de l'espoir de qch.,** to hold out the hope of sth. to s.o.; to flatter s.o. with the hope of sth. **4.** to flatter; **f. qn d'un beau discours,** to flatter, compliment, s.o. in a fine speech; **f. qn sur son bel esprit,** to flatter s.o. on his wit; **être flatté de qch.,** to feel flattered by sth.; **je suis flatté (de ce) qu'il m'ait invité,** I'm flattered that he asked me; **peintre qui flatte ses modèles,** painter who flatters his sitters; **f. le portrait de qn,** to draw a flattering portrait of s.o. **5.** (*a*) **f. un cours d'eau,** gradually to divert a stream; **f. les vagues,** to break the force of the waves (by a slope); (*b*) **il faut f. la sauce pour la faire sortir,** you've got to coax the sauce out.

se flatter, to flatter oneself, to delude oneself; to imagine; **elle se flattait de réussir,** she flattered herself, felt sure, that she would succeed; **elle se flattait de le revoir,** she fondly hoped to see him again; **il se flatte qu'on a besoin de lui,** he flatters himself that he is indispensable; **celui qui se flatte décourage les flatteurs,** to blow your own trumpet discourages others from flattering you; **se f. de son habileté,** to congratulate oneself on one's cleverness; **se f. de générosité, d'avoir fait qch.,** to take credit to oneself, *F:* to pat oneself on the back, for generosity, for doing sth.; **Londres se flatte d'être la plus grande ville du monde,** London prides itself on being the largest city in the world.

flatterie [flatri], *s.f.* (*a*) flattery, blandishment; (*b*) *pl.* **flatteries,** undiscriminating praise, flattering remarks.

flatteur, -euse [flatœːr, -øːz]. **1.** *a.* (*a*) pleasing, pleasant (taste, verse, etc.); -fond (hope); (*b*) flattering (remark, etc.). **2.** *s.* flatterer; sycophant.

flatteusement [flatøzmɑ̃], *adv.* flatteringly.

flatueux, -euse [flatɥø, -øːz], *a. O:* flatulent, producing flatulence; *F:* windy (food, etc.); **colique flatueuse,** flatulent colic.

flatulence [flatylɑ̃ːs], *s.f. Med:* flatulence; *F:* wind.

flatulent [flatylɑ̃], *a. Med:* flatulent.

flatuosité [flatɥozite], *s.f. Med:* flatus; *F:* wind.

flavanone [flavanɔn], *s.f. Ch:* flavanone.

flavanthrène [flavɑ̃trɛn], *s.m. Ch:* flavanthrone, flavanthrene.

flave [flaːv], *a.* pale yellow; pale blond.

flavescence [flavɛs(s)ɑ̃s], *s.f. Vit: etc:* flavescence.

flavescent [flavɛs(s)ɑ̃], *a.* flavescent, yellowish.

Flavien [flavjɛ̃], *Pr.n.m.* Flavian.

flavine [flavin], *s.f. Ch:* flavin.

flavone [flavɔn], *s.f. Ch:* flavone.

flavonol [flavɔnɔl], *s.m. Ch:* flavonol.

flavopurpurine [flavopyrpyrin], *s.f. Ch:* flavopurpurin.

fléau, -aux [fleo], *s.m.* **1.** *Agr:* flail; *A: Arm:* **f. d'armes,** flail, morning star. **2.** scourge; plague, pest, curse, bane; **Attila, le f. de Dieu,** Attila, the scourge of God; **la guerre est un terrible f.,** war is a dreadful curse, a dreadful calamity; **ici les lapins sont un f.,** here the rabbits are a curse, a pest; *F:* **c'est un vrai f.!** he's a regular menace; *B:* **l'Éternel frappa Pharaon de grands fléaux,** the Lord plagued Pharaoh with great plagues. **3.** (*a*) beam, arm (of balance); (*b*) bar (of door); (*c*) *Hyd.E:* lever with counterweight (for lock gates); (*d*) (coolie's) pole.

fléchage [fleʃaːʒ], *s.m.* arrowing (direction).

flèche[1] [flɛʃ], *s.f.* **1.** (*a*) arrow; *Lit:* shaft; **fer de f.,** arrow-head; *F:* **les flèches de la satire,** the shafts of satire; **faire f. de tout bois,** to use every means to attain an end, to leave no stone unturned; **je ne sais plus de quel bois faire f.,** I don't know which way to turn; *Prov:* **tout bois n'est pas bon à faire f.,** you cannot make a silk purse out of a sow's ear; (*b*) **f. (de direction, indicatrice),** direction sign, arrow(head); *Aut:* **f. de direction,** trafficator; (*c*) *Ch: Ph: etc:* pointer (of balance); (*d*) *Bot:* **f. d'eau,** arrow-head; (*e*) *Miner:* **flèches d'amour,** Cupid's darts, Venus's hair stone, rutilated quartz; (*f*) *Av:* **angle de f.,** sweepback angle; **ailes en f.,** swept-back wings; **f. de l'aile,** wing sweep-back; **avion à f. variable,** (variable) sweep wing aircraft; (*g*) **des prix qui montent en f.,** rocketing prices; **montée en f. des prix et des salaires,** wage-price spiral; *F:* **partir en f., partir, filer comme une f.,** to shoot off; **arriver, entrer, en f.,** to blow in. **2.** (*a*) spire (of church, etc.); leading shoot (of tree); (*b*) jib, boom (of crane); balance-bar (of lock-gate); swipe-beam (of drawbridge); sweep (of horse-gear); *Civ.E:* **f. de levage,** gin pole; (*c*) *Nau:* (i) **f. d'un mât,** pole of a mast; **mât de f.,** topmast, pole-mast, mast-head; **mât de f. d'artimon,** mizzen topmast; (ii) topsail (of cutter); **f. en cul,** gaff topsail; (*d*) beam (of plough); pole (of carriage); trail (of gun); (*e*) **cheval de f.,** head horse; **chevaux en f.,** horses driven tandem; *Nau:* **remorquer en f.,** to tow astern; *F:* **être en f.,** (i) to be in an awkward position; (ii) to be prominent, supreme; (*f*) *Geog:* **f. littorale,** spit; **f. isthme,** tombolo. **3.** (*a*) *Geom:* sagitta, versed sine; *Arch: Eng: etc:* rise (of arch); rise of camber (of road); *Ball:* maximum ordinate, culminating point, highest point of trajectory (of projectile); *Av:* camber (of airfoil profile); *N.Arch:* camber (of deck, etc.); **f. relative,** camber ratio; *N.Arch:* **f. de barrot,** beam camber; (*b*) sag, dip (of cable, etc.); set, deflection, amount of flexion (of girder, spring); compression (of spring); bowing (of crankshaft); **faire f.,** to sag, dip.

flèche[2], *s.f.* flitch (of bacon).

fléché [fleʃe], *a. Fr.C:* **ceinture fléchée,** sash with arrow design.

flécher [fleʃe], *v.tr.* **1.** *Breed:* (*of ram*) to tup (ewe). **2.** to arrow (road, direction).

fléchette [fleʃɛt], *s.f. Games:* dart; *A.Mil:* aerial dart.

fléchier [fleʃje], s.m. arrow-maker.

fléchière [fleʃjɛːr], s.f. Arch: arrowheaded leaf; Bot: arrow-head.

fléchir [fleʃiːr]. 1. v.tr. (a) to bend; f. le genou (devant qn), to bend, bow, the knee (to s.o.); (b) Anat: to flex (the arm, etc.); (c) to move (s.o.) to pity, to mercy; les larmes ne le fléchiront pas, tears will not move him (to pity); se laisser f. aux prières de qn, to be swayed, touched, by s.o.'s entreaties; to relent at s.o.'s entreaties. 2. v.i. (a) to give way, bend; ses jambes, les troupes, fléchissaient, his legs, the troops, were giving way; câble qui fléchit dans son milieu, cable that sags in the middle; (b) (of sound, current, etc.) to weaken; son attention fléchit, his attention flags; les prix fléchissent, prices are sagging, going down, becoming easier; son talent fléchit, his talent is falling off; le nombre des passagers a un peu fléchi, the number of passengers shows a slight falling off. 3. v.tr. or i. to inflect.

fléchissant [fleʃisɑ̃], a.m. Mec: moment f., bending moment.

fléchissement [fleʃismɑ̃], s.m. 1. bending (of the knee, etc.). 2. (a) yielding, bending (of girder, etc.); sagging (of cable, etc.); deflection; (b) f. de son, d'intensité de lumière, de courant, weakening of sound, of intensity of light, of current; f. de dépôts en banque, d'un talent, falling off of bank deposits, of a talent; Av: f. de l'aile, wing droop; Med: f. de l'organisme, fall in resistance of the organism; (c) Com: falling, sagging, easing (of prices).

fléchisseur [fleʃisœːr], a. & s.m. Anat: (muscle) f., flexor.

fléchois, -oise [fleʃwa, -waːz], a. & s. Geog: (native, inhabitant) of La Flèche.

flector [flɛktɔːr], s.m. flexible joint.

flegmatique [flɛgmatik], a. phlegmatic. 1. lymphatic (person, temperament, etc.). 2. calm, imperturbable, stolid.

flegmatiquement [flɛgmatikmɑ̃], adv. phlegmatically, imperturbably, stolidly.

flegme [flɛgm], s.m. 1. (a) A.Med: phlegm; (b) Med: phlegm. 2. coolness, stolidness, imperturbability, impassivity, phlegm; avoir un grand f., être d'un grand f., to be very cool, very self-possessed. 3. Ch: Brew: phlegma.

flegmon [flɛgmɔ̃], s.m. Med: phlegmon.

flegmoneux, -euse [flɛgmɔnø, -øːz], a. Med: phlegmonic, phlegmonous.

flein [flɛ̃], s.m. chip-basket; punnet.

flémard, flemmard, -arde [flemaːr, -ard]. P: 1. a. idle, indolent, lazy. 2. s. idler, slacker.

flémarder, flemmarder [flemarde], v.i. P: to laze, idle, slack.

flème, flemme [flɛm], s.f. P: laziness, slackness; slacking; il a la f., he has a lazy fit, does not feel up to work; battre, tirer, sa f., to idle away one's time, to slack about; j'ai la f. de le faire, d'y aller, I can't be bothered with it, to do it, to go (there); ça me donne la f., I can't be bothered to do it.

flémer, flemmer [fleme], v.i. (je flème, n. flémons; je flèmerai) P: = FLÉMARDER.

flénu [fleny], a. & s.m. Min: bituminous (coal).

fléole [fleɔl], s.f. Bot: phleum; F: cat's-tail grass; f. des prés, timothy grass, meadow cat's-tail grass.

Flessingue [flesɛ̃ːg], Pr.n. Geog: Flushing.

flet [flɛ], s.m. Ich: flounder.

flétan [fletɑ̃], s.m. Ich: halibut.

flétrir[1] [fletriːr], v.tr. to fade, wilt; to make (colours, etc.) fade; to wither up (flowers, etc.); f. les espérances de qn, to blight s.o.'s hopes; linge flétri, soiled linen; les chagrins lui ont flétri le cœur, grief has withered his heart.

se flétrir, (of colours, etc.) to fade; (of flowers, etc.) to fade, wither, wilt; les mains flétries de la malade, the patient's wasted hands; seins flétris, shrunken breasts.

flétrir[2], v.tr. 1. to brand (convict, etc.); to stigmatize (crime, etc.). 2. to sully, stain; f. le nom, la réputation, de qn, to sully s.o.'s good name, to cast a slur on s.o.'s character.

flétrissant[1] [fletrisɑ̃], a. fading, withering, wilting.

flétrissant[2], a. dishonouring, sullying; affaire flétrissante, degrading affair.

flétrissement [fletrismɑ̃], s.m. fading; withering (of plants).

flétrissure[1] [fletrisyːr], s.f. fading; withering (of flowers).

flétrissure[2], s.f. 1. (a) brand (on a criminal); (b) branding. 2. (moral, etc.) blemish, blot, stigma.

flette [flɛt], s.f. (a) A: shallop; (b) punt or barge.

flettner [flɛtnɛːr], s.m. Av: trimming tab; régler les flettners, to trim the tabs.

fleur [flœːr], s.f. 1. flower; (a) blossom, bloom; Hort: bouton à f., flower bud; arbre en fleur(s), tree in blossom, in flower; cultiver des fleurs, to grow flowers; fleurs des champs, wild flowers; l'aubépine est en f., the may is out; ni fleurs, ni couronnes, no flowers by request; tissu à fleurs, flowered material; fleurs de rhétorique, flowers of rhetoric; Med: tisane des quatre fleurs, infusion of mallow, mountain cat's foot, colt's foot and red poppy; Bot: f. d'amour, columbine; love lies bleeding; larkspur; f. d'Arménie, sweet william; f. aux dames, f. de Pâques, pasque flower; f. de la Saint-Jean, yellow bedstraw; f. du soleil, dyer's weed, yellow weed, weld; f. de soleil, star jelly; f. des veuves, purple, sweet, scabious; Her: f. de lis, fleur de lis, lys; F: f. de macadam, street walker; se couvrir de fleurs, to cover oneself in glory; couvrir qn de fleurs, jeter des fleurs à qn, to praise s.o. highly, profusely; faire une f. à qn, to do s.o. an unexpected favour; s'amener comme une f., to drop in unexpectedly; être f. bleue, to be romantic; (b) être dans, à, la f. de l'âge, to be in the prime of life; dans la première f. de la jeunesse, in the flower, bloom, of youth; être dans la f. de la santé, to be blooming with health; la fine f. de la race, the flower of the race; la f. de l'armée, the flower, pick, of the army; F: la f. des pois, the pick of the bunch; (c) bloom (on peaches, grapes); (d) fleurs (du soufre sur le caoutchouc, etc.), bloom; f. d'antimoine, de soufre, flowers of antimony, of sulphur; f. de cobalt, de zinc, cobalt, zinc, bloom; f. du tan, flowers of tan; f. d'émeri, flour emery; fleurs de vin, flowers of wine; f. de farine, pure wheaten flour; Arch: f. de chapiteau, rosette (of Corinthian capital); (e) P: f. (de virginité), virginity, U.S: cherry. 2. (= SURFACE) (a) prep.phr. à f. de, on the surface of, on a level with; à f. d'eau, at water level; Nau: between wind and water; (of submarine) awash; (of ship) with deck awash, on the point of sinking; rocher à f. d'eau, rock that is awash; voler à f. d'eau, to skim the water; Ten: balle à f. de corde, ball that just grazes, skims, the net; blocs de pierre éparpillés à f. de sol, rocks lying loosely upon the soil; émotions, beauté, à f. de peau, skin-deep emotions, beauty; avoir les nerfs à f. de peau, to be on edge; j'ai les nerfs à f. de peau, I'm on edge, my nerves are on edge; yeux à f. de tête, prominent eyes; F: goggle eyes; enfoncer un clou à f. de bois, to drive in a nail flush with the wood; P: être à f., to be broke, skint; (b) Tan: hair side, grain side (of skin); grain split (of hide). 3. pl. Nau: rung heads; bordages des fleurs, bilge planks. 4. pl. Med: F: fleurs blanches, leucorrhoea; F: whites.

fleurage [flœraːʒ], s.m. 1. (a) Mill: fine bran; (b) flouring (of bread before baking); (c) (potato) meal. 2. floral pattern (on cloth, carpet).

fleuraison [flœrɛzɔ̃], s.f. flowering; time of flowering.

fleurant [flœrɑ̃], a. (of flowers) scented, perfumed, fragrant; smelling (of sth.).

fleurdelisé [flœrdəlize], a. Her: fleury; lilied; étendard f., lilied, lily, banner.

fleurdeliser [flœrdəlize], v.tr. 1. to decorate, ornament (sth.) with fleurs-de-lis. 2. A: to brand (a criminal) with a fleur-de-lis.

fleuré [flœre], a. Her: fleury.

fleurée [flœre], s.f. Dy: f. (du bleu indigo) flurry.

fleurer [flœre]. 1. v.i. to smell, to be fragrant; rose qui ne fleure pas, rose that has no scent; f. la violette to smell of violets; Cu: (plat) qui fleure le thym, (dish) with a smell of thyme; f. le pédantisme, to smack of pedantry. 2. v.tr. Bak: to flour (oven-peel, etc.).

fleuret [flœrɛ], s.m. 1. (a) (fencing) foil; discussion à fleurets mouchetés, discussion, argument, with kid gloves on; (b) Min: plain chisel; drill(-bit), cutting-bit, borer, jumper; Petroleum Ind: f. d'amorçage, shot borer. 2. Tex: (a) f. de coton, de laine, first-quality cotton, wool; (b) floss silk, ferret.

fleureter [flœrte], v.i. (je fleurette, n. fleuretons; je fleuretterai) A: to talk sweet nothings; to flirt (avec qn, with s.o.).

fleurette [flœrɛt], s.f. (a) A: floweret, small flower; (b) conter f. à qn, to say sweet nothings to s.o., to flirt with s.o.

fleurettiste [flœretist], s.m. & f. Fenc: foil-play expert.

fleuri [flœri], a. 1. (a) in bloom; in flower, in blossom; (b) decorated with flowers; Her: (of plant) flowered (gules, etc.); avoir la boutonnière fleurie, (i) to have a flower in one's buttonhole; (ii) F: to wear a decoration. 2. flowery (path, etc.); flowery, florid (style); la saison fleurie, spring; Pâques fleuries, Palm Sunday; Arch: gothique f., flamboyant gothic; Mus: contrepoint f., florid counterpoint; teint f., florid complexion; A: barbe fleurie, white flowing beard.

fleuriau, -iaux [flœrjo], s.m. N.Arch: (framing) ribband.

fleurir [flœriːr]. 1. v.i. (a) (of plants) to flower, bloom, blossom, blow; to burst into bloom; (of pers.) to come out in spots, pimples; le soleil fait f. les roses, the sun brings out the roses; F: menton qui commence à f., chin that is getting downy; (b) (pr.p. florissant; p.d. il florissait) to flourish, prosper; art qui florissait au dix-huitième siècle, art that flourished in the eighteenth century. 2. v.tr. to decorate (table) with flowers; to deck (s.o.) out with flowers; f. une tombe, to lay flowers on a grave; des églantiers fleurissent la muraille, the wall is covered with wild roses in bloom; f. sa boutonnière, to put a flower in one's buttonhole; qui vous a fleuri ainsi? (i) who gave you all these flowers? (ii) who gave you that buttonhole? f. son langage, to use flowery, florid, language.

fleurissant [flœrisɑ̃], a. in bloom; in flower, in blossom.

fleuriste [flœrist], s.m. & f. florist. 1. flower grower. 2. dealer in flowers; flower seller. 3. artificial-flower maker. 4. flower painter. 5. a. jardin, jardinier, f., flower garden, flower grower.

fleuromètre [flœrɔmɛtr], s.m. Civ.E: fluorometer.

fleuron [flœrɔ̃], s.m. 1. Bot: small flower; floret (of compositae, etc.). 2. flower-shaped ornament; rosette; fleuron; Arch: finial; Her: fleuron; Bookb: Typ: (small) floral ornament; fleuron; F: c'est encore un f. à sa couronne, that's another feather in his cap; Louis XIV vit se détacher les plus beaux fleurons de sa couronne, Louis XIV saw the loss of the brightest jewels of his crown.

fleuronné [flœrɔne], a. 1. Bot: floreted. 2. Arch: etc: ornamented with flower-work, with fleurons; flowered. 3. Her: f. et contre-f., flory counter-flory.

fleuronner [flœrɔne]. 1. v.i. (a) (of plants) to produce florets; (b) to blossom. 2. v.tr. to ornament (sth.) with flower-work.

fleuve [flœːv], s.m. (large) river; f. côtier, short coastal river; lit d'un f., river bed; F: un f. de sang, a river of blood; un f. de larmes, a flood of tears; le f. de la vie, the course, current, of life; Geog: le f. Jaune, the Yellow River; Jur: fleuves internationaux, international waterways; B: les fleuves de Babylone, the waters of Babylon; attrib. roman f., roman-fleuve, saga (novel); s'il se met à raconter sa vie c'est un roman f., he'll tell you the story of his life in seventeen volumes.

Flewelling [flevəliŋ], Pr.n. W.Tel: montage F., Flewelling circuit.

flexibilité [flɛksibilite], s.f. flexibility; pliability (of disposition); suppleness (of body).

flexible [flɛksibl̩]. 1. a. (a) flexible, bendable, pliable; (of golf club) whippy; tuyau f., hose pipe; (b) caractère f., pliable, pliant, accommodating disposition, nature; esprit f., adaptable mind, intelligence. 2. s.m. El: flexible lead, flex; Mec.E: Bowden wire; Ind: hose pipe; E: flexible coupling.

flexicaule [flɛksikoːl], a. Bot: having a flexuous stalk.

flexion [flɛksjɔ̃], s.f. 1. (a) flexion, deflexion, bending, sagging; moment, effort, essai, de f., bending moment, stress test; (b) Mec: buckling, collapse (of rod, etc.). 2. Ling: inflexion (of word); les flexions du verbe, the inflexions of the verb; langue à flexions, inflected language; f. casuelle, case-ending.

flexionnel, -elle [flɛksjɔnɛl], a. Ling: flexional (termination, language, etc.).

flexueux, -euse [flɛksɥø, -øːz], a. flexuous, winding; Bot: flexuose.

flexuosité [flɛksɥozite], s.f. flexuosity.

flexure [flɛksyːr], s.f. Geol: flexure, fold; Oc: f. continentale, continental slope.

flibot [flibo], s.m. Nau: A: flyboat.

flibuste [flibyst], s.f. (a) buccaneering, freebooting, piracy; (b) Coll. pirates; Hist: (organized) pirates, buccaneers in the West Indies.

flibuster [flibyste]. 1. v.i. to freeboot, buccaneer; occ. to be a crook. 2. v.tr. P: to pinch, steal (sth.).

flibusterie [flibystri], s.f. 1. piracy, buccaneering. 2. P: pinching, stealing.

flibustier [flibystje], *s.m.* **1.** (*a*) pirate, freebooter, buccaneer, filibuster; (*b*) privateer; (*c*) gunrunner. **2.** (*a*) cheat, crook, swindler; (*b*) highwayman, brigand.
flic [flik], *s.m. P:* policeman, cop, bobby; **f. de la route,** speed-cop.
flicaille [flikɑːj], *s.f. P:* cops, the fuzz, *U.S:* bulls.
flic flac [flikflak], *s.m.* **1.** crack (of whip); slap, smack. **2.** heel-and-toe dance, clog dance.
flicflaquer [flikflake], *v.i.* to crack like a whip.
flinders [flɛ̃dɛːr], *s.m. Nau:* flinders bar(s).
flindersia [flindɛrsja], *s.m. Bot:* flindersia.
flingot [flɛ̃go], **flingue** [flɛ̃ːg], *s.m. P:* (*a*) humane killer; (*b*) *Mil:* rifle; (*c*) firearm, gun.
flinguer [flɛ̃ge], *v.tr. P:* to shoot (s.o.), to bump (s.o.) off.
flinkite [flɛ̃kit], *s.f. Miner:* flinkite.
flint(-glass) [flint(glɑːs)], *s.m. Opt: Glassm:* flint glass.
flion [flijɔ̃], *s.m. Moll: F:* sunset shell.
flip [flip], *s.m.* (*drink*) flip.
flip-flap [flipflap], *s.m.inv.* handspring.
flip-flop [flipflɔp], *s.m. Elcs:* flip-flop.
flipot [flipo], *s.m. Carp: etc:* Dutchman; strengthening piece; odd piece (let in to hide a flaw, etc.).
flipper [flipœːr], *s.m. F:* pinball.
flirt [flœrt], *s.m. F:* **1.** flirtation, flirting; **avoir un f. avec qn,** to have a flirtation with s.o.; **j'ai le f. en horreur,** I loathe flirting; *Pol:* **un f. avec l'opposition,** a flirtation with the opposition. **2. mon f.,** my boyfriend, girlfriend; the boy, girl, I'm going out with; **un de mes anciens flirts,** an old flame of mine. **3.** *a. O:* flirtatious.
flirtage [flœrtaːʒ], *s.m.* (*rare*) **1.** flirting. **2. un f.,** a flirtation.
flirtation [flœrtasjɔ̃], *s.f. F:* flirtation.
flirter [flœrte], *v.i.* to flirt; *Pol:* to flirt (with a party, etc.).
flirteur, -euse [flœrtœːr, -øːz], (*a*) *a.* flirtatious; (*b*) *s.* flirt, philanderer.
floc[1] [flɔk]. **1.** *int.* plop! flop! **2.** *s.m.* (*a*) thud; (*b*) splash (into water).
floc[2], *s.m.* tassel (of aiguillette, etc.).
flocage [flɔkaːʒ], *s.m. Tex:* flocking.
flocculus, -li [flɔkylyːs, -li], *s.m.* **1.** *Anat:* flocculus. **2.** *Astr: pl.* **flocculi,** flocculi.
floch, floche[1] [flɔʃ], *s.m. Cards:* (*at poker*) flush.
floche[2], *a.* **1.** (*a*) *A:* soft, flabby; (*b*) dull, muffled (sound). **2.** flossy; **lin f.,** floss flax, linen floss; flourishing thread; **soie f.,** floss silk.
floche[3], *s.f.* **1.** *Cost:* tassel. **2.** *Tex:* organzine.
flockage [flɔkaːʒ], *s.m. Tex:* flocking.
flock-book [flɔkbuk], *s.m. Husb:* flock book; *pl. flock-books.*
flocon [flɔkɔ̃], *s.m.* (*a*) flake; **la neige tombe à gros flocons,** the snow is falling in large flakes; **flocon d'écume,** foam flake; **flocons d'avoine,** porridge oats; **céréales en flocons,** cereals, breakfast foods; *Fr.C:* **flocons de maïs,** cornflakes; (*b*) **f. de laine,** tuft, flock, of wool; (*c*) *Ch:* flocculus, floccule; (*d*) *Metall:* **flocons,** flakes.
floconnage [flɔkɔnaːʒ], *s.m. Tex:* flocking.
floconnement [flɔkɔnmɑ̃], *s.m.* **1.** forming into (i) flakes; (ii) floccules. **2.** fleeciness (of material).
floconner [flɔkɔne], *v.i.* **1.** to form into flakes, to flake. **2.** *Ch: etc:* to form into floccules; to become flocculent; to flocculate.
floconneux, -euse [flɔkɔnø, -øːz], *a.* **1.** fleecy, fluffy (cloth, etc.); flocculate. **2.** *Ch: etc:* flocculent (precipitate). **3.** *Paperm:* cloudy; **papier f.(par transparence),** cloudy paper.
floculant [flɔkylɑ̃], *s.m. Ph:* flocculant, flocculating agent.
floculat [flɔkyla], *s.m. Ph:* flocculate.
floculation [flɔkylasjɔ̃], *s.f. Ch:* flocculation (of colloidal solution); **réaction de f.,** flocculation reaction; flocculation test.
floculé [flɔkyle], *s.m. Ph:* flocculate.
floculer [flɔkyle], *v.i. Ch:* (*of colloidal solution*) to flocculate.
floculeux, -euse [flɔkylø, -øːz], *a. Ch:* flocculose (precipitate, etc.).
floe [flɔ], *s.m. Oc:* (ice) floe.
flondre [flɔ̃dr], *s.m. Ich: F:* flounder.
flonflon [flɔ̃flɔ̃], *s.m.* **1.** fol-de-rol (of a refrain). **2.** blare, pom pom pom (of a band and its big drum). **3.** chorus (of song, operetta, etc.). **4.** popular, cheap, song, music, tune.
flonger [flɔ̃ʒe], *v.i. P:* to lurch, to stagger.
flopée [flɔpe], *s.f. A:* shower of blows; *P:* large quantity, lashings (of sth.); crowd (of people, of things).
floquet [flɔkɛ], *s.m. Cost:* small (silk) tassel.
floraison [flɔrɛzɔ̃], *s.f.* flowering, blossoming, blooming, (in)florescence.
floral, -aux [flɔral, -o], *a.* floral; *Bot:* **feuille florale,** floral leaf; **jeux floraux,** floral games (literary competitions held yearly at Toulouse).
Floralies [flɔrali], *s.f.pl.* (*a*) *Rom.Ant:* Floralia; (*b*) floral festival; flower show.
flore[1] [flɔːr], *s.m. Nau: A:* grease, tallow.
Flore[2]. **1.** *Pr.n.f. Myth:* Flora. **2.** *s.f. Bot:* flora; *Med:* **f. intestinale,** intestinal flora.
floréal [flɔreal], *s.m. Fr.Hist:* eighth month of the French Republican calendar (April-May).
florée [flɔre], *s.f. Ind:* flurry.
florence [flɔrɑ̃ːs]. **1.** *s.m. Tex:* Florence, sarsenet. **2.** *s.f. Fish:* **(crin de) f.,** silkworm gut, silk gut.
florencé [flɔrɑ̃se], *a. Her:* (fleur-de-lis) florencée.
florensite [flɔrɑ̃sit], *s.f. Miner:* florencite.
florentin, -ine [flɔrɑ̃tɛ̃, -in], *a. & s.* **1.** *Geog:* Florentine. **2.** *s.f.* **florentine;** *Tex:* (*a*) Florentine, twilled silk; (*b*) Florentine drill, French twill. **3.** *a.* **récipient f.,** Florentine flask, receiver; **(gâteau) f.,** (type of) almond cake; **baiser f.,** French, deep, kiss.
florer [flɔre], *v.tr. Nau: A:* to grease (ship).
florès [flɔrɛs], *used only in the phr. F:* **faire f.,** to prosper; to shine (in society); to be in vogue.
floribond [flɔribɔ̃], *a. Bot:* floriferous.
floribunda [flɔribɔ̃da], *s.m. Hort:* **rosier f.,** floribunda rose.
florican [flɔrikɑ̃], *s.m. Orn:* florican.
floricole [flɔrikɔl], *a. Ent:* flower-dwelling.
floriculture [flɔrikyltyːr], *s.f.* floriculture, flower growing.
Floride [flɔrid], *Pr.n.f. Geog:* Florida.
floridées [flɔride], *s.f.pl. Algae:* Florideae, the red algae.
floridien, -ienne [flɔridjɛ̃, -jɛn], *a. & s. Geog:* Floridian, Floridan.
florifère [flɔrifɛːr], *a.* floriferous, flower-bearing; **plante très f.,** prolific flowerer.
floriforme [flɔrifɔrm], *a.* floriform, flower-shaped.
florilège [flɔrilɛːʒ], *s.m.* (*a*) florilegium, anthology of verse; (*b*) anthology, collection (of music, etc.); (*c*) **votre devoir est un f. d'impropriétés,** your exercise is a tissue of mistakes.
florin [flɔrɛ̃], *s.m. Num:* florin; *F:* **herbe à mille florins,** lesser centaury.
floripare [flɔripaːr], *a. Bot:* floriparous.
florir [flɔriːr], *v.i.* to flower, blossom.
florissant [flɔrisɑ̃], *a.* flourishing, prosperous (business, etc.); **d'une santé florissante,** in the best of health, hale and hearty.
floriste [flɔrist], *s.m. & f.* florist, student of the flora of a country.
floristique [flɔristik], *a.* floristic.
florule [flɔryl], *s.f. Bot:* florule, florula.
flos-ferri [flɔsferi], *s.m.inv. Miner:* flos ferri.
flot [flo], *s.m.* **1.** (*a*) wave; *Poet:* billow; **apaiser les flots,** to still the waves; **f. de la marée,** tidal wave; (*b*) **f. de dentelle, de rubans,** cascade of lace, of ribbons; (*c*) **(marée de) f.,** rising tide, flood-tide, flood; **demi-flot,** half-tide; **bassin à f.,** wet dock, flooding dock; **portes de f.,** gates of a tidal basin; **étale de f.,** slack water (at flood or ebb of the tide); (*d*) *F:* **flots de larmes,** floods of tears; **un f. de larmes lui monta aux yeux,** the tears welled up into her eyes; **un f. de sang lui monta au visage,** a flush rose to his cheek; **flots de sang,** streams, torrents, of blood; **un f. de gens dans la rue,** a stream, multitude, of people in the street; **f. pressé d'hommes,** surging mass, crowd, of men; **f. tumultueux d'idées,** flood, torrent, of confused ideas; **arrêter le f. de(s) voitures,** to hold up the stream of traffic; **lancer un f. d'injures à la tête de qn,** to launch a torrent of abuse at s.o., **la mort de Louis XVII a fait couler des flots d'encre,** a great deal of ink has been spilt over the death of Louis XVII; *adv.phr.* **à flots,** in torrents, in crowds, in plenty; **entrer, sortir, à flots,** to stream in, out; **couler à flots,** to gush out; **les rayons du soleil entraient à flots par la fenêtre,** the sun's rays came flooding through the window. **2.** floating; **jeter du bois à f. perdu,** to float wood down-stream; *adv.phr:* **à f.,** afloat; **mettre un navire à f.,** (i) to set a ship afloat, to launch a ship; (ii) to refloat, float off, a ship; **(re)mise à f.,** refloating, floating off; *F:* **mettre une société à f.,** to launch, float, a company; **remettre qn à f.,** to set s.o. up in funds, to restore s.o.'s fortunes; **rester à f.,** to remain afloat (after collision, etc.); **choses de f. et de mer,** flotsam and jetsam. **3.** *A:* timber-raft; drive (of timber).
flottabilité [flɔtabilite], *s.f.* buoyancy; **f. aérostatique,** aerostatic buoyancy; **ballonnet de f.,** buoyancy bag; **caisson, réservoir, de f.,** buoyancy tank; **chambre de f.,** buoyancy chamber, compartment (of air-cushion vehicle).
flottable [flɔtabl], *a.* **1.** (*of river*) navigable, floatable (for rafts of wood). **2.** (*of wood, etc.*) floatable, buoyant.
flottage [flɔtaːʒ], *s.m.* **1.** floating, driving, running, (of timber) down a river; **f. à bûches perdues,** floating; **f. en train,** rafting; **bois de f.,** raftwood; **train de f.,** timber-raft. **2.** flo(a)tation (of ore).
flottaison [flɔtɛzɔ̃], *s.f.* **1.** floating. **2.** *Nau:* (*a*) boot-topping, plane of flo(a)tation (of ship); (*b*) **(ligne de) f.,** floating line; water line, mark; Plimsoll line, Plimsoll mark; **f. en différence,** trimmed waterline; **longueur à la f.,** water line length; **f. en charge,** load line, load watermark; **f. lège,** light watermark; *N.Artil:* **viser à la f.,** to aim at the water line.
flottant [flɔtɑ], *a.* (*a*) floating; *Aut: Nau:* (*of cargo*) afloat; **moteur f.,** floating engine; **île flottante,** floating island; **robe flottante,** flowing robe; **manteau f.,** loose coat; **pantalon f.,** baggy trousers; **cheveux flottants,** flowing hair; **filet f.,** drift-net; *Orn:* **plumes flottantes,** plumes (of ostrich, etc.); *Fin: Ins:* **dette, police, flottante,** floating debt, policy; **titres flottants,** shares on the market; (*b*) irresolute, undecided (mind); **avoir une volonté flottante,** to be wavering or infirm of purpose; **personnalité flottante,** an elusive, evasive, personality; **marcher d'un pas f.,** to walk with wavering steps.
flottard[1] [flɔtaːr], *s.m. F:* naval cadet.
flottard[2], *a. F:* watery; **sauce flottarde,** thin gravy.
flottation [flɔtasjɔ̃], *s.f. Ind:* flo(a)tation process (for ores, etc.).
flotte[1] [flɔt], *s.f.* **1.** (*a*) fleet; **f. de commerce, marchande,** merchant fleet; **f. de guerre,** naval forces; **f. de ligne, de combat,** battle fleet; **f. aérienne,** air fleet; *F:* **f. de gens,** crowds, swarms, of people; (*b*) the navy; **son fils est dans la f.,** his son is in the navy. **2.** *F:* (*a*) water, rain; **il tombe de la f.,** it's pouring with rain; **tomber dans la f.,** to fall into the water; **boire de la f.,** to drink water; (*b*) soup.
flotte[2], *s.f.* **1.** float, (of net, fishing hook, cable, etc.); (mooring) buoy. **2.** *Veh:* (drag-)washer (of wheel hub). **3.** *Tex:* skein (of silk).
flotté [flɔte]. **1.** *a.* (*a*) **bois f.,** (i) driftwood; (ii) raftwood; (*b*) **pré f.,** water meadow. **2.** *s.m. Tex:* loose thread (in the weave).
flottement [flɔtmɑ̃], *s.m.* undulation; wavering, swaying (of line of troops, etc.); flapping (of flag); wobble, slack (of chain); *Aut:* **f. des roues,** shimmy, wheel wobble; **les flottements du cœur humain,** the wavering, vacillation, irresolution, of the human heart; **il y eut un moment de f.,** there was a moment's hesitation.
flotter [flɔte]. **1.** *v.i.* (*a*) to float; **bois qui flotte,** wood that floats; **faire f. un objet,** to buoy up, float, an object; (*b*) **ses cheveux flottent sur ses épaules,** her hair hangs loosely over, about, her shoulders; **ses cheveux flottaient au gré du vent,** her hair streamed on the breeze; **pavillon qui flotte dans l'air,** flag that floats in the breeze; **un drapeau flotte sur le clocher,** a flag waves over the steeple; **il flotte dans ses vêtements,** his clothes hang loosely around him; (*c*) to waver, hesitate; to be irresolute; (of line of troops, etc.) to sway, to waver; **f. de pensée en pensée,** to let one's mind run from one thing to another; **f. entre l'espérance et la crainte,** to waver, fluctuate, between hope and fear; **les prix flottent entre . . . et . . .,** prices fluctuate between . . . and. . . . **2.** *v.tr.* **f. du bois,** to float, drive, run, timber (down a stream); **f. un câble,** to float a cable. **3.** *v.impers. F:* **il flotte,** it's raining, it's pouring.
flotteron [flɔt(ə)rɔ̃], *s.m.* small float (of fishing line, etc.).
flotteur [flɔtœːr], *s.m.* **1.** raftsman (in charge of floated timber). **2.** (*a*) float (of fishing-line, seaplane, carburettor, etc.); buoyancy chamber (of torpedo); pontoon (of floating bridges); *Av:* **flotteurs en catamaran,** twin floats (of seaplane); (*b*) *Plumb:* ball (of ball-tap, etc.); **robinet à f.,** ball-cock; *Mch:* **f. d'alarme,** boiler float; (*c*) anchor buoy; (*d*) **f. de natation,** (pair of) waterwings; (*e*) *Algae:* air bladder, float.
flottille [flɔtiːj], *s.f.* (*a*) *Navy:* flotilla; **conducteur de f.,** flotilla leader; (*b*) **f. de pêche,** fishing fleet.
flou [flu]. **1.** *a.* woolly (outline, sound, idea, etc.); hazy, blurred (horizon); *Opt:* unsharp, fuzzy (image); (image) out of focus; **pensée floue,** vague idea; **cheveux flous,** soft, fluffy, hair; **robe floue,** loose-fitting dress; **peinture floue,** blurred, fuzzy, painting; *Lit:* **personnage f.,** nebulous character; *Cin: Th:* **éclairage donnant des ombres à contours flous,** soft lighting. **2.** *s.m.*

(*a*) blur, softness, woolliness, fuzziness (of outline); unsharpness (of image); *Phot:* **f. chromatique,** chromatic softness; **f. artistique,** soft-focus effect; *T.V:* **f. d'image,** blooming; (*b*) **le f.,** dressmaking (as opposed to tailoring). **3.** *adv.* **c'est peint trop flou,** the painting is woolly.

flouer [flue], *v.tr. F:* to swindle (s.o.); **f. qn de qch.,** to swindle, do, diddle, cheat, s.o. out of sth.; **on m'a floué,** I've been had, done.

flouerie [fluri], *s.f. F:* **1.** swindling, cheating. **2.** swindle.

flouette [fluɛt], *s.f. Nau:* weather-cock.

floueur, -euse [fluœːr, -øːz], *s. F:* swindler.

flous(s)e [flus], *s.m. P:* cash, lolly.

flouve [fluːv], *s.f. Bot:* **f. odorante,** (sweet) vernal grass.

flouze [fluːz], *s.m. P:* cash, lolly.

fluage [flyaːʒ], *s.m. Metall:* creep; flow (of plastics); **f. à la presse,** extrusion.

fluatation [flyatasjɔ̃], *s.f. Const:* surface water-proofing (with fluates).

fluate [flyat], *s.m. Ch:* (*a*) *A:* fluoride; (*b*) fluosilicate, fluate.

fluaté [flyate], *a. Ch:* **chaux fluatée,** calcium fluoride, fluorite.

flucérine [flyserin], *s.f. Miner:* fluocerine.

fluctuant [flyktɥɑ̃], *a.* fluctuating, varying; *Med:* fluctuant (tumour, etc.).

fluctuation [flyktɥasjɔ̃], *s.f.* fluctuation; *Med:* fluctuation (in abcess, etc.); *Biol:* fluctuation; **fluctuations du marché,** market fluctuations; **fluctuations du change,** fluctuations in exchange; *Mec.E:* **f. de charge,** variation of load.

fluctuer [flyktɥe], *v.i.* (*a*) (*rare*) to waver; (*b*) *Fin: etc:* to fluctuate.

fluctueux, -euse [flyktɥø, -øːz], *a.* unstable; rough, choppy (sea).

flué [flye], *a. Paperm:* unsized (paper); *Metall:* **métal f.,** extruded metal; *Med:* **humeur fluée,** running matter.

fluellite [flyɛlit], *s.f. Miner:* fluellite.

fluence [flyɑ̃ːs], *s.f.* (*a*) lapse, passage (of time); (*b*) *Atom.Ph:* fluence (of particles); **f. énergétique,** energy fluence.

fluent [flyɑ̃], *a.* flowing; *Civ.E: etc:* **terrain f.,** loose soil; *Med:* **hémorroïdes fluentes,** bleeding piles.

fluer [flye], *v.i.* **1.** to flow; **la mer flue et reflue,** the sea flows and ebbs. **2.** *Med:* (*of pus*) to run; (*of haemorrhoids*) to bleed. **3.** *Metall:* to creep.

fluet, -ette [flyɛ, -ɛt], *a.* thin, slender (person, column, etc.); of slight build; **voix fluette,** thin voice.

flueurs [flyœːr], *s.f.pl. Med:* **1.** menses; *F:* (monthly) periods. **2. f. blanches,** leucorrhea.

fluidal, -aux [flɥidal, -o], *a. Geol:* **texture fluidale,** fluidal texture.

fluide [flɥid], *a. & s.m.* fluid. **1.** *a. F:* **style f.,** flowing style; **pensée f.,** elusive thought; **la circulation était intense mais f.,** the traffic was heavy but kept moving; **une situation f.,** a fluid situation. **2.** *s.m.* **f. à viscosité constante,** Newtonian fluid; **f. réfrigérant, f. de refroidissement, f. caloporteur,** coolant; **mécanique des fluides,** fluid mechanics; **f. de frein,** brake fluid; **f. électrique,** electric fluid.

fluidement [flɥidmɑ̃], *adv.* fluidly, like a fluid; flowingly.

fluidifiant [flɥidifjɑ̃], *s.m.* (*a*) *Ind:* thinning agent, thinner; (*b*) *a. & s.m. Pharm:* expectorant.

fluidification [flɥidifikasjɔ̃], *s.f. Petroleum Ind:* fluxing.

fluidifier [flɥidifje], *v.tr.* (*pr.sub. & p.d.* **n. fluidifiions**) to fluidify; *Metall:* to flux.

fluidique [flɥidik], *a.* fluidic.

fluidisation [flɥidizasjɔ̃], *s.f. Tchn:* fluidization.

fluidiser [flɥidize], *v.tr. Tchn:* to fluidize; *Atom.Ph:* **réacteur à combustible fluidisé,** fluidized reactor.

fluidité [flɥidite], *s.f.* **1.** fluidity; flowingness (of language). **2.** *Pol.Ec:* free interplay of supply and demand. **3.** *Aut:* **f. de la circulation,** steady flow of traffic.

flume [flym], *s.m. Gold-min:* flume.

fluoaluminate [flyɔalyminat], *s.m.* fluoaluminate.

fluoborate [flyɔbɔrat], *s.m.* fluoborate.

fluoborique [flyɔbɔrik], *a.* fluoboric.

fluocérine [flyɔserin], **fluocérite** [flyɔserit], *s.f. Miner:* fluocerine, fluocerite.

fluophosphate [flyɔfɔsfat], *s.m.* fluophosphate.

fluor [flyɔːr], *s.m. Ch:* fluorine; *Miner:* **spath f.,** fluorspar, fluorite; *Paleont:* **test du f.,** fluorine test.

fluoranthene [flyɔrɑ̃tɛn], *s.m.* fluoranthene.

fluoration [flyɔrasjɔ̃], *s.f. Ch:* fluoridation.

fluoré [flyɔre], *a. Ch:* containing fluorine.

fluorène [flyɔrɛn], *s.m. Ch:* fluorene.

fluorescéine [flyɔrɛs(s)ein], *s.f. Ch:* fluorescein.

fluorescence [flyɔrɛs(s)ɑ̃ːs], *s.f.* fluorescence; **éclairage par f.,** fluorescent, strip, lighting.

fluorescent [flyɔrɛs(s)ɑ̃], *a.* fluorescent; **éclairage f.,** fluorescent, strip, lighting; *T.V:* **écran f.,** fluorescent screen.

fluorhydrate [flyɔridrat], *s.m. Ch:* hydrofluoride.

fluorhydrique [flyɔridrik], *a. Ch:* hydrofluoric (acid).

fluorifère [flyɔrifɛːr], *a. Ch:* containing fluorine.

fluorimètre [flyɔrimɛtr], *s.m.* fluorimeter.

fluorine [flyɔrin], *s.f. Miner:* fluorspar, fluorite, calcium fluoride.

fluorographie [flyɔrɔgrafi], *s.f.* fluorography.

fluoromètre [flyɔrɔmɛtr], *s.m.* fluorometer; fluorophotometer.

fluoroscope [flyɔrɔskɔp], *s.m. X Rays:* fluoroscope.

fluoroscopie [flyɔrɔskɔpi], *s.f. X Rays:* fluoroscopy.

fluorose [flyɔroːz], *s.f. Vet:* fluorosis.

fluoruration [flyɔryrasjɔ̃], *s.f. Ch:* fluoridation.

fluorure [flyɔryːr], *s.m. Ch:* fluoride.

fluosilicate [flyɔsilikat], *s.m.* fluosilicate.

fluosilicique [flyɔsilisik], *a.* fluosilicic (acid).

fluosulfonique [flyɔsylfɔnik], *a.* fluosulphonic (acid).

fluotournage [flyɔturnaːʒ], *s.m. Metalw:* rotary extrusion, hydrospinning.

flush [flœʃ], *s.m. Cards:* (*poker*) flush; **la quinte f.,** straight flush.

flustre [flystr], *s.f. Z:* flustra; sea mat.

flustridés [flystride], *s.m.pl. Z:* Flustridae.

flûte[1] [flyt], *s.f.* **1.** (*a*) flute; **grande f.,** concert flute; **petite f.,** piccolo; **f. tierce,** flute in E flat; **f. traversière,** transverse, German, flute; **f. à bec,** fipple flute; *esp.* recorder; **f. de Pan,** Pan-pipe, Pan's pipe, Pandean pipe; *Th:* **la F. enchantée,** the Magic Flute; *Carp:* **joint en bec de f.,** scarf; *F:* **ajustez, accordez, vos flûtes,** settle your differences; *Prov:* **ce qui vient de la f. s'en va par le tambour,** easy come easy go; **être du bois dont on fait les flûtes,** to be pliable, easily influenced; (*b*) flutist, flautist, flute. **2.** (*a*) long thin loaf of French bread; (*b*) tall champagne or beer glass, flute glass; (*c*) slender taper-necked bottle *esp.* (i) hock bottle; (ii) Moselle bottle; (*d*) *pl. F:* (thin) legs, shanks; **jouer des flûtes, se tirer des flûtes,** to run, to show a clean pair of heels; (*e*) *Tex:* (tapestry) shuttle, flute; (*f*) *Com:* (cheese or butter) taster. **3.** *int: P:* = ZUT.

flûte[2], *s.f. Nau: A:* store ship; **navire armé en f.,** boat armed *en flûte,* carrying only half its guns.

flûté [flyte], *a.* like a flute; fluty; **voix flûtée,** (i) soft, melodious, flute-like, voice; (ii) piping voice; *Mus:* **sons flûtés,** harmonics (on stringed instruments).

flûteau, -eaux [flyto], *s.m.* **1.** (*a*) whistle, pipe; (*b*) mirliton, *U.S:* kazoo. **2.** *Bot:* water plantain.

flûter [flyte]. **1.** *v.i.* (*a*) *A:* to play the flute; *F:* **envoyer f. qn,** to send s.o. to hell; (*b*) (*of blackbird*) to flute. **2.** *v.tr.* **f. un litre,** to swig off a litre.

flûteur [flytœːr], *s.m. Orn:* piping crow, flutebird.

flûtiau, -iaux [flytjo], *s.m. Mus:* whistle, pipe.

flûtiste [flytist], *s.m. & f.* flutist, flautist, flute player, flute.

flutter [flœtœːr], *s.m. Av: Med:* flutter.

fluvial, -iaux [flyvjal, -jo]. **1.** *a.* fluvial; **voie fluviale,** waterway; **pêche fluviale,** river fishing; **agents de la brigade fluviale, police fluviale,** river police; **canonnière fluviale,** river gunboat. **2.** *s.f.pl. Bot:* **fluviales,** Fluviales.

fluviatile [flyvjatil], *a.* fluviatile; **mollusques fluviatiles,** river, freshwater, molluscs.

fluvio(-)glaciaire [flyvjɔglasjɛːr], *a. Geol:* fluvio-glacial; **cailloutis f.(-)g.,** fluvio-glacial gravel.

fluviographe [flyvjɔgraf], *s.m. Geog:* fluviograph.

fluvio(-)marin [flyvjɔmarɛ̃], *a. Geol:* fluviomarine.

fluviomètre [flyvjɔmɛtr], *s.m. Geog:* fluviometer.

fluviométrique [flyvjɔmetrik], *a.* fluviometric.

flux [fly], *s.m.* **1.** flow; (*a*) **f. de paroles,** flow of words, garrulity; **un f. de sang lui monta au visage,** a flush, blush, rose to his cheeks; **f. continu d'émigrants,** unceasing stream of emigrants; (*b*) flow, flood (of the tide); **le f. et le reflux,** the ebb and flow; *Pol: F:* **le f. et le reflux des partis,** the swing of the pendulum; *Mch:* **f. alternatif,** alternating flow (of steam). **2.** *Cards:* flush; **être à f.,** to be flush. **3.** *Med:* flux; **f. de ventre,** diarrhoea; **f. de sang,** dysentery; **f. plasmatique rénal,** renal plasma flow; **f. menstruel,** menstrual flow. **4.** *Ch: Metall:* flux; *Petroleum Ind:* flux (oil). **5.** (*a*) *El:* flux (in conductor), flow (of current); **f. magnétique,** magnetic flux, current; **f. de dispersion,** stray flux, leakage flux; **f. de réaction,** reaction flux; (*b*) *Opt:* **f. lumineux,** luminous flux; light flux; (*c*) *Atom.Ph:* flux, flow (of radiation); **f. électronique,** electron flow, stream; **f. ionique,** ion flow; **f. de neutrons,** neutron flux. **6.** *Av:* **turbo-réacteur à double f.,** turbo-fan; **turbo-réacteur à simple f.,** turbo-jet.

fluxage [flyksaːʒ], *s.m. Tchn:* **fluxing.**

fluxer [flykse], *v.tr. Tchn:* to flux.

fluximètre [flyksimɛtr], *s.m. Ph:* fluxmeter, flux-graph.

fluxion [flyksjɔ̃], *s.f.* **1.** (*a*) *Med:* fluxion, inflammation; **f. à la joue,** swollen cheek; **f. dentaire,** gumboil; *F:* **f. de poitrine,** inflammation of the lungs, pneumonia; **vous allez attraper une f. de poitrine,** you'll catch your death of cold; (*b*) *Vet:* **f. périodique des yeux,** periodic ophthalmia, moon blindness. **2.** *Mth: A:* **méthode des fluxions,** method of fluxions.

fluxionnaire [flyksjɔnɛːr], *a. Vet:* **étalon f.,** moon-blind stallion.

fluxmètre [flyksmɛtr], *s.m. Ph:* fluxmeter.

flysch [fliʃ], *s.m. Geol:* flysch.

fob [fɔb], *a.inv. Com:* (**vente**) **f.,** f.o.b., free on board.

foc [fɔk], *s.m. Nau:* jib; **grand f.,** main jib, outer jib; **faux f.,** middle jib; **petit f.,** fore staysail; inner jib; **f. d'artimon,** mizzen-topmast staysail; **bâton de f.,** jib-boom.

focal, -aux [fɔkal, -o]. **1.** *a.* (*a*) *Geom: Opt:* focal; **axe f.,** focal axis; **distance, longueur, focale,** focal distance, length; **plan f.,** focal plane; *Phot:* **obturateur f.,** focal-plane shutter; (*b*) *Med:* **infection focale,** focal infection. **2.** *s.f. Geom: Opt:* **focale,** focal distance, length, focal line.

focalisation [fɔkalizasjɔ̃], *s.f. Opt: Elcs:* focusing; *Mth:* convergence.

focaliser [fɔkalize], *v.tr. Opt: Phot: Elcs:* to focus.

focimètre, focomètre [fɔsimɛtr, fɔkɔ-], *s.m. Opt:* focometer, focimeter.

focimétrique, focométrique [fɔsimetrik, fɔkɔ-], *a. Phot: Opt:* focusing (view-finder, etc.).

focquier [fɔkje], *s.m. Nau:* jibman.

focus [fɔkys], *a. Elcs:* (tube) **f.,** x-ray (tube).

fœhn [føn], *s.m. Meteor:* fœhn, föhn.

fœne [fen], *s.m. Ent:* foenus.

foène, foëne, foesne [fwɛn], *s.f.* **1.** *Fish:* grains, fish-gig, eel-prong, pronged harpoon. **2.** *Min:* alligator grab.

foéner, foëner [fwene], *v.tr.* (**je foène, n. foénons; je foénerai**) to spear (fish).

foéneur, foëneur [fwenœːr], *s.m.* spear-fisher.

fœtal, -aux [fetal, -o], *a. Biol:* f(o)etal; **annexes fœtales,** fœtal membranes; *Med:* **rythme f.,** embryocardia.

fœtalisation [fetalizasjɔ̃], *s.f. Biol:* f(o)etalization.

fœticide [fetisid], *Jur: a.* f(o)eticidal; *s.m.* f(o)eticide.

fœtus [fetys], *s.m. Z:* f(o)etus.

fofolle [fɔfɔl], *a.f. F:* flighty; foolish.

foggara [fɔgara], *s.m.* irrigation tunnel.

foi [fwa], *s.f.* faith. **1.** (*pledged word, honour*) (*a*) **acheteur de bonne f.,** genuine purchaser, bona fide purchaser; **il est de bonne f.,** he is quite sincere; **de bonne f. dites-nous votre opinion,** tell us your honest opinion, your candid opinion; **je pensais en toute bonne f. que . . .,** I honestly thought that . . .; **mauvaise f.,** (i) dishonesty, insincerity; (ii) unfairness; **de mauvaise f.,** mala fide; **témoin de bonne, de mauvaise, f.,** truthful, dishonest, witness; **jurer sur, par, sa f.,** to swear on one's honour; **engager sa f.,** to plight one's troth; to pledge one's word; **f. jurée,** sworn word; **f. conjugale,** marital fidelity; **manquer de f. à qn,** to break faith with s.o.; **manque de f.,** breach of faith; **ma f., oui!** upon my word, yes! indeed yes! **ma f., on n'y peut rien,** well, it cannot be helped; **f. d'honnête homme, de traducteur, etc.,** on my word as a gentleman, as a man of honour, as a translator, etc.; **sur la f. de sa lettre,** on the strength of his letter; *Mil:* **être prisonnier sur sa f.,** to be a prisoner on parole; (*b*) *Hist:* fealty; **homme de f.,** vassal. **2.** belief, trust, confidence; **avoir f. en qn, en qch.,** to have faith, to believe, in s.o., in sth.; **avoir f. en l'avenir,** to have confidence in the future; **ajouter f., attacher f., à une nouvelle,** to credit, to believe (in), a piece of news; **prêter f. à une revendication,** to admit a claim; **témoin digne de f.,** trustworthy, reliable, credible, witness; **renseignements dignes de f.,** information worthy of credence; reliable information; **texte qui fait f.,** authentic text; **le document fait f. que . . .,** the document attests the fact that . . .; **le cachet de la poste fera f.,** = must be postmarked not later than . . .; *Jur:* **en f. de quoi,** in witness, in testimony, whereof; **ligne de f.,** zero alignment (of optical instruments); *Artil:* visual line of sight; *Nau:* lubber's point

(of the compass); *Av:* lubber line. 3. (religious) faith, belief; **renoncer à la f. de ses pères,** to renounce the faith of one's forefathers; **acte, article, de f.,** act, article, of faith; **il est de f. que Jésus-Christ s'est fait homme,** it is (an article) of faith that Jesus Christ became man; **profession de f.,** (i) profession of faith; (ii) *Pol: F:* candidate's address, statement of policy; *F:* **il n'a ni f. ni loi,** he fears neither God nor man; **il n'y a que la f. qui sauve,** faith is everything; **la f. du charbonnier,** blind belief.

foie [fwa], *s.m.* 1. liver; **maladie de f.,** liver complaint; **huile de f. de morue,** cod-liver oil; *Vet:* **pourriture du f.,** liver rot; *Cu:* **f. gras,** foie gras; *F:* **avoir des jambes en pâté de f.,** to have cotton-wool legs; **se ronger les foies,** to eat one's heart out; *P:* **avoir les foies blancs,** to be a funk, a coward, lily-livered; **avoir les foies,** to be in a funk. 2. *Ch:* **f. d'antimoine, de soufre,** liver of antimony, of sulphur. 3. *inv.* **épagneul f. et blanc,** liver-and-white spaniel.

foie-de-bœuf [fwadbœf], *s.m.*, **foie-de-chêne** [fwadʃɛn], *s.m. Fung:* fistulina, beef-steak fungus; *pl. foies-de-bœuf, -de chêne.*

foin[1] [fwɛ̃], *s.m.* 1. hay; **foins fauchés,** new-mown hay; **faire les foins,** to make hay; **tas de f.,** haycock; **meule de f.,** haystack; **graine de f. (recueillie au grenier),** hayseed; **rhume des foins,** hay fever; *F:* **faire ses foins,** to make money; **mettre du f. dans ses bottes,** to feather one's nest; *P:* **faire du f.,** to make a din; *F:* **faire un f. de tous les diables,** to make a great song and dance (about sth.); **être bête à manger du f.,** to be as dumb as an ox; *P:* **coucher dans les foins,** to roll, tumble, in the hay; *F:* **quand il n'y a plus de f. dans le ratelier,** when the money runs out. 2. choke) (of artichoke).

foin[2], *int. O:* pooh! bah! **f. de . . .,** a fig for . . .; *A:* a murrain on . . .; **faire f. des convenances,** to snap one's fingers at etiquette.

foine [fwan], *s.f. Fish:* grains, fish-gig, eel-prong, pronged harpoon.

foinette [fwanɛt], *s.f. Agr:* small iron fork.

foirade [fwarad], *s.f. P:* (*a*) squitters; (*b*) jitters; (*c*) disaster, flop.

foirage [fwarɑːʒ], *s.m. Mec.E:* **f. des filets d'un écrou,** stripping of a screw; *P:* **c'est un vrai f.,** it's a real flop.

foirail [fwarɑːj], **foiral** [fwaral], *s.m. Dial:* fair-ground, market-place.

foire[1] [fwaːr], *s.f.* 1. fair; *Com:* trade fair; *U.S:* farmer's market; **f. aux chevaux,** horse fair; **f. de louage,** mop (fair); **f. aux plaisirs,** fun fair; **le champ de f.,** the fair ground; **quelle f.!** what a mess! what a crowd! **c'est une f., ici,** this place is a beargarden; **f. d'empoigne,** free-for-all; **la f. n'est pas sur le pont,** there is no hurry; *Mus: A:* **f. des enfants,** toy symphony. 2. *A:* fairing.

foire[2], *s.f. P:* diarrhoea; **attraper la f.,** to get diarrhoea.

foire-échantillon [fwarreʃɑ̃tijɔ̃], *s.f.* trade fair; *pl. foires-échantillons.*

foire-exposition [fwarɛkspozisjɔ̃], *s.f. Com:* (international) exhibition; *pl. foires-expositions.*

foirer [fware], *v.i.* 1. *P:* (i) to have diarrhoea, *P:* squitters; (ii) to be in a funk; (iii) to funk it. 2. *F:* (*a*) **vis qui foire,** screw that won't bite; *v.tr.* **f. un écrou,** to strip a nut; (*b*) *Artil:* **fusée qui foire,** fuse that hangs fire; (*c*) **cordage qui foire,** rope that is fraying; (*d*) *Civ.E:* **tranchée qui foire,** trench that caves in; (*e*) to fail, flop.

foireux, -euse [fwarø, -øːz]. *P:* 1. *a.* (*a*) suffering from diarrhoea; (*b*) funky, in a funk; (*c*) **film f.,** dud film; film that flopped; (*d*) *Civ.E:* **terrain f.,** soft, unstable ground, ground liable to cave in. 2. *s.* coward.

foirol(l)e [fwarɔl], *s.f. Bot:* annual mercury, French mercury, garden mercury.

fois [fwa], *s.f.* 1. time, occasion; **une fois,** once; **il y avait, il était, une f. . . .,** once upon a time there was . . .; **deux f.,** twice; **deux f. autant,** twice as much; **trois f. quatre font douze,** three times four is twelve; *F:* **je vous l'ai dit vingt f., cent f.,** I have told you so dozens of, hundreds of, times; **trois f. plus grand que . . .,** three times as big as . . .; **trois f. plus de confiture, de livres, que . . .,** three times as much jam, as many books as . . .; **voilà trois f. qu'il revient, c'est la troisième f. qu'il revient,** this is the third time he's come back; **encore une f.,** once more, once again; **y regarder à deux f. pour faire qch.,** to think twice before doing sth.; **une (bonne) f. (pour toutes),** once and for all; **cette f.,** on this occasion, this time; **je vous le permets pour cette f.,** you may do it this once; **une autre f.,** another time, on another occasion; **d'autres f.,** at other times; **par deux f.,** not (only) once, but twice; **ne pas se faire dire une chose deux f.,** not to have to be told twice to do a thing; **combien de f.?** how many times? how often? **j'en ai pris deux f.,** I had two helpings; **une f. sa résolution prise . . .,** once he had made up his mind . . .; **la première f. que je l'ai vu,** the first time I saw him; **faire beaucoup en une f.,** to do a great deal at once, at one sitting; **il faut le boire en une f.,** you must drink it at one go; **toutes les f. que . . .,** every time that, whenever . . .; **chaque f. que . . .,** each time that, whenever . . .; **pour une f. tu as raison,** you are right for once; **pour une f. que j'avais de bonne cartes, il y avait maldonne,** the one time I got good cards there was a misdeal; *adv.phr.* **à la f.,** at one and the same time; **ne parlez pas tous à la f.,** don't all speak at once, together; **faire deux choses à la f.,** to do two things at once; **elle riait et pleurait à la f.,** she was laughing and crying at the same time; **elle m'attire et me repousse à la f.,** she both, at once, attracts and repels me. 2. *P:* **des f.** (*a*) sometimes, now and then; (*b*) **vous n'auriez pas des f. . . .,** you haven't by any chance got . . .; **des f. qu'il viendrait vous voir,** in case he should come, if he should happen to come, to see you; (*c*) *Iron: F:* **non, mais des f.!** well, that's a bit thick! well, I'm blowed!

foison [fwazɔ̃], *s.f.* abundance, plenty, great numbers; *F:* lots, heaps; *used chiefly in the adv.phr.,* **à f.,** plentifully, abundantly, in abundance; **partout des fleurs à f.,** everywhere flowers galore, in profusion; **trésors à f.,** a profusion, a multitude, of treasures; **jardin où tout pousse à f.,** garden in which everything grows riotously.

foisonnant [fwazɔnɑ̃], *a.* 1. abundant, plentiful. 2. swelling; **masse foisonnante de cadavres,** festering mass of dead bodies.

foisonnement [fwazɔnmɑ̃], *s.f.* 1. swelling, expansion (of lime, etc., when moistened); increase in volume (of quarried stone); *El:* **f. (des plaques d'accumulateurs),** growth. 2. buckling (of metal). 3. *F:* **sa lettre était un f. de fautes d'orthographe,** his letter was swarming with spelling mistakes.

foisonner [fwazɔne], *v.i.* 1. to abound (**de, en,** in, with); **fleurs qui foisonnent dans les bois,** flowers that abound, grow in profusion, in the woods; **la lande foisonne de gibier,** the heath is alive, swarms, teems, with game; *F:* **le livre foisonne de fautes d'impression,** the book is full of misprints. 2. (*a*) (*of animals*) to breed rapidly, to increase; (*b*) (*of earth, lime, etc.*) to increase in volume, to swell, to expand; (*c*) to fester (and swell). 3. (*of metals, etc.*) to buckle.

fol [fɔl], *a. See* FOU.

folâtre [fɔlɑːtr], *a.* playful, lively, sprightly.

folâtrement [fɔlɑtrəmɑ̃], *adv.* playfully, in a lively, sprightly, way.

folâtrer [fɔlɑtre], *v.i.* to romp, frolic, gambol, play about; to play the fool.

folâtrerie [fɔlɑtrəri], *s.f.* 1. playfulness, sportiveness, sprightliness. 2. frolic, romp.

folding [fɔldiŋ], *a. & s.m.* folding (camera); **f. mixte,** plate-and-film camera.

foliacé [fɔljase], *a.* foliaceous, leaf-like.

foliaire [fɔljɛːr], *a. Bot:* foliar; **organe f.,** leaf-organ.

foliation [fɔljasjɔ̃], *s.f.* 1. *Bot:* foliation; (*a*) leafing; (*b*) vernation; arrangement of the leaves, phyllotaxy. 2. *Geol:* foliation.

folichon, -onne [fɔliʃɔ̃, -ɔn], *a.* (*a*) playful, light-hearted; **propos folichons,** light, frivolous talk; (*b*) (*usu. with neg. const.*) *F:* **ce n'est pas f.,** it's not very exciting, interesting; it's not much fun.

folichonner [fɔliʃɔne], *v.i.* 1. to play about, to lark about; to play the fool. 2. to flirt, to play around (with women).

folichonnerie [fɔliʃɔnri], *s.f.* 1. (*a*) playing about, larking about; sportiveness; (*b*) flirting. 2. (*a*) lark, frolic, romp; (*b*) light, silly, talk, behaviour.

folichonneur, -euse [fɔliʃɔnœːr, -øːz], *s.* one who indulges in light, frivolous, silly, behaviour; **vieux f.,** gay old dog.

folie [fɔli], *s.f.* 1. madness; *Med:* **f. à deux,** folie à deux; **f. circulaire,** folie circulaire; **accès de f.,** fit of madness; **f. du suicide,** suicidal mania; **f. des grandeurs,** delusions of grandeur, megalomania; **être pris de f.,** to go mad; **atteint de f. furieuse,** raving mad; **avoir un grain de f.,** to be slightly crazy, a bit touched; **aimer qn à la f.,** to be madly in love with s.o., to love s.o. to distraction; **il aime la chasse à la f.,** he is mad on hunting; **il a la f. des fleurs,** he is mad on flowers, he has a mania for flowers. 2. folly; piece of folly, act of folly; (*a*) **c'est f. à lui de sortir par cette pluie,** it is idiocy, sheer madness, on his part to go out in this rain; **il a eu la f. de . . .,** he was silly enough to . . .; (*b*) **les folies de la jeunesse,** the follies of youth; **dire des folies,** to talk wildly, extravagantly; **faire des folies,** (i) to act irrationally, to commit acts of extravagance; (ii) to have one's fling; **quel magnifique cadeau, vous avez fait des folies!** what a magnificent present, you really shouldn't have done it! **je viendrai dîner demain, mais surtout ne faites pas de folies,** I'll come to dinner tomorrow, but don't do anything too elaborate; *F:* (*of woman*) **faire des folies de son corps,** to sleep around; (*c*) **chienne en f.,** bitch on heat. 3. *A:* (*a*) folly; fool (in cap and bells); (*b*) folly (= country pleasure-house).

folié [fɔlje], *a. Bot:* foliate(d); *Ch:* foliated.

foliipare [fɔliipaːr], *a. Bot:* **bourgeon f.,** leaf-bud.

folio [fɔljo], *s.m. Typ: etc:* folio.

foliole [fɔljɔl], *s.f. Bot:* leaflet, foliole.

foliolé [fɔljɔle], *a. Bot:* foliolate.

foliot [fɔljo], *s.m. Hor:* foliot.

foliotage [fɔljɔtaːʒ], *s.m.* (i) foliation; (ii) pagination (of book).

foliotation [fɔljɔtasjɔ̃], *s.f. Pal:* foliation.

folioter [fɔljɔte], *v.tr.* (i) to folio, (ii) to paginate (book).

folioteur [fɔljɔtœːr], *s.m.* **folioteuse** [fɔljɔtøːz], *s.f.* numbering machine.

foliotocol [fɔljɔtɔkɔl], *s.m. Orn:* emerald cuckoo.

folique [fɔlik], *a. Ch:* folic (acid).

folium [fɔljɔm], *s.m. Mth:* folium; **f. de Descartes,** folium of Descartes.

folklore [fɔlklɔːr], (*a*) folklore; (*b*) folk songs, country dancing, local traditions.

folklorique [fɔlklɔrik], *a.* (*a*) folkloric; **danses folkloriques,** country dancing, folk dancing, folk-dances; (*b*) **village f.,** picturesque, fairy-tale, village.

folklorisme [fɔlklɔrism], *s.m.* study of folklore.

folkloriste [fɔlklɔrist], *s.m.* folklorist, student of folklore.

folk-singer [fɔlksiŋgœːr], *s.* folk singer; *pl. folk-singers.*

folk-song [fɔlksɔ̃g], *s.m.* (modern) folk song; *pl. folk-songs.*

folle[1]. *See* FOU.

folle[2], *s.f. Fish:* square fishing net; **demi-f.,** very fine fishing net interleaved between two tramelnets.

folle-avoine [fɔlavwan], *s.f. Bot:* wild oat; *pl. folles-avoines.*

follement [fɔlmɑ̃], *adv.* madly. 1. foolishly, unwisely; **entrer f. dans une entreprise,** to enter rashly upon an undertaking; **aimer f. qn,** to be madly, desperately, in love with s.o. 2. extravagantly; **s'amuser f.,** to have a glorious, wonderful, time.

follet, -ette[1] [fɔlɛ, -ɛt], *a.* 1. merry, lively; *F:* **elle est un peu follette,** she's a bit foolish, slightly crazy; **esprit f.,** elfish spirit, sprite, (hob)goblin; **feu f.,** will-o'-the-wisp, Jack-o'-lantern; *F:* **c'est un vrai feu f.,** he is like quick-silver. 2. **poil f.,** down (of bird, of boy's face); **cheveux follets,** stray lock(s) of hair.

follette[2], *s.f. Bot:* orach.

folliculaire [fɔl(l)ikylɛːr]. 1. *a. Physiol:* follicular. 2. *s.m. Pej: Lit:* penny-a-liner, hack writer.

follicule [fɔl(l)ikyl], *s.m. Bot: Anat:* follicle, follicules; **follicules de séné,** senna pods.

folliculeux, -euse [fɔl(l)ikylø, -øːz], *a. Bot: Physiol:* folliculose, follicular.

folliculine [fɔl(l)ikylin], *s.f.* 1. *Bio-Ch:* folliculin. 2. *Z:* folliculina.

folliculite [fɔl(l)ikylit], *s.f. Med: Vet:* folliculitis.

folliculo-stimuline [fɔl(l)ikylɔstimylin], *s.f.* follicle-stimulating hormone.

fomen(ta)teur, -trice [fɔmɑ̃(ta)tœːr, -tris], *s.* fomenter, stirrer up (of trouble).

fomentation [fɔmɑ̃tasjɔ̃], *s.f.* 1. *A: Med:* fomentation. 2. **f. de guerres intestines,** fomentation, stirring up, of civil wars.

fomenter [fɔmɑ̃te], *v.tr.* 1. *A: Med:* to foment. 2. **f. la sédition,** to foment sedition; **f. des troubles, la discorde,** to foster a disturbance, to stir up strife; **f. le désordre,** to promote disorder; **f. une querelle entre . . . et . . .,** to stir up a quarrel between . . . and . . .

fonçage [fɔ̃saːʒ], *s.m.* 1. bottoming, heading (of a cask). 2. **f. d'un pieu,** driving of a pile; **f. de puits,** well boring, sinking; *Min:* shaft sinking. 3. slate cutting. 4. *Cu:* lining (of pastry tin, etc.). 5. plain-colour sizing (of wallpaper).

fonçailles [fɔ̃sɑːj], *s.f.pl.* (*a*) head (of cask); (*b*) cane, straw, bottom (of chair); (*c*) bed boards.

foncé [fɔ̃se], *a.* 1. dark (colour); **une robe de couleur foncée,** a dark-coloured dress; **des rubans bleu f.,** dark-blue ribbons, ribbons of a deep blue. 2. *Carp:* **trou f.,** hole drilled part way through a plank.

foncée [fɔ̃se], *s.f. Min:* bed, layer (of slate).

foncement [fɔ̃smɑ̃], *s.m.* = FONÇAGE.

foncer [fɔ̃se], *v.* (je fonçai(s); n. fonçons) **1.** *v.tr.* (*a*) **f. un tonneau,** to bottom, fit a bottom to, a cask; to head a cask; (*b*) to sink, drive (in) (pile, etc.); to sink, bore (well, mine-shaft); (*c*) to deepen, darken, the colour of (sth.); (*d*) *Cu:* to line (tin, etc.) with pastry, etc.; (*e*) *Tex:* to depress pedal (in hand weaving). **2.** *v.i.* (*a*) **f. sur qn,** to rush, charge, swoop (down), upon s.o.; (*of bull, footballer*) to charge s.o.; (*of serpent*) to strike s.o.; *abs.* to strike; **les vaisseaux ennemis foncèrent sur nous,** the enemy ships bore down upon us; **ils ont foncé dans un arbre,** they ran smack into a tree; (*b*) *F:* to speed along; to forge ahead; to throw oneself (enthusiastically) into sth.; **f. dans le brouillard,** to go ahead blindly, regardless; (*c*) (*of whale*) to sound; (*d*) to deepen, darken (in colour).

se foncer, to grow darker, deeper (in colour).

foncet [fɔ̃sɛ], *s.m. Const:* escutcheon, keyplate.

fonceur, -euse [fɔ̃sœːr, -øːz], *s.* **1.** (well-)sinker, borer. **2.** (*a*) plain-colour sizer (of wallpapers); (*b*) *Paperm:* coater. **3.** *s.f.* **fonceuse,** *Paperm:* coater, coating machine. **4.** *s. F:* dynamic, go-ahead, person.

foncier, -ière[1] [fɔ̃sje, -jɛːr], *a.* **1.** concerning, pertaining to, the land; **propriété foncière,** landed property; real estate; **le propriétaire f.,** the ground landlord; **rente foncière,** ground rent; **impôt f.,** land tax; **crédit f.,** loan bank (granting loans on landed property); land bank; **contribution foncière des propriétés bâties,** property tax; **contribution foncière des propriétés non bâties,** *F:* **impôt f.,** land tax; **régime f.,** system of land tenure; **administrateur f.,** land agent; estate agent; **cabinet d'administrateur f.,** estate agency. **2.** deep-seated, fundamental; **homme d'un égoïsme f.,** man selfish to the core; **bon sens f.,** innate common sense.

foncière[2], *s.f. Min:* bed, layer, of slate.

foncièrement [fɔ̃sjɛrmɑ̃], *adv.* fundamentally, at (the) bottom, thoroughly; **le système est f. mauvais,** the system is radically wrong; **il était f. bon,** he was naturally of a kind disposition.

fonçoir [fɔ̃swaːr], *s.m. Metalw:* sharp-faced hammer.

fonction [fɔ̃ksjɔ̃], *s.f.* **1.** function; office; (*a*) **f. publique,** (i) public office; (ii) *Coll.* officials; **hautes fonctions,** high office; **prendre ses fonctions, entrer en fonctions,** to take up, enter upon, begin, one's duties; to take up one's appointment; to take office; **demeurer en fonctions,** to remain, continue, in office; **préparé aux fonctions publiques,** trained for public office; **quelle f. remplissez-vous?** what position do you hold? **il est, de par ses fonctions, responsable de . . .,** he is ex officio responsible for . . .; **faire f. de . . .,** to serve, act, as . . .; **exercer les fonctions de . . .,** to serve, act, as . . .; **lieutenant faisant f. de capitaine,** lieutenant acting (as) captain; **logement et voiture de f.,** accommodation and car provided; **adjectif qui fait f. d'adverbe,** adjective that is used as an adverb; (*b*) **fonctions de l'estomac, du cœur,** functions of the stomach, of the heart; (*c*) *Typ:* work other than typesetting and composing. **2.** *Mth: etc:* function; **f. inverse,** inverse function; **en f. de,** according to, with respect to; *Mth:* in terms of, as a function of; **exprimer une quantité en f. d'une autre,** to express one quantity in terms of, as a function of, another; **lorsque *x* est f. de *y*,** when *x* varies as *y*, is a dependent variable of *y*; **courbe de la viscosité en f. de la température,** graph of viscosity in terms of temperature; **la valeur de la force électromotrice est f. du taux de la variation du courant,** the value of the electromotive force is dependent upon the rate of change of the current; **la résistance est f. de la pression,** resistance is a function of pressure; **les variations du chômage se sont produites en f. de l'indice général des prix,** unemployment figures have moved, varied, according to the price index; **le bon marché est f. de l'abondance,** cheapness is conditional upon abundance; **le moyen de transport doit être f. du genre de marchandises,** the means of transport should vary according to the type of goods carried; **les appointements offerts seront f. de l'expérience,** the salary offered will be commensurate with, according to, in accordance with, experience.

fonctionnaire [fɔ̃ksjɔnɛːr], *s.* **1.** official, *esp.* civil servant; *Lit:* functionary; **hauts fonctionnaires,** higher officials, higher civil servants; **moyens fonctionnaires,** senior officials, senior civil servants; **petits fonctionnaires,** minor officials, minor civil servants. **2.** *s.m. Typ:* printing-shop worker (other than compositor or typesetter).

fonctionnalisme [fɔ̃ksjɔnalism], *s.m.* functionalism.

fonctionnaliste [fɔ̃ksjɔnalist], *a.* functionalist; **l'architecture f.,** functionalist architecture.

fonctionnariat [fɔ̃ksjɔnarja], *s.m.* (state of) being a civil servant.

fonctionnarisation [fɔ̃ksjɔnarizasjɔ̃], *s.f.* **1.** organizing on the lines of the civil service. **2.** state of being organized on the lines of the civil service.

fonctionnariser [fɔ̃ksjɔnarize], *v.tr.* **1.** to treat (employees) as civil servants. **2.** to organize on the lines of the civil service. **3.** to deal with in the official manner; *F:* to tie up in red tape.

fonctionnarisme [fɔ̃ksjɔnarism], *s.m.* officialism, officialdom; functionarism; *F:* red tape.

fonctionnel, -elle [fɔ̃ksjɔnɛl], *a.* functional; *Psy:* **psychologie fonctionnelle,** functional psychology, functionalism; *Path:* **trouble f.,** functional disorder; *Art: Furn:* functional.

fonctionnellement [fɔ̃ksjɔnɛlmɑ̃], *adv.* functionally.

fonctionnement [fɔ̃ksjɔnmɑ̃], *s.m.* (*a*) functioning, working (of government, of plan, of the organs, etc.); procedure (of court of law); **bon f. de l'administration,** efficiency, smoothness, of administration; **participer au f. d'une assemblée,** to participate, take part, in the work of an assembly; (*b*) *E:* operation, running, working (of a machine, etc.); **f. automatique,** automatic operation; push-button operation; **f. en duplex,** duplex operation; **f. en tandem,** tandem working; **en f.,** in action, operating, working; **en cours de f., pendant le f.,** while running, while working; **en (bon) état de f.,** in (good) running order, in (good) working order; **s'assurer du bon f. d'un mécanisme,** to see, to make sure, that a mechanism works freely, properly; **condition de f.,** operating condition; **cycle de f.,** operating cycle; **f. cyclique, périodique,** cyclic operation, cycling; **diagramme de f.,** operating diagram; **limites de f.,** operating limits; **période, temps, de bon f.,** operating time, time between failures; **charge de f.,** operating load; **coûts de f.,** operating costs; *Mch:* **pression de f.,** working pressure; (*of machine, etc.*) **entrer en f.,** to begin working.

fonctionner [fɔ̃ksjɔne], *v.i.* **1.** (*of committee, etc.*) to function. **2.** to act, work; **machine qui fonctionne bien,** machine that runs, works, well; **est-ce que les freins fonctionnent?** are the brakes working? **les trains ne fonctionnent plus,** the trains are no longer running; **la pompe ne fonctionne pas,** the pump is not acting, is out of order; **les freins n'ont pas fonctionné,** the brakes failed to work, to act; **quand le cœur ne fonctionne plus,** when the heart ceases to beat; **faire f. une machine,** to run, work, a machine; *El:* **f. sur courant continu,** to operate on direct current.

fond [fɔ̃], *s.m.* **1.** (*a*) bottom; crown (of hat); seat (of chair, trousers); bottom, head (of cask); bottom (of artichoke); back (of the throat); **f. d'un puits,** bottom of a well; **abîme sans f.,** bottomless chasm; **mettre un f. à une chaise,** to bottom a chair; **remettre un f. à un pantalon,** to reseat a pair of trousers; **f. de lit,** bed boards; **f. de plateau,** tray cloth; **fond d'une bouteille,** punt of a bottle; **boîte à double f., à f. intermédiaire,** box with a false bottom; **casserole à f. de cuivre,** copper-bottomed saucepan; *Mch:* **f. de cylindre, de chaudière,** cylinder head, boiler head; **f. arrière de chaudière,** back plate of a boiler; **f. d'une serrure,** plate of a lock; **au f. du cœur,** at the bottom of one's heart, deep down; **du f. du cœur,** from the bottom of one's heart; **au f. il était très flatté,** in his heart of hearts, deep down, he was extremely gratified; **regarder qn au f. des yeux,** to look s.o. straight in the eyes; **aller au f. d'une affaire,** to get to the bottom of a matter; **nous touchons au f. du problème,** we have got to the root of the problem; **descendre au f. des choses,** to get down to bed rock, to rock bottom; **il possède le f. de cette matière,** he has sound knowledge of the subject; **le f. de la coupe,** the dregs of the cup; **f. de bouteille,** dregs; **f. de café,** coffee grout, *F:* grounds; *F:* **racler les fonds de tiroir,** to scrape the barrel; **f. d'un bateau,** bottom of a boat; **bateau à f. plat,** flat-bottomed boat; **double f. (d'un navire),** double bottom; **f. de cale,** bilge; *F:* **être à f. de cale,** to be completely broke; *Geol:* **f. de bateau,** syncline; **f. de bateau renversé,** anticline; (*b*) bottom, bed (of the ocean); **f. de sable,** sandy bottom; **donner f.,** to cast anchor, to moor; (*of anchor*) **prendre f.,** to bite, grip; **s'envoyer par le f.,** to scuttle one's ship, to send a ship to the bottom; **grands fonds,** ocean deeps; **hauts, petits, fonds,** shallows, white water; **par de grands fonds,** in deep water; **courant de f.,** undertow; **mer du f.,** ground swell; **trouver, prendre, le f.,** to sound, to take soundings; **trouver le f. en sondant,** to strike ground; **il y a cent brasses de f.,** there are a hundred fathoms of water; **par cinquante brasses de f.,** at a depth of fifty fathoms; **se maintenir par des fonds suffisants,** to keep in safe soundings; *Swim:* **le grand f.,** the deep end (of swimming pool); **le petit f.,** the shallow end; *Mch:* **f. de course,** lower dead-centre (of piston); *adv.phr.* **à fond,** thoroughly; **chausser les étriers à f.,** to put one's feet well home in the stirrups; **visser une pièce à f.,** to screw a piece home; *Aut:* **enfoncer une pédale à f.,** to press a pedal home; **à f. de train,** at top speed; *Sp:* **partir à f.,** to start all out; **pousser une attaque à f.,** to push an attack home; **connaître un sujet à f.,** to have a thorough knowledge of a subject; **connaître à f. l'économie politique,** to be an expert on economics; **il connaît son métier à f.,** he is a master of his craft, he knows his trade thoroughly, through and through; **examiner qch. à f.,** to go thoroughly into sth., to sift (evidence) thoroughly; **interroger qn à f.,** to question s.o. closely, exhaustively; **se lancer à f. dans une description,** to plunge headlong into a description. **2.** foundation; **bâtir sur un f. solide,** to build on a solid foundation; **rebâtir une maison de f. en comble,** to rebuild a house from top to bottom; **être ruiné de f. en comble,** to be completely ruined; **accusation sans f.,** baseless, unfounded, charge, accusation; *Jur:* **défense sans f.,** peremptory defence; **f. de vérité,** substratum of truth; **il y a un f. d'amertume dans ses écrits,** there is an underlying bitterness in his writing; **discours avec un f. d'humour,** speech with an undercurrent, underlying vein, of humour; **il y a en lui un f. de faiblesse,** there is a strain of weakness in him; *Needlew:* **broderie sur f. de soie,** embroidery on a silk foundation, on a silk ground; *Tex:* **f. d'un tissu,** background colour of a (printed) material; **f. de robe,** (under) slip, foundation slip; **faire f. sur qn, sur qch.,** to rely, depend, on s.o., sth.; **je fais peu de f. sur lui,** I have little trust in him; I am not counting on him; **le f. et la forme,** the form and the substance; **je n'aime ni la forme ni le f. de sa lettre,** I like neither the form nor the substance of his letter; *Jur:* **f. d'un procès,** main issue of a suit; **le f. de la cause est en état,** the case is at issue upon its merits; **le f. de cette politique,** the essential features of this policy; **être d'accord sur le f.,** to agree on the basic issues; **homme qui manque de f.,** man who (i) lacks steadfastness of purpose, (ii) is shallow-minded, (iii) lacks stamina; **cheval qui a du f.,** horse that has good bottom, horse with staying power; **course de (grand) f.,** long distance race; (*skiing*) cross-country race; **coureur de f.,** long-distance runner, swimmer; **question de f.,** fundamental question; *Journ:* **article de f.,** leading article, leader; *Mus:* **jeu de f.,** pipe stop (of organ), foundation stop, diapason stop; **bruit de f.,** (i) scratching (of gramophone needle); (ii) *Cin: W.Tel:* background noise; **f. sonore, musical,** background music; *Th: Toil:* **f. de teint,** make-up foundation; *adv.phr.* **au f., dans le f.,** fundamentally, basically; **au f. vous avez raison,** fundamentally, you're right; **au f. ce n'est pas un mauvais sujet,** he's all right basically; **il a un bon f.,** he's good at heart, he's basically good. **3.** back, furthermost part, far end, upper or lower end (of enclosed space); **f. d'une boutique,** back of a shop; **fonds de boutique,** oddments, old stock; **au (fin) f. du désert, de l'Asie,** in the heart of the desert, of Asia; **glacé jusqu'au f. des os,** frozen to the very marrow (of one's bones); **f. d'un tableau,** background of a picture; *Typ: Bookb:* **petit f.,** back edge (of page); **petit f. (marge intérieure),** back margin, inner margin; **grand f. (marge extérieure),** outer margin; *Nau:* **f. d'une voile,** bunt of a sail; *Phot:* **f. d'atelier,** studio background; *Th:* **le f.,** backdrop; **toile de f.,** back cloth, background; **servir de f. à . . .,** to serve as a background to . . .; **ligne de f.,** (i) *Ten:* base line; (ii) *Fish:* ground, bottom, line; *Ten:* **jeu de f.,** baseline play; *Mch:* **mettre les feux au f.,** to bank the fires. **4.** *Cu:* stock; **f. blanc, f. brun,** white, brown, stock; **f. de volaille,** chicken stock.

fondage [fɔ̃daːʒ], *s.m. Metall:* melting, smelting (of metals).

fondamental, -aux [fɔ̃damɑ̃tal, -o], *a.* fundamental; basic, underlying, (principle); **pierre fondamentale,** foundation stone; **couleurs fondamentales,** primary colours; **la recherche fondamentale,** basic research; *Mus:* **note fondamentale,** *s.f.* **fondamentale,** fundamental, pedal-note (of wind instrument); **basse fondamentale, son f.,** root, generator (of chord); *Ph:* **oscillation fondamentale,** natural oscillation.

fondamentalement [fɔ̃damɑ̃talmɑ̃], *adv.* fundamentally; basically; at the base; at the core; **système f. mauvais,** system radically unsound.

fondamentalisme [fɔ̃damɑ̃talism], *s.f. Rel.H:* fundamentalism.

fondamentaliste [fɔ̃damɑ̃talist], *a. & s. Rel.H:* fundamentalist.

fondant [fɔ̃dɑ̃]. **1.** *a.* (*a*) melting; **température de la glace fondante,** temperature of melting ice; **poire fondante,** pear that melts in the mouth; juicy, luscious pear; (*b*) *Vet:* resolvent (ointment, etc.); (*c*) *A:* **tableaux fondants,** dissolving views; *Phot:* **vues fondantes,** dissolving views. **2.** *s.m.* (*a*) *Metall:* flux; (*b*) (i) fondant; (ii) fondant icing; (iii) plain chocolate; (*c*) *Ind:* **f. d'un émail,** base of an enamel; (*d*) *Vet:* resolvent.

fondateur, -trice [fɔ̃datœːr, -tris], *s.* founder (of business, etc.); *Fin:* promoter, founder (of company); **parts de f.,** founder's shares.

fondation [fɔ̃dasjɔ̃], *s.f.* **1.** (*a*) founding, foundation (of empire, hospital, etc.); **de f.,** from the start; **cela est de f.,** it's traditional, the traditon; it has always been like that; (*b*) (fund for) endowment, foundation (of hospital, prize, etc.); (*c*) (endowed) establishment, institution; foundation. **2.** (*a*) *Const:* foundation; **jeter les fondations d'une maison,** to lay the foundations of a house; **fondations sur radier, fondations en cuvelage,** floating foundations; (*b*) *Mch:* **plaque de f.,** bed plate.

fonde[1] [fɔ̃ːd], *s.f. Nau:* bottom; anchorage.

fonde[2], *s.f. A.Mil:* (i) sling; (ii) projectile of engine of war.

fondé [fɔ̃de]. **1.** *a.* (*a*) founded, grounded, reasonable, justified; **doutes bien fondés,** well-founded, well-grounded, fully justified, suspicions; **mes soupçons n'étaient pas fondés, étaient mal fondés,** my suspicions were groundless, were unjust; **la police est bien fondée à le croire coupable,** the police have good reason to believe him guilty; **nous ne sommes pas fondés à leur refuser ce droit,** we are not entitled to refuse them this right; **êtes-vous f. à refuser?** are you justified in refusing? **qu'est-ce qu'il y a de f. dans ces bruits (qui courent)?** what grounds are there for these reports? (*b*) funded (debt). **2.** *s.m.* **f. de pouvoir,** (i) *Jur:* agent (holding power of attorney); proxy; (ii) *Com:* manager, managing director; (iii) chief clerk, signing clerk; **il est le f. de pouvoir de . . .,** he holds a power of attorney for . . .; **f. de procuration spéciale et authentique,** attorney.

fondement [fɔ̃dmɑ̃], *s.m.* **1.** (*a*) *Const:* substructure; foundation; base; **jeter les fondements d'un édifice,** to lay the foundations of a building; **fondements d'une montagne,** base of a mountain; **ébranlé jusque dans ses fondements,** shaken to its foundations; (*b*) **critique qui manque de f.,** baseless criticism; **dénué de f.,** without foundation; **soupçons sans f.,** baseless, groundless, suspicions; unfounded suspicions. **2.** (*a*) *Anat: Med:* fundament; (*b*) *F:* buttocks, bottom.

fonder [fɔ̃de], *v.tr.* (*a*) to found, lay the foundations of (building, business, etc.); **f. un immeuble sur de la roche,** to build on a rock foundation; **immeuble fondé sur radier,** building on floating foundations; **f. une ville, un empire,** to found a town, an empire; **f. une société,** to float a company; **f. un journal,** to start a newspaper; **f. un commerce, une maison de commerce,** to start, set up, a business; **f. un foyer,** to get married, set up a household; **f. ses espérances sur qch.,** to ground, base, build, one's hopes on sth.; (*b*) *Fin:* to fund (debt).

se fonder. se f. sur qch., to place one's reliance on sth.; to build upon (promise, etc.); **je me fonde sur ce que vous venez de dire,** I am basing myself on, I take my stand on, what you have just said; **sur quelles preuves vous fondez-vous?** what evidence are you going on? **sur quoi se fonde-t-il pour nier que . . .?** what are his grounds for denying that . . .? **un espoir qui se fondait sur une information fausse,** a hope that was based, founded, on misinformation.

fonderie [fɔ̃dri], *s.f.* **1.** (*a*) smelting; (*b*) founding, casting (of metals). **2.** (*a*) smelting works; (*b*) foundry; **f. (de fer),** ironworks; **f. de cuivre,** (i) copper-smelting works; (ii) brass-foundry; **f. de cloches, de canons,** bell-foundry, gun-foundry; (*c*) (i) melting-house; (ii) melting-vat, (for wax).

fondeur [fɔ̃dœːr], *s.m.* **1.** (*a*) smelter; (*b*) (metal-) founder, caster; **f. de cloches,** bell-founder, -caster; **f. en cuivre,** brass-founder; **f. en bronze,** bronze-founder; **f. en médailles,** medal-caster. **f. en caractères, f. typographe,** type-founder. **2.** iron-merchant. **3.** *Sp:* cross-country skier; long-distance runner, swimmer, etc.

fondeuse [fɔ̃døz], *s.f.* (*machine*) caster.

fondis [fɔ̃di], *s.m.* subsidence; hole in the ground (due to subsidence).

fondoir [fɔ̃dwaːr], *s.m.* (tallow-)melting house; (tallow) melter.

fondouk [fɔ̃duk], *s.m.* Arab inn, fonduk.

fondre [fɔ̃ːdr]. **1.** *v.tr.* (*a*) to smelt (ore); (*b*) to melt (snow, wax, lead, etc.); to melt down (metal, etc.); **f. deux fils ensemble,** to fuse two wires together; *El:* **f. un fusible,** to blow a fuse; (*c*) to cast, found (bell, gun, etc.); (*d*) to dissolve, melt (salts, sugar, etc.); *Med:* to disperse (swelling, etc.); (*e*) **f. des teintes,** to blend colours; *Cin:* **f. une scène dans la suivante,** to dissolve a scene into the following one; (*f*) *Com:* **f. deux compagnies en une seule,** to amalgamate two companies. **2.** *v.i.* (*a*) to melt; **le beurre fond au soleil,** butter melts in the sun; *El:* **le fusible fond,** the fuse blows; **faire f. un fusible,** to blow a fuse; **faire f. le lard de baleine (pour la mise en tonneaux),** to try out (oil from) blubber; **mon cœur fondit de pitié,** my heart melted with pity; *F:* **l'argent lui fond entre les mains,** money melts in his hands, he spends money like water; **il fond à vue d'œil,** he is getting thinner every day; **mes économies fondent à vue d'œil,** my savings are rapidly diminishing, melting away; *Sp: F:* **se faire f.,** to train down; (*b*) (*of salts, sugar, etc.*) to melt, dissolve; **f. en larmes,** to dissolve in(to) tears. **3.** *v.i.* to pounce, swoop down (upon the prey, etc.); *F:* **f. sur qn,** to pounce, bear down, upon s.o.

se fondre. 1. = FONDRE 2 (*a*); **l'armée se fondait dans le désert,** the army was melting away in the desert. **2.** (*a*) to mix, merge, blend; **ces couleurs se fondent bien,** these colours blend well; **silhouette qui se fond dans le lointain,** outline that melts, vanishes, fades in the distance; (*b*) (*of companies, etc.*) to amalgamate.

fondrière [fɔ̃dri(j)ɛːr], (*a*) hollow (in ground); (*b*) bog, quagmire, swamp, morass; *Fr.C:* **f. de mousse,** muskeg; (*c*) muddy or slushy hole (in road).

fondrilles [fɔ̃driːj], *s.f.pl. Cu:* sediment, crust (on pan).

fonds [fɔ̃], *s.m.* **1.** (*a*) **f. de terre,** estate (piece of) land; *Jur:* tenement, hereditament; **cultiver un f.,** to cultivate a piece of land; (*b*) (*in museum*) bequest. **2.** (*a*) **f. de commerce,** business, goodwill; **f. de commerce à vendre,** business for sale (as a going concern); *Publ:* **ouvrage de f.,** copyright work forming part of the goodwill of a publishing house; (*b*) stock(-in-trade); **avoir un f. de science,** to have a stock of knowledge; **il a du f.,** there is something in him; **chaque nation a son f. de chansons populaires,** each nation has its heritage of folk songs; (*c*) *occ. found as a misspelling for* FOND 2. **3.** (*a*) funds; **fournir les f. d'une entreprise,** to supply the capital for an undertaking; *Com:* **faire les f.,** to provide for a bill of exchange; **mettre des f. dans une entreprise,** to invest money in a business; **mise de f.,** (i) putting up of capital, money; (ii) paid-in capital; **ma première mise de f. fut de £100,** my initial outlay was £100; **rentrer dans ses f.,** to get one's outlay, one's money, back; **appel de f.,** call upon shareholders; **f. disponibles,** abilities; **mangez vos revenus, mais ne touchez pas au f.,** spend your income, but don't touch your capital; (*b*) fund (for special purpose); **f. secrets,** secret service fund; **f. de roulement,** working capital, trading capital, wage fund, cash reserve; **f. d'assurance contre le chômage involontaire,** unemployment fund; **F. Monétaire International,** International Monetary Fund; **f. commun,** pool; (*c*) means, resources; **vivre sur ses f.,** to live on one's means, capital; **placer son argent à f. perdu,** to purchase a life annuity; *F:* **prêt à f. perdu,** loan without security; *Adm:* **subvention à f. perdu,** capital grant; **être en f.,** to be in funds; **je ne suis pas, ne suis guère, en f. à présent,** I am (a bit) short of money at present, I am not very flush at present, I'm a bit tight at the moment; (*d*) *pl. Fin:* stocks, securities, funds; **f. d'État, f. publics,** Government stock(s); **f. consolidés,** funded, consolidated, debt; *F:* consols.

fondu, -ue [fɔ̃dy]. **1.** *a.* (*a*) melted (butter, etc.); molten (lead, etc.); (*b*) **couleurs bien fondues,** well-blended colours; (*c*) *s.m.* **le f. de ces pastels,** the mellowness of these pastels. **2.** *a.* cast (brass, etc.). **3.** *s.m. Cin:* dissolve; **ouverture en f.,** fade-in, fading in, dissolve-in; **fermeture en f.,** fade-out, dissolve-out; **f. enchaîné,** lap dissolve, cross fade; **f. au gris,** fade grey; **f. soutenu,** fade under. **4.** *s.f. Cu:* **fondue,** fondu(e); **fondue bourguignonne,** meat fondue.

fonger [fɔ̃ʒe], *v.i. def.* (*pr.p.* **fongeant**) *Typ:* (*of paper*) to soak up the ink.

fongia [fɔ̃ʒja], **fongie** [fɔ̃ʒi], *s.f. Coel:* fungia, mushroom coral.

fongibilité [fɔ̃ʒibilite], *s.f. Jur:* fungible nature (of sth.).

fongible [fɔ̃ʒibl̩], *a. Jur:* fungible.

fongicide [fɔ̃ʒisid]. **1.** *a.* fungicidal. **2.** *s.m.* fungicide.

fongicole [fɔ̃ʒikɔl], *a. Ent:* fungus-dwelling.

fongiforme [fɔ̃ʒifɔrm], *a.* fungiform; mushroom-shaped.

fongique [fɔ̃ʒik], *a.* fungic, fungal; *Med:* **intoxication f.,** fungus poisoning.

fongistatique [fɔ̃ʒistatik], *a.* mycostatic, fungistatic.

fongivore [fɔ̃ʒivɔːr], *a.* fungivorous, fungus-feeding.

fongoïde [fɔ̃gɔid], *a.* fungoid (tumour, etc.).

fongosité [fɔ̃gɔzite], *s.f. Med:* fungosity.

fongueux, -euse [fɔ̃gø, -øːz], *a. Med:* fungous (growth, etc.).

fongus [fɔ̃gyːs], *s.m. Med: Vet:* fungus (growth).

fontaine [fɔ̃tɛn], *s.f.* **1** (*a*) spring; pool (of running water); *Myth:* **la F. de Jouvence,** the Fountain of Youth; *Prov:* **il ne faut jamais dire: f., je ne boirai pas de ton eau,** we never know what the future holds for us; you never can tell; (*b*) spring, source, well; **f. jaillissante,** spout well; **f. de boue,** mud spring; *Geol:* **f. ardente,** fire well; **f. intermittente,** intermittent spring. **2.** fountain; **les fontaines Wallace,** the Wallace drinking fountains (in Paris); *F:* **ouvrir la f.,** to start weeping; *F:* to turn on the taps. **3.** cistern; **f. filtrante, de ménage,** (household) filter; **f. d'arrosage,** water-can (of grindstone). **4.** *Cu:* **faire une f. dans la farine, mettre la farine en f.,** to make a well, a hollow, in the flour. **5.** *Fish:* head cavity (of sperm whale). **6.** *N.Arch:* **f. de bossoir,** davit pedestal, davit stand.

fontainier [fɔ̃tenje], *s.m.* **1.** fountain-maker, filter-maker; dealer in, erector of, repairer of, fountains, filters, pumps, etc. **2.** *Adm:* turncock. **3.** well borer, sinker.

fontanelle [fɔ̃tanɛl], *s.f. Anat:* fontanel(le) (of the cranium).

fontange [fɔ̃tɑ̃ːʒ], *s.f. A.Cost:* fontange.

Fontarabie [fɔ̃tarabi], *Pr.n. Geog:* Fuenterrabia.

fonte[1] [fɔ̃ːt], *s.f.* **1.** (*a*) melting; **f. des neiges,** melting, thawing, of the snow; **eaux de f.,** melt-water; (*b*) *Hort:* **f. des semis,** damping-off (of seedlings); (*c*) *Hist:* **fontes d'argenterie,** melting down of plate; (*d*) smelting (of ore); (*e*) casting, founding; **jeter du métal en f.,** to cast metal; **pièces de f.,** castings; **brut de f.,** rough cast, (just) as cast; **venu de f. (avec),** cast integral (with), cast in one piece (with); **cylindres venus de f. ensemble,** cylinders cast in one piece. **2.** (*a*) reduced metal (which collects in crucible of furnace); (*b*) **(fer de) f., f. de fer, f. moulée,** cast iron; **fonte (en gueuse, brute),** pig (iron); **f. de moulage,** foundry pig; **f. alliée,** alloy cast iron; **f. d'acier,** cast steel; **f. aciérée,** semi-steel; **f. blanche,** white (pig) iron; **f. grise, entectique,** grey (pig) iron; **f. noire,** black (pig) iron; **f. truitée,** mottled (pig) iron; **f. douce,** soft (cast, pig) iron; **f. dure,** hard (cast, pig) iron; **f. d'affinage,** converter pig, conversion pig; **f. malléable,** malleable (cast, pig) iron; **f. spéculaire,** spiegel; **f. trempée (en coquille),** chilled (cast) iron; **pièce en f.,** casting; **poêle en f.,** cast-iron stove; **saumon de f.,** iron pig. **3.** *Typ:* fount.

fonte[2], *s.f.* **1.** (saddle) holster (for pistol, revolver). **2.** *A: Aut:* leather pocket.

fontenaisien, -ienne [fɔ̃tnezjɛ̃, -jɛn], *a. & s. Geog:* (native, inhabitant) of (i) Fontenay-aux-Roses; (ii) Fontenay-le-Comte.

fontenier [fɔ̃tenje], *s.m.* = FONTAINIER.

fontinal, -aux [fɔ̃tinal, -o], *a.* **projet f.,** scheme for the supply of drinking water.

fontinalis [fɔ̃tinalis], *s.m. Moss:* fontinalis; water moss.

fontis [fɔ̃ti], *s.m.* subsidence.

fonts [fɔ̃], *s.m.pl. Ecc:* **f. (baptismaux),** font; **tenir un enfant sur les f. (baptismaux),** to stand sponsor, godfather, godmother, to a child; *F:*

A: **tenir qn sur les f.,** (i) to put searching questions to s.o.; (ii) to have much to say about s.o.

foot [fut], *s.m. F:* (*a*) soccer; (*b*) **jouer au f.,** to kick a ball about, play beach football; **jouer au p'tit f.,** to play pin-table football.

football [futbol, -bɔl], *s.m.* (association) football; *F:* **f.-association,** soccer.

footballeur, footballer [futbolœːr], *s.m.* footballer.

footing [futiŋ], *s.m.* walking (training or exercise); **avant le petit déjeuner une heure de f.,** an hour's constitutional before breakfast; **course de f.,** walking race.

for[1] [fɔːr], *s.m.* **1.** *A:* tribunal. **2. le f. intérieur,** the conscience; **dans, en, son f. intérieur,** in his heart of hearts, in his innermost heart; **dans mon f. intérieur je n'étais pas sans inquiétude,** within myself, inwardly, I was somewhat anxious. **3. f. ecclésiastique,** temporal jurisdiction of the church.

for[2], *s.m. A.Jur:* **privilège du f.,** benefit of clergy.

for[3], *a.inv. Com:* free on rail.

forable [fɔrabl̩], *a. Min:* drillable.

forage [fɔraːʒ], *s.m.* **1.** drilling, boring (of metal, well, etc.); sinking (of well); *Surg:* opening (of obstructed canal); **surveillant de f.,** driller; *F:* tool pusher; *Min:* **tige de f.,** drill-pipe; **installation de f.,** drilling rig; **tour de f.,** derrick; **f. à curage, continu, à injection,** hydraulic circulation system; **f. à la grenaille,** shot-drilling; **f. de reconnaissance,** wildcatting. **2.** borehole, drill hole; **f. de reconnaissance,** wildcat (well).

forain, -aine [fɔrɛ̃, -ɛn]. **1.** *a.* (from) outside, foreign; **propriétaire f.,** non-resident landowner; *Nau:* **mouillage f.,** open berth; **rade foraine,** open roadstead. **2.** *a. & s.* itinerant; **théâtre f., spectacle f.,** travelling theatre, travelling show (at a fair); **(acteur) f.,** strolling player; **fête foraine,** fun fair; **(marchand) f.,** (i) packman, pedlar, hawker; *Jur:* itinerant vendor; (ii) stall keeper, booth keeper (at a fair, etc.); *A:* **photographie foraine,** tintype, ferrotype, photography.

foramen [fɔramɛn], *s.m. Anat:* foramen; *Bot:* micropyle.

foraminé [fɔramine], *a. Anat:* foraminate(d); perforated.

foraminifères [fɔraminifɛːr], *s.m.pl. Prot: Paleont:* Foraminifera.

forant [fɔrɑ̃], *s.m. N.Arch:* stage pole (in shipyard).

forban [fɔrbɑ̃], *s.m.* corsair, pirate, buccaneer; (*of financier, etc.*) bandit; **f. littéraire,** pirate, plagiarist.

forbannir [fɔrbaniːr], *v.tr. A.Jur:* to banish.

forbannissement [fɔrbanismɑ̃], *s.m. A.Jur:* banishment.

forbésite [fɔrbezit], *s.f. Miner:* forbesite.

forçable [fɔrsabl̩], *a.* (position) that can be forced, stormed.

forcade [fɔrkad], *s.f. Fish:* oyster-fishing with a fork.

forçage [fɔrsaːʒ], *s.m.* **1.** *Hort:* forcing (of plant, etc.). **2.** *Num:* excess in weight (of coin). **3.** *Ven:* running down (of stag), bringing to bay.

forcalquiérien, -ienne [fɔrkalkjerjɛ̃, -jɛn], *a. & s. Geog:* (native, inhabitant) of Forcalquier.

forçat [fɔrsa], *s.m.* **1.** *A:* galley slave; **chaîne de forçats,** chain-gang. **2.** convict; *F:* **mener une vie de f.,** to drudge and slave.

force [fɔrs], *s.f.* **1.** strength, force, vigour; (*a*) **f. d'une personne, d'un mur, d'une corde, du vent,** strength of a person, of a wall, of a rope, of the wind; **f. d'âme,** strength (in adversity); **f. de caractère,** strength of character; **s'il avait plus de f. de caractère,** if he had more backbone; **les fabricants sont la f. du pays,** manufacturers are the backbone of the country; **mourir dans la f. de l'âge,** to die in the prime of life, in the full vigour of manhood; **être à bout de forces,** to be exhausted, at the end of one's tether; **reprendre des, ses, forces,** to regain strength, to recruit (one's strength); **ranimer, réparer, les forces de qn,** to revive s.o.'s strength; **travailler de toutes ses forces, de toute sa f.,** to work with all one's strength, to work all out, for all one is worth; **y aller de toutes ses forces,** to go at it tooth and nail, hammer and tongs, for all one is worth; **elle se débattait de toutes ses forces,** she fought like a wildcat; **elle n'avait plus la f. de répondre,** she had no strength left to answer; **en f.,** by brute force; (*of pers., animal*) **taillé en f.,** powerfully built; *Const:* **(jambe de) f.,** force piece, strut; *Mec:* **f. de résistance à la tension,** tensile strength; (*b*) **il est d'une belle f. au tennis,** he is a crack tennis player; **ils sont de f. (égale),** they are equally matched, well matched; **boxeur de première f.,** first-rate, first-class, boxer; **il est de f. à vous renverser,** he is strong enough to overthrow you; **se sentir de f. à soutenir la lutte,** to feel equal to the contest; **vous n'êtes pas de f. à vous mesurer avec lui,** you are no match for him; he is too much for you; **je ne me sens pas de f. à faire cela,** I don't feel up to, equal to, doing it; **vous sentez-vous de f. à faire vingt kilomètres à pied?** are you game for a twenty-kilometre walk? **tour de f.,** tour de force, feat (of strength or skill); **travailleur de f.,** heavy worker; (*c*) force, violence; **f. majeure,** circumstances outside one's control, force majeure; **faire appel à la f.,** to resort to force; **faire qch. de vive f.,** to do sth. by sheer, main, force; **entrer, pénétrer, de f., par f., dans une maison,** to force one's way into a house; **entrer de f. dans l'ascenseur,** to squash into the lift; **faire entrer qch. de f. dans qch.,** to force sth. into sth.; **retenir qn de f.,** to detain s.o. forcibly; **faire f. sur (un câble, etc.)** to bring a strain on (a cable, etc.); *Nau:* **faire f. de voiles,** to carry a press of sail(s), to cram on sail, to crowd on (all) sail; **faire f. de rames,** to row, pull, hard; **f. lui fut d'obéir,** he was obliged to obey, he had no alternative, no option, but to obey; **f. était d'accepter,** one could not avoid accepting, one had to accept; **f. resta à la police,** the police won the day; **céder à la f.,** to act under duress; to be forced to yield, to give way; **verser une somme par f.,** to pay a sum of money under compulsion; to be forced to hand over a sum of money; **ma femme voulait à toute f. faire appeler un médecin,** my wife was all for calling in a doctor; *Prov:* **la f. prime le droit; f. passe droit,** might is right; *adv.phr.* **de gré ou de f.,** willy-nilly; by fair means or foul; **de toute f. il nous faut . . .,** we absolutely must . . .; **à toute f.,** in spite of all opposition; **il veut à toute f. entrer,** he is determined to get in, he is bent on getting in; **il faut à toute f. les retrouver,** we must find them again at all costs. **2.** (*a*) force (of a blow, of the wind); force, strength, drift (of a current); force, power (of a waterfall); force, cogency (of an argument); **les forces de la nature,** the forces of nature; **s'exprimer avec f.,** to express oneself forcefully; **par la f. des choses,** through, by, the force of circumstances; **dans toute la f. du mot,** in every sense, acceptation, of the word; **c'était la f. du sang qui les rapprochait,** it was the call of blood that drew them together; (*b*) *Mec: Ph:* **f. accélératrice, f. d'accélération,** accelerating force; **f. composante,** component force; **forces concourantes,** concurrent forces; **composition des forces,** composition of forces; **f. d'inertie,** vis inertiae, inertia; **f. vive,** kinetic energy, momentum; **acquérir de la f. vive,** to gather momentum; **f. de Lorentz,** Lorentz force; **f. en chevaux,** horse power; **f. mécanique,** mechanical force; **f. motrice,** motive power, (horse) power; driving, moving, propelling, power; **f. motrice de la vapeur,** steam power; **f. locomotrice,** locomotive power; **f. propulsive,** propelling, propulsive, force; **f. de traction,** (i) tractive power (of locomotive, etc.); (ii) tensile load, stress (on material); **f. tensorielle,** tensor force; **f. tangentielle, f. appliquée à la circonférence,** peripheral force; **f. déviante,** deflecting force (on indicator, etc.); **f. fléchissante,** deflecting force (on beam, etc.); **f. répulsive,** repelling, repellent, repulsive, force, power; force of repulsion; **f. d'attraction,** attraction, attractive force; **f. portante (d'un aimant),** carrying force, lifting capacity, power (of magnet); **f. élévatoire,** lifting power, capacity; *Av:* **f. de sustentation,** lifting force, power; *Av: Aer:* **f. ascensionnelle,** static lift, buoyancy; (*c*) *El:* **f. électrique,** electric power; *F:* **la force,** power; **prise de f.,** power point; **ligne de transport de f.,** power cable, power line; **f. électromotrice,** electromotive force; **f. thermo-électrique,** thermo-electromotive force; **f. magnétique,** magnetic force; **f. magnétomotrice,** magneto-motive force; (*d*) *Atom.Ph:* **f. nucléaire,** nuclear force; **f. nucléaire d'attraction, de répulsion,** nuclear attraction, repulsion; **f. (nucléaire) centrale, non centrale,** central, non-central, (nuclear) force; **f. de cohésion,** cohesive force, power; **f. disruptive,** disruptive force, fission-producing force; **f. d'échange,** exchange force; (*e*) **f. d'un régiment,** strength of a regiment. **3.** (*a*) *Mil: etc:* **la f. armée,** the military; **faire appel à la f. armée,** to call out the military, the troops; **les forces armées, les forces militaires,** the armed forces; the services; **composition des forces armées,** force structure; **planification des forces armées,** force planning; **forces aériennes,** air forces; **f. de protection aérienne,** air cover; **forces aéronavales,** fleet air arm, naval air force; *U.S:* naval air arm; **forces navales,** naval forces, sea forces; **forces terrestres,** ground forces, land forces; **forces affectées,** assigned forces; **forces prévues pour affectation,** earmarked forces; **f. d'intervention,** (i) *Mil:* mobile force, field force; (ii) *Navy:* task force; **f. de frappe,** striking force; **les forces en présence,** the opposing forces; **victorieux contre des forces supérieures,** victorious against odds; **nous étions là, nous sommes arrivés, en force(s),** we turned out, arrived, in (full) force; (*b*) **la force publique, les forces de police, les forces de l'ordre,** the police force. **4.** *a.inv.* **f. gens,** a great number of, a lot of, (very) many, people; **boire f. bière,** to drink large amounts, considerable quantities, of beer. **5.** (*a*) *adv.phr.* **à f.** (i) *A:* very much, extremely; (ii) *F:* finally; **à f. il a fini par y arriver,** he finally arrived; he finally got it; (*b*) *prep.phr.* **à f. de;** (i) by dint of, by means of; **à f. de travailler il a réussi,** by dint of hard work he succeeded; **à f. de volonté,** by sheer force of will; **à force de travailler on s'épuise,** through too much work you become exhausted; **à f. de mille peines on remit l'embarcation à flot,** with an enormous amount of trouble the boat was floated off; **à f. de répéter,** by constant repetition; **cela finit par lasser à f. d'être répété,** things become tiring through constant repetition; **il s'est enroué à f. de crier,** he shouted himself hoarse; (ii) **lever un fardeau à f. de bras,** to lift a weight by sheer strength (of arm).

forcé [fɔrse], *a.* forced. **1.** (*a*) **emprunt f.,** compulsory loan; **vente forcée,** forced sale; **culture forcée des légumes,** forcing of vegetables; *Mch:* **tirage f.,** forced, artificial, draught; *Av:* **atterrissage f.,** forced landing; *Jur:* **travaux forcés,** hard labour; **mariage f.,** *F:* shotgun wedding; (*b*) *Mil:* **avancer à marches forcées,** to advance by forced marches. **2.** strained; **cœur f.,** strained heart; **exemple f.,** far-fetched example; **rire f.,** forced, unnatural, laugh; **sourire f.,** forced, wry, smile; **amabilité forcée,** affected, put-on, amiability. **3.** *F:* **c'est f.!** it's inevitable!

forcement [fɔrsəmɑ̃], *s.m.* **1.** (*a*) forcing; **introduire qch. à f.,** to force sth. in; (*b*) forcing open, breaking open; **f. de blocus,** blockade running. **2.** *Adm:* **f. en, de, recettes,** compulsion to make good the taxes officials have failed to collect. **3.** *Rail:* emergency addition of carriages to a regular passenger train.

forcément [fɔrsemɑ̃], *adv.* perforce. **1.** under compulsion; **ne faire la guerre que f.,** to make war only under compulsion; **c'est f. que je vous quitte,** I am leaving you because I must. **2.** necessarily, inevitably; **vous réussirez f.,** you are bound to succeed; **ce qu'il dit n'est pas f. ce qu'il pense,** what he says is not necessarily what he thinks.

forcené, -ée [fɔrsəne]. **1.** *a.* frantic, mad; **une rage forcenée le secouait,** he was shaking with furious rage; **nationalisme f.,** exaggerated, insane, nationalism, nationalism run mad. **2.** *s.* madman, madwoman; person out of his, her, senses, mind; **se conduire comme un f.,** to carry on like a madman.

forcener [fɔrsəne], *v.i.* (*of storm, etc.*) to rage; *A:* to run mad.

forceps [fɔrsɛps], *s.m. Obst: Ent:* forceps.

forcer [fɔrse], *v.tr.* (**je forçai(s); n. forçons**) to force. **1.** to compel; **f. un vote,** to coerce an assembly into voting a measure; **f. la main à qn,** to force s.o.'s hand; **f. le respect de qn,** to compel respect from s.o.; **son travail force notre admiration,** his work compels our admiration; **f. qn à,** *occ.* **de, faire qch.,** to force, compel, s.o. to do sth.; **f. une nation à entrer en guerre,** to force a nation into war; **il me força à accepter un pourboire,** he forced a tip into my hand; **on les força de payer,** they were made to pay; (*in the passive usu. with* **de**) **être forcé de faire qch.,** to be forced to do sth.; (*but*) **j'y suis bien forcé,** I cannot avoid (doing) it. **2.** (*a*) **forcer qn, qch.,** to deal violently with, to do violence to, s.o., sth.; **f. une femme,** to violate, rape, a woman; **f. un planton,** to force a sentry; *F:* **f. la consigne,** to force one's way in, to disregard orders; **f. un obstacle,** to overcome an obstacle; **f. l'ennemi,** to break through the enemy; **f. un poste,** to take a post by storm, by force; **f. une serrure,** to force a lock; **f. le couvercle,** to wrench the lid open; **f. la caisse,** to break into the till; **f. une porte,** to break open a door; **f. sa prison,** to break jail; **f. la porte de qn,** to force one's way in; **f. les lois,** to strain the law; **f. le sens,** to strain, twist the meaning; *Lit:* **je ne veux point f. ton inclination,** I want to leave you free to marry whom you choose; I don't want to force a husband on you; (*of horse*) **f. la main,** to bolt; *Nau:* **f. la quaran-**

taine, to break the quarantine regulations; **f. le blocus**, to run the blockade; *Mth:* **f. un chiffre**, to correct the last figure (to give a result to so many places of decimals); (*b*) to strain (mast); to bend (connecting-rod, etc.); to buckle (plate); **se f. l'épaule**, to wrench, strain, one's shoulder; **se f. le cœur**, to strain one's heart; **f. sa voix**, to force one's voice; *F:* **f. la note**, to overdo it; **f. un cheval**, to overwork, override, cram, a horse; **f. la marche, le pas**, to force the pace, increase one's pace, to step out; **f. l'allure**, to increase speed; **f. des fleurs**, to force flowers; *Ven:* **f. un cerf**, to run down a stag, to bring a stag to bay; (*c*) **f. la dose d'un médicament**, to increase the dose of a medicine; *Phot:* **f. la durée de pose**, to increase the exposure. **3.** *v.i.* (*a*) **f. de voiles**, to crowd on, cram on, sail; **f. sur les avirons**, to strain at the oars; **f. de vitesse**, to increase speed; **le vent force**, the wind is rising; **il avait forcé sur le whisky**, he had overdone the whisky; *Cards:* (*at bridge*) **f. sur l'annonce de qn**, to overcall, to over-bid, s.o.; (*b*) *F:* **cette porte force**, this door is sticking, jamming.

se forcer. **1.** to overstrain oneself; **se forcer en portant un fardeau**, to strain, rick, oneself carrying sth. heavy. **2. je me suis forcé pour ne rien dire**, I did violence to my feelings, I restrained my feelings, and said nothing; **se forcer à rire**, to force a laugh.

forcerie [fɔrsəri], *s.f. Hort:* (*a*) forcing house, hothouse; **f. de raisins**, vinery; (*b*) forcing bed.

forces [fɔrs], *s.f.pl. A: Tls:* spring shears.

forcet [fɔrsɛ], *s.m.* whipcord.

forceur, -euse [fɔrsœːr, -øːz], *s.* forcer; (*a*) **f. de blocus**, blockade runner; (*b*) producer of forced vegetables, flowers, etc.

forcière [fɔrsjɛːr], *s.f. Pisc:* breeding-pool.

forcine [fɔrsin], *s.f.* bulge at the junction of a major branch with the trunk of a tree.

forcing [fɔrsiŋ], *s.m.* **1.** *Sp:* sustained pressure. **2.** *Cards:* forcing.

forcipressure [fɔrsiprɛsyːr], *s.f. Surg:* forcipressure.

forcipule [fɔrsipyl], *s.f. Arach:* chelicera.

forcir [fɔrsiːr], *v.i. F:* **1.** to get fat; to put on weight. **2.** (*of a child*) to grow (strong); **le vent forcit**, the wind grows stronger, is strengthening. **3.** (*of young horse, dog*) to furnish.

forclore [fɔrklɔːr], *v.tr.* (*used only in the infinite and p.p.* **forclos**) *Jur:* **1.** to foreclose (mortgage). **2.** to bar, preclude, estop (**de**, from).

forclusion [fɔrklyzjɔ̃], *s.f.* estoppel; *Jur:* **1.** foreclosure (of mortgage). **2.** barring, preclusion (**de**, from).

forer [fɔre], *v.tr.* to drill, bore, perforate; **f. un puits**, to sink a well; **f. pour rechercher du pétrole**, to drill for oil; **f. un tunnel à travers . . .**, to drive a tunnel through . . .; **f. un canon**, to bore a gun; **machine à f.**, (machine) drill; **clef forée**, piped key.

forerie [fɔr(ə)ri], *s.f.* **1.** *Ind:* drilling shop. **2.** (*a*) drill press, drilling machine; (*b*) gun lathe. **3.** boring (of gun barrel).

forestage [fɔrɛstaːʒ], *s.m.* **1.** right of pasturage in a forest; forest right. **2.** *A:* cheminage. **3.** quit rent; forest due.

forestier, -ière [fɔrɛstje, -jɛːr]. **1.** *a.* pertaining to a forest; **exploitation forestière**, lumbering; **massif f.**, forest-clad mountain group; (**garde**) **f.**, forester, forest ranger; **maison forestière**, forester's lodge. **2.** *s.m.* forester.

foret [fɔrɛ], *s.m.* (*a*) drill, bit; **f.** (**de dentiste**), (dentist's) drill; **f. à droite, à gauche**, right-hand, left-hand, drill; **f. à angle**, angle drill, corner drill; **f. à hélice, f. hélicoïdal**, twist drill; **f. à langue d'aspic, f.** (**en**) **fer de lance**, flat drill, arrow-headed drill, spearhead drill; **f. à** (**l'**)**archet**, drill with bow; **f. à rallonge**, extension drill; **f. flexible**, snake drill; **f. à centrer**, centre drill; **f. aléseur**, reamer bit; **f. pour tour**, chuck drill; **perceuse à forets multiples**, gang driller; **queue de f.**, drill shank; **f. à queue conique**, taper-shank twist drill; **course du f.**, drill stroke; (*b*) **f. à bois**, gimlet; **f. de charpentier**, auger; (*c*) (brace) bit; **f. à centre, à téton**, centre bit.

forêt [fɔrɛ], *s.f.* forest; **forêts sèches**, dry deciduous forests; **f. tropicale décidue**, deciduous tropical forest; **f. des moussons**, monsoon forest; **f. épineuse**, thorn forest; **f. primitive**, primeval forest; **région couverte de forêts**, forested region, country; **connaissance de la f.**, woodcraft; *Adm:* **le service des Eaux et Forêts** = the Forestry Commission; *Prov:* **l'arbre vous cache la f.**, you can't see the wood for the trees; **une f. de mâts**, a forest of masts; **f. de cheveux**, shock, thick crop, of hair; *Arch:* **f. de comble**, timbering (of cathedral, etc.); *Geog:* **la F.-Noire**, the Black Forest; *A:* **c'est une vraie f. de Bondy**, it's a regular Hounslow Heath.

foretage [fɔrtaːʒ], *s.m.* rent for quarrying rights.

forêtain [fɔrɛtɛ̃], *s.m. Dial:* orchardist.

forêt-galerie [fɔrɛgalri], *s.f.* gallery-forest; *pl. forets-galeries.*

forêt-parc [fɔrɛpark], *s.f. For: Geog:* open forest; *pl. forêts-parcs.*

foreur [fɔrœːr], *s.m.* borer, driller; **f. de puits artésiens**, Artesian-well engineer; *Petroleum Ind:* **f. d'exploration**, wildcatter.

foreuse [fɔrøːz], *s.f.* **1.** drill(ing machine), machine drill; **f. à appui**, breast drill; **f. à main**, hand drill; **f. à diamant, à pointe de diamant**, diamond drill. **2.** *Min: etc:* rock drill; **f. à câble**, churn drill.

forézien, -ienne [fɔrezjɛ̃, -jɛn], *a. & s. Geog:* (native, inhabitant) of (i) Feurs, (ii) the Forez region.

forfaire [fɔrfɛːr]. **1.** *v.ind.tr.* (*conj. like* FAIRE; *used only in the infinitive, the compound tenses, and occ. the pr.ind.sg.*) to be false to (sth.); **f. à son devoir**, to fail in one's duty; **f. à l'honneur**, to forfeit one's honour; **f. à sa parole**, to break one's word. **2.** *v.tr. A:* (*a*) to forfeit (possessions); (*b*) to incur (fine).

forfait[1] [fɔrfɛ], *s.m.* heinous crime.

forfait[2], *s.m.* contract; **avoir un f. pour l'exécution de travaux**, to have a contract for the carrying out of some work; **à f.**, on a contract basis; **travail à f.**, (i) work by contract, contract work; (ii) (*for workman*) job work; **prix à f.**, price as per contract; lump sum; **acheter, vendre, qch. à f.**, to buy, sell, sth. (i) outright, (ii) as a job lot; **vente à f.**, (i) outright sale; (ii) *St.Exch:* selling of futures; **endossement à f.**, endorsement without recourse; **voyage à f.**, inclusive, package, tour, *U.S:* all-expense tour; *Post:* **affranchi à f.**, bulk-rate prepaid.

forfait[3], *s.m. Turf: etc:* fine, forfeit (paid for scratching a horse); **déclarer f. pour un cheval**, to scratch a horse; **match gagné par f.**, match won by default; *F:* walk-over; **déclarer f.**, (i) *Sp: etc:* to withdraw from a competition; (ii) to give up; to back out; to throw in one's hand.

forfaitaire [fɔrfɛtɛːr], *a.* contractual; **marché f.**, (transaction by) contract, outright purchase; **paiement f.**, lump sum; **acheter qch. à un prix f.**, to buy sth. outright; **prix f.**, contract price; price of a job lot; all-in price; *F:* **voyage à prix f.**, package tour; *Const: etc:* **convention f.**, contract (for work).

forfaitairement [fɔrfɛtɛrmɑ̃], *adv.* contractually.

forfaiteur [fɔrfɛtœːr], *s.m.* maladministrator; *A:* prevaricator.

forfaiture [fɔrfɛtyːr], *s.f.* **1.** misuse, abuse (of authority); maladministration; *A:* prevarication. **2. f. au devoir, à l'honneur**, breach of duty, of honour; **je ne saurais, sans une véritable f., me dérober à cette obligation**, I cannot, without a definite breach of faith, shirk this obligation. **3.** *A:* felony (of a vassal to his lord).

forfanterie [fɔrfɑ̃tri], *s.f.* impudent boast(ing); bragging, piece of brag; braggadocio; *F:* line-shooting.

forficule [fɔrfikyl], *s.f. Ent:* forficula; earwig.

forficulidés [fɔrfikylide], *s.m.pl. Ent:* Forficulidae.

forgage [fɔrgaːʒ], **forgagement** [fɔrgaʒmɑ̃], *s.m. Jur:* debtor's equity of repurchase of goods sold by process of law.

forge [fɔrʒ], *s.f.* **1.** (*a*) forge, smith's hearth; **f. portative, de campagne**, portable forge; **f. à ventilateur**, fan forge; **f.** (**à la**) **catalane**, Catalan forge; **feu de f.**, forge hearth; **brut de f.**, rough forged; as forged; **venu de f.** (**avec**), forged integral (with), in one piece (with); **pièce de f.**, forging; **grosse pièce de f.**, heavy forging; **petite pièce de f.**, light forging; (*b*) **f. maréchale**, smithy; **mener un cheval à la f.**, to take a horse to the blacksmith's; **ouvrage de f.**, smith's work; **f. de serrurier**, locksmith's workshop; (*c*) forging mill. **2.** (*a*) *A: usu.pl.* ironworks; **maître de forges**, ironmaster; (*b*) **le Comité des Forges**, the French association of heavy industries (employers).

forgeable [fɔrʒabl̩], *a.* forgeable (metal).

forgeage [fɔrʒaːʒ], *s.m. Metalw:* forging, smithing; **f. par matriçage**, die forging; **f. par choc**, impact, drop, forging; **f. par compression**, compression forging; **f. par martelage**, hammer forging; **f. par refoulement**, upset forging, upsetting; **f. par roulage**, roll forging.

forgement [fɔrʒəmɑ̃], *s.m. A: Metalw:* forging.

forger [fɔrʒe], *v.* (**je forgeai(s)**; **n. forgeons**) to forge. **1.** *v.tr.* (*a*) **f. à chaud, à froid**, to forge hot, cold; **fer forgé**, wrought iron; **acier forgé au pilon**, hammered steel; **presse à f.**, forging press; *F:* **f. des vers**, to hammer out verse; **f. les fers** (**de qn**), to enslave (s.o.); *Prov:* **c'est en forgeant qu'on devient forgeron**, practice makes perfect; (*b*) **f. un document**, to forge a document; **f. une histoire, une excuse**, to fabricate, make up, invent, a story, an excuse; **f. des nouvelles**, to invent, manufacture, news; **f. des mots**, to coin words; **f. une accusation contre qn**, to concoct, trump up, a charge against s.o.; **se f. des arguments spécieux**, to trump up specious arguments; **il se forge une félicité sans nuages**, he conjures up visions of cloudless bliss. **2.** *v.i.* (*of horses*) to forge, click, overreach.

forgerie [fɔrʒəri], *s.f.* **1.** *A:* forging, smith's work, smithery, smithing. **2.** forgery, forged document.

forgeron [fɔrʒərɔ̃], *s.m.* **1.** (*a*) (black)smith; (*b*) iron-smith. **2.** *Amph: F:* **f. du Brésil**, Brazilian (black)smith (tree frog). **3.** *Ich: F:* (*a*) John Dory; (*b*) chaetodon, butterfly fish.

forgeur, -euse [fɔrʒœːr, -øːz], *s.* **1.** inventor, maker up, fabricator (of news, of lies); coiner (of words). **2.** *s.m.* blacksmith's assistant, apprentice. **3.** *s.f.* **forgeuse**, forging-press.

forjet [fɔrʒɛ], *s.m.*, **forjeture** [fɔrʒətyːr], *s.f.* **1.** *Arch:* projection; part of building jutting out. **2.** forward bulge (of wall, etc.).

forjeter [fɔrʒəte] (*conj. like* JETER) **1.** *v.tr. Arch:* to construct (wall, etc.) with projections. **2.** *v.i.* (*a*) *Arch:* to project, to jut out; (*b*) (*of wall, etc.*) to bulge out.

se forjeter, (*a*) *Arch:* to project; (*b*) to bulge out.

forlan, -ane [fɔrlɑ̃, -an]. **1.** *a. & s. Geog:* Friulian. **2.** *s.f. Danc:* **forlane**, forlana.

forlancer [fɔrlɑ̃se], *v.tr. Ven: O:* to start (quarry).

forligner [fɔrliɲe], *v.tr.* **1.** *A:* to disgrace one's ancestors, ancestry. **2.** *Lit:* to forfeit one's honour.

forlonger [fɔrlɔ̃ʒe], *v.tr. Ven:* to get ahead of.

formage [fɔrmaːʒ], *s.m. Tchn:* shaping, forming; moulding; **f. par étirage**, forming by drawing.

formal [fɔrmal], *s.m. Ch:* formal.

formaldéhyde [fɔrmaldeid], *s.m. occ. s.f. Ch:* formaldehyde.

formaline [fɔrmalin], *s.f. Ch:* formalin.

formalisation [fɔrmalizasjɔ̃], *s.f.* formalization.

formaliser [fɔrmalize], *v.tr.* to formalize; **logique formalisée**, formal logic.

se formaliser, to take offence; **se f. de qch.**, to take offence, umbrage, at sth.; to take exception to sth.; **il s'est formalisé qu'on ne l'ait pas invité, de ce qu'on ne l'avait pas invité**, he took offence at not being invited.

formalisme [fɔrmalism], *s.m.* **1.** formalism; **f. administratif**, red tape. **2.** *Art: Phil:* formalism.

formaliste [fɔrmalist]. **1.** *a.* formal, formalistic, stiff, punctilious, precise (mind, etc.). **2.** *s.* (*a*) formalist, precisian; conventionalist; stickler for formalities; (*b*) *Phil:* formalist.

formalité [fɔrmalite], *s.f.* **1.** formality, formal procedure; **remplir une f.**, to comply with a formality, to observe a formality; **c'est une pure f.**, it is a mere matter of form; *F:* **sans autre f., sans plus de f.**, without further ado. **2.** *F:* ceremony, ceremoniousness; *esp.* **sans formalité(s)**, without ceremony.

formamide [fɔrmamid], *s.m. Ch:* formamide.

formant [fɔrmɑ̃], *s.m. Ling: Ac:* formant.

formante [fɔrmɑ̃ːt], *s.f. Ling:* formant.

formariage [fɔrmarjaːʒ], *s.m. Mediev.Hist:* marriage out of rank or condition.

format [fɔrma], *s.m.* (*a*) format, form and size (of book); format, size (of paper); **f. de poche**, pocket size; (*b*) *Phot:* size (of plates); **appareil de petit f.**, miniature camera; (*c*) *T.V:* **f. d'images**, aspect ratio of pictures; *Cin:* **f. standard**, standard gauge; (*d*) *Com:* **f. réduit**, small size; **grand f.**, king-size (cigarettes, etc.).

formateur, -trice [fɔrmatœːr, -tris]. **1.** *a.* formative, which forms, fashions; *Ling:* **éléments formateurs**, formative elements. **2.** *s.* former, maker, fashioner; *A:* **Dieu f. de tout ce qui est**, God, maker of all that is.

formatif, -ive [fɔrmatif, -iːv], *a.* formative (suffix, etc.).

formation [fɔrmasjɔ̃], *s.f.* formation. **1.** (*a*) forming; formation; development, production; making up (of trains, plans, etc.); setting (of fruit, etc.); *Com:* striking (of balance); **la f. du monde**, the creation of the world; **f. du caractère**, moulding of character; **les années de f.**, the formative years; **époque, âge, de la f.**, puberty; **une nation en voie de f.**, a nation in the making; **f. de mauvaises habitudes**, formation of bad habits; **f. d'une pellicule à la surface d'un liquide**, formation of a film on the surface of a liquid; *T.V:* **f. de l'image**, image forming; (*b*) education; training; **f. professionnelle**, professional training; **f. professionnelle des adultes**, further education for adults; **je suis historien de f.**, I am a(n) historian

by training; *Av:* **f. des pilotes,** training of pilots; *Mil:* **f. des cadres comme instructeurs,** training of officers and non-commissioned officers as instructors; (*c*) formation (of a language); **la f. du pluriel,** the formation of the plural; **mot de f. récente,** word of recent origin; **mot de, d'une, f. savante,** word of learned origin. **2.** (*a*) make-up (of train, etc.); structure (of rock, etc.); *Geol:* **f. quaternaire,** quaternary formation; **f. sédimentaire,** sedimentary stratum, deposit; (*b*) *Mil: etc:* formation, disposition; **f. articulée,** flexible formation; **f. diluée,** deployed, loose, formation; **f. dispersée,** open formation; **f. dense, f. groupée,** dense formation; **f. serrée,** close formation; **f. en profondeur,** formation in depth; **f. d'approche,** approach formation; **f. d'attaque,** attack formation; **f. de combat,** battle formation, *U.S:* combat formation; **f. de marche, de route,** march, route, road, formation; **f. de défilé,** march-past, *Av:* fly-past, review, formation; **avions en f. triangulaire,** aircraft in triangular formation; (*c*) *Mil: etc:* unit, formation; **f. blindée,** armoured formation; **f. sanitaire,** medical unit; **f. aérienne,** air (force) unit; **formations auxiliaires,** auxiliary units; **se heurter à des formations ennemies,** to run into enemy units, formations; (*d*) *Mil:* **unité de f.,** reserve unit, unit formed on mobilization; (*e*) *Sp:* line-up; (*f*) *Mus:* (pop) group.

formazyle [fɔrmazil], *s.m. Ch:* formazyl.

forme [fɔrm], *s.f.* **1.** form, shape; *pl. F:* (woman's) curves; **le fond et la f. (d'un discours, etc.),** the substance and the form; **formes d'un navire,** lines of a ship; **formes fines,** clean lines; **la statue prend f.,** the statue is taking shape; **des idées prennent f. dans mon esprit,** ideas are taking shape in my mind; **en f. de cloche, d'œuf,** bell-shaped, egg-shaped; **jardin en f. de triangle,** garden in the shape of a triangle; **des arbres de toutes les formes,** trees of all shapes; **donner à l'argile la f. d'une urne,** to shape the clay into an urn; **Jupiter prit la f. d'un cygne,** Jupiter assumed the form of a swan; **un homme de formes athlétiques,** a man of athletic build; **vêtement qui prend la f. du corps, qui épouse les formes,** close-fitting garment; **par la f. il ressemblait à une barrique,** he was shaped like a barrel; **sous la f. d'une nymphe,** in the form, shape, of a nymph; **statistiques sous f. de tableau,** statistics in tabular form; **étudier une affaire sous toutes ses formes,** to consider a matter in all its aspects; *Surv:* **lignes de f. (du terrain),** form lines (of ground); *Pharm:* **à prendre sous la f. de pilules,** to be taken in the form of pills; **sans f.,** shapeless, formless; *A:* **dire qch. par f. d'avertissement,** to say sth. by way of warning. **2.** form, method, of procedure; (*a*) **la quittance est en bonne f.,** the receipt is in order, in proper form; **un reçu en bonne et due f.,** a regular receipt; **formes juridiques,** legal formalities; **les formes établies,** the established procedure; **arrêt cassé pour vice de f.,** judgement quashed on a technical point, on a point of law; **renvoyer qn sans autre f. de procès,** to dismiss s.o. without ceremony; **avertir qn dans les formes,** to give s.o. formal, due, warning; **faire qch. dans les formes,** to do sth. with due ceremony; **pour la f.,** as a matter of form; for form's sake; for the sake of appearances; **question pour la f.,** rhetorical question; **l'invitation est de pure f.,** the invitation is purely, entirely, formal, a matter of form; (*b*) *pl.* manners; **avoir des formes,** to be polite, well-mannered; **manquer de formes,** to be ill-mannered; **c'est un homme qui manque de formes,** he lacks polish; **y mettre les formes,** to be polite; to use tact; (*c*) **être en f.,** to be in form, in condition; **ne pas être en f., être en petite f.,** to be in poor form; **être en pleine f.,** *F:* **être dans une f. à tout casser,** to be in cracking form; **être au meilleur de sa f.,** to be at the top of one's form; **plus en f. que jamais,** in better form than ever; **équipe bien en f.,** team at the top of its form; **l'équipe vient en f.,** the team is getting into form, is coming on. **3.** *Ind:* former, forming block; mould (for cheese, etc.); *Bootm:* (i) last; (ii) shoe tree; *Hatm:* (i) block; (ii) body; (iii) (*of woman's hat*) shape, hood; (iv) crown; *Paperm:* mould, form; **papier à f.,** hand-made paper; **chapeau haut de f.,** top hat; *Dressm:* **jupe en f.,** flared skirt. **4.** (*a*) (bed of sand, etc. under paving stones); (*b*) **f. d'un lièvre,** hare's form. **5.** *Nau:* dock; **f. sèche,** dry dock; **f. de radoub,** graving dock; **f. flottante,** floating dock. **6.** *Typ:* form(e); **serrer une f.,** to lock up a form. **7.** *Vet:* ringbone. **8.** (*a*) *A.Furn:* upholstered form, seat; (*b*) *Ecc.Arch:* choir stall. **9.** *Mth:* quantic.

formé [fɔrme], *a.* formed, full-grown; (*of fruit*) set; **enfant bien f.,** well-formed, well-developed, child; **jeune fille formée,** girl who has arrived at puberty.

forme-écluse [fɔrmeklyːz], *s.f. Nau:* dry dock (with flood-gates at both ends); *pl. formes-écluses.*

formel, -elle [fɔrmɛl], *a.* **1.** formal, strict, express, precise, categorical (rule, order, etc.); **témoignage f.,** positive statement; **promesse formelle,** distinct promise, promise in so many words; **défense formelle,** strict prohibition; **mise en demeure formelle de faire qch.,** peremptory call, summons, or notice to do sth.; **donner un démenti f. à une accusation,** to give a flat, categorical, denial to a charge; **veto f.,** absolute veto. **2.** formal, superficial; **politesse formelle,** formal politeness. **3.** *Lit:* **beauté formelle,** beauty of form (of poem, etc.); *Phil:* **cause formelle,** formal cause.

formellement [fɔrmɛlmɑ̃], *adv.* formally; **il est f. interdit de . . .,** it is absolutely, strictly, expressly, forbidden to . . .; **promettre f.,** to promise distinctly, faithfully.

formène [fɔrmɛn], *s.m. A.Ch:* formene, methane, marsh-gas.

former [fɔrme], *v.tr.* to form. **1.** to make, create; *Gram:* to form (the plural, etc.); **f. une société,** to form a company; **f. des vœux,** to make vows; **f. un projet,** to form, draw up, a plan; **f. des objections,** to raise, formulate, objections; **vapeurs qui forment les nuages,** vapour that forms, composes, the clouds; **les os et les muscles qui forment le corps,** the bones and muscles of which the body is made up, constituted; **les murs forment un carré,** the walls form a square; *Mil:* **f. le carré,** to form square; *Tp:* **f. un numéro,** to dial a number; *Rail:* **f. un train,** to make up a train. **2.** to shape fashion, frame; (*a*) **f. une urne,** to fashion an urn; **f. son style sur celui de X,** to model one's style on X's, on that of X; **lettres mal formées,** badly formed, shaped, letters; (*b*) to bring up, educate (child); to train (pilots, etc.); to school (horse); *Hort:* to train (fruit tree); **f. le caractère d'un enfant,** to mould a child's character; **il a été formé à une rude école,** he has been brought up in a hard school; **son métier l'a formé à être patient,** his job has taught him patience; **cette université a formé des hommes remarquables,** this university has turned out some remarkable men; (*c*) *Tchn:* to form (metal, plastics, etc.); **presse à f.,** forming press.

se former, to form; to take form; **la compagnie se forma en ligne,** the company formed into line; **il se forme un orage,** a storm is gathering; **nos plans se forment,** our plans are taking shape; **le fruit se forme,** the fruit is setting; **l'équipe se forme,** the team is shaking down, is getting into form, is getting into shape; **se f. aux affaires,** to acquire a business training; to get into the way of business; **le train se forme à Toulouse,** the train is made up at Toulouse; **des croûtes se forment autour de la plaie,** scabs are forming, appearing, around the wound.

formeret [fɔrmərɛ], *a. & s.m. Arch:* **(arc) formeret,** wall-rib (of vaulting), formeret.

formette [fɔrmɛt], *s.f. A.Furn:* small bench; small stall (in church).

formeur [fɔrmœːr], *s.m. Ind:* (*pers.*) former.

formiamide [fɔrmjamid], *s.m. Ch:* formamide.

formiate [fɔrmjat], *s.m. Ch:* formate.

Formica [fɔrmika], *s.m. R.t.m:* Formica.

formicage [fɔrmikaːʒ], *s.m. Orn:* anting.

formica-leo [fɔrmikaleo], *s.m. Ent:* myrmeleon; ant-lion.

formicant [fɔrmikɑ̃], *a. Med:* formicant (pulse).

formicariidés [fɔrmikariide], *s.m.pl. Orn:* Formicariidae.

formication [fɔrmikasjɔ̃], *s.f. Med:* formication.

formicidés [fɔrmiside], *s.m.pl. Ent:* Formicidae.

formidable [fɔrmidabl], *a.* (*a*) fearsome, formidable; **conséquences formidables à envisager,** consequences fearful to consider; (*b*) *F:* tremendous; **c'est f.!** well, I never! **elle est f.,** she's (i) fantastic, (ii) smashing, a smasher.

formidablement [fɔrmidabləmɑ̃], *adv.* formidably, tremendously.

formier [fɔrmje], *s.m.* **1.** *Bootm:* last-maker. **2.** *Hatm:* blocker. **3.** *A:* cloth placed on the seat of a bench.

formique [fɔrmik], *a. Ch:* formic (acid).

formogène [fɔrmɔʒɛn], *a.* formol-producing.

formoir [fɔrmwaːr], *s.m. Leath:* smoothing-stick.

formol [fɔrmɔl], *s.m. Ch: Com:* formol; *Leath:* **tannage au f.,** formaldehyde tanning.

formolage [fɔrmɔlaːʒ], *s.m. Ch:* formolizing.

formoler [fɔrmɔle], *v.tr. Ch: Med:* to formolize.

formosan, -ane [fɔrmɔzɑ̃, -an], *a. & s.* **1.** *Geog:* Formosan, Taiwanese. **2.** *Ling: a.* **les parlers formosans,** Formosan, the Formosan languages.

Formose [fɔrmoːz], *Pr.n.f. Geog:* Formosa, Taiwan.

formulable [fɔrmylabl̩], *a.* formul(at)able; that can be formulated; **demande difficilement f.,** request difficult to put into words.

formulaire [fɔrmylɛːr], *s.m.* **1.** (*a*) collection of formulae, formulary; (*b*) pharmacopoeia. **2.** (printed) form, questionnaire.

formulation [fɔrmylasjɔ̃], *s.f.* formulation, expressing (of one's feelings, etc.).

formule [fɔrmyl], *s.f.* **1.** (*a*) *Mth: Ch: Pharm: etc:* formula; *Pharm:* recipe; *F:* **c'est la bonne f.,** that's just what the doctor ordered; **f. dentaire,** dental formula; *Ch:* **f. empirique,** empiric formula; **f. de constitution, rationnelle, développée,** constitutional, structural, graphic, rational formula; (*b*) (set) form of words; (turn of) phrase; formula; **f. finale, f. de politesse,** formal ending used in correspondence; *often Pej:* **f. politique,** political formula; (*c*) **la f. d'un service médical fondé sur . . .,** the type of medical service based upon . . . **2.** *Adm: etc:* (printed) form (to be filled up); *Post:* telegraph form; **f. d'effet de commerce,** form for bill of exchange; **f. de chèque,** cheque form, blank cheque; **f. de quittance(s),** printed form of receipt; **remplir une f.,** to fill up a form.

formuler [fɔrmyle], *v.tr.* (*a*) to formulate; to express (thought, etc.) in a formula; **f. un acte,** to draw up a document in due form, to formulate a document; *Ph: Ch: Mth:* **f. une loi,** to reduce a law to a formula, to formulate a law; *Med:* **f. une ordonnance,** to write out a prescription; (*b*) **f. un souhait,** to express a wish; to put a wish into words; **f. sa position, sa pensée,** to define one's position, one's thought; **f. une plainte,** to lodge, bring forward, a complaint; **f. une proposition,** to formulate a proposal; **f. une règle,** to lay down a rule; **f. ses griefs,** to set forth clearly one's grievances, to state one's grievances categorically.

formyle [fɔrmil], *s.m. Ch:* formyl.

fornicateur, -trice [fɔrnikatœːr, -tris], *s.* fornicator; *f.* fornicatress, *occ.* fornicatrix.

fornication [fɔrnikasjɔ̃], *s.f.* fornication.

fornice [fɔrnis], *s.f. Bot:* fornix.

forniquer [fɔrnike], *v.i.* to fornicate; *F:* to have (sexual) intercourse.

fornix [fɔrniks], *s.m. Anat:* fornix.

Fornoue [fɔrnu], *Pr.n. Geog:* Fornovo di Taro.

forpaiser [fɔrpeze], *v.i.* (*of domestic animal*) to graze outside its normal pasture; (*of wild animal*) to lie up in a distant pasture (when hunted).

forpaisson [fɔrpesɔ̃], *s.m.* offence of grazing pigs in woodland (without permission).

fors [fɔːr], *prep. Lit:* except, save.

forstérite [fɔrsterit], *s.f. Miner:* forsterite.

forsythia [fɔrsitja], *s.m. A:* **forsythie** [fɔrsiti], *s.f. Bot:* forsythia.

fort [fɔːr]. I. *a.* **1.** (*a*) strong; **f. comme un Turc, comme un bœuf,** as strong as a horse; **recourir à la manière forte,** to have recourse to strong action, to violence; **partisans de la manière forte,** partisans of, believers in, strong measures, violent action; **je suis plus f. des bras que vous,** I am stronger in the arms than you; *Equit:* **cheval f. en bouche,** hard-mouthed horse; *Nau:* **navire f. de côté,** stiff ship; **trouver plus f. que soi,** to meet one's match; **être f. de qch.,** to rely on sth. for one's strength, confidence, assurance; to get one's strength from sth.; **f. de mon innocence je ne prenais pas garde aux accusations,** in the full assurance of my own innocence I took no notice of the accusations; **f. de la popularité dont il jouissait,** strong in the popularity he enjoyed; **f. de votre aide précieuse,** strengthened, supported, by your valuable help; **c'est une forte tête,** (i) he, she, is a very able person; (ii) he, she, is very stubborn; (iii) he, she, has a good head (for drink); **esprit f.,** (i) *A:* free-thinker rationalist; (ii) sceptic; non-conformist; **être f. en mathématiques,** to be good at mathematics; **il est plus f. que moi en français,** he is better at French than I am; **pas très f.,** not very able; *F:* **être f. en thème,** to be (i) good at school work, a bookworm, (ii) a swot; **il est le plus f. de sa classe,** he's the best in his form; **être f. à tous les jeux,** to be good at games; *P:* **f. en gueule,** loud-mouthed; *Fin:* **devise forte,** strong currency; **semelle forte,** stout sole; **terre forte,** heavy soil; **tabac f.,** strong tobacco; **beurre f.,** rancid butter; **avoir une forte odeur,** to have a strong smell; to smell high; **forte nourriture,** high diet; **boissons fortes,** strong drink;

forte fièvre, high fever; **fortes chaleurs,** intense heat; **vent f.,** high wind; *Nau:* **forte brise,** stiff breeze, moderate gale; **pluie forte,** heavy rain; **forte mer,** heavy sea, surging sea; **d'une voix forte,** in a loud voice; *Mus:* **temps f.,** strong beat; **c'est plus f. que moi!** I can't help it! *F.* **c'est (par) trop f.!** it's really too bad! that's a bit thick! *F:* **c'est un peu f.!** *P:* **c'est un peu f. de café, de chicorée!** that's a bit thick, a bit steep! *F:* **en voilà une forte!** (i) well . . .! that's beyond anything! well, of all things . . .! (ii) of all the colossal lies . . .! **ce qu'il y a de plus f., c'est que . . .,** (i) the most outrageous, (ii) the best, part of it is that . . .; (*b*) **ville, place, forte,** fortified town; fortress; (*c*) **se faire f. de faire qch.,** to engage, undertake, to do sth. (**fort** *may remain inv.*) **elles se font f., fortes, de le retrouver,** they undertake to find him again; *Jur:* **se porter f.** (*inv.*) **pour qn,** to stand as security for s.o., to answer for s.o. **2.** large; **femme forte,** stout woman; **avoir le nez un peu f.,** to have rather a large nose; **lèvres fortes,** full lips; **bois f.,** stout timber; **forte barbe,** heavy beard; **il y avait une forte rosée,** there was a heavy dew; **les blés sont forts,** there is a heavy crop of wheat; *N.Arch:* **navire f. en bois,** ship of heavy scantling; **une trop forte commande,** an unduly large order; **forte somme,** large sum of money; **fortes ressources,** ample means; **forte différence,** great difference; **forte dose,** powerful dose; **f. buveur,** heavy drinker; **forte perte,** heavy loss; **perdre une forte somme,** to lose heavily; **dans une forte mesure,** to a considerable extent; **forte hausse, baisse, des prix,** sharp, big, rise, drop, in prices; **forte pente,** steep gradient; **armée forte de cinq mille hommes,** army of five thousand men, five thousand strong; **navire f. en artillerie,** ship with heavy ordnance; *Com:* **prix f.,** full price, catalogue price, advertised price; published price; *P:* **il a pris une forte cuite,** he got thoroughly sozzled.

II. **fort,** *adv.* **1.** strongly; **frapper f.,** to strike hard; **tirer f. la sonnette,** to pull the bell hard; **la pluie tombe plus f.,** the rain is coming down harder; **les affaires ne vont pas f.,** business is in a bad way; *F:* **y aller f.,** (i) to go hard at it; (ii) to exaggerate; to overdo it; **crier f.,** to shout loudly; **crier de plus en plus f.,** to shout louder and louder. **2.** very, extremely; **il a été f. mécontent,** he was highly, extremely, displeased; **vous vous trompez f.,** you are greatly mistaken; **j'ai f. à faire,** I have a great deal to do.

III. **fort,** *s.m.* **1.** (*a*) strong part; forte (of blade, etc.); **le f. et le faible de son caractère,** the strong and weak points of his character; **étudier le f. et le faible d'une question,** to study every aspect of a question; **du f. au faible,** altogether, all told; by and large; **le f. d'un bois,** the heart of a wood; **le f. de l'hiver,** the depth, the dead, of winter; **au (plus) f. du combat,** in the thick of the fight, at the height of the action; **au f. de la dispute,** when the argument was at its height; **au f. de la fièvre, de l'été,** in the height of the fever, of summer; **au plus f. de l'épidémie,** at the height of the epidemic; **le plus f. est fait,** the most difficult part is done; **faire le plus f. d'un ouvrage,** to break the back of a piece of work; **la politesse n'est pas son f.,** politeness is not his strong point, his forte; **la poésie n'est pas mon f.,** poetry is not my line; (*b*) *N.Arch:* main breadth (of ship); **largeur au f.,** extreme beam, extreme width (of ship); (*c*) (*bowls*) **f. (de la boule),** bias. **2.** (*a*) strong man; **les forts des Halles,** the market porters; (*b*) *Sch: F:* **f. en thème,** (i) able pupil; bookworm; (ii) swot; (*c*) *Prov:* **la raison du plus f. est toujours la meilleure,** might is right. **3.** (*a*) fort, stronghold; redoubt; **f. d'arrêt,** barrier fort; **f. maritime,** coastal-defence fort; (*b*) *Ven:* cover.

fortage [fɔrtaːʒ], *s.m.* rent for quarrying rights.

forte [fɔrte], *adv. & s.m.inv. Mus:* forte.

fortement [fɔrtəmɑ̃], *adv.* strongly; stoutly; vigorously; **frapper f. sur une note,** to strike a note hard; **secouer qch. f.,** to shake sth. hard; **un nœud f. serré,** a tightly pulled knot; **insister f. sur qch.,** to insist firmly, strongly, on sth.; **f. épicé,** highly spiced; **f. irrité,** greatly irritated.

forteresse [fɔrtərɛs], *s.f.* fortress, fortified place, stronghold; *Lit:* fastness; **une des dernières forteresses du paganisme,** one of the last strongholds of paganism; *Av. A:* **f. volante,** flying fortress.

fortiche [fɔrtiʃ], *a.&s.P:* **c'est (un) f., il est f.,** (i) he's a tough guy; (ii) he's smart, he knows the ropes.

fortifiable [fɔrtifjabl], *a.* fortifiable.

fortifiant [fɔrtifjɑ̃]. **1.** *a.* fortifying, strengthening; **l'air f. de la mer,** the bracing sea air; **nourriture fortifiante,** strengthening food. **2.** *s.m.* tonic.

fortificateur [fɔrtifikatœːr], *s.m. A:* fortifier (of port, town, etc.).

fortification [fɔrtifikasjɔ̃], *s.f.* fortification. **1.** fortifying (of town, etc.). **2.** defence work(s); **les fortifications,** the fortifications (of a town); **f. rasante,** low-level fortification; **f. de campagne,** field fortification, work(s); **f. improvisée, f. de fortune, f. provisoire, f. passagère,** hasty field fortification; **f. permanente,** permanent fortification; **f. maritime,** coastal fortifications.

fortifié [fɔrtifje], *a.* fortified (town, port, etc.).

fortifier [fɔrtifje], *v.tr.* (*p.d. & pr.sub.* **n. fortifiions, v. fortifiiez**) **1.** to strengthen, fortify; **f. un mur,** to strengthen, support, a wall; **exercice qui fortifie le corps,** exercise that strengthens, braces up, invigorates, the body; **l'air de la mer vous fortifiera,** the sea air will set you up; **f. qn dans une résolution,** to support s.o. in a resolution; **f. les soupçons de qn,** to confirm s.o.'s suspicions; **f. de jeunes plantes,** to harden (off) seedlings. **2.** *Mil:* to fortify (town, etc.).

se fortifier. 1. to become stronger; **sa santé s'est fortifiée,** he has grown more robust. **2.** *Mil:* to raise a line of defences; to entrench oneself.

fortifs (les) [lefɔrtif], *s.f.pl. P:* the Fortifications (of Paris).

fortin [fɔrtɛ̃], *s.m.* small fort, fortlet, fortalice, fortin.

fortiori (a) [afɔrsjɔri], *loc.adv.* all the more so, *a fortiori.*

fortis [fɔrtis], *s.m.* drystone-walled terrace on hillside.

fortisan [fɔrtizɑ̃], *s.m. Tex:* fortisan.

fortissimo [fɔrtisimo], *adv. & s.m.inv. Mus:* fortissimo.

fortitude [fɔrtityd], *s.f. Lit:* fortitude.

fortrait [fɔrtrɛ], *a.* foundered (horse).

fortraiture [fɔrtrɛtyːr], *s.f. Vet:* founder (of horse).

fortran [fɔrtrɑ̃], *s.m.* (*computers*) fortran.

fortuit [fɔrtɥi], *a.* fortuitous; chance; **rencontre fortuite entre lui et sa sœur,** chance, casual, meeting between him and his sister; **cas f.,** (i) accidental case, accident; (ii) *Jur:* act of God, fortuitous event; *Golf:* **eau fortuite,** casual water.

fortuité [fɔrtɥite], *s.f.* fortuitousness, fortuity.

fortuitement [fɔrtɥitmɑ̃], *adv.* fortuitously, by chance, accidentally.

fortune [fɔrtyn], *s.f.* **1.** (*a*) fortune, chance, luck; **les caprices de la f.,** the caprices of fortune; **coup de f.,** stroke of luck; **tenter (la) f.,** to try one's luck; **jouer sa vie sur un coup de f.,** to stake one's life on a chance; **s'attacher à la f. de qn,** to throw in one's lot with s.o.; *Lit:* **depuis qu'il s'est attaché à ma f.,** since he has linked his fortunes with mine; **compagnons de f.,** chance companions; **officier de f.,** officer risen from the ranks; **venez dîner à la f. du pot,** come and take pot luck; **dispositif de f.,** makeshift; **pont de f.,** emergency bridge; **installation de f.,** temporary, makeshift, rough and ready, installation; **lit de f.,** makeshift bed, shakedown; **réparations de f.,** makeshift, emergency, repairs; *Aut: etc:* roadside repairs; **faire à une voiture des réparations de f.,** to tinker up a car; **disposez-vous de moyens de f.?** have you anything you can make shift with? anything you can make do with? *Nau:* **mât, gouvernail, gréement, de f.,** jury mast, jury rudder, jury rig(ging); **(voile de) f.,** cross-jack (foresail); **feu de f.,** flare-up (light); *M.Ins:* **f. de mer,** (i) perils of the sea, sea risks; accidents at sea; (ii) goods on which a maritime lien applies; (*b*) *A:* **rencontrer qn de f., par f.,** to meet s.o. by chance. **2.** (*a*) (i) *A:* piece of good luck, fortune; **il n'a pas de f.,** he is unlucky; (ii) **il eut la f. de . . .,** he had the good fortune to . . .; *Prov:* **la f. vient en dormant,** good luck comes when you are not looking for it; **à fou f., la f. rit aux sots,** fortune favours fools, fools have the best luck; (*b*) *A:* amorous adventure; **un homme à bonnes fortunes,** a Don Juan; (*c*) **mauvaise f.,** misfortune; **revers de f.,** reverse (of fortune), setback; **avoir la bonne, la mauvaise, f. de rencontrer qn,** to have the good, bad, luck to meet s.o.; (*d*) *A:* **faire contre mauvaise f. bon cœur,** to be steadfast in the face of adversity. **3.** fortune, wealth; **arriver à la f.,** to become wealthy, rich; **faire f.,** to make one's fortune, a fortune; *F:* to make one's pile; **le mot a fait f.,** the remark made a hit; **avoir de la f.,** to be well off; to be a person of means; **quelle est sa f.?** how much is he worth? how rich is he? **être l'artisan de sa f.,** to be a self-made man; **c'est à cet incident qu'il dut sa f.,** this incident was the making of him; **aller chercher f. en Amérique,** to go and seek one's fortune in America; **ses bijoux valent une f.,** her jewels are worth a fortune; **se retirer après f. faite,** to retire after making one's fortune, *F:* one's pile.

fortuné [fɔrtyne], *a.* **1.** fortunate, happy, successful; *Gr.Myth:* **les îles Fortunées,** the Fortunate Islands, the Islands of the Blest. **2.** rich, well-off, well-to-do; **les gens fortunés,** the moneyed classes; **veuve peu fortunée,** widow of slender means.

forum [fɔrɔm], *s.m.* **1.** *Rom.Ant:* forum. **2.** forum; meeting(-place); open discussion. **3.** politics; **les luttes du f.,** political struggles.

forure [fɔryːr], *s.f.* boring, bore(-hole); *esp.* pipe (of a key).

fosa [fɔza], **fossa** [fɔsa], *s.m. Z:* fossa, foussa.

fossane [fɔsan], *s.f. Z:* fossane.

fosse [foːs], *s.f.* **1.** pit, hole; *Oc:* (ocean) deep; trough; *Sp:* (jumping) pit; *Ven:* pit (trap); *Aut:* **f. (de réparation),** inspection pit; **f. de scieur,** saw pit; **f. de coulée,** foundry pit, casting pit; **f. de tanneur, à tan,** bark pit; **f. aux ours,** bear pit; *A:* bear-garden; **f. aux lions,** lions' den; *Husb:* **f. à fumier et à purin,** midden pit, cesspit; *Hyg:* **f. d'aisances,** cesspool; **f. septique,** septic tank; **f. d'égout,** sullage pit; **f. d'infiltration,** soakage pit; **f. mobile, portable,** portable latrine, lavatory; *Artil:* **f. de recul,** recoil pit; *Mch:* **f. du volant,** wheel race; *Nau:* **f. aux mâts,** mast-timber pond; *Th:* **f. d'orchestre,** orchestra pit; *Geol:* **f. d'effondrement,** rift valley; trough fault. **2.** grave; **f. commune,** pauper's grave, potter's field; *F:* **avoir un pied dans la f., être au bord de la f.,** to have one foot in the grave. **3.** *Anat:* fossa; **f. canine,** canine fossa; **fosses nasales,** nasal fossae; **f. iliaque,** iliac fossa; **f. gutturale,** fauces; **fosses orbitaires,** orbital cavities; orbits. **4.** *Min:* pit.

fossé [fose], *s.m.* **1.** (*a*) ditch, trench, drain; **les fossés le long de la route,** the ditches along the road; **entretien des haies et fossés,** hedging and ditching; **f. d'irrigation,** water-trench; **f. de captage,** catch-drain; **f. collecteur,** feeder; **creuser des fossés,** to trench, to ditch; *Hyd.E:* **f. de réception,** catchwater drain; *For: etc:* **f. d'arrêt (pour les chenilles, les feuilles, etc.),** trap-ditch (for caterpillars, leaves, etc.); (*b*) *Fort:* moat, fosse; **château entouré d'un f.,** moated castle; *F:* **sauter le f.,** to take the plunge, to cross the Rubicon, *esp.* to get married; *Prov:* **ce qui tombe dans le f. est pour le soldat,** findings (is) keepings. **2.** *Geol:* trough; **f. d'effondrement,** rift valley; **f. tectonique,** tectonic valley. **3.** gulf, rift (between persons).

fosserage [fosəraːʒ], *s.m. Vit:* first ploughing of a vineyard.

fosserer [fosəre], *v.tr. Vit:* to plough (vineyard).

fossette [fosɛt, fɔ-], *s.f.* small cavity; (*a*) pit, chuck-hole (in game of marbles); **jouer à la f.,** to play at chucks, at pits; (*b*) dimple; **ses joues à fossettes,** her dimpled cheeks; (*c*) *Anat:* fossa; **f. sous-maxillaire,** sub-maxillary fossa; (*d*) *Geol: etc:* socket.

fosseur [fosœːr], *s.m. A.Mil:* pioneer.

fossile [fosil, fɔ-], *a. & s.m.* **1.** (*a*) fossil; *Paleont:* **f. remanié,** derived fossil; (*b*) **l'homme f.,** fossil man. **2.** *F:* (*a*) **un vieux f.,** an old fossil; (*b*) fossilized (ideas, etc.).

fossilifère [fosilifɛːr, fɔ-], *a.* fossiliferous, fossil-bearing.

fossilisateur, -trice [fosilizatœːr, -tris, fɔ-], *a. Geol:* (*of soil constituents*) fossilizing, that promotes fossilization.

fossilisation [fosilizasjɔ̃, fɔ-], *s.f.* fossilization.

fossiliser [fosilize, fɔ-], *v.tr.* to fossilize.

se fossiliser, to fossilize; to become fossilized.

fossoir [foswaːr], *s.m. Vit:* vineyard plough, hoe.

fossoyage [foswajaːʒ, fɔ-], *s.m.* **1.** trenching, ditching. **2.** grave-digging.

fossoyer [foswaje, fɔ-], *v.tr.* (**je fossoie, n. fossoyons; je fossoierai**) to trench, drain, ditch (field, etc.).

fossoyeur, -euse [foswajœːr, fɔ-, -øːz]. **1.** *s.m.* grave-digger. **2.** *Ent:* (*a*) *a.* fossorial, burrowing (insect); (*b*) *s.m.* sexton beetle. **3.** *s.f.* **la fossoyeuse,** death.

fossure [fosyːr], *s.f. Vit:* first ploughing of a vineyard.

fou [fu], **fol, folle** [fɔl], *the form* **fol,** *used in the m. before a vowel within the word group, is confined to senses* 1. (*b*) *and* (*e*). **1.** *a.* (*a*) mad, demented, insane, crazy; **f. à lier,** raving mad, crazy; *F:* stark staring mad, as mad as a hatter; **cette nuit terrible l'avait rendue folle,** that dreadful night had driven her out of her mind; **vous êtes f.,** you're mad, crazy; **il n'est pas assez f. pour . . .,** he's not mad, stupid, enough to . . .; *F:* **il n'est pas f.,** he's no fool; **il était f. de douleur,** he was mad, frantic, (i) with pain, (ii) with grief; **vous me rendez f.,** you are driving me mad, you drive me to distraction; **il y a de quoi devenir f.,** it's enough to drive you mad; **f. de joie,** beside one-

self with joy; **être f., folle, de qn,** to be madly in love with s.o.; to dote on s.o.; **elle était folle de son neveu,** she doted on her nephew; **elle était ce soir-là d'une gaieté folle,** that evening she was in (very) high spirits, she was madly happy; **f. de terreur,** wild with fear; *F:* **il est f. de peinture,** he's mad about painting; (*b*) foolish, extravagant, silly; **des illusions folles,** wild delusions; **les vierges folles,** the foolish virgins; *A:* **folle de son corps,** wanton; **un fol espoir,** a foolish, mad, hope; *Lit:* (*pseudo-archaic*) **les tourbillonnements fols des feuilles,** the mad dance, the wild whirlings, of the leaves; *Prov:* **de f. juge brève sentence,** a fool's bolt is soon shot; (*c*) excessive (in size, number), prodigious, enormous; **succès f.,** tremendous, wild, success; **mal de tête f.,** splitting headache; **il gagne un argent f.,** he makes pots of money; **à une allure folle,** at a breakneck speed; **il y avait un monde f.,** there was a fearful crowd, a tremendous crowd; the place was crowded; **dépenser un argent f.,** to spend an exorbitant amount of money; **un prix f.,** an extravagantly, exorbitantly, high price; *F:* **c'est f. ce que c'est cher!** it's madly expensive! it costs the earth! *F:* **c'est f. ce qu'on s'amuse!** aren't we having fun! isn't it wonderful! *F:* **c'est f. ce qu'elle peut être dynamique,** it's extraordinary how dynamic she is; (*d*) not under control; out of control; **des mèches folles tombaient sur son front,** wisps of hair were hanging down over her forehead; **herbes folles,** rank weeds; **balance folle,** unsteady balance; *Mec.E:* **poulie folle,** loose pulley; **roue folle,** idle wheel, idler; free wheel; *Nau:* **vent f.,** unsteady, baffling, wind; **aiguille (de compas) folle,** crazy (compass) needle; *Med:* **jambe folle,** partially paralysed leg (with uncontrollable movements); **train, camion, f.,** runaway train, lorry; **f. rire,** uncontrollable laughter; (*e*) *Jur:* **folle enchère,** re-auctioning of goods not taken by the purchaser at a previous auction; **fol appel,** unreceivable appeal, appeal dismissed as an abuse of the process of justice. **2.** *s.* (*never* **fol**) (*a*) madman, madwoman, lunatic; **f. furieux,** raving lunatic, maniac; **devenir f. furieux,** to go berserk; *A:* **maison de fous,** lunatic asylum, madhouse; **on se croirait dans une maison de fous,** you would think this was Bedlam; it's a regular madhouse; *Lit:* **la folle du logis,** the imagination; **f. du volant,** reckless driver, speed merchant; (*b*) (court) fool, jester; *A:* **le pape des fous,** the Abbot of Unreason; (*c*) **une vieille folle,** a silly old woman; **les vieux fous sont plus fous que les jeunes,** there's no fool like an old fool; **courir comme un f.,** to run like a madman; (*d*) **faire le f.,** to play the fool; **plus on est de fous plus on rit,** the more the merrier. **3.** *s.m.* (*a*) *Chess:* bishop; (*b*) *Orn:* *F:* **f. (de Bassan),** gannet; booby; **f. à pieds bleus,** blue-footed booby.

fouace [fwas], *s.f. Cu:* = girdle cake.

fouacier [fwasje], *s.m.* baker of *fouaces.*

fouage [fwa:ʒ], *s.m. Feud:* hearth-tax.

fouaille [fwɑ:j], *s.f. Ven:* fourail.

fouaillée [fwɑje], *s.f. O:* thrashing, whipping, flogging; *F:* lathering, larruping.

fouailler [fwɑje], *v.tr.* (*a*) *O: Lit:* to flog, lash (with a whip); to punish (horse); (*b*) to lash (with the tongue); to castigate (vice, etc.); (*c*) (*of horse*) **f. de la queue,** to lash its tail.

fouailleur [fwɑjœ:r], *s.m.* flogger.

fouanne [fwa:n], *s.f. Fish:* grains, fishgig, pronged harpoon.

fouarre [fwa:r], *s.m. A:* straw.

foucade [fukad], *s.f. O: & Lit:* passing whim, fancy; **travailler par foucades,** to work by fits and starts.

Foucault [fuko], *Pr.n. El:* **courants de F.,** Foucault currents, eddy currents.

fouchtra [fuʃtra]. **1.** *int. Dial:* = FICHTRE, FOUTRE. **2.** *a.m. & s.m. P:* (native, inhabitant) of Auvergne.

foudre[1] [fudr̥], *s.* **1.** (*a*) *f.* (*& A: m.*) thunderbolt, lightning; **la f. est tombée à . . .,** the lightning struck at . . .; **maison frappée de la f.,** house struck by lightning; **coup de f.,** (i) lightning discharge; (ii) thunderbolt; (iii) *A:* unexpected event or disaster, bolt from the blue; (iv) *F:* love at first sight; **ç'a été le coup de f. de part et d'autre,** they fell head over heels in love; (*b*) *m.* **les foudres de Jupiter,** Jove's thunderbolts, thunders; (*c*) *f.* **les foudres romaines,** the thunders of the Vatican; **les foudres de l'Église,** excommunication, anathema; (*d*) *m. Mil:* (*in Fr. army*) forked lightning badge (of staff officers); *Her:* thunderbolt. **2.** *m. A: or Iron:* **un f. de guerre,** a great captain; **f. d'éloquence,** powerful orator.

foudre[2], *s.m.* tun, hogshead, large cask; **le f. d'Heidelberg,** the Heidelberg Tun.

foudrier [fudrije], *s.m. Coop:* tun maker.

foudroiement [fudrwamɑ̃], *s.m.* striking (down) (of sth., of s.o.) by lightning, by a thunderbolt; blasting (of sth.).

foudroyage [fudrwaja:ʒ], *s.m. Min:* **f. après sous-cavage,** undercut caving; **f. intégral,** total caving.

foudroyant [fudrwajɑ̃], *a.* **1. Jupiter f.,** Jupiter wielder of thunderbolts, Jupiter Fulgator; *Rom.Hist:* **la Foudroyante,** the Thundering Legion. **2.** (*a*) striking (down), terrifying, crushing; **attaque foudroyante,** smashing attack; **nouvelle foudroyante,** overwhelming, crushing, news; *F:* thunderbolt; **regard f.,** withering look; **lancer un regard f. à qn,** to look daggers at s.o.; (*b*) of lightning speed; *Med:* fulminating, fulminant, foudroyant; **progrès foudroyants d'une industrie,** lightning progress of an industry; **il y eut des conversions foudroyantes,** there were lightning conversions; *Aut:* **reprise foudroyante,** lightning pick-up; terrific acceleration; *Fb:* **shoot f.,** cannon-ball shot.

foudroyer [fudrwaje], *v.* (**je foudroie, n. foudroyons; je foudroierai**) **1.** *v.tr.* to strike down (by lightning), to blast; **arbre foudroyé,** blasted tree, tree struck by lightning; **l'apoplexie l'a foudroyé,** he was struck down by apoplexy; *F:* **en quelques salves l'artillerie foudroya le village,** with a few rounds the artillery battered the village into ruins; **elle le foudroya d'un regard,** she withered him with a glance; **cette nouvelle m'a foudroyé,** I was thunderstruck, dumbfounded, by the news; **f. ses adversaires,** to confound, crush, one's opponents. **2.** *v.i. A:* to hurl thunderbolts, to thunder; *F:* to fulminate.

fouée [fwe], *s.f.* **1.** (*a*) fire (of baker's oven); (*b*) = girdle cake. **2.** faggot, bundle of sticks. **3.** *Ven:* night fowling; *A:* bat-fowling.

fouëne, fouène [fwɛn], *s.f. Fish:* grains, fishgig, pronged harpoon.

fouet [fwɛ], *s.m.* **1.** birch(-rod); **donner le f. à un enfant,** to birch a child. **2.** (*a*) whipcord; (*b*) whip; **donner le f. à qn,** to whip, flog, s.o.; to give s.o. a whipping, a flogging; **la peine du f.,** the penalty of the lash; *Sch:* **la punition du f.,** flogging; **coup de f.,** (i) cut, lash (of whip); (ii) fillip, stimulus (to the system), shot in the arm; (iii) whipping, whip, lashing, surging (of cable); flapping (of sail); (iv) *Med:* tearing of ligament, of muscle-fibre; (v) *Nau:* jerking; *F:* **donner un coup de f. à la circulation,** to stimulate the circulation; **faire claquer son f.,** (i) to crack one's whip; (ii) *F:* to blow one's own trumpet; **le f. de la satire,** the lash of satire; *Cu:* **f. à battre les œufs, f. à œufs,** egg-whisk; *Artil:* **tir de plein f.,** direct fire; **coup de plein f.,** direct hit; **collision de plein f.,** head-on collision; **percuter de plein f.,** to collide head-on; **entrer de plein f. dans qch.,** to run smack into sth.; **il était éclairé de plein f. par la lune,** he was in the full light of the moon. **3.** loose, mobile, part of sth.; tip (of bird's wing); *Nau:* tail (of pulley); *Ven:* (dog's) tail, stern; *Hort:* runner (of strawberry plant); *Tex:* **f. de chasse,** picking-stick (of loom). **4.** *Ich:* **fouet (ruban),** ribbon-fish. **5.** *Rept:* *F:* grass snake.

fouettage [fwɛta:ʒ], *s.m.* whipping (of horses, etc.); beating, whisking (of liquids).

fouettant [fwɛtɑ̃], *a.* stimulating, exciting.

Fouettard [fwɛta:r], *Pr.n.m.* **le Père F.,** (*as threat to naughty child*) the bogyman.

fouette [fwɛt], *s.f. Fish:* **pêche à la f.,** whipping.

fouetté [fwete]. **1.** *a.* whipped (cream, etc.); whisked (eggs, etc.). **2.** *s.m. Danc:* fouetté.

fouettée [fwete], *s.f.* whipping, spanking; **administrer une f. à un enfant,** to spank a child.

fouettement [fwɛtmɑ̃], *s.m.* cutting, lashing, beating, whipping; *esp.* flapping (of sail); surging (of cable); lashing, whipping (of rod, etc.); lashing (of rain).

fouette-queue [fwɛtkø], *s.m. F: Rept:* mastigure; *pl. fouette-queues.*

fouetter [fwete], *v.tr.* **1.** (*a*) to whip, flog, lash (horse, person); to beat, whisk (eggs); to whip (cream); *Fr.C:* **crème à f.,** whipping cream; *A:* **fouettez, cocher!** drive on, whip up, coachman! **fouette, cocher!** off we go! fire away! **il n'y a pas là de quoi f. un chat,** there's nothing to make such a fuss about; **avoir d'autres chats,** *A:* **d'autres chiens, à f.,** to have other fish to fry; **le vent nous fouettait la neige au visage,** the wind was beating the snow in our faces; *v.tr. & i.* **la pluie fouette (contre) les vitres,** the rain is lashing against the panes; (*b*) to excite, stimulate; **l'exercice fouette le sang,** exercise stimulates the blood, sends the blood pulsing through the veins; **spectacle qui fouette le sang,** sight that makes the blood boil; **brise qui fouette le sang,** breeze that makes the blood tingle; **fouetté par le désir de . . .,** incited, spurred on, stimulated, by the desire, wish, to . . .; (*c*) *abs. Mec.E:* (*of moving part*) to lash, whip; (*of cable*) to surge; *Nau:* (*of mast*) to shake; (*of sail*) to flap. **2.** (*a*) *Bookb: etc:* to tie (book) up (with whipcord); *Nau:* **f. une bosse,** to pass a stopper; (*b*) *Vet:* **f. un bélier,** to castrate a ram (by ligature of the testicles). **3.** *v.i. P:* (*a*) to stink; **ça fouette dans ton escalier,** your staircase stinks (to high heaven); **f. du goulot,** to have a bad breath; (*b*) to be in a funk.

fouetteur, -euse [fwɛtœ:r, -ø:z], *s.* **1.** *a. Sch: A:* **frère f.,** lay-brother who carried out whipping of pupils. **2.** *s.* whipper, flogger.

fou-fou [fufu], *a.m. F:* foolish; idiotic; *s.a.* FOFOLLE.

fougade [fugad], *s.f.* **1.** *A:* whim, fancy. **2.** *Cu:* (sort of) curry.

fougasse [fugas], *s.f.* **1.** *Mil: A:* fougasse, small mine. **2.** *A:* intrigue, underhand trick. **3.** = girdle cake.

fouge [fu:ʒ], *s.f.* plants rooted up (by wild boar).

fouger [fuʒe], *v.i.* (*of swine, boar, etc.*) to root, rout; *Agr:* to plough up (grass).

fougeraie [fuʒrɛ], *s.f.* fern-patch, patch of ferny ground; fernbrake.

fougerais, -aise [fuʒrɛ, -ɛ:z], *a. & s. Geog:* (native, inhabitant) of Fougères.

fougère [fuʒɛ:r], *s.f.* (*a*) *Bot:* fern; **f. à l'aigle, f. grand aigle,** bracken; **f. arborescente,** tree fern; **f. mâle,** male fern; **f. femelle,** lady fern, female fern; (*b*) *Const: Carp:* **à brin de f., en f.,** herringbone (tiling, etc.); (*c*) *Glassm: A:* **cendre de f.,** fern-ash.

fougerole [fuʒrɔl], *s.f.* small fern.

fougon [fugɔ̃], *s.m. Hist:* clay hearth (on board a galley).

fougue[1] [fug], *s.f.* (*a*) fire, spirit, passion; **f. de la jeunesse,** ardour, heat, fire, enthusiasm, of youth; **f. des passions,** heat of passion; **cheval plein de f.,** high-mettled, mettlesome, fiery, spirited, horse; **équipe pleine de f.,** team full of dash; (*b*) (*of tree*) running to wood.

fougue[2], *s.f.* (*a*) *A:* squall; (*b*) *Nau:* **perroquet de f.,** mizzen topsail, jigger topsail; **mât (de perroquet) de f.,** mizzen topmast.

fougueusement [fugøzmɑ̃], *adv.* ardently, spiritedly, impetuously.

fougueux, -euse [fugø, -ø:z], *a.* (*a*) fiery, ardent, spirited; **caractère f.,** passionate, impetuous, nature; **coursier f.,** fiery, high-spirited, steed; **race au sang f.,** hot-blooded race; (*b*) (tree) that runs to wood.

fouguiste [fugist], *s.m. A:* cartridge-maker.

fouillage [fuja:ʒ], *s.m. Agr:* breaking up of the subsoil, subsoil ploughing.

fouille [fu:j], *s.f.* **1.** excavation, (*a*) digging, trenching, excavating; **f. en sous-œuvre,** excavation for underpinning; (*b*) excavation, pit, trench cut; hole (for planting tree, etc.); **f. blindée,** timbered excavation; **f. à ciel ouvert,** open pit; *Mil:* **abri à f. ouverte,** cut and cover shelter; (*c*) *usu. pl. Archeol:* dig, excavations; **les fouilles de Pompéi,** the excavations at Pompeii; **faire des fouilles dans un endroit,** to excavate a site. **2.** (*a*) **f. d'un suspect, des poches de qn,** search(ing) of a suspected person, of s.o.'s pockets; (*b*) *P:* pocket.

fouillé [fuje], *a.* **travail très f.,** work showing great research, going into great detail; elaborate work; *Phot:* **cliché très f.,** negative with fine definition.

fouille-au-pot [fujopo], *s.m.inv. P:* **1.** (*a*) kitchen-boy; (*b*) bad cook. **2.** fussy, meddlesome, husband.

fouillement [fujmɑ̃], *s.m. A:* (*a*) digging, excavating; (*b*) searching.

fouille-merde [fujmɛrd], *s.m.inv. Ent: F:* dung-beetle.

fouiller [fuje]. **1.** *v.tr.* (*a*) to dig, excavate, trench; to burrow into (the ground); *A:* **machine à f.,** excavating machine; *Art:* **f. une sculpture,** to undercut a sculpture; (*b*) to search; **f. qn,** to search s.o.; to go through s.o.'s pockets; *U.S:* to frisk s.o.; **f. les malles de qn,** to go through s.o.'s trunks; **f. un tiroir,** to ransack a drawer; **f. un bois,** to scour, comb, a wood; **ses yeux fouillaient la salle,** he scanned the house; **son regard fouilla l'ombre,** he peered into the darkness; **f. un problème,** to go thoroughly into a problem; **f. son style,** to elaborate one's style; **f. le terrain,** (i) *Mil:* to explore, search, the ground (by observation, patrol, etc.); (ii) *Artil:* to search the ground (with gunfire). **2.** *v.i.* (*a*) **f. sous le terrain,** to undermine; (*b*) **f. dans une**

armoire, to search, rummage, in a cupboard; **f. sous le lit,** to rummage under the bed; **elle fouillait dans la poubelle pour retrouver sa bague,** she was fishing in the dustbin to find her ring; **f. pour trouver qch.,** to rummage, forage, for sth.; **f. (dans) tout Paris pour trouver un livre,** *F:* to ransack Paris for a book; **f. dans les archives,** to burrow into, to explore, the archives; **f. dans le village,** to nose, poke, about the village; **f. dans le cœur humain,** to explore the human heart; **f. dans le passé de qn,** to rake up s.o.'s past.

se fouiller, to go through one's pockets; *P:* **tu peux te f.!** nothing doing! you'll be lucky!

fouilleur, -euse [fujœːr, -øːz], *s.* **1.** *(a)* excavator, digger; *(b)* rummager, searcher; **f. de poches,** pickpocket; *(c) s.f. Cust:* **fouilleuse,** woman-searcher (of women-suspects). **2.** *s.f.* **fouilleuse;** *(a)* subsoil plough; *(b)* excavator. **3.** *s.m. Ven:* wild boar.

fouillis [fuji], *s.m.* **1.** jumble, mess, muddle, litter (of papers, etc.); tumble (of rocks); tangle (of brushwood, etc.). **2.** *Fish:* small mud-worm (used as bait).

fouillot [fujo], *s.m. Locksm:* door-knob hole (of lock); serrure à f., spring-lock.

fouillouse [fujuːz], *s.f. A: P:* purse, pocket.

Fouilly-les-Oies [fujilezwa], *Pr.n.* **sortir de F.-l.-O.,** to come from the back of beyond, *U.S:* the backwoods, *Aust:* the backblocks.

fouinard [fwinaːr], *a. F:* *(a)* inquisitive, nosy; *s.* Nosy Parker; snooper; *(b)* sly, sneaking; *(c) A:* cowardly, given to ratting.

fouinasser [fwinase], *v.i. P:* to nose about; to poke one's nose into other people's business; to snoop.

fouine[1] [fwin], *s.f.* **1.** *Agr:* long pitchfork. **2.** *Fish:* grains, fishgig, pronged harpoon.

fouine[2], *s.f. Z:* white-breasted marten, stone marten, beech marten; *F:* **à figure de f.,** weasel-faced; **des yeux de f.,** ferrety eyes.

fouiner [fwine], *v.i.* **1.** *F:* to ferret, to nose about; to nose into, poke one's nose into, other people's business. **2.** *P:* *(a)* to slip off, slink away; *(b)* to rat.

fouinette [fwinɛt], *s.f. Agr:* small iron fork.

fouineur, -euse [fwinœːr, -øːz], *F:* *(a) a. & s.* inquisitive, nosy (person); *(b) s.* bargain-hunting collector; bargain hunter.

fouir [fwiːr], *v.tr.* to dig (underground); **f. un puits,** to dig, excavate, a well; **animaux qui fouissent le sol, la vase,** animals that burrow in the soil, the mud.

fouissage [fwisaːʒ], *s.m.,* **fouissement** [fwismɑ̃], *s.m.* digging, burrowing.

fouisseur, -euse [fwisœːr, -øːz], *a. & s.* burrowing (animal); burrower; **guêpe, abeille, fouisseuse,** digger wasp, digger bee.

foulage [fulaːʒ], *s.m.* **1.** fulling, milling (of cloth, leather). **2.** pressing, crushing, treading (of grapes). **3.** *Med:* kneading (by masseur). **4.** *Metall:* ramming (of sand, etc.). **5.** *Typ:* impression; **cylindre de f.,** impression cylinder; **excès, trop, de f.,** over-impression. **6.** *(computers)* embossment.

Foulahs [fula], *s.m.pl. Ethn:* Fulah(s), Fellata(s).

foulant [fulɑ̃], *a.* *(a)* pressing, crushing; *Tex:* fulling; **pompe foulante,** force-pump, forcing pump; *(b) P:* **ce n'est pas bien f.,** it's not hard work.

foulard [fulaːr], *s.m.* **1.** *Tex:* foulard, silk. **2.** *(a)* silk scarf; *(b)* silk handkerchief. **3.** *Tex:* **f. d'apprêt, f. gommeur,** sizing machine.

foulardage [fulardaːʒ], *s.m. Tex:* sizing.

foularder [fularde], *v.tr. Tex:* to size (cloth).

foule [ful], *s.f.* **1.** *(a)* pressing, crushing; fulling, milling (of cloth, leather); *(b)* fulling-room. **2.** crowd; throng (of people); **psychologie des foules,** mob psychology; **la f. se pressait partout,** everywhere was crowded, it was crowded, there were crowds, everywhere; **accourir, se rendre, en f. à un spectacle,** to crowd, flock, throng, to a play; **ils sont entrés en f.,** they came crowding in; **faire f. autour de qn,** to crowd round s.o.; **magasin qui fait f.,** shop that draws crowds; **se mettre au-dessus de la f.,** to rise above the common herd; **servi par une f. de domestiques,** waited on by a host of servants: *F:* **elle a une f. de cousins,** she has a whole crowd of cousins, she has cousins galore; **f. d'idées,** host of ideas; **une f. de doutes se présentait, se présentaient, à son esprit,** doubts crowded upon his mind; **des souvenirs m'assaillirent en f.,** memories crowded in on me. **3.** *Fr.C:* migration (of caribou). **4.** *Tex:* shed, space (between two lines of warp threads). **5.** *Hist:* *(jousting)* **combat à la f.,** mêlée, mellay.

foulé [fule]. **1.** *a.* *(a)* pressed, crushed; *(b)* fulled (cloth); **drap non f.,** unmilled cloth; *(c)* sprained, strained (foot, wrist). **2.** *s.m. Tex:* light-weight summer cloth.

foulée [fule], *s.f.* **1.** *Const:* tread (of stair). **2.** *(a)* print, tread (of horse's hoof); *(b) usu. pl.* stride; **parcourir les guérets à longues foulées,** to stride over the fields; *Rac:* **allonger sa f.,** to step out, lengthen one's stride; **rester dans la f.,** to lie behind (another runner); **faire qch. d'une seule f.,** to do sth. at one go; *(c) pl. Ven:* foil, spoor, slot, track (of game). **3. f. de soufflet,** compression of bellows. **4.** *Tan:* pile of skins (to be fulled at one time).

foulement [fulmɑ̃], *s.m.* pressing, crushing.

fouler [fule], *v.tr.* **1.** to press; *(a)* **f. une robe,** to crush, crumple, rumple, a dress; **f. l'herbe,** to trample (down), tread down, the grass; *Winem:* **f. le raisin,** to tread, press, crush, the grapes; **f. qch. aux pieds,** to tread, trample, sth. under foot; *F:* **f. qn aux pieds,** to ride rough-shod over s.o.; *(b) Tex:* to full (cloth); *(c) Metall:* to ram (sand, etc.). **2.** *(a)* to sprain, strain, wrench, twist; **se f. le poignet,** to sprain one's wrist; **se f. l'épaule,** to strain, wrench, one's shoulder; *F:* **ne pas se f. la rate,** *P:* **ne pas se la f.,** to take things easy, to take it easy; *(b)* (i) to override (horse); (ii) *(of saddle)* to gall (horse).

se fouler, *F:* *(a)* to put oneself out, to take pains; *(b)* to hurry; **ne pas se f.,** to take it easy; **il n'a pas à se f.,** he has a soft job; *Ind:* **travailler sans se f.,** to go slow.

foulerie [fulri], *s.f. Tex:* fulling-mill, fullery.

fouleur, -euse [fulœːr, -øːz], *s.* **1.** *Tex:* fuller. **2.** wine presser. **3.** *s.f.* **fouleuse,** fulling machine.

fouloir [fulwaːr], *s.m.* **1.** *Tex:* *(a)* beater, fulling stock; *(b)* fulling mill. **2.** wine press; treading vat. **3.** (dentist's) filling instrument. **4.** *Metall:* rammer.

foulon [fulɔ̃], *s.m. Tex:* **1.** fuller; **chardon à f.,** fuller's teasel, fuller's weed; **terre à f.,** fuller's earth. **2. (moulin à) f.,** fulling mill. **3.** *Ent:* *(a)* June beetle; *(b) Dial:* *(Normandy),* (i) wasp; (ii) hornet.

foulonnage [fulɔnaːʒ], *s.m. Tex:* fulling.

foulonner [fulɔne], *v.tr. Tex:* to full (cloth).

foulonnier [fulɔnje], *s.m.* **1.** *Tex:* *(a)* fuller, fulling-mill worker; *(b)* fuller, owner of fulling-mill. **2.** *Ent: Dial:* *(Normandy)* hornet.

Fouloups [fulup], *s.m.pl. Ethn:* Felup, Fulup.

foulque [fulk], *s.f. Orn:* **f. (macroule),** coot; **f. à crête,** crested coot; **f. noire,** common coot, bald coot, baldicoot.

foultitude [fultityd], *s.f. F: Hum:* multitude; crowd.

foulure [fulyːr], *s.f.* **1.** *(a)* sprain, wrench; **f. au genou,** sprained knee; **se donner une f.,** to give oneself a wrench; *F:* **il ne se donnera pas de f.,** he won't hurt himself with overwork; he won't break his back over it; *(b) Equit:* saddle-gall (of horse). **2.** *Tan:* fulling, milling (of skins).

four [fuːr], *s.m.* **1.** *(a)* (kitchen, baker's) oven; **f. à gaz, f. électrique,** gas, electric, oven; *Mil: etc:* **f. de campagne,** field oven; **mettre qch. au f.,** to put sth. in the oven; **faire cuire qch. au f.,** to bake, roast, sth.; **vaisselle allant au f.,** ovenware; **plat allant au f.,** ovenproof (baking) dish; *Cu:* **pommes de terre au f.,** baked potatoes; **noir comme dans un f.,** pitch black; **il y fait chaud comme dans un f.,** it's baking hot here, it's like an oven in here; *Prov:* **on ne peut être au f. et au moulin,** you can't be in two places at once; *Sch: F:* **f. à bachot,** crammer; *(b) Cu:* **petits fours,** petits fours. **2.** *(a) Ind: etc:* kiln; furnace; **f. à chaux,** lime kiln; **f. à briques,** brick kiln; **f. de campagne,** brick clamp; **f. à carboniser,** charcoal burner; **f. à sécher le houblon,** oast house; **f. à chauffer les rivets,** rivet heater; **f. à ciment,** cement kiln; **f. à coke,** coke oven; **f. de verrerie,** glass furnace; **f. de traitement thermique,** heat-treat oven; **f. à griller, f. de grillage,** roasting kiln; **f. à recuire, f. de recuite,** annealing furnace; **f. à tremper,** tempering furnace; **f. de fusion,** smelting furnace, smelter (for ore); melting furnace (for metal); **f. de séchage,** drying oven, drying kiln, dryer; **f. de cémentation, f. à cémenter,** cementation furnace; cementing, carburizing, furnace; **f. de coupellation, f. à coupeller,** cupellation, cupel furnace; cupelling furnace; **f. de puddlage, f. à puddler,** puddling furnace; **f. à creuset(s),** pot, crucible, furnace; **f. à récupération, à récupérateur,** recuperating, recuperative, furnace; **f. à réverbère,** reverberatory (furnace); **f. à sole, f. Martin,** open-hearth furnace; **f. basculant,** tilting furnace; **f. rotatif,** revolving kiln, furnace; **f. à air chaud,** hot-blast stove; **f. solaire,** solar furnace; *(petroleum refining)* **f. de fractionnement, de distillation,** topping still; **f. de grillage à moufle,** muffle roasting furnace; **f. Pasteur,** pasteurizer; *(b)* **f. électrique,** electric furnace, oven; **f. à arc,** arc furnace; **f. à induction,** induction furnace; **f. à résistance,** resistance furnace; **f. (à) basse fréquence,** low-frequency furnace; **f. (à) haute fréquence,** radio-frequency furnace. **3.** *Geol:* **f. à cristaux,** geode. **4.** *F: esp: Th:* failure, flop; **la pièce fit, fut un, f.,** the play was a flop. **5.** *P:* wide-open mouth; gape.

fourbature [furbatyːr], *s.f. Vet:* founder; laminitis.

fourbe[1] [furb], *s.f. A:* **1.** imposture, deceit. **2.** swindle, piece of roguery.

fourbe[2]. **1.** *a.* cheating, double-dealing, two-faced, swindling (person). **2.** *s.* cheat, rogue, swindler, double-dealer.

fourber [furbe], *v.tr. A:* *(a)* to cheat, swindle; *(b)* to deceive.

fourberie [furbəri], *s.f.* **1.** imposture, deceit, cheating, double-dealing, underhand dealing; **maître en f.,** out-and-out swindler. **2.** cheat, swindle, piece of underhand dealing.

fourbi [furbi], *s.m. F:* *(a) Mil:* kit; *(b)* (collection of) rubbish; **je vais me débarrasser de tout le f.,** I'm going to get rid of this rubbish, lock, stock and barrel; **(et) tout le f.,** the whole lot, the whole bag of tricks; *(c)* gadget, thing; **comment appelez-vous ce f.-là?** what's this thing called? *(d)* **un sale f.,** a rotten job; **il connaît le f.,** he knows all the tricks; he knows what he's about.

fourbir [furbir], *v.tr.* to furbish, clean, rub up, polish up, shine up (metal).

fourbissage [furbisaːʒ], *s.m.* furbishing, cleaning, rubbing up, polishing, shining up (of metal); *Mil: Nau: F:* spit and polish; **faire le f.,** to clean the brass-work.

fourbisseur [furbisœːr], *s.m.* *(a)* sword furbisher; *(b) A:* sword cutler.

fourbissure [furbisyːr], *s.f.* = FOURBISSAGE.

fourbu [furby], *a.* *Vet:* *(of horse)* foundered, broken-down; *F:* *(of pers.)* tired out, dead tired, dead beat, dog-tired, done up, fagged (out).

fourbure [furbyːr], *s.f. Vet:* founder; laminitis.

fourc [furk], *s.m.* fork (of branches of tree).

fourcade [furkad], *s.f. Fish:* oyster-fishing with a fork.

fourcat [furka], *s.m. N.Arch:* crutch. **1.** cant frame, timber. **2. f. d'ouverture,** lowest transom.

fourche [furʃ], *s.f.* fork. **1.** *(a)* **f. à foin, à fourrage,** hay fork, pitchfork; **f. à bêcher, de jardinier,** garden fork; **remuer le sol à la f.,** to fork the ground; **chariot (élévateur) à f.,** fork-lift truck; *F:* **traiter qn à la f.,** to treat s.o. roughly; to ill-treat s.o.; *F:* **faire qch. à la f.,** to do sth. all anyhow; *(b) Mec.E:* fork, yoke; **f. de bicyclette,** bicycle fork; *Cy:* **f. élastique,** spring fork; **tête de f. de motocyclette,** forkhead; **f. de roue,** wheel fork; **articulation à f.,** fork link; **f. à articulation,** fork joint; **f. de joint universel,** universal-joint yoke; **f. de réglage,** adjusting yoke; **f. d'embrayage,** clutch fork; **f. de débrayage (de courroie de transmission),** belt fork, strap fork; *Av:* **f. d'articulation (du train avant),** hinge fork. **2.** *(a) Tail:* fork, crotch, crutch (of trousers); *(b)* **arbre, chemin, qui fait la fourche,** tree, road, that branches, forks; **la route fait fourche à . . .,** the road branches off, divides, at . . .; **chemin à f.,** bifurcated, forked, road; **la f. de deux routes,** the forking of a road; **à f.,** Y-shaped.

fourché [furʃe], *a.* forked (lever, etc.); furcate (branch, etc.).

fourchée [furʃe], *s.f.* pitchforkful (of hay, etc.).

fourche-fière [furʃfjeːr], *s.f.* long-handled pitch-fork; *pl. fourches-fières.*

fourchement [furʃəmɑ̃], *s.m.* fork(ing), dividing (of tree, road, etc.).

fourcher [furʃe]. **1.** *v.i.* *(of roads, etc.)* to fork, divide, branch; *F:* **la langue lui a fourché,** he made a slip of the tongue. **2.** *v.tr.* *(a)* **f. le sol,** to fork the ground; to dig the ground with a fork; *(b) Chess:* **f. deux pièces avec un cavalier,** to fork two pieces with a knight.

fourchetée [furʃəte], *s.f.* table-forkful.

fourchet [furʃɛ], *s.m.* **1.** *Agr:* two-pronged fork. **2.** *(a)* fork (of bough, etc.); *(b) Tail:* fork, crotch, crutch (of trousers). **3.** *Vet:* foot rot.

fourchette [furʃɛt], *s.f.* **1.** (table) fork, dinner fork; **f. à découper,** carving fork; **f. à griller le pain,** toasting fork; **f. à homard,** lobster pick; **repas à la f.,** knife-and-fork meal; **manger au hasard de la f.,** to take pot luck; *F:* **il a un joli coup de f., c'est une bonne f.,** he's got a large appetite, he's a good trencherman; *F:* **manger qch. avec la f. du père Adam,** to eat sth. with one's fingers; *Mil: P:* **charge à la f.,** bayonet charge; *Games: P:* **marquer à la f.,** to mark up more points than one has scored; *Wr:* **donner le coup de f. à qn,** to gouge s.o.'s eyes; *P:* **vol à la**

f., pickpocketing. 2. (*a*) *Artil:* bracket; **prendre une cible en f., à la f.,** to bracket a target; **prise en f.,** bracketing; **régler le tir à la f.,** to range by bracketing; **resserrer la f.,** to reduce, shorten, the bracket; **tirer à la f.,** to straddle; (*b*) *Cards:* tenace; **être pris en f.,** to be caught in a tenace; (*c*) (*statistics*) bracket; **f. de salaire,** wage bracket. 3. (*a*) wishbone (of fowl); (*b*) frog (of horse's hoof). 4. (*a*) claw (of cartridge extractor); (*b*) beam- or pan-support (of balance); (*c*) *Mec.E:* belt-guide, -shifter; **f. de débrayage,** clutch throw-out fork; *Aut:* **f. de commande de changement de vitesse, f. de baladage,** (gear-change) selector fork; (*d*) *Carp: Mec.E: etc:* **assemblage à f.,** slit-and-tongue junction; (*e*) rest (for taking aim with gun); (*f*) *Veh:* futchel(l) (of carriage); tongue-hounds (of wagon); (*g*) fourchette (of glove).

fourchon [furʃɔ̃], *s.m.* 1. fork (of bough). 2. prong, tine (of pitchfork); **fourche à trois fourchons,** three-pronged fork.

fourchu [furʃy], *a.* forked, bifurcated; Y-shaped; **chemin f.,** bifurcating path; **langue fourchue,** divided, forked, tongue; **perche fourchue,** forked pole; **piquet f.,** cleft stick; **menton f.,** cleft chin; **pied f.,** cloven hoof; *F:* **il a le pied f.,** he's an ill-disposed type; *Mus:* **doigté f.,** cross-fingering (on wind instrument); *Gym:* **faire l'arbre f.,** to walk on one's hands.

fourchure [furʃyːr], *s.f.* (*place where a tree, road, etc., forks*) fork; forking.

fourgat [furga], *s.m. O: P:* receiver (of stolen goods), fence.

fourgon[1] [furgɔ̃], *s.m.* poker, (fire)rake, pricker; *Prov:* **la pelle se moque du f.,** it is (a case of) the pot calling the kettle black.

fourgon[2], *s.m.* van, wag(g)on; (*a*) *Road Veh:* **f. automobile,** (i) motor van; (ii) motor hearse; **f. bancaire,** bullion van, *U.S:* armored car; **f. de déménagement,** furniture van, pantechnicon; **f. de livraison,** delivery van; *Adm:* **f. des postes,** mail van; **f. cellulaire,** police van; (*b*) *Mil:* (general service) wag(g)on, vehicle; **les fourgons,** the wagon train; **revenir en France dans les fourgons de l'ennemi,** to come back to France in the wake of the enemy; (*c*) *Rail:* **f. de chemin de fer,** railway van, guard's van; **f. à bagages,** luggage van; **f. à marchandises,** goods wagon, goods van; *U.S:* goods truck; **f. à bestiaux,** cattle truck, box, *U.S:* box car; **f. à frein,** brake van; **f. de tête,** front (brake) van; **f. de queue,** rear (brake) van, guard's van.

fourgonner [furgɔne]. 1. *v.i.* to poke, rake, the fire (of furnace, baker's oven, etc.); *F:* **f. dans un tiroir, dans une armoire,** to poke about, rummage about, in a drawer, in a cupboard. 2. *v.tr.* to poke, prick (the fire).

fourgonnette [furgɔnɛt], *s.f. Aut:* light van.

fourgue [furg], *s.m. P:* receiver (of stolen goods), fence.

fourguer [furge], *v.tr. P:* (*a*) to sell, flog (stolen goods); (*b*) to sell, flog (sth.) cheaply.

fouriérisme [furjerism], *s.m. Pol.Ec:* Fourierism, associationism.

fouriériste [furjerist], *s.m. Pol.Ec:* Fourierist, associationist.

fourmariérite [furmarjerit], *s.f. Miner:* fourmarierite.

fourme [furm], *s.f.* (type of) cheese (made in Auvergne).

fourmi [furmi], *s.f. Ent:* (*a*) ant; **f. rouge, f. fauve,** wood ant, red ant; **f. ailée,** winged ant, ant-fly; **f. amazone,** Amazon ant; **f. champignonniste,** market-gardening ant; **f. à parasol,** parasol ant; **f. esclavagiste,** slave ant; **f. maçonne,** mason ant; **f. à miel,** honey ant; **f. moissonneuse,** harvesting ant; **f. de visite,** visiting ant; *F:* **avoir des fourmis dans les jambes,** to have a tingling, pins and needles, in one's legs; *F:* **j'ai des fourmis dans le pied,** my foot has gone to sleep; *F:* **avoir des œufs de fourmis sous les pieds,** to have ants in one's pants; (*b*) **f. blanche,** termite, white ant; (*c*) *F:* busy and thrifty person; **un travail de f.,** an intricate and laborious job.

fourmiesien, -ienne [furmizjɛ̃, -jɛn], *a. & s. Geog:* (native, inhabitant) of Fourmies.

fourmilier [furmilje], *s.m.* 1. *Z:* anteater; **petit f. arboricole,** two-toed anteater; **f. marsupial,** marsupial anteater. 2. *Orn:* ant thrush, ant catcher.

fourmilière [furmiljɛːr], *s.f.* 1. (*a*) anthill, ant's nest; (*b*) **toute la f. se précipitait sur l'agresseur,** all the ants (of the anthill) were rushing at the attacker; **toute la f. était agitée,** all the ants were, the whole anthill was, in a state of agitation; (*e*) **cette ville est une f.,** the town is a seething mass of activity; **cette f. de gens qui passaient vite,** that seething, swarming, mass of hurrying people. 2. *Vet:* spongy horn (of horse's pumiced foot); pumiced foot.

fourmi-lion [furmiljɔ̃], *s.m. Ent:* ant-lion; *pl. fourmis-lions.*

fourmillant [furmijɑ̃], *a.* swarming, teeming, seething (**de,** with).

fourmillement [furmijmɑ̃], *s.m.* 1. swarming (of ants, etc.); **un f. d'embarcations,** a swarm, crowd, of boats; **le f. de la foule,** the seething, swarming, of the crowd. 2. pricking, tingling, sensation; pins and needles; *Med:* formication.

fourmiller [furmije], *v.i.* 1. to swarm; to teem; to move hither and thither; **ouvrage qui fourmille de fautes,** work that teems with, abounds in, mistakes; **l'avenue fourmillait de voitures,** the avenue was alive with cars; **le plancher fourmillait d'insectes,** the floor was crawling with insects; **les vers fourmillaient dans ce fromage,** the cheese was alive with maggots. 2. **le pied me fourmille,** I've pins and needles in my foot.

fournage [furnaːʒ], *s.m. A:* charge made for baking bread, for roasting joint.

fournaise [furnɛːz], *s.f.* furnace; **cette chambre est une (vraie) f.,** this room's like a furnace, like an oven.

fourneau, -eaux [furno], *s.m.* 1. (*a*) furnace (of boiler, etc.); **f. de forge,** forging furnace; **f. d'une pipe,** bowl of a pipe; (*b*) **f. de cuisine,** (kitchen) range; **f. à gaz,** gas stove, cooker; (*c*) *Metall: Ind:* **f. à lunettes, f. à deux foyers,** spectacle furnace, furnace with two hearths; **f. atomique,** atomic furnace; **décharger un f., jeter bas les feux d'un f.,** to draw a furnace; **mettre un f. hors feu,** to blow down a furnace; **haut f.,** blast furnace; **haut f. blindé,** armoured, cased, blast furnace; **blindage de haut f.,** armour, casing, of blast furnace; **haut f. enveloppé,** blast furnace with chamber hearth; **haut f. à creuset ouvert,** blast furnace with open hearth; **allumer un haut f.,** to blow in a furnace; **décharger un haut f.,** to blow out a furnace; (*d*) **f. à charbon,** charcoal kiln, pit, pile. 2. *Mil: Min:* **f. de mine,** mine chamber, blast hole. 3. *P:* **va donc, f.!** you idiot!

fournée [furne], *s.f.* ovenful (of bread, pottery, etc.); batch (of loaves, etc.); charge (of kiln, blast furnace); **f. cuite,** kiln (of baked bricks, etc.), baking; burning (of bricks, etc.); **pain de la première f.,** bread from the first baking; (*b*) *usu. Iron:* **une f. de sénateurs,** a bevy, batch, of senators; **la première f. de touristes,** the first batch, contingent, of tourists; **une belle f. de prisonniers,** a fine batch of prisoners.

fourni [furni], *a.* 1. well-stocked; full; **une table bien fournie,** a loaded table; **une librairie bien fournie,** a well-stocked bookshop. 2. thick (hair, forest, etc.); bushy (beard, etc.); **barbe peu fournie,** thin beard. 3. *Sp:* **champ f.,** big field of starters.

fournier, -ière [furnje, -jɛːr], *s.* 1. (*a*) baker; owner of a public bakehouse; (*b*) oven-man. 2. *s.m. Orn:* oven bird.

fournil [furni(l)], *s.m.* 1. bakehouse. 2. *A:* wash-house (with copper).

fournilles [furniːj], *s.f.pl.* firewood, brushwood.

fourniment [furnimɑ̃], *s.m.* (*a*) *A.Arms:* powder flask; (*b*) (soldier's) equipment, accoutrements.

fournir [furniːr], *v.tr.* 1. (*a*) *A:* to complete, to fill; **f. des sacs, une somme d'argent,** to fill up sacks, to complete, make up, a sum of money; (*b*) (*of horse*) **f. une belle carrière,** to run well; **cheval qui fournit toute la carrière,** horse that completes the full course; **f. sa carrière, une longue carrière,** to have a long career; to live to a great age. 2. (*a*) to supply, furnish, provide; to find (sentries, fatigue party, a security); **f. qch. à qn, f. qn de qch.,** to supply s.o. with sth.; **tant par mois, tout f.,** so much a month, all found; **la maison est bien fournie en argenterie et en linge,** the house is well equipped, well supplied, with cutlery and linen; **f. des renseignements à qn,** to provide, furnish, s.o. with information; **f. un rapport, un compte rendu,** to make, give in, a report; to give an account (of sth.); **je peux f. les documents,** I can produce the documents; **cela me fournira l'occasion de . . .,** that will give me the opportunity to . . .; *Com:* **f. une lettre de crédit sur qn,** to issue a letter of credit on s.o.; **ce magasin nous fournit tous les produits d'épicerie,** this shop supplies us with all our groceries; **poulet qui fournit deux repas,** chicken that makes two meals; **f. une maison en vin, etc.,** to supply a house with wine, etc.; *abs.* **f. sur la caisse de qn,** to draw on s.o.; (*b*) **vignoble qui fournit un bon vin,** vineyard that yields, produces, a good wine; **école qui fournit des spécialistes,** school that produces, turns out specialists; **f. un effort considérable,** to make a considerable effort; **le travail qu'il a fourni,** the amount of work he has done; *Sp:* **f. un jeu remarquable,** to play an outstanding game. 3. *v.ind.tr.* **f. aux dépenses,** to defray the expenses; **f. aux besoins de qn,** to supply s.o.'s wants; **je ne saurais f. à tous,** I cannot serve everybody's turn; *Cards:* **f. à la couleur demandée,** to follow suit; **f. à trèfle,** to follow the lead in clubs, the club lead.

se fournir. 1. **bois, barbe, qui commence à se f.,** wood, beard, that is beginning to grow thick. 2. (*a*) **se f. de qch.,** to provide oneself with sth.; (*b*) *Com:* **il se fournit chez nous,** he is a customer of ours, we supply him.

fournissement [furnismɑ̃], *s.m. Fin:* 1. contribution in shares (to a company); holding in shares. 2. repartition account.

fournisseur, -euse [furnisœːr, -øːz], *s.* (*a*) supplier, purveyor, caterer; **f. de l'armée,** army contractor; **f. du Gouvernement,** Government contractor; **f. de thé,** dealer in tea, tea dealer; **f. de navires, de la marine,** ships' chandler; **pharmacien f. breveté de Sa Majesté,** chemist by special appointment to His, Her, Majesty; (*b*) **les fournisseurs,** the tradesmen; **entrée des fournisseurs,** tradesmen's entrance.

fourniture [furnityːr], *s.f.* 1. supplying, providing, furnishing; *Adm:* procurement; **(ceci) ne fait pas partie de la f.,** (this) is not included in the contract; **façon et f. d'une robe,** making of and supplying of materials for a dress. 2. (*a*) *Cu:* seasoning (of dish); (*b*) *Mus:* furniture stop (of organ); mixture (stop); sesquialtera. 3. *pl.* (*a*) supply of goods, supplies, requisites; **fournitures pour la photographie,** photographic materials, supplies; **fournitures pour chapeaux,** hat trimmings; **fournitures de navires,** ships' chandlery; **fournitures de bureau,** office equipment; (office) stationery; *Com:* **marché de fournitures,** supply contract, contract for supplies; (*b*) **fournitures de dentiste,** dentist's equipment.

fourpan [furpɑ̃], *s.m.* door-knob hole.

fourrage[1] [furaːʒ], *s.m.* 1. *Nau:* serving, keckling (of cable). 2. *Tail:* lining fur.

fourrage[2], *s.m.* 1. (*a*) *Husb: etc:* forage, fodder, provender; **f. (en) sec,** dry fodder, hay; **f. (en) vert,** green fodder; grass; soiling crop; **donner le f. aux bêtes,** to fodder the cattle; (*b*) *Fish:* **poisson f.,** live fish bait. 2. *Mil:* foraging; **aller au f.,** to forage; **faire du f. (dans un champ),** to gather fodder. 3. foraging party.

fourragement [furaʒmɑ̃], *s.m.* 1. foraging. 2. pillaging.

fourrager[1] [furaʒe], *v.* (**n. fourrageons; je fourrageai(s)**) 1. *v.i.* (*a*) *O:* to forage; **f. au sec, au vert,** to forage for hay, for grass; *F:* **f. dans des papiers,** to rummage, forage, among papers; **f. dans les œuvres d'autrui,** to plagiarize, *F:* crib, from the works of others; (*b*) to foray. 2. *v.tr.* (*a*) **f. un champ,** to clear a field (of all its produce); (*b*) to pillage, ravage (country); **comme vous avez fourragé mes dentelles!** how you have rumpled my lace! **cheveux fourragés par le vent,** hair blown about by the wind.

fourrager[2], **-ère** [furaʒe, -ɛːr]. 1. *a.* (*a*) pertaining to forage; **(corde) fourragère,** forage rope; (*b*) **plantes fourragères,** fodder crops; **graine fourragère,** grass seed. 2. *s.f.* **fourragère,** (*a*) field sown with fodder crop; **f. de luzerne,** field of lucerne; (*b*) hay cart, hay wag(g)on; (*c*) *Mil:* general service wagon; aiglet or lanyard (worn by certain units round the left shoulder as a military distinction); shoulder braid; (*d*) *Aut: A:* luggage carrier, grid.

fourrageur [furaʒœːr], *s.m.* 1. *Mil: A:* forager; **cavaliers dispersés en fourrageurs,** cavalry in open, extended, order. 2. (*a*) pillager, marauder; (*b*) *F:* plagiarist.

fourrageux, -euse [furaʒø, -øːz], *a.* suitable for fodder; **paille fourrageuse,** fodder straw.

fourré [fure]. 1. *a.* (*a*) lined (coat, gloves, etc.); fur-lined; thick (wood); thickly wooded (country); **chocolats fourrés à la crème,** chocolate creams; **bonbon f.,** sweet with a soft centre; *F:* **c'est un innocent f. de malice,** he is not such a fool as he looks; (*b*) **paix fourrée,** hollow peace, sham peace; **médaille fourrée, bijou f.,** plated medal, jewellery; *Fenc:* **coup f.,** exchanged hit, double hit; **porter un coup f. à qn,** to deal s.o. a backhanded blow; (*c*) *F:* **être toujours f. chez qn,** to be constantly at s.o.'s house; **il est toujours f. chez nous,** he is never away from our house; he is never off our doorstep. 2. *s.m.* (*a*) thicket; brake; *Ven:* cover; (*b*) jungle.

fourreau, -eaux [furo], *s.m.* (*a*) sheath, cover, case; *Cost:* sheath dress; **f. d'une épée,** sheath, scabbard, of a sword; **tirer l'épée du f.,** to unsheathe, bare, one's sword; **remettre l'épée au**

f., to sheathe, put up, one's sword; *A: F:* **coucher dans son f.**, to sleep in one's clothes; **f. pour fusil de chasse**, gun case; **f. de parapluie**, umbrella sheath, case; (*b*) *Mec.E:* sleeve (for sliding spindle, etc.); quill (for shaft, etc.); **entraînement par f.**, quill drive; **f. d'avance**, feed sleeve (of lathe, etc.); **joint à f.**, expansion, expanding, joint; *Hyd.E:* **f. de pompe**, priming pipe of pump; *I.C.E:* **soupapes à fourreaux**, sleeve valves; **f. de distribution**, valve sleeve; *Mch:* **f. de cylindre**, liner of cylinder; *Nau:* **piston à f.**, trunk piston; (*c*) *Anat:* sheath (of horse, bull, etc.).

fourre-duvet [furdyvɛ], *s.m. Sw.Fr:* eiderdown case, cover; *pl. fourre-duvets.*

fourre-oreiller [furɔrɛje], *s.m. Sw.Fr:* pillowcase, pillowslip; *pl. fourre-oreillers.*

fourrer [fure], *v.tr.* **1.** (*a*) to cover, coat, line, with fur; **manteau fourré d'hermine**, coat lined with ermine; *A:* **se f.**, to wrap oneself up in furs; (*b*) *A:* **f. une médaille d'or**, to coat, plate, a medal with gold; (*c*) *Mec.E:* **f. un assemblage**, to pack a joint; *Nau:* **f. un câble**, to serve, keckle, a cable. **2.** *F:* to stuff, cram; **f. une lettre dans sa poche**, to stuff, shove, a letter into one's pocket; **f. ses mains dans ses poches**, to stuff, bury, one's hands in one's pockets; **il le fourra sous son oreiller**, he tucked it under his pillow; **je ne sais plus où je les ai fourrés**, I forget where I stowed them away; **je les avais fourrés dans le coin**, I had stuck them in, bundled them into, the corner; **où est-il allé se f.?** where ever has he hidden himself? **je ne savais où me f.**, I didn't know where to hide; **chercher quelque trou où se f.**, to be looking for a job (without much hope of success); **f. son nez partout, dans les affaires d'autrui**, to poke one's nose into everything, into other people's business; **se f. dans la conversation**, to butt into the conversation; **f. des bonbons à un enfant**, (i) to cram a child, (ii) to stuff a child's pockets, with sweets; *P:* **s'en f. jusque-là**, to gorge; **il me fourre du latin et du grec**, he crams me with Latin and Greek; **f. qn dedans**, (i) to let s.o. down badly, to take s.o. in, to have s.o.; (ii) to run s.o. in; **se f. le doigt dans l'œil**, to make a mistake; **f. qn à la porte**, to bundle s.o. out of the house.

fourre-tout [furtu], *s.m.inv.* **1.** lumber room. **2.** hold-all (for travelling).

fourreur [furœːr], *s.m.* **1.** furrier. **2. naturaliste f.**, taxidermist.

fourrier [furje], *s.m.* **1.** *A:* (*a*) harbinger (sent on in front of a monarch, etc.); (*b*) forerunner, precursor (of death, etc.). **2.** (*a*) *Mil:* quartermaster sergeant; (*b*) *Navy:* writer.

fourrière [furjɛːr], *s.f.* **1.** (animal, car) pound; **mettre un chien en f.**, to put a dog in the pound, to impound a dog; **mise en f.**, impounding, poundage; **frais de f.**, poundage. **2.** *Agr:* headland (in ploughing).

fourrure [furyːr], *s.f.* **1.** (*a*) fur, skin; **manteau de f.**, fur coat; **f. de peau de mouton**, sheepskin (coat, rug, etc.); *Her:* **les fourrures**, the heraldic furs (vair, ermine, etc.); (*b*) hair, coat (of heavy-coated animal); **f. plate**, short-haired fur. **2.** filling, lining, material; (*a*) **f. d'un assemblage**, fur, packing, of a joint; *Mec.E:* **f. d'antifriction**, antifriction lining, bushing; *Aut:* **f. de frein**, brake lining; (*b*) *Civ.E: Const:* blocking piece, filler block, filler slip. **3.** *Nau:* (i) keckling, service; (ii) junk.

fourvoiement [furvwamɑ̃], *s.m.* **1.** (*a*) misleading, leading astray; (*b*) losing of one's way, going astray. **2.** (moral) error, going astray.

fourvoyer [furvwaje], *v.tr.* (**je fourvoie, n. fourvoyons; je fourvoierai**) (*a*) to mislead; to lead (s.o.) astray; (*b*) *v.i. or abs. Ven:* to follow the wrong trail.

se fourvoyer. 1. to lose oneself, to lose one's way; to go astray. **2.** to go right off the track, to be entirely mistaken; **être fourvoyé**, to be on the wrong track, the wrong tack.

foussa [fusa], *s.m. Z:* fossa, foussa.

foutaise [futɛːz], *s.f. P:* (*a*) rot, rubbish; **tout ça c'est de la f., des foutaises**, that's a lot of (bloody) rot; (*b*) **on s'est quitté pour des foutaises**, we parted over a mere trifle, something that didn't matter a bit.

fouteau, -eaux [futo], *s.m. F:* beech(tree).

foutelaie [futlɛ], *s.f.* beech plantation; beech grove.

foutoir [futwaːr], *s.m. P:* messy room, place; pigsty; **quel f.!** what a shambles!

foutral, -als [futral], *a. P:* extraordinary.

foutraque [futrak], *a. F:* mad, loony, cracked.

foutre [futr̥], *v.tr.* (*p.p.* **foutu**; *pr.ind.* **je fous, n. foutons**; *p.d.* **je foutais**; *fu.* **je foutrai**) **1.** *P:* (*a*) **f. qch. par terre**, to chuck sth. on the ground; (*b*) **f. un coup de pied à qn**, to kick s.o.; (*c*) **il ne fout rien de toute la journée**, he does damn all from one day's end to another; **qu'est-ce que ça me fout?** what the hell do I care? (*d*) **f. le camp**, to do a bunk, to scram; (*e*) **fous-moi la paix!** (i) can't you (bloody well) leave me alone; bugger off! (ii) shut up! shut your ugly gob! **2.** *V:* to f . . k. **3.** *int. V:* hell and damnation! what the bloody hell! good God! (*Note: even in sense* **1** *this verb is not used in polite society, neither is* **se foutre** *and the derivatives of the verb*).

se foutre, *P:* (*a*) **il s'en fout complètement**, he doesn't care a damn; (*b*) **est-ce que vous vous foutez de moi?** are you trying to make a fool of me?

foutrement [futr(ə)mɑ̃], *adv. P:* (*intensive*) **f. bon**, bloody good.

foutriquet [futrikɛ], *s.m. P:* little squit, little squirt.

foutu [futy], *a. P:* (*a*) **f. caractère**, bloody-minded person; **dans un f. état**, in an awful, rotten, state; (*b*) **c'est un type f.**, he's done for; he'll never do any good; **la mayonnaise est foutue**, the mayonnaise is spoilt, done for; (*c*) **être mal f.**, to feel (i) (bloody) tired, (ii) out of sorts, lousy; (iii) to be badly dressed; (*d*) **il n'est même pas f. de réussir**, he just isn't capable of making the grade; **il est f. de venir quand nous ne serons pas là**, he'll bloody well turn up when we aren't here.

fovéa [fɔvea], *s.f. Anat:* fovea.

fovéal [fɔveal], *a. Anat:* foveal.

fovéolaire [fɔveɔlɛːr], *a.* foveolar.

fovéole [fɔveɔl], *s.f. Anat: Bot:* foveola, small pit.

fovéolé [fɔveɔle], *a. Biol: Bot:* foveolate, pitted.

Fowler [fulɛːr], *Pr.n.* **1.** *Pharm:* **liqueur de F.**, arsenical solution, Fowler's solution. **2.** *Av:* **volet F.**, Fowler flap.

fowlérite [fulerit], *s.f. Miner:* fowlerite.

fox [fɔks], *s.m.* **1.** *F:* fox terrier. **2.** *Vit:* foxy taste (of wine).

foxé [fɔkse], *a. Vit:* foxy.

fox-hound [fɔksaund], *s.m. Ven:* foxhound; *pl. fox-hounds.*

foxien, -ienne [fɔksjɛ̃, -jɛn], *a. & s. Geog:* (native, inhabitant) of Foix.

fox-terrier [fɔkstɛrje], *s.m.* fox terrier; **f.-t. à poil lisse, à poil dur**, smooth-haired, wire-haired, fox terrier; *pl. fox-terriers.*

fox-trot [fɔkstrɔt], *s.m.inv. Danc:* foxtrot.

foyard [fwajaːr], *s.m. F:* beech (tree).

foyer [fwaje], *s.m.* **1.** fire(place), hearth, grate; firebox (of steam engine); **(tapis, devant, de) f.**, hearthrug; **marbre du f.**, hearthstone; **le feu flambait dans le f.**, the fire was blazing on the hearth; **f. de forge**, smith's hearth, fire-pot; **f. catalan**, Catalan forge; **f. de chaudière**, boiler furnace; **f. mécanique**, mechanical stoker; *Hort:* **f. fumigène**, smudge pot. **2.** (*a*) **f. de chaleur**, source of heat; **f. d'un incendie**, seat of a fire; *Geol:* **f. réel (centre d'un séisme), f. sismique**, centrum, seismic focus; **un f. d'érudition**, a centre of learning; (*b*) *Med:* focus, seat (of disorder); **f. d'infection, f. infectieux**, centre of infection; **f. de corruption, d'intrigue**, hotbed of corruption, of intrigue. **3.** (*a*) hearth, home; **le f. familial**, the home; **f. détruit**, broken home; **les joies du f. (domestique)**, the joys of home life; **rentrer dans ses foyers**, to come (back) home; to come back to one's native land; **rendre des prisonniers à leurs foyers**, to get or send prisoners back to their homes; **f. du soldat**, soldiers' club; **f. d'étudiants**, students' union, club, centre; (*b*) *Th:* **f. du public**, foyer; **f. des artistes**, green room. **4.** *Mth: Ph:* focus (of lens, curve, etc.); *Phot:* **appareil à f. fixe**, fixed-focus camera; **mettre au f. la lampe d'un phare**, to focus, set, a headlight, a searchlight; *Opt:* **verres à double f.**, bifocal lenses, bifocals.

frac [frak], *s.m. Cost:* dress coat.

fracas [frakɑ], *s.m.* (*a*) din; (sound of a) crash; **le f. des armes**, the clash of arms; **le f. du tonnerre**, the noise of thunder; **le vase tomba et se brisa avec f.**, the vase fell and broke with a crash; the vase crashed to the ground; **les brisants grondent avec f. sur la plage**, the breakers are thundering on the beach; **dans le f. de la bataille**, in the din of the battle; *F:* **faire du f.**, to kick up a row; (*b*) **sans f.**, quietly; **à grand f.**, ostentatiously; **livre qui a fait du f.**, book that made, caused, a sensation; **il a essayé de partir avec le moins de f. possible**, he tried to leave with the least possible disturbance, as quietly, discreetly, as possible.

fracassant [frakasɑ̃], *a.* **bruit f.**, shattering noise; **victoire fracassante**, smashing, resounding, victory; **déclaration fracassante**, startling announcement.

fracassement [frakasmɑ̃], *s.m.* (*rare*) smashing, shattering.

fracasser [frakase], *v.tr.* to smash (sth.) to pieces; to shatter (sth.); **il eut le bras droit fracassé**, his right arm was shattered.

se fracasser, to crash, smash, to pieces.

fraction [fraksjɔ̃], *s.f.* **1.** *A:* breaking; *Ecc:* **la f. du pain**, the breaking, fraction, of the (eucharistic) bread. **2.** (*a*) *Mth:* fraction; **f. ordinaire**, vulgar fraction; **f. décimale**, decimal fraction; **f. périodique**, recurring decimal; **f. de f.**, compound fraction; **petites parties d'une f.**, partial fractions, part fractions; **pendant une f. de seconde**, for a fraction of a second; **moteur à f. de cheval**, fractional horse power engine; *Atom.Ph:* **f. de tassement**, packing fraction; **f. molaire**, mole fraction; (*b*) part, portion; (political) group; **une f. importante de l'Assemblée a voté contre le projet de loi**, a substantial proportion of the House voted against the bill.

fractionnaire [fraksjɔnɛːr], *a.* fractional; fractionary; **nombre, expression, f.**, mixed number, improper fraction.

fractionnateur [fraksjɔnatœːr], *s.m. Ch: etc:* fractionating column.

fractionnel, -elle [fraksjɔnɛl], *a.* that causes division; **activité fractionnelle au sein d'un parti**, activity that causes a split within a (political) party; **l'exclusion d'un militant pour travail f.**, the exclusion of a militant member for splinter tactics.

fractionnement [fraksjɔnmɑ̃], *s.m.* **1.** dividing-up; splitting into parts, into portions; *Rail:* **f. d'un train**, division of a train (into two or more parts); **le f. de la propriété**, the splitting up of the estate. **2.** *Ch: Ind:* (*a*) fractional distillation, fractionation; (*b*) cracking (of oil, etc.).

fractionner [fraksjɔne], *v.tr.* **1.** to divide into (fractional) parts; to split (up) (shares, etc.); *Mth:* to fractionize (expression); **f. le voyage**, to break the journey (into stages); **f. le paiement de qch.**, to pay for sth. in instalments. **2.** *Ch: Ind:* (*a*) to fractionate (distillation); **distillation fractionnée**, fractional distillation; (*b*) to crack (mineral oils).

se fractionner, to split up; to divide into groups.

fractionnisme [fraksjɔnism], *s.m. Pol:* splitting, splinter, tactics (within a party).

fractionniste [fraksjɔnist], *s.m. or f. Pol:* member of a splinter group (within a party).

fractocumulus [fraktɔkymylyːs], *s.m. Meteor:* fractocumulus.

fractonimbus [fraktɔnɛ̃byːs], *s.m. Meteor:* fractonimbus.

fractostratus [fraktɔstratyːs], *s.m. Meteor:* fractostratus.

fracturation [fraktyrasjɔ̃], *s.f. Petroleum Min:* (artificial) fracturing of strata.

fracture [fraktyːr], *s.f.* **1.** (*a*) breaking open, forcing (of lock, door, etc.); (*b*) *Ling:* breaking (of vowel); fracture. **2.** (*a*) fracture (of bone); **f. comminutive**, comminuted fracture; **f. simple, multiple**, simple, multiple, fracture; **f. balistique**, gunshot fracture; **f. compliquée, ouverte**, compound, open, fracture; **f. présumée**, suspected fracture; **réduire une f.**, to reduce, set, a fracture; (*b*) *Geol:* fracture.

fracturer [fraktyre], *v.tr.* **1.** to force (lock); to break open (door, till, safe). **2.** to fracture, break; **se f. la jambe**, to break one's leg; **crâne fracturé**, fractured skull.

se fracturer, *Geol: etc:* to fracture, break.

fragile [fraʒil], *a.* **1.** fragile; flimsy; brittle (glass, etc.); **f. comme le cristal**, as brittle as glass; (*on parcel, etc.*) **fragile**, fragile; with care. **2.** (*of pers.*) delicate; fragile; **avoir l'estomac f.**, to have a weak stomach, digestion; **santé f.**, delicate, poor, health. **3. autorité f.**, unstable authority; authority which is not firmly established; **prospérité f.**, insecure prosperity; **bonheur f.**, precarious happiness; **hypothèse f.**, flimsy, ill-founded, hypothesis; **fortune f.**, unstable fortune.

fragilement [fraʒilmɑ̃], *adv.* fragilely, weakly; **puissance f. établie**, precariously established power.

fragilisation [fraʒilizasjɔ̃], *s.f.* **1.** (metal) fatigue. **2.** (*of pers.*) (state of) becoming fragile, delicate.

fragiliser [fraʒilize], *v.tr.* to cause (s.o.) to become fragile, delicate; **les événements récents l'ont fragilisée**, recent events have made her frail, delicate.

fragilité [fraʒilite], *s.f.* **1.** fragility; brittleness (of glass, etc.); *Metalw:* embrittlement; **f. de revenu**, temper brittleness. **2.** frailty, fragility (of health); weakness; **la f. des choses humaines**, the instability of human affairs; **f. d'une hypothèse**, flimsiness of an hypothesis.

fragment [fragmɑ̃], *s.m.* (*a*) fragment; broken piece; chip (of stone, etc.); splinter (of broken bone); **f. de chanson,** snatch, scrap, of a song; (*b*) extract (from a book); **publier des fragments historiques,** to publish a book of historical extracts; (*c*) **ce f. de ma vie que je passe sous silence,** this episode in my life to which I make no allusion; **connaître la vérité par fragments,** to know only part of the truth.

fragmentaire [fragmɑ̃tɛːr], *a.* fragmentary, fragmental; in fragments.

fragmentairement [fragmɑ̃tɛrmɑ̃], *adv.* (*a*) in fragments; partially; (*b*) little by little; progressively.

fragmentation [fragmɑ̃tasjɔ̃], *s.f.* (*a*) fragmenting, fragmentation; breaking up (of an empire, etc.); (*b*) *Biol:* **f. (chromosomique),** fragmentation; (*c*) *Geol:* fragmental deposition.

fragmenter [fragmɑ̃te], *v.tr.* to divide (sth.) into fragments; to split (sth.) up; **f. le travail entre plusieurs collaborateurs,** to divide the work between several fellow-workers; **f. un empire,** to break up an empire; **f. la publication d'un ouvrage,** to publish a work in parts.

fragon [fragɔ̃], *s.m. Bot:* ruscus; **f. épineux,** butcher's broom, knee holly.

fragrance [fragrɑ̃ːs], *s.f.* fragrance, perfume.

fragrant [fragrɑ̃], *a.* fragrant, sweet-smelling.

frai [frɛ], *s.m.* **1.** abrasion, wear (of coins); **f. artificiel,** sweating. **2.** (*a*) (i) spawning (of fishes); (ii) spawning season; (*b*) spawn; **f. de grenouille,** frog's spawn; (*c*) *Pisc:* fry.

fraîchement [frɛʃmɑ̃], *adv.* **1.** coolly; **accueillir qn f.,** to receive s.o. coldly; *F:* **comment ça va?—comme le temps, f.,** how are you?—not too hot, like the weather. **2.** freshly, recently; **terre f. remuée,** freshly turned soil; **f. peint,** newly, freshly, painted; **f. débarqué à Paris,** recently arrived in Paris.

fraîcheur [frɛʃœːr], *s.f.* freshness. **1.** coolness, chilliness; **dans la f. du soir,** in the cool of the evening; **la f. des soirées d'automne,** the chilliness of the autumn evenings; *O:* **attraper une f.,** to catch a chill. **2. la f. des fleurs, de son teint,** the freshness, bloom, of the flowers, of her complexion; **jeunes femmes dans toute leur f.,** young women in the bloom of youth; **beauté qui n'est plus de la première f.,** beauty that has lost its bloom; **viande de première f.,** fresh-killed meat; **poisson de première f.,** freshly landed fish; **légumes de première f.,** fresh-picked vegetables; **f. d'esprit,** freshness of approach. **3.** *Nau:* cats-paw, light air.

fraîchin [frɛʃɛ̃], *s.m.* smell of fresh fish.

fraîchir [frɛʃiːr], *v.i. Meteor:* to freshen. **1.** to grow colder; *impers.* **il fraîchit,** it is getting cooler. **2. le vent fraîchit,** the wind is freshening, it is blowing fresh.

fraie [frɛ], *s.f.*, **fraieson** [frɛzɔ̃], *s.f. Ich:* spawning time, season.

frainte [frɛ̃ːt], *s.f. Ind:* (*a*) waste, loss (in manufacturing processes); (*b*) loss in transit.

frairie [frɛri], *s.f.* **1.** *A:* jollification, merry-making; **être de f.,** to be one of a jovial party, to feast. **2.** *Dial:* village feast(day), fair.

frais¹, fraîche [frɛ, frɛʃ]. **1.** *a.* fresh; (*a*) cool; **vent f.,** cool wind; **un petit vent f.,** a little chill wind; **robe fraîche,** cool dress; *P:* **me voilà frais!** I'm in a pretty mess! in a pretty fix! (*b*) *Nau:* **vent f.,** fresh gale; **(vent) grand f.,** stormy gale; *adv.* **il vente grand f.,** it is blowing up for a gale; (*c*) new, recent; **événement de fraîche date,** event of recent date, recent event; **ils sont mariés de fraîche date,** they are recently married; **troupes fraîches,** fresh troops; **œufs frais,** new-laid eggs; **pain f.,** fresh, new, bread; **eau fraîche,** (i) freshly drawn water; (ii) cold water; **nouvelles fraîches,** fresh news; **avoir la mémoire fraîche d'un fait,** to have the recollection of a fact fresh in one's mind; *P.N:* **peinture fraîche,** wet paint; **encre encore fraîche,** ink still wet; *Equit:* **bouche fraîche,** moist mouth (of horse); (*with adv. force*) **roses toutes fraîches cueillies,** freshly gathered roses; **dahlia f. épanoui, rose fraîche épanouie,** dahlia, rose, in its first bloom; **une Anglaise fraîche débarquée,** a newly-landed Englishwoman; (*d*) **teint, visage, f.,** fresh complexion; *F:* **f. comme l'œil, comme une rose, comme un gardon,** as fresh as a daisy, as a rose, as paint; **elle était fraîche comme une rose,** she was as radiant as a rose; **deux belles filles, grandes et fraîches,** two handsome girls, tall and radiant; **f. et dispos,** hale and hearty, in good fettle; **f. et dispos pour le travail,** fit and ready for work. **2.** (*a*) *s.m.* **prendre le f. sur le balcon,** to take the air, to enjoy the cool of the evening, on the balcony; **mettre du vin au f.,** to put wine in a cool place, in the cool; **à mettre au frais,** to be kept cool, in a cool place; *adv.phr.* **de f.,** freshly; **rasé de f.,** fresh-shaven; **peint de f.,** freshly painted; **il était ganté de f.,** he wore new gloves; (*b*) *s.f.* **la fraîche,** the cool of the day; **sortir à la fraîche,** to go out in the cool of the evening; *A:* (*vendor's cry*) **à la fraîche!** (i) fresh fish for sale! (ii) buy my cool drinks!

frais², *s.m.pl.* expenses, cost; **faux f.,** (i) incidental, contingent, expenses; contingencies; (ii) *Jur:* untaxable costs; **menus f.,** (i) petty expenses, petty cash; (ii) pocket money; **f. d'un procès,** costs of a lawsuit; **être condamné aux f.,** to be ordered to pay costs; **faire les f. de qch.,** to bear the cost, the expense, of sth.; **supporter tous les f. d'une entreprise,** to finance an undertaking; **faire, couvrir, ses f.,** (i) to cover one's expenses, to get back one's money, one's outlay; (ii) to get out of a transaction without loss; (iii) (*of enterprise*) to pay its way; **faire les f. de la conversation,** (i) to contribute a large share of the talk; (ii) to be the subject of the conversation; **faire tous les f. de la conversation,** to do all the talking; **le golf et le bridge font les f. du repas,** golf and bridge supply conversation for the meal, keep the meal going; **faire qch. à ses f.,** to do sth. at one's own expense; **à grands f., à peu de f.,** at great, at little, cost; expensively; inexpensively; **il aime inviter les gens à ses f., et (il) n'aime pas à être invité aux f. d'autrui,** he likes to invite people (and to pay for them), and he dislikes being invited (and paid for); **repartir sur nouveaux f.,** to make a fresh start; **rentrer dans ses f.,** to get one's money back; **se mettre en f.,** to go to expense; **ne vous mettez pas en f. pour elle,** do not put yourself out for her; **se mettre en f. pour plaire,** to lay oneself out to please; **faire des f.,** to lay oneself out to please; **ne faites pas de f. pour le dîner,** don't run to any expense over the dinner; **j'en suis pour mes f.,** I've had all my trouble for nothing, I've got nothing for my pains; *F:* **arrêter les f.,** to give up, to throw in the sponge; *Com: Ind:* **f. à payer, f. échus,** outstanding expenses; **f. accessoires,** accessory expenses; **f. accessoires de courtage,** expenses in connection with brokerage; **f. d'amortissement,** (i) amortization, amortizement, charges; (ii) (amount written off for) depreciation, reserve for depreciation (of building, plant, etc.); **f. accidentels,** incidental expenses; **f. fixes, f. permanents,** fixed charges; standing costs, expenses, charges; **f. d'administration, de gestion,** administrative costs, management expenses; **f. divers,** sundry charges, sundries; **f. généraux,** overhead charges, expenses, overheads; standing expenses, charges; **compte de f. généraux,** charges account; **f. de bureau,** office expenses; **f. d'entreposage, de magasinage,** storage (charges), warehouse charges; **f. de manutention,** handling costs, expenses; **f. de transport,** transport charges; **f. de premier établissement,** initial capital expenditure; **f. d'installation,** initial, preliminary, expenses; **total des f. effectués, encourus,** total expenses incurred; **exempt de f., sans f.,** free of charge; (*on bill*) no expenses; *Ind:* **f. de lancement (d'une fabrication),** set-up costs; **f. de main d'œuvre,** labour costs, expenses; **f. d'outillage,** tooling-up expenses; **f. d'entretien (du matériel, etc.),** upkeep, maintenance, expenses; cost of upkeep, of maintenance; **f. d'exploitation,** operating costs; **f. de transformation,** conversion costs; *Nau:* **f. d'agence,** agency fees, attendance fees; **f. de chaland,** lighterage; **f. de pilotage,** pilotage; **f. de remorquage,** towage; **f. de port,** port charges; **f. de grue,** cranage; *Adm:* **f. de bureau,** office allowance; **f. de représentation,** entertainment allowance; *Adm: Com:* **f. de déplacement,** *Mil:* **f. de route,** travel allowance; travelling expenses; **f. de séjour,** living expenses; *F:* **aux f. de la princesse,** at the expense of the government, the firm; *F:* on the house; *Jur:* **f. de justice,** court costs; **f. d'expertise,** survey fees; *Sch:* **f. de scolarité, f. scolaires,** school fees.

fraisage [frɛzaːʒ], *s.m.* **1.** *Metalw:* (*a*) milling (of surface); **f. d'angle,** angle milling; **f. de côté, f. latéral,** side milling; **f. de face,** face milling; **f. de forme,** form milling; **f. des rainures,** slot milling; **f. en bout,** end milling; **f. en plan,** plane milling; **sabot de f.,** milling shoe; **tête de f.,** milling head; (*b*) countersinking (of hole). **2.** *Dent:* drilling.

fraise¹ [frɛːz], *s.f.* (*a*) strawberry; **f. des bois,** wood strawberry; **f. ananas,** pine strawberry; **arbre à fraises,** strawberry tree; **f. du désert,** fruit of a kind of cactus; **aller aux fraises,** (i) to go strawberry picking; (ii) *F:* (*of man and girl*) to go for a walk in the woods; *P:* **sucrer les fraises,** (i) to tremble (all over); (ii) to be gaga; *a.inv.* **rubans f. (écrasée),** (crushed) strawberry ribbons; (*b*) *F:* naevus; **avoir une f. sur la joue,** to have a strawberry mark on one's cheek; (*c*) *P:* face, mug; **amener sa f.,** to blow in; **ramener sa f.,** (i) to butt into the conversation; (ii) to shove one's opinions down people's throats.

fraise², *s.f.* **1.** (*a*) *Z:* mesentery (of animal); (*b*) *Cu:* (calf's) ruffle. **2.** (*a*) *A.Cost:* ruff, fraise; (*b*) wattle (of turkey). **3.** *Fort:* fraise. **4.** *Ven:* coronet (of stag's horn). **5.** *Mec.E: etc:* (*a*) milling cutter, tool; mill; **f. d'angle, f. biconique,** angle cutter, mill; angular cutter; **f. de côté, f. latérale,** side mill; **f. de face, f. plane, f. à surfacer,** face cutter, mill; **f. de forme,** formed cutter; **f. en bout,** end mill; **f. en bout à deux arêtes de coupe,** two-lipped end mill; **f. hélicoïdale,** spiral-fluted mill, cutter with a lead; **f. à dents fraisées,** milled-tooth cutter; **f. à lames rapportées,** inserted-tooth cutter; **f. à queue,** shank-type cutter, cutter with shank; **f. à profiler, f. commune,** profile cutter; **f. à fileter,** thread-milling cutter; **f. à rainurer,** slot mill, cutter; slotting cutter; **f. à dégrossir, à finir, les rainures,** roughing, finishing, slot mill; **f. à tailler les engrenages,** gear cutter; **f. à dégrossir, à finir, les engrenages,** roughing, finishing, gear cutter; **f. à tailler les crémaillères,** rack-tooth cutter; **f. ébaucheuse,** stocking cutter; **enlever à la f.,** to mill off; **travailler une pièce à la f.,** to mill, bore, out a part; (*b*) **fraise (conique),** countersink; **f. conique mâle,** pipe reamer; **f. simple,** plain countersink; **f. à couteau,** snail countersink; **f. taillée, f. à roder, f. champignon,** rose bit, countersink; (*c*) *Dent: Surg:* bur, drill; **f. chirurgicale,** surgical bur, bone bur; **f. à extrémité mousse,** non-end-cutting bur; **f. à fissure,** fissure bur; **f. (à) double taille,** cross-cut bur; (*d*) *Civ.E:* rock drill.

fraise-mère [frɛzmɛːr], *s.f. Mec.E:* (i) hob (for cutting worm); (ii) gear-milling cutter, thread-milling cutter; *pl. fraises-mères.*

fraiser¹ [frɛze], *v.tr.* **1.** to fold (sth.) into a ruff; to frill, to goffer. **2.** *Mec.E:* (*a*) to mill; **f. entre pointes,** to mill between centres; **machine à f.,** milling machine, miller; **machine à f. les engrenages, les filetages,** gear-milling, thread-milling, machine; **machine à f. les rainures,** keyway milling machine; (*b*) to countersink (hole); (*c*) *Dent:* to drill. **3.** *Fort:* to provide with a fraise.

fraiser², *v.tr.* to knead (dough).

fraiseraie [frɛzrɛ], *s.f.* strawberry field; strawberry bed.

fraise-scie [frɛzsi], *s.f. Mec.E:* metal-slitting saw; *pl. fraises-scies.*

fraisette [frɛzɛt], *s.f. A.Cost:* small ruff.

fraiseur, -euse [frɛzœːr, -øːz], *Mec.E:* **1.** *s.m.* (*pers.*) miller, milling machine operator. **2.** *s.f.* **fraiseuse,** miller, milling-machine; *F: Civ.E:* rotary snow plough; **f. automatique,** automatic milling machine; **f. à commande manuelle, f. à main,** hand-(operated) milling machine; **f. à reproduire,** copying milling machine; **f. de fabrication,** manufacturing milling machine; **f. d'outillage,** tool (room) milling machine.

fraisier [frɛzje], *s.m.* **1.** strawberry plant; **f. élevé,** hautbois strawberry plant. **2.** strawberry grower.

fraisière [frɛzjɛːr], *s.f. Hort: A:* strawberry field; strawberry bed.

fraisiériste [frɛzjerist], *s.m.* strawberry grower.

fraisil [frɛzi(l)], *s.m.* coal cinders; small coal (from forge); breeze.

fraisoir [frɛzwaːr], *s.m. Tls:* **1.** wood drill. **2.** countersink (bit).

fraissine [frɛsin], *s.f.* ash grove, plantation.

fraisure [frɛzyːr], *s.f.* **1.** countersunk hole, countersink. **2.** *Fort:* row of fraises.

framboise [frɑ̃bwaːz], *s.f.* raspberry.

framboisé [frɑ̃bwaze], *a.* raspberry-flavoured.

framboiser [frɑ̃bwaze], *v.tr.* to flavour (sth.) with raspberry.

framboiseraie [frɑ̃bwazrɛ], *s.f.* raspberry field; raspberry bed.

framboisier [frɑ̃bwazje], *s.m.* raspberry cane.

framboisière [frɑ̃bwazjɛːr], *s.f.* raspberry bed.

framée [frame], *s.f. A.Arms:* framea, javelin (of the Franks).

franc¹ [frɑ̃], *s.m.* franc; **donnez-moi pour vingt francs d'essence, s'il vous plaît,** twenty francs' worth of petrol, please.

franc², franche [frɑ̃, frɑ̃ːʃ], *a.* **1.** free; **f. arbitre** [frɑ̃karbiːtr], free will; **f. de tout droit,** duty-free, free of duty; **f. d'impôts,** exempt from taxation; **f. de port,** post-free; (*of railway parcels*) carriage paid; *Cust:* **zone franche,** free zone; *Nau:* **f. d'avaries,** free of average; **avoir part franche dans une affaire,** to share in the profits of a business without contributing to the expenses; **navire f. d'eau,** ship free of water; **la pompe est franche,** the pump is sucking, is dry; *Fb:* **coup f.,** free

kick; *Nau:* **port f.**, free port; *Mil:* **corps f.**, commando (unit); **avoir ses coudées franches**, to have (i) elbow room, (ii) a free hand; **à f. étrier**, at full gallop. **2.** *(a)* frank; open (admiration, etc.); candid; outspoken; **dire la franche vérité**, to speak the simple truth; **situation franche**, clear, unequivocal, position; **il est f. comme l'or**, he is as frank, as candid, as a child; **avoir son f. parler**, to speak one's mind; **il aime son f. parler**, he is an outspoken man; **c'est net et f.**, it's all open and above-board; **y aller de f. jeu**, to go about it openly, to be quite straightforward about it; **jouer jeu f., f. jeu (avec, contre, qn)**, (i) to play a straightforward game; (ii) to play the (square) game, to play fair (with s.o.); to play above-board, to act on the square; **laissez-moi f. jeu!** give me a fair chance! **saut f.**, clean jump (at hurdles, etc.); *adv.* **pour parler f.**, frankly speaking; candidly speaking; *(b)* real, true, downright; **beurre f.**, pure butter; **cassure franche**, clean break; **coupure franche**, sharp gap, sharp cut-off (on ground, material, etc.); **c'est un f. Breton**, he's a true Breton; **un vert f.**, a pure green; **une franche canaille**, an arrant, downright, out and out, scoundrel; **f. buveur**, heavy drinker; **joie franche**, unmixed joy; **vin f.**, unadulterated, pure, wine; **vin f. de goût**, wine clean to the taste; natural tasting wine; *Arb:* **arbre f. de pied**, ungrafted, maiden, tree; *Const:* **pierre franche**, sound stone; *Nau:* **barre franche**, tiller; *Nau:* **vent f.**, steady wind; *(c)* complete, whole; **huit jours francs**, eight clear days; *(d)* *Cards:* **cinq levées franches**, five quick tricks, five tricks straight off.

franc³, franque [frɑ̃, frɑ̃:k]. **1.** *Hist:* *(a)* *a.* Frankish; *(b)* *s.* Frank. **2.** *s.* *(in Levantine use)* European, Frank. **3.** *a. Ling: A:* **langue franque**, lingua franca.

français, -aise [frɑ̃sɛ, -ɛ:z]. **1.** *a.* French. **2.** *s.* Frenchman, Frenchwoman; **les Français**, the French; **deux F.**, two Frenchmen. **3.** *s.m.* **le f.**, (the) French (language); **parler f.**, (i) to speak French; (ii) to speak clearly, intelligibly; to express oneself clearly; *F:* **vous ne comprenez pas le f.?** don't you understand plain French, plain language? *F:* **en bon f.**, to put it more clearly, more simply; *F:* **parler f. comme une vache espagnole**, to speak broken, pidgin, French; *Sch:* **le f. fondamental**, basic French. **4.** **à la française**, in the French style, manner; **jardin à la française**, formal garden.

franc-alleu [frɑ̃kalø], *s.m. Hist:* freehold land, allodium, freehold; *pl. francs-alleux.*

franc-blaquet [frɑ̃blakɛ], *s.m. Ich: F:* sprat; *pl. francs-blaquets.*

franc-bord [frɑ̃bɔ:r], *s.m.* **1.** *Nau:* freeboard; **navire haut de f.-b.**, ship high out of the water; **f.-b. en eau douce**, fresh water freeboard; **marques de f.-b.**, freeboard marks. **2.** *Nau:* **construit à f.-b.**, carvel built. **3.** strip of public land (beyond towpath bordering a river); *pl. francs-bords.*

franc-bourgeois [frɑ̃burʒwa], *s.m. Hist:* freeman; *pl. francs-bourgeois.*

franc-canton [frɑ̃kɑ̃tɔ̃], *s.m. Her:* canton; *pl. francs-cantons.*

franc-comtois, -oise [frɑ̃kɔ̃twa, -wa:z], *a. & s. Geog:* (native, inhabitant) of Franche-Comté; *pl. francs-comtois.*

France [frɑ̃:s], *Pr.n.f. Geog:* France; **la F. est bornée par . . .**, France is bounded by . . .; **en F.**, in France; **je suis de F.**, I am from France; **les vins de F.**, French wines; **les rois de F.**, the kings of France, the French kings; *Hist:* **la F. libre**, Free France; **la F. combattante**, Fighting France.

franc-fief [frɑ̃fjɛf], *s.m. Hist:* frank-fee; *pl. francs-fiefs.*

franc-filin [frɑ̃filɛ̃], *s.m. Nau:* white rope; *pl. francs-filins.*

Francfort [frɑ̃kfɔ:r], *Pr.n. Geog:* Frankfurt; *Cu:* **saucisse de F.**, frankfurter; *Anthr:* **plan de F.**, Frankfurt horizontal.

francfortois, -oise [frɑ̃kfɔrtwa, -wa:z], *Geog:* *(a)* *a.* Frankfurt; *(b)* *s.* Frankfurter.

franchement [frɑ̃ʃmɑ̃], *adv.* **1.** frankly, candidly, openly, undisguisedly; readily, unhesitatingly; **j'accepte f. vos excuses**, I unreservedly accept your apology; **parler f.**, to speak candidly, frankly; to use plain language; **laissez-moi vous dire f. ce que je pense**, let me speak my mind; **il est f. athée**, he is openly, avowedly, an atheist; **mouvement exécuté f.**, movement boldly carried out; **cheval qui saute f.**, horse that is a clean jumper. **2.** really, quite; **c'était f. stupide**, it was sheer stupidity; **c'était f. de ma faute**, it was really my fault; **j'en suis f. dégoûté**, I am heartily sick of it; **f. non!** (quite) frankly, no!

franchir [frɑ̃ʃi:r], *v.tr.* **1.** *(a)* to clear (obstacle); to jump (over) (ditch, wall); to shoot (rapids); to run past (danger signal); to exceed (limit of credit, etc.); to get over (difficulty); **f. le fossé d'un saut**, to jump over the ditch; to jump clean over the ditch; **l'escadron franchit l'arête**, the squadron topped the ridge; *(b)* to pass through, to cross; **f. le Rubicon**, to cross, pass, the Rubicon; **f. un canal**, to pass, go, through a canal; **f. la grille du jardin**, to go through the garden gate; **f. le seuil**, to step over, cross, the threshold; **f. le salon**, to cross, pass through, the drawing-room; **le train franchit le tunnel**, the train is passing through the tunnel; *Av:* **f. le mur du son**, to break (through) the sound barrier; **il a franchi la quarantaine**, he has turned forty. **2.** *(a)* **f. une pompe**, to free, clear, a pump; *(b)* **f. un vaisseau, une voie d'eau**, to pump a ship dry. **3.** *v.i. Nau:* *(of wind)* to veer aft.

franchise [frɑ̃ʃi:z], *s.f.* **1.** *(a)* freedom; **octroyer à une ville une charte de f.**, to grant a city a charter (of freedom); *(b)* *Hist:* **les franchises d'une ville**, the franchises of a town; *(c)* *Hist:* (i) right of sanctuary; (ii) sanctuary, asylum; *(d)* *(diplomatic, etc.)* immunity. **2.** exemption; **importer, faire entrer, qch. en f.**, to import sth. free of duty, duty free; **admission en f.**, free admission; **entrée en f. de . . .**, free import of . . .; **bagages en f.**, free (allowance of) luggage; *Post:* **en f. (postale)** = O.H.M.S., official paid; **f. militaire**, on active service, O.A.S.; **f. de port**, franking privilege. **3.** *Ins:* accidental damage excess. **4.** frankness, openness, candour, outspokenness; **parler avec f.**, to speak frankly, candidly; **avouer en toute f. que . . .**, to confess quite frankly, quite openly, that . . .; **j'aime la f.**, I like plain speaking.

franchissable [frɑ̃ʃisabl], *a.* that can be crossed, passed; passable (river, etc.); negotiable (hill, etc.); *Rail:* (signal) that can be passed (after the train has halted for a certain time).

franchissement [frɑ̃ʃismɑ̃], *s.m.* clearing (of obstacle); jumping (of ditch, etc.); crossing, passing (of river, etc.); *Mil:* **capacité de f.**, *(of tank)* trench, ditch, crossing capacity; spanning capacity, ability; **f. de vive force**, forced crossing (of river); **f. par surprise**, surprise crossing (of river); **exercice de f. de cours d'eau**, river crossing exercise; **échelle de f.**, trench ladder.

franc-homme [frɑ̃kɔm], *s.m. Hist:* freeman; *pl. francs-hommes.*

francien, -ienne [frɑ̃sjɛ̃, -jɛn]. **1.** *a.* concerning, related to, the Ile-de-France. **2.** *s.m. Ling:* Francien.

francique [frɑ̃sik], *s.m. A.Ling:* Frankish.

francisant, -ante [frɑ̃sizɑ̃, -ɑ̃:t], *s.* student of, specialist in, French.

francisation [frɑ̃sizasjɔ̃], *s.f.* **1.** Francization, gallicizing (of foreign word, etc.). **2.** *Nau:* Francization, registry as a French ship; **acte de f.**, certificate of Francization, of registry (as a French ship).

franciscain, -aine [frɑ̃siskɛ̃, -ɛn]. **1.** *a. & s.m. Ecc:* Franciscan. **2.** *s.f. Ecc:* **franciscaine**, (Poor) Clare.

franciscanisant, -ante [frɑ̃siskanizɑ̃, -ɑ̃:t], *s.* student of Saint Francis of Assisi.

franciser [frɑ̃size], *v.tr.* **1.** to Francize, gallicize (foreign word, etc.). **2.** *Nau:* to register (a ship) as French.

se franciser, to become quite French, to adopt French ways.

francisque [frɑ̃sisk], *s.f. A.Arms:* francisc(a), Frankish battle-axe.

francium [frɑ̃sjɔm], *s.m. Ch:* francium.

franc-juge [frɑ̃ʒy:ʒ], *s.m. Hist:* member of the Sainte-Vehme; *pl. francs-juges.*

franc-maçon [frɑ̃masɔ̃], *s.m.* freemason; *pl. francs-maçons.*

franc-maçonnique [frɑ̃masɔnik], *a.* masonic; *pl. franc-maçonniques.*

franc-maçonnerie [frɑ̃masɔnri], *s.f.* freemasonry; *F:* **la f.-m. des grandes écoles** = the old-boy network.

franc-mariage [frɑ̃marja:ʒ], *s.m. A.Jur:* marriage between free subjects (as opposed to serfs).

franco¹ [frɑ̃ko]. **1.** *adv.* *(a)* free, carriage free; **f. (de port)**, carriage paid, postage paid; **livré f.**, delivery free (of charge), post(age) paid; **catalogue f. sur demande**, catalogue sent free on request; **f. (à) bord**, free on board, F.O.B.; **f. quai**, free alongside ship, F.A.S.; free on quay, at wharf, *U.S:* ex quay, ex wharf; **f. gare**, free on train, on rail; **f. valeur**, free of payment; *(b)* *F:* readily, unhesitatingly; **vas-y f.!** go ahead! **2.** *s.m. St.Exch:* single commission (on double operation).

franco-² [frɑ̃ko], *comb.fm.* Franco-; **franco-allemand**, Franco-German.

Franco-Américain, -aine [frɑ̃koamerikɛ̃, -ɛn], *s. Fr.C:* Franco-American (French-speaking Canadian emigrated to New England).

François [frɑ̃swa], *Pr.n.m.* Francis, Frank; **saint F. d'Assise**, Saint Francis of Assisi; *P:* **faire le coup du père F. à qn**, (i) to (waylay and) throttle s.o. (with a silk handkerchief); to garrotte s.o. *(from a ruffian of this name, notorious for the trick)*; (ii) to betray s.o.

Françoise [frɑ̃swa:z], *Pr.n.f.* Frances.

François-Joseph [frɑ̃swaʒozɛf], *Pr.n.m. Geog:* **l'archipel F.-J.**, Franz Josef Land.

francolin [frɑ̃kɔlɛ̃], *s.m. Orn:* francolin; black partridge.

francolite [frɑ̃kɔlit], *s.f. Miner:* francolite.

Franconie [frɑ̃kɔni], *Pr.n.f. Hist:* Franconia; **Haute, Moyenne, Basse, F.**, Upper, Middle, Lower, Franconia.

franconien, -ienne [frɑ̃kɔnjɛ̃, -jɛn], *a. & s. Hist:* Franconian.

francophile [frɑ̃kɔfil], *a. & s.* francophile.

francophilie [frɑ̃kɔfili], *s.f.* francophilia.

francophobe [frɑ̃kɔfɔb], *a. & s.* francophobe.

francophobie [frɑ̃kɔfɔbi], *s.f.* francophobia.

francophone [frɑ̃kɔfɔn], *a. & s.* French-speaking (person).

francophonie [frɑ̃kɔfɔni], *s.f.* *(a)* (the state of) being French-speaking; *(b)* the French-speaking countries.

franco-provençal, -aux [frɑ̃kɔprɔvɑ̃sal, -o], *a. & s.m. Ling:* Franco-Provençal.

franc-parler [frɑ̃parle], *s.m.* frankness, candour; plainness, bluntness, of speech; plain speaking; **jeune homme qui a le f.-p.**, outspoken youth; **permettez-moi mon f.-p.**, allow me to speak quite frankly, quite candidly; *(often without the hyphen. See* FRANC² *2).*

franc-quartier [frɑ̃kartje], *s.m. Her:* quarter; *pl. francs-quartiers.*

franc-salé [frɑ̃sale], *s.m. Hist:* *(a)* right to buy or sell salt without paying tax; *(b)* allocation of free salt (granted to certain privileged people).

franc-saure [frɑ̃sɔ:r], *s.m.* salted dried herring; *pl. francs-saures.*

franc-servant [frɑ̃sɛrvɑ̃], *s.m. Hist:* freeman (as opposed to serf); *pl. francs-servants.*

franc-tenancier [frɑ̃tənɑ̃sje], *s.m. Hist:* freeholder, franklin; *pl. francs-tenanciers.*

franc-tireur [frɑ̃tirœ:r], *s.m. Mil:* franc-tireur, irregular combatant, guerrilla; sniper; *pl. francs-tireurs.*

frange [frɑ̃:ʒ], *s.f.* *(a)* fringe; **rideaux à franges**, fringed curtains; **franges d'épaulettes**, bullions; *(b)* **f. (de cheveux)**, fringe; *(c)* *Opt:* **f. d'interférence**, interference fringe, rings; **franges de Fresnel**, diffraction fringes; *Anat:* **f. synoviale**, synovial ligament, fold, fringe; *(d)* **les franges du sommeil**, the borderline of sleep.

frangé [frɑ̃ʒe], fringed; **pantalon f.**, frayed trousers; **petite baie frangée d'écume**, bay fringed with foam.

frangeant [frɑ̃ʒɑ̃], *a. Geog:* **récif f.**, fringing reef.

franger [frɑ̃ʒe], *v.tr.* **(je frangeai(s); n. frangeons)** to fringe, to border.

frangible [frɑ̃ʒibl], *a.* frangible, breakable, brittle.

frangin, -ine [frɑ̃ʒɛ̃, -in], *s. P:* *(a)* brother, sister; *(b)* fellow, *F:* guy; *(c)* *s.f.* **frangine**, girl, *F:* bird.

frangipane [frɑ̃ʒipan], *s.f.* **1.** frangipane (perfume). **2.** *Cu:* frangipane.

frangipanier [frɑ̃ʒipanje], *s.m. Bot:* plumiera, frangipani, frangipane; **f. à fleurs rouges**, red jasmine.

franglais [frɑ̃glɛ], *s.m. F:* Franglais.

frangule [frɑ̃gyl], *s.f. Bot:* alder buckthorn, black alder.

franguline [frɑ̃gylin], *s.f. Ch:* frangulin.

frankéniacées [frɑ̃kenjase], *s.f.pl. Bot:* Frankeniaceae.

frankénie [frɑ̃keni], *s.f. Bot:* frankenia; sea heath.

franklinisation [frɑ̃klinizasjɔ̃], *s.f. Med:* Franklinization.

franklinite [frɑ̃klinit], *s.f. Miner:* franklinite.

franque. *See* FRANC³.

franquette [frɑ̃kɛt], *s.f. used only in* **à la bonne f.**, simply, without ceremony; **faire qch. à la bonne f.**, to do things in a simple, homely, way; **homme à la bonne f.**, easy-going sort of man; **venez dîner chez nous à la bonne f.**, come and take pot luck with us.

franquisme [frɑ̃kism], *s.m. Pol:* Francoism.

franquiste [frɑ̃kist]. *Pol:* **1.** *a.* pro-Franco. **2.** *s.m. & f.* supporter of Franco.

frappage [frapa:ʒ], *s.m.* **1.** stamping; striking (of medal, coin); minting (of coins). **2.** chilling (of wine, etc.); putting on the ice.

frappant [frapɑ̃], *a.* striking, remarkable; **manquement f. à une règle,** conspicuous violation of a rule; **ressemblance frappante,** striking resemblance; **d'une façon frappante,** strikingly, in a striking manner.

frappe[1] [frap], *s.f.* **1.** (*a*) striking, minting (of coins); (*b*) *Typwr:* striking (of the keys); touch; **six impressions en une seule f.,** six copies at one go; **erreur, faute, de f., fausse f.,** typing error; (*c*) *Baseball:* hit. **2.** impression, stamp (on coin, etc.). **3.** *Typ:* set of matrices. **4.** (*a*) striking face, top die (of power hammer); (*b*) sound bow (of bell). **5.** *Mil:* **première, deuxième, f.,** first, second, strike; **puissance de f.,** strike, striking, power; **force de f.,** strike, striking, force.

frappe[2], *s.f. P:* hooligan; **c'est une sale petite f.,** he's a filthy little bastard.

frappé [frape]. **1.** *a.* (*a*) struck; **f. d'horreur, de douleur,** horrorstruck, horrorstricken; grief-stricken; **f. d'étonnement,** struck with amazement; (*b*) *Tex:* (*of material*) solid and close-woven; (*c*) (*of wine, etc.*) chilled; **café f.,** iced coffee; **whisky f.,** whisky on the rocks; (*d*) *P:* crazy, barmy, loony. **2.** *s.m.* (*a*) *Mus:* down beat; (*b*) *Danc:* frappé.

frappe-cocktail [frapkɔktɛl], *s.m. A:* cocktail-shaker; *pl. frappe-cocktails.*

frappe-devant [frapdəvɑ̃], *s.m.inv. Tls: Metalw:* sledgehammer.

frappement [frapmɑ̃], *s.m.* (action of) striking; blow; *B.Hist:* **f. du rocher,** striking of the rock.

frapper [frape], *v.tr.* **1.** (*a*) to strike, hit; **f. légèrement,** to tap; **f. qn du poing,** to hit s.o. with one's fist; *F:* to thump s.o.; **f. la table du poing,** to strike the table with one's fist, to bang one's fist on the table; **f. des mains, dans ses mains,** to clap (one's hands); **f. qn avec la main,** to slap s.o.; **elle le frappa au visage,** she struck him in the face; **se f. les cuisses,** to slap one's thighs; **f. un coup,** to strike a blow; **f. un grand coup,** to make a dramatic move; **f. des marchandises d'un droit,** to impose, levy, a duty on goods; **f. qn d'une punition,** to impose a punishment on s.o.; **son qui me frappa l'oreille,** sound that struck, caught, my ear, that fell upon my ear; **f. l'air de ses cris,** to make the air ring with one's cries; *Mus:* **f. un accord,** to strike a chord; **le malheur qui nous frappe,** the misfortune that has overtaken us; **la crise économique qui nous frappe,** the economic crisis from which we are suffering; *Town P:* **f. d'alignement,** to instruct to conform to, to subject to, the building line; **être frappé d'une maladie, d'une mort soudaine,** to be stricken with a disease, to be struck down by sudden death; **être frappé de mutisme,** to be struck dumb; **f. qn d'étonnement,** to strike s.o. with amazement; **ce qui me frappa le plus ce fut . . .,** what struck, impressed, me most was . . .; *abs.* **ce qui frappe chez lui est que . . .,** the striking thing about him is that . . .; **f. la porte,** to slam the door; *abs.* **f. à la porte,** to knock at the door; **f. doucement à la porte,** to tap at the door; **f. deux coups,** to give a double knock; **on frappa à la porte,** there was a knock, a tap, at the door; **on frappe,** there's a knock; **entrer sans f.,** to walk straight in; **je le reconnais à sa façon de frapper,** I know him by his knock; **f. du pied, du talon,** to stamp (one's foot); *Th:* **f. les trois coups,** to give the three classic knocks (before the curtain goes up); *s.a.* JUSTE 3; (*b*) to stamp; to strike (medal, coin); to mint (coins); to stamp, emboss, goffer (wallpaper, etc.); to block (leather, etc.); **f. ses initiales sur . . .,** to stamp one's initials on . . .; (*c*) to punch (out), cut out (paper pattern, etc.); (*d*) to type (letter, etc.). **2.** *Nau:* to bend, frap; **f. une drisse,** to bend a halyard; **f. un signal,** to bend on a signal; **f. un cordage sur un câble,** to make a rope fast to a cable. **3.** to ice; to chill (wine, etc.); **f. le champagne,** to put the champagne on ice.

se frapper, *F:* (*a*) to get flustered, put out; (*b*) to become demoralized, alarmed, *F:* panicky; to panic; **ne vous frappez pas,** don't panic; don't get excited.

frappeur, -euse [frapœːr, -øːz], *s.* **1.** (*a*) hitter, striker; *Metalw:* hammerman, striker; **f. de rivets,** rivet striker; *Psychics:* **esprit f.,** (i) rapping spirit; (ii) poltergeist; (*b*) stamper; embosser (of wall-paper, etc.); (*c*) cutter-out, puncher (of paper patterns, etc.). **2.** *s.m.* (*a*) *Metalw:* striking hammer, striker; **f. pneumatique,** pneumatic hammer; **f. pneumatique (à mater),** pneumatic caulking tool; (*b*) *W.Tel:* tapper.

frase [fraːz], *s.f.* (baker's) scraper.

fraser [fraze], *v.tr.* to knead (dough).

frasil [frazil], *s.m. Fr.C: Geog:* frazil (ice).

frasnien [franjɛ̃], *a. & s.m. Geol:* Frasnian.

frasque [frask], *s.f.* prank, escapade.

frater [fratɛːr], *s.m. A: F:* **1.** lay brother. **2.** barber's, surgeon's, assistant.

fraternel, -elle [fratɛrnɛl], *a.* fraternal, brotherly; **il s'est montré très f. avec moi,** he adopted a very brotherly attitude towards me.

fraternellement [fratɛrnɛlmɑ̃], *adv.* fraternally, like brothers, in a brotherly fashion.

fraternisation [fratɛrnizasjɔ̃], *s.f.* fraternization, fraternizing.

fraterniser [fratɛrnize], *v.i.* to fraternize (**avec,** with).

fraternité [fratɛrnite], *s.f.* fraternity; brotherhood; **il y a entre eux une f. d'esprit,** they are of similar outlook, they look at things in the same way.

fratricide[1] [fratrisid]. **1.** *s.m. & f.* fratricide. **2.** *a.* fratricidal.

fratricide[2], *s.m.* (crime of) fratricide.

fratrie [fratri], *s.f. Gr.Ant:* phratry.

fraudatoire [frodatwaːr], *a.* fraudulent.

fraude [froːd], *s.f.* **1.** fraud, deception, piece of trickery; **commettre une f.,** to commit a fraud; *Jur:* **f. civile,** fraud, wilful misrepresentation; **f. pénale,** cheating; **f. fiscale,** tax evasion; *adv.phr.* **en f.,** (i) fraudulently, unlawfully; (ii) secretly; **entrer, passer, qch. en f.,** to smuggle sth. in, to smuggle sth. through the customs. **2.** fraudulence, deceit; **par f.,** under false pretences.

frauder [frode]. **1.** *v.tr.* (*a*) to defraud, cheat, swindle (s.o.); **f. les droits de douane, f. la douane,** to defraud the customs, to smuggle; (*b*) **lait fraudé,** adulterated milk. **2.** *v.i.* to cheat.

fraudeur, -euse [frodœːr, -øːz], *s.* **1.** defrauder, cheat, swindler. **2.** smuggler.

frauduleusement [frodyløzmɑ̃], *adv.* fraudulently, by fraud.

frauduleux, -euse [frodylø, -øːz], *a.* fraudulent; *Jur:* **banqueroute frauduleuse,** fraudulent bankruptcy; **coupable de manœuvres frauduleuses,** guilty of fraud; *Publ:* **édition frauduleuse,** pirated edition.

fraxinelle [fraksinɛl], *s.f. Bot:* fraxinella; *F:* false dittany, *U.S:* gas plant.

fraxinicole [fraksinikɔl], *a.* that grows on ash trees.

fraye [frɛːj], *s.f.* **1.** (*a*) *Tchn:* groove (on knife handle); (*b*) rut (made in road by passage of vehicles). **2.** *Orn: Dial:* thrush.

frayement [frɛ(j)mɑ̃], *s.m.* **1.** tracing, clearing (of path). **2.** *Vet:* galling (of horse, etc.).

frayer [freje], *v.* (**je fraye, je fraie, n. frayons; je frayerai, je fraierai**) **1.** *v.tr.* (*a*) to scrape, rub; **la roue m'a frayé la cuisse,** the wheel scraped, grazed, my thigh; *Ven:* (*of stag*) **f. son bois aux arbres,** to fray its head against a tree; **f. des pièces d'or,** (i) (*through use*) to wear away gold coins; (ii) (*fraudulently*) to sweat gold coins; *Vet:* **f. un cheval,** to gall a horse; (*b*) **f. un chemin,** to open up, trace out, clear, a path; to blaze a trail; **le chemin frayé,** the beaten track; **se f. un passage,** (i) to clear a way (for oneself), (ii) to effect an entrance; to force, break, one's way in; **se f. un chemin, se f. route, à travers la foule,** to force, fight, thrust, carve, push, one's way through a crowd; to elbow, to shoulder, one's way through the crowd; to get through the crowd; **se f. péniblement un chemin dans la neige,** to plough (one's way) through the snow; **se f. un chemin à travers des difficultés,** to battle one's way through difficulties; **f. la voie à qn,** to clear, pave, the way for s.o. **2.** *v.i.* (*a*) (*of fishes*) to spawn; (*b*) **f. avec qn,** to consort with, associate with, frequent, s.o.; **je ne fraye pas avec eux,** I don't mix with them; **ils ne frayent pas ensemble,** they have nothing to do with each other; **f. avec l'aristocratie,** to hobnob with the aristocracy; (*c*) (*of coins, etc.*) to wear away, to wear thin.

frayère [frɛjɛːr], *s.f.* spawning ground; redd.

frayeur [frɛjœːr], *s.f.* fright; fear, dread (**de,** of); **pousser un cri de f.,** to give a frightened cry, shout; to cry out with fear; **vous me faites mourir de f.,** you frighten me to death; **être en proie à la f.,** to be overcome by, with, fear; *F:* to be frightened to death.

frayoir [frɛjwaːr], *s.m. Ven:* (*a*) mark made by stag's antlers on tree; (*b*) tree against which the stag frays his head.

fredaine [frədɛn], *s.f.* prank, escapade; **faire des fredaines,** to sow one's wild oats.

Frédéric [frederik], *Pr.n.m.* Frederick.

fredon [frədɔ̃], *s.m. A:* **1.** *Mus:* (*a*) trill; roulade; flourish; (*b*) song; chorus. **2.** (*a*) *Cards:* brelan; (*b*) *Hum:* threesome, group of three people.

fredonnement [frədɔnmɑ̃], *s.m.* humming (of tune).

fredonner [frədɔne], *v.tr.* to hum (tune, song).

free-drop [fridrɔp], *s.m. Av:* free drop; **larguer (qch.) en f.-d.,** to free-drop (sth.).

freesia [frizja], *s.m.,* **freesie** [frizi], *s.f. Bot:* freesia.

freezer [frizœːr], *s.m. F:* freezing compartment, freezer (of refrigerator).

frégatage [fregataːʒ], *s.m. N.Arch:* tumble home.

frégate [fregat], *s.f.* **1.** *Navy:* frigate; **f. lance-engins,** guided missile destroyer; **capitaine de f.,** commander. **2.** *Orn:* frigate (bird); **pétrel f.,** frigate petrel, *U.S:* white-faced petrel; **f. superbe,** magnificent frigate bird; man o' war bird.

frégate-école [fregatekɔl], *s.f. A:* training ship; *pl. frégates-écoles.*

frégaton [fregatɔ̃], *s.m.* **1.** *A.Nau:* Venetian frigate. **2.** *Navy: F:* commander.

frein [frɛ̃], *s.m.* **1.** (*a*) bit; (*in wider sense*) bridle; **ronger son f.,** (*of horse*) to champ the bit; *F:* (*of pers.*) to fret, chafe, under restraint, to champ the bit; **mettre un f. aux désirs de qn,** to curb, bridle, s.o.'s desires; **avidité, curiosité, sans f.,** unbridled, uncurbed, cupidity, curiosity; (*of passions, imagination, etc.*) **ne plus connaître de f.,** to break loose from all restraint; to run riot; (*b*) *Anat:* fraenum; **f. de la langue,** string(s) of the tongue; (*c*) *Ent:* frenulum. **2.** (*a*) brake; friction band; **f. sur jante,** rim brake; **f. à ruban, à collier, à bande,** band-brake; **f. à sabots,** shoe brake; **f. à patin,** electro-magnetic brake; **f. à main, f. de stationnement,** hand brake; **f. à pédale, au pied,** foot brake; **f. sur l'embrayage,** clutch brake; *Rail: etc:* **f. à vide,** vacuum brake; **f. à air (comprimé),** air brake; **volant (de manœuvre) de f.,** brake wheel; **f. à vis,** screw brake; **f. (à commande) mécanique,** mechanical brake, power brake; **f. de secours, f. de détresse,** emergency brake; *Cy:* **câble de f.,** brake wire; **f. dans le moyeu, à rétropédalage,** back-pedalling brake; *Aut:* **freins sur quatre roues,** four-wheel brakes; **freins sur roues avant,** front-wheel brakes; **f. à disque,** disc brake; **f. à tambour,** drum brake; **le principe du f. moteur,** the principle of engine braking; **serrer, mettre, le f.,** to apply the brake, to brake; **desserrer, ôter, le f.,** to release the brake; **serrage (à fond) du f.,** brake (full) on; **desserrage du f.,** brake off; **bloquer, caler, les freins,** to jam (on) the brakes; **donner un brusque coup de f.,** to clap on, jam on, the brake; **donner un coup de f. à qn,** to pull s.o. up short; **donner un coup de f. (à une entreprise),** to put a brake (on an undertaking); to bring (sth.) to a sudden halt; **servir de f. aux activités de qn,** to act as a brake, as a check, upon s.o.'s activities; to restrain s.o.'s activities; (*b*) *Artil:* **f. de tir,** recoil buffer, brake; **f. hydraulique,** hydraulic buffer; **f. de bouche,** muzzle brake; (*c*) *Aut:* **f. de direction,** steering damper; **f. de débrayage,** clutch stop; (*d*) *Av:* **f. aérodynamique,** air brake; **f. de l'hélice,** airscrew brake; **f. de piqué,** dive brake; (*e*) *Mec:* **f. d'écrou,** nut lock.

freinage [frɛnaːʒ], *s.m.* **1.** (*a*) *Veh:* braking; applying, putting on, the brake; brake application, braking action; **f. à récupération, f. rétroactif,** regenerative braking; **f. brusqué, f. brutal,** sudden application of the brake, jamming on of the brake; **distance de f.,** braking distance; **couple de f.,** brake torque; **effort de f.,** braking pull; **puissance de f.,** braking effect; **essai de f.,** braking test; *Av:* **f. aérodynamique,** aerodynamic braking; *Av: etc:* **parachute de f.,** brake parachute, braking, drag, parachute; (*b*) (*skiing*) stemming; **f. en chasse-neige,** snowplough stemming with two skis; **f. unilatéral,** single stemming; **angle de f.,** stemming angle; (*c*) *Mec: Aerodynamics:* deceleration, negative acceleration (of atom, spacecraft, etc.); **effet de f.,** damping; *Atom.Ph:* **rayonnement de f.,** bremsstrahlung; *Av:* **f. à l'atterrissage,** landing deceleration; (*of spacecraft*) **f. lors de la rentrée dans l'atmosphère,** re-entry deceleration; (*d*) *W.Tel:* **grille de f.,** suppressor grid. **2.** brake system; brakes (collectively); *Aut:* **f. intégral, f. sur quatre roues,** four-wheel braking system, brakes; **f. conjugué,** coupled, interacting, brakes.

freindre [frɛ̃dr], *v.i.* (*conj. like* ENFREINDRE) *Com:* (*of cereals in store, goods in transit*) to lose weight.

freiner [frene], *v.tr.* **1.** (*a*) **f. une roue,** to brake, apply the brake(s) to, a wheel; (*b*) *abs.* to put on the brakes; **f. brusquement,** to jam on the brakes; (*c*) *Mec. etc:* to decelerate. **2.** to curb (inflation, etc.); **f. la production,** to check, restrain, production.

freinomètre, frénomètre [frenɔmɛtr], *s.m.* brake-testing machine.

freineur [frenœːr], *s.m. Rail: etc:* brakesman.

freinte [frɛ̃ːt], *s.f.* (*a*) *Tex:* waste (during manufacturing processes); (*b*) *Com: Ind:* loss in weight (during transit, manufacture).

fréjus [freʒyːs], *s.m.* reed (*esp.* of quality suitable for making fishing rod).

fréjussien, -ienne [freʒysjɛ̃, -jɛn], *a. & s. Geog:* (native, inhabitant) of Fréjus [freʒyːs].

frelampier [frəlɑ̃pje], *s.m. Ecc: A:* lamplighter (in monastery).

frelatage [frəlataːʒ], *s.m.*, **frelatement** [frəlatmɑ̃], *s.m.*, **frelaterie** [frəlatri], *s.f.* adulteration (of food, wine, etc.).

frelater [frəlate], *v.tr.* to adulterate (food, wine, etc.); to doctor (a product); **ces lectures frelatent le goût,** this sort of reading debases one's taste; **cela n'est pas frelaté,** this is perfectly genuine.

frelateur, -euse [frəlatœːr, -øːz], *s.* adulterator.

frêle [frɛ(ː)l], *a.* frail, weak (health, person); delicate (person); fragile (stem, etc.); **une f. espérance,** a feeble, faint, hope.

freloche [frəlɔʃ], *s.f.* (gauze) butterfly net.

frelon [frəlɔ̃], *s.m.* **1.** *Ent:* hornet. **2.** *O:* (*pers.*) idler; sponger; drone.

freluche [frəlyʃ], *s.f.* **1.** tuft (of tassel, etc.). **2.** gossamer (thread).

freluquet [frəlykɛ], *s.m. F:* (*pers.*) young whipper-snapper; conceited young puppy.

frémir [fremiːr], *v.i.* **1.** (*to vibrate*) **le vent frémit dans les arbres,** the wind is sighing in the trees; **les feuilles frémissent,** the leaves are rustling; **l'eau frémit dans la bouilloire,** the water is simmering, singing, in the kettle; **faire f. les cordes d'une harpe,** to run one's fingers over the strings of a harp; **les cordes frémissent,** the strings are quivering. **2.** to quiver, tremble, shake, quake, shudder; **f. de tous ses membres,** to tremble, quiver, in every limb; **f. de crainte,** to shake, quiver, with fear; **ça me fait f. quand j'y pense,** it gives me the shivers, makes me shudder, to think of it; **f. d'impatience,** to quiver with impatience; **f. de colère,** to shake with anger.

frémissant [fremisɑ̃], *a.* **1.** rustling (leaves); simmering (water); sighing, soughing (wind). **2.** trembling, quivering, shaking; throbbing; **tout f. de joie,** quivering, trembling, with joy.

frémissement [fremismɑ̃], *s.m.* **1.** (*a*) rustle, rustling (of leaves, etc.); simmering (of water); sighing, soughing (of wind); (*b*) *Med:* fremitus; **f. cataire, vibratoire,** purring tremor (of the heart). **2.** (*a*) shuddering, quaking, quivering; throbbing; (*b*) shudder, tremor, quiver; **un f. parcourut la salle,** a tremor went through the audience.

frênaie [frenɛ], *s.f.* ash plantation.

frêne [frɛ(ː)n], *s.m.* ash (tree or timber).

frénésie [frenezi], *s.f.* (*a*) *A.Med:* frenzy, madness; **tomber en f., dans une f.,** to fall into a frenzy, into a fit of madness; (*b*) agitation, frenzy; **applaudir avec f.,** to applaud frantically, enthusiastically.

frénétique [frenetik], *a.* (*a*) *A.Med:* frenzied, mad (person); *s.* madman, madwoman; (*b*) frantic; passionate; violent; **applaudissements frénétiques,** frantic applause; **danser de la manière f. de certains danseurs,** to dance in the frenzied fashion of certain dancers.

frénétiquement [frenetikmɑ̃], *adv.* frenziedly, frantically, frenetically, madly.

frénomètre [frenɔmɛtr̥], *s.m.* brake-testing machine.

Fréon [freɔ̃], *s.m. R.t.m: Ch:* Freon.

fréquemment [frekamɑ̃], *adv.* frequently, repeatedly, often; **il lui arrive f. d'oublier,** he is apt to forget.

fréquence [frekɑ̃ːs], *s.f.* **1.** frequency; **f. d'une épidémie,** prevalence, frequent occurrence, of an epidemic; *Med:* **f. du pouls,** frequency, quickness, rapidity, of the pulse; pulse-rate; **la f. des enlèvements d'enfants a ému l'opinion publique,** public opinion has been roused by the frequency of child kidnapping. **2.** (*a*) *Ph:* **fréquence (d'un mouvement ondulatoire),** frequency (of wave motion); **f. limite,** threshold frequency; **graphique des fréquences,** frequency curve; **table des fréquences,** frequency table; **taux de f.,** frequency rate; (*b*) *Elcs: W.Tel:* (i) **basse, haute, f.,** low, high, frequency; **très haute f.,** very high frequency (V.H.F.); **f. ultra-haute,** ultra-high frequency; **f. moyenne, f. intermédiaire,** intermediate frequency; **f. commune,** common frequency; **f. fondamentale,** fundamental frequency; **f. unique,** spot frequency; **f. utile,** effective frequency; **f. passante,** filter frequency; **f. porteuse, f. de courant porteur,** carrier frequency; **f. acoustique, f. audible, f. musicale,** audio frequency; **f. de récurrence, de répétition (des impulsions),** (pulse) recurrence, repetition, frequency; **f. radio (électrique),** radio frequency; **f. de fonctionnement,** operating frequency; (ii) *T.V:* **f. de ligne,** line frequency; **f. de trame,** frame frequency; **f. d'image,** picture, vision, frequency; *T.V: Radar:* **f. de balayage,** scanning frequency, scanning sweep; **f. vidéo,** video frequency; (iii) **bande de fréquences,** frequency band; **gamme de fréquences,** frequency range; **gamme des fréquences audibles,** audio range; **jeu de fréquences,** frequency complement; **lot de fréquences,** frequency block; **intervalle de f.,** frequency spacing; **étalon de f.,** frequency standard; **contrôleur de f.,** frequency controller, monitor; **indicateur de f.,** frequency indicator, indicating dial; **changeur de f.,** frequency changer, converter; **diversité de f.,** frequency diversity; **diviseur de f.,** frequency divider; **multiplicateur de f.,** frequency multiplier; **doubleur, tripleur, de f.,** frequency doubler, tripler; **déplacement, dérive, de f.,** frequency shift, drift; **libération de fréquences,** frequency clearing; **répartition des fréquences,** frequency allotment.

fréquencemètre [frekɑ̃smɛtr̥], *s.m. El.E:* frequency meter.

fréquent [frekɑ̃], *a.* **1.** (*a*) frequent; **comme il est f. dans leur milieu,** as often happens in their milieu; (*b*) **j'en fais un f. usage,** I often use it. **2.** *Med:* **pouls f.,** quick, rapid, pulse.

fréquentable [frekɑ̃tabl̥], *a.* (person) pleasant to meet; frequentable (place); (place) that is pleasant to visit; *F:* **c'est un type peu f.,** he's impossible; I wouldn't be seen dead with him.

fréquentatif, -ive [frekɑ̃tatif, -iːv], *a. Gram:* frequentative (verb, etc.).

fréquentation [frekɑ̃tasjɔ̃], *s.f.* frequentation, frequenting; (*a*) **f. des théâtres,** frequent visits to the theatre; **la f. des Parisiens a fait beaucoup de bien aux hôteliers de cette ville,** the hotel keepers of this town have derived considerable benefit from the frequent visits of Parisians; **f. assidue des conférences,** regular attendance at lectures; (*b*) **homme de f. difficile,** man whom it is very difficult to approach, with whom one cannot easily get on intimate terms; **f. des artistes, des gens du monde,** association with artists, with society people; **éviter les mauvaises fréquentations,** to avoid bad company; **on juge les gens par leur f. quotidienne,** people are judged by the company that they keep; (*c*) *Ecc:* **f. des sacrements,** frequentation of the sacraments; *O:* **f. des œuvres classiques,** habitual reading of the classics, of classical literature.

fréquenté [frekɑ̃te], *a.* much visited, crowded (place); **hôtel bien f.,** hotel with a good (= *respectable*) clientele; **endroit mal f.,** place of evil repute, with a bad reputation; **plage très fréquentée,** popular, crowded, beach; **port très f., route très fréquentée,** busy port, road.

fréquenter [frekɑ̃te]. **1.** *v.tr.* to frequent; (*a*) **f. un lieu,** to frequent a place, to visit a place frequently; **je fréquentais un petit externat,** I attended a small day school; **f. un auteur,** to study, read, an author; *Ecc:* **f. les sacrements,** to frequent the sacraments; (*b*) **f. qn,** (i) to associate with, (ii) to visit, s.o.; to be on visiting terms with s.o.; **quels gens fréquente-t-il?** what company does he keep? **nous ne fréquentons pas les mêmes milieux,** we don't move in the same set, circles; **mon frère les fréquente beaucoup,** my brother sees a good deal of them; *F:* **il l'a fréquentée pendant deux ans avant de se marier,** he was going out with her for two years before they got married; *abs. F:* **il fréquente,** he's practically engaged. **2.** *v.i.* (*a*) *O: Lit:* **f. chez qn, dans des familles riches,** to be on visiting terms with s.o., with wealthy people; to be a frequent visitor at s.o.'s house; (*b*) *F:* **ce sont des gens qui ne fréquentent pas,** they are unsociable.

frère [frɛːr], *s.m.* **1.** (*a*) brother; **f. germain,** full brother; **frères jumeaux,** twin brothers; **frères siamois,** Siamese twins; **f. de lait,** foster brother; *s.a.* CONSANGUIN 1, UTÉRIN; **les frères Martin,** the Martin brothers; *Com:* **Martin frères,** Martin Bro(ther)s; **ils se ressemblent comme des frères,** they look so alike they might be brothers; **frères d'armes,** brothers-in-arms; *Hist:* (*W. Indian pirates*) **frères de la côte,** brethren of the Coast; (*b*) *Ecc:* **mes très chers frères,** dearly beloved brethren; **nos frères en Jésus-Christ,** our brethren in Christ, our fellow-Christians; (*c*) **f. maçon,** *F:* **frère trois points,** freemason; (*d*) *F:* **tu es un f.,** you're a true, real, friend; **un faux f.,** a false friend; a traitor; **vieux f.!** old chap! **2.** *Ecc:* friar; **f. lai,** lay brother; **frères des écoles chrétiennes,** brothers of the christian schools; *abs.* **il a été élevé chez les frères** = he went to a school run by priests. **3.** *Nau:* sister ship, twin ship; *F:* **j'ai vu le f. de ton vase chez un antiquaire,** I saw the twin of your vase in an antique shop.

frérot [frero], *s.m. F:* little brother.

fresaie [frəzɛ], *s.f. Orn: F:* barn owl, screech owl.

fresque [frɛsk], *s.f. Art:* fresco; **peinture à f.,** painting in fresco; *Lit: etc:* **son œuvre est une vaste f. de la vie au XIXe siècle,** his works present a vast panorama of life in the 19th century.

fresquiste [frɛskist], *a. & s.m.* (**peintre**) **f.,** fresco painter.

fressure [fresyːr], *s.f.* pluck (of calf, sheep, etc.); *Cu:* **f. d'agneau, de porc,** lamb's fry, pig's fry.

fret [frɛ], *s.m.* freight. **1.** freightage (for sea, air, road, transport); **payer le f.,** to pay the freight; *Rail: etc:* **f. à la mesure, au poids,** freight by measure, by weight. **2.** chartering; **prendre un navire à f.,** to charter a ship; **donner un navire à f.,** to freight (out) a ship. **3.** load, cargo (of ship, aircraft, lorry); **prendre du f.,** to take in freight, to embark cargo; **f. de sortie, de retour,** outward freight, home freight; **faux f.,** dead freight.

frètement [frɛtmɑ̃], *s.m.* freighting, chartering (of ship).

fréter[1] [frete], *v.tr.* (**je frète; je fréterai**) **1.** to freight (out) (ship). **2.** (*rare*) (= AFFRÉTER) to charter (ship, aircraft); *O:* to hire (vehicle). **3.** to equip, fit out (ship).

fréter[2], *v.i.* to hoe up the weeds (in a wheatfield).

fréteur [fretœːr], *s.m.* ship-owner; transporter (of goods by sea).

frétillant [fretijɑ̃], *a.* **1.** (*of fish, etc.*) wriggling, wrigly; (*of dog's tail*) wagging. **2.** full of life, quivering with life; lively, frisky; **un petit vieux f.,** a brisk little old man.

frétillement [fretijmɑ̃], *s.m.* **1.** wriggling (of fish, etc.); wagging (of tail). **2.** fidgeting, quivering (from excitement, etc.).

frétiller [fretije], *v.i.* (*of fishes, etc.*) to wriggle; **le chien frétille de la queue,** the dog is wagging its tail; **l'enfant frétille d'impatience,** the child is fidgeting, quivering, with impatience; *F:* **la langue lui frétille,** he is itching to speak.

frétillon [fretijɔ̃], *s.m. F: O:* fidget, fidgety-Phil.

fretin [frətɛ̃], *s.m.* (*a*) *Fish:* fry; **menu f.,** small fry; (*b*) (**menu**) **f.,** (i) object of no value; rubbish; (ii) person of small account, small fry; **la police n'a arrêté que le menu f.,** the police arrested only the small fry; **il ne reste que du f.,** there is nothing left but oddments, remnants.

frettage [frɛtaːʒ], *s.m.* (*a*) binding, hooping; fitting of a collar or ferrule (on sth.); (*b*) *Civ.E:* reinforcement (of concrete).

frette[1] [frɛt], *s.f.* (binding) hoop, collar, ferrule; band (of axle, etc.); *A.Arms:* coronal (of lance); **f. de moyeu,** nave ring (of wheel); *El.E:* **f. du collecteur,** commutator hoop; **f. d'induit,** armature binding; *Aut:* **f. de friction,** brake lock; *Artil:* **f. de renfort,** outer tube (of gun).

frette[2], *s.f. Arch: Her:* fret.

fretté[1] [frete], *a.* **1.** ferruled, iron-shod (stake); hooped, iron-banded (concrete).

fretté[2], *a. Her:* fretty.

fretter [frete], *v.tr.* to bind (sth.) with a ring, with a ferrule; to band, hoop (sth.); **canon fretté en fil(s) d'acier,** wire(wound) gun.

freudien, -ienne [frødjɛ̃, -jɛn], *a. Psy:* Freudian.

freudisme [frødism], *s.m. Med: Psy:* Freud(ian)-ism.

freux [frø], *s.m. Orn:* (**corbeau**) **f.,** rook; **colonie de f.,** rookery.

friabilité [fri(j)abilite], *s.f.* friability, friableness.

friable [fri(j)abl̥], *a.* friable, crumbly.

friand, -ande [fri(j)ɑ̃, -ɑ̃ːd]. **1.** *a.* (*a*) fond of delicacies; **être f. de sucreries,** to be very fond of sweets, to have a sweet tooth; **être f. de compliments,** to be avid for compliments; (*b*) *A:* **morceau f.,** dainty morsel, tasty morsel. **2.** *s. A: or Dial:* dainty feeder; epicure. **3.** *s.m. Cu:* (*a*) meat pie (made with puff pastry); (*b*) small (almond) cake.

friandise [fri(j)ɑ̃diːz], *s.f.* **1.** *A:* daintiness, love of good food, epicurism. **2.** dainty, delicacy, titbit.

Fribourg [fribuːr], *Pr.n. Geog:* **1.** Freiburg. **2.** Fribourg.

fribourgeois, -oise [friburʒwa, -waːz], *a. & s. Geog:* (native, inhabitant) of (i) Freiburg, (ii) Fribourg.

fric [frik], *s.m. P:* dough, lolly; **aboule ton f.,** come on, fork out, cough up.

fricadelle [frikadɛl], *s.f. Cu:* (*a*) fried mince ball; (*b*) (*E. France*) (type of) pork liver sausage.

fricandeau, -eaux [frikɑ̃do], *s.m. Cu:* fricandeau, larded veal braised.

fricassé, -ée [frikase]. **1.** *a. Cu:* fricasseed. **2.** *s.f.* **fricassée,** (*a*) *Cu:* fricassee; (*in Belg.*) bacon omelette; (*b*) *P:* **fricassée de museaux,** hugs and kisses.

fricasser [frikase], *v.tr.* (*a*) *Cu:* to fricassee; (*b*) to embezzle; *A:* **f. tout son bien,** to squander, run through, all one's property.

fricasseur, -euse [frikasœːr, -øːz], *s. A: Cu:* (*a*) preparer of fricassees; (*b*) indifferent cook; *A:* **f. d'héritages,** squanderer of legacies; prodigal.

fricatif, -ive [frikatif, -iːv]. *Ling:* **1.** *a.* fricative (consonant, etc.). **2.** *s.f.* **les fricatives,** fricatives, fricative consonants; **fricative sourde,** voiceless fricative as in hiss; **fricative sonore,** voiced fricative as in buzz.

fric-frac [frikfrak], *s.m. P:* burglary; *pl. fric-frac(s).*

friche [friʃ], *s.f.* waste land, fallow land; (*of land*) **rester, être, en f.,** to lie fallow; (*of land*) **retomber en f.,** to be laid fallow; **esprit resté en f.,** undeveloped mind.

frichti [friʃti], *s.m. P:* meal; food, grub.

fricot [friko], *s.m. Cu: F:* made-up dish; stew; **faire le f.,** to do the cooking; **l'odeur du f. montait,** there was a smell of cooking.

fricotage [frikɔtaːʒ], *s.m. F:* **1.** (*a*) stewing; cooking; (*b*) underhand practices; wangling; wire-pulling; **f. des comptes,** cooking of accounts. **2.** feasting. **3.** *Mil:* shirking (of duties).

fricoter [frikɔte], *v.tr. & i. F:* **1.** (*a*) to stew; to cook; **f. un lapin,** to stew a rabbit; **elle fricote bien,** she's a good cook; **elle aime à f.,** she's fond of cooking; (*b*) *A:* **f. tout son bien,** to squander one's fortune. **2.** (*a*) to act on the sly; **je me demande ce qu'il fricote,** I wonder what he's cooking up, he's up to; **f. des comptes,** to cook accounts; (*b*) to make a bit on the side. **3.** *Mil:* to shirk, to mike.

fricoteur, -euse [frikɔtœːr, -øːz], *F:* **1.** *a. & s.* (person) (i) fond of cooking, (ii) fond of good living. **2.** *s.* (*a*) wangler, fiddler; (*b*) embezzler. **3.** *s. Mil:* shirker.

friction [friksjɔ̃], *s.f.* **1.** (*a*) *Med:* rubbing, chafing (of the limbs, etc.); *Sp:* rub-down; **brosse, gant, à f.,** flesh brush, glove; (*b*) dry shampoo, scalp massage. **2.** *Mec:* friction; *Mec.E:* **embrayage à f.,** friction clutch; *Exp:* **amorce à f.,** friction primer tube. **3.** *Geol:* **brèche de f.,** friction, fault, breccia. **4.** friction, disagreement.

frictionnel, -elle [friksjɔnɛl], *a.* **1.** frictional; *Hyd.E:* **perte frictionnelle,** friction head. **2.** *Pol. Ec:* **chômage f.,** temporary unemployment (of worker who has a waiting period between finishing one employment and starting another).

frictionner [friksjɔne], *v.tr.* **1.** (*a*) to rub, chafe (**avec,** with); **f. qn,** to give s.o. a rub down; **se f. la jambe avec de l'huile,** to rub one's leg with oil; (*b*) **f. la tête de qn,** to give s.o. a dry shampoo, a scalp massage. **2.** to friction glaze (paper).

frictionneur [friksjɔnœːr], *a.m. Paperm:* **cylindre f.,** friction roller.

Fridolin [fridɔlɛ̃], *s.m. P:* German, Jerry, Kraut.

friedélite [fridelit], *s.f. Miner:* friedelite.

frigard [frigaːr], *s.m.* soused herring.

Frigidaire [friʒidɛːr], *Pr.n.m. R.t.m:* Frigidaire, refrigerator; *F:* **mettre un projet en F.,** to put a plan into cold storage.

frigidarium [friʒidarjɔm], *s.m. Rom.Ant:* frigidarium.

frigide [friʒid], *a.* **1.** *esp. Lit:* cold, icy; **marbre f.,** ice-cold marble. **2.** (*a*) *Physiol:* frigid; (*b*) **accueil f.,** frigid welcome.

frigidement [friʒidmɑ̃], *adv.* frigidly, coldly.

frigidité [friʒidite], *s.f.* **1.** coldness (of marble, etc.). **2.** *Physiol:* frigidity.

frigo [frigo]. **1.** *s.m. F:* fridge, refrigerator. **2.** *s.m. P:* frozen, chilled, meat. **3.** *a. P:* **il fait f.,** it's freezing (cold).

frigorie [frigɔri], *s.f. Ph.Meas:* negative kilo-(gramme) calorie.

frigorifère [frigɔrifɛːr], *s.m.* cold store, refrigerator.

frigorification [frigɔrifikasjɔ̃], *s.f.* refrigerating, chilling (of meat).

frigorifié [frigɔrifje], *a.* frozen; chilled (meat, etc.); *F:* **nous étions frigorifiés,** we were frozen stiff.

frigorifier [frigɔrifje], *v.tr.* to refrigerate.

frigorifique [frigɔrifik], *a.* refrigerating, chilling; frigorific; **installation, matériel, f.,** refrigerating plant; **appareil f.,** refrigerator; **mélange f.,** freezing mixture; **navire f.,** refrigerated ship; **train f.,** insulated train; **wagon f.,** refrigerator van; **entrepôt f.,** *s.m.* **f.,** cold store; *A: Nau:* **les frigorifiques,** the refrigerator.

frigorifuge [frigɔrifyːʒ], *a.* insulating (substance) (used in the refrigerating industry).

frigorifuger [frigɔrifyʒe], *v.tr.* to insulate (for refrigeration).

frigorigène [frigɔriʒɛn], *a. & s.m.* (**fluide**) **f.,** refrigerating fluid; refrigerant; **agent f.,** coolant.

frigorimètre [frigɔrimɛtr], *s.m. Meteor:* frigorimeter; katathermometer.

frigoriste [frigɔrist], *s.m.* refrigerating engineer.

frigothérapie [frigɔterapi], *s.f. Med:* frigotherapy.

frigousse [frigus], *s.f. A: P:* feast, (*or simply*) dish.

frileusement [friløzmɑ̃], *adv.* cosily, snugly; huddled up; **f. enveloppée dans ses fourrures,** snugly wrapped up in her furs; **se serrer f. contre qn,** to snuggle up against s.o.; **il ramena f. sur ses genoux la couverture,** with a shiver (of cold) he pulled the rug up over his knees.

frileux, -euse [frilø, -øːz]. **1.** *a.* chilly; (*a*) *A: & Lit:* cold (weather, wind, etc.); (*b*) sensitive to the cold, susceptible to cold, feeling the cold; *s.* **un f., une frileuse,** a chilly person; **je suis très frileuse,** I feel the cold terribly. **2.** *s.f.* **frileuse,** head shawl. **3.** *s.m. or f. Orn: F:* redbreast, robin.

frilinge [frilɛ̃ːʒ], *s.m. Hist:* (Saxon) freeman.

friller [frije], *v.i. Tchn:* to bubble, to be on the point of boiling.

frimaire [frimɛːr], *s.m. Hist:* third month of the French Republican calendar (November-December).

frimas [frimɑ], *s.m. Lit:* (hoar-)frost; rime; **le f. des ans,** the hoar of years; *Poet:* **les f.,** winter-(time); *A:* **poudré à f.,** with white-powdered hair.

frime [frim], *s.f. F:* sham, pretence, make-believe; **tout ça c'est de la f.,** that's all sham, all window-dressing, *F:* all bunkum, all eyewash; **faire qch. pour la f.,** (i) to do sth. for appearances' sake; (ii) to make a pretence of doing sth.

frimer [frime], *v.i. P:* (*a*) to pretend; (*b*) **f. bien,** to look well, to cut a dash; (*c*) to look at, stare at.

frimousse [frimus], *s.f. F:* (*usu. of child, girl*) (nice little) face; **quelle jolie petite f.!** what a sweet little face; **la f. blanche du chaton,** the little white face of the kitten.

fringale [frɛ̃gal], *s.f. F:* pang of hunger, keen appetite; **avoir la f.,** to be ravenous, starving; **brise de mer qui vous donne la f.,** sea breeze that puts a keen edge on one's appetite; **avoir une f. de divertissements,** to hanker after pleasure.

fringant [frɛ̃gɑ̃], *a.* brisk, spirited, lively, frisky (horse); smart, dashing (person); **un air f.,** a brisk, lively, appearance.

fringillaire [frɛ̃ʒilɛːr], *s.m.*, **fringille** [frɛ̃ʒil], *s.m. Orn:* finch.

fringillidés [frɛ̃ʒilide], *s.m.pl. Orn:* Fringillidae.

fringot(t)ement [frɛ̃gɔtmɑ̃], *s.m.* chirping (of chaffinch).

fringot(t)er [frɛ̃gɔte], *v.i.* (*of chaffinch*) to chirp.

fringuer [frɛ̃ge], *v.* **1.** *v.i. A:* (*a*) to prance; to frisk; to skip about; (*b*) to cut a dash. **2.** *v.tr. P:* to dress (s.o.); **bien fringué,** well dressed; **il s'était bien fringué pour sortir,** he'd got himself up all ready to go out.

fringues [frɛ̃ːg], *s.f.pl. P:* clothes, togs.

frinson [frɛ̃sɔ̃], *s.m. Orn: F:* greenfinch.

frio [frio], *a. P:* **il fait f.,** it's freezing (cold).

Frioul (le) [ləfriul], *Pr.n.m. Geog:* Friuli.

frioulan [friulɑ̃], *s.m. Ling:* Friulian.

frioulien, -ienne [friuljɛ̃, -jɛn], *a. & s. Geog:* Furlanian, Frioulian.

fripe [frip], *s.f. P:* food, grub (*esp.* anything that can be spread on bread *e.g.* butter, jam).

fripé [fripe], *a.* (*a*) crumpled (garment); (*b*) wrinkled (face).

friper[1] [fripe], *v.tr.* to crumple, crush, crease (dress, etc.).

se friper, (*of garment*) to get crushed, crumpled; (*of face, etc.*) to become wrinkled.

friper[2], *v.tr. P: A:* to gobble up (sth.); to cram (sth.) down; **f. un legs,** to run through a legacy.

friperie [fripri], *s.f.* **1.** (*a*) secondhand goods (*esp.* clothes, furniture); (*b*) rubbish, trumpery, frippery. **2.** (*a*) secondhand (clothes) business; (*b*) secondhand (clothes) shop. **3.** shed, warehouse (for storing sugar cane).

fripier, -ière [fripje, -jɛːr], *s.* secondhand dealer; old-clothes man, woman; wardrobe dealer.

fripon, -onne [fripɔ̃, -ɔn]. **1.** *s.* (*a*) *A:* rogue, rascal, knave; **à f., f. et demi,** set a thief to catch a thief; (*b*) *F:* **petit f.! petite friponne!** you naughty little boy, girl! you little wretch! **2.** *a. F:* mischievous (child, smile, etc.).

friponneau, -eaux [fripɔno], *s.m.* (*a*) *A:* young gallant; (*b*) *F:* mischievous little boy.

friponner [fripɔne], *v.tr. A:* to rob (s.o.); to cheat (s.o.).

friponnerie [fripɔnri], *s.f. A:* **1.** roguery, knavery. **2.** piece of roguery, of knavery; knavish trick.

fripouille [fripuːj], *s.f.* (*a*) *A:* rabble; riff-raff; (*b*) *F:* swindler; rotter; bad lot.

fripouillerie [fripujri], *s.f. F:* (*a*) swindling; cheating; dirty dealing; (*b*) swindle, dirty deal.

friquet [frikɛ], *s.m.* **1.** *Orn: F:* tree sparrow. **2.** (*a*) skimmer (used for jam-making); (*b*) **f. liturgique,** (silver, etc.) strainer (for communion wine). **3.** (*a*) *F:* whippersnapper; (*b*) *P:* informer, nark.

frire [friːr], *v.tr. & i. def.* (*has only p.p.* **frit**; *pr.ind.* **je fris, tu fris, il frit,** *no pl.*; *imp.* **fris**; *fu.* **je frirai**; *for the v.tr. the parts wanting are supplied by* **faire frire**) to fry; **je fris, fais f., des pommes de terre, du poisson,** I am frying potatoes, fish; **f. qch. à l'huile,** to fry sth. in oil; **les pommes de terre sont en train de f.,** the potatoes are frying; **poêle à f.,** frying pan; **pâte à f.,** batter; *F:* **n'avoir pas de quoi f.,** to have nothing to eat; *F:* **il n'y a rien à f. dans cette affaire,** there is nothing to be got out of this business.

frisant [frizɑ̃], *a.* **lumière frisante,** oblique light.

frise[1] [friːz], *s.f.* **1.** *Arch:* frieze. **2.** *Const:* plank, board (destined to make blocks for parquet flooring); **f. de parquet,** framing strip (for parquet flooring). **3.** *N.Arch:* **f. d'éperon,** trail board. **4.** *Th:* **les frises,** the borders, sky pieces.

frise[2], *s.f. Tex:* **1.** frieze; dreadnought, fearnought (cloth). **2.** friezing machine.

Frise[3], *Pr.n.f. Geog:* Friesland; *Mil:* **chevaux de f.,** (i) *A:* chevaux de frise; (ii) (any form of) portable wire entanglement.

frisage [frizaːʒ], *s.m.* **1.** *O:* curling, waving (of hair, etc.). **2.** trellis work (made of thin strips of wood).

frisé [frize]. **1.** *a.* curly; crisp (hair); **cheveux frisés naturellement,** naturally curly hair; **laitue frisée,** curly lettuce; **velours f.,** uncut velvet; terry; *Husb:* **poule frisée,** frizzle fowl; *s.m.* (*1939-45 War*) **un f.,** a German. **2.** *s.m. Needlew:* **f. d'or, d'argent,** gold, silver, thread, wire (for embroidery borders).

frise-beurre [frizbœːr], *s.m.inv. in pl. Dom.Ec:* butter shaper.

frisée [frize], **friselée** [frizle], *s.f. Hort:* crinkle (of potatoes), potato mosaic.

friselis [friz(ə)li], *s.m.* (*a*) rustle, rustling (of leaves); (*b*) lapping (of water).

friser [frize]. **1.** (*a*) *v.tr.* to curl, wave; **f. les cheveux de qn, f. qn,** to curl s.o.'s hair; **fer à f.,** curling tongs; **f. au, avec le, fer,** to curl with an iron; **f. du drap,** to crimp cloth; (*b*) *v.i.* (*of hair, etc.*) to curl; (*c*) *abs. Typ:* **presse qui frise,** press that slurs, mackles. **2.** *v.tr.* to touch, skim; **la balle lui a frisé le visage,** the bullet grazed his face; **f. la prison,** to scrape clear of prison; *F:* to sail near the wind; **f. un accident,** to have a narrow escape; **il frisait la soixantaine,** he was close on, bordering on, sixty; he was getting on towards sixty; **hardiesse qui frise l'insolence,** boldness that verges, borders, on insolence.

se friser, (*of horse*) to brush, to interfere.

frisette[1] [frizɛt], *s.f.* ringlet, small curl.

frisette[2], *s.f. Const:* narrow plank, board.

frisoir [frizwaːr], *s.m. A:* **1.** hair curler, curling pin. **2.** curling-tongs.

frisolée [frizɔle], *s.f. Hort:* crinkle (of potatoes); **f. (mosaïque),** potato mosaic.

frison[1] [frizɔ̃], *s.m.* **1.** (*a*) wave (of curl); curl (of hair); **porter les cheveux en frisons,** to wear curls; (*b*) *Paperm:* wave of colour (in marbled paper). **2.** (*a*) floss silk; (*b*) *pl.* scraps, waste; wood wool; clippings (of sheet metal); shavings. **3.** *Typ:* slur, blue, mackle.

frison[2], *s.m. A: Nau:* can.

frison[3], **-onne** [frizɔ̃, -ɔn], *a. & s. Geog:* Frisian; **vache frisonne,** Friesian cow.

frisotter [frizɔte]. **1.** *v.tr.* **f. les cheveux de qn, f. qn,** to curl lightly, to crimp, frizz, s.o.'s hair. **2.** *v.i.* (*a*) (*of hair, etc.*) to curl; to be frizzy; (*b*) *Typ:* (*of press*) to slur slightly.

frisque [frisk], *a. A:* lively, brisk.

frisquet, -ette[1] [friskɛ, -ɛt], *a. F:* chill(y); **il fait f.,** it is a bit chilly, a bit parky; *s.m.* **le f. du petit jour,** the chilliness, nip, of the early morning air.

frisquette[2] [friskɛt], *s.f. Typ:* frisket (of hand-press).

frisselis [fris(ə)li], *s.m.* rustle, rustling (of leaves).

frisson [frisɔ̃], *s.m.* (*a*) shiver (from cold); **avoir le f.,** to shiver; *F:* to have the shivers; **le f. m'a pris,** I was taken with a shivering fit; (*b*) shudder, thrill; **j'en ai le f.,** it makes me shudder; *F:* it gives me the shudders, the shivers; **cela donne le f.,** it makes one shudder; **un f. lui passa dans le dos,** a cold shiver went down his back; (*c*) **f. de plaisir,** thrill of pleasure; **f. d'impatience,**

quiver of impatience; **f. de crainte**, chill of fear; (*d*) *Med:* **frissons (symptomatiques)**, rigor.

frissonnant [frisɔnɑ̃], *a.* shivering (with cold, fright); shuddering (with horror); quivering (horse, etc.); *Cu:* (*of liquid*) simmering.

frissonnement [frisɔnmɑ̃], *s.m.* **1.** shivering; shuddering; quivering. **2.** slight shiver, shudder, quiver.

frissonner [frisɔne], *v.i.* (*a*) to shiver, shudder; **f. de froid, d'horreur,** to shiver with cold, to shudder with horror; (*b*) **f. de joie**, to be thrilled with delight; (*c*) to quiver (with impatience).

frisure [frizyːr], *s.f.* (*a*) curling (of the hair, etc.), curliness; **f. naturelle, artificielle,** natural, artificial, curliness, curl; **la f. du vent**, the shivering of the wind; (*b*) *pl.* curls; ringlets.

frit, frite [fri, frit], *a.* **1.** fried; **poisson f.**, fried fish; **pommes de terre frites**, *s.f.* **frites**, chipped potatoes, chips, French fried potatoes; *F:* French fries; (*on menu*) **bifteck frites**, steak and chips. **2.** *F:* **il est f.**, he's done for, he's had it; **tout est f.**, it's all up.

friteau, -eaux [frito], *s.m. Cu:* (*a*) (type of) fritter; (*b*) **f. de poulet**, chicken fried in batter.

friterie [fritri], *s.f.* **1.** fish-frying room, fish-cooking room (in fish-canning factory). **2.** (i) fried food; (ii) fish and chip stall.

friteur, -euse [fritœːr, -øːz]. **1.** *s.* (*a*) vendor of fish and chips, of fried foods; (*b*) (*pers.*) fryer (in fish-canning factory). **2.** *s.f. Dom.Ec:* **friteuse**, deep fryer; **(faire) cuire à la friteuse**, to deep fry.

fritillaire [fritil(l)ɛːr], *s.f. Bot:* fritillary; **f. damier, f. méléagride**, snake's head.

fritons [fritɔ̃], *s.m.pl.* greaves, cracklings (of rendered pork or goose fat).

frittage [fritaːʒ], *s.m. Ind:* calcining, roasting; calcination; *Metall:* sintering; *Glassm:* fritting.

fritte [frit], *s.f. Ind:* **1.** calcining, roasting. **2.** (*a*) calcined, roasted, ore, etc.; (*b*) *Glassm:* frit.

fritter [frite], *v.tr. Ind:* to calcine, roast (carbonates, etc.); *Metall:* to sinter; *Glassm:* to frit.

frittons [fritɔ̃], *s.m.pl.* greaves, cracklings (of rendered pork, or goose fat).

friture [frityːr], *s.f.* **1.** (*a*) frying (of foods); **panier à f.**, frying basket; (*b*) *Tp: W.Tel:* **(bruits de) f.**, crackling (noise), sizzling (noises); sizzle. **2.** (*a*) fried food, fry, *esp.* fried fish; (*b*) **servir une f.**, to serve a dish of fried fish (*esp.* small fish, whitebait). **3.** fat, oil (for frying). **4.** (*in Belg.*) chip stall.

friturier, -ière [frityrje, -jɛːr], *s.* keeper of a fish and chip shop; fish fryer; seller of fried foods.

Fritz [frits], *s.m. Hist:* German soldier; *F:* (1914 and 1939) Fritz; **les F.**, Jerry; **un F.**, a Jerry.

frivole [frivɔl], *a.* frivolous; **occupation f.**, frivolous, futile, occupation; **querelle f.**, futile quarrel; **je la trouve plutôt f.**, I find her rather frivolous.

frivolement [frivɔlmɑ̃], *adv.* frivolously.

frivolité [frivɔlite], *s.f.* **1.** frivolity; (*a*) frivolousness; shallowness (of mind); (*b*) trifle. **2.** (*a*) *Needlew:* tatting; **faire de la f.**, to tat; **col en f.**, tatted collar; (*b*) *Com:* **frivolités**, (fancy) trimmings.

froc [frɔk], *s.m.* **1.** (monk's) (i) cowl, (ii) frock, gown; **porter le f.**, to be a monk; **quitter le f., jeter le f. aux orties,** (i) (*of monk*) to unfrock oneself, to throw one's frock away; (ii) to change one's profession. **2.** *P:* trousers.

frocard [frɔkaːr], *s.m. Pej:* monk.

froid [frwa, -ɑ]. **I.** *a.* **1.** (*a*) cold (in temperature); **vent, temps, bain, f.**, cold wind, weather, bath; **j'ai les mains froides comme la glace**, my hands are frozen, like ice; **mains froides et moites**, cold clammy hands; **chambre froide**, (i) cold room; (ii) (*refrigerating*) chilling chamber; (*b*) **moteur f.**, cold engine; **repas f.**, cold meal; **viandes froides**, cold meat; **à table! tout va être f.!** come along! the food will all get cold! **2.** (*a*) cold, unresponsive, (person); chilly (manner); **accueil f.**, cold, frigid, reception; **sourire f.**, frigid smile; **être d'une politesse froide**, to be frigidly polite; **se montrer, être, f. avec qn**, to treat s.o. coldly, coolly, in a distant manner; **garder la tête froide**, to keep cool (and collected); **cela me laisse f.**, it leaves me cold; **style f.**, frigid, stiff, style; lifeless style; **tons froids**, cold tints; *Equit:* **cheval f.**, unresponsive horse; **épaules froides**, stiff shoulders (of horse); **ces promesses me laissent f.**, these promises leave me cold; *v.phr:* **battre f. à qn**, to cold-shoulder s.o.; **ne sentir ni f. ni chaud pour qn.**, to be, feel, indifferent about s.o.; **cela n'y fera ni chaud ni f.**, it won't do any good or any harm: *Hist:* **la guerre froide**, the phoney war (1939-40); (*b*) *Physiol:* (sexually) cold, frigid.

II. **à froid,** *adv.phr.* in the cold state; **soluble à f.**, soluble when cold; **martelé à f.**, cold-hammered; **martelage à f.**, coldhammering; **ciseau à f.**, cold chisel; **laminage à f.**, cold rolling; *Surg:* **opérer à f.**, to operate cold, between (the patient's) attacks; *Sp:* **prendre un adversaire à f.**, to catch, tackle, an opponent unawares; **s'emporter à f.**, to pretend to be moved, worked up; **des gens qui parlent à f. de leurs crimes**, people who can speak calmly, without emotion, of the crimes they have committed.

III. **froid,** *s.m.* **1.** cold; **le chaud et le f.**, heat and cold; **la saison des grands froids**, the cold season; **cinq degrés de f.**, five degrees of frost; **coup, vague, de f.**, cold snap; *Med:* **coup de f.**, chill; **prendre f.**, to catch a chill, a cold; **il est mort de f.**, he was frozen to death; *F:* **je meurs, crève, de f.**, I'm freezing (to death), I'm dying of cold; **il va mourir de f.**, he'll catch his death of cold; **il fait f.**, it is cold; *F:* **il fait un f. de canard, de chien, de loup,** it's bitterly cold, freezing; **cela m'a fait, donné, f. (dans le dos)**, it gave me the shivers; it sent cold shivers down my spine; **avoir f.**, to be, feel, cold; **avoir f. aux mains**, to have cold hands; **elle n'a pas f. aux yeux**, (i) she's very determined; she'll stick at nothing; (ii) she's got plenty of cheek, of nerve; (iii) she's a terror. **2. l'industrie du f.**, refrigerating, the refrigerating industry; **f. artificiel, industriel**, (industrial) refrigeration; *Ph:* **pôle du f.**, absolute zero. **3.** (*a*) coldness; **il y a du f. entre eux, ils sont en f.**, they're not on the best of terms; **vivre en f. avec qn**, not to get on with s.o.; **l'incident a jeté un f. sur les invités**, the incident put a damper on the company; (*b*) lifelessness (of style).

froidement [frwadmɑ̃], *adv.* **1.** coldly, frigidly; **accueillir qn f.**, to receive s.o. coldly. **2. regarder f. la mort**, to look calmly on death. **3. il écrit trop f.**, his style lacks warmth.

froideur [frwadœːr], *s.f.* **1.** *O:* coldness (of temperature). **2.** coldness; (*a*) chilliness, frigidity (of manner); **il y a de la f. entre eux**, there is a coldness, a coolness, between them; (*b*) irresponsiveness; **contempler le spectacle avec f.**, to look coldly on, to look on coldly; (*c*) frigidity (of style). **3.** *Physiol:* (sexual) frigidity.

froidure [frwadyːr], *s.f.* **1.** *A: & Lit:* coldness (*usu.* of atmospheric conditions); the cold season, cold weather; **se défendre contre la f.**, to protect oneself against the cold. **2.** *Med:* frostbite.

froissable [frwasabl̩], *a.* **1.** creaseable. **2.** easily hurt, easily offended.

froissant [frwasɑ̃], *a.* hurtful to the feelings; slighting (behaviour); wounding to the susceptibilities.

froissé [frwase], (*a*) *a.* offended, hurt, ruffled; **j'ai été très f. de sa réponse**, I was very much hurt at his answer; **d'un air f.**, with a slight show of annoyance; (*b*) (*of dress, etc.*) creased, crumpled.

froissement [frwasmɑ̃], *s.m.* **1.** (slight) bruising (of some part of the body); rumpling, crumpling (of paper, cloth, etc.); rustling, rustle (of newspapers, of silk); jostling (in crowd); **f. d'intérêts**, slight conflict, clash, of interests. **2.** giving or taking offence; ruffling of susceptibilities; **éprouver des froissements**, to suffer slights, to feel slighted; **pour éviter tous froissements**, in order to avoid wounding any susceptibilities.

froisser [frwase], *v.tr.* **1.** to bruise slightly (hand, muscle, etc.); **se f. la jambe en tombant**, to bruise, strain, one's leg in falling; *A:* être **froissé dans la foule**, to be jostled in the crowd. **2.** to crease (material); to crumple (paper, material); to rumple (hair, etc.). **3. f. qn**, to offend, give offence to, s.o.; to hurt, ruffle, s.o.'s feelings; **f. les opinions de qn**, to come into conflict with s.o.'s opinions; **cela ne vous froisse pas que je (vous) le dise?** you don't mind my mentioning it?

se froisser, to take offence, to take umbrage (**de**, at); to take exception (**de**, to); **il se froisse facilement**, he takes offence easily, he's very thin-skinned; **il ne se froisse jamais**, he never takes anything the wrong way, never takes offence at anything.

froissure [frwasyːr], *s.f.* slight bruise (of hand, muscle, etc.); crumple, rumple (in piece of paper, silk, etc.).

frôlement [frolmɑ̃], *s.m.* slight rubbing, brushing (**contre**, against); light touch(ing); **le f. des branches**, the rubbing of the branches against one another; *Med:* **bruit de f.**, rustling; **f. hydatique**, hydatic fremitus.

frôler [frole], *v.tr.* to touch lightly (with a glancing motion); to brush, rub; **f. qn en passant**, to brush (against) s.o.; **une balle lui frôla le bras**, a bullet grazed his arm; **f. un avion**, to buzz an aircraft; **il a frôlé la mort**, he very nearly died, he only just escaped death.

frôleur, -euse [frolœːr, -øːz]. **1.** *a.* caressing. **2.** *s.f.* **frôleuse**, coquette. **3.** *s.m.* sexual pervert (with a morbid desire for physical contact with women).

fromage [frɔmaːʒ], *s.m.* **1.** cheese; **f. bien fait**, ripe cheese; **f. blanc, f. gras**, cream cheese; **f. de Chester**, Cheshire cheese; **f. de chèvre**, goat's milk cheese; **f. bleu**, blue cheese; **f. fondu, industriel**, processed cheese; **tarte au f. blanc**, cheesecake; **rôtie au f.**, toasted cheese, Welsh rarebit, Welsh rabbit; *P:* **il a là un gentil petit f.**, that's a nice sinecure, cushy job, soft job, he's got. **2.** *Cu:* **f. de cochon**, pork brawn; **f. de tête**, brawn, collared head, potted head, *U.S:* head-cheese.

fromagé [frɔmaʒe], *a. Cu:* cheese-flavoured.

fromageon [frɔmaʒɔ̃], *s.m.* cream cheese (of ewes' milk).

fromager[1] [frɔmaʒe], *v.tr. Cu:* to add cheese to (a sauce, etc.).

fromager[2], **-ère** [frɔmaʒe, -ɛːr]. **1.** *a.* pertaining to cheese-making; **l'industrie fromagère**, the cheese industry. **2.** *s.* (i) cheesemonger; (ii) cheese maker. **3.** *s.m.* cheese basket, drainer, mould. **4.** *s.m. Bot:* silk-cotton tree, bombax.

fromagerie [frɔmaʒri], *s.f.* cheesemongery; **acheté dans une f.**, bought at a cheesemonger's.

fromageux, -euse [frɔmaʒø, -øːz], *a.* cheese-like.

fromagier, -ière [frɔmaʒje, -jɛːr]. **1.** *a.* cheese (industry). **2.** *s.f.* **fromagière**, cheese dish.

froment [frɔmɑ̃], *s.m.* **1.** wheat; **pain de f.**, wheaten bread (of first quality). **2. faux f.**, false oat. **3. f. rampant, f. des chiens, des haies**, couch grass.

fromentacé [frɔmɑ̃tase], *a.* (*of plant such as couch grass*) wheat-like.

fromentage [frɔmɑ̃taːʒ], *s.m. Hist:* levy of wheat (made by feudal squire).

fromental, -aux [frɔmɑ̃tal, -o]. **1.** *a.* wheat-bearing (plain, etc.). **2.** *s.m. F:* false oat; onion grass, couch grass, twitch; tall meadow oat.

fromentée [frɔmɑ̃te]. **1.** *s.f.* frumenty. **2.** *a.f.* **robe f.**, wheat-coloured coat (of cow).

fromenteux, -euse [frɔmɑ̃tø, -øːz], *a.* rich in wheat.

fromentier, -ière [frɔmɑ̃tje, -jɛːr], *a.* wheat-producing.

frometon [frɔmtɔ̃], *s.m.*, **fromgi** [frɔmʒi], *s.m. P:* cheese.

fronce [frɔ̃ːs], *s.f.* (*a*) (accidental) pucker; crease (in paper, etc.); **faire des fronces à une feuille**, to crease or pucker a sheet; (*b*) *Needlew:* gather, fold-in; **jupe à fronces**, gathered skirt.

froncé [frɔ̃se]. **1.** *a.* (*a*) wrinkled; puckered; *Needlew:* gathered; (*b*) severe; angry. **2.** *s.m. Needlew:* flounce.

froncement [frɔ̃smɑ̃], *s.m.* wrinkling, puckering (*esp.* of the brows); **f. de(s) sourcils**, frown; scowl.

froncer [frɔ̃se], *v.tr.* (**je fronçai(s); n. fronçons**) (*a*) to wrinkle, pucker; **f. les sourcils**, to knit one's brows, to frown; **il me lança un mauvais regard, en fronçant les sourcils**, he scowled at me; **f. les lèvres**, to pucker, purse, one's lips; (*b*) *Needlew:* to gather.

se froncer, to pucker (up).

fronceur [frɔ̃sœːr], *s.m.* (*sewing-machine*) gatherer.

froncis [frɔ̃si], *s.m. Needlew:* gathers, gathering; *Laund:* rucking (of linen).

fronçure [frɔ̃syːr], *s.f.* **1.** (*a*) wrinkling, puckering, rucking; (*b*) *Needlew:* gathering (of dress, etc.). **2.** (*a*) pucker; (*b*) gather.

frondaison [frɔ̃dɛzɔ̃], *s.f.* **1.** foliation, leafing, frondescence. **2.** foliage, leaves.

fronde[1] [frɔ̃ːd], *s.f. Bot:* **1.** frond. **2.** (*a*) foliation, frondescence; (*b*) foliage.

fronde[2], *s.f.* **1.** (*a*) sling; **pierre à f.**, sling stone; *Ph:* **thermomètre à f., thermomètre-f.**, whirled thermometer; (*b*) (toy) catapult; (*c*) *Surg:* splint (for fractured jaw); (*d*) *Dent:* casting machine. **2.** *Hist:* **la F.**, (i) the insurrection, (ii) the party, of the Fronde (1648-53).

fronder [frɔ̃de]. **1.** *v.tr.* (*a*) to sling (stone, etc.); to fling (stone, etc.) with a sling, a catapult; *abs.* to use a sling; (*b*) to hit (s.o.) with a sling. **2.** *v.i.* (*a*) *Hist:* to be a member of the Fronde; (*b*) **f. contre qn**, *v.tr.* **f. qn**, to criticize s.o.; to attack s.o.; (*c*) to complain, grouse.

frondescence [frɔ̃dɛs(s)ɑ̃ːs], *s.f. Bot:* frondescence.

frondescent [frɔ̃dɛs(s)ɑ̃], *a. Bot:* frondescent.

frondeur, -euse [frɔ̃dœːr, -øːz]. **1.** *s.* (*a*) slinger; (*b*) *Hist:* member of the Fronde; (*c*) critic of the authorities; *F:* grouser. **2.** *a.* critical (of the authorities); irreverent, given to criticizing, to insubordination.

frondicole [frɔ̃dikɔl], *a.* leaf-dwelling (insect).

frondifère [frɔ̃difɛːr], *a. Bot:* frondiferous.

front [frɔ̃], *s.m.* 1. forehead, brow; **f. fuyant,** receding forehead; **donner du f. contre un réverbère,** to butt, run, into a lamp-post; **le f. courbé sur son travail,** his head bowed down over his work; **marcher le f. haut,** to walk with one's head high; **montrer un f. serein,** to show an unruffled countenance; **f. d'airain,** brazen face; **et vous avez le f. de me dire cela!** you have the face, the impudence, the cheek, to tell me that! **de quel f. osez-vous faire cela?** how can you have the face to do it? 2. face, front (of building, of troops on parade, etc.); brow (of hill); *Mil:* **f. de bataille, d'action,** battle front; **le f.,** the front, the front line; **se trouver au f., sur le f.,** to be at the front; **soldats du f.,** front-line troops; **f. d'opérations,** front of operations; **opérations sur de grands fronts,** operations on wide fronts; **f. à battre,** frontage to be covered by fire, to be swept; **f. à tenir,** frontage to be held; **f. mouvant,** fluid front; **f. stabilisé,** stabilized front; *Min:* **f. de taille,** working face; coal face; **f. d'avancement,** heading face; **f. à deux ailes,** double stope; *Meteor:* **f. chaud, froid,** warm, cold, front; **f. de mer,** (i) (sea) front; (ii) water front; (iii) *Mil:* coastal fortifications; *Ph:* **f. d'onde,** front of wave; *Pol:* **f. commun,** united front, common front; **f. populaire,** popular front; **faire f. à qn, qch.,** to face, resist, s.o., sth.; *abs.* **faire f.,** to face sth.; to resist, to stand fast. 3. **de f.,** (*a*) *adv. phr.* abreast; **mener trois chevaux de f.,** to drive three horses abreast; **mener plusieurs choses de f.,** to have several things on hand at once, many irons in the fire; *Mil:* **marche de f.,** march in line; *Nau:* **en ligne de f.,** line abreast; (*b*) *adj.phr.* frontal, front; **vue de f.,** front view; **attaque de f.,** frontal attack; (*c*) *adv.phr.* **heurter qn, qch., de f.,** to run slap into s.o., sth.

frontail [frɔ̃taːj], *s.m. Harn:* forehead strap, headband.

frontal, -aux [frɔ̃tal, -o]. 1. *a.* frontal, front; **os f.,** frontal bone; **veine frontale,** frontal vein; *Med:* **miroir f.,** head mirror; *Phot:* **lentille frontale,** front lens; *Mec.E:* **palier f.,** end bearing. 2. *s.m.* (*a*) *Anat:* frontal bone; (*b*) *Harn:* forehead strap, head band; (*c*) *A.Arm:* visor (of sallet); (*c*) *Arch:* small pediment; (*e*) *Tls:* frontal hammer, frontal helve.

frontalier, -ière [frɔ̃talje, -jɛːr]. 1. *a.* **régions frontalières,** border regions, frontier regions. 2. *s.* (i) inhabitant of frontier zone; (ii) frontier worker (who crosses a frontier daily to go to his, her, work).

frontalité [frɔ̃talite], *s.f. Art:* frontality.

fronteau, -eaux [frɔ̃to], *s.m.* 1. (*a*) *Ecc:* frontlet (of nun); phylactery, frontlet (of Jew); (*b*) *Harn:* forehead strap, headband. 2. *Arch:* small pediment. 3. *Artil:* **f. de mire,** fore-sight (of gun); dispart-sight, dispart. 4. *N.Arch:* (*a*) breast beam; (*b*) breastwork; (*c*) break bulkhead; (*d*) **f. d'écoutille,** headledge; (*e*) **f. de dunette,** poop break. 5. *Ecc:* altar frontal.

frontel [frɔ̃tɛl], **frontier** [frɔ̃tje], *s.m. Ecc:* altar frontal.

frontière [frɔ̃tjɛːr]. 1. *s.f.* (*a*) frontier (line); border(line); boundary; **reculer les frontières d'un état,** to extend the frontiers of a state; **les habitants de la f.,** the inhabitants of the frontier zone; **commission de délimitation de(s) frontière(s),** boundary commission; frontier commission; **rectification de f.,** frontier rectification, adjustment; boundary adjustment; (*b*) *Ph:* **f. diffuse,** diffuse boundary; (*c*) **les frontières de la bienséance,** the limits of decency. 2. *Cost:* (*in Savoie*) head-dress, coiffe. 3. *a.* **ville f.,** frontier town; **gare f.,** frontier station; **borne f.,** boundary stone.

frontignan [frɔ̃tiɲɑ̃], *s.m.* Frontignan (wine).

Frontin [frɔ̃tɛ̃], *s.m.* knavish valet (of the old French comedy).

frontispice [frɔ̃tispis], *s.m.* 1. *Arch: A:* frontispiece, main façade (of building). 2. (*a*) frontispiece (of book); (*b*) title page.

frontogénèse [frɔ̃toʒ(e)nɛːz], *s.f. Meteor:* frontogenesis.

frontolyse [frɔ̃toliːz], *s.f. Meteor:* frontolysis.

fronton [frɔ̃tɔ̃], *s.m.* 1. *Arch:* (*a*) fronton, pediment; (*b*) ornamental front, façade; (*c*) *Sp:* (i) fronton (of pelota court); (ii) pelota court. 2. *A: Nau:* upper stern-rails.

fronto-pariétal, -aux [frɔ̃toparjetal, -o], *a. Anat:* fronto-parietal.

frottage [frɔtaːʒ], *s.m.* (transitive action of) rubbing; friction, chafing (of limb, etc.); polishing (of floors, furniture, etc.); scouring (of metal, etc.).

frottant [frɔtɑ̃], *a.* rubbing. 1. polishing. 2. in frictional contact; **surface frottante,** rubbing surface.

frotté [frɔte]. 1. *a. Art:* scumbled (background). 2. *s.m.* = FROTTIS. 3. *s.f.* **frottée;** (*a*) *P:* hiding, thrashing; (*b*) **f. d'ail,** crust of bread rubbed with garlic.

frottement [frɔtmɑ̃], *s.m.* (intransitive action of) rubbing. 1. (*a*) chafing; *Harn:* **pièce de f.,** galling leather; *Med:* **bruit de f.,** pleural rub; *Phot:* **marques de f.,** stress marks; (*b*) **avancer lentement avec un f. de pieds,** to shuffle slowly along. 2. *Mec.E:* (*a*) friction; **force de f.,** frictional force, force of friction; **f. de roulement, de glissement,** rolling friction, sliding friction; **plaque de f.,** friction plate; *El.E:* **bague de f.,** slip ring; *Av:* **f. superficiel,** skin friction; **user qch. par le f.,** to abrade sth.; to wear sth. down; **usure par le f.,** abrasion; (*b*) fit (of parts); **f. doux,** easy fit; **f. dur, à refus,** tight fit; **ajuster à f.,** to adjust to an exact fit. 3. contact (with other people); **f. d'intérêts,** clash of interests.

frotter [frɔte]. 1. *v.tr.* to rub; **f. deux pierres l'une contre l'autre,** to rub two stones together; **se f. les mains,** to rub one's hands; **se f. la jambe d'huile,** to rub one's leg with oil; **f. un membre engourdi,** to chafe a numbed limb; **f. le parquet avec un chiffon,** to rub up, polish, the floor with a rag; **parquet frotté à la cire,** waxed floor; **f. qch. à l'émeri,** to rub up, polish, clean, sth. with emery paper; *Nau:* **f. les coutures d'une voile,** to rub down the seams of a sail; **f. une allumette,** to strike a match; **f. les pieds en marchant,** to shuffle along; *A: F:* **f. qn, f. l'échine à qn,** to thrash, drub, s.o.; to dust s.o.'s jacket; **on l'a frotté comme il faut,** he has had a proper hiding, tanning; **f. les oreilles à qn,** to warm s.o.'s ears; **f. son nez à, dans, qch.,** to poke one's nose into sth. 2. *v.i.* **la roue frotte contre le frein,** the wheel rubs, grinds, against the brake. 3. *v.tr. Art:* to scumble (sky, background); **fond frotté de bleu,** the background scumbled with blue; **être frotté de latin,** to have a smattering of Latin.

se frotter. 1. **se f. contre qch.,** to rub against sth. 2. **se f. à qn,** to associate with s.o.; **se f. aux artistes,** to mix, rub shoulders, with artists. 3. **se f. à qn, à qch.,** to come up against s.o., sth.; **il ne fait pas bon (de) se f. à lui,** it is unwise to interfere with him; **qui s'y frotte s'y pique,** gather thistles, expect prickles; **ne vous y frottez pas!** be careful! **ne vous (y) frottez pas à le critiquer,** you had better avoid criticizing him.

frotteur, -euse [frɔtœːr, -øːz], *s.* 1. (*pers.*) floor polisher. 2. *s.m.* (*a*) *El.E:* sliding contact, (contact-)brush; (*b*) *El.E:* (collecting) shoe (of tram, etc.); **f. prenant le rail par en dessous,** underrunning type of collecting shoe; (*c*) *Mec.E: etc:* (i) friction piece; (ii) cam, wiper. 3. *s.f.* **frotteuse,** (mechanical) floor polisher.

frottis [frɔti], *s.m.* 1. (*a*) *Art:* scumble; *Mapdrawing:* hill-shading; (*b*) *Med: etc:* smear (for microscopic examination). 2. scratch (on mirror, etc.). 3. **prendre un f. d'une inscription, etc.,** to take a rubbing of an inscription, etc.

frottoir [frɔtwaːr], *s.m.* 1. rubber, polisher, polishing cloth, polishing pad; rough towel; scrubbing brush; **f. de barbier,** razor wipe; **f. d'une boîte d'allumettes,** striking surface of a match-box. 2. (*a*) friction plate (of slide mounting); (*b*) *El.E:* brush (of dynamo).

frotton [frɔtɔ̃], *s.m. Typ:* frotton.

frotture [frɔtyːr], *s.f.* layer of dead wood (on tree trunk).

frouer [frue], *v.tr. Ven:* to call (birds).

frou-frou, froufrou [frufru], *s.m.* 1. rustle, rustling, swish, frou-frou (of silk dress, etc.); rustle, rustling (of leaves); *Tchn:* scroop (of silk); *F: A:* **faire du f.-f.,** to make a great display, a great show; to show off. 2. *Orn: F:* humming-bird; *pl. frous-frous, froufrous.*

froufroutant [frufrutɑ̃], *a.* (*of silk, etc.*) rustling, swishing.

froufrouter [frufrute], *v.i.* (*of silk, etc.*) to rustle, swish; *F: A:* (*of pers.*) to make a display, to show off.

froussard, -arde [frusaːr, -ard], *a.* & *s. P:* funky, cowardly (person); **c'est un f., il est f.,** he's a (bit of a) funk.

frousse [frus], *s.f. P:* funk, fear; **avoir la f.,** to be in a funk, to have cold feet, to have the wind up; to have the jitters; **il a eu une sainte f.,** he's been in a blue funk; **flanquer la f. à qn,** to put the wind up s.o.

fructescent [fryktɛs(s)ɑ̃], *a.* fructescent, fruitbearing.

fructiculteur [fryktikyltœːr], *s.m.* orchardman, orchardist; fruit grower.

fructiculture [fryktikyltyːr], *s.f.* orcharding; fruit growing.

fructidor [fryktidɔːr], *s.m. Hist:* twelfth month of the Fr. Republican calendar (August-September).

fructifère [fryktifɛːr], *a.* fructiferous, fruitbearing.

fructifiant [fryktifjɑ̃], *a.* fruitful, productive.

fructification [fryktifikasjɔ̃], *s.f.* 1. fructification, fructifying. 2. fruition (of idea, etc.).

fructifier [fryktifje], *v.i.* to fructify, to bear fruit; **son travail commence à f.,** his work is beginning to bear fruit, to produce good results; **faire f. son argent,** to lay out one's money to advantage.

fructiforme [fryktifɔrm], *a.* fructiform, fruit-like.

fructose [fryktoːz], *s.m. Ch:* fructose.

fructuaire [fryktɥɛːr], *s.m. Rom.Jur:* usufructuary.

fructueusement [fryktɥøzmɑ̃], *adv.* fruitfully, profitably.

fructueux, -euse [fryktɥø, -øːz], *a.* fruitful, advantageous, profitable; **commerce f.,** profitable business.

fructule [fryktyl], *s.m. Bot:* fructule, fruitlet; drupel (of raspberry, etc.).

fructuosité [fryktɥozite], *s.f.* fruitfulness, profitableness.

frugal, -aux [frygal, -o], *a.* frugal (person, meal, etc.).

frugalement [frygalmɑ̃], *adv.* frugally.

frugalité [frygalite], *s.f.* frugality.

frugifère [fryʒifɛːr], *a.* fructiferous, frugiferous, fruit-bearing.

frugivore [fryʒivɔːr], *Z:* (*a*) *a.* fructivorous, frugivorous, fruit-eating (animal); **les chauves-souris frugivores,** the fruit bats; (*b*) *s.* fruit-eater.

fruit[1] [frɥi], *s.m.* fruit. 1. **f. à noyau,** stone fruit; **arbre à f.,** fruit tree; **producteur de fruits,** orchardist, fruit grower; **porter f.,** to bear fruit; **exemple qui portera f.,** example that will bear fruit; **fruits d'été,** summer fruit; **fruit(s) sec(s)** dried fruit; **un f. sec.,** (i) a student who has failed to qualify for a profession; (ii) a failure. 2. (*a*) **les fruits de la terre,** the fruits of the earth; *Cu:* **fruits de mer** = seafood; *Lit:* **le f. de ses entrailles,** the fruit of her womb; (*b*) **les fruits de la paix,** the fruits, advantages, of peace; **quel f. espérez-vous en tirer?** what results do you expect to derive from it? **étudier avec f.,** to study to good purpose, with good result, profitably; **le f. de nos travaux,** the outcome of our labours; **sans f.,** fruitlessly; fruitless; *Jur:* **fruits civils, naturels,** emblements; *s.a.* PENDANT I 1.

fruit[2], *s.m. Civ.E: etc:* batter (of wall, abutment, etc.); **avoir du f.,** to batter.

fruitarien, -ienne [frɥitarjɛ̃, -jɛn], *a.* & *s.* fruitarian.

fruité [frɥite], *a.* 1. (*of wines, etc.*) fruity, tasting of the fruit; **huile d'olive fruitée,** full-flavoured olive oil. 2. *Her:* fructed.

fruitelet [frɥitlɛ], *s.m.* fruit-shaped knob (on cover of soup tureen).

fruiter [frɥite], *v.i.* to fruit, to bear fruit.

fruiterie [frɥitri], *s.f.* 1. storeroom for fruit. 2. (*a*) fruiterer's, greengrocer's, shop; (*b*) fruit business, greengrocery.

fruiteux, -euse [frɥitø, -øːz], *a.* fruity (port, etc.).

fruitier[1], **-ière** [frɥitje, -jɛːr]. 1. *a.* (*a*) fruit-bearing; **arbre f.,** fruit tree; (*b*) *Furn:* **une armoire de bois f.,** a wardrobe in cherry wood, pear wood. 2. *s.* fruiterer, greengrocer. 3. *s.m.* (*a*) store room for fruit; apple loft; **f. portatif,** fruit-storing stand; (*b*) orchard. 4. *s.f.* **fruitière,** co-operative cheese dairy (gruyère production).

fruitier[2], *s.m.* **bureau en f.,** bureau with writing flap.

frumentacé [frymɑ̃tase], *a.* (*of plant*) cultivated for its grain.

frumentaire [frymɑ̃tɛːr]. *Rom.Ant:* 1. *a.* **lois frumentaires,** wheat (distribution) laws. 2. *s.m.* member of the secret police.

frusquer [fryske], *v.tr. P:* to dress, clothe.

frusques [frysk], *s.f.pl. P:* clothes, togs, duds; **toutes ses f.,** all one's clothes; **mettre ses belles f.,** to put on one's glad rags; **de vieilles f.,** cast-off clothing, cast-offs; **f. d'occasion,** slops; **apportez vos f. de football,** bring (along) your football things.

frusquin [fryskɛ̃], *s.m. P:* **tout son (saint) f.,** all one's clothes and money.

fruste [fryst], *a.* (*a*) (*of coins, statue, etc.*) worn, defaced; (*b*) rough, unpolished; **marbre encore f.,** rough-hewn marble; (*c*) (*of pers.*) rough, unmannerly; (*of work of art, etc.*) rough, primitive; **manières frustes,** rough manners; **style f.,** unpolished style.

frustratif, -ive [frystratif, -iːv], *a.* frustrative.

frustrant [frystrɑ̃], *a.* frustrating.

frustration [frystrasjɔ̃], *s.f.* frustration. 1. disappointing (of s.o.'s hopes, etc.). 2. cheating,

defrauding (of one's creditors, etc.). 3. *Psy:* frustration.

frustratoire [frystratwa:r], *a.* frustrative.

frustrer [frystre], *v.tr.* 1. to frustrate, disappoint; **f. qn dans son espoir, f. l'espoir de qn,** to frustrate s.o.'s hopes; **f. qn de sa proie,** to balk s.o. of his prey; **se voir frustré d'un droit,** to be denied a right; **espérance frustrée par la mort,** hope thwarted by death. 2. **f. qn de qch.,** to defraud s.o. of sth.; **on m'a frustré de mes biens,** I have been cheated out of my property.

frustule [frystyl], *s.m. Algae:* frustule (of diatom).

frutescent [frytɛs(s)ɑ̃], *a. Bot:* frutescent, shrubby.

fruticetum [frytisetɔm], *s.m.* fruticetum; shrubbery.

fruticuleux, -euse [frytikylø, -ø:z], *a. Bot:* fruticose; fruticulose; **lichens f.,** fruticose lichens.

frutiqueux, -euse [frytikø, -ø:z], *a. Bot:* frutescent, shrubby.

fucacé [fykase], *Algae:* 1. *a.* fucoid. 2. *s.f.* **fucacée,** fucoid; *pl.* **fucacées,** Fucaceae.

fucales [fykal], *s.f.pl. Algae:* Fucales.

fuchsia [fyksja, *F:* fyʃja], *s.m. Bot:* fuchsia.

fuchsien [fyksjɛ̃], *a. Alg:* **fonctions, relations, fuchsiennes,** Fuchsian group.

fuchsine [fyksin], *s.f. Dy:* fuchsine.

fuchsite [fyksit], *s.f. Miner:* fuchsite.

fuchsone [fyksɔn], *s.f. Ch:* fuchsone.

fucoïde [fykɔid], *a. & s.m. Algae:* fucoid.

fucoïdées [fykɔide], *s.f.pl. Algae:* Fucoideae, Phacophyceae.

fucose [fyko:z], *s.m. Ch:* fucose.

fucoxanthine [fykɔksɑ̃tin], *s.f. Bio-Ch:* fucoxanthin.

fucus [fyky:s], *s.m. Algae:* fucus; *F:* sea wrack, rock weed; **f. court,** flat wrack.

fuégien, -ienne [fɥeʒjɛ̃, -jɛn], *a. & s. Geog:* Fuegian.

fuel (-oil) [fjul (ɔjl)], *s.m.* fuel oil; **f.-o. domestique, léger, fluide,** domestic fuel oil.

fugace [fygas], *a.* (*a*) fugacious, fleeting, fugitive, evanescent, transient; **lubie f.,** passing whim; **mémoire f.,** poor, unretentive, memory; (*b*) *Bot:* fugacious; (*c*) *Med:* **symptômes fugaces,** transitory symptoms.

fugacité [fygasite], *s.f. Lit:* fugacity, evanescence, transience.

fugitif, -ive [fyʒitif, -i:v], *a.* 1. fugitive, fleeing; **le couple f.,** the runaway couple; *s.* **un f., une fugitive,** a fugitive, a runaway; *Mil:* an escaper. 2. **désir f.,** transitory, passing, desire; **passion fugitive,** fleeting, ephemeral, passion; **mémoire fugitive,** short memory; **couleur fugitive,** fugitive, loose, colour; *Mil: Navy:* **but f.,** fleeting target; *Lit:* **pièces fugitives,** fugitive pieces.

fugitivement [fyʒitivmɑ̃], *adv.* fugitively.

fugue [fyg], *s.f.* 1. *Mus:* fugue. 2. *Psy:* fugue. 3. flight, escapade; **faire une fugue,** to break out; to run away from home (for a few days); **faire une f. à Paris,** to run off to Paris for a few days.

fugué [fyge], *a. Mus:* fugued, fugal (style, passage, etc.).

fuguette [fygɛt], *s.f. Mus:* fughetta.

fugueur, -euse [fygœ:r, -ø:z], *s. Psy:* person subject to fugues.

fuie [fɥi], *s.f. A:* dovecot.

fuir [fɥi:r], *v.* (*pr.p.* **fuyant;** *p.p.* **fui;** *pr.ind.* **je fuis, n. fuyons, ils fuient;** *p.d.* **je fuyais;** *p.h.* **je fuis;** *fu.* **je fuirai**) 1. *v.i.* (*a*) to flee, fly, run away; **f. devant l'ennemi,** to fly from, before, the enemy; **ils fuirent se cacher dans les buissons,** they ran away and hid in the bushes; **flâneurs que la pluie fait f.,** loiterers whom the rain disperses, puts to flight; **le ruisseau fuit dans la vallée,** the stream races down the valley; **les arbres de la route fuyaient à nos côtés,** the trees by the roadside whizzed past us; **le temps fuit,** time flies; time is flying; **à mesure que les années fuient,** as the years slip by; **les heures fuient,** the hours are slipping by; *Nau:* **f. (devant le vent),** to scud, run, before the wind; *s.a.* SEC 3; (*b*) (*of horizon, etc.*) to recede; **front qui fuit,** receding forehead; (*c*) (*in discussion, etc.*) to shift one's ground, to run away from the point, to evade the issue; (*d*) (*of ground*) to give way; (*e*) (*of tap, cask, etc.*) to leak; *Civ.E:* (*of pipe*) to bleed; **le vin fuit,** the wine is running out. 2. *v.tr.* to shun, avoid; **f. le danger,** to shun danger; **tout le monde le fuit,** everybody avoids him, he is shunned by everybody; **f. le regard de qn,** to avoid s.o.'s eye.

fuite [fɥit], *s.f.* 1. (*of pers.*) (*a*) flight, running away (**devant,** from); absconding; **prendre la f.,** to take (to) flight, to turn tail, to take to one's heels; **être en f.,** to be on the run; **f. d'un prisonnier,** escape of a prisoner; **mettre l'ennemi en f.,** to put the enemy to flight; to rout the enemy; **f. de toute une nation,** exodus of a whole nation; *F:* **la f. des cerveaux,** the brain drain; (*b*) *Jur:* **f. du domicile conjugal,** elopement, desertion; *Aut:* **délit de f.,** failure to report an accident; **écrasé par une voiture qui a pris la f.,** run over by a hit-and-run driver; (*c*) *F:* **la f.,** (i) *Mil:* the end of military service; (ii) *Sch:* the holidays; (*d*) evasion, avoidance (of difficulties, etc.); **user de fuites,** to evade the issue. 2. (*of thg*) (*a*) **la f. des galaxies,** the flight of the galaxies; **f. des capitaux à l'étranger,** flight of capital abroad; **la f. devant la livre,** the flight from the pound; **la f. du temps,** the passage of time; (*b*) (i) leak; escape (of steam, etc.); **f. de gaz,** escape, leakage, bleeding, of gas; **f. d'eau,** leaking of water; *El:* **f. de courant,** wastage of current; *W.Tel:* **condensateur de f.,** grid-leak condenser; bypass condenser; **résistance de f.,** grid-leak resistance; (ii) **boucher une f. dans un tuyau,** to stop up a leak in a pipe; **il y a une f. à la chaudière,** the boiler is leaking; (*c*) *Hyd.E:* **écluse de f.,** tail lock, tail race; (*d*) leakage (of official secrets, etc.); (*e*) *Art:* **point de f.,** vanishing point; **ligne de f.,** vanishing trace.

fuitif, -ive [fɥitif, -i:v], *a. Lit:* fugitive.

fulcracé [fylkrase], *a. Bot:* fulcrate.

fulcre [fylkr̥], **fulcrum** [fylkrɔm], *s.m. Z: Bot:* fulcrum.

fulcré [fylkre], *a. Bot:* **branche fulcrée,** prop root.

fulgore [fylgɔ:r], *s.m. Ent:* fulgorid; *pl.* **fulgores,** Fulgora, the fulgorids.

fulgorides [fylgɔrid], *s.m.pl. Ent:* Fulgoridae.

fulgurant [fylgyrɑ̃], *a.* fulgurating, flashing (like lightning); *Med:* **douleurs fulgurantes,** lightning pains; **lancer un regard f. à qn,** to look daggers at s.o.

fulguration [fylgyrasjɔ̃], *s.f.* 1. (*a*) *Meteor:* lightning; (*b*) *Metall:* fulguration, flashing. 2. *Med:* (*a*) fulguration, lightning stroke; (*b*) electrotherapy.

fulgurer [fylgyre], *v.i.* 1. to fulgurate, flash. 2. *Med:* to treat by electrotherapy.

fulgurite [fylgyrit], *s.f. Geol:* fulgurite.

fuligineux, -euse [fyliʒinø, -ø:z], *a.* 1. fuliginous, smoky, sooty; mirky, murky, dingy (sky, etc.); **flamme fuligineuse,** smoky flame; **rhétorique fuligineuse,** obscure rhetoric. 2. *Med:* covered with sordes.

fuliginosité [fyliʒinozite], *s.f.* 1. murkiness, smokiness; dinginess. 2. *pl. Med:* sordes (in typhoid fever, etc.).

fuligule [fyligyl], *s.f. Orn:* (*a*) **f. morillon,** tufted duck; **f. nyroca,** white-eyed pochard, ferruginous duck; **f. milouinan,** scaup duck; **f. milouin,** pochard; (*b*) *pl.* **fuligules,** Filigulinae.

fulmar [fylma:r], *s.m. Orn:* fulmar (petrel).

fulmicoton [fylmikɔtɔ̃], *s.m. Exp:* gun cotton, pyroxylin.

fulminaire [fylminɛ:r], *a.* fulminous.

fulminant [fylminɑ̃], *a.* fulminating, fulminant; menacing; **yeux fulminants,** flashing eyes; *Rom.Hist:* **la Fulminante,** the Thundering Legion; *Ch:* **poudre fulminante,** fulminating powder.

fulminate [fylminat], *s.m. Ch:* fulminate; *Sm.a:* **capsule de f.,** cartridge cap.

fulmination [fylminasjɔ̃], *s.f. Ch: Ecc: etc:* fulmination.

fulminatoire [fylminatwa:r], *a.* fulminating; detonating.

fulminer [fylmine]. 1. *v.tr. Ecc:* to fulminate (Papal bull, etc.); **f. des reproches contre qn,** to launch violent reproaches against s.o. 2. *v.i.* (*a*) *Ecc:* to fulminate; **f. contre un abus,** to fulminate, inveigh, against an abuse; (*b*) *Ch: etc:* to fulminate, detonate.

fulminique [fylminik], *a. Ch:* fulminic (acid).

fulvène [fylvɛn], *s.m. Ch:* fulvene.

fumable [fymabl̥], *a.* smokable (cigar, etc.).

fumade [fymad], *s.f.,* **fumage**[1] [fyma:ʒ], *s.m.,* **fumaison**[1] [fymezɔ̃], *s.f. Agr:* 1. dunging, dressing, manuring (of land). 2. (animal) manure, dressing; **fumages peu abondants,** light dressings.

fumage[2], *s.m.,* **fumaison**[2], *s.f.* 1. smoking, smoke-curing (of fish, meat, etc.). 2. (process of) giving a gilt finish to silver (by smoke application).

fumagine [fymaʒin], *s.f. Bot:* fumagine.

fumant [fymɑ̃], *a.* (*a*) smoking; **cendres fumantes,** smoking ashes; **rôti f.,** smoking-hot joint; **acide sulfurique f.,** fuming sulphuric acid; **f. de colère,** fuming with anger; (*b*) **potage f.,** steaming soup; **chevaux fumants (de sueur),** steaming, smoking, horses; *Lit:* **mains encore fumantes de sang,** hands still reeking with blood; (*c*) *F:* terrific, sensational.

fumariacées [fymarjase], *s.f.pl. Bot:* Fumariaceae.

fumarique [fymarik], *a. Ch:* fumaric (acid).

fumarol(l)e [fymarɔl], *s.f. Geog:* fumarole.

fumart [fyma:r], *s.m. Dial:* polecat.

fumature [fymaty:r], *s.f. Agr:* manuring (of soil by pasturing flocks and herds).

fumé [fyme]. 1. *a.* (*a*) smoked, smoke-cured (fish, meat, etc.); (*b*) **verre f.,** smoked glass; **verres fumés,** sunglasses. 2. *s.m. Engr:* (*a*) smoke proof; (*b*) block-maker's proof.

fume-cigare [fymsiga:r], *s.m.inv.* cigar-holder.

fume-cigarette [fymsigarɛt], *s.m.inv.* cigarette-holder.

fumée [fyme], *s.f.* 1. (*a*) smoke; **casque à f.,** smoke-helmet; **charbon sans f.,** smokeless coal; **rideau de f.,** smoke screen; **plafond noirci par la f.,** smoky ceiling; *Ball:* **poudre sans f.,** smokeless powder; **noir de f.,** lamp-black; **la f. (de tabac) vous gêne-t-elle?** do you mind my smoking? **partir, s'en aller, en f.,** to dissolve into thin air; to peter out; **toutes les choses de ce monde ne sont que f.,** all things in this world are but vanity, but idle dreams; *Prov:* **il n'y a pas de f. sans feu,** there is no smoke without fire; (*b*) steam (of soup, etc.); vapour (of marsh); fumes (of charcoal, etc.); *pl.* **les fumées du vin,** the fumes of wine; (*c*) *pl.* **fumées,** *Ven:* dung. 2. *a.inv.* **gris fumées,** smoke-grey, smoke-colour.

fumer[1] [fyme], *v.tr.* (*a*) *Agr:* to dung, manure (land, etc.); (*b*) *A:* **f. ses terres,** (i) (*of noble*) to marry a rich bourgeois wife; (ii) to be buried on one's property.

fumer[2]. 1. *v.i.* (*a*) to smoke; **lampe qui fume,** smoking lamp; (*b*) (*of soup, food, etc.*) to steam; (*of horse*) to steam, smoke; **f. de colère,** *F:* **f.,** to fume, to rage. 2. *v.tr.* to smoke; (*a*) **f. du poisson,** to smoke-cure fish; (*b*) **f. du tabac, une pipe,** to smoke tobacco, a pipe; **après le dîner nous avons fumé tranquillement,** after dinner we had a quiet smoke; **défense de f.,** no smoking; (*c*) *abs.* **cigare qui fume bien,** cigar that smokes well.

fumerie [fymri], *s.f.* 1. smoking (of tobacco); **après les liqueurs et la f.,** after liqueurs and a smoke. 2. **f. d'opium,** opium den.

fumerolle [fymrɔl], *s.f. Geol:* 1. fumarole, smoke-hole (of volcano). 2. smoke, vapour, exhalation (coming from the fumarole).

fumeron [fymrɔ̃], *s.m.* piece of half-kilned charcoal, smoky charcoal.

fumet [fymɛ], *s.m.* 1. (pleasant) smell (of food cooking); bouquet (of wine). 2. *Ven:* scent. 3. *Cu:* highly-flavoured concentrate (for adding to sauces, etc.).

fumeterre [fymtɛ:r], *s.f. Bot:* fumitory.

fumeur, -euse[1] [fymœ:r, -ø:z], *s.* 1. (*a*) smoker; *Rail:* (*on window*) **fumeurs,** smoking (compartment); **grand f.,** heavy smoker; (*b*) **f. de poisson,** fish-smoker, fish-curer. 2. *Rail: F:* smoking compartment; *F:* smoker.

fumeux, -euse[2] [fymø, -ø:z], *a.* 1. smoky, smoking; **lampe fumeuse,** smoky lamp; **idées fumeuses,** hazy, woolly, ideas. 2. heady (wine).

fumier [fymje], *s.m.* 1. stable-litter, manure, dung; **f. bien fait, consumé,** well-rotted, well-decayed, manure; **trou, fosse, à f.,** dung-pit. 2. dunghill, manure heap; **mourir sur le f.,** to die in squalor. 3. *P:* **espèce de f.!** you bastard!

fumière [fymjɛ:r], *s.f.* dunghill, dungheap.

fumifuge [fymify:ʒ]. 1. *a.* smoke-preventing, -expelling. 2. *s.m.* smoke preventer.

fumigant [fymigɑ̃], *s.m.* fumigant.

fumigateur [fymigatœ:r], *s.m.* fumigator.

fumigation [fymigasjɔ̃], *s.f.* fumigation; **faire des fumigations de soufre,** to fumigate with sulphur.

fumigatoire [fymigatwa:r], *a.* fumigating, fumigatory.

fumigène [fymiʒɛn]. 1. *a.* smoke-producing; **obus f.,** smoke shell; **bombe f.,** smoke bomb. 2. *s.m.* smoke producer.

fumiger [fymiʒe], *v.tr.* (**je fumigeais, n. fumigeons**) to fumigate.

fumiste [fymist], *s.m.* 1. *Tchn:* (*pers.*) stove setter. 2. *F:* (*a*) practical joker; (*b*) humbug, fraud; *a.* **il est un peu f.,** he's a bit of a fraud.

fumisterie [fymistəri], *s.f.* 1. stove setting. 2. *F:* practical joke; hoax; **ce beau programme est une vaste f.,** this fine programme is nothing but eyewash, is a complete fraud.

fumivore [fymivɔ:r]. 1. *a.* smoke-consuming; **foyer f.,** smokeless fireplace, furnace. 2. *s.m.* smoke absorber.

fumivorité [fymivɔrite], *s.f.* (*a*) efficiency in smoke absorption, removal (of an apparatus); (*b*) (*of fireplace, etc.*) quality of not smoking.

fumoir [fymwa:r], *s.m.* 1. smoking-room (of hotel, etc.). 2. smoke room, smoke(-curing) house (for meat, fish, etc.).

fumosité [fymozite], *s.f.* smokiness.

fumure [fymyːr], *s.f.* (*a*) dung, manure; (*b*) dunging, manuring (of field).
funaire [fynɛːr], *s.m. Bot:* cord moss.
funambule [fynɑ̃byl], *s.m. & f.* **1.** funambulist, tightrope walker. **2.** *Z:* palm squirrel.
funambulesque [fynɑ̃bylɛsk], *a.* **1.** funambulatory. **2.** fantastic, grotesque (story, etc.).
funaria [fynarja], *s.m. Bot:* cord moss.
fune [fyn], *s.f. Nau:* rope; *esp.* **f. de tente,** ridge rope; ridge pole (of tent or awning); *Fish:* **f. de seine,** drag rope of a seine; **f. de chalut,** trawl warp.
funèbre [fynɛbr̥], *a.* **1.** funeral (ceremony, etc.); *Mus:* **hymne, chant, f.,** dirge; **marche f.,** funeral march, dead march; **couche f.,** death bed; **pompes funèbres,** undertaking; **cloche f.,** knell. **2.** funereal, dismal, gloomy (aspect, expression, etc.).
funèbrement [fynɛbrəmɑ̃], *adv.* funereally, dismally, gloomily.
funer [fyne], *v.tr. Nau: A:* to rig (mast, etc.).
funérailles [fyneraːj], *s.f.pl.* **1.** (elaborate) funeral (ceremonies); **f. nationales,** state funeral; **f. militaires,** military funeral. **2.** *int. F:* (*S. of Fr.*) **oh, f.!** oh blast! oh no! (look who's coming!).
funéraire [fynerɛːr], *a.* funeral, funerary; **pierre f.,** tombstone; **drap f.,** pall; **frais funéraires,** funeral expenses.
funeste [fynɛst], *a.* (*a*) deadly, fatal; **accident f.,** fatal accident; **coup f.,** mortal, deadly, blow; **écueil f. à de nombreux navires,** reef on which many ships have foundered; (*b*) fatal, disastrous, catastrophic; **erreurs funestes,** fatal, catastrophic, lamentable, errors; **cela peut avoir des suites funestes,** that may have disastrous consequences; **influence f.,** disastrous influence; **politique f. aux intérêts du pays,** policy fatal to the interests of the country; **mauvais temps f. aux récoltes,** bad weather catastrophic for the harvest; (*c*) *Lit:* funereal, sombre, gloomy; that evokes death; **des cyprès funestes,** sombre, sad, cypresses.
funestement [fynɛstəmɑ̃], *adv.* fatally, mortally.
fungia [fœ̃ʒja], **fungie** [fœ̃ʒi], *s.f. Coel:* fungia, mushroom coral.
funiculaire [fynikylɛːr]. **1.** *a.* (*a*) funicular (railway); (*b*) *Anat: Med:* funicular; (*c*) *Mec:* **polygone f.,** funicular (polygon). **2.** *s.m.* funicular (railway). **3.** *s.f. Mth:* catenary, funicular curve.
funicule [fynikyl], *s.m. Bot:* funicle, funiculus.
funiculé [fynikyle], *a. Bot:* funiculate.
funiculite [fynikylit], *s.f. Med:* funiculitis.
funifère [fynifɛːr], *a.* having funicular appendices.
funiforme [fynifɔrm], *a. Miner:* funiform, cord-shaped.
funin [fynɛ̃], *s.m. Nau:* (untarred) rope.
fur [fyːr], *s.m. A:* rate; *now used only in the adv. phr.* **au f. et à mesure,** (in proportion) as, progressively; **on inspecte les articles et on les emballe au f. et à mesure,** the articles are inspected and packed as the inspection proceeds, as soon as they are ready; **on peut fournir ces articles au f. et à mesure des besoins,** these articles can be supplied as (they are) wanted; **envoyez-moi l'argent au f. et à mesure que vous le recevrez,** send me the money (as fast) as you receive it; **payer qn au f. et à mesure de l'ouvrage,** to pay s.o. as the work proceeds.
furanne [fyran], *s.m. Ch:* furan(e).
furannose [fyranoːz], *s.m. Bio-Ch:* furanose.
furet [fyrɛ], *s.m.* **1.** (*a*) *Z:* ferret; **chasse au f.,** ferreting; **chasser au f.,** to go ferreting; **jeu du f.,** (*various games of the type of*) hunt-the-slipper; (*b*) inquisitive person; *F:* nosy parker, Paul Pry. **2.** pipe-cleaner. **3.** *Atom.Ph:* rabbit.
furetage [fyrtaːʒ], *s.m.* **1.** ferreting (for rabbits). **2.** searching; *F:* rummaging, nosing about (for sth.).
fureter [fyrte], *v.* (**je furette, n. furetons; je furetterai**) **1.** *v.i.* (*a*) to ferret, hunt with ferrets, go ferreting; (*b*) **f. dans les armoires,** to ferret, pry about, nose about, rummage, in the cupboards. **2.** *v.tr.* (*a*) to ferret (rabbit-burrow, etc.); (*b*) **f. des papiers,** to ferret, nose about, rummage, among papers.
fureteur, -euse [fyrtœːr, -øːz], *s.* **1.** ferreter. **2.** searcher, rummager; *F:* nosy parker, Paul Pry; *a.* **yeux fureteurs,** prying eyes.
fureur [fyrœːr], *s.f.* **1.** fury, rage, wrath; **être en f.,** to be in a rage; **se mettre, entrer, en f.,** to get, fly, into a rage, into a passion; **exciter la f. de qn,** excite, stir up, s.o.'s anger. **2.** fury, passion; **f. poétique,** poetic frenzy; **les fureurs de l'amour,** the transports of passion; **aimer qn, qch., avec f., à la f.,** to be passionately fond of s.o., sth.; to be passionately in love with s.o.; **avoir la f. de bâtir,** to have a craze for building, to be building mad **chanson qui fait f. à présent,** song that is all the rage, all the go, at present; **chanson qui a fait f.,** song that created a furore; **la f. de la tempête,** the fury of the storm; **déchaîner les fureurs de la guerre,** to let loose the fury of war.
furfur [fyrfyːr], *s.m. Med:* furfur.
furfuracé [fyrfyrase], *a. Med:* furfuraceous.
furfural [fyrfyral], *s.m. Ch:* furfural, furfuraldehyde.
furfurane [fyrfyran], *s.m. Ch: A:* furfuran(e).
furfure [fyrfyːr], *s.f. Med:* furfur.
furfurol(e) [fyrfyrɔl], *s.m. Ch: A:* furfurol(e).
furfuryle [fyrfyril], *s.m. Ch:* furfuryl.
furfurylidène [fyrfyrilidɛn], *s.m. Ch:* furfurylidene.
furibard [fyribaːr], *a. F:* furious.
furibond [fyribɔ̃], *a.* furious, full of fury; **elle lui lança un regard f.,** she glared at him, looked daggers at him; *s.* **se conduire comme un f.,** to behave like a madman.
furie [fyri], *s.f.* **1.** (*a*) *Myth:* **les Furies,** the Furies; (*b*) **c'est une f.,** she's a termagant, a fury. **2.** (*a*) fury, rage; **se battre avec f.,** to fight furiously; *Hist:* **la f. française,** the dash of the French soldiery, the *furia francese*; **taureau en f.,** infuriated, mad, bull; **entrer, se mettre, en f.,** to become furious; **la f. de la tempête,** the fury of the storm; **la f. des timbres-poste,** the craze for stamp-collecting; (*b*) **applaudir avec f.,** to applaud frantically. **3.** *Z:* **les furies,** the emballonurid bats.
furieusement [fyrjøzmɑ̃], *adv.* **1.** furiously, passionately. **2.** *F:* extremely, tremendously; **il est f. bavard,** he's a tremendous talker; **travailler f.,** to work furiously, *F:* like blazes.
furieux, -ieuse [fyrjø, -jøːz], *a.* **1.** furious, raging; in a passion; **être f. contre qn,** *F:* **après qn,** to be furious, in a rage, *F:* wild, with s.o.; **rendre qn f.,** to make s.o. furious; to enrage, infuriate, s.o.; **tigre f.,** infuriated, mad, tiger; **tempête furieuse,** raging, howling, tempest; **galop f.,** wild, mad, gallop; *Her:* **taureau f.,** bull rampant; *s.* **un f., une furieuse,** a madman, madwoman; *s.a.* FOLIE 1, FOU 2. **2.** (*intensive*) *F:* **c'est un f. mangeur,** he's a tremendous, prodigious, eater; **j'avais une furieuse envie de le faire,** I was mad keen to do it.
furile [fyril], *s.m. Ch:* furil(e).
furilique [fyrilik], *a. Ch:* furilic (acid).
furin [fyrɛ̃], *s.m. A: Nau:* high seas; **mener un vaisseau en f.,** to pilot a ship into the open.
furnariidés [fyrnariide], *s.m.pl. Orn:* Furnariidae.
furoïne [fyrɔin], *s.f. Ch:* furoin.
furol(l)e [fyrɔl], *s.f. A: or Dial:* Jack-o'-lantern, will-o'-the-wisp.
furon [fyrɔ̃], *s.m. Z:* young ferret.
furoncle [fyrɔ̃ːkl̥], *s.m. Med:* furuncle; *F:* boil.
furonculeux, -euse [fyrɔ̃kylø, -øːz], *a. Med:* furuncular, furunculous.
furonculose [fyrɔ̃kyloːz], *s.f. Med:* furunculosis.
furtif, -ive [fyrtif, -iːv], *a.* furtive, stealthy; **elle me regarda d'un œil f.,** she glanced furtively at me; **d'un pas f.,** with a stealthy tread, stealthily.
furtivement [fyrtivmɑ̃], *adv.* furtively, stealthily; **regarder qn f.,** to glance furtively, to peep, at s.o.; **entrer, sortir, f.,** to creep, steal, in, out.
furyle [fyril], *s.m. Ch:* furyl.
fusain [fyzɛ̃], *s.m.* **1.** *Bot:* euonymus, spindle tree, prickwood. **2.** (*a*) drawing charcoal, charcoal pencil, fusain; **dessiné au f.,** drawn in charcoal; (*b*) charcoal sketch. **3.** *Min:* fusain.
fusainiste [fyzɛnist], *s.m.* artist in charcoal, fusinist.
fusaïole [fyzajɔl], *s.f. Tex: Archeol:* spindle-whorl.
fusant [fyzɑ̃], *a. Exp:* fusing; **composition fusante,** fuse composition; *Artil:* **obus fusant,** time shell; **tir f.,** time-fuse fire.
fusariose [fyzarjoːz], *s.f. Med:* fusariosis, fusariose.
fusarol(l)e [fyzarɔl], *s.f. Arch:* fusarole.
fuscine [fysin], *s.f.* **1.** *Myth:* (Neptune's) trident. **2.** *A:* (fisherman's or gladiator's) trident.
fuseau, -eaux [fyzo], *s.m.* **1.** *Tex:* spindle; **f. de quenouille,** distaff; **f. pour dentelles,** lace bobbin; **f. de dentellière,** lacemaker's bones; **fuseaux de la chaîne,** passive bobbins; *F:* **jambes de, en, f.,** spindly legs; **il peut à peine se tenir sur ses fuseaux,** he can hardly keep on his pins. **2.** *Biol:* nucleus spindle; *Anat:* **f. de l'émail (d'une dent),** enamel spindle (of tooth). **3.** (*a*) *Geom:* spherical lune; (*b*) **f. horaire,** time belt, zone; hour zone; standard time belt; (*c*) *Aer:* gore (of balloon). **4.** *Mec.E:* (*a*) **f. de lanterne,** stave of a trundle; (*b*) **f. de chaîne,** link-pin of a roller-chain. **5.** (*a*) taper; **effilé en forme de f.,** tapered; *Hort:* **(arbre en) f.,** quenouille-trained fruit tree; (*b*) *pl. Cost:* ski(ing) trousers; tapered trousers. **6.** *Av:* pod (for engine, weapon, etc.).
fusée [fyze], *s.f.* **1.** (*a*) spindleful (of thread); (*b*) *Mec.E:* spindle (of shaft, axle); spindle, barrel (of capstan, winch); *Aut:* stub axle; *Nau:* **f. de vergue,** yard arm; (*c*) tang (of foil or rapier blade); (*d*) loom (of oar); (*e*) fusee chain (of watch); (*f*) *Med:* fistula; (*g*) *Vet:* splinter (of bone). **2.** *Ball: Pyr:* rocket; (*a*) *Pyr:* rocket, flare, light; **f. éclairante,** flare; **f. éclairante à parachute,** parachute flare; **f. de signalisation, f.-signal,** signal rocket, flare; rocket signal; **f. traçante,** tracer rocket; **f. volante,** sky rocket; **f. à pétard,** maroon; **pistolet lance-f., à f.,** signalling pistol, flare-pistol; **lancer une f.,** to fire, shoot, a rocket; to throw a flare; (*b*) *Ball:* (i) **f. à un étage, f. monoétage,** one-stage rocket; **f. mère,** first-stage rocket; **f. à deux, à trois, étages,** two-, three-stage rocket; **f. chimique,** chemical rocket; **f. à liquides, à propergol liquide,** liquid-propellent rocket; **f. à poudre, à propergol solide,** solid-propellent rocket; **f. (à propulsion) électrique,** electric rocket; **f. (à propulsion) ionique,** ion(-drive) rocket; **f. à plasma,** plasma(-drive) rocket; **f. à photons,** photon(-drive) rocket; **f. (à propulsion) nucléaire,** (thermodynamic) nuclear rocket, **lancer une f.,** to launch a rocket; (ii) **f. d'appoint,** booster; **f. individuelle,** man rocket, personal rocket; **f. météo(rologique),** meteorological rocket, weather rocket; **f. postale,** mail-carrying rocket; **f. sonde,** sounding rocket, probe (rocket); **avion (à) f.,** rocket-propelled aircraft; **f. engin,** missile; **f. de radar, de proximité,** homing missile; **f. porteuse,** carrier rocket; (iii) *Nau:* **f. porte-amarre,** life(-saving) rocket. **3.** *Exp: Artil: etc:* fuse (of shell, bomb, etc.); **f. de culot,** base fuse; **f. d'ogive,** nose, point, fuse; **f. à percussion, f. percutante,** percussion fuse, impact fuse, concussion fuse; **f. instantanée,** instantaneous fuse, direct-action fuse; **f. à retard(ement), f. à effet retardé, f. à temps,** delay-(action) fuse, time fuse; **f. à double effet,** double-action fuse, time and percussion fuse; **f. à mouvement d'horlogerie,** mechanical time fuse; **f. à plateau,** disc fuse; **f. de proximité,** proximity fuse; **f. auto-destructrice,** self-destroying fuse; **chapeau, coiffe, de f.,** fuse cap, cover; **corps de f.,** fuse body, case; **réglage de la f.,** fuse setting; **extrapolation de la f.,** fuse prediction (in anti-aircraft fire); **régler, extrapoler, une f.,** to set, predict, a fuse; **insérer une f. dans un obus, dans une bombe,** to fuse a shell, a bomb. **4.** (*a*) *Mus: A:* (vocal) run; (*b*) *F:* **de longues fusées de rire,** long ripples of laughter. **5.** *Her:* fusil.
fusée-détonateur [fyzedetɔnatœːr], *s.f.* detonating, explosive, fuse; *pl. fusées-détonateurs.*
fusée-parachute [fyzeparaʃyt], *s.f.* parachute flare; *pl. fusées-parachutes.*
fusée-sonde [fyzesɔ̃ːd], *s.f. Av:* sounding rocket; *pl. fusées-sondes.*
fusel [fyzɛl], *s.m. Dist:* **huile de f.,** fusel oil.
fuselage [fyzlaːʒ], *s.m. Av:* fuselage, air frame; body (of aircraft); **f. à treillis,** lattice fuselage; **f. limousine,** passenger-carrying fuselage; **avion à f. porteur,** lifting-body aircraft.
fuselé [fyzle], *a.* **1.** (*a*) spindle-shaped; tapering; **doigts fuselés,** tapering, slender, fingers; (*b*) streamlined; *N.Arch:* faired; *Av:* fusiform. **2.** *Her:* fusilly.
fuseler [fyzle], *v.tr.* (**je fuselle, n. fuselons; je fusellerai**) (*a*) to shape like a spindle, to taper; (*b*) to streamline.
fuséologue [fyzeɔlɔg], *s.m.* (space) rocket specialist.
fuser [fyze], *v.i.* **1.** (*of colours*) to spread, run; **la lumière fuse par la fenêtre,** (i) the light streams in by the window; (ii) the light streams out of the window; **une colère glacée fusait dans son regard,** an icy wave of anger spread over his face; **les chants fusent de partout,** songs break, burst, out everywhere. **2.** (*a*) to fuse, melt; (*b*) to slake; **chaux fusée,** air-slaked lime; (*c*) *Ch:* to crackle, deflagrate; *F:* to fizz. **3.** *Pyr:* (*of fuse, etc.*) to burn slowly.
fuserolle [fyz(ə)rɔl], *s.f. Arch:* fusarole.
fusette [fyzɛt], *s.f.* (cardboard, plastic) cotton reel.
fusibilité [fyzibilite], *s.f.* fusibility.
fusible [fyzibl̥]. **1.** *a.* fusible, easily melted. **2.** *s.m. El.E:* fuse; fuse wire; **f. de sûreté,** safety fuse, cut-out; **f. à lame,** strip fuse; **f. à bouchon,** plug fuse; **f. pour haute tension,** high-voltage protector; **f. à cartouche,** cartridge fuse; **f. de compteur,** house service fuse, cut-out; **f. de ligne,** line fuse; **boîte à fusibles,** fuse box; **le f. est fondu,** the fuse has gone, we've blown a fuse.

fusiforme [fyzifɔrm], *a.* fusiform; spindle-shaped; slender.

fusil [fyzi], *s.m.* **1.** steel (of tinder-box); **pierre à f.,** flint. **2.** (*a*) (sharpening) steel; (*b*) whetstone. **3.** gun; (*a*) **f. de chasse,** sporting gun, fowling piece, shotgun; **f. à chiens extérieurs,** hammer gun; **f. à aiguille,** needle gun; **f. à bascule,** hinged breech loader, drop-down gun; **f. à deux coups,** (i) double-barrelled gun; (ii) *Cost: F:* drainpipe trousers; **f. à un coup,** single-barrelled gun, single loader; **f. à air comprimé,** air gun; **f. harpon,** harpoon gun; *Hist:* **f. à mèche,** matchlock; **f. à pierre,** flintlock; *Mil: etc:* **f. (rayé),** rifle; **f. automatique, f. semi-automatique,** automatic, semi-automatic, gun, rifle; **f. à chargeur,** *O:* **f. à répétition,** magazine rifle; **f. de dotation, f. réglementaire,** service, regulation, rifle; *A:* **f. de munition,** service gun; **changer son f. d'épaule,** (i) *Mil:* to change arms; (ii) to change one's opinions; (*c*) **coup de f.,** (i) gunshot, musket-shot; **il fut tué d'un coup de f.,** he was shot; **j'entendis un coup de f.,** I heard the report of a gun, of a rifle; (ii) *P:* barefaced overcharging; fleecing (in restaurants, hotels, etc.); **essuyer le coup de f.,** to be stung, fleeced; (*d*) *F:* (*pers.*) **c'est un de nos meilleurs fusils,** he's one of our best shots.

fusilier [fyzilje], *s.m.* fusilier; **f. marin,** *approx.* = Royal marine.

fusilier-voltigeur [fyziljevɔltiʒœːr], *s.m.* rifleman; *pl.* **fusiliers-voltigeurs.**

fusillade [fyzijad], *s.f.* **1.** fusillade, rifle fire. **2.** (military) execution, shooting (of spy, etc.).

fusiller [fyzije], *v.tr.* **1.** (*a*) to shoot (down) (men); **on se fusillait presque à bout portant,** they shot at each other almost at point-blank range; **f. qn du regard,** to look daggers at s.o.; (*b*) to execute (spy, etc.) (by shooting); to shoot (spy); (*c*) *F:* **f. une auto,** to ruin a car (through bad driving); **vous allez f. tout le bazar,** you are going to mess up, spoil, the whole show. **2. f. un couteau,** to sharpen a knife on the steel.

fusilleur [fyzijœːr], *s.m.* member of a firing squad.

fusil-mitrailleur [fyzimitrajœːr], *s.m.* automatic rifle, light automatic; light machine gun; *pl.* **fusils-mitrailleurs.**

fusiniste [fyzinist], *s.m.* artist in charcoal, fusinist.

fusion [fyzjɔ̃], *s.f.* **1.** (*a*) fusion, melting (by heat); **point de f.,** melting-point; **fer en f.,** molten iron; **entrer en f.,** to begin to melt; **eaux de f. (d'un**

glacier), outwash; (*b*) smelting, melt (of ore, iron, etc.); (*c*) *Atom.Ph:* fusion. **2.** dissolving, melting (of sth. in a liquid). **3.** coalescing (of ideas, etc.); *Fin:* merger; **f. entre deux compagnies,** etc., amalgamation of two companies, etc.; **opérer une f.,** to amalgamate; *Cin:* **opérer la f. de deux scènes,** to fade one scene into another.

fusionnement [fyzjɔnmɑ̃], *s.m.* amalgamation, fusion (of two parties, etc.).

fusionner [fyzjɔne], *v.tr., i. & pr.* (*a*) *Com: Pol: etc:* to amalgamate, unite, merge; **f. deux listes (électorales),** to combine two lists; **f. deux idées,** to coalesce, blend, two ideas; (*b*) *Rail:* to join up (two trains).

fusionniste [fyzjɔnist], *s.m. & f. Com: Pol: etc:* fusionist.

fusocellulaire [fyzosɛlylɛːr], *a. Med:* fusocellular (tumour).

fustanelle [fystanɛl], *s.f. Cost:* fustanelle, fustanella, (Greek) kilt.

fustet [fystɛ], *s.m. Bot:* fustet, smoke tree, Venetian sumac.

fustibale [fystibal], *s.f. A.Arms:* fustibal, staff sling.

fustigation [fystigasjɔ̃], *s.f.* fustigation, thrashing, beating.

fustiger [fystiʒe], *v.tr.* (**je fustigeai(s), n. fustigeons**) to fustigate, thrash, beat.

fusuline [fyzylin], *s.f. Paleont:* fusulina.

fusulinidés [fyzylinide], *s.m.pl. Paleont:* Fusulinidae.

fût [fy], *s.m.* **1.** stock (of rifle, plane, anvil, etc.); handle (of saw, racquet, etc.); brace (for bit); **f. à rochet,** ratchet brace. **2.** (*a*) shaft (of column, chimney); stem (of candelabra); post (of crane); standard (of jack, etc.); shank (of rivet); stick (of violin bow); (*b*) *Arb:* bole (of tree); **à f. court, long,** short-boled, long-boled; **arbre à f. plein,** non-tapering tree; **arbre à f. décroissant,** tapering tree. **3.** (*a*) cask, barrel, tun; drum (for oil, etc.); **tirer de la bière du f.,** to draw beer from the wood; **bière détaillée du fût,** draught beer; (*b*) body (of box, jack, etc.); (organ-) chest; **f. d'un tambour,** barrel, body, of a drum.

futaie [fytɛ], *s.f.* wood, forest (of full-grown trees); **f. de châtaigniers,** chestnut-grove; **demi-f.,** forest of trees from 40 to 60 years old; **arbre de haute f.,** full-grown tree, timber tree; **bois de haute f.,** wood of timber trees (of 100 to 200 years old); **forêt de haute f.,** open forest.

futaille [fytaːj], *s.f.* **1.** cask, tun; *Nau:* **pattes à futailles,** can-hook slings. **2.** casks (collectively); **f. en botte,** shook; **mettre une f. en botte,** to shook (a barrel).

futaine [fytɛn], *s.f. Tex:* fustian.

futainier [fytɛnje], *s.m.* (i) manufacturer, (ii) seller, of fustian.

futal [fytal], *s.m. P:* (pair of) trousers.

futé [fyte], *a.* (*a*) sharp, smart, astute, crafty; sly; **enfant f.,** sharp child; **f. comme un renard,** cunning as a fox; **s. c'est une petite futée,** she's a sly, crafty, little creature; (*b*) **air f.,** spiteful look, appearance.

futée [fyte], *s.f. Carp:* stopping (made of glue and sawdust); mastic.

futile [fytil], *a.* futile, trivial, trifling; frivolous (person); idle (pretext); **homme f.,** trifler; **incident f.,** trifling incident; **s'irriter pour des sujets futiles,** to get annoyed over trifles; **le prétexte le plus f.,** the most futile, trifling, pretext.

futilement [fytilmɑ̃], *adv.* futilely.

futilité [fytilite], *s.f.* **1.** futility. **2. s'occuper à des futilités,** to trifle; to busy oneself with trifles; **dire des futilités,** to say polite nothings.

futur [fytyːr]. **1.** *a.* (*a*) future; **la vie future,** the life to come; **f. acheteur, abonné,** intending purchaser, subscriber; (*b*) *s: P:* **mon f., ma future,** my intended (husband, wife); *P:* my young man, my young lady; **sa future bru,** his future daughter-in-law. **2.** *s.m.* (*a*) *Gram:* future (tense); **verbe au f.,** verb in the future; (*b*) *Phil:* future, futurition, futurity.

futurisme [fytyrism], *s.m. Art:* futurism.

futuriste [fytyrist], *Art:* **1.** *a.* futurist(ic). **2.** *s.* futurist.

futurition [fytyrisjɔ̃], *s.f.* futurition.

fuxéen, -enne [fykseɛ̃, -ɛn], *a. & s. Geog:* (native, inhabitant) of Foix.

fuyant [fɥijɑ̃], *a.* **1.** fleeing, flying (animal, etc.); fleeting (moment). **2.** receding (forehead, line); *Art:* **échelle fuyante,** reducing, diminishing, vanishing, scale; *Aut:* **ligne fuyante,** streamline; *s.m.* **les fuyants d'un tableau,** the perspective lines, the perspective, of a picture. **3. yeux fuyants,** shifty eyes.

fuyard, -arde [fɥijaːr, -ard]. **1.** *a.* (*of animal*) shy, timid, that runs away. **2.** *s.* (*a*) (panic-stricken) fugitive; runaway; (*b*) *F:* person who backs out of an engagement, an appointment.

fy [fi], *s.m. Vet:* kind of (animal) leprosy.

G

G, g [ʒe], *s.m.* the letter G, g; *Tp:* G comme Gaston, G for George; *Meteor:* couche G, G region (of ionosphere).

gabalitain, -aine [gabalitɛ̃, -ɛn], *a. & s. Geog:* (native, inhabitant) of the Gévaudan region.

Gabaon [gabaɔ̃], *Pr.n.m. B.Hist:* Gibeon.

Gabaonite [gabaɔnit], *s.m. & f. B.Hist:* Gibeonite.

gabarage [gabaraʒ], *s.m. Nau:* lighterage.

gabardine [gabardin], *s.f.* **1.** *Tex:* gabardine. **2.** *Cost:* (gabardine) raincoat.

gabare [gabaːr], *s.f.* **1.** *Nau:* (a) sailing barge; lighter; (b) transport vessel, store ship, scow. **2.** drag-net.

gabaret [gabarɛ], *s.m. Fish:* (small) drag-net.

gabariage [gabarjaʒ], *s.m. N.Arch:* shaping, moulding (of armour plate).

gabarier[1] [gabarje], *s.m. Nau:* **1.** skipper (of barge). **2.** lighterman, bargee.

gabarier[2], *v.tr.* **1.** *N.Arch:* to shape, mould. **2.** *Metalw:* to gauge (metal plate).

gabarieur [gabarjœːr], *s.m.* **1.** *N.Arch:* (ship's) draughtsman. **2.** *Ind:* template maker.

gabarit [gabari], *s.m.* **1.** (a) *N.Arch:* (i) model (of ship), mould (of ship's part); (ii) plan scantling; g. de membrure, frame mould; forme sur g., moulded form; (b) *Const:* outline (of building). **2.** (a) *Mec.E: etc:* template, templet, gauge, jig, former; g. de mécanicien, engineer's jig; g. d'assemblage, de montage, assembly jig, assembling gauge; g. de fraisage, milling jig; g. de perçage, drill template, drilling gauge; g. de traçage, contour template, marking template; g. passe-partout, master template, master gauge; g. de contrôle, de vérification, control, inspection, gauge; trim template; tour à g., copying lathe; (b) *El.E:* g. de bobinage, winding former; (c) *Dent:* g. d'occlusion, occlusal template (for artificial teeth); (d) *Rail:* g. de chargement, loading gauge, tunnel gauge; g. limite de chargement, maximum structure, maximum moving dimensions (of rolling stock); g. de courbe, curve gauge; g. d'écartement (des voies), rail gauge, track gauge; gauge template; g. d'usure des rails, wear and tear gauge; (e) *F: usu. Pej:* des gens de son g., people of his sort, people like him; c'est un homme de petit g., he's a half pint, a little runt of a man; c'est un homme de grand g., he's a great hulk of a man; *s.a.* FEU 4.

gabarit-obstacle [gabariɔpstak]], *s.m. Rail:* minimum dimensions, clearance (under bridge, etc.); *pl. gabarits-obstacles.*

gabarre [gabaːr], *s.f.* = GABARE.

gabbro [gabro], *s.m. Geol: Art:* gabbro.

gabegie [gabʒi], *s.f.* **1.** *O:* intrigue, trickery; *pl.* underhand dealings, hole-and-corner dealings. **2.** waste; muddle; disorder.

gabelage [gablaʒ], *s.m. Hist:* (a) time during which the salt was in store before sale; (b) official mark put on salt in store.

gabeleur [gablœːr], **gabeleux** [gablø], **gabelou** [gablu], *s.m.* **1.** *Hist:* collector of the salt tax, exciseman. **2.** *Pej:* custom-house officer.

gabelier [gabəlje], *s.m. Hist:* salt-tax officer, inspector.

gabelle [gabɛl], *s.f. Hist:* **1.** salt tax. **2.** (salt) excise. **3.** building in which the salt was bonded.

gaber [gabe], *v.i. & tr. A: & Hum:* to joke; to make fun of (s.o.).

Gabès [gabɛs], *Pr.n. Geog:* Gabes.

gabet [gabɛ], *s.m. Leath:* punch.

gabeur [gabœːr], *s.m. A:* railer, scoffer.

gabian [gabjɑ̃], *s.m. Dial:* (*Atlantic coast*) seagull.

gabie [gabi], *s.f.* (a) *A.Nau:* half-top; (b) *W.Tel:* cross-piece (for aerial).

gabier [gabje], *s.m. A.Nau:* topman; g. breveté, able(-bodied) seaman.

gabion [gabjɔ̃], *s.m.* **1.** (a) *Mil:* gabion; g. clayonné, wicker gabion; g. farci, sap roller; *Hyd.E:* gabion. **2.** *Agr:* (rough two-handled) basket. **3.** *Ven:* hide, blind.

gabionnade [gabjɔnad], *s.f. A: Mil:* gabionade, line of gabions.

gabionnage [gabjɔna:ʒ], *s.m. Mil:* gabionage, (i) gabion entrenching; (ii) gabioned parapet, gabionade.

gabionner [gabjɔne], *v.tr. Mil:* to gabion (trench, etc.).

gable, gâble [gɑ:bl], *s.m. Arch:* **1.** gable. **2.** (triangular) window canopy.

Gabon (le) [ləgabɔ̃], *Pr.n.m. Geog:* Gabon.

gabonais, -aise [gabɔnɛ, -ɛːz], *a. & s. Geog:* Gabonese.

gabord [gabɔːr], *s.m. Nau:* garboard (strake); tôle de g., garboard plate.

gabot [gabo], *s.m. Ich:* exocoetus; *F:* flying fish.

gabre [gabr], *s.m. Orn: F:* (a) cock partridge; (b) turkey cock.

Gabriel [gabri(j)ɛl], *Pr.n.m.* Gabriel.

gaburon [gabyrɔ̃], *s.m. Nau:* fish-front (of mast).

gâchage [gaʃaːʒ], *s.m.* **1.** mixing (of mortar, etc.). **2.** spoiling, bungling; wasting. **3.** *A:* rinsing (of linen). **4.** harrowing.

gâche[1] [gaːʃ], *s.f.* **1.** trowel. **2.** *Cu:* (cook's) spatula.

gâche[2], *s.f.* **1.** *Locksm:* (a) (box) staple, keeper (of lock); (b) (latch) catch; g. de verrou, bolt-clasp; (b) striking box, plate; strike box (of spring bolt). **2.** notch (for pawl). **3.** *Const: etc:* wall hook, clip; saddle (fastening wire on pole, etc.).

gâche[3], *s.f. P:* cushy job.

gâchée [gaʃe], *s.f. Const:* batch (of cement, concrete).

gâcher [gaʃe], *v.tr.* **1.** (a) to mix, wet, temper; g. du mortier, to mix mortar; g. la chaux, to slack lime; g. serré, to temper (clay, etc.) hard; (b) *A:* to rinse (linen in running water). **2.** (a) to spoil (sheet of paper, etc.); to bungle (job); g. une besogne, to botch, mess up, a piece of work; g. le métier, (i) to undercut; to sell below market price; (ii) to do more than is strictly necessary; (b) to waste; g. une fortune, to squander, *F:* play ducks and drakes with, a fortune; g. son temps, to waste one's time; g. sa vie, (i) to waste one's life, (ii) to ruin one's life, to make a mess of one's life, to go to the dogs. **3.** *Agr:* to harrow (corn, in the spring).

gâchette [gaʃɛt], *s.f.* **1.** *Sm.a:* (a) tumbler, sear (of gun lock); (b) trigger; *F:* avoir la g. facile, to be trigger-happy. **2.** follower, spring catch (of lock). **3.** *Mec.E:* pawl. **4.** *Elcs:* gate.

gâcheur, -euse[1] [gaʃœːr, -øːz], *a. & s.* **1.** *a.* (a) bungling; (b) undercutting. **2.** *s.* (a) bungler, botcher; (b) undercutter; *pl.* cheap labour. **3.** *s.m.* (mason's, carpenter's) labourer, mate.

gâcheux, -euse[2] [gaʃø, -øːz], *a.* **1.** muddy, miry (road, etc.). **2.** damaged (fruit).

gâchis [gaʃi], *s.m.* **1.** wet mortar. **2.** (a) mud; slush; (b) quel g.! what a mess! nous voilà dans un beau g.! we're in a fine mess! faire un beau g. de sa vie, to make a hash, a mess, of one's life; g. politique, political muddle, confusion.

gâchoir [gaʃwaːr], *s.m. Cer:* vat for mixing potter's clay.

gadarénien, -ienne [gadarenjɛ̃, -jɛn], *a. & s. B.Hist:* Gadarene.

gade [gad], *s.m. Ich:* gade, gadoid.

gadelle [gadɛl], *s.f. Bot: Fr.C:* red currant.

gadget [gadʒɛt], *s.m. F:* gadget.

gadidés [gadide], *s.m.pl. Ich:* Gadidae.

gadiformes [gadifɔrm], *s.m.pl. Ich:* Gadiformes.

gadille [gadiːj], *s.f. Orn: F:* robin.

gadin [gadɛ̃], *s.m.* **1.** *Fish:* float. **2.** *P:* head, *F:* nut; ramasser un g., to come a cropper; y aller du g., to lose one's head, to be guillotined.

gaditan, -ane [gaditɑ̃, -an], *a. & s. Geog:* (native, inhabitant) of Cadiz.

gadoïde [gadɔid], *a. & s.m. Ich:* gadoid.

gadolinite [gadɔlinit], *s.f. Miner:* gadolinite.

gadolinium [gadɔlinjɔm], *s.m. Ch:* gadolinium.

gadouard [gaduaːr], *s.m.* scavenger.

gadoue [gadu], *s.f.* **1.** (a) night soil, sewage sludge (used as manure); (b) mud, slush, slime; (c) *P:* je suis dans une belle g., I am in a mess. **2.** *P:* (a) shit; (b) prostitute, tart.

gadzarts [gadzaːr], *s.m.inv. Sch: F:* (= gars des Arts) student or former student of an École des Arts et Métiers.

Gaël [gaɛl], *s.m. Ethn:* Gael.

gaélique [gaelik], *a. Ethn: Ling:* Gaelic; *s.m.* le g., Gaelic.

Gaète [gaɛt], *Pr.n. Geog:* Gaeta.

gaffe [gaf], *s.f.* **1.** (a) boathook; (b) *Fish:* gaff; *P:* avaler sa g., to die, to kick the bucket. **2.** *F:* blunder, faux pas; faire une g., to put one's foot in it; to make a a bad break; to drop a clanger; to drop a brick. **3.** (a) *Mil: A:* faire la g., porter g., to be on sentry duty; (b) *P:* faire g., to take care; to be on the look-out; fais g.! look out! watch it! **4.** *P:* prison warder; *P:* screw.

gaffeau, -eaux [gafo], *s.m. Fish:* gaff (hook).

gaffer [gafe]. **1.** *v.tr.* (a) to hook (floating object, etc.); (b) *Fish:* to gaff (salmon, etc.). **2.** *v.i. F:* (a) *Row:* to catch a crab; (b) to make a faux pas; to put one's foot in it; to drop a clanger; to drop a brick. **3.** *v.i. P:* to look (at), to observe; gaffe un peu! have a butcher's! have a dekko!

gaffeur, -euse [gafœːr, -øːz], *s. F:* blunderer; blundering fool; c'est un g., he's always putting his foot in it.

gag [gag], *s.m. Th: Cin: F:* gag.

gaga [gaga], *F:* **1.** *s.m.* dodderer, driveller. **2.** *a.inv.* gaga, doddering, senile.

gage [gaːʒ], *s.m.* **1.** *Com: Jur:* (a) pledged chattels; pawned article; pledge, pawn, security; contrat de g., bailment; laisser qch. pour g., to leave sth. as security, on deposit; mettre qch. en g., to pawn, pledge, sth.; mise en g., pawning, pledging; prêteur sur gages, pawnbroker; ma montre est en g., my watch is in pawn; lettre de g., (i) mortgage bond; (ii) debenture bond; (b) (of pers.) surety; rester en g., to remain as surety. **2.** (a) token, sign; g. d'amour, love token; cette victoire, g. de beaucoup d'autres, this victory, that gave promise of many others; (b) *A:* jeter devant qn le g. du combat, to throw down the gage (of battle) to s.o. **3.** forfeit; jouer aux gages, to play at forfeits. **4.** *pl.* wages, pay; être aux gages de qn, to be employed by s.o.; tueur à gages, hired assassin; *Cin: etc:* auteur à gages fixes, staff writer; *A:* casser qn aux gages, to discharge s.o.

G:1

gagé [gaʒe], *a.* **1.** *Jur:* secured (loan); **meubles gagés,** furniture under distraint; **recettes non gagées,** unassigned, unpledged, revenue. **2.** *A:* **commis g.,** salaried clerk; **homme g.,** hired man.

gagéa [gaʒea], **gagée** [gaʒe], *s.f. Bot:* star of Bethlehem.

gager [gaʒe], *v.tr.* **(je gageai(s); n. gageons) 1.** *(a) A:* to wager, bet; *(b) F:* **je gagerais que . . .,** I'd bet that . . .; **j'en gagerais ma tête à couper,** I'd bet anything you like, I'd bet my bottom dollar. **2.** *A:* *(a)* to pay wages to (s.o.); *(b)* to hire (servant). **3.** to guarantee, secure (loan, etc.).

gagerie [gaʒri], *s.f. Jur:* security of a pledge (*used esp. in* SAISIE-GAGERIE).

gageur, -euse [gaʒœ:r, -ø:z]. **1.** *s. A:* wagerer. **2.** *a. Ins:* **police gageuse,** wager policy.

gageure [gaʒy:r], *s.f.* *(a)* wager; long shot; *(b)* **payer une g.,** to pay a wager; *(c)* **c'est une g., cela ressemble à une g.,** it's impossible; you can hardly believe it; the odds are dead against it.

gagiste [gaʒist], *s.m.* **1.** *(a) Th:* supernumerary actor; *F:* super; *(b) A.Mil:* musician not on the strength; *(c) Pej:* wage-earner. **2.** *Jur:* *(a)* pledger, pawner; *(b)* **(créancier) gagiste,** pledgee, pledge holder, tied creditor.

gagnable [gaɲabl], *a.* (*rare*) **1.** obtainable, procurable. **2.** reclaimable (land).

gagnage [gaɲa:ʒ], *s.m. A: or Dial:* *(a) Husb:* pasturage; *(b) Ven:* browsing land, browsing ground.

gagnant, -ante [gaɲɑ̃, -ɑ̃:t]. **1.** *a.* winning (ticket, etc.); **partir g.,** (i) to start favourite; (ii) to be a sure winner; **jouer g.,** to bet on a certainty. **2.** *s.* winner.

gagne-denier [gaɲ(ə)dənje], *s.m. A:* **1.** (day-) labourer; casual worker. **2.** cadger; *pl. gagne-deniers.*

gagnepain [gaɲ(ə)pɛ̃], *s.m. A.Arm:* gauntlet.

gagne-pain [gaɲ(ə)pɛ̃], *s.m.inv.* **1.** (means of) living; livelihood; **la truelle d'un maçon est son g.-p.,** a mason makes his living by his trowel. **2.** breadwinner; support (of the family).

gagne-petit [gaɲ(ə)pəti], *s.m.inv.* **1.** person earning a pittance; *a.* **esprit g.-p.,** small-shopkeeper attitude of mind. **2.** *A:* (itinerant) knife grinder. **3.** *A:* cheapjack.

gagne-place [gaɲ(ə)plas], *s.m. F:* space-saver; *pl. gagne-places.*

gagner [gaɲe], *v.tr.* **1.** *(a)* to earn; **g. de l'argent,** to earn money; **g. mille francs par mois,** to earn a thousand francs a month; **g. gros,** (i) to make big money; (ii) to make large profits; **g. sa vie, g. de quoi vivre,** to earn one's living; **il a bien gagné son avancement,** he has earned his promotion; **ce que je gagne suffit à nos besoins,** I earn enough to keep us; **il gagne bien sa vie,** he earns a good salary, makes a good living, good money; **il l'a bien gagné,** (i) he's earned it; (ii) *F:* it serves him right; *(b)* to gain; to be the gainer (à, by); **g. du temps,** (i) to save time; (ii) to gain time; **chercher à g. du temps,** to play for time; **il a gagné deux kilos,** he's gained, put on, two kilos; **c'est autant de gagné, c'est toujours ça de gagné,** (i) that's so much gained, so much to the good; (ii) at least that's settled; **g. au change,** to benefit by the exchange; **j'ai gagné à la hausse générale des prix,** I have benefited by the general rise in prices; **g. à faire qch.,** to profit by doing sth.; **j'y gagnerai,** I shall gain by it; **g. à être connu,** to improve on acquaintance; **nous ne gagnerons rien à attendre,** there is nothing to be gained by waiting; **votre réputation y gagnera,** it will add to your credit; **et moi, qu'est-ce que j'y gagne?** and what do I get out of it? and where do I come in? **2.** *(a)* to win, gain (a victory); *Mil:* to take (a town); *(b)* **g. la partie, la course,** to win the game, the race; **g. mille francs à qn,** to win a thousand francs from s.o.; **g. un lot à une loterie,** to win a prize in a lottery; **donner gagné à qn,** to throw up the cards, to admit, acknowledge, defeat; **g. dans un fauteuil,** to (have a) walk over; **g. haut la main,** to win in a canter; to win hands down; *(c)* **g. qn à une cause,** to win over s.o. to a cause; **g. qn à une idée,** to sell s.o. an idea; **g. la confiance de qn,** to win, gain, s.o.'s confidence; **sa générosité lui a gagné beaucoup d'amis,** his generosity won him many friends; **g. les témoins,** to bribe the witnesses; **g. sur qn qu'il fasse qch.,** to prevail on s.o. to do sth.; *Equit:* **g. la volonté d'un cheval,** to break a horse; *(d)* to get, catch (a disease, etc.); **maladie qui se gagne,** infectious disease; **j'y ai gagné un gros rhume,** all I got out of it was a heavy cold. **3.** *A:* **g. qn,** to best s.o. (at a game). **4.** to reach, arrive at; **g. le haut,** to reach the top; **g. son domicile,** to reach home; **g. le village à la nuit,** to get to the village at nightfall; **g. les montagnes,** to escape to the mountains; **g. sa propre chambre,** to retire to one's own room; *Nau:* **g. un port,** to fetch into a port; **g. le port,** to fetch into port; *s.a.* LARGE 2; *A:* **g. au pied,** to run away, to take to one's heels. **5.** *(a)* to gain on, overtake; **se laisser g.,** to let oneself be caught up; **g. un navire,** to gain on, overhaul, a ship; **g. le devant,** to forge ahead, to take the lead; **la nuit nous gagna,** darkness overtook us; **le feu, l'épidémie, gagne,** the fire, the epidemic, is spreading; **g. du terrain,** (i) to gain ground; (ii) to reclaim land (from the sea, etc.); **la mer gagne du terrain,** the sea is encroaching on the land; **g. une marche sur qn,** to steal a march on s.o.; *Nau:* **g. à la bordée,** to gain ground on the tack; **le mécontentement gagne de force,** the discontent is mounting; **ce rire contagieux gagna tous les convives,** this laughter infected all the guests; **nous fûmes gagnés par cette vague d'enthousiasme,** we were caught up in this wave of enthusiasm; **un vertige le gagna,** a fit of giddiness came over him; **la faim nous gagnait,** we were getting hungry; **gagné par le sommeil, par les larmes,** overcome by sleep, with tears; *Nau:* (i) **g. (dans) le vent, g. au vent,** to gain the wind, to draw ahead against the wind, to fetch to windward; (*of ship*) to claw her way to windward; (ii) **g. le vent, le dessus du vent, sur . . .,** to get the weather-gauge of . . .; **g. le vent d'une pointe,** to weather a headland; **g. de l'avant,** to forge ahead; *(b) Med:* to spread; **l'enflure a gagné la gorge,** the swelling has spread to the throat. **6.** (*of horse*) **g. à la main,** to pull. **7.** *Ven:* (*of deer*) to browse.

gagneur, -euse [gaɲœ:r, -ø:z], *s.* **1.** gainer, earner (of money). **2.** winner. **3.** *s.f. P:* **gagneuse,** well-paid prostitute.

gahnite [ganit], *s.f. Miner:* gahnite.

gai [ge], *a.* **1.** gay; *(a)* merry, lively (person, song); (person) in good spirits; cheery (voice); **g. comme un pinson,** bright as a lark; happy as a sandboy; **avoir l'esprit g.,** to be of a cheerful disposition; **cheval g.,** lively horse; **g. et dispos,** in high spirits; *F:* alive and kicking; **g. compagnon,** boon companion; *F:* **être un peu g.,** to be tipsy, to be tight, to be merry; **avoir le vin g.,** to be merry in one's cups; *Iron:* **ça va être g.!** that *will* be nice! *(b)* bright, cheerful (room, colour, etc.); **vert g.,** light green; *(c)* amusing (talk, stories). **2.** (*of bolt, key, etc.*) free, easy, having play; loose; **tenon trop g. dans sa mortaise,** tenon that has too much play in its mortise; *Fish:* **hareng g.,** shotten herring; *Her:* **cheval g.,** horse without saddle or bridle.

gaïac [gajak], *s.m. Bot:* guaiacum; **résine de g.,** (gum) guaiacum; **(bois de) g.,** lignum vitae.

gaïacol [gajakɔl], *s.m. Ch:* guaiacol.

gaiement [gemɑ̃], *adv.* gaily, cheerfully; merrily, brightly.

gaieté [gete], *s.f.* (*the spelling* **gaîté** *is no longer used*) **1.** gaiety, mirth, cheerfulness, blitheness; **vous n'êtes pas d'une g. folle!** you're not over-cheerful! **être d'une g. folle, déborder de g.,** to be bubbling over with high spirits; **reprendre sa g.,** to recover one's spirits, to perk up; *F:* to buck up; **de g. de cœur,** of one's own free will; *F:* **être en g.,** to be tipsy, merry. **2.** *pl. A:* *(a)* escapades; *F:* larks; *(b)* jollities, frolics; *(c)* **dire des gaietés,** to be somewhat free in one's conversations, to tell club stories, to crack broad jokes.

Gaïkovar [gaikɔva:r], *s.m.* Gaekwar (of Baroda).

gail [ga:j], *s.m. P:* horse, nag.

gaillard, -arde[1] [gaja:r, -ard]. **1.** *a.* *(a)* strong, well, vigorous; **frais et g.,** hale and hearty; **il se sentait g.,** he felt in good form; *F:* full of beans; **il était tout à fait g. quand je l'ai vu,** he was alive and kicking when I saw him; *(b) O:* merry, lively, cheery; *(c)* spicy, risqué (story, remark); *(d)* fresh (wind), cool (weather). **2.** *s.* *(a) s.m.* (i) hearty, vigorous, type; **un grand et solide g.,** a great strapping young man; (ii) *F:* shy customer; *A:* **un vert g.,** a rip; *(b) s.f.* (i) **une grande gaillarde,** a strapping young woman; (ii) *F:* **c'est une gaillarde,** she's a bit of a tart. **3.** *(a) a. A:* **château g.,** fortress; *(b) s.m. Nau:* (*in sailing vessel*) **g. d'avant,** forecastle; **g. d'arrière,** poop; **pont de g.,** forecastle deck; **haut de g.,** deep-waisted. **4.** *s.f.* **gaillarde;** *(a) Danc:* galliard; *(b) Typ:* eight-point type; brevier.

gaillarde[2], *s.f. Bot:* gaillardia.

gaillardement [gajardəmɑ̃], *adv.* **1.** gaily, good-humouredly. **2.** boldly, bravely, gallantly.

gaillardie [gajardi], *s.f. Bot:* gaillardia.

gaillardise [gajardi:z], *s.f.* **1.** *O:* gaiety; jollity. **2. conter des gaillardises,** to tell risqué stories, naughty stories; to crack broad jokes.

gaille [ga:j], *s.m. P:* horse, nag.

gaillet [gajɛ], *s.m. Bot:* cheese rennet, yellow bedstraw; **g. accrochant,** turkey grass, goose grass, cleavers, catchweed.

gailleterie [gaj(ɛ)tri], *s.f.* small coal, beans and nuts; cobbles.

gailleteux, -euse [gajtø, -ø:z], *a. Coal Min:* (seam) yielding a high percentage of small coal.

gailletin [gajtɛ̃], *s.m.* nuts (of coal).

gaillette [gajɛt], *s.f.* cobbles (of coal).

gain [gɛ̃], *s.m.* **1.** winning (of contest, war, etc.); *Jur:* **avoir g. de cause,** to win one's case; **donner g. de cause à qn,** to decide in favour of s.o.; **il y a chances égales de g. et de perte,** it's an even chance, there's a fifty-fifty chance. **2.** *(a)* gain, profit; **avoir l'amour du g.,** to be obsessed with making profits, money; *(b)* earnings; *Jur:* **g. de la femme mariée,** wife's earned income; **g. fortuit,** capital gain; **g. de survie,** income, capital, etc., due to survivor; *(c)* winnings; **les gains de la soirée,** the evening's winnings; **être en g.,** to be in pocket; *(d)* **un g. de temps,** a saving of time; **g. retiré d'une lecture,** profit acquired from reading. **3.** *El: Elcs: etc:* gain; **g. en courant,** current gain; **g. en tension,** voltage magnification; *Elcs:* **g. d'étage,** stage gain; **à g. élevé,** high-gain; *Atom.Ph:* **g. de régénération,** breeding gain.

gainage [gɛna:ʒ], *s.m.* *(a) Mec.E: Civ.E: etc:* casing, sheathing, sleeving; *(b) Atom.Ph:* canning, casing, cladding (of fuel, etc.).

gaine [gɛn], *s.f.* **1.** *(a)* cover, case; casing, wrapping, *U.S:* jacket; **g. d'une momie,** mummy case; **g. en cuir,** leather case; **g. à matériel (pour parachutages),** container; **g. métallique,** metallic sheath, sleeve; **câble sous g.,** sheathed cable; **g. souple,** flexible sheath; **g. tubulaire,** quill; *Av:* **g. de protection des commandes,** control casing; *Atom.Ph:* **g. de combustible,** fuel can(ning), clad(ding), sheath; **g. d'électrons, d'ions,** electron, ion, sheath; *El.E:* **g. de faisceau de câble,** conduit; *Aut:* **gaines de ressorts,** spring gaiters; *(b) Anat:* sheath (of muscle, tendon artery); *(c) Bot:* sheath; ocrea (round stem); *(d) Cost:* foundation (garment); corset; roll-on; girdle; *A:* **g. de hanches,** suspender belt; *(f) Geol:* gangue, matrix. **2.** *Arch:* terminal. **3.** *Artil:* priming tube (of melinite shell). **4.** *Const: Min: etc:* (ventilation) shaft, passage, duct; **(réseau de) g. isolante,** insulating sleeve; **g. de chauffe,** heating flue, hot-air pipe. **5.** hem (of flag); tabling; edging (of sail).

gaine-combinaison [gɛnkɔ̃binɛzɔ̃], *s.f. Cost:* corselet; *pl. gaines-combinaisons.*

gaine-culotte [gɛnkylɔt], *s.f. Cost:* pantie girdle; *pl. gaines-culottes.*

gainer [gene], *v.tr.* **1.** to sheath; **articles gainés cuir,** articles covered, cased, in leather. **2.** *Nau:* to hem, table (a sail); to edge (a flag).

gainerie [gɛnri], *s.f.* **1.** sheath making, scabbard making, case making; casing trade, shop. **2.** *Aut:* interior fittings.

gainier, -ière [genje, -jɛ:r]. **1.** *s.* sheath maker, scabbard maker, case maker. **2.** *s.m. Bot: F:* Judas tree.

gaîté [gete], *s.f. O: see* GAIETÉ.

gaize [gɛ:z], *s.f. Miner:* gaize.

gal [gal], *s.m. Ph:* gal.

gala [gala], *s.m.* gala, fête; **en habit, toilette, de g.,** (i) in gala dress, in full dress; (ii) in one's Sunday best; **dîner en grand g.,** to dine in state; to dine with great ceremony.

Galaad[1] [galaad], *Pr.n.m. B.Geog:* Gilead.

Galaad[2], *Pr.n.m. Lit:* Galahad.

galactagogue [galaktagɔg], *a. & s.m. Biol:* galactagogue, galactogogue.

galactane [galaktan], *s.f. Biol:* galactan.

galactique [galaktik], *a.* galactic.

galactite [galaktit], *s.f. Miner:* galactite.

galactites [galaktit], *s.f.pl. Bot:* Galactia.

galactocèle [galaktɔsɛl], *s.m. Obst:* galactocele.

galactogène [galaktɔʒɛn], **galactogogue** [galaktɔgɔg], *a. & s.m. Biol:* galactagogue, galactogogue; milk-producing (gland, etc.).

galactomètre [galaktɔmɛtr], *s.m.* lactometer.

galactonique [galaktɔnik], *a.* galactonic (acid).

galactophage [galaktɔfa:ʒ], *a. Biol:* galactophagous.

galactophore [galaktɔfɔ:r]. **1.** *a.* galactophorous; **vaisseau g.,** galactophore, milk duct. **2.** *s.m.* galactophorus, artificial nipple.

galactophorite [galaktɔfɔrit], *s.f. Med:* galactophoritis.

galactopoïèse [galaktɔpɔjɛ:z], *s.f. Biol:* galactopoiesis, galactopoieses.

galactopoïétique [galaktɔpɔjetik], *a. Biol:* galactopoietic.

galactorrhée [galaktɔre], *s.f. Med:* galactorrh(o)ea.
galactose [galaktoːz], *s.f. Ch:* galactose.
galactosémie [galaktɔzemi], *s.f. Med:* galactosemia.
galactosurie [galaktɔzyri], *s.f. Med:* galactosuria.
galactozyme [galaktɔzim], *s.m. Bio-Ch:* galactozyme.
galago [galago], *s.m. Z:* galago; bush-baby.
Galalithe [galalit], *s.f. R.t.m:* Galalith.
galamment [galamɑ̃], *adv.* gallantly, like a gentleman; (*a*) politely, courteously; (*b*) *A:* **habillé g.,** elegantly dressed; (*c*) bravely, honourably; **se tirer g. d'une affaire,** to come out of an affair with honour.
galand [galɑ̃], *s.m. A:* **g. de feuillée,** brigand, gentleman, brother, of the (green) woods.
galandage [galɑ̃daːʒ], *s.m.* (*a*) *Const:* brick partition; (*b*) half-timbered construction (with brickwork in between the beams).
galanga [galɑ̃ga], *s.m.* **1.** *Bot:* galingale. **2.** *Pharm:* galanga(l).
galant[1] [galɑ̃]. **1.** *a.* (*a*) *A:* gay, elegant; **costume g.,** stylish costume; **votre costume est du dernier g.,** your dress is the last thing in elegance; (*b*) attentive to women, gallant [ga'lant]; **homme g.,** ladies' man; **vers galants,** love poems; (*c*) **femme galante,** (i) woman of loose morals; (ii) kept prostitute, woman; *A:* **fête galante,** gay party or entertainment (*esp.* of wantons); **intrigue galante,** love affair; (*d*) *O:* **g. homme,** man of honour, gentleman; **traiter qn en g. homme, agir en g. homme à l'égard de qn, avec qn,** to treat s.o. in a gentlemanly fashion; **façon d'agir de g. homme,** handsome treatment; **se conduire en g. homme,** to behave like a gentleman; **s'il est tant soit peu g. homme, il fera des excuses,** if he is anything of a gentleman he will apologize; *Mus:* **style g.,** rococco style. **2.** *s.m.* lover, gallant, ladies' man; philanderer; **faire le g. auprès d'une dame,** to court, pay court to, a lady; to flirt with a lady; *A:* **vert g.,** (i) gentleman of the (green) woods; (ii) lusty young (or elderly) man; gay spark; gallant.
Galant[2], *Pr.n.m. Mediaeval Lit:* Wayland.
galanterie [galɑ̃tri], *s.f.* **1.** politeness (*esp.* to ladies); **montrer de la g. auprès des femmes,** to be attentive to women. **2.** *usu. pl.* (*a*) love affair, intrigue; (*b*) pretty speech; **dire des galanteries à une dame,** to pay compliments to a lady.
galantin [galɑ̃tɛ̃], *s.m. Pej: O:* (over-assiduous) ladies' man; **vieux g.,** amorous old dodderer.
galantine [galɑ̃tin], *s.f. Cu:* galantine.
galantiser [galɑ̃tize], *v.tr. & i. A:* to pay compliments; to say sweet nothings (to) (a lady).
galapiat [galapja], *s.m. F:* good-for-nothing; loafer; rough, tough; **un petit g.,** a little wretch; a young tough.
galate [galat], *a. & s. B.Hist:* Galatian.
Galatée [galate], *Pr.n.f. Myth:* Galatea.
galathée [galate], *s.f. Crust:* galathea, squat lobster.
Galatie [galasi], *Pr.n.f. A.Geog:* Galatia.
galaxie [galaksi], *s.f. Astr:* galaxy; the Milky Way; **g. bleue,** blue stellar objects.
galaxiidés [galaksiide], *s.m.pl. Ich:* Galaxiidae.
galaxite [galaksit], *s.f. Miner:* galaxite.
galazyme [galazim], *s.m. Bio-Ch:* galactozyme.
galbanum [galbanɔm], *s.m.* **1.** *A.Pharm:* galbanum. **2.** *F: A:* **du g.,** false pretences.
galbe [galb], *s.m.* **1.** *Arch:* entasis (of column). **2.** curve (of furniture, baluster, etc.); curved lines, curves, contour (of the human figure); sweep, outline, lines (of car); **avoir du g.,** to be shapely, well-proportioned; to have a good figure.
galbé [galbe], *a.* (*a*) *Arch:* (*of column*) with entasis; (*b*) shapely; well-proportioned; (*c*) *Aut: etc:* **glace de sécurité galbée,** curved safety glass.
galber [galbe], *v.tr.* (*a*) to construct (column) with entasis; (*b*) to give curves to (vase, chest of drawers, etc.); (*c*) *Tchn:* to curve, bend (lightly) (sheet metal).
galbeux, -euse [galbø, -øːz], *a. A:* **1.** curved, rounded. **2.** *P:* stylish, smart.
galbeur [galbœːr], *s.m.* metal worker (who bends sheet metal).
galbord [galbɔːr], *s.m. Nau:* garboard (strake).
galbule [galbyl], *s.m. Bot:* galbulus (of cypress).
galbulidés [galbylide], *s.m.pl. Orn:* Galbulidae.
gale [gal], *s.f.* **1.** (*a*) *Med:* scabies; **g. bédouine,** prickly heat; **g. du ciment,** bricklayer's itch; **arbre à la g.,** poison ivy, poison oak; (*b*) *F:* scold, shrew (of a woman). **2.** *Vet:* scab, mange. **3.** *Bot:* scurf, scale. **4.** defect (in cloth); defect, worm hole (in timber).
galé [gale], *s.m. Bot:* sweet gale, bog myrtle, Dutch myrtle.
galéasse [galeas], *s.f. Nau: A:* large Venetian galley; galleass.
galée [gale], *s.f.* **1.** *Nau: A:* galley. **2.** *Typ:* composing galley; **g. à coulisse,** slice galley.
galéga [galega], *s.m. Bot:* goat's rue.
galéiforme [galeifɔrm], *a. Bot:* galeiform, galeate.
galéjade [galeʒad], *s.f.* (*originally S. of Fr. Dial:*) tall story; **débiter, dire, des galéjades à qn,** to pull s.o.'s leg.
galéjer [galeʒe], *v.i.* to tell tall stories.
galène [galɛn], *s.f.* **1.** *Miner:* galena, sulphide of lead, lead glance; **g. de fer,** wolfram. **2.** *W.Tel: A:* (galena) crystal; **poste à g.,** crystal set.
galénique [galenik], *a.* (*a*) *Hist. of Med:* Galenic; (*b*) *Pharm:* **médicament g.,** galenical (preparation).
galénisme [galenism], *s.m. Hist. of Med:* Galenism.
galéniste [galenist], *s.m. Hist. of Med:* Galenist.
galénobismuthite [galenɔbizmytit], *s.f. Miner:* galenobismutite.
galéocerdo [galeɔsɛrdo], *s.m. Ich:* galeocerdo.
galeopithecus [galeɔpitekyːs], **galéopithèque** [galeɔpitɛk], *s.m. Z:* galeopithecus, flying lemur.
galéopsis [galeɔpsis], *s.m. Bot:* hemp nettle, stinking nettle.
galère [galɛːr], *s.f.* **1.** (*a*) galley, slave ship; **vogue la g.!** let the worst happen! **mais que diable allait-il faire dans cette g.?** but what the hell was he doing there? whatever took him there? (spoken by Géronte in Molière's *Les Fourberies de Scapin*); *Nau:* **avirons en g.!** rest on your oars! (*b*) *A:* convict ship; *pl.* hulks; **condamné aux galères,** sentenced to penal servitude; **la maison est une vraie g.,** this place is a hell upon earth. **2.** (mason's) barrow, trolley. **3.** crucible furnace. **4.** *Mil: etc:* tow rope, drag rope. **5.** *Moll:* Portuguese man-of-war. **6.** *Tls:* long plane; *Hort:* small hoe.
galerie [galri], *s.f.* **1.** (*a*) gallery; long room; **g. de portraits,** portrait gallery; **les galeries du Louvre,** the galleries of the Louvre; (*b*) *A:* gallery (round tennis court); **faire g.,** to sit out; to be a looker-on; (*c*) arcade, covered walk; (*d*) **g. marchande,** shopping centre; (*e*) *Fr.C:* porch. **2.** balcony, gallery; *Th:* **première g.,** dress circle; **seconde g.,** upper circle; **troisième g.,** gallery; *F:* the gods; **jouer pour la g.,** to play to the gallery; *Nau:* **g. de poupe,** stern gallery, stern-walk; **fausse g.,** badge. **3.** (*a*) *Min:* gallery, drift, level, road, drivage; **g. d'avancement,** heading; **g. en direction,** drift(way); **g. de traînage,** drawing road; **g. principale,** mother gate; **g. simple,** single entry; **g. à siphon,** blind level; **g. à flanc de coteau,** adit; **les galeries,** the levels; **g. transversale,** cross heading; **g. d'aérage,** ventilating course; *Mil:* **g. d'écoute,** listening gallery; *El.E:* **g. des câbles,** cable tunnel; (*b*) run (of mole); **g. de termites,** termite gallery. **4.** (*a*) cornice, moulding, beading (on furniture); (*b*) fret (of hearth fire); fender, curb; (*c*) *Aut:* roof rack; (*d*) shelf rail.
galérien [galerjɛ̃], *s.m.* (*a*) rower on a galley, galley slave; **travailler comme un g.,** to work like a galley slave; (*b*) convict; *F:* **mener une vie de g.,** to lead a dog's life.
galerne [galɛrn], *s.f. Nau:* **vent de g.,** wind from the west-north-west.
galérucinés [galerysine], *s.m.pl. Ent:* Galerucidae.
galet [galɛ], *s.m.* **1.** (*a*) pebble; **galets de chaussée,** cobblestones; *A:* **jeu de galets,** shovelboard, shuffleboard; *Anthr:* **civilisation du g. aménagé,** pebble culture; (*b*) *pl.* shingle; **plage de galets,** shingly beach; shingle beach. **2.** *Mec.E:* roller, runner, pulley, (rail)wheel; (*a*) **g. à boudin, à joue,** flanged roller, (rail)wheel; **g. à une joue, à un seul boudin,** single-flanged roller, (rail) wheel; **g. à double boudin, à deux joues,** double-flanged roller, (rail)wheel; **g. à boudin central,** centre-flange roller, (rail)wheel; **couronne de galets,** roller ring; **goujon de g.,** roller pin; (*b*) **g. de roulement,** travelling, running wheel; rail wheel; runner; **g. d'entraînement,** striking roller, pulling sprocket; **g. de guidage, g. guide,** guide roller, idle(r) roller, idle(r) pulley, idle(r) wheel; jockey pulley, jockey roller; **g. de guidage de câble,** cable pulley; **g. de guidage de courroie,** belt guide, belt idler; **g. de pression, g. presseur,** pressure roller, idle(r) roller; **g. de tension, g. tendeur,** tensioning pulley, idle(r) roller, idler sprocket; **g. de poussoir,** tappet roller; **g. de came,** cam follower; *Cin:* **galets presseurs, galets guide-film,** idle rollers; *Mil:* **g.-support de chenille,** track-supporting roller (of tank). **3.** *Fish:* float (of net).
galetas [galtɑ], *s.m.* (*a*) garret, attic; (*b*) hovel.
galettard [galɛtaːr], *a. P:* rich, rolling (in it).
galeton [galtɔ̃], *s.m. Dial:* buckwheat pancake.
galetouse [galtuːz], *s.f. P:* bowl; mess tin, dixie.
galette [galɛt], *s.f.* **1.** (*a*) *Cu:* buckwheat pancake; kind of biscuit; girdle cake; **g. des Rois,** Twelfth-night cake; **g. aux pommes,** apple tart; *F:* **plat comme une g.,** flat as a pancake; (*b*) *Nau:* ship's biscuit; *Mil:* biscuit. **2.** (*a*) hard, thin, mattress; *Mil: P:* biscuit; (*b*) *Pyr:* press-cake; slab (of explosive); (*c*) *Artil:* pad (of obturator); (*d*) *Metalw: F:* blank; **g. de roue,** wheel blank; *W.Tel:* **self en g.,** slab coil, slab inductance, pancake coil. **3.** *P:* money, brass. **4.** *P:* (*of pers.*) nonentity; idiot; clumsy, ham-handed, type.
galetteux, -euse [galɛtø, -øːz], *a. P:* rich, rolling (in it).
galettière [galɛtjɛːr], *s.f. Dial:* frying pan (for cooking pancakes).
galeux, -euse [galø, -øːz], *a.* (*child, etc.*) with the itch; mangy (dog); scurfy (tree); **plaie galeuse,** sore caused by the itch; **brebis galeuse,** (i) scabby sheep; (ii) black sheep (of the family, etc.); **société galeuse,** rotten society; *Tchn:* **verre g.,** spotty glass.
galfâtre [galfɑːtr], *s.m.* (*rare*) good-for-nothing.
galgal, *pl.* **-als** [galgal], *s.m. Archeol:* cairn, barrow.
galgale [galgal], *s.f. Nau:* India stuff.
galhauban [galobɑ̃], *s.m. Nau:* back stay.
galibot [galibo], *s.m. Min:* (*N. France*) pit boy.
Galice [galis], *Pr.n.f. Geog:* Galicia (Spain).
Galicie [galisi], *Pr.n.f. Geog:* Galicia (in Poland).
galicien, -ienne [galisjɛ̃, -jɛn], *a. & s. Geog:* Galician (of Spain or Poland).
galidia [galidja], **galidie** [galidi], *s.f. Z:* galidia.
galidiinés [galidiine], *s.m.pl. Z:* the Malagasy mongooses.
Galien [galjɛ̃], *Pr.n.m.* Galen.
Galilée[1] [galile], *Pr.n.f. B.Geog:* Galilee.
Galilée[2], *Pr.n.m. Hist:* Galileo.
galiléen, -éenne [galileɛ̃, -ɛn], *a. & s. B.Hist:* Galilean.
galimafrée [galimafre], *s.f. Cu:* (*a*) hash; (*b*) *A:* badly-prepared food.
galimatias [galimatjɑ]. **1.** *a. A:* obscure, unintelligible. **2.** *s.m.* gibberish.
galine [galin], *s.f. Sp:* (*Ice hockey*) puck.
galion [galjɔ̃], *s.m. Nau:* galleon; *A:* **quand mes galions seront arrivés,** when my ship comes home.
galiote [galjɔt], *s.f. Nau:* **1.** *A:* gal(l)iot. **2.** (covered-in) canal barge. **3.** bar securing the hatchway cover; thwart carling.
galipette [galipɛt], *s.f. F:* somersault; **faire la g.,** to turn a somersault; **faire des galipettes,** to be up to one's tricks.
galipot [galipo], *s.m.* **1.** *Com:* galipot, white resin. **2.** *Nau:* blacking. **3.** *Fr.C:* **courir le g.,** to go on a spree; to gad about.
galipoter [galipɔte], *v.tr. Nau:* to black down.
gallamine [galamin], *s.f. Med:* gallamine (triethiodide).
gallate [gal(l)at], *Ch:* gallate.
galle [gal], *s.f. Bot:* gall(nut); **g. de chêne,** oak apple; **noix de g.,** nut gall; **g. en grain de groseille (des feuilles du chêne),** oak spangle.
galléine [galein], *s.f. Ch:* gallein.
gallérie [galeri], *s.f. Ent:* bee moth.
Galles [gal], *Pr.n.f. Geog:* **le pays de G.,** Wales; **la G. du Nord,** North Wales; **Prince de G.,** (i) Prince of Wales; (ii) *Tex:* Prince of Wales check.
galliambe [gal(l)iɑ̃ːb], *a. Pros:* galliambic.
gallec [gal(l)ɛk], *s.m.* **1.** French-speaking Breton (of *haute Bretagne*). **2.** (French) dialect of the *haute Bretagne.*
gallican, -ane [gal(l)ikɑ̃, -an], *a. & s. Ecc:* Gallican.
gallicaniser [gal(l)ikanize], *v.tr.* to convert to Gallicanism.
gallicanisme [gal(l)ikanism], *s.m. Ecc:* Gallicanism.
gallicaniste [gal(l)ikanist], *s.m. Ecc:* Gallicanist.
gallicisme [gal(l)isism], *s.m.* French turn or phrase, idiom of the French language; gallicism.
gallicole [gal(l)ikɔl], *Ent:* **1.** *a.* gallicolous. **2.** *s.m.* gallicola.
gallidés [gal(l)ide], **galliformes** [galifɔrm], *s.m.pl. Orn:* Galliformes.
gallinacé [gal(l)inase], *Orn:* **1.** *a.* gallinaceous, gallinacean. **2.** *s.m.pl.* **gallinacés,** Gallinaceae, Gallinaceans.
galline [gal(l)in], *a.f.* (*rare*) *Orn:* **l'espèce g.,** the galline species.
gallinette [gal(l)inɛt], *s.f. Fung:* clavaria.
Gallion [galjɔ̃], *Pr.n.m. B.Hist:* Gallio.
gallioniste [galjɔnist], *s.m.* indifferentist.
galliote [galjɔt], *s.f. Bot:* herb bennet.

gallique[1] [gal(l)ik], *a. Hist:* Gallic, of Gaul.

gallique[2], *a. Ch:* gallic (acid).

gallium [galjɔm], *s.m. Ch:* gallium.

gallo- [gal(l)ɔ], *pref.* Gallo-; **Gallo-belge,** Gallo-Belgian.

gallo [gal(l)o]. **1.** *s.m.* (*a*) (*f.* **gallèse,** *occ.* **gallote**) (French-speaking) Breton of *haute Bretagne*; (*b*) *Ling:* (French) dialect spoken in *haute Bretagne*. **2.** *a.* **pays g.,** area in which the *gallo* dialect is spoken.

gallois, -oise [galwa, -wa:z]. **1.** *a.* Welsh; **charbon g.,** Welsh coal. **2.** *s.* Welshman, Welshwoman; **les G.,** the Welsh. **3.** *Ling:* **le g.,** Welsh.

gallomane [gal(l)ɔman], *a. & s.* gallomaniac.

gallomanie [gal(l)ɔmani], *s.f.* gallomania.

gallon [gal(l)ɔ̃], *s.m. Meas:* gallon.

gallophile [gal(l)ɔfil], *a.* gallophile.

gallophilisme [gal(l)ɔfilism], *s.m.* gallophilism.

gallophobe [gal(l)ɔfɔb], *a. & s.* (*rare*) gallophobe; anti-French.

gallophobie [gal(l)ɔfɔbi], *s.f.* (*rare*) gallophobia.

gallo-romain [gal(l)ɔrɔmɛ̃], *a.* Gallo-Roman; *pl. gallo-romain(e)s.*

gallup [galœp], *s.m.* Gallup poll.

galochard [galɔʃa:r], *a. F:* **menton g.,** nutcracker chin.

galoche [galɔʃ], *s.f.* **1.** (*a*) clog (with leather upper); *F:* **menton en g.,** nutcracker chin; *P:* **vieille g.,** old fogey; (*b*) overshoe, galosh, *U.S:* rubber. **2.** *Nau:* (*a*) snatch block; (*b*) chock, fairlead. **3.** *P:* French kiss.

galocher [galɔʃe], *v.i.* to clop around.

galocherie [galɔʃri], *s.f.* factory making *galoches.*

galochier [galɔʃje], *s.m.* maker of *galoches.*

galon [galɔ̃], *s.m.* **1.** braid, galloon; **g. de finition,** upholstery binding. **2.** *pl. Mil:* (N.C.O.'s) stripes; (officer's) bands, gold braid; *Navy:* (officer's) stripes; (*in Merchant Service*) bands; **priver qn de ses galons,** to reduce s.o. to the ranks; **rendre ses galons,** to resign one's rank; *F:* **prendre du g.,** (i) to be promoted; (ii) to move up in the world; *F:* **arroser ses galons,** to celebrate one's promotion. **3.** *Nau:* band (over seam of sail).

galonnard [galɔna:r], *s.m. Mil: P:* officer.

galonné [galɔne], *s.m. P:* (non-commissioned) officer.

galonner [galɔne], *v.tr.* to trim, ornament, with braid or lace; to braid, lace; **habit galonné d'or,** coat laced, gallooned, with gold; gold-laced coat.

galonnier [galɔnje], *s.m.* (gold, silver) lace maker.

galop [galo], *s.m.* **1.** gallop; **prendre le g.,** to break into a gallop; **au g. (allongé),** at a gallop; **au grand g.,** at a full gallop; **au g. de manège,** at a hand gallop; **au petit g.,** at a canter; **aller au grand g.,** to ride full gallop; **faire aller un cheval au grand g.,** to gallop a horse; **aller au petit g.,** to canter along; **faire un petit g.,** to have a canter; **faire aller un cheval au petit g.,** to canter a horse; **partir au g.,** to gallop away; **faire qch. au g.,** to gallop, rush, through sth.; to scamp sth.; **faire déjeuner qn au g.,** to rush s.o. through lunch; **quelques lignes au grand g.,** a few lines in hot haste. **2.** *Danc:* galop. **3.** *Mch:* **mouvement de g.,** hunting (of locomotive). **4.** *A: P:* scolding, ticking off. **5.** *Med:* **bruit de g.,** gallop rhythm.

galopade [galɔpad], *s.f.* **1.** *Equit:* (*a*) galloping, gallop; canter; **faire une g.,** to have a gallop; **son imagination prend la g.,** his imagination runs away with him; **expédier son repas à la g.,** to bolt one's meal; (*b*) gal(l)opade; (*c*) space galloped over; **il n'y a qu'une g.,** it is only a short distance from here. **2.** *Danc: A:* gal(l)opade.

galopant [galɔpɑ̃], *a.* runaway; **démographie galopante,** runaway increase in population; **phtisie galopante,** galloping consumption.

galope [galɔp], *s.f.* **1.** *Bookb:* (*a*) hatching; (*b*) hatching iron. **2.** *adv.phr.* **traverser la France à la g.,** to tear, dash, rush, through France.

galopée [galɔpe], *s.f.* hurry, rush; **travail fait d'une g.,** rushed work.

galoper [galɔpe]. **1.** *v.i.* (*a*) to gallop; **se mettre à g.,** to break into a gallop; (*b*) to gallop around; to rush around; (*c*) **g. en lisant,** to skim (through a book). **2.** *v.tr.* (*a*) **g. un cheval,** to gallop a horse; (*b*) to pursue, chase (s.o.); **g. les rues, la campagne,** to scour the streets, the countryside (in search of sth.); *A:* **g. une femme,** to be pressing in one's attentions to a woman; (*c*) *F:* to plague (s.o.); **la peur me galope,** I'm haunted by fear. **3.** *v.ind.tr.* **g. après qn, qch.,** to run after s.o., sth.; **je ne galope pas après le vin,** I don't make a rush for wine; I'm not all that keen on wine.

galopeur, -euse [galɔpœ:r, -ø:z]. **1.** *a.* galloping. **2.** *s.* (*horse*) galloper. **3.** *s.f. F:* **galopeuse,** second-hand (of watch, clock).

galopin, -ine [galɔpɛ̃, -in], *s.* **1.** (*a*) errand boy, girl; (*b*) *F:* (i) (street) urchin; (ii) child, brat; (*c*) *s.m.* young scamp. **2.** *s.m. Mec.E:* (*a*) idler, loose pulley; (*b*) jockey wheel. **3.** *s.m. F:* stirrup cup.

galopiner [galɔpine], *v.i.* to run wild in the streets.

galoubet [galubɛ], *s.m.* three-holed (fipple-)flute (of Provence).

galtonia [galtonia], *s.m. Bot:* galtonia, Cape hyacinth.

galtouse [galtu:z], *s.f. P:* money, *F:* dough, lolly.

galuchat [galyʃa], *s.m.* shark skin, shagreen (for case-making).

galuchatisé [galyʃatize], *a. Leath:* shagreened; shagreen-like; greenish.

galure [galy:r], **galurin** [galyrɛ̃], *s.m. P:* hat; *P:* titfer.

galvanique [galvanik], *a.* galvanic (cell, etc.); **plaqué g.,** electro-plate; **dorure g.,** electro-gilding.

galvaniquement [galvanikmɑ̃], *adv.* by galvanizing.

galvanisateur [galvanizatœ:r], *s.m.* = GALVANISEUR.

galvanisation [galvanizasjɔ̃], *s.f.* (*a*) galvanization, galvanizing; (*b*) *El:* galvanism.

galvaniser [galvanize], *v.tr.* **1.** to galvanize (corpse, etc.); to give new life to (undertaking, etc.); to stimulate, galvanize (a crowd, etc.). **2.** *Metall:* to galvanize; (i) to (electro-)plate; (ii) to zinc; **tôle galvanisée,** galvanized (sheet-)iron.

galvaniseur [galvanizœ:r], *s.m. Metalw:* galvanizer.

galvanisme [galvanism], *s.m. Med:* galvanism.

galvano- [galvano]. **1.** *pref.* galvano-; **galvanocaustique,** galvanocaustic; **galvanomagnétique** galvanomagnetic. **2.** *s.m.* **galvano,** *Typ: F:* electrotype plate; *F:* electro.

galvanocautère [galvanɔkotɛ:r], *s.m. Surg:* galvanocautery.

galvanofaradisation [galvanɔfaradizasjɔ̃], *s.f.* galvanofaradization.

galvanomètre [galvanɔmɛtr], *s.m. El:* galvanometer; **g. apériodique,** dead-beat, aperiod galvanometer; **g. à torsion,** torsion galvanometer; **g. à miroir, à réflexion,** mirror, reflexion, galvanometer; **g. balistique,** ballistic galvanometer; **g. thermique, à fil chaud,** hot-wire galvanometer; **g. en dérivation, à résistance shunt,** shunted galvanometer; **g. à cadre,** loop galvanometer; **g. à cadre mobile,** moving coil galvanometer.

galvanométrique [galvanɔmetrik], *a.* galvanometric.

galvanoplaste [galvanɔplast], *s.m.* (*a*) electroplater; (*b*) electrotyper.

galvanoplastie [galvanɔplasti], *s.f.* galvanoplasty; electro-deposition; *Ind:* electroplating; *Typ:* electrotyping.

galvanoplastique [galvanɔplastik], *a.* galvanoplastic.

galvanoponcture [galvanɔpɔ̃kty:r], *s.f.* galvanopuncture.

galvanoscope [galvanɔskɔp], *s.m.* galvanoscope; *Tg:* (linesman's) detector.

galvanotype [galvanɔtip], *s.m. Typ:* electrotype.

galvanotypie [galvanɔtipi], *s.f. Typ:* electrotyping.

galvardine [galvardin], *s.f. A.Cost:* gaberdine.

galvaudage [galvoda:ʒ], *s.m.* (*rare*) compromising (of one's reputation); prostitution (of one's talents).

galvauder [galvode]. **1.** *v.tr. A:* to botch (work). **2.** *v.tr.* to compromise (reputation); to bring into disrepute; to prostitute (one's talents). **3.** *v.i. O:* to idle; to loaf around.

se galvauder, to let oneself down; **se g. dans une affaire louche,** to compromise one's reputation by taking part in a shady deal.

galvaudeur, -euse [galvodœ:r, -ø:z], **galvaudeux, -euse** [galvodø, -ø:z], *s. F: O:* vagrant; good-for-nothing.

gamache [gamaʃ], *s.f. A.Cost:* spatterdash, gaiter, gamash.

gamai(s), gamay [gamɛ], *s.m. Vit:* common Burgundy vine, grape.

gambade [gɑ̃bad], *s.f.* leap, gambol; *Equit:* gambade; *pl.* capers, antics; **faire des gambades,** to gambol, to cut capers.

gambader [gɑ̃bade], *v.i.* to leap, caper; to frisk (about); to gambol.

gambadeur, -euse [gɑ̃badœ:r, -ø:z], *s.* gamboller, caperer.

gambe [gɑ̃:b], *s.f.* **1.** *pl. Nau:* futtock-shrouds. **2.** *A.Mus:* **viole de g.,** viol(a) da gamba.

gamberger [gɑ̃bɛrʒe], *v.i. & tr. P:* (*a*) to understand, to catch on; (*b*) to imagine, to get it into one's head (that . . .).

gambette[1] [gɑ̃bɛt], *s.m. Orn:* redshank.

gambette[2], *s.f. P:* leg; **jouer, se tirer, des gambettes,** to run away, to beat it; **tricoter des gambettes,** (i) to hoof it, to beat it; (ii) to dance.

gambeyer [gɑ̃beje], *v.tr. & i. Nau:* **1.** to gybe. **2.** to dip (lugsail when going about).

gambi [gɑ̃bi], *s.m. Nau: F:* midshipman; *F:* middy.

Gambie [gɑ̃bi], *Pr.n.f. Geog:* The Gambia.

gambier[1] [gɑ̃bje], *s.f.* clay pipe (made in the form of a head); *P:* **tête à g.,** ugly mug.

gambier[2], *s.m. Bot: Com:* gambier, pale catechu.

gambier[3], *s.m. Glassm:* holder (for supporting container of molten glass).

gambier[4], *v.tr. Nau:* = GAMBEYER.

gambillard [gɑ̃bija:r], *s.m. O: Th:* **chanteur g.,** song-and-dance artist.

gambille [gɑ̃bi:j], *s.f. P:* **1.** *pl.* **gambilles,** legs, pins. **2.** (*a*) dance, hop; (*b*) dance hall.

gambiller [gɑ̃bije], *v.i.* **1.** (*a*) *F: A:* to wiggle one's legs (as one sits dangling them); (*b*) *P:* to dance (to a lively rhythm), to jig about; to shake a leg. **2.** *Nau:* = GAMBEYER.

gambilleur, -euse [gɑ̃bijœ:r, -ø:z], *s. F: O:* (*a*) frequenter of dance halls; (*b*) political mountebank.

gambir [gɑ̃bi:r], *s.m. Pharm:* gambier, pale catechu.

gambit [gɑ̃bi], *s.m. Chess:* (*a*) gambit; (*b*) **(pion de) g.,** gambit pawn.

gambusie [gɑ̃byzi], *s.f. Ich:* gambusia.

gamelle [gamɛl], *s.f.* **1.** *Mil: Navy:* (*a*) *A:* (communal) mess bowl; (*b*) (i) mess kettle, dixie, dixy; (ii) mess tin; **chef de g.,** mess sergeant; **manger à la g.,** to eat in the mess; (*c*) *P:* **ramasser une g.,** to come a cropper. **2.** *Min:* pan.

gamelot [gamlo], *s.m. Nau:* (mess-)kid; piggin.

gamétange [gametɑ̃:ʒ], *s.m. Biol:* gametangium, gametangia.

gamète [gamɛt], *s.m. Biol:* gamete.

gamétocide [gametɔsid], *s.m. Med:* gametocide.

gamétocyte [gametɔsit], *s.m. Biol:* gametocyte.

gamétogénèse [gametɔʒenɛ:z], *s.f. Biol:* gametogenesis.

gamétophyte [gametɔfit], *s.m. Bot:* gametophyte.

gamin, -ine [gamɛ̃, -in]. **1.** *s.* (*a*) *s.m. A:* errand boy; (*b*) *A:* street urchin, street arab; (*c*) *F:* (i) child, brat; (ii) lively, mischievous, child; (iii) son, daughter; **une gamine de dix ans,** a girl of ten; **mon g. va aller en Allemagne,** my boy's going to Germany; (*of man*) **ce n'est qu'un grand g.,** he's just a big schoolboy. **2.** *a.* (*a*) lively, mischievous; (*b*) **elle est encore gamine,** she's still just a child; (*c*) **un petit chapeau g.,** a saucy little hat.

gaminer [gamine], *v.i.* (*rare*) to play around in a lively, mischievous, manner; to behave like a child.

gaminerie [gaminri], *s.f.* childish prank, trick; childish behaviour; **il a passé l'âge de ces gamineries,** he's too old to behave in such a childish way.

gamma [gam(m)a], *s.m.* (*a*) *Gr.Alph:* gamma; (*b*) *Phot:* (development factor) gamma; **g. infini,** gamma infinity; (*c*) *Astr:* **point g.,** first point of Aries; (*d*) *Metall:* **fer g.,** gamma iron; (*e*) *Atom.Ph:* **particule g.,** gamma particle; **rayons g.,** gamma rays; **radiation, rayonnement, g.,** gamma radiation; **cascade de rayons g.,** gamma cascade; **flux de rayons g.,** gamma flux; **g. de capture,** capture gamma; **g. instantané,** prompt gamma; **détecteur (de rayons) g.,** gamma monitor; **appareil, équipement, d'irradiation g.,** gamma irradiation plant; **pasteurisation par irradiation g.,** gamma-ray pasteurization.

gammacisme [gam(m)asism], *s.m. Med:* gammacism.

gammaglobuline [gam(m)aglɔbylin], *s.f. Biol:* gamma globulin.

gammagraphie [gam(m)agrafi], *s.f.* gamma radiography, gammagraphy; **g. industrielle,** industrial gammagraphy.

gammamètre [gam(m)amɛtr], *s.m.* gamma (-radiation) meter.

gammare [gam(m)a:r], *s.m.* **1.** *Crust:* gammarid, camaron, *F:* shore skipper, sand hopper. **2.** school (of whales).

gammaridés [gam(m)aride], *s.m.pl. Crust:* Gammaridae.

gammathérapie [gam(m)aterapi], *s.f.* gamma-therapy, gamma-ray therapy.

gamme [gam], *s.f.* **1.** *Mus:* scale, gamut; **faire des gammes,** to practise scales; **changer de g.,** to alter one's tone, to change one's tune, to climb down; *A:* **chanter sa g. à qn,** to give s.o. a good

dressing-down, to upbraid s.o. 2. range, series, scale; **g. des couleurs,** colour scale; *Phot.Engr:* **g. d'épreuves trichromes,** set of progressive proofs; *Atom.Ph:* **g. d'énergie,** energy range; **toute la g. des sensations,** the whole gamut, range, of sensations; *F:* **toute la g.!** the whole lot (of them)!

gammée [game], *a.f.* **croix g.,** gammadion, fylfot; swastika.

gammexane [gam(m)εksan], *s.m. Ch:* gammexane.

gamo- [gamɔ], *pref.* gamo-; **gamomanie,** gamomania; **gamophylle,** gamophyllous.

gamocarpellé [gamɔkarpεle], *a. Bot:* syncarpous.

gamogénèse [gamɔʒenεːz], *s.f. Biol:* gamogenesis.

gamogénétique [gamɔʒenetik], *a. Biol:* gamogenetic.

gamolépis [gamɔlepis], *s.m. Bot:* gamolepis.

gamone [gamɔn], *s.f. Biol:* gamone.

gamonte [gamɔ̃ːt], *s.m. Biol:* gamont.

gamopétale [gamɔpetal], *a. Bot:* gamopetalous.

gamopétalie [gamɔpetali], *s.f. Bot:* gamopetaly.

gamophobie [gamɔfɔbi], *s.f. Med:* gamophobia.

gamosépale [gamɔsepal], *a. Bot:* gamosepalous.

gamotropisme [gamɔtrɔpism], *s.m. Z:* gamotropism.

ganache [ganaʃ], *s.f.* **1.** (lower) jaw, jowl, ((i) of horse, (ii) *P:* of person); **cheval chargé de g.,** heavy-headed horse. **2.** *F:* (*a*) fool, idiot; good-for-nothing; (*b*) **vieille g.,** old fogey, buffer. **3.** low padded armchair.

ganacherie [ganaʃri], *s.f. F:* stupidity; incapacity, incompetence.

ganachisme [ganaʃism], *s.m. F:* hopeless incompetence (of old fools).

Gand [gɑ̃], *Pr.n.m. Geog:* Ghent.

gandin [gɑ̃dε̃], *s.m. F: A:* dandy, masher.

gandoura [gɑ̃dura], *s.f. Cost:* gandoura(h).

gang [gɑ̃ːg], *s.m. F:* (*a*) gang; (*b*) racket; **le g. de l'alcool,** the rum racket.

ganga [gɑ̃ga], *s.m. Orn:* pin-tailed grouse; **g. cata,** pin-tailed sand grouse; **g. des sables, g. unibande,** black-bellied sand grouse; **g. du Sénégal,** spotted sand grouse.

gangave [gɑ̃gaːv], *s.f. Nau:* gangava.

Gange (le) [ləgɑ̃ːʒ], *Pr.n.m. Geog:* the (river) Ganges.

gangétique[gɑ̃ʒetik], *a. Geog:* Gangetic (delta, etc.).

gangliectomie [gɑ̃gliεktɔmi], *s.f. Surg:* gangli(on)ectomy.

gangliforme [gɑ̃glifɔrm], *a.* gangliform.

ganglion [gɑ̃gli(j)ɔ̃], *s.m.* **1.** *Anat:* ganglion; **g. nerveux,** ganglion cell; **ganglions lymphatiques,** lymphatic glands, lymph glands. **2.** (*a*) *Med:* **g. synovial,** ganglion; (*b*) *Vet:* spavin.

ganglionnaire [gɑ̃gli(j)ɔnεːr], *a. Anat:* ganglionary, ganglionic; **états ganglionnaires de l'enfance,** swollen glands in childhood.

ganglionné [gɑ̃gli(j)ɔne], *a.* gangli(on)ated.

gangrène [gɑ̃grεn], *s.f.* **1.** *Med:* gangrene, mortification; **g. sèche, humide, sénile,** dry, humid, senile, gangrene; **g. gazeuse,** gas gangrene; **g. des os,** necrosis. **2.** *Bot:* canker. **3.** *F:* rot, corruption.

gangrené [gɑ̃grəne], *a.* **1.** *Med:* gangrenous, gangrened. **2.** *F:* corrupt.

gangrener [gɑ̃grəne, -grene], *v.tr.* (**il gangrène; il gangrènera**) **1.** *Med:* to gangrene, to cause to mortify. **2.** to corrupt.

se gangrener. **1.** to mortify, gangrene; to become gangrened. **2.** to become corrupted.

gangreneux, -euse [gɑ̃grənø, -øːz], *a.* **1.** *Med:* gangrenous, gangrened. **2.** *Bot:* cankerous.

gangster [gɑ̃gstεːr], *s.m. F:* gangster; hooligan.

gangstérisme [gɑ̃gsterism], *s.m. F:* gangsterism; hooliganism.

gangue [gɑ̃ːg], *s.f.* **1.** *Miner:* gang(ue), matrix (of precious stone, etc.). **2.** *Min:* attle, deads, gang(ue). **3.** *Med:* sclerosis (of tissues surrounding tumour, etc.).

gangueill [gɑ̃gœːj], *s.f.* fishing net (used for eels).

gangui [gɑ̃gi], *s.m.* (Mediterranean) fishing net.

gannet [ganε], *s.m. Orn:* gannet, solan goose.

gannister [ganistεːr], *s.m. Miner:* ganister.

ganoïde [ganɔid], *Ich:* **1.** *a.* ganoid (scale). **2.** *s.m.pl.* **ganoïdes,** Ganodei, Ganoids.

ganomalite [ganɔmalit], *s.f. Miner:* ganomalite.

ganophyllite [ganɔfilit], *s.f. Miner:* ganophyllite.

ganse [gɑ̃ːs], *s.f.* **1.** (*a*) braid, (plaited) cord, gimp, edging; piping (cord); (*b*) **g. de cheveux,** plait of hair. **2.** (*a*) rope handle; loop; (*b*) *Nau:* eye becket.

ganser [gɑ̃se], *v.tr.* **g. un chapeau, un siège,** to trim a hat, edge a chair, with cord; **g. une couture,** to pipe a seam.

gansette [gɑ̃sεt], *s.f.* small cord, edging.

gant [gɑ̃], *s.m.* **1.** glove; *Arm:* gauntlet; (*a*) **mettre ses gants,** to draw on, pull on, one's gloves; **gants en suède, en tissu,** suède gloves, fabric gloves; **gants de chamois,** chamois-leather gloves; **gants de daim,** doe-skin gloves; **gants de buffle,** riding gloves; **gants fourrés,** lined gloves; **gants de caoutchouc,** rubber gloves; **cela vous va comme un g.,** it fits you like a glove; **philanthrope en gants blancs,** kid-glove philanthropist; **il faut prendre des gants pour l'approcher,** one has to handle him with kid gloves (on); **jeter le g. à qn,** to throw down the gauntlet to s.o.; **relever le g.,** to take up the gauntlet, to accept the challenge; **souple comme un g.,** good-natured, easy-going; (*b*) **gants de boxe,** boxing-gloves; *F:* **prendre part à une polémique sans mettre les gants,** to join in a controversy without the gloves; **gants d'escrime,** fencing-gloves; *Mil:* **gants moufles,** mittens; (*c*) *Toil:* **g. de toilette** = face flannel, *U.S:* washcloth, washrag; **g. de crin,** flesh glove, friction glove. **2.** *A:* (*a*) *pl.* glove money; gratuity; **avoir les gants de qch.,** to be the first to do, think of, sth.; **se donner les gants de qch.,** to take the credit for sth.; (*b*) *P:* (*of woman*) **perdre ses gants,** to lose her virginity. **3.** (*a*) *Bot:* **g. de bergère, (de) Notre-Dame,** (i) foxglove; (ii) columbine; (iii) throatwort; (*b*) *Spong:* **g. de Neptune,** glove sponge.

gantelé [gɑ̃tle], *a.* gauntleted; **la main gantelée,** the mailed fist.

gantelée [gɑ̃tle], *s.f. Bot:* (*a*) foxglove; (*b*) campanula trachelium, throatwort, nettle-leaved bell-flower.

gantelet [gɑ̃tlε], *s.m.* **1.** gauntlet. **2.** hand leather (of shoemaker, etc.). **3.** bandage (for the hand).

ganteline [gɑ̃tlin], *s.f. Bot:* = GANTELÉE.

gant-éponge [gɑ̃tepɔ̃ːʒ], *s.m.* = face flannel; *pl. gants-éponges.*

ganter [gɑ̃te], *v.tr.* **1.** (*a*) to glove; **être bien gantée,** to be well gloved; **main gantée de blanc,** white-gloved hand; (*b*) **g. du sept,** to take sevens in gloves. **2.** (*of gloves*) to fit. *F:* **ça me gante,** that suits me down to the ground, fits my bill.

se ganter. **1.** to put, pull, draw, slip, on one's gloves. **2. chez qui vous gantez-vous?** where do you buy your gloves? **elle se gante bien,** she is always well-gloved.

ganterie [gɑ̃tri], *s.f.* **1.** (*a*) glove-making, gloving; (*b*) glove trade. **2.** (*a*) glove factory; (*b*) glove shop; (*c*) (*in store*) glove counter, department. **3.** glove wear.

gantier, -ière [gɑ̃tje, -jεːr]. **1.** *s.* glover. **2.** *a.* **ouvrière gantière,** glove-factory hand. **3.** *s.f. A:* **gantière,** (i) glove box; (ii) glove tray.

gant-jaune [gɑ̃ʒon], *s.m. A:* dandy; *pl. gants-jaunes.*

gantois, -oise [gɑ̃twa, -waːz], *a.* & *s. Geog:* (native, inhabitant) of Ghent.

Ganymède [ganimed], *Pr.n.m. Myth:* Ganymede.

gapençais, -aise [gapɑ̃sε, -εːz], **gapençois, -oise** [gapɑ̃swa, -waːz], *a.* & *s. Geog:* (native, inhabitant) of Gap.

gapette [gapεt], *s.f. P:* cap.

garage [garaːʒ], *s.m.* **1.** (*a*) docking (of boats); (*b*) dock, basin (of canal, river); **g. à sec,** dry basin. **2.** *Rail:* shunting, side-tracking; **voie de g.,** siding; *F:* **mettre, ranger (qn, qch.) sur une voie de g.,** to shelve (s.o., sth.). **3.** (*rare*) garaging, parking (of cars, etc.). **4.** (*a*) garage; **g. à plusieurs étages,** multi-storey car park; **g. de canots,** boathouse; **g. d'autobus,** bus depot; **g. d'avions,** (aircraft) hangar; *Rail:* **g. de machines,** engine shed; (*b*) passing place (on narrow road); (*c*) *Mil:* turnout, bypass (in trenches).

garagiste [garaʒist], *s.m. Aut:* (*a*) garage keeper, proprietor; (*b*) garage mechanic.

garaie [garε], *s.f. Nau:* (*on river, canal*) berthing (of craft to let another pass).

garamond [garamɔ̃], *s.m. Typ:* Garamond.

garançage [garɑ̃saːʒ], *s.m. A.Dy:* dyeing with madder.

garance [garɑ̃ːs], *s.f.* **1.** *Bot:* (*a*) madder, madder-wort; (*b*) *F:* **petite g., g. de chien,** squinancy wort. **2.** (*a*) madder (dye); (*b*) madder(-red); *a.inv.* **les pantalons garance,** the red trousers of the French (pre-1914) infantry, etc.; *P: A:* **il en pince pour la g.,** he's all for a soldier's life; **toutes les filles en pincent pour la g.,** all the girls love a soldier.

garancer [garɑ̃se], *v.tr. A.Dy:* to madder, to dye with madder.

garanceur [garɑ̃sœːr], *s.m. A. Dy:* madder worker.

garancière [garɑ̃sjεːr], *s.f.* **1.** madder field. **2.** *A.Dy:* (madder) dye works.

garant[1], -ante [garɑ̃, -ɑ̃ːt], *s.* (*a*) guarantor, surety, bail; **g. d'une dette,** surety for a debt; **se rendre, se porter, g. de qn,** (i) to answer for s.o.; (ii) to go bail for s.o.; **je m'en porte g.,** I can vouch for it; **elle vous en est garante,** she gives you her word for it; **je me porte g. qu'il ne lui sera fait aucun mal,** I pledge myself that he won't come by any harm; I will be responsible for his safety; **prendre qn à g. de qch.,** to call s.o. to witness sth.; **être g. de ses faits,** to be answerable for one's actions; *a.* **puissance garante,** guaranteeing power; (*b*) authority, guarantee; **je cite pour g. les Écritures saintes,** I'm quoting the Scriptures as my authority; **son intérêt est le g. de sa discrétion,** his interest is the best guarantee of his discretion, is a warrant for his discretion.

garant[2], *s.m.* **1.** *Nau:* (tackle)fall. **2.** *Bootm:* eyelet.

garanti, -ie[1] [garɑ̃ti], *s. Jur:* guarantee (= receiver of guaranty).

garantie[2] [garɑ̃ti], *s.f.* **1.** (*a*) guarantee (**contre,** against); **les garanties constitutionnelles,** the constitutional guarantees; **les garanties individuelles,** laws for the protection of individuals; **prendre des garanties contre les abus,** to insure against abuses; **s'entourer de garanties,** to obtain safeguards; (*b*) guarantee, pledge (of execution of contract); guaranty (of payment); **g. bancaire,** bank guarantee; **g. d'exécution,** contract bond; **fonds déposés, détenus, en g.,** funds lodged, held, as security; **verser une somme en g.,** to leave a deposit; **donner sa montre en g.,** to pledge one's watch; **donner une g. pour qn,** to stand security for s.o.; **pour plus de g. . . .,** for a more secure guarantee . . .; **g. accessoire,** collateral security; *Fin:* **g. de la circulation,** backing of the currency; (*c*) *Com:* warranty, guarantee (of quality, etc.); **avec g.,** warranted, guaranteed; **sans g.,** unwarranted; **lettre de g. d'indemnité,** letter of indemnity; *Adm:* **le bureau des garanties,** the assay office. **2.** *Fin:* underwriting; **syndicat de g.,** underwriters; **contrat de g.,** underwriting contract.

garantir [garɑ̃tiːr], *v.tr.* **1.** (*a*) to warrant, guarantee; **g. une dette,** to guarantee a debt; **créance garantie,** secured debt; **g. un cheval de tout défaut,** to warrant a horse free from vice; **pendule garantie (pour) deux ans,** clock guaranteed for two years; **g. un fait,** to vouch for a fact; *pred.* **je le garantis honnête,** I can vouch for his honesty; **je vous garantis qu'il viendra,** I'm sure he'll come; (*b*) *Fin:* to underwrite (issue of shares, etc.). **2.** to shelter, protect; **ce vieux sac me garantit de la pluie,** this old sack helps to keep out the rain; **se g. contre le froid,** to protect oneself against the cold. **3.** (*a*) *Jur:* **g. qn contre . . .,** to indemnify s.o. from, against . . .; (*b*) **g. une maison contre l'incendie,** to secure, insure, a house against fire.

garantissement [garɑ̃tismɑ̃], *s.m.* guaranteeing.

garantisseur [garɑ̃tisœːr], *s.m.* guarantor.

garbure [garbyːr], *s.f. Cu:* (*S.W.Fr.*) soup made with cabbage, bacon and conserve of goose.

garce [gars], *s.f.* (*a*) *A:* (*f. of* **gars**) girl; (*b*) *P:* prostitute, tart; **fils de g.,** son of a bitch; (*c*) *P:* disagreeable, bitchy, girl, woman; (*d*) *P:* **une belle g.,** a smasher; (*e*) *P:* **cette g. de vie,** this bloody (awful) life.

garcette [garsεt], *s.f. Nau:* **1.** gasket, becket; **g. de tournevire,** (rope)nipper; **g. de ris,** reef point. **2.** rope end, rope's end, cat-o'-nine-tails.

garçon [garsɔ̃], *s.m.* **1.** (*a*) boy; **elle est accouchée d'un g.,** she gave birth to a son; **école de garçons,** boys' school; **traiter qn en petit g.,** to treat s.o. like a child; **tu es un grand g.,** you're a big boy now; **c'est un g. manqué,** she's a tomboy; (*b*) son; **il est venu avec ses deux garçons,** he came with his two sons, boys. **2.** young man; **g. d'honneur,** best man, groomsman; **garçons (de la fête),** stewards; **un bon, brave, g.,** a good sort; **un beau, un joli, g.,** a handsome young man; **un mauvais g.,** a bad lot; *Pej:* **mon g., voulez-vous . . .,** young man, do you mind . . . **3.** bachelor; **il est encore g.,** he's still single, still a bachelor; **vieux g.,** old bachelor; confirmed bachelor; **appartement de g.,** bachelor flat; **vivre en g.,** to live as a bachelor. **4.** (*a*) *A:* servant; workman; employee; (*b*) (assistant) caretaker; cleaner; messenger; **g. de salle,** auctioneer's messenger; **g. de bureau,** office boy, (office) messenger; **g. de courses,** errand boy; **g. de recette,** bank messenger, walk clerk; **g. boucher,** butcher's boy; **g. coiffeur,** hairdresser's assistant; **g. boulanger,** baker's man, assistant; **g. (de café, de bar),** (bar) waiter; **g. (de comptoir),** barman; (*in restaurant*) **g.!** waiter! **g. d'écurie,** groom; *A:* (*at inn*) (h)ostler; (*in hotel*) **g. d'étage,** boots; floor waiter; **g. d'ascenseur,** lift boy, liftman; **g. de cuisine,** kitchen boy, kitchen porter; *Nau:* **g. de cabine,** (cabin) steward; **g. de pont,** deck steward.

garçonne [garsɔn], *s.f.* bachelor girl.

garçonner [garsɔne], *v.i. F:* **1.** to lead a (rackety) bachelor's life. **2.** (*of girl*) to behave like a tomboy.

garçonnet [garsɔnɛ], *s.m.* **1.** *F:* little boy. **2.** *Com:* **taille g.,** youth's size.

garçonnier, -ière [garsɔnje, -jɛːr]. **1.** *a.* **habitudes garçonnières,** (i) bachelor habits; (ii) (woman's) mannish habits. **2.** *s.f.* **garçonnière,** bachelor's establishment; bachelor flat.

gardannais, -aise [gardanɛ, -ɛːz], *a. & s.* (native, inhabitant) of Gardanne.

garde[1] [gard], *s.m. & f.* (*a*) keeper; *Hist: Adm:* **G. des Sceaux** = Lord Chancellor; *Hist:* **G. des Archives** = Master of the Rolls; (*b*) guard; watchman; *Mil:* sentry; **g. de nuit,** night watchman; **g. champêtre,** rural policeman; **g. du corps,** bodyguard; **g. forestier,** forester, ranger keeper, forest warden; *Hist: Pol:* (*in China*) **Gardes rouges,** Red guards; (*c*) *s.f.* (i) nurse; (ii) nanny; **g. de nuit,** (privately employed) night nurse; (*d*) *Mil:* guardsman; **g. à cheval,** horse guardsman; **g. à pied,** foot guardsman; **gardes du corps,** lifeguards; **g. (républicain) mobile,** mobile guard; member of security police.

garde[2], *s.f.* **1.** (*a*) guardianship, care, protection, custody (of a person); care (of thing); **chien de g.,** watchdog; **chien de bonne g.,** good watchdog; **commettre qch. à la g. de qn,** to entrust s.o. with (the care of) sth.; **être sous bonne g.,** to be in safe custody, keeping; **avoir qch. en garde,** to have charge of sth.; **que Dieu nous ait en g.,** may God protect us, may we remain in God's keeping; **prendre qn en sa g.,** to take s.o. under one's protection, to take charge of s.o.; **je laisse les enfants à, sous, votre g.,** I am leaving the children in your charge; *Jur:* **g. des enfants,** custody of the children (after divorce); (*b*) nursing; **faire des gardes,** to go out nursing, to do nursing; (*c*) guarding, protection (of frontier, machinery, etc.); *Rail:* **plaque de g.,** guard plate (of locomotive); *Nau:* **(palan de) g.,** vang; (*d*) *Veh: Aut:* clearance; **g. (au sol),** ground clearance; *Av:* **g. de l'hélice,** airscrew ground clearance; (*e*) keeping; **vin de g.,** good keeping wine; **ces fruits ne sont pas de g.,** this fruit won't keep; **de bonne g.,** worth keeping. **2.** (*a*) watch(ing); **g. à vue,** close watch; **faire la g.,** to keep watch; **faire bonne g.,** to keep a sharp look-out, to keep a good watch; (*b*) care, guard; **mettre qn en g. contre qch.,** to put s.o. on his guard against sth.; *Fenc:* **se mettre en g.,** to take one's guard; **se remettre en g.,** to recover; **remise en g.,** recovery; **en g.!** on guard! **être, se tenir, sur ses gardes,** to be on one's guard; to look out; **g. à toi!** look out! *A. & Lit:* **n'avoir g. de faire qch.,** to be far from doing sth.; **je n'eus g. de le désabuser,** I took good care not to undeceive him; **nous nous en donnons bien de g.,** far from us such a thought. **3. prendre g.,** (*a*) **prendre g. à qn, à qch.,** to beware of s.o., of sth.; **prenez g. aux orties!** look out for the nettles; mind the nettles! **prenez g.!** take care! (*b*) **prendre g. à qch.,** to attend to, be careful of, to notice, sth.; **je n'avais pas pris g. que le car dépassait l'arrêt,** I had not noticed that the bus was running past the stop; **un fait auquel on n'a pas pris g.,** a fact that has been left out of consideration; **je n'y prendrais pas g.,** I should take no notice of it; I should not take any notice of it; **faire qch. sans y prendre g.,** to do sth. without meaning it, inadvertently; (*c*) (i) *O:* **prendre g. à faire qch.,** to be careful to do sth.; to take good care to do sth.; (ii) **prendre g. de ne pas faire qch.,** to be careful not to do sth.; **prenez g. à, de, ne pas vous perdre,** be careful not to get lost, mind you don't get lost; (*d*) *O:* **prendre g. de faire qch.,** to be careful not to do sth.; **prenez g. de tomber,** mind you don't fall; (*e*) **prendre g. que . . . (ne)** + *sub.*, to be careful, to take care that (sth. does not happen); **prenez g. qu'il (ne) vous voie,** take care he doesn't see you. **4.** guard; (*a*) **soldat de g. à la porte,** soldier on guard at the door; **être de g.,** to be on guard, *Nau:* on duty; **descendre de g.,** to come off guard, off duty; **descente de g.,** coming off guard; **monter la g.,** (i) to mount guard; (ii) to go on guard; **"à la g.!"** "guard turn out!"; **sergent de g.,** sergeant in charge of the quarter guard, guard commander; *Navy:* **embarcation de g.,** guard boat; (*b*) **le corps de g., la g.,** the guard; **histoire de corps de g.,** barrack-room story; **g. montante,** new guard, relieving guard; **g. descendante,** old guard; **appeler la g.,** to call out the guard; **faire sortir la g.,** to turn out the guard; **g. du drapeau,** colour party, colour escort, colour guard; **g. d'honneur,** guard of honour; (*c*) **la g.,** the Guards; **la g. à cheval,** the Horseguards; **la g. à pied,** the Footguards; **la g. du corps,** the Lifeguards, the bodyguards; **la G. républicaine,** the Republican Guard (of Paris); **la G. mobile** = security (state) police; *A:* **la G. nationale,** the National Guard; **la G. nationale à cheval** = the Yeomanry; *Hist:* **la G. impériale,** (Napoleon's) Imperial Guard; *Rom.Hist:* **la g. prétorienne,** the Pretorian guard; **la vieille g.,** the old brigade; (*d*) *Mil:* **(salle de) g.,** guard room; (*e*) *A:* the watch; **crier à la g.,** to cause a commotion, to make a fuss. **5.** *Cards:* covering card, guard. **6.** (*a*) (hilt) guard (of sword, foil); **g. en coquille,** basket hilt; **enfoncer son épée jusqu'à la g.,** to run one's sword in up to the hilt; **s'enferrer jusqu'à la g.,** to give oneself away completely, to be left without a leg to stand on; *F:* **s'en donner jusqu'à la g., jusqu'aux gardes,** to stuff oneself full; (*b*) ward (of lock). **7.** *Bookb:* **(feuille, page, de) g.,** (i) flyleaf; (ii) end paper. **8.** *Nau:* **g. montante, descendante,** check spring ahead, astern.

gardé [garde], *a.* guarded; *Rail:* **passage à niveau g.,** level-crossing gate with keeper, manned level crossing; *Cards:* **roi g., dame gardée,** guarded king, queen; **toute(s) proportion(s) gardée(s),** all things considered.

garde-à-vous [gardavu], *s.m.* no *pl. Mil:* (position of) attention; **être, se tenir, au g.-à-v.,** to stand at attention; **au g.-à-v.,** at attention; **se mettre vivement au g.-à-v.,** to spring to attention; **g.-à-v.!** attention! 'shun!

garde-barrière [gard(ə)barjɛːr], *s.m. & f.* gate-keeper (at level-crossing); *pl. gardes-barrière(s).*

garde-bébé [gard(ə)bebe], *s.m. & f.* baby-sitter, sitter-in; *pl. gardes-bébés.*

garde-bœuf [gard(ə)bœf], *a. & s.m. Orn:* **(héron) g.-b.,** buff-backed heron, cattle egret; *pl. gardes-bœuf(s).*

garde-bois [gard(ə)bwa], *s.m.* forester, ranger, keeper, forest warden; *pl. garde(s)-bois.*

garde-boue [gard(ə)bu], *s.m.inv.* mudguard (of bicycle, etc.); *A:* splash board, dashboard (of vehicle).

garde-boutique [gard(ə)butik], *s.m F:* (*a*) *Orn: A:* kingfisher; (*b*) *Com:* unsaleable article; *pl. garde-boutiques.*

garde-bras [gard(ə)brɑ], *s.m.inv. A.Arm:* brace.

garde-but [gard(ə)by], *s.m. Fb:* goalkeeper; *pl. gardes-but.*

garde-canal [gard(ə)kanal], *s.m.* lock keeper; *pl. gardes-canal, -canaux.*

garde-cendre(s) [gard(ə)sɑ̃dr], *s.m.inv.* **1.** ashpan (of fireplace). **2.** fender.

garde-chaîne [gard(ə)ʃɛn], *s.m.inv.* chain-guard.

garde-chasse [gard(ə)ʃas], *s.m.* gamekeeper; *pl. gardes-chasse(s).*

garde-chiourme [gard(ə)ʃjurm], *s.m.* (*a*) *A:* warder (of convict-gang); galley-sergeant; (*b*) **un vrai g.-c.,** a regular slave-driver; *pl. gardes-chiourme.*

garde-corps [gard(ə)kɔːr], *s.m.inv.* **1.** parapet, balustrade. **2.** railing, side rail, guard rail, hand rail (of bridge, etc.); *Nau:* **g.-c. arrière,** stern rail. **3.** *Nau:* (*a*) life line, man rope; (*b*) capstan swifter.

garde-côte [gard(ə)koːt], *s.m.* **1.** coastguard; *pl. gardes-côtes.* **2.** (*a*) coastguard vessel; (*b*) coast-defence ship; *pl. garde-côtes.*

garde-couche [gard(ə)kuʃ], *s.f.* (monthly) nurse; *pl. gardes-couches.*

garde-crotte [gard(ə)krɔt], *s.m.inv. in pl.* = GARDE-BOUE.

garde-cuisse [gard(ə)kɥis], *s.m. A:* leg guard (worn in jousts, tournaments); *pl. garde-cuisse, garde-cuisses.*

garde-doigts [gard(ə)dwa], *s.m.inv. Sp:* batting glove.

garde-feu [gard(ə)fø], *s.m.* **1.** fireman (in theatre, etc.); *pl. gardes-feu.* **2.** *inv.* (*a*) fender; (*b*) fire guard; (*c*) fire screen; (*d*) *For:* **tranchée g.-f.,** fire line, trace.

garde-filin [gard(ə)filɛ̃], *s.m. N.Arch:* rope guard; *pl. garde-filins.*

garde-flanc(s) [gard(ə)flɑ̃], *s.m.* **1.** *Mil:* flanking cavalry squadron; *pl. gardes-flancs.* **2.** *inv: Harn:* side leather, side pad.

garde-fou [gard(ə)fu], *s.m.* **1.** parapet, balustrade. **2.** railing, handrail (of bridge, etc.); *pl. garde-fous.*

garde-française [gard(ə)frɑ̃sɛːz], *s.m. Hist:* soldier of the *gardes-françaises* (infantry regiment of the King's household, disbanded 1789).

garde-frein(s) [gard(ə)frɛ̃], *s.m. Rail:* brakesman; *pl. gardes-frein(s).*

garde-frontière [gard(ə)frɔ̃tjɛːr], *s.f.* frontier guard; *pl. gardes-frontière.*

garde-gouttes [gard(ə)gut], *s.m.inv. Ind:* splash guard; *Mec.E:* oil guard.

garde-guichet [gard(ə)giʃɛ], *s.m. Cr:* wicket keeper; *pl. gardes-guichet.*

garde-hélice [gardelis], *s.m.* propeller guard; *pl. garde-hélices.*

garde-jambe [gard(ə)ʒɑ̃ːb], *s.m. Harn: Cr:* leg guard; *Cr: Hockey: etc:* pad; *pl. garde-jambes.*

garde-jupe [gard(ə)ʒyp], *s.m.inv. Cy:* dress guard.

garde-ligne [gard(ə)liɲ], *s.m. Rail:* track watchman; *pl. gardes-ligne(s).*

garde-magasin [gardmagazɛ̃], *s.m.* **1.** (*a*) warehouseman; (*b*) *Mil:* storekeeper, barrack-sergeant; *Navy:* yeoman; *pl. gardes-magasin(s).* **2.** *inv:* = GARDE-BOUTIQUE.

garde-main [gard(ə)mɛ̃], *s.m.* hand shield; *pl. garde-main(s).*

garde-malade [gardmalad]. **1.** *s.m.* male nurse. **2.** *s.f.* (sick) nurse; *pl. des gardes-malade(s).*

garde-manche [gard(ə)mɑ̃ːʃ], *s.m.* (over)sleeve, cuff protector; *pl. garde-manche(s).*

garde-manège [gard(ə)manɛːʒ], *s.m.* riding-school keeper; *pl. gardes-manège(s).*

garde-manger [gard(ə)mɑ̃ʒe], *s.m.inv.* **1.** *A:* larder, pantry. **2.** (meat) safe. **3.** *P:* stomach, bread basket.

garde-marine [gard(ə)marin], *s.m. Navy: A:* midshipman; *pl. gardes-marine.*

garde-meuble [gard(ə)mœbl], *s.m.* (*a*) furniture repository, warehouse; (*b*) lumber room; *pl. garde-meubles.*

garde-mites [gard(ə)mit], *s.m.inv. Mil: F:* stores orderly.

Gardénal [gardenal], *s.m. Pharm: R.t.m:* Gardenal, Luminal, phenobarbital, phenobarbitone.

garde-nappe [gard(ə)nap], *s.m.* **1.** dinner mat, table mat. **2.** doily. **3.** (table-)runner; *pl. garde-nappe(s).*

gardénia [gardenja], *s.m.,* **gardénie** [gardeni], *s.f. Bot:* gardenia.

garde-noble [gard(ə)nɔbl], *s.m.* gentleman of the Papal Guard; *pl. gardes-nobles.*

garde-notes [gard(ə)nɔt], *s.m.inv.* filing jacket, portfolio.

garden-party [gardɛnparti], *s.f.* garden party; *pl. garden-parties.*

garde-pavé [gard(ə)pave], *s.m.inv.* kerb, curb, (of pavement); kerbstone.

garde-pêche [gard(ə)pɛʃ], *s.m.* **1.** water bailiff; river keeper, watcher; *pl. gardes-pêche.* **2.** *inv:* (*a*) (river) conservancy boat; (*b*) (sea-)fishery service vessel; fishery protection vessel.

garde-place [gard(ə)plas], *s.m. Rail:* **1.** holder (for reservation ticket); **(ticket) g.-p.,** reservation ticket. **2.** (office for) reservation of seats; *pl. garde-places.*

garde-port [gard(ə)pɔːr], *s.m.* wharfmaster (on river); *pl. gardes-port(s).*

garde-poussière [gard(ə)pusjɛːr], *s.m.inv.* dust guard.

garder [garde], *v.tr.* to keep. **1.** to guard, protect; to keep watch over (s.o., sth.); **g. les portes (de la ville),** to guard, keep, the gates (of the city); **que les anges te gardent!** may angels guard you! **g. qn d'un danger,** to protect s.o. from a danger; **g. la boutique,** to look after, mind, the shop; **g. un troupeau,** to tend a flock; *F:* **dites donc, nous n'avons pas gardé les cochons ensemble!** don't be so familiar! don't take liberties! **g. les enfants,** to mind the children; **g. qn à vue,** to keep a close watch on s.o.; *F:* **g. le mulet,** to be kept waiting; *F:* **g. les manteaux, les balles,** (i) to be on duty; (ii) to stay at home doing nothing (while others are enjoying themselves); *A: F:* **en donner à g. à qn,** to pull a fast one on s.o. **2.** (*a*) to retain; **g. un vêtement,** (i) to keep a garment; (ii) to keep on a garment; **g. qn à dîner,** to keep s.o. to dinner, to make s.o. stay to dinner; **g. qn en otage,** to keep, detain, s.o. as a hostage; (*b*) to preserve; **g. une poire pour la soif,** to put by, keep, something for a rainy day; **g. une somme intacte,** to keep a sum of money intact; **g. les apparences,** to keep up appearances; **g. ses illusions, son innocence,** to keep one's illusions, one's innocence; **g. son sang-froid,** to keep cool (and collected); **g. rancune à qn,** to harbour resentment against s.o.; *F:* **la g. bonne à qn,** to owe s.o. a grudge; **g. le sourire,** to keep smiling; **g. son sérieux,** to keep a straight face; **g. les yeux baissés,** to keep one's eyes down, lowered; **viande qui ne se garde pas bien,** meat that does not keep well; **dans la famille se gardent certaines traditions,** certain traditions are preserved in the family. **3.** to remain in (a place); **g. la chambre,** to keep, stay, in one's room; **g. le lit,** to be laid up, to be confined to, have to stay in, bed; **être obligé de g. le lit,** to be confined to one's bed. **4.** to observe, respect; **g. les commandements,** to keep the commandments; **g. un**

secret, sa parole, to keep a secret, one's word; **il n'a pas gardé sa parole,** he has broken his word.

se garder. 1. to protect oneself; **garde-toi!** look out (for yourself)! *Cards:* se g. à trèfle, to keep a guard in clubs; *F:* se g. à carreau, to take every precaution, to be on one's guard. 2. (*a*) se g. de qn, de qch., to beware of s.o., sth.; (*b*) se g. de faire qch., to take care not to do sth.; **gardez-vous (bien) de le perdre,** mind you don't lose it! take care not to lose it! **je m'en garderai bien!** I shall do no such thing! *F:* not if I know it! **il se garde bien de livrer ses secrets,** he's very careful not to give away his secrets; **se g. de paroles inutiles,** to talk to the point.

garde-rats [gard(ə)ra], *s.m.inv. Nau:* rat guard.

garderie [gard(ə)ri], *s.f.* 1. beat, domain, of one ranger, keeper. 2. day nursery. 3. boarding kennel (for pets).

garde-rivière [gard(ə)rivjɛːr], *s.m.* river policeman; *pl. gardes-rivière.*

garde-robe[1] [gard(ə)rɔb], *s.f.* 1. wardrobe (= (i) piece of furniture; (ii) clothes); *A:* **grand maître de la g.-r.** = Master of the Robes. 2. *A:* (*a*) water closet, privy, w.c.; **brosse à g.-r.,** lavatory brush; (*b*) commode, nightstool; (*c*) *Med:* faeces, stool(s), motion. 3. *Bot:* southernwood; *pl. garde-robes.*

garde-robe[2], *s.m. A:* (lady's) apron, overall; *pl. garde-robes.*

garde-rôle [gard(ə)roːl], *s.m. Hist:* = Keeper of the Rolls; *pl. gardes-rôle(s).*

garde-roue [gard(ə)ru], *s.m. A:* 1. splasher, splashboard (of carriage). 2. paddle-box (of steamer); *pl. garde-roues.*

garde-scellés [gard(ə)sele], *s.m. Hist:* Keeper of the Seals; *pl. gardes-scellés.*

garde-soleil [gard(ə)sɔlɛːj], *s.m.inv. Opt:* lens shade.

garde-temps [gard(ə)tɑ̃], *s.m.inv. Ind:* timing apparatus; chronometer.

gardeur, -euse [gardœːr, -øːz]. 1. *s.* keeper, tender (of animals); herdsman; **g. de cochons,** swineherd; **gardeuse d'enfant,** (i) baby farmer; (ii) mother's help. 2. *a.* **mémoire gardeuse de détails,** memory retentive of detail.

garde-voie [gard(ə)vwa], *s.m. Rail:* track watchman; *pl. gardes-voie.*

garde-vue [gard(ə)vy], *s.m.inv.* 1. eyeshade. 2. lampshade, candle shade.

gardian [gardjɑ̃], *s.m.* cowherd (in Camargue).

gardien, -ienne [gardjɛ̃, -jɛn], *s.* (*a*) guardian, keeper; watchman; caretaker (of public building, etc.); (museum) attendant; warder (of prison); (car-park) attendant; **g. de plage,** lifeguard; **g. de la paix,** policeman (in a town); *Sp:* **g. (de but),** goalkeeper; *Ecc:* **(père) g.,** (Father) Superior (of religious community); **g. des intérêts publics,** protector of the public interest; **se poser g. de l'ordre,** to set oneself up as an upholder of public order; (*b*) *a.* **ange g.,** (i) guardian angel; (ii) *F:* bodyguard.

gardiennage [gardjɛnaːʒ], *s.m.* 1. guarding (of bridges, railways, etc., in time of war). 2. conservancy (of harbours). 3. caretaking.

gardon[1] [gardɔ̃], *s.m. Ich:* roach; **g. rouge,** red-eye, rudd.

gardon[2], *s.m. Geog: Dial:* (*in Cévennes*) (mountain) torrent.

gardonneau, -eaux [gardɔno], *s.m. Ich:* young roach.

gare[1] [gaːr], *int.* look out! out of the way! mind yourself! **g. dessous!** look out below! down there! *F:* **gare la bombe!** look out for squalls! **g. à lui . . .,** woe betide him . . ., he's got it coming to him . . .; *A:* **g. l'eau!** mind the slops! look out below! *esp. Scot:* gardy loo! **sans crier g.,** without warning; *P:* **à la g.!** scram!

gare[2], *s.f.* 1. *Nau:* (*a*) siding (of river, canal); (*b*) (canal) wharf; basin, dock, (in river, canal). 2. (*a*) (railway) station; **g. (de voyageurs),** passenger station; **g. de marchandises,** goods station, *U.S:* freight depot; **g. d'attache,** home station; **g. de correspondance, de bifurcation, d'embranchement,** junction; **g. de transit, de raccordement,** transfer station; **g. de tête de ligne, g. terminus, g. en cul-de-sac,** terminus, terminal (station); **g. maritime,** harbour station, maritime station, terminal; **g d'arrivée,** (i) (*passengers*) arrival station; (ii) (*goods*) receiving station; **g. de départ,** departure station; **g. d'expédition, g. expéditrice,** forwarding station, despatch station; **g. de destination, g. destinataire,** destination station; **(colis à prendre) en g.,** (parcel) to be (left till) called for; *Com:* **prix (en) g. départ,** at-station price; **g. de triage,** marshalling yard; **chef de g.,** stationmaster; **le train entre en g.,** the train is coming in; **le train est en g.,** the train is in, has arrived; *Mil:* **commissaire de g.,** railway traffic officer (R.T.O.), *U.S:* railroad transportation officer; **g. de ravitaillement,** supply station, rail head; **g. de ravitaillement en munitions,** ammunition rail head; **g. origine d'étapes,** rail head; **g. régulatrice,** regulating, regulation, station; **g. d'embarquement, de débarquement,** entraining, detraining, station; (*b*) **g. routière,** bus, coach, station; **g. routière (de marchandises),** road haulage depot; **g. dépôt de matériaux,** (contractor's) yard, store; **g. aérienne,** air terminal.

garenne [garɛn], *s.f.* 1. (rabbit) warren; **g. privée, forcée,** (collection of) hutches (for breeding rabbits); **lapin de g.,** *F:* **un g.,** wild rabbit. 2. (fishing) preserve. 3. *A:* **tabac en g.,** tobacco in bond.

garer [gare], *v.tr.* 1. to garner; **g. les récoltes,** to get in the harvest. 2. to dock (vessel). 3. to shunt (train) on to a siding. 4. (*a*) to put (car) into the garage; to garage (car); to put (aeroplane) into the hangar; (*b*) to park (car); *F:* **j'ai de la peine à me g.,** I find it difficult to park; it's a job to find a parking place.

se garer. 1. to get out of the way **(de,** of); to stand aside; **se g. d'une explosion,** to take cover; **garez-vous!** (i) stand aside! (ii) take cover! *F:* **garez-vous des femmes!** keep out of the way, steer clear, of women! *F:* **être garé des voitures,** to be prudent. 2. (*of car, canal barge, etc.*) to pull to one side. 3. (*of trains*) to shunt on to a siding; **wagons garés,** stabled wagons. 4. *P:* to sober up.

gareur [garœːr], *s.m. Rail:* shunter.

gargamelle [gargamɛl], *s.f. P:* throat.

gargantua [gargɑ̃tɥa], *s.m. F:* glutton, guzzler (*from the Gargantua of Rabelais*); **un appétit, un repas de G.,** a gargantuan appetite, meal.

gargantuesque [gargɑ̃tɥɛsk], *a.* gargantuan (meal, etc.).

gargariser [gargarize], *v.tr.* to gargle (one's throat); *P:* **se g. le sifflet,** to w(h)et one's whistle.

se gargariser, to gargle; *F:* **se g. avec, de, qch.,** to revel in sth.

gargarisme [gargarism], *s.m.* 1. gargle, throat wash. 2. gargling.

gargoine [gargwan], *s.f. P:* throat; **se rincer la g.,** to whet one's whistle.

gargot [gargo], *s.m.* 1. (small) (poor quality) restaurant. 2. slaughterer (of pigs).

gargote [gargɔt], *s.f.* cheap, poor quality, restaurant.

gargoter [gargɔte], *v.i.* 1. *A:* to be a messy eater. 2. to cook badly. 3. to frequent poor restaurants.

gargotier, -ière [gargɔtje, -jɛːr], *s.* 1. keeper of poor restaurant. 2. poor cook.

gargouillade [garguјad], *s.f. Danc:* gargouillade.

gargouillage [garguјaːʒ], *s.m. P:* jumble of words; confused noise.

gargouille [garguːj], *s.f.* 1. (*a*) (water)spout (of roof gutter, of pump); (*b*) *Arch:* gargoyle. 2. (*a*) (street) gutter; (*b*) culvert, drain (of embankment). 3. *Metall:* waste-gas main.

gargouillement [gargujmɑ̃], *s.m.* 1. (*a*) gurgling, bubbling (of water); (*b*) squelch (of wet shoes). 2. rumbling (of the bowels, stomach), tummy rumbles.

gargouiller [garguje], *v.i.* 1. (*a*) (*of water*) to gurgle, bubble; (*b*) *F:* (*of shoes in the wet*) to squelch; **sol qui gargouille sous les pas,** squelchy, squishy, ground. 2. (*of the bowels, stomach*) to rumble. 3. *F:* to paddle (in the gutter).

gargouillette [gargujɛt], *s.f.* = GARGOULETTE.

gargouillis [garguji], *s.m.* (*a*) bubbling, gurgling (of water); (*b*) squelch(ing) (of wet shoes).

gargoulette [gargulɛt], *s.f. Cer:* water cooler, goglet, gugglet.

gargousse [gargus], *s.f. Artil:* (i) cartridge (of big gun); (ii) cartridge bag; **g. à blanc,** blank cartridge; **g. sans poudre,** dummy cartridge.

gargoussier [gargusje], *s.m. Artil:* cartridge case.

gargoylisme [gargɔilism], *s.m. Med:* gargoylism.

garibaldi [garibaldi], *s.m. A:* 1. garibaldi shirt, blouse. 2. garibaldi cap.

garibaldien [garibaldjɛ̃], *s.m. Hist:* Garibaldian.

garide [garid], *s.f. Bot:* xerophilous vegetation (of Rhone and certain Alpine valleys).

garigue [garig], *s.f. Geog:* gar(r)igue.

garnement [garnəmɑ̃], *s.m.* 1. *A:* scapegrace, rogue, good-for-nothing. 2. **(mauvais) g.,** scamp; wretch (of a child); *F:* bad lot.

garni [garni]. I. *a.* 1. (*a*) **bourse bien garnie,** well-lined purse; **maison bien garnie,** well-appointed house; **chevelure bien garnie,** thick head of hair; *Hatm:* **chapeaux garnis, non garnis,** trimmed, untrimmed, hats; *Rail:* **voiture garnie** = first class carriage (with well-upholstered seats); *P:* **elle est bien garnie,** she's well upholstered; (*b*) *Cu:* **plat g.,** meat with vegetables; **choucroute garnie,** sauerkraut with sausages; **assiette garnie,** dish of assorted *charcuterie,* (cold sausages, etc.); (*c*) *Metall:* **g. d'anti-friction,** Babbit-lined. 2. *usu. Pej:* **chambre garnie,** bed-sittingroom; **chambres garnies,** furnished apartments.

II. **garni,** *s.m.* 1. filling (piece); (*a*) *Const:* packing; (*b*) *Carp:* sliver, splinter; (*c*) *Nau:* rounding (of rope). 2. *usu. Pej:* furnished room(s); bed-sittingroom(s), bed-sitter(s); **loger en g.,** to live in lodgings, *F:* in digs; **loueur en g.,** keeper of furnished apartments.

garniérite [garnjerit], *s.f. Miner:* garnierite.

garnir [garniːr], *v.tr.* 1. to strengthen, protect; **bien garni contre le froid,** well protected against the cold; **g. une position, une place de guerre,** to occupy, man, a position; to garrison a stronghold. 2. to furnish, provide **(de,** with); **g. une boutique,** to stock a shop; **g. qn d'argent,** to provide s.o. with money; **g. une porte de verrous,** to furnish a door with bolts; **g. une porte de clous,** to stud a door with nails; **g. de verre la crête d'un mur,** to set the top of a wall with broken glass; **g. qch. à l'intérieur,** to line sth.; **garni de feutre,** felt-lined; **nid garni de mousse,** nest lined with moss; **coffret garni de . . .,** case fitted (out) with . . .; **salle garnie de monde,** (i) room full of people; (ii) *Th:* large audience; **elle se tenait à côté de la table à thé toute garnie,** she stood by the fully-laid tea table; **g. un navire d'hommes,** to man a ship; **g. une lampe,** to fill a lamp (with oil); **g. une chaudière,** to stoke a boiler; *F:* **il se garnit bien le ventre,** he keeps his belly well lined. 3. (*a*) to trim (dress, hat, etc.); **broche garnie de perles,** brooch set with pearls; *O:* **g. un service,** to decorate a dinner table with flowers; *Cu:* **g. un plat,** to garnish a dish; (*b*) *Harn:* to harness (horse). 4. *Tchn:* (*a*) to garret (joints); to stuff (chair, etc.); to lag (boiler); to pack (piston); **g. un frein,** to line a brake; *Phot:* **g. un châssis,** to load, fill, a slide; *Nau:* (i) **g. un mât, le cabestan,** to rig a mast, the capstan; **g. une manœuvre au cabestan,** to bring, take, a rope to the capstan; **g. une voile,** to bend the gear of a sail; **g. les perroquets,** to put on the top-gallant gear; (ii) **g. une manœuvre,** to serve, round, whip, a rope; **g. un anneau de bitord,** to graft a ring; *Fish:* **g. un hameçon,** to bait a hook; (*b*) *Tex:* to raise the nap on, to nap, teasel, teazle, raise (cloth).

se garnir, to fill **(de,** with); **la salle commence à se g.,** the room, *Th:* the house, is beginning to fill.

garnisaire [garnizɛːr], *s.m. A:* bailiff's man.

garnison [garnizɔ̃], *s.f.* 1. garnishing; **pièce de garnison,** ornament brazed on (to a piece of jewellery). 2. *Mil:* (*a*) garrison; **mettre une g. dans une ville,** to garrison a town; **vie de g.,** garrison life; **ville de g.,** garrison town; **être en g., tenir g., dans une ville,** to be garrisoned, in garrison, stationed, in a town; **la ville resta sans g.,** the town remained ungarrisoned, without a garrison; (*b*) station; **le bataillon va changer de g.,** the battalion is about to change station.

garnisonner [garnizɔne], *v.tr. A:* to garrison.

garnissage [garnisaːʒ], *s.m.* 1. (*a*) garnishing, furnishing, trimming, facing (of coat); filling-in (of flaws in wood); packing (of piston); lagging (of boiler); (*b*) (*material*) packing, stuffing; *Metall:* **g. basique,** basic lining (of furnace). 2. *Tex:* napping, teaseling, teazling, raising (of cloth).

garnissement [garnismɑ̃], *s.m.* (action of) furnishing (house, etc.).

garnisseur, -euse [garnisœːr, -øːz], *s.* 1. garnisher, trimmer (of hats, dresses, etc.); fitter (of cases, etc.); filler (of lamps). 2. *Tex:* napper, teaseler, teazler, gigger. 3. *s.f. Tex:* **garnisseuse,** teazling, napping, machine.

garniture [garnityːr], *s.f.* 1. furniture, fittings; (*a*) mountings (of a rifle); rigging (of a ship); (metal) furnishings (of chest of drawers, etc.); **g. de lit,** bedding; **garnitures d'une serrure,** wards of a lock; **garnitures mobiles,** tumblers; **g. des ancres, d'une pompe,** anchor, pump, gear; **g. d'une pompe à incendie,** hose of a fire engine; **g. intérieure d'une voiture,** upholstery of a car; (*b*) *Typ:* furniture. 2. (*a*) trimming, decoration (of hat, dress, etc.); (*b*) trimming(s); (*c*) *Pyr:* **g. (de fusée volante),** decoration. 3. (complete) set (of buttons, diamonds, ornaments, etc.); **g. de feu, de foyer,** fire irons **g. de cheminée,** mantelpiece ornaments; **g. de bureau,** desk set, writing set; **g. de toilette,** toilet set; **g. de poulies,** set of pulleys. 4. *Const:*

filling, garreting (of masonry); **g. de comble,** roofing. **5.** *Cu:* garnish(ing) (of dish); vegetables, etc. (accompanying meat); spread, filling (for sandwiches, etc.); (*in restaurant*) **changement de g.,** change of vegetables. **6.** (*a*) *Mch:* packing (of stuffing box); stuffing (piece); (packing) ring (of piston); **boîte à g.,** stuffing box; **g. de métal blanc,** babitting; (*b*) lagging (of boiler); (*c*) *Aut: etc:* **g. de frein,** brake lining; brake pad (of disc brake); **g. d'embrayage,** clutch lining; (*d*) *Nau:* serving, rounding (of rope).

garno [garno], *s.m. P: A:* (*a*) lodgings, digs; (*b*) hotel.

garonnais, -aise [garɔnɛ, -ɛːz], *a. Geog:* of the Garonne basin.

garou[1] [garu], *s.m.*, **garouette** [garwɛt], *s.f. Bot:* **1.** spurge flax. **2. g. des bois,** mezereon, spurge olive.

garou[2], *s.m.* (= LOUP-GAROU) werewolf; *F:* **courir le g.,** to make a night of it; to prowl about at night.

garrigue [garig], *s.f. Geog:* garrigue (of Mediterranean area).

garrocher [garɔʃe], *v.tr. Fr.C: P:* to throw (stones, etc.).

garrot[1] [garo], *s.m.* **1.** *Surg:* tourniquet, garrot. **2.** racking stick, woolding stick; **g. d'une scie,** tongue of a (frame)saw. **3. supplice du g.,** gar(r)otting, gar(r)otte; **faire subir le supplice du g. à qn,** to gar(r)otte s.o.

garrot[2], *s.m.* withers (of horse); **blessé au g.,** witherwrung.

garrot[3], *s.m. Orn:* **g. arlequin,** harlequin duck; **g. albéole,** buffel-headed duck; **g. à l'œil d'or, canard g.,** garrot, goldeneye; **g. d'Islande,** Barrow's goldeneye.

garrottage [garɔtaːʒ], *s.m.* gar(r)otting.

garrotte [garɔt], *s.f.* gar(r)otte, gar(r)otting.

garrotté [garɔte], *a. Vet:* witherwrung (horse).

garrotter [garɔte], *v.tr.* **1.** to rack down (goods on a truck, etc.). **2.** to pinion (prisoner, etc.); **solidement garrotté,** bound hand and foot. **3.** to gar(r)otte, strangle.

garrulité [garylite], *s.f.* garrulousness, garrulity.

gars [gɑ], *s.m. F:* boy; (young) man; **un petit g.,** a little boy, chap; **un beau g.,** a fine, handsome young man; **un brave g.,** a good sort; **un drôle de g.,** an odd type; **allons-y, les gars!** come on, boys! **eh les gars!** hullo! what ho! (chaps)! (*to child*) **bonjour, mon petit g.!** hullo young man!

garsotte, garzotte [garsɔt, garzɔt], *s.f. Orn: F:* teal.

garzette [garzɛt], *s.f. Orn:* **aigrette g.,** little egret.

Gascogne [gaskɔɲ], *Pr.n.f. Geog:* Gascony; **le Golfe de G.,** the Bay of Biscay.

gascon, -onne [gaskɔ̃, -ɔn]. **1.** *a. & s. Ethn:* Gascon; *F:* **faire le Gascon,** to boast, to brag; **la lessive du G.,** turning the tablecloth (instead of laying a clean one); **une offre de g.,** a hollow promise; **s'en tirer en G.,** to wangle one's way out of it. **2.** *s.m.* the Gascon dialect.

gasconisme [gaskɔnism], *s.m.* Gascon pronunciation, turn of phrase.

gasconnade [gaskɔnad], *s.f.* **1.** boasting, bragging. **2.** (piece of) brag, tall story; **raconter des gasconnades,** to boast, brag.

gasconner [gaskɔne], *v.i.* **1.** to speak with a Gascon accent. **2.** to boast, brag.

gas(-)oil [gɑzwal, -ɔjl], *s.m.* Diesel oil; gas oil; **g. de chauffe,** (fuel) oil.

Gaspard [gaspaːr]. **1.** *Pr.n.m.* Jasper. **2.** *s.m. P: A:* cunning fellow, artful dodger. **3.** *s.m. P:* rat.

gaspillage [gaspijaːʒ], *s.m.* **1.** squandering, wasting (of money, etc.); **habitudes de g.,** wastefulness. **2. pas de gaspillages!** don't be wasteful! **3.** *Min:* **g. du gisement,** gophering.

gaspiller [gaspije], *v.tr.* to waste, squander (money); *F:* to blue (money); **g. du papier, du drap,** to waste, spoil, paper, cloth; **g. son temps,** to fritter away one's time, to waste one's time; **g. sa vie,** to make a mess of one's life.

se gaspiller, to be wasted, to run to waste.

gaspilleur, -euse [gaspijœːr, -øːz], (*a*) *s.* spendthrift, waster; (*b*) *a.* **il est très g.,** he is very wasteful.

gassendiste [gasɛ̃dist], *s.m. Phil.Hist:* Gassendist.

gaster [gastɛːr], *s.m. A: Hum:* **Messer G.,** the stomach, the inner man.

gastéria [gasterja], *s.m. Bot:* gasteria.

gastéromycètes [gasterɔmisɛt], *s.f.pl. Fung:* Gasteromyceteae, Gasteromycetes.

gastérophiles [gasterɔfil], *s.m.pl. Ent:* Gast(e)rophilidae, the bot flies.

gastéropode [gasterɔpɔd], *Moll:* **1.** *a.* gasteropodous. **2.** *s.m.* gasteropod; *pl.* **gastéropodes,** Gast(e)ropoda.

gastérostéidés [gasterɔsteide], *s.m.pl. Ich:* Gasterosteidae.

Gaston [gastɔ̃], *Pr.n.m.* Gaston.

gastralgie [gastralʒi], *s.f. Med:* gastralgia, stomach pains.

gastralgique [gastralʒik], *a.* (*a*) *Med:* gastralgic; (*b*) dyspeptic.

gastrectomie [gastrɛktɔmi], *s.f. Surg:* gastrectomy.

gastrectomiser [gastrɛktɔmize], *v.i. & tr. Surg:* to perform a gastrectomy (on).

gastrine [gastrin], *s.f. Physiol:* gastrin.

gastrique [gastrik], *a.* gastric; **suc g.,** gastric juice; **toux g.,** stomach cough; **embarras g.,** stomach upset, bilious attack; **léger embarras g.,** touch of indigestion; **j'ai de l'embarras g.,** my stomach is out of order.

gastrite [gastrit], *s.f. Med:* gastritis.

gastr(o)- [gastro], *pref.* gastr(o)-; **gastro-hépatique,** gastro-hepatic.

gastrobranche [gastrɔbrɑ̃ːʃ], *s.m. Ich:* **g. aveugle,** hag(fish).

gastrocèle [gastrɔsɛl], *s.f. Surg:* gastrocele.

gastrochaena [gastrɔkena], *s.m. Moll:* Gastrochaena.

gastro-colique [gastrɔkɔlik], *a. Anat:* gastrocolic; *pl. gastro-coliques.*

gastro-colite [gastrɔkɔlit], *s.f. Med:* gastrocolitis.

gastro-duodénal, -aux [gastrɔdɥɔdenal, -o], *a. Med:* gastroduodenal.

gastro-duodénostomie [gastrɔdɥɔdenɔstɔmi], *s.f. Surg:* gastroduodenostomy.

gastrodynie [gastrɔdini], *s.f. Med:* gastrodynia.

gastro-entérique [gastrɔɑ̃terik], *a. Med:* gastroenteric; *pl. gastro-entériques.*

gastro-entérite [gastrɔɑ̃terit], *s.f. Med:* gastroenteritis; *pl. gastro-entérites.*

gastro-entérocolite [gastrɔɑ̃terɔkɔlit], *s.f. Med:* gastro-enterocolitis.

gastro-entérologie [gastrɔɑ̃terɔlɔʒi], *s.f. Med:* gastro-enterology.

gastro-entérologue [gastrɔɑ̃terɔlɔg], *s.m. Med:* gastro-enterologist; *pl. gastro-entérologues.*

gastro-entéroptôse [gastrɔɑ̃terɔptoːz], *s.m. Med:* gastro-enteroptosis.

gastro-entérostomie [gastrɔɑ̃terɔstɔmi], *s.f. Surg:* gastroenterostomy.

gastro-épiploïque [gastrɔepiplɔik], *a. Anat:* gastroepiploic; *pl. gastro-épiploïques.*

gastro-hépatite [gastrɔepatit], *s.f. Med:* gastro-hepatitis.

gastro-intestinal, -aux [gastrɔɛ̃testinal, -o], *a.* gastrointestinal.

gastro-jéjunal, -aux [gastrɔʒeʒynal, -o], *a. Anat:* gastrojejunal.

gastro-jéjunostomie [gastrɔʒeʒynɔstɔmi], *s.f. Surg:* gastrojejunostomy.

gastrolithe [gastrɔlit], *s.m. Crust:* gastrolith.

gastrologie [gastrɔlɔʒi], *s.f.* gastrology.

gastrologique [gastrɔlɔʒik], *a.* gastrological.

gastrolyse [gastrɔliːz], *s.f. Surg:* gastrolysis.

gastromane [gastrɔman], *s.m.* glutton.

gastromycètes [gastrɔmisɛt], *s.m.pl. Fung:* Gast(e)romycetes.

gastronome [gastrɔnɔm], *s.m.* **1.** gastronome. **2.** writer on gastronomy.

gastronomie [gastrɔnɔmi], *s.f.* gastronomy.

gastronomique [gastrɔnɔmik], *a.* gastronomical.

gastropexie [gastrɔpɛksi], *s.f. Surg:* gastropexy.

gastropodes [gastrɔpɔd], *s.m.pl. Moll:* Gast(e)ropoda.

gastroptôse [gastrɔptoːz], *s.f. Med:* gastroptosis.

gastrorragie [gastrɔraʒi], *s.f. Med:* gastrorrhagia, haemorrhage of the stomach.

gastrorrhée [gastrɔre], *s.f. Med:* gastrorrhea.

gastroscope [gastrɔskɔp], *s.m. Med:* gastroscope.

gastroscopie [gastrɔskɔpi], *s.f. Med:* gastroscopy.

gastrospasme [gastrɔspasm], *s.m.* gastrospasm.

gastrostomie [gastrɔstɔmi], *s.f. Surg:* gastrostomy.

gastrotomie [gastrɔtɔmi], *s.f. Surg:* gastrotomy.

gastrotriches [gastrɔtriʃ], *s.m.pl. Ann:* Gastrotricha.

gastro-vasculaire [gastrɔvaskylɛːr], *a.* gastrovascular; *pl. gastro-vasculaires.*

gastrula [gastryla], *s.f. Biol:* gastrula.

gastrulation [gastrylasjɔ̃], *s.f. Biol:* gastrulation.

gat [gɑ], *s.m.* quay steps.

gât [gɑ], *s.m.* (drainage) gat.

Gat(h) [gat], *Pr.n.m. A.Geog:* Gath.

gatangier [gatɑ̃ʒje], *s.m. Ich:* spotted dogfish.

gate [geit], *s.f. Elcs:* gate.

gâté [gɑte], *a.* spoilt; (*a*) damaged; **fruit g.,** damaged fruit; **œufs gâtés,** rotten, addled, eggs; **viande gâtée,** tainted meat; **dents gâtées,** decayed teeth; (*b*) **enfant g.,** (i) spoilt, pampered, child; (ii) pet, favourite; **l'enfant g. de la famille,** the blue-eyed boy (of the family); **l'enfant g. de la fortune,** the spoiled darling of fortune; *s.m. P:* **c'est un petit g.,** he's a lucky man.

gâteau, -eaux [gɑto], *s.m.* **1.** cake; (open) tart; (cold, sweet) pudding; **gros g. à la crème,** gâteau, *pl.* gâteaux; **g. sec,** (i) (sweet) biscuit; (ii) plain cake; **g. de riz** = rice pudding; **g. des Rois,** Twelfth-night cake; *F:* **papa g.,** (i) fond, easy-going, over-indulgent, parent; (ii) friend of the family who spoils the children; (iii) (*girl's wealthy older friend*) sugar daddy; *F:* **marraine g.,** fairy godmother; **on ne peut pas manger le g. à midi tout en le gardant pour le dîner,** you can't have your cake and eat it; *F:* **c'est du g.,** it's a piece of cake; *F:* **partager le g., avoir part au g.,** to share the profit, the loot; to have one's slice of the cake. **2.** (*a*) lump, cake (of any material); disc (of gun cotton, etc.); *Surg:* pledget; (*b*) *Ap:* **g. de miel,** honeycomb; **g. de cire,** wax comb foundation; (*c*) **g. de bouse,** cow pat(ch).

gâte-bois [gɑtbwɑ], *s.m.inv.* **1.** *F:* bungling carpenter **2.** *Ent:* goat moth.

gâte-cuir [gɑtkɥiːr], *s.m.inv. F:* bungling shoemaker.

gâte-maison [gɑtmɛzɔ̃], *s.m. Pej: F: A:* over-industrious servant; *pl. gâte-maison(s).*

gâte-métier [gɑtmetje], *s.m.inv. O:* (*a*) person who works for less than the standard wage; (*b*) undercutter (of prices).

gâte-papier [gɑtpapje], *s.m.inv. O: F:* scribbler; writer of trash.

gâte-pâte [gɑtpɑːt], *s.m.inv. F:* **1.** bad baker, pastrycook. **2.** botcher.

gâter [gɑte], *v.tr.* to spoil. **1.** to damage; **g. un vêtement,** to spoil a garment; **la grêle gâte le blé,** hail damages wheat; **les mouches gâtent la viande,** flies taint the meat; **g. le goût, le jugement, de qn,** to corrupt s.o.'s taste, s.o.'s judgment; **cela ne gâte rien,** that won't do any harm; **il a tout gâté,** he has spoiled everything, made a hash of everything; **g. le plaisir de qn,** to spoil s.o.'s pleasure; **détails qui gâtent le tableau,** details that spoil the picture; **cette histoire m'a gâté l'appétit,** that story has spoilt my appetite; *Com:* **g. le métier,** to spoil the market; *abs.* **malade qui gâte,** patient who wets, fouls, his bed. **2.** to pamper; **son mari la gâte,** her husband spoils her; **g. ses enfants,** to spoil one's children, to over-indulge one's children.

se gâter, to deteriorate; **le poisson se gâte facilement,** fish easily goes bad; **le fruit se gâte,** the fruit is spoiling; **le temps se gâte,** the weather is breaking up; it is turning wet; **les affaires se gâtent,** things are going wrong.

gâterie [gɑtri], *s.f.* **1.** over-indulgence (to faults of others); spoiling (of children); **accoutumé aux gâteries de sa mère,** accustomed to be indulged, coddled, by his mother. **2.** *pl.* treats, goodies (for children).

gâte-sauce [gɑtsoːs], *s.m.inv. F:* **1.** cook who spoils the food. **2.** kitchen boy.

gâte-tout [gɑttu], *s.m.inv. F:* muddler; spoil-sport.

gâteur, -euse[1] [gɑtœːr, -øːz], *s. A:* **1.** spoiler, waster (of material); **g. de papier,** scribbler, writer of trash. **2.** spoiler (of children).

gâteux, -euse[2] [gɑtø, -øːz]. **1.** *s.* (*a*) patient, imbecile, who fouls his, her, bed; (*b*) dotard. **2.** *a.* senile, gaga; in one's second childhood. **3.** *s.f. Cost:* **gâteuse,** full-skirted coat.

gâtine [gɑtin], *s.f. Geog:* gâtine, sterile marshland.

gâtisme [gɑtism], *s.m.* (*a*) incontinence (of urine, etc.); (*b*) senility, senile decay; **tomber dans le g.,** to become senile.

gatte [gat], *s.f.* **1.** *Nau:* manger. **2.** *Tchn:* drip tray, *U.S:* drip pan.

gattilier [gatilje], *s.m. Bot:* agnus castus, chaste tree.

gau [go], *s.m. P:* louse; *pl. gaus.*

gauche [goːʃ], *a.* **1.** (*a*) warped, crooked; out of true; skew (surface, etc.); (*b*) *Tchn:* warping. **2.** awkward, clumsy (person, manner); unhandy (person); bungling (attempt); **g. aux caresses,** awkward at caressing. **3.** left; (*a*) **main g.,** left hand; **rive g.,** left bank (of river); **côté g.,** (i) near side (of a horse); (ii) *Aut:* (*in Eng., etc.*) near side (*in Fr., U.S: etc.*) off side; (*b*) *s.f.* **assis à ma g.,** seated on my left; **mon voisin de g.,** my left-hand neighbour; **le tiroir de g.,** the left-hand drawer; *Nau:* **changer de route sur la g.,** to alter course to port; (*c*) *s.m.* (= *poing gauche*) *Box:* **feinter du g.,** to feint with the left; (*d*) *Pol:* (i) *s.f.* **la Gauche,** the Left; (ii) **(politique) de g.,** leftwing (politics); **homme de g.,** leftist. **4.** *adv. phr.* (*a*) **à g.,** (i) on the left(-hand side), to the

left; **tournez à g.,** turn left; **la première rue à g.,** the first street on the left; **le coin à g. de la feuille,** the left-hand corner of the sheet; **emprunter à droite et à g.,** to borrow right and left, right, left and centre; *F:* **mettre de l'argent à g.,** to put money by; *P:* **passer l'arme à g.,** to go west, to peg out; *Nau:* **à g. (la barre)!** port (the helm)! *A:* starboard the helm! *Ven:* **coup de fusil à g.,** left; (ii) (in a) counter-clockwise (direction); **vis, hélice, à pas de g.,** left-handed screw; left-hand airscrew; (iii) *A:* amiss, wrongly; **prendre l'affaire à g.,** to take a warped view of the matter; (*b*) *F:* **jusqu'à la g.,** (i) to the end, to the last; (ii) right up to the hilt; **ils nous ont eu jusqu'à la g.,** they cheated us right, left and centre.

gauchement [goʃmɑ̃], *adv.* awkwardly, clumsily.

gaucher, -ère [goʃe, -ɛːr]. **1.** *a.* & *s.* left-handed (person). **2.** *s.* left-hander; *Box:* southpaw.

gaucherie [goʃri], *s.f.* **1.** left-handedness. **2.** awkwardness, clumsiness, *gaucherie.* **3. commettre des gaucheries,** to fumble; to be awkward; to make blunders.

gauchi [goʃi], *a.* out of true, out of truth; **meule gauchie,** untrue grindstone.

gauchir [goʃiːr], *v.i.* **1.** *A:* (*a*) to turn aside, to swerve; (*b*) to flinch, give way; to dodge (blow). **2.** *A:* to equivocate, quibble. **3.** *v.i.* & *pr.* (*of wood, etc.*) to warp, wind; to shrink out of truth, out of true; (*of iron*) to buckle. **4.** *v.tr.* to give camber, batter, to (sth.). **5.** *v.tr. Av:* **g. l'aileron,** to warp the aileron; to bank.

gauchisant, -ante [goʃizɑ̃, -ɑ̃ːt], *a.* & *s. Pol:* leftish.

gauchisme [goʃism], *s.m.Pol:* leftism.

gauchissement [goʃismɑ̃], *s.m.* **1.** warping, winding, buckling, getting out of true. **2.** *Av:* warping (of aileron); banking; **commande de g.,** warp(ing) control.

gauchiste [goʃist], *a.* & *s. Pol:* leftist.

gaucho [goʃo], *s.m.* gaucho (of S. America); cowboy.

gaudage [godaːʒ], *s.m.* dyeing with weld.

gaude [goːd], *s.f.* **1.** *Bot:* yellow weed, dyer's weed, weld. **2.** *A:* & *Dial: pl.* **gaudes** = polenta; *U.S:* cornmeal mush.

gauder[1] [gode], *v.tr.* to dye with weld.

gauder[2] **(se), gaudir (se)** [səgodiːr], *v.pr. A.* & *F:* **1.** to enjoy oneself, to have a jolly time. **2. se gaudir de qn,** to laugh at, make fun of, s.o.

gaudissement [godismɑ̃], *s.m.* enjoyment (*esp.* of gross pleasures).

gaudisserie [godisri], *s.f. A.* & *F:* (*a*) broad mirth; (*b*) ribald joke.

gaudisseur, -euse [godisœːr, -øːz], *s. A: F:* joker, wag.

gaudriole [godri(j)ɔl], *s.f. F:* broad joke; light-hearted remark; **dires des gaudrioles,** (i) to tell spicy stories; to crack broad jokes; (ii) to be larking around.

gaudrioler [godri(j)ɔle], *v.i. F:* (*a*) to tell spicy stories; to crack broad jokes; (*b*) to lark around.

gaufrage [gofraːʒ], *s.m.* **1.** embossing (of leather, etc.); goffering, fluting (of linen); corrugating, chequering (of sheet iron); crinkling, puckering (of paper); *Bookb:* blocking (of cover). **2.** embossed work; corrugation(s); goffers, fluting, chequered pattern.

gaufre [goːfr], *s.f.* **1. g. de miel,** honeycomb; **g. de cire,** wax comb-foundation. **2.** *Cu:* waffle, gauffer, gofer; **moule à gaufres,** (i) waffle iron; (ii) *P:* pock-marked face; (iii) *P:* dolt, idiot.

gaufré [gofre], *a.* **cuir g.,** stamped leather.

gaufrer [gofre], *v.tr.* **1.** (*a*) to figure, emboss (leather, velvet, etc.); *Bookb:* to block (cover); (*b*) **g. à la paille,** to goffer, flute, crimp (linen); **fer à g.,** goffering iron; (*c*) to corrugate (iron, paper); to crinkle (paper). **2.** *Tex:* to diaper (cloth).

gaufrette [gofrɛt], *s.f. Cu:* wafer (biscuit).

gaufreur, -euse [gofrœːr, -øːz], *s.* **1.** stamper, gofferer, embosser. **2.** *s.f.* **gaufreuse;** (*a*) *Tchn:* embossing press; (*b*) *Cu:* pastry crimper.

gaufrier [gofri(j)e], *s.m. Cu:* waffle iron.

gaufroir [gofrwaːr], *s.m.* (hand) embossing press.

gaufrure [gofryːr], *s.f.* **1.** stamped design (on leather, etc.). **2.** goffering (on linen). **3. cheveux à gaufrures,** crimped hair.

gaulage [golaːʒ], *s.m.* beating (of fruit trees, of walnut trees).

gaule[1] [goːl], *s.f.* **1.** (long thin) pole, stick; **g. de pavillon,** (small) flagstaff; **g. de pompe,** pump spear. **2.** (one-piece) fishing rod; *F:* **les chevaliers de la g.,** the knights of the rod; the angling fraternity. **3.** (riding) switch; withe.

Gaule[2] *Pr.n.f. A.Geog:* Gaul; **la G. cisalpine,** Cisalpine Gaul.

gaulée [gole], *s.f.* (*a*) beating (of fruit trees); (*b*) fruit brought down at one beating; (*c*) *P:* beating, thrashing (of person).

gauler [gole], *v.tr.* **1.** to beat, thrash (fruit tree, walnut tree). **2.** *P:* to pinch, to nab (s.o.).

gaulette [golɛt], *s.f.* **1.** withe, switch. **2.** thin slat.

gaulis [goli], *s.m.* **1.** plantation (of young trees); sapling wood. **2.** coppice, copse, thicket. **3.** brush(wood). **4.** branches fit for cutting (in brushwood).

gaullisme [golism], *s.m. Pol.Hist:* Gaullism.

gaulliste [golist], *a.* & *s.m. Pol:* Gaullist, follower of de Gaulle.

gaulois, -oise [golwa, -waːz]. **1.** *a.* Gallic, of Gaul; **esprit g.,** (broad) Gallic humour; **contes g.,** spicy stories. **2.** *s.* (*a*) **les G.,** the Gauls; (*b*) **le g.,** (the) Gallic (tongue). **3.** *s.f. R.t.m:* **gauloise,** a popular brand of cigarette.

gauloiserie [golwazri], *s.f.* broad joke; spicy story.

gault [go], *s.m. Geol:* gault.

gaulthérie [goteri], *s.f. Bot:* gaultheria; **g. du Canada,** partridge berry, checker berry, wintergreen.

gaulthériline [goterilin], *s.f.* gaultheria oil.

gaupe [goːp], *P: A:* slut; trollop.

gaur [goːr], *s.m. Z:* gaur.

gauss [goːs], *s.m. El.Meas:* gauss.

gausser (se) [səgose], *v.pr.* **se g. de qn,** to laugh at, make fun of, s.o.; to sneer at s.o.

gausserie [gosri], *s.f. F:* mockery; sneering; making fun of s.o.

gausseur, -euse [gosœːr, -øːz]. **1.** *s.* mocker; sneerer. **2.** *a.* mocking, sneering.

gaussien, -ienne [goːsjɛ̃, -jɛn], *a. Mth:* Gaussian.

gaussmètre [gosmɛtr], *s.m.* gaussmeter.

Gautier [gotje], *Pr.n.m.* Walter.

Gauvain [govɛ̃], *Pr.n.m.* Gawain, Gavin; Ywain.

gavache [gavaʃ], *s.m. Dial:* (*in Languedoc*) dirty skunk, miserable worm of a man.

gavage [gavaːʒ], *s.m.* (*a*) cramming (of poultry); (*b*) *Med:* forcible feeding (*esp.* of babies); (*c*) *F:* gorging, stuffing.

gave[1] [gaːv], *s.f. F:* crop (of birds).

gave[2], *s.m. Geog:* (mountain) torrent (in the Pyrenees).

gavée [gave], *s.f.* charge of food (in cramming); *P:* **en avoir une g.,** (i) to be stuffed, crammed (with food); (ii) to be fed up; to have had a bellyful.

gaver [gave], *v.tr.* to cram (poultry); *Med:* to feed (s.o.) forcibly; *F:* **se g. de nourriture,** to gorge; to stuff oneself with food; **g. un élève,** to cram a pupil (for an examination).

gaveur, -euse [gavœːr, -øːz]. **1.** *s.* (*pers.*) crammer (of poultry). **2.** *s.f.* **gaveuse;** (*a*) (poultry) crammer, cramming apparatus; (*b*) *Av:* booster pump.

gavial, -als [gavjal], *s.m. Rept:* gavial, gharial.

gavian [gavjɑ̃], **gavion**[1] [gavjɔ̃], *s.m. Orn: F:* seagull.

gaviidés [gaviide], *s.m.pl. Orn:* Colymbidae, the divers.

gavion[2] [gavjɔ̃], **gaviot** [gavjo], *s.m. A: P:* throat; **j'en ai jusqu'au g.,** I'm stuffed full.

gavot, -ote [gavo, -ɔt], *a.* & *s. Geog:* (native, inhabitant) of Gap, of the Gap region.

gavotte [gavɔt], *s.f. Danc: Mus:* gavotte.

gavroche [gavrɔʃ], *s.m. A:* street arab (of Paris), ragamuffin (*from the character in V. Hugo's* **Les Misérables**).

gayal, -als [gajal], *s.m. Z:* gayal.

gay-lussite [gelysit], *s.f. Miner:* gaylussite.

gaz [gɑːz], *s.m.* gas; (*a*) *Ch:* **g. naturel,** natural gas; **gisement de g. (naturel),** gas field; **g. des marais,** marsh gas; **g. dégénéré, non dégénéré,** degenerate, non-degenerate, gas; **g. noble,** noble gas; **g. parfait,** ideal gas; **g. délétère,** deleterious gas; **g. inerte,** inert gas; **g. inflammable,** (in)flammable gas; **g. occlus,** occluded gas; **g. organique,** organic gas; **g. rare,** rare gas; **g. raréfié,** rarefied gas; **g. étouffant, g. méphitique,** choke damp; **g. toxique,** foul, poisonous, gas; **dégagement de g.,** emission of gas; *Elcs:* **g. électronique,** electron gas; *Atom.Ph:* **g. radioactif,** radioactive gas; (*b*) *Ind:* **g. combustible,** fuel gas; **g. de combustion, g. de carneau,** flue gas; **g. de pétrole,** oil gas, petroleum gas; **g. de four à coke,** coke-oven gas; **g. de haut fourneau,** blast-furnace gas; **g. de gazogène, g. pauvre,** producer gas; **g. à l'eau,** water gas; **g. d'échappement (de haut fourneau, etc.),** exhaust gas, escape gas; burnt gas; **g. perdus,** waste gases; **g. résiduels,** residual gases; **bouteille à g., tube de g. comprimé,** gas cylinder; **épurateur de g.,** gas cleaner; (*c*) (i) **g. d'éclairage,** lighting gas, illuminating gas; coal gas; **g. de ville,** town gas; **machine fonctionnant au g. de de ville,** machine running on town gas; **faire mettre, poser, le g.,** to have the gas laid on; **les conduites de g. sont posées,** *F:* **le g. est mis, est posé,** the gas is laid on; **faire la cuisine au g.,** to cook by gas; **ouvrir, fermer, le g.,** to turn on, turn off, the gas; **baisser, lever, le g.,** to turn down, turn up, the gas; **cuisinière à g.,** gas cooker; **fourneau à g.,** gas stove; **réchaud à g.,** gas ring; *O:* **lustre à g.,** gasolier; *St.Exch:* **valeurs de g.,** gas stocks; (ii) gas company; **employé du g.,** gas-board employee; (iii) *P:* **allumer son g.,** to wake up, to (sit up and) take notice; **éteindre son g.,** to die, to snuff it; (*d*) *Dent:* **g. hilarant, g. nitreux,** laughing gas; (*e*) *Mil:* **g. de combat,** war gas; **guerre des g.,** gas warfare; **g. asphyxiant, g. toxique,** asphyxiating gas; *F:* poison gas; **g. mortel,** lethal gas; **g. persistant,** persistent gas; **g. fugace,** non-persistent gas; **g. insidieux,** gas with delayed effect; **g. irritant, g. toxique spécialisé,** irritant gas; **g. lacrymogène,** tear gas; **g sternutatoire,** sneeze gas, nose-irritant gas; **g. suffocant,** choking gas, lung-irritant gas; **g. vésicant,** blister gas; **attaque par g.,** gas attack; **alerte aux g.,** gas alarm; **fin d'alerte (aux g.),** gas clear; **consignes relatives aux g.,** gas discipline; **lâcher, lancer, des g. (asphyxiants),** to release gas; **mode de lancement de g.,** method of releasing gas; **épandage de g.,** gas spraying; **obus à g.,** gas shell; **défense contre les g.,** defence against gas; **matériel, équipement, de protection contre les g.,** gas equipment; **rideau de protection contre les g.,** gas curtain; **détecteur de g.,** gas detector; **chambre à g.,** gas-chamber; *Mil:* **passage dans la chambre à g.,** gas-chamber exercise, test; (*f*) *I.C.E:* **g. tonnant,** explosive mixture; **ouvrir, mettre, les g.,** to open the throttle; *F:* to step on the gas; **à pleins g.,** with the throttle full open; flat out; **g. d'échappement,** exhaust fumes; *F:* **il y a de l'eau dans le g.,** there's a snag in this; (*g*) *Med:* **avoir des g.,** to suffer from flatulence; *F:* from wind; **lâcher un g.,** to break wind.

gazage [gɑzaːʒ], *s.m.* (action of) gassing (men); *Tex:* (action of) gassing (linen).

gaze [gɑːz], *s.f.* (*a*) (i) gauze; (ii) butter muslin; **g. métallique,** wire gauze; *Med:* **g. oxygénée,** antiseptic gauze, sterilized gauze; (*b*) thin veil; *A:* **raconter les choses sans g.,** to tell the story without any reticence.

gazé[1] [gɑze], *s.m.,* **gazée** [gɑze], *s.f. Ent: F:* black-veined white (butterfly).

gazé[2], **-ée.** **1.** *a.* & *s.* gassed (soldier, troops). **2.** *a. Tex:* **fil g.,** gassed thread.

gazéifiable [gɑzeifjabl], *a.* gasifiable, volatile.

gazéificateur [gɑzeifikatœːr], *s.m.* **1.** aerator (for water, etc.). **2.** flare lamp.

gazéification [gɑzeifikasjɔ̃], *s.f.* **1.** *Ch:* gasification; **g. du charbon,** coal distillation. **2.** aeration (of mineral waters).

gazéifier [gɑzeifje], *v.tr.* (*pr.sub.* & *p.d.* **n. gazéifions, v. gazéifiiez**) **1.** *Ch:* to gasify, volatilize; to reduce (sth.) to the gaseous state. **2.** to aerate (mineral waters, wine).

se gazéifier, to gasify.

gazéiforme [gɑzeifɔrm], *a.* gasiform.

gazelle [gazɛl], *s.f. Z:* gazelle; **g. africaine, dorcas,** dorcas; **g. du Tibet,** goa, Tibetan gazelle.

gazelle-girafe [gazɛlʒiraf], *s.f. Z:* gerenuk; long-necked antelope; *pl. gazelles-girafes.*

gazer[1] [gɑze], *v.tr.* (*a*) to cover with gauze; (*b*) *A:* to draw a veil over (sth.); to gloss over (details, etc.).

gazer[2]. **1.** *v.tr.* (*a*) to gas (troops); (*b*) *Tex:* to gas (linen). **2.** *v.i. F:* (*a*) to move at top speed; to step on the gas; (*b*) **ça gaze!** everything's O.K.! we're doing fine! **comment ça va?—ça gaze!** how's things?—Fine! **ça gaze?** all right? everything O.K.? **j'ai bien gazé à l'examen,** everything went like a house on fire at the exam.

gazetier [gaz(ə)tje], *s.m. A:* **1.** gazette-writer, journalist. **2.** *F:* newsmonger.

gazette [gazɛt], *s.f.* gazette, news sheet; **la G. des tribunaux,** the Police Gazette; *F:* **lire la g.,** (i) to watch other people eating; (ii) (*of horse*) to be off its feed; *F:* **vieille g.,** stale news; *F:* (*of pers.*) **c'est une vraie g.,** he (she) can always tell you the latest news.

gazeur [gɑzœːr], *s.m. Tex:* gasser.

gazeux, -euse [gɑzø, -øːz], *a.* **1.** gaseous; *El:* **lampe à atmosphère gazeuse,** gas-filled lamp; *Ph: Ch:* **échanges gazeux,** gaseous exchanges. **2.** aerated (water, etc.); fizzy (drink); **limonade gazeuse,** sparkling lemonade.

gazier[1], **-ière** [gɑzje, -jɛːr], *s.* worker in gauze.

gazier[2], **-ière.** **1.** *a.* **l'industrie gazière,** the gas industry. **2.** *s.m.* (*a*) employee at gas works; (*b*) gas fitter; (*c*) *P:* geezer, bloke.

gazifère [gazifɛːr], a. & s.m. gas-making (apparatus).

gazillon [gazijɔ̃], s.m. Tex: light gauze.

gazinière [gazinjɛːr], s.f. F: gas cooker.

gazoduc [gazɔdyk], s.m. gas pipeline.

gazogène [gazɔʒɛn]. 1. a. (a) gas-producing; (b) aerating. 2. s.m. (a) gas producer, gas generator; g. à vent, g. soufflé, pressure gas producer; g. à acétylène, acetylene generator; gaz de g., producer gas; (b) aerator (of mineral water, etc.).

gaz-oil [gazwal, gazɔjl], s.m. = GAS-OIL.

gazoline [gazɔlin], s.f. gasolene, gasoline.

gazomètre [gazɔmɛtr̥], s.m. gasometer, gas holder.

gazométrie [gazɔmetri], s.f. gasometry.

gazométrique [gazɔmetrik], a. gasometric.

gazon [gazɔ̃], s.m. 1. (a) (fine, short) grass; turf, sward; (b) lawn; P.N: défense de marcher sur le g., keep off the grass; danser sur le g., to dance on the lawn, on the grass; couper, tondre, le g., to cut the grass, the lawn; P: se faire tondre le g., to get one's hair cut; P: se ratisser le g., to comb one's hair; P: ne pas avoir de g. sur la prairie, sur la terrasse, to be as bald as a coot. 2. turf, sod; Golf: touffe de g., divot; lever des gazons, to cut turf; Hort: terre de g., loam. 3. Bot: g. d'Olympe, (mountain) thrift; g. mousse, mossy saxifrage.

gazonnage [gazɔnaːʒ], s.m., **gazonnement** [gazɔnmɑ̃], s.m. 1. turfing, sodding. 2. edging with turf.

gazonnant [gazɔnɑ̃], a. Bot: c(a)espitose, growing in tufts.

gazonné, -ée [gazɔne]. 1. a. grass-covered, turfed. 2. s.f. Hort: gazonnée, square of turf.

gazonner [gazɔne]. 1. v.tr. to cover with turf, to turf. 2. v.i. (of land) to become covered with grass.

gazonneux,-euse [gazɔnø, -øːz], a. turfy, covered with turf; grassy.

gazoscope [gazɔskɔp], s.m. Min: gasocope.

gazouillant [gazujɑ̃], a. warbling, chirping, twittering (bird); le ruisseau g., the babbling, purling, brook.

gazouillement [gazujmɑ̃], s.m. twittering, warbling, chirping (of birds); babbling, murmuring (of running water); prattle, prattling (of children).

gazouiller [gazuje], v.i. 1. (of bird) to twitter, warble, chirp; (of water) to babble, murmur, purl; (of child) to prattle; with cogn. acc. la source gazouille un doux murmure, the spring babbles gently on; enfant qui gazouille sa prière, child lisping his prayer. 2. P: (as if from gaz) to stink, to hum.

gazouilleur, -euse [gazujœːr, -øːz], a. & s. warbling, twittering (bird); babbling (stream); prattling (child).

gazouillis [gazuji], s.m. twittering (of birds); murmuring (of running water).

Gê [ʒe], Pr.n.f. Gr.Myth: Gaea.

geai [ʒɛ], s.m. Orn: g. (des chênes), jay; g. bleu, blue jay; g. de montagne, nuthatch; le g. paré des plumes du paon, the jackdaw in borrowed feathers.

géant, -ante [ʒeɑ̃, -ɑ̃ːt]. 1. s. (a) giant, giantess; Gym: pas de g., giant's stride; avancer à pas de g., to make great strides forward; to make spectacular progress; Geog: la Chaussée des Géants, the Giant's Causeway; (b) les géants de l'art, the great masters; F: les géants du football, the football giants, the great stars of football; F: les géants de la route, the competitors in the Tour de France. 2. a. gigantic; arbre g., giant tree; Com: carton g., giant (size) packet; T.V: écran g., large screen.

géanticlinal, -aux [ʒeɑ̃tiklinal, -o], Geol: 1. a. geanticlinal. 2. s.m. geanticline.

géantisme [ʒeɑ̃tism], s.m. Med: gigantism, giantism.

géaster, géastre [ʒeaster, ʒeastr̥], s.m. Fung: geaster, geastrum.

gecko [ʒeko], s.m. Rept: gecko; g. des murailles, des murs, wall, Moorish, gecko; g. diurne de Madagascar, Madagascar green gecko; g. des rochers, rock gecko; g. à queue épineuse, (Australian) spiny-tailed gecko; gekko g., tokay; g. verruqueux, g. à doigts en disques, Turkish gecko.

geckonidés [ʒekɔnide], s.m.pl. Rept: Geckonidae, Gekkonidae.

gédanite [ʒedanit], s.f. Miner: gedanite.

Gédéon [ʒedeɔ̃], Pr.n.m. B.Hist: Gideon.

gédinnien [ʒedinjɛ̃], a. & s.m. Geol: Gedinnian.

gédrite [ʒedrit], s.f. Miner: gedrite.

géhenne [ʒeɛn], s.f. (a) Gehenna, Hell; (b) A: torture (of prisoners); (c) sa vie est une g., his life is a hell upon earth; pendant deux jours je ne sortis pas de cette g., for two days I did not leave that place of torture.

géhenner [ʒeɛne], v.tr. A: to torture.

gehlénite [ʒəlenit], s.f. Miner: gehlenite.

Geiger-Müller [ʒeʒɛrmylɛːr], Pr.n. Atom.Ph: compteur de G.(-M.), Geiger(-Müller) counter.

geignant [ʒɛɲɑ̃], a. whimpering, whining, fretful.

geignard, -arde [ʒɛɲaːr, -ard], F: 1. a. fretful, (given to) whining; grumbling, peevish. 2. s. whiner, grizzler.

geignement [ʒɛɲmɑ̃], s.m. 1. whining, whimpering, grumbling. 2. whine, whimper; (feeble) groan.

geigneur, -euse [ʒɛɲœːr, -øːz], s. (habitual) whiner, (eternal) grizzler.

geikielite [ʒekjelit], s.f. Miner: geikielite.

geindre[1] [ʒɛ̃ːdr̥], v.i. (pr.p. geignant; p.p. geint; pr.ind. je geins, il geint, n. geignons, ils geignent; p.d. je geignais; p.h. je geignis; fu. je geindrai) to whine, whimper; to fret, complain; to grizzle.

geindre[2], s.m. baker's assistant.

géique [ʒeik], a. Ch: Agr: geic (acid).

geisha [gaiʃa, gɛʃa], s.f. geisha.

gel [ʒɛl], s.m. 1. frost, freezing. 2. Ch: gel; colloid.

gélatine [ʒelatin], s.f. gelatin(e); Exp: g. détonante, g. explosive, blasting gelatine, gum dynamite.

gélatiné [ʒelatine], a. gelatinized.

gélatiner [ʒelatine], v.tr. to gelatinize, to coat with gelatine.

gélatineux, -euse [ʒelatinø, -øːz], a. gelatinous.

gélatinifier [ʒelatinifje], v.tr. to gelatinate, to gelatinize.

gélatiniforme [ʒelatinifɔrm], a. gelatiniform, gelatinoid.

gélatinisant [ʒelatinizɑ̃], s.m. 1. Exp: gelatinizing agent. 2. Tchn: plasticizer.

gélatinisation [ʒelatinizasjɔ̃], s.f. gelatinization.

gélatiniser [ʒelatinize], v.tr. 1. to gelatinize (dynamite). 2. to coat (glass plate, etc.) with gelatine.

gélatino-bromure [ʒelatinobrɔmyːr], s.m. Ch: Phot: gelatino-bromide; Phot: papier au g.-b., bromide paper.

gélatino-chlorure [ʒelatinoklɔryːr], s.m. Ch: Phot: gelatino-chloride; papier au g.-c., gaslight paper.

gélation [ʒelasjɔ̃], s.f. gelation.

gelé [ʒ(ə)le], a. 1. frozen; F: je suis absolument g., I'm absolutely frozen. 2. (a) frost-bitten (nose, toe); (b) (plant, fruit) nipped by the frost; frost-nipped; (c) cold, indifferent; public g., unreceptive audience. 3. Fin: dettes gelées, frozen debts; capitaux gelés, frozen capital. 4. P: (a) drunk; P: canned; (b) surprised, bowled over; (c) (= no longer possible) c'est g.! we've had it!

géléchie [ʒeleʃi], s.f. Ent: gelechid.

géléchiidés [ʒeleʃiide], s.m.pl. Ent: Gelechiidae.

gelée [ʒ(ə)le], s.f. 1. frost; forte g., hard frost; g. blanche, hoar frost, hoar; white frost; rime; temps à la g., frosty weather; brûlé par la g., frost-nipped. 2. (a) Cu: jelly; g. de veau, de poulet, veal, chicken, jelly; g. de groseilles, red currant jelly; (b) Ap: g. royale, royal jelly; (c) Toil: g. pour les ongles, nail paste.

geler [ʒ(ə)le], v. (je gèle, n. gelons; je gèlerai) 1. v.tr. to convert into ice; to freeze; froid qui gèle les conduites d'eau, cold that freezes the water pipes. 2. v.i. (a) to become frozen; to freeze; l'étang a gelé d'un bout à l'autre, the pond has, is, frozen over; les vignes vont g., the vines will be nipped (by the frost); on gèle dans cette salle, this room is like an ice-house, is icy cold; (b) impers. il gèle dur, à pierre fendre, it is freezing hard; il a gelé blanc cette nuit, there was a white frost last night; il a gelé à dix degrés, there were ten degrees of frost.

se geler. 1. to freeze, solidify. 2. je me suis gelé à vous attendre, I've got frozen waiting for you.

geleur [ʒəlœːr], s.m. used in Saint Marc est un grand g. de vignes, the vines are often nipped by the frost on Saint Mark's day.

gélidiales [ʒelidjal], s.f.pl. Algae: Gelidiales.

gélidium [ʒelidjɔm], s.m. Algae: gelidium.

gélif, -ive [ʒelif, -iːv], a. 1. frost-cleft, frost-riven (tree, stone). 2. huile gélive, oil that freezes easily.

gélifiant [ʒelifjɑ̃], a. Ch: gelling; pouvoir g., gelling power.

gélification [ʒelifikasjɔ̃], s.f. 1. Bot: gelification. 2. Ch: gelling, gelation.

gélifier (se) [səʒelifje], v.pr. Ch: to gel.

gélignite [ʒeliɲit], s.f. Exp: gelignite.

géline [ʒelin], s.f. 1. A: hen. 2. Ich: megrim.

gelinotte [ʒ(ə)linɔt], s.f. 1. Orn: g. (des bois), hazel grouse; g. des prairies, pinnated grouse (of N. America), prairie chicken, prairie grouse; g. des Pyrénées, pintail, pintailed sand grouse. 2. fattened pullet.

géliturbation [ʒelityrbasjɔ̃], s.f. Geog: cryoturbation.

gélivation [ʒelivasjɔ̃], s.f. Geog: congelifraction, frost weathering (of rocks).

gélivité [ʒelivite], s.f. gelivity, liability to crack (through frost).

gélivure [ʒelivyːr], s.f. frost crack, cleft (in stone, earth); heart shake (in wood).

Gélon [ʒelɔ̃], Pr.n.m. Gr.Hist: Gelo.

gélose [ʒeloːz], s.f. Ch: gelose; agar-agar.

gélosique [ʒelɔzik], a. gelosic; charbon gélosique, boghead coal.

gélule [ʒelyl], s.f. Pharm: capsule.

gelure [ʒəlyːr], s.f. Med: frostbite.

gémara (la) [laʒemara], s.f. Rel.H: the Gemara.

gémarique [ʒemarik], a. Gemaric.

gématrie [ʒematri], s.f. gematria.

gémeau, -eaux, -elle [ʒemo, -ɛl], s. 1. A: twin. 2. s.m.pl. Astr: les Gémeaux, Gemini, the Twins.

gémellaire [ʒemɛlɛːr], a. gemellary, twin; grossesse g., twin pregnancy.

gémellipare [ʒemɛlipaːr], a. Med: gemelliparous.

gémination [ʒeminasjɔ̃], s.f. 1. Biol: Dent: gemination. 2. Sch: g. de classes, grouping, combination, of forms. 3. Ling: gemination (of vowel, consonant, syllable).

géminé [ʒemine], a. 1. Biol: geminate, twin (leaves, etc.); Ch: geminate; Arch: colonnes géminées, twin columns; fenêtres géminées, gemel windows. 2. Sch: (a) classes géminées, forms taught together; (b) écoles géminées, mixed, co-educational, schools. 3. Ling: consonnes, voyelles, géminées, geminated, doubled, consonants, vowels; geminates.

géminer [ʒemine], v.tr. to geminate.

gémir [ʒemiːr], v.i. to groan, moan, wail; g. de douleur, to groan with pain; je gémissais de les voir (faire cela), I could have wept to see them (doing that); g. sous le joug de la tyrannie, to groan under the yoke of tyranny; le vent gémit dans la forêt, the wind moans through the forest; g. de ses péchés, to bewail one's sins; g. sur son sort, to bemoan one's fate; la charrette gémit sous le fardeau, the cart is groaning under the load; notre voiture montait la côte en gémissant, our carriage creaked its way up the hill.

gémissant [ʒemisɑ̃], a. moaning, wailing; essieu g., creaking axle.

gémissement [ʒemismɑ̃], s.m. groan(ing), moan(ing); wail(ing); pousser un profond g., to give, utter, a deep groan; le g. de la forêt, the moaning of the forest.

gémisseur, -euse [ʒemisœːr, -øːz]. 1. a. wailing, moaning. 2. s. wailer, moaner.

gemmage [ʒɛm(m)aːʒ], s.m. tapping (of trees for resin).

gemmail, -aux [ʒɛm(m)aːj, -o], s.m. (non-leaded) stained glass window.

gemmation [ʒɛm(m)asjɔ̃], s.f. Biol. gemmation.

gemme [ʒɛm], s.f. 1. Miner: (a) gem; precious stone; (b) a. gemmeous; pierre g., gem stone; sel g., rock salt. 2. Arb: pine resin. 3. Biol: gemma. 4. Bot: (a) (leaf) bud; (b) offset bulb.

gemmé [ʒɛm(m)e], a. 1. gemmed, jewelled. 2. Arb: tapped (for resin).

gemmer [ʒɛm(m)e]. 1. v.i. (of trees) to bud, to gemmate. 2. v.tr. to tap (trees for resin).

gemmeur [ʒɛm(m)œːr], s.m. Arb: tapper.

gemmifère [ʒɛm(m)ifɛːr], a. Bot: Miner: gemmiferous; gravier g., diamond-bearing gravel.

gemmiflore [ʒɛm(m)iflɔːr], a. Bot: gemmiflorate.

gemmiforme [ʒɛm(m)ifɔrm], a. Bot: gemmiform, bud-shaped.

gemmipare [ʒɛm(m)ipaːr], a. Biol: gemmiparous.

gemmiparité [ʒɛm(m)iparite], s.f. Biol: gemmiparous reproduction.

gemmiste [ʒɛm(m)ist], s.m. artist who makes (non-leaded) stained glass windows.

gemmologie [ʒɛm(m)ɔlɔʒi], s.f. gemmology.

gemmologiste [ʒɛm(m)ɔlɔʒist], s.m. gemmologist.

gemmule [ʒɛm(m)yl], s.f. Bot: gemmule.

gémonies (les) [leʒemɔni], s.f.pl. Rom.Ant: the Gemonies; Lit: traîner, vouer, qn aux g., to hold s.o. up to public obloquy.

gempylidés [ʒɑ̃pilide], s.m.pl. Ich: Gempylidae, the snake mackerels.

gemsbok [gɑ̃sbɔk], s.m. Z: gemsbok.

génal, -aux [ʒenal, -o], a. Anat: genal, cheek (muscle, etc.).

gênant [ʒɛnɑ̃], a. 1. in the way; salon rempli de meubles gênants, drawing room cluttered up with furniture, drawing room in which you can't move for furniture; les jupes longues sont gênantes, long skirts are a nuisance, are awkward, get in one's way. 2. embarrassing, awkward (situation, silence); (of pers.) annoying.

génappe [ʒenap], s.m. Tex: genappe.

gencive [ʒɑ̃siːv], s.f. (a) Anat: gum; gencives enflées, swollen gums; abcès à la g., gumboil; (b) pl. P: jaw(s); un coup dans les gencives, a punch on the jaw.

gendarme [ʒɑ̃darm], s.m. 1. (a) Hist: (i) cavalryman; (ii) (extended meaning) soldier, man at arms; (b) gendarme, member of the state police force, approx. = police constable; gendarmes à cheval = mounted police; gendarmes motocyclistes, motorcycle police; être arrêté par les gendarmes, to be arrested, taken into custody (by the police); (of children) jouer aux gendarmes et aux voleurs, to play at cops and robbers; F: dormir en g., to sleep with one eye open; (c) F: (of woman) martinet; faire le g., to boss people about; (d) chapeau de g., (i) A.Cost: gendarme's two-pointed hat; (ii) F: paper hat. 2. flaw (in jewel). 3. Geol: rock pinnacle, gendarme. 4. Fung: g. noir, boletus aereus. 5. F: spark (from crackling fire). 6. Cu: F: (a) red herring; (b) (Swiss) flat, dry sausage.

gendarmer (se) [səʒɑ̃darme], v.pr. to be up in arms (against s.o., a proposal, etc.); il n'y a pas de quoi se g., there's nothing to get worked up about.

gendarmerie [ʒɑ̃darməri], s.f. 1. (a) (in Fr.) the state police force; (b) la G. royale du Canada, the Royal Canadian Mounted Police. 2. barracks, headquarters (of the gendarmes).

gendarmeux, -euse [ʒɑ̃darmø, -øːz], a. flawy (diamond, etc.).

gendelettre [ʒɑ̃dlɛtr̥], s.m. F: Iron: man of letters.

gendre [ʒɑ̃ːdr̥], s.m. son-in-law.

gène [ʒɛn], s.m. Biol: gene; g. dominant, récessif, dominant, recessive, gene.

gêne [ʒɛ(ː)n], s.f. 1. A: (physical or moral) torture; mettre qn à la g., to torture s.o.; to put s.o. on the rack; se mettre l'esprit à la g., to rack one's brains. 2. discomfort, constraint, embarrassment; avoir de la g. dans la respiration, to have difficulty in breathing; ressentir de la g. en la présence de qn, to feel ill at ease in s.o.'s presence; vous ne me causerez aucune g., you won't inconvenience me in the least; sans g., unconstrained, unconventional, free and easy; il est sans g.! he's a cool customer! he doesn't stand on ceremony! 3. want, financial embarrassment, pressure; être dans la g., to be in financial difficulties; to be badly off, hard up; ils sont dans une grande g., they can hardly keep body and soul together; F: they are on their beam ends.

gêné [ʒene], a. 1. embarrassed, ill at ease; se sentir g., to feel awkward; sourire g., embarrassed smile; il n'est pas g., he's never embarrassed; he's got no inhibitions; he doesn't mind what he does; silence g., awkward silence, uneasy silence. 2. in financial difficulties; hard up.

généalogie [ʒenealɔʒi], s.f. 1. genealogy, pedigree, descent; pedigree (of cattle, horses, etc.); se vanter d'une longue g., to boast a long descent, an ancient lineage. 2. (science of) genealogy.

généalogique [ʒenealɔʒik], a. genealogical; arbre g., family tree, genealogical tree; pedigree; Breed: livre g., stud book (of horses); herd book (of cattle).

généalogiquement [ʒenealɔʒikmɑ̃], adv. genealogically.

généalogiste [ʒenealɔʒist], s.m. & f. genealogist.

génécologie [ʒenekɔlɔʒi], s.f. Biol: genecology.

génépi [ʒenepi], s.m. Bot: (in Alps) (a) wormwood; (b) g. (musqué), musk milfoil, genepi.

gêner [ʒene], v.tr. 1. (a) A: to torture; (b) to constrict, cramp; (of garment) to pull, drag, pinch; manteau qui gêne aux entournures, coat too tight under the arms; mes souliers me gênent, my shoes pinch, are too tight; on est gêné ici, we're cramped here; we're too crowded here. 2. to hinder, obstruct, impede; to be in (s.o.'s) way; to interfere with (an activity); g. la navigation, to obstruct, interfere with, navigation; g. la circulation, to hold up the traffic; g. la circulation du sang, to impede the circulation of the blood; g. la vue, to obstruct, block, the view; cette valise vous gêne-t-elle? is this bag in your way? être gêné par la myopie, to be handicapped by short sight; être gêné pour respirer, pour exprimer ses pensées, to have difficulty in breathing, in expressing one's ideas. 3. to inconvenience, embarrass; cela vous gênerait-il de me prêter cent francs? would it be a nuisance for you to lend me 100 francs? could you manage to lend me 100 francs? cela vous gênerait-il que je revienne demain? I hope it won't disturb, bother, you, be awkward for you, put you out, if I come back tomorrow; le froid ne me gêne pas, I don't mind the cold; la fumée (de tabac) vous gêne-t-elle? do you mind my smoking? does my smoking upset, disturb, you? cette perte d'argent nous a gênés, losing this money has made things difficult for us; cela me gênerait de le rencontrer, it would be awkward for me to meet him.

se gêner. 1. to put oneself under some restraint; to put oneself out; je ne me suis pas gêné pour le lui dire, I didn't hesitate to tell him so; I made no bones about telling him so; il ne se gêne pas avec nous, he doesn't stand on ceremony with us, he makes himself at home; F: faut pas se g., no need to ask; Iron: il ne se gêne pas! he's not backward in coming forward! Iron: ne vous gênez pas! that's right! make yourself at home! 2. to put oneself to inconvenience; (a) en vous gênant un peu vous pourrez tous vous asseoir, by squeezing up a little you will all be able to sit down; mais oui, je puis le faire sans me g., but of course I can do it without any trouble; it's no trouble for me to do it; (b) il s'est gêné pour leur prêter l'argent, he went short to lend them the money; nous avons dû nous g. un peu, we had to economize, draw in our horns, a bit.

général, -ale, -aux [ʒeneral, -o]. 1. a. (a) general (rule, ideas, appearance, etc.); le consentement g., common consent; l'opinion générale, the prevailing, general, opinion; affirmation par trop générale, sweeping statement; en règle générale, as a general rule; d'une façon générale, generally speaking, broadly speaking; inspecteur g., inspector general; Ecc: concile g., general council; Th: répétition générale, dress rehearsal; quartier g., headquarters; Physiol: circulation générale, systemic circulation; (Fr.Hist: & Channel Is.) états généraux, states general; Pol.Ec: commerce g., total, global, trade (including entrepôt trade); (b) officier g., (i) Mil: etc: general officer; (ii) Navy: flag officer; adv.phr. en g., in general, generally, taken all round; (i) inclusively, universally; en g. et en particulier, in general and in particular; (ii) as a rule, generally speaking, roughly speaking, in the main, for the most part; l'Anglais en g. s'imagine que . . ., the average Englishman imagines that . . . 2. s.m. (a) the general; procéder du g. au particulier, to go from the general to the particular; conclure du particulier au g., to make (rash) generalizations; (b) (i) Mil: general; g. de brigade, brigadier; g. de division, major general; g. de corps d'armée, lieutenant general; g. d'armée, general; (ii) Mil.Av: g. de brigade aérienne, air commodore; g. de division aérienne, air vice-marshal; g. de corps d'armée aérienne, air marshal; g. d'armée aérienne, air chief marshal; (c) Ecc: general (of Jesuits, Dominicans). 3. s.f. générale; (a) madame la générale, the general's wife; (b) Ecc: notre abbesse est générale de tout l'ordre, our abbess is general of the order; (c) alarm call; battre la générale, to call to arms; to sound the alarm; Navy: to beat for action; (d) Th: la générale, dress rehearsal.

généralat [ʒenerala], s.m. Mil: Ecc: 1. rank of general. 2. (duration of) generalship. 3. Mil: A: area under the command of a general.

généralement [ʒeneralmɑ̃], adv. generally; homme g. estimé, man generally esteemed; g. parlant, generally speaking, on the whole, broadly speaking; voilà l'idée qu'on se fait g. de votre fortune, this is the sort of notion people have of your fortune.

généralisable [ʒeneralizabl̥], a. generalizable.

généralisant [ʒeneralizɑ̃], a. generalizing.

généralisateur, -trice [ʒeneralizatœːr, -tris]. 1. a. generalizing (mind, method). 2. s. generalizer.

généralisation [ʒeneralizasjɔ̃], s.f. 1. generalizing. 2. generalization.

généraliser [ʒeneralize], v.tr. to generalize.

se généraliser, to become general, to come into general use; (of habit, etc.) to spread.

généralissime [ʒeneralisim], s.m. generalissimo, commander-in-chief.

généraliste [ʒeneralist], s. Med: general practitioner.

généralité [ʒeneralite], s.f. generality. 1. la g. des hommes, the generality of men; dans la g. des cas . . ., in most cases . . . 2. s'en tenir à des généralités, to confine oneself to generalities. 3. Hist: treasury subdivision of old France.

générateur, -trice [ʒeneratœːr, -tris]. 1. a. generating (machine, line, function); generative (force, organ); productive (de, of); ambiance génératrice de crime, environment that breeds crime; Mus: son g., fundamental tone, generator (of chord, vibrating, body, etc.); El.E: station, usine, génératrice, generating station, generating plant; power house; Mch: chaudière génératrice, s.m. générateur, steam boiler. 2. s.m. generator; (a) Ch: Ind: g. d'acétylène, d'oxygène, acetylene generator, oxygen generator; g. de, à, gaz, gas generator, gas producer; gasifier; Ph: etc: g. de bruit(s), noise generator; g. d'ultra-sons, ultrasonic generator; Atom.Ph: g. de neutrons, de protons, neutron generator, proton generator; Mil: etc: g. de fumée, g. fumigène, smoke generator; Mch: g. (de vapeur), (steam) boiler, steam generator; (b) El: g. d'électricité, electric generator; g. électrostatique, electrostatic generator; g. à induction, induction generator; Elcs: g. d'impulsions, pulse generator; g. d'impulsions codées, pulse coder; g. de signaux, Elcs: signal(ling) generator; T.V: colour coder. 3. s.f. génératrice, (a) generator, generating set, de courant, current generator; El: génératrice dynamo; génératrice auxiliaire, booster generator; génératrice polymorphique, multiple-current generator; génératrice à main, hand-driven generator; Av: génératrice mue par le vent, wind-driven generator; génératrice, couplée au, mue par le, moteur, engine-driven generator; Rail: génératrice couplée aux essieux, axle generator; Atom.Ph: génétratrice nucléaire, nuclear-power reactor; (b) Mth: génératrice, generating line (of surface); generatrix.

génératif, -ive [ʒeneratif, -iːv], a. generative.

génération [ʒenerasjɔ̃], s.f. 1. (act of) generation, generating; la g. des métaux, the formation of metals; la g. d'une idée, the originating of an idea; g. de la vapeur, generation, production, of steam; Nat.Hist: g. spontanée, spontaneous generation. 2. (a) la g. de Noé, the generations, descendants, of Noah; descendant à la sixième g., descendant six generations removed; (b) la g. actuelle, the present generation, the present age; la jeune g., the younger generation; la g. montante, qui monte, the rising generation; les générations futures, future generations; de g. en g., from generation to generation; (c) Tchn: generation; Mil: g. d'armes, weapon family.

générer [ʒenere], v.tr. (je génère, n. générons; je générerai) 1. to generate, engender. 2. to generate, produce (electricity, steam, etc.).

généreusement [ʒenerøzmɑ̃], adv. generously; nobly (treated); liberally (rewarded); munificently, without stint.

généreux, -euse [ʒenerø, -øːz], a. 1. noble, generous (soul); cœur g., warm heart; vin g., generous wine, wine with a fine bouquet. 2. (a) liberal, generous, munificent, open-handed, bountiful, bounteous; unstinted (help, etc.); il est trop g., he is too free with his money; verser une contribution généreuse, to contribute liberally, generously; terre généreuse, fertile soil; (b) elle a des formes généreuses, she is built on generous lines. 3. s. (a) A: brave, courageous, person; (b) generous person.

générique [ʒenerik]. 1. a. generic (term, etc.). 2. s.m. Cin: credit titles, credits.

génériquement [ʒenerikmɑ̃], adv. generically.

générosité [ʒenerozite, -ro-], s.f. generosity. 1. (a) A: nobility, magnanimity; (b) liberality, open-handedness, munificence; avec g., generously; (c) body, generousness (of a wine). 2. pl. acts of generosity.

Gênes [ʒɛ(ː)n], Pr.n.f. Geog: Genoa.

genèse [ʒənɛːz], s.f. genesis, origin, birth; la g. des mondes, the origin of the universe; g. d'une idée, birth of an idea; B: la G., (the Book of) Genesis; la g. de l'histoire, history in the making.

génésiaque [ʒenezjak], a. genesiac(al); genesitic.

génésique [ʒenezik], a. Physiol: genetic (instinct etc.).

genestrol(l)e [ʒənɛstrɔl], s.f. Bot: F: dyer's greenweed.

genet [ʒ(ə)nɛ], s.m. A: jennet (horse).

genêt [ʒ(ə)nɛ], s.m. Bot: genista, esp. broom; g. épineux (needle) furze, gorse, whin; g. des teinturiers, dyer's greenweed, dyer's broom, woadwaxen; g. d'Espagne, rush-leaved broom.

généthliaque [ʒenetljak]. 1. a. Astr: Lit: genethliac(al). 2. s.m. Poet: genethliacon.

généticien, -ienne [ʒenetisjɛ̃, -jɛn], s. geneticist.

genêtière [ʒ(ə)nɛtjɛːr], s.f. broom field.

génétique [ʒenetik]. (a) a. genetic; (b) s.f. genetics.

génétiquement [ʒenetikmɑ̃], adv. genetically.

génétisme [ʒenetism], s.m. Psy: genetism.

génétiste [ʒenetist], s.m. & f. 1. geneticist. 2. believer in geneticism.

genette[1] [ʒənɛt], s.f. Bot: (a) dyer's broom; (b) narcissus.

genette², *s.f. Z:* genet (civet); **g. de Madagascar,** Malagasy civet.
genette³, *s.f.* **1.** *Harn:* Turkish bit. **2.** *Equit:* **monter à la g.,** to ride with short stirrups.
gêneur, -euse [ʒɛnœːr, -øːz], *s. F:* (*a*) spoil-sport; intruder; nuisance, troublesome interrupter; (*b*) *F:* (*where two are company*) gooseberry; **je ne veux pas être un g., une gêneuse,** I don't want to play gooseberry.
Genève [ʒ(ə)nɛ(ː)v]. *Pr.n.f. Geog:* Geneva; *Hist:* **la Convention de G.,** the Geneva Convention; **la croix de G.,** the Geneva cross; *Bot:* **pin de G.,** Norway pine.
Geneviève [ʒənvjɛːv], *Pr.n.f.* Genevieve, Winifred.
genevois, -oise [ʒənvwa, ʒnɛv-, -waːz], *a. & s.* Genevese, Genevan.
genévrette [ʒənevrɛt], *s.f.*, **genevrette** [ʒən(ə)-vrɛt], *s.f.* (*drink*) genevrette.
genévrier [ʒ(ə)nevrie], *s.m. Bot:* juniper (tree); **g. de Virginie,** (common red) cedar (tree); **g. oxycèdre,** cade.
genévrière [ʒ(ə)nevriɛːr], *s.f.* juniper plantation.
géni [ʒeni], *a.inv. Anat:* genial; **apophyses g.,** genial apophyses, process.
génial, -aux [ʒenjal, -o], *a.* inspired, full of genius; **œuvre géniale,** work of genius; **idée géniale,** brilliant idea.
génialement [ʒenjalmɑ̃], *adv.* brilliantly; in a brilliant manner; with genius.
génialité [ʒenjalite], *s.f.* (quality of) genius; brilliancy, inspired cleverness (of invention, etc.).
géniculation [ʒenikylasjɔ̃], *s.f. Nat.Hist:* geniculation.
géniculé [ʒenikyle], *a.* geniculate; kneed; *Anat:* **corps g.,** geniculate body; **ganglion g.,** geniculate ganglion; *Bot:* **tige géniculée,** geniculate stem.
génie [ʒeni], *s.m.* **1.** (*a*) (guardian) spirit; (presiding) genius; **son mauvais g.,** his evil genius; **invoquer le g. de la Liberté,** to invoke the spirit of Liberty; (*b*) **un g. sortit de la bouteille,** a genie sprang, leapt, out of the bottle; **les génies des contes arabes,** the genii, the jinn, of the Arabian Nights. **2. homme de g.,** man of genius; **g. très marqué pour les mathématiques,** genius for mathematics; **suivre son g.,** to follow the bent of one's genius. **3.** characteristic, spirit, essence, nature, character; **le g. d'une langue,** the genius, essence, of a language; **le g. du christianisme,** the spirit of christianity; **le g. des Français,** the genius of the French, the spirit of France. **4.** (*pers.*) genius; **ce ne sont pas des génies,** they are no geniuses. **5.** *Tchn:* (*a*) **g. civil,** (i) civil engineering (industry); (ii) civil engineers (as a body); **g. aéronautique,** (i) aeronautical engineering; (ii) aeronautical engineers; **g. atomique,** (i) atomic, nuclear, engineering; (ii) atomic, nuclear, engineers; **g. chimique,** (i) chemical engineering; (ii) chemical engineers; **g. maritime,** (i) marine, naval, architecture; naval construction; (ii) marine, naval, architects; corps of naval constructors; **g. rural,** (i) agricultural engineering; (ii) agricultural engineers; (*b*) **g. militaire,** (i) military engineering; (ii) military engineers (as a body); **le Corps du Génie, le Génie** = the Royal Engineers, the Engineers; *U.S:* the Corps of Engineers, the Engineer Corps; **bataillon, compagnie, du g.,** engineer battalion, company; **g. de combat,** field engineers; *U.S:* combat engineers; **bataillon, compagnie, du g. de combat,** engineer field battalion, company; *U.S:* engineer combat battalion, company; **g. divisionnaire,** divisional engineers; **compagnie de parc, d'entrepôt, du g.,** engineer park, depot, company; **g. aéroporté,** airborne engineers; **g. de l'air,** aviation, air, engineers; **bataillon, compagnie, du g. de l'air,** aviation engineer *or* engineer aviation battalion, company; **officier du g.,** engineer officer; **soldat du g.,** engineer; **sapeur du g.,** engineer sapper; **matériel du g.,** engineer material, engineer stores.
génien, -ienne [ʒenjɛ̃, -jɛn], *a. Anat:* pertaining to the chin; **apophyse génienne,** genial process.
génieux [ʒenjø], *s.m.* **1.** (large) breakfast cup and saucer. **2.** earthenware casserole (with handle).
genièvre [ʒənjɛːvr], *s.m.* **1.** *Bot:* (*a*) juniper berry; (*b*) juniper (tree). **2.** gin, hollands, geneva; **g. allemand,** schnapps. **3.** *Pharm:* **essence de g.,** juniper oil.
genièvrerie [ʒənjɛvrəri], *s.f.* gin factory.
génio(-)glosse [ʒenjɔglɔs], *Anat:* **1.** *a.* genioglossal. **2.** *s.m.* genioglossus.
génio(-)hyoïdien [ʒenjɔjɔidjɛ̃], *a. & s.m. Anat:* genio-hyoid.
génioplastie [ʒenjɔplasti], *s.f. Surg:* genioplasty.
génipayer [ʒenipeje], *s.m. Bot:* genip (tree).
génisse [ʒenis], *s.f.* (*a*) heifer; (*b*) *P:* cow (of a woman).

génistéine [ʒenistein], *s.f. Ch:* genistein.
génital, -aux [ʒenital, -o], *a.* genital; **les organes génitaux,** the genitals.
géniteur, -trice [ʒenitœːr, -tris]. **1.** *s.m. Z:* sire; *s.f.* dam. **2.** *s. Hum:* father, mother, *f.* genetrix; **nos géniteurs,** our parents.
génitif [ʒenitif], *s.m. Gram:* genitive (case); **au g.,** in the genitive.
génito-crural, -aux [ʒenitɔkryral, -o], *a. Anat:* genito-crural.
génitoires [ʒenitwaːr], *s.m.pl. A:* testicles.
génito-urinaire [ʒenitɔyrinɛːr], *a. Anat:* genito-urinary.
génocide [ʒenɔsid], *s.m.* genocide.
génoïde [ʒenɔid], *s.m. Biol:* genoid.
génodermatose [ʒenɔdɛrmatoːz], *s.f. Med:* genodermatosis.
génois, -oise [ʒenwa, -waːz], *a. & s.* **1.** *Geog:* Genoese. **2.** *s.f.* (*a*) **génoise,** Genoese cake, pastry (made with almonds); (*b*) *Const:* (*in Mediterranean countries*) eaves formed by three rows of tiles.
génol [ʒenɔl], *s.m. Phot:* metol.
génome [ʒenɔm], *s.m. Biol:* genome.
génomère [ʒenɔmɛːr], *s.m. Biol:* genomere.
genope [ʒ(ə)nɔp], *s.f. Nau:* (break)stop; racking; **casser les genopes,** to break the stops (of a flag).
genoper [ʒ(ə)nɔpe], *v.tr. Nau:* **1.** to stop, rack, frap (ropes, etc.). **2.** *v.i.* (*of rope*) to jam; to get jammed.
génotype [ʒenɔtip], *s.m. Biol:* genotype.
génotypique [ʒenɔtipik], *a. Biol:* genotypical.
genou, -oux [ʒ(ə)nu], *s.m.* **1.** knee; (*a*) **enfoncé jusqu'aux genoux dans la boue,** knee-deep in mud; **avoir les genoux en dedans,** to be knock-kneed; **se mettre à genoux, fléchir le(s) genou(x),** to bend the knee, to kneel down, to drop on one's knees; **un g. à, en, terre,** on one knee; **être à genoux,** to be kneeling, on one's knees; **demander pardon à genoux,** to beg for pardon on one's bended knees; **à genou(x)!** down on your knee(s)! kneel down; *Mil: A:* **genou à terre!** on the knee! **tomber à genoux,** to fall on one's knees; **se jeter aux genoux de qn,** to go down on one's knees to s.o.; **être aux genoux de qn,** (i) to worship, adore, s.o.; (ii) to be completely under s.o.'s thumb; **tenir un enfant sur ses genoux,** to hold a child on one's knees, in one's lap; **sur les genoux des dieux,** in the lap of the gods; **être sur les genoux,** to be dog-tired; **tenir son g. dans ses mains;** to nurse one's knee; *F:* **avoir la tête comme un g.,** to be as bald as a coot; **ronds de genoux,** 'knees' (in one's trousers); *P:* **g. creux,** shirker; (*b*) *Vet:* **g. creux, de mouton,** hollow knee, sheep knee; **g. de bœuf,** ox knee; **g. de veau,** thick knee. **2.** *Mec.E:* **(joint à) g.,** (i) elbow joint; (ii) ball-and-socket joint; (iii) toggle joint; **g. d'un tuyau,** elbow (joint) of a pipe. **3.** *Row: Nau:* loom (of oar). **4.** *N.Arch:* (*a*) knee; (*b*) futtock.
genou-allonge [ʒ(ə)nualɔ̃ːʒ], *s.m. N.Arch:* futtock; *pl. genoux-allonges.*
genouillé [ʒənuje], *a. Anat:* **corps genouillés,** geniculate bodies; *Bot:* **tige genouillée,** geniculate stem.
genouillère [ʒ(ə)nujɛːr], *s.f.* **1.** (*a*) *A.Arm:* **genouillère,** knee piece; (*b*) knee pad, knee guard, knee cap; knee bandage; (horse's) knee cap; **bottes à genouillères,** top boots, jack boots. **2.** *Mec.E:* **articulation à g.,** knuckle joint, ball-and-socket joint; toggle joint; *Metalw:* **presse à g.,** toggle press. **3.** *Fort: genouillere; Mil:* firing step.
génovéfain [ʒenɔvefɛ̃], *a. Ecc:* **religieux génovéfains,** canonici of St Genevieve.
génovéfine [ʒenɔvefin], *s.f. Ecc: A:* daughter of St Genevieve.
genre [ʒɑ̃ːr], *s.m.* **1.** genus, family, race, kind; **le g. humain,** the human race, humanity, mankind; *Phil:* **le g. et la différence,** genus and differentia. **2.** kind, manner, sort, way; **monde de tous les genres,** people of all kinds, of all classes, of every sort, type, description; **quel g. de vie mène-t-il?** what kind of a life does he lead? **toutes les tentatives de ce g. ont échoué,** all such attempts have failed; **s'occuper d'un g. d'articles,** to deal in a line of goods; **mon g. de commerce,** my line of business; **c'est plus dans son g.,** that's more in his line; **c'est un artiste dans son g.,** he is an artist in his way; **très bon dans son g.,** very good of its kind; **vin blanc g. sauternes,** white wine of the Sauterne type; **étui g. maroquin,** case in imitation morocco; **dans le genre de . . .,** (much) like . . .; **un peu dans le g. de . . .,** rather like . . .; **tout à fait dans le g. de . . .,** very much like . . .; **elle portait une robe dans le g. de celle-ci,** she wore a dress rather like this one; *F:* **ce n'est pas mon g.,** (i) he, she, is not the kind of person I like; (ii) it's just not me. **3.** (artistic, literary) style, manner; **le g. comique,** comedy; **le g. tragique,** tragedy; **le g. gothique,** the Gothic style, order; **peinture de g.,** genre painting; *Art:* **modèle pour tableaux de g.,** character model; **tableaux de g.,** subject picture; *Mus:* **morceau de g.,** characteristic piece; **scènes de g.,** typical scenes. **4.** manners, fashion, taste; **c'est bon, mauvais, g.,** it is good, bad, form, in good, bad, taste; **elle a du g.,** she's got a style about her; **se donner du g., faire du g.,** to put on airs; to be affected; **ce n'est pas son g.,** that's not like him, her; *O:* **ces chapeaux sont tout à fait le dernier g.,** these hats are quite the latest thing. **5.** *Gram:* gender.
gens¹ [ʒɑ̃], *s.m.pl.* (*was originally feminine, being the plural of* GENT, *q.v., and most attributive adjectives preceding* gens *still take the feminine form, the word group being nevertheless felt as masculine*—**ces bonnes gens sont venus me trouver; heureux les petites gens éloignés des grandeurs! quels sont ces gens? quels** *or* **quelles sont ces bonnes gens? tout** *varies according as the attributive adjective has a distinct feminine ending or not:* **toutes ces bonnes gens,** *but* **tous ces pauvres gens; jeunes gens,** *and the compounds of group* 2(*b*) *below, never have a feminine adjective;* **de bons petits jeunes gens; les malheureux gens de lettres.**) **1.** people, folk(s), men and women; **il y avait peu de g. dans la salle,** there were few people in the hall; *Th:* there was a poor house; **beaucoup de g., bien des g., l'ont vu,** many people have seen it; **qui sont ces gens-là?** who are these people? *A:* **bon logement pour bêtes et gens,** good accommodation for man and beast; **il y a des g. qui . . .,** there are people who . . ., some people . . .. **2.** (*a*) **jeunes g.,** (i) young people; adolescents; (ii) young men; (*b*) **g du monde,** society people; **g. de bien,** honest folk; **g. d'église,** (i) clergy(men), priests, (ii) church(y) people; **g. de lettres,** men of letters; **g. de mer,** sailors; **g. d'épée,** (i) soldiers, (ii) nobles; **g. de robe,** lawyers; **g. de théâtre,** the acting profession; **g. du voyage, du cirque,** circus people; **les g. du pays,** *F:* the locals; (*c*) **petites gens,** (i) humble people; (ii) petty(-minded) people; (*d*) *Nau:* **les g. de quart,** the watch; (*e*) *O:* servants, domestics; retinue; attendants, retainers, people; **g. de maison,** servants; **les g. du Cardinal,** (i) the Cardinal's train, retinue; (ii) the Cardinal's people, following, supporters. **3.** nations, peoples; **le droit des g.,** the law of nations.
gens² [ʒɛ̃ːs], *s.f. Rom.Ant:* gens, family.
Genséric [ʒɛ̃serik], *Pr.n.m. Hist:* Genseric.
gent¹ [ʒɑ̃], *s.f. A:* (*still occ. used humorously after the manner of La Fontaine*) tribe, race, brood; **la g. qui porte crête,** the denizens of the poultry yard, the crested folk; **la g. moutonnière,** the woolly race, the sheep; **la g. ailée,** the feathered tribe, the world of birds.
gent², *a. A:* gentle, tender; **le g. berger,** the gentle shepherd.
genthite [ʒɑ̃tit], *s.f. Miner:* genthite.
gentian(ac)ées [ʒɑ̃sjan(as)e], *s.f.pl. Bot:* Gentianaceae.
gentianales [ʒɑ̃sjanal], *s.f.pl. Bot:* Gentianales.
gentiane [ʒɑ̃sjan], *s.f.* **1.** *Bot:* gentian; **g. acaule,** gentianella; **g. de Bavière,** Bavarian gentian; **g. des marais,** autumn bells, windflower. **2.** gentian bitters.
gentianine [ʒɑ̃sjanin], *s.f. Ch:* gentianin.
gentil¹, -ille [ʒɑ̃ti, -iːj], *a.* **1.** *A:* noble; **g. cavalier,** noble gallant; **gentille dame,** gentle lady. **2.** (*a*) pretty, pleasing, nice; **un gentil enfant** (*no 'liaison'* [ʒɑ̃tiɑ̃fɑ̃]), a pretty child; **n'est-ce pas qu'elle est gentille?** isn't she pretty? isn't she nice? **un g. petit chapeau,** a nice little hat; **elle a été très gentille pour, avec, moi,** she was very kind to me; **c'est g. à vous de m'écrire,** it is very kind, very nice, of you to write to me; **c'est g. de votre part,** it is very kind of you; **il s'est montré très g.,** he proved very kind, helpful; **il fait le g.,** he is making himself very pleasant; *Iron:* **je vous trouve g.!** a nice fellow you are! (*b*) **sois gentil(le),** (i) be a good boy, a good girl; (ii) (*to older people*) be an angel, be a dear; (*c*) *F:* **une gentille somme,** a considerable sum of money; (*d*) *Bot:* **bois g.,** mezereon, spurge olive.
gentil², *s.m. Hist:* gentile.
gentilé [ʒɑ̃tile], *s.m. A:* gentilitial name.
gentilhomme [ʒɑ̃tijɔm], *s.m. A:* man of gentle birth, gentleman; **foi de g.!** on the honour of a gentleman; **g. de service,** groom, gentleman, in waiting; **g. de la chambre,** groom of the bed-chamber; **g. de la Chambre du Roi,** gentleman

of the Privy Chamber; *pl. gentilshommes* [ʒɑ̃tizɔm].

gentilhommerie [ʒɑ̃tijɔmri], *s.f. A:* **1.** *Coll.* gentry; (the) quality. **2.** condition of a gentleman, gentility.

gentilhommesque [ʒɑ̃tijɔmɛsk], *a. A: adv.phr.* **à la g.,** in a genteel manner like the gentry.

gentilhommière [ʒɑ̃tijɔmjɛːr], *s.f.* (*a*) country seat, manor house; (*b*) *Belg:* boarding house for men.

gentilisme [ʒɑ̃tilism], *s.m. Rel:* gentilism.

gentilité [ʒɑ̃tilite], *s.f. Coll.* heathendom; the gentiles.

gentillâtre [ʒɑ̃tijɑːtr̥], *s.m. A:* (*a*) squireen; (*b*) *Pej:* would-be gentleman.

gentillesse [ʒɑ̃tijɛs], *s.f.* **1.** (*a*) prettiness, graciousness, engaging manner, sweetness of manner, pretty ways, pleasant disposition; (*b*) **auriez-vous la g. de . . .,** would you be so kind as to . . .; **il a été plein de g. pour moi,** he showed me great kindness; **il abuse de votre g.,** he takes advantage of your kindness, your good nature. **2.** *pl. A:* gracious words, deeds; **dire des gentillesses à une dame,** to say nice things, sweet nothings, to a lady; to make pretty speeches to a lady.

gentillet, -ette [ʒɑ̃tijɛ, -ɛt], *a.* rather nice; pretty-ish; **enfant g.,** engaging child; **elle était jeune et gentillette,** she was young and pretty.

gentillien, -ienne [ʒɑ̃tijɛ̃, -jɛn], *a. & s.* (native, inhabitant) of Gentilly.

gentiment [ʒɑ̃timɑ̃], *adv.* nicely; pleasantly; **causer g.,** to have a pleasant talk together; **elle me fait g. compagnie,** she's kind enough to keep me company; *Iron:* **vous voilà g. arrangé!** that's a nice mess you're in!

gentiobiose [ʒɑ̃tjɔbjoːz], *s.m. Ch:* gentiobiose.

gentiopicrine [ʒɑ̃tjɔpikrin], *s.f. Ch:* gentiopicrin.

gentisate [ʒɑ̃tizat], *s.m. Ch:* gentisate.

gentisine [ʒɑ̃tizin], *s.f. Ch:* gentisin.

gentisique [ʒɑ̃tizik], *a. Ch:* gentisic (acid).

gentleman [dʒɛntləmən, ʒɑ̃tləman], *s.m.* gentleman; **g. de naissance,** a born gentleman; *pl. gentlemen.*

gentleman-farmer [ʒɑ̃tləmanfarmœːr, dʒɛn-], *s.m.* gentleman-farmer; *pl. gentlemen-farmers.*

gentleman-rider [ʒɑ̃tləmanraidœːr, dʒɛn-], *s.m. Rac:* amateur jockey; *pl. gentlemen-riders.*

gentry [dʒɛntri], *s.f.* gentry.

génuflexion [ʒenyflɛksjɔ̃], *s.f. Ecc:* genuflexion; **faire une g.,** to genuflect, to bend the knee.

géo- [ʒeɔ], *pref.* geo-; *Bot:* **géoblaste,** geoblast; *Astr:* **géocyclique,** geocyclic.

géobiologie [ʒeɔbjɔlɔʒi], *s.f.* geobiology.

géobiontes [ʒeɔbjɔ̃ːt], *s.m.pl. Biol:* geobionts.

géoblaste [ʒeɔblast], *s.m. Bot:* geoblast.

géobotanique [ʒeɔbɔtanik], *s.f.* geobotany.

géocentrique [ʒeɔsɑ̃trik], *a. Astr:* geocentric.

géocérite [ʒeɔserit], *s.f. Miner:* geocerite.

géochimie [ʒeɔʃimi], *s.f.* geochemistry.

géochimique [ʒeɔʃimik], *a.* geochemical.

géochimiste [ʒeɔʃimist], *s.m. & f.* geochemist.

géochronologie [ʒeɔkrɔnɔlɔʒi], *s.f.* geochronology.

géocichle [ʒeɔsikl̥], *s.m. Orn:* ground thrush.

géoclase [ʒeɔklɑːz], *s.f. Geol:* fault.

géocratique [ʒeɔkratik], *a.* geocratic.

géocronite [ʒeɔkrɔnit], *s.f. Miner:* geocronite.

géocyclique [ʒeɔsiklik], *a.* geocyclic.

géode [ʒeɔd], *s.f. Geol:* geode, druse.

géodésie [ʒeɔdezi], *s.f.* geodesy, surveying.

géodésien [ʒeɔdezjɛ̃], *s.m.* geodesist.

géodésique [ʒeɔdezik], (*a*) *a.* geodetic(al), geodesic; **arc g.,** geodetic arc; *Surv:* **point g.,** triangulation point; **ligne g.,** geodesic line, geodesic; (*b*) *s.m.* geodesic.

géodésiste [ʒeɔdezist], *s.m.* geodesist.

géodimètre [ʒeɔdimɛtr̥], *s.m.* geodimeter.

géodique [ʒeɔdik], *a. Geol:* geodic.

géodynamique [ʒeɔdinamik]. **1.** *a.* geodynamic. **2.** *s.f.* geodynamics.

Geoffroi [ʒɔfrwa, -ɑ], *Pr.n.m.* Godfrey, Geoffrey.

géogénie [ʒeɔʒeni], *s.f.* geogeny.

géognosie [ʒeɔgnozi], *s.f.* geognosy.

géographe [ʒeɔgraf], *s.m. & f.* geographer; **ingénieur g.,** surveyor.

géographie [ʒeɔgrafi], *s.f.* (*a*) geography; **g. économique,** economic geography; **g. humaine,** anthropo-geography, human geography; (*b*) *Sch:* geography book.

géographique [ʒeɔgrafik], *a.* geographic(al); **carte g.,** map; **dictionnaire g.,** gazetteer.

géographiquement [ʒeɔgrafikmɑ̃], *adv.* geographically.

géoïde [ʒeɔid], *s.m.* geoid.

géoïdique [ʒeɔidik], *a.* geoidal.

geôlage [ʒolaːʒ], *s.m. A:* gaol-fee(s).

geôle [ʒoːl], *s.f. A: & Lit:* **1.** gaol, jail; prison. **2.** gaoler's lodge.

geôlier [ʒolje], *s.m. A: & Lit:* gaoler, jailer, turnkey.

geôlière [ʒoljɛːr], *s.f. A: & Lit:* **1.** gaoler's wife. **2.** female gaoler, wardress.

géologie [ʒeɔlɔʒi], *s.f.* geology.

géologique [ʒeɔlɔʒik], *a.* geological.

géologiquement [ʒeɔlɔʒikmɑ̃], *adv.* geologically.

géologue [ʒeɔlɔg], *s.m. & f.* geologist.

géomagnétique [ʒeɔmaɲetik], *a.* geomagnetic.

géomagnétisme [ʒeɔmaɲetism], *s.m.* geomagnetism.

géomancie [ʒeɔmɑ̃si], *s.f.* geomancy.

géométral, -aux [ʒeɔmetral, -o]. **1.** *a.* flat (projection, elevation) (as opposed to perspective view). **2.** *s.m.* flat projection.

géomètre [ʒeɔmɛtr̥]. **1.** *s.m.* geometer, geometrician; **arpenteur g.,** (land) surveyor. **2.** *s.f. Ent:* geometer (moth); geometrid moth; **g. du bouleau,** peppered moth.

géométrides [ʒeɔmetrid], **géométridés** [ʒeɔmetride], *s.m.pl. Ent:* Geometridae, the geometrical moths.

géométrie [ʒeɔmetri], *s.f.* (*a*) geometry; **g. plane,** plane geometry; **g. analytique,** analytical, coordinate, geometry; **g. dans l'espace, à trois dimensions,** solid, three-dimensional, geometry; geometry of space; **g. descriptive,** descriptive geometry; (*b*) *Mec.E: etc:* geometry, arrangement of parts; *Aut:* **g. de la direction,** steering geometry; *Atom.Ph:* **bonne, mauvaise, g.,** good, poor, geometry (of reactor, irradiation, etc.); **g. normale,** standard geometry; **g. du réseau (du réacteur),** lattice design, lattice pitch (of reactor); (*c*) *Av:* **avion à g. fixe,** fixed-geometry aircraft; **avion à g. variable,** variable-geometry aircraft.

géométrique [ʒeɔmetrik], *a.* geometric(al); **progression g.,** geometrical progression; **exactitude g.,** mathematical exactness.

géométriquement [ʒeɔmetrikmɑ̃], *adv.* geometrically.

géométrisation [ʒeɔmetrizasjɔ̃], *s.f.* geometrization, geometrizing; reduction (of sth.) to geometrical terms.

géométriser [ʒeɔmetrize], *v.tr.* to geometrize.

géomorphique [ʒeɔmɔrfik], *a.* geomorphic.

géomorphogénèse [ʒeɔmɔrfɔʒenɛːz], *s.f.* geomorphogenesis.

géomorphogénie [ʒeɔmɔrfɔʒeni], *s.f.* geomorphogeny.

géomorphologie [ʒeɔmɔrfɔlɔʒi], *s.f.* geomorphology.

géomorphologique [ʒeɔmɔrfɔlɔʒik], *a.* geomorphologic(al).

géomorphologue [ʒeɔmɔrfɔlɔg], *s.m. & f.* geomorphologist.

géomyidés [ʒeɔmjide], *s.m.pl. Z:* Geomyidae, the gophers.

géonoma [ʒeɔnɔma], *s.m. Bot:* geonoma.

géophage [ʒeɔfaːʒ]. **1.** *a.* geophagous. **2.** *s.m. & f.* geophagist.

géophagie [ʒeɔfaʒi], *s.f.* geophagy.

géophile [ʒeɔfil], *s.m. Ent:* geophilus.

géophone [ʒeɔfɔn], *s.m.* geophone, sound detector; *Geog:* **emplacement du g.,** seismic observation point.

géophysicien, -ienne [ʒeɔfizisjɛ̃, -jɛn], *s.* geophysicist.

géophysique [ʒeɔfizik]. **1.** *a.* geophysical. **2.** *s.f.* geophysics.

géophyte [ʒeɔfit], *s.f. Bot:* geophyte.

géopoliticien [ʒeɔpɔlitisjɛ̃], *s.m.* geopolitician.

géopolitique [ʒeɔpɔlitik], *s.f.* geopolitics.

géoponie [ʒeɔpɔni], *s.f.* agriculture.

géoponique [ʒeɔpɔnik]. **1.** *a.* geoponic(al), agricultural. **2.** *s.f.* geoponics.

géopotentiel, -ielle [ʒeɔpɔtɑ̃sjɛl], *a.* **cote géopotentielle,** geopotential (of a point).

géorama [ʒeɔrama], *s.m.* georama.

Georges [ʒɔrʒ]. **1.** *Pr.n.m.* George. **2.** *s.m. Av: F:* George, automatic pilot.

Georgette [ʒɔrʒɛt], *Pr.n.f.* Georgina, Georgiana; *Tex:* **crêpe g.,** georgette.

Géorgie [ʒeɔrʒi], *Pr.n.f. Geog:* Georgia (i) in Russia; (ii) in U.S.A.; **G. du Sud,** South Georgia (Tierra del Fuego).

géorgien, -ienne [ʒeɔrʒjɛ̃, -jɛn], *a. & s. Geog:* Georgian.

Géorgiques (les) [leʒeɔrʒik], *s.f.pl. Lt.Lit:* the Georgics (of Virgil); **la première Géorgique,** the first Georgic.

géostationnaire [ʒeɔstasjɔnɛːr], *a.* geostationary, synchronous (orbit, satellite, etc.).

géostatique [ʒeɔstatik]. **1.** *s.* geostatic. **2.** *s.f.* geostatics.

géostrophique [ʒeɔstrɔfik], *a. Meteor:* geostrophic.

géosynclinal, -aux [ʒeɔsɛ̃klinal, -o], *Geol:* **1.** *a.* geosynclinal. **2.** *s.m.* geosyncline.

géotaxie [ʒeɔtaksi], *s.f. Biol:* geotaxis, geotaxy.

géothermal, -aux [ʒeɔtɛrmal, -o], *a.* geothermal.

géothermie [ʒeɔtɛrmi], *s.f.* geothermics.

géothermique [ʒeɔtɛrmik], *a.* geothermic, geothermal; **énergie g.,** geothermic energy, power.

géothermomètre [ʒeɔtɛrmɔmɛtr̥], *s.m.* geothermometer.

géotrichose [ʒeɔtrikoːz], *s.f. Med:* geotrichosis.

géotropique [ʒeɔtrɔpik], *a. Bot:* geotropic.

géotropisme [ʒeɔtrɔpism], *s.m. Bot:* geotropism.

géotrupe [ʒeɔtryp], *s.m. Ent:* geotrupes.

Gépides [ʒepid], *Pr.n.m.pl. Hist:* Gepides.

gérance [ʒerɑ̃ːs], *s.f.* **1.** (*a*) management, direction (of business, newspaper, etc.); (*b*) managership, administratorship; (*c*) (duration of) managership. **2.** board of governors, of directors.

géraniacées [ʒeranjase], *s.f.pl. Bot:* Geraniaceae.

géraniol [ʒeranjɔl], *s.m. Ch:* geraniol.

géranium [ʒeranjɔm], *s.m.* **1.** *Bot:* geranium, crane's bill; **g. des prés,** meadow crane's bill; **g. à feuilles d'aconit,** Alpine crane's bill; **g. robertin,** herb Robert. **2.** *Hort:* pelargonium; *F:* geranium; **g. lierre,** trailing pelargonium; *F:* ivy-leaved geranium.

gérant, -ante [ʒerɑ̃, -ɑ̃ːt], *s.* **1.** manager, director; manageress, managing director (of company); **g. d'immeubles,** landlord's agent; *a. Journ:* **rédacteur g.,** managing editor. **2.** *Nau:* ship's husband.

géranyle [ʒeranil], *s.m. Ch:* geranyl.

Gérard [ʒeraːr], *Pr.n.m.* Gerald.

gerbable [ʒɛrbabl̥], *a.* stackable.

gerbage [ʒɛrbaːʒ], *s.m.* **1.** binding (of sheaves); sheaving. **2.** stacking, piling (of casks, bales).

gerbe [ʒɛrb], *s.f.* **1.** sheaf (of corn); **mettre le blé en gerbes,** to sheaf the corn; **g. d'étincelles,** shower of sparks; **g. d'eau** (fan-shaped) spray of water; splash; column of water (raised by shell, etc.); **les oiseaux s'envolent en g.,** the birds rise and fan out; **g. de fleurs,** sheaf of flowers (at funeral). **2.** *Mil:* cone of fire; **g. de dispersion,** cone of dispersion; **g. de trajectoires,** pencil, sheaf, of trajectories; *Atom.Ph:* **g. cosmique,** cosmic-ray shower. **3.** *Pyr:* gerb(e). **4.** *Her:* garb.

gerbée [ʒɛrbe], *s.f.* **1.** fodder straw (with a little corn left in it). **2.** corn cut in the green (for fodder). **3.** rye straw (for hats, chairs, etc.).

gerber [ʒɛrbe], *v.tr.* **1.** (*a*) to bind, sheave (corn, etc.); (*b*) *v.i.* **blé qui gerbe bien,** corn that is tillering, stooling, well. **2.** to stack, pile (barrels, crates, shells). **3. g. un fort,** to bombard a fort. **4.** *P:* (*a*) to vomit; (*b*) to condemn; **g. à la passe, à la faux,** to condemn to death.

gerbeur, -euse [ʒɛrbœːr, -øːz], *s.* **1.** (*pers.*) (*a*) binder of sheaves; (*b*) stacker (of barrels, etc.). **2.** stacker, stacking machine; *a.* **chariot g.,** fork-lift truck.

gerbier [ʒɛrbje], *s.m.* **1.** stack (of corn). **2.** *A:* movable shelter to protect corn.

gerbière [ʒɛrbjɛːr], *s.f.* **1.** harvest wag(g)on. **2.** pile of sheaves.

gerbille [ʒɛrbij], *s.f. Z:* gerbil.

gerbillon [ʒɛrbijɔ̃], *s.m. Agr:* small sheaf.

gerboise [ʒɛrbwaːz], *s.f.* (*a*) *Z:* jerboa; (*b*) *B:* cony, daman.

gerce [ʒɛrs], *s.f.* **1.** (*a*) crack, fissure (in wood); (*b*) cracked plank; (*c*) crack, chap (in the skin); **avoir des gerces aux mains,** to have chapped hands. **2.** *Ent:* clothes moth. **3.** *P:* girl.

gercé [ʒɛrse], *a.* cracked, cleft; **bois g.,** shaky wood; **bateau g.,** leaky boat; **mains gercées,** chapped hands.

gercement [ʒɛrs(ə)mɑ̃], *s.m.* cracking (of wood); chapping (of hands).

gercer [ʒɛrse], *v.tr.* (**il gerçait; il gerça**) to crack (wood, the soil); to chap (the hands, etc.); *v.i.* **la terre gerce,** the earth is cracking.

se gercer, (*of skin*) to crack, chap; (*of wood*) to cranny, to become shaky.

gerçure [ʒɛrsyːr], *s.f.* crack, cleft, fissure, flaw; chap (in skin); *Tchn:* shake, flaw (in wood); hair crack, hair line (in metal).

gerçuré [ʒɛrsyre], *a.* shaky, cracked (timber).

gerenuk [ʒɛrənyk], *s.m. Z:* gerenuk.

gérer [ʒere], *v.tr.* (**je gère, n. gérons; je gérerai**) **1.** to manage, run (newspaper, hotel, estate); **g. les affaires de qn,** to manage s.o.'s business; **g. une tutelle,** to administer the estate of a ward; **mal g. ses finances,** to mismanage one's finances. **2.** *Jur:* **se g. créancier,** to come forward as creditor.

gerfaut [ʒɛrfo], *s.m. Orn:* gyrfalcon, gerfalcon; **g. blanc,** Greenland falcon; **g. d'Islande,** Iceland falcon.

gérhardtite [gerartit], *s.f. Miner:* gerhardtite.

gériatre [ʒerjatr̥], *s.m. & f. Med:* geriatrist.

gériatrie [ʒerjatri], *s.f. Med:* geriatrics.

germain[1], **-aine** [ʒɛrmɛ̃, -ɛn], *Hist:* **1.** *a.* Germanic, Teutonic. **2.** *s.* German, Teuton.

germain[2], **-aine**, *a. Jur:* **frère g.**, own brother, full brother, brother german; **sœur germaine**, own sister, full sister, sister german; **cousin g.**, cousin german, own cousin, first cousin.

germandrée [ʒɛrmɑ̃dre], *s.f. Bot:* germander; **g. petit chêne**, wall germander.

Germanie [ʒɛrmani], *Pr.n.f. Hist:* Germania.

germanique [ʒɛrmanik]. **1.** *a. Hist:* (*a*) Germanic, Teutonic; (*b*) **l'Empire g.**, the German Empire. **2.** *s.m. Ling:* Germanic.

germanisant [ʒɛrmanizɑ̃]. **1.** *a.* Germanizing (influence, etc.). **2.** *s.m.* student of Germanic, of German.

germanisation [ʒɛrmanizasjɔ̃], *s.f.* Germanization, Germanizing; Teutonization.

germaniser [ʒɛrmanize], *v.tr.* to Germanize (one's name, etc.); to Teutonize.

germanisme [ʒɛrmanism], *s.m. Ling:* Germanism; Teutonism; *esp. Ling:* German phrase, idiom.

germaniste [ʒɛrmanist], *s.m. & f. Ling:* Germanist, German scholar.

germanite [ʒɛrmanit], *s.f. Miner:* germanite.

germanium [ʒɛrmanjɔm], *s.m. Ch:* germanium.

germanophile [ʒɛrmanɔfil], *a. & s.m. & f.* Germanophile.

germanophilie [ʒɛrmanɔfili], *s.f.* Germanophilia.

germanophobe [ʒɛrmanɔfɔb]. **1.** *a.* Germanophobic. **2.** *s.* Germanophobe.

germanophobie [ʒɛrmanɔfɔbi], *s.f.* Germanophobia.

germe [ʒɛrm], *s.m. Biol:* germ; **g. d'une pomme de terre**, eye of a potato; (*of potatoes*) **pousser des germes**, to sprout; **g. d'un œuf**, t(h)read of an egg; *Ph:* **g. de cristallisation**, crystal nucleus; **g. d'une idée**, germ of an idea; **les germes de la corruption**, the seeds of corruption; **étouffer une rébellion dans le g.**, to crush a rebellion in the bud; *Vet:* **g. de fève**, mark of mouth (of horse).

germen [ʒɛrmɛn], *s.m. Biol:* germen.

germer [ʒɛrme], *v.i.* to germinate; to shoot, spring (up); (*of potatoes*) to sprout; **orge germé**, sprouted barley; **un doute germa dans son esprit**, a doubt germinated, sprang up, in his mind.

germicide [ʒɛrmisid]. **1.** *s.m.* germicide. **2.** *a.* germ-destroying.

germinal, -aux [ʒɛrminal, -o]. **1.** *a. Biol:* germinal; **feuille germinale**, seed leaf. **2.** *s.m. Hist:* seventh month of the French Republican calendar (March-April).

germinateur, -trice [ʒɛrminatœːr, -tris], *a.* germinative.

germinatif, -ive [ʒɛrminatif, -iːv], *a. Biol:* germinative, germinal; **plasma g.**, germ plasm.

germination [ʒɛrminasjɔ̃], *s.f. Biol:* germination.

germoir [ʒɛrmwaːr], *s.m.* **1.** *Hort:* hot bed, seed bed. **2.** *Brew:* malthouse floor.

germon [ʒɛrmɔ̃], *s.m. Ich:* albacore; **g. atlantique**, long-finned albacore, long-finned tuna.

géromois, -oise [ʒeromwa, -waːz], *a. & s. Geog:* (native, inhabitant) of Gérardmer.

Gérone [ʒerɔn], *Pr.n. Geog:* Gerona.

gérondif [ʒerɔ̃dif], *s.m. Gram:* **1.** gerund. **2.** gerundive; **au gérondif**, in the gerund(ive).

géronte [ʒerɔ̃ːt], *s.m.* **1.** *Th:* the 'old man' in French classical comedy. **2.** credulous old man, old fool.

gérontisme [ʒerɔ̃tism], *s.m.* senile decay, dotage.

gérontocratie [ʒerɔ̃tɔkrasi], *s.f.* gerontocracy.

gérontocratique [ʒerɔ̃tɔkratik], *a.* gerontocratic.

gérontologie [ʒerɔ̃tɔlɔʒi], *s.f.* gerontology.

gérontologue [ʒerɔ̃tɔlɔg], *s.m.* gerontologist, specialist in gerontology.

gérontophilie [ʒerɔ̃tɔfili], *s.f.* gerontophilia.

géro-psychiatrie [ʒerɔpsikjatri], *s.f.* geriatric psychiatry.

gerrhosaurinés [ʒerɔsɔrine], *s.m.pl. Rept:* Gerrhosauridae.

gerris [ʒɛri], *s.m. Ent:* water strider.

gersdorffite [gɛrzdɔrfit], *s.f. Miner:* gersdorffite.

gerseau [ʒɛrso], *s.m. Nau:* grummet, gromet.

Gertrude [ʒɛrtryd], *Pr.n.f.* Gertrude.

Gervais [ʒɛrvɛ], *Pr.n.m.* Gervase.

gérydines [ʒeridin], *s.f.pl. Ent:* Gerydinae.

gerzeau [ʒɛrzo], *s.m. Bot: F:* corn cockle.

gésier [ʒezje], *s.m. Orn: Ent:* gizzard; *P:* **recevoir un coup dans le g.**, to get one in the bread-basket, one below the belt.

gésine [ʒezin], *s.f. A:* confinement, lying-in; **femme en g.**, woman brought to bed, lying in child-bed.

gésir [ʒeziːr], *v.i. def.* (*used only in the following forms: pr.p.* **gisant**; *pr.ind.* **il gît, n. gisons, vous gisez, ils gisent**; *p.d.* **je gisais**, etc.) (*of pers.*) to lie (helpless or dead); (*of thg*) to lie; **il gisait dans son sang**, he was lying, weltering, in his blood; (*on gravestone*) **ci-gît, ci-gisent . . .**, here lies, here lie . . .; **c'est là que gît le lièvre**, that's the point, there's the rub; **savoir où gît le lièvre**, to know where the trouble lies; *Nau:* **l'île gît N.N.E.**, the island lies N.N.E.; **la côte gît nord et sud**, the coast runs north and south.

gesnériacées [ʒɛsnerjase], *s.f.pl. Bot:* Gesner(i)aceae.

gesse [ʒɛs], *s.f. Bot:* vetch, everlasting pea; **g. odorante**, sweet pea; **g. velue**, hairy vetchling.

Gessen [ʒɛsɛn], *Pr.n. B.Hist:* **la terre de G.**, the land of Goshen.

gessien, -ienne [ʒɛsjɛ̃, -jɛn], *a. & s. Geog:* (native, inhabitant) of Gex.

gestaltisme [gɛʃtaltism], *s.m. Phil:* gestaltism.

gestaltiste [gɛʃtaltist], *a. & s.m. & f. Phil:* gestaltist.

gestapo [gɛstapo], *s.f. Pol.Hist:* Gestapo.

gestation [ʒɛstasjɔ̃], *s.f. Physiol:* period of gestation, pregnancy; **projet en g.**, plan in embryo.

gestatoire [ʒɛstatwaːr], *a. Ecc:* **chaise g.**, gestatorial chair.

geste[1] [ʒɛst], *s.m.* **1.** gesture, motion, movement; **d'un g. large il nous fit entrer**, he waved us in, showed us in, with a flourish; **d'un g. de la main**, with a wave, a motion, of the hand; **d'un g. il me fit asseoir**, he motioned me to a chair; **écarter qn d'un g.**, to wave s.o. aside; **faire un g.**, to make a gesture; **faire un g. d'impatience**, to make a gesture, a movement, of impatience; **il n'a même pas fait un g. pour m'aider**, he didn't lift a finger to help me; **(faites) un g. et vous êtes mort**, move a finger and you are a dead man; **g. de résignation**, shrug of resignation; **joindre le g. à la parole**, to suit the action to the word; **le langage des gestes**, the language of gesture; sign language; *Mil:* **commandements au g.**, command by arm, hand, signal; *Ten: etc:* **perfectionner son g.**, to perfect one's action. **2. beau g., g. de sympathie**, handsome gesture, gesture of sympathy.

geste[2], *s.f.* **1.** *Lit:* **(chanson de) g.**, chanson de geste, mediaeval verse-chronicle (of heroic exploits). **2. faits et gestes**, doings, exploits; **rendre compte de ses faits et gestes**, to give an account of oneself; **on observe vos faits et gestes**, your behaviour is being watched.

gesticulaire [ʒɛstikylɛːr], *a.* gesticulatory.

gesticulateur, -trice [ʒɛstikylatœːr, -tris], *s.* (*rare*) gesticulator.

gesticulation [ʒɛstikylasjɔ̃], *s.f.* gesticulating, gesticulation.

gesticulatoire [ʒɛstikylatwaːr], *a.* gesticulatory.

gesticulé [ʒɛstikyle], *a.* expressed in gestures.

gesticuler [ʒɛstikyle], *v.i.* to gesticulate.

gestion [ʒɛstjɔ̃], *s.f.* (*a*) management (of business, works, etc.); conduct (of affairs); administration, control; **g. administrative**, administration; **g. autonome**, independent administration, management; **à g. autonome**, independently administered, operated; **g. des deniers publics**, administration of public funds; **g. financière d'une affaire**, financial administration of a business; **bonne g.**, good administration, good management; **mauvaise g.**, maladministration, bad management, mismanagement; *Ind:* **g. de la production**, production control; **g. de stock**, inventory control; **problèmes de g. de stock**, inventory problems; (*computers*) **g. automatisée**, automated management; **g. de fichiers**, file maintenance; (*b*) administratorship; **rendre compte de sa g.**, to render an account of one's administration; *Jur:* **ordonner une g.**, to make an administration order.

gestionnaire [ʒɛstjɔnɛːr]. **1.** *a.* **administration g.**, administration by agent, factor; **compte g.**, management account. **2.** *s.* manager, administrator, *f.* manageress, administratrix; *Adm:* official in charge (of service); **g. de stock**, inventory manager.

gestuel, -elle [ʒɛstɥɛl], (*a*) *a. Art:* **peinture gestuelle**, action painting; (*b*) *s.f.* **la gestuelle des sourds-muets**, the sign language of deaf-mutes.

Gètes [ʒɛt], *s.m.pl. A.Hist:* Getae.

Gethsémani [ʒɛtsemani], *Pr.n. B.Hist:* Gethsemane.

getter [gɛtər], *s.m. Elcs:* getter.

Gétules [ʒetyl], *s.m.pl. A.Hist:* Getulians.

Gétulie [ʒetyli], *Pr.n.f. A.Hist:* Getulia.

geyser [ʒezɛːr], *s.m. Geog:* geyser.

geysérien, -ienne [ʒezerjɛ̃, -jɛn], *a.* geyseral, geyseric.

geysérite [ʒezerit], *s.f. Miner:* geyserite.

Ghana [gana], *Pr.n.m. Geog:* Ghana.

ghanéen, -éenne [ganeɛ̃, -eɛn], *a. & s. Geog:* Ghanaian.

ghassoulien, -ienne [gasuljɛ̃, -jɛn], *a. Prehist:* Ghassulian.

ghât [gɑːt], *s.m. Indian Civ:* ghat.

Ghâtes (les) [legɑːt], *Pr.n.f.pl. Geog:* the Ghats.

ghee [gi], *s.m.* ghee.

ghetto [gɛt(t)o], *s.m.* ghetto.

ghilde [gild], *s.f. Hist: etc:* guild.

ghy [gi], *s.m.* = GHEE.

gi [ʒi], *adv. P:* yes! O.K.!

giaour [ʒjauːr], *s.m.* giaour.

gibberella [ʒiberɛla], *s.m. Fung:* gibberella.

gibbérelline [ʒiberɛlin], *s.f. Bot:* gibberellin.

gibbeux, -euse [ʒib(b)ø, -øːz], *a.* **1.** gibbous; **parties gibbeuses de la lune**, gibbosities of the moon. **2.** humped, hunch-backed.

gibbon [ʒib(b)ɔ̃], *s.m. Z:* gibbon (ape).

gibbosité [ʒib(b)ozite], *s.f.* **1.** gibbosity. **2.** hump.

gibbsite [ʒibzit], *s.f. Miner:* gibbsite.

gibecière [ʒibsjɛːr], *s.f.* **1.** *A:* belt purse. **2.** game bag, pouch. **3.** *A:* wallet; (school) satchel.

gibelet [ʒible], *s.m. A:* gimlet; *F:* **avoir un coup de g.**, to be a little cracked.

Gibelin [ʒiblɛ̃], *s.m. Hist:* Ghibelline.

gibelotte [ʒiblɔt], *s.f.* fricassee of rabbit (cooked in white wine).

giberne [ʒibɛrn], *s.f.* **1.** (*a*) *A:* cartridge-pouch; **enfant de g.**, child born to a soldier on active service; (*b*) **chaque soldat a son bâton de maréchal dans sa g.**, every soldier carries a marshal's baton in his knapsack. **2.** (bandsman's) wallet **3.** *A:* (school) satchel.

gibet [ʒibɛ], *s.m.* **1.** *A:* gibbet, gallows. **2.** *Tchn:* **g. de puisatier**, shear legs.

gibier [ʒibje], *s.m.* game (= wild animals); **gros g.**, big game; **menu g.**, small game; **g. à poil**, ground game; game animals; **g. à plumes**, game birds; **g. d'eau**, wild fowl; *F:* **du g. très mêlé**, a very mixed bag; *F:* **g. de potence**, *A:* **de galère**, gallows bird, jail bird; **un vrai g. de potence**, one of the greatest rogues unhanged; *F:* **ce n'est pas de son g.**, (i) it's not his line; (ii) it's not his cup of tea; **voilà mon g.**, that's what I'm after; **c'est le g. rêvé des voleurs**, it's fair game for any thief.

giboulée [ʒibule], *s.f.* **1.** sudden shower (*usu.* with snow or hail); **giboulées de mars** = April showers. **2.** *F:* shower of blows, drubbing.

gibouler [ʒibule], *v.impers. F:* to rain in showers.

giboyer[1] [ʒibwaje], *v.i.* (**je giboie, n. giboyons; je giboierai**) *A:* to go, spend one's time, shooting; to go out with a gun; to pot at small game.

giboyer[2], *s.m. A: F:* grub-street journalist; (*from Augier's play* **"Le Fils de Giboyer,"** 1862).

giboyeur [ʒibwajœːr], *s.m.* **1.** *A:* sportsman, man who likes to go out with a gun. **2.** provider of game for the markets.

giboyeux, -euse [ʒibwajø, -øːz], *a.* abounding in game; well stocked with game; **pays g.**, good game country.

gibus [ʒibys], *s.m.* crush hat, opera hat (from the name of the inventor).

giclage [ʒiklaːʒ], *s.m. I.C.E:* spraying (of petrol); **carburateur à g.**, spray carburettor, jet carburettor.

giclée [ʒikle], *s.f.* **1.** spirt, squirt (of water, blood); *F:* burst (of machine-gun fire). **2.** *I.C.E:* spray (of petrol into carburettor).

giclement [ʒikləmɑ̃], *s.m.* splashing up, squelching (of mud, etc.); squirting, spirting (of blood, etc.).

gicler [ʒikle], *v.i.* **1.** to squirt out; to spout forth; (*of blood, etc.*) to spirt (out); **faire g. de l'eau de Seltz dans un verre**, to squirt soda water into a glass. **2.** to splash up; **les roues faisaient g. la boue**, the wheels splashed up the mud. **3.** *P:* to run off.

giclet [ʒiklɛ], *s.m. Bot:* squirting cucumber.

gicleur [ʒiklœːr], *s.m. I.C.E:* (spray) nozzle; atomizer, jet; **g. du carburateur**, carburettor jet; **g. de ralenti**, pilot jet; **g. principal**, main jet, power jet; **g. auxiliaire**, auxiliary jet; **g. d'accélération**, accelerating jet; **g. à jets multiples**, multiple-jet nozzle; **g. de départ**, starting, warming-up, jet; **le g. est noyé**, the jet is submerged, flooded.

giclure [ʒiklyːr], *s.f.* mark, splash (left by splashing liquid).

giennois, -oise [ʒjɛnwa, -waːz], *a. & s. Geog:* (native, inhabitant) of Gien.

giffard [ʒifaːr], *s.m. Mch:* (Giffard) injector.

gifle [ʒifl], *s.f.* **1.** (*a*) slap in the face; box on the ear; **donner, appliquer,** *F:* **flanquer, une g. à qn**, to slap s.o.'s face; *F:* **recevoir une fameuse g.**, to get a regular stinger; *F:* **tête à gifles**, face one would like to slap; unpleasant sullen face; (*b*) insult, (public) humiliation. **2.** kick (of rifle).

gifler [ʒifle], *v.tr.* (*a*) to slap, smack, (s.o.'s) face; to box (s.o.'s) ears; **je le giflai de mon gant,** I slapped him in the face with my glove; **visage giflé par le vent,** face lashed by the wind; (*b*) **mots qui giflent,** humiliating words.
gigacycle [ʒigasikl̩], *Elcs: s.m.* gigacycle.
gigahertz [ʒigaɛrts], *s.m. Meas:* gigahertz.
gigantesque [ʒigɑ̃tɛsk], *a. & s.m.* gigantic.
gigantesquement [ʒigɑ̃tɛskəmɑ̃], *adv.* gigantically.
gigantisme [ʒigɑ̃tism], *s.m. Med:* gigantism, giantism.
gigantoblaste [ʒigɑ̃tɔblast], *s.m.* gigantoblast.
gigantolite [ʒigɑ̃tɔlit], *s.f. Miner:* gigantolite.
gigantomachie [ʒigɑ̃tɔmaʃi], *s.f. Myth:* gigantomachia, battle of the giants.
gigantopithèque [ʒigɑ̃tɔpitɛk], *s.m. Paleont:* gigantopithecus.
gigantostracés [ʒigɑ̃tɔstrase], *s.m.pl. Paleont:* Gigantostraca.
gigartinales [ʒigartinal], *s.f.pl. Algae:* Gigartinales.
Gigogne [ʒigɔɲ], *s.f.* **la mère G.,** = the Old Woman who lived in a shoe; **une mère G.,** the mother of a large and ever-increasing family; **table g.,** nest of tables; **lit g.,** trundle, truckle, bed; **poupée g.,** nest of (Russian) dolls; *Ball:* **fusée g.,** multi-stage rocket; *Navy:* **navire g.,** mother ship.
gigolette [ʒigɔlɛt], *s.f. P: A:* young woman of easy virtue.
gigolo [ʒigɔlo], *s.m. F:* gigolo.
gigot [ʒigo], *s.m.* **1.** leg of mutton; *A.Cost:* **manche à g.,** leg of mutton sleeve. **2.** *pl.* hind legs (of horse).
gigoté [ʒigɔte], *a.* **cheval, chien, bien, mal, g.,** horse, dog, strong, weak, in the hind legs.
gigotement [ʒigɔtmɑ̃], *s.m. F:* jerking, flinging about (one's limbs).
gigoter [ʒigɔte], *v.i. F:* **1.** to kick, fling about, jerk around (one's legs, arms); (*to child*) **ne gigote pas!** don't wriggle! don't fidget! **2.** (*of dying animal*) to give a convulsive jerk.
gigue[1] [ʒig], *s.f. Danc:* jig.
gigue[2], *s.f. Sm.a:* **g. de crosse,** cheek layer (of butt of rifle).
gigue[3], *s.f.* (*a*) haunch (of venison); (*b*) *pl. F:* legs, stumps, pins; **avoir de grandes gigues,** to be long-legged; (*c*) **une grande g.,** a long-legged, gawky, young woman, a beanpole.
giguer [ʒige], *v.i. F: O:* to jig, dance; to caper.
Gilbert [ʒilbɛːr]. **1.** *Pr.n.m.* Gilbert. **2.** *s.m. El. Meas:* gilbert.
gilde [gild], *s.f. Hist: etc:* guild.
gilet [ʒilɛ], *s.m.* (*a*) waistcoat, vest; **g. droit, croisé,** single-breasted, double-breasted, waistcoat; **g. ouvert,** low-cut waistcoat; **g. fermé,** high-cut waistcoat; **tissu pour gilets,** waistcoating; **g. de travail, à manches,** sleeved vest; **venir pleurer sur le g. de qn,** to weep on s.o.'s shoulder; (*b*) **g. de sauvetage,** life jacket; **g. d'armes,** fencing jacket; *A:* **donner un g. à qn,** to beat s.o. thoroughly, give s.o. a thorough beating (at fencing, at a game); (*c*) (*man's undergarment*) **g. (de corps, de peau, de dessous, hygiénique),** (under)vest, singlet, *U.S:* undershirt; **g. de coton, de nylon,** cotton, nylon, vest; (*d*) (woman's) cardigan.
giletier, -ière [ʒiltje, -jɛːr]. **1.** *a.* **ceinture giletière,** cummerbund vest. **2.** *s.* waistcoat maker, waistcoat hand. **3.** *s.f.* **giletière,** watch chain, watch guard.
gill [ʒil], *s.m. Tex:* gill.
Gilles [ʒil]. **1.** *Pr.n.m.* Giles. **2.** *s.m. A:* **gille(s),** Tom Fool; clown, ninny (in popular drama); *F: A:* **faire gille(s),** (i) to slip away (from the company), (ii) to abscond, (iii) to go bankrupt.
gillotage [ʒilɔtaːʒ], *s.m. A:* photozincography (as first practised by F. Gillot).
gillsage [ʒilsaːʒ], *s.m. Tex:* gilling.
Gilsonite [ʒilsɔnit], *s.f. Miner:* uintaite, Gilsonite (*R.t.m.*)
gimb(e)lette [ʒɛ̃blɛt], *s.f. Cu:* jumble, jumbal, ring-biscuit.
gin [dʒin, ʒin], *s.m.* gin.
gindre [ʒɛ̃ːdr̩], *s.m.* baker's assistant.
gingembre [ʒɛ̃ʒɑ̃ːbr̩], *s.m.* (*a*) *Bot:* ginger; (*b*) **g. confit,** crystallized ginger; **racine de g.,** ginger race.
gingeole [ʒɛ̃ʒɔl], *s.f. Bot:* jujube.
gingeolier [ʒɛ̃ʒɔlje], *s.m. Bot:* jujube tree.
gingin [ʒɛ̃ʒɛ̃], *s.m. F:* common sense; **avoir du g.,** to have gumption, nous.
ginginer [ʒɛ̃ʒine], *v.i. A: P:* (*a*) to ogle; (*b*) **g. des hanches,** to swing a saucy hip.
gingival, -aux [ʒɛ̃ʒival, -o], *a.* gingival; of the gums.
gingivectomie [ʒɛ̃ʒivɛktɔmi], *s.f. Surg:* gingivectomy.
gingivite [ʒɛ̃ʒivit], *s.f. Med:* gingivitis; **g. expulsive,** pyorrhea; **g. gravidique,** pregnancy gingivitis; **g. scorbutique,** scorbutic gingivitis.
gingko [ʒɛ̃ko], *s.m. Bot:* ginkgo.
ginglet [ʒɛ̃glɛ], *s.m. F:* = GINGUET 2.
ginglyme [ʒɛ̃glim], *s.m. Anat:* ginglymus, hinge joint.
ginguelet [ʒɛ̃glɛ], *s.m. F:* = GUINGUET 2.
ginguer [ʒɛ̃ge], *v.i.* (*of cow*) to fling out.
ginguet, -ette [ʒɛ̃gɛ, -ɛt]. **1.** *a. A: F:* weak, poor, thin (wine, style); of little value; **femme ginguette,** pretty doll (of a woman). **2.** *s.m. A:* (*a*) thin wine; (*b*) (unpretentious) local wine. **3.** *s.m.* pawl (of capstan, etc.).
ginkgo [ʒɛ̃ko], *s.m. Bot:* ginkgo.
ginkgoales [ʒɛ̃kwal], *s.f.pl. Bot:* Ginkgoales.
ginnerie [ʒinri], *s.f. Tex:* ginnery.
ginseng [ʒɛ̃sɑ̃], *s.m. Bot: etc:* ginseng.
giobertite [ʒjɔbɛrtit], *s.f. Miner:* giobertite, magnesite.
giorno (à) [adʒjɔrno], *adv.phr.* **éclairage à g.,** brilliant illumination; **éclairé à g.,** brilliantly lighted.
girafe [ʒiraf], *s.f.* **1.** (*a*) *Z:* giraffe; *F:* **peigner la g.,** to waste one's time; to do damn all; (*b*) *F:* lanky, long-necked woman; beanpole. **2.** (*a*) *Cin:* boom (of microphone); *F:* giraffe; (*b*) *Civ.E:* tip wagon (with lateral tip); (*c*) (*in Normandy*) square fishing net; (*d*) *F:* high diving-board.
girafeau, -eaux [ʒirafo], **girafon** [ʒirafɔ̃], *s.m.* baby giraffe.
giraffidés [ʒirafide], *s.m.pl. Z:* Giraffidae.
giralducien, -ienne [ʒiraldysjɛ̃, -jɛn], *a.* of Giraudoux.
girande [ʒirɑ̃ːd], *s.f.* girandole (of water-jets or of rockets).
girandole [ʒirɑ̃dɔl], *s.f.* **1.** girandole, chandelier; *Pyr:* girandole. **2.** epergne, centre-piece (for table). **3.** cluster (of blooms); girandole (of jewels). **4.** *Bot:* **g. d'eau,** water horse-tail.
girasol [ʒirasɔl], *s.m.* **1.** *Miner:* girasol, fire opal. **2.** *Bot:* sunflower.
giration [ʒirasjɔ̃], *s.f.* gyration; *Nau:* **cercle de g.,** turning circle (of ship); **essai de g.,** turning trial; **achever une g.,** to finish a turn; **rayon de g.,** radius of gyration, of turn.
giratoire [ʒiratwaːr], *a.* gyratory (movement, traffic, etc.); roundabout (traffic); **sens, carrefour, g.,** roundabout.
giraumon(t) [ʒiromɔ̃], *s.m. Hort: F:* pumpkin.
giraviation [ʒiravjasjɔ̃], *s.f.* gyroaviation.
giravion [ʒiravjɔ̃], *s.m. Av:* gyroplane; rotary-wing aircraft; rotating wing aircraft; rotor aircraft.
girelle[1] [ʒirɛl], *s.f. Cer:* revolving table (of potter's wheel).
girelle[2], *s.f. Ich:* girella, rainbow wrasse, gold-sinny wrasse, goldfinny wrasse.
girie [ʒiri], *s.f. P:* whining; bellyaching; fuss; **assez de giries!** stop whining, fussing! **faire des giries,** (i) to bellyache; (ii) to put on airs.
girl [gœrl], *s.f.* chorus girl; showgirl.
girodyne [ʒirɔdin], *s.m. Av:* autogyro.
girofle [ʒirɔfl̩], *s.m. Bot:* clove; **un clou de g.,** a clove; **huile de g.,** oil of cloves.
giroflée [ʒirɔfle], *s.f. Bot:* **g. des jardins, grande g.,** stock(-gilly flower); **g. quarantaine,** ten-week stock; **g. jaune, des murailles,** wallflower; *P:* **une g. (à cinq feuilles, à cinq branches),** a slap in the face.
giroflier [ʒirɔfli(j)e], *Bot:* clove tree.
girol(l)e [ʒirɔl], *s.f. Bot:* **1.** skirret. **2.** chanterelle (mushroom).
giron [ʒirɔ̃], *s.m.* **1.** lap; **tenir un enfant dans son g.,** to hold a child in one's lap; **le g. de l'Église,** the bosom of the Church. **2.** *Arch:* tread (board) (of step); **marches avec 15 cm. de g.,** steps with a 15 cm. tread. **3.** *Mec.E:* loose handle, handle case (of windlass, etc.). **4.** loom (of oar). **5.** *Her:* gyron.
girond [ʒirɔ̃], *a. P:* (*usu. of woman*) nice and plump; easy on the eye; **ce qu'elle est gironde!** she's the goods, a bit of all right.
Gironde [ʒirɔ̃ːd]. **1.** *Pr.n.f. Geog:* the (river) Gironde. **2.** *s.f. Hist:* **la Gironde,** the Girondist party, the Girondins (during the Revolution).
girondin, -ine [ʒirɔ̃dɛ̃, -in], (*a*) *Hist: a. & s.* Girondist, Girondin; (*b*) *a.* **le vignoble g.,** the vineyards of Gironde.
gironné [ʒirɔne], *a.* **1.** *Const:* **marches gironnées,** winding steps; **tuile gironnée,** triangular tile. **2.** *Her:* gyronny.
gironner [ʒirɔne], *v.tr.* to hammer out (metal); **g. un chaudron,** to round the bottom of a cauldron; **g. un escalier,** to trace the design for a winding staircase.
girouette [ʒirwɛt], *s.f.* (*a*) weathercock; vane; **g. à fumée,** (revolving) chimney cowl; chimney jack; *F:* **graisser la g. (avant de souffler dessus),** to pave the way; (*b*) *F:* (*of pers.*) weathercock.
girouette-anémomètre [ʒirwɛtanemɔmɛtr̩], *s.f.* speed and direction anemometer; *pl. girouettes-anémomètres.*
girouetter [ʒirwɛte], *v.i.* to veer, to turn round, to chop and change.
girouetterie [ʒirwɛtri], *s.f.* fickleness, chopping and changing.
gisant [ʒizɑ̃]. **1.** *a.* (*of pers.*) lying (helpless or dead); *For:* **bois g.,** felled timber; fallen trunks; *Nau:* **navire g.,** stranded vessel; *Mill:* **(meule) gisante,** nether millstone, bedstone, bedder. **2.** *s.m.* gisant, recumbent figure (on tomb).
giselle [ʒizɛl], *s.f. Tex:* giselle.
gisement [ʒizmɑ̃], *s.m.* **1.** (*a*) *Geol:* layer, bed, deposit, stratum; **g. pétrolifère,** petroleum deposit, oil field; (*b*) *Min:* (i) lode, vein; (ii) lie of the lodes; **gisements houillers,** coal measures; (*c*) *Archeol:* **g. préhistorique,** prehistoric site. **2.** (*a*) *Nau: etc:* bearing; *Av:* **g. grossier,** coarse bearing; **g. à la boussole,** compass bearing; **g. magnétique,** magnetic bearing; **g. par rapport au nord du quadrillage (de la carte),** grid bearing; **g. vrai,** true bearing; **g. inverse,** reverse bearing; **g. relatif,** relative bearing; **relever un g.,** to take a bearing; **relèvement d'un g.,** taking of a bearing, position finding; **tracer un g.,** to plot a bearing; (*radar*) **indicateur de g.,** plan position indicator; (*b*) *Nau:* **connaître le g. de la côte,** to know how the coast lies, to know the lie of the coast; (*c*) *Artil:* lateral deflection; **g. corrigé,** corrected lateral deflection.
gismondine [ʒizmɔ̃din], **gismondite** [ʒizmɔ̃dit], *s.f. Miner:* gismondine, gismondite.
gisoir [ʒizwaːr], *s.m.* sleeping quarters (of pigsty).
gisorcien, -ienne [ʒizɔrsjɛ̃, -jɛn], *a. & s. Geog:* (native, inhabitant) of Gisors.
gîtage [ʒitaːʒ], *s.m. Const:* joisting.
gitan, -ane [ʒitɑ̃, -an], *s.* **1.** (Spanish) gipsy; gitano, *f.* gitana. **2.** *s.f. R.t.m:* **Gitane,** type of popular French cigarette.
gîte[1] [ʒit], *s.m.* **1.** (*a*) resting place, lodging; **n'avoir pas de g.,** to be homeless; **revenir au g.,** to return to one's old home; **retour au g.,** homing; *Mil: A:* **g. d'étapes,** road post (on line of communication); (*b*) lair (of deer); form, seat (of hare); **trouver un lièvre au g.,** to find a hare sitting. **2.** (*a*) *Const: etc:* joist, sleeper (of floor, of artillery platform); (*b*) stratum, bed, deposit (of ore, etc.); **gîtes houillers,** coal measures; (*c*) nether millstone. **3.** leg of beef; **g. à la noix,** silverside; *P:* **ça, c'est dans le g.!** that's a little bit of all right!
gîte[2], *s.f. Nau:* **1.** list(ing); (*of ship*) **avoir, prendre, de la g.,** to have, take, a list; to list, to heel (over); **donner de la g. sur tribord,** to list to starboard. **2.** bed (of stranded vessel).
gîter [ʒite]. **1.** *v.i.* (*a*) *A: F:* to lodge, *A:* lie; **nous avons bien gîté,** we were well lodged; **où gitez-vous?** where do you hang out? (*b*) (*of animal*) to couch; (*of bird*) to perch; (*c*) (*of ship*) (i) to run aground; (ii) to list, heel. **2.** *v.tr. A:* to house, shelter (s.o.); to put (s.o.) up.
se gîter, (*a*) *A: F:* to take up one's abode, one's quarters; (*b*) (*of animal*) to find shelter; to bed.
githago [ʒitago], *s.m. Bot:* corn cockle.
giton [ʒitɔ̃], *s.m.* catamite.
gitonogamie [ʒitɔnɔgami], *s.f. Bot:* geitonogamy.
givétien, -ienne [ʒivetjɛ̃, -jɛn], *a. & s.m. Geol:* Givetian.
givetois, -oise [ʒivtwa, -waːz], *a. & s. Geog:* (native, inhabitant) of Givet.
givordin, -ine [ʒivɔrdɛ̃, -in], *a. & s. Geog:* (native, inhabitant) of Givors.
givrage [ʒivraːʒ], *Av: etc:* icing.
givre[1] [ʒiːvr̩], *s.m.* **1.** hoar frost, white frost. **2.** (*a*) frost (forming in refrigerator, etc.); (*b*) sugar crystals (on crystallized fruit, etc.).
givre[2], *s.f. Her:* wyvern.
givré [ʒivre], *a.* **1.** frosty; covered with hoar frost; *Av:* iced up. **2.** (*of preserved fruit, etc.*) covered with sugar crystals; *Cu:* **orange givrée,** frozen orange filled with sorbet. **3.** *P:* (*a*) drunk, high, stoned; (*b*) mad, nuts, batty.
givrée [ʒivre], *s.f.* (imitation) frost (for Christmas trees, etc.).
givrer [ʒivre], *v.tr.* (*a*) to cover (sth.) with hoar frost; *Av:* to ice up; (*b*) to frost (Christmas tree, cake, etc.); (*c*) *P:* **se g.,** to get drunk, sozzled.
givreux, -euse [ʒivrø, -øːz], *a.* **1.** frosted over. **2.** (*of diamonds, etc.*) with icy flecks.
givrure [ʒivryːr], *s.f.* icy fleck (in diamond, etc.).
glabelle [glabɛl], *s.f. Anat:* glabella.

glabre [glɑːbr], *a. Nat.Hist:* glabrous, smooth; **visage g.,** (i) hairless face; (ii) clean-shaven face; **à visage g.,** clean-shaven.

glabrisme [glabrism], *s.m. Bot:* glabrousness.

glaçage [glasaːʒ], *s.m.* (*a*) glazing, glossing; surfacing (of paper); (*b*) *Cu:* icing, frosting; (*c*) freezing (of refrigerator, etc.); refrigeration (of food).

glaçant [glasɑ̃], *a.* freezing (cold); icy (coldness, wind); chilling, frigid (manner, reception).

glace [glas], *s.f.* **1.** ice; **cube de g.,** ice cube; *Fr.C:* **sur g.,** on the rocks; **glaces de fond,** bottom ice, ground ice, anchor ice; **g. flottante,** floating ice, drift ice; **g. pourrie,** cat ice; **banc de g.,** ice floe; **champ de g.,** ice field; **clarté des glaces,** ice blink; **navire retenu, pris, par les glaces,** ice-bound ship; **hiver sans g.,** ice-free winter; **le thermomètre est à g.,** the thermometer is at freezing point; **les saints de g.,** the Ice Saints, the Icemen (i.e. the Saints who are commemorated on May 11, 12, 13, *viz.* St Mamertus, St Pancras, St Servatius); the blackthorn winter; **ferré à g.,** (i) (*of horse*) rough-shod; (ii) (*of pers.*) knowledgeable, well up (in a subject); (*of pers.*) **être de g.,** to have a chilly, frigid, manner; **un accueil de g.,** a frigid reception. **2.** (*a*) glass; **g. (de vitrine),** plate glass; **assurance des glaces de magasin,** plate-glass insurance; **uni comme une g.,** as smooth as glass; *Phot:* **g. dépolie,** focusing screen; *Arch:* **panneau de g.,** glass panel (in door, etc.); (*b*) (looking) glass, mirror; **g. à main,** hand mirror; **se coiffer devant la g.,** to do one's hair in front of the mirror; **salle des glaces,** hall of mirrors; *P:* **passer devant la g.,** (i) to stand the round (of drinks) (after losing game); (ii) *Jur:* to be up before the beak; (iii) to be done out of one's share; (*c*) *Aut: etc:* window; **baisser la g.,** to open, lower, the window; **lever, remonter, la g.,** to raise, close, shut, the window; (*d*) *Aut: A:* **g. brise-vent,** windscreen; (*e*) *Mch:* **g. du cylindre,** cylinder face; **g. du tiroir,** slide-face, facing. **3.** *Cu:* (*a*) (*meat jelly on egg*) glaze; (*b*) (sugar) icing; (*c*) ice (cream); **g. à la vanille, aux fraises,** vanilla, strawberry, ice. **4.** *Lap:* flaw (in diamond).

glacé [glase], *a.* **1.** (*a*) frozen (river, etc.); (*b*) chilled, icy, cold; **je me sentis g.,** a chill came over me; **j'ai les pieds glacés,** my feet are (as) cold as ice; **g. jusqu'aux os,** chilled to the bone; **politesse glacée,** frigid, freezing, frosty, icy, stony, politeness; **regard g.,** stony stare; **jeter un regard g. à qn,** to look coldly, frigidly, at s.o.; **colère glacée,** suppressed anger; (*c*) **trempe g.,** chilling (of cast iron); (*d*) iced (coffee, etc.). **2.** glazed, glossy; **papier g.,** smooth glazed, glossy, paper; *Paperm:* **papiers glacés,** bright enamels; **gants glacés,** glacé-kid gloves; **soie glacée,** watered silk; **fil g.,** glazed thread; *Phot:* **épreuve glacée,** glossy print; *Cu:* **fruits glacés,** crystallized fruits; **cerises glacées,** glacé cherries. **3.** *s.m.* (*a*) glaze, gloss (of paper, materials, gloves, pottery); (*b*) = boiled sweet.

glacer [glase], *v.tr.* (**je glaçai(s); n. glaçons**) **1.** (*a*) to freeze; **le froid a glacé l'étang,** the cold has made the pond freeze; **cela me glace le sang,** it makes my blood run cold; **cela me glace le cœur,** it chills my heart; **g. l'enthousiasme,** to chill, damp, enthusiasm; (*b*) to ice (water, champagne); (*c*) *Cu:* to ice, frost (cake, etc.). **2.** to glaze (thread, meat, pastry, etc.); to surface (paper); *Ind:* to polish (rice); *Art:* **g. un tableau,** to scumble, glaze, a picture; *Phot:* **g. une épreuve,** to glaze a print. **3.** *Dressm:* **g. une doublure,** to tack in, baste on, a lining.

se glacer, to freeze; **le ruisseau se glace rarement,** the stream rarely freezes; **mon sang se glaça (d'effroi, d'épouvante) à ce spectacle,** my blood froze, ran cold, at the sight; **sens glacés d'effroi,** senses numbed with terror.

glacerie [glasri], *s.f.* **1.** (*a*) glass works; mirror factory; (*b*) glass trade. **2.** (*a*) ice-cream factory; (*b*) ice-cream trade.

glaceur [glasœːr], *s.m. Tchn:* **1.** glazer (of material, paper). **2.** (*a*) glazing, rolling, machine; (*b*) glazer, glazing pad.

glaceux, -euse [glasø, -øːz], *a. Lap:* flawy.

glaciaire [glasjɛːr], *a. Geol:* glacial; **érosion g.,** glacial erosion; **période g.,** ice age, glacial age.

glaciairiste [glasjɛrist], *s.m.* = GLACIÉRISTE.

glacial, -als *or* **-aux** [glasjal, -o], (*the pl. of the adj. is rarely used*) **1.** *a.* icy (temperature); frosty (air); frigid; **vent g.,** icy, cutting, bitter, wind; **zone glaciale,** arctic region; **politesse glaciale, abord g.,** icy, chilly, chilling, chill, frigid, politeness, manner; **regarder qn d'un œil g.,** to give s.o. an icy look; **style g.,** frigid style. **2.** *s.f. Bot:* **glaciale,** ice plant.

glacialement [glasjalmɑ̃], *adv.* icily, frigidly.

glaciation [glasjasjɔ̃], *s.f.* glaciation.

glacié [glasje], *a. Geol:* glaciated.

glacier[1] [glasje], *s.m. Geol:* glacier; **g. encaissé, g. de vallée (du type alpin),** valley glacier, Alpine glacier; **g. continental,** continental ice sheet; **bleu g.,** ice-blue.

glacier[2], *s.m.* **1.** ice-cream (i) manufacturer, (ii) retailer; **pâtissier g., g. confiseur,** confectioner (who also sells ice-cream). **2.** *A:* (i) manufacturer, (ii) seller, of mirrors, plate-glass.

glacière [glasjɛːr], *s.f.* **1.** (*a*) *A:* ice house, ice pit; (*b*) *F:* **cette chambre est une vraie g.!** this room's a real ice house! **2.** (*a*) ice box; *Rail:* refrigerator van; (*b*) *F:* (*incorrect use*) refrigerator; (*c*) insulated picnic bag. **3.** mass of ice; **g. naturelle,** ice cave.

glaciériste [glasjerist], *s.m.* (*a*) student of glaciers; (*b*) *Mount:* specialist at, in, climbing on ice.

glaciologie [glasjɔlɔʒi], *s.f. Geol:* glaciology.

glaciologiste [glasjɔlɔʒist], **glaciologue** [glasjɔlɔg], *s.m. & f. Geol:* glaciologist.

glacis [glasi], *s.m.* **1.** (*a*) slope, bank; *Const:* (i) ramp; (ii) weathering; *Geog: Fort:* glacis; *Coke-making:* wharf (upon which the coke-oven is emptied); **g. couverts de neige,** snow-covered slopes; (*b*) *Farr:* surface (of horse's hoof). **2.** *Art:* scumble, glaze. **3.** *Dressm:* tacking, basting.

glaçoire [glaswaːr], *s.f. Cu:* sugar sifter, sugar dredge.

glaçon [glasɔ̃], *s.m.* (*a*) block of ice; ice floe; *pl.* drift ice, broken ice (on river); (*b*) icicle; (*c*) ice cube; **whisky sec aux glaçons,** whisky on the rocks; (*d*) *F:* **cette femme est un vrai g.!** what an iceberg that woman is! **c'est un g.!** he's, she's, a cold fish!

glaçure [glasyːr], *s.f. Cer:* glaze; **g. stannifère,** tin glaze; **g. plombifère,** lead glaze.

gladiateur [gladjatœːr], *s.m.* gladiator; **combats de gladiateurs,** gladiatorial fights.

gladiatorial, -aux [gladjatɔrjal, -o], *a.* gladiatorial.

gladié [gladje], *a. Bot:* gladiate, sword-shaped.

gladite [gladit], *s.f. Miner:* gladite.

glaïeul [glajœl], *s.m. Bot:* gladiolus, sword grass, sword lily; **g. des marais,** sword flag.

glairage [glɛraːʒ], *s.m, Bookb:* glairing.

glaire [glɛːr], *s.f.* **1.** (*a*) white of egg, glair; *Bookb:* glair; (*b*) mucus, phlegm; *Med:* glair. **2.** *Lap:* flaw (in diamond, etc.).

glairer [glere], *v.tr. Bookb:* to glair (book cover).

glaireux, -euse [glɛrø, -øːz], *a.* glaireous, glairy; **gorge glaireuse,** throat full of phlegm.

glairine [glɛrin]. *s.f. Ch:* glairin.

glairure [glɛryːr], *s.f. Bookb:* glair.

glaisage [glɛzaːʒ], *s.m. Min:* (*a*) claying (of bore hole); (*b*) coffering (of shaft).

glaise [glɛːz], *s.f.* clay, loam; *Hyd.E:* puddled clay, puddle, puddling; **terre glaise,** (i) clay, (ii) potter's clay.

glaiser [gleze], *v.tr.* **1.** *Agr:* to clay; to dress (soil) with clay. **2.** to line (sth.) with clay; to loam; *Min:* to coffer (shaft); *Hyd.E:* to puddle, pug (reservoir).

glaiseux, -euse [glɛzø, -øːz]. **1.** *a.* clayey, loamy; **sol g.,** clay soil, stiff soil. **2.** *s.m. P:* peasant, clodhopper.

glaisière [glɛzjɛːr], *s.f.* clay pit.

glaive [glɛːv], *s.m.* **1.** *Lit. & Poet:* glaive, sword, blade; *A:* **la puissance du g.,** the power of life and death. **2.** *Ich: F:* swordfish.

glanage [glanaːʒ], *s.m.* gleaning.

gland [glɑ̃], *s.m.* **1.** (*a*) *Bot:* acorn; **g. de terre,** ground nut, peanut; (*b*) *pl. Agr:* mast. **2.** tassel (of curtain, etc.); acorn (of sword-knot); **orné de glands,** tasselled. **3.** *Anat:* glans. **4.** *Mch:* **g. de presse-étoupe,** stuffing gland. **5.** *Moll:* **g. de mer,** acorn shell. **6.** *P:* clot, stupid person.

glandage [glɑ̃daːʒ], *s.m.* **1.** (*a*) area where acorns are gathered; (*b*) gathering acorns; right to gather acorns. **2.** *Med: Vet:* inflammation of gland in the throat.

glande [glɑ̃ːd], *s.f. Anat: Bot:* gland; **g. lacrimale,** lachrymal gland; **glandes lymphatiques,** lymphatic glands; **glandes à sécrétion interne,** ductless glands; *F:* **avoir des glandes au cou,** to have swollen glands; *Rept:* **g. venimeuse,** poison gland; *Moll:* **g. du noir,** ink bag (of cuttlefish); *Ent:* **g. cirière,** wax gland.

glandé [glɑ̃de], *a.* **1.** *Her:* acorned. **2.** *Vet:* glandered.

glandée [glɑ̃de], *s.f.* **1.** acorn crop, mast, pannage. **2.** acorn harvest; **faire la g.,** to gather, get in, the acorns.

glander [glɑ̃de], *v.i. P:* to loiter, to kick one's heels.

glandifère [glɑ̃difɛːr], *a. Bot:* glandiferous, acorn-bearing.

glandiforme [glɑ̃difɔrm], *a.* glandiform. **1.** acorn-shaped. **2.** gland-like.

glandivore [glɑ̃divɔːr], *a.* acorn-eating.

glandouiller [glɑ̃duje], *v.i. P:* to loiter, to kick one's heels.

glandulaire [glɑ̃dylɛːr], *a.* glandular.

glandule [glɑ̃dyl], *s.f. Anat:* glandule.

glanduleux, -euse [glɑ̃dylø, -øːz], *a.* glandulous.

glandulifère [glɑ̃dylifɛːr], *a.* glanduliferous.

glane [glan], *s.f.* **1.** (*a*) gleaning; **faire la g.,** to glean; (*b*) *pl.* gleanings; (*c*) *pl. F:* pickings. **2. g. d'oignons,** string, rope, of onions; **g. de poires,** cluster of pears. **3.** *Hist:* collection of tithes.

glanement [glan(ə)mɑ̃], *s.m.* (action of) gleaning.

glaner [glane], *v.tr.* (*a*) to glean; (*b*) to gather (wild flowers, fruit); to pick up (things strewn around); **g. le bois tombé,** to gather sticks (for firewood); (*c*) **il y a beaucoup à g. dans ce livre,** a great deal can be learnt, gleaned, from this book.

glaneur, -euse [glanœːr, -øːz], *s.* gleaner.

glanure [glanyːr], *s.f.* gleaning(s); **glanures prises dans les journaux,** gleanings from the newspapers; newspaper cuttings.

glaphique [glafik], *s.m. Miner:* steatite.

glapir [glapiːr], *v.i.* (*of puppy, F: of pers.*) to yelp, yap; (*of fox*) to bark.

glapissant [glapisɑ̃], *a.* yapping, yelping (dog); **voix glapissante,** shrill voice.

glapissement [glapismɑ̃], *s.m.* yapping, yelping (of puppies); barking (of foxes).

glaréole [glareɔl], *s.f. Orn:* glareole; pratincole; **g. à collier,** (collared) pratincole; **g. à ailes noires,** black-winged pratincole.

glaréolidés [glareɔlide], *s.m.pl. Orn:* Glareolidae, the pratincoles.

Glaris [glaris], *Pr.n. Geog:* Glarus.

glaronais, -aise [glarɔnɛ, -ɛːz], *a. & s. Geog:* (native, inhabitant) of Glarus.

glas [glɑ], *s.m.* (*a*) knell; **sonner le g.,** to toll the knell, the passing bell; **nouvelle qui sonne le g. de bien des espérances,** news that puts an end to many hopes; (*b*) salvo of guns (at military or State funeral).

glass [glas], *s.m. P:* drink, snifter.

glatir [glatiːr], *v.i.* (*of eagle*) to scream.

Glauber [globɛːr], *Pr.n.m. Pharm:* **sel de G.,** Glauber's salt(s).

glaubérite [globerit], *s.f. Miner:* glauberite.

glaucescence [glosɛs(s)ɑ̃ːs], *s.f. Bot:* glaucescence.

glaucescent [glosɛs(s)ɑ̃], *a. Bot:* glaucescent.

glaucière [glosjɛːr], *s.f.,* **glaucienne** [glosjɛn], *s.f. Bot:* glaucium; **glaucienne jaune,** yellow-horned poppy.

glaucochroïte [glokɔkrɔit], *s.f. Miner:* glaucochroite.

glaucodot [glokɔdo], *s.m. Miner:* glaucodot.

glaucomateux, -euse [glokɔmatø, -øːz], *a.* glaucomatous.

glaucome [glokɔm, -kom], *s.m. Med:* glaucoma.

glaucomys [glokɔmis], *s.m. Z:* glaucomys.

glauconie [glokɔni], **glauconite** [glokɔnit], *s.f. Miner:* glauconite; green earth.

glauconieux, -ieuse [glokɔnjø, -jøːz], *a.* glauconitic.

glauconifère [glokɔnifɛːr], *a.* glauconiferous.

glaucophane [glokɔfan], *s.f. Miner:* glaucophane.

glauque [gloːk]. **1.** *a.* glaucous, bluey-green; **yeux glauques,** sea-green eyes. **2.** *s.f. Bot:* sea milk-wort.

glaux [glo], *s.m. Bot:* milkwort.

glaviot [glavjo], *s.m.* **1.** *A.Arms:* small sword. **2.** *P:* spit, spittle, gob.

glaviotter [glavjɔte], *v.i. P:* to spit, to gob.

glèbe [glɛb], *s.f.* **1.** clod (of earth), sod. **2.** (*a*) *A. & Lit:* soil, land (under cultivation); glebe; **le laboureur penché sur la g.,** the peasant bending over the soil; (*b*) *Hist:* feudal land; **attaché à la g.,** bound to the soil.

gléc(h)ome [glekɔm], *s.m. Bot:* glec(h)oma, ground ivy.

gleichenia [glekenja], *s.m. Bot:* Gleichenia.

glène[1] [glɛn], *s.f. Anat:* glene, socket.

glène[2], *s.f. Nau:* coil (of rope); **g. plate,** Flemish coil; **filer sa g.,** to drop one's coil.

glène[3], *s.f. Fish:* creel.

gléner [glene], *v.tr.* (**je glène, n. glénons; je glénerai**) *Nau:* to coil (rope).

glénoïdal, -aux [glenɔidal, -o], *a.,* **glénoïde** [glenɔid], *a. & s.f.,* **glénoïdien, -ienne** [glenɔidjɛ̃, -jɛn], *a. Anat:* **1.** *a.* glenoid. **2.** *s.f.* **glénoïde,** glenoid cavity.

glette [glɛt], *s.f. Com:* litharge.

gley [glɛ], *s.m. Geol:* gley.

gliadine [gliadin], *s.f. Bio-Ch:* gliadin.

gline [glin], *s.f. Fish:* creel.
gliome [glijɔm], *s.m. Med:* glioma.
gliridés [gliride], *s.m.pl. Z:* Gliridae, the dormice.
gliron [glirɔ̃], *s.m. Dial:* dormouse.
glissade [glisad], *s.f.* **1.** slip; (*a*) **faire une g.,** (i) to slip; (ii) to make a faux pas; (*b*) *Av:* **g. sur l'aile,** side slip; **g. sur la queue,** tail dive. **2.** (*a*) sliding; **faire une g.,** to have a slide; (*b*) *Mount:* glissade; (*c*) *Danc:* glide; glissade; (*d*) *Mus:* (i) portamento; (ii) rapid scale passage (produced by running finger along the keys of the piano). **3.** slide (on snow or ice).
glissage [glisa:ʒ], *s.m.* sliding down (of cut timber in the mountains).
glissance [glisɑ̃:s], *s.f.* slipperiness (*esp.* of road).
glissant [glisɑ̃], *a.* **1.** slippery (eel, pavement, etc.); **il fait g.,** it's slippery (walking); **être sur un terrain g.,** to be on delicate, slippery, ground. **2.** sliding; **porte glissante,** sliding door; *Mec.E:* **joint g.,** sliding joint, slip joint, expansion joint; *Mth:* **vecteur g.,** sliding vector.
glissé [glise]. **1.** *a.* **carte glissée,** palmed card. **2.** *s.m. Danc:* glissade, glide.
glissée [glise], *s.f.* sliding, shifting.
glissement [glismɑ̃], *s.m.* (*a*) sliding, slipping; slip; *Civ.E:* **angle de g. (d'un remblai),** batter (of an embankment); (*b*) gliding, glide; *Av:* side-slipping, skidding; (*c*) *Mec.E:* creeping (of belt); (*d*) *Elcs:* **g. de fréquence,** frequency variation; (*e*) *Geol: Geog:* **g. (vertical),** fault slip; **surface de g.,** slickenside; **g. de terrain,** landslide; landslip; (*f*) *St.Exch:* gradual falling away; *Ling:* **g. de sens,** shift in meaning; *Pol:* **g. à gauche, vers la gauche, au profit des gauches,** swing to the left.
glisser [glise]. I. *v.i.* **1.** (*a*) to slip; **le couteau lui a glissé des mains,** the knife slipped from his hands; **j'ai glissé sur une flaque d'huile,** I slipped on a patch of oil; **g. sur une peau de banane,** to slip on a banana skin; **à mon entrée il se laissa g. de sur la table,** when I came in he slipped off the table; (*b*) (*of wheel*) to skid; *Av:* **g. sur l'aile,** to side-slip; (*c*) *Mec.E:* (*of belt*) to creep; (*d*) *Aut:* **g. à droite** = to filter to the left, (*in U.S: etc.*) to the right; (*e*) *Danc:* to glissade. **2.** to slide (on ice, on lubricated surface); **faire g.,** to slide (part of machine, etc.); **se laisser g. le long d'une corde,** to slide down a rope; **g. le long de la rampe,** to slide down the banisters; **g. dans le péché,** to slide into sin; *P:* **se laisser g.,** to die, to peg out. **3.** to glide (over the water, etc.); **un sourire ironique glissa sur ses lèvres,** he gave a brief ironic smile. **4. g. sur qch.** (*a*) to make little impression on sth.; to glance off sth.; **l'épée lui glissa sur les côtes,** the sword merely grazed his ribs; the sword glanced off his ribs; (*b*) to touch lightly on (subject); **glissons (là-dessus)!** we won't dwell on that; let's leave that (for the moment); let that pass; I, we, won't insist.
II. **glisser,** *v.tr.* **1.** (*a*) **g. qch. dans la poche de qn,** to slip sth. into s.o.'s pocket; **on a glissé la commode contre l'autre mur,** we pushed the chest of drawers over against the other wall; **la porte s'entrouvrit et un petit enfant glissa un œil,** the door half opened and a small child peeped in; **g. un œil vers qn,** to sneak a glance at s.o.; **g. un mot à qn,** to slip a note to s.o.; **g. un mot à l'oreille de qn,** to drop a word in s.o.'s ear; **impossible de g. un mot!** I couldn't get a word in edgeways. **2.** *Knitting:* **g. une maille,** to slip a stitch.
se glisser, to glide, creep, steal (**dans,** into); **se g. dans son lit,** to slip, creep, into bed; **se g. dans la société,** to worm one's way into society; **il s'est glissé bien des fautes dans ce livre,** many errors have crept into this book; **glose qui s'est glissée dans le texte,** gloss that has slipped into the text.
glissette [glisɛt], *s.f. Geom:* glissette.
glisseur, -euse [glisœ:r, -ø:z], *s.* **1.** (*a*) slider (on ice, snow); (*b*) *A:* **bateau g.,** hydroplane boat. **2.** *s.m.* (*a*) *Mch:* slide block; (*b*) *Av:* glider; (*c*) *Mth:* sliding vector.
glissière [glisjɛ:r], *s.f.* **1.** groove, slide; **porte à glissières,** sliding door; **à g.,** skid-mounted; *Row:* **banc à glissières,** sliding seat. **2.** (*a*) *Mch:* (slipper) guide, slipper, slide bar, guide rod; *Artil:* recoil slide; *Mec.E: pl.* shears (of lathe); *Veh: etc:* **glissières de la glace,** window guides; *Cin:* **g. (de la bande),** pad; **voie de g.,** slide face; *Oil Min:* **g. de forage,** drilling jar; (*b*) *Av: etc:* cable guide; (*c*) (*alongside road*) crash barrier. **3.** *Ind:* shoot (for coal, etc.).
glissoir [gliswa:r], *s.m.* **1.** *Mch:* slide, sliding block. **2.** *For:* timber slide, shoot. **3.** flume (of a mill).
glissoire [gliswa:r], *s.f.* **1.** slide (on ice or snow). **2.** timber slide, shoot.
global, -aux [glɔbal, -o], *a.* total, aggregate, inclusive, gross, global (sum, etc.); lump (payment); **capital g.,** total capital; *Nau:* **déplacement g.,** gross displacement; **tonnage g.,** total tonnage; *Sch:* **méthode globale,** global method (of teaching reading).
globalement [glɔbalmɑ̃], *adv.* in the aggregate, in the lump, in bulk.
globalité [glɔbalite], *s.f.* universality (of theory).
globe [glɔb], *s.m.* **1.** (*a*) globe, sphere; **faire le tour du g.,** to go round the globe, round the world; **le g. du soleil,** the orb of the sun; (*b*) orb (of regalia); *Her:* mound. **2. g. de lampe,** lamp-globe; **g. électrique,** electric-light globe; **g. d'une pendule,** glass shade of a clock; **statuette sous g.,** statuette under glass. **3.** *Anat:* **g. de l'œil,** eyeball, globe of the eye. **4.** *Meteor:* **g. de feu, g. fulminant,** fire ball, globe lightning. **5.** *Med:* **g. hystérique,** *globus hystericus,* choking sensation (associated with hysteria); **g. vésical,** vesical distention (caused by retention of urine).
globe-trotter [glɔbtrɔtœ:r], *s.m.* globe trotter; *pl. globe-trotters.*
globeux, -euse [glɔbø, -ø:z], *a. Bot:* globose.
globicéphales [glɔbisefal], *s.m.pl. Z:* globicephala; *F:* pilot whales, caa'ing whales, blackfish.
globigérine [glɔbiʒerin], *s.f. Prot:* globigerina; *pl.* Globigerinae; *Geol:* **boue à globigérines,** globigerina ooze.
globigérinidés [glɔbiʒerinide], *s.m.pl. Prot:* Globigerinidae.
globine [glɔbin], *s.f. Bio-Ch:* globin.
globique [glɔbik], *a.* **globoïdale** [glɔbɔidal], *a.f.* globular; **vis g.,** hour-glass screw.
globoïde [glɔbɔid], *s.m. Bot:* globule.
globulaire [glɔbylɛ:r]. **1.** *a.* (*a*) globular (in shape); *Geol:* spherulitic; (*b*) *Med:* **numération g.,** blood count. **2.** *s.f. Bot:* globe daisy, globularia.
globulariacées [glɔbylarjase], *s.f.pl. Bot:* Globulariaceae.
globulation [glɔbylasjɔ̃], *s.f. Metall:* spheroidizing.
globule [glɔbyl], *s.m.* **1.** (*a*) globule (of air, water); drop (of water); (*b*) *Physiol:* (blood) corpuscle; **g. blanc,** leukocyte, white corpuscle; **g. rouge,** erythrocyte, red corpuscle; **g. du pus,** pus cell; (*c*) *Pharm:* globule, small pill; (*d*) *Biol:* **g. polaire,** polar body. **2.** air hole (in metals, etc.).
globuleux, -euse [glɔbylø, -ø:z], *a.* globular; globulous, globulose; **yeux g.,** protruding eyes.
globulin [glɔbylɛ̃], *s.m. Physiol:* hematoblast, blood platelet.
globuline [glɔbylin], *s.f. Ch:* globulin.
globulinurie [glɔbylinyri], *s.f. Med:* globulinuria.
globulolyse [glɔbylɔli:z], *s.f. Med:* hemolysis.
globus pallidus [glɔbyspalidys], *s.m. Anat:* globus pallidus.
glockenspiel [glɔkɛnspil], *s.m. Mus:* glockenspiel.
gloire [glwa:r], *s.f.* **1.** glory; **il fut la g. de son siècle,** he was the glory of his age; **titres de g.,** titles to fame; **Salomon dans toute sa g.,** Solomon in all his glory; **se couvrir de g.,** to cover oneself with glory; **rendre g. à Dieu,** to give glory to God, to glorify God; **g. à Dieu!** glory be to God! **rendre g. à la vérité,** to testify to the truth; **travailler pour la g.,** to work for nothing, for love; *F:* **parti pour la g.,** a little tight, slightly elevated, slightly fuddled, well away. **2.** boast, pride; vainglory; **se faire g. de qch.,** to glory in sth., to pride oneself on sth.; **se faire g. de faire qch.,** to take a pride, to glory, in doing sth.; **mettre sa g. à, en, qch.,** to boast of, glory in, sth. **3.** glory, halo, aureole, nimbus, gloriole. **4.** *Pyr:* fixed sun.
glome [glɔm], *s.m. Z: Anat:* glome.
glomérule [glɔmeryl], *s.m. Biol:* glomerule, tuft.
glomérulé [glɔmeryle], *a. Biol:* glomerulate.
glomérulonéphrite [glɔmerylɔnefrit], *s.f. Med:* glomerulonephritis.
glomus [glɔmy:s], *s.m.Anat:* glomus; **g. carotidien,** glomus caroticum.
gloria [glɔrja], *s.m.* **1.** *Ecc:* *Gloria* ((i) *Patri,* (ii) *in excelsis*). **2.** *F: O:* (*a*) coffee or tea served with spirits; (*b*) small coffee-cup.
gloriette [glɔrjɛt], *s.f.* **1.** summer-house, arbour. **2.** fancy bird cage.
glorieusement [glɔrjøzmɑ̃], *adv.* **1.** gloriously. **2.** proudly.
glorieux, -euse [glɔrjø, -ø:z], *a.* **1.** glorious (reign, etc.); **les g. martyrs,** the glorious martyrs; **les g.,** the saints in glory; *Theol:* **corps g.,** glorified body. **2.** vainglorious, proud; **g. de qch.,** vain, conceited, about, sth.; **g. comme un paon,** as proud, vain, as a peacock. **3.** *s.m.* boaster, braggart; **faire le g.,** to brag, to swagger.
glorificateur, -trice [glɔrifikatœ:r, -tris], *s.* praiser, glorifier, panegyrist.
glorification [glɔrifikasjɔ̃], *s.f.* glorification.
glorifier [glɔrifje], *v.tr.* (*p.d. & pr.sub.* **n. glorifiions, v. glorifiiez**) to praise, glorify, magnify; to crown with glory; *Ecc:* **que ton nom soit glorifié!** hallowed be thy name.
se glorifier, to boast; **se g. de qch., de faire qch.,** to glory in sth., in doing sth.; to boast of sth., of doing sth.
gloriole [glɔrjɔl], *s.f.* **1.** notoriety, vainglory; **pour la g.,** for the sake of kudos; **faire de la g.,** to talk big. **2. conter toutes ses petites glorioles,** to recount all one's petty triumphs.
glose [glo:z], *s.f.* **1.** gloss, commentary; **g. marginale,** marginal note. **2.** comment, criticism; **dire la vérité sans g.,** to speak the truth and nothing but the truth; *F:* **craindre les gloses du public,** to be afraid of what people will say.
gloser [gloze]. **1.** *v.tr.* to gloss, expound (text). **2.** *v.i. A. & F:* **g. de, sur, qch.,** to find fault with sth., to carp at sth.; to gossip (unkindly) about sth.; **toute la ville en glosait,** the whole town was talking about it.
gloseur, -euse [glozœ:r, -ø:z], *s. A:* quiz, gossip; carper.
glossaire [glɔsɛ:r], *s.m.* **1.** glossary, dictionary. **2.** vocabulary (of a language).
glossalgie [glɔsalʒi], *s.f. Med:* glossalgia.
glossateur [glɔsatœ:r], *s.m. A:* writer of glosses; glossator, glossist, glossarist; commentator.
glosse [glɔs], *s.f. Ent:* glossa.
glossématique [glɔsematik], *s.f. Ling:* glossematics.
glossème [glɔsɛm], *s.m. Ling:* glosseme.
glossette [glɔsɛt], *s.f. Pharm:* glossette.
glossien, -ienne [glɔsjɛ̃, -jɛn], *a. Anat:* glossal.
glossine [glɔsin], *s.f. Ent:* glossina, tsetse fly.
glossique [glɔsik], *a.* = GLOSSIEN.
glossite [glɔsit], *s.f. Med:* glossitis.
glossodynie [glɔsɔdini], *s.f. Med:* glossodynia, glossalgia.
glossographe [glɔsɔgraf], *s.m.* glossographer.
glossographie [glɔsɔgrafi], *s.f.* glossography.
glossolalie [glɔsɔlali], *s.f.* glossolalia.
glossologie [glɔsɔlɔʒi], *s.f. Med: Ling: Phil:* glossology.
glossophage [glɔsɔfa:ʒ], *s.m. Z:* glossophaga.
glosso-pharyngien, -ienne [glɔsofarɛ̃ʒjɛ̃, -jɛn], *a. Anat: etc:* glossopharyngeal.
glossoplégie [glɔsɔpleʒi], *s.f. Med:* glossoplegia.
glossotomie [glɔsɔtɔmi], *s.f. Surg:* glossotomy.
glottal, -aux [glɔt(t)al, -o], *a. Ling: Anat:* glottal.
glotte [glɔt], *s.f. Anat:* glottis; *Ling:* **coup de g.,** glottal catch, glottal stop.
glottique [glɔt(t)ik], *a.* glottal, glottic.
glouglou [gluglu], *s.m.* **1.** glug-glug, gurgle, bubbling (of liquor issuing from bottle); **faire g.,** to gurgle, to bubble. **2.** gobble (of turkey); coo (of pigeon).
glouglouter [gluglute], *v.i.* **1.** (*of liquid*) to gurgle, bubble. **2.** (*of turkey*) to gobble.
gloussant [glusɑ̃], *a.* clucking (hen, etc.).
gloussement [glusmɑ̃], *s.m.* clucking, cluck (of hen); gobbling, gobble (of turkey); chuckling, chuckle, chortle (of person).
glousser [gluse], *v.i.* (*of hen*) to cluck; (*of turkey*) to gobble; (*of pers.*) to chuckle, to gurgle; to chortle.
glouteron [glutrɔ̃], *s.m. Bot:* **1.** burdock, burr; **g. épineux,** lesser burdock, burweed. **2.** bed-straw.
glouton, -onne [glutɔ̃, -ɔn]. **1.** *a.* greedy, gluttonous. **2.** *s.* (*a*) glutton, gormandizer; **c'est un petit g.,** he's a regular little pig; (*b*) *s.m. Z:* glutton, wolverine.
gloutonnement [glutɔnmɑ̃], *adv.* gluttonously; ravenously, greedily; *F:* like a pig.
gloutonnerie [glutɔnri], *s.f.* gluttony, gourmandism.
gloxinia [glɔksinja], *s.m.inv.,* **gloxinie** [glɔksini], *s.f. Bot:* gloxinia.
glu [gly], *s.f.* (*a*) bird lime; **enduire des ramilles de g.,** to lime twigs; **prendre des oiseaux à la g.,** to lime birds; **être pris à la g.,** to be inveigled, caught in a trap; **il a de la g. aux mains,** money sticks to his fingers; (*b*) **g. marine,** marine glue; *Bot:* **arbre à la g.,** holly; (*c*) *Ent:* (snail, etc.) slime; **glandes à g.,** slime glands.
gluant [glyɑ̃], *a.* sticky, gummy, gluey; *F:* **il est g.,** he sticks to you like a leech.
gluau, -aux [glyo], *s.m.* **1.** lime twig, snare; **tendre des gluaux aux oiseaux,** to set snares for the birds. **2.** *P:* phlegm, gob.
glucagon [glykagɔ̃], *s.m. Ch:* glucagon.
glucamine [glykamin], *s.f. Ch:* glucamine.
glucide [glysid], *s.m.* glucid(e).

glucidique [glysidik], *a. Ch: Biol:* **aliments glucidiques**, carbohydrates.
glucine [glysin], *s.f. Ch:* beryllia, beryllium oxide.
glucinium [glysinjɔm], *s.m. Ch:* glucin(i)um, beryllium.
glucite [glysit], *s.f.*, **glucitol** [glysitɔl], *s.m.* glucitol.
glucocorticoïde [glykokɔrtikɔid], *s.m. Bio.-Ch:* glucocorticoid.
glucomètre [glykɔmɛtr], *s.m. Brew:* glucometer, saccharometer.
gluconate [glykɔnat], *s.m.* gluconate.
gluconique [glykɔnik], *a. Ch:* gluconic (acid).
glucoprotéide [glykɔprɔteid], *s.m.*, **glucoprotéine** [glykɔprɔtein], *s.f.* glucoprotein, glycoprotein.
glucopyrannose [glykɔpiranoːz], *s.m. Ch:* glucopyranose.
glucosamine [glykozamin], *s.f. Ch:* glucosamine.
glucosan(n)e [glykozan], *s.m. Ch:* glucosan.
glucose [glykoːz], *s.m. occ. s.f.* glucose, grape sugar; **g. sanguin**, blood sugar.
glucoserie [glykozri], *s.f.* glucose factory.
glucoside [glykozid], *s.m. Ch:* glucoside.
glucosurie [glykozyri], *s.f. Med:* glucosuria; diabetes mellitus.
gluer [glye], *v.tr.* to lime (twigs); **cela vous glue les mains**, it makes one's fingers sticky.
glui [glɥi], *s.m.* thatching straw (from rye).
glumacé [glymase], *Bot:* **1.** *a.* glumaceous. **2.** *s.f.pl.* **glumacées**, Glumaceae.
glume [glym], *s.f.* (*a*) *Bot:* glume; (*b*) *Agr:* chaff.
glumé [glyme], *a. Bot:* glumose.
glumelle [glymɛl], *s.f. Bot:* glumella, lemma.
glumiflores [glymiflɔːr], *s.f.pl. Bot:* Glumiflorae.
glutamine [glytamin], *s.f. Ch:* glutamine.
glutamique [glytamik], *a. Ch:* glutamic.
glutarique [glytarik], *a. Ch:* glutaric.
glutathion [glytatjɔ̃], *s.m. Ch:* glutathione.
gluten [glytɛn], *s.m.* gluten; **pain de g.**, gluten bread.
glutinatif, -ive [glytinatif, -iːv], *a.* agglutinative, binding.
glutination [glytinasjɔ̃], *s.f.* agglutination, binding, caking.
glutineux, -euse [glytinø, -øːz], *a.* glutinous.
glutinosité [glytinozite], *s.f.* glutinosity.
glycémie [glisemi], *s.f. Med:* glycemia.
glycérat [glisera], **glycéré** [glisere], *s.m. Pharm:* glycerite, glycerole; solution in glycerine; **g. de tannin**, glycerine of tannic acid; *F:* glycerine and tannin.
glycère [glisɛːr], *s.f. Ann:* glycera.
glycéride [gliserid], *s.f. Ch:* glyceride.
glycérie [gliseri], *s.f. Bot:* glyceria, sweet grass; **g. flottante**, manna grass, float grass.
glycérine [gliserin], *s.f. Ch:* glycerin(e), glycerol.
glycériné [gliserine], *a. Pharm: etc:* glycerized.
glycériner [gliserine], *v.tr.* to rub (sth.) over, treat (sth.), with glycerin(e).
glycérique [gliserik], *a. Ch:* **acide g.**, glyceric acid.
glycérol [gliserɔl], *s.m. Ch:* glycerol.
glycérolé [gliserɔle], *s.m.* = GLYCÉRÉ.
glycérophosphate [gliserɔfɔsfat], *s.m. Ch: Pharm:* glycerophosphate.
glycérophosphorique [gliserɔfɔsfɔrik], *a. Ch:* glycerophosphoric (acid).
glycéryle [gliseril], *s.m. Ch:* glyceryl.
glycidique [glisidik], *a. Ch:* glycidic (acid).
glycin [glisɛ̃], *s.m.*, **glycine**[1] [glisin], *s.f. Phot:* glycin(e).
glycine[2], *s.f. Bot:* wistaria.
glycine[3], *s.f. Ch:* glycocoll, glycin.
glyco- [gliko, -o], *pref.* glyco-; *Ch:* **glycogénase**, glycogenase.
glycocolle [glikokɔl], *s.m. Ch:* glycocoll, glycin, gelatin sugar.
glycogène [glikɔʒɛn], *s.m. Ch:* glycogen.
glycogénèse [glikɔʒenɛːz], *s.f.*, **glycogénie** [glikɔʒeni], *s.f. Physiol:* glycogenesis.
glycogénique [glikɔʒenik], *a. Physiol:* glycogenic.
glycol [glikɔl], *s.m. Ch:* glycol.
glycolique [glikɔlik], *a. Ch:* glycolic (acid).
glycolyse [glikɔliːz], *s.f. Physiol:* glycolysis.
glycolytique [glikɔlitik], *a. Physiol:* glycolytic.
glyconien, -ienne [glikɔnjɛ̃, -jɛn], **glyconique** [glikɔnik], *a. Gr.Pros:* glyconic (metre, verse).
glycoprotéide [glikɔprɔteid], *s.m. Ch:* glucoprotein, glycoprotein.
glycosamine [glikɔzamin], *s.f. Ch:* glucosamine.
glycoside [glikɔzid], *s.f. Ch:* glycoside.
glycosurie [glikɔzyri], *s.f. Med:* glycosuria.
glycosurique [glikɔzyrik], *a. Med:* glycosuric.
glycuronique [glikyrɔnik], *a. Ch:* glycuronic (acid).
glycuronurie [glikyrɔnyri], *s.f. Med:* glycuresis.
glycyméridés [glisimeride], *s.m.pl. Moll:* Glycymeridae.
glycyphage [glisifaːʒ], *s.m. Ent:* glycyphagus.
glycyrrhizine [glisirizin], *s.f. Ch:* glycyrrhizin.
glyoxal [gliɔksal], *s.m. Ch:* glyoxal.
glyoxaline [gliɔksalin], *s.f. Ch:* glyoxaline.
glyoxime [gliɔksim], *s.f. Ch:* glyoxime.
glyoxylique [gliɔksilik], *a. Ch:* glyoxylic (acid).
glyphe [glif], *s.m. Arch:* glyph, groove, channel.
glyptique [gliptik], *Art:* **1.** *a.* glyptic. **2.** *s.f.* glyptics.
glyptodon [gliptɔdɔ̃], *s.m.*, **glyptodonte** [gliptɔdɔ̃ːt], *s.m. Paleont:* glyptodon.
glyptographie [gliptɔgrafi], *s.f.* glyptography.
glyptologie [gliptɔlɔʒi], *s.f.* glyptology.
glyptothèque [gliptɔtɛk], *s.f.* **1.** collection of carved gems. **2.** museum of sculpture.
gmelina [gmelina], *s.m. Bot:* gmelina.
gmélinite [gmelinit], *s.f. Miner:* gmelinite.
gnaf [ɲaf], *s.m. P:* (*a*) cobbler, shoemender; (*b*) bungler; (*c*) rotter, stinker.
gnangnan [ɲɑ̃ɲɑ̃], *F:* **1.** *a.inv.* flabby, lackadaisical, spineless, wet. **2.** (*a*) *s.m. or f.* spineless person, wet; (*b*) *s.m.* drivel.
gnaphale [gnafal], *s.m. Bot:* cudweed.
gnathion [gnatjɔ̃], *s.m. Anthr:* gnathion.
gnathique [gnatik], *a. Anthr:* gnathic; **indice g.**, gnathic index.
gnathobdellidés [gnatɔbdɛlide], *s.m.pl. Ent:* Gnathobdellida.
gnatologie [gnatɔlɔʒi], *s.f. Dent:* gnathology.
gnathopode [gnatɔpɔd], *s.m. Crust:* gnathopod.
gnathostomes [gnatɔstɔm], *s.m.pl. Z:* Gnathostomata.
gnaule [ɲoːl], *s.f. P:* brandy, spirits, rotgut.
gneiss [gnɛs], *s.m. Geol:* gneiss.
gneissique [gnɛsik], *a. Geol:* gneissic.
gnétacées [gnetase], *s.f.pl. Bot:* Gnetaceae.
gnétales [gnetal], *s.f.pl. Bot:* Gnetales.
gnète [gnɛt], *s.m. Bot:* gnetum.
gniaf(fe) [ɲaf], *s.m. P:* (*a*) cobbler, shoemender; (*b*) bungler; (*c*) rotter, stinker.
gniaffer [ɲafe], *v.tr. A: P:* to bungle, botch, foozle (piece of work).
gniaule, gniole [ɲoːl], *s.f. P:* brandy, spirits, rotgut.
gnocchi [ɲɔki], *s.m. Cu:* gnocchi.
gnognot(t)e [ɲɔɲɔt], *s.f. P:* **1.** trash, rubbish; **ce n'est pas de la g.**, that's something like. **2.** trifle; **c'est de la g.**, that's just chicken feed.
gnole, gnôle [ɲoːl], *s.f. P:* brandy, spirits, rotgut.
gnome [gnoːm], *s.m.* gnome.
gnomide [gnɔmid], *s.f.* gnomide.
gnomique [gnɔmik], *a.* gnomic (poet, aorist).
gnomon [gnɔmɔ̃], *s.m.* **1.** gnomon. **2.** sundial.
gnomonique [gnɔmɔnik]. **1.** *a.* gnomonic (column, etc.). **2.** *s.f.* gnomonics; the art of making sundials.
gnon [ɲɔ̃], *s.m. P:* blow, biff, punch.
gnophos [gnɔfɔs], *s.m. Ent:* annulet (moth).
gnose [gnoːz], *s.f.* **1.** *Theol:* gnosis. **2.** *Rel.H:* gnosticism.
gnoséologie [gnozeɔlɔʒi], *s.f.* gnoseology.
gnosie [gnozi], *s.f. Phil:* gnosis.
gnosique [gnozik], *a. Phil:* gnostic.
gnosticisme [gnɔstisism], *s.m.* gnosticism.
gnostique [gnɔstik], *a. & s.* gnostic.
gnou [gnu], *s.m. Z:* gnu, wildebeest.
gnouf [ɲuf], *s. P:* **1.** *s.m.* prison, clink, jug, cooler. **2.** *s.f. Sch: the École normale des sciences.*
go [go], *used in the adv.phr. F:* **tout de go. 1.** easily, without a hitch; **avaler qch. tout de go**, to swallow sth. at a gulp; **répondre tout de go**, to answer straight off. **2.** without ceremony, all of a sudden; **je l'embrassai tout de go**, I kissed her where she stood, there and then.
goal [goːl], *s.m. F: Fb:* **1.** *A:* goal. **2.** goalkeeper.
goal-average [golaveraːʒ], *s.m. Sp:* goal average; *pl. goal-averages.*
goal-keeper [golkipœːr], *F:* goalkeeper; *pl. goal-keepers.*
gobage [gɔbaːʒ], *s.m.* **1.** *P:* (*a*) infatuation, fancy (de, for); (*b*) snobbishness. **2.** *Fish:* ripple (made on water by fish catching insect).
gob(b)e[1] [gɔb], *s.f.* ball, bolus; (*a*) poison ball (for destroying animals); (*b*) food ball, cob (for fattening poultry); (*c*) wool-ball (in sheep).
gobe[2], *s.f.* cave (in chalk cliffs of the English Channel).
gobe[3], *s.m. Fish:* net (placed across small coastal streams to catch migratory fish).
gobe-la-lune [gɔblalyn], *s.m.inv. in pl. P:* simpleton, boob, dope.
gobelet [gɔblɛ], *s.m.* **1.** (*a*) goblet, cup; **verre g.**, tumbler; **g. d'une bouteille isolante**, screw cap of a vacuum flask; *Phot: etc:* **g. gradué**, graduated measure; (*b*) *Pyr:* rocket case; (*c*) **joueur de gobelets**, thimblerigger; **tour de g.**, conjuring trick (with glasses); (*d*) **g. de gland**, acorn cup. **2.** *pl. Bot:* **gobelets**, pennywort.
gobeleterie [gɔblɛtri], *s.f.* **1.** hollow glass (i) factory, (ii) trade. **2.** hollow glassware.
gobeletier [gɔblətje], *s.m.* manufacturer of, dealer in, glassware.
gobelin [gɔblɛ̃], *s.m.* goblin, hobgoblin, imp.
Gobelins (les) [legɔblɛ̃], *Pr.n.m.pl.* the State factory of Gobelin tapestry (in Paris).
gobelot(t)er [gɔblɔte], *v.i. F:* (*a*) *A:* to sip, drink slowly; (*b*) to have a good blow-out.
gobelot(t)eur [gɔblɔtœːr], *s.m. A:* boozer, tippler.
gobe-mouches [gɔbmuʃ], *s.m.inv.* **1.** *Orn:* flycatcher; **g.-m. brun**, brown flycatcher; **g.-m. narcisse**, Narcissus flycatcher; **g.-m. noir**, pied flycatcher; **g.-m. nain, rougeâtre**, red-breasted flycatcher; **g.-m. gris**, spotted flycatcher; **g.-m. à collier**, white-collared flycatcher; **g.-m. royal**, crested flycatcher; **g.-m. de paradis**, paradise flycatcher; **g.-m. américain**, tyrant, king bird, field martin. **2.** (*device for catching flies*) fly catcher. **3.** *Bot:* flytrap; sundew. **4.** *F:* simpleton, boob, dope.
gober [gɔbe], *v.tr.* (*a*) to swallow, gulp down (oyster, raw egg, etc.); to bolt (food); **œuf à g.**, new-laid egg (suitable for swallowing raw); **g. l'appât, le morceau, la mouche**, to swallow, rise to, the bait; *F:* **gober des mouches**, to stand gaping; to waste one's time; (*b*) (*of fish*) to catch (insect, on surface of water); (*c*) *F:* to believe (blindly); **g. des louanges**, to swallow flattery; **il gobe tout ce qu'on lui dit**, he believes everything he's told; (*d*) *F:* to have a strong liking for (s.o.), to be gone on (s.o.); **les élèves le, la, gobent**, the pupils think no end of him, adore her.
se gober, *F:* to think a lot of oneself, to think no small beer of oneself; **il se gobe dans ce rôle**, he fancies himself in the part; **elle se gobe énormément**, she's awfully stuck up.
goberge [gɔbɛrːʒ], *s.m.* **1.** *Carp: A:* caul (for pressing). **2.** mattress support.
goberger (se) [səgɔbɛrʒe], *v.pr.* (**je me gobergeai(s); n.n. gobergeons**) **1.** *A:* **se g. de qn**, to make fun of s.o. **2.** *F:* (*at a meal*) to do oneself well, proud.
gobet [gɔbɛ], *s.m.* **1.** (*a*) *A:* piece of meat, mouthful of meat, gobbet; (*b*) piece of meat difficult to sell. **2.** *Ven:* (*of hawk*) **prendre (un oiseau) au g.**, to pounce upon (partridge, etc.); *F: A:* **prendre qn au g.**, to take s.o. by surprise, to nab s.o. **3.** *F: A:* simpleton.
gobetage [gɔbtaːʒ], *s.m. Const:* **1.** rough-casting. **2.** rendering, roughing-in (in plastering). **3.** stopping (of cracks); pointing (of walls, etc.).
gobeter [gɔbte], *v.tr.* (**je gobette, n. gobetons; je gobetterai**) *Const:* **1.** to rough-cast. **2.** to render (with plaster). **3.** to stop (cracks); to point (wall, etc.).
gobetis [gɔbti], *s.m. Const:* **1.** rough-cast. **2.** rendering, roughing-in coat (of plaster). **3.** stopping; pointing.
gobette [gɔbɛt], *s.f.* **1.** *Dial:* (little) girl. **2.** *P:* (*a*) (*in Fr. prison*) wine ration; (*b*) **payer la g.**, to pay for the drinks.
gobeur, -euse [gɔbœːr, -øːz], *s.* **1.** gulper, swallower (of oysters, etc.). **2.** *F:* simpleton, dope; **g. de fausses nouvelles**, credulous person; *a.* **il est très g.**, he is easily taken in; he'll swallow anything.
gobichonner [gɔbiʃɔne], *v.i. P: A:* to feast, to guzzle, to eat and swill.
gobichonneur, -euse [gɔbiʃɔnœːr, -øːz], *s. A:* **1.** guzzler. **2.** reveller.
gobie [gɔbi], *s.m. Ich:* (common sand) goby; **g. brun**, rock goby; **g. noir**, black goby, groundling; **g. des marais**, mudskipper.
gobiesocidés [gɔbisɔside], *s.m.pl. Ich:* Gobiesocidae.
gobiesox [gɔbizɔks], *s.m. Ich:* gobiesox.
gobiidés [gɔbiide], *s.m.pl. Ich:* Gobiidae.
gobille [gɔbiːj], *s.f.* **1.** *Games:* marble, alley taw. **2.** *Exp:* triturating ball.
gobin [gɔbɛ̃], *s.m. F: A:* hunchback.
gobinisme [gɔbinism], *s.m.* gobinism.
gobseck [gɔbsɛk], *s.m. A:* miser, usurer (*from the character in Balzac's novel of that name*).
godage [gɔdaːʒ], *s.m.* puckering, dragging (of cloth, garment); cockling (of paper).
godaille [gɔdɑːj], *s.f. F:* feast, revel, guzzle, blow-out.
godailler [gɔdɑje], *v.i. F:* **1.** (*a*) to pub-crawl; (*b*) to guzzle. **2.** (*of cloth*) to pucker; (*of paper*) to cockle.
godailleur [gɔdɑjœːr], *s.m. F:* (*a*) pub-crawler; (*b*) guzzler.

godasse [gɔdas], *s.f. P:* boot.
goddam [gɔd(d)am], *s.m. F: A:* Englishman; *pl. goddem.*
gode [gɔd], *s.m. Ich: F:* gade.
godefiche [gɔdfiʃ], *s.f. Moll: F:* scallop.
Godefroi, Godefroy [gɔdfrwɑ, -a], *Pr.n.m.* Godfrey.
godelureau, -eaux [gɔdlyro], *s.m. Pej: F:* (*a*) elegant young idler; **c'est un g.,** he thinks he's God's gift to women; (*b*) skirt-chaser.
godenot [gɔdno], *s.m. A:* **1.** juggler's puppet, joker. **2.** *F:* misshapen little man.
goder [gɔde], *v.i.* (*of cloth*) to pucker, to ruck (up); (*of paper*) to cockle; (*of trousers*) **g. aux genoux,** to bag at the knees.
godet [gɔdɛ], *s.m.* **1.** (*a*) (i) (wooden) bowl; (drinking) cup, mug, drinking horn; (ii) *P:* glassful; **boire un g.,** to swig, knock back, a glassful; (*b*) **g. à couleur,** saucer for mixing water colours; pan (of moist colour); **g. de rechange,** refill (for powder compact, etc.); **g. de support,** insulator (for telegraph wires, for piano); **g. à huile,** waste-oil cup (of machine); drip receiver; **g. graisseur,** lubricating cup; **g. d'une pipe,** bowl of a pipe; (*c*) *Mec.E: etc:* socket (for foot of machine, etc.); *A.Mil:* bucket (of colour-belt, for butt of lance, etc.); *Fish:* holder, support (for fishing rod); (*d*) *Min:* skip; (*e*) *Hyd.E:* (noria) scoop; bucket (of dredger, excavator, waterwheel); **roue à godets,** overshot wheel; **chaîne à godets,** scoop chain; (*f*) *Bot:* cup (of acorn); calyx (of flower); (*g*) *Hort:* small flower pot. **2.** (*a*) pucker, ruck (in cloth, garment); (*b*) *Dressm:* (i) flare; (ii) gore; **à godets,** (i) flared; (ii) gored.
godétia [gɔdesia], *s.f.,* **godétie** [gɔdesi], *s.f. Bot:* godetia.
godiche [gɔdiʃ], **godichon, -onne** [gɔdiʃɔ̃, -ɔn], *F:* **1.** *a.* (*a*) stupid, silly, batty; (*b*) awkward, clumsy, ham-handed. **2.** *s.m. & f.* (*a*) simpleton, dope; (*b*) lout; lump; **quelle godiche, cette fille!** what a lump (of a girl)!
godille [gɔdiːj], *s.f.* **1.** (*a*) stem oar; scull; **aller à la g.,** to (single-)scull; **faire aller un canot à la g.,** to (single-)scull a boat; **(faire qch.) à la g.,** (to do sth.) without rhyme or reason; (*b*) *pl.* pair of sculls. **2.** *Skiing:* wedeln, godille.
godiller [gɔdije], *v.i.* to (single-)scull; to single.
godilleur [gɔdijœːr], *s.m.* sculler.
godillot [gɔdijo], *s.m.* (*a*) (military) boot; (*b*) hobnailed boot; (*c*) *F:* shapeless old shoe.
godiveau, -eaux [gɔdivo], *s.m. Cu:* (*a*) forcemeat; (*b*) forcemeat ball; (*c*) paste for *quenelles.*
godron [gɔdrɔ̃], *s.m.* **1.** *Arch:* gadroon, godroon. **2.** *pl. Metalw:* boss beading. **3.** *Cost:* (*a*) pleat, goffer; *pl.* fluting; (*b*) goffering iron.
godronnage [gɔdrɔnaːʒ], *s.m.* **1.** *Arch:* gadrooning. **2.** *Metalw:* bossing; milling (of the head of a screw). **3.** *Dressm:* goffering.
godronné [gɔdrɔne], *a.* **1.** *Arch:* gadrooned. **2.** *Metalw:* milled (screw head, etc.). **3.** *Dressm:* pleated, fluted, frilled.
godronner [gɔdrɔne], *v.tr.* **1.** *Arch:* to gadroon; to ornament (gold cup, etc.) with bosses. **2.** to mill (head of screw, etc.). **3.** *Dressm:* to goffer, flute.
godure [gɔdyːr], *s.f.* pucker, ruck.
goéland [gɔelɑ̃], *s.m. Orn:* (sea)gull; **g. argenté, à manteau bleu,** herring gull; **g. bourgmestre,** glaucous, burgomaster, gull; **g. cendré,** common gull, *U.S:* short-billed gull; **g. rieur,** black-headed gull; **g. tridactyle,** kittiwake; **g. d'Audouin,** Audouin's gull; **g. marin, g. à manteau noir,** great black-backed gull; **g. brun,** lesser black-backed gull; **g. railleur, à tête grêle,** slender-billed gull; **g. à tête noire,** great black-headed gull; **g. leucoptère, à ailes blanches,** Iceland gull.
goélette [gɔelɛt], *s.f.* **1.** *Nau:* (*a*) schooner; **g. franche,** fore-and-aft schooner; **g. carrée, à huniers,** topsail schooner; (*b*) **(voile) g.,** trysail; **g. de cape,** storm trysail. **2.** *Orn:* sea swallow.
goémon [gɔemɔ̃], *s.m.* seaweed; **goémons épaves,** (sea) wrack, knotted wrack; **g. jaune,** fucus, brown algae, brown wrack; **g. jaune vésiculeux,** bladder wrack; **g. jaune denticulé,** serrated wrack; **g. noir,** channelled wrack; **niveau des goémons jaunes, des petits goémons noirs,** fucus zone; Pelvetia zone.
goémonier, -ière [gɔemɔnje, -jɛːr]. **1.** *a.* of, relating to, seaweed; **récolte goémonière,** crop of seaweed. **2.** *s.m.* (*a*) gatherer of seaweed; (*b*) boat used for gathering seaweed.
Gœttingue [gœtɛ̃ːg], *Pr.n.m. Geog:* Göttingen.
goethite [gœtit], *s.f. Miner:* goethite.

gogaille [gɔgɑːj], *s.f. P: A:* revel, feasting; **être en g.,** to be on the spree.
gogo[1] **(à)** [agogo], *adv.phr. F:* galore; **livres à g.,** books galore; **être à g.,** to be in clover; **avoir de l'argent à g.,** to have money to burn.
gogo[2], *s.m. F:* easy dupe, gullible fool, sucker.
goguenard, -arde [gɔgnaːr, -ard]. **1.** *a.* facetious; bantering; joking; sarcastic; jeering. **2.** *s.* joker; facetious person; sarcastic person; **c'est un g.,** he likes to make fun of people; **faire le g.,** to be facetious.
goguenarder [gɔgnarde], *v.i.* to banter; to be facetious; to be sarcastic; to jeer; to make fun of people.
goguenarderie [gɔgnard(ə)ri], *s.f. A:* = GOGUENARDISE.
goguenardise [gɔgnardiːz], *s.f.* banter(ing); sarcasm; sarcastic remarks; jeering; making fun of people.
goguenau, -eaux [gɔgno], *s.m.,* **goguenot** [gɔgno], *s.m.* **1.** (*a*) cider jug; (*b*) *A:* (Algerian troops') camp kettle. **2.** (*a*) pan (of night-commode); pail (of latrines); (*b*) *P:* (i) chamber pot, po, jerry; (ii) *pl.* latrines, *P:* bog, *U.S:* john.
goguette [gɔgɛt], *s.f.* **1.** (*a*) *A:* = glee club; (*b*) *F:* **être en g.,** to be (a little) tight, merry. **3.** *A:* **chanter goguette(s) à qn,** to insult s.o.
goï [gɔj], *s.m. Jewish Rel:* goy; *pl.* goïm.
goinfrade [gwɛ̃frad], *s.f. F:* (regular) gorge; good blowout.
goinfre [gwɛ̃ːfr], *s.m. F:* guzzler, greedyguts.
goinfrer [gwɛ̃fre], *v.i. F:* to guzzle, gorge.
goinfrerie [gwɛ̃frəri], *s.f.* gluttony, guzzling.
goitre [gwaːtr], *s.m.* goitre.
goitreux, -euse [gwatrø, -øːz]. **1.** *a.* goit(e)rous (neck, swelling, person). **2.** *s.* goit(e)rous person.
Golconde [gɔlkɔ̃ːd], *Pr.n.f.* Golconda.
gold-point [gɔldpɔint], *s.m. Fin:* gold point; **maintenir le change au-dessus du g.-p.,** to maintain the exchange above the gold point.
golf [gɔlf], *s.m.* **1.** golf; **g. miniature,** miniature golf; **(terrain de) g.,** golf links. **2.** *Cost:* (*a*) sports jersey, jumper; (*b*) **en tenue de g.,** in plus fours.
golfe [gɔlf], *s.m.* **1.** gulf, bay; **le Courant du G.,** the Gulf-stream; **le Grand G. Australien, de l'Australie,** the Great Australian Bight. **2.** *Anat:* (*a*) sinus; (*b*) bulb.
golfeur, -euse [gɔlfœːr, -øːz], *s.* golfer.
golfier [gɔlfje], *s.m.* (*in Newfoundland*) inshore fisherman.
Golgotha [gɔlgɔta], *Pr.n.m.* Golgotha.
Goliath [gɔljat]. **1.** *Pr.n.m.* (*a*) Goliath; (*b*) *s.m.* goliath, giant. **2.** *s.m. Ent:* goliath beetle.
golmelle, golmette, golmotte [gɔlmɛl, gɔlmɛt, gɔlmɔt], *s.f. Fung:* ruffled agaric, parasol mushroom; reddish amanita.
gombo [gɔ̃bo], *s.m. Bot:* gumbo, lady's finger.
Goménol [gɔmenɔl], *s.m. R.t.m:* soothing oil; petroleum jelly.
gomina [gɔmina], *s.f. F:* solid brilliantine, hair dressing.
gominer (se) [sәgɔmine], *v.pr.* to plaster down one's hair (with brilliantine, etc.).
gommage [gɔmaːʒ], *s.m.* **1.** gumming. **2.** *Mch: I.C.E:* sticking, gumming (of valves, pistons). **3.** toning down, smoothing out.
gomme [gɔm], *s.f.* **1.** (*a*) gum; **g. arabique,** gum arabic; **g. laque,** shellac; *A:* **g. explosive,** explosive gelatine; (*b*) *Comest:* **pastille, boule, de g.,** gum; **g. à mâcher,** chewing gum. **2.** (*a*) **g. (élastique, à crayon, à effacer),** (india)rubber, eraser; **g. à encre,** ink eraser; (*b*) *F:* **histoire à la g.,** pointless tale; **individu à la g.,** flabby type; *St.Exch:* **transactions à la g.,** bogus transactions. **3.** (*a*) *Med:* gumma; (*b*) *Arb:* (*disease of fruit trees*) gum, gummosis. **4.** *P:* (*a*) *O:* **la (haute) g.,** the smart set; **faire de la g.,** to swank; (*b*) **mettre la g.,** to get a move on; to go all out; to pull out all the stops; *Aut:* to step on the gas.
gommé [gɔme], *a.* gummed, gummy; **papier g.,** sticky paper; *Med:* **taffetas g.,** medicated gauze (dressing).
gomme-ammoniaque [gɔmamɔnjak], *s.f.* gum ammoniac; *pl. gommes-ammoniaques.*
gomme-gutte [gɔmgyt], *s.f.* gamboge; *pl. gommes-guttes.*
gomme-laque [gɔmlak], *s.f.* shellac; *pl. gommes-laques.*
gommelaqué [gɔmlake], *a.* shellacked.
gommelaquer [gɔmlake], *v.tr.* to shellac, to lacquer.
gommement [gɔm(ə)mɑ̃], *s.m.* gumming.
gommer [gɔme], *v.tr.* **1.** to gum. **2.** to erase, rub out. **3.** to mix with gum. **4.** (*of elasticized underwear*) to streamline (the figure). **5.** *v.i. Mec.E:* to stick, jam, gum; **piston gommé,** gummed piston.

gomme-résine [gɔmrezin], *s.f.* gum resin; *pl. gommes-résines.*
gommette [gɔmɛt], *s.f.* small sticker.
gommeux, -euse [gɔmø, -øːz]. **1.** *a.* (*a*) gummy, sticky; **plante gommeuse,** gum-yielding plant; (*b*) *Med:* gummatous (tumour, etc.). **2.** *P:* (*a*) over-dressed; would-be smart; (*b*) *s.m. & f.* flashy dresser, *U.S:* dude; **ce n'est qu'un petit g., une petite gommeuse,** he, she, only thinks of what he, she, can put on his, her, back. **3.** *s.f. A:* **gommeuse,** singer (in *café-concert*). **4.** *s.f.* **gommeuse,** machine for the manufacture of gummed paper.
gommier [gɔmje], *s.m. Bot:* gum tree; **g. (bleu),** eucalyptus; **g. doux,** sweet gum (tree).
gommifère [gɔmifɛːr], *a.* gummiferous, gum-bearing, -yielding.
gommo-résineux, -euse [gɔmɔrezinø, -øːz], *a.* gum-resinous.
gommose [gɔmoːz], *s.f. Arb:* (*disease in fruit trees*) gummosis, gum.
Gomorrhe [gɔmɔːr], *Pr.n. B.Hist:* Gomorrha.
gomorrhéens [gɔmɔreɛ̃], *s.m.pl. B.Hist:* the people of Gomorrha.
gomphose [gɔ̃foːz], *s.f. Anat:* gomphosis.
gonade [gɔnad], *s.f. Biol:* gonad.
gonadique [gɔnadik], *a. Biol:* gonadal.
gonadostimuline [gɔnadɔstimylin], *s.f.* gonadotrop(h)in.
gonadotrope [gɔnadɔtrɔp], *a. Physiol:* gonadotrop(h)ic.
gonadotrophine [gɔnadɔtrɔfin], *s.f.* gonadotrop(h)in.
gonalgie [gɔnalʒi], *s.f. Med:* pain in the knee.
gonce, goncesse [gɔ̃ːs, gɔ̃sɛs], *s. P:* = GONZE, GONZESSE.
gond [gɔ̃], *s.m.* (*a*) hinge pin (of door); **mettre une porte sur ses gonds,** to hang a door; **enlever une porte de ses gonds,** to take a door off its hinges; **porte hors des, de ses, gonds,** door off its hinges; *F:* **sortir (hors) de ses gonds,** to lose one's temper, get into a tantrum; *F:* to fly off the handle, to blow one's top; (*b*) pin, pintle (of hook-and-eye hinge of rudder).
gonder [gɔ̃de], *v.tr.* to hinge (door); **porte gondée à faux,** door hung off the straight.
gondolage [gɔ̃dɔlaːʒ], *s.m.* warping (of wood); cockling, curling (of paper); buckling (of sheet iron, etc.); blistering (of paint).
gondolant [gɔ̃dɔlɑ̃], *a. P:* side-splitting, uproarously funny (story, etc.).
gondole [gɔ̃dɔl], *s.f.* **1.** (*a*) gondola; (*b*) *Aer:* nacelle, gondola (of balloon). **2.** *Civ.E:* (paved) gutter. **3.** *Med:* eye bath. **4.** *Com:* (*in supermarket, etc.*) island, gondola. **5.** *Furn:* gondola chair.
gondolé [gɔ̃dɔle], *a.* **1.** buckled, warped, out of true, truth; cockled, wavy (paper, etc.). **2.** blistered.
gondolement [gɔ̃dɔlmɑ̃], *s.m.* = GONDOLAGE.
gondoler [gɔ̃dɔle], *v.i.* (*of wood*) to warp; (*of paper*) to cockle, curl; (*of sheet iron*) to buckle; (*of car bumper, etc.*) to crumple up; (*of paint, varnish*) to blister.
se gondoler, *P:* to double up, split one's sides, shake, with laughter.
gondolier [gɔ̃dɔlje], *s.m.* gondolier.
Gondvana, Gondwana [gɔ̃(d)vana], *Pr.n.m. Geol:* **le continent du G.,** Gondwanaland.
gone, gonesse [gɔn, gɔnɛs], *s. F: Dial:* (*in Lyons and region*) (*a*) kid, brat; (*b*) fellow, chap, bloke.
gonelle [gɔnɛl], *s.f. Ich:* butterfly blenny, gunnel, butterfish.
gonfalon [gɔ̃falɔ̃], *s.m.,* **gonfanon** [gɔ̃fanɔ̃], *s.m. A:* gonfalon, banner, streamer.
gonfalonier [gɔ̃falɔnje], *s.m.,* **gonfanonier** [gɔ̃fanɔnje], *s.m. A:* gonfalonier.
gonflable [gɔ̃flabl̩], *a.* inflatable.
gonflage [gɔ̃flaːʒ], *s.m. Aut: etc:* (*a*) inflation; **g. excessif,** over-inflation; (*b*) tyre pressure; **vérification du g. des pneus,** checking of tyre pressures; **tableau de gonflages,** table of tyre pressures.
gonflant [gɔ̃flɑ̃], *a.* **coiffure gonflante,** bouffant hairstyle; **jupon g.,** full petticoat
gonflé [gɔ̃fle], *a.* **1.** (*of sail*) full. **2. yeux gonflés,** puffy eyes; **visage g.,** bloated face; **riz g.,** puffed rice; **g. d'orgueil,** puffed up with pride; **avoir le cœur g.,** to be sad. **3.** (*a*) sure of oneself; full of oneself, self-important; *F:* stuck-up; *F:* **t'es g.,** you've got a nerve; **g. à bloc,** (i) keyed-up; (ii) sure of oneself; (*b*) *Aut: F:* **moteur g.,** hotted-up, souped-up, engine. **4. prix gonflés,** exaggerated prices.

gonflement [gɔ̃fləmɑ̃], *s.m.* **1.** (*a*) inflating, inflation (of tyres, balloon); **g. exagéré, excessif,** over-inflation; **g. insuffisant,** under-inflation; (*b*) distension (of stomach); swelling. **2.** swell (in gun barrel, etc.); bulge (on surface). **3.** *Min:* **g. (du mur, de la sole),** creep.

gonfler [gɔ̃fle]. **1.** *v.tr.* (*a*) to inflate, distend; to blow up, pump up (tyre); to puff out, blow out, bulge (one's cheeks); to puff (rice); **le vent gonfle les voiles,** the wind fills the sails; **les pneus ne sont pas assez gonflés,** the tyres are down; (*b*) to swell; **torrent gonflé par les pluies,** torrent swollen by the rains; (*c*) *Aut: F:* to hot up, soup up (an engine). **2.** *v.i. & pr.* (*a*) to become inflated; (*of stomach*) to become distended; **son cœur se gonfla,** he felt a lump in his throat; **yeux gonflés de larmes,** eyes swollen with tears; (*b*) *Nau:* (*of sail*) to belly.

gonfleur [gɔ̃flœːr], *s.m. Aut:* (tyre) inflator; air line; (air) pump.

gong [gɔ̃g], *s.m.* **1.** gong. **2.** *Av:* **g. sonique,** sonic boom.

gongonner [gɔ̃gɔne], *v.i. F:* (*of garment*) to pucker; to sit badly.

gongoresque [gɔ̃gɔrɛsk], *a. Lit.Hist:* gongoresque; *Pej:* cultist.

gongorisme [gɔ̃gɔrism], *s.m. Lit.Hist:* gongorism; *Pej:* cultism.

gongoriste [gɔ̃gɔrist]. **1.** *a.* gongoresque (style, etc.); *Pej:* cultist. **2.** *s.m. Lit.Hist:* gongorist; admirer of Gongora; *Pej:* cultist.

goniatites [gɔnjatit], *s.f.pl. Paleont:* goniatites.

gonidial, -aux [gɔnidjal, -o], *a. Bot:* gonidial.

gonidie [gɔnidi], *s.f. Bot:* gonidium.

gonio [gɔnjo], *s.m. Nau: F:* (*a*) direction finder, radiogoniometer; (*b*) direction finding, location (by radio).

goniocote [gɔnjɔkɔt], **goniocotes** [gɔnjɔkɔtɛs], *s.m. Ent:* goniocotes.

goniodes [gɔnjɔdɛs], *s.m. Ent:* Goniodes.

goniomètre [gɔnjɔmɛtr̥], *s.m. Surv: etc:* goniometer, position finder, direction finder; angle gauge; *Artil:* dial sight; **g. boussole,** aiming circle; *Cryst:* **g. à réflexion,** reflecting goniometer; **g. d'application,** contact goniometer.

goniomètre-boussole [gɔnjɔmɛtr̥busɔl], *s.m. Surv:* aiming circle; **g.-b. à prisme,** prismatic compass; *pl. goniomètres-boussoles.*

goniométrie [gɔnjɔmetri], *s.f.* goniometry, position finding, direction finding.

goniométrique [gɔnjɔmetrik], *a.* goniometric(al), position-finding, direction-finding.

gonion [gɔnjɔ̃], *s.m. Anat:* gonion.

goniopholis [gɔnjɔfɔlis], *s.m. Paleont:* goniopholis.

gonioscopie [gɔnjɔskɔpi], *s.f. Med:* gonioscopy.

gonne [gɔn], *s.f.* barrel, drum (for tar, etc.).

gonnelle [gɔnɛl], *s.f. Ich:* gunnel, blenny, butter-fish.

gonochorie [gɔnɔkɔri], *s.f.*, **gonochorisme** [gɔnɔkɔrism], *s.m. Biol:* gonochorism.

gonochorique [gɔnɔkɔrik], *a. Biol:* gonochorismal.

gonochorisme [gɔnɔkɔrism], *s.m. Biol:* gonochorism.

gonococcie [gɔnɔkɔksi], *s.f. Med:* gonococcal infections.

gonocoque [gɔnɔkɔk], *s.m. Bac: Med:* gonococcus.

gonophore [gɔnɔfɔːr], *s.m. Biol:* gonophore.

gonoplax [gɔnɔplaks], *s.m. Crust:* gonoplax, the angular crabs.

gonorrhée [gɔnɔre], *s.f. Med:* gonorrhoea.

gonorrhéique [gɔnɔreik], *a. Med:* gonorrhoeal.

gonosome [gɔnɔzɔm], *s.m. Z:* gonosome.

gonotome [gɔnɔtɔm], *s.m. Z:* gonotome.

gonozoïde [gɔnɔzɔid], *s.m. Z:* gonozooid.

gonse, gonsesse [gɔ̃ːs, gɔ̃sɛs], *s. P:* = GONZE, GONZESSE.

gonys [gɔnis], *s.m. Orn:* gonys.

Gonzague [gɔ̃zag], *Pr.n.m. Hist:* Gonzaga.

gonze [gɔ̃ːz], *s.m. P:* man, bloke, type, guy.

gonzesse [gɔ̃zɛs], *s.f. P:* woman, girl, bird, (bit of) skirt, *U.S:* broad, babe.

gopher [gɔfɛːr], *s.m. B.Hist:* **bois de g.,** gopher wood.

goral [gɔral], *s.m. Z:* goral.

gord [gɔːr], *s.m.* **1.** *Fish:* kiddle, stake net. **2.** *Min:* (*in N. of Fr.*) (*in coal mine*) clay.

gordiacés [gɔrdjase], **gordiens** [gɔrdjɛ̃], *s.m.pl. Ann:* Gordiacea.

gordien [gɔrdjɛ̃], *a.m.* Gordian (knot); **trancher le nœud g.,** to cut the Gordian knot.

gordonite [gɔrdɔnit], *s.f. Miner:* gordonite.

gorenflos, gorenflot [gɔrɑ̃flo], *s.m. Cu:* sponge cake soaked in rum or kirsch.

goret [gɔrɛ], *s.m.* **1.** (*a*) piglet; (*b*) *F:* (i) dirty little urchin; (ii) filthy pig (of a man). **2.** *Nau: A:* scrub broom, hog. **3.** (*a*) *A:* chief assistant to (i) cobbler, shoemender, (ii) hatter; (*b*) *O:* general assistant to cobbler, shoemender.

goretage [gɔrtaːʒ], *s.m. Nau: A:* hogging, scrubbing.

goreter [gɔrte], *v.tr.* (**je gorette, n. goretons; je goretterai**) *Nau: A:* to hog down (hull).

gorfou [gɔrfu], *s.m. Orn:* crested penguin, rock hopper.

gorge [gɔrʒ], *s.f.* **1.** (*a*) throat, neck; **couper la g. à qn,** to cut s.o.'s throat; **empoigner qn par la g.,** to seize s.o. by the throat; **il me serrait la g.,** he held me by the throat; **je le tiens à la g.,** (i) I've got him by the throat; (ii) I have him at my mercy; (*b*) bosom, bust (of woman); *A:* (**tour de**) **g.,** yoke (of garment); **g. d'un pigeon,** pigeon's breast. **2.** throat, gullet; **avoir mal à la g., avoir un mal de g.,** to have a sore throat; **exhalaisons qui vous prennent à la g.,** fumes that catch your throat; *F:* **il me reste en travers de la g.,** I can't stomach him; *F:* **s'arroser la g.,** to wet one's whistle; **avoir un serrement de g.,** to gulp; **avoir la gorge serrée,** to have a lump in one's throat; **sa g. se serra,** a lump came into his throat; he gulped; **crier à pleine g.,** to shout at the top of one's voice; **avaler qch. à pleine g.,** to gulp sth. down; **rire à g. déployée,** to laugh heartily; to roar, shout, scream, with laughter. **3.** *Ven:* gorge, contents of stomach; **rendre g.,** (i) to bring up food, to vomit; (ii) *F:* to have to cough up; **g. chaude,** tit-bit from prey given to hawk; **faire des gorges chaudes de qn,** to have a good laugh at s.o. **4.** (*a*) *Geog:* gorge; (*b*) *Fort:* gorge. **5.** groove; *Arch:* quirk, gorge; *I.C.E:* groove (for piston ring); *Mec.E: etc:* groove, notch, score (of pulley); swallow (of sheave); furrow (of screw); **roue à g.,** double-flanged wheel; **g. d'étanchéité,** seal groove; *Arch:* **moulure à g.,** grooved moulding. **6.** *Const:* throat (of chimney). **7.** neck, journal (of axle); neck (of gun, cartridge-case); roller (of map). **8.** tumbler (of lock). **9.** *Bootm:* riser (of the heel).

gorgé [gɔrʒe], *a.* gorged, replete; *F:* **g. d'or,** bursting with money; *Vet:* **jambe gorgée,** swollen leg (of horse); *Ven:* **chien bien g.,** full-throated hound.

gorge-blanche [gɔrʒəblɑ̃ːʃ], *s.f. Orn:* whitethroat; *pl. gorges-blanches.*

gorge-bleue [gɔrʒəblø], *s.f. Orn:* bluethroat; **g.-b. à miroir roux,** red-spotted bluethroat; **g.-b. à miroir blanc,** white-spotted bluethroat; *pl. gorges-bleues.*

gorge-de-pigeon [gɔrʒdəpiʒɔ̃], *a.inv. & s.m.* dove-coloured shot (silk).

gorgée [gɔrʒe], *s.f.* mouthful (of wine, etc.); gulp; **petite g.,** sip; **avaler qch. d'une g.,** to swallow sth. at one draught, gulp; **boire son vin à petites gorgées,** to sip one's wine.

gorge-jaune [gɔrʒəʒoːn], *s.f. Orn:* yellowthroat; *pl. gorges-jaunes.*

gorge-noire [gɔrʒənwaːr], *s.f. Orn:* redstart; *pl. gorges-noires.*

gorger [gɔrʒe], *v.tr.* (**je gorgeai(s); n. gorgeons**) **1.** to stuff, gorge; **se g. de nourriture,** to fill oneself up with food, to gorge; **il s'est gorgé de lectures,** he stuffed himself up with reading; he devoured books. **2.** *Husb:* to cram (fowls).

gorgeret [gɔrʒərɛ], *s.m.* **1.** *Ent:* terminal point of sting (of bee, wasp). **2.** *Orn: Dial:* robin.

gorgerette [gɔrʒərɛt], *s.f.* **1.** *A:* front, gorget (for lady's dress). **2.** *Orn:* blackcap.

gorgerin [gɔrʒərɛ̃], *s.m.* **1.** *A.Arm:* gorgerin, gorget, throat-piece (of helmet). **2.** *Arch:* quirk, gorge, gorgerin.

gorget [gɔrʒɛ], *s.m. Tls:* moulding plane.

gorgonaires [gɔrgɔnɛːr], *s.m.pl. Coel:* Gorgonacea.

Gorgone [gɔrgɔn], *s.f.* **1.** *Myth:* Gorgon. **2.** *Coel:* **g. éventail,** sea-fan.

gorgonidés [gɔrgɔnide], *s.m.pl. Coel:* Gorgoniidae.

gorgonie [gɔrgɔni], *s.f. Coel:* gorgonia.

Gorgonzola [gɔrgɔ̃zɔla]. **1.** *Pr.n. Geog:* Gorgonzola. **2.** *s.m.* (*also* **fromage de G.**), Gorgonzola (cheese).

gorille [gɔriːj], *s.m.* **1.** *Z:* gorilla. **2.** *F:* strong-arm man, bodyguard.

Gorkhalis [gɔrkali], *s.m.pl. Ethn:* Gurkhas.

Goshen [gɔʃɛn], *Pr.n.m. B.Hist:* Goshen.

gosier [gozje], *s.m.* throat; (i) gullet, (ii) windpipe; **s'éclaircir le g.,** to clear one's throat; **g. harmonieux,** harmonious voice; **rire à plein g.,** to laugh loudly, heartily; **j'ai le g. très étroit,** I have a very small throat; *Anat:* **isthme du g.,** isthmus of the fauces; *F:* **grand g.,** glutton; **s'humecter le g.,** to moisten one's throat; *F:* to wet one's whistle; **avoir le g. pavé, ferré, de fer blanc,** to have a throat of cast iron.

goslarite [gɔzlarit], *s.f. Miner:* goslarite.

gosse [gɔs], *s.m. & f.*, *A:* **gosselin, -ine** [gɔslɛ̃, -in], *s. F:* youngster, kid; nipper; *P:* **c'est ma g.,** she's my girl.

gosser [gɔse], *v.tr. Fr.C: F:* to whittle.

Goth [go], *Pr.n.m. Hist:* Goth.

gotha [gɔta], *s.m. Hist:* (German) bomber, gotha.

Gothembourg, Gothenbourg [gɔtɑ̃buːr], *Pr.n.m. Geog:* Gothenburg.

Gothie [gɔti], *Pr.n.f. Geog:* (Swedish) Gotland.

gothique [gɔtik]. **1.** *a.* (*a*) Gothic; **caractères gothiques,** Gothic type, black letter, German text; (*b*) *F: O:* old-fashioned; barbarous. **2.** *s.m. Arch: Ling:* Gothic; *Art:* **g. troubadour,** Gothick. **3.** *s.f. Typ:* black letter, Old English.

gotique [gɔtik], *s.m. Ling:* Gothic.

goton [gɔtɔ̃], *s.f. F: A:* **1.** country girl. **2.** loose woman; prostitute. **3.** (ridiculously) over-dressed woman.

gouache[1] [gwaʃ], *s.f. Art:* gouache; **peindre à la g.,** to paint in gouache.

gouache[2], *s.f. A:* partridge.

gouacher [gwaʃe], *v.tr.* to paint in gouache.

gouaille [gwɑːj], *s.f. O:* (*a*) banter; jeering; (*b*) irony.

gouailler [gwɑje]. **1.** *v.tr. O:* to mock, jeer at (s.o.). **2.** *v.i.* to joke.

gouaillerie [gwɑjri], *s.f.* joking, banter.

gouailleur, -euse [gwɑjœːr, -øːz]. **1.** *a.* facetious; mocking, bantering (tone). **2.** *s.* facetious person; joker.

gouailleusement [gwɑjøzmɑ̃], *adv.* facetiously; by way of a joke.

goualante [gwalɑ̃ːt], *s.f. P:* song.

goualer [gwale], *v.tr. & i. P:* (*a*) to sing; (*b*) to gossip; to spread tales.

goualeur, -euse [gwalœːr, -øːz], *s. P:* singer.

gouape [gwap], *s.f. P:* nasty bit of work; louse; *P:* bastard.

gouaper [gwape], *v.i. P: A:* (*a*) to loaf; (*b*) to live a disreputable life.

goudron [gudrɔ̃], *s.m.* tar; **g. de gaz, de houille,** coal tar; **g. de bois,** wood tar; **g. minéral,** asphalt; bitumen; **g. à calfater,** (navy) pitch; **bac de réfrigération de g.,** tar-cooler box; *Med:* **eau de g.,** tar water.

goudronnage [gudrɔnaːʒ], *s.m.* tarring.

goudronner [gudrɔne], *v.tr.* **1.** to tar; *Nau:* to pay; **toile goudronnée,** tarpaulin; **papier goudronné,** tar-lined paper. **2. huile goudronnée,** gummed oil.

goudronnerie [gudrɔnri], *s.f.* **1.** tar works. **2.** tar shed.

goudronneur [gudrɔnœːr], *s.m.* (*pers.*) tar sprayer, tar spreader.

goudronneuse[1] [gudrɔnøːz], *s.f.* tar sprayer; tar-spraying machine; asphalt distributor.

goudronneux, -euse[2] [gudrɔnø, -øːz], *a.* (*a*) tarry; (*b*) **huile goudronneuse,** gummy oil.

goudronnier [gudrɔnje], *s.m.* (*a*) tar manufacturer; (*b*) dealer in tar.

gouet [gwɛ], *s.m.* **1.** billhook. **2.** *Bot:* wild arum; lords and ladies.

gouffre [gufr̥], *s.m.* (*a*) gulf, pit, abyss; **g. béant,** yawning chasm; **tomber dans un g. de maux,** to be plunged into misfortune; **c'est un g. (que cet homme-là)!** money just slips through his fingers! **un g. de tous les vices,** a sink of iniquity; (*b*) whirlpool, vortex; (*c*) *Geol:* swallowhole; (*d*) *Oc:* cauldron.

gouge[1] [guːʒ], *s.f. Tls:* **1.** gouge, hollow chisel; **g. à ébaucher,** turning gouge, round tool; **g. à nez rond, g. à cuiller,** spoon gouge, drill; **g. triangulaire,** corner chisel, parting tool. **2.** barrel plane.

gouge[2], *s.f.* **1.** *A:* whore. **2.** *Dial:* (*a*) farm-girl; (*b*) (i) wife; (ii) daughter.

gouger [guʒe], *v.tr.* (**je gougeai(s); n. gougeons**) to gouge; to scoop out; *Nau:* **pomme gougée,** (i) seizing truck, shroud truck, (ii) comb-cleat; fair lead(er).

gougère [guʒɛːr], *s.f.* sort of cheese cake.

gougette [guʒɛt], *s.f. Tls:* small gouge.

gougnotte [guɲɔt], *s.f. P:* lesbian.

gouin, gouine [gwɛ̃, gwin], *s.* **1.** *s.m. A: F:* bad lot. **2.** *s.f. P:* lesbian.

goujat [guʒa], *s.m.* **1.** (*a*) *A:* camp follower; (*b*) *A. & Dial:* mason's apprentice; hodman. **2.** boor, lout.

goujaterie [guʒatri], *s.f.* ungentlemanly, loutish (i) behaviour, (ii) action.

goujatisme [guʒatism], *s.m.* ungentlemanly, loutish, behaviour.

goujon[1] [guʒɔ̃], *s.m. Ich:* gudgeon; **g. de mer,** black goby; *F:* **avaler le g.,** (i) to swallow the bait, (ii) to die.

goujon², *s.m.* **1.** (*a*) *Const:* **g. (pour pierres),** gudgeon, joggle (in stonework); (*b*) projecting stud; *Carp:* tenon, joggle (on foot of post, etc.); **g. à ressort,** spring stud; **g. de mât de tente,** tent-pole spike; (*c*) *Mec.E:* **g. prisonnier,** stud bolt; **g. de fixation,** set screw, stud bolt. **2.** (*a*) *Carp:* coak; **g. perdu, g. prisonnier,** dowel (pin); (*b*) *Mec.E:* **g. de jonction,** assembling pin; **g. d'assemblage, de repérage, g. repère,** locating (dowel) pin; **g. de charnière,** pin, pintle, of a hinge; **g. de chaîne (de bicyclette),** link pin; **g. d'arbre,** gudgeon of a shaft; **g. de bielle,** connecting-rod gudgeon; **g. d'un cylindre oscillant,** trunnion of an oscillating cylinder.

goujonnage [guʒɔnaːʒ], *s.m.* dowelling.

goujonner¹ [guʒɔne], *v.tr. F:* to cheat, do (s.o.); **on vous a goujonné,** you've been had.

goujonner², *v.tr. Carp:* to coak, to dowel; *Const:* to joggle; *Mec.E:* to pin, to bolt; **g. des planches,** to dowel planks together; **plaques goujonnées,** keyed plates.

goujonnière [guʒɔnjɛːr], *a. Ich:* **perche g.,** pope, ruff.

goujonnoir [guʒɔnwaːr], *s.m.* dowelling jig.

goujure [guʒyːr], *s.f.* channel, groove; *Nau:* score (in pulley, block, dead-eye).

goulache, goulasch [gulaʃ], *s.f. Cu:* (Hungarian) goulash.

gouldie [guldi], *s.f. Orn:* gouldia; *F:* thorn-tail.

goule¹ [gul], *s.f.* ghoul.

goule², *s.f. A. & P:* throat; mouth.

goulée [gule], *s.f.* **1.** *F:* big mouthful, gulp. **2.** *Metall:* channel (from furnace to mould).

goulet [gulɛ], *s.m.* narrow part, neck (of object); gully (in mountains); narrow gorge; *Const:* neck gutter (of roof); *Nau:* gut, bottleneck, narrows (of harbour); **g. d'étranglement,** (i) narrow passage (in gorge); (ii) bottleneck; **le G. de Brest,** the Brest Channel.

goulette [gulɛt], *s.f.* = GOULOTTE.

goulot [gulo], *s.m.* **1.** neck (of bottle); spout (of watering-can); **boire au g.,** to drink (straight) from the bottle; *Aut:* **g. d'étranglement,** bottleneck. **2.** *P:* gullet, mouth; **se rincer le g.,** to take a drink; **repousser du g.,** to have foul breath.

goulotte [gulɔt], *s.f.* **1.** spout (of coal-hopper, etc.); shoot, chute. **2.** channel.

goulu, -ue [guly]. **1.** (*a*) *a.* greedy, gluttonous; (*b*) *a. F:* **pois goulus,** sugar peas; (*c*) *s.* (i) glutton; (ii) *P: A: s.f.* **goulue,** large-mouthed woman. **2.** *s.m.* (*a*) *Ich: F:* **g. de mer,** shark; (*b*) *Z: F:* glutton, wolverine. **3.** *s.f.pl.* **goulues,** wide-jawed blacksmith's tongs.

goulûment [gulymɑ̃], *adv.* greedily, voraciously; **manger g.,** to eat ravenously, to gobble one's food.

goum [gum], *s.m.* **1.** (*among the Arabs*) tribe, family. **2.** *Fr. Mil.Hist:* (*in N. Africa*) goum, Arab unit.

goumi [gumi], *P:* cosh.

goumier [gumje], *s.m. Fr. Mil.Hist:* goum(ier).

goundou [gundu], *s.m. Med:* goundou.

goupil [gupi], *s.m. A:* fox; *Lit:* Reynard the Fox.

goupille [gupiːj], *s.f.* **1.** (linch)pin; keeper pin; gudgeon; forelock; **g. fendue,** split pin, forelock pin; cotter; **g. d'arrêt,** stop bolt, stop pin; **g. conique,** taper pin; **g. de cisaillement,** shear pin; **g. cylindrique,** cylindrical pin; **g. d'entraînement,** dog pin; **g. de montage,** locating pin; **cheville à g.,** forelock bolt; *Artil:* **g. de sûreté (de fusée),** fuse safety-pin; **mettre une g. à qch.,** to pin, key, sth. **2.** *Navy:* **g. de sel,** soluble plug (of a mine).

goupiller [gupije], *v.tr.* **1.** *Tchn:* to pin, key; **g. un écrou,** to cotter a bolt. **2.** *P:* to contrive, wangle (sth.).

se goupiller, *F:* **ça se goupille bien, mal,** it's going, turning out, well, badly.

goupillon [gupijɔ̃], *s.m.* **1.** *Ecc:* aspergillum, sprinkler (for holy water); *A:* **le sabre et le g.,** the Army and the Church. **2.** brush (for gum, lamp, bottle); **g. nettoie-pipes,** pipe cleaner.

goupillonner [gupijɔne], *v.tr.* to clean (with a bottle-brush).

goupiner [gupine], *v.tr. & i. P:* **1.** to work, slog. **2.** to steal, pinch.

gour¹ [guːr], *s.m.pl.* (*used generally for the sing.*) *Geog:* eroded hill (in Sahara), gara, *pl.* gour.

gour², *s.m. Geog:* pool (in river, cave).

goura [gura], *s.m. Orn:* goura.

gourami [gurami], *s.m. Ich:* gourami(es), paradise fish.

gourance [gurɑ̃ːs], *s.f. P:* **1.** mistake, boob. **2.** **avoir des gourances,** to be suspicious, to smell a rat.

gourbet [gurbɛ], *s.m. Bot:* beach grass, marram (grass).

gourbi [gurbi], *s.m.* **1.** (Arab) hut, shack. **2.** *Mil: F:* (*a*) shelter, shack; **baraque-g.,** wattle hut; (*b*) funk hole.

gourbillage [gurbijaːʒ], *s.m. Nau:* countersinking.

gourbiller [gurbije], *v.tr. Nau:* to countersink.

gourd¹ [guːr], *a.* **1.** (*a*) numb(ed) (with cold); stiff, swollen (with cold); (*b*) *F:* **ne pas avoir les bras gourds,** to be ready with one's fists; **ne pas avoir les mains gourdes,** to be quick (with one's hands). **2.** *Agr:* **blé g.,** wheat swollen by the rain.

gourd², *s.m. Geog:* pool (in river, cave).

gourde [gurd], *s.f.* **1.** *Bot:* gourd. **2.** (*a*) calabash, gourd, water bottle; (*b*) **g. d'eau-de-vie,** flask of brandy. **3.** *F:* idiot, dimwit, dope; *a.* stupid, dim-witted, blockheaded.

gourdin [gurdɛ̃], *s.m.* **1.** club, cudgel, bludgeon; **faire faire qch. à qn à coups de g.,** to bludgeon s.o. into doing sth. **2.** *Nau: A:* rope's end.

gourdiner [gurdine], *v.tr.* to cudgel, thrash, beat.

goure [guːr], *s.f. P:* **1.** *A: Pharm:* adulterated drug. **2.** take-in; **vol à la g.,** confidence trick.

gourer [gure], *v.tr. P:* **1.** *A:* to adulterate, doctor (drugs). **2.** to cheat, trick, to pull a fast one on (s.o.).

se gourer, *P:* (*a*) to be wrong, to be off beam; (*b*) to make a bloomer; (*c*) **se g. de qn,** to mistrust, be suspicious of, *U.S:* leary of, s.o.

goureur, -euse [gurœːr, -øːz], *s. A: P:* **1.** maker, seller, of adulterated drugs. **2.** cheat.

gourg [guːr], *s.m. Geog:* pool (in river, cave).

gourgandine [gurgɑ̃din], *s.f.* **1.** *F:* loose woman. **2.** *Moll:* venus shell; *Com:* cockle.

gourgandiner [gurgɑ̃dine], *v.tr. F:* to chase after (women); to chase (the skirts).

gourgane [gurgan], *s.f. F:* horse bean; *pl. Nau:* dried beans.

gourganier [gurganje], *s.m. P: O:* old sailor, old salt, old shellback.

gourgouran [gurgurɑ̃], *s.m. Tex:* Indian silk (fabric).

Gourien, -ienne [gurjɛ̃, -jɛn], *a. & s. Geog:* Gurian.

gourmade [gurmad], *s.f. A: F:* slap, cuff; **se donner des gourmades,** to come to blows.

gourmand, -ande [gurmɑ̃, -ɑ̃ːd]. **1.** *a.* (*a*) *A:* greedy, gluttonous; (*b*) **être g.,** to appreciate good food; **g. de friandises,** (passionately) fond of sweet things; **être g. d'honneurs,** to hanker after honours; (*c*) *Agr:* **herbes gourmandes,** parasitical weeds; *Hort:* **branches gourmandes,** suckers; epicormic branches. **2.** (*a*) *s. A:* gourmand, glutton; (*b*) *s.* gourmand; gourmet; (*c*) *s.m. Hort:* (i) sucker; (ii) *F:* **(pois) g.,** sugar pea.

gourmander [gurmɑ̃de]. **1.** *v.i. A:* to gormandize, guzzle. **2.** *v.tr.* (*a*) to rebuke; (*b*) *A:* to treat roughly; *Equit:* **g. la bouche d'un cheval,** to saw at a horse's mouth.

gourmandise [gurmɑ̃diːz], *s.f.* **1.** greediness, gluttony; gourmandism; **le péché de g.,** the sin of gluttony; **manger avec g.,** to eat greedily. **2.** *often pl.* sweetmeats, dainties, good things to eat; **le chocolat est une g. que l'on n'a pas tous les jours,** chocolate is a treat which we don't have every day.

gourme [gurm], *s.f.* **1.** *Med:* (*a*) impetigo; (*b*) teething rash. **2.** *Vet:* strangles; **jeter sa g.,** (i) (*of horse*) to run at the nose; (ii) *F:* (*of pers.*) to sow one's wild oats.

gourmé [gurme], *a.* stiff, starched, stuck-up, affected (manner).

gourmer [gurme], *v.tr.* **1.** to put a curb-chain on (horse). **2.** *A: F:* to pommel, pummel, punch (s.o.); to knock (s.o.) about.

se gourmer, to be stiff, starched (in one's manners); to be affected.

gourmet [gurmɛ], *s.m.* **1.** *A:* wine taster. **2.** (*a*) gourmet; epicure; (*b*) connoisseur.

gourmette [gurmɛt], *s.f.* **1.** *Harn:* curb (chain); **fausse g.,** lip strap; **mors à g.,** chain bit; **lâcher la g. à un cheval, à qn,** to give a horse its head; to give s.o. a free rein, a free hand. **2.** (*a*) curb watch chain; (*b*) chain bracelet. **3.** *Tchn:* polishing chain.

gournable [gurnabl], *s.f. N.Arch:* treenail.

gournabler [gurnable], *v.tr.* to treenail.

gournaud [gurno], *s.m. Ich: F:* grey gurnard.

gourou [guru], *s.m. Hindu Rel:* guru.

gouspin [guspɛ̃], *s.m. P:* (*a*) young rascal, little devil; (*b*) good-for-nothing, guttersnipe.

gouspiner [guspine], *v.i. P:* (*of child*) to run loose in the streets.

goussant [gusɑ̃], *A: a. & s.m.*, **goussaut** [guso], *a. & s.m.* thick-set, stocky (horse, dog, person); **(cheval) g.,** cob; **petit homme g.,** stocky little man.

gousse [gus], *s.f.* pod, shell, husk (of peas, etc.); **g. de pois,** pea pod; **g. d'ail,** clove of garlic; **g. de vanille,** vanilla bean.

goussepain [guspɛ̃], *s.m. P:* = GOUSPIN.

gousset [gusɛ], *s.m.* **1.** *A:* armpit. **2.** fob pocket; waistcoat pocket; trouser pocket; **avoir le g. bien garni, vide,** to have one's pockets well-lined; to be cleaned out, (stony) broke. **3.** *Mec.E: etc:* (shoulder) bracket, stay plate, gusset (plate); **g. en équerre,** angle plate; **g. de coin,** corner bracket; shoulder bracket; **g. venu d'emboutissage,** integral gusset. **4.** *Her:* gusset.

goût [gu], *s.m.* taste. **1.** (sense of) taste; **avoir le g. fin,** to have a fine palate; **dépravation du g.,** spoiling the palate; *P:* **perdre le g. du pain,** to die, to peg out; **faire passer le g. du pain à qn,** (i) to murder s.o.; to do away with s.o.; (ii) to make s.o. want to give up. **2.** flavour, taste; bouquet (of wine); **g. de terroir,** native tang; **cela a le g. de . . .,** it tastes like . . .; **donner du g. à un mets,** to flavour a dish; **sans g.,** tasteless(ly); **manque de g.,** tastelessness. **3** (*pleasure in, preference for, sth.*) *Cu:* **ajouter du sucre et du citron selon son g.,** add sugar and lemon to taste; **le g. des affaires,** a liking for business; **g. passager,** passing fancy; **le g. du jour,** the reigning fashion; **avoir du g. pour, le g. de, qch.,** to have a taste for sth.; **acquérir un g. pour qch., prendre g. à qch.,** to acquire, develop, a taste for sth.; **prendre g. à la chimie,** to take to chemistry; **il a un g. naturel pour la chimie,** he has a natural taste for chemistry; **chacun (à) son g., à chacun son g., des goûts et des couleurs on ne discute pas,** everyone to his taste, there's no accounting for taste; **donner à qn le g. de, pour, qch.,** to give s.o. a taste for sth.; **avoir des goûts de luxe,** to have expensive tastes; **une maison à mon g.,** a house to my liking; **elle n'est pas à mon g.,** I don't care for her; **ces opinions ne sont pas à mon g.,** I don't hold with these opinions; **faire qch. par g.,** to do sth. from inclination; **je ne vis pas ici par g.,** I don't live here from choice; **affaire de g.,** matter of taste. **4.** (*discernment, right judgment*) **g. parfait,** perfect taste; **parole d'un g. douteux,** remark in doubtful taste; **avoir du g.,** to have good taste; **les gens de g.,** people of taste; **mauvais g.,** (i) bad taste; (ii) lack of taste; (iii) bad form; **elle s'habille avec g.,** she has a good dress sense, a flair for clothes; *Mus:* **notes de g.,** grace notes. **5.** style, manner; **peint dans le g. de Watteau,** painted in the Watteau manner; **quelque chose dans ce g.-là,** something of that sort, in that style.

goûter [gute]. **I.** *v.tr.* **1.** (*a*) to taste (food); **avaler qch. sans le g.,** to swallow sth. without tasting it; (*b*) (*of cook, etc.*) to taste, try, sample (food, drink). **2.** to enjoy, appreciate, relish; **g. la musique,** to enjoy music; **pièce goûtée par la galerie, du public,** piece that appeals to the gallery, to the public; **il goûtait beaucoup cette simple vie de famille,** he enjoyed this simple family life; **je goûte assez votre conseil,** I am rather inclined to take your advice. **3. g. de qch.,** (i) to taste sth. for the first time, (ii) to taste of, enjoy (s.o.'s hospitality, etc.); *Prov:* **qui goûte de tout se dégoûte de tout,** he who tastes of everything tires of everything. **4. g. à qch.,** to taste sth.; to take a little of sth.; **goûtez donc à ce vin!** just try this wine! **elle a goûté à tous les plaisirs de la vie,** she has tasted all life's pleasures. **5.** *abs.* (*a*) to take a snack (between meals); (*b*) to picnic; **nous emporterons de quoi g.,** we shall take a snack with us.

II. **goûter,** *s.m.* (=) (afternoon) tea; (*to child*) **as-tu emporté ton g.?** have you got your (afternoon) snack? **g. d'enfants,** children's party.

goûteur, -euse [gutœːr, -øːz]. **1.** *s.* taster. **2.** *a. F:* tasty.

goutte [gut], *s.f.* **1.** drop (of liquid); **g. à g.,** drop by drop; (*of liquid*) **tomber g. à g.,** to drip; **c'est une g. d'eau dans la mer,** it is a drop in the ocean, in the bucket; **il suait à grosses gouttes,** beads of perspiration stood on his forehead; **il tombait quelques gouttes,** it was spitting with rain; **grosses gouttes de pluie sur le sol,** heavy drops of rain, splashes of rain, on the ground; *s.a.* SE RESSEMBLER. **2.** spot, splash (of colour); speck; fleck; **oiseau parsemé de gouttes blanches,** bird speckled with white. **3.** *F:* (*a*) small quantity, sip, sup; **prendre une g. de bouillon,** to take a sip, just a mouthful, of soup; **g. de cognac,** dash of brandy (in sauce); *A:* **(œuvre de) la g. de lait,** milk dispensary; (*b*) nip, drop (of brandy, etc.); **il aime la g.,** he likes a drop of spirits; **boire la g.,** to tipple, to nip; **boire, prendre, une g.,** to have a nip; *F:* **il a bu une g.,** (i) he was nearly drowned, (ii) he had a heavy loss, (iii) (*of actor*) he got hissed, *F:* got the bird. **4.** *adv.phr.* **ne . . . g.,** not at all (*thus used today only with* **comprendre, entendre, voir**); **je n'entends**

g. à ce que vous dites, I don't understand in the least what you are saying; **je n'y vois g.,** (i) I can't see a thing; (ii) I can't make anything of it; **on n'y voyait g.,** you couldn't see your hand before your face. **5.** *Arch:* gutta. **6.** *Metall:* **g. froide,** (i) blister (in casting), (ii) bead (in ingot). **7.** *Meteor:* **g. froide, chaude,** cold, warm, air mass. **8.** *Paperm:* water stain. **9.** *pl. Pharm:* drops; **gouttes pour le nez,** nasal drops. **10.** *Med:* (*a*) gout; (*b*) *A:* **g. sciatique,** sciatica; **g. militaire,** gleet.

goutte-à-goutte [gutagut], *s.m.inv. Med:* drip; **g.-à-g. intraveineux,** intravenous drip; **g.-à-g. rectal,** Murphy drip.

goutte-d'eau [gutdo], *s.f.* **1.** (*a*) *Lap:* colourless topaz; (*b*) diamond tear drop. **2.** *Const:* drip; *pl. gouttes-d'eau.*

goutte-de-lin [gutdəlɛ̃], *s.f. Bot: F:* dodder; *pl. gouttes-de-lin.*

goutte-de-sang [gutdəsɑ̃], *s.f. Bot: F:* pheasant's-eye; *pl. gouttes-de-sang.*

goutte-de-suif [gutdəsɥif], *s.f. El.E:* stud, contact point (of switchboard); *Mec.E:* **tête en g.-de-s.,** button-head (of rivet); *pl. gouttes-de-suif.*

gouttelette [gutlɛt], *s.f.* droplet, tiny drop, globule.

goutter [gute], *v.i.* to drip.

gouttereau, -eaux [gutro], *a. Arch:* **mur g.,** wall that carries the gutter.

goutteux, -euse [gutø, -øːz], *a. & s.* **1.** *Med:* gouty (subject). **2.** *Bot: F:* **herbe aux goutteux,** goutweed.

gouttière [gutjɛːr], *s.f.* **1.** *Const:* (*a*) (roof) gutter; (rainwater) guttering; (*b*) *pl.* eaves; **chat de g.,** common domestic cat; alley cat; **les chats sur les gouttières,** the cats on the tiles. **2.** (*a*) spout, rain pipe; *F:* **j'ai une g. dans ma chambre,** the ceiling in my room's leaking; (*b*) shoot, chute. **3.** (*a*) groove (of bone, sword, rapier); *Ven:* gutter; *A.Veh:* rain-strap (over carriage-door); (*b*) **gouttières des jugulaires,** jugular gutters (of horse). **4.** (*a*) *Surg:* cradle, (cradle-like) splint; (*b*) trough (for rocket, for handling ammunition); *Artil:* trough slide (of recoil gear). **5.** fore-edge (of book). **6.** *N.Arch:* (*a*) (inner) waterway; (*b*) **g. de hublot,** eyebrow, wriggle; (*c*) **g. renversée,** (i) shelf (piece), (ii) stringer.

gouvernable [guvɛrnabl̩], *a.* governable, manageable; **peu g.,** unmanageable.

gouvernail [guvɛrnaːj], *s.m.* **1.** (*a*) *Nau:* rudder, helm; **g. compensé, à double safran,** balanced rudder; **g. de fortune,** jury rudder; **g. suspendu,** underhung rudder; **monter, démonter, le g.,** to ship, unship, the rudder; **roue du g.,** (steering) wheel; **tenir le g.,** to be at the wheel, at the helm; to steer; **prendre le g.,** to take the helm; **effet de g.,** steerage way; **g. de plongée,** horizontal rudder (of submarine); **g. de profondeur,** diving rudder, plane, hydroplane; (*b*) *Av:* **g. vertical, de direction,** vertical rudder; **g. d'altitude, de profondeur,** horizontal rudder; elevator; elevating plane; **axe du g.,** rudder-post. **2.** *Nau:* **g. de drisse,** backstay traveller. **3.** flier, fantail (of windmill).

gouvernance [guvɛrnɑ̃ːs], *s.f. Hist:* governance, governorship.

gouvernant [guvɛrnɑ̃], *a.* (*a*) governing, ruling; (party) in power; (*b*) *s. usu.pl.* **les gouvernants et les gouvernés,** the governors and the governed; **des gouvernants de rencontre,** a makeshift government.

gouvernante [guvɛrnɑ̃ːt], *s.f.* **1.** *Hist:* (woman) governor, ruler (of province, etc.); regent. **2. Madame la G.,** the wife of the governor. **3.** (i) housekeeper (of bachelor, widower, priest); (ii) housekeeper (of hotel). **4.** *A:* governess.

gouvernat [guvɛrna], *s.m.* **1.** governorate. **2.** governorship.

gouverne [guvɛrn], *s.f.* **1.** (*a*) guidance, direction; **pour vous servir de g.,** to serve as your guiding principle; **pour votre g.,** for your guidance; (*b*) *Nau:* steering; **aviron de g.,** steer(ing) oar. **2.** *Av:* **gouvernes,** movable surfaces, control surfaces; **g. de direction,** rudder; **g. de profondeur,** elevator; **g. combinée aileron-profondeur,** elevon; **g. compensée,** balanced surface.

gouverneau [guvɛrno], *s.m. Paperm:* (*pers.*) supervisor.

gouvernement [guvɛrnəmɑ̃], *s.m.* **1.** (*a*) government, management, direction, administration (of household, business, state, etc.); **g. monarchique,** monarchic(al) government; **commission de g.,** governing commission; (*b*) governorship; *Mil:* command (of fortified position); (*c*) *Nau:* steering, handling (of boat). **2.** (the) government; (the) Cabinet; **le g. français, britannique,** the French, British, government; **les membres du g. se sont réunis,** a cabinet meeting was held. **3.** Government House.

gouvernemental, -aux [guvɛrnəmɑ̃tal, -o], *a.* governmental; statutory; **le parti g.,** the government party.

gouvernementalisme [guvɛrn(ə)mɑ̃talism], *s.m.* governmentalism.

gouverner [guvɛrne], *v.tr.* **1.** *Nau:* to steer, handle (ship); **g. en route,** to steer the course; **g. sur un port,** to steer, stand, head, for a port; to bear in with a port; **g. à la lame,** to steer by the sea; **g. d'après le vent,** to steer by the wind; **gouvernez droit!** steady! **gouvernez comme ça!** keep her so! **appareil, machine, à g.,** steering-gear, -engine. **2.** (*a*) to govern, rule, control, direct; **Dieu gouverne l'univers,** God is the ruler of the universe; **g. ses passions,** to control, govern, one's passions; **g. un cheval,** to control, manage, a horse; *Tchn:* **mouvement gouverné par un pendule,** movement regulated, governed, controlled, by a pendulum; (*b*) *A:* to tutor. **3.** (*a*) to manage, administer; **bien g. ses ressources,** to make the most of, to husband, one's resources; (*b*) to govern (country). **4.** *Gram:* **verbe qui gouverne l'accusatif,** verb that governs, takes, the accusative. **5.** *v.i. Nau:* **navire qui ne gouverne plus,** ship that refuses to steer, that no longer answers to the helm.

gouverneur [guvɛrnœːr], *s.m.* **1.** governor (of province, bank, etc.); commanding officer (of fortified position); **g. général,** governor-general; *Fr.C:* **lieutenant g.,** lieutenant governor. **2.** *A:* (*a*) tutor; (*b*) guardian; (*c*) steersman. **3.** (*a*) *Paperm:* supervisor; (*b*) *Min:* (*Central Fr.*) foreman. **4.** *Ich:* pilot fish.

gouvernorat [guvɛrnɔra], *s.m.* **1.** governorate. **2.** governorship.

goy(e) [gɔj], *s. Jewish Rel:* goy; *pl. goyim.*

goyasite [gɔjazit], *s.f. Miner:* goyazite.

goyau, -aux [gwajo], *s.m. Min:* small gallery (in which it is impossible to stand upright); **g. d'aérage,** ventilation shaft.

goyave [gɔjaːv], *s.f. Bot:* guava (fruit); **confiture de g.,** guava jelly.

goyavier [gɔjavje], *s.m. Bot:* guava (tree).

goyot [gwajo], *s.m.* = GOYAU.

Graal (le) [ləgraːl], *s.m. Medieval Lit:* the (Holy) Grail, the Sangreal.

grabat [graba; -ɑ], *s.m.* mean bed, litter (of straw, rags, etc.); pallet; **mourir sur un g.,** to die in abject poverty; **être sur le g.,** (i) *A:* to be laid up, to be ill; (ii) to be reduced to poverty, to be ruined.

grabataire [grabatɛːr], *a. & s.m. & f. A:* bed-ridden (person).

graben [grabɛn], *s.m. Geol:* graben, rift valley.

grabuge [grabyːʒ], *s.m. F:* quarrel, (noisy) squabble, row, rumpus; **faire du g.,** to kick up a row, a shindy; to create; **il y aura du g.,** there'll be ructions, the hell of a row.

grâce [grɑːs], *s.f.* **1.** grace, gracefulness, charm; (*a*) **les grâces de la femme,** feminine charm; **elle met de la g. dans tout,** she does everything gracefully; **avoir bonne g. à faire qch.,** to do sth. in a graceful manner; **il a bonne g. à cheval,** he is a graceful rider; **danser avec g.,** to dance gracefully; **faire des grâces à qn,** to make a fuss of s.o., to be all over s.o.; **elle fait des grâces devant le miroir,** she's preening herself in front of the mirror; (*b*) **de bonne g.,** willingly, readily; **de mauvaise g.,** unwillingly, ungraciously; **il serait de mauvaise g. de refuser,** it would be ungracious, in bad taste, to refuse; **faire qch. avec mauvaise g.,** to do sth. with a bad grace; (*c*) *Myth:* **les trois Grâces,** the three Graces. **2.** favour; **trouver g. devant qn, auprès de qn,** to find favour in s.o.'s eyes; **se mettre dans, entrer dans, obtenir, les bonnes grâces de qn,** to get into favour with s.o., to get into s.o.'s good graces, *F:* into s.o.'s good books; **perdre les bonnes grâces de qn,** to fall out of favour, from grace, with s.o.; **rentrer en g.,** to reingratiate oneself (**auprès de,** with); **s'efforcer de gagner les bonnes grâces de qn,** to curry favour with s.o.; **de g.!** for pity's sake! for goodness' sake! **grâce!** mercy! **3.** (*a*) (act of) grace; **faire une g. à qn,** to do s.o. a favour, a kindness; **les grâces de Dieu,** the blessings of God; **demander une g. à qn, solliciter une g. de qn,** to ask a favour of s.o.; **coup de g.,** finishing stroke, quietus, coup de grâce; **donner le coup de g. à un animal,** to put an animal out of its pain; **c'est trop de grâces que vous me faites!** you really are too kind! *Com:* **jours, terme, de g.,** days of grace; **demander huit jours de g.,** to beg for a week's grace; (*b*) *Theol:* divine aid, favour, grace; **en état de g.,** in a state of grace; **l'an de g. 1802,** the year of grace 1802; **à la g. de Dieu,** (i) trusting to Providence, trusting in God, (ii) we must trust in God; **il fut abandonné à la g. de Dieu,** (i) he was abandoned to the mercy of God, (ii) *F:* he was left to sink or swim. **4.** (*a*) *Jur:* free pardon; **lettre(s) de g.,** reprieve; **faire g. à qn,** to grant s.o. a free pardon; *F:* **je vous fais g. cette fois-ci,** I will let you off this time; (*b*) **demander g., crier g.,** to cry for mercy; **faire g. de qch. à qn,** to spare s.o. sth., *F:* to let s.o. off sth.; **je vous fais g. du reste,** (i) you needn't do, say, any more; (ii) I'll spare you the rest; *Iron:* **faites-moi g. de vos explications!** that's quite enough of your explanations! **demander g. pour qn,** to intercede, to ask for mercy for s.o. **5.** thanks; (*a*) *pl.* (*after meal*) grace, thanks; **rendre grâces à qn de qch.,** to thank s.o. for sth.; **action de grâce(s),** thanksgiving; (*b*) *prep. phr.* **g. à,** thanks to, owing to; **g. à votre aide,** thanks to your help; **g. à Dieu,** (i) thanks be to God; (ii) with God's help, by God's grace. **6.** *Bot: F:* **g. des eaux,** frog bit. **7.** *Games: A:* **jeu de grâces,** the graces.

graciable [grasjabl̩], *a.* pardonable.

gracier [grasje], *v.tr.* (*p.d. & pr.sub.* **n. graciions, v. graciiez**) to pardon, reprieve.

gracieusement [grasjøzmɑ̃], *adv.* **1.** gracefully, becomingly. **2.** graciously, kindly. **3.** gratuitously, without payment.

gracieuser [grasjøze], *v.tr. A:* greet s.o. effusively. **se gracieuser,** *A:* to put on airs and graces.

gracieuseté [grasjøzte], *s.f.* **1.** graciousness, affability, kindness. **2. faire une g. à qn,** to do s.o. a kindness, a favour; **ce serait une g. de votre part de . . .,** it would be an act of kindness, a graceful action, on your part to . . .. **3.** *A:* gratuity.

gracieux, -euse [grasjø, -øːz], *a.* **1.** graceful, pleasing (figure, style, etc.). **2.** (*a*) gracious (manner, etc.); **sourire g.,** charming smile; **g. envers ses inférieurs,** affable to his inferiors; (*b*) **mesure gracieuse en faveur de qn,** measure of grace in favour of s.o.; (*c*) free (of charge); *adv. phr.* **à titre g.,** as a favour, gratis, free of charge; **exemplaire envoyé à titre g.,** complimentary, presentation, copy; **billet donné à titre g.,** complimentary ticket. **3. notre g. souverain,** our gracious Sovereign.

gracilaire [grasilɛːr], *s.m. Ent:* gracilarid moth.

gracilariidés [grasilariide], *s.m.pl. Ent:* Gracilariidae.

gracile [grasil], *a.* slender (stalk, etc.); gracile, slim; **voix g.,** thin voice.

gracilité [grasilite], *s.f.* **1.** slenderness, slimness (of figure). **2.** thinness (of voice).

Gracques (les) [legrak], *Pr.n.m.pl. Rom.Hist:* the Gracchi.

gradation [gradasjɔ̃], *s.f.* gradation, gradual process; **avec une g. lente,** by slow degrees; **par g.,** gradually; *Rh:* **procéder par g. (ascendante),** to work up to a climax; **g. inverse, descendante,** anticlimax.

grade [grad], *s.m.* **1.** rank, dignity, degree, grade; **titulaires de grades élevés,** higher-grade officials; **détenir un g.,** to hold a rank. **2.** (university) degree; **prendre ses grades,** to take one's degree; to graduate. **3.** (*a*) *Mil:* rank; **g. effectif,** actual rank; **g. honoraire,** brevet rank; **g. honorifique,** honorary rank; **g. (à titre) définitif, temporaire,** substantive, permanent, rank; temporary rank; **le plus élevé en g.,** the senior in rank; **monter en g.,** to be promoted; **obtenir le g. de commandant,** to obtain one's majority; (*b*) *Navy:* rating; (*c*) *F:* **en prendre pour son g.,** to get hauled over the coals; **il en a eu pour son g.,** he got precisely what he was asking for, just what he deserved. **4.** *Mth:* grade. **5.** grade (of lubricating oil, engine oil).

gradé [grade], *s.m.* **1.** *Mil:* non-commissioned officer, N.C.O.; **gradés et soldats,** rank and file; **tous les gradés,** all ranks (commissioned and non-commissioned). **2.** *Navy:* rated man; **les gradés,** the petty officers.

grader[1] [grade], *v.tr.* (*rare*) *Mil:* **g. un soldat,** to raise a soldier from the ranks, to give a soldier a stripe.

grader[2] [gradɛːr], *s.m. Civ.E:* grader.

gradient [gradjɑ̃], *s.m.* gradient; **g. thermique, de température,** temperature gradient; **g. de pression,** pressure gradient; **g. de vitesse,** speed, velocity, gradient; *Geol:* **g. géothermique,** geothermal gradient; *El:* **g. du potentiel,** potential gradient; **g. de tension,** voltage gradient; *Meteor:* **vent du g.,** gradient wind; *Biol:* **g. (physiologique),** gradient.

gradin [gradɛ̃], *s.m.* **1.** (*a*) step, tier, stepped row of seats; **gradins d'un amphithéâtre,** tiers, gradin(e)s, of an amphitheatre; **collines disposées en gradins,** hills rising tier upon tier; stepped hills; **g. d'autel,** altar gradin(e); *Mil:* **g. de tir,** fire step; *F:* **quand j'étais sur les gradins,** when I was at school; (*b*) *Min:* stope; **gradins droits,** underhand stopes; **gradins renversés,** overhand stopes; (*c*) altar (of graving dock). **2.** *Tchn:* **assemblage à gradins,** joggle-joining; **poulie à gradins,** cone pulley, step pulley; stepped pulley; **lentille à gradins,** corrugated lens; *El.E:* **disposer les balais en gradins,** to stagger the brushes (of a dynamo).

gradine [gradin], *s.f. Tls: Sculp:* gradine.

gradualité [gradɥalite], *s.f.* gradualness; gradual character (of change, etc.).

graduateur [gradɥatœːr], *s.m.* **1.** graduator (of thermometers, etc.). **2.** *El.E:* **g. de tension,** voltage regulator.

graduation [gradɥasjɔ̃], *s.f. Ph:* **1.** graduating (of scale). **2.** graduation. **3.** scale.

gradué, -ée [gradɥe]. **1.** *a.* (*a*) graduated; **verre g.,** measuring glass; graduated measure, *U.S:* graduate; **échelle graduée,** graduated scale; (*b*) graded, progressive (exercises, etc.). **2.** *s. Sch: A:* graduate.

graduel, -elle [gradɥɛl]. **1.** *a.* gradual, progressive; *Ecc:* **psaume g.,** gradual psalm. **2.** *s.m. Ecc:* gradual.

graduellement [gradɥɛlmɑ̃], *adv.* gradually, by degrees.

graduer [gradɥe], *v.tr.* **1.** to graduate, calibrate (thermometer, etc.). **2.** to grade (studies, etc.). **3.** *A:* to confer a degree upon (s.o.).

gradueuse [gradɥøːz], *s.f.* pattern designer (for standard-sized clothes).

graffigner [grafiɲe], *v.tr. P:* to scratch, claw.

graffite [grafit], *s.m.*, **graffiti** [grafiti], *s.m.* (*the pl.* **graffiti** *is now used increasingly as a sing.*) *Art:* graffito; *pl. graffites, graffiti.*

graille [grɑːj], *s.f.* **1.** *Orn: F:* crow. **2.** *P:* food, grub.

graillement [grɑjmɑ̃], *s.m.* **1.** (*a*) raucousness (of voice); (*b*) huskiness (caused by phlegm). **2.** hawk (of phlegm). **3.** hoarse sound.

grailler [grɑje], *v.i.* **1.** (*a*) to shout in a raucous voice (like a crow); (*b*) to speak huskily. **2.** to hawk up phlegm. **3.** *P:* to eat; *P:* to nosh.

graillon[1] [grɑjɔ̃], *s.m.* **1. sentir le g.,** to smell of burnt fat; to taste greasy. **2.** *pl.* (*a*) *A:* scraps (of broken meat); (*b*) *Sculp:* chippings (of stone).

graillon[2], *s.m. P:* clot of phlegm; *P:* gob.

graillonnement [grɑjɔnmɑ̃], *s.m.* hawking up (of phlegm); hawk.

graillonner[1] [grɑjɔne], *v.i. Cu:* to smell of burnt fat.

graillonner[2], *v.i. F:* to hawk up phlegm; to hawk.

graillonneur[1], **-euse** [grɑjɔnœːr, -øːz]. **1.** *a.* (dish) that (i) smells of, (ii) contains, burnt fat. **2.** *A:* (*a*) *s.* seller of scraps (from the table); (*b*) *s.f.* **graillonneuse,** bad cook.

graillonneur[2], **-euse,** *s. P:* person who is always hawking up phlegm.

grain[1] [grɛ̃], *s.m.* **1.** (*a*) grain; **g. de blé,** grain of wheat; **g. d'orge,** barleycorn; *Anat:* **grains d'orge,** seed bodies (in joints); **g. de moutarde, de grenade,** mustard, pomegranate, seed; **le bon g. finit toujours par lever,** quality will tell in the end; (*b*) corn; *Husb:* hard food (for poultry); **le g., les grains,** corn, cereals; the grain crop; **la récolte des grains,** the corn, cereal, harvest; **entrepôt de g.,** granary; **poulet de g.,** corn-fed chicken; *F:* **être dans le g.,** to be in clover. **2. g. de café,** coffee bean; **g. de poivre,** peppercorn; **g. de raisin,** grape; **g. de beauté,** beauty spot, mole. **3.** particle, atom; (*a*) **g. de sel, de sable, de poudre,** grain of salt, sand, powder; **g. de poussière,** speck, particle, of dust; **g. d'électricité,** electron; **réduire qch. en grains,** to granulate, grind, sth.; *Ball:* **poudre à gros grains,** pebble powder; (*b*) **g. de coquetterie, de jalousie,** touch of coquetry, jealousy; **g. de méchanceté,** hint, touch, of spite(fulness); (*c*) *F:* **il a un g.,** he's not quite right in the head, he's a bit cracked, he's not all there; (*d*) *F:* **avoir son g.,** to be tight, fuddled; (*e*) *A.Meas:* grain (= 0,053 gramme). **4.** (*a*) bead; (*b*) *Sm.a:* **g. d'orge,** bead; *Ball:* **g. de plomb,** pellet; (*c*) *I.C.E: El:* **grains platinés,** platinum points; (*d*) *Metall:* **g. d'essai,** button; (*e*) *Pharm:* pellet. **5.** (*a*) grain, texture (of substance); rough side (of skin, etc.); **côté g. du cuir,** grain side of leather; **contre le g.,** against the grain; **g. fin, dense,** close grain; **à gros grains,** coarse-grained; **à grains fins, serrés,** close-grained; fine-grained; **cassure à grains,** granular fracture; **cuir gros g.,** coarse-grained leather; **ruban gros g.,** petersham; *Phot:* **g. fin,** fine grain; **gros g.,** coarse grain; (*b*) pock mark. **6.** *Tls:* (stonemason's) chisel. **7.** *Mec.E:* (*a*) bush(ing), lining (of bearing, etc.); necking; (*b*) cam roller.

grain[2], *s.m. Nau:* squall; gust of wind; **g. épais,** thick squall; **g. noir,** black squall; **g. blanc,** white squall; **fort g. de pluie,** heavy rainstorm; **essuyer un g.,** to meet with a squall; **parer un g.,** to steer clear of a squall; **veiller au g.,** to look out for squalls; **temps à grains,** squally weather.

grainasse [grɛnas], *s.f. Nau:* gust of wind.

grain-d'orge [grɛ̃dɔrʒ], *s.m.* **1.** *Tls: Carp:* (*a*) routing-plane; (*b*) diamond-point chisel; (*c*) barleycorn (between mouldings). **2.** *Nau:* (*a*) filling, gore; (*b*) cleat. **3.** *F:* sty(e) (in the eye); *pl. grains-d'orge.*

graine [grɛn], *s.f.* **1.** seed (of plants); **g. de lin,** linseed; **g. de moutarde,** mustard seed; **g. de paradis,** grains of paradise, Guinea grains, Malaguetta pepper; **g. de Perse,** common buckthorn seed; *Pharm:* **g. à vers,** wormseed; **g. de girofle,** cardamom; **g. d'anis,** aniseed; **monter en g.,** to run to seed, to seed; (*of flax*) to boll; *F:* (*of girl*) to be on the wrong side of thirty; *F:* **en prendre la g.,** to profit from s.o.'s example; *F:* **casser la g.,** to eat, to have a bite; *F:* **c'est une mauvaise g.,** he's a bad lot. **2. graines de vers à soie,** silkworms' eggs; graine.

grainé [grɛne], *a.* **1.** (*of soap*) salted out. **2.** *Crust:* (*of female lobster, etc.*) bearing eggs.

graineler [grɛnle], *v.tr.* to grain (paper, leather).

grainer [grɛne], *v.tr.* **1.** *Engr:* to mull (zinc plate). **2.** to granulate, corn (metal, etc.). **3.** to grain (paper, leather). **4.** *P:* to eat.

graineterie [grɛntri], *s.f.* seed trade; seed shop, seed merchant's.

grainetier, -ière [grɛntje, -jɛːr], *s.* corn chandler.

grainetis [grɛnti], *s.m. Num:* milled edge, milling, graining.

grainier, -ière [grɛnje, -jɛːr], *s.* **1.** seed merchant; corn-chandler; **g.-fleuriste,** seedsman. **2.** *s.m. Bot:* collection of seeds.

graisin [grɛzɛ̃], *s.m. Glassm:* cullet.

graissage [grɛsaːʒ], *s.m.* (*a*) greasing, oiling, lubrication (of wheels, etc.); **g. automatique,** automatic lubrication; **à g. automatique,** self-lubricating; **g. à compte-gouttes,** drop-feed lubrication; **g. par gravité,** gravity-feed lubrication; **g. par barbotage, par projection,** splash lubrication; **g. par brouillard d'huile,** spray lubrication; **g. sous pression,** pressure greasing; *I.C.E:* **g. par mélange,** petroil lubrication; *Aut: A:* **g. central,** one-shot lubrication; **huile de g.,** lubricating oil; **trou de g.,** oil hole; **bague de g.,** oiling ring; **circuit de g.,** lubrication system; **douille de g.,** oiling sleeve; **schéma (du circuit) de g.,** lubrication chart; *F:* **g. de patte,** palm-greasing (bribery); (*b*) *Typ:* blue, smearing; **g. non adhérent,** scum; **g. par mouillage insuffisant,** tinting.

graisse [grɛs], *s.f.* **1.** (*a*) grease, fat; **tache de g.,** grease spot; *B:* **la g. de la terre,** the fatness of the earth; **g. de ménage,** (i) cooking fat; (ii) oleomargarine; **g. de rognon,** suet; **g. de rôti,** dripping; **g. de porc,** lard; **g. de baleine,** blubber; **(faire) fondre de la g.,** to melt, try down, fat; *F:* **prendre de la g.,** to put on fat; *F:* **c'est une boule de g.,** he's, she's, a little dumpling (of a person); **boniments à la g. d'oie, à la g. de chevaux de bois,** blarney; bluff; (*b*) *Pharm:* **g. balsamique,** benzoinated lard; **g. de laine,** lanoline; (*c*) lubricating) grease; **g. pour essieux,** axle grease; **g. graphitée,** graphite grease, **g. à température de fluage élevée,** high melting-point grease, **g. consistante,** cup grease, hard, solid, thick, grease; **g. anti-gel, g. incongelable,** non-freezing grease, lubricant; **g. pour engrenages,** gear lubricant; **g. anti-rouille,** rust preventer; *Mil:* **g. d'armes,** rifle oil; *Nau:* **g. de coq,** slush; **g. pour graissage forcé,** grease-gun grease, pressure-gun grease; **pistolet, pompe, injecteur, à g.,** grease gun; **étanche à la g.,** grease-sealed; (*d*)*Typ:* thickness of type; (*e*) *P:* money, lolly; (*f*) *P:* **de haute g.,** bawdy; (*g*) *P:* cheating (at cards, etc.); (*h*) *P:* **g. d'abattage,** force. **2. g. minérale,** crude paraffin, mineral jelly. **3.** ropiness (of wine); **tourner à la g.,** to get ropy.

graisser [grɛse], *v.tr.* **1.** to grease, oil, lubricate; **g. ses chaussures,** to oil, dub, one's boots; *F:* **g. ses bottes,** to prepare (i) for a long journey, (ii) for the other world; **g. la patte à,** *occ.* **de, qn,** to bribe s.o.; to oil, grease, s.o.'s palm; to square s.o.; **g. la marmite,** to pay one's footing. **2. métal qui graisse la lime,** metal that clogs the file. **3.** to soil (one's clothes, etc.) with grease; to grease (one's clothes); *abs.* **onguent qui ne graisse pas,** non-greasy ointment. **4.** *Typ:* to blur, smear; **g. par mouillage insuffisant,** to tint; **g. par frottement,** to rub. **5.** *v.i.* (*of wine*) to become ropy.

graisseur, -euse [grɛsœːr, -øːz], *s. Mec.E:* **1.** (*pers.*) greaser, oiler. **2.** *s.m.* greaser, lubricator; grease cup; nipple; **g. à bague,** ring oiler; **g. à graisse,** grease gun; **g. à aiguille,** needle lubricator; **g. centrifuge,** banjo oiler; **g. à godet,** grease-cup; **g. à trombone,** telescope lubricator; **g. compte-gouttes,** drip-feed lubricator; **g. coup de poing,** hand-pump lubricator; **g. par gravité,** gravity-feed lubricator; **g. à, sous, pression,** forced-feed lubricator. **3.** *a.* **godet g.,** grease box; **balai g.,** oil brush; **anneau g.,** oil ring; **palier g.,** self-lubricating plummer block; **pistolet g.,** grease gun.

graisseux, -euse [grɛsø, -øːz], *a.* **1.** (*a*) greasy, oily, unctuous; (*b*) fatty, adipose (tissue). **2.** ropy (wine).

graissin [grɛsɛ̃], *s.m. Fish:* bait (made of sardine heads).

graissoir [grɛswaːr], *s.m.* grease rag, oiling rag.

grallaire [gralɛːr], *s.f. Orn:* ant-shrike; **g. à tête rousse,** chestnut-crowned ant-pitta.

gralle [gral], *s.m. Orn: A:* wader.

Gram [gram], *Pr.n. Bac:* **liqueur de G.,** Gram's solution; **g. positif, négatif,** gram-positive, -negative.

gramen [gramɛn], *s.m. Bot:* lawn grass.

graménite [gramenit], *s.f. Miner:* gramenite.

gramicidine [gramisidin], *s.f. Bac:* gramicidin.

graminacées [graminase], *s.f.pl. Bot:* Graminaceae.

graminé [gramine]. **1.** *a. Bot:* graminaceous. **2.** *s.f.pl.* **graminées,** Graminaceae.

graminiforme [graminifɔrm], *a. Bot:* graminiform.

graminologie [graminɔlɔʒi], *s.f. Bot:* graminology.

grammaire [gram(m)ɛːr], *s.f.* (*a*) grammar; **contre la g.,** ungrammatical; (*b*) **une g. française,** a French grammar (book); **g. du cinéma,** (book of) the conventions of the cinema; **g. musicale,** (book of) the rules of music.

grammairien, -ienne [gram(m)ɛrjɛ̃, -jɛn], *s.* grammarian.

grammatical, -aux [gram(m)atikal, -o], *a.* grammatical.

grammaticalement [gram(m)atikalmɑ̃], *adv.* grammatically.

grammaticalisation [gram(m)atikalizasjɔ̃], *s.f.* grammaticalization.

grammaticaliser [gram(m)atikalize], *v.tr.* to grammaticalize.

grammaticalité [gram(m)atikalite], *s.f.* grammaticalness.

grammatiste [gram(m)atist], *s.m.* pedant, grammatist.

grammatite [gram(m)atit], *s.f. Miner:* tremolite, grammatite.

gramme[1] [gram], *s.m. Meas:* gram(me) (= 0·0353 oz.).

gramme[2], *s.f. El:* gramme-dynamo.

gramme-équivalent [gramekivalɑ̃], *s.m. Ch:* gramme-equivalent; *pl. gramme-équivalents.*

gramme-force [gramfɔrs], *s.m. Ph:* gram weight; *pl. grammes-force.*

gramme-poids [grampwɑ], *s.m. Ph:* gram weight; *pl. grammes-poids.*

gramophone [gramɔfɔn], *s.m. A:* gramophone.

grand, grande [grɑ̃, grɑ̃ːd], *a.* **1.** (*a*) tall (in stature), large, big (in size); **homme g.,** tall man; **un g. homme blond,** a tall, fair man; **un petit homme pas plus g. que ça,** a little man only so high; **grande ville,** large town; **grande échelle,** tall, long, ladder; **grands bras, grandes jambes,** long arms, long legs; **grands pieds,** big feet; **grande distance,** great distance; **assez g.,** biggish, fair-sized; **plus g. que nature,** larger than life; **ses yeux s'ouvrirent tout grands,** his eyes opened wide; **plaine d'une grande étendue,** wide, broad, plain; **une grande heure,** a full, good, hour; *Opt:* **g. angle de champ,** wide (angle of) field; **un g. A,** a capital A; **l'amour avec un grand A,** love with a capital L; **le G. Montréal,** Greater Montreal; *s.a.* AIR I. 1, MER; (*b*) chief, main; **g. chemin,** main road, highway, high road; **la Grande rue,** the High Street, *U.S:* Main Street; **grandes marées,** spring tides; *s.m.* **le g. de l'eau,** high-water mark; *Nau:* **le g. mât,** the mainmast; **la grande messe,** high mass; **g. ressort,** mainspring; **les grandes vacances,** the long vacation, the summer holidays; **les grands commis,** the higher civil servants; *Geom:* **g. axe d'une ellipse,** major axis of an ellipse; (*c*) **quand tu seras g.,** when you are grown up, when you are old enough; **elle se fait grande,** (i) she is growing

up; (ii) she is growing tall; **les grandes personnes,** the grown-ups; **plante déjà grande,** fully-grown plant; *Sch:* **les grandes classes,** the upper forms; **un g. garçon,** a big boy; **son g. frère,** his big brother; (*d*) *adv.* **faire g.,** do things in a big way, on a large scale; **voir g.,** to have big ideas; **œil g. ouvert, yeux grands ouverts,** wide-open eye(s); **porte(s) grande(s) ouverte(s),** wide-open door(s); *adv.phr.* **en g.,** (i) on a large scale, (ii) full size; **faire les choses en g.,** to do things on a grand scale; **statue en g.,** life-size statue; **se faire peindre en g.,** to have one's portrait painted life-size; **reproduction en g.,** enlarged copy; **ouvrir toutes les fenêtres en g.,** to open all the windows wide; **ouvrir un robinet en g.,** to turn a tap full on; *Nau:* **amenez en g.,** lower amain; **arriver en g.,** to bear round. **2.** (*of number, quantity*) large, many; **pas g. monde,** not many people; **je n'ai pas g. argent,** I haven't a lot of money; **le g. public,** the general public; **dans le plus g. détail,** in the fullest detail; **en grande partie,** largely, to a great extent, in a great measure. **3.** (*of worth, rank, fame*) **les grands hommes,** great men; **un g. homme,** a great man; **g. seigneur,** great nobleman; **de grande naissance,** of noble birth; **le g. monde,** (high) society; **g. concert,** grand concert; **le g. air de** *la Tosca*, the great aria in *La Tosca*; **g. dîner,** grand dinner; **grands vins,** high-class wines; **Alexandre le G.,** Alexander the Great; **se donner de grands airs,** to give oneself airs; **une grande dame,** a great lady, a grand lady; **le G. Hôtel,** the Grand (Hotel); **g. feu d'artifice,** grand display of fireworks; *s.m.* **donner dans le g.,** to be high and mighty; to be fond of display; *Hist:* **Monsieur le G.** (= **grand écuyer**), the Master of the Horse. **4.** (*of moral, intellectual, qualities*) **grandes pensées,** great, noble, thoughts; **se montrer g.,** to show oneself magnanimous; **la grande manière,** the grand manner. **5.** great; **une grande découverte,** a great discovery; **ils sont grands amis,** they are great friends; **grande différence,** wide, great, difference; **avec g. plaisir, de g. cœur,** with great pleasure, very willingly; **avec le plus g. plaisir,** with the greatest pleasure; **avec la plus grande facilité,** with the greatest, utmost, ease; **g. froid,** severe cold; **il fait g. jour,** it is broad daylight; **il est g. temps de partir,** it is high time we were off; **grandes pluies,** heavy rains; **g. vent,** high wind; **grands explosifs,** high explosives; **g. bruit,** loud noise; **ce fut un g. remue-ménage,** there was a great bustle, a great upheaval; **g. buveur,** hard drinker; **les grands blessés,** the seriously wounded, the bad cases; **les grands infirmes,** the badly disabled; **ils sont dans une grande misère,** they are in great poverty; **à mon g. étonnement, à mon g. regret, à ma grande surprise,** much to my astonishment, much to my regret, much to my surprise; **à ma grande horreur,** to my utter horror; **grande jeunesse,** extreme youth; **excusez la grande liberté,** if it isn't asking too much; (*at seaside resort, etc.*) **la grande semaine,** gala week; *Tex:* **couleur g. teint,** fast dye. **6.** *s.* (*a*) *Spanish Hist: m.* grandee; (*b*) **grands et petits,** old and young; **contes pour grands et petits,** tales for grown-ups and children; *Sch:* **les grand(e)s,** the senior boys, girls; (*c*) **les grands de la terre,** the great ones of the earth, of this world; **les grands,** great men; (*d*) *Pol:* **les Grands,** the Great Powers; **les quatre Grands,** the big Four (France, Great Britain, U.S.A., U.S.S.R.).

grand' [grɑ̃], *a. A:* (*used in comb. fms for* **grande**- *and now replaced by* **grand-**) grand-.

grand-angulaire [grɑ̃tɑ̃gylɛːr], *a. & s.m. Opt:* wide-angle (lens, field-glass, etc.); *pl. grand(e)s-angulaires.*

Grand(-)Belt [grɑ̃bɛlt], *Pr.n.m. Geog:* the Great Belt (of the Baltic).

grand-calot [grɑ̃kalo], *s.m. Mil: P:* brass hat; *pl. grands-calots.*

grand'chambre [grɑ̃ʃɑ̃bʀ], *s.f. Navy: A:* wardroom; *pl. grand'chambres.*

grand-chantre [grɑ̃ʃɑ̃tʀ], *s.m.* precentor; *pl. grands-chantres.*

grand-chose [grɑ̃ʃoːz]. **1.** *indef. pron. m.inv.* (*usu. coupled with* **pas** *or* **sans**) **il ne fait pas g.-c.,** he doesn't do much; **il ne sera, ne fera, jamais, g.-c.,** he'll never amount to much; **cela ne fait pas g.-c.,** it's of no great importance, it doesn't matter much; it has little effect; **sans que cela fasse g.-c.,** without its mattering much; without any great effect; **elle ne vaut pas g.-c.,** she's no better than she should be; **cela ne vaut pas g.-c.,** it's not worth much; **je ne pense pas g.-c. de ce livre,** I don't think much of this book. **2.** *s. F:* **un, une, pas g.-c.,** a good-for-nothing; a poor sort; a wet.

grand-croix [grɑ̃krwɑ, -a]. **1.** *s.f.inv.* Grand Cross (of the Legion of Honour). **2.** *s.m.* Knight Grand Cross; *pl. grands-croix.*

grand-crosse [grɑ̃krɔs], *s.f. Golf: O:* driver; *pl. grands-crosses.*

grand-duc [grɑ̃dyk], *s.m.* **1.** grand duke. **2.** *Orn:* **g.-d. (d'Europe),** eagle owl; great horned owl; **g.-d. ascalaphe,** desert eagle owl. **3.** *F:* **faire la tournée des grands-ducs,** to go round the night clubs; *pl. grands-ducs.*

grand-ducal, -aux [grɑ̃dykal, -o], *a.* grand-ducal.

grand-duché [grɑ̃dyʃe], *s.m.* grand duchy; *pl. grands-duchés.*

Grande-Bretagne [grɑ̃dbrətaɲ], *Pr.n.f. Geog:* Great Britain.

grande-duchesse [grɑ̃ddyʃɛs], *s.f.* grand duchess; *pl. grandes-duchesses.*

grand-écoute [grɑ̃tekut], *s.f. Nau:* main-sheet; *pl. grand-écoutes.*

Grande-Grèce [grɑ̃dgrɛs], *Pr.n.f. A.Geog:* Magna Graecia.

grandelet, -ette [grɑ̃dlɛ, -ɛt], *a.* tallish; quite, fairly, big.

grandement [grɑ̃dmɑ̃], *adv.* **1.** grandly, nobly; **faire les choses g.,** to do things lavishly, in a lavish style, on a grand scale. **2.** greatly, largely; **se tromper g.,** to be greatly mistaken; **avoir g. raison,** to be altogether right; **avoir g. le temps,** to have ample time; **il est g. temps de . . .,** it is high time to . . .; **avoir g. de quoi vivre,** to have plenty to live on, to be amply provided for.

grandesse [grɑ̃dɛs], *s.f. Spanish Hist:* grandeeship.

grandet, -ette [grɑ̃dɛ, -ɛt], *a.* tallish, biggish; quite, fairly, tall, big.

grandeur [grɑ̃dœːr], *s.f.* **1.** (*a*) size; height (of tree); bulk (of parcel); **échelle de grandeurs,** scale of sizes; **étoile de troisième g.,** star of the third magnitude; **g. nature,** full-size(d); life-size(d); (*b*) loudness (of noise); (*c*) extent (of voyage); scale (of undertaking). **2.** greatness; (*a*) importance; magnitude (of offence); grandeur (of conception); *s.a.* FOLIE 1; (*b*) majesty, splendour, grandeur; **la g. de Rome,** the greatness of Rome; **au faîte de la g. humaine,** at the summit of human grandeur; **édifice empreint de g.,** noble building; **regarder qn du haut de sa g.,** to look down on s.o.; (*c*) nobility (of character, etc.). **3. sa G.,** his Highness; **sa G. l'archevêque,** his Grace the Archbishop; **sa G. l'évêque,** his Lordship the Bishop; **votre G.,** your Highness; your Grace; your Lordship.

grand-garde [grɑ̃gard], *s.f. Mil: A:* outpost picket (with supports); *pl. grand-gardes.*

grand-guignolesque [grɑ̃giɲɔlɛsk], *a.* over-melodramatic; **situation g.-g.,** melodramatic situation; situation worthy of the *Grand Guignol*; *pl. grand-guignolesques.*

grand-halte [grɑ̃dalt], *s.f. Mil:* main halt; battle practice firing; *pl. grand-haltes.*

grand-hune [grɑ̃yn], *s.f. Nau:* main-top; *pl. grand-hunes.*

grandiloquence [grɑ̃dilɔkɑ̃ːs], *s.f.* grandiloquence.

grandiloquent [grɑ̃dilɔkɑ̃], *a.* grandiloquent.

grandiose [grɑ̃djoːz], (*a*) *a.* grand, imposing; grandiose; **spectacle g.,** imposing, awe-inspiring, spectacle; (*b*) *s.m.* grandiose, imposing, appearance; magnificence.

grandiosement [grɑ̃djozmɑ̃], *adv.* in a grand, grandiose, manner; magnificently, imposingly.

grandir [grɑ̃diːr]. **1.** *v.i.* (*a*) (i) to grow tall; (ii) to grow up; **il a grandi,** he has grown, he is taller; **il a grandi l'année dernière,** he shot up last year; **g. de plus en plus,** to grow taller and taller; **faire g. le blé,** to make the corn grow; **en grandissant,** as one grows up, as one grows older; (*b*) **g. en sagesse,** to grow in wisdom; **son influence grandit,** his influence increases, is growing; **la rumeur grandissait,** the rumour was growing, was spreading. **2.** *v.tr.* (*a*) to make (sth.) greater, to increase; **ses talons la grandissent,** her heels add to her height, make her look taller; **se grandir en se haussant sur la pointe des pieds,** to make oneself taller by standing on tiptoe; (*b*) **ses malheurs l'ont grandi,** he is all the greater for his misfortunes; (*c*) to magnify; **g. un incident,** to magnify, exaggerate, an incident; **les enfants grandissent ce qui les entoure,** children imagine things around them to be larger than they really are.

grandissant [grɑ̃disɑ̃], *a.* growing, increasing; **tempête grandissante,** rising storm; **il l'attendait avec une impatience grandissante,** he was waiting for him (it, her) with growing impatience.

grandissement [grɑ̃dismɑ̃], *s.m.* (*a*) growth, increase; (*b*) *Opt:* magnification.

grandissime [grɑ̃disim], *a. F:* lordly (personage); immense (pleasure); tremendous (thump).

grand(-)livre [grɑ̃liːvʀ], *s.m.* **1.** *Com:* ledger; **g.-l. d'achats,** goods-bought ledger; **g.-l. de ventes,** goods-sold ledger; **porter qch. au g.-l.,** to post (up) an item. **2. le G.-L.,** the Great Book of the Public Debt; *pl. grands-livres.*

grand-maman [grɑ̃mamɑ̃], *s.f. F:* grandmamma, grandma, granny; *pl. grand(s)-mamans.*

grand-mère [grɑ̃mɛːr], *s.f.* (*a*) grandmother; *F:* **est-ce que je te demande si ta g.-m. fait du vélo?** mind your own business! (*b*) *F:* old woman; **des contes de g.-m.,** old wives' tales; *pl. grand(s)-mères.*

grand-messe [grɑ̃mɛs], *s.f. Ecc:* high mass; *pl. grand(s)-messes.*

grand-oncle [grɑ̃tɔ̃ːkl], *s.m.* great-uncle, grand-uncle; *pl. grands-oncles.*

grand-papa [grɑ̃papa], *s.m. F:* grandpapa, grandad; *pl. grands-papas.*

grand-peine (à) [agrɑ̃pɛn], *adv.phr.* with great difficulty.

grand-père [grɑ̃pɛːr], *s.m.* grandfather; *pl. grands-pères.*

grand-porte [grɑ̃pɔrt], *s.f.* gateway; *pl. grand-portes.*

grand-prêtre [grɑ̃prɛːtʀ], *s.m.* high priest; *pl. grands-prêtres.*

grand-rade [grɑ̃rad], *s.f. Nau:* outer roadstead, outer harbour; *pl. grand-rades.*

grand-raison [grɑ̃rɛzɔ̃], *s.f.* no *pl.* good reason; **avoir g.-r. de faire qch.,** to have every reason for doing sth.

grand-route [grɑ̃rut], *s.f.* highway, high road, main road; *pl. grand-routes.*

grand-rue [grɑ̃ry], *s.f.* high street, main street; *pl. grand-rues.*

grands-parents [grɑ̃parɑ̃], *s.m.pl.* grandparents.

grand-tante [grɑ̃tɑ̃ːt], *s.f.* great aunt; *pl. grand(s)-tantes.*

grand-teint [grɑ̃tɛ̃], *s.m.inv. Dy:* fast dye.

grand-tente [grɑ̃tɑ̃ːt], *s.f. Nau:* main awning; *pl. grand-tentes.*

grand-vergue [grɑ̃vɛrg], *s.f. Nau:* mainyard; *pl. grand(s)-vergues.*

grand-voile [grɑ̃vwal], *s.f. Nau:* mainsail; *pl. grand(s)-voiles.*

grange [grɑ̃ːʒ], *s.f.* barn; **mettre le blé en g.,** to garner the corn; **battre le blé en g.,** to thresh the corn by hand.

grangée [grɑ̃ʒe], *s.f.* barnful; **une g. de blé,** a barnful of wheat; enough wheat to fill a barn.

granifère [granifɛːr], *a. Bot:* graniferous.

graniforme [granifɔrm], *a. Bot: Anat:* graniform.

Granique (le) [ləgranik], *Pr.n.m. A.Geog:* Granicus.

granit [grani(t)], **granite** [granit], *s.m.* granite; **g. à deux micas,** binary granite, granulite; **cœur de g.,** heart of stone.

granitaire [granitɛːr], *a.* granite-like.

granité [granite], *s. & a. Tex:* pebble weave; *Cer:* **surface granitée,** (black and) crackle finish; **verre g.,** pebble glass.

graniter [granite], *v.tr.* to paint in imitation of granite.

graniteux, -euse [granitø, -øːz], *a.* granitic; granite (formation).

granitier [granitje], *s.m.* stonemason, stone cutter (who works in granite).

granitique [granitik], *a.* granitic.

granitisation [granitizasjɔ̃], *s.f. Geol:* granitization.

granito [granito], *s.m. Const:* terrazzo.

granitoïde [granitɔid], *a.* granitoid.

granivore [granivɔːr]. **1.** *a.* granivorous. **2.** *s.* granivore, seed-eater.

granodiorite [granɔdjɔrit], *s.f. Miner:* granodiorite.

grantia [grɑ̃tja], *s.m. Spong:* grantia.

granulaire [granylɛːr], *a.* granular.

granularité [granylarite], *s.f. Phot:* granularity.

granulat [granyla], *s.m. Civ.E:* aggregate.

granulateur [granylatœːr], *s.m.* granulator; granulating machine (for gunpowder, etc.).

granulation [granylasjɔ̃], *s.f.* **1.** (*a*) granulation; (*b*) *Exp:* corning, graining (of powder). **2.** *pl. Med:* granulations.

granulatoire [granylatwaːr], *s.m.* granulator (of metals), granulating machine.

granule [granyl], *s.m.* granule.

granulé [granyle]. **1.** *a.* granulated. **2.** *s.m.* pellet; product in granular form; **g. chocolaté,** granulated chocolate.

granuler [granyle], *v.tr.* **1.** to granulate; *Exp:* to grain, corn (powder). **2.** *Engr:* to stipple.

granuleux, -euse [granylø, -øːz], *a.* granular, granulous; *Biol:* **cellule granuleuse,** granule cell.

granulie [granyli], *s.f. Med:* granulitis.

granulite [granylit], *s.f. Miner:* granulite.
granulitique [granylitik], *a.* granulitic.
granulocyte [granylɔsit], *s.m. Physiol:* granulocyte.
granulo-graisseux, -euse [granylɔgrɛsø, -ø:z], *a. Med:* granulo-adipose.
granulomatose [granylɔmato:z], *s.f. Med:* granulomatosis.
granulome [granylɔm], *s.m. Med:* granuloma.
granulométrie [granylɔmetri], *s.f.* granulometry.
granulométrique [granylɔmetrik], *a.* granulometric.
granulopénie [granylɔpeni], *s.f. Med:* granulopenia, granulocytopenia.
granulose [granylo:z], *s.f. Ch: Physiol:* granulose.
granulosité [granylozite], *s.f. Cin: Phot: etc:* coarseness of grain; granularity.
granvillais, -aise [grɑ̃vilɛ, -ɛ:z], *a. & s. Geog:* (native, inhabitant) of Granville.
grape(-)fruit [grɛpfrut], *s.m. Bot:* grapefruit, pomelo.
graphe [graf], *s.m.* graph; **g. orienté,** oriented graph.
graphème [grafɛm], *s.m. Ling:* grapheme.
graphie [grafi], *s.f.* **1.** writing. **2.** method of writing. **3.** (*philology*) graphy.
graphier [grafje], *s.m. Rail:* indicator board (showing arrivals, departures, hours of work of train personnel).
graphiola [grafjɔla], *s.m. Fung:* graphiola.
graphique [grafik]. **1.** *a.* (*a*) graphic (sign, method); graphical (method); diagrammatic (representation); **dessin g.,** diagram; (*b*) *Geol:* graphic (granite, etc.). **2.** *s.m.* diagram; graph; graphic table; (patient's) temperature chart; **g. à barres, à bandes,** bar chart; **g. à secteurs,** pie chart; **g. d'écoulement, de débit,** flow diagram, chart; **g. de marche,** (i) *Mch:* running, working, diagram; (ii) *Mil:* march diagram; **g. figuratif,** pictogram. **3.** *s.f.* graphics; graphic arts.
graphiquement [grafikmɑ̃], *adv.* graphically; by means of diagrams; **figurer une courbe g.,** to plot a curve.
graphiquer [grafike], *v.tr.* to draw a diagram of (sth.); to graph, plot.
graphisme [grafism], *s.m.* method, style, of writing; style of drawing.
graphiste [grafist], *s.m. & f.* graphic artist.
graphitage [grafita:ʒ], *s.m.* graphitizing, graphitization.
graphite [grafit], *s.m.* graphite, blacklead, plumbago; **g. de cornue,** retort graphite; **g. colloïdal,** colloidal graphite; *Metall:* **g. de fourneau,** kish.
graphité [grafite], *a.* **huile graphitée,** graphite oil.
graphiter [grafite], *v.tr.* to graphitize; (*computers*) to mark-sense.
graphiteux, -euse [grafitø, -ø:z], *a.* (*a*) *Geol:* graphitic; (*b*) *Metall:* (*of pig iron*) kishy.
graphitique [grafitik], *a.* graphitic, plumbaginous.
graphitisation [grafitizasjɔ̃], *s.f.* graphitization.
graphiure [grafjy:r], *s.m. Z:* graphiure.
graphologie [grafɔlɔʒi], *s.f.* graphology.
graphologique [grafɔlɔʒik], *a.* graphological.
graphologue [grafɔlɔg], *s.m. or f.* graphologist.
graphomanie [grafɔmani], *s.f. Med:* graphomania.
graphomètre [grafɔmɛtr], *s.m.* graphometer; circumferentor.
graphométrie [grafɔmetri], *s.f.* graphometry.
graphométrique [grafɔmetrik], *a.* graphometric.
graphoscope [grafɔskɔp], *s.m.* graphoscope.
graphotypie [grafɔtipi], *s.f. Engr:* graphotype.
grappe[1] [grap], *s.f.* **1.** (*a*) cluster, bunch (of grapes, currants, dates); **g. de (deux ou trois) cerises,** cherry bob; **g. de lierre,** cluster of ivy; **g. d'oignons,** string of onions; **mordre à la g.,** to jump at the offer; (*b*) cluster, group (of people). **2.** *Bot:* raceme. **3.** *pl.* (*a*) *Med:* condylomata; (*b*) *Vet:* (horses') grapes; (*c*) *Anat:* **glandes en grappes,** acinous glands.
grappe[2], *s.f.* ground madder.
grappeler [graple], *v.tr.* (**je grappelle, n. grappelons; je grappellerai**) to arrange in bunches or clusters.
grapper [grape], *v.tr.* to grind (madder).
grapperie [grapri], *s.f. Hort:* **1.** grape growing. **2.** vinery.
grappier, -ière [grapje, -jɛ:r]. **1.** *a.* that produces bunches (of grapes). **2.** *s.m. Tchn:* granular residue (obtained when slaking lime).
grappillage [grapija:ʒ], *s.m.* **1.** gleaning (of grapes). **2.** *F:* (*a*) making of petty profits; (*b*) picking and stealing, scrounging.
grappiller [grapije], *v.tr. & i.* **1.** to glean (in vineyard). **2.** *F:* (*a*) to make petty (illicit) profits; to make sth. on the side; (*b*) to pilfer, cadge, scrounge.
grappilleur, -euse [grapijœ:r, -ø:z], *s.* **1.** gleaner (in vineyard). **2.** *F:* pilferer, cadger, scrounger; maker of petty (illicit) profits.
grappillon [grapijɔ̃], *s.m.* small bunch, cluster (of grapes, etc.).
grappin [grapɛ̃], *s.m.* **1.** (*a*) *Nau:* grapnel, hook, grappling anchor; *A:* **grappins d'abordage,** grappling irons; (*b*) **g. à main,** drag, creeper; (*c*) *Hyd.E:* grab dredger; grab; (*d*) clutch (of crane); (*e*) (lumberman's) cant hook, gripper, peavie, peav(e)y; *F:* **mettre le g., sur qch., qn,** to hook, lay hands on, get hold of, sth., s.o.; (*f*) *Petroleum Ind:* **g. de repêchage,** tool grab. **2.** *Const:* anchor tie, anchor iron; anchor. **3.** *pl.* climbing irons.
grappiner [grapine], *v.tr.* (*a*) to grapple (with grappling irons); (*b*) *Fish:* to catch (fish) (with a multi-hook fishhook); (*c*) *Glassm:* to clean (molten glass).
grappu [grapy], *a.* laden with grapes; heavy-clustered (branch, etc.).
graptolit(h)e [graptɔlit], *s.m. Paleont:* graptolite; *pl.* **les graptolites,** Graptolitoidea.
gras, grasse [grɑ, grɑ:s], *a.* **1.** (*a*) fat (meat); fatty (tissues); **matières grasses,** fats; (*b*) rich (food); **régime g.,** meat diet; **potage g., potage au g.,** meat soup; *Ecc:* **jour g.,** meat day; **les jours g.,** Sunday, Monday and Tuesday before Ash Wednesday; **mardi g.,** Shrove Tuesday; **la semaine grasse,** Shrovetide; **faire g., manger g ,** to eat meat (*esp.* on a fast day); **g. pâturages,** rich pastures; **fromage g.,** full cream cheese; (*c*) *s.m.* fat (of meat). **2.** (*a*) fat, stout (person); *s.* **les g. et les maigres,** fat and thin people; **g. comme un porc,** as fat as a pig; *A:* **en serez-vous plus g.?** will you be any the richer for it? **tourner au gras,** to put on fat; **être g. comme un cent de clous,** to be as thin as a lath, to be nothing but a bag of bones; (*b*) fatted, fat (animal); plump (pullet); **tuer le veau g.,** to kill the fatted calf. **3.** (*a*) greasy, oily (rag, hair, etc.); **eaux grasses,** (i) dishwater; (ii) swill, swillings; **vernis g.,** oil varnish; *Th:* **crayon g.,** stick of grease paint; **blanc g.,** white greasepaint; *s. A:* **entretenir le mécanisme au g.,** to keep the machinery well greased; (*b*) pinguid; *Ch:* **acide g.,** fatty acid; *Toil:* **crème grasse,** cream for dry skins. **4.** thick; (*a*) **boue grasse,** thick, slimy, mud; **il fait g. à marcher,** it is slippery under foot; **vin g.,** ropy wine; **toux grasse,** loose, phlegmy, cough; **voix grasse,** oily voice; **avoir le parler g.,** to have a thick voice; **parler g.,** (i) = GRASSEYER; (ii) to talk smut; **conte g.,** broad story; **un rire g.,** a belly laugh; *adv.* **rire g.,** to give a deep chuckle, a hearty laugh; **temps g.,** thick, foggy, weather; *Vet:* **cheval qui a la vue grasse,** dim-sighted horse; (*b*) **poutre grasse,** thick beam; **plante grasse,** succulent (plant); *Typ:* **caractères g.,** heavy, bold(-faced), type; **trait g.,** heavy line; *s.m.* **écrire en g.,** to write with a bold stroke; *Mec.E:* **g. sur la largeur,** allowance in width; *Const:* **g. d'une poutre,** excessive thickness, waste, of a beam; *Const:* **équerrage (en) g.,** standing bevelling; *F:* **il n'y en a pas g.,** there's not much of it; *s.m.* **le g. de la jambe,** the calf of the leg; **le g. du pouce,** the thick of the thumb; *s.a.* MATINÉE 1. **5.** soft; (*a*) **contours g.,** softened, woolly, outlines; (*b*) **pierre grasse,** soft stone. **6.** (*a*) heavy, pinguid, clayey (soil); (*b*) rich (coal, limestone); **charbon g.,** bituminous coal. **7.** *s.m. Geol:* **g. de cadavre,** mineral, mountain, tallow; hatchettine, hatchettite, adipocerite.
gras-double [grɑdubl], *s.m. Cu:* tripe.
grassement [grɑsmɑ̃], *adv.* **1. vivre g.,** to live in plenty, on the fat of the land; **rire g.,** to laugh heartily. **2. récompenser qn g.,** to reward s.o. handsomely, generously.
grasserie [grasri], *s.f. Ser:* grasserie, jaundice.
grasset, -ette [grasɛ, -ɛt]. **1.** *a. O: F:* plump (person, chicken); chubby (child). **2.** *s.m.* (*a*) stifle (joint) (of horse); (*b*) *Cu:* thin flank; (*c*) *Amph:* tree-frog. **3.** *s.f. Bot:* **grassette,** butterwort.
grasseyement [grasɛjmɑ̃], *s.m.* (*a*) strongly marked r (in speech); (*b*) exaggerated rolling of uvular r.
grasseyer [grasɛje], *v.i. Ling:* (*a*) to speak with a strongly marked r (unfamiliar to the listener); (*b*) to speak with a strong uvular r, to roll one's r's.
grasseyeur, -euse [grasejœ:r, -ø:z], *s.* person who rolls his, her, r's.
grassois, -oise [graswa, -wa:z], *a. & s. Geog:* (native, inhabitant) of Grasse.
grassouillet, -ette [grasujɛ, -ɛt], *a. F:* plump (person); chubby (child).
grateron [gratrɔ̃], *s.m. Bot:* goose grass, catchweed, scratchweed.
gratianopolitain, -aine [grasjanɔpɔlitɛ̃, -ɛn], *a. & s. Geog:* (native, inhabitant) of the Grésivaudan region.
graticulation [gratikylasjɔ̃], *s.f. Draw:* graticulation.
graticule [gratikyl], *s.m.* framework of squares (for enlargement, etc., of maps, plans); graticule; **amorce de g.,** graduation tick.
graticuler [gratikyle], *v.tr.* to divide (drawing, etc.) into squares; to graticulate.
Gratien [grasjɛ̃], *Pr.n.m. Hist:* Gratian.
gratifiant [gratifjɑ̃], *a. Psy:* gratifying.
gratification [gratifikasjɔ̃], *s.f.* **1.** (*a*) gratuity, tip; **donner une g. au porteur,** to tip the porter; (*b*) bonus, bounty; **g. du jour de l'an** = (i) Christmas box, (ii) Christmas bonus; (*c*) *Mil: Navy:* **g. de première mise,** outfit allowance; **g. de réforme,** temporary wound pension. **2.** *Psy:* gratification.
gratifier [gratifje], *v.tr.* (*p.d. & pr.sub.* **n. gratifiions, v. gratifiiez**) **1.** (*a*) to present (**qn de qch.,** s.o. with sth.); **g. la commune d'une statue,** to present the parish with a statue; (*b*) *abs. Psy:* to gratify (s.o.); to give (psychological) satisfaction (to s.o.). **2.** *Iron:* **être gratifié d'une amende,** to be landed with a fine; **être gratifié des erreurs d'un autre,** to have s.o. else's mistakes attributed to oneself; to be landed with s.o. else's mistakes; **g. un garnement d'une bonne paire de gifles,** to give a naughty child, to reward a naughty child with, a couple of good slaps.
gratin [gratɛ̃], *s.m.* **1.** (*a*) *Cu: O:* burnt portion adhering to the pan; (*b*) raspings, (seasoned) breadcrumbs, *gratin*; **au g.,** (cooked) with breadcrumbs and grated cheese; (*c*) dish cooked *au gratin*; *F:* **le g.,** the upper crust (of society); the best (of anything); the pick of the basket; **le g. du g. de la société parisienne,** the cream of Paris society. **2.** friction surface (of matchbox).
gratiné, -ée [gratine]. **1.** *a.* (*a*) *Cu:* sprinkled with breadcrumbs and cheese, *au gratin*; **sole gratinée,** sole *au gratin*; **chou-fleur g.,** cauliflower cheese; (*b*) *F:* **une addition gratinée,** a bill to beat all bills, an enormous bill; **c'est g.!** it's a bit much! **2.** *s.m. Cu:* dish cooked *au gratin*; *s.f.* **gratinée,** (onion) soup *au gratin.*
gratiner [gratine], *Cu:* **1.** *v.i. O:* to stick to the side of the pan. **2.** *v.tr.* to cook (sth.) *au gratin.*
gratiole [grasjɔl], *s.f. Bot:* gratiola; hedge hyssop.
gratis [gratis]. **1.** *adv.* (*a*) gratis, for nothing, free of charge; **entrée g.,** admission free; no charge for admission; (*b*) gratuitously; without provocation. **2.** *a.* free (ticket, etc.).
gratitude [gratityd], *s.f.* gratitude, gratefulness; thankfulness.
gratouiller [gratuje]. *F:* (*a*) *v.tr.* to scrape, scratch; (*b*) *v.i.* to itch.
grattage [grata:ʒ], *s.m.* **1.** *Tex:* teaseling, napping, raising. **2.** (*a*) scraping (off); (*b*) erasure (of writing); scratching out; (*c*) *Surg:* scraping (of a bone).
gratte [grat], *s.f.* **1.** (mason's or painter's) scraper; (caulker's) chisel. **2.** *F:* pickings, perquisites, rake-off; perks; fringe benefits; profits on the side; **faire de la g.,** to get pickings; to get a rake-off; to make a bit on the side. **3.** *Fr.C:* (snow) plough.
gratteau [grato], *s.m. Tls:* scratcher.
gratte-boësse [gratbwɛs], *s.f.,* **gratte-bosse** [gratbɔs], *s.f.,* scratch brush; *pl. gratte-boësses, -bosses.*
gratte-boësser [gratbwɛse], *v.tr.* to scratch-brush.
gratte-ciel [gratsjɛl], *s.m.inv.* skyscraper.
gratte-cul [gratky], *s.m.inv. Bot: F:* hip.
gratte-dos [grat(ə)do], *s.m.inv.* back-scratcher.
grattée [grate], *s.f. P:* thrashing, (good) hiding.
gratte-fond [gratfɔ̃], *s.m. Tls:* scraper (for cleaning stone surfaces); *pl. gratte-fonds.*
gratte-huile [gratɥil], *a.inv. A: I.C.E:* **bague g.-h.,** scraper-ring (of piston).
gratteler [gratle], *v.tr.* (**je grattelle, n. grattelons; je grattellerai**) to score (plate of metal, etc.) for surfacing.
gratteleux, -euse [gratlø, -ø:z], *a. Med: F: A:* suffering from (i) the itch, (ii) ciliary blepharitis.
grattelle [gratɛl], *s.f. Med: F: A:* (*a*) (slight) itch; (*b*) ciliary blepharitis.
grattement [grat(ə)mɑ̃], *s.m.* **1.** scratching. **2.** *F:* itching.
gratte-miettes [gratmjɛt], *s.m.inv.* (crumb) grater.
gratte-ongles [gratɔ̃:gl], *s.m.inv.* manicure knife.
gratte-paille [gratpɑ:j], *s.m.inv. Orn: F:* hedge warbler, hedge sparrow, dunnock.
gratte-papier [gratpapje], *s.m.inv.* **1.** *Pej:* pen-pusher. **2.** (lawyer's) copying clerk; **un emploi de g.-p.,** a clerking job.

gratte-pavé [gratpave], *s.m.inv. P: O:* ragman, muckworm.
gratte-pieds [gratpje], *s.m.inv.* (metal) doormat.
gratter [grate], *v.tr.* **1.** (*a*) to scrape (metal surface, etc.); **g. la terre,** (i) to turn over the soil (superficially); (ii) to cultivate the soil, to grow crops; **g. légèrement la terre pour y semer des graines,** to rake over the ground (lightly) (in order) to plant seeds; **g. le papier,** (i) *Pej:* to be a pen-pusher; to work as a clerk; (ii) *F:* to cover a lot of paper; *abs.* **plume qui gratte,** scratchy pen; (*b*) to scratch (with nails, claws, etc.); **chat qui gratte le sol,** cat that is scratching up the soil, the earth; (*of horse*) **g. (la terre) du pied,** to paw the ground; **se g. la tête, l'oreille,** to scratch one's head, one's ear; **se g.,** (i) to scratch oneself; (ii) to give oneself something to think about; *P:* **tu peux toujours te g.!** you can whistle for it! nothing doing! *F:* **ça me gratte terriblement,** it makes me itch like nobody's business; *s.a.* CUIRE 2, DÉMANGER; (*c*) *Tex:* to teasel, raise, nap (of cloth); to brush up (wool); **laine grattée,** brushed wool; (*d*) **g. le fond d'un navire,** to grave a ship; (*e*) **vin qui gratte le gosier,** wine that rasps the throat; *F:* **donnez-moi (à boire) qch. qui gratte,** give me sth. with a kick in it. **2.** to erase, scratch out (a word, etc.). **3.** *F:* (*a*) **g. les fonds de tiroir,** to scrape the bottom of the barrel; **g. le pavé,** to scrape, pick up, a living in the gutter; to be desperately poor, on the brink of starvation; (*b*) to make a bit on the side; **c'est une affaire où il n'y a pas grand-chose à g.,** you can't make much out of that, there's not much to be had out of that. **4.** *Cy: Aut: F:* to overtake, pass (a competitor, another car); **il ne songe qu'à g. les autres voitures,** his one aim is to pass everything else on the road. **5.** *v.i.* (*a*) **g. à la porte,** to scratch at the door; (*b*) **g. du violon, g. de la guitare,** to scrape on the fiddle, to strum away on the guitar; (*c*) *P:* to work.
gratteron [gratrɔ̃], *s.m. Bot:* goose grass, catchweed, scratchweed.
gratte-tube [grattyb], *s.m.* tube, pipe, cleaner, scraper; *pl. gratte-tubes.*
gratteur, -euse [gratœːr, -øːz], *s.* **1.** (*a*) (*pers.*) scratcher; *F:* **g. de papier** = GRATTE-PAPIER; (*b*) *Tex:* teaseler, napper. **2.** *Civ.E:* scraper loader.
grattoir [gratwaːr], *s.m.* scraper; *Typ:* slice; **g. de bureau,** erasing knife, scraper-eraser; **g. à peinture,** paint scrubber; *Plumb:* **g. triangulaire,** shave hook.
grattoire [gratwaːr], *s.f. Locksm:* lock cleaner.
grattons [gratɔ̃], *s.m.pl.* **1.** greaves (of rendered fat). **2.** lumps (in powdered matter).
grattouiller [gratuje]. *F:* (*a*) *v.tr.* to scrape, scratch; (*b*) *v.i.* to itch.
grattures [gratyːr], *s.f.pl.* scrapings (of brass, etc.).
gratuit [gratɥi], *a.* gratuitous; (*a*) free (of charge); **école, consultation, gratuite,** free school, free consultation; **à titre g.,** gratis, free of charge; (*b*) **insulte gratuite,** gratuitous, unprovoked, insult; **supposition gratuite,** gratuitous assumption, unfounded supposition; *Phil:* **acte g.,** inconsequent action, *acte gratuit.*
gratuité [gratɥite], *s.f.* gratuitousness; exemption from payment; **la g. de l'enseignement,** the fact that education is free.
gratuitement [gratɥitmɑ̃], *adv.* gratuitously; (*a*) for nothing, free of charge; (*b*) without cause, wantonly, without provocation.
grau [gro], *s.m. Geog:* (*a*) salt-water pool; small lagoon; (*b*) (*in Languedoc*) channel joining lagoon to the sea; (*c*) (*in Languedoc*) estuary (of short coastal river).
grauwacke [grovak], *s.f. Miner:* greywacke, graywacke.
gravatier [gravatje], *s.m.* rubbish carter.
gravatif, -ive [gravatif, -iːv], *a. Med:* (*of pain*) dragging, bearing-down.
gravats [grava], *s.m.pl.* (*a*) screenings (of plaster); (*b*) rubbish (from demolitions).
grave[1] [graːv]. **I.** *a.* **1.** *A:* heavy; *still used in Ph:* **mouvement d'un corps g.,** motion of a heavy body. **2.** (*a*) grave, serious, (mistake, face); grave, solemn (tone); sober (face, countenance); (*b*) important, weighty (business); (*c*) **blessure g.,** severe wound; **subir une g. opération,** to undergo a serious operation; **hélas! il y eut plus g.,** alas! there was worse to come; **la guerre offre des risques trop graves pour qu'on les traite à la légère,** the risks of war are too serious to be treated lightly; **il serait g. que** + *sub.,* it would be a serious matter if . . .. **3.** *Mus: etc:* **note g., voix g.,** low(-pitched), deep, full-toned, note, voice. **4.** *Gram:* **accent g.,** grave accent.
II. grave, *s.m.* **1.** *Ph: A:* **les graves,** heavy bodies. **2. le g. et le plaisant,** matters grave and gay; **passer du g. au doux,** to pass from grave to gay. **3.** low(-pitched), deep, note.
grave[2], *s.f.* **1.** gravel beach, strand (of Newfoundland cod fisheries). **2.** *Geog:* **les Graves,** gravelly region of the Gironde.
gravé [grave], *a.* (*a*) **pierre gravée,** engraved stone; **image gravée,** graven image; (*b*) (*of metals*) pitted; (*c*) (*of pers.*) pock-marked.
gravelage [gravlaːʒ], *s.m.* (*a*) gravelling (of roads, etc.); (*b*) gravel.
gravelé [gravle], (*a*) *a.* **allée gravelée,** gravel path; (*b*) *a. & s.f. Com:* **(cendre) gravelée,** pearl ash.
graveler [gravle], *v.tr.* (**je gravelle, n. gravelons; je gravellerai**) to gravel, cover with gravel.
gravelet [gravlɛ], *s.m.* (quarryman's) small chisel.
graveleusement [gravløzmɑ̃], *adv.* licentiously.
graveleux, -euse [gravlø, -øːz], *a.* **1.** gravelly (soil); gritty (pencil, pear). **2.** smutty (story, song). **3.** *Med: A:* (*a*) suffering from gravel; (*b*) (urine) showing traces of gravel.
gravelin [gravlɛ̃], *s.m. F:* (common) oak (tree).
gravelinois, -oise [gravlinwa, -waːz], *a. & s. Geog:* (native, inhabitant) of Gravelines.
gravelle [gravɛl], *s.f.* **1.** *Med: A:* gravel. **2.** deposit (in wine bottles). **3.** *Fr.C: P.N:* loose chippings, *U.S:* gravel.
gravelot [gravlo], *s.m. Orn:* **grand g.,** ringed plover; **petit g.,** little ringed plover; **g. à collier interrompu,** Kentish plover, *U.S:* snowy plover; **g. à double collier,** killdeer plover; **g. mongol,** greater sand plover.
gravelure [gravlyːr], *s.f.* smutty saying, story; *pl.* indecencies.
gravement [gravmɑ̃], *adv.* **1.** gravely, solemnly, soberly. **2.** seriously (ill); **il s'est g. trompé,** he was seriously, greatly, mistaken. **3.** *Mus:* **morceau qui doit être exécuté g.,** piece that should be played in slow tempo.
graver [grave], *v.tr.* to cut, engrave, carve (material, design on material); *Rec:* to record; **g. sur bois,** to engrave on wood; **g. à l'eau-forte,** to etch; **g. en relief,** to emboss; **g. un coin en creux,** to sink a die; **g. une bouche à feu,** to chase a gun; **gravé par le feu,** burnt in; **cela reste gravé dans ma mémoire,** it remains graven on my memory.
se graver. 1. *Mil:* (*of gun barrel*) to become scored. **2. incident qui s'est gravé dans ma mémoire,** incident that has remained graven on my memory, that has stuck in my memory.
graves[1] [graːv], *s.m. Vit:* Graves (wine); **une bouteille de g.,** a bottle of Graves.
Graves[2], *Pr.n. Med:* **maladie de G.,** Graves' disease, exophthalmic goitre.
gravétien, -ienne [gravesjɛ̃, -jɛn], **gravettien, -ienne** [gravɛtjɛ̃, -jɛn], *a. Prehist:* Gravettian.
gravette [gravɛt], *s.f.* **1.** *F:* lobworm, lugworm. **2.** (type of) oyster (of Arcachon area).
graveur [gravœːr]. **1.** *s.m.* engraver; carver (on stone, etc.); **g. à l'eau-forte,** etcher; **g. sur bois,** wood engraver; **g. en creux,** die sinker. **2.** *a.* **bain g.,** etching bath.
gravide [gravid], *a.* gravid, pregnant.
gravidique [gravidik], *a.* relating to, or caused by, pregnancy.
gravidité [gravidite], *s.f.* gravidity, pregnancy.
gravidocardiaque [gravidɔkardjak], *a.* gravidocardiac.
gravier [gravje], *s.m.* **1.** gravel, grit; **terrain de g.,** gravelly soil; **g. sableux,** hoggin; **couvrir un chemin de g.,** to gravel a path. **2.** *usu. pl. Med: A:* gravel.
gravière [gravjɛːr], *s.f.* **1.** gravel pit. **2.** *Orn: F:* ringed plover. **3.** *Agr:* mixed sowing of vetch and lentils.
gravifique [gravifik], *a. Ph: O:* **l'attraction g.,** (the force of) gravity.
gravillon [gravijɔ̃], *s.m.* fine gravel; grit; *P.N:* **gravillons,** loose chippings.
gravillonnage [gravijɔnaːʒ], *s.m.* fine-gravelling; gritting.
gravillonner [gravijɔne], *v.tr.* to (fine-)gravel (path, etc.); to grit, spread grit on (a road).
gravillonneur [gravijɔnœːr], *s.m.* (*machine*) crusher (for making chippings).
gravillonneuse [gravijɔnøːz], *s.f.* (*machine*) gravel spreader; grit spreader; gritter.
gravillonnière [gravijɔnjɛːr], *s.f.* (fine) gravel pit.
gravimètre [gravimɛtr], *s.m. Ph:* gravimeter.
gravimétrie [gravimetri], *s.f.* gravimetry.
gravimétrique [gravimetrik], *a.* (*a*) gravimetric(al); *Ch:* **analyse g.,** gravimetric analysis; (*b*) *Min:* gravitational (method of prospecting).
gravir [graviːr]. **1.** *v.i.* **g. sur qch.,** to climb, clamber, on to sth. **2.** *v.tr.* to climb; to ascend (mountain); to mount (ladder); **g. un échelon social,** to climb a rung of the social ladder.
gravitant [gravitɑ̃], *a.* gravitating.
gravitation [gravitasjɔ̃], *s.f.* gravitation; gravitational pull.
gravité [gravite], *s.f.* **1.** *Ph:* gravity; **g. spécifique,** specific gravity; **centre de g.,** centre of gravity; **triage par g.,** sorting by gravity; **alimentation par g.,** gravity feed; **alimenté par g.,** gravity-fed. **2.** (*a*) gravity, seriousness; soberness (of bearing); **garder, perdre, sa g.,** to preserve, lose, one's gravity; (*b*) severity, seriousness (of illness); seriousness (of operation); **blessure sans g.,** slight wound; **quelle est la g. de sa blessure?** how serious is his injury? **3.** *Mus:* low pitch, deepness (of note).
graviter [gravite], *v.i.* **1.** to gravitate (**vers,** towards). **2.** to revolve (**autour de,** round); **les planètes gravitent autour du soleil,** the planets revolve round the sun; **g. autour de la terre,** to orbit the earth; **g. autour de qn que l'on admire,** to hover, revolve, around s.o. one admires.
gravoir [gravwaːr], *s.m.* graver's tool; graver.
gravois [gravwa], *s.m.pl. O:* (*a*) screenings (of plaster); (*b*) rubbish (from demolitions).
gravure [gravyːr], *s.f.* **1.** engraving; (*a*) **g. sur bois de fil,** wood cutting; **g. sur bois de bout,** wood engraving; **g. sur pierre,** stone engraving, lithography; **g. en creux,** (i) intaglio engraving, incised work, (ii) die sinking; *Typ:* **g. de caractères,** letter cutting; (*b*) **g. en taille-douce,** copperplate engraving; **g. à l'eau-forte, g. en creux,** etching; **g. en relief,** line work, half-tone work; **g. au trait,** line work; **g. en simili,** half-tone work; **g. à la manière noire,** mezzotint; **g. au pointillé,** stipple, stippling; **g. en couleurs,** colour printing. **2.** print, picture, engraving, etching; **g. en taille-douce, g. sur cuivre,** copperplate; **g. sur bois,** woodcut; wood engraving; **g. en couleurs,** colour print; **livre plein de gravures,** book full of illustrations; **g. hors texte,** full-page plate; **g. avant la lettre,** proof before letters; **marchand de gravures,** print seller. **3.** carving (on stone, wood, etc.). **4.** *Rec:* recording.
graylois, -oise [grɛlwa, -waːz], *a. & s. Geog:* (native, inhabitant) of Gray.
gré [gre], *s.m.* **1.** liking, taste; **à mon g., selon mon g.,** (i) to my liking, to my taste, (ii) in my opinion; **je m'habille à mon g.,** I dress to please myself, as I please; **il trouva une chambre à son g.,** he found a room that suited him, a room to his liking, taste; **au g. de mes désirs,** (i) just as I could wish, (ii) to my heart's content. **2.** will, pleasure; **passage à supprimer au g. de l'exécutant,** passage which may be cut out at the artist's pleasure, *ad lib;* **se marier contre le g. de son père,** to get married against one's father's wishes; **bail renouvelable au g. du locataire,** lease renewable at the option of the tenant; **de mon propre g., de mon plein g.,** of my own free will, of my own accord; **de bon g.,** willingly; gladly; **de mauvais g.,** reluctantly; **elle va et vient à son (bon) g.,** she comes and goes as she pleases; **bon g. mal g.,** whether we like it or not; willy-nilly; **de g. ou de force,** willy-nilly; by fair means or foul; **au g. des flots,** at the mercy of the waves; **de g. à g.,** by (mutual) agreement; **vendre de g. à g.,** to sell by private contract; *Com: F:* **billets placés de g.,** bills on tap. **3.** (*a*) **savoir (bon) g. à qn de qch., de faire qch.,** to be grateful to s.o. for sth., for doing sth.; **ce dont je vous sais le plus de g., le g. le plus profond, c'est . . .,** what I am most (deeply) grateful to you for is . . .; **savoir peu de g., mauvais g., à qn de qch., de faire qch.,** to be annoyed with s.o. about sth., for doing sth.; to take sth. badly; (*b*) *A:* **prendre qn, qch., en g.,** (i) to conceive a liking for s.o., sth., (ii) to take sth. in good part.
gréage [greaːʒ], *s.m. Nau:* (action of) rigging.
grèbe [grɛb], *s.m. Orn:* grebe; **g. huppé, grand g.,** great crested grebe; **petit g., g. castagneux,** little grebe, dabchick; **g. à cou noir,** black-necked, *U.S:* eared, grebe; **g. jougris, g. à joues grises,** red-necked, *U.S:* Holboell's, grebe; **g. esclavon, oreillard,** Slavonian, *U.S:* horned, grebe.
grebiche [grəbiʃ], *s.f.* **1.** file number (of MS, etc.). **2.** loose-leaf binder. **3.** metallic edging, trimming (on fancy leather goods, on skirt, etc.). **4.** printer's imprint.
grec, grecque [grɛk]. **1.** *a.* Greek, *occ.* Grecian; (*a*) (*of ancient Greece*) **les orateurs grecs,** the Greek orators; **coiffure à la grecque,** hair done in the Grecian style; **profil g.,** Grecian profile; (*b*) **Église grecque,** Greek Orthodox church; (*c*) *P:* **vol à la grecque,** confidence-trick. **2.** *s.* (*a*) Greek (ancient or modern); **une Grecque,** a

Greek woman; (*b*) *P:* **un grec,** (i) a (card-) sharper, a Greek, a rook, (ii) a welsher. **3.** *s.m. Ling:* **le g.,** (the) Greek (language); **le g. moderne,** modern Greek. **4.** *s.f.* **grecque;** (*a*) *Arch: Art:* Greek key-pattern, Greek border; (*b*) (bookbinder's) saw. **5.** *a. & s.m. Dial:* (*Mediterranean area*) **(vent) g.,** north-easterly wind.

grécage [greka:ʒ], *s.m. Bookb: A:* saw-cutting.

grécal(e) [grekal], *s.m. Dial:* (*Corsica*) north-easterly wind.

Grèce [grɛs], *Pr.n.f.* **1.** *Geog:* Greece. **2.** *P: A:* **la G.,** the world of rogues and sharpers; = Alsatia.

grécisant, -ante [gresizɑ̃, -ɑ̃:t], *s.* (*a*) lover of things Greek; (*b*) *Ecc:* partisan of the Greek Orthodox ritual.

gréciser [gresize]. **1.** *v.tr.* to Hellenize, to Gr(a)ecize; **g. une phrase,** to give a Greek turn to a phrase. **2.** *v.i.* to use Greek phrases.

grécisation [gresizasjɔ̃], *s.f.* Hellenization.

grécité [gresite], *s.f.* (*a*) Greekness, Greek spirit; Gr(a)ecism; Hellenism; **disputer la g. d'une expression,** to argue as to whether an expression is Greek; (*b*) **haute g.,** classical Greek; **basse g.,** Hellenistic Greek.

gréco- [grekɔ], *pref.* gr(a)eco-; **grécomanie,** gr(a)ecomania.

gréco-bouddhique [grekɔbudik], *a.* **art g.-b.,** Graeco-buddhist art; *pl. gréco-bouddhiques.*

gréco-latin, -ine [grekɔlatɛ̃, -in], *a. Ling:* Gr(a)eco-Latin; *pl. gréco-latin(e)s.*

grécomanie [grekɔmani], *s.f.* gr(a)ecomania.

gréco-romain, -aine [grekɔrɔmɛ̃, -ɛn], *a.* Gr(a)eco-Roman; *pl. gréco-romain(e)s.*

gréco-slave [grekɔsla:v], *a.* Gr(a)eco-Slavonic, *pl. gréco-slaves.*

grecquage [greka:ʒ], *s.m. Bookb:* saw-cutting.

grecque. *See* GREC.

grecquer [greke], *v.tr. Bookb:* to saw-cut (book).

gredin, -ine [grədɛ̃, -in], *s.* **1.** *A:* beggar; vagrant. **2.** (*a*) rogue, scoundrel; (*b*) *F:* rascal, wretch; **petit g.!** you little wretch! you little horror!

gredinerie [grədinri], *s.f.* low, mean, underhand, unscrupulous, (i) behaviour, (ii) action.

gréement [gremɑ̃], *s.m. Nau: Av:* **1.** rigging; **g. dormant, fixe,** standing rigging; **g. courant,** running rigging; **capeler le gréement,** to send up the rigging. **2.** rig (of ship); *Y:* **g. Marconi,** Bermudian rig. **3.** gear (of boat, etc.); **g. d'une pompe,** pump gear.

greenockite [grinɔkit], *s.f. Miner:* greenockite.

greenovite [grinɔvit], *s.f. Miner:* greenovite.

gréer [gree], *v.tr. Nau: Av:* (*a*) to rig (mast, vessel, etc.); **gréé en carré,** square-rigged; **g. une pompe,** to rig a pump; *P:* **se gréer,** to rig, tog, oneself out; to tog up; (*b*) to sling (hammock, nets); (*c*) **g. une vergue,** to send up a yard; to cross a yard.

gréeur [greœ:r], *s.m. Nau:* rigger.

greffage [grɛfa:ʒ], *s.m.* **1.** *Hort:* grafting. **2.** *Nau:* making of horseshoe knot, of cut-splice.

greffe[1] [grɛf], *s.f.* **1.** (*a*) *Arb: Hort:* graft, scion, slip; (*b*) *Surg:* graft (of skin, tissue, etc.); transplant (of organ); **g. autoplastique,** autoplastic graft, autograft; **g. hétéroplastique,** heteroplastic graft, heterograft; **g. homoplastique,** homoplastic graft, homograft; **g. cutanée,** skin graft; **g. dermo-épidermique,** split-skin graft; **g. épidermique,** epidermal graft; **g. osseuse,** bone graft; **g. du cœur,** heart graft, transplant; **g. du rein, des reins,** kidney graft, transplant; **opéré de la g. du cœur, patient ayant subi la g. du cœur,** heart transplant patient. **2.** grafting; (*a*) *Arb:* **g. par rameau détaché,** (ordinary) grafting; **g. par œil détaché,** budding; **g. par approche,** grafting by approach, inarching; **g. en fente simple,** cleft grafting; **g. en fente à cheval,** saddle grafting; **g. en fente anglaise,** whip grafting; **g. en couronne,** crown grafting; **g. en écusson,** shield grafting, shield budding; (*b*) *Surg:* **g. de la cornée,** corneal grafting; **g. épidermique,** skin grafting. **3.** *Nau:* (*a*) horse-shoe; (*b*) cut-splice.

greffe[2], *s.m.* **1.** *Jur:* office of the clerk of the court; record office (of court). **2.** *Fin:* registry (of joint-stock company).

greffer [grefe], *v.tr.* (*a*) *Arb: Hort:* to graft; (*b*) *Surg:* to graft (skin); **g. un rein,** to transplant a kidney; (*c*) **g. un nouveau chapitre à un roman,** to insert an additional chapter into a novel.

greffeur [grefœ:r], *s.m. Arb: Hort:* grafter, budder.

greffier [grefje], *s.m.* **1.** *Jur:* clerk (of the court). **2.** *Adm: Fin:* registrar. **3.** *Const:* **g. du bâtiment** = clerk of the Board of Works. **4.** *F:* cat.

greffoir [grɛfwa:r], *s.m.* grafting knife.

greffon [grɛfɔ̃], *s.m.* (*a*) *Arb: Hort:* graft, scion, slip; (*b*) *Surg:* graft, transplant; **rejet du g.,** graft rejection.

grégaire [gregɛ:r], **grégarien, -ienne** [gregarjɛ̃, -jɛn], *a.* gregarious.

grégarines [gregarin], *s.f.pl. Prot:* Gregarinida.

grégarisme [gregarism], *s.m.* gregariousness.

grège [grɛ:ʒ], *a.* raw (silk).

grégeois [greʒwa], *a.m. A:* (= GREC) **feu g.,** Greek fire.

Grégoire [gregwa:r], *Pr.n.m.* Gregory; **saint G. de Nazianze,** St Gregory Nazianzen.

grégorien, -ienne [gregɔrjɛ̃, -jɛn], *a.* Gregorian (chant, etc.).

grègues [grɛg], *s.f.pl. A:* trunk hose; breeches; *F:* **tirer ses g.,** to make oneself scarce, to cut and run.

greisen [graizɛn], *s.m. Geol:* greisen.

grêlage [grɛla:ʒ], *s.m.* (*comb making*) grailing.

grêle[1] [grɛ(:)l], *a.* slender, thin (leg, stalk, etc.); **voix g.,** thin, high-pitched, voice; *Anat:* **intestin g.,** small intestine.

grêle[2], *s.f.* **1.** (*a*) hail; **orage accompagné de g.,** hailstorm; (*b*) **g. de coups, de balles,** hail, shower, of blows, of bullets. **2.** pock marks.

grêle[3], *s.f.* (*comb maker's*) grail.

grêlé [grele], *a.* **1.** pock-marked, (pock-)pitted. **2.** *Her:* (*of coronet*) set with pearls.

grêler[1] [grele]. **1.** *v.impers.* **il grêle,** it hails; *v.i.* **les malheurs ont grêlé sur ma tête,** misfortunes have hailed down, poured down, on me. **2.** *v.tr.* to damage, destroy (crops, etc.) by hail. **3.** *v.tr.* to pock-mark.

grêler[2], *v.tr.* (*comb making*) to grail.

grelet [grəlɛ], *s.m. Tls:* (miner's) pickaxe; (mason's) gurlet.

grêlet, -ette [grɛlɛ, -ɛt], *a.* rather slender; smallish, puny.

grelette [grəlɛt], *s.f. Tls:* fretwork file.

grêleux, -euse [grɛlø, -ø:z], *a.* haily (weather, season).

grelichonne [grəliʃɔn], *s.f.* (mason's) trowel.

grêlifuge [grɛlify:ʒ], *a.* anti-hail (device).

grelin [grəlɛ̃], *s.m. Nau:* warp cablet, hawser; **g. de remorque,** tow rope; **en g.,** cable-laid; **s'amarrer avec quatre grelins,** to make fast with four warps.

grêlon [grɛlɔ̃], *s.m.* hailstone.

grelot [grəlo], *s.m.* **1.** (*a*) (small globular) bell; sleigh bell; cow bell; *A:* **attacher le g.,** to bell the cat; *F:* **faire sonner son g.,** to put one's word in; to make oneself conspicuous; *P:* **avoir les grelots,** to have the wind up, to be in a blue funk; (*b*) **les grelots du carnaval,** the gay uproar of the carnival; (*c*) *F:* (ceaseless) chatter; (*d*) *P:* testicle; (*e*) *A.Cost:* **g. de dolman,** button of hussar jacket. **2.** *Bot:F:* **g. blanc** snow-drop.

grelottant [grəlɔtɑ̃], *a.* **1.** shivering, shaking (with cold, fear, etc.). **2.** jingling.

grelotte [grəlɔt], *s.f. P:* funk; **avoir la g.,** to have the wind up, to be in a blue funk.

grelottement [grəlɔtmɑ̃], *s.m.* (*a*) shivering; (*b*) tinkling, jingling (like bells).

grelotter [grəlɔte], *v.i.* **1.** to tremble, shake, shiver (with cold, fear, etc.); **il grelottait de froid,** he was shaking with cold; **g. de peur,** to be trembling with fear, to shake in one's shoes; *with cogn. acc.* **g. la fièvre,** to be shaking with fever. **2.** to jingle, tinkle.

greluche [grəlyʃ], *s.f. P:* woman.

greluchon [grəlyʃɔ̃], *s.m. P: O:* (*a*) fancy man; (*b*) lounge-lizard.

greluchonne [grəlyʃɔn], *s.f.* (mason's) trowel.

grément [gremɑ̃], *s.m. A:* = GRÉEMENT.

grémial, -iaux [gremjal, -jo], *s.m. Ecc:* gremial.

grémil [gremil], *s.m. Bot:* gromwell.

gremille [grəmi:j], *s.f. Ich:* pope, ruff.

grenadage [grənada:ʒ], *s.m. Mil:* grenading; attack with hand grenades; *Navy:* depth-charging.

grenade[1] [grənad], *s.f.* **1.** *Bot:* pomegranate (fruit). **2.** (*a*) *Mil:* grenade; **g. à blanc, g. inerte, fausse g.,** dummy grenade; **g. d'exercice,** practice grenade, drill grenade; **g. à main,** hand grenade; **g. à manche,** stick-grenade; **g. à fusil,** *O:* **g. V.B. (Vivien-Bessière),** rifle grenade; **lance-grenade(s),** grenade thrower; **g. défensive, g. à fragmentation,** fragmentation grenade; **g. offensive,** offensive grenade; **g. adhésive,** sticky grenade; **g. éclairante,** illuminating grenade, light grenade; **g. fumigène,** smoke grenade; **g. incendiaire,** incendiary grenade; (*b*) *Navy:* **g. sous-marine,** depth charge. **3.** grenade ornament (on uniform, etc.).

Grenade[2], *Pr.n.f. Geog:* **1.** Granada (Spain). **2.** Grenada (Windward Islands).

grenadeur [grənadœ:r], *s.m. Navy:* depth-charge rails.

grenadier[1] [grənadje], *s.m. Bot:* pomegranate (tree).

grenadier[2], *s.m. Mil:* (*a*) *A. & Br.Army:* grenadier; **un vrai g.,** a tall, well-built man; **boire comme un g.,** to drink like a fish; *P:* **tirer au g.,** to swing the lead; (*b*) (1914-18) bomber; (*c*) *F:* tall, masculine woman; amazon.

grenadière [grənadjɛ:r], *s.f. Mil:* **1.** *A:* grenade pouch. **2.** band (of rifle); (*of rifle*) **à la grenadière,** slung; **anneau g.,** band swivel.

grenadille [grənadi:j], *s.f.* **1.** *Bot:* granadilla. **2.** *Com:* red ebony, grenadillo.

grenadin[1], -ine[1] [grənadɛ̃, -in], *a. & s. Geog:* (native, inhabitant) of (i) Granada; (ii) Grenada.

grenadin[2], *s.m.* **1.** *Cu:* braised (larded) veal. **2.** *Orn:* African finch. **3.** *Hort:* grenadin.

grenadine[2] [grənadin], *s.f.* **1.** *Tex: Exp:* grenadine. **2.** grenadine, pomegranate (syrup).

Grenadines (les) [lɛgrənadin], *Pr.n. Geog:* the Grenadines, the Grenadine Islands.

grenage [grəna:ʒ], *s.m.* granulation, granulating; shotting.

grenaillage [grənɑja:ʒ], *s.m. Tchn:* shot-blasting.

grenaille [grənɑ:j], *s.f.* **1.** refuse grain, tailings. **2.** granular metal; shot; **g. de plomb,** lead shot; **g. d'acier trempé,** chilled shot; **en g.,** granulated (tin, etc.). **3.** *Tp:* granular filling (of capsule); **g. de charbon,** carbon granules. **4.** *P.N:* (*in Belgium*) **grenailles errantes,** loose chippings.

grenaillement [grənɑjmɑ̃], *s.f.* granulation, granulating, shotting.

grenailler [grənɑje], *v.tr.* to granulate (metal, wax, etc.); to shot (metal), to shot-blast.

se grenailler, to granulate; to shot.

grenailleuse [grənɑjø:z], *s.f.* shot-blasting machine.

grenaison [grənɛzɔ̃], *s.f.* seeding, corning (of cereals, etc.).

grenasse [grənas], *s.f. Nau:* gust of wind, of rain.

grenat [grəna]. **1.** *s.m. Lap:* garnet; **g. almandin,** almandite; **g. calcifère,** grossularite; **g. magnésien,** pyrope; **g. jaune,** cinnamon stone. **2.** *a.inv.* garnet-red.

grenatifère [grənatifɛ:r], *a.* garnet-bearing (rock).

grenatite [grənatit], *s.f. Miner:* garnet-rock.

grené [grəne]. **1.** *a.* stippled. **2.** *s.m.* stipple; **gravure en g.,** stipple(d) engraving.

greneler [grənle], *v.tr.* (**je grenelle**) to grain (paper, leather).

grener [grəne], *v.* (**je grène, n. grenons; je grènerai**) **1.** *v.i.* (*of cereals, etc.*) to seed; to corn. **2.** *v.tr.* (*a*) to corn, granulate (gunpowder); to shred (wax); to grain (salt); (*b*) to grain (paper, leather); (*c*) *Engr:* to stipple.

greneté [grənte], *s.m.* (*goldsmith's work*) pellet moulding.

greneter [grənte, grɛnte], *v.tr.* to mill (coin).

grèneterie [grɛntri], *s.f.* **1.** (*a*) corn trade, corn chandlery; (*b*) seed trade. **2.** corn chandler's, seedsman's (shop).

grenetier [grənətje], *s.m. Hist:* manager of a salt warehouse.

grènetier, -ière [grɛntje, -jɛ:r], *s.* (*a*) corn chandler; (*b*) seedsman, -woman.

grènetis [grɛnti], *s.m. Num:* milled edge, milling, graining (of coin).

grènetoir [grɛntwa:r], *s.m. Tchn:* milling cutter, milling machine (for coins).

grenettes [grənɛt], *s.f.pl.* (*a*) *Com: Dy:* Avignon, French, berries; (*b*) *Min:* beans; (*c*) *Exp:* (powder) screenings.

grèneture [grɛnty:r], *s.f.* (*a*) milled edge, milling, graining (of coin); (*b*) pellet moulding (on gold, silver).

greneur [grənœ:r], *s.m. Engr: Typ:* (*pers.*) grainer; stippler.

grenier [grənje], *s.m.* **1.** (*a*) granary, storehouse; *Hist:* **greniers d'abondance,** public granaries; (*b*) grain-producing, cereal-producing, area, region; **l'Égypte était le g. de l'ancien monde,** Egypt was the granary of the ancient world; (*c*) **g. à foin, à grain,** hay loft, corn loft; (*c*) *P:* **g. à puces,** (i) cat; (ii) dog. **2.** attic, garret; **chercher qch. de la cave au g.,** to hunt for sth. from cellar to garret, high and low. **3.** *Nau:* (*a*) dunnage; **faire son g.,** to lay the dunnage; to dunnage; (*b*) **charger du grain en g.,** to ship grain in bulk.

Grenoble [grənɔbl], *Pr.n. Geog:* Grenoble; *F: Iron:* **faire à qn la conduite de G.,** (i) to give s.o. the order of the boot; (ii) to give s.o. a rough handling, a warm reception.

grenoblois, -oise [grənɔblwa, -wa:z], *a. & s. Geog:* (native, inhabitant) of Grenoble.

grenoir [grənwa:r], *s.m.* granulator; granulating machine.

grenouillage [grənuja:ʒ], *s.m. F:* **1.** (*a*) wangle; shady deal; (*b*) wangling; shady dealing. **2.** embezzlement.

grenouillard [grənuja:r], *s.m.* **1.** *Orn: F:* buzzard. **2.** *P:* (*a*) teetotaller; (*b*) cold-water fiend.

grenouille [grənu:j], *s.f.* **1.** (*a*) frog; **g. agile,** agile frog; **g. bœuf, g. mugissante, g. taureau,** bullfrog; **g. des bois,** (American) wood frog; **g. cornue (sud-américaine),** (South American) escuerzo; **g. fouisseuse australienne,** water-reservoir frog; **g. des fraises,** strawberry frog; **g. géante du Cameroun,** goliath frog; **g. arboricole de Java,** Javan flying frog; **g. léopard,** leopard frog; **g. oxyrhine,** moor frog; **g. persillée,** parsley frog; **g. poilue,** hairy frog; **g. rousse,** common frog; **g. de Sibérie,** Siberian frog; **g. verte,** edible frog; **g. volante indo-malaise,** Indo-Malayan flying frog; *F:* **jeter une pierre dans la mare aux grenouilles,** (i) to put the cat among the pigeons; (ii) to drop a brick; (*b*) *F:* **g. de bénitier,** bigoted churchwoman, church hen. **2.** (*a*) *F:* frog-shaped money box; (*b*) *P:* mess funds, club money, cash box, funds (of a society); **manger, bouffer, faire sauter, la g.,** to make off with the funds, the cash (box). **3.** *Civ.E:* frog rammer.

grenouiller [grənuje], *v.i. F:* **1.** (*a*) to paddle, splash (in the water); (*b*) to drink water; to be a teetotaller. **2.** to wangle; to go in for shady dealings.

grenouillère [grənujɛ:r], *s.f.* **1.** (*a*) marsh, swamp; froggery; *F:* damp, unhealthy, house, spot; (*b*) *F:* (i) paddling pool; (ii) bathing place (in a river). **2.** *Hyd.E:* strainer (of pump).

grenouillet [grənujɛ], *s.m. Bot: F:* **1.** = GRENOUILLETTE 2. **2.** Solomon's seal.

grenouillette [grənujɛt], *s.f.* **1.** *F:* green frog. **2.** *Bot: F:* (*a*) frog-bit; (*b*) water crowfoot. **3.** *Med:* ranula, *F:* frog-tongue.

grenter [grɑ̃te], *v.tr.* to mill, grain, pellet, mould (precious metals).

grenu [grəny], *a.* **1.** (*a*) (*of corn*) grainy, full of grain; (*b*) **huile grenue,** clotted oil. **2.** (*a*) granular (fracture, etc.); (*b*) grained (leather, etc.); (*c*) coarse-grained, crystalline (salt). **3.** *s.m.* granularity (of marble, etc.).

grenure [grəny:r], *s.f.* **1.** *Art:* stippling, stipple. **2.** *Leath:* grain(ing).

grep [grɛp], *s.m. Geol: Dial:* (*S.W. Fr.*) hardpan.

grès[1] [grɛ], *s.m.* **1.** sandstone; **g. rouge,** red sandstone; **g. bigarré,** Bunter, new red, sandstone; **g. falun,** shelly sandstone; **g. dur,** grit; **g. grossier,** sandstone grit; **g. à bâtir, de construction,** freestone, brownstone; **g. à meule,** millstone grit; **g. à pavés,** paving stone; **g. vert,** greensand; **g. mamelonné,** sarsen stone. **2. poterie de g., g. cérame,** stoneware; **g. flambé,** glazed earthenware; **cruche de g.,** stone jug; **g. salé,** salt-glazed earthenware.

grès[2], *s.m.* **1.** *Ser:* sericin, silk glue. **2.** *Ven:* grinder (of wild boar).

grésage [greza:ʒ], *s.m. Tchn:* polishing (on a grindstone).

grèserie [grɛzri], *s.f.* **1.** (*a*) sandstone quarry; (*b*) sandstone. **2.** stoneware factory; pottery.

gréseur [grezœ:r], *s.m.* (sandstone) quarryman.

gréseux, -euse [grezø, -ø:z], *a.* **1.** gritty, sandy. **2. roches gréseuses,** sandstones.

grésier [grezje], *s.m.* (sandstone) quarryman.

grésière [grezjɛ:r], *s.f.* sandstone quarry, grit-(rock) quarry.

grésil [grezi(l)], *s.m.* **1.** *Meteor:* sleet; frozen rain. **2.** pounded glass; *Glassm:* cullet.

grésillement[1] [grezijmɑ̃], *s.m.* pattering (of sleet).

grésillement[2], *s.m.* **1.** crackling (of fire); chirping (of crickets); sizzling (of frying pan). **2.** shrivelling (up).

grésiller[1] [grezije], *v.impers.* to sleet; **il grésille,** there's sleet falling.

grésiller[2]. **1.** *v.i.* (*a*) (*of fire*) to crackle; (*of flame*) to sputter; (*of frying pan, of gas*) to sizzle; (*of candle*) **mourir en grésillant,** to sputter out; (*b*) (*of crickets*) to chirp. **2.** *v.tr.* to shrivel up, to scorch (leather, etc.).

se grésiller, (*of leather, etc.*) to shrivel up.

grésillon[1] [grezijɔ̃], *s.m.* **1.** *Com:* small coke. **2.** *A:* small bruise. **3.** clamp, fastening (of chest).

grésillon[2], **-onne** [grezijɔ̃, -ɔn], *a. & s. Geog:* (native, inhabitant) of the Ile de Groix.

grésoir [grezwa:r], *s.m. Tls:* grinder (for glass).

gresserie [grɛsri], *s.f.* **1.** sandstone quarry. **2.** (*a*) stoneware; (*b*) stoneware trade.

gressier [grɛsje], *s.m.* (sandstone) quarryman.

gressin [grɛsɛ̃, grɛ-], *s.m. Cu:* bread stick.

grève [grɛ:v], *s.f.* **1.** (*a*) strand, (sea) shore, (sandy) beach; **g. de galets,** shingle, shingly, beach; **vagues qui déferlent sur la g.,** waves breaking on the shore; (*b*) (sandy) bank (of river); **les grèves de la Loire,** the sandbanks of the Loire; *Hist:* **la (place de) G.,** the Strand (open space on the banks of the Seine where dissatisfied workmen used to assemble); (*c*) *Geol:* stony soil (of periglacial origin); (*d*) *Civ.E:* coarse sand (used for mortar). **2.** (*from* 1 (*b*)) strike (of workers); walkout; **se mettre en g.,** to go, come out, on strike; to take strike action; **faire g.,** to strike, to be on strike; **lancer un ordre de g., ordonner une g.,** to call a strike; **g. d'avertissement, g. symbolique,** token strike; **g. des bras croisés,** sit-down strike; **g. générale,** general strike; **g. perlée,** (i) go-slow strike; (ii) sabotage; scamping (of work); **faire la g. perlée,** to go slow; *F:* to ca'canny; **g. sauvage,** wildcat strike; **g. de solidarité, de sympathie,** sympathy strike, strike in sympathy; **g. surprise,** lightning strike; **g. sur le tas,** sit-down strike; stay-in strike; **g. tournante,** staggered strike; **g. du zèle,** work-to-rule strike, working to rule; **faire la g. du zèle,** to work to rule; **piquet de g.,** strike picket; **briseur de g.,** strike breaker; (*of prisoners*) **faire la g. de la faim,** to go on hunger strike.

grevé, -ée [grəve]. **1.** *a.* (*a*) entailed (estate); **héritier g.,** heir of entail; (*b*) mortgaged (building, etc.). **2.** *s.* heir of entail.

grever [grəve], *v.tr.* (**je grève, n. grevons; je grèverai**) **1.** to burden, encumber; **héritage grevé de dettes,** encumbered estate, inheritance burdened with debts; **se grever pour doter sa fille,** to encumber one's estate to give one's daughter a dowry; **forêt grevée d'usages,** burdened forest; **grevé d'un impôt,** saddled with a tax. **2.** *Jur:* (*a*) to entail (estate); (*b*) to mortgage (real property). **3.** *Adm:* to lay, impose, a rate on (a building).

grèves [grɛ:v], *s.f.pl. A.Arm:* greaves.

gréviculteur [grevikyltœ:r], *s.m.* (*rare*) strike leader.

grevillea [grevilea], *s.m. Bot:* grevillea.

gréviste [grevist]. **1.** *s.m. & f.* striker; **g. de la faim,** hunger-striker. **2.** *a.* **mouvement g.,** strike movement.

grèze [grɛ:z], *s.f.* **1.** *Dial:* (*Charente area*) stony soil. **2.** *Geol:* **g. litée,** patterned ground (of periglacial origin).

gribouillage [gribuja:ʒ], *s.m.* **1.** *Art:* daub. **2.** scrawl; scribble; sprawling hand(writing).

Gribouille [gribu:j], *Pr.n.m.* (popular type of) simpleton, nitwit, clot; **suivre une politique de G.,** to jump out of the frying pan into the fire.

gribouiller [gribuje]. **1.** *v.i.* to draw badly; to daub; **empêcher un enfant de g. sur les murs,** to stop a child drawing, scribbling, on the walls. **2.** *v.tr.* (*a*) to paint (daubs); (*b*) to write (sth.) illegibly, in a confused manner; **message gribouillé,** illegible message.

gribouillette [gribujɛt], *s.f. A:* (children's) scrambling; **jeter des sous à la g.,** to make children scramble for pennies, to throw pennies for a scramble; *F:* **faire qch. à la g.,** to do sth. in a scrambling fashion; **jeter son cœur à la g.,** to bestow one's heart at random.

gribouilleur, -euse [gribujœ:r, -ø:z], *s.* **1.** dauber, daubster. **2.** scribbler, scrawler.

gribouillis [gribuji], *s.m.* = GRIBOUILLAGE.

gribouri [griburi], *s.m. Ent: F:* common vine-grub.

griche-dents [griʃdɑ̃], *s.f.inv. F:* turnip-lantern.

grief[1] [gri(j)ɛf]. **1.** grievance, ground for complaint; **avoir un g. contre qn,** to have a grievance against s.o.; **faire g. à qn de qch.,** to harbour resentment against s.o. on account of sth., to hold sth. against s.o.; **le seul g. qu'on puisse faire à votre projet, c'est que . . .,** the only objection that can be made to your plan is that . . .; **on me fait g. d'avoir soutenu M. . . .,** I have never been forgiven for supporting Mr. . . . **2.** *Jur: pl.* **griefs,** statement of grounds of an appeal.

grief[2], **griève** [gri(j)ɛ:v], *a. A:* grave, serious.

grièvement [gri(j)ɛvmɑ̃], *adv.* severely, badly (wounded); deeply (offended).

grièveté [gri(j)ɛvte], *s.f. A:* grievousness, severity (of wound); heinousness (of offence).

griffade [grifad], *s.f.* scratch, stroke (of the claw); **donner une g. à qn,** to claw, scratch, s.o.

griffage [grifa:ʒ], *s.m. For:* marking, notching, blazing (of sapling).

griffard [grifa:r], *s.m. F:* cat, moggy.

griffe[1] [grif], *s.f.* **1.** (*a*) claw (of tiger, etc.); talon (of hawk); (*of cat*) **se faire les griffes, faire ses griffes,** to sharpen its claws; **coup de g.,** scratch; **donner un coup de g. à qn,** (i) to claw, scratch, s.o.; (ii) *F:* to have a dig at s.o.; **sortir ses griffes,** to show fight; **tomber sous les griffes de qn,** to fall into s.o.'s clutches; *Prov:* **à la g. on connaît le lion,** by his mark you may know him; (*b*) *Mec.E: Tls: etc:* claw, clip, clamp; **g. de plateau de tour,** jaw of lathe chuck; **g. de blocage,** clamping handle; **g. d'embrayage,** coupling-dog, -claw; **griffes de prise directe,** direct-drive dogs; **g. de bec de lampe,** glass holder, globe holder (of lamp); *Sm.a:* **g. de l'extracteur,** extractor hook; **marteau à g.,** claw-hammer; **accouplement, embrayage, à griffes,** claw coupling, claw clutch; *Carp:* **g. d'établi,** bench stop; **g. à papiers,** paper clip, fastener; **griffes de monteur,** climbing irons; *Nau:* **nœud de g.,** marlinspike hitch; (*c*) toe (of horseshoe); (*d*) *Bot:* tendril (of vine); crown (of asparagus); (*e*) *Tex:* griff (of loom). **2.** (*a*) stamped signature; (*b*) (signature) stamp; (*c*) (*on clothes*) label. **3.** *For:* (bark) blaze.

griffe[2], *a. & s. Ethn:* griffe.

griffe-bineuse [grifbinø:z], *s.f.* claw cultivator, Dutch hoe; *pl. griffes-bineuses.*

griffer [grife], *v.tr.* **1.** to scratch, claw. **2.** to stamp (circular, etc.) with a signature. **3.** *For:* to mark, notch, blaze (sapling). **4.** to secure (sth.) with a clamp.

griffet [grifɛ], *s.m. Orn: F:* swallow.

griffeton [griftɔ̃], *s.m. Mil: P:* infantryman, foot-slogger.

griffon[1] [grifɔ̃], *s.m.* **1.** griffon, gryphon. **2.** griffon (terrier). **3.** *Orn:* tawny vulture, griffon vulture. **4.** *Fish:* double hook.

griffon[2], *s.m.* mineral water spring.

griffonnage [grifɔna:ʒ], *s.m.* **1.** scribbling. **2.** (*a*) scrawl, scribble, doodle; (*b*) rough sketch.

griffonnement [grifɔnmɑ̃], *s.m. Art:* (*a*) preliminary sketch, rough sketch; (*b*) wax, clay, model.

griffonner [grifɔne], *v.tr.* **1.** to scrawl, scribble (off) letter, etc.); *abs.* to scribble, scrawl; to doodle; **toute la journée il griffonnait sur ses genoux,** he sat scribbling away all day. **2.** to sketch (sth.) roughly.

griffonneur, -euse [grifɔnœ:r, -ø:z], *s.* scribbler; **c'est un infatigable g.,** he never stops scribbling.

griffonnis [grifɔni], *s.m.* pen-and-ink sketch.

grifton [griftɔ̃], *s.m. Mil: P:* soldier.

griffu [grify], *a.* **patte griffue,** clawed foot; **main griffue,** claw of a hand, talon.

griffure [grify:r], *s.f.* scratch.

grignard [griɲa:r], *s.m.* hard sandstone.

grigne [griɲ], *s.f.* **1. g. du pain,** tender undercrust alongside the slash in a loaf. **2.** kink, pucker (in felt, etc.).

grigner [griɲe], *v.i.* (*of felt*) to pucker, crinkle up.

grignon [griɲɔ̃], *s.m.* **1.** hard overcrust of a loaf. **2.** *pl. Agr:* (olive) oil cake.

grignotage [griɲɔta:ʒ], *s.m.*, **grignotement** [griɲɔtmɑ̃], *s.m.* nibbling.

grignoter [griɲɔte], *v.tr.* to nibble (at) sth., to pick at (food); **g. son capital,** to eat into one's capital; *F:* **il trouve toujours à g. qch.,** he always manages to make a bit on the side.

grignoteur, -euse [griɲɔtœ:r, -ø:z], *s.* **1.** (*pers.*) nibbler. **2.** *s.f. Tls:* **grignoteuse,** nibbling machine.

grigou [grigu], *s.m. F:* miser, old screw; skinflint.

gri-gri [grigri], *s.m. Ent: F:* cricket; *pl. gris-gris.*

gri(-)gri [grigri], *s.m.* (West African) amulet.

gril [gri(l)], *s.m.* **1.** (*a*) *Cu:* grid(iron), grill, griller, *U.S:* broiler; **faire cuire qch. sur le g.,** to grill sth.; (*of meat*) **cuire sur le g.,** to grill; (*b*) *Hist:* grill (as instrument of torture); **être sur le g.,** (i) to be on the grill; (ii) *F:* to be on tenterhooks, on the rack. **2.** *Hyd.E:* grating (protecting sluice gate); *Rail:* gridiron (track); *Nau:* **g. de carénage,** gridiron; *Th:* **le g.,** the upper flies. **3.** *Anat:* **g. costal,** rib cage.

grillade [grijad], *s.f. Cu:* **1.** grilling, *U.S:* broiling; **mettre qch. à la g.,** to grill, broil, sth. **2.** grill, grilled meat, *esp.* grilled steak; *Fr.C:* grilled chop, cutlet; *A:* **g. de pain,** piece of toast.

grillage[1] [grija:ʒ], *s.m.* **1.** *Cu:* (*a*) grilling, *U.S:* broiling (of meat); *A:* toasting (of bread); (*b*) roasting, burning (of nuts, etc.). **2.** (*a*) *Ch:* calcining; (*b*) *Metall:* roasting (of ores). **3.** *Tex:* singeing. **4.** *El: F:* (*a*) short circuit; (*b*) burning out (of lamp, bulb, etc.).

grillage[2], *s.m.* (*a*) (metal) grating, open metal-work, latticework; **g. en fil de fer,** wire netting; (*b*) *Mch:* grate, grid (of boiler furnace); (*c*) *Civ.E: Const:* grillage (for foundations); (*d*) *El:* grid, frame (of accumulator plate); (*e*) *Ten:* stop-netting.

grillager [grijaʒe], *v.tr.* (**je grillageai(s); n. grillageons**) **1.** to fit latticework, a grill(e), on to (window, etc.); **fenêtre grillagée de fer,** window latticed with iron; **porte grillagée coulissante,** sliding lattice door; **verre grillagé,** wired glass. **2.** to surround (court, etc.) with

wire netting. **3.** to lay down a grillage for (building).

grillageur [grijaʒœːr], *s.m.* (i) maker, (ii) erector, of latticework, wire netting.

grille [griːj], *s.f.* **1.** (*a*) (iron) bars; grill(e) (of convent parlour); trellis; grating, screen, netting; **mettre (qn), être, sous les grilles (d'une prison),** to put (s.o.), to be, behind (prison) bars; **g. de comptoir,** counter grille (of bank, etc.); **g. d'une porte,** grille, spy hole, of a door; (*b*) **g. ouvrante, g. d'entrée,** iron gate, entrance gate (to grounds, etc.); *P:* **repeindre sa g. (en rouge),** to have one's monthly period, to have the curse; (*c*) railings (round monument, etc.); **séparé de la rue par une g.,** railed off from the road; (*d*) grating, grate (of sink, drain, etc.); rack (of turbine); **g. filtre,** mesh filter; *Mch:* **tiroir à g.,** gridiron valve; (*e*) **la g. du foyer,** the bars of the grate; the fire grate; *Ind:* **g. tournante,** revolving grate; **g. oscillante, g. à secousses,** jigging grate; *Ch:* **g. à analyse,** combustion furnace; (*f*) bearing (of stirrup). **2.** *Aut:* gate (quadrant); **secteur à g.,** visible gate; **g. de radiateur,** radiator grille, false front of radiator. **3.** *El:* grid ((i) of accumulator, (ii) of electron tube); **courant de g.,** grid current; *W.Tel:* **lampe à cinq grilles,** pentagrid tube; **g. (d'une triode),** auxiliary electrode; **condensateur de la g.,** grid condenser; **g. d'arrêt, g. suppresseuse,** suppressor grid; **g. d'arrêt, g. de protection,** shield grid; **g. chauffante,** heating grid; **circuit, courant, tension, de g.,** grid circuit, current, voltage; **commande de g.,** grid control; **polarisation de g.,** grid bias; **tension de g.,** grid voltage; **amplitude de tension de g.,** grid swing. **4.** (cipher) stencil. **5.** pattern (of crossword).

grille-corbeille [grijkɔrbɛːj], *s.f.* grille holder (of solid fuel burner); *pl. grilles-corbeilles.*

grille-écran [grijekrɑ̃], *s.f. Elcs:* screen grid; *W.Tel:* **lampe à g.-é.,** screen-grid lamp; *pl. grilles-écrans.*

grille-marron(s) [grijmarɔ̃], *s.m.* chestnut roaster; *pl. grille-marrons.*

grille-midi [grijmidi], *s.m. Bot: F:* rock rose.

grille-pain [grijpɛ̃], *s.m.inv.* toaster.

griller[1] [grije]. **1.** *v.tr.* (*a*) to grill, *U.S:* broil (meat); to toast (bread); to roast (coffee, almonds, chestnuts); (*b*) *Metall:* to roast, calcine (ore); (*c*) *Tex:* to singe. **2.** *v.tr.* (*a*) to scorch, burn; **se g. les cheveux,** to singe one's hair; *F:* **g. une cigarette,** *P:* **en g. une,** to smoke a cigarette; (*b*) *El:* to burn out (a lamp); *Mec.E:* **coussinet grillé,** burnt-out bearing; *P:* **il est grillé,** his game's up; he's been found out, shown up; *P:* **c'est une affaire grillée,** it's in the soup, it's no go; (*c*) (*of sun, frost*) to scorch (vegetation); *F:* **le feu lui grillait le visage,** the fire was making his face burn, was scorching his face; (*d*) *F: Sp:* **g. un concurrent,** to race past a competitor; to leave a competitor standing; *Com:* **se faire g. par un concurrent,** to be outstripped by a competitor; *Aut:* **g. un signal, le feu rouge,** to shoot, jump, the lights; (*of bus, train*) **g. une étape, une station,** to go past a stop (without stopping). **3.** *v.i.* (*a*) *Cu:* (*of meat*) to grill; (*of bread*) to toast; *F:* **près de la porte on gelait, à côté de feu on grillait,** the people near the door were freezing, while those by the fire were roasting; (*b*) **g. d'impatience,** to be burning with impatience; **g. d'envie de faire qch.,** to be burning, bursting, to do sth.; **il grillait de prendre la parole,** he was itching to speak; (*c*) (*in guessing games, etc.*) to be warm.

griller[2], *v.tr.* **1.** (*a*) to rail in, rail off (garden, tomb, etc); (*b*) to grate, bar (window, etc.). **3.** to shut up, imprison (s.o.).

grillet [grijɛ], *s.m. Ent: F:* cricket.

grilleté [grijəte], *a. Her:* belled (hawk, etc.).

grilleur, -euse [grijœːr, -øːz], *s.* **1.** *Cu:* griller, roaster. **2. g. de minerai,** ore roaster.

grilloir [grijwaːr], *s.m. Cu:* griller, roaster.

grillon [grijɔ̃], *s.m. Ent:* cricket; **g. de boulangerie, g. domestique,** domestic cricket; **g. des champs,** field cricket; **le g. du foyer,** the cricket on the hearth.

grillon-taupe [grijɔ̃toːp], *s.m. Ent:* mole-cricket; *pl. grillons-taupes.*

grill-room [grilrum], *s.m.* grill (room); *pl. grill-rooms.*

grillure [grijyr], *s.f. Bot:* grey rot (of vine leaf).

grilse [grils], *s.m. Ich:* grilse.

grimaçant [grimasɑ̃], *a.* **1.** grimacing, grinning (face, etc.). **2.** ill-fitting (garment); full of creases.

grimace [grimas], *s.f.* (*a*) grimace; **faire la g.,** (i) (*in disgust*) to make a face; (ii) (*in disappointment*) to pull a long face; **faire la g., des grimaces, à qn,** to make, pull, faces at s.o.; **faire la g. à une offre,** to give an offer an unfavourable reception; **faire une g. de douleur,** to wince; *Prov:* **on n'apprend pas à un vieux singe à faire des grimaces,** you can't teach an old dog new tricks; (*b*) crease, pucker, wrinkle (in clothing); **manteau qui fait la g.,** coat that puckers; (*c*) **faire des grimaces,** to put on airs; to mince; to simper; (*d*) *Sculp:* grotesque figure (on choir stalls, etc.).

grimacer [grimase], *v.i.* (**je grimaçai(s); n. grimaçons**) (*a*) to grin, to make faces; *with cogn. acc.* **g. un sourire,** to force a smile; to give a wry smile; (*b*) (*of garments*) to pucker, crease; (*c*) to simper, mince.

grimaceries [grimasri], *s.f.pl.* (*a*) grimaces, grimacing; (*b*) affectation.

grimacier, -ière [grimasje, -jɛːr]. **1.** *a.* (*a*) grimacing, grinning; (*b*) affected; **demoiselle grimacière,** affected, mincing, girl. **2.** *s.* (*a*) affected person; (*b*) hypocrite, humbug.

grimage [grimaːʒ], *s.m. Th:* (action of) making up.

grimaud[1] [grimo], *s.m. A:* ignoramus; scribbler.

grimaud[2], *a. A:* sulky.

grimaudage [grimodaːʒ], *s.m.,* **grimauderie** [grimodri], *s.f. A:* (pedantic) verbiage; drivelling.

grime [grim], *s.m. Th:* dotard, old fogey; **jouer les grimes,** to play old men.

grimer [grime], *v.tr. Th:* **g. un acteur,** to make up an actor; **g. qn en vieillard,** to make s.o. up as an old man.

se grimer, to make up (one's face).

grimoire [grimwaːr], *s.m.* **1.** *A:* wizard's book of spells; black book; *A:* book of gramarye. **2.** gibberish, mumbo-jumbo. **3.** scrawl, unintelligible scribble.

grimpant [grɛ̃pɑ̃]. **1.** *a.* climbing (animal); climbing, trailing, creeping (plant); creeping (salt); **rose grimpante,** climbing rose; **plante grimpante,** creeper, climbing plant, *U.S:* vine. **2.** *s.m. P:* trousers, pants.

grimpart [grɛ̃paːr], *s.m. Orn: F:* tree creeper.

grimpée [grɛ̃pe], *s.f.* (stiff) climb.

grimpement [grɛ̃pmɑ̃], *s.m. Ch:* creep(ing).

grimper[1] [grɛ̃pe], *v.i.* **1.** to climb (up), clamber (up); **il a, est, grimpé sur la muraille,** he climbed (up) the wall; **g. à une corde, à un mât (en s'aidant des genoux et des pieds),** to swarm up a rope, up a pole; **g. à un arbre (à la force des bras et des jambes),** to shin up a tree; **g. au pouvoir,** to climb to power; *v.tr.* **g. une montagne, un escalier,** to climb a mountain, a flight of stairs. **2.** (*of plants, liquids*) to creep; (*of plants*) to climb; to trail.

grimper[2], *s.m.* rope-climbing exercises.

grimpereau, -eaux [grɛ̃pro], *s.m. Orn:* **g. (des bois),** tree creeper; **g. des jardins,** short-toed tree creeper; **g. de muraille,** wall creeper.

grimpette [grɛ̃pɛt], *s.f.* **1.** steep climb; steep path. **2.** climbing iron.

grimpeur, -euse [grɛ̃pœːr, -øːz]. **1.** *a.* (*a*) *Z:* climbing, scansorial (bird, organ); (*b*) **appareil g.,** set of climbing irons. **2.** *s.m. Z:* climber. **3.** *s. Sp:* climber; *s.m. Cy:* hill climber, hill-climbing specialist.

grincement [grɛ̃smɑ̃], *s.m.* grinding, creaking, grating (of door, wheels, etc.); **g. de dents,** grinding, gnashing, of teeth; **le g. de la craie sur le tableau,** the squeaking of the chalk on the blackboard.

grincer [grɛ̃se], *v.i.* (**je grinçai(s); n. grinçons**) (*a*) (*of door, wheels, etc.*) to grate; to grind; to creak; **g. des dents,** to grind, grit, gnash, one's teeth; **scie qui fait g. les dents,** saw that sets one's teeth on edge; **la charrette montait la côte en grinçant,** the cart creaked its way up the hill; **porte qui grince sur ses gonds,** creaking door; **plume qui grince sur le papier,** scratchy pen; **les cimes des pins grincent en se heurtant,** the pine tops creak as they knock against each other; **remarque grinçante,** caustic remark; **sourire grinçant,** grim smile; (*b*) (*of bat*) to squeak.

grinche [grɛ̃ːʃ], *O:* **1.** *a. F:* crabbed, sour-tempered. **2.** *P:* (*a*) *s.m.* thief, burglar; (*b*) *s.f.* **la grinche,** light-fingered gentry.

grincher [grɛ̃ʃe]. **1.** *v.i.* (*a*) *O:* (*of bread*) to blister; (*b*) to protest, growl, snarl. **2.** *v.tr. P:* to steal, scrounge.

grincheux, -euse [grɛ̃ʃø, -øːz]. **1.** *a.* grumpy, bad-tempered; whining, complaining. **2.** *s.* grumbler, grouser.

grinchu [grɛ̃ʃy], *a. P: O:* = GRINCHEUX.

grinette [grinɛt], *s.f. Orn: F:* young corncrake.

gringalet [grɛ̃galɛ], (*a*) *s.m.* (i) (little) shrimp (of a man, boy); (ii) whipper-snapper; (*b*) *a.* puny.

gringole [grɛ̃gɔl], *s.f. Her:* head of serpent.

gringolé [grɛ̃gɔle], *a. Her:* gringoly, gringolée.

gringotter [grɛ̃gɔte]. **1.** *v.i.* to warble, twitter. **2.** *v.tr.* **g. un air,** to hum a tune.

gringue [grɛ̃ːg], *s.m. P:* **faire du g. à qn,** to make a pass at s.o.

gringuenaude [grɛ̃gnoːd], *s.f. O: F:* **1.** clot of dirt; (nose-, etc.) picking. **2.** toothsome morsel, picking (of cake, meat, etc.).

griot[1], **-otte**[1] [gri(j)o, -ət], *s.* (*W. Africa*) (*a*) *Ethn:* griot; (*b*) witch doctor cum minstrel.

griot[2], *s.m. Mill:* seconds.

griotte[2] [gri(j)ɔt], *s.f.* **1.** *Bot:* morello (cherry). **2.** *Miner:* griotte (marble).

griottier [gri(j)ɔtje], *s.m. Bot:* morello cherry (tree).

grip [grip], *s.m. Rail: etc:* grip (of cable car).

griphite [grifit], *s.f. Miner:* griphite.

grippage [gripaːʒ], *s.m. Mch:* (*a*) rubbing, friction (of surfaces); (*b*) seizing, seizure, binding, jamming (of bearing, piston, valve, etc.); (*c*) abrasion, scoring (of bearing, etc.).

grippal, -aux [gripal, -o], *a. Med:* influenzal; **catarrhe g.,** influenza cold.

grippe [grip], *s.f.* **1** dislike, aversion; **prendre qn en g., se prendre de g. contre qn,** to take, conceive, a dislike to s.o. **2.** *Med:* influenza; *F:* flu; *U.S:* grippe; **g. gastro-intestinale,** gastric influenza; **g. asiatique,** Asian flu.

grippé [gripe], *a.* **1.** suffering from influenza; **être g.,** to have influenza. **2.** *Med:* pinched, drawn (face) (symptomatic of peritonitis, etc.). **3.** *Mec.E:* seized-up.

grippe-argent [griparʒɑ̃], *s.m.inv. A: F:* sharper, shark.

grippement [gripmɑ̃], *s.m.* **1.** *Mch:* = GRIPPAGE. **2.** *Med:* **g. de la face,** pinched features.

grippeminaud [grip(ə)mino], *s.m. Lit:* **1.** pussy-(cat); grimalkin. **2.** sleek, smooth-faced, man; plausible individual.

gripper [gripe]. **1.** *v.tr.* (*a*) *A:* to seize, pounce upon, clutch, snatch; (*b*) *Mec.E:* to seize up, jam (mechanism). **2.** *v.i. & pr.* (*a*) (*of material*) to crinkle (up), wrinkle, pucker; (*b*) *Mec.E:* (*of bearings*) (i) to run hot, get hot; (ii) to seize (up); to bind, jam; (iii) to become abraded, scored; to furrow.

se gripper. (*a*) *A:* **se g. contre qn,** to take a dislike to s.o.; (*b*) (*of mechanism*) to jam, to clog up, to seize up.

grippe-sou [gripsu], *s.m. F:* grasping old miser, skinflint, money-grubber; *pl. grippe-sou(s).*

grippure [gripyːr], *s.f. Mec.E:* **1.** seizing up. **2.** abrasion, furrow, score (in bearing, etc.).

gris [gri]. **1.** *a.* (*a*) grey, *U.S:* gray; **jupe grise,** grey skirt; **g. de poussière,** grey with dust; **papier g.,** (coarse) brown paper; (*b*) (*compound a.inv. & s.m.; if the compound includes another colour adj. they are usu. linked with a hyphen*) **g. perle, g.-de-perle,** pearl grey; **g. (de) fer, g. d'acier,** iron grey, steel grey; **g. ardoise,** slate-grey; **g.-bleu,** blue-grey; **g. bleuté,** blueish grey; **g. souris,** mouse colour; **g. truité, moucheté,** flea-bitten grey; **g. anthracite,** charcoal grey; **des chevaux g. pommelé,** dapple-grey horses, dapple greys; **une robe g. clair,** a light grey dress; *Hairdr:* **g. fumé, g. pompadour, g. argent,** smoke-grey, pompadour grey, silver-grey (tint, wash); (*c*) grey-haired, grey-headed; **à trente ans elle était toute grise,** at thirty she was quite grey; **barbe grise,** grey beard; (*d*) *Anat:* **matière, substance, grise,** grey matter; (*e*) **vin g.,** rosé wine (of Anjou, Lorraine, etc.); (*f*) **temps g.,** cloudy, dull, grey, hazy, weather; **ciel g.,** grey, overcast, sky; **il fait g.,** the weather is grey, dull, cloudy, overcast; (*g*) **l'éminence grise,** the power behind the throne; (*h*) **faire grise mine,** to look anything but pleased; **faire grise mine à qn,** to give s.o. a poor welcome, the cold shoulder; **pensées grises,** dark thoughts; **en voir de grises,** to have a rough time of it, to get more than one bargains for; **en faire voir de grises à qn,** to give s.o. a rough time, to lead s.o. a dance; (*i*) *F:* (slightly) tipsy, fuddled; **un peu g.,** a bit high. **2.** *s.m.* (*a*) grey (colour); **le g. est peu salissant,** grey doesn't show the dirt; **peint en g.,** painted grey; **habillé de g.,** dressed in grey; *s.a.* 1. (*b*); (*b*) **un g.,** a grey horse; (*c*) (= **tabac g.**) **un paquet de g.** = a packet of shag.

grisaille [grizaːj], *s.f.* **1.** *Art:* (*a*) grisaille; **bleu g.,** neutral blue; (*b*) pencil sketch on grey-tinted paper; (*c*) (*oil painting*) first sketch with shadows laid in; (*d*) *Engr:* tint drawing; **les grisailles du soir sur l'estuaire,** the greyness of the evening over the estuary; **au soleil couchant la salle se remplit de grisaille(s),** at sunset the room fills with grey shadows. **2.** grizzled wig. **3.** *Bot: F:* grey poplar. **4.** *Tex:* pepper-and-salt (cloth).

grisailler [grizɑje]. **1.** *v.tr.* (*a*) to paint (sth.) grey; (*b*) to paint (sth.) in grisaille. **2.** *v.i.* to turn, become, grey, to grey.

grisant [grizɑ̃], *a.* intoxicating; heady; exhilarating; **succès g.,** intoxicating success; **cette joie grisante de se sentir libre,** the exhilarating pleasure of feeling free.

grisard, grisart [grizaːr], *s.m.* **1.** *Bot:* grey poplar. **2.** *Z: F:* badger. **3.** hard sandstone.

grisâtre [grizɑːtr̥], *a.* greyish.

grisbi [grizbi], *s.m. P:* dough, lolly.

gris-bleu [griblø], *a.inv. & s.m.inv.* blue-grey, grey-blue.

grisbock [gribɔk], *s.m. Z:* grysbok.

gris-brun [gribrœ̃], *a.inv. & s.m.inv.* browny-grey, brownish-grey, grey-brown.

gris-de-perle [grid(ə)pɛrl], *a.inv. & s.m.inv.* pearl-grey, pearly-grey.

grisé [grize], *s.m.* **1.** *Engr:* (grey) tint, wash; **g. (en hachures),** hachuring. **2. cliché du g.,** tint block.

Grisélidis [grizelidis], *Pr.n.f. Lit:* Griselda.

griséofulvine [grizeofylvin], *s.f. Ch:* griseofulvin.

griser [grize], *v.tr.* **1.** to paint, tint, with grey; to grey. **2.** to make (s.o.) tipsy, fuddled; **le cognac me grisa,** the brandy went to my head; **grisé par le succès,** intoxicated by, with, success; **grisé d'une facile victoire,** intoxicated with, by, an easy victory.

se griser, to get tipsy, fuddled; **se g. de rêves,** to luxuriate in, on, dreams; to be carried away by dreams.

griserie [grizri], *s.f.* **1.** tipsiness, intoxication. **2.** intoxication, exhilaration, excitement.

griset [grizɛ], *s.m.* **1.** *Orn:* young finch. **2.** *Ich: F:* (*a*) grey shark, cow shark; (*b*) sea bream. **3.** *Fung: F:* wood blewit.

grisette [grizɛt], *s.f.* **1.** *A:* cheap, grey (i) dress-material, (ii) dress. **2.** *A:* young (grey-clad) milliner, etc., of easy virtue; *grisette*; **la g.!** the jade! **3.** *Orn:* whitethroat. **4.** *Fung: F:* (*a*) sheathed agaric; (*b*) clouded agaric. **5.** building stone (of the Beaucaire region).

gris-gris [grigri], *s.m.* grigri, greegree, (West-African) amulet.

gris-jaune [griʒon], *a.inv. & s.m.inv.* yellowish-grey.

grisollement [grizɔlmɑ̃], *s.m.* song (of the lark).

grisoller [grizɔle], *v.i.* (*of lark*) to carol, sing, warble.

grison[1], **-onne** [grizɔ̃, -ɔn]. **1.** *a. A:* grey, grey-headed, grizzled. **2.** *s.m. A:* (*a*) grey-beard; (*b*) donkey; (*c*) confidential servant; (*d*) grey monk. **3.** *s.m.* hard limestone.

grison[2], **-onne,** *a. & s.* **1.** *Geog:* (native, inhabitant) of the Canton of Grisons. **2.** *s.m.* Romanche (language).

grisonnant [grizɔnɑ̃], *a.* turning grey, going grey, greying; touched with grey.

grisonnement [grizɔnmɑ̃], *s.m.* **1.** (*of the hair*) turning grey, growing grey, greying. **2.** painting, staining, (of sth.) grey.

grisonner [grizɔne]. **1.** *v.i.* (*of pers., of the hair*) to grow grey, to go grey, to grey; (*of hair*) to be touched with grey. **2.** *v.tr.* to paint, stain, (sth.) grey.

Grisons [grizɔ̃], *Pr.n.m.pl. Geog:* **le Canton des G.,** the Canton of Grisons.

grisotte [grizɔt], *s.f.* clock (on stockings).

grisou [grizu], *s.m. Min:* **(feu) g.,** fire damp, (pit) gas; **coup de g.,** fire-damp explosion.

grisou-dynamite [grizudinamit], *s.f. Min.Exp:* grisoutine.

grisoumètre [grizumɛtr̥], *s.m. Min:* fire-damp detector.

grisoumétrie [grizumetri], *s.f. Min:* fire-damp detection (with estimate of quantity present).

grisou-naphtalite [grizunaftalit], *s.f. Min.Exp:* grisounite.

grisouscope [grizuskɔp], *s.m. Min:* = safety lamp.

grisouscopie [grizuskɔpi], *s.f. Min.* fire-damp detection (with rough estimate of quantity present).

grisouteux, -euse [grizutø, -øːz], *a. Min:* liable to fire-damp; fiery, gassy (mine).

gris-vert [grivɛːr], *a.inv. & s.m.inv.* greeny-grey, greenish grey, grey-green.

grive [griːv], *s.f.* **1.** *Orn:* thrush; **g. à ailes rousses,** dusky thrush; **g. dorée,** (i) White's thrush, golden mountain thrush; (ii) golden oriole; **g. draine, g. de gui,** missel-, mistle-, thrush; **g. ermite,** hermit thrush; **g. à gorge noire,** black-throated thrush; **g. à gorge rousse,** red-throated thrush; **g. à joues grises,** grey-cheeked thrush; **g. litorne,** fieldfare; **g. mauvis,** redwing; **g. micolore,** Tickell's thrush; **g. musicienne,** song thrush; **g. de Naumann,** Naumann's thrush, red-tailed fieldfare; **g. obscure,** eyebrowed, dark, thrush; **g. petite,** olive-backed thrush; **g. sifflante,** whistling thrush; **g. superbe,** jewel thrush; **g. de Swainson,** Swainson's thrush; **g. de Wilson,** Wilson's thrush; *Bot: F:* **arbre à grives,** rowan, mountain ash; *Prov:* **faute de grives on mange des merles,** beggars can't be choosers; half a loaf is better than no bread; *F:* **soûl comme une g.,** dead drunk. **2.** *P:* (*a*) *A:* war; (*b*) (i) the army; (ii) military service.

grivelage [grivlaːʒ], *s.m.* (*a*) (action of) ordering a meal (in a restaurant) without having the money to pay for it; (*b*) small illicit profit; *F:* making a bit on the side.

grivelé [grivle], *a.* speckled (plumage).

griveler [grivle], *v.* (**je grivèle, n. grivelons; je grivèlerai**) **1.** *v.i. F: A:* to appropriate small sums of money; to make a bit on the side. **2.** *v.tr.* **g. un repas,** to sneak a meal in a restaurant.

grivèlerie [grivɛlri], *s.f. Jur:* (offence consisting of) ordering a meal (at a restaurant) without having the money to pay for it.

griveleur [grivlœːr], *s.m.* **1.** *A:* dishonest administrator. **2.** person who sneaks a meal in a restaurant.

grivelure [grivlyːr], *s.f.* grey speckled colour.

grivet [grivɛ], *s.m. Z:* grivet, green monkey.

griveton [grivtɔ̃], *s.m. Mil: P:* soldier.

grivette [grivɛt], *s.f. Orn:* small thrush.

grivois, -oise[1] [grivwa, -waːz], *a. & s.* **1.** *s.m. A:* German soldier (in the service of France). **2.** *s. A:* free-spoken, lusty, person. **3.** *a.* licentious, loose, broad (story, song, joke).

grivoise[2] [grivwaːz], *s.f. A:* (type of) snuff box (with grinder).

grivoiser [grivwaze], *v.tr. A:* to grind (with a *grivoise*).

grivoiserie [grivwazri], *s.f.* broad joke; blue story; smutty story; licentious gesture; **conter des grivoiseries,** to talk smut.

grizzlé [grizle], *a.* **ours g.,** grizzly bear.

grizzli, grizzly [grizli], *s.m. Z:* grizzly (bear).

grœnendael [grønɑ̃dɛl], *s.m. Z:* Grœnendael (sheep dog).

Groenland [grɔɛnlɑ̃(:d), grɔɛ̃-], *Pr.n.m. Geog:* Greenland; **au G.,** in Greenland.

groenlandais, -aise [grɔɛnlɑ̃dɛ, grɔɛ̃-, -ɛːz]. **1.** *a. Geog:* of, belonging to Greenland; Greenlandic. **2.** *s.* Greenlander. **3.** *s.m. Ling:* Greenlandic.

grog [grɔg], *s.m.* grog; toddy.

groggy [grɔgi], *a. Box: F:* groggy.

grognard, -arde [grɔɲaːr, -ard], *F:* **1.** *a.* grumbling, growling; given to grousing. **2.** *s.* (*a*) grumbler, grouser; (*b*) *Hist:* soldier of Napoleon's Old Guard; veteran.

grognasse [grɔɲas], *s.f. P:* (*a*) ugly, unpleasant, (old) woman; bitch; (*b*) prostitute, tart.

grognasser [grɔɲase], *v.i. P:* to grumble.

grogne [grɔɲ], *s.f. F:* grumbling, grousing.

grognement [grɔɲmɑ̃], *s.m.* **1.** (*a*) (i) grunting (of pig, *F:* of pers.); (ii) grunt; (*b*) (i) growling (of dog, *F:* of pers.); (ii) growl; **pousser un g., faire entendre un g.,** to grunt; to growl, to give a grunt, a growl. **2.** *F:* (*a*) grumbling, grousing; (*b*) (i) snarling; (ii) snarl; **il se redressa avec un g.,** he sprang up with a snarl.

grogner [grɔɲe], *v.i.* **1.** (*a*) (*of pig, F: of pers.*) to grunt; (*b*) (*of dog, F: of pers.*) to growl. **2.** to grumble, to grouse; *with cogn. acc.* **g. un refus,** to growl out a refusal; **g. des insultes,** to mutter insults.

grognerie [grɔɲri], *s.f.* grumbling, growling, grousing.

grogneur, -euse [grɔɲœːr, -øːz]. **1.** *a.* grumbling, grousing; **figure grogneuse,** sulky, disagreeable face. **2.** *s.* grumbler, grouser.

grognon [grɔɲɔ̃]. **1.** *s.m. or f.* grumbler, grouser; **c'est une vieille g.,** she's an old grumbler. **2.** *a.* (*f.* **grognon** *or* **grognonne**), grumbling, peevish; **c'est une femme g., grognonne,** she's a grumbler; **moue grognonne,** peevish expression.

grognonner [grɔɲɔne], *v.i.* **1.** to grunt. **2.** (*a*) to grouse, to grumble; (*b*) to be peevish.

grognonnerie [grɔɲɔnri], *s.f.* (*rare*) grumbling, grousing; peevishness; **des grognonneries continuelles,** constant grumbling.

groin [grwɛ̃], *s.m.* **1.** (*a*) snout (of pig, etc.); (*b*) *F:* ugly mug. **2.** *Civ.E:* head of a groyne.

groise [grwaːz], *s.f. Geol:* stony soil (of periglacial origin).

groisil [grwazi(l)], *s.m. Glassm:* cullet.

groizillon, -onne [grwɑzijɔ̃, -ɔn], *a. & s. Geog:* (native, inhabitant) of the île de Groix.

grole[1], **grolle**[1] [grɔl], *s.f. Orn: Dial:* (*a*) crow; (*b*) rook; (*c*) jackdaw.

grole[2], **grolle**[2], *s.f. P:* shoe; **traîner la g.,** to walk aimlessly.

groles, grolles [grɔl], *s.f.pl. P:* **avoir les g.,** to have the wind up, to be in a blue funk.

grolle[3], *s.f. A:* drinking mug (with lid).

groller [grɔle], *v.i. A: F:* to croak, grouse.

groma [grɔma], *s.f. Rom.Ant:* surveyor's measuring rod.

gromatique [grɔmatik], *a. Rom.Ant: Surv:* **instruments gromatiques,** gromatical instruments.

gromie [grɔmi], *s.f. Prot:* gromia.

grommeler [grɔmle], *v.i.* (**je grommelle, n. grommelons; je grommellerai**) to grumble, mutter; *with cogn. acc.:* **g. un juron,** to mutter an oath.

grommellement [grɔmɛlmɑ̃], *s.m.* grumbling, muttering; rumbling (of thunder, etc.).

grondable [grɔ̃dabl̥], *a.* (child) who deserves a scolding; (action) that might give rise to complaint.

grondant [grɔ̃dɑ̃], *a.* **1.** (*a*) scolding; (*b*) growling, snarling. **2.** rumbling, muttering, roaring (waves, storm, etc.).

grondée [grɔ̃de], *s.f.* scolding.

grondement [grɔ̃dmɑ̃], *s.m.* **1.** grow(ling), snarl(ing) (of dog, etc.). **2.** rumble, rumbling (of thunder); muttering (of gathering storm); roaring (of the storm); booming (of the waves, of the breakers); **g. du canon,** roar, boom(ing), of guns.

gronder [grɔ̃de]. **1.** *v.i.* (*a*) (*of dog, etc.*) to growl, snarl; (*b*) (*of thunder, etc.*) to rumble; (*of storm, etc.*) to boom, to roar; **les brisants se précipitent en grondant,** the breakers are thundering; (*c*) **g. contre qn,** to grumble at s.o., to find fault with s.o. **2.** *v.tr.* to scold; **g. qn sur qch., au sujet de qch.,** to scold, reprimand, s.o. for sth.; **g. qn d'avoir fait qch.,** to scold s.o. for doing sth.; **si je manque mon train, je vais être grondé,** if I miss my train I'll catch it.

gronderie [grɔ̃dri], *s.f.* (severe) scolding; rating.

grondeur, -euse [grɔ̃dœːr, -øːz]. **1.** *a.* grumbling, scolding; **parler d'un ton g.,** to speak irritably, in a scolding voice; **femme grondeuse,** nagging, scolding, wife, woman. **2.** *s. O:* grumbler; *f.* scold, shrew.

grondin [grɔ̃dɛ̃], *s.m. Ich:* **g. (rouge),** red gurnet, red gurnard; **g. gris,** grey gurnard; hardhead.

Groningue [grɔnɛ̃ːg], *Pr.n.f. Geog:* Groningen.

groom [grum], *s.m.* **1.** *Equit: A:* groom. **2.** (*in hotel*) page, buttons, *U.S:* bellhop, bell boy.

gros, grosse [gro, groːs]. **1.** *a.* (*a*) big, bulky, stout, coarse, heavy; **grosse femme,** big, stout, woman; **monsieur g. et gras,** portly gentleman; **g. morceau,** large piece; lump; **grosse corde,** thick, stout, rope; **g. drap,** coarse cloth; **g. pull-over,** chunky sweater; **fil grosse épaisseur,** heavy wire; **poutre grosse d'un pied,** beam a foot across; **g. bout,** thick end (of stick, etc.); **g. caractères,** large characters (in writing); **g. murs,** main walls (of building); **g. moteur,** high-powered, heavy, engine; **g. tour,** heavy lathe; **grosse pièce de forge,** heavy forging; **g. doigt du pied,** big toe; **grosses lèvres,** thick lips; **g. souliers,** stout, strong, shoes; **grosse toile,** coarse linen; **g. vin,** coarse wine; **g. sel,** coarse salt; **grosse viande,** butcher's meat; **affaire de g. bon sens,** matter of plain common sense; **un peu g.,** not very subtle; a bit too obvious; **c'est un peu g.!** that's a bit much! **g. rire,** (i) loud laugh, (ii) coarse laugh, broad laugh; **grosse gaieté,** broad humour; **grosse voix,** gruff voice; big voice; *P:* **g. cul,** (i) *Mil:* = shag (tobacco); (ii) heavy lorry; **g. mot,** coarse expression, foul word, swearword; **allons, pas de gros mots!** come now, no bad language! **grosse indélicatesse,** piece of gross impropriety; **grosse cavalerie,** heavy cavalry; **grosse somme,** large sum; **ce n'est pas une grosse affaire,** (i) it's only a small business, deal; (ii) it's no great matter, not very difficult; *Cards: etc:* **jouer g. (jeu),** to play for high stakes; **on ne fait pas de bien grosses parties,** we do not play for very high stakes; **c'est avec la France que nous faisons la plus grosse partie de nos affaires,** the bulk of our business is done with France; **g. mangeur,** great eater, hearty eater; **g. appétit,** hearty appetite; **avoir la grosse faim,** to be very hungry; **g. rhume,** heavy, violent, cold; **grosse fièvre,** high fever; **un g. kilo,** a good kilo; **grosse faute,** gross, serious, mistake; **faire la grosse besogne,** to do the heavy work, the rough work; **grosse mer,** heavy sea, high sea; **la mer était grosse,** there was a high sea running, the sea was running high; **la rivière est grosse,** the river is swollen; **g. temps,** stormy, bad, weather; stress of weather; **grosse averse, grosse pluie,** heavy shower, heavy rain; **g. vent,** high wind, strong

gale; **g. bourgeois,** solid, substantial, citizen; **g. propriétaire,** big landowner; **grosse héritière,** wealthy heiress; *F:* **les g. bonnets,** *P:* **les grosses légumes,** the top brass; *s.a.* BRAS 1, CŒUR 2, ŒIL 3; (*b*) *A:* **femme grosse,** pregnant woman; **elle est grosse de trois mois,** she is three months pregnant; **action grosse de danger, grosse de conséquences,** action fraught with danger, big, pregnant, with consequences; **paroles grosses de meurtre,** words pregnant with murder; **yeux g. de larmes,** eyes big, swollen, with tears; (*c*) *adv.* **gagner g.,** to earn a great deal, to make big money; **il eût donné g. pour . . .,** he would have given a lot, anything, to . . .; **il y a g. à parier qu'il ne viendra pas,** a hundred to one he won't come! **2.** *s.m.* & *f.* (*a*) *F:* large, fat, person; **un bon g.,** a fat, good-tempered man; **un g. plein de soupe,** a well-fed type; **eh bien, mon g.!** well, old man! old chap! (*b*) *P:* rich, influential, person; **les petits payent pour les g.,** the small man stands the racket while the rich get away with it. **3.** *s.m.* (*a*) bulk, mass, chief part, biggest or thickest part; **g. d'un mât,** thick end of a mast; **g. de l'avant-bras,** swell of the forearm; **le g. de la cargaison,** the bulk of the cargo; **le g. de l'armée, de la flotte,** the main body of the army, of the fleet; **le g. du peuple,** the mass, bulk, of the people; **le g. d'une doctrine,** the essential part of a doctrine; **le plus g. est fait,** the hardest part of the job is done; I, we, have broken the back of the work; **g. de l'été, de l'hiver,** height of summer, depth of winter; *Nau:* **gros de l'eau,** high water at spring-tide; (*b*) **en gros;** (i) roughly, broadly, approximately, on the whole, in the main; **en très g.,** very roughly; **évaluation en g.,** rough estimate; (ii) **dépenser cent francs tout en g.,** to spend a hundred francs in all, altogether, all told; (iii) **écrire en g.,** to write in large characters; **écrit en g.,** writ(ten) large; (iv) **acheter en g.,** to buy in bulk; (*c*) *Com:* wholesale (trade); **faire le g. et le détail,** to deal wholesale and retail; **marchand en g.,** wholesale dealer, wholesaler; **boucher en g.,** wholesale butcher; (*d*) *A:* **un g. de prisonniers allemands travaillait dans le champ,** a party of German prisoners was working in the field. **4.** *s.f.* **grosse;** (*a*) roundhand (writing); **écrire en grosse,** to engross; **plume de grosse,** broad-nibbed pen; (*b*) *Mar.Ins:* **grosse (aventure),** bottomry; **contrat de grosse,** bottomry bond; **à la grosse (aventure),** on bottomry; **prêt à la grosse,** bottomry loan; (*c*) *Com:* gross, twelve dozen; **six grosses de plumes,** six gross pens; (*d*) *Jur:* engrossed document, engrossment, written instrument; **grosse (exécutoire),** first authentic copy (of agreement or title).

gros-argentin [grozarʒɑ̃tɛ̃], *s.m. Ich: F:* dealfish, ribbon fish; *pl. gros-argentins.*

gros-bec [grobɛk], *s.m. Orn:* **g.-b. (casse-noyaux),** hawfinch, grosbeak; *pl. gros-becs.*

gros-bleu [groblø], *a.* & *s.m.inv.* dark blue.

gros-bout [grobu], *s.m. Cu:* chump end (of loin); *pl. gros-bouts.*

groseille [grozɛːj], *s.f.* **1. g. à grappes,** (red, white) currant; **g. noire,** blackcurrant; **sirop de groseille(s),** red currant syrup; **une g. à l'eau,** red-currant syrup and soda water; **gelée de groseille(s),** red-currant jelly. **2. g. à maquereau, g. verte,** gooseberry.

groseillier [grozeje], *s.m.* **1.** currant bush; **g. noir,** blackcurrant bush; **g. sanguin,** bloody, red-flowering, currant. **2. g. à maquereau,** gooseberry bush; **g. d'Amérique,** Barbados gooseberry.

gros-grain [grogrɛ̃], *s.m. Tex:* grogram, grosgrain; *pl. gros-grains.*

gros-guillaume [grogijoːm], *s.m.* **1.** (type of) reddish-coloured table grape. **2.** *F: A:* (coarse) farmhouse bread. **3.** *Ich: Dial:* (*Brittany*) (type of) skate; *pl. gros-guillaumes.*

gros-guilleri [grosgijəri], *s.m. Orn: F:* house sparrow; *pl. gros-guilleris.*

Gros-Jean [groʒɑ̃], *s.m. A: F:* man of low degree, Hodge; *Prov:* **le voilà G.-J. comme devant!** the beggar is back to his hedge again! **c'est G.-J. qui en remontre à son curé,** it's like teaching your grandmother to suck eggs.

gros-mollet [groməlɛ], *s.m. F:* lump fish, lump sucker; *pl. gros-mollets.*

gros-œil [grozœːj], *s.m. Ich: F:* anableps, stargazer; *pl. gros-œils.*

gros-pêne [gropeːn], *s.m.* dead lock (of safety lock); *pl. gros-pênes.*

Gros-René [grorəne], *s.m. A:* confidential servant; (*from the character in Molière's* **Le Dépit amoureux**).

grosse-écale [grosekal], *s.f. Tchn:* odd-sized paving stone; *pl. grosses-écales.*

grossement [grosmɑ̃], *adv.* **1.** roughly speaking, on the whole. **2. blaguer un peu g.,** to be a trifle broad in one's humour.

grosserie [grosri], *s.f.* **1.** *A:* wholesale trading. **2.** (*a*) *A:* hardware, ironmongery; (*b*) silver tableware. **3.** *Tchn: coll.* edge tools.

grossesse [grosɛs], *s.f.* pregnancy; **g. gémellaire,** twin pregnancy; **robe de g.,** maternity dress.

grossette [grosɛt], *s.f. Const:* return (of door, window, lining).

grosseur [grosœːr], *s.f.* **1.** (*a*) size, bulk, volume; thickness (of lips, etc.); (*b*) (*of pers.*) stoutness, fatness. **2.** *Med:* swelling, tumour, growth; **avoir une g. au cou,** to have a swelling on the neck.

grossier, -ière [grosje, -jɛːr]. **1.** *a.* (*a*) coarse, rough (food, cloth, etc.); **peuples encore grossiers,** peoples still in a primitive state of civilization; (*b*) **stupidité grossière,** rank stupidity; **ignorance grossière,** gross, crass, ignorance; **faute grossière,** glaring blunder; **n'avoir qu'une idée grossière de qch.,** to have only a crude, rough, idea of sth.; (*c*) rude, unmannerly (**envers,** to); vulgar, coarse, gross; **air g.,** uncouth appearance; **g. personnage,** ill-mannered person; **il a été on ne peut plus g.,** he was most rude; it would be difficult to imagine anything ruder; **langage g.,** coarse language; **plaisanterie grossière,** coarse, ribald, joke; (*d*) unrefined; **avoir des goûts grossiers,** to have coarse tastes; **traits grossiers,** coarse features; *s.m.* **éviter le g. dans ses écrits,** to avoid coarseness in one's writing; (*e*) *Geol:* **calcaire g.,** limestone rich in fossils; **sable grossier,** coarse-grained sand. **2.** *a.* & *s.m. A:* wholesale (dealer).

grossièrement [grosjɛrmɑ̃], *adv.* **1.** coarsely, roughly; **table g. façonnée,** roughly-made table; **esquisser g. un plan,** to make a rough sketch. **2.** (*a*) uncouthly; rudely; boorishly; coarsely; (*b*) **louer g. qn,** to give s.o. fulsome praise. **3. se tromper g.,** to be grossly mistaken. **4. répondre g.,** to answer rudely; to give an offensive answer; to be rude (to s.o.).

grossièreté [grosjɛrte], *s.f.* **1.** (*a*) coarseness, roughness (of object); (*b*) rudeness, vulgarity, coarseness (of manner, etc.); unmannerliness, boorishness; (*c*) grossness, glaring nature (of mistake). **2. dire des grossièretés à qn,** to say rude things to s.o.; to be rude, offensive, to s.o.; *F:* **pas de grossièretés,** keep it, the party, clean!

grossir [grosiːr]. **1.** *v.tr.* to enlarge, increase, swell, magnify; **torrent grossi par les pluies,** torrent swollen by the rain; **g. les défauts de qn, un incident,** to magnify, exaggerate, s.o.'s faults, an incident; **objet grossi trois fois,** object magnified three times; **vue grossie,** enlarged sketch (of machine, etc.); **g. sa voix,** to put a threatening note into one's voice. **2.** (*a*) *v.i.* to increase, swell; to grow bigger, larger; **il grossit chaque jour,** he grows stouter, puts on weight, every day; **le vent, la mer, grossit,** the wind, sea, is rising, is becoming high, is getting up; **les objets grossissent en se rapprochant,** objects grow larger as they come nearer; (*b*) *v.i.* & *pr.* **la foule (se) grossissait,** the crowd was increasing; **se g. de qch.,** to be increased, swelled, by sth.

grossissant [grosisɑ̃], *a.* **1.** growing, swelling; **dette grossissante,** growing debt. **2.** magnifying, amplifying, enlarging (lens, etc.); **verre g.,** magnifying glass, magnifier.

grossissement [grosismɑ̃], *s.m.* **1.** increase in size, swelling. **2.** (*a*) magnifying, enlargement (of object through lens, etc.); (*b*) magnification, amplification, magnifying power (of lens, etc.); **g. 10,** magnification × 10; **g. maximal, optimal,** maximum, optimum, magnification; **jumelles à fort g.,** high-power field glasses.

grossiste [grosist], *s.m.* & *f.* wholesaler.

grossium [grosjəm], *s.m. P:* important business man, big shot, tycoon.

grosso-modo [grosomədo], *adv.* roughly (speaking); **raconter l'affaire g.-m.,** to give a rough, summary, account of the matter.

grossoyer [groswaje], *v.tr.* (**je grossoie, n. grossoyons; je grossoierai**) to engross (document).

grossulaire [grosylɛːr], *s.f.,* **grossularite** [grosylarit], *s.f. Miner:* grossularite.

gros-ventre [grovɑ̃tr], *s.m. Vet: F:* coccidiosis (of rabbit).

grotesque [grɔtɛsk]. **1.** *a.* (*a*) *Art: etc:* grotesque; (*b*) ludicrous, ridiculous, absurd, grotesque. **2.** *s.m. or f. Arch: Art:* grotesque (ornament). **3.** *s.m.* & *f.* grotesque person; figure of fun; freak.

grotesquement [grɔtɛskəmɑ̃], *adv.* grotesquely, ridiculously, absurdly.

grothite [grotit], *s.f. Miner:* grothite.

grotte [grɔt], *s.f.* grotto, (underground) cave; **la G. de Fingal,** Fingal's Cave.

grou [gru], *s.m.,* **grouette** [gruɛt], *s.f.* gravelly soil (suitable for cultivating vines).

grouillant [grujɑ̃], *a.* crawling, alive, seething (**de,** with); **vers grouillants,** crawling, wriggling, worms; **barbe grouillante de vermine,** beard crawling with vermin; **rue grouillante (de monde),** street swarming, alive, with people; **foule grouillante,** teeming crowd.

grouillement [grujmɑ̃], *s.m.* **1.** swarming, crawling, wriggling; **g. de piétons,** swarming mass of pedestrians; **le g. des vers,** the wriggling of worms. **2. g. des intestins,** rumbling of the bowels. **3.** *Cin:* swarming (of image).

grouiller [gruje], *v.i.* **1.** to crawl, swarm, be alive (**de,** with); **fromage qui grouille de vers,** cheese crawling, alive, with maggots; **leurs habits grouillaient (de vermine),** their clothes were alive with vermin; **cette ville grouille de soldats,** the town is swarming with, overrun with, soldiers; **la foule grouillait dans la rue,** the crowd was swarming in the street, the street was teeming, swarming, with people. **2.** *A:* to move. **3.** *Cin:* (*of image*) to swarm.

se grouiller, *P:* to hurry up, to look alive, to get going; to stir one's stumps; **dis-lui de se g.,** tell him to get a move on; **grouille (-toi)!** buck up! get cracking! get busy!

grouillis(-grouillot) [gruji(grujo)], *s.m. F:* crowd, swarm, seething mass (of worms, people, etc.).

grouillot [grujo], *s.m. St.Exch: F:* messenger (boy); errand boy.

grouiner [grwine], *v.i.* (*of pig*) to grunt.

groulasse [grulas], **groule** [grul], *s.f. P:* errand girl.

group [grup], *s.m. Bank: Com:* sealed bag of cash, of specie (for transmission to or from branch office).

groupage [grupaːʒ], *s.m.* **1.** *Com:* collecting, bulking (of parcels). **2.** *Med: etc:* **g. sanguin,** blood grouping.

groupe [grup], *s.m.* **1.** (*a*) group (of people, things); clump (of trees, etc.); battery (of lights); cluster (of stars, etc.); party (of people); **lampes disposées en groupes de trois,** lamps arranged in groups of three; **ils arrivaient par groupes de deux ou trois,** they arrived in twos and threes; **les invités s'en allèrent par petits groupes,** the guests straggled off; **touristes répartis en cinq groupes,** tourists divided into five parties, groups; **un petit g. attendait près de la porte,** a small group of people was waiting near the door; *Pol.Ec: Ind: etc:* **g. de travail,** working party; study group; **g. d'étude,** study group; seminar; *Pol:* **g. d'extrême droite,** ultra-conservative group; group of the extreme right; **g. de pression,** pressure group; *Med:* **g. sanguin,** blood group; **détermination du g. sanguin,** blood grouping; **g. témoin,** control group (of patients, etc.); (*b*) **g. scolaire,** (multilateral) school block; (*c*) *Nat.Hist:* division; (*d*) *Mus:* group (of notes joined at the stems, or sung to one syllable); (*e*) *Trans:* **g. mobile,** mobile unit. **2.** (*a*) *Mec.E:* bank (of machines, instruments, etc.); unit, block (of mechanical elements); *Ind:* **g. de chaudières,** bank of boilers; *Mch: I.C.E:* **g. moteur, g. motopropulseur,** power plant, power unit, motor plant, motor unit; **g. propulsif,** propelling [illegible]; *I.C.E:* **g. de(s) cylindres,** cylinder block; **g. de turbines,** turbine set; **g. moto-pompe,** motor-pump set; *Av:* **g. réacto-propulseur,** jet power plant; **g. des servitudes de bord,** ancillary power unit; (*b*) *El.E:* set; **g. électrogène,** generating set, unit; **g. convertisseur,** converter set, motor-generator set; **g. auxiliaire,** auxiliary set; **g. de relais,** relay set; (*c*) *Atom.Ph:* **g. de séparation (des isotopes, etc.),** (isotope, etc.) separation unit; **g. de diffusion,** diffusion unit; (*d*) (*computers*) **g. de bits consécutifs, g. de positions binaires,** byte; **g. de deux bits,** dibit; **g. d'erreurs,** error burst; (*e*) *Rail:* **g. de changements de voie,** set of points. **3.** *Mil:* (*a*) (*organic unit*) **g. de combat,** squad; **demi-g.,** section, *U.S:* half squad; **g. d'artillerie,** battery, *U.S:* (artillery) battalion; **g. d'aviation** (*transport air unit only*), squadron (of transport aircraft); **g. d'État-Major,** Army Headquarters Wing; **g. moto,** motor-cycle unit; (*b*) **g. d'armées,** army group; **g. d'intervention,** mobile force, task force; **g. franc,** commando; *Av:* **vol de g.,** formation flying.

groupement [grupmɑ̃], *s.m.* **1.** (*a*) grouping, arranging in groups; **g. des enfants d'après l'âge,** classification of children by age groups; (*statistics*) **g. de données,** classification, grouping, of data; **g. de matériel de guerre sur un point**

stratégique, concentration of war material at a strategic point; (*b*) *Ind: Com:* pooling (of interests, etc.); (*c*) *El:* connection, connecting up, coupling, arrangement (of cells, etc.). **2.** group (of thgs., people); (*a*) **g. politique,** political group; **g. de consommateurs,** consumers' group; **s'opposer à de puissants groupements d'intérêts,** to be in opposition to powerful groups of interests; **g. syndical,** trade union bloc; (*b*) *Ind:* pool; (*c*) *Mil:* group, formation; **g. tactique,** tactical grouping; **g. tactique (de) toutes armes,** task force; **g. temporaire,** temporary formation; **g. d'infanterie,** brigade group, *U.S:* battle group; **sous-g. d'infanterie,** battalion group; *Mil.Av:* **g. des moyens militaires de transport aérien,** air transport group. **3.** *Artil: etc:* (shot) group(ing), (shot) pattern; **tir de g.,** grouping practice; **point moyen du g.,** centre of dispersion, of impact; **densité du g.,** density of grouping; **g. collectif, individuel,** grouping (of shots) by a body of men, by a single man; **g. horizontal, vertical,** grouping (of shots) on a horizontal, on a vertical, target.

grouper [grupe], *v.tr.* **1.** to group; to arrange (in groups); **g. des efforts,** to concentrate efforts; **g. des moyens,** to pool resources. **2.** *Com:* **g. des colis,** to collect parcels (for forwarding in bulk). **3.** *El:* to connect up, join up, group, couple (cells, etc.). **4.** *Med:* **g. un malade,** to determine a patient's blood group. **5.** *Arch:* to pair (columns).

se grouper, to form a group; to gather; to bunch (together); **se g. autour du feu,** to gather round the fire; **ils se tenaient groupés à la porte,** they stood in a knot at the door, they clustered round the door; **se g. autour d'un chef,** to gather, rally, round a leader.

groupeur [grupœːr], *s.m. Com:* forwarding agent.

groupuscule [grupyskyl], *s.m. Pej: F:* bunch, small group (of people).

grouse [gruːz], *s.m. or f. Orn:* grouse.

gruau[1] [gryo], *s.m.* **1.** (*a*) (finest) wheat flour; **pain de g.,** fine wheaten bread; (*b*) coarse ground wheat flour; **g. d'avoine,** (i) groats; (ii) oatmeal. **2.** *Cu:* gruel.

gruau[2], **-aux,** *s.m.* **1.** *Orn:* young crane. **2.** *Mec.E:* small crane.

gruauter [gryote], *v.tr.* to grind (wheat, oats).

grue [gry], *s.f.* **1.** *Orn:* crane; **g. antigone,** sarus crane; **g. blanche américaine,** whooping crane; **g. blanche de Mandchourie,** Manchurian crane; **g. cendrée,** common crane; **g. couronnée,** crowned crane; **g. de Numidie,** demoiselle crane; **g. de paradis,** paradise crane; **g. sibérienne,** Asiatic white crane; *F:* **faire le pied de g. (à attendre qn),** to kick, cool, one's heels (waiting for s.o.); to be kept waiting, to wait about, hang about, (at the door, etc.) for s.o.; **cou de g.,** long scraggy neck. **2.** *F:* (*a*) **grande g.,** great gawk of a woman; (*b*) woman of easy virtue; tart; **une jeune femme très g.,** a very flashy young woman; (*c*) *A:* fool, simpleton. **3.** (*a*) *Mec.E: Const: etc:* crane; **g. à main,** hand crane; **g. à vapeur,** steam crane; **g. à volée, à flèche, à bras,** jib crane; **g. à colonne, à fût,** pillar crane; **g. à pivot,** revolving crane; **g. transportable, g. roulante,** travelling crane, loco crane; **g. à portique,** gantry crane; **g. chevalet,** Goliath crane; **g. d'applique, à potence, à console,** wall crane; **g. hydraulique,** hydraulic crane, water crane; **g. de chargement,** (i) loading hoist; (ii) *Artil:* loading davit (of heavy gun); **g. marteau,** hammer-head crane; **g. à contrepoids,** balance crane; **g. à benne preneuse,** grabbing crane; **g. volante, g. du ciel,** flying crane; **g. flottante,** floating crane; **g. à flotteur,** pontoon crane; **conducteur de g.,** crane driver; **frais, droits, de g.,** cranage; *Cin:* **g. de prise de vue,** crane; (*b*) *Rail:* **g. alimentaire, g. d'alimentation,** water pillar, water crane.

gruer [grye], *v.tr.* to grind (wheat, oats).

grugeage [gryʒaːʒ], *s.m. Metall: Glassm:* notching.

grugeoir [gryʒwaːr], *s.m. Tls:* notcher.

grugeon [gryʒɔ̃], *s.m.* lump (of soft sugar).

gruger [gryʒe], *v.tr.* (**je grugeai(s); n. grugeons**) **1.** *A:* to crunch (piece of sugar, etc.); to crumble (glass). **2.** (*a*) *A:* to eat (up), swallow; **g. qn sans merci,** to eat s.o. out of house and home; (*b*) to swindle, exploit (s.o.).

grugerie [gryʒri], *s.f.* swindling; exploitation.

grugeur, -euse [gryʒœːr, -øːz], *s.* swindler, shark; exploiter.

gruidés [gryide], *s.m.pl. Orn:* Gruidae, the cranes.

gruiformes [gryifɔrm], *s.m.pl. Orn:* Gruiformes.

grume [grym], *s.f.* **1.** bark (left on felled tree); **bois en g.,** rough timber; undressed timber. **2.** log. **3.** *Dial:* grape.

grumeau, -eaux [grymo], *s.m.* **1.** (finely divided) curd (of milk, soap, etc.); **se mettre en grumeaux, former des grumeaux,** to curdle. **2. grumeaux de sel,** specks of salt; salty deposit. **3.** *Geol:* (soil) aggregate.

grumeler (se) [səgrymle], *v.pr.* (**il se grumelle; il se grumellera**) to clot, curdle.

grumeleux, -euse [grymlø, -øːz], *a.* **1.** curdled. **2. poire grumeleuse,** gritty pear. **3.** (*of soil*) friable.

grumelure [grymlyːr], *s.f. Metall:* cavity (in casting).

grumier [grymje], *s.m.* timber lorry.

grünérite [grynerit], *s.f. Miner:* grünerite.

gruon [gryɔ̃], *s.m. Orn:* young crane.

gruppetto [grupɛto], *s.m. Mus:* turn, gruppetto; *pl. gruppetti.*

grutier [grytje], *s.m. Mec.E:* crane driver, crane operator.

gruyère [gryjɛːr], *s.m.* Gruyere (cheese).

grylle [griːj], *s.m.* gryllos.

gryllidés [grilide], *s.m.pl. Ent:* Gryllidae.

grylloblattides [grilɔblatid], *s.m.pl. Ent:* Grylloblattodea.

gryphée [grife], *s.f. Paleont: Moll:* gryphaea.

grypocères [gripɔsɛːr], *s.m.pl. Ent:* skippers.

grypose [gripoːz], *s.f. Med:* gryposis.

guacharo [gwaʃaro], *s.m. Orn:* oilbird, guacharo.

guadalcazarite [gwadalkazarit], *s.f. Miner:* guadalcazarite.

guadeloupéen, -éenne [gwadlupeɛ̃, -een], *a. & s. Geog:* (native, inhabitant) of Guadeloupe.

guais [gɛ], *a. Fish:* **hareng g.,** shotten herring.

guanaco [gwanako], *s.m. Z:* guanaco.

Guanches [gwɑ̃ʃɛs], *s.m.pl. Hist: Ethn:* Guanches.

guaner [gwane], *v.tr.* to guano (field).

guanidine [gwanidin], *s.f. Ch:* guanidine.

guanier, -ière [gwanje, -jɛːr], *a.* relating to guano; guaniferous.

guanine [gwanin], *s.f. Ch:* guanine.

guano [gwano], *s.m.* guano.

guanyle [gwanil], *s.m. Ch:* guanyl.

guarani [gwarani], *s.m. Ling:* Guarani.

guarinite [gwarinit], *s.f. Miner:* guarinite.

Guatemala (le) [ləgwatemala], *Pr.n.m. Geog:* Guatemala.

guatémaltèque [gwatemaltɛk], *a. & s.m. or f. Geog:* Guatemalan.

gué[1] [ge], *s.m.* ford; **pierres de g.,** stepping stones; **passer une rivière à g.,** to ford a river; to wade through a river; **sonder le g.,** to throw out a feeler, to see how the land lies; **changer d'attelage au milieu du g.,** to change, swap, horses in midstream.

gué[2], *int. A:* (*in old songs*) = hey! nonny-nonny!

guéable [geabl̩], *a.* fordable (river); **non g.,** unfordable.

guebli [gɛbli], *s.m. Meteor:* (*in Algeria, Tunisia*) sirocco.

Guèbre [gɛbr̩], *s.m. Rel: O:* Guebre, Gheber, Parsee.

guède [gɛd], *s.f. Bot:* woad, pastel.

guéder [gede], *v.tr.* (**je guède, n. guédons; je guéderai**) **1.** *Dy: A:* to woad, to steep (material) in woad. **2.** *F: A:* **se g. de boisson,** to steep, soak, oneself in drink; to soak; **g. qn de nourriture,** to stuff, cram, s.o. with food.

guédoufle [geduf̩l], *s.f.* twin oil and vinegar bottle.

guéer [gee], *v.tr.* **1.** *O:* to ford (stream); to wade through (stream). **2.** *A:* to soak or rinse (linen in a stream). **3.** to water (horse).

Gueldre [gɛldr̩]. *Pr.n.f. Geog:* **1. la G.,** Gelderland, Guelders (in Holland). **2.** Geldern, Guelders (in Germany). **3.** *Bot:* **rose de G.,** guelder rose.

gueldrois, -oise [gɛldrwa, -waːz], *a. & s.* (native, inhabitant) of (i) Gelderland, (ii) Geldern.

guelfe [gɛlf], *s.m. Hist:* Guelph.

guelfisme [gɛlfism], *s.m. Hist:* Guelphism.

guelmois, -oise [gɛlmwa, -waːz], *a. & s. Geog:* (native, inhabitant) of Guelma (Algeria).

guelta [gɛlta], *s.f. Geog:* (*in Sahara*) pool (in dry river bed); water hole.

guelte [gɛlt], *s.f. Com:* commission, percentage (on sales).

Guenièvre [gənjɛːvr̩], *Pr.n.f. Lit:* Guinever(e).

guenille [gəniːj], *s.f.* **1.** tattered garment, old rag; **en guenilles,** in rags (and tatters). **2.** worthless object; rubbish; *Lit:* **g. si l'on veut, ma g. m'est chère,** call it trash, if you will, but my trash is dear to me. **3.** *Lit:* decrepit (old) man.

guenilleux, -euse [gənijø, -øːz], *a.* ragged, (clad) in rags, tattered.

guenillon [gənijɔ̃], *s.m.* (*a*) piece of rag; (*b*) *A:* **g. de papier,** scrap of paper.

guenipe [gənip], *s.f. F:* (*a*) slut, slattern; (*b*) tart.

guenon [gənɔ̃], *s.f.* **1.** *Z:* (*a*) *A:* long-tailed monkey; **g. à long nez,** proboscis monkey; (*b*) she-monkey (in general). **2.** *F:* ugly woman, fright. **3.** *P:* (*a*) prostitute; (*b*) **la g.,** the mistress, the manageress, the old woman.

guenuche [gənyʃ], *s.f.* **1.** small she-monkey. **2.** *F:* (small) ugly woman, little fright.

guépard [gepaːr], *s.m. Z:* cheetah.

guêpe [gɛ(ː)p], *s.f.* **1.** *Ent:* wasp; **g. maçonne,** mason wasp, mud dauber; **taille de g.,** wasp-waist. **2.** artful, crafty, woman; *F:* **pas folle, la g.!** you won't get the better of her (him)!

guépéou [gepeu], *s.m. Russian Adm: A:* Ogpu.

guêpier [gepje], *s.m.* **1.** wasps' nest, vespiary; *F:* **donner, tomber, se fourrer, dans un g.,** to stir up a hornets' nest. **2.** wasp trap. **3.** *Orn:* **g. (d'Europe),** bee-eater; **g. de Perse,** blue-cheeked bee-eater.

guêpière [gepjɛːr], *s.f. Cost:* wasp waister, wasp-waisted corset.

guépiot [gepjo], *s.m.* cheetah cub.

Guerchin (le) [ləgɛrʃɛ̃], *Pr.n.m. Hist. of Art:* Guercino.

guère [gɛːr], *adv.* (*always with neg. expressed or understood*) hardly (any), not much, not many, only a little, only a few; **je ne l'aime g.,** I don't care much for him; **je ne la vois g.,** I don't see much of her, I see very little of her, I hardly ever see her; **le voyez-vous?—g.!** do you see him?—not very often! very little! **cet appel n'a eu g. de succès,** the appeal met with very little success; **il n'a g. d'argent,** he hasn't much money; he has hardly any money; **vous n'en avez g. non plus,** you haven't (got) much either; **il n'a g. d'amis,** he has hardly any, very few, friends; **il ne mange g. que du pain,** he hardly eats anything but bread; **il n'y a g. que lui qui puisse vous aider,** he's about the only man who can help you; **il ne tardera g. à venir,** he will not be long in coming; **il n'a g. moins de trente ans,** he is not far short of, not much under, thirty; **ne plus g.,** (i) hardly any more; (ii) not much longer; **il n'en reste plus g.,** there is hardly any left; **il ne tardera plus g.,** he won't be long now; **il n'y a g. plus de six ans,** it is barely more than six years ago; *F:* **il n'y a g.,** quite recently; **il ne s'en faut (de) g.,** there is not much wanting, it's not far short; **est-il mort?—il ne s'en faut guère,** is he dead?—pretty nearly; **si ce n'est pas un charlatan, il ne s'en faut g.,** if he isn't a quack he's next door to (being) one; **sans g. avoir d'amis, il était respecté,** although he had very few, only a few, friends, he was respected.

guéret [gere], *s.m. Agr:* (*a*) ploughed land; (*b*) fallow land; (*c*) *pl. Lit: Poet:* **les guérets,** the fields.

guérétois, -oise [geretwa, -waːz], *a. & s. Geog:* (native, inhabitant) of Guéret.

guéréza [gereza], *s.m. Z:* guereza, white-mantled colobus.

guéridon [geridɔ̃], *s.m.* **1.** pedestal table. **2.** *A: Nau:* (bailing) scoop.

guérilla [gerija], *s.f.* **1.** guer(r)illa warfare. **2.** band, troop, of guer(r)illas.

guérillero [gerijero], *s.m.* guer(r)illa (irregular soldier).

guérir [geriːr]. **1.** *v.tr.* (*a*) to cure, heal (s.o.); to restore (s.o.) to health; *B:* **et dès ce moment-là sa fille fut guérie,** and her daughter was made whole from that very hour; **se g. de ses préjugés,** to overcome one's prejudices; **g. qn d'une habitude,** to cure, break, s.o. of a habit; (*b*) **g. un rhume,** to cure a cold; **g. une brûlure,** to heal a burn; *F:* **cela ne guérit rien,** that's no cure, that doesn't help much. **2.** *v.i.* (*a*) to recover one's health; to be cured, restored to health; to recover; **g. de la fièvre,** to get over, recover from, a fever; **il n'en guérira pas,** he won't get over it; (*b*) (*of wound, etc.*) to heal; **mon bras guérit lentement,** my arm is slowly mending, healing, getting better.

guérison [gerizɔ̃], *s.f.* **1.** recovery; **en voie de g.,** on the way to recovery. **2.** (*a*) cure (of disease); **faire des guérisons,** to effect cures; (*b*) healing (of wound).

guérissable [gerisabl̩], *a.* (*a*) curable; (*b*) that can be healed.

guérisseur, -euse [gerisœːr, -øːz]. **1.** *s.* (*a*) (*pers.*) healer; (*b*) quack (doctor); (*c*) faith healer; (*d*) **les Anglais considèrent la mer comme une grande guérisseuse,** the English consider the sea to be a great healer. **2.** *a.* healing.

guérite [gerit], *s.f.* **1.** *Mil:* sentry box. **2.** cabin, shelter (for watchman, etc.); look-out turret (on castle walls, etc.); **g. de grue,** cab, house, of a crane; *Rail:* **g. à signaux, pour aiguilles,** signal box, cabin; **g. d'un wagon,** look-out (seat) of a van. **3.** hooded (wicker) chair. **4.** *Nau:* (*a*) **g. de la hune,** rim of the top; (*b*) **g. de manche à vent,** opening of a wind-sail.

Guernesey [gɛrnəzɛ], *Pr.n.m. Geog:* Guernsey; *Husb:* **vache de G.**, Guernsey (cow).

guernesiais, -aise [gɛrnəzjɛ, -ɛːz], *a. & s. Geog:* (native, inhabitant) of Guernsey.

guerre [gɛːr], *s.f.* war, warfare. **1.** (*a*) **g. moderne,** modern warfare; **g. classique,** conventional warfare; **g. chaude, froide,** hot, cold, war; **g. sur terre,** land warfare; **g. aérienne, g. dans les airs,** air warfare; **g. atomique,** atomic warfare; **g. bactériologique,** bacteriological warfare, germ warfare; **g. chimique,** chemical warfare; **g. électronique,** electronic warfare; **g. des nerfs,** war of nerves; **g. psychologique,** psychological warfare; **g. radiologique,** radiological warfare; **g. localisée,** local, contained, war; **g. générale,** general war; **g. planétaire, g. universelle,** global war; **g. limitée,** limited war(fare); **g. totale,** total war(fare); **g. préventive,** preventive war; **g. éclair,** lightning war, blitzkrieg, *F:* blitz; **petite g.,** (i) minor war; minor operations; (ii) manœuvres; sham fighting; **g. en rase campagne,** open warfare, field warfare; **g. de mouvement,** mobile warfare; **g. d'embuscade,** bush warfare, guerilla warfare; **g. de rues,** street fighting; **g. de positions,** static warfare; **g. de tranchées,** trench warfare; **g. de siège,** siege warfare; **g. dans le désert,** desert warfare; **g. dans la brousse,** bush, jungle, warfare; **g. dans les régions arctiques,** arctic warfare; **g. en montagne,** mountain warfare; *Navy:* **g. navale, g. sur mer,** naval warfare; **g. sous-marine,** submarine warfare; **g. anti-sous-marine,** anti-submarine warfare; **g. au commerce, g. de course,** commerce-destroying, *A:* privateering; **g. civile,** civil war; **g. révolutionnaire,** revolutionary war; **g. subversive, g. non classique,** unconventional war, subversive war; **g. nationale,** people's war; **g. sainte,** holy war; **se mettre en g.,** to go to war; **être en g. avec, contre . . .,** to be at war with . . .; **en temps de g.,** in time of war, in wartime; **en pleine g.,** in the midst of war; **faire la g. à, contre, un pays,** to wage war, make war, on, against, a country; **faire la g. avec qn,** to serve (i) with, (ii) under, s.o.; **faire la bonne g.,** to fight fair, *F:* to play the game; **c'est de bonne g.,** it's quite fair; **s'en aller en g.,** to go to the wars; **usé par la g.,** war-worn; **à la g. comme à la g.,** (i) one must take the rough with the smooth; (ii) we, you, have got to rough it; *A:* **le Ministère de la G.,** *F:* **la G.,** *A:* the War Department, the War Office; **usine de g.,** munitions factory; (*b*) *Hist:* **la g. de Trente ans,** the Thirty Years War; **la Grande Guerre,** the Great War; **la première, la deuxième, g. mondiale,** World War I, II; **la drôle de g.,** the phoney war (1939-40). **2.** (*a*) strife, contention, quarrel, feud; **faire la g. à qn sur, au sujet de, qch.,** to fight s.o. over sth.; **g. à outrance, à mort,** war to the knife; **une g. à mort entre deux familles,** a deadly feud between two families; **être en g. ouverte avec, contre, qn,** to be openly at war with s.o.; *Com:* **g. des prix, des tarifs,** price, tariff, war; **g. de plume,** paper warfare; **nom de g.,** assumed name; pen name; *adv.phr.* **de g. lasse j'y consentis,** for the sake of peace and quiet I gave in; *Prov:* **qui terre a g. a.,** riches lead to lawsuits; (*b*) **les éléments en g.,** the elements at war.

guerrier, -ière [gɛrje, -jɛːr]. **1.** *a.* warlike, martial; *Lit:* **travaux guerriers,** toils of war; **danse guerrière,** war dance. **2.** *s.m.* warrior. **3.** *s.f.* **guerrière,** amazon.

guerroyant [gɛrwajɑ̃], *a.* bellicose, pugnacious; *F:* always on the warpath; *A:* **humeur guerroyante,** warlike temper.

guerroyer [gɛrwaje], (**je guerroie, n. guerroyons; je guerroierai**) (*a*) *A: v.tr.* **g. le roi,** to take up arms against the king; (*b*) *v.i.* to war, to wage war, to fight (**contre,** against).

guerroyeur, -euse [gɛrwajœːr, -øːz]. **1.** *s.* fighter. **2.** *a.* fighting (spirit, mood).

guet [gɛ], *s.m.* **1.** watch(ing); lookout; **être au g.,** to be on the watch; **avoir l'œil au g.,** to keep a sharp lookout; **avoir l'œil et l'oreille au g.,** to keep one's eyes and ears open; *Mil: etc:* **poste de g.,** lookout post; **réseau, système, de g.,** watch net, watch system; *Nau:* **service du g.,** coastguard service; **faire le g.,** (i) to be on the watch; (ii) to go the rounds; **chien de bon g.,** good watchdog. **2.** *A:* **le g.,** the watch, the patrol; the constables of the watch; **les bourgeois durent faire le g.,** the burgesses had to do the patrolling; **mot du g.,** password, watchword. **3.** *A:* flourish of trumpets.

guet-apens [gɛtapɑ̃], *s.m.* **1.** (*a*) ambush; snare, trap; *Mil:* ambuscade; **attirer qn dans un g.-a.,** to ambush s.o.; **tomber dans un g.-a.,** to fall into an ambush, into a trap; **être victime d'un g.-a.,** to be ambushed, to fall into an ambush; (*b*) **le coup d'État fut un g.-a. contre la République,** the coup d'état was an attack against the republic. **2.** *Jur:* lying in wait; **meurtre par g.-a.,** murder with felonious intent; **de g.-a.,** with premeditation; *pl. guets-apens* [gɛtapɑ̃].

guète [gɛt], *s.f.* = GUETTE.

guêtre [gɛ(ː)tr̥], *s.f.* **1.** gaiter; **demi-guêtres, guêtres de ville,** spats; *F:* **tirer ses guêtres,** to take to one's heels, to scram; **traîner ses guêtres partout,** to loaf about; *A:* **il y laissa ses guêtres,** he died there (*esp.* on the field of battle). **2.** *Aut:* gaiter, patch (for punctured tyre).

guêtrer [getre], *v.tr.* to gaiter; to put gaiters on (s.o.).

se guêtrer, to put on one's gaiters.

guêtrier, -ière [getri(j)e, -(j)ɛːr], *s.* gaiter maker.

guêtron [gɛtrɔ̃], *s.m. A:* spat, short gaiter; anklet.

guette [gɛt], *s.f.* **1.** *A. & Dial:* watch; **chien de bonne g.,** good watchdog; *Fr.C:* **faire la g.,** to watch for fowl. **2.** *A:* watch-tower (of castle). **3.** *A:* watchman.

guetter [gete], *v.tr.* (*a*) to lie in wait for, to be on the lookout for, to watch for (s.o.); (*b*) to mark down (adversary); (*c*) **g. l'occasion,** to watch one's opportunity; **il guettait que l'occasion se présentât,** he was watching, waiting, for the opportunity to occur.

guetteur [getœːr], *s.m.* **1.** *A:* watchman, watcher. **2.** *Mil: Nau:* lookout (man) (in trenches, etc.); **poste de guetteurs,** lookout post; **g. sémaphorique,** coast signalman. **3.** fire watcher. **4.** *a.* **guetteur, -euse,** watching.

gueugueule [gœgœl], *s.f. P:* pretty face; **ça, c'est g.!** she's easy on the eye! she's a good-looker!

gueulante [gœlɑ̃t], *s.f. P:* uproar; **pousser une g.,** (i) to shout, to yell; (ii) to sing loudly in chorus; (iii) to shout together in protest.

gueulard, -arde [gœlaːr, -ard]. **1.** *a. & s.* (*a*) *A. & Dial:* gluttonous (person); glutton, guzzler; (*b*) *F:* loud-voiced, loud-mouthed (person). **2.** *s.m.* (*a*) *F: Nau:* speaking trumpet; *W.Tel:* extra-loud loudspeaker; (*b*) mouth (of sewer); mouth, throat (of blast furnace); muzzle (of gun); **g. de mine,** pithead; *Metall:* **gaz de g.,** waste gases. **3.** *a.* hard-mouthed (horse).

gueule [gœl], *s.f.* **1.** (*a*) mouth (of carnivorous animal, dog, pike, some other large fish); *F:* (*of dog*) **donner de la g.,** to bark; *Ven:* (*of hounds*) **chasser de g.,** to give tongue; (*of puppy*) **faire sa g.,** to begin to eat solid food; to be growing up; (*b*) *P:* mouth (of pers.); **c'est un fort en g., une grande g.,** he's got far too much to say for himself; he doesn't know how to keep his trap shut; **jeter des injures à pleine g.,** to bawl out abuse; **donner de la g.,** to shout; **coups de g.,** slanging match; **(vas-tu fermer) ta g.!** shut up! belt up! **être porté sur la g.,** to be fond of eating and drinking; **s'en mettre plein la g.,** to stuff, to guzzle; **dépenser beaucoup pour la g.,** to spend a lot on food (and drink); **se soûler la g.,** to get drunk; **avoir la g. de bois,** to have a hangover; **une fine g.,** a gourmet; (*c*) *P:* face, mug; **avoir une sale g.,** (i) to have an ugly mug; (ii) to look rotten, to look down in the mouth; (iii) to look a nasty customer; **faire sa, la, g.,** to sulk; to pull a long face; **il m'a fait la g.,** he's given me the cold shoulder; **casser la g. à qn,** to bash s.o.'s face in; **se casser la g.,** (i) to spoil one's beauty; (ii) to come a cropper; *Mil:* **les Gueules cassées,** soldiers with serious facial injuries; (*in N.Fr.*) **gueules noires,** (coal) miners; (*d*) *F:* **avoir de la g.,** to have an air about one; **ce tableau a de la g.,** that's some picture; **ce chapeau a une drôle de g.,** that's a queer sort of hat. **2.** mouth (of sack, well, bottle, tunnel, etc.); muzzle (of gun); fire hole (of furnace); *Hyd.E:* **g. bée,** open sluice, (cylindrical) opening; *adv.phr.* (*of mill*) **marcher à g. bée,** to work with all sluice-gates open.

gueule-de-four [gœldəfuːr], *s.m. Orn: F:* long-tailed tit; *pl. gueules-de-four.*

gueule-de-lion [gœldəljɔ̃], *s.f. Bot: F:* snapdragon; *pl. gueules-de-lion.*

gueule-de-loup [gœldəlu], *s.f.* **1.** *Bot: F:* snapdragon. **2.** (*a*) *Const:* (chimney) cowl, chimney jack; turn-cap; (*b*) *Mch:* (exhaust) muffler. **3.** *Carp:* rounded groove. **4.** *Nau:* blackwall hitch; *pl. gueules-de-loup.*

gueule-de-raie [gœldərɛ], *s.f. Nau:* cat's paw (knot); *pl. gueules-de-raie.*

gueulée [gœle], *s.f.* **1.** (*of animal, P: of pers.*) large mouthful; (*of animal*) **chercher sa g.,** to hunt, search, for food. **2.** *Fish:* bite (at bait). **3.** *F:* shout; uproar.

gueulement [gœlmɑ̃], *s.m. P:* shout, yell; **il a poussé un g. de souffrance,** he let out a yell of pain.

gueuler [gœle]. **1.** *v.i. P:* to bawl, shout; **faire g. la radio,** to turn the radio on full blast. **2.** *v.tr.* (*a*) to bawl out (song, orders, etc.); (*b*) *Ven:* (*of hound*) to seize, catch (quarry).

gueules [gœl], *s.m. Her:* gules.

gueuleton [gœltɔ̃], *s.m. P:* feast, spread, blow-out, tuck-in; banquet; **c'était un g. à tout casser,** it was a hell of a blow-out; **nous avons fait un bon petit g.,** we did ourselves damn well.

gueuletonner [gœltɔne], *v.i. P:* to guzzle, to have a good blow-out.

gueulette [gœlɛt], *s.f.* **1.** *Glassm:* opening (in furnace). **2.** *P:* pretty face.

gueulin [gœlɛ̃], *s.m. Fish:* bait (consisting of pieces of fish).

gueuloir [gœlwaːr], *s.m.* **1.** *F:* mouth, throat (considered as an instrument for the production of voice); **je l'ai relu avec le g. qui lui sied,** I read it over again in the right tone of voice, with the expression it needed; **il s'est levé pour dilater son g.,** he got up to give his throat a bit of exercise. **2.** *P:* loudspeaker.

gueusaille [gøzɑːj], *s.f. P:* rabble, riff-raff, scum.

gueusailler [gøzɑje], *v.i. P:* **1.** to live like a beggar. **2.** to hobnob with the rabble.

gueusard, -arde [gøzaːr, -ard], *s.* (*the f. is rarely used*) *F:* scoundrel, wretch.

gueusat [gøza], *s.m. Metall:* small pig.

gueuse[1] [gøːz], *s.f. Metall:* **1. g. de fonte,** pig; **g. des mères,** sow; **fer en g., g. de fer,** pig(iron); *Nau:* kentledge; **g. d'athlétisme,** heavy weight. **2.** pig mould.

gueuser [gøze], *A: F:* **1.** *v.i.* to beg; to be a beggar. **2.** *v.tr.* **g. son pain,** to beg, cadge, one's bread.

gueuserie [gøzri], *s.f. A:* **1.** (*a*) beggary, destitution; (*b*) begging, mendicity. **2.** wretched affair, poor show.

gueuset [gøzɛ], *s.m. Metall:* small pig.

gueusette [gøzɛt], *s.f. Bootm:* container (in which the colour tinting the vamps is put).

gueux, -euse[2] [gø, -øːz]. **1.** *s.* (*a*) beggar, tramp, vagabond; **vie de g.,** beggarly existence; *A: F:* **g. revêtu,** beggar on horseback; *Hist:* **g. de mer,** sea-beggar; (*b*) *F:* **mon g. de neveu,** my scamp of a nephew; (*c*) *Bot: F:* **herbe aux g.,** wild clematis, traveller's joy. **2.** *s.f.* **gueuse,** (*a*) (i) *A:* prostitute; (ii) *F:* **courir la gueuse,** to go wenching, to chase the skirts; to lead a wild life; (*b*) *F:* **la Gueuse,** the Republic. **3.** *s. A:* **gueux, gueuse,** (earthenware) foot-warmer (burning peat or charcoal). **4.** *a.* poor, poverty-stricken; **g. comme un rat d'église,** as poor as a church mouse.

Gugusse [gygys], *Pr.n.m. & s.m. F:* (= AUGUSTE) the funny man (at the circus).

gui[1] [gi], *s.m. Bot:* mistletoe.

gui[2], *s.m. Nau:* **1.** boom; **g. de la brigantine,** spanker boom. **2.** guy(rope).

Gui[3], *Pr.n.m.* Guy; *Hist. of Mus:* **G. d'Arezzo,** Guido d'Arezzo.

guib [gib], *s.m. Z:* guib, guiba, harnessed antelope; bushbuck.

guibolle [gibɔl], *s.f. P:* leg; *P:* pin; **jouer des guibolles,** to stir one's stumps.

guibre [gibr̥], *s.f. N.Arch:* cutwater; knee of the (ship's) head; **étrave à g.,** cutwater stem; *A:* **figure de g.,** figurehead.

guichart [giʃaːr], *s.m.* **1.** *Ecc.Cost:* band (of scapular). **2.** *Games:* (tip) cat.

guiche [giʃ], *s.f.* **1.** (*a*) *A.Arm:* shield strap; guige; (*b*) *Ven:* baldric (of hunting horn). **2.** *Ecc.Cost:* side bands (on habit of Carthusian monk). **3.** *Games:* (*N.Fr.*) (tip) cat. **4.** (*a*) *A:* side curl; love lock, kiss curl; (*b*) *pl.* curls (on the forehead, temples).

guichet [giʃɛ], *s.m.* **1.** (*a*) wicket (gate) (of prison, etc.); (*b*) spy hole, grille, judas, grating (in door); shutter (of confessional); service hatch (in restaurant, etc.); **g. de dépense,** buttery hatch; **g. des lépreux,** lepers' squint (in church). **2.** turnstile; entrance gate; *Rail:* (platform) barrier. **3.** (*a*) *Bank: Post:* position, *U.S:* wicket; **payer à ses guichets,** to pay over the counter; **g. fermé,** position closed; (*b*) booking office (window); *Th:* box office (window); **jouer à guichets fermés,** to play (i) before an invited audience, with admission by invitation, (ii) with all seats reserved in advance, (iii) to capacity, (iv) to members only; *P:* **les guichets sont fermés!** no go! nothing doing! not on your Nellie! **4.** slit, mouth (of letter box). **5.** *Cr:* wicket; **gardien de g., garde-g.,** wicket keeper; **c'est Martin qui est au g.,** Martin's in, Martin's batting (now), Martin is at the wicket.

guichetier [giʃtje], *s.m.* **1.** turnkey (of prison). **2.** booking clerk; box-office assistant; counter clerk (in bank); counter assistant, clerk (in post office).

guidage [gidaːʒ], *s.m. Mec.E:* **1.** (*a*) guiding (of moving part); (*b*) centring (on boring lathe). **2.** guides, guide rails, bars (of pile-driver monkey, etc.); sliding path. **3.** (*a*) *Elcs: etc:* guidance; **console, pupitre, de g.,** guidance console; **opérateur, servant, de g.,** guidance operator; **signaux de g.,** guidance signals; **g. en direction,** directional guidance; **g. à mi-course,** mid-course guidance; **g. terminal,** terminal guidance; **g. programmé,** pre-set guidance; **g. par fil,** wire guidance; **g. par inertie,** inertial guidance; **g. par infra-rouges,** infra-red guidance; **g. par tête chercheuse, auto-g.,** homing guidance; **tête de g.,** homing head; **g. par télécommande,** command guidance; **g. par mise sur vecteur,** vectoring guidance; **g. sur faisceau (électro-magnétique), g. par ondes dirigées,** beam-rider, beam-riding, guidance; **g. (radio-)astronomique, g. par visée astronomique,** (radio-)celestial guidance; (radio-)stellar guidance; **g. mixte par inertie et visée astronomique,** stellar-inertial, celestial-inertial, guidance; *Av:* **g. par radio-maillage, par radio-mailles,** grid-guidance; (*b*) *Anat:* **g. condylien,** condylar guidance, guide, condyle guidance.

guide[1] [gid], *s.m.* **1.** (*a*) (tourist, museum) guide; **g. de montagne,** mountain guide; (*b*) *Mil:* guide; *Mil.Hist:* soldier of the Guides (under the Empire); (*c*) guide, counsellor; **en tout sa sœur était son g.,** his sister was his guide in everything; **n'avoir d'autre g. que son caprice,** to have no other guide but one's whims; (*d*) *s.f.* girl guide; **g. aînée,** ranger; (*in Fr.*) **Guides de France,** Catholic girl guides. **2.** guide (book). **3.** *Tchn:* **g. de courroie,** belt-guide; **g. de sonnette,** guide post of a pile-driving ram; *Carp:* **g. d'onglet,** mitre fence (of saw); *I.C.E:* **g. de clapet,** valve-guide; *Mch:* **g. de la tête du piston,** slide bar, cross-head guide; *Nau:* **g. de drisse,** traveller; *Elcs:* **g. d'ondes,** wave guide; *El.E:* **g. de câble,** cable guide.

guide[2], *s.f. Equit:* rein; **grandes guides,** lead reins; **leçons de guide,** driving lessons; **tenir bien les guides,** to be a good driver, to drive well; **conduire à grandes guides,** to drive (i) tandem, (ii) four-in-hand; **mener la vie à grandes guides,** to live in lavish style; to go the pace; (*of pers.*) **c'est une fine g.,** he's a fine whip.

Guide[3] (le) [ləgid], *Pr.n.m. Hist. of Art:* Guido Reni.

guide-âne [gidɑːn], *s.m.* **1.** (*a*) book of standing instructions (in office, etc.); (*b*) (elementary) handbook of instructions ("how to do it"). **2.** writing lines, black lines (supplied with writing pad, etc.). **3.** *Tchn:* toother (used in the manufacture of combs); *pl. guide-âne(s).*

guideau, -eaux [gido]. **1.** *s.m. Fish:* **g. (de rivière),** kiddle. **2.** *Hyd:* guide vane.

guide-coke [gidkɔk], *s.m.inv.* coke sheet (in coke ovens).

guide-courroie [gidkurwa], *s.m. Mch:* strap guide, belt guide; *pl. guide-courroie(s).*

guide-feuilles [gidfœj], *s.m.inv. Typ:* taker-in.

guide-fil [gidfil], *s.m.inv. Tex:* reed.

guide-fil(s) [gidfil], *s.m. El.E:* cable guide; **tube g.-f.,** cable conduit; *pl. guide-fils.*

guide-lame [gidlam], *s.m.inv.* guard (of mowing machine).

guide-papier [gidpapje], *s.m. Typewr:* paper guide.

guider [gide], *v.tr.* to guide, conduct, direct, lead (s.o.); to drive (car, horse); to steer (boat); **g. un aveugle à travers une rue,** to lead a blind man across a street, to help a blind man to cross the street; **cavalier guidant son cheval,** rider leading his horse; *B:* **l'étoile qui guida les rois mages,** the star that guided the wise men; **c'est ce terrible désastre qui me guidait,** it was that terrible disaster that showed me the way (I should take); **g. un enfant dans le choix d'une carrière,** to advise, guide, a child in the choice of a career; **(avion, etc.) guidé par radio,** radio-controlled (aircraft, etc.).

guide-rope [gidrɔp], *s.m. Aer:* trail rope; drag; *pl. guide-ropes.*

guidon [gidɔ̃], *s.m.* **1.** *Cy:* handlebar; *F:* **moustaches en g. de bicyclette, de vélo de course,** handlebar moustache. **2.** *Mil:* (*a*) guidon, camp colour; (*b*) foresight, bead (of gun, rifle); **g. fin, plein,** fine, full, sight. **3.** *Nau:* (*a*) pennant, pendant (of senior officer, etc.); (*b*) burgee. **4. g. de renvoi,** reference mark (in book).

guidonnage [gidɔnaːʒ], *s.m. Min:* **1.** guiding (of cables, etc.). **2.** guides (of cable, of cage, etc.).

guifette [gifɛt], *s.f. Orn:* tern; **g. épouvantail, noire,** black tern; **g. moustac, à moustaches,** whiskered tern; **g. à ailes blanches, g. leucoptère,** white-winged black tern.

guignard, -arde [giɲaːr, -ard], *s.* **1.** *F:* unlucky person, Jonah. **2.** *s.m. Orn:* dotterel.

guigne[1] [giɲ], *s.f.* heart-cherry, gean; **g. noire,** black heart-cherry, blackheart; *F:* **se soucier de qch. comme d'une g.,** not to care a fig, a rap, a damn, a button, about sth.

guigne[2], *s.f. F:* bad luck; **porter la g. à qn,** to bring s.o. bad luck; **avoir la g.,** to be up against it; to be out of luck.

guigner [giɲe], *v.tr.* (*a*) to give a surreptitious glance at (sth.); *Cards:* **g. le jeu du voisin,** to look over one's opponent's hand; **g. une femme au passage,** to steal a glance at a woman (as she goes by); *abs.* **g. de l'œil, du coin de l'œil,** to give sidelong glances; (*b*) to look enviously at sth.; to want (sth.) (badly); **g. un héritage,** to covet a legacy; **g. un beau parti,** to be all out for a good match (= rich husband or wife).

guignette [giɲɛt], *s.f. Orn:* **g. perlée,** spotted sandpiper.

guignier [giɲje], *s.m.* heart-cherry(tree), gean.

guignol [giɲɔl], *s.m.* **1.** (*a*) = Punch; (*b*) = Punch and Judy show; puppet show; *Th:* **grand g.,** Grand Guignol; *F:* **faire le g.,** to play, act, the fool; (*c*) *P:* policeman, cop. **2.** *Av. etc:* (*a*) king post (of aircraft); (*b*) **g. d'angle,** bell crank; (*c*) **g. d'aileron,** aileron lever; **g. de béquille,** tail-skid lever; **g. de gouverne de direction,** rudder horn, rudder lever; **g. de gouverne de profondeur,** elevator lever; (*d*) *Mch:* travelling block.

guignolet [giɲɔlɛ], *s.m.* cherry brandy.

guignon [giɲɔ̃], *s.m. F: O:* bad luck (*esp.* in gambling); **je suis en g.,** I'm out of luck; my luck is out; **avoir du g.,** to have a run of bad luck.

guignonnant [giɲɔnɑ̃], *a. F: O:* provoking, irritating, aggravating.

guignot [giɲo], *s.m. Orn: F:* finch.

guilandine [gilɑ̃din], *s.f. Bot:* guilandina; bonduc (tree).

guilde [gild], *s.f.* **1.** *Hist:* g(u)ild; **g. de commerçants,** merchant guild. **2.** (record, book, etc.) club.

guil(e)din [gildɛ̃], *s.m. A:* gelding.

guili-guili [giligili], *s.m. F:* **faire g.-g. à un enfant,** to tickle, chuck, a child under the chin.

guillage [gijaːʒ], *s.m. Brew:* fermenting.

guillante [gijɑ̃ːt], *a.f.* **bière g.,** fermenting beer.

Guillaume [gijoːm]. **1.** *Pr.n.m.* William. **2.** *s.m. Tls:* rabbet(ing) plane; rabbet; **g. à onglet,** mitre plane; **g. à canneler,** fluting plane.

guilledin [gildɛ̃], *s.m. A:* gelding.

guilledou [gijdu], *s.m. F:* (*used only in*) **courir le g.,** (i) (*of man*) to run after the girls; to chase skirts; to be on the look-out for amorous interludes; (ii) (*of girl, woman*) to be a flirt; to have an eye for the opposite sex.

guillemeter [gijmɔte], *v.tr.* (**je guillemette, n. guillemetons; je guillemetterai**) *Typ: etc:* to put (word, passage) in inverted commas, in quotation marks; to quote (word, passage).

guillemets [gijmɛ], *s.m.pl. Typ:* inverted commas, quotation marks; *F:* quotes; **ouvrir les g.,** to open (the) inverted commas; **fermer les g.,** to close the inverted commas; **ouvrez, fermez les g.,** quote, unquote; **mettre une phrase entre g., encadrer une phrase de g.,** to put a sentence in inverted commas; **mots entre g.,** words quoted.

guillemot [gijmo], *s.m. Orn:* guillemot; **g. de Troïl, à capuchon,** common guillemot, *U.S:* common murre; **g. à miroir blanc,** black guillemot; **g. bridé,** bridled guillemot; **g. de Brünnich,** Brünnich's guillemot.

guiller [gije], *v.i.* (*of beer*) to work, ferment.

guilleret, -ette [gijrɛ, -ɛt], *a.* lively, gay, brisk (person, tune); broad, risqué (joke).

guillerettement [gijrɛtmɑ̃], *adv.* gaily, briskly.

guilleri [gijri], *s.m.* chirp, cheep, twitter (of sparrows).

guillochage [gijɔʃaːʒ], *s.m.* **1.** *Metalw:* (rose-) engine turning, chequering. **2.** = GUILLOCHIS.

guilloche [gijɔʃ], *s.f. Metalw:* rose-engine tool, chequering tool.

guilloché [gijɔʃe], *a.* **1.** engine-turned. **2. poulie guillochée,** bushed pulley.

guillocher [gijɔʃe], *v.tr.* to ornament with guilloches, to guilloche; to chequer; **tour à g.,** rose engine.

guillocheur [gijɔʃœːr], *s.m. Metalw:* (rose-)engine turner.

guillochis [gijɔʃi], *s.m. Art:* guilloche (pattern), chequered pattern (on gold, silver, etc.).

guillochure [gijɔʃyːr], *s.f. Metalw:* rose-engine ornamentation, chequering.

guillotinade [gijɔtinad], *s.f. A:* **1.** guillotining. **2.** mass guillotining, guillotining in batches.

guillotine [gijɔtin], *s.f.* **1.** (*a*) guillotine; (*b*) guillotining, decapitation; (*c*) *P:* **g. sèche,** solitary confinement. **2. fenêtre à g.,** sash window; **obturateur à g.,** drop shutter (of camera). **3.** guillotine (for cutting paper); **cisailles à g.,** guillotine shears.

guillotiné, -ée [gijɔtine], *a. & s.* guillotined (person); **le cadavre d'un g.,** the corpse of a man who has been guillotined.

guillotinement [gijɔtinmɑ̃], *s.m.* guillotining.

guillotiner [gijɔtine], *v.tr.* to guillotine.

guillotineur [gijɔtinœːr], *s.m.* guillotiner.

guimauve [gimoːv], *s.f.* (*a*) *Bot:* marsh mallow; (*b*) *F:* (i) bad poetry; (ii) mediocre song; **g. blonde,** insipid writing; (*c*) *Cu:* **(pâte de) g.,** marshmallow.

guimbarde [gɛ̃bard], *s.f.* **1.** Jew's harp, Jew's trump. **2.** *F:* **vieille g.,** ramshackle old vehicle, old rattletrap, old boneshaker, jalopy. **3.** *Tls:* router plane, grooving plane, plough.

guimées [gime], *s.f.pl. Paperm:* treble lines.

guimpage [gɛ̃paːʒ], *s.m. Tex:* gimping.

guimpe [gɛ̃ːp], *s.f.* **1.** (nun's) wimple. **2.** chemisette, tucker.

guimper [gɛ̃pe], *v.tr. Tex:* to gimp.

guinche [gɛ̃ːʃ], *s.m. P:* (*a*) (low-class) dance hall; (*b*) (public) dance, hop.

guincher [gɛ̃ʃe], *v.i. P:* to dance.

guindage [gɛ̃daːʒ], *s.m.* **1.** *Mec.E:* (*a*) hoisting (by windlass); (*b*) hoisting tackle, hoist. **2.** *Mil: etc:* (i) racking down, rack lashing; (ii) riband (of pontoon bridge).

guindant [gɛ̃dɑ̃], *s.m. Nau:* **1.** hoist, drop (of signal); hoist (of sail). **2.** hound(ing) (of lower mast).

guindas [gɛ̃dɑs], *s.m. Nau:* horizontal capstan, windlass.

guinde [gɛ̃ːd], *s.f.* **1.** hand(-operated) crane; *Th:* hoist (for shifting decor). **2.** *P:* car.

guindé [gɛ̃de], *a.* **1.** stiff, strained, unnatural; *F:* starchy (person); affected (language, etc.); academic, over-studied, stilted, stiff (style); **jeune homme g.,** (stiff and) starchy young man; *Th:* **g. dans un rôle,** stilted, affected, in a part. **2.** *Nau:* (*of anchor*) aweigh.

guindeau, -eaux [gɛ̃do], *s.m. Nau:* windlass; **barre de g.,** handspike; **g. à vapeur,** donkey (engine), steam winch.

guinder [gɛ̃de], *v.tr.* **1.** (*a*) to hoist, raise (with a windlass); to windlass; *Th:* to hoist (decor); (*b*) *Nau:* to send up, sway up (mast). **2.** *Mil: etc:* to rack down, lash down (bridge lashing, etc.).

se guinder. 1. *A:* to hoist oneself, to climb. **2.** to adopt a superior manner; **le récit se guinde un peu,** the (style of the) narrative is becoming somewhat strained, stiff. **3.** *Ven:* (*of bird*) to mount out of sight.

guinderesse [gɛ̃drɛs], *s.f. Nau:* mast rope, top rope.

guindrage [gɛ̃draːʒ], *s.m. Tex:* **1.** length of skein (of silk). **2.** reeling, spooling (of silk).

guindre [gɛ̃ːdr], *s.m. Tex:* small loom (used for doubling silk yarn).

Guinée [gine]. **1.** *Pr.n.f. Geog:* Guinea; **G. espagnole, portugaise,** Spanish, Portuguese, Guinea; **le golfe de G.,** the Gulf of Guinea; *Bot: F:* **herbe de G.,** Guinea grass. **2.** *s.f.* (*a*) *Num: A:* guinea; (*b*) *Tex: A:* Guinea cloth, Guinea cotton.

guinéen, -enne [gineɛ̃, -ɛn], *a. & s. Geog:* Guinean.

guingampois, -oise [gɛ̃gɑ̃pwa, -waːz], *a. & s. Geog:* (native, inhabitant) of Guingamp.

guingan [gɛ̃gɑ̃], *s.m. Tex:* gingham.

guingois [gɛ̃gwa], *s.m.* (*a*) *A:* skew; **esprit dans lequel il y a du g.,** crooked, warped, mind; **esprit de g.,** cross-grained disposition; (*b*) (*still used in*) *adv.phr.* **de g.,** askew, out of the straight; lop-sided; **chapeau de g.,** hat all askew; **tout va de g.,** everything's going wrong.

guinguet, -ette[1] [gɛ̃gɛ, -ɛt], *a.* (*of wine*) acid.

guinguette[2] [gɛ̃gɛt], *s.f.* **1.** (suburban) café (with music and dancing, *usu.* in the open). **2.** *A:* cottage in the country.

guinguettier [gɛ̃gɛtje], *s.m.* keeper of a *guinguette.*

guinois, -oise [ginwa, -waːz], *a. & s. Geog:* (native, inhabitant) of Guines.

guinot [gino], *s.m. Orn: F:* finch.

guiorer [gjɔre], *v.i.* (*of mouse*) to squeak.

guipage [gipaːʒ], *s.m.* (*action of, material for*) winding, taping, wrapping, lapping, covering; *El:* **fil à g. simple, double,** single-, double-lapped wire; **à g. en coton,** cotton-covered; *Mch:* **g. isolant,** insulating sleeve, wrapping.

guiper [gipe], *v.tr.* to wind (about); to tape, wrap, lap; *El.E: etc:* **g. un fil,** to cover a wire; **fil guipé coton,** cotton-lapped wire.

guipon [gipɔ̃], *s.m.* (a) *Nau:* tar brush, mop; pitch mop; (b) *Paint:* long-handled brush.

guipure [gipyːr], *s.f.* **1.** point lace, pillow lace. **2.** *El.E:* wrapping, lapping (of cable, etc.).

guirlandage [girlɑ̃daːʒ], *s.m. El.E:* wrapping, covering (for cables).

guirlande [girlɑ̃d], *s.f.* **1.** garland, festoon, wreath; **g. de perles,** rope of pearls; (*of ropes, etc.*) **faire g.,** to sag. **2.** mousing (of rope), mouse; marling. **3.** *N.Arch:* breast hook, fore hook.

guirlander [girlɑ̃de], *v.tr.* **1.** to garland, festoon; to hang (sth.) with garlands, with festoons. **2.** *Nau:* to mouse (hook, etc.); to marl down (rope).

guisard, -arde [gizaːr, -ard], *a. & s. Geog:* (native, inhabitant) of Guise [gɥiːz].

guisarme [gɥizarm], *s.f. A.Arms:* guisarme.

guise[1] [giːz], *s.f.* manner, way, fashion; **faire qch. à sa g.,** to do sth. in one's own way, in one's own time; **faire, agir, à sa g.,** to have one's (own) way; to do as one pleases; to go one's own way; to take one's own course; **à votre g.!** please yourself! **en g. de,** (i) by way of; (ii) instead of; **se servir d'un poignard en g. de couteau,** to use a dagger for, as, a knife; **des caisses en g. de chaises,** boxes by way of chairs.

guise[2], *s.f. Games:* tip cat.

guitare [gitaːr], *s.f.* **1.** *Mus:* guitar; **g. hawaïenne,** Hawaiian guitar; *A: F:* **c'est toujours la même g.,** it's the same old story. **2.** *Ich: F:* guitar fish. **3.** *Fish:* **corde à g.,** gimp.

guitariste [gitarist], *s.m. & f.* guitarist, guitar player.

Guite [git], *Pr.n.f. F:* (= MARGUERITE) Peggy; Peg.

guit-guit [gitgit], *s.m. Orn:* guitguit, honey creeper; **g.-g. bleu,** blue honey creeper.

guitoune [gitun], *s.f.* **1.** *Mil: P:* (a) dug-out, funk-hole, shelter; (b) tent; **coucher sous la g.,** to sleep under canvas. **2.** (*in Algeria*) hut, cottage.

guivre [giːvr̩], *s.f. Her:* serpent devouring a babe.

guivré [givre], *a. Her:* bearing a guivre.

gulaire [gylɛːr], *a. Anat:* gular, pertaining to the upper throat; **poche g.,** gular pouch (in frogs, etc.).

gulden [guldən], *s.m. Num:* guilder.

gulonique [gylɔnik], *a. Ch:* gulonic (acid).

gulose [gyloːz], *s.m. Ch:* gulose.

gulpes [gylp], *s.m.pl. Her:* golps.

gumène [gymɛn], *s.f. Her:* cable.

gummifère [gym(m)ifɛːr], *a. Bot:* gummiferous, gum-bearing, gum-yielding.

gummite [gymit], *s.f. Miner:* gummite.

gunitage [gynitaːʒ], *s.f. Const:* guniting.

gunite [gynit], *s.f. Const:* gunite.

guniter [gynite], *v.tr. Const:* to gunite.

guniteuse [gynitøːz], *s.f. Const:* cement gun.

gunnère [gynɛːr], *s.f. Bot:* prickly rhubarb, gunnera.

guppy [gypi], *s.m. Ich:* guppy.

guse [gyːz], *s.f. Her:* guze.

gustatif, -ive [gystatif, -iːv], *a.* gustative, gustatory (nerve, etc.).

gustation [gystasjɔ̃], *s.f.* gustation, tasting.

Gustave [gystaːv], *Pr.n.m.* Gustavus.

gutta-percha [gytaperka], *s.f.* gutta-percha; **g.-p. dentaire,** dental gutta-percha.

guttation [gytasjɔ̃], *s.f. Bot:* guttation.

guttère [gytɛːr], *s.f. Orn:* crested guinea fowl.

guttier [gytje], *s.m. Bot:* gamboge tree.

guttiféracées [gytiferase], *s.f.pl. Bot:* Guttiferae, Clusiaceae.

guttifère [gytifɛːr], *Bot:* (a) *a.* guttiferous; (b) *s.m.pl.* **guttifères,** Guttiferae.

guttiforme [gytiform], *a.* guttiform, guttate.

guttural, -aux [gytyral, -o]. **1.** *a. Anat: Ling:* guttural; **voix gutturale,** guttural, throaty, voice; *s.a.* FOSSE 3. **2.** *s.f.* **gutturale;** *Ling:* guttural.

gutturalement [gytyralmɑ̃], *adv.* gutturally; throatily.

Guy [gi], *Pr.n.m.* Guy; *Ecc:* **Saint G.,** Saint Vitus; *Med:* **danse de Saint G.,** St Vitus's dance.

guyanais, -aise [gɥijanɛ, -ɛːz], *a. & s. Geog:* Guianese.

Guyane (la) [lagɥijan], *Pr.n.f. Geog:* Guiana; **G. française,** French Guiana; *Hist:* **G. britannique,** British Guiana.

Guyenne (la) [lagɥijɛn], *Pr.n.f. A.Geog:* Guienne.

guyot [gijo], *s.m. Geol:* guyot.

guzla [gyzla], *s.f. Mus:* gusla, gusle, gousle, guzla.

gy [ʒi], *adv. P: O:* = OUI.

Gygès [ʒiʒɛs], *Pr.n.m. A.Hist:* Gyges.

gymkana [ʒimkana], *s.m.* gymkhana.

gymnase [ʒimnaːz], *s.m.* gymnasium.

gymnasiarque [ʒimnazjark], *s.m.* **1.** *Gr.Ant: Sch:* gymnasiarch. **2.** *Sp:* professional gymnast.

gymnaste [ʒimnast], *s.m.* gymnast; **g. sportif,** gymnast and all-round athlete.

gymnastique [ʒimnastik]. **1.** *a.* gymnastic. **2.** *s.f.* (a) gymnastics; **faire de la g.,** (i) to do gymnastics; (ii) to go in for gymnastics; **g. rythmique,** eurhythmics; *Med:* **g. passive,** passive movements; **g. corrective,** remedial gymnastics; **g. respiratoire,** breathing exercises; *F:* **il m'a fait faire une drôle de g.,** he put me through my paces more than somewhat; (b) **g. matinale,** morning exercises; *F:* daily dozen; (b) *Sch: F:* gymnasium.

gymnique [ʒimnik]. **1.** *a.* gymnic. **2.** *s.f.* science of gymnastics.

gymnite [ʒimnit], *s.f. Miner:* gymnite.

gymnoblaste [ʒimnoblast], *a. Nat.Hist:* gymno-blastic.

gymnoblastiques [ʒimnoblastik], *s.m.pl. Z:* Gymnoblastea.

gymnocarpe [ʒimnɔkarp], *a. Bot:* gymnocarpous.

gymnodactyle [ʒimnɔdaktil], *s.m. Rept:* gymno-dactylus.

gymnodonte [ʒimnɔdɔ̃ːt], *a. & s.m. Ich:* gymno-dont.

gymnoglosse [ʒimnɔglɔs], *a. Moll:* gymno-glossate.

gymnogyne [ʒimnɔʒin], *a. Bot:* gymnogynous.

gymnolémates [ʒimnɔlemat], *s.m.pl. Z:* Gymno-laemata.

gymnophiones [ʒimnɔfjɔn], *s.m.pl. Z:* Gymno-phiona.

gymnorhine [ʒimnɔrin], *s.m. Orn:* gymnorhina; piping crow.

gymnosome [ʒimnɔsɔm], *a. Moll:* gymnosomate, gymnosom(at)ous.

gymnosophie [ʒimnɔzɔfi], *s.f.* gymnosophy.

gymnosophiste [ʒimnɔzɔfist], *s.m. & f.* gymnoso-phist.

gymnosperme [ʒimnɔspɛrm]. **1.** *a. Bot:* gymno-spermous. **2.** *s.m.* gymnosperm.

gymnospermé [ʒimnɔspɛrme], *a. Bot:* gymno-spermous.

gymnospermie [ʒimnɔspɛrmi], *s,f. Bot:* gymno-spermy.

gymnostome [ʒimnɔstɔːm]. **1.** *a. Bot:* gymno-stomous. **2.** *s.m.pl. Z:* **gymnostomes,** Gymno-stomata.

gymnote [ʒimnɔt], *s.m. Ich:* gymnotus; *F:* electric eel.

gymnure [ʒimnyːr], *s.m. Z:* rat-shrew; **g. chinois,** Chinese shrew-hedgehog.

gynandre [ʒinɑ̃:dr̩], *a. Bot:* gynandrous.

gynandrie [ʒinɑ̃dri], *s.f. Bot:* gynandry.

gynandroïde [ʒinɑ̃drɔid], *a. & s.f. Med:* gynan-droid.

gynandromorphe [ʒinɑ̃drəmɔrf], *Ent:* (a) *a.* gynandromorphous; (b) *s.m.* gynandromorph.

gynandromorphisme [ʒinɑ̃drəmɔrfism], *s.m. Ent:* gynandromorphism.

gynécée [ʒinese], *s.m. Cl.Ant: Bot:* gynaeceum.

gynéco- [ʒinekɔ, -o], *comb. fm.* gynaeco-; **gynéco-cratie,** gynaecocracy.

gynécologie [ʒinekɔlɔʒi], *s.f.* gynaecology.

gynécologique [ʒinekɔlɔʒik], *a.* gynaecological.

gynécologiste [ʒinekɔlɔʒist], *s.m. & f.,* **gyné-cologue** [ʒinekɔlɔg], *s.m. & f.* gynaecologist.

gynécomastie [ʒinekɔmasti], *s.f. Med:* gynaeco-mastia, gynaecomasty.

gynécopathie [ʒinekɔpati], *s.f.* gynaecopathy.

gynérion [ʒinerjɔ̃], *s.m. Bot:* gynerium; **g. argenté,** pampas grass.

gyn(o)- [ʒin(o), -(o)], *pref.* gyn(o)-; **gynodioïque,** gynodioecious; **gynobase,** gynobase.

gynobasique [ʒinɔbazik], *a. Bot:* gynobasic.

gynocardique [ʒinɔkardik], *a. Ch:* gynocardic (acid).

gynodioïque [ʒinɔdiɔik], *a. Bot:* gynodioecious.

gynogénèse [ʒinɔʒenɛːz], *s.f. Biol:* gynogenesis.

gynogénétique [ʒinɔʒenetik], *a.* gynogenetic.

gynomonoïque [ʒinɔmɔnɔik], *a. Bot:* gynomo-noecious.

gynophore [ʒinɔfɔːr], *s.m. Bot:* gynophore.

gynostème [ʒinɔstɛm], *s.m. Bot:* column, gyno-stemium (in orchids).

gypaète [ʒipaet], *s.m. Orn:* **g. barbu,** bearded vulture, lammergeyer.

gyps [ʒips], *s.m. Orn:* **g. fauve,** griffon(-vulture).

gypse [ʒips], *s.m.* **1.** *Miner:* gypsum, plaster-stone. **2.** *Com:* plaster of Paris.

gypseux, -euse [ʒipsø, -øːz], *a. Miner:* gypseous.

gypsifère [ʒipsifɛːr], *a. Miner:* gypsiferous, gypsum-bearing.

gypsographie [gipsɔgrafi], *s.f. Engr:* gypso-graphy.

gypsophile [ʒipsɔfil], *s.f. Bot:* gypsophila.

gyrie [ʒiri], *s.f. P:* whining; bellyaching; fuss; **assez de gyries!** stop whining! **faire des gyries,** (i) to bellyache; (ii) to put on airs.

gyrin [ʒirɛ̃], *s.m. Ent:* gyrinus; gyrinid, whirligig beetle.

gyrinidés [ʒirinide], *s.m.pl. Ent:* Gyrinidae.

gyro [ʒiro], *s.m. Av: F:* gyroscope.

gyro- [ʒiro], *comb.fm.* gyro-; **gyrodactyle,** gyro-dactyle; **gyromancie,** gyromancy.

gyrocompas [ʒirɔkɔ̃pa], *s.m. Nau: Av:* gyro compass.

gyrodirectionnel [ʒirɔdirɛksjɔnɛl], *s.m. Av:* direc-tional gyro.

gyrohorizon [ʒirɔɔrizɔ̃], *s.m.* gyro horizon.

gyrolite [ʒirolit], *s.f. Miner:* gyrolite.

gyromancie [ʒirɔmɑ̃si], *s.f.* gyromancy.

gyromètre [ʒirɔmɛtr̩], *s.m.* gyrometer, rate gyro.

gyromitre [ʒiromitr̩], *s.m. Fung:* gyromitra.

gyropilote [ʒiropilot], *s.m. Av:* gyropilot, auto-matic pilot.

gyroplane [ʒiroplan], *s.m. Av.Hist:* gyroplane.

gyroscope [ʒiroskɔp], *s.m.* gyroscope; *Av:* **g. direc-tionnel,** directional gyroscope; **g. d'assiette,** trim gyroscope.

gyroscopie [ʒiroskɔpi], *s.f.* gyroscopics.

gyroscopique [ʒiroskɔpik], *a.* gyroscopic (top, etc.); *Nau:* **compas g.,** gyro compass; *Av:* **appareil g. de pilotage,** gyropilot; **horizon g.,** gyro horizon.

gyrostabilisateur [ʒirɔstabilizatœːr], *s.m.* gyro-stabilizer.

gyrostat [ʒirɔsta], *s.m.* gyrostat.

gyrostatique [ʒirɔstatik], *a.* gyrostatic.

gyrovague [ʒirɔvag], *s.m. Ecc.Hist:* gyrovague.

H

Words beginning with an "aspirate" h are shown by an asterisk.

H, h [aʃ], *s.m. & f.* (the letter) H, h; **h muet(te),** 'mute' h; **h aspiré(e), 'aspirate' h;** *s.a.* ASPIRER 2. (The *h* is never sounded in standard French.) *Tp:* **H comme Henri,** H for Harry; *Mil: etc:* **l'heure H,** zero hour (of operation timetable); **bombe H,** H bomb.

*****ha** [ɑ], *int.* 1. ah! 2. (*as laughter*) ha, ha! ha! ha! haw haw! 3. *s.m.inv.* **pousser des ha,** to cry ha!

*****hâ** [ɑ], *s.m. Ich:* tope.

habab(s) [abab]. 1. *a. & s. Ethn:* Habab. 2. *s.m. Ling:* **le h.,** Habab.

Habacuc [abakyk], *Pr.n.m. B.Hist:* Habakkuk.

*****habanera** [abanera], *s.f. Danc:* habanera.

habeas corpus [abeaskɔrpys], *s.m. Eng. Jur:* Habeas Corpus Writ.

habenaria [abenarja], *s.f. Bot:* habenaria.

habile [abil], *a.* (*a*) clever, skilful, able, resourceful, capable (workman, etc.); cunning, smart, artful, crafty (rogue, etc.); **mains habiles,** skilled hands; **façonner qch. d'une main h.,** to fashion sth. skilfully, with a cunning hand; **h. en tous les arts,** skilled in all the arts; **h. dans un métier, à faire qch.,** clever at a trade, at doing sth.; adept in sth.; **h. à travailler le bois,** skilled in woodwork; **être h. à la vente,** to be a good hand, to be smart, at selling things; **flatteur h.,** adroit flatterer; (*b*) *Jur:* **h. à succéder,** able, competent, qualified, to inherit; (*c*) *s.m. or f. Lit:* clever, astute, person.

habilement [abilmã], *adv.* cleverly, skilfully, ably, capably, resourcefully; *Lit:* promptly.

habileté [abilte], *s.f.* (*a*) ability, skill, skilfulness; **h. à faire qch.,** skill in doing sth.; **h. technique,** technical skill, ingenuity; (*b*) cleverness, smartness; **surpasser qn en h.,** to outwit s.o.; (*c*) *in the pl.* abilities; skilful manœuvres; **les habiletés du métier,** the tricks of the trade.

habilitant [abilitã], *a. Jur:* **lettres habilitantes,** enabling letters.

habilitation [abilitasjɔ̃], *s.f. Jur:* **h. de qn à faire qch.,** enabling of s.o. to do sth.

habilité [abilite], *s.f. Jur:* ability, competency, title; **avoir h. à hériter,** to be entitled to succeed.

habiliter [abilite], *v.tr. Jur:* **h. qn à faire qch.,** to enable, entitle, s.o. to do sth.; **compagnie seule habilitée pour développer une région,** company alone entitled, empowered, to develop a district.

habillable [abijabl], *a.* (*of pers.*) for whom it is easy to find suitable clothes; (*of things*) easy to arrange, adorn; *Com:* package.

habillage [abijaʒ], *s.m.* 1. preparing, preparation; (*a*) *Cu:* dressing; drawing and trussing (of poultry); cleaning (of fish); trimming (of meat); (*b*) *Arb:* pruning, trimming (of trees); (*c*) fitting, assembling, putting together (of watch, etc.); (*d*) *Typ:* (i) packing of cylinder; (ii) type run round a block; (*e*) *Tchn:* (*of boiler, etc.*) lagging; *Av:* covering; (*f*) *Tan:* tawing (of chamois and thin leather). 2. (*a*) *Com:* get-up, packaging (of goods); (*b*) *Nau:* appointments (of ship).

habillé [abije], *a.* 1. (*a*) dressed; *Mil:* fully, properly, dressed; **h. en femme,** dressed up, got up, as a woman; **habillé(e) de, en, bleu,** dressed in blue; **habillée d'un tailleur,** dressed in a suit; (*b*) clad; **h. chaudement,** warmly clad, dressed; (*c*) *Mec.E:* encased; *Typ:* packed (cylinder); *Const:* **un mur h. de bois,** a wall faced with wood. 2. (*of clothes*) smart, formal; *F:* dressy; **robe**

habillée, smart dress; **soirée habillée,** formal, full dress, *F:* dressy, occasion. 3. *s.m. Z: F:* **h. de soie,** pig.

habillement [abijmã], *s.m.* 1. clothing, dressing; effets d'h., wearing apparel, clothing; *Nau: F:* **le magasin d'h.,** the slop-room; *F:* the slops; *Mil:* **magasin d'h.,** clothing, equipment, store; **revue d'h.,** clothing inspection; **l'industrie de l'h.,** the clothing trade; *F:* the Rag Trade. 2. clothes, dress; **h. complet,** suit of clothes.

habiller [abije], *v.tr.* 1. to prepare; (*a*) *Cu:* to dress (meat, fowl); to draw and truss (poultry); to clean (fish); to trim (meat); (*b*) *Arb:* to prune, trim (tree); (*c*) to put (watch, etc.) together, to assemble (parts); *Typ:* **h. une gravure,** to run type round a block; *Typ:* **h. un châssis,** to fit up, equip, a chassis. 2. (*a*) to dress; **h. un enfant en soldat,** to dress up a child as a soldier; *F:* **h. qn,** to speak ill of s.o.; **h. qn de (la) belle façon,** to give s.o. a good dressing-down; (*b*) to clothe; to provide (s.o.) with clothes; **quel tailleur vous habille?** who is your tailor? **robe qui habille bien,** becoming, smart, dress; **h. qn de façon disgracieuse,** to dress s.o. up in unbecoming clothes; **h. ses pensées en phrases,** to clothe one's thoughts in words. 3. to cover (up), wrap up; **h. des meubles de housses,** to put loose covers on furniture; *Typ:* **h. le cylindre,** to pack the cylinder; *Com:* **h. un article pour la vente,** to get up, label, box, package, an article for sale.

s'habiller. 1. (*a*) to dress; to put one's things on; (*of priest, etc.*) to robe; **s'h. de noir,** to dress in black; **s'h. en femme,** to dress up as a woman; (*b*) **s'h. sur mesure,** en confection, to have one's clothes made to measure, to buy one's clothes ready made. 2. to dress (for dinner, for the evening); **il s'habille bien,** he dresses well, he's always well dressed.

habilleur, -euse [abijœːr, -øːz], *s.* 1. *Dressm: Th:* dresser. 2. *Tan:* dresser, tawer (of chamois leather); *Fish:* dresser.

habillure [abijyːr], *s.f.* join (in wire netting).

habit [abi], *s.m.* 1. dress, costume; *pl.* clothes, **mettre ses habits,** to put on one's clothes; **h. complet,** suit of clothes; **marchand d'habits,** old-clothes man; **son bel h. du dimanche,** his Sunday best; **h. de cour,** court dress; **habits royaux,** royal robes; **en h. ecclésiastique,** in clerical attire, garb. 2. (*a*) coat; **mettre h. bas,** (i) to take off one's coat; (ii) *F:* to die; **h. de cheval,** riding habit; *A: F:* **les habits rouges,** the redcoats (English soldiers); **h. vert,** member of the *Académie française*; (*b*) **h. de soirée,** *F:* **h. à queue de pie, en queue de morue,** (evening) dress-coat, swallowtail coat, tails; **être en h.,** to be in evening dress; in tails; *Mil: Navy:* in mess dress; **se mettre en h. pour dîner,** to dress for dinner. 3. (monk's, nun's) habit; (monk's) frock; **prendre l'h.,** to take the habit, to enter religion; (i) to become a monk; (ii) to take the veil; **prise d'h.,** taking (i) of the habit, (ii) of the veil; *s.a.* MOINE 1.

habitabilité [abitabilite], *s.f.* habitability, fitness for habitation.

habitable [abitabl], *a.* habitable, fit for habitation, liv(e)able.

habitacle [abitakl], *s.m.* 1. *B.Lit:* habitation, dwelling-place. 2. *Nau:* binnacle; **h. à compensateurs,** compensating binnacle. 3. (*a*) *Av:*

h. du pilote, du passager, cockpit; (*b*) *Aut:* (i) top; (ii) passenger space.

habitant, -ante [abitã, -ãːt], *s.* 1. (*a*) inhabitant; resident, dweller; **ville de 10,000 habitants,** town of 10,000 inhabitants; **les habitants de la forêt, des airs,** the denizens of the forest, of the air; (*b*) occupier (of house); (*c*) inmate (of house); **loger chez l'h.,** (i) *Mil:* to be billeted with the locals; (ii) to rent a room, to be put up, in s.o.'s house; (*d*) *P:* louse; *F:* maggot (in fruit, etc.). 2. (*in West Indies*) colonial settler, planter; (*in Canada*) habitant; small-scale farmer; *attrib.* (*inv.*): *Fr.C:* **style h.,** habitant style.

habitat [abita], *s.m.* 1. habitat (of animal, plant); biotope. 2. accommodation (of people).

habitation [abitasjɔ̃], *s.f.* 1. habitation; (*a*) dwelling, inhabiting; **taxe d'h.,** inhabited house duty; (*b*) *Jur:* cohabitation; (*c*) occupancy (of house). 2. (*a*) dwelling(-place), residence, abode; *Jur:* house, tenement; **n'avoir point d'h.,** to have no fixed abode; **(maison d')h.,** dwelling-house, dwelling; **immeuble d'h.,** residential building; **avoir son h. à . . .,** to reside at . . .; **h. à loyer modéré, H.L.M.** = council house; council flats; (*up to 1947*) **h. à bon marché, H.B.M.** = council house; **h. rurale,** farmhouse; (*b*) (*in West Indies*) colonial settlement, plantation; (*c*) **aire d'h.,** habitat (of animal, plant).

habité [abite], *a.* inhabited; **vol non h.,** unmanned space flight; **vaisseau spatial h.,** manned spacecraft; *F:* **fromage h.,** cheese that is alive (with maggots); **fruit h.,** maggoty fruit.

habiter [abite]. 1. *v.tr.* (*a*) to inhabit, to dwell in, live in (a place); **h. une jolie maison,** to live in an attractive house; **cette pièce n'a jamais été habitée,** this room has never been lived in; **pays peu habité,** sparsely inhabited country; (*b*) to occupy (house); (*c*) (*of idea, devil, etc.*) to possess; **il a toujours été habité de, par, la même conviction,** he was always obsessed by the same conviction; **cette idée l'habite,** this idea fills his thoughts; *B:* **habité par un démon,** possessed with, of, a devil. 2. *v.i.* (*a*) to live, reside, dwell; to have one's home (à, at); **h. à la ville, à la campagne,** to live in (the) town, in the country; **h. en Italie,** to live in Italy; **aller h. à la campagne,** to move into the country; **h. (dans la) rue Lebeau, (sur l')avenue Pasquier,** to live in, *U.S:* on, rue Lebeau, avenue Pasquier; (*b*) *Jur:* **h. avec qn,** to live, cohabit, with s.o.

habituable [abitɥabl], *a.* that can be habituated, accustomed (à, to).

habitude [abityd], *s.f.* (*a*) habit, custom, practice, use; **habitudes de propreté,** cleanliness; **la force de l'h.,** the force of habit; **faire qch. par pure h.,** to do sth. from mere habit, by sheer force of habit; **poussé par l'h. . . .,** from sheer force of habit . . .; *Prov:* **l'h. est une seconde nature,** use is second nature; **prendre, contracter, l'h. de faire qch.,** to acquire, start, the habit of doing sth.; to grow, get, into the habit of doing sth.; to fall into the way of doing sth.; **se faire une h. de . . .,** to make it one's practice to . . .; **avoir l'h., avoir pour h., de faire qch.,** to be in the habit of doing sth.; **il n'a pas l'h. de surfaire,** he is not given to overcharging; **n'ayant pas l'h. de courir . . .,** being unaccustomed to running

. . .; **son cheval a la vilaine h. de se cabrer,** his horse has a nasty trick of rearing; **prendre de mauvaises habitudes,** to get into bad habits; **avoir des habitudes de paysan,** to behave like a peasant; **adopter les habitudes d'un pays,** to adopt the customs of a country; **ne prenez pas l'h. de jouer aux cartes,** don't make a habit of playing cards; **ce n'est pas une h. chez moi,** I don't make a habit of it; **ce n'est pas dans mes habitudes,** it is not what I am accustomed to; **est-ce que j'avais l'h. de me plaindre?** was I in the habit of grumbling? **vous ne vous exercez pas autant que vous en aviez l'h.,** you don't practise as much as you used to; **habitude (du corps),** habit (of body); **à, selon, suivant son h.,** as is, was, his, her, custom; **se défaire d'une h.,** to get out of a habit; **perdre l'h. de fumer,** to get out of the way of, to give up, smoking; **faire perdre une h. à qn,** to break s.o. of a habit; **cela tournera en h.,** it will grow into a habit; **je suis un homme d'h.,** I am a man of settled habits; *adv.phr.* **d'h.,** usually, ordinarily; **comme d'h.,** as usual; **arriver plus tôt que d'h.,** to arrive earlier than usual; *adj.phr. A:* **ses vêtements d'h.,** his usual clothes; (*b*) knack; **c'est une affaire d'h.,** it's just a matter of knack; **je n'en ai plus l'h.,** I'm out of practice; (*c*) **avoir des, ses, habitudes (dans une maison),** to be a constant caller (at a house); to be very much at home (in a friend's house).

habitudinaire [abitydinɛːr], *s. Theol:* person who habitually commits the same sins.

habitué, -ée [abitɥe]. **1.** *a.* non-beneficed, unbeneficed (priest). **2.** *s.* (*a*) frequenter; habitual visitor; regular attendant; regular customer; habitué; **h. du cinéma,** cinema-goer; **c'est un h. de la maison,** he's a friend of the family; (*b*) non-beneficed priest.

habituel, -elle [abitɥɛl], *a.* usual, customary, regular; habitual (**à,** to); **un mal h.,** a customary evil; **avec sa courtoisie habituelle,** with his usual courtesy; **notre garçon h.,** our regular waiter; *F:* **c'est l'histoire habituelle, le coup h.,** it's the old story all over again, it's the same old story.

habituellement [abitɥɛlmɑ̃], *adv.* habitually, usually, regularly.

habituer [abitɥe], *v.tr.* to accustom, habituate, make familiar; **h. qn à qch.,** to accustom s.o. to sth.; **h. qn à faire qch.,** *A:* **de faire qch.,** to get s.o. into the habit of doing sth.; **h. qn à la fatigue,** to inure s.o. to fatigue; **h. un chien à obéir,** to train a dog in obedience.

s'habituer, to get used, to get, grow, accustomed, to become used (**à,** to); **nous y sommes habitués,** we are used to it; **s'h. à faire qch.,** to accustom oneself to do sth.; to get into the habit of doing sth.; **s'h. au froid,** to inure oneself to cold, to get inured to cold.

habitus [abitys], *s.m. Nat.Hist: Physiol:* habit(us).

***hâbler** [ɑble], *v.i. Lit:* to boast, brag; to talk big; to draw the long bow.

***hâblerie** [ɑbləri], *s.f.* **1.** bragging, boasting, braggadocio. **2.** exaggerated statement, piece of brag.

***hâbleur, -euse** [ɑblœːr, -øːz], *s.* boaster, braggart; **faire le h.,** to talk big; *attrib.* **parler h.,** big talk.

***haboob** [abub], *s.m. Meteor:* haboob; dust-, sand-, storm (in Africa).

habrocome [abrɔkɔm], *s.m. Z:* abrocome.

habromanie [abrɔmani], *s.f. Psy:* habromania, cheromania.

habronème [abrɔnɛm], *s.m. Vet:* habronema worm.

habronémose [abrɔnemoːz], *s.f. Vet:* habronemiasis, habronemosis.

***Habsbourg** [apsbuːr], *Pr.n.m. Hist:* **la maison de H.,** the House of Hapsburg.

Haceldama [asɛldama], *Pr.n.m. B:* Aceldama.

***hachage** [aʃaːʒ], *s.m.* chopping, cutting.

***hachard** [aʃaːr], *s.m.* (tinman's) shears, block shears.

***hache** [aʃ], *s.f.* ax(e); **h. à main,** hatchet; **h. de bûcheron,** felling axe; **h. de fendage, h. à fendre,** cleaving axe; **h. de charpentier,** adze; **h. de tonnelier,** howel; *A.Nau:* **h. d'abordage,** pole-axe; **coup de h.,** blow, stroke, with the axe; **fait, taillé, à coups de h.,** (i) rough-hewn, hacked out; (ii) *F:* done in a rough and ready fashion; *A. Arms:* **h. d'armes,** battle-axe, war-axe; **h. de guerre,** tomahawk; **enterrer, déterrer, la h. de guerre,** to bury, dig up, the hatchet; **aller au bois sans h.,** to set out unprepared; **pièce de terre en h.,** part of an estate dovetailing into another; enclave; **périr sous la h.,** to be sent to the scaffold; **porter la h. dans les dépenses publiques,** to axe, to apply the axe to, public expenditure.

***haché** [aʃe], *a.* **1.** (*a*) minced; (*b*) staccato, jerky (style, etc.); (*c*) **mer hachée,** cross sea; choppy sea. **2.** (cross-)hatched, hachured. **3.** hackly, jagged (outline).

***hache-fourrage** [aʃfuraːʒ], *s.m.inv.* (power-driven) foddercutter.

***hache-légumes** [aʃlegym], *s.m.inv. Cu:* vegetable-cutter, -mincer.

***hachement** [aʃmɑ̃], *s.m.* **1.** chopping, cutting, hacking. **2.** rough-hewing, hacking out.

Hachémite [aʃemit], *a. & s.* Hashimite, Hashemite.

***hache-paille** [aʃpɑːj], *s.m.inv. Agr:* chaffcutter.

***hacher** [aʃe], *v.tr.* **1.** (*a*) to chop (up); to hash (meat, etc.); **h. menu qch.,** to chop sth. up small; to mince sth.; *F:* **h. qn menu comme chair à pâté,** to make mincemeat of s.o.; *F:* **elle se laisserait h. pour vous,** she would allow herself to be chopped up alive for your sake; **le détachement s'est fait h. en pièces,** the detachment was cut to pieces; **visage haché de rides profondes,** face scored with deep wrinkles; (*b*) to hack (up), mangle (joint, manuscript, etc.); **récoltes hachées par la grêle,** crops cut up by the hail; (*c*) **discours haché par des quintes de toux,** speech interrupted by fits of coughing. **2.** *Engr: Mapm:* to (cross-)hatch, to hachure (drawing).

***hachereau, -eaux** [aʃro], *s.m.* hatchet, small axe.

***hachette** [aʃɛt], *s.f.* **1.** hatchet; **h. à marteau,** hammer-head hatchet. **2.** *Ich:* bleak.

***hacheur** [aʃœːr], *s.m.* chopper; *Pej:* **hacheurs de paille,** German speaking people, Alsatians.

***hache-viande** [aʃvjɑ̃ːd], *s.m.inv. Cu:* mincing-machine; mincer.

***hachis** [aʃi], *s.m. Cu:* (*a*) minced meat, forcemeat; *F:* **faire un h. d'un livre,** to make mincemeat of a book; (*b*) mince; **h. de veau,** minced veal; (*c*) hash; **en h.,** hashed; minced; **h. parmentier =** cottage pie, shepherd's pie; **h. d'échalotes, d'herbes,** chopped shallots, herbs.

***hashisch** [aʃiʃ], *s.m.* has(c)hish, bhang.

***hashischin** [aʃiʃɛ̃], *s.m.* **1.** has(c)hish-smoker, -eater. **2.** *Hist:* assassin.

***hachischine** [aʃiʃin], *s.f.* has(c)hish extract, resin.

***hachischisme** [aʃiʃism], *s.m.* has(c)hish intoxication.

***hachoir** [aʃwaːr], *s.m.* **1.** *Cu:* (*a*) chopping knife, chopper; (*b*) (i) chopping board; (ii) butcher's block. **2.** chopping machine, mincing machine; mincer. **3.** *Agr:* chaffcutter.

***hachot** [aʃo], *s.m.* small billhook.

***hachotte** [aʃɔt], *s.f.* (*a*) (slater's) lath hatchet; (*b*) (cooper's) adze.

***hachurateur** [aʃyratœːr], *s.m. Mapm:* device for hatching.

***hachure** [aʃyːr], *s.f. Engr: Mapm:* hatching, hachure; **carte en hachures,** hachured map; **système de hachures,** hatching, hachuring.

***hachurer** [aʃyre], *v.tr. Engr: Mapm:* to hatch, hachure (drawing, etc.); **vitres hachurées d'eau,** windows streaked with water.

hacienda [asjɛnda; asjẽda], *s.f.* hacienda.

***hack** [ak], *s.m. Turf:* hack.

***hacquebute** [akbyt], *s.f. A.Arm:* hackbut, harquebus.

***haddock** [adɔk], *s.m. Cu:* smoked haddock.

hadal [adal], *a. Oc:* **profondeurs hadales,** depths of over 6000 metres.

***hade** [ad], *s.f. Dial:* (*in S. of Fr.*) fairy.

hadène [adɛn], *s.m. Ent:* hadena (lepida).

Hadès [adɛs], *Pr.n.m. Gr.Myth:* Hades.

***hadith** [adit], *s.m Rel.H:* hadith, hadit; *pl. hadits, hadiths.*

***hadj** [a(d)ʒ], ***hadji** [adʒi], *s.m.* Hadji, Hajji (Mussulman who has made his pilgrimage to Mecca).

Hadrien [adriɛ̃], *Pr.n.m. Rom.Hist:* Hadrian; **mur d'H.,** Hadrian's Wall.

hadrome [adrɔm], *s.m. Bot:* hadrome.

hadromérides [adrɔmerid], *s.m.pl. Spong:* Hadromerina.

hadron [adrɔ̃], *s.m. Atom.Ph:* high-energy particle such as meson, nucleon, etc.

Hadullamite [adylamit], *s.m. or f. B.Lit:* Adullamite.

haemanthus [emɑ̃tyːs], *s.m. Bot:* haemanthus.

haematoxylon [ematɔksilɔ̃], *s.m. Arb: Bot:* **1.** haematoxylon. **2.** red dye from logwood.

haemoprotéidés [emɔprɔteide], *s.m.pl. Ent:* Haemoproteidae.

Hændel [ɛndɛl], *Pr.n.m. Mus.Hist:* Handel.

hafnium [afniɔm], *s.m. Ch:* hafnium.

***hagard** [agaːr], *a.* **1. faucon h.,** haggard. **2.** haggard, wild(-looking) (appearance, etc.); drawn (face).

***hagardement** [agardəmɑ̃], *adv.* in a wild manner, wildly.

***haggis** [agis], *s.m. Scot: Cu:* haggis.

hagiographe [aʒjɔgraf]. **1.** *a.* hagiographal; *B.Lit:* **les Livres hagiographes,** the Hagiographa. **2.** *s.m.* hagiographer.

hagiographie [aʒjɔgrafi], *s.f.* hagiography.

hagiographique [aʒjɔgrafik], *a.* hagiographic(al).

hagiologie [aʒjɔlɔʒi], *s.f.* hagiology.

hagiologique [aʒjɔlɔʒik], *a.* hagiologic(al).

hagiorite [agjɔrit], *a.* **moine h.,** Mount Athos monk.

***haha** [ɑ(h)ɑ], *int. & s.m.* **1.** *int.* (*denotes surprise, interest, etc.*) oh, really! ha-ha! **2.** *s.m.* surprise obstacle (ha-ha, haw-haw; sunk fence).

***hai** [e], *int.* = HÉ.

***haï(e)** [aj], *int.* (*denotes sudden twinge of pain*) ow! ouch!

Haïderabad [ajderabad], *Pr.n.m. Geog:* Hyderabad.

haidingérite [edɛ̃ʒerit], *s.f. Miner:* haidingerite.

haïdouk [ajduk], *s.m. Hist:* heyduck.

***haie** [ɛ], *s.f.* **1.** (*a*) hedge(row); **h. vive,** quickset hedge; **h. morte,** dead hedge; **h. barbelée,** barbed-wire (i) fence, (ii) entanglement; **entretien des haies et fossés,** hedging and ditching; **entourer un jardin d'une h.,** to hedge a garden; **chemin bordé, non bordé, de haies,** fenced, unfenced, road; (*b*) hurdle; *Sp:* **course de haies,** (short-distance) hurdle race; *F:* the hurdles; (*c*) line, row (of trees, etc.); hedge (of police, of troops); **faire, former, la haie,** to line the streets (or any processional route); **h. d'honneur,** guard of honour. **2.** *Agr:* beam (of plough).

***haïe** [ɑːj], *int.* (*to horse*) gee-up!

haïk [aik], *s.m.* hai(c)k, cloak (of Arab, *Mil:* of spahi).

***haillon**[1] [ajɔ̃], *s.m.* rag (of clothing); **être en haillons,** to be in rags and tatters.

***haillon**[2], *s.m. Dial:* wattle and daub hut (providing shelter for slate quarriers).

***haillonneux, -euse** [ɑjɔnø, -øːz], *a.* ragged, tattered.

***haim, *hain** [ɛ̃], *s.m. Dial:* **1.** *Fish:* hook. **2.** *Nau:* boathook.

***Hainaut** [ɛno], *Pr.n.m. Geog: Hist:* Hainault.

***haine** [ɛ(ː)n], *s.f.* hatred (**de, contre,** of); detestation; *Lit:* hate; **avoir la h. de qch., de qn; avoir qch., qn, en h.,** to hate, detest, sth., s.o.; **sa h. de, pour, la guerre,** his hatred of war; **prendre qch., qn, en h.,** to conceive a strong aversion for sth., s.o.; **s'attirer la h. de qn,** to incur s.o.'s hatred; **la h. qu'il vous porte,** his hatred for you, of you; the hatred that he bears you; **en h. de qch., de qn,** out of hatred of sth., of s.o., for s.o.; *Lit:* **exposé à toutes les haines,** exposed to widespread odium; **soulever la h. universelle,** to excite universal hatred.

***haineusement** [ɛnøzmɑ̃], *adv.* in a tone, with a look, of bitter hatred; heinously.

***haineux, -euse** [ɛnø, -øːz], *a.* full of hatred; heinous; **regard h.,** look of bitter hatred; **joie haineuse,** joy caused, inspired, by hatred.

***hainuyer, -ère** [ɛnɥije, -ɛːr], *a. & s. Geog:* (native inhabitant) of Hainault.

***hair** [ɛːr], *s.m. Ven:* one-year-old stag.

***haïr** [aiːr], *v.tr.* (**je hais** [ɛ], **tu hais, il hait, n. haïssons,** etc.; *imp.* **hais;** *otherwise regular*) to hate, detest (s.o., sth.); **h. qn comme la peste,** to hate s.o. like poison, like the plague; to loathe s.o.; **h. qn à mort,** to have a mortal hatred of s.o.; **être haï de, par, qn,** to be hated by s.o.; **elle hait qu'on la voie,** she hates to be seen; *F:* **je ne hais pas un bon dîner,** I have no aversion, no objection, *F:* I wouldn't say no, to a good dinner; **h. qn d'avoir fait qch.,** to hate s.o. for doing sth.; **je me hais d'avoir consenti,** I hate myself for consenting.

***haire**[1] [ɛːr], *s.f.* **1.** hair-shirt. **2.** *Tex:* (*a*) hair-cloth; (*b*) rough sackcloth.

***haire**[2], *s.f. A:* back-plate (of fining-furnace).

***haïssable** [aisabl], *a.* hateful, detestable.

***haïsseur, -euse** [aisœːr, -øːz], *s. & a. A:* hater.

***Haïti** [aiti], *Pr.n. Geog:* Haiti.

***haïtien, -ienne** [aitjɛ̃, -sjɛ̃, -jɛn], *a. & s. Geog:* Haitian.

***haje** [aʒe], *s.m. Rept:* haje.

***hakim** [akim], *s.m.* (*in Arabia*) Muslim physician and philosopher; hakim; *pl. hakims, hukama.*

halabe [alab], *s.f. Tex:* silk produced by *nephila madagascariensis.*

halabé [alabe], *s.m. Ent: nephila madagascariensis.*

halacaridés [alakaride], *s.m. pl. Arach:* Halacaridae.

***halage** [alaːʒ], *s.m.* (*a*) warping, hauling (of ship); **cale à h.,** hauling-slip; (*b*) towing; **chemin, corde, de h.,** towpath; towing-line; **h. à la cordelle,** tracking; *Jur:* **servitude de h.,** obligation (on owners whose properties adjoin a navigable

waterway) to maintain a towpath; **chemin de contre h.**, footpath.
*__halbi__ [albi], _s.m. Dial:_ fermented drink made of apples and pears.
*__halbran__ [albrɑ̃], _s.m. Orn:_ young wild-duck; flapper.
*__halbrené__ [albrəne], _a._ 1. broken-feathered. 2. _A: F:_ knocked up, fagged out.
*__halbrener__ [albrəne], _v._ (**je halbrène, n. halbrenons; je halbrènerai**) 1. _v.i._ to go duck-shooting. 2. _v.tr._ to clip the wings of (falcon).
__halcyon__ [alsjɔ̃], _s.m. Orn:_ halcyon, kingfisher.
*__halde__ [ald], _s.f. Min:_ 1. dump(heap); **h. de scories,** slag dump; **h. de déblais,** waste heap. 2. mouth (of mine).
*__hale__ [ɑːl], _s.m._ tow-line, -rope (of canal barge).
*__hâle__ [ɑːl], _s.m._ 1. (_a_) burning, tanning, browning (of skin by weather); sunburn; (_b_) tan, sunburnt complexion; **prendre facilement le h.,** to tan easily. 2. (_a_) hot, dry wind; (_b_) cold, shrivelling, wind.
*__hâlé__ [ɑle], _a._ 1. sunburnt, tanned, weather-beaten (complexion, etc.); **h. comme un romanichel,** brown as a berry. 2. (_of vegetation_) burnt up; shrivelled up, nipped.
*__hale-à-bord__ [ɑlabɔːr], _s.m.inv. Nau:_ inhaul.
*__hale-avant__ [ɑlavɑ̃], _s.m.inv. Nau:_ guy (hauling forward the lower topsail yard).
*__hale-bas, halebas__ [ɑlbɑ], _s.m.inv. Nau:_ down-haul, inhaul, inhauler (of flag, etc.).
*__hale-bouline__ [ɑlbulin], _s.m. F: Nau:_ land-lubber, bad sailor; _pl. hale-boulines._
*__hale-breu__ [ɑlbrø], _s.m.inv. Nau:_ (_a_) tricing-line, tripping-line; (_b_) heel-rope (of mast).
*__hale-dedans__ [ɑldədɑ̃], _s.m.inv. Nav:_ inhaul.
*__hale-dehors__ [ɑldəɔːr], _s.m.inv. Nau:_ (jib) out-haul.
__haléfis__ [alefi], _s.m. Lap:_ corner facet.
__haleine__ [alɛn], _s.f._ breath; (_a_) **avoir l'h. fraîche,** to have sweet breath; **avoir l'h. mauvaise, fétide,** to have offensive, bad, breath; **retenir son h.,** to hold one's breath; **attendre en retenant son h.,** to wait in breathless suspense; **tout d'une h.,** (i) all in one breath, in (one and) the same breath; (ii) at one go; **il ne fait pas une h. de vent,** not a breath of air is stirring; (_b_) wind; **avoir l'h. bonne, avoir de l'h.,** to have plenty of wind; **avoir l'h. courte,** to be short-winded; **il a l'h. courte,** he is soon at the end of his tether, he soon runs dry; **(re)prendre h.,** (i) to take breath; (ii) to recover one's breath, to get one's second wind; **perdre h.,** to get out of breath, to lose one's breath; **courir à perdre h.,** to run till one is out of breath; **discuter à perdre h.,** to argue non-stop; **faire perdre h. à qn,** to put s.o. out of breath; **ça m'a coupé l'h.,** it made me gasp; **hors d'h.,** out of breath, breathless; **hors d'h. d'avoir couru,** breathless with running; **travail de longue h.,** long and exacting task; **politique de longue h.,** long-term policy; **en h.,** in good condition, in good fettle, in good form; **mettre qn en h. pour qch.,** to put s.o. in the right mood, in the right disposition, for sth.; **tenir qn en h.,** (i) to hold s.o. breathless, to hold s.o.'s attention, to keep s.o. on the alert, in suspense; (ii) to keep s.o. in training; **se tenir en h.,** to keep oneself fit; to keep one's hand in.
__hale(i)née__ [alɔne, -lɛn-], _s.f._ strong breath (_usu._ unpleasant); whiff (of drink, etc.); **je m'avançai au milieu d'hale(i)nées de vin et de tabac,** I made my way among strong smells of wine and tobacco.
__hale(i)ner__ [alɔne, -lɛn-], _v.tr._ (**j'halène, n. halenons; j'halénerai; j'haleine, n. haleinons; j'haleinerai**) _A:_ 1. **h. qn,** to smell s.o.'s breath. 2. (_of hound_) to scent (quarry); _F:_ **h. un dessein,** to get wind of a plot. 3. (_a_) **le dragon halenait des flammes,** the dragon breathed out flames; (_b_) _v.i._ to pant, snort; to puff.
*__haler__[1] [ale], _v.tr._ 1. (_a_) to warp (ship); (_b_) to tow (barge, etc.); **h. à la cordelle,** to track (barge, etc.); (_c_) **h. une embarcation au sec,** to haul up a boat (on the beach). 2. _Nau:_ to pull, haul in, heave (rope, etc.); **h. en dedans, h. bas,** to haul in, down; **h. bas un pavillon,** to haul down a flag; _v.i._ **h. sur une manœuvre,** to haul, pull, on a rope; to heave at a rope. 3. _Nau:_ (_a_) **h. le vent,** to sail closer to the wind; (_b_) (_of the wind_) **h. arrière, le travers,** to haul aft, on the beam; **h. l'ouest,** to veer, shift, to the west.
*__haler__[2] [ale], _v.tr. Ven:_ to halloo (hounds) on (to the pursuit); _F:_ **h. les chiens après qn,** to set the dogs on s.o.
*__hâler__ [ɑle], _v.tr._ 1. (_of sun, etc._) to burn, brown, tan (s.o.). 2. (_of sun, etc._) to burn up (vegetation); (_of cold wind_) to shrivel up, nip (vegetation).
se hâler, to get sunburnt.
__halesia__ [alezja], _s.m. Bot:_ halesia.
*__haletant__ [altɑ̃], _a._ panting, breathless, out of breath; gasping (for breath); _F:_ puffing and blowing; **poitrine haletante,** heaving chest.
*__halètement__ [alɛtmɑ̃], _s.m._ panting; gasping; _F:_ puffing and blowing.
*__haleter__ [alte], _v.i._ (**je halète, n. haletons; je halèterai**) 1. to pant; to gasp (for breath); _F:_ to puff (and blow). 2. _A:_ **h. après les honneurs, après les richesses,** to pant after honours, after wealth.
*__haleur, -euse__ [ɑlœːr, -øːz], _s._ 1. (_a_) hauler; (_b_) (boat-)tower; **h. à la cordelle,** tracker. 2. _s.m._ steam winch.
*__half-track__ [alftrak], _s.m._ half-track vehicle.
__Halicarnasse__ [alikarnas], _Pr.n. A.Geog:_ Halicarnassus.
__halichère__ [aliʃɛːr], _s.m. Z:_ halichoerus.
__halicondri(d)e__ [alikɔ̃dri(d)], _s.f. Spong:_ halichondria.
__halicte__ [alikt], _s.m. Ent:_ halictus.
__halictes__ [alikt], _s.m.pl. Ent:_ Halictidae.
__halieutique__ [aljøtik]. 1. _a._ halieutic. 2. _s.f._ halieutics. 3. _s.m. pl. Gr.Lit:_ **les Halieutiques,** (Oppian's) Halieutica.
__halieutiste__ [aljøtist], _s.m._ 1. person connected with fishing. 2. person who sells fishing tackle.
*__halin__ [ɑlɛ̃], _s.m._ tow(ing)-rope, -line; heaving-line.
__haliotide__ [aljɔtid], __haliotis__ [aljɔtis], _s.f. Conch:_ haliotis, ear-shell; _Moll:_ abalone.
__halioti(di)dés__ [aljɔti(di)de], _s.m.pl. Moll:_ Haliotidae.
__halite__ [alit], _s.f. Miner:_ halite, rock salt.
__halitherium__ [aliterjɔm], _s.m. Paleont:_ halitherium.
__halitueux, -euse__ [alitɥø, -øːz], _a. Med: etc:_ moist, clammy, halituous (skin).
*__hall__ [ɔl], _s.m._ 1. (palatial) entrance hall; (hotel) lounge. 2. (_a_) _Ind:_ bay, shop, room; **h. des machines,** engine-room, -shop; **h. de montage,** assembly shop; (_b_) _Aut:_ open garage; (_c_) **h. de gare,** glass-roofed railway, etc., station concourse.
*__hallage__ [alaːʒ], _s.m. Com:_ market dues.
__hallali__ [alali], _s.m. Ven:_ mort; **sonner l'h.,** to blow the mort; **assister à l'h.,** to be in at the death, at the finish.
*__halle__ [al], _s.f._ 1. (covered) market; **h. aux poissons,** fish market; **les Halles (centrales),** the Central Market (in Paris); **sur la place de la h.,** in the market-place; _F:_ **langage des halles** = billingsgate; **mandataire aux Halles,** inside broker (in the Paris Halles, etc.); **Les Halles,** district in Paris (where the covered market was before it was removed to the suburbs); **h. aux blés,** corn exchange; **h. aux vins,** wine market; _A:_ **h. aux draps,** cloth-hall; _Arch:_ **église-halle,** hall-church. 2. _A:_ = HALL.
*__hallebarde__ [albard], _s.f. A.Arms:_ halberd, halbert; bill; _F:_ **il pleut, tombe, des hallebardes,** it's raining cats and dogs, in buckets; it's pouring.
*__hallebardier__ [albardje], _s.m. A.Mil:_ halberdier.
*__hallier__[1] [alje], _s.m._ 1. market-watchman. 2. stall-keeper (in the markets).
*__hallier__[2], _s.m._ (_a_) thicket, copse, brake; (_b_) _pl._ brushwood.
*__hallier__[3], _s.m. Ven:_ trammel(-net).
__hallomégalie__ [alɔmegali], _s.f. Path:_ hypertrophy of the hallux.
*__hallope__ [alɔp], _s.m. Fish:_ (large) dragnet.
__halloysite__ [alɔjzit], _s.f. Miner:_ halloysite.
*__hallstattien__ [alʃtatjɛ̃], _a. & s.m. Prehist:_ Hallstatt(an).
__hallucinant__ [al(l)ysinɑ̃], _a._ hallucinating (drug, etc.); haunting; **pensée hallucinante,** haunting thought; **ressemblance hallucinante,** striking, stunning, similarity, resemblance.
__hallucination__ [al(l)ysinasjɔ̃], _s.f._ hallucination, delusion; **être en proie à une h.,** to be under a hallucination; _Psy:_ **h. psychique,** pseudohallucination.
__hallucinatoire__ [al(l)ysinatwaːr], _a._ hallucinatory.
__halluciné, -ée__ [al(l)ysine], _a. & s._ hallucinated; _F:_ moonstruck (person).
__halluciner__ [al(l)ysine], _v.tr._ to hallucinate.
__hallucinogène__ [alysinɔʒɛːn], _Pharm:_ 1. _s.m._ hallucinogen. 2. _a._ hallucinogenic.
__hallucinose__ [alysinoːz], _s.f. Psy:_ hallucinosis.
__hallus, hallux valgus__ [alys, alyksvalgys], _s.m. Path:_ hallux valgus.
*__halma__ [alma], _s.m. Games:_ halma.
__halmature__ [almatyːr], _s.m. Z:_ wallaby.
*__halo__ [alo], _s.m._ 1. (_a_) _Meteor:_ halo; _F:_ **la gare s'annonce par un h. sur le ciel,** a patch of light in the sky shows that the station is quite near; (_b_) halo, areola (of nipple). 2. (_a_) _Opt:_ blurring; (_b_) _Med:_ glaucomatous halo, ring; (_c_) _Phot:_ halation.
*__halobate__ [alɔbat], _s.m. Ent:_ halobates.
*__halobios__ [alɔbjɔs], _s.m. Biol:_ halobiont.
*__halochimie__ [alɔʃimi], _s.f. Ch:_ chemistry of salts, halology.
__halogénation__ [alɔʒenasjɔ̃], _s.f. Ch:_ halogenation.
__halogénant__ [alɔʒenɑ̃], __halogène__ [alɔʒɛn], _Ch:_ 1. _a._ halogenous. 2. _s.m._ halogen.
*__halogénure__ [alɔʒenyːr], _s.m. Ch:_ halide; **h. d'alkyle,** alkyl halide; **h. alcalin,** alkal metal halide; **h. d'argent,** silver halide.
*__halographie__ [alɔgrafi], _s.f. Ch:_ halography; description of salts.
__haloïdation__ [alɔidasjɔ̃], _s.f. Ch:_ halogenation.
__haloïde__ [alɔid], _a. & s.m. Ch:_ haloid.
*__haloir, *hâloir__ [ɑlwaːr], _s.m._ 1. hemp kiln. 2. (cheese) drying-room.
*__halologie__ [alɔlɔʒi], _s.f. Ch:_ treatise on salts.
*__halomètre__ [alɔmɛtr], _s.m._ 1. _Ch:_ salt gauge. 2. _Cryst:_ halometer.
*__halométrie__ [alɔmetri], _s.f._ 1. _Ch:_ gauging of salts. 2. halometry.
__halomorphe__ [alɔmɔrf], _a. Geol:_ halomorphic.
*__halophile__ [alɔfil], _a. Bot:_ halophilous.
__halophyte__ [alɔfit], _Bot:_ 1. _a._ halophytic. 2. _s.f._ halophyte.
*__halosaure__ [alɔzoːr], _s.m. Ich:_ halosaurus.
*__halosel__ [alɔsɛl], _s.m. Ch:_ haloid.
*__halot__ [alo], _s.m._ rabbit-hole, -burrow.
__halotolérant__ [alɔtɔlerɑ̃], _a. Biol:_ euryhaline.
*__halotechnie__ [alɔtɛkni], _s.f. Ch:_ halotechny.
__halotrichite__ [alɔtriʃit, -kit], _s.f. Miner:_ halotrichite, feather-alum.
*__halte__ [alt], _s.f._ 1. stopping, stop, halt; **faire une h.,** to make a halt; to halt; to come to a halt, to a stop; **faire h.,** (i) _Mil:_ to halt, (ii) _Rail:_ (_of train_) to stop, to call (at station); **faire faire h. à une troupe,** to halt a troop; _Mil:_ **h. horaire** = regular halt after fifty minutes' marching (in infantry); **grande h.,** mealtime halt. 2. (_a_) stopping place, resting place; (_b_) _Rail:_ halt, wayside station. 3. _int._ **h.(-là)!** stop! _Mil:_ halt!
*__halter__ [alte], _v.i. O:_ to stop, to come to a stop.
__haltère__ [altɛːr], _s.m._ 1. dumb-bell; bar-bell; **faire des haltères,** to do dumb-bell exercises. 2. _pl. Ent:_ poisers (of diptera).
*__halte-repas__ [alt(ə)rəpɑ], _s.f. Mil:_ halt for food; _pl. haltes-repas._
__haltérophile__ [alterɔfil], _s.m._ weight lifter.
__haltérophilie__ [alterɔfili], _s.f._ weight lifting.
*__hamac__ [amak], _s.m. Nau: etc:_ hammock; **crocher, décrocher, un h.,** to sling, unsling, a hammock; **h. à cadre, à l'anglaise,** cot.
*__hamada__ [amada], _s.f. Geol:_ ham(m)ada.
__hamadryade__ [amadri(j)ad], _s.f._ 1. _Gr.Myth:_ hamadryad, dryad, wood nymph, tree nymph. 2. _Rept:_ hamadryas, hamadryad, king-cobra.
__hamadryas__ [amadri(j)as], _s.m. Z:_ hamadryad, Arabian baboon.
__hamamélidacées__ [amamelidase], _s.f.pl. Bot:_ Hamamelidacea.
__hamamélis__ [amamelis], _s.m. Bot:_ hamamelis, witch hazel.
*__hambergite__ [ɑ̃bɛrʒit], _s.f. Miner:_ hambergite.
*__Hambourg__ [ɑ̃buːr]. 1. _Pr.n.m. Geog:_ Hamburg. 2. _s.m._ (i) keg (of salted fish), (ii) beer cask.
*__hambourgeois, -oise__ [ɑ̃burʒwa, -waːz], _Geog:_ 1. _a._ of Hamburg. 2. (_a_) _s._ Hamburger; (_b_) _s.m. F:_ plain clothes (police)man. 3. _s.f._ **hambourgeoise,** special taffeta for ribbons and dresses.
__hamburger__ [ɑ̃byrʒɛːr, -gœːr], _s.m. Cu:_ hamburger.
*__hameau, -eaux__ [amo], _s.m._ hamlet; _Mil:_ **h. stratégique,** fortified hamlet.
__hameçon__ [amsɔ̃], _s.m._ (fish)hook; **h. sans œillet,** blind hook; **garnir un h.,** to bait a hook; **prendre un poisson à l'h.,** to hook a fish; **prendre l'h.,** (_of fish_) to take the hook; _F:_ (_of pers._) to swallow the bait; **mordre à l'h.,** to rise to the bait.
__hameçonné__ [amsɔne], _a._ 1. (_of fish_) caught on a hook, hooked; (_of pers._) enticed, allured (by). 2. (_of line, etc._) fitted with hooks. 3. _Bot: etc:_ barbed (spike, etc.).
__hameçonner__ [amsɔne], _v.tr._ 1. to hook (fish). 2. to put hooks on (line).
*__hamelia__ [amelja], _s.m. Bot:_ hamelia.
__hamiltonia__ [amiltɔnja], _s.m. Bot:_ Hamiltonia.
__hamiltonien, -ienne__ [amiltɔnjɛ̃, -jɛn], _a. Phil: Mth:_ Hamiltonian.
__haminée__ [amine], _s.f. Moll:_ Haminoea.
__hamitique__ [amitik], _a. & s.m. Ling:_ Hamitic.
__hamlinite__ [ɑ̃linit], _s.f. Miner:_ hamlinite.
*__hammam__ [amam], _s.m._ Turkish baths.
*__hammerless__ [amœrlɛs], _s.m._ hammerless (gun).

***hampe**[1] [ɑ̃:p], *s.f.* **1.** (*a*) staff, pole (of flag, etc.); stave, shaft (of spear, halbert); (*b*) handle (of brush, etc.); shank (of fish-hook). **2.** *Bot:* scape, stem; **h. (florale)**, spike. **3.** *Typ:* vertical line of the letters t, h, p, etc.; ascender, or descender of a letter (as the case may be).
***hampe**[2], *s.f. Cu:* (*a*) thin flank (of beef); (*b*) breast of venison.
***hampé** [ɑ̃pe], *a.* mounted (on staff).
***hampette** [ɑ̃pɛt], *s.f.* handle (of brush, etc.); shank (of fish-hook).
***hamster** [amstɛ:r], *s.m.* (*a*) *Z:* hamster; **h. roux,** golden hamster; (*b*) *F:* hoarder (of food in times of scarcity).
hamule [amyl], *s.m. Ent: Biol:* hamulus.
hamuleux, -euse [amylø, -ø:z], *a. Bot:* hamular.
***han** [ɑ̃], *int.* (*sound of breath accompanying violent effort*) **pousser un h. à chaque coup,** to give a grunt at every stroke, at every breath; (*uttered by a man handling an axe, sledgehammer, etc.*) huh!
Hanak [anak], *Pr.n.m. B.Lit:* Anak.
***hanap** [anap], *s.m. A:* goblet, tankard, hanap.
***hanapier** [anapje], *s.m. A:* hanaper.
***hanche** [ɑ̃:ʃ], *s.f.* **1.** hip; **les (deux) poings sur les hanches,** (with his) hands on (his) hips; with arms akimbo; **avoir les hanches larges,** to have large hips; to be broad-hipped; *F:* **mettre le poing sur la h.,** to strike an attitude; **tour de hanches,** (i) hip measurement; (ii) *Wr:* cross-buttock; *Dressm:* **fausses hanches,** hip-pads. **2.** (*a*) haunch (of horse); *pl.* hind-quarters; (*b*) hook (of ox, etc.); (*c*) coxa (of insect); (*d*) *Cer:* rounded centre (of pot, urn, etc.). **3.** *Mec.E: etc:* **hanches d'une chèvre,** sheers, sheer-legs. **4.** *Nau:* quarter (of ship); **h. sous le vent,** lee quarter; **h. du vent,** weather quarter; **par la h.,** on the quarter.
***hanché** [ɑ̃ʃe], *a.* (*at drill*) **dans la position hanchée,** (standing) at ease; **prendre la position hanchée,** to stand at ease.
***hanchement** [ɑ̃ʃmɑ̃], *s.m. Lit:* the projecting of one hip (to strike an attitude); *Sculp:* Gothic slouch, slouching from the hips.
***hancher** [ɑ̃ʃe], *v.i.* **1.** to move the hips (in walking). **2.** to stand with the weight of the body on one leg. **3.** to limp from the hip. **4.** *v.tr.* to make (a statue) stand with the weight on one leg (thus forming a Gothic slouch), to give a Gothic slouch to (a statue).
se hancher, (i) (*at drill*) to stand at ease; (ii) to strike an attitude.
***hand-ball** [ɑ̃dbal], *s.m. Sp:* handball; **h.-b. à sept.,** indoor handball; **h.-b. à onze,** field handball.
***handicap** [ɑ̃dikap], *s.m.* (*a*) *Sp:* handicap; (*b*) handicap, disadvantage; **combler le h.,** to overcome the handicap; **il bégayait mais il a réussi à vaincre ce h.,** he used to stutter but he managed to overcome this handicap.
***handicapage** [ɑ̃dikapa:ʒ], *s.m. Sp:* handicapping.
handicapé, -ée [ɑ̃dikape], *a. & s.* handicapped (person); **enfant h.,** handicapped child; **h. physique,** physically handicapped; **les handicapés,** the handicapped, the disabled.
***handicaper** [ɑ̃dikape], *v.tr.* (*a*) *Sp:* to handicap; (*b*) to handicap, to put at a disadvantage.
***handicapeur** [ɑ̃dikapœ:r], *s.m. Sp:* handicapper.
***hanebane** [anban], *s.f. Bot:* henbane.
***hanet** [anɛ], *s.m.* **1.** tent rope. **2.** *Nau:* (*a*) reef line, point, nettle; (*b*) **les hanets de hamac,** the hammock lashings.
***hangar** [ɑ̃ga:r], *s.m.* **1.** (open) shed, shelter; **h. à marchandises,** goods depot; **h. à bateaux,** boathouse; **h. de dock, de quai,** dock shed, transit shed. **2.** *Av:* hangar; **h. orientable,** revolving hangar; **h. démontable,** portable hangar; **aire de h.,** hangar floor.
Hankéou [ɑ̃keu], *Pr.n.m. Geog:* Hankow.
***hanneton** [antɔ̃], *s.m.* (*a*) *Ent:* cockchafer, maybug; **h. vert,** rose-beetle, rose-chafer; **h. de la Saint-Jean,** garden chafer; *F:* **avoir un h. dans le plafond,** to have a bee in one's bonnet; *F:* **il est étourdi comme un h., c'est un vrai h.,** he's (completely) scatterbrained; *F:* **un froid qui n'est pas piqué des hannetons,** intense cold; (*b*) *Tex:* **soucis d'h., sourcils de h.,** tufted fringes.
***hannetonnage** [antɔna:ʒ], *s.m.* clearing (trees) of cockchafers.
***hannetonner** [antɔne]. **1.** *v.tr.* to clear (trees) of cockchafers. **2.** *v.i.* (*a*) to destroy cockchafers; (*b*) *F:* to be absentminded; to say, do, the wrong thing.
Hannon [anɔ̃], *Pr.n.m. Hist:* Hanno.
***hannuyer, -ère** [anɥije, -ɛ:r], *a. & s. Geog:* (native, inhabitant) of Hainault.

***Hanovre** [anɔ:vr], *Pr.n.m. Geog:* (town of) Hanover; **le H.,** (the state of) Hanover.
***hanovrien, -enne** [anɔvri(j)ɛ̃, -ɛn], *a. & s. Geog:* Hanoverian.
***hansar(d)** [ɑ̃sa:r], *s.m. Tls:* pit-saw, cross-cut saw.
***hansart** [ɑ̃sa:r], *s.m. Dial:* (*W.Fr.*) butcher's chopper.
***hanse**[1] [ɑ̃:s], *s.f. Hist:* Hanse; **la H.,** the Hanseatic league, the Hanse towns.
***hanse**[2], *s.f. Ind:* pin-shank.
***hanséate** [ɑ̃seat], *a. & s. Hist:* (native, inhabitant) of one of the Hanse towns.
***hanséatique** [ɑ̃seatik], *a. Hist:* Hanseatic; **la Ligue h.,** the Hanseatic League.
***hanté** [ɑ̃te], *a.* haunted (house, etc.).
***hantement** [ɑ̃tmɑ̃], *s.m. A:* **1.** frequenting, haunting. **2.** haunting memory.
***hanter** [ɑ̃te], *v.tr.* (*a*) *O: Lit:* to frequent, haunt; **h. la mauvaise compagnie,** to keep bad company; *Prov:* **dis-moi qui tu hantes et je te dirai qui tu es,** a man is known by the company he keeps; (*b*) (*of ghost*) to haunt (house); (*c*) (*of idea, etc.*) to obsess (s.o.); **l'idée du suicide le hante,** he is obsessed by the idea of suicide; **les rêves qui hantent son sommeil,** the dreams that haunt his sleep; **être hanté par une idée,** to be obsessed by an idea, to have an idea on the brain.
***hanteur, -euse** [ɑ̃tœ:r, -ø:z], *s. Lit:* haunter, frequenter.
***hantise** [ɑ̃ti:z], *s.f.* **1.** *A:* frequentation, intimacy. **2.** haunting memory; obsession; *Psy:* perseveration.
***Haourân (le)** [ləaurɑ:n], *Pr.n.m. Geog:* Jebel Hauran.
***Haoussa** [ausa], ***Haousa** [auza]. **1.** *Pr.n.m. Geog:* Hausaland. **2.** *s.m.pl.* **les Haoussas,** the Hausas. **3.** *s.m. Ling:* **le h.,** (the) Hausa (language).
***hapalemur** [apaləmy:r], *s.m. Z:* gentle(-)lemur.
***hapalidés** [apalide], *s.m.pl. Z:* Hapalidae.
***hapalotidés** [apalɔtide], *s.m.pl. Z:* Dipopidae; kangaroo-rat family.
hapax (legomenon) [apaks (legɔmenɔn)], *s.m. Ling:* hapax (legomenon); *pl. hapax (legomena).*
haplobiontique [aplɔbjɔ̃tik], *a. Biol:* haplobiontic.
haplographie [aplɔgrafi], *s.f.* haplography.
haploïde [aplɔid], *a. Biol:* haploid.
haploïdie [aplɔidi], *s.f. Biol:* haploidy.
haplologie [aplɔlɔʒi], *s.f. Gram: Phonetics:* haplology.
haplome[1] [aplom], *s.m. Biol:* genom.
haplome[2], *s.m. Ecc:* haploma.
haplomes [aplom], *s.m.pl. Ich:* Haplomi.
haplomitose [aplɔmito:z], *s.f. Biol:* haplomitosis.
haplonte [aplɔ̃:t], *s.m. Biol:* haplont.
haplopétale [aplɔpetal], *a. Bot:* haplopetalous.
haplophase [aplɔfɑ:z], *s.f. Biol:* haplophase.
***happant** [apɑ̃], *a.* (*of clay, etc.*) adhesive, adhering (when damped).
***happe** [ap], *s.f.* **1.** (*a*) *Carp: etc:* (i) cramp, (joiner's) dogs; (ii) G cramp; (*b*) *Metall:* crucible tongs; (*c*) *Const:* cramp iron. **2.** staple; **anneau à h.,** ring and staple. **3.** handle, ear, lug (of boiler, etc.). **4.** *Veh:* clout (of axle).
***happelourde** [aplurd], *s.f. A:* **1.** imitation jewel; piece of paste. **2.** *F:* (*a*) showy (but unsound) horse; (*b*) person blessed with more good looks than sense.
***happement** [apmɑ̃], *s.m.* **1.** snapping (up), seizing, snatching. **2.** adhering, clinging, sticking (of clay, of cigarette, to the lips, etc.).
***happer** [ape]. **1.** *v.tr.* (*of birds, etc.*) to snap up, snatch, seize, catch (insects, etc.); **ma robe fut happée par la porte,** my dress caught in the door; *F:* **être happé par un gendarme,** to be nicked by the fuzz; **auto happée par un train,** car caught by a train (at level crossing). **2.** *v.i.* **h. à la langue, aux lèvres,** to stick, adhere, cling, to the tongue, to the lips.
***happeur** [apœ:r], *s.m.* **1.** clip (for papers). **2.** person who snatches at everything within reach, grabber.
haptène [aptɛn], *s.m. Bio-Ch:* hapten(e).
haptique [aptik], *a. Physiol:* haptic.
haptoglobine [aptɔglɔbin], *s.f. Bio-Ch:* haptoglobin.
haptomètre [aptɔmɛtr], *s.m. Med:* haptometer.
haptophore [aptɔfɔ:r], *s.f. Biol: Ch:* haptophore.
haptotropisme [aptɔtrɔpism], *s.m. Biol:* haptotropism.
***haque** [ɑk], *s.f.* **1.** *Agr:* strong dibbler for planting vines. **2.** *Fish:* **harengs à la h.,** salted herring used as bait.
***haquebute** [akbyt], *s.f. A.Arm:* hackbut, harquebus.

***haquebutier** [akbytje], *s.m. A.Mil:* hackbuteer, hackbutter.
***haquenée** [akne], *s.f.* (*a*) *A:* palfrey; (*b*) hack, quiet horse; ambling mare; **aller à la h.,** to amble along; *F:* **une grande h.,** a tall gawky woman; *A:* **aller sur la h. des cordeliers,** to go, ride, on Shanks's mare.
***haquet** [akɛ], *s.m.* (narrow) dray (for casks); *Mil:* **h. à bateau, à ponton,** pontoon wag(g)on; **h. à main,** hand cart.
***haquetier** [aktje], *s.m.* drayman.
hara-kiri [arakiri], *s.m.* hara-kiri; *pl. hara-kiris.*
***harangue** [arɑ̃:g], *s.f.* (*a*) harangue; speech; (*b*) *F:* (i) boring speech; (ii) sermon, telling-off.
***haranguer** [arɑ̃ge], *v.tr.* (*a*) to harangue; (*b*) *F:* to lecture (s.o.); *abs. F:* to hold forth; to spout.
***harangueur** [arɑ̃gœ:r], *s.m.* (*a*) *A:* orator, speaker; (*b*) *Pej:* speechifier, tub-thumper; **grand h. de foules,** great mob orator.
***haras** [arɑ], *s.m.* **1.** stud farm, horse-breeding establishment, haras. **2.** stud.
***harassant** [arasɑ̃], *a.* tiring, fatiguing.
***harasse** [aras], *s.f.* (large) crate (for glass, etc.); skip.
***harassé** [arase], *a.* tired, worn-out, exhausted.
***harassement** [arasmɑ̃], *s.m.* **1.** (*a*) harassing, worrying; (*b*) harassment. **2.** fatigue, exhaustion.
***harasser** [arase], *v.tr.* (*a*) to tire (out), exhaust; to override (horse); (*b*) to harass, worry.
se harasser, to tire oneself; to worry.
***harcelage** [arsəla:ʒ], *s.m. O:* = HARCÈLEMENT.
***harcelant** [arsəlɑ̃], *a.* harassing, harrying, tormenting, worrying; **besoin h.,** impelling need.
***harcèlement** [arsɛlmɑ̃], *s.m.* **1.** (act of) harassing, harrying, tormenting, badgering; *Mil:* **tir de h.,** harassing fire; **guerre de h.,** guerilla war. **2.** torment, worry.
***harceler** [arsəle], *v.tr.* (**je harcelle, n. harcelons; je harcèlerai**) to harass, worry, torment; to harry, to keep (the enemy under pressure; to bait (an animal); *Av: F:* to buzz (an aircraft); **h. qn de questions,** to badger, ply, pester, plague, s.o. with questions; **h. qn pour obtenir qch.,** to pester s.o. in order to obtain sth.; **harcelé de tous côtés,** hard pressed on all sides; **être harcelé par ses créanciers,** to be dunned, harried, by one's creditors; **elle le harcèle de querelles,** she is always at him, always nagging at him.
***harcèlerie** [arsɛlri], *s.f. A:* worry, persecution.
***harceleur, -euse** [arsəlœ:r, -ø:z]. **1.** *a.* harassing, worrying. **2.** *s.* tormentor, harasser, worrier.
***harde**[1] [ard], *s.f.* (*a*) *Ven:* herd, bevy (of roe deer); sounder (of swine); (*b*) flock (of birds of prey); (*c*) herd (of wild horses, of wild animals).
***harde**[2], *s.f. Ven:* **1.** leash (for hounds). **2.** set of two, four, or six hounds coupled together.
***hardé** [arde], *a.m.* soft-shelled (egg).
***harder**[1] [arde], *v.tr. Ven:* to leash, couple (hounds in twos, fours, or sixes).
***harder**[2] **(se)**, *v.pr.* (*a*) (*of deer*) to herd; (*b*) (*of hunted stag*) to seek refuge in the herd.
***hardes** [ard], *s.f.pl.* **1.** (*a*) *A.Jur:* personal belongings; (*b*) *Nau:* everything contained in a sailor's trunk. **2.** (worn) clothes, wearing apparel; *F:* togs; **marchand(e) de h.,** old-clothes man, wardrobe dealer.
***hardi** [ardi], *a.* (*a*) bold, hardy, audacious; daring, fearless; **il est assez h. avec les femmes,** he is not shy with women; **écriture hardie,** bold hand(writing); **imagination hardie, talent h.,** inventive imagination, talent; **parler h.,** open, daring, way of talking; (*of artist*) **avoir le pinceau h.,** to wield a bold brush; **h. à agir,** bold to act; **décolleté h.,** provoking neckline; *s.a.* COQ[1]; (*b*) rash, venturesome (undertaking, etc.); (*c*) impudent, brazen; *F:* **h. comme un page,** as impudent as a cock-sparrow, as bold as brass; (*d*) *int.* courage! now for it! go it!
***hardiesse** [ardjɛs], *s.f.* **1.** boldness, hardihood; (*a*) daring, pluck; **prendre la h. de faire qch.,** to make so bold as to do sth., to take the liberty of doing sth.; **h. des lignes d'un tableau,** boldness of outline in a picture; (*b*) impudence, effrontery; **il a eu la h. de m'écrire,** he had the audacity, the cheek, to write to me; **pardonnez-moi ma h.,** excuse my saying so . . .. **2.** (*a*) bold, daring, act; **style plein de hardiesses,** style full of audacities; (*b*) (*usu. in pl.*) piece of effrontery, bold speech.
***hardillier** [ardilje], *s.m. Tapestry:* metal hook (used in the making of tapestries).
***hardiment** [ardimɑ̃], *adv.* boldly, hardily; (*a*) fearlessly, confidently; *Art:* **sujet traité h.,** subject boldly treated; (*b*) impudently.

***hardware** [ardwɛːr], *s.m.* (*computers*) hardware.
harelde [arɛld], *s.f. Orn:* **h. de Miquelon,** long-tailed duck, *U.S:* old squaw.
***harem** [arɛm], *s.m.* harem, *F:* **promener un h. avec soi,** to be always surrounded by women.
***hareng** [arɑ̃], *s.m.* herring; **h. bouffi,** bloater; **h. (salé et) fumé, h. doux,** kipper; **h. saur,** red herring; **pêche, industrie du h.,** herring fishery, industry; *s.a.* CAQUE, GUAIS, SERRÉ 1; *F:* **la mare aux harengs,** the herring pond; *F:* **être sec comme un h.,** to be as skinny, thin, as a rail; *P:* **hareng (saur),** policeman.
***harengade** [arɑ̃gad], *s.f.* **1.** *Fish:* drift net (for catching herrings); herring net. **2.** bucketful of salted herrings or sardines.
***harengaison** [arɑ̃gɛzɔ̃], *s.f.* (*a*) herring season; (*b*) (season's) catch of herrings, herring harvest.
***harengère** [arɑ̃ʒɛːr], *s.f.* **1.** (female) fishmonger. **2.** *Pej:* fish-woman, fishwife.
***harengerie** [arɑ̃ʒri], *s.f.* herring market.
***harenguet** [arɑ̃gɛ], *s.m. Ich:* sprat.
***harengueux** [arɑ̃gø], *s.m.*, ***harenguier** [arɑ̃gje], *s.m.* **1.** herring boat. **2.** herring fisher.
***harenguière** [arɑ̃gjɛːr], *s.f.* herring net.
***haret** [arɛ], *a.m.* **chat h.,** (i) wild cat; (ii) domestic cat run wild; feral cat.
***harfang** [arfɑ̃], *s.m.* great white owl; **h. des neiges,** snowy owl.
harfleurais, -aise [arflœrɛ, -ɛːz], **harfleurois, -oise** [arflœrwa, -waːz], *a. & s. Geog:* (native, inhabitant) of Harfleur.
***hargne** [arɲ], *s.f.* bad temper, surly disposition, peevishness.
***hargneusement** [arɲøzmɑ̃], *adv.* peevishly, cantankerously; naggingly; viciously.
***hargneux, -euse** [arɲø, -øːz], *a.* snarling (dog); peevish, cross, cross-grained, cantankerous, crusty, snappy (person); nagging (woman); ill-tempered, vicious (horse).
***haricot** [ariko], *s.m.* **1.** *Cu:* **h. de mouton,** Irish stew, haricot mutton. **2.** (*a*) **h. blanc,** haricot bean, kidney bean, *U.S:* bush bean; **h. vert,** French bean; **h. d'Espagne,** scarlet runner; **h. à rames, à filets,** runner bean; **h. sauteur,** Mexican jumping bean; **h. de Lima,** sugar bean, Lima bean; **haricots beurre,** butter beans; **haricots secs,** dried beans; *F:* **jouer avec des haricots,** to play for nothing, for love; *P:* **des haricots!** not a sausage! nuts! *P:* **courir sur le h. à qn,** to pester, plague, s.o.; *P:* **la fin des haricots,** the bloody limit; (*b*) (i) *Med:* kidney tray; (ii) **table h.,** kidney table; (*c*) *Adm:* *F:* island (at road junction).
***haricoter** [arikɔte], *v.i. A:* *F:* (*a*) to play for small stakes, for love; (*b*) to do business, speculate, in a small way.
***haridelle** [aridɛl], *s.f. F:* (*a*) old horse, screw, crock; (*b*) *F:* tall gaunt woman.
***harka** [arka], *s.f.* (*a*) *Mil:* (Arab) special contingent; (*b*) *Mil.Hist:* (*in N. Africa*) native auxiliary contingent.
***harki** [arki], *s.m. Mil:* member of a *harka.*
***harle** [arl], *s.m. Orn:* merganser, sawbill; **h. piette,** smew; **h. huppé,** red-breasted merganser; **h. couronné,** hooded merganser; **h. bièvre, grand h.,** goosander, *U.S:* American merganser.
Harlem [arlɛm], *Pr.n. Geog:* Haarlem; *U.S:* Harlem.
harmattan [armatɑ̃], *s.m. Meteor:* harmattan.
harmonica [armɔnika], *s.m.* **1.** harmonica, musical glasses. **2. h. (à bouche),** mouth organ.
harmonicorde [armɔnikɔrd], *s.m. A.Mus:* harmonichord.
harmonie [armɔni], *s.f.* **1.** (*a*) harmony, consonance; accord, agreement; **h. des couleurs,** harmony, balance, of colours; **tout était en h. dans la pièce,** everything in the room was in keeping; **conduite en h. avec . . .,** conduct in keeping with . . ., of a piece with . . .; **être en h. avec qch.,** to be in accordance with sth.; to fit in with sth.; **cette action n'est pas en h. avec son caractère,** this action is not in keeping, not consistent, with his character; **mettre un texte en h. avec un autre,** to bring one text into harmony with another; **vivre en h.,** to live in harmony, harmoniously; **la forme est en parfaite h. avec le fond,** the manner is perfectly attuned to the matter; *Pros:* **h. imitative,** representation of ideas by means of sounds or rhythm; *Ling:* **h. vocalique,** vowel harmony; (*b*) harmoniousness. **2.** *Mus:* (*a*) harmony; **table d'h.,** sounding-board (of piano, etc.); *A.Phil:* **l'h, céleste,** the music of the spheres, the harmony of the spheres; (*b*) (i) brass and reed band; (ii) wind section (of orchestra).
harmonier [armɔnje], *v.tr.* = HARMONISER.
harmonieusement [armɔnjøzmɑ̃], *adv.* harmoniously; (*a*) melodiously; (*b*) fittingly; (*c*) peaceably; **nous vivons assez h.,** we manage to rub along together.
harmonieux, -euse [armɔnjø, -øːz], *a.* (*a*) harmonious, melodious, tuneful (sound); (*b*) harmonious (discussion, arrangement, etc.); **couleurs harmonieuses,** colours that harmonize, that blend well; **peu h.,** inharmonious, discordant.
harmoniphon(e) [armɔnifɔn], *s.m. A.Mus:* harmoniphon.
harmonique [armɔnik]. **1.** *a.* (*a*) *Mus:* *Mth:* harmonic (scale, progression, etc.); **série h.,** harmonic series; **division h.,** harmonic division; **analyse h.,** harmonic analysis; **analyseur h.,** harmonic analyser; **composante, distorsion, h.,** harmonic component, distortion; **sons harmoniques,** harmonics; (*b*) *Anat:* **suture h.,** harmonic suture. **2.** *s.m. Mus:* harmonic; **harmoniques inférieurs,** sub-harmonics, undertones; **harmoniques supérieurs,** first harmonics, overtones; **h. (d'ordre) élevé,** higher harmonic.
harmoniquement [armɔnikmɑ̃], *adv. Mus:* *Mth:* harmonically.
harmonisateur, -trice [armɔnizatœːr, -tris], *s.* harmonizer.
harmonisation [armɔnizasjɔ̃], *s.f.* (*a*) harmonization, harmonizing; (*b*) bringing into line; (*c*) *Ling:* **h. vocalique,** vowel harmony.
harmoniser [armɔnize], *v.tr.* **1.** to harmonize, attune (ideas); to bring (plans, activities) into line; to match (colours). **2.** *Mus:* (*a*) to harmonize (melody, etc.); (*b*) to voice (pipe or stop of an organ).
s'harmoniser, to be in keeping, to harmonize, agree (**avec,** with); (*of colours*) **s'h. avec qch.,** to match, to tone in with, sth.; **lois qui s'harmonisent avec les tendances du jour,** laws in keeping, in harmony, with the tendencies of the day.
harmoniste [armɔnist], *s.m. & f.* **1.** *Mus:* (*a*) harmonist; (*b*) voicer (of organ). **2.** *s.m.pl. Rel:* **harmonistes,** Harmonites, Rappists.
harmonistique [armɔnistik], *s.f. Rel:* harmonistic(s).
harmonium [armɔnjɔm], *s.m.* harmonium.
harmoniumiste [armɔnjɔmist], *s.m. & f. A:* harmonium player, performer on the harmonium.
harmonogramme [armɔnɔgram], *s.m. Ind:* graph showing methods for planning production in a satisfactory way, thus making optimum use of manpower and material.
harmotome [armɔtɔm], *s.m. Miner:* harmotome, cross-stone.
***harnachement** [arnaʃmɑ̃], *s.m.* **1.** harnessing (of horse, etc.). **2.** (*a*) harness, trappings; (*b*) saddlery. **3.** *F:* (heavy, absurd) rig-out.
***harnacher** [arnaʃe], *v.tr.*, (*a*) to harness; (*b*) *F:* **h. qn d'une manière ridicule,** to dress s.o. up like a guy.
***harnacherie** [arnaʃri], *s.f.* harness-making, saddlery.
***harnacheur** [arnaʃœːr], *s.m. A:* **1.** harness-maker; saddler. **2.** groom.
***harnais** [arnɛ], *s.m.* **1.** (*a*) harness; **un h.,** a set of harness; **h. d'attelage,** draught harness; **h. agricole,** light harness for draught horse; **course sous h.,** harness racing; **cheval de h.,** draught-horse, cart-horse; (*b*) saddlery. **2.** (*a*) (i) *A:* harness; armour, accoutrements, military equipment; (ii) uncomfortable clothes; ridiculous get-up; (iii) *P:* any clothes, *F:* togs; (*b*) **blanchi sous le h.,** grown grey in the job; **reprendre le h.,** to get into harness again; to get back to work again. **3. h. de pêche,** fishing-tackle. **4.** *Mec.E:* **h. d'engrenages,** train of gear wheels; gearing. **5.** *Tex:* (loom-)harness, mounting. **6.** *Ind:* **h. de sécurité,** safety harness.
***harnaque** [arnak], *s.m. A:* *F:* fake.
***harnois** [arnwa, arnɛ], *s.m. A:* = HARNAIS.
***haro** [aro], *int. & s.m.* **(clameur de) h.,** outcry, hue and cry; **crier h.,** to raise a hue and cry; **faire h. sur qn,** to denounce s.o.
harouelle [arwɛl], *s.f. Fish:* cod line.
harpagon [arpagɔ̃], *s.m.* skinflint, miser; (*from the chief character in Molière's* L'Avare).
***harpail** [arpaːj], *s.m.*, ***harpaille** [arpaːj], *s.f.* **1.** herd of hinds and young deer. **2.** *A:* gang of marauders.
***harpailler**[1] [arpaje], *v.i. Ven:* (*of hounds following doe, hind*) to be on the wrong scent.
***harpailler**[2] **(se)** *v.pr. A:* *F:* to quarrel, wrangle, squabble.
***harpaye** [arpɛ(j)], *s.m. Orn:* marsh-harrier.
***harpe**[1] [arp], *s.f. Mus:* harp; **jouer, pincer, de la h.,** to play the harp; **h. éolienne,** Aeolian harp.
***harpe**[2], *s.f.* **1.** *Ven:* (hound's) claw. **2.** *Const:* (*a*) toothing-stone; *pl.* **les harpes,** the tooth(ing); (*b*) **h. de fer,** corner iron; forked tie.
***harpe**[3], *s.f. Moll:* harpa, harp shell.
***harpé** [arpe], *a.* clean-flanked (horse, hound).
***harpeau, -eaux** [arpo], *s.m. Nau:* grappling iron.
***harpe-luth** [arplyt], *s.f. Mus:* harp lute, harp guitar; *pl. harpes-luths.*
***harper**[1] [arpe], *v.i. Mus:* *A:* to harp.
***harper**[2], *v.tr.* to grip, clutch, grab; to grapple with (s.o.).
***harpidés** [arpide], *s.m.pl. Moll:* Harpidae.
***harpie** [arpi], *s.f.* **1.** (*a*) *Myth:* harpy; (*b*) *F:* (i) harpy, (ii) shrew, hell-cat. **2.** (*a*) *Orn:* harpy (-eagle); crested, spotted, eagle; (*b*) *Z:* harpy (-bat).
***harpigner (se)** [sәarpiɲe], ***harpiller (se)** [sәarpije], *v.pr. A:* (*a*) to quarrel, wrangle; (*b*) to come to fisticuffs.
***harpin** [arpɛ̃], *s.m.* boathook.
***harpiste** [arpist], *s.m. & f.* (*a*) harpist (in orchestra, etc.); (*b*) harper.
***harpoise** [arpwaːr], *s.f.* harpoon line.
***harpoise** [arpwaːz], *s.f.* harpoon head.
***harpon** [arpɔ̃], *s.m.* **1.** harpoon; **pêche, chasse (sous-marine) au h.,** (underwater) spear fishing. **2.** (two-handled) cross-cut saw. **3.** *Const:* (*a*) toothing-stone; (*b*) wall staple. **4.** *Min:* centre spear; **h. à câble,** spear; *Oil Ind:* grapple, fishing hook.
***harponnage** [arpɔnaːʒ], *s.m.*, ***harponnement** [arpɔnmɑ̃], *s.m.* harpooning.
***harponner** [arpɔne], *v.tr.* **1.** to harpoon. **2.** *P:* (*a*) to arrest, *P:* collar, pinch (s.o.); (*b*) to stop (s.o.); **se faire h.,** to get caught, cornered.
***harponneur** [arpɔnœːr], *s.m.* harpooner.
***harpye** [arpi], *s.f.*, ***harpyia** [arpija], *s.f. Z:* harpy bat, harpy.
***hart** [aːr], *s.f.* **1.** (*a*) withe (for hurdling, etc.); (*b*) band, binder (for bundling faggots, etc., together). **2.** *A:* rope, noose (for hanging); **sous peine de la h.,** under penalty of the gallows; **les six bourgeois se présentèrent la h. au col,** the six burgesses presented themselves with ropes about their necks.
hartine [artin], **hartite** [artit], *s.f. Miner:* hartite.
haruspication [aryspikasjɔ̃], *s.f. Rom.Ant:* haruspication, haruspicy.
haruspice [aryspis], *s.m. Rom.Ant:* haruspex.
harveyage [arvɛjaːʒ], *s.m. Metall:* **1.** Harvey process, harveyizing. **2.** hard-faced part (of armour-plate, etc.).
harveyé [arveje], *a.* harveyized.
harveyer [arveje], *v.tr. Metall:* to harveyize (steel).
***hasard** [azaːr], *s.m.* **1.** (*a*) chance, luck, accident; **coup de h.,** (i) stroke of luck, (ii) fluke; **par un coup de h.,** by a mere chance; **rencontre de h.,** chance meeting, accidental meeting; **emplette de h.,** chance purchase; **jeu de h.,** game of chance; *A:* **de h.,** secondhand; *P:* **gibier de h.,** woman picked up by a man; pick-up; **manger au h. de la fourchette,** to take pot luck; **au h. des circonstances,** according to circumstances; **c'est un exemple que j'ai pris au h. de mes lectures,** it is an example I came across in the course of my reading; **ne rien laisser au h.,** to leave nothing to chance; **se fier au h.,** to trust to luck; **ce n'est que par le plus grand des hasards que . . .,** it was only by the merest chance that . . .; **c'est un h. qu'il ait réussi,** his success was due to a fluke; **le h. fit que** + *ind. or sub.*, chance so ordained that . . .; luck would have it that . . .; *adv.phr.* **au hasard,** at a guess, haphazardly, at random; **frapper au h.,** to strike blindly; **choix fait au h.,** random choice, selection; **numéro tiré au h.,** random number; **par h.,** by accident, by chance; **par pur h.,** by pure, sheer, accident; **comme par h.,** casually; **si par h. vous le voyez,** if you (should) happen to see him; **sauriez-vous son adresse par h.?** do you by any chance know his address? do you happen to know his address? **découvrir la vérité par h.,** to stumble upon the truth; (*b*) risk, danger, hazard; **courir le h.,** to run the hazard, the risk; **au h. d'un refus, de tout perdre,** at the risk of a refusal, of losing everything; **à tout h.,** (i) at all hazards; (ii) on the off chance; (iii) just in case, as a precaution; **les hasards de la guerre,** the hazards of war. **2.** *Games:* (*a*) *Golf:* hazard; (*b*) *Ten: etc:* (*of ball*) **faire h.,** to break.
***hasardé** [azarde], *a.* **1.** hazardous, risky, rash, foolhardy (undertaking, etc.); indiscreet (words, etc.); **chanson hasardée,** risky song; *A:* **blond h.,** reddish (hair). **2.** *Cu:* *A:* (*of meat, etc.*) too long hung; tainted.
***hasardément** [azardemɑ̃], *adv. A:* in a risky, hazardous, manner.

hasarder H : 6 haut

***hasarder** [azarde], *v.tr.* to risk, venture, hazard (one's life, etc.); h. une opinion, to venture an opinion; to venture upon an opinion; h. de se faire des ennemis, to run the risk of making enemies.

se hasarder, to take risks; to run risks; se trop h., to take too many risks; se h. à, *A:* de, faire qch., to venture to do sth.; il ne faut pas se h. (tout) seul dans la jungle, one should not go alone into the jungle.

***hasardeusement** [azardøzmɑ̃], *adv.* haphazardly; hazardously; foolhardily.

***hasardeux, -euse** [azardø, -ø:z], *a.* 1. (*a*) dangerous, hazardous, perilous, risky; (*b*) toit h., shaky roof. 2. *A:* daring, venturesome, foolhardy.

***hasardise** [azardi:z], *s.f. A:* rash step, dubious undertaking.

***haschisch** [aʃiʃ], *s.m.* has(c)hish, bhang.

***hase** [ɑ:z, a:z], *s.f. Z:* (*a*) doe hare; (*b*) doe (of wild rabbit).

hasidim [asidim], *s.m.pl. Jew.Rel:* Has(s)idim.

hasparrandais, -aise [asparɑ̃dɛ, -ɛ:z], *a. & s. Geog:* (native, inhabitant) of Hasparren [asparɛn].

hast [ast], *s.m. A:* shaft; arme d'h., shafted weapon; pike, spear; thrusting weapon.

hastaire [astɛ:r], **hastat** [asta], *s.m. Rom.Mil. Hist:* spearman.

***haste** [ast], *s.f.* 1. *A.Arms:* lance, spear, pike. 2. stem (of letters t, f, etc.).

***hasté** [aste], *a. Bot:* hastate (leaf, etc.).

***hastifolié** [astifɔlje], *a. Bot:* hastate.

***hastiforme** [astifɔrm], *a.* lanciform, lanceolate; hastate.

***hatchettine** [atʃɛtin], *s.f.*, ***hatchettite** [atʃɛtit], *s.f. Miner:* hatchettine, hatchettite.

***hâte**[1] [ɑ:t], *s.f.* haste, hurry; mettre trop de h. dans qch., to be in too much of a hurry over sth.; faire h., to hurry, make haste; avoir h. de faire qch., (i) to be in a hurry, in haste, to do sth.; (ii) to be eager, to long, to do sth.; j'ai h. de partir, I am in a hurry to leave; avoir trop h., mettre trop de h., à gagner de l'argent, to be in too great a hurry, too much in a hurry, to make money; to want to get rich quickly; *adv.phr.* à la hâte, in a hurry, hastily, hurriedly; je reçus un billet écrit à la h., I received a note written in haste, a hasty note; préparatifs faits à la h., hurried preparations; déjeuner à la h., to make a hurried breakfast; to hurry over one's breakfast; calcul fait à la h., rough and ready calculation; casernes bâties à la h., rushed-up barracks; avec h., en h., hastily, in haste; en toute h., with all possible speed, post-haste, in a tearing hurry; revenir en toute h., to hurry back; to rush, tear, back; monter, descendre, en toute h., to rush, hurry, up, down; se rendre en toute h. à . . ., to go at top speed to . . .; agir sans h., to act without haste, deliberately, with deliberation.

***hâte**[2], *s.f. Cu:* spit.

***hâté** [ɑte], *a.* forward (season, etc.); forced (fruit); rushed (work).

***hâtelet** [ɑtlɛ], *s.m. Cu:* skewer.

hâtelette [ɑtlɛt], *s.f. Jewel:* small (ornamental) brooch.

***hatelette** [ɑtlɛt], *s.f.*, ***hatelle** [ɑtɛl], *s.f. Cu:* small bird, kidney, etc., roasted on a skewer.

***hâter** [ɑte], *v.tr.* to hasten; to hurry (sth.) on; to push (sth.) forward; h. la procédure, to accelerate proceedings; h. la besogne, to expedite the work; h. le pas, to quicken one's pace, to hurry up; h. le dîner, to put the dinner forward, to hurry up with the dinner; h. des fraises, to force strawberries.

se hâter, to hasten, hurry; se h. de faire qch., to make haste to do sth., to lose no time in doing sth.; se h. de suivre qn, to hurry after s.o.; il se hâta de sortir, d'entrer, de monter, de descendre, he rushed out, in, up, down; on se hâta tant que tout fut prêt le lendemain, they put on so much speed that everything was ready the next day; *Prov:* hâtez-vous lentement, more haste less speed; slow and sure! easy does it.

hâtereau, -eaux [ɑtro], *s.m. Cu:* liver ball wrapped in a caul.

***hâtier** [ɑtje], *s.m. Cu:* spit-rack.

***hâtif, -ive** [ɑtif, -i:v], *a.* (*a*) forward, early (spring, fruit, etc.); premature (decision); precocious (plant, fruit); (*b*) hasty, hurried, sudden, ill-considered (measure, etc.).

***hâtiveau, -eaux** [ɑtivo], *s.m. Hort:* early fruit, vegetable; *esp.* early pear, hasting pear.

***hâtivement** [ɑtivmɑ̃], *adv.* (*a*) prematurely, early; (*b*) hastily, in a hurry; without due consideration.

***hâtiveté** [ɑtivte], *s.f. A:* earliness, precociousness (of fruit, etc.).

hattérie [ateri], *s.f. Rept:* hatteria, tuatara.

***hauban** [obɑ̃], *s.m.* (*a*) *Nau:* shroud; h. bâtard, swifter; grands haubans, main rigging, main shrouds; haubans de fortune, preventer shrouds; (*b*) guy, stay; fil de h., stay, guy, bracing, wire; h. en fil (métallique, souple), wire stay, guy; h.-chaîne, chain stay; h. de rappel, straining stay; tendeur de h., stay tightener; *Nau:* haubans de cheminée, funnel stays, funnel guys; *Av:* h. de croisillonnage, bracing-wire; *Oil Min:* h. tendeur, span wire (on drilling rig); *Civ.E:* pont à haubans, cable-stayed bridge.

***hauban(n)age** [obana:ʒ], *s.m.* guying, staying, bracing; *Av:* h. des ailes, wing bracing; câble de h., *usu.* câble d'h., tie.

***hauban(n)er** [obane], *v.tr.* to guy, stay, brace (post, etc.).

***haubergeon** [obɛrʒɔ̃], *s.m. A.Mil.Cost:* haubergeon.

***haubergier** [obɛrʒje], *s.m.* hauberk maker.

***haubert** [obɛ:r], *s.m. A.Mil.Cost:* hauberk, shirt of mail, coat of mail; *Hist:* fief de h., knight's fee; service de h., knight service.

haubourdinois, -oise [oburdinwa, -wa:z], *a. & s. Geog:* (native, inhabitant) of Haubourdin.

hauérite [oerit], *s.f. Miner:* hauerite.

***hausse** [o:s], *s.f.* 1. rise, rising; (*a*) température en h., rising temperature; baromètre à la h., en h., barometer on the rise; les affaires sont à la h., things are looking up; (*b*) *Com: Fin:* rise; marché orienté à la h., rising market; h. des prix, advance, inflation, of prices; inflated prices; les prix sont à la h., prices are hardening; marchandises en h., goods on the rise; la h. du prix du blé, the rise in the price of wheat; les blés ont subi une h. considérable, wheat has gone up considerably (in price); il y a h. sur les blés, there is an advance on wheat; jouer à la h., to speculate on a rising market, to bull the market, to go a bull; spéculateur à la h., bull; tendance à la h., bullish tendency; provoquer une h. factice, to rig the market; *s.a.* OPÉRATEUR 1. 2. (*a*) prop, block, stand; placer des hausses sous les pieds d'un meuble, to raise, prop up, a piece of furniture; (*b*) *Typ:* (i) underlay; mettre les hausses, to underlay the type; (ii) overlay. 3. level raiser; *Hyd.E:* flush-board, flash board, shutter. 4. *Mil:* (*a*) *Sm.a:* (back)sight (of rifle); h. de combat, à trou, à œilleton, battle sight, peep sight, aperture sight; h. à charnière, leaf sight; h. à curseur, back sight with leaf and slide; h. à tambour, drum backsight; pied de h., backsight bed; planche de h., backsight leaf; curseur de h., backsight slide; poussoir de curseur de h., backsight slide catch; mettre la h. à 400 mètres, to set the sight, to sight, at 400 metres; (*b*) *Artil:* (i) tangent scale, (tangent) sight; (ii) sighting gear; (*c*) elevation, range; grande h., petite h., high, low, range; angle de h., angle of elevation; tambour des hausses, elevation, sight, drum. 5. *Ap:* super hive; *F:* super. 6. *Mus:* h. de l'archet, nut of the bow.

***hausse-col** [oskɔl], *s.m. A.Mil.Cost:* gorget; *pl. hausse-col(s).*

***haussement** [osmɑ̃], *s.m.* 1. raising (of wall, of one's voice, etc.); h. du niveau d'une rivière, banking (up) of a river. 2. lifting; *esp.* h. d'épaules, shrug(ging) of the shoulders, shrug.

***hausse-pied** [ospje], *s.m.* 1. *A:* (carriage) step. 2. *Ven:* (wolf, etc.) trap. 3. *Ven:* first falcon flown at a heron to make it rise. 4. step (on spade); *pl. hausse-pied(s).*

***hausse-queue** [oskø], *s.m.inv. Orn: F:* wagtail.

***hausser** [ose]. 1. *v.tr.* to raise; (*a*) to make higher; h. une maison de deux étages, to raise a house two storeys; h. un mur, to heighten a wall; h. les prix, to raise, put up, advance, prices; h. la voix, to raise one's voice; *Mus:* h. un chant, to set a song higher; h. un chant d'un demi-ton, to set a song a semitone up, to raise a song a semitone; (*b*) to lift; h. qn sur son dos, to lift, hoist, s.o. on to one's shoulders; h. les épaules, to shrug one's shoulders; h. le store, to pull up, raise, the blind; *s.a.* COUDE 1. 2. *v.i.* (*a*) to rise; (*of prices*) to go up, advance; faire h. les prix, to send up, force up, the prices; *A:* la rivière a haussé, the river has risen; (*b*) *Nau:* (*of land, etc.*) to raise (over the horizon).

se hausser. 1. to raise oneself; se h. sur la pointe des pieds, to stand on tiptoe; se h. pour voir, to crane one's neck; se h. jusqu'à qn, to raise oneself, to rise, to s.o.'s level; *A:* il veut se h., he is trying to push himself. 2. *A:* le temps se hausse, the clouds are lifting, the weather is clearing.

***haussette** [osɛt], *s.f.* 1. side planks (of cart). 2. *Hyd.E:* shutter (of water-gate).

***haussier** [osje], *s.m. St. Exch: F:* bull.

***haussière** [osjɛ:r], *s.f.* 1. *Nau:* hawser. 2. rails (of cart).

haussmannite [osmanit], *s.f. Miner:* hausmannite.

***haussoir** [oswa:r], *s.m.*, ***haussoire** [oswa:r], *s.f. Hyd.E:* floodgates, sluice.

haustorie [ostɔri], *s.f. Fung:* haustorium.

***haut** [o]. I. *a.* 1. high; (*a*) tall (grass, etc.); lofty (building, etc.); towering (cliff); homme h. de taille, de haute taille, tall man; le mur est h. de six pieds, the wall is six foot high; *F:* il est h. comme trois pommes, he's pint-sized, he's knee-high to a grasshopper; chambre haute de plafond, lofty room; maison haute de quatre étages, house four storeys high; hautes terres, highlands; hautes eaux, high water; haute mer, open sea, high seas; navire de haute mer, sea-going ship; à mer haute, at high water, at high tide; (*b*) exalted, important, great; high-class; le Très-H., the Most High (God); les hautes parties contractantes, the high contracting parties; de h. rang, of high rank; h. fonctionnaire, highly-placed official; amis en h. lieu, friends in high places, influential friends; de hauts faits, deeds of valour; la haute finance, la haute banque, (i) high finance, (ii) the financiers, bankers; la haute cour de justice, the High Court of Justice; haute couture, haute couture; haute cuisine, haute cuisine; le h. comique, high comedy; les hautes cartes, the high cards, the picture cards; (*c*) raised; marcher la tête haute, to carry one's head high; voix haute, (i) loud voice; (ii) high voice; lire à haute voix, to read aloud; à haute et intelligible voix, in a loud and clear voice; jeter de hauts cris, (i) to utter loud cries; (ii) to make a great fuss; les prix sont hauts, prices are high; (*d*) (*to a high degree*) tenir qn en haute estime, to hold s.o. in high esteem; avoir une haute opinion de soi-même, to have a high opinion of oneself; haute autorité morale, lofty moral authority; haute trahison, high treason; haute insolence, the height of insolence; être h. en couleur, (i) to have a high colour, a florid complexion; (ii) to be a colourful character; style h. en couleur, highly-coloured style; les hauts temps, remote antiquity; les hautes latitudes, high latitudes; *Mch:* haute pression, high, heavy, pressure; *W.Tel:* haute fréquence, high frequency; (*e*) *A:* far forward; le carême est h. cette année, Easter is late this year. 2. upper, higher; les hauts étages, the upper storeys; les hautes branches, the upper branches, the top branches; le plus h. étage, the top floor; la plus haute branche, the topmost branch; les hautes classes, (i) the upper classes (of society); (ii) the higher, upper, top, forms (of school); the upper school; *Hist:* une haute dame, a lady of noble, high, birth; les hautes mathématiques, higher mathematics; *Geog:* le h. Canada, Upper Canada; le h. Rhin, the upper Rhine; la Haute Écosse, the Highlands (of Scotland); *Nau:* les hautes voiles, the upper sails; the kites.

II. **haut,** *adv.* 1. high (up), above, up; h. dans les airs, high up in the skies; h. les mains! hands up! *s.a.* MAIN 1; h. les bras! commence work! h. les cœurs! keep up your courage! *sursum corda! A:* h. le pied! off you go! be off! parler h., to speak loudly; parlez plus h.! speak up! speak out! parler, penser, tout h., to talk, think, aloud; rêver tout h., to dream aloud, to talk in one's sleep; dire qch. tout h., to say sth. aloud; dire qch. bien h., to assert sth. loudly; estimer qch. h., to set a high value on sth.; condamner h. et ferme, to condemn utterly; *A:* h. cravaté, wearing a high stock; un homme h. placé, a man in a high position; oiseau h. perché, bird perched on high; h. jambé, long in the leg; *F:* h. sur patte, (i) (*of animal*) long in the leg; (ii) (*of car*) high-slung; h. assis, sitting in a high chair; h. voûté, high-vaulted; viser h., to aim high; prétendre trop h., to aim too high; voler h., to fly high; les dépenses montent h., expenditure is running high; *Cards:* couper h., to trump high; *Nau:* (*of ship*) avoir ses huniers h., to have her topsails set; *Nau:* l'ancre est h., the anchor is up; *s.a.* LÀ-HAUT, PENDRE 1. 2. back; remonter plus h. (dans le temps), to go further back; aussi h. qu'on remonte dans l'histoire, as far back in history as we can go; on a déjà vu plus h. que . . ., we saw above that . . .; comme il est dit plus h., as aforesaid; as has been indicated above, earlier; cité, indiqué, mentionné, énoncé, plus h., mentioned above, mentioned earlier.

III. **haut,** *s.m.* 1. height; le mur a six pieds de h., the wall is six foot high; traiter qn de (son)

h., to patronize s.o.; **regarder qn du h. de sa grandeur,** to look down on s.o.; **tomber de (son) h.,** (i) to fall flat on the ground, (ii) to fall from one's high position; **tomber de h.,** to be very much taken aback; to be dumbfounded, *F:* flabbergasted; to gasp (at the news). **2.** top, upper part; *Cost:* (i) top, bodice (of dress); (ii) (*separate garment*) top; **le h. de la page, de l'escalier,** the head, top, of the page, of the stairs; **être au h. de l'échelle,** to be at the top of the ladder, of the tree; **sur le h. des collines,** on the hill-tops; *s.a.* PAVÉ 2; (*on packing cases*) **h.,** this side up; **h. du bras,** upper arm; **h. de la table,** head of the table; **h. de la rue,** top of the street; **c'était au plus h. du jour,** it was high noon; **les hauts et les bas,** the ups and downs (of life, of illness, etc.); *Mth:* **courbe concave vers le h.,** curve concave upwards; *Nau:* **h. du mât,** mast-head; **h. de l'eau,** high water, top of the flood; **les hauts (d'un navire),** the topsides, upper works; *Nau:* **cargaison arrimée dans les hauts,** cargo stowed on top; *Typ:* **h. de casse,** upper case, *F:* caps; *Mch:* **h. de course,** top of stroke, upper dead-centre (of piston); **l'étage du h.,** the top floor; **le h. d'une côte,** the brow of a hill; **il se jeta du h. de la falaise, de l'arbre,** he flung himself from the cliff, down from the tree; **gloire à Dieu au plus h. des cieux,** Glory to God in the Highest; *Ten:* **servir par le h.,** to serve overarm; *F:* **aller par h. et par bas,** to be sick and to have diarrhoea. **3.** *adv.phr.* **de h. en bas,** (i) downwards, (ii) from top to bottom; **chercher qch. de h. en bas,** to look high and low for sth.; **regarder qn de h. en bas,** to look at s.o. contemptuously, to look down on s.o.; **traiter qn de h. en bas,** to treat s.o. in a condescending manner, superciliously, in a high and mighty way; to put on airs with s.o.; *F:* **le prendre de h.,** to put on airs; **du h. en bas,** from top to bottom; **en h.,** (i) above, *Nau:* aloft; (ii) upstairs; *Nau:* **en h. tout le monde!** all hands on deck! **en h. les gabiers!** away aloft! **son âme est allée en h.,** his soul is gone aloft, to heaven; **portez cela en h.,** carry that upstairs; **regarder en h.,** to look upwards; **révélation d'en h.,** revelation from on high; **un ordre d'en h.,** an order from high quarters; **pays d'en h.,** upland; *prep.phr.* **en h. de,** at the top of. **4.** *s.f. P:* **la haute,** the upper classes; the upper crust; **elle est de la haute,** she's ever so genteel.

***hautain**[1] [otɛ̃], *a.* **1.** *A:* lofty, noble. **2.** proud, haughty; **air h.,** lordly air. **3.** (*of bird of prey*) lofty, that soars high.

***hautain**[2], *s.m. Vit:* espalier-trained vine.

***hautainement** [otɛnmɑ̃], *adv.* proudly, haughtily.

***hautaineté** [otɛnte], *s.f.* haughtiness.

***hautbois** [obwɑ], *s.m. Mus:* **1.** oboe. **2.** oboe player, oboist.

***hautboïste** [obɔist], *s.m. & f. Mus:* oboe player; oboist.

***haut-commissaire** [okɔmisɛːr], *s.m. Adm:* high commissioner; *pl. hauts-commissaires.*

***haut-de-chausse(s)** [odʃoːs], *s.m. Cost: A:* breeches, trunk hose; *F:* (*of wife*) **porter le h.-de-c.,** to wear the breeches; *pl. hauts-de-chausse(s).*

***haut-de-forme** [odfɔrm], *s.m.* top hat; *pl. hauts-de-forme.*

***haute-contre** [otkɔ̃ːtr], *s.f.* counter-tenor, alto (voice); *pl. hautes-contre.*

***haute-futaie** [otfytɛ], *s.f.* timber forest; *pl. hautes-futaies.*

***haute-lice, -lisse** [otlis], *s.f.* high-warp tapestry; *pl. hautes-lices, -lisses.*

***haute-lissier, -ière** [otlisje, -jɛr], *s.* weaver specializing in high-warp tapestries.

***hautement** [otmɑ̃], *adv.* **1.** highly; **h. estimé,** highly esteemed. **2.** (*a*) loudly; **annoncer qch h.,** to proclaim sth. loudly; (*b*) openly, boldly, in no uncertain tones; **je lui ai dit h. ma façon de penser,** I told him straight out what I thought. **3.** loftily, nobly; **penser h.,** to have lofty thoughts.

***haute-taille** [ottɑːj], *s.f. Mus:* light tenor; *pl. hautes-tailles.*

***hauteur** [otœːr], *s.f.* **1.** (*a*) height, elevation; altitude (of star, triangle, etc.); **h. du soleil,** altitude of the sun; **h. observée, vraie,** observed, true, altitude; **tour qui a cent pieds de h.,** tower a hundred feet high; *Av:* **prendre de la h.** to climb; **h. d'appui,** breast height, elbow height; **à h. d'appui,** breast-high, elbow-high; **le peu de h. du plafond,** the lowness of the ceiling; **elle tomba de (toute) sa h.,** (i) she fell flat; (ii) she was staggered, taken aback; *Ball:* **écart en h.,** vertical deviation; **à la h. de qch.,** abreast of, level with, sth.; **à la h. de l'œil,** at eye level; **être à la h. d'une tâche,** to be equal to a task, *F:* to be up to a job; **poète à la h. de Virgile,** poet on a level with Virgil; **arriver à la h. d'un adversaire,** to draw level with an opponent; **se trouver, se montrer, à la h. de la situation,** to prove equal to the task, to rise to the occasion; **il est à la h. des idées actuelles,** he is abreast of the times; *Sch:* **vos compositions sont à la h.,** your papers are up to the mark, up to standard; *F:* **être à la h.,** to be up to scratch; *F:* **dîner à la h.,** slap-up dinner; **la voiture s'arrêta à la h. du numéro 128,** the car stopped opposite number 128; *Nau:* **à la h. du cap Horn,** off, abreast of, Cape Horn; **vasistas à h. du plafond,** fanlight on a level with the ceiling; **table à h. variable,** adjustable table; **cheveux relevés en h.,** hair taken up on top of the head; *Typ:* **h. en papier,** height to paper (of type); *Dressm:* **h. du dos** = length of back; **saut en h.,** high jump; (*b*) depth; **h. d'un arc de pont,** depth of a bridge arch; **h. sous clef,** rise (of arch); **h. libre, de passage,** headroom (of arch, etc.); *Av:* **h. libre,** clearance; *Const:* **h. d'assise,** thickness of a course; **h. d'eau,** (i) depth, (ii) *Hyd.E:* head, of water; *Mec.E:* **h. du pas d'une vis,** lead of a screw; **h. de chute (d'un pilon, etc.),** drop (of stamp, etc.); (*c*) *Mus:* pitch (of note); (*d*) loftiness (of ideas, etc.); **la h. de ses vues,** his high ideals. **2.** haughtiness, arrogance; **traiter qn avec h.,** to treat s.o. arrogantly, in an arrogant manner; **regarder qn de toute sa h.,** to look at s.o. with utter contempt. **3.** (*a*) high place; eminence, rising ground, hill; hilltop; *Mapm:* **échelle des hauteurs,** vertical scale; (*b*) **Gloire à Dieu dans les hauteurs,** Glory to God in the Highest.

***haut-fond** [ofɔ̃], *s.m.* shoal, shallow (in sea or river); *Oc:* shelf; *pl. hauts-fonds.*

***haut(-)fourneau** [ofurno], *s.m. Metall:* blast furnace; *pl. hauts(-)fourneaux.*

***hautin** [otɛ̃], *s.m. Vit:* espalier-trained vine.

***haut-jointé, -ée** [oʒwɛ̃te], *a.* (*of horse*) long-legged, long-pasterned; *pl. haut-jointé(e)s.*

***haut-le-cœur** [olkœːr], *s.m.inv.* (*a*) heave (of stomach); **avoir des h.-le-c.,** to retch, to feel sick; (*b*) disgust; repulsion; **cela me donne des h.-le-c.,** it disgusts me, *F:* it makes my gorge rise, my stomach heave.

***haut-le-corps** [olkɔːr], *s.m.inv.* sudden start, jump; **faire, marquer, un h.-le-c.,** (i) to start, to give a sudden start; (ii) (*of horse*) to buck, shy.

***haut-le-pied** [olpje]. **1.** *s.m.inv.* (*a*) vagabond, tramp; (*b*) **faire, partir, h.-le-p.,** (i) (*of horse*) to bolt, (ii) *F:* to decamp. **2.** *a.inv.* (i) *Mil:* (*of horse, etc.*) spare, in reserve; (ii) *Rail:* (*of engine*) running light; *F:* wild-cat (engine); (*of train*) empty. **3.** *adv.* in haste, quickly; **manger h.-le-p.,** to snatch a meal.

***haut-mal** [omal], *s.m.* no *pl. Med: F:* epilepsy.

***haut-monté, -ée** [omɔ̃te], *a.* (*of horse*) long-legged, long-pasterned; *pl. haut-monté(e)s.*

***haut-parleur** [oparlœːr], *s.m. W.Tel:* loud-speaker; amplifier (in stations, at public meetings, etc.); **h.-p. à pavillon,** horn loud-speaker; **h.-p. à cône,** cone loudspeaker; **h.-p. à bobinage mobile, h.-p. (électro)dynamique,** moving-coil loudspeaker; **h.-p. électrostatique,** electrostatic loudspeaker; **réception en h.-p.,** reception (i) on a loudspeaker, (ii) of loud-speaker strength; *W.Tel: etc:* **h.-p. de cabine, témoin, de contrôle,** projection-room monitor, monitor speaker; *pl. haut-parleurs.*

***haut-pendu** [opɑ̃dy], *s.m. Nau:* (*a*) insulated nimbus; (*b*) passing squall; *pl. hauts-pendus.*

***haut-perché, -ée** [opɛrʃe], *a.* (*of horse*) long-legged; *pl. haut-perché(e)s.*

***haut-relief** [orəljef], *s.m. Art:* high relief, alto-relievo; *pl. hauts-reliefs.*

***hauturier, -ière** [otyrje, -jɛːr]. **1.** *a.* of the high seas; **pêche hauturière,** deep-sea fishing; **navigation hauturière,** ocean navigation; **aviation hauturière,** naval aviation. **2.** *s.m.* **(pilote) h.,** deep-sea pilot, "proper pilot."

***haut-volant** [ovɔlɑ̃], *a. & s.m. Orn:* high-flying (pigeon); *pl. haut-volants.*

***haüyne** [ayin], *s.f. Miner:* hauyne, hauynite.

***havage** [avaːʒ], *s.m. Min:* **1.** cutting, bossing, kirving; undercutting. **2.** cut; undercut. **3.** *Civ.E:* shaft-sinking by means of a caisson pile.

***havanais, -aise** [avanɛ, -ɛːz]. **1.** *a. & s. Geog:* Havanese. **2.** *s.f.* **havanaise,** *Danc:* habanera.

***Havane** [avan]. **1.** *Pr.n.f. Geog:* **la H.,** Havana. **2.** (*a*) *s.m.* Havana (cigar); (*b*) *a.inv.* light brown colour; **cuir h.,** brown leather; **maroquinerie en h.,** leather goods in tan.

***hâve** [ɑːv], *a.* haggard, emaciated, gaunt (face); sunken (cheeks).

***havée** [ave], *s.f. Min:* cut.

***haveneau, -eaux** [avno], ***havenet** [avnɛ], *s.m.* shrimping net.

***haver** [ave], *v.tr. Min:* to (under)cut, (under)hole.

***haveron** [avrɔ̃], *s.m. Bot:* wild oats.

***Havers** [avɛːr], *Pr.n.m. Anat:* **canaux de H.,** Haversian canals.

***haversien, -ienne** [avɛrsjɛ̃, -jɛn], *a. Anat:* Haversian; **système h.,** Haversian system (of bone).

***haveur** [avœːr], *s.m. Min:* (coal-)cutter, under-cutter, hewer.

***haveuse** [avøːz], *s.f. Min:* coal-cutter, coal-cutting machine, undercutter; **h. à pic, à percussion,** pick, puncher, coal-cutting machine.

***havildar** [avildaːr], *s.m. Mil.* (*India*): havildar.

***havir** [aviːr], *Cu:* **1.** *v.tr.* to scorch, burn (meat, bread, etc.). **2.** *v.i. & pr.* (*of meat, etc.*) to catch, burn.

havrais, -aise [ɑvrɛ, -ɛːz], *a. & s. Geog:* (native, inhabitant) of Le Havre.

***havre** [ɑːvr]. **1.** *s.m.* (*a*) harbour, haven, port; (*b*) cove. **2.** *Pr.n.m. Geog:* **Le H.,** Le Havre.

***havresac**[1] [ɑvrəsak], *s.m.* (*a*) *A: Mil:* knapsack, pack; (*b*) haversack; (workman's) tool bag.

***havresac**[2], *s.m.,* ***havresat** [ɑvrəsa], *s.m. Metall:* hammer scale.

havrits [avri], *s.m.pl. Min:* fakes, rashings.

Hawaï [awaj(i)], *Pr.n. Geog:* Hawaii; **les îles H.,** the Hawaiian Islands.

hawaïen, -ïenne [awajɛ̃, -jɛn], *a. & s. Geog:* Hawaiian; *Mus:* **guitare hawaïenne,** Hawaiian guitar; ukulele; *Geol:* **éruption hawaïenne,** Hawaiian eruption.

***haworthia** [awɔrtja], *s.m. Bot:* haworthia.

***haye** [aːj], *s.f. Agr:* beam (of plough).

***Haye (la)** [laɛ], *Pr.n.f. Geog:* the Hague; *Hist:* **les Actes, les Conventions, de la H.,** the Hague Conventions; **la Conférence de la H.,** the Hague Conference.

***hayette** [ajɛt], *s.f.* **1.** *Agr:* small hoe (for weeding hedges). **2.** *Ven:* (*esp. in Normandy*) small hedge.

***hayon** [ajɔ̃], *s.m.* **1.** (*a*) forage ladder (of hay cart); (*b*) back door of a commercial vehicle. **2.** market stall. **3.** (*in W. of France*) wattle enclosure used as a shelter.

hazebrouckois, -oise [azbrukwa, -waːz], *a. & s. Geog:* (native, inhabitant) of Hazebrouck.

***hé** [e], *int.* **1.** (*to call attention*) hullo! hi there! I say! **2.** (*surprise*) hey! what! **3. hé! hé!** well, well! **4.** *O:* **hé bien . . .,** well . . . .

***head** [ed], *s.m. Geol:* Head.

***heaume** [oːm], *s.m.* **1.** *Arm:* helm(et); **h. en calotte,** bas(i)net. **2.** *A.Num:* heaume; **h. d'argent, gros h.,** silver gros heaume.

***heaumier, -ière** [omje, -jɛːr], *s. A:* maker, seller, of helmets; *f.* wife of the *heaumier.*

héautoscopie [eotɔskɔpi], *s.f. Psy:* abnormal perception of one's body as alienated from oneself.

hebdomadaire [ɛbdɔmadɛːr]. **1.** *a.* weekly. **2.** *s.m.* weekly (paper), magazine.

hebdomadairement [ɛbdɔmadɛrmɑ̃], *adv.* weekly, once a week.

hebdomadier, -ière [ɛbdɔmadje, -jɛːr], *s. Ecc:* hebdomadary.

Hébé [ebe], *Pr.n.f. Myth:* Hebe.

hébéphrénie [ebefreni], *s.f. Med: O:* hebephrenia.

hébéphrénique [ebefrenik], *a. & s. Med: O:* hebephrenic.

héberge [ebɛrʒ], *s.f. Jur:* point of disjunction; point at which a party wall ceases to be common.

hébergement [ebɛrʒ(ə)mɑ̃], *s.m.* lodging; (*a*) sheltering, entertaining; (*b*) shelter, entertainment; (*c*) overnight charge, charge for a night at Youth Hostels.

héberger [ebɛrʒe], *v.tr.* **(j'hébergeai(s); n. hébergeons) 1.** to harbour; to lodge, shelter (and feed); to entertain (s.o.); to offer hospitality, a home, to (s.o.); **h. les moissons,** to store crops in a barn (after harvest). **2.** *Const:* to build against a party wall.

hébergeur, -euse [ebɛrʒœːr, -øːz], *s.* shelterer, entertainer, harbourer.

hébertisme [ebɛrtism], *s.m. Gym:* developing the body through open air games and sports (such as walking, swimming, etc.).

hébétant [ebetɑ̃], *a.* dulling, stupefying.

hébété [ebete], *a.* dazed, vacant, bewildered (expression); **h. de douleur,** stupefied, dulled, with grief; **il avait l'air h.,** he seemed to be in a daze; **regarder qn d'un air h.,** to stare, gape, at s.o.; *s.* **il agit comme un h.,** he acts as if he were in a daze.

hébétement [ebɛtmɑ̃], *s.m.* stupefaction, dazed condition.

hébéter [ebete], *v.tr.* **(j'hébète, n. hébétons; j'hébéterai)** to dull, deaden, stupefy (the senses, etc.); to daze.

s'hébéter à force de boire, to drink oneself stupid; **s'h. dans l'oisiveté,** to go to seed through idleness.

hébétude [ebetyd], *s.f.* **1.** *Med:* hebetude. **2.** dazed, stunned, condition; **frapper qn d'h.,** to daze, dumbfound, s.o.; **h. de l'ivresse,** drunken stupor; **vivre dans une douce h.,** to live in a state of lethargic content.

hébotomie [ebɔtɔmi], *s.f. Surg:* hebeosteotomy, pubiotomy.

hébraïque [ebraik], *a.* Hebraic, Hebrew.

hébraïsant [ebraizɑ̃], *s.m.* Hebraist.

hébraïser [ebraize], *v.i.* to hebraize; to study Hebrew.

hébraïsme [ebraism], *s.m.* Hebraism.

hébraïste [ebraist], *s.m.* Hebraist; Hebrew scholar.

hébreu, -eux [ebrø]. **1.** *a.m.* (**hébraïque** *is used for the f.*); Hebrew; *s.* **un Hébreu,** a Hebrew. **2.** *s.m. Ling:* **l'h.,** Hebrew; *F:* **c'est de l'h. pour moi,** that's all Greek to me.

hébridais, -aise [ebridɛ, -ɛːz], *a. & s. Geog:* Hebridean.

Hébrides (les) [lezebrid], *Pr.n.f.pl. Geog:* the Hebrides.

Hécate [ekat], *Pr.n.f. Gr.Myth:* Hecate.

hec [ɛk], *s.m.* lower half of a stable door; heck.

hécatombe [ekatɔ̃ːb], *s.f.* (*a*) hecatomb; (*b*) great slaughter; **les hécatombes de la route,** the toll of the roads; *Sch:* **faire une h. de candidats,** to slaughter, plough, the candidates wholesale.

hécatonstyle [ekatɔ̃stil], *Arch:* (*a*) *a.* with a hundred columns; (*b*) *s.m.* hecatonstylon.

***hechtia** [ɛktja], *s.m. Bot:* hechtia.

hectare [ɛktaːr], *s.m.* hectare (10,000 square metres = 2.47 acres).

hecté [ɛkte], *s.f. A.Num:* hecte.

hecticité [ɛktisite], *s.f. Med:* hecticity.

hectique [ɛktik], *a. Med:* hectic (fever).

hecto- [ɛktɔ]. **1.** *pref.* hecto-; **hectocotyle,** hectocotyle. **2.** *s.m. F:* **hecto** [ɛkto], abbreviation for (i) HECTOGRAMME; **je prendrai deux hectos d'olives,** I'll have 200 grammes of olives; (ii) HECTOLITRE; **il a vendu 20 hectos de vin,** he sold 2,000 litres of wine.

hectogramme [ɛktɔgram], *s.m.* hectogramme.

hectographe [ɛktɔgraf], *s.m.* (= AUTOCOPISTE) hectograph.

hectographie [ɛktɔgrafi], *s.f.* hectographic reproduction.

hectographier [ɛktɔgrafje], *v.tr.* (*p.d. & pr.sub:* **n. hectographiions, v. hectographiiez**) to hectograph (circular, etc.).

hectolitre [ɛktɔlitr̥], *s.m.* hectolitre.

hectomètre [ɛktɔmɛtr̥], *s.m.* hectometre.

hectométrique [ɛktɔmetrik], *a.* hectometric.

hectopièze [ɛktɔpjɛːz], *s.m. Ph.Meas:* bar.

hectowatt [ɛktɔwat], *s.m. El:* hectowatt.

hectowatt(-)heure [ɛktɔwatœːr], *s.m. El:* hectowatt-hour; *pl. hectowatts-heure.*

Hécube [ekyb], *Pr.n.f. Gr.Lit:* Hecuba.

hédenbergite [edɛ̃bɛrʒit], *s.f. Miner:* hedenbergite.

hédéracé [ederase], *a. & s. Bot:* hederaceous; *s.f.pl.* **hédéracées,** Araliaceae.

hédéragénine [ederaʒenin], *s.f. Ch:* hederagenin.

hédérine [ederin], *s.f. Ch:* hederin.

hédonisme [edɔnism], *s.m.* hedonism.

hédoniste [edɔnist]. **1.** *s.m. & f.* hedonist. **2.** *a.* hedonistic; hedonic(al).

hédonistique [edɔnistik], *a.* hedonistic.

hédrocèle [edrɔsɛl], *s.f. Med:* hedrocele.

hedychium [edikjɔm], *s.m. Bot:* hedychium.

hégélianisme [egeljanism, -ʒ-], *s.m. Phil:* Hegelianism.

hégélien, -ienne [egeljɛ̃, -ʒ-, -jɛn], *a. & s. Phil:* Hegelian.

hégémonie [eʒemɔni], *s.f.* hegemony, supremacy.

hégire [eʒiːr], *s.f. Moham.Rel:* Hegira.

heiduque [ejdyk], *s.m. Hist:* heyduck.

***heimatlos** [aimatloːs], *a. & s.m.inv.* stateless (person).

***heimatlosat** [aimatloza], *s.m.* statelessness.

***hein** [ɛ̃], *int.* (*a*) (*expressing surprise*) eh? what? (*b*) (= **n'est-ce pas**) **il fait beau aujourd'hui, hein?** fine day, isn't it?

hélas [elaːs], *int.* alas!

helcion [elsjɔ̃], *s.m. Moll:* blue-rayed limpet.

Hélène [elɛn], *Pr.n.f.* Helen, Helena; Ellen; *Gr.Ant:* **H. de Troie, H., épouse de Ménélas,** Helen of Troy; *Hist:* **H., mère de Constantin,** Helena, the mother of Constantine.

hélénine [elenin], *s.f. Pharm:* helenin.

helenium [elenjɔm], *s.m. Bot:* helenium; *F:* sneezeweed.

hélépole [elepɔl], *s.f. A.Arms:* helepole, helepolis.

***héler** [ele], *v.tr.* (**je hèle, n. hélons; je hélerai**) to hail, call (s.o., a boat, a taxi); *Nau:* to speak (a ship).

Héli [eli], *Pr.n.m. B.Hist:* Eli.

hélianthe [eljɑ̃ːt], **helianthus** [eljɑ̃tyːs], *s.m. Bot:* helianthus, sunflower; **h. tubéreux,** Jerusalem artichoke.

hélianthème [eljɑ̃tɛm], **helianthemum** [eljɑ̃temɔm], *s.m. Bot:* helianthemum, rock-rose.

hélianthine [heljɑ̃tin], *s.f. Ch:* helianthin(e); methyl orange.

héliaque [eljak], *a. Astr:* heliac(al); **lever, coucher, h.,** heliacal rising, setting.

hélibus [elibyːs], *s.m. Av:* helibus.

hélice [elis], *s.f.* **1.** (*a*) *Geom:* helix, spiral line; **escalier en h.,** winding, spiral, staircase; (*b*) *Anat:* helix, rim of the outer ear; (*c*) *Arch:* helix (of Corinthian capital, etc.). **2.** (*a*) *Mec.E:* Archimedean screw; conveyance worm; *Petroleum Ind:* **hélices,** helical packing (used in refining plants); **tarière en h.,** twist drill; **h. à vis,** spiral conveyor; (*b*) *Nau: Av:* propeller; *Nau:* screw; *Av: O:* airscrew; **propulseur à h.,** screw propeller; **h. à pas à droite, à pas à gauche,** right-hand(ed), left-hand(ed), propeller; **h. à pas constant, à pas variable,** constant-pitch, variable-pitch, propeller; **h. (à pas) réversible,** reversible(-pitch) propeller; **arbre porte-h.,** propeller shaft; **moyeu d'h.,** propeller boss, hub; *Nau:* **h. (de loch),** rotator; **vapeur à une h., à deux, trois, hélices,** single-screw, twin-screw, triple-screw, steamer; **h. à trois ailes, à trois pales,** three-bladed propeller; **h. à ailes rapportées,** built-up propeller; **h. à ailes articulées,** feathering screw; **h. en tunnel, h. sous voûte,** tunnel screw, propeller; **cage d'h.,** propeller frame; **remous de l'h.,** propeller wash; *Av:* **h. propulsive,** pusher propeller; **h. tractive,** tractor propeller; **h. sustentatrice,** lifting, sustaining, propeller; rotor; **h. freinante,** braking propeller; **h. à pas réglable, à pas commandé,** controllable (-pitch) propeller; **h. à pas réglable au sol,** adjustable-pitch propeller; ground-adjustable propeller; **h. à mise en drapeau complète, totale,** full-feathering propeller; **h. à mise en drapeau rapide,** quick-feathering propeller; **h. en drapeau,** feathered propeller; **mettre une h. en drapeau,** to feather a propeller; **h. armée,** propeller with capped ends, tips; **h. à cardan, h. orientable,** swivelling propeller; **h. carénée,** ducted propeller; **h. de service,** working propeller; **h. en moulinet,** windmilling propeller; **h. à réducteur,** geared-down propeller; **couple de l'h.,** propeller torque; **arbre d'h.,** propeller shaft; **régulateur d'h.,** propeller governor; **casserole d'h.,** propeller hub spinner; **souffle d'h.,** propeller slipstream; **mettre en marche l'h.,** to swing the propeller; (*c*) *Fish:* spinner. **3.** *Moll:* helix; **h. aquatique,** water snail, pond snail.

héliciculteur [elisikyltœːr], *s.m.* breeder, raiser, of edible snails.

héliciculture [elisikyltyːr], *s.f.* breeding, raising of edible snails.

hélicidés [eliside], *s.m.pl. Moll:* Helicidae.

hélicien, -ienne [elisjɛ̃, -jɛn], *a. Anat:* of the helix; **muscles héliciens,** helicis major and minor muscles.

héliciforme [elisifɔrm], *a. Nat.Hist:* heliciform, spiral.

hélicine [elisin], *s.f. Moll:* helicina.

hélico [eliko], *s.m. F:* helicopter.

hélico-centripète [elikɔsɑ̃tripɛt], *a. Av:* inward-flow (turbine); *pl. hélico-centripètes.*

hélicoïdal, -aux [elikɔidal, -o], *a.* helicoid(al), helical, spiral; *Tls:* **mèche hélicoïdale,** twist drill; *Mec.E:* **transporteuse hélicoïdale,** screw, spiral, conveyor; *Hyd.E:* **turbine hélicoïdale,** downward-flow, axial-flow, turbine.

hélicoïde [elikɔid], *a. & s.m. Geom:* helicoid.

hélicon[1] [elikɔ̃], *s.m. Mus:* helicon.

Hélicon[2], *Pr.n.m. Geog:* (Mount) Helicon.

héliconie [elikɔni], *s.f. Ent:* heliconian.

héliconides [elikɔnid], *s.m.pl. Ent:* Heliconiidae.

hélicoptère [elikɔptɛːr], *s.m. Av:* helicopter; rotorcraft; **h. à éjection d'air comprimé en bout de pales,** pressure-jet helicopter; rotor-tip jet-helicopter; **h. à turbine à gaz,** gas turbine helicopter; **h. à voilure auxiliaire,** helicopter with an auxiliary rotor.

hélicoptère-grue [elikɔptɛːrgry], *s.m. Av:* heavy-lift helicopter; *pl. hélicoptères-grues.*

hélicotrème [helikɔtrɛm], *s.m. Anat:* helicotrema.

héligare [eligaːr], *s.f.* helicopter station.

hélio- [eljɔ, -o], *pref.* helio-; **héliofuge,** heliofugal; **héliothérapie,** heliotherapy.

hélio [eljo], *s.f. F:* photogravure.

héliocentrique [eljɔsɑ̃trik], *a. Astr:* heliocentric.

héliochromie [eljɔkrɔmi], *s.f.* heliochromy, colour photography.

héliocopris [eljɔkɔpris], *s.m. Ent:* giant copris, dung-beetle.

héliodinides [eljɔdinid], *s.m.pl. Ent:* Heliodinidae.

Héliodore [eljɔdɔːr], *Pr.n.m. Gr.Lit:* Heliodorus.

héliodore[2], *s.m. Miner:* heliodor.

héliodyne [eljɔdin], *s.m. Opt:* solar furnace.

hélio-électrique [eljɔelɛktrik], *a. Ph: Elcs:* helio-electric, photoelectric; *pl. hélio-électriques.*

Héliogabale [eljɔgabal], *Pr.n.m. Rom.Hist:* Heliogabalus.

héliographe [eljɔgraf], *s.m. Meteor: Surv:* heliograph; **h. enregistreur,** sunshine recorder.

héliographie [eljɔgrafi], *s.f.* heliography. **1.** description of the sun. **2.** *Tchn:* process engraving.

héliographique [eljɔgrafik], *a. Tchn:* **1.** process-(work, etc.). **2. papier h.,** printing paper (for blue prints, etc.).

héliograveur [eljɔgravœːr], *s.m.* photogravure worker.

héliogravure [eljɔgravyːr], *s.f.* photogravure.

héliolite [eljɔlit], *s.f. Miner:* heliolite.

hélio-marin [eljɔmarɛ̃], *a. Med:* **centre h.-m.,** children's sea-side convalescent home where heliotherapy is used; *pl. hélio-marin(e)s.*

héliomètre [eljɔmɛtr̥], *s.m. Astr:* heliometer.

héliométrique [eljɔmetrik], *a. Astr:* heliometric.

hélion [eljɔ̃], *s.m. Atom.Ph:* helium nucleus.

héliophile [eljɔfil], *a.* heliophilous, sun-loving (plant, etc.).

héliopile [eljɔpil], *s.f. Ph:* solar battery.

hélioscope [eljɔskɔp]. **1.** *s.m. Astr:* helioscope, solar prism; **h. de polarisation,** polarizing prism. **2.** *a.* helioscopic.

héliostat [eljɔsta], *s.m.* **1.** *Astr: Surv:* heliostat. **2.** *Mil:* heliograph.

héliothérapie [eljɔterapi], *s.f. Med:* heliotherapy; sun-ray treatment.

héliotrope [eljɔtrɔp], *s.m.* **1.** (*a*) *Bot:* heliotrope, turnsole; (*b*) *a.inv.* heliotrope(-coloured). **2.** *Miner:* heliotrope, bloodstone. **3.** *Surv:* heliotrope; heliostat; heliograph.

héliotropine [eljɔtrɔpin], *s.f. Ch:* heliotropin; piperonal.

héliotropique [eljɔtrɔpik], *a. Bot:* heliotropic.

héliotropisme [eljɔtrɔpism], *s.m. Bot:* heliotropism; **à h. négatif,** apheliotropic (root, leaf).

héliport [elipɔːr], *s.m.* heliport, air-stop, rotor stop.

héliportage [elipɔrtaːʒ], *s.m. Mil:* transport (of troops, goods) by helicopter.

héliporté [elipɔrte], *a.* transported by helicopter, helicopter-borne.

hélitransport [elitrɑ̃spɔːr], *s.m. Av:* transport by helicopter.

hélitransporté [elitrɑ̃spɔrte], *a. Av:* (i) transported by helicopter; (ii) (*of goods*) conveyed by helicopter.

hélium [eljɔm], *s.m. Ch:* helium.

hélix [eliks], *s.m. Anat:* helix (of the ear).

Hellade [elaːd, ɛl-], *Pr.n.f. A.Geog:* Hellas, Greece.

helladique [eladik, ɛl-], *a. Gr.Hist:* Helladic.

helladotherium [eladɔterjɔm], ɛl-], *s.m. Paleont:* helladotherium.

hellandite [elɑ̃dit, ɛl-], *s.f. Miner:* hellandite.

hellanodice [elanɔdis, ɛl-], *s.m. Gr.Ant:* hellanodic, judge at the Olympic Games.

hellébore [elebɔːr, ɛl-], *s.m. Bot:* hellebore.

helléborine [eleborin, ɛl-], *s.f. Bot:* helleborine.

hellène [elɛn, ɛl-]. **1.** *a.* Hellenic, Greek. **2.** *s.* (*a*) Hellene, Greek; (*b*) *Rel.H:* pagan.

hellénique [elenik, ɛl-]. **1.** *a. Hist:* Hellenic. **2.** *s.f. pl.* **les Helléniques,** the Hellenica (of Xenophon).

hellénisant [elenizɑ̃, ɛl-], *a.* **1.** Hellenist. **2.** Hellenizing (Jew).

hellénisation [elenizasjɔ̃, ɛl-], *s.f.* Hellenization.

helléniser [elenize, ɛl-], *v.tr. & i.* to Hellenize.

s'helléniser, to become Hellenized.

hellénisme [elenism, ɛl-], *s.m.* Hellenism.

helléniste [elenist, ɛl-], *s.m. & f.* **1.** Hellenist. **2.** Hellenizing Jew.

hellénistique [elenistik, ɛl-], *a.* Hellenistic.

***heller** [ɛlɛːr], *s.m. A.Num:* heller.

Hellespont (l') [lelɛspɔ̃], *Pr.n.m. A.Geog:* the Hellespont.

helminthagogue [ɛlmɛ̃tagɔg]. **1.** *a. Med:* helminthagogic, vermifugal. **2.** *s.m.* vermifuge.

helminthe [ɛlmɛ̃ːt], *s.m.* helminth, (intestinal) worm.

helminthiase [ɛlmɛ̃tjaːz], *s.f. Med: Vet:* helminthiasis.

helminthique [ɛlmɛ̃tik], *a. & s.m. Med:* helminthic.

helminthoïde [ɛlmɛ̃tɔid], *a.* helminthoid, vermiform.

helminthologie [εlmε̃tɔlɔʒi], *s.f. Nat.Hist: Med:* helminthology.

hélobiales [elɔbjal], *s.m.pl. Bot:* Helobiae, Naiadales.

hélodée [elɔde], *s.f. Bot:* elodea.

hélodermatidés [elɔdermatide], *s.m.pl. Rept:* Helodermatidae.

héloderme [elɔderm], *s.m. Rept:* heloderma; Gila monster.

Héloïse [elɔiːz], *Pr.n.f.* Heloise.

hélopeltis [elɔpeltis], *s.m. Ent:* Helopeltis.

hélophyte [elɔfit], *s.f. Bot:* helophyte.

hélotarse [elɔtars], *s.m. Orn:* bateleur (eagle).

helvelle [εlvεl], *s.f. Fung:* turban-top.

helvète [εlvεt]. **1.** *a. Ethn:* Helvetian. **2.** *s.m.pl. Hist:* les Helvètes, the Helvetii.

Helvétie [εlvesi], *Pr.n.f. Geog: A. & Poet:* Helvetia.

helvétien, -ienne [εlvesjε̃, -jεn]. **1.** *a. & s.* Helvetian, Swiss. **2.** *a. & s.m. Geol:* Helvetian.

helvétique [εlvetik], *a.* Helvetic (canton, *Hist:* Republic); **le gouvernement h.,** the Swiss government.

helvétisme [εlvetism], *s.m.* Swiss French turn of phrase, expression.

helvine [εlvin], *s.f. Miner:* helvin(e), helvite.

helxine [εlksin], *s.f. Bot:* helxine.

***hem** [εm], *int.* (a)hem! hm!

hém(o)- [em(ɔ)], *pref.* haem(o)-; **hémine,** haemin.

hémagglutinine [emaglytinin], *s.f. Physiol:* h(a)emagglutinin.

hémal, -aux [emal, -o], *a. Physiol:* h(a)emal; **arc h.,** h(a)emal arch.

hémalopie [emalɔpi], *s.f. Med:* h(a)emopthalmia.

hémangiectasie [emɑ̃ʒjektazi], *s.f. Path:* h(a)emangiectasia, haemangiectasis.

hémangiomatose [emɑ̃ʒɔmatoːz], *s.f. Med:* h(a)emangiomatosis.

hémangiome [emɑ̃ʒɔm], *s.m. Med:* h(a)emangioma.

hémapophyse [emapɔfiːz], *s.f.* h(a)emapophysis.

hémarthrose [emartroːz], *s.f. Med:* h(a)emarthrosis.

hématémèse [ematemεːz], *s.f. Med:* h(a)ematemesis.

hématidrose [ematidroːz], *s.f. Med:* h(a)ematidrosis.

hématie [emati], *s.f. Physiol:* red blood corpuscle, erythrocyte; **h. nucléée,** erythroblast.

hématimètre [ematimεtr̩], *s.m.* blood-count cell.

hématimétrie [ematimetri], *s.f. Med:* h(a)ematimetry.

hématine [ematin], *s.f. Biol:* h(a)ematin.

hématite [ematit], *s.f. Miner:* h(a)ematite; **h. rouge,** red iron(-ore); **h. brune,** limonite.

hémat(o)- [emat(ɔ), -o], *pref.* h(a)emat(o)-; **hématémèse,** h(a)ematemesis; **hématique,** h(a)ematic; **hématocyste,** h(a)ematocyst.

hématoblaste [ematoblast], *s.m. Physiol:* h(a)ematoblast; blood platelet.

hématocèle [ematɔsεl], *s.f. Med:* h(a)ematocele.

hématocrite [ematɔkrit], *s.m. Physiol:* hematocrit.

hématocyste [ematɔsist], *s.f.* h(a)ematocyst.

hématocytologie [ematɔsitɔlɔʒi], *s.f. Med:* h(a)emocytology.

hématogène [ematɔʒεn], *s.m. Bio-Ch:* h(a)ematogen.

hématoïde [ematɔid], *a.* h(a)ematoid.

hématoïdine [ematɔidin], *s.f. Bio-Ch:* h(a)ematoidin.

hématolite [ematɔlit], *s.f. Miner:* h(a)ematolite.

hématologie [ematɔlɔʒi], *s.f. Med: Biol:* h(a)ematology.

hématologique [ematɔlɔʒik], *a. Med: Biol:* h(a)ematologic(al).

hématologiste [ematɔlɔʒist], **hématologue** [ematɔlɔg], *s.m. & f.* h(a)ematologist.

hématolyse [ematɔliːz], *s.f.* h(a)ematolysis.

hématome [ematoːm], *s.m. Med:* h(a)ematoma.

hématomètre [ematɔmεtr̩], *s.m. Med:* h(a)ematometra.

hématomyélie [ematɔmjeli], *s.f. Path:* h(a)ematomyelia.

hématophage [ematɔfaːʒ], *a. & s.m.* **1.** *a.* (a) *Ent:* blood-sucking (insect); (b) h(a)ematophagous. **2.** *s.m.* (a) h(a)ematophagus; (b) *Biol:* h(a)emophagocyte.

hématophagie [ematɔfaʒi], *s.f. Biol: Med:* h(a)ematophagia, h(a)ematophagy.

hématopoïèse [ematɔpɔjeːz], *s.f. Med: Physiol:* h(a)emopoiesis.

hématoporphyrine [ematɔpɔrfirin], *s.f. Bio-Ch:* h(a)ematoporphyrin.

hématoscope [ematɔskɔp], *s.m. Med:* h(a)ematoscope.

hématose [ematoːz], *s.f. Physiol:* h(a)ematosis.

hématosine [ematozin], *s.f. Biol:* h(a)ematin.

hématozoaire [ematɔzɔeːr], *s.m. Med:* h(a)ematozoon.

hématurie [ematyri], *s.f. Med:* h(a)ematuria, black-water fever.

hémélytre [emelitr̩], *Ent:* **1.** *a.* hemelytral. **2.** *s.f.* hemelytron.

héméralope [emeralɔp], *Med:* **1.** *s.m. & f.* nyctalope. **2.** *a.* nyctalopic.

héméralopie [emeralɔpi], *s.f. Med:* nyctalopia.

héméralopique [emeralɔpik], *a. Med:* nyctalope.

hémérobe [emerɔb], *s.m. Ent:* hemerobius, the lace-wing.

hémérocalle [emerɔkal], *s.f.,* **hémérocallis** [emerɔkalis], *s.m. Bot:* hemerocallis, day-lily.

hémérologue [emerɔlɔg], *s.* (a) calendar maker; (b) person who deals with anything connected with the calendar.

hémérologie [emerɔlɔʒi], *s.f.* hemerology, art of calendar making.

hémérotempérature [emerɔtɑ̃peratyːr], *s.f. Bot:* hemerotemperature; daylight temperature.

hémérothèque [emerɔtεk], *s.f.* newspaper library.

hémi- [emi], *pref.* hemi-; **hémicarpe,** hemicarp; **hémicéphalique,** hemicephalic.

hémiacétal [emiasetal], *s.m. Ch:* hemi-acetal.

hémiagueusie [emiagøzi], *s.f. Med: Psy:* hemiageusia.

hémialgie [emialʒi], *s.f. Med:* hemialgia, *esp.* migraine.

hémianesthésie [emianεstezi], *s,f. Med:* hemianaesthesia.

hémianop(s)ie [emianɔp(s)i], *s.f. Med:* hemianopia, hemianopsia.

hémiatrophie [emiatrɔfi], *s.f. Med:* hemiatrophy.

hémicarpe [emikarp], *s.m. Bot:* hemicarp.

hémicellulose [emisεlyloːz], *s.f. Bio-Ch:* hemicellulose.

hémicéphalique [emisefalik], *a.* hemicephalic.

hémic(h)ordés [emikɔrde], *s.m.pl. Biol:* Hemichorda(ta).

hémichorée [emikɔre], *s.f. Psy: Med:* hemiballismus, unilateral chorea.

hémicranie [emikrani], *s.f. Med:* hemicrania, migraine.

hémicristallin [emikristalε̃], *a. Miner:* hemicrystalline.

hémicryptophyte [emikriptɔfit], *s.f. Bot:* hemicryptophyte.

hémicycle [emisikl̩], *s.m. Arch:* hemicycle; **en h.,** semicircular (vault, arch, etc.); *F:* **dans l'h. de la Chambre,** on the floor of the Chamber (of Deputies).

hémicyclique [emisiklik], *a.* hemicyclic; semicircular.

hémicylindrique [emisilε̃drik], *a.* hemicylindrical, semicylindrical.

hémidrose [emidroːz], *s.f. Med:* hemidrosis.

hémièdre [emiεdr̩], *Cryst:* **1.** *a.* hemihedral. **2.** *s.m.* hemihedron.

hémiédrie [emiedri], *s.f. Cryst:* hemihedrism.

hémiédrique [emiedrik], *a. Cryst:* hemihedral, hemihedric.

hémimétabole [emimetabɔl], *Ent:* **1.** *a.* hemimetabolic, hemimetabolous. **2.** *s.m.pl.* **hémimétaboles,** Hemimetabola.

hémi-mimie [emimimi], *s.f. Psy:* hemi-facial expression, mimicry.

hémine [emin], *s.f. Bio-Ch:* hemin.

hémione [emjɔn], *s.m. Z:* hemione, dziggetai, kiang.

hémiopie [emiɔpi], *s.f. Med:* hemiopia.

hémiparasite [emiparazit], *s.m. Biol:* hemiparasite.

hémiparésie [emiparezi], *s.f. Med:* hemiparesis.

hémiplégie [emipleʒi], *s.f. Med:* hemiplegia.

hémiplégique [emipleʒik], *a. & s. Med:* hemiplegic.

hémiptère [emiptεːr], *Ent:* **1.** *a.* hemipterous, hemipteral, hemipteran. **2.** *s.m.* hemipter, hemipteran; *pl.* **hémiptères,** Hemiptera, Hemipters.

hémiptéroïdes [emipterɔid], *s.m.pl. Ent:* Hemiptera.

hémisphère [emisfεːr], *s.m.* hemisphere; **l'h. nord, sud,** the northern, southern, hemisphere; *Anat:* **les hémisphères cérébraux,** the cerebral hemispheres; **hémisphères cérébelleux,** cerebellar hemispheres.

hémisphérectomie [emisferεktɔmi], *s.f. Surg:* hemispherectomy.

hémisphérique [emisferik], *a.* hemispheric(al), semispheric(al); **à tête h.,** round-headed (bolt, etc.).

hémisphéroïde [emisferɔid]. **1.** *a.* hemispheroidal. **2.** *s.m.* hemispheroid.

hémistiche [emistiʃ], *s.m. Pros:* hemistich.

hémitriptère [emitriptεːr], *s.m. Ich:* hemitripterus, sea-raven.

hémitrope [emitrɔp], *a. Cryst:* twinned, hemitropic (felspar).

hémitropie [emitrɔpi], *s.f. Cryst:* hemitropism, twin crystallization; **axe d'h.,** twin axis; **plan d'h.,** twin plane.

hém(o)- [em(o)], *pref.* h(a)em(o)-; **hémine,** h(a)emin; **hémophilie,** h(a)emophilia.

hémochromatose [emɔkromatoːz], *s.f. Med:* h(a)emochromatosis.

hémoclasie [emɔklazi], *s.f. Med:* h(a)emoclasia.

hémoconcentration [emɔkɔ̃sɑ̃trasjɔ̃], *s.f. Path:* h(a)emoconcentration.

hémoconie [emɔkɔni], *s.f. Med:* h(a)emoconia.

hémoculture [emɔkyltyːr], *s.f.* h(a)emoculture, blood culture.

hémocyanine [emɔsjanin], *s.f. Biol: Ch:* h(a)emocyanin.

hémocytoblaste [emɔsitoblast], *s.m. Med:* h(a)emocytoblast.

hémocytomètre [emɔsitɔmεtr̩], *s.m.* h(a)emocytometer.

hémodiagnostic [emɔdjagnɔstik], *s.m. Med:* h(a)emodiagnosis.

hémodromomètre [emɔdromɔmεtr̩], *s.m.* h(a)emodromometer.

hémodynamique [emɔdinamik], *s.f.* h(a)emodynamics.

hémogénie [emɔʒeni], *s.f. Med:* h(a)emogenia, pseudoh(a)emophilia.

hémogénique [emɔʒenik], *a. Med:* h(a)emogenic.

hémoglobine [emɔglɔbin], *s.f. Physiol:* h(a)emoglobin.

hémoglobinémie [emɔglɔbinemi], *s.f. Med:* h(a)emoglobin(a)emia.

hémoglobinomètre [emɔglɔbinɔmεtr̩], *s.m.* h(a)emoglobinometer.

hémoglobinurie [emɔglɔbinyri], *s.f. Med:* h(a)emoglobinuria.

hémogramme [emɔgram], *s.m. Med:* h(a)emogram(me).

hémolyse [emɔliːz], *s.f. Med:* h(a)emolysis.

hémolysine [emɔlizin], *s.f. Ch: Physiol:* h(a)emolysin.

hémolytique [emɔlitik], *a. Ch: Physiol:* h(a)emolytic.

hémopathie [emɔpati], *s.f. Med:* h(a)emopathy.

hémopéricarde [emɔperikard], *s.m. Physiol:* (h(a)emopericardium.

hémopéritoine [emɔperitwan], *s.m. Physiol:* h(a)emoperitoneum.

hémophile [emɔfil], *Med:* **1.** *a.* h(a)emophilic. **2.** *s.m. & f.* h(a)emophiliac; *F:* bleeder.

hémophilie [emɔfili], *s.f. Med:* h(a)emorrhagic diathesis; h(a)emophilia.

hémophilique [emɔfilik], *s.m. & f. Med:* h(a)emophilic.

hémoprotéidés [emɔprɔteide], *s.m.pl. Ent:* H(a)emoproteidae.

hémoptysie [emɔptizi], *s.f. Med:* h(a)emoptysis, spitting of blood.

hémoptysique [emɔptizik], *a. Med:* h(a)emoptysical.

hémorragie [emɔraʒi], *s.f. Med:* h(a)emorrhage; bleeding; *Pol.Ec:* **l'h. des réserves d'or,** the heavy drain on the gold reserve.

hémorragique [emɔraʒik], *a. Med:* h(a)emorrhagic.

hémorroïdaire [emɔrɔideːr], *Med:* **1.** *a.* h(a)emorroïdal. **2.** *s.* sufferer from h(a)emorrhoids, person who suffers from h(a)emorrhoids.

hémorroïdal, -aux [emɔrɔidal, -o], *a. Med:* h(a)emorrhoidal; **flux hémorroïdaux,** bleeding of piles.

hémorroïdes [emɔrɔid], *s.f.pl. Med:* h(a)emorrhoids, piles; *in sg.* pile, marisca; **hémorroïdes sèches,** blind piles; **faire l'ablation d'une hémorroïde,** to remove a pile.

hémostase [emɔstaːz], *s.f. Physiol:* h(a)emostasia.

hémostatique [emɔstatik], *Med: Surg:* **1.** *a.* h(a)emostatic; **pince h.,** h(a)emostat, artery clip. **2.** *s.m.* h(a)emostat; h(a)emostatic.

hémothèque [emɔtεk], *s.f. Med:* **1.** blood storage room. **2.** blood bank.

hémothorax [emɔtɔraks], *s.m. Physiol:* h(a)emothorax.

hémotoxine [emɔtɔksin], *s.f. Ch: Physiol:* h(a)emotoxin, h(a)emolysin.

hendayais, -aise [ɑ̃daje, -εːz], *a. & s. Geog:* (native, inhabitant) of Hendaye.

hendéc(a)- [ε̃dek(a)], *pref.* hendec(a)-; **hendécandre,** hendecandrous.

hendécagone [ε̃dekagɔn], *Geom:* **1.** *a.* hendecagonal. **2.** *s.m.* hendecagon.

hendécasyllabe [ε̃dekasil(l)ab], *Pros:* **1.** *a.* hendecasyllabic. **2.** *s.m.* hendecasyllable.

hendécasyllabique [ɛ̃dekasil(l)abik], *a. Pros:* hendecasyllabic.
hénioque [enjɔk], *s.m. Ich:* whip-fish.
***henné** [ɛn(n)e], *s.m. Bot: Toil:* henna; **se faire teindre les cheveux au h.,** to have one's hair henna'd.
hennebontais, -aise [ɛnbɔ̃tɛ, -ɛːz], *a. & s. Geog:* (native, inhabitant) of Hennebont.
***hennin** [ɛnɛ̃], *s.m. A.Cost:* hennin.
***hennir** [ɛniːr], *v.i.* to whinny; to neigh.
***hennissant** [ɛnisɑ̃], *a.* whinnying, neighing.
***hennissement** [ɛnismɑ̃], *s.m.* (*a*) whinnying, neighing; (*b*) whinny, neigh.
***hennuyer, -ère** [ɛnɥije, -ɛːr], *a. & s. Geog:* (native, inhabitant) of Hainault.
Hénoch [enɔk], *Pr.n.m.* Enoch.
Henri [ɑ̃ri], *Pr.n.m.* Henry.
Henriette [ɑ̃rjɛt], *Pr.n.f.* Henrietta.
henriquinquiste [ɑ̃rikɛ̃kist], *s. Hist:* legitimist, *i.e.* supporter of the Count de Chambord (dynastically Henri V).
***hep** [ɛp], *int.* hi! hey! hi there!
henry [ɑ̃ri], *s.m. El:* henry (unit of self-induction); *pl. henrys.*
héparine [eparin], *s.f. Ch: Med:* heparin.
hépatalgie [epatalʒi], *s.f. Med:* hepatalgia.
hépatectomie [epatɛktɔmi], *s.f. Surg:* hepatectomy.
hépatique [epatik]. **1.** *a. Anat: etc:* hepatic. **2.** (*a*) *s.m. Pharm:* hepatic; (*b*) *s.m. & f.* person suffering from a liver complaint. **3.** *s.f. Bot:* hepatica; *F:* liverwort; **h. terrestre, des fontaines,** stone-liverwort.
hépatisation [epatizasjɔ̃], *s.f. Med:* hepatization.
hépatiser (s') [sepatize], *v.pr.* (*of lungs*) to become hepatized.
hépatisme [epatism], *s.m. Med:* hepatism.
hépatite [epatit], *s.f.* **1.** *Med:* hepatitis. **2.** *Miner:* hepatite.
hépatocèle [epatɔsɛl], *s.f. Med:* hepatocele.
hépatocirrhose [epatɔsiroːz], *s.f. Med:* cirrhosis of the liver.
hépatogastrite [epatɔgastrit], *s.f. Med:* hepatogastritis.
hépatologie [epatɔlɔʒi], *s.f. Med: Anat: Physiol:* hepatology.
hépatomégalie [epatɔmegali], *s.f. Med:* hepatomegaly.
hépatonéphrite [epatɔnefrit], *s.f. Med:* hepatonephritis.
hépatopexie [epatɔpɛksi], *s.f. Surg:* hepatopexy.
hépatorragie [epatɔraʒi], *s.f. Med:* hepatorrhagia.
hépatorraphie [epatɔrafi], *s.f. Surg:* hepatorrhaphy.
hépatorrhexie [epatɔrɛksi], *s.f. Med:* hepatorrhexis.
hépatoscopie [epatɔskɔpi], *s.f. Ant:* hepatoscopy.
hépiale [epjal], *s.m. Ent:* (*a*) hepialus, hepialid, swift; **h. du houblon,** ghostmoth; (*b*) *a.* hepialid (moth).
hépialides [epjalid], *s.m.pl. Ent:* Hepialidae; *F:* the swifts.
hept(a)- [ɛpt(a)], *pref.* hept(a)-; **heptagyne,** heptagynous; **heptapétale,** heptapetalous.
heptacorde [ɛptakɔrd]. *Mus:* **1.** *a.* seven-stringed. **2.** *s.m.* heptachord (instrument, scale).
heptaèdre [ɛptaɛːdr], *s.m. Geom:* heptahedron.
heptaédrique [ɛptaedrik], *a. Geom:* heptahedral.
heptagonal, -aux [ɛptagɔnal, -o], *a. Geom:* heptagonal.
heptagone [ɛptagɔn], *Geom:* **1.** *a.* heptagonal. **2.** *s.m.* heptagon.
Heptaméron (l') [lɛptamerɔ̃], *s.m. Lit.Hist:* the Heptameron.
heptamètre [ɛptamɛtr̥], *s.m. Pros:* heptameter.
heptane [ɛptan], *s.m. Ch:* heptane.
heptaphylle [ɛptafil], *a. Bot:* heptaphyllous.
heptarchie [ɛptarʃi], *s.f. Hist:* heptarchy.
heptarchique [ɛptarʃik], *a.* heptarchic(al).
heptasyllabe [ɛptasil(l)ab], *a. Pros:* heptasyllabic.
Heptateuque (l') [lɛptatøk], *s.m. B:* the Heptateuch.
heptavalent [ɛptavalɑ̃], *a. Ch:* septivalent, heptavalent.
heptène [ɛptɛn], *s.m. Ch:* heptene.
heptode [ɛptɔd], *s.f. Elcs:* heptode.
heptose [ɛptoːz], *s.m. Ch:* heptose.
heptyle [ɛptil], *s.m. Ch:* heptyl.
heptylène [ɛptilɛn], *s.m. Ch:* heptylene.
heptylique [ɛptilik], *a. Ch:* heptylic.
heptyne [ɛptin], *s.m. Ch:* heptyne.
Héraclée [erakle], *Pr.n.f. Geog:* Heraclea.
Héraclès [eraklɛːs], *Pr.n.m. Myth:* Herakles, Heracles.
Héraclides (les) [lezeraklid], *s.m.pl. Myth:* the Heraclidae; **un héraclide,** a Heraclid.
Héraclite [eraklit], *Pr.n.m. Gr.Phil:* Heraclitus.
héraclitéen, -enne [erakliteɛ̃, -ɛn], *a. Phil:* Heraclitean, Heraclitic.
Héraklès [eraklɛːs], *Pr.n.m.* = HÉRACLÈS.
héraldique [eraldik]. **1.** *a.* heraldic; armorial; **l'art, la science, h.,** heraldry, blazonry. **2.** *s.f.* heraldry.
héraldiste [eraldist], *s.m. & f.* heraldist.
hérapathite [erapatit], *s.f. Miner:* herapathite.
hérau(l)derie [ero(l)dəri], *s.f.* heraldry.
***héraut** [ero], *s.m.* (*a*) herald; (*b*) herald, *Lit:* harbinger (of spring, etc.).
herbacé [ɛrbase], *a. Bot:* herbaceous; **bordure herbacée,** herbaceous border; *Oc: Biol:* **la zone herbacée,** the Laminarian zone (of coastal waters).
herbage [ɛrbaːʒ], *s.m.* **1.** grassland; pasture; meadow(land). **2.** grass, herbage. **3.** *Cu:* green vegetables.
herbagement [ɛrbaʒmɑ̃], *s.m. Husb:* putting (of animals) out to grass.
herbager[1] [ɛrbaʒe], *v.tr.* **(j'herbageai(s); n. herbageons)** *Husb:* to put (animals) out to grass.
herbager[2], **-ère** [-ɛːr], *s.* grazier.
herbageux, -euse [ɛrbaʒø, -øːz], *a.* grassy (plain, etc.).
herbe [ɛrb], *s.f.* **1.** herb, plant, weed; **herbes potagères,** green vegetables; **fines herbes,** herbs (for seasoning); **omelette aux fines herbes,** omelette, fines herbes; **herbes marines,** seaweed; **mauvaise h.,** weed; *F:* **c'est une mauvaise h.,** he's a bad lot, a ne'er-do-well; *s.a.* CROÎTRE; **jardin couvert d'herbes,** garden overrun with weeds, that has run to waste; *F:* **sur quelle h. avez-vous marché?** what's the matter with you? *Prov:* **à chemin battu il ne croît pas d'h.,** there are too many people plying that trade already. **2.** grass; **brin d'h.,** blade of grass; **faire de l'h.,** to cut grass (for rabbit, etc.); **mettre un cheval à l'h.,** to turn a horse out to grass; **couper l'h. sous le pied à qn,** to take the wind out of s.o.'s sails, to cut the ground from under s.o.'s feet; **déjeuner sur l'h.,** to picnic; **nous avons déjeuné sur l'h.,** we had an alfresco lunch; *F:* **manger l'h. par la racine,** to push up the daisies; *Golf:* **être dans l'h. longue,** to be in the rough. **3. en h.,** green, unripe (corn, etc.); in the blade; **poète en h.,** budding poet; **diplomate en h.,** diplomatist in embryo; *s.a.* BLÉ. **4.** *Bot:* (*common names*) **h. aux abeilles,** meadow sweet; **h. amère, h. aux vers,** tansy; **h. d'amour,** mignonette; **h. aux ânes,** evening primrose; **h. aux boucs, à l'hirondelle,** greater celandine; **h. cachée,** broomrape; **h. carrée, de siège,** water betony; **h. aux centaures,** centaury; **h. à cent goûts,** mugwort; **h. aux chantres,** hedge mustard; **h. aux charpentiers,** (i) milfoil, yarrow; (ii) orpin(e), live-long; **h. aux chats,** catmint, *U.S:* catnip; **h. des chevaux,** henbane; **h. au cœur, aux poumons,** lungwort; **h. au coq,** costmary; **h. à la coupure,** (i) orpin(e), live-long; (ii) sneezewort; **h. aux cuillers,** scurvy grass; **h. aux écrouelles,** (i) burweed; (ii) figwort; **h. aux écus,** moneywort; **h. empoisonnée,** deadly nightshade; **h. à éternuer,** sneezewort; **h. de fic, aux hémorroïdes,** figwort, pilewort, lesser celandine; **h. à foulon,** soapwort; **h. aux goutteux,** gout-weed; **h. aux gueux,** wild clematis, traveller's joy; **h. de Guinée,** Guinea grass; **h. à jaunir,** (i) dyer's green weed; (ii) yellow weed; **h. au lait,** (i) milkwort; (ii) euphorbia; **h. à loup,** wolf's bane, monk's hood; **h. aux mamelles,** nipplewort; **h. aux massues,** club moss; **h. à mille florins,** lesser centaury; **h. aux mites,** moth-mullein; **h. de Pâques, du vent,** pasque flower; **h. au pauvre homme,** hedge hyssop; **h. aux perles,** gromwell; **h. aux poux,** lousewort; **h. à la puce,** poison ivy; **h. aux puces,** flea-bane; **h. à la rate,** hart's-tongue fern; **h. à la rosée,** sundew; **h. sacrée,** vervain; **h. de saint-Christophe,** baneberry; **h. de saint-Jacques,** ragwort; **h. de saint-Jean,** St John's wort; **h. sans couture,** adder's tongue; **h. à sétons,** green hellebore; **h. à soleil,** sunflower; **h. des sorciers,** thorn apple; **h. à la tache,** water avens; **h. du tonnerre,** houseleek; **h. aux verrues,** (i) *Moss:* wartwort, (ii) *Bot:* wartwort, wart weed; **h. aux vipères,** viper's bugloss; **h. vivante,** sensitive plant; **h. à la Trinité,** liverwort; **h. aux cinq coutures,** rib-wort, -grass; **h. aux voituriers,** orpin(e), live-long; **h. sainte,** bastard balm; **h. sacrée, à tous les maux,** verbena, wild vervain; **h. à l'éléphant,** elephant grass; **h. aux teigneux,** burdock.
herbeiller [ɛrbɛje], *v.i. Ven:* (*of boar*) to feed.
herber [ɛrbe], *v.tr. Tex:* to bleach (linen) on the grass; to croft, grass (linen).
herberie [ɛrbəri], *s.f.* **1.** bleaching ground (for linen). **2.** grass-market.
herbette [ɛrbɛt], *s.f.* (*a*) lawn grass; (*b*) *Poet:* (green)sward.
herbeux, -euse [ɛrbø, -øːz], *a.* grassy, grass-grown.
herbicide [ɛrbisid], *s.m.* weedkiller.
herbier [ɛrbje], *s.m.* **1.** (*a*) herbal; (*b*) herbarium; hortus siccus. **2.** *Agr:* loft, shed, for cut grass. **3.** *Bot:* water plant community; **h. de zostères,** zostera bed, bed of eelgrass.
herbière [ɛrbjɛːr], *s.f.* **1.** herb woman, herb seller. **2.** paunch, rumen (of ruminants).
herbivore [ɛrbivɔːr], *Z:* **1.** *a.* herbivorous, grass-eating. **2.** *s.m.* herbivore; *pl.* **les herbivores,** the Herbivora.
herborisateur, -trice [ɛrbɔrizatœːr, -tris], *s.* herborizer, plant gatherer, botanizer.
herborisation [ɛrbɔrizasjɔ̃], *s.f.* **1.** herborizing, botanizing. **2.** botanizing excursion.
herborisé [ɛrbɔrize], *a. Miner:* arborized, dendritic (agate, etc.).
herboriser [ɛrbɔrize], *v.i.* (*a*) to herborize; to go botanizing; to botanize; (*b*) to gather plants, herbs.
herboriseur [ɛrbɔrizœːr], *s.m.* herborizer, plant-gatherer, botanizer.
herboriste [ɛrbɔrist], *s.m. & f.* herbalist.
herboristerie [ɛrbɔristəri], *s.f.* **1.** herbalist's shop. **2.** herb trade.
herbu, -ue [ɛrby]. **1.** *a.* grassy; **chemin h.,** grass-grown road. **2.** *s.f.* **herbue;** (*a*) light grazing land; (*b*) *Vit:* loam; (*c*) *Metall:* clay flux. **3.** *s.m. Oc:* mud flat (consolidated by vegetation).
***herchage** [ɛrʃaːʒ], *s.m.* (*N. of Fr.*) *Min:* haulage (of coal); putting.
***herche** [ɛrʃ], *s.f. Min:* wag(g)on; tram, skip, tub.
***hercher** [ɛrʃe], *v.i. Min:* to haul (coal); to put (the tubs).
***hercheur** [ɛrʃœːr], *s.m.* (*N. of Fr.*) *Min:* haulage man, haulage boy; putter.
hercogamie [ɛrkɔgami], *s.f. Bot:* hercogamy.
Herculanum [ɛrkylanɔm], *Pr.n.m. A.Geog:* Herculaneum.
Hercule [ɛrkyl]. **1.** *Pr.n.m. Myth: Astr:* Hercules; **travail d'H.,** Herculean task; *Geog: A:* **les Colonnes d'H.,** the Pillars of Hercules. **2.** *s.m.* **(homme taillé en) h.,** powerfully built man; **un hercule de foire,** a (professional) strong man. **3.** *s.m. Ent: F:* **h. des Antilles,** Hercules beetle.
herculéen, -enne [ɛrkyleɛ̃, -ɛn], *a.* Herculean (strength, etc.).
hercynien, -ienne [ɛrsinjɛ̃, -jɛn], *a. Geol:* Hercynian.
hercynite [ɛrsinit], *s.f. Miner:* hercynite.
***herd-book** [(h)ərdbuk], *s.m. Husb:* herd-book; *pl. herd-books.*
herdérite [ɛrderit], *s.f. Miner:* herderite.
***hère** [ɛːr], *s.m.* **1.** *F:* **un pauvre h.,** a poor, unlucky, creature (lacking in character, devoid of means); a poor blighter; **pauvre h.!** poor devil! **2.** *Ven:* young stag.
héréditaire [ereditɛːr], *a.* hereditary (charge, prince, disease); (disease) that runs in the family.
héréditairement [ereditɛrmɑ̃], *adv.* hereditarily.
héréditarisme [ereditarism], *s.m. Biol:* hereditarianism; **partisan de l'h.,** hereditarian.
hérédité [eredite], *s.f.* **1.** *Jur: Biol:* hereditary principle; heredity; **h. d'influence,** telegony. **2.** right of inheritance, heirship. **3.** *A:* inheritance, heritage, succession, estate; *A.Jur:* **expilation d'h.,** depredation of decedent's estate.
hérédoataxie [eredɔataksi], *s.f. Med:* heredo-ataxia.
hérédosyphilis [eredɔsifilis], *s.f. Med:* heredo-syphilis.
hérédosyphilitique [eredɔsifilitik], *a. Med:* (i) heredito-syphilitic; (ii) heredosyphilitic.
hérésiarque [erezjark], *s.m.* heresiarch.
hérésie [erezi], *s.f.* heresy.
héréticité [eretisite], *s.f.* heretical character (of book, etc.).
hérétique [eretik]. **1.** *a.* heretical. **2.** *s.* heretic.
héricart [erikar], *s.f. Hort:* variety of large strawberry.
hérissé [erise], *a.* **1.** bristling; (*a*) **les cheveux hérissés de terreur,** his hair on end with fright; *F:* **homme toujours h.,** man who is always up in arms, who always has his back up; (*b*) **carré h. de baïonnettes,** square bristling with bayonets; **l'affaire est hérissée de difficultés,** the business bristles with difficulties, is beset with difficulties. **2.** (*a*) spiky (hair); bristly (moustache); *Bot:* prickly (stem, fruit); (*b*) shaggy, rough (hair, etc.); **cheval h.,** rough-coated horse.
***hérissement** [erismɑ̃], *s.m.* bristling.
***hérisser** [erise], *v.tr.* **1.** (*a*) to erect, to bristle (up); (*of bird*) **h. ses plumes,** to ruffle up, put up, its feathers; (*b*) to make to bristle; to cover, surround, with spikes; **h. un bastion de pieux,** to

protect a bastion with sharp stakes; **de hautes montagnes hérissent toute cette région,** high mountains give a rugged appearance to the whole of this region; **il a été hérissé par cette remarque,** this remark made him bristle; *F:* **h. sa conversation de malices,** to lard, pepper, one's conversation with sly digs. 2. *Const:* to rough-cast (wall).

se hérisser, to bristle (up), to become erect; (*of hair*) to stand on end; *F:* (*of pers.*) to get one's back up; *F:* **ça m'a fait h. les cheveux,** it made my hair stand on end; **ne vous hérissez pas,** don't bristle up.

***hérisson** [erisɔ̃], *s.m.* 1. (*a*) *Z:* hedgehog; (*b*) **h. de mer,** (i) *Echin:* sea urchin, (ii) *Ich:* porcupine fish; (iii) *Ann:* sea-mouse; (*c*) *F:* cross-grained person, person who is always on the defensive. 2. (*a*) row of spikes (on wall, etc.); *Mil:* chevaux de frise; (*b*) bottle-drainer. 3. *Mec.E:* sprocket wheel; pin wheel; **h. de côté,** crown wheel. 4. (*a*) (sweep's) flue-brush; (*b*) bottle-brush. 5. (*a*) *A:* spiked toll-bar or town-gate; (*b*) *Agr:* toothed cylinder, toothed roller; (*c*) *Tex:* urchin (of carding machine). 6. chestnut husk, bur. 7. *Mil:* (*fortified position*) hedgehog. 8. *Civ.E:* subgrade, foundation (of road).

hérissonnage [erisɔnaːʒ], *s.m.* 1. *Const:* rough-casting (of wall). 2. *Civ.E:* subgrading (of a road).

***hérissonne** [erisɔn], *s.f.* 1. *Z:* female hedgehog. 2. *Ent:* woolly bear (caterpillar). 3. *Z:* Erinaceus.

***hérissonner** [erisɔne], *v.tr.* to roughcast (wall).

héritable [eritabl̥], *a. Jur: A:* heritable (property).

héritage [eritaːʒ], *s.m.* inheritance, heritage; **part d'h.,** portion; **recueillir son h.,** to come into one's property; **faire un h.,** to receive a legacy; to come into money; **faire un petit h.,** to come into a small legacy; **il lui échut un h.,** he was left a legacy; **oncle à h.,** uncle from whom one has expectations; **dissiper son h.,** to squander one's patrimony; **h. de honte,** legacy of shame.

hériter [erite], *v.* to inherit. 1. *v.i.* (*a*) **h. d'une fortune,** to inherit, succeed, to come into, a fortune; *abs.* **c'est lui qui a hérité,** he came into the property; the estate devolved upon him, devolved to him; (*b*) *F:* to get; **il a hérité de dix jours de prison,** he got ten days' imprisonment; **il a hérité de tous les défauts de son père,** he has inherited all his father's failings. 2. *v.tr.* **h. qch. de qn,** to inherit sth. from s.o.; *abs.* **h. de qn,** to inherit s.o.'s estate, to become s.o.'s heir.

héritier, -ière [eritje, -jɛːr], *s.* heir, *f.* heiress; **h. de qch., de qn,** heir to sth., to s.o.; **h. présomptif,** (i) *Jur:* next-of-kin; (ii) heir apparent; **h. légitime,** heir-at-law, rightful heir; **se montrer le digne h. de la gloire de ses ancêtres,** to prove a worthy heir to the glory of one's line; *F:* **épouser une héritière,** to marry a gold mine.

hermaphrodisme [ɛrmafrɔdism], *s.m. Biol: Bot:* hermaphrod(it)ism.

Hermaphrodite [ɛrmafrɔdit]. 1. *Pr.n.m. Gr. Myth:* Hermaphroditus. 2. *s.m.* hermaphrodite. 3. *a.* hermaphrodite, hermaphroditic.

herme [ɛrm], *s.m.* (*in S. of Fr.*) sterile, unproductive, strip of land.

hermella [ɛrmela], **hermelle** [ɛrmɛl], *s.f. Ann:* sabellid.

herméneute [ɛrmenøt], *s.m. Ecc:* hermeneut.

herméneutique [ɛrmenøtik], *Phil:* 1. *a.* hermeneutic(al). 2. *s.f.* hermeneutics.

Hermès [ɛrmɛs]. 1. *Pr.n.m. Gr.Myth:* Hermes. 2. *s.m.* herm, terminal figure.

herméticité [ɛrmetisite], *s.f.* 1. (air-, water-, light-)tightness; imperviousness. 2. esotericism.

hermétique [ɛrmetik], *a.* 1. hermetic (philosophy, alchemy). 2. tight (-closed), hermetically sealed; **joint h.,** (air-, water-)tight joint; *Phot:* **rideau h.,** light-tight shutter. 3. *Arch:* **colonne h.,** hermetic column.

hermétiquement [ɛrmetikmɑ̃], *a.* (*a*) hermetically (sealed, etc.); (*b*) *F:* tight(-shut), close(-shut).

hermétisme [ɛrmetism], *s.m.* 1. hermetism, hermeticism, hermetics. 2. abstruseness, obscurity (of text, etc.).

hermétiste [ɛrmetist], *s.m.* follower of the Hermetic philosophy, hermetist; alchemist.

hermine [ɛrmin], *s.f.* 1. *Z:* stoat, ermine. 2. *Com:* ermine (fur); **fourré d'h.,** ermined; *F:* **avoir la blancheur de l'h.,** to be as pure as snow. 3. *Her:* ermine. 4. **l'h.,** the ceremonial robe of French magistrates and professors; **endosser l'h.,** to take up a career as magistrate, professor.

herminé [ɛrmine], *a. Her:* ermine(d); white powdered with black tufts.

herminer [ɛrmine], *v.tr.* to line, edge, (garment) with ermine.

herminette [ɛrminɛt], *s.f.* 1. fawn-coloured ermine (used for cravats, caps, etc.). 2. *Tls: Carp:* adze; *Coop:* howel.

Herminie [ɛrmini], *Pr.n.f.* Erminia.

hermitage [ɛrmitaːʒ], *s.m.* = ERMITAGE.

hermite [ɛrmit], *s.m.* = ERMITE.

hermitien, -ienne [ɛrmisjɛ̃, -jɛn], **hermitique** [ɛrmitik], *a. Math:* **matrice hermitienne, h.,** square matrix.

hermodactylus [ɛrmɔdaktilyːs], *s.m. Bot:* hermodactyl(us).

Hermondures [ɛrmɔ̃dyːr], *Pr.n.m.pl. Hist:* Hermunduri.

***herniaire** [ɛrnjɛːr]. 1. *a.* hernial (tumour, etc.); **bandage h.,** truss. 2. *s.f. Bot:* rupture wort; **h. glabre,** glabrous rupture-wort.

***hernie** [ɛrni], *s.f.* 1. *Med:* (*a*) hernia, rupture; **h. inguinale,** inguinal hernia; bubonocele; **h. étranglée,** strangulated hernia; (*b*) **h. du poumon,** hernia of the lung; (*c*) **h. discale,** slipped disk. 2. *Aut: Cy:* bulge, swelling (in tyre). 3. *Hort:* club-root; finger-and-toe (of cabbage, turnip).

***hernié** [ɛrnje], *a.* protruding (bowel).

***hernieux, -euse** [ɛrnjø, -øːz], *a.* suffering from hernia, ruptured.

***herniole** [ɛrnjɔl], *s.f. Bot:* rupture wort.

***hernute** [ɛrnyt], *s.m. Rel.H:* Moravian brother, Herrnhuter.

Héro [ero], *Pr.n.f. Gr.Myth:* Hero.

Hérode [erɔd], *Pr.n.m.* Herod.

Hérodiade [erɔdjad], *Pr.n.f.* Herodias.

hérodien [erɔdjɛ̃], *s.m. Jew.Hist:* Herodian.

Hérodote [erɔdɔt], *Pr.n.m. Gr.Lit:* Herodotus.

héroïcité [erɔisite], *s.f.* (*rare*) heroicalness.

héroï-comique [erɔikɔmik], *a.* heroi-comic, mock-heroic; *pl. heroï-comiques.*

héroïde [erɔid], *s.f.* heroic verse.

héroïne[1] [erɔin], *s.f.* heroine.

héroïne[2], *s.f. Ch:* heroin(e).

héroïnomanie [erɔinɔmani], *s.f. Path:* heroin addiction, heroinism.

héroïque [erɔik], *a.* heroic(al); **remède h.,** heroic remedy, kill-or-cure remedy.

héroïquement [erɔikmɑ̃], *adv.* heroically.

héroïser [erɔize], *v.tr.* to heroize; to treat (s.o. as a hero.

héroïsme [erɔism], *s.m.* heroism.

***héron**[1] [erɔ̃], *s.m. Orn:* heron; **h. cendré,** common heron; **h. pourpré,** purple heron; **h. crabier,** squacco heron; **h. garde-bœuf(s),** cattle egret; **h. ardoise,** African black heron.

Héron[2], *Pr.n.m. Gr.Ant:* **H. l'Ancien,** Hero of Alexandria.

***héronneau, -eaux** [erɔno], *s.m. Orn:* young heron.

héronnier, -ière [erɔnje, -jɛːr], *a. & s.f.* 1. *a.* skinny, long-legged; **jambe héronnière,** lanky leg. 2. *s.f.* **héronnière,** heronry.

***héros** [ero], *s.m.* hero; **devenir le h. du jour,** to become the hero of the hour; *F:* **h. de salon,** carpet-knight; **jouer au, se prendre pour un, h.,** to indulge in heroics.

***herpe** [ɛrp], *s.f. A:* 1. *N.Arch:* **h. de poulaine,** head-rail; **h. de guibre,** headboard. 2. *pl. Jur:* **herpes marines,** natural treasures thrown up by the sea (coral, ambergris, seaweed, etc.).

herpès [ɛrpɛs], *s.m. Med:* herpes, tetter; cold sore; **h. tonsurant,** ringworm; **h. cataménial,** herpes menstrualis; **h. récidivant,** recurrent herpes.

herpétiforme [ɛrpetifɔrm], *a. Med:* herpetiform.

herpétique [ɛrpetik], *a. Med:* herpetic.

herpétisme [ɛrpetism], *s.m. Med:* herpetism.

herpétologie [ɛrpetɔlɔʒi], *s.f.* herpetology.

herpétologique [ɛrpetɔlɔʒik], *a.* herpetologic.

herpétologiste [ɛrpetɔlɔʒist], *s.m.* herpetologist.

***hersage** [ɛrsaːʒ], *s.m. Agr:* harrowing.

***herschage** [ɛrʃaːʒ], *s.m. Min:* haulage (of coal); putting.

herschélite [ɛrʃelit], *s.f. Miner:* herschelite.

***herse** [ɛrs], *s.f.* 1. *Agr:* harrow; **h. à semer,** drill harrow; **h. roulante,** revolving harrow; **h. en fascines,** bush harrow; **h. à chaînons,** chain harrow; **h. à disques,** disc-harrow. 2. *A.Fort:* portcullis, herse; **porte munie d'une h.,** portcullised gateway. 3. *Const:* **herses de (la) croupe,** hip cross-beams (of roof). 4. (*a*) *Ecc:* (taper-) hearse; (*b*) *pl. Th:* stage lights, battens. 5. balloon anchor.

***hersement** [ɛrsmɑ̃], *s.m. Agr:* harrowing.

***herser** [ɛrse], *v.tr. Agr:* to harrow; to drag (field).

***herseur** [ɛrsœːr], *s.m. Agr:* harrower.

***hersillon** [ɛrsijɔ̃], *s.m. A.Mil:* caltrop.

hertz [ɛrts], *s.m. El.E:* hertz, cycle per second.

hertzien, -ienne [ɛrtsjɛ̃, -jɛn], *a. El:* hertzian (wave, etc.); *W.Tel:* **câble h.,** radio link; **réseau h.,** radio relay system.

Herzégovine [ɛrzegɔvin], *Pr.n.f. Hist:* Herzegovina.

herzégovinien, -ienne [ɛrzegɔvinjɛ̃, -jɛn], *a. & s. Hist:* Herzegovinian.

herzenbergite [ɛrzɛ̃bɛrʒit], *s.f. Miner:* herzenbergite.

hesdinois, -oise [edinwa, -waːz], *a. & s. Geog:* (native, inhabitant) of Hesdin.

Hésiode [ezjɔd], *Pr.n.m. Gr.Lit:* Hesiod.

hésione [ezjɔn], *s.f. Ann:* hesione.

hésionidés [ezjɔnide], *s.m.pl. Ann:* Hesionidae.

hésitant [ezitɑ̃], *a. & s.* hesitating, wavering, undecided (character, etc.); faltering (voice, footsteps); halting, *F:* shilly-shally (policy, etc.).

hésitation [ezitasjɔ̃], *s.f.* hesitation, hesitancy, wavering; **parler avec h.,** to speak hesitatingly; **sans h.,** unhesitatingly, without faltering; **non sans h.,** not without misgivings; **h. à faire qch.,** backwardness in doing sth.; **plus d'hésitations!** *F:* no more shilly-shallying! get on with it!

hésiter [ezite], *v.i.* 1. to hesitate, waver; **h. sur qch.,** to hesitate over sth.; **h. sur ce qu'on fera,** to hesitate as to what one will do; **il hésitait, ne sachant s'il devait,** he hesitated, not knowing whether he should; **h. dans ses croyances,** to waver in one's beliefs; **h. à, pour, faire qch.,** to hesitate, be reluctant, to do sth., to be shy of doing sth.; to be backward in doing sth.; to hold back; *F:* to shilly-shally; **il n'hésite devant rien,** he hesitates at nothing, nothing daunts him; **h. entre deux partis,** to hesitate between two causes; **il n'y a pas à h.,** there is no room for hesitation. 2. to, hesitate, falter (in speaking, etc.).

hespérétine [ɛsperetin], *s.f. Ch:* hesperitin, hesperetin.

Hespérides [ɛsperid], *Pr.n.f.pl. Gr.Myth:* the Hesperides; **le Jardin des H.,** the Garden of the Hesperides.

hespéridés [ɛsperide], *s.m.pl.,* **hespéries** [ɛsperi], *s.f.pl. Ent:* skippers.

hespéridine [ɛsperidin], *s.f. Ch:* hesperidin.

hespérornis [ɛsperɔrnis], *s.m. Paleont:* hesperornis.

***Hesse** [ɛs], *Pr.n.f. Geog:* Hesse, Hessen; *Ent:* **mouche de H.,** Hessian fly.

***hessian** [esjɑ̃], *s.m. Tex:* hessian; burlap.

hessite [ɛs(s)it], *s.f. Miner:* hessite.

***hessois, -oise** [ɛswa, -waːz], *a. & s. Geog:* Hessian.

hésychasme [ezikasm], *s.f. Rel.H:* Hesychasm.

hésychaste [ezikast], *s. Rel.H:* Hesychast.

hétaire [etɛːr], *s.m. Gr.Ant:* hetaeria, hetairia.

hétaïre [etaiːr], *s.f. Gr.Ant:* hetaera, hetaira.

hétairie [etɛri], *s.f. Gr.Ant:* hetaeria, hetairia.

hétairisme [etɛrism], *s.m. Gr.Ant: Anthr:* hetaerism, hetairism.

Hétéens [eteɛ̃], *s.m.pl. A.Hist:* Hittites.

hétère [etɛːr], *s.f. Gr.Ant:* hetaeria, hetairia.

hétér(o)- [eter(ɔ), -o], *pref.* heter(o)-; **hétérochrome,** heterochromous; **hétérandre,** heterandrous.

hétéroatome [eterɔatɔm], *s.m. Ch:* heteroatom.

hétéroatomique [eterɔatɔmik], *a. Ch:* heteroatomic.

hétéroblastique [eterɔblastik], *a. Biol:* heteroblastic.

hétérocarpe [eterɔkarp], *a. Bot:* heterocarpous.

hétérocéphale [eterɔsefal], *s.m. Z:* (East African) naked mole-rat; heterocephalus glaber.

hétérocercie [eterɔsɛrsi], **hétérocerquie** [eterɔsɛrki], *s.f. Ich:* heterocercality.

hétérocères [eterɔsɛːr], *s.m.pl. Ent:* Heterocera.

hétérocerque [eterɔsɛrk], *a. Ich:* heterocercal (tail).

hétérochrome [eterɔkroːm], *a.* heterochromous.

hétérochromosome [eterɔkromozoːm], *s.m. Biol:* heterochromosome.

hétérochronie [eterɔkrɔni], *s.f.* heterochronism, heterochrony.

hétérochronisme [eterɔkrɔnism], *s.m. Biol:* heterochronism, heterochrony.

hétéroclite [eterɔklit], *a.* 1. *Gram:* heteroclite, irregular (noun, etc.). 2. unusual, strange, odd, queer, eccentric; **mélange h.,** incongruous medley; **bâtiment h.,** patchwork building; nondescript building.

hétérococcales [eterɔkɔkal], *s.f.pl. Algae:* Heterococcales.

hétérocyclique [eterɔsiklik], *a. Ch:* heterocyclic.

hétérodon [eterɔdɔ̃], *s.m. Rept:* heterodon.

hétérodontes [eterɔdɔ̃ːt], *s.m.pl. Moll:* Heterodonta.

hétérodoxe [eterɔdɔks], *a.* heterodox, unorthodox.

hétérodoxie [eterɔdɔksi], *s.f.* heterodoxy.

hétérodrome [eterɔdrɔm], *a. Mec:* heterodromous.

hétérodyname [eterɔdinam], *a. Biol: Ent:* heterodynamic.

hétérodyne [eterɔdin], *a. & s.f. W.Tel:* heterodyne (receiver).

hétérogame [eterɔgam], *a. Biol: Bot:* heterogamous.

hétérogamétie [eterɔgamesi], *s.f. Biol:* heterogamety.

hétérogamie [eterɔgami], *s.f. Biol: Bot:* heterogamy.

hétérogène [eterɔʒɛn], *a.* (*a*) heterogeneous, dissimilar; (*b*) incongruous (collection, etc.); mixed (society).

hétérogénéité [eterɔʒeneite], *s.f.* heterogeneousness, heterogeneity.

hétérogénèse [eterɔgenɛːz], *s.f. Biol:* heterogenesis.

hétérogénie [eterɔʒeni], *s.f. Biol:* heterogeny.

hétérogénite [eterɔʒenit], *s.f. Miner:* heterogenite.

hétérogonie [eterɔgɔni], *s.f. Biol:* heterogony.

hétérogreffe [eterɔgrɛf], *s.f. Biol: Surg:* heterograft.

hétérogyne [eterɔʒin], *a. Biol:* heterogynous.

hétérolysine [eterɔlizin], *s.f. Bio-Ch:* heterolysine.

hétéromère [eterɔmɛːr], (*a*) *a. Biol:* heteromerous; (*b*) *s.m.pl. Ent:* **hétéromères,** Heteromera.

hétérométabole [eterɔmetabɔl], *a. Ent:* heterometabolic, heterometabolous.

hétéromorphe [eterɔmɔrf], *a. Bot: Ch:* heteromorphous, heteromorphic.

hétéromorphie [eterɔmɔrfi], *s.f.,* **hétéromorphisme** [eterɔmɔrfism], *s.m.* heteromorphism.

hétéromorphite [eterɔmɔrfit], *s.f. Miner:* heteromorphite.

hétéromorphose [eterɔmɔrfoːz], *s.f. Biol:* heteromorphosis.

hétéromyidés [eterɔmiide], *s.m.pl. Z:* Heteromyidae.

hétéroneures [eterɔnœːr], *s.m.pl. Ent:* Heteroneura.

hétéronome [eterɔnɔm], *a.* heteronomous.

hétéronomie [eterɔnɔmi], *s.f. Eth:* heteronomy.

hétéronyme [eterɔnim], *s.m.* **1.** ghosted work. **2.** ghost(-writer).

hétéropage [eterɔpaːʒ], *a. Biol: Ter:* heteropagus.

hétérophile [eterɔfil], *a. Biol:* heterophile.

hétérophorie [eterɔfɔri], *s.f. Opt:* heterophoria.

hétérophtalmie [eterɔftalmi], *s.f. Anat:* heterophthalmus.

hétérophyllie [eterɔfili], *s.f. Bot:* heterophylly.

hétérophytique [eterɔfitik], *a. Bot:* heterophytic; **plante h.,** heterophyte.

hétéroplasie [eterɔplazi], *s.f. Med:* heteroplasia.

hétéroplastie [eterɔplasti], *s.f. Surg:* heteroplasty.

hétéropodes [eterɔpɔd], *s.m.pl. Moll:* Heteropoda.

hétéropolaire [eterɔpɔlɛːr], *a. Ch:* heteropolar.

hétéroptère [eterɔptɛːr], *a. & s. Ent:* **1.** *a.* heteropterous. **2.** *s.m.pl.* **hétéroptères,** Heteroptera.

hétérosexuel, -elle [eterɔsɛksɥɛl] *a. & s.* heterosexual.

hétéroside [eterɔzid], *s.m. Ch:* heteroside; **h. flavonique,** flavonoid glycoside.

hétérosis [eterɔzis], *s.f. Biol:* heterosis.

hétérosome [eterɔzoːm]. **1.** *s.m. Biol:* heterochromosome. **2.** *s.m.pl. Ich:* **hétérosomes,** Heterosomata.

hétérosporé [eterɔspɔre], *a. Bot:* heterosporous, heterosporic.

hétérosporie [eterɔspɔri], *s.f. Bot:* heterospory.

hétérostatique [eterɔstatik], *a. El:* heterostatic.

hétérostylie [eterɔstili], *s.f. Bot:* heterostyly.

hétérotherme [eterɔtɛrm], *a. Z:* poecilothermal.

hétérotrophe [eterɔtrɔf], *a. Biol: etc:* heterotrophic.

hétérotrophie [eterɔtrɔfi], *s.f. Biol:* heterotrophism.

hétérotypique [eterɔtipik], *a. Biol:* heterotypic(al).

hétérozygote [eterɔzigɔt], *a. & s.m. Biol:* **1.** *a.* heterozygotic. **2.** *s.m.* heterozygote.

hetman [ɛtmɑ̃], *s.m.* (cossack) hetman.

***hêtraie** [ɛtrɛ], *s.f.* (*a*) beech grove; (*b*) beech plantation.

***hêtre** [ɛ(ː)tr], *s.m.* beech (tree or timber); **h. rouge, pourpre,** copper beech; **h. blanc,** hornbeam; **bois de hêtres,** beech wood; beeches.

***heu**[1] [ø], *int.* (*a*) ah! (*b*) (*doubt*) h'm! (*c*) (*indifference, contempt*) pooh! hmph! (*d*) (*in hesitating speech*) . . . er . . ..

***heu**[2], **heux,** *s.m. Nau:* hoy.

heuchère [øʃɛːr], *s.f. Bot:* heuchera.

***heulandite** [ølɑ̃dit], *s.f. Miner:* heulandite.

heur [œːr], *s.m. A. & Lit:* luck, chance; *usu.* good luck; **il n'est qu'h. et malheur,** it is the way of the world; we must take the rough with the smooth; **heurs et malheurs d'un soldat de plomb,** joys and sorrows of a tin soldier; *Iron:* **je n'ai pas l'h. de la connaître,** I have not the pleasure of her acquaintance; **il a l'h. de vous plaire,** he has taken your fancy.

heure [œːr], *s.f.* hour; (*a*) **à toutes heures du jour,** at all hours of the day; **heures d'affluence, de pointe,** rush, peak, hours; **heures creuses,** off-peak hours, slack time; **la fuite des heures,** the flight of time; **d'h. en h.,** hour by hour; every hour, hourly; **un gaulliste de la première h.,** a Gaullist from the start; **l'homme de la dernière h.,** the man who saves the situation at the eleventh hour; **à la dernière h.,** at the last minute, the eleventh hour; *Journ:* **la dernière h.,** (i) the latest news; intelligence; (ii) stop-press news; **une h. d'horloge,** a full hour; an hour by the clock; **j'ai attendu une bonne h.,** I waited a full hour, for fully an hour; *F:* **voilà une h. que je t'attends!** I've been waiting hours, ages, for you! **trois bons quarts d'h.,** a good three-quarters of an hour; **une petite h.,** rather less than an hour; **cent kilomètres à l'h.,** a hundred kilometres an hour; engager qn à l'h., to employ s.o. by the hour, at time rates; **travail à l'h.,** time work; **être payé à l'h.,** to be paid by the hour, by time (rates); **homme à l'h.,** casual labourer; *F:* **s'embêter à cent sous de l'h.,** to be bored stiff; **h. de main-d'œuvre, d'ouvrier,** man(-) hour; **la semaine de 40 heures,** the 40-hour week; **heures supplémentaires,** overtime; **tous les frais de travail hors d'heures seront payés par . . .,** all overtime to be paid by . . .; **faire des heures,** to put in time; **je fais ce travail en dehors de mes heures de bureau,** I do this work out of office hours; **à mes heures perdues,** in my spare time; (*b*) (*time on the clock*) **l'h. de Greenwich,** Greenwich mean time; **h. astronomique,** sidereal time; **h. du fuseau,** standard time; **h. légale,** civil, official, time; **h. d'été,** *Fr.C:* **h. avancée,** summer time, *U.S:* daylight saving time; *Nau:* **h. du bord,** ship's time; *F:* **se mettre à la même h. que qn,** to bring oneself up to date, to catch up with s.o.; *F:* **le parti communiste est à l'h. de la Russie,** the Communist party takes its cue from Russia; **quelle h. est-il?** what's the time? what time is it? **quelle h. avez-vous?** what time do you make it? **la radio donne l'h. à midi,** the radio gives the time (signal) at 12 o'clock; *F:* **je ne vous demande pas l'h. (qu'il est),** mind your own business; it's nothing to do with you; **cinq heures moins dix,** ten (minutes) to five; **je prends le train de neuf heures,** I catch, take, the nine o'clock train; **le train part à dix heures cinquante,** the train leaves, goes, at ten fifty, at ten (minutes) to eleven; **à deux heures du matin,** at two (o'clock) in the morning; **où serai-je demain à cette heure-ci?** where shall I be this time tomorrow? **à une h. avancée (de la journée),** late in the day; **à une h. peu avancée de l'après-midi,** early in the afternoon; **jouer au bridge jusqu'à pas d'h.,** to play bridge until all hours; **à cinq heures juste(s), sonnant(es), topant(es),** on the stroke of five; **mettre sa montre à l'h.,** to set one's watch (right), to put one's watch on time; **avancer, retarder, l'h.,** to put the clock forward, back; *Ecc:* **livre d'heures,** Book of Hours; (*c*) (*appointed time*) **l'h. du dîner,** dinner time; **l'h. d'aller se coucher,** bedtime; **h. suprême, dernière,** hour of death; **son h. est venue, a sonné,** his time has come, he is about to die; *Aut: etc:* **h. d'éclairage,** lighting-up time; *Mil:* **l'h. H,** zero hour; **prendre h. avec qn,** to fix (the time of) an appointment with s.o.; **à l'h. dite,** at the appointed, agreed, time; **être à l'h.,** to be punctual, to be on time; **il est toujours à l'h.,** he's always on time; he's never late; **arriver à l'h. exacte,** to arrive prompt to the minute, dead on time; **il est l'h., c'est l'h.,** (i) the hour has come; (ii) the hour is striking; (iii) time is up; **faire tout à ses heures,** to have one's own fixed times for doing things; **libre de le faire à son h.,** free to do it when one likes, in one's own time; (*d*) (*present time*) **pour l'h.,** for the present, for the time being; **la question de l'h.,** the question of the hour; **problèmes de l'h.,** current problems; **l'h. n'est pas à badiner,** this is no time for trifling; **à l'h. qu'il est,** (i) by this time; (ii) nowadays; now; *esp. U.S:* presently; **il est couché à cette h.,** he has gone to bed by now; (*e*) time, period; *Sch:* **h. de cours,** period; **nous avons connu des heures agréables,** we have known good times (together); **il y eut une h. où . . .,** there was a time when . . .; **cette mode a eu son h.,** this fashion has had its day; **venir à son h.,** to appear, come, happen, at the right time, moment; **j'attends mon h.,** I'm biding my time; (*f*) *adv. phrs.* **de bonne h.,** (i) early, in good time; (ii) at an early period; **il est de trop bonne h. pour rentrer,** it's too early to go home; **se lever de bonne h.,** to get up early; to be an early riser; **son génie se manifesta de bonne h.,** his genius was apparent at an early age; **de meilleure h.,** earlier; **faire qch. sur l'h.,** to do sth. at once, right away; **je vais le faire dès cette h.,** I'll do it at once, *U.S:* right now; **à toute h.,** at any time; at all hours of the day; *P.N:* **casse-croûte à toute h.,** snacks served at any time; **tout à l'h.,** (i) a few minutes ago; (ii) soon, in a few minutes; **à tout à l'h.!** so long! see you later! (*g*) *int.* **à la bonne h.!** well done! good (for you)! that's right! fine! that's better! that's the spirit!

heure-lampe [œrlɑ̃ːp], *s.f. A: El.Meas:* lamp-hour; *pl. heures-lampe.*

heurette [œrɛt], *s.f.* **1.** (i) *A:* the half-hour; (ii) *Dial:* not quite an hour. **2.** small Book of Hours.

heureusement [œrøzmɑ̃, ørø-], *adv.* happily; (*a*) successfully; (*b*) luckily, fortunately; **h. que j'étais là,** it is a good thing that I was there, fortunately I was there; **la France est un des pays les plus h. situés,** France is one of the most happily situated countries; (*c*) **commencer h.,** to begin auspiciously; (*d*) **des pensées h. exprimées,** well expressed thoughts.

heureux, -euse [œrø, ørø, -øːz], *a.* **1.** happy; **h. comme un poisson dans l'eau,** as happy as a sand-boy, as happy as a bird on the tree; **h. comme un roi,** as happy as a king; **vivre h. avec une petite rente,** to live contentedly, happily, on a small income; **une heureuse ignorance,** blissful ignorance; *F:* **il vit comme un imbécile h.,** he lives in blissful ignorance; **h. du bonheur des autres,** rejoicing in the happiness of others; **je suis très h. de vous faire savoir que . . .,** I am very happy, pleased, to inform you, I have much pleasure in informing you, that . . .; **je suis heureux de noter que . . .,** I note with satisfaction that . . ., I am glad, pleased, to note that . . .; **je suis très h. d'assister à . . .,** it give me great pleasure to be present at . . .; **elle était tout heureuse de ce qu'il l'accompagnait,** she was overjoyed that he was coming with her; **je suis infiniment h. que vous y consentiez,** I am so glad that you agree; **nous serions h. que vous acceptiez,** we should be glad if you would accept; *s.* **vous avez fait un h.,** you have made one man happy; **les h. du jour,** the rich. **2.** (*a*) successful; **négociations heureuses,** successful negotiations; **l'issue heureuse des négociations,** the successful outcome of the negotiations; (*b*) lucky, favoured; **h. au jeu, en amour,** lucky at cards, in love; **vous avez la main heureuse,** you are always lucky; **h. en enfants,** blest in his children; **une chute heureuse,** a lucky fall; **le feu roi, d'heureuse mémoire,** the late king, of blessed memory; *B:* **h. les pauvres en esprit,** blessed are the poor in spirit. **3.** (*a*) favourable, lucky, fortunate; **c'est fort h. pour vous,** that's very lucky for you; **c'est h., il est fort h., que vous soyez libre,** it is a (very) good thing, a good job, that you are free; **il est h. pour lui que . . .,** it is well, fortunate, for him that . . .; **par un h. accident . . .,** by a fortunate accident . . .; **être dans une situation heureuse,** to be in a fortunate position; (*b*) **début h.,** auspicious beginning. **4.** felicitous, happy, apt (phrase, etc.).

heuristique [œristik], (*a*) *a.* heuristic (method); (*b*) *s.f.* heuristics.

***heurt** [œːr], *s.m.* **1.** shock, blow, knock, bump; **h. des armes,** clash of arms; **heurt des couleurs,** colours that clash; **tout s'est fait sans h.,** everything went smoothly. **2.** *Vet:* mark (of blow); bruise. **3.** *Civ.E:* crown (of bridge, roadway); back (of bridge).

heurté [œrte], *a.* **1.** *Art: Phot:* contrasty, hard (negative, etc.). **2.** *Lit:* abrupt or halting (style). **3.** jarring, harsh (sound). **4. mer heurtée,** choppy sea.

***heurtement** [œrt(ə)mɑ̃], *s.m.* clashing, clash; **h. de voyelles,** hiatus.

***heurtequin** [œrtəkɛ̃], *s.m. Veh:* collar, hurter (of axle).

***heurter** [œrte], *v.tr. & i.* **1.** (*a*) to knock (against), run against, run into (s.o., sth.); **h. qn dans la rue,** to run against, jostle, collide with, bump into, s.o. in the street; **se h. la tête à, contre, qch.,** to knock one's head against sth.; **h. de la tête contre une muraille,** to run one's head against a wall; **h. du pied contre une pierre,** to stub one's toe, to stumble, against a stone; *Nau:* **h. un récif,** to hit a rock; **h. une mine,** to strike a mine; (*b*) **h. à la porte,** to knock at the door; **on a heurté deux coups,** I heard two knocks. **2.** to shock, offend (s.o.'s feelings, etc.); **h. des intérêts, toutes les idées reçues,** to go against,

run counter to, interests, all conventions; **h. de front une nation,** to come into direct collision with, give offence to, a nation. **3. h. un tableau, un cliché,** to accentuate the contrasts in a picture, in a negative.

se heurter. 1. se h. à, contre, qn, to run (slap) into s.o.; **venir se h. contre qn,** to collide with s.o., *F:* to barge into s.o.; **se h. à, contre, qch.,** to bang against sth.; **se h. à une difficulté,** to come up against a difficulty. **2.** to collide; **les deux autos se sont heurtées,** the two cars collided; **les deux navires se sont heurtés,** the two ships ran foul of one another; **ici nos intérêts se heurtent,** here our interests clash; **les deux béliers se heurtèrent de front,** the two rams came full butt into each other.

***heurtoir** [œrtwa:r], *s.m.* **1.** door knocker. **2.** (*a*) door stop; (*b*) *Mec.E:* (i) catch, stop; (ii) driver, tappet; (*c*) *Rail:* (i) buffer; (ii) bumping post (of siding). **3.** *Hyd.E:* sill (of lock gate, etc.).

***heuse**[1] [ø:z], *s.f.* plunger, bucket (of pump).

heuse[2], *A.Cost:* hose.

***hévé** [eve], *s.m. O:* hevea.

hévéa [evea], *s.m. Bot:* hevea.

hex(a)- [egz(a)], *pref.* hexa-; **hexacanthe,** hexacanthous.

hexachlorocyclohexane [egzaklɔrɔsiklɔegzan], *s. Ch:* hexachlorocyclohexane.

hexacontane [egzakɔ̃tan], *s.m. Ch:* hexacontane.

hexacoralliaires [egzakɔraljɛ:r], *s.m.pl. Geol:* hexacoralla.

hexacorde [egzakɔrd], *s.m. Mus:* hexachord.

hexacosane [egzakozan], *s.m. Ch:* hexacosane.

hexactinellidés [egzaktinɛlide], *s.m.pl. Spong:* Hexactinellida; Hyalospongiae.

hexadécane [egzadekan], *s.m. Ch:* hexadecane.

hexaèdre [egzaɛdr̥], *Geom:* **1.** *a.* hexahedral. **2.** *s.m.* hexahedron.

hexaédrique [egzaedrik], *a. Geom:* hexahedral.

hexafluorure [egzaflyɔry:r], *s.m. Ch:* hexafluoride; **h. d'uranium,** uranium hexafluoride.

hexagonal, -aux [egzagɔnal, -o], *a. Geom:* hexagonal.

hexagone [egzagɔn], *Geom:* **1.** *a.* hexagonal. **2.** *s.m.* hexagon; *Pr.n. F:* l'H., France.

hexagyne [egzaʒin], *a. Bot:* hexagynian, hexagynous.

hexamètre [egzamɛtr̥], *Pros:* **1.** *a.* hexametric(al). **2.** *s.m.* hexameter.

hexamoteur [egzamɔtœ:r], *a. & s.m.* **(avion) h.,** six-engined aircraft.

hexanche [egzɑ̃:ʃ], *s.m. Ich:* hexanchus.

hexandre [egzɑ̃:dr̥], *a. Bot:* hexandrous.

hexane [egzan], *s.m. Ch:* hexane.

hexanitrodiphénylamine [egzanitrɔdifenilamin], *s.f. Exp:* hexanitrodiphenylamine.

hexaples [egzapl̥], *s.m.pl. B.Lit:* hexapla.

hexapode [egzapɔd], *a. & s.m. Ent:* hexapod(ous); *s.m.pl.* **les hexapodes,** Hexapoda, insects (in the strict sense).

hexapodie [egzapɔdi], *s.f. Pros:* hexapody.

hexapolaire [egzapɔlɛ:r], *a. El.E: etc:* six-pole (stator, etc.).

hexaréacteur [egzareaktœ:r], *a. Av:* six turbo-jet aircraft.

hexastyle [egzastil], *a. & s.m. Arch:* hexastyle.

hexasyllabe [egzasil(l)ab], *a. Pros:* hexasyllabic.

hexatétraèdre [egzatetraɛdr̥], *s.m. Cryst:* hex(a)tetrahedron.

Hexateuque (l') [legzatø:k], *s.m. B.Lit:* the Hexateuch.

hexatomique [egzatɔmik], *a. Ch:* hexatomic.

hexavalent [egzavalɑ̃], *a. Ch:* hexavalent, sexivalent.

hexène [egzɛn], *s.m. Ch:* hexene.

hexet [egzɛ], *s.m.* (*computers*) six-bit byte.

hexogène [egzɔʒɛn], *s.m. Ch:* hexogen.

hexosane [egzɔzan], *s.m. Ch:* hexosan.

hexose [egzo:z], *s.m. Ch:* hexose.

hexyl [egzil], *s.m. Exp:* dipicrylamine.

hexyle [egzil], *s.m. Ch:* hexyl.

hexylène [egzilɛn], *s.m. Ch:* hexylene.

hexylique [egzilik], *a.* **alcool h.,** hexyl alcohol; **acide h.,** hexilic acid.

hexyne [egzin], *s.m. Ch:* hexyne.

heyduque [ɛdyk], *s.m. Hist:* heyduck.

hiatal, -aux [jatal, -o], *a. Med:* hiatal.

hiatus [jatys, ja-], *s.m.* **1.** gap, break (in narrative, in genealogical tree, etc.). **2.** *Pros: Anat:* hiatus.

hibernacle [ibɛrnakl̥], *s.m.* **1.** *Biol: etc:* hibernacle, hibernaculum; *Bot:* winter-lodge. **2.** (*rare*) winter quarters.

hibernal, -aux [ibɛrnal, -o], *a.* hibernal (germination, etc.); winter-flowering (plant); wintry (temperature); **sommeil h.,** hibernation.

hibernant [ibɛrnɑ̃], *a.* hibernating (animal).

hibernation [ibɛrnasjɔ̃], *s.f.* hibernation; *Med:* **h. artificielle,** artificial hibernation.

hiberner [ibɛrne], *v.i.* to hibernate.

hibernien, -ienne [ibɛrnjɛ̃, -jɛn], *a. & s. A:* Hibernian, Irish.

hibiscus [ibisky:s], *s.m. Bot:* hibiscus.

***hibou, -oux** [ibu], *s.m. Orn:* owl; **jeune h.,** owlet; **h. du Cap,** Algerian marsh owl; **h. brachyote, des marais,** short-eared owl; **h. grand-duc,** eagle-owl; **h. moyen-duc,** long-eared owl; **h. petit-duc,** scops owl; **h. pêcheur, kétupa,** Asian fish-owl; *F:* **un vieux h.,** an old recluse; *F:* **avoir des yeux de h.,** to have owlish eyes; **nid de hiboux,** old deserted house.

***hic** [ik], *s.m. F:* the main difficulty; *used in the phr.* **voilà le hic!** that's the snag!

hickory [ikɔri], *s.m. Bot:* hickory, shell-bark.

hidalgo [idalgo], *s.m.* hidalgo.

hiddénite [idenit], *s.f. Miner:* hiddenite.

***hideur** [idœ:r], *s.f.* (*a*) hideousness; (*b*) hideous sight; *F:* (*of woman*) **quelle h.!** what a fright!

***hideusement** [idøzmɑ̃], *adv.* hideously.

***hideux, -euse** [idø, -ø:z], *a.* (*a*) hideous; **h. à voir,** hideous-looking; (*b*) *F:* repulsive (character, etc.).

hidrosadénite [idrɔsadenit], *s.f. Med:* hidrosadenitis, hidradenitis.

***hie** [i], *s.f.* **1.** (paviour's) beetle, (earth)rammer, punner. **2.** *Civ.E:* pile driver, pile-driving machine.

hièble [jɛbl̥], *s.f. occ. s.m. Bot:* dwarf elder, bloodwort, *F:* ground elder.

hiémal, -aux [iemal, je-, -o], *a.* hiemal; winter (solstice, etc.).

hiémation [jemasjɔ̃], *s.f.* **1.** wintering. **2.** *Bot:* winter growth (of certain plants).

***hiement** [imɑ̃], *s.m. Civ.E:* ramming, punning; pile-driving.

***hier**[1] [ie], *v.* (*p.d. & pr.sub.* **n. hiions, v. hiiez**) **1.** *v.tr.* to ram down (paving stones). **2.** *v.i.* to creak.

hier[2] [iɛ:r, jɛ:r]. **1.** *adv.* yesterday; **h. (au) matin,** yesterday morning; **h. (au) soir,** last night; **d'h. en huit,** a week from yesterday; **il y a eu h. huit jours,** yesterday week; **le journal d'h.,** yesterday's paper; **je ne suis arrivé que d'h.,** I arrived only yesterday; **cela n'est que d'h.,** it is quite recent; *F:* **il est né d'h.,** he's still very green; *F:* **je ne suis pas né d'h.,** I wasn't born yesterday; **homme d'h.,** upstart, nobody. **2.** *s.m.* **vous aviez toute la journée d'h. pour vous décider,** you had all yesterday to make up your mind.

***hiérarchie** [jerarʃi], *s.f.* (*a*) hierarchy; **h. sociale,** social hierarchy; *R.C.Ch:* **la H. romaine,** the Roman Hierarchy; (*b*) *Mil: Adm:* classification of grades; ranking; **h. de commandement,** chain, line, of command.

***hiérarchique** [jerarʃik], *a.* hierarchical; **par (la) voie h.,** through (the) official channels, through the usual channels.

***hiérarchiquement** [jerarʃikmɑ̃], *adv.* hierarchically; through the usual channels.

***hiérarchisation** [jerarʃizasjɔ̃], *s.f.* hierarchization.

***hiérarchiser** [jerarʃize], *v.tr.* (*a*) to form, manage (state, etc.) on the hierarchical system; (*b*) **h. le personnel,** to grade the staff.

hiératique [jeratik], *a.* hieratic (style, writing, etc.).

hiératiquement [jeratikmɑ̃], *adv.* hieratically.

hiératiser [jeratize], *v.tr. Art:* to conventionalize (attitude, etc.) according to religious tradition.

hiér(o)- [jer(ɔ)], *pref.* hier(o)-; **hiérocratie,** hierocracy; **hiérographe,** hierographer.

hiéroglyphe [jerɔglif], *s.m.* (*a*) hieroglyph; (*b*) *pl.* hieroglyphics.

hiéroglyphique [jerɔglifik], *a.* hieroglyphic(al); **signes hiéroglyphiques,** hieroglyphics.

hiérogramme [jerɔgram], *s.m.* hierogram.

hiérographie [jerɔgrafi], *s.f.* hierography.

hiérographique [jerɔgrafik], *a.* hierographic(al).

hiéronymite [jerɔnimit], *s.m. Rel.H:* Hieronymite.

hiérophante [jerɔfɑ̃:t], *s.m. Gr.Ant:* hierophant.

hiérosolymitain, -aine [jerɔsɔlimitɛ̃, -ɛn], *a. & s.*, **hiérosolymite** [jerɔsɔlimit], *a. & s. Geog:* Hierosolymitan; of Jerusalem.

hi-fi [ifi], *a. W.Tel: etc: F:* hi-fi, high-fidelity.

***high-life** [ajlajf, *P:* iglif, iʃlif], *s.m. O: F:* high life; world of fashion.

***hi-han** [iɑ̃], *int. & s.m. onomat.* (donkey's) hee-haw; **faire h.-h.,** to hee-haw.

hi hi [ii], *int. onomat.* (*sound of tittering*) tee-hee! tehee! he(e) he(e)!

***hilaire**[1] [ilɛ:r], *a. Bot: Anat:* hilar.

Hilaire[2], *Pr.n.m.* Hilary.

hilarant [ilarɑ̃], *a.* mirth-provoking; *Ch:* **gaz h.,** laughing gas.

hilare [ila:r], *a.* hilarious, mirthful; in a jovial mood.

hilarité [ilarite], *s.f.* hilarity, mirth, laughter; **provoquer l'h. générale,** to raise a general laugh; to set the company laughing.

Hildegarde [ildəgard], *Pr.n.f.* Hildegard.

Hildegonde [ildəgɔ̃:d], *Pr.n.f.* Hildegond.

***hile** [il], *s.m. Anat: Bot:* hilum; *Anat:* transverse fissure, porta (of the liver).

hiloire [ilwa:r], *s.f. N.Arch:* **1.** binding-strake (of deck); **h. renversée,** hatch carling. **2. h. de panneau,** hatch-coaming; **h. transversale,** ledge. **3.** *Row:* weatherboard.

hilote [ilɔt], *s.m.* = ILOTE.

Himalaya (l') [limalaja], *Pr.n.m. Geog:* Himalaya; **les monts Himalaya,** the Himalayas.

himalayen, -enne [imalajɛ̃, -ɛn], *a. & s. Geog:* Himalayan.

himanthales [imɑ̃tal], *s.m. Algae:* thong-weeds.

***hindi** [ɛ̃di, indi], *s.m. Ling:* Hindi.

hindou, -oue [ɛ̃du], *a. & s. Ethn:* Hindu.

hindouisme [ɛ̃duism], *s.m.* Hinduism.

Hindoustan [ɛ̃dustɑ̃], *Pr.n.m. Geog:* Hindustan.

hindoustani [ɛ̃dustani], *s.m. Ling:* Hindustani.

hinterland [ɛ̃tɛrlɑ̃:d], *s.m.* hinterland.

hipolais [ipɔlɛs], *s.m. Orn:* **h. ictérine,** icterine warbler.

hipparion [ip(p)arjɔ̃], *s.m. Paleont:* hipparion.

Hipparque [ip(p)ark], *Pr.n.m. Gr.Hist:* Hipparchus.

hippiatre [ip(p)ia:tr̥], *s.m. A:* farrier; horse doctor.

hippiatrie [ip(p)jatri], *s.f. A:* veterinary art, farriery.

hippiatrique [ip(p)jatrik]. **1.** *a. Vet:* concerning farriery. **2.** *s.f.* = HIPPIATRIE.

***hippie** [ip(p)i], *a. & s. F:* hippie.

hippique [ip(p)ik], *a.* relating to horses, equine; **concours h.,** (i) horse show; (ii) race meeting; *Belg:* **agence h.,** betting shop.

hippisme [ip(p)ism], *s.m.* horse racing.

hippobosque [ip(p)ɔbɔsk], *s.m. Ent:* horse tick.

hippocampe [ip(p)ɔkɑ̃:p], *s.m.* **1.** *Gr.Myth: Anat:* hippocampus. **2.** *Ich:* hippocampus, sea horse.

hippocastanacées [ip(p)ɔkastanase], *s.f.pl. Bot:* Hippocastanaceae.

Hippocrate [ip(p)ɔkrat], *Pr.n.m. Gr.Ant:* Hippocrates; *Med:* **serment d'H.,** Hippocratic oath; *Surg:* **bonnet d'H.,** capeline (bandage), mitra hippocratis; *s.a.* CORDE 3.

hippocratique [ip(p)ɔkratik], *a.* Hippocratic; *Med:* **facies h.,** Hippocratic countenance; *facies hippocratica*; **doigts hippocratiques,** Hippocratic fingers.

hippocratisme [ip(p)ɔkratism], *s.m. Med:* hippocratism.

Hippocrène [ip(p)ɔkrɛn], *Pr.n.f. Gr.Ant:* Hippocrene.

hippodrome [ip(p)ɔdro:m], *s.m.* **1.** hippodrome, circus. **2.** race-course.

hippogriffe [ip(p)ɔgrif], *s.m. Myth:* hippogriff, hippogryph.

hippolithe [ip(p)ɔlit], *s.f. Vet:* hippolith.

hippologie [ip(p)ɔlɔʒi], *s.f.* hippology; care and management of horses.

hippologique [ip(p)ɔlɔʒik], *a.* concerning hippology.

Hippolyte [ip(p)ɔlit]. **1.** *Pr.n.m. Gr.Lit:* Hippolytus. **2.** *Pr.n.f. Gr.Myth:* Hippolyta.

hippomane [ip(p)ɔman]. **1.** *a.* mad on horses. **2.** *s.m.* (*a*) lover of horses; (*b*) great rider.

hippomobile [ip(p)ɔmɔbil], *a.* horse-drawn (vehicle).

hippophaé [ip(p)ɔfae], *s.m. Bot:* hippophaë.

hippophage [ip(p)ɔfa:ʒ]. **1.** *a.* hippophagous. **2.** *s.m.* hippophagist.

hippophagie [ip(p)ɔfaʒi], *s.f.* hippophagy.

hippophagique [ip(p)ɔfaʒik], *a.* **boucherie h.,** horse butcher('s).

hippopotame [ip(p)ɔpɔtam], *s.m. Z:* hippopotamus.

hippotechnie [ip(p)ɔtɛkni], *s.f.* science of breeding, management and training of horses.

hippotraginés [ip(p)ɔtraʒine], *s.m.pl. Z:* Hippotraginae.

hippotrague [ip(p)ɔtrag], *s.m. Z:* hippotragus; **h. à la robe noire,** sable antelope; **h. rouan,** roan hippotragus.

hippurique [ip(p)yrik], *a. Physiol:* **acide h.,** hippuric acid.

hircin [irsɛ̃], *a.* hircine, goatish.

hirnéole [irneɔl], *s.f. Fung:* Jew's ear.

hironde [irɔ̃:d], *s.f. Carp:* dovetail.

hirondeau, -eaux [irɔ̃do], *s.m. Orn:* young swallow.

hirondelle [irɔ̃dɛl], *s.f.* **1.** (*a*) *Orn:* swallow; **h. de fenêtre,** house martin; **h. de rivage,** sand

martin, *U.S:* bank swallow; **h. rousseline,** red-rumped swallow; **h. des rochers,** crag martin; **h. de cheminée,** swallow, *U.S:* barn swallow; **h. de mer,** (common) tern, sea swallow; **h. des marais,** pratincole; *Prov:* **une h. ne fait pas le printemps,** one swallow does not make a summer; *Cu:* **nid d'h.,** bird's nest; *s.a.* HERBE 4; (*b*) *Ich:* **h. de mer,** (i) swallow-fish; (ii) Ray's bream; (*c*) *Th: F:* gatecrasher (who slips in during the entr'acte, *esp.* at dress rehearsals). **2.** small river steamboat (for passengers). **3.** axle-tree band. **4.** *F:* cycle cop.

hirondinées [irɔ̃dine], *s.f.pl. Orn:* Hirundinidae.

hirsute [irsyt], *a.* **1.** hirsute, hairy, shaggy, unkempt. **2.** *F:* rough, boorish.

hirsutisme [irsytism], *s.m. Anat: Med:* hirsutism.

hirudinées [irydine], *s.f.pl. Ann:* Hirudinidae.

hirudi(ni)culture [irydi(ni)kylty:r], *s.f.* leech-breeding.

hirundinidés [irœ̃dinide], *s.m.pl. Orn:* Hirundinidae, the swallows.

Hispanie [ispani], *Pr.n.f. A.Geog:* Hispania.

hispanique [ispanik], *a.* Hispanic, Spanish.

hispanisant [ispanizɑ̃], *s.m.* (i) student of Spanish; (ii) expert on Spain.

hispanisme [ispanism], *s.m. Ling:* Hispanicism.

hispano-américain, -aine [ispanɔamerikɛ̃, -ɛn], *a. & s. Geog:* Hispano-American, Spanish-American; *pl. hispano-américain(e)s.*

hispano-arabe [ispanɔarab], **hispano-moresque** [ispanɔmɔrɛsk], *a. Ethn: Art:* Hispano-Moresque, Hispano-Moorish; *pl. hispano-arabes, -moresques.*

hispide [ispid], *a.* **1.** *Bot: Ent:* hispid. **2.** hairy, rough.

***hissage** [isa:ʒ], *s.m.* hoisting (up, in), pulling up; running up (of signal); **machine de h.,** winding-engine, hoist(ing engine).

***hisser** [ise], *v.tr.* to hoist (up), pull up; *Nau:* to hoist (up), trice (up) (sail); to hoist in (boat); to run up (signal); to sway up (yard); *F:* **h. qn sur son cheval,** to hoist s.o. on to his horse; **hissez!** up with it! hoist away! *Nau:* up sails! sway away! **h. un pavillon à bloc,** to hoist a flag right up! **o! hisse!** yo-heave-ho! yoho!

se hisser, se h. jusqu'à la fenêtre, to pull, hoist, oneself up to the window; **se h. le long du mur,** to climb up the wall; **se h. sur la pointe des pieds,** to stand on tiptoe.

histamine [istamin], *s.f. Physiol: Med:* histamine.

histaminique [istaminik], *a. Physiol: Med:* histaminic.

hister [istɛ:r], *s.m. Ent:* hister, beetle.

histérides [isterid], *s.m.pl. Ent:* Histeridae (family of beetles).

histidine [istidin], *s.f. Biol: Physiol:* histidine.

histioïde [istiɔid], *a. Physiol:* histioid, histoid.

histo- [istɔ], *pref.* histo-; **histoblaste,** histoblast; **histotomie,** histotomy.

histoblaste [istɔblast], *s.m. Ent:* histoblast (cell, or cell group); imaginal disk.

histochimique [istɔʃimik], *a.* histochemical.

histogène [istɔʒɛn], *Biol: etc:* **1.** *a.* histogenic. **2.** *s.m.* histogene.

histogénèse [istɔʒenɛ:z], *s.f. Biol: etc:* histogenesis, histogeny.

histogénie [istɔʒeni], *s.f. Biol: etc:* histogenesis, histogeny.

histogénique [istɔʒenik], *a. Biol: etc:* histogenic.

histogramme [istɔgram], *s.m. Statistics:* histogram.

histoire [istwa:r], *s.f.* **1.** (*a*) history; **h. du moyen âge,** medieval history; **tableau, peintre, d'h.,** historical painting, painter; **livre d'h.,** history-book; **l'h. sainte,** sacred history, Bible history; **c'est dans l'h. sainte,** it is in the Bible; **les à-côtés de l'h., la petite h.,** sidelights on history, the petty details of history; **nous faisons l'h.,** we are making history; (*b*) **h. naturelle,** natural history; (*c*) *Sch:* history book; **apportez vos histoires de France,** bring your French histories. **2.** story, tale, narrative; **histoires de chiens,** dog stories; **h. de marin,** sailor's yarn; **livre d'histoires,** story book; **h. de fous,** shaggy dog story; **raconter de longues histoires,** to spin long yarns; **h. qui n'est pas pour les jeunes filles,** story that is not fit for children; *F:* **c'est toujours la même h.,** it's the old, old story; **c'est stupide, cette h.-là,** the whole thing, affair, is silly; **le plus beau de l'h., c'est que . . .,** the best of the story, of the business, is that . . .; **les histoires de la ville,** the tittle-tattle of the town; *F:* **il est sorti h. de prendre un peu l'air,** he went out merely, just, to get a breath of fresh air; **"J'ai mal à la tête," dit il, histoire de changer de sujet,** "I've got a headache," he said, by way of changing the subject; *s.a.* RIRE 2; *F:* **en voilà une histoire!** (i) what a blow! (ii) what a lot of fuss! what a song and dance! **c'est toute une h.,** (i) it's a long story; (ii) it's no end of a job; *Iron:* **la belle h.!** what about it? is that all? **3.** *F:* fib, story; **tout ça c'est des histoires,** that's all bunkum; it's all my eye (and Betty Martin); **faire courir des histoires sur le compte de qn,** to spread rumours about s.o. **4.** *F:* **faire des histoires, un tas d'histoires,** to make a fuss, a to-do; **faire des histoires à qn,** to put difficulties in s.o.'s way, to make trouble for s.o.; **avoir des histoires avec qn,** to fall foul of, to be at loggerheads with, s.o.; **il faut éviter d'avoir des histoires,** you, we, must keep out of trouble; *F:* **pas d'histoires!** no fuss! **sans histoires,** (i) uneventful, (ii) trouble-free; **a-t-on besoin de tant d'histoires pour se vêtir?** do you have to make such a fuss about getting dressed? **5.** *F:* **qu'est-ce que c'est que cette h.-là?** what's that thing?

histologie [istɔlɔʒi], *s.f.* histology.

histologique [istɔlɔʒik], *a.* histological.

histologiste [istɔlɔʒist], *s.m.* histologist.

histolyse [istɔli:z], *s.f. Biol: Physiol:* histolysis.

histopathologie [istɔpatɔlɔʒi], *s.f.* histopathology.

histoplasmose [istɔplasmo:z], *s.f. Med:* histoplasmosis.

historicisme [istɔrisism], *s.m.* historicism.

historicité [istɔrisite], *s.f.* historicity; genuineness (of event, etc.).

historié [istɔrje], *a.* historiated (initials, etc.); illuminated (Bible, etc.); storied (urn, window, etc.).

historien, -ienne [istɔrjɛ̃, -jɛn], *s.* (*a*) historian; (*b*) narrator.

historier [istɔrje], *v.tr.* (*p.d. & pr.sub.* **n. historiions, v. historiiez**) to illustrate, embellish, illuminate (Bible, etc.); *F:* **h. un récit,** to embellish, touch up, a story.

historiette [istɔrjɛt], *s.f.* anecdote; short story, short tale.

historiographe [istɔrjɔgraf], *s.m.* historiographer, chronicler.

historiographie [istɔrjɔgrafi], *s.f.* historiography.

historique [istɔrik]. **1.** *a.* historic(al); *F:* **c'est h.,** it actually happened; *Th:* **pièce h.,** (i) *A:* history, (ii) costume play; *Gram:* **présent h.,** historic present; (*of building*) **être classé (comme) monument h.,** to be scheduled as an ancient monument, as a place of historic interest. **2.** *s.m.* historical record; historical account, recital of the facts (of a discovery, etc.); **faire l'h. des événements du mois dernier,** to give a chronological account of last month's events; *Mil:* **h. du régiment,** regimental records, history.

historiquement [istɔrikmɑ̃], *adv.* **1.** historically. **2.** *A:* **réciter qch. h.,** to relate sth. accurately, as it actually happened.

historisant [istɔrizɑ̃], *a.* historicist.

historisme [istɔrism], *s.* **1.** historism, historicism. **2.** historicity.

histotoxique [istɔtɔksik], *a. & s.m. Biol:* **1.** *a.* histotoxic. **2.** *s.m.* histotoxin.

histozyme [istɔzim], *s.m. Bio-Ch:* histozyme.

histrion [istriɔ̃], *s.m.* (*a*) histrion, play-actor; (*b*) second-rate (play-)actor; (*c*) *F:* (*political, etc.*) mountebank.

histrionique [istriɔnik], *a.* histrionic; theatrical, stagy.

histrionner [istriɔne], *v.i. Pej:* (*a*) to be a second-rate (play-)actor; (*b*) to behave histrionically.

hitlérien [itlerjɛ̃], *a.* Hitlerite; **gouvernement h.,** Hitler government.

hitlérisme [itlerism], *s.m.* Hitlerism.

Hittite [itit], *A.Hist:* **1.** *a. & s.* Hittite. **2.** *s.m.* the Hittite language.

hittitologue [ititɔlɔg], *s.m. & f.* Hittitologist.

hiver [ivɛ:r], *s.m.* winter; **en h.,** in winter; *Lit:* **à l'h.,** at the onset of winter; **temps d'h.,** wintry weather; **par un beau jour d'h.,** on a fine winter's day; **vêtements d'h.,** winter clothing; **sports d'h.,** winter sports; **quartiers d'h.,** winter quarters; **jardin d'h.,** winter garden; **passer l'h. à la ville,** to winter in town; *Lit:* **il compte soixante hivers,** he has seen sixty winters; *s.a.* ÉTÉ[1]; *Nau:* **mât, bâton, d'h.,** stump top-gallant mast; *F:* **le bonhomme H.,** Jack Frost.

hivernage [ivɛrna:ʒ], *s.m.* **1.** (*a*) wintering (of cattle, etc.); (*b*) laying up (of ships) for the winter; (*c*) *Husb:* final ploughing (before winter). **2.** (*a*) winter season; (*b*) rainy season (in tropics). **3.** winter quarters; *Nau:* winter harbour. **4.** *Husb:* winter fodder.

hivernal, -aux [ivɛrnal, -o], *a.* winter (cold, etc.); wintry (weather); *Mount:* **ascension hivernale,** *s.f.* **hivernale,** winter ascent.

hivernant, -ante [ivɛrnɑ̃, -ɑ̃:t], *a.* wintering; *s.* winter visitor, winterer (on the Riviera, etc.).

hiverné [ivɛrne], *a. Nau:* **côtes hivernées,** snow-covered coast.

hiverner [ivɛrne]. **1.** *v.i.* to winter; to go into winter quarters; (*of ship*) to lie up (for the winter). **2.** *v.tr.* (*a*) to shelter (cattle) for winter; to winter (cattle); (*b*) to plough (field) before winter.

s'hiverner, *A:* to inure oneself, get inured, to the cold.

***hmm** [m], *int.* hum! hm!

***ho** [o], *int.* **1.** (*to call, summon*) hi! *Nau:* **ho, du canot!** boat ahoy! **2.** (*surprise*) oh!

***hoazin** [oazin], ***hoatzin** [oatzin], *s.m. Orn:* hoatzin, hoactzin, hoacin; *F:* stinkbird.

***hobby** [ɔbi], *s.m.* hobby.

hobereau, -eaux, -eaute [ɔbro, -o:t], *a. & s.* **1.** *a.* **la vieille race hobereaute,** the old race of squires. **2.** *s.* (*sarcastically*) small landed proprietor. **3.** *s.m. Orn:* **(faucon) h.,** hobby.

hoc [ɔk], *s.m. Games:* hoc.

hocco [ɔko], *s.m. Orn:* **h. commun,** crested curassow; **h. à casque,** galeated curassow, cashew bird.

***hochage** [ɔʃa:ʒ], *s.m. Dial:* shaking down (of cider apples).

***hoche** [ɔʃ], *s.f.* notch, nick (on tally, etc.); dent (on blade).

***hochement** [ɔʃmɑ̃], *s.m.* shaking, tossing; **h. de tête,** (i) shake of the head; (ii) nod; (iii) (*of pers. or horse*) toss of the head.

***hochepot** [ɔʃpo], *s.m. Cu:* rich meat and vegetable stew; **h. flamand,** same dish cooked in beer.

***hochequeue** [ɔʃkø], *s.m. Orn:* wagtail.

***hocher**[1] [ɔʃe]. **1.** *v.tr. Dial:* to shake (fruit-trees, etc.). **2.** *v.tr. & i.* **h. (de) la tête,** (i) to shake one's head; (ii) to nod; (iii) (*of pers. or horse*) to toss the head; **h. la queue,** (*of birds*) to wag the tail; **cheval qui hoche du nez, de la bride,** horse that tosses its head; *F:* **h. du nez,** to shake one's head in disapproval.

***hocher**[2], *v.tr.* to notch, nick (tally, etc.); to dent (blade); *Dressm:* to pink.

***hochet** [ɔʃɛ], *s.m.* **1.** (*a*) (child's) rattle or coral; (*b*) bauble, toy. **2.** broad-bladed spade.

***hocheur** [ɔʃœ:r], *s.m. Z:* white-nosed monkey.

***hockey** [ɔkɛ], *s.m. Sp:* (*a*) hockey; **h. sur glace,** *Fr.C:* **h.,** ice hockey, *U.S:* hockey; **partie de h.,** hockey game, match; **joueur de h.,** (ice) hockey player; (*b*) *Fr.C:* (ice-) hockey stick.

***hockeyeur** [ɔkɛjœ:r], *s.m.* (ice-)hockey player.

hodomètre [ɔdɔmɛtr], *s.m.* hodometer, odometer; pedometer.

hodoscope [ɔdɔskɔp], *s.m. Elcs:* hodoscope.

hodotermes [ɔdɔtɛrm], *s.m.pl. Ent:* Hodotermites.

hodotermitidés [ɔdɔtɛrmitide], *s.m.pl. Ent:* Hodotermitidae.

hœrnésite [œrnezit], *s.f. Miner:* hoernesite.

hoffman(n)esque [ɔfmanɛsk], *a.* reminiscent of the Tales of Hoffman; Hoffmannesque; weird.

Hoggar [ɔgar], *Pr.n.m. Geog:* Ahaggar.

***hogner** [ɔɲe], *v.i. A. & Dial:* to mutter, grumble; (*of dog*) to growl.

hoir [wa:r], *s.m. A.Jur:* heir.

hoirie [wari], *s.f. A.Jur:* inheritance, succession; **avance, avancement, d'h.,** settlement of portion by anticipation; advancement.

hol- [ɔl], *pref.* hol(o)-.

***holà** [ɔla], *int.* **1.** hallo! **2.** stop! hold on! not so fast! enough! whoa (back)! **mettre le h.,** to interfere (in a fight); **il est venu mettre le h.,** he came to restore order; **mettre le h. au désordre,** to check the disorder, to put a stop to disorder.

holandrique [ɔlɑ̃drik], *a. Biol:* holandric.

holarctique [ɔlarktik], *a. Biol: Geog:* holarctic (region).

holding [ɔldiŋ], *s.m. Fin:* holding; **société h.,** holding company.

***hold-up** [ɔldœp], *s.m. F:* hold-up.

holectypus [ɔlɛktipy:s], *s.f. Paleont:* holectypoid.

holectypidés [ɔlɛktipide], *s.m.pl. Paleont:* Holectypina.

hôlement [olmɑ̃], *s.m.* hooting (of owl).

***hôler** [ole], *v.i.* (*of owl*) to hoot.

holisme [ɔlism], *s.m. Biol: Phil:* holism.

***hollandais, -aise** [ɔlɑ̃dɛ, -ɛ:z]. **1.** *a.* Dutch; *Cu:* **sauce hollandaise,** hollandaise (sauce). **2.** *s.* Dutchman, Dutchwoman; Netherlander; *occ.* Hollander; *Mus:* **le H. volant,** The Flying Dutchman; *Ch:* **liqueur des H.,** Dutch liquid oil. **3.** *s.m. Ling:* **le h.,** Dutch.

***Hollande** [ɔlɑ̃:d]. **1.** *Pr.n.f. Geog:* Holland. **2.** *s.m.* (*a*) **(fromage de) Hollande,** Dutch cheese; (*b*) *Paperm:* Dutch paper. **3.** *s.f.* (*a*) *Tex:* Holland (cambric); (*b*) *Cer:* Delft ware.

***hollandé** [ɔlɑ̃de], *a. Tex:* **batiste hollandée,** holland.
***hollandite** [ɔlɑ̃dit], *s.f. Miner:* hollandite.
holmium [ɔlmjɔm], *s.m. Ch:* holmium.
hol(o)- [ɔl(ɔ)], *pref.* hol(o)-; **holacanthe,** holacanthous; **holoèdre,** holohedron.
holoaxe [ɔlɔaks], *a. Cryst:* holoaxial.
holoblastique [ɔlɔblastik], *a. Biol:* holoblastic.
holocarpe [ɔlɔkarp], *a. Bot:* holocarpic, holocarpous.
holocauste [ɔlɔkost], *s.m.* holocaust; (i) burnt-offering; (ii) sacrifice; **s'offrir en h.,** to sacrifice oneself.
holocène [ɔlɔsɛn], *a. & s.m. Geol:* Holocene, Recent (epoch).
holocéphale [ɔlɔsefal], *Ich:* **1.** *a.* holocephalous. **2.** *s.m.pl.* **holocéphales,** holocephala, chimaera.
holocrine [ɔlɔkrin], *a. Biol:* holocrine (gland).
holocristallin [ɔlɔkristalɛ̃], *a. Miner:* holocrystalline.
holodiscus [ɔlɔdiskyːs], *s.m. Bot:* holodiscus.
holoèdre [ɔlɔɛdr], *Cryst:* **1.** *a.* holohedral. **2.** *s.m.* holohedron.
holoédrie [ɔlɔedri], *s.f. Cryst:* holohedrism, holosymmetry.
holoédrique [ɔlɔedrik], *a. Cryst:* holohedral.
hologramme [ɔlɔgram], *s.m. Opt: Phot:* hologram.
holographe [ɔlɔgraf], *a.* holograph(ic) (will).
hologénèse [ɔlɔʒenɛːz], *s.f. Biol:* hologenesis.
holographie [ɔlɔgrafi], *s.f.* **1.** holograph, holographic document. **2.** *Opt: Phot:* holography.
holographique [ɔlɔgrafik], *a. Opt: Phot:* holographic.
holométabole [ɔlɔmetabɔl], *a. Ent:* holometabolous (insect).
holomètre [ɔlɔmɛtr], *s.m. Astr: etc:* holometer.
holomorphe [ɔlɔmɔrf], *a. Mth:* holomorphic.
holomorphose [ɔlɔmɔrfoːz], *s.f. Biol:* holomorphosis.
holoparasite [ɔlɔparazit], *a. & s.m. Biol:* **1.** *a.* holoparasitic. **2.** *s.m.* holoparasite.
Holopherne [ɔlɔfɛrn], *Pr.n.m. B.Hist:* Holophernes, Holofernes.
holophrastique [ɔlɔfrastik], *a. Ling:* holophrastic.
holophtalme [ɔlɔftalm], *a. Ent:* holoptic.
holoplancton [ɔlɔplɑ̃ktɔ̃], *s.m. Biol:* holoplankton.
holopneustique [ɔlɔpnøstik], *a. Ent: Biol:* holopneustic.
holoptychius [ɔlɔptikjys], *s.m. Ich:* holoptychius.
holoside [ɔlɔsid], *s.m. Bio-Ch:* holoside.
holosidère [ɔlɔsidɛːr], *s.m. Miner:* holosiderite.
holosté, -ée [ɔlɔste]. **1.** *a. Nat.Hist:* holosteous; *Bot:* **stellaire holostée,** stichwort. **2.** *s.f. Bot:* **holostée,** holosteum.
holostéens [ɔlɔsteɛ̃], *s.m.pl. Ich:* Holostei.
holostérique [ɔlɔsterik], *a.* holosteric (barometer).
holothrix [ɔlɔtriks], *s.m. Bot:* holothrix.
holothurides [ɔlɔtyrid], *s.m.pl. Echin:* Holothur(i)oidea.
holothurie [ɔlɔtyri], *s.f. Echin:* holothurian, sea slug, sea cucumber.
holotriches [ɔlɔtriʃ], *s.m.pl. Z:* Holotricha.
holotype [ɔlɔtip], *s.m. Biol:* holotype.
***holsteinois, -oise** [ɔlstɛnwa, -waːz], *Geog:* **1.** *a.* of Holstein. **2.** *s.* Holsteiner.
***hom** [hm, hɔm], *int.* hum! hm!
homalonotus [ɔmalɔnɔtyːs], *s.m. Paleont:* Homalonotus.
***homard** [ɔmaːr], *s.m.* **1.** lobster; **h. femelle,** hen lobster; **h. épineux,** crayfish; *F:* **nez et menton en patte de h.,** nut-cracker nose and chin; **devenir rouge comme un h.,** to flush or blush scarlet. **2.** *Mil: P:* spahi.
***homarderie** [ɔmardəri], *s.f. Fish:* lobster-ground.
homardier [ɔmardje], *s.m. Fish:* lobster boat.
homatropine [ɔmatrɔpin], *s.f. Pharm:* homatropine.
***Hombourg** [ɔ̃buːr], *Pr.n. Geog:* Homburg.
hombre [ɔ̃ːbr], *s.m. Cards:* (game of) ombre.
***home** [oːm], *s.m.* **1.** home. **2. h. d'enfants,** children's home.
homélie [ɔmeli], *s.f.* homily; sermon; *F:* **faire une h. à qn,** to read s.o. a lecture.
homéo- [ɔmeɔ], *pref.* homeo-, homoeo-, homoio-.
homéomorphe [ɔmeɔmɔrf], *a. Cryst: Mth:* hom(o)eomorphic, hom(o)eomorphous.
homéomorphie [ɔmeɔmɔrfi], *s.f. Cryst: Mth:* hom(o)eomorphism.
homéopathe [ɔmeɔpat], *Med:* **1.** *a.* hom(o)eopathic. **2.** *s.m.* hom(o)eopath.
homéopathie [ɔmeɔpati], *s.f.* hom(o)eopathy.
homéopathique [ɔmeɔpatik], *a.* hom(o)eopathic.
homéopathiquement [ɔmeɔpatikmɑ̃], *adv.* hom(o)eopathically.
homéostasie [ɔmeɔstazi], *s.f. Psy: etc:* hom(o)eostasis.
homéostat [ɔmeɔsta], *s.m. Tchn:* hom(o)eostatic machine.
homéostatique [ɔmeɔstatik], *a.* hom(o)eostatic.
homéotéleute [ɔmeɔteløt], *s.f. Pros:* hom(o)eoteleuton.
homéotherme [ɔmeɔtɛrm], *Z:* **1.** *a.* homoiothermic, hom(o)eothermic; **les vertébrés homéothermes,** the warm-blooded vertebrates. **2.** *s.m.* homoiotherm, hom(o)eotherm, warm-blooded creature.
homéotypique [ɔmeɔtipik], *a. Biol:* hom(o)eotypic(al).
Homère [ɔmɛːr], *Pr.n.m. Gr.Lit:* Homer.
homéride [ɔmerid], *s.m.* Homerid.
homérique [ɔmerik], *a.* Homeric (poem, laughter).
homicide[1] [ɔmisid]. **1.** *s.m. & f.* homicide; **h. point ne seras,** thou shalt not kill; *Jur:* **h. de soi-même,** *felo de se.* **2.** *a.* (*a*) homicidal; (*b*) *Poet:* **un fer h.,** a murderous weapon.
homicide[2], *s.m. Jur:* homicide (as a crime); **h. volontaire,** wilful homicide; murder; *U.S:* first degree murder; **h. excusable,** justifiable homicide; **h. par imprudence, h. involontaire,** manslaughter (through negligence), *U.S:* second degree murder; **h. involontaire (au cours d'une rixe),** chance-medley; **h. sans préméditation,** culpable homicide, manslaughter; **h. accidentel,** death by misadventure.
homicidé [ɔmiside], *a. Jur:* **personne homicidée,** person murdered.
homilétique [ɔmiletik]. **1.** *a.* homiletic(al). **2.** *s.f.* homiletics.
homiliaire [ɔmiljɛːr], *s.m.* homiliary.
homilite [ɔmilit], *s.f. Miner:* homilite.
homing [homiŋ], *s.m. Av:* homing (navigation).
hominiens [ɔminjɛ̃], *s.m.pl. Z:* Hominidae.
hommage [ɔmaːʒ], *s.m.* **1.** homage; **faire, rendre, h. à qn,** (i) to do, render, homage, to do, make pay, obeisance, to s.o.; (ii) to pay a tribute to s.o.; **rendre à qn l'h. d'une découverte,** to give s.o. full credit for a discovery; to render homage to s.o. for a discovery. **2.** *pl.* respects, compliments; **présenter ses hommages à une dame,** (i) to pay one's respects, (ii) to send one's compliments, to a lady; **présentez mes hommages à Madame X,** my respects, my compliments, to Mrs X. **3.** tribute, token (of respect, esteem); **faire h. de qch. à qn,** to offer sth. to s.o. as a token of esteem; **h. de l'éditeur, exemplaire en h.,** complimentary copy, presentation copy; **h. de l'auteur,** with the author's compliments; (*of book published to honour a professor, etc.*) **h. au Professeur X,** studies in honour of Professor X.
hommagé [ɔmaʒe], *a. A:* (*of land*) held by right of homage.
hommager [ɔmaʒe], *s.m. A:* homager.
hommasse [ɔmas], *a. F:* (*of woman*) masculine, mannish; **manière, brusquerie, h.,** rough, unrefined, manner.
homme [ɔm], *s.m.* man. **1.** (*a*) mankind; **l'h. propose et Dieu dispose,** man proposes, God disposes; **on reconnaît la main de l'h.,** one can tell the human hand, the hand of man; **tous les hommes,** all men, all mankind; **de mémoire d'h.,** within living memory; **le Fils de l'h.,** the Son of Man; **les droits de l'h.,** the rights of man, human rights; (*b*) (*opposed to woman or boy*) **se montrer un h.,** to show oneself a man; **soyez (un) h.!** be a man! **homme fait,** grown man; *Com:* **rayon hommes,** men's department; **nous avons eu une réunion entre hommes,** we had a stag-party; **jeune h.,** *see* JEUNE 1; **se battre h. à h.,** to fight man to man; **parler à qn d'h. à h.,** to speak to s.o. as man to man; *P:* **mon h.,** my husband, *P:* my man; **h. à femmes,** lady-killer; *s.a.* ÂGE 1; (*c*) (individual, *pl. hommes or gens, q.v.*) **il n'est pas, ce n'est pas, mon h.,** he is not the man for me; **trouver son h.,** to meet one's match; **h. à tout faire,** man of all work; **h. à procès,** litigious man; **il n'est pas h. à souffrir un affront,** he's not the man to stand being insulted; **h. d'État,** statesman; **h. de cheval,** horseman; **h. de mer,** seafaring man; *Mil:* **h. du rang,** *O:* **h. de troupe,** private (soldier), *U.S:* enlisted man; **six cents hommes,** six hundred men, six hundred other ranks; *Ind: etc:* **h. de journée, de peine,** (day-) labourer; **employer cent hommes,** to employ a hundred hands; *Nau:* **les hommes (d'équipage),** the crew, the hands, the ship's company; **h. de vigie,** look-out man; *s.a.* AFFAIRE 3, ARGENT 2, ARMÉE 1, BIEN II 1, 2, BRAVE 2, ÉPÉE 1, LETTRE 4, LOI 1, MONDE 1, PAILLE 1, PAUVRE 1, POLITIQUE 1, RUE 1; (*d*) *Z:* **h. des bois,** orang-utan; (*e*) **l'abominable h. des neiges,** the abominable snowman; (*f*) *Rail:* **l'h.-mort,** dead-man's handle. **2.** *Equit:* **h. de bois,** dumb jockey.
homme-affiche [ɔmafiʃ], *s.m.,* **homme-sandwich** [ɔmsɑ̃dwi(t)ʃ], *s.m.* sandwich man; *pl. hommes-affiches, -sandwichs.*
homme-canon [ɔmkanɔ̃], *s.m.* **1.** (*Post Office*) head of the blind duty. **2.** human cannon ball (in circus); *pl. hommes-canons.*
homme-Dieu (l') [lɔmdjø], *s.m. Theol:* the God-man.
homme-fusée [ɔmfyze], *s.m.* man rocket; *pl. hommes-fusées.*
homme-grenouille [ɔmgrənuːj], *s.m. Nau:* frogman; *pl. hommes-grenouilles.*
hommelette [ɔmlɛt], *s.f. P:* feeble man, weed.
homme-orchestre [ɔmɔrkɛstr], *s.m.* (*a*) one-man band; (*b*) *F:* Pooh-Bah; *pl. hommes-orchestres.*
homme-serpent [ɔmsɛrpɑ̃], *s.m.* contortionist; *pl. hommes-serpents.*
homo- [ɔmɔ], *pref.* homo-; **homoplastie,** homoplasty; **homotaxique,** homotaxial.
homocentrique [ɔmɔsɑ̃trik], *a. Geom:* homocentric, concentric.
homocerque [ɔmɔsɛrk], *a. Ich: Z:* homocercal.
homochrome [ɔmɔkroːm], *a. Nat.Hist:* procryptic.
homochromie [ɔmɔkromi], *s.f. Nat.Hist:* procrypsis.
homocinétique [ɔmɔsinetik], *a. Mec.E:* **joint h.,** Hooke's joint.
homocyclique [ɔmɔsiklik], *a. Ch:* homocyclic.
homodrome [ɔmɔdroːm], *s. Bot:* homodromous, homodromal.
homodyname [ɔmɔdinam], *a. Biol: Ent:* homodynamic.
homœo-, homéo- [ɔmeɔ], *pref.* homoeo-, homeo- homoio-; **homéotherme,** hom(o)eo-thermal; **homœomère,** hom(o)eomerous.
homofocal, -aux [ɔmɔfɔkal, -o], *a. Opt:* homofocal.
homogame [ɔmɔgam], *a. Bot:* homogamous.
homogamétique [ɔmɔgametik], *a. Biol:* homogametic.
homogamie [ɔmɔgami], *s.f. Biol:* homogamy.
homogénat [ɔmɔʒena], *s.m. Biol:* homogenate.
homogène [ɔmɔʒɛn], *a.* homogeneous; *Metall:* **acier h.,** cast steel, ingot steel.
homogénéisateur, -trice [ɔmɔʒeneizatœːr, -tris], *a. & s.* **1.** *a.* homogenizing (machine, etc.). **2.** *s.* homogenizer.
homogénéisation [ɔmɔʒeneizasjɔ̃], *s.f.* homogenization.
homogénéiser [ɔmɔʒeneize], *v.tr.* to homogenize; **lait homogénéisé,** homogenized milk.
homogénéité [ɔmɔʒeneite], *s.f.* homogeneousness, homogeneity.
homogènement [ɔmɔʒɛnmɑ̃], *adv.* homogeneously.
homogénésie [ɔmɔʒenezi], *s.f. Biol:* homogenesis.
homogénie [ɔmɔʒeni], *s.f. Biol:* homogeny.
homogramme [ɔmɔgram], *s.m. Ling:* homograph.
homographe [ɔmɔgraf]. (*a*) *s.m.* homograph; (*b*) *a.* homographic.
homographie [ɔmɔgrafi], *s.f. Ling: Geom:* homography.
homographique [ɔmɔgrafik], *a. Ling: Geom:* homographic.
homogreffe [ɔmɔgrɛf], *s.f. Surg: Biol:* homograft.
homolatéral, -aux [ɔmɔlateral, -o], *a. Anat:* homolateral, ipsilateral.
homolécithique [ɔmɔlesitik], *a. Biol:* homolecithal.
homologatif, -ive [ɔmɔlɔgatif, -iːv], *a. Jur:* homologative, confirmative.
homologation [ɔmɔlɔgasjɔ̃], *s.f. Jur:* confirmation, *Scot:* homologation (of deed, etc., by the court); probate (of will); official approval; *Sp:* ratification (of record, etc.); *Hort:* licensing, prescribing (of a new variety); *Ind:* **h. d'un prototype,** type approval, type certification.
homologie [ɔmɔlɔʒi], *s.f. Biol: Geom: etc:* homology.
homologique [ɔmɔlɔʒik], *a. Biol: Geom: etc:* homological.
homologue [ɔmɔlɔg], *Biol: Geom: etc:* **1.** *a.* homologous. **2.** (*a*) *s.m.* homologue; (*b*) *s.m. & f. F:* opposite number.
homologuer [ɔmɔlɔge], *v.tr. Jur:* **1.** to confirm, endorse, *Scot:* homologate (deed, etc.); to ratify (decision); to grant probate of (will). **2.** (*a*) to obtain legal ratification of (document, etc.); **h. un testament,** to prove a will; (*b*) *Adm:* **prix homologués,** authorized charges. **3.** to recognize, to confirm; *Sp:* to ratify (sporting records); **record homologué,** official record. **4.** *Hyg: Med:* to authorize (drugs, equipment).
homomorphe [ɔmɔmɔrf], *a. Mth: Biol:* homomorphic.

homomorphisme [ɔmɔmɔrfism], *s.m. Biol: Math:* homomorphism, homomorphy.
homoncule [ɔmɔ̃kyl], *s.m.* **1.** homunculus. **2.** *F:* manikin, dwarf.
homoneures [ɔmɔnœːr], *s.m.pl. Ent:* Homoneura.
homonyme [ɔmɔnim], *Ling:* **1.** *a.* homonymous. **2.** *s.m.* (*a*) homonym; (*b*) *F:* namesake.
homonymie [ɔmɔnimi], *s.f. Ling:* homonymy.
homoousien [ɔmɔuzjɛ̃], *a. & s. Rel:* Homoousian.
homopétale [ɔmɔpetal], *a. Bot:* homopetalous.
homophone [ɔmɔfɔn]. **1.** *a. Ling: Mus:* homophonous, homophonic. **2.** *s.m. Ling:* homophone.
homophonie [ɔmɔfɔni], *s.f. Ling: Mus:* homophony.
homopolaire [ɔmɔpɔlɛːr], *a. Biol: El:* homopolar.
homoptère [ɔmɔptɛːr], *Ent:* **1.** *a.* homopterous. **2.** *s.m.pl.* **les homoptères,** Homoptera.
homosexualité [ɔmɔsɛksɥalite], *s.f.* homosexuality.
homosexuel, -elle [ɔmɔsɛksɥɛl], *a.* homosexual.
homothermal, -aux [ɔmɔtɛrmal, -o], *a. Ph:* homothermal.
homothétie [ɔmɔtesi], *s.f. Geom:* similarity (in construction and position); **centre d'h.,** centre of similarity.
homothétique [ɔmɔtetik], *a. Geom:* homothetic; **réduction h.,** scaling down.
homotope [ɔmɔtɔp], *a. Mth:* homotopic.
homotopie [ɔmɔtɔpi], *s.f. Mth:* homotopy.
homotrope [ɔmɔtrɔp], *a. Bot:* homotropous, homotropal.
homotype [ɔmɔtip], *Biol:* **1.** *a.* homotypic(al). **2.** *s.m.* homotype.
homozygote [ɔmɔzigɔt], *Biol:* **1.** *a.* homozygous. **2.** *s.m.* homozygote.
homozygotie [ɔmɔzigɔsi], *s.f. Biol:* homozygosis, homozygosity.
homuncule [ɔmɔ̃kyl], *s.m.* **1.** homunculus. **2.** *F:* manikin, dwarf.
***hon!** [ɔ̃], *int. A:* (*denoting displeasure, threat*), ha!
***honchets** [ɔ̃ʃɛ], *s.m.pl. Games:* spillikins, jackstraws.
***hondurien, -ienne** [ɔ̃dyrjɛ̃, -jɛn], *a. & s. Geog:* (native, inhabitant) of Honduras.
***honfleurais, -aise** [ɔ̃flœrɛ, -ɛːz], **honfleurois, -oise** [ɔ̃flœrwa, -waːz], *a. & s. Geog:* (native, inhabitant) of Honfleur.
hongnette [ɔ̃nɛt], *s.f.* = HOUGNETTE.
***hongre** [ɔ̃ːgr]. **1.** *a.m.* gelded, castrated (horse). **2.** *s.m.* gelding.
***hongreline** [ɔ̃grəlin], *s.f. A.Cost:* (*a*) man's fur-lined winter coat; (*b*) woman's long-line bodice.
***hongrer** [ɔ̃gre], *v.tr. Vet:* to geld, castrate.
***hongreur** [ɔ̃grœːr], *s.m.* gelder.
***Hongrie** [ɔ̃gri], *Pr.n.f. Geog:* Hungary.
***hongroierie** [ɔ̃grwari], *s.f.* Hungarian-leather manufacture, trade, works.
***hongrois, -oise** [ɔ̃grwa, -waːz], *a. & s. Geog: Ling: etc:* Hungarian.
***hongroyage** [ɔ̃grwajaːʒ], *s.m.* Hungarian-leather manufacture, trade, works.
***hongroyer** [ɔ̃grwaje], *v.tr.* (**je hongroie, n. hongroyons; je hongroierai**) to dress, taw, (leather) by the Hungarian method.
***hongroyeur, -euse** [ɔ̃grwajœːr, -øːz], *s.* tanner, tawer, of Hungarian leather.
honnête [ɔnɛ(ː)t], *a.* **1.** honest, honourable, upright; **homme h., h. homme,** honest man; **honnêtes gens,** honest, decent, people; **une famille des plus honnêtes,** a highly respectable family; **fille h.,** straight, decent, girl; **peu h.,** dishonourable; *s.m.* **il s'est toujours attaché à l'h.,** he always put honesty first. **2.** courteous, well-bred, civil, polite; *A:* **h. homme,** gentleman; **être h. envers, avec, qn,** to be civil to s.o.; **vous êtes vraiment trop h.,** you are really too kind; **façons peu honnêtes,** uncivil, impolite, manners. **3.** decent, seemly, becoming (behaviour, etc.); **attitude peu h.,** unseemly, unbecoming, attitude; **il n'est pas h. de se louer soi-même,** you shouldn't blow your own trumpet. **4.** reasonable, moderate, fair (price, etc.); **moyens honnêtes,** fair means; **procédés honnêtes,** square, fair, dealings; **jouir d'une h. aisance,** to be comfortably off, to enjoy a decent competency; **vivre dans une h. aisance,** to live in modest comfort.
honnêtement [ɔnɛtmɑ̃], *adv.* **1.** honestly, honourably, uprightly; **h. parlant,** frankly speaking. **2.** courteously, civilly, politely. **3.** decently, becomingly. **4.** reasonably, fairly, squarely.
honnêteté [ɔnɛtte], *s.f.* **1.** honesty, uprightness, integrity. **2.** (*a*) courtesy, civility, politeness; (*b*) polite action; **faire mille honnêtetés à qn,** to be extremely polite to s.o. **3.** decency, propriety, decorum; seemliness; modesty (in woman). **4.** reasonableness, fairness, fair dealing.
honneur [ɔnœːr], *s.m.* honour. **1.** (*a*) **homme d'h.,** man of honour, honourable man; **il est l'h. incarné,** he is the soul of honour; **engager son h.,** to stake one's honour; **être engagé d'h. à faire qch.,** to be bound in honour, in honour bound, to do sth.; *s.a.* S'ENGAGER 1; **soutenir l'h. du corps,** to show *esprit de corps*; *s.a.* POINT[1] 6; **déclarer sur l'h. que. . .,** to state on one's honour that. . .; **(ma) parole d'h!** on my word of honour! *F: Sch:* honour bright! **se faire h. de qch., de faire qch.,** to be proud of sth., proud to do sth.; **piquer qn d'h.,** to put s.o. (up)on his mettle; **mettre son h. à faire qch., se piquer d'h.,** to make it a point of honour, to feel in honour bound, to do sth.; **tenir à h. de faire qch.,** (i) to consider it an honour to be allowed to do sth.; (ii) to consider oneself in honour bound to do sth.; **faire qch. en tout h.,** to do sth. in all good faith; **je ne peux pas en tout h., accepter cet argent,** I cannot in all honesty accept this money; **en tout bien tout h.,** fair and square, fair and above-board; **affaire d'h.,** affair of honour, duel; **faire une réparation d'h. à qn,** to make a full apology to s.o.; **dette d'h.,** debt of honour; **perdre qn d'h.,** to ruin s.o.'s honour; *s.a.* CHAMP[1] 1, LÉGION; (*b*) *Lit:* (*of woman*) chastity, honour; **rendre l'h. à une femme,** to restore a woman's honour; (*c*) **assis à la place d'h.,** occupying the seat of honour; **cour d'h. (d'un lycée, etc.),** main quadrangle (of a lycée), main courtyard; **la table d'h.,** = the high table (at university); **salle d'h.,** (i) main hall; (ii) *Mil:* regimental hall (for trophies); **avoir, tenir, la place d'h.,** to have pride of place; **escalier d'h.,** grand staircase; *Mil: etc:* **garde d'h.,** guard of honour; *s.a.* DAME[1] 1, DEMOISELLE 1, GARÇON 2, PAS[1] 1, VIN 1. **2.** (*honourable distinction*) (*a*) **réception en l'h. de qn,** reception in honour of s.o., party to meet s.o.; **apéritif d'h. pour. . .,** cocktail party in honour of. . .; **hôte d'h.,** chief guest; **président d'h.,** honorary president; **faire h. à qn,** to do honour to, to honour, s.o.; *F:* **faire h. au dîner,** to do justice to the dinner; **voulez-vous me faire l'h. de dîner chez moi?** will you do me the honour of dining with me? **à qui ai-je l'h. (de parler, monsieur)?** (i) to whom have I the honour, the pleasure, of speaking? (ii) *Iron:* you have the advantage of me, sir; **j'ai l'h. de vous faire savoir que. . .,** I beg to inform you that. . .; **on m'a fait l'h. de cette découverte,** I have been credited with this discovery; **mettre une coutume en h.,** to bring a custom into honour; **être en h. chez qn,** to be held in high honour by s.o.; *F:* **en quel h. vous voit-on ici?** (i) what brings you here? (ii) what right have you to be here? *Games:* **à vous l'h.,** your honour; **jouer pour l'h.,** to play for love; *Golf:* **avoir l'h.,** to have the honour; (*b*) credit; **faire h. à son pays,** to be an honour, a credit, to do credit, to one's country; **cela lui fait grand h.,** it reflects great credit on him; **cela fait h. à son courage,** that speaks well for his courage; **on doit dire à leur h. que. . .,** it must be said to their credit that. . .; **il en est sorti à son h.,** he came out of it with credit, with flying colours; **c'est tout à son h.,** this redounds to his credit, this is all to his credit; **son refus est tout à son h.,** it speaks well for him, it is greatly to his credit, his honour, that he did not accept; **h. à lui!** all honour to him! **le cricket est à l'h. en Angleterre,** cricket holds a place of honour in England; *s.a.* SEIGNEUR 1. **3.** *pl.* (*a*) regalia (at coronation, etc.); (*b*) (marks of esteem) **rendre les derniers honneurs, les honneurs suprêmes, à qn,** to pay the last tribute to s.o.; **faire (à qn) les honneurs de la maison,** to do the honours of the house (to s.o.); *Mil:* **rendre les honneurs à qn,** to present arms, to give, pay (military) honours, to s.o.; **se retirer d'une forteresse avec tous les honneurs de la guerre,** to leave a fortress with all the honours of war. **4. faire h. à sa signature,** to honour one's signature; **faire h. à ses affaires,** to meet one's obligations; *Com:* **faire h. à une traite,** to honour, meet, a bill; **ne pas faire h. à un effet,** to dishonour a bill; **acceptation par h.,** acceptance (of a bill) for honour. **5.** *Games:* (*a*) *Cards:* **les honneurs,** honours; **quatre d'honneurs,** four by honours; **honneurs partagés,** honours even; (*b*) **partie d'h.,** deciding game or match; (*c*) (*bowling*) **h. simple,** spare; **h. double,** strike. **6.** *Nau:* **ranger (des rochers, un navire) à l'h.,** to pass dangerously close to (rocks, ship). **7.** *Her:* **lieu d'h.,** honour point.
***honnir** [ɔniːr], *v.tr. A:* to cover with disgrace; to disgrace, to dishonour; to shame; to revile; **hon(n)i soit qui mal y pense,** evil be to him who evil thinks; **honni de tous,** spurned by all.
***honnissement** [ɔnismɑ̃], *s.m. A:* scorning, spurning; reviling.
***honnisseur** [ɔnisœːr], *s.m. A:* scorner, spurner; reviler.
Honolulu [ɔnɔlyly], *Pr.n.m.* Honolulu.
honorabilité [ɔnɔrabilite], *s.f.* (*a*) honourable character; (*b*) respectability; (*c*) standing (of a firm).
honorable [ɔnɔrabl̩], *a.* (*a*) honourable; **mention h.,** honourable mention (at show, etc.); (*Engl.*) **le très H. . . .,** the Right Honourable. . .; **vieillesse h.,** respected old age; *Vit:* **année h.,** vintage year; *s.a.* AMENDE 2, PIÈCE 2; (*b*) respectable, reputable (family, profession, etc.); creditable (performance, work); **maison h.,** firm of high standing; **peu honorable,** hardly respectable; disreputable; **fortune h.,** respectable competence.
honorablement [ɔnɔrabləmɑ̃], *adv.* (*a*) honourably, with honour; **vivre h.,** to live respectably; **h. enterré,** interred with (due) honour; **famille h. connue,** family of good repute; **traiter qn h.,** to treat s.o. honourably, to do the right thing by s.o.; (*b*) **s'acquitter h.,** to acquit oneself creditably, with credit.
honoraire [ɔnɔrɛːr]. **1.** *a.* honorary (duty, member, etc.); **professeur h.,** emeritus professor; *Mil:* **colonel h.,** brevet colonel. **2.** *s.m.pl. occ. sg.* fee(s) (of professional man); honorarium; (lawyer's) retainer; (author's) royalty.
honorariat [ɔnɔrarja], *s.m.* (*a*) honorary membership; (*b*) *Mil:* brevet rank.
Honoré [ɔnɔre], *Pr.n.m.* Honoratus.
honorer [ɔnɔre], *v.tr.* **1.** (*a*) to honour (s.o.); to respect (s.o.'s good qualities, etc.); *Com.Corr:* **votre honorée du. . .,** your favour of the. . .; **mon honoré confrère,** my respected colleague; **tes père et mère honoreras,** honour thy father and mother; (*b*) to do honour to (s.o.); **h. qn de sa présence, de sa confiance, d'une invitation,** to honour, favour, s.o. with one's presence, with one's confidence, with an invitation; **h. une cérémonie de sa présence,** to grace a ceremony with one's presence; **votre confiance m'honore,** I'm honoured by your confidence; (*c*) *Com: Fin:* to honour, meet, retire (bill); **ne pas h. une traite,** to dishonour a bill; *Com: Jur:* **refuser d'honorer (un contrat),** to repudiate (a contract). **2.** to be an honour to, do credit to (s.o., sth.); to reflect honour on (s.o.); **démarche qui vous honore,** step that does you credit.
s'honorer, (*a*) to gain distinction; (*b*) to consider oneself honoured; **s'h. d'avoir fait qch.,** to be proud of, to pride oneself (up)on, having done sth.
honorifique [ɔnɔrifik], *a.* **1.** honorary (title, rank, etc.); **accepter une distinction h.,** to accept an honour. **2.** honorific (phrase of Eastern languages). **3.** *A:* **droits honorifiques,** right to a seat of honour (in church, etc.).
honorifiquement [ɔnɔrifikmɑ̃], *adv.* honorifically.
Honorine [ɔnɔrin], *Pr.n.f.* Honour, Honora, *F:* Norah.
***honte** [ɔ̃ːt], *s.f.* **1.** (*a*) (sense of) shame; **avoir perdu toute h., tout sentiment de h.,** *A:* **avoir toute h. bue,** to be lost, dead, to all sense of shame; to be past all sense of shame; **h. à vous!** shame (on you)! **sans h.,** shameless; **avoir h.,** to be ashamed; **vous devriez avoir h.!** you ought to be ashamed of yourself! **avoir h. de faire qch.; avoir, éprouver, de la h. à faire qch.,** to be, feel, ashamed to do sth.; **avoir h. de qn,** to be ashamed of s.o.; **faire h. à qn,** to make s.o. ashamed, to put s.o. to shame; **vous me faites h.,** I am ashamed of you; **faire h. à sa famille,** to shame one's family, to be a disgrace to one's family; **vous nous faites rougir de h.,** you put us to the blush; **je lui ai fait h. de son ingratitude,** I told him he ought to be ashamed of his ingratitude; (*b*) **fausse h., mauvaise h.,** self-consciousness, bashfulness. **2.** (cause of) shame, disgrace, dishonour; **couvrir qn de h.,** to cover s.o. with shame, with disgrace; to bring shame on s.o.; **quelle h.!** what a shame! for shame! **avouer qch. à sa h.,** to confess sth. to one's shame; **faire, être, la h. de qn,** to be a disgrace to, to disgrace, s.o.; **c'est une h. qu'il ait été acquitté,** it is a scandal that he should have been acquitted; **ces taudis sont la h. de la ville,** these slums are a disgrace, a reproach, to the town; *A: F:* **il en sera pour sa courte h.,** he is sure to

get snubbed, to come back with a flea in his ear. 3. *F: A:* **faire mille hontes à qn,** to shower reproaches on s.o., to revile s.o.

***honteusement** [ɔ̃tøzmɑ̃], *a.* 1. shamefully; (*a*) disgracefully; (*b*) ignominiously; **s'en aller h.,** to slink away. 2. bashfully, shamefacedly.

***honteux, -euse** [ɔ̃tø, -ø:z], *a.* 1. ashamed; **être h. d'avoir fait qch.,** to be ashamed of having done sth.; **je suis h. qu'on vous ait oublié,** I am ashamed that you were forgotten. 2. bashful, shamefaced, sheepish; **d'un air h.,** sheepishly; **les pauvres honteux,** the uncomplaining poor; the proud poor; *Prov:* **jamais h. n'eut belle amie,** faint heart never won fair lady, none but the brave deserve the fair. 3. shameful, disgraceful (conduct, etc.); **c'est h.!** it's a shame! **c'est d'autant plus h. à vous,** all the more shame to you. 4. **parties honteuses,** pudenda; *Path:* **maladies honteuses,** venereal diseases.

***hoodoo** [udu], *s.m. Anthr:* hoodoo, voodoo.

***hop** [ɔp], *int.* **allons hop!** now then jump! **allez hop!** out you go! *P:* hop it!

hopcalite [ɔpkalit], *s.f. Ch:* hopcalite.

hopéite [ɔpeit], *s.f. Miner:* hopeite.

hôpital, -aux [ɔpital, -o], *s.m.* 1. (*a*) hospital; infirmary; **salle d'h.,** ward; **faire les hôpitaux,** to walk the wards; **h. municipal, h. départemental,** hospital administered by the town, by the *département*; **h. psychiatrique,** mental hospital; **h. de contagieux,** isolation hospital; *Mil:* **h. auxiliaire,** Red Cross hospital; **h. de campagne,** field hospital; **h. de garnison,** garrison, *U.S:* station, hospital; **h. d'évacuation,** (casualty) clearing station, clearing hospital; **h. de l'intérieur,** base hospital; **h. mixte,** civil hospital in which certain wards are reserved for military cases; *Med:* **pourriture d'h.,** hospital gangrene; (*b*) *Navy:* **h. du bord,** sick-bay; **navire h.,** hospital ship; (*c*) *Ser:* cocoonery for under-developed silkworms. 2. *A:* (= HOSPICE 2) poor-house; **h. des orphelins,** orphans' home; **finir ses jours à l'h.,** to end one's days in the workhouse; *F:* **prendre le chemin de l'h.,** to be on the road to ruin, to go to the dogs. 3. *Hist:* **ordre de l'H.,** order of the Knights Hospitallers.

hoplite [ɔplit], *s.m. Gr.Ant:* hoplite.

***hoquet** [ɔkɛ], *s.m.* 1. hiccough, hiccup; **avoir le h.,** to have the hiccups; **il s'excusa entre deux hoquets,** he hiccuped out an apology. 2. (*a*) gasp (of surprise, terror, etc.); **avoir un h. d'étouffement, de surprise,** to catch one's breath; **être au dernier h.,** to be at one's last gasp; (*b*) **h. de nausée,** keck; (*c*) *Lit:* shock, jolt. 3. *A.Mus:* hocket.

***hoqueter** [ɔkte], *v.i.* (**je hoquette, n. hoquetons; je hoquetterai**) to hiccup; to have the hiccups.

***hoqueton** [ɔktɔ̃], *s.m.* 1. (*a*) *Hist: Cost:* haqueton, acton; jack; (*b*) *A:* smock-frock. 2. *A:* archer, yeoman.

Horace [ɔras], *Pr.n.m.* 1. *Rom.Hist:* Horatius; **les Horaces,** the Horatii. 2. (*a*) *Lt.Lit:* Horace; (*b*) *Engl. dramatic Lit:* Horatio.

horacien, horatien, -ienne [ɔrasjɛ̃, -jɛn], *a.* Horatian.

horaire [ɔrɛ:r]. 1. *a.* (*a*) horary; **signal h.,** time signal; **boule h.,** time-ball; **compteur h.,** time meter; **lignes horaires (d'un cadran solaire),** hour-lines; *Astr:* **cercle h.,** horary circle, hour circle; **fuseau h.,** time belt, time zone; standard time belt; **angle h. local, sidéral,** local, sidereal, hour angle; *Rail:* **tableau h.,** timetable; (*b*) hourly; **vitesse h.,** speed per hour; *Ind:* **débit h.,** hourly output, output per hour; **puissance h.,** output per hour. 2. *s.m.* schedule; timing; *Rail: etc:* time-table; *Rail:* **horaires types,** standard working time-tables; *F:* **être dans l'h.,** to be on time; *Rac:* **arriver à un contrôle selon l'h.,** to arrive at a check point on schedule (in long-distance road race).

***horde** [ɔrd], *s.f.* horde (of nomads, etc.); *F:* **h. (de créanciers),** swarm, host (of creditors, etc.).

hordéacé [ɔrdease], **hordéiforme** [ɔrdeifɔrm], *a. Bot:* hordeaceous.

hordéine [ɔrdein], *s.f. Bio-Ch:* hordein.

hordénine [ɔrdenin], *s.f. Pharm:* hordenine.

hordeum [ɔrdeɔm], *s.m. Bot:* hordeum.

***horion** [ɔrjɔ̃], *s.m.* blow, punch, knock; **recevoir des horions,** to get knocked about.

horizon [ɔrizɔ̃], *s.m.* 1. (*a*) horizon, skyline; **à l'h., au-dessus de l'h.,** on the horizon, on the sky-line; **reculer l'h. de ses connaissances,** to widen the bounds of one's knowledge; **l'h. politique se rembrunit,** the political outlook is darkening; **tour d'h. politique,** political survey; **ouvrir des horizons nouveaux,** to open up new horizons; (*b*) *Surv: etc:* **h. vrai, artificiel,** true, artificial, horizon; *Av:* **h. gyroscopique,** artificial horizon; **barre d'h.,** horizon bar (of flight director). 2. *Art:* **(ligne d')h.,** vanishing line. 3. **h. géologique,** geological horizon.

horizonner [ɔrizɔne], *v.tr.* (*rare*) to bound, limit (the view, etc.).

horizontal, -aux [ɔrizɔ̃tal, -o]. 1. *a.* horizontal; level; **se mettre dans la position horizontale,** to assume a horizontal position; to lie down. 2. *s.f.* **horizontale;** (*a*) horizontal line; (*b*) *P:* prostitute, tart; **elle fait l'horizontale,** she earns her money on her back.

horizontalement [ɔrizɔ̃talmɑ̃], *adv.* horizontally; (*in crosswords*) across.

horizontalité [ɔrizɔ̃talite], *s.f.* horizontality.

horloge [ɔrlɔ:ʒ], *s.f.* 1. (*a*) clock (*esp.* town or church clock); **h. comtoise, de parquet,** grandfather('s) clock; **h. à poids,** weight-driven clock; **h. à ressort,** spring-clock; *Tp:* **l'h. parlante,** the speaking clock; **h. à quartz,** quartz crystal clock; **h. électronique,** electronic clock; *Ind: etc:* **h. mère, centrale, principale,** master clock; **h. réceptrice,** slave clock; **h. atomique, moléculaire,** atomic clock; **h. électrique,** electric clock; **il est deux heures à l'h., l'h. marque deux heures,** it is two by the clock, the clock is pointing to two; **j'ai attendu une bonne heure d'h.,** I waited for a full hour by the clock; **dormir neuf heures d'h.,** to sleep for nine solid hours; *s.a.* RÉGLÉ 2; (*b*) *A:* **h. à eau, d'eau,** water-clock; **h. à, de, sable,** hour-glass; **h. solaire,** sundial; (*c*) **jeu de l'h.,** clock-golf. 2. *Ent:* **h. de la mort,** death-watch (beetle).

horloger, -ère [ɔrlɔʒe, -ɛ:r]. 1. *a.* horological; **l'industrie horlogère,** the clock-making industry. 2. *s.* clock and watch maker.

horlogerie [ɔrlɔʒri], *s.f.* 1. clock and watch making; **mouvement d'h.,** clockwork; **entraîné, mû, par un mouvement d'h.,** clockwork-driven; **mécanisme d'h. à retardement,** clockwork delay mechanism (of bomb, etc.). 2. (*a*) clock trade, watch trade; (*b*) clockmaker's shop; **vous trouverez cela dans une h.,** you will find that at a clockmaker's. 3. *coll.* clocks and watches.

horminum [ɔrminɔm], *s.m. Bot:* horminum.

***hormis** [ɔrmi], *prep.* (*no liaison;* **hormis elle** [ɔrmiɛl]) except, but, save; **tous h. cinq,** all but five, all with the exception of five; **personne h. vous,** no one but you; no one besides yourself; **je risquerais tout h. (de) lui déplaire,** I would risk everything, except his displeasure; *conj.phr.* **hormis que** + *ind.,* except that, save that; apart from the fact that; **je n'ai rien remarqué h. qu'il était présent,** I noticed nothing, except that he was there; *A:* **h. que . . . ne** + *sub.,* unless, except; **les dames ne dansaient point, h. qu'elles n'en fussent priées par le roi,** the married ladies did not dance, unless they were requested by the king.

hormonal, -aux [ɔrmɔnal, -o], *a. Physiol:* hormonal; of, relating to, hormones; **insuffisance hormonale,** hormone deficiency; **sous contrôle h.,** hormone dependent.

hormone [ɔrmɔn], *s.f. Physiol:* hormone; *Med:* **prescrire des hormones à qn,** to prescribe hormones, hormone treatment, for s.o.

hormonothérapie [ɔrmɔnɔterapi], *s.f. Med:* hormonotherapy.

***hornblende** [ɔrnblɛ̃:d], *s.f. Miner:* hornblende.

***hornblendite** [ɔrnblɛ̃dit], *s.f. Miner:* hornblendite.

hornéophyton [ɔrneɔfitɔ̃], *s.f. Paleont:* horneophyton.

horodateur [ɔrɔdatœ:r], *s.m. Ind:* time clock, time recorder; time-stamp.

horographe [ɔrɔgraf], *s.m.* horographer.

horographie [ɔrɔgrafi], *s.f.* horography, dialling.

horographique [ɔrɔgrafik], *a.* relating to horography.

horokilométrique [ɔrɔkilɔmetrik], *a.* relating to time spent and distance covered.

horologe [ɔrɔlɔ:ʒ], *s.m. Rel:* horologion.

horométrie [ɔrɔmetri], *s.f.* horometry, horology.

horométrique [ɔrɔmetrik], *a.* horometric(al), horologic(al).

horoptère [ɔrɔptɛ:r], *s.m. Opt:* horopter.

horoptérique [ɔrɔpterik], *a.* horopteric.

horoscope [ɔrɔskɔp], *s.m.* horoscope; **faire, dresser, tirer, l'h. de qn,** to cast s.o.'s horoscope.

horoscopie [ɔrɔskɔpi], *s.f.* horoscopy.

horoscopique [ɔrɔskɔpik], *a.* horoscopic(al).

horreur [ɔr(r)œ:r], *s.f.* horror. 1. (feeling of) horror; **à ma grande h.,** to my unspeakable horror; **conte à faire h.,** horrifying story; **cela faisait h. à voir,** it was horrible to see; **frappé d'h.,** horror-stricken; **ce spectacle nous glaça d'h.,** this sight petrified us with horror. 2. repugnance, disgust, detestation, abhorrence, horror; **faire h. à qn,** to horrify s.o., to fill s.o., with horror, be repulsive to s.o.; **avoir qn, qch., en h., avoir h. de qn, de qch.,** to have a horror of s.o., of sth.; to hate, detest, abhor, abominate, s.o., sth.; **j'ai h. d'y penser,** I dread to think of it; **il avait en h. qu'on le dupât,** he hated to be taken in; **être en h. à qn,** to be held in abhorrence by s.o.; *A.Ph:* **la Nature a h. du vide,** Nature abhors a vacuum. 3. (quality of) horror, awfulness; **silence plein d'h.,** silence full of horror, awful silence. 4. (*a*) (cause, object, of) horror; **quelle h.!** (i) what a shocking thing! (ii) what an awful looking object! **quelle h. d'enfant!** what a horrid child! **oh, la petite h.!** the (or you) horrid thing! (*b*) **les horreurs de la guerre,** the horrors of war; **commettre des horreurs,** to commit atrocities; **dire des horreurs de qn,** to say horrid things about s.o.; **il m'a dit des horreurs,** he has been saying dreadful things to me.

horrible [ɔr(r)ibl], *a.* horrible, horrifying, awful, shocking, fearful, frightful, *F:* horrid; **spectacle h.,** ghastly, gruesome, sight; **h. à voir,** awful to behold; appalling; *F:* **il fait un froid h.,** it is awfully cold; **whisky h.,** vile whisky.

horriblement [ɔr(r)ibləmɑ̃], *adv.* horribly, dreadfully, fearfully, frightfully, shockingly; **j'ai joué h. (mal),** I played awfully badly.

horrifiant [ɔr(r)ifjɑ̃], *a.* horrifying.

horrifier [ɔr(r)ifje], *v.tr.* (*p.d. & pr.sub.* **n. horrifiions, v. horrifiiez**) *F:* to horrify; **être horrifié de qch.,** to be horrified at sth.; **je m'en allai horrifié,** I went away horrorstricken.

horrifique [ɔr(r)ifik], *a. A: F:* horrific, hair-raising.

horripilant [ɔr(r)ipilɑ̃], *a.* 1. *A:* hair-raising (adventure). 2. *F:* exasperating, maddening.

horripilateur [ɔr(r)ipilatœ:r], *a. Anat:* **muscle !** , erector pili muscle.

horripilation [ɔr(r)ipilasjɔ̃], *s.f.* 1. *Med:* horripilation, goose-flesh. 2. *F:* exasperation; revulsion, recoil (**contre,** from).

horripilement [ɔr(r)ipilmɑ̃], *s.m. F:* exasperation; revulsion, recoil (**contre,** from).

horripiler [ɔr(r)ipile], *v.tr.* 1. *A:* to give (s.o.) goose-flesh; to make (s.o.'s) flesh creep. 2. to exasperate (s.o.); to set (s.o.'s) nerves on edge.

***hors** [ɔr], *prep.* (*liaison with* r; **hors elle** [ɔrɛl]) 1. (*a*) out of, outside; **h. (la) barrière,** without the gates; **longueur h. tout,** over-all length; **h. pointe,** off-peak (hours); **h. taxe,** exclusive of tax; **h. d'usage,** worn out, obsolete; *Mil:* **compagnie h. rang,** special detachment; **fourneau h. feu,** furnace out of blast; *s.a.* COURANT 2, JEU 2, LIGNE 1, LOI 1, SERVICE 1; (*b*) except; **tous h. un seul,** all but one; *F:* all bar(ring) one; *O:* **je sors tous les jours h. quand il pleut,** I go out every day except when it rains; *conj.phr.* **hors que** + *ind.,* except that, save that; **je ne sais rien h. qu'elle vous aime,** I know nothing save that she loves you; *A:* **hors que . . . ne** + *sub.,* unless, except; **h. qu'il ne soit mort, il reviendra,** except he be dead, he will return. 2. *prep.phr.* **hors de** out of, outside (of); (*a*) **h. de la ville,** outside the town; **nous voilà h. de la forêt,** we have come right through the forest; **nous voilà h. de l'hiver,** winter is over; **dîner h. de chez soi,** to dine out; **hors d'ici!** get out (of here)! **hors d'haleine,** out of breath; **hors de combat,** (i) (*of gun, ship, etc.*) out of action; (ii) (*of man*) disabled; **matériel h. de service,** scrapped material; *Fb:* **hors des touches,** out of touch; **être hors d'affaire,** to have got through one's difficulties; (*of sick person*) to be out of danger; *Com:* **mettre un associé h. d'intérêt,** to buy out a partner; **h. d'inquiétude,** relieved of anxiety; **h. de portée,** out of reach; **h. de portée de fusil,** out of range; **sévère dans l'exercice de ses fonctions, h. de là très indulgent,** severe in the performance of his office, otherwise very indulgent; **h. de là point de salut,** without it there is no hope of salvation; **être hors de soi,** to be beside oneself (with rage, etc.); **cela le met h. de lui,** it makes him wild; it drives him frantic, to distraction; **c'est h. de prix,** it's prohibitive; *s.a.* CAUSE 2, COUR 2, PORTÉE 3, VOIX 1; (*b*) **h. de le battre,** unless they had beaten him, short of beating him. 3. *adj. phr.* **hors d'œuvre,** (i) *Arch:* out of the alignment, projecting; (ii) *Lap:* (*of precious stone*) unmounted, unset; **pièce h. d'œuvre,** extra room built out; **mesure h. d'œuvre,** outside measurement; *s.a.* ESCALIER, HORS-D'ŒUVRE.

***horsain** [ɔrsɛ̃, ɔrzɛ̃], *s.m.* (*Norman Dial:*) outsider (referring to s.o. not born in Normandy).

***hors-bord** [ɔrbɔ:r], *s.m.inv.* outboard motor boat; *F:* speedboat; **moteur h.-b.,** outboard motor.

***hors-caste** [ɔrkast], *s.m. & f. inv.* outcaste, outcast.

***hors-concours** [ɔrkɔ̃kuːr]. **1.** *adv.* hors concours, out of competition; **mettre h.-c.,** to disqualify (for superiority). **2.** *a.inv.* (*a*) not allowed to compete; hors concours; ineligible; (*b*) above competition, unrivalled, hors concours. **3.** *s.m.inv.* person, exhibit, ineligible for competition (because of superiority).

***hors-d'œuvre** [ɔrdœːvr], *s.m.inv.* **1.** (*a*) *Arch:* annexe, outwork; (*b*) *F:* irrelevant matter, extraneous chapter (in book, etc.). **2.** *Cu:* hors-d'œuvre; **les hors-d'œuvre,** the hors-d'œuvres.

horsfordite [ɔrsfɔrdit], *s.f. Miner:* horsfordite.

***hors-jeu** [ɔrʒø], *s.m.inv. Sp:* off-side.

***hors-la-loi** [ɔrlalwa], *s.m.inv.* outlaw.

***hors-ligne** [ɔrliɲ], *s.m.inv. Civ.E:* patch of land outside the boundary (of projected public highway).

***hors-montoir** [ɔrmɔ̃twaːr], *s.m.* no *pl.* (**côté**) **h.-m.,** off side (of horse).

***hors-œuvre** [ɔrœːvr], *s.m.inv.* external dimensions.

***hors-programme** [ɔrprɔgram], (*a*) *a.inv. Sch:* outside the syllabus, extra-curricular; (*b*) *s.m. inv. Cin:* supplementary film.

***hors-série** [ɔrseri], *a.inv.* (*a*) **voiture h.-s.,** non-series car; (*b*) out of the ordinary.

***horst** [ɔrst], *s.m. Geol:* horst.

***hors-texte** [ɔrtɛkst], *s.m.inv. Bookb:* (inset) plate.

***hors-tout** [ɔrtu], *a.inv.* overall (length).

hortensia [ɔrtɑ̃sja], *s.m. Bot:* hydrangea.

horticole [ɔrtikɔl], *a.* horticultural; flower-(show, etc.).

horticulteur [ɔrtikyltœːr], *s.m.* horticulturist.

horticultural, -aux [ɔrtikyltyral, -o], *a.* horticultural.

horticulture [ɔrtikyltyːr], *s.f.* horticulture, gardening; **exposition d'h.,** flower-show.

hortillon [ɔrtijɔ̃], *s.m.* **1.** = HORTILLONNAGE 1. **2.** market gardener (of an *hortillonnage*).

hortillonnage [ɔrtijɔnaːʒ], *s.m.* (*in lower Somme valley*) **1.** intensively cultivated marshland market garden (drained by canals). **2.** cultivation of *hortillonnages.*

hortillonneur [ɔrtijɔnœːr], *s.m.* market gardener (of an *hortillonnage*).

hortonolite [ɔrtɔnɔlit], *s.f. Miner:* hortonolite.

hosanna [ɔzan(n)a]. **1.** *int.* hosanna! **2.** *s.m.* (cry of) hosanna; song of praise; **entonner des hosannas à la louange de qn,** to sing, trumpet, s.o.'s praises.

hosannière [ɔzanjɛːr], *a.f.* **croix h.,** cross at the foot of which the hosanna was sung on Palm Sunday.

hospice [ɔspis], *s.m.* **1.** hospice (on the Saint-Bernard, etc.). **2.** (*a*) almshouse, old people's home; (*b*) home for incurables; (*c*) *A:* **h. des aliénés,** lunatic asylum; **h. des enfants trouvés, des enfants assistés,** foundling hospital; **mourir à l'h.,** to die in the poorhouse. **3.** *F: A:* (= HÔPITAL 1) hospital.

hospitalier[1], **-ière** [ɔspitalje, -jɛːr], *a.* hospitable (person, house); *P:* **elle a la cuisse hospitalière,** she's of easy virtue, she's a bit of a tart; *P:* **maison (très) hospitalière,** brothel.

hospitalier[2], **-ière,** *a.* pertaining to hospices and hospitals; **religieux h.,** *s.m.* **hospitalier,** hospitaller; **sœur hospitalière,** *s.f.* **hospitalière,** Sister of Mercy; **cité hospitalière,** hospital centre; **centre h. universitaire** = teaching hospital; **service h.,** ward (in an hospital); *Freemasonry: s.m.* **hospitalier,** officer in charge of fund for charitable works.

hospitalièrement [ɔspitaljɛrmɑ̃], *adv.* hospitably.

hospitalisation [ɔspitalizasjɔ̃], *s.f.* **1.** (*a*) hospitalization; ordering, admission, to a home or hospital; (*b*) hospital care or treatment. **2.** converting (of house, etc.) into a hospital.

hospitalisé, -ée [ɔspitalize], *s.* **1.** inmate (of home, etc.); almsman, -woman. **2.** (in-)patient.

hospitaliser [ɔspitalize], *v.tr.* **1.** to send, admit (s.o.) to a nursing home, to a hospital; to hospitalize (s.o.). **2.** to convert (house, etc.) for hospital purposes.

hospitalisme [ɔspitalism], *s.m.* **1.** *Med: Psy:* hospitalism. **2.** *Med:* cross infection, *U.S:* intrahospital surinfection.

hospitalité [ɔspitalite], *s.f.* **1.** hospitality; **accorder l'h. à qn,** to show s.o. hospitality; *F:* to put s.o. up; *Adm: A:* **établissement d'h. de nuit,** casual ward. **2.** *Pol:* asylum.

hospitalo-universitaire [ɔspitalɔynivɛrsitɛːr], *a.* **centre h.-u.** = teaching hospital; *pl. hospitalo-universitaires.*

hospodar [ɔspɔdaːr], *s.m. Hist:* hospodar.

host [ɔst], *s.m. Mil.Hist:* army (in feudal times).

hosta [ɔsta], *s.m. Bot:* hosta.

hosteau, -eaux [ɔsto], *s.m. Mil: P:* **1.** hospital. **2.** prison.

hostellerie [ɔstɛlri], *s.f.* fashionable country inn.

hostie [ɔsti], *s.f.* **1.** *Jew.Ant: Lit:* victim, offering (for sacrifice). **2.** *Ecc:* (eucharistic) host.

hostile [ɔstil], *a.* hostile; unfriendly (action); **être h. à, envers, qn,** to be hostile, opposed, adverse, to s.o.; **les journaux hostiles au gouvernement,** the papers opposed, hostile, to the Government; **la maison lui demeurait h.,** the house still made him feel uneasy.

hostilement [ɔstilmɑ̃], *adv.* in a hostile manner, hostilely.

hostilité [ɔstilite], *s.f.* **1.** hostility (**contre,** to); enmity, ill-will; **acte d'h.,** act of war; **l'h. des journaux,** the unfriendliness of the press. **2.** *pl.* hostilities; **au commencement des hostilités,** on the outbreak of hostilities.

***hostise** [ɔstiːz], *s.f. Hist:* = *HÔTISE.

hosto [ɔsto], *s.m. Mil: P:* **1.** hospital. **2.** prison.

hôte, hôtesse [oːt, otɛs, ɔtɛs], *s.* **1.** host, *f.* hostess; (*a*) entertainer (of guests); **robe d'hôtesse,** hostess gown; **faire bon visage d'h. à qn,** to give s.o. a warm, cordial, greeting; (*b*) innkeeper; landlord, landlady (of tavern, etc.); **compter sans son h.,** to reckon without one's host; **dîner à la table d'h.,** to dine at the *table-d'hôte*; (*c*) *Av:* **hôtesse de l'air,** air-hostess; **hôtesse médicale de l'air,** air nurse. **2.** (*a*) (*f.* **hôte**) guest, visitor; **h. payant,** paying guest; **h. d'honneur,** chief guest; (*b*) *Lit:* dweller; **les hôtes du lieu,** the dwellers on the spot; **hôtes d'un hospice,** inmates of an almshouse. **3.** *s.m. Biol:* host, **h. intermédiaire,** intermediate, intermediary, host. **4.** *A.Jur:* person who came to settle in a *hôtise.*

hôtel [otɛl, ɔt-], *s.m.* **1.** (*a*) **h. (particulier),** mansion, town house, private residence; *s.a.* MAÎTRE 1; (*b*) *Hist:* **l'h. (du roi),** the Royal Household; (*c*) *Eng.Jur:* **hôtels de cour,** Inns of Court. **2.** public building; **h. de ville,** town-hall, guildhall; **L'H. des Monnaies,** the Mint; **H. des Postes,** General Post Office; **L'H. des Invalides,** the Military Pensioners Hospital; **H. de la Police,** (*in Paris*) police headquarters; **h. maternel,** hostel for (working) unmarried mothers; **L'H. des ventes,** the general auction rooms (in Paris); **la collection fut envoyée à l'H. des ventes,** the collection came under the hammer. **3.** (*a*) hotel, hostelry; **descendre à l'h.,** to put up at a hotel; **h. de passe,** hotel used as a call-house; (*b*) **h. meublé, garni,** residential hotel (providing lodging but not board), *U.S:* rooming house; *often Pej:* apartments, lodgings.

hôtelage [otəlaːʒ], *s.m. Hist:* rent paid to lord for the right to stay on his land.

hôtel-Dieu [otɛldjø], *s.m.* hospital (in many French towns); *pl. hôtels-Dieu.*

hôtelier, -ière [otəlje, -jɛːr], *s.* **1.** (*a*) innkeeper; hotel-keeper; landlord, landlady; host, hostess of an inn; hotelier (of large hotel); (*b*) *a.* **l'industrie hôtelière,** the hotel trade. **2.** *Ecc: Hist:* hosteller (of monastery).

hôtellerie [otɛlri], *s.f.* **1.** hostelry, inn. **2.** guest quarters (of an abbey or convent). **3. l'h.,** the hotel trade.

hôtesse. *See* HÔTE.

***hôtise** [otiːz], *s.f. Hist:* small estate granted to foreigners by lord (in order to repopulate and recultivate his lands).

***hotte** [ɔt], *s.f.* **1.** (*a*) basket (carried on the back); dosser, pannier; **h. de maçon,** hod; (*b*) *Ven:* **porter la h.,** (*of hare, stag*) to be near its end. **2.** *Const:* (*a*) head (of rain-water drain-pipe); (*b*) hood (of forge, laboratory, over fire-place); canopy (over fire-place); **fausse h.,** canopy with purely decorative function. **3.** *Ind:* (feeding) hopper, boot. **4. h. à draguer,** dredging-bucket.

***hottée** [ɔte], *s.f.* (*a*) basketful, dosserful; (*b*) hodful; (*c*) *F:* large quantity.

***hottentot, -ote** [ɔtɑ̃to, -ɔt], *a. & s. Ethn:* Hottentot.

***hotter** [ɔte], *v.tr.* to carry (the grapes, etc.) in a *hotte.*

***hottereau, -eaux** [ɔtro], *s.m.,* ***hotteret** [ɔtrɛ], *s.m.* small *hotte.*

***hotteur, -euse** [ɔtœːr, -øːz], *s.,* ***hottier, -ière** [ɔtje, -jɛːr], *s.* carrier (of grapes from vineyard, etc.).

***hottoir** [ɔtwaːr], *s.m.* waste tip (of slate-quarry).

***hotu** [ɔty], *s.m. Ich:* beaked carp, nose-carp.

***hou** [u], *int.* **1.** boo! **hou! hou! voici le loup!** wolf! wolf! **2. hou! la vilaine!** shame on you, naughty girl!

***houache** [waʃ], ***houaiche** [wɛːʃ], *s.f. Nau:* **1.** wake, track (of vessel); wash. **2.** (i) stray line, (ii) stray mark, forerunner (of log).

***houage** [uaːʒ], *s.m.* hoeing.

***houari** [uari], *s.m. Nau:* (**voile à**) **h.,** shoulder-of-mutton sail, sliding-gunter sail.

***houblon** [ublɔ̃], *s.m. Bot: Brew:* hop(s); **tige, sarment, liane, de h.,** hop-bine, -bind; **h. blanc,** white-bine; **h. rouge,** red-bine; **cueillir le h.,** to pick the hops, to hop; **cueilleur, -euse de h.,** hop-picker, hopper; **cueillette du h.,** hop-picking; hopping; **perche à h.,** hop-pole.

***houblonnage** [ublɔnaːʒ], *s.m. Brew:* (action of) hopping (beer).

***houblonner** [ublɔne], *v.tr. Brew:* to hop (beer); **bière peu houblonnée,** mild beer.

***houblonnier, -ière** [ublɔnje, -jɛːr]. **1.** *a.* hop (-growing) (district, etc.). **2.** *s.m.* hop grower. **3.** *s.f.* **houblonnière,** hop garden, hop field.

houcre [ukr], *s.f. Nav.Hist:* seventeenth century fishing boat.

houdan [udɑ̃], *s.f. Husb:* Houdan.

houdanais, -aise [udanɛ, -ɛːz], *a. & s. Geog:* (native, inhabitant) of Houdan.

***houe** [u], *s.f. Tls:* hoe.

***houement** [umɑ̃], *s.m.* hoeing.

***houer** [we], *v.tr.* to hoe.

***houette** [wɛt], *s.f.* small hoe.

***houeur** [uœːr], *s.m.* hoer.

Hougli, Hougly, (l') [lugli], *Pr.n.m. Geog:* the (River) Hooghly.

***hougnette** [uɲɛt], *s.f.* (sculptor's) broach-chisel.

hougre [ugr], *s.m. Nau:* = HOURQUE.

***houille** [uːj], *s.f.* **1.** (pit-)coal; **mine de h.,** coal-mine, -pit; colliery; **extraction de la h.,** coal-getting, -winning; **h. de chaudière,** steam-coal; **h. à vapeur sans fumée,** smokeless steam-coal; **h. brune,** brown coal, lignite; **h. maigre, sèche, non collante,** lean coal, non-caking coal; **h. grasse, collante,** soft, bituminous, coal; caking coal; cannel-coal, **h. demi-grasse,** semi-bituminous coal; **h. flambante,** splint coal; **h. brillante,** vitrain; *s.a.* MARÉCHALE. **2. h. blanche,** hydro-electric power; **h. bleue,** tide-power; **h. verte,** stream-power; **h. incolore, azur, atmosphérique,** wind-power; **h. d'or,** solar power; **h. rouge,** geothermic energy.

***houiller, -ère** [uje, -ɛːr], *a.* (*a*) carboniferous, coal-bearing; **dépôt, bassin, h.,** coal bed, basin; **gîte h.,** coal field; (*b*) **production houillère,** output of coal.

***houillère** [ujɛːr], *s.f.* coal-pit; colliery; **exploitation (de(s) houillère(s),** coalmining.

***houilleur** [ujœːr], *s.m.* collier, (coal)miner, pitman.

***houilleux, -euse** [ujø, -øːz], *a. Geol:* carboniferous, coal-bearing.

***houillification** [ujifikasjɔ̃], *s.f. Geol:* carbonization (of vegetable matter).

***houillifier (se)** [səujifje], *v.pr. Geol:* (*of vegetable matter*) to carbonize.

***houka(h)** [uka], *s.m.* hookah.

***houle** [ul], *s.f.* (*a*) swell, surge (of sea); **grosse h.,** heavy swell; **h. battue,** cross sea; **h. de fond,** ground-swell; **h. longue,** roller; (*b*) rippling (of corn field, etc.).

***houler** [ule], *v.i.* (*of the sea, etc.*) to swell, surge.

***houlette** [ulɛt], *s.f.* **1.** (*a*) (shepherd's) crook; **prendre qn sous sa h.,** to take s.o. under one's wing; **h. d'un parapluie,** crook of an umbrella; (*b*) *A:* (bishop's) crozier. **2.** spatula-shaped implement, *esp. Hort:* trowel, spud; *Metall:* hand-ladle.

***houleux, -euse** [ulø, -øːz], *a.* swelling, surging, heavy, angry (sea); *Nau:* rather rough (sea); *F:* **foules houleuses,** surging, tumultuous, crowds; **réunion houleuse,** stormy meeting.

***houleviche** [ulviʃ], *s.f. Fish:* strong trammel-net.

***houlque** [ulk], *s.f. Bot:* holcus; **h. laineuse,** velvet-grass, meadow soft-grass; *F:* Yorkshire fog.

***houp** [up], *int.* **allons h.!** now then, heave! **saute, h.!** jump, (h)up! **houp-là!** upsidaisy! oops!

***houpée** [upe], *s.f.* = HOUPPÉE.

***houper** [upe], *v.tr.* **1.** to give (horse, dog) the word of command to jump. **2.** *Ven:* to hollo.

***houppe** [up], *s.f.* **1.** (*a*) bunch, tuft (of feathers, wool, etc.); pompon; **h. à poudrer,** powder-puff; **boîte à houppe,** puff-box; (*b*) tassel, bob. **2.** (*a*) tuft, crest (of hair); topknot; **en h.,** tufted; (*b*) (bird's) tuft, crest (of feathers); (*c*) crest (of tree). **3.** *Cryst: Opt:* brush; absorption figure; **houppes d'Haidinger,** Haidinger's brushes.

***houppé** [upe], *a.* tufted, crested.

***houppée** [upe], *s.f.* **1.** choppy sea; popply sea. **2.** spray, foam (on crest of wave); **prendre la h.,** to drop into or step out of a small boat as she hangs on the top of the wave.

***houppelande** [uplɑ̃:d], *s.f.* (*a*) *A:* (warmly lined) greatcoat or cloak; (coachman's) box-coat; (*b*) cosy outdoor over-garment (*esp.* as worn by priest); surcoat.

***houpper** [upe], *v.tr.* **1.** to tuft; to trim (sth.) with tufts, with pompons. **2.** *Tex:* to comb)wool).

***houppette** [upɛt], *s.f.* **1.** small tuft (of wool, feathers). **2.** powderpuff.

***houppier** [upje], *s.m.* **1.** manufacturer of pompons, tassels, etc. **2.** *For:* crown (of tree).

***houppifère** [upifɛ:r]. **1.** *a.* tufted. **2.** *s.m. Orn:* euplocomus; **h. ignicolore,** fire-back.

***houque** [uk], *s.f.* = HOULQUE.

***hourd** [u:r], *s.m.* **1.** *A:* (*a*) *Fort:* hoarding; (*b*) scaffold, covered stand (round tournament ground). **2.** (sawyer's) trestle.

***hourdage** [urda:ʒ], *s.m. Const:* **1.** (*a*) rough-casting; (*b*) nogging, pugging, hollow brick-work. **2.** rough masonry or plaster-work, rubble-work.

***hourder** [urde], *v.tr. Const:* (*a*) to rough-cast (wall, etc.); (*b*) to nog, pug (framework).

***hourdir** [urdir], *v.tr.* to rough-cast with mortar.

***hourdis** [urdi], *s.m.* **1.** *Const:* = HOURDAGE. **2.** *N.Arch:* **barre de h.,** (deck) transom.

***houret** [urɛ], *s.m. Ven:* worthless dog; mongrel, cur.

***houri**[1] [uri], *s.m.* coasting lugger.

***houri**[2], *s.f. Moham.Rel:* houri.

***hourque** [urk], *s.f. Nau:* **1.** howker, hooker. **2.** *F:* cranky ship, cranky old tub.

***hourra** [ura], *int. & s.m.* hurrah! huzza! **pousser trois hourras,** to give three cheers.

***hourvari** [urvari], *s.m.* **1.** *Ven:* (*a*) cast-back (of hunted game); back-cast; (*b*) huntsman's call to hounds to cast back. **2.** (*a*) backcast, backset; (*b*) uproar, tumult; (*c*) *Meteor:* violent squall (in the West Indies).

***housard** [uza:r], *s.m. A:* = HUSSARD.

***housarde** [uzard], *s.f.* **1.** = HUSSARDE. **2.** *Pej:* unfeminine woman.

***housé** [uze], *a. A:* **être tout h.,** to have one's boots all covered with mud, to be in a bedraggled condition.

***houseau, -eaux** [uzo], *s.m.* **1.** large pin. **2.** *A:* greave.

***houseaux** [uzo], *s.m.pl. A:* spatterdashes, leggings, long leather gaiters; *F: A:* **il y laissa ses h.,** he died there.

***houspillement** [uspijmɑ̃], *s.m.* **1.** hustling, jostling, knocking about, rough handling. **2.** abusing, rating; *F:* hauling over the coals.

***houspiller** [uspije], *v.tr.* **1.** to hustle (s.o.); to knock, *F:* bash, (s.o.) about; to jostle; to handle (s.o.) roughly; to bully (s.o.), *F:* to rough-house (s.o.). **2.** to abuse, rate (s.o.); to haul (s.o.) over the coals.

***houspilleur, -euse** [uspijœ:r, -ø:z], *s.* hustler, jostler; bully.

***houssage**[1] [usa:ʒ], *s.m.* covering (of furniture).

***houssage**[2], *s.m.* dusting, whisking (of furniture, etc.).

***houssaie, *houssaye** [usɛ], *s.f.* holly-plantation, -grove.

***housse** [us], *s.f.* **1.** (*a*) covering, furniture cover; (protecting) bag; loose cover; *Aut:* (i) spare tyre cover; (ii) car cover, (iii) seat cover; *Av:* propeller cover; **h. à vêtements,** protective bag (for clothing); **drap h.,** fitted sheet; (*b*) dust-sheet. **2.** *Harn:* (*a*) housing, horse-cloth; *A:* sumpter-cloth (of pack-horse); (*b*) (sheepskin) pad (of collar). **3.** *Veh:* hammer-cloth. **4.** *Cer:* rough shape (of piece of pottery).

***housseau, -eaux** [uso], *s.m.* = HOUSEAU.

***houssée** [use], *s.f. Harn:* sheepskin (used for pad of collar, etc.).

***housser**[1] [use], *v.tr.* to cover up, to put covers on (furniture, etc.).

***housser**[2], *v.tr.* to dust (furniture).

***housset** [usɛ], *s.m.*, ***houssette**[1] [usɛt], *s.f.* spring-lock, snap-lock (of box, trunk).

***houssette**[2], *s.f.* **1.** *Her:* charge on a shield representing soldier's boot. **2.** Persian silk.

***houssière** [usjɛ:r], *s.f. For:* holly-plantation, -grove.

***houssine** [usin], *s.f.* (*a*) switch (for beating furniture); (*b*) (riding-) switch.

***houssiner** [usine], *v.tr.* to switch, beat (clothes, etc.); **h. son cheval,** to touch up one's horse.

***houssoir** [uswa:r], *s.m.* feather-brush, -duster; whisk.

***housson** [usɔ̃], *s.m. Bot:* butcher's-broom, knee-holly.

houst(e) [ust], *int.* = OUSTE.

houstonia [ustɔnja], *s.f. Bot:* houstonia.

***housure** [uzy:r], *s.f. Ven:* trail of droppings left along hedges, etc. by wild boar.

***houvet** [uvɛ], *s.m. Crust: F:* edible crab.

***houx** [u], *s.m. Bot:* holly; **petit h.** = HOUSSON.

houzard [uza:r], *s.m.*, **houzarde** [uzard], *s.f. A:* = HUSSARD, HUSSARDE.

***houzeau, -eaux** [uzo], *s.m. Harn:* large needle with one end in form of a ring.

***hova** [uv], *a. & s.m. & f. Ethn:* Hova.

***hovenia** [ɔvenja], *s.m. Bot:* hovenia.

***hovercraft** [ɔvɛrkraft], *s.m. Trans:* hovercraft.

howea [ɔvea], *s.m. Bot:* howea.

howlite [ɔvlit], *s.f. Miner:* howlite.

hoya [waja], *s.m. Bot:* hoya.

***hoyau, -aux** [wajo, ojo], *s.m.* **1.** *Agr:* mattock, grubbing-hoe. **2.** *Min:* pickaxe.

***huage** [ya:ʒ], *s.m. Coll. Ven:* hallooing, whooping.

***huaille** [yɑ:j], *s.f. A:* mob, rabble, riff-raff.

***huard** [ya:r], *s.m. Orn:* **1.** black-throated diver. **2.** osprey.

Hubert [ybɛ:r], *Pr.n.m.* Hubert.

***hublot** [yblo], *s.m. Nau:* scuttle, sidelight, port-hole; air-port; **verre de h.,** bull's eye; **faux h.,** dead-light; **bonnette de h.,** wind-catcher, wind-scoop; **h. fixe,** fixed light, non-opening light; *Av:* **h. largable,** escape hatch.

hubnérite [ybnerit], *s.f. Miner:* hu(e)bnerite.

***huche** [yʃ], *s.f.* **1.** kneading-trough. **2.** bin; **h. à blé,** corn-bin; **la h. (à, au pain),** the bread bin, pan, hutch. **3.** (*a*) *Ind:* hopper; bin-hopper (of flour mill); (*b*) hutch (for washing ore). **4.** fish tank. **5.** *A:* casing (of turbine).

huchée [yʃe], *s.f. A:* **1.** (*a*) cry, shout; (*b*) crying, shouting. **2.** *Ven:* call on the horn.

***hucher**[1] [yʃe], *v.tr. Ven: A:* (*a*) to call (the hounds); (*b*) *abs.* to wind the horn.

***hucher**[2], *s.m.* bin maker.

***hucher**[3] **(se)**, *v.pr. F:* = SE JUCHER.

***hucherie** [yʃri], *s.f.* chest making, bin making.

***huchet** [yʃɛ], *s.m. A:* hunting-horn; *Her:* hunter's horn (without sling).

***huchier** [yʃje], *s.m.* maker of (wooden) hutches.

***hue** [y], *int.* (*to horse*) gee (up!) (*esp.* turn to the right); *F:* **l'un tire à hue et l'autre à dia,** they are not pulling together; **il n'entend ni à hue ni à dia,** you can't make him listen to reason; he won't listen to anyone.

huée [ye, ɥe], *s.f.* **1.** *Ven:* shouting, hallooing, whoop(ing). **2.** (*a*) boo, hoot; (*b*) *pl.* booing, hooting; jeering, jeers; **quitter la scène au milieu des huées,** to be hooted, booed, off the stage; **la foule le poursuivait de ses huées,** the crowd hooted after him.

huemal [yemal], *s.m. Z:* huemal, guemal, Andean deer.

***huer** [ye, ɥe]. **1.** *v.i.* (*a*) *Ven: etc:* to shout, halloo, whoop; (*b*) (*of owl*) to hoot. **2.** *v.tr.* to hoot, boo (actor, etc.); *Sp:* to barrack (player).

huéron [ɥerɔ̃], *s.m. Orn:* hoopoe.

***huerta** [wɛrta], *s.f. Geog:* huerta.

***huet** [yɛ], *s.m.*, ***huette** [yɛt], *s.f. Orn:* = HULOTTE.

***hueur** [yœ:r; ɥœ:r], *s.m.* **1.** shouter. **2.** hooter, booer.

hugolâtre [ygɔlɑ:tr], *s.m. & f.*, **hugophile** [ygɔfil], *s.m. & f.* devotee of Victor Hugo.

hugolesque [ygɔlɛsk], *a. Lit:* Hugoesque.

hugolien, -ienne [ygɔljɛ̃, -jɛn], *a.* relating to Victor Hugo.

***huguenot, -ote** [ygno, -ɔt], *a. & s.* **1.** *Hist:* Huguenot, Calvinist. **2.** *Dom.Ec:* **(marmite) huguenote,** pipkin; *Cu:* **œufs à la huguenote,** eggs cooked in mutton gravy. **3.** *Hist.Num:* money of little value.

***huguenoterie** [ygnɔtri], *s.f. Hist:* Huguenot party or faction.

***huguenotisme** [ygnɔtism], *s.m. Hist:* Huguenotism.

***Hugues** [yg], *Pr.n.m.* Hugh, Hugo.

***huhau** [yo], *int.* gee up! gee-ho!

hui [ɥi], *adv.* (*a*) *A:* to-day; **dès hui,** this very day; *Jur:* **ce jour d'hui,** to-day, this day; (*b*) *Dial:* **le jour d'h.,** today; *s.a.* AUJOURD'HUI.

huilage [ɥila:ʒ], *s.m.* **1.** oiling, lubrication, greasing. **2.** *Metall:* oil-tempering.

huile [ɥil], *s.f.* oil. **1. h. comestible,** edible oil; **h. végétale,** vegetable oil; **h. solaire,** sun-tan oil; **h. de cuisine, à frire, de ménage,** cooking oil; **cuisine à l'h.,** oil cookery; **frit à l'h.,** fried in oil; **h. à salade,** salad oil; **h. de lin,** linseed oil; **h. cuite,** boiled oil; **couleurs à l'h.,** oil colours; **peinture à l'h.,** oil painting; **portrait à l'h.,** portrait in oils; **h. douce,** sweet oil; **h. brute,** crude oil; **h. de graissage,** lubricating oil, machine oil; **h. à brûler, d'éclairage, lampante,** lamp oil; *F:* **ouvrage qui sent l'h.,** work that smells of the midnight oil, laboured piece of work; *O:* **verser de l'h. sur les plaies,** to pour oil on troubled waters; **jeter de l'h.,** to be dressed with studied elegance, in an affected way; **il n'y a plus d'h. dans la lampe,** his life is flickering out; **tache d'h.,** oil stain; *F:* **mauvais exemple qui fait tache d'h.,** bad example that spreads; *F:* **h. de bras, de coude,** elbow grease; **jeter de l'h., verser de l'h. sur le feu,** to add fuel to the fire; **il tirerait de l'h. d'un mur,** there is nothing he can't do; he can turn everything to account; **on tirerait plutôt de l'h. d'un mur que de l'argent de cet homme-là,** it is easier to get blood out of a stone than money from that man; *P:* **les huiles,** the big shots, the high-ups, the top brass; **être dans les huiles,** to be influential; *Ecc:* **les huiles saintes,** the holy oil (for the administration of extreme unction, etc.); *s.a.* AMANDE, 1, COLZA 2, COTRET, CROTON, NOIX 1, OLIVE 1, PAVOT. **2. h. animale,** animal oil; **h. de pied de bœuf,** neat's foot oil; **h. de baleine,** train oil, whale oil; **h. de blanc de baleine,** sperm oil, spermaceti, cetaceum; **h. de foie de morue,** cod-liver oil. **3. h. minérale,** mineral oil; **h. de naphte,** naphta; *Tchn:* **h. de machine,** engine oil; **h. siccative,** quick drying oil; **h. soufflée,** blown oil, condensed oil; **h. sulfurée,** sulphurized oil; **h. sulfonée,** sulphonated oil; **h. de base,** stock oil, base stock; **h. blanche,** white oil; **h. de coupe,** (metal) cutting oil, coolant; **h. de lavage,** wash oil; **h. de paraffine,** paraffin oil; **h. de pétrole,** rock oil, paraffin; **moteur à h. lourde,** heavy-oil engine. **4. h. essentielle,** essential oil; **h. de ricin,** castor oil; **h. de girofle,** oil of cloves; **huile de fusel,** fusel oil; **h. de Canton,** tung oil, China wood oil; *s.a.* VITRIOL.

huilé [ɥile], *a.* oiled; **manteau en toile huilée,** oiled raincoat, *U.S:* oiled slicker.

huiler [ɥile]. **1.** *v.tr.* to oil; (*a*) to lubricate, grease; (*b*) to dress with oil. **2.** *v.i. Bot:* to exude oil.

huilerie [ɥilri], *s.f.* **1.** (vegetable-)oil mill. **2.** oil store.

huileux, -euse [ɥilø, -ø:z], *a.* oily, greasy.

huilier [ɥilje], *s.m.* **1.** (*a*) oilcan; (*b*) oil and vinegar cruet. **2.** oilman, oil manufacturer, dealer.

huilière [ɥiljɛ:r], *s.f. Nau:* oilcan.

***huir** [yir], *v.i. Orn:* (*of kite*) to call.

huis [ɥi], *s.m. A:* door; *still used in* **entretien à h. clos,** conversation behind closed doors; private interview; *Jur:* **entendre une cause à h. clos,** to hear a case *in camera*; **rendre un jugement à h. ouvert,** to pronounce judgment in open court; *the h is 'aspirate' in* **ordonner le h. clos,** (i) to clear the court; (ii) to order a case to be heard *in camera*; **demander le h. clos,** to ask that a case shall be tried *in camera.*

huisserie [ɥisri], *s.f. Const:* door frame, casing.

huissier [ɥisje], *s.m.* **1.** (gentleman) usher. **2.** *Jur:* (*a*) process server = sheriff's officer, bailiff; (*b*) **h. audiencier,** court usher. **3.** *A:* joiner, *esp.* one who made doors.

***huit** [ɥit]. **1.** *num. a.inv. & s.m.inv.* eight; (*as card. adj. before a noun or adj. beginning with a consonant sound* [ɥi]; *otherwise always* [ɥit]) **huit (petits) garçons** [ɥi(pti)garsɔ̃], eight (little) boys; **huit** [ɥit] **hommes,** eight men; **j'en ai huit** [ɥit], I have eight; **le huit mai,** the eighth of May; **Charles Huit,** Charles the Eighth; **le h. de cœur,** the eight of hearts; **au chapitre h. de . . .,** in the eighth chapter of . . .; *Artil:* **pièce de h.,** eight-pounder; **h. jours,** a week; **tous les h. jours,** every week; once a week; **(d')aujourd'hui en h.,** today week; **de demain en h.,** tomorrow week; **donner ses h. jours à qn,** (*of master or servant*) to give s.o. a week's notice. **2.** *s.m.* [ɥit] (*a*) = HUIT-DE-CHIFFRE(S) 2 and 3; (*b*) *Aut: etc:* **h. de ressort,** spring shackle; (*c*) *Row:* **le h.,** bow (oarsman); (*d*) (*of workman*) **être du premier h.,** to be on first shift; (*e*) **faire des h.,** to sprinkle water in figures of eight (on floor to lay the dust); (*f*) (*at fun fair*) **le grand h.,** the big dipper.

***huitain** [ɥitɛ̃], *s.m. Pros:* octave, octet.

***huitaine** [ɥitɛn], *s.f.* **1.** (about) eight; **une h. de francs,** some eight francs, eight francs or so. **2.** week; **dans une h. de jours,** in a week or so, a week from now; **dans la h.,** in the course of the week; **sous h.,** within a week; **à h.,** a week from that day, today; **affaire remise à h.,** case adjourned for a week; **payer sa h. à qn,** to pay s.o. his week's wages; *Ind:* **mettre le personnel en h.,** to close down for a week; **mettre des ouvriers en h.,** to lock out some men for a week. **3.** (small) eight-day clock.

***huitante** [ɥitɑ̃:t], *num.a.inv.* (*Swiss and Belgian usage*) eighty.

***huitantième** [ɥitɑ̃tjɛm], *num.a.* (*Swiss and Belgian usage*) eightieth.

***huit-de-chiffre(s)** [ɥidəʃifr], *s.m.* **1.** figure of eight. **2.** figure-of-eight bandage. **3.** *Tls:* figure-of-eight calipers, hour-glass calipers, double calipers; *pl. huits-de-chiffres.*

***huitième** [ɥitjɛm]. **1.** *num. a. & s.* eighth. **2.** *s.m.* eighth (part); **trois huitièmes,** three eighths. **3.** *s.m.* eight; (*a*) *Sp:* **être en h. de finale,** to be in the last eight; (*b*) *Cards:* (*at piquet*) a hand of eight cards of the same colour. **4.** *s.f. Sch:* **(classe de) h.** = second form of junior school; **être en h.,** to be in the second form.

***huitièmement** [ɥitjɛmmɑ̃], *adv.* eighthly, in the eighth place.

***huit-pieds** [ɥipje], *s.m.inv. Mus:* eight-foot stop (of organ).

huître [ɥi:tr], *s.f.* **1.** oyster; **h. perlière, à perle,** pearl oyster; **huîtres du pays,** natives; **h. portugaise,** Portuguese oyster (*gryphaea angulata*). **2.** *P:* (*a*) gob, spit; (*b*) fool, mug.

***huit-reflets** [ɥir(ə)flɛ], *s.m.inv. F:* top hat.

huîtrier, -ère [ɥitrije, -ɛ:r]. **1.** *a.* of, pertaining to, oysters; **industrie huîtrière,** oyster farming. **2.** *s.m. Orn:* **h.(-pie),** oyster-catcher. **3.** *s.f.* **huîtrière,** oyster bed.

***hulotte** [ylɔt], *s.f. Orn:* common wood owl, brown owl, hoot-owl; **h. chat-huant,** tawny owl.

***hululation** [ylylasjɔ̃], *s.f.*, ***hululement** [ylylmɑ̃], *s.m.* ululation (of owls); tu-whit, to-whoo; hoot(ing).

***hululer** [ylyle], *v.i.* (*of owl*) to ululate; to hoot, to tu-whoo.

***hum** [œm], *int.* hem! hm!

***humage** [yma:ʒ], *s.m.* (action of) inhaling.

humagne [ymaɲ], *s.m.* white vine grown in Valais.

humain [ymɛ̃], *a.* **1.** human; **le genre h., les (êtres) humains,** human beings, humans; **sciences humaines,** social sciences; *Mus:* **voix humaine,** vox humana (stop of organ); *s.a.* RESPECT. **2.** humane.

humainement [ymɛnmɑ̃], *adv.* **1.** humanly. **2.** humanely.

humanisable [ymanizabl̥], *a.* that can become gentler, more human.

humanisant [ymanizɑ̃], *a.* humanizing.

humanisation [ymanizasjɔ̃], *s.f.* humanization, humanizing.

humaniser [ymanize], *v.tr.* **1.** to humanize; to make human. **2.** to humanize; to make (s.o.) more humane, gentler; to civilize. **3. h. une doctrine,** to popularize a doctrine.

s'humaniser. 1. to become human. **2.** (*a*) to become more humane, gentler; (*b*) *F:* to become more sociable. more human; to thaw.

humanisme [ymanism], *s.m.* **1.** *Hist: Lit: Phil:* humanism. **2.** *Lit: Sch:* classical studies.

humaniste [ymanist]. **1.** *s.m.* humanist; classical scholar. **2.** *a.* humanistic.

humanistique [ymanistik], *a. Pal:* **écriture h.,** (*script used by fifteenth century Italian humanists*) *littera antiqua.*

humanitaire [ymanitɛ:r], *a. & s.* humanitarian; **œuvre h.,** humane task.

humanitarisme [ymanitarism], *s.m.* humanitarianism.

humanité [ymanite], *s.f.* **1.** humanity; (*a*) human nature; *F:* **payer le tribut à l'h.,** (i) to yield to temptation; (ii) to pay the debt of nature; (*b*) mankind; (*c*) kindness, benevolence, humaneness. **2.** *pl.* humanities; *Sch:* **les classes d'humanités,** the classical side (of school); **faire ses humanités,** to receive a good classical education.

humantin [ymɑ̃tɛ̃], *s.m. Ich:* spine shark, orynotus.

humate [ymat], *s.m. Ch:* humate.

humble [œ̃:bl], *a.* humble, lowly; meek; **à mon h. avis,** in my humble opinion; **votre très h. serviteur,** your very humble servant; **h. de cœur,** humble of heart, humble-hearted; **humbles ressources,** slender means.

humblement [œ̃bləmɑ̃], *adv.* humbly.

humboldtine [œ̃bɔldtin], *s.f. Miner:* humboldtine.

humboldtite [œ̃bɔldtit], *s.f. Miner:* humboldtite.

humectage [ymɛkta:ʒ], *s.m. Ind:* moistening, wetting, damping.

humectant [ymɛktɑ̃]. **1.** *a.* moistening, wetting. **2.** *a. & s.m. A.Med:* humectant.

humectation [ymɛktasjɔ̃], *s.f.* **1.** (*a*) moistening, wetting, damping; (*b*) *A.Med:* humectation. **2.** moistness, dampness.

humecter [ymɛkte], *v.tr.* to damp, moisten; *F:* **s'h. le gosier,** to wet one's whistle.

s'humecter, to become moist, damp; to moisten.

humecteur [ymɛktœ:r], *s.m. Civ.E: etc:* wetting or moistening appliance of machine; *Com: Post:* **h. digital,** finger moistener.

***humer** [yme], *v.tr.* **1.** (*rare*) to suck in, up; to take in; **h. son café,** to sip one's coffee; **h. un œuf,** to swallow, gulp down, an egg (raw). **2.** to inhale, sniff; **h. l'air frais,** to inhale, breathe in, the fresh air; **h. le parfum d'une fleur,** to smell a flower; **h. une prise,** to take a pinch of snuff.

huméral, -aux [ymeral, -o], *a. Anat:* humeral (ligment, etc.); *Ecc:* **voile h.,** humeral veil.

huméro-cubital [ymerɔkybital], *a. Anat:* humero-cubital; *pl. huméro-cubitaux, -ales.*

huméro-métacarpien, -ienne [ymerɔmetakarpjɛ̃, -jɛn], *a. Anat:* humero-metacarpal.

humérus [ymery:s], *s.m. Anat:* humerus.

humescent [ymɛs(s)ɑ̃], *a.* slightly damp, dampish.

humeur [ymœ:r], *s.f.* **1.** (*a*) *A.Med:* humour; (*b*) *pl. A.Med:* tissue-fluids, body-fluids; **humeurs froides,** scrofula; (*c*) *Anat:* **h. aqueuse, h. vitrée,** aqueous humour, vitreous humour (of the eye). **2.** (*a*) humour, mood, spirits; **bonne h.,** good humour; **être de bonne, belle, h.,** to be in a good mood; **être d'excellente h.,** to be in high spirits; **sourire de bonne h.,** good-humoured smile; **répondre avec bonne h.,** to answer good-humouredly; **être de mauvaise h., d'une h. de chien,** to be in a bad temper, out of sorts, in a bad mood; **de méchante h.,** in a (bad) temper, grumpy; **répondre avec mauvaise h.,** to answer testily, irritably; to snap back; **être d'une h. noire,** (i) to feel depressed, to have a fit of the blues; (ii) to be in a bad temper; *s.a.* MASSACRANT; **être d'h. à refuser net,** to be in the mood to refuse point blank; **être en h. de faire qch.,** to be in the mood to do sth.; to feel like doing sth.; **en h. de lire,** in a reading mood; **je ne suis pas, ne me sens pas, d'h. à rire,** *O:* **en h. de rire,** I am in no laughing mood, in no humour for laughing; I don't feel like laughing; (*b*) temper; **avoir l'h. vive,** to be quick-tempered; **homme d'h. égale,** even-tempered man; **h. inégale,** uneven temper; **accès d'h.,** fit of temper; **incompatibilité d'h.,** incompatibility of temperament; (*c*) (ill-)humour; **mouvement d'h.,** outburst of temper, of petulance; **montrer de l'h.,** to show (ill-)temper; **avoir de l'h.,** to be in a temper; **avec h.,** testily, irritably; **épancher son h. sur qn,** to vent one's spleen on s.o.; (*d*) *Psy:* **trouble de l'h.,** maniac phase, depressive phase (in melancholia, etc.). **3.** *occ.* = HUMOUR.

humeux, -euse [ymø, -ø:z], *a.* humic, humous.

humicole [ymikɔl], *a. Biol: Nat.Hist:* (*of an organism*) living in humus or dead leaves.

humide [ymid], *a.* damp, moist, humid; watery, wet; **maison h., draps humides,** damp house, sheets; **couloir sombre et h.,** dark, dank passage; **temps h. et chaud,** muggy weather; **temps h. et froid,** raw weather; *St.Exch:* **pieds humides,** outside brokers.

humidement [ymidmɑ̃], *adv.* damply, moistly, humidly.

humidificateur [ymidifikatœ:r], *s.m.* humidor (in a spinning mill); *Dom.Ec:* humidifier.

humidification [ymidifikasjɔ̃], *s.f.* damping, moistening, humidification.

humidifier [ymidifje], *v.tr.* (*p.d. & pr.sub.* **n. humidifiions, v. humidifiiez**) to damp, moisten, to humidify.

humidité [ymidite], *s.f.* humidity, damp(ness), moisture, moistness, wet(ness); (*on packet*) **craint l'h.,** to be kept dry; **taches d'h.,** mildew; **taché d'h.,** mildewed; **chargé d'h.,** heavy with moisture; **h. relative, absolue,** relative, absolute, humidity; **teneur en h.,** moisture content.

humifère [ymifɛ:r], *a.* humus-bearing.

humification [ymifikasjɔ̃], *s.f.* humification.

humifié [ymifje], *a.* (*of soil*) in which organic matter has been reduced to humus; humified.

humifuse [ymify:z], *a. Bot:* humifuse.

humigène [ymiʒɛn], *a.* humus producing (matter).

humiliant [ymiljɑ̃], *a.* humiliating, mortifying; humiliatory.

humiliation [ymiljasjɔ̃], *s.f.* humiliation, mortification; **essuyer une h.,** to suffer an affront, to be humiliated.

humilier [ymilje], *v.tr.* (*p.d. & pr.sub.* **n. humiliions, v. humiliiez**) (*a*) *Ecc:* to humble, to fill with humility; (*b*) to humiliate (s.o.); to make (s.o.) feel small.

s'humilier. s'h. jusqu'à faire qch., to stoop to doing sth.; **s'h. devant qn,** to cringe to s.o.; *F:* to eat humble pie; **s'h. devant Dieu,** to humble oneself before God.

humilité [ymilite], *s.f.* humility, humbleness; **en toute h.,** most humbly, in all humility.

humine [ymin], *s.f. Ch:* humin, humic acid.

humique [ymik], *a. Ch:* humic (acid).

humite [ymit], *s.f. Miner:* humite.

humivore [ymivɔ:r], *a. Nat.Hist:* humus-eating.

humoral, -aux [ymɔral, -o], *a. A.Med:* humoral (disorder, etc.).

humoresque [ymɔrɛsk], *s.f. Mus:* humoresque.

humorisme [ymɔrism], *s.m. A.Med:* humoralism.

humoriste [ymɔrist]. **1.** *a.* (*a*) *A.Med:* humoralistic; (*b*) humorous (writer, etc.). **2.** *s.* (*a*) *A.Med:* humoralist; (*b*) humorist.

humoristique [ymɔristik], *a.* humorous (talker, writer, etc.); **dessin h.,** cartoon; **dessinateur h.,** cartoonist; **il se croit h.,** he thinks he's witty.

humoristiquement [ymɔristikmɑ̃], *adv.* humorously.

humour [ymu:r], *s.m.* humour; **h. noir,** (i) sick humour; (ii) bitter, sardonic, humour.

humulène [ymylɛn], *s.m. Ch:* humulene.

humuline [ymylin], *s.f. Brew:* drink made from rum and hops.

humulus [ymyly:s], *s.m. Bot:* humulus, hop.

humus [ymy:s], *s.m.* humus, leaf mould, vegetable mould.

***Hun** [œ̃], *s.m.Hist:* Hun.

***hune** [yn], *s.f. Nau:* top; **h. militaire,** fighting-top; **h. de vigie,** crow's nest; **grande h.,** maintop; **mât de h.,** topmast; **oh(é) de la h.!** aloft there! **h. de direction de tir,** fire-control top.

***hunier** [ynje], *s.m. Nau:* topsail; **grand h.,** main topsail; **petit h.,** fore-topsail; **h. d'artimon,** mizzen-topsail; **h. fixe,** lower mizzen-topsail; **h. volant,** upper mizzen-topsail.

***Huningue** [ynɛ̃:g], *Pr.n. Geog:* Hüningen.

***hunnique** [ynik], *a. Hist:* Hunnic, Hunnish; relating to the Huns.

***hunter** [œntœ:r, -tɛ:r], *s.m. Equit:* hunter.

***huot** [yo], *s.m. Orn: F:* wood owl.

***huppe**[1] [yp], *s.f. Orn:* **h. (d'Europe),** hoopoe.

***huppe**[2], *s.f.* tuft, crest (of bird); **alouette à h.,** tufted lark; *F: A:* **rabattre la h. à qn,** to take s.o. down a peg; *cp.* HOUPPE.

***huppe**[3], *s.f. Carp:* white rot (in timber).

***huppé** [ype], *a.* **1.** *Orn:* tufted, crested. **2.** *F:* (*a*) smart, well-dressed, in high society; **c'est qn de très h.,** he's very rich; (*b*) *A:* smart, cute.

***huppe-col** [ypkɔl], *s.m. A:* humming-bird; *pl. huppe-cols.*

***huque** [yk], *s.f. A.Cost:* (i) woman's coat with a hood; (ii) man's doublet.

***hurasse** [yras], *s.m.* helve-ring (of pickaxe, etc.).

***hure** [y:r], *s.f.* **1.** (*a*) shaggy, tousled, head; *F:* **ne fais pas la h.,** don't look so boarish, boorish; (*b*) head (of boar, etc.); jowl (of salmon); **h. de sanglier,** boar's head; (*c*) *Her:* (i) boar's head; (ii) dolphin's head; (*d*) *P:* head, mug; **se gratter la h.,** to shave. **2.** *Cu:* potted head; brawn, *U.S:* head cheese. **3.** (long-handled) brush; Turk's head wall-brush.

***hurf(e)** [œrf], *a. P:* tip-top.

***hurlant** [yrlɑ̃], *a.* howling, yelling, roaring.

***hurlée** [yrle], *s.f.* howling (of wolf).

***hurlement** [yrləmɑ̃], *s.m.* howl(ing) (*esp.* of wolf or dog); yell(ing), roar(ing) (of dog, etc.); **pousser un h.,** to give a howl; **hurlements de rage,** angry yells, roars of anger; **pousser un h. de rage,** to utter a roar of rage, to roar with rage; **pousser des hurlements lugubres,** to howl dismally; **le h. de la tempête,** the howling, roaring, of the storm.

***hurler** [yrle]. **1.** *v.i.* (*of dog, wolf*) to howl; (*of wind, storm*) to roar; (*of pers.*) to howl, roar, yell; **h. de rage,** to howl with rage; **se mettre à h.,** to set up a howl; *F:* **couleurs qui hurlent,** colours that do not harmonize, *F:* that shriek at one another; **h. avec les loups,** to cry with the pack; to do in Rome as Rome does, as the Romans do. **2.** *v.tr.* to roar out, bawl out (song, speech, etc.).

***hurleur, -euse** [yrlœ:r, -ø:z]. **1.** *a.* howling, yelling; **derviche h.,** howling dervish. **2.** *s.* howler, yeller. **3.** *s.m.* (*a*) *Z:* howler (monkey); **h. de Panama,** mantled howler (of Panama); (*b*) *W.Tel: F:* extra-loud loudspeaker.

hurlu [yrly], *s.m.* white mustard.

hurluberlu [yrlybɛrly], *a. & s.* harum-scarum; scatterbrain(ed); happy-go-lucky (person).

***huron, -onne** [yrɔ̃, -ɔn]. **1.** *a. & s. Ethn:* Huron. **2.** *s.m. F: A:* boor, churl.

***Huronie** [yrɔni], *Pr.n.f. Fr.C:* Huron country.

***huronien, -ienne** [yrɔnjɛ̃, -jɛn], *a. & s.m. Geol:* Huronian.

***hurrah** [ura], *int. & s.m.* hurrah.

hurricane [yrikan], *s.m.* hurricane (in West Indies).

***huso** [yzo], *s.m. Ich:* huso, huchen.

***hussard** [ysa:r]. **1.** *s.m. Mil:* hussar; **bonnet de h.,** busby. **2.** *a. F:* unceremonious.

***hussarde** [ysard], *s.f.* **1.** hussarde (dance). **2. à la h.,** (*a*) *adv.phr.* cavalierly, brusquely, unceremoniously; (*b*) *adj.phr.* **pantalon à la h.,** full trousers; *A:* peg-top trousers; **culotte à la h.,** riding-breeches; **bottes à la h.,** riding-boots.

*hussarder [ysarde], *v.i. Pej:* to act brusquely and unceremoniously in courtship.

*hussite [ysit], *s.m. Rel.H:* Hussite.

hutia [ytja], *s.m. Z:* hutia.

*hutin [ytɛ̃], *a.m. A:* headstrong; quarrelsome; Le Hutin, nickname of Louis X (of France).

*hutinet [ytinɛ], *s.m. Coop:* cooper's mallet.

*hutte [yt], *s.f. (a)* hut, shed, shanty, cabin; h. de terre, mud hut, *U.S:* sod house; *(b) Ven:* la h., the shooting of wild-fowl from a hide.

*hutteau, -eaux [yto], *s.m.* small hide (for shooting).

*hutter (se) [sœyte], *v.pr.* to build a hut and live in it; to hut.

*hutteur [ytœːr], *s.m.,* ***huttier** [ytje], *s.m.* wild-fowler.

*huve [yːv], *s.f. A.Cost:* starched linen coif worn by women.

Huygens [ɥiʒɛ̃ːs], *Pr.n. Opt:* **principe de H.,** Huygens', Huyghens' principle.

Hyacinthe [jasɛ̃ːt]. **1.** *Pr.n.m. Myth:* Hyacinthus. **2.** *s.f. (a) Bot: A:* (= JACINTHE) hyacinth; *(b) Miner:* hyacinth, jacinth; **h. citrine,** jargoon. **3.** *a.inv.* hyancinthine; purplish-blue.

hyacinthine [jasɛ̃tin], *s.f. Miner:* variety of hyacinth.

Hyades (les) [lezjad], *s.f.pl. Myth: Astr:* the Hyades.

hyænarctos [jenarktɔs], *s.m. Paleont:* hyaenarctos.

hyænodon [jenɔdɔ̃], *s.m. Paleont:* hyaenodon.

hyænodontidés [jenɔdɔ̃tide], *s.m.pl. Paleont:* Hyaenodontidae.

hyalin [jalɛ̃, jal-], *a. Bot: Miner:* hyaline, glassy; **quartz h.,** rock-crystal.

hyalite [jalit; jal-], *s.f.* **1.** *Miner:* hyalite, water-opal. **2.** *Glassm:* hyalithe.

hyalogène [jalɔʒɛn, jal-], *s.m. Ch:* hyalogen.

hyalograph [jalɔgraf-, jal-], *s.m. Glass Engr:* hyalograph.

hyalographie [jalɔgrafi, jal-], *s.f. Glass Engr:* hyalography.

hyaloïde [jalɔid, jal-], *a. Anat: etc:* hyaloid (membrane, etc.).

hyaloïdien, -ienne [jalɔidjɛ̃, -jɛn; jal-], *a. Anat:* pertaining to the hyaloid membrane; hyaloid.

hyalonème [jalɔnɛːm, jal-], *s.m. Spong:* hyalonema.

hyalophane [jalɔfan, jal-], *s.f. Miner:* hyalophane.

hyaloplasme [jalɔplasm], *s.m. Biol:* hyaloplasm(a).

hyalosidérite [jalɔsiderit, jal-], *s.f. Miner:* hyalosiderite.

hyalotechnie [jalɔtɛkni, jal-], *s.f.,* **hyalurgie** [jalyrʒi; jal-]. *s.f.* glass-making; technics of glass.

hyalotechnique [jalɔtɛknik, jal-], **hyalurgique** [jalyrʒik, jal-], *a.* pertaining to glass-making; l'industrie h., the glass industry.

hyalotékite [jalɔtekit, jal-], *s.f. Miner:* hyalotekite.

hyaluronidase [jalyrɔnidaːz, -jal], *s.f. Biol:* hyaluronidase.

hyaluronique [jalyrɔnik, jal-], *a. Bio-Ch:* acide h., hyaluronic acid.

Hybléen, -éenne [ibleɛ̃, -ɛɛn], *a. & s. A.Geog:* **1.** *a.* Hyblaean (honey, etc.). **2.** *s.* inhabitant of Hybla.

hybridation [ibridasjɔ̃], *s.f. Hort: Biol:* hybridization; cross-breeding; *Bio-Ch:* h. cellulaire, nuclear hybridization.

hybride [ibrid], *a. & s.m. Biol: Ling:* hybrid; *Bio-Ch:* orbitale h., hybrid orbital, orbit.

hybrider [ibride], *v.tr. Biol:* to hybridize, to cross.

hybridisme [ibridism], *s.m. Biol:* hybridism; hybridity.

hybridité [ibridite], *s.f. Biol: Ling:* hybridity, hybrid character.

hydarthrose [idartroːz], *s.f. Med:* hydrarthrosis; h. du genou, *F:* water on the knee.

hydantoïne [idɑ̃tɔin], *s.f. Ch:* hydantoin.

hydantoïque [idɑ̃tɔik], *a. Ch:* acide h., hydantoic acid.

hydatide [idatid], *s.f. Med:* hydatid; *Anat:* (in male) h. sessile, pédiculée, de Morgagni, sessile, stalked, hydatid of Morgagni.

hydatidocèle [idatidɔsɛl], *s.f. Med:* hydatidocele.

hydatique [idatik], *a. Med:* hydatic; kyste h., hydatid (cyst).

hydatisme [idatism], *s.m. Med:* hydatism.

hydne [idn], *s.m. Fung:* hydnum.

hydrachne [idrakn], *s.f. Arach:* hydrachnid, water-spider, water-mite.

hydrachnidés [idraknide], *s.m.pl. Arach:* Hydrachnidae.

hydracide [idrasid], *s.m. Ch:* hydracid.

hydragogue [idragɔg], *a. & s.m. Med:* hydragogue, hydragog.

hydraires [idrɛːr], *s.m.pl. Coel:* Hydroida, Hydroidea.

hydramnios [idramnjɔs], *s.m. Obst:* hydramnios, hydramnion.

hydrangea [idrɑ̃ʒea], **hydrangelle** [idrɑ̃ʒɛl], *s.f. Bot:* hydrangea.

hydrangées [idrɑ̃ʒe], *s.f.pl. Bot:* Hydrangeaceae, *F:* hydrangeas.

hydrante [idrɑ̃ːt], *s.m. Z:* hydranth.

hydrargillite [idrarʒilit], *s.f. Miner:* hydrargillite.

hydrargyre [idrarʒiːr], *s.m. Ch: A:* mercury, quicksilver.

hydrargyrique [idrarʒirik], *a. Pharm:* hydrargyric, mercurial.

hydrargyrisme [idrarʒirism], *s.m. Med:* mercurialism.

hydrastine [idrastin], *s.f. Pharm:* hydrastine.

hydratable [idratabl], *a.* hydratable.

hydratant [idratɑ̃], *a.* hydrating; *Toil:* **crème hydratante,** moisturizing cream.

hydratation [idratasjɔ̃], *s.f. Ch:* hydration.

hydrate [idrat], *s.m. Ch:* hydrate, hydroxide; h. de chaux, de calcium, calcium hydrate, calcium hydroxide; h. de potasse, caustic potash; h. de soude, caustic soda; h. de carbone, carbohydrate.

hydraté [idrate], *a. Ch:* hydrated, hydrous; baryte hydratée, barium hydrate.

hydrater [idrate], *v.tr. Ch:* to hydrate.

s'hydrater, to hydrate; to become hydrated.

hydrateur [idratœːr], *s.m. Fr.C:* vegetable container (in refrigerator).

hydraule [idrol], *s.f. A.Mus:* hydraulus, hydraulic organ.

hydraulicien [idrolisjɛ̃], *s.m.* hydraulic engineer, hydraulician.

hydraulicité [idrolisite], *s.f.* **1.** *Const:* hydraulicity. **2.** *Geog:* coefficient of flow (of a river).

hydraulico-électrique [idrolikoelɛktrik], *a.* water-power electrical (plant, etc.); *pl.* hydraulico-électriques.

hydraulico-pneumatique [idrolikɑpnɔmatik], *a.* machine h.-p., hydraulic jack, press; *pl.* hydraulico-pneumatiques.

hydraulique [idrolik]. **1.** *a.* hydraulic (machine, press, cement, engineer, etc.); force h., hydraulic power, water power; roue h., water wheel; usine h., water works; énergie h., hydroelectric power; *Mec.E:* à commande h., hydraulically operated; commande h., hydraulic control; manœuvre h., hydraulic working (of gun, etc.); vérin h., hydraulic actuator, jack; bélier h., hydraulic ram; *Aut:* freins hydrauliques, hydraulic brakes; *Av: etc:* circuit h., hydraulic system. **2.** *s.f. (a)* hydraulics; *(b)* hydraulic engineering; ingénieur en h., hydraulic engineer.

hydrauliquement [idrolikmɑ̃], *adv.* hydraulically; machine commandée h., hydraulically-operated machine.

hydrauliste [idrolist], *s.m.* hydraulic engineer.

hydraviation [idravjasjɔ̃], *s.f.* marine aviation.

hydravion [idravjɔ̃], *s.m.* seaplane, hydroplane; h. à flotteurs, seaplane with floats, *U.S:* floatplane; h. à coque, flying-boat.

hydrazide [idrazid], *s.f. Ch:* hydrazide.

hydrazine [idrazin], *s.f. Ch:* hydrazine.

hydrazo- [idrazo], *pref. Ch:* hydraz(o)-; **hydrazotoluène,** hydrazotoluene.

hydrazoïque [idrazɔik], *a. & s.m. Ch:* hydrazoic (acid).

hydrazone [idrazon], *s.f. Ch:* hydrazone.

hydre [idr], *s.f. Myth: Astr: Coel:* hydra.

hydrémie [idremi], *s.f. (rare) Med:* hydraemia.

hydrie [idri], *s.f. Gr.Ant:* hydria, water-pitcher, water-pot.

hydrindène [idrɛ̃dɛn], *s.m. Ch:* hydrindene, indan.

hydriote [idri(j)ɔt], *a. & s. Geog:* Hydriote; (native) of Hydra.

hydrique [idrik]. **1.** *a.* hydrous; épidémie d'origine h., epidemic due to the water, to the water supply. **2.** *a.suff. Ch: (a)* hydro-; chlorhydrique, hydrochloric (acid); *(b)* -hydric; sulfhydrique, sulphydric (acid, etc.).

hydr(o)- [idr(ɔ), -(o)], *pref.* hydr(o)-; **hydrocyanique,** hydrocyanic; **hydrargyre,** hydrargyrum.

hydroa [idrɔa], *s.m. Med:* hydroa.

hydroaérien, -ienne [idrɔaerjɛ̃, -jɛn], *a.* station hydroaérienne, seaplane base.

hydroaérique [idrɔaerik], *a. Med:* hydroaeric; (bruit) h., (noise) characteristic of a cavity full of liquids and gases; (image) h., X-ray showing such a cavity.

hydroaéroplane [idrɔaerɔplan], *s.m. A:* = HYDRAVION.

hydroaéroport [idrɔaerɔpɔːr], *s.m.* seaplane base.

hydroaromatique [idrɔarɔmatik], *a. Ch:* hydroaromatic.

hydrobase [idrɔbaːz], *s.f.* seaplane base.

hydrobatidés [idrɔbatide], *s.m.pl. Orn:* Hydrobatidae.

hydrobromate [idrɔbrɔmat], *s.m. A.Ch:* hydrobromate; hydrobromide.

hydrocachexie [idrɔkaʃɛksi], *s.f. Vet:* cachexia aquosa, edematous ancylostomiasis.

hydrocarbonate [idrɔkarbɔnat], *s.m. Ch:* hydrocarbonate; *Miner:* h. de magnésie, hydromagnesite.

hydrocarbone [idrɔkarbɔn], *s.m. Ch:* hydrocarbon, carbohydrate.

hydrocarboné [idrɔkarbɔne], *a. Ch:* hydrocarbonic.

hydrocarbure [idrɔkarbyːr], *s.m. Ch:* hydrocarbon.

hydrocaule [idrɔkol], *s.m. Z:* group of hydrocauli.

hydrocèle [idrɔsɛl], *s.f. Med:* hydrocele.

hydrocellulose [idrɔselyloːz], *s.f. Ch:* hydrocellulose.

hydrocéphale [idrɔsefal], *a. & s. Med:* hydrocephalic, hydrocephalous (subject).

hydrocéphalie [idrɔsefali], *s.f. Med:* hydrocephalus, hydrocephaly; *F:* water on the brain.

hydrocérame [idrɔseram], *s.m. Dom.Ec:* hydroceramic pottery vessel.

hydrocéramique [idrɔseramik], *a. Cer:* hydroceramic.

hydrocérusite [idrɔseryzit], *s.f. Miner:* hydrocerusite.

hydrocharidacées [idrɔkaridase], *s.f.pl. Bot:* hydrocharitaceae.

hydrochœridés [idrɔkeride], *s.m.pl. Z:* Hydrochoeridae.

hydrochore [idrɔkɔːr], *a. Bot:* hydrochore.

hydroclasseur [idrɔklasœːr], *s.m. Ph: Ind:* hydraulic classifier.

hydrocolloïde [idrɔkɔl(l)ɔid], *s.m. Dent:* hydrocolloid.

hydrocoralliaires [idrɔkɔralje:r], *s.f.pl. Coel:* Hydrocorallia, Hydrocorallinae, Hydrocorallina.

hydrocortisone [idrɔkɔrtizɔn], *s.f. Biol: Pharm:* hydrocortisone.

hydrocotyle [idrɔkɔtil], *s.f. Bot:* hydrocotyle; *F:* pennywort, water-cup.

hydrocution [idrɔkysjɔ̃], *s.f. Med:* loss of consciousness or death through sudden immersion in cold water.

hydrocyon [idrɔsjɔ̃], *s.m. Ich:* hydrocyon, tiger-fish.

hydrodésulfuration [idrɔdesylfyrasjɔ̃], *s.f. Petroleum Ind:* hydrodesulfurization, hydrodesulfurizing.

hydrodynamique [idrɔdinamik]. **1.** *a.* hydrodynamic(al); *(of fish, whales)* streamlined (for efficient underwater movement); les cétacés ont une forme remarquablement h., whales are wonderfully streamlined. **2.** *s.f.* hydrodynamics.

hydro(-)électricité [idrɔelektrisite], *s.f.* hydro(-)electricity.

hydro(-)électrique [idrɔelɛktrik], *a.* hydro(-)electric.

hydro-extracteur [idrɔɛkstraktœːr], *s.m. Ind:* hydro-extractor; centrifugal drying machine; *pl.* hydro-extracteurs.

hydrofoil [idrɔfoil], *s.m. Nau:* hydrofoil (boat).

hydrofuge [idrɔfyːʒ]. **1.** *a.* waterproof, damp-proof; *(of coat, etc.)* rain-proof; *Const:* couche h., damp-course. **2.** *s.m.* water repellent.

hydrofuger [idrɔfyʒe], *v.tr.* (j'hydrofugeai(s); n. hydrofugeons) to waterproof, rain-proof (garment, etc.).

hydrogame [idrɔgam], *a. Bot:* water-pollinated.

hydrogamie [idrɔgami], *s.f. Bot:* pollination by water.

hydrogel [idrɔʒɛl], *s.m. Ch: Ph:* hydrogel.

hydrogénation [idrɔʒenasjɔ̃], *s.f. Ch:* hydrogenation.

hydrogène [idrɔʒɛn], *s.m. Ch:* hydrogen; h. lourd, heavy hydrogen, deuterium.

hydrogéné [idrɔʒene], *a.* hydrogenated.

hydrogéner [idrɔʒene], *v.tr.* to hydrogenate, hydrogenize.

hydrogénèse [idrɔʒenɛːz], *s.f. Geog:* hydrology, ground-water hydrology.

hydrogéologie [idrɔʒeɔlɔʒi], *s.f.* hydrogeology.

hydroglisseur [idrɔglisœːr], *s.m.* hydroglider; hydroplane (motor boat); speedboat.

hydrographe [idrɔgraf]. **1.** *a. & s.m. Navy:* (ingénieur) h., hydrographer; navire h., survey vessel. **2.** *s.m.* hydrograph.

hydrographie [idrɔgrafi], *s.f.* hydrography; faire l'h. d'une mer, to chart a sea; *A:* école d'h., training college for the officers of the merchant service.

hydrographier [idrɔgrafje], *v.tr.* (*p.d.* & *pr.sub.* **n. hydrographiions, v. hydrographiiez**) to survey (coast); to chart (sea).
hydrographique [idrɔgrafik], *a.* hydrographic(al); **bassin h.,** drainage basin, catchment-basin; *Navy:* **le service h.,** the survey department.
hydroïde [idrɔid], *a.* & *s.m. Coel:* hydroid.
hydrolaccolithe [idrɔlakɔlit], *s.m. Geol:* hydrolaccolith.
hydrolase [idrɔlaːz], *s.f. Biol:* hydrolase.
hydrolat [idrɔla], *s.m. Pharm:* aromatic, medicated, water.
hydrolithe [idrɔlit], *s.f. Ch:* hydrolith.
hydrologie [idrɔlɔʒi], *s.f. Med: Geog:* hydrology.
hydrologique [idrɔlɔʒik], *a.* hydrological; **régime h. (d'un cours d'eau),** river régime.
hydrologiste [idrɔlɔʒist], **hydrologue** [idrɔlɔg], *s.m.* & *f.* hydrologist.
hydrolyse [idrɔliːz], *s.f. Ind: Ch:* hydrolysis.
hydrolyser [idrɔlize], *v.tr.* to hydrolize, to hydrolyse.
hydromagnésite [idrɔmaɲezit], *s.f. Miner:* hydromagnesite.
hydromancie [idrɔmɑ̃si], *s.f.* hydromancy.
hydromante [idrɔmɑ̃ːt], *s.f. Amph:* hydromantes.
hydromécanique [idrɔmekanik]. **1.** *a.* hydraulic; **industrie h.,** hydraulic engineering. **2.** *s.f.* hydromechanics, hydraulics.
hydroméduse [idrɔmedyːz], *s.f. Coel:* hydromedusa; **les hydroméduses,** the Hydromedusae.
hydromel [idrɔmɛl], *s.m.* hydromel; **h. vineux,** mead, vinous hydromel.
hydrométallurgie [idrɔmetal(l)yrʒi], *s.f.* hydrometallurgy.
hydrométéore [idrɔmeteɔːr], *s.m. Meteor:* hydrometeor.
hydromètre [idrɔmɛtr], *s.m.* **1.** *Ph: Ind:* (= ARÉOMÈTRE) hydrometer. **2.** *Oc: etc:* depth-gauge; *esp.* pneumatic depth recorder. **3.** *Hyd.E:* hydrometrograph, current meter. **4.** *Ent:* water spider.
hydrométridés [idrɔmetride], *s.m.pl. Ent:* Hydrometridae.
hydrométrie [idrɔmetri], *s.f. Ph:* hydrometry.
hydrométrique [idrɔmetrik], *a.* hydrometric(al).
hydrominéral, -aux [idrɔmineral, -o], *a.* **Vichy est une station hydrominérale,** Vichy is a spa; **l'industrie hydrominérale,** the mineral-water industry.
hydromorphe [idrɔmɔrf], *a. Geol:* hydromorphic.
hydromoteur [idrɔmɔtœːr], *s.m.* hydromotor.
hydromys [idrɔmis], *s.m. Z:* hydromys.
hydronéphrose [idrɔnefroːz], *s.f. Med:* hydronephrosis.
hydronymie [idrɔnimi], *s.f.* hydronymy.
hydropéricarde [idrɔperikard], *s.m. Med:* hydropericardium.
hydrophane [idrɔfan], *Miner:* **1.** *s.f.* hydrophane. **2.** *a.* hydrophanous.
hydrophidés [idrɔfide], *s.m.pl. Rept:* Hydrophi(i)dae.
hydrophile [idrɔfil], *a.* **1.** absorbent (cotton-wool, etc.). **2.** *Ent:* (*a*) hydrophilous; (*b*) *s.m.* hydrophilus; **h. brun,** water-devil.
hydrophilides [idrɔfilid], *s.m.pl.* Hydrophilidae.
hydrophilie [idrɔfili], *s.f. Biol: Ch: Ph:* hydrophilism, hydrophily.
hydrophilisation [idrɔfilizasjɔ̃], *s.f. Tex:* hydrophilizing.
hydrophilite [idrɔfilit], *s.f. Miner:* hydrophilite.
hydrophis [idrɔfis], *s.m. Rept:* hydrophis, water-snake.
hydrophobe [idrɔfɔb], *Med: Ch:* **1.** *a.* hydrophobic. **2.** *s.* hydrophobic subject.
hydrophobie [idrɔfɔbi], *s.f.* **1.** *Med: O:* hydrophobia, rabies. **2.** *Ch:* hydrophobic property (of molecule, etc.).
hydrophobique [idrɔfɔbik], *a. Med: Ch:* hydrophobic.
hydrophone [idrɔfɔn], *s.m.* hydrophone.
hydrophore [idrɔfɔːr], *a.* **1.** *Z:* hydrophoric. **2.** *Archeol:* hydrophoric.
hydrophories [idrɔfɔri], *s.f.pl. Gr.Ant:* Hydrophoria.
hydrophtalmie [idrɔftalmi], *s.f. Med:* hydrophtalmia, hydrophtalmos.
hydrophyllacées [idrɔfilase], *s.f.pl. Bot:* Hydrophyllaceae.
hydrophylle [idrɔfil], *s.f. Bot:* water-leaf; hydrophyllum.
hydrophyton [idrɔfitɔ̃], *s.m. Coel:* hydrophyton.
hydropigène [idrɔpiʒɛːn], *a. Med:* hydropigenous.
hydropique [idrɔpik], *Med:* **1.** *a.* dropsical; hydropic(al). **2.** *s.* dropsical subject.
hydropisie [idrɔpizi], *s.f. Med:* dropsy.
hydroplanage [idrɔplanaːʒ], *s.m. Aut:* aquaplaning.
hydroplane [idrɔplan], *s.m. A: Av:* hydroplane, seaplane.
hydroplaner [idrɔplane], *v.i. Av:* to taxi along (on water); to hydroplane.
hydropneumatique [idrɔpnømatik], *a.* **1.** *Artil:* hydropneumatic (buffer). **2.** *Aut:* **suspension, frein, h.,** hydropneumatic suspension, brake.
hydropneumothorax [idrɔpnømɔtɔraks], *s.m. Med:* hydropneumothorax.
hydroponique [idrɔpɔnik], *a.* hydroponic; **culture h.,** hydroponics, *F:* soilless gardening.
hydropotes [idrɔpɔtɛs], *s.m. Z:* Chinese water deer.
hydropsyché [idrɔpsiʃe], *s.f. Ent:* hydropsyche.
hydroptère [idrɔptɛːr], *s.m.* hydrofoil.
hydroquinone [idrɔkinɔn], *s.f. Ch: Phot:* hydroquinone, quinol.
hydrorachis [idrɔraʃis], *s.m. Med:* rachischis, spina bifida.
hydrorrhée [idrɔre], *s.f. Path:* hydrorrhea.
hydroscope [idrɔskɔp], *s.m.* water-diviner; dowser.
hydroscopie [idrɔskɔpi], *s.f.* water-divining; dowsing.
hydrosilicate [idrɔsilikat], *s.m. Ch:* hydrosilicate.
hydroski [idrɔski], *s.m. Navy:* hydroski.
hydrosol [idrɔsɔl], *s.m. Ch:* hydrosol.
hydrosoluble [idrɔsɔlybl], *a. Ch:* water-soluble.
hydrosome [idrɔzoːm], *s.m. Coel:* hydrosome.
hydrosphère [idrɔsfɛːr], *s.f. Geog:* hydrosphere.
hydrostat [idrɔsta], *s.m. Hyd.E:* hydrostat.
hydrostaticien [idrɔstatisjɛ̃], *s.m.* hydrostatics engineer.
hydrostatimètre [idrɔstatimɛtr], *s.m. Surv: Hyd.E:* hydrostatic level, water-level.
hydrostatique [idrɔstatik]. **1.** *a.* hydrostatic(al); **niveau h.,** (i) *Geol:* water table; (ii) water level (in well). **2.** *s.f.* hydrostatics.
hydrosulfate [idrɔsylfat], *s.m. Ch:* hydrosulphide.
hydrosulfite [idrɔsylfit], *s.m. Ch:* hydrosulphite.
hydrosulfureux [idrɔsylfyrø], *a.m. Ch:* **acide h.,** hydrosulphurous acid.
hydrotalcite [idrɔtalsit], *s.f. Miner:* hydrotalcite.
hydrotaxie [idrɔtaksi], *s.f. Biol:* hydrotaxis.
hydrotechnique [idrɔtɛknik], *s.f.* water-supply engineering.
hydrothèque [idrɔtɛk], *s.f. Z:* hydrotheca.
hydrothérapeute [idrɔterapøt], *s. Med:* hydrotherapist.
hydrothérapeutique [idrɔterapøtik], **hydrothérapie** [idrɔterapi], *s.f.* hydrotherapeutics, hydrotherapy, water cure.
hydrothérapique [idrɔterapik], *a.* hydrotherapeutic; **établissement h.,** hydropathic establishment, *F:* hydro.
hydrothérapiste [idrɔterapist], *s.m.* & *f.* hydrotherapist.
hydrothermal, -aux [idrɔtermal, -o], *a.* hydrothermal.
hydrothermique [idrɔtɛrmik], *a.* **1.** hydrothermal. **2. centrale h.,** thermo-electric power station.
hydrothorax [idrɔtɔraks], *s.m. Med:* hydrothorax.
hydrotimétrie [idrɔmetri], *s.f. Ch:* hydrometry.
hydrotraitement [idrɔtrɛtmɑ̃], *s.m. Petroleum Ind:* hydro-treating.
hydrotropisme [idrɔtrɔpism], *s.m. Bot:* hydrotropism.
hydrotypie [idrɔtipi], *s.f. Phot:* hydrotype.
hydroxamique [idrɔksamik], *a. Ch:* **acide h.,** hydroxamic acid.
hydroxy- [idrɔksi-], *pref. Ch:* hydrox- hydroxy-.
hydroxyde [idrɔksid], *s.m. Ch:* hydroxide.
hydroxylamine [idrɔksilamin], *s.f. Ch:* hydroxylamine.
hydroxyle [idrɔksil], *s.m. Ch:* hydroxyl.
hydroxylé [idrɔksile], *a. Ch:* hydroxylated.
hydrozoaires [idrɔzɔɛːr], *s.m.pl. Coel:* Hydrozoa.
hydrure [idryːr], *s.m. Ch:* hydride; **h. lourd,** deuteride.
hyène [jɛn], *s.f. Z:* hyena; **h. tachetée,** spotted hyena.
hyénidés [jenide], *s.m.pl. Z:* Hyaenidae.
hyérois, -oise [jerwa, -waːz], *a.* & *s. Geog:* (native) of Hyères.
Hygie [iʒi], *Pr.n.f. Myth:* Hygeia.
hygiène [iʒjɛn], *s.f.* hygiene; **h. publique,** public health, sanitation; **h. industrielle,** industrial welfare; **conférence d'h.,** health conference; **articles d'h. en caoutchouc,** rubber goods; **h. alimentaire,** nutrition; **mauvaise h. alimentaire,** malnutrition.
hygiénique [iʒjenik], *a.* hygienic; healthy; sanitary; **peu h.,** unhealthy (work); unsanitary (building); **papier h.,** toilet-paper; **serviette h.,** sanitary towel.
hygiéniquement [iʒjenikmɑ̃], *adv.* hygienically, healthily; sanitarily.
hygiénisme [iʒjenism], *s.m.* sanitarianism.
hygiéniste [iʒjenist], *s.m.* hygienist, sanitarian, public health specialist; **expert h.,** health expert; **h. alimentaire,** nutritionist.
hygr(o)- [igr(ɔ), -(o)], *pref.* hygr(o)-; **hygrologie,** hygrology; **hygrophile,** hygrophile.
hygrographe [igrɔgraf], *s.m.* hygrograph.
hygrology [igrɔlɔʒi], *s.f. Ph:* hygrology.
hygroma [igrɔma], *s.m. Med:* hygroma; **h. du genou,** *F:* housemaid's knee.
hygromètre [igrɔmɛtr], *s.m. Ph:* hygrometer; **h. à cheveu,** hair hygrometer; **h. à condensation,** dew-point hygrometer; **h. enregistreur,** hygrograph.
hygrométricité [igrɔmetrisite], *s.f. Ph:* **1.** humidity. **2.** humidity-absorption index.
hygrométrie [igrɔmetri], *s.f. Ph:* hygrometry, hygroscopy.
hygrométrique [igrɔmetrik], *a. Ph:* hygrometric(al); **degré h.,** relative humidity.
hygronastie [igrɔnasti], *s.f. Bot:* hygronasty.
hygrophile [hygrɔfil], *a. Bot: Geog:* hygrophile; **la forêt h.,** the tropical rain forest.
hygroscope [igrɔskɔp], *s.m. Ph:* hygroscope.
hygroscopie [igrɔskɔpi], *s.f. Ph:* hygroscopy.
hygroscopique [igrɔskɔpik], *a.* (*a*) hygroscopic(al); (*b*) slightly deliquescent (salt).
hygrostat [igrɔsta], *s.m. Ph:* hygrostat.
hygrotropisme [igrɔtrɔpism], *s.m. Ent: etc:* hygrotropism.
hylémyie [ilemi], *s.f. Ent:* hylemya.
***hylidés** [ilide], *s.m.pl. Amph:* Hylidae, the tree frogs.
hylo- [ilɔ, -o], *pref.* hylo-; **hylogénie,** hylogeny; **hylotome,** hylotomous.
hylobates [ilɔbatɛs], *s.m. Z:* gibbon.
hylobatidés [ilɔbatide], *s.m.pl. Z:* Hylobates.
hylobie [ilɔbi], *s.m. Ent:* **h. du sapin,** pine-weevil.
hylochère [ilɔʃɛːr], *s.m. Z:* giant forest hog.
hylozoïsme [ilɔzɔism], *s.m. Phil:* hylozoism.
hylozoïste [ilɔzɔist], *a.* & *s. Phil:* hylozoist.
Hymen [imɛn]. **1.** *Pr.n.m. Myth:* Hymen. **2.** *s.m.* (*a*) *Poet:* marriage; (*b*) *Anat:* hymen, maidenhead.
hyménal, -aux [imenal, -o], **hyménéal, -aux** [imeneal, -o], *a. Anat:* hymenal.
hyménée [imene], *s.m.* **1.** *Gr.Ant:* nuptial song. **2.** *Poet:* marriage.
hyménéen, -enne [imeneɛ̃, -ɛn], *a.* hymenean.
hyménium [imenjɔm], *s.m. Fung:* hymenium; *pl. hyménia.*
hyménomycètes [imenɔmisɛt], *s.m.pl. Fung:* hymenomycetes.
hyménophyllées [imenɔfil(l)e], *s.f.pl. Bot:* Hymenophyllaceae, *F:* filmy ferns.
hyménoptère [imenɔptɛːr], *Ent:* **1.** *a.* hymenopterous. **2.** *s.m.pl.* **hyménoptères,** Hymenoptera.
hyménoptéroïdes [imenɔpterɔid], *s.m.pl. Ent:* Hymenopteroidea.
hyménoptérologie [imenɔpterɔlɔʒi], *s.f. Ent:* hymenopterology.
hyménoptérologue [imenɔpterɔlɔg], *s. Ent:* hymenopterist, hymenopterologist.
Hymette (l') [limɛt], *Pr.n.m. Geog:* (Mount) Hymettus.
hymnaire [imnɛːr], *s.m.* hymn book, hymnal, hymnary.
hymne [imn]. **1.** *s.m.* song (of praise), patriotic song, hymn; **h. national,** national anthem. **2.** *s.f. Ecc:* hymn.
hymnographe [imnɔgraf], *s.m.* hymn-writer; hymnographer.
hymnologie [imnɔlɔʒi], *s.f.* hymnology.
hynobiidés [inɔbiide], *s.m.pl. Amph:* Hynobiidae.
hyoglosse [iɔglɔs, jo-], *a.* & *s.m. Anat:* **1.** *a.* hyoglossal. **2.** *s.m.* hyoglossus.
hyoïde [iɔid, jo-], *a.* & *s.m. Z: Anat:* hyoid (bone).
hyoïdien, -ienne [iɔidjɛ̃, -jɛn, jo-], *a. Anat:* hyoid(ean); *Z:* **arc h.,** the second postoral visceral arch of higher vertebrates.
hyomandibulaire [iɔmɑ̃dibylɛːr, jo-], *a.* & *s.m. Anat:* **1.** *a.* hyomandibular. **2.** *s.m.* hyomandibula, hyomandibular.
hyosciamine [iɔsjamin, jo-], *s.f. Pharm:* hyoscyamine.
hyoscine [iɔsin], *s.f. Ch:* hyoscine.
hyoscyamus [iɔsjamys], *s.m. Bot:* Hyoscyamus.
hyotherium [iɔterjɔm], *s.m. Paleont:* Hyotherium.
hypallage [ipal(l)aːʒ], *s.m. Rh:* hypallage.
hy(pa)panté [i(pa)pɑ̃te], *s.f. Eastern Orthodox Ch:* Hypapante.
Hypatie [ipati], *Pr.n.f. Hist:* Hypatia.
hyper- [ipɛr], *pref.* hyper-; **hyperchlorhydrie,** hyperchlorhydria.
hyperacousie [ipɛrakuzi], *s.f. Path:* hyperacousia.

hyperactif, -ive [iperaktif, -i:v], *a.* hyperactive.
hyperactivité [iperaktivite], *s.f.* hyperactivity.
hyperalgésie [iperalʒezi], *s.f. Path: Med:* hyperalgesia.
hyperalgésique [iperalʒezik], *a. Path: Med:* hyperalgesic.
hyperbate [iperbat], *s.f. Rh:* hyperbaton, inversion.
hyperbole [iperbɔl], *s.f.* 1. *Rh:* hyperbole, exaggeration; overstatement. 2. *Geom:* hyperbola.
hyperbolique [iperbɔlik], *a. Rh: Geom:* hyperbolic(al).
hyperboliquement [iperbɔlikmã], *adv. Rh:* hyperbolically.
hyperboloïde [iperbɔlɔid], *a. & s.m. Geom:* 1. *a.* hyperboloidal. 2. *s.m.* hyperboloid.
hyperboréal, -aux [iperbɔreal, -o], *a. O: Lit:* hyperboreal.
hyperborée [iperbɔre], **hyperboréen, -enne** [iperbɔreɛ̃, -ɛn], *a.* hyperborean.
hypercharge [iperʃarʒ], *s.f. Atom.Ph:* hypercharge.
hyperchlorhydrie [iperklɔridri], *s.f. Med:* hyperchlorhydria; gastric hyperacidity.
hypercompoundage [iperkɔ̃paunda:ʒ], *s.m. El.E:* overcompounding.
hypercompounder [iperkɔ̃paunde], *v.tr. El.E:* to overcompound.
hypercritique [iperkritik]. 1. *a.* hypercritical, over-critical. 2. *s.m.* hypercritic, severe critic. 3. *s.f.* hypercriticism.
hyperdulie [iperdyli], *s.f. Theol:* hyperdulia.
hyperémie, hyperhémie [iperemi], *s.f. Med:* hyperaemia, congestion.
hyperémier (s') [siperemje], *v.pr. Med:* to become congested; **organe hyperémié**, congested organ.
hyperémotivité [iperemotivite], *s.f. Med: Psy:* hyperemotivity.
hyperénergie [iperenɛrʒi], *s.f. Path:* hyperenergy.
hyperespace [iperɛspas], *s.m. Mth:* hyperspace.
hyperesthésie [iperɛstezi], *s.f. Med:* hyperaesthesia.
hyperfin [iperfɛ̃], *a. Opt:* hyperfine (structure).
hyperfocal, -aux [iperfɔkal, -o], *a. Phot:* hyperfocal (distance).
hyperfréquence [iperfrekã:s], *s.f.* ultra high frequency, very high frequency; *pl.* microwaves; **récepteur d'hyperfréquences**, microwave receiver.
hypergénèse [iperʒenɛ:z], *s.f. Med: Biol:* hypergenesis.
hyperglobulie [iperglobyli], *s.f. Path:* hyperglobulinemia.
hyperglycémiant [iperglisemjã], *a. Med:* hyperglysemic.
hyperglycémie [iperglisemi], *s.f. Med:* hyperglycemia.
hypergol [ipergɔl], *s.m. Rockets:* hypergol.
hypéricacées [iperikase], *s.f.pl. Bot:* Hypericaceae.
hyperinsulinisme [iperɛ̃sylinism], *s.m. Med:* hyperinsulinism.
hyperkératose [iperkerato:z], *s.f. Path:* hyperkeratosis.
hyperlordose [iperlɔrdo:z], *s.f. Med:* hyperlordosis.
hyperlourd [iperlur], *a. Atom.Ph:* **hydrogène h.**, tritium; **eau hyperlourde**, a compound of oxygen and tritium.
hypermarché [ipermarʃe], *s.m.* hypermarket.
hypermétamorphose [ipermetamɔrfo:z], *s.f. Ent:* hypermetamorphosis.
hypermètre [ipermɛtr], *A.Pros:* 1. *s.m.* hypermeter. 2. *a.* hypermetric(al).
hypermétrope [ipermetrɔp], *a. Med:* hypermetropic.
hypermétropie [ipermetrɔpi], *s.f. Med:* hypermetropia, long-sightedness.
hypermnésie [ipermnezi], *s.f. Psy:* hypermnesia.
hypernerveux, -euse [ipernɛrvø, -ø:z], *a.* highly-strung.
hypéron [iperɔ̃], *s.m. Atom.Ph:* hyperon, heavy meson.
hyperoodon [iperɔɔdɔ̃], *s.m. Z:* hyperoodon, bottle-nosed whale, bottle-nose, beaked whale.
hyperorganisme [iperɔrganism], *s.m. Phil: Sociology:* organicism.
hyperparasite [iperparazit], *s.m. & a. Biol:* 1. *a.* hyperparasitic. 2. *s.m.* hyperparasite.
hyperpiésie [iperpjezi], *s.f. Med:* hyperpiesis, high blood pressure.
hypersécrétion [ipersekresjɔ̃], *s.f. Med:* hypersecretion.
hypersensibilisation [ipersãsibilizasjɔ̃], *s.f. Phot:* hypersensitizing (of plate).
hypersensibilité [ipersãsibilite], *s.f.* over-sensitiveness, hypersensitiveness, super-sensitiveness.
hypersensible [ipersãsibl], *a.* hypersensitive, over-sensitive; supersensitive (person, *Phot:* plate).

hypersensitif, -ive [ipersãsitif, -i:v], *a. & s.* hypersensitive, over-sensitive, supersensitive (person, etc.).
hypersonique [ipersɔnik], *a. Ph: Av:* hypersonic; **vitesses hypersoniques**, hypersonic speeds.
hypersustentateur, -trice [ipersystãtatœ:r, -tris], *Av:* 1. *a.* **dispositif h.**, high-lift device; **volet-h.**, high-lift flap. 2. *s.m.* high-lift device.
hypersustentation [ipersystãtasjɔ̃], *s.f. Av:* lift increasing, increase, by lift-flap device.
hypertélie [iperteli], *s.f. Z:* hypertely.
hypertendu [ipertãdy], *a. & s. Med:* hypertensive (patient); (person) suffering from high blood pressure.
hypertension [ipertãsjɔ̃], *s.f. Med:* hypertension; **h. artérielle**, high blood pressure.
hyperthyroïdie [ipertirɔidi], *s.f. Med:* hyperthyrosis.
hypertonie [ipertɔni], *s.f. Ch: Physiol:* hypertonus, hypertonicity.
hypertonique [ipertɔnik], *a. Ph: Ch:* hypertonic; **solution h.**, hypertonic salt solution.
hypertrichose [ipertriko:z], *s.f. Med:* hypertrichosis.
hypertrophie [ipertrɔfi], *s.f. Med:* hypertrophy; **h. des amygdales**, enlarged tonsils; *F:* **h. administrative**, the proliferation of civil servants.
hypertrophié [ipertrɔfje], *a. Med:* hypertrophied; **amygdales hypertrophiées**, enlarged tonsils.
hypertrophier (s') [sipertrɔfje], *v.pr. Med:* to hypertrophy.
hypertrophique [ipertrɔfik], *a. Med:* hypertrophic, hypertrophous.
hyperventilation [ipervãtilasjɔ̃], *s.f. Med:* hyperventilation.
hypervitaminose [ipervitamino:z], *s.f. Med:* hypervitaminosis.
hypèthre [ipɛtr], *a. Archeol:* hypaethral, hypethral.
hyphaene, hyphène [ifɛn], *s.m. Bot:* hyphaene, doom palm.
hyphe [if], *s.m. Fung:* hypha.
hypholome [ifɔlɔm], *s.m. Fung:* hypholoma.
hyphomycètes [ifɔmisɛt], *s.m. Fung:* hyphomycetes.
hyphydrogame [ifidrɔgam], *a. Bot:* below the water (pollination).
hyphydrogamie [ifidrɔgami], *s.f. Bot:* hyphydrogamy.
hypnagogique [ipnagɔʒik], *a. Psy:* hypnagogic.
hypne [ipn], *s.f. Moss:* hypnea.
hypnopédie [ipnɔpedi], *s.f.* hypnopedia, sleep learning.
hypnose [ipno:z], *s.f. Med:* hypnosis; **h. provoquée**, induced hypnosis.
hypnotique [ipnɔtik], *a. & s. Pharm: Psy:* hypnotic; *s.m. Pharm:* hypnotic, narcotic.
hypnotiser [ipnɔtize], *v.tr.* to hypnotize.
hypnotiseur, -euse [ipnɔtizœ:r, -ø:z]. 1. *a.* hypnotizing, hypnotic. 2. *s.* hypnotist.
hypnotisme [ipnɔtism], *s.m.* hypnotism.
hypnotoxine [ipnɔtɔksin], *s.f. Biol:* hypnotoxin.
hypo- [ipɔ], *pref.* hypo-; **hypogyne**, hypogynous.
hypoazoteux, -euse [ipɔazɔtø, -ø:z], *a. Ch:* hyponitrous.
hypoazotique [ipɔazɔtik], *a. Ch:* hyponitric.
hypocagne [ipɔka:ɲ], *s.f. Sch: F:* first-year class preparing to compete for entrance to the *École Normale Supérieure.*
hypocagneux, -euse [ipɔkaɲø, -ø:z], *s.f. Sch:* student in the *hypocagne.*
hypocauste [ipɔkost], *s.m. Rom.Ant:* hypocaust.
hypocentre [ipɔsãtr], *s.m.* hypocentre.
hypocéphale [ipɔsefal], *s.m.* 1. *Archeol:* hypocephalus. 2. *Ent:* capricorn beetle of Brazil.
hypochlorate [ipɔklɔrat], *s.m. Ch:* hypochlorate.
hypochloreux, -euse [ipɔklɔrø, -ø:z], *a. Ch:* **acide h.**, hypochlorous acid.
hypochlorique [ipɔklɔrik], *a. Ch:* hypochloric.
hypochlorite [ipɔklɔrit], *s.m. Ch:* hypochlorite.
hypochlorurie [ipɔklɔryri], *s.f. Path:* hypochloruria.
hypochlorydrie [ipɔklɔridri], *s.f. Med:* hypochlorhydria.
hypochromatopsie [ipɔkrɔmatɔpsi], *s.f. Opt:* deficient colour perception.
hypocondre [ipɔkɔ̃:dr]. 1. *s.m. Anat:* hypochondrium; hypochondriac area. 2. *a. & s. =* HYPOCONDRIAQUE.
hypocondriaque [ipɔkɔ̃drijak]. 1. *a.* hypochondriac(al); *Lit:* melancholy, depressed. 2. *s.* hypochondriac.
hypocondrie [ipɔkɔ̃dri], *s.f.* hypochondria.
hypocoristique [ipɔkɔristik]. 1. *a.* hypocoristic. 2. *s.m.* hypocorism, hypocoristic.
hypocras [ipɔkra:s], *s.m.* hippocras.
hypocrisie [ipɔkrizi], *s.f.* hypocrisy; cant.

hypocrite [ipɔkrit]. 1. *a.* hypocritical. 1. *s.m. & f.* hypocrite.
hypocritement [ipɔkritmã], *adv.* hypocritically.
hypocycloïdal, -aux [ipɔsiklɔidal, -o], *a. Mec.E: Geom:* hypocycloidal.
hypocycloide [ipɔsiklɔid], *s.f. Geom:* hypocycloid.
hypoderme [ipɔdɛrm], *s.m.* 1. *Anat: Bot: etc:* hypoderm(a); hypodermis. 2. *Ent:* warble fly, gadfly; hypoderma.
hypodermie [ipɔdɛrmi], *s.f. Med:* hypodermic treatment, therapy.
hypodermique [ipɔdɛrmik], *a. Med: Bot:* hypodermic.
hypodermose [ipɔdɛrmo:z], *s.f. Vet:* hypodermosis, warble fly infestation.
hypoesthésie [ipɔɛstezi], *s.f. Med:* hypaesthesia.
hypogastre [ipɔgastr], *s.m. Anat:* hypogastrium, hypogastric region.
hypogastrique [ipɔgastrik], *a. Anat:* hypogastric; **ceinture h.**, abdominal belt; **plexus nerveux h.**, hypogastric plexus.
hypogé [ipɔʒe], *a. Geol:* hypogeal, hypogean, underground; **eau hypogée**, juvenile water; *Bot:* hypogeous (cotyledon).
hypogée [ipɔʒe], *s.m. Archeol:* hypogeum.
hypogène [ipɔʒɛn], *a. Geol:* hypogene.
hypoglosse [ipɔglɔs], *a. & s.m. Anat:* hypoglossal (nerve).
hypoglycémiant [ipɔglisemjã], *a. & s.m. Med: Pharm:* hypoglycemic (drug).
hypoglycémie [ipɔglisemi], *s.f. Med:* hypoglycemia.
hypoglycémique [ipɔglisemik], *a. Med:* hypoglycemic (coma).
hypogonadisme [ipɔgɔnadism], *s.m. Path:* hypogonadism; eunuchoidism.
hypogyne [ipɔʒin], *a. Bot:* hypogynous.
hypoïde [ipɔid], *a. Mec.E:* hypoid; **engrenage h.**, crown-wheel and pinion; hypoid (gear).
hypokhâgne [ipɔkaɲ], *s.f. Sch: F: =* HYPOCAGNE.
hypokhâgneux, -euse [ipɔkaɲø, -ø:z], *s. Sch: F: =* HYPOCAGNEUX, -EUSE.
hypolaïs [ipɔlais], *s.f. Orn:* warbler; **h. ictérine**, icterine warbler; **h. polyglotte**, melodious warbler; **h. russe**, booted warbler; **h. pâle**, olivaceous warbler; **h. des oliviers**, olive-tree warbler.
hypologie [ipɔlɔʒi], *s.f. Path:* hypologia.
hypomane [ipɔman], *s. Med: Psy:* person suffering, sufferer, from hypomania.
hypomanie [ipɔmani], *s.f. Med: Psy:* hypomania.
hyponomeute [ipɔnɔmø:t], *s.m. Ent:* ermine moth.
hypoparathyroïdie [ipɔparatirɔidi], *s.f. Path:* hypoparathyroidism.
hypopharynx [ipɔfarɛ̃ks], *s.m. Ent: Anat:* hypopharynx.
hypophosphate [ipɔfɔsfat], *s.m. Ch:* hypophosphate.
hypophosphite [ipɔfɔsfit], *s.m. Ch:* hypophosphite.
hypophosphoreux, -euse [ipɔfɔsfɔrø, -ø:z], *a. Ch:* hypophosphorous.
hypophosphorique [ipɔfɔsfɔrik], *a.m. Ch:* hypophosphoric.
hypophysaire [ipɔfize:r], *a. Anat:* hypophyseal, hypophysial, relating to the hypophysis; *Med:* **insuffisance h.**, hypopituitarism.
hypophyse [ipɔfi:z], *s.f. Anat:* hypophysis; pituitary body.
hypopituitarisme [ipɔpityitarism], *s.m. Med:* hypopituitarism.
hyposcenium [ipɔsenjɔm], *s.m. Gr.Ant: Th:* hyposcenium.
hyposécrétion [ipɔsekresjɔ̃], *s.f. Med:* hyposecretion.
hypostase [ipɔsta:z], *s.f. Ling: Phil: Theol:* hypostasis.
hypostatique [ipɔstatik], *a. Phil: Theol:* hypostatic; *Biol:* **gène h.**, hypostatic gene; *Path:* **congestion h.**, hypostatical congestion.
hypostyle [ipɔstil], *a. Arch:* hypostyle, pillared (hall, etc.).
hyposulfate [ipɔsylfat], *s.m. Ch:* dithionate; *A:* hyposulphate.
hyposulfite [ipɔsylfit], *s.m. Ch:* hyposulphite, thiosulphate; **h. de soude**, sodium thiosulphate, hyposulphite of soda; *Phot: F:* hypo.
hyposulfureux [ipɔsylfyrø], *a.inv. Ch:* thiosulphuric.
hypotaupe [ipɔto:p], *s.f. Sch: F:* first-year class preparing for the *École Polytechnique.*
hypotendu [ipɔtãdy], *a. & s. Med:* hypotensive (patient); (person) suffering from low blood pressure.
hypotension [ipɔtãsjɔ̃], *s.f. Med:* hypotension; **h. artérielle**, low blood pressure; *Surg:* **h. contrôlée**, controlled hypotension.

hypoténuse [ipɔtenyːz], s.f. Geom: hypotenuse; **le carré de l'h.**, the square on the hypotenuse.

hypothalamus [ipɔtalamyːs], s.m. Anat: hypothalamus.

hypothécable [ipɔtekabl], a. mortgageable.

hypothécaire [ipɔtekɛːr]. 1. a. pertaining to mortgage; **prêt h.**, loan on mortgage; **contrat h.**, mortgage deed; **créancier h.**, mortgagee; **débiteur h.**, mortgagor; **lettre h.**, letter of hypothecation. 2. s. holder of mortgage; mortgagee.

hypothécairement [ipɔtekɛrmɑ̃], adv. Jur: by, on, mortgage.

hypothénar [ipɔtenaːr], a.inv. Anat: (éminence) h., hypothenar.

hypothèque [ipɔtɛk], s.f. 1. mortgage; **terre grevée d'hypothèques**, burdened estate; **franc, libre, d'hypothèques**, unencumbered, unmortgaged; **avoir une h. sur une maison**, to have a bond, a mortgage, on a house; **h. en premier rang**, first mortgage; **prendre une h.**, to raise a mortgage; **prêt sur h.**, mortgage loan; **obligations de première h.**, first-mortgage bonds; **purger une h.**, to pay off, clear off, redeem, a mortgage; **h. générale**, blanket mortgage; **h. sur biens meubles**, chattel mortgage; **conservateur des hypothèques**, registrar of mortgages; **prendre une h. sur l'avenir**, to mortgage one's future; **lever l'h.**, to remove all hindrances. 2. handicap.

hypothéquer [ipɔteke], v.tr. (j'hypothèque, n. hypothéquons, j'hypothéquerai) 1. to mortgage (estate, etc.); **h. des titres**, to hypothecate, mortgage, securities; to lodge stock as security. 2. to secure (debt) by mortgage. 3. **h. son avenir**, to mortgage one's future. 4. F: **être bien hypothéqué** (i) to be seriously ill, to be in a bad way; (ii) to be in a hole, to be in a jam.

hypothermal, -aux [ipɔtɛrmal, -o], a. Geol: hypothermal.

hypothermie [ipɔtɛrmi], s.f. Med: hypothermia, low temperature; Surg: **h. provoquée**, hypothermia.

hypothèse [ipɔtɛːz], s.f. Phil: etc: hypothesis, assumption; theory; **faire des hypothèses**, to make suppositions; to form theories; **envisager la pire des hypothèses**, to assume the worst; **dans l'h. où**, on the assumption, on the supposition, that; supposing that; **dans, selon, cette h.**, on this assumption; **en toute h.**, in any case; s.a. ÉPREUVE, I (a); TEST.

hypothétique [ipɔtetik], a. hypothetic(al), assumed.

hypothétiquement [ipɔtetikmɑ̃], adv. hypothetically.

hypothyroïdie [ipɔtirɔidi], s.f. Med: hypothyroidism.

hypotonie [ipɔtɔni], s.f. Med: hypotonus, hypotonia.

hypotonique [ipɔtɔnik], a.Med:Ph:Ch: hypotonic.

hypotrophie [ipɔtrɔfi], s.f. Med: hypotrophy.

hypotypose [ipɔtipoːz], s.f. Rh: hypotyposis.

hypovitaminose [ipɔvitaminoːz], s.f. hypovitaminosis.

hypsides [ipsid], s.m.pl. Ent: Hypsidae.

hypsogramme [ipsɔgraːm], s.m. Elcs: diagram showing the variations of power-distribution, intensity, etc., of a transmitter; (computers) level diagram.

hypsographie [ipsɔgrafi], s.f. hypsography.

hypsomètre [ipsɔmɛtr], s.m. Surv: hypsometer, thermo-barometer.

hypsométrie [ipsɔmetri], s.f. hypsometry, altimetry.

hypsométrique [ipsɔmetrik], a. hypsometric(al); **courbe h.**, contour line; **carte h.**, contour map.

hyracoïdes [irakɔid], s.m.pl. Z: Hyracoidea.

hyrax [iraks], s.m. Z: hyrax; pl. hyraxes, hyraces.

Hyrcanie [irkani], Pr.n.f. A.Geog: Hyrcania.

hyrcanien, -ienne [irkanjɛ̃, -jɛn], a. A.Geog: Hyrcanian.

hysope [izɔp], s.f. Bot: hyssop.

hystarazine [istarazin], s.f. Ch: hystarazin.

hystéralgie [isteralʒi], s.f. Med: hysteralgia.

hystérectomie [isterɛktɔmi], s.f. Surg: hysterectomy.

hystérèse [isterɛːz], s.f., **hystérésis** [isterezis], s.f. Magn: hysteresis, magnetic lag; **courbe d'h.**, hysteresis curve.

hystérie [isteri], s.f. Med: hysteria; **h. collective**, mass hysteria; Vet: **h. canine**, canine hysteria.

hystériforme [isteriform], a. Psy: hysteriform.

hystérique [isterik], a. & s. Med: hysterical; **boule h., globe h.**, globus histericus. 2. s. hysterical, hysteric, person.

hystérisme [isterism], s.m. hystericism (in literature, etc.).

hystérite [isterit], s.f. Med: hysteritis.

hystérocèle [isterɔsɛl], s.f. Med: hysterocele.

hystérogène [isterɔʒɛn], a. hysterogenic, hysterogenous.

hystérographie [isterɔgrafi], s.f. Med: hysterography.

hystérotomie [isterɔtɔmi], s.f. Surg: hysterotomy; **h. abdominale**, Caesarean operation.

hystolyse [istɔliːz], s.f. Biol: hystolysis.

hystricidés [istriside], s.m.pl. Z: Hystricidae.

hystricomorphes [istrikɔmɔrf], s.m.pl. Z: Hystricomorpha.

I

I, i [i], *s.m.* **1.** (the letter) I, i; *Tp:* **I comme Irma,** I for Isaac; **droit comme un i,** bolt upright; **mettre les points sur les i,** to speak plainly, unambiguously; to emphasize (sth.); to dot one's i's (and cross one's t's); **n'être bon qu'à mettre les points sur les i,** to be unable to rise above trifling details. **2. i grec,** (the letter) Y, y.

Iahvé [jave], *Pr.n.m.* Yahweh, Jehovah.

iakoute [jakut]. **1.** *a. & s. Ethn:* Yakut. **2.** *s.m. Ling:* Yakut.

Iakoutsk [jakutsk], *Pr.n. Geog:* Yakutsk.

iambe [jã:b], *s.m. Pros:* **1.** (*a*) iamb, iambus; (*b*) iambic. **2.** *pl.* satirical poem (*usu.* written in alternate twelve and eight foot lines).

iambélégiaque [jãbeleʒjak], *a. A.Pros:* vers i., iambelegus.

iambique [jãbik], *a. Pros:* iambic (line, verse).

iatrochimie [jatrɔʃimi], *s.f. A.Med:* iatrochemistry.

iatrogénie [jatrɔʒeni], *s.f.* iatrogenicity.

iatrophysique [jatrɔfizik], *s.f. A.Med:* iatrophysics.

ibère [ibɛ:r]. **1.** *a. & s.m. or f. Ethn:* Iberian. **2.** *s.m. Ling:* Iberian.

ibéride [iberid], *s.f. Bot:* iberis, *F:* candytuft.

Ibérie [iberi], *Pr.n.f. A.Geog:* Iberia ((i) modern Spain, (ii) modern Georgia).

ibérien, -ienne [iberjɛ̃, -jɛn], *a. Ethn:* Iberian.

ibérique [iberik], *a. Geog:* Iberian; **la péninsule i.,** the Iberian peninsula.

ibéris [iberis], *s.m. Bot:* Iberis.

ibériste [iberist], *s.* scholar specializing in the study of the Iberians, the Basques and their civilizations.

ibérite [iberit], *s.f. Miner:* iberite.

ibéro-américain, -aine [iberɔamerikɛ̃, -ɛn], *a. & s.* Latin-American, *esp.* Spanish-American; *pl.* **ibéro-américains, -aines.**

ibéro-celtique [iberɔsɛltik], *a. Ethn:* Ibero-Celtic; *pl.* **ibéro-celtiques.**

ibex [ibɛks], *s.m. Z:* ibex.

ibidem, ib. [ibidɛm], *adv.* ibidem, ibid., ib.

ibidorhynque [ibidɔrɛ̃:k], **ibidorhynchus** [ibidɔrɛ̃kys], *s.m. Orn:* ibidorhyncha; ibis-bill.

ibis [ibis], *s.m. Orn:* ibis; **i. falcinelle,** glossy ibis; **i. rouge,** scarlet ibis; **i. sacré,** sacred ibis.

Ibos [ibo], *s.m.pl. Ethn:* the Ibo(s).

iboga [ibɔga], *s.m. Bot:* iboga.

ibsénien, -ienne [ipsenjɛ̃, -jɛn], *Lit:* **1.** *a.* in the style, manner, of Ibsen; Ibsenian. **2.** *s.* Ibsenite.

ibsénisme [ipsenism], *s.m. Lit:* Ibsenism.

Icabod [ikabɔd], *Pr.n.m. B.Hist:* Ichabod.

icaque [ikak], *s.f. Bot:* **1.** (**prune d')i.,** coco plum. **2.** coco plum (tree), icaco.

icaquier [ikakje], *s.m. Bot:* coco plum (tree), icaco.

Icare [ika:r], *Pr.n.m. Gr.Myth:* Icarus.

Icarie [ikari], *Pr.n.f. A.Geog:* Icaria.

icarien, -ienne [ikarjɛ̃, -jɛn]. **1.** *a.* **la mer icarienne,** the Icarian sea. **2.** *s. Fr.Hist:* follower of the communist Cabet (author of *Le Voyage en Icarie*); Icarian. **3.** *a.* **jeux icariens,** trapeze acrobatics.

iceberg [isberg, ajsbɛrg], *s.m.* iceberg.

ice-boat [ajsbot], *s.m.* iceboat; *pl.* ice-boats.

icefield, icefjeld [ajsfild], *s.m. Geog:* ice(-)field.

icelui [isəlɥi], **icelle** [isɛl], **iceux** [isø], **icelles** [isɛl], *pron. & a. A. & Jur:* = CELUI(-CI), CELLE (-CI), CEUX(-CI), CELLES(-CI).

Icènes [isɛn], *s.m.pl.,* **Icéniens** [isenjɛ̃], *s.m.pl. Hist:* Iceni.

---

ichneumon [iknømɔ̃], *s.m.* **1.** *Z:* ichneumon, Pharaoh's rat. **2.** *Ent:* ichneumon (fly).

ichneumonidés [iknømɔnide], *s.m.pl. Ent:* Ichneumonidae, Ichneumonides.

ichnographie [iknɔgrafi], *s.f.* ichnography; ground plan, ichnograph.

ichnographique [iknɔgrafik], *a.* ichnographic(al); plan i., ground plan, ichnograph.

ichnologie [iknɔlɔʒi], *s.f.* ichnology.

ichor [ikɔ:r], *s.m. Gr.Myth: Med:* ichor.

ichoreux, -euse [ikɔrø, -ø:z], *a. Med:* ichorous.

Ichthys [iktis], *s.m. Ecc:* Ichthys, Ichthus.

icht(h)yo- [iktjɔ, -o, ikti], *comb. fm.* (*Note: although some of the words which follow may be spelt* ichtyo- *or* ichthyo-, *the spelling* ichtyo- *has been adopted throughout*) ichthyo-; **ichtyomorphe,** ichthyomorphic.

ichtyobdelle [iktjɔbdɛl], *s.f. Ann:* ichthyobdella.

ichtyocaude [iktjɔko:d], *s.f. Nau:* device like a fishtail serving as propeller in certain ships.

ichtyocolle [iktjɔkɔl]. **1.** *s.f.* fish-glue, isinglass, ichthyocol, ichthyocolla; **i. en cœur,** leaf isinglass; **i. en livre,** book isinglass; **i. en lyre,** lyre isinglass. **2.** *s.m. Ich:* beluga.

ichtyodonte [iktjɔdɔ̃:t], *s.f. Paleont:* ichthyodont.

ichtyodorulite [iktjɔdɔrylit], *s.f. Paleont:* ichthyodorulite, ichthyodorylite.

ichtyographie [iktjɔgrafi], *s.f.* ichthyology.

ichtyoïde [iktjɔid], *a.* ichthyoid.

ichtyol (ammonium) [iktjɔl(amɔnjɔm)], *s.m. Pharm:* ichthyol, ichthammol.

ichtyologie [iktjɔlɔʒi], *s.f.* ichthyology.

ichtyologique [iktjɔlɔʒik], *a.* ichthyologic(al).

ichtyologue [iktjɔlɔg], **ichtyologiste** [iktjɔlɔʒist], *s.m. & f.* ichthyologist.

ichtyomorphe [iktjɔmɔrf], *a.* ichthyomorphic.

ichtyophage [iktjɔfa:ʒ]. **1.** *a.* ichthyophagous, fish-eating. **2.** *s.* ichthyophagist. **3.** *s.pl. A.Civ:* ichtyophages, Ichthyophagi.

ichtyophagie [iktjɔfaʒi], *s.f.* ichthyophagy.

ichtyptérygie [iktjpteriʒi], *s.f. Z:* ichthyopterigium; *pl.* -ia.

ichtyptérygiens [iktjpteriʒjɛ̃], *s.m.pl. Paleont: A:* Ichthyopterigia.

ichtyornis [iktjɔrnis], *s.m. Paleont:* ichthyornis.

ichtyosaure [iktjɔsɔ:r], *s.m. Paleont:* ichthyosaurus; ichthyosaur.

ichtyosauriens [iktjɔsɔrjɛ̃], *s.m.pl. Paleont:* Ichthyosauria.

ichtyose [iktjo:z], *s.f. Med:* ichthyosis, fish-skin disease, porcupine disease.

ichtyotoxine [iktjɔtɔksin], *s.f.* ichthyotoxin.

ici [isi], *adv.* **1.** here; **i. et là,** here and there; **venez i.,** come here; (*to dog*) **i., Médor!** here, Médor! **les gens d'i.,** the people (who live) here, *F:* the locals; **je ne suis pas d'i.,** I'm a stranger here, I don't live here, I'm not from here; **i.-bas,** here below, on earth; **hors d'i.!** get out of here! clear out! scram! **il y a vingt kilomètres d'i. à Paris,** it's twenty kilometres (from here) to Paris; **c'est à dix minutes d'i.,** it's ten minutes away; **c'est un vin d'i.,** it's a local wine; **il habite par i., près d'i.,** he lives near here, around here; **passez par i.,** this way, please; **c'est i.,** it's here; this is the place; **veuillez signer i.,** sign here, please; **c'est une glacière i.,** this (room, etc.) is like an icehouse; **le car vient jusqu'i.,** the bus comes as far as here, as far as this; *Tp:* **i. Thomas,** Thomas speaking; *W.Tel:* **i. Radio Luxembourg,** this is Radio Luxembourg.

---

2. now; at this point; **jusqu'i.,** up to now, hitherto; **d'i.,** from today; from this time, from now on; **d'i. (à) lundi,** between now and Monday, by Monday; **d'i. (à) deux jours,** within the next two days; **d'i. là on verra,** by then we shall see; **d'i. peu,** before long; **dans un mois d'i.,** in a month's time; **on ne le verra pas d'i. (à) longtemps,** we shan't see him for a long time now; **d'i. (à ce) que cela se fasse, on a le temps d'attendre,** it will be a long time before anything is done, we shall have to wait for that to get done; *F:* **d'i. (à ce) que vous ayez fini, je serai parti,** by the time you've finished, I shall be gone.

icône [ikoːn, -ɔn], *s.f. Ecc:* icon, ikon.

iconique [ikɔnik], *a.* iconic, ikonic (statue, etc.).

icono- [ikɔnɔ-], *pref.* icono-; **iconomanie,** iconomania.

iconoclasie [ikɔnɔklazi], *s.f.,* **iconoclasme** [ikɔnɔklasm], *s.m.* iconoclasm.

iconoclaste [ikɔnɔklast]. **1.** *a.* iconoclastic. **2.** *s.m.* iconoclast.

iconoclastie [ikɔnɔklasti], *s.f.* iconoclasm.

iconogène [ikɔnɔʒɛn], *s.m. Phot:* eikonogen.

iconographe [ikɔnɔgraf], *s.m. & f.* iconographer.

iconographie [ikɔnɔgrafi], *s.f.* iconography.

iconographique [ikɔnɔgrafik], *a.* iconographic(al).

iconolâtre [ikɔnɔlɑ:tr], *s.m. & f. Rel.H:* iconolater.

iconolâtrie [ikɔnɔlɑtri], *s.f.* iconolatry; image worship.

iconologie [ikɔnɔlɔʒi], *s.f.* iconology.

iconologique [ikɔnɔlɔʒik], *a.* iconological.

iconologiste [ikɔnɔlɔʒist], **iconologue** [ikɔnɔlɔg], *s.m. & f.* iconologist.

iconomanie [ikɔnɔmani], *s.f.* iconomania.

iconomètre [ikɔnɔmɛtr], *s.m. Phot:* iconometer, view meter.

iconométrie [ikɔnɔmetri], *s.f. Phot:* iconometry.

iconophile [ikɔnɔfil], *s.m. & f.* collector of statues, of prints; iconophile.

iconoscope [ikɔnɔskɔp], *s.m.* **1.** *Phot:* viewfinder. **2.** *T.V:* iconoscope.

iconostase [ikɔnɔstɑ:z], *s.f. Ecc.Arch:* iconostasis.

iconothèque [ikɔnɔtɛk], *s.f.* iconographical section (of museum, library), print room.

icosaèdre [ikɔzaɛ:dr], *Geom:* **1.** *a.* icosahedral. **2.** *s.m.* icosahedron.

icosagone [ikɔzagɔn], *Geom:* **1.** *a.* icosagonal. **2.** *s.m.* icosagon.

ictère [iktɛːr], *s.m.* **1.** *Med:* icterus, jaundice; **i. des enfants,** yellow gum; **i. vrai, biliphéique,** true jaundice; **i. grave,** malignant jaundice; **i. bleu,** blue jaundice, cyanosis. **2.** *Bot:* icterus. **3.** *Orn:* icterus; American oriole.

ictéridés [ikteride], *s.m.pl. Orn:* Icteridae.

ictérigène [ikterizɛn], *a. Med:* icterogenic.

ictérique [ikterik], *Med:* **1.** *a.* (*a*) icteric(al) (disorder); (*b*) jaundiced (pers., eyes, etc.). **2.** *s.* sufferer from jaundice.

icterus [ikterys], *s.m. Orn:* icterus.

icticyon [iktisjɔ̃], *s.m. Z:* icticyon; bushdog.

ictus [iktys], *s.m.* ictus. **1.** *Pros: etc:* stress. **2.** *Med:* (apoplectic) stroke; (epileptic) fit.

idalie [idali], *s.f. Ent:* idalia.

idante [idɑ̃:t], *s.m. Biol:* idant.

ide[1] [id], *s.m. Ich:* ide, orfe.

ide[2], *s.m. Biol:* id.

idéal [ideal]. **1.** *a.* (*pl.* **idéaux** [ideo]) ideal; **un monde i.,** an ideal world; **le beau i.,** the ideal of beauty; **un mari i.,** an ideal husband. **2.** *s.m.*

(*pl.* **idéals, idéaux**) ideal; **se rallier à d'autres idéals,** to rally to other ideals; **elle était l'i. de la beauté,** she was ideally beautiful. 3. *s.m. Mth:* ideal.

idéalement [idealmã], *adv.* ideally.

idéalisation [idealizasjɔ̃], *s.f.* idealization, idealizing.

idéaliser [idealize], *v.tr.* to idealize.

idéalisme [idealism], *s.m.* idealism.

idéaliste [idealist]. 1. *a.* idealistic. 2. *s.m. & f.* idealist.

idéalité [idealite], *s.f.* ideality. 1. idealness. 2. tendency to idealize. 3. *pl.* vague ideals, dreams of what might be. 4. *A:* idealism.

idéat [idea], *s.m. Psy:* ideate.

idéation [ideasjɔ̃], *s.f. Psy:* ideation.

idéationnel, -elle [ideasjɔnɛl], *a. Psy:* ideational.

idée [ide], *s.f.* 1. idea; (*a*) (mental) conception; notion; **avoir une haute i. de son devoir,** to have an exalted idea of one's duty; **je n'en ai pas la moindre i.,** I haven't the least, the faintest, idea, the remotest conception; **vous vous êtes fait une i. fausse de ma situation de fortune,** you have (formed) a wrong notion, idea, of my means, of my financial position; **a-t-on i. d'une chose pareille?** can you imagine it? who would have thought it? **on n'a pas (l')i. de faire une chose pareille!** fancy anyone doing such a thing! **on n'a pas i. de cela,** you can't imagine it; **en voilà une i.!** what an idea! **quelle i.!** the (very) idea! *F:* **où il est? mais au café, cette i.!** where he is? but at the pub, of course! **i. de génie, i. lumineuse,** brilliant idea, brainwave; **bonne i.!** good idea! **avoir l'i. de faire qch.,** to hit upon the idea of doing sth.; **quelle bonne i. que vous soyez venu!** what a good idea of yours to come! **qu'est-ce qui vous a donné l'i. de venir?** what gave you the idea of coming? *F:* **il y a de l'i.,** you've got something there; **avoir une i. de derrière la tête,** to have an idea at the back of one's mind; **j'ai (l')i. que . . ,** I have an idea, I rather fancy, that . . . ; **l'i. m'est venue que . . ,** it has occurred to me that . . . ; **l'i. me vint tout à coup que . . ,** it flashed on me, it flashed through my mind, that . . . ; *F:* **j'ai comme une i. qu'il va venir ce soir,** I've some sort of idea that he'll come tonight; **laissez-moi rassembler mes idées,** let me collect my thoughts; **laissez-moi suivre le fil de mes idées,** let me follow the thread of my thoughts; **donner des idées à qn,** to put ideas into s.o.'s head; **vous pouvez chasser cette i. de votre esprit,** you can dismiss that idea from your mind; **le nez de M. Wilson et ses oreilles donnent, évoquent, l'i. d'un lapin,** Mr Wilson's nose and ears suggest a rabbit, are suggestive of a rabbit; **femme à idées,** woman of, with, ideas; (*b*) imagination; **essayez de vous faire une i. de notre situation,** try to imagine our position; **voir qch. en i.,** to see sth. in the mind's eye; **pays des idées,** world of fancy; **se faire des idées,** to imagine things; **c'est une i. que vous vous faites,** it's mere fancy; **i. fixe,** obsession, idée fixe; (*c*) view, opinion; **avoir une haute i. d'un tableau,** to have a high opinion of a picture; **je n'ai pas une bien haute i. de son travail,** I don't think much of his work; **avoir des idées arrêtées sur qch.,** to have set ideas, very decided views, on sth.; **agir selon son i., faire à son i.,** to act according to one's own ideas; **faites à votre i.,** do as you think best, as you think fit; **en faire à son i.,** to do just what one likes; **changer d'i.,** to change, alter, one's mind, one's opinion; (*d*) whim, fancy; **comme l'i. m'en prend,** just as the fancy takes me; **avoir des idées noires,** to have (a fit of) the blues, to be depressed; **étudier l'anglais dans, avec, l'i. de s'établir à l'étranger,** to study English with the idea of, with a view to, settling abroad; **il faut la laisser se marier à son i.,** we must let her marry according to her fancy, her own idea. 2. mind; **j'ai dans l'i. que . . ,** I have a notion that . . . ; **il me vient à l'i. que . . ,** it occurs to me that . . . ; **il ne me vint pas à l'i. que . . ,** it never entered my head that . . . ; **je ne peux pas lui ôter cela de l'i.,** I can't get that out of his mind; **cela m'est sorti de l'i.,** it has gone clean out of my mind, head; **il me revient à l'i., en l'i., que je l'ai laissé à la maison,** now I remember that I left it at home. 3. *F:* very small quantity; **une i. de vanille,** just a suspicion of vanilla; **ruban une i. trop bleu,** ribbon a thought too blue.

idée-force [idefɔrs], *s.f. Psy:* idée-force; *pl.* **idées-forces.**

idéen, -enne [ideɛ̃, -ɛn], *a. & s. Gr.Ant:* Idaean, from Mount Ida.

idéer [idee], *v.tr. Psy:* to ideate.

idem [idɛm], *adv.* idem, id.; ditto.

idempotent [idãpɔtã], *a. Mth:* idempotent.

identifiable [idãtifjabl], *a.* identifiable.

identificateur, -trice [idãtifikatœːr, -tris]. 1. *a.* identifying, identificatory. 2. *s.m.* (computers) identifier.

identification [idãtifikasjɔ̃], *s.f.* identifying, identification; *Mil: Av:* authentication; **signal, code, d'i.,** authentication signal, code; **dispositif, matériel, électronique d'i.,** identification friend or foe (I.F.F.); *Av:* **feu d'i.,** identification light; *Med:* **i. des types (de bactéries ou de virus),** typing.

identifier [idãtifje], *v.tr.* (*p.d. & pr.sub.* n. **iden-tifiions, v. identifiiez**) to identify. 1. to make identical, to consider as identical. 2. to establish the identity of (s.o., sth.). **s'identifier à une cause, à un parti,** to identify oneself, to become identified, with a cause, with a party; **Molière s'identifie avec le personnage d'Alceste,** Molière himself may be identified with the character of Alceste; **le lecteur s'identifie avec le héros du roman,** the reader identifies himself with the hero of the novel.

identique [idãtik] (*a*) *a.* identical, the very same; **projet i. au nôtre,** plan identical with ours; *Nau:* **bâtiments identiques,** sister ships; (*b*) *s.m.* **le principe des identiques,** the principle of the identical; *Typ:* **impression en i.,** offset.

identiquement [idãtikmã], *adv.* identically.

identité [idãtite], *s.f.* identity. 1. **i. de signification de deux termes,** identity of meaning of two terms. 2. *Mil:* **plaque d'i.,** identification disk, identity disk; **bracelet d'i.,** identity bracelet, identification bracelet; *Adm:* **carte d'i.,** identity card; **pièces d'i.,** identification papers; **payable sur présentation de pièces d'i.,** payable on proof of identity; **établir son i.,** to prove one's identity; **le Bureau d'i., l'I. judiciaire** = the Criminal Records Office. 3. *Mth:* identity. 4. *Phil:* **le principe d'i.,** the identity principle, the law of identity.

idéogramme [ideogram], *s.m.* ideogram, ideograph, picture symbol.

idéographie [ideografi], *s.f.* ideography.

idéographique [ideografik], *a.* ideographic(al).

idéologie [ideolɔʒi], *s.f.* 1. *Phil:* ideology. 2. *Pej:* ideology, vague theorizing, impractical views. 3. *Pol:* ideology; **la révolution du xxe siècle est d'abord une politique et une i.,** the 20th-century revolution is first and foremost a policy and an ideology.

idéologique [ideolɔʒik], *a.* ideological.

idéologue [ideolɔg], *s.m.* 1. ideologist. 2. ideologue, theorist, visionary.

idéo-moteur, -trice [ideomotœːr, -tris], *a. Psy:* ideomotor; *pl.* **idéo-moteurs, -trices.**

ides [id], *s.f.pl. Rom.Ant:* ides.

idiacanthus [idjakãtyːs], *s.m. Ich:* idiacanthus.

idioblaste [idjoblast], *s.m. Biol:* idioblast.

idiochromatique [idjokromatik], *a.* idiochromatic.

idiochromosome [idjokromozoːm], *s.m. Biol:* idiochromosome.

idiocyclophane [idjosiklofan], *a. Cryst:* idio-(cyclo)phanous.

idio-électrique [idjoelektrik], *a.* idio-electric; *pl.* **idio-électriques.**

idiogame [idjogam], *a. Bot:* idiogamous.

idiogamie [idjogami], *s.f. Bot:* idiogamy.

idioglossie [idjoglɔsi], *s.f. Med:* idioglossia.

idiogramme [idjogram], *s.m. Biol:* idiogram.

idiomatique [idjomatik], *a.* idiomatic; **expression i.,** idiom.

idiome [idjoːm], *s.m.* (*a*) idiom, dialect; (*b*) language.

idiomorphe [idjomorf], *a. Geol:* idiomorphic.

idiomusculaire [idjomyskyleːr], *a. Anat:* idio-muscular.

idiopathie [idjopati], *s.f.* idiopathy.

idiopathique [idjopatik], *a.* idiopathic(al).

idiophone [idjofɔn], *s.m. Mus:* idiophone.

idioplasme [idjoplasm], *s.m. Biol:* idioplasm.

idiorrythmie [idjoritmi], *s.f. Rel:* idiorrythmism, idiorrythmy.

idiosome [idjozoːm], *s.m. Biol:* idiosome.

idiostatique [idjostatik], *a. El:* idiostatic.

idiosyncrasie [idjosɛ̃krazi], *s.f. Med:* idiosyncrasy.

idiosyncrasique [idjosɛ̃krazik], *a.* idiosyncratic.

idiot, -ote [idjo, -ɔt]. 1. *a.* (*a*) *Med:* idiot (child, etc.); (*b*) idiotic, absurd, mad; senseless (joke, etc.); **réflexion idiote,** idiotic remark; **ce serait i. de refuser,** it would be mad, absurd, to refuse; **si vous êtes assez i. pour le croire,** if you're stupid enough to believe it; **c'est i.!** it's absurd. 2. *s.* (*a*) *Med:* idiot, imbecile; **i. congénital,** congenital idiot; *F:* **l'i. du village,** the village idiot; (*b*) idiot, fool, *F:* clot, dope; **me prenez-vous pour un i.?** do you take me for a fool? **faire l'i.,** to act, play, the fool; *F:* **espèce d'i.!** you clot!

idiotement [idjotmã], *adv.* idiotically, stupidly.

idiotie [idjosi], *s.f.* 1. *Med:* (*a*) idiocy, imbecility; **i. congénitale,** congenital idiocy; (*b*) mental deficiency. 2. (*a*) stupidity (of pers., etc.); **l'i. du public,** the stupidity of the public; (*b*) stupid action, saying; **ne dites pas d'idioties!** don't talk rubbish! **ce journal est rempli d'idioties,** this paper is full of nonsense; **faire une i.,** to do sth. stupid; (*c*) *F:* stupid, rubbishy, book, film.

idiotifier [idjotifje], *v.tr.* to make stupid; to stupefy.

idiotique [idjotik], *a.* idiomatic (expression, etc.).

idiotiser [idjotize], *v.tr.* (*rare*) 1. to reduce (s.o.) to a state of imbecility. 2. to daze, to stupefy.

idiotisme[1] [idjotism], *s.m.* 1. *Med:* idiocy. 2. *A:* stupidity.

idiotisme[2], *s.m. Ling:* idiom, idiomatic expression, phrase.

idiste [idist], *Ling:* 1. *a.* idoistic. 2. *s.m. or f.* idoist.

idite [idit], *s.f.*, **iditol** [iditɔl], *s.m. Ch:* idite, iditol.

ido [ido], *s.m. Ling:* ido.

idocrase [idokraːz], *s.f. Miner:* idocrase.

idoine [idwan], *a.* (*a*) *A: or Jur:* fit, able; suitable, proper; *Jur:* **apte et i. à tester,** fit and competent to make a will; (*b*) *Hum:* **voilà l'homme i.,** there's the very man (for the job, etc.); **c'est i. et adéquat,** it fills the bill.

idolâtre [idolɑːtr]. 1. *a.* idolatrous; **être i. de qn, de qch.,** to idolize, to be passionately fond of, s.o., sth. 2. *s.* idolater, *f.* idolatress.

idolâtrement [idolatrəmã], *adv.* (*rare*) idola-trously.

idolâtrer [idolatre], *v.* to idolize. 1. *v.i.* to worship idols, to practise idolatry. 2. *v.tr.* to be passionately fond of (s.o., sth.); **i. son corps,** to worship one's body; **i. ses enfants,** to idolize one's children.

idolâtrie [idolatri], *s.f.* idolatry; **aimer qn jusqu'à l'i.,** to idolize, worship, s.o.

idolâtrique [idolatrik], *a.* idolatrous.

idole [idol], *s.f.* (*a*) idol, image; **adorer des idoles,** to worship idols; **culte des idoles,** idolatry; **faire une i. de qn,** to idolize s.o.; **faire son i. de l'argent,** to worship money, to make a god of money; **ne vous tenez pas là comme une i.,** don't stand there like a wooden image; (*b*) idol (of the public; (*c*) *s.m. or f. A:* phantom, shadow.

Idoménée [idomene], *Pr.n.m. Gr.Lit:* Idomeneus.

idonéité [idoneite], *s.f. Ecc:* idoneity.

idonique [idonik], *a. Ch:* idonic (acid).

idosaccharique [idosakarik], *a. Ch:* idosaccharic.

idose [idoːz], *s.m. Ch:* idose.

idothée [idote], **idothea** [idotea], *s.f. Crust:* idothea.

idrialite [idrijalit], *s.f. Miner:* idrialite.

Idumée [idyme], *Pr.n.f. A.Geog:* Idumaea.

iduméen, -enne [idymeɛ̃, -ɛn], *a. & s.* Idumaean.

idylle [idil], *s.f.* (*a*) *Lit:* idyll; (*b*) idyll, romance; **i. entre deux jeunes gens,** romance between two young people.

idyllique [idilik], *a.* idyllic.

idylliste [idilist], *s.m.* idyllist.

ièble [jɛbl], *s.f. Bot:* dwarf elder.

-iel, -ielle [jɛl], *a.suff.* -ial; **circonstanciel,** circum-stantial; **présidentiel,** presidential; **torrentiel,** torrential.

Iéna [jena], *Pr.n. Geog:* Jena.

iénois, -oise [jenwa, -waːz], *a. & s. Geog:* (native, inhabitant) of Jena.

if [if], *s.m.* 1. *Bot:* yew (tree); **if du Canada,** ground hemlock. 2. (*a*) triangular frame (for illumination lights, for signals, etc.); *Ecc:* taper-hearse; (*b*) draining rack (for bottles).

igame [igam], *s.m.* (see I.G.A.M.E.) = inspecteur général de l'Administration en mission extra-ordinaire), administrator in charge of the prefects of a large district.

igamie [igami], *s.f.* territory administered by an *igame.*

igloo, iglou [iglu], *s.m.* igloo.

Ignace [iɲas], *Pr.n.m.* Ignatius; **I. de Loyola,** Ignatius Loyola.

ignacien [iɲasjɛ̃], *s.m. Rel.H:* Ignatian, *Pej:* Jesuit.

igname [iɲam], *s.f. Bot:* yam, Indian potato.

ignare [iɲaːr]. 1. *a.* ignorant, illiterate. 2. *s.m. or f.* ignoramus.

igné [iɲe], *a.* 1. *Lit:* fiery. 2. *Geol:* igneous (rock, etc.).

ignescent [iɲɛs(s)ã], *a.* ignescent.

ignicole [iɲikɔl]. 1. *a.* fire-worshipping. 2. *s.m. or f.* fire-worshipper.

ignicolle [iɲikɔl], *a.* with flame-coloured neck or back.

ignicolore [ignikɔlɔːr], *a.* of a bright metallic red; *Orn:* **houppifère i.**, fireback, firebacked pheasant.

ignifère [ignifɛːr], *a.* igniferous.

ignifugation [ignifygasjɔ̃], *s.f.* fireproofing (of wood, etc.).

ignifuge [ignifyːʒ]. **1.** *a.* (*a*) non-inflammable, fire-resisting, fireproof; *U.S:* fire-resistant; (*b*) **grenade i.**, fire extinguisher. **2.** *s.m.* fireproof, fireproofing, material.

ignifugeant [ignifyʒɑ̃]. **1.** *a.* fireproofing (bath, etc.). **2.** *s.m.* fireproofing agent.

ignifugé [ignifyʒe], *a.* fireproofed (material).

ignifugeage [ignifyʒaːʒ], *s.m.* fireproofing.

ignifuger [ignifyʒe], *v.tr.* **(j'ignifugeai(s); n. ignifugeons)** to fireproof.

ignigène [igniʒɛn], *a.* ignigenous.

ignimbrite [ignɛ̃brit], *s.f. Geol:* ignimbrite.

ignimbritique [ignɛ̃britik], *a. Geol:* **éruption i.**, acid lava eruption.

ignipuncture [ignipɔ̃ktyːr], *s.f. Med:* heat cauterization; ignipuncture.

igniteur [ignitœːr], *s.m. El:* ignitor.

ignition [ignisjɔ̃], *s.f.* (state of) ignition; (*cp.* ALLUMAGE = act of ignition); **mettre qch. en i.**, to ignite sth.

ignitron [ignitrɔ̃], *s.m. El:* ignitron.

ignitubulaire [ignitybylɛːr], *a. Mch:* **chaudière i.**, fire-tube boiler.

ignivome [ignivɔm, -voːm], *a. Lit:* ignivomous, fire-emitting (volcano, dragon, etc.).

ignivore [ignivɔːr]. **1.** *a.* ignivorous, fire-eating. **2.** *s.m. & f.* fire-eater.

ignobilité [iɲɔbilite], *s.f.* **1.** *A:* low birth. **2.** ignobility, baseness.

ignoble [iɲɔbḷ], *a.* **1.** *A:* low-born. **2.** (*a*) ignoble; base (person); vile, disgraceful, unspeakable (conduct, etc.); (*b*) wretched, filthy (dwelling, etc.); (*c*) *Ven:* untrainable (hawk); **oiseau i.**, ignoble, short-winged, hawk.

ignoblement [iɲɔbləmɑ̃], *adv.* ignobly; basely, disgracefully.

ignominie [iɲɔmini], *s.f.* ignominy, shame, disgrace.

ignominieusement [iɲɔminjøzmɑ̃], *adv.* ignominiously.

ignominieux, -ieuse [iɲɔminjø, -jøːz], *a.* ignominious, shameful, disgraceful.

ignorable [iɲɔrabḷ], *a.* the ignorance of which is excusable.

ignoramment [iɲɔramɑ̃], *adv. A:* ignorantly.

ignorance [iɲɔrɑ̃ːs], *s.f.* **1.** ignorance; **par i.**, through, out of, ignorance; **laisser qn dans l'i. de qch.**, to keep s.o. in ignorance of sth., in the dark about sth.; **les siècles d'i.**, the dark ages; **peuple plongé dans l'i.**, benighted people; *Jur:* **prétendre cause d'i.**, to plead ignorance. **2.** *pl.* errors, mistakes, blunders.

ignorant, -ante [iɲɔrɑ̃, -ɑ̃ːt]. **1.** *a.* (*a*) ignorant; **élève i.**, ignorant pupil; **i. en latin**, unacquainted with Latin; who has not learnt Latin; (*b*) **i. de qch.**, ignorant of sth.; **l'homme est i. de sa destinée**, no man can tell what the future has in store for him; man is ignorant of his destiny; **il était i. des événements récents**, he did not know what had happened recently. **2.** *s.* ignoramus; **faire l'i.**, to affect ignorance.

ignorantin [iɲɔrɑ̃tɛ̃], (*a*) *a. & s.m. Rel.H:* **(frère) i.**, Ignorantine (friar); (*b*) *s. F:* ignoramus.

ignorantisme [iɲɔrɑ̃tism], *s.m.* ignorantism, obscurantism.

ignorantissime [iɲɔrɑ̃tisim], *a. F:* supremely ignorant.

ignorantiste [iɲɔrɑ̃tist], *a. & s.* ignorantist, obscurantist.

ignoré [iɲɔre], *a.* unknown; neglected; **plaisir i.**, unknown pleasure; **vivre i.**, to live in obscurity; **visiteur de marque qui souhaite que son séjour reste i.**, distinguished visitor who hopes to stay incognito; **i. de, par, ses contemporains**, (i) unknown to, (ii) ignored by, passed over by, his contemporaries.

ignorer [iɲɔre], *v.tr.* **1.** (*a*) not to know; to be ignorant of (sth.); to know nothing of (sth.); **il semble i. le prix du temps**, he doesn't seem to know the value of time; **il ignore tout de . . .**, he knows nothing whatever about . . .; **j'ignore complètement ses projets**, I'm completely in the dark about his plans; **nul n'est censé i. la loi**, ignorance of the law is no excuse; **je n'ignore pas les difficultés**, I am not blind to the difficulties; **j'ignore où je suis né**, I do not know where I was born; **il ignore qui je suis**, he does not know who I am; **j'ignore le latin**, I don't know any Latin; **il ignore le bonheur**, he has never known happiness; **ne pas i. qch.**, to be fully, well, aware of sth.; (*b*) **s'i. soi-même**, to be unaware of one's own nature; not to know oneself; **charme qui s'ignore**, unconscious charm; (*c*) (*of pers.*) (i) *A:* **chercher à se faire i.**, to attempt to avoid recognition; (ii) **i. qn**, to ignore, to snub, s.o.; (*d*) *abs.* **le savant sait qu'il ignore**, the true scholar is aware of his own ignorance; (*e*) *v.i. O:* **ne pas i. de qch.**, to be aware of sth. (*now rarely used except in* **pour que, afin que, nul, personne, n'en ignore**), so that nobody may remain in ignorance (of the fact). **2.** (*a*) (*rare*) **il ignorait vous avoir fait tant de peine**, he did not know that he had caused you so much trouble; (*b*) **i. que** (+ *sub. or* + *ind. when the fact is presented as a reality*), not to know that . . .; **j'ignorais qu'il fût arrivé**, I did not know that he had arrived; **j'ignorais que la ville avait été ravagée par un désastre**, I did not know that the town had been ravaged by a disaster; **ignoriez-vous qu'il fût de retour?** didn't you know that he had returned? **je n'ignore pas qu'il a voulu me suivre**, I am not unaware that he wanted to follow me; **personne n'ignore que l'affaire est importante**, there is nobody who does not know, nobody is unaware, that the matter is important; (*c*) **j'ignorais si vous viendriez**, I didn't know whether you were coming.

iguane [igwan], *s.m. Rept:* iguana; **faux i. australien**, lace lizard; **i. à queue épineuse**, spinytail iguana; **i. des haies**, fence lizard; **i. à queue carénée**, keeltail iguana.

iguanidés [igwanide], *s.m.pl. Rept:* Iguanidae.

iguanien, -ienne [igwanjɛ̃, -jɛn]. *Rept:* **1.** *a.* iguanian. **2.** *s.m.pl.* **iguaniens**, Iguania, iguanians.

iguanodon [igwanɔdɔ̃], *s.m. Paleont:* iguanodon.

igue [iːg], *s.f. Geol:* (*in the Causses*) jama.

ihléite [ileit], *s.f. Miner:* ihleite.

ijolit(h)e [iʒɔlit], *s.f. Geol:* ijolite.

ikse [iks], *s.m.* (the letter) x.

il, ils [il]. **1.** *pers. pron. nom. m. unstressed when preceding the vb; clings to the vb or its adjunct*; (*P: often* [i] *before a cons. or after the vb*) (*of pers.*) he, they; (*of thg*) it, they; (*of ship*) she, they; **il danse, ils chantent**, he dances, they sing; **il nous connaît**, he knows us; **où est-il?** where is he? **sont-ils arrivés?** have they come? **il ne vous a rien dit?—qui ça, il?** did he tell you nothing?—who do you mean, he? **c'est à vous ce bracelet? qu'il est joli!** is this bracelet yours? isn't it pretty! **c'est un beau navire et il s'appelle "Reine,"** she's a fine ship and she is called "Queen." **2.** *inv.* it, there; (*a*) (*anticipatory subject of vbs used impersonally*) **il est, il doit être, six heures**, it is, must be, six o'clock; **il est honteux de mentir**, it is shameful to lie; **il est facile de s'en assurer**, it is easy to make sure; **il est vrai que j'étais là**, it is true that I was there; **il arriva deux bataillons d'infanterie**, two battalions of infantry arrived; **il était une fois une fée**, once upon a time there was a fairy; (*b*) (*with impers. vbs*) **il pleut, il neige**, it is raining, it is snowing; **il est tard**, it is late; **il faut partir**, it's time to go; **il y a quelqu'un à la porte**, there is some one at the door; **y en a-t-il de reste?** is there any left?

il- [il(l)], *pref.* (*used before words beginning with* **l**) *expressing negation*; **illégitime**, illegitimate; **illicite**, illicit, unlawful; **illimité**, unlimited.

ilang-ilang [ilɑ̃ilɑ̃], *s.m. Bot:* ylang-ylang, ilang-ilang.

ildefonsite [ild(ə)fɔ̃sit], *s.f. Miner:* tantalite.

île [i(ː)l], *s.f.* **1.** (*a*) island, *Poet: & in Pr.n.* isle; **habiter dans une î.**, to live on an island; **î. rattachée**, tied island; **î. coralienne**, coral island; **î. de cordon libre**, barrier island; **l'î. de Man**, the Isle of Man; **l'î. de Wight**, the Isle of Wight; **les îles Anglo-Normandes**, the Channel Islands; **les îles du Vent**, the Windward Islands; **les îles sous le Vent**, the Leeward Islands; *A:* **l'I. de France**, Mauritius; *A:* **les Iles**, the West Indies; (*b*) *Cu:* **î. flottante**, floating island. **2.** *A:* block of houses. **3.** *Petroleum Min:* **î. de forage**, offshore drilling rig.

iléite [ileit], *s. Med:* ileitis.

iléo-cæcal [ileosekal], *a. Anat:* ileo-caecal; **valvule iléo-cæcale**, ileo-caecal valve; *pl. iléo-cæcaux, -cales.*

iléo-colique [ileɔkolik], *a. Anat:* ileo-colic; *pl. iléo-coliques.*

iléo-colostomie [ileɔkɔlɔstɔmi], *s.f. Surg:* ileocolostomy; *pl. iléo-colostomies.*

iléo-cystoplastie [ileɔsistɔplasti], *s.f. Surg:* ileocystoplasty; *pl. iléo-cystoplasties.*

iléo-iléostomie [ileɔileɔstɔmi], *s.f. Surg:* ileo-ileostomy; *pl. iléo-iléostomies.*

iléon [ileɔ̃], *s.m. Anat:* ileum.

iléo-sigmoïdostomie [ileɔsigmɔidɔstɔmi], *s.f. Surg:* ileosigmoidostomy; *pl. iléo-sigmoïdostomies.*

iléostomie [ileɔstɔmi], *s.f. Surg:* ileostomy.

iles [il], *s.m.pl. Anat:* ilia, flanks.

ilésite [ilezit], *s.f. Miner:* ilesite.

îlet [ilɛ], *s.m.*, **îlette** [ilɛt], *s.f.* **1.** *A:* small island. **2.** (*in Réunion*) hamlet.

iléum [ileɔm], *s.m. Anat:* ileum.

iléus [ileyːs], *s.m. Med:* ileus; acute, chronic, intestinal obstruction.

ilex [ilɛks], *s.m. Bot:* ilex. **1.** holly. **2.** holm oak.

Iliade (l') [liljad], *s.f. Gr.Lit:* the Iliad.

iliaque[1] [iljak], *a. Gr.Hist:* relating to Ilium, Ilian, Iliac.

iliaque[2], *a. Anat:* iliac; **os i.**, hip bone; **muscle i.**, iliacus.

ilicacées [ilikase], **ilicinées** [ilisine], *s.f.pl. Bot:* Ilicaceae.

îlien, -ienne [iljɛ̃, -jɛn] (*esp. on Breton coast*). **1.** *a.* island (tradition, etc.). **2.** *s.* islander.

ilio-lombaire [iljɔlɔ̃bɛːr], *a. Anat:* ilio-lumbar; *pl. ilio-lombaires.*

ilion[1] [iljɔ̃], *s.m. Anat:* ilium.

Ilion[2], *Pr.n.m. A.Geog:* Ilium, Troy.

ilio-pectiné [iljɔpɛktine], *a.* iliopectineal; *pl. ilio-pectiné(e)s.*

ilio-pubien, -ienne [iljɔpybjɛ̃, -jɛn], *a.* iliopubic; *pl. ilio-pubiens, -iennes.*

ilium [iljɔm], *s.m. Anat:* ilium.

illabourable [il(l)aburabḷ], *a.* untillable.

illacérable [il(l)aserabḷ], *a.* untearable.

illatif, -ive [il(l)atif, -iːv], *a. Gram: Log:* illative.

illation [il(l)asjɔ̃], *s.f. Log:* illation.

illécèbre [il(l)esɛbr], *s.f. Bot:* whorled knotgrass, knotwort.

illégal, -aux [il(l)egal, -o], *a.* illegal, unlawful; *Mil: etc:* **absence illégale**, absence without leave; A.W.O.L.

illégalement [il(l)egalmɑ̃], *adv.* illegally, unlawfully.

illégaliste [il(l)egalist], *a. & s. Pol:* (person) who favours illegal action.

illégalité [il(l)egalite], *s.f.* illegality. **1.** unlawfulness. **2.** unlawful act.

illégitime [il(l)eʒitim]. **1.** *a.* illegitimate (child, etc.); unlawful (marriage, etc.); unwarranted (claim, etc.); spurious (title). **2.** *s.f. F:* mistress.

illégitimement [il(l)eʒitim(ə)mɑ̃], *adv.* illegitimately, unlawfully.

illégitimité [il(l)eʒitimite], *s.f.* illegitimacy (of child); unlawfulness (of marriage); unwarranted nature (of claim); spuriousness (of title).

illésé [il(l)eze], *a.* uninjured, unhurt.

illettré, -ée [il(l)ɛtre, il(l)etre], *a. & s.*, illiterate, uneducated (person).

illibéral, -aux [il(l)iberal, -o], *a.* illiberal; (*a*) narrow-minded; (*b*) avaricious, mean; (*c*) restrictive of freedom.

illibéralité [il(l)iberalite], *s.f.* illiberality; (*a*) narrow-mindedness; (*b*) meanness, lack of generosity.

illicite [il(l)isit], *a.* illicit, unlawful; *Sp:* **coup i.**, foul (stroke, blow, etc.).

illicitement [il(l)isitmɑ̃], *adv.* illicitly, unlawfully.

illico [iliko], *adv. F:* at once, then and there; here and now.

illimitable [il(l)imitabḷ], *a.* illimitable, boundless.

illimitation [il(l)imitasjɔ̃], *s.f. A. & Lit:* unlimitedness; absence of limits.

illimité [il(l)imite], *a.* unlimited, boundless, unbounded; **congé i.**, indefinite leave; *Fin:* **responsabilité illimitée**, unlimited liability.

illimiter [il(l)imite], *v.tr.* (*rare*) not to limit, not to set bounds to.

illipé [il(l)ipe], *s.m. Bot:* illipe; **beurre, huile, d'i.**, illipe butter, mahua butter.

illiquéfié [il(l)ikefje], *a.* unliquefied.

illiquide [il(l)ikid], *a. Fin:* unrealizable, unmarketable, tied up, unavailable, frozen (assets).

illisibilité [il(l)izibilite], *s.f.* illegibility; unreadableness.

illisible [il(l)izibḷ], *a.* **1.** illegible, unreadable (writing, etc.). **2.** unreadable (book, etc.).

illisiblement [il(l)isibləmɑ̃], *adv.* illegibly.

illogicité [il(l)ɔʒisite], *s.f.* illogicality; inconsequence; inconsistency (of reasoning).

illogique [il(l)ɔʒik], *a.* illogical; inconsequent; inconsistent.

illogiquement [il(l)ɔʒikmɑ̃], *adv.* illogically; inconsistently.

illogisme [il(l)ɔʒism], *s.m.* **1.** illogicality. **2.** *pl.* illogicalities; inconsistencies.

illudérite [il(l)yderit], *s.f. Miner:* zoisite.

illuminable [il(l)yminabḷ], *a.* illuminable. **1.** that can be lit up. **2. l'âme est i.**, the soul may be illuminated, enlightened.

illuminant [il(l)yminɑ̃]. **1.** *a.* illuminant, illuminating. **2.** *s.m.* illuminant.

illuminateur [il(l)yminatœːr], *s.m.* **1.** illuminator (of building, etc.). **2.** illuminer (of the soul or mind); enlightener.

illuminatif, -ive [il(l)yminatif, -iːv], *a. Theol:* illuminative.

illumination [il(l)yminasjɔ̃], *s.f.* illumination. **1.** (*a*) lighting (of town, room, etc.); **i. de plafond,** ceiling illumination; **i. par projecteurs,** flood-lighting; (*b*) *pl.* lights, illuminations. **2.** (inward) light; enlightenment; inspiration.

illuminé, -ée [il(l)ymine], *s.* (*a*) *Rel.H:* Illuminee; *s.m.pl.* **illuminés,** Illuminati; (*b*) *F:* (i) crank; (ii) *a.* cranky.

illuminer [il(l)ymine], *v.tr.* **1.** (*a*) to illuminate (for festivity); (*b*) to light up; **la lune en son plein illuminait la route,** the full moon lit up the road; **visage illuminé d'un sourire de triomphe,** face lit up by a triumphant smile. **2.** (*a*) *Rel: Phil:* to enlighten, illumine; (*b*) *A:* to give sight to (the blind).

s'illuminer, to light up; **ses yeux s'illuminèrent de joie,** his eyes lit up with joy.

illuminisme [il(l)yminism], *s.m. Rel.H:* Illuminism.

illuministe [il(l)yminist], (*a*) *a.* illuministic; (*b*) *s.* Illuminist.

illusion [il(l)yzjɔ̃], *s.f.* **1.** (*a*) illusion; **i. optique,** optical illusion; **se nourrir d'illusions,** to cherish illusions; **se leurrer d'illusions,** to delude oneself; **se bercer d'illusions, de douces illusions,** to live in a fool's paradise; **se faire i. à soi-même,** to deceive oneself; to pretend to oneself; **se faire i. sur soi-même,** to have illusions about oneself; (*b*) *Tex:* tulle **i.,** illusion. **2.** delusion; **être dans l'i., se faire i.,** to labour under a delusion; **il ne se faisait aucune i. à cet égard,** he had no illusions on that point; **ses promesses nous ont fait i.,** we were led astray by his promises.

illusionnable [il(l)yzjɔnabl̩], *a.* easily deluded.

illusionnant [il(l)yzjɔnɑ̃], *a.* **1.** illusory. **2.** delusive, delusory.

illusionner [il(l)yzjɔne], *v.tr.* to delude, deceive; **la distance nous illusionne sur la forme des objets,** distance give one illusions as to the shape of objects.

s'illusionner, to labour under a delusion; to delude oneself; to deceive oneself.

illusionnisme [il(l)yzjɔnism], *s.m.* **1.** tendency to cherish illusions. **2.** art of the illusionist; conjuring.

illusionniste [il(l)yzjɔnist], *s.m. & f.* illusionist, conjurer.

illusoire [il(l)yzwaːr], *a.* illusory (promise, etc.); illusive; **le sens de la vue est le plus i.,** the sense of sight is the most illusive.

illusoirement [il(l)yzwarmɑ̃], *adv.* illusively; illusorily.

illustrateur [il(l)ystratœːr], *s.m.* **1.** illustrator (of books, etc.). **2.** *A:* **i. d'une ville,** one who has brought renown to, shed lustre upon, a town; an honour to his (native) town.

illustration [il(l)ystrasjɔ̃], *s.f.* **1.** *A:* (*a*) rendering illustrious; shedding of lustre (upon town, etc.); **ces victoires contribuèrent à l'i. de son règne,** these victories added lustre to his reign; (*b*) celebrated person; celebrity; **on avait convié toutes les illustrations de la ville,** all the people of note in the town had received invitations. **2.** *Art:* illustration; (*a*) illustrating; *Publ:* art work; (*b*) picture; *Typ:* cut; **i. en couleur,** coloured illustration. **3.** (*a*) annotating, expounding, elucidation (of a text, etc.); (*b*) *A: pl.* notes, scholia.

illustre [il(l)ystr̩], *a.* illustrious, famous, renowned.

illustré [il(l)ystre]. **1.** *a.* illustrated; **abondamment i.,** profusely illustrated. **2.** *s.m.* illustrated magazine.

illustrement [il(l)ystrəmɑ̃], *adv.* illustriously.

illustrer [il(l)ystre], *v.tr.* **1.** *A: or Lit:* to render illustrious; **région illustrée par ses vins,** district renowned, famous, for its wines; **ouvrage qui l'a illustré,** work that has made him celebrated, famous; **dialecte illustré par plusieurs œuvres littéraires,** dialect that boasts several literary works. **2.** to illustrate (book, etc.); **carte postale illustrée,** picture postcard. **3.** (*a*) to make clear, throw light upon, annotate, elucidate (obscure text, etc.); **i. la définition d'un mot par des citations,** to illustrate, explain, the definition of a word by means of quotations; (*b*) *Theol:* to enlighten.

s'illustrer, *A:* to become famous (**par,** for, through); to win fame, renown.

illustrissime [il(l)ystrisim], *a.* most illustrious.

illutation [il(l)ytasjɔ̃], *s.f.* **1.** *Const:* coating with mud; luting. **2.** *Med:* mud bath; mud cure.

illuter [il(l)yte], *v.tr. Med:* to bathe (patient) in mud, to illutate.

illuvial, -aux [il(l)yvjal, -o], *a. Geol:* illuvial.

illuviation [il(l)yvjasjɔ̃], *s.f. Geol:* illuviation.

illuvion [il(l)yvjɔ̃], **illuvium** [il(l)yvjɔm], *s.m. Geol:* illuvium.

Illyrie [il(l)iri], *Pr.n.f. Hist:* Illyria.

illyrien, -ienne [il(l)irjɛ̃, -jɛn], *a. & s.* Illyrian.

illyrique [il(l)irik], *a.* Illyric.

illyrisme [il(l)irism], *s.m. Hist:* the Illyrian movement.

ilménite [ilmenit], *s.f. Miner:* ilmenite.

ilménorutile [ilmenɔrytil], *s.m. Miner:* ilmenorutile.

îlot [ilo], *s.m.* **1.** islet, small island. **2.** (*a*) block (of houses); (*World War II*) **chef d'i.,** air-raid warden; (*b*) **ces villages de pêcheurs, petits îlots de cabanes,** these fishing villages, little islands, groups, of huts; (*c*) *Mil:* **i. de resistance,** pocket, point, of resistance; **î. de résistance aux autorités d'occupation,** nucleus of resistance against the occupation authorities. **3.** *Med:* **ilots pancréatiques, de Langerhans,** islands of Langerhans. **4.** super-structure, island, (of aircraft carrier).

ilote [ilɔt], *s.m. Gr.Hist:* helot.

îlotier [ilotje], *s.m.* policeman who supervises a block of houses.

ilotisé [ilɔtize], *a.* reduced to a state of helotism, helotized.

ilotisme [ilɔtism], *s.m.* (*a*) *Gr.Hist:* helotism, helotry; (*b*) state of abjection, of ignorance.

ilvaïte [ilvait], *s.f. Miner:* ilvaite.

ilysanthes [ilizɑ̃tɛs], *s.m. Bot:* ilysanthes; false hedge hyssop.

im- [im, ɛ̃], *pref.* im-, un-; **immaculé,** immaculate; **immérité,** unmerited.

image [imaːʒ], *s.f.* image. **1.** (*a*) reflection; **voir son i. dans l'eau,** to see one's reflection in the water; (*b*) *Opt:* **i. réelle,** real image; **i. virtuelle,** virtual image; **i. blanche,** ghost image; *Phot:* **i. latente,** latent image; (*c*) *Cin: T.V:* frame; *Cin:* **i. normale,** normal key, plain-key, middle-key, picture; **i. très lumineuse,** high-key picture; **i. sombre,** low-key picture; *T.V:* **i. de télévision,** television picture; **i. double, i. fantôme,** echo, ghost, double, image; **émission à 25 images par seconde,** emission at 25 frames per second; (*d*) **i. radar,** radar picture, display; **i. fantôme,** ghost image; **i. de fond, i. parasite,** clutter; **i. panoramique,** plan-position-indicator picture. **2.** likeness, representation; (*a*) **l'i. vivante de son père,** the living image of his father; **Dieu créa l'homme à son i.,** God created man in his own image; (*b*) statue; **culte des images,** image worship; (*c*) picture; figure; **livre d'images,** picture book; **il dessina l'i. d'un chat,** he drew the figure of a cat; **i. d'Épinal,** an early form of strip cartoon; **ça fait i. d'Épinal,** it's rather naïve; **écriture en images,** pictorial writing; **être sage comme une i.,** to be as good as gold; (*of pers.*) **c'est une belle i.,** she's like a (beautiful) doll, she's about as approachable as a statue; (*d*) *Num:* image. **3.** (*a*) mental picture, idea, expression; **i. persistante, consécutive,** after(-)image; **expression qui fait i.,** vivid, colourful, expression; **agité par l'i. d'un malheur possible,** disturbed by the idea of a possible accident; (*b*) (public) image (of politician, product, etc.). **4.** simile; metaphor. **5.** *Psy:* **i. affective,** imago. **6.** *Ent:* imago.

imagé [imaʒe], *a.* vivid, picturesque (style, etc.); full of imagery.

image-orthicon [imaʒɔrtikɔ̃], *s.m. T.V:* image orthicon; *pl. images-orthicons.*

imager[1] [imaʒe], *v.tr.* (**j'imageai(s); n. imageons**) to colour (style, speech).

imager[2], **-ère** [imaʒe, -ɛːr], *s. A:* (i) manufacturer of, (ii) dealer in, picture-sheets, colour-prints.

imagerie [imaʒri], *s.f.* **1.** imagery. **2.** (i) manufacture of, (ii) trade in, (colour) prints.

imagier, -ière [imaʒje, -jɛːr], *s.* **1.** *A:* (*a*) drawer of pictures (for the trade); (*b*) seller of colour prints. **2.** *A:* image-maker, -carver (*esp.* for church decoration).

imaginable [imaʒinabl̩], *a.* imaginable, thinkable, conceivable; **le plus haut degré i.,** the highest degree imaginable; **tous les malheurs possibles et imaginables,** every conceivable misfortune.

imaginaire [imaʒinɛːr]. **1.** (*a*) *a.* imaginary; fancied; make-believe; *Mth:* imaginary (root, etc.); **valeur i.,** imaginary, fictitious, value; **malade i.,** hypochondriac; **conte i.,** fanciful tale; **maux imaginaires,** fancied ills, imaginary ills; (*b*) *s.m.* imaginary; **le réel cède la place à l'i.,** the real gives way to the imaginary, to make-believe. **2.** *s.f. Mth:* imaginary quantity.

imaginal, -aux [imaʒinal, -o], *a. Ent:* imaginal; **disques imaginaux,** imaginal disks, buds.

imaginateur, -trice [imaʒinatœːr, -tris], *s.* imaginer.

imaginatif, -ive [imaʒinatif, -iːv]. **1.** *a.* imaginative (faculty, person, etc.). **2.** *s.* imaginative person, person with imagination. **3.** *s.f. A. & Lit:* **imaginative,** imagination.

imagination [imaʒinasjɔ̃], *s.f.* imagination; (*a*) conception; **figurez-vous, par un effort d'i., que . . .,** picture to yourself, by a stretch of imagination, that . . .; **voir qch. en i.,** to see sth. in one's mind's eye, in one's imagination; **cela dépasse l'i.!** it's beyond belief! **imaginations d'un poète,** a poet's fantasies; (*b*) fancy, invention, **de pure i.,** baseless, unfounded, devoid of foundation; **c'est pure i.,** it is only fancy; **se faire des imaginations,** to fancy, imagine, all sorts of things.

imaginer [imaʒine], *v.tr.* to imagine. **1.** to conceive, invent, devise; **i. un projet, une méthode,** to devise, think out, a scheme, a method; **i. un dispositif,** to contrive, think up, a device; **bien imaginé,** well thought out; **c'est lui qui l'a imaginé,** he's the one who devised it, thought it out; **il imagina de renforcer . . .,** the idea struck him to strengthen . . ., he thought out a plan for strengthening . . .. **2.** (*a*) to fancy, picture; **imaginez (-vous) un peu le plaisir que cela m'a fait,** just imagine the pleasure it gave me; **comme on peut (se) l'i. . . .,** as may (well) be imagined . . .; **tout ce qu'on peut i. de plus beau, la plus belle chose qu'on puisse i.,** the finest thing imaginable; **rien de plus drôle ne saurait s'i.,** nothing funnier could be imagined; **vous n'imaginez pas comme nous sommes heureux,** you can't imagine how happy we are; **je n'imagine pas pourquoi vous le permettriez,** I can't imagine why you should allow it; **vous plaisantez, j'imagine,** you must be joking; (*b*) (= **s'imaginer**) **gardez-vous d'i. que vous soyez jolie,** don't make the mistake of thinking you are pretty.

s'imaginer, *v.tr.pr.* to delude oneself with the thought, the fancy (that . . .); to think, fancy, suppose (that . . .); **elle s'imagine que tout le monde l'admire,** she thinks, fancies, that everyone admires her; **il ne faut pas vous i. que . . .,** you must not imagine that . . .; **n'allez pas vous i. que . . .,** don't run away with the idea that . . .; **elle s'est imaginé que . . .,** she got an idea (into her head) that . . .; **je m'étais imaginé faire fortune,** I had thought I should make a fortune; **il s'imagine tout savoir,** he fancies he knows everything.

imagisme [imaʒism], *s.m. Eng.Lit:* imagism.

imagiste [imaʒist], *s.m. & f.* **1.** = IMAGIER, -IÈRE. **2.** *Eng.Lit:* imagist.

imago [imago], *s.f.* **1.** *Ent:* imago; *Fish:* **i. rousse,** red spinner. **2.** *Psy:* imago.

imam, iman [imɑ̃], *s.m. Moham.Rel:* ima(u)m.

imamat [imama], **imanat** [imana], *s.m. Moham. Rel:* imamate.

imbasculable [ɛ̃baskylabl̩], *a.* that cannot be overturned.

imbâti [ɛ̃bati], *a.* **1.** not built, unbuilt. **2.** not built over, upon; **terrains imbâtis,** building land.

imbattable [ɛ̃batabl̩], *a.* invincible; unbeatable (race-horse); **prix imbattables,** competitive, unbeatable, prices.

imbattu [ɛ̃baty], *a.* unbeaten (champion); unbroken (record).

imbécile [ɛ̃besil]. **1.** *a.* (*a*) *Med:* (i) imbecile; (ii) mentally retarded; (*b*) silly, idiotic, *F:* half-witted; **remarque i.,** idiotic remark. **2.** *s.m. & f.* (*a*) *Med:* imbecile; (*b*) idiot, fool; **le premier i. venu vous dira cela,** any fool will tell you that; **i. que je suis!** what an idiot I am! **faire l'i.,** to play, act, the fool; *F:* **espèce d'i.!** you bloody fool!

imbécilement [ɛ̃besilmɑ̃], *adv.* idiotically, foolishly.

imbécillité [ɛ̃besilite], *s.f.* **1.** (*a*) imbecility, feebleness of mind; (*b*) silliness, stupidity. **2.** *F:* stupid action, speech; **commettre des imbécillités,** to do foolish things; to act idiotically; **dire des imbécillités,** to talk nonsense, *F:* to talk (utter) rot.

imber [ɛ̃bɛːr], *s.m. Orn:* great northern diver; ember (goose), common loon.

imberbe [ɛ̃bɛrb], *a.* **1.** beardless (chin, boy, etc.); **au menton i.,** smooth-chinned; **mains imberbes,** hairless hands; *Pej:* **jeune homme i.,** raw youth, callow youth. **2.** (*of fish*) without barbels.

imbiber [ɛ̃bibe], *v.tr.* **1.** **i. qch. de qch.,** to soak, steep, sth. in sth. to imbue, impregnate, sth.

with sth.; **imbibé d'eau,** wet; **i. une éponge,** to wet a sponge; **linge imbibé d'huile,** oil-soaked rag; **être imbibé de préjugés,** to be steeped in, imbued with, prejudice. **2.** (*of liquid*) to permeate, drench, soak (sth.). **3.** to soak up, absorb, imbibe (sth.); *abs. F:* **trop i.,** to drink too much; *F:* to be a soak.

s'imbiber. 1. to become saturated (**de,** with); to absorb; **le gâteau s'imbibe de rhum,** the cake soaks up the rum; **s'i. de préjugés,** to become steeped in prejudice. **2.** (*of liquids*) to become absorbed, to sink in; **la teinture s'imbibe dans la laine,** the dye soaks into the wool.

imbibition [ɛ̃bibisjɔ̃], *s.f.* **1.** soaking; *Tchn:* impregnation. **2.** absorption; *Tchn:* imbibition (*e.g.* of water by roots); **eau d'i.,** soakage water.

imboire [ɛ̃bwaːr], *v.tr.* (*conj. like* BOIRE) *A: except for occ. use of infin. and p.p.* (*See* IMBU) (*a*) *Tchn:* to smear, coat (with grease, etc.); (*b*) to absorb (ideas, etc.).

imbriago [ɛ̃brijagɔ], *s.m. Ich: F:* imbriago; gurnard.

imbricatif, -ive [ɛ̃brikatif, -iːv], *a. Bot:* imbricative.

imbrication [ɛ̃brikasjɔ̃], *s.f.* imbrication; overlap(ping) (of tiles, scales, etc.); imbricated work; *Dent:* **i. des dents,** overlapping (of) teeth, tooth crowding.

imbrim [ɛ̃brim], *s.m. Orn:* great northern diver; ember(goose), common loon.

imbriquant [ɛ̃brikɑ̃], *a.* overlapping, imbricating (tile, etc.).

imbriqué [ɛ̃brike]. **1.** *a.* imbricate(d), overlapping; tegulated (armour); **tortue imbriquée,** hawksbill turtle; *Geol:* **structure imbriquée,** imbricate structure. **2.** *s.f. Bot:* **imbriquée,** imbricate aestivation.

imbriquer [ɛ̃brike], *v.tr.* to imbricate, to overlap; (*computers*) to interleave.

s'imbriquer, (*a*) to overlap; **des tuiles qui s'imbriquent parfaitement,** tiles with perfect overlap; **des questions économiques qui s'imbriquent dans les questions politiques,** economic questions that overlap with political matters.

imbrisable [ɛ̃brizabl̩], *a.* unbreakable.

imbroglio [ɛ̃brɔ(l)jo, ɛ̃brɔglijo], *s.m.* imbroglio; *pl. imbroglios.*

imbrûlable [ɛ̃brylabl̩], *a.* unburnable, fireproof.

imbrûlé [ɛ̃bryle], (*a*) *a.* unburnt; (*b*) *s.m. usu. pl.* **une forte proportion d'imbrûlés,** a high proportion of unburnt residue; (*c*) *a. & s.m. Ch:* sliver.

imbu [ɛ̃by]. **1.** *a.* imbued, soaked; **papier i. d'huile,** (i) oily paper; (ii) oiled paper; **i. de sa personne,** full of one's own importance; **i. de préjugés,** steeped in, imbued with, prejudice. **2.** *s.m.* flatness, dullness, streakiness (of paint).

imbuvable [ɛ̃byvabl̩], *a.* (*a*) undrinkable, not fit to drink; (*b*) *F:* (*of pers.*) insufferable.

imidazole [imidazɔl], *s.m. Ch:* imidazol(e).

imide [imid], *s.m. Ch:* imid(e).

imidoacide [imidoasid], *s.m. Ch:* imido acid.

imidoéther [imidoetɛːr], *s.m. Ch:* imido ether.

imidogène [imidoʒɛn], *s.m. Ch:* imidogen.

imine [imin], *s.f. Ch:* imin(e).

iminoéther [iminoetɛːr], *s.m. Ch:* imono ether.

imitable [imitabl̩]. *a.* **1.** imitable, **2.** deserving, worthy, of imitation.

imitateur, -trice [imitatœːr, -tris]. **1.** *s.* (*a*) imitator; **les disciples et les imitateurs de ce grand homme,** the disciples and the imitators of this great man; (*b*) *Th:* impersonator. **2.** *a.* imitative, imitating; **l'enfant humain est beaucoup plus i. que l'enfant singe,** the human child is more imitative, has greater gifts of imitation, than the young monkey.

imitatif, -ive [imitatif, -iːv], *a.* imitative (word, art, animal).

imitation [imitasjɔ̃], *s.f.* imitation. **1.** (*a*) imitating, copying; **arts d'i.,** imitative arts; **défier toute i.,** to defy imitation; **à l'i. de qn, de qch.,** in imitation, on the model, of s.o., of sth.; **l'I. de Jésus-Christ,** the Imitation of Christ; *Mus:* (*in counterpoint*) **i. régulière, canonique, contrainte,** exact imitation; **i. par mouvement contraire,** imitation in contrary motion; (*b*) mimicking; *Th:* impersonation; (*c*) forging (of signature, etc.); counterfeiting (of money). **2.** (*a*) copy; **bijoux en i.,** imitation, costume, jewellery; **manteau (en) i. loutre,** imitation sealskin coat; *Com:* coney seal coat; **pièce qui est une i. du français,** play taken from the French; (*b*) forgery, counterfeit.

imiter [imite], *v.tr.* to imitate; (*a*) **l'enfant imite ce qu'il voit,** a child imitates what it sees; **i. les vertus de ses ancêtres,** to follow the (good) example of one's ancestors; **i. le cri d'un animal,** to imitate the cry of an animal; **il leva son verre et tout le monde l'imita,** he raised his glass and everyone followed suit, did likewise; (*b*) to mimic; to take (s.o.) off; *Th:* to impersonate (s.o.); **il imitait le patron à s'y méprendre,** he could take off the boss to the life; (*c*) *Lit: etc:* to take (a style) as one's model; to copy; **celui qui n'a pas commencé par i. ne sera jamais original,** the man who does not begin by imitating will never be original; **son ouvrage est imité de l'espagnol,** his work is modelled on the Spanish; *Pej:* **ceux qui imitent servilement,** servile imitators; plagiarists; **le peintre et le poète imitent les couleurs de la nature,** the painter and the poet reproduce the colours of nature; (*d*) **des peintures sur fond d'or imitant la mosaïque,** paintings on a gold background in imitation of mosaics, to give an effect of mosaic; (*e*) to forge (signature); to counterfeit (coin).

imma [ima], *s.m.* red ochre.

immaculé [im(m)akyle], *a.* immaculate; stainless, unspotted; undefiled; *Theol:* **l'Immaculée Conception,** the Immaculate Conception.

immanence [im(m)anɑ̃ːs], *s.f.* immanence.

immanent [im(m)anɑ̃], *a.* immanent; **ce n'est que justice immanente,** it's only a just retribution.

immanentisme [im(m)anɑ̃tism], *s.m. Phil:* immanentism.

immanentiste [im(m)anɑ̃tist], *a. & s.m. & f. Phil:* immanentist.

immangeable [ɛ̃mɑ̃ʒabl̩], *a.* (*a*) uneatable; (*b*) inedible.

immaniable [ɛ̃manjabl̩], *a.* **1.** unmanageable, intractable; unworkable (ship). **2.** unwieldy, unhandy.

immanœuvrable [ɛ̃manœvrabl̩], *a. Nau:* unmanageable, unworkable (vessel).

immanquable [ɛ̃mɑ̃kabl̩], *a.* **1.** (target, etc.) that cannot be missed. **2.** certain, unavoidable, inevitable (event, etc.).

immanquablement [ɛ̃mɑ̃kabləmɑ̃], *adv.* inevitably, without fail, for certain; **ils périront i.,** they are bound to perish.

immarcescible [ɛ̃marsɛsibl̩], *a. Lit:* unfading, incorruptible.

immariable [ɛ̃marjabl̩], *a.* unmarriageable.

immatérialiser [im(m)aterjalize], *v.tr.* to immaterialize.

immatérialisme [im(m)aterjalism], *s.m. Phil:* immaterialism.

immatérialiste [im(m)aterjalist], *s.m. & f.* immaterialist.

immatérialité [im(m)aterjalite], *s.f.* immateriality.

immatériel, -ielle [im(m)aterjɛl], *a.* **1.** immaterial, unsubstantial. **2.** intangible (assets, etc.).

immatériellement [im(m)aterjɛlmɑ̃], *adv.* immaterially.

immatriculation [im(m)atrikylasjɔ̃], *s.f.* **1.** registering, registration (of deed, of rolling stock, etc.); *Aut:* **plaque d'i.,** number plate; **numéro d'i.,** registration number. **2.** enrolment, enrolling; *Mil: etc:* taking on the strength.

immatricule [im(m)atrikyl], *s.f.* **1.** registration (of deed, etc.). **2.** registration number, certificate.

immatriculer [im(m)atrikyle], *v.tr.* to enter (s.o., sth.) on a register. **1.** to register (document, car, rolling stock, etc.); **une voiture immatriculée 8789 UK 75,** a car with registration number 8789 UK 75. **2.** to enrol (s.o.); *Mil: etc:* to enter (man) on the strength; *Adm:* **il y a deux millions d'immatriculés,** there are two million (annuitants, etc.) on the registers.

immature [im(m)atyːr], *a. Biol: etc:* immature; **les cellules immatures sont nombreuses dans les tumeurs malignes,** immature cells are numerous in malignant tumours.

immaturité [im(m)atyrite], *s.f.* immaturity.

immédiat [im(m)edja(t)], *a.* immediate. **1.** (*a*) direct (cause, successor, etc.); *Ch:* **analyse immédiate,** proximate analysis; *Phil:* **connaissance immédiate,** immediate knowledge; (*b*) close at hand; near; **dans le voisinage i. de . . .,** in close vicinity to . . ., in the immediate vicinity of . . .; *Mil:* **contre-attaque immédiate,** local counter-attack; (*c*) urgent (question, etc.). **2.** without delay; **exiger une réponse immédiate,** to demand an immediate answer; **dans un avenir i.,** in the immediate future; **(mécanisme) à action immédiate,** quick-action, quick-acting (mechanism). **3.** *s.m.* immediate future; **dans l'i.,** in the immediate future.

immédiatement [im(m)edjatmɑ̃], *adv.* immediately. **1.** without interval; **il me précède, me suit, i.,** he is next before me, next after me. **2.** directly, at once, forthwith; **i. après,** directly afterwards. **3.** *Phil:* without intermediary.

immédiateté [im(m)edjat(ə)te], *s.f. Phil: A.Jur:* immediacy.

immédité [im(m)edite], *a.* un(pre)meditated.

immémorable [im(m)emɔrabl̩], *a.* not worthy to be remembered, not memorable.

immémorant [im(m)emɔrɑ̃], *a. A:* forgetful.

immémoré [im(m)emɔre], *a.* unremembered, forgotten.

immémorial, -iaux [im(m)emɔrjal, -jo], *a.* immemorial; **de temps immémoriaux,** time out of mind; from, since, time immemorial.

immémorialement [im(m)emɔrjalmɑ̃], *adv.* (*rare*) immemorially; from time immemorial.

immense [im(m)ɑ̃ːs], *a.* **1.** immeasurable, boundless. **2.** immense, vast, huge; *F:* **c'est i.,** it's great, wonderful; *adv.* **voir i.,** to have visions of vast possibilities; to envisage things on a large scale.

immensément [im(m)ɑ̃semɑ̃], *adv.* immensely, hugely; **i. riche,** enormously rich.

immensité [im(m)ɑ̃site], *s.f.* **1.** immensity, infinity. **2.** vastness, immense extent; boundlessness; boundless space; **l'i. de l'océan,** the vastness of the ocean.

immensurable [im(m)ɑ̃syrabl̩], *a.* immensurable, immeasurable.

immerger [im(m)ɛrʒe], *v.tr.* (**j'immergeai(s); n, immergeons**) **1.** (*a*) to immerse, plunge, dip; *Tg:* **i. un câble,** to lay a cable; *Ind: etc:* **i. des déchets,** to get rid of, dispose of, wastes into the sea; **bois qui résiste longtemps immergé,** wood that lasts well under water; (*b*) to drop (a body) overboard (in funeral at sea), to bury at sea; to commit (a body) to the deep. **2.** *Astr:* to occult.

s'immerger. 1. (*of ship*) to settle. **2.** *Astr:* to be occulted.

immérité [im(m)erite], *a.* unmerited, undeserved.

imméritoire [im(m)eritwaːr], *a.* unmeritorious.

immersif, -ive [im(m)ɛrsif, -iːv], *a. Ph: Ch:* by (means of) immersion.

immersion [im(m)ɛrsjɔ̃], *s.f.* **1.** immersion, dipping; *Tg:* laying (of cable); *Astr:* occultation; *Opt:* **objectif à i.,** immersion objective; *Nau:* **sonar à i. variable,** variable-depth sonar; *Ind: etc:* **i. des déchets,** disposal of wastes into the sea. **2.** submergence, submersion (of submarine); **vitesse en i.,** speed submerged. **3.** *Nau:* committal (of body) to the deep.

immesurable [ɛ̃məzyrabl̩], *a.* immeasurable.

immesuré [ɛ̃məzyre], *a.* unmeasured.

immettable [ɛ̃mɛtabl̩], *a.* unwearable; unfit to wear; **ton pardessus est vraiment i.,** your coat's really not fit to put on, to wear.

immeuble [im(m)œbl̩], *Jur:* **1.** *a.* real, fixed; **biens immeubles,** real estate or property. **2.** *s.m.* (*a*) real estate, landed property, realty; **vente d'immeubles,** property sale; **placer son argent en immeubles,** to invest in house property; (*b*) house, block of flats; (*c*) (business) premises.

immigrant, -ante [im(m)igrɑ̃, -ɑ̃ːt], *a. & s.* immigrant.

immigration [im(m)igrasjɔ̃], *s.f.* immigration; **pays d'i.,** country open to immigrants; **agent du service de l'i.,** immigration officer.

immigré, -ée [im(m)igre], *s.* immigrant, settler.

immigrer [im(m)igre], *v.i.* to immigrate.

imminence [im(m)inɑ̃ːs], *s.f.* imminence (of danger, etc.).

imminent [im(m)inɑ̃], *a.* imminent, impending (danger, etc.); **votre ruine est imminente,** you are on the verge of ruin.

immiscer [im(m)ise], *v.tr.* (**j'immisçai(s); n. immisçons**) to mix up, involve (s.o.) (**dans,** in).

s'immiscer. 1. s'i. dans une affaire, to interfere in, meddle with, in, a matter; to intrude; to poke one's nose into sth.; *A:* **s'i. de faire qch.,** to take it upon oneself to do sth. **2.** *Jur:* **s'i. dans une succession,** to assume a succession.

immiscibilité [im(m)isibilite], *s.f.* immiscibility.

immiscible [im(m)isibl̩], *a.* immiscible; that will not mix together.

immiséricordieux, -euse [im(m)izerikɔrdjø, -øːz], *a. A:* merciless, pitiless; hard-hearted.

immixtion [im(m)ikstjɔ̃], *s.f.* **1. i. dans une affaire,** unwarrantable interference in, with, a matter; **i. dans les affaires d'autrui,** meddling with other people's business, *F:* busybodying, nosey-parkerism. **2.** *Jur:* **i. dans une succession,** assumption of a succession.

immobile [im(m)ɔbil], *a.* **1.** motionless, still, unmoved; **visage i.,** set face; **rester complètement i.,** to stand stock-still. **2.** immovable; firm, steadfast (in danger, etc.).

immobilier, -ière [im(m)ɔbilje, -jɛːr], *a. Jur:* real; **biens immobiliers,** *s.m.* **immobilier,** real estate, landed estate, realty; *Scot:* heritage; **héritier i.,** heir to the real estate; **vente immobilière,** sale of

property; **société immobilière,** building society; **agence immobilière,** estate agency; **agent i.,** estate agent.

immobilisation [im(m)ɔbilizasjɔ̃], *s.f.* **1.** immobilization, immobilizing (of army, fractured limb, etc.); *Av:* **période d'i.,** grounding time. **2.** (*a*) *Jur:* conversion (of personal) into real estate; *Fin:* capitalization (of expenditure). **3.** *Com:* (*a*) locking up, tying up, tie-up (of capital); (*b*) *pl.* **immobilisations,** fixed assets, capital assets; **faire de grosses immobilisations,** to carry heavy stocks.

immobilisé [im(m)ɔbilize], *a.* (*a*) immobilized; **elle était immobilisée (à la maison) pour cause d'infirmité,** she was housebound by illness; **hélice immobilisée,** disabled propeller; (*b*) fixed (assets); (*c*) *a.* & *s.m. Mil:* (man) not called up, in a reserved occupation.

immobiliser [im(m)ɔbilize], *v.tr.* **1.** to immobilize; (*a*) to bring to a standstill; (*b*) to secure (fractured limb, etc.) against motion; to fix (sth.) in position. **2.** *Jur:* to convert (personalty) into realty. **3.** *Com:* to lock up, tie up (capital).

s'immobiliser, to cease to move, to come to a stop; *Mec:* (*of moving body*) to come to rest.

immobilisme [im(m)ɔbilism], *s.m.* opposition to progress, ultra-conservatism.

immobiliste [im(m)ɔbilist]. **1.** *a.* opposed to progress. **2.** *s.m.* & *f.* ultra-conservative, die-hard.

immobilité [im(m)ɔbilite], *s.f.* immobility, motionlessness; fixity; **i. politique,** ultra-conversatism; *Mil:* **garder l'i.,** to remain at attention, to stand at attention.

immodération [im(m)ɔderasjɔ̃], *s.f.* immoderation, immoderateness.

immodéré [im(m)ɔdere], *a.* immoderate, excessive, inordinate; **rires immodérés,** unrestrained, uncontrolled, laughter; **usage i. de l'alcool,** excessive consumption of alcohol.

immodérément [im(m)ɔderemɑ̃], *adv.* immoderately, excessively, inordinately; unrestrainedly; **boire i.,** to drink to excess.

immodeste [im(m)ɔdɛst], *a. O:* immodest, shameless; unmaidenlike (girl); unmaidenly (behaviour).

immodestement [im(m)ɔdɛstəmɑ̃], *adv.* immodestly, without shame.

immodestie [im(m)ɔdɛsti], *s.f. O:* **1.** immodesty, shamelessness. **2.** immodest act.

immolateur [im(m)ɔlatœːr], *s.m. A.* & *Lit:* immolator, sacrificer.

immolation [im(m)ɔlasjɔ̃], *s.f. Lit:* immolation, sacrifice; **les immolations de la Terreur,** the holocausts under the Terror.

immoler [im(m)ɔle], *v.tr. Lit:* to immolate, sacrifice; **i. ses enfants aux idoles,** to sacrifice, offer up, one's children to idols; **i. tout aux intérêts de sa famille,** to sacrifice everything in the interests of one's family.

immonde [im(m)ɔ̃ːd], *a.* **1.** *Rel:* unclean (animal, spirit, etc.). **2.** (*a*) (unspeakably) foul; filthy; **taudis i.,** filthy hovel; (*b*) disgusting; obscene.

immondice [im(m)ɔ̃dis], *s.f.* **1.** *Theol: A:* impurity. **2.** *pl.* dirt, refuse, street sweepings; **dépôt d'immondices,** rubbish shoot, tip; *P.N:* **défense de déposer des immondices,** shoot no rubbish, tipping (of rubbish) prohibited.

immontable [ɛ̃mɔ̃tabl̩], *a.* (horse) that no one can mount; unrideable (horse).

immoral, -aux [im(m)ɔral, -o], *a.* immoral; corrupt; **roman i.,** licentious novel.

immoralement [im(m)ɔralmɑ̃], *adv.* immorally.

immoralisme [im(m)ɔralism], *s.m. Phil:* immoralism.

immoraliste [im(m)ɔralist], *a.* & *s.m.* & *f. Phil:* immoralist.

immoralité [im(m)ɔralite], *s.f.* immorality; licentiousness, licentious nature (of a novel, etc.).

immortalisateur, -trice [im(m)ɔrtalizatœːr, -tris], *s.* immortalizer.

immortalisation [im(m)ɔrtalizasjɔ̃], *s.f.* immortalization.

immortaliser [im(m)ɔrtalize], *v.tr.* to immortalize.

immortaliseur [im(m)ɔrtalizœːr], *s.m.* immortalizer.

immortalité [im(m)ɔrtalite], *s.f.* immortality.

immortel, -elle [im(m)ɔrtɛl]. **1.** *a.* immortal (life, etc.); everlasting, undying, imperishable (fame, etc.); **les dieux immortels,** the immortal gods. **2.** *s.* immortal; *Lit:* god, goddess; **les immortels,** the immortals, *esp.* the members of the Académie Française. **3.** *s.f. Bot:* **immortelle,** everlasting (flower); immortelle.

immortellement [im(m)ɔrtɛlmɑ̃], *adv.* immortally, everlastingly, for ever.

immotivé [im(m)ɔtive], *a.* unmotived, unmotivated, groundless.

immuabilité [im(m)ɥabilite], *s.f.* immutability.

immuable [im(m)ɥabl̩], *a.* immutable, unalterable; fixed, unchanging, rigid; **règle i.,** hard-and-fast rule.

immuablement [im(m)ɥabləmɑ̃], *adv.* immutably, unalterably.

immun [im(m)œ̃], *s.m. Med:* immunized person.

immunigène [im(m)yniʒɛn], *a. Med:* immunogenic, immunizing (power).

immunisant [im(m)ynizɑ̃], *a. Med: Vet:* immunizing, protective (serum).

immunisation [im(m)ynizasjɔ̃], *s.f. Med: etc:* immunization.

immuniser [im(m)ynize], *v.tr. Med:* to immunize (s.o.) (**contre,** against), to render (s.o.) immune (**contre,** to, from).

immunisine [im(m)ynizin], *s.f. Biol:* immunisin.

immuniste [im(m)ynist], *s.m. or f. A.Jur:* immunist.

immunité [im(m)ynite], *s.f.* immunity; (*a*) privilege; **i. parlementaire,** parliamentary immunity (of members while the House is sitting); **i. diplomatique,** diplomatic immunity; (*b*) franchise, exemption, from taxation; (*c*) *Med:* **i. contre une maladie,** immunity to, from, a disease.

immunochimie [im(m)ynoʃimi], *s.f.* immunochemistry.

immunoélectrophorèse [im(m)ynoelɛktrɔfɔrɛːz], *s.f.* immunoelectrophoresis.

immunogène [im(m)ynɔʒɛn], *a. Med:* immunogenic, immunizing.

immunogénétique [im(m)ynɔʒenetik], *s.f. Med:* immunogenetics.

immunologie [im(m)ynɔlɔʒi], *s.f.* immunology.

immunologique [im(m)ynɔlɔʒik], *a.* immunological.

immunologiste [im(m)ynɔlɔʒist], *s.m.* & *f.* immunologist.

immuno-réaction [im(m)ynoreaksjɔ̃], *s.f. Med:* immunoreaction, immune reaction; *pl. immuno-réactions.*

immunothérapie [im(m)ynoterapi], *s.f. Med:* immunotherapy.

immuno(-)transfusion [im(m)ynotrɑ̃zfyzjɔ̃], *s.f. Med:* immunotransfusion; *pl. immuno-transfusions.*

immun-sérum [im(m)œserɔm], *s.m. Med:* immune serum; *pl. immun-sérums.*

immuration [im(m)yrasjɔ̃], *s.f. Rel.H:* immuring, immurement.

immutabilité [im(m)ytabilite], *s.f.* immutability, fixity, unalterableness.

impact [ɛ̃pakt], *s.m.* (*a*) impact; shock; collision; **point d'i.,** point of impact; **l'i. de la nouvelle,** the impact of the news; (*b*) *Artil:* hit; (*c*) *Av:* touch-down; **point d'i.,** touch-down point.

impacter [ɛ̃pakte], *v.tr. Surg:* to impact.

impaction [ɛ̃paksjɔ̃], *s.f. Surg:* impaction.

impair [ɛ̃pɛːr]. **1.** *a.* (*a*) odd, uneven (number, etc.); *s.m.* **jouer à pair ou i.,** to play at odd or even; **les jours impairs,** Monday, Wednesday, and Friday; **le côté i. d'une rue,** the odd-numbered side of a street; *Rail:* **voie impaire,** down line; (*b*) *Anat:* single, azygous (bone, etc.); *O:* **organe i.,** unpaired organ. **2.** *s.m.* blunder, bloomer, bad break; **commettre un i.,** to drop a brick; to put one's foot in it.

impala [ɛ̃pala], *s.m. Z:* impala.

impalpabilité [ɛ̃palpabilite], *s.f.* impalpability.

impalpable [ɛ̃palpabl̩], *a.* impalpable, intangible.

impaludation [ɛ̃palydasjɔ̃], *s.f. Med:* impaludation.

impaludé [ɛ̃palyde], *a.* malarial (swamp, etc.); (*of pers.*) suffering from malaria.

impaludisme [ɛ̃palydism], *s.m. Med:* malaria.

impanation [ɛ̃panasjɔ̃], *s.f. Theol:* impanation.

impané [ɛ̃pane], *a. Theol:* impanate.

imparable [ɛ̃parabl̩], *a.* unstoppable; unavoidable; *Fb:* **shoot i.,** unstoppable shot; **des sortilèges imparables,** spells against which there is no protection.

imparcouru [ɛ̃parkury], *a.* untrodden, untraversed.

impardonnable [ɛ̃pardɔnabl̩], *a.* unpardonable, unforgivable; **vous êtes i. d'avoir oublié,** it is unforgivable of you to have forgotten.

impardonné [ɛ̃pardɔne], *a.* unpardoned, unforgiven.

imparfait [ɛ̃parfɛ], *a.* **1.** incomplete (cure, etc.); imperfect, incomplete (knowledge); *A:* unfinished, uncompleted (book, etc.). **2.** (*a*) imperfect, defective; *Mus:* imperfect (cadence); (*b*) **l'homme est i.,** man is imperfect, is not perfect; **toute philosophie est imparfaite,** no philosophy is perfect. **3.** *a.* & *s.m. Gram:* imperfect (tense); **verbe à l'i.,** verb in the imperfect.

imparfaitement [ɛ̃parfɛtmɑ̃], *adv.* imperfectly.

imparidigité [ɛ̃paridiʒite], *a. Z:* imparidigitate, perissodactyl(e), perissodactylate, perissodactylous, odd-toed.

imparipenné [ɛ̃paripɛnne], *a. Bot:* imparipinnate.

imparisyllabe [ɛ̃parisil(l)ab], **imparisyllabique** [ɛ̃parisil(l)abik], *a. Lt.Gram:* imparisyllabic.

imparité [ɛ̃parite], *s.f.* **1.** inequality, disparity, imparity. **2.** *Mth:* oddness (of number).

impartagé [ɛ̃partaʒe], *a.* **1.** undivided (estate, etc.). **2.** unshared (sorrow, etc.).

impartageable [ɛ̃partaʒabl̩], *a.* **1.** indivisible. **2.** that cannot be shared, unsharable.

impartial, -iaux [ɛ̃parsjal, -jo], *a.* impartial, unbiassed, fair-minded, unprejudiced; even-handed (justice); **opinion impartiale,** impartial opinion.

impartialement [ɛ̃parsjalmɑ̃], *adv.* impartially.

impartialité [ɛ̃parsjalite], *s.f.* impartiality, fair-mindedness; **reconnaître, en toute i., que . . .,** to acknowledge, in all fairness, that . . .

impartir [ɛ̃partiːr], *v.tr.* (**j'impartis, n. impartissons**) (*used only in inf., pres. indicative & p.p.*) (*a*) *Jur:* to grant (right, favour), to assign (task) (**à,** to); **la responsabilité qui m'est impartie,** the responsibility that is delegated to me, that falls on me; **la loi vous impartit un délai de trois jours,** the law allows you three days' grace; **délai imparti,** time limit; (*b*) **les dons que la nature nous a impartis,** the gifts which nature has bestowed on us.

impassable [ɛ̃pɑsabl̩], *a.* impassable (barrier); unfordable (river).

impasse [ɛ̃pɑːs], *s.f.* impasse. **1.** blind alley, dead end, *cul-de-sac*; *P.N:* **i.,** no through road. **2.** position from which there is no escape; deadlock; **se trouver dans une i.,** to find oneself in a dilemma, *F:* in a fix, in a hole; **sortez-moi de cette i.,** get me out of this fix; **aboutir à une i.,** to come to a deadlock; **i. électorale,** electoral deadlock; *Fin:* **i. budgétaire,** budget deficit. **3.** *Cards:* **faire une i.,** to finesse; **jouer dans les impasses du mort,** to play through a tenace in dummy.

impassibilité [ɛ̃pasibilite], *s.f.* (*a*) *Theol:* impassibility; (*b*) impassibility, impassiveness.

impassible [ɛ̃pasibl̩], *a.* impassive. **1.** unmoved, unperturbed; imperturbable; calm and collected; unconcerned; **rester i. (devant le malheur),** to keep a stiff upper lip. **2.** (*a*) unimpressionable (judge, etc.); (*b*) callous.

impassiblement [ɛ̃pasibləmɑ̃], *adv.* impassively.

impastation [ɛ̃pastasjɔ̃], *s.f.* impastation.

impatiemment [ɛ̃pasjamɑ̃], *adv.* impatiently.

impatience [ɛ̃pasjɑ̃ːs], *s.f.* **1.** *Lit:* impatience, intolerance (**de,** of); **i. du joug,** chafing under the yoke. **2.** (*a*) impatience; **avec i.,** impatiently; (*b*) eagerness; **avoir une grande i. de faire qch.,** to be all impatience, most eager, to do sth.; **attendre qch. avec i.,** to long for sth., to be impatient to have sth. **3.** *pl.* (*a*) fits of impatience; (*b*) **avoir des impatiences dans les jambes,** to have the fidgets, to be itching to get going.

impatiens [ɛ̃pasjɛ̃s], *s.f. Bot:* balsamine, impatiens.

impatient [ɛ̃pasjɑ̃]. **1.** *a.* impatient; (*a*) *Lit:* intolerant (**de,** of); **i. du joug,** chafing under the yoke; (*b*) impatient; **d'un air i.,** impatiently; (*c*) eager, desirous; **être i. de faire qch.,** to be eager, anxious, all agog, to do sth.; **i. de partir,** impatient to be gone. **2.** *s.f. Bot:* **impatiente,** balsamine, impatiens.

impatientant [ɛ̃pasjɑ̃tɑ̃], *a.* annoying, provoking.

impatienter [ɛ̃pasjɑ̃te], *v.tr.* to make (s.o.) lose patience, to provoke (s.o.); **il m'impatiente,** I have no patience with him; **vous m'impatientez avec vos folies,** I have no patience with all your foolishness; **je suis impatienté qu'on ne fasse rien,** it tries my patience to see that nothing is done.

s'impatienter, to lose patience; to grow impatient; **s'i. de qch., contre qn,** to be impatient with sth., with s.o.; **s'i. de faire qch.,** (i) to be impatient to do sth.; (ii) to grow tired of doing sth.

impatronisation [ɛ̃patrɔnizasjɔ̃], *s.f.* (*a*) setting (of s.o.) in authority (over a household, etc.); (*b*) assumption of authority, self-assertion (in office, in another person's household).

impatroniser [ɛ̃patrɔnize], *v.tr.* **1.** to set (stranger) in authority (over one's household, over subordinates). **2.** to introduce and impose (practice); to set (fashion).

s'impatroniser, to make one's authority, one's influence, felt; to obtain a footing; *F:* to get one's foot in (somewhere); to assert oneself; **s'i. chez qn,** to take over the husband's, the wife's, place in a household.

impavide [ɛ̃pavid], *a. Lit:* impavid, fearless, undismayed, undaunted.
impayable [ɛ̃pɛjabl̩], *a.* **1.** inestimable, invaluable, priceless. **2.** *F:* highly amusing, killingly funny, killing; **tour i.,** priceless joke; **vous êtes i.!** you're the limit!
impayé [ɛ̃peje], *a.* (*a*) unpaid (debt, etc.); (*b*) *a.* & *s.m.* dishonoured (bill).
impeccabilité [ɛ̃pɛkabilite], *s.f.* impeccability; (*a*) *A:* sinlessness; (*b*) faultlessness (of attire, etc.).
impeccable [ɛ̃pɛkabl̩], *a.* impeccable. **1.** *A:* not liable to sin. **2.** (*a*) infallible; (*b*) impeccable, faultless (style, taste, etc.); flawless (technique).
impeccablement [ɛ̃pɛkabləmɑ̃], *adv.* impeccably, flawlessly.
impécunieux, -euse [ɛ̃pekynjø, -ø:z], *a.* impecunious.
impécuniosité [ɛ̃pekynjozite], *s.f.* impecuniosity.
impédance [ɛ̃pedɑ̃:s], *s.f. El:* impedance; **bobine d'i.,** choking coil, choke; **i. acoustique,** acoustic(al) impedance; **i. d'onde,** wave impedance; **i. de charge, d'utilisation,** load impedance; **i. d'entrée, de sortie,** input, output, impedance; **i. négative,** expedance.
impédimenta [ɛ̃pedimɛ̃ta], *s.m.pl.* impedimenta.
impénétrabilité [ɛ̃penetrabilite], *s.f.* **1.** impenetrability; imperviousness. **2.** inscrutableness, inscrutability (of s.o.'s purpose, etc.).
impénétrable [ɛ̃penetrabl̩], *a.* **1.** impenetrable (forest, etc.); **i. à l'eau,** impervious to water; **nation i. à l'influence étrangère,** nation impenetrable to, by, foreign influence, impervious to foreign influence; **cœur i.,** heart of steel. **2.** inscrutable (face); unfathomable (mystery, etc.); close (silence, secret).
impénétrablement [ɛ̃penetrabləmɑ̃], *adv.* impenetrably, inscrutably, imperviously.
impénétré [ɛ̃penetre], *a.* **1.** unpenetrated (forest, etc.). **2.** unsolved, unfathomed (mystery, etc.).
impénitence [ɛ̃penitɑ̃:s], *s.f.* impenitence, impenitency; unrepentance; obduracy; **mourir dans l'i. finale,** to die in final impenitence.
impénitent [ɛ̃penitɑ̃], *a.* impenitent, unrepentant; obdurate; **buveur i.,** hardened drinker.
impenne [ɛ̃pɛn], **impenné** [ɛ̃pɛnne], *Orn:* **1.** *a.* impennate. **2.** *s.m.pl.* **impennes,** Impennes.
impensable [ɛ̃pɑ̃sabl̩], *a.* unthinkable.
impenses [ɛ̃pɑ̃:s], *s.f.pl. Jur:* expenses incurred for the maintenance or improvement of property; **i. et améliorations,** upkeep and improvements; **i. nécessaires,** maintenance expenses; **i. utiles,** expenditure on improvements (which give increased value to the property); **i. voluptuaires,** expenditure on luxury items (which do not increase the value of the property).
imper [ɛ̃pɛ:r], *s.m. F:* (= IMPERMÉABLE) mac.
impérant [ɛ̃perɑ̃], *a. Astrol:* dominant (sign).
imperata [ɛ̃perata], *s.m. Bot:* imperata.
impératif, -ive [ɛ̃peratif, -i:v]. **1.** (*a*) *a.* imperious, imperative, peremptory (tone, etc.); *Jur:* mandatory (law); (*b*) *s.m.* imperative; requirement; *Phil:* **i. catégorique,** categorical, moral, imperative. **2.** *Gram:* (*a*) *a.* & *s.m.* imperative (mood, etc.); **à l'i.,** in the imperative; (*b*) *a.* imperatival (force, etc.).
impérativement [ɛ̃perativmɑ̃], *adv.* imperatively.
impératoire [ɛ̃peratwa:r], *s.f. Bot:* imperatoria; masterwort.
impératrice [ɛ̃peratris], *s.f.* empress.
imperceptibilité [ɛ̃pɛrsɛptibilite], *s.f.* imperceptibility.
imperceptible [ɛ̃pɛrsɛptibl̩], *a.* imperceptible, unperceivable, undiscernible; intangible; **i. à l'œil nu,** invisible to the naked eye; **un sourire i.,** a scarcely perceptible smile, a shadow of a smile.
imperceptiblement [ɛ̃pɛrsɛptibləmɑ̃], *adv.* imperceptibly.
imperdable [ɛ̃pɛrdabl̩], *a.* that cannot be lost; **un procès i.,** a safe case; **un match i.,** a sure win.
imperfectibilité [ɛ̃pɛrfɛktibilite], *s.f.* imperfectibility.
imperfectible [ɛ̃pɛrfɛktibl̩], *a.* imperfectible, not perfectible.
imperfectif, -ive [ɛ̃pɛrfɛktif, -i:v], *a. Gram:* imperfective.
imperfection [ɛ̃pɛrfɛksjɔ̃], *s.f.* imperfection. **1.** incompletion, incompleteness. **2.** (*a*) defectiveness, faultiness; (*b*) defect, fault, flaw, blemish.
imperforation [ɛ̃pɛrfɔrasjɔ̃], *s.f.* imperforation.
imperforé [ɛ̃pɛrfɔre], *a.* imperforate (anus, nose, etc.).
impérial, -aux [ɛ̃perjal, -o]. **1.** *a.* imperial; **Sa Majesté Impériale,** His, Her, Imperial Majesty. **2.** *s.m.pl. Hist:* **les Impériaux,** the Imperials (troops of the Holy Roman Emperor). **3.** *s.f.* **impériale:** (*a*) top, tester (of four-poster bed); (*b*) top (deck) (of bus, etc.); **autobus à i.,** double-decker bus; **monter à l'i.,** to go on top, upstairs; **les voyageurs d'i.,** the upstairs, top-deck, passengers; (*c*) imperial; tuft (on lower lip) (as worn by Napoleon III); (*d*) *Bot:* (*also* **couronne impériale**) crown imperial; (*e*) *Cards:* (*also* **série impériale**) the four court cards of one suit.
impérialement [ɛ̃perjalmɑ̃], *adv.* imperially.
impérialisme [ɛ̃perjalism], *s.m.* imperialism.
impérialiste [ɛ̃perjalist]. **1.** *a.* imperialistic. **2.** *s.m.* & *f.* imperialist.
impérieusement [ɛ̃perjøzmɑ̃], *adv.* (*a*) imperiously, haughtily; (*b*) urgently, imperatively.
impérieux, -euse [ɛ̃perjø, -ø:z], *a.* imperious. **1.** haughty, lordly, domineering; peremptory (tone, etc.). **2.** urgent, imperative, pressing (necessity, etc.); **c'est mon devoir i. de . . .,** it is my bounden duty to . . . .
impérissable [ɛ̃perisabl̩], *a.* imperishable, undying, unperishing.
impérissablement [ɛ̃perisabləmɑ̃], *adv.* imperishably.
impéritie [ɛ̃perisi], *s.f.* incapacity, incompetence (due to inexperience).
impermanence [ɛ̃pɛrmanɑ̃:s], *s.f.* impermanence, impermanency.
impermanent [ɛ̃pɛrmanɑ̃], *a.* impermanent.
imperméabilisant [ɛ̃pɛrmeabilizɑ̃], *a.* & *s.m.* waterproofing (compound).
imperméabilisation [ɛ̃pɛrmeabilizasjɔ̃], *s.f.* (water)proofing.
imperméabiliser [ɛ̃pɛrmeabilize], *v.tr.* to (water)proof (cloth).
imperméabilité [ɛ̃pɛrmeabilite], *s.f.* impermeability; imperviousness (**à**, to).
imperméable [ɛ̃pɛrmeabl̩]. **1.** *a.* impervious (**à**, to); impermeable; water-repellent; **i. à l'eau,** waterproof, watertight; **i. au gaz, à la lumière,** gas-tight, light-proof; **i. à la poussière,** dust-proof. **2.** *s.m. Cost:* raincoat, waterproof, mackintosh.
impermutabilité [ɛ̃pɛrmytabilite], *s.f. Fin:* unexchangeability, inconvertibility (of securities).
impermutable [ɛ̃pɛrmytabl̩], *a. Fin:* unexchangeable, inconvertible (security).
impersévérance [ɛ̃pɛrseverɑ̃:s], *s.f.* want of perseverance.
impersévérant [ɛ̃pɛrseverɑ̃], *a.* unpersevering.
impersonnalité [ɛ̃pɛrsɔnalite], *s.f.* impersonality.
impersonnel, -elle [ɛ̃pɛrsɔnɛl], *a.* impersonal (style, verb, etc.).
impersonnellement [ɛ̃pɛrsɔnɛlmɑ̃], *adv.* impersonally.
impersuadé [ɛ̃pɛrsɥade], *a.* unpersuaded.
impersuasible [ɛ̃pɛrsɥazibl̩], *a.* unpersuadable.
impertinemment [ɛ̃pɛrtinamɑ̃], *adv.* **1.** *Jur:* irrelevantly. **2.** impertinently, pertly, rudely.
impertinence [ɛ̃pɛrtinɑ̃:s], *s.f.* impertinence. **1.** *Jur:* irrelevance. **2.** (*a*) pertness, rudeness; (*b*) piece of impertinence; **dire des impertinences (à qn),** to be impertinent (to s.o.).
impertinent, -ente [ɛ̃pɛrtinɑ̃, -ɑ̃:t]. **1.** *a. Jur:* impertinent, irrelevant. **2.** *a.* & *s.* impertinent, *F:* cheeky (person).
imperturbabilité [ɛ̃pɛrtyrbabilite], *s.f.* imperturbability.
imperturbable [ɛ̃pɛrtyrbabl̩], *a.* imperturbable, unruffled.
imperturbablement [ɛ̃pɛrtyrbabləmɑ̃], *adv.* imperturbably.
imperturbé [ɛ̃pɛrtyrbe], *a.* unperturbed.
impesanteur [ɛ̃pəzɑ̃tœ:r], *s.f. Ph:* weightlessness.
impétigineux, -euse [ɛ̃petiʒinø, -ø:z], *a. Med:* impetiginous.
impétigo [ɛ̃petigo], *s.m. Med:* impetigo; (*of Rugby players*) scrum-pox.
impétrable [ɛ̃petrabl̩], *a. Jur:* obtainable (by petition); *A:* impetrable.
impétrant, -ante [ɛ̃petrɑ̃, -ɑ̃:t], *s.* **1.** *Jur:* grantee (of title, living, diploma, etc.). **2.** *F:* (*incorrectly*) petitioner.
impétration [ɛ̃petrasjɔ̃], *s.f.* impetration (of living, etc.; *Theol:* of grace).
impétrer [ɛ̃petre], *v.tr.* (**j'impètre, n. impétrons; j'impétrerai**) to impetrate, obtain (living, title, diploma, etc., from the competent authority).
impétueusement [ɛ̃petɥøzmɑ̃], *adv.* impetuously.
impétueux, -euse [ɛ̃petɥø, -ø:z], *a.* (*a*) impetuous; hot-headed, impulsive; vehement; *s.* **jeunes impétueux,** young hotheads; (*b*) **torrent i.,** rushing, raging, torrent; **vent i.,** blustering wind.
impétuosité [ɛ̃petɥozite], *s.f.* impetuosity; impulsiveness.
impeuplé [ɛ̃pœple], *a. A:* unpopulated.
impie [ɛ̃pi], *a.* impious, ungodly; blasphemous; *s.* **les impies,** the impious, the ungodly.
impiété [ɛ̃pjete], *s.f.* **1.** (*a*) impiety, godlessness; ungodliness; (*b*) impiousness (of a wish or action). **2.** (*a*) blasphemy; (*b*) impious deed.
impitoyabilité [ɛ̃pitwajabilite], *s.f.* pitilessness (**à, envers,** towards).
impitoyable [ɛ̃pitwajabl̩], *a.* (*a*) pitiless (**à, envers, pour,** towards); ruthless, merciless, unmerciful; **être i. sur les moindres fautes,** to be merciless about the slightest mistakes; (*b*) relentless, inexorable, unrelenting.
impitoyablement [ɛ̃pitwajabləmɑ̃], *adv.* (*a*) pitilessly, ruthlessly, mercilessly, unmercifully; (*b*) relentlessly, unrelentingly.
implacabilité [ɛ̃plakabilite], *s.f.* implacability, unrelentingness.
implacable [ɛ̃plakabl̩], *a.* implacable, relentless, unpardoning, unrelenting (**à, pour, à l'égard de,** towards); **mal i.,** incurable disease.
implacablement [ɛ̃plakabləmɑ̃], *adv.* implacably.
implacentaire [ɛ̃plasɑ̃tɛ:r], *Z:* **1.** *a.* implacental. **2.** *s.m.pl.* **implacentaires,** Implacentalia.
implant [ɛ̃plɑ̃], *s.m. Med:* implant; **i. endo-osseux,** intraosseous implant; *Dent:* **i. prothétique,** implant denture.
implantation [ɛ̃plɑ̃tasjɔ̃], *s.f.* (*a*) planting, implantation; introduction; **l'i. des Arabes en Espagne,** the settling, establishment, of the Arabs in Spain; **l'i. d'une industrie dans une région,** the setting up, establishment, of an industry in a region; (*b*) pegging out, laying out (of ground plan); (*c*) layout (of factory, equipment, etc.); (*d*) *Surg:* grafting; *Med: Dent:* implantation.
implanté [ɛ̃plɑ̃te], *s.m. Hairdr:* laying out, arrangement (of hair on wig).
implanter [ɛ̃plɑ̃te], *v.tr.* (*a*) to plant; to introduce, to establish; to implant (idea, etc.); **i. un usage dans un milieu,** to establish a custom in a milieu; **i. un complexe métallurgique,** to set up, establish, a metallurgical complex; **certains végétaux implantent leurs racines à une profondeur considérable,** certain plants establish their roots at a considerable depth; (*b*) *Const:* to peg out (ground plan); (*c*) *Surg:* to graft; *Med:* to implant.
s'implanter, to take root; **le gui s'implante dans le pommier,** mistletoe attaches itself to the apple tree; *F:* **s'i. chez qn,** to plant, foist, oneself on s.o.
implanteur [ɛ̃plɑ̃tœ:r], *s.m. Surv:* chainman's assistant, picket man.
impleuré [ɛ̃plœre, -øre], *a. A:* unwept, unlamented.
implexe [ɛ̃plɛks], *a. Lit:* intricate, complex (plot, etc.).
impliable [ɛ̃pli(j)abl̩], *a.* (*a*) unbendable, not foldable; unpliant; (*b*) stubborn, unpliable, unyielding (nature, etc.).
implication [ɛ̃plikasjɔ̃], *s.f.* **1.** *Jur:* implication (**dans**, in). **2.** *Log:* (*a*) *A:* contradiction (between two propositions); (*b*) implication.
implicite [ɛ̃plisit], *a.* implicit; (*a*) implied (intention, condition, etc.); (*b*) absolute (faith, confidence).
implicitement [ɛ̃plisitmɑ̃], *adv.* implicitly; (*a*) by implication, impliedly; (*b*) unquestioningly.
impliquer [ɛ̃plike], *v.tr.* **1.** to implicate, involve; **être impliqué dans une mauvaise affaire,** to be mixed up in a bad business; **véhicule impliqué (dans un accident),** vehicle involved (in an accident); **difficultés impliquées dans une théorie,** difficulties involved in a theory. **2.** to imply; *Log:* **i. contradiction,** to imply a contradiction.
implorable [ɛ̃plɔrabl̩], *a.* open to entreaty.
implorant [ɛ̃plɔrɑ̃], *a.* imploring; **d'un ton i.,** imploringly.
implorateur, -trice [ɛ̃plɔratœ:r, -tris]. **1.** *s.* implorer, beseecher. **2.** *a.* imploring.
imploration [ɛ̃plɔrasjɔ̃], *s.f.* imploring, imploration, entreaty.
implorer [ɛ̃plɔre], *v.tr.* to implore, beseech, entreat (s.o.); **i. la protection, le secours, de qn,** to beg for s.o.'s protection, s.o.'s help; **j'implore Dieu, le ciel, de ne pas avoir à rester longtemps ici,** I'm praying to God (that) I won't have to stay here long.
imploser [ɛ̃ploze], *v.i.* to implode.
implosif, -ive [ɛ̃plozif, -i:v], *a.* & *s.f. Ling:* implosive.
implosion [ɛ̃plozjɔ̃], *s.f.* implosion; **faire i.,** to implode.
imployable [ɛ̃plwajabl̩], *a.* unbending, inflexible.
impluviosité [ɛ̃plyvjozite], *s.f.* rainlessness, lack of rain.
impluvium [ɛ̃plyvjɔm], *s.m. Rom.Ant:* impluvium.
impolarisable [ɛ̃pɔlarizabl̩], *a. El:* impolarizable (battery).

impoli [ɛ̃pɔli], *a.* (*a*) impolite, unmannerly, ill-mannered, uncivil, rude, discourteous (**envers, avec,** to); **enfant i.,** rude, ill-mannered, child; **il est i. d'arriver en retard,** it is impolite, discourteous, to arrive late; *s.* **vous êtes un i.,** you've no manners; (*b*) *A:* unpolished (speech, civilization, etc.).
impoliment [ɛ̃pɔlimɑ̃], *adv.* uncivilly, impolitely, discourteously, rudely.
impolitesse [ɛ̃pɔlitɛs], *s.f.* **1.** impoliteness; (*a*) discourtesy, incivility; (*b*) rudeness, unmannerliness, lack of manners, ill-breeding. **2.** act of discourtesy, of rudeness, breach of (good) manners; **faire une i. à qn,** to behave discourteously to s.o.; to be rude to s.o.
impolitique [ɛ̃pɔlitik], *a.* impolitic, ill-advised.
impolitiquement [ɛ̃pɔlitikmɑ̃], *adv.* ill-advisedly, in an impolitic manner.
impollu [ɛ̃pɔl(l)y], *a. A. & Lit:* pure, unspotted.
impollué [ɛ̃pɔl(l)ɥe], *a.* unpolluted.
impondérabilité [ɛ̃pɔ̃derabilite], *s.f.* **1.** imponderability. **2.** weightlessness.
impondérable [ɛ̃pɔ̃derabl]. **1.** *a.* imponderable. **2.** *s.m.pl.* **impondérables,** intangible factors, imponderables.
impondéré [ɛ̃pɔ̃dere], *a.* **1.** unweighed, ill-considered (action). **2.** (nature) lacking stability.
impopulaire [ɛ̃pɔpylɛːr], *a.* unpopular.
impopularité [ɛ̃pɔpylarite], *s.f.* unpopularity.
imporosité [ɛ̃pɔrɔzite], *s.f.* impermeability, imporosity, imporousness.
importable[1] [ɛ̃pɔrtabl], *a.* importable, that may be imported.
importable[2], *a. F:* unwearable; (dress, etc.) not fit to wear.
importance [ɛ̃pɔrtɑ̃ːs], *s.f.* importance; (*a*) consequence, moment, weight; **affaire d'i.,** important matter; **l'affaire est d'i.,** the matter is of some importance; **l'i. des intérêts en jeu,** the importance of the interests at stake; **de peu d'i.,** of little importance, of no great significance; **sans i.,** unimportant; trifling (matter); **événement de la première i., de toute i.,** event of outstanding importance, all-important event; **avoir de l'i.,** to be important, of importance; **point qui a de l'i.,** point of importance; **tout cela a peu d'i.,** all that amounts to little; **cela n'a pas d'i.,** it's of no importance, of no consequence; **cela n'a pas la moindre i.,** it doesn't matter a bit, in the least; **le mouvement prend de l'i.,** the movement is gaining ground; **mettre, attacher, prêter, de l'i. à qch.,** to attach importance to sth.; **attacher trop d'i. à des riens,** to make too much of trifles; (*b*) size, extent; **une ville de cette i.,** a town of that size; **usine de moyenne i.,** medium-sized factory; **quelle est l'i., de la production d'aluminium en France?** what is the French output of aluminium? how much aluminium does France produce? *Rail:* **i. du retard,** number of minutes late; **fixer l'i. d'une délégation,** to settle the number of members of a delegation; **i. d'une blessure,** extent of a wound; **i. du dommage,** extent of the damage; **i. d'un bassin houiller,** extent of a coal bed; **l'assurance varie selon l'i. de la voiture,** the insurance varies according to the size of the car; (*c*) *adv.phr.* **tancer qn d'i.,** to give s.o. a good scolding, a good talking-to; *F:* **rosser qn d'i.,** to thrash s.o. soundly; (*d*) social importance, position, standing; **i. d'une maison,** standing of a firm; (*e*) *Pej:* self-importance; **être pénétré de son i.,** to be full of one's own importance; **il était enclin à croire à son i.,** he was inclined to think too much of his own importance, significance; **faire l'homme d'i.,** to act big.
important, -ante [ɛ̃pɔrtɑ̃, -ɑ̃ːt]. **1.** *a.* (*a*) important, significant; **peu i.,** unimportant; **rôle i.,** important rôle, part; **la partie la plus importante du travail a été entreprise par . . .,** the main, most important, part of the work was undertaken by . . .; **rien d'i. à signaler,** nothing of significance to report; **il est i. de faire vite,** it is important to act quickly; **personnage i.,** important, influential, man; (*b*) large; considerable, important; **ville importante,** large town; **une somme importante,** a considerable sum of money; **la recette a atteint un chiffre i.,** the takings, the proceeds, reached a high, considerable, figure; **nous ne pouvons pas vous accorder un crédit plus i.,** we cannot allow you credit beyond this figure, beyond these figures; **vente peu importante,** small sale; **une aviation importante,** a large air force; **un retard i.,** a considerable delay; (*c*) *a. & s.* self-important (person); **se prendre pour qn d'i.,** to have an exaggerated idea of one's own importance, to be full of one's own importance; **faire l'i.,** to give oneself airs; to act big, to throw one's weight about. **2.** *s.m.* **l'i.,** the important point, the main thing.
importateur, -trice [ɛ̃pɔrtatœːr, -tris]. **1.** *s.* importer. **2.** *a.* importing (firm, etc.).
importation [ɛ̃pɔrtasjɔ̃], *s.f.* importation. **1.** importing (of goods); **maison d'i.,** importing firm; **commerce d'i.,** import trade; **licence d'i.,** import licence. **2.** (*thing imported*) import.
importer[1] [ɛ̃pɔrte], *v.tr.* (*a*) to import (goods); **la France importe du café,** France is an importer of coffee; **i. de la main-d'œuvre,** to import (foreign) labour; **les bois de Norvège s'importent en France,** Norwegian timber is imported into France; *abs.* **i. en contrebande,** to smuggle; (*b*) to introduce (custom, fashion, epidemic, etc.) (into a country); **le normand, idiome importé en Angleterre par Guillaume le Conquérant,** Norman-French, a language introduced into England by William the Conqueror; **l'eucalyptus, arbre importé d'Australie,** the eucalyptus, a tree introduced from Australia.
importer[2], *v.i.* (*used mainly in the third pers. sing. and plural*) to be of importance, of consequence; to matter, to signify. **1. les choses qui importent,** the things that matter; **ce n'est pas le fond mais la façon de le traiter qui importe,** it is not the subject but its treatment that is the (important) thing; **que m'importe la vie!** what is life to me! **2.** *impers.* **il importe que** + *sub.,* it is essential that . . .; **il importe à tout le monde de le faire,** it is incumbent on everyone to do so; **il m'importe beaucoup que vous y alliez,** it is very important to me that you should go; **il importe peu que . . ., peu importe que . . .,** it doesn't matter much whether . . .; **peu m'importe,** I don't mind, it's all the same to me; **peu m'importe ce qu'on en pensera,** I don't care what people will think; **n'importe,** no matter, never mind; **qu'importe?** what does it matter? **qu'importe qu'il vienne ou ne vienne pas, qu'il vienne ou non?** what does it matter, signify, whether he comes or not? **que m'importe?** what do I care? **faire qch. n'importe comment, où, quand,** to do something no matter how, where, when; to do sth. anyhow, anywhere, any time; **de n'importe quel point de vue je ne pouvais excuser . . .,** from whatever, whichever, point of view, I could not excuse . . ., look at it as I would, I could not excuse . . .; **n'importe quelle autre personne,** anybody else; **venez à n'importe quelle heure de la journée,** come at any time of the day; **venez n'importe quel jour,** come any day; **n'importe qui,** any one (at all), no matter who; **n'importe qui de sérieux vous dira que . . .,** any serious-minded, responsible, person will tell you that . . .; **n'importe quoi,** anything, no matter what; **il fait plus pour eux que n'importe qui,** he does more for them than any man living, any man alive; *F:* **ce n'est pas n'importe qui,** he's somebody; he's not a mere nobody; **donnez-moi n'importe lequel,** give me any one of them, whichever you like.
import-export [ɛ̃pɔrɛkspɔːr], *s.f. Com:* import-export.
importun, -une [ɛ̃pɔrtœ̃, -yn]. **1.** *a.* importunate; obtrusive, troublesome, tiresome, bothersome (person); harassing (thought, etc.); unseasonable (request); unwelcome (visitor, attentions); **je crains de vous être i.,** I'm afraid I'm disturbing you. **2.** *s.* pest, intruder; nuisance (of a man, of a woman).
importunément [ɛ̃pɔrtynemɑ̃], *adv.* importunately, obtrusively.
importuner [ɛ̃pɔrtyne], *v.tr.* to importune; (*a*) to bother, pester (s.o.); to obtrude oneself on (s.o.), to badger (s.o.); **être importuné par ses créanciers,** to be dunned by one's creditors; (*b*) to annoy, trouble, inconvenience (s.o.); **j'espère que je ne vous importune pas,** I hope I am not disturbing you; **le bruit des cloches m'importune,** the noise of bells disturbs me; **ses visites nous importunent,** his visits are a nuisance; **je ne vous importunerai pas des détails,** I shan't trouble you with the details, inflict the details on you.
importunité [ɛ̃pɔrtynite], *s.f.* importunity. **1.** obtrusiveness; **obtenir une faveur de qn à force d'i.,** to wring a favour from s.o., out of s.o.; to badger s.o. into granting a favour. **2. les importunités de ses créanciers,** the dunning(s) of his creditors.
imposable [ɛ̃pozabl], *a.* (*a*) taxable (person, income, goods); (*b*) rateable, assessable (property).
imposant [ɛ̃pozɑ̃], *a.* imposing (figure, ceremony); commanding, stately, dignified (figure, etc.); **le caractère i. du paysage,** the grandeur of the landscape.
imposé, -ée [ɛ̃poze]. **1.** *a.* (*a*) (*of task, etc.*) prescribed, allotted, set; (*of price*) laid down; recommended; (*of goods, etc.*) taxed; (*b*) (*skating, etc.*) **figures imposées,** compulsory figures. **2.** *s.* (*a*) taxpayer; (*b*) ratepayer.
imposer [ɛ̃poze]. I. *v.tr.* **1.** (*a*) *Ecc:* to lay on (hands); (*b*) *Typ:* to impose (sheet). **2.** to give, assign; **imposer un nom à un enfant,** to give a child a name. **3.** to impose, prescribe; to set (task); **i. des conditions à qn,** to impose conditions on s.o.; to lay down conditions, to dictate terms, to s.o.; **i. une règle,** to lay down, enforce, a rule; **je m'impose comme règle absolue de . . .,** I lay it down as, make it, an absolute rule to . . .; **ils m'ont imposé de partir,** they made me, forced me to, leave; **i. (le) silence à qn,** to enjoin silence on s.o.; **i. son opinion à qn,** to thrust, foist, one's opinion on s.o.; **i. sa manière de voir,** to carry one's point; **i. ses confidences à qn,** to force one's confidence upon s.o.; **i. du respect à qn,** to inspire s.o. with respect; **i. le respect,** to command respect; **l'élection a imposé l'union des Gauches,** the election has compelled the parties of the Left to come together; **procédé qui impose des pressions très élevées,** process that calls for, necessitates, very high pressures; **s'i. un labeur,** to undertake a task; **s'i. de faire qch.,** to make it a duty to do sth.; **l'obligation à lui imposée,** the obligation laid upon him; *Ecc:* **i. l'antienne,** to give the note for the antiphon. **4.** (*a*) *Jur:* **i. une charge à qn,** to lay a charge on s.o.; **charges imposées au légataire,** charges falling on the legatee; *Adm:* **i. des droits sur qch.,** to impose, put, a tax on sth., to tax sth.; **être lourdement imposé,** to be heavily taxed; (*b*) **i. qn,** (i) to tax s.o., (ii) to rate s.o.; **i. une ville,** to levy a contribution on a town; **i. qch.,** to make sth. taxable; **i. les automobiles,** to tax cars; **i. un immeuble,** to levy a rate on a building; to assess a building.
II. **imposer,** *v.i.* **1. (en) i.,** to inspire respect, awe; **(en) i. à qn,** to impress s.o.; **sa fermeté m'en imposa,** his firmness filled me with respect, impressed me. **2. (en) i. à qn,** to impose on s.o.; to deceive s.o., to take s.o. in; **i. à la crédulité de qn,** to play on s.o.'s credulity.
s'imposer. 1. to assert oneself; to compel recognition; to take the lead; **s'i. à l'attention,** to command attention; to obtrude oneself; **la conviction s'imposa à mon esprit que . . .,** the conviction forced itself upon me that . . .; it was borne in upon me that . . .; **une mauvaise habitude s'impose peu à peu,** a bad habit gains on one. **2. s'i. à qn, chez qn,** to foist, thrust, force, oneself upon s.o. **3.** to be indispensable; **la discrétion s'impose,** discretion is imperative, is essential; **cette séparation s'impose,** this separation is called for; **l'amabilité s'impose aux commerçants,** a shopkeeper needs a pleasant manner; **une visite au Louvre s'impose,** you, we, simply must visit the Louvre, *F:* a visit to the Louvre is a must.
imposeur [ɛ̃pozœːr], *s.m. Typ:* form man, form setter.
imposition [ɛ̃pozisjɔ̃], *s.f.* **1.** (*a*) laying on, *Ecc:* imposition (of hands); (*b*) *Typ:* imposing, imposition. **2.** giving, assigning (of name, etc.). **3.** imposing, laying down (of conditions); setting, prescribing (of task). **4.** (*a*) imposition, putting on (of tax); taxation; (*b*) assessment (of property); **année d'i.,** taxable year. **5.** (*a*) tax, duty; **catégorie d'i.,** tax bracket; (*b*) rates.
impossibilité [ɛ̃pɔsibilite], *s.f.* impossibility. **1. il y a i. à cela,** it is impossible that it should be so, this is impossible; **être dans l'i. matérielle de faire qch.,** (i) to find it impossible to do sth.; (ii) to be unavoidably prevented from doing sth.; **mettre qn dans l'i. de faire qch.,** to make it impossible for s.o. to do sth.; **il est de toute i. qu'il vienne à le savoir,** it is impossible that he should come to know of it, for him to come to know of it; *Jur:* **défense fondée sur l'i. de faire autrement,** plea of necessity; **alléguer, plaider, l'i. de faire autrement,** to urge the plea of necessity. **2. accomplir des impossibilités,** to accomplish impossibilities, to do the impossible.
impossible [ɛ̃pɔsibl], *a.* impossible. **1. c'est i.,** it's impossible, it's out of the question; **cela m'est i.,** it's not possible for me, I cannot; **il m'est i. de le faire,** I can't do it; **il m'est i. de ne pas croire que . . .,** I cannot help believing that . . .; **il m'aurait été i. de rester,** I could not have remained; **projet i. à exécuter, qu'il est i. d'exécuter,** impossible, impracticable, unrealistic, unfeasible, plan; **chose i. à faire,**

unfeasible thing; **c'est i. à faire,** it can't be done; **il a fait l'i. pour nous secourir,** he did his utmost, did everything possible, moved heaven and earth, to help us; **homme i. à émouvoir,** man who cannot be moved; **il est i. qu'il revienne en temps voulu,** he cannot possibly be back in time; **vous lui rendez la vie i.,** you're making life impossible for him; **on ne peut pas faire l'i.,** *Prov:* **à l'i. nul n'est tenu,** one can't do the impossible, you can't put a quart into a pint pot; *adv.phr.* **par i.,** against all possibility; **si par i. il est encore vivant,** if, to suppose the impossible, by any remote chance, he is still alive. **2.** *F:* (*a*) extravagant, absurd (hat, etc.); **rentrer à des heures impossibles,** to come home at all hours (of the night); **il a fallu nous lever à une heure i.,** we had to get up at an unearthly hour; (*b*) **vous êtes i.!** you're impossible! you're the end! **enfant i.,** enfant terrible.

imposte [ɛ̃pɔst], *s.f. Arch:* (*a*) impost (of bearing arch); springer; (*b*) transom, dormant-tree; (*c*) transom window, fanlight.

imposteur [ɛ̃pɔstœːr], *s.m.* impostor; **les hommes sont tous des imposteurs,** men are all deceivers.

imposture [ɛ̃pɔstyːr], *s.f.* **1.** imposture, imposition, deception, trickery. **2.** imposture, lie, piece of trickery.

impôt [ɛ̃po], *s.m.* **1.** tax, duty; **i. foncier,** land tax; **i. sur le revenu,** income tax; **i. progressif,** graduated income tax; **i. supplémentaire sur le revenu,** supertax; **i. retenu à la base, à la source,** (i) pay as you earn (tax), P.A.Y.E.; (ii) tax deducted at source; **i. sur le capital,** capital levy; **i. sur les plus-values, sur les gains de fortune,** capital gains tax; **i. sur le chiffre d'affaires,** turnover tax; **i. du timbre,** stamp duty; **i. direct, indirect,** direct, indirect, tax; **taxes et impôts,** taxes and dues; **payer mille francs d'impôts,** to pay a thousand francs in taxes; **mettre un i. sur qch., frapper qch. d'un impôt,** to tax sth.; to levy a tax on sth.; *F:* **l'i. du sang,** the obligation to serve (in war), the blood tax; *s.a.* ABONNEMENT 1. **2.** taxes, taxation.

impotence [ɛ̃pɔtɑ̃ːs], *s.f.* helplessness, lameness, infirmity.

impotent, -ente [ɛ̃pɔtɑ̃, -ɑ̃ːt]. **1.** *a.* helpless, crippled; **être i. de la jambe gauche,** to be lame in, to have lost the use of, the left leg. **2.** *s.* cripple; helpless invalid.

impoursuivi [ɛ̃pursɥivi], *a.* unpursued, not followed up.

impraticabilité [ɛ̃pratikabilite], *s.f.* impracticability, impracticableness; unpracticalness.

impraticable [ɛ̃pratikabl̩], *a.* **1.** impracticable, unfeasible, unworkable; unpractical; out of the question. **2.** (*a*) impassable; **chemin i. aux automobiles,** road unfit for motor traffic; (*b*) uninhabitable (room, etc.); (country) impossible (for tourists, etc.); *Sp:* (*of football ground, etc.*) unplayable, unfit for play. **3.** *A:* (*of pers.*) unsociable; difficult to live with.

impratique [ɛ̃pratik], *a.* unpractical.

impratiqué [ɛ̃pratike], *a.* unfrequented, untrodden (path, etc.).

imprécateur, -trice [ɛ̃prekatœːr, -tris]. **1.** *a.* that curses, calls down curses. **2.** *s.* curser.

imprécation [ɛ̃prekasjɔ̃], *s.f.* imprecation, curse; **lancer, proférer,** *A:* **faire, des imprécations contre qn,** to curse s.o., to call down curses on s.o.

imprécatoire [ɛ̃prekatwaːr], *a.* imprecatory.

imprécaution [ɛ̃prekosjɔ̃], *s.f. Lit:* want of precaution; incautiousness.

imprécis [ɛ̃presi], *a.* lacking in precision. **1.** vague, unprecise, imprecise, indefinite (terms, etc.); inexplicit. **2.** inaccurate.

imprécisable [ɛ̃presizabl̩], *a.* not precisely determinable, statable.

imprécisé [ɛ̃presize], *a.* not definitely determined, stated.

imprécision [ɛ̃presizjɔ̃], *s.f.* imprecision, lack of precision. **1.** looseness (of terminology, etc.); vagueness (of statement, etc.); **laisser un point dans l'i.,** to leave a point undetermined. **2.** inaccuracy (of aim, etc.).

imprégnable [ɛ̃preɲabl̩], *a.* impregnatable.

imprégnant [ɛ̃preɲɑ̃]. **1.** *a.* impregnating. **2.** *s.m.* impregnant.

imprégnation [ɛ̃preɲasjɔ̃], *s.* **1.** impregnation, permeation; **i. du bois par la créosote,** impregnation of wood with creosote. **2.** *Biol:* (*a*) *A:* impregnation, fecundation; (*b*) telegony.

imprégné [ɛ̃preɲe], *a.* impregnated; **i. de faux principes,** impregnated with false principles; **regard i. de tristesse,** look full of sadness.

imprégner [ɛ̃preɲe], *v.tr.* (**j'imprègne, n. imprégnons; j'imprégnerai**) to impregnate (**de,** with). **1.** to permeate (tissue, wood, etc.). **2.** (*a*) *Biol: A:* to fecundate; (*b*) **dès sa jeunesse il avait été imprégné de ces principes,** from his youth he had been impregnated with these principles, these principles had been instilled into him.

s'imprégner, to become saturated (**de,** with); **s'i. d'eau,** to soak up, soak in, water; **s'i. d'idées nouvelles,** to become impregnated with new ideas.

imprenable [ɛ̃prənabl̩], *a.* impregnable (fortress, etc.); **vue i.,** view that cannot be obstructed, unspoilable view.

impréparation [ɛ̃preparasjɔ̃], *s.f.* unpreparedness (**à,** for).

impresario [ɛ̃presarjo], *s.m.* impresario; business manager (for film star, etc.).

imprescriptibilité [ɛ̃prɛskriptibilite], *s.f. Jur:* imprescriptibility, indefeasibility (of a right, etc.).

imprescriptible [ɛ̃prɛskriptibl̩], *a. Jur:* imprescriptible, indefeasible (right, etc.).

impresse [ɛ̃prɛs], *a.f. Phil:* **idées impresses,** *a posteriori* ideas.

impressible [ɛ̃prɛsibl̩], *a. Phil:* impressible.

impressif, -ive [ɛ̃prɛsif, -iːv], *a. A:* impressive (speech, etc.).

impression [ɛ̃prɛsjɔ̃], *s.f.* **1.** pressing; pressure; **i. du vent,** pressure, force, of the wind. **2.** impressing; (*a*) *Tex: etc:* printing; **i. de coton, sur coton,** calico printing; (*b*) *Typ:* printing (off), striking off; **i. directe,** direct printing; **i. offset,** offset printing; **i. à la gélatine,** gelatine printing; **i. au minimum de pression,** kiss impression; **i. au vol,** on-the-fly printing; **i. typographique,** letterpress printing; **livrer un ouvrage à l'i.,** to have a work printed; **livre à l'i.,** book in the press; **à temps pour l'i.,** in time for press; **faute d'i.,** misprint; **i. en couleurs,** colour printing; **i. en creux,** copperplate printing; (*computers*) **i. à la volée,** on-the-fly printing, printing in flight; *Phot:* **double i.,** double exposure; (*c*) stamping (of coins); (*d*) **i. au fer chaud,** branding; (*e*) *Paint:* priming; (*f*) **l'i. des (saints) stigmates (de Saint François),** the impression of the (Holy) Stigmata (of St Francis). **3.** impression, impress; (*a*) **i. d'un cachet sur la cire,** impression of a seal upon wax; **i. de pas sur le sol,** footprints, footmarks, footsteps, on the ground; (*b*) *Publ:* **troisième i. d'un livre,** third impression third printing, of a book; (*c*) *Engr: etc:* print; **i. en couleurs,** colour print; (*d*) impress (on coin); (*e*) mark, brand (of branding iron); (*f*) *Paint:* priming (coat). **4.** (*a*) (mental) impression; **la ville donne une i. de tristesse,** the town gives an impression of sadness; **dites-nous vos impressions,** tell us your impressions; **quelle i. vous a-t-elle faite?** *F:* **vous a-t-elle fait?** how did she impress you? how does she strike you? **son discours fit une grande i.,** his speech made, created, a great impression; **faire i.** to make an impression; **son discours fit i.,** his speech was very impressive, went home; **faire bonne, mauvaise, i.,** to make a good, bad, impression; **cela fera i.,** it will cause a sensation; **le spectacle lul fit i.,** he was impressed by the scene; **j'ai l'i. de l'avoir déià vu,** I seem to have seen him before, I fancy, I've got an idea, it strikes me, that I've seen him before; (*b*) *Ling:* **i. sémantique,** sign process.

impressionnabilité [ɛ̃prɛsjɔnabilite], *s.f.* **1.** impressionability, impressibility. **2.** *Ch: Phot:* sensitivity.

impressionnable [ɛ̃prɛsjɔnabl̩], *a.* **1.** impressionable, impressible. **2.** *Ch: Phot:* sensitive (plate, etc.); **papier i.,** sensitized paper.

impressionnant [ɛ̃prɛsjɔnɑ̃], *a.* impressive; moving (sight, voice); sensational (news); **la recette a baissé dans des proportions impressionnantes,** there has been an appalling drop in the takings; **effet i.,** spectacular effect; **il était i.,** he made a striking picture.

impressionner [ɛ̃prɛsjɔne], *v.tr.* **1.** (*a*) to impress, affect, move; to make an impression upon (s.o.); **j'ai été très impressionné,** I was very much impressed; *abs.* **spectacle qui impressionne péniblement,** sight that makes a painful impression; (*b*) *F:* to upset, frighten. **2.** (*a*) to act on (the retina); to produce an image on (sensitized paper, etc.); (*b*) *Rec:* to make a recording on (a tape).

s'impressionner, to be strongly affected (by piece of news, etc.); **ne vous impressionnez pas,** don't make too much of it, don't get alarmed about it; don't panic; **elle s'impressionne facilement,** she is easily upset.

impressionnisme [ɛ̃prɛsjɔnism], *s.m. Art:* impressionism.

impressionniste [ɛ̃prɛsjɔnist], *a. & s.m. & f. Art:* impressionist.

imprévisibilité [ɛ̃previzibilite], *s.f.* unforeseeableness, unpredictability.

imprévisible [ɛ̃previzibl̩], *a.* unforeseeable, unpredictable.

imprévision [ɛ̃previzjɔ̃], *s.f.* lack of foresight; improvidence.

imprévoyable [ɛ̃prevwajabl̩], *a.* unforeseeable, unpredictable.

imprévoyance [ɛ̃prevwajɑ̃ːs], *s.f.* lack of foresight, improvidence.

imprévoyant [ɛ̃prevwajɑ̃], *a.* lacking in foresight; improvident.

imprévu [ɛ̃prevy]. **1.** *a.* unforeseen, unlooked-for, unexpected; **événement i.,** unexpected occurrence, bolt from the blue. **2.** *s.m.* (*a*) unexpected character (of event); (*b*) unforeseen events, acts of God; **tenir compte de l'i.,** to allow for contingencies; **parer à l'i.,** to provide against accidents, against emergencies; **sauf i., à moins d'i.,** barring accidents, unless something unforeseen happens; **en cas d'i.,** in case of an emergency, of a contingency; should a contingency arise; **imprévus,** unforeseen expenses, contingencies.

imprimabilité [ɛ̃primabilite], *s.f.* printing quality (of paper).

imprimable [ɛ̃primabl̩], *a.* printable.

imprimage [ɛ̃primaːʒ], *s.m.* drawing (of gold).

imprimant, -ante [ɛ̃primɑ̃, -ɑ̃ːt]. **1.** *a. Typ:* printing (drum). **2.** *s.f.* **imprimante,** printer (of computer).

imprimatur [ɛ̃primatyːr], *s.m.inv.* imprimatur (granted by bishop, university, etc.).

imprimé [ɛ̃prime]. **1.** *a.* printed. **2.** *a. Ph.Geog:* **méandre i.,** entrenched meander. **3.** *s.m.* printed paper, book; **remplir un i.,** to fill in a form; *Post:* **imprimés,** printed matter; **tarif imprimés,** printed-paper rate; **service des imprimés,** book post; **département, catalogue, des imprimés (dans une bibliothèque),** department, catalogue, of printed books. **4.** *s.m. Tex:* print.

imprimer [ɛ̃prime], *v.tr.* **1.** to communicate (direction, etc.) to (sth.); **i. le mouvement à un corps,** to impart, transmit, motion to a body, to set a body in motion; *Lit:* **i. le respect,** to inspire respect; **à tout ce qu'elle porte elle imprime sa personalité,** she stamps her personality upon everything she wears. **2.** (*a*) to (im)print, impress, stamp (sth. on sth.); **i. un cachet sur la cire,** to stamp, impress, a seal upon wax; (*b*) to (im)print (material); **indienne imprimée,** printed calico; print; (*c*) *Elcs:* **circuit imprimé,** printed circuit. **3.** *Typ:* to print; **presse à i.,** printing press; **cette machine imprime 80 feuilles par minute,** this machine runs off eighty copies a minute; *F:* **i. qn,** to publish s.o.'s works, to publish s.o.; **il aime à se faire i., à se voir imprimé,** he likes to see himself in print; **le livre est imprimé,** the book is in print. **4.** *Paint:* to prime, ground (canvas, etc.).

imprimerie [ɛ̃primri], *s.f.* **1.** (art of) printing; **l'i. a changé la face du monde,** the invention of printing changed the face of the world; **caractères d'i.,** type; **encre d'i.,** printing ink. **2.** (*a*) printing house, printing works, (printing) press; **I. nationale,** State Press; **livre à l'i.,** book in the press, book printing; (*b*) printing plant.

imprimerie-librairie [ɛ̃primrilibrɛri], *s.f.* printing and publishing house; *pl. imprimeries-librairies.*

imprimeur [ɛ̃primœːr], *s.m.* **1.** (*a*) (master) printer; **i. libraire,** printer and publisher; (*b*) (working) printer. **2.** *Tex:* **i. d'indiennes,** calico printer. **3.** **i. lithographe,** lithographer. **4.** *a.* **cylindre i.,** printing drum.

imprimeuse [ɛ̃primøːz], *s.f.* small printing machine; hand press.

imprimure [ɛ̃primyːr], *s.f.* **1.** *Paint:* priming, grounding. **2.** playing-card printer's stencil.

improbabilité [ɛ̃prɔbabilite], *s.f.* **1.** improbability, unlikelihood. **2.** **ce sont là des improbabilités,** these are unlikely contingencies; these things are not likely to happen.

improbable [ɛ̃prɔbabl̩], *a.* improbable, unlikely; **nous attendions le passage i. d'un taxi,** we were waiting on the off chance for a taxi.

improbablement [ɛ̃prɔbabləmɑ̃], *adv.* improbably.

improbant [ɛ̃prɔbɑ̃], *a.* unconvincing.

improbateur, -trice [ɛ̃prɔbatœːr, -tris]. *Lit:* **1.** *a.* disapproving; **murmure i.,** murmur of disapproval. **2.** *s.* disapprover, censurer.

improbatif, -ive [ɛ̃prɔbatif, -iːv], *a. Lit:* disapproving; (sign) of disapproval.

improbation [ɛ̃prɔbasjɔ̃], *s.f. Lit:* (strong) disapproval; disapprobation; **sa conduite a encouru l'i. générale,** his conduct has been censured by everybody.

improbe [ɛ̃prɔb], *a.* (*rare*) dishonest, unprincipled.

improbité [ɛ̃prɔbite], *s.f. Lit:* 1. dishonesty, improbity; lack of integrity. 2. dishonest act.

improductibilité [ɛ̃prɔdyktibilite], *s.f.* unproducibleness.

improductible [ɛ̃prɔdyktibl̩], *a.* unproducible.

improductif, -ive [ɛ̃prɔdyktif, -iːv], *a.* unproductive (land, etc.); non-productive (assets); **argent i.,** money lying idle.

improductivement [ɛ̃prɔdyktivmɑ̃], *adv.* unproductively.

improductivité [ɛ̃prɔdyktivite], *s.f.* unproductiveness.

improfitable [ɛ̃prɔfitabl̩], *a.* unprofitable, unremunerative.

improgressif, -ive [ɛ̃prɔgrɛsif, -iːv], *a.* unprogressive.

impromptu [ɛ̃prɔ̃pty]. 1. *adv.* without preparation, impromptu. 2. *a.* (*often inv.*) unpremeditated (departure, etc.); impromptu (meal, etc.); extempore, off the cuff (speech, etc.); *adv.phr.* **à l'i.,** off-hand, on the spur of the moment. 3. *s.m. Th: Mus:* impromptu.

impromulgué [ɛ̃prɔmylge], *a.* unpromulgated.

imprononçable [ɛ̃prɔnɔ̃sabl̩], *a.* unpronounceable.

impropère [ɛ̃prɔpɛːr], *s.m. Ecc:* (*R.C. Liturgy*) the Reproaches, the Improperia.

impropice [ɛ̃prɔpis], *a.* unpropitious, unfavourable, inauspicious.

improportionnel, -elle [ɛ̃prɔpɔrsjɔnɛl], *a.* (*of numbers*) without any common ratio.

impropre [ɛ̃prɔpr̩], *a.* (*a*) incorrect, wrong (term, expression); (*b*) **i. à qch., à faire qch.,** unfit, unsuitable, for sth., unsuitable for doing sth.; **i. au service militaire,** unfit for military service; **i. à la consommation,** unfit for human consumption; (*c*) improper (diphthong, derivation).

improprement [ɛ̃prɔprəmɑ̃], *adv.* incorrectly, improperly, wrongly.

impropriété [ɛ̃prɔpri(j)ete], *s.f.* (*a*) impropriety; incorrectness; (*b*) incorrect use of a word.

improspère [ɛ̃prɔspɛːr], *a.* (*rare*) unprosperous.

improuvable [ɛ̃pruvabl̩], *a.* unprovable.

improuvé [ɛ̃pruve], *a.* unproved; *Jur:* not proven.

improuver [ɛ̃pruve], *v.tr. A:* to disapprove of (sth.).

improvisade [ɛ̃prɔvizad], *s.f. A:* improvisation; **parler à l'i.,** to speak extempore, *F:* off the cuff.

improvisateur, -trice [ɛ̃prɔvizatœːr, -tris], *s.* (*a*) *Mus:* improviser, improvisator; *improv(v)isatore, -trice,* extempore player; (*b*) writer of impromptu verses; (*c*) extempore speaker; *Th: F:* ad-libber.

improvisation [ɛ̃prɔvizasjɔ̃], *s.f. Mus: etc:* improvisation. 1. improvising, extemporizing, extempore playing; *Th: F:* ad-libbing. 2. extemporization (on organ, etc.); impromptu poem; extempore speech.

improvisé [ɛ̃prɔvize], *a.* extemporaneous, off the cuff (speech, etc.); impromptu (dance); *Sp:* scratch (team).

improviser [ɛ̃prɔvize], *v.tr.* 1. to improvise; **i. un bal,** to arrange a dance at a moment's notice, on the spur of the moment, an impromptu dance; **i. un discours,** to make an impromptu, extempore speech; **i. un mât et une voile,** to rig up a jury mast and sail. 2. *abs.* (*a*) to speak extempore, *F:* to ad-lib; (*b*) *Mus:* **i. à l'orgue,** to improvise, extemporize, on the organ.

improviste (à l') [alɛ̃prɔvist], *adv.phr.* unexpectedly, unawares, without a moment's warning; **prendre qn à l'i.,** to take s.o. unawares; **prendre l'ennemi à l'i.,** to take the enemy by surprise; **survenir à l'i.,** to turn up unexpectedly; **visite à l'i.,** surprise visit.

imprudemment [ɛ̃prydamɑ̃], *adv.* imprudently, rashly, incautiously, unadvisedly.

imprudence [ɛ̃prydɑ̃ːs], *s.f.* imprudence. 1. rashness; **quelle i. de votre part!** how imprudent of you! **pas d'i.!** be careful! *Jur:* **homicide par i.,** manslaughter (by negligence). 2. imprudent act; **commettre une i.,** to be guilty of an imprudence; **commettre des imprudences,** to act rashly, imprudently.

imprudent, -ente [ɛ̃prydɑ̃, -ɑ̃ːt]. 1. *a.* imprudent, foolhardy, rash, reckless; unwise; venturesome; unwary, incautious. 2. *s.* imprudent, rash, reckless, person; dare-devil.

impubère [ɛ̃pybɛːr], *a. Jur:* under the age of puberty.

impuberté [ɛ̃pybɛrte], *s.f.* impuberty.

impubliable [ɛ̃pybli(j)abl̩], *a.* unpublishable.

impublié [ɛ̃pybli(j)e], (*a*) *a.* unpublished; (*b*) *s.m.* unpublished manuscript.

impudemment [ɛ̃pydamɑ̃], *adv.* shamelessly; impudently; **mentir i.,** to lie shamelessly, brazenly, unblushingly.

impudence [ɛ̃pydɑ̃ːs], *s.f.* 1. impudence; (*a*) effrontery; (*b*) shamelessness. 2. (*a*) piece of impudence, of effrontery; (*b*) shameless action, remark.

impudent, -ente [ɛ̃pydɑ̃, -ɑ̃ːt], *a. & s.* 1. shameless, immodest, unblushing (person, action). 2. impudent, insolent (person).

impudeur [ɛ̃pydœːr], *s.f.* shamelessness. 1. immodesty, lewdness. 2. effrontery, shameless audacity.

impudicité [ɛ̃pydisite], *s.f.* 1. unchastity, impudicity, lewdness. 2. indecent act, lewd act, indecency.

impudique [ɛ̃pydik]. 1. *a.* unchaste, immodest (person); lewd, indecent (act, song, etc.). 2. *s. B:* whoremonger; harlot.

impudiquement [ɛ̃pydikmɑ̃], *adv.* unchastely, lewdly, immodestly.

impugnation [ɛ̃pyɲasjɔ̃], *s.f. A:* impugning, impugnment.

impugner [ɛ̃pyɲe], *v.tr. A:* to impugn.

impuissance [ɛ̃pɥisɑ̃ːs], *s.f.* 1. impotence, impotency, powerlessness, helplessness; **i. à faire qch.,** powerlessness, inability, to do sth.; **je suis dans l'i. de le sauver,** it is beyond my power to save him; **l'i. de ses efforts,** the futility of his efforts. 2. *Med:* impotence, impotency.

impuissant [ɛ̃pɥisɑ̃], *a.* 1. (*a*) impotent, powerless, helpless (person); **i. à faire qch.,** powerless to do sth.; (*b*) unavailing, futile, ineffective (effort, etc.). 2. *Med:* impotent.

impulser [ɛ̃pylse], *v.tr.* to give impulse to, to impel.

impulseur [ɛ̃pylsœːr], *s.m.* (*a*) impeller (of pump, etc.); (*b*) *Av: etc:* thruster; **i. d'apogée, de périgée,** apogee thruster, perigee thruster; **i. de rentrée (dans l'atmosphère),** re-entry thruster; **i. de lacet,** yaw thruster.

impulsif, -ive [ɛ̃pylsif, -iːv], *a.* impulsive (force, character, etc.).

impulsion [ɛ̃pylsjɔ̃], *s.f.* (*a*) *Mec:* impulse; **force d'i.,** impulsive force; (*b*) *Atom.Ph:* momentum (of particle); **i. du spin,** spin momentum; **i. orbitale,** orbital momentum; **i. neutronique,** neutron burst, neutron pulse; (*c*) *El: Elcs: etc:* **i. de courant,** current impulse; rush, surge, of current; **i. d'ouverture,** break impulse; **i. de fermeture,** make impulse; **i. de tension,** potential pulse, voltage pulse; **conformateur d'impulsions,** pulse shaper; **émission d'impulsions,** pulsing; **générateur d'impulsions,** pulse generator; **interrupteur d'impulsions,** pulse chopper; **compteur d'impulsions,** pulse counter; **analyseur d'amplitude d'impulsions,** pulse height analyser; **ondes fonctionnant, travaillant, en régime d'impulsions,** pulsed waves; *W.Tel:* **transmetteur à impulsions,** impact transmitter; **i. d'accord,** tuning pulse; (*d*) (radar) pulse; (sonar) ping; **émetteur d'impulsions sonar,** pinger; **durée d'i. (de) sonar,** ping length; **radar à impulsions,** pulse radar; **radar à modulation d'i.,** pulse-modulated radar; **i. de fixation,** gating pulse, strobe pulse; **i. parasite,** pulse strike; **train d'impulsions,** pulse train; (*e*) impulse, impulsion, impetus; **donner de l'i. au commerce,** to give a stimulus, an impulse, to trade; **les affaires ont reçu une nouvelle i.,** business has received fresh impetus, shows renewed activity. 2. (*a*) impulse; **êtres d'i.,** creatures of impulse; **sous l'i. du moment,** under the impulse of the moment, on the spur of the moment; (*b*) prompting; **sous l'i. de qui cela s'est-il fait?** at whose instance, at whose prompting, was it done? who was behind it?

impulsion-obsession [ɛ̃pylsjɔ̃ɔbsɛsjɔ̃], *s.f. Psy:* obsessive impulse; *pl. impulsions-obsessions.*

impulsivement [ɛ̃pylsivmɑ̃], *adv.* impulsively.

impulsivité [ɛ̃pylsivite], *s.f.* impulsiveness.

impunément [ɛ̃pynemɑ̃], *adv.* with impunity.

impuni [ɛ̃pyni], *a.* unpunished; **laisser une attaque impunie,** to allow an attack to pass unpunished; (*of crime*) **rester i.,** to go unpunished.

impunissable [ɛ̃pynisabl̩], *a.* unpunishable.

impunité [ɛ̃pynite], *s.f.* impunity; **voler les idées de qn en toute i.,** to steal s.o.'s ideas with impunity.

impur, -ure [ɛ̃pyːr]. 1. *a.* (*a*) impure; foul, tainted; mixed; **eau impure,** cloudy, muddy, water; **de naissance impure,** of tainted stock; (*b*) *Rel:* unclean (flesh, spirit); (*c*) immoral; **femme impure,** woman of loose morals; **geste i.,** lewd gesture; **langage i.,** foul language. 2. (*a*) *s.* person of loose morals; (*b*) *s.f. A:* **impure,** prostitute.

impurement [ɛ̃pyrmɑ̃], *adv.* impurely, lewdly; immorally.

impureté [ɛ̃pyrte], *s.f.* 1. (*a*) impurity, foulness (of water, etc.); (*b*) *Rel:* uncleanness; (*c*) (moral) impurity, unchastity, lewdness, immorality; (*c*) (*computers*) impurity; **i. acceptrice,** acceptor impurity. 2. *pl.* (*a*) impurities (in water, etc.); *Paperm:* contraries; (*b*) *A:* **livre plein d'impuretés,** book full of obscenities.

impurifié [ɛ̃pyrifje], *a.* unpurified.

imputabilité [ɛ̃pytabilite], *s.f.* imputability.

imputable [ɛ̃pytabl̩], *a.* 1. imputable, ascribable, attributable (à, to); **aucun blâme ne lui est i.,** no blame attaches to him; **manque de compression i. à une soupape faussée,** lack of compression attributable, due, to a bent valve. 2. chargeable; **frais imputables sur un compte,** expenses chargeable to an account. 3. *Theol:* **les mérites du Christ sont imputables aux croyants,** the righteousness of Christ is imputable to believers.

imputatif, -ive [ɛ̃pytatif, -iːv], *a. Theol:* imputative (righteousness, etc.).

imputation [ɛ̃pytasjɔ̃], *s.f.* 1. imputation, charge; **imputations calomnieuses,** slanderous charges. 2. (*a*) *Com: Fin:* charge, charging (up) (of expenses, etc.); **i. d'une somme sur une quantité,** deduction of a sum from a quota; (*b*) *Jur:* **i. de paiement (sur une dette),** appropriation of moneys (to a debt); **un débiteur peut déterminer l'i. de ses paiements,** a debtor may specify the application of his payments. 3. *Theol:* imputation, application (of the righteousness of Christ, etc.).

imputer [ɛ̃pyte], *v.tr.* 1. (*a*) to impute, ascribe, attribute; **i. un crime à un innocent,** to impute a crime to an innocent person; **les faits à lui imputés,** the actions imputed to him; **i. la faute à qn,** to lay the blame at s.o.'s door; **la faute doit en être imputée à . . .,** the blame falls on . . .; **i. un malheur à l'imprudence de qn,** to ascribe a disaster, to put a disaster down, to s.o.'s imprudence; **imputez-le à mon ignorance,** put it down to my ignorance; **i. à qn d'avoir fait qch.,** to charge s.o. with having done sth., with doing sth.; *A:* **i. qch. à péché à qn,** to count sth. for sin to s.o.; *A:* **ne me l'imputez pas à crime,** do not set it down against me as a crime; **ne me l'imputez pas pour faiblesse,** do not put it down to weakness on my part; (*b*) *Theol:* to impute (righteousness, guilt). 2. *Com: Fin:* **i. qch. sur qch.,** (i) to deduct sth. from sth., (ii) to charge sth. to sth.; **i. des frais à, sur, un compte,** to charge expenses to an account; **i. une somme au compte de qch.,** to charge a sum on sth.; **i. un paiement à une certaine dette,** to assign, apply, a payment to a particular debt.

imputrescibilisation [ɛ̃pytrɛs(s)ibilizasjɔ̃], *s.* prevention of decay.

imputrescibilité [ɛ̃pytrɛs(s)ibilite], *s.f.* imputrescibility.

imputrescible [ɛ̃pytrɛs(s)ibl̩], *a.* imputrescible, incorruptible; rot-proof; **rendre de la colle i.,** to stop paste from going bad.

in- [in, ɛ̃], (before *l* **il-** [il], before *b, m, p,* **im-** [im, ɛ̃], before *r* **ir-** [ir]), *pref. expresses negation,* in-, im-, il-, ir-; un-; **illiquéfié,** unliquefied; **illesté,** without ballast; **illibéralisme,** illiberalism; **impitoyabilité,** pitilessness; **inamissible,** inamissible; **inamusable,** unamusable; **indétachable,** undetachable; **invigilance,** unwatchfulness; **irréalisation,** failure to realize; **irrémissibilité,** irremissibility; **irrespect,** disrespect.

inabondance [inabɔ̃dɑ̃ːs], *s.f.* (*rare*) dearth, scarcity (**de,** of).

inabordable [inabɔrdabl̩], *a.* (*a*) unapproachable, inaccessible (coast, person, etc.); (*b*) unattackable (position, etc.); (*c*) prohibitive (price).

inabordé [inabɔrde], *a.* unapproached, unvisited (island, etc.).

inabrité [inabrite], *a.* unsheltered, unprotected.

inabrogé [inabrɔʒe], *a.* unrepealed.

inabrogeable [inabrɔʒabl̩], *a.* unrepealable.

inabsous, -oute [inapsu, -ut], *a.* unabsolved, unpardoned.

inabstinence [inapstinɑ̃ːs], *s.f.* intemperance.

inaccentué [inaksɑ̃tɥe], *a. Gram: Ling:* 1. unaccented (vowel). 2. unstressed (syllable, etc.).

inacceptable [inaksɛptabl̩], *a.* unacceptable; objectionable.

inacceptation [inaksɛptasjɔ̃], *s.f.* non-acceptance.

inaccepté [inaksɛpte], *a.* unaccepted, declined.

inaccessibilité [inaksɛsibilite], *s.f.* inaccessibility, unapproachableness; *Geog:* **pôle d'i.,** pole of inaccessibility.

inaccessible [inaksɛsibl̩], *a.* 1. inaccessible; unapproachable; *F:* ungetatable; **dans une région i.,** *F:* at the back of beyond; **poste i. à ceux qui n'ont pas de grades universitaires,** post for which those who have no university degree

are ineligible. **2. forêt i. aux rayons du soleil,** forest into which the rays of the sun cannot penetrate; **boîte i. à la lumière,** light-tight box; **i. à la pitié,** inaccessible to pity, incapable of pity; **i. à la flatterie,** proof against flattery.

inacclimaté [inaklimate], *a.* unacclimatized.

inaccommodable [inakɔmɔdabl̩], *a. A:* irreconcilable (facts); unadjustable (quarrel, etc.).

inaccompagné [inakɔ̃paɲe], *a.* unaccompanied.

inaccompli [inakɔ̃pli], *a.* unaccomplished, unfinished, unfulfilled.

inaccomplissement [inakɔ̃plismɑ̃], *s.m.* nonfulfilment, non-accomplishment.

inaccordable [inakɔrdabl̩], *a.* **1.** (*a*) irreconcilable (facts); (parties) unwilling to come to terms; (*b*) untunable (instrument). **2.** ungrantable, inadmissible (request, etc.).

inaccostable [inakɔstabl̩], *a.* (*esp. of pers.*) unapproachable, difficult of access.

inaccoutumance [inakutymɑ̃:s], *s.f.* **1.** *A. & Lit:* unaccustomedness. **2.** *Med:* **i. à un médicament,** non-addictive quality of a drug.

inaccoutumé [inakutyme], *a.* unaccustomed. **1.** unused (à, to). **2.** unusual.

inaccusable [inakyzabl̩], *a.* beyond the reach of accusation; unimpeachable.

inachevé [inaʃve], *a.* unfinished, uncompleted.

inachèvement [inaʃɛvmɑ̃], *s.m.* failure to finish, to complete (work); incompletion.

inacquérable [inakerabl̩], *a.* unacquirable.

inacquitté [inakite], *a.* (*a*) undischarged (criminal, debt, etc.); (*b*) unreceipted (bill).

inactif, -ive [inaktif, -i:v], *a.* inactive. **1.** idle, not in action; *Ch: etc:* **corps i.,** inert body; *Com:* **marché i.,** dull market; **fonds inactifs,** capital lying idle, unemployed capital. **2.** indolent, sluggish, inert, idle.

inactinique [inaktinik], *a. Ph:* inactinic; *Phot:* **éclairage i.,** safe light; **lampe, lanterne, i.,** safe lamp.

inaction [inaksjɔ̃], *s.f.* inaction, idleness; *Com:* dullness (of market).

inactivation [inaktivasjɔ̃], *s.f. Med:* inactivation (of a serum).

inactivement [inaktivmɑ̃], *adv.* (*a*) inactively; (*b*) indolently; **vivre i.,** to lead an idle, lazy, life.

inactiver [inaktive], *v.tr. Med:* to inactivate (a serum).

inactivité [inaktivite], *s.f.* **1.** inactivity; *Ch:* inertness; *Com:* dullness (of market); **période d'i.,** period of inactivity, idle period; *Com:* dead period; *Ind:* down time. **2.** (*of civil servant, etc.*) **être mis en i.,** to be out of work, unemployed.

inactuel, -elle [inaktɥɛl], *a.* out-of-date; of another age; not in the news.

inadaptable [inadaptabl̩], *a.* unadaptable.

inadaptation [inadaptasjɔ̃], *s.f.* **1.** maladjustment. **2.** *Ph.Geog:* antecedence (of drainage system).

inadapté, -ée [inadapte], *a. & s.* maladjusted; **enfant i.,** maladjusted child; **il est i.,** he is a (social) misfit; **les inadaptés,** the social misfits; **la ré-éducation des inadaptés,** the re-education of the maladjusted; **mener une vie inadaptée à ses besoins,** to lead a life unsuited to one's needs, that is not in conformity with one's needs; **vieillards inadaptés aux exigences de la vie moderne,** old people who cannot cope with the demands of modern life.

inadéquat [inadekwa], *a.* inadequate.

inadéquation [inadekwasjɔ̃], *s.f.* inadequacy.

inadhérent [inaderɑ̃], *a.* inadherent, inadhesive.

inadmissibilité [inadmisibilite], *s.f.* **1.** inadmissibility (of evidence, request). **2.** *Sch:* failure to qualify at the written examination.

inadmissible [inadmisibl̩], *a.* **1.** inadmissible, objectionable (request, etc.); **votre proposition est i.,** your proposal is out of the question; **il serait i. que les hostilités reprissent,** it would be unthinkable for hostilities to be resumed; **c'est i.!** who ever heard of such a thing! **2. candidat i.,** candidate who has not qualified at the written examination.

inadmission [inadmisjɔ̃], *s.f.* non-admission, refusal of admission.

inadvertance [inadvɛrtɑ̃:s], *s.f.* **1.** inadvertence, inadvertency, unwariness; **par i.,** inadvertently, by an oversight; through carelessness, by mistake. **2.** (*a*) oversight, mistake; (*b*) lapse of memory, of attention.

inadvertant [inadvɛrtɑ̃], *a.* (*rare*) inadvertent, heedless, careless.

inaffecté [inafekte], *a.* **1.** unaffected (style, etc.). **2.** unallocated (room, etc.).

inaffection [inafɛksjɔ̃], *s.f.* lack of affection; coldness.

inaffouillable [inafujabl̩], *a. Civ.E:* water-resisting (lining of canal, etc.).

inaguerri [inageri], *a.* untrained, unseasoned, raw (troops).

inajournable [inaʒurnabl̩], *a.* that cannot be postponed, adjourned.

inaliénabilité [inaljenabilite], *s.f. Jur:* inalienability, inalienableness; indefeasibility, indefeasibleness (of right).

inaliénable [inaljenabl̩], *a. Jur:* inalienable, untransferable, unassignable (property, right, etc.); indefeasible (right); **rendre un legs i.,** to tie up a succession.

inaliénablement [inaljenabləmɑ̃], *adv.* inalienably; indefeasibly.

inaliénation [inaljenasjɔ̃], *s.f. Jur:* inalienability, inalienableness.

inaliéné [inaljene], *a. Jur:* unalienated.

inalliable [inaljabl̩], *a.* **1.** incompatible (ideas, etc.). **2.** *Metall:* that cannot be alloyed, nonalloyable.

inalpage [inalpa:ʒ], *s.m.* (*in Savoy*) moving up to summer pastures.

inalper (s') [sinalpe], *v.pr.* (*in Savoy*) to move up (with flocks and herds) to summer pastures.

inaltérabilité [inalterabilite], *s.f.* **1.** resistance to deterioration; permanence; fastness (of colour). **2.** (*a*) unalterableness (of planetary motion, etc.); (*b*) unfailingness (of good humour, etc.).

inaltérable [inalterabl̩], *a.* **1.** that does not deteriorate, undeteriorating; **i. à l'air ou à l'eau,** unaffected by air or water, weather-resisting; **santé i.,** iron constitution; **couleur i.,** fast colour; **métal i.,** non-corrosive metal. **2.** (*a*) unalterable (course of the stars, etc.); (*b*) unfailing, unvarying (good humour, etc.).

inaltéré [inaltere], *a.* unspoilt, unimpaired, undeteriorated; (*of stone, etc.*) unweathered.

inamendable [inamɑ̃dabl̩], *a.* unimprovable (land).

inamiable [inamjabl̩], *a.* unamiable.

inamical, -aux [inamikal, -o], *a.* unfriendly.

inamicalement [inamikalmɑ̃], *adv.* in an unfriendly manner.

inamissible [inamisibl̩], *a. Theol:* inamissible.

inamovibilité [inamɔvibilite], *s.f. Adm:* fixity of tenure; irremovability (of judge, etc.).

inamovible [inamɔvibl̩], *a.* irremovable. **1.** (*a*) holding appointment for life; *F:* **il est vraiment i.,** he's a fixture, you'll never shift him; (*b*) (post) held for life. **2.** fixed, built in; **agencements inamovibles (d'un bâtiment),** fixtures; **(pièce) i.,** non-detachable (part).

inanalysable [inanalizabl̩], *a.* that cannot be analysed.

inanimé [inanime], *a.* **1.** (*a*) inanimate; **le monde i.,** inanimate nature; (*b*) *Gram:* inanimate (gender). **2.** (*a*) inanimate, lifeless; **corps i.,** inanimate, dead, body; (*b*) senseless, unconscious; **tomber i.,** to fall down unconscious, in a faint. **3.** lifeless, lacking animation; **la place était vide, le port i.,** the square was empty, the port without life; **regard i.,** dull, lifeless, stare; *Lit:* **style i.,** lifeless flat, style; *Com:* **marché i.,** dull market.

inanisation [inanizasjɔ̃], *s.f. Med:* innutrition.

inanité [inanite], *s.f.* **1.** (*a*) *A:* emptiness, void; (*b*) inanity, futility. **2.** inane remark.

inanitiation [inanisjasjɔ̃], *s.f. Med:* innutrition.

inanition [inanisjɔ̃], *s.f.* (*a*) *O:* innutrition; (*b*) inanition, starvation; **mourir d'i.,** to die of starvation, to starve to death; **tomber d'i.,** to collapse from starvation; **le commerce serait mort d'i.,** trade would have been starved out of existence.

inapaisable [inapɛzabl̩], *a.* inappeasable, unappeasable (hunger, etc.); unslakable, unquenchable (thirst); (grief) that nothing can assuage, that nothing can soothe; not to be assuaged.

inapaisé [inapeze], *a.* unappeased (hunger, etc.); unslaked, unquenched (thirst); unassuaged (grief, etc.).

inapercevance [inapɛrsəvɑ̃:s], *s.f.* lack of perception.

inaperçu [inapɛrsy], *a.* (*a*) unseen, unperceived, unobserved; (*b*) unnoticed, unremarked; **passer i.,** to escape notice; to pass unnoticed; (*of mistake, etc.*) to escape detection, to pass undetected.

inapparent [inaparɑ̃], *a.* unapparent; inconspicuous.

inappétence [inapetɑ̃:s], *s.f.* (*a*) *Med:* lack of appetite, inappetence; (*b*) **i. sexuelle,** lack of sexual desire; frigidity.

inapplicabilité [inaplikabilite], *s.f.* inapplicability.

inapplicable [inaplikabl̩], *a.* inapplicable; **théorie i.,** impracticable theory; **loi, décret, i.,** law, decree, which cannot be applied, put into effect.

inapplication [inaplikasjɔ̃], *s.f.* **1.** lack of assiduity, of application; inapplication; **réprimander un élève pour son i.,** to reprimand a pupil for lack of application, for inattention. **2. i. d'une loi,** failure to put a law into effect; leaving of a law in abeyance; **l'i. d'un système ne prouve pas qu'il soit inapplicable,** the failure to make use of a system does not prove that it is impracticable.

inappliqué [inaplike], *a.* **1.** lacking in application, careless; **élève i.,** inattentive pupil. **2.** unapplied (method, etc.); (law) in abeyance; dormant.

inappréciable [inapresjabl̩], *a.* **1.** inappreciable (quantity, etc.); **i. à l'œil,** not discernible by, not perceptible to, the eye. **2.** inestimable, invaluable, priceless; **services inappréciables,** invaluable services; **bonheur i.,** inestimable happiness.

inappréciablement [inapresjabləmɑ̃], *adv.* inappreciably.

inapprécié [inapresje], *a.* unappreciated.

inapprenable [inaprənabl̩], *a.* unlearnable.

inapprêté [inaprete], *a.* unprepared, uncooked, (food, etc.); undressed (cloth, etc.); unrehearsed (speech, etc.); **style i.,** easy, unstudied, style.

inappris [inapri], *a.* unlearnt (lesson, etc.).

inapprivoisable [inaprivwazabl̩], *a.* untamable.

inapprivoisé [inaprivwaze], *a.* untamed; wild (bird, etc.); shy.

inapprochable [inaprɔʃabl̩], *a.* unapproachable.

inapprouvé [inapruve], *a.* unapproved (of).

inapte [inapt]. **1.** *a.* (*a*) inapt, unapt; unfit (à, for); unsuited (à, to); **i. aux affaires,** unfit for, unsuited for, unsuited to, business; **il était i. à se faire apprécier,** he was incapable of making himself appreciated; (*b*) *Mil:* **être déclaré i.,** to be declared unfit for full military service; **i. à faire campagne,** unfit for active service. **2.** *s.m.* **les inaptes,** the unfit; the incapacitated.

inaptitude [inaptityd], *s.f.* unaptness, inaptness, inaptitude; unfitness (à, for); incapacity (for work, military service, etc.).

inarmé [inarme], *a.* unarmed, without arms.

inarrangeable [inarɑ̃ʒabl̩], *a.* unarrangeable; (dispute) that cannot be adjusted.

inarticulable [inartikylabl̩], *a.* unpronounceable.

inarticulation [inartikylasjɔ̃], *s.f.* inability to articulate (clearly).

inarticulé [inartikyle]. **1.** *a.* (*a*) inarticulate (sound, etc.); (*b*) not jointed; *Z: etc:* inarticulate(d). **2.** *s.m.pl. Z:* **inarticulés,** Inarticulata.

inassermenté [inasɛrmɑ̃te], *a.* unsworn; *Hist:* nonjuring (priest).

inasservi [inasɛrvi], *a.* unsubdued, unenslaved.

inassiduité [inasidɥite], *s.f.* lack of assiduity.

inassiégeable [inasjeʒabl̩], *a.* unbesiegeable.

inassignable [inasiɲabl̩], *a.* unassignable, unassigned (cause, etc.).

inassimilable [inasimilabl̩], *a.* inassimilable, unassimilable.

inassisté [inasiste], *a.* not in receipt of national assistance.

inassorti [inasɔrti], *a.* ill-assorted, ill-matched.

inassortissable [inasɔrtisabl̩], *a.* unmatchable; that cannot be matched.

inassouvi [inasuvi], *a.* unsatiated, unappeased, unsatisfied, unsated (hunger, desire); unslaked, unquenched (thirst).

inassouvissable [inasuvisabl̩], *a.* insatiable, insatiate, unappeasable, unsatisfiable, unquenchable.

inassouvissement [inasuvismɑ̃], *s.m.* **1.** nonsatisfaction (of desire, etc.). **2.** *pl. Psy:* unsatisfied instincts.

inassujetti [inasyʒeti], *a.* **1.** (*a*) unsubjected (à, to); (*b*) unsubdued. **2.** unfixed, loose (rope end, etc.).

inassuré [inasyre], *a.* unassured, uncertain (success, etc.).

inattaquable [inatakabl̩], *a.* unassailable, unattackable (position, etc.); unquestionable (right, etc.); *Ch: etc:* **i. par les acides, aux acides,** acid-proof, acid-resisting; unattacked by acids; incorrodible.

inattaqué [inatake], *a.* unattacked; unassailed; unquestioned.

inatteignable [inatɛɲabl̩], *a.* unattainable; unreachable.

inattendu [inatɑ̃dy], *a.* unexpected, unlooked for, unforeseen.

inattentif, -ive [inatɑ̃tif, -i:v], *a.* inattentive (à, to); unobservant, careless, heedless (à, of); **élève i.,** inattentive pupil; **lecteur i.,** careless reader; **i. aux avertissements,** taking no notice of the warnings.

inattention [inatɑ̃sjɔ̃], *s.f.* (*a*) inattention (à, to); carelessness; negligence, unobservance (à, of);

(*b*) **faute d'i.,** careless mistake; slip; **par i.,** through an oversight.

inattesté [inatɛste], *a.* unattested.

inaudible [inodibl̩], *a.* inaudible.

inaugural, -aux [inogyral, -o], *a.* inaugural (address, etc.); **voyage i.,** maiden voyage, trip.

inaugurateur, -trice [inogyratœːr, -tris], *s.* inaugurator.

inauguration [inogyrasjɔ̃], *s.f.* inauguration; opening (of fête, port, etc.); unveiling (of statue); **discours d'i.,** inaugural address; **faire l'i. de . . .,** to inaugurate . . .; to open (fête, new hall, etc.).

inaugurer [inogyre], *v.tr.* to inaugurate, dedicate (building, etc.); to unveil (statue, etc.); to open (fête, port, etc.); to usher in (epoch, etc.); **l'assemblée inaugurera ses travaux . . .,** the assembly will begin its work . . .; **i. un navire,** to put a ship into service, into commission; **i. une politique nouvelle,** to initiate a new policy; **i. une mode,** to launch a fashion; *F:* **i. un nouvel appartement,** to give a house-warming (party); *F:* **i. un nouveau chapeau,** to wear a hat for the first time.

inauthenticité [inotɑ̃tisite], *s.f.* unauthenticity.

inauthentique [inotɑ̃tik], *a.* unauthentic, not genuine.

inaverti [inavɛrti], *a.* (*a*) unwarned; unadmonished; (*b*) uninformed, inexperienced, unexperienced.

inavouable [inavwabl̩], *a.* unavowable, unacknowledgeable; **projet i.,** plan which one dare not acknowledge; **un métier i.,** a job that one is ashamed to mention; **douleurs inavouables,** sorrows to which one cannot confess; **un livre i.,** a book of which one is ashamed to acknowledge the authorship.

inavouablement [inavwabləmɑ̃], *adv.* unacknowledgeably.

inavoué [inavwe], *a.* unacknowledged; unconfessed, unavowed; sneaking (liking, etc.); **crime i.,** hidden, unconfessed, crime; **jalousie inavouée,** secret, unacknowledged, jealousy.

inbreeding [inbridiŋ], *s.m. Husb:* inbreeding.

Inca [ɛ̃ka], *s.m. & a.inv. Hist:* Inca.

incaguer [ɛ̃kage], *v.tr.* (*a*) to cover with excrement; (*b*) *A:* to scorn.

incalcinable [ɛ̃kalsinabl̩], *a. Ch: etc:* that cannot be calcined, not calcinable.

incalculable [ɛ̃kalkylabl̩], *a.* incalculable, beyond computation; **nombre i. de . . .,** countless number of . . .; **conséquences incalculables,** incalculable consequences.

incalculablement [ɛ̃kalkylabləmɑ̃], *adv.* incalculably.

incalescence [ɛ̃kalɛs(s)ɑ̃ːs], *s.f.* incalescence.

incalomniable [ɛ̃kalɔmnjabl̩], *a.* beyond the reach of calumny.

incamération [ɛ̃kamerasjɔ̃], *s.f. Ecc.Hist:* incameration.

incamérer [ɛ̃kamere], *v.tr. Ecc.Hist:* to annexe to the Pope's domain.

incandescence [ɛ̃kɑ̃dɛs(s)ɑ̃ːs], *s.f.* (*a*) incandescence; **bec de gaz à i.,** incandescent gas burner; *El:* **lampe à i.,** incandescent lamp; **i. résiduelle,** after-glow; (*b*) flaring up (of passion).

incandescent [ɛ̃kɑ̃dɛs(s)ɑ̃], (*a*) incandescent; **charbon i.,** white-hot coal; (*b*) aflame (with passion, etc.); glowing (imagination).

incanescent [ɛ̃kanɛs(s)ɑ̃], *a. Bot:* canescent.

incantation [ɛ̃kɑ̃tasjɔ̃], *s.f.* incantation.

incantatoire [ɛ̃kɑ̃tatwaːr], *a.* magical, spellbinding; spell-like; incantatory.

incapable [ɛ̃kapabl̩]. **1.** *a. & s.m. or f.* incapable, inefficient, incompetent (person); **ma bonne est i.,** my maid is (completely) incompetent, is no good, no use; **c'est un parfait i.,** he's completely incapable, *F:* he can't do a thing (right). **2.** *a.* (*a*) **i. de faire qch.,** (i) incapable of doing sth.; (ii) unable to do sth.; (iii) unfit to do sth.; **i. de parler,** incapable of speech, unable to speak; **i. d'une petitesse,** incapable of a mean action; **je ne le croirais pas i. de faire cela,** I wouldn't put it past him to do that; **je me sens i. d'une tâche de si longue haleine,** I feel unequal to (undertaking) so long a job; **navire i. de prendre la mer,** unseaworthy ship; (*b*) *A:* **terre i. de rien produire,** land incapable of producing anything. **3.** *a. & s.m. or f.* (person) under a disability; **i. de tester,** disqualified from making, not competent to make, a will; **les (majeurs) incapables,** the legally incapacitated.

incapacitant [ɛ̃kapasitɑ̃], *s.m. Mil:* incapacitant.

incapacité [ɛ̃kapasite], *s.f.* **1.** incapacity, incapability, unfitness, inefficiency, incompetency (of person). **2. i. de faire qch.,** incapability of doing sth., incapacity for doing sth.; **i. de se rendre compte des faits,** inability to realize the facts. **3.** (*a*) *Jur:* disability, incapacity; **en état d'i. légale,** declared incapable of managing his own affairs; **frapper qn d'i.,** to incapacitate, disqualify, s.o.; (*b*) *Adm:* **i. permanente,** permanent disablement; **i. partielle,** partial disablement; **i. de travail,** industrial disablement.

incapaciter [ɛ̃kapasite], *v.tr.* to incapacitate.

incarcérable [ɛ̃karserabl̩], *a.* (*a*) liable to imprisonment, imprisonable; (*b*) (*of animal*) impoundable.

incarcération [ɛ̃karserasjɔ̃], *s.f.* **1.** incarceration, imprisonment. **2.** *Med: A:* incarceration (of hernia).

incarcérer [ɛ̃karsere], *v.tr.* (**j'incarcère, n. incarcérons; j'incarcérerai**) (*a*) to incarcerate, imprison (s.o.); **faire i. qn,** (i) to have s.o. sent to prison; (ii) to send s.o. to prison, to gaol; to lodge s.o. in gaol; **être incarcéré,** to be sent to prison, to gaol; (*b*) to impound (animal).

s'incarcérer, *Med: A:* (*of hernia, etc.*) to become incarcerated, strangulated.

incardination [ɛ̃kardinasjɔ̃], *s.f. Ecc:* incardination.

incardiné [ɛ̃kardine], *a.m. Ecc:* incardinated (priest).

incarnadin [ɛ̃karnadɛ̃], *a. & s.m. Lit:* incarnadine.

incarnat [ɛ̃karna]. **1.** *a.* rosy, pink; flesh-coloured. **2.** *s.m.* rosy tint (of dawn); rosiness (of complexion); carnation; bloom (of youth); blush (of rose).

incarnation [ɛ̃karnasjɔ̃], *s.f.* **1.** (*a*) *Theol:* incarnation (of Christ); (*b*) **il est l'i. de tous les vices,** he is the embodiment of all the vices. **2.** *Med:* ingrowing (of the nails).

incarné [ɛ̃karne], *a.* **1.** (*a*) *Theol:* incarnate; **le Verbe incarné,** the Word Incarnate; (*b*) **la vertu incarnée,** the personification, embodiment, of virtue; *F:* **c'est le diable i.,** he's the devil incarnate. **2. ongle i.,** ingrowing nail.

incarner [ɛ̃karne], *v.tr.* (*a*) to incarnate, embody; *Myth:* **Zeus, incarné sous la forme d'un cygne,** Zeus, who had taken the form of a swan; (*b*) **i. une idée dans une œuvre,** to embody an idea in a book; **l'agent diplomatique incarne la souveraineté de l'État,** the diplomatic agent personifies the sovereignty of the state; (*c*) *Th: etc:* to play the part of, the rôle of.

s'incarner. **1.** to become incarnate, embodied; *Theol:* **le Verbe s'est incarné,** the Word became flesh; **tous nos espoirs s'incarnent en vous,** all our hopes are bound up in you. **2.** (*of nail*) to grow in.

incartade [ɛ̃kartad], *s.f.* **1.** (verbal) attack, outburst; **faire une i. contre qn,** to break into a violent tirade against s.o. **2.** freak, prank, indiscretion. **3.** *Equit:* sudden swerve (of horse).

incasique [ɛ̃kazik], *a. Hist:* Inca.

incassable [ɛ̃kɑsabl̩], *a.* unbreakable.

incélébré [ɛ̃selebre], *a.* uncelebrated; unsung (victory).

incendiaire [ɛ̃sɑ̃djɛːr]. **1.** *a.* incendiary (bomb, speech); inflammatory (speech, etc.). **2.** *s.* (*of pers.*) (*a*) incendiary; arsonist; *Psy:* pyromaniac; (*b*) firebrand.

incendie [ɛ̃sɑ̃di], *s.m.* **1.** (*a*) (outbreak of) fire; conflagration; burning (of a town, etc.); **i. de forêt,** forest fire; **poste d'i.,** fire station; *Nau:* **postes d'i.,** fire quarters; **échelle à incendie,** fire escape; **pompe à i.,** fire engine; **service d'i.,** fire-protection organization; **i. volontaire, par malveillance,** arson, incendiarism, fire-raising; **provoquer un i.,** (i) to cause, start, a fire; (ii) to commit arson; **l'hôtel a été détruit par un i.,** the hotel was burnt down, was destroyed by fire; **i. de mine,** pit fire, underground fire; (*b*) **l'i. du soleil couchant,** the blaze of the setting sun; (*c*) **la Serbie, brandon d'un i. européen,** Serbia, the brand that set Europe ablaze. **2.** *A:* eruption (of volcano).

incendié, -ée [ɛ̃sɑ̃dje]. **1.** *a.* (*a*) (*of house, etc.*) (i) on fire, burning; (ii) burnt down; (*b*) **le plateau tout i. de soleil,** the plateau all ablaze with sunlight. **2.** *s.* victim of a fire.

incendier [ɛ̃sɑ̃dje], *v.tr.* (*p.d. & pr.sub.* **n. incendiions, v. incendiiez**) (*a*) to set (house, forest, etc.) on fire; to set fire to (sth.), to fire (sth.); to burn (sth.) down; (*b*) **i. le monde pour satisfaire son ambition,** to set the world ablaze to satisfy one's own ambition; **i. l'imagination de qn,** to fire s.o.'s imagination; (*c*) **cela lui incendia la gorge,** it made his throat burn, feel as if it were on fire; (*d*) **le soleil couchant qui incendie la montagne,** the setting sun that sets the mountain ablaze, makes the mountain look as if it were on fire; (*e*) *P:* to blow (s.o.) up, to give (s.o.) hell.

in-cent-vingt-huit [ɛ̃sɑ̃vɛ̃tɥit], *a. & s.m.inv. Typ:* (in) 128mo.

incération [ɛ̃serasjɔ̃], *s.f.* inceration.

incérer [ɛ̃sere], *v.tr.* (**j'incère, n. incérons**) to incerate.

incertain [ɛ̃sɛrtɛ̃], *a.* uncertain, doubtful; dubious (result, etc.); (*a*) **temps i.,** unsettled, broken, weather; **bleu i.,** undecided blue; *s.* **préférer le certain à l'i.,** to prefer a certainty to an uncertainty; *Fin:* **donner l'i.,** to quote uncertain; (*b*) (*of pers.*) **i. de qch.,** (i) uncertain of, about, sth.; (ii) undecided about sth.; **i. de ce qu'il faut faire,** uncertain what to do; **j'étais i. si je devais intervenir,** I was dubious (as to) whether I should interfere; (*c*) unreliable; undependable; fidgety (horse).

incertifié [ɛ̃sɛrtifje], *a.* uncertified.

incertitude [ɛ̃sɛrtityd], *s.f.* (*a*) uncertainty, incertitude, doubt; dubiousness (of result, etc.); **i. du temps,** unsettled state of the weather; (*b*) indecision, perplexity (of mind); **être dans l'i.,** to be in a state of uncertainty, of doubt; **l'i. règne au sujet de . . .,** there is uncertainty, uncertainty prevails, regarding . . .; **après une longue i.,** after a long period of suspense; **i. quant à l'avenir,** uncertainty about, as to, the future; (*c*) *Atom.Ph:* **principe d'i. (d'Heisenberg),** Heisenberg's uncertainty principle.

incessamment [ɛ̃sɛsamɑ̃], *adv.* **1.** *A. & Lit:* unceasingly, incessantly. **2.** immediately, without delay, at once, forthwith, as soon as possible; **j'arriverai i.,** you may expect me at any moment.

incessant [ɛ̃sɛsɑ̃], *a.* unceasing, incessant, ceaseless; unintermitting, unremitting; **d'incessantes récriminations,** endless, never-ending, recriminations.

incessibilité [ɛ̃sesibilite], *s.f. Jur:* inalienability (of right).

incessible [ɛ̃sesibl̩], *a. Jur:* (*a*) inalienable (right); (*b*) not negotiable, unassignable, untransferable.

inceste[1] [ɛ̃sɛst], *a. & s.m. & f. A:* incestuous (person).

inceste[2], *s.m.* incest.

incestueusement [ɛ̃sɛstɥøzmɑ̃], *adv.* incestuously.

incestueux, -euse [ɛ̃sɛstɥø, -øːz], *a. & s.* incestuous (person).

inchangé [ɛ̃ʃɑ̃ʒe], *a.* unchanged (price, etc.).

inchangeable [ɛ̃ʃɑ̃ʒabl̩], *a.* unchangeable.

inchantable [ɛ̃ʃɑ̃tabl̩], *a.* unsingable.

inchâtié [ɛ̃ʃɑtje], *a.* unchastised, unpunished.

inchauffable [ɛ̃ʃofabl̩], *a.* unheatable; **ces grandes pièces sont inchauffables,** one just can't heat these large rooms.

inchavirabilité [ɛ̃ʃavirabilite], *s.f.* uncapsizability.

inchavirable [ɛ̃ʃavirabl̩], *a.* uncapsizable; self-righting (lifeboat, etc.).

inchoatif, -ive [ɛ̃kɔatif, -iːv], *a. & s.m. Gram:* inceptive, inchoative (verb, etc.).

inchoation [ɛ̃kɔasjɔ̃], *s.f.* inchoation, origination.

incicatrisable [ɛ̃sikatrizabl̩], *a.* that will not cicatrize, heal (up); ever-open (wound to the feelings, etc.).

incidemment [ɛ̃sidamɑ̃], *adv.* incidentally.

incidence [ɛ̃sidɑ̃ːs], *s.f.* **1.** *A:* happening, event. **2.** *Tchn:* incidence; **angle d'i.,** (i) *Opt:* angle of incidence; (ii) *Av:* angle of attack, of incidence (to air current); (iii) *Nau:* angle of attack (of wind on sail); (iv) angle of entry (of torpedo); (v) *Mec.E:* angle of relief (of tool); *Ph: Opt:* **i. brewstérienne,** angle of polarization; *Av:* **indicateur d'i.,** trim indicator; **angle d'i. critique,** angle of stall; *Ball:* **i. rasante,** grazing incidence, small angle of incidence. **3.** influence; repercussion; impact; **l'i. des salaires sur les prix de revient,** the effect, repercussion, of wage levels on production costs. **4.** *Med:* incidence (of disease).

incident, -ente [ɛ̃sidɑ̃, -ɑ̃ːt]. **1.** *a.* (*a*) incidental (question, etc.); *Gram:* parenthetical (clause); (*b*) *Opt:* incident (ray). **2.** *s.m.* incident; (*a*) occurrence, happening; (*b*) *Jur:* point of law; **multiplier les incidents,** to bring forward endless points; to cavil; (*c*) difficulty, hitch, mishap; (*computers*) alert; **faire naître des incidents,** to create difficulties; **i. technique,** technical hitch; **i. de fonctionnement,** malfunction; breakdown; *Sm.a: etc:* **i. de tir,** stoppage of fire; **i. diplomatique,** diplomatic incident; **i. de frontière,** frontier incident; **voyage sans i.,** trouble-free journey; **nous y sommes arrivés sans i.,** we arrived, got there, safely; (*d*) *Lit: Th:* episode. **3.** *s.f.* **incidente,** parenthetical clause.

incidentaire [ɛ̃sidɑ̃tɛːr], *Jur:* **1.** *a.* quibbling pettifogging. **2.** *s.* quibbler, pettifogger.

incidentel, -elle [ɛ̃sidɑ̃tɛl], *a.* incidental (circumstance, etc.).

incidenter [ɛ̃sidɑ̃te], *v.i.* (*a*) *Jur:* to raise a point (or points) of law, of procedure; (*b*) to make difficulties, to quibble.

incinérateur [ɛ̃sineratœːr], *s.m.* incinerator; **i. d'ordures,** dust destructor, refuse destructor.

incinération [ɛ̃sinerasjɔ̃], *s.f.* (*a*) incineration; *Ch: etc:* **capsule à i.,** incineration dish; (*b*) cremation, *U.S:* incineration (of the dead).

incinérer [ɛ̃sinere], *v.tr.* (**j'incinère, n. incinérons; j'incinérerai**) (*a*) to incinerate; to burn to ashes; (*b*) to cremate, *U.S:* to incinerate (the dead).

incipit [ɛ̃sipit], *s.m.inv. Lit: Mus: etc:* incipit.

incirconcis [ɛ̃sirkɔ̃si], *a.* (*a*) *Jewish Rel:* uncircumcised; *s.m.pl.* **les incirconcis,** the uncircumcised, the Gentiles; (*b*) *s.m. A:* sinner.

incirconcision [ɛ̃sirkɔ̃sizjɔ̃], *s.f.* **1.** uncircumcision. **2.** *A:* **i. du cœur,** obduracy of heart.

incirconscriptible [ɛ̃sirkɔ̃skriptibl̩], *a.* **1.** *Geom:* uncircumscribable. **2.** illimitable.

incirconscrit [ɛ̃sirkɔ̃skri], *a.* uncircumscribed; unlimited.

inconspect [ɛ̃sirkɔ̃spɛ(kt)], *a.* uncircumspect.

incirconspection [ɛ̃sirkɔ̃spɛksjɔ̃], *s.f.* lack of circumspection.

incise [ɛ̃siːz], *s.f. Gram:* interpolated clause, incidental clause.

inciser [ɛ̃size], *v.tr.* to incise, cut; to make an incision in (sth.); *Surg:* to buttonhole; **i. un furoncle,** to cut into, to lance, a boil; **i. un pin,** to tap a pine tree (for resin).

inciseur [ɛ̃sizœːr], *s.m.* **1.** *Arb:* tool for ringing or tapping trees. **2.** surgeon's knife.

incisif, -ive [ɛ̃sizif, -iːv]. **1.** *a.* incisive, sharp, cutting (remark, etc.). **2.** *Anat:* (*a*) *a.* incisal, incisive; **os i.,** incisive bone; (*b*) *s.f.* **incisive,** incisor (tooth); **incisive conoïde,** peg-shaped incisor; **incisive en forme de pelle,** shovel-shaped incisor.

incision [ɛ̃sizjɔ̃], *s.f.* incision. **1.** (*a*) cutting; *Arb:* **i. annulaire,** ringing, girdling (of tree); **i. d'un pin,** tapping of a pine tree (for resin); (*b*) *Surg:* incision; dissection; **i. rayonnante,** radiating incision; **i. d'un furoncle,** lancing of a boil. **2.** cut; *Arb:* **i. annulaire,** ring, girdle (cut into bark of tree); *Surg:* **i. chirurgicale,** operation wound; **faire une i.,** to incise, to make an incision.

incisivement [ɛ̃sizivmɑ̃], *adv.* incisively, sharply.

incisure [ɛ̃sizyːr], *s.f.* (*a*) *Anat:* incisure; (*b*) *Bot:* incising.

incitable [ɛ̃sitabl̩], *a.* incitable.

incitant [ɛ̃sitɑ̃]. **1.** *a.* inciting, stimulating. **2.** *s.m. Med:* stimulant.

incitateur, -trice [ɛ̃sitatœːr, -tris]. **1.** *a.* inciting (agent, etc.). **2.** *s.* inciter (à, to); instigator.

incitatif, -ive [ɛ̃sitatif, -iːv], *a.* inciting.

incitation [ɛ̃sitasjɔ̃], *s.f.* (*a*) inciting, incitement (à, to); instigation; (*b*) *Physiol:* excitation.

inciter [ɛ̃site], *v.tr.* to incite, urge (on), instigate (s.o.); **i. qn au mal,** to incite s.o. to do wrong; **i. qn à faire qch.,** to incite s.o. to do sth.; to prompt s.o. to do sth.; *F:* to egg s.o. on; **i. qn à la réserve,** to urge s.o. to be cautious; **le charme du paysage les incitera probablement à y faire un séjour,** the delightful scenery will probably tempt them to stay; **ce temps n'incite pas au travail,** this weather is not conducive to work.

incivil [ɛ̃sivil], *a.* uncivil, impolite, rude, discourteous.

incivilement [ɛ̃sivilmɑ̃], *adv.* uncivilly, rudely.

incivilisable [ɛ̃sivilizabl̩], *a.* uncivilizable.

incivilisé [ɛ̃sivilize], *a.* uncivilized.

incivilité [ɛ̃sivilite], *s.f.* **1.** incivility, impoliteness, rudeness, discourtesy. **2.** piece of incivility, rude remark; discourtesy.

incivique [ɛ̃sivik], *a.* **1.** unpatriotic; with no sense of civic duty. **2.** *Hist:* (*World War II, in Belgium*) collaborationist; *s.m. or f.* collaborator.

incivisme [ɛ̃sivism], *s.m.* **1.** lack of patriotism; lack of (any sense of) good citizenship. **2.** *Hist:* (*World War II, in Belgium*) collaboration.

inclairvoyant [ɛ̃klɛrvwajɑ̃], *a.* shortsighted (policy, adviser, etc.).

inclassable [ɛ̃klɑsabl̩], *a.* unclass(ifi)able, nondescript.

inclémence [ɛ̃klemɑ̃ːs], *s.f.* inclemency (of weather); severity (of weather, pers. judgement).

inclément [ɛ̃klemɑ̃], *a.* **1.** *Poet:* unmerciful (fates, etc.). **2.** inclement (weather); severe (judgement, judge, weather, etc.).

inclinable [ɛ̃klinabl̩], *a.* tilting, canting, inclinable (table, stand, etc.); reclining (chair, seat, etc.).

inclinaison [ɛ̃klinɛzɔ̃], *s.f.* **1.** (*a*) tilting, canting; **dispositif d'i.,** tilting device; (*b*) incline, gradient, slope (of hill, etc.); inclination (of line, star); pitch, slant (of roof, etc.); tilt (of camera, hat, etc.); heel, list (of ship); rake (of mast, of bow or stern); *Aut:* of steering column); dip (of magnetic needle, of stratum, lode); angle (of trajectory); elevation (of barrel, gun, etc.); skew (of propeller blade); *Nau:* steeve (of bowsprit); declivity (of launching ways); *Dent:* **i. incisive,** incisal inclination; *Const:* **comble à forte, faible, i.,** high-pitched, low-pitched, roof; *Av:* **angle d'i.,** angle of bank; angle of roll; **aiguille d'i.,** dipping needle. **2.** (= INCLINATION) nod (of the head).

inclinant [ɛ̃klinɑ̃], *a.* **1.** inclining, sloping. **2.** inclinable (à, to); **i. à la dévotion,** devotionally inclined; **i. à faire qch.,** prone to do sth.

inclination [ɛ̃klinasjɔ̃], *s.f.* inclination. **1.** bending, bow(ing) (of body); nod (of head); **faire une profonde i.,** to make a low bow. **2.** (*a*) bent, propensity; **avoir de l'i., se sentir d'i., à faire qch.,** to be, feel, inclined to do sth.; **avoir, se sentir, de l'i. pour qn, qch.,** to like, have a liking for, s.o., sth.; (*b*) attachment, love; **mariage d'i.,** marriage of affection, love match; **faire un mariage d'i.,** to marry for love; **la chasse est son i. dominante,** hunting is his favourite pursuit; he is especially fond of hunting.

incliné [ɛ̃kline], *a.* **1.** inclined; (*a*) **la tête inclinée,** with bowed head; **arbres à têtes inclinées chacune de son côté,** trees with heads nodding in different directions; (*b*) sloping, tilting; **planche inclinée,** cant board; **plan i.,** (i) inclined plane; (ii) *Ind: etc:* shoot (for goods, etc.). **2. i. à, vers, qch., à faire qch.,** inclined, disposed, to sth., to do sth.

incliner [ɛ̃kline]. **1.** *v.tr.* to incline; (*a*) to slant, slope, cant; *Nau:* **i. la route vers le nord, etc.,** to edge to the north, etc.; (*b*) to tip up; to tilt; (*c*) to bend, bow (the head, etc.); (*d*) **i. qn à faire qch.,** to predispose, influence, s.o. in favour of doing sth.; **son cœur l'inclinait à la miséricorde,** his heart inclined him to pity. **2.** *v.i.* (*a*) (*of wall, etc.*) to lean, slope; (*of ship*) to list; (*b*) **i. à la pitié,** to incline, be disposed, to pity; **i. à faire qch.,** to be, feel, inclined to do sth.; **i. à croire que . . .,** to incline to the belief that . . .; **Louis inclinait vers, pour, une alliance avec l'Espagne,** Louis inclined towards an alliance with Spain.

s'incliner. **1.** to slant, slope; *Nau:* (*of ship*) to heel (over); *Av:* to bank; **le rivage s'incline vers la mer,** the shore shelves down to the sea. **2.** (*a*) **s'i. sur qn,** to bend over s.o.; (*b*) to bow (down); to make one's bow (on retiring, etc.); **s'i. devant qn,** to bow before s.o.; **s'i. devant les arguments de qn,** to bow, yield, to s.o.'s arguments; **s'i. devant la volonté de qn,** to defer to s.o.'s will; **s'i. devant une décision,** to bow to a decision; to abide by a decision; **s'i. devant les faits,** (i) to bow to the inevitable; (ii) to bow to the evidence; **je m'incline devant ce qu'il a accompli,** I take my hat off to him for what he has accomplished; **j'ai dû m'i.,** I had to give in.

inclinomètre [ɛ̃klinɔmɛtr̩], *s.m.* inclinometer.

inclure [ɛ̃klyːr], *v.tr.* (*conj. like* CONCLURE *except p.p.* **inclus,** *but little used except in p.p.*) **1.** to enclose (document in letter, etc.). **2.** *Jur:* to insert (clause in contract, etc.).

inclus [ɛ̃kly], *a.* **1.** (*a*) enclosed (in letter, etc.); *s.f.* **l'incluse,** the enclosed (note); *s.a.* CI-INCLUS; (*b*) **jusqu'à la page 5 incluse,** up to and including page 5. **2.** (*a*) *Bot:* **étamines incluses,** included stamens; (*b*) *Dent:* **dent incluse,** impacted tooth.

inclusif, -ive [ɛ̃klyzif, -iːv], *a.* inclusive.

inclusion [ɛ̃klyzjɔ̃], *s.f.* **1.** (*a*) enclosing (of document in letter, etc.); (*b*) inclusion (of consequence in theory, etc.); (*c*) insertion (of clause, etc.). **2.** *Miner: Cryst:* inclusion; *Dent:* impaction (of tooth).

inclusivement [ɛ̃klyzivmɑ̃], *adv.* inclusively; **du vendredi au mardi i.,** from Friday to Tuesday inclusive.

incoagulable [ɛ̃kɔagylabl̩], *a.* incoagulable.

incoercibilité [ɛ̃kɔɛrsibilite], *s.f.* incoercibility.

incoercible [ɛ̃kɔɛrsibl̩], *a.* incoercible; **soif i.,** uncontrollable thirst; **rire i.,** irrepressible laughter.

incognito [ɛ̃kɔɲito, -gn-]. **1.** *adv.* incognito; **voyager i.,** to travel incognito. **2.** *s.m.* **garder l'i.,** to preserve one's incognito; *pl. incognitos.* **3.** *adv. A:* in secret; unbeknown to anyone.

incognoscible [ɛ̃kɔgnɔs(s)ibl̩], *a. Phil:* unknowable, incognizable.

incohérence [ɛ̃kɔerɑ̃ːs], *s.f.* incoherence, incoherency (of particles, of speech, of thought); disjointedness (of speech, etc.).

incohérent [ɛ̃kɔerɑ̃], *a.* **1.** *Ph:* incoherent. **2.** incoherent, inconsistent, rambling, disjointed (speech, etc.).

incohésif, -ive [ɛ̃kɔezif, -iːv], *a.* incohesive.

incohésion [ɛ̃kɔezjɔ̃], *s.f.* (*a*) *Ph:* incohesion; (*b*) lack of cohesion (in party, etc.).

incoiffable [ɛ̃kwafabl̩], *a.* (*of hair*) impossible to keep in order.

incoinçable [ɛ̃kwɛ̃sabl̩], *a.* (*a*) (*of fastening*) nonjamming, that cannot jam, stick; (*b*) *F:* (*of pers.*) who cannot be stumped, floored, faulted.

incollable [ɛ̃kɔlabl̩], *a. F:* (*pers.*) who cannot be stumped, floored, faulted.

incolore [ɛ̃kɔlɔːr], *a.* colourless (crystal, style, etc.).

incombant [ɛ̃kɔ̃bɑ̃], *a. Bot:* incumbent (anther).

incomber [ɛ̃kɔ̃be], *v.i.* (*used only in third pers.*) **i. à qn,** to devolve on, be incumbent on, s.o.; **les devoirs qui lui incombent,** the duties which fall on him; **chacun s'acquitta de la tâche qui lui incombait,** each one did his part; **la responsabilité incombe à l'auteur,** the responsibility lies, rests, with the author; **c'est au traducteur qu'il incombe de . . .,** it is the translator's responsibility to . . .; **c'est à moi qu'incomba le devoir de le ramener,** the duty of bringing him back fell upon me; **c'est là la tâche qui nous incombe,** this is the task before us; *impers.* **il nous incombe à tous de . . .,** it is the duty of all of us, it is for all of us, to . . .; **il m'incombe de pourvoir à ses besoins,** it is my duty to provide for his needs, it falls to me to provide for his needs; *Jur:* **pièce qui incombe à un dossier,** document which belongs to a dossier.

incombustibilité [ɛ̃kɔ̃bystibilite], *s.f.* incombustibility.

incombustible [ɛ̃kɔ̃bystibl̩], *a.* incombustible, noninflammable, uninflammable; fireproof.

incomestible [ɛ̃kɔmɛstibl̩], *a.* inedible.

incommensurabilité [ɛ̃kɔm(m)ɑ̃syrabilite], *s.f.* incommensurability.

incommensurable [ɛ̃kɔm(m)ɑ̃syrabl̩], *a.* **1.** *Mth:* incommensurable (avec, with); incommensurate; **racine i.,** irrational root. **2.** immeasurable, huge.

incommensurablement [ɛ̃kɔm(m)ɑ̃syrabləmɑ̃], *adv.* **1.** incommensurably. **2.** immeasurably.

incommerçable [ɛ̃kɔmɛrsabl̩], *a. Com: Fin:* unnegotiable, not negotiable.

incommodant [ɛ̃kɔmɔdɑ̃], *a.* incommoding, unpleasant, disagreeable, annoying.

incommode [ɛ̃kɔmɔd], *a.* **1.** inconvenient; incommodious (room, etc.); uncomfortable (chair, position, etc.); unhandy, clumsy, awkward (tool, etc.); **objet i. à porter, à manier,** unwieldy object; **petite table i. pour écrire,** small table awkward for writing at. **2.** *A:* troublesome, disagreeable (person); unpleasant (smell, etc.); *Jur:* **établissements incommodes,** buildings for carrying on noisy or noxious trades.

incommodé [ɛ̃kɔmɔde], *a.* **1.** ill at ease; **être i. par la chaleur,** to feel the heat. **2.** *A:* (*a*) short of cash; (*b*) **être i. d'un bras,** to have lost the full use of an arm; *Nau:* **navire i.,** crippled ship.

incommodément [ɛ̃kɔmɔdemɑ̃], *adv.* inconveniently; uncomfortably, awkwardly.

incommoder [ɛ̃kɔmɔde], *v.tr.* **1.** to inconvenience, incommode, hinder, disturb (s.o.); **la fumée ne vous incommode pas?** you don't mind my smoking? **s'i. pour être agréable à qn,** to go out of one's way to oblige s.o.; **est-ce que ma chaise vous incommode?** is my chair in your way? **cela vous incommoderait-il de me prêter cent francs?** would it inconvenience you, be any inconvenience to you, would it put you out, to lend me a hundred francs? **2.** (*of food, etc.*) to make (s.o.) unwell; to disagree with (s.o.); to upset (s.o.).

incommodité [ɛ̃kɔmɔdite], *s.f.* **1.** (*a*) inconvenience; incommodiousness; (*b*) discomfort; awkwardness (of situation). **2.** *A:* (*a*) indisposition; (children's) ailment; **les incommodités de la vieillesse,** the infirmities of old age; (*b*) (financial) embarrassment.

incommodo [ɛ̃kɔmɔdo], *s.m. Jur:* **enquête de commodo et i.,** public, administrative, inquiry.

incommuable [ɛ̃kɔm(m)ɥabl̩], *a. A:* incommutable.

incommunicabilité [ɛ̃kɔmynikabilite], *s.f.* incommunicableness, incommunicability.

incommunicable [ɛ̃kɔmynikabl̩], *a.* incommunicable.

incommutabilité [ɛ̃kɔmytabilite], *s.f. Jur:* indefeasibility (of right, property).

incommutable [ɛ̃kɔmytabl̩], *a. Jur:* **1.** nontransferable (property); indefeasible (right). **2.** (owner) who cannot be dispossessed; absolute (owner).

incomparabilité [ɛ̃kɔ̃parabilite], *s.f.* incomparableness, peerlessness.

incomparable [ɛ̃kɔ̃parabl̩], *a.* incomparable, unrivalled, peerless, matchless.

incomparablement [ɛ̃kɔ̃parabləmɑ̃], *adv.* incomparably, beyond compare.

incompatibilité [ɛ̃kɔ̃patibilite], *s.f.* incompatibility (of duties, etc.); (*computers*) non-conjunction; **i. d'humeur,** incompatibility of temperament.

incompatible [ɛ̃kɔ̃patibl̩], *a.* incompatible, inconsistent, at variance (**avec,** with); **fonctions, humeurs, incompatibles,** incompatible posts, temperaments; **absolument i. avec la situation actuelle,** utterly inappropriate to the present, the existing, situation.

incompatiblement [ɛ̃kɔ̃patibləmɑ̃], *adv.* incompatibly.

incompensable [ɛ̃kɔ̃pɑ̃sabl̩], *a.* **1.** that cannot be compensated, repaid; not compensable. **2.** (compass) that cannot be compensated.

incompensé [ɛ̃kɔ̃pɑ̃se], *a.* uncompensated ((i) loss, etc., (ii) pendulum, compass).

incompétemment [ɛ̃kɔ̃petamɑ̃], *adv.* incompetently.

incompétence [ɛ̃kɔ̃petɑ̃:s], *s.f.* incompetence, incompetency (of person, tribunal); **i. à faire qch.,** lack of authority to do sth.; *Jur:* **réclamer l'i.,** to put in a plea in bar of trial.

incompétent [ɛ̃kɔ̃petɑ̃], *a.* incompetent; (*a*) inefficient; (*b*) *Jur:* not qualified, unqualified (to try case); (*c*) **i. en matière d'art,** incompetent in the matter of art, ignorant of art; **i. à faire qch.,** incompetent to do sth.

incomplet, -ète [ɛ̃kɔ̃plɛ, -ɛt], *a.* incomplete, unfinished; *Mil:* under strength.

incomplètement [ɛ̃kɔ̃plɛtmɑ̃], *adv.* incompletely.

incomplétude [ɛ̃kɔ̃pletyd], *s.f. Psy:* (sense of) inadequacy; (sense of) unfulfilment.

incomplexe [ɛ̃kɔ̃plɛks], *a.* incomplex, simple (syllogism, etc.).

incompréhensibilité [ɛ̃kɔ̃preɑ̃sibilite], *s.f.* incomprehensibility.

incompréhensible [ɛ̃kɔ̃preɑ̃sibl̩], *a.* incomprehensible; **c'est i.,** I can't make it out.

incompréhensiblement [ɛ̃kɔ̃preɑ̃sibləmɑ̃], *adv.* incomprehensibly.

incompréhensif, -ive [ɛ̃kɔ̃preɑ̃sif, -i:v], *a.* uncomprehending; obtuse (mind, etc.).

incompréhension [ɛ̃kɔ̃preɑ̃sjɔ̃], *s.f.* incomprehension, lack of understanding; obtuseness.

incompressibilité [ɛ̃kɔ̃prɛsibilite], *s.f.* incompressibility.

incompressible [ɛ̃kɔ̃prɛsibl̩], *a.* incompressible.

incomprimé [ɛ̃kɔ̃prime], *a.* uncompressed.

incompris [ɛ̃kɔ̃pri], *a.* misunderstood; unappreciated; *s.* **je suis un(e) incompromis(e),** no one has ever understood me.

incomptable [ɛ̃kɔ̃tabl̩], *a.* uncountable, incomputable; innumerable; **pendant des siècles incomptables,** during untold centuries; **pouls i.,** pulse which cannot be counted.

inconcessible [ɛ̃kɔ̃sɛsibl̩], *a.* ungrantable; (favour etc.) that cannot be granted.

inconcevabilité [ɛ̃kɔ̃s(ə)vabilite], *s.f.* inconceivability.

inconcevable [ɛ̃kɔ̃s(ə)vabl̩], *a.* inconceivable, unthinkable, unimaginable; **il est i. qu'il soit acquitté,** it is unthinkable that he should be acquitted.

inconcevablement [ɛ̃kɔ̃s(ə)vabləmɑ̃], *adv.* inconceivably.

inconciliabilité [ɛ̃kɔ̃siljabilite], *s.f.* irreconcilability, incompatibility (of theories, etc.).

inconciliable [ɛ̃kɔ̃siljabl̩], *a.* **1.** irreconcilable, incompatible (theories, etc.) (**avec,** with). **2. plaideurs inconciliables,** litigants who will not come to terms.

inconciliablement [ɛ̃kɔ̃siljabləmɑ̃], *adv.* irreconcilably.

inconciliant [ɛ̃kɔ̃siljɑ̃], *a.* unconciliating, unconciliatory.

inconciliation [ɛ̃kɔ̃siljasjɔ̃], *s.f.* refusal to come to terms, to be conciliated.

inconcluant [ɛ̃kɔ̃klyɑ̃], *a.* inconclusive (argument, etc.).

incondensable [ɛ̃kɔ̃dɑ̃sabl̩], *a. & s.m.* uncondensable (gas).

inconditionnalisme [ɛ̃kɔ̃disjɔnalism], *s.m.* unconditionality, unconditionalness.

inconditionné [ɛ̃kɔ̃disjɔne], *a. & s.m. Psy:* unconditional; unconditioned.

inconditionnel, -elle [ɛ̃kɔ̃disjɔnɛl], *a.* unconditional (consent); absolute (liability, etc.); *Pol: etc:* unwavering (supporter).

inconditionnellement [ɛ̃kɔ̃disjɔnɛlmɑ̃], *adv.* unconditionally.

inconducteur, -trice [ɛ̃kɔ̃dyktœ:r, -tris], *a. El:* non-conducting.

inconduite [ɛ̃kɔ̃dɥit], *s.f.* loose living, laxity of conduct; *Jur:* misconduct.

Inconel [ɛ̃kɔnɛl], *s.m. Metall: R.t.m:* Inconel.

inconfessé [ɛ̃kɔ̃fese], *a. Ecc:* **mourir i.,** to die without confession, unconfessed, unshriven.

inconformité [ɛ̃kɔ̃fɔrmite], *s.f.* inconformity, unconformity (**avec,** to, with).

inconfort [ɛ̃kɔ̃fɔ:r], *s.m.* discomfort.

inconfortable [ɛ̃kɔ̃fɔrtabl̩], *a.* uncomfortable.

inconfortablement [ɛ̃kɔ̃fɔrtabləmɑ̃], *adv.* uncomfortably.

incongédiable [ɛ̃kɔ̃ʒedjabl̩], *a.* that, who, cannot be dismissed.

incongelable [ɛ̃kɔ̃ʒ(ə)labl̩], *a.* uncongealable, unfreezable; non-freezing.

incongru [ɛ̃kɔ̃gry], *a.* **1.** incongruous, foolish (remark, etc.); out of place. **2.** improper, unseemly (question, etc.). **3.** *A:* ungrammatical.

incongruent [ɛ̃kɔ̃grɥɑ̃], *a. Anat:* incongruent.

incongruité [ɛ̃kɔ̃grɥite], *s.f.* **1.** (*a*) incongruity, incongruousness, absurdity; (*b*) impropriety, unseemliness, unbecomingness, tactlessness (of behaviour). **2.** (*a*) incongruity; foolish, tactless, improper, remark, action; malapropism; (*b*) *A:* mistake in grammar.

incongrûment [ɛ̃kɔ̃grymɑ̃], *adv.* (*a*) incongruously; (*b*) improperly.

inconnaissable [ɛ̃kɔnɛsabl̩], *a. & s.m.* unknowable, **l'avenir est i.,** we do not know what the future has in store for us; **être curieux de l'i.,** to be curious about the unknowable, about things which cannot be known.

inconnaissance [ɛ̃kɔnɛsɑ̃:s], *s.f.* ignorance, incognizance.

inconnu, -ue [ɛ̃kɔny]. **1.** *a.* unknown (**de, à,** to); **i. de tout le monde,** unknown to all; **un procédé à lui i.,** process unknown to him. **2.** *s.* (*a*) unknown person; (i) stranger; (ii) (mere) nobody; *Jur:* **mandat contre i.,** warrant against a person or persons unknown; (*b*) *s.m.* (the) unknown; **l'i. des événements,** the uncertainty of events; **faire un saut dans l'i.,** to take a leap in the dark; **le grand i.,** fate, destiny. **3.** *s.f. Mth:* **inconnue,** unknown (quantity).

inconquérable [ɛ̃kɔ̃kerabl̩], *a.* unconquerable; impregnable.

inconquis [ɛ̃kɔ̃ki], *a.* unconquered (province, etc.).

inconsciemment [ɛ̃kɔ̃sjamɑ̃], *adv.* unconsciously, unknowingly.

inconscience [ɛ̃kɔ̃sjɑ̃:s], *s.f.* **1.** unconsciousness. **2.** unawareness, obliviousness (of sth.); failure to realize (sth.); **c'était de l'i. pure,** it was sheer thoughtlessness; you, he, etc., just didn't think.

inconsciencieux, -ieuse [ɛ̃kɔ̃sjɑ̃sjø, -jø:z], *a.* unconscientious.

inconscient, -ente [ɛ̃kɔ̃sjɑ̃, -ɑ̃:t]. **1.** *a.* (*a*) unconscious; **la vie inconsciente des plantes,** the unconscious life of plants; **effort i.,** unconscious effort; **geste i.,** unconscious, mechanical, gesture; (*b*) **i. de ce qui se passe autour de lui,** oblivious of what is going on around him. **2.** *s.* thoughtless person; **agir en i.,** to act without thinking, without reflection. **3.** *s.m. Psy:* **l'i.,** the unconscious.

inconséquemment [ɛ̃kɔ̃sekamɑ̃], *adv.* inconsistently, inconsequently, inconsequentially.

inconséquence [ɛ̃kɔ̃sekɑ̃:s], *s.f.* (*a*) inconsistency, inconsequence, irrelevance; **un tissu d'inconséquences,** a tissue of absurdities, of inconsistencies, of irrelevancies; (*b*) inconsequentiality; (*c*) **une i.,** an indiscretion, *F:* a bloomer.

inconséquent [ɛ̃kɔ̃sekɑ̃], *a.* (*a*) inconsistent, inconsequent (reasoning, etc.); (*b*) irresponsible, inconsequential (reasoning, behaviour, person); rash, unguarded (words); scatterbrained (person); rambling (speech).

inconservable [ɛ̃kɔ̃sɛrvabl̩], *a.* unpreservable.

inconsidération [ɛ̃kɔ̃siderasjɔ̃], *s.f. A:* **1.** lack of consideration; thoughtlessness, inconsiderateness. **2. tomber dans l'i.,** to fall from one's high estate, from honour; to fall into disrepute.

inconsidéré [ɛ̃kɔ̃sidere], *a.* thoughtless. **1.** inconsiderate (person). **2.** unconsidered, ill-considered, rash (act).

inconsidérément [ɛ̃kɔ̃sideremɑ̃], *adv.* inconsiderately, thoughtlessly.

inconsistance [ɛ̃kɔ̃sistɑ̃:s], *s.f.* **1.** unsubstantiality, lack of firmness; looseness (of soil, etc.); softness (of mud); flabbiness (of nature). **2.** inconsistency (of person, act).

inconsistant [ɛ̃kɔ̃sistɑ̃], *a.* **1.** unsubstantial; lacking in body, in firmness; soft (mud, etc.); loose soil, etc.); flabby (nature). **2.** inconsistent (conduct, person).

inconsolable [ɛ̃kɔ̃sɔlabl̩], *a.* inconsolable, unconsolable (person, grief); disconsolate (person); **elle est i. de sa perte,** she cannot get over her loss.

inconsolablement [ɛ̃kɔ̃sɔlabləmɑ̃], *adv.* inconsolably, disconsolately.

inconsolé [ɛ̃kɔ̃sɔle], *a.* unconsoled, uncomforted.

inconsommable [ɛ̃kɔ̃sɔmabl̩], *a.* **1.** *Pol.Ec:* indestructible, permanent (capital, *e.g.* land). **2.** unfit for consumption; inedible. **3.** *Jur:* (marriage) that cannot be consummated.

inconsommé [ɛ̃kɔ̃sɔme], *a.* **1.** unconsummated (marriage, etc.). **2.** unconsumed (food, etc.); *Mil:* unexpended.

inconstance [ɛ̃kɔ̃stɑ̃:s], *s.f.* **1.** inconstancy, fickleness. **2.** changeableness (of weather); *Biol:* instability (of type); variability.

inconstant [ɛ̃kɔ̃stɑ̃], *a.* **1.** inconstant, fickle (disposition); **joueur i.,** erratic player. **2.** changeable (weather); *Biol:* variable (type).

inconstatable [ɛ̃kɔ̃statabl̩], *a.* unverifiable, unprovable.

inconstitutionnalité [ɛ̃kɔ̃stitysjɔnalite], *s.f.* unconstitutionality.

inconstitutionnel, -elle [ɛ̃kɔ̃stitysjɔnɛl], *a.* unconstitutional.

inconstitutionnellement [ɛ̃kɔ̃stitysjɔnɛlmɑ̃], *adv.* unconstitutionally.

incontentable [ɛ̃kɔ̃tɑ̃tabl̩], *a.* ungratifiable, unsatisfiable, that cannot be gratified, that nothing can satisfy.

incontestabilité [ɛ̃kɔ̃tɛstabilite], *s.f.* **1.** incontestability, undeniableness; *Ins:* **clause d'i.,** incontestability clause. **2.** incontestable fact.

incontestable [ɛ̃kɔ̃tɛstabl̩], *a.* incontestable, undeniable, indubitable, indisputable; beyond all question; **il est i. que c'est de sa faute,** it is beyond question, there is no doubt whatever, that it is his fault.

incontestablement [ɛ̃kɔ̃tɛstabləmɑ̃], *adv.* incontestably, undeniably, indubitably; beyond all question; unquestionably.

incontesté [ɛ̃kɔ̃tɛste], *a.* uncontested, undisputed.

incontinence [ɛ̃kɔ̃tinɑ̃:s], *s.f.* incontinence; (*a*) unchastity; (*b*) lack of restraint; **être adonné, porté, à l'i.,** to be given to excesses; **i. de langage,** *A:* **de langue,** loquacity, garrulousness; (*c*) *Med:* **i. d'urine,** incontinence of urine; **i. nocturne,** enuresis, bed-wetting.

incontinent[1] [ɛ̃kɔ̃tinɑ̃], *a.* (*a*) incontinent, unchaste; (*b*) unrestrained; (*c*) *Med:* incontinent.

incontinent[2], *adv. A: or Lit:* at once, forthwith, straightway; *A:* incontinent(ly).

incontinuité [ɛ̃kɔ̃tinɥite], *s.f.* lack of continuity, discontinuity.

incontrit [ɛ̃kɔ̃tri], *a.* uncontrite.

incontrôlable [ɛ̃kɔ̃trolabl̩], *a.* difficult to verify, to check; unverifiable, uncheckable.

incontrôlé [ɛ̃kɔ̃trole], *a.* **1.** unchecked, unverified. **2.** uncontrolled; uncontrollable; **gestes incontrôlés,** uncontrolled, wild, gesticulations.

incontroversable [ɛ̃kɔ̃trɔvɛrsabl̩], *a.* incontrovertible, indisputable.

incontroversé [ɛ̃kɔ̃trɔvɛrse], *a.* uncontradicted, uncontroverted, undisputed.

inconvenable [ɛ̃kɔ̃vnabl̩], *a.* unsuitable, not fitting (**à,** for, to).

inconvenablement [ɛ̃kɔ̃vnabləmɑ̃], *adv.* unsuitably.

inconvenance [ɛ̃kɔ̃vnɑ̃:s], *s.f.* **1.** impropriety, indecorousness, unseemliness; **se conduire avec i.,** to behave in an ill-bred manner. **2.** breach of (good) manners; **dire des inconvenances,** to make ill-placed, indiscreet, remarks.

inconvenant [ɛ̃kɔ̃vnɑ̃], *a.* improper, indecorous; **propos inconvenants,** unseemly, ill-bred, remarks; **question inconvenante,** indelicate, indiscreet, question; **être dans une tenue inconvenante pour recevoir qn,** to be unsuitably dressed to receive s.o.; **il est vraiment i.,** he doesn't know how to behave, he has no manners.

inconvénient [ɛ̃kɔ̃venjɑ̃], *s.m.* (*a*) *A:* disaster; calamity; (*b*) disadvantage, drawback; **c'est vous qui en subirez les inconvénients,** it's you who will suffer the drawbacks (of it); **situation qui entraîne des inconvénients graves,** situation giving rise to serious disadvantages; **nous partirons ce soir si vous n'y voyez pas d'i.,** we'll leave this evening, if you see no objection (to it), if you've nothing against it; **pouvez-vous sans i. me prêter ce livre?** would it be convenient for you to lend me this book? **nous pouvons sans i. modifier notre itinéraire,** we can change our route without any inconvenience; **n'y a-t-il pas d'i. à laisser cet enfant jouer près de la rivière?** is there no risk, danger, in letting the child play near the river? **cela ne va pas sans quelques inconvénients,** it's not an unmixed blessing; **les avantages et les inconvénients (de qch.),** the advantages and disadvantages (of sth.); the pros and cons (of a course of action);

générosité sans i. pour notre bourse, generosity that makes no call on our purse; **toute chose a ses inconvénients,** everything has its disadvantages; **parer à, éviter, un i.,** to take steps to avoid, to overcome a difficulty.

inconversible [ɛ̃kɔ̃vɛrsibl̩], *a. Log:* inconvertible (proposition).

inconverti [ɛ̃kɔ̃vɛrti], *a.* unconverted, unregenerate.

inconvertible [ɛ̃kɔ̃vɛrtibl̩], *a.* **1.** inconvertible (paper money, etc.). **2.** *Log:* inconvertible. **3.** *A:* = INCONVERTISSABLE.

inconvertissable [ɛ̃kɔ̃vɛrtisabl̩], *a.* beyond hope of conversion, past praying for.

incoordination [ɛ̃koɔrdinasjɔ̃], *s.f.* incoordination; (*a*) lack of co-ordination; (*b*) *Med:* ataxia; **i. motrice,** locomotor ataxia.

incorporable [ɛ̃kɔrpɔrabl̩], *a.* incorporable.

incorporalité [ɛ̃kɔrpɔralite], *s.f.* incorporeality, incorporeity (of angels, *Jur:* of a right).

incorporation [ɛ̃kɔrpɔrasjɔ̃], *s.f.* incorporation; (*a*) **i. des jaunes d'œufs dans du sucre,** blending of egg yolks with sugar; (*b*) **i. d'un territoire à un empire,** incorporation of a territory into an empire; **i. d'une minorité ethnique,** absorption of an ethnic minority; **i. d'un terrain à un domaine,** incorporation of a piece of land into an estate; (*c*) *Ling:* incorporation; (*d*) *Ecc:* incardination; (*e*) *Mil:* **i. des conscrits dans un régiment,** bringing of conscripts on to the strength of a regiment; *abs.* **i. à vingt ans,** conscription at the age of twenty; **sursis d'i.,** deferment of call-up; **centre d'i.,** recruiting depot, *U.S:* inducting center.

incorporé [ɛ̃kɔrpɔre]. **1.** *a.* built-in; integral with; **armoire incorporée,** built-in cupboard; **i. à l'ordinateur,** built into the computer. **2.** *s.m. Mil:* recruit (to a regiment, etc.).

incorporéité [ɛ̃kɔrpɔreite], *s.f.* incorporeity.

incorporel, -elle [ɛ̃kɔrpɔrɛl], *a.* incorporeal (being, *Jur:* right); *Jur:* **biens incorporels,** intangible property.

incorporer [ɛ̃kɔrpɔre], *v.tr.* to incorporate; (*a*) **i. des œufs à,** *occ.* **avec, une sauce,** to blend, mix, incorporate, eggs into a sauce; **substance qui s'incorpore facilement à une autre,** substance that blends well with another one; (*b*) to incorporate (territory, etc.); to build in (cupboard, etc.); **i. un terrain à un domaine,** to incorporate a piece of land in an estate; **i. un paragraphe dans un chapitre,** to incorporate, insert, a paragraph in a chapter; **i. qn dans un groupe,** to introduce s.o. into a group; **tout de suite elle fut incorporée à la famille,** she became one of the family straight away; (*b*) *Mil:* to bring (men) on to the strength; **i. des recrues dans un bataillon,** to draft recruits into a battalion.

incorrect [ɛ̃kɔrɛkt], *a.* incorrect. **1.** (*a*) inaccurate, wrong; **solution incorrecte,** wrong solution; **citation incorrecte,** misquotation; (*b*) untrue; (*c*) defective, faulty; (*of machinery, etc.*) **montage i.,** faulty assembly. **2.** (*a*) contrary to etiquette, to the prevailing fashion; **tenue incorrecte,** (i) slovenly dress; (ii) hardly decent attire; (iii) unsuitable clothes (for the occasion); (*b*) (*of pers.*) impolite, ill-mannered, rude; **être i. avec qn,** to treat s.o. in an ill-mannered, off-hand, fashion; **être i. avec son concurrent,** to deal unfairly with one's (business) competitor.

incorrectement [ɛ̃kɔrɛktəmɑ̃], *adv.* (*a*) incorrectly; **écrire i.,** to write ungrammatically; **écrire un mot i.,** to mis-spell a word; **citer un auteur i.,** to misquote an author; (*b*) **se conduire i. avec qn,** to treat s.o. (i) unfairly, (ii) in an ill-mannered fashion.

incorrection [ɛ̃kɔrɛksjɔ̃], *s.f.* **1.** (*a*) incorrectness, inaccuracy, error; (*b*) slovenliness, unsuitability (of attire); (*c*) lack of (good) manners, of savoir-faire; impoliteness. **2.** (*a*) *Gram: etc:* incorrect expression; (*b*) impolite, ill-mannered, action; **l'élève a été renvoyé à la suite d'une grave i. envers le professeur,** the pupil was expelled for being exceedingly rude to the master; **ce retard est une grave i.,** this delay is very ill-mannered; constitutes a serious breach of manners; (*c*) *Com:* unfair, dubious, transaction.

incorrigibilité [ɛ̃kɔriʒibilite], *s.f.* incorrigibility.

incorrigible [ɛ̃kɔriʒibl̩], *a.* incorrigible (child, etc.); irreclaimable, *F:* hopeless (drunkard, etc.); past praying for; (*of minor*) **prétendu i.,** charged with incorrigibility; **paresse i.,** incorrigible laziness.

incorrigiblement [ɛ̃kɔriʒibləmɑ̃], *adv.* incorrigibly; **il est i. bavard,** he's an incorrigible gossip.

incorrompu [ɛ̃kɔr(r)ɔ̃py], *a.* uncorrupted.

incorruptibilité [ɛ̃kɔr(r)yptibilite], *s.f.* incorruptibility.

incorruptible [ɛ̃kɔr(r)yptibl̩], *a.* incorruptible; (*a*) proof against corruption, against decay; (*b*) unbribable; (*c*) *s.m. Hist:* **l'I.,** the (Sea-green) Incorruptible (Robespierre).

incorruptiblement [ɛ̃kɔr(r)yptibləmɑ̃], *adv.* incorruptibly.

incorruption [ɛ̃kɔr(r)ypsjɔ̃], *s.f.* incorruption.

incouvé [ɛ̃kuve], *a.* unhatched (egg).

incréable [ɛ̃kreabl̩], *a.* uncreatable.

incrédibilité [ɛ̃kredibilite], *s.f.* incredibility.

incrédulité [ɛ̃kredylite], *s.f.* **1.** incredulity; **avec i.,** incredulously. **2.** *Theol:* unbelief.

incrédule [ɛ̃kredyl]. **1.** *a.* (*a*) incredulous (**à l'égard de,** of); sceptical; **i. à mes paroles,** doubting my words; (*b*) *Theol:* unbelieving. **2.** *s.* unbeliever, infidel.

incréé [ɛ̃kree], *a.* uncreate(d), increate.

incrément [ɛ̃kremɑ̃], *s.m. Mth: Pol.Ec: A:* increment.

increscent [ɛ̃krɛs(s)ɑ̃], *a. Bot:* accrescent; increscent.

increvable [ɛ̃krəvabl̩], *a.* (*a*) unpuncturable, puncture-proof (tyre); *F:* **c'est un tuyau i.,** it's straight from the horse's mouth; (*b*) *P:* indefatigable, tireless.

incriminable [ɛ̃kriminabl̩], *a.* **1.** (person) liable to prosecution. **2.** indictable (offence).

incrimination [ɛ̃kriminasjɔ̃], *s.f.* **1.** incriminating, crimination, charging. **2.** accusation, charge; indictment.

incriminé, -ée [ɛ̃krimine], *a. & s.* accused.

incriminer [ɛ̃krimine], *v.tr. Jur:* **1.** to (in)criminate, accuse, indict, charge (s.o.); **c'est toujours moi qu'on incrimine,** it is always I who get the blame; **il faut i. la cuisine d'aujourd'hui,** modern cookery is to blame; **l'article incriminé,** the article complained of, the object of the complaint. **2. i. la conduite de qn,** to condemn s.o.'s conduct, behaviour.

incristallisable [ɛ̃kristalizabl̩], *a.* uncrystallizable.

incritiquable [ɛ̃kritikabl̩], *a.* beyond criticism; uncriticizable; not worth criticizing.

incrochetable [ɛ̃krɔʃtabl̩], *a.* unpickable (lock); burglar-proof (safe).

incroyable [ɛ̃krwajabl̩]. **1.** *a.* (*a*) incredible, unbelievable; beyond belief; **récit i.,** incredible tale; *F:* **en conter d'incroyables,** to tell tall stories; **il est i. de penser que . . .,** it is incredible, unbelievable, to think that . . .; **il est i. que** + *sub.*, it is unbelievable, inconceivable, that . . .; (*b*) incredible, extraordinary; **il est d'une paresse i.,** he's incredibly lazy; **c'est un type i.!** he's an incredible, extraordinary, person! **surmonter d'incroyables difficultés,** to overcome incredible, tremendous, difficulties. **2.** (*a*) *s.m.* **l'i.,** the incredible, the unbelievable; (*b*) *s. Hist:* incroyable (beau or belle of the French Directoire period).

incroyablement [ɛ̃krwajabləmɑ̃], *adv.* incredibly, unbelievably; beyond belief; **il est i. paresseux,** he is incredibly lazy, lazy beyond belief.

incroyance [ɛ̃krwajɑ̃:s], *s.f.* unbelief.

incroyant, -ante [ɛ̃krwajɑ̃, -ɑ̃:t]. **1.** *a.* unbelieving. **2.** *s.* unbeliever.

incrustant [ɛ̃krystɑ̃], (*a*) *a.* petrifying (well, etc.); *Ind: Mch:* hard (water); (*b*) *s.m.* petrifying agent.

incrustation [ɛ̃krystasjɔ̃], *s.f.* incrustation. **1.** (*a*) encrusting; *Join:* inlaying; *Const:* overlaying, lining (of wall, etc.); (*b*) *Mch:* furring (up) (of boiler). **2.** (*a*) *Miner:* crust; (*b*) inlaid work; **avec incrustations de nacre,** inlaid with mother of pearl; (*c*) *Dressm:* insertion; **i. de dentelle,** lace inlay; (*d*) *Mch:* **incrustations de chaudière,** fur(ring); boiler scale; **revêtu d'incrustations,** encrusted; furred (boiler); **enlever les incrustations d'une chaudière,** to scale a boiler; (*e*) *pl. Med:* chalkstones (in joints, etc.); (*f*) *Dent:* inlay; **i. en céramique, en or,** porcelain inlay; gold inlay; **i. vestibulaire,** facing.

incrustement [ɛ̃kryst(ə)mɑ̃], *s.m. Const:* overlay (in wall, etc.).

incruster [ɛ̃kryste], *v.tr.* **1.** to encrust; *Join: Furn:* to inlay (**de,** with); *Const:* to overlay, line (wall, etc.); *Dressm:* **i. une robe,** to make up a dress with insertions. **2.** to encrust, form a crust on (sth.); (*of water*) to fur (pipes, etc.).

s'incruster. 1. to become encrusted, to fur (up); **chaudière incrustée,** furred boiler. **2.** (*a*) **préjugés qui s'incrustent dans l'esprit,** prejudices that become engrained in the mind; (*b*) *F:* to dig oneself in; to overstay one's welcome; **quand on l'invite, il s'incruste,** once invited you can't get rid of him.

incrusteur [ɛ̃krystœ:r], *s.m.* inlayer; **i. sur bois,** marquetry inlayer.

incubateur, -trice [ɛ̃kybatœ:r, -tris]. **1.** *a.* incubating (apparatus, etc.). **2.** *s.m.* (*a*) *Husb: Med:* incubator; (*b*) *Pisc:* grille.

incubation [ɛ̃kybasjɔ̃], *s.f.* (*a*) incubation, hatching (of eggs); *Ap:* **cellule d'i.,** brood cell; (*b*) sitting (of hens); (*c*) *Med:* **période d'i.,** incubation period (of disease).

incube[1] [ɛ̃kyb], *s.m.* incubus; nightmare.

incube[2], *a. Bot:* incubous (leaf).

incuber [ɛ̃kybe], *v.tr.* to incubate, hatch out (eggs).

incuisable [ɛ̃kɥizabl̩], *a.* uncookable.

incuit [ɛ̃kɥi], *a.* uncooked; underdone.

inculcation [ɛ̃kylkasjɔ̃], *s.f.* inculcating, inculcation.

inculpabilité[1] [ɛ̃kylpabilite], *s.f.* blamelessness, guiltlessness.

inculpabilité[2], *s.f.* liability to be charged (with an offence).

inculpable [ɛ̃kylpabl̩], *a.* (*a*) *Jur:* chargeable, indictable, inculpatable; (*b*) blameworthy.

inculpation [ɛ̃kylpasjɔ̃], *s.f.* indictment, charge, inculpation; **i. de vol,** indictment for theft, on a charge of theft.

inculpé, -ée [ɛ̃kylpe], *a. & s. Jur:* **l'i.,** the accused, the prisoner (in the widest sense); **i. de complicité,** charged with, indicted for, indicted on a charge of, complicity.

inculper [ɛ̃kylpe], *v.tr.* to indict, charge, inculpate; **i. qn de coups et blessures, d'avoir commis un vol,** to charge s.o. with assault and battery, with committing a theft.

inculquer [ɛ̃kylke], *v.tr.* to inculcate (**à,** in); to instil (**à,** into); **i. une leçon,** to inculcate a lesson, to point a moral; **i. de force ses idées à des enfants,** to force one's ideas upon children.

inculte [ɛ̃kylt], *a.* (*a*) uncultivated, wild (garden, etc.); waste (land); (*b*) **barbe i.,** unkempt beard; (*c*) (*of pers.*) rough, unpolished; uneducated.

incultivable [ɛ̃kyltivabl̩], *a.* untillable, uncultivable, irreclaimable (land).

incultivé [ɛ̃kyltive], *a.* (*a*) untilled, uncultivated (land, etc.); (*b*) uncultured (mind, etc.).

inculture [ɛ̃kylty:r], *s.f.* **1.** lack of culture (in person). **2.** lack of cultivation; **l'état d'i. de ces terres,** the neglected condition of this land.

incunable [ɛ̃kynabl̩]. **1.** *a.* (book) printed early (before A.D. 1500); incunabular (book). **2.** *s.m.* early printed book, incunable; incunabulum, *pl.* incunabula.

incurabilité [ɛ̃kyrabilite], *s.f.* incurability, incurableness.

incurable [ɛ̃kyrabl̩]. **1.** *a.* incurable (disease, etc.). **2.** *s.* incurable (person); **hospice des Incurables, les Incurables,** home for incurables.

incurablement [ɛ̃kyrabləmɑ̃], *adv.* incurably.

incurie [ɛ̃kyri], *s.f.* carelessness, negligence, lack of care, slackness.

incurieux, -ieuse [ɛ̃kyrjø, -jø:z], *a.* incurious (**de,** of); lacking in curiosity.

incuriosité [ɛ̃kyrjozite], *s.f.* lack of curiosity, incuriosity.

incursif, -ive [ɛ̃kyrsif, -i:v], *a.* incursive.

incursion [ɛ̃kyrsjɔ̃], *s.f.* inroad, foray, raid, incursion; **faire des incursions dans tout le pays,** to overrun the land; **faire une i. dans le domaine de la poésie, de la science,** to make an excursion into the realm of poetry, of science.

incurvable [ɛ̃kyrvabl̩], *a.* that can curve, bend; **tige i.,** pliable stem.

incurvariides [ɛ̃kyrvariid], *s.m.pl. Ent:* Incurvariidae.

incurvation [ɛ̃kyrvasjɔ̃], *s.f.* incurvation; bend; sag.

incurvé [ɛ̃kyrve], incurvate(d); curved; **table à pieds incurvés,** table with curved legs; **ligne incurvée,** (i) concave, (ii) convex, line.

incurver [ɛ̃kyrve], *v.tr.* to incurvate, incurve; to bend, to curve; **i. les pieds d'une table,** to give a table curved legs.

incus [ɛ̃ky:s], *s.m. Meteor:* incus.

incuse [ɛ̃ky:z], *a.f. & s.f.* (**médaille**) **i.,** incuse (medal).

indaguer [ɛ̃dage], *v.i.* (*in Belgium*) to institute a criminal investigation.

indamine [ɛ̃damin], *s.f. Ch:* indamine.

indane [ɛ̃dan], *s.f. Ch:* indan, hydrindene.

indanthrène [ɛ̃dɑ̃trɛn], *s.m. Dy:* indanthrene.

indatable [ɛ̃databl̩], *a.* that cannot be dated.

indazine [ɛ̃dazin], *s.f. Ch:* indazine.

indazole [ɛ̃dazɔl], *s.m. Ch:* indazole.

Inde [ɛ̃:d]. **1.** *Pr.n.f. Geog:* (*a*) India; *Hist:* **l'I. anglaise,** British India; **la compagnie anglaise des Indes,** the East India company; **les races de l'I.,** the Indian races; (*b*) **les Indes,** the Indies; **les Indes occidentales,** the West Indies; **les Indes orientales, les grandes Indes,** the East Indies; *A:* **la mer des Indes,** the Indian Ocean; (*c*) **bois d'I.,**

logwood; **cochon d'I.,** guinea-pig; **marron d'I.,** horse chestnut; *s.a.* ŒILLET 2. **2.** *s.m.* indigo (blue).

indébrouillable [ɛ̃debrujabl̩], *a.* (*a*) (skein, etc.) that cannot be unravelled or disentangled; (*b*) inextricable, tangled (situation, etc.).

indécachetable [ɛ̃dekaʃtabl̩], *a.* (envelope) that cannot be opened without detection.

indécemment [ɛ̃desamɑ̃], *adv.* indecently.

indécence [ɛ̃desɑ̃:s], *s.f.* **1.** indecency, immodesty. **2. commettre des indécences,** to commit acts of indecency.

indécent [ɛ̃desɑ̃], *a.* **1.** indecent, improper; immodest. **2.** indecorous; **les facéties sont indécentes à un juge,** facetiousness is unbecoming in a judge.

indéchiffrable [ɛ̃deʃifrabl̩], *a.* **1.** indecipherable (inscription); illegible (writing). **2.** unintelligible, incomprehensible, obscure; (*of pers.*) impenetrable, inscrutable.

indéchiffré [ɛ̃deʃifre], *a.* undeciphered.

indéchirable [ɛ̃deʃirabl̩], *a.* untearable, tear-proof.

indéchiré [ɛ̃deʃire], *a.* untorn.

indécis [ɛ̃desi], *a.* **1.** undecided, unsettled, open (question, etc.); doubtful (victory, success, etc.); vague (light, outline, etc.); blurred (outline); **bataille indécise,** drawn battle; *Games:* **partie indécise,** drawn game, draw. **2.** (*of pers.*) (*a*) **être i. quant au parti à prendre,** to be undecided, in two minds, how to act; (*b*) irresolute, hesitating; wavering; (*c*) *s.m.* **c'est un i.,** he's somebody who can never make his mind up.

indécision [ɛ̃desizjɔ̃], *s.f.* **1.** indecision, irresolution; **être dans l'i. du parti à prendre,** to be undecided how to act, as to what course to take. **2.** uncertainty.

indécisivement [ɛ̃desizivmɑ̃], *adv.* indecisively.

indéclinabilité [ɛ̃deklinabilite], *s.f. Gram:* indeclinableness.

indéclinable [ɛ̃deklinabl̩], *a.* **1.** *A:* that cannot be refused, declined; (responsibility, etc.) that cannot be shirked. **2.** *Gram:* indeclinable.

indécollable [ɛ̃dekɔlabl̩], *a.* that cannot be unglued, unstuck.

indécomposable [ɛ̃dekɔ̃pozabl̩], *a.* indecomposable, irresolvable (element, etc.).

indécomposé [ɛ̃dekɔ̃poze], *a.* undecomposed.

indécousable [ɛ̃dekuzabl̩], *a.* that cannot come unsewn; non-ripping (seam).

indécouvrable [ɛ̃dekuvrabl̩], *a.* undiscoverable.

indécrassable [ɛ̃dekrasabl̩], *a.* = INDÉCROTTABLE.

indécrit [ɛ̃dekri], *a.* undescribed.

indécrottable [ɛ̃dekrɔtabl̩], *a.* **1.** uncleanable. **2.** *F:* incorrigible, irretrievable, past praying for; hopeless (dunce, etc.).

indédoublable [ɛ̃dedublabl̩], *a.* **1.** *Ch: etc:* indecomposable (body). **2.** *Phot:* unconvertible (anastigmat).

indéfectibilité [ɛ̃defɛktibilite], *s.f. Theol:* indefectibility (of the church, etc.).

indéfectible [ɛ̃defɛktibl̩], *a.* **1.** *Theol:* indefectible; **amitié i.,** indestructible friendship. **2.** *Pol.Ec:* **actif i.,** non-wasting assets.

indéfectiblement [ɛ̃defɛktibləmɑ̃], *adv.* indefectibly.

indéfendable [ɛ̃defɑ̃dabl̩], *a.* indefensible (town, opinion).

indéfendu [ɛ̃defɑ̃dy], *a.* undefended.

indéfini [ɛ̃defini], *a.* **1.** (*a*) indefinite; **congé i.,** indefinite leave; *Gram:* **pronom i.,** indefinite pronoun; *A:* **passé i.,** indefinite past (tense); perfect (tense); **modes indéfinis,** infinite parts (of the verb); (*b*) *Bot:* indefinite (inflorescence, etc.). **2.** undefined.

indéfiniment [ɛ̃definimɑ̃], *adv.* indefinitely; **ajourner une affaire i.,** to adjourn a case *sine die.*

indéfinissable [ɛ̃definisabl̩], *a.* indefinable, undefinable (term, etc.); indeterminate (colour, etc.); undefinable (feeling); (man, feeling, pain) difficult to describe; enigmatic (person, smile, etc.).

indéfinité [ɛ̃definite], *s.f.* indefiniteness.

indéformable [ɛ̃defɔrmabl̩], *a.* indeformable; that will not lose its shape; *Aer:* rigid (airship).

indéfrichable [ɛ̃defriʃabl̩], *a.* (land) that cannot be cleared; waste (land).

indéfriché [ɛ̃defriʃe], *a.* uncleared (land).

indéfrisable [ɛ̃defrizabl̩]. **1.** *a.* (hair) that will not come out of curl. **2.** *s.f. Hairdr: O:* permanent wave; **i. à froid,** cold perm; home perm.

indégonflable [ɛ̃degɔ̃flabl̩], *a.* undeflatable.

indéhiscence [ɛ̃deis(s)ɑ̃:s], *s.f. Bot:* indehiscence.

indéhiscent [ɛ̃deis(s)ɑ̃], *a. Bot:* indehiscent.

indélébile [ɛ̃delebil], *a.* indelible (ink, stain, etc.).

indélébilement [ɛ̃delebilmɑ̃], *adv.* indelibly.

indélébilité [ɛ̃delebilite], *s.f.* indelibility.

indélégable [ɛ̃delegabl̩], *a.* (power) that cannot be delegated, indelegable.

indélibéré [ɛ̃delibere], *a.* undeliberated, unconsidered (proceeding, etc.).

indélicat [ɛ̃delika], *a.* (*a*) indelicate, coarse (nature, etc.); tactless (action); (*b*) dishonest, unscrupulous (cashier, etc.); **procédés indélicats,** sharp practices.

indélicatement [ɛ̃delikatmɑ̃], *adv.* (*a*) indelicately; (*b*) unscrupulously.

indélicatesse [ɛ̃delikatɛs], *s.f.* **1.** (*a*) indelicacy; tactlessness; (*b*) unscrupulousness. **2.** (i) indelicate, tactless, (ii) unscrupulous, action; *F:* embezzlement.

indémaillable [ɛ̃demajabl̩], *a.* ladderproof, nonladder, non-run, mesh (stocking).

indémêlable [ɛ̃demɛlabl̩], *a.* that cannot be unravelled, disentangled.

indemne [ɛ̃dɛmn], *a.* **1.** (*a*) without loss; without (material or moral) damage; **sortir i. d'une affaire délicate,** to come out of an awkward business with one's reputation undamaged; (*b*) undamaged, unscorched, unsinged, etc.; (*c*) uninjured, unhurt, unscathed, scatheless, unscarred, etc.; **le pilote et son passager sont indemnes,** the pilot and his passenger are uninjured, unhurt; are without a scratch. **2. plaie i. de tout germe morbide,** wound free from any morbid germ.

indemnisable [ɛ̃dɛmnizabl̩], *a.* entitled to compensation.

indemnisation [ɛ̃dɛmnizasjɔ̃], *s.f.* indemnification; compensation.

indemniser [ɛ̃dɛmnize], *v.tr.* to indemnify; to compensate; **i. qn d'une perte,** to compensate s.o. for a loss; **i. qn en argent,** to pay s.o. compensation in cash.

indemnitaire [ɛ̃dɛmnitɛ:r], *s.m. & f.* receiver of an indemnity, of compensation; indemnitee.

indemnité [ɛ̃dɛmnite], *s.f.* (*a*) indemnity, indemnification, compensation (for loss sustained); **i. de guerre,** war indemnity; **i. en argent,** pecuniary compensation; compensation in cash; **demander une i. (en dommages-intérêts),** to put in a claim (for damages); (*b*) compensation to other party, penalty (for delay, non-delivery, etc.); *Nau:* **i. pour surestarie,** demurrage; (*c*) *Adm:* allowance; grant; additional pay, extra pay; **i. de vie chère, de cherté de vie,** cost-of-living allowance; **i. de résidence,** living allowance; **i. de logement,** housing allowance; **i. de fonction(s),** acting allowance; **i. de chef de famille, i. de salaire unique,** marriage allowance; **i. de charges de famille,** family allowance; **i. de chômage,** unemployment benefit, *F:* dole; **i. de maladie,** sickness benefit; **i. pour accidents de travail,** industrial injuries benefit; **i. journalière,** daily, per diem, allowance; **i. de route, de déplacement,** travelling expenses, allowance; **i. kilométrique,** mileage allowance; *Nau:* **i. pour temps gagné,** despatch money; *Jur:* **i. de déplacement,** conduct money (paid to a witness); *Pol:* **i. parlementaire,** salary of a member of parliament; *Mil: etc:* **i. d'entrée en campagne,** war-outfit allowance; **i. de table,** mess allowance.

indémontable [ɛ̃demɔ̃tabl̩], *a.* that cannot be taken to pieces.

indémontrable [ɛ̃demɔ̃trabl̩], *a.* undemonstrable, unprovable.

indémontré [ɛ̃demɔ̃tre], *a.* undemonstrated, not proved.

indène [ɛ̃dɛn], *s.m. Ch:* indene.

indéniable [ɛ̃denjabl̩], *a.* undeniable; **il est i. que,** *usu.* + **ind.,** it is undeniable that . . ..

indéniablement [ɛ̃denjabləmɑ̃], *adv.* undeniably.

indénone [ɛ̃denɔn], *s.f. Ch:* indone.

indénouable [ɛ̃denwabl̩], *a.* that cannot be untied; (mystery) that cannot be unravelled.

indentation [ɛ̃dɑ̃tasjɔ̃], *s.f.,* **indenture** [ɛ̃dɑ̃ty:r], *s.f.* indentation (of coast, etc.); re-entrant.

indenté [ɛ̃dɑ̃te], *a.* indented (coastline, etc.).

indépendamment [ɛ̃depɑ̃damɑ̃], *adv.* independently (de, of); **l'avancement se fait selon les capacités i. de l'ancienneté,** promotion goes by ability irrespective of seniority.

indépendance [ɛ̃depɑ̃dɑ̃:s], *s.f.* **1.** independence (de, à l'égard de, of); **i. législative,** legislative independence; home rule; local autonomy; **faire preuve d'i.,** to show independence, self-reliance. **2. il s'était acquis une modeste i.,** he had acquired small independent means.

indépendant, -ante [ɛ̃depɑ̃dɑ̃, -ɑ̃:t]. **1.** *a.* (*a*) independent (de, of); free; **circonstances indépendantes de ma volonté,** circumstances beyond my control; **avoir une fortune indépendante,** to be independent; **état i.,** free state; (*b*) self-reliant; (*c*) *Aut:* **roues (avant) indépendantes,** independent (front-wheel) suspension; *Mth:* **vecteur i.,** free vector; (*d*) self-contained (apparatus, flat, etc.); (*e*) *Gram:* misrelated, unrelated (particle). **2.** *s.* independent person; *Pol:* Independent; *Rel.H:* **les Indépendants,** the Independents.

indépensé [ɛ̃depɑ̃se], *a.* unexpended, unspent.

indéplissable [ɛ̃deplisabl̩], *a.* permanently pleated (skirt, etc.).

indéracinable [ɛ̃derasinabl̩], *a.* **1.** that cannot be uprooted. **2.** ineradicable (prejudice, etc.).

indéraciné [ɛ̃derasine], *a.* uneradicated (abuse, etc.).

indéraillable [ɛ̃derajabl̩], *a. Rail:* (*of locomotive*) not likely to leave the rails.

indéréglable [ɛ̃dereglabl̩], *a.* fool-proof (mechanism, etc.); that cannot get out of order.

indescriptible [ɛ̃dɛskriptibl̩], *a.* indescribable, beyond description; that beggars description.

indescriptiblement [ɛ̃dɛskriptibləmɑ̃], *adv.* indescribably.

indésirable [ɛ̃dezirabl̩], *a. & s.* undesirable.

indesserrable [ɛ̃desɛrabl̩], *a.* **1.** unyielding (grip, grasp). **2. écrou i.,** self-locking nut, lock nut.

indestituable [ɛ̃dɛstitɥabl̩], *a.* irremovable (from office).

indestructibilité [ɛ̃dɛstryktibilite], *s.f.* indestructibility, indestructibleness.

indestructible [ɛ̃dɛstryktibl̩], *a.* indestructible.

indestructiblement [ɛ̃dɛstryktibləmɑ̃], *adv.* indestructibly.

indétecté [ɛ̃detɛkte], *a.* undetected.

indéterminable [ɛ̃detɛrminabl̩], *a.* indeterminable, unascertainable.

indétermination [ɛ̃detɛrminasjɔ̃], *s.f.* indetermination. **1.** indefiniteness. **2.** irresoluteness, irresolution.

indéterminé [ɛ̃detɛrmine], *a.* **1.** undetermined, indeterminate, indefinite; *Mth:* **problème i.,** *s.m.* **indéterminé,** indeterminate problem. **2.** irresolute, undetermined, undecided.

indéterminisme [ɛ̃detɛrminism], *s.m. Phil:* indeterminism.

indéterministe [ɛ̃detɛrminist], *a. & s. Phil:* indeterminist.

indétonant [ɛ̃detɔnɑ̃], *a.* inexplosive (mixture).

indétraquable [ɛ̃detrakabl̩], *a.* fool-proof (mechanism).

indétrempable [ɛ̃detrɑ̃pabl̩], *a.* (*of steel*) that keeps its temper; heat-resisting.

indéveloppable [ɛ̃devlɔpabl̩], *a. Geom:* skew (surface).

indevinable [ɛ̃d(ə)vinabl̩], *a.* unguessable.

indeviné [ɛ̃d(ə)vine], *a.* unguessed.

indévissable [ɛ̃devisabl̩], *a. Mec.E:* self-locking (nut).

indévot [ɛ̃devo], *a.* undevout, indevout (person, posture, etc.); irreligious (person).

indévotion [ɛ̃devosjɔ̃], *s.f.* indevotion, irreligion.

index [ɛ̃dɛks], *s.m.* **1.** (*a*) forefinger, index (finger); **tenir qch. entre le pouce et l'i.,** to hold sth. between one's finger and thumb; to hold sth. with, in, one's fingers; (*b*) pointer (of balance, etc.); indicator, finger; **i. radioactif,** radium illuminated pointer; (*c*) **i. du prix, du coût, de la vie,** cost of living index, consumer's price index. **2.** (*a*) index (of book); **faire l'i. d'un livre,** to index a book; (*b*) *R.C.Ch:* **Index (librorum prohibitorum), l'I. (expurgatoire),** (the) (Expurgatory) Index; **mettre un livre à l'I.,** to put a book on the Index; **mettre qch. à l'i.,** to prohibit sth., to put sth. on the prohibited list, on the black list; to blacklist sth.; **mettre qn à l'i.,** to put s.o. on the black list; to blacklist s.o.

indexage [ɛ̃dɛksa:ʒ], *s.m.* indexing.

indexation [ɛ̃dɛksasjɔ̃], *s.f.* **1.** (card-)indexing. **2.** *Pol.Ec:* pegging of prices (in relation to certain products).

indexer [ɛ̃dɛkse], *v.tr.* **1.** to index. **2.** *Pol.Ec:* to peg (prices) (in relation to certain products); **salaires indexés au coût de la vie,** wages geared to the cost of living.

indianaïte [ɛ̃djanait], *s.f. Miner:* indianaite.

indianisation [ɛ̃djanizasjɔ̃], *s.f.* Indianization.

indianiser [ɛ̃djanize], *v.tr.* to Indianize.

indianisme [ɛ̃djanism], *s.m.* Indianism.

indianiste [ɛ̃djanist], *s.m. & f.* Indianist, *esp.* Sanskrit scholar.

indianite [ɛ̃djanit], *s.f. Miner:* indianite.

indianologie [ɛ̃djanɔlɔʒi], *s.f.* Amerindian studies.

indic [ɛ̃dik], *s.m. P:* nark; stool pigeon.

indical, -aux [ɛ̃dikal, -o], *a.* indicial, indicatory.

indican [ɛ̃dikɑ̃], *s.m. Ch:* indican.

indicanurie [ɛ̃dikanyri], *s.f. Med:* indicanuria.

indicateur, -trice [ɛ̃dikatœ:r, -tris]. **1.** *a.* indicatory; **faits indicateurs de qch.,** facts indicative of sth.; **(doigt) i.,** forefinger, index finger; **poteau i.,** signpost; **plaque indicatrice (de route),** direction panel, road sign; *Rail:* direction board;

El.E: **tableau i.,** annunciator board; **lampe indicatrice,** tell-tale lamp; *Com: etc:* **chiffre i.,** index number. **2.** *s.* informer, (police) spy. **3.** *s.m.* (railway) timetable; guide; (street) directory. **4.** *s.m. Tchn:* indicator, tell-tale; pointer (of weather-glass, etc.); (*a*) **i. à cadran,** dial gauge; **i. lumineux,** visual indicator, luminous pointer; tell-tale lamp; **i. de niveau d'eau,** (i) *Min: etc:* water-level indicator; (ii) *Mch:* water gauge, water indicator; *I.C.E:* **i. de niveau (de carburant),** (fuel) gauge; *Rail:* **i. de pente, de rampe,** gradient indicator, post; (*b*) *Mec: Ph:* **i. de contrainte,** stress indicator; **i. de flexion,** deflection indicator; **i. de tension,** tension indicator; **i. de vide,** vacuum gauge; (*c*) *Mch:* indicator (of power and correct working); gauge (of boiler); pointer; **i. de pression (de vapeur),** pressure gauge, steam gauge; **i. (du nombre) de tours,** revolution indicator, counter, pointer; *Mch: Veh:* **i. de vitesse,** speed indicator, tachometer; *Aut:* speedometer; **diagramme d'i., i. de courbes,** indicator diagram, card; **relever un tracé d'i.,** to take an indicator card; (*d*) *Av:* **i. de pente,** (in)clinometer; glide path localiser; **i. de pente à bille,** ball (in)clinometer; **i. de pente latérale,** bank indicator; **i. de pente longitudinale,** fore-and-aft (in)clinometer; **i. de virage et de pente,** turn-and-bank indicator; **i. d'altitude,** altimeter; **i. de baisse de pression,** pressure-drop warning light; **i. de densité,** densitometer; **i. de dérive,** drift indicator; **i. de débit,** flowmeter; **i. de vitesse relative, i. de vitesse par rapport à l'air,** air-speed indicator; **i. de vitesse d'air,** anemometer; **i. automatique de route,** course-line computer, offset-course computer; **i. (gyroscopique) de cap,** directional indicator; **i. (gyroscopique) de direction,** direction indicator, directional gyro(scope); **i. de position (par rapport au) sol,** ground position indicator, G.P.I.; (*spacecraft*) **i. d'attitude,** attitude indicator; (*e*) *Nau:* **i. d'angle de barre,** rudder-angle indicator, tiller tell-tale; **i. d'assiette,** trim indicator; **i. de tirant d'eau,** draught indicator, gauge; (*f*) *El:* **i. de pertes,** leak(age), fault-detector; **i. de pointe,** maximum demand indicator, peak indicator; **i. de tension,** voltage indicator; (*g*) *Tp:* **i. d'appel,** call indicator; **i. de durée,** chargeable-time indicator; (*h*) *Elcs:* indicator; (*radar*) display; **i. panoramique (radar),** plan position indicator, P.P.I.; **i. de site,** elevation display; **i. de veille,** surveillance display; *Av: Elcs:* **i. de direction,** to-from indicator; *T.V: W.Tel:* **i. de direction,** direction finder; **i. d'occupation,** studio warning sign; (*i*) *Atom.Ph:* indicator, monitor, tracer; **i. de radiation(s),** radiation counter; radiation detector, monitor; survey meter; **i. isotopique,** isotopic indicator, tracer; **i. radioactif,** radioactive indicator, tracer; tracer element; **i. de pertes, d'échappement,** leak detector. **5.** *s.m. Orn:* honey guide. **6.** *s.f. Geom:* **indicatrice,** indicatrix.

indicatif, -ive [ɛ̃dikatif, -iːv]. **1.** *a.* indicative (de, of); indicatory. **2.** *a.* & *s.m. Gram:* **(mode) i.,** indicative (mood); **à l'i.,** in the indicative. **3.** *s.m. Tg: W.Tel: etc:* **i. d'appel,** call sign, call signal, call number; **i. littéral,** code letter; **i. numérique,** numerical code; *Tp:* **i. (départemental),** (dialling) code, prefix; *W.Tel:* **i. du poste,** station signal; **i. (musical),** signature tune (of programme); **annuaire des indicatifs des émetteurs amateurs,** Radio Amateur Call Book.

indication [ɛ̃dikasjɔ̃], *s.f.* indication. **1.** (*a*) indicating, pointing out; (*b*) drawing up (of procedure, etc.). **2.** (*a*) (i) (piece of) information; *Jur:* **fausse i. de revenu,** false declaration of income; *Mil: Av:* **i. de service,** conventional signal; (ii) **à titre d'i.,** for your, my, guidance; (*b*) sign, token (of guilt, etc.); clue (to sth.); (*c*) mark; **i. de terrain,** landmark; **indications topographiques,** survey marks, data; (*d*) *Tp:* **appel avec i. de durée (I.D.),** advise duration charge call. **3.** *esp. pl.* instruction(s); **indications du mode d'emploi,** directions for use; **selon les indications données,** as directed; **voici quelques indications supplémentaires,** here are some further particulars; **sauf i. contraire . . .,** except where, unless, otherwise stated . . .; *Th:* **indications scéniques,** stage directions.

indicatoridés [ɛ̃dikatɔride], *s.m.pl. Orn:* Indicatoridae, the honey guides.

indice [ɛ̃dis], *s.m.* **1.** indication, sign; mark, token; *Nau:* landmark; **condamner qn sur les indices les plus faibles,** to condemn s.o. with hardly anything to go upon, on the flimsiest of evidence; **action qui est l'i. d'une belle âme,** action that betokens a noble soul; **il n'y a pas de meilleur i. du tempérament d'un homme que ce qu'il trouve risible,** nothing shows a man's character better than what he laughs at, what he finds amusing; *W.Tel: T.V:* **i. de popularité,** popularity rating (of programme); *Nau:* **indices que la terre est proche,** signs that point to the proximity of land; *Min:* **indices de pétrole,** oil shows. **2.** *Mth: Ph: Ch: etc:* (i) index (number); (ii) factor, coefficient; (iii) rating; *Alg:* **i. dans l'interligne inférieur,** sub-index; *Ac:* **i. d'affaiblissement sonore,** sound-reduction factor; *Ball:* **i. de résistance balistique,** ballistic coefficient; *Opt:* **i. de réfraction,** index of refraction, refractive index; *Ch:* **i. d'acide,** acid number; **i. de brome,** bromine number; *Ch: etc:* **i. de détonation,** knock-rating (of petrol); **i. d'octane,** octane rating, number; *El: Elcs:* **i. de glissement amont,** pushing figure; **i. de glissement aval,** pulling figure; **i. de pulsation,** pulse number; *Anthr:* **i. céphalique,** cephalic, cranial, index; **i. dentaire,** dental index; *Pol.Ec:* **i. du coût de la vie,** cost of living index; **i. des prix de gros, de détail,** wholesale, retail, price index; **i. pondéré** weighted index.

indiciaire [ɛ̃disjɛːr], *a.* indicial; **classement i.,** index classification.

indicible [ɛ̃disibl̩], *a.* (*a*) inexpressible, beyond words, unutterable; untold (suffering); unspeakable (grief, rage); (*b*) indescribable; **c'est d'une bêtise i.,** it's a piece of unutterable stupidity.

indiciblement [ɛ̃disibləmɑ̃], *adv.* inexpressibly; unutterably.

indicolite, *s.f. Miner:* indicolite, blue tourmaline.

indiction [ɛ̃diksjɔ̃], *s.f.* **1.** *Rom.* & *Ecc. Hist:* (cycle, era, of) indiction; **i. première, seconde, septième,** first, second, seventh, indiction. **2.** *Ecc:* proclamation (of fast); convocation (of council).

indien, -ienne [ɛ̃djɛ̃, -jɛn]. **1.** (*a*) *a.* & *s.* Indian (of India, of America); **l'océan i.,** the Indian Ocean; (*b*) *a.* **en file indienne,** in single file. **2.** *s.f.* **indienne:** (*a*) *Tex:* (i) printed calico, print; (ii) chintz; (*b*) *Swim:* overarm stroke.

indiennage [ɛ̃djɛnaːʒ], *s.m.* calico printing (process).

indiennerie [ɛ̃djɛnri], *s.f.* (*a*) printed cotton-goods industry; calico printing; (*b*) printed cotton goods.

indienneur, -euse [ɛ̃djɛnœːr, -øːz], *s.* manufacturer of, worker in, printed cotton goods; calico printer.

indifféremment [ɛ̃diferamɑ̃], *adv.* indifferently; (*a*) with indifference; (*b*) without discrimination, equally.

indifférence [ɛ̃diferɑ̃ːs], *s.f.* **1.** indifference, lack of interest; unconcern; apathy; heartlessness; **i. aux événements,** indifference to, lack of interest in, what is, was, happening; **une totale i. pour lui-même,** a total lack of interest in his own welfare; **i. devant le, en face du, en présence du, danger,** unconcern in the face of danger; **i. aux malheurs des autres,** indifference to the misfortunes of others. **2.** *Ch:* indifference; (*a*) inertness (of a body); (*b*) neutrality (of a salt, etc.).

indifférenciation [ɛ̃diferɑ̃sjasjɔ̃], *s.f. Psy:* (*a*) inability to differentiate; (*b*) lack of differentiation.

indifférencié [ɛ̃diferɑ̃sje], *a.* undifferentiated.

indifférent [ɛ̃diferɑ̃], *a.* **1.** (*a*) indifferent (à, to); unaffected (à, by); unconcerned; apathetic; **se montrer i. au sort de qn,** to show indifference to s.o.'s fate, to appear unconcerned about s.o.'s fate; **rester i. à tout,** to take no interest in anything; **il m'est i.,** I am, feel, indifferent about him; he is nothing to me; **je lui suis i.,** (i) I am indifferent to him; (ii) he is, feels, indifferent about me; **les hommes lui sont indifférents,** she won't look at a man; men mean nothing to her; (*b*) cold, insensible, emotionless (heart, etc.); **regarder qch. d'un œil i.,** to look coldly at sth.; to look coldly on. **2.** *Ch:* indifferent; (*a*) inert (body); (*b*) neutral (salt, solution, etc.). **3.** immaterial, unimportant; **cela m'est i.,** it's all the same, quite immaterial, to me; I don't care either way; **il m'est i. de faire cela ou autre chose,** it is a matter of indifference to me, all one to me, whether I do that or something else; **il est i. d'y aller ou de ne pas y aller,** it doesn't matter whether one, he, etc., goes or not; **tout lui est i.,** all things are alike to him; **parler de choses indifférentes,** to engage in small talk. **4.** *Fish:* **poissons indifférents,** fish for which there is no close season.

indifférentisme [ɛ̃diferɑ̃tism], *s.m.* indifferentism.

indifférentiste [ɛ̃diferɑ̃tist], *s.m.* or *f.* indifferentist.

indifférer [ɛ̃difere], *v.tr. def. used in 3rd pers. sing.* & *pl. with pronoun complement only* **(il indiffère, il indifféra)** *F:* **cela m'indiffère,** that leaves me indifferent; I couldn't care less about it.

indiffusible [ɛ̃difyzibl̩], *a.* (*a*) *Ph:* unsusceptible of diffusion, non-diffusing; (*b*) *Biol:* (substance) that does not disperse; undispersing.

indigénat [ɛ̃diʒena], *s.m. Hist:* **1.** right of citizenship (as formerly conceded to natives, *e.g.* in Algeria). **2.** *coll.* native population (of colony).

indigence [ɛ̃diʒɑ̃ːs], *s.f.* (*a*) *A:* lack (of sth.); (*b*) poverty, indigence, want, penury; **tomber dans l'i., être réduit à l'i.,** be reduced to poverty, to fall on evil days; **i. d'idées,** penury, lack, of ideas.

indigène [ɛ̃diʒɛn]. **1.** *a.* (*a*) indigenous (à, to); aboriginal; native (population, troops); **flore i.,** indigenous flora; (*b*) home-grown (produce). **2.** *s.* native (*esp.* of foreign country, of colony).

indigent, -ente [ɛ̃diʒɑ̃, -ɑ̃ːt]. **1.** *a.* (*a*) poor, needy, necessitous, poverty-stricken, indigent; (*b*) **végétation indigente,** scanty vegetation; **imagination indigente,** lack of imagination. **2.** *s.* poor person; *Adm: O:* pauper; **les indigents,** the poor; the destitute.

indigéré [ɛ̃diʒere], *a.* undigested.

indigeste [ɛ̃diʒɛst], *a.* **1.** indigestible; stodgy (food). **2.** undigested; confused, ill-arranged, heavy (book, etc.); crude (work).

indigestibilité [ɛ̃diʒɛstibilite], *s.f.* indigestibility.

indigestible [ɛ̃diʒɛstibl̩], *a.* indigestible.

indigestion [ɛ̃diʒɛstjɔ̃], *s.f.* indigestion; **avoir une i.,** to have (an attack of) indigestion; *F:* **j'en ai une i.,** I'm fed up with it.

indigestionner [ɛ̃diʒɛstjɔne], *v.tr.* to give (s.o.) indigestion; *F:* to make (s.o.) fed up.

indigète [ɛ̃diʒɛt], *a. Rom.Ant:* **dieux indigètes,** local patron deities.

indigitamenta [ɛ̃diʒitamɑ̃ta], *s.m.pl. Rom.Ant:* indigitamenta.

indignation [ɛ̃diɲasjɔ̃], *s.f.* indignation; **éprouver une vive i. de, devant, la conduite de qn,** to feel highly indignant at s.o.'s conduct; **soulever l'i. de qn,** to make s.o. indignant; **d'un ton d'i., avec i.,** indignantly.

indigne [ɛ̃diɲ], *a.* unworthy. **1.** (*a*) undeserving; **i. de qch., de faire qch.,** unworthy of sth., to do sth.; **elle est i. qu'on fasse rien pour elle,** she is not worth helping; she doesn't deserve to be helped; **i. de la confiance du public,** undeserving of public confidence; (*b*) *Jur:* **i. de succéder,** disqualified, debarred, from succeeding, from inheriting. **2.** shameful (action, conduct); **conduite i. d'un honnête homme,** conduct unworthy of an honest man; **c'est i.!** it's outrageous! **conduite i. d'un frère, d'une sœur, d'un père, d'une mère, d'un roi,** unbrotherly, unsisterly, unfatherly, unmotherly, unkingly, behaviour; **i. d'un Anglais,** un-English.

indigné [ɛ̃diɲe], *a.* roused to indignation, indignant (de, at); **d'un air, d'un ton, i.,** indignantly; **tout le monde en est i.,** every one is up in arms about it; **être i. que** + *sub.*, **de ce que** + *ind.*, to be indignant that . . .; **regarder qn d'un œil i.,** to glare at s.o.

indignement [ɛ̃diɲmɑ̃], *adv.* **1.** unworthily. **2.** shamefully, infamously.

indigner [ɛ̃diɲe], *v.tr.* to rouse (s.o.) to indignation, to make (s.o.) indignant; **cela m'indigne,** it makes my blood boil.

s'indigner, to become indignant, to be indignant; **s'i. de, contre, qch., qn,** to be indignant at sth., with s.o.; **s'i. que** + *sub.*, **de ce que** + *ind.*, to be indignant that . . .; **je m'indigne de voir ce crime impuni,** it makes me furious to see this crime go unpunished.

indignité [ɛ̃diɲite], *s.f.* **1.** (*a*) unworthiness; *Jur:* **exclu d'une succession pour cause d'i.,** debarred from succeeding; *Hist:* **i. nationale,** a punishment imposed in France on those guilty of collaboration with the Germans during the 1939-45 war; (*b*) baseness, vileness (of an action). **2.** infamous action; **souffrir des indignités,** to suffer indignities, humiliations; **c'est une i.!** it is outrageous! it's an outrage! it's a scandal!

indigo [ɛ̃digo], *s.m.* **1.** indigo; *Ch: Ind:* **blanc, bleu, brun, d'i.,** indigo white, indigo blue, indigo brown; *a.inv.* **des rubans indigo,** indigo-blue ribbons. **2.** indigo plant.

indigofera [ɛ̃digɔfera], *s.m. Bot:* indigofera.

indigoïde [ɛ̃digɔid], *a. Ch:* indigoid.

indigoterie [ɛ̃digɔtri], *s.f.* indigo (i) plantation, (ii) factory.

indigotier [ɛ̃digɔtje], *s.m.* **1.** *Bot:* indigo plant. **2.** indigo manufacturer, worker.

indigotine [ɛ̃digɔtin], *s.f. Ch:* indigotin.

indique[1] [ɛ̃dik], *a. Ch:* indic.

indique[2], *a. A:* Indian.

indique-fuites [ɛ̃dikfɥit], *s.m.inv.* (gas-fitter's) leak detector.

indiquer [ɛ̃dike], *v.tr.* **1.** to indicate; (*a*) to point to, point (out); **i. qch. du doigt,** to point to sth., to point sth. out (with one's finger); **i. le chemin à qn,** to show s.o. the way; **développer ce qui n'est qu'indiqué,** to expatiate on what is merely hinted at; (*b*) to mark, show; **le compteur indique cent,** the meter reads one hundred; **i. le poids d'une façon précise,** to show the exact weight; **point indiqué sur la carte,** point shown on the map; **la maison indiquée sur le bordereau ci-joint,** the firm mentioned on the accompanying, enclosed, slip; **comme indiqué ci-dessous,** as noted below; **i. exactement l'emplacement (de groupes blindés ennemis),** to pin-point (groups of enemy armour); (*c*) to show, tell; **indiquez-moi un bon médecin,** can you tell me of a good doctor; (*d*) to betoken; **tout dans la maison indique un goût raffiné,** everything in the house shows good taste; **toutes ses paroles indiquent sa sincérité,** all his words show his sincerity; **cela indique chez lui une grande lâcheté,** it argues great cowardice in him; **cela indique de l'intelligence,** it shows, demonstrates, intelligence; **comme son nom l'indique,** as its name implies; (*e*) to appoint, name (a day, etc.); **i. l'heure d'un rendez-vous,** to fix the time of an appointment; **à l'heure indiquée,** at the appointed time; *Rail: etc:* **arriver à l'heure indiquée,** to arrive at the scheduled time; (*f*) to draw up (a procedure, etc.); to dictate, prescribe, lay down (a line of action, etc.); **conduite indiquée par les circonstances,** conduct dictated by the circumstances; **c'était indiqué,** it was the obvious thing to do; **un sujet de plaisanterie tout indiqué,** a ready-made subject for jokes; **nous nommerons X; il est tout à fait indiqué pour ce poste,** we shall appoint X; he's the very man, *the* man, for the job; **cela ne paraît pas très indiqué,** it wouldn't appear very advisable; **un smoking serait tout à fait indiqué,** a dinner jacket seems the most suitable, appropriate; (*g*) *Art: Lit:* to outline, sketch (features, plot, etc.). **2.** *A:* to denounce (s.o.), to inform against (s.o.).

indirect [ɛ̃dirɛkt], *a.* **1.** (*a*) indirect (route, line of descent, tax, *Artil:* fire, *Gram:* object, etc.); collateral (heirs); *Gram:* **discours i.,** indirect speech, oratio obliqua; **éclairage i.,** concealed lighting; **contributions indirectes,** indirect taxation; (*b*) *Jur:* circumstantial (evidence). **2.** *Pej:* **attaque indirecte,** covert attack; *F:* backhander; **moyens indirects,** crooked, underhand, methods.

indirectement [ɛ̃dirɛktəmɑ̃], *adv.* indirectly.

indirigeable [ɛ̃diriʒabl̩], *a.* (*a*) ungovernable; (*b*) incontrollable.

indirubine [ɛ̃dirybin], *s.f. Ch:* indirubin(e).

indiscernabilité [ɛ̃disɛrnabilite], *s.f.* indiscernibility, indiscernibleness.

indiscernable [ɛ̃disɛrnabl̩], *a.* indistinguishable; indiscernible; **deux feuilles indiscernables,** two indistinguishable leaves; **des nuances indiscernables,** scarcely perceptible nuances; *s. Phil:* **principe (de l'identité) des indiscernables,** principle of (the identity of) indiscernibles.

indisciplinable [ɛ̃disiplinabl̩], *a.* indisciplinable, intractable.

indiscipline [ɛ̃disiplin], *s.f.* indiscipline, lack of discipline.

indiscipliné [ɛ̃disipline], *a.* undisciplined, unruly; out of hand.

indiscret, -ète [ɛ̃diskrɛ, -ɛt]. **1.** *a.* (*a*) *A:* (i) indiscreet, imprudent, unguarded; (ii) lacking in moderation; **faire un usage i. de qch.,** to use sth. without moderation, to excess; (*b*) indiscreet, (over-)curious, *F:* nosy (person); tactless (question); **il ne se rend pas compte qu'il est i.,** he doesn't realize that he's indiscreet; **à l'abri des regards indiscrets,** safe from curious, prying, eyes; **est-il i. de vous demander ce que vous comptez faire?** I hope I'm not being indiscreet in asking you what you are going to do; **zèle i.,** misplaced zeal; (*c*) indiscreet; (*pers.*) who gives away secrets; **gare aux langues indiscrètes!** beware of indiscreet people, of people whose tongues run away with them; **je me méfie des oreilles indiscrètes,** I'm on my guard against eavesdroppers. **2.** *s.* (*a*) indiscreet, tactless, meddlesome, person; *F:* nosey parker; (*b*) blabber; teller of secrets; eavesdropper, listener at doors; **c'est un fameux i.!** he's terribly indiscreet! he's not someone you can trust with a secret!

indiscrètement [ɛ̃diskrɛtmɑ̃], *adv.* indiscreetly.

indiscrétion [ɛ̃diskresjɔ̃], *s.f.* indiscretion. **1.** indiscreetness; **sans i., pourquoi . . .?** if it's not indiscreet, if it's a fair question, why . . .? **peut-on vous demander sans i. . . .?** would it be indiscreet, rude, to ask . . .? do you mind my asking . . .? **2.** indiscreet action, remark; **il lui échappe des indiscrétions,** he blurts out (i) tactless things, (ii) secrets; **elle s'est rendue coupable de quelques indiscrétions,** she has been guilty of some indiscretions.

indiscutabilité [ɛ̃diskytabilite], *s.f.* indisputability.

indiscutable [ɛ̃diskytabl̩], *a.* indisputable, unquestionable; obvious; **il est i. que . . .,** it is beyond argument that . . .

indiscutablement [ɛ̃diskytabləmɑ̃], *adv.* indisputably, unquestionably; beyond a doubt.

indiscuté [ɛ̃diskyte], *a.* (*a*) undiscussed, undebated; (*b*) unquestioned, beyond doubt.

indispensabilité [ɛ̃dispɑ̃sabilite], *s.f.* indispensability, indispensableness.

indispensable [ɛ̃dispɑ̃sabl̩], *a.* indispensable (**à qn,** to s.o.; **à, pour, qch.,** for sth.; **pour faire qch.,** for doing sth.). **1.** obligatory; **engagement i.,** engagement there is no getting out of. **2.** essential (**à,** to); absolutely necessary; (object) not to be dispensed with; **il est i. que j'aie votre autorisation écrite,** it is essential that I should have your authorization in writing; **il s'imagine qu'il est i.,** he imagines that he is indispensable; **il nous est i.,** we can't spare him; *s.m.* **ne prenez que l'i.,** don't take more than is strictly necessary; **réduire la durée de son séjour à l'i.,** to stay no longer than is strictly necessary.

indispensablement [ɛ̃dispɑ̃sabləmɑ̃], *adv.* indispensably.

indisponibilité [ɛ̃dispɔnibilite], *s.f.* **1.** *Jur:* inalienability. **2.** unavailability, unavailableness (of funds, of man for a duty).

indisponible [ɛ̃dispɔnibl̩], *a.* **1.** *Jur:* inalienable (property); entailed (estate). **2.** (*a*) *Adm:* not available (for duty, etc.); (*b*) unavailable (capital, etc.); (*car, etc.*) out of commission.

indisposé [ɛ̃dispoze], *a.* **1.** (*a*) indisposed, unwell, poorly, ailing; out of sorts; **se sentir vaguement i.,** to feel off colour; (*b*) *F:* (*of woman*) **être indisposée,** to have one's period, *F:* the curse. **2. i. contre qn,** unfriendly to s.o.; ill-disposed towards s.o.

indisposer [ɛ̃dispoze], *v.tr.* **1.** to make (s.o.) unwell; (*of food, etc.*) to upset (s.o.), to disagree with (s.o.). **2.** to make (s.o.) ill-disposed, hostile; to estrange, antagonize (s.o.); **i. qn contre qn,** to set s.o. against s.o.

indisposition [ɛ̃dispozisjɔ̃], *s.f.* **1.** (*a*) indisposition, illness, upset; (*b*) *F:* monthly period, *F:* the curse. **2.** *A:* unfriendly disposition (**envers, pour,** towards).

indisputable [ɛ̃dispytabl̩], *a.* indisputable, incontestable, incontrovertible, unquestionable.

indisputablement [ɛ̃dispytabləmɑ̃], *adv.* indisputably, incontestably, incontrovertibly, unquestionably.

indisputé [ɛ̃dispyte], *a.* undisputed, unquestioned.

indissociable [ɛ̃dis(s)ɔsjabl̩], *a.* indissociable (**de,** from).

indissolubilité [ɛ̃dis(s)ɔlybilite], *s.f.* **1.** insolubility (of salt, etc.). **2.** indissolubility (of marriage, etc.).

indissoluble [ɛ̃dis(s)ɔlybl̩], *a.* **1.** insoluble (salt, etc.). **2.** indissoluble (bond, friendship).

indissolublement [ɛ̃dis(s)ɔlybləmɑ̃], *adv.* indissolubly.

indistinct [ɛ̃distɛ̃(:kt)], *a.* indistinct; (*a*) not kept separate; (*b*) hazy, blurred; faint (inscription); dim (light); **bruits indistincts,** indistinct noises.

indistinctement [ɛ̃distɛ̃ktəmɑ̃], *adv.* indistinctly; (*a*) indiscriminately; **tous les Français i.,** all Frenchmen, without distinction; (*b*) hazily, vaguely; faintly; dimly; **voir qch. indistinctement,** to see sth. vaguely, indistinctly; **parler i.,** to speak indistinctly.

indistinction [ɛ̃distɛ̃ksjɔ̃], *s.f.* **1.** indistinctness, vagueness. **2.** *occ.* lack of distinction.

indistingué [ɛ̃distɛ̃ge], *a.* **1.** not discriminated. **2.** undistinguished.

indistinguible [ɛ̃distɛ̃gibl̩], *a.* indistinguishable (**de,** from).

indium [ɛ̃djɔm], *s.m. Ch:* indium.

individu [ɛ̃dividy], *s.m.* **1.** *Nat.Hist: Jur: etc:* individual; *F:* **soigner son i., avoir soin de son i.,** to look after oneself well; to look after number one. **2.** *F: usu. Pej:* individual, person, fellow; **un i. de mauvaise mine,** an unprepossessing type; **quel est cet i.?** who is this fellow? **un i. louche,** a shady customer; **salle remplie d'individus louches,** room filled with suspicious characters.

individualisation [ɛ̃dividɥalizasjɔ̃], *s.f.* individualization.

individualiser [ɛ̃dividɥalize], *v.tr.* to individualize; to specify, particularize (case, etc.).

s'individualiser, to assume an individuality, to take on individual characteristics.

individualisme [ɛ̃dividɥalism], *s.m.* individualism.

individualiste [ɛ̃dividɥalist]. **1.** *a.* individualistic. **2.** *s.m. or f.* individualist.

individualité [ɛ̃dividɥalite], *s.f.* individuality.

individuation [ɛ̃dividɥasjɔ̃], *s.f. Phil:* individuation.

individuel, -elle [ɛ̃dividɥɛl]. **1.** *a.* (*a*) individual; personal (liberty, etc.); private (fortune, etc.); **tables individuelles,** separate tables; **agir à titre i.,** to act in an individual capacity; *Sp:* **athlète i.,** unattached athlete; *Nau:* **cabine individuelle,** single cabin; (*b*) *Jur:* several (liability, etc.); *Pol:* **scrutin i.,** uninominal voting. **2.** *s.m.* (*a*) **l'i. et le collectif,** the individual and the collective; (*b*) *Sp:* unattached athlete, player.

individuellement [ɛ̃dividɥɛlmɑ̃], *adv.* **1.** individually, personally, in person. **2.** *Jur:* severally.

indivis [ɛ̃divi], *a. Jur:* **1.** undivided, joint (estate). **2.** joint (owners); **propriétaire i.,** parcener, coparcener; **bien(s) i.,** indivisum; **par i.,** jointly.

indivisaire [ɛ̃divizɛ:r], *s.m. & f. Jur:* joint owner; parcener, coparcener.

indivisé [ɛ̃divize], *a.* undivided.

indivisément [ɛ̃divizemɑ̃], *adv. Jur:* jointly.

indivisibilité [ɛ̃divizibilite], *s.f.* indivisibility.

indivisible [ɛ̃divizibl̩], *a.* **1.** indivisible. **2.** *Jur:* joint (obligation, etc.).

indivisiblement [ɛ̃divizibləmɑ̃], *adv.* **1.** indivisibly. **2.** jointly.

indivision [ɛ̃divizjɔ̃], *s.f. Jur:* joint possession; parcenary, coparcenary.

indivulgable [ɛ̃divylgabl̩], *a.* unrevealable.

in-dix-huit [indizɥit], *a. & s.m.inv. Typ:* decimo-octavo, (in) eighteenmo.

indo-afghan, -ane [ɛ̃doafgɑ̃, -an], *a. & s. Ethn:* Indo-Afghan; *pl. indo-afghan(e)s.*

indo-aryen, -yenne [ɛ̃doarjɛ̃, -jɛn], *a. & s. Ling:* Indo-Aryan; *pl. indo-aryens, -yennes.*

Indo-Chine, Indochine [ɛ̃dɔʃin; ɛ̃do-], *Pr.n.f. Geog:* Indo-china.

indo-chinois, indochinois, -oise [ɛ̃dɔʃinwa, -wa:z; ɛ̃do-], *a. & s.* Indochinese; *pl. indo(-)chinois(es).*

indocile [ɛ̃dɔsil], *a.* intractable, unmanageable, disobedient, indocile; **caractère i. au joug,** nature that will brook, stand, no restraint.

indocilement [ɛ̃dɔsilmɑ̃], *adv.* intractably.

indocilité [ɛ̃dɔsilite], *s.f.* intractableness, intractability, indocility.

indocte [ɛ̃dɔkt], *a. A:* unlearned, unlettered.

indo-européen, -enne [ɛ̃doøropeɛ̃, -ɛn], *a. & s. Ethn: Ling:* Indo-European; *pl. indo-européens, -ennes.*

indo-gangétique [ɛ̃dogɑ̃ʒetik], *a.* Indo-Gangetic plain, etc.); *pl. indo-gangétiques.*

indogène [ɛ̃dɔʒɛn], *s.m. Ch:* indogen.

indogénide [ɛ̃dɔʒenid], *s.m. Ch:* indogenid(e).

indo-germanique [ɛ̃dɔʒɛrmanik], *a. Ling:* Indo-Germanic; *pl. indo-germaniques.*

indo-iranien, -ienne [ɛ̃doiranjɛ̃, -jɛn], *a. & s.m. Ling:* Indo-Iranian; *pl. indo-iraniens, -iennes.*

indole [ɛ̃dɔl], *s.m. Ch:* indol(e), ketol.

indolemment [ɛ̃dɔlamɑ̃], *adv.* indolently, apathetically.

indolence [ɛ̃dɔlɑ̃:s], *s.f.* **1.** indolence, apathy. **2.** *Med:* indolence, painlessness (of tumour, etc.).

indolent, -ente [ɛ̃dɔlɑ̃, -ɑ̃:t]. **1.** *a.* (*a*) indolent, apathetic; (*b*) *Med:* painless, indolent (tumour). **2.** *s.* sluggard, slacker.

indoline [ɛ̃dɔlin], *s.f. Ch:* indolin(e).

indolore [ɛ̃dɔlɔ:r], *a.* painless.

indomptable [ɛ̃dɔ̃tabl̩], *a.* unconquerable (nation); untam(e)able (animal); unmanageable (horse); indomitable (pride); ungovernable, uncontrollable (passion).

indomptablement [ɛ̃dɔ̃tabləmɑ̃], *adv.* unconquerably, indomitably; uncontrollably.

indompté [ɛ̃dɔ̃te], *a.* unconquered (nation); untamed (animal); uncontrolled (passion).

Indonésie [ɛ̃dɔnezi], *Pr.n.f. Geog:* Indonesia.

indonésien, -ienne [ɛ̃dɔnezjɛ̃, -jɛn], *a. & s. Geog: Ethn:* Indonesian.

indophénine [ɛ̃dɔfenin], *s.f. Ch:* indophenin.

indophénol [ɛ̃dɔfenɔl], *s.m. Ch:* indophenol.

indo-portugais, -aise [ɛ̃dopɔrtygɛ, -ɛ:z], *a. & s.m. Ling:* Indo-Portuguese; *pl. indo-portugais(es).*

indosé [ɛ̃doze], *a. Ch:* trace (element).

indou, -oue [ɛ̃du], *a. & s. Ethn:* = HINDOU.

indouisme [ɛ̃duiʃm], *s.m. Rel:* = HINDOUISME.

Indou-Kouch [ɛ̃dukuʃ], *Pr.n.m.,* **Indou-Koh** [ɛ̃duko], *Pr.n.m. Geog:* Hindu-Kush.

Indoustan [ɛ̃dustɑ̃], *Pr.n.m. Geog:* = HINDOUSTAN.

in-douze [induːz], *a. & s.m.inv. Typ:* duodecimo, (in) twelvemo.

indoxyle [ɛ̃dɔksil], *s.m. Ch:* indoxyl.

indoxyle-sulfurique [ɛ̃dɔksilsylfyrik], *a. Ch:* indoxylsulphuric.

indoxylique [ɛ̃dɔksilik], *a. Ch:* indoxylic.

indoxylurie [ɛ̃dɔksilyri], *s.f. Med:* indoxyluria.

indri(s) [ɛ̃dri], *s.m. Z:* indri; **i. babacoto, i. sans queue,** babacoote.

indrisidés [ɛ̃driside], *s.m.pl. Z:* Indridae.

indu [ɛ̃dy], *a.* **1.** *Jur: (of money)* not owed, not due; *s.m.* **paiement de l'i.,** payment of money not owed. **2.** *(a)* undue (haste, etc.); unseasonable (remark, etc.); **rentrer à une heure indue,** to come home at a disgraceful time of night; **il rentre à des heures indues,** he comes home at all hours of the night; **familiarités indues,** unwarranted familiarities; *(b) Adm:* against the regulations.

indubitable [ɛ̃dybitabl̩], *a.* beyond doubt, indubitable, unquestionable; **il est i. qu'il a raison,** he is undoubtedly right.

indubitablement [ɛ̃dybitabləmɑ̃], *adv.* indubitably, undoubtedly, unquestionably.

inductance [ɛ̃dyktɑ̃:s], *s.f. El:* inductance; *(a)* coefficient of self-induction; *(b)* inductance coil; **i. avec noyau de fer,** iron-core inductance; **i. sans fer,** air-core inductance; **i. propre,** self-inductance; *W.Tel:* **i. de syntonisation,** (aerial) tuning inductance.

inductancemètre [ɛ̃dyktɑ̃smɛtr̩], *s.m. El:* inductometer, impedometer.

inducteur, -trice [ɛ̃dyktœ:r, -tris]. **1.** *a. (a) El:* inductive (capacity, etc.); inducing (current); **pouvoir i. spécifique,** specific inductive capacity; dielectric constant; **fil i.,** inducing wire, primary wire; *(b) Log:* inductive. **2.** *s.m. (a) El:* inductor; field magnet (of dynamo); *(b) Physiol:* **i. de l'ovulation,** inducer of ovulation.

inductif, -ive [ɛ̃dyktif, -i:v], *a. (a) Log:* inductive (method); *(b) El:* **couplage i.,** inductive coupling, inductance coupling; **réaction inductive,** inductive feedback, inductance feedback; **relais i.,** induction relay.

inductile [ɛ̃dyktil], *a. Metall:* inductile.

inductilité [ɛ̃dyktilite], *s.f. Metall:* inductility.

induction [ɛ̃dyksjɔ̃], *s.f.* induction. **1.** *Log: (a)* **raisonner par i.,** to reason by induction, inductively; *(b)* conclusion, inference. **2.** *(a) El:* **i. électrique, magnétique,** electric, magnetic, induction; **i. mutuelle,** mutual induction; **i. propre,** self-induction; **courant d'i.,** induced current; **bobine d'i.,** inductor coil, induction coil, field-magnet coil; **moteur d'i.,** induction motor; **pont d'i.,** inductance bridge; **coefficient d'i.,** inductance; *(b) Metall: etc:* **four d'i.,** induction furnace; **soudage par i.,** induction welding; **chauffage par i.,** induction heating; *(e) Atom.Ph:* **i. nucléaire,** nuclear induction; *(d) Biol:* induction. **3.** *Med:* conduciveness; *Dent:* **i. de la carie,** caries conduciveness.

inductivité [ɛ̃dyktivite], *s.f. El:* inductivity.

inductomètre [ɛ̃dyktɔmɛtr̩], *s.m. El:* inductometer.

induire [ɛ̃dɥi:r], *v.tr. (pr.p.* **induisant;** *p.p.* **induit;** *pr.ind.* **j'induis, n. induisons, ils induisent;** *p.h.* **j'induisis;** *fu.* **j'induirai) 1.** *usu. Pej:* to induce; **i. qn à faire qch.,** to lead, induce, tempt, s.o. to do sth.; to beguile s.o. into doing sth.; **ne nous induisez pas en tentation,** lead us not into temptation; *abs.* **ces calques peuvent i. en contresens,** these calques can lead to mistranslation. **2.** *Log:* to infer, induce (conclusion). **3.** *El:* to induce (a current).

induit [ɛ̃dɥi]. **1.** *a.* induced; *El:* **courant i.,** induced current; **circuit i.,** induced, secondary, circuit; *Atom.Ph:* **radio-activité induite,** induced radioactivity; *Mch:* **tirage i.,** induced draught (in boiler, etc.). **2.** *s.m. El: (a)* induced circuit; **charge d'i.,** induced charge; *(b)* armature (of large dynamo, etc.); **enroulement d'i.,** armature winding; **i. en anneau,** ring armature; **i. en tambour,** drum armature; **i. à barres,** bar-wound armature; **i. à rainures,** slotted armature; **ouverture d'i.,** armature gap; **courant d'i.,** armature current; **noyau d'i.,** armature core.

indulgence [ɛ̃dylʒɑ̃:s], *s.f.* **1.** indulgence, leniency; **avec i.,** indulgently, leniently; **avoir, montrer, de l'i. envers qn, pour qn,** to be indulgent to s.o.; to show forbearance to s.o.; to make allowances for s.o. **2.** *Ecc:* indulgence; **i. plénière,** plenary indulgence; *Hist:* **vente d'indulgences,** sale of indulgences.

indulgencier [ɛ̃dylʒɑ̃sje], *v.tr. (p.d. & pr.sub.* **n. indulgenciions, v. indulgenciiez)** *Ecc:* to attach an indulgence to, to indulgence (rosary, etc.).

indulgent [ɛ̃dylʒɑ̃], *a.* indulgent, lenient, kind, condoning, long-suffering; **être i. à, pour, envers, qn,** to be indulgent to, lenient with, s.o.; to bear with s.o.; **se montrer i.,** to make allowances.

induline [ɛ̃dylin], *s.f. Ch:* indulin(e).

indult [ɛ̃dylt], *s.m. Ecc:* indult.

indultaire [ɛ̃dyltɛ:r], *s.m. Ecc:* beneficiary by virtue of an indult.

indûment [ɛ̃dymɑ̃], *adv. (a)* unduly, improperly; *(b) Adm:* without permission.

induration [ɛ̃dyrasjɔ̃], *s.f.* **1.** *Geol:* induration. **2.** *Med:* induration ((i) hardening of tissue; (ii) hardened tissue).

induré [ɛ̃dyre], *a.* indurated, hardened; *Med:* sclerous.

indurer [ɛ̃dyre], *v.tr. Geol: Med:* to indurate, harden.

s'indurer, *(of tumour, etc.)* to indurate, harden.

Indus [ɛ̃dy:s], *Pr.n.m. Geog:* the (river) Indus.

induse [ɛ̃dy:z], *s.f.,* **indusie** [ɛ̃dyzi], *s.f.* **1.** *Bot:* indusium (of frond, etc.). **2.** *Geol:* **calcaires à induses,** indusial limestone.

indusié [ɛ̃dyzje], *a. Bot:* indusiate(d).

industrialisation [ɛ̃dystri(j)alizasjɔ̃], *s.f.* industrialization.

industrialiser [ɛ̃dystri(j)alize], *v.tr.* to industrialize; **pays industrialisé,** advanced, industrialized, country.

s'industrialiser, *(of trade, etc.)* to become industrialized.

industrialisme [ɛ̃dystri(j)alism], *s.m.* industrialism.

industrialiste [ɛ̃dystri(j)alist]. **1.** *a.* industrial. **2.** *s.m. & f.* industrialist.

industrie [ɛ̃dystri], *s.f.* **1.** *(a)* activity; industry (of bees, etc.); *(b) A:* ingenuity, cleverness, skill; **vivre d'i.,** to live by one's wits. **2.** *(a)* industry; manufacturing; **la grande i.,** large-scale industry; **la petite i.,** (i) home industries; (ii) small-scale industry; **l'i. lourde, légère,** heavy, light, industry; **i. de transformation,** processing industry; **l'i. minière,** the mining industry; **l'i. mécanique,** engineering; **l'i. métallurgique,** the metallurgical industry; **l'i. automobile,** the motor industry; **l'i. du bâtiment,** the building trade; **l'i. de la chaussure,** the boot and shoe industry; **l'i. de pointe,** advance technology industry; **l'i. du spectacle,** the entertainments industry, show business; *(b)* **diriger une i. prospère,** to run a successful business.

industrie-clef [ɛ̃dystrikle], *s.f.* key industry; *pl. industries-clefs.*

industriel, -elle [ɛ̃dystri(j)ɛl]. **1.** *a.* industrial (product, centre, school, etc.); **établissement i., société industrielle,** manufacturing firm; **région, zone, industrielle,** industrial zone; **alcool i.,** industrial alcohol; **diamant i.,** bo(a)rt; **les chefs industriels,** the captains of industry; *F:* **en quantité industrielle,** in huge numbers, in large quantities. **2.** *s.m.* manufacturer; industrialist.

industriellement [ɛ̃dystri(j)ɛlmɑ̃], *adv.* industrially; **vins produits i.,** mass-produced wines.

industrier (s') [sɛ̃dystri(j)e], *v.pr. (p.d. & pr.sub.* **n.n. industriions; v.v. industriiez)** to employ, busy, oneself; **s'i. à faire qch.,** (i) to set to work to do sth.; (ii) to work hard at sth.; (iii) to use one's wits to get sth. done.

industrieusement [ɛ̃dystri(j)øzmɑ̃], *adv.* **1.** busily, actively, industriously. **2.** *A:* skilfully, ingeniously.

industrieux, -euse [ɛ̃dystri(j)ø, -ø:z], *a.* **1.** *Lit:* skilful, ingenious. **2.** *A:* busy, active; **ville industrieuse,** (i) busy, (ii) industrial, town.

induts [ɛ̃dy], *s.m.pl. Ecc:* clerics in full vestments (assisting celebrant at High Mass).

induvial, -aux [ɛ̃dyvjal, -o], *a. Bot:* induvial.

induvies [ɛ̃dyvi], *s.f.pl. Bot:* induviae.

induvié [ɛ̃dyvje], *a. Bot:* induviate.

inébranlable [inebrɑ̃labl̩], *a.* unshak(e)able; *(a)* immovable, solid, firm (wall, etc.); *(b)* resolute, constant, steadfast, unyielding, adamant (person, etc.); unswerving (purpose, etc.); unflinching, unwavering (courage); **i. à la violence,** not to be shaken by violence.

inébranlablement [inebrɑ̃labləmɑ̃], *adv.* unshak(e)ably; immovably, steadfastly, unswervingly.

inébranlé [inebrɑ̃le], *a.* unshaken, unmoved.

inébriant [inebriɑ̃]. **1.** *a.* intoxicating, inebriating. **2.** *s.m.* intoxicant, inebriant.

inéchangeable [ineʃɑ̃ʒabl̩], *a.* unexchangeable.

inéclairci [ineklɛrsi], *a.* unelucidated, unexplained.

inéclairé [ineklere], *a.* unlighted, unlit (passage, etc.); unenlightened (mind, etc.).

inéconomique [inekɔnɔmik], *a.* uneconomical.

inécoutable [inekutabl̩], *a. F:* unbearable; impossible (to listen to).

inécouté [inekute], *a.* unlistened to.

inécrit [inekri], *a.* unwritten.

inédifiant [inedifjɑ̃], *a.* unedifying.

inédit [inedi]. **1.** *a. (a)* (previously) unpublished (book, etc.); *(b)* unprecedented; new, original (show, plan). **2.** *s.m. (a)* (previously) unpublished work; *(b)* **l'i.,** the new, the original.

inéditable [ineditabl̩], *a.* unpublishable; unsuitable for publication.

inéducable [inedykabl̩], *a.* ineducable; unteachable.

ineffabilité [inefabilite], *s.f.* ineffability, ineffableness, unutterableness.

ineffable [inefabl̩], *a.* ineffable, unutterable, beyond expression.

ineffablement [inefabləmɑ̃], *adv.* ineffably, unutterably.

ineffaçable [inefasabl̩], *a.* ineffaceable (mark, memory, etc.); indelible, unremovable (stain, etc.).

ineffaçablement [inefasabləmɑ̃], *adv.* ineffaceably, indelibly.

ineffacé [inefase], *a.* uneffaced; unobliterated.

ineffectif, -ive [inefɛktif, -i:v], *a.* ineffective.

ineffectué [inefɛktɥe], *a.* not effected, unperformed.

inefficace [inefikas], *a.* ineffective, ineffectual (measure); inefficacious, useless (remedy).

inefficacement [inefikasmɑ̃], *adv.* ineffectually, ineffectively.

inefficacité [inefikasite], *s.f.* ineffectualness, ineffectiveness; inefficacy (of prayers, remedy).

inefficient [inefisjɑ̃], *a. F:* inefficient.

inégal, -aux [inegal, -o], *a.* **1.** unequal (parts, etc.); **enfants inégaux en âge,** children of unequal age. **2.** *(a)* uneven, rough (ground); *(b)* irregular (pulse, etc.); shifting, changeable (wind); **d'une humeur inégale,** of an uneven, unequable, temper; **homme d'un caractère i.,** crotchety individual, man of uncertain temper.

inégalable [inegalabl̩], *a.* matchless, peerless, incomparable; **elle est i.,** she has no equal.

inégalé [inegale], *a.* unequalled, unmatched, unrivalled.

inégalement [inegalmɑ̃], *adv. (a)* unequally, unevenly; **charge répartie i.,** unevenly distributed load; *(b)* irregularly.

inégalité [inegalite], *s.f.* **1.** inequality, disparity (entre, between); **les inégalités sociales,** social inequalities. **2.** *(a)* unevenness, inequality (of ground); **inégalités de terrain,** uneven surface of the ground; **les inégalités du chemin,** the bumpiness of the road; the bumps in the road; *(b)* **i. d'humeur,** capriciousness; unevenness; crotchetiness (of temper); **endurer les inégalités d'humeur de qn,** to bear with s.o.'s uneven temper. **3.** *Mth: Astr:* inequality; **l'i.** $x > y$, the inequality $x > y$.

inélasticité [inelastisite], *s.f.* inelasticity.

inélastique [inelastik], *a.* inelastic; lacking in elasticity.

inélégamment [inelegamɑ̃], *adv.* inelegantly.

inélégance [inelegɑ̃:s], *s.f.* inelegance, inelegancy; lack of elegance; **inélégances de style,** inelegancies of style.

inélégant [inelegɑ̃], *a.* inelegant; **il serait i. d'insister,** it would be discourteous, would show a lack of delicacy, to insist.

inéligibilité [ineliʒibilite], *s.f.* ineligibility.

inéligible [ineliʒibl̩], *a.* ineligible.

inéluctabilité [inelyktabilite], *s.f.* ineluctability.

inéluctable [inelyktabl̩], *a.* ineluctable; **destin i.,** inescapable doom.

inéluctablement [inelyktabləmɑ̃], *adv.* ineluctably.

inéludable [inelydabl̩], *a.* that cannot be eluded, inescapable.

inemployable [inɑ̃plwajabl̩], *a.* unemployable; unusable.

inemployé [inɑ̃plwaje], *a.* unemployed, unused (time, capital, etc.).

inénarrable [inenarabl̩], *a.* indescribable; **chapeau i.,** impossible hat; *F:* **c'est dommage que vous ne l'ayez pas vu; c'était i.!** it was a shame you didn't see it; it was priceless!

inénarrablement [inenarabləmɑ̃], *adv.* indescribably.

inencrassable [inɑ̃krasabl̩], *a. Ind: etc:* non-fouling.

inengendré [inɑ̃ʒɑ̃dre], *a.* unbegotten.

inensemencé [inɑ̃smɑ̃se], *a.* unsown, unsowed (field).

inentamable [inɑ̃tamabl̩], *a.* impenetrable.

inentamé [inɑ̃tame], *a.* intact; uncut (loaf, etc.); **foi inentamée,** unshaken faith; *Mil:* **front i.,** unbroken front.

inentendu [inɑ̃tɑ̃dy], *a.* unheard.

inépanoui [inepanwi], *a.* unopened (flower).

inéprouvé [inepruve], *a.* **1.** untried, unproved, untested. **2.** not yet experienced, felt.

inepte [inɛpt], *a.* **1.** inept, foolish, stupid, silly, idiotic (remark, etc.). **2.** *A:* without aptitude (**à**, for).
ineptement [inɛptəmɑ̃], *adv.* ineptly, foolishly, idiotically.
ineptie [inɛpsi], *s.f.* ineptitude. **1.** ineptness, folly, stupidity (of remark, etc.). **2. dire des inepties,** to talk nonsense; *F:* to blether.
inépuisable [inepɥizabl̩], *a.* (*a*) inexhaustible; (*b*) never-failing, unfailing (patience, etc.); **homme i. en ressources,** man of endless resource.
inépuisablement [inepɥizabləmɑ̃], *adv.* inexhaustibly; unfailingly.
inépuisé [inepɥize], *a.* unexhausted, unspent.
inépuré [inepyre], *a.* unpurified, unrefined (oil, etc.).
inéquation [inekwasjɔ̃], *s.f. Mth:* inequation.
inéquilibré [inekilibre], *a.* unbalanced (electrical phases, etc.); unequilibrated.
inéquitable [inekitabl̩], *a.* inequitable, unfair.
inéquitablement [inekitabləmɑ̃], *adv.* inequitably, unfairly.
inerme [inɛrm], *a. Bot:* inerm(ous), destitute of spines or prickles; *Ann:* **ténia i.,** unarmed tapeworm.
inerrance [inɛrɑ̃:s], *s.f.* inerrancy, infallibility.
inertance [inɛrtɑ̃:s], *s.f. Ac:* inertance.
inerte [inɛrt], *a.* (*a*) inert (mass, etc.); sluggish (nature, appetite, etc.); dull (intelligence); *Ch:* indifferent, actionless (body); (*b*) **résistance i.,** passive resistance.
inertie [inɛrsi], *s.f.* **1.** (*a*) *Mec: etc:* inertia; **force d'i.,** inertia, *vis inertiae*; **moment d'i.,** moment of inertia; **i. de masse,** mass inertia; **i. thermique,** thermal inertia, temperature lag; **démarreur à i.,** inertia starter; *Aer: Ball: etc:* **navigation à, par, i.,** inertial navigation; **guidage par i.,** inertial guidance; (*b*) **se déplacer, se mouvoir, par i.,** to coast; *Aer: Ball:* **méthode d'i.,** coasting method. **2.** inertia, sluggishness, dullness, inertness (of mind, body); listlessness (of mind); **opposer de l'i. à qch.,** to offer passive resistance to sth.; *Med:* **i. utérine,** (uterine) inertia.
inertiel, -ielle [inɛrsjɛl], *a.* (*a*) inertial; **guidage i.,** inertial guidance; **navigation inertielle,** inertial navigation; (*b*) *Aer: Ball:* **vol i.,** coasting flight.
inescation [inɛskasjɔ̃], *s.f.* (*witchcraft*) inescation.
inescomptable [inɛskɔ̃tabl̩], *a. Fin:* undiscountable.
inésite [inezit], *s.f. Miner:* inesite.
inespérable [inɛsperabl̩], *a.* not to be hoped for.
inespéré [inɛspere], *a.* unhoped-for, unexpected, unlooked-for.
inespérément [inɛsperemɑ̃], *adv.* contrary to all hope.
inessayé [inesɛje], *a.* **1.** unattempted. **2.** untried, untested.
inessentiel, -ielle [inesɑ̃sjɛl], *a.* inessential.
inesthétique [inɛstetik], *a.* unaesthetic, inaesthetic.
inestimable [inɛstimabl̩], *a.* inestimable, invaluable, priceless.
inestimé [inɛstime], *a.* unesteemed, unvalued, unprized.
inétanche [inetɑ̃:ʃ], *a.* **i. à l'eau,** not watertight; **i. à l'air,** untight to air.
inétendu [inetɑ̃dy], *a.* unextended.
inétirable [inetirabl̩], *a.* undrawable (metal).
inétudié [inetydje], *a.* unstudied (pose, grace, style).
inévaluable [inevalɥabl̩], *a.* impossible to estimate, evaluate; not evaluable.
inévitable [inevitabl̩], *a.* **1.** unavoidable (accident, engagement, etc.); **c'est i.,** it can't be avoided, there's nothing else for it. **2.** inevitable (result); **c'est i.,** it's inevitable, it's bound to happen; **il est i. qu'on vous fasse un procès,** you are bound to be sued.
inévitablement [inevitabləmɑ̃], *adv.* **1.** unavoidably. **2.** inevitably.
inexact [inegzakt], *a.* **1.** inexact, inaccurate, incorrect; wrong (amount, etc.); unreliable (figures, etc.); **esprit i.,** inaccurate mind. **2.** (*a*) unpunctual (official, etc.); (*b*) **i. à remplir ses devoirs,** remiss, slack, lax (in one's duty).
inexactement [inegzaktəmɑ̃], *adv.* **1.** inaccurately; incorrectly; wrongly. **2.** unpunctually.
inexactitude [inegzaktityd], *s.f.* **1.** inaccuracy, inexactitude; (*a*) inaccurateness, incorrectness, inexactness; unreliability (of results, etc.); (*b*) (instance of) inaccuracy; mistake. **2.** (*a*) unpunctuality; (*b*) **i. à remplir ses devoirs,** remissness, slackness; laxity (in one's duties).
inexaucé [inegzose], *a.* unheard, unanswered (prayer, etc.); ungratified, unfulfilled (desire).
inexcitabilité [inɛksitabilite], *s.f. Physiol:* inexcitability.
inexcitable [inɛksitabl̩], *a. Physiol: etc:* unexcitable, inert.
inexcusable [inɛkskyzabl̩], *a.* inexcusable (person or action); unwarrantable (action).
inexcusablement [inɛkskyzabləmɑ̃], *adv.* inexcusably; unwarrantably.
inexécutable [inegzekytabl̩], *a.* inexecutable, impracticable; unworkable (plan, etc.); (order) that cannot be carried out.
inexécuté [inegzekyte], *a.* unperformed, unexecuted; unfulfilled (promise); (order) not carried out.
inexécution [inegzekysjɔ̃], *s.f.* non-performance, non-execution, inexecution; non-fulfilment (of promise).
inexécutoire [inegzekytwa:r], *a.* unenforceable, non-enforceable.
inexercé [inegzɛrse], *a.* **1.** unexercised, untrained, undrilled. **2.** unpractised, unskilled (**à,** in); inexperienced (eye, etc.).
inexhaustible [inegzostibl̩], *a.* inexhaustible.
inexigibilité [inegziʒibilite], *s.f.* non-exigibility.
inexigible [inegziʒibl̩], *a.* **1.** inexigible (debt). **2.** *Fin:* not due.
inexistant [inegzistɑ̃], *a.* non-existent.
inexistence [inegzistɑ̃:s], *s.f.* non-existence, inexistence.
inexorabilité [inegzɔrabilite], *s.f.* inexorability (of fate, etc.).
inexorable [inegzɔrabl̩], *a.* inexorable, unrelenting; **être i. aux prières de qn,** to be unmoved by s.o.'s entreaties.
inexorablement [inegzɔrabləmɑ̃], *adv.* inexorably, unrelentingly.
inexpérience [inɛksperjɑ̃:s], *s.f.* inexperience, want of experience.
inexpérimenté [inɛksperimɑ̃te], *a.* **1.** inexperienced (leader, etc.); unpractised, unskilled (hand, etc.). **2.** untried, untested (process).
inexpert [inɛkspɛ:r], *a.* inexpert, unpractised, unskilled (**dans, en,** in).
inexpiable [inɛkspjabl̩], *a.* inexpiable, unatonable.
inexpié [inɛkspje], *a.* unatoned, unexpiated.
inexplicabilité [inɛksplikabilite], *s.f.* unaccountableness.
inexplicable [inɛksplikabl̩], *a.* inexplicable, unexplainable, unaccountable; **c'est i.,** there is no accounting for it.
inexplicablement [inɛksplikabləmɑ̃], *adv.* inexplicably, unaccountably.
inexplicite [inɛksplisit], *a.* inexplicit.
inexpliqué [inɛksplike], *a.* unexplained, unaccounted for, never yet accounted for.
inexploitable [inɛksplwatabl̩], *a.* not exploitable; unworkable (mine); uncultivable (land); unprofitable (undertaking).
inexploité [inɛksplwate], *a.* unexploited; unworked, (mine, etc.); undeveloped (land); unharnessed (energy, power); **ressources inexploitées,** untapped resources.
inexplorable [inɛksplɔrabl̩], *a.* inexplorable, unexplorable.
inexploré [inɛksplɔre], *a.* unexplored.
inexplosible [inɛksplozibl̩], *a.* (boiler, etc.) that cannot explode.
inexplosif, -ive [inɛksplozif, -i:v], *a.* non-explosive (substance).
inexposable [inɛkspozabl̩], *a.* that cannot be exposed, defined.
inexposé [inɛkspoze], *a.* unexposed, unstated (reasons, etc.).
inexpressif, -ive [inɛksprɛsif, -i:v], *a.* inexpressive (phrase, word, etc.); expressionless (face, etc.).
inexpressivité [inɛksprɛsivite], *s.f.* inexpressiveness.
inexprimable [inɛksprimabl̩], *a.* inexpressible; (joy, etc.) beyond words; unutterable.
inexprimablement [inɛksprimabləmɑ̃], *adv.* inexpressibly.
inexprimé [inɛksprime], *a.* unexpressed, unuttered.
inexpugnabilité [inɛkspygnabilite], *s.f.* impregnability, unexpugnability.
inexpugnable [inɛkspygnabl̩], *a. Mil:* impregnable, inexpugnable; storm-proof (fortress, etc.); (place) that cannot be stormed.
inextensibilité [inɛkstɑ̃sibilite], *s.f.* inextensibility.
inextensible [inɛkstɑ̃sibl̩], *a.* inextensible, non-extensile, non-stretching.
in extenso [inɛkstɛ̃so], *Lt.adv.phr.* in extenso, in full.
inextinguible [inɛkstɛ̃g(ɥ)ibl̩], *a.* inextinguishable, unquenchable (fire, thirst, etc.); irrepressible, uncontrollable (laughter).
inextirpable [inɛkstirpabl̩], *a.* ineradicable, inextirpable.
in extremis [inɛkstremis], *Lt.adv.phr.* in extremis, at the last extremity.
inextricabilité [inɛkstrikabilite], *s.f.* inextricability, inextricableness.
inextricable [inɛkstrikabl̩], *a.* inextricable; (hopelessly) entangled.
inextricablement [inɛkstrikabləmɑ̃], *adv.* inextricably.
infaillibiliste [ɛ̃fajibilist], *s. Theol:* infallibilist.
infaillibilité [ɛ̃fajibilite], *s.f.* infallibility.
infaillible [ɛ̃fajibl̩], *a.* infallible. **1.** unerring. **2.** certain, sure, unfailing (remedy, etc.).
infailliblement [ɛ̃fajibləmɑ̃], *adv.* infallibly. **1.** unerringly. **2.** certainly, unfailingly.
infaisable [ɛ̃fəzabl̩], *a.* unfeasible, infeasible; impracticable.
infalsifiable [ɛ̃falsifjabl̩], *a.* that cannot be forged, counterfeited, falsified; unfalsifiable.
infamant [ɛ̃famɑ̃], *a.* **1.** defamatory. **2.** ignominious, dishonourable; *Jur:* **peine infamante,** penalty involving loss of civil rights (*e.g.* banishment).
infâme [ɛ̃fɑ:m], *a.* infamous (deed, life, person); foul (deed); unspeakable (behaviour); vile, squalid (slum); *s. Hist: Lit:* **écrasons l'i.!** let us crush the Beast!
infamie [ɛ̃fami], *s.f.* **1.** infamy, dishonour, disgrace; *A:* **noter qn d'i.,** to brand s.o. with infamy, with dishonour; **être noté d'i. comme escroc,** to be branded as a swindler. **2.** infamous thing, action, statement; vile, foul, deed; **commettre une i.,** to be guilty of an infamy; *pl.* **dire des infamies à qn, sur le compte de qn,** to vilify s.o., to slander s.o.
infant, -ante [ɛ̃fɑ̃, -ɑ̃:t], *s. Spanish Hist:* infante, *f.* infanta.
infanterie [ɛ̃fɑ̃tri], *s.f. Mil:* infantry; **soldat d'i.,** infantryman; **i. légère,** light infantry; **i. portée,** lorry-borne infantry; **i. motorisée,** motorized infantry; **i. aéroportée, i. de l'air,** airborne infantry; **i. aérotransportée,** air-transported infantry; **i. à pied,** dismounted infantry; **i. de marine,** Marine Light Infantry; *A:* **i. de ligne,** line infantry, infantry of the line.
infanticide[1] [ɛ̃fɑ̃tisid]. **1.** *s.m. & f.* infanticide; child-murderer. **2.** *a.* infanticidal.
infanticide[2], *s.m.* infanticide; child-murder.
infantile [ɛ̃fɑ̃til], *a.* (*a*) infantile (disease, etc.); **mortalité i.,** infant mortality; **psychiatrie i.,** child psychiatry; *O:* **paralysie i.,** infantile paralysis; (*b*) *Geol:* **stade i.,** youthful stage (of erosion).
infantilisme [ɛ̃fɑ̃tilism], *s.m.* infantilism, retarded development.
infarctus [ɛ̃farkty:s], *s.m. Med:* infarct, infarction; **i. du myocarde,** myocardial infarction; coronary thrombosis.
infatigabilité [ɛ̃fatigabilite], *s.f.* indefatigability, tirelessness.
infatigable [ɛ̃fatigabl̩], *a.* indefatigable, untiring, tireless, unsparing in one's efforts; *Lit:* **i. à faire le bien,** never wearied in well-doing.
infatigablement [ɛ̃fatigabləmɑ̃], *adv.* indefatigably, untiringly, tirelessly.
infatuation [ɛ̃fatɥasjɔ̃], *s.f.* (*a*) *A:* infatuation (**de,** with, for, over); **être dans une grande i. de qch.,** to be infatuated with sth.; (*b*) self-conceit.
infatué [ɛ̃fatɥe], *a.* (*a*) *A:* infatuated (**de,** with); (*b*) conceited; (over-)pleased with oneself; **i. de soi-même,** eaten up with self-conceit, full of one's own importance.
infatuer [ɛ̃fatɥe], *v.tr. A:* to infatuate.
s'infatuer, (*a*) *O:* **s'i. de qn, qch.,** to become infatuated with s.o., sth.; (*b*) **s'i. (de soi-même),** to become full of one's own importance, to become conceited.
infécond [ɛ̃fekɔ̃], *a.* barren, sterile (animal, land, mind, etc.); unfruitful (suggestion, etc.).
infécondité [ɛ̃fekɔ̃dite], *s.f.* barrenness, sterility, unfruitfulness, fruitlessness.
infect [ɛ̃fɛkt], *a.* (*a*) that smells, tastes, objectionable; **odeur infecte,** stench, stink; **goût i.,** objectionable, nasty, taste; **boue infecte,** putrid, stinking, mud; (*b*) *F:* bad (of its kind); **café i.,** filthy coffee; **repas i.,** rotten, revolting, meal; **temps i.,** filthy, foul, weather; (*c*) repugnant; **roman i.,** novel beneath contempt; **il a été i. avec ses amis,** he treated his friends abominably; *F:* **c'est un type i.,** he's a stinker.
infectant [ɛ̃fɛktɑ̃], *a.* infectious, infecting (miasma, virus).
infecter [ɛ̃fɛkte], *v.tr.* to infect; (*a*) *Med:* **malade contagieux qui infecte ses proches,** patient who spreads contagion; **i. une plaie,** to infect a wound; (*b*) to poison (the atmosphere); to contaminate; to pollute; **source infectée,** polluted, contaminated, spring; **les usines contribuent à i. l'air des grandes villes,** factories contribute to the pollution of the air in large

cities; **les cadavres en décomposition infectaient la ville sinistrée,** the rotting corpses were polluting the ruins of the town; (*c*) **il nous infecte avec, de, son haleine,** his breath smells terrible; *F:* he stinks us out with his breath; *abs.* **cadavre qui infecte,** corpse that stinks; *with cogn. acc.* **il infecte le tabac,** he stinks, reeks, of tobacco; **salle qui infecte le cigare,** room reeking of cigars; (*d*) **ce vice infecte tous les âges,** this vice contaminates every age; **le désir de plaire infecte toutes ses actions,** all his actions are marred by his desire to please; **livres qui infectent les mœurs,** books that corrupt morals.

s'infecter, to go, become, turn, septic.

infectieux, -euse [ɛ̃fɛksjø, -øːz], *a. Med:* infectious (disease, etc.).

infection [ɛ̃fɛksjɔ̃], *s.f.* **1.** (*a*) infection; corruption; putrefaction; (*b*) *Med:* infection; **répandre, transmettre, l'i.,** to spread the infection; **i. latente,** latent infection; **foyer d'i.,** focus, centre, of infection; **i. purulente,** pyaemia, pyohemia; **i. bactérienne, i. microbienne,** bacterial infection; **i. virale,** virus infection. **2.** (*a*) stench, stink; **il sort de cet égout une i. insupportable,** there's an intolerable stench coming from this drain; **c'est une i. ici!** what a stink! what a foul smell! (*b*) *F:* **c'est une i.!** it's revolting, abominable! it's below anything! it's the end!

infectiosité [ɛ̃fɛksjɔzite], *s.f. Med:* infectivity, infectiveness.

infélicité [ɛ̃felisite], *s.f. Lit:* unhappiness, misfortune, infelicity.

inféodation [ɛ̃feɔdasjɔ̃], *s.f. A.Jur:* infeudation, enfeoffment.

inféoder [ɛ̃feɔde], *v.tr. A.Jur:* to enfeoff.

s'inféoder à un parti, to give one's allegiance to a party, to become an adherent of a party.

infère [ɛ̃fɛːr], *a. Bot:* inferior (calyx, etc.).

inférence [ɛ̃ferɑ̃ːs], *s.f. Log:* inference. **1.** inferring. **2.** conclusion.

inférer [ɛ̃fere], *v.tr.* (**j'infère, n. inférons; j'inférerai**) to infer (de, from); **j'infère de ces témoignages que . . .,** I gather from the evidence that . . ..

inférieur, -eure [ɛ̃ferjœːr], *a.* inferior. **1.** (*a*) lower; **partie inférieure (de qch.),** (i) lower part, (ii) under part (of sth.); **lèvre inférieure,** lower lip; **mâchoire inférieure,** bottom jaw; **les membres inférieurs,** the lower limbs, the legs; **couche inférieure,** bottom layer; **les étages inférieurs de la maison,** the lower floors, storeys, of the house; **i. au niveau de la mer,** below sea level; (*of temperature, etc.*) **i. à la normale,** below normal; (*b*) *Geog:* **la Loire inférieure,** the lower (course of the) Loire; **la vallée inférieure du Rhône,** the lower Rhone valley; (*c*) *Astr:* **les planètes inférieures,** the inferior planets. **2.** (*a*) **d'un rang i.,** of a lower rank, lower in rank; **position inférieure,** subordinate position; **elle ne lui est i. en rien,** she is in no way inferior to him; **roman i. à ce que l'on pouvait attendre de l'auteur,** novel below the standard one might expect from the author; **il leur est i. en science,** he is less learned; less knowledgeable than they are; **humilié de se voir i. à un plus jeune,** humiliated by finding oneself the subordinate of a younger man; **il n'a pas été i. à sa tâche,** he proved himself equal to the job; *Sch:* **les classes inférieures,** the lower forms; (*b*) poor; **des marchandises inférieures,** goods of poor quality; (*c*) **6 est i. à 8,** 6 is less than 8; **note inférieure à douze,** mark below twelve; **être i. de mille Fr. à la somme prévue,** to fall short of the sum expected by a thousand Frs; **des troupes inférieures en nombre,** outnumbered troops; (*d*) *Phil:* **concept i.,** lower concept; (*e*) **les animaux inférieurs,** the lower animals. **3.** *s.* inferior, subordinate; **être l'i. de qn,** to be s.o.'s inferior; **traiter qn en i.,** to treat s.o. as an inferior, as a subordinate; **le directeur est courtois avec ses inférieurs,** the director treats his subordinates with courtesy.

inférieurement [ɛ̃ferjœrmɑ̃], *adv.* **1.** in a lower position; on the under side. **2.** in an inferior manner; less well.

infériorisation [ɛ̃ferjɔrizasjɔ̃], *s.f.* (action of) giving (s.o.) a feeling of inferiority.

inférioriser [ɛ̃ferjɔrize], *v.tr.* to give (s.o.) a feeling of inferiority.

infériorité [ɛ̃ferjɔrite], *s.f.* **1.** (*a*) inferiority; **i. du nombre, numérique, en nombre,** numerical inferiority, inferiority in numbers; **i. dans la conversation,** inferiority (to others) in conversation; **sa myopie le met dans un état d'i.,** he is handicapped by his short sight; **maintenir qn dans un état d'i.,** to keep s.o. in a subordinate position; *Psy:* **complexe d'i.,** inferiority complex; (*b*) **i. de niveau,** difference (= drop) in level. **2.** handicap.

infermentescible [ɛ̃fɛrmɑ̃tɛs(s)ibl̩], *a.* unfermentable.

infernal, -aux [ɛ̃fɛrnal, -o], *a.* infernal. **1. les puissances infernales,** the powers of hell; **les régions infernales,** the infernal regions. **2.** devilish, diabolical; (*a*) **un vacarme i., un bruit i.,** an infernal din, *F:* a hell of a din, of a row; **le cycle i. des salaires et des prix,** the vicious wage-price spiral; **il fait une chaleur infernale,** it's as hot as hell; (*b*) **machination infernale,** devilish, diabolical, trick; **la ruse infernale d'un mari jaloux,** the diabolical cunning of a jealous husband; (*c*) *Mil: etc:* **machine infernale,** (i) *A:* infernal engine; (ii) booby trap. **3.** *F:* **cet enfant est i.,** this child's a little devil; **un métier i.,** a hellish job, the devil of a job; **c'est i.!** it's hellish! it's sheer hell! **4.** *A.Med:* **pierre infernale,** lunar caustic.

infernalement [ɛ̃fɛrnalmɑ̃], *adv.* infernally, devilishly.

inférobranche [ɛ̃ferɔbrɑ̃ːʃ], *s.m. Moll:* inferobranch; *pl.* **inférobranches,** Inferobranchiata.

infertile [ɛ̃fɛrtil], *a.* infertile, unfertile, unfruitful, barren (land, vine, etc.).

infertilisable [ɛ̃fɛrtilizabl̩], *a.* incapable of fertilization; unfertilizable.

infertilisé [ɛ̃fɛrtilize], *a.* unfertilized.

infertilité [ɛ̃fɛrtilite], *s.f.* infertility; unfruitfulness, barrenness.

infestation [ɛ̃fɛstasjɔ̃], *s.f. Med:* infestation.

infester [ɛ̃fɛste], *v.tr.* (*of vermin, etc.*) to infest, overrun; (*of bandits, etc.*) to ravage, infest (a region); (*of ghosts*) to haunt; **des brigands infestaient les routes,** the roads were infested with highwaymen; **des pirates infestaient les côtes,** the coasts were ravaged by pirates; **des souris infestent la maison,** the house is overrun by mice.

infeutrable [ɛ̃føtrabl̩], *a.* which does not felt, does not get matted.

infibulation [ɛ̃fibylasjɔ̃], *s.f. Anthr: Vet:* infibulation.

infibuler [ɛ̃fibyle], *v.tr. Anthr: Vet:* to infibulate.

infidèle [ɛ̃fidɛl], *a.* **1.** (*a*) unfaithful; disloyal; **être i. à son roi, son maître,** to be disloyal to one's king, one's master; **ami i.,** false friend; **mari, femme, i.,** unfaithful husband, wife; (*b*) *O:* dishonest; defaulting (cashier, etc.); (*c*) **être i. à sa promesse,** to break one's promise, one's word; **i. à son devoir,** negligent of one's duty; (*d*) misleading; incorrect; **mémoire i.,** untrustworthy memory; **compte rendu i.,** inaccurate, inexact, account; **traducteur i., traduction i.,** inaccurate translator, translation; *s.f.pl. Lit:* **les belles infidèles,** elegant inaccuracies (of translation). **2.** *Rel:* (*a*) unbelieving; (*b*) *s.m. & f.* infidel, unbeliever.

infidèlement [ɛ̃fidɛlmɑ̃], *adv.* unfaithfully. **1.** faithlessly. **2.** incorrectly, inaccurately.

infidélité [ɛ̃fidelite], *s.f.* **1.** (*a*) infidelity (**envers,** to); unfaithfulness; (*b*) *O:* dishonesty; (*c*) inaccuracy (in translation, etc.); (*d*) (religious) unbelief. **2.** (act of) infidelity; (*a*) **faire des infidélités à sa femme,** to be unfaithful to one's wife; (*b*) breach of trust; (*c*) **infidélités de traduction,** inaccuracies in translation.

infiltrat [ɛ̃filtra], *s.m. Med:* infiltrate.

infiltration [ɛ̃filtrasjɔ̃], *s.f.* infiltration. **1.** percolation, seepage; *Med:* infiltration (of fluid); **i. du tissu par un épanchement sanguin,** infarction; *Geol:* **eau d'i.,** percolating, seepage, water; *Hyd.E:* **perte d'i. d'un canal,** leakage loss of a canal. **2.** filtering through (of traffic, of attacking troops, etc.); *Mil:* **infiltrations (ennemies),** infiltration; **l'i. communiste,** communist infiltration.

infiltrer [ɛ̃filtre], *v.tr.* to infiltrate. **1.** (*a*) to cause (fluid) to filter, to percolate (**dans,** into); (*b*) **i. une idée, un soupçon, dans l'esprit de qn,** to instil(l) an idea, a suspicion, into s.o.'s mind. **2.** (*of fluid*) to filter, to percolate into (tissue, rock, etc.); to seep into (ground).

s'infiltrer. 1. (*a*) (*of fluid*) to infiltrate, percolate, seep (**dans,** into; **à travers,** through); to soak in, filter in; *Med:* to infiltrate; (*b*) (*of idea, etc.*) to trickle in, filter in, soak in; *Lit:* **un soupçon s'infiltra dans mon esprit,** a suspicion crept, found its way, into my mind; **ces idées s'infiltrent partout,** these ideas are infiltrating everywhere. **2.** (*of troops, etc.*) to infiltrate, to progress, advance, by infiltration; **des groupes de manifestants s'infiltraient dans la ville,** groups of demonstrators infiltrated into the town.

infime [ɛ̃fim], *a.* **1.** lowly, mean (rank, etc.); **occuper un rang i. dans la société,** to occupy an insignificant place in society. **2.** tiny, minute, negligible; **majorité i.,** infinitesimal majority; **détails infimes,** minute details.

infimité [ɛ̃fimite], *s.f.* (*rare*) **1.** lowliness, meanness (of birth, etc.). **2.** tininess, minuteness.

infini [ɛ̃fini]. **1.** *a.* infinite; (*a*) **Dieu est i.,** God is infinite; **la justice divine est infinie,** divine justice is infinite; (*b*) boundless, immeasurable (space, etc.); never-ending, eternal, endless (bliss, etc.); innumerable (favours, etc.); **cela vous fera un bien i.,** it will do you a world of good. **2.** *s.m.* **l'i.,** the infinite; *A:* **calcul de l'i.,** infinitesimal calculus; *Phot:* **régler à l'i.,** to focus for infinity; *adv.phr.* **à l'i.,** to infinity, ad infinitum; **ne remettez pas à l'i.,** don't keep putting things off.

infiniment [ɛ̃finimɑ̃], *adv.* infinitely; (*a*) *Mth:* **le calcul des i. petits,** the infinitesimal calculus; (*b*) extremely; **i. plus intelligent,** infinitely more intelligent; **se sentir i. mieux,** to feel very much better; **se donner i. de peine,** to give oneself an infinite amount of trouble; **il a i. plus d'argent que vous,** he has much more money than you; **cela vaut i. mieux,** that is infinitely better; **je regrette i.,** I'm terribly sorry.

infinité [ɛ̃finite], *s.f.* (*a*) *Mth: etc:* infinity; (*b*) **l'i. de l'espace,** the infinity, infinitude, boundlessness, of space; **une i. de raisons,** endless reasons, a whole host of reasons; **une i. de gens étaient venus,** a whole crowd of people had come; **notre vue s'étend sur une i. de toitures,** we look out on to a wilderness of roofs.

infinitésimal, -aux [ɛ̃finitezimal, -o], *a.* (*a*) *Mth:* infinitesimal (part, etc.); **calcul i.,** infinitesimal calculus; (*b*) **quantité infinitésimale,** infinitesimal, negligible, amount.

infinitésime [ɛ̃finitezim], *a. & s.f.* (*rare*) infinitesimal(ly small) (object).

infinitif, -ive [ɛ̃finitif, -iːv], *a. & s.m. Gram:* infinitive (mood); **proposition infinitive,** infinitive clause; **à l'i.,** in the infinitive.

infinitude [ɛ̃finityd], *s.f.* infinitude (de, of).

infirmable [ɛ̃firmabl̩], *a. Jur:* that may be invalidated or reversed (on appeal).

infirmatif, -ive [ɛ̃firmatif, -iːv], *a. Jur:* invalidating, nullifying.

infirmation [ɛ̃firmasjɔ̃], *s.f. Jur:* invalidation; nullification; quashing.

infirme [ɛ̃firm]. **1.** *a.* (*a*) infirm (old man, etc.); (*b*) disabled, crippled; **il est i. du bras gauche,** he is crippled in the left arm; (*c*) *Lit:* weak, feeble, frail (body, spirit, etc.); **l'esprit est prompt mais la chair est i.,** the spirit is willing but the flesh is weak. **2.** *s.m. & f.* (*a*) invalid; (*b*) cripple; **les grands infirmes,** the badly disabled.

infirmer [ɛ̃firme], *v.tr.* **1.** (*a*) to reveal, show up, the weakness of (proof, argument, etc.); **i. les titres de gloire de qn,** to call in question s.o.'s title to fame; (*b*) to weaken (s.o.'s authority); (*c*) to weaken, invalidate (evidence, claim). **2.** (*a*) *Jur:* to annul, quash (judgment); to set (verdict) aside; (*b*) to cancel (letter, etc.).

infirmerie [ɛ̃firməri], *s.f.* (*a*) *A:* infirmary, hospital (for old people); (*b*) (*in school, prison, etc.*) infirmary; (*in school*) sanatorium; sick room; sick bay; (*in the Navy*) sick bay, sick berth; *F:* **cette maison est une véritable i.!** this house is just like a hospital! (*c*) *Ven:* (*in kennels*) sick bay.

infirmier, -ière [ɛ̃firmje, -jɛːr]. **1.** *s.m.* (i) male nurse, *Mil:* medical orderly; *Navy:* sick-berth attendant; (ii) ambulance man. **2.** *s.f.* **infirmière,** (hospital) nurse; **infirmière diplômée** = state-registered nurse; **infirmière en chef,** matron; **infirmière visiteuse,** district nurse; *Mil:* **l'infirmière-major,** the head nurse.

infirmité [ɛ̃firmite], *s.f.* (*a*) infirmity (of body or mind); (*b*) physical disability; **i. permanente, i. temporaire,** permanent, temporary, disablement; (*c*) *Lit:* weakness, frailty.

infixe [ɛ̃fiks], *s.m. Ling:* infix.

infixer [ɛ̃fikse], *v.tr. Ling:* to infix (letter, syllable).

inflammabilité [ɛ̃flamabilite], *s.f.* inflammability, *Tchn: U.S:* flammability.

inflammable [ɛ̃flamabl̩], *a.* inflammable; (*a*) ignitable; easily set on fire; combustible; *Tchn: U.S:* flammable; (*b*) easily excited; **imagination i.,** easily kindled imagination.

inflammateur, -trice [ɛ̃flamatœːr, -tris]. **1.** *a.* inflammatory (projectile, etc.). **2.** *s.m. Exp: etc:* ignition apparatus, igniter.

inflammation [ɛ̃flamasjɔ̃], *s.f.* **1.** inflammation, ignition, firing (of explosives, etc.); **i. spontanée,** spontaneous combustion; self-ignition; **point d'i.,** (i) flash point (of mineral oil); (ii) *I.C.E:* hot spot. **2.** *Med:* inflammation. **3.** *A:* anger, irritation.

inflammatoire [ɛ̃flamatwaːr], *a. Med:* inflammatory.

inflation [ɛ̃flasjɔ̃], *s.f. Pol.Ec:* inflation; **i. galopante,** galloping inflation; **i. fiduciaire,** inflation of the currency; **politique d'i.,** inflationary policy; **tendances à l'i.,** inflationary tendencies.
inflationnisme [ɛ̃flasjɔnism], *s.m.* inflationism.
inflationniste [ɛ̃flasjɔnist], (*a*) *s.m. & f.* inflationist; (*b*) *a.* inflationary; **politique i.,** inflationary, inflationist, policy; **le danger i.,** the danger of inflation.
infléchi [ɛ̃fleʃi], *a.* **1.** inflected, bent (ray, etc.); *Bot:* inflexed (stamen, etc.). **2.** *Gram:* inflected (vowel, etc.).
infléchir [ɛ̃fleʃiːr], *v.tr.* **1.** to bend, inflect, curve (ray, etc.). **2.** to change the direction, orientation, of; **essayer d'i. la politique du gouvernement,** to try to modify, to change, government policy.
s'infléchir. 1. to bend, deviate; *Opt:* (*of ray*) to be inflected; *Bot:* (*of stamen, etc.*) to become inflexed. **2.** (*of structure, beam*) to cave in.
infléchissable [ɛ̃fleʃisabl̩], *a.* (*a*) unbendable, rigid; (*b*) that cannot be moved to pity; unfeeling, hard-hearted.
inflectif, -ive [ɛ̃flɛktif, -iːv], *a. Ling:* inflective.
inflexe [ɛ̃flɛks], *a. Bot:* inflexed.
inflexibilité [ɛ̃flɛksibilite], *s.f.* inflexibility; unyieldingness; rigidity; **l'i. d'un essieu,** the rigidity of an axle; **l'i. de son caractère,** his inflexible, unyielding, nature.
inflexible [ɛ̃flɛksibl̩], *a.* inflexible, unbending; rigid; unyielding; **rester i.,** to refuse to be influenced; to stick to one's point of view; **il fut i.,** he was adamant; **demeurer i. dans une résolution,** to stick to a resolution; **i. à toutes les prières,** unmoved by all entreaties; **i. dans ses principes,** unyielding, unswerving, in his principles; **volonté i.,** iron will; **règle i.,** rigid rule.
inflexiblement [ɛ̃flɛksibləmɑ̃], *adv.* inflexibly; inexorably.
inflexion [ɛ̃flɛksjɔ̃], *s.f.* inflexion, inflection. **1.** (*a*) *Mth: Opt: etc:* bend(ing); inflexion; change of direction (of curve, ray); *Mth:* **point d'i.,** point of change of curve; point of inflexion; (*b*) act of bending; **légère i. du corps devant l'autel,** slight bow before the altar. **2.** modulation (of voice). **3.** *Ling: Gram:* inflection.
inflexionnel, -elle [ɛ̃flɛksjɔnɛl], *a.* inflectional, inflexional.
inflictif, -ive [ɛ̃fliktif, -iːv], *a. Jur:* inflictive (penalty).
infliction [ɛ̃fliksjɔ̃], *s.f. Jur:* infliction (of penalty) (à, upon).
infliger [ɛ̃fliʒe], *v.tr.* (**j'infligeai(s); n. infligeons**) to inflict; **i. une peine à qn,** to inflict, impose, a penalty on s.o.; **i. des dommages à qch.,** to cause damage to sth.; **i. une défaite à l'ennemi,** to inflict a defeat upon the enemy; **i. un affront à qn,** to snub, slight, s.o.; **il nous a infligé sa présence,** he inflicted himself on us, *F:* we were landed with him.
inflorescence [ɛ̃flɔrɛs(s)ɑ̃ːs], *s.f. Bot:* inflorescence.
influençable [ɛ̃flyɑ̃sabl̩], *a.* susceptible to influence, influenceable.
influence [ɛ̃flyɑ̃ːs], *s.f.* influence; **exercer une i. sur qch., sur qn,** to have, exercise, an influence on sth., on s.o.; **sous l'i. de qn,** under the influence of s.o.; **il a beaucoup d'i.,** he has plenty of influence, he is very influential; **sphère d'i.,** sphere of influence; **il s'efforce de l'obtenir à l'i.,** he's doing his best to get it by influence, by graft; **trafic d'i.,** corrupt practice; *El:* **machine à i.,** influence machine; *Civ.E:* **ligne d'i.,** influence line; *Artil: Ball:* **fusée à i., fonctionnant par i.,** influence fuse, proximity fuse.
influencer [ɛ̃flyɑ̃se], *v.tr.* (**j'influençai(s); n. influençons**) **1.** to influence; to put pressure upon (s.o.); **les journaux qui influencent l'opinion,** the papers that influence public opinion. **2.** to act on, have an influence on (s.o., sth.); **les hormones influencent l'organisme tout entier,** hormones have an influence on the whole organism.
influent [ɛ̃flyɑ̃], *a.* influential; **avoir des amis influents,** to have influential friends, to have friends at court; **peu i.,** uninfluential, without influence.
influenza [ɛ̃flyɑ̃za, -ɛ̃za], *s.f. O:* influenza.
influer [ɛ̃flye]. **1.** *v.i.* **i. sur qn,** to influence s.o., to exercise, have, (an) influence on, over, s.o.; **i. sur qch.,** to have an effect, an influence, on sth.; **i. sur le résultat,** to affect the result. **2.** *v.tr. A:* to cause (sth.) to flow, penetrate, into (sth.); **Dieu influe le bien dans tout ce qu'il fait,** God breathes good into all that He does.
influx [ɛ̃fly], *s.m.*, **influxion** [ɛ̃flyksjɔ̃], *s.f.* **1.** influx (of ideas, etc.). **2.** *Physiol:* **i. nerveux,** nerve impulse.
in-folio [infɔljo]. **1.** *a.inv.* **volume in-f.,** (in-) folio volume. **2.** *s.m.inv.* folio; folio book.

infondé [ɛ̃fɔ̃de], *a.* unfounded (fears, etc.).
infondibuliforme [ɛ̃fɔ̃dibylifɔrm], *a. Anat: Bot:* infundibular, infundibuliform, funnel-shaped.
inforçable [ɛ̃fɔrsabl̩], *a.* that cannot be forced; unforceable.
informant [ɛ̃fɔrmɑ̃], *a.* informative, inspiring, vitalizing (influence).
informateur, -trice [ɛ̃fɔrmatœːr, -tris], *s.* (*a*) informant; **journaliste i.,** police-news reporter; (*b*) informer; (police) spy.
informaticien, -ienne [ɛ̃fɔrmatisjɛ̃, -jɛn], *s.* computer expert, specialist; information specialist; data-processing expert; **ingénieur i.,** computer engineer.
informatif, -ive [ɛ̃fɔrmatif, -iːv], *a.* **1.** informative, informatory. **2.** *Jur:* invalidating.
information [ɛ̃fɔrmasjɔ̃], *s.f.* (*a*) inquiry; *Jur:* preliminary investigation (of a case); **ouvrir une i.,** to begin legal proceedings; **les faits qui résultent des informations,** the facts established by the inquiry; **prendre des informations (sur qn),** to make inquiries (about s.o.); (*b*) information; news; *W.Tel: T.V: Journ:* **informations,** news (bulletin); **Ministère de l'I.,** Ministry of Information; **Commissariat à l'I.** = Central Office of Information; **service d'informations,** information service; *Journ:* **service des informations,** reporting staff, *esp.* police-news staff; *Petroleum Min:* **informations provenant du sondage,** doghouse dope; **l'ampleur de ses informations nous étonne,** the extent of his information astonishes us; (*c*) *Elec:* (*computers, radar*) (**éléments d'**) **i.** data (for processing by computer); **i. codée,** coded data; **affichage, présentation, de l'i., des informations,** data display, data presentation; **collecte, recueil, de l'i., des informations,** data collection; **exploitation, interprétation, de l'i., des informations,** data handling; **traitement de l'i., des informations,** data processing; **i. alphanumérique,** alphanumeric data; **bit d'i.,** information bit.
informatique [ɛ̃fɔrmatik]. **1.** *s.f.* (*a*) information processing, data processing; **i. de gestion,** business data processing; **i. médicale,** medical computing; **i. hospitalière,** hospital data processing; **centre d'i.,** data-processing, information-processing, centre; **cours d'i.,** computer course, data-processing course; **école d'i.,** computer school, data-processing school; **professeur d'i.,** data-processing instructor; **directeur d'i.,** data-processing manager; (*b*) **l'i.,** the information-processing industry, the data-processing industry; (*c*) **le monde de l'i.,** (i) the computer world, the data-processing world; (ii) the computer field, the data-processing field. **2.** *a.* **matériel i.,** computer equipment; **réseau i.,** information network; **service i.,** information-processing department, data-processing department.
informatisation [ɛ̃fɔrmatizasjɔ̃], *s.f.* computerization.
informatiser(s') [(s)ɛ̃fɔrmatize], *v.tr. & pr.* to computerize.
informe [ɛ̃fɔrm], *a.* **1.** (*a*) formless, unformed, shapeless (mass, etc.); half-formed (thought, etc.); crude (plan); (*b*) ill-formed, unshapely; mis-shapen (monster, etc.). **2.** *Jur:* (document, etc.) not complying with the requirements of the law, not in order; irregular, informal.
informé [ɛ̃fɔrme]. **1.** *a.* (well-)informed; **dans les milieux bien informés,** in well-informed circles; **mal i.,** misinformed; not very knowledgeable. **2.** *s.m. Jur:* result of inquiry; **renvoyer une cause à plus ample i.,** to defer a case for further inquiry; **jusqu'à plus ample i.,** until further notice.
informel, -elle [ɛ̃fɔrmɛl], *a. Art:* abstract.
informer [ɛ̃fɔrme]. **1.** *v.tr.* (*a*) **i. qn de qch.,** to inform s.o. of sth.; to acquaint s.o. with (a fact); **on l'a informé que le paquet était retrouvé,** he was told that the parcel was found; **i. l'autorité,** to give notice to the authorities; **veuillez m'en i.,** please let me know; (*b*) *Phil: A:* to inform, mould, vitalize, animate. **2.** *v.i. Jur:* (*a*) **i. d'un crime, sur un crime,** to investigate a crime, to inquire into a crime; (*b*) **i. contre qn,** to inform against s.o.; to lay information against s.o.
s'informer, to make inquiries; **s'i. de qch.,** to inquire about sth.; **s'i. de la santé de qn,** to inquire, ask, after s.o.('s health); **je ne me suis pas informé de, sur, ce qu'il comptait faire,** I did not inquire what he proposed to do; **s'i. auprès de qn si . . .,** to inquire of s.o. whether . . .; **en s'informant on apprit que le bruit était faux,** on inquiry the rumour proved false; **chercher à s'i.,** to try to get information, to try to find out (about things).

informité [ɛ̃fɔrmite], *s.f.* lack of form, formlessness.
informulé [ɛ̃fɔrmyle], *a.* unformulated.
infortifiable [ɛ̃fɔrtifjabl], *a.* unfortifiable; that cannot be fortified.
infortune [ɛ̃fɔrtyn], *s.f.* (*a*) misfortune, bad luck; **s'apitoyer sur l'i. d'autrui,** to sympathize with the misfortunes of others; **pour comble d'i.,** as a crowning misfortune; **compagnons d'i.,** companions in adversity; fellow-sufferers; **tomber dans l'i.,** to meet with misfortune; *Lit:* to fall on evil days; (*b*) misfortune, piece of bad luck; (*c*) *F:* **i. conjugale,** marital infidelity.
infortuné [ɛ̃fɔrtyne], *a.* unfortunate, ill-fated, unlucky, unhappy; *s.* unfortunate person.
infra [ɛ̃fra], *adv.* infra; **se reporter i.,** see below.
infra- [ɛ̃fra], *pref.* **1.** infra-; **infra-axillaire,** infra-axillary. **2.** sub-, under-; **infrastructure,** substructure, understructure.
infra-acoustique [ɛ̃fraakustik], *a.* sub-audio; *pl. infra-acoustiques.*
infra-axillaire [ɛ̃fraaksilɛːr], *a.* infra-axillary; *pl. infra-axillaires.*
infracambrien, -ienne [ɛ̃frakɑ̃brjɛ̃, -jɛn], *a. & s.m. Geol:* Pre-Cambrian.
infraclusion [ɛ̃fraklysjɔ̃], *s.f. Dent:* infraclusion.
infracteur, -trice [ɛ̃fraktœːr, -tris], *s.* infringer, breaker (of the law, of a treaty).
infraction [ɛ̃fraksjɔ̃], *s.f.* infraction. **1.** infringement; **i. de droits,** infringement of rights; **i. à un traité,** infringement of a treaty; **i. aux droits d'autrui,** infringement on the rights of others. **2.** offence; **i. à la loi,** breaking the law; **i. au devoir,** breach of duty; **i. à un ordre,** violation of an order; **être en i.,** to be committing an offence; **contravention pour i. au code de la route,** summons for a motoring offence; **commettre une i. au bon goût,** to commit an offence against good taste.
infradien [ɛ̃fradjɛ̃], *a. Biol:* **rythme i.,** circadian rhythm.
infradyne [ɛ̃fradin], *s.m. W.Tel:* infradyne.
infralapsaire [ɛ̃fralapsɛːr], *s.m. Rel.H:* infralapsarian, sublapsarian.
infralapsarisme [ɛ̃fralapsarism], *s.m. Rel.H:* infralapsarianism, sublapsarianism.
infralias [ɛ̃fralias], *s.m. Geol:* Lower Lias.
infraliasique [ɛ̃fraliazik], *a. Geol:* Lower Liassic.
infranchissable [ɛ̃frɑ̃ʃisabl̩], *a.* impassable (barrier, etc.); insuperable (difficulty).
infrangible [ɛ̃frɑ̃ʒibl̩], *a.* infrangible.
infra-noir [ɛ̃franwaːr], *a. T.V:* infra-black; *pl. infra-noir(e)s.*
infra-paginal [ɛ̃frapaʒinal], *a.* **note infra-paginale,** footnote.
infraposition [ɛ̃frapɔzisjɔ̃], *s.f.* infraposition.
infra(-)rouge [ɛ̃fraruːʒ], *a. & s.m. Opt:* (*a*) *a.* infra-red; **lampe à rayons infra(-)rouges,** infra-red lamp; *Aut: etc:* **séchage à l'i.,** infra-red drying; (*b*) *s.m.* infra-red rays, radiation.
infra-son [ɛ̃frasɔ̃], *s.m.* infrasonic vibration; *pl. infra-sons.*
infra-sonore [ɛ̃frasɔnɔːr], *a.* infrasonic; *pl. infra-sonores.*
infrastructure [ɛ̃frastryktyːr], *s.f.* **1.** *Civ.E:* (*a*) substructure, understructure; underframe (of bridge, etc.); bed (of roadway, etc.); (*b*) *Adm: Pol.Ec:* infrastructure. **2.** *Tchn: Mil.E:* infrastructure, basic equipment (of railways, hospitals, etc.); ground environment (of radar system, air defence, etc.); *Av:* **i. aérienne,** ground organization, ground environment; **i. de défense aérienne,** air-defence ground environment.
infravirus [ɛ̃fraviryːs], *s.m. Med:* filterable virus.
infréquence [ɛ̃frekɑ̃ːs], *s.f.* infrequency, rareness.
infréquent [ɛ̃frekɑ̃], *a.* infrequent, rare.
infréquentable [ɛ̃frekɑ̃tabl̩], *a.* (*of place*) that one would not visit; (*of pers.*) with whom one would not mix, *F:* impossible.
infréquenté [ɛ̃frekɑ̃te], *a.* unfrequented.
infroissabilité [ɛ̃frwasabilite], *s.f. Tex:* crease resistance.
infroissable [ɛ̃frwasabl̩], *a. Tex: etc:* uncreasable, crease-resisting; uncrushable.
infructueusement [ɛ̃fryktɥøzmɑ̃], *adv.* fruitlessly; unprofitably, without success.
infructueux, -euse [ɛ̃fryktɥø, -øːz], *a.* (*a*) unfruitful, barren (land, etc.); (*b*) fruitless, unavailing, unsuccessful (efforts, etc.); (*c*) unprofitable (investment, etc.).
infule [ɛ̃fyl], *s.f. Rom.Ant: etc:* infula.
infumable [ɛ̃fymabl], *a.* (*a*) unsmokable (cigar, etc.); (*b*) *P:* unbearable (person).
infundibuliforme [ɛ̃fɔ̃dibylifɔrm], *a. Anat: Bot:* infundibular, infundibuliform, funnel-shaped.
infundibulum [ɛ̃fɔ̃dibylɔm], *s.m. Anat:* infundibulum.

infus [ɛ̃fy], *a.* infused, inborn, innate, intuitive (knowledge, etc.); **il croit avoir la science infuse,** he thinks he knows everything without having learnt it, by instinct.

infusé [ɛ̃fyze], *s.m. Pharm:* infusion.

infuser [ɛ̃fyze], *v.tr.* to infuse. **1.** to instil; **i. une nouvelle vie à qn,** to put, infuse, new life into s.o. **2. i. à froid,** to steep, macerate (herbs, etc.).

s'infuser, to infuse; (*of tea*) to draw; **faire i. le thé,** to infuse the tea; **laisser i. le thé,** to let the tea draw; **thé trop infusé,** stewed tea.

infusibilité [ɛ̃fyzibilite], *s.f.* infusibility, non-fusibility.

infusible [ɛ̃fyzibl̩], *a.* infusible, non-fusible, non-melting.

infusion [ɛ̃fyzjɔ̃], *s.f.* infusion. **1.** *Ecc:* affusion (as a form of baptism). **2.** *Theol:* instillation (of truth, etc.). **3.** (*a*) infusing (of herbs, tea); **i. à froid,** steeping (of herbs, etc.); (*b*) decoction; **une i. de camomille,** an infusion of camomile; camomile tea.

infusoire [ɛ̃fyzwaːr], *a.* & *s. Prot: O:* infusorian; *s.m.pl.* **infusoires,** Infusoria; *Geol:* **terre à infusoires,** *Com:* **terre d'infusoires,** infusorial earth; diatomite.

ingagnable [ɛ̃gaɲabl̩], *a.* that cannot be won; doomed to failure; hopeless (case).

ingambe [ɛ̃gɑ̃ːb], *a.* active, nimble; sprightly; brisk; **vieillard i.,** old man who is still active, still a good walker.

ingélif, -ive [ɛ̃ʒelif, -iːv], *a.* frost-proof.

ingénier (s') [sɛ̃ʒenje], *v.pr.* (*p.d.* & *pr.sub.* **n.n ingéniions, v.v. ingéniiez**) **s'i. à faire qch., pour faire plaisir à qn,** to exercise one's wits, strain one's ingenuity, in order to do sth., in order to please s.o.; **s'i. à plaire,** to contrive to please, to make an effort to please.

ingénierie [ɛ̃ʒenjəri], *s.f. Ind:* (*a*) study and development of projects; (*b*) project-study department.

ingénieur [ɛ̃ʒenjœːr], *s.m.* (*a*) (graduate, qualified) engineer; **i. civil,** engineer employed in the private sector; **i. d'État,** engineer employed in the public sector; **art, science, de l'i.,** engineering; **i. constructeur, i. des travaux publics,** civil engineer; **i. des ponts et chaussées,** civil engineer (in government employment); **i. des mines,** mining engineer; **i. électricien, i. électro-mécanicien,** electrical engineer; **i. mécanicien,** mechanical engineer; **i. électronicien,** electronics engineer; **i. radio(télégraphiste),** radio engineer; *Cin:* **i. du son,** sound engineer; **i. chimiste,** chemical engineer; **i. opticien,** optical engineer; **i. hydraulicien,** hydraulic engineer; **i. de l'aéronautique,** aeronautical engineer; **i. (du génie) rural,** agricultural engineer; **i. agronome,** agronomist; *Nau:* **i. de la marine, i. maritime,** naval architect, shipbuilder; **i. du génie maritime, i. des constructions navales,** naval constructor; **i. mécanicien, i. des constructions mécaniques, de la marine,** marine engineer, naval engineer; **i. de l'artillerie navale,** naval ordnance officer; (*b*) **i. géographe, i. topographe,** surveyor; topographer; **i. hydrographe,** marine surveyor; hydrographer; *Mil:* **Corps des Ingénieurs géographes** = the Ordnance Survey; (*c*) specialist, expert, engineer; **i. conseil,** (i) engineering consultant, consulting engineer; (ii) (*for patent rights*) patent engineer; **i. d'études, i. projecteur,** design engineer; **i. des méthodes,** industrial engineer; **i. en organisation,** work study engineer; **i. (chargé) des mises au point,** development engineer; **i. (chargé) des recettes, i. réceptionnaire,** acceptance engineer; **i. commercial, i. chef du service des ventes,** sales engineer.

ingénieusement [ɛ̃ʒenjøzmɑ̃], *adv.* ingeniously, cleverly.

ingénieux, -euse [ɛ̃ʒenjø, -øːz], *a.* ingenious, clever (person, scheme, piece of apparatus); **i. à plaire,** expert at pleasing; **i. à tourner les difficultés,** clever at getting round difficulties, at dodging difficulties.

ingéniosité [ɛ̃ʒenjozite], *s.f.* ingenuity, ingeniousness (of person or thing); cleverness (of person).

ingénu, -ue [ɛ̃ʒeny]. **1.** *a.* ingenuous, artless, simple, naïve, unsophisticated; **faire l'i.,** to affect simplicity; **réponse ingénue,** naïve reply; **franchise ingénue,** unsophisticated frankness. **2.** *s.f.* **ingénue,** (*a*) naïve, unsophisticated, girl; (*b*) *Th:* ingénue.

ingénuité [ɛ̃ʒenɥite], *s.f.* ingenuousness, naïveness, artlessness, simplicity; **remarque faite en toute i.,** remark made quite ingenuously.

ingénument [ɛ̃ʒenymɑ̃], *adv.* ingenuously, naïvely, simply, in an unsophisticated manner; **faire i. confiance à un escroc,** to be naïve enough to trust a crook.

ingérence [ɛ̃ʒerɑ̃ːs], *s.f.* (unwarrantable) interference, meddling; **i. dans une affaire,** unwarranted intervention in a matter; **i. des autorités dans les entreprises particulières,** interference of the authorities in private enterprise.

ingérer [ɛ̃ʒere], *v.tr.* (**j'ingère, n. ingérons; j'ingérerai**) *Physiol:* to ingest; to introduce (food) into the stomach; *F:* **i. un bon dîner,** to stow away a good dinner.

s'ingérer. 1. s'i. dans une affaire, to interfere in, meddle with, a matter; *A:* **s'i. de faire qch.,** to take it upon oneself, to presume, to do sth. **2. s'i. dans un emploi,** to edge, push, one's way into a job.

ingesta [ɛ̃ʒɛsta], *s.m.pl. Physiol:* ingesta.

ingestion [ɛ̃ʒɛstjɔ̃], *s.f. Physiol:* ingestion, consumption; *Biol:* **i. intracellulaire,** phagocytosis.

inglorieusement [ɛ̃glɔrjøzmɑ̃], *adv.* ingloriously.

inglorieux, -euse [ɛ̃glɔrjø, -øːz], *a.* inglorious.

ingluvial, -aux [ɛ̃glyvjal, -o], *a. Orn:* ingluvial.

ingluvie [ɛ̃glyvi], *s.f. Orn:* pellet (of bird of prey).

ingouvernable [ɛ̃guvɛrnabl̩], *a.* **1.** ungovernable, unruly; **enfant i.,** unmanageable child. **2.** unmanageable, uncontrollable (ship, etc.); (ship) that will not steer.

ingrat, -ate [ɛ̃gra, -at], *a.* **1.** ungrateful (**envers,** to, towards); **i. aux bienfaits,** ungrateful for favours. **2.** (*a*) unproductive, unprofitable, poor, meagre (soil, etc.); **tâche ingrate,** thankless task; **semer en terre ingrate,** to sow on stony ground; (*b*) unpromising, barren (subject of research, etc.). **3.** (*a*) unpleasing, disagreeable, repellent; hard (work, etc.); intractable (material, etc.); (*b*) unattractive (appearance, etc.); **visage i.,** plain, *U.S:* homely, face; **voix ingrate,** unpleasant voice; **l'âge i.,** the awkward age. **4.** *s.* ungrateful person; heartless person.

ingratement [ɛ̃gratmɑ̃], *adv.* ungratefully.

ingratitude [ɛ̃gratityd], *s.f.* **1.** ingratitude, ungratefulness. **2.** thanklessness, unprofitableness (of task, etc.); unproductiveness (of soil).

ingravissable [ɛ̃gravisabl̩], *a.* unclimbable, unscalable (hill, etc.).

ingrédient [ɛ̃gredjɑ̃], *s.m.* ingredient, constituent.

ingressif, -ive [ɛ̃gresif, -iːv], *a. Gram:* ingressive.

ingression [ɛ̃grɛsjɔ̃], *s.f.* **1.** *Astr:* ingress. **2.** intrusion, encroachment (of sea, etc.). **3.** *Dent:* impaction.

ingriffable [ɛ̃grifabl̩], *a.* scratch-proof; *Com:* "will not scratch."

ingriste [ɛ̃grist], *s.m.* & *f. Art:* follower, disciple, of Ingres.

inguéable [ɛ̃geabl̩], *a.* unfordable.

inguérissable [ɛ̃gerisabl̩], *a.* (*a*) incurable; (*b*) inconsolable (grief).

inguinal, -aux [ɛ̃gɥinal, -o], *a. Anat:* inguinal.

ingurgitation [ɛ̃gyrʒitasjɔ̃], *s.f.* ingurgitation, swallowing.

ingurgiter [ɛ̃gyrʒite], *v.tr.* (*a*) to make (s.o.) swallow (sth.); **la potion qu'on lui a ingurgitée,** the dose (of medicine) that he was made to swallow, that was poured down his throat; (*b*) *F:* to swallow (greedily and in large quantities); **i. un litre de vin,** to gulp down, knock back, a litre of wine; **il a ingurgité son dîner,** he wolfed his dinner; **i. des huîtres,** to swallow, gulp down, oysters (whole); (*c*) *F:* **on me faisait de force i. le latin,** they stuffed me with Latin.

inhabile [inabil], *a.* (*a*) unfitted (**à,** to); **i. à parler en public,** unaccustomed to public speaking; *Jur:* **i. à tester,** incompetent to make a will; **i. à voter,** not qualified to vote; (*b*) clumsy; incompetent; incapable; inefficient; **ouvrier i.,** incompetent workman.

inhabilement [inabilmɑ̃], *adv.* unskilfully; awkwardly.

inhabileté [inabilte], *s.f.* lack of skill (**à faire qch.,** in doing sth.); clumsiness, awkwardness; incompetence.

inhabilité [inabilite], *s.f. Jur:* legal incapacity, disability; **i. à succéder,** incompetency to succeed; **i. du mineur à tester,** incompetency of a minor to make a will.

inhabiliter [inabilite], *v.tr. Jur:* to disqualify (**à faire qch.,** from doing sth.).

inhabitable [inabitabl̩], *a.* uninhabitable (region, house, etc.); **cette maison est i.,** this house is not fit to live in.

inhabitation [inabitasjɔ̃], *s.f.* unoccupied condition (of house, etc.); **l'i. d'un bâtiment amène sa dégradation,** when a building is unoccupied it falls into disrepair.

inhabité [inabite], *a.* uninhabited; untenanted (house); **vol i.,** unmanned (space) flight.

inhabitude [inabityd], *s.f.* unaccustomedness (**de,** to).

inhabitué [inabitɥe], *a.* unaccustomed; **i. aux privations,** unused to privations; **ses cheveux inhabitués au peigne,** her hair which was never combed.

inhabituel, -elle [inabitɥɛl], *a.* unusual.

inhalant [inalɑ̃], *a.* inhalant, inhaling.

inhalateur, -trice [inalatœːr, -tris]. **1.** *a.* inhaling (apparatus). **2.** *s.m.* inhaling apparatus; inhaler; inhalator; **i. d'oxygène,** oxygen-breathing apparatus.

inhalation [inalasjɔ̃], *s.f.* inhalation. **1.** inhaling. **2.** *Med:* (*thg to be inhaled*) inhalant.

inhaler [inale], *v.tr.* to inhale (ether, etc.).

inharmonie [inarmɔni], *s.f.* disharmony, discordance (of sounds, etc.).

inharmonieusement [inarmɔnjøzmɑ̃], *adv.* inharmoniously; discordantly.

inharmonieux, -ieuse [inarmɔnjø, -jøːz], *a.* inharmonious, disharmonious, discordant; **voix inharmonieuse,** unmusical voice; **couleurs inharmonieuses,** colours that clash.

inharmonique [inarmɔnik], *a. Mus:* inharmonic.

inhérence [inerɑ̃ːs], *s.f.* inherence, inherency (**à,** in).

inhérent [inerɑ̃], *a.* inherent (**à,** in).

inhibage [inibaːʒ], *s.m. Pyr:* addition of an inhibitor (to explosive).

inhibé, -ée [inibe], *a.* **1.** *Physiol: Psy:* inhibited; *s.* inhibited person, person with inhibitions. **2.** *Ch:* **huile inhibée,** inhibited oil.

inhiber [inibe], *v.tr.* **1.** *Jur: A:* to prohibit. **2.** *Physiol: Psy:* to inhibit. **3.** *Ch: etc:* to inhibit, retard (reaction). **4.** (*computers*) to blind.

inhibiteur, -trice [inibitœːr, -tris]. **1.** *a. Anat: Psy:* inhibitory (reflex, nerve, etc.); **influence inhibitrice,** inhibitory, inhibiting, influence. **2.** *s.m. Ch: etc:* inhibitor; protective agent; **i. de corrosion,** corrosion inhibitor; **i. de catalyse métallique,** metal deactivator; **i. de polymérisation,** short stop.

inhibitif, -ive [inibitif, -iːv], *a. Physiol: Psy:* inhibitory; **cause inhibitive,** inhibiting cause.

inhibition [inibisjɔ̃], *s.f.* **1.** *Jur:* prohibition; **défenses et inhibitions sont faites de . . .,** the parties are prohibited from + *ger.* **2.** *Psy: Med:* inhibition; **mort par i.,** death from inhibition. **3.** *Ch: etc:* inhibition.

inhibitoire [inibitwaːr], *a.* **1.** *Jur:* inhibitory, prohibitory. **2.** *Psy: Med:* inhibitory.

inhomogène [inɔmɔʒɛn], *a.* inhomogeneous.

inhospitalier, -ière [inɔspitalje, -jɛːr], *a.* inhospitable.

inhospitalité [inɔspitalite], *s.f.* inhospitality, inhospitableness.

inhumain [inymɛ̃], *a.* inhuman; unfeeling, cruel; **un cri i.,** an inhuman, unearthly, cry; *F:* **elle n'est pas inhumaine,** she's not inhuman, by no means frigid; *s. Lit: A:* **ma belle inhumaine,** my fair cruel one.

inhumainement [inymɛnmɑ̃], *adv.* inhumanly.

inhumanité [inymanite], *s.f.* inhumanity; cruelty, unfeelingness.

inhumation [inymasjɔ̃], *s.f.* burial, interment; *Archeol:* inhumation.

inhumer [inyme], *v.tr.* to bury, inter; *Adm:* **permis d'i.,** permission to bury, to dispose of, a body.

inimaginable [inimaʒinabl̩], *a.* unimaginable; inconceivable, unthinkable.

inimaginé [inimaʒine], *a.* unimagined; unthought of.

inimitable [inimitabl̩], *a.* inimitable; matchless.

inimitablement [inimitabləmɑ̃], *adv.* inimitably.

inimité [inimite], *a.* never yet imitated.

inimitié [inimitje], *s.f.* **1.** enmity, hostility, ill-feeling; **avoir de l'i. pour qn,** to be on bad terms with s.o., to dislike s.o.; **causer de l'i. entre deux personnes,** to create bad blood between two persons. **2.** hostility, unfriendliness (between animals or animal races).

inimprimable [inɛ̃primabl̩], *a.* unprintable; unpublishable.

inimprimé [inɛ̃prime], *a.* unprinted.

ininflammabilité [inɛ̃flamabilite; -flɑ-], *s.f.* non-inflammability, uninflammability; *U.S:* non-flammability.

ininflammable [inɛ̃flamabl̩; -flɑ-], *a.* non-inflammable, uninflammable; *U.S:* non-flammable; fireproof; *Cin:* non-flam; *A:* **film i.,** safety film.

ininstructif, -ive [inɛ̃stryktif, -iːv], *a.* uninstructive.

inintelligemment [inɛ̃tɛl(l)iʒamɑ̃], *adv.* unintelligently.

inintelligence [inɛ̃tɛl(l)iʒɑ̃ːs], *s.f.* lack of intelligence; unintelligence; obtuseness.

inintelligent [inɛ̃tɛl(l)iʒɑ̃], *a.* unintelligent; obtuse.

inintelligibilité [inɛ̃tɛl(l)iʒibilite], *s.f.* unintelligibility.

inintelligible [inɛ̃tɛl(l)iʒibl̩], *a.* unintelligible; **le passage est i.,** the passage is unintelligible, makes no sense; *s.m.* **attacher un sens à l'i.,** to make sense out of nonsense.

inintelligiblement [inɛ̃tɛl(l)iʒibləmɑ̃], *adv.* unintelligibly.

inintentionnel [inɛ̃tɑ̃sjɔnɛl], *a.* unintentional.

inintentionnellement [inɛ̃tɑ̃sjɔnɛlmɑ̃], *adv.* unintentionally.

inintéressant [inɛ̃terɛsɑ̃], *a.* uninteresting.

ininterprétable [inɛ̃tɛrpretabl̩], *a.* uninterpretable.

ininterprété [inɛ̃tɛrprete], *a.* uninterpreted.

ininterrompu [inɛ̃tɛrɔ̃py], *a.* uninterrupted, unintermitting; unbroken (sleep, etc.); **progrès i.,** steady, uninterrupted, progress.

ininterruption [inɛ̃tɛrypsjɔ̃], *s.f.* lack of interruption, continuity, uninterruptedness.

inion [injɔ̃], *s.m. Anat:* inion.

inique [inik], *a.* iniquitous.

iniquement [inikmɑ̃], *adv.* iniquitously.

iniquité [inikite], *s.f.* iniquity. **1.** iniquitousness; flagrant injustice. **2.** iniquitous action.

initial, -aux [inisjal, -o]. **1.** *a.* (*a*) initial (letter, cost, etc.), **vitesse initiale,** initial velocity; *Box:* **round i.,** first round; (*b*) *Com:* **prix i.,** starting price; (*c*) *Bot:* **cellule initiale,** *s.f.* **initiale,** initial; meristematic cell. **2.** *s.f.* **initiale,** initial (letter).

initialement [inisjalmɑ̃], *adv.* initially.

initialer [inisjale], *v.tr. A:* to initial (document).

initiateur, -trice [inisjatœːr, -tris]. **1.** *s.* initiator; (*a*) originator, pioneer (of scheme, etc.); **être l'i. de qch.,** to initiate sth.; (*b*) instructor (of neophyte, novice, etc.). **2.** *a.* initiatory (rite, ceremony, etc.).

initiation [inisjasjɔ̃], *s.f.* initiation (à, into); **rites d'i.,** initiatory, initiation, rites; **ce livre est une excellente i. à la musique,** this book is an excellent introduction, approach, to music; *Ch:* **i. d'une réaction,** initiation of a reaction.

initiatique [inisjatik], *a.* initiative; initiatory.

initiative [inisjatiːv], *s.f.* initiative; **i. privée,** private initiative, private enterprise; **la commission dispose d'une grande i.,** the commission has wide powers of initiative; **l'i. dans l'édition est chose extrêmement rare,** in publishing initiative is a very rare thing; **sur l'i. de X,** on X's initiative; **prendre l'i. d'une réforme,** to initiate a reform; **prendre l'i. de faire qch.,** to take the initiative in doing sth., **prendre une i. au sujet de qch.,** to take action, to take the initiative, about sth.; **droit d'i.,** right of initiative; *Pol:* right to propose legislation; **le parlement a l'i. des lois,** parliament has the right to introduce bills, to propose legislation; *Mil: etc:* **garder l'i.,** to keep the initiative; **faire qch. de sa propre i.,** to do sth. on one's own initiative, *F:* off one's own bat; **nous souhaitons le succès à cette i. intéressante,** we wish this interesting initiative, venture, experiment, every success; **défaut, manque, d'i.,** lack of initiative; **il n'a aucune i.,** he's got no initiative; **syndicat d'i.,** tourist office, bureau.

initié, -ée [inisje], *s.* (*a*) initiate; (*b*) *F:* person in the know.

initier [inisje], *v.tr.* (*p.d. & pr.sub.* **n. initiions, v. initiiez**) (*a*) to initiate (s.o.), to receive (s.o.) among the initiates; (*b*) **i. qn à un secret,** to initiate, *F:* let, s.o. into a secret; **i. qn à une science, aux procédés d'un art,** to initiate s.o. in a science, in an art; **c'est moi qui l'ai initié au grec,** it was I who introduced him to Greek; **je l'ai initié à la conduite de l'affaire,** I taught him how to run the business.

s'initier, to learn, to be learning; *F:* to get to learn; **s'i. aux détails d'un commerce,** to get to know the details of a business.

injectable [ɛ̃ʒɛktabl̩], *a.* injectable.

injecté [ɛ̃ʒɛkte], *a.* **1.** congested, inflamed, injected; **yeux injectés de sang, de bile,** bloodshot, jaundiced, eyes. **2. bois i.,** impregnated, *esp.* creosoted, wood.

injecter [ɛ̃ʒɛkte], *v.tr.* **1. i. un liquide dans une cavité, dans une veine,** to inject a fluid into a cavity, into a vein; **i. une antitoxine à une bête,** to inject an animal with antitoxin; *Pol.Ec:* **i. du capital,** to inject capital. **2.** (*a*) **i. une cavité, une veine (de, avec, un liquide),** to inject a cavity, a vein (with a fluid); (*b*) **i. le bois,** to impregnate, *esp.* to creosote, wood.

s'injecter, (*of eyes, etc.*) to become bloodshot, injected.

injecteur, -trice [ɛ̃ʒɛktœːr, -tris]. **1.** *a.* injecting (tube, etc.). **2.** *s.m.* injector; *Mec.E: etc:* atomizer; burner; (engine) injector; *Av: Aut: etc:* (injection, spray) nozzle; **i. multijet,** multiple jet nozzle; **i. d'huile,** oil spud; *Civ.E:* **i. de ciment,** cement injector; *Atom.Ph:* **i. d'électrons,** electron injector.

injection [ɛ̃ʒɛksjɔ̃], *s.f.* **1.** (*a*) injection, injecting; *Mch:* admission (of water, etc.); **pompe à i.,** injection pump; **condensation par i.,** jet condensation; **capacité d'i.,** injectivity; *I.C.E:* **moteur à i. (directe),** (direct) injection engine; *Mec.E:* **rampe principale, auxiliaire, d'i.,** main, pilot, fuel pipe (of turbo jet); (*b*) impregnation, impregnating, creosoting (of wood); **usine d'i. des bois,** wood preserving plant; (*c*) *Med:* injection; **i. intramusculaire,** intramuscular injection; **i. intraveineuse,** intravenous injection; **i. hypodermique,** sous-cutanée, hypodermic, subcutaneous, injection; **i. sous-périostée,** subperiostal injection; **i. sus-périostée,** supraperiostal injection; **i. spinale,** spinal injection; (*d*) *Const:* grouting; **trou d'i.,** grout hole; *Petroleum Ind:* **i. de boue,** mud grouting; (*e*) *Geol:* injection; intrusion (of rock); **roche d'i.,** intruded rock; (*f*) *Pol.Ec:* **i. de capital,** injection of capital. **2.** (*matter injected*) injection.

injonctif, -ive [ɛ̃ʒɔ̃ktif, -iːv], *a. Jur: Gram:* injunctive.

injonction [ɛ̃ʒɔ̃ksjɔ̃], *s.f.* injunction; *Jur:* **i. de la cour,** order of the court; **i. à qn de s'abstenir de . . .,** injunction against s.o. restraining him from ..

injouable [ɛ̃ʒwabl̩], *a.* unplayable (music, ball, etc.); unperformable, unactable (play).

injudicieusement [ɛ̃ʒydisjøzmɑ̃], *adv.* injudiciously.

injudicieux, -euse [ɛ̃ʒydisjø, -øːz], *a.* injudicious.

injure [ɛ̃ʒyːr], *s.f.* **1.** wrong, injury; *Jur:* tort; **pardon des injures,** forgiveness of injuries; **faire i. à qn,** to wrong s.o.; **faire à qn l'i. de croire que . . .,** to insult s.o. by thinking that . .; **l'i. des ans,** the ravages of time; **i. à toute justice,** violation of all justice; *Jur:* **i. grave,** injury or slander so serious as to form a ground for divorce. **2.** insulting word or remark; insult; *pl.* abuse; **dire, débiter, des injures à qn,** to use insulting language to s.o.; to abuse, slang, s.o.; **accabler qn d'injures,** to shower abuse on s.o.; **en venir aux injures,** to descend to abusive language.

injurier [ɛ̃ʒyrje], *v.tr.* (*p.d. & pr.sub.* **n. injuriions, v. injuriiez**) to abuse, insult (s.o.); to call (s.o.) names, to use abusive language to (s.o.); **i. la mémoire de qn,** to insult s.o.'s memory; **i. son propre siècle,** to disparage, belittle, speak slightingly, of one's own century.

injurieusement [ɛ̃ʒyrjøzmɑ̃], *adv.* **1.** injuriously, insultingly. **2.** *Jur:* tortiously.

injurieux, -euse [ɛ̃ʒyrjø, -øːz], *a.* **1.** (*a*) *A:* hurtful, harmful (à, to); (*b*) *Jur:* tortious. **2.** insulting, abusive, injurious (language); derisive (laughter).

injuste [ɛ̃ʒyst]. **1.** *a.* (*a*) unjust, unfair (**envers, avec, pour,** to); **être i. envers qn,** to wrong s.o.; (*b*) unrighteous (person); (*c*) *A:* unjustified. **2.** *s.m.* **le juste et l'i.,** right and wrong.

injustement [ɛ̃ʒystəmɑ̃], *adv.* (*a*) unjustly, unfairly; wrongfully; (*b*) unrighteously.

injustice [ɛ̃ʒystis], *s.f.* **1.** injustice, unfairness (**envers,** to, towards). **2. faire une i. à qn,** to do s.o. an injustice, to wrong s.o.; **je n'aime pas les injustices,** I don't like injustice; **ce sont là des injustices flagrantes,** these are cases of flagrant injustice.

injustifiable [ɛ̃ʒystifjabl̩], *a.* unjustifiable, unwarrantable, inexcusable.

injustifié [ɛ̃ʒystifje], *a.* unjustified, unwarranted; *Mil: etc:* **réclamation injustifiée,** frivolous complaint.

inlandsis [inlɑ̃dsis], *s.m. Geog:* (continental) ice sheet; ice cap.

inlassable [ɛ̃lɑsabl̩], *a.* untiring, unflagging, unwearying (efforts, etc.); tireless (man, horse).

inlassablement [ɛ̃lɑsabləmɑ̃], *adv.* untiringly, tirelessly.

inlay [inlei], *s.m. Dent:* filling, *U.S:* (dental) inlay.

innavigabilité [in(n)avigabilite], *s.f.* **1.** unnavigability (of waters). **2.** unseaworthiness (of ship).

innavigable [in(n)avigabl̩], *a.* **1.** unnavigable, innavigable (waters). **2.** unseaworthy (ship).

inné [in(n)e], *a.* innate, inborn (quality, etc.); *Phil:* **idées innées,** innate ideas.

innégociable [in(n)egɔsjabl̩, ɛ̃-], *a. Com:* not negotiable.

innéisme [in(n)eism], *s.m. Phil:* innatism.

innéité [in(n)eite], *s.f.* innateness.

innervation [in(n)ɛrvasjɔ̃], *s.f. Physiol:* innervation.

innervé [in(n)ɛrve], *a. Bot:* nerveless (leaf).

innerver [in(n)ɛrve], *v.tr. Physiol:* to innervate; *F:* to be the nerve centre (of sth.).

innettoyable [in(n)ɛtwjabl̩], *a.* that cannot be cleaned.

innocemment [inɔsamɑ̃], *adv.* innocently; in all innocence.

innocence [inɔsɑ̃ːs], *s.f.* innocence. **1.** (*guiltlessness*) **protester de son i.,** to protest one's innocence; **avoir la conviction de l'i. de l'accusé,** to be convinced of the innocence of the accused. **2.** (*a*) (*sinlessness*) **l'i. d'une sainte vie,** the innocence of a holy life; (*b*) innocence; naïveté; **abuser de l'i. de qn,** to take advantage of s.o.'s innocence; **l'âge d'i.,** the age of innocence; **en toute i.,** in all innocence; (*c*) innocence; virginity; **perdre son i.,** to lose one's innocence. **3.** harmlessness (of joke, drug, etc.).

innocent, -ente [inɔsɑ̃, -ɑ̃ːt]. **1.** (*a*) *a.* innocent, not guilty; **tout homme est présumé i. jusqu'à ce qu'il ait été déclaré coupable,** a man is presumed innocent until he has been proved guilty; (*b*) *s.* innocent person; **un i. condamné,** an innocent man condemned. **2.** (*a*) *a.* innocent, pure, holy; **vie innocente,** blameless, virtuous, life; **i. comme un enfant,** as innocent as a child; (*b*) *s.* innocent person (*esp.* a young child); *Ecc:* **les (saints) Innocents,** the Holy Innocents; **la fête, le jour, des saints Innocents,** Innocents' Day, Childermas. **3.** (*a*) *a.* innocent; naïve; simple; **il est bien i. de croire à cela,** he's very naïve to believe that; (*b*) *s.* simpleton, naïve person; **ne fais pas l'i.!** don't pretend you don't understand! **l'i. du village,** the village idiot; *Prov:* **aux innocents les mains pleines,** (i) fortune favours fools; (ii) beginners have all the luck. **4.** *a.* innocent, harmless, inoffensive; **plaisanterie innocente,** harmless, inoffensive, joke; **mensonge i.,** white lie; **drogue innocente,** harmless medicine; **jeux innocents,** parlour games, (games of) forfeits. **5.** *Pr.n.m.* (Pope) Innocent. **6.** *a. & s.f. Cost: A:* **(robe à) l'innocente,** maternity dress.

innocenter [inɔsɑ̃te], *v.tr.* **1. i. qn (d'une accusation),** to clear s.o. (of a charge); to declare s.o. not guilty. **2.** to excuse, justify (conduct, etc.).

innocuité [in(n)ɔkɥite], *s.f.* innocuousness, harmlessness; *Med:* **essai d'i.,** safety test.

innombrable [in(n)ɔ̃brabl̩], *a.* innumerable, numberless, countless; untold (generations); **livres innombrables,** books without number; **l'armée i. de Darius,** the teeming army of Darius.

innombrablement [in(n)ɔ̃brabləmɑ̃], *adv.* innumerably.

innom(m)é [in(n)ɔme], *a.* unnamed, nameless; not yet named; *Jur:* **contrat i.,** innominate contract.

innominé [in(n)ɔmine], *a. Anat:* innominate, unnamed (bone, artery); **os i.,** hip-bone, os innominatum.

innommable [in(n)ɔmabl̩], *a.* (*a*) unnamable; (*b*) **un i. tas d'ordures,** a disgusting, an unspeakable, heap of rubbish; **conduite i.,** unspeakable behaviour.

innovateur, -trice [in(n)ɔvatœːr, -tris]. **1.** *a.* innovating, innovative. **2.** *s.* innovator.

innovation [in(n)ɔvasjɔ̃], *s.f.* innovation.

innover [in(n)ɔve], *v.i.* to innovate, to introduce changes, innovations; to break new ground; **i. à qch.,** to make innovations, changes, in sth.; *v.tr.* **on n'innove jamais rien ici,** there are never any changes, nothing ever changes, here.

inobéissant [inɔbeisɑ̃], *a.* disobedient, noncompliant.

inobligeant [inɔbliʒɑ̃], *a.* disobliging, unobliging.

inobservable [inɔpsɛrvabl̩], *a.* **1.** that cannot be observed, that cannot be complied with. **2.** inobservable, hardly perceptible.

inobservance [inɔpsɛrvɑ̃ːs], *s.f.* non-observance, unobservance, inobservance (of fasts, of medical orders, etc.); failure to observe (orders, etc.).

inobservation [inɔpsɛrvasjɔ̃], *s.f.* non-observance, disregard (of the law); non-compliance (**de,** with); **i. d'une promesse,** non-adherence to a promise; failure to keep a promise.

inobservé [inɔpsɛrve], *a.* unobserved. **1.** (*of rules, etc.*) not kept, not complied with. **2.** unnoticed.

inobstrué [inɔpstrye], *a.* unobstructed, free from obstructions.

inocclusion [inɔklyzjɔ̃], *s.f. Dent:* malocclusion.

inoccupation [inɔkypasjɔ̃], *s.f.* lack of occupation, unemployment, inoccupation.

inoccupé, -ée [inɔkype], unoccupied. **1.** *a. & s.* idle, unemployed (person). **2.** *a.* vacant (seat, house); uninhabited (house).

inocérame [inɔseram], **inoceramus** [inɔseramyːs], *s.m. Paleont:* inoceramus.

in-octavo [inɔktavo], *a. & s.m.inv. Typ:* octavo.

inoculabilité [inɔkylabilite], *s.f. Med:* inoculability.

inoculable [inɔkylabl], *a. Med:* inoculable.

inoculateur, -trice [inɔkylatœːr, -tris], *s. Med:* inoculator.

inoculation [inɔkylasjɔ̃], *s.f. Med:* inoculation; **i. curative,** curative inoculation.

inoculer [inɔkyle], *v.tr.* **1.** (*a*) **i. une maladie à qn,** to infect s.o. with a disease; **i. au peuple une doctrine nouvelle,** to implant a new doctrine in the people; **elle nous a inoculé sa gaieté,** she has infected us with her gaiety; (*b*) *Med:* **i. un virus à qn,** to inoculate s.o. with a virus. **2. i. qn (contre une maladie),** to inoculate s.o. (against a disease).

inodore [inɔdɔːr], *a.* inodorous, odourless; (*a*) scentless (rose, etc.); (*b*) free from effluvia; *A:* **cabinet i.,** hygienic water-closet.

inoffensé [inɔfɑ̃se], *a.* not offended; **il est i.,** he hasn't taken offence.

inoffensif, -ive [inɔfɑ̃sif, -iːv], *a.* inoffensive; harmless; innocuous; **plaisanterie inoffensive,** harmless joke; *Med:* **dose inoffensive,** safe dose.

inoffensivement [inɔfɑ̃sivmɑ̃], *adv.* inoffensively, harmlessly.

inofficiel, -ielle [inɔfisjɛl], *a.* unofficial.

inofficiellement [inɔfisjɛlmɑ̃], *adv.* unofficially.

inofficieusement [inɔfisjøzmɑ̃], *adv. Jur:* inofficiously.

inofficieux, -euse [inɔfisjø, -øːz], *a. Jur:* inofficious (testament, etc.).

inofficiosité [inɔfisjɔzite], *s.f. Jur:* inofficiosity.

inomissible [inɔmisibl̩], *a.* that cannot, should not, be omitted.

inondable [inɔ̃dabl̩], *a.* (*of land*) (*a*) liable to inundation; (*b*) easily flooded.

inondation [inɔ̃dasjɔ̃], *s.f.* (*a*) inundation; flood; *Mil:* **tendre une i.,** to flood an area; **i. causée par la fonte des neiges,** flood, flooding, caused by snow melting; **i. de brochures,** flood, deluge, of pamphlets; (*b*) (action of) flooding; *Petroleum Ind:* water flooding; **l'i. du marché par des produits étrangers,** the flooding of the market with foreign produce.

inondé, -ée [inɔ̃de]. **1.** *a.* flooded; **pays i.,** flooded countryside, country under water; **visage i. de larmes, de pleurs,** face streaming with tears; **i. de lumière,** suffused with light; **ville inondée de sang,** town bathed in blood, swimming with blood; **i. d'invitations,** snowed under with invitations. **2.** *s.* flood victim.

inonder [inɔ̃de], *v.tr.* (*a*) to inundate, flood (fields, etc.); to glut (the market); **les articles en matière plastique inondent le marché,** the market is being flooded with plastic goods; (*b*) to soak, drench; **nous avons été inondés par l'averse,** we were soaked by the shower; (*c*) **la foule inonda le terrain (de jeu),** the crowd swarmed over, invaded, the pitch; (*d*) *Petroleum Min:* to flood (well, to force out the last of the oil).

inopérable [inɔperabl̩], *a. Surg:* inoperable (tumour, patient).

inopérant [inɔperɑ̃], *a.* (*a*) *Jur:* inoperative, invalid; (*b*) ineffectual (remedy).

inopiné [inɔpine], *a.* sudden, unexpected, unforeseen.

inopinément [inɔpinemɑ̃], *adv.* suddenly, unexpectedly.

inopportun [inɔpɔrtœ̃], *a.* **1.** inopportune. **2.** unseasonable, ill-timed (remark, etc.).

inopportunément [inɔpɔrtynemɑ̃], *adv.* **1.** inopportunely. **2.** unseasonably.

inopportunité [inɔpɔrtynite], *s.f.* **1.** inopportuneness, inopportunity. **2.** unseasonableness, untimeliness; gratuitousness (of a remark, etc.); **i. d'une démarche,** poor timing of a move.

inopposable [inɔpozabl̩], *a. Jur:* that cannot be opposed; incontestable.

inorganique [inɔrganik], *a.* inorganic (body, chemistry; *Ling:* letter or sound).

inorganisable [inɔrganizabl̩], *a.* unorganizable.

inorganisation [inɔrganizasjɔ̃], *s.f.* lack of organization.

inorganisé [inɔrganize], *a.* (*a*) disorganized; (*b*) *Biol:* unorganized; (*c*) *Pol.Ec:* unorganized, non-union (labour).

inosculation [inɔskylasjɔ̃], *s.f. Anat: Surg:* inosculation.

inosite [inɔzit], *s.f.,* **inositol** [inɔzitɔl], *s.m. Ch:* inosite, inositol.

inostensible [inɔstɑ̃sibl̩], *a.* inostensible.

inostensiblement [inɔstɑ̃sibləmɑ̃], *adv.* inostensibly.

inotrope [inɔtrɔp], *a. Physiol:* inotropic.

inoubliable [inubli(j)abl̩], *a.* unforgettable, never-to-be-forgotten.

inoublié [inubli(j)e], *a.* unforgotten, not forgotten.

inouï [inui, inwi], *a.* (*a*) *Lit:* unheard of; never heard before; never known of before; **sauts d'harmonie inouïs,** harmonic intervals hitherto unknown; (*b*) unheard of, extraordinary, outrageous (behaviour); **avec une violence inouïe,** with incredible, unprecedented, violence; **la vogue inouïe de ce chanteur,** the extraordinary, incredible, vogue of this singer; **il est i. de faire cela!** whoever heard of anyone doing that! *F:* **il est i.,** he's incredible; *F:* he has to be seen to be believed; *P:* **il a un culot i.,** he's got the hell of a nerve.

inouïsme [inuism, -w-], *s.m. A: F:* unheard-ofness; **l'i. de son costume,** the outrageousness of her get-up.

inox [inɔks], *a. & s.m. F:* **(acier) i.,** stainless (steel).

inoxydable [inɔksidabl̩], *a.* unoxidizable, non-corrodible; rustproof; **acier i.,** *s.m.* **inoxydable,** stainless steel; **couteau i.,** stainless steel knife.

inoxydé [inɔkside], *a.* unoxidized.

in(-)pace [inpase], *s.m.inv.* dungeon (in convent, where prisoners were immured for life).

in partibus [inpartibyːs], *adj.phr.* (*a*) *Ecc.Hist:* **évêque in p.,** bishop in partibus (infidelium); (*b*) *F:* (*of minister, professor, etc.*) titular; in name (only).

in petto [inpeto, inpɛtto], *adv.phr.* (*a*) in one's inmost heart; secretly; (*b*) *Ecc:* **nommé in p. au cardinalat,** nominated cardinal in petto.

in-plano [inplano], *s.m.inv. Typ:* broadsheet, broadside; **format in-p.,** atlas size.

inqualifiable [ɛ̃kalifjabl̩], *a.* unqualifiable, beyond words; **agression i.,** unjustifiable act of aggression; **conduite i.,** unspeakable behaviour.

in-quarante-huit [ɛ̃karɑ̃tɥit], *a. & s.m.inv. Typ:* (in) forty-eightmo.

inquart [ɛ̃kaːr], *s.m.,* **inquartation** [ɛ̃kartasjɔ̃], *s.f. Metall:* (in)quartation (of gold with silver).

inquarter [ɛ̃karte], *v.i. Metall:* to make a silver-gold alloy (in the proportion 3:1).

in-quarto [inkwarto], *a. & s.m.inv. Typ:* quarto (sheet, volume).

in-quatre-vingt-seize [inkatrəvɛ̃sɛːz], *a. & s.m.inv. Typ:* (in) ninety-sixmo.

inquiet, -ète [ɛ̃kjɛ, -ɛt], *a.* (*a*) restless, fidgety; **sommeil i.,** troubled, broken, sleep; (*b*) anxious, apprehensive, uneasy; worried; **i. sur qch., de qn, sur le compte de qn,** uneasy, worried, about sth., s.o.; **se sentir i. au sujet de qch.,** to feel ill at ease about sth.; **il s'est montré très i. à votre égard,** he showed great concern about you; **avoir l'esprit i.,** to be uneasy in one's mind; **conscience inquiète,** uneasy conscience; **âme inquiète,** unquiet soul; (*c*) **i. de faire qch.,** anxious to do sth.; (*d*) *s. Med:* **un i.,** an anxious person, a worrier.

inquiétant [ɛ̃kjetɑ̃], *a.* disquieting, alarming, disturbing, upsetting (news, etc.).

inquiètement [ɛ̃kjɛtmɑ̃], *adv. A: Lit:* uneasily, anxiously, unquietly.

inquiéter [ɛ̃kjete], *v.tr.* **(j'inquiète, n. inquiétons; j'inquiéterai) 1.** (*a*) *Lit:* to disturb (s.o.'s peace, etc.); (*b*) **depuis son acquittement, la police ne l'a plus inquiété,** since he was acquitted, he has no longer been bothered, troubled, by the police; (*c*) **i. l'ennemi,** to worry, harass, the enemy. **2.** to make (s.o.) anxious; to trouble, disturb, worry (s.o.); **sa santé m'inquiète,** I'm worried about his health; **vous m'inquiétez,** you worry me, make me worried; I'm worried, anxious, about you. **3.** *Jur:* **i. qn dans la possession de qch.,** to challenge s.o.'s right to sth.

s'inquiéter, to become anxious, to worry, to get uneasy **(de, au sujet de,** about); **ne vous inquiétez pas à son sujet,** don't worry about him, over him; **ne vous inquiétez pas de cela, que cela ne vous inquiète pas,** don't worry, *F:* don't bother your head, about that; **je ne m'inquiète guère de ce qu'on dit,** I don't mind what they say; I am not concerned about what they say; **il s'inquiète de ce qu'on ne lui réponde pas,** he is worrying about not having received an answer; **il s'inquiète que vous (ne) vous ennuyiez,** he is afraid you find it very dull; **sans s'i. des conséquences,** without considering, thinking about, the consequences; **vous êtes-vous inquiété de l'heure du train?** have you enquired, asked, about the time of the train?

inquiétude [ɛ̃kjetyd], *s.f.* **1.** (*a*) *A. & Lit:* agitation; restlessness; *O: F:* **avoir des inquiétudes dans les jambes,** to feel twitchings in one's legs; (*b*) *Med:* anxiety. **2.** anxiety; concern, misgivings, uneasiness; **son état inspire les plus vives inquiétudes,** his condition is causing great anxiety; **rassurer toutes les inquiétudes,** to remove all anxieties; **dissiper les inquiétudes de qn, tirer qn de son i.,** to set s.o.'s mind at ease; **état d'inquiétude,** state of anxiety; anxious state of mind; **je suis sans inquiétude,** I have no misgivings; my mind is easy; **être sans i. au sujet de qch.,** to be unconcerned about sth.; **éprouver quelques inquiétudes,** to have a few qualms.

inquilin [ɛ̃kɥilɛ̃], *Nat.Hist:* (*a*) *a.* inquiline, inquilinous; (*b*) *s.m.* inquiline.

inquilinisme [ɛ̃kɥilinism], *s.m. Nat.Hist:* inquilinism.

inquisiteur, -trice [ɛ̃kizitœːr, -tris]. **1.** *s.m.* (*a*) *Ecc.Hist:* inquisitor; (*b*) *F:* snooper. **2.** *a.* (*a*) inquisitorial (tribunal, etc.); (*b*) inquisitive, prying (glance, etc.).

inquisitif, -ive [ɛ̃kizitif, -iːv], *a.* (*a*) *Phil:* speculative (philosophy); (*b*) inquisitive; inquisitorial.

inquisition [ɛ̃kizisjɔ̃], *s.f.* inquiry, inquisition; *Ecc.Hist:* **l'I.,** the Inquisition.

inquisitionner [ɛ̃kizisjɔne], *v.tr. A:* to search, examine (goods, etc.).

inquisitoire [ɛ̃kizitwaːr], *a. Jur:* inquisitorial (procedure).

inquisitorial, -aux [ɛ̃kizitɔrjal, -o], *a.* inquisitorial.

inracontable [ɛ̃rakɔ̃tabl̩], *a.* untellable; **joies inracontables,** joys that cannot be put into words; **une série d'aventures inracontables,** a series of unrelatable adventures; **c'est un film i.,** it is impossible to tell the plot of this film.

inrouillable [ɛ̃rujabl̩], *a.* rustless (steel, etc.).

insaisissabilité [ɛ̃sezisabilite, ɛ̃se-], *a. Jur:* immunity from seizure, from distraint, from attachment.

insaisissable [ɛ̃sezisabl̩, ɛ̃se-], *a.* **1.** (*a*) that cannot be grasped; (*b*) difficult to catch; elusive (person, meaning); (*c*) imperceptible (sound, difference); **i. à l'œil nu,** imperceptible to the naked eye. **2.** *Jur:* not distrainable, not attachable.

insalifiable [ɛ̃salifjabl̩], *a. Ch:* not salifiable.

insalissable [ɛ̃salisabl̩], *a.* unsoilable, dirt-proof.

insalivation [ɛ̃salivasjɔ̃], *s.f. Physiol:* insalivation.

insalubre [ɛ̃salybr̩], *a.* insalubrious (climate); unhealthy (climate, occupation, etc.); insanitary (dwelling, etc.).

insalubrement [ɛ̃salybrəmɑ̃], *adv.* unhealthily.

insalubrité [ɛ̃salybrite], *s.f.* insalubrity, unhealthiness; insanitariness.

insane [ɛ̃san], *a.* insane.

insanité [ɛ̃sanite], *s.f.* insanity. **1.** madness. **2.** insane act, saying; **débiter des insanités,** to talk utter nonsense.

insapide [ɛ̃sapid], *a. A:* tasteless (food, drink, etc.).

insatiabilité [ɛ̃sasjabilite], *s.f.* insatiability.

insatiable [ɛ̃sasjabl̩], *a.* insatiable (appetite, greed, curiosity, etc.); unquenchable (thirst); **être i. de richesses,** to have an insatiable desire for wealth; **i. dans ses ambitions,** insatiable in his ambition, of insatiable ambition.

insatiablement [ɛ̃sasjabləmɑ̃], *adv.* insatiably.

insatisfaction [ɛ̃satisfaksjɔ̃], *s.f.* sense of frustration, of dissatisfaction; **la lecture de ce livre m'a laissé dans l'i.,** the book left me with a sense of frustration.

insatisfait [ɛ̃satisfɛ], *a.* (*a*) (*of pers.*) dissatisfied; *s.* **c'est un (éternel) i.,** he's always dissatisfied, he's never satisfied; (*b*) unsatisfied (desire, curiosity, etc.); **une femme insatisfaite,** a frustrated woman.

insaturable [ɛ̃satyrabl̩], *a.* insaturable, non-saturable.

insaturation [ɛ̃satyrasjɔ̃], *s.f. Ch:* non-saturation.

insaturé [ɛ̃satyre]. **1.** *a.* unsaturated. **2.** *s.m. Ch:* unsaturate.

insciemment [ɛ̃sjamɑ̃], *adv.* (*rare*) unknowingly, unconsciously, unwittingly.

inscripteur, -trice [ɛ̃skriptœːr, -tris], (*a*) *a.* recording (device, etc.); **tambour i.,** drum recorder; (*b*) *s.m.* keyboard (of adding machine, etc.).

inscriptible [ɛ̃skriptibl̩], *a.* (*a*) *Geom:* inscribable; (*b*) **nom. i. dans une liste,** name suitable for entering on a list.

inscription [ɛ̃skripsjɔ̃], *s.f.* **1.** (*a*) writing down, inscribing; entering, recording (in diary, account book, etc.); **i. des détails sur qch.,** taking down, noting, entering, of the details of sth.; (*b*) registration, enrolling, enrolment; **droit d'i.,** registration fee, entrance fee; **feuille d'i.,** entry form; **prendre son i.,** to enter one's name; *Jur:* **i. hypothécaire,** registry, registration, of mortgages; **propriété libre de toute i.,** unencumbered estate; **i. de faux,** plea of forgery; *Rail:* **i. des colis, des bagages,** booking, registration, of luggage; (*c*) *Sch:* entry; matriculation; **prendre ses inscriptions à l'université** = (i) to enter, matriculate, (ii) to follow a course, at the university; (*d*) *Fr. Navy:* **i. maritime,** seaboard conscription, seamen's registration, for the navy; (*e*) *Rail:* **i. des courbes,** taking of curves (by train); (*f*) *Rec: A:* **i. sur cire,** wax recording. **2.** (*a*) inscription (on tomb, etc.); entry (in account book, etc.); **i. marginale,** marginal note; **i. en creux, en**

relief, sunken, embossed, lettering; (*b*) directions (on signpost, etc.); notice. 3. (*a*) *Fin:* scrip; **i. sur le grand-livre,** (French) Treasury scrip; (*b*) *St.Exch:* **i. à la cote,** quotation in the list.

inscrire [ɛ̃skriːr], *v.tr.* (*pr.p.* **inscrivant;** *p.p.* **inscrit;** *pr.ind.* **j'inscris, il inscrit, n. inscrivons;** *p.d.* **j'inscrivais;** *p.h.* **j'inscrivis;** *fu.* **j'inscrirai)** 1. (*a*) to inscribe, write down; **i. tous les détails sur son carnet,** to write down, enter, take down, all the details in one's note-book; **inscrivez-moi pour cent francs,** put me down for a hundred francs; **i. une question à l'ordre du jour,** to place a question on the agenda; *Sch:* **les matières inscrites au programme,** the subjects prescribed; (*b*) to register (marriage, etc.); to enrol (s.o.); to enter (s.o.'s) name; **se faire i. à un cours,** to enter, put down, one's name, to enrol, register, for a course; **se faire i. pour un concours,** to go in for a competition; **je suis inscrit pour le concours,** I am entered for the competition; *Ind:* **i. (un employé) à l'arrivée,** to book in (an employee); **i. l'heure de sortie (d'un employé),** to book out . . .; *War Adm:* (*rationing*) **s'inscrire chez un commerçant,** to register with a tradesman; *Fin:* **valeur inscrite à la cote officielle,** listed stock; **valeur non inscrite,** unlisted stock; **la dette inscrite,** the Consolidated Debt. 2. to inscribe, engrave (epitaph, etc.). 3. *Geom:* to inscribe (triangle, etc.) **(dans, in).**

s'inscrire, (*a*) to put down one's name; (*b*) to have oneself registered; *Jur:* **s'i. en faux contre qch.,** to indict sth. as false, to dispute the validity of sth.; (*c*) *Rail:* **la machine devra s'i. sans difficultés en courbes de 150 mètres de rayon,** the engine should take curves of 150 metres radius without any difficulty; (*d*) **cette décision s'inscrit dans le cadre de la politique gouvernementale,** this decision fits into, is in keeping with, the general pattern of the government's policy.

inscrit, -ite [ɛ̃skri, -it]. 1. *a.* (*a*) *Mth:* inscribed; (*b*) enrolled, registered (voter, etc.). 2. (*a*) *s.* registered voter; (*b*) *s.m. Navy:* **i. maritime,** seaman registered for service in the navy.

inscrivant [ɛ̃skrivɑ̃], *a. Jur:* that requires registration (for mortgage).

inscrutabilité [ɛ̃skrytabilite], *s.f.* inscrutability, inscrutableness; unfathomableness (of divine purposes, etc.).

inscrutable [ɛ̃skrytabl̩], *a.* inscrutable, unfathomable.

inscrutablement [ɛ̃skrytabləmɑ̃], *adv.* inscrutably.

insculper [ɛ̃skylpe], *v.tr.* to stamp; to hallmark.

insécabilité [ɛ̃sekabilite], *s.f.* indivisibility.

insécable [ɛ̃sekabl̩], *a.* indivisible.

insecouable [ɛ̃səkwabl̩], *a.* unshak(e)able.

insectarium [ɛ̃sɛktarjɔm], *s.m.* insectarium.

insecte [ɛ̃sɛkt], *s.m. Ent:* insect; **les insectes,** Insecta; **i.(-)brindille,** stick insect.

insecticide [ɛ̃sɛktisid], *a. & s.m.* insecticide, insect killer; **poudre i.,** insect powder.

insectier [ɛ̃sɛktje], *s.m.* specimen case (for insects).

insectifuge [ɛ̃sɛktifyːʒ], *a. & s.m.* insectifuge, insect repellant.

insectillice [ɛ̃sɛktilis], *a.* insect-attracting.

insectivore [ɛ̃sɛktivoːr], *Z:* 1. *a.* insectivorous. 2. *s.m.* insect eater, insectivore; *pl.* **insectivores,** Insectivora.

insectologie [ɛ̃sɛktɔlɔʒi], *s.f.* insectology.

insécurité [ɛ̃sekyrite], *s.f.* insecurity.

in-seize [insɛːz], *a. & s.m.inv. Typ:* (in) sixteenmo.

inselberg [inselbɛrg], *s.m. Geol:* inselberg.

inséminateur, -trice [ɛ̃seminatœːr, -tris], *s.m. & f.* inseminator.

insémination [ɛ̃seminasjɔ̃], *s.f.* **i. (artificielle),** (artificial) insemination.

inséminé [ɛ̃semine], *a. Bot:* seedless (fruit).

inséminer [ɛ̃semine], *v.tr.* to inseminate (artificially).

insénescence [ɛ̃senɛs(s)ɑ̃ːs], *s.f. Biol:* senescence.

insensé, -ée [ɛ̃sɑ̃se], *a.* (*a*) mad, insane; *s.* madman, -woman; (*b*) senseless, insensate, stupid, foolish (action, etc.); **c'est i. qu'il sorte par le temps qu'il fait,** it is sheer madness for him to go out in this weather; (*c*) rash, extravagant, wild, *F:* hare-brained (scheme, etc.).

insensément [ɛ̃sɑ̃semɑ̃], *adv.* madly; senselessly.

insensibilisateur [ɛ̃sɑ̃sibilizatœːr], *s.m. Med:* 1. anaesthetic. 2. anaesthetizing apparatus.

insensibilisation [ɛ̃sɑ̃sibilizasjɔ̃], *s.f.* insensibilization; anaesthetization.

insensibiliser [ɛ̃sɑ̃sibilize], *v.tr. Med:* to insensibilize, anaesthetize.

insensibilité [ɛ̃sɑ̃sibilite], *s.f.* insensitiveness; (*a*) insensibility; (*b*) indifference, callousness **(envers,** to); (*c*) (sexual) coldness; frigidity; (*d*) **i. aux couleurs,** colour-blindness; (*e*) lack of sensitiveness (of boiler-governor, etc.); **i. au magnétisme,** insensitiveness to magnetism.

insensible [ɛ̃sɑ̃sibl̩], *a.* insensible. 1. (*a*) insensitive, insensate, insentient; (*b*) indifferent **(à,** to); unfeeling; callous **(à,** to); **il est i. au froid,** he is insensible, indifferent, to cold; he doesn't feel the cold; **i. à la flatterie,** proof against flattery; **il se montra i. à toutes leurs prières,** he was deaf to all their prayers; (*c*) **i. à l'amour,** insensible to love; frigid; (*d*) **i. aux couleurs,** colour-blind; (*e*) *Equit:* hard-mouthed (horse); hard (mouth). 2. imperceptible; hardly perceptible (difference, etc.).

insensiblement [ɛ̃sɑ̃sibləmɑ̃], *adv.* imperceptibly, by slow degress, insensibly.

insensitif, -ive [ɛ̃sɑ̃sitif, -iːv], *a. W.Tel: O:* insensitive (spot on crystal).

inséparabilité [ɛ̃separabilite], *s.f.* inseparability, inseparableness.

inséparable [ɛ̃separabl̩]. 1. *a.* inseparable; *s.* **ce sont deux inséparables,** they are always together, they are inseparable. 2. *s.m.pl. Orn:* lovebirds.

inséparablement [ɛ̃separabləmɑ̃], *adv.* inseparably.

inséquent [ɛ̃sekɑ̃], *a. Geol:* insequent.

insérable [ɛ̃serabl̩], *a.* insertable.

insérer [ɛ̃sere], *v.tr.* **(j'insère, n. insérons; j'insérerai)** to insert; **i. une clause dans un contrat,** to insert a clause in an agreement; **i. une annonce dans un journal,** to insert, put, an advertisement in a paper; **prière d'i.,** (i) for publication (in your columns); (ii) *F:* publisher's blurb (accompanying review copies); **prière d'i. dans les journaux belges,** Belgian papers please copy.

s'insérer, (*a*) to be attached to; (*b*) to fit in.

insermenté [ɛ̃sɛrmɑ̃te], *a. & s.m. Hist:* non-juring (priest).

insertion [ɛ̃sɛrsjɔ̃], *s.f.* 1. insertion; **tarif des insertions,** advertising rates; *El:* **i. des résistances,** switching-in of resistances. 2. *Anat: Needlew: etc:* insertion. 3. *Tchn:* insert. 4. *Pol:* **i. sociale,** sociological integration.

insexué [ɛ̃sɛksɥe], **insexuel, -elle** [ɛ̃sɛksɥɛl], *a.* asexual.

insidieusement [ɛ̃sidjøzmɑ̃], *adv.* insidiously.

insidieux, -euse [ɛ̃sidjø, -øːz], *a.* (*a*) insidious (advice, disease); (*b*) crafty (lawyer); (*c*) **remarques insidieuses,** insidious remarks.

insigne[1] [ɛ̃siɲ], *a.* 1. distinguished, remarkable, conspicuous; **général i. par ses services,** general distinguished for his services; **faveur i.,** signal favour. 2. *Pej:* notorious; arrant (liar, etc.); **traître i.,** arch-traitor; **indiscrétion i.,** blazing, glaring, indiscretion; **mensonge i.,** glaring lie.

insigne[2], *s.m.* distinguishing mark; badge; **i. sportif,** sporting emblem; badge; **insignes (de la royauté, etc.),** insignia (of royalty, etc.); *Mil:* **i. de grade,** badge of rank; **i. (d'officier d'état-major),** tab.

insignifiance [ɛ̃siɲifjɑ̃ːs], *s.f.* 1. insignificance, unimportance. 2. vacuousness (of speech, etc.).

insignifiant [ɛ̃siɲifjɑ̃], *a.* 1. insignificant, unimportant; nominal (rent); trivial, trifling (loss, sum). 2. vacuous (face, remark).

insincère [ɛ̃sɛ̃sɛːr], *a.* insincere.

insincérité [ɛ̃sɛ̃serite], *s.f.* insincerity.

insinuant [ɛ̃sinɥɑ̃], *a.* insinuating, insinuative; **manières insinuantes,** ingratiating manner.

insinuatif, -ive [ɛ̃sinɥatif, -iːv], *a. A:* insinuative.

insinuation [ɛ̃sinɥasjɔ̃], *s.f.* insinuation. 1. introduction (*e.g.* of probe into wound). 2. innuendo.

insinuer [ɛ̃sinɥe], *v.tr.* to insinuate. 1. to introduce, insert (gently); **i. le doigt dans une plaie,** to introduce one's finger into a wound, to probe a wound with one's finger; **i. de bons principes à qn,** to instil good principles into s.o. 2. to hint at (sth.); **que voulez-vous i.?** what are you hinting at? *F:* what are you getting at? **i. à qn que . . .,** to insinuate to s.o. that . . .; **i. à qn de faire qch.,** to insinuate, give a hint, to s.o. that he ought to do sth.

s'insinuer, (*a*) to penetrate; to creep in, into; to steal in, into; **s'i. dans les bonnes grâces de qn,** to insinuate oneself into s.o.'s favour; **s'i. à la cour,** to worm one's way into court circles; **l'eau s'insinue partout,** water penetrates, permeates, everywhere; **s'i. entre les voitures,** to thread one's way through the traffic; (*b*) *Rac:* to nick in.

insipide [ɛ̃sipid], *a.* insipid; (*a*) tasteless (dish, etc.); (*b*) dull, flat, uninteresting (conversation, etc.); tame (story, ending); **quel dénouement i.!** what a flat, wishy-washy, ending!

insipidité [ɛ̃sipidite], *s.f.* insipidity, insipidness; (*a*) tastelessness (of food, etc.); (*b*) dullness, flatness (of conversation); tameness (of ending, etc.).

insistance [ɛ̃sistɑ̃ːs], *s.f.* insistence **(à faire qch.,** on doing sth.); **mettre une grande i. à qch., à faire qch.,** to insist strongly on sth., on doing sth.; **avec i.,** emphatically, insistently; **il affirme avec i. l'avoir vu,** he insists that he saw it; *Ling:* **accent d'i.,** emphasis (on a word or syllable).

insistant [ɛ̃sistɑ̃], *a.* insistent; stubborn; *Orn:* **pouce i.,** insistent hind toe.

insister [ɛ̃siste], *v.i.* to insist; **i. sur un fait,** to dwell, lay stress, on a fact; **je n'insisterai pas là-dessus,** I will not labour the point; **on a trop insisté sur ces détails,** these details have been overstressed; **on n'insistera jamais assez là-dessus,** this cannot be over-emphasized; one cannot accord too much importance to this; **i. sur ses demandes,** to stand out for, insist on, persist in, one's claims; **i. sur les avantages de . . .,** to dwell on the advantages of . . .; **i. pour avoir une réponse immédiate,** to press for an immediate answer; **i. pour,** *A:* **à, faire qch.,** to insist on doing sth.; **i. pour que qch. se fasse,** to insist on sth. being done, that sth. should be done; **i. auprès de qn,** to take a matter up strongly with s.o.; **i. auprès de qn sur la nécessité de faire qch.,** to urge on s.o. the necessity of doing sth.; **n'insistez pas trop,** don't be too insistent; don't push the matter too far.

insobriété [ɛ̃sɔbri(j)ete], *s.f. A:* insobriety; intemperance.

insociabilité [ɛ̃sɔsjabilite], *s.f.* unsociability, insociability, unsociableness.

insociable [ɛ̃sɔsjabl̩], *a.* unsociable.

insocial, -aux [ɛ̃sɔsjal, -o], *a.* unsocial; **les insociaux,** the social misfits.

in-soixante-douze [inswasɑ̃tduːz], *a. & s.m.inv. Typ:* (in) seventy-twomo.

in-soixante-quatre [inswasɑ̃tkatr̩], *a. & s.m.inv. Typ:* (in) sixty-fourmo.

insolateur [ɛ̃sɔlatœːr], *s.m.* solar furnace.

insolation [ɛ̃sɔlasjɔ̃], *s.f.* insolation. 1. (*a*) *Phot: O:* daylight printing; (*b*) sun-bathing; treatment of disease by sun-baths. 2. (*a*) *Med:* insolation, sunstroke; **être frappé d'i.,** to get a touch of the sun; to succumb to the heat; (*b*) *Hort: Arb:* sun scald; (*c*) *Arb:* **fente d'i.,** sun crack. 3. (*amount of solar heat received by the earth*) insolation.

insolemment [ɛ̃sɔlamɑ̃], *adv.* insolently; impudently.

insolence [ɛ̃sɔlɑ̃ːs], *s.f.* 1. insolence; (*a*) impertinence; impudence; **répondre avec i.,** to answer insolently; (*b*) overbearing manner, arrogance. 2. **c'est une i. de sa part,** it is a piece of impudence on his part; **trêve d'insolences!** enough of your insolence!

insolent, -ente [ɛ̃sɔlɑ̃, -ɑ̃t]. 1. *a.* (*a*) insolent, impertinent, impudent, *F:* cheeky **(envers, avec,** to); (*b*) overbearing (in victory, success); (*c*) extraordinary, that defies all bounds; **étaler une santé insolente,** to be bursting with health; **luxe i.,** indecent, blatant, luxury. 2. *s.* insolent fellow, impudent girl, woman.

insoler [ɛ̃sɔle], *v.tr.* to insolate; to expose (sth.) to the sun; *Phot: O:* to print by daylight.

s'insoler, to sunbathe.

insolidité [ɛ̃sɔlidite], *s.f.* insolidity, unsoundness.

insolite [ɛ̃sɔlit], *a.* unusual, unwonted; strange; peculiar; **mots nouveaux et insolites,** new and strange words; **bruit i.,** strange, extraordinary, noise; **tenue i. pour la saison,** odd, strange, clothes for the time of year.

insolubiliser [ɛ̃sɔlybilize], *v.tr.* to render insoluble.

insolubilité [ɛ̃sɔlybilite], *s.f.* 1. insolubility (of substance). 2. insolubleness, insolvability, unsolvableness (of problem).

insoluble [ɛ̃sɔlybl̩], *a.* 1. insoluble (substance). 2. insoluble, insolvable, unsolvable; **problème i. à l'esprit humain,** problem insoluble by the human mind; **situation i.,** deadlock.

insolvabilité [ɛ̃sɔlvabilite], *s.f. Com:* insolvency; *Jur:* **acte manifeste d'i. (entraînant la faillite),** act of bankruptcy.

insolvable [ɛ̃sɔlvabl̩], *a. Com:* insolvent.

insomniaque [ɛ̃sɔmnjak]. 1. *a.* sleepless; suffering from insomnia. 2. *s.m. & f.* insomniac.

insomnie [ɛ̃sɔmni], *s.f.* 1. insomnia, sleeplessness, wakefulness; **nuit d'i.,** sleepless night. 2. **fréquentes insomnies,** frequent fits of insomnia.

insomnieux, -ieuse [ɛ̃sɔmnjø, -jøːz]. 1. *s.* insomniac. 2. *a.* sleepless; suffering from insomnia.

insondabilité [ɛ̃sɔ̃dabilite], *s.f.* 1. unsoundableness, unfathomableness (of ocean, etc.). 2. unfathomability, unfathomable nature (of mystery, etc.).

insondable [ɛ̃sɔ̃dabl̩], *a.* 1. unsoundable, unfathomable, fathomless (ocean, etc.); bottomless (pit). 2. unfathomable (mystery); impenetrable,

incomprehensible (grief). **3.** immense, infinite; **bêtise i.,** abysmal stupidity; **une i. maladresse,** unbelievable, unimaginable, clumsiness.

insondé [ɛ̃sɔ̃de], *a.* unfathomed, unprobed (abyss, mystery, etc.).

insonore [ɛ̃sɔnɔːr], *a. Cin: etc:* **1.** soundproof (studio, etc.). **2.** insulating, sound-absorbing (material).

insonorisation [ɛ̃sɔnɔrizasjɔ̃], *s.f. Cin: etc:* sound damping; insulation (of sound camera); soundproofing.

insonorisé [ɛ̃sɔnɔrize], *a.* sound-proof(ed).

insonoriser [ɛ̃sɔnɔrize], *v.tr. Cin: W.Tel: etc:* to insulate, sound-proof (studio, etc.).

insonorité [ɛ̃sɔnɔrite], *s.f.* lack of sonority.

insouciamment [ɛ̃susjamɑ̃], *adv.* unconcernedly; heedlessly; jauntily.

insouciance [ɛ̃susjɑ̃ːs], *s.f.* (*a*) freedom from care; unconcern, insouciance; jauntiness; **avec i.,** unconcernedly; jauntily; (*b*) thoughtlessness, casualness.

insouciant [ɛ̃susjɑ̃], *a.* (*a*) careless, free from care, unconcerned, insouciant; jaunty (air, manner); **l'enfance insouciante,** carefree childhood; **i. du péril,** careless of danger; (*b*) insouciant, thoughtless, casual, remiss, easy-going; *s.* **c'est un i., une insouciante,** he's, she's, an irresponsible, easy-going, person.

insoucieusement [ɛ̃susjøzmɑ̃], *adv.* inconcernedly; heedlessly; jauntily.

insoucieux, -euse [ɛ̃susjø, -øːz], *a.* heedless (**de,** of); **être i. du lendemain,** to give no thought to the morrow; **i. de l'avenir,** regardless of the future; **i. de ses intérêts,** neglectful of his interests; **leur gaieté insoucieuse,** their irresponsible gaiety.

insoudable [ɛ̃sudabl̩], *a. Metalw:* that cannot be welded, soldered; not weldable.

insouffrable [ɛ̃sufrabl̩], *a. F:* insufferable, unbearable (person); intolerable (behaviour).

insoumis, -ise [ɛ̃sumi, -iːz], *a.* **1.** unsubdued, unsubjugated (people, etc.). **2.** (*a*) unsubmissive, refractory, unruly, intractable (child, etc.); **jeunesse insoumise,** rebellious youth; (*b*) *a. & s.m. Mil:* absentee (conscript or reservist); (*c*) *a. & s.f. Adm: A:* **(fille) insoumise,** unregistered prostitute.

insoumission [ɛ̃sumisjɔ̃], *s.f.* insubordination, unsubmissiveness; *Mil:* failure (of conscript or reservist) to join or rejoin the colours; *Adm: A:* failure to register (on the part of a prostitute).

insoupçonnable [ɛ̃supsɔnabl̩], *a.* beyond suspicion; above suspicion.

insoupçonné [ɛ̃supsɔne], *a.* unsuspected (**de,** by); **richesses insoupçonnées,** undreamt-of, unthought-of, wealth.

insoutenable [ɛ̃sutnabl̩], *a.* **1.** untenable (opinion, position, etc.); unwarrantable, unmaintainable (assertion, etc.); indefensible (position, etc.). **2.** unbearable, insupportable, unendurable (agony, etc.).

inspecter [ɛ̃spɛkte], *v.tr.* to inspect (troops, school, works, etc.); to survey (field of battle, etc.).

inspecteur, -trice [ɛ̃spɛktœːr, -tris], *s.* inspector (of schools); inspector (of police, etc.); overseer (of works, etc.); shop-walker; surveyor (of mines, etc.); **i. de la sûreté,** detective inspector; **i. du travail,** factory inspector; **i. des mines,** inspector of mines; **i. sanitaire,** (i) public-health officer; (ii) sanitary inspector; **i. des contributions directes,** assessor, inspector, of taxes; **i. des contributions indirectes** = inspector of Customs and Excise; *Jur:* **magistrat inspecteur,** visiting magistrate; *Mil: etc:* **i. général,** inspector general; *Rail:* **i. de mouvement,** section superintendent; *Sch:* **i. d'Académie,** school inspector (one is assigned to each *departement* = H.M.I.); **i. (de l'Enseignement) primaire,** primary-school inspector (one is assigned to each *arrondissement*).

inspection [ɛ̃spɛksjɔ̃], *s.f.* **1.** (*a*) inspection, inspecting; examination, examining; survey; *Mil:* muster parade; **faire l'i. de,** to inspect, examine; **passer l'i. (d'une compagnie, etc.),** to inspect (a company, etc.); *Adm:* **i. du travail,** factory inspection; **ordre d'i.,** inspecting order; (*b*) tour of inspection. **2.** inspectorship, inspectorate; **obtenir une i.,** to receive an appointment as inspector, to be appointed inspector. **3.** body, board, of inspectors; inspectorate.

inspectorat [ɛ̃spɛktɔra], *s.m. Adm:* inspectorate. **1.** inspectorship. **2.** *coll.* the body, board, of inspectors.

inspirant [ɛ̃spirɑ̃], *a.* inspiring (example, etc.).

inspirateur, -trice [ɛ̃spiratœːr, -tris]. **1.** *a.* (*a*) *Anat:* inspiratory (muscle, etc.); (*b*) inspiring (thought, etc.). **2.** *s.* (*a*) inspirer (of a deed, of a person); instigator (of plot); the man, woman, behind (the movement, etc.); (*b*) (*thg*) inspiring force.

inspiration [ɛ̃spirasjɔ̃], *s.f.* inspiration. **1.** *Physiol:* inspiration, breathing in, inhaling. **2.** (*a*) suggestion, prompting; **sous l'i. du moment,** on the spur of the moment; **il a eu l'heureuse i. de . . .,** he had the happy idea of . . . (+ *ger.*); **i. soudaine,** sudden inspiration, *F:* brainwave; **se diriger par les inspirations des autres,** to act on the suggestions of others; (*b*) **poésie pleine d'i.,** inspired verse.

inspiratoire [ɛ̃spiratwaːr], *a. Physiol:* inspiratory.

inspiré, -ée [ɛ̃spire]. **1.** *a.* (*a*) inspired (writing, poet, etc.); (*b*) **bien, mal, i.,** well advised; ill advised. **2.** *s.* mystic; visionary; fanatic.

inspirer [ɛ̃spire], *v.tr.* to inspire. **1.** (*a*) to breathe into; **i. de l'air dans les poumons d'un noyé,** to breathe, pump, air into the lungs of a drowned man; (*b*) **i. qch. à qn,** to inspire s.o. with sth.; **i. l'amour de la beauté à qn,** to inspire s.o. with a love of beauty; **i. du courage aux troupes,** to inspire the troops with courage; **i. une idée à qn,** to instil an idea into s.o.; **i. le respect,** to inspire respect; *A:* **i. à qn de faire qch.,** to prompt s.o. to do sth.; **i. la révolte,** to instigate rebellion; (*c*) **i. qn,** to inspire s.o., to give inspiration to s.o.; to prompt s.o. to action; **inspiré par la jalousie,** prompted, actuated, by jealousy; **la muse qui m'a inspiré,** the Muse to whom I owe my inspiration; (*d*) **être inspiré de faire qch.,** to be inspired to do sth.; (*e*) **inspiré de,** inspired by; **contes inspirés de la vie des animaux,** tales drawn from, inspired by, animal life; **régime inspiré du principe de liberté,** régime imbued with the spirit of liberty. **2.** to breathe in, inhale (air, smoke, etc.).

s'inspirer de qn, de qch., to take, draw, one's inspiration from s.o., from sth.

instabilité [ɛ̃stabilite], *s.f.* instability; (*a*) shakiness, unsteadiness; *Nau:* crankiness (of ship); (*b*) inconstancy, fickleness, uncertainty (of fortune, etc.); precariousness (of situation); flightiness (of disposition); **éléments d'i. (dans le cours des changes, etc.),** disturbing factors (in the rate of exchange, etc.); (*c*) *Ch:* instability, lability (of salt, etc.); (*d*) *Psy: Med:* instability; **i. mentale,** mental instability.

instable [ɛ̃stabl̩]. **1.** *a.* (*a*) shaky, unsteady, *F:* wobbly (table, etc.); *Nau:* unstable, cranky (ship); **équilibre i.,** unstable equilibrium; **gouvernement i.,** unstable, shaky, government; (*b*) unstable, unreliable (person, nature, etc.); flighty (disposition); wavering (politician, etc.); **population i.,** shifting population; (*c*) changeable (weather); (*d*) *Ch:* unstable, labile (salt, etc.); (*e*) *Elcs:* astable; (*f*) *Med:* **diabète i.,** uncontrolled diabetes. **2.** *s.m. & f.* (*a*) unreliable, capricious, person; (*b*) (emotionally) unstable person.

instablement [ɛ̃stabləmɑ̃], *adv.* unsteadily.

installage [ɛ̃stalaːʒ], *s.m. Mil:* = kit inspection.

installateur [ɛ̃stalatœːr], *s.m.* **1.** *Ecc:* inductor (of prelate). **2.** *Ind:* fitter; installer (of central heating, etc.).

installateur-décorateur [ɛ̃stalatœrdekɔratœːr], *s.m.* = plumber and decorator, *F:* builder; *pl. installateurs-décorateurs.*

installation [ɛ̃stalasjɔ̃], *s.f.* installation. **1.** installing; (*a*) **i. d'un juge, d'un évêque,** installation of a judge, of a bishop; **i. d'un curé,** induction of a *curé*; (*b*) setting up (of machine, etc.); fitting up, equipping, equipment (of workshop); fixing (of curtains, etc.); **i. du chauffage central, de l'électricité,** installation of central heating, of electricity; (*c*) *Nau:* stowing (of gear, etc.); (*d*) setting up house; **fêter son i.,** to give a house-warming party. **2.** (*a*) appointments (of flat, etc.); fittings, equipment (of workshop, etc.); **installations sanitaires,** sanitary arrangements; **installations électriques,** electrical equipment, fittings, installations; **venez voir mon i.,** come and see how I've fitted up my flat, house, etc.; (*b*) *Ind: etc:* plant; unit; equipment; fittings; **i. d'aérage, de forge,** ventilation plant, forging plant; **i. d'épuration,** purifying plant; **i. frigorifique,** refrigerating plant; *Min:* **i. de forage,** boring plant, drilling rig; **installations de surface,** surface equipment; *Aut:* **i. de lavage,** washing bay; **i. d'éclairage,** lighting plant; **i. (de lumière) électrique,** electric (light) installation, plant; **i. téléphonique,** telephone installation; **i. téléphonique privée,** private (telephone) exchange; *Elcs:* **installations radar,** radar installations, facilities; **i. (de) radio(télégraphie),** wireless, radio, installation, station, set; *Av:* **installations aériennes,** air installations; **installations au sol,** ground installations, facilities; **installations de contrôle aérien,** air-control installations, facilities; *Nau:* **installations à bord,** ship's equipment, installations; **installations à terre,** shore equipment, installations; **installations de pont,** deck fittings; **installations portuaires,** port installations, facilities; harbour facilities; **installations de carénage,** docking installations, facilities; **installations de chargement et de déchargement des navires,** ship-loading and -unloading facilities; **installations de déchargement des pétroliers,** tanker-discharge facilities; **installations assurant la rotation des navires, permettant aux navires de reprendre la mer,** turn-round facilities; *Nau: Av: etc:* **installations de sauvetage,** rescue equipment; *Rail:* **i. de chargement et de déchargement des wagons,** rail loading and unloading facilities.

installé [ɛ̃stale], *a. F:* in a comfortable position, comfortably off.

installer [ɛ̃stale], *v.tr.* to install; (*a*) **i. un président, un évêque,** to install a president, a bishop; **i. un curé,** to induct a *curé*; (*b*) **i. qn dans un fauteuil,** to make s.o. comfortable in an armchair; *F:* **installez-vous!** make yourself at home! *Mil:* **i. une batterie sur une hauteur,** to plant a battery on a height; (*c*) to set up, install (machine, etc.); to fit up, equip (factory, etc.); to fix (curtains, etc.); **chambres installées avec tout le confort moderne,** rooms fitted with all modern conveniences; **maison bien installée,** well-appointed house; (*d*) to establish, arrange, settle; **i. qn dans une maison,** to establish s.o. in a house; **i. sa famille à la campagne,** to settle one's family in the country; (*e*) *Nau:* to stow (gear, etc.); (*f*) *v.i. P:* **en i.,** to show off.

s'installer, to install oneself; to settle (down); to make oneself at home, *F:* to park oneself; **s'i. dans un fauteuil,** to settle oneself in an armchair; **s'i. à la campagne,** to go and live, to settle, in the country; **s'i. comme médecin,** to set up as a doctor; **s'i. dans le mensonge,** to be caught up in a chain of lies.

installeur [ɛ̃stalœːr], *s.m. F:* swank.

instaminé [ɛ̃stamine], *a. Bot:* without stamens.

instamment [ɛ̃stamɑ̃], *adv.* (to request) insistently, earnestly; (to beg) hard; **on demande i. un médecin,** a doctor is urgently required; **le parti travailliste demande i. que l'on prenne une décision,** the Labour Party is pressing for a decision.

instance [ɛ̃stɑ̃ːs], *s.f.* **1.** (*a*) (i) *A:* instancy, solicitation; (ii) **demander qch. à qn avec i.,** to beg, plead with, s.o. for sth.; (*b*) *pl.* requests, entreaties; **devant les instances de sa famille de,** as his family begged, *F:* badgered, him to; under pressure from his family to; **céder aux instances de qn,** to yield, give away, to s.o.'s requests; (*c*) *Jur:* process, suit; **introduire une i. (en justice),** to institute an action, proceedings; **introduire une i. en divorce,** to start divorce proceedings; **affaire en i.,** case on the cause list; **pièces en i.,** documents pertaining to the case (before the court); **tribunal d'i.** = magistrate's court; **tribunal de grande i.,** *A:* **de première i.** = county court; **juge d'i.** = Justice of the Peace; police-court magistrate; **acquitté en seconde i.,** acquitted on appeal; (*d*) authority; **les instances internationales,** international authorities. **2.** immediacy; **proposition de loi en i.,** bill on the eve of presentation; **être en i. de départ pour . . .,** to be on the point of departure, about to leave, for . . .; **étudiant en i. de congé,** student on the point of going on holiday; **soldat en i. de réforme,** soldier awaiting discharge; **aucune décision n'a été prise; tout est encore en i.,** no decision has been taken; everything is still pending, still under discussion. **3.** *Psy:* instance.

instant[1] [ɛ̃stɑ̃], *a.* pressing, urgent; **péril i.,** imminent danger.

instant[2], *s.m.* moment, instant; **à chaque i., à tout i.,** continually, at every moment; **par instants,** off and on, on and off, from time to time; **un i. de délai,** a moment's delay; **c'est l'affaire d'un i.,** it won't take a moment; **il ne se demanda pas un i. ce qui pourrait en résulter,** he never once asked himself what the outcome might be; **pendant un i. personne ne bougea,** for a moment nobody moved; **un i.!** wait a moment! wait a bit! just a moment! *adv.phr.* **à l'i.,** (i) a moment ago; (ii) immediately, at once; **je l'apprends à l'i.,** I have only just heard of it; **je descends à l'i.,** I'll be down in a moment; **toujours prêt à partir à l'i.,** always ready to start at short notice, at a moment's notice; **je l'attends d'un i. à l'autre,** I expect him any minute, at any moment; **je l'ai vu il y a un i.,** I saw him a moment ago; **pour l'i.,**

for the moment; **dans un i.**, in a (short) while; **en un i.**, in no time, quickly, swiftly; **un soin de tous les instants**, unremitting, ceaseless, care; **dès l'i. que** + *ind.*, (i) from the moment when . . .; (ii) since, seeing that . . ..

instantané [ɛ̃stɑ̃tane]. **1.** *a.* instantaneous (death, etc.); sudden (fright, etc.); *El:* **valeur instantanée**, instantaneous value. **2.** *s.m. Phot:* snapshot.

instantanéité [ɛ̃stɑ̃taneite], *s.f.* instantaneousness, instantaneity.

instantanément [ɛ̃stɑ̃tanemɑ̃], *adv.* instantaneously; at once, (done) in a moment.

instar de (à l') [alɛ̃stardə], *prep.phr.* after the fashion, manner, of; like; **coiffure à l'i. des Grecs**, hair dressed in imitation of the Greeks, in Greek fashion; **à l'i. de Narcisse je regardais . . .**, like Narcissus I looked at . . ..

instaurateur, -trice [ɛ̃stɔratœːr, -tris], *s.* founder, establisher.

instauration [ɛ̃stɔrasjɔ̃], *s.f.* founding (of republic, of liberty); setting up.

instaurer [ɛ̃stɔre], *v.tr.* to found (research centre, etc.); to set up (form of worship, republic, etc.); **i. des mesures, une méthode**, to initiate, adopt, measures, a method; **i. le règne de la justice**, to establish a reign of justice.

instigateur, -trice [ɛ̃stigatœːr, -tris], *s.* instigator (**de**, of); inciter (**de**, to); **qui a été l'i. de ce crime?** who is at the bottom of this crime?

instigation [ɛ̃stigasjɔ̃], *s.f.* instigation, incitement (**à**, to); **agir, faire qch., à l'i. de qn**, to act, to do sth., at, on, s.o.'s instigation, on s.o.'s advice, under the influence of s.o.

instiguer [ɛ̃stige], *v.tr.* (*a*) *A:* **i. qn à faire qch.**, to incite, prompt, s.o. to do sth.; (*b*) (*in Belgium*) to instigate.

instillation [ɛ̃stilasjɔ̃], *s.f. Med:* instillation (of drops).

instiller [ɛ̃stile], *v.tr.* (*a*) *Med:* to instil; **i. une lotion dans l'œil**, to drop some lotion into the eye; (*b*) **i. le courage à qn**, to instil courage into s.o.

instinct [ɛ̃stɛ̃], *s.m.* instinct; **les animaux ont l'i. de (leur propre) conservation**, animals have the instinct of self-preservation; **avoir l'i. de la musique**, to have a natural aptitude for music; *adv.phr.* **par i., d'i.**, by instinct, instinctively.

instinctif, -ive [ɛ̃stɛ̃ktif, -iːv], *a.* instinctive.

instinctivement [ɛ̃stɛ̃ktivmɑ̃], *adv.* instinctively, by instinct.

instinctuel, -elle [ɛ̃stɛ̃ktyɛl], *a.* instinctual.

institué, -ée [ɛ̃stitɥe], *s. Jur:* legatee, devisee.

instituer [ɛ̃stitɥe], *v.tr.* to institute; (*a*) to establish, set up, found (institution, etc.); to lay down (a rule); **i. une enquête**, to institute an inquiry; **i. des poursuites contre qn**, to institute, initiate, proceedings against s.o.; (*b*) to appoint (official, etc.); *Jur:* **i. un héritier**, to appoint an heir; *pred.* **i. qn héritier**, to appoint s.o. as one's heir, to institute s.o.; (*c*) to initiate (experiment).

s'instituer, (*of custom, etc.*) to become established.

institut [ɛ̃stity], *s.m.* **1.** institute, institution; **l'I. (national de France)**, the Institute (composed of the five Academies). **2.** *Ecc:* (*a*) (monastic) order; (*b*) rule (of monastic order). **3.** *Sch:* institute, institution, college. **4. i. de coupe**, (high-class) tailoring establishment; **i. de beauté**, beauty parlour.

institutes [ɛ̃stityt], *s.f.pl. Jur:* **les I. de Justinien**, the Institutes of Justinian.

instituteur, -trice [ɛ̃stitytœːr, -tris], *s.* **1.** *A:* founder, foundress, institutor (of religious order, of hospital, etc.). **2.** (*a*) (school)teacher, (primary) schoolmaster, schoolmistress; (*b*) *s.f.* **institutrice**, governess; **institutrice à domicile**, visiting governess; **institutrice à demeure**, resident governess.

institution [ɛ̃stitysjɔ̃], *s.f.* institution. **1.** (*a*) instituting, establishing; **usages d'i.**, man-made customs; (*b*) *Jur:* appointing (of heir). **2.** (*thing instituted*) (*a*) **les caisses d'épargne sont une i. utile**, savings banks are a useful institution; (*b*) (*educational, etc.*) establishment; independent, private, school; (*c*) **institutions sociales**, social services; (*d*) *Fr.Adm:* **population des institutions**, the total number of conscripted soldiers in barracks, inmates of mental hospitals, and monks and nuns in religious institutions; (*e*) **les institutions**, the establishment. **3.** *A:* education.

institutionnalisation [ɛ̃stitysjɔnalizasjɔ̃], *s.f.* institutionalization.

institutionnaliser [ɛ̃stitysjɔnalize], *v.tr.* to institutionalize.

institutionnalisme [ɛ̃stitysjɔnalism], *s.m.* institutionalism.

institutionnel, -elle [ɛ̃stitysjɔnɛl], *a.* institutional.

instructeur [ɛ̃stryktœːr]. **1.** *s.m.* instructor, teacher; *Mil:* **sergent i.**, sergeant instructor, drill sergeant; **i. d'équitation**, riding master. **2.** *a. Jur:* **juge i.**, examining magistrate.

instructif, -ive [ɛ̃stryktif, -iːv], *a.* instructive.

instruction [ɛ̃stryksjɔ̃], *s.f.* instruction. **1.** (*a*) direction; guidance; *Elcs:* instruction; *Ecc:* **i. pastorale**, (bishop's) pastoral letter (on a point of doctrine, etc.); (*b*) *pl.* instructions, directions, orders; **instructions permanentes**, standing instructions, orders, *U.S:* standing operation procedure; **conformément aux instructions**, as directed, as requested; *Nau:* **instructions cachetées**, sealed orders; **instructions nautiques**, sailing directions, instructions; **livret d'instructions**, instruction manual (of a car, etc.); **aux termes des instructions qui lui avaient été données, la commission était chargée de . . .**, under its terms of reference the commission was instructed to . . .. **2.** (*a*) education, schooling; *Mil:* training (of troops, etc.); *Mil:* **i. prémilitaire**, preparatory training; **i. pratique, théorique**, practical, educational, training; **programme d'i.**, training syllabus; **degré d'i.**, *Sch:* standard of education; *Mil:* standard of training; *Sch:* **i. primaire**, primary education; **i. professionnelle**, vocational training; **avoir de l'i.**, to be well informed, well educated; **sans i.**, uneducated; (*b*) lesson; **tirer des instructions salutaires de qch.**, to draw useful lessons from sth. **3.** *Jur:* (*a*) preliminary investigation (of case); **ouvrir une i.**, to open a judicial inquiry; **juge d'i.**, examining magistrate; **code d'i. criminelle**, code of criminal procedure; (*b*) **i. écrite**, written statements (of a case).

instruction-machine [ɛ̃stryksjɔ̃maʃin], *s.f. Elcs:* instruction code; *pl. instructions-machines.*

instruire [ɛ̃strɥiːr], *v.tr.* (*pr.p.* **instruisant**; *p.p.* **instruit**; *pr.ind.* **j'instruis, il instruit, n. instruisons**; *p.d.* **j'instruisais**; *p.h.* **j'instruisis**) **1. i. qn de qch.**, to inform s.o. of sth.; **il m'instruisit de sa situation**, he told me how he was situated; **instruit de mon malheur il m'offrit son aide**, having heard of my misfortune he offered to help me. **2.** (*a*) to teach, educate, instruct; **i. qn dans, en, qch., à faire qch.**, to instruct s.o. in sth., how to do sth.; **i. un commis à tenir les livres**, to teach a clerk to keep books, to instruct a clerk in book-keeping; **instruit par l'expérience**, having learnt from experience; (*b*) to train (troops, horse, etc.); to drill (troops). **3.** *Jur:* to examine, investigate (a case); *abs.* **i. contre qn**, to get up the case against s.o.

s'instruire. **1.** to acquire knowledge; to improve one's mind; to educate oneself; **on s'instruit à tout âge**, one can always learn something (new); it's never too late to learn; **homme qui s'est instruit tout seul**, self-educated man. **2.** to get information; **s'i. des circonstances exactes**, to find out the exact circumstances.

instruit [ɛ̃strɥi], *a.* **1.** (*a*) educated, learned; well-read; **homme i.**, scholarly man; man of learning; scholar; **fort i. dans un sujet**, well versed in a subject, *F:* very well up in a subject; **il est un peu i. en physique**, he has some knowledge of physics; **jeune fille très instruite**, highly educated girl; **homme peu i.**, poorly educated man, man who has had little schooling; (*b*) trained (soldier, etc.). **2. i. de qch.**, acquainted with sth.; aware of sth.; **être i. d'une affaire**, to know all about a matter.

instrument [ɛ̃strymɑ̃], *s.m.* instrument; (*a*) implement, tool; **i. tranchant**, edge tool; **i. à finir**, finishing tool, finisher, trimmer; **i. de précision**, precision instrument; **i. de mesure**, measuring instrument; **i. de travail**, implement; **i. de dessin**, drawing instrument; **i. de navigation**, navigation(al) instrument; **i. d'optique**, optical instrument; **instruments nautiques**, nautical instruments; *Artil: Sm.a:* **i. de pointage**, aiming instrument, device; *Av:* **instruments de bord**, (aircraft) instruments, airborne instruments; **les instruments de bord (d'un appareil)**, aircraft instrumentation; **i. à lecture tête haute, tête basse**, head-up, head-down, instrument, display; **approche aux instruments**, instrument approach; **atterrissage aux instruments**, instrument landing; **vol aux instruments**, instrument flying, flight; **règles de vol aux instruments**, instrument flight rules; *Surv:* **i. de levés, i. topographique**, surveying instrument; **i. de nivellement**, levelling instrument; *Surg:* **i. de chirurgie, i. chirurgical**, surgical instrument; **i. coupant, tranchant**, cutting instrument; **i. tranchant à biseau unique, à double biseau**, single-bevelled, bi-bevelled, cutting instrument; **i. rotatif**, rotary instrument; **inventions susceptibles de se transformer en instruments de mort**, inventions that can easily turn into instruments of death; *Lit:* **instruments de guerre**, instruments of war; **servir d'i. à la vengeance de qn**, to serve as the instrument, the tool, of s.o.'s vengeance; **se faire l'i. d'un parti, d'une cause**, to be the upholder of a party, of a cause; (*b*) *Mus:* (musical) instrument; **i. à anche**, reed instrument; **i. à vent**, wind instrument; **i. à cordes**, stringed instrument; (*c*) *Jur:* (legal) instrument (deed, contract, writ, etc.); **i. de mariage**, certificate of marriage; **instruments de paiement légaux**, legal tender.

instrumentaire [ɛ̃strymɑ̃tɛːr], *a. Jur:* **témoin i.**, witness to a deed; *Scot:* instrumentary witness; **notaire i.**, attesting notary; *Nau:* **officier i.**, officer acting as registrar (on board ship).

instrumental, -aux [ɛ̃strymɑ̃tal, -o], *a.* instrumental (cause, music; *Gram:* case); **concert vocal et i.**, vocal and instrumental concert.

instrumentalisme [ɛ̃strymɑ̃talism], *s.m. Phil:* instrumentalism.

instrumentation [ɛ̃strymɑ̃tasjɔ̃], *s.f.* **1.** *Mus:* scoring, instrumentation, orchestration. **2.** *Tchn:* (*a*) automatic control instruments, apparatus (*esp.* at petroleum refinery); (*b*) the study and design of such apparatus.

instrumenter [ɛ̃strymɑ̃te]. **1.** *v.i. Jur:* to draw up a document, a deed; to instrument; **i. contre qn**, to order proceedings to be taken against s.o. **2.** *v.tr. Mus:* to score, instrument (opera, etc.). **3.** *v.tr. Petroleum Ind:* to equip (refinery) with automatic control equipment.

instrumentiste [ɛ̃strymɑ̃tist], *s.m. & f.* (*a*) *Mus:* instrumentalist, instrumental performer; (*b*) *Surg:* theatre nurse.

insu [ɛ̃sy], *s.m. used in the prep.phr.* **à l'i. de**, without the knowledge of; **marié à l'i. de ses parents**, married without his parents' knowledge; **à mon insu**, unknown to me; without my knowledge; behind my back; **à l'i. de tout le monde**, unknown to anyone; without anyone being the wiser.

insubmersibilité [ɛ̃sybmɛrsibilite], *s.f.* insubmersibility.

insubmersible [ɛ̃sybmɛrsibl̩], *a.* insubmersible, unsinkable, non-sinkable (lifeboat, etc.).

insubordination [ɛ̃sybɔrdinasjɔ̃], *s.f.* insubordination.

insubordonné [ɛ̃sybɔrdɔne], *a.* insubordinate (soldier, etc.); disobedient, undisciplined (pupil, etc.).

insubstantiel, -elle [ɛ̃syptɑ̃sjɛl], *a.* insubstantial, unsubstantial.

insuccès [ɛ̃syksɛ], *s.m.* lack of success; failure; miscarriage (of plan); **entreprise vouée à l'i.**, enterprise (fore)doomed to failure; **i. total**, total failure.

insuffisamment [ɛ̃syfizamɑ̃], *adv.* insufficiently; inadequately; **i. vêtu**, scantily, thinly, clad; **i. nourri**, underfed; **i. gonflé**, under-inflated (tyre, etc.).

insuffisance [ɛ̃syfizɑ̃ːs], *s.f.* **1.** (*a*) insufficiency, deficiency; **il y a i. de blé**, there is a deficiency, a shortage, of wheat; **suppléer avec du cidre à l'i. de vin**, to eke out the wine with cider; **i. de personnel**, shortage of staff; **i. de moyens**, inadequacy of means; **i. d'une carte**, inadequacy of a map; *Jur:* **clôture pour i. d'actif**, closing of bankruptcy proceedings when assets are insufficient to defray legal expenses; (*b*) *Med:* insufficiency; **i. mécanique du cœur**, heart failure. **2. l'i. du personnel**, the incapacity, incompetence, inefficiency, of the staff.

insuffisant [ɛ̃syfizɑ̃], *a.* insufficient. **1.** inadequate (means, clothing, etc.); **poids i.**, short weight; **nourriture insuffisante**, insufficient food; malnutrition; **lumière insuffisante**, inadequate light; **gonflage i. (d'un pneu, etc.)**, under-inflation. **2.** incapable, incompetent; **i. à faire qch.**, not equal to doing sth.; **i. dans un emploi**, not equal to a position, unequal to the job; **chef i.**, incompetent leader.

insufflateur [ɛ̃syflatœːr], *s.m.* **1.** *Med:* insufflator, throat sprayer, nose sprayer. **2.** *Ind: Mch:* blower.

insufflation [ɛ̃syflasjɔ̃], *s.f.* **1.** *Med:* insufflation, spraying (of nose, throat); **i. pulmonaire**, artificial respiration. **2.** inflation, blowing up (of toy balloon, etc.).

insuffler [ɛ̃syfle], *v.tr.* **1.** (*a*) to insufflate; **i. de l'air dans qch.**, to blow, breathe, force, air into sth.; **i. à qn un grand enthousiasme**, to inspire s.o. with great enthusiasm; (*b*) *Med:* to spray (the throat, etc.). **2.** to inflate, blow up (bladder, toy balloon, etc.).

insulaire [ɛ̃sylɛːr]. **1.** *a.* insular. **2.** *s.* islander.

insularité [ɛ̃sylarite], *s.f.* insularity.

insulinase [ɛ̃sylinaːz], *s.f. Ch: Biol:* insulinase.

Insulinde (l') [ɛ̃sylɛ̃:d], *Pr.n.f. Geog:* the Indian Archipelago, the East Indies.
insuline [ɛ̃sylin], *s.f. Med:* insulin.
insulinothérapie [ɛ̃sylinɔterapi], *s.f. Med:* insulinization, insulin treatment.
insultant [ɛ̃syltɑ̃], *a.* insulting, offensive.
insulte [ɛ̃sylt], *s.f.* **1.** insult; **faire une i. à qn,** to insult s.o.; **i. à la justice,** outrage on justice; **une i. au bon sens,** an insult to common sense. **2.** *A.Mil:* **place exposée aux insultes de l'ennemi,** place open to enemy attack.
insulté, -ée [ɛ̃sylte], *s.* person who has received an insult, injured party.
insulter [ɛ̃sylte]. **1.** *v.tr.* to insult, affront (s.o.). **2.** *v.ind.tr.* (*a*) **i. au malheur,** to jeer at misfortune; (*b*) **i. à qch.,** to be an insult to sth.; **i. au bon goût,** to insult good taste. **3.** *v.tr. A.Mil:* to storm.
insulteur, -euse [ɛ̃syltœ:r, -ø:z]. **1.** *a.* insulting. **2.** (*a*) *s.* insulter; (*b*) *s.m. Rom.Ant:* reviler, insulter (in triumphal procession).
insupportable [ɛ̃sypɔrtabl̩], *a.* unbearable, unendurable (pain); intolerable (conduct); insufferable (person, arrogance); provoking (child); **il est i.,** he's very aggravating, impossible, infuriating; **il est i. à tous,** he is a nuisance to everybody; **sa conduite est i.,** his conduct is impossible.
insupportablement [ɛ̃sypɔrtabləmɑ̃], *adv.* unbearably; insufferably.
insupporter [ɛ̃sypɔrte], *v.i. Lit:* (*only used in third pers.*) to be intolerable (**à**, to).
insurgé, -ée [ɛ̃syrʒe], *a. & s.* insurgent, insurrectionist, rebel; **être i. contre qn,** to be in insurrection against s.o.; to be up in arms against s.o..
insurgents [ɛ̃syrʒɑ̃], *s.m.pl. Hist:* (the American) insurgents (in the War of Independence).
insurger (s') [sɛ̃syrʒe], *v.pr.* (**je m'insurgeai(s); n.n. insurgeons**) to rise (in rebellion); to revolt, to rebel (**contre,** against); **faire i. une nation,** to rouse a nation (to rebellion); **s'i. contre une proposition,** to flare up at a proposal; **s'i. contre un abus,** to rise, take up arms, against an abuse.
insurmontable [ɛ̃syrmɔ̃tabl̩], *a.* insurmountable, insuperable (barrier, difficulty); unconquerable (aversion).
insurmontablement [ɛ̃syrmɔ̃tabləmɑ̃], *adv.* insurmountably, insuperably.
insurpassable [ɛ̃syrpɑsabl̩], *a.* unsurpassable.
insurrection [ɛ̃syr(r)ɛksjɔ̃], *s.f.* insurrection, rising, rebellion; **en état d'i.,** insurgent; **en pleine i. contre . . .,** in open insurrection against . . ..
insurrectionnel, -elle [ɛ̃syr(r)ɛksjɔnɛl], *a.* insurrectional, insurrectionary (troops, etc.); (spirit, etc.) of revolt; **gouvernement i.,** rebel government.
insurrectionner (s') [sɛ̃syr(r)ɛksjɔne], *v.pr.* to rise up, rebel (**contre,** against).
intact [ɛ̃takt], *a.* intact; (*a*) untouched; undamaged, unbroken, whole; *F:* **se relever i. (après une chute),** to get up unhurt (after a fall); (*b*) unsullied, unblemished (reputation, etc.); (*c*) **le problème reste i.,** the problem remains unsolved; (*d*) (*of woman*) virgin.
intaillable [ɛ̃tɑjabl̩], *a. Lap:* that cannot be intagliated.
intaille [ɛ̃tɑ:j], *s.f. Lap:* intaglio ((i) work, (ii) gem).
intaillé [ɛ̃tɑje], *a. Lap: Eng:* intagliated.
intailler [ɛ̃tɑje], *v.tr. Lap:* to intaglio.
intangibilité [ɛ̃tɑ̃ʒibilite], *s.f.* intangibility, intangibleness.
intangible [ɛ̃tɑ̃ʒibl̩], *a.* **1.** intangible (being, cause). **2. intérêts intangibles,** sacred interests, sacrosanct interests.
intarissable [ɛ̃tarisabl̩], *a.* inexhaustible (well, imagination, etc.); perennial (spring); *F:* long-winded (orator); endless (chatter, etc.); unfailing (fund of humour, etc.); **il est i. sur ce sujet,** he could talk for ever on this subject; **il est i. en éloges à votre égard,** he cannot say enough in your praise; **larmes intarissables,** tears that cannot be checked; **mine i.,** inexhaustible mine.
intarissablement [ɛ̃tarisabləmɑ̃], *adv.* inexhaustibly; endlessly.
intégrable [ɛ̃tegrabl̩], *a. Mth:* integrable.
intégral, -aux [ɛ̃tegral, -o], *a.* **1.** integral, entire, complete, whole, full-scale; **paiement i.,** payment in full; **texte i.,** full text; **édition intégrale,** (complete and) unabridged edition; **réforme intégrale,** sweeping reform; **jouissance intégrale de . . .,** full enjoyment of . . .. **2.** *Mth:* (*a*) **calcul i.,** integral calculus; (*b*) *s.f.* **intégrale,** (i) *Mth:* integral; **intégrale linéaire,** line integral; **intégrale de surface,** surface integral; (ii) **l'orchestre symphonique X vient d'enregistrer l'intégrale des symphonies de Beethoven,** the X Symphony Orchestra has just made a recording of all Beethoven's symphonies.
intégralement [ɛ̃tegralmɑ̃], *adv.* wholly, entirely, completely, fully, in full; **rembourser i. une somme,** to repay a sum in full; **traiter une question i.,** to deal with the whole question, with the question in full.
intégralité [ɛ̃tegralite], *s.f.* **1.** integrality, entireness, wholeness; **poser une question dans son i.,** to propound a question as a whole. **2.** whole; **payer l'i. de son loyer,** to pay the whole of one's rent.
intégrant [ɛ̃tegrɑ̃], *a.* integral, integrant (part, etc.); **faire partie intégrante de,** to be part and parcel of, to be an integral part of.
intégrateur [ɛ̃tegratœ:r], *a. & s.m.* **1.** *a.* integrating; **calculateur i.,** integrating computer; **compteur i.,** integrating meter; **wattmètre i.,** integrating wattmeter. **2.** *s.m. Mth: Elcs:* integrator, integraph; *Atom.Ph:* integrator, scaler; *TV:* colour decoder; *Atom.Ph:* **i. de courant ionique,** ion-current integrator.
intégration [ɛ̃tegrasjɔ̃], *s.f.* **1.** *Mth:* integration; **signe d'i.,** integral sign; **i. par parties,** integration by parts. **2.** vertical trustification (of allied industries). **3.** *Physiol:* integration. **4.** *Pol:* integration.
intégrationniste [ɛ̃tegrasjɔnist], *s.m. & f. Pol:* integrationist.
intègre [ɛ̃tɛgr̩], *a.* upright, honest, just, righteous.
intégré [ɛ̃tegre], *a.* (*a*) (*of pers.*) integrated, assimilated; (*b*) integrated (machine, etc.); *Elcs:* **circuits intégrés,** integrated circuits.
intègrement [ɛ̃tɛgrəmɑ̃], *adv.* uprightly, justly, honestly.
intégrer [ɛ̃tegre], *v.tr.* (**j'intègre, n. intégrons; j'intégrerai**) **1.** *Mth:* to integrate. **2.** to integrate, incorporate (**à, dans,** into). **3. s'i.,** to combine with, to join; *Pol:* (*of party*) **s'i. dans une majorité,** to combine with, a majority. **4.** *v.i. Sch: F:* **i. à une grande École,** to get into a *grande École.*
intégrifolié [ɛ̃tegrifɔlje], *a. Bot:* integrifolious.
intégrité [ɛ̃tegrite], *s.f.* integrity. **1.** completeness, entirety, wholeness; **maintenir l'i. du territoire national, de l'Église,** to preserve the integrity of the national territory, of the Church. **2.** uprightness, honesty, righteousness.
intellect [ɛ̃tɛl(l)ɛkt], *s.m. Phil:* intellect, understanding.
intellectif, -ive [ɛ̃tɛl(l)ɛktif, -i:v], *Phil:* **1.** *a.* intellective. **1.** *s.f. A:* **intellective,** intellect.
intellection [ɛ̃tɛl(l)ɛksjɔ̃], *s.f. Phil:* intellection, perception, understanding, comprehension.
intellectualisation [ɛ̃tɛl(l)ɛktɥalizasjɔ̃], *s.f.* intellectualization.
intellectualiser [ɛ̃tɛl(l)ɛktɥalize], *v.tr.* to intellectualize.
intellectualisme [ɛ̃tɛl(l)ɛktɥalism], *s.m. Phil:* intellectualism.
intellectualiste [ɛ̃tɛl(l)ɛktɥalist], *a. & s.m. & f.* intellectualist.
intellectualité [ɛ̃tɛl(l)ɛktɥalite], *s.f.* intellectuality, intellectualness.
intellectuel, -elle [ɛ̃tɛl(l)ɛktɥɛl]. **1.** *a.* intellectual (faculty, person); **travail i.,** brain work; **paresse intellectuelle,** mental laziness; **fatigue intellectuelle,** mental fatigue. **2.** *s.* intellectual, scholar; brain worker; professional man, woman; *Pej:* highbrow.
intellectuellement [ɛ̃tɛlɛktɥɛlmɑ̃], *adv.* intellectually.
intelligemment [ɛ̃tɛliʒamɑ̃], *adv.* intelligently.
intelligence [ɛ̃tɛliʒɑ̃:s], *s.f.* **1.** understanding, comprehension; **avoir l'i. de plusieurs langues,** to have a knowledge, a command, an understanding, of several languages; **son i. des problèmes de la vie,** his understanding of the problems of life; **avoir l'i. des affaires,** (i) to have a good knowledge of business; (ii) to have a good head for business; **donner à qn l'i., d'un passage,** to explain a passage to s.o.; **pour l'i. de ce qui va suivre . . .,** in order to understand what follows . . ., for the clearer comprehension of what follows . . .. **2.** intelligence, intellect; brain power; **enfant à l'i. éveillée,** quick, clever, child; **i. de premier ordre,** intellect of the first order; **aiguiser l'i. de qn,** to sharpen s.o.'s wits. **3.** (*a*) (mutual) understanding, agreement, *in the phrs:* **être, vivre, en bonne, mauvaise, i. avec qn,** to be, live, on good, bad, terms with s.o.; **ces tribus vivent en bonne i.,** these tribes live on a friendly basis; **être d'i. avec qn,** to have an understanding, be in collusion, with s.o.; **ils sont d'i.,** there is an understanding between them; they are hand in glove; they play into each other's hands; **cela s'est fait d'i. avec lui,** it was done with his connivance; **nous avions décidé de communiquer le résultat de l'entrevue au moyen de signes d'i.,** we had decided to give the result of the interview by means of signs; (*b*) *pl.* **entretenir des intelligences avec qn,** to keep up a secret correspondence with s.o.; **pratiquer, avoir, des intelligences avec l'ennemi,** to be in (secret) communication, to have dealings, with the enemy.
intelligent [ɛ̃tɛliʒɑ̃], *a.* (*a*) intelligent; bright, clever (pupil); *F:* brainy; **être i. pour les affaires,** to have a good head for business; **il est i.,** *F:* he has brains; he's all there; (*b*) understanding.
intelligentsia, intelligentzia [ɛ̃tɛliʒɛn(t)sia], *s.f.* intelligentsia.
intelligentiel, -elle [ɛ̃tɛliʒɑ̃sjɛl], *a.* intelligential.
intelligibilité [ɛ̃tɛliʒibilite], *s.f.* intelligibility, intelligibleness.
intelligible [ɛ̃tɛliʒibl̩], *a.* (*a*) intelligible, understandable; (*b*) audible, clear, distinct.
intelligiblement [ɛ̃tɛliʒibləmɑ̃], *adv.* (*a*) intelligibly, plainly; (*b*) audibly, clearly, distinctly.
intempéramment [ɛ̃tɑ̃peramɑ̃], *adv.* intemperately.
intempérance [ɛ̃tɑ̃perɑ̃:s], *s.f.* intemperance; (*a*) excess, lack of moderation (**de langage,** in language); **habitudes d'i.,** intemperate habits; **i. de langue,** intemperance of speech; (*b*) insobriety; drunkenness.
intempérant [ɛ̃tɑ̃perɑ̃], *a.* intemperate.
intempéré [ɛ̃tɑ̃pere], *a.* unrestrained, immoderate.
intempérie [ɛ̃tɑ̃peri], *s.f.* **1.** *A:* (*a*) disorder (of stomach, etc.); (*b*) inclemency (of weather). **2.** *pl.* **intempéries,** bad weather; **exposé aux intempéries,** exposed to the elements; **imperméable aux intempéries,** weather-proof.
intempérisme [ɛ̃tɑ̃perism], *s.m. Geol:* weathering.
intempestif, -ive [ɛ̃tɑ̃pɛstif, -i:v], *a.* untimely, ill-timed, unseasonable (remark, etc.); inopportune (arrival, etc.); premature; *Aut:* **avertissement i.,** incorrect signalling; **le système est à toute épreuve et empêche toute ouverture intempestive de la valve,** the system is foolproof and prevents any inadvertent opening of the valve.
intempestivement [ɛ̃tɑ̃pɛstivmɑ̃], *adv.* unseasonably, inopportunely; at the wrong moment.
intempestivité [ɛ̃tɑ̃pɛstivite], *s.f.* untimeliness, unseasonableness.
intemporalité [ɛ̃tɑ̃pɔralite], *s.f.* timelessness.
intemporel, -elle [ɛ̃tɑ̃pɔrɛl], *a.* (*a*) timeless, of all time; **le vrai et le faux sont intemporels,** truth and falsehood are timeless; (*b*) immaterial; *Art:* **lumière intemporelle,** suffused light.
intenable [ɛ̃tnabl̩], *a.* (*a*) untenable, unmaintainable (position, etc.); (fortress, etc.) that cannot be defended; (*b*) intolerable; **chaleur i.,** unbearable heat; **rendre la vie i. à qn,** to make life intolerable for s.o.; to make s.o.'s life a burden; *F:* **enfant i.,** uncontrollable child.
intendance [ɛ̃tɑ̃dɑ̃:s], *s.f.* intendance, intendancy. **1.** (*a*) stewardship (of estate); (*b*) managership; (*c*) *Sch:* bursarship. **2.** *Fr.Hist:* administration (of province). **3.** (*a*) *Mil:* **le service de l'i.,** the commissariat, the Quartermaster General's Department; **l'Intendance Militaire** = the Royal Army Service Corps (R.A.S.C.), *U.S:* the Quartermaster Corps; **l'Intendance (Service de la Solde),** the Royal Army Pay Corps, *U.S:* the Finance Department; (*b*) *Navy:* (naval) paymaster's department.
intendant [ɛ̃tɑ̃dɑ̃], *s.m.* intendant. **1.** (*a*) steward, bailiff; (*b*) manager; (*c*) *Sch:* bursar. **2.** *Fr. Hist:* administrator (of province). **3.** *Mil:* senior administrative officer of the Quartermaster General's staff.
intendante [ɛ̃tɑ̃dɑ̃:t], *s.f.* **1.** (*a*) steward's wife; (*b*) *Sch:* (woman) bursar. **2.** *Fr.Hist:* wife of the Administrator (of a province). **3.** *Ecc:* Mother Superior (of certain convents).
intense [ɛ̃tɑ̃:s], *a.* intense; severe (cold, pain, etc.); heavy (gunfire); high (fever); intensive (propaganda); deep (blue, red, etc.); **maladie i.,** severe form of illness; **le vert i. des tropiques,** the rich green of the tropics; *El:* **courant i.,** (i) strong current, (ii) heavy flow (of current); **temps d'un froid i.,** intensely cold weather; **vie intense,** strenuous life; **circulation i.,** dense, heavy, traffic; **plaisir i.,** intense pleasure; **les heures les plus intenses de la vie,** the most intense moments of one's life.
intensément [ɛ̃tɑ̃semɑ̃], *adv.* intensely; with intensity; intensively.
intensif, -ive [ɛ̃tɑ̃sif, -i:v], *a.* (*a*) intensive (cultivation, etc.); *El:* **courant i.,** heavy flow of current; *Ind:* **feu i.,** hot fire; (*b*) *a. & s.m. Gram:* intensive (verb, pronoun).
intensification [ɛ̃tɑ̃sifikasjɔ], *s.f.* intensification.
intensifier [ɛ̃tɑ̃sifje], *v.tr.* (*p.d. & pr.sub.* **n. intensifiions, v. intensifiiez**) to intensify.

intensimètre [ɛ̃tɑ̃simɛtr̥], *s.m. Atom.Ph:* intensitometer, dose-rate meter.

intensité [ɛ̃tɑ̃site], *s.f.* **1.** intensity, intenseness; brilliancy (of light); loudness (of sound); force (of wind); depth (of colour); strength (of current); density (of magnetic field); **i. d'un sentiment,** intensity, depth, of an emotion; **donner plus d'i. à une expression,** to add emphasis to an expression; *El:* **i. efficace,** effective current; **i. nominale, minimale,** rated, trace, current; **i. de fermeture, d'ouverture,** pick-up, drop-out, current; **i. résiduelle,** residual current; **i. du courant en ampères,** amperage; **i. de chargement,** rate of charging (of an accumulator); **i. d'un champ perturbateur,** (i) *El:* perturbing-field strength; (ii) *W.Tel:* radio-noise field intensity; *Ac:* **i. acoustique,** acoustic intensity; loudness; *Opt:* **i. de la lumière, i. lumineuse,** intensity, brilliancy, of light; **i. lumineuse (en bougies),** candle power; **i. lumineuse d'une jumelle,** light-transmitting capacity of field glasses; *Atom.Ph:* **i. d'activation,** intensity of activation; **i. d'irradiation,** dose rate; **i. de radioactivité,** intensity of radioactivity; **i. de rayonnement,** radiation intensity; **i. neutronique,** neutron intensity, density. **2.** *Ling:* **accent d'i.,** stress.

intensivement [ɛ̃tɑ̃sivmɑ̃], *adv.* intensively.

intenter [ɛ̃tɑ̃te], *v.tr. used only in Jur:* **i. une action, un procès, à, contre, qn,** to bring, enter, an action, to institute proceedings, against s.o.

intention [ɛ̃tɑ̃sjɔ̃], *s.f.* intention; (*a*) purpose, design; *Jur:* intent; **avec i. délictueuse,** with malicious intent; **sans mauvaise i.,** with no ill intent; **avoir l'i., avoir pour i., de faire qch.,** to intend to do sth., to mean to do sth.; to plan to do sth.; **je n'ai nullement l'i. d'accepter,** I have no intention of accepting; **je n'en avais pas l'i.,** I did not mean it; **il n'avait nullement l'i. de nous manquer de respect,** he meant no disrespect; **il a de bonnes intentions, ses intentions sont bonnes,** he means well; **quelles sont vos intentions?** (i) what are your intentions? (ii) what do you mean to do? **cela n'a jamais été mon i.,** I never meant it; that was never what I meant, intended; **son i. arrêtée de (faire) construire,** his determination to build; **je n'ai pas l'i. de rester ici,** I do not contemplate, I have no intention of, staying here; **j'avais l'i. de faire le trajet à pied,** I was going to walk (it); **dans l'i. de faire qch.,** with a view to doing sth.; with the intention of doing sth.; with the purpose of doing sth.; **cette lettre était, avait été, écrite dans l'i. de l'irriter,** the letter was meant to irritate him; **faire qch. dans la meilleure i.,** to do sth. with the best intentions; **faire qch. avec i.,** to do sth. deliberately, on purpose; **sans i.,** unintentionally; **sans i. de faire qch.,** with no intention of doing sth.; **intentions au sujet de qch.,** intentions with regard to sth.; (*b*) will, wish; **mon i. est que vous le fassiez,** I wish you to do it; I intend, mean, you to do it; **accepter l'i. pour le fait,** to take the will for the deed; *Prov:* **c'est l'i. qui fait l'action, l'i. est réputée pour le fait,** it is the intention that counts; **l'enfer est pavé de bonnes intentions,** the road to hell is paved with good intentions; *prep.phr.* **à l'i. de,** in honour of; for the sake of; for; **une quête à l'i. des aveugles,** a collection in aid of the blind; **voici une écharpe que j'ai achetée à votre i.,** here's a scarf I bought especially for you; **faire une toilette de dimanche à l'i. de qn,** to put on one's best clothes in honour of s.o.; **les enfants ne manquent pas de livres écrits à leur i.,** there is no lack of books written specially for children; **cette remarque est à votre i.,** that remark is aimed at you, that's a dig at you; *Ecc:* **dire une messe à l'i. (spéciale) de qn, de qch.,** to say a mass for a special intention; (*c*) *Surg:* **réunion par première, seconde, i.,** healing, reunion, by first, second, intention.

intentionnalité [ɛ̃tɑ̃sjɔnalite], *s.f. Psy:* intentionality.

intentionné [ɛ̃tɑ̃sjɔne], *a. used only in* (*a*) **bien, mal, i.,** well-, ill-disposed (**envers,** towards); **mieux i.,** better disposed; (*b*) **personne, démarche, bien intentionnée,** well-intentioned person, step; well-meaning person.

intentionnel, -elle [ɛ̃tɑ̃sjɔnɛl], *a.* **1.** intentional, wilful, deliberate. **2.** *Jur:* **délit i.,** misdemeanour with intent; **poser au jury la question intentionnelle,** to ask the jury whether the act was committed with intent; to put the question of intent to the jury.

intentionnellement [ɛ̃tɑ̃sjɔnɛlmɑ̃], *adv.* intentionally, wilfully, deliberately, designedly.

inter- [ɛ̃tɛr], *pref.* inter-; **intercellulaire,** intercellular.

inter [ɛ̃tɛːr], *s.m. F:* **1.** *Fb:* **i. droit, gauche,** inside right, left; **les inters,** the insides, the inside forwards. **2.** *Tp:* = trunks.

interaction [ɛ̃tɛraksjɔ̃], *s.f.* (*a*) interaction; interplay; reciprocal action; **entrer en i.,** to interact; (*b*) *Ph: W.Tel: etc:* interaction; **composante d'i.,** component of interaction; *Atom.Ph:* **i. de particules,** particle interaction; **i. tensorielle,** tensor interaction; *Mth:* **espace d'i. de révolution,** cylindrical interaction space; (*c*) *Av:* interference.

interagir [ɛ̃tɛraʒiːr], *v.i.* to interact.

interallié [ɛ̃tɛralje], *a.* interallied.

interambulacraire [ɛ̃tɛrɑ̃bylakrɛːr], *a. Z:* interambulacral.

interambulacre [ɛ̃tɛrɑ̃bylakr̥], *s.m. Z:* interambulacrum.

interaméricain [ɛ̃tɛramerikɛ̃], *a.* inter-American.

interandin [ɛ̃tɛrɑ̃dɛ̃], *a. Geog:* inter-Andean.

interarabe [ɛ̃tɛrarab], *a.* Pan-Arab.

interarmées [ɛ̃tɛrarme], *a.inv. Mil:* combined, joint (action) (of the different services).

interarmes [ɛ̃tɛrarm], *a.inv. Mil:* combined (staff, operation, etc.).

interarticulaire [ɛ̃tɛrartikylɛːr], *a. Anat:* interarticular.

interastral, -aux [ɛ̃tɛrastral, -o], *a.* interstellar (space).

interatomique [ɛ̃tɛratɔmik], *a.* interatomic (space, etc.).

interattraction [ɛ̃tɛratraksjɔ̃], *s.f.* mutual attraction.

inter-auriculaire [ɛ̃tɛrɔrikylɛːr], *a. Anat:* interauricular.

intercadence [ɛ̃tɛrkadɑ̃ːs], *s.f. Med:* intercadence (of pulse).

intercadent [ɛ̃tɛrkadɑ̃], *a. Med:* intercadent (pulse).

intercalaire [ɛ̃tɛrkalɛːr], *a.* **1.** *Chr:* intercalary (day, year, etc.); *Med:* **jours intercalaires,** days of intermission (of fever). **2.** intercalated; *Bookb:* **feuille i.,** interpolated sheet; **feuillet i.,** inset; *Surv:* **ligne i.,** form-line; *Agr:* **culture i.,** cover crop. **3.** *s.m.* guide card, guide (of card index, etc.).

intercalation [ɛ̃tɛrkalasjɔ̃], *s.f.* **1.** intercalation, interpolation, insertion; *Chr:* intercalation; *El:* switching in (of resistance); *Geol:* interstratification; **i. gazifère,** gas streak; **i. de grès,** band of sandstone. **2.** *pl. Typ:* special sorts.

intercalé [ɛ̃tɛrkale], *a.* inserted; *Gram:* **proposition intercalée,** interpolated, incidental, clause.

intercaler [ɛ̃tɛrkale], *v.tr.* to intercalate (day in year, etc.); to interpolate, insert (item in bill, etc.); *F:* to sandwich (sth.) in; *El:* to cut in, switch in (resistance, etc.); **i. des citations dans un discours,** to intersperse, sprinkle, lard, a speech with quotations; **s'i. entre deux personnes,** to slip in between two people; *Rail:* **on a intercalé le wagon-restaurant entre deux voitures de première,** the dining car was put in between two first class coaches.

intercapillaire [ɛ̃tɛrkapil(l)ɛːr], *a.* intercapillary.

intercéder [ɛ̃tɛrsede], *v.tr.* (*conj. like* CÉDER) to intercede, plead; **i. auprès de qn pour qn,** to intercede with s.o. on s.o.'s behalf.

intercellulaire [ɛ̃tɛrsɛlylɛːr], *a.* intercellular.

intercensitaire [ɛ̃tɛrsɑ̃sitɛːr], *a.* intercensal, between two censuses.

intercentre [ɛ̃tɛrsɑ̃tr̥], *s.m. Biol:* intercentrum.

intercepter [ɛ̃tɛrsɛpte], *v.tr.* to intercept (letter, message, aircraft, etc.); to shut out (light, etc.); *Sp:* to tackle (opponent); *Mch:* to cut off, shut off (steam); **i. les fuyards,** to head off the fugitives.

intercepteur [ɛ̃tɛrsɛptœːr], *s.m. Av:* **1.** interceptor, spoiler. **2.** interceptor (fighter), interception aircraft.

interception [ɛ̃tɛrsɛpsjɔ̃], *s.f.* interception; *Fb. etc:* tackle; *Mch:* shutting off (of steam); *Mil: Av:* interception; *W.Tel:* **i. des émissions,** monitoring; **opérateur d'i.,** monitor.

intercesseur [ɛ̃tɛrsɛsœːr], *s.m.* intercessor (**auprès de,** with; **pour,** on behalf of); mediator.

intercession [ɛ̃tɛrsɛsjɔ̃], *s.f.* intercession (**auprès de,** with; **pour,** on behalf of); mediation.

interchange [ɛ̃tɛrʃɑ̃ːʒ], *s.m. Biol:* interchange.

interchangeabilité [ɛ̃tɛrʃɑ̃ʒabilite], *s.f.* interchangeability (of parts); interchangeableness.

interchangeable [ɛ̃tɛrʃɑ̃ʒabl̥], *a.* interchangeable.

interchanger [ɛ̃tɛrʃɑ̃ʒe], *v.tr.* to interchange.

intercinèse [ɛ̃tɛrsinɛːz], *s.f. Biol:* (*of cell*) interkinesis; rest stage (between two nuclear divisions).

intercirculation [ɛ̃tɛrsirkylasjɔ̃], *s.f. Rail:* intercommunication (between coaches).

interclasse [ɛ̃tɛrklɑːs], *s.m. or f. Sch:* (short) break (between two classes).

interclassement [ɛ̃tɛrklɑsmɑ̃], *s.m. Elcs:* (*computer*) collation.

interclasser [ɛ̃tɛrklɑse], *v.tr. Elcs:* (*of computer*) to collate.

interclasseuse [ɛ̃tɛrklɑsøːz], *s.f. Elcs:* collator (of computer).

interclubs [ɛ̃tɛrklyb], *a.inv.& s.m.inv.Sp:* interclub.

intercolonial, -aux [ɛ̃tɛrkɔlɔnjal, -o], *a.* intercolonial.

intercolumnaire [ɛ̃tɛrkɔlɔmnɛːr], *a. Anat:* intercolumnar.

intercom [ɛ̃tɛrkɔm], *s.m.* intercom, intercommunication system.

intercommunal, -aux [ɛ̃tɛrkɔmynal, -o], *a.* belonging to, shared by, several *communes.*

intercommunication [ɛ̃tɛrkɔmynikasjɔ̃], *s.f.* intercommunication; *Rail:* alarm system; **voie d'i.,** line of communication.

intercommunion [ɛ̃tɛrkɔmynjɔ̃], *s.f. Ecc:* intercommunion.

intercompréhension [ɛ̃tɛrkɔ̃preɑ̃sjɔ̃], *s.f.* mutual comprehension.

interconfessionnalisme [ɛ̃tɛrkɔ̃fɛsjɔnalism], *s.f. Ecc:* interdenominationalism.

interconfessionnel, -elle [ɛ̃tɛrkɔ̃fɛsjɔnɛl], *a. Ecc:* interconfessional, interdenominational.

interconnecté [ɛ̃tɛrkɔnɛkte], *a.* (*of power stations*) connected (up).

interconnecter [ɛ̃tɛrkɔnɛkte], *v.tr. El:* to connect (up) (circuits); *Elcs:* to attach, hook up (computers).

interconnexion [ɛ̃tɛrkɔnɛksjɔ̃], *s.f. El:* interconnection; *Elcs:* attachment, hook-up (of computers).

intercontinental, -aux [ɛ̃tɛrkɔ̃tinɑ̃tal, -o], *a.* intercontinental; **fusée intercontinentale, engin i.,** intercontinental ballistic missile.

intercostal, -aux [ɛ̃tɛrkɔstal, -o], *a. Anat:* intercostal.

intercotidal, -aux [ɛ̃tɛrkɔtidal, -o], *a. Geog:* **zone intercotidale,** intertidal zone (of shore).

intercourse [ɛ̃tɛrkurs], *s.f. Nau:* free intercourse (between stated ports of two countries).

intercroisé [ɛ̃tɛrkrwaze, -wa-], *a.* intersected, interwoven; crisscross(ed).

intercurrence [ɛ̃tɛrkyrɑ̃ːs], *s.f. Med: etc:* intercurrence (of disorder).

intercurrent [ɛ̃tɛrkyrɑ̃], *a. Med: etc:* intercurrent (disorder).

intercycle [ɛ̃tɛrsikl̥], *s.m.* (*computers*) intercycle.

interdentaire [ɛ̃tɛrdɑ̃tɛːr], *a. Dent:* interdental.

interdental, -aux [ɛ̃tɛrdɑ̃tal, -o], *a. Ling:* interdental.

interdépartemental, -aux [ɛ̃tɛrdepartəmɑ̃tal, -o], *a.* interdepartmental.

interdépartementalement [ɛ̃tɛrdepartəmɑ̃talmɑ̃], *adv.* **résoudre un problème i.,** to solve a problem interdepartmentally.

interdépendance [ɛ̃tɛrdepɑ̃dɑ̃ːs], *s.f.* interdependence.

interdépendant [ɛ̃tɛrdepɑ̃dɑ̃], *a.* interdependent.

interdiction [ɛ̃tɛrdiksjɔ̃], *s.f.* interdiction. **1.** prohibition, forbidding; *Jur:* **i. de séjour,** prohibition from entering certain towns, areas; local banishment; *Nau:* **i. faite à un navire de quitter un port,** refusal to allow a ship to leave a port; *Av:* **i. de vol,** grounding (of aircraft); **i. des essais atomiques,** atomic test ban; *Artil:* **tir d'i.,** standing barrage fire. **2.** *Jur:* (*a*) state of minority declared by court; deprival of control over money; **frapper un aliéné d'i.,** to impose judicial interdiction on an insane person; **i. d'un aliéné,** certifying of a lunatic; **demande en i.,** petition (i) of lunacy, (ii) that a spendthrift be deprived of control over his estate; (*b*) **i. légale, civile, judiciaire,** suspension, (temporary) deprivation, of civil rights; (*c*) *Adm:* suspension from duty; (*d*) *Ecc:* interdict. **3.** *Nau:* danger buoy.

interdigital, -aux [ɛ̃tɛrdiʒital, -o], *a.* interdigital.

interdire [ɛ̃tɛrdiːr], *v.tr.* (*conj. like* DIRE, except *pr.ind.* **v. interdisez** and *imp.* **interdisez**) **1.** to forbid, prohibit; (*a*) **i. qch. à qn,** to forbid s.o. sth.; *Av:* **i. (un avion) de vol,** to ground (an aircraft); **la passerelle est interdite aux voyageurs,** passengers are not allowed on the bridge; **l'importation des allumettes est interdite,** the import of matches is prohibited; **il nous est interdit de révéler . . .,** we are not allowed to reveal, disclose . . .; **il n'est pas interdit de penser que . . .,** one might perhaps be forgiven for thinking that . . .; *P.N:* **entrée interdite (au public),** no admittance; *P.N:* **passage interdit,** no thoroughfare; *P.N:* **sens interdit,** no entry, *U.S:* do not enter; **cette zone reste interdite à toute installation militaire,** this zone remains a prohibited area for all military works; **i. l'entrée de sa maison à qn,** to forbid s.o. one's house;

questions interdites à nos recherches, questions into which we are forbidden to enquire, questions that are forbidden; **pièce interdite par la censure,** play banned by the censor; **livre interdit à l'affichage,** book banned (for political reasons) from being advertised or displayed; **i. à qn de faire qch.,** to prohibit s.o. from doing sth., to forbid s.o. to do sth.; **s'i. le vin,** to give up (drinking) wine; (*b*) **i. qn de ses fonctions,** to suspend s.o. from the execution of his duties; (*c*) **i. un magistrat,** to suspend a magistrate; **i. un prêtre,** to lay a priest under an interdict; *Jur:* **faire i. qn,** to have s.o. declared incapable of managing his own affairs; **i. qn en démence,** to declare s.o. insane; **aliéné interdit,** certified lunatic; insane person under restraint; (*c*) *Wr:* to bar (a hold). **2.** to disconcert, nonplus, bewilder.

s'interdire, to become confused; to be disconcerted, put out.

interdisciplinaire [ɛ̃tɛrdisipline:r], *a.* **recherches interdisciplinaires,** combined research project (undertaken by several scientific research groups, etc.).

interdit, -e [ɛ̃tɛrdi]. **1.** *a.* disconcerted, nonplussed, bewildered; taken aback, put out; **il les regarda i. et bouche bée,** he gazed at them in open-mouthed bewilderment; he gaped at them. **2.** *s. Jur:* (*a*) prodigal, lunatic, or convict under judicial disability; (*b*) **i. de séjour,** ex-convict prohibited from entering a certain area; *Av:* **i. de vol,** grounded. **3.** *s.m.* (*a*) *Ecc:* interdict; **frapper qn, qch., d'i.,** to lay s.o., sth., under an interdict; **mettre un pays en i.,** to interdict a country; **lever l'i.,** to raise, remove, the interdict; (*b*) *Anthr:* taboo.

interdunaire [ɛ̃tɛrdyne:r], *a. Geog:* between (the) dunes.

interdune [ɛ̃tɛrdyn], *s.f. Geog:* trough (between dunes).

interépineux, -euse [ɛ̃terepinø, -ø:z], *a. Anat:* interspinal; **muscle i.,** interspinalis.

intéressant [ɛ̃teresɑ̃], *a.* **1.** (*a*) interesting; **livre i.,** interesting book; **visage i.,** interesting face; **détail i.,** interesting, curious, detail; **sa pâleur lui donne un air i.,** her paleness is rather attractive; **elle s'accusait, s'en voulait, de s'être montrée une compagne peu intéressante,** she blamed herself for having been, proved, a dull, uninteresting, companion; (*b*) **chercher à se rendre i.,** to try to make oneself interesting, to draw attention to oneself; *s.* **faire l'i.,** to show off. **2.** (*worthy of consideration*) (*a*) **ces gens-là ne sont pas intéressants,** these people are not our sort, *F:* not our cup of tea; I, we, have nothing in common with those people; *F:* **c'est un individu, un type, peu i.,** he's a shady, dubious, character; **ce n'est pas un type i.,** I've no time for him; (*b*) **elle est dans une position intéressante,** she's pregnant, she's in an interesting condition. **3.** advantageous; remunerative; **il serait i. de s'en assurer,** it would be a good thing to make sure of it, to ascertain the facts; **prix intéressants,** attractive, advantageous, prices; **j'ai refusé la situation, qui était peu intéressante,** I turned down the job, which was not very well paid.

intéressé [ɛ̃terese], *a.* **1.** interested; **être i. dans une entreprise,** to have a financial interest in a venture; **i. à faire qch.,** interested, concerned, in doing sth.; **i. à ce que qch. se fasse,** interested in sth. being done; **les parties intéressées,** *s.* **les intéressés,** the interested parties, the persons concerned; **les premiers intéressés,** those most directly affected; **c'est vous le premier i.,** you are the most closely concerned. **2.** selfish, self-seeking; **amour i.,** cupboard love; **agir dans un but i.,** to have an axe to grind; **jouer un jeu i.,** to play for one's own hand.

intéressement [ɛ̃teresmɑ̃], *s.m. Com: Ind:* profit-sharing (scheme).

intéresser [ɛ̃terese], *v.tr.* to interest; (*a*) **i. qn dans son commerce,** to give s.o. a financial interest, a partnership, in the business; **i. les employés (aux bénéfices),** to initiate a profit-sharing scheme; *Cards: etc:* **i. le jeu,** to play for a stake; *F:* to put a bit on (the game); (*b*) to affect, concern; **cela m'intéresse peu,** that hardly concerns me, hardly affects me; **blessure qui intéresse le poumon,** wound that affects, implicates, the lung; **question qui intéresse le bien-être du pays,** question that affects the welfare of the country; **question qui intéresse le monde entier,** question in which the whole world is concerned; question of world-wide interest; (*c*) to be interesting to (s.o.); **sujet qui m'intéresse beaucoup,** subject which interests me greatly, in which I am greatly interested; subject that appeals to me; **ceci peut vous i.,** this may be, prove, of interest to you; **voici qch. qui vous intéressera, qui est susceptible de vous i.,** here's sth. in your line; *F:* **être intéressé par qch.,** to be interested in sth.; *F: Iron:* **continue, tu m'intéresses,** go on, I'm listening; (*d*) **i. qn à une cause,** to interest s.o. in a cause; to win s.o. over to a cause.

s'intéresser, (*a*) **s'i. dans une affaire,** to become interested in, to put money into, a venture; (*b*) **s'i. à qn, à qch.,** to take, feel, an interest in s.o., in sth.; to interest oneself in s.o., in sth.; to concern oneself with sth.; to be interested in s.o., in sth.; **j'étais présent, mais personne ne s'est intéressé à moi,** I was there, but no one took any notice of me.

intérêt [ɛ̃terɛ], *s.m.* interest. **1.** share, stake (in business, etc.); **avoir un i. au jeu,** (i) to have a stake in the game; (ii) to have an axe to grind; **mettre qn hors d'i.,** to buy, pay, s.o. out. **2.** advantage, benefit; **il y a i. à . . .,** it is desirable to . . .; **reconnaître l'i. d'un compromis,** to see the advantage of a compromise; **il y a tout i., le plus haut i., à ce qu'il le fasse,** it is most desirable that he should do it; **il est de mon i. de le faire, j'ai i. à le faire,** it is in my interest to do it; **consulter son i.,** to consult one's own interest, *F:* to have an eye to the main chance; **je parle sans i.,** I am speaking disinterestedly, I am not speaking from interested motives; **agir dans son i.,** to act in, for, one's own interest; **i. personnel,** self-interest; **i. bien entendu,** enlightened self-interest; **il l'a fait par i.,** he has done it out of self-interest; **son i. le guide,** he is governed by his mercenary outlook; **il a fait un mariage d'i.,** he married for money; **il sait où se trouve son i.,** he knows where his advantage lies, *F:* which side his bread is buttered; **agir au mieux des intérêts de qn,** to act in s.o.'s best interests; **l'i. public,** public interest; **voyager dans l'i. de sa santé,** to travel for the benefit of one's health; **agir dans l'i. commun des peuples,** to act for the common good of the people; **l'i. de la population exige . . .,** the welfare of the population requires . . .; *Rail:* **ligne d'i. local,** (i) branch line, local line, (ii) light railway. **3.** (feeling of) interest; **porter i. à qn,** to take an interest in s.o.; **ressentir de l'i. pour qn,** to feel interested in s.o.; **prendre de l'i. à qch.,** to take an interest in sth.; **cela est sans i. pour moi,** I am not interested; **livre sans i., dépourvu d'i.,** uninteresting book. **4.** *Fin:* **i. simple, composé,** simple, compound, interest; **placer son argent à 5% d'i.,** to invest one's money at 5% interest; **somme qui porte i.,** sum that bears interest; **prêt à i.,** loan bearing interest; **emprunter à i.,** to borrow at interest; **(cotation d'actions) sans intérêts,** (quotation of shares) ex-dividend; **intérêt(s) couru(s),** accrued interest; **intérêts à échoir,** accruing interest; **intérêts échus,** outstanding interest; **valeurs à intérêts,** interest-bearing securities; **valeurs à i. fixe,** fixed-interest securities; *St.Exch:* **i. de report,** contango. **5.** *Gram:* **pronom expressif d'i. atténué,** pronoun in the ethic dative.

interétages [ɛ̃tɛreta:ʒ], *attrib. a.inv.* interstage (operation, etc. in multistage rocket); **connecteur i.,** interstage relay.

interface [ɛ̃tɛrfas], *s.f. Ph: Ch:* interface; *Cryst:* interplanar crystal facing.

interfacial, -iaux [ɛ̃tɛrfasjal, -jo], *a. Ph: etc:* interfacial; **tension interfaciale,** interfacial tension; **région interfaciale,** interface region.

interférence [ɛ̃tɛrferɑ̃:s], *s.f.* **1.** (*a*) *Ph:* interference; *Opt:* **franges d'i.,** interference rings; (*b*) *W.Tel:* **interférences,** interference; **i. des ondes sonores,** interference fading; **i. des bandes latérales,** monkey chatter; **i. entre voies,** interchannel interference; **i. radar,** radar interference; (*c*) *Tp:* thump (of circuit); (*d*) *Atom.Ph:* **i. électronique, neutronique,** electron, neutron, interference; (*e*) *Dent:* **i. des cuspides,** cuspal interference. **2.** interference, intervention.

interférent [ɛ̃tɛrferɑ̃], *a. Ph:* interfering (rays, etc.).

interférentiel, -ielle [ɛ̃tɛrferɑ̃sjɛl], *a. Ph:* interferential.

interférer [ɛ̃tɛrfere], *v.i.* (**il interfère; il interférait; il interférera**) **1.** *Ph:* (*of light waves, etc.*) to interfere. **2. leurs initiatives risquent d'i.,** there is a risk that their initiatives will interfere with each other.

interféromètre [ɛ̃tɛrferɔmɛtr], *s.m. Ph:* interferometer.

interférométrie [ɛ̃tɛrferɔmetri], *s.f.* interferometry.

interféron [ɛ̃tɛrferɔ̃], *s.m. Biol:* interferon.

interfibrillaire [ɛ̃tɛrfibrijɛ:r], *a. Biol:* interfibrillar.

interfluve [ɛ̃tɛrfly:v], *s.m. Geog:* interfluve.

interfoliacé [ɛ̃tɛrfɔljase], *a. Bot:* interfoliaceous.

interfoliage [ɛ̃tɛrfɔlja:ʒ], *s.m.* interleaving (of book).

interfoliaire [ɛ̃tɛrfɔljɛ:r], *a. Bot:* interfoliaceous.

interfolier [ɛ̃tɛrfɔlje], *v.tr.* (*p.d. & pr.sub.* **n. interfoliions, v. interfoliiez**) to interleave; to interpage (book, etc.).

interfractionnel, -elle [ɛ̃tɛrfraksjɔnɛl], *a. Pol: etc:* (resolution, etc.) supported by several groups.

interfrange [ɛ̃tɛrfrɑ̃:ʒ], *s.m. Opt:* distance between interference rings.

intergalactique [ɛ̃tɛrgalaktik], *a. Astr:* intergalactic.

interglaciaire [ɛ̃tɛrglasjɛ:r]. **1.** *a. Geol:* interglacial (deposit, etc.). **2.** *s.m.* interglacial (age, period).

intergouvernemental, -aux [ɛ̃tɛrguvɛrnəmɑ̃tal, -o], *a.* intergovernmental.

intergroupe [ɛ̃tɛrgrup], *s.m. Pol: etc:* joint committee.

interguerre (l') [lɛ̃tɛrgɛ:r], *s.m. F:* the inter-war years.

intérieur [ɛ̃terjœ:r]. **1.** *a.* (*a*) interior, inner (room, harbour, etc.); internal (part, etc.); **cour intérieure,** inner court; **sac (à main) avec glace intérieure,** handbag with mirror inside; **mer, navigation, intérieure,** inland sea, navigation; *Nau:* **cabine intérieure,** *Navy:* **chambre intérieure,** inboard cabin; (*b*) inward (feelings, etc.); **vie intérieure,** inner life; **une voix intérieure me disait . . .,** a voice within me said . . .; *A:* **homme i.,** man who lives within himself; *s.a.* FOR; (*c*) domestic (administration, etc.); **législation intérieure,** municipal law; **commerce i.,** home trade, inland trade; **la politique intérieure de la France,** the home policy of France; **(tarif d')affranchissement en régime i.,** inland postage rate. **2.** *s.m.* (*a*) interior, inside; **place d'i.,** inside seat (of bus, etc.); **à l'i.,** inside, on the inside; **à l'i. de la gare,** inside the station; **la porte était verrouillée à l'i.,** the door was bolted on the inside; **une voix à l'i. me cria d'entrer,** a voice from inside shouted to me to come in; *Nau:* **à l'i. du bord,** inboard; **l'i. du pays,** the interior of the country; **dans l'i. du pays, inland; les villes de l'i.,** the inland towns; **une fois débarqués, nous nous dirigeâmes vers l'i.,** once landed, we started up country; (*b*) *A:* inner nature, inmost thoughts; (*c*) home, house; **vie d'i.,** home life, domestic life; **homme d'i.,** stay-at-home; **femme d'i.,** domesticated woman; **sa femme est (une) bonne femme d'i.,** his wife is a good housekeeper; **une cousine dirige son i.,** a cousin manages his house; **elle ignore tout de la direction d'un i.,** she knows nothing of housekeeping; **avoir un i. bien tenu,** to have a well-kept home; **chaussures d'i.,** house shoes; *Art:* **peintre d'intérieurs,** painter of interiors, of scenes of domestic life; (*d*) home (country); **marché de l'i.,** home markets; *Post:* **colis à destination de l'i.,** inland parcels; *Adm:* **le Ministère de l'I.** = the Home Office; **le Ministre de l'I.** = the Home Secretary. **3.** *s.m. Fb:* **intérieur gauche,** inside left (player).

intérieurement [ɛ̃terjœrmɑ̃], *adv.* inwardly, internally, inside, within; **rire i.,** to laugh to oneself; **je me disais i. que . . .,** I said to myself that . . ..

intérim [ɛ̃terim], *s.m.* interim; **dans l'i.,** in the interim, (in the) meanwhile; *Fin:* **dividende par i.,** interim dividend; **commander par i.,** to exercise temporary command; **secrétaire par i.,** interim secretary; **faire l'i. (de qn),** to deputize (for s.o.); to act as locum tenens; **assurer l'i.,** to carry on (during vacancy or absence); to take over s.o.'s duties temporarily.

intérimaire [ɛ̃terimɛ:r]. **1.** *a.* temporary, provisional (duty, official, etc.); *Pol:* **cabinet i.,** caretaker cabinet; **directeur i.,** acting manager; **personnel i.,** personnel from a firm supplying temporary staff; **dividende, rapport, i.,** interim dividend, report; **protection i. d'un ouvrage,** ad interim copyright. **2.** *s.* official holding temporary appointment; deputy; locum tenens; *F:* temporary.

intérimairement [ɛ̃terimɛrmɑ̃], *adv.* temporarily, provisionally, ad interim.

intérimat [ɛ̃terima], *s.m.* (*a*) duties ad interim; (*b*) provisional government.

interindividuel, -elle [ɛ̃tɛrɛ̃dividɥɛl], *a.* interindividual; personal (relationships); **psychologie interindividuelle,** study of personal relationships.

intériorisation [ɛ̃terjɔrizasjɔ̃], *s.f.* interiorization.

intérioriser [ɛ̃terjɔrize], *v.tr.* to interiorize.

intériorité [ɛ̃terjɔrite], *s.f.* inwardness, interiority.

interjacent [ɛ̃tɛrʒasɑ̃], *a.* interjacent.

interjectif, -ive [ɛ̃tɛrʒɛktif, -iːv], *a.* interjectional, interjectory (phrase, etc.); interjaculatory (remark, etc.).

interjection [ɛ̃tɛrʒɛksjɔ̃], *s.f.* **1.** *Gram:* interjection. **2.** *Jur:* **i. d'appel,** lodging of an appeal.

interjectivement [ɛ̃tɛrʒɛktivmɑ̃], *adv.* interjectionally.

interjeter [ɛ̃tɛrʒəte], *v.tr.* (*conj. like* JETER) *Jur:* **i. appel (d'un jugement),** to appeal, to bring an appeal (against a judgment); to give notice of appeal.

interlignage [ɛ̃tɛrliɲaːʒ], *s.m. Typ:* leading out.

interligne [ɛ̃tɛrliɲ]. **1.** *s.m.* (*a*) space between two lines; *Typewr:* spacing; *Mus:* space (on the stave); **dans les interlignes,** between the lines; *Typewr:* **écrit à simple, double, i.,** typed in single, double, spacing; **page tapée sans i.,** single-spaced page; **i. réglable,** adjustable line space; **levier d'i.,** line spacer; **pointeau d'i.,** line-space gauge; (*b*) interlineation. **2.** *s.f. Typ:* lead.

interligner [ɛ̃tɛrliɲe], *v.tr.* **1.** to write between the lines of (a text); to interline. **2.** *Typ:* to lead out (type); **texte interligné,** leaded matter; **texte non interligné,** matter set solid.

interlinéaire [ɛ̃tɛrlineɛːr], *a.* interlinear (translation, etc.).

interlinéation [ɛ̃tɛrlineasjɔ̃], *s.f.* interlineation, interlining.

interlinguistique [ɛ̃tɛrlɛ̃gwistik]. **1.** *a. Ling:* interlingual; interlinguistic. **2.** *s.f.* interlinguistics.

interlobaire [ɛ̃tɛrlɔbɛːr], *a.* interlobar.

interlobulaire [ɛ̃tɛrlɔbylɛːr], *a.* interlobular.

interlock [ɛ̃tɛrlɔk]. **1.** *s.m.* (*a*) *Tex:* interlock machine; (*b*) *El:* interlock. **2.** *a.* **tissu i.,** interlock.

interlocuteur, -trice [ɛ̃tɛrlɔkytœːr, -tris], *s.* **1.** interlocutor, *f.* interlocutress; speaker (engaged in conversation); **mon i.,** the person with whom I was talking. **2.** questioner.

interlocution [ɛ̃tɛrlɔkysjɔ̃], *s.f.* interlocution.

interlocutoire [ɛ̃tɛrlɔkytwaːr]. **1.** *a.* interlocutory (judgment); provisional (order). **2.** *s.m.* interlocutory judgment, decree; provisional order; *Scot:* interlocutor (if provisional).

interlope [ɛ̃tɛrlɔp]. **1.** *s.m. A.Com: Nau:* interloper; smuggler; blockade-runner. **2.** *a.* (*a*) unauthorized, illegal, dishonest, shady (trade, trader); (*b*) suspect, dubious, shady (house, society, etc.).

interloqué [ɛ̃tɛrlɔke], *a.* disconcerted, nonplussed, abashed; **il resta i.,** he was taken aback.

interloquer [ɛ̃tɛrlɔke], *v.tr.* **1.** *Jur:* (*a*) **i. une affaire,** to award an interlocutory decree in a case; (*b*) to pronounce an interlocutory decree against (s.o.). **2.** to disconcert, nonplus (s.o.); to throw (s.o.) off his balance; to take (s.o.) aback.

s'interloquer, to be overcome by shyness; to get nervous (at examinations, etc.).

interlude [ɛ̃tɛrlyd], *s.m. Mus: Th:* interlude.

interlunaire [ɛ̃tɛrlynɛːr], *a.* interlunar, interlunary (period).

intermariage [ɛ̃tɛrmarjaːʒ], *s.m.* intermarriage.

intermaxillaire [ɛ̃tɛrmaksil(l)ɛːr], *a. Anat: Z:* intermaxillary (bone, etc.).

intermède [ɛ̃tɛrmɛd], *s.m.* **1.** *A:* medium, intermediary; **par l'i. de qch.,** through the medium, agency, of sth. **2.** *Th:* (*a*) interlude; (*b*) *A:* one-act opera. **3.** time interval; interruption; interlude; **le jour d'été polaire, sans i. de nuit,** the summer day of the polar regions, uninterrupted by night; **son séjour à la campagne avait été un i. agréable,** his stay in the country had been a pleasant interlude.

intermédiaire [ɛ̃tɛrmedjɛːr]. **1.** *a.* intermediate, intermediary, intervening (state, time, etc.); **distance i., plan i.,** middle distance; **une date i. entre . . . et . . .,** some date between . . . and . . .; **commerce i.,** middleman's business; *Mec.E:* **arbre i.,** countershaft; *Aut:* **arbre i. de changement de vitesse,** lay-shaft. **2.** *s.m.* agent, intermediary, go-between; *Com:* middleman. **3.** *s.m.* intermediary, agency, (inter)medium; (*a*) **par l'i. de qn,** through the instrumentality of s.o., through, via, s.o.; **par l'i. de la presse,** through the medium of the press; (*b*) *I.C.E:* **i. de poussoir,** tappet; *Phot:* **i. pour plaques,** plate carrier, adapter; (*c*) *Mec.E:* step-up gear, step-down gear; (*d*) *Dent:* **i. de bridge,** pontic. **4.** *s.m.* **passer d'une idée à l'autre sans i.,** to pass from one idea to another without transition.

intermédiat [ɛ̃tɛrmedja], *a.* intermediate (time).

intermenstruel, -elle [ɛ̃tɛrmɑ̃stryɛl], *a. Physiol:* intermenstrual.

intermétallique [ɛ̃tɛrmetalik], *a.* intermetallic.

intermezzo [ɛ̃tɛrmɛdzo], *s.m. Mus:* intermezzo.

interminable [ɛ̃tɛrminabl], *a.* interminable (journey, speech); endless (task); never-ending (complaint, task).

interminablement [ɛ̃tɛrminabləmɑ̃], *adv.* interminably, endlessly.

interministériel, -ielle [ɛ̃tɛrministerjɛl], *a.* interministerial; connecting, involving, several ministries.

intermission [ɛ̃tɛrmisjɔ̃], *s.f.* intermission; (*a*) **sans i.,** without intermission, uninterruptedly; (*b*) *Med:* intermission (of fever, etc.).

intermittence [ɛ̃tɛrmitɑ̃ːs], *s.f.* intermittency, intermittence; *Cards:* gap (in sequence); **par intermittence(s),** intermittently; *Gaming:* **jouer l'i.,** to back a different colour, number, at each coup.

intermittent [ɛ̃tɛrmitɑ̃], *a.* intermittent (fever, stream, gunfire, etc.); irregular (pulse); *El:* **courant i.,** make-and-break current; *Ind:* **main-d'œuvre d'emploi i.,** casual labour; **employé i.,** casual worker.

intermodulation [ɛ̃tɛrmɔdylasjɔ̃], *s.f.* intermodulation, cross modulation.

intermoléculaire [ɛ̃tɛrmɔlekylɛːr], *a.* intermolecular.

intermonde [ɛ̃tɛrmɔ̃ːd], *s.m. Phil:* intermundane space.

intermusculaire [ɛ̃tɛrmyskylɛːr], *a.* intermuscular.

internat [ɛ̃tɛrna], *s.m.* **1.** (*a*) living-in (system, period); *Sch:* boarding; (*b*) *Med:* resident medical studentship. **2.** boarding school. **3.** boarders, resident students (collectively); *Sch:* **maître d'i.** = housemaster.

international, -ale, -aux [ɛ̃tɛrnasjɔnal, -o]. **1.** *a.* international; **droit i.,** international law. **2.** (*a*) *s.m. Sp:* international (player); (*b*) *s.f.* **l'Internationale;** (i) the International Working Men's Association; the International; (ii) the Internationale.

internationalement [ɛ̃tɛrnasjɔnalmɑ̃], *adv.* internationally.

internationalisation [ɛ̃tɛrnasjɔnalizasjɔ̃], *s.f.* internationalization.

internationaliser [ɛ̃tɛrnasjɔnalize], *v.tr.* to internationalize.

internationalisme [ɛ̃tɛrnasjɔnalism], *s.m.* internationalism.

internationaliste [ɛ̃tɛrnasjɔnalist], *a. & s.m. & f.* internationalist.

internationalité [ɛ̃tɛrnasjɔnalite], *s.f.* internationality.

interne [ɛ̃tɛrn]. **1.** *a.* (*a*) internal (organ, etc.); inward (purity, etc.); **côté i.,** inner side; *Geom:* **angle i.,** interior angle; *Gram:* **accusatif de l'objet i.,** cognate accusative; *s.a.* COMBUSTION; (*b*) *Jur:* **droit i.,** municipal law; (*c*) *Sch:* **élève i.,** boarder. **2.** *s.* (*a*) *Sch:* boarder; (*b*) *Med:* = house physician, house surgeon, *U.S:* intern.

interné, -ée [ɛ̃tɛrne]. **1.** *a.* interned. **2.** *s.* internee, interned person.

internement [ɛ̃tɛrnəmɑ̃], *s.m.* internment (of alien); confinement (of madman); seclusion (of carrier pigeons).

interner [ɛ̃tɛrne], *v.tr. Adm:* to intern (alien, vessel, etc.); to shut up, confine (madman); to seclude (carrier pigeons).

internissable [ɛ̃tɛrnisabl], *a.* untarnishable.

internodal, -aux [ɛ̃tɛrnɔdal, -o], *a. Bot:* internodal.

internonce [ɛ̃tɛrnɔ̃ːs], *s.m. Ecc:* internuncio.

internonciature [ɛ̃tɛrnɔ̃sjatyːr], *s.f. Ecc:* internuncioship.

internucléaire [ɛ̃tɛrnykleɛːr], *a.* internuclear.

interocéanique [ɛ̃terɔseanik], *a.* interoceanic.

interocepteur [ɛ̃terɔseptœːr], *Physiol: Psy:* **1.** *a.* interoceptive. **2.** *s.m.* interoceptor.

interoceptif, -ive [ɛ̃terɔseptif, -iːv], *a. Physiol:* interoceptive.

interoculaire [ɛ̃terɔkylɛːr], *a. Ent:* interocular (antennae).

interoperculaire [ɛ̃terɔpɛrkylɛːr], *s.m. Ich:* interopercle, interoperculum.

interosseux, -euse [ɛ̃terɔsø, -øːz], *a.* interosseous; *Surg:* **couteau i.,** catling.

interpapillaire [ɛ̃tɛrpapilɛːr], *a. Anat:* interpapillary.

interpariétal, -aux [ɛ̃tɛrparjetal, -o], *a. Anat:* interparietal.

interparlementaire [ɛ̃tɛrparləmɑ̃tɛːr], *a. Pol:* interparliamentary; **commission i.,** joint committee (of both Houses).

interparticulaire [ɛ̃tɛrpartikylɛːr], *a. Atom.Ph:* interparticle.

interpédonculaire [ɛ̃tɛrpedɔ̃kylɛːr], *a. Anat:* interpeduncular.

interpellateur, -trice [ɛ̃tɛrpɛlatœːr, -tris], *s.* interpellator; heckler.

interpellation [ɛ̃tɛrpɛlasjɔ̃], *s.f.* **1.** (*a*) (sharp, peremptory) questioning; (*b*) (sharp) question; interpellation, interruption (at meeting, etc); heckling. **2.** (*a*) challenge; *Mil: etc:* **laisser passer qn sans i.,** to let s.o. pass unchallenged; (*b*) *Jur:* peremptory question (to witness, etc.); (*c*) *Fr.Pol.Hist:* interpellation (to minister).

interpeller [ɛ̃tɛrpɛle], *v.tr.* **1.** to call upon (s.o.), to challenge (s.o.); to heckle (s.o.); **i. un passant,** (i) *Mil:* (*of sentry*) to challenge s.o. (passing); (ii) to stop s.o. and speak to him; to accost s.o.; **les deux automobilistes s'interpellaient grossièrement,** the two drivers were exchanging insults. **2.** *Pol:* to put a question to (a minister, etc.); to interpellate.

interpénétration [ɛ̃tɛrpenetrasjɔ̃], *s.f. Pol.Ec: etc:* interpenetration.

interpénétrer [ɛ̃tɛrpenetre], *v.tr.* to interpenetrate.

s'interpénétrer, to interpenetrate; **ces deux facteurs s'interpénètrent,** these two factors are interdependent.

interphase [ɛ̃tɛrfɑːz], *s.f. Biol:* interphase.

Interphone [ɛ̃tɛrfɔn], *s.m. R.t.m:* Interphone, Intercom.

interplanétaire [ɛ̃tɛrplanetɛːr], *a.* interplanetary; **fusée i.,** space rocket; **voyage i.,** space flight.

Interpol [ɛ̃tɛrpɔl], *s.m.* Interpol.

interpolaire [ɛ̃tɛrpɔlɛːr], *a. El:* interpolar (circuit, etc.).

interpolateur, -trice [ɛ̃tɛrpɔlatœːr, -tris], *s.* interpolator.

interpolation [ɛ̃tɛrpɔlasjɔ̃], *s.f.* interpolation.

interpoler [ɛ̃tɛrpɔle], *v.tr.* to interpolate; *Mth:* **i. une fonction,** to interpolate a function.

interponctuation [ɛ̃tɛrpɔ̃ktyasjɔ̃], *s.f. A: Gram:* points of suspension.

interposé [ɛ̃tɛrpoze], *a.* interposed; *Jur:* **personne interposée,** (i) third person fraudulently replacing one of the interested parties; intermediary (in illegal donation); (ii) intermediary.

interposer [ɛ̃tɛrpoze], *v.tr.* to interpose, place (entre, between); **i. son autorité pour faire faire qch.,** to interpose, use, one's authority to have sth. done.

s'interposer, to interpose, intervene; to come between; **ne vous interposez pas,** don't intervene.

interposition [ɛ̃tɛrpozisjɔ̃], *s.f.* **1.** (*a*) interposition; (*b*) *Jur:* **i. de personne,** (fraudulent) putting forward of a third party; use of an intermediary (in a donation). **2.** intervention.

interprétable [ɛ̃tɛrpretabl], *a.* interpretable.

interprétariat [ɛ̃tɛrpretarja], *s.m.* interpretership.

interprétateur, -trice [ɛ̃tɛrpretatœːr, -tris], *s.* interpreter.

interprétatif, -ive [ɛ̃tɛrpretatif, -iːv], *a.* **1.** interpretative, explanatory (note, etc.); **clause interprétative,** interpretation clause. **2.** assumed (permission); taken for granted.

interprétation [ɛ̃tɛrpretasjɔ̃], *s.f.* **1.** interpreting (of speech, etc.). **2.** (*a*) interpretation; *Mil: etc:* **i. du renseignement,** interpretation of intelligence, of information; **fausse i., i. erronée,** misinterpretation, misconstruction (of statement, etc.); **donner une fausse i. (à qch.),** to misinterpret [(passage, etc.); to put a false construction on (s.o.'s actions, etc.); (*b*) *Mus: Th:* rendering, interpretation. **3.** *Th:* cast (of a play).

interprète [ɛ̃tɛrprɛt], *s.m. & f.* **1.** interpreter; **servir d'i. à qn, auprès d'une assemblée,** to act as interpreter to s.o., to a meeting; *Jur:* **i. juré,** official, sworn, interpreter; *Mil:* **i. auprès d'une division,** interpreter to, with, a division. **2.** expounder, expositor (of text, etc.); exponent, interpreter (of music, theatrical part, etc.); *Th:* **les interprètes,** the cast.

interpréter [ɛ̃tɛrprete], *v.tr.* (**j'interprète, n. interprétons; j'interpréterai**) to interpret; (*a*) to act as interpreter; **i. un discours,** to interpret a speech; (*b*) to explain, expound (text, etc.); to interpret (intelligence, information); **bien, mal, i. une action,** to put the right construction, a wrong construction, on an action; **mal i. les paroles de qn,** (i) to misunderstand, (ii) to garble, misinterpret, s.o.'s words; **il ne faut pas mal i. ces observations,** you should not take these remarks amiss, you should not misinterpret these remarks; **i. autrement . . .,** to put another construction on . . .; **comment interprétez-vous les faits?** how do you interpret the facts? *Mil: etc:* **i. des signaux,** to read, make out, signals; **mal i. un signal,** to misread a signal; (*c*) *Mus: Th:* to render (work, part).

interprofessionnel, -elle [ɛ̃tɛrprɔfɛsjɔnɛl], *a.* interprofessional.

interpsychologie [ɛ̃tɛrpsikɔlɔʒi], *s.f.* the study of personal relationships.

interradius [ɛ̃tɛrradjyːs], *s.m. Z:* interradium, interambulacrum.

interrané [ɛ̃tɛrane], *a. Bot:* subterranean (plant).

interrègne [ɛ̃tɛrrɛɲ], *s.m.* interregnum.

interrogateur, -trice [ɛ̃tɛrɔgatœːr, -tris]. **1.** *a.* interrogative, interrogatory, inquiring, questioning; **d'un ton i.,** in an interrogative tone, in a tone of inquiry; **il me lança un regard i.,** he gave me a questioning look. **2.** *s.* (*a*) questioner, interrogator; (*b*) *Sch:* (oral) examiner; (*c*) *s.m. W.Tel: Tp:* interrogator.

interrogateur-répondeur [ɛ̃tɛrɔgatœrrepɔ̃dœːr], *s.m. Elcs:* interrogator-responser; *pl. interrogateurs-répondeurs.*

interrogatif, -ive [ɛ̃tɛrɔgatif, -iːv], *a. & s. Gram:* interrogative (pronoun, sentence, etc.).

interrogation [ɛ̃tɛrɔgasjɔ̃], *s.f.* interrogation. **1.** questioning; putting of a question; *Gram:* **point d'i.,** question-mark, *U.S:* interrogation point. **2.** question, query, inquiry; *Sch:* oral test; *F:* oral; **i. écrite,** written answers (to questions).

interrogativement [ɛ̃tɛrɔgativmɑ̃], *adv.* interrogatively, questioningly.

interrogatoire [ɛ̃tɛrɔgatwaːr], *s.m.* (*a*) *Jur:* interrogatory, examination (of defendant, etc.); **i. contradictoire d'un témoin,** (examination and) cross-examination of a witness; (*b*) *Mil: etc:* interrogation, questioning (of prisoners).

interroger [ɛ̃tɛrɔʒe], *v.tr.* (**j'interrogeai(s); n. interrogeons**) (*a*) to examine, interrogate (witness, etc.); to examine (candidate); **i. qn sur la chimie, en chimie,** to question s.o. on chemistry; to examine s.o. in chemistry; **i. qn du regard,** to look at s.o. inquiringly, to give s.o. a questioning look; *Jur:* **i. contradictoirement,** to (examine and) cross-examine; (*b*) to consult (history, etc.); to sound (one's conscience); **i. les faits,** to consider, examine, the facts.

s'interroger, to ask oneself, to wonder (**sur,** about; **si,** whether, if).

interrompre [ɛ̃tɛrɔ̃ːpr], *v.tr.* (*conj. like* ROMPRE) (*a*) to interrupt (s.o., a conversation); *abs. F:* to cut in, to chip in; **sans vous i. . . .,** I don't mean to interrupt you . . ., excuse my interrupting . . .; **veuillez bien ne pas nous i.,** please don't interrupt; **i. la conversation, la méditation, de qn,** to break in upon the conversation, upon s.o.'s meditation; (*b*) to intercept, interrupt (flow of river, etc.); (*c*) to stop, suspend (traffic, etc.); to cut short (s.o., conversation); to break off (negotiations, etc.); to break up (conference); to break (journey) (**à,** at); *El:* to break, cut off, switch off (the current); *Mch:* to cut off, shut off (steam); *El.E:* **i. et rétablir,** to make and break; **il interrompit un instant sa lecture,** he stopped reading for a moment; **i. son travail,** to break off work.

s'interrompre, to break off, to stop (in a speech, etc.); **s'i. de parler, de chanter,** to stop, break off, talking, singing; **il s'interrompit un moment dans sa lecture,** he stopped reading for a moment.

interrompu [ɛ̃tɛrɔ̃py], *a.* interrupted, broken off; **non i.,** unbroken, continuous; **sommeil i.,** broken sleep; **propos interrompus,** (i) desultory talk; (ii) *Games:* cross questions and crooked answers; *Mus:* **cadence interrompue,** interrupted cadence. *Cards:* **partie interrompue,** unfinished game; *El:* **enroulement i.,** split winding.

interrupteur, -trice [ɛ̃tɛryptœːr, -tris]. **1.** *a.* interrupting, interruptory. **2.** *s.* interrupter. **3.** *s.m.* (*a*) *El:* switch; contact breaker, circuit breaker; **i. à lames, à couteau,** knife switch; **i. à culbuteur, à bascule,** tumbler switch; **i. à poire,** pear switch; **i. instantané,** quick-break switch; **i. va-et-vient,** two-way switch; **i. à tambour,** drum switch; **i. de démarrage,** starter switch; **i. à flotteur,** float switch; **i. à mercure,** mercury switch; **i. à (bouton) poussoir,** push button switch; **i. à relais,** relay switch; **i. bipolaire,** two-pole, double-pole, switch; **i. principal,** master switch; **i. à bras articulé,** toggle switch; **i. d'excitation,** field (break-up) switch; **i. d'urgence, de secours,** emergency switch; **i. de fin de course,** limit switch; **i. de sécurité, de sûreté,** safety switch; **i. général,** power switch; **i. rotatif,** rotary switch, turn-button switch; **i. (de) secteur,** mains switch; **i. unipolaire, i. monopolaire,** single-pole switch; **i. à minuterie,** time clock switch; **i. de télécommande,** remote control switch; **i. à gradation de lumière,** dimmer; (*b*) cut-out; **i. double,** double cut-out; **i. à maximum, de surcharge,** overload cut-out.

interrupteur-disjoncteur [ɛ̃tɛryptœrdisʒɔ̃ktœːr], *s.m. El.E:* cut-out; *pl. interrupteurs-disjoncteurs.*

interrupteur-distributeur [ɛ̃tɛryptœrdistribytœːr], *s.m. I.C.E:* make-and-break, distributor (of ignition); *pl. interrupteurs-distributeurs.*

interruptif, -ive [ɛ̃tɛryptif, -iːv], *a.* interruptive, interruptory.

interruption [ɛ̃tɛrypsjɔ̃], *s.f.* (*a*) interruption (of s.o., of conversation); breaking in (on conversation); **pas d'interruptions, s'il vous plaît!** please don't interrupt! (*b*) interruption; intercepting (of flow of river, etc.); (*c*) stoppage, cessation, break; severance (of communication, etc.); breaking off (of negotiations, etc.); *Mch:* shutting off (of steam); *El:* disconnection, switching off; breaking (of current), *U.S:* outage; **i. sans étincelles,** sparkless breaking; **i. du travail,** stoppage of work, cessation from work; **notre correspondance a subi une longue i.,** there has been a long break in our correspondence; **sans i.,** unceasingly, without a break; **j'y travaille avec des interruptions,** I work at it off and on.

inter-saison [ɛ̃tɛrsɛzɔ̃], *s.f. Sp: etc:* off season; *pl. inter-saisons.*

interscapulaire [ɛ̃tɛrskapylɛːr], *a. Anat:* interscapular.

interscapulothoracique [ɛ̃tɛrskapylɔtɔrasik], *a. Surg:* interscapulothoracic.

interscolaire [ɛ̃tɛrskɔlɛːr], *a.* inter-school (competition, etc.).

intersecté [ɛ̃tɛrsɛkte], *a.* **1.** *Arch:* intersecting, interlacing. **2.** *Geom:* intersected (line, etc.).

intersecter [ɛ̃tɛrsɛkte], *v.tr.* to intersect.

intersecteur [ɛ̃tɛrsɛktœːr], *s.m.* (*computers*) AND element.

intersection [ɛ̃tɛrsɛksjɔ̃], *s.f.* (*a*) *Geom: etc:* intersection; **point d'i.,** point of intersection; (*b*) crossing, intersection (of roads, tracks); (*c*) *Surv:* intersection, *U.S:* foresight (by compass bearings); **faire l'i. d'une contrée,** to traverse a country; **carte faite par i.,** traverse map.

intersertal, -aux [ɛ̃tɛrsɛrtal, -o], *a. Geol:* intersertal.

intersession [ɛ̃tɛrsesjɔ̃], *s.f.* (parliamentary) recess.

intersexualité [ɛ̃tɛrsɛksɥalite], *s.f. Biol:* intersexualism, intersexuality.

intersexué, -ée [ɛ̃tɛrsɛksɥe], *Biol:* **1.** *a.* intersexual; hermaphrodite; bisexual. **2.** *s.* **un, une, intersexué(e),** an intersex (individual), a hermaphrodite, a bisexual (individual).

intersidéral, -aux [ɛ̃tɛrsideral, -o], *a.* intersidereal, interstellar, outer (space); **course intersidérale,** space race.

intersigne [ɛ̃tɛrsiɲ], *s.m.* portent.

interspécifique [ɛ̃tɛrspesifik], *s.* interspecific.

interstellaire [ɛ̃tɛrstel(l)ɛːr], *a. Astr:* interstellar (space, etc.); **voyage i.,** space flight.

interstérile [ɛ̃tɛrsteril], *a. Biol:* mutually infecund.

interstérilité [ɛ̃tɛrsterilite], *s.f. Biol:* mutual infecundity.

interstice [ɛ̃tɛrstis], *s.m.* **1.** interstice; chink, cleft; *Mch:* **fuite par les interstices,** clearance losses (in turbine, etc.). **2.** *pl. Ecc:* (*R.C.Ch.*) interstices (between the reception of the various degrees of orders).

interstitiel, -ielle [ɛ̃tɛrstisjɛl], *a. Anat: etc:* interstitial.

interstratification [ɛ̃tɛrstratifikasjɔ̃], *s.f. Geol:* interstratification.

interstratifier [ɛ̃tɛrstratifje], *v.tr. Geol:* to interstratify.

intersubjectif, -ive [ɛ̃tɛrsybʒɛktif, -iːv], *a. Psy:* **communication intersubjective,** intersubjective communication.

intersubjectivité [ɛ̃tɛrsybʒɛktivite], *s.f. Psy:* intersubjectivity.

intersyndical, -aux [ɛ̃tɛrsɛ̃dikal, -o], *a. Ind: etc:* inter-union.

intersystole [ɛ̃tɛrsistɔl], *s.f. Physiol:* heart-beat interval.

intertidal, -aux [ɛ̃tɛrtidal, -o], *a. Geog:* intertidal.

intertitre [ɛ̃tɛrtitr̥], *s.m. Journ:* subtitle.

intertransversaire [ɛ̃tɛrtrɑ̃svɛrsɛːr], *a. Anat:* intertransverse, intertransversal, intertransversary.

intertrigineux, -euse [ɛ̃tɛrtriʒinø, -øːz], *a. Med:* intertriginous.

intertrigo [ɛ̃tɛrtrigo], *s.m. Med:* intertrigo.

intertropical, -aux [ɛ̃tɛrtrɔpikal, -o], *a.* intertropical.

Intertype [ɛ̃tɛrtip], *s.f. Typ: R.t.m:* Intertype.

interurbain [ɛ̃tɛryrbɛ̃], *a.* interurban; *Tp:* **relations, lignes, interurbaines,** trunk connections, trunk lines; *s.m. Tp:* trunks.

intervalle [ɛ̃tɛrval], *s.m.* interval. **1.** (*a*) distance, interval, gap, space (**entre,** between); **sentinelles disposées à des intervalles de cent mètres,** sentries posted a hundred yards apart; **i. sur route,** road space; (*b*) *El.E:* clearance (space) (in dynamo, etc.); **i. d'allumage,** starter gap; **i. d'éclatement, de déchargement,** gap; **i. de fréquence,** frequency spacing; **i. d'impulsions,** pulse spacing, interval; *Tg:* **i. de manipulation,** spacing interval; (*c*) *Ph: Mec.E:* range, interval; **i. d'ébullition,** boiling range; **i. d'absorption,** absorption range; **i. angulaire,** angular range, interval; *Atom.Ph:* **i. de recouvrement,** overlap region; (*d*) *Mus:* **i. simple, redoublé,** simple, compound, interval. **2.** period (of time); **visites à de longs intervalles,** visits at long intervals; visits few and far between; **par intervalles,** at intervals, on and off, now and then, intermittently; **dans l'i. je vais . . .,** in the meantime I shall . . .; **ils étaient partis dans l'i.,** by then, by that time, they had gone.

intervenant, -ante [ɛ̃tɛrvənɑ̃, -ɑ̃ːt]. **1.** *a. Jur: etc:* intervening, intermediate. **2.** *s.* intervening party, intervener; *Com:* acceptor (of bill) for honour.

intervenir [ɛ̃tɛrvəniːr], *v.i.* (*conj. like* VENIR; *the aux. is* **être**) **1.** to intervene; (*a*) to interpose; to take action; to step in; **i. pour prendre la défense de qn,** to intervene in defence of s.o.; **i. dans une querelle,** to intervene, act as mediator, in a quarrel; **i. dans une conversation,** to break in on a conversation, *F:* to butt in; **je jugeai qu'il était temps d'i.,** I thought it was time for me to intervene, to take a hand; **faire i. qn,** to bring in s.o.; to call in s.o.; to appeal to s.o.; **faire i. la force armée,** to call out the military; **le prix de la colle intervient dans le coût de la reliure,** the price of glue affects the cost of binding; **faire i. un député, un parlementaire, en sa faveur,** to ask a Member of Parliament to sponsor one's application, one's claim, to use his influence on one's behalf; **une théorie qui fait i. la gravité,** a theory which involves, involving, gravity; (*b*) *Jur:* **i. à un contrat,** to intervene in, become a third party to, an agreement; (*c*) to interfere; **i. dans un pays voisin,** to intervene in the affairs of a neighbouring country. **2.** *impers.* to happen, occur, arise; **un grand changement est intervenu,** meanwhile a great change has taken place; **un accord est intervenu sur . . .,** an agreement has been reached, concluded, arrived at, on . . .; **il intervint un jugement,** judgment was pronounced.

intervention [ɛ̃tɛrvɑ̃sjɔ̃], *s.f.* **1.** (*a*) intervening, intervention; **i. chirurgicale,** surgical intervention, operation; **l'i. de la force armée,** the intervention of the military; **offre d'i.,** offer of mediation; *Mil.Av:* **i. aérienne,** strike; (*b*) *Jur:* intervention, becoming a third party (in a contract, etc.); **paiement par i.,** payment on behalf of a third party; *Com:* **acceptation par i.,** acceptance (of protested bill) for honour; (**acte d') i.,** act of honour; *Com:* **i. à protêt,** intervention on protest; (*c*) **l'i. de M. X a été accueillie favorablement,** Mr X's speech was favourably received; **i. parlementaire,** sponsoring of claims, of applications (by members of Parliament). **2.** interference.

interventionnisme [ɛ̃tɛrvɑ̃sjɔnism], *s.m. Pol: etc:* interventionism.

interventionniste [ɛ̃tɛrvɑ̃sjɔnist], *s.m. & f. Pol: etc:* interventionist.

interventriculaire [ɛ̃tɛrvɑ̃trikylɛːr], *a. Anat:* interventricular.

interversibilité [ɛ̃tɛrvɛrsibilite], *s.f. Mth:* invertibility.

interversible [ɛ̃tɛrvɛrsibl̥], *a.* invertible.

interversion [ɛ̃tɛrvɛrsjɔ̃], *s.f.* inversion, transposition (of order, of dates, of seasons); *Ch:* (optical) inversion (of polarization of sugar, etc.); *Mth:* inversion; *Geol:* inversion (of strata).

intervertébral, -aux [ɛ̃tɛrvɛrtebral, -o], *a. Anat:* intervertebral; **disque i.,** (intervertebral) disk.

intervertir [ɛ̃tɛrvɛrtiːr], *v.tr.* **1.** to invert, transpose; to reverse (the order of . . .); **maintenant les rôles sont intervertis,** now the tables are turned. **2.** *Ch:* to invert (polarization of a carbohydrate); **sucre interverti,** invert sugar.

interview [ɛ̃tɛrvju], *s.f.* **1.** interview; **i. de M. Wilson,** interview with Mr Wilson. **2.** interviewing.

interviewé, -ée [ɛ̃tɛrvju(v)e], *a. & s.* (person) interviewed.

interviewer[1] [ɛ̃tɛrvju(v)e], *v.tr.* to interview.

interviewer[2] [ɛ̃tɛrvju(v)œːr], *s.m.* interviewer.

intervilles [ɛ̃tɛrvil], *a.inv.* interurban.

intervision [ɛ̃tɛrvizjɔ̃], *s.f.* closed-circuit television.

intervocalique [ɛ̃tɛrvɔkalik], *a. Ling:* intervocalic.

interzonal, -aux [ɛ̃tɛrzɔnal, -o], *a.* interzonal, interzone.

intestable [ɛ̃tɛstabl̩], *a. Jur:* unqualified to make a will.

intestat [ɛ̃tɛsta], *a.inv. Jur:* **mourir i., décéder i.,** to die intestate; **succession ab i.,** intestate estate; **hériter ab i.,** to succeed to an intestate estate.

intestin¹ [ɛ̃tɛstɛ̃], *a.* internal; domestic, civil (war, etc.).

intestin², *s.m. Anat:* intestine(s); **gros i.,** large intestine; **i. grêle,** small intestine; **i. antérieur, i. pré-oral,** foregut.

intestinal, -aux [ɛ̃tɛstinal, -o], *a.* intestinal; **affection intestinale,** intestinal, bowel, affection; *Vet:* **vers intestinaux,** worms.

intima [ɛ̃tima], *s.m. Anat:* intima.

intimation [ɛ̃timasjɔ̃], *s.f.* **1.** intimation; notification (**d'un ordre,** of an order); *Jur:* **i. de vider les lieux,** notice to quit; **faire des intimations aux partis,** to notify, summon, the parties. **2.** *Jur:* notice of appeal.

intime [ɛ̃tim], *a.* intimate. **1.** interior, inward, deep-seated (conviction, grief, etc.); **pensées intimes,** inmost thoughts; **sens i. d'un passage,** inner meaning of a passage; **les recoins les plus intimes du cœur,** the inmost recesses of the heart; **blesser les sentiments les plus intimes de qn,** to wound s.o.'s inmost feelings. **2.** close (*a*) **services en rapport i. avec l'armée,** departments closely linked with the army; **mélange i.,** intimate mixture; (*b*) **ami i.,** particular, intimate, close, friend; **dîner i.,** quiet dinner; dinner between old friends; **leur petit salon est plus i.,** their living-room is more homelike, more cosy; **conversation i.,** heart-to-heart talk; *s.* **un, une, i.,** an intimate friend, a close friend, a bosom friend; **ses intimes savent que . . .,** his intimates know that . . .; **les David et leurs intimes,** the David circle; (*c*) *Jur:* **preuve de relations intimes,** evidence that intimacy took place; (*d*) **hygiène i.,** personal hygiene; (*e*) **secrétaire i.,** private secretary.

intimé, -ée [ɛ̃time], *s. Jur:* respondent, defendant (before Court of Appeal).

intimement [ɛ̃tim(ə)mɑ̃], *adv.* intimately; closely.

intimer [ɛ̃time], *v.tr.* **1. i. qch. à qn,** to intimate sth. to s.o., to give s.o. (formal) notice of sth., to notify s.o. of sth.; **i. à qn l'ordre de partir,** to give s.o. notice to go; *Jur:* **faire i. un appel à qn,** to give s.o. notice of appeal. **2.** *Jur:* **i. qn,** to cite, summons, s.o. to appear, before the Court of Appeal.

intimidable [ɛ̃timidabl̩], *a.* easily intimidated.

intimidant [ɛ̃timidɑ̃], *a.* intimidating, awe-inspiring.

intimidateur, -trice [ɛ̃timidatœːr, -tris]. **1.** *a.* intimidating, intimidatory. **2.** *s.* intimidator.

intimidation [ɛ̃timidasjɔ̃], *s.f.* intimidation; *esp. Jur:* threatening; undue influence; **système d'i.,** system of intimidation.

intimider [ɛ̃timide], *v.tr.* (*a*) to intimidate, frighten; to cow; to make (s.o.) shy, self-conscious; **il nous intimidait,** we stood in awe of him; **être, se sentir, intimidé en présence de qn,** to be, feel, self-conscious, to feel nervous, in s.o.'s presence; **la sévérité de son regard m'a intimidé,** his stern looks put me off; **nullement intimidé,** nothing daunted; (*b*) *Jur:* to threaten; to exert undue influence on (s.o.); *F:* to browbeat, bully (s.o.).

s'intimider, to become shy, self-conscious, nervous; **ne vous intimidez pas,** don't be frightened.

intimisme [ɛ̃timism], *s.m. Lit: Art:* intimism.

intimiste [ɛ̃timist], *a. & s.m. & f. Lit: Art:* intimist; **poésie i.,** intimist poetry.

intimité [ɛ̃timite], *s.f.* **1.** inward parts, depths (of one's being, etc.); **dans l'i. de la conscience il se rendait compte que . . .,** his inner conscience told him that . . .. **2.** intimacy; (*a*) close connection (between actions, etc.); intimacy (of mixture, etc.); (*b*) closeness (of friendship, contact); **lier i. avec qn,** to become intimate with s.o.; (*c*) **l'i. du chez-soi,** the privacy of one's home; **dans l'i.,** in private (life); **introduire qn dans son i.,** to introduce s.o. into (the bosom of) one's family; **le mariage fut célébré dans la plus stricte i.,** it was a very quiet wedding; **les obsèques auront lieu dans la plus stricte i.,** the funeral will be private; **il avait des goûts d'i.,** he enjoyed home life.

intinction [ɛ̃tɛ̃ksjɔ̃], *s.f. Ecc:* intinction.

intine [ɛ̃tin], *s.m. Bot:* intine.

intirable [ɛ̃tirabl̩], *a. Typ:* that cannot be printed, run off.

intitulation [ɛ̃titylasjɔ̃], *s.f.* (*a*) giving a title to (a book); (*b*) title (of book).

intitulé [ɛ̃tityle], *s.m.* title (of document, of book, etc.); heading (of chapter, etc.); *Jur:* premises (of deed); **i. d'un acte,** abstract of title of an act.

intituler [ɛ̃tityle], *v.tr.* to entitle, give a title to (book, document, person, etc.); **article intitulé . . .,** article headed . . ..

s'intituler, (*a*) to be entitled; **ce livre s'intitule** *Standard Dictionary*, this book is entitled *Standard Dictionary*; (*b*) *often Pej:* to call oneself; **s'i. baron,** to call oneself a baron.

intolérabilité [ɛ̃tɔlerabilite], *s.f.* intolerableness, intolerability.

intolérable [ɛ̃tɔlerabl̩], *a.* intolerable, insufferable, unbearable, unendurable; **vie i.,** life that is not worth living.

intolérablement [ɛ̃tɔlerabləmɑ̃], *adv.* intolerably, unbearably.

intolérance [ɛ̃tɔlerɑ̃ːs], *s.f.* intolerance; **avoir trop d'i. pour les faiblesses de qn,** to be too intolerant of s.o.'s failings; *Med:* **i. d'un remède,** inability to tolerate a remedy, allergy, intolerance, to a remedy.

intolérant [ɛ̃tɔlerɑ̃], *a.* intolerant (**de,** of).

intolérantisme [ɛ̃tɔlerɑ̃tism], *s.m.* religious, political, intolerance.

intonation [ɛ̃tɔnasjɔ̃], *s.f.* intonation. **1.** *Mus:* (*a*) opening phrase (of plainsong melody); (*b*) modulation (of voice). **2.** modulation, pitch, ring (of the voice); **sa réponse n'avait pas l'i. de la vérité,** his answer did not ring true.

intondu [ɛ̃tɔ̃dy], *a.* unshorn.

intorsion [ɛ̃tɔrsjɔ̃], *s.f. Bot: etc:* intorsion; twisting.

intortus [ɛ̃tɔrtyːs], *s.m. Meteor:* mare's tail cirrus.

intouchable [ɛ̃tuʃabl̩]. **1.** *a.* untouchable; *F:* sacrosanct. **2.** *s.m. & f.* (*in India*) untouchable.

intoxicant [ɛ̃tɔksikɑ̃], *a. Med:* poisonous, toxic.

intoxication [ɛ̃tɔksikasjɔ̃], *s.f.* (*a*) *Med:* intoxication, poisoning; **i. alimentaire,** food poisoning; (*b*) intoxication, over-elation; (*c*) poisoning (of mind, etc.); *Mil: Pol:* deception; **mesures d'i.,** deceptive measures; **plan d'i.,** deception plan.

intoxiquer [ɛ̃tɔksike], *v.tr.* (*a*) *Med:* to poison; (*esp. of food, etc.*) to cause auto-intoxication; (*b*) to poison (mind, etc.).

intra- [ɛ̃tra], *pref.* intra-; **intrahépatique,** intrahepatic; **intramusculaire,** intramuscular; **intra-utérin,** intra-uterine; **intravaginal,** intravaginal.

intra-artériel, -ielle [ɛ̃traarterjɛl], *a.* intra-arterial; *intra-artériel(le)s.*

intra-articulaire [ɛ̃traartiklɛːr], *a.* intra-articular; *pl. intra-articulaires.*

intra-atomique [ɛ̃traatɔmik], *a. Atom.Ph:* intra-atomics; *pl. intra-atomiques.*

intra-aural, -aux [ɛ̃traɔral, -o], *a.* intra-aural.

intracardiaque [ɛ̃trakardjak], *a.* intracardiac.

intracellulaire [ɛ̃traselylɛːr], *a. Biol:* intracellular.

intracérébral, -aux [ɛ̃traserebral, -o], *a. Med: etc:* intracerebral (injection, etc.).

intracervical, -aux [ɛ̃trasɛrvikal, -o], *a.* intracervical.

intra-champ [ɛ̃traʃɑ̃], *s.m. Sp:* (*baseball*) infield; *pl. intra-champs.*

intracrânien, -ienne [ɛ̃trakrɑnjɛ̃, -jɛn], *a. Anat:* intracranial.

intradermique [ɛ̃tradɛrmik], *a. Anat:* intradermic, intradermal.

intradermo-réaction [ɛ̃tradɛrmɔreaksjɔ̃], *s.f. Med:* intradermal reaction; *pl. intradermo-réactions.*

intrados [ɛ̃trado], *s.m.* (*a*) *Arch:* inner surface, soffit, intrados (of arch); (*b*) *Av:* under surface (of wing); face (of propeller blade); **panneau d'i.,** lower skin panel; **radiateur d'i.,** under-wing radiator; **volet d'i.,** split flap.

intraduisible [ɛ̃tradɥizibl̩], *a.* untranslatable, that can hardly be translated.

intraduit [ɛ̃tradɥi], *a.* untranslated.

intraépithélial, -aux [ɛ̃traepiteljal, -o], *a. Anat:* intraepithelial.

intraglaciaire [ɛ̃traglasjɛːr], *a. Geol:* intraglacial.

intrahépatique [ɛ̃traepatik], *a. Anat:* intrahepatic.

intraitable [ɛ̃trɛtabl̩], *a.* (*a*) intractable, unmanageable; (*b*) obstinate, stiff-necked, uncompromising; adamant; **vertu i.,** inflexible virtue.

intramédullaire [ɛ̃tramedyl(l)ɛːr], *a. Anat:* intramedullary.

intramercuriel, -ielle [ɛ̃tramɛrkyrjɛl], *a. Astr:* intra-mercurial; *pl. intra-mercuriel(le)s.*

intramoléculaire [ɛ̃tramɔlekylɛːr], *a. Ph:* intramolecular.

intramontagnard [ɛ̃tramɔ̃taɲaːr], **intramontagneux, -euse** [ɛ̃tramɔ̃taɲø, -øːz], *a. Geog:* intramontane.

intra-muros [ɛ̃tramyroːs]. **1.** *adv.* within the (city) walls. **2.** *a.inv.* intramural (district, etc.).

intramusculaire [ɛ̃tramyskylɛːr], *a.* intramuscular.

intransférable [ɛ̃trɑ̃sferabl̩], *a.* untransferable; *Jur:* unassignable (right, etc.).

intransigeance [ɛ̃trɑ̃ziʒɑ̃ːs], *s.f.* intransigence, intransigency; uncompromisingness; strictness.

intransigeant, -ante [ɛ̃trɑ̃ziʒɑ̃, -ɑ̃ːt]. **1.** *a.* intransigent (in politics); uncompromising, strict (moral code, etc.); peremptory (tone); **politique intransigeante,** policy of no compromise; **sur ce point il est i.,** on this point he is adamant. **2.** *s. Pol:* intransigent(ist); diehard.

intransitif, -ive [ɛ̃trɑ̃zitif, -iːv], *a. & s.m. Gram:* intransitive.

intransitivement [ɛ̃trɑ̃zitivmɑ̃], *adv. Gram:* intransitively.

intransitivité [ɛ̃trɑ̃zitivite], *s.f. Gram:* intransitivity, intransitiveness.

intransmissible [ɛ̃trɑ̃smisibl̩], *a.* intransmissible.

intransportable [ɛ̃trɑ̃spɔrtabl̩], *a.* (*a*) untransportable; (*b*) (*of wounded man*) unfit to travel, to be moved.

intranucléaire [ɛ̃tranykleɛːr], *a.* intranuclear.

intra-oculaire [ɛ̃traɔkylɛːr], *a. Anat:* intraocular; *pl. intra-oculaires.*

intrapelvien, -ienne [ɛ̃trapɛlvjɛ̃, -jɛn], *a. Anat:* intrapelvic.

intrapilaire [ɛ̃trapilɛːr], *a. El:* internal (current, etc.).

intrapleural, -aux [ɛ̃traplœral, -o], *a. Anat:* intrapleural.

intra-rachidien, -ienne [ɛ̃traraʃidjɛ̃, -jɛn], *a. Anat:* intraspinal, intrathecal; *pl. intra-rachidiens, -iennes.*

intrasolaire [ɛ̃trasɔlɛːr], *a.* intrasolar.

intraspécifique [ɛ̃traspesifik], *a.* intraspecific.

intratellurique [ɛ̃tratelyrik], *a. Geol:* intratelluric.

intrathoracique [ɛ̃tratɔrasik], *a. Anat:* intrathoracic.

intra-utérin [ɛ̃trayterɛ̃], *a. Anat:* intra-uterine; *pl. intra-utérins, -ines.*

intravasculaire [ɛ̃travaskylɛːr], *a.* intravascular.

intraveineux, -euse [ɛ̃travenø, -øːz], *a.* intravenous.

intraversable [ɛ̃travɛrsabl̩], *a.* untraversable, that cannot be crossed.

intraversé [ɛ̃travɛrse], *a.* untraversed (plain, etc.); untrodden (ways).

in-trente-deux [intrɑ̃tdø], *a. & s.m.inv. Typ:* (in) thirty-twomo.

in-trente-six [intrɑ̃tsis], *a. & s.m.inv. Typ:* (in) thirty-sixmo.

intrépide [ɛ̃trepid], *a.* intrepid, dauntless, undaunted, bold, fearless (hero, etc.); **menteur i.,** brazen(-faced) liar; **i. à nier l'évidence même,** brazen in denial of patent facts.

intrépidement [ɛ̃trepidmɑ̃], *adv.* intrepidly, fearlessly; dauntlessly, nothing daunted.

intrépidité [ɛ̃trepidite], *s.f.* intrepidity, dauntlessness, fearlessness; **avec i.,** fearlessly; **son i. à attaquer,** his fearlessness, boldness, in attack.

intrication [ɛ̃trikasjɔ̃], *s.f. Nat.Hist:* intrication.

intrigailler [ɛ̃trigaje], *v.i.* to engage in petty intrigue.

intrigant, -ante [ɛ̃trigɑ̃, -ɑ̃ːt]. **1.** *a.* intriguing, scheming, designing. **2.** *s.* intriguer, schemer, wire-puller.

intrigue [ɛ̃trig], *s.f.* intrigue. **1.** (*a*) plot, scheme; **homme d'i.,** man of intrigue; adventurer; **une i. de cour,** a court intrigue; *Pol:* **intrigues de couloirs,** lobbying; (*b*) (love) affair, intrigue; **avoir une i. avec une femme mariée,** to have an affair with a married woman. **2.** *Lit: Th:* plot (of play, novel, etc.); **i. secondaire,** subordinate plot, sub-plot; *Lit.Hist:* **comédie d'i.,** comedy depending chiefly on intricacy of plot; comedy of intrigue.

intrigué [ɛ̃trige], *a.* puzzled, curious, mystified; intrigued; **elle était intriguée par ces visites,** she was intrigued by these visits.

intriguer [ɛ̃trige]. **1.** *v.tr.* (*a*) to puzzle; to rouse the curiosity of (s.o.); to intrigue (s.o.); **ça l'a intrigué,** that intrigued him, got him guessing; (*b*) *Lit: Th:* to elaborate, work up, the plot of (book, etc.); (*c*) *abs.* **ce qui intrigue, c'est que . . .,** the intriguing thing is that . . .. **2.** *v.i.* to scheme, plot, intrigue; **i. pour qn,** to intrigue, scheme, on s.o.'s behalf; *F:* to pull wires for s.o.

s'intriguer, *A:* (*a*) to be puzzled, intrigued; (*b*) **s'i. pour qn,** to scheme, plot, for s.o.; (*c*) **s'i. partout,** to meddle officiously in everything; to poke one's nose into everything.

intrinsèque [ɛ̃trɛ̃sɛk], *a.* intrinsic (value, defect, *Anat:* muscle, etc.); specific (value).

intrinsèquement [ɛ̃trɛ̃sɛkmɑ̃], *adv.* intrinsically, specifically.

intriqué [ɛ̃trike], *a.* (*a*) intricate, criss-cross (pattern, etc.); (*b*) *Nat.Hist:* intricate (fibres, etc.).

intro- [ɛ̃trɔ], *pref.* intro-; **introfléchi,** introflexed.

introducteur, -trice [ɛ̃trɔdyktœːr, -tris], s. 1. (a) introducer (of person, of the potato into France, etc.); innovator (of fashion, etc.); (b) usher (at a reception); (at court) i. des ambassadeurs, etc., master of ceremonies. 2. s.m.pl. St.Exch: F: the shop.

introductif, -ive [ɛ̃trɔdyktif, -iːv], a. introductory, introductive.

introduction [ɛ̃trɔdyksjɔ̃], s.f. introduction. 1. (a) insertion (of probe in wound, etc.); Mch: admission, induction (of steam, gas, etc.); (b) (computers) i. manuelle, manual input; (c) introducing, bringing in (of s.o. into s.o.'s presence, of goods into country, etc.); lettre d'i., (letter of) introduction (de la part de, from; auprès de, to); (d) Jur: i. d'instance, writ of summons, first process); (e) St.Exch: bringing out (of shares); actions à l'i., F: shop shares. 2. (a) introductory matter, chapter; preliminary piece (to play, etc.); après quelques mots d'i. . . ., after a few introductory words . . .; (b) i. à la physique, an introduction to physics, a first course in physics; (c) Mus: introduction (to symphony, etc.).

introductoire [ɛ̃trɔdyktwaːr], a. introductory.

introduire [ɛ̃trɔdɥiːr], v.tr. (pr.p. introduisant; p.p. introduit; pr.ind. j'introduis, il introduit, n. introduisons; p.h. j'introduisis; fu. j'introduirai) to introduce; (a) to insert, put (key in lock, etc.); s'i. entre deux personnes, to get in between two people; (b) (computers) to input; (c) to bring in (goods, new ideas, etc.); to admit, let in (steam, etc.); St.Exch: to introduce, bring out (shares); i. un nouveau sujet de conversation, to introduce a fresh subject of conversation; i. une mode, to introduce, launch, a fashion; Jur: i. une instance, to present a plea; P.N: il est défendu d'i. des chiens, no dogs allowed; (d) to present, usher in, show in (stranger, etc.); introduisez ce monsieur, show the gentleman in; il fut introduit au salon, he was shown into the drawing room; il fut introduit auprès du baron, he was shown, ushered, into the baron's presence.

s'introduire, to get in, enter; les voleurs se sont introduits dans la cuisine, the thieves got into, found their way into, the kitchen; abus qui s'est introduit dans l'État, abuse that has crept into the State; s'i. dans le monde, to worm one's way into society; l'eau s'introduit partout, the water is penetrating everywhere.

introfléchi [ɛ̃trɔfleʃi], a. introflexed.

introït [ɛ̃trɔit], s.m. Ecc: introit.

introjection [ɛ̃trɔʒɛksjɔ̃], s.f. Psy: introjection.

intromission [ɛ̃trɔmisjɔ̃], s.f. Ph: Bot: intromission, absorption (of air, water, etc.).

intronisation [ɛ̃trɔnizasjɔ̃], s.f. 1. enthroning, enthronement (esp. of bishop). 2. establishment (of system, doctrine, etc.).

introniser [ɛ̃trɔnize], v.tr. 1. to (en)throne (king, bishop). 2. to set up, establish (new religion, etc.).

s'introniser, (a) s'i. chez qn, to establish oneself in s.o.'s household; (b) (of custom, etc.) to become established, to assert itself.

introrse [ɛ̃trɔrs], a. Bot: introrse.

introspecter (s') [sɛ̃trɔspɛkte], v.pr. to introspect, to be introspective.

introspectif, -ive [ɛ̃trɔspɛktif, -iːv], a. introspective.

introspection [ɛ̃trɔspɛksjɔ̃], s.f. introspection.

introublé [ɛ̃truble], a. undisturbed.

introuvable [ɛ̃truvabl̩], a. (a) undiscoverable, not to be found; l'assassin reste i., the murderer remains undiscovered; bénéficiaire i., untraceable beneficiary; pendant la guerre la bière était i., beer was unobtainable during the war; (b) the like of which is not to be found; matchless, incomparable.

introversion [ɛ̃trɔvɛrsjɔ̃], s.f. Psy: introversion.

introverti, -ie [ɛ̃trɔvɛrti], a. Psy: introverted; s. introvert.

intrure [ɛ̃tryːr], v.tr. A: (p.p. intrus) to intrude (s.o.); il l'avait intruse dans notre société, he had intruded her upon our company, upon us; he had foisted her upon us.

s'intrure, A: il s'était intrus dans la réunion, he had intruded his presence, pushed his way, into the meeting.

intrus, -use [ɛ̃try, -yːz]. 1. a. intruding. 2. s. (a) intruder; F: gatecrasher; (b) Ecc: unqualified priest; (c) Jur: trespasser.

intrusif, -ive [ɛ̃tryzif, -iːv], a. Geol: intrusive.

intrusion [ɛ̃tryzjɔ̃], s.f. (a) intrusion; faire i. dans une société, auprès de qn, to intrude upon a company, upon s.o.; i. dans une affaire, interference in a matter; (b) Jur: trespass; (c) Geol: intrusion; roches d'i., intrusive rocks.

intubation [ɛ̃tybasjɔ̃], s.f. Med: intubation.

intuitif, -ive [ɛ̃tɥitif, -iːv], a. intuitive.

intuition [ɛ̃tɥisjɔ̃], s.f. intuition; avoir l'i. de qch., to have an intuition of sth.; par i., intuitively.

intuitionnisme [ɛ̃tɥisjɔnism], s.m. intuitionalism.

intuitionniste [ɛ̃tɥisjɔnist], s.m. & f. intuitionalist.

intuitivement [ɛ̃tɥitivmɑ̃], adv. intuitively.

intumescence [ɛ̃tymɛs(s)ɑ̃ːs], s.f. swelling (up), intumescence.

intumescent [ɛ̃tymɛs(s)ɑ̃], a. beginning to swell, intumescent.

intussusception [ɛ̃tys(s)ys(s)ɛpsjɔ̃], s.f. Physiol: Surg: intussusception, introsusception.

inula [inyla], s.f. Bot: inula.

inulase [inylaːz], s.f. Bio-Ch: inulase.

inule [inyl], s.f. Bot: inula, elecampane.

inuline [inylin], s.f. Ch: inulin.

inusable [inyzabl̩], a. impossible to wear out; everlasting.

inusité [inyzite], a. (a) unusual, uncommon; (b) not in common use.

inusuel, -elle [inyzɥɛl], a. Lit: unusual.

inutile [inytil]. 1. a. (a) useless (work, article); unavailing, unprofitable (work); vain (effort); wasteful (expenditure); je suis i. ici, I'm of no use here; perdre son temps en discours inutiles, to waste one's breath; je sais qu'il est (parfaitement) i. de s'adresser à vous, I know it's quite hopeless appealing to you; les bouches inutiles, the useless members of society; (b) needless, unnecessary; c'est i.! (i) it's no good! (ii) you needn't trouble; i. de dire que . . ., needless to say, no need to say, that . . .; i. à vous d'attendre, you needn't wait; i. d'attendre, it's no good waiting; il est i. qu'il m'écrive, he needn't write to me, it is no use his writing to me; je juge, j'estime, i. de raconter . . ., I see no object, no point, in relating . . .; histoire i. à remémorer, story not worth raking up. 2. s. les inutiles, the useless members of society; the drones.

inutilement [inytilmɑ̃], adv. (a) uselessly, unavailingly, to no purpose, in vain; (b) needlessly, unnecessarily.

inutilisable [inytilizabl̩], a. (a) unserviceable, unusable; (b) worthless; unemployable (man).

inutilisé [inytilize], a. unutilized; untapped (resources, etc.).

inutilité [inytilite], s.f. 1. (a) inutility, uselessness, unprofitableness, futility; (b) needlessness, unnecessariness; (c) A: laisser qn dans l'i., to leave s.o. unemployed. 2. pl. superfluous, useless things; apprendre des inutilités, to learn useless things.

invagination [ɛ̃vaʒinasjɔ̃], s.f. invagination, intussusception.

invaginé [ɛ̃vaʒine], a. invaginate(d).

invaginer [ɛ̃vaʒine], v.tr. to invaginate.

invaincu [ɛ̃vɛ̃ky], a. unconquered; unvanquished; unbeaten; Mount: sommet i., unconquered, unscaled, peak; Turf: cheval i., unbeaten horse.

invalidable [ɛ̃validabl̩], a. Jur: (election, etc.) that can be invalidated.

invalidation [ɛ̃validasjɔ̃], s.f. Jur: invalidation (of document, election, etc.); unseating (of elected member).

invalide [ɛ̃valid]. 1. a. (a) invalid, infirm; disabled (soldier, etc.); F: table invalide, rickety old table; (b) Jur: invalid (will, etc.); null and void. 2. s. (a) invalid; (b) s.m. disabled soldier, pensioner; invalides civils, civil pensioners; l'Hôtel des Invalides, s.m.pl. les Invalides, the army pensioners' hospital (in Paris). 3. s.m.pl. A: invalides, (invalid) pension; F: A: avoir ses invalides, to be ending one's days in honourable retirement.

invalider [ɛ̃valide], v.tr. 1. Jur: to invalidate (will, election, etc.); to quash (election); to unseat (an elected member). 2. abs. Med: to cripple.

invalidité [ɛ̃validite], s.f. 1. (a) infirmity; Adm: disablement, disability; coefficient d'i., degree of disablement; pension d'i., disability pension; s.a. ASSURANCE 3; (b) chronic ill health; invalidism. 2. Jur: invalidity (of will, etc.).

invar [ɛ̃vaːr], s.m. Metall: invar (metal); invar steel.

invariabilité [ɛ̃varjabilite], s.f. invariability, invariableness.

invariable [ɛ̃varjabl̩], a. invariable, unvarying, unchanging, constant; Gram: particule i., invariable particle.

invariablement [ɛ̃varjabləmɑ̃], adv. invariably.

invariance [ɛ̃varjɑ̃ːs], s.f. Mth: invariance.

invariant [ɛ̃varjɑ̃], s.m. Mth: invariant, constant.

invasion [ɛ̃vazjɔ̃], s.f. 1. invading, invasion; armée d'i., invading army. 2. invasion, inroad; faire une i. dans un pays, to invade a country; faire i. chez qn, to invade s.o.'s house, to descend on s.o.; l'eau faisait i. de toutes parts, the water was coming in on all sides; l'i. du mauvais goût, the outbreak of bad taste. 3. Med: invasion (of disease). 4. infestation (of parasites).

invective [ɛ̃vɛktiːv], s.f. (a) invective; (b) pl. abuse; se répandre en invectives contre qn, to break into a torrent of abuse against s.o.

invectiver [ɛ̃vɛktive]. 1. v.i. i. contre qn, to inveigh against s.o.; to rail at, against, s.o.; i. contre le vice, to denounce vice. 2. v.tr. to abuse (s.o.); to use abusive language to (s.o.); to hurl abuse at (s.o.).

invendable [ɛ̃vɑ̃dabl̩], a. unsaleable, unmarketable, unmerchantable.

invendu [ɛ̃vɑ̃dy]. 1. a. unsold. 2. s.m.pl. invendus, unsold goods; unsold copies (of newspapers, etc.).

invengé [ɛ̃vɑ̃ʒe], a. unavenged, unrevenged.

inventaire [ɛ̃vɑ̃tɛːr], s.m. inventory; (a) faire, dresser, un i., to draw up an inventory; i. d'entrée (dans un immeuble), ingoing inventory; i. de sortie (d'un immeuble), outgoing inventory; i. de bord, (i) Nau: ship's inventory; (ii) Av: inventory of aircraft equipment and furniture; sous bénéfice d'i., (i) Jur: under beneficium inventorii; (ii) conditionally, with reservations; accepter une succession sous bénéfice d'i., to accept an estate without liability to debts beyond the assets descended; Com: Ind: système d'i. permanent, continuous review system; (b) Com: stock list; (établissement, levée, d') inventaire, stocktaking; faire, dresser, l'i., to take stock; soldes après i., stocktaking sale; (c) Book-k: i. (comptable), accounts; book inventory; i. de fin d'année, de fin d'exercice, accounts for, to the end of, the financial year; livre d'i., des inventaires, balance book; (d) Fin: valuation (of investments, securities, etc.); (e) list, schedule; survey (of ancient monuments, paintings, etc.).

inventer [ɛ̃vɑ̃te], v.tr. to invent; (a) to find out, discover; il n'a pas inventé la poudre, he will never set the Thames on fire; (b) to devise, contrive (machine, excuse, etc.); F: to dream up; to make up (story, etc.); to coin (phrase); i. une histoire, F: un bobard, to spin a yarn; histoire inventée (à plaisir), trumped-up story, pure fabrication; (c) abs. i. de faire qch., (i) to take it into one's head to do sth.; (ii) to hit on the idea of doing sth.

inventeur, -trice [ɛ̃vɑ̃tœːr, -tris]. 1. s. (a) inventor, discoverer (of process, etc.); (b) l'i. de ce bruit, the author of this rumour; (c) Jur: finder (of lost object, etc.). 2. a. inventive (mind, etc.).

inventif, -ive [ɛ̃vɑ̃tif, -iːv], a. inventive (mind, etc.).

invention [ɛ̃vɑ̃sjɔ̃], s.f. 1. (a) invention, inventing; l'i. du téléphone, the invention of the telephone; nécessité est mère d'i., necessity is the mother of invention; vivre d'i., to live by one's wits; (b) invention, inventiveness, imagination; artiste qui manque d'i., artist lacking in imagination; avoir l'i. du détail, to have the faculty for inventing details. 2. (thing invented) (a) invention; inventions pratiques, l'avion, le téléphone, etc., practical inventions, such as aircraft and the telephone; brevet d'i., patent (for an invention); F: toutes ces inventions du diable! all these inventions of the devil! F: sa dernière i., his latest craze; (b) invention, fabrication, lie; ce bruit est une pure i., this rumour is pure invention; sa maladie est une i., he's only pretending to be ill; pure i. tout cela! that's sheer invention! nothing but make-believe! 3. A: finding, discovery; still used in (a) Ecc: I. de la (Sainte) Croix, Invention of the Cross; (b) Jur: i. d'un trésor, finding of treasure trove.

inventivité [ɛ̃vɑ̃tivite], s.f. inventiveness.

inventorier [ɛ̃vɑ̃tɔrje], v.tr. (p.d. & pr.sub. n. inventoriions, v. inventoriiez) 1. (a) to inventory, make a list, an inventory, of, to inventorize (goods, etc.); abs. to take stock; (b) to value (goods, bills, etc.); (c) to classify (facts, etc.). 2. to enter (article) on an inventory, on a stock list.

inventoriste [ɛ̃vɑ̃tɔrist], s.m. & f. inventory maker.

invérifiable [ɛ̃verifjabl̩], a. unverifiable (rumour, etc.).

invérifié [ɛ̃verifje], a. unverified (statement, etc.).

inversable [ɛ̃vɛrsabl̩], a. that cannot overturn, that cannot upset; bateau i., uncapsizable boat; self-righting boat.

inverse [ɛ̃vɛrs]. 1. a. inverse, inverted, opposite, contrary; en sens i. (de qch.), in the opposite direction (to sth.); en ordre i., in the reverse order; action i., back action; Mec.E: pas i., reverse pitch; Nau: (of two ships) faire route i., to steer on an opposite course; Mth: en raison i. de qch., in inverse ratio to sth.; Book-k:

écriture i., contra entry, set-off; *Geol:* faille i., reversed fault. 2. *s.m.* opposite, reverse; faire l'i. de ce qui est commandé, to do the very opposite of what one is told to do; ensuite c'est l'i. qui se produit, then the process is reversed; à l'i. du bon sens, (in a manner) contrary to reason; against the dictates of common sense; unreasonably. 3. *s.f.* (*a*) *Log:* inverse, contrapositive; (*b*) *Mth:* inverse (function, etc.); reciprocal; l'i. de . . ., the reciprocal of . . .; (*c*) *Ph: Opt:* i. optique, optical isomer.

inversement [ɛ̃vɛrsəmɑ̃], *adv.* inversely; conversely.

inverser [ɛ̃vɛrse]. 1. *v.tr.* (*a*) to reverse (current, image, result, etc.); *I.C.E:* carburateur inversé, down-draught carburettor; (*b*) *Gram:* to invert (subject, object, etc.). 2. *v.i.* (*of electric current, etc.*) to reverse, to flow the opposite way.

inverseur [ɛ̃vɛrsœːr], *s.m.* (*a*) *Mec.E:* reverser, reversing device, lever, handle, etc.; *Mch:* i. de marche, reverse gear; i. réducteur, reverse reduction gear; *Av:* i. de poussée, thrust reverser (of jet engine); (*b*) *El.E:* i. du courant, current reverser, throw-over switch; change-over switch; i. de marche, reversing switch; i. bipolaire, two-way switch; i. de poles, pole changer; (*c*) *Opt:* erector (in telescope).

inversible [ɛ̃vɛrsibl̩], *a.* reversible (film, emulsion).

inversif, -ive [ɛ̃vɛrsif, -iːv], *a. Gram: etc:* inversive.

inversion [ɛ̃vɛrsjɔ̃], *s.f.* 1. (*a*) *Gram: Mus: Mil: Mth: etc:* inversion; *Geol:* i. du relief, inversion of relief, inverted relief; (*b*) transposition. 2. (*a*) *Mec.E:* reversing, reversal; *Mch:* i. de marche, reversing; levier d'i. de marche, reversing lever; i. du sens de rotation, reversing of the direction of rotation; *Av:* i. de la poussée, thrust reversal, reverse thrust (of jet engine); (*b*) *El.E:* reversal (of current, etc.); i. de phase, phase reversal or inversion; i. de poles, pole changing, polarity reversal, inversion; (*c*) inversion; *Biol:* i. chromosomique, chromosome inversion; *Ch:* i. des hydrates de carbone, carbohydrate inversion; i. du sucre, inversion of sugar; (*d*) *Typ:* procédé d'i., offset reversal process; (*e*) *Typewr:* levier d'i. de marche de ruban, ribbon reverse key. 3. *Phot:* reversal, reversion (of film from positive to negative); *Cin:* film par i., reversal film. 4. *Psy:* i. sexuelle, sexual inversion; homosexuality.

invertase [ɛ̃vɛrtɑːz], *s.f. Bio-Ch:* invertase, sucrase, invertin, inverting enzyme.

invertébré [ɛ̃vɛrtebre], *a. & s.m. Z:* invertebrate; *s.m.pl.* invertébrés, Invertebrata.

inverti, -ie [ɛ̃vɛrti]. 1. *a. Ch:* sucre i., invert sugar. 2. *s. Psy:* sexual pervert; invert.

invertine [ɛ̃vɛrtin], *s.f. Bio-Ch:* invertin, invertase, sucrase.

invertir [ɛ̃vɛrtiːr], *v.tr.* 1. to reverse (motion, electric current, etc.). 2. *Opt:* to invert, reverse, erect, the image of (object). 3. to reverse, change the order of (troops, etc.).

investi [ɛ̃vɛsti], *a.* capitaux investis, funded capital.

investigateur, -trice [ɛ̃vɛstigatœːr, -tris]. 1. *a.* investigating, inquiring, investigatory; searching (glance). 2. *s.* investigator, inquirer.

investigation [ɛ̃vɛstigasjɔ̃], *s.f.* investigation, inquiry; faire des investigations sur qch., to inquire into, investigate, sth.

investir[1] [ɛ̃vɛstiːr], *v.tr.* to invest; i. qn d'une fonction, to invest, vest, s.o. with an office; i. qn de l'autorité suprême, to invest s.o. with supreme authority; i. qn d'une mission, to entrust s.o. with a mission; les fonctions dont la cour est investie, the duties which fall to the court; i. qn de sa confiance, to give s.o. one's full confidence; *Ecc:* i. qn d'un bénéfice, to institute s.o. to a benefice.

investir[2], *v.tr.* to beleaguer, hem in, invest (town, etc.).

investir[3], *v.tr.* to invest (money); i. des capitaux à l'étranger, to invest capital abroad.

investissement[1] [ɛ̃vɛstismɑ̃], *s.m. Mil:* investment, beleaguerment (of fortress); armée d'i., investing army, beleaguering army.

investissement[2], *s.m.* (*a*) investment, investing (of capital); investissements à l'étranger, investments abroad; (*b*) *Psy:* emotional investment (in s.o., sth.).

investisseur [ɛ̃vɛstisœːr], *s.m. Fin:* investor.

investiture [ɛ̃vɛstityːr], *s.f.* 1. investiture; induction (of bishop, etc.). 2. *Jur: A:* livery of seizin. 3. *Pol:* nomination (of candidate). 4. *Pol:* vote taken by the Lower House in favour of a new Prime Minister nominated by the President of the Republic.

invétéré [ɛ̃vetere], *a.* inveterate; deeply rooted (hatred, etc.); confirmed, irreclaimable (drunkard, criminal); intractable (disease); caractère i. d'une maladie, inveteracy of a disease.

invétérer (s') [sɛ̃vetere], *v.pr.* (il s'invétère; il s'invétérera) (*of evil, etc.*) to take deep root, to become inveterate; laisser (s')i. une maladie, to let a disease go too far, become inveterate.

inviable [ɛ̃vjabl̩], *a.* inviable.

invigilant [ɛ̃viʒilɑ̃], *a. Lit:* unwatchful.

invigoration [ɛ̃vigɔrasjɔ̃], *s.f. Physiol:* invigoration.

invincibilité [ɛ̃vɛ̃sibilite], *s.f.* invincibility, invincibleness; unconquerableness.

invincible [ɛ̃vɛ̃sibl̩], *a.* invincible, unconquerable (hero, etc.); insuperable (difficulty).

invinciblement [ɛ̃vɛ̃sibləmɑ̃], *adv.* invincibly.

in-vingt-quatre [invɛ̃tkatr̩], *a. & s.m.inv. Typ:* (in) twenty-four-mo.

inviolabilité [ɛ̃vjɔlabilite], *s.f.* inviolability, inviolacy, inviolateness; sacredness (of office, etc.); *Jur:* i. des députés, freedom of members of parliament from arrest and legal proceedings.

inviolable [ɛ̃vjɔlabl̩], *a.* 1. inviolable; sacred (office, etc.). 2. burglar-proof (lock).

inviolablement [ɛ̃vjɔlabləmɑ̃], *adv.* inviolably.

inviolé [ɛ̃vjɔle], *a.* inviolate; unbroken (vow); village i. par la civilisation citadine, village untouched by urban civilization; *Mount:* sommet i., unscaled height, peak.

invisibilité [ɛ̃vizibilite], *s.f.* invisibility.

invisible [ɛ̃vizibl̩], *a.* 1. invisible; *Needlew:* blind (hemming); i. à l'œil nu, invisible to the naked eye; filet i., invisible hairnet. 2. (person) never to be seen; il restait i., he, it, was nowhere to be seen, nothing could be seen of him, of it.

invisiblement [ɛ̃viziblәmɑ̃], *adv.* invisibly.

invitant [ɛ̃vitɑ̃]. 1. *a.* attractive, inviting. 2. *s.m. Sp:* les invitants, the challengers.

invitation [ɛ̃vitasjɔ̃], *s.f.* invitation; i. à déjeuner, à prendre le thé, invitation to lunch, to tea; venir sur l'i. de qn, to come at s.o.'s invitation, at s.o.'s request; venir sans i., to come uninvited; *Tg:* i. à transmettre, "ready" signal; i. à répéter, "repeat" signal.

invitatoire [ɛ̃vitatwaːr], *s.m. Ecc:* invitatory (psalm).

invite [ɛ̃vit], *s.f.* 1. invitation, inducement (à, to); romancier indifférent aux invites de l'écran, novelist indifferent to the enticements of the screen. 2. *Cards:* lead; call (for a suit); i. d'atouts, call for trumps; répondre à l'i. de qn, (i) to return s.o.'s lead, (ii) *F:* to respond to s.o.'s advances. 3. *Fenc:* invite.

invité, -ée [ɛ̃vite], *s.* guest; visitor; i. à un mariage, wedding guest.

inviter [ɛ̃vite], *v.tr.* to invite. 1. i. qn à dîner, to invite, ask, s.o. to dinner; être déjà invité pour ce soir, to be already engaged, booked, for this evening; c'est vous qui l'avez i. à venir ici, it was you who asked him here; i. qn à entrer, to ask s.o. in. 2. (*a*) i. le désastre, to court disaster; (*b*) i. qn à faire qch., (i) to invite, request, s.o. to do sth., (ii) to urge, tempt, s.o. to do sth.; ce beau temps invite à la promenade, this fine weather tempts one to go for a walk; *Cards:* i. atout, to call for trumps.

inviteur, -euse [ɛ̃vitœːr, -øːz]. 1. *a.* hospitable. 2. *s.* host, hostess.

invitré [ɛ̃vitre], *a. Cer: etc:* unvitrified.

invivable [ɛ̃vivabl̩], *a. F:* unbearable, intolerable; (*a*) impossible to live with; (*b*) impossible to live in.

invocateur, -trice [ɛ̃vɔkatœːr, -tris], *s.* invoker.

invocation [ɛ̃vɔkasjɔ̃], *s.f.* invocation.

invocatoire [ɛ̃vɔkatwaːr], *a.* invocatory.

invoisé [ɛ̃vwaze], *a. Ling:* unvoiced.

involontaire [ɛ̃vɔlɔ̃tɛːr], *a.* involuntary. 1. unintentional, undesigned. 2. unwilling (spectator, etc.).

involontairement [ɛ̃vɔlɔ̃tɛrmɑ̃], *adv.* involuntarily. 1. unintentionally, undesignedly. 2. unwillingly.

involucelle [ɛ̃vɔlysɛl], *s.m. Bot:* involucel.

involucral, -aux [ɛ̃vɔlykral, -o], *a. Bot:* involucral.

involucre [ɛ̃vɔlykr̩], *s.m. Bot:* involucre.

involucré [ɛ̃vɔlykre], *a. Bot:* involucrate.

involuté [ɛ̃vɔlyte], *a.* involute(d) (leaf, etc.).

involutif, -ive [ɛ̃vɔlytif, -iːv], *a.* (*a*) *Bot:* involutive; (*b*) *Mth:* matrice involutive, reciprocal matrix.

involution [ɛ̃vɔlysjɔ̃], *s.f.* 1. *A:* involvement, intricacy (of procedure, etc.). 2. (*a*) *Bot: Mth: etc:* involution; *Obst:* i. utérine, involution of the womb; (*b*) *Biol:* involution, degeneration.

invoquer [ɛ̃vɔke], *v.tr.* 1. (*a*) to call upon, to invoke (the aid of) (the Deity, etc.); *Lit:* i. la Muse, to invoke the Muse; i. le témoignage de qn, to call s.o. to witness; i. l'aide de la justice, to appeal to the law; (*b*) to invoke, call forth (a spirit). 2. i. une raison, un motif, to put forward a reason, a motive; documents invoqués dans un litige, documents invoked, called for, referred to, in a suit.

invraisemblable [ɛ̃vrɛsɑ̃blabl̩], *a.* unlikely, improbable, beyond all probability, hard to believe; histoire i., tall story, impossible story, story that is hard to swallow; il est i. qu'il n'en sache rien, it is hard to believe that he knows nothing about it; chapeau i., incredible hat; ces Américains sont invraisemblables, these Americans are really incredible, extraordinary, fantastic; c'est i.! it's unbelievable! *s.m.* l'i. est quelquefois vrai, truth is sometimes stranger than fiction.

invraisemblablement [ɛ̃vrɛsɑ̃blabləmɑ̃], *adv.* improbably.

invraisemblance [ɛ̃vrɛsɑ̃blɑ̃ːs], *s.f.* 1. unlikelihood, unlikeliness, improbability. 2. fact, statement, hard to believe; récit plein d'invraisemblances, story full of improbabilities, that won't hold water; tissu d'invraisemblances, tissue of improbabilities, of impossibilities.

invulnérabilité [ɛ̃vylnerabilite], *s.f.* invulnerability.

invulnérable [ɛ̃vylnerabl̩], *a.* invulnerable.

invulnérablement [ɛ̃vylnerabləmɑ̃], *adv.* invulnerably.

inyoite [injɔit], *s.f. Miner:* inyoite.

iodargyrite [jɔdarʒirit], *s.f. Miner:* iodyrite, iodargyrite, iodite.

iodate [jɔdat], *s.m. Ch:* iodate.

iode [jɔd], *s.m.* 1. *Ch:* iodine; *Pharm:* teinture d'i., (tincture of) iodine. 2. *El:* lampe à i., tungsten lamp.

ioder [jɔde], *v.tr. Med: Phot:* to iodize; to coat with, soak in, iodine, iodide; to iodate.

iodeux, -euse [jɔdø, -øːz], *a. Ch:* iodous (acid, etc.).

iodhydrate [jɔdidrat], *s.m. Ch:* hydriodide, iodhydrate.

iodhydrine [jɔdidrin], *s.f. Ch:* iodhydrin, iodohydrin.

iodhydrique [jɔdidrik], *a. Ch:* hydriodic, iodhydric.

iodifère [jɔdifɛːr], *a.* iodiferous.

iodique [jɔdik], *a. Ch:* iodic.

iodisme [jɔdism], *s.m. Med:* iodism.

iodite [jɔdit], *s.f. Miner:* iodite.

iodler [jɔdle], *v.i.* to yodel, *U.S:* to warble.

iodleur [jɔdlœːr], *s.m.* yodeller.

iodobenzène [jɔdɔbɛ̃zɛn], *s.m. Ch:* iodobenzene.

iodobromite [jɔdɔbrɔmit], *s.f. Miner:* iodobromite.

iodoforme [jɔdɔfɔrm], *s.m. Pharm:* iodoform.

iodoformé [jɔdɔfɔrme], *a.* iodoformized (gauze, etc.).

iodomercurate [jɔdɔmɛrkyrat], *s.m. Ch:* iodomercurate.

iodométrie [jɔdɔmetri], *s.f. Ch:* iodometry.

iodométrique [jɔdɔmetrik], *a. Ch:* iodometric.

iodonium [jɔdɔnjɔm], *s.m. Ch:* iodonium.

iodosé [jɔdɔze], *a. Ch:* iodoso-.

iodosobenzène [jɔdɔzɔbɛ̃zɛn], *s.m. Ch:* iodosobenzene.

iodotannique [jɔdɔtanik], *a. Pharm:* iodotannic.

ioduration [jɔdyrasjɔ̃], *s.f. Ch:* iodization.

iodure [jɔdyːr], *s.m. Ch:* iodide.

iodurer [jɔdyre], *v.tr. Ch: Med: Phot:* to iodize, iodate (with iodide).

iodyrite [jɔdirit], *s.f. Miner:* iodyrite, iodite.

iolite [jɔlit], *s.f. Miner:* iolite.

ion [jɔ̃], *s.m. Ph: Ch:* ion; i. d'hydrogène, hydrogen ion; i. gazeux, gaseous ion; i. primaire, secondaire, primary, secondary, ion; nombre volumique d'ions, ion density; source d'ions, ion source, ion gun; *Atom.Ph:* i. du réseau, lattice ion; accélérateur d'ions, ion accelerator; échangeur d'ions, ion exchanger.

ion-gramme [jɔ̃gram], *s.m.* gram(me) ion, ion gram(me); *pl. ions-grammes.*

Ionie [jɔni], *Pr.n.f. A.Geog:* Ionia.

ionien, -ienne [jɔnjɛ̃, -jɛn], *a. & s. Geog:* Ionian; la mer Ionienne, the Ionian Sea; *Mus:* mode i., Ionian mode; *Phil:* école ionienne, Ionian school.

ionique[1] [jɔnik], *a. Arch: etc:* Ionic (order, etc.).

ionique[2], *a. Ph. etc:* ionic; *attrib.* ion; accélération i., ion acceleration; bombardement i., ion bombardment; courant i., ion current; conduction i., ionic conduction; densité i., ion density; faisceau i., ion beam; chauffage par bombardement i., ion-bombardment heating, ionic heating; à chauffage par bombardement i., ionic-heated; *Mec.E:* propulsion i., ion(ic) propulsion; moteur i., ion(ic) engine; moteur-fusée i., ion(ic) rocket.

ionisable [jɔnizabl̩], *a. Ph:* ionizable.

ionisant [jɔnizɑ̃]. 1. *s.m. El: Ph: Ch:* ionizer. 2. *a.* ionizing.

ionisateur [jɔnizatœːr], *s.m.* ionizer.

ionisation [jɔnizasjɔ̃], *s.f. Elcs: Ph: Ch:* ionization; **chambre d'i.,** ionization chamber, cloud chamber; **courant d'i.,** ionization current; **i. colonnaire,** columnar ionization; **i. par choc,** collision, impact, ionization; **i. par rayonnement,** radiation ionization; **i. (d'origine) thermique,** thermal ionization; **i. volumétrique,** volume ionization; **potentiel d'i.,** ionization potential.

ioniser [jɔnize], *v.tr. Ph: Ch:* to ionize.

ionomètre [jɔnɔmɛtr], *s.m.* ionometer.

ionone [jɔnɔn], *s.f. Ch:* ionone.

ionophorèse [jɔnɔfɔrɛːz], *s.f. Ch: etc:* iontophoresis.

ionosphère [jɔnɔsfɛːr], *s.f. Meteor:* ionosphere.

ionosphérique [jɔnɔsferik], *a.* ionospheric; **enregistreur i.,** ionospheric recorder; **couche i.,** ionosphere layer.

iota [jɔta], *s.m. Gr.Alph:* iota; *F:* **pas un i.,** not a bit, not an iota; not one jot or tittle; **il n'y manque pas un i.,** there's not an iota missing; **il ne s'est pas écarté d'un i. de ses instructions,** he didn't depart by a hair's breadth from his instructions.

iotacisme [jɔtasism], *s.m. Ling:* iotacism.

iouler [jule], *v.i. O:* to yodel, *U.S:* to warble.

iouleur [julœːr], *s.m. O:* yodeller.

iourte [jurt], *s.f.* yourt, yurt.

ioutre [jutr], *s.m. P: Pej:* Jew, *P:* yid.

ipécacuana [ipekakɥana], *s.m., F:* **ipéca** [ipeka], *s.m. Pharm:* ipecacuanha, ipecac.

Iphigénie [ifiʒeni], *Pr.n.f. Gr.Lit:* Iphigenia.

ipomée [ipɔme], *s.f. Bot:* ipomea; **i. bonne-nuit,** moon-flower.

ipréau, -éaux [ipreo], *s.m. Bot: F:* white poplar.

iproniazide [iprɔnjazid], *s.f. Med:* iproniazid.

ipséité [ipseite], *s.f. Phil:* ipseity.

iradé [irade], *s.m. (in Turkey)* irade; decree.

Irak [irak], *Pr.n.m. Geog:* Iraq, Irak.

irakien, -ienne [irakjɛ̃, -jɛn], *a. & s. Geog:* Iraqi, Iraki.

Iran (l') [lirɑ̃], *Pr.n.m. Geog:* Iran.

iranien, -ienne [iranjɛ̃, -jɛn]. **1.** *Geog: a. & s.* Iranian. **2.** *Ling: a. & s.m.* Iranian.

iranisant [iranizɑ̃], *s.m.* student of Iranian history, literature, languages.

Iraq [irak], *Pr.n.m. Geog:* Iraq, Irak.

iraquien, -ienne [irakjɛ̃, -jɛn], *a. & s. Geog:* Iraqi, Iraki.

irascibilité [iras(s)ibilite], *s.f.* irascibility, irascibleness, hot temper.

irascible [irasibl̩], *a.* irascible, easily angered, irritable, *F:* peppery.

irbis [irbi(s)], *s.m. Z:* ounce, snow leopard.

ire [iːr], *s.f. A:* anger, ire (of the gods).

irénarque [irenark], *s.m. Rom.Hist:* irenarch.

Irène[1] [irɛn], *Pr.n.f.* Irene.

irène[2], *s.f. Orn:* irena.

Irénée [irene], *Pr.n.m.* (Saint) Irenaeus.

irénique [irenik], *a.* irenic.

irénisme [irenism], *s.m. Rel.H:* irenicism.

iréniste [irenist], *s.m. Rel:* irenicist.

iridacé, -ée [iridase], *Bot:* **1.** *a.* iridaceous. **2.** *s.f.pl.* **iridacées,** Iridaceae.

iridectomie [iridɛktɔmi], *s.f. Surg:* iridectomy.

iridencleisis [iridɑ̃kleizis], *s.m. Med:* iridencleisis.

iridescence [iridɛs(s)ɑ̃ːs], *s.f.* iridescence.

iridescent [iridɛs(s)ɑ̃], *a.* iridescent.

iridié [iridje], *a.* iridic; iridium, iridio-; **platine i.,** iridioplatinum; **vis iridiée,** iridium-pointed screw.

iridien, -ienne [iridjɛ̃, -jɛn], *a. Med:* iridian.

iridier [iridje], *v.tr. Metall:* to iridize.

iridique [iridik], *a. Ch:* iridic.

iridite [iridit], *s.f. Ch:* iridite.

iridium [iridjɔm], *s.m. Ch:* iridium.

iridochoroïdite [iridɔkɔrɔidit], *s.f. Med:* iridochoroiditis.

iridocyclite [iridɔsiklit], *s.f. Med:* iridocyclitis.

irido-diagnostic [iridodjagnɔstik], *s.m. Med:* iridodiagnosis.

iridodialyse [iridɔdjaliːz], *s.f. Med:* iridodialysis.

iridodonèse [iridɔdɔnɛːz], **iridodonésis** [iridɔdɔnezis], *s.f. Med:* iridodonesis.

irido-kératite [iridɔkeratit], *s.f. Med:* iridokeratitis.

iridomyrmex [iridɔmirmɛks], *s.m. Ent:* iridomyrmex.

iridoplégie [iridɔpleʒi], *s.f. Med:* iridoplegia, iridoparalysis.

iridosclérectomie [iridɔsklerɛktɔmi], *s.f. Surg:* iridosclerectomy.

iridosmine [iridɔsmin], *s.f. Miner:* iridosmine, iridosmium.

iridotomie [iridɔtɔmi], *s.f. Surg:* iridotomy.

irien, -ienne [irjɛ̃, -jɛn], *a. Anat:* iridal, iridial, iridian, iridic.

Iris [iris]. **1.** *Pr.n.f. Myth:* Iris. **2.** *s.m. (a)* iris; *A:* rainbow(-like play of colours); prismatic halo; *(b) Anat:* iris (of eye); *Phot:* **diaphragme i.,** iris diaphragm. **3.** *s.m. Bot:* iris, *F:* flag; **i. jaune, des marais,** yellow iris, (water) flag; **i. fétide, i.-gigot,** gladdon, roast-beef plant, stinking iris; *Pharm: etc:* **racine d'i.,** orris root; **racine d'i. pulvérisée,** orris powder.

irisable [irizabl̩], *a.* capable of iridescence.

irisation [irizasjɔ̃], *s.f.* iridescence, irisation.

irisé [irize], *a.* iridescent, irisated, irised; rainbow-coloured; **aspect i.,** iridescence (of plumage, etc.).

iriser [irize], *v.tr.* to make iridescent.

s'iriser, to become iridescent.

iritis [iritis], *s.f. Med:* iritis.

Irkoutsk [irkutsk], *Pr.n.m. Geog:* Irkutsk.

irlandais, -aise [irlɑ̃dɛ, -ɛːz]. **1.** *a.* Irish. **2.** *s.* Irishman; Irishwoman, Irish girl; **les I.,** the Irish. **3.** *s.m. Ling:* Irish, Erse.

Irlande [irlɑ̃ːd], *Pr.n.f. Geog:* Ireland; **I. du Nord,** Northern Ireland; **d'I.,** Irish.

irone [irɔn], *s.f. Ch:* irone.

ironie [irɔni], *s.f.* irony; **par une i. du sort,** by an irony of fate; **l'i. des choses,** *F:* the cussedness of things.

ironique [irɔnik], *a.* ironic(al); **faire des compliments ironiques à qn,** to compliment s.o. with one's tongue in one's cheek.

ironiquement [irɔnikmɑ̃], *adv.* ironically; with one's tongue in one's cheek.

ironiser [irɔnize]. **1.** *v.tr.* to speak ironically, derisively, of (s.o., sth.). **2.** *v.i.* to speak ironically, to be ironical (sur, about).

ironisme [irɔnism], *s.m.* irony, ironic method (in debate).

ironiste [irɔnist], *s.m. & f.* ironist.

iroquois, -oise [irɔkwa, -waːz], *a. & s.* Iroquois (Indian); *A: F:* **drôle d'I.,** rum old card; **quel I.!** what a boor!

irraccommodable [ir(r)akɔmɔdabl̩], *a.* unmendable.

irrachetable [ir(r)aʃtabl̩], *a.* unredeemable, irredeemable (funds, etc.).

irracheté [ir(r)aʃte], *a.* unredeemed.

irracontable [ir(r)akɔ̃tabl̩], *a.* unrepeatable, untellable.

irradiance [ir(r)adjɑ̃ːs], *s.f.* radiance.

irradiant [ir(r)adjɑ̃], *a.* irradiant.

irradiateur, -trice [ir(r)adjatœːr, -tris]. **1.** *a.* irradiative. **2.** *s.m. Atom.Ph:* irradiator.

irradiation [ir(r)adjasjɔ̃], *s.f.* **1.** *Ph: Med:* irradiation; exposure; **i. aiguë,** acute exposure, irradiation; **i. brève, i. de courte durée,** short irradiation; **i. directe,** direct exposure; **i. par contact,** contact irradiation; **i. prolongée, i. de longue durée,** protracted irradiation; **i. superficielle,** surface irradiation; *Atom.Ph:* **i. admissible,** permissible exposure; **i. neutronique,** neutron irradiation; **i. du combustible (dans le cœur du réacteur),** (core-) fuel irradiation, exposure; **niveau d'i. du combustible,** fuel-irradiation level; **i. (profonde) par rayons X,** (deep) X-ray irradiation. **2.** *Phot:* halation.

irradié, -iée [ir(r)adje], *s.* person exposed to, suffering from, atomic radiation.

irradier [ir(r)adje]. **1.** *v.i.* to radiate; **lumière qui irradie d'une source,** light radiating from a source; **la douleur irradiait du côté gauche,** the pain was spreading on the left side; **routes qui irradient autour de Paris,** roads that spread out around Paris. **2.** *v.tr.* to expose to (atomic) radiation.

irraisonnable [ir(r)ɛzɔnabl̩], *a.* irrational, unreasoning.

irraisonné [ir(r)ɛzɔne], *a.* unreasoned.

irrassasiable [ir(r)asazjabl̩], *a.* insatiable (de, for); **appétit i. de dispute,** insatiable passion for wrangling.

irrationalisme [ir(r)asjɔnalism], *a.m.* irrationalism.

irrationaliste [ir(r)asjɔnalist], *a. & s.m. & f.* irrationalist.

irrationalité [ir(r)asjɔnalite], *s.f.* irrationality.

irrationnel, -elle [ir(r)asjɔnɛl], *a.* **1.** irrational (action, etc.). **2.** *Mth:* **quantité irrationnelle,** irrational quantity.

irrationnellement [ir(r)asjɔnɛlmɑ̃], *adv.* irrationally.

irrattrapable [ir(r)atrapabl̩], *a.* irretrievable.

irréalisable [ir(r)realizabl̩], *a.* unrealizable; *(a)* unattainable, impracticable, unfeasible; *(b) Fin:* **biens irréalisables,** unrealizable property.

irréalisé [ir(r)ealize], *a.* unrealized.

irréaliste [ir(r)ealist]. **1.** *a.* unrealistic. **2.** *s.m. & f.* unrealist.

irréalité [ir(r)ealite], *s.f.* unreality.

irrecevabilité [ir(r)əsəvabilite], *s.f.* inadmissibility.

irrecevable [ir(r)əsəvabl̩], *a.* inadmissible (evidence, etc.); unacceptable (theory, etc.); *Jur:* **être déclaré i. en son action,** to be non-suited.

irrécompensable [ir(r)ekɔ̃pɑ̃sabl̩], *a.* that cannot be adequately recompensed; beyond reward, unrequitable.

irrécompensé [ir(r)ekɔ̃pɑ̃se], *a.* unrequited, unrewarded.

irréconciliabilité [ir(r)ekɔ̃siljabilite], *s.f.* irreconcilability.

irréconciliable [ir(r)ekɔ̃siljabl̩], *a.* irreconcilable, unreconcilable.

irréconciliablement [ir(r)ekɔ̃siljabləmɑ̃], *adv.* irreconcilably.

irréconcilié [ir(r)ekɔ̃silje], *a.* unreconciled.

irrécouvrable [ir(r)ekuvrabl̩], *a.* irrecoverable, unrecoverable (loss, etc.); **créance i.,** bad debt.

irrécupérable [ir(r)ekyperabl̩]. *(a) a.* irreparable, irremediable (loss, etc.); non recoverable; *(b) s.m.* misfit.

irrécusable [ir(r)ekyzabl̩], *a.* unimpeachable, unexceptionable, irrecusable (evidence, etc.); (authority, etc.) beyond exception; unchallengeable (juryman, evidence).

irrécusablement [ir(r)ekyzabləmɑ̃], *adv.* unimpeachably, unexceptionably.

irrédente [ir(r)edɑ̃ːt], *a.f. Pol.Hist:* Irredentist (province).

irrédentisme [ir(r)edɑ̃tism], *s.m. Pol.Hist:* Irredentism.

irrédentiste [ir(r)edɑ̃tist], *a. & s.m. & f. Pol.Hist:* Irredentist.

irréductibilité [ir(r)edyktibilite], *s.f.* irreducibleness, irreducibility.

irréductible [ir(r)edyktibl̩], *a.* **1.** irreducible (equation, dislocation, etc.); **hernie i.,** irreducible hernia; **fraction i.,** fraction in its lowest terms. **2.** indomitable; **se montrer i. sur un article,** to adhere strictly to a clause; **attachement i.,** unshakeable attachment (to s.o.); **opposition i.,** relentless opposition. **3.** *s.m. & f.* diehard.

irréduit [ir(r)edɥi], *a.* unreduced (fracture).

irréel, -elle [ir(r)eɛl], *a.* unreal.

irréfléchi [ir(r)efleʃi], *a.* **1.** unconsidered, thoughtless (action). **2.** hasty, rash, unthinking, unreflecting, irresponsible (person).

irréflexion [ir(r)eflɛksjɔ̃], *s.f.* thoughtlessness, heedlessness; **faire qch. par i.,** to do sth. without thinking.

irréformable [ir(r)efɔrmabl̩], *a.* **1.** irreformable, unreformable, incorrigible. **2.** *Jur:* irrevocable, irreformable (decision, etc.).

irréformé [ir(r)efɔrme], *a.* unrevoked (decision).

irréfragabilité [ir(r)efragabilite], *s.f.* irrefragability; undeniability.

irréfragable [ir(r)efragabl̩], *a.* irrefragable; unanswerable; undeniable; *Hist:* **le Docteur i.,** the Irrefragable Doctor (Alexander of Hales).

irréfragablement [ir(r)efragabləmɑ̃], *adv.* irrefragably, undeniably.

irréfrangible [ir(r)efrɑ̃ʒibl̩], *a. Opt:* irrefrangible (rays).

irréfrénable [ir(r)efrenabl̩], *a.* irrepressible.

irréfutable [ir(r)efytabl̩], *a.* irrefutable, indisputable.

irréfutablement [ir(r)efytabləmɑ̃], *adv.* irrefutably, unanswerably.

irréfuté [ir(r)efyte], *a.* unrefuted.

irrégularité [ir(r)egylarite], *s.f.* **1.** *(a)* irregularity (of building, of conduct); *(b)* unpunctuality; *(c) Mec.E:* **i. du couple moteur,** torque variation. **2. irrégularités (de conduite, de terrain),** irregularities (of conduct, of the ground); *Adm: Com:* **irrégularités d'écriture,** falsifying, *F:* cooking, of accounts.

irrégulier, -ière [ir(r)egylje, -jɛːr]. **1.** *a. (a)* irregular (shape, verb, pulse, troops, etc.); erratic (life, pulse); straggling (building); **sommeil i.,** broken sleep; **vie irrégulière,** disorderly, irregular, loose, life; *Aut:* **freinage i.,** unequal, uneven, braking; *Mil:* **absence irrégulière,** absence without leave; *(b)* unpunctual. **2.** *s.m.* guerrillero, guer(r)illa, partisan; *esp. pl.* irregulars.

irrégulièrement [ir(r)egyljɛrmɑ̃], *adv.* **1.** irregularly. **2.** unpunctually.

irréligieusement [ir(r)eliʒjøzmɑ̃], *adv.* irreligiously.

irréligieux, -ieuse [ir(r)eliʒjø, -jøːz], *a.* irreligious.

irréligion [ir(r)eliʒjɔ̃], *s.f.* irreligion; irreligiousness.

irréligiosité [ir(r)eliʒjozite], *s.f.* irreligiosity.

irremboursable [ir(r)ɑ̃bursabl̩], *a. (a)* not repayable; *(b)* unredeemable.

irrémédiable [ir(r)emedjabl̩], *a.* irremediable (ill, loss); irretrievable (loss); incurable (disease); irreparable (injury); **c'est i.**, there is no going back on it; it is beyond remedy, past recall.
irrémédiablement [ir(r)emedjabləmɑ̃], *adv.* irremediably, irreparably; hopelessly; irretrievably.
irrémissible [ir(r)emisibl̩], *a.* irremissible, unremittable (crime, etc.); unpardonable (crime).
irrémissiblement [ir(r)emisibləmɑ̃], *adv.* irremissibly, without remission.
irrémission [ir(r)emisjɔ̃], *s.f.* irremission, irremissibleness.
irremplaçable [ir(r)ɑ̃plasabl̩], *a.* irreplaceable.
irremplissable [ir(r)ɑ̃plisabl̩], *a.* that cannot be (i) filled, (ii) fulfilled.
irrémunérable [ir(r)emynerabl̩], *a.* beyond remuneration, compensation, payment; for which no compensation, remuneration, can be given.
irrémunéré [ir(r)emynere], *a.* unremunerated; unpaid.
irréparable [ir(r)eparabl̩], (*a*) *a.* irreparable; beyond repair; irrevocable; irretrievable (loss, mistake); (*b*) *s.m.* **commettre l'i.**, to do sth. irrevocable.
irréparablement [ir(r)eparabləmɑ̃], *adv.* irreparably; irretrievably; irrevocably.
irrépréhensible [ir(r)epreɑ̃sibl̩], *a.* irreprehensible; blameless, above reproach.
irrépréhensiblement [ir(r)epreɑ̃sibləmɑ̃], *adv.* irreprehensibly.
irreprésentable [ir(r)əprezɑ̃tabl̩], *a.* (play) that cannot be staged, produced; unstageable.
irrépressible [ir(r)epresibl̩], **irréprimable** [ir(r)eprimabl̩], *a.* irrepressible.
irréprimé [ir(r)eprime], *a.* unrepressed.
irréprochabilité [ir(r)eprɔʃabilite], *s.f.* irreproachableness.
irréprochable [ir(r)eprɔʃabl̩], *a.* irreproachable; blameless; faultless (attire, etc.); **ouvrage i. de style**, work irreproachable in style; **il a toujours été i. dans sa conduite**, he was always irreproachable, beyond reproach, in his behaviour.
irréprochablement [ir(r)eprɔʃabləmɑ̃], *adv.* irreproachably; blamelessly; faultlessly.
irreproductif, -ive [ir(r)əprɔdyktif, -i:v], *a.* unproductive (consumption, etc.).
irrésistibilité [ir(r)ezistibilite], *s.f.* irresistibility, irresistibleness.
irrésistible [ir(r)ezistibl̩], *a.* irresistible; **il est i.**, (i) he's irresistible, full of charm; (ii) *F:* he's a scream.
irrésistiblement [ir(r)ezistibləmɑ̃], *adv.* irresistibly.
irrésolu [ir(r)ezɔly], *a.* **1.** irresolute, wavering (nature, etc.); faltering (steps, etc.). **2.** unsolved (problem, etc.).
irrésoluble [ir(r)ezɔlybl̩], *a.* **1.** irresolvable (nebula). **2.** insoluble, unsolvable (problem, etc.).
irrésolument [ir(r)ezɔlymɑ̃], *adv.* irresolutely.
irrésolution [ir(r)ezɔlysjɔ̃], *s.f.* irresolution, indecision, wavering, irresoluteness.
irrespect [ir(r)ɛspɛ], *s.m.* disrespect; pertness.
irrespectueusement [ir(r)ɛspɛktɥøzmɑ̃], *adv.* disrespectfully; pertly.
irrespectueux, -euse [ir(r)ɛspɛktɥø, -ø:z], *a.* disrespectful (**pour, envers**, to, towards); *F:* cheeky (child).
irrespirable [ir(r)ɛspirabl̩], *a.* unbreathable, irrespirable (air, etc.).
irresponsabilité [ir(r)ɛspɔ̃sabilite], *s.f.* irresponsibility.
irresponsable [ir(r)ɛspɔ̃sabl̩], *a.* irresponsible (agent, etc.); **il est i.**, he is not accountable for his actions; *s.m.Jur:* **les irresponsables (pénalement)**, the mental defectives.
irrétractable [ir(r)etraktabl̩], *a.* irretractable (confession, etc.).
irrétrécissabilité [ir(r)etresisabilite], *s.f.* unshrinkableness (of material).
irrétrécissable [ir(r)etresisabl̩], *a.* unshrinkable (material, etc.).
irrévélable [ir(r)evelabl̩], *a.* unrevealable, undisclosable, that cannot be revealed.
irrévélé [ir(r)evele], *a.* unrevealed, undisclosed.
irrévéremment [ir(r)everamɑ̃], *adv.* irreverently.
irrévérence [ir(r)everɑ̃:s], *s.f.* irreverence.
irrévérencieusement [ir(r)everɑ̃sjøzmɑ̃], *adv.* irreverently; disrespectfully.
irrévérencieux, -euse [ir(r)everɑ̃sjø, -ø:z], *a.* disrespectful; *F:* cheeky.
irrévérent [ir(r)everɑ̃], *a.* irreverent; disrespectful.
irréversibilité [ir(r)eversibilite], *s.f.* irreversibility.
irréversible [ir(r)eversibl̩], *a.* non-reversible; *Mec.E:* irreversible (gear, etc.); non-reversing; **manuellement i.**, with no manual reversing mechanism; *Aut:* **direction i.**, irreversible steering; **le cours de l'histoire est i.**, the course of history is irreversible; you can't put the clock back.
irrévocabilité [ir(r)evɔkabilite], *s.f.* irrevocability, irrevocableness.
irrévocable [ir(r)evɔkabl̩], *a.* irrevocable; **obligation i.**, binding agreement; **prendre un parti i.**, to commit oneself to a policy; **décision i.**, irrevocable decision; *Jur:* **décret i.**, decree absolute.
irrévocablement [ir(r)evɔkabləmɑ̃], *adv.* irrevocably.
irrigable [ir(r)igabl̩], *a.* (*a*) irrigable; (*b*) floodable; **prairie i.**, water meadow.
irrigateur, -trice [ir(r)igatœ:r, -tris]. **1.** *s.m.* (*a*) garden hose; street hose; (*b*) water cart; (*c*) *Med:* irrigator (for wounds); (*d*) *Med: Hyg:* enema; douche. **2.** *a.* irrigating (canal, etc.).
irrigation [ir(r)igasjɔ̃], *s.f.* **1.** *Agr:* (*a*) irrigation; **canal d'i.**, irrigation canal; (*b*) flooding. **2.** *Med: Hyg:* irrigation, spraying (of wound, etc.); douching (of womb, etc.); **i. du côlon**, colonic irrigation.
irrigatoire [ir(r)igatwa:r], *a.* irrigatory.
irriguer [ir(r)ige], *v.tr.* **1.** *Agr:* (*a*) to irrigate; (*b*) to flood. **2.** *Med:* to irrigate, spray (wound); to douche (womb, etc.).
irrisor [ir(r)izɔ:r], *s.m. Orn: A:* irrisor; wood hoopoe.
irritabilité [ir(r)itabilite], *s.f.* irritability. **1.** sensitiveness, reaction to stimulus. **2.** irritableness (of temper); testiness, touchiness.
irritable [ir(r)itabl̩], *a.* irritable. **1.** (*a*) sensitive (skin, etc.); (*b*) (organ) reacting to a stimulus. **2.** easily provoked (person); testy, touchy.
irritant[1] [ir(r)itɑ̃]. **1.** *a.* irritating, exasperating, aggravating. **2.** *a.* & *s.m. Med:* irritant.
irritant[2], *a. Jur:* irritant; **clause irritante**, irritant clause.
irritatif, -ive [ir(r)itatif, -i:v], *a. Med:* irritating, irritative.
irritation [ir(r)itasjɔ̃], *s.f.* irritation. **1.** irritating. **2.** annoyance, vexation; **être en proie à une vive i.**, to be seething with anger. **3.** *Med:* inflammation.
irrité [ir(r)ite], *a.* irritated. **1.** angry (**contre**, with at); **i. qu'on le fît attendre, de ce qu'on le faisait attendre**, angry at being kept waiting. **2.** *Med:* inflamed (wound).
irriter [ir(r)ite], *v.tr.* to irritate. **1.** to annoy, provoke, aggravate (s.o.); to tease (dog, etc.); to bait (bull, bear); **i. qn contre qn**, to set s.o. against s.o. **2.** to excite (passions, etc.); **bruit qui irrite les nerfs**, irritating noise, noise that gets on one's nerves. **3.** *Med:* to inflame (wound, etc.).
s'irriter. **1.** to grow angry (**contre qn**, with, at, s.o.; **de qch.**, at sth.); **s'i. pour des sujets futiles**, to get annoyed over trifles; **prompt à s'i.**, quick-tempered; **je m'irrite de me lever de si bonne heure le matin**, it makes me angry getting up so early in the morning. **2.** (*of sore, etc.*) to become irritated, inflamed.
irroration [ir(r)ɔrasjɔ̃], *s.f.* (*a*) exposure to dew; (*b*) sprinkling, spraying.
irrorer [ir(r)ɔre], *v.tr.* to spray.
irrotationnel, -elle [ir(r)ɔtasjɔnɛl], *a. Ph: Mth:* irrotational.
irruption [ir(r)ypsjɔ̃], *s.f.* irruption; (*a*) invasion, raid; **faire i. dans une salle**, to burst, *F:* barge, into a room; **la foule fit i. sur le terrain de jeu**, the crowd rushed, swarmed, on to the ground; (*b*) overflow, flood (of river); inrush (of water); **i. de la mer**, tidal wave.
Isaac [izaak], *Pr.n.m.* Isaac.
Isabelle [izabɛl]. **1.** *Pr.n.f.* Isabel(la). **2.** *a.inv.* biscuit-coloured, cream-coloured, isabelline; **cheval i.**, light-bay horse. **3.** *s.m.* (*a*) biscuit-colour, Isabella colour; (*b*) light-bay horse.
isadelphe [izadɛlf], *a. Bot:* isadelphous.
isagogique [izagɔʒik]. **1.** *a.* isagogic. **2.** *s.f.* isagogics.
isagone [izagɔn], *a. Mth:* equiangular.
Isaïe [izai], *Pr.n.m. B.Hist:* Isaiah.
isallobare [izalɔba:r], *s.f. Meteor:* isallobar.
isallobarique [izalɔbarik], *a. Meteor:* isallobaric.
isallotherme [izalɔtɛrm], *s.f. Meteor:* isallotherm.
isanémone [izanemɔn], *s.f. Meteor:* isanemone.
isanomale [izanɔmal], *s.f. Meteor:* isanomal.
isard [iza:r], *s.m. Z:* izard, wild goat (of the Pyrenees).
isatide [izatid], *s.m. Bot:* isatis.
isatine [izatin], *s.f. Ch:* isatin.
isatique [izatik], *a. Ch:* isatic.
isatis[1] [izatis], *s.m. Bot:* isatis.
isatis[2], *s.m. Z:* arctic fox; blue fox.
isatogénique [izatɔʒenik], *a. Ch:* isatogenic.
Isaurie [izɔri], *Pr.n.f. A.Geog:* Isauria.
isaurien, -ienne [izɔrjɛ̃, -jɛn]. **1.** *a. Hist:* Isaurian (dynasty). **2.** *s. A.Geog:* **les Isauriens**, the Isaurians.
isba [izba], *s.f.* isba(h).
Iscariote [iskarjɔt], *Pr.n.m.* (Judas) Iscariot.
iscariotisme [iskarjɔtism], *s.m.* Iscariotism.
ischémie [iskemi], *s.f. Med:* ischaemia.
ischémier [iskemje], *v.tr. Med:* to cause ischaemia (in organ, etc.).
ischémique [iskemik], *a. Med:* ischaemic.
ischiatique [iskjatik], *a. Anat:* ischiatic.
ischio-caverneux [iskjɔkavernø], *Anat:* **1.** *a. inv.* ischiocavernous. **2.** *s.m.* ischiocavernosus.
ischion [iskjɔ̃], *s.m. Anat:* ischium.
ischiote [iskjɔt], *a.* & *s. Geog:* (native, inhabitant) of Ischia.
ischurie [iskyri], *s.f. Med:* ischuria.
Isée [ize], *Pr.n.m. Gr.Ant:* Isaeus.
Isengrin [izɑ̃grɛ̃], *Pr.n.m.* Isengrin (the wolf in the *Roman de Renart*).
isentropique [izɑ̃trɔpik], *a. Ph:* isentropic.
isérine [izerin], *s.f. Miner:* iserine.
iséthionique [izetjɔnik], *a. Ch:* isethionic.
isiaque [izjak]. **1.** *a.* Isiac(cal). **2.** *s.m.* Isiac, priest of Isis.
Isidore [izidɔ:r], *Pr.n.m.* Isidore.
isinglass [izɛ̃glas], *s.m.* isinglass.
Islam [islam], *s.m. Rel:* Islam.
islamique [islamik], *a.* Islamic, Islamitic.
islamisant [islamizɑ̃], *s.m.* Islamist, specialist in Islamic studies.
islamisation [islamizasjɔ̃], *s.f.* Islamization; conversion to Islam.
islamiser [islamize], *v.tr.* to Islamize.
islamisme [islamism], *s.m.* Islamism.
islamite [islamit], *s.m.* & *f.* Islamite, Islamist.
islandais, -aise [islɑ̃dɛ, -ɛ:z], *Geog:* **1.** *a.* Icelandic. **2.** (*a*) *s.* Icelander; (*b*) *s.m. Ling:* **l'i.**, Icelandic. **3.** *s.m. F:* sailor engaged in the Iceland fisheries.
Islande [islɑ̃:d], *Pr.n.f. Geog:* Iceland.
Ismaël [ismaɛl], *Pr.n.m. B.Hist:* Ishmael.
Ismaélien [ismaeljɛ̃], **Ismaïlien** [ismailjɛ̃], *s.* Ismaili (Moslem).
ismaélisme [ismaelism], **ismaïlisme** [ismailism], *s.m.* Ismailism.
Ismaélites [ismaelit], **Ismaïlites** [ismailit], *s.m.pl.* Ishmaelites.
is(o)- [iz(ɔ)], *pref.* iso-. **1.** **isobryé**, isobryous; **isocarpe**, isocarpous; **isadelphe**, isadelphous. **2.** **isobutane**, isobutane.
iso-agglutination [izɔaglytinasjɔ̃], *s.f. Med:* isoagglutination.
isoamyle [izɔamil], *s.m. Ch:* isoamyl.
isoamylique [izɔamilik], *a. Ch:* isoamylic.
isoapiol [izɔapjɔl], *s.m. Ch:* isoapiol.
iso-anticorps [izɔɑ̃tikɔr], *s.m. Med:* isoantibody.
isobare [izɔba:r], **isobarique** [izɔbarik], **isobarométrique** [izɔbarɔmetrik], *a. Meteor:* isobaric, isobarometric; **courbe i., ligne i.**, *s.f.* **isobare**, isobaric curve, isobar; *Atom.Ph:* **spin isobarique**, isobaric spin.
isobase [izɔba:z], *s.f. Geol:* isobase.
isobathe [izɔbat]. **1.** *a.* isobathic. **2.** *s.f.* isobath.
isobornéol [izɔbɔrneɔl], *s.m. Ch:* isoborneol.
isobronte [izɔbrɔ̃:t], *s.f. Meteor:* isobront(on).
isobutane [izɔbytan], *s.m. Ch:* isobutane.
isobutène [izɔbytɛn], **isobutylène** [izɔbitilɛn], *s.m. Ch:* isobutylene.
isobutyle [izɔbytil], *s.m. Ch:* isobutyl.
isocalorique [izɔkalɔrik], *a.* isocaloric.
isocarde [izɔkard], *s.f. Moll:* isocardia.
isocèle [izɔsɛl], *a. Geom:* isosceles (triangle).
isocéphalie [izɔsefali], *s.f.* isocephaly.
isocéphalique [izɔsefalik], *a.* isocephalic.
isochimène [izɔkimɛn], *Meteor:* **1.** *a.* isocheimal, isochimenal (line). **2.** *s.f.* isocheim.
isochore [izɔkɔ:r], *a.* isochoric.
isochromatique [izɔkrɔmatik], *a. Opt: Phot:* isochromatic.
isochrome [izɔkrɔm], *a. Mec:* isochromatic.
isochrone [izɔkrɔn], **isochronique** [izɔkrɔnik]. **1.** *a. Mec: Geol:* isochronous, isochronal, isochronic. **2.** *s.f. Geol: Meteor:* **isochrone**, isochrone.
isochronisme [izɔkrɔnism], *s.m. Mec: Physiol: etc:* isochronism.
isocinchoméronique [izɔsɛ̃kɔmerɔnik], *a. Ch:* isocinchomeronic.
isoclase [izɔkla:z], **isoclasite** [izɔklazit], *s.m. or f. Miner:* isoclasite.
isoclinal, -aux [izɔklinal, -o], *a. Geol:* isoclinal.
isocline [izɔklin], *Surv: etc:* **1.** *a.* isoclinal (line). **2.** *s.f.* isoclinal (line), isoclinic.
isoclinique [izɔklinik], *a.* isoclinal, isoclinic.
isocolloïde [izɔkɔlɔid], *s.m.* isocolloid.
isocolon [izɔkɔlɔ̃], *s.m. Ling:* isocolon.

isocorie [izɔkɔri], s.f. Med: isocoria.
isocraquage [izɔkrakaːʒ], s.m. Petroleum Ind: isocracking.
Isocrate [izɔkrat], Pr.n.m. Gr.Hist: Isocrates.
isocyanate [izɔsjanat], s.m. Ch: isocyanate.
isocyanique [izɔsjanik], a. Ch: isocyanic.
isocyclique [izɔsiklik], a. Ch: isocyclic.
isodactyle [izɔdaktil], a. Z: isodactylous.
isodactylie [izɔdaktili], s.f. isodactylism.
isodiabatique [izɔdjabatik], a. Ph: isodiabatic.
isodiaphère [izɔdjafɛːr], a. Atom.Ph: noyaux iso-**diaphères**, isodiapheres.
isodimorphe [izɔdimɔrf], a. Cryst: isodimorphic.
isodimorphisme [izɔdimɔrfism], s.m. Cryst: isodimorphism.
isodome [izɔdɔm], a. Arch: isodomic, isodomous.
isodomon [izɔdɔmɔ̃], s.m. Arch: isodomum, isodomon.
isodonte [izɔdɔ̃ːt], a. Z: isodont(ous).
isodose [izɔdoːz], a. Med: Atom.Ph: etc: **courbe i.**, isodose curve; **carte, graphique, d'isodoses**, isodose map, pattern.
isodyname [izɔdinam], a. (dietetics) isodynamic.
isodynamie [izɔdinami], s.f. isodynamia.
isodynamique [izɔdinamik], a. Magn: Mec: isodynamic.
isoélectrique [izɔelɛktrik], a. isoelectric.
isoète [izɔɛt], s.m. Bot: isoetes, quill-wort.
isoeugénol [izɔøʒenɔl], s.m. isoeugenol.
isogame [izɔgam], a. Bot: isogamous.
isogamie [izɔgami], s.f. Bot: isogamy.
isogène [izɔʒɛn], a. Opt: homocentric.
isogéotherme [izɔʒeɔtɛrm], a. **ligne i.**, isogeotherm.
isoglosse [izɔglɔs], a. Ling: isoglossal.
isogonale [izɔgɔnal], a. Mth: isogonal.
isogone [izɔgɔn], **isogonique** [izɔgɔnik], a. Geom: Magn: isogonal, isogonic.
isogroupe [izɔgrup], a. Med: of the same blood group.
isohaline [izɔalin], a. & s.f. Oc: isohaline, isohalsine.
isohyète [izɔjɛt], Meteor: 1. a. isohyetal. 2. s.m. isohyet.
isoïonique [izɔjɔnik], a. Ch: isoionic.
isolable [izɔlabl], a. 1. isolable. 2. insulatable.
isolant [izɔlɑ̃]. 1. a. (a) isolating; Ling: **langues isolantes**, isolating languages; (b) insulating; **bouteille isolante**, vacuum flask; **cabine isolante**, soundproof box; El.E: **ruban i.**, insulating tape. 2. s.m. (a) insulating substance, insulator, insulant; insulation material; (b) Const: damp-proofing compound.
isolat [izɔla], s.m. isolate.
isolateur, -trice [izɔlatœːr, -tris]. 1. a. (a) El: insulating; (b) Const: **plaques isolatrices**, damp-coursing. 2. s.m. insulator; El.E: **i. à cloche**, petticoat insulator; **i. à suspension**, suspension insulator; **i. (à) haute tension**, high-voltage, high-tension, insulator; **i. d'arrêt**, shackle insulator, strain insulator; **i. de ligne**, line, section, insulator; **i. d'étincelles**, spark box; Elcs: **i. d'antenne**, antenna insulator; **i. de poulie (d'antenne)**, bobbin insulator; **i. haute fréquence**, radio-frequency insulator; W.Tel: etc: **i. d'entrée de poste, i. de traversée**, lead-in insulator.
isolation [izɔlasjɔ̃], s.f. El: insulation; Ac: **i. acoustique, phonique**, soundproofing; **i. thermique**, heat insulation.
isolationnisme [izɔlasjɔnism], s.m. isolationism.
isolationniste [izɔlasjɔnist], a. & s.m. & f. isolationist.
isolé [izɔle], a. 1. isolated, detached (house, etc.); lonely, remote (spot, etc.); isolated (protest, etc.); Gram: **participe i.**, misrelated, unrelated, participle; **il se tient i. de la foule**, he stands aloof from the crowd; Mil: **homme i.**, s. **un isolé**, (i) unattached man, casual, (ii) man travelling alone; **division isolée**, independent division. 2. El: insulated (cable, etc.).
isolement [izɔlmɑ̃], s.m. 1. isolation; **politique du splendide i.**, policy of splendid isolation; **hôpital d'i.**, isolation hospital; Mch: etc: **robinet d'i.**, isolating valve; **i. phonique, sonore**, acoustic isolation; sound isolation. 2. El: insulation; **défaut d'i.**, faulty insulation; **mauvais i.**, leakage; **i. corrodé**, burnt insulation; **ruban d'i.**, insulating tape.
isolément [izɔlemɑ̃], adv. separately, individually; **vivre i.**, (i) to live solitarily, alone, (ii) (of husband and wife, etc.) to live apart; Adm: Mil: **hommes voyageant i.**, men travelling singly.
isoler [izɔle], v.tr. 1. to isolate (de, d'avec, from); **se trouver isolé**, to find oneself cut off (from other troops, etc.); **i. un quartier**, to seal off an area; **on isola la rue par un cordon de police**, the street was sealed, cordoned, off by the police.

2. (a) El.E: to insulate; **i. au mica**, to insulate with mica; (b) Ch: to isolate (element, etc.).
s'isoler. 1. to become isolated, separated. 2. to separate oneself, live apart, hold aloof (from society).
isoleucine [izɔløsin], s.f. Ch: isoleucine.
isologue [izɔlɔg], Ch: 1. a. isologous. 2. s.m. isolog(ue).
isoloir [izɔlwar], s.m. 1. El: insulator; insulating stool; Tg: **i. à cloche**, bell-shaped insulator; cup, petticoat, insulator. 2. polling booth.
isomère [izɔmɛːr]. 1. a. Ch: Bot: etc: isomerous, isomeric. 2. s.m. Ch: isomer.
isomérie [izɔmeri], s.f., **isomérisme** [izɔmerism], s.m. Ch: isomerism; **i. cis-trans**, (i) cis-trans isomerism; (ii) syn-anti isomerism.
isomérisation [izɔmerizasjɔ̃], s.f. isomerization.
isométrique [izɔmetrik], a. Cryst: Geom: isometric(al); perspective **i.**, isometric perspective.
isomorphe [izɔmɔrf]. 1. a. Cryst: Mth: etc: isomorphous, isomorphic. 2. s.m. isomorph.
isomorphie [izɔmɔrfi], s.f., **isomorphisme** [izɔmɔrfism], s.m. isomorphism.
isonèphe [izɔnɛf], Meteor: 1. a. isonephelic. 2. s.f. isoneph.
isoniazide [izɔnjazid], s.f. isoniazid.
isonicotinique [izɔnikɔtinik], a. Ch: isonicotinic.
isonitrile [izɔnitril], s.m. Ch: isonitrile.
isonomie [izɔnɔmi], s.f. Cryst: Pol: isonomy.
isooctane [izɔɔktan], s.m. Ch: isooctane.
isopache [izɔpaʃ], s.f. Geol: isopachyte.
isoparaffine [izɔparafin], s.f. isoparaffin.
isopelletiérine [izɔpɛl(ə)tjerin], s.f. Ch: isopelletierine.
isopentane [izɔpɛ̃tan], s.m. Ch: isopentane.
isopérimètre [izɔperimɛtr], a. Geom: isoperimetric(al).
isophane [izɔfan], a. Biol: isophanal.
isophtalique [izɔftalik], a. Ch: isophthalic.
isoplèthe [izɔplɛt], a. **ligne i.**, isopleth, isoline.
isopode [izɔpɔd], Crust: 1. a. isopodous. 2. s.m. isopod; pl. **isopodes**, Isopoda.
isoprène [izɔprɛn], s.m. Ch: isoprene.
isopropényle [izɔprɔpenil], s.m. Ch: isopropenyl.
isopropyle [izɔprɔpil], s.m. Ch: isopropyl.
isopropylique [izɔprɔpilik], a. isopropyl (alcohol).
isoptères [izɔptɛːr], s.m.pl. Ent: Isoptera, the termites.
isoquinoléine [izɔkinɔlein], s.f. Ch: isoquinoline.
Isorel [izɔrɛl], s.m. R.t.m: Const: hardboard.
isoséiste [izɔseist], **isosiste** [izɔsist], Geol: 1. a. isoseismal, isoseismic. 2 s.f. isoseist, isoseismal.
isospin [izɔspin], s.m. Atom.Ph: isotopic spin.
isospondyles [izɔspɔ̃dil], s.m.pl. Ich: Isospondyli.
isosporé [izɔspɔre], a. Bot: isosporous.
isostasie [izɔstazi], s.f. Geol: isostasy; isostacy.
isostatique [izɔstatik], a. isostatic.
isostémone [izɔstemɔn], a. Bot: isostemonous.
isostère [izɔstɛːr], a. isosteric.
isostérie [izɔsteri], s.f. Ch: isosterism.
isotèle [izɔstel], s.m. Gr.Hist: isoteles.
isotélie [izɔsteli], s.f. Gr.Hist: isotely.
isothère [izɔtɛːr], a. Meteor: isotheral (line).
isotherme [izɔtɛrm], Meteor: 1. a. isothermal (line). 2. s.f. isotherm.
isothermique [izɔtɛrmik], a. isothermic.
isotone [izɔtɔn], a. Atom.Ph: isotone.
isotonie [izɔtɔni], s.f. Ph: isotonicity.
isotonique [izɔtɔnik], a. Ph: isotonic; Med: **solution i.**, isotonic solution.
isotope [izɔtɔp], s.m. Ch: Ph: isotope; **i. stable, instable**, stable, unstable, isotope; **i. radioactif**, radioactive isotope; **i. traceur**, tracer isotope, isotopic tracer; **i. père**, parent isotope; **séparation des isotopes**, isotope separation.
isotopie [izɔtɔpi], s.f. Ch: isotopy.
isotopique [izɔtɔpik], a. Ph: Ch: isotopic; **déplacement i.**, isotopic shift; Atom.Ph: **courant i.**, isotopic flow; **rapport i.**, abundance ratio of isotopes; **séparation i.**, isotopic separation; **spin i.**, isotopic spin.
isotron [izɔtrɔ̃], s.m. Atom.Ph: isotron.
isotrope [izɔtrɔp], a. Ch: Ph: isotropic.
isotropie [izɔtrɔpi], s.f. Ch: Ph: isotropy, isotropism.
isotropique [izɔtrɔpik], a. Mth: isotropic.
isotype [izɔtip], a. Cryst: isotypic(al).
isovalérianique [izɔvalerjanik], **isovalérique** [izɔvalerik], a. Ch: isovaleric.
isovireur [izɔvirœːr], a.m. Phot: self-toning (paper).
isoxazole [izɔksazɔl], s.m. Ch: isoxazole.
Ispahan [ispaɑ̃], Pr.n. Geog: Isfahan.
Israël [israɛl], Pr.n.m. Israel.
israélien, -ienne [israeljɛ̃, -jɛn], a. & s.m. & f. Geog: Israeli.

Israélite [israelit], B.Hist: 1. s.m. & f. Israelite, Jew. 2. a. Israelitish (woman, etc.); Israelitic (history, etc.).
issant, -ante [isɑ̃, -ɑ̃ːt], a. Her: (lion, etc.) issuant.
issoldunois, -oise [isɔldynwa, -waːz], a. & s. Geog: (native, inhabitant) of Issoudun.
issologue see ISOLOGUE.
issorien, -ienne [isɔrjɛ̃, -jɛn], a. & s. Geog: (native, inhabitant) of Issoire.
issoudunois, -oise [isudynwa, -waːz], a. & s. Geog: (native, inhabitant) of Issoudun.
issu [isy], a. descended (de, from); born (de, of); **i. de sang royal**, of royal descent; **philosophie issue du découragement**, philosophy born of discouragement; **la France issue de 1789**, the France born of 1789; **élèves issus de l'enseignement technique**, products of technical education.
issue [isy], s.f. 1. exit, way out; outlet (of tunnel, etc.); **i. de secours**, emergency exit; **chemin sans i.**, cul-de-sac, dead end; **trouver une i. à une impasse**, to find a way out of a deadlock; **ménager une i. à l'eau (d'un réservoir)**, to construct an outlet channel for the water (in a reservoir); **se ménager une i.**, to prepare a loophole of escape, a way out. 2. issue, end, conclusion; outcome; **l'affaire a eu une i. heureuse**, the matter ended happily, had a happy ending; **je ne sais pas quelle en sera l'i.**, I don't know how the matter will end, how things will go, what the upshot of it will be; **la seule i. possible est le recours aux armes**, the only solution is recourse to arms; **changer l'i. de la bataille**, to turn the tide of the battle; **à l'i. de**, at the end of; **à l'i. de la réunion**, at the end of the meeting, when the meeting broke up. 3. pl. (a) Mill: **issues de blé**, sharps, middlings; (b) by-products of butchery (leather, horns, hoofs, etc.).
Istamboul, Istanboul, Istanbul [istɑ̃bul], Pr.n. Geog: Istambul.
isthme [ism], s.m. Geog: Anat: etc: isthmus; **L'i. de Suez**, the Isthmus of Suez.
isthmien, -ienne [ismjɛ̃, -jɛn], a., **isthmique** [ismik], a. Isthmian, isthmic (canal, games, etc.).
Istrie [istri], Pr.n.f. Geog: Istria.
istrien, -enne [istriɛ̃, -ɛn], a. & s. Geog: Istrian.
isubre [izybr], s.m. Z: Altai wapiti.
itabirite [itabirit], s.f. Miner: itabirite.
itacisme [itasism], s.m. Ling: (Gr.): itacism.
itaconique [itakɔnik], a. Ch: itaconic.
itague [itag], s.f. Nau: tie; **i. d'un corps-mort**, chain pendant of moorings; **palan sur i.**, runner and tackle; **i. d'affourchage**, dip rope, clear hawse pendant.
italianisant, -ante [italjanizɑ̃, -ɑ̃ːt], s. Italianist.
italianisation [italjanizasjɔ̃], s.f. Italianization.
italianiser [italjanize]. 1. v.tr. to Italianize. 2. v.i. to affect Italian speech, manners.
s'italianiser, to become Italianized.
italianisme [italjanism], s.m. Ling: Italianism, Italicism, Italian phrase, idiom.
Italie [itali], Pr.n.f. Geog: Italy.
italien, -ienne [italjɛ̃, -jɛn]. 1. a. & s. (a) Geog: Italian; (b) **à l'italienne**, in the Italian style, manner; Cu: served with chopped mushrooms; **cuisine à l'italienne**, Italian cooking; **table à l'italienne**, table with sliding leaves; **volet à l'italienne**, awning blind; Bookb: **format, reliure, à l'italienne**, oblong format. 2. s.m. Ling: Italian. 3. s.m.pl. Th: A: **les Italiens**, the Italian Opera (in Paris).
italiote [italjɔt], a. & s. Ethn: Italiot.
italique [italik]. 1. a. Ethn: etc: Italic (race, languages, etc.). 2. a. & s.m. Typ: italic (type); **imprimer un mot en i.**, to print a word in italic.
italiqué [italike], a. Typ: italicized.
italo- [italɔ], comb.fm. Italo-; **i.-byzantin**, Italo-Byzantine; **i.-celtique**, Italo-Celtic.
itea [itea], s.m. Bot: itea.
item [itɛm]. 1. adv. item, likewise, also. 2. s.m. inv. A: item, article (in account); **voilà l'i.**, there's the rub!
itératif, -ive [iteratif, -iːv], a. 1. Jur: reiterated, repeated (prohibition, etc.). 2. Gram: iterative, frequentative (verb). 3. (computers) **opération itérative**, iterative operation.
itération [iterasjɔ̃], s.f. reiteration, repetition; iteration; (computers) **compteur, nombre d'itérations**, cycle criterion; **effectuer des itérations**, to iterate.
itérativement [iterativmɑ̃], adv. repeatedly; over and over again.
itérer [itere], v.i. & tr. (j'itère, n. itérons; j'itérerai(s)), to repeat, reiterate.
ithaginis [itaʒinis], s.m. Orn: ithagene, blood pheasant.
Ithaque [itak], Pr.n.f. A.Geog: Ithaca.
ithomiides [itɔmiid], s.m.pl. Ent: Ithomiidae.